P9-DBT-235

# Greek-English Lexicon

# A Greek-English Lexicon

COMPILED BY

HENRY GEORGE LIDDELL

AND

ROBERT SCOTT

---

REVISED AND AUGMENTED THROUGHOUT BY

SIR HENRY STUART JONES

WITH THE ASSISTANCE OF

RODERICK McKENZIE

AND WITH THE COOPERATION OF
MANY SCHOLARS

With a revised supplement
1996

CLARENDON PRESS · OXFORD

*Oxford University Press, Walton Street, Oxford* OX2 6DP
*Oxford New York*
*Athens Auckland Bangkok Bombay*
*Calcutta Cape Town Dar es Salaam Delhi*
*Florence Hong Kong Istanbul Karachi*
*Kuala Lumpur Madras Madrid Melbourne*
*Mexico City Nairobi Paris Singapore*
*Taipei Tokyo Toronto*
*and associated companies in*
*Berlin Ibadan*

*Oxford is a trade mark of Oxford University Press*

*Published in the United States by*
*Oxford University Press Inc., New York*



*First edition published 1843*
*Second edition 1845*
*Third edition 1849*
*Fourth edition 1855*
*Fifth edition 1861*
*Sixth edition 1869*
*Seventh edition 1882*
*Eighth edition 1897*
*New (ninth) edition completed 1940*
*New Supplement added 1996*



*British Library Cataloguing in Publication Data*
*Data available*

*Library of Congress Cataloging in Publication Data*
*Liddell, Henry George, 1811–1898.*
*A Greek-English lexicon / compiled by Henry George Liddell and Robert Scott.—Rev. and augm. throughout / by Sir Henry Stuart Jones with the assistance of Roderick McKenzie and with the co -operation of many scholars.*
*p. cm.*
*"With a supplement, 1996."*
*Includes bibliographical references and index.*
*1. Greek language—Dictionaries—English. I. Scott, Robert, 1811–1887. II. Jones, Henry Stuart, 1867–1939. III. McKenzie, Roderick, 1887–1937. IV. Title.*
*PA445.E5L6 1996 483'.21—dc20 95–32369 CIP*
*ISBN 0–19–864226–1 (hc : alk. paper)*

1 3 5 7 9 10 8 6 4 2

*Printed in Great Britain*
*on acid-free paper by*
*The Bath Press, Avon*

# PREFACE 1925

MORE than eighty years have passed since the first edition of the famous Lexicon upon which the present work is based was published by the Clarendon Press. Henry George Liddell and Robert Scott—the latter a Craven and Ireland Scholar—were both placed in the First Class in the Oxford list of 1833, both having been born in 1811. In 1835 Scott became a Fellow of Balliol and in the following year Liddell was elected to a Studentship of Christ Church. It appears that Mr. Talboys, an Oxford bookseller and publisher, first approached Scott with a proposal that a Greek-English Lexicon, based on that of Franz Passow, should be compiled, and that Scott made his acceptance conditional on the consent of Liddell to join in the work; at any rate, it was Talboys who first undertook the publication, which was taken over after his retirement by the Clarendon Press. There is, however, some ground for thinking that William Sewell, who had been an examiner in the Schools of 1833, suggested the idea to Liddell and Scott; and Liddell mentions in his correspondence the encouragement which the project received from Dean Gaisford.

The Lexicon of Passow, which the Oxford scholars took as the basis of their work, was itself founded upon that of Johann Gottlob Schneider, the editor of Theophrastus, the first edition of which had appeared in 1797–8. Passow had laid down, in his Essay on *Zweck, Anlage, und Ergänzung griechischer Wörterbücher*, published in 1812, the canons by which the lexicographer should be guided, amongst which the most important was the requirement that citations should be chronologically arranged in order to exhibit the history of each word and its uses. In obedience to this principle, Passow based his work on a special study of the Early Epic vocabulary, and the relatively full treatment of Homeric usage is a legacy bequeathed by him to Liddell and Scott which has persisted throughout the successive editions of their work. The first edition of his Lexicon appeared in 1819, and his expressed intention was to expand the work gradually by incorporating successively the results of special studies of Early Lyric Poetry, the Ionic Prose of Herodotus and Hippocrates, the Attic dramatists, and the Attic Prose writers: but little change was made in his second and third editions (1825 and 1827), and the fourth (1831), in which the Early Lyric poets and Herodotus received fuller recognition, was the first in which he felt himself at liberty to omit the name of Schneider from his title-page and also the last to appear in his lifetime. He died in 1833 in his forty-seventh year.

In the meantime two attempts had been made to adapt the *Thesaurus Linguae Graecae* of Henri Estienne to modern uses. The first of these was the result of the activities of Abraham Valpy, and was largely the work of E. H. Barker of Trinity College, Cambridge. It was completed in nine folio volumes, published in 1819–28, and reproduced the text of Stephanus' *Thesaurus*, interlarded with a mass of copious but ill-digested information. The first volume met with vigorous and not undeserved criticism on the part of Bishop Blomfield in an article in the *Quarterly Review* (vol. xxii, pp. 302 ff.) which is marred by a lavish display of *odium philologicum*. The editors, however, profited by the Bishop's strictures, and his prophecy that a work in which 139 columns were devoted to the word *ἄγαλμα* would run to fifty volumes and attain to completion in 1889 was signally falsified. The work labours under the serious disadvantage of retaining the etymological arrangement of Stephanus,[1] which forces the reader to make a laborious search for any compound or derived word.

This mistake was avoided by the compilers of the Paris *Thesaurus*, the publication of which was begun in 1831 by Firmin-Didot, and was placed under the general editorship of Karl Benedict Hase. This enterprise was also subjected to criticism in the *Quarterly Review* (vol. li, pp. 144 ff.) by J. R. Fishlake (the translator of Buttmann's *Lexilogus*) on the ground of its unwieldy bulk; but the association of the brothers Wilhelm and Ludwig Dindorf at an early stage of the work[2] enabled it to be carried through in thirty-four years, and its vast collections of material, though often ill-arranged and unevenly treated, were largely drawn upon by Liddell and Scott in their successive editions.

The first of these appeared in 1843; it was a quarto volume of 1,583 pages, priced at 42*s.*, and 6,000 copies were printed. A second, revised and enlarged, was called for in 1845, and the editors acknowledged their indebtedness to the German lexicon of Wilhelm Pape, which had appeared almost simultaneously with their own. In 1849 a third edition, corrected, but not substantially enlarged, was published, and six years later came the fourth, revised throughout. This marks a considerable advance on its predecessors, and much additional material was inserted; but the writers specially recognized were still chiefly those of the early classical period, including the Lyric poets, the authors of the Hippocratean writings, and the Attic orators. The editors now felt justified in omitting the name of Passow from their title-page. Eight thousand copies of this edition were printed, and the price was reduced to 30*s.* After another interval of six years the fifth edition, 'revised and augmented', appeared in 1861, and use was made of the greatly enlarged fifth edition of Passow, published by Valentin Rost and Friedrich Palm and completed in 1857, while the philological information was recast in the light of G. Curtius' *Griechische Etymologie* (1858). There were 10,000 copies of this edition, priced at 31*s.* 6*d.* The sixth is dated in 1869; it was again considerably augmented, the number of pages being increased from 1,644 to 1,865, and the verbal forms were more fully given with the aid of Veitch's *Greek Verbs, irregular and defective* (2nd ed., 1866). Of this edition 15,000 copies were printed, and the price was raised to 36*s.* Fourteen years later appeared a seventh edition, revised by Liddell, whose Preface is dated October 1882; the page was enlarged, and this made a reduction in the number to 1,776 possible. Bonitz's Index to Aristotle (1870) and Roehl's Index to *CIG* (1877) were largely drawn upon, and help was received from American scholars—Professors Drisler, Goodwin, and Gildersleeve—especially in regard to the particles and the technical terms of Attic law. This edition was stereotyped, and from time to time reprinted. Finally, in 1897, there was published an eighth edition, in which such corrections were made as could be inserted without altering the pagination. This made it impossible to take full account of such new sources as the *Ἀθηναίων Πολιτεία*, but there was a short list of Addenda, containing references to this work and to inscriptions published in the *Journal of Hellenic Studies*. Liddell appears to have been engaged for some years after the publication of the seventh edition on a lexicographical study of inscriptions; Sir William Thiselton-Dyer has kindly placed at my disposal two volumes of an interleaved edition of the abridged Lexicon in which his collections of material, largely drawn from the *Corpus Inscriptionum Atticarum* and Roehl's *Inscriptiones Graecae Antiquissimae*, are contained; but he seems to have laid the work aside in his later years, and he died in 1898, at the age of 87, a few months after the appearance of the eighth edition.

[1] In 1812 Passow himself had advocated the retention of Stephanus' arrangement; but he fortunately abandoned it in favour of the alphabetical principle.

[2] Their names appeared on the title-page of Part IV (containing *β*), which appeared concurrently with the second half of *α*.

Some five years later the Delegates of the Clarendon Press were invited to consider the revision of the Lexicon with a view to the incorporation of the rapidly growing material supplied by newly discovered texts on stone and papyrus, for which room might be found by the adoption of more compendious methods of reference; and a conference took place in March 1903, for which Ingram Bywater prepared a memorandum on the projected revision, advice being sought from Henry Jackson, Sir Richard Jebb, J. E. B. Mayor, and Arthur Sidgwick. The Delegates received the project favourably and it was hoped that Mr. Sidgwick might be able to act as editor. Contributions were invited in his name and a fair amount of material was collected, including a large number of notes and suggestions by Professor Leeper of Melbourne. Amongst other English and American scholars whose contributions were of considerable extent may be named the Rev. M. A. Bayfield and Prof. C. J. Goodwin, and particularly Mr. Herbert W. Greene, of whose services to the Lexicon more will be said presently. Mr. Sidgwick was, however, prevented by his duties as a teacher and afterwards by the failure of his health from commencing the work of revision.

In the meantime two more ambitious schemes had been initiated. At the second general assembly of the International Association of Academies, held in London in May 1904, Sir Richard Jebb submitted on behalf of the British Academy a scheme for the compilation of a new Thesaurus of Ancient Greek up to the early part of the seventh century A.D.; and after a discussion in which the difficulty and magnitude of the enterprise were emphasized[1] a Committee of Inquiry, consisting of Sir R. C. Jebb, Professors Diels, Gomperz, Heiberg, Krumbacher, Leo, and M. Perrot, with power to co-opt, was appointed to consider method, means, and preliminary questions in connexion with the proposal. In 1905 Prof. P. Kretschmer was added to the Committee, which drafted a memorandum on the question of establishing a periodical '*Archiv*' and an office for the collection of slips. At the close of the year Jebb, who had acted as Chairman, died, and was replaced in 1906 by Gomperz, while Bywater was added to the Committee, which, at a meeting held at Vienna in May, decided to constitute itself a permanent and independent body.

The difficulties of the project had been incisively stated by Diels in an article published in the *Neue Jahrbücher* for 1905,[2] in the course of which he wrote as follows:

> Any one who bears in mind the bulk of Greek literature, which is at least 10 times as great [as that of Latin], its dialectical variations, its incredible wealth of forms, the obstinate persistence of the classical speech for thousands of years down to the fall of Constantinople, or, if you will, until the present day: who knows, moreover, that the editions of almost all the Greek classics are entirely unsuited for the purposes of slipping, that for many important writers no critical editions whatever exist: and who considers the state of our collections of fragments and special Lexica, will see that at the present time all the bases upon which a Greek Thesaurus could be erected are lacking.
>
> But even if we were to assume that we possessed such editions and collections from Homer down to Nonnus, or (as Krumbacher proposed in London) down to Apostolius, and further that they had all been worked over, slipped, or excerpted by a gigantic staff of scholars, and that a great house had preserved and stored the thousands of boxes, whence would come the time, money, and power to sift these millions of slips and to bring Νοῦς into this Chaos? Since the proportion of Latin to Greek Literature is about 1 : 10, the office work of the Greek Thesaurus would occupy at least 100 scholars. At their head there would have to be a general editor, who, however, would be more of a general than an editor. And if this editorial cohort were really to perform its task punctually, and if the Association of Academies, which, as is well known, has not a penny of its own, were to raise the ten million marks necessary for the completion of (say) 120 volumes; and if scholars were to become so opulent that they could afford to purchase the *Thesaurus Graecus* for (say) 6,000 marks—how could one read and use such a monstrosity?

---

[1] Krumbacher was anxious to include Byzantine Greek in the ambit of the new Thesaurus.

[2] p. 692; Diels had already expressed his views in his *Elementum* (1899), p. ix sqq.

Diels's own solution was the compilation, not of one, but of ten Thesauri, representing the main branches of Greek Literature, Epic, Lyric, Tragic, Comic, Philosophical, Historical, Mathematical and Technical, Medical, Grammatical, and Jewish-Christian, each of which, he thought, would equal the Latin Thesaurus in bulk![1]

The majority of the members of the Committee, however, were still of the opinion that a foundation should be laid for the Thesaurus by the preparation of full slips for the whole of Greek literature on the method which had been adopted for the Latin Thesaurus, and made a recommendation in this sense to the third assembly of the International Association of Academies, held at Vienna in May 1907. The Association invited the British Academy (represented at Vienna by Bywater) to prepare a specimen for submission to the meeting which was to be held in 1910; but a Committee appointed by the Academy to consider this proposal, consisting of Bywater, H. Jackson, S. H. Butcher, and Sir F. Kenyon, reported in the following sense:

> They (the Committee) are not convinced that the *modus operandi* suggested for the projected Greek Thesaurus is the best possible. They think (*a*) that the Latin Thesaurus would not provide a proper scale and model; (*b*) that the mechanical slipping of Greek texts, besides being as is confessed a huge undertaking, would not serve as a satisfactory basis, inasmuch as it would give results difficult to manipulate and of questionable value. Rather, as recommended by M. Paul Meyer at the discussion in May 1904, they would suggest as a more promising plan that of the *New English Dictionary*.

In the face of this report, the British Academy felt that it was useless to proceed with the scheme, and it was tacitly dropped.

At about the date when the project of a *Thesaurus Graecus* was finally abandoned, a proposal was made by a group of Greek scholars for the preparation of a Lexicon of the Greek language—Ancient, Medieval, and Modern—the publication of which should commence in 1921 as a memorial of the Centenary of Greek independence. The Greek Government took the scheme under its patronage, and in November 1908 a Commission was appointed by royal decree, at the head of which was the veteran scholar Kontos, who was succeeded on his death by Hatzidakis. Krumbacher, in one of his latest articles in the *Byzantinische Zeitschrift*,[2] criticized the project, and advised the Greek scholars to confine themselves in the first instance to the Modern tongue; and though this recommendation was not, as it seems, formally adopted, the preliminary publications of the Commission consist mainly in a series of studies of the modern dialects, which appear as supplements to Ἀθηνᾶ, and it would appear that a Lexicon of Medieval and Modern Greek is contemplated in the first instance.

When it became clear that Mr. Sidgwick would be unable to carry out the revision of the Lexicon, the Delegates of the Clarendon Press invited me to undertake the work, which I did in the autumn of 1911, having been elected by Trinity College to a Research Fellowship which I continued to hold (except for a short period during the war) until my election to the Camden Professorship of Ancient History at the close of 1919. It was hoped at first that the preparation of a revised text might be completed in five years; but before the work had progressed very far it became clear that a more drastic revision than was suggested by a cursory examination would be necessary. Moreover, such large gaps (especially in technical subjects) remained to be filled if the new edition was to be adequate to the needs of modern scholarship—to say nothing of the large mass of new material awaiting incorporation—that the time allotted was evidently insufficient for more than a preliminary revision of Liddell and Scott's text, which would afterwards have to be worked up into a largely re-written Lexicon with the contributions of specialists and others whose help might be enlisted.

[1] A similar suggestion had been made more than half a century earlier by F. A. Wolf in his *Vorlesungen über die Altertumswissenschaft* i p. 187.

[2] xviii (1909), 708 ff.

Such assistance has been placed at my disposal with a generosity for which I cannot find words adequate to express my gratitude; nor would it be possible within the limits of this preface to enumerate all those who have supplied corrections of, or suggested improvements in, the text of the eighth edition. Mention, however, must be made of those who undertook special researches in aid of the revision.

Taking the more technical subjects first, the most laborious task was that of revising and amplifying the vocabulary of Medicine. It is interesting to recall the fact that many years ago the late Dr. Greenhill, of Trinity College, projected a Lexicon of Greek Medicine, for which he collected a certain amount of material in the shape of references arranged on slips and worked up a small portion of it in a series of articles in the *Medico-Chirurgical Journal.* He proposed to the Delegates that he should collaborate with M. Daremberg in preparing his Lexicon, but the suggestion did not meet with their approval, and Dr. Greenhill proceeded no further; his collection of slips passed after his death into the possession of the Royal College of Surgeons. It was clearly necessary that the field should be resurveyed, and I was fortunate enough to secure the services of Dr. E. T. Withington, who took up residence in Oxford and has worked untiringly on this difficult subject. He has read for lexicographical purposes the whole of the extant remains of Greek medical literature, and there is scarcely a page in the Lexicon which does not bear traces of his handiwork.[1]

For the subject of Botany, again, expert assistance was indispensable. Sir William Thiselton-Dyer, F.R.S., has for a long while been collecting material for a Glossary of Greek plants, and the publication of Max Wellmann's edition of Dioscorides, completed in 1914, has furnished a reliable critical text of the most important author in this branch of literature. Sir William Dyer has been most generous in placing the results of his study of Greek plant-names at my disposal, and his identifications are not likely to be disputed. A number of them had already been communicated to Sir Arthur Hort for use in his edition of Theophrastus' *Historia Plantarum.*[2]

The province of Greek Mathematics belongs in a special sense to Sir Thomas Heath, F.R.S., whose *History of Greek Mathematics* and editions of Euclid, Apollonius of Perga, Aristarchus of Samos, and Diophantus mark him out as the first authority in this subject. He has found leisure to contribute a large number of notes of the greatest value on Greek mathematical terms. To take an obvious instance, it will be seen that the eighth edition of Liddell and Scott recognizes the word ἀσύμπτωτος only in a Medical sense illustrated by a quotation (not quite accurately translated) from Hippocrates; Sir Thomas Heath has supplied the materials for a history of the use from which the modern *asymptote* is derived.

In the domain of Natural History Professor D'Arcy Thompson's help has enabled me to correct a number of mistakes made by previous lexicographers. His *Glossary of Greek Birds* has been in constant use, and his version of the *Historia Animalium* in the Oxford translations of Aristotle to a large extent supplies the want of a glossary of the Animal Kingdom.

In the field of Astronomy and Astrology I have to thank Mr. Edmund J. Webb for reading the *Almagest* of Ptolemy and other astronomical writings, and thereby greatly increasing the accuracy of the Lexicon in these matters. For the Astrological vocabulary a glossary was drafted by the Rev. C. T. Harley Walker, and the ground has also (as above mentioned) been worked over by Dr. Withington; but in this thorny subject difficulties frequently arise, for which Professor A. E. Housman, when appealed to, never fails to provide a solution.

[1] Dr. Withington has also found time to deal with the Alchemists and Astrologers, including the extensive collections of the *Catalogus Codicum Astrologorum.*

[2] Sir Arthur Hort has himself rendered aid in the difficult task of interpreting the Greek of Theophrastus

Amongst technical writings must be classed those of the tacticians and military engineers. The first were studied for my purposes by the late Mr. C. D. Chambers; the latter group, whose works are often very difficult of interpretation, have been read (together with other authors) by Mr. F. W. Hall.

Besides these highly specialized branches of study, there were large tracts of literature which it was needful to explore, but which a single editor could not hope to cover unaided. In the matter of papyri, for example, he might be able to deal with the newly recovered literary texts such as the *Ἀθηναίων Πολιτεία*, Bacchylides, Herodas, Cercidas, and the recently found fragments of the Early Lyric poets and Callimachus, but the great mass of non-literary papyri, especially those concerned with the technique of law and administration in Ptolemaic and Roman Egypt, required to be dealt with by those specially versed in the new science of papyrology. The Ptolemaic papyri were therefore read, partly by Mr. Edgar Lobel (who dealt with the Petrie collection) and partly by Professor Jouguet of Lille, those of the Roman period by Professor Martin of Geneva. Mr. H. Idris Bell of the British Museum has supplied valuable notes on recent papyrological publications and on unedited documents in the British Museum Collection.[1] For the vocabulary of the Inscriptions little could be done by the editor except to revise the existing references to Boeckh's *Corpus Inscriptionum Graecarum*—no light task, seeing that so many of the stones have been re-examined and may be studied in improved texts—and to supplement these corrected citations by illustrations from collections such as those of Dittenberger[2] or Michel or the *Griechische Dialektinschriften*, with the aid of Herwerden's *Lexicon Suppletorium*, a work unfortunately marred by constant inaccuracy of reference, which it is charitable to ascribe to lack of the minute care required in lexicographical proof-reading. I was therefore compelled to invoke the aid of Mr. M. N. Tod, to whom I owe an incalculable debt for his services in this field. Mr. Tod has for several years read with an eye to the improvement of the Lexicon every epigraphical publication which has appeared, such for example as the later volumes of the *Inscriptiones Graecae*, Cagnat's *Inscriptiones Graecae ad res Romanas pertinentes*, the *Tituli Asiae Minoris*, and the special publications of the inscriptions of Delphi, Ephesus, Magnesia, Miletus, and Priene, and has excerpted the whole of the periodical literature in which inscriptions are to be found, so that it is hard to believe that any new material of real importance which has accrued since 1911 can have escaped his methodical scrutiny. I have also received help in epigraphical matters from Professor M. Cary and Miss C. A. Hutton.

Turning to Literature proper, it soon became clear that while the references to Plato and Aristotle needed careful revision and some amplification,[3] the terminology of the later schools of Philosophy had never been adequately treated by lexicographers. Neither Usener's *Epicurea* nor von Arnim's *Stoicorum Veterum Fragmenta* possesses an index; and Mr. (now Professor) J. L. Stocks generously undertook to remedy this defect, and to supply me with a vocabulary of the important technical terms of the Stoic and Epicurean schools (including in his survey of the latter such later works as the tracts or other remains of Philodemus, Polystratus, Demetrius Lacon, Diogenianus, and Diogenes of Oenoanda). Unfortunately his work was interrupted by the Great War, and on his return from service Mr. Stocks found himself unable to work up the material which he had collected within the

[1] The first part of Preisigke's *Wörterbuch der griechischen Papyrusurkunden* appeared after the sheets of Part I had been printed off, but has been used for Addenda.

[2] The appearance of a third edition of the *Sylloge Inscriptionum Graecarum*, completed in 1924, has necessitated the alteration of a large number of references. The pitfalls which beset the path of the lexicographer may be exemplified by the fact that on the first revision the word ἀπόπλωσις was illustrated by *SIG*²929.127, and this was altered by the concordance-table to *SIG*³685.127: fortunately it was discovered in time that the word had disappeared in the later text!

[3] Bonitz's *Index to Aristotle* and Ast's *Lexicon Platonicum* are no longer all-sufficing guides. Such words as μορυχώτερον (which should be read in Arist. *Metaph.* 987ᵃ10) and τεράμων (which there is reason to think once stood in the text of Pl. *Sph.* 221a, though it is not mentioned by Burnet) are addenda.

necessary limits of time. His notes on Stoic terminology were therefore transferred to Mr. A. C. Pearson, who carried the work a stage further, but found, after his appointment to the Regius Professorship of Greek at Cambridge, that he would not have time to complete it. Professor E. V. Arnold of Bangor, who is retiring from his post, hopes to find the leisure necessary for this much-needed work.

In dealing with the vocabulary of Epicurus and his school Mr. Stocks found that for an adequate treatment it would be necessary to obtain access to the transcripts of the fragments of the περὶ φύσεως and other writings made by Wilhelm Crönert and used by him in his revision of Passow's Lexicon, of which more will be said presently. Crönert (who had spent some time in England as a prisoner of war in 1917–19) very kindly acceded to a request which I made to him at the suggestion of von Wilamowitz-Moellendorff and generously placed his transcripts at the disposal of Mr. Stocks, who visited him in Germany and made full use of this valuable material.

The peculiar vocabulary of the later Platonists has not hitherto received the attention which it deserves in Lexica; it is worthy of note that even in the seventh edition (1883) Liddell and Scott stated that the word μετεμψύχωσις (which is absent from the Paris Thesaurus and appears in Rost and Palm with the note 'Clem.Al. (?)') 'seems to be of no authority', though in the eighth edition an example of its use is cited from Proclus' Commentary on the *Republic* of Plato. As a matter of fact, this word can be quoted from ten authors besides Proclus.[1] Professor Burnet, who in his edition of the *Phaedo* drew attention to some of these passages, added: 'Hippolytus, Clement and other Christian writers say μετενσωμάτωσις ("reincarnation") which is accurate but cumbrous'; but the implication that this word belongs to Patristic Greek is misleading. It is found in Plotinus and in later Platonists such as Hierocles and Proclus. Again, such a characteristic use as that of ἄτοπος in the philosophical sense of 'non-spatial' has escaped lexicographers. In dealing with this branch of literature I have received help from various scholars, notably Professor A. E. Taylor; and the late Mr. M. G. Davidson read the *Enneads* of Plotinus, the abstruse work of Damascius περὶ ἀρχῶν, and other treatises. The extant commentaries on the works of Aristotle of course belong to this school of thought, and Mr. W. D. Ross kindly undertook to supply notes on their vocabulary with the aid of the excellent indices of the Berlin edition and with the collaboration of certain of the Oxford translators;[2] the bulk of this work, however, fell upon his own shoulders.

Another branch of literature demanding special study was that of the magical and mystical writings—the *Corpus Hermeticum*, the magical papyri, the *Tabellae Defixionum*, and such like. This field was carefully worked over by Mr. Walter Scott, whose notes dealt very fully with the difficult words often found in these sources.

For the New Testament the intensive study of theologians has done great things in recent times, and the results of their labours are readily accessible; for the ordinary purposes of revision such Lexica as those of Ebeling and Zorell are generally sufficient; while for the illustration of Biblical usage from Hellenistic and later Greek we have a most valuable aid in Moulton and Milligan's *Vocabulary of the Greek Testament*, which (within its natural limits) may almost be regarded as a Lexicon of the κοινή as a whole. I owe a deep debt of gratitude to Professor Milligan for supplying advance proofs of the *Vocabulary*, the fifth part of which has just been published. Prof. A. H. McNeile and the Rev. A. Llewellyn Davies have advised me in matters relating to the LXX, Hexapla, etc.

Turning to post-classical Greek literature in general, help was received from various scholars (amongst whom may be named Mr. Ronald Burn and Mr. C. E. Freeman, who excerpted several of the less familiar writers), but such merits as the new edition may

[1] D. S. 10. 6, Gal. 4. 763, Alex. Aphr. *de An.* 27. 18, Porph. *Abst.* 4. 16, Herm. ap. Stob. 1. 49. 69 (tit.), Sallust. 20, Hieronym. *Ep.* 124. 4. *Theol. Ar.* 40, Serv. ad Verg. *Aen.* 3. 68, Sch. Iamb. *Protr.* 14.

[2] Two of these, Mr. Erwin Webster and Mr. Gibson, lost their lives in the Great War.

possess in virtue of largely increased illustration and more accurate interpretation of the ancient texts will in the main be due to the self-effacing and monumental labours of Mr. Herbert W. Greene, sometime Fellow of Magdalen. Amongst the materials placed at my disposal when I began my editorial work in 1911 were twenty-four volumes of notes compiled by Mr. Greene as contributions to the Lexicography of authors mainly (though not by any means entirely) of post-Alexandrian date, including Lucian, the Anthology, all the later Epic poets, the *Scriptores Erotici*, Aelian, Philostratus, and others. From that time onwards Mr. Greene has not ceased to read and excerpt the remains of later Greek literature, including the works of practically every non-technical writer of importance from Polybius to Procopius. The twenty-four volumes have grown to nearly eighty, and many of the notes which they contain are elaborate dissertations constituting an important contribution to Classical Scholarship. Valuable aid has also been received from Professor W. A. Goligher, who read the minor Greek historians, Mr. J. M. Edmonds, who supplied a vocabulary of the Greek Lyric poets, Mr. J. H. A. Hart, who is compiling an *index verborum* to Philo, Professor A. W. Mair and Mr. M. T. Smiley, whose notes on Callimachus have been of great use, and other scholars, such as Professors J. A. Platt, A. Souter, R. L. Dunbabin, and W. L. Lorimer, Mr. T. W. Allen, Mr. A. H. Smith, Mr. G. Middleton, and the late Mr. G. E. Underhill, to all of whom special thanks are due. The advice of Mr. Edgar Lobel has been constantly sought and freely given, especially in regard to the remains of Early Lyric poetry and the ancient lexicographers.

The procedure of revision was briefly as follows. At the outset the Clarendon Press supplied a paste-up of the eighth edition in columns, and the first step was to note in the margin the essential alterations of the text and the most important additions. After this had been done, a second paste-up in columns was made, and the marginalia of the first were fused with newly accumulated material and recast in a form suitable for publication; but it was found that the copy thus produced would present great difficulties to the printer, and that a clean copy based on the use of short sections of Liddell and Scott's text treated as a proof was required. When I became Camden Professor at the beginning of 1920 it became necessary to provide me with assistance in my editorial work, and Mr. R. McKenzie of Trinity College (now Fereday Fellow of St. John's College) was appointed Assistant-Editor by the Delegates of the Press. Apart from his arduous labour in putting my drafts into final shape and in arranging and working in a large mass of accumulated material, Mr. McKenzie has been able to render inestimable service to the Lexicon on the philological side. After careful consideration it was decided that etymological information should be reduced to a minimum. A glance at Boisacq's *Dictionnaire étymologique de la langue grecque* will show that the speculations of etymologists are rarely free from conjecture; and the progress of comparative philology since the days of G. Curtius (whose *Griechische Etymologie* was the main source drawn upon by Liddell and Scott) has brought about the clearance of much rubbish but little solid construction. Some assured results, however, have been attained, and the etymologies presented in the text have in almost every case been approved by Mr. McKenzie.

The space required for the incorporation of new material without an excessive increase in the bulk of the Lexicon has been saved partly by abbreviations and compendious methods of printing, partly by certain limitations of scope. Liddell and Scott, though they originally intended their work to be a Lexicon of Classical Greek,[1] admitted a number of words from Ecclesiastical and Byzantine writers, for many of which no reference was given except the symbols 'Eccl.' and 'Byz.' After due consideration it has been decided to exclude both Patristic and Byzantine literature from the purview of the present edition. It would

[1] This appears from letters written in 1877 by Dean Liddell to Mr. Falconer Madan (who kindly placed them at my disposal) with reference to J. E. B. Mayor's well-known articles on Greek Lexicography in the *Journal of Philology*.

have manifestly been impossible to include more than a small and haphazard selection of words and quotations from these literatures, which would therefore have had to be treated quite differently from the remains of Classical Greek, where (it may be hoped) sufficient illustration has been given of the vocabulary and usage of all writers of importance, accompanied by precise and easily verifiable references. There is, moreover, in preparation a Lexicon of Patristic Greek (including Christian poetry and inscriptions) under the editorship of Dr. Darwell Stone, which will, it is hoped, be printed when the publication of the present work is concluded.[1] For the Byzantine vocabulary we shall have to wait for the Modern Greek Lexicon to which allusion has already been made, but it will hardly be denied that some time-limit was called for, and this has been fixed roughly at A. D. 600 in order to include the historians and poets of the reign of Justinian, though such writers as the scholiasts, grammarians, and others who preserve the fragmentary remains of ancient scholarship must naturally be taken into account in their own province.

The present volume will not challenge comparison in scale with the revision of Passow's *Wörterbuch der griechischen Sprache* by Wilhelm Crönert, of which three parts, extending as far as ἀνά, appeared in 1912–14. This monument of Herculean toil will, if and when it is completed (a consummation for which all lovers of learning will devoutly pray), bulk about three times as large as Liddell and Scott; in fact, this estimate may be exceeded if Crönert is able to carry out the plan foreshadowed in the preface to his second part, where he looks forward to the gradual expansion of his work as it proceeds (after the manner of Passow) by means of a fuller treatment of post-Classical Greek. Crönert's work has been criticized by Kretschmer,[2] who regards it as too ambitious in scope and unlikely to be completed within a reasonable period of time, and would prefer a Lexicon on a somewhat smaller scale as a preliminary to the *Thesaurus Linguae Graecae* which must remain for a long while to come a pious aspiration. It may be hoped that the present work will do something to supply this need, and that it may be found to possess some compensating advantages denied to the larger Lexicon of Crönert, such as the provision of exact references for every word cited from an author and fuller and more representative quotations from the later literature, e.g. from such authors as Plotinus.[3]

My best thanks are due to those scholars who are generously devoting their time to the reading of the proof-sheets and the verification of references, especially to the authors originally read by them for the purposes of the Lexicon. Some of these have already been named, such as Sir W. Thiselton-Dyer, Professors D'Arcy Thompson, A. E. Taylor, A. C. Pearson, and J. L. Stocks, Mr. Herbert Greene, Mr. Tod, Dr. Withington, Mr. Ross, and Mr. F. W. Hall. Lieut.-Col. Farquharson's scrutiny of the quotations from Plato and Aristotle is producing important results; and Messrs. C. and G. M. Cookson, Mr. W. W. How, and the Rev. W. Evans are doing valuable work in maintaining the standard of accuracy. The Editor's task is naturally heavy, especially in view of the fact that the progress of scholarship tends to make the text originally drafted for the Press out of date or to bring fresh material to light. Such publications as Ulrich Wilcken's *Urkunden der*

[1] Christian authors are of course frequently cited as the source of classical quotations, and such treatises as those of Porphyry and Julian *Against the Christians* are reconstructed from Patristic writings.

[2] In *Glotta* vi pp. 300 ff.

[3] A comparison of the art. ἀμφίβιος in Crönert-Passow with that of the present work will illustrate the difference of method. Crönert, on the other hand, gives the lexicographical tradition of the ancient grammarians very fully. For this it would not have been possible to find room; nor, indeed, has it yet been thoroughly sifted and critically edited. The deaths of Wentzel, Leopold Cohn, and Egenolff, and the migration of Bethe and Reitzenstein to more succulent pastures, have brought the two great enterprises of the firm of Teubner—the *Corpus Grammaticorum Graecorum* and that of the ancient Lexica—to a premature end. De Stefani's edition of the *Etymologicum Gudianum* is, however, in course of appearing, and it is understood that Drachmann is editing the remains of the Glossary of 'Cyril' (see Pauly-Wissowa, *Realencyclopädie* xii 175).

*Ptolemäerzeit* furnish more accurate readings of Papyri and necessitate changes or deletions,[1] and I must place on record my gratitude to Professor Wilcken for kindly undertaking to verify and correct references to documents in the yet unpublished portions of his work,[2] as also to Mr. J. U. Powell for permitting me to use and refer to the proofs of his *Collectanea Alexandrina*, shortly about to appear. Professor J. Bidez and Mr. A. D. Knox kindly sent me advanced proofs of the editions of the *Epistles of Julian* and of Herodas in which they have collaborated. The care and accuracy shown by the Press readers have been altogether exceptional.

It has, I hope, been made abundantly clear that the new edition of Liddell and Scott's Lexicon is in reality the work of many hands, and represents a great sacrifice of leisure and an earnest devotion to Greek learning on the part of the present generation of scholars, and that not in this country alone. I would fain hope that in the world of science at least (which has, or should have, no frontiers) it may further in some small degree the restoration of the comity of nations.

H. STUART JONES.

[1] For example, ἀντιπατάσσω was cited by me from *PPar.* 40, but the reference was deleted from the proof when it was found that in *UPZ* 12 Wilcken read ὠνηλάται ὄντες for ἀντιπατάσσοντες !

[2] This should cause little inconvenience to the user of the Lexicon, as Part I of *UPZ* contains concordance-tables for the whole work.

# POSTSCRIPT 1940

THE Delegates of the Oxford University Press, in issuing the tenth and last part of the revised edition of Liddell and Scott's Greek Lexicon, wish to express their deep gratitude to all who have assisted in carrying this undertaking to a conclusion. They greatly regret that neither the Editor Sir Henry Stuart Jones, who died on 29 June 1939, nor the Assistant Editor Mr. Roderick McKenzie, who died on 24 June 1937, survived to see the work completed. McKenzie saw the main body of the work to its end, and himself wrote the long article on *ὡς*; Sir Henry was at work on the Addenda and Corrigenda up to within a fortnight of his death and had almost put them into shape. The work done by these two men could not be overrated. Sir Henry was the ideal Editor; his wide range of knowledge and his exact scholarship, his persistent devotion to his task even in periods of ill health, his tactful assiduity in consulting experts and his skill in co-ordinating their results, gave the work at once its consistency and its elasticity. McKenzie, to whom fell the arrangement, in their ultimate form, of most of the articles, provided a fine complement; his great knowledge of comparative philology, his laborious accuracy, and his tireless patience, gave his contribution inestimable value.

In the Preface published in 1925 Stuart Jones sketched the history of the work up to the publication of *ἀποβαίνω*, and recorded the signal services given by many scholars to the work in its formative stages. To that nothing need now be added. But Jones went on to thank the scholars who were 'generously devoting their time to the reading of proof-sheets and the verification of references'. It is important that the nature of this work should be understood. The procedure adopted, when work was resumed after the Four Years' War, was this: McKenzie wrote out Jones's corrections on a 'paste-up' of the previous edition. This was the 'copy'; and fresh material was to some extent incorporated in it from time to time. But as succeeding sections of the alphabet were revised and set up in type, proofs were sent to the volunteer helpers, whose labours, in the event, went far beyond mere verification; in their hands and the editors' the work was very largely recast. The method has obvious advantages, and the peculiar excellences of the revised lexicon owe much to its adoption. But inevitably it prolonged the process of gestation. The period of publication, 1925–40, was actually longer than the period of copy-writing, 1911–24, even although the earlier period was interrupted by the war, and in the later period there were two editors instead of one.

Of those who were named in the original Preface as having embarked on the labour of proof-reading, some are dead: notably Sir William T. Thiselton-Dyer, A. C. Pearson, and Herbert Greene.[1] Others have lived to see the work to its end. These, and not these alone, have more than doubled the debt of gratitude which, fifteen years ago, Jones could not 'find words adequate to express'.

Unhappily neither editor lived to prepare a final list of acknowledgements. McKenzie died suddenly in 1937. Jones, though he lived to see the end in sight, left no material for the brief 'epilogue' which it had been agreed he should furnish. It would be impossible now to produce a complete or balanced account of the labours of the proof-readers and verifiers without undertaking inquiries which the circumstances of the time make difficult. The list which follows does not attempt discrimination. Special mention must, however, be made of the prolonged and arduous labours of Mr. M. N. Tod of Oriel College on the inscriptions; of Lt.-Col. A. S. L. Farquharson of University College on Plato and Aristotle;

[1] Greene's notebooks (see the 1925 Preface, p. x) are in the Bodleian.

of Dr. E. T. Withington of Balliol College on the medical writers; of Sir D'Arcy Thompson of St. Andrews on natural history; and of the late Sir Thomas Heath on mathematics and astrology.

The proofs were read also, in whole or in part, by the following: Mr. P. V. M. Benecke of Magdalen College; Mr. F. H. Colson of St. John's College, Cambridge; Mr. Christopher Cookson of Magdalen College; Prof. E. S. Forster of Sheffield University; Mr. E. T. D. Jenkins of University College, Aberystwyth; Mr. Edgar Lobel of the Queen's College; Mr. W. L. Lorimer of St. Andrews; Prof. J. F. Mountford of Liverpool University; Mr. Maurice Platnauer of Brasenose College; Sir David Ross, Provost of Oriel College; Prof. A. E. Taylor of Edinburgh; and by the late F. W. Hall, A. E. Housman, A. C. Pearson, J. A. Smith, and J. L. Stocks. As press reader from the beginning of the work Mr. T. Bruce has made a special contribution to its accuracy.

The Addenda and Corrigenda issued with the several parts have been greatly enlarged, and are now consolidated in a single list. Of these, the proofs were read by Dr. H. Idris Bell of the British Museum, Prof. G. R. Driver of Magdalen College, and Prof. Paul Maas of Königsberg, as well as by some of those who have been named above.

The Addenda owe much to the reviews and private communications of Dr. Ernest Harrison of Trinity College, Cambridge; of Prof. Maas; of Prof. R. Pfeiffer of Munich (it is noted with pleasure that both Prof. Maas and Prof. Pfeiffer are now resident in Oxford); of Prof. K. Latte of Hamburg; of Prof. W. Schmid of Tübingen; of Herr Pfarrer P. Katz of Coblenz, and of many other scholars.

Both in the Addenda and in the main work the principle of anonymity has been applied to original contributions that appear first in the Lexicon, and it was the intention of the Editors that those who made them should be free at any later time to claim their own discoveries.

Miss Margaret Alford, who bears an honoured name, helped Sir Henry Stuart Jones in the compilation of the Addenda, and since his death, with the collaboration of Professor Maas in the final stages, has performed the laborious duty of preparing the Addenda for Part 10 and of correcting proofs of the whole.

It is impossible now, as it was impossible in 1925, to name all who have contributed to the improvement of the great lexicon. The sacrifice of leisure, and the devotion to Greek learning, of which Jones then wrote, have been nobly sustained by a generation of scholars, and the monument of unselfish industry is at last complete.

CLARENDON PRESS, OXFORD.
*June*, 1940.

# NOTE 1968

THE *Addenda et Corrigenda* printed in this revised edition of Liddell and Scott when it was first issued complete in 1940 have now been withdrawn. They are replaced by the *Supplement*, the history and scope of which are explained in the Preface to it. The lists 'I. Authors and Works (Additional)' and 'V. General List of Abbreviations (*Addenda et Corrigenda*)' have also been withdrawn from the preliminary pages of the main Lexicon, as their function is now performed by the lists prefaced to the *Supplement*.

# AIDS TO THE READER

## A. LISTS OF ABBREVIATIONS, ETC.

THE lists which follow are designed to make it easy for the reader to trace the quotations given in the Lexicon. The general list of abbreviations (V) gives references, where needed, to one or other of the lists (I–IV) in which the expansion will be found; but the abbreviated names of authors have not been inserted in List V unless their alphabetical position in List I is different from that of the full name (e.g. A. = Aeschylus). List V also contains the expansion of all abbreviations used without explanation in List I. The names of authors are in general printed in roman type, the titles of their works (given in alphabetical order under the author's name) in italics, which are also used for the titles of collections and periodical publications.

The list of authors (I) is not intended to furnish a bibliography of Greek Literature, but to indicate the editions which have been followed in respect of the form of reference, i.e. pagination, numeration of books, chapters, sections, lines, fragments, &c.; where the form adopted in the Lexicon differs from that of the edition cited (e.g. where the pagination of an earlier editor is used, but may be found in the margin of a later edition) the fact is stated. It will be understood that the reading adopted in the edition cited is not necessarily given (or referred to) in the Lexicon. For the convenience of readers a few editions of the fragments of individual authors have been named in the list, even when the remains of the author have been cited from the sources of the quotations. Where no abbreviation follows the author's name the full name is used in the Lexicon, and where no date is given it is to be understood that evidence to determine it is lacking. No attempt has in general been made to indicate which of the works attributed to an author are to be regarded as spurious.

In the description of the editions used 'OCT' is added to show that the work is one of the Oxford Classical Texts (*Scriptorum Classicorum Bibliotheca Oxoniensis*); similarly 'T.' indicates the smaller Teubner Series (*Bibliotheca Scriptorum Graecorum et Romanorum Teubneriana*), 'D.' the Didot editions, and 'Loeb' the Loeb Classical Library.

## B. METHODS OF REFERENCE

Where the works of an author have been divided into recognized chapters and sections these are usually given, and the orators are (when possible) cited by speech and section; but references by page are given in accordance with custom to Aristotle (Bekker), the commentators on Aristotle (Berlin edition), Plato (Stephanus), Philo (Mangey), Plutarch's *Moralia* (Wyttenbach), Galen (Kühn, except for certain recently edited treatises), Athenaeus (Casaubon), Julian (Spanheim), and Themistius (Hardouin). Page-references to other authors are in general introduced by 'p.' and followed by the initial of the editor's name; if not, the facts are stated in List I. The symbol '*Fr.*' (= *Fragment*) is generally used where the remains of an author consist partly of complete works and partly of quotations; a simple number denotes a fragment drawn from one of the collections indicated in List I. Where supplementary or recent but uncompleted collections are quoted, the initial of the editor (e.g. 'D.' for Demiańczuk, 'J.' for Jacoby) is added to the number of the fragment. The annotations of ancient commentators are cited either by reference to the passage discussed or as substantive works: thus 'Ulp. ad D.' followed by reference to speech and section, but 'Did. *in D.*' cited by column and line of papyrus.

# I. AUTHORS AND WORKS

**Abydenus** Historicus [Abyd.] ii A. D. (?)
Ed. C. Müller, *FHG* iv p. 279.
**Aceratus** Epigrammaticus [Acerat.]
v. *Anthologia Graeca.*
**Acesander** Historicus [Acesand.] iii or ii B.C.
Ed. C Müller, *FHG* iv p. 285.
**Achaeus** Tragicus [Achae.] v B.C.
Ed. A. Nauck, *TGF* p. 746.
**Achilles Tatius** Astronomus [Ach.Tat.] iii A.D. (?)
*Introductio in Aratum*, ed. E. Maass, *Commentariorum in Aratum reliquiae*, Berlin 1898, p. 25. [*Intr.Arat.*]
**Achilles Tatius** Scriptor Eroticus [Ach.Tat.] iv A.D. (?)
Ed. R. Hercher, *Erotici* i p. 37.
**Acusilaus** Historicus [Acus.] v B.C.
Ed. F. Jacoby, *FGrH* i p. 47.
**Adaeus** Epigrammaticus i A.D.
v. *Anthologia Graeca.*
**Adamantius** Physiognomonicus [Adam.] iv A.D.
Ed. R. Förster, *Scriptores Physiognomonici*, Leipzig (T.) 1893, i p. 297.
**Aelianus** [Ael.] ii/iii A.D.
Ed. R. Hercher, Leipzig (T.) 1864–87.
*Ep.* = *Epistulae* (ed. R. Hercher, *Epistolographi*, p. 17)
*Fr.* = *Fragmenta*
*NA* = *De Natura Animalium* (excerpts in Ar.Byz.*Epit.*)
*Tact.* = *Tactica* (ed. H. Köchly & W. Rüstow, *Griechische Kriegsschriftsteller*, Leipzig 1855)
*VH* = *Varia Historia*
**Aelius Dionysius** Grammaticus [Ael.Dion.] ii A.D.
Ed. E. Schwabe, *Aelii Dionysii et Pausaniae Atticistarum Fragmenta*, Leipzig 1890.
**Aemilianus** Epigrammaticus [Aemil.] i A.D.
v. *Anthologia Graeca.*
**Aeneas Gazaeus** Rhetor [Aen.Gaz.] v/vi A.D.
*Epistulae*, ed. R. Hercher, *Epistolographi*, p. 24. [*Ep.*]
*Theophrastus*, ed. J. F. Boissonade, Paris 1836. [*Thphr.*]
**Aeneas Tacticus** [Aen.Tact.] iv B.C.
Ed. R Schöne, Leipzig (T) 1911.
**Aesara** Philosophus [Aesar.]
Apud Stobaeum.
**Aeschines** Orator [Aeschin.] iv B.C.
Ed. F. Blass, Leipzig (T.) 1896.
*Ep.* = *Epistulae*
**Aeschines Socraticus** Philosophus [Aeschin.Socr.] iv B.C.
Ed. H. Dittmar, Berlin 1912.
**Aeschrio** Lyricus iv B.C.
Ed. T. Bergk, *PLG* ii p. 516.
**Aeschylus** Tragicus [A.] vi/v B.C.
Ed. A. Sidgwick, Oxford (OCT).
Scholia, ed. W. Dindorf in editione Aeschyli, Oxford 1851.
Scholia in Aeschyli Persas, ed. O. Dähnhardt, Leipzig (T.) 1894.
*A.* = *Agamemnon*
*Ch.* = *Choephori*
*Eleg.* = *Fragmenta Elegiaca*, ed. T. Bergk, *PLG* ii p. 240.
*Eu.* = *Eumenides*
*Fr.* = *Fragmenta*, ed. A. Nauck, *TGF* p. 3; new fragments, marked A, B, &c., ed. H. W. Smyth, *American Journal of Philology*, xli (1920) p. 101.
*Pers.* = *Persae*
*Pr.* = *Prometheus Vinctus*
*Supp.* = *Supplices*
*Th.* = *Septem contra Thebas*
**Aeschylus Alexandrinus** Tragicus [Aesch.Alex.] iii B.C.
Ed. A. Nauck, *TGF* p. 824.
**Aesopus** Fabularum Scriptor [Aesop.]
Ed. C. Halm, Leipzig (T.) 1889.
*Prov.* = *Proverbia*, ed. E. L. von Leutsch & F. G. Schneidewin, *Paroemiographi* ii p. 228.
**Aethlius** Historicus v B.C. (?)
Ed. C. Müller, *FHG* iv p. 287.
**Aëtius** Medicus [Aët.] vi A.D.
Editio Aldina, Venice 1534 (Lib. i–viii); Lib. vii 1–90, ed. J. Hirschberg, Leipzig 1899; Lib. ix, ed. S. Zervos, Ἀθηνᾶ xxiii (1911) p. 265; Lib. xi, ed. C. Daremberg & C. E. Ruelle, *Rufus*, Paris 1879, p. 85; Lib. xii, ed. G. A. Kostomiris, Paris 1892; Lib. xiii (parts), xv, ed. S. Zervos, Ἀθηνᾶ xviii (190[illegible]) p. 241, xxi (1909) p. 3; Lib. xvi, ed. S. Zervos, Leipzig 190[illegible]
**Africanus, Julius** Historicus [Afric.] ii/iii A.[illegible]
*Cest.* = Κεστοί in *POxy.* 412.
**Agaclytus** Historicus [Agaclyt.]
Ed. C. Müller, *FHG* iv p. 288.
**Agatharchides** Geographus [Agatharch.] ii B.C.
Ed. C. Müller, *GGM* i p. 111.
*Fr.Hist.* = *Fragmenta Historica*, ed. C. Müller, *FHG* iii p. 190.
**Agathemerus** Geographus [Agathem.] post Posidonium.
Ed. C. Müller, *GGM* ii p. 471.
**Agathias** Historicus et Epigrammaticus [Agath.] vi A.D.
Ed. L. Dindorf, *HGM* ii p. 132.
v. *Anthologia Graeca.*
**Agathinus** Medicus [Agathin.] i A.D.
Apud Oribasium.
**Agatho** Tragicus v B.C.
Ed. A. Nauck, *TGF* p. 763.
**Agathocles** Historicus [Agathocl.]
Ed. C. Müller, *FHG* iv p. 288.
**Agis** Epigrammaticus
v. *Anthologia Graeca.*
**Aglaïas** Elegiacus i A.D.
Ed. U. Cats Bussemaker, *Poetae Bucolici et Didactici*, p. 97, Paris (D.) 1850.
**Albinus** Philosophus [Alb.] ii A.D.
*Introductio in Platonem*, ed. C. F. Hermann, *Plato*, vol. vi, Leipzig (T.) 1892, p. 147. [*Intr.*]
**Alcaeus** Comicus [Alc.Com.] v/iv B.C.
Ed. T. Kock, *CAF* i p. 756; suppl. J. Demiańczuk, *Supp. Com.* p. 7.
**Alcaeus** Lyricus [Alc.] vii/vi B.C.
Ed. T. Bergk, *PLG* iii p. 147; suppl. E. Diehl, *Supp. Lyr.*[3] p. 10. [*Supp.*]
**Alcaeus Messenius** Epigrammaticus [Alc.Mess.] iii/ii B.C.
v. *Anthologia Graeca.*
**Alcidamas** Rhetor [Alcid.] iv B.C.
Ed F. Blass, *Antipho*, Leipzig (T.) 1892, p. 183.
*Od.* = Ὀδυσσεύς.
*Soph.* = περὶ σοφιστῶν
**Alcinous** Philosophus [Alcin.]
*Introductio in Platonem*, ed. C. F. Hermann, *Plato*, Leipzig (T.) 1892, vol. vi, p. 152. [*Intr.*]
**Alciphro** Epistolographus [Alciphr.] iv A.D.
Ed. M. A. Schepers, Leipzig (T.) 1905. (Cited acc. to numeration of earlier edd.)
**Alcmaeon** Philosophus v B.C.
Ed. H. Diels, *Vorsokr.* i p. 131.
**Alcman** Lyricus [Alcm.] vii B.C.
Ed. T Bergk, *PLG* iii p. 14.
**Alexander** Comicus [Alexand.Com.]
Ed. T. Kock, *CAF* iii p. 372.
**Alexander Aetolus** Elegiacus [Alex.Aet.] iii. B.C.
Ed. J. U. Powell, *Coll. Alex.* p. 121.
**Alexander Aphrodisiensis** Philosophus [Alex.Aphr.] iii A.D.
*de An.* = *de Anima liber*, ed. I. Bruns (*Supplementum Aristotelicum* ii *pars* i), Berlin 1887.
*Fat.* = *de Fato*, ed. I. Bruns (*Supplementum Aristotelicum* ii *pars* ii), Berlin 1892.
*Febr.* = *de febribus*, ed. J. L. Ideler, *Physici et Medici Graeci Minores*, Berlin 1841, i p. 81.
*in APr.* = *in Aristotelis Analyticorum Priorum librum I commentarium*, ed. M. Wallies (*Comm. in Arist. Graeca* ii *pars* i), Berlin 1883.
*in Metaph.* = *in Aristotelis Metaphysica commentaria*, ed. M. Hayduck (*Comm. in Arist. Graeca* i), Berlin 1891.
*in Mete.* = *in Aristotelis Meteorologicorum libros commentaria*, ed. M. Hayduck (*Comm. in Arist. Graeca* iii *pars* ii), Berlin 1899.
*in SE* = *in Aristotelis Sophisticos Elenchos commentarium*, ed. M. Wallies (*Comm. in Arist. Graeca* ii *pars* iii), Berlin 1898.
*in Sens.* = *in librum de sensu commentarium*, ed. P. Wendland (*Comm. in Arist. Graeca* iii *pars* i), Berlin 1901.
*in Top.* = *in Aristotelis Topicorum libros octo commentaria*, ed. M. Wallies (*Comm. in Arist. Graeca* ii *pars* ii), Berlin 1891.
*Mixt.* = *de Mixtione*, ed. I. Bruns (*Supplementum Aristotelicum* ii *pars* ii), Berlin 1892.

*Pr.* = *Problemata*, ed. J. L. Ideler, *Physici et Medici Graeci Minores*, Berlin 1841, i p. 3.
*Pr. Anecd.* = προβλήματα ἀνέκδοτα, ed. U. Cats Bussemaker, *Aristotelis Opera*, vol. iv (Paris (D.) 1857), p. 291.
*Quaest.* = *Quaestiones*, ed. I. Bruns (*Supplementum Aristotelicum* ii *pars* ii), Berlin 1892.

**Alexander Ephesius** Epicus [Alex.Eph.] i B.C.
Ed. J. A. F. A. Meineke, *Analecta Alexandrina*, Berlin 1843, p. 371.

**Alexander Polyhistor** Historicus [Alex.Polyh.] i B.C.
Ed. C. Müller, *FHG* iii p. 206.

**Alexander** Rhetor [Alex.] ii A.D.
*De Figuris*, ed. L. Spengel, *Rhet.* iii p. 7. [*Fig.*]
περὶ ῥητορικῶν ἀφορμῶν, ed. L. Spengel, op. cit., p. i. [*Rh.*]

**Alexander Trallianus** Medicus [Alex.Trall.] vi A.D.
Ed. T. Puschmann, Vienna 1878–9; Nachträge, ed. T. Puschmann, Berlin 1886.
*Febr.* = *de febribus*
*Verm.* = *epistula de vermibus*

**Alexis** Comicus [Alex.] iv B.C.
Ed. T. Kock, *CAF* ii p. 297.

**Alpheus** Epigrammaticus [Alph.] i A.D.
v. *Anthologia Graeca*.

**Alypius** Musicus [Alyp.] iii (iv?) A.D.
Ed. C. Jan, *Musici Scriptores Graeci*, Leipzig (T.) 1895, p. 367.

**Amipsias** Comicus [Amips.] v/iv B.C.
Ed. T. Kock, *CAF* i p. 670; suppl. J. Demiańczuk, *Supp. Com.* p. 7.

**Ammianus** Epigrammaticus [Ammian.] ii A.D.
v. *Anthologia Graeca*.

**Ammianus Marcellinus** Historicus [Amm.Marc.] iv A.D.
Ed. C. U. Clark, L. Traube, W. Heraeus, Berlin 1910–15.

**Ammonius** Epigrammaticus [Ammon.] v A.D. (?)
v. *Anthologia Graeca*.

**Ammonius** Grammaticus [Ammon.] i/ii A.D.
περὶ ὁμοίων καὶ διαφόρων λέξεων, ed. L. C. Valckenaer[2], Leipzig 1822. [*Diff.*]

**Ammonius** Philosophus [Ammon.] v A.D.
*in APr.* = *in Aristotelis Analyticorum Priorum librum I commentarium*, ed. M. Wallies (*Comm. in Arist. Graeca* iv *pars* vi), Berlin 1899.
*in Cat.* = *in Aristotelis Categorias commentarius*, ed. A. Busse (*Comm. in Arist. Graeca* iv *pars* iv), Berlin 1895.
*in Int.* = *in Aristotelis de Interpretatione commentarius*, ed. A. Busse (*Comm. in Arist. Graeca* iv *pars* v), Berlin 1897.
*in Porph.* = *in Porphyrii Isagogen sive V voces*, ed. A. Busse (*Comm. in Arist. Graeca* iv *pars* iii), Berlin 1891.

**Amphis** Comicus iv B.C.
Ed. T. Kock, *CAF* ii p. 236.

**Anacharsis** Epistolographus [Anach.] i B.C. (?)
Ed. R. Hercher, *Epistolographi*, p. 102.

**Anacreon** Lyricus [Anacr.] vi B.C.
Ed. T. Bergk, *PLG* iii p. 253.

**Anacreontea** [*Anacreont.*]
Ed. C. Preisendanz, Leipzig (T.) 1912; cited by T. Bergk's numeration, *PLG* iii p. 296.

**Ananius** Lyricus [Anan.] vi B.C.
Ed. T. Bergk, *PLG* ii p. 501.

**Anaxagoras** Philosophus [Anaxag.]. v B.C.
Ed. H. Diels, *Vorsokr.* i p. 375.

**Anaxandrides** Comicus [Anaxandr.] iv B.C.
Ed. T. Kock, *CAF* ii p. 135; suppl. J. Demiańczuk, *Supp. Com.* p. 7.

**Anaxandrides** Historicus [Anaxandr.Hist.] iii B.C. (?)
Ed. C. Müller, *FHG* iii p. 106 (perperam 'Alexandrides').

**Anaxarchus** Philosophus [Anaxarch.] iv B.C.
Ed. H. Diels, *Vorsokr.* ii p. 144.

**Anaxilas** Comicus [Anaxil.] iv B.C.
Ed. T. Kock, *CAF* ii p. 264.

**Anaximander** Historicus [Anaximand.Hist.] iv B.C.
Ed. F. Jacoby, *FGrH* i p. 159.

**Anaximander** Philosophus [Anaximand.] vi B.C.
Ed. H. Diels, *Vorsokr.* i p. 14.

**Anaximenes** Philosophus [Anaximen.] vi B.C.
Ed. H. Diels, *Vorsokr.* i p. 22.

**Anaxippus** Comicus [Anaxipp.] iv B.C.
Ed. T. Kock, *CAF* iii p. 296.

**Andocides** Orator [And.] v/iv B.C.
Ed. F. Blass[4] (C. Fuhr), Leipzig (T.) 1913.

**Andromachus** Poeta Medicus [Androm.] i A.D.
Apud Galenum.

**Andron** Historicus iv B.C.
Ed. F. Jacoby, *FGrH* i p. 161.

**Andronicus** Epigrammaticus [Andronic.]
v. *Anthologia Graeca*.

**Andronicus Rhodius** Philosophus [Andronic.Rhod.] i B.C.
*De Passionibus*, ed. X. Kreuttner, Heidelberg 1885; ed. K. Schuchardt, Darmstadt 1883; cited by page of F. W. A. Mullach, *FPG* iii p. 570.

**Androtion** Historicus [Androt.] iv B.C.
Ed. C. Müller, *FHG* i p. 371.

**Anecdota Graeca** e codd. MSS. Bibl. reg. Parisin., ed. L. Bachmann, Leipzig 1828–9. [*An.Bachm.*]

**Anecdota Graeca** ed. I. Bekker, 3 vols., Berlin 1814–21. [*AB*]

**Anecdota Graeca** e codd. MSS. Bibl. Oxon., ed. J. A. Cramer, 4 vols., Oxford 1835–7. [*An.Ox.*]

**Anecdota Graeca** e codd. MSS. Bibl. Reg. Parisiensis, ed. J. A. Cramer, 4 vols., Oxford 1839–41. [*An.Par.*]

**Anecdota Graeca et Latina** [*Anecd.Stud.*]
Ed. R. Schoell & G. Studemund, Leipzig 1886.

**Anonymus** vel **Anonymi** [Anon.]
*Fig.* = Anonymi *de Figuris*, ed. L. Spengel, *Rhet.* iii pp. 110, 171, 174.
*Geog.Comp.* = *Geographiae Expositio Compendiaria*, ed. C. Müller, *GGM* ii p. 494.
*in Cat.* = *Anonymi in Aristotelis Categorias paraphrasis*, ed. M. Hayduck (*Comm. in Arist. Graeca* xxiii *pars* ii), Berlin 1883.
*in EN* = *Anonymi in Ethica Nicomachea commentaria*, ed. G. Heylbut (*Comm. in Arist. Graeca* xx), Berlin 1892.
*in Prm.* = *Anonymi Commentarius in Platonis Parmenidem*, ed. W. Kroll in *Rh. Mus.* xlvii (1892) 599.
*in Rh.* = *Anonymi in Artem Rhetoricam commentaria*, ed. H. Rabe (*Comm. in Arist. Graeca* xxi *pars* ii), Berlin 1896.
*in SE* = *in Sophisticos Elenchos paraphrasis*, ed. M. Hayduck (*Comm. in Arist. Graeca* xxiii *pars* iv), Berlin 1884.
*in Tht.* = *Anonymi Commentarius in Platonis Theaetetum*, ed. H. Diels & W. Schubart, *BKT* ii, Berlin 1905.
*Incred.* = Anonymus, περὶ ἀπίστων, ed. N. Festa (post Palaephatum (q. v.), p. 88), Leipzig (T.) 1902.
*Trop.* = Anonymi, περὶ τρόπων, ed. L. Spengel, *Rhet.* iii pp. 207, 227.

**Anonymus Londnensis** [Anon.Lond.] i A.D.
*Anonymi Londinensis ex Aristotelis Iatricis Menoniis et aliis medicis eclogae*, ed. H. Diels (*Supplementum Aristotelicum* iii *pars* i), Berlin 1893.

**Anonymus Rhythmicus** [Anon.Rhythm.]
*Oxy.* = *POxy.* 9.

**Anonymus Vaticanus** [Anon.Vat.]
Paradoxographus Vaticanus Rohdii, ed. O. Keller, *Rerum Naturalium Scriptores* i, Leipzig (T.) 1877, p. 106.

**Antagoras** Elegiacus [Antag.] iii B.C.
Ed. J. U. Powell, *Coll. Alex.* p. 120.

**Antenor** Historicus ii B.C. (?)
Ed. C. Müller, *FHG* iv p. 305.

**Anthemius** Paradoxographus [Anthem.] vi A.D.
Ed. A. Westermann, Παραδοξογράφοι, Brunswick-London 1839, p. 149.

**Anthologia Graeca**
(Names of epigrammatists, where found in codd., are added in brackets.)
*Anthologia Palatina, Planudea*, ed. F. Dübner, Paris (D.) 1864–72; ed. H. Stadtmüller, vols. i, ii (1), iii (1) (all published), Leipzig (T.) 1894–1906. [*AP*, *APl.*]
*Appendix nova epigrammatum*, ed. E. Cougny, Paris (D.) 1890. [*App.Anth.*]

**Anticlides** Historicus [Anticl.] iii B.C. (?)
Ed. C. Müller, *SRAM* p. 147.

**Antidotus** Comicus [Antid.] iv B.C.
Ed. T. Kock, *CAF* ii p. 410.

**Antigonus Carystius** Paradoxographus [Antig.] iii B.C.
*Mirabilia*, ed. O. Keller, *Rerum Naturalium Scriptores* i, Leipzig (T.) 1877, p. 1. [*Mir.*]

**Antigonus Nicaeanus** Astrologus [Antig.Nic.]
Apud Hephaestionem Astrologum.

**Antimachus Colophonius** Elegiacus et Epicus [Antim.] v/iv B.C.
*Fragmenta Elegiaca*, ed. T. Bergk, *PLG* ii p. 289. [*Eleg.*]
*Fragmenta Epica*, ed. G. Kinkel, *EGF* p. 273. [Antim.]; suppl. J. U. Powell, *Coll. Alex.* p. 249. [Antim.Col.]

**Antiochus Atheniensis** Astrologus [Antioch.Astr.] ii A.D.
Ed. A. Olivieri, *Cat. Cod. Astr.* i 108; ed. F. Boll, ib. vii 107.

**Antiochus** Epigrammaticus [Antioch.]
v. *Anthologia Graeca*.

**Antiochus** Historicus [Antioch.Hist.] v B.C.
Ed. C. Müller, *FHG* i p. 181.

**Antipater Sidonius** Epigrammaticus [Antip.Sid.] ii B.C.
v. *Anthologia Graeca*.

**Antipater Tarsensis** Stoicus [Antip.*Stoic.*] ii B.C.
Ed. H. von Arnim, *SVF* iii p. 244.

**Antipater Thessalonicensis** Epigrammaticus [Antip.Thess.] i B.C.
v. *Anthologia Graeca*.

**Antiphanes** Comicus [Antiph.] iv B.C.
Ed. T. Kock, *CAF* ii p. 12; suppl. J. Demiańczuk, *Supp. Com.* p. 8.

**Antiphanes Macedo** Epigrammaticus [Antiphan.] i A.D.
v. *Anthologia Graeca*.

**Antiphanes Megalopolitanus** Epigrammaticus [Antiphan.] i A.D.
v. *Anthologia Graeca*.

**Antiphilus** Epigrammaticus [Antiphil.] i A.D.
v. *Anthologia Graeca.*

**Antipho** Orator v B.C.
Ed. T. Thalheim, Leipzig (T.) 1914.

**Antipho Sophista** [Antipho Soph.] v B.C.
Ed. H. Diels, *Vorsokr.* ii p. 289.

**Antipho** Tragicus [Antipho Trag.] iv B.C.
Ed. A. Nauck, *TGF* p. 792.

**Antisthenes** Rhetor [Antisth.] iv B.C.
Ed. F. Blass (post Antiphontem), Leipzig (T.) 1892.
*Aj.* = Αἴας
*Od.* = Ὀδυσσεύς

**Antistius** Epigrammaticus [Antist.] i A.D.
v. *Anthologia Graeca.*

**Antoninus Liberalis** Mythographus [Ant.Lib.] ii A.D. (?)
Ed. E. Martini, *Mythographi Graeci* ii (1), Leipzig (T.) 1896.

**Antonius Argivus** Epigrammaticus [Anton.Arg.]
v. *Anthologia Graeca.*

**Antonius Diogenes** Scriptor Eroticus [Ant.Diog.] i or ii A.D.
Ed. R. Hercher, *Erotici* i p. 231.

**Antyllus** Medicus [Antyll.] ii A.D.
Apud Oribasium.

**Anubion** Poeta Astrologus [Anub.] i A.D.
Ed. H. Köchly (post Manethonem), Leipzig (T.) 1858.

**Anyte** Epigrammatica [Anyt.] iv/iii B.C.
v. *Anthologia Graeca.*

**Aphthonius** Rhetor [Aphth.] iv/v A.D.
Προγυμνάσματα, ed. L. Spengel, *Rhet.* ii p. 19. [*Prog.*]

**Apion** Grammaticus i A.D.
Ed. A. Ludwich in *Philol.* lxxiv (1917) p. 205, lxxv (1919) p. 9.

**Apollinarius** Epigrammaticus [Apollinar.] ii A.D. (?)
v. *Anthologia Graeca.*

**Apollodorus** Comicus [Apollod.Com.] iv/iii B.C.
Ed. T. Kock, *CAF* iii p. 288.
(Fragmenta utrum ad Apollodorum Carystium an ad Geloum pertineant incertum.)

**Apollodorus Carystius** Comicus [Apollod.Car.] iv/iii B.C.
Ed. T. Kock, *CAF* iii p. 280; suppl. J. Demiańczuk, *Supp. Com.* p. 8.

**Apollodorus Gelous** Comicus [Apollod.Gel.] iv/iii B.C.
Ed. T. Kock, *CAF* iii p. 278.

**Apollodorus** Mythographus [Apollod.] i A.D. (?)
*Bibliotheca*, ed. R. Wagner, *Mythographi Graeci* i, Leipzig (T.) 1894; cited without title.
*Epitome*, ed. R. Wagner, op. cit., p. 173. [*Epit.*]
*Fragmenta Historica*, ed. C. Müller, *FHG* i p. 428. [Hist.]

**Apollodorus Damascenus** Mechanicus [Apollod.] ii A.D.
Πολιορκητικά, Ed. R. Schneider, *Abhandlungen der Göttinger Gesellschaft der Wissenschaften* (*Phil.-hist. Klasse*), 1908. [*Poliorc.*] (Cited by Wescher's page, given in Schneider's margin.)

**Apollodorus** Lyricus [Apollod.Lyr.]
Ed. T. Bergk, *PLG* iii p. 378.

**Apollodorus Seleuciensis** Stoicus [Apollod.*Stoic.*] ii B.C.
Ed. H. von Arnim, *SVF* iii p. 259.

**Apollonides** Epigrammaticus [Apollonid.] i A.D.
v. *Anthologia Graeca.*

**Apollonides** Tragicus [Apollonid.Trag.]
Ed. A. Nauck, *TGF* p. 825.

**Apollonius** Biographus [Apollon.]
*Vit.Aeschin.* = *Vita Aeschinis*, ed. F. Blass (ante Aeschinem).

**Apollonius** Paradoxographus [Apollon.] ii B.C. (?)
*Mirabilia*, ed. O. Keller, *Rerum Naturalium Scriptores* i, Leipzig (T.) 1877, p. 43. [*Mir.*]

**Apollonius Citiensis** Medicus [Apollon.Cit.] i B.C.
Ed. H. Schöne, Leipzig 1896.

**Apollonius Dyscolus** Grammaticus [A.D.] ii A.D.
Ed. R. Schneider & G. Uhlig, Leipzig 1878–1910.
*Adv.* = *de Adverbiis*; cited by Schneider's page and line.
*Conj.* = *de Conjunctionibus*; cited by Schneider's page and line.
*Pron.* = *de Pronominibus*; cited by Schneider's page and line.
*Synt.* = *de Syntaxi*; cited by Bekker's page and line, given in Uhlig's margin.

**Apollonius Pergaeus** Geometra [Apollon.Perg.] iii/ii B.C.
*Conica*, ed. J. L. Heiberg, Leipzig (T.) 1891. [*Con.*]

**Apollonius** Medicus [Apollon.] i A.D.
Apud Galenum.

**Apollonius Rhodius** Epicus [A.R.] iii B.C.
Ed. R. C. Seaton, Oxford (OCT).

**Apollonius** Sophista [Apollon.] i/ii A.D.
*Lexicon Homericum*, ed. I. Bekker, Berlin 1833. [*Lex.*]

**Apollonius Tyanensis** Epistolographus [Ap.Ty.] i A.D.
*Epistulae*, ed. C. L. Kayser, *Philostratus* i p. 345. [*Ep.*]

**Apollophanes** Comicus [Apolloph.] v B.C.
Ed. T. Kock, *CAF* i p. 797; suppl. J. Demiańczuk, *Supp. Com.* p. 9.

**Apollophanes** Stoicus [Apolloph.*Stoic.*] iii B.C.
Ed. H. von Arnim, *SVF* i p. 90.

**Apostolius** Paroemiographus [Apostol.] xv A
Ed. E. von Leutsch & F. G. Schneidewin, *Paroemiograph* p. 233.

**Appianus** Historicus [App.] ii A
Ed. L. Mendelssohn & P. Viereck, Leipzig (T.) 1879–1905.
*BC* = *Bella Civilia*
*Gall.* = Κελτική
*Hann.* = Ἀννιβαϊκή
*Hisp.* = Ἰβηρική
*Ill.* = Ἰλλυρική
*Ital.* = Ἰταλική
*Mac.* = Μακεδονική
*Mith.* = Μιθριδάτειος
*Praef.* = *Praefatio*
*Pun.* = Λιβυκή
*Reg.* = Βασιλική
*Sam.* = Σαυνιτική
*Sic.* = Σικελική
*Syr.* = Συριακή

**Apsines** Rhetor [Aps.]
*Rh.* = *Ars Rhetorica*, ed. C. Hammer, in L. Spengel, *Rhet.* i² (2), Leipzig (T.) 1894, p. 217.

**Apuleius** Scriptor Botanicus [Apul.] iv A.D. (?)
*Herbarium*, Basel 1560. [*Herb.*]

**Aquila** Interpres Veteris Testamenti [Aq.] ii A.D.
Ed. F. Field, *Origenis Hexapla*, Oxford 1875; cf. Vetus Testamentum.

**Arabius** Epigrammaticus [Arab.] vi A.D.
v. *Anthologia Graeca.*

**Araros** Comicus [Arar.] v/iv B.C.
Ed. T. Kock, *CAF* ii p. 215.

**Aratus** Epicus [Arat.] iv/iii B.C.
Ed. E. Maass, Berlin 1893.
Scholia, ed. E. Maass, *Commentariorum in Aratum reliquiae*, Berlin 1898.

**Arcadius** Grammaticus [Arc.] iv A.D. (?)
Ed. E. H. Barker, Leipzig 1820; ed. M. Schmidt, Ἐπιτομὴ τῆς καθολικῆς προσῳδίας Ἡρωδιανοῦ, Jena 1860: cited by Barker's page, given in Schmidt's margin.

**Arcesilaus** Comicus [Arcesil.] v B.C.
Ed. J. Demiańczuk, *Supp. Com.* p. 10.

**Archedicus** Comicus [Arched.] iv/iii B.C.
Ed. T. Kock, *CAF* iii p. 276.

**Archedemus Tarsensis** Stoicus [Arched.*Stoic.*] iii B.C. (?)
Ed. H. von Arnim, *SVF* iii p. 262.

**Archemachus** Historicus [Archemach.]
Ed. C. Müller, *FHG* iv p. 314.

**Archestratus** Epicus [Archestr.] iv B.C.
Ed. P. Brandt, *Corpusculum poesis Epicae Graecae ludibundae* i p. 114, Leipzig (T.) 1888.

**Archias** (unus vel plures) Epigrammaticus [Arch.] i B.C.
v. *Anthologia Graeca.*

**Archias Junior** Epigrammaticus [Arch.Jun.]
v. *Anthologia Graeca.*

**Archigenes** Medicus [Archig.] ii A.D.
Apud Galenum, Aëtium, Oribasium.

**Archilochus** Lyricus [Archil.] vii B.C.
Ed. T. Bergk, *PLG* ii p. 383; suppl. E. Diehl, *Supp. Lyr.*³ p. 4. [*Supp.*]

**Archimedes** Geometra [Archim.] iii B.C.
Ed. J. L. Heiberg, ed. 2, Leipzig (T.) 1910–15.
*Aequil.* = περὶ ἰσορροπιῶν
*Aren.* = ψαμμίτης
*Bov.* = πρόβλημα βοεικόν
*Circ.* = κύκλου μέτρησις
*Con.Sph.* = περὶ κωνοειδέων καὶ σφαιροειδέων
*Eratosth.* = πρὸς Ἐρατοσθένην ἔφοδος
*Fluit* = περὶ τῶν ὀχουμένων
*Fr.* = *Fragmenta*
*Quadr.* = τετραγωνισμὸς παραβολῆς
*Sph.Cyl.* = περὶ σφαίρας καὶ κυλίνδρου
*Spir.* = περὶ ἑλίκων
*Stom.* = στομάχιον

**Archimelus** Epigrammaticus [Archimel.] iii B.C.
v. *Anthologia Graeca.*

**Archippus** Comicus [Archipp.] v/iv B.C.
Ed. T. Kock, *CAF* i p. 679; suppl. J. Demiańczuk, *Supp. Com.* p. 10.

**Archytas Amphissensis** Epicus [Archyt.Amph.] iii B.C.
Ed. J. U. Powell, *Coll. Alex.* p. 23.

**Archytas Tarentinus** Philosophus [Archyt.] iv B.C.
Ed. H. Diels, *Vorsokr.* i p. 322.

**Aretaeus** Medicus [Aret.] ii A.D.
Ed. K. Hude, *CMG* ii, Leipzig 1923.
*CA* = ὀξέων νούσων θεραπευτικόν
*CD* = χρονίων νούσων θεραπευτικόν
*SA* = περὶ αἰτιῶν καὶ σημείων ὀξέων παθῶν
*SD* = περὶ αἰτιῶν καὶ σημείων χρονίων παθῶν

**Arion** Lyricus vi B.C.
Ed. T. Bergk, *PLG* iii p. 79.

**phron** Lyricus iv B.C.
Ed. T. Bergk, *PLG* iii p. 595.
**istaenetus** Rhetor [Aristaenet.]
Ed. Hercher, *Epistolographi*, p. 133.
**istagoras** Comicus [Aristag.] v B.C.
Ed. T. Kock, *CAF* i p. 710.
**istagoras** Historicus [Aristag.Hist.] iv B.C.
Ed. C. Müller *FHG* ii p. 98.
**ristarchus** Grammaticus [Aristarch.] iii/ii B.C.
Apud Scholia in Homerum.
**ristarchus Samius** Astronomus [Aristarch.Sam.] iii B.C.
Ed. Sir T. L. Heath, Oxford 1913.
**ristarchus** Tragicus [Aristarch.Trag.] v B.C.
Ed. A. Nauck, *TGF* p. 728.
**risteas** Epicus [Aristeas Epic.] vi B.C.
Ed. G. Kinkel, *EGF* p. 243.
**Aristeas Judaeus** ii B.C. (?)
Ed. P. Wendland, Leipzig (T.) 1900.
**Aristias** Tragicus v B.C.
Ed. A. Nauck, *TGF* p. 726.
**Aristides** Rhetor [Aristid.] 129–189 A.D.
Ed. S. Jebb, 2 vols., Oxford 1722–30; ed. W. Dindorf, 3 vols., Leipzig 1829; ed. B. Keil, vol. ii (all published), Berlin 1898.
*Or.* = *Orationes*, cited by speech and section, if from Keil; the rest cited without title by Jebb's vol. and page (given in margin of Dindorf).
*Rh.* = *τέχναι ῥητορικαί*, ed. L. Spengel, *Rhet.* ii p. 457; cited by Spengel's page.
Scholia, ed W. Dindorf, op. cit.; ed. W. Frommel, Frankfort 1826.
**Aristides Milesius** Historicus [Aristid.Mil.] ii B.C.
Ed. C. Müller, *FHG* iv p. 320.
**Aristides Quintilianus** Musicus [Aristid.Quint.] iii A.D. (?)
Ed. A. Jahn, Berlin 1882.
**Aristippus** Philosophus [Aristipp.] v/iv B.C.
Cited from sources; cf. F. W. A. Mullach, *FPG* ii p. 405.
**Aristo** Epigrammaticus i B.C. (?)
v. *Anthologia Graeca.*
**Aristo Chius** Stoicus [Aristo *Stoic.*] iii B.C.
Ed. H. von Arnim, *SVF* i p. 75.
**Aristobulus** Historicus [Aristobul.] iv B.C.
Ed. C. Müller, *SRAM* p. 94.
**Aristocles** Epigrammaticus [Aristocl.]
Apud Aelianum.
**Aristocles** Historicus [Aristocl.Hist.] i B.C./i A.D.
Ed. C. Müller, *FHG* iv p. 329.
**Aristocles** Philosophus [Aristocl.] ii A.D.
Apud Eusebium; cf. F. W. A. Mullach, *FPG* iii p. 206.
**Aristodemus** Historicus [Aristodem.] i B.C.
Ed. C. Müller, *FHG* iii p. 307.
**Aristodicus** Epigrammaticus [Aristodic.] iii or ii B.C.
v. *Anthologia Graeca.*
**Aristomenes** Comicus [Aristomen.] v/iv B.C.
Ed. T. Kock, *CAF* i p. 690.
**Aristonous** Lyricus iii B.C.
Ed. J. U. Powell, *Coll. Alex.* p. 162.
**Aristonymus** Comicus [Aristonym.] v/iv B.C.
Ed. T. Kock, *CAF* i p. 668.
**Aristonymus** Gnomologus [Aristonym.]
Apud Stobaeum.
**Aristophanes** Comicus [Ar.] v/iv B.C.
Ed. F. W. Hall & W. M. Geldart, Oxford (OCT); suppl. J. Demiańczuk, *Supp. Com.* p. 11.
*Ach.* = *Acharnenses*
*Av.* = *Aves*
*Ec.* = *Ecclesiazusae*
*Eq.* = *Equites*
*Fr.* = *Fragmenta*
*Lys.* = *Lysistrata*
*Nu.* = *Nubes*
*Pax*
*Pl.* = *Plutus*
*Ra.* = *Ranae*
*Th.* = *Thesmophoriazusae*
*V.* = *Vespae*
Scholia, ed. W. Dindorf in editione Aristophanis, Oxford 1835–8.
**Aristophanes Boeotus** Historicus [Aristoph.Boeot.] iv B.C.
Ed C. Müller, *FHG* iv p. 337.
**Aristophanes Byzantinus** Philosophus [Ar.Byz.] iii/ii B.C.
*Epit.* = *Historiae Animalium Epitome subiunctis Aeliani Timothei aliorumque eclogis*, ed. Spyridon P. Lambros (*Supplementum Aristotelicum* i *pars* i), Berlin 1885.
**Aristopho** Comicus iv B.C.
Ed. T. Kock, *CAF* ii p. 276.
**Aristoteles** Philosophus [Arist.] iv B.C.
Ed. I. Bekker, Berlin 1831–70.
*APo.* = *Analytica Posteriora*
*APr.* = *Analytica Priora*
*Ath.* = *Ἀθηναίων Πολιτεία*, ed. Sir F. G. Kenyon, Oxford (OCT).
*Aud.* = *de Audibilibus*
*Cael.* = *de Caelo*
*Cat.* = *Categoriae*
*Col.* = *de Coloribus*
*de An.* = *de Anima*
*Div.Somn.* = *de Divinatione per Somnia*
*EE* = *Ethica Eudemia*
*EN* = *Ethica Nicomachea*
*Ep* = *Epistulae*, *ed* R. Hercher, *Epistolographi*, p. 170.
*Fr.* = *Fragmenta*, ed. V. Rose, Leipzig (T.) 1886.
*GA* = *de Generatione Animalium*
*GC* = *de Generatione et Corruptione*
*HA* = *Historia Animalium*
*IA* = *de Incessu Animalium*
*Insomn.* = *de Insomniis*
*Int.* = *de Interpretatione*
*Juv.* = *de Juventute*
*LI* = *de Lineis Insecabilibus*
*Long* = *de Longaevitate*
*MA* = *de Motu Animalium*
*MM* = *Magna Moralia*
*Mech.* = *Mechanica*
*Mem.* = *de Memoria*
*Metaph.* = *Metaphysica*
*Mete.* = *Meteorologica*
*Mir.* = *Mirabilia*
*Mu.* = *de Mundo*
*Oec.* = *Oeconomica*
*PA* = *de Partibus Animalium*
*Pepl.* = *Peplus* (*Fr.* 640).
*Ph.* = *Physica*
*Phgn.* = *Physiognomonica*
*Po.* = *Poetica*
*Pol.* = *Politica*
*Pr.* = *Problemata*
*Resp.* = *de Respiratione*
*Rh.* = *Rhetorica*
*Rh.Al.* = *Rhetorica ad Alexandrum*
*SE* = *Sophistici Elenchi*
*Sens.* = *de Sensu*
*Somn.Vig.* = *de Somno et Vigilia*
*Spir.* = *de Spiritu*
*Top.* = *Topica*
*VV* = *de Virtutibus et Vitiis*
*Vent.* = *de Ventis*
*Xen.* = *de Xenophane*
**Aristoxenus** Musicus [Aristox.] iv B.C.
*Fragmenta Historica*, ed. C. Müller, *FHG* ii p. 269. [*Fr.Hist.*]
*Harmonica*, ed. H. S. Macran, Oxford 1902. [*Harm.*] (Cited by Meibom's page, given in Macran's margin.)
*Rhythmica*, ed. R. Westphal, *Aristoxenos von Tarent Melik und Rhythmik*, vol ii, Leipzig 1893. [*Rhyth.*]
**Arius Didymus** Doxographus [Ar.Did.] i B.C.
Ed. H. Diels, *Doxographi Graeci*, Berlin 1879, p. 447.
**Arrianus** Historicus [Arr.] ii A.D.
*Alan.* = *Expeditio contra Alanos*, ed. R. Hercher & A. Eberhard, *Arriani Scripta Minora*, Leipzig (T.) 1885.
*An.* = *Anabasis*, ed. A. G. Roos, Leipzig (T.) 1907.
*Cyn.* = *Cynegeticus*, ed. Hercher-Eberhard (v. supr.).
*Epict.* = *Epicteti Dissertationes*, ed. H. Schenkl, Leipzig (T.) 1894.
*Fr.* = *Fragmenta Historica*, ed. C. Müller, *FHG* iii p. 586.
*Ind.* = *Indica*, ed. Hercher-Eberhard (v. supr.).
*Peripl.M.Eux.* = *Periplus maris Euxini*, ed. Hercher-Eberhard (v. supr.).
*Tact.* = *Tactica*, ed. Hercher-Eberhard (v. supr.).
**Artemidorus Daldianus** Onirocriticus [Artem.] ii A.D.
Ed. R. Hercher, Leipzig 1864.
**Artemidorus Tarsensis** Epigrammaticus [Artemid.] i B.C.
v. *Anthologia Graeca.*
**Artemo** Epigrammaticus
v. *Anthologia Graeca.*
**Artemones** Historici
Ed. C. Müller, *FHG* iv p. 340.
**Arusianus Messius** Grammaticus [Arus.Mess.] iv/v A.D.
Ed. H. Keil, *Gramm. Lat.* vii p. 437.
**Ascensio Isaiae** [*Ascens.Is.*]
Ed. B. P. Grenfell and A. S. Hunt, *PAmh.* I. I.
**Asclepiades** Epigrammaticus [Asclep.] iii B.C.
v. *Anthologia Graeca.*
**Asclepiades Junior** Medicus [Asclep.Jun.] i/ii A.D.
Apud Galenum.
**Asclepiades Myrleanus** Historicus [Asclep.Myrl.] ii/i B.C.
Ed. C. Müller, *FHG* iii p. 298.
**Asclepiades Prusensis** Medicus [Asclep.] ii/i B.C.
Apud Galenum.
**Asclepiades Tragilensis** Historicus [Asclep.Tragil.] iv B.C.
Ed. F. Jacoby, *FGrH* i p. 166.
**Asclepiodotus** Tacticus [Ascl.] i B.C.
Ed. H. Köchly & W. Rüstow, *Griechische Kriegsschriftsteller*, Leipzig 1855; ed. W. A. Oldfather, v. Onosander. [*Tact.*]

**Asclepius** Philosophus [Ascl.] vi A.D.
*in Metaph.* = *in Aristotelis Metaphysicorum libros* A–Z *commentaria*, ed. M. Hayduck (*Comm. in Arist. Graeca* vi *pars* ii), Berlin 1888.

**Asius** Lyricus vii/vi B.C.
Ed. T. Bergk, *PLG* ii p. 406.

**Aspasius** Philosophus [Asp.] ca. 110 A.D.
*in EN* = *in Ethica Nicomachea commentaria*, ed. G. Heylbut (*Comm. in Arist. Graeca* xix *pars* i), Berlin 1889.

**Astrampsychus** Onirocriticus [Astramps.] ii A.D.
*Onir.* = *Onirocritica*, ed. N. Rigalt (post Artemidorum), Paris 1603.
*Orac.* = *Oracula*, ed. R. Hercher, Berlin 1863.

**Astydamas** Tragicus [Astyd.] iv B.C.
Ed. A. Nauck, *TGF* p. 777.
*Fragmentum Elegiacum*, ed. T. Bergk, *PLG* ii p. 326. [*Eleg.*]

**Athanis** Historicus iv B.C.
Ed. C. Müller, *FHG* ii p. 81.

**Athenaeus** Epigrammaticus [Ath.]
v. *Anthologia Graeca.*

**Athenaeus** Grammaticus [Ath.] ii/iii A.D.
Ed. G. Kaibel, 3 vols., Leipzig (T.) 1887–90.
*Epit.* = *Epitome*, ed. J. Schweighäuser, Strassburg 1801–7.

**Athenaeus** Mechanicus [Ath.Mech.]
Ed. C. Wescher, *Poliorcétique des Grecs*, Paris 1867 (page and line).

**Athenaeus** Medicus [Ath.Med.] i A.D.
Apud Oribasium.

**Athenio** Comicus iii B.C.
Ed. T. Kock, *CAF* iii p. 369.

**Athenodorus Tarsensis** Historicus [Athenodor.Tars.] i B.C.
Ed. C. Müller, *FHG* iii p. 485.

**Atilius Fortunatianus** Grammaticus Latinus [Atil.Fort.] iv A.D. (?)
Ed. H. Keil, *Gramm. Lat.* vi p. 278.

**Attalus** Grammaticus [Attal.] ii B.C.
Ed. E. Maass, *Commentariorum in Aratum reliquiae*, Berlin 1898, p. 3. [*in Arat.*]

**Atticus** Philosophus [Attic.] ii A.D.
Apud Eusebium.

**Ausonius** Poeta Latinus [Aus.] iv A.D.
Ed. R. Peiper, Leipzig (T.) 1886.
*Ep.* = *Epistulae*
*Epigr.* = *Epigrammata*
*Idyll.* = *Idyllia*

**Autocrates** Comicus [Autocr.] v/iv B.C.
Ed. T. Kock *CAF* i p. 806.

**Autolycus** Astronomus [Autol.] iv B.C.
Ed. F. Hultsch, Leipzig (T.) 1885.

**Automedon** Epigrammaticus [Autom.] i A.D.
v. *Anthologia Graeca.*

**Axionicus** Comicus [Axionic.] iv B.C.
Ed. T. Kock, *CAF* ii p. 411.

**Axiopistus** Poeta Ethicus [Axiop.] iv/iii B.C.
Ed. J. U. Powell, *Coll. Alex.* p. 219.

**Babrius** Fabularum Scriptor [Babr.] ii A.D.
Ed. O. Crusius, Leipzig (T.) 1897.

**Bacchius** Musicus [Bacch.]
*Harm.* = Εἰσαγωγὴ τέχνης μουσικῆς, ed. C. Jan, *Musici Scriptores Graeci*, Leipzig (T.) 1895, p. 292.

**Bacchylides** Lyricus [B.] v B.C.
Ed. Sir R. C. Jebb, Cambridge 1905.
*Scolia*, in *POxy.* 1361. [*Scol.Oxy.*]

**Balbilla** Lyrica [Balbill.] ii A.D.
v. *Epigrammata Graeca* in II.

**Barbucallos** Epigrammaticus [Barb.] vi A.D.
v. *Anthologia Graeca.*

**Bassus, Lollius** Epigrammaticus [Bass.] i A.D.
v. *Anthologia Graeca.*

**Bato** Comicus iii B.C.
Ed. T. Kock, *CAF* iii p. 326.

**Bato Sinopensis** Historicus [Bato Sinop.] ii B.C.
Ed. C. Müller, *FHG* iv p. 347.

**Batrachomyomachia** [Batr.]
Ed. T. W. Allen, *Homeri Opera* v, Oxford (OCT), p. 168.

**Berosus** Historicus [Beros.] iv/iii B.C.
Ed. C. Müller, *FHG* ii p. 495.

**Besantinus** Epigrammaticus [Besant.] ii A.D.
v. *Anthologia Graeca.*
*Ara* = *AP* 15.25.

**Bianor** Epigrammaticus i B.C./i A.D.
Idem qui et Statyllius Flaccus, q. v.
v. *Anthologia Graeca.*

**Bias** Lyricus vi B.C.
Ed. T. Bergk, *PLG* iii p. 199. [*Fr.Lyr.*]

**Bion** Bucolicus ii B.C.
Ed. U. von Wilamowitz-Möllendorff², *Bucolici Graeci*, Oxford (OCT).

**Biotus** Tragicus
Ed. A. Nauck, *TGF* p. 825.

**Bito** Mechanicus iii or ii B
Ed. C. Wescher, *Poliorcétique des Grecs*, Paris 1867 (page a line).

**Blaesus** Comicus [Blaes.]
Ed. G. Kaibel, *CGF* p. 191.

**Boeo sive Boeus** Epicus ii B.C. (
Ed. J. U. Powell, *Coll. Alex.* p. 23.

**Boethus** Epigrammaticus [Boeth.] i A.
v. *Anthologia Graeca.*

**Boethus Sidonius** Stoicus [Boeth.*Stoic.*] ii B.
Ed. H. von Arnim, *SVF* iii p. 265.

**Brutus** Epistolographus [Brut.] i B.
*Ep.* = *Epistula*, ed. R. Hercher. *Epistolographi*, p. 177.

**Butherus** Philosophus [Buther.]
Apud Stobaeum.

**Caelius Aurelianus** Medicus [Cael.Aur.] v A.D
Ed. C. Amman, Amsterdam 1709.
*CP* = *Celeres Passiones*
*TP* = *Tardae Passiones*

**Callias** Epigrammaticus [Call.]
v. *Anthologia Graeca.*

**Callias** Comicus [Call.Com.] v/iv B.C.
Ed. T. Kock, *CAF* i p. 693; suppl. J. Demiańczuk, *Supp. Com.* p. 27.

**Callias** Historicus [Call.Hist.] iv/iii B.C.
Ed. C. Müller, *FHG* ii p. 382.

**Callicratidas** Philosophus [Callicrat.]
Apud Stobaeum.

**Callicter** Epigrammaticus
Interdum scribitur Cillactor.
v. *Anthologia Graeca.*

**Callimachus** Epicus [Call.] iii B.C.
Ed. O. Schneider, 2 vols., Leipzig 1870–3; ed. A. W. Mair, London (Loeb) 1921; *Fragmenta nuper reperta*, ed. R. Pfeiffer, ed. major, Bonn 1923.
*Aet.* = *Aetia*
*Ap.* = *Hymnus in Apollinem*
*Cer.* = *Hymnus in Cererem*
*Del.* = *Hymnus in Delum*
*Dian.* = *Hymnus in Dianam*
*Epigr.* = *Epigrammata*
*Fr.* = *Fragmenta*
*Fr.anon.* = *Fragmenta anonyma*
*Hec.* = *Hecale*
*Iamb.* = *Iambi*
*Jov.* = *Hymnus in Jovem*
*Lav.Pall.* = *Lavacrum Palladis*
*Sos.* = *Sosibii Victoria*
Note.—*Aet.*, *Hec.*, *Iamb.* generally refer to Mair's edition; fragments cited from Pfeiffer's edition are distinguished by the initial 'P.'

**Callinicus** Rhetor [Callinic.Rh.] iii A.D.
Ed. H. Hinck (post Polemonem), Leipzig (T.) 1873.

**Callinus** Epicus [Callin.] vii B.C.
Ed. T. Bergk, *PLG* ii p. 3.

**Callistratus** Historicus [Callistr.Hist.] i B.C.
Ed. C. Müller, *FHG* iv p. 353.

**Callistratus** Sophista [Callistr.] iv A.D.
Ed. C. Schenkl & Aem. Reisch (post Philostratum Minorem), Leipzig (T.) 1902.
*Stat.* = *Statuarum descriptiones*

**Callixinus** Historicus [Callix.] iii B.C. (?)
Ed. C. Müller, *FHG* iii p. 55.

**Candidus** Historicus v A.D.
Ed. L. Dindorf, *HGM* i p. 441.

**Cantharus** Comicus [Canthar.] v B.C.
Ed. T. Kock, *CAF* i p. 764; suppl. J. Demiańczuk, *Supp. Com.* p. 28.

**Carcinus** Tragicus [Carc.] v B.C.
Ed. A. Nauck, *TGF* p. 797.

**Carmen Aureum** [*Carm.Aur.*]
Ed. E. Diehl, *Anthologia Lyrica* ii, Leipzig (T.) 1923, p. 186.

**Carmina Popularia** [*Carm.Pop.*]
Ed. T. Bergk, *PLG* iii p. 654.

**Carneiscus** Philosophus [Carneisc.] iv/iii B.C.
Ed. W. Crönert, *Kolotes und Menedemos*, Leipzig 1906, p. 60.

**Carphyllides** Epigrammaticus [Carph.]
v. *Anthologia Graeca.*

**Carystius** Historicus [Caryst.] ii B.C.
Ed. C. Müller, *FHG* iv p. 356.

**Cassius** Medicus [Cass.] iii A.D.
Προβλήματα, ed. J. L. Ideler, *Physici et Medici Graeci Minores*, Berlin 1841, i p. 144. [*Pr.*]

**Cassius Felix** Medicus [Cass.Fel.] iv A.D.
Ed. V. Rose, Leipzig (T.) 1879.

**Castorio** Lyricus iv/iii B.C.
Ed. T. Bergk, *PLG* iii p. 634.

**alogus Codicum Astrologorum** [*Cat.Cod.Astr.*]
d. F. Cumont et alii, Brussels 1898– ; cited by vol. and page.
**es** Philosophus [Ceb.] i A.D.
d. K. Praechter, Leipzig (T.) 1893.
**sus** Medicus [Cels.] i A.D.
d. F. Marx, Leipzig 1915.
**sus** Philosophus [Cels.] ii A.D.
pud Origenem.
**phalio** Historicus ii A.D.
Ed. C. Müller, *FHG* iii p. 625.
**phisodorus** Comicus [Cephisod.] v/iv B.C.
Ed. T. Kock, *CAF* i p. 800.
**rcidas** Iambographus [Cerc.] iii B.C.
Ed. J. U. Powell, *Coll. Alex.* p. 201.
**rcopes** [Cercop.]
Ed. T. W. Allen, *Homeri Opera* v, Oxford (OCT), p. 159.
**erealius** Epigrammaticus [Cereal.] i/ii A.D. (?)
v. *Anthologia Graeca.*
**ertamen Homeri et Hesiodi** [Certamen]
Ed. T. W. Allen, *Homeri Opera* v, Oxford (OCT), p. 225.
**haeremon** Historicus [Chaerem.Hist.] i A.D.
Ed. C. Müller, *FHG* iii p. 495.
**haeremon** Tragicus [Chaerem.] iv B.C.
Ed. A. Nauck, *TGF* p. 781.
**hamaeleon** Grammaticus [Chamael.]
Apud Athenaeum.
**haracteres Epistolici** [*Epist.Charact.*]
*Demetrii et Libanii qui feruntur τύποι ἐπιστολικοί et ἐπιστολιμαῖοι χαρακτῆρες*, ed. V. Weichert, Leipzig (T.) 1910.
**Charax** Historicus ii A.D. (?)
Ed. C. Müller, *FHG* iii p. 636, iv p. 669.
**Chares** Historicus iv B.C.
Ed. C. Müller, *SRAM* p. 114.
**Chares** Iambographus [Chares Iamb.] iv/iii B.C.
Ed. J. U. Powell, *Coll. Alex.* p. 223.
**Chares** Tragicus [Chares Trag.]
Ed. A. Nauck, *TGF* p. 826.
**Chariclides** Comicus [Chariclid.]
Ed. T. Kock, *CAF* iii p. 393.
**Charisius** Grammaticus Latinus [Charis.] iv A.D.
Ed. H. Keil, *Gramm. Lat.* vol. i.
**Charito** Scriptor Eroticus ii A.D. (?)
Ed. R. Hercher, *Erotici* ii p. 3.
**Charixenes** Medicus [Charixen.] ii A.D.
Apud Galenum.
**Charon** Historicus v B.C.
Ed. C. Müller, *FHG* i p. 32, iv p. 627.
**Charondas** Philosophus [Charond.] (vii B.C.)
Apud Stobaeum.
**Chilo** Lyricus vi B.C.
Ed. T. Bergk, *PLG* iii p. 199.
**Chio** Epistolographus (iv B.C.)
Ed. R. Hercher, *Epistolographi*, p. 194.
**Chionides** Comicus [Chionid.] v B.C.
Ed. T. Kock, *CAF* i p. 4.
**Choerilus** Epicus [Choeril.] v B.C.
Ed. G. Kinkel, *EGF* p. 265.
**Choerilus** Tragicus [Choeril.Trag.] v B.C.
Ed. A. Nauck, *TGF* p. 719.
**Choeroboscus** Grammaticus [Choerob.] iv/v A.D.
*περὶ ὀρθογραφίας*, ed. Cramer, *An. Ox.* ii p. 167.
*περὶ τρόπων*, ed. L. Spengel, *Rhet.* iii p. 244. [Rh.]
*Scholia in Hephaestionem*, ed. W. Consbruch, post Hephaestionem, p. 177. [*in Heph.*]
*Scholia in Theodosii Canones*, ed. A. Hilgard, 2 vols., Leipzig 1889–94. [*in Theod.*]
**Choricius** Rhetor [Chor.] vi A.D.
Ed. J. F. Boissonade, Paris 1846.
*Brum.* = *εἰς τὰ Ἰουστινιανοῦ Βρουμάλια*, ed. R. Förster, *Ind. Lect. Vratisl.* 1891/2, Breslau 1891.
*Lyd.* = *Λυδοί*, ed. R. Förster, op. cit.
*Milt.* = *Μιλτιάδης*, ed. R. Förster, *Ind. Lect. Vratisl.* 1892/3, Breslau 1892.
*Proc.* = *Ἐπιθαλάμιος εἰς Προκόπιον*, ed. R. Förster, *Ind. Lect. Vratisl.* 1891/2, Breslau 1891.
*Zach* = *Ἐπιθαλάμιος εἰς Ζαχαρίαν*, ed. R. Förster, op. cit.
Note.—Other orations cited from periodicals, *Hermes* xvii (1883), *Jahrb.* ix (1894), *Philol.* liv (1895), *Rev. Phil.* i (1877), *Rh. Mus.* xxxvii (1882), xlix (1894), or from Reiske's *Libanius*, vol. iv, pp. 512, 771.
**Chrysippus** Stoicus [Chrysipp.*Stoic.*] 281–208 B.C.
Ed. H. von Arnim, *SVF* ii and iii pp. 1–194.
**Chrysippus Tyanensis** Rei Coquinariae Scriptor [Chrysipp. Tyan.] i A.D.
Apud Athenaeum.
**Cicero, M. Tullius** Orator et Philosophus [Cic.] i B.C.
*Acad.* = *Academica*, ed. O. Plasberg, Leipzig (T.) 1922.
*Att.* = *Epistulae ad Atticum*, ed. L. C. Purser, Oxford (OCT).
*Brut.* = *Brutus*, ed. A. S. Wilkins, Oxford (OCT).
*Fam.* = *Epistulae ad Familiares*, ed. L. C. Purser, Oxford (OCT).
*Fin.* = *de Finibus*, ed. T. Schiche, Leipzig (T.) 1915.
*ND* = *de Natura Deorum*, ed. O. Plasberg, Leipzig (T.) 1917.
*Off.* = *de Officiis*, ed. C. Atzert, Leipzig (T.) 1923.
*Orat.* = *Orator*, ed. A. S. Wilkins, Oxford (OCT).
*QF* = *Epistulae ad Quintum Fratrem*, ed. L. C. Purser, Oxford (OCT).
*Top.* = *Topica*, ed. W. Friedrich, Leipzig (T.) 1893.
*Tusc.* = *Tusculanae Disputationes*, ed. M. Pohlenz, Leipzig (T.) 1918.
**Cillactor**, v. Callicter
**Claudianus** Epigrammaticus [Claudian.] iv/v A.D.
v. *Anthologia Graeca.*
**Claudius Iolaus** Historicus [Claud.Iol.]
Ed. C. Müller, *FHG* iv p. 362.
**Cleaenetus** Tragicus [Cleaenet.] iv B.C.
Ed. A. Nauck, *TGF* p. 807.
**Cleanthes** Stoicus [Cleanth.*Stoic.*] 331–233 B.C.
Ed. H. von Arnim, *SVF* i p. 103.
Poetical fragments, ed. J. U. Powell, *Coll. Alex.* p. 227.
**Clearchus** Comicus [Clearch.Com.] iv B.C.
Ed. T. Kock, *CAF* ii p. 408.
**Clearchus** Historicus [Clearch.] iv/iii B.C.
Ed. C. Müller, *FHG* ii p. 302.
**Clemens Alexandrinus** Theologus [Clem.Al.] ii/iii A.D.
Ed. O. Stählin, Leipzig 1905–9.
*Paed.* = *Paedagogus*
*Protr.* = *Protrepticus*
*Strom.* = *Stromateis*
**Cleobulina** Lyrica vi B.C.
Ed. T. Bergk, *PLG* ii p. 62.
**Cleobulus** Lyricus [Cleobul.] vi B.C.
Ed. T. Bergk, *PLG* iii p. 201.
**Cleomedes** Astronomus [Cleom.] ii A.D.
Ed. H. Ziegler, Leipzig (T.) 1891.
**Cleon Siculus** Lyricus [Cleon Sic.]
Ed. T. Bergk, *PLG* ii p. 363.
**Cleonides** Musicus [Cleonid.] ii A.D.
*Harm.* = *Introductio Harmonica*, ed. C. Jan, *Musici Scriptores Graeci*, Leipzig (T.) 1895, p. 179; ed. H. Menge, *Euclidis Opera* viii, Leipzig (T.) 1916, p. 186.
**Cleopatra** Medica
Apud Galenum.
**Cleostratus** Poeta Philosophus [Cleostrat.] iv/iii B.C. (?)
Ed. H. Diels, *PPF* p. 19.
**Clidemus** (vel **Clitodemus**) Historicus [Clidem. vel Clitodem.] iv B.C.
Ed. C. Müller, *FHG* i p. 359.
**Clinias** Philosophus [Clin.] iv B.C.
Apud Stobaeum.
**Clitarchus** Gnomologus [Clitarch.]
*Sententiae*, ed. A. Elter, *Index Lect. Hib.* . . . Bonn 1892. [*Sent.*]
**Clitarchus** Historicus [Clitarch.] iv B.C.
Ed. C. Müller, *SRAM* p. 74.
**Clitodemus**, v. Clidemus
**Clitomachus** Philosophus [Clitom.] ii B.C.
Apud Stobaeum.
**Clitopho** Historicus
Ed. C. Müller, *FHG* iv p. 367.
**Clytus** Historicus iv/iii B.C.
Ed. C. Müller, *FHG* ii p. 333.
**Codex Justinianus** [*Cod.Just.*] iv/vi A.D.
Ed. P. Krüger, *Corpus Juris Civilis* ii[9], Berlin 1915.
**Codex Theodosianus** [*Cod.Theod.*] v A.D.
Ed. T. Mommsen & P. M. Meyer, Berlin 1895; ed. P. Krüger, Berlin 1923.
**Colotes** Philosophus [Colot.] iv/iii B.C.
*In Platonis Euthydemum*, *In Platonis Lysin*, ed. W. Crönert, *Kolotes und Menedemos*, Leipzig 1906. [*in Euthd.*, *in Ly.*]
**Coluthus** Epicus [Coluth.] v/vi A.D.
Ed. W. Weinberger (post Tryphiodorum), Leipzig (T.) 1896.
**Comica Adespota** [*Com.Adesp.*]
Ed. T. Kock, *CAF* iii p. 397; suppl. J. Demiańczuk, *Supp. Com.* p. 89, O. Schroeder, *Novae Comoediae fragmenta in papyris reperta exceptis Menandreis*, Bonn 1915.
**Conon** Historicus i B.C./i A.D.
Ed. F. Jacoby, *FGrH* i p. 190.
**Corinna** Lyrica [Corinn.] vi B.C.
Ed. T. Bergk, *PLG* iii p. 543; suppl. E. Diehl, *Supp. Lyr.*[3] p. 48. [*Supp.*]
**Cornelius Longus** Epigrammaticus [Corn.Long.]
v. *Anthologia Graeca.*
**Cornutus** Philosophus [Corn.] i A.D.
*de Natura Deorum*, ed. C. Lang, Leipzig (T.) 1881. [*ND*]
*Ars Rhetorica*, ed. C. Hammer, in L. Spengel, *Rhet.* i[2] (2), Leipzig (T.) 1894, p. 352. [*Rh.*]
**Corpus Hermeticum** [*Corp.Herm.*]
*Hermetica*, ed. W. Scott, Oxford 1924.

**Crantor** Philosophus Academicus iv/iii B.C.
Cited from sources; cf. F. W. A. Mullach, *FPG* iii p. 131.
**Craterus** Historicus [Crater.] iv/iii B.C.
Ed. C. Müller, *FHG* ii p. 617.
**Crates** Comicus [Crates Com.] v B.C.
Ed. T. Kock, *CAF* i p. 130; suppl. J. Demiańczuk, *Supp. Com.* p. 29.
**Crates** Historicus [Crates Hist.]
Ed. C. Müller, *FHG* iv p. 369.
**Crates Thebanus** Poeta Philosophus [Crates Theb.] iv B.C.
Ed. H. Diels, *PPF* p. 207.
*Ep.* = *Epistulae*, ed. R. Hercher, *Epistolographi*, p. 199.
**Crateuas** Botanicus ii/i B.C.
*Fragmenta*, ed. M. Wellmann (post Dioscoridem), vol. iii, p. 144. [*Fr.*]
**Cratinus** Comicus [Cratin.] v B.C.
Ed. T. Kock, *CAF* i p. 11; suppl. J. Demiańczuk, *Supp. Com.* p. 30.
**Cratinus Junior** Comicus [Cratin.Jun.] iv B.C.
Ed. T. Kock, *CAF* ii p. 289.
**Cratippus** Historicus [Cratipp.] v/iv B.C.
Ed. B. P. Grenfell et A. S. Hunt, post *Hellenica Oxyrhynchia.*
**Creon** Historicus
Ed. C. Müller, *FHG* iv p. 371.
**Crinagoras** Epigrammaticus [Crin.] i B.C./i A.D.
v. *Anthologia Graeca.*
**Crinis** Stoicus
Ed. H. von Arnim, *SVF* iii p. 268.
**Critias** Philosophus, Tragicus, Elegiacus [Critias] v B.C.
Ed. H. Diels, *Vorsokr.* ii p. 308.
**Crito** Comicus [Crito Com.] ii B.C.
Ed. T. Kock, *CAF* iii p. 354.
**Crito** Medicus i/ii A.D.
Apud Galenum.
*Fragmenta Historica*, ed. C. Müller, *FHG* iv p. 373. [Crito Hist.]
**Crito** Philosophus
Apud Stobaeum.
**Crobylus** Comicus [Crobyl.] iv B.C.
Ed. T. Kock, *CAF* iii p. 379.
**Ctesias** Historicus [Ctes.] v/iv B.C.
Ed. C. Müller (post Herodotum Dindorfii), Paris (D.) 1844.
**Cydias** Lyricus v B.C. (?)
Ed. T. Bergk, *PLG* iii p. 564.
**Cyllenius** Epigrammaticus [Cyllen.] i A.D. (?)
v. *Anthologia Graeca.*
**Cypria** [Cypr.]
Ed. T. W. Allen, *Homeri Opera* v, Oxford (OCT), p. 116.
**Cyrilli Glossarium** [Cyr.]
Ed. M. Schmidt (post Hesychium, vol. iv, p. 362), Jena 1862.
**Cyrillus** Epigrammaticus [Cyrill.] i A.D. (?)
v. *Anthologia Graeca.*
**Cyrus, Flavius** Epigrammaticus v A.D.
v. *Anthologia Graeca.*

**Daimachus** Historicus iii B.C.
Ed. C. Müller, *FHG* ii p. 440.
**Damagetus** Epigrammaticus [Damag.] iii B.C.
v. *Anthologia Graeca.*
**Damascius** Philosophus [Dam.] v/vi A.D.
*Isid.* = *Vita Isidori*, ed. Westermann, v. Diogenes Laertius.
*Pr.* = *de Principiis*, ed. C. A. Ruelle, Paris 1889.
**Damianus** Opticus [Damian.]
*Opt.* = *Optica*, ed. R. Schöne, Berlin 1897.
**Damocharis** Epigrammaticus [Damoch.] vi A.D.
v. *Anthologia Graeca.*
**Damocrates** Poeta Medicus [Damocr.] i A.D.
Apud Galenum.
**Damocritus** Historicus [Damocrit.] i B.C. or i A.D. (?)
Ed. C. Müller, *FHG* iv p. 377.
**Damon** Historicus
Ed. C. Müller, *FHG* iv p. 377.
**Damostratus** Epigrammaticus [Damostr.]
v. *Anthologia Graeca.*
**Damoxenus** Comicus [Damox.] iv/iii B.C.
Ed. T. Kock, *CAF* iii p. 348.
**David** Philosophus vi A.D.
*in Porph.* = *in Porphyrii Isagogen commentarium*, ed. A. Busse (*Comm. in Arist. Graeca* xviii *pars* ii), Berlin 1904.
*Proll.* = *Prolegomena Philosophiae*, ed. A. Busse (ibid.).
**Deiochus** Historicus [Deioch.]
Ed. C. Müller, *FHG* ii p. 17.
**Demades** Orator [Demad.] iv B.C.
Ed. F. Blass (v. Dinarchus).
*Fr.* = *Fragmenta*, ed. H. Sauppe, *Orat. Att.* ii p. 312.
**Demetrius** Astrologus [Demetr.]
Apud Palchum.
**Demetrius** Comicus Novae Comoediae [Demetr.Com.Nov.] iv/iii B.C.
Ed. T. Kock, *CAF* iii p. 357.

**Demetrius** Comicus Veteris Comoediae [Demetr.Com.Vet.] v/iv
Ed. T. Kock, *CAF* i p. 795.
**Demetrius Apamensis** Medicus [Demetr.Apam.]
Apud Caelium Aurelianum et Soranum.
**Demetrius Lacon** Philosophus [Demetr.Lac.]
Ed. W. Crönert, *Kolotes und Menedemos*, Leipzig 1906, p. 1 ed. V. de Falco, Naples 1923.
**Demetrius Phalereus** Rhetor [Demetr.] iv B
*Eloc.* = *Demetrius on Style*, ed. W. Rhys Roberts, Cambridge 19
**Demetrius Phalereus** Historicus [Dem.Phal.] iv B.
Ed. C. Müller, *FHG* ii p. 362.
**Demetrius Troezenius** Poeta Philosophus [Demetr.Troez.] i B.C./i A.D. (
Ed. H. Diels, *PPF* p. 224.
**Demochares** Historicus [Democh.] iv/iii B.
Ed. C. Müller, *FHG* ii p. 445.
**Democritus** Epigrammaticus [Democr.]
v. *Anthologia Graeca.*
**Democritus** Philosophus [Democr.] v B.C
Ed. H. Diels, *Vorsokr.* ii p. 10.
Pseudo-**Democritus** Alchemista [Ps.-Democr.]
Ed. M. Berthelot, *Collection des anciens alchimistes grecs*, p. 41.
**Democritus Ephesius** Historicus [Democr.Eph.]
Ed. C Müller, *FHG* iv p. 383.
**Demodocus** Lyricus [Demod.] vi B.C.
Ed. T. Bergk, *PLG* ii p. 65.
**Demon** Historicus iv/iii B.C.
Ed. C. Müller, *FHG* i p. 378, iv pp. 626, 646.
**Demonicus** Comicus [Demonic.]
Ed. T. Kock, *CAF* iii p. 375.
**Demophilus** Gnomologus [Demoph.]
*Sent.* = *Sententiae*, ed. J. C. Orelli, *Opuscula Graecorum Veterum Sententiosa* i p. 37, Leipzig 1819; cf. H. Schenkl, *Wien. Stud.* viii (1886), p. 262.
*Sim.* = *Similitudines*, ed. F. W. A. Mullach, *FPG* i p. 485; cf. A. Elter, *Gnomica Homoeomata* v, Bonn 1900.
**Demosthenes** Orator [D.] 384–322 B.C.
Ed. F. Blass, Leipzig (T.) 1888–92; ed. S. H. Butcher & W. Rennie, Oxford (OCT).
*Ep.* = *Epistulae*
*Prooem.* = *Prooemia*
**Demosthenes Bithynus** Epicus [Dem.Bith.] iii B.C. (?)
Ed. J. U. Powell, *Coll. Alex.* p. 25.
**Demosthenes Ophthalmicus** Medicus [Dem.Ophth.] i A.D.
Apud Aëtium.
**Dercylus** Historicus [Dercyl.]
Ed. C. Müller, *FHG* iv p. 386.
**Dexippus** Historicus [Dexipp.] iii A.D.
Ed. L. Dindorf, *HGM* i p. 165.
**Dexippus** Philosophus [Dexipp.] iv A.D.
*in Cat.* = *in Aristotelis Categorias commentarium*, ed. A. Busse (*Comm. in Arist. Graeca* iv *pars* ii), Berlin 1888.
**Diagoras** Lyricus [Diagor.] v B.C.
Ed. T. Bergk, *PLG* iii p. 562.
**Dialexeis** [*Dialex.*] ca. 400 B.C.
Anonymi Δισσοὶ Λόγοι, ed. H. Diels, *Vorsokr.* ii p. 334.
**Dicaearchus** Geographus [Dicaearch.] iv B.C.
Ed. C. Müller, *GGM* i p. 97.
**Dicaearchus** Historicus [Dicaearch.Hist.] iv B.C.
Ed. C. Müller, *FHG* ii p. 225.
**Dicaeogenes** Tragicus [Dicaeog.] iv B.C.
Ed. A. Nauck, *TGF* p. 775.
**Didymus** Grammaticus [Did.] i B.C.
*in D.* = *Commentary on Demosthenes*, ed. H. Diels & W. Schubart (*BKT* i), Berlin 1904; cited by col. and line.
**Dieuches** Medicus [Dieuch.]
Apud Oribasium.
**Dieuchidas** Historicus [Dieuchid.] iv B.C.
Ed. C. Müller, *FHG* iv p. 388.
**Digesta** [*Dig.*]
Ed. T. Mommsen & P. Krüger, *Corpus Juris Civilis* i[13], Berlin 1920.
**Dinarchus** Orator [Din.] iv/iii B.C.
Ed. (cum Demadis fragmentis) F. Blass, Leipzig (T.) 1888.
*Fr.* = *Fragmenta*, ed. H. Sauppe, *Orat. Att.* ii p. 321.
**Dinias** Historicus iii B.C.
Ed. C. Müller, *FHG* iii p. 24.
**Dinolochus** Comicus [Dinol.] v B.C.
Ed. G. Kaibel, *CGF* p. 149.
**Dinon** Historicus iv B.C.
Ed. C. Müller, *FHG* ii p. 88.
**Dio Cassius** Historicus [D.C.] ii/iii A.D.
Ed. U. P. Boissevain, Berlin 1895–1901; cited by the numeration of the earlier editions.
**Dio Chrysostomus** Sophista [D.Chr.] i/ii A.D.
Ed. Guy de Budé, Leipzig (T.) 1916, 1919.
**Diocles** Epigrammaticus [Diocl.] i A.D.
v. *Anthologia Graeca.*

**[Dio]cles** Comicus [Diocl.Com.] v B.C.
[E]d. T. Kock, *CAF* i p. 766; suppl. J. Demiańczuk, *Supp. Com.* p. 39.
**[Dio]cles** Medicus [Diocl.*Fr.*]
[E]d. M. Wellmann (*Fragmentsammlung der griechischen Ärzte* i p. 117), Berlin 1901.
**[Di]odorus** Comicus [Diod.Com.] iv B.C.
[E]d. T. Kock, *CAF* ii p. 420.
**[Di]odorus** Epigrammaticus [Diod.] i B.C./i A.D.
[I]dem qui et Zonas, q.v.; v. *Anthologia Graeca.*
**[Di]odorus** Rhetor [Diod.Rh.]
Ed. H. Hinck (post Polemonem), Leipzig (T.) 1873, p. 51.
**[Di]odorus Atheniensis** Periegeta [Diod.Ath.] iv B.C.
Ed. C. Müller, *FHG* ii p. 353.
**[D]iodorus Siculus** Historicus [D.S.] i B.C.
Ed. I. Bekker, L. Dindorf, F. Vogel (C. Th. Fischer), Leipzig (T.) 1888–1906.
**[D]iodorus Tarsensis** Epigrammaticus [Diod.Tars.] i B.C./i A.D.
v. *Anthologia Graeca.*
**[D]iogenes Apolloniates** Philosophus [Diog.Apoll.] v B.C.
Ed. H. Diels, *Vorsokr.* i p. 416.
**[D]iogenes Atheniensis** Tragicus [Diog.Ath.]
Ed. A. Nauck, *TGF* p. 776.
**Diogenes Babylonius** Stoicus [Diog.Bab.*Stoic.*] ii B.C.
Ed. H. von Arnim, *SVF* iii p. 210.
**Diogenes Cynicus** Philosophus [Diog.] iv B.C.
*Ep.* = *Epistulae*, ed. R. Hercher, *Epistolographi*, p. 235; cf. F. W. A. Mullach, *FPG* ii p. 299
**Diogenes Laertius** [D.L.] iii A.D. (?)
*Diogenis Laertii de clarorum philosophorum vitis . . libri decem . .* [ed.] C. G. Cobet: accedunt *Olympiodori, Ammonii, Iamblichi, Porphyrii et aliorum vitae Platonis, Aristotelis, Pythagorae, Plotini et Isidori*, Ant. Westermanno, et *Marini vita Procli* J. F. Boissonadio edentibus, Paris (D.) 1862.
*Epigrammata*: v. *Anthologia Graeca.*
**Diogenes Oenoandensis** Epicureus [Diog.Oen.] ii A.D.
Ed. Iohannes William, Leipzig (T.) 1907.
**Diogenes Sinopensis** Tragicus [Diog.Sinop.] iv B.C.
Ed. A. Nauck, *TGF* p. 807.
**Diogenianus** Paroemiographus [Diogenian.]
Ed. E. L. von Leutsch & F. G. Schneidewin, *Paroemiographi* i p. 177, ii p. 1.
**Diogenianus Epicureus** [Diogenian.Epicur.] ii B.C. (?)
Ed. Alfred Gercke, *Jahrbücher für klassische Philologie, Suppl.* xiv p. 748.
**Diomedes** Grammaticus [Diom.]
Ed. H. Keil, *Gramm. Lat.* i, Leipzig 1857, p. 299.
**Dionysius** Comicus [Dionys.Com.] iv B.C.
Ed. T. Kock, *CAF* ii p. 423.
**Dionysius** Epigrammaticus [Dionys.]
v. *Anthologia Graeca.*
**Dionysius** Rerum Naturalium Scriptor [Dionys.]
*Av.* = *de Avibus* (Paraphrasis Oppiani Ἰξευτικῶν), ed. F. S. Lehrs (post Oppianum, q.v.).
**Dionysius** Tragicus [Dionys.Trag.] iv B.C.
Ed. A. Nauck, *TGF* p. 793.
**Dionysius Byzantius** Geographus [Dion.Byz.] ii/iv A.D. (?)
*de Bospori navigatione*, ed. C. Wescher, Paris 1874; cited by section.
**Dionysius Calliphontis filius** Geographus [Dion.Calliph.] i B.C./i A.D.
Ed. C. Müller, *GGM* i p. 238.
**Dionysius Chalcus** Elegiacus [Dionys.Eleg.] v B.C.
Ed. T. Bergk, *PLG* ii p. 262.
**Dionysius Halicarnassensis** [D.H.] i B.C.
*Antiquitates Romanae*, ed. C. Jacoby, Leipzig (T.) 1885–1905; cited without title.
*Opuscula*, ed. H. Usener, L. Radermacher, Leipzig (T.) 1899, 1904.
*Amm.* 1, 2 = *Epistula ad Ammaeum* 1, 2
*Comp.* = *de Compositione Verborum*
*Dem.* = *de Demosthene*
*Din.* = *de Dinarcho*
*Is.* = *de Isaeo*
*Isoc.* = *de Isocrate*
*Lys.* = *de Lysia*
*Orat.Vett.* = *de Oratoribus Veteribus*
*Pomp.* = *Epistula ad Pompeium*
*Rh.* = *Ars Rhetorica*
*Th.* = *de Thucydide*
*Vett.Cens.* = *de Veterum Censura*, ed. J. Hudson, Oxford 1704.
**Dionysius Heracleota** Stoicus [Dionys.*Stoic.*] iii B.C.
Ed. H. von Arnim, *SVF* i p. 93.
**Dionysius Minor** Elegiacus [Dionys.Minor]
Ed. T. Bergk, *PLG* ii p. 324.
**Dionysius Periegeta** [D.P.]
Ed. G. Bernhardy (cum commentariis Eustathii), Leipzig 1828; cf. C. Müller, *GGM* ii p. 102.
**Dionysius Samius** Historicus [Dionys.Sam.] ii B.C. (?)
Ed. F. Jacoby, *FGrH* i p. 178.

**Dionysius Thrax** Grammaticus [D.T.] ii B.C.
Ed. G. Uhlig, Leipzig 1883; cited by Bekker's page, given in Uhlig's margin.
Scholia in Dionysium Thracem, ed. A. Hilgard, *Grammatici Graeci* i *pars* iii, Leipzig 1901.
**Diophanes** Epigrammaticus [Diophan.]
v. *Anthologia Graeca.*
**Diophantus** Mathematicus [Dioph.] iii A.D.
Ed. P. Tannery, Leipzig (T.) 1893, 1895.
**Dioscorides** Epigrammaticus [Diosc.] iii B.C.
v. *Anthologia Graeca.*
**Dioscorides** Historicus [Diosc.Hist.] iv B.C.
Ed. C. Müller, *FHG* ii p. 192.
**Dioscorides (Dioscurides)** Medicus [Dsc.] i A.D.
*de Materia Medica*, ed. M. Wellmann, Berlin 1906–14; cited without title.
*Alex.* = *Alexipharmaca*; *Ther.* = *Theriaca*; ed. K. Sprengel, *Dioscorides* (vols. xxv and xxvi of *Medici Graeci*, ed. C. G. Kühn), Leipzig 1829.
*Eup.* = περὶ Εὐποριστῶν, ed. Wellmann (v. supr.).
**Dioscorides Glossator** [Diosc.Gloss.]
Apud Galenum.
**Diotimus** Epigrammaticus [Diotim.] iii B.C. (?)
v. *Anthologia Graeca.*
**Diotogenes** Philosophus [Diotog.]
Apud Stobaeum.
**Dioxippus** Comicus [Diox.]
Ed. T. Kock, *CAF* iii p. 358.
**Diphilus** Comicus [Diph.] iv/iii B.C.
Ed. T. Kock, *CAF* ii p. 541; suppl. J. Demiańczuk, *Supp. Com.* p. 40.
**Diphilus Siphnius** Rerum Naturalium Scriptor [Diph.Siph.] iii B.C.
Apud Athenaeum.
**Dius** Philosophus
Apud Stobaeum.
**Diyllus** Historicus [Diyll.] iii B.C.
Ed. C. Müller, *FHG* ii p. 360, iii p. 198.
**Donatus, Aelius** Grammaticus Latinus [Donat.] iv A.D.
Ed. H. Keil, *Gramm. Lat.* iv p. 353.
**Dorio** Rerum Naturalium Scriptor i B.C.
Apud Athenaeum.
**Dorotheus** Astrologus [Doroth.] ii A.D.
Ed. H. Koechly (post Manethonem, q.v.); suppl. *Cat. Cod. Astr.*
**Dosiadas** Epigrammaticus [Dosiad.] iii B.C.
v. *Anthologia Graeca.*
*Ara* = *AP* 15. 26.
**Dosiades** Historicus [Dosiad.Hist.]
Ed. C. Müller, *FHG* iv p. 399.
**Dositheus** Grammaticus Latinus [Dosith.] iv A.D. (?)
Ed. H. Keil, *Gramm. Lat.* vii p. 363.
**Dromo** Comicus iv B.C.
Ed. T. Kock, *CAF* ii p. 419.
**Duris** Epigrammaticus iv/iii B.C.
v. *Anthologia Graeca.*
**Duris** Historicus iv/iii B.C.
Ed. C. Müller, *FHG* ii p. 466.

**Ecphantides** Comicus [Ecphantid.] v B.C.
Ed. T. Kock, *CAF* i p. 9.
**Ecphantus** Pythagoreus [Ecphant.]
Apud Stobaeum.
**Elegiaca Alexandrina Adespota** [*Eleg.Alex.Adesp.*]
Ed. J. U. Powell, *Coll. Alex.* p. 130.
**Elias** Philosophus vi A.D.
*in Cat.* = *in Aristotelis Categorias commentaria*, ed. A. Busse (*Comm. in Arist. Graeca* xviii *pars* i), Berlin 1900.
*in Porph.* = *in Porphyrii Isagogen commentaria* (ibid.).
**Empedocles** Poeta Philosophus [Emp.] v B.C.
Ed. H. Diels, *PPF* p. 74.
*Sphaer.* = *Sphaera*, ed. E. Maass, *Commentariorum in Aratum reliquiae*, pp. 154, 199.
**Enoch** Judaeus [1*Enoch*] ii/i B.C.
Ed. R. H. Charles, Oxford 1912.
**Ephippus** Comicus [Ephipp.] iv B.C.
Ed. T. Kock, *CAF* ii p. 250.
**Ephorus** Historicus [Ephor.] iv B.C.
Ed. C. Müller, *FHG* i p. 234, iv pp. 626, 641; suppl. F. Bilabel, *Die kleineren Historikerfragmente auf Papyrus*, Bonn 1923, p. 7.
**Epica Alexandrina Adespota** [*Epic.Alex.Adesp.*]
Ed. J. U. Powell, *Coll. Alex.* p. 71.
**Epicharmus** Comicus [Epich.] v B.C.
Ed. G. Kaibel, *CGF* p. 88.
Pseudepicharmea, v. Axiopistus.
**Epicrates** Comicus [Epicr.] iv B.C.
Ed. T. Kock, *CAF* ii p. 282.
**Epictetus** Philosophus [Epict.] i/ii A.D.
Ed. H. Schenkl, Leipzig (T.) 1894.
*Ench.* = *Enchiridion*
*Fr.* = *Fragmenta*
*Gnom.* = *Gnomologium*

**Epicurus** Philosophus [Epicur.] iv/iii B.C.
Ed. H. Usener, *Epicurea*, Leipzig 1887 (*Epistulae*, *Fragmenta*, *Sententiae*); ed. P. von der Mühll, Leipzig (T.) 1922 (*Epistulae*, *Sententiae*, *Gnomologium Vaticanum*).
*Dial.* 1413 = *Dialogus*, in *PHerc.* 1413 (ined.)
*Ep.* = *Epistulae*
*Fr.* = *Fragmenta*
*Nat.* = *De rerum natura*, partim ined. (cited by book [2, 11, 14, 15, or 28] and col. or *Fr.*: unnumbered books cited as *Nat.Herc.* followed by No. of papyrus and col. or *Fr.*: portions edited by Gomperz in *Wien. Stud.* i (1879) p. 27 cited by No. of line, followed by 'G.').
*Sent.* = *Sententiae* (κύριαι δόξαι)
*Sent.Vat.* = *Gnomologium Vaticanum*, ed. Wotke-Usener, *Wien. Stud.* X (1888) pp. 175–201 = Usener, *Kleine Schriften* i p. 297; ed. P. von der Mühll (v. supr.).
NOTE.—Unedited papyri are cited from transcripts furnished by W. Crönert.

**Epigenes** Comicus [Epig.] iv B.C.
Ed. T. Kock, *CAF* ii p. 416.

**Epigoni**
Ed. T. W. Allen, *Homeri Opera* v, Oxford (OCT), p. 115.

**Epigonus** Epigrammaticus [Epig.]
v. *Anthologia Graeca*.

**Epilycus** Comicus [Epil.] v/iv B.C. (?)
Ed. T. Kock, *CAF* i p. 803; suppl. J. Demiańczuk, *Supp. Com.* p. 40.

**Epimenides** Philosophus [Epimenid.] vi B.C.
Ed. H. Diels, *Vorsokr.* ii p. 185.

**Epinicus** Comicus [Epin.] ii B.C.
Ed. T. Kock, *CAF* iii p. 330.

**Erasistratus** Medicus [Erasistr.] iii B.C.
Apud Galenum.

**Eratosthenes** Epicus [Eratosth.] iii B.C.
Ed. J. U. Powell, *Coll. Alex.* p. 58.
*Cat.* = Καταστερισμοί, ed. A. Olivieri, *Mythographi Graeci* iii (1), Leipzig (T.) 1897.

**Eratosthenes Scholasticus** Epigrammaticus [Eratosth.] vi A.D.
v. *Anthologia Graeca*.

**Erinna** Lyrica [Erinn.]
Ed. T. Bergk, *PLG* iii p. 141.

**Eriphus** Comicus [Eriph.] iv B.C.
Ed. T. Kock, *CAF* ii p. 428.

**Erotianus** Grammaticus [Erot.] i A.D.
Ed. E. Nachmanson, Göteborg (Uppsala) 1918.

**Erycius** Epigrammaticus [Eryc.] i B.C.
v. *Anthologia Graeca*.

**Etruscus** Epigrammaticus [Etrusc.]
v. *Anthologia Graeca*.

**Etymologicum Genuinum** [*Et.Gen.*]
Ineditum; cf. R. Reitzenstein, *Geschichte der griechischen Etymologika*, Leipzig 1897, p. 1 ff.

**Etymologicum Gudianum** [*Et.Gud.*]
Ed. E. L. de Stefani, fasc. 1 (A–B), fasc. 2 (B–Z), Leipzig 1909, 1920; ed. F. W. Sturz, Leipzig 1818.
*z* = Cod. Par. Suppl. Gr. 172.

**Etymologicum Magnum** [*EM*]
Ed. T. Gaisford, Oxford 1848.

**Euangelus** Comicus [Euang.]
Ed. T. Kock, *CAF* iii p. 376.

**Eubulides** Comicus [Eubulid.]
Ed. T. Kock, *CAF* ii p. 431.

**Eubulus** Comicus [Eub.] iv B.C.
Ed. T. Kock, *CAF* ii p. 164; suppl. J. Demiańczuk, *Supp. Com.* p. 40.

**Euclides** Geometra [Euc.] iii B.C.
Ed. J. L. Heiberg & H. Menge, Leipzig (T.) 1883–1916.
*Elementa*, cited without title
*Dat.* = *Data*
*Fr.* = *Fragmenta*
*Opt.* = *Optica*
*Phaen.* = *Phaenomena*
*Sect.Can.* = *Sectio Canonis*

**Eucrates** Historicus [Eucrat.]
Ed. C. Müller, *FHG* iv p. 407.

**Eudemus** Philosophus [Eudem.] iv B.C.
Cited from sources. Cf. F. W. A. Mullach, *FPG* iii p. 222; Spengel, *Eudemi Rhodii Fragmenta*, Berlin 1866.

**Eudoxus** Astronomus [Eudox.] iv B.C.
*Ars* = *Ars astronomica*, ed. F. Blass, Kiel 1887 (cited by col. and line).

**Eudoxus** Comicus [Eudox.Com.]
Ed. T. Kock, *CAF* iii p. 332.

**Eugaeon** Historicus v B.C.
Ed. C. Müller, *FHG* ii p. 16, iv p. 653 [fort. Euagon].

**Eugenes** Epigrammaticus
v. *Anthologia Graeca*.

**Eumelus** Epicus [Eumel.] viii B.C. (?)
Ed. G. Kinkel, *EGF* p. 185.

**Eunapius** Historicus [Eun.] iv/v A.D.
*Hist.* = *Fragmenta Historica*, ed. L. Dindorf, *HGM* i p. 205.
*VS* = *Vitae Sophistarum*, ed. J. F. Boissonade (post Philostrat ed. Westermann), Paris (D.) 1849.

**Eunicus** Comicus [Eunic.] v B.C.
Ed. T. Kock, *CAF* i p. 781.

**Euodus** Epigrammaticus [Euod.]
v. *Anthologia Graeca*.

**Euphorio** Epicus [Euph.] iii B.C.
Ed. J. U. Powell, *Coll. Alex.* p. 28.
*Fr.Hist.* = *Fragmenta Historica*, ed. C. Müller, *FHG* iii p. 71.

**Euphro** Comicus iii B.C.
Ed. T. Kock, *CAF* iii p. 317.

**Euphronius** Lyricus [Euphron.] iii B.C.
Ed. J. U. Powell, *Coll. Alex.* p. 176.

**Eupithius** Epigrammaticus
v. *Anthologia Graeca*.

**Eupolis** Comicus [Eup.] v B.C.
Ed. T. Kock, *CAF* i p. 258; suppl. J. Demiańczuk, *Supp. Com.* p. 41

**Euripides** Tragicus [E.] v B.C.
Ed. G. G. A. Murray, Oxford (OCT). Fragments, ed. A. Nauck, *TGF* p. 363, and H. von Arnim, *Supplementum Euripideum*, Bonn 1913 (titles of plays cited from this work are distinguished by an asterisk):
*Alc.* = *Alcestis*
*Andr.* = *Andromache*
**Antiop.* = *Antiope*
**Archel.* = *Archelaus*
*Ba.* = *Bacchae*
**Cret.* = *Cretes*
*Cyc.* = *Cyclops*
*El.* = *Electra*
*Ep.* = *Epistulae*, ed. R. Hercher, *Epistolographi*, p. 275.
*Epigr.* = *Epigrammata*, ed. T. Bergk, *PLG* ii p. 265.
*Fr.* = *Fragmenta*
*HF* = *Hercules Furens*
*Hec.* = *Hecuba*
*Hel.* = *Helena*
*Heracl.* = *Heraclidae*
*Hipp.* = *Hippolytus*
*Hyps.* = *Hypsipyle*, ed. A. S. Hunt, *Tragicorum Graecorum Fragmenta Papyracea*, Oxford (OCT).
*IA* = *Iphigenia Aulidensis*
*IT* = *Iphigenia Taurica*
*Ion*
*Med.* = *Medea*
**Melanipp.Capt.* = *Melanippe Captiva*
**Melanipp.Sap.* = *Melanippe Sapiens*
**Oen.* = *Oeneus*
*Or.* = *Orestes*
*Ph.* = *Phoenissae*
**Phaëth.* = *Phaëthon*
**Pirith.* = *Pirithous*
*Rh.* = *Rhesus*
**Sthen.* = *Stheneboea*
*Supp.* = *Supplices*
*Tr.* = *Troades*
Scholia in Euripidem, ed. W. Dindorf, 4 vols., Oxford 1863; ed. E. Schwarz, 2 vols., Berlin 1887, 1891.

**Euryphamus** Pythagoreus [Euryph.]
Apud Stobaeum; cf. F. W. A. Mullach, *FPG* ii p. 15.

**Eusebius** Historicus [Eus.Hist.] iii A.D.
Ed. L. Dindorf, *HGM* i p. 201.

**Eusebius Caesariensis** Scriptor Ecclesiasticus [Eus.] iv A.D.
*DE* = *Demonstratio Evangelica*, ed. I. A. Heikel, Leipzig 1913.
*PE* = *Praeparatio Evangelica*, ed. E. H. Gifford, Oxford 1903.

**Eusebius Myndius** Philosophus [Eus.Mynd.]
Ed. F. W. A. Mullach, *FPG* iii p. 7.

**Eustathius** Episcopus Thessalonicensis [Eust.] xii A.D.
*Commentarii ad Homeri Iliadem et Odysseam, ad fidem exempli Romani [editi]*, 7 vols., Leipzig 1825–30.
See also Dionysius Periegeta.

**Eustathius Epiphaniensis** Historicus [Eust.Epiph.] v A.D.
Ed. L. Dindorf, *HGM* i p. 354.

**Eustratius** Philosophus [Eustr.] xi/xii A.D.
*in APo.* = *in Analyticorum Posteriorum librum secundum commentarium*, ed. M. Hayduck (*Comm. in Arist. Graeca* xxi *pars* i), Berlin 1907.
*in EN* = *in Ethica Nicomachea commentaria*, ed. G. Heylbut (*Comm. in Arist. Graeca* xx), Berlin 1892.

**Euthycles** Comicus [Euthycl.]
Ed. T. Kock, *CAF* i p. 805.

**Eutocius** Mathematicus [Eutoc.] vi A.D.
Commentarii in Archimedem et Apollonium Pergaeum (qq. v.).

**Eutolmius** Epigrammaticus [Eutolm.] vi A.D.
v. *Anthologia Graeca*.

**Eutychianus** Historicus [Eutych.] iv A.D.
Ed. L. Dindorf, *HGM* i p. 365.

**Evenus** Elegiacus [Even.] v B.C.
Ed. T. Bergk, *PLG* ii p. 269.

**...ekiel** Poeta Judaeus [Ezek.] ii B.C.
*Exag.* = *Exagoge*, ed. K. Kuiper, *Mnemosyne* xxviii (1900) p. 237.

**...vorinus** Historicus [Favorin.] ii A.D.
Ed. C. Müller, *FHG* iii p. 577.

**...vorinus** Philosophus [Favorin.]
Apud Stobaeum.

**...estus** Grammaticus Latinus [Fest.] ii A.D.
Ed. W. M. Lindsay, Leipzig (T.) 1913.

**...irmicus Maternus** Astrologus [Firm.] iv A.D.
Ed. W. Kroll & F. Skutsch, Leipzig (T.) 1897, 1913.

**...laccus** Epigrammaticus; v. Statyllius, Tullius

**...ortunatianus** Rhetor [Fortunat.*Rh.*] iv A. D. (?)
Ed. C. Halm, *Rhetores Latini Minores*, p. 79, Leipzig 1863.

**...ronto, M. Cornelius** Scriptor Latinus ii A.D.
*Ep.* = *Epistulae*, ed. S. A. Naber, Leipzig 1867; ed. C. R. Haines, London & New York (Loeb) 1919–20.

**Gabrielius** Epigrammaticus [Gabriel.] vi A.D.
v. *Anthologia Graeca.*

**Gaetulicus, Cn. Lentulus** Epigrammaticus [Gaet.] i A.D.
v. *Anthologia Graeca.*

**Galenus** Medicus [Gal.] ii A.D.
Ed. C. G. Kühn, Leipzig 1821–33 (cited by vol. and p.); ed. H. Diels et alii, *CMG* v 4 (2), 9 (1, 2), Leipzig 1918– (in progress): the following works (cited by title) are separately edited in the editions named:
*Anim.Pass.* = περὶ ψυχῆς παθῶν κτλ., ed. J. Marquardt, *Galeni Scripta Minora* i p. 1, Leipzig (T.) 1884.
*Consuet.* = περὶ ἐθῶν, ed. I. Müller, *Scripta Minora* (v. supr.) ii p. 9.
*Inst.Log.* = εἰσαγωγὴ διαλεκτική, ed. C. Kalbfleisch, Leipzig (T.) 1896.
*Libr.Ord.* = περὶ τῆς τάξεως τῶν ἰδίων βιβλίων, ed. I. Müller, *Scripta Minora* (v. supr.) ii p. 80.
*Libr.Propr.* = περὶ τῶν ἰδίων βιβλίων, ib. p. 91.
*Med.Phil.* = ὅτι ὁ ἄριστος ἰατρὸς καὶ φιλόσοφος, ib. p. 1.
*Mixt.* = περὶ κράσεων, ed. G. Helmreich, Leipzig (T.) 1904.
*Nat.Fac.* = περὶ φυσικῶν δυνάμεων, ed. G. Helmreich, *Scripta Minora* iii p. 101.
*Opt.Doctr.* = περὶ τῆς ἀρίστης διδασκαλίας, ed. J. Marquardt, ib. i p. 82.
*Parv.Pil.* = περὶ τοῦ διὰ τῆς σμικρᾶς σφαίρας γυμνασίου, ib. p. 93.
*Phil.Hist.* = φιλόσοφος ἱστορία, ed. H. Diels, *Doxographi Graeci*, Berlin 1879.
*Protr.* = προτρεπτικός, ed. J. Marquardt, *Scripta Minora* i p. 103.
*Sect.Intr.* = περὶ αἱρέσεων τοῖς εἰσαγομένοις, ed. G. Helmreich, ib. iii p. 1.
*Subf.Emp.* = *Subfiguratio Empirica*, ed. M. Bonnet, Bonn 1872.
*Thras.* = Θρασύβουλος, ed. G. Helmreich, *Scripta Minora* iii p. 33.
*UP* = *de Usu Partium*, ed. G. Helmreich, Leipzig (T.) 1907–9.
*Vict.Att.* = περὶ λεπτυνούσης διαίτης, ed. C. Kalbfleisch, *CMG* v (4), Leipzig 1923.
The work *De placitis Hippocratis et Platonis* (cited by vol. and p. of Kühn) has been re-edited by I. Müller, Leipzig 1874.

**Gallus** Epigrammaticus i B.C. (?)
v. *Anthologia Graeca.*

**Gaudentius** Musicus [Gaud.*Harm.*]
Ed. C. Jan, *Musici Scriptores Graeci*, Leipzig (T.) 1895, p. 327.

**Gauradas** Epigrammaticus
v. *Anthologia Graeca.*

**Gellius, Aulus** Grammaticus Latinus [Gell.] ii A.D.
Ed. C. Hosius, Leipzig (T.) 1903.

**Geminus** Astronomicus [Gem.] i B.C.
Ed. C. Manitius, Leipzig (T.) 1898.
*Calend.* = *Calendarium*, ed. C. Wachsmuth (post Lyd. *Ost.*, p. 181).

**Geminus** Epigrammaticus; v. Tullius Geminus.

**Geoponica** [*Gp.*]
Ed. H. Beckh, Leipzig (T.) 1895.

**Germanicus Caesar** Epigrammaticus [Germ.] i B.C./i A.D
v. *Anthologia Graeca.*

**Glaucus Atheniensis** Epigrammaticus [Glauc.]
v. *Anthologia Graeca.*

**Glaucus Nicopolitanus** Epigrammaticus [Glauc.]
v. *Anthologia Graeca.*

**Glossaria** [*Gloss.*]
Ed. G. Loewe, G. Goetz & F. Schoell, *Corpus Glossariorum Latinorum*, Leipzig 1888–1924.

**Gorgias** Rhetor et Sophista [Gorg.] v B.C.
Ed. H. Diels, *Vorsokr.* ii p. 235.
*Hel.*, *Pal.* = *Helena*, *Palamedes*, ed. F. Blass (post Antiphontem, q. v.).

**Gorgon** Historicus
Ed. C. Müller, *FHG* iv p. 410.

**Gregorius Corinthius** Grammaticus [Greg.Cor.] xii A.D.
Ed. G. H. Schaefer, Leipzig 1811.
*Trop.* = περὶ τρόπων, ed. L. Spengel, *Rhet* iii p. 215.

**Gregorius Cyprius** Paroemiographus [Greg.Cypr.] xiii A.D.
Ed. E. L. von Leutsch & F. G. Schneidewin, *Paroemiographi* i p. 349, ii p. 53.

**Hadrianus** Rhetor [Hadr.Rh.] ii A.D.
Ed. H. Hinck (post Polemonem, p. 44), Leipzig (T.) 1873.

**Hadrianus Imperator** Epigrammaticus [Hadr.] ii A.D.
v. *Anthologia Graeca.*

**Hanno** Geographus translated iv B.C.
*Per pl.* = *Periplus*, ed. C. Müller, ***GGM* i p. 1.**

**Harmodius** Historicus [Harmod.]
Ed. C. Müller, *FHG* iv p. 411.

**Harpocratio** Grammaticus [Harp.] i or ii A.D.
Ed. W. Dindorf, Oxford 1853.

**Harpocratio** Medicus et Astrologus [Harp.Astr.] i A.D.
in *Cat. Cod. Astr.*

**Hecataeus Abderita** Historicus [Hecat.Abd.] iii B.C.
Ed. C. Müller, *FHG* ii p. 384.

**Hecataeus Milesius** Historicus [Hecat.] vi/v B.C.
Ed. F. Jacoby, *FGrH* i p. 1.

**Hedyle** Epigrammatica
Apud Athenaeum.

**Hedylus** Epigrammaticus [Hedyl.] iii B.C.
v. *Anthologia Graeca.*

**Hegemon** Comicus et Parodus [Hegem.] v B.C.
Ed. T. Kock, *CAF* i p. 700; ed. P. Brandt, *Corpusculum poesis epicae ludibundae* i p. 42, Leipzig (T.) 1888.

**Hegesander** Historicus [Hegesand.]
Ed. C. Müller, *FHG* iv p. 412.

**Hegesianax** Epicus [Hegesian.] ii B.C.
Ed. J. U. Powell, *Coll. Alex.* p. 8.

**Hegesias** Historicus
Ed. C. Müller, *SRAM* p. 138.

**Hegesippus** Comicus [Hegesipp.Com.] iii B.C.
Ed. T. Kock, *CAF* iii p. 312.

**Hegesippus** Epigrammaticus [Hegesipp.]
v. *Anthologia Graeca.*

**Heliodorus** Scriptor Eroticus [Hld.] iii A.D.
Ed. W. A. Hirschig, *Erotici*, p. 223, Paris (D.) 1856.

**Heliodorus** Medicus [Heliod.] i/ii A.D.
Apud Oribasium.

**Heliodorus** Periegeta [Heliod.Hist.]
Ed. C. Müller, *FHG* iv p. 425.

**Heliodorus** Philosophus [Heliod.]
*in EN* = *in Ethica Nicomachea paraphrasis*, ed. G. Heylbut (*Comm. in Arist. Graeca* xix *pars* ii), Berlin 1889.

**Helladius** Epigrammaticus [Hellad.] ii A.D. (?)
v. *Anthologia Graeca.*

**Helladius** [Hellad.]
Apud Photium (*Bibl.*, cod. 279).

**Hellanicus** Historicus [Hellanic.] v B.C.
Ed. F. Jacoby, *FGrH* i p. 104.

**Hellenica Oxyrhynchia** [*Hell.Oxy.*]
Cum Theopompi et Cratippi fragmentis, ed. B. P. Grenfell & A. S. Hunt, Oxford (OCT).

**Hemerologium Florentinum** [*Hemerolog.Flor.*]
= *Histoire de l'Acad. roy. des Inscr. et Belles-lettres avec Mém. de litt.*, Paris, t. xlvii, 1809, pp. 66–84.

**Heniochus** Comicus [Henioch.]
Ed. T. Kock, *CAF* ii p. 431.

**Hephaestio** Astrologus [Heph.Astr.] iv A.D.
in *Cat. Cod. Astr.*
Bk. i, ed. A. Engelbrecht, Vienna 1887.

**Hephaestio** Grammaticus [Heph.]
*Hephaestionis Enchiridion cum commentariis veteribus*, ed. M. Consbruch, Leipzig (T.) 1906; cited without title.
*Poëm.* = περὶ ποιημάτων, ed. M. Consbruch, ibid. p. 62.
Scholia, ibid. p. 79; ed. R. Westphal, *Scriptores Metrici Graeci* i p. 95, Leipzig (T.) 1866.

**Heraclas** Medicus [Heracl.]
Apud Oribasium.

**Heraclides** Comicus [Heraclid.Com.] iv B.C.
Ed. T. Kock, *CAF* ii p. 435.

**Heraclides** Historicus [Heraclid.]
*Pol.* = περὶ πολιτειῶν, ed. V. Rose, in Arist. *Fr.* pp. 370–86.

**Heraclides Cumaeus** Historicus [Heraclid.Cum.] iv B.C.
Ed. C. Müller, *FHG* ii p. 95.

**Heraclides Lembus** Historicus [Heraclid.Lemb.] ii B.C.
Ed. C. Müller, *FHG* iii p. 167.

**Heraclides Ponticus** Historicus [Heraclid.Pont.] iv B.C.
Ed. C. Müller, *FHG* ii p. 197; cf. O. Voss, *De Heraclidis Pontici vita et scriptis*, Rostock 1896.

**Heraclides Sinopensis** Epigrammaticus [Heraclid.Sinop.]
v. *Anthologia Graeca.*

**Heraclides Tarentinus** Medicus [Heraclid.] i B.C.
Apud Galenum.

**Heraclitus** [Heraclit.] i A.D. (?)
*All.* = *Allegoriae* = *Quaestiones Homericae*, ediderunt societatis philologae Bonnensis sodales, prolegomena scripsit F. Oelmann, Leipzig (T.) 1910.

**Heraclitus** Epigrammaticus [Heraclit.] iii B.C.
*Anthologia Graeca.*

**Heraclitus** Paradoxographus [Heraclit.]
*Incred.* = *de incredibilibus*, ed. N. Festa, *Mythographi Graeci* iii (2), Leipzig (T.) 1902.

**Heraclitus** Philosophus [Heraclit.] vi/v B.C.
Ed. H. Diels, *Vorsokr.* i p. 67.
*Ep.* = *Epistulae*, ed. R. Hercher, *Epistolographi*, p. 280.

**Herillus Carthaginiensis** Stoicus [Herill.*Stoic.*] iii B.C.
Ed. H. von Arnim, *SVF* i p. 91.

**Hermes Trismegistus** [Herm.]
Apud Stobaeum: see also *Corpus Hermeticum.*

**Hermesianax** Elegiacus [Hermesian.] iv/iii B.C.
Ed. J. U. Powell, *Coll. Alex.* p. 96.

**Hermias** Historicus [Herm.Hist.] iv B.C.
Ed. C. Müller, *FHG* ii p. 80.

**Hermias** Iambographus [Herm.Iamb.] iii B.C. (?)
Ed. J. U. Powell, *Coll. Alex.* p. 237.

**Hermias Alexandrinus** Philosophus [Herm.] v A.D.
*in Phdr.* = *in Platonis Phaedrum scholia*, ed. P. Couvreur, Paris 1901; cited by Ast's pages, given in Couvreur's margin.

**Hermippus** Comicus [Hermipp.] v B.C.
Ed. T. Kock, *CAF* i p. 224; suppl. J. Demiańczuk, *Supp. Com.* p. 53.
*Iamb.* = *Fragmenta Iamborum*, ed. T. Bergk, *PLG* ii p. 505.

**Hermippus** Historicus [Hermipp.Hist.] iii/ii B.C.
Ed. C. Müller, *FHG* iii p. 35.

**Hermocles** Lyricus [Hermocl.] iv/iii B.C.
Ed. J. U. Powell, *Coll. Alex.* p. 173.

**Hermocreon** Epigrammaticus [Hermocr.]
v. *Anthologia Graeca.*

**Hermodorus** Epigrammaticus [Hermod.]
v. *Anthologia Graeca.*

**Hermogenes** Rhetor [Hermog.] ii A.D.
Ed. H. Rabe, Leipzig (T.) 1913.
*Id.* = περὶ ἰδεῶν
*Inv.* = περὶ εὑρέσεως
*Meth.* = περὶ μεθόδου δεινότητος
*Prog.* = προγυμνάσματα
*Stat.* = περὶ τῶν στάσεων

**Hermon** vel **Hermonax** Epicus
Ed. J. U. Powell, *Coll. Alex.* p. 251.

**Hero** Mechanicus ii/i B.C. (?)
Ed. W. Schmidt, H. Schöne, J. L. Heiberg, Leipzig (T.) 1899–1914; *Belopoeica*, ed. R. Schneider, Metz 1907; spurious treatises (distd. by asterisk), ed. F. Hultsch, Berlin 1864.
*Aut.* = *Automatopoetica*
*Bel.* = *Belopoeica*
**Deff.* = *Definitiones*
*Dioptr.* = *Dioptra*
**Geep.* = *Liber Geeponicus*
**Geom.* = *Geometrica*
**Mens.* = *Mensurae*
*Metr.* = *Metrica*
*Spir.* = (*Spiritalia*) *Pneumatica*
**Stereom.* = *Stereometrica*

**Herodas** Mimographus [Herod.] iii B.C.
Ed. W. Headlam & A. D. Knox, Cambridge 1922.

**Herodianus** Grammaticus [Hdn.] ii A.D.
Hdn.Gr. = *Herodiani Technici reliquiae*, ed. A. Lentz, Leipzig 1867–70 (cited by vol. and p.).
Hdn.*Epim.* = *Partitiones*, ed. J. F. Boissonade, London 1819.
Hdn.*Philet.* = *Philetaerus*, ed. Pierson, with Moeris, q. v.
Hdn.*Vers.* = *de Versibus*, ed. W. Studemund, *Jahrbücher für klassische Philologie* xcv (1867) p. 618.

**Herodianus** Historicus [Hdn.] iii A.D.
Ed. K. Stavenhagen, Leipzig (T.) 1922.

**Herodianus** Rhetor [Hdn.]
*Fig.* = *de Figuris*, ed. L. Spengel, *Rhet.* iii p. 83.

**Herodorus** Historicus [Herodor.] v/iv B.C.
Ed. F. Jacoby, *FGrH* i p. 215.

**Herodotus** Historicus [Hdt.] v B.C.
Ed. C. Hude, Oxford (OCT).
Ps.-Hdt.*Vit.Hom.* = *Vita Homeri*, ed. T. W. Allen, *Homeri Opera* v, Oxford (OCT), p. 192.

**Herodotus** Medicus [Herod.Med.] i A.D.
Apud Oribasium.
Cf. R. Fuchs, *Rheinisches Museum* xlix (1894) p. 532, l (1895) p. 576, lviii (1903) p. 69, *Festschrift zu J. Vahlens 70. Geburtstag*, p. 147 sq.; M. Wellmann, *Hermes* xl (1905) p. 580, xlviii (1913) p. 141.

**Herophilus** Medicus [Herophil.] iii B.C.
Apud Galenum.

**Hesiodus** Epicus [Hes.]
Ed. A. Rzach, editio tertia, Leipzig (T.) 1913.
*Fr.* = *Fragmenta*
*Op.* = *Opera et Dies*
*Sc.* = *Scutum Herculis*
*Th.* = *Theogonia*

**Hesychius Milesius** Historicus [Hsch.Mil.] vi A.D.
Ed. C. Müller, *FHG* iv p. 143.

**Hesychius** Lexicographus [Hsch.] v A.D.
Ed. M. Schmidt, Jena 1858–68.

**Hicesius** Medicus [Hices.] i
Apud Athenaeum.

**Hierocles** Facetiarum Scriptor [Hierocl.] iv A.D.
Ed. A. Eberhard, *Philogelos: Hieroclis et Philagrii facetiae*, Be[rlin] 1869. [*Facet.*]

**Hierocles** Historicus [Hierocl.Hist.] iii A.D.
Ed. C. Müller, *FGH* iv p. 429.

**Hierocles Platonicus** Philosophus [Hierocl.] v A.
*in CA* = *in Carmen Aureum*, ed. F. W. A. Mullach, *FPG* i 408.
*Prov.* = *de providentia*, apud Photium; cited by Bekker's page.

**Hierocles Stoicus** Philosophus [Hierocl.] i/ii A.
Ed. H. v. Arnim, *BKT* iv (1906); cited by Arnim's page.

**Hieronymus Cardianus** Historicus [Hieronym.Hist.] iv/iii B.
Ed. C. Müller, *FHG* ii p. 450.

**Himerius** Sophista [Him.] iv A.D.
Ed. F. Dübner, Paris (D.) 1849 (post Philostratum, ed. Westermann).
*Ecl.* = *Eclogae*
*Or.* = *Orationes*

**Hippagoras** Historicus
Ed. C. Müller, *FHG* iv p. 430.

**Hipparchus** Astronomicus [Hipparch.] ii B.C.
Ed. C. Manitius, Leipzig (T.) 1894.

**Hipparchus** Comicus [Hipparch.Com.] iii B.C. (?)
Ed. T. Kock, *CAF* iii p. 272.

**Hipparchus** Philosophus Pythagoreus [Hipparch.]
Apud Stobaeum; cf. F. W. A. Mullach, *FPG* ii p. 16.

**Hippias Eleus** Historicus et Sophista v B.C.
Ed. F. Jacoby, *FGrH* i p. 156; ed. H. Diels, *Vorsokr.* ii p. 282.

**Hippias Erythraeus** Historicus [Hippias Erythr.]
Ed. C. Müller, *FHG* iv p. 431.

**Hippiatrica** [*Hippiatr.*]
*Veterinariae Medicinae libri duo*, ed. S. Grynaeus, Basel 1537; ed. E. Oder & C. Hoppe, Leipzig (T.) 1924.

**Hippocrates** Medicus [Hp.] v B.C.
Ed. E. Littré, 10 vols., Paris 1839–61; ed. H. Kuehlewein, vols. i–ii (all published), Leipzig 1894, 1902.
*Acut.* = περὶ διαίτης ὀξέων
*Acut.*(*Sp.*) = περὶ διαίτης ὀξέων (νόθα)
*Aër.* = περὶ ἀέρων ὑδάτων τόπων
*Aff.* = περὶ παθῶν
*Alim.* = περὶ τροφῆς
*Anat.* = περὶ ἀνατομῆς
*Aph.* = ἀφορισμοί
*Art.* = περὶ ἄρθρων ἐμβολῆς
*de Arte* = περὶ τέχνης
*Carn.* = περὶ σαρκῶν
*Coac.* = Κωακαὶ προγνώσιες
*Cord.* = περὶ καρδίης
*Decent.* = περὶ εὐσχημοσύνης
*Dent.* = περὶ ὀδοντοφυΐης
*Dieb.Judic.* = περὶ κρισίμων ἡμερέων
*Ep.* = ἐπιστολαί
*Epid.* = ἐπιδημίαι
*Fist.* = περὶ συρίγγων
*Flat.* = περὶ φυσῶν
*Foet.Exsect.* = περὶ ἐγκατατομῆς ἐμβρύου
*Fract.* = περὶ ἀγμῶν
*Genit.* = περὶ γονῆς
*Gland.* = περὶ ἀδένων
*Haem.* = περὶ αἱμορροΐδων
*Hebd.* = περὶ ἑβδομάδων, ed. W. H. Roscher, *Die Hippokratische Schrift von der Siebenzahl*, Paderborn 1913.
*Hum.* = περὶ χυμῶν
*Insomn.* = περὶ ἐνυπνίων
*Int.* = περὶ τῶν ἐντὸς παθῶν
*Judic.* = περὶ κρισίων
*Jusj.* = ὅρκος
*Lex* = νόμος
*Liqu.* = περὶ ὑγρῶν χρήσιος
*Loc.Hom.* = περὶ τόπων τῶν κατὰ ἄνθρωπον
*Medic.* = περὶ ἰητροῦ
*Mochl.* = μοχλικόν
*Morb.* = περὶ νούσων
*Morb.Sacr.* = περὶ ἱερῆς νούσου
*Mul.* = γυναικεῖα
*Nat.Hom.* = περὶ φύσιος ἀνθρώπου
*Nat.Mul.* = περὶ γυναικείης φύσιος
*Nat.Puer.* = περὶ φύσιος παιδίου
*Oct.* = περὶ ὀκταμήνου
*Off.* = κατ᾽ ἰητρεῖον
*Oss.* = περὶ ὀστέων φύσιος
*Praec.* = παραγγελίαι
*Prog.* = προγνωστικόν
*Prorrh.* = προρρητικόν
*Salubr.* = περὶ διαίτης ὑγιεινῆς

*Septim.* = περὶ ἑπταμήνου
*Septim.(Sp.)* = περὶ ἑπταμήνου (second treatise)
*Steril.* = περὶ ἀφόρων
*Superf.* = περὶ ἐπικυήσιος
*Ulc.* = περὶ ἑλκῶν
*VC* = περὶ τῶν ἐν κεφαλῇ τρωμάτων
*VM* = περὶ ἀρχαίης ἰητρικῆς
*Vict.* = περὶ διαίτης
*Vid.Ac.* = περὶ ὄψιος
*Virg.* = περὶ παρθενίων

**Hippodamus** Pythagoreus [Hippod.]
Apud Stobaeum.

**Hippolytus** Scriptor Ecclesiasticus [Hippol.] iii A.D.
*Haer.* = *Refutatio Omnium Haeresium*, ed. P. Wendland, Leipzig 1916.

**Hippon** Philosophus v B.C.
Ed. H. Diels, *Vorsokr.* i p. 288.

**Hipponax** Iambographus [Hippon.] vi B.C.
Ed. T. Bergk, *PLG* ii p. 460.

**Hippothoon** Tragicus
Ed. A. Nauck, *TGF* p. 827.

**Hippys** Historicus v B.C. (?)
Ed. C. Müller, *FHG* ii p. 12.

**Historiae Augustae Scriptores** [*Hist.Aug.*]
*Scriptores Historiae Augustae*, ed. H. Peter², Leipzig (T.) 1884.

**Homerus** Epicus [Hom.]
Ed. D. B. Monro & T. W. Allen, Oxford (OCT).
Batr. = Batrachomyomachia (q.v.), Il. = Ilias, Od. = Odyssea } sine auctoris nomine laudantur.
*Epigr.* = *Epigrammata*, ed. D. B. Monro, Oxford 1896. [Hom. *Epigr.*]
*Hymni*, v. Hymni Homerici.
Scholia in Homeri Iliadem, ed. W. Dindorf, 4 vols., Oxford 1874; vols. v and vi, ed. E. Maass, Oxford 1887–8.
Scholia in Homeri Odysseam, ed. W. Dindorf, Oxford 1855.

**Honestus** Epigrammaticus [Honest.] i B.C. (?)
v. *Anthologia Graeca.*

**Horapollo** [Horap.] iv A.D. (?)
*Hieroglyphica*, ed. J. C. de Pauw, Utrecht 1727; ed. C. Leemans, Amsterdam 1835.

**Hymni Homerici** [*h.Hom.*]
Ed. T. W. Allen, *Homeri Opera* v, Oxford (OCT).
*h.Ap.* = *hymnus ad Apollinem*
*h.Bacch.* = *hymnus ad Bacchum*
*h.Cer.* = *hymnus ad Cererem*
*h.Mart.* = *hymnus ad Martem*
*h.Merc.* = *hymnus ad Mercurium*
*h.Pan.* = *hymnus ad Panem*
*h.Ven.* = *hymnus ad Venerem*

**Hymni Magici** [*Hymn.Mag.*]
Ed. G. Parthey, *Abh. Berl. Akad.* 1865, p. 109 sqq.; cf. C. Wessely, *Denkschr. Wien. Akad., philol.-hist. Kl.* xxxvi (2) (1888) p. 27: v. Orphica.

**Hymnus ad Idaeos Dactylos** [*Hymn.Id.Dact.*] iv B.C.
Ed. J. U. Powell, *Coll. Alex.* p. 171.

**Hymnus ad Isim** [*Hymn.Is.*]
*IG* 12(5).739.

**Hymnus Curetum** [*Hymn.Curet.*] iii B.C. (?)
Ed. J. U. Powell, *Coll. Alex.* p. 160.

**Hyperides** Orator [Hyp.] iv B.C.
Ed. F. G. Kenyon, Oxford (OCT).
*Ath.* = *adv. Athenogenem*
*Dem.* = *adv. Demosthenem*
*Epit.* = *Epitaphius*
*Eux.* = *pro Euxenippo*
*Fr.* = *Fragmenta*
*Lyc.* = *pro Lycophrone*
*Phil.* = *adv. Philippum*

**Hypsicles** Astronomus [Hypsicl.] ii B.C.
Ed. C. Manitius, Dresden 1888.

**Iamblichus** Philosophus [Iamb.] iv A.D.
*Comm.Math.* = *de communi mathematica scientia*, ed. N. Festa, Leipzig (T.) 1891.
*in Nic.* = *in Nicomachi arithmeticam introductionem*, ed. H. Pistelli, Leipzig (T.) 1894 (cited by page).
*Myst.* = *de Mysteriis*, ed. G. Parthey, Berlin 1857.
*Protr.* = *Protrepticus*, ed. H. Pistelli, Leipzig (T.) 1888.
*VP* = *de vita Pythagorica*, ed. A. Nauck, Leipzig 1884.

**Iamblichus** Scriptor Eroticus [Iamb.*Bab.*] ii A.D.
Ed. R. Hercher, *Erotici* i p. 217.

**Ibycus** Lyricus [Ibyc.] vi B.C.
Ed. T. Bergk, *PLG* iii p. 235.
*Oxy.* = *POxy.* 1790.

**Idomeneus** Historicus iii B.C.
Ed. C. Müller, *FHG* ii p. 489.

**Ilias** [Il.]
v. Homerus.

**Ilias Parva** [Il.Parv.]
Ed. T. W. Allen, *Homeri Opera* v, Oxford (OCT), p. 127.

**Iliu Persis** [Il.Pers.]
Ed. T. W. Allen, *Homeri Opera* v, Oxford (OCT), p. 137.

**Ion Chius**
*Fragmenta Elegiaca*, ed. T. Bergk, *PLG* ii p. 251. [Ion Eleg.]
*Fragmenta Historica*, ed. C. Müller, *FHG* ii p. 44. [Ion Hist.]
*Fragmenta Lyrica*, ed. T. Bergk, *PLG* ii p. 255. [Ion Lyr.]
*Fragmenta Tragica*, ed. A. Nauck, *TGF* p. 732. [Ion Trag.]

**Iophon** Tragicus v B.C.
Ed. A. Nauck, *TGF* p. 761.

**Irenaeus** Epigrammaticus [Iren.] vi A.D.
v. *Anthologia Graeca.*

**Isaeus** Orator [Is.] iv B.C.
Ed. T. Thalheim, Leipzig (T.) 1903.

**Isidorus** Tragicus [Isid.Trag.]
Ed. A. Nauck, *TGF* p. 829.

**Isidorus Aegeates** Epigrammaticus [Isid.Aeg.]
v. *Anthologia Graeca.*

**Isidorus Characenus** Geographus [Isid.Char.] i B.C./i A.D.
Ed. C. Müller, *GGM* i p. 244.

**Isidorus Hispalensis** Grammaticus [Isid.] vi/vii A.D.
*Etym.* = *Etymologiae*, ed. W. M. Lindsay, Oxford (OCT).

**Isidorus Scholasticus** Epigrammaticus [Isid.] vi A.D.
v. *Anthologia Graeca.*

**Isigonus** Paradoxographus [Isig.] ii/i B.C. (?)
Ed. C. Müller, *FHG* iv p. 435.

**Isocrates** Orator [Isoc.] v/iv B.C.
Ed. F. Blass, 2 vols., Leipzig (T.) 1889–98.
*Ep.* = *Epistulae*

**Ister** Historicus iii B.C.
Ed. C. Müller, *FHG* i p. 409.

**Isyllus** Lyricus [Isyll.] iii B.C.
Ed. J. U. Powell, *Coll. Alex.* p. 132 (= *IG* 4.950).

**Joannes Alexandrinus** Grammaticus [Jo.Alex. vel Jo.Gramm.] vi A.D.
Idem qui Philoponus (q.v.).
Compendium περὶ διαλέκτων, ed. O. Hoffmann, *Die griechischen Dialekte* ii, Göttingen 1893, p. 204. [Jo.Gramm.*Comp.*]
τονικὰ παραγγέλματα. ed. W. Dindorf, Leipzig 1825. [Jo.Alex.]

**Joannes Diaconus** Grammaticus [Jo.Diac.]
Ed. T. Gaisford, *Poetae Graeci Minores*, vol. iii, p. 448.

**Joannes Gazaeus** [Jo.Gaz.] vi A.D.
Ed. P. Friedländer, Leipzig–Berlin 1912.

**Josephus** Historicus [J.] i A.D.
Ed. S. A. Naber, Leipzig (T.) 1888–96.
*AJ* = *Antiquitates Judaicae*
*Ap.* = *contra Apionem*
*BJ* = *Bellum Judaicum*
*Vit.* = *Vita*

**Juba, Rex Mauretaniae** Historicus i B.C./i A.D.
Ed. C. Müller, *FHG* iii p. 465.

**Julianus Imperator** [Jul.] iv A.D.
Ed. F. C. Hertlein, Leipzig (T.) 1875–6.
*ad Ath.* = *Epistula ad Athenienses*
*ad Them.* = *Epistula ad Themistium*
*Caes.* = *Caesares*
*Ep.* = *Epistulae*, ed. J. Bidez & F. Cumont, Paris 1922.
*Gal.* = *contra Galilaeos*, ed. C. J. Neumann, Leipzig 1880.
*Mis.* = *Misopogon*
*Or.* = *Orationes*

**Julianus Aegyptius** Epigrammaticus [Jul. vel Jul.Aegypt.] vi A.D.
v. *Anthologia Graeca.*

**Julianus Laodicensis** Astrologus [Jul.Laod.] v/vi A.D.
v. *Catalogus Codicum Astrologorum.*

**Juncus** Philosophus [Junc.] ii A.D. (?)
Apud Stobaeum.

**Justinianus** Imperator [Just.] vi A.D.
*Constitutio* Δέδωκεν, ed. P. Krüger, *Corpus Juris Civilis* i[13], Berlin 1920. [*Const.*Δέδωκεν]
*Constitutio 'omnem'*, ed. P. Krüger, op. cit. [*Const.omnem*]
*Edicta*, ed. R. Schoell et W. Kroll, *Corpus Juris Civilis* iii[4], Berlin 1905. [*Edict.*]
*Novellae*, ed. R. Schoell et W. Kroll, op. cit. [*Nov.*]

**Juvenalis, D. Junius** Poeta Latinus [Juv.] i A.D.
Ed. S. G. Owen, Oxford (OCT) (post Persium).

**Laco** Epigrammaticus
v. *Anthologia Graeca.*

**Lamprocles** Lyricus [Lamprocl.] v B.C.
Ed. T. Bergk, *PLG* iii p. 554.

**Lasus** Lyricus vi B.C.
Ed. T. Bergk, *PLG* iii p. 376.

**Leo Philosophus** Epigrammaticus [Leo Phil.] v A.D.
v. *Anthologia Graeca.*

**Leonidas** Epigrammaticus [Leon.] iii B.C.
v. *Anthologia Graeca.*

**Leonidas** Medicus [Leonid.] i/ii A.D.
Apud Oribasium.
**Leonidas Alexandrinus** Epigrammaticus [Leon.] i A.D.
v. *Anthologia Graeca.*
**Leontius** Epigrammaticus [Leont.] vi A.D.
v. *Anthologia Graeca.*
**Leontius** Mathematicus [Leont. *in Arat.*] vii A.D.
Ed. E. Maass, *Commentariorum in Aratum reliquiae*, Berlin 1898, p. 559.
**Lesbonax** Grammaticus [Lesb.Gramm.] ii A.D.
Ed. R. Müller, Leipzig 1900.
**Lesbonax** Rhetor [Lesb.Rh.] ii A.D.
Ed. F. Kiehr, Leipzig 1907.
**Leucippus** Philosophus [Leucipp.] v B.C.
Ed. H. Diels, *Vorsokr.* ii p. 1.
**Leucon** Comicus v/iv B.C.
Ed. T. Kock, *CAF* i p. 703.
**Lexicon Messanense** [*Lex.Mess.*]
Ed. H. Rabe, *Rh. Mus.* xlvii (1892) p. 404; l (1895) p. 148.
**Lexicon Rhetoricum** [*Lex.Rhet.*]
Apud Aelium Dionysium et Eustathium.
**Lexicon Rhetoricum Cantabrigiense** [*Lex.Rhet.Cant.*]
Ed. M. H. E. Meier, Halle 1844; ed. E. O. Houtsma, Leyden 1870.
**Lexicon Sabbaiticum** [*Lex.Sabb.*]
Ed. A. Papadopulos-Kerameus, Petersburg 1892.
**Lexicon de Spiritu** [*Lex.deSpir.*]
Ed. L. C. Valckenaer (post Ammonium).
**Lexicon Vindobonense** [*Lex.Vind.*]
Ed. A. Nauck, Petersburg 1867.
**Libanius** Sophista [Lib.] iv A.D.
Ed. R. Foerster, Leipzig (T.) 1903–1923.
*Arg.D.* = *Argumenta Orationum Demosthenicarum* (viii p. 600)
*Chr.* = *Chriae* (viii p. 63)
*Comp.* = *Comparationes* (viii p. 334)
*Conf.* = *Confirmationes* (viii p. 138)
*Decl.* = *Declamationes* (v–vii)
*Def.Leg.* = *Defensio Legis* (viii p. 568)
*Descr.* = *Descriptiones* (viii p. 460)
*Enc.* = *Encomia* (viii p. 216)
*Ep.* = *Epistulae* (x, xi)
*Eth.* = *Ethopoeiae* (viii p. 372)
*Fab.* = *Fabulae* (viii p. 24)
*Loc.* = *Loci Communes* (viii p. 158)
*Narr.* = *Narrationes* (viii p. 33)
*Or.* = *Orationes* (i–iv)
*Ref.* = *Refutationes* (viii p. 123)
*Sent.* = *Sententiae* (viii p. 106)
*Thes.* = *Theses* (viii p. 550)
*Vit.* = *Vituperationes* (viii p. 282)
**Licymnius** Lyricus [Licymn.] iv B.C.
Ed. T. Bergk, *PLG* iii p. 598.
**Limenius** Lyricus [Limen.] ii B.C.
Ed. J. U. Powell, *Coll. Alex.* p. 149.
**Linus** Epicus
Apud Stobaeum.
**Lollius Bassus** Epigrammaticus [Loll.] i A.D.
v. *Anthologia Graeca*; cf. Bassus.
**Longinus** Rhetor [Longin.] (iii A.D.)
Ed. A. O. Prickard, Oxford (OCT); cited without title.
*Fr.* = *Fragmenta*, ed. C. Hammer in L. Spengel, *Rhet.* i² (2), Leipzig (T.) 1894, p. 213.
*Proll.Heph.* = *Prolegomena ad Hephaestionis Euchiridion*, ed. M. Consbruch (post Hephaestionem), Leipzig (T.) 1906, pp. 81 ff.
*Rh.* = *Ars Rhetorica*, ed. C. Hammer, op. cit., p. 179.
**Longus** Scriptor Eroticus iii A.D. (?)
Ed. R. Hercher, *Erotici* i p. 239.
**Lucianus** Sophista ii A.D.
Ed. C. Jacobitz, 3 vols., Leipzig (T.) 1896–7; ed. J. Sommerbrodt, 3 vols. [all published], Berlin 1886–99; ed. N. Nilén, Leipzig (T.) 1906–.
Scholia in Lucianum, ed. H. Rabe, Leipzig (T.) 1906.
*Abd.* = *Abdicatus*
*Alex.* = *Alexander*
*Am.* = *Amores*
*Anach.* = *Anacharsis*
*Apol.* = *Apologia*
*Asin.* = *Asinus*
*Astr.* = *de Astrologia*
*Bacch.* = *Bacchus*
*Bis Acc.* = *Bis Accusatus*
*Cal.* = *Calumniae non temere credendum*
*Cat.* = *Cataplus*
*Charid.* = *Charidemus*
*Cont.* = *Contemplantes*
*Cyn.* = *Cynicus*
*DDeor.* = *Dialogi Deorum*
*DMar.* = *Dialogi Marini*
*DMeretr.* = *Dialogi Meretricii*
*DMort.* = *Dialogi Mortuorum*
*Dem.Enc.* = *Demosthenis Encomium*
*Demon.* = *Demonax*
*Deor.Conc.* = *Deorum Concilium*
*Dips.* = *Dipsades*
*Dom.* = *de Domo*
*Electr.* = *Electrum*
*Ep.Sat.* = *Epistulae Saturnales*
*Eun.* = *Eunuchus*
*Fug.* = *Fugitivi*
*Gall.* = *Gallus*
*Halc.* = *Halcyon*
*Harm.* = *Harmonides*
*Herc.* = *Hercules*
*Herm.* = *Hermotimus*
*Herod.* = *Herodotus*
*Hes.* = *Hesiodus*
*Hipp.* = *Hippias*
*Hist.Conscr.* = *Quomodo historia conscribenda sit*
*Icar.* = *Icaromenippus*
*Im.* = *Imagines*
*Ind.* = *adversus Indoctum*
*JConf.* = *Juppiter Confutatus*
*JTr.* = *Juppiter Tragoedus*
*Jud.Voc.* = *Judicium Vocalium*
*Laps.* = *pro Lapsu inter Salutandum*
*Lex.* = *Lexiphanes*
*Luct.* = *de Luctu*
*Macr.* = *Macrobii*
*Merc.Cond.* = *de Mercede Conductis*
*Musc.Enc.* = *Muscae Encomium*
*Nav.* = *Navigium*
*Nec.* = *Necyomantia*
*Ner.* = *Nero*
*Nigr.* = *Nigrinus*
*Ocyp.* = *Ocypus*
*Par.* = *de Parasito*
*Patr.Enc.* = *Patriae Encomium*
*Peregr.* = *de Morte Peregrini*
*Phal.* 1, 2 = *Phalaris* 1, 2
*Philopatr.* = *Philopatris* [Ps.-Luc.]
*Philops.* = *Philopseudes*
*Pisc.* = *Piscator*
*Pr.Im.* = *pro Imaginibus*
*Pro Merc.Cond.* = *pro Mercede Conductis*
*Prom.* = *Prometheus*
*Prom.Es* = *Prometheus es in verbis*
*Pseudol.* = *Pseudologista*
*Rh.Pr.* = *Rhetorum praeceptor*
*Sacr.* = *de Sacrificiis*
*Salt.* = *de Saltatione*
*Sat.* = *Saturnalia*
*Scyth.* = *Scytha*
*Sol.* = *Soloecista*
*Somn.* = *Somnium sive Vita Luciani*
*Symp.* = *Symposium*
*Syr.D.* = *de Syria Dea*
*Tim.* = *Timon*
*Tox.* = *Toxaris*
*Trag.* = *Tragodopodagra*
*Tyr.* = *Tyrannicida*
*VH* 1, 2 = *Verae Historiae* 1, 2
*Vit.Auct.* = *Vitarum Auctio*
*Zeux.* = *Zeuxis*
**Lucillius** Epigrammaticus [Lucill.] i A.D.
v. *Anthologia Graeca.*
**LXX**
v. Vetus Testamentum.
**Lycophron** Tragicus [Lyc.] iii B.C.
Ed. E. Scheer (cum scholiis), Berlin 1881–1908.
*Fr.* = *Fragmenta Tragica*, ed. A. Nauck, *TGF* p. 817.
**Lycophronides** Lyricus [Lycophronid.] iii B.C. (?)
Ed. T. Bergk, *PLG* iii p. 633.
**Lycurgus** Orator [Lycurg.] iv B.C.
Ed. F. Blass, Leipzig (T.) 1899.
*Fragmenta*, ed. H. Sauppe, *Orat. Att.* ii p. 258.
**Lycus** Historicus iv/iii B.C.
Ed. C. Müller, *FHG* ii p. 370.
**Lydus, Joannes Laurentius** Historicus [Lyd.] vi A.D.
*de Magistratibus populi Romani*, ed. R. Wünsch, Leipzig (T.) 1903. [*Mag.*]
*de Mensibus*, ed. R. Wünsch, Leipzig (T.) 1898. [*Mens.*]
*de Ostentis*, ed. C. Wachsmuth, Leipzig (T.) 1897. [*Ost.*]
**Lynceus** Comicus [Lync.]
Ed. T. Kock, *CAF* iii p. 274.
Cetera fragmenta apud Athenaeum.
**Lyrica Adespota** [*Lyr.Adesp.*]
Ed. T. Bergk, *PLG* iii p. 689.

**rica Alexandrina Adespota** [*Lyr.Alex.Adesp.*]
Ed. J. U. Powell, *Coll. Alex.* p. 177.

**sias** Orator [Lys.] v B.C.
Ed. C. Hude, Oxford (OCT).
*Fragmenta*, ed T. Thalheim, Leipzig (T.) 1901. [*Fr.*]; ed. H. Sauppe, *Orat. Att.* ii p. 170. [*Fr.* . . S.]

**ysimachides** Historicus [Lysimachid.]
Ed. C. Müller, *FHG* iii p. 340.

**ysimachus** Historicus [Lysim.] ii or i B.C.
Ed C. Müller, *FHG* iii p. 334.

**ysippus** Comicus [Lysipp.] v B.C.
Ed. T. Kock, *CAF* i p. 700.

**ysis** Philosophus
*Ep.* = *Epistula*, v. Pythagorae et Pythagoreorum Epistulae.

**acarius** Paroemiographus [Macar.] xv A.D.
Ed. E. L. von Leutsch & F. G. Schneidewin, *Paroemiographi* ii p. 135.

**Macedonius** Epigrammaticus [Maced.] i A.D. (?)
v. *Anthologia Graeca.*

**Macedonius** Lyricus [Maced.]
*Paean*, ed. J. U. Powell, *Coll Alex.* p. 138. [*Pae*]

**Macedonius Thessalonicensis** Epigrammaticus [Maced.] vi A.D.
v. *Anthologia Graeca.*

**Macho** Comicus iii B.C.
Ed. T. Kock, *CAF* iii p 324.
Cetera fragmenta apud Athenaeum.

**Macrobius** Grammaticus [Macr.] iv/v A.D.
*Exc.* = *Excerpta Grammatica*, ed. H. Keil, *Gramm. Lat.* v p. 595.
*Sat.* = *Saturnalia*, ed. F. Eyssenhardt[2], Leipzig (T.) 1893.

**Maecius** Epigrammaticus [Maec.] i A.D. (?)
v. *Anthologia Graeca.*

**Magnes** Comicus [Magn.] v B.C.
Ed. T. Kock, *CAF* i p. 7; suppl. J. Demiańczuk, *Supp. Com.* p. 54.

**Magnus** Epigrammaticus iv A.D. (?)
v. *Anthologia Graeca.*

**Magnus** Historicus [Magnus Hist.] iv A.D.
Ed. L. Dindorf, *HGM* i p. 365.

**Maiistas** Epicus [Maiist.] iii B.C.
Ed. J. U. Powell, *Coll. Alex.* p. 68 (= *IG* 11(4).1299).

**Malchus** Historicus [Malch.] iv A.D.
Ed. L. Dindorf, *HGM* i p. 383.

**Mamercus** Elegiacus [Mamerc.]
Ed. T. Bergk, *PLG* ii p. 325.

**Manetho** Astrologus [Man.] iv A.D. (?)
Ed. H. Koechly (with Dorotheus and Anubion), Leipzig (T.) 1858.

**Manetho** Historicus [Man.Hist.] iii B.C.
Ed. C. Müller, *FHG* ii p. 511.

**Mantissa Proverbiorum** [*Mantiss.Prov.*]
Ed. E. L. von Leutsch & F. G. Schneidewin, *Paroemiographi* ii p. 745.

**Marcellinus** Biographus [Marcellin.] iv A.D. (?)
*Vita Thucydidis*, ed. H. Stuart Jones (ante Thucydidem), Oxford (OCT). [*Vit.Thuc.*]

**Marcellinus** Medicus [Marcellin.] ii A.D. (?)
*Puls.* = *de Pulsibus*, ed. H. Schöne, *Festschrift zur 49. Versammlung deutscher Philologen und Schulmänner*, Basel 1907.

**Marcellus Sidetes** Poeta Medicus [Marc.Sid.] ii A.D.
Ed. M. Schneider, *Commentationes philologae quibus O. Ribbeckio . . . congratulantur discipuli*, Leipzig 1888, p. 115.

**Marcianus** Geographus [Marcian.] iv/v A.D.
Ed. C. Müller, *GGM* i p. 515. [*Peripl.*]
*Epit.* = Artemidori Epitome, ed. C. Müller, ib. p. 574.

**Marcus Antoninus** Imperator [M.Ant.] ii A.D.
Ed. J. H. Leopold, Oxford (OCT).

**Marcus Argentarius** Epigrammaticus [Marc.Arg.] vi A.D.
v. *Anthologia Graeca.*

**Margites**
Ed. T. W. Allen, *Homeri Opera* v, Oxford (OCT), p. 152.

**Maria** Alchemista [Maria Alch.] ii A.D. (?)
Apud Olympiodorum et Zosimum.

**Marianus** Epigrammaticus [Marian.] v/vi A.D.
v. *Anthologia Graeca.*

**Marinus** Biographus [Marin.] v/vi A.D.
*Procl.* = *Vita Procli*, ed. J. F. Boissonade (post Cobeti Diogenem Laertium), Paris (D.) 1862.

**Marius Victorinus** Grammaticus Latinus [Mar.Vict.] iv A.D.
Ed. H. Keil, *Gramm. Lat.* vi p. 1.

**Martialis** Epigrammaticus Latinus [Mart.] i A.D.
Ed. W. M. Lindsay, Oxford (OCT).

**Martianus Capella** Grammaticus Latinus [Mart.Cap.] v A.D.
Ed. F. Eyssenhardt, Leipzig (T.) 1866.

**Matro** Parodius iv B.C.
*Conv.* = *Convivium*, ed. P. Brandt, *Corpusculum poesis epicae ludibundae* i, Leipzig (T.) 1888, p. 60.
*Parod.Fr.* = *Parodiarum Fragmenta*, op. cit. p. 91.

**Maximus** Astrologus [Max.] i B.C. (?)
Ed. A. Ludwich, Leipzig (T.) 1877.
*Epit.* = *Epitome*, ed. A. Ludwich, op. cit., p. 79.

**Maximus Tyrius** Sophista [Max.Tyr.] ii A.D.
Ed. H. Hobein, Leipzig (T.) 1910 (cited by the numeration of F. Dübner, post Theophrastum, Paris (D.) 1840).

**Megasthenes** Historicus [Megasth.] iv/iii B.C.
Ed. C. Müller, *FHG* ii p. 397.

**Meges** Medicus i A.D.
Apud Oribasium.

**Melampus** Scriptor de divinatione [Melamp.]
*περὶ ἐλαιῶν τοῦ σώματος μαντική πρὸς Πτολεμαῖον*, ed. J. G. F. Franz, *Scriptores Physiognomiae Veteres*, Altenburg 1780.
*περὶ παλμῶν*, ed. H. Diels, *Abh. Berl.Akad.*, 1907; cf. *PRyl.* 1. 28.

**Melanippides** Lyricus [Melanipp.] v B.C.
Ed. T. Bergk, *PLG* iii p. 589.

**Melanthius** Historicus [Melanth.Hist.] iv B.C. (?)
Ed. C. Müller, *FHG* iv p. 444.

**Melanthius** Tragicus [Melanth.Trag.]
Ed. A. Nauck, *TGF* p. 760.

**Meleager** Epigrammaticus [Mel.] i B.C.
v. *Anthologia Graeca.*

**Melinno** Lyrica i A.D. (?)
Apud Stobaeum.

**Melissa**
*Ep.* = *Epistula*, v Pythagorae et Pythagoreorum Epistulae.

**Melissus** Philosophus [Meliss.] v B.C.
Ed. H. Diels, *Vorsokr.* i p. 176.

**Memnon** Historicus [Memn.] i A.D.
Ed. C. Müller, *FHG* iii p. 525.

**Menaechmus** Historicus [Menaechm.] iii B.C.
Ed. C. Müller, *SRAM* p. 145.

**Menander** Comicus [Men.] iv/iii B.C.
Ed. T. Kock, *CAF* iii p. 3; suppl. J. Demiańczuk, *Supp. Com.* p. 54.
*Menandrea*, ed. A. Körte[2], Leipzig (T.) 1912:
*Epit.* = Ἐπιτρέποντες
*Georg.* = Γεωργός
*Her.* = Ἥρως
*Inc.* 1, 2 = *Fabula incerta* 1, 2
*Kith.* = Κιθαριστής
*Kol.* = Κόλαξ
*Kon.* = Κωνεαζόμεναι
*Mis.* = Μισούμεναι
*Mon.* = Μονόστιχοι, ed. A. Meineke, *Fragmenta Comicorum Graecorum* iv (1841) p. 340
*Per.* = Περινθία
*Phasm.* = Φάσμα
*Pk.* = Περικειρομένη
*Sam.* = Σαμία

**Menander** Rhetor [Men.Rh.] iii A.D.
Ed. L. Spengel, *Rhet.* iii p. 329.

**Menander Ephesius** Historicus [Men.Eph.]
Ed. C. Müller, *FHG* iv p. 445.

**Menander Protector** Historicus [Men.Prot.] vi A.D.
Ed. L. Dindorf, *HGM* ii p. 1.

**Menecles Barcaeus** Historicus [Menecl.] ii B.C.
Ed. C. Müller, *FHG* iv p. 448.

**Menecrates** Comicus [Menecr.]
Ed. J. Demiańczuk, *Supp. Com.* p. 63.

**Menecrates Ephesius** Poeta Philosophus [Menecr.Eph.] iv B.C.
Ed. H. Diels, *PPF* p. 171.

**Menecrates Xanthius** Historicus [Menecr.Xanth.] iv/iii B.C.
Ed. C. Müller, *FHG* ii p. 343.

**Menemachus** Medicus [Menemach.] i A.D.
Apud Oribasium.

**Menesthenes** Historicus [Menesth.]
Ed. C. Müller, *FHG* iv p. 451.

**Menetor** Historicus
Ed. C. Müller, *FHG* iv p. 452.

**Menippus** Epistolographus [Menipp.] iii B.C.
*Epistulae*, ed. R. Hercher, *Epistolographi*, p. 400. [*Ep.*]

**Meno** Medicus iv B.C.
*Iatr.* = *Iatrika*
v. Anonymus Londinensis.

**Menodotus Samius** Historicus [Menodot.] iii B.C. (?)
Ed. C. Müller, *FHG* iii p. 103.

**Mesomedes** Lyricus [Mesom.] ii A.D.
Ed. C. Jan, *Musici Scriptores Graeci*, Leipzig (T.) 1899, p. 454, *Suppl.* p. 46.
*Mus.* = *Hymnus in Musam*
*Nem.* = *Hymnus in Nemesin*
*Sol.* = *Hymnus in Solem*

**Metagenes** Comicus [Metag.] v B.C.
Ed. T. Kock, *CAF* i p. 704.

**Metrodorus** Epigrammaticus [Metrod.] iv A.D.
v. *Anthologia Graeca.*

**Metrodorus** Philosophus [Metrod.] iv/iii B.C.
Ed. A. Körte, *Jahrbücher für klassische Philologie, Suppl.* xvii p. 529, Leipzig 1890.

**Metrodorus** *(continued)*
*Herc.* 831 = Papyrus Herculanensis 831; ed. A. Körte, op. cit., pp. 571 ff.

**Metrodorus Chius** Philosophus [Metrod.Chius] v B.C.
Ed. H. Diels, *Vorsokr.* ii p. 140.

**Metrodorus Scepsius** Historicus [Metrod.Sceps.] i B.C.
Ed. C. Müller, *FHG* iii p. 203.

**Michael Ephesius** Philosophus [Mich.] xi/xii A.D.
*in EN* = *in Ethica Nicomachea commentarium*, ed. G. Heylbut (*Comm. in Arist. Graeca* xx), Berlin 1892; *in librum quintum Ethicorum Nicomacheorum commentarium*, ed. M. Hayduck (*Comm. in Arist. Graeca* xxii *pars* iii), Berlin 1901.
*in PA* = *in libros de Partibus Animalium, de Animalium Motione, de Animalium Incessu commentaria*, ed. M. Hayduck (*Comm. in Arist. Graeca* xxii *pars* ii), Berlin 1904.
*in PN* = *in Parva Naturalia commentaria*, ed. P. Wendland (*Comm. in Arist. Graeca* xxii *pars* i), Berlin 1903.

**Michaelius** Epigrammaticus vi A.D. (?)
v. *Anthologia Graeca.*

**Mimnermus** Lyricus [Mimn.] vi B.C.
Ed. T. Bergk, *PLG* ii p. 25.

**Mimnermus** Tragicus [Mimn.Trag.]
Ed. A. Nauck, *TGF* p. 829.

**Minucianus** Rhetor [Minuc.] ii A.D.
Ed. C. Hammer in L. Spengel, *Rhet.* i² (2), Leipzig (T.) 1894, p. 340.

**Mithradates** Epistolographus [Mithr.] (i B.C.)
Ed. R. Hercher, *Epistolographi*, p. 177.

**Mnasalcas** Epigrammaticus [Mnasalc.] iii B.C.
v. *Anthologia Graeca.*

**Mnaseas** Historicus iii/ii B.C.
Ed. C. Müller, *FHG* iii p. 149.

**Mnesimachus** Comicus [Mnesim.] iv B.C.
Ed. T. Kock, *CAF* ii p. 436.

**Mnesitheus Atheniensis** Medicus [Mnesith.Ath.] iii B.C.
Apud Oribasium.

**Mnesitheus Cyzicenus** Medicus [Mnesith.Cyz.]
Apud Oribasium; fortasse idem qui Atheniensis.

**Moeris** Grammaticus [Moer.] ii A.D.
Ed. J. Pierson, Leyden 1759.

**Moero** Epica iii B.C.
Ed. J. U. Powell, *Coll. Alex.* p. 21.

**Molpis** Historicus
Ed. C. Müller, *FHG* iv p. 453.

**Moschio** Gnomologus
Γνῶμαι, ed. H. Schenkl (post Epictetum), p. 481. [*Gnom.*]

**Moschio** Paradoxographus
Apud Athenaeum.

**Moschio** Tragicus [MoschioTrag.] iv B.C.
Ed. A. Nauck, *TGF* p. 812.

**Moschus** Bucolicus [Mosch.] ii B.C.
Ed. U. von Wilamowitz-Möllendorff², *Bucolici Graeci*, Oxford (OCT).

**Moses** Alchemista ii A.D. (?)
Ed. M. Berthelot, *Collection des anciens alchimistes grecs*, Paris 1888, p. 139.

**Mucius Scaevola** Epigrammaticus [Muc.Scaev.]
v. *Anthologia Graeca.*

**Mundus Munatius** Epigrammaticus [Mund.]
v. *Anthologia Graeca.*

**Musaeus** Epicus [Musae.] v/vi A.D.
Ed. A. Ludwich, Bonn 1912.

**Musaeus** Philosophus [Musae.]
Ed. H. Diels, *Vorsokr.* ii p. 179. [*Fr.* .. D.]

**Musicius** Epigrammaticus [Music.]
v. *Anthologia Graeca.*

**Musonius** Philosophus [Muson.] i A.D.
Ed. O. Hense, Leipzig (T.) 1905.
*Ep.* = *Epistula* in R. Hercher, *Epistolographi*, p. 401.

**Myia**
*Ep.* = *Epistula*, v. Pythagorae et Pythagoreorum Epistulae.

**Myrinus** Epigrammaticus [Myrin.]
v. *Anthologia Graeca.*

**Myro** Historicus
Ed. C. Müller, *FHG* iv p. 460.

**Myrsilus** Historicus [Myrsil.]
Ed. C. Müller, *FHG* iv p. 455.

**Myrtilus** Comicus [Myrtil.] v B.C.
Ed. T. Kock, *CAF* i p. 253.

**Naumachius** Epicus [Naumach.] ii A.D.
Apud Stobaeum.

**Nausicrates** Comicus [Nausicr.] iv B.C.
Ed. T. Kock, *CAF* ii p. 295; suppl. J. Demiańczuk, *Supp. Com.* p. 64.

**Nausiphanes** Philosophus [Nausiph.] iv/iii B.C.
Ed. H. Diels, *Vorsokr.* ii p. 155.

**Neanthes** Historicus [Neanth.] iii B.C.
Ed. C. Müller, *FHG* iii p. 2.

**Nearchus** Historicus [Nearch.]
Ed. C. Müller, *SRAM* p. 58.

**Nechepso** Astrologus [Nech.] ii B.C.
*Nechepsonis et Petosiridis fragmenta magica*, ed. E. Ri (*Philologus* vi *Suppl.* (1891–3) pp. 325–94): etiam apud Vetti Valentem.

**Neophron** Tragicus [Neophr.] v B
Ed. A. Nauck, *TGF* p. 729.

**Neoptolemus** Epicus [Neoptol.] iii/ii B
Ed. J. U. Powell, *Coll. Alex.* p. 27.

**Nepualius (Neptunalius, Neptunianus)**
Ed. W. Gemoll, Striegau 1884; cf. *Rh. Mus.* xlviii (1893) xlv (1890) 70.

**Nessas** Philosophus v B.
Ed. H. Diels, *Vorsokr.* ii p. 140.

**Nestor** Epigrammaticus iii A.
v. *Anthologia Graeca.*

**Nicaenetus** Epicus [Nicaenet.] ii B.C
Ed. J. U. Powell, *Coll. Alex.* p. 1.

**Nicander** Epicus [Nic.] ii B.C
Ed. O. Schneider, with scholia edited by H. Keil, Leipzig, 1856
*Alex.* = *Alexipharmaca*
*Ther.* = *Theriaca*
Scholia vetera ed. H. Bianchi, *Stud. Ital.* xii (1904) p. 321.

**Nicarchus** Epigrammaticus [Nicarch.] i A.D.
v. *Anthologia Graeca.*

**Nicias** Epigrammaticus [Nic.] iii B.C.
v. *Anthologia Graeca.*

**Nico** Comicus
Ed. T. Kock, *CAF* iii p. 389.

**Nicochares** Comicus [Nicoch.] iv B.C.
Ed. T. Kock, *CAF* i p. 770; suppl. J. Demiańczuk, *Supp. Com.* p. 64.

**Nicocles** Historicus [Nicocl.]
Ed. C. Müller, *FHG* iv p. 464.

**Nicodemus** Epigrammaticus [Nicod.]
v. *Anthologia Graeca.*

**Nicolaus** Comicus [Nicol.Com.] iv B.C. (?)
Ed. T. Kock, *CAF* iii p. 383.

**Nicolaus** Rhetor [Nicol.]
*Prog.* = *Progymnasmata*, ed. J. Felten, Leipzig (T.) 1913.

**Nicolaus Damascenus** Historicus [Nic.Dam.] i B.C.
Ed. L. Dindorf, *HGM* i p. 1.
*Vit.Caes.* = *Vita Caesaris*

**Nicomachus** Comicus [Nicom.Com.]
Ed. T. Kock, *CAF* iii p. 386.

**Nicomachus** Tragicus [Nicom.Trag.]
Ed. A. Nauck, *TGF* p. 762.

**Nicomachus Gerasenus** Mathematicus [Nicom.] ii A.D.
*Ar.* = *Arithmetica Introductio*, ed. R. Hoche, Leipzig (T.) 1866.
*Harm.* = *Harmonicum Enchiridium*, ed. C. Jan, *Musici Scriptores Graeci*, Leipzig (T.) 1895, p. 237.
*Exc.* = *Excerpta*, ib., p. 266.

**Nicopho** Comicus v/iv B.C.
Ed. T. Kock, *CAF* i p. 775.

**Nicostratus** Comicus [Nicostr.Com.] iv B.C.
Ed. T. Kock, *CAF* ii p. 219; suppl. J. Demiańczuk, *Supp. Com.* p. 66.

**Nicostratus** Philosophus [Nicostr.]
Apud Stobaeum.

**Niger, Sextius** Medicus
Apud Plinium et Dioscoridem.

**Nonius Marcellus** Grammaticus Latinus iv A.D.
Ed. W. M. Lindsay, Leipzig (T.) 1903.

**Nonnus** Epicus [Nonn.] iv/v A.D. (?)
*D.* = *Dionysiaca*, ed. A. Ludwich, Leipzig (T.) 1909, 1911.

**Nossis** Epigrammatica [Noss.] iii B.C. (?)
v. *Anthologia Graeca.*

**Nosti**
Ed. T. W. Allen, *Homeri Opera* v, Oxford (OCT), p. 140.

**Novum Testamentum**
Ed. A. Souter, Oxford 1910.
*Act.Ap.* = Acts of the Apostles
*Apoc.* = Apocalypse
*Ep.Col.* = Epistle to the Colossians
1, 2 *Ep.Cor.* = 1st, 2nd Epistle to the Corinthians
*Ep.Eph.* = Epistle to the Ephesians
*Ep.Gal.* = Epistle to the Galatians
*Ep.Hebr.* = Epistle to the Hebrews
*Ep.Jac.* = Epistle of James
1, 2 *Ep.Jo.* = 1st, 2nd Epistle of John
*Ep.Jud.* = Epistle of Jude
1, 2 *Ep.Pet.* = 1st, 2nd Epistle of Peter
*Ep.Phil.* = Epistle to the Philippians
*Ep.Philem.* = Epistle to Philemon
*Ep.Rom.* = Epistle to the Romans
1, 2 *Ep.Thess.* = 1st, 2nd Epistle to the Thessalonians
1, 2 *Ep.Ti.* = 1st, 2nd Epistle to Timothy
*Ep.Tit.* = Epistle to Titus
*Ev.Jo.* = Gospel according to John
*Ev.Luc.* = Gospel according to Luke
*Ev.Marc.* = Gospel according to Mark
*Ev.Matt.* = Gospel according to Matthew

**[Nu]menius Apamensis** Platonicus [Numen.] ii A.D.
[A]pud Eusebium; cf. F. W. A. Mullach, *FPG* iii p. 153.
**[Nu]menius Heracleota** Poeta Didacticus [Numen.] iii B.C.
[A]pud Athenaeum.
**[Ny]mphis** Historicus iii B.C.
[E]d. C. Müller, *FHG* iii p. 12.
**[N]ymphodorus** Historicus [Nymphod.]
Ed. C. Müller, *FHG* ii p. 375.

**[O]cellus Lucanus** Philosophus [Ocell.] i B.C. (?)
Ed. F. W. A. Mullach, *FPG* i p. 383.
**[O]dyssea** [Od.]
v. Homerus.
**[O]enomaus** Philosophus [Oenom.] ii A.D.
Apud Eusebium.
**[O]lympiodorus** Alchemista [Olymp.Alch.] iv A.D. (?)
Ed. M. Berthelot, *Collection des anciens alchimistes grecs*, Paris 1888, p. 75.
**[O]lympiodorus** Historicus [Olymp.Hist.] v A.D.
Ed. L. Dindorf, *HGM* i p. 450.
**[O]lympiodorus** Philosophus [Olymp.] vi A.D.
*in Alc.* = *in Platonis Alcibiadem commentarii*, ed. F. Creuzer, Frankfurt 1820–25.
*in Cat.* = *in Categorias commentarium*, ed. A. Busse (*Comm. in Arist. Graeca* xii *pars* i), Berlin 1902.
*in Grg.* = *in Platonis Gorgiam commentaria*, ed. A. Jahn, in *Neue Jahrbücher für Philologie, Suppl.* xiv (1848) p. 104.
*in Mete.* = *in Aristotelis Meteora commentaria*, ed. W. Stüve (*Comm. in Arist. Graeca* xii *pars* ii), Berlin 1900.
*in Phd.* = *in Platonis Phaedonem commentaria*, ed. W. Norvin, Leipzig (T.) 1913.
*in Phlb.* = *in Platonis Philebum scholia*, ed. G. Stallbaum, in editione Philebi, Leipzig 1820.
*Proll.* = *Prolegomena*, ed. A. Busse (*Comm. in Arist. Graeca* xii *pars* i), Berlin 1902.
*Vit.Pl.* = *Vita Platonis*; v. Diogenes Laertius.
**Onatas** [Onat.]
Apud Stobaeum.
**Onosander (Onasander)** Tacticus [Onos.] i A.D.
Ed. W. A. Oldfather, *Aeneas Tacticus, Asclepiodotus, Onasander*, with an Engl. tr. by members of the Illinois Greek Club, Lond. &c. (Loeb) 1923.
**Ophelio** Comicus [Ophel.] iv B.C.
Ed. T. Kock, *CAF* ii p. 293.
**Oppianus Anazarbensis** Epicus [Opp.] ii/iii A.D.
*H.* = *Halieutica*, ed. F. S. Lehrs, in *Poetae Bucolici et Didactici*, &c., Paris (D.) 1851.
**Oppianus Apamensis** Epicus [Opp.] iii A.D.
*C.* = *Cynegetica*, ed. P. Boudreaux, Paris 1908.
(*Ix.* = *Ixeutica*, only in paraphrase; v. Dionysius.)
Scholia in Oppianum, ed. U. C. Bussemaker, Paris (D.) 1847.
**Oracula Chaldaica** [*Orac.Chald.*]
*Thomae Stanleii Historia Philosophiae Orientalis*, ed. J. Clericus, Amsterdam 1690.
**Oribasius** Medicus [Orib.] iv A.D.
Ed. U. C. Bussemaker & C. Daremberg, 6 vols., Paris 1851–76.
*Eup.* = *Euporista*
*Fr.* = *Fragmenta*
*inc.* = *liber incertus*
*Syn.* = *Synopsis*
**Origenes** Theologus iii A.D.
Ed. P. Koetschau, Leipzig 1899.
*Cels.* = *contra Celsum*
**Orion** Lexicographus v A.D.
Ed. F. W. Sturz (= *Etymologicum Magnum*, vol. iii), Leipzig 1820.
**Orphica** [Orph.]
Ed. E. Abel, Leipzig & Prague 1885.
*A.* = *Argonautica*
*H.* = *Hymni*
*L.* = *Lithica*
*Fr.* = *Fragmenta*, ed. O. Kern, Berlin 1922.

**Paean Delphicus** [*Pae.Delph.*] ii B.C.
Ed. J. U. Powell, *Coll. Alex.* p. 141.
**Paean Erythraeus** [*Pae.Erythr.*] iv B.C.
Ed. J. U. Powell, *Coll. Alex* pp. 136, 140.
**Palaephatus** Paradoxographus [Palaeph.]
Ed. N. Festa, in *Mythographi Graeci* iii (2), Leipzig (T.) 1902.
**Palchus** Astrologus [Palch.] v or vi A.D.
in *Cat. Cod. Astr.*
**Palladas** Epigrammaticus [Pall.] vi A.D.
v. *Anthologia Graeca*.
**Palladius** Medicus [Pall.]
*in Hp.* = *in Hippocratem*, ed. F. R. Dietz, Königsberg 1834.
*in Hp.Fract.* = *in librum Hippocratis de fracturis*, ed. R. Charterius, *Hippocratis et Galeni Opera*, vol. xii, Paris 1679.
**Pamphila** Historica i A.D.
Ed. C. Müller *FHG* iii p. 520.

**Pamphilus** Epigrammaticus [Pamphil.]
v. *Anthologia Graeca*.
**Pamphilus** Medicus [Pamphil.]
Apud Galenum.
**Pancrates** Epicus [Pancrat.] ii A.D.
Apud Athenaeum.
*Oxy.* = *POxy.* 1085.
**Pancrates** Epigrammaticus [Pancrat.]
v. *Anthologia Graeca*.
**Panyasis** Epicus [Panyas.]
Ed. Kinkel, *EGF* p. 253; suppl. J. U. Powell, *Coll. Alex.* p. 248.
**Pappus** Mathematicus [Papp.] iii A.D. (?)
Ed. F. Hultsch, Berlin 1876–1878; cited by page.
**Parmenides** Poeta Philosophus [Parm.] vi/v B.C.
Ed. H. Diels, *PPF* p. 48.
**Parmenio** Epigrammaticus [Parmen.]
v. *Anthologia Graeca*.
**Parmeno** Epigrammaticus
v. *Anthologia Graeca*.
**Parmeno** Iambographus iii B.C. (?)
Ed. J. U. Powell, *Coll. Alex.* p. 237.
**Parrhasius** Elegiacus [Parrhas.] v iv B.C.
Ed. T. Bergk, *PLG* ii p. 320.
**Parthenius** Mythographus [Parth.] i B.C.
Ed. E. Martini, *Mythographi Graeci* ii (1) *Suppl.*, Leipzig (T.) 1902.
**Patrocles Thurius** Tragicus [Patrocl.]
Ed. A. Nauck, *TGF* p. 830.
**Paulus Aegineta** Medicus [Paul.Aeg.] vii A.D.
Ed. J. L. Heiberg, *CMG* ix, Leipzig 1921–1924; Bk. vi ed. R. Briau, Paris 1855.
**Paulus Alexandrinus** Astrologus [Paul.Al.] iv A.D.
Ed. A. Schato, Wittenberg 1586 (cited by signature and page of quaternion, as: *G.* 3).
**Paulus Silentiarius** Epigrammaticus [Paul.Sil.] vi A.D.
v. *Anthologia Graeca*.
**Pausanias** Periegeta [Paus.] ii A.D.
Ed. H. Hitzig & H. Bluemner, Leipzig 1896–1910.
**Pausanias Damascenus** Historicus [Paus.Dam.] iv A.D. (?)
Ed. L. Dindorf, *HGM* i p. 154.
**Pausanias Grammaticus** [Paus.Gr.]
Ed. E. Schwabe; v. Aelius Dionysius.
**Pediasimus** [Pediasim.]
Ed. R. Wagner (post Apollodorum), *Mythographi Graeci* i, Leipzig (T.) 1894.
**Pelagius** Alchemista [Pelag.Alch.] iii A.D.
Ed. M. Berthelot, *Collection des anciens alchimistes grecs*, Paris 1888, p. 253.
**Pempelus** Philosophus [Pempel.]
Apud Stobaeum.
**Perictione** Philosophus [Perict.]
Apud Stobaeum.
**Periplus Maris Rubri** [*Peripl.M.Rubr.*] i A.D.
Ed C. Müller, *GGM* i p. 257; ed. B. Fabricius, 2 Aufl., Leipzig 1883.
**Persaeus Citieus** Stoicus [*Pers.Stoic.*] iii B.C.
Ed. H. von Arnim, *SVF* i p. 96.
*Fragmenta Historica*, ed. C. Müller, *FHG* ii p. 623. [*Fr.Hist.*]
**Perses** Epigrammaticus [Pers.]
v. *Anthologia Graeca*.
**Persius** Poeta Latinus [Pers.] i A.D.
Ed. S. G. Owen[2], Oxford (OCT).
**Petosiris** Astrologus [Petos.]
Ed. E. Riess, v. Nechepso; etiam apud Vettium Valentem.
**Petronius** [Petron.]
Ed. F. Buecheler, Berlin 1862; ed. sextam curavit W. Heraeus, 1922.
**Petrus Patricius** Historicus [Petr.Patr.] vi A.D.
Ed. L. Dindorf, *HGM* i p. 425.
**Phaedimus** Epigrammaticus [Phaedim.] ii B.C.
v. *Anthologia Graeca*.
**Phaënnus** Epigrammaticus [Phaënn.] ii B.C. (?)
v. *Anthologia Graeca*.
**Phaestus** Epicus [Phaest.]
Ed. J. U. Powell, *Coll. Alex.* p. 28.
**Phalaecus** Epigrammaticus [Phal.] iii B.C.
v. *Anthologia Graeca*.
**Phalaris** Epistolographus [Phalar.] (vi B.C.)
*Ep.* = *Epistulae*, ed. R. Hercher, *Epistolographi*, p. 439.
**Phanias** Epigrammaticus [Phan.]
v. *Anthologia Graeca*.
**Phanias** Historicus [Phan.Hist.] iv/iii B.C.
Ed. C. Müller, *FHG* ii p. 293.
**Phanocles** Elegiacus [Phanocl.] iii B.C. (?)
Ed. J. U. Powell, *Coll. Alex.* p. 106.
**Phanodemus** Historicus [Phanod.] iv B.C.
Ed. C. Müller, *FHG* i p. 366.
**Pherecrates** Comicus [Pherecr.] v B.C.
Ed. T. Kock, *CAF* i p. 145; suppl. J. Demiańczuk, *Supp. Com.* p. 66.
**Pherecydes Lerius** Historicus [Pherecyd.] vi B.C.
Ed. F. Jacoby, *FGrH* i p. 58.

**Pherecydes Syrius** Philosophus [Pherecyd.Syr.] vi B.C.
Ed. H. Diels, *Vorsokr.* ii p. 198.
**Philagrius** Medicus [Philagr.] iii/iv A.D.
Apud Aëtium et Oribasium.
**Philemo** Comicus [Philem.] iv/iii B.C.
Ed. T. Kock, *CAF* ii p. 478; suppl. J. Demiańczuk, *Supp. Com.* p. 71.
**Philemo Junior** Comicus [Philem.Jun.] iii B.C. (?)
Ed. T. Kock, *CAF* ii p. 540.
**Philetaerus** Comicus [Philetaer.] v/iv B.C.
Ed. T. Kock, *CAF* ii p. 230; suppl. J. Demiańczuk, *Supp. Com.* p. 72.
**Philetas** (vel **Philitas**) Elegiacus [Philet.] iv/iii B.C.
Ed J. U. Powell, *Coll. Alex.* p. 90.
Fragmenta glossarii, cited from sources.
**Philippides** Comicus [Philippid.] iv/iii B.C.
Ed. T. Kock, *CAF* iii p. 301.
**Philippus** Comicus [Philipp.Com.] iv B.C.
Ed. T. Kock, *CAF* ii p. 215.
**Philippus** Epigrammaticus [Phil.] i A.D.
v. *Anthologia Graeca.*
**Philiscus** Comicus [Philisc.Com.]
Ed. T. Kock, *CAF* ii p. 443.
**Philiscus** Tragicus [Philisc.Trag.]
Ed. A. Nauck, *TGF* p. 819.
**Philistus** Historicus [Philist.] v/iv B.C.
Ed. C. Müller, *FHG* i p. 185, iv pp. 625, 639.
**Phillis** Historicus
Ed. C. Müller, *FHG* iv p. 476.
**Philo** Epicus [Ph.Epic.]
Apud Eusebium.
Ed. A. Ludwich, *De Philonis carmine Graeco-Iudaico commentatio*, Königsberg 1900.
**Philo** Mechanicus [Ph.] iii/ii B.C.
*Bel.* = (*Belopoeica*) *Exzerpte aus Philons Mechanik*, ed. H. Diels & E. Schramm, *Abh. Berl. Akad.* 1919, No. 12; cited by page and line of Wescher, given in margin.
**Philo Byblius** Historicus [Ph.Bybl.] i/ii A.D.
Ed. C. Müller, *FHG* iii p. 560.
**Philo Byzantius** Paradoxographus [Ph.Byz.]
*Mir.* = *de Septem Miraculis*, ed. R. Hercher (post Aelianum), Paris (D.) 1858.
**Philo Judaeus** [Ph.]
Ed. L. Cohn & P. Wendland (S. Reiter), Berlin 1896–1915.
*Fr.* = *Fragmenta*, ed. J. Rendel Harris, Cambridge 1886.
**Philo Tarsensis** Medicus [Ph.Tars.]
Apud Galenum.
**Philochorus** Historicus [Philoch.] iv B.C.
Ed. C. Müller, *FHG* i p. 385, iv p. 646.
**Philocles** Tragicus [Philocl.]
Ed. A. Nauck, *TGF* p. 759.
**Philodamus Scarpheus** Lyricus [Philod.Scarph.] iv B.C.
Ed. J. U. Powell, *Coll. Alex.* p. 165.
**Philodemus** Philosophus [Phld.] i B.C.
*Acad.Ind.* = *Academicorum Index*, ed. S. Mekler, Berlin 1902. [p. . . M.]
*D.* 1, 3 = περὶ θεῶν α′, γ′, ed. H. Diels, *Abhandlungen der Berliner Akademie*, 1916, 1917. [Col. or *Fr.*]
*Herc.* = *Herculanensia Volumina, Collectio altera*, Naples 1862–76, (i.e. partim inedita) (ex apographis W. Crönert). [No. of papyrus, Col. or *Fr.*]
*Hom.* = περὶ τοῦ καθ' Ὅμηρον ἀγαθοῦ βασιλέως, ed. A. Olivieri, Leipzig (T.) 1909.
*Ind.Sto.* = *Stoicorum Index Herculanensis*, ed. D. Comparetti, *Riv. Fil.* iii (1875). [Col. or *Fr.*]
*Ir.* = *de Ira*, ed. C. Wilke, Leipzig (T.) 1914.
*Lib.* = περὶ παρρησίας, ed. A. Olivieri, Leipzig (T.) 1914.
*Mort.* = *de Morte*, ed. D. Bassi, *Papiri Ercolanesi*, Milan 1914. [Col.]
*Mus.* = *de Musica*, ed. J. Kemke, Leipzig (T.) 1884.
*Oec.* = περὶ οἰκονομίας, ed. C. Jensen, Leipzig (T.) 1906.
*Piet.* = *de Pietate*, ed. T. Gomperz, *Herkulanische Studien* ii, Leipzig 1866. [Col. or *Fr.*]
*Po.* = περὶ ποιημάτων, ed. A. Hausrath, *Jahrbücher für klassische Philologie, Suppl.* xvii (1880) p. 211; ed. T. Gomperz, *Philodem und die aesthetischen Schriften der Herkulanensischen Bibliothek, Sitzungsberichte der Wiener Akademie*, cxxiii (1891): ed. C. Jensen, *Philodemos über die Gedichte, fünftes Buch*, Berlin 1923. [No. of book (where known, otherwise No. of papyrus), Col. or *Fr.*]
*Rh.* = *Volumina Rhetorica*, ed. S. Sudhaus, 2 vols., Leipzig (T.) 1892, 1896, *Suppl.* 1895. [Cited by vol. and p.]
*Sign.* = περὶ σημείων καὶ σημειώσεων, ed. T. Gomperz, *Herkulanische Studien* i, Leipzig 1865. [Col. or *Fr.*]
*Sto.* = περὶ τῶν Στωικῶν, ed. W. Crönert, *Kolotes und Menedemos*, Leipzig 1906, pp. 53 sqq. [Col. or *Fr.*]
*Vit.* = περὶ κακιῶν ι′, ed. C. Jensen, Leipzig (T.) 1911.
**Philodemus Gadarensis** Epigrammaticus [Phld.] i B.C.
Videtur idem fuisse ac philosophus.
v. *Anthologia Graeca.*

**Philolaus** Philosophus [Philol.] v/iv B.C.
Ed. H. Diels, *Vorsokr.* i p. 301.
**Philomnestus** Historicus [Philomnest.]
Ed. C. Müller, *FHG* iv p. 477.
**Philonides** Comicus [Philonid.] v B.C.
Ed. T. Kock, *CAF* i p. 254; suppl. J. Demiańczuk, *Supp. Com.* p. 73.
**Philoponus, Joannes** Philosophus [Phlp.] vi A.D.
Idem qui Joannes Alexandrinus, q.v.
*in APo.* = *in Aristotelis Analytica Posteriora commentaria*, ed. M. Wallies (*Comm. in Arist. Graeca* xiii *pars* iii), Berlin 1909.
*in APr.* = *in Aristotelis Analytica Priora commentaria*, ed. M. Wallies (*Comm. in Arist. Graeca* xiii *pars* ii), Berlin 1905.
*in Cat.* = *Philoponi* (*olim Ammonii*) *in Aristotelis Categorias commentarium*, ed. A. Busse (*Comm. in Arist. Graeca* xiii *pars* i) Berlin 1898.
*in de An.* = *in Aristotelis de Anima libros commentaria*, ed. M. Hayduck (*Comm. in Arist. Graeca* xv), Berlin 1897.
*in GA* = *Philoponi* (*Michaelis Ephesii*) *in libros de Generatione Animalium commentaria*, ed. M. Hayduck (*Comm. in Arist. Graeca* xiv *pars* iii), Berlin 1903.
*in GC* = *in Aristotelis libros de Generatione et Corruptione commentaria*, ed. Hieronymus Vitelli (*Comm. in Arist. Graeca* xiv *pars* ii), Berlin 1897.
*in Mete.* = *in Aristotelis Meteorologicorum librum primum commentarium*, ed. M. Hayduck (*Comm. in Arist. Graeca* xiv *pars* i), Berlin 1901.
*in Ph.* = *in Aristotelis Physica commentaria*, ed. Hieronymus Vitelli (*Comm. in Arist. Graeca* xvi, xvii), Berlin 1887–8.
**Philostephanus** Comicus [Philosteph.Com.]
Ed T. Kock, *CAF* iii p. 393.
**Philostephanus** Historicus [Philosteph.Hist.]
Ed. C. Müller, *FHG* iii p. 28.
**Philostratus** Sophista [Philostr.] ii/iii A.D.
Ed. C. L. Kayser, Leipzig (T.) 1870, 1871.
*Dial.* = Διαλέξεις
*Ep.* = *Epistulae*
*Her.* = *Heroicus*
*VA* = *Vita Apollonii*
*VS* = *Vitae Sophistarum*
*Gym.* = *de gymnastica*, ed. J. Jüthner, Leipzig & Berlin 1909.
*Im.* = *Philostrati majoris imagines*, ed. O. Benndorf, C. Schenkl, Leipzig (T.) 1893.
**Philostratus Junior** Sophista [Philostr.Jun.] iii A.D.
*Im.* = *Imagines*, ed. C. Schenkl, Aemilius Reisch, Leipzig (T.) 1902.
**Philoxenus** Epigrammaticus [Philox.] iii B.C.
v. *Anthologia Graeca.*
**Philoxenus** Grammaticus [Philox.Gramm.] i B.C.
Ed. H. Funaioli, *Grammaticae Romanae Fragmenta*, vol. i, Leipzig (T.) 1907, p. 443.
**Philoxenus** Lyricus [Philox.] v/iv B.C.
Ed. T. Bergk, *PLG* iii p. 601.
**Philumenus** Medicus [Philum.] iii A.D.
*Ven.* = *de Venenatis Animalibus*, ed. M. Wellmann, Berlin 1908; etiam apud Oribasium et Aëtium.
**Philyllius** Comicus [Philyll.] v B.C.
Ed. T. Kock, *CAF* i p. 781; suppl. J. Demiańczuk, *Supp. Com.* p. 73.
**Phintys** Pythagoreus [Phint.]
Apud Stobaeum.
**Phlegon Trallianus** Paradoxographus [Phleg.] ii A.D.
Ed. O. Keller, *Rerum naturalium scriptores Graeci minores*, vol. i, Leipzig (T.) 1877.
*Mir.* = *Miracula*
*Macr.* = *Macrobii*
*Olymp.* = *Olympiades*
*Fragmenta Historica*, ed. C. Müller, *FHG* iii p. 602. [*Fr.Hist.*]
**Phocylides** Lyricus [Phoc.] vi B.C.
Ed. T. Bergk, *PLG* ii p. 68.
**Phoebammon** Rhetor [Phoeb.] v/vi A.D.
*Fig.* = *de Figuris*, ed. L. Spengel, *Rhet.* iii p. 41.
**Phoenicides** Comicus [Phoenicid.] iii B.C.
Ed. T. Kock, *CAF* iii p. 333.
**Phoenix** Iambographus [Phoen.] iii B.C.
Ed. J. U. Powell, *Coll. Alex.* p. 231.
**Photius** Lexicographus, etc. [Phot.] ix A.D.
*Lexicon*, ed. S. A. Naber, Leiden, 1864–65 (cited without title).
*Der Anfang des Lexikons des Photios*, ed. R. Reitzenstein, Leipzig & Berlin 1907 (cited thus: Phot. p. . . R.).
*Bibl.* = *Bibliotheca*, = J.-P. Migne, *Patrologia Graeca*, vol. ciii, Paris 1860 (cited by Bekker's pages).
**Phrynichus** Atticista [Phryn.] ii A.D.
Ed. W. G. Rutherford, London 1881.
*PS* = *Praeparatio Sophistica*, ed. I. de Borries, Leipzig (T.) 1911.
**Phrynichus** Comicus [Phryn.Com.] v B.C.
Ed. T. Kock, *CAF* i p. 369; suppl. J. Demiańczuk, *Supp. Com.* p. 74.

**[Ph]rynichus** Tragicus [Phryn.Trag.] vi/v B.C.
[E]d. A. Nauck, *TGF* p. 720.
[F]ragmenta Lyrica, ed. T. Bergk, *PLG* iii p. 561. [Phryn.Lyr.]
**[Ph]ylarchus** Historicus [Phylarch.] iii B.C.
Ed. C Müller. *FHG* i p. 334; iv p. 645.
**[Ph]ylotimus** Medicus [Phylotim.]
Apud Athenaeum.
**[Pi]ndarus** Lyricus [Pi.] v B.C.
Ed. O. Schroeder, Leipzig 1900.
*O.*, *P.*, *N.*, *I.* = *Olympian, Pythian, Nemean, Isthmian Odes; Fr.* = *Fragmenta.*
*Dith.Oxy.* = *Dithyrambi*, in *POxy.* 1604.
*Pae.*, *Parth.* = *Paeanes*, *Parthenia*, ed. E. Diehl, *Supp. Lyr.*³ p. 52.
Scholia, ed A. Boeckh, in editione Pindari, Berlin 1811–21; Scholia Vetera, ed. A. B. Drachmann, Leipzig (T.) 1903, 1910.
**[P]isander** Epicus [Pisand.]
Ed G. Kinkel, *EGF* i, Leipzig (T.) 1877, p. 248.
**[P]ittacus** Lyricus [Pittac.] vi B.C.
Ed. T. Bergk, *PLG* iii p. 198.
**Placita Philosophorum** [*Placit.*]
Ed. H. Diels, *Doxographi Graeci*, Berlin 1879, p. 273.
**Plato** Comicus [Pl.Com.] v/iv B.C.
Ed. T. Kock, *CAF* i p. 601; suppl. J. Demiańczuk, *Supp. Com.* p. 76.
**Plato** Philosophus [Pl.] v/iv B.C.
Ed. J. Burnet, Oxford (OCT).
*Alc.* 1, 2 = *Alcibiades* 1, 2
*Amat.* = *Amatores*
*Ap.* = *Apologia*
*Ax.* = *Axiochus*
*Chrm.* = *Charmides*
*Clit.* = *Clitopho*
*Cra.* = *Cratylus*
*Cri.* = *Crito*
*Criti.* = *Critias*
*Def.* = *Definitiones*
*Demod.* = *Demodocus*
*Ep.* = *Epistulae*
*Epigr.* = *Epigrammata*, ed. T. Bergk, *PLG* ii p. 295
*Epin.* = *Epinomis*
*Erx.* = *Eryxias*
*Euthd* = *Euthydemus*
*Euthphr.* = *Euthyphro*
*Grg.* = *Gorgias*
*Hipparch.* = *Hipparchus*
*Hp.Ma.*, *Mi.* = *Hippias Major, Minor*
*Ion*
*Just.* = *De Justo*
*La.* = *Laches*
*Lg.* = *Leges*
*Ly.* = *Lysis*
*Men.* = *Meno*
*Min.* = *Minos*
*Mx.* = *Menexenus*
*Phd.* = *Phaedo*
*Phdr.* = *Phaedrus*
*Phlb.* = *Philebus*
*Plt.* = *Politicus*
*Prm.* = *Parmenides*
*Prt.* = *Protagoras*
*R.* = *Respublica*
*Sis.* = *Sisyphus*
*Smp.* = *Symposium*
*Sph.* = *Sophista*
*Thg.* = *Theages*
*Tht.* = *Theaetetus*
*Ti.* = *Timaeus*
*Virt.* = *De Virtute*
Scholia, ed. C. F. Hermann, *Platonis Dialogi*, vol. vi, Leipzig (T.) 1892.
**Plato Junior** Epigrammaticus [Pl.Jun.]
v. *Anthologia Graeca.*
**Platonius** Grammaticus [Platon.]
*De Differentia Comoediarum*, etc., ed. G. Kaibel, *CGF* p. 3. [*Diff. Com.*]
**Plautus** Comicus Latinus [Plaut.] iii/ii B.C.
Ed. W. M. Lindsay, Oxford (OCT).
**Plinius** Rerum Naturalium Scriptor [Plin.] i A.D.
*HN* = *Historia Naturalis*, ed. C. Mayhoff, 5 vols., Leipzig (T.) 1892–1909.
**Plotinus** Philosophus [Plot.] iii A.D.
Ed. R. Volkmann, Leipzig (T.) 1883–4.
**Plutarchus** Biographus et Philosophus [Plu.] i/ii A.D.
*Moralia* ed. G. N. Bernardakis, 7 vols., Leipzig (T.) 1888–96; cited by vol. (2) and page of Wyttenbach: *Vitae Parallelae*, ed. C. Sintenis, 5 vols., Leipzig (T.) 1881–65; ed. C. Lindskog & K. Ziegler, Leipzig (T.), i (1) (1914), i (2) (1914), iii (1) (1915).
*Aem.* = *Aemilius Paulus*
*Ages.* = *Agesilaus*
*Agis*
*Alc.* = *Alcibiades*
*Alex.* = *Alexander*
*Ant.* = *Antonius*
*Arat.* = *Aratus*
*Arist.* = *Aristides*
*Art.* = *Artoxerxes*
*Brut.* = *Brutus*
*CG* = *C. Gracchus*
*Caes.* = *Caesar*
*Cam.* = *Camillus*
*Cat. Ma.*, *Mi.* = *Cato Major, Minor*
*Cic.* = *Cicero*
*Cim.* = *Cimon*
*Cleom.* = *Cleomenes*
*Comp.* = *Comparatio* [followed by two names]
*Cor.* = *Coriolanus*
*Crass.* = *Crassus*
*Daed.* = *de Daedal's Plataeensibus* (vol. vii, p. 43 B.)
*Dem.* = *Demosthenes*
*Demetr.* = *Demetrius*
*Dio*
*Eum.* = *Eumenes*
*Fab.* = *Fabius Maximus*
*Flam.* = *Flamininus*
*Fr.* = *Fragmenta* (vol. vii, pp. 1–149 B.); *Fr.inc.* = *Fragmenta incerta*, ib., pp. 150–2.
*in Hes.* = *Commentarii in Hesiodum* (vol. vii, p. 5 B.)
*Lib.* = *de Libidine et Aegritudine* (vol. vii, p. 1 B.)
*Luc.* = *Lucullus*
*Lyc.* = *Lycurgus*
*Lys.* = *Lysander*
*Mar.* = *Marius*
*Marc.* = *Marcellus*
*Metr.* = *de Metris* (vol. vii, p. 465 B.)
*Nic.* = *Nicias*
*Nob.* = *pro Nobilitate* (vol. vii, p. 194 B.)
*Num.* = *Numa*
*Oth.* = *Otho*
*Pel.* = *Pelopidas*
*Per.* = *Pericles*
*Phil.* = *Philopoemen*
*Phoc.* = *Phocion*
*Pomp.* = *Pompeius*
*Prov.* = *Proverbia* (ed. von E. L. Leutsch & F. G. Schneidewin, *Paroemiographi* i p. 321)
*Publ.* = *Publicola*
*Pyrrh.* = *Pyrrhus*
*Rom.* = *Romulus*
*Sert.* = *Sertorius*
*Sol.* = *Solon*
*Strom.* = Στρωματεῖς (vol. vii, p. 37 B.)
*Sull.* = *Sulla*
*TG* = *Tiberius Gracchus*
*Them.* = *Themistocles*
*Thes.* = *Theseus*
*Tim.* = *Timoleon*
Ps.-Plu.*Fluv.* = *de Fluviis* (vol. vii, p. 282 B.).
Ps.-Plu.*Vit.Hom.* = *Vita Homeri*, ed. T. W. Allen, *Homeri Opera* v, Oxford (OCT), p. 192.
**Poeta** *de herbis* [Poet. *de herb.*]
Ed. F. S. Lehrs, in *Poetae Bucolici et Didactici*, Paris (D.) 1851, p. 169 bis.
**Polemo** Historicus [Polem.Hist.] ii B.C.
Ed. C. Müller, *FHG* iii p. 108.
**Polemo** Physiognomonicus [Polem.*Phgn.*]
Ed. R. Förster, *Scriptores physiognomonici Graeci et Latini* i, Leipzig (T.) 1893, p. 427.
**Polemo Sophista** [Polem.] i/ii A.D.
*Declamationes*, ed. H. Hinck, Leipzig (T.) 1873.
*Call.* = *Callimachus*
*Cyn* = *Cynegirus*
**Poliochus** Comicus [Polioch.]
Ed. T. Kock, *CAF* iii p. 390.
**Pollianus** Epigrammaticus [Poll.] ii A.D. (?)
v. *Anthologia Graeca.*
**Pollux** Grammaticus [Poll.] ii A.D.
Bks. i–v ed. Bethe, Leipzig 1900: complete in W. Dindorf, Leipzig 1824.
**Polus** Philosophus
Apud Stobaeum.
**Polyaenus** Historicus [Polyaen.] ii A.D.
Ed. J. Melber, Leipzig (T.) 1887.
**Polyaenus, Julius** Epigrammaticus [Polyaen.] i B.C. (?)
v. *Anthologia Graeca.*
**Polybius** Historicus [Plb.] ii B.C.
Ed. T. Büttner-Wobst, Leipzig (T.) 1882–1905.
*Fr.* = *Fragmenta*

**Polybius Sardianus** Rhetor [Plb.Rh.]
Ed. L. Spengel, *Rhet.* iii p. 105.

**Polycharmus** Historicus [Polycharm.]
Ed. C. Müller, *FHG* iv p. 479.

**Polyclitus** Philosophus [Polyclit.] v/iv B.C.
Ed. H. Diels, *Vorsokr.* i p. 294.

**Polycrates** Historicus [Polycr.]
Ed. C. Müller, *FHG* iv p. 480.

**Polystratus** Epicureus [Polystr.] iii B.C.
Ed. C. Wilke, Leipzig (T.) 1905 (cited by page).

**Polystratus** Epigrammaticus [Polystr.]
v. *Anthologia Graeca.*

**Polyzelus** Comicus [Polyzel.] v/iv B.C.
Ed. T. Kock, *CAF* i p. 789; suppl. J. Demiańczuk, *Supp. Com.* p. 82.

**Pompeius** Epigrammaticus [Pomp.] i A.D.
v. *Anthologia Graeca.*

**Pompeius Macer** Tragicus [Pomp.Mac.]
Ed. A. Nauck, *TGF* p. 830.

**Porphyrius Tyrius** Philosophus [Porph.] iii A.D.
*Abst.* = *de Abstinentia,* ed. A. Nauck$^{2}$, *Porphyrii Opuscula,* Leipzig (T.) 1886.
ad Il. (Od.) = *Quaestionum Homericarum ad Iliadem* (*Odysseam*) *pertinentium reliquiae,* ed. H. Schrader, Leipzig 1880–82, 1890.
*Antr.* = *de Antro Nympharum,* ed. A. Nauck$^{2}$, *Porphyrii Opuscula,* Leipzig (T.) 1886.
*Chr.* = *adversus Christianos,* ed. A. von Harnack, *Abh. Berl. Akad.* 1916.
*Fr.Hist.* = *Fragmenta Historica,* ed. C. Müller, *FGH* iii p. 688.
*Gaur.* = *ad Gaurum* (πῶς ἐμψυχοῦται τὰ ἔμβρυα), ed. T. Kalbfleisch, *Abh. Berl. Akad.* 1895.
*in Cat.* = *in Aristotelis Categorias commentarium,* ed. A. Busse (*Comm. in Arist. Graeca* iv *pars* i p. 55), Berlin 1887.
*in Harm.* = *in Ptolemaei Harmonica,* ed. J. Wallis (post Ptolemaeum).
*in Ptol.* = *in Ptolemaei Tetrabiblon,* Basel 1559 (cited by page).
*Intr.* = *Isagoge sive quinque voces,* ed. A. Busse (*Comm. in Arist. Graeca* iv *pars* i p. 1), Berlin 1887.
*Marc.* = *ad Marcellam,* ed. A. Nauck$^{2}$, *Porphyrii Opuscula,* Leipzig (T.) 1886.
*Plot.* = *Vita Plotini,* ed. A. Westermann, v. Diogenes Laertius; ed. R. Volkmann, v. Plotinus.
*Sent.* = *Sententiae ad intelligibilia ducentes,* ed. B. Mommert, Leipzig (T.) 1907.
*VP* = *Vita Pythagorae,* ed. A. Nauck$^{2}$, *Porphyrii Opuscula,* Leipzig (T.) 1886.

**Posidippus** Comicus [Posidipp.] iii B.C.
Ed. T. Kock, *CAF* iii p. 335.

**Posidippus** Epigrammaticus [Posidipp.] iii B.C.
v. *Anthologia Graeca.*

**Posidonius** Historicus [Posidon.] ii/i B.C.
Ed. C. Müller, *FHG* iii p. 245.

**Posidonius** Medicus [Posidon.] iii/iv A.D.
Apud Aëtium.

**Pratinas** Lyricus et Tragicus [Pratin.] vi/v B.C.
Fragmenta Lyrica, ed. T. Bergk, *PLG* iii p. 557. [Lyr.]
Fragmenta Tragica, ed. A. Nauck, *TGF* p. 726. [Trag.]

**Praxagoras** Historicus [Praxag.] iv A.D.
Ed. L. Dindorf, *HGM* i p. 438.

**Praxilla** Lyrica [Praxill.] v B.C.
Ed. T. Bergk, *PLG* iii p. 566.

**Priscianus** Grammaticus [Priscian.] v/vi A.D.
*Inst.* = *Institutio,* ed. M. Hertz & H. Keil, *Gramm. Lat.*, vols. ii & iii, Leipzig 1855–9.

**Priscianus Lydus** Philosophus [Prisc.Lyd.] vi A.D.
Ed. I. Bywater (*Supplementum Aristotelicum* i *pars* ii), Berlin 1886.

**Priscus** Historicus [Prisc.] v A.D.
Ed. L. Dindorf, *HGM* i p. 275.

**Proclus** Philosophus [Procl.] v A.D.
ad Hes.*Op.* = ad Hesiodi *Opera et Dies,* ed. T. Gaisford, *Poetae Graeci Minores,* vol. iii, p. 9.
*Chr.* = *Chrestomathia,* ed. T. W. Allen, *Homeri Opera* v, Oxford (OCT), p. 99.
*H.* = *Hymni,* ed. E. Abel (post Orphica, p. 276).
*Hyp.* = *Hypotyposis astronomicarum positionum,* ed. C. Manitius, Leipzig (T.) 1909.
*in Alc.* = *in Platonis Alcibiadem,* ed. F. Creuzer, Frankfurt 1820.
*in Cra.* = *in Platonis Cratylum commentaria,* ed. G. Pasquali, Leipzig (T.) 1908.
*in Euc.* = *in primum Euclidis librum commentarius,* ed. G. Friedlein, Leipzig (T.) 1873.
*in Prm.* = *in Platonis Parmenidem commentarii,* ed. G. Stallbaum, Leipzig 1840.
*in R.* = *in Platonis Rempublicam commentarii,* ed. W. Kroll, 2 vols., Leipzig (T.) 1899, 1901.
*in Ti.* = *in Platonis Timaeum commentarii,* ed. E. Diehl, 3 vols., Leipzig (T.) 1903, 1904, 1906.
*Inst.* = *Institutio Theologica,* ed. F. Dübner, in F. Creuzer & G. Moser, *Plotinus,* pp. li–cxvii, Paris (D.) 1855.
*Inst.Phys.* = *Institutio Physica,* ed. A. Ritzenfeld, Leipzig ( 1912.
*Par.Ptol.* = *Paraphrasis Ptolemaei Tetrabiblou,* ed. L. Allati Basel 1554 (cited by page).
*Theol.Plat.* = περὶ τῆς κατὰ Πλάτωνα θεολογίας, ed. Aem. Port Hamburg 1618.

**Procopius Caesariensis** Historicus [Procop.] vi A.
Ed. J. Haury, Leipzig (T.) 1905–13.
*Aed.* = *de Aedificiis*
*Arc.* = *Historia Arcana*
*Goth.* = *de Bello Gothico*
*Pers.* = *de Bello Persico*
*Vand.* = *de Bello Vandalico*

**Procopius Gazaeus** Rhetor [Procop.Gaz.] v/vi A.D.
Ed. J. F. Boissonade, *Choricius,* Paris 1846, pp. 129–78.
*Ecphr.* = ἔκφρασις ὡρολογίου, ed. H. Diels, *Abh. Berl. Akad.* 1917 No. 7 (cited by Boissonade's page, given in margin).
*Ep.* = *Epistulae,* ed. R. Hercher, *Epistolographi,* p. 533.
*Pan.* = *Panegyricus in Anastasium,* ed. I. Bekker et B. G. Niebuhr, cum Dexippo et aliis, Bonn 1829 (cited by page); cf. C. Kemp, *Procopii Gazaei in Imp. Anastasium Panegyricus,* Bonn 1918.

**Prodicus** Philosophus [Prodic.] v B.C.
Ed. H. Diels, *Vorsokr.* ii p. 267.

**Promathidas** Historicus [Promathid.] i B.C.
Ed. C. Müller, *FHG* iii p. 201.

**Protagoras** Philosophus [Protag.] v B.C.
Ed. H. Diels *Vorsokr.* ii p. 219.

**Protagoridas** Historicus [Protagorid.] ii B.C.
Ed. C. Müller, *FHG* iv p. 484.

**Proxenus** Historicus [Proxen.] iii B.C.
Ed. C. Müller, *FHG* ii p. 461.

**Psalms of Solomon** [*Psalm.Solom.*] i B.C.
Ed. H. E. Ryle & M. R. James, Cambridge 1891.

**Pseudo-Callisthenes** Historicus [Ps.-Callisth.]
Ed. C. Müller, *SRAM* p. 1 bis.

**Pseudo-Phocylidea** [Ps.-Phoc.] i A.D. (?)
Ed. T. Bergk, *PLG* ii p. 74.

Note.—The spurious works of other authors cited with the prefix 'Pseudo-' will be found under the names of the several authors.

**Ptolemaeus** Epigrammaticus [Ptol.]
v. *Anthologia Graeca.*

**Ptolemaeus** Mathematicus [Ptol.] ii A.D.
Ed. J. L. Heiberg, Leipzig (T.) 1898–1907; works included in this edition are marked with an asterisk.
**Alm.* = *Almagest* = *Syntaxis Mathematica*
**Anal.* = περὶ ἀναλήμματος
*Calend.* = *Calendarium,* ed. C. Wachsmuth, v. Lyd. *Ost.*
**Fr.* = *Fragmenta*
*Geog.* = *Geographia* (lib. i–iii, ed. C. Müller, C. T. Fischer, Paris 1883–1901; ed. F. A. Nobbe, Leipzig 1843–5).
*Harm.* = *Harmonica,* ed. J. Wallis, *Opera Mathematica* iii, Oxford 1699.
**Hyp.* = Ὑποθέσεις
**Inscr.Can.* = *Inscriptio Canobi*
*Judic.* = περὶ κριτηρίου, ed. J. Bullialdus, Paris 1663; ed. F. Hanow, Leipzig (Progr. Küstrin) 1870; cited by page of B., given in margin of H.
**Phas.* = Φάσεις
**Planisph.* = *Planisphaerium*
**Pseph.* = ψηφοφορία
*Tetr.* = *Tetrabiblos,* ed. J. Camerarius, Nürnberg 1535, cited by page of reprint, Basel 1553 (with Lat. transl. by P. Melanchthon).
Ps.-Ptol. *Centil.* = *Centiloquium* (καρπός), post *Tetrabiblon* editum.
Scholia in Ptolemaei Tetrabiblon, Basel 1559; v. Porphyrius.

**Ptolemaeus Ascalonita** [Ptol.Ascal.]
Ed. G. Heylbut, *Hermes* xxii (1887) p. 388.

**Ptolemaeus Chennos** [Ptol. Chenn.] c. 100 A.D.
Cited from sources; cf. A. Chatzis, *Der Philosoph und Grammatiker Ptolemaios Chennos,* Paderborn 1914.

**Ptolemaeus Euergetes II** Historicus [Ptol.Euerg.] ii B.C.
Ed. C. Müller, *FHG* iii p. 186.

**Ptolemaeus Megalopolitanus** Historicus [Ptol.Megalop.]
Ed. C. Müller, *FHG* iii p. 66.

**Pyrgio** Historicus
Ed. C. Müller, *FHG* iv p. 486.

**Pythaenetus** Historicus [Pythaen.]
Ed. C. Müller, *FHG* iv p. 487.

**Pythagoras** Philosophus [Pythag.] vi/v B.C.
Ed. H. Diels, *Vorsokr.* i p. 27, cf. p. 341.

**Pythagorae et Pythagoreorum Epistulae** [Pythag. *Ep.*]
Ed. R. Hercher, *Epistolographi,* p. 601. Cf. Melissa, Myia, Theano.

**Pythocles** Historicus [Pythocl.]
Ed. C. Müller, *FHG* iv p. 488.

**Python** Tragicus iv B.C.
Ed. A. Nauck, *TGF* p. 810.

**intilianus** Rhetor Latinus [Quint.] i A.D.
:d. E. Bonnell, Leipzig (T.) 1884–9; ed. L. Radermacher, Leipzig (T.) 1907–.
*Inst.* = *Institutio Oratoria*
**intus Smyrnaeus** Epicus [Q.S.] iv A.D. (?)
Ed. A. Zimmermann, Leipzig (T.) 1891.

**etores Graeci** [Rh.]
Ed. Ch. Walz, 9 vols., Stuttgart 1832–6.
**hetorius** Astrologus [Rhetor.] vi A.D.
in *Cat. Cod. Astr.*
**hianus** Epicus [Rhian.] iii B.C.
Ed. J. U. Powell, *Coll. Alex.* p. 9.
**hinthon** Comicus [Rhinth.] iii B.C.
Ed. G. Kaibel, *CGF* p. 183.
**ufinus** Epigrammaticus [Rufin.]
v. *Anthologia Graeca.*
**Rufus** Medicus [Ruf.] ii A.D.
Ed. C. Daremberg & C. E. Ruelle, Paris 1879.
*Anat.* = ἀνατομή
*Onom.* = περὶ ὀνομασίας
*Ren.Ves.* = *de renum et vesicae affectionibus*
*Sat.Gon.* = *de satyriasmo et gonorrhoea*
*Syn.Puls.* = *synopsis de pulsibus*
**Rufus** Rhetor [Ruf.Rh.]
Ed. C. Hammer, in L. Spengel, *Rhet.* i[2] (2), p. 399.
**Rutilius Lupus** Rhetor [Rutil.]
Ed. C. Halm, *Rhetores Latini Minores*, Leipzig 1863, p. 3.

**Sabinus, Tullius** Epigrammaticus [Tull.Sab.] i A.D. (?)
v. *Anthologia Graeca.*
**Sacerdos, Marius Plotius** Grammaticus Latinus [Sacerd.] iii/iv A.D.
Ed. H. Keil, *Gramm. Lat.* vi p. 416.
**Sallustius** Philosophus [Sallust.] iv A.D.
Ed. F. W. A. Mullach, *FPG* iii p. 28.
**Samus** Epigrammaticus iii B.C.
v. *Anthologia Graeca.*
**Sannyrio** Comicus [Sannyr.] v B.C.
Ed. T. Kock, *CAF* i p. 793; suppl. J. Demiańczuk, *Supp. Com.* p. 83.
**Sappho** Lyrica [Sapph.] vii/vi B.C.
Ed. Th. Bergk, *PLG* iii p. 82.
*Supp.* = Papyrus fragments in E. Diehl, *Supp. Lyr.*[3] p. 29.
*Oxy.* = Papyrus fragments in *POxy.*, cited by No. of Papyrus.
**Satyrus** Epigrammaticus [Satyr.] i B.C. (?)
v. *Anthologia Graeca.*
**Satyrus** Historicus [Satyr.] iii B.C.
Ed. C. Müller, *FHG* iii p. 159.
*Vit.Eur.* = *Vita Euripidis, POxy.* 1176.
**Scamon** Historicus
Ed. C. Müller, *FHG* iv p. 489.
**Scholia**
See under several authors.
**Sciras** Comicus iii B.C.
Ed. G. Kaibel, *CGF* p. 190.
**Scolia** [*Scol.*]
Ed. T. Bergk, *PLG* iii p. 643.
**Scylax** Geographus [Scyl.] iv B.C. (?)
Ed. C. Müller, *GGM* i p. 15.
**Scymnus** Geographus [Scymn.] ii B.C.
Ed. C. Müller, *GGM* i p. 196.
**Scythinus** Epigrammaticus [Scythin.]
v. *Anthologia Graeca.*
**Scythinus Teius** Poeta Philosophus [Scythin.] iv B.C.
Ed. H. Diels, *PPF* p. 169.
**Secundus** Gnomologus [Secund.] ii A.D.
*Sent.* = *Sententiae*, ed. F. W. A. Mullach, *FPG* i p. 512.
**Seleucus** Grammaticus et Historicus [Seleuc.]
Cited from sources; cf. C. Müller, *FHG* iii p. 500.
**Seleucus** Lyricus [Seleuc.Lyr.]
Ed. J. U. Powell, *Coll. Alex.* p. 176.
**Semonides** Iambographus [Semon.] vii/vi B.C. (?)
Ed. T. Bergk, *PLG* ii p. 441 (ubi perperam 'Simonides').
**Semus** Historicus
Ed. C. Müller, *FHG* iv p. 492.
**Seneca, L. Annaeus** i A.D.
*QN* = *Quaestiones Naturales*, ed. A. Gercke, Leipzig (T.) 1907.
**Serapio** Astrologus ii/i B.C. (?)
in *Cat. Cod. Astr.*
**Serapio** Epigrammaticus
v. *Anthologia Graeca.*
**Serapio** Tragicus
Ed. A. Nauck, *TGF* p. 831.
**Serenus** Geometra [Seren.] iv A.D.
*Opuscula*, ed. J. L. Heiberg, Leipzig (T.) 1896.
*Sect.Con.* = *Sectio Coni*
*Sect.Cyl.* = *Sectio Cylindri*
**Serenus** Gnomologus [Seren.]
Apud Stobaeum.

**Servius** Grammaticus Latinus [Serv.] iv A.D.
*In Vergilii carmina commentarii*, ed. G. Thilo & H. Hagen, Leipzig 1878–1902.
**Severus** Medicus [Sever.] iv A.D.
*Clyst.* = *de Clysteribus*, ed. F. R. Dietz, Königsberg 1836.
**Severus** Philosophus [Sever.] ii A.D.
Apud Eusebium.
**Sextus** Pythagoreus [Sext.]
*Sent.* = *Sententiae*, ed. A. Elter, Bonn 1891–2.
**Sextus Empiricus** Philosophus [S.E.] ii A.D.
Ed. H. Mutschmann, Leipzig (T.) 1912–; ed. I. Bekker, Berlin 1842.
*M.* = *adversus Mathematicos*
*P.* = Πυρρώνειοι ὑποτυπώσεις
**Silenus** Historicus [Silen.] iii/ii B.C.
Ed. C. Müller, *FHG* iii p. 100.
**Simmias** (vel **Simias**) Elegiacus [Simm.] iii B.C.
Ed. J. U. Powell, *Coll. Alex.* p. 109.
**Simon Atheniensis**
*Eq.* = *de forma et delectu equorum*, ed. F. Ruehl, *Xenophontis Scripta Minora*, p. 193, Leipzig (T.) 1912.
**Simonides** Lyricus [Simon.] vi/v B.C.
Ed. T. Bergk, *PLG* iii p. 382.
**Simplicius** Philosophus [Simp.] vi A.D.
*in Cael.* = *in Aristotelis de Caelo commentaria*, ed. J. L. Heiberg (*Comm. in Arist. Graeca* vii), Berlin 1894.
*in Cat.* = *in Aristotelis Categorias commentarium*, ed. C. Kalbfleisch (*Comm. in Arist. Graeca* viii), Berlin 1907.
*in de An.* = *in libros Aristotelis de Anima commentaria*, ed. M. Hayduck (*Comm. in Arist. Graeca* xi), Berlin 1882.
*in Epict.* = *in Epictetum commentaria*, ed. F. Dübner (post Theophrasti Characteras), Paris (D.) 1840.
*in Ph.* = *in Aristotelis Physica commentaria*, ed. H. Diels (*Comm. in Arist. Graeca* ix and x), Berlin 1882–95.
**Simylus** Comicus [Simyl.]
Ed. T. Kock, *CAF* ii p. 444.
**Socrates Argivus** Historicus [Socr.Arg.]
Ed. C. Müller, *FHG* iv p. 496.
**Socrates Cous** Historicus [Socr.Cous]
Ed. C. Müller, *FHG* iv p. 499.
**Socrates Rhodius** Historicus [Socr.Rhod.] i B.C.
Ed. C. Müller, *FHG* iii p. 326.
**Socratis et Socraticorum Epistulae** [Socr.*Ep.*] (v/iv B.C.)
Ed. R. Hercher, *Epistolographi*, p. 609.
**Solon** Lyricus [Sol.] vi B.C.
Ed. T. Bergk, *PLG* ii p. 34: new fragments cited apud Arist. *Ath.*
**Sopater** Comicus [Sopat.] iv B.C.
Ed. G. Kaibel, *CGF* p. 192.
**Sopater** Gnomologus [Sopat.] iv A.D.
Apud Phot. *Bibl.* cod. 161.
**Sopater** Rhetor [Sopat.Rh.] v A.D.
Ed. Ch. Walz, *Rhetores Graeci* (Stuttgart 1832–6) iv, v p. 1, viii p. 1.
**Sophilus** Comicus [Sophil.] iv B.C. (?)
Ed. T. Kock, *CAF* ii p. 444.
**Sophocles** Tragicus [S.] v B.C.
Tragoediae, ed. A. C. Pearson, Oxford (OCT).
*Aj.* = *Ajax*
*Ant.* = *Antigone*
*El.* = *Electra*
*Eleg.* = *Elegiae*, ed. T. Bergk, *PLG* ii p. 243.
*Fr.* = *Fragmenta*, ed. A. C. Pearson, Cambridge 1917.
*OC* = *Oedipus Coloneus*
*OT* = *Oedipus Tyrannus*
*Ph.* = *Philoctetes*
*Tr.* = *Trachiniae*
**Sophonias** Philosophus [Sophon.] xiv A.D.
*in de An.* = *in libros Aristotelis de Anima paraphrasis*, ed. M. Hayduck (*Comm. in Arist. Graeca* xxiii pars i), Berlin 1883.
**Sophron** Comicus [Sophr.] v B.C.
Ed. G. Kaibel, *CGF* i p. 152; suppl. J. Demiańczuk, *Supp. Com.* p. 125.
**Soranus** Medicus [Sor.] ii A.D.
Ed. V. Rose, Leipzig (T.) 1882.
*Fasc.* = *de fasciis*, ed. R. Charterius *Opera Hippocratis et Galeni*, vol. xii, p. 505, Paris 1679 (cited by vol. and p.).
*Fract.* = *de signis fracturarum*, ed. J. L. Ideler, *Physici et Medici Graeci Minores* i p. 248, Berlin 1841.
**Sosibius** Historicus [Sosib.] iii B.C.
Ed. C. Müller, *FHG* ii p. 625.
**Sosicrates** Comicus [Sosicr.]
Ed. T. Kock, *CAF* iii p. 391.
**Sosicrates** Historicus [Sosicr.Hist.]
Ed. C. Müller, *FHG* iv p. 500.
**Sosicrates Rhodius** Historicus [Sosicr.Rhod.]
Ed. C. Müller, *FHG* iv p. 501.
**Sosipater** Comicus [Sosip.] iii B.C. (?)
Ed. T. Kock, *CAF* iii p. 314.
**Sosiphanes** Tragicus [Sosiph.] ii B.C.
Ed. A. Nauck, *TGF* p. 819.

**Sositheus** Tragicus [Sosith.]
Ed. A. Nauck, *TGF* p. 821.

**Sostratus** Historicus [Sostrat.]
Ed C. Müller, *FHG* iv p. 504; ed. F. Jacoby, *FGrH* i p. 186.

**Sosylus** Historicus [Sosyl.] iii/ii B.C.
Ed. F. Bilabel, *Die kleineren Historikerfragmente auf Papyrus*, Bonn 1923, p. 29.

**Sotades** Comicus [Sotad.Com.]
Ed. T. Kock, *CAF* ii p. 447; suppl. J. Demiańczuk, *Supp. Com.* p. 83.

**Sotades** Lyricus [Sotad.] iii B.C.
Ed. J. U. Powell, *Coll. Alex.* p. 238.

**Sotion** Paradoxographus i/ii A.D.
Ed. A. Westermann, Παραδοξογράφοι, Brunswick–London 1839, p. 183 (cited by page).

**Speusippus** Philosophus [Speus.] iv B.C.
Cited from sources; cf. F. W. A. Mullach, *FPG* iii p. 75.

**Sphaerus** Historicus [Sphaer. Hist.]
Ed. C. Müller, *FHG* iii p. 20.

**Sphaerus** Stoicus [Sphaer.*Stoic.*] iii B.C.
Ed. H von Arnim, *SVF* i p. 139.

**Stadiasmus** sive **Periplus Maris Magni** [*Stad.*] i B.C./i A.D.
Ed. C. Müller, *GGM* i p. 427.

**Staphylus** Historicus [Staphyl.]
Ed. C Müller, *FHG* iv p. 505.

**Statyllius Flaccus** Epigrammaticus [Stat.Flacc.] i B.C /i A.D.
Idem qui Bianor, q.v.

**Stephanus** Comicus [Steph.Com.] iv/iii B.C.
Ed. T Kock, *CAF* iii p. 360.

**Stephanus** Medicus [Steph.] vii A.D.
*in Gal.*, *in Hp.* = *in Galenum, in Hippocratem*, ed. F. R. Dietz, Königsberg 1834.

**Stephanus** Philosophus [Steph.] vii A.D.
*in Int.* = *in librum Aristotelis de Interpretatione commentarium*, ed M. Hayduck (*Comm. in Arist. Graeca* xviii *pars* iii), Berlin 1885.
*in Rh.* = *in Artem Rhetoricam commentaria*, ed. H. Rabe (*Comm. in Arist. Graeca* xxi *pars* ii), Berlin 1896.

**Stephanus Byzantius** [St.Byz.] v A.D. (?)
Ed. A. Meineke, vol i (all published), Berlin 1849.

**Stesichorus** Lyricus [Stesich.] vii/vi B.C.
Ed. T. Bergk, *PLG* iii p. 205.

**Stesimbrotus** Historicus [Stesimbr.] v B.C.
Ed. C Müller, *FHG* ii p. 52

**Sthenidas** Philosophus [Sthenid.]
Apud Stobaeum.

**Stobaeus, Joannes** [Stob.] v A.D.
Ed. C. Wachsmuth & O. Hense, 5 vols., Berlin 1884–1912.
*App.* = *Appendix* to the ed. of T Gaisford, vol. iv, Oxford 1822.
Scholia, ed. A. H. L. Heeren, *Stobaeus*, Göttingen 1792–1801.

**Stoicorum Veterum Fragmenta** [*Stoic.*]
Ed. H. von Arnim, Leipzig 1903 (cited by vol. and page).

**Strabo** Geographus [Str.] i B.C./i A.D.
Ed. G. Kramer, Berlin 1844–52.
*Chr.* = *Chrestomathiae* (cited by bk. and section as given in C. Müller, *GGM* ii p. 529).

**Strato** Comicus [Strato Com.] iii B.C. (?)
Ed. T. Kock, *CAF* iii p. 361.

**Strato** Epigrammaticus [Strat.] ii A.D.
v. *Anthologia Graeca.*

**Strattis** Comicus [Stratt.] v B.C.
Ed. T. Kock, *CAF* i p. 711; suppl. J. Demiańczuk, *Supp. Com.* p. 84.

**Suetonius** Grammaticus et Historicus Latinus [Suet.] ii A.D.
Ed. M. Ihm, Leipzig (T.) 1908.
περὶ βλασφημιῶν, ed. E. Miller, *Mélanges de littérature grecque*, Paris 1868, p. 413.

**Suidas** Lexicographus [Suid.] x A.D.
Ed. G. Bernhardy, Halle 1853.

**Sulpicius Maximus** Epicus [Sulp.Max.] i A.D.
*IG* 14. 2012.

**Susario** Comicus [Sus.] vi B.C.
Ed. T. Kock, *CAF* i p. 3.

**Symmachus** Interpres Veteris Testamenti [Sm.] ii/iii A.D.
Ed. F Field, *Origenis Hexapla*, Oxford 1875.

**Synesius** Alchemista [Syn.Alch.] iv A.D.
Ed. M. Berthelot, *Collection des anciens alchimistes grecs*, Paris 1888, p. 75.

**Syrianus** Philosophus et Rhetor [Syrian.] v A.D.
*in Hermog.* = *in Hermogenem commentaria*, ed. H. Rabe, Leipzig (T.) 1892–3.
*in Metaph.* = *in Metaphysica commentaria*, ed. W. Kroll (*Comm. in Arist. Graeca* vi *pars* i), Berlin 1902.

**Teleclides** Comicus [Telecl.] v B.C
Ed. T. Kock, *CAF* i p. 209; suppl. J. Demiańczuk, *Supp. Com.* p. 86

**Teles** Philosophus iii B.C.
Ed. O. Hense², Tübingen 1909.

**Telesilla** Lyrica [Telesill.] vi/v B.C.
Ed. T. Bergk, *PLG* iii p. 380.

**Telestes** Lyricus [Telest.] iv B
Ed. T. Bergk. *PLG* iii p. 627.

**Terentianus Maurus** Grammaticus Latinus [Ter Maur.] ii A.
Ed. H. Keil, *Gramm. Lat.* vol. vi p. 313.

**Terentius Scaurus** Grammaticus Latinus [Ter.Scaur.] ii A.
Ed. H. Keil, *Gramm. Lat.* vii p. 1.

**Terpander** Lyricus [Terp.] vii B.
Ed. T. Bergk, *PLG* iii p. 7.

**Teucer Babylonius** Astrologus i A.D. (
Ed. F. Boll, *Sphaera*, Leipzig 1903, pp. 6, 31.

**Teucer Cyzicenus** Historicus
Ed. C. Müller, *FHG* iv p. 508.

**Thales** Philosophus [Thal.] vi B.C
Ed. H. Diels, *Vorsokr.* i p. 1; *fragmentum lyricum*, ed. T. Bergk *PLG* iii p. 200.

**Thallus, Antonius** Epigrammaticus i B.C./i A.D
v. *Anthologia Graeca.*

**Theaetetus** Epigrammaticus [Theaet.] iii B.C.
v. *Anthologia Graeca.*

**Theagenes** Historicus [Theagen.]
Ed. C. Müller, *FHG* iv p. 509.

**Theages** Philosophus [Theag.]
Apud Stobaeum.

**Theano**
*Ep.* = *Epistulae*, v. Pythagorae et Pythagoreorum Epistulae.

**Thebaïs**
Ed. T. W. Allen, *Homeri Opera* v, Oxford (OCT), p. 112.

**Themiso** Historicus [Themiso Hist.]
Ed. C. Müller, *FHG* iv p. 511.

**Themiso** Medicus i B.C.
Apud Galenum.

**Themistius** Sophista [Them.] iv A.D.
*in APo.* = *Aristotelis Analyticorum Posteriorum paraphrasis*, ed. M. Wallies (*Comm. in Arist. Graeca* v *pars* i), Berlin 1900.
*in APr.* = *in Aristotelis Analyticorum Priorum librum I paraphrasis*, ed. M. Wallies (*Comm. in Arist. Graeca* xxiii *pars* iii), Berlin 1884.
*in de An.* = *in libros Aristotelis de Anima paraphrasis*, ed. R Heinze (*Comm. in Arist. Graeca* v *pars* iii), Berlin 1899.
*in Ph.* = *in Aristotelis Physica paraphrasis*, ed. H. Schenkl (*Comm. in Arist. Graeca* v *pars* ii), Berlin 1900.
*in PN* = *Themistii (Sophoniae) in Parva Naturalia commentarium*, ed. P. Wendland (*Comm. in Arist. Graeca* v *pars* vi), Berlin 1903.
*Or.* = *Orationes*, ed. W. Dindorf, Leipzig 1832; cited by page of Hardouin.

**Themistocles** Epistolographus [Themist.] v B.C.
*Ep.* = *Epistulae*, ed. R. Hercher, *Epistolographi*, p. 741.

**Theocles** Lyricus [Theocl.] iv/iii B.C.
Ed. J. U. Powell, *Coll. Alex.* p. 173.

**Theocritus** Poeta Bucolicus [Theoc.] iii B.C.
Ed. U. von Wilamowitz-Möllendorff², *Bucolici Graeci*, Oxford (OCT).
*Beren.* = *Coma Berenices*
*Ep.* = *Epigrammata*
Scholia, ed. C. Wendel, Leipzig (T.) 1914.

**Theodectes** Tragicus [Theodect.] iv B.C.
Ed. A. Nauck, *TGF* p. 801.

**Theodoridas** Epigrammaticus [Theodorid.] iii B.C.
v. *Anthologia Graeca.*

**Theodorus** Epigrammaticus [Theod.]
v. *Anthologia Graeca*

**Theodosius Alexandrinus** Grammaticus [Theodos.] iv A.D. (?)
*Can.* = *Canones*, ed. A. Hilgard, in *Grammatici Graeci*, *pars* iv, vol. i, Leipzig 1889.
Spuria, ed. C. W. Göttling, Leipzig 1822. [Theodos.Gr.]

**Theodotion** Interpres Veteris Testamenti [Thd.] ii A.D. (?)
F. Field, *Origenis Hexapla*, Oxford 1875.

**Theognetus** Comicus [Theognet.]
Ed T Kock, *CAF* iii p. 364.

**Theognis** Elegiacus [Thgn.] vi B.C.
Ed. T. Bergk, *PLG* ii p. 117.

**Theognis** Tragicus [Thgn.Trag.] v/iv B.C.
Ed. A Nauck. *TGF* p. 769.

**Theognis Rhodius** Historicus [Thgn.Hist.]
Ed. C. Müller, *FHG* iv p. 514.

**Theognostus** Grammaticus [Theognost.] ix A.D.
*Can.* = *Canones*, ed. J. A Cramer, *An. Ox.*, vol. ii.

**Theologumena Arithmeticae** [*Theol.Ar.*]
[Iamblichus], *Theologumena Arithmeticae*, ed. V. de Falco, Leipzig (T.) 1922; cited by Ast's pages (in margin).

**Theolytus** Epicus [Theolyt.]
Ed. J. U. Powell, *Coll. Alex.* p. 9.

**Theon** Epigrammaticus
v. *Anthologia Graeca.*

**Theon** Rhetor i/ii A.D. (?)
*Prog.* = *Progymnasmata*, ed. L. Spengel, *Rhet.* ii p. 59.

**[Th]eon Gymnasiarcha** Medicus [Theon Gymn.]
[A]pud Galenum
**[Th]eon Smyrnaeus** Philosophus [Theo Sm.] ii A.D.
[E]d. E. Hiller, Leipzig (T.) 1878.
*[i]n Ptol.* = *in Ptolemaeum*, ed. Halma, *Œuvres de Ptolémée*, tom. v, Paris 1821.
**[Th]eophanes** Epigrammaticus [Theoph.]
v. *Anthologia Graeca.*
**[Th]eophilus** Comicus [Theophil.]
Ed. T. Kock, *CAF* ii p. 473.
**[T]heophrastus** Philosophus [Thphr.] iv/iii B.C.
Ed. F. Wimmer, Leipzig (T.) 1854–62; *HP*, *Od.*, *Sign.*, ed. Sir Arthur Hort, London and New York (Loeb) 1916.
*CP* = *de Causis Plantarum*
*Char.* = *Characteres*, ed. H. Diels, Oxford (OCT).
*Fr.* = *Fragmenta*
*HP* = *Historia Plantarum*
*Ign.* = *de Igne*
*Lap.* = *de Lapidibus*
*Lass.* = *de Lassitudine*
*Metaph.* = *Metaphysica*, ed. H. Usener, Bonn 1890.
*Od.* = *de Odoribus*
*Sens.* = *de Sensu*
*Sign.* = *de Signis Tempestatum*
*Sud.* = *de Sudore*
*Vent.* = *de Ventis*
*Vert.* = *de Vertigine*
**Theopompus** Comicus [Theopomp.Com.] v B.C.
Ed. T. Kock, *CAF* i p. 733; suppl. J. Demiańczuk, *Supp. Com.* p. 86.
**Theopompus** Historicus [Theopomp.Hist.] iv B.C.
Ed. B. P. Grenfell & A. S. Hunt, v. *Hellenica Oxyrhynchia.*
**Theopompus Colophonius** Epicus [Theopomp.Coloph.]
Ed. J. U. Powell, *Coll. Alex.* p. 28.
**Thespis** Tragicus vi/v B.C.
Ed. A. Nauck, *TGF* p. 832.
**Thomas** Epigrammaticus [Thom.] vi A.D.
v. *Anthologia Graeca.*
**Thomas Magister** Grammaticus [Thom.Mag.] xiii/xiv A.D.
Ed. F. Ritschl, Halle 1832.
**Thrasymachus** [Thrasym.] iv B.C.
Ed. H. Diels, *Vorsokr.* ii p. 276.
**Thucydides** Historicus [Th.] v B.C.
Ed. H. Stuart Jones, Oxford (OCT).
**Thugenides** Comicus [Thugen.]
Ed. T. Kock, *CAF* iii p. 377; suppl. J. Demiańczuk, *Supp. Com.* p. 87.
**Thyillus** Epigrammaticus [Thyill.] i B.C.
v. *Anthologia Graeca.*
**Thymocles** Epigrammaticus [Thymocl.]
v. *Anthologia Graeca.*
**Tiberius** Rhetor [Tib.]
*Fig.* = *de Figuris*, ed. L. Spengel, *Rhet.* iii p. 59.
**Tiberius Illustrius** Epigrammaticus [Tib.Ill.] i A.D. (?)
v. *Anthologia Graeca.*
**Timaeus** Grammaticus [Tim.]
*Lex.* = *Lexicon Platonicum*, ed. C. F. Hermann, *Platonis Dialogi*, vol. vi, Leipzig (T.) 1892.
**Timaeus** Historicus [Timae.] iv/iii B.C.
Ed. C. Müller, *FHG* i p. 193, iv pp. 625, 640.
**Timaeus Locrus** Philosophus [Ti.Locr.]
Ed. C. F. Hermann, post Platonis Timaeum, Leipzig (T.) 1852.
**Timagenes** Historicus [Timag.] i B.C.
Ed. C. Müller, *FHG* iii p. 317.
**Timo Phliasius** Poeta Philosophus iii B.C.
Ed. H. Diels, *PPF* p. 173.
**Timocles** Comicus [Timocl.] iv B.C.
Ed. T. Kock, *CAF* ii p. 451; suppl. J. Demiańczuk, *Supp. Com.* p. 88.
**Timocreon** Lyricus [Timocr.] v. B.C.
Ed. T. Bergk, *PLG* iii p. 536.
**Timostratus** Comicus [Timostr.] ii B.C.
Ed. T. Kock, *CAF* iii p. 355.
**Timotheus** Comicus [Tim.Com.] iv/iii B.C. (?)
Ed. T. Kock, *CAF* ii p. 450.
**Timotheus** Lyricus [Tim.] v/iv B.C.
Ed. U. von Wilamowitz-Möllendorff, Leipzig 1903.
*Fr.* = *Fragmenta*
*Pers.* = *Persae*
**Timotheus Gazaeus** Philosophus [Tim.Gaz.]
v. Aristophanes Byzantinus, Philosophus.
**Titanomachia** [Titanomach.]
Ed. T. W. Allen, *Homeri Opera* v, Oxford (OCT), p. 110.
**Tragica Adespota** [*Trag.Adesp.*]
Ed. A. Nauck, *TGF* p. 837.
**Trophilus** [Trophil.]
Apud Stobaeum.
**Tryphiodorus** Epicus [Tryph.]
Ed. W. Weinberger, v. Coluthus.

**Trypho** Grammaticus i B.C.
*Fr.* = *Fragmenta*, ed. A. von Velsen, Berlin 1853.
*Pass.* = Excerpta περὶ παθῶν, ed. R. Schneider, Progr. Gymn. Duisburg, Leipzig 1895.
*Trop.* = περὶ τρόπων, ed. L. Spengel, *Rhet* iii p. 189.
**Tullius Flaccus** Epigrammaticus [Tull.Flacc.]
v. *Anthologia Graeca.*
**Tullius Geminus** Epigrammaticus [Tull.Gem.]
v. *Anthologia Graeca.*
**Tullius Laurea** Epigrammaticus. [Tull.Laur.] i B.C.
v. *Anthologia Graeca.*
**Tullius Sabinus**, v. Sabinus.
**Tymnes** Epigrammaticus [Tymn.]
v. *Anthologia Graeca.*
**Tyrtaeus** Elegiacus [Tyrt.] vii B.C.
Ed. T. Bergk, *PLG* ii p. 8.
**Tzetzes, Joannes** Grammaticus [Tz.] xii A.D.
ad Hes.*Op.* = ad Hesiodi *Opera et Dies*, ed. T. Gaisford, *Poetae Graeci Minores*, vol. iii.
ad Lyc. = ad Lycophronem, ed. E. Scheer, v. Lycophron.
*Diff. Poet.* = περὶ διαφορᾶς ποιητῶν, ed. G. Kaibel, *CGF* p. 34.
*H.* = *Historiarum variarum chiliades*, ed. T. Kiessling, Leipzig 1826.
*Proll.Com.* = *Prolegomena de Comoedia Graeca*, ed. G. Kaibel, *CGF* p. 17.
*Trag.Poes.* = *De Tragica Poesi*, ed. G. Kaibel, op. cit., p. 43.

**Ulpianus** Grammaticus [Ulp.] iii A.D.
*Commentary on Demosthenes*, ed. H. Wolf, Basel 1572.
**Uranius** Historicus [Uran.] i B.C. (?)
Ed. C. Müller, *FHG* iv p. 523.

**Varro, M. Terentius** Historicus et Grammaticus Latinus i B.C.
*LL* = *de Lingua Latina*, ed. G. Goetz & F. Schoell, Leipzig 1910.
*RR* = *Res Rusticae*, ed. G. Goetz, Leipzig (T.) 1912.
*Sat.Men.* = *Saturae Menippeae*, ed. F. Buecheler, post Petronium (q.v.)
**Velius Longus** Grammaticus Latinus [Vel.Long.] ii A.D.
Ed. H. Keil, *Gramm. Lat.* vii p. 37.
**Vettius Valens** Astrologus [Vett.Val.] ii A.D.
Ed. W. Kroll, Berlin 1908 (cited by page and line).
**Vetus Testamentum Graece redditum** [LXX]
Ed. H. B. Swete, ed. 3, Cambridge 1901.
A. Versiones ab Origene collectae
Ed. F. Field, *Origenis Hexapla*, Oxford 1875.
Al. = ἄλλοι
Aq. = Aquila (q.v.)
Heb. = Ἑβραῖος
Quint. = Quinta
Sext. = Sexta
Sm. = Symmachus (q.v.)
Thd. = Theodotion (q.v.)
B. Libri singuli his siglis notantur :—
*Am.* = *Amos*
*Ba.* = *Baruch*
*Bel*
*Ca.* = *Canticles*
1, 2 *Ch.* = 1, 2 *Chronicles*
*Da.* = *Daniel*
*De.* = *Deuteronomy*
*Ec.* = *Ecclesiastes*
*Ep.Je.* = *Epistle of Jeremiah*
*Es.* = *Esther*
1, 2 *Es.* = 1, 2 *Esdras*
*Ex.* = *Exodus*
*Ez.* = *Ezekiel*
*Ge.* = *Genesis*
*Hb.* = *Habakkuk*
*Hg.* = *Haggai*
*Ho.* = *Hosea*
*Is.* = *Isaiah*
*Jb.* = *Job*
*Jd.* = *Judges*
*Je.* = *Jeremiah*
*Jl.* = *Joel*
*Jn.* = *Jonah*
*Jo.* = *Joshua*
*Ju.* = *Judith*
1–4 *Ki.* = 1–4 *Kings*
*La.* = *Lamentations*
*Le.* = *Leviticus*
*Ma.* = *Malachi*
1–4 *Ma.* = 1–4 *Maccabees*
*Mi.* = *Micah*
*Na.* = *Nahum*
*Ne.* = *Nehemiah*
*Nu.* = *Numbers*
*Ob.* = *Obadiah*
*Pr.* = *Proverbs*
*Prec.Man.* = *Prayer of Manasses*

**Vetus Testamentum** (*continued*)
*Ps.* = *Psalms*
*Ru.* = *Ruth*
*Si.* = *Ecclesiasticus* (*Siracides*)
*Su.* = *Susanna*
*To* = *Tobit*
*Wi.* = *Wisdom of Solomon*
*Za.* = *Zechariah*
*Ze.* = *Zephaniah*

**Vita Philonidis Epicurei** [*Vit.Philonid.*]
= *PHerc.* 1044, ed. W. Crönert, *Berl. Sitzb.* xli (1900); cited by page of offprint (942–959 = 1–18).

**Vitae Homeri** [*Vit.Hom.*]
Ed. T. W. Allen, *Homeri Opera*, Oxford (OCT), v p. 245.

**Vitruvius** Scriptor de Architectura Latinus [Vitr.] i B.C.
Ed. F. Krohn, Leipzig (T.) 1912.

**Xanthus** Historicus [Xanth.] v B.C.
Ed. C. Müller *FHG* i p. 36, iv pp. 623, 628.

**Xenagoras** Historicus [Xenag.]
Ed. C. Müller, *FHG* iv p. 526.

**Xenarchus** Comicus [Xenarch.] iv B.C.
Ed. T. Kock, *CAF* ii p. 467.

**Xeno** Comicus
Ed. T. Kock, *CAF* iii p. 390.

**Xenocles** Tragicus [Xenocl.] v B.C.
Ed. A. Nauck, *TGF* p. 770.

**Xenocrates** Medicus (apud Oribasium) [Xenocr.] i A.D.
Ed. J. L. Ideler, *Physici et Medici Graeci Minores* i p. 121, Berlin 1841.

**Xenophanes** Poeta Philosophus [Xenoph.] vi B.C.
Ed. H. Diels, *PPF* p. 20.

**Xenophon** Historicus [X.] v/iv B.C.
Ed. E. C. Marchant, Oxford (OCT).
*Ages.* = *Agesilaus*
*An.* = *Anabasis*
*Ap.* = *Apologia Socratis*
*Ath.* = *Respublica Atheniensium*
*Cyn.* = *Cynegeticus*
*Cyr.* = *Institutio Cyri* (*Cyropaedia*)
*Ep.* = *Epistulae*, ed. R. Hercher, *Epistolographi*, p. 788.
*Eq.* = *de Equitandi ratione*
*Eq.Mag.* = *de Equitum magistro*
*HG* = *Historia Graeca* (*Hellenica*)
*Hier.* = *Hiero*
*Lac.* = *Respublica Lacedaemoniorum*
*Mem.* = *Memorabilia*
*Oec.* = *Oeconomicus*
*Smp.* = *Symposium*
*Vect.* = *de Vectigalibus*

**Xenophon Ephesius** Scriptor Eroticus [X.Eph.] ii A.D. (
Ed. R. Hercher, *Erotici* i p. 327.

**Zaleucus** [Zaleuc.] (vii B.C
Apud Stobaeum.

**Zelotus** Epigrammaticus [Zelot.]
v. *Anthologia Graeca.*

**Zeno Citieus** Stoicus [Zeno *Stoic.*] iv/iii B.C
Ed. H. von Arnim, *SVF* i p. 1.

**Zeno Eleaticus** Philosophus [Zeno Eleat.] v B.C
Ed. H. Diels, *Vorsokr.* i p. 165.

**Zeno Tarsensis** Stoicus [Zeno Tars.*Stoic.*] iii/ii B.C
Ed. H. von Arnim, *SVF* iii p. 209.

**Zenobius** Paroemiographus [Zen.] ii A.D.
Ed. E. L. von Leutsch & F. G. Schneidewin, *Paroemiographi* i p. 1.

**Zenodotus** Grammaticus [Zenod.] iv/iii B.C.
Apud Scholia in Homerum.

**Zonaeus** Rhetor [Zonae.]
*Fig.* = *de Figuris*, ed L. Spengel, *Rhet.* iii p. 161.

**Zonaras** Lexicographus [Zonar.]
Ed. J. A. H. Tittmann, Leipzig 1808.

**Zonas** Epigrammaticus [Zon.] i B.C./i A.D.
Idem qui et Diodorus Sardianus, q.v.

**Zopyrus** Historicus [Zopyr.Hist.]
Ed. C. Müller, *FHG* iv p. 531.

**Zopyrus** Medicus [Zopyr.] i A.D.
Apud Oribasium.

**Zosimus** Alchemista [Zos.Alch.] iii/iv A.D.
Ed. M. Berthelot, *Collection des anciens alchimistes grecs*, Paris 1888, p. 107.

**Zosimus** Epigrammaticus [Zos.]
v. *Anthologia Graeca.*

**Zosimus** Historicus [Zos.] v A.D.
Ed. L. Mendelssohn, Leipzig 1887.

# II. EPIGRAPHICAL PUBLICATIONS

*Anatolian Studies* = *Anatolian Studies presented to Sir W. M. Ramsay*, Manchester 1923.

Arangio-Ruiz et Olivieri *Inscr. Gr.* = V. Arangio-Ruiz et A. Olivieri, *Inscriptiones Graecae Siciliae et infimae Italiae ad ius pertinentes*, Milan 1925.

*BMus.Inscr.* = *Ancient Greek Inscriptions in the British Museum*, Oxford 1874–1916.

Baillet *Inscr. des tombeaux des rois* = J. Baillet, *Inscriptions grecques et latines des tombeaux des rois à Thèbes*, Le Caire 1920–23.

Benndorf-Niemann *Reisen in Lykien* = O. Benndorf & G. Niemann, *Reisen in Lykien und Karien*, Vienna 1884.

*Buckler Anat. Studies* = *Anatolian Studies presented to W. H. Buckler*, ed. W. M. Calder & J. Keil, Manchester 1939.

*CIG* = A. Boeckh, *Corpus Inscriptionum Graecarum*, Berlin 1828–77.

*CIJud.* = *Corpus Inscriptionum Iudaicarum*, ed. J.-B. Frey: vol. i (Europe), Rome 1936.

*CIL* = *Corpus Inscriptionum Latinarum*, Berlin 1862–.

*Chron.Lind.* = *Chronicle of Lindos*, ed. Chr. Blinkenberg, *Die Lindische Tempelchronik*, Bonn 1915; ed. F. Jacoby, *FGrH* ii p. 1005.

*Corinth* = *Corinth, results of excavations conducted by the American School of Classical Studies at Athens*, Cambridge, Massachusetts 1929–; vol. viii Part i, *Greek Inscriptions*, ed. B. D. Meritt, 1931.

Cumont *Fouilles de Doura-Europos* = F. Cumont, *Fouilles de Doura-Europos* (1922–3), Paris 1926.

Dain *Inscr. du Louvre* = A. Dain, *Inscriptions grecques du musée du Louvre: Les textes inédits*, Paris 1933.

*Delph.*3(1),(2),.. = *Fouilles de Delphes*, tome iii: *Épigraphie.* Paris 1909–. (École française d'Athènes.)

Demitsas Μακεδ. = M. G. Demitsas, Ἡ Μακεδονία κτλ., vol. i (all published), Athens 1896.

Dessau *ILS* = H. Dessau, *Inscriptiones Latinae Selectae*, Berlin 1892–1916.

*Dura*[1], *Dura*[2]... = *The Excavations at Dura-Europos. Preliminary Report of First* (*Second...*) *Season of Work*, ed. P. V. C. Bauer, M. I. Rostovtzeff, A. R. Bellinger, and others, Yale University Press 1929–.

Durrbach *Choix d'inscrr. de Délos* = F. Durrbach, *Choix d'inscriptions de Délos*, Paris 1921.

*Edict.Diocl.* = *Edictum Diocletiani*, ed. T. Mommsen & H. Blümner, *Der Maximaltarif des Diocletian*, Berlin 1893; suppl. *CIL* iii pp. 1926 ff., 2208 ff, 2328[57] ff.: cited where possible by Mommsen's chaps. & lines, recently found portions by place of discovery (*Aeg.* = Aegira; *Clit.* = Clitor; *Delph.* = Delphi; *Troez.* = Troezen); *Geronthr.* = *IG*5(1)1115; *Gyth.* = 5(1)1148.

*Eph.Epigr.* = *Ephemeris Epigraphica, Corporis Inscriptionum Latinarum Supplementum*, Berlin 1872–.

*Ephes.*2,3,.. = *Forschungen in Ephesos, veröffentlicht vom Oesterreichischen Archaeologischen Institute*. Bde. 2, 3, Vienna 1912, 1923; 4(1), 1932; 4(2), Baden bei Wien 1937.

*Epigr Gr.* = G. Kaibel, *Epigrammata Graeca ex lapidibus conlecta*, Berlin 1878.

*Foed.Delph.Pell.* = *Foedus inter Delphos et Pellanenses*, ed. B.

Haussoullier, *Traité entre Delphes et Pellana*, Paris 1917; *Schwyzer* (q.v.) No. 328[a].

*DI* = *Sammlung der griechischen Dialekt-Inschriften*, ed. H. Collitz et alii, Göttingen 1884–1915.

*erasa* = *Gerasa, City of the Decapolis*, ed. C. H. Kraeling, New Haven, Connecticut, 1938.

aussoullier *Milet* = B. Haussoullier, *Études sur l'histoire de Milet et du Didymeion*, Paris 1902.

euzey-Daumet *Mission Arch. de Macédoine* = L. Heuzey et H. Daumet, *Mission Archéologique de Macédoine*, Paris 1876.

*listria* = V. Pârvan, *Histria*, Part iv, Bucarest 1916; Part vii, Bucarest 1923.

*G* = *Inscriptiones Graecae.*

vol. i = *Inscriptiones Atticae anno Euclidis vetustiores*, ed. A. Kirchhoff, 1873: *Supplementa, indices* 1877, 1887, 1891 [= *Corpus Inscriptionum Atticarum*, vol. i *et* vol. iv *pars* i fasc. i–iii].

*IG*1[2] = *IG* vol. i ed. minor, ed. F. Hiller von Gaertringen, 1924.

vol. ii = *Inscriptiones Atticae aetatis quae est inter Euclidis annum et Augusti tempora*, ed. U. Koehler [5 parts, 1877, 1883, 1888, 1893 (*indices* by J. Kirchner), 1895 (*supplementa*) = *Corpus Inscriptionum Atticarum*, vol. ii *partes* i–iv et vol. iv *pars* ii].

vol. iii = *Inscriptiones Atticae aetatis Romanae*, ed W. Dittenberger, *pars* i 1878, *pars* ii 1882, *pars* iii (v. *Tab. Defix.*) 1897 [= *Corpus Inscriptionum Atticarum*, vol. iii *partes* i, ii, *et Appendix*].

*IG*2[2] = *Voluminum* ii et iii *editio minor*, ed. J. Kirchner, *pars* i fasc. i 1913, fasc. ii 1916; *pars* ii fasc. i (1370–1695) 1927, fasc. ii (1696–2788) 1931; *pars* iii fasc. i (2789–5219) 1935.

vol. iv = *Inscriptiones Argolidis*, ed. M. Fraenkel, 1902 [= *Corpus Inscriptionum Graecarum Peloponnesi et insularum vicinarum*, vol. i].

*IG*4[2] = *Voluminis* iv *editio minor*, fasc. i = *Inscriptiones Epidauri*, ed. F. Hiller von Gaertringen, 1929.

vol. v fasc. i = *Inscriptiones Laconiae et Messeniae*, ed. W. Kolbe, 1913; fasc. ii = *Inscriptiones Arcadiae*, ed. F. Hiller von Gaertringen, 1913.

vol. vii = *Inscriptiones Megaridis et Boeotiae*, ed. W. Dittenberger, 1892 [= *Corpus Inscriptionum Graecarum Graeciae Septentrionalis*, vol. i].

vol. ix *pars* i = *Inscriptiones Phocidis, Locridis, Aetoliae, Acarnaniae, insularum maris Ionii*, ed. W. Dittenberger, 1897 [= *Corpus Inscriptionum Graecarum Graeciae Septentrionalis*, vol. iii *pars* i]; *pars* ii = *Inscriptiones Thessaliae*, ed. O. Kern, 1908.

*IG*9[2] = Voluminis ix *partis* i *editio minor*, fasc. i = *Inscriptiones Aetoliae*, ed. G. Klaffenbach, 1932.

vol. xi = *Inscriptiones Deli*: fasc. ii, ed. F. Dürrbach, 1912; fasc. 3 cited as *Inscr. Délos* (q.v.); fasc. iv, ed. P. Roussel, 1914.

vol. xii = *Inscriptiones insularum maris Aegaei praeter Delum*: fasc. i, *Inscriptiones Rhodi, Chalces, Carpathi cum Saro, Casi*, ed. F. Hiller von Gaertringen, 1895.

fasc. ii, *Inscriptiones Lesbi, Nesi, Tenedi*, ed. W. Paton, 1899.

fasc. iii, *Inscriptiones Symes, Teutlussae, Teli, Nisyri, Astypalaeae, Anaphes, Therae et Therasiae, Pholegandri, Meli, Cimoli*, ed. F. Hiller von Gaertringen, 1898; *Supplementa*, ed. F. Hiller von Gaertringen 1904.

fasc. v, *Inscriptiones Cycladum*: *pars* i, *Inscriptiones Cycladum praeter Tenum*, ed. F. Hiller von Gaertringen, 1903; *pars* ii, *Inscriptiones Teni insulae*, ed. F. Hiller von Gaertringen, 1909.

fasc. vii, *Inscriptiones Amorgi et insularum vicinarum*, ed. J. Delamarre, 1908.

fasc. viii, *Inscriptiones insularum maris Thracici*, ed. C. Fredrich, 1909.

fasc. ix, *Inscriptiones Euboeae*, ed. E. Ziebarth, 1915.

vol. xiv = *Inscriptiones Siciliae et Italiae additis Galliae Hispaniae Britanniae Germaniae inscriptionibus*, ed. G. Kaibel, 1890.

*IGRom.* = *Inscriptiones Graecae ad res Romanas pertinentes*, ed. R. Cagnat et alii, Paris, vol. i 1911, iii 1906, iv 1927.

*IPE* = *Inscriptiones orae septentrionalis Ponti Euxini*, ed. B. Latyshev, Petersburg 1885–1901: 1[2] = vol. i, second edition, 1916.

*Inscr.Cos* = *The Inscriptions of Cos*, ed. W. R. Paton & E. L. Hicks, Oxford 1891.

*Inscr.Cret.* = *Inscriptiones Creticae opera et consilio Friderici Halbherr collectae. I. Tituli Cretae mediae praeter Gortynios. Curavit Margarita Guarducci.* Rome 1935.

*Inscr.Cypr.* = Cyprian Inscriptions in O. Hoffmann, *Die griechischen Dialekte*, vol. i, Göttingen 1891.

*Inscr.Délos* = Nos. 290–371, 372–509, ed. F. Durrbach, Paris 1926, 1929 (*Acad. des Inscriptions et Belles-Lettres*). [The numeration is continued from *IG*11(2).] Nos. 1400–96 [an interval is left after the nos. of *IG*11(4)] ed. F Durrbach & P. Roussel, 1935. Nos. 1497–2879 (2 pts.) ed. P. Roussel & M. Launey, 1937.

*Inscr. gr. et lat. de la Syrie* = *Inscriptions grecques et latines de la Syrie*; I. Commagène et Cyrrhestique, ed. L. Jalabert & R. Mouterde, Paris 1929.

*Inscr.Magn.* = *Die Inschriften von Magnesia am Maeander*, ed. O. Kern, Berlin 1900.

*Inscr.Mus.Alex.* = E. Breccia, *Iscrizioni greche e latine* (*Catal. gen. des antiq. égypt. du musée d'Alexandrie*, 57), 1911.

*Inscr.Olymp.* = *Olympia: die Ergebnisse der... Ausgrabung: Textband* v, *Die Inschriften*, ed. W. Dittenberger & K. Purgold, Berlin 1896.

*Inscr.Perg.* = *Die Inschriften von Pergamon* (in *Altertümer von Pergamon* viii), ed. M. Fraenkel, Berlin 1890–1895.

*Inscr.Prien.* = *Die Inschriften von Priene*, ed. F. Hiller von Gaertringen, Berlin 1906.

Keil-Premerstein *Erster* (*zweiter, dritter*) *Bericht* = J. Keil & A. von Premerstein, *Bericht über eine* (*eine zweite, eine dritte*) *Reise in Lydien* (*Denkschriften der Wiener Akademie, phil.-hist. Klasse*, LIII, 2. *Abh.*, LIV, 2. *Abh.*, LVII, 1. *Abh*), Vienna 1908, 1911, 1914.

*LF, LW* = Philippe Le Bas, W. H. Waddington & P. Foucart, *Voyage Archéologique en Grèce et en Asie Mineure*, Paris 1847–70.

*Leg.Gort.* = *Leges Gortynensium* (*GDI* 4991, *Schwyzer* 179).

*Leg.Sacr.* = *Leges Graecorum Sacrae*, ed. J. de Prott & L. Ziehen, Leipzig fasc. i 1896, fasc. ii (1) 1906.

MacDowell *Stamped Objects from Seleucia* = R. H. MacDowell, *Stamped & Inscribed Objects from Seleucia on the Tigris* (Univ. of Michigan Studies, Humanistic Series, vol. xxxvi), Ann Arbor 1935.

Maiuri *Nuova Silloge* = A. Maiuri, *Nuova Silloge Epigrafica di Rodi e Cos*, Firenze 1925.

*MAMA* = *Monumenta Asiae Minoris Antiqua*, vol. i, ed. W. M. Calder, Manchester-London 1928 (Publications of the American Society for Archaeological Research in Asia Minor); vol. iii, ed. J. Keil & A. Wilhelm, 1931; vol. iv, ed. W. H. Buckler, W. M. Calder, W. K. C. Guthrie, 1933; vol. v, ed. C. W. M. Cox & A. Cameron, 1937; vol. vi, ed. W. H. Buckler & W. M. Calder, 1939 (iii–vi Manchester).

*Marm.Par.* = *Marmor Parium* (*IG*12(5).444) ed. F. Jacoby, *Das Marmor Parium*, Berlin 1904, and *FGrH* ii p. 992.

*Mél.Bidez* = *Mélanges Bidez* (*Annuaire de l'Institut de philologie et d'histoire orientales*, tome ii), Brussels 1934.

*Mél.Glotz* = *Mélanges Gustave Glotz*, Paris 1932.

*Mél.Navarre* = *Mélanges offerts à M. Octave Navarre par ses élèves et ses amis*, Toulouse 1935.

*Michel* = C. Michel, *Recueil d'inscriptions grecques*, Brussels 1900: Supplements i, ii, Brussels 1912, 1927.

*Milet* = *Milet. Ergebnisse der Ausgrabungen und Untersuchungen seit dem Jahre 1899*, herausg. von Theodor Wiegand (*Königliche Museen zu Berlin*), 1906–. *Milet*3 = *Milet* Bd. I Heft iii; for other parts Band and Heft are given.

*Milet*6,7 = *Sechster* (*siebenter*) *vorläufiger Bericht über die in Milet und Didyma unternommenen Ausgrabungen, Abh. Berl. Akad.* 1908 Anhang I, 1911 Anh. I.

*Mon.Anc.Gr.* = *Monumenti Ancyrani versio Graeca* (*Res Gestae Divi Augusti*, ed. E. Diehl[3], Bonn 1918).

*Mon.Piot* = *Monuments et mémoires publiés par la fondation Piot*, Paris 1894–.

*Mueller-Bees* = N. Mueller & N. A. Bees, *Die Inschriften der jüdischen Katakombe am Monteverde zu Rom*, Leipzig 1919.

Myres *Cesnola Coll.* = J. L. Myres, *Handbook of the Cesnola Collection of Antiquities from Cyprus*, New York 1914.

*Naukratis* = *Naukratis.* Pt. i by [Sir] W. M. Flinders Petrie, London 1886, Pt. ii by E. A. Gardner, 1888 (*Egypt Exploration Fund, Memoirs* iii, vi).

*OGI* = *Orientis Graeci Inscriptiones Selectae*, ed. W. Dittenberger, Leipzig 1903–5.

Pelekides *Thessalonica* = S. Pelekides, Ἀπὸ τὴν πολιτεία καὶ τὴν κοινωνία τῆς ἀρχαίας Θεσσαλονίκης, Salonika 1934.

Petersen-Luschan *Reisen in Lykien* = E. Petersen & F. von Luschan, *Reisen in Lykien, Milyas und Kibyratis*, Vienna 1889.

*Princeton Exp.Inscr.* = *Publications of the Princeton University Archaeological Expeditions to Syria in 1904–5 and 1909*: Division III, *Greek and Latin Inscriptions*, Leyden, Section A by E. Littmann, D. Magie, & D. R. Stuart, 1921; Section B by W. K. Prentice, 1922.

Puchstein *Epigr.Gr.* = O. Puchstein, *Epigrammata Graeca in Aegypto reperta*, Strassburg 1880.

Ramsay *Cities and Bishoprics* = [Sir] W. M. Ramsay, *Cities and Bishoprics of Phrygia*, Oxford 1895–7.

Ramsay *Studies in Eastern Rom. Prov.* = *Studies in the History and Art of the Eastern Provinces of the Roman Empire*, ed. [Sir] W. M. Ramsay, Aberdeen 1906.

Robert *Collection Froehner* = *Collection Froehner* (Bibliothèque nationale. Département des médailles et des antiques), i. *Inscriptions grecques*, ed. L. Robert, Paris 1936.

Robert *Ét. Anat.* = L. Robert, *Études Anatoliennes*, Paris 1937 (*Études orientales publiées par l'institut français d'archéologie de Stamboul* No. v).

Roussel *Cultes Égyptiens* = P. Roussel, *Les Cultes égyptiens à Délos*, Nancy 1916.

Ruppel *T. von Dakke* = W. Ruppel, *Der Tempel von Dakke*, vol. 3, Cairo 1930 (*Service des Antiquités d'Égypte*).
*Rüsch* = E. Rüsch, *Grammatik der delphischen Inschriften* i, Berlin 1914 (*Epigraphischer Anhang*, pp. 312–31).
*SIG* = *Sylloge Inscriptionum Graecarum*, ed. W. Dittenberger, editio tertia, Leipzig 1915–24. (*SIG*² = editio altera, 1898–1901.)
*Sardis* 7(1) = *Sardis, Publications of the American Society for the Excavation of Sardis*, Vol. vii, *Greek and Latin Inscriptions*, Part I, by W. H. Buckler and D. M. Robinson, Leyden 1932.
*Schwyzer* = E. Schwyzer, *Dialectorum Graecarum Exempla epigraphica potiora*, Leipzig 1923.
*Stud.Pont.* = *Studia Pontica*, Brussels 1903–: vol. iii *Recueil des inscriptions grecques et latines du Pont et de l'Arménie*, publ. par J. G. C. Anderson, F. Cumont, H. Grégoire, fasc. i (1910).
*Supp.Epigr.* = *Supplementum Epigraphicum Graecum*, adjuvantibus P. Roussel, A. Salač, M. N. Tod, E. Ziebarth, ed. J. J. E. Hondius, Leyden 1923–.
Swoboda *Denkmäler* = *Denkmäler aus Lykaonien, Pamphylien u. Isaurien*, herausgegeben von H. Swoboda, J. Keil, und F. Kno[ll], Brünn etc., 1935.
*TAM* = *Tituli Asiae Minoris*, vol. ii fasc. i, ed. E. Kalinka, Vien[na] 1920; fasc. ii, 1930.
*Tab.Defix.* = *Defixionum Tabellae in Attica regione repertae*, e[d.] R. Wuensch (*IG*3 *pars* iii).
*Tab.Defix.Aud.* = *Defixionum Tabellae quotquot innotuerunt*, ed[.] A. Audollent, Paris 1904.
*Tab.Heracl.* = *Tabulae Heracleenses* (*IG*14.645, *Schwyzer* 62–3).
*Test.Epict.* = *Testamentum Epictetae* (*IG*12(3).330, *Michel* 1001 *Schwyzer* 227); cited by col. and line.
*Wiegand Mnemos.* = *Mnemosynon Theodor Wiegand dargebracht*, Munich 1938.
Wood *Ephesus* = J. T. Wood, *Discoveries at Ephesus*, London 1877.

# III. PAPYROLOGICAL PUBLICATIONS

*BGU* = *Berliner griechische Urkunden* (*Ägyptische Urkunden aus den Königlichen Museen zu Berlin*), Berlin 1895–.
*BKT* = *Berliner Klassikertexte, herausgegeben von der Generalverwaltung der Kgl. Museen zu Berlin*, Berlin 1904–.
*Berichtigungsl.* = *Berichtigungsliste der griechischen Papyrusurkunden aus Ägypten*: I. F. Preisigke, Hefte 1 & 2, Strassburg 1913; Hefte 3 & 4, Berlin & Leipzig 1922; II. F. Bilabel, Heidelberg 1931, 1933.
Bilabel 'Οψαρτ. = F. Bilabel, 'Οψαρτυτικά *und Verwandtes* (*Sitzungsberichte d. Heidelberger Akademie der Wissenschaften, Phil.-hist. Kl.* 1919, 23. *Abh.*), Heidelberg 1920.
*CPHerm.* = *Corpus Papyrorum Hermopolitanorum* i, ed. C. Wessely (*Studien zur Paläogr. u. Papyruskunde* v), Leipzig 1905.
*CPR* = *Corpus Papyrorum Raineri Archiducis Austriae*, vol. i, *Griechische Texte*, ed. C. Wessely, Wien 1895; cf. *PRain.*(*NS*).
Διηγήσεις = Διηγήσεις *di poemi di Callimaco in un papiro di Tebtynis*, a cura di M. Norsa e G. Vitelli, Firenze 1934: cited by column and line; ed. A. Vogliano *PUniv.Milan.* i. 18.
Frisk *Bankakten* = *Bankakten aus dem Faijûm nebst anderen Berliner Papyri*, ed. H. Frisk (*Göteborgs Kungl. Vetenskaps- och Vitterhets-Samhälles Handlingar, femte följden, Ser.A. Band 2 No. 2*), Göteborg 1931.
*Herc.* (following an author's name) = Herculaneum papyri, cited by No. of papyrus and column or fragment from *Herculanensium Voluminum quae supersunt, Collectio altera*, Naples 1862–76, D. Bassi, *Herculanensium Voluminum, Collectio tertia*, fasc. i, Milan 1914, and other publications; 'Epicureus *Herc*...p...V.' refers to *Epicuri et Epicureorum scripta*.., ed. A. Vogliano (v. I (Add.) s.v. Epicurus).
*Kapsomenakis* = S. G. Kapsomenakis, *Voruntersuchungen zu einer Grammatik der Papyri der nachchristlichen Zeit*, Munich 1938.
Meyer *Ostr.* = Ostraca in *P.Meyer* (q.v.).
Mitteis *Chr.*, Wilcken *Chr.* = L. Mitteis & U. Wilcken, *Grundzüge und Chrestomathie der Papyruskunde*, Leipzig & Berlin 1912.
Möller *Pap.Berl.Mus.* = S. Möller, *Griechische Papyri aus dem Berliner Museum*, Göteborg 1929.
*Ostr.* = U. Wilcken, *Griechische Ostraka aus Ägypten und Nubien*, Leipzig & Berlin 1899.
*Ostr.Bodl.* = J. G. Tait, *Greek Ostraca in the Bodleian Library and other collections*, I, London 1930 (cited by No. of part and No. of ostracon).
*Ostr.Mich.* = L. Amundsen, *Greek Ostraca in the University of Michigan Collection*, Part I, Texts (= University of Michigan Studies, Humanistic Series, vol. xxxiv), Ann Arbor 1935.
*Ostr.Strassb.* = *Griechische und griechisch-demotische Ostraka der Universitäts- und Landesbibliothek zu Strassburg*, ed. P. Viereck, Berlin 1923.
*Ostr.Wilbour* = C. Préaux, *Les ostraca grecs de la Collection Charles-Edwin Wilbour au Musee de Brooklyn*, New York 1935.
*PAberd.* = *Catalogue of Greek & Latin papyri & ostraca in the possession of the University of Aberdeen*, ed. E. G. Turner (*Aberdeen Univ. Studies* No. 116), 1939.
*PAlex.* = *Papyrus ptolémaïques du Musee d'Alexandrie*, ed. G. Botti, *Bull.Soc.Alex.* First Series No. 2 (1899) p. 65.
*PAmh.* = *Amherst Papyri*, ed. B. P. Grenfell & A. S. Hunt, 2 vols., London 1900–1; cited by No. of vol., papyrus, and line.
*PAntin.* = *the Antinoe Papyrus* of Theocritus in *Two Theocritus Papyri*, ed. A. S. Hunt & J. Johnson, London 1930.
*PAvrom.* = *Parchments of the Parthian period from Avroman in Kurdistan*, ed. E. H. Minns, *JHS* xxxv (1915) p. 22.
*PBaden* = F. Bilabel, *Veröffentlichungen aus den badischen Papyrus-Sammlungen*, Heft 2 and Heft 4, *Griechische Papyri*, Heidelberg 1923, 1924.
*PBasel* = *Papyrusurkunden der öffentlichen Bibliothek der Universität zu Basel*, I. *Urkunden in griechischer Sprache*, ed. E. Rabel (*Abh. Gött. Gesellsch.* Neue Folge, vol. xvi, No. 3), Berlin 1917.
*PBerl.Leihg.* = *Berliner Leihgabe griechischer Papyri*, herausgegeben vom griechischen Seminar der Universität Uppsala durch T. Kalén, Uppsala 1932.
*PBerol.* = Berlin Papyri, cited by inventory No. (*PBerol.* 6926, 7927ᵛ = B. Lavagnini, *Eroticorum Graecorum Fragmenta Papyracea*, Leipzig (T.) 1922, pp. 1ff., 21ff.).
*PBouriant* = *Les papyrus Bouriant*, ed. P. Collart, Paris 1926.
*PBremen* = U. Wilcken, *Die Bremer Papyri* (*Abhandlungen der Preussischen Akademie der Wissenschaften*, 1936, Phil.-hist. Klasse No. 2), Berlin 1936.
*PCair.* = Cairo Papyri cited by catalogue No. from B. P. Grenfell & A. S. Hunt, *Greek Papyri, Catalogue général des Antiquités égyptiennes du Musée du Caire*, vol. x, Nos. 10001–10869, Oxford 1903.
*PCair.Preis.* = F. Preisigke, *Griechische Urkunden des ägyptischen Museums zu Kairo* (*Schriften der wissenschaftlichen Gesellschaft zu Strassburg*, Heft 8), Strassburg 1911.
*PCair.Zen.* = C. C. Edgar, *Zenon Papyri*, 4 vols. (*Catal. gén. des Antiq. égypt. du Musée du Caire*, 79) 1925–31: digits indicating 59(000) omitted in refs., thus 2 = 59002.
*PCornell* = *Greek Papyri in the Library of Cornell University*, ed. W. L. Westermann & C. J. Kraemer, New York 1926.
*PEdgar* = C. C. Edgar, *Selected papyri from the archives of Zenon, Annales du Service des Antiquités de l'Égypte*, Nos. 1–10 in vol. xviii (1918) pp. 159–82; Nos. 11–21, ib. pp. 224–44; Nos. 22–36, vol. xix (1920) pp. 13–36; Nos. 37–48, ib. pp. 81–104; Nos. 49–54, vol. xx (1920) pp. 19–40; Nos. 55–64, ib. pp. 181–206; Nos. 65–6, vol. xxi (1921) pp. 89–109; Nos. 67–72, vol. xxii (1922) pp. 209–31; Nos. 73–76, vol. xxiii (1923) pp. 73–98; Nos. 77–88, ib. pp. 187–209; Nos. 89–104, vol. xxiv (1924) pp. 17–52.
*PEleph.* = *Elephantine Papyri*, ed. O. Rubensohn, *Ägyptische Urkunden aus den Kgl. Museen zu Berlin: Griechische Urkunden*: Sonderheft, Berlin 1907.
*PEnteux.* = *Publications de la Société royale égyptienne de Papyrologie, Textes et Documents*, i, 'Εντεύξεις.., ed. O. Guéraud, Cairo 1931–2.
*PFay.* = B. P. Grenfell, A. S. Hunt, D. G. Hogarth, *Fayûm Towns and their Papyri*, London 1900.
*PFlor.* = *Papiri Fiorentini, documenti pubblici e privati dell'età romana e bizantina*: I ed. G. Vitelli, Milano 1906; II ed. D. Comparetti, 1908–11; III ed. G. Vitelli, 1915.
*PFrankf.* = H. Lewald, *Griechische Papyri aus dem Besitz des rechtswissenschaftlichen Seminars der Universität Frankfurt* (*Sitzungsberichte der Heidelberger Akademie der Wissenschaften, Phil.-hist. Kl.* 1920, 14. *Abh.*).
*PFreib.* = *Mitteilungen aus der Freiburger Papyrussammlung*, in *Sitzungsberichte der Heidelberger Akademie der Wissenschaften, Phil.-hist. Klasse*, 1914, 2. *Abh.*, 1916, 10. *Abh.*
*PGand*, *PSorb.* } = *Quelques papyrus des collections de Gand et de Paris*, ed. M. Hombert, *Revue belge de Philologie et d'Histoire* iv (1925), 633–76: republished in *Sammelb.* iii.
*PGen.* = *Les papyrus de Genève* transcrits et publiés par Jules Nicole, Geneva 1896, 1900.
*PGiss.* = *Griechische Papyri im Museum des oberhessischen Geschichtsvereins zu Giessen*, Bd. I, Hefte 1–3, ed. O. Eger, E. Kornemann, P. M. Meyer, Leipzig etc. 1910–12.
*PGnom.* = *Der Gnomon des Idios Logos* (*BGU* v (1) 1210) ed. W. Schubart 1919.
*PGoodsp.* = E. J. Goodspeed, *A group of Greek papyrus texts* (*Class. Phil.* i, 1906, p. 167).
*PGoodsp.Cair.* = E. J. Goodspeed, *Greek papyri from the Cairo*

Museum .. (*Decennial publications of the University of Chicago*, 1st series, vol. v p. 3), Chicago 1904.

*PGot.* = H. Frisk, *Papyrus grecs de la Bibl. Municipale de Gothembourg*, Göteborg 1929.

*PGrad.* = G. Plaumann, *Griechische Papyri der Sammlung Gradenwitz* (*Sitzungsberichte der Heidelberger Akademie der Wissenschaften*, 1914, 15. *Abh.*).

*PGrenf.* 1. = B. P. Grenfell, *An Alexandrian erotic fragment and other Greek papyri chiefly Ptolemaic*, Oxford 1896.

2. = B. P. Grenfell & A. S. Hunt, *New Classical Fragments and other Greek and Latin papyri*, 1897.

*PGurob* = *Greek papyri from Gurob*, ed. J. G. Smyly (Royal Irish Academy, Cunningham Memoirs, No. 12, Dublin-London 1921).

*PHal.* = Halle Papyri = *Dikaiomata: Auszüge aus alexandrinischen Gesetzen und Verordnungen in einem Papyrus des Philologischen Seminars der Universität Halle, mit einem Anhang..herausgegeben von der Graeca Halensis..*, Berlin 1913.

*PHamb.* = P. M. Meyer, *Griechische Papyrusurkunden der Hamburger Stadtbibliothek* (*Staats- und Universitätsbibliothek* 1924), Bd. 1, Leipzig etc. 1911–24.

*PHarris* = *The Rendel Harris Papyri*, ed. J. Enoch Powell, Cambridge 1936.

*PHaw.* = *The Hawara Papyri*, ed. [Sir] W. M. Flinders Petrie, *Hawara, Biahmu, and Arsinoe*, 1889: in part re-edited by J. G. Milne, *Arch. Pap.* v (1913) p. 378: *PHaw.* 80 and 81 re-edited by U. Wilcken in *Genethliakon für C. Robert*, Berlin 1910, p. 191.

*PHeid.* = *Veröffentlichungen aus der Heidelberger Papyrussammlung* (vol. i = A. Deissmann, *Die Septuaginta-Papyri und andere altchristliche Texte*, 1905; vol. iii (1) = C. H. Becker, *Papyri Schott-Reinhardt*, i, 1906).

*PHib.* = *Hibeh Papyri*, Part I, ed. B. P. Grenfell & A. S. Hunt, London 1906.

*PHolm.* = *Papyrus Graecus Holmiensis*, ed. O. Lagercrantz, Uppsala 1913.

*PIand.* = *Papyri Iandanae: cum discipulis edidit* Carolus Kalbfleisch, Leipzig & Berlin 1912–.

*PJena* = *Jenaer Papyrus-Urkunden*, ed. F. Zucker & F. Schneider, Jena 1926.

*PKaran.* = E. J. Goodspeed, *Papyri from Karanis* (*Univ. of Chicago: Studies in Classical Philology*, vol. iii), Chicago 1902.

*PKlein Form.* = *Stud.Pal.* (q.v.) iii, viii.

*PLeid.* = C. Leemans, *Papyri Graeci musei antiquarii publici Lugduni-Batavi*, tom. i Leiden 1843; tom. ii 1885.

*PLeid.U.* = *Somnium Nectanebi*, ed. B. Lavagnini, *Eroticorum Graecorum Fragmenta Papyracea*, Leipzig (T.) 1922, p. 37: = *UPZ* 81.

*PLeid.V.*, v. *PMag.Leid.V.*

„ *W.*, v. „ „ *W.*

*PLeid.X.* = chemical papyrus in *PLeid.* (q.v.) vol. ii: reprinted in M. Berthelot, *Archéologie et Histoire des Sciences* (Paris 1906), pp. 269–306 (= *Comptes rendus des séances de l'Acad. des Sciences*, tom. xlix): cited by Berthelot's sections.

*PLille* = *Institut papyrologique de l'université de Lille: Papyrus grecs* publiés sous la direction de Pierre Jouguet.., Paris 1907–28.

*PLips.* = L. Mitteis, *Griechische Urkunden der Papyrussammlung zu Leipzig*, vol. i, 1906.

*PLit.Lond.* = H. J. M. Milne, *Catalogue of the Literary Papyri in the British Museum*, London 1927.

*PLond.* = *Greek papyri in the British Museum*, vols. i and ii ed. F. G. Kenyon, vol. iii ed. F. G. Kenyon & H. I. Bell, vols. iv and v ed. H. I. Bell, London 1893–; unpublished papyri (*PLond. ined.*) are cited by inventory No.

*PLond.* 1821, ed. H. I. Bell & W. E. Crum, *Aegyptus* vi (1925) pp. 177–226.

*PLond.*1912–29 = H. I. Bell, *Jews and Christians in Egypt*, London 1924.

*PMag.* = *Papyri Graecae Magicae*, herausgegeben und übersetzt von K. Preisendanz, 2 vols., Leipzig & Berlin 1928, 1931.

*PMag.Berol.* = G. Parthey, *Zwei griechische Zauberpapyri des Berliner Museums*, *Abh. Berl. Akad.* 1865 pp. 109–80; cf. W. Kroll, *Philol.* liv (1895) p. 564 (= *PMag.* 1, 2).

*PMag.Leid.V.* = *Papyrus magica musei Lugdunensis Batavi*, ed. A. Dieterich, *Jahrb. f. kl. Phil.*, Suppl. xvi (1888) pp. 793–818; cited by column and line (= *PMag.* 12).

*PMag.Leid.W.* = Leiden magical papyrus *W.*, ed. A. Dieterich, *Abraxas* (*Festschrift..Hermann Usener..*Bonn), Leipzig 1891; cited by page and line of the papyrus, as in Leemans' edition (= *PMag.* 13, cited by column and line).

*PMag.Lond.* = *PLond.*1.46, 121, etc.

*PMag.Par.*1,2 = C. Wessely, *Wiener Denkschr.* xxxvi (2) (1888) pp. 44–126, pp. 139–148; partly in A. Dieterich, *Eine Mithrasliturgie*, Leipzig 1903, pp. 1ff., and A. Deissmann, *Light from the Ancient East*, London 1919, pp. 258 ff. (= *PMag.*4, 3).

*PMag.Rain.* = C. Wessely, *Wiener Denkschr.* xlii (2) (1893) p. 65.

*PMagd.* = *Papyrus de Magdola*, rééd...par Jean Lesquier, Paris 1912 (*PLille* II 2–4); republished in *PEnteux.*

*PMasp.* = Jean Maspéro, *Papyrus grecs d'époque byzantine*, in *Catalogue général des antiquités égyptiennes du Musée du Caire*, I (Nos. 67001–67124) 1911, II (Nos. 67125–67278) 1913, III (Nos. 67279–67359) 1916. Digits indicating 67(000) omitted in refs., thus, 2 = 67002.

*PMed.Lond.* = *London Medical Papyrus*, No. 155, ed. C. Kalbfleisch in *Papyri graecae Musei Britannici et Musei Berolinensis*, Rostock 1902.

*PMed.Strassb.* = *Papyri Argentoratenses Graecae*, ed. C. Kalbfleisch, *Index lectionum in Academia Rostochiensi* 1901.

*PMerton* = H. Idris Bell & C. H. Roberts, *Catalogue of the Greek papyri in the collection of Wilfred Merton*, London, vol. i 1949.

*PMeyer* = P. M. Meyer, *Griechische Texte aus Ägypten*: 1. *Papyri des neutestamentlichen Seminars der Universität Berlin*; 2. *Ostraka der Sammlung Deissmann*, Berlin (Leipzig) 1916.

*PMich.* = *University of Michigan papyri*, published in *Trans. Am. Ph. Ass.* liii (1922) p. 134.

*PMich.*iii = *Michigan Papyri* vol. iii: Miscellaneous Papyri, edited by J. G. Winter (= University of Michigan Studies, Humanistic Series, vol. xl), Ann Arbor 1936.

*PMich.Teb.* = *Michigan Papyri* vol. ii: Papyri from Tebtunis, in two volumes, Part I, ed. A. E. R. Boak (= University of Michigan Studies, Humanistic Series, vol. xxviii), Ann Arbor 1933.

*PMich.Zen.* = *Zenon papyri in the University of Michigan collection*, ed. C. C. Edgar (= University of Michigan Studies, Humanistic Series, vol. xxiv), Ann Arbor 1931.

*PMilan.* = *Papiri Milanesi*, ed. A. Calderini (Pubbl. di 'Aegyptus', S. Scient., vol. i), Parte i, Collezione Jacovelli-Vita, Milano, Università Cattolica del Sacro Cuore, 1928.

*PMilan.R.Univ.* = *PUniv. Milan.* (q.v.).

*PMilan.*17 = Commentario ad Antimaco da Colofone, ed. A. Vogliano, *PUniv Milan.* i. 17.

*PMonac.* = A. Heisenberg & L. Wenger, *Byzantinische Papyri* (*Veröffentlichungen aus der Papyrus-Sammlung der K. Hof- und Staatsbibliothek zu München* I), Leipzig 1914.

*POsl.* = *Papyri Osloenses*, ed. S. Eitrem, Oslo 1925–.

*POxy.* = *Oxyrhynchus Papyri*, ed. B. P. Grenfell & A. S. Hunt, London 1898–.

*PPar.* = W. Brunet de Presle, *Notices et extraits des papyrus grecs du musée du Louvre et de la bibliothèque impériale* xviii (2), Paris 1865.

*PPar.Wess.* = C. Wessely, *Die Pariser Papyri des Fundes von El Faijûm* (*Wiener Denkschr.* xxxvii (2) (1889) pp. 97 ff.).

*PPetr.* = *The Flinders Petrie Papyri..*, Pt. 1, ed. J. P. Mahaffy (Royal Irish Academy, Cunningham Memoirs, No. 8); Pt. 2, ed. J. P. Mahaffy (ibid., No. 9); Pt. 3, ed. J. P. Mahaffy & J. G. Smyly (ibid., No. 11), Dublin 1891–1905.

*PPrincet.* = *Papyri in the Princeton University Collections*, vol. I ed. A. C. Johnson and H. B. van Hoesen (= Johns Hopkins University Studies in Archaeology No. 10), Baltimore 1931; vol. II ed. E. H. Kase (= Princeton University Studies in Papyrology No. 1), Princeton 1936.

*PRain.* (*NS*) = *Mitteilungen aus der Papyrussammlung der Nationalbibliothek in Wien* (*Papyrus Erzherzog Rainer*). Neue Serie I i (1932), ed. H. Gerstinger; I ii (1939), ed. H. Oellacher; cf. *CPR.*

*PRein.* = *Papyrus grecs et démotiques..*, ed. Théodore Reinach, Paris 1905.

*PRev.Laws* = B. P. Grenfell, *Revenue Laws of Ptolemy Philadelphus*, Oxford 1896.

*PRoss.-Georg.* = *Papyri Russischer und Georgischer Sammlungen*, herausgegeben von Gregor Zereteli, bearbeitet von G. Zereteli, O. Krüger, P. Jernstedt, Tiflis 1925–35.

*PRyl.* = *Catalogue of the Greek papyri in the John Rylands Library at Manchester*, vol. i 1911, ed. A. S. Hunt; vol. ii 1915, ed. A. S. Hunt, J. de M. Johnson, V. Martin; vol. iii 1938, ed. C. H. Roberts.

*PSI* = *Papiri greci e latini* (*Pubblicazioni della Società italiana per la ricerca dei papiri greci e latini in Egitto*), Firenze 1912–; cited by No. of vol., papyrus, and line.

*PSorb.* (i.e. Papyri in the Sorbonne), v. *PGand.*

*PStrassb.* = F. Preisigke, *Griechische Papyrus der kaiserlichen Universitäts- und Landesbibliothek zu Strassburg*, 2 vols., Strassburg (afterwards Leipzig) 1906–20.

*PTaur.* = V. A. Peyron, *Papyri graeci regii Taurinensis musei Aegyptii*, Turin 1826–7.

*PTeb.* = *Tebtunis Papyri*, ed. B. P. Grenfell, A. S. Hunt, J. G. Smyly, E. J. Goodspeed, London & New York, vol. i 1902, vol. ii 1907, vol. iii pt. i 1933, pt. 2 (ed. A. S. Hunt, J. G. Smyly, C. C. Edgar; London & Univ. of California Press) 1938.

*PThead.* = *Papyrus de Théadelphie*, éd. par Pierre Jouguet, Paris 1911.

*PTheb.Bank* = U. Wilcken, *Aktenstücke aus der Kgl. Bank zu Theben* (*Abh. Berl. Akad.* 1886).

*PUniv.Giss.* = H. Kling and others, *Mitteilungen aus der Papyrussammlung der Giessener Universitätsbibliothek*, 1924–.

*PUniv.Milan.* = A. Vogliano, *Papiri della R. Università di Milano*, vol. i, Milan 1937.

*PVarsov.* = G. Manteuffel, *Papyri Varsovienses*, Warsaw 1935.

*PVat.* 11 = *Il Papiro Vaticano Greco* 11 (1. Φαβωρίνου περὶ φυγῆς; 2. *Registri Fondiari della Marmarica*), ed. M. Norsa & G. Vitelli, Città del Vaticano, Biblioteca Apostolica Vaticana 1931. (*Studi e Testi* 53.)

*PWarren* = *The Warren Papyri*, ed. A. S. Hunt, cited from *Studi in onore di S. Riccobono* ii, Palermo 1932, pp. 521–5, and *Aegyptus* xiii (1933) pp. 241–6.

*PWürzb.* = *Mitteilungen aus der Würzburger Papyrussammlung*, von Ulrich Wilcken (*Abhandlungen der Preussischen Akademie der Wissenschaften*, 1933, Phil.-hist. Klasse No. 6), Berlin 1934.

*PZen.Col.* = *Zenon papyri: business papers of the 3rd century B.C.*, ed. W. L. Westermann and E. S. Hasenoehrl, New York, vol. i (*Columbia Papyri, Greek Series*, vol. iii) 1934.

*Raccolta Lumbroso* = *Raccolta di Scritti in onore di G. Lumbroso*, Milan 1925.

*Sammelb.* = *Sammelbuch griechischer Urkunden aus Ägypten* (both inscriptions and papyri), Bde. i, ii ed. F. Preisigke, Strassburg (later Berlin & Leipzig) 1913–22; Bd. iii (6001–7269) [illegible] F. Bilabel, Berlin & Leipzig 1926–7; Bd. iv (7270–7514), Bd [illegible] Heft 1 (7515–7654) ed. F. Bilabel, Heidelberg 1931, 1934.

*Stud.Pal.* = C. Wessely, *Studien zur Paläographie und Papyr*[illegible]*kunde*, Leipzig 1901–.

*Studi Riccobono*, v. *PWarren.*

*Theb.Ostr.* = *Theban Ostraca*..Pt. iii: *Greek texts*, by J. G. Miln[illegible] Toronto (Oxford) 1913.

Thunell *Sitologenpapyri* = K. Thunell, *Sitologen-Papyri aus d. Berlin*[illegible] *Museum*, Uppsala 1924; republished in *PBerl. Leihg.*

*UPZ* = U. Wilcken, *Urkunden der Ptolemäerzeit*: I. *Papyri a*[illegible] *Unterägypten*, Berlin & Leipzig 1922; II. *Papyri aus Oberägypten*[illegible] 1935–.

Wilcken *Chr.*, v. Mitteis *Chr.*

# IV. PERIODICALS

NOTE.—(*a*) Periodicals are cited by No. of vol. except where otherwise stated. (*b*) References to periodicals (unless otherwise explained in the context) are to inscriptions published therein.

*AEM* = *Archäologisch-epigraphische Mittheilungen aus Oesterreich-Ungarn*, 1877–97.

*AJA* = *American Journal of Archaeology*, second series, 1897–.

*AJP* = *American Journal of Philology*, 1880–.

*Abh.Berl.Akad.* = *Abhandlungen der Preussischen Akademie der Wissenschaften* (Berlin), earlier *der Koeniglichen Akademie der Wissenschaften zu Berlin* (cited by Jahrgang).

*Aegyptus*, Milan 1920–.

*Aevum* = *Aevum, rassegna di scienze storiche*, etc. (Università Cattolica del Sacro Cuore), Milan 1927–.

*Africa Italiana* = *Africa Italiana, collezione di monografie*, Rome 1925–.

*Africa Italiana Riv.* = *Africa Italiana, rivista di storia e d'arte*, Bergamo 1927–.

*Albania* = *Albania: revue d'archéologie, d'histoire, d'art et des sciences appliquées en Albanie et dans les Balkans*, i, ii, Milan etc., iii–, Paris 1925–.

*Ann.Épigr.* = *L'Année épigraphique*, published in *Revue Archéologique* (cited by year).

*Annales du Service* = *Annales du Service des Antiquités de l'Égypte*, 1899–.

*Annuario* = *Annuario della regia Scuola Archeologica di Atene*, 1914–.

*Arch.Anz.* = *Archäologischer Anzeiger*, in *Jahrb.* (q.v.).

'Αρχ.Δελτ. = 'Αρχαιολογικὸν Δελτίον, 1915– (cited by year).

'Αρχ.'Εφ. = 'Αρχαιολογικὴ 'Εφημερίς, 1910– (cited by year).

*Arch.Pap.* = *Archiv für Papyrusforschung*, 1900–.

*Arch f.Religionswiss.* = *Archiv für Religionswissenschaft*, Freiburg im Breisgau 1898–.

*Atene e Roma*, 1898–.

*Ath.Mitt.* = *Mitteilungen des deutschen archäologischen Instituts, Athenische Abteilung*, 1876–.

'Αθηνᾶ, 1889–.

*Atti Acc. Napoli* = *Atti della Reale Accademia di Archeologia ecc., Napoli, Nuova Serie*, 1910–.

*Ausonia* = *Ausonia, Rivista della Società italiana di archeologia e storia dell'arte*, 1906–.

*BCH* = *Bulletin de Correspondance Hellénique*, 1877–.

*BphW* = *Berliner philologische Wochenschrift*, 1881–1920. Cf. *Phil. Wochenschr.*

*BSA* = *Annual of the British School at Athens*, 1895–.

*Berl.Sitzb.* = *Sitzungsberichte* (*Monatsberichte* before 1882) *der Preussischen Akademie der Wissenschaften* (Berlin) (cited by year).

*Bull.Comm.Arch.Com.* = *Bullettino della Commissione Archeologica Comunale di Roma*, Rome 1872–.

*Bull.Inst Arch.Bulg.* = *Bulletin de l'Institut archéologique bulgare*, Sophia 1921–

*Bull.Inst.Ég.* = *Bulletin de l'institut égyptien*, cinquième série, Cairo 1907–18.

*Bull.Inst.Franç.* = *Bulletin de l'Institut Français d'Archéologie Orientale*, Le Caire 1901–.

*Bull.Soc.Alex.* = *Bulletin de la Société Archéologique d'Alexandrie*, Alexandria. First Series 1898–1902 (Nos. 1–5); Nouv. Série (vol. i, No. 6–) 1904– (cited by volume).

*Byz.-neugr.Jahrb.* = *Byzantinisch-neugriechische Jahrbücher*, 1920–.

Βυζάντιον = Βυζάντιον, *Revue internationale des études byzantines*, Paris 1924–.

*CQ* = *Classical Quarterly*, 1907–.

*CR* = *Classical Review*, 1887–.

*CRAcad.Inscr.* = *Comptes rendus de l'Académie des Inscriptions et Belles-Lettres* (cited by year).

*Clara Rhodos* = *Clara Rhodos, studi e materiali pubbl. a cura dell'Istituto storico-archeologico di Rodi*, Rhodes 1928–.

*Class.Phil.* = *Classical Philology*, Chicago 1906–.

*Dacia* = *Dacia: recherches et découvertes archéologiques en Roumanie, publ. sous la dir. de* V. Pârvan, Bucarest 1927–.

*Docum. ant. dell'Africa Italiana* = *Documenti antichi dell'Africa Italiana*, Bergamo 1932–.

'Ελληνικά = 'Ελληνικά, ἱστορικὸν περιοδικὸν δημοσίευμα, Athens 1928–.

*Eos, Commentarii Societatis Philologae Polonorum*, Lwów 1894–.

'Εφ.'Αρχ. = 'Εφημερὶς 'Αρχαιολογική, περίοδος τρίτη, 1883–1909 (cited by year).

'Ηπειρωτικὰ χρονικά, 1926–.

*Eranos* = *Eranos: Acta philologica Suecana*, 1906–.

*Ét.de Pap.* = *Société royale égyptienne de papyrologie: Études de Papyrologie*, Le Caire 1932–.

*Glotta*, 1907–.

*Gött.gel.Anz.* = *Göttingische gelehrte Anzeigen* (cited by year).

*Gött.Nachr.* = *Nachrichten der Gesellschaft der Wissenschaften zu Göttingen* (cited by year).

*Harv.Theol.Rev.* = *Harvard Theological Review*, 1908–.

*Hermes*, 1866–.

*Hesperia* = *Hesperia: Journal of the American School of Classical Studies at Athens*, Cambridge, Mass. 1932–.

*Historia* = *Historia, studi storici per l'antichità classica*, 1–9, Milan & Rome 1927–35.

*Istros* = *Istros: revue roumaine d'archéologie et d'histoire ancienne*, Bucarest 1934–.

*Izv.Arch.Comm.* = Извѣстія археологической Комиссіи русской академіи наукъ (Reports of the Archaeological Commission of the Russian Academy of Sciences), Petrograd 1901–18.

*JEA* = *Journal of Egyptian Archaeology*, 1914–.

*JHS* = *Journal of Hellenic Studies*, 1880–.

*JRS* = *Journal of Roman Studies*, 1911–.

*Jahrb.* = *Jahrbuch des* (*kaiserlich*) *deutschen archäologischen Instituts*, 1886– (contains *Arch. Anz.*).

*Jahresh.* = *Jahreshefte des österreichischen archäologischen Institutes*, 1898–; *Beibl.* = *Beiblatt.*

*Klio* = *Klio, Beiträge zur alten Geschichte*, 1901–.

*L'Ant.Cl.* = *L'Antiquité Classique*, Louvain 1932–.

*Leipz.Stud.* = *Leipziger Studien zur klassischen Philologie*, 1878–95.

*Liv.Ann.* = *Liverpool Annals of Archaeology and Anthropology*, 1908–.

*Mél. de l'éc. fr. de Rome* = *Mélanges d'archéologie et d'histoire: École française de Rome*, Paris & Rome 1881–.

*Mélanges Beyrouth* = *Mélanges de l'Université Saint-Joseph*, Beyrouth (*Liban*), Beyrouth 1906–.

*Mém.Inst.Franç.* = *Mémoires publiés par les membres de l'Institut français d'archéologie orientale du Caire*, Le Caire 1902–.

*Mnemos* = *Mnemosyne*, 1852–.

*Mon.Ant.* = *Monumenti antichi pubblicati per cura della Reale Accademia dei Lincei*, 1890–.

Μουσ.Σμυρν. = Μουσεῖον [Σμυρναῖον] καὶ βιβλιοθήκη τῆς Εὐαγγελικῆς Σχολῆς, Smyrna 1875–86 (cited by year).

*Mus.Belg.* = *Musée Belge*, 1897–.

*Not.Scav.* = *Notizie degli Scavi*, Serie v, 1904–.

*Notiz.Arch.* = *Notiziario Archeologico del Ministero delle Colonie*, Milan-Rome 1915–.

*Papers of Amer. School at Athens* = *Papers of the American School of Classical Studies at Athens*, Boston 1882 (publ. 1885)–1897.

*Phil Wochenschr.* = *Philologische Wochenschrift* (incorporating *Berliner philologische Wochenschrift* and *Wochenschrift für klassische Philologie*), 1921–.

*Philol.* = *Philologus*, 1841–.

Πολέμων = Πολέμων, ἐπιστημονικὸν ἀρχαιολογικὸν περιοδικόν, Athens 1929 (only vol. i published, but there are offprints from vol. ii).

ρακτικὰ 'Ακ.'Αθ. = Πρακτικὰ τῆς 'Ακαδημίας 'Αθηνῶν, 1926–.
DAP = *Quarterly of the Department of Antiquities in Palestine*, London 1931–.
ecueil de Travaux = *Recueil de Travaux relatifs à la philologie et à l'archéologie égyptiennes et assyriennes*, 1870–.
end. Pont. Accad. Arch. = *Rendiconti della Pontificia Accademia Romana di Archeologia*, 1921/2–.
Rev Arch = *Revue Archéologique* (cited by year).
Rev.Bibl. = *Revue Bi lique internationale*, Paris 1892–.
Rev.Épigr. = *Revue Épigraphique*, 2 vols., 1913–14 (all published).
Rev.Ét.Gr. = *Revue des Études grecques*, 1888–.
Rev.Hist.Rel. = *Revue de l'histoire des religions*, Paris 1880–.
Rev.Phil = *Revue de Philologie*, Nouv. Série 1877–1926, Troisième Sér. 1927–.
Rh.Mus. = *Rheinisches Museum*, Neue Folge, Frankfurt 1842–1920.
Riv.Fil = *Rivista di Filologia*, 1873–.
Riv.Ist.Arch. = *Rivista del R. Istituto d'Archeologia e Storia dell'Arte*, Rome 1929–.
Röm Mitt. = *Mitteilungen des deutschen archäologischen Instituts, Römische Abteilung*, 1886–.
Sitzb.Heidelb.Akad. = *Heidelberg. Akademie der Wissenschaften. Sitzungsberichte* (*phil.-hist. Klasse*) 1910– (cited by year).
Sokrates = *Sokrates*, Neue Folge, Berlin 1913–24.
Stud.Ital. = *Studi italiani di filologia classica*, nuova serie i–, Florence 1920–.
Syria, Paris 1920–.
Trans.Am.Phil Ass. = *Transactions of the American Philological Association*, 1869–.
Univ. of Eg. Fac. Bull. = *Université Égyptienne, Faculty of Arts Bulletin*, Cairo 1933–.
WkP = *Wochenschrift für klassische Philologie*, 1884–1920. Cf. *Phil. Wochenschr.*
Wien.Sitzb. = *Sitzungsberichte der (Kaiserlichen) Akademie der Wissenschaften in Wien, Philosophisch-historische Klasse*, 1849–.
Wien.Stud. = *Wiener Studien*, 1879–.
Wiener Denkschr. = *Denkschriften der Akademie der Wissenschaften in Wien, Phil.-hist. Klasse*, 1850– (cited by year).
Yale Class. Studies = *Yale Classical Studies*, 1928–.
Zeitschr.d.Savigny-Stiftung = *Zeitschrift der Savigny-Stiftung für Rechtsgeschichte, romanistische Abteilung*, 1880–.

# V. GENERAL LIST OF ABBREVIATIONS

NOTE.—This list contains:

(1) Abbreviations used in the Lexicon or in Lists I–IV, but not explained in those lists.

(2) Abbreviations explained in List I but out of their alphabetical order. For all names of authors List I is to be consulted; the note 'v. I' has been added only to names of works cited without an author's name.

(3) All abbreviations explained in Lists II–IV, with references to those lists.

It does not contain titles of works given in List I under the author's name or under Anonymus.

A. = Aeschylus
*AB* = *Anecdota Graeca*, v. I
A D. = Apollonius Dyscolus
*AEM*, v. IV
*AJA*, v. IV
*AJP*, v. IV
*AP*, *APl.*, v. *Anthologia Graeca*
A.R. = Apollonius Rhodius
*Abh.Berl.Akad.*, v. IV.
abs. = absolute, absolutely
acc. = accusative
acc. to = according to
Act. = Active
*Act.Ap.* = *Acts of the Apostles*
ad loc. = ad locum
Adj. = Adjective
Adv., Advbs. = Adverb, Adverbs
Aeol. = Aeolic
Aesch.Alex. = Aeschylus Alexandrinus
afterwds. = afterwards
Agath. = Agathias
Al. = ἄλλοι, v. Vetus Testamentum
al. = alibi (i.e. elsewhere in the same author)
Alc. = Alcaeus
Alcm. = Alcman
Alex. = Alexis, *when followed directly by a number, otherwise* = Alexander
Amm.Marc. = Ammianus Marcellinus
*An.Ox.*, *Par.* = *Anecdota Oxoniensia, Parisiensia*, v. I
anap. = anapaests
Anat. = in Anatomy
*Anatolian Studies*, v. II
And. = Andocides
*Anecd.Stud.* = *Anecdota Graeca et Latina*, ed. R. Schoell & G. Studemund, v. I
*Ann.Épigr.*, v. IV
*Annales du Service*, v. IV
*Annuario*, v. IV
Ant.Diog. = Antonius Diogenes
Ant.Lib. = Antoninus Liberalis
Antip. = Antipater
Antiph. = Antiphanes
aor. = aorist
ap. = apud (quoted in)
Ap.Ty. = Apollonius Tyanensis
*Apoc.* = *Apocalypse*
Apollon. = Apollonius
App. = Appianus
*App.Anth.*, v. *Anthologia Graeca*
Appellat. = Appellative
apptly. = apparently
Ar. = Aristophanes
Ar.Byz. = Aristophanes Byzantinus
Ar.Did. = Arius Didymus
Arc. = Arcadius *or* Arcadian dialect
Arch. = Archias
*Arch.Anz.*, v. IV
'Αρχ.Δελτ., v. IV
'Αρχ.'Εφ., v. IV
*Arch.Pap.*, v. IV
Archit. = in Architecture
Arg. = Argive *or* Argument
Arist. = Aristoteles
Aristoph. = Aristophanes (the Homeric critic)
Arm. = Armenian
Art. = Article
Ascl. = Asclepiodotus *or* Asclepius
Asclep. = Asclepiades
Asp = Aspasius
Astrol. = in Astrology
*Atene e Roma*, v. IV
Ath. = Athenaeus
*Ath.Mitt.*, v. IV
'Αθηνᾶ, v. IV
Att. = Attic dialect
augm. = augment
Aus. = Ausonius
*Ausonia*, v. IV
Avest. = Avestan

B. = Bacchylides
*BCH*, v. IV
*BGU*, v. III
*BKT*, v. III
*BMus.Inscr.*, v. II
*BpW*, v IV
*BSA*, v. IV
Bacch. = Bacchius
Benndorf-Niemann *Reisen in Lykien*, v. II
*Berl.Sitzb.*, v. IV
Bgk. = Bergk
Bilabel 'Οψαρτ., v III
Blomf. = Blomfield
Boeot. = Boeotian dialect
Buttm. = Philipp Buttmann
Byz. = Byzantine

*CAF* = T. Kock, *Comicorum Atticorum Fragmenta*, 3 vols., Leipzig 1880–8
*CGF* = G. Kaibel, *Comicorum Graecorum Fragmenta*, vol. i fasc. i (all published), Berlin 1899
*CIA*, v. *IG* in II
*CIG*, v. II
*CIL*, v. II
*CMG* = *Corpus Medicorum Graecorum*, Leipzig 1908–
*CPHerm.*, v. III
*CPR*, v. III
*CQ*, v. IV
*CR*, v. IV
*CRAcad.Inscr.*, v. IV
c. gen. pers., etc. = cum genitivo personae, etc.
ca. = circa
Call. = Callimachus
Call.Com. = Callias Comicus
Call.Hist. = Callias Historicus
Callin. = Callinus
*Carm.* = *Carmen, Carmina*, v. I
Cerc. = Cercidas
Cercop. = Cercopes, v. I
Certamen, v. I
cf. = confer, conferatur
*Chron.Lind.*, v. II
cj. = conjecture, conjectured by
Cleobul. = Cleobulus
*Cod.* = *Codex*, v. I
cod., codd. = codex, codices
cogn. = cognate
coll. *or* collect. = collective
*Coll.Alex.* = J. U. Powell, *Collectanea Alexandrina*, Oxford 1925
collat. = collateral
Com. = Comedy, Comic, in the language of the Comic writers
*Com.Adesp.*, v. I
*Comm.in Arist.Graeca* = *Commentaria in Aristotelem Graeca*
Comp. = Comparative
compd. = compound
compos. = composition
*Const.Δέδωκεν*, v. Justinianus
*Const.omnem*, v. Justinianus
Conj. = Conjunction
conj. = conjunctive
constr = construction
contr. = contracted, contraction
copul. = copulative
Corc. = Corcyra, Corcyraean
*Corp.Herm.*, v. I
correl. = correlative
Cret. = Cretan
Cypr. = Cypria (v. I) *or* Cyprian dialect

D. = Demosthenes
D.C. = Dio Cassius
D.Chr. = Dio Chrysostomus
D.H. = Dionysius Halicarnassensis
D.L. = Diogenes Laertius
D.P. = Dionysius Periegeta
D.S. = Diodorus Siculus
D.T. = Dionysius Thrax
Dam. = Damascius
dat. = dative
Decr. = Decretum
defect. = defective
*Delph.* 3(1), (2), v. II
Dem.Bith. = Demosthenes Bithynus
Dem.Ophth. = Demosthenes, Ophthalmicorum Scriptor
Dem.Phal. = Demetrius Phalereus, Historicus
demonstr. = demonstrative
Dep. = Deponent Verb
deriv. = derived, derivation, derivative
Desiderat. = Desiderative
difft. = different
*Dig.* = *Digesta*, v. I
Dim. = Diminutive
Din. = Dinarchus
Dind. = Dindorf (W. *or* L.)
Diog. = Diogenes
Dion.Byz. = Dionysius Byzantius
Dioph. = Diophantus
dissim. = dissimilated
dist., distd., distn. = distinct, distinguished, distinction
disyll. = disyllable
Docum. = Documentum
Dor. = Doric
downwds. = downwards
Dsc. = Dioscorides Medicus
dub., dub. l., dub. sens. = dubious, dubia lectio, dubio sensu

E. = Euripides
*EGF* = G. Kinkel, *Epicorum Graecorum Fragmenta* i (all published), Leipzig (T.) 1877
*EM* = *Etymologicum Magnum*
e.g. = exempli gratia
Ecphant. = Ecphantus

ed. = edited by
edd. = editors
*Edict. Diocl.*, v. II
*Eleg. Alex. Adesp.*, v. I
ellipt. = elliptically
Elmsl. = Elmsley
elsewh. = elsewhere
enclit. = enclitic
Ep. = Epice, in the Epic dialect
*Ep.* = *Epistula*, rarely *Epigram*
*Ep. Col.*, etc. = Epistle to the Colossians, etc., v. Novum Testamentum
'Εφ.'Αρχ., v. IV
*Eph. Epigr.*, v. II
*Ephes.* 2, v. II
Epic. = Epicus
*Epic. Alex. Adesp.*, v. I
Epid. = Epidaurus
Epig. = Epigenes *or* Epigonus
Epigoni, v. I
Epigr. = Epigram
*Epigr. Gr.*, v. II
Epin. = Epinicus
*Epist. Charact.* = *Characteres Epistolici*, v. I
*Epistolographi* = R. Hercher, *Epistolographi Graeci*, Paris (D.) 1873
epith. = epithet
equiv. = equivalent
*Eranos*, v. IV
*Erotici* = R. Hercher, *Erotici Scriptores Graeci*, Leipzig (T.) 1858–9
esp. = especially
*Et. Gen.* = *Etymologicum Genuinum*
*Et. Gud.* = *Etymologicum Gudianum*
etc. = et cetera (i.e. in other authors)
etym. = etymology, etymologically
Eub. = Eubulus
Euc. = Euclides
Eup. = Eupolis
Euph. = Euphorio
euph. *or* euphon. = euphonic
euphem. = euphemistic, euphemistically
Eust. = Eustathius
Eustr. = Eustratius
*Ev. Jo.*, etc. = Gospel according to John, etc., v. Novum Testamentum
exc. = except
exclam. = exclamation
expl., expld. = explanation, explained

*FGrH* = F. Jacoby, *Fragmente der griechischen Historiker*, Berlin 1923–
*FHG* = C. Müller, *Fragmenta Historicorum Graecorum*, 5 vols., Paris (D.) 1841–70
*FPG* = F. W. A. Mullach, *Fragmenta Philosophorum Graecorum*, 3 vols., Paris (D.) 1860–81
f. l. = falsa lectio
fem. = feminine
fin. = sub finem
Foed. = Foedus
*Foed. Delph. Pell.*, v. II
folld. = followed
foreg. = foregoing
fort. = fortasse
*Fr.* = Fragment
fr. = from
freq. = frequent, frequently
Frequentat. = Frequentative Verb
fut. = future

*GDI*, v. II
*GGM* = C. Müller, *Geographici Graeci Minores*, Paris (D.) 1855–61
Gal. = Galenus
gen. *or* genit. = genitive
Geom. = in Geometry
Germ. = German
*Gloss.* = *Glossaria*, v. I
*Glotta*, v. IV
Goth. = Gothic
*Gött. gel. Anz.*, v. IV
*Gött. Nachr.*, v. IV.
*Gp.* = *Geoponica*, v. I
Gr. = Greek
Gramm. = Grammarians, in the language of the Grammarians
*Gramm. Lat.* = H. Keil, *Grammatici Latini*, Leipzig 1855–80

*HGM* = L. Dindorf, *Historici Graeci Minores*, Leipzig (T.) 1870–1
*h. Ap.*, etc. = *Hymnus ad Apollinem*, etc., v. sq.
*h. Hom.* = *hymni Homerici*
Halic. = Halicarnassus
Haussoullier *Milet*, v. II
Hdn. = Herodianus
Hdt. = Herodotus
Heb. = 'Εβραῖος, v. Vetus Testamentum
Hebr. = Hebrew
*Hell. Oxy.* = *Hellenica Oxyrhynchia*, v. I
*Hemerolog. Flor.*, v. I
Heracl. = Heraclas
*Herc.*, v. III
Herm. = Hermann, Hermes, *or* Hermias
*Hermes*, v. IV
Herod. = Herodas
Herod. Med. = Herodotus Medicus
Hes. = Hesiodus
heterocl. = heteroclite
heterog. = heterogeneous
hex. = hexameters
*Hippiatr.*, v. I
*Hist. Aug.* = *Historiae Augustae Scriptores*, v. I
Hld. = Heliodorus, Scriptor Eroticus
Hp. = Hippocrates
Hsch. = Hesychius
*Hymn.* = *Hymnus*, *Hymni*, v. I
hyperdor. = hyperdorian

I.-E., I.-Eur. = Indo-European
*IG*, v. II
*IGRom.*, v. II
*IPE*, v. II
i.e. = id est
ib. = ibidem (i.e. in the same work)
ibid. = ibidem (i.e. in the same passage)
Icel. = Icelandic
Id. = Idem
Il. = Iliad
imper. = imperative
impers. = impersonal
impf. = imperfect
inc loc. = incerto loco
ind. *or* indic. = indicative
indecl. = indeclinable
indef. = indefinite
inf. = infinitive
init. = ad initium
Inscr. = Inscription
*Inscr. Cos*, *Cypr.*, etc., v. II
insep. = inseparable
instr. = instrumental
intens. = intensive
interp. *or* interpol. = interpolated
interpr. = interpreted, interpretation
interrog. = interrogative
intr. = intransitive
Ion. = Ionic
irreg. = irregular
Is. = Isaeus
Iterat. = Iterative
*Izv. Arch. Comm.*, v. IV

J. = Josephus
*JHS*, v. IV
*JRS*, v. IV
*Jahrb.*, v. IV
*Jahresh.*, v. IV
Jo. = Joannes
Jusj. = Jusjurandum

Keil-Premerstein, v. II
*Klio*, v. IV

*LF*, *LW*, v. II
l. = lege
l. c., ll. cc. = loco citato, locis citatis
Lacon. = Laconian
Lat. = Latin
*Leg. Gort.*, v. II
*Leg. Sacr.*, v. II
leg. = legendum
*Leipz. Stud.*, v. IV
lengthd. = lengthened
Leon. = Leonidas (two epigrammatists)
Leonid. = Leonidas Medicus
Lett. = Lettish
Lex = Lex (law)
*Lex.* = Lexicon, v. I
lit. = literally, literal
Lit. Crit. = in Literary Criticism
Lith. = Lithuanian
*Liv. Ann.*, v. IV
Lob. = C. A. Lobeck
loc. = locative
Lyc. = Lycophron
Lyr. = Lyricus, Lyric poetry
*Lyr. Adesp.*, v. I
*Lyr. Alex. Adesp.*, v. I
Lys. = Lysias
Lysim. = Lysimachus

M. Ant. = Marcus Antoninus, v. Marcus
ME., MHG., etc. = Middle English, Middle High German, etc.
Magn. = Magnes
Man. = Manetho
*Mantiss. Prov.*, v. I
Mar. Vict. = Marius Victorinus
Marc. Arg. = Marcus Argentarius
Marc. Sid. = Marcellus Sidetes
Margites, v. I
*Marm. Par.*, v. II
masc. = masculine
Math. = in Mathematics
Med. = Medium, Middle
Medic. = in medical writers
Megar. = Megarian
Megalop. = Megalopolis
Mein. = Meineke
Mel. = Meleager
Meliss. = Melissus
Men. = Menander
Mess. = Messenian
metaph. = metaphorically, metaphorical
metaplast. = metaplastice
metath. = metathesis
metr. = metrically
metri gr. = metri gratia
*Michel*, v. II
*Milet.* 3, 6, 7, v. II
Mitteis *Chr.*, v. III
*Mnemos.*, v. IV
Mod. = modern
Moer. = Moeris
*Mon. Anc. Gr.*, v. II
*Mon. Ant.*, v. IV
Mosch. = Moschus
Μουσ Σμυρν., v. IV
*Mus. Belg.*, v. IV
Music. = in musical writers

*NT* = Novum Testamentum
n. pr. = nomen proprium
neg. = negative
neut. *or* n. = neuter
Nic. = Nicander *or* Nicias
Nic. Dam. = Nicolaus Damascenus
nom. = nominative
Nosti, v. I
*Not. Scav.*, v. IV

OE. = Old English
*OGI*, v. II
OHG. = Old High German
OIr. = Old Irish
Od. = Odyssey
oft. = often
opp. = opposed to
opt. = optative
Orac. = Oraculum
*Orat. Att.* = J. G. Baiter and H. Sauppe, *Oratores Attici*, Zurich 1839–50
orat. obliq. = oratio obliqua
Oratt. = Oratores Attici
Orchom. = Orchomenos
orig. = originally
Osc. = Oscan
*Ostr.*, v. III
*Ostr. Strassb.*, v. III
*Oxy.* = *POxy.*, q. v. (III)
oxyt. = oxytone

*PAlex.* and other abbrevs. beginning with *P*, v. III
*PLG* = T. Bergk, *Poetae Lyrici Graeci*[4], Leipzig 1882 (reprint 1914–15)
*PPF* = H. Diels, *Poetarum Philosophorum Fragmenta*, Berlin 1901
Pall. = Palladius *or* Palladas
Pamph. = Pamphylian
Pap. = Papyrus
paratrag. = paratragoedia
Parm. = Parmenides
Parmen. = Parmenio
parod. = parody
*Paroemiographi* = E. L. von Leutsch & F. G. Schneidewin, *Corpus Paroemiographorum Graecorum*, Göttingen 1839–51
parox. = paroxytone
part. = participle
partit. = partitive
Pass. = Passive
Patron. = Patronymic
pecul. = peculiar
perh. = perhaps
*Peripl. M. Rubr.*, v. I
perispom. = perispomenon
pers., person. = person, personal
Petersen-Luschan *Reisen in Lykien*, v. II
pf. *or* perf. = perfect
Ph. = Philo
Phan. = Phanias
Phil. = Philippus Epigrammaticus
*Phil. Wochenschr.*, v. IV
Philet. = Philetas
Philipp. Com. = Philippus Comicus
Philol. = Philolaus
*Philol.*, v. IV
Philonid. = Philonides; for *Vit. Philonid.* v. infr.
Philos. = in Philosophy
Phld. = Philodemus Philosophus
Phlp. = Philoponus
Phoen. = Phoenix
Pi. = Pindarus
pl. = plural
Pl. = Plato
*Placit.*, v. I
Plb. = Polybius
Plin. = Pliny
plpf. = pluperfect
Poet. = Poeta, poetical
Pors. = Porson
post-Hom. = post-Homeric
pr. n. = proper name
Prep. = Preposition
pres. = present
Prisc. = Priscus Historicus
Prisc. Lyd. = Priscianus Lydus
Priscian. *Inst.* = Priscianus Grammaticus, *Institutio*

iv. = privative
rob. = probable, probably
rob. for = probably to be read instead of
rob. l. = probable reading
Pron. = Pronoun
rop. = properly
roparox. = proparoxytone
roperisp. = properispomenon
rov. = proverbially, proverbial

Q.S. = Quintus Smyrnaeus
q. v., qq. v. = quod vide, quae vide
qn. = question
Quint. = Quintilianus *or* Quinta Versio (v. Vetus Testamentum)

radic. = radical
Ramsay *Cities and Bishoprics*, v. II
*Recueil de Travaux*, v. IV
reflex. = reflexive
regul. = regular, regularly
relat. = relative
rest. = restoration
*Rev. Arch.*, v. IV
*Rev. Épigr.*, v. IV
*Rev. Ét. Gr.*, v. IV
*Rev. Phil.*, v. IV
Rh. = Rhetores Graeci, ed. Walz
*Rh. Mus.*, v. IV
Rhet. = Rhetorical, Rhetoric
*Rhet.* = L. Spengel, *Rhetores Graeci*, 3 vols., Leipzig (T.) 1853-6: i pars ii, iterum ed. C. Hammer 1894
*Riv. Fil.*, v. IV
Roussel *Cultes Égyptiens*, v. II
Ruf. = Rufus
Rufin. = Rufinus
Ruhnk. = Ruhnken
*Rüsch*, v. II

S. = Sophocles
S.E. = Sextus Empiricus
*SIG*, v. II
*SRAM* = C. Müller, *Scriptores Rerum Alexandri Magni*, Paris (D., post Arrianum) 1846
*SVF* = H. von Arnim, *Stoicorum Veterum Fragmenta*, Leipzig 1903
s. v. = sub voce
s. v. l. = si vera lectio
*Sammelb.*, v. III
sc. = scilicet
Sch. = Scholia; see under several authors
Schneid. = Schneider
Schw. = Schweighäuser
*Schwyzer*, v. II
*Scol.* = *Scolia*
sens.obsc. = sensu obsceno
Sext. = Sextus Philosophus *or* Sexta Versio (v. Vetus Testamentum)
sg. = singular
shd = should
shortd. = shortened
signf. = signification
Skt. = Sanskrit
Slav. = Slavonic
Sm. = Symmachus
sq., sqq. = sequens, sequentia
St.Byz. = Stephanus Byzantius
*Stad.* = *Stadiasmus*, v. I
*Stoic.* = *SVF*, q. v.
Str. = Strabo
strengthd. = strengthened
sts. = sometimes
*Stud. Ital.* = *Studi italiani di filologia classica*, 1893–
*Stud. Pal.*, v. III
*Stud. Pont.*, v. II
sub. = subaudi
subj. = subjunctive
Subst. = Substantive
Sup. = Superlative
*Supp. Com.* = J. Demiańczuk, *Supplementum Comicum*, Cracow 1912
*Supp. Epigr.*, v. II
*Supp. Lyr.* = E. Diehl, *Supplementum Lyricum*[3], Bonn 1917
suppl. = supplement
Surg. = in Surgery
susp., susp. l. = suspected, suspecta lectio
syll. = syllable
sync. = syncopated
Syngr. = Syngrapha
synon. = synonymous
Syrac. = Syracuse, Syracusan

*TAM*, v. II
*TGF* = A. Nauck, *Tragicorum Graecorum Fragmenta*[2], Leipzig 1889
t.t. = technical term
*Tab. Defix.*, v. II
*Tab. Defix. Aud.*, v. II
*Tab. Heracl.*, v. II
Tarent. = Tarentum, Tarentine
termin. = termination
Test. = Testimonium
*Test. Epict.*, v. II
Th. = Thucydides
Thd. = Theodotion
*Theb. Ostr.*, v. III
Thebaïs, v. I
Them. = Themistius
Themist. = Themistocles
Theo Sm. = Theon Smyrnaeus
Theoc. = Theocritus
Theod. = Theodorus
*Theol. Ar.*, v. I
Thess. = Thessalian
Thgn. = Theognis
Thphr. = Theophrastus
Ti. Locr. = Timaeus Locrus
Tim. = Timotheus Lyricus
Tim. Com. = Timotheus Comicus
Tim. Gaz. = Timotheus Gazaeus
Tim. *Lex.* = Timaeus Grammaticus
tit. = titulus
Titanomach. = Titanomachia, v. I
tm. = tmesis
Trag. = Tragic, Tragedy, in the language of the Tragic writers
*Trag. Adesp.*, v. I
trans. = transitive
trisyll. = trisyllable
Tryph. = Tryphiodorus
Tull. Sab. = Sabinus (q. v.), Tullius
Tyrrhen. = Tyrrhenian

*UPZ*, v. III
Umbr. = Umbrian
usu. = usually

v. = vide; *also* voce *or* vocem
v. h. v. = vide hanc vocem
v. l., vv. ll. = varia lectio, variae lectiones
Ved. = Vedic
verb. Adj. = verbal Adjective
*Vit. Philonid.* = *Vita Philonidis Epicurei*, v. I
voc. = voce, vocem; *also* vocative
*Vorsokr.* = H. Diels, *Fragmente der Vorsokratiker*[4], Berlin 1922

*WkP*, v. IV
*Wien. Stud.*, v. IV
*Wiener Denkschr.*, v. IV
Wilcken *Chr.*, v. III

X. = Xenophon
X. Eph. = Xenophon Ephesius
Xenoph. = Xenophanes

*Zeitschr. d. Savigny-Stiftung*, v. IV
Zen. = Zenobius
Zon. = Zonas

# VI. SIGNS, ETC.

*, to denote words not actually extant.

=, equal *or* equivalent to, the same as.

( ) Between these brackets stand the Etymological remarks.

[ ] Between these brackets stand the Prosodial remarks.

The Hyphen has for the most part been used without regard to etymology, to represent that group of letters which is common to two or more consecutive words.

⊛, to denote words which also appear in the Supplement.

# A

## A — ἄβαρις

**A α, ἄλφα** (q.v.), τό, indecl., first letter of the Gr. alphabet: as Numeral, α′ = εἷς and πρῶτος, but ͵α = 1,000.

⊛**ἀ–**, as insep. Prefix in compos.: I. α στερητικόν (Sch.Od. .279, etc., cf. Eust.985.16), expressing *want* or *absence* (cf. Arist. *Metaph.*$1022^{b}32$), as σοφός wise, ἄσοφος *un*wise: for n̥, the weak form of the negative *ne*, commonly used in the formation of adjs. and advbs., very rarely in that of vbs. and substs., cf. ἀδώτης, ἀτιμάω, ἀτίω. Before a vowel it usu. appears as ἀν– (exc. where ϝ or *spiritus asper* has been lost, as ἄ-οινος, ἄ-υπνος, when it sts. coalesces with the following vowel, as ἀργός = ἀ-ϝεργός): the forms ἀνάεδνος, ἀνάελπτος are probably misspelt for ἀν-έϝεδνος, –έϝελπτος. Adjs. formed with it freq. take gen., esp. in Trag., cf. ἀλαμπὲς ἡλίου, = ἄνευ λάμψεως ἡλίου, S.*Tr.*691. [ᾰ, exc. in adjs. which begin with three short syllables, which have ᾱ in Ep., and freq. also in Lyr., Trag., and Com.; ἀθάνατος invariably has ᾱθ.] II. α ἀθροιστικόν (Eust. 641.61; τὸ ἄλφα σημαίνει πολλαχοῦ τὸ ὁμοῦ Pl.*Cra.*405c), properly ἁ– since it represents *sm̥-* (cf. ἅμα, εἷς = *sems*), and so in ἁπλόος, ἁθρόος: but freq. ἀ– by dissimilation from following aspirate, as ἄ-λοχος, and hence by analogy in ἄ-κοιτις, etc., q.v.: sts. in the form ὀ–, as in ὄπατρος, ὀγάστριος, ὄζυξ. [ᾰ.] III. α ἐπιτατικόν (Eust. 641.61), strengthening the force of compds., as ἀ-τενής; prob. identical in etymology with II, from which it is distinguished by Gramm., who sts. confuse it with I; v. ἀδάκρυτος. [ᾰ.]

**ἀ–** as a prothetic vowel, usually before a double consonant, as ἀ βληχρός, ἀ-σπαίρω; sts. before a single consonant, as ἀ-μέλγω; before a vowel where ϝ is lost, as ἀ-ϝείδω. [ᾰ.]

**ἆ**, exclamation expressing pity, envy, contempt, etc., in Hom. always ἆ δειλέ, ἆ δειλώ, ἆ δειλοί, Il.11.441, 17.443, Od.20.351, cf. Thgn.351, Theoc.*Ep.*6; also in Lyr., Archil.135, and Trag., A.*Ag.* 1087, etc.; in reproofs or warnings, ἆ, μηδαμῶς .. S.*Ph.*1300, cf. *OT*1147, E.*Hel.*445, etc.:—freq. with adj., ἆ μάκαρ Thgn.1013, Choeril.1; ἆ τάλας Semon.7.76, cf. B.15.30; ἆ τρισευδαίμων Id.3. 10; rarely alone, Ar.*Ra.*759; sts. doubled, ἆ ἆ A.*Pr.*114,566, Ar. *V.*1379.—Rare in Prose, Pl.*Hp.Ma.*293a (Euclus ap.Sch. ad loc. is said to have used it = νῦν).

**ἃ ἅ** or **ἆ ἆ**, to express laughter, *ha ha*, E.*Cyc.*157, Pl.Com.16 (prob. l.), etc.; ἃ ἃ δασυνθὲν γέλωτα δηλοῖ Hsch., Phot., Eust.855.19.

**ἄα**· σύστημα ὕδατος, Hsch., Phot., cf. *Et.Gud.* II. v. ἄας.

⊛**ἀάατος**, ον, (ἀάω) in Il. ⏑ – – ⏑, *not to be injured, inviolable*, νῦν μοι ὄμοσσον ἀ. Στυγὸς ὕδωρ 14.271. II. in Od. ⏑ – ⏑ ⏑, ἄεθλος ἀ. ἐκτετέλεσται 22.5, cf. 21.9, prob. *unimpeachable*, i.e. *decisive.* III. later, *invincible.* κάρτος ἀάᾰτος A.R.2.77. (ἀάϝατος, cf. sq., Hsch.)

**ἀάβακτοι**· ἀβλαβεῖς, Hsch.; cf. **ἀάβηκτον**· μέλαν, ἀβλαβές, *Et. Gud.* (–βυκτον Cyr.)

⊛**ἀᾱγής**, ές, *unbroken, hard*, Od.11.575, Theoc.24.123, etc. (ἀϝαγής, cf. ἄγνυμι.) [First α short ll. cc., long A.R.3.1251, Q.S.6.596.]

**ἄαδα**· ἔνδεια (Lacon.), Hsch. **ἀαδεῖν**· ὀχλεῖν, ἀπορεῖν, *Et.Gud.*, cf. Hsch., Phot.p.3R. (prob. for ἀ-ϝαδεῖν, cf. ἀαδής). **ἀαδένη** (ἀαδέν *Et.Gud.*, Cyr.)· ὑεία κόπρος, Hsch. **ἀαδής**, ές, (for ἀ-ϝαδής) *unpleasant*, cj. for ἀδαής in Thgn.296.

⊛**ἀάζω**, *breathe with the mouth wide open*, Arist.*Pr.*$964^{a}11$. (Onomatopoeic word, for ἀᾶζω, make the sound *aha!*)

**ἄαθι**· αὐτόθι, Cyr.

**ἀάκατος**· τριακάς (Cypr.), *Et.Gud.* **ἀακίδωτος**, ον, (ἀκίς) *barbless*, Cyr. **ἄακτος**, ον, = ἀαγής, Hsch., *Et.Gud.* **ἀάλιον**· ἄτακτον, Apollon.*Lex.*, cf. Hsch.: ἀ.· ἄπληκτον, *Et.Gud.* **ἀανές** (ἄνω)· οὐ τελεσθησόμενον, Hsch.:—also **ἀάνης**· χρήσιμος, Id., *Et.Gud.*

**ἄανθα**, ἡ, a kind of *ear-ring*, Alcm.120, Ar.*Fr.*926.

**ἀάπλετος**, ον, lengthd. Ep. for ἄπλετος, v.l. in Q.S.1.675.

⊛**ἄαπτος**, ον, (ἅπτομαι) *not to be touched, resistless, invincible*, χεῖρες Hom. (mostly in Il., as 1.567), Hes.*Op.*148; κῆτος ἄ. Opp.*H.*5.629. (Ar.Byz. read ἄεπτος (q.v.) in Hom.; cf. ἀπτοεπής.)

⊛**ἄᾱς**, *to-morrow* or *the day after to-morrow*, gen. of ἄα, = ἠώς, read by Zenod. for ἠοῦς in Il.8.470 (cf. Sch.Ven.); as Adv. in Boeot., Hsch.; cf. ἀές.

**ἀασι-φόρος**· βλάβην φέρων, Hsch., *Et.Gud.*, cf. *EM*1.49. ⊛**–φρονία**, ἡ, *folly*, Phot.p.4R. **–φροσύνη, –φρων**, v. ἀεσι–.

**ἀάσκει**· βλάπτει, Hsch.

**ἀασμός**, ὁ, (ἀάζω) *breathing out, expiration*, Arist.*Pr.*$964^{a}18$.

**ἀάσπετος, ἀάσχετος**, v. sub ἄσπετος, ἄσχετος.

**ἀάστονα**· ἀνεύφραντα, Hsch.

**ἀατήρ**, ῆρος, ὁ, *dishonourer*, ἀλλοτρίων λεχέων Man.4.56 s.v.l.

**ἄᾰτος**, contr. **ἆτος**, ον, (ἄω) *insatiate*, c. gen., ἄατος πολέμοιο Hes. *Th.*714; Ἄρης ἆτος πολέμοιο Il.5.388; μάχης ἆτόν περ ἐόντα 22. 218: abs., ἄατος ὕβρις A.R.1.459. [First syll. short in Hes., long in A.R.]

**ἄᾱτος**, ον, = ἄητος (q.v.), Q.S.1.217.

**ἀάτυλον**· ἀβλαβές, Hsch.

**ἀάω**, Ep. Verb (twice in Trag., v. infr.), used by Hom. in aor. Act. ἄᾰσα (ᾄᾰσαν Od.10.68, later ἄᾰσε prob. in Matro *Conv.*29) contr. ἆσα, Med. ἀᾰσάμην (ἀᾱσατο, v.l. ἀάσσατο, Il.9.537) contr. ἀσάμην, Pass. ἀάσθην: pres. only in 3 sg. Med. ἀᾶται Il.19.91:—*hurt, damage*, always in reference to the mind, *mislead, infatuate*, of the effects of wine, sleep, divine judgements, etc., ἄασάν μ' ἕταροί τε κακοὶ πρὸς τοῖσί τε ὕπνος Od.10.68; ἆσέ με δαίμονος αἶσα κακὴ καὶ .. οἶνος 11.61; φρένας ἄασε οἴνῳ 21.297; of love, θαλερὴ δέ μιν ἄασε Κύπρις Epic. ap.Parth.21.2; inf. ἆσαι A.*Fr.*417; part. ἄσας S.*Fr.*628:—Med., Ἄτη ἣ πάντας ἀᾶται Il.19.91:—Pass., Ἄτης, ᾗ πρῶτον ἀάσθην Il. 19.136, cf. Hes.*Op.*283, *h.Cer.*258. II. Intr. in aor. Med., *to be infatuated, act foolishly*, ἀασάμην Il.9.116, etc.; ἀάσατο δὲ μέγα θυμῷ ib.537, 11.340; καὶ γὰρ δή νύ ποτε Ζεὺς ἄσατο 19.95, Aristarch., v.l. Ζῆν' ἄσατο (sc. Ἄτη), cf. Sch.Ven. ad loc.; εἴ τί περ ἀασάμην A.R.1.1333; ἀασάμην .. ἄτην 2.623. (ἀϝάω, cf. ἀτάω.)

**ἄβα**· τρόχος, ἡ βοή, Hsch. **ἀβάγητρον**· λεπτόν, Hsch., cf. ἀβαήρ. **ἄβαγνα**· ῥόδα ἀμάραντα (Maced.), Hsch. **ἀβάδιστος**, ον, *untrodden*, πόντος Sch.Opp.*H.*2.526. **ἄβαζος**· ἥσυχος, Suid. **ἀβαήρ**· ὁ λεπτός, Suid. **ἀβάθ**· διδάσκαλος (Cypr.), Hsch. ⊛**ἀβάθματα**· στρέμματα, Hsch.

**ἀβᾰθής**, ές, (βάθος) *not deep*, φάλαγξ Arr.*Tact.*5.6; *in single rank*, ἡ ἐφ' ἑνὸς ἀ. τάξις ib.17.5, ἕλκεα Aret.*SA*1.9, Gal.11.127. 2. Geom., *without depth*, ἐπιφάνεια S.E.*P.*3.43, cf. Simp.*in Ph.*572.25.

**ἄβαθρος**, ον, *without foundation*, Cyr.

**ἀβαίνω**· στένω, οἰμώζω, Cyr.

⊛**ἀβᾰκέω**, (ἀβακής) *to be speechless*, only in aor., οἱ δ' ἀβάκησαν πάντες *said nothing, took no heed*, Od.4.249.

**ἀβακηνούς**· τοὺς γυναικὶ μὴ ὁμιλήσαντας, Phot., *AB*323.

⊛**ἀβᾰκής**, ές, (βάζω) *speechless*: hence, *calm, gentle*, ἀβάκην (Aeol. acc.) τὰν φρέν' ἔχω Sapph.72. Adv. –κέως, εὕδοντι Poet.ap.*EM*2.57: —also **ἀβακήμων** Hsch., **ἄβαξ** *Lex.Rhet.*ap.Eust.1494.64.

⊛**ἀβάκητον**· ἀνεπίφθονον, Hsch., Phot.

**ἀβᾰκίζομαι**, = ἀβακέω, Anacr.74.

⊛**ἀβάκιον**, τό, = ἄβαξ I.1a, Lys.*Fr.*50, Alex.15.3, Plb.5.26.13. b. = ἄβαξ I.1b, Plu.*Cat.Mi.*90. 2. = ἄβαξ I.2, Poll.10.150. 3. pl., *slabs* (?) in theatre, Suid. s.v. ἄβαξι.

⊛**ἀβᾰκίσκος**, ὁ, Dim. of ἄβαξ, *small stone for inlaying*, in mosaic work, Moschio ap.Ath.5.207c.

**ἀβακλή**· ἅμαξα, Cyr.

**ἀβακοειδής**, ές, *like an* ἄβαξ, Sch.Theoc.4.61.

⊛**ἄβακτον**· τὸν μὴ μακαριστόν (Dor.), Phot., *AB*323; cf. σαβάκτης.

⊛**ἀβάκχευτος**, ον, *uninitiated in Bacchic orgies*, E.*Ba.*472: generally, *joyless*, Id.*Or.*319:—in late Prose, Luc.*Lap.*3, Jul.*Or.*7.221d.

**ἀβακχίωτος**, ον, *having no part in Bacchus, undrinkable*, ὄμβρος, i.e. salt spray, Tim.*Pers.*72.

⊛**ἄβᾰλε** [ᾱβ], properly ἆ βάλε, expressing a wish, *O that ..!* c. indic., Call.*Fr.*455; c. inf., *AP*7.699, $IPE1^{2}$.519 (Chersonesus); cf. βάλε.

**ἀβαμβάκευτος**, ον, *not seasoned*, of food, Pyrgion ap.Ath.4.143e.

⊛**ἄβαξ** [ᾰ], ἄκος, ὁ, *slab, board*: 1. *reckoning-board*, used for counting votes, Arist.*Ath.*69.1. b. *board* sprinkled with sand or dust for drawing geometrical diagrams, S.E.*M.*9.282, Iamb.*Protr.* 34 (pl.), *VP*5.22. 2. *dice-board*, Caryst.3. 3. *sideboard*, Ammon.*Diff.*1. 4. *trencher, plate*, Cratin.86, cf. *BCH*29.510 (Delos, iii B.C.). II. in Lat. form *abacus*, *slab* on capital of column, Vitr.3.5.5. 2. *marble wall-slab*, Id.7.3.10. III. v. ἀβακής.

**ἀβάπτιστος**, ον, (βαπτίζω) *not to be dipped, that will not sink*, ἀ. ἅλμας, of a net, Pi.*P.*2.80; ναῦς *EM*811.26; τρύπανον trepan *with a guard, to stop it from going too deep*, Gal.10.447. II. *not drenched with liquor*, Plu.2.686b.

**ἄβαπτος**, ον, (βάπτω) of iron, *not tempered*, Hsch., Suid.

**ἀβαρβάριστος**, ον, *without barbarisms*, *Lex.Vind.*294. Adv. –τως *EM*331.37. **ἀβάρβαρος**, f.l. for ἀβόρβορος, q.v.

⊛**ἀβαρής**, ές, (βάρος) *without weight*, Arist.*Cael.*$277^{b}19$; ἀβαρῆ εἶναι ἀέρα καὶ πῦρ Zeno *Stoic.*1.27, cf. Chrysipp.*Stoic.*2.143, Plot. 6.9.9, etc.; *light*, γῆ *AP*7.461 (Mel.): metaph., ἀ. χρῆμα *a light* matter, *Com.Adesp.*158; παρρησία .. μαλακὴ καὶ ἀ. Plu.2.59c; of the pulse, Archig.ap.Gal.8.651. II. *not offensive*, ὀσμαί Aret.*CA*2.3; of persons, *not burdensome*, ἀ. ἑαυτὸν τηρεῖν, παρέχειν, 2*Ep.Cor.*11.9, *CIG*5361.15 (Berenice). Adv. –ρῶς *without giving offence*, Simp.*in Epict.*p.85 D.; *without taking offence*, ib.p.88 D.

**ἄβαρις**, (βᾶρις) *having no boat, landsman*, Hsch. **ἀβαριστάν**· γυναικιζομένην (Cypr.), Id. ⊛**ἀβαρκνᾷ**· κομᾷ (Maced.), but **ἄβαρ-**

κνα· λιμός, Id. **ἀβαρλεῖται·** ταράσσεται, κροτεῖ, Id. **ἀβάρνου·** στένε, Id. **ἀβαρταί,** = πτηναί (Cypr.), Id. **ἀβαρύ,** = ὀρίγανον (Maced.), Id. **ἀβάς·** εὐήθης; also = ἱερὰ νόσος (Tarent.), Id. **ἀβάσαι·** ἀριστῆσαι, καὶ ἀρθῆναι, Id.

**⊛ἀβασάνιστος,** ον, *not tortured*, ἀ. θνῄσκειν J.*BJ*1.32.3, cf. Plu.2.273c; κημοῖς ὑπερφὰν ἀ. Ael.*NA*13.9. Adv. -τως *without pain*, βλέπειν τὸν ἥλιον ib.10.14. 2. *untried, unexamined*, ἀ. τι ἐᾶσαι Antipho 1.13; ἀπολιπεῖν Plb.4.75.3; παραλείπειν Plu.2.59c. Adv. -τως *without due examination*, Th.1.20, Plu.2.28b.

**ἀβασίλευτος,** ον, *not ruled by a king*, Th.2.80, X.*HG*5.2.17: generally, *free from rule*, Plu.2.1125d, Artem.1.8.

**ἀβασκάνιστος,** ον, *free from malice*, perh. to be read for ἀβασάν-, Plu.2.755d.

**ἀβάσκᾰνος,** ον, (βασκαίνω) *free from envy*, Teles p.56.1 H.; τὸ ἀ. Ph.1.252; *unprejudiced*, μάρτυς J.*BJ*1.9.4. Adv. -νως M.Ant.1.16.

**⊛ἀβάσκαντος,** ον, *secure against enchantments, free from harm*, *CIG*5053, 5119 (Nubia), *Cat.Cod.Astr.*7.234; esp. of children, *BGU* 8.11, al., *POxy.*300 (i A.D.):—in act. sense, *acting as a charm* or *protection against witchcraft*, ἀ. ἀνθρώποις καὶ ζῴοις v.l. in Dsc.3.91. Adv. -τως, ὑγιαίνειν *POxy.*292 (i A.D.), cf. *AP*11.267. II. Act., *not harming*, *PMag.Leid.W.*18.7.

**⊛ἀβάστακτος,** ον, (βαστάζω) *not to be borne* or *carried*, Plu.*Ant.*16; *not removable*, σημεῖον *IGRom.*4.446 (Perg.). Adv. -τως Hsch.

**ἄβαστον·** ἄβατον, Hsch.

**ἀβατόομαι,** Pass., *to be made desert*, Lxx *Je.*29.20(21).

**⊛ἄβᾰτος,** ον, also η, ον Pi.*N.*3.21:—*untrodden*, ἐρημία A.*Pr* 2 codd.; *impassable*, of mountains, Hdt.4.25, 7.176, S.*OT*719, etc.: ἀβάτου τῆς Ἑλλάδος οὔσης διὰ τὸν πόλεμον Isoc.3.33; of a river, *not fordable*, X.*An.*5.6.9; ἅλς Pi. l. c.; ὕλη Str.5.4.5; εἶναι εἰς ἄβατον to be made *desolate*, Lxx *Je.*29.17, al.: metaph., *inaccessible*, τὸ πόρσω σοφοῖς ἄ. κἀσόφοις Pi.*O.*3.44; οἰκίαι ἄ. τοῖς ἔχουσι μηδὲ ἕν Aristopho 3; ἀ. ποιεῖν τὰς τραπέζας Anaxipp.3; [τὸ ἀγαθὸν] ἐν ἀβάτοις ὑπεριδρυμένον Procl. *in Alc.*p.319C. 2. of holy places, *not to be trodden*, S.*OC*167, 675; ἕρπει πλοῦτος.. ἐς τἄβατα καὶ πρὸς βέβηλα Id.*Fr.*88.7, cf. Porph.*Abst.*4.11; ἄ. ἱερόν Pl.*La.*183b; ἀβατώτατος ὁ τόπος (sc. οἱ τάφοι) Arist.*Pr.*924ᵃ5: metaph., *pure, chaste*, ψυχή Pl.*Phdr.*245a. b. as Subst., ἄβατον, τό, *adytum*, Theopomp.Hist.313, *IG*4.952 (Epidaur.), etc.; = *bidental*, Διὸς καταιβάτου ἄ. ib.2.1659b. 3. metaph., φύσις ἄ. οἴκτῳ Ph.2.53. 4. of a horse, *not ridden*, Luc.*Zeux.*6; of female animals, Id.*Lex.*19. 5. ἄβατον, τό, a plant eaten pickled, Gal.6.623. II. Act., ἄ. πόνος a plague *that hinders walking*, i.e. gout, Luc.*Ocyp.*36; ὑποδήματα Phot., Suid. s. v. ἀναξυρίδας.

**ἀβᾰφής,** ές, = ἄβαπτος, v. sub ἀναφής:—also -ος, ον, *Gloss.*

**ἄβδελον·** ταπεινόν, Hsch.

**ἀβδέλυκτος,** ον, (βδελύσσω) *not to be abominated*, A.*Fr.*137.

**Ἀβδηρίτης** [ῑ], ου, ὁ *a man of Abdera* in Thrace, the *Gothamite* of antiquity, prov. of simpletons, D.17.23:—Adj. **Ἀβδηριτικός,** ή, όν, *like an Abderite*, i.e. *stupid*, Cic.*Att.*7.7.4, Luc.*Hist.Conscr.*2.

**ἄβδης,** ὁ, said by Hsch. to mean *scourge* in Hippon.98.

**⊛ἀβέβαιος,** ον, *unreliable*, of remedies, Hp.*Aph.*2.27; ἀβεβαιότατον ὧν κεκτήμεθα (sc. πλοῦτος) Alex.281, cf. Men.128; ὀφθαλμὸς ἀ. *unsteady*, Arist.*HA*492ᵃ12: metaph., τύχη Democr.176, cf. Plb.15.34.2; αἰτία Epicur.*Ep.*3p.65U.; φιλία Arist.*EE*1236ᵇ19; τὸ ἀ. = ἀβεβαιότης, Hierocl. *in CA*2p.422 M., Heraclit.*Ep.*7; ἐξ ἀβεβαίου from *an insecure position*, Arr.*An.*1.15.2. 2. of persons, *unstable, fickle*, D.58.63, Arist.*EN*1172ᵃ9. Adv. -ως Men.*Georg.Fr.*2.

**ἀβεβαιότης,** ητος, ἡ, *instability*, τῆς τύχης Plb.30.10.1; of persons, D.S.14.9, cf. Ph.1.276.

**⊛ἀβέβηλος,** ον, *sacred, inviolable*, Plu.*Brut.*20, cf. *Cam.*30; of persons, *pure*, *Inscr.Prien.*113.67.

**ἄβεις·** ἔχεις, Hsch. **ἀβέλιος,** i.e. ἀϝέλιος, Cret. for ἥλιος, ἥλιος, Hsch.

**ἄβελλον·** ταπεινόν, Hsch.

**ἀβελτέρειος,** α, ον, lengthd. for ἀβέλτερος, as ἡμετέρειος for ἡμέτερος, Hdn.Gr.1.137; prob. (for -ίου) in Anaxandr.12 (Dind.).

**ἀβελτερεύομαι,** *play the fool*, Epicur.*Nat.*89G.

**ἀβελτερία,** ἡ, *silliness, fatuity*, Pl.*Tht.*174c, *Smp.*198d, D.19.98, Arist.*Pol.*1315ᵃ3, etc.; ἀ. καὶ νωθρότης Id.*Rh.*1390ᵇ30; pl., Phld.*Lib.*p.41O.

**ἀβελτεροκόκκυξ,** υγος, ὁ, *silly fellow*, Pl.Com.64.

**ἀβέλτερος,** ον, (α, ον Pl.*Phlb.*48c) *silly, stupid*, Ar.*Nu.*1201, Antiph.324, Pl.*R.*409c, etc.; δόξαι Polystr.p.29W.; πρός τι Anaxandr.21; ἀ. τι παθεῖν D.19.338: c. inf., ἀ. ἀντιτείνειν Hierocl. *in CA* 10p.434M.: irreg. Comp. ἀβελτερέστερος (s. v. l.) Gal.18(2).337: Sup. -ώτατος Ar.*Ra.*989; of Margites, Hyp.*Lyc.*7. Adv. -ρως Polystr. l. c., Plu.2.127e. (Comic formation, cf. βέλτερος.)

**ἀβέρβηλον·** πολύ, ἐπαχθές, μέγα, βαρύ, ἀχάριστον, μάταιον, Hsch., cf. -λος ἀκατάστατος, Suid.; cf. ἀβύρβηλος.

**ἀβηδών,** i.e. ἀϝηδών, for ἀηδών (prob. Lacon.), Hsch. **⊛ἀβήρ,** i.e. ἀϝήρ, Lacon. word for οἴκημα στοὰς ἔχον, Id.; cf. αὐήρ. **ἀβήρει·** ᾄδει, **ἀβηροῦσιν·** ᾄδουσιν, Id. **ἀβής·** ἀναίσχυντος, ἀνόσιος, Id. **ἀβήσσει·** ἐπινοεῖ, Id.

**⊛ἀβίαστος,** ον, (βιάζομαι) *unforced, without force* or *violence*, Pl.*Ti.*61a; τὸ ἀ. φυλάξει *shall maintain order*, *PThead.*19.21. 2. *unstrained, unaffected*, χάρις D.H.*Dem.*38. 3. *not liable to compulsion*, ἀ. τὸ ἀπαθές Porph.ap.Eus.*PE*5.10. 4. *irresistible*, Sch.Opp.*H.*2.8. 5. Adv. -τως Arist.*MA*703ᵃ22, Aët.9.28, Simp. *in Epict.*p.117D.

**ἀβίβαστος,** ον, = ἄβατος, *POxy.*1380.115, *Gloss.*

**ἀβίβλης,** ου, ὁ, *without books*, Tz.*H.*6.407, 475.

**⊛ἄβιδα·** ἀνδρεῖον, Hsch.

**ἄβιν·** ἐλάτην, οἱ δὲ πεύκην, Hsch. **ἀβίολη·** σπέρμα ἐμφερές, Id.

**ἄβιος,** ον (A), = ἀβίωτος, βίος *AP*7.715 (Leon.). 2. *not t[o be] survived*, αἰσχύνη Pl.*Lg.*873c. II. *without a living, starvi[ng]*, Luc.*D.Mort.*15.3, Man.4.113, Vett.Val.46.12; ἄτεκνος καὶ ἄ. προώλης, an imprecatory form in *CIG*3915.46 (Hierapolis). I[II.] perh. *having no fixed subsistence, nomad*, Ἱππημολγῶν γλακτοφ[ά]γων ἀβίων τε Il.13.6 (various expl. in Nic.Dam.p.145 D.); but pr[ob.] Ἀβίων, pr. n., cf. Arr.*An.*4.1.1, Str.7.3.2, etc.; Ἀ. Σαυρομάται *M[...]* *Belg.*16.70 (Attic, ii A.D.).

**ἄβιος,** ον (B), (α intensive) *wealthy*, Antipho Soph.43.

**ἀβίοτος,** ον, *making life unliveable*, κατακονὰ ἀ. βίου, ἀ. βίου τύ[χα] E.*Hipp.*821, 868; βίοτος *AP*9.574 (v. l. κοὺ βίοτον).

**ἀβίυκτον** (-ηκ- cod.)· ἐφ' οὗ οὐκ ἐγένετο βοὴ ἀπολλυμένου, Hsc[h.] (For ἀϝίυκτον, cf. ἰύζω.)

**ἀβιωτοποιός,** όν, *making life insupportable*, Sch.E.*Hipp.*821.

**ἀβίωτος,** ον, (βιόω) *not to be lived, insupportable*, ἀ. πεποίηκε τὸ[ν] βίον Ar.*Pl.*969; ἀ. ζῶμεν βίον Philem.93.7, cf. 90.7, Boeth.*Stoic.*3.266; ἀ. χρόνον βιοτεῦσαι E.*Alc.*242; ἀ. φέρ' ἔσεσθαι τὸν βίον αὐτ[ῷ] D.21.131; ἀ. ἡγουμένων τὸ καταγνωσθῆναι Phld.*Mort.*35:—ἀβίωτό[ν] [ἐστι] *life is intolerable*, Pl.*R.*407a; ἀ. ζῆν Id.*Lg.*926b; ἀ. ἡμῖν E.*Io[n]* 670. Adv. ἀβιώτως, ἔχειν Plu.*Dio*6; αἰσχρῶς καὶ ἀ. διατεθῆναι Id. *Sol.*7. II. ἀβίωτον, τό, = κώνειον, Ps.-Dsc.4.78.

**ἀβλάβ-εια,** ἡ, *freedom from harm*, σαρκός Plu.2.1090b; for A.*Ag.*1024 v. εὐλάβεια. II. Act., *harmlessness*, Cic.*Tusc.*3.8.16. **⊛-ής,** ές, *without harm*, i.e., I. Pass., *unharmed, unhurt*, Sapph.*Supp.*1.1, Pi.*O.*13.27, *P.*8.54, A.*Th.*67, X.*Cyr.*4.1.3, Pl.*R.*342b, etc.; ζώσαν ἀβλαβεῖ βίῳ S.*El.*650. Adv. ἀβλαβῶς, Ion. -έως, *safely*, ζώειν Thgn.1154; ἔχειν Dexipp.p.148 D., cf. Arr.*An.*6.19.2: Sup. -έστατα X.*Eq.*6.1:—*securely*, ἐδήσατο σάνδαλα *h.Merc.*83. II. Act., *not harming, harmless, innocent*, ξυνουσία A.*Eu.*285; ἡδοναί Pl.*R.*357b, etc.; ἀ. σπασμοί *doing no serious injury*, Hp.*Epid.*1.6; τὸ πρὸς ἀνθρώπους ἀ. Phld.*Piet.*65: c. gen., ἀ. τῶν πλησίον Porph.*Sent.*32: c. dat., Eus.Mynd.1. Adv. -ῶς, c. dat., *without harm to*, τῇ γαστρί Metrod.41. 2. *averting* or *preventing harm*, ὕδωρ Theoc.24.98:—in Pl.*Lg.*953b we have the act. and pass. senses conjoined, ἀ. τοῦ δρᾶσαί τε καὶ παθεῖν. 3. in treaties, *without violating the terms*, ἀβλαβῶς σπονδαῖς ἐμμένειν, coupled with δικαίως and ἀδόλως, Th.5.18 and 47: so in Adj., ξύμμαχοι πιστοὶ.. καὶ ἀ. *IG*1.33. -ία, ἡ, poet. for ἀβλάβεια II, ἀβλαβίῃσι νόοιο *h.Merc.*393; Ἀβλαβίαι personified, *SIG*1014.67 (Erythrae); sg. in later Prose, Phld.*Piet.*28.

**ἀβλαβύνιον·** σειρὰ πλεκομένη παρ' Αἰγυπτίοις ἐκ βύβλων ⟨πρὸς⟩ κάθαρσιν οὖσα, Hsch. **ἀβλαδέως·** ἡδέως, Id. (cf. βλαδαρός). **ἀβλάξ·** λαμπρῶς (Cypr.), Id.

**ἄβλαπτος,** ον, = ἀβλαβής II, Nic.*Th.*488. Adv. -τως Orph.*H.*64.10.

**ἄβλαροι·** ξύλα, Hsch. **ἄβλας·** ἀσύνετος, Hsch. (ἀβλής Cyr.).

**ἀβλαστ-έω,** *not to run to leaf*, Thphr.*CP*1.20.5. II. *not to germinate*, of seeds, Id.*Ign.*44. -ος, ον, *not growing out*, of fibre, Id.*HP*1.2.5:—also -ής, ές, *not growing*, ib.2.2.8; of seeds, *not germinating*, 8.11.7; of places, *unfruitful*, ἐδάφη *CP*2.4.1; τόποι *Gp.*9.9.4 (Comp.): metaph., ἀ. πρὸς ἀρετήν Plu.2.38c; πλοῦτος ἄ. Them.*Or.*18.221d. -ητος, ον, *not striking from cuttings*, v.l. Thphr.*CP*1.3.2.

**ἄβλαυτος,** ον, (βλαύτη) *unslippered*, Opp.*C.*4.369, Philostr.Jun.*Im.*5.

**ἀβλεμής,** ές, (βλεμεαίνω) *feeble*, Nic.*Al.*82; in Lit. Crit. [τὸ πρᾶγμα] ἀβλεμὲς προσπίπτει falls *flat*, Longin.29.1. Adv. ἀβλεμέως, πίνων drinking *intemperately*, Panyas.13.8.

**ἀβλεννής,** ές, (βλέννα) without *mucus*, Apollon.*Lex.*51.32 (glossed by ἄχυμος); as name of fish, = βελόνη II, Diph.Siph.ap.Ath.8.355f.

**ἀβλεπτ-έω,** *overlook, disregard*, τὸ πρέπον Plb.30.6.4, Anon.ap. Suid.; Pass., τὰ -ηθέντα Hp.*Decent.*13. -ῆ· τὸν ἀβλεπτεῦντα, Hsch. -ημα, τό, *mistake, oversight*, Plb.*Fr.*90, Arr.*Epict.Fr.*12. -ος, ον, = ἀτέκμαρτος, Sch.Opp.*H.*1.773. 2. Astrol., = ἀσύνδετος, Firm.2.23.7.

**⊛ἀβλέφᾰρος,** ον, *without eyebrows*, *AP*11.66 (Antiphil.).

**ἀβλεψία,** ἡ, *blindness*, metaph., Suet.*Claud.*39, Hierocl. *in CA*25 p.477M.: c. gen., *failure to see*, Polystr.p.31W. II. *invisibility*, *PMag.Leid.W.*7.5.

**ἄβληρα,** i.e. ἄϝληρα, for αὔληρα, εὔληρα (q. v.), Hsch.

**ἀβλής,** ῆτος, ὁ, ἡ, (βάλλω) *not thrown* or *shot*, ἰὸν ἀβλῆτα an arrow *not yet used*, Il.4.117; cf. A.R.3.279.

**ἀβλήτηρες·** μάρτυρες, Hsch.

**ἄβλητος,** ον, *not hit* (by missiles), opp. ἀνούτατος, Il.4.540.

**ἀβληχής,** ές, (βληχή) *without bleatings*, ἐπαύλιον *AP*9.149 (Antip.).

**ἀβληχρής,** ές, gen. έος, = ἀβληχρός, *mild, soothing*, Nic.*Th.*885.

**ἀβληχρός,** ά, όν, (α euphon., βληχρός, q. v.):—*weak, feeble*, of Aphrodite's hand, Il.5.337; τείχεα 8.178; θάνατος an *easy* death in ripe old age, opp. a *violent* one, Od.11.135, 23.282; πόνος Epicur.*Sent.Vat.*4; κῶμα A.R.2.205; πυρετός Procop.*Pers.*2.22.

**⊛ἀβλοπές·** ἀβλαβές, Hsch. **⊛ἀβλοπία,** ἡ, Cret. = ἀβλάβεια, *GDI* 4986 (Gortyn), 5125 (Oaxos), cf. Hsch.

**ἀβοαί·** εὐχαί, Hsch.

**ἀβοατί, -ατος,** Dor. for ἀβοητί, -ητος.

ἀβοηθ-ησία, ἡ, *helplessness*, Lxx *Si.*51.10. ⊛-ητος, ον; *af-fording of no help, without remedy, incurable*, of disease, Hp.*Acut.*(*Sp.*)33; πάθος Plu.2.454d; of wounds, Plb.1.81.5, etc.; *fatal*, of poisons, Thphr.*HP*9.16.6; ἀ. ἔχειν τὴν ἐπικουρίαν, *unserviceable, useless*, D.S.20.42; νὺξ ἀ. Gal.19.481. Adv. -τως Dsc.*Ther.*12, Gal. 122. II. of persons, *helpless*, Lxx *Ps.*87(88).6, Plu.*Arat.*2, Epict.*Ench.*24; γυνὴ χήρα καὶ ἀ. *BGU*970.8 (ii A.D.). III. Act., *unhelpful*, ἀφιλανθρωπία -ήτους ποιεῖ Phld.*Oec.*p.68J.

ἀβοηθί, Adv. *without assistance*, prob. in Euph.54.2.

ἀβοητί, Dor. -ᾱτί, Adv. (βοάω) *without summons*, Pi.*N.*8.9.

ἀβόητος, Dor. -ᾱτος, ον, (βοάω) *not loudly lamented*, *Epigr.Gr.* 40 (Smyrna). 2. *not noised abroad*, [κλέος] οὐκ ἀ. *IG*2.4174.

⊛ἀβολαία (-βαλ- cod.)· συγγραφή, ὁμολογία, Hsch. ἀβολεῖς· περιβολαί (Sicel.), Hsch.

ἀβολέω, later Ep. for ἀντιβολέω, *meet*, A.R.3.1145; Ep. aor. ἀβόλησαν Id.2.770, Call.*Fr.*455.

ἀβολ-ητύς, ύος, ἡ, *a meeting*, Ion. word, Antim.[108]. -ήτωρ, ορος, ὁ, *one who meets*, Id.58.

⊛ἀβόλλα, ἡ, = Lat. *abolla, thick woollen cloak*, *Peripl.M.Rubr.*6, *CPR*1.27 (ii A.D.).

⊛ἄβολος, ον, (βολή) *that has not shed his foal-teeth*, of a young horse, S.*Fr.*408, Pl.*Lg.*834c, Stratt.52, Arist.*HA*576b15, *IG*2.978: also of an old horse, *that no longer sheds them*, *AB*322. 2. ἄβολα, τά, *an unlucky throw* of the dice, Poll.7.204.

ἀβόρβορος, ον, *without filth*, ψαλὶς οὐκ ἀ. S.*Fr.*367 (-βάρβ- codd.).

Ἀβοριγῖνες, οἱ, = Lat. *aborigines*, D.H.1.9, al.

ἄβορος, ον, *greedy*, Hdn.Gr.ap.Sch.Il.8.178.

ἀβοσκ-ής, ές, (βόσκω) *unfed, fasting*, Nic.*Th.*124. -ητος, ον, *pastureless*, ὄρη Babr.45.10, cf. Eust.307.27.

ἄβοστοι· οἱ αἴτησιν ὑπὸ Λακώνων, Hsch.

ἄβοτος, ον, (βόσκω) *without pasture*, Hsch.

ἀβουκόλητος, ον, (βουκολέω) *untended*: metaph., *unheeded*, ἀ. τοὐτ' ἐμῷ φρονήματι A.*Supp.*929.

ἀβουλ-εί, Adv. *inconsiderately*, Suid.:—also -ί, Ph.1.124.

ἀβούλευτος, ον, *ill-advised, inconsiderate*. Adv. -τως Lxx 1*Ma.* 5.67.

⊛ἀβουλ-έω, *to be unwilling*, Pl.*R.*437c: c. acc. inf., Id.*Ep.*347a:—c. acc., *dislike, object to*, D.C.55.9. II. *not to will*, οὐ γὰρ -ῶν ἐνεργεῖ *without willing*, Plot.6.8.13, cf. ib.21. ⊛-ητος, ον, (βούλομαι) *involuntary*, Pl.*Lg.*733d, Ph.1.561; ἀ. καρδίας κίνησις, ἔκκρισις Gal.2.610, Aët.13.56. Adv. -τως Asclep.Cypr.ap.Porph.*Abst.*4.15, Plu.2.631c, S.E.*P.*1.19. II. *not according to one's wish* or *will*, τὰ ἀ. Zeno *Stoic.*1.53; τύχη Phld.*Mort.*33, cf. Ph.2.392, Plu.2. 599b. -ία, ἡ, *ill-advisedness, thoughtlessness*, Pi.*O.*10.41, Hdt.7. 210, Antipho 4.2.6, Men.16.9 D, etc.; ἐπαρθέντες ἀβουλίῃ Hdt.7.9. γ'; ἐξ ἀ. πεσεῖν, ἀβουλίᾳ πεσεῖν S.*El.*398,429: pl., A.*Th.*750, Hdt. 8.57. 2. *irresolution*, Th.5.75; *indecision*, Democr.119. ⊛-ος, ον, *inconsiderate, ill-advised*, S.*Ant.*1026, Men.*Pk.*382, *Anacreont.*12. 4; τέκνοισι Ζῆν' ἄβουλον *taking no thought* for them, *unfeeling*, S.*Tr.* 140, cf. *El.*546, E.*Heracl.*152: Comp., Th.1.120.7: Sup., Plu.*Dio*43. Adv. -ως Hdt.3.71; οὐκ ἀ. Pherecr.143.6; ἀ. καὶ ἀθέως Antipho 1. 23: Sup. ἀβουλότατα Hdt.7.9.β', Plb.*Fr.*92.

ἀβουσκολεῖ· θορυβεῖ, Hsch.

ἀβούτης, ου, ὁ, (βοῦς) *without oxen*, i.e. *poor*, Hes.*Op.*451.

ἄβουτον· τὴν οὐλίαν (Arg.), Hsch.

⊛ἄβρα, ἡ, *favourite slave*, Men.64.3, al., Lxx *Ge.*24.61, *Ex.*2.5, al., Plu.*Caes.*10, Aristaen.1.22, Luc.*Tox.*14. (Prob. Semitic; written by some Gramm. ἅβρα, cf. *AB*322.)

ἀβράβεσθαι· ἁβρύνεσθαι, Hsch.

ἀβραμίδιον, τό, Dim. of sq., Xenocr.78.

ἀβρᾱμίς, or ἄβραμις, ιδος, ἡ (also ἀβραβίς, *PLond.ined.*2184 (iii A.D.)), kind of *mullet*, salted in Egypt, Ath.7.312b, *PLond.ined.* 2143 (ii A.D.), Opp.*H.*1.244.

⊛ἀβραμύας, ὁ, *throw at dice*, Hsch. ἀβράνας, Celtic word = κερκοπίθηκος, Id. ἀβρανίδας· κροκευτούς (Lacon.), Id.

⊛ἄβραχος, ον, prob. = ἄβροχος, *not steeped*, στροβίλια *PMag.Berol.* 1.245.

⊛ἄβρεκτος, ον, = ἄβροχος, Hp.*Aff.*52, Plu.2.381c, Mosch.2.114.

ἀβρεμής· ἀβλεπτής (Cypr.), Hsch.

ἀβρίζομαι, Med. or Pass., = ἁβρύνομαι, Hsch. (in Lacon. form -ἰδδ-).

ἀβρῖθής, ές, *of no weight*, βάρος μὲν οὐκ ἀβριθὲς E.*Supp.*1125.

ἄβρικτος, ον, (βρίζω) *wakeful*, Hsch., Suid.:—ἀβρίξ, Adv., Hsch.

ἀβρινά· κεκαθαρμένα, Hsch. ἀβριστήν· μαστιγίαν, Id.

ἁβρο-βάτης, ου, ὁ, *softly* or *delicately stepping*, A.*Pers.*1072; Subst. in B.3.48. -βιος, ον, *living delicately, effeminate*, Ἴωνες B.17.2, cf. Plu.*Demetr.*2 (Sup.), D.P.968, Alciphr.1.12. -βόστρυχος, ον, = ἁβροκόμης, Tz.*H.*1.230. -γοος, ον, *wailing womanishly*, A.*Pers.*541. -δαις, ὁ, ἡ, *luxurious*, ἁβρόδαιτι τραπέζῃ Archestr. *Fr.*61.1. -δίαιτα, ἡ, *luxurious living*, a faulty compd., *AB*322, Suid., Ael.*VH*12.24 (in lemmate). -δίαιτος, ον, *living delicately*, ἁβροδιαίτων Λυδῶν ὄχλος A.*Pers.*41, cf. Epigr.ap.Clearch.4: τὸ ἁ. *effeminacy*, Th.1.6, Ath.12.513c; ἁ. βίος, *luxurious*, Diog.Oen.23. Adv. -τως Ph.1.324. -είμων, ον, (εἷμα) *softly clad*, *Com.Adesp.* 1275. -καρπον, = ἁβρότονον, Hsch.

⊛ἁβρο-κόμης, ου, ὁ, *with luxuriant foliage*, φοῖνιξ E.*Ion* 920, *IT* 1099. II. *with delicate hair*, Orph.*H.*56.2, Nonn.*D.*13.91, al.; (with play on both meanings) *AP*12.256 (Mel.):—also -κομος, ον, Nonn.*D.*13.456, Man.2.446.

ἀβρομία· σκοτεία, Hsch.

ἀβρόμιος, ον, *without Bacchus* *AP*6.291 (Antip.).

ἁβρομίτρης, ου, ὁ, *with dainty girdle*, Hsch.

ἄβρομος, ον, (ἀ collect.) *joining in a shout*, Il.13.41; taken by Aristarch. to mean *noisy* (ἀ intens.). 2. (ἀ priv.) *noiseless*, κῦμα A.R.4.153. II. v. ἄβρωμος.

ἁβροπάρθενοι χοροί, *consisting of delicate maidens*, *Lyr.Alex.Adesp.* 22.

ἁβρο-πέδῑλος, ον, *soft-sandalled*, Ἔρως *AP*12.158 (Mel.). ⊛-πενθής, ές, v. ἀκροπενθής. -πέτηλος, ον, *with soft leaves*, Jo.Gaz.*Ecphr.* 2.2. -πηνος, ον, (πήνη) *of delicate texture*, Lyc.863. -πλουτος, ον, *richly luxuriant*, χαίτη E.*IT*1148.

⊛ἁβρός, ά, όν, poet. also ός, όν:—*graceful, delicate, pretty*, παρθένος Hes *Fr.*218; παῖς, Ἔρως Anacr.17, 65; ἅβραι Χάριτες Sapph.60; esp. of the body, σῶμα, πούς, etc., Pi.*O.*6.55, E.*Tr.*506; neut. pl., ἁβρὰ παρηΐδος *Ph.*1486; of women, A.*Fr.*313, S.*Tr.*523; ἁ. ἄθυρμα, of a pet dog, *IG*14.1647 (Lipara): of things, *splendid*, στέφανος, κῦδος, πλοῦτος Pi.*I.*8.65, *O.*5.7, *P.*3.110: of style, *graceful, pretty*, λόγος Hermog.*Id.*2.5; freq. with a notion of disparagement, *dainty, luxurious*; hence, ἁβρὰ παθεῖν live *delicately*, Sol.24.4, Thgn.474; a common epithet of Asiatics, Hdt.1.71, etc.; Ἰώνων ἁβρὸς.. ὄχλος Antiph. 91; Ἀγάθυρσοι -ότατοι ἀνδρῶν Hdt.4.104. Adv. ἁβρῶς, ψάλλειν Anacr.17; ὑμνεῖν Stesich.37; βαίνειν step *delicately*, Sapph.5, E.*Med.* 831: neut. sg. as Adv., ἁβρὸν βαίνοντες E.*Med* 1164; neut. pl., ἁβρὰ γελᾶν *Anacreont.*41.3, 42.5: Comp. ἁβροτέρως, ἔχειν Hld.1.17.— Chiefly poet., never in old Ep.; rare in early Prose, X.*Smp.*4.44, Pl.*Smp.*204c, Clearch.4. [ᾰ by nature, cf. E.*Med.*1164, *Tr.*820.]

ἁβροσία, ἡ, = ἁβροσύνη, Sch.E.*Or.*349.

ἁβροσταγής, ές, (στάζω) *dropping rich unguents*, μέτωπον Anon. ap.Suid. s.v. ἁβρός.

ἁβροσύνη, ἡ, = ἁβρότης, Sapph.79, E.*Or.*349, Xenoph.3.1 (pl.).

ἁβρόσφυρος, ον, *with delicate ankles*, Ναΐδες *Lyr.Alex.Adesp.*3.3.

ἀβροτάζω, *miss*, c. gen., only in aor. 1 subj., μήπως ἀβροτάξομεν (Ep. for -ωμεν) ἀλλήλοιιν Il.10.65:—Subst. ἀβρόταξις, εως, ἡ, *error*, Hsch., Eust.789.52: Adj. ἀβροτήμων, ον, *erring*, in Hsch., *AB*322. (For ἀμ(β)ρ-τάζω, cf. ἀμβροτ-εῖν, ἁμαρτ-εῖν.)

⊛ἁβρότης, ητος, ἡ, *splendour, luxury*, δόμους ἁβρότατος houses *of luxury*, i.e. *luxurious*, Pi.*P.*11.34, cf. B.*Fr.*26; τῇ Μήδων στολῇ καὶ ἁβρότητι X.*Cyr.*8.8.15, cf. Pl.*Alc.*1.122c, E.*Ba.*968; οὐκ ἐν ἁβρότητι κεῖσαι thou art not in a position *to be fastidious*, Id.*IA*1343; also, ἁβρότατος ἔπι in *the freshness of youth*, Pi.*P.*8.89. II. of style, *sweetness, charm*, Hermog.*Id.*1.12.

ἁβρότῑμος, ον, *delicate and costly*, προκαλύμματα A.*Ag.*690 (lyr.).

ἀβροτίνη, ἡ, = ἁμαρτωλή, Hsch.; cf. ἀβροτάζω.

ἁβροτόν-ινος, η, ον, *made of* ἁβρότονον, ἔλαιον Dsc.1.50. -ίτης οἶνος wine *prepared with* ἁβρότονον, Dsc.5.52.

⊛ἁβρότονον or ἀβρ-, τό, *wormwood*, *Artemisia arborescens*, Thphr. *HP*6.7.3, Nic.*Th.*92, etc.; ἁ. ἄρρεν, *southernwood*, *Artemisia fragrans*, Gal.11.804; ἁ. θῆλυ, *lavender cotton*, *Santolina Chamaecyparissus*, Dsc.3.24; written ἀβούτονον Ps.-Dsc. l.c.

ἄβροτος, ον, also η, ον, = ἄμβροτος (q.v.), *holy*, in Hom. only once, νὺξ ἀβρότη Il.14.78; ἀβρότη alone = νύξ, Eust. ad loc. II. *without men, deserted of men*, ἀβρότον εἰς ἐρημίαν v.l. for ἄβατον A.*Pr.*2, as quoted by Sch.Ven.Il.14.78.

ἁβροχαίτης, ου, ὁ, = ἁβροκόμης, *Anacreont.*41.8.

ἀβροχ-έω, *not to be inundated*, *BGU*973.14, *PFay.*33 (ii A.D.), etc. -ία, ἡ, *want of rain, drought*, Men.Eph.ap.J.*AJ*8.13.2, Heph.*Astr.*1.23, S.E.*M.*9.203. 2. in Egypt, *failure of the inundation* of the Nile, *OGI*56.15 (pl., iii B.C.), cf. *CPHerm.*119 ii 22 (iii A.D.). ⊛-ικός, ή, όν, = ἄβροχος, *PFlor.*286.23 (vi A.D.). -ιστος, ον, = foreg., *PGoodsp.*15.22 (iv A.D.). -ος, ον, (βρέχω) *unwetted, unmoistened*, Aeschin.2.21, Nic.*Th.*339, Sotion p.183 W.; κατὰ πόντον ἀ. ἀΐσσεις Mosch.2.143 (v.l. ἄτρομος): c. gen., ἅλμης Nonn.*D.*1.75. Adv. -χως *without getting wet*, Lib.*Or.*11.217. 2. *wanting rain, waterless*, πεδία E.*Hel.*1485; Ἀρκαδίη Call.*Jov.*19. 3. *not inundated*, *PHib.*1.85 (iii B.C.), *BGU*455 (i A.D.), etc.

⊛ἁβροχίτων [ῐ], ωνος, ὁ, ἡ, *in soft tunic, softly clad*, *AP*9.538; epith. of Dionysus, *Inscr.Cos*5.11; εὐνὰς ἁβροχίτωνας beds *with soft coverings*, A.*Pers.*543.

ἄβρυνα (ἄβρ- Hsch.), τά, *mulberries* (Cypr.), Parth.ap.Ath.2. 51f, cf. *AB*224.

ἁβρ-υντής, οῦ, ὁ, *coxcomb, fop*, Adam.1.23. ⊛-ύνω, (ἁβρός) *make delicate, treat delicately*, μὴ γυναικὸς ἐν τρόποις ἐμὲ ἅβρυνε A.*Ag.* 919: *deck out*, εἰς γάμον ἁβρῦναί τινα *AP*6.281 (Leon.):—Med. or Pass., *live delicately*; hence, *wax wanton, give oneself airs*, ἁβρύνεται γὰρ πᾶς τις εὖ πράσσων πλέον A.*Ag.*1205, cf. S.*OC*1339; ἐκαλλυνόμην τε καὶ ἡβρυνόμην ἄν Pl.*Ap.*20c: c. dat. rei, *pride, plume oneself on* a thing, οὐχ ἁβρύνομαι τῷδ' E.*IA*858; ἡβρύνετο τῷ βραδέως διαπράττειν X.*Ages.*9.2; οἷς ὁ τῶν γυναικῶν ἁβρύνεται βίος Clearch.9.

ἄβρυστος· ἢ ἄβροστος ἢ ὁ βιβρωσκόμενος, Hsch. ἀβρυτός, = βρύσσος, Id.

ἄβρωμα, τό, *a woman's garment*, Hsch.

⊛ἄβρωμος, ον, *free from smell*, Diph.Siph.ap.Ath.8.355b, Xenocr. 9, Dsc.1.16, Aët.9.1. (ἄβρομος is a common v.l.)

Ἅβρων, ωνος, ὁ, *Abron*, an Argive, proverbial for luxurious living, Ἅβρωνος βίος Suid., Zen.1.4.

ἀ-βρώς, ῶτος, ὁ, ἡ, *not devoured*; hence, *not bitten* by mosquitoes, *AP*9.764 (Paul. Sil.). ⊛-βρωσία, ἡ, *want of food, fasting*, Poll.

6.39. ⊛-**βρωτος**, ον, (βιβρώσκω) *uneatable, not good for food*, κρέα Ctes.*Fr.*57.26, cf. Arist.*HA*618ᵃ1, Phanias Hist.34, Thphr.*HP*3.12.2; ὀστᾶ Men.129. 2. *not eaten*, Nic.*Fr.*74.44; οὐδὲν ἄ. περιλείποντες Porph.*Abst.*2.27:—of wood, *not eaten* by worms, Thphr.*HP* 5.1.2. II. of persons, *without eating*, S.*Fr.*967; ἄ., ἄποτος Charito 6.3.

**Ἄβῡδος**, ἡ, *Abydos*, on the Asiatic side of the Hellespont:—**Ἀβυδόθεν**, Adv. *from Abydos*, Il.4.500; **Ἀβυδόθι**, *at Abydos*, 17.584:—Adj. **Ἀβυδηνός**, ή, όν, *of* or *from Abydos*, Ath.13.572e, etc.: prov., Ἀ. ἐπιφόρημα a dessert *of Abydos*, i. e. *something unpleasant*, variously expl., Zen.1.1, etc.; μὴ εἰκῇ τὴν Ἄβυδον (sc. πατεῖν) Paus.Gr.*Fr.*2: **Ἀβυδοκόμης** (Ἀβυδηνοκώμης or -κόμος Zen. 1.1), ου, ὁ, = ὁ ἐπὶ τῷ συκοφαντεῖν κομῶν, Ar.*Fr.*733.

**ἀβύθητος**, ον, = sq., Sch.Opp.*H.*2.216.

**ἄβυθος**, ον, = ἄβυσσος, εἴς τινα ἄ. φλυαρίαν Pl.*Prm.*130d (sed leg. εἴς τινα βυθὸν φλυαρίας).

**ἀβύρ-βηλος**, = ἀβέρ-, Hsch., Phot., Suid.; **-βητος**, *EM*4.52.

**ἀβύρσευτος**, ον, *untanned*, Sch.Il.2.527.

**ἀβυρτ-άκη** [ᾰκ], ἡ, *sour sauce of leeks, cress, and pomegranate-seeds*, Pherecr.181, Theopomp.Com.17, Alex.141.13, Nymphod.19, Polyaen.4.3.32. **-ακοποιός**, όν, *making* ἀβυρτάκη, Demetr. Com.Nov.1.5. **-ακώδης**, ες, *like* ἀβυρτάκη, Hsch. s. v. νεοδάρτης.

**ἄβυσσος**, ον, *bottomless, unfathomed*, πηγαί Hdt.2.28; ἄτης ἄβυσσον πέλαγος A.*Supp.*470; χάσματα E.*Ph.*1605; λίμνη Ar.*Ra.*137: generally, *unfathomable, boundless*, πλοῦτος A.*Th.*948; ἀργύριον Ar. *Lys.*174; φρένα Δίαν καθορᾶν, ὄψιν ἄβυσσον A.*Supp.*1058. II. ἡ ἄ. *the great deep*, Lxx *Ge.*1.2, etc.: *the abyss, underworld*, *Ev. Luc.*8.31, *Ep.Rom.*10.7, *Apoc.*9.1, etc.; *the infinite void*, *PMag.Par.* 1.1120, cf. *PMag.Lond.*121.261.

**ἀβῶ**· ἐπινοῶ, Cyr.; fut. ἀβήσω, Id.: **ἀβώ**, v. ἀβώρ.

**ἀβωλόκοπος**, ον, *not hoed*, Poll.1.246.

**ἄβωλος**, ον, *not mixed with clods of earth*, πυρός, etc., *PTeb.*370.13 (ii A.D.), etc.

**ἀβώρ**, i.e. ἀϝώρ, Lacon. for ἠώς, and **ἀβώ** = πρωΐ, Hsch.

**ἄβως** or **ἀβῶς**, (βοή) *speechless*, Hsch., *EM*4.54. (Ion. form.)

**ἀγ**, apoc. form of ἀνά before κ, γ, χ. v. ἀνά init.

**ἀγα-**, intensive prefix, *very*, as ἀγα-κλεής, etc., cf. ἄγαν. (Prob. for *mga*, reduced form of μέγα.)

**ἄγᾱ**, Dor. for ἄγη.

**ἀγάασθαι, ἀγάασθε**, Ep. forms from ἄγαμαι, Od.

⊛**ἀγάζηλοι**· μεγαλόζηλοι, οἱ δὲ φθονεροί, *EM*5.29.

⊛**ἀγάζω**, (ἄγαν) *exalt overmuch*, τὰ θεῶν μηδὲν -ειν A.*Supp.*1061, cf. S.*Fr.*968. II. Med., *honour, adore*, λοιβαῖσιν Pi.*N.*11.6, cf. Orph.*A.*64.

**ἀγαθάγγελος**, *bringing good tidings*, trans. of Persian Οἰβάρας, Nic.Dam.p.53.14 D.

**ἀγαθαίνω**, = -ύνω, Simp. *in Epict.*p.70 D.

**ἀγαθειίκελος**, ον, *like the good*, Hdn.*Epim.*187.

⊛**ἀγαθίδιον**, τό, Dim. of ἀγαθίς, Paul.Aeg.2.57, Hsch. s. v. τολύπη.

**ἀγαθικός**, ή, όν, = ἀγαθός, Epich.99.

**ἀγᾰθίς**, ίδος (ῐ Hdn.Gr.2.18), ἡ, *ball of thread*, Pherecyd.148 J., Aen.Tact.31.19, Orib.*Fr.*57, etc.; ἀγαθῶν ἀγαθίδες, prov., *quantities of goods*, *Com.Adesp.*827. II. = σησαμίς, Hsch., Eust.1366.33.

**ἀγαθο-γονία**, ἡ, *production of good*, Iamb. *in Nic.*82.22. **-δαιμονέω**, Astrol., *occupy the house of* ἀγαθοδαίμων III, Vett.Val.62.20, Paul.Al.*O.*3: **-δαιμονητικός**, ή, όν, *belonging thereto*, Jul.Laod. in *Cat.Cod.Astr.*5.184. **-δαιμονισταί**, οἱ, *guests who drink only to the* ἀγαθὸς δαίμων (cf. δαίμων): hence, *moderate drinkers*, Arist. *EE*1233ᵇ3: **-δαιμονιασταί**, a club of such drinkers, *IG*12(1).161 (Rhodes). ⊛**-δαίμων**, ονος, ὁ, *the good Genius*, less correct for ἀγαθὸς δαίμων, A.D.*Adv.*60.15, *PMag.Leid.W.*17.25. II. *an Egyptian serpent*, *Hist.Aug.Elag.*28, Philum.*Ven.*29. III. Astrol., *propitious region* (east of μεσουράνημα), Vett.Val.135.32. **-δοσία**, ἡ, (δόσις) *the giving of good*, Alex.Aphr. *in Metaph.* 707.19. **-δότης**, ου, ὁ, *the giver of good*, Diotog.ap.Stob.4.7.62. Adv. -δότως Eustr. *in EN*387.11. ⊛**-ειδής**, ές, *like good, seeming good*, opp. ἀγαθός, Pl.*R.*509a, etc. II. *having the form of good*, Plot.1.7.1, al., Jul.*Or.*4.135a, Procl.*Inst.*25: Comp., Iamb.*Protr.*4: Sup., Marin.*Procl.*27. ⊛**-εργασία**, ἡ, = ἀγαθοεργία, Procop.*Aed.*1.7. **-εργέω**, *do good* or *well*, 1*Ep.Ti.*6.18: contr. **-ουργέω**, *Act.Ap.*14.17. **-εργία**, Ion. -ίη, contr. -ουργία, ἡ, *good deed, service*, Hdt.3.154,160, Jul.*Or.*4.135d. 2. *beneficence*, Procl. *in Cra.*pp.13,90 P. **-εργός** (contr. **-ουργός**, Plu.2.1015e, Procl.*Inst.*122), όν, *doing good*, Jul.*Or.*4.144d, Dam. *Isid.*296, Procl. *in Alc.*p.54 C.:—οἱ Ἀ., at Sparta, *Commissioners sent on foreign service*, Hdt.1.67. **-θέλεια**, ἡ, *desire of good*, Anon.ap.Suid. **-θελής**, ές, *benevolent*, Antigonus ap.Heph.*Astr.* 2.18, *Gloss.* **-λογέω**, *use fair words*, Eust.378.30. **-ποιέω**, *do good*, *Ev.Marc.*3.4, S.E.*M.*11.70, Aesop.66. 2. ἀ. τινά *do good to*, *Ev.Luc.*6.33: c. dupl. acc., Lxx *Nu.*10.32, Aristeas 242: τινί Lxx 2*Ma.*1.2. 3. *make good*, τι Plot.6.7.22; τὰ κακά *Corp.Herm.* 9.4. 4. Astrol., *make favourable*, Vett.Val.203.32: Pass., Jul.Laod. in *Cat.Cod.Astr.*5(1).185. b. *exert beneficent influence*, Procl. *Par.Ptol.*292. II. *do well, act rightly*, 1*Ep.Pet.*2.15. **-ποίησις**, ἡ, *well-doing*, Eustr. *in EN*17.25. **-ποιία**, ἡ, = foreg., 1*Ep. Pet.*4.19, al. II. *propitious influence*, Vett.Val.164.17, Ptol.*Tetr.* 38. **-ποιός**, όν, *beneficent*, Lxx *Si.*42.14, Plu.2.368b, Porph.*Marc.* 17; of the King of Persia, Men.Prot.p.16 D.: c. gen., -ποιὲ τῆς οἰκουμένης *PMag.Lond.*122.16. II. Astrol., *exerting beneficent influence*, Ptol.*Tetr.*19, Artem.4.59, *PMag.Lond.*46.48, etc. b. *creating the Good*, Dam.*Pr.*33.

⊛**ἀγᾰθός** [ᾰγ], ή, όν, Lacon. ἀγασός Ar.*Lys.*1301, Cypr. ἀζα *GDI*57:—*good*: I. of persons, 1. *well-born, gen*[tle], opp. κακός, δειλός, οἷά τε τοῖς ἀγαθοῖσι παραδρώωσι χέρηες Od. 324, cf. Il.1.275; ἀφνειός τ' ἀ. τε Il.13.664, cf. Od.18.276; πατ[ρὸς] δ' εἴμ' ἀγαθοῖο, θεὰ δέ με γείνατο μήτηρ Il.21.109, cf. Od.4.611; κα[κῶν] ἐξ ἀ. Thgn.190, cf. 57 sq.; πραῢς ἀστοῖς, οὐ φθονέων ἀγαθοῖς Pi. 3.71, cf. 2.96, 4.285; τίς ἂν εὔπατρις ὧδε βλάστοι; οὐδεὶς τῶν ἀ. κτ... S.*El.*1082; οἵ τ' ἀ. πρὸς τῶν ἀγενῶν κατανικῶνται Id.*Fr.*84; τοὺς ... γενεῖς γὰρ κἀγαθοὺς . . φιλεῖ Ἄρης ἐναίρειν ib.649, cf. E.*Alc.*600, a[l.]; ἀγαθοὶ καὶ ἐξ ἀγαθῶν Pl.*Phdr.*274a:— in political sense, *aristocra*[tic], esp. in the phrase καλοὶ κἀγαθοί (v. sub καλοκἀγαθός). [2.] *brave, valiant*, since courage was attributed to Chiefs and Noble[s], Il.1.131, al.; τῷ κ' ἀγαθὸς μὲν ἔπεφν', ἀγαθὸν δέ κεν ἐξενάριξεν 21.280, cf. Hdt.5.109, etc. 3. *good, capable*, in reference to ability, ... βασιλεύς Il.3.179; ἰητήρ 2.732; θεράπων 16.165, 17.388; πύκτ[ης] Xenoph.2.15; ἰητρός Hp.*Prog* 1; προβατογνώμων A.*Ag* 795; ἀρ... χοντες Democr.266: freq. with qualifying words. ἀ. ἐν ὑσμίνῃ Il.13.314; βοὴν ἀ. 2.408,563, al.; πύξ Od.11.300; βίην Il.6.478; γνώ[μην] S.*OT*687; πᾶσαν ἀρετήν Pl.*Lg.*899b, cf. *Alc.*1.124e; τέχνη[ν] Id.*Prt.*323b; τὰ πολέμια, τὰ πολιτικά, Hdt.9.122, Pl.*Grg.*516b, etc. more rarely c. dat., ἀ. πολέμῳ X.*Oec.*4.15: with Preps., ἄνδρες ἀ. περὶ τὸ πλῆθος Lys.13.2; εἴς τι Pl.*Alc.*1.125a; πρός τι Id.*R.*407e; c. inf., ἀ. μάχεσθαι Hdt.1.136; ἱππεύεσθαι 1.79; ἀ. ἱστάναι *good at weighing*, Pl.*Prt.*356b. 4. *good*, in moral sense, first in Thgn.438, cf. Heraclit.104, S.*El.*1082, X.*Mem.*1.7.1, Pl.*Ap.*41d, etc.; ψυχῆς ἀγαθῆς πατρὶς ὁ ξύμπας κόσμος Democr.247: freq. with other Adjs., ὁ πιστὸς κἀ. S.*Tr.*541; δικαίων κἀ. ib.1050:—ironical, τὸν ἀ. Κρέοντα Id.*Ant.*31. 5. ὦ 'γαθέ, *my good friend*, as a term of gentle remonstrance, Pl.*Prt.*311a. etc. 6. ἀ. δαίμων, v. sub δαίμων; ἀ. τύχη, v. sub τύχη; ἀ. θεός = Lat. *bona dea*, Plu.*Caes.*9, *Cic.*19. II. of things, 1. *good, serviceable*, Ἰθάκη . . ἀ. κουροτρόφος Od.9.27, etc.; ἀ. τοῖς τοκεῦσι, τῇ πόλει X.*Cyn.*13.17: c. gen., εἴ τι οἶδα πυρετοῦ ἀ. *good for* it, Id. *Mem.*3.8.3; ἑλκῶν Thphr.*HP*9.11.1. 2. of outward circumstances, αἰδὼς οὐκ ἀ. κεχρημένῳ ἀνδρὶ παρεῖναι Od.17.347; εἰπεῖν εἰς ἀγαθόν *to good purpose*, Il.9.102; ὁ δὲ πείσεται εἰς ἀ. περ *for his own good end*, 11.789; οὐκ ἀγαθὸν πολυκοιρανίη 2.204:— ἀγαθόν [ἐστι], c. inf., *it is good* to do so and so. Il.7.282, 24.130, Od.3.196, etc. 3. *morally good*, πρῆξις Democr.177; ἔργα Emp.112.2, cf. *Ep.Rom.*2.7, etc. 4. ἀγαθόν, τό, *good, blessing, benefit*, of persons or things, ὦ μέγα ἀ. σὺ τοῖς φίλοις X.*Cyr.*5.3.20; φίλον, ὁ μέγιστον ἀ. εἶναί φασι Id.*Mem.*2.4.2, cf. Ar.*Ra.*74, etc; as term of endearment for a baby, *blessing!, treasure!*, Men.*Sam.*28:—ἀγαθόν τινα δεδρακέναι, πεποιηκέναι confer *a benefit* on . . , Th.3.68, Lys.13.92; ἐπ' ἀγαθῷ τινος for one's *good*, Th.5.27, X.*Cyr.*7.4.3; ἐπ' ἀ. τοῖς πολίταις Ar.*Ra.*1487; οὐκ ἐπ' ἀ. *for no good end*, Th.1.131; ἐπ' οὐδενὶ ἀ. τῆς Ἑλλάδος X.*HG*5.2.35:—in pl., ἡ ἐπ' ἀγαθοῖς γεναμένη (sic) κατασπορά *PFlor.*21.10 (iii A.D.):—τὸ ἀ. or τἀ., *the good*, Epich.171.5, cf. Pl.*R.*506b, 508e, Arist.*Metaph.*1091ᵃ31, etc.:—in pl., ἀγαθά, τά, *goods of fortune, treasures, wealth*, Hdt.2.172, Lys.13.91, X.*Mem.*1.2.63, etc.; ἀγαθὰ πράττειν *fare well*, Ar.*Av.*1706; also, *good things, dainties*, Thgn.1000, Ar.*Ach.*873, etc.: *good qualities*, τοῖς ἀ., οἷς ἔχομεν ἐν τῇ ψυχῇ Isoc.8.32, cf. Democr.37; *good points*, of a horse, εἰ τἄλλα πάντα ἀ. ἔχοι, κακόπους δ' εἴη X.*Eq.* 1.2. III. Comp. and Sup. are usu. supplied from other stems, viz. Comp. ἀμείνων, ἀρείων, βελτίων, κρείσσων (κάρρων), λωΐων (λῴων), Ep. βέλτερος, λωΐτερος, φέρτερος:—Sup. ἄριστος, βέλτιστος, κράτιστος, λώϊστος (λῷστος), Ep. βέλτατος, κάρτιστος, φέρτατος, φέριστος:—later, reg. Comp. ἀγαθώτερος Lxx *Jd.*11.25, 15.2, D.S.*Fr.*12, Plot. 5.5.9, Diod.Rh.p.53.9 H.: Sup. ἀγαθώτατος D.S.16.85, Hld.5.15, etc. (-ότατος *POxy.*1757.26 (ii A.D.)). IV. Adv. usually εὖ, q.v.: ἀγαθῶς Hp.*Off.*9, Arist.*Rh.*1388ᵇ6, Lxx 1*Ki.*20.7. (Etym. dub. (ὅτι ἄγει ἡμᾶς ἐπὶ τὸν ὀρθὸν βίον *Stoic.* 3.49); perh. cognate with ἄγαμαι, hence *admirable*.)

**ἀγάθοσμον**· τήλινον (sc. ἔλαιον), *EM*5.34, Hsch. (prob. l.).

**ἀγαθοσύμβουλος**, *benesuasor*, *Gloss.*

**ἀγαθότης**, ητος, ἡ, *goodness*, Lxx *Wi.*1.1, Ph.1.50, Alex.Aphr. *in Metaph.*695.37, Plot.4.8.6, Sallust.3, etc.; as a form of address, ἡ σὴ ἀ. Jul.*Ep.*12,86.

**ἀγαθοτυχέω**, Astrol., *occupy the house of* ἀγαθὴ τύχη, Vett.Val.83.20; ἀγ. πρὸς . . *Cat.Cod.Astr.*1.118.

**ἀγαθουργέω, -ουργία, -ουργός**, v. ἀγαθοεργ-.

**ἀγαθο-φανής**, ές, *appearing good, hypocritical*, Democr.82. **-φόρος**, ον, *bearing good tidings*, *PMag.Par.*1.3166; -φόρον, τό, *Cat. Cod.Astr.*2.170. **-φρων**, ον, gen. -ονος, (φρήν) *well-disposed*, Ptol. *Tetr.*163.

**ἀγαθόω**, *do good to one*, τινί or τινά Lxx 1*Ki.*25.31, *Si.*49.9. 2. *make good*, Numen.ap.Eus.*PE*11.22 (Pass.).

**ἀγάθ-υνσις**, ἡ, *making good*, Eustr. *in EN*276.32. ⊛**-ύνω**, first and freq. in Lxx: I. *honour, magnify*, 3*Ki.*1.47, *Ps.*50(51).18: *adorn*, τὴν κεφαλήν 4*Ki.*9.30. 2. *cheer*, ἀγαθυνάτω σε ἡ καρδία *Ec.*11.9:—Pass., *to be of good cheer, rejoice greatly*, 2*Ki.*13.28, *Da.*6.23, al. II. *make good*, Alex.Aphr. *in Metaph.*707.11, al., Procl.*Inst.*13,122: Pass., Simp. *in Epict.*p.6 D., al. b. Astrol., *make beneficent*, in Pass., Doroth. in *Cat.Cod.Astr.*2.196, Jul.Laod.ib. 4.24. III. *do good to*, τινά Heliod. *in EN*86.41. IV. *do good, do well*, Lxx *Ps.*35(36).3; τινί (v.l. τινά) to one, ib.124(125).4.

**ἀγάθωμα**, τό, *embodiment of the good*, Procl. *in Prm.*p.863S.

**ἀγαθωσύνη**, ἡ, *goodness, kindness*, Lxx *Jd.*9.16, al., *Ep.Rom.*15. *Ep.Eph.*5.9.

**ἀγαίομαι**, Ep. and Ion. for ἄγαμαι, only pres. and impf.: I. bad sense (cf. ἄγη II), 1. c. acc. rei, *to be indignant at*, ἀγαιομένου κακὰ ἔργα Od.20.16: *look on with jealousy* or *envy*, οὐδ' ἀγαίομαι ὧν ἔργα Archil.25. 2. c. dat. pers., *to be wroth* or *indignant with*, . . Ζεὺς αὐτὸς ἀγαίεται Hes.*Op.*333; ἀγαιόμενοί τε καὶ φθονέοντες τῇ Hdt.8.69 (cf. Sch.Od.20.16). II. in good sense, *admire*, Opp.*H.*4.138; abs. in part., A.R.1.899, 3.1016; οἴνῳ ἀγαιομένη ὄμφῳ Διός Orph.*Fr.*204: ἀγαίετο θυμός Hes.*Fr.*81.4.

**ἀγαῖος**, α, ον (A), *enviable*, Hsch., *AB*334, *EM*8.50.

**ἀγαῖος**, α, ον (B), (ἄγω) *leading the procession*, μόσχος, dub. in *IG*²438.203 (Delphi).

**ἀγα-κλεής**, ές, voc. -κλεές Il.17.716, al.: Ep. gen. ἀγακλῆος Il.16.38, nom. pl. ἀγακλῆεῖς Man.3.324: shortened acc. sing. ἀγακλέα Pi.*P.*9.106, *I.*1.34; dat. ἀγακλέϊ *APl.*5.377; acc. pl. ἀγακλέας Antim. *Eleg.*2:—*very glorious, famous*, in Il. always of men, as 16.738, 13.529; later of places and things, ναός, Δᾶλος, B.15.12, Pi.*Pae.*4.12; παιάν ib.5.48.—Ep. and Lyr. word (not in Od.), exc. in Adv. ἀγακλεῶς, Hp.*Praec.*12. **-κλειτός**, ή, όν, = foreg., of men, Il.2.564, Hes.*Th.*1016, etc. 2. of things, ἀ. ἑκατόμβη Od.3.59; πάθος S.*Tr.*854 (lyr.). **-κλυμένη**, poet. fem. = sq., Antim. *Eleg.*4. **-κλυτός**, όν, = -κλειτός, Il.6.426, Hes.*Th.*945, etc. 2. of things, ἀ. δώματα Od.3.388, 7.3,46. **-κτῐμένη**, poet. fem. = ἐϋκτιμένη, *well-built* or *placed*, πόλις Pi.*P.*5.81.

**ἀγᾰλακτία**, ἡ, *want of milk*, Autocr.3.

**ἀγάλακτος** [γᾰ], ον, (α priv., γάλα) *giving no milk*, Hp.*Nat. Puer.*30, cf. Call.*Ap.*52. 2. *getting no milk*, A.*Ag.*718. 3. νομαὶ ἀγάλακτοι pastures *bad for milch cattle*, Gal.6.346. II. (α collect.) = ὁμογάλακτος, Hsch.; also **ἀγαλακτοσύνη**, = συγγένεια, Id.

**ἀγάλαξ**, ακτος, ὁ, ἡ, = foreg. I, only in pl. ἀγάλακτες, Call.*Ap.*52. II. = foreg. II, Hsch., Suid.

**ἀγαλλί-ᾱμα**, τό, *transport of joy*, Lxx *Ps.*31(32).7, etc. **-ᾱσις**, εως, ἡ, *great joy, exultation*, Lxx *Jb.*8.21, al., *Ev.Luc.*1.14,44, 1*Enoch* 5.9, Ps.-Callisth.2.22. **-άω**, late form of ἀγάλλομαι, *rejoice exceedingly*, *Apoc.*19.7 (v.l. ἀγαλλιώμεθα); ἠγαλλίασα *Ev.Luc.*1.47, cf. *POxy.*1592.4 (iii/iv A.D.):—more common as Dep. ἀγαλλιάομαι, Lxx*Is.*12.6, al.: fut. -άσομαι *Ps.*5.11: aor. ἠγαλλιασάμην *Ps.*15(16).2, *Ev.Jo.*8.56; ἠγαλλιάσθην ib.5.35.—This family of words seems also to have been used *in malam partem*, **ἀγαλλιάζει**· λοιδορεῖται, **ἀγάλλιος**· λοίδορος, **ἀγαλμός**· λοιδορία, Hsch., cf. *EM*7.8.

**ἀγαλλίς**, ίδος, ἡ, *dwarf iris, Iris attica*, *h.Cer.*7,426:—also **ἀγαλλιάς**, ἡ, Nic.*Fr.*74.31.

**ἀγάλλω** [ᾰ], Pi.*O.*1.86b, Ar.*Th.*128, etc.: fut. ἀγᾰλῶ Ar.*Pax* 399, Theopomp.Com.47: aor. ἤγηλα D.C.44.48, etc., subj. ἀγήλω Hermipp. 8, inf. ἀγῆλαι E.*Med.*1027:—Pass., only pres. and impf. in early writers: aor. 1 inf. ἀγαλθῆναι D.C.51.20:—*glorify, exalt*, Pi. l. c., *N.*5.43: esp. *pay honour to* a god, ἄγαλλε Φοῖβον Ar.*Th.*128, cf. Pl. *Lg.*931a; ἀ. τινὰ θυσίαισι Ar.*Pax* l. c.; φέρε νῦν, ἀγήλω τοὺς θεούς Hermipp. l. c.; θεοὺς καρποῖς Xenocr.ap.Porph.*Abst.*4.22:—*adorn*, γαμηλίους εὐνάς E. l. c.:—Med. in act. sense, εὔιον ἀγαλλόμεναι θεόν E.*Ba.*157:—Pass., *glory, exult in* a thing, c. part., τεύχεσ' δ' Ἕκτωρ . . ἔχων ὤμοισιν ἀγάλλεται Il.17.473; νικῶν Archil.66.4; ἣν ἕκαστος πατρίδα ἔχων . . ἀ. Th.4.95; but mostly c. dat., ἵπποισιν καὶ ὄχεσφιν ἀγαλλόμενος Il.12.114; πτερύγεσσι 2.462; νῆες . . ἀ. Διὸς οὔρῳ Od.5.176; Μοῦσαι . . ἀ. ὀπὶ καλῇ Hes.*Th.*68; ἀσπίδι Archil.6; ἑορταῖς E.*Tr.*452: in Prose, τῷ οὐνόματι ἠγάλλοντο Hdt.1.143, cf. Th.2.44, Pl.*Tht.*176b; ἀλλοτρίοις πτεροῖς ἀ. *strut* in borrowed plumes, Luc.*Ap.*4; ἐπί τινι Th.3.82, X.*Cyr.*8.4.11; διὰ τἆλλα καὶ ὅτι . . D.C.66.2: c. acc., *AP*7.378 (Apollonid.): abs., Hdt.4.64, 9.109, Hp.*Art.*35, E.*Ba.*1197.

**ἄγαλμα**, ατος, τό, acc. to Hsch. πᾶν ἐφ' ᾧ τις ἀγάλλεται, *glory, delight, honour*, Il.4.144, etc.; κεφάλαισιν ἀνδρῶν ἀγάλματα (sc. λόφοι) Alc.15; χώρας ἄ., of an ode, Pi.*N.*3.13, cf. 8.16; of children, τέκνον δόμων ἄ. A.*Ag.*208; εὐκλείας τέκνοις ἄ. conversely, of a father, S.*Ant.*704; Καδμεΐας νύμφας ἄ., addressed to Bacchus, ib.1115; ματέρος ἄ. φόνιον, of slain sons, E.*Supp.*371; ἀγάλματ' ἀγορᾶς *mere ornaments* of the agora, Id.*El.*388, cf. Metagen.10.3; rare in Prose, Pl.*Ti.*37c. 2. *pleasing gift*, esp. for the gods, ἄ. θεῶν Od.8.509, of a bull adorned for sacrifice, ib.3.438; of a tripod, Hdt.5.60, al.; generally, = ἀνάθημα, *IG*1.373[12a], etc.; Χάρης εἰμὶ . . ἄ. τοῦ Ἀπόλλωνος *GDI*5507 (Miletus); ἄνθηκεν ἄ. Simon.155; so, Ἑκάτης ἄ. . . κύων, because sacred to her, E.*Fr.*968, = Ar.*Fr.*594a; ἄ. Ἀΐδα, of a tombstone, Pi.*N.*10.67. 3. *statue in honour of a god*, Hdt.1.131, 2.42,46, Lys.6.15 (pl.):—τὸ τοῦ Διὸς ἄ., opp. εἰκόνες of men, Isoc. 9.57, cf. *Michel*545 (Phrygia, ii B.C.), etc.; as an object of worship, A.*Th.*258, *Eu.*55, S.*OT*1379, Pl.*Phdr.*251a:—*sculpture*, μήτε ἄ. μήτε γραφή Arist.*Pol.*1336[b]15. 4. *statue* (more general than ἀνδριάς, q. v.), Pl.*Men.*97d, etc.:—also, *portrait, picture*, ἐξαλειφθεῖσ' ὡς ἄ. E.*Hel.*262. 5. generally, *image*, τῶν ἀιδίων θεῶν Pl.*Ti.*37c; νεφέλης E.*Hel.*705; μητρός *Trag.Adesp.*126; Ἄρεως Polemo *Call.* 52:—expressed by painting or words, Pl.*Smp.*216e, cf. *R.*517d; *hieroglyphic sign*, Plot.5.8.6.

**ἀγαλμ-ατίας**, ου, ὁ, *like a statue, beautiful as one*, Philostr.*VS*2. 25.6. **-άτιον**, τό, Dim. of ἄγαλμα, *IG*4.1588 (Attic, fr. Aegina, v B.C.), Theopomp.Com.47, Polycharm.5, Plu.*Lyc.*25, etc. **-ατίτης**, ὁ, = λιθοκόλλα, Hsch.

**ἀγαλματο-γλύφος**, ὁ, = *sculptor*, Vett.Val.4.12, *Rev.Ét.Gr.*19.265 (Aphrodisias). **-ποιέω**, *make statues*, Poll.7.108: Pass., *have a statue made of oneself*, Steph. *in Rh.*280.10. **-ποιητικός**, όν, ἡ, *of* or *for statuary*, Jul.*Gal.*235c: -κή, ἡ, *sculpture*, [Gal.]14. 686. **-ποιΐα**, ἡ, *sculptor's art*, Philostr.*VS*1.11.2, Porph.*Abst.* 2.49. **-ποιικός**, = -ποιητικός, Poll.1.13: -ποιϊκόν, τό, *sculptor's fee*, *IG*1.324. **-ποιός**, ὁ, *sculptor*, Hdt.2.46, Pl.*Prt.*311c, etc.; γραφεῖς ἢ ἀ. Arist.*Pol.*1340[a]38.

**ἀγαλματ-ουργία**, ἡ, = ἀγαλματοποιΐα, Max.Tyr.33.3. **-ουργικός**, ή, όν, = ἀγαλματοποιικός, ibid. **-ουργός**, όν, = ἀγαλματοποιός, Poll.1.12.

**ἀγαλματο-φορέω**, *carry an image in one's mind, bear impressed upon one's mind*, Ph.1.16, al.; Pass., 2.136. **-φόρος**, ον, *carrying an image in one's mind*, Hsch. **-φώρας**, ὁ, *temple-robber*, *Jahresh.*2.197 (Elis, iv B.C.).

**ἀγαλματ-όω**, *make into an image*, Lyc.845. **-ώδης**, ες, *like a statue*, f.l. in Gal.*UP*11.13.

**ἀγαλμητόν**· ἀσθενές, Hsch. **ἀγαλμός**, v. ἀγαλλιάω.

**ἀγαλμο-ειδής**, ές, f.l. for ἀγλαο-, q. v. **-τύπευς**, έως, *maker of statues*, Man.4.569.

**ἀγάλοχον**, τό, *eagle-wood, Aquilaria malaccensis*, Dsc.1.22, etc.

**ἄγαλσις**, ἡ, *rejoicing*, *EM*9.52.

**ἄγᾰμαι** [ᾰ], 2 pl. ἄγασθε Od.5.129, Ep. ἀγάασθε ib.119; Ep. inf. ἀγάασθαι 16.203: impf. ἠγάμην Pl.*R.*367e, X.*Smp.*8.8, Ep. 2 pl. ἠγάασθε Od.5.122: fut. Ep. ἀγάσσομαι Od.4.181; later, ἀγασθήσομαι Them.*Or.*27.335d, Themist.*Ep.*8: aor. ἠγασάμην Hom., D.18. 204, Plu.*Fab.*18, etc.; Ep. ἠγάσσατο or ἀγάσσατο Il.3.181,224; after Hom. the pass. ἠγάσθην prevails, Hes.*Fr.*93.2, Sol.33, etc. (Perh. cognate with ἀγα-, q. v.) [ἄγᾰμαι, but ἠγάασθε metri grat., Od. l. c.] I. abs., *wonder*, μνηστῆρες δ' . . ὑπερφιάλως ἀγάσαντο Od.18.71, etc.; c. part., Ὀδυσῆος ἀγασσάμεθ' εἶδος ἰδόντες Il.3. 224. 2. more freq. c. acc., *admire* a person or thing, τὸν δ' ὁ γέρων ἠγάσσατο Il.3.181; ὥς σέ, γύναι, ἄγαμαι Od.6.168; μῦθον ἄ. Il.8.29; τὸ προορᾶν ἄ. σευ Hdt.9.79; ὑμέων ἀγάμεθα τὴν προνοίην Id.8.144; οὐκ ἄγαμαι ταῦτ' ἀνδρὸς ἀριστέως E.*IA*28; ταῦτα ἀγασθεὶς X.*Cyr.*2.3.19, cf. Isoc.4.84, etc.: c. acc. pers. et gen. rei, *admire* one *for* a thing, Pl.*R.*426d, X.*Cyr.*2.3.21. 3. c. gen., *wonder at* freq. in Com., ἄγαμαι δὲ λόγων Ar.*Av.*1744; ἄ. κεραμέως αἴθωνος Eup.21D.; ἄ. σοῦ στόματος, ὡς . . Phryn.Com.10:—also in Prose, X.*Mem.*2. 6.33, Pl.*Euthd.*276d, etc. 4. c. gen. pers., foll. by part., *wonder at* one's doing, ἄ. Ἐρασίνου οὐ προδιδόντος Hdt.6.76.β'; ἀ. αὐτοῦ εἰπόντος Pl.*R.*329d, etc.; ἄ. τινος ὅτι, . . διότι . . , Id.*Hp.Ma.*291e, X.*Mem.*4.2.9, etc. 5. c. dat., *to be delighted with* a person or thing, Hdt.4.75, Pl.*Smp.*179c, X.*Cyr.*2.4.9; later, ἐπί τινι D.*Ep.*2. 11, Menetor Hist.1, Phalar.*Ep.*79. II. in bad sense, *feel envy, bear a grudge*, c. dat. pers., εἰ μή οἱ ἀγάσσατο Φοῖβος Ἀπόλλων Il. 17.71; ἀγασσάμενοι [μοι] περὶ νίκης 23.639; with inf. added, *to be jealous* of one *that* . . , σχέτλιοί ἐστε, θεοί, . . οἵ τε θεαῖς ἀγάασθε παρ' ἀνδράσιν εὐνάζεσθαι Od.5.119, 23.211; foll. by a relat., ἔφασκε Ποσειδάων' ἀγάσεσθαι ἡμῖν, οὕνεκα . . 8.565:—Pass. aor. ἠγάσθην Hes.*Fr.* 93.2, dub. in E.*HF*845. 2. c. acc., *to be jealous of, angry at* a thing, ἀγασσάμενοι κακὰ ἔργα Od.2.67; of Gods, 4.181, cf. 23.64. Cf. ἀγαίομαι.

**Ἀγαμέμνων**, ονος, ὁ, *Agamemnon*, Hom., etc.: Ἀγαμέμνονος δαίς, of a fatal feast, Eust.1507.60:—also epith. of Zeus at Sparta, Staphylus Hist.10, Eust.168.10.—Adj. **Ἀγᾰμεμνόνεος**, έα, εον, Hom., also **-όνειος**, εία, ειον, and **-όνιος**, ία, ιον, Pi., A.: Patron. **-ονίδης**, ου, ὁ, *Agamemnon's son*, Orestes, Od.1.30, S.*El.*182.

**ἀγᾰμένως**, Adv. part. pres. of ἄγαμαι, *with admiration* or *respect*, ἀ. λέγειν Arist.*Rh.*1408[a]18; ἀ. τὸν λόγον ἀπεδέξατο Pl.*Phd.*89a.

**ἀγάμ-ετος**, ον, = ἄγαμος, S.*Fr.*970:—also **-ητος**, ον, *Com.Adesp.* 315. **-ία**, ἡ, *single estate, celibacy*, Plu.2.491e. **-ίου δίκη** action against a bachelor *for not marrying*, Plu.*Lys.*30, cf. Poll. 3.48; ἀγαμίου ζημία Aristo*Stoic.*1.89. **-ος**, ον, *unmarried, single*, prop. of the man, whether bachelor or widower (ἄνανδρος being used of the woman), Il.3.40, X.*Smp.*9.7, etc.; ζῶ δὲ Τίμωνος βίον, ἄγαμον, ἄδουλον Phryn.Com.18:—of the woman, A.*Supp.*143, S.*OT*1502, E.*Or.*205. Adv. -ως Sch. ad loc. II. γάμος ἄ. *marriage that is no marriage, fatal marriage*, S.*OT*1214, E.*Hel.*690.

**ἄγαν**, Adv. *very much*, chiefly Aeol. Dor. and Trag., not in Hom., rare in Ion., as Hdt.2.173, Hp.*Art.*4, al., Democr.222; freq. in bad sense, *too much*:—prov., μηδὲν ἄ. Pi.*Fr.*216 (attributed to Chilo by Arist.*Rh.*1389[b]4); μηδὲν ἄ. σπεύδειν Thgn.335:—with Verbs, ἄ. διαστρέψαι Hp.*Fract.*8; ἄ. ἐλευθεροστομεῖν A.*Pr.*182; ἄ. τι ποιεῖν Pl.*R.*563e:—with Adjs. either preceding or following, ἄ. κοῦφος Hp.*Art.*4; ἄ. βαρύς A.*Pers.*515; πιθανὸς ἄ. Id.*Ag.*485; with Sup., ἄ. ἀγριωτάτους *far* the most savage, Ael.*NA*1.38, cf. 8.13:—with Adv., ὑπερθύμως ἄ. A.*Eu.*824; ἄ. οὕτω S.*Ph.*598; ὠμῶς ἄ. X.*Vect.* 5.6:—with a Subst., ἡ ἄ. χρημάτων συναγωγή Democr.222; ἡ ἄ. σιγή S.*Ant.*1251; ἡ ἄ. ἐλευθερία Pl.*R.*564a; without Art., εἰς ἄ. δουλείαν ib. (Cf. ἀγα-.) [ἀγᾶν Thgn.219, Orac.ap.Hdt.4.157, A.*Eu.* 121, etc.; in late poets, ἀγᾶν *AP*5.215.6 (Agath.), 10.51 (Pall.), cf. Eust.1433 fin.]

**ἄγανα**· σαγήνην (Cypr.), Hsch. (Prob. ἀγάνα.)

**ἀγᾰνακτ-έω**, properly in physical sense, *feel a violent irritation*, of the effects of cold on the body, Hp.*Liqu.*2, cf. Heliod.ap.Orib.46. 7.8; of wine, *ferment*, Plu.2.734e; so metaph., ζεῖ τε καὶ ἀ., of the soul, Pl.*Phdr.*251c. II. metaph., *to be displeased, vexed*, μηδ' ἀγανάκτει Ar.*V.*287; esp. *show outward signs of grief*, κλάων καὶ ἀ.

Pl.*Phd.*117d; τὰ σπλάγχν' ἀγανακτεῖ Ar.*Ra.*1006, etc.; ἀ. ἐνθυμούμενος.. And.4.18:—foll. by a relat., ἀ. ὅτι.. Antipho 4.2.1, Lys. 3.3; ἀ. εἰ.., ἐάν.. And.1.139, Pl.*La.*194a. **2.** c. dat. rei *to be vexed at* a thing, θανάτῳ Pl.*Phd.*63b, etc.; c. acc. neut., ib.64a; ἀ. ταῦτα, ὅτι.. Id.*Euthphr.*4d; ἀ. ἐπί τινι Lys.1.1, Isoc.16.49, etc.; ὑπέρ τινος Pl.*Euthd.*283e, etc.; περί τινος Id.*Ep.*349d; διά τι Id. *Phd.*63c; πρός τι Epict.*Ench.*4, M.Ant.7.66; and sts. c. gen. rei, *AB*334. **3.** *to be vexed at* or *with* a person, τινί X.*HG*5.3.11; πρός τινα Plu.*Cam.*28, Diog.Oen.68; κατά τινος Luc.*Tim.*18:—c. part., *to be angry at*, ἀ. ἀποθνήσκοντας Pl.*Phd.*62e, cf. 67d. **III.** Med. in act. sense, aor. part. -ησάμενος Luc.*Somn.*4; prob. in Palaeph.40; ἠγανάκτηνται τῷ πράγματι Hyp.*Fr.*70. **-ησις**, εως, ἡ, *physical pain and irritation*, ἀ. περὶ τὰ οὖλα, of the irritation caused by teething, Pl.*Phdr.*251c. **II.** *vexation*, ἀγανάκτησιν ἔχει Th.2.41, cf. 2*Ep.Cor.*7.11, Plot.4.4.19:—of God, *wrath*, Porph. *Marc.*7, Jul.*Gal.*171e. **-ητέον**, *one must complain*, Plot.4.8.7. **-ητικός**, ή, όν, *apt to be vexed, irritable, peevish*, Pl.*R.*604e, 605a (v.l. ἀγανακτικός). **-ητός**, ή, όν, *vexatious*, Pl.*Grg.* 511b. **-ικός**, ή, όν, = ἀγανακτητικός (q.v.), Luc.*Pisc.*14. Adv. -κῶς M.Ant.11.13.

**ἀγάνεται**· πραγματεύεται, χρῆται, Hsch. **ἀγάνημαι**· ἀσχάλλω, ἀγανακτῶ, Id. **ἀγανίδα**· ἀτρέμας, Id. (fort. -ηδά).

**ἀγάννα**· ἅμαξα ἱερά· καὶ ἡ ἐν οὐρανῷ ἄρκτος, *Et.Gud.*, cf. Hsch.

***ἀγάννῐφος**, ον, *much snowed on, snow-capt*, Ὄλυμπος Il.1.420; ἄκρα Epich.130.

**ἀγᾰνοβλέφαρος**, ον, *mild-eyed*, Πειθώ Ibyc.5, cf. *AP*9.604 (Nossis).

**ἀγανόμματος**, ον, *mild-eyed*, *Lyr.Alex.Adesp.*20.

**ἀγᾰνόρειος, ἀγᾰνορία**, Dor. for ἀγην-.

***ἀγᾰνός**, ή, όν (ἀγανοῖσιν is corrupt in *Il.Parv.*6), poet. Adj. *mild, gentle*, of persons or their words and acts, ἀ. καὶ ἤπιος ἔστω σκηπτοῦχος βασιλεύς Od.2.230, 5.8; ἀ. ἐπέεσσιν Il.2.164, 180, etc.; μύθοις ἀ. Od.15.53; εὐχωλῇς Il.9.499, Od.13.357; δώροισι Il.9.113; Ἀτθίς Sapph.*Supp.*25.15; λόγοις Pi.*P.*4.101; ὀφρύι ib.9.38; Trag. only in A.*Ag.*101; αὐλῶν ἀγαναὶ φωναί Mnesim.4.56. **2.** in Hom. freq. of the shafts of Apollo and Artemis, as *bringing an easy death*, ἀλλ' ὅτε γηράσκωσι.., Ἀπόλλων Ἀρτέμιδι ξὺν οἷς ἀγανοῖς βελέεσσιν ἐποιχόμενος κατέπεφνεν Od.15.411, cf. 3.280, Il.24.759, etc.: Sup. ἀγανώτατος Hes.*Th.*408, Pi.*Fr.*149, Them.*Or.*20.234a. Adv. -νῶς Anacr.51.1, E.*IA*601: Comp. ἀγανώτερον, βλέπειν Ar. *Lys.*886.—Poet. and late Prose, Them. l.c.

***ἄγᾰνος**, ον, (ἄγνυμι) *broken*, ξύλον ἄ. sticks *broken for firewood*, S.*Fr.*231.

**ἀγανο-φροσύνη**, ἡ, *gentleness, kindliness*, Il.24.772, Od.11.202. **-φρων**, ον, gen. ονος, poet. Adj. *gentle of mood*, Il.20.467, Cratin.238; Ἡσυχία Ar.*Av.*1321.

***ἀγανῶπις**, ιδος, ἡ, (ὤψ) *mild-eyed*, Marcell.Sid.80, cf. Hsch.

**ἀγάνωτος**, ον, (γανόω) *not enamelled* or *lacquered*, Posidon.Medic. ap.Paul.Aeg.7.20, Zos.Alch.p.220 B.

***ἀγάομαι**, Ep. collat. form of ἄγαμαι, only part. ἀγώμενος, *admiring*, Hes.*Th.*619; and opt. ἀγήσα(ι)το Alc.14:—ἄγασθε is the right reading in Od.5.129.

**ἀγαπάζω**, Ep. and Lyr. form of ἀγαπάω, Hom.; Dor. 3 pl. -οντι Pi.*I.* 4(5).54: Ep. impf. ἀγάπαζον A.R.4.1291:—also in Med., Hom.; Dor. impf. ἀγαπάζοντο Pi.*P.*4.241:—Pass., Diotog.ap.Stob.4.7.62:—only in pres. and impf., exc. aor. act. ἀγαπάξαι Callicrat.ap.Stob.4.28.18:—*treat with affection, receive with outward signs of love*, ὡς δὲ πατὴρ ὃν παῖδα.. ἀγαπάζει, ἐλθόντ' ἐξ ἀπίης γαίης δεκάτῳ ἐνιαυτῷ Od.16.17; νεμεσσητὸν δέ κεν εἴη ἀθάνατον θεὸν ὧδε βροτοὺς ἀγαπαζέμεν ἄντην Il.24.464; νέκυν E.*Ph.*1327:—Med. in abs. sense, *show signs of love, caress*, κύνεον ἀγαπαζόμενοι κεφαλήν τε καὶ ὤμους Od. 21.224: c. acc., like Act., Pi.*P.* l.c.; τινὰ δώροις A.R.4.416. **2.** *welcome, receive gratefully*, τιμαὶ καλλίνικον χάρμ' ἀγαπάζοντι Pi.*I.* l.c.

***ἀγαπάω** (Dor. -έω Archyt.ap.Stob.3.1.110), Ep. aor. ἀγάπησα Od.23.214: pf. ἠγάπηκα Isoc.15.147, etc. **I.** *greet with affection* (cf. foreg.), once in Hom., Od. l.c.:—in Trag. only *show affection for* the dead, ὅτ' ἠγάπα νεκρούς E.*Supp.*764, cf. *Hel.*937:—Pass., *to be regarded with affection*, ξένων εὐεργεσίαις ἀγαπᾶται Pi.*I.*5(6).70:—generally, *love*, ὥσπερ.. οἱ ποιηταὶ τὰ αὑτῶν ποιήματα καὶ οἱ πατέρες τοὺς παῖδας ἀγαπῶσι Pl.*R.*330c, cf. *Lg.*928a; ὡς λύκοι ἄρν' ἀγαπῶσ' Poet.ap.*Phdr.*241d; ἀ. τοὺς ἐπαινέτας ib.257e; ἐπιστήμην, τὰ χρήματα, etc., Id.*Phlb.*62d, al.; τούτους ἀγαπᾷ καὶ περὶ αὑτὸν ἔχει D.2.19; ὁ μέγιστον ἀγαπῶν δι' ἐλάχιστ' ὀργίζεται Men.659; esp. of children, αὐτὸν ἐτιθηνούμην ἀγαπῶσα Id.*Sam.*32, etc.:—Pass., Pl.*Plt.*301d, etc.; ὑπὸ τῶν θεῶν ἠγαπῆσθαι D.61.9; ὑπὸ τοῦ Φθᾶ *OGI*90.4 (Rosetta, ii B.C.); so in Lxx of the love of God for man and of man for God, *Is.*41.8, *De.*11.1, al., cf. *Ev.Jo.*3.21, *Ep.Rom.*8.28:—as dist. fr. φιλέω (q.v.) implying regard rather than affection, but the two are interchanged, cf. X.*Mem.*2.7.9 and 12; φιλεῖσθαι defined as ἀγαπᾶσθαι αὐτὸν δι' αὑτόν Arist.*Rh.*1371$^a$21:—seldom of sexual love, for ἐράω, Arist.*Fr.*76, Luc.*J.Tr.*2; ἀ. ἑταίραν Anaxil.22.1 (but ἀ. ἑταίρας *to be fond of* them, X.*Mem.*1.5.4; ἐρωτικὴν μέμψιν ἡ ἀγαπωμένη λύει dub. in Democr.271):—of brotherly love, *Ev.Matt.*5.43, al. **2.** *persuade, entreat*, Lxx 2*Ch.*18.2. **3.** *caress, pet*, Plu.*Per.*1. **II.** of things, *to be fond of, prize, desire*, Pl.*Lys.*215a,b, etc.; τὰ χρήματα *R.* 330c; μᾶλλον τὸ σκότος ἢ τὸ φῶς *Ev.Jo.*3.19; *prefer*, τὰ Φιλίππου δῶρα ἀντὶ τῶν κοινῇ τοῖς Ἕλλησι συμφερόντων D.18.109:—Pass., λιθίδια τὰ ἀγαπώμενα *highly prized, precious stones*, Pl.*Phd.*110d. **III.** *to be well pleased, contented*, once in Hom., οὐκ ἀγαπᾷς ὃ ἕκηλος.. μεθ' ἡ[μῖν] δαίνυσαι; Od.21.289; freq. in Att., ἀγαπᾶν ὅτι.. Th.6.36; m[ore] commonly, ἀ. εἰ.. *to be well content* if.., Lys.12.11, Pl.*R.*450a, a[l.;] ἐάν.. ib.330b, cf. Ar.*V.*684, Pl.*Grg.*483c, al. **2.** c. part., τιμώμενος Pl.*R.*475b, cf. Isoc.12.8, Antiph.169: c. inf., οὐκ ἀ. τῶν ἴσ[ων] τυγχάνειν τοῖς ἄλλοις Isoc.18.50, cf. D.55.19, Hdn.2.15.4, Alcip[hr.] 3.61, Luc.*D.Mort.*12.4, etc. **3.** c. dat. rei, *to be contented wi[th]*, ἀ. τοῖς ὑπάρχουσιν ἀγαθοῖς Lys.2.21; τοῖς πεπραγμένοις D.1.14. c. acc. rei, *tolerate, put up with*, μηκέτι τὴν ἐλευθερίαν ἀ. Isoc.4.140; τὰ παρόντα D.6.15; τὸ δίκαιον Pl.*R.*359a (Pass.), cf. Aris[t.] *Rh.*1398$^a$23. **5.** rarely c. gen., ἵνα.. τῆς ἀξίας ἀγαπῶσιν *may [be] content with* the proper price, Alex.125.7. **6.** abs., *to be co[n]tent*, ἀγαπήσαντες Lycurg.73, cf. Luc.*Nec.*17. **7.** c. inf., *to b[e] fond of* doing, *wont* to do, like φιλέω, τοὺς Λυκίους ἀγαπῶντας τὸ τρ[ί]χωμα φορεῖν Arist.*Oec.*1348$^a$29, cf. Lxx *Ho.*12.7.

***ἀγάπ-η**, ἡ, *love*, Lxx *Je.*2.2, *Ca.*2.7, al.; ἀ. καὶ μῖσος *Ec* 9.1; dub. l. in *PBerol.*9859 (ii B.C.), Phld.*Lib.*p.52 O.; of the love of husband and wife, Sch.Ptol.*Tetr.*52. **2.** esp. *love* of God for man and of man for God, Lxx *Wi.*3.9, Aristeas 229; φόβος καὶ ἀ. Ph.1.283, cf. *Ep.Rom.*5.8, 2*Ep.Cor.*5.14, *Ev.Luc.*11.42, al.:—also *brotherly love, charity*, 1*Ep.Cor.*13.1, al. **II.** in pl., *love-feast*, 2*Ep.Pet.* 2.13, *Ep.Jud.*12. **III.** *alms, charity*, *PGen.*14 (iv/v A.D.). **IV.** ἀγάπη θεῶν, title of Isis, *POxy.*1380.109 (ii A.D.). **-ημα**, τό, *darling*, of a person, Crates Theb.*Fr.*12, cf. Suet.*Gramm.*3, *Epigr. Gr.*1023 (Talmis):—generally, *delight*; of a dainty dish, λίχνων ἀνδρῶν ἀ. Axionic.4.6; φίλον ὥραισιν ἀ. *Lyr.Alex.Adesp.*24. **-ήνωρ**, ορος, ὁ, ἠνορέην ἀγαπῶν, *loving manliness, manly*, epith. of heroes, Il.8.114, etc. **-ησις**, εως, ἡ, *affection*, Arist.*Metaph.*980$^a$22, Pl. *Def.*413b, Clearch.39, Lxx *Ho.*11.12, al., Aristeas 44, Phld.*Lib.*p. 38 O., Plu.*Per.*24, etc. **-ησμός**, ὁ, = foreg., Men.453. **-ητέος**, α, ον, *to be loved, desired*, Pl.*R.*358a. **-ητικός**, ή, όν, *affectionate*, Plu.*Sol.*7; περὶ τὰ τέκνα M.Ant.1.13, etc. Adv. -κῶς Ph.2.216, Sch.E.*Ph.*309. ***-ητός**, ή, όν, Dor. -ᾱτός, ά, όν, *that wherewith one must be content* (cf. ἀγαπάω III), hence of only children, μοῦνος ἐὼν ἀ. Od.2.365; Ἑκτορίδην ἀ. Il.6.401, cf. Od.4.817, Sapph. 85, Ar.*Th.*761, Pl.*Alc.*1.131e; Νικήρατος.. ὁ τοῦ Νικίου ἀ. παῖς D.21. 165, cf. Arist.*Pol.*1262$^b$23, *EE*1233$^b$2; αὕτη μονογενὴς αὐτῷ ἀγαπητή Lxx *Jd.*11.34, cf. *To.*3.10, *Ev.Marc.*12.6 (but cf. also II 2), etc.; ἀγαπητός· μονογενής, Hsch.:—so of things, Arist.*Rh.*1365$^b$16; δαπίδιον ἓν ἀ. Hipparch.Com.1; προβάτιον Men.319.3. **2.** *to be acquiesced in* (as the least in a choice of evils), And.3.22, J.*BJ*5.10.3:—hence, ἀγαπητόν [ἐστι] *one must be content*, εἰ.., ἐάν.. Pl.*Prt.*328b, X.*Oec.* 8.16, D.18.220, Arist.*Metaph.*1076$^a$15, etc.; c. inf., *EN*1171$^a$20. **II.** of things, *desirable*, ἤθη X.*Mem.*3.10.5; βίος Pl.*Phlb.*61e (Sup.). **2.** of persons, *beloved*, ἀδελφὲ ἀγαπητέ Lxx *To.*3.10: in letters, as a term of address, *Ep.Rom.*12.19, cf. *PGrenf.*2.73, etc. **III.** Adv. -τῶς *gladly, contentedly*, Pl.*Lg.*735d, D.19.219, etc. **2.** *just enough to content one, barely, scarcely*, Pl.*Lys.*218c; ἀ σωθῆναι Lys. 6.45, cf. Diph.89.2, etc.

**ἀγαπώντως**, = ἀγαπητῶς, Pl.*Lg.*735d, Numen.ap.Eus.*PE*14.5.

**ἀγᾰρῐκόν**, τό, name for various *tree-fungi*, Dsc.3.1, etc.: ἀ. ἄρρεν, *Boletus Agaricum*; ἀ. θῆλυ, *Agaricus dryinus*; ἀ. μέλαν, *fly agaric*, *Amanita muscaria*, l.c. [ᾰγ Damocr.ap.Gal.14.96 (iamb.): ᾱγ Androm.ap.Gal.14.39 (hex.).]

**ἀγαρράπτει** τε· ἔφθορεν, Hsch.

**ἄγαρρις**, ἡ, (ἀγείρω) *meeting*, *IG*14.759.12 (Naples), Hsch.

**ἀγάρροος**, ον, contr. -ρρους, ουν, (ῥέω) *strong-flowing*, Ἑλλήσποντος Il.2.845, 12.30; πόντος h.*Cer.*34; Τίγρις *AP*7.747 (Lib.), cf. Q.S. 10.174.

**ἀγάς**· ἡ πτῶσις τοῦ ἀστραγάλου, Hsch.

**ἀγασθενής**, ές, (σθένος) *very strong*, Opp.*C.*2.2, *Epigr.Gr.*1052 (Stratonicea):—in Il. only as pr. n. Ἀγασθένης.

**ἄγασις**, ἡ, *rejoicing*, *EM*9.52; *envy*, Hsch. (ἄγασσις cod.).

**ἄγασμα**, τό, (ἄγαμαι) *object of adoration*, S.*Fr.*971 (pl.).

***ἀγάστονος**, ον, *much groaning*, of the sea, Od.12.97, h.*Ap.*94: *loud-wailing, lamentable*, A.*Th.*99, cf. *AP*14.123; πόνος Naum.ap. Stob.4.22.32.

***ἀγαστός**, ή, όν, (ἄγαμαι) later form of Hom. ἀγητός, *admirable*, A.*Fr.*268; οὐκέτι μοι βίος ἀ. E.*Hec.*168; ἐκεῖνο δὲ κρίνω τοῦ ἀνδρὸς ἀ. X.*HG*2.3.56, cf. *An.*1.9.24, Plu.*Aem.*22, Procop.*Aed.*1.4. Adv. -τῶς, prob. in S.*Ichn.*243, cf. X.*Ages.*1.24. (Pure Att. θαυμαστός.)

**ἀγάστωρ**, ορος, ὁ, ἡ, (ἀ copul., γαστήρ, cf. ἀδελφός) *from the same womb*: pl., *twins*, Hsch.: generally, *near kinsman*, Lyc.264.

**ἀγασυλλίς**, ίδος, ἡ, the plant which produces ἀμμωνιακόν, *Ferula marmarica*, Dsc.3.84.

**ἀγάσυρτος**, ὁ, '*swept and garnished*' (σύρω), epith. given to Pittacus by Alc.37B, cf. D.L.1.81.

***ἀγᾱτός**, ή, όν, = ἀγαστός, v.l. in h.*Ap.*515, (ἀγᾰ-) Theoc.1.126.

**ἀγαυός**, ή, όν, in Hom. almost always of kings or heroes, *illustrious, noble*, κήρυκες Il.3.268; Περσεφόνεια Od.11.213; πομπῆες *noble* guides, 13.71, cf. Pi.*P.*4.72; once in Trag., Πέρσαις ἀγαυοῖς A.*Pers.*986 (lyr.): Sup. -ότατος Od.15.229. **2.** of things, *brilliant, glorious*, δῶρον h.*Merc.*442; θρόος Pi.*Pae.*9.36; esp. of stars, Arat.71, al., Man.2.14 (Sup.):—in late Prose, Hierocl.*in CA*4 p.425 M. (Perh. α intens., γαίω, cf. Hdn.Gr.2.166.)

***ἀγαυρ-ίᾱμα**, τό, *insolence*, Lxx *Ba.*4.34, Hsch., *AB*325. ***-ιάομαι**, *to be insolent*, Lxx *Jb.*3.14: Act., *EM*6.38.

**ἀγαύρισμα**, τό, kind of wrestling, Eust.1444.8.

**ἀγαυρός**, ά, όν, = γαῦρος with α euphon., *stately, proud*, ταῦρος Hes.

.832; δένδρον Nic.*Th.*832 (Sup.). Adv. Sup. -ότατα Hdt.7.57. 2. Ion., euphem. for a beggar, *EM*0.30, Suid.

**ἀγάφθεγκτος**, ον, (φθέγγομαι) *loud-sounding*, ἀοιδαί Pi.*O.*6.91.

**ἀγάω**, = ἀγάζομαι, Alcm.121.

**ἄγγᾰρα**, τά, *daily stages of the* ἄγγαροι, *EM*7.17.

**ἀγγᾰρ-εία**, ἡ, *impressment for the public service*, *OGI*665.21 (pl.), Arr.*Epict.*4.1.79; in pl. = *cursus publicus*, *SIG*880.53 (Pizus, A.D.). **-ευτής**, οῦ, ὁ, *one who impresses*, Hsch. s. v. ἀγγαρεύεαι. II. *impressed workman, labourer*, *PSI*200.2 (vi A.D.); ὁ ἐπιείμενος τῶν ἀ. *PLand.*24.1 (vi A.D.). **-εύω**, *press one to serve as* ἄγγαρος, generally, *press into service*, *Ev.Matt.*5.41, 27.32, *OGI* 665.24; κτήνη, πλοῖα *PTeb.*5.182, 252 (ii B.C.), cf. *PPetr.*2 p.64 (ii B.C.):—Pass., *to be pressed into service*, Men.440: metaph., *to be constrained*, Procop.*Arc.*13. **-ήιος**, ὁ, Ion. form of ἄγγαρος, Hdt.3.126. II. Subst. **-ήιον**, τό, *posting-system*, Id. 8.98.

***ἄγγᾰρος**, ὁ, in Persia, *mounted courier*, for carrying royal despatches, Hdt.3.126, X.*Cyr.*8.6.17, Theopomp.Hist.106, etc. 2. term of abuse (= φορτηγός), ἄ. ὄλεθρος Men.2D., cf. Lib.*Or.*1. 129. II. as Adj., ἄ. πῦρ the *courier* flame, of beacon fires, A.*Ag.* 282; ἄ. ἡμίονοι *posting-mules*, Lib.*Or.*18.143. (Assyr. *agarru*, 'hired labourer'.)

**ἀγγαροφορέω**, *bear as an* ἄγγαρος, Procop.*Arc.*30, *Aed.*2.4; generally, 'toil and moil', Men.10D.

**ἄγγατος**· τὸ εἰς ἀναδενδράδα ξύλον. Hsch.

**ἀγγείδιον**, τό, Dim. of ἀγγεῖον, Thphr.*HP*9.6.4, Hero*Spir.*1.6, Damocr.ap.Gal.13.41 (prob. l.), *BGU*590.8 (ii A.D.). II. *gallbladder*, Ruf.*Anat.*30.

**ἀγγειο-λογέω**, *take up a vein and operate upon it*, c. acc., interp. in Sor.1.85, cf. Paul.Aeg.6.5: —hence Subst. **-λογία**, ἡ, Antyll. or Heliod.ap.Orib.45.18.32, Aët.7.95.

***ἀγγεῖον**, Ion. **-ήιον**, τό, *vessel* for holding liquid or dry substances (τοῦτο.. ξηροῖς καὶ ὑγροῖς.. ἐργασθέν, ἀγγεῖον δὴ μιᾷ κλήσει προσφθεγγόμεθα Pl.*Plt.*287e); of metal, ἀργύρεα ἀ. silver *jars* or *vases* for water, Hdt.1.188; ἀργυρᾶ καὶ χαλκᾶ ἀ. Plu.2.695b; ἐν ἀ. χαλκῷ *mortar*, Thphr.*Lap.*60; ξύλινα ἀ. *tubs*, Hdt.4.2; *vessels* for holding money, in a treasury, Id.2.121.β′; for masons' use, Th.4.4; ὀστράκινα ἀ. Hp.*Mul.*2.193, Lxx *La.*4.2; *pails* or *buckets* used by firemen, Plu.*Rom.*20; *sacks* of leather, θύλακοι καὶ ἄλλα ἀ. X.*An.* 6.4.23; τὰς ῥαφὰς τῶν ἀ. Plu.*Lys.*16; for corn, Lxx *Ge.*42.25; for wine, Lxx 1*Ki.*25.18; for bread, 1*Ki.*9.7; *box* for petitions, *PTaur.* 1ii6 (ii B.C.), etc. 2. *receptacle, reservoir*, X.*Oec.*9.2, Pl.*Lg.* 845e; *bed* of the sea, Pl.*Criti.*111a. 3. *coffin, sarcophagus*, *IG* 12(2).494 (Lesbos), *BSA*17.227 (Pamphyl.), etc. II. of the human or animal body, *vessel, cavity*, Hp.*Morb.*4.37, Arist.*HA*521ᵇ6, *PA*680ᵇ33; of the veins, Id.*HA*511ᵇ17, al.; the lungs, Id.*GA*787ᵇ3; the female breast, Id.*PA*692ᵃ12; *afterbirth*, Sor.2.57; of plants, *capsule*, Thphr.*HP*1.11.1:—later, *the body* itself, M.Ant.3.3, cf. Secund. *Sent.*7.

**ἀγγειοτομία**, ἡ, *section of a vein*, Paul.Aeg.6.31.

**ἀγγειώδης**, ες, *like a vessel, hollow*, Arist.*PA*671ᵃ23, Eudem.*Fr.* 44, M.Ant.10.38.

***ἀγγελία**, Ion. and Ep. **-ίη**, ἡ, (ἄγγελος) *message, tidings*, as well the substance as the conveyance thereof, Il.18.17, Od.2.30, etc.; ἀ. λέγουσα τάδε Hdt.2.114; ἀγγελίην φάτο, ἀπόφασθε, ἀπέειπε, Il.18.17, 9.422, 7.416; φέρειν 15.174; πέμπειν Hdt.2.114; ἐσπέμπειν 3.69; τὰς ἀ. ἐσφέρειν 1.114, 3.77: —ἐμὴ ἀ. *a report of* me, *concerning* me, Il.19.337; ἀ. τινός *a message about* a person or thing, ἀγγελίην πατρὸς φέρει ἐρχομένοιο *news of* thy father's coming, Od.1. 408; ἀνέρος αἴθονος ἀ. S.*Aj.*222; ἀ. τῆς Χίου ἀφικνεῖται Th.8.15; ἦλθε ἀ. τῶν πόλεων ὅτι ἀφεστᾶσι Id.1.61: ἀ. ἦλθον ἐκ τῶν πολεμίων X.*Cyr.*6.2.14; with Verbs of motion, ἀγγελίην ἐλθεῖν Il.11. 140: Ep. in gen., τευ ἀγγελίης.. ἤλυθες Il.13.252; ἀγγελίης οἰχνεσκε 15.640; ἤλυθε σεῦ ἕνεκ' ἀγγελίης (i.e. ἀγγελίης σοῦ ἕνεκα) 3.206; ἀγγελίης πωλεῖται Hes.*Th.*781:—wrongly expl. by Sch.Il., Apollon.*Lex.* as a masc. Subst. ἀγγελίης. 2. *announcement, proclamation*, Pi.*P.*2.4: *command, order*, *h.Cer.*448, Pi.*O.*3.28, cf. Od.5.150, 7.263. 3. 'Α. personified as daughter of Hermes, Pi. *O.*8.82. II. *messenger*, Ἶρις ἀ. v.l. Hes.*Th.*781.

**ἀγγελια-φορέω**, *bear messages*, Sch.A.*Pr.*969. ***-φόρος**, Ion. **ἀγγεληφ-**, ον, *messenger*, Hdt.1.120, Arist.*Mu.*398ᵃ31, Luc. *Sacr.*8, etc.: esp. *Persian chamberlain*, Hdt.3.118.

***ἀγγελικός**, ή, όν, *of* or *for a messenger*, ῥῆσις Phryn.*PS* p.45 B. b. *conveying information*, πάθος, of sensation, Gal.19. 378. 2. *angelic*, τάξις, νοῦς Procl.*in Ti.*1.341, 3.126 D.; γένος Hierocl.*in CA* 2 p.423 M. Adv. -κῶς Procl.*in Ti.*3.192D.: opp. δαιμονίως, Id.*in Cra.*p.71 P. II. ἀ. ὄρχησις Sicilian pantomimic dance at banquets, Ath.14.629e, cf. Poll.4.103, and v. ἄγγελος II; perh. from Ἄγγελος a name of Hecate, cf. Ath. l.c., Poll. l.c., Hsch.

**ἀγγελιώτης**, ου, ὁ, *messenger*, *h.Merc.*296, Call.*Jov.*68, *Hec.*1.1.6, Nonn.*D.*13.36: fem. **ἀγγελιῶτις**, ιδος, Call.*Del.*216.

***ἀγγέλλω**, (ἄγγελος): impf. ἀγγέλλεσκον Hsch.: Ep. and Ion. fut. ἀγγελέω Il.9.617, Hdt., Att. ἀγγελῶ, Dor. -ίω (ἀν-) *Tab.Heracl.*1.118: aor. 1 ἤγγειλα Hom., Att.: pf. ἤγγελκα Plb.35.4.2, (κατ-) Lys.25.30, (εἰσ-) Lycurg.1, (περι-) D.21.4:—**Med.** (v. infra): aor. ἠγγειλάμην (ἐπ-) Hdt.6.35, Pl.*Grg.*458d:—**Pass.**, fut. ἀγγελθήσομαι (ἀπ-) D.19. 324, later ἀγγελήσομαι (ἀν-) Lxx *Ps.*21(22).30: aor. ἠγγέλθην Hdt., Att.: pf. ἤγγελμαι A.*Ch.*774, Th.8.97: plpf. ἄγγελτο v.l. in Hdt. 7.37:—aor. 2 Pass. ἠγγέλην is found *IG*1.27b (ἐπ-), E.*IT*932, and became usual in Hellenistic Gk., cf. Lxx *Jo.*2.2 (ἀπ-), Plu.*Ant.*68, Hdn.3.7.1, etc.: aor. 2 Act. ἤγγελον is rare even in late writers, as (παρ-) App.*BC*1.121 without impf. as v.l., though in *AP*7.614 (Agath.) ἀγγελέτην is required by the metre:—*bear a message*, ὦρτο δὲ Ἶρις.. ἀγγελέουσα Il.8.409; τινί Od.4.24, 15.458: c. inf., οἵ κε.. κείνοις ἀγγείλωσι.. οἰκόνδε νέεσθαι *may bring* them *word* to return home, 16.350, cf. *EM*6.52: c. acc. inf., κήρυκες δ'.. ἀγγελλόντων.. γέροντας λέξασθαι Il.8.517. 2. c. acc. rei, *announce, report*, ἐσθλά Il.10.448; φάος ἠοῦς Od.13.94; Ποσειδάωνι πάντα τάδε Il. 15.159:—in Prose, μή τι νεώτερον ἀγγέλλεις; Pl.*Prt.*310b; prov., οὐ πόλεμον ἀγγέλλεις 'that's good news', Id.*Phdr.*242b; ἀγγέλλωμεν ἐς πόλιν τάδε; E.*Or.*1539; πρὸς τίν' ἀγγεῖλαί με χρὴ λόγους; Id.*Supp.* 399. 3. c. acc. pers., *bring news of..*, εἴ κέ μιν ἀγγείλαιμι Od.14.120; later, ἀ. περί τινος S.*El.*1111:—dependent clauses are added with a Conj., ἤγγειλ' ὅττι ῥά οἱ πόσις ἔκτοθι μίμνε Il.22.439; ἀ. ὡς.. E.*IT*704, D.18.169; ὁθούνεκα.. S.*El.*47:—also in part., ἢ καὶ θανόντ' ἤγγειλαν; ib.1452; Κῦρον ἐπιστρατεύοντα.. ἤγγειλεν X.*An.*2.3.19, cf. *Cyr.*6.2.15; with ὡς, πατέρα τὸν σὸν ἀγγελῶν ὡς οὐκέτ' ὄντα S.*OT*955; ἠγγείλας ὡς τεθνηκότα Id.*El.*1341. II. Med., only pres., Τεύκρῳ ἀγγέλλομαι εἶναι φίλος *I announce myself* to him as a friend, Id.*Aj.*1376. III. Pass., *to be reported of*, ἐπὶ τὸ πλεῖον Th.6.34: c. part., ζῶν ἢ θανὼν ἀγγέλλεται S.*Tr.*73, cf. E. *Hec.*591, Th.3.16, X.*HG*4.3.13: c. inf., ἤγγελται ἡ μάχη ἰσχυρὰ γεγονέναι Pl.*Chrm.*153b, cf. X.*Cyr.*5.3.30:—ἠγγέλθη τοῖς στρατηγοῖς, ὅτι φεύγοιεν that.., Id.*HG*1.1.27:—ἐπὶ τοῖς ἠγγελμένοις Th.8.97. (ἀπ-αγγέλλω is more common in Oratt.)

**ἄγγελμα**, τό, *message, tidings*, E.*Or.*876, Th.7.74, etc.

***ἄγγελος**, ὁ, ἡ, *messenger, envoy*, Il.2.26, etc.; δι' ἀγγέλων ὁμιλέειν τινί Hdt.5.92.ζ′, cf. *SIG*229.25 (Erythrae):—prov., Ἀράβιος ἄ., of a loquacious person, Men.32. 2. generally, *one that announces* or *tells*, e.g. of birds of augury, Il.24.292, 296; Μουσῶν ἄγγελος, of a poet, Thgn.769; ἄγγελε ἔαρος.. χελιδοῖ Simon.74; ἄ. ἄφθογγος, of a beacon, Thgn.549; of the nightingale, ὄρνις.. Διὸς ἄ. S.*El.*149: c. gen. rei, ἄ. κακῶν ἐμῶν Id.*Ant.*277; ἄγγελον γλῶσσαν λόγων E.*Supp.*203; αἴσθησις ἡμῖν ἄ. Plot.5.3.3; neut. pl., ἄγγελα νίκης Nonn.*D.*34.226. 3. *angel*, Lxx *Ge.*28.12, al., *Ev.Matt.*1. 24, al., Ph.2.604, etc. 4. in later philos., *semi-divine being*, ἡλιακοὶ ἄ. Jul.*Or.*4.141b, cf. Iamb.*Myst.*2.6, Procl.*in R.*2.243K.; ἄ. καὶ ἀρχάγγελοι *Theol.Ar.*43.10, cf. Dam.*Pr.*183, al.: also in mystical and magical writings, Herm.ap.Stob.1.49.45, *PMag Lond.*46.121, etc. II. title of Artemis at Syracuse, Hsch.

**ἀγγέλτειρα**, ἡ, fem., = foreg., prob. in Orph.*H.*78.3.

**ἀγγελτικός**, ή, όν, *premonitory*: c. gen., τεράστια συμφορᾶς ἀ. Heracl.*Alleg.*42; τοῦ μέλλοντος Porph.*Abst.*3.3: ἀ. ζῴδια Jul.Laod. in *Cat.Cod.Astr.*5(1).192.

**ἀγγέριος**· ἄγγελος, Hsch. **ἀγγεράκομον**· σταφυλήν, Id.

**ἀγγοθήκη**, ἡ, *receptacle for vessels*, Ath.5.210c, cf. ἐγγυθήκη.

**ἀγγοπήνια**· τὰ τῶν μελισσῶν κηρία. Hsch., Suid. **ἀγγόρπη**· ᾧ τοὺς ἐλέφαντας τύπτουσι σιδήρῳ, Hsch.

***ἄγγος**, εος, τό, *vessel* to hold liquids, e.g. wine, Od.16.13, cf. 2. 289; milk, Il.16.643; *vat* for the vintage, Hes.*Op.*613; *pitcher*, Hdt. 5.12, E.*El.*55; *bucket, pail*, Hdt.4.62; *wine-bowl*, E.*IT*953, 960. II. for dry substances, *cradle*, Hdt.1.113, E.*Ion*32, 1337; *casket*, S.*Tr.* 622; *cinerary urn*, Id.*El.*1118, 1205; *coffin*, *CIG*3573 (Assos). III. of parts of the body, e.g. *womb*, Hp.*Epid.*6.5.11, v. Gal. ad loc.; τρόφιμον ἄ. *stomach*, Tim.*Pers.*73. IV. *shell* of the κάραβος, Opp. *H.*2.406. V. *cell* of a honey-comb, *AP*9.226 (Zonas).

**ἄγγουρος**, kind of *cake* or *tart*, Hsch. **ἀγγριάς**· τοὺς ἐρεθισμούς· οἱ δὲ τὰς ἀνίας, Orion ap.*EM*6.40, cf. Hsch. **ἀγγρίζειν**· ὑφαιρεῖσθαι (cf. ἀγρέω), ἐρεθίζειν, Hsch., *EM*7.28. **ἀγγρίς**· ὀδύνη, Suid. **ἀγγρισμός**, *irritatio*, *Gloss.* **ἀγγριστής**, *irritator*, ib.

**ἄγγων**, ωνος, ὁ, *Frankish javelin*, Agath.2.5.

**ἄγδην**, Adv. (ἄγω) *by carrying*, ἄγδην σύρειν Luc.*Lex.*10.

**ἄγε, ἄγετε**, imper. of ἄγω, used as Adv., *come on!* freq. in Hom., who mostly strengthens it, εἰ δ' ἄγε, νῦν δ' ἄγε, ἄγε δή, ἀλλ' ἄγε, in Att. freq. ἄγε νύν Ar.*Eq.*1011, etc.; before 1 and 2 pers. pl., ἄγε δὴ τραπείομεν Il.3.441; ἄγε δὴ στέωμεν 11.348; ἄγε τάμνετε Od.3.332; ἀλλ' ἄγε, Πέρσαι, φροντίδα θώμεθα A.*Pers.*140; ἄγε δὴ καὶ χορὸν ἄψωμεν Id.*Eu.*307; rarely before 1 sg., ἄγε δὴ.. ἀριθμήσω Od.13.215; before 3 pl., ἀλλ' ἄγε, κήρυκες.. λαὸν.. ἀγειρόντων Il.2.437; in Prose, ἄγε τοίνυν.. σκοπῶμεν X.*Cyr.*5.5.15; foll. by ὅπως c. fut., Ar.*Ec.*149; abs., E.*Cyc.*590:—also, ἄγετε,.. λύσασθε A.*Ch.*803; ἄγετε with 1 pl., Il.2.139, Od.1.76, Ar.*Lys.*665; with 1 sg., Od.22.139: cf. ἄγι.

**ἀγέγωνος**, ον, *speechless*, πέτρα Epigr. in *AEM*6.6 (Callatis).

***ἄγεθλον**, τό, (ἄγω) *sacrificial victim*, *GDI*1266 (Pamphyl.).

**ἄγει**, Dor. = ἄγρει, *An.Ox.*1.71.

**ἄγειος**, ον, (γῆ) *landless*, corrupt in A.*Supp.*858.

**ἀγείρᾰτος**, ον, poet. for ἀγέραστος, Hdn.Gr.2.269.

***ἀγείρω**, Aeol. ἀγέρρω *EM*8.13: fut. ἀγερῶ *IG*5(1).1447.16 (Messene, ii B.C.): aor. 1 ἤγειρα, Ep. ἄγειρα Od.14.285:—Med., aor. 1 ἠγειράμην A.R.4.1335, (συν-) Od.14.323, Ael.*VH*4.14:—**Pass.**, aor. 1 ἠγέρθην Hom.: pf. ἀγήγερμαι App.*BC*2.134: plpf. ἀγήγερτο Id.*Mith.*108, Ep. 3 pl. ἀγηγέρατο Il.4.211, App.*Hisp.*40.—Hom. has shortened pres. ἀγέρεσθαι (al. ἀγερέσθαι) Od.2.385 (also in later Ep., A.R.3.895, etc., cf. *IG*14.1389 i 35), aor. 2 ἀγέροντο Il.18.245, part. ἀγρόμενος 2.481, etc.:—*gather together*, λαὸν ἀγείρων Il.4.377, etc.; ἐνθάδ' ἀπὸ.. πολίων ἤγειρα ἕκαστον 17.222; so in Att., τὸν ἐς Θήβας στόλον S.*OC*1306, Th.1.9; τὸ Ἑλλάδος στράτευμα S.*El.*695;

στρατιάν X.*An*.3.2.13, cf. App.*Mith*.84; εἰς μίαν οἴκησιν ἀ. κοινωνούς Pl.*R*.369c:—Pass., *gather, assemble*, Il.2.52, Od.2.8, etc.; ἀγρόμενοι σύες *herded* swine, Od.16.3; θυμὸς ἐνὶ στήθεσσιν ἀγέρθη, ἐς φρένα θυμὸς ἀγέρθη Il.4.152, 22.475 (cf. ἐγείρω). II. of things, *collect, gather*, δημόθεν ἄλφιτα.. καὶ αἴθοπα οἶνον ἀγείρας Od.19.197; πολὺν βίοτον καὶ χρυσὸν ἀγείρων 3.301; πολλὰ δ' ἄγειρα χρήματα 14.285:—so in Med., ἀγειρόμενοι κατὰ δῆμον 13.14. 2. *collect by begging*, ὡς ἂν πύρνα κατὰ μνηστῆρας ἀγείροι 17.362, cf. Hdt.1.61; ἀφ' ὧν ἀγείρει καὶ προσαιτεῖ D.8.26:—abs., *collect money* for the gods, Νύμφαις ἀ. A.*Fr*.168, cf. Hdt.4.35, Pl.*R*.381d, *SIG*1015.26 (Halicarnassus); esp. for Cybele, Luc.*Alex*.13, cf. μητραγύρτης:—abs., *go about begging*, Philostr.*VA*5.7, Man.6.299, Max.Tyr.19.3, etc. 3. *put things together, accumulate arguments*, as in a speech, A.*Ch*.638. 4. ὀφρύας εἰς ἓν ἀ. *frown*, *AP*5.299 (Paul. Sil.).—Rare in good Prose.

**ἀγείσωτος,** ον, *without cornice*, *EM*8.55.

**ἀγείτης·** ὑβριστής, Hsch., *EM*8.51. (Perh. f.l. for ἀλείτης.)

**ἀγείτων,** ον, gen. ονος, *neighbourless*, πάγος A.*Pr*.272; οἶκος φίλων ἀ. E.*El*.1130; ἄφιλος καὶ ἀ. Plu.2.423e.

**⊛ἀγελάζομαι,** Pass., *to be gregarious, flock*, Arist.*HA*597$^{b}$7, 610$^{b}$2, Nic.Dam.p.151D.; ἐς τὴν ἤπειρον Men.Prot.p.49D.:—Act., ἀγελάσαι· κομίσαι, Hsch.

**⊛ἀγελαιοκομικός,** ή, όν, (κομέω) *pertaining to cattle-breeding*: ἡ ἀγελαιοκομική (sc. τέχνη) *the art of breeding and keeping cattle*, Pl.*Plt*.275e sq., 299d.

**⊛ἀγελαῖος,** α, ον, (ἀγέλη) *belonging to a herd*, in Hom. always with βοῦς, Il.11.729, Od.10.410, al., cf. S.*Aj*.175; βοσκήματα E.*Ba*.677; αἱ ἀ. τῶν ἵππων, i.e. brood-mares, X.*Eq*.5.8. II. *in herds* or *shoals, gregarious*, ἰχθύες Hdt.2.93; ἀγελαῖα, τά, *gregarious animals*, Pl.*Plt*.264d; opp. μοναδικά, σποραδικά, Arist.*HA*487$^{b}$34, *Pol*.1256$^{a}$23; πολιτικὸν ὁ ἄνθρωπος ζῷον πάσης μελίττης καὶ παντὸς ἀ. ζῴου μᾶλλον ib.1253$^{a}$8. 2. *of the common herd*, ἀ. ἄνθρωποι, opp. ἄρχοντες, Pl.*Plt*.268a; hence, *common, ordinary*, ἀ. ἰσχάδες Eup.374; ἄρτοι Pl.Com.76; κεραμίδες *SIG*$^{2}$587.209, cf. *Ath.Mitt*.22.182 (Lebad.):—σοφισταί Isoc.12.18, νῆσοι Philostr.*Im*.2.17; proparox. in this sense, Eust.1752.63.

**ἀγελαιο-τροφία,** ἡ, *keeping of herds*, Pl.*Plt*.261e. **-τροφικός,** ή, όν, *of* or *fit for* ἀγελαιοτροφία: ἡ -κή, = foreg., Pl.*Plt*.267b. **-τρόφος,** ον, *keeping herds*, Max.Tyr.26.6, al.

**ἀγελαιών,** ῶνος, ὁ, *a place for herds* (τὰ ἀγελαῖα), *pasture*, Suid.

**ἀγέλαοι,** οἱ, *members of an* ἀγέλη II, *GDI*4952 (Dreros).

**⊛ἀγελ-αρχέω,** *lead a herd* or *company*, Ph.1.679: c. gen., 1.658, Plu.*Galb*.17. **⊛-άρχης,** ου, ὁ, (ἄρχω) *leader of a flock* or *herd*, Procl. *in Cra*.p.38P.; ἀ. ταῦρος Luc.*Am*.22: generally, *leader, captain*, Plu.*Rom*.6; τῶν φιλοσοφίας ἐραστῶν Procl. *in Prm*.p.526S.:—also **-αρχος,** ὁ, dub. l. in Ph.2.144. **-αρχία,** ἡ, *IGRom*.3.648 (Idebessus, ii A.D.):—Adj. **⊛-αρχικός,** prob. l. for -ιανός, ibid.

**ἀγέλασμα,** ατος, τό, *gathering, crowd*, νούσων Procl.*H*.7.44.

**ἀγελ-αστέω,** *to be* ἀγέλαστος, Heraclit.*Ep*.7.2,9. **-αστί,** Adv. *without laughter*, Pl.*Euthd*.278e, Thphr.*Fr*.124, Plu.2.727a.

**ἀγελαστικός,** ή, όν, *gregarious, social*, Ph.2.202, Max.Tyr.21.7.

**ἀγέλαστος,** ον, (γελάω) *not laughing, grave, gloomy*, *h.Cer*.200; ἀ. πρόσωπα βιαζόμενοι A.*Ag*.794; of the orator Crassus, Lucil ap. Cic.*Fin*.5.30, cf. Vett.Val.75.11: metaph., Σίβυλλα ἀγέλαστα φθεγγομένη Heraclit.92; ἀ. φρήν A.*Fr*.290; βίος Phryn.Com.18; ἀ. πέτρα, stone at Eleusis on which Demeter sat, *SIG*$^{2}$587.183, Apollod.1.5.1. II. Pass., *not to be laughed at, not trifling*, ξυμφοραί A.*Ch*.30, v.l. Od.8.307.

**ἀγελάτης,** Dor. **-άτας,** ου, ὁ, chief of an ἀγέλη II, Heraclid.*Pol*.15. II. = ἔφηβος, Hsch. (cod. ἀγελάστους), cf. *GDI*5142 (Oaxos).

**⊛ἀγελείη,** ἡ, Ep. epith. of Athena, = ἄγουσα λείαν, *driver of spoil, the forager*, Il.6.269, etc., cf. Hes.*Sc*.197. II. ἀγελεία, ἡ, mystical name of *Seven*, *Theol.Ar*.42.30.

**⊛ἀγέλ-η,** ἡ, (ἄγω) *herd*, of horses, Il.19.281; elsewhere in Hom. always of oxen and kine, Il.11.678, etc., cf. βούνομος:—also, *any herd* or *company*, συῶν ἀ. Hes.*Sc*.168; ἀ. παρθένων Pi.*Fr*.112; μαινάδων E.*Ba*.1022; πτηνῶν ἀγέλαι S.*Aj*.168, E.*Ion*106; *shoal* of fish, Opp.*H*.3.639: metaph., πόνων ἀγέλαι E.*HF*1276:—also in Pl.*R*.451c, Arist.*HA*570$^{a}$27, etc., but rare in early Prose. II. in Crete and at Sparta, *bands* in which boys were trained, Ephor.64, Plu.*Lyc*.16, Heraclid.*Pol*.15, *GDI*4952 (Dreros), etc.; νέων ἀ. *Epigr.Gr*.223.8 (Miletus); ἀϊθέων ib.239 (Smyrna). III. = ἀστρικαὶ σφαῖραι *Theol.Ar*.43.6. **-ηδόν,** Adv. (ἀγέλη) *in herds* or *companies*, Il.16.160, Hdt.2.93, *AP*9.24 (Leon.), etc.:—also **-ηδά,** Arat.965, 1079. **-ηθεν,** Adv. (ἀγέλη) *from a herd*, A.R.1.356, 406. **-ῆτις,** ἴδος, ἡ, pecul. fem. of ἀγελαῖος, Numen.ap.Ath.7.327b. II. = ἀγελείη, Corn.*ND*20. **-ηκόμος,** ον, *keeping herds*, Nonn.*D*.47.208. **-ήτης,** ου, ὁ, *belonging to a herd*, βοῦς Suid.; cf. ἀγελάτης. **-ητρόφος,** ὁ, *horse-keeper*, Poll.1.181 (v.l. ἀγελο-). **-ηφι,** Ep. dat. of ἀγέλη, Il.2.480. **-ίζει·** ἀθροίζει, *gregat*, Gloss. **-ικός,** ή, όν, *of the flock*, πρόβατα *Sammelb*.4322.9 (i A.D.). **-ισμός,** ὁ, gloss on ἀγελαῖος, Sch.Opp.*C*.1.240.

**ἀγέλοιος,** ον, *not laughable*, οὐκ ἀγέλοιον *no bad joke*, Henioch.4.6. Adv. -ως *Arg*.1 Ar.*Ra*.

**ἄγελος,** ου, ὁ, = ἀγέλη III, *Theol.Ar*.43.6.

**ἀγέμιστος,** ον, *not put on board ship*, στέμφυλα, *PAvrom*.1$^{b}$34 (i B.C.).

**ἄγεν,** Ep. for ἐάγησαν, v. sub ἄγνυμι, Il.4.214.

**ἀγενεᾱλόγητος,** ον, *of unrecorded descent*, *Ep.Heb*.7.3.

**ἀγένεια,** ἡ, (ἀγενής) *low birth*, Arist.*Pol*.1317$^{b}$40.

**⊛ἀγένειος,** ον, (γένειον) *beardless, boyish*; ἀγένειόν τι εἰρηκέναι speak *like a boy*, Luc.*J.Tr*.29; τὸ ἀ. Id.*Eun*.9. Adv. -είως, ἔχ Philostr.*VS*1.8.1. II. ἀγένειοι, οἱ, *boys* within the age to en for certain prizes at the games, Pi.*O*.8.54, 9.89, cf. Ar.*Eq*.1373, L 21.4, Pl.*Lg*.833c, *IG*2.965, al., Paus.6.6.3. III. (γενεά) *chi less*, *GDI*1891.29 (Delph.), Hsch.

**⊛ἀγεν-ής,** ές, (γενέσθαι) *unborn, uncreated*, Pl.*Ti*.27c. II. *no family, ignoble*, opp. ἀγαθός, S.*Fr*.84, cf. *POxy*.33$^{v}$5.5 (ii A.D. of things, οὐκ ἀγενεῖς στίχοι Sch.Od.11.568; cf. *AB*336, St.By s.v. Ἀνακτορεία. III. *childless*, Is.2.10, cf. Harp. (ἄπα codd.). **-ησία,** ἡ, *uncreatedness*, τοῦ κόσμου Simp. *in Cae* 139.24. **-ητος,** ον, (γενέσθαι) *uncreated, unoriginated*, Parm 8.3, Heraclit.50; of the elements, Emp.7; ἀρχή Pl.*Phdr*.245d, c Arist.*Cael*.281$^{b}$26, al. Adv. -τως Plu.2.1015b (prob.), Syr. *in Metaph* 146.1, Dam.*Pr*.409. II. *not having happened*, Gorg.*Pal*.23; τ γὰρ φανθὲν τίς ἂν δύναιτ' ἂν ἀγένητον ποιεῖν; S.*Tr*.743; ἅπαντα τὰ πρῶτον ἦλθ' ἅπαξ Id.*Fr*.860; ἀγένητα ποιεῖν, ἅσσ' ἂν ᾖ πεπραγμένα Agatho 5; αἰτίαι ἀ. *groundless* charges, Aeschin.3.225; διαβολαί Al ciphr.3.58; ὕπνοι ἀ. *baseless* dreams, Phld.*D*.1.22; ὧν οὐδὲν.. ἀ. *was left undone*, Isoc.20.8. III. translator's error for Lat. *infectus, dyed*, *Edict.Diocl*.24.13.

**ἀγένν-εια** (in Mss. often ἀγένεια or ἀγεννία), ἡ, *meanness, baseness*, Arist.*Virt.Vit*.1251$^{b}$16, Plb.30.9.1, al., Phld.*Herc*.1457.4. II. *sordidness*, opp. πολυτέλεια, D.S.33.7. **-ής,** ές, (γέννα) = ἀγενής II (q.v.), *low-born*, Hdt.1.134 (Comp.), Pl.*Prt*.319d, etc.; οἱ ἀ., opp. οἱ γενναῖοι, Arist.*Pol*.1296$^{b}$22, etc.; of a cock, Pl.*Tht*.164c, Men.223.13. 2. of things, *sordid*, Hdt.5.6, Pl.*Grg*.465b, 513d, al.; βωμολοχεύματ' Ar.*Pax*748; οὐδὲν ἀ. Dem.21.152. Adv. -νῶς E.*IA*1458, Pl.Com.46.6.—In Pl. mostly with neg., οὐκ ἀ. *Chrm*.158c, etc. **-ησία,** ἡ, *uncreatedness*, opp. γένεσις, τῆς ὕλης Herm. ap.Stob.1.11.2. **-ητος,** ον, (γεννάω) *unbegotten, unborn*, ἀ. τότ' ἦ S.*OC*973: *unoriginated*, Pl.*Ti*.52a. Adv., ἀναιτίως καὶ ἀ. Plu.2.1015b codd. 2. *non-existent*, αἰτία Aret.*SD*2.11. II. = ἀγεννής, *low-born, mean*, S.*Tr*.61. III. Act., *not productive*, Thphr.*CP*6.10.1. Adv. -τως *without leaving issue*, *Epigr.Gr*.333a (Perg.). **-ία,** v. sub ἀγέννεια. **-ίζω,** *act like an* ἀγεννής, Teles p.6.4H.

**ἀγέομαι,** Dor. for ἡγέομαι: τὰ ἁγημενα *custom, prescription*, Orac. ap.D.43.66.

**ἀγέραστος,** ον, (γέρας) *without a gift of honour, unrecompensed*, Il.1.119, Hes.*Th*.395; ἀ. τύμβος, ὄνομα E.*Hec*.115, *Ba*.1378; ἀπελθεῖν ἀ. Luc.*Tyr*.3: c. gen., θυέων ἀ. A.R.3.65:—cf. ἀγείρᾰτος.

**ἀγέρδα** (ἀγέραα cod.)· ἄπιος, ὄγχνη, Hsch.

**ἀγερέθω,** v. sub ἠγερέθομαι.

**ἄγερθεν,** Dor. and Ep. 3 pl. aor. 1 Pass. of ἀγείρω.

**⊛ἀγερ-μός,** ὁ, *collection of money for the service of the gods* (cf. ἀγείρω II.2), *SIG*1015.27 (Halicarnassus), D.H.2.19 (with v.l. ἀγυρμός), Ath.8.360d, Poll.3.111. II. *the call-to-arms* of the Greeks against Troy, Arist.*Po*.1451$^{a}$27. III. metaph., *collection*, of wisdom and experience, Ael.*VH*4.20. **-μοσύνη,** ἡ, = ἄγερσις, Opp.*C*.4.251. **-σῐκύβηλις** [ῠ], ὁ, *mendicant priest*, Cratin.62. (From κύβηλις II, not Κυβέλη.) **⊛-σις,** εως, ἡ, *gathering, mustering*, στρατιῆς Hdt.7.5, 48. II. = πανήγυρις, *SIG*$^{2}$660.3 (Miletus, iii B.C., pl.). **-της,** Dor. **-τας,** ὁ, *collector of dues*, *IG*14.423 i35 (Tauromenium).

**ἀγερωπεῖ** (-ύπτει cod.)· ἐφορᾷ, ἀσπαστὸν ἡγεῖται, Hsch., cf. *Et.Gud.*, *EM*8.29. **ἀγερώσσει·** ἀγρυπνεῖ, Hsch., *Et.Gud*.

**⊛ἀγερ-ωχία,** ἡ, *arrogance*, Plb.10.35.8, D.Chr.32.9; in good sense, *high-heartedness*, Ps.-Callisth.3.25. II. *revelry*, Lxx *Wi*.2.9; pl., *feats of mastery*, Philostr.*VA*2.28. **⊛-ωχος** [ᾰ], ον, poet. Adj. (used also in late Prose, v. infr.), in Hom. always in good sense, *high-minded, lordly*, Τρῶες, Ῥόδιοι, Μυσοί, Il.3.36, 2.654, 10.430, cf. Alcm.122, B.5.35; βάτραχοι Batr.145; once of a single man, viz. Periclymenus, Od.11.286, Hes.*Fr*.14; of *noble* actions, ἀ. ἔργματα Pi.*N*.6.34; νίκη *O*.10(11).79; πλούτου στεφάνωμ' ἀ. *lordly* crown of wealth, *P*.1.50; *high-spirited*, Philostr.*Im*.2.2, al.; ἀγέρωχα σκιρτᾶν ib.32; -ότερα γυμνάσια Id.*Gym*.46. II. later in bad sense, *arrogant*, Archil.154, Alc.120, *Com.Adesp*.162, Lxx 3*Ma*.1.25; ἀ. ὄνος Luc.*Asin*.40; of things, φυτόν *Anacreont*.53.42. Adv. -χως *AP*9.745 (Anyte), Plb.2.8.7: Comp. -ότερον Id.18.34.3.

**Ἀγεσίλαος, Ἀγεσίλας,** v. sub Ἀγησίλαος.

**⊛ἀγεσίφρων·** τὰς ὀφρῦς ἐπαίρων, Hsch. (fort. -οφρύων).

**ἀγέστρατος,** ὁ, ἡ, *host-leading*, Ἀθήνη Hes.*Th*.925; ἦχος, αὐλός, Nonn.*D*.26.15, 28.28.

**ἁγέτης, ἁγέτις,** Dor. for ἡγ-.

**ἀγετοί·** θαυμαστοί, ἔνδοξοι, Hsch. **ἀγέτρια·** μαῖα (Tarent.), Id. (perh. for ἀγρέτρια, cf. ἀγρέω). **ἀγευστί,** gloss on ἀπαστί, Id.

**ἀγευστία,** ἡ, *fasting*, Sch.Ar.*Nu*.621.

**ἄγευστος,** ον, (γεύομαι) Act., *not tasting* or *having tasted*, πλακοῦντος Pl.Com.113; ἰχθύων Luc.*Sat*.28: metaph., οἷσι κακῶν ἄ. αἰών S.*Ant*.583; ἐλευθερίας ἄ. Pl.*R*.576a; τῶν τερπνῶν X.*Mem*.2.1.23; τοῦ καλοῦ Arist.*EN*1179$^{b}$15; τῶν ἀγαθῶν Phld.*Ir*.p.60W.; προβλήματα ἀμφιβολίας καὶ ζητήσεως ἄ. Alex.Aphr.*Pr.Praef*.:—abs., *without eating*, ἄποτοι καὶ ἄ. Luc.*Tim*.18. II. Pass., *tasteless*, Arist.*de An*.422$^{a}$30. 2. *untasted*, Plu.2.731d, Porph.*Abst*.2.27.

**ἀγεωμέτρητος,** ον, of persons, *ignorant of geometry*, Arist.*APo*.77$^{b}$13; ἀ. μηδεὶς εἰσίτω, Inscr. on Plato's door, Elias *in Cat*.118.18, cf. Phlp. *in de An*.117.29. Adv. -τως Anon. *in SE*29.35. 2. of blems, *not geometrical*, Arist.*APo.*$77^{b}17$. II. *not measured* or *surveyed*, prob. in *PTeb.*87.84 (ii B.C.).

**ἀγεωργ-ησία**, ἡ, *bad husbandry*, Thphr.*CP*2.15.1. **-ητος**, ον, *uncultivated*, Thphr.*CP*1.16.2, *PPar.*63.6 (ii B.C.), *SIG*685.73 (Magnesiae, ii B.C.), D.S.2.36, Ph.1.564, etc. **-ίου δικάζεσθαι** bring an action *for neglect of tillage*, Phryn.*PS*p.33 B.

***ἄγη**, Dor. **ἄγᾱ** [ἄγ], ἡ, (ἄγαμαι) *wonder, amazement*, Hom. only in phrase ἄγη μ' ἔχει Il.21.221, Od.3.227, 16.243: glossed by τιμή, σεβασμός, Hsch. II. *envy, malice*, φθόνῳ καὶ ἄγῃ χρεώμενος Hdt.6.61: of the gods, *jealousy*, μή τις ἄγα θεόθεν κνεφάσῃ A.*Ag.* 131: pl. ἄγαις, = ζηλώσεσιν, Id.*Fr.*85.

***ἀγή** (A), Dor. **ἀγά** [ᾱγ], ἡ, (ἄγνυμι) *breakage*: 1. *fragment, splinter*, ἀγαῖσι κωπῶν A.*Pers.*425; πρὸς ἁρμάτων τ' ἀγαῖσι E.*Supp.* 693. 2. κύματος ἀγή *place where* the wave *breaks, beach*, A.R.1. 554, Numen.ap.Ath.7.305a. 3. *curve, bending*, ὄφιος, ποταμοῦ, Arat.668,729 (v.l.):—hence Böckh cj. ἀγάν (for ἄγαν) Pi.*P.*2.82, in the sense of *crooked arts, deceit.* 4. *wound*, Hsch.

**ἀγή** (B), ἡ, (ἄγω) = ἀγωγή, ξύλων *Michel*1359.17 (Chios).

**ἄγη**, Ep. for ἐάγη, v. sub ἄγνυμι.

***ἀγηθής**, ές, *joyless*, cj. in S.*Tr.*869.

***ἀγηλᾰτ-έω**, *drive out one accursed* or *polluted*, esp. *one guilty of sacrilege and murder*, Hdt.5.72, S.*OT*402, Arist.*Ath.*20.3:—also **-ίζω**, *EM*10.34.

**ἀγήλᾰτος**, ον, (ἄγος, ἐλαύνω) *driving out a curse*, ἀ. μάστιξ, i.e. lightning *which consumes and so purifies*, Lyc.436.

**ἄγημα**, τό, (from ἄγω, or perh. Dor. for ἥγημα; Boeot. **ἄγειμα**, *BCH*18.534 (Thisbe)) *anything led, division, corps* of an army, of the Lacedaemonians, X.*Lac.*11.9, 13.6: in the Macedonian army, *the Guard*, Plb.5.65.2, Arr.*An.*1.1.11; τῶν ἱππέων τὸ ἄ. ib.4.24.1; τῶν πεζῶν τὸ ἄ. 2.8.3; τῶν ἐλεφάντων Phylarch.1: in the armies of the Ptolemies, etc., *PPetr.*3p.22 (iii B.C.), Plu.*Eum.*7, App.*Syr.*32, cf. Ael.Dion.*Fr.*8; βασιλικὸν ἄ. Plb.5.82.4. II. name of a district in the Heracleopolite nome, *PHib.*101.3, *PTeb.*2.38.4.

***ἀγηνόρειος**, Dor. **ἀγᾱνόρ-**, α, ον, = ἀγήνωρ, A.*Pers.*1026.

***ἀγην-ορέω** [ᾰ], *to be valiant*, Nonn.*D.*12.206, 37.338, al. **-ορία**, ἡ, *manliness, courage*, of men, Il.22.457; *arrogance, pride*, in pl., 9.700; sg., Nonn.*D.*42.384, *AP*10.75.7 (Pall.), etc.; of a lion, Il. 12.46. ***-ωρ**, Dor. **ἀγάνωρ**, ορος, ὁ, ἡ, (ἀγα-, ἀνήρ) poet. Adj. *manly, heroic*, θυμός Il.2.276, 12.300; κραδίη καὶ θυμὸς ἀ. 9.635, etc.; βίῃ καὶ ἀγήνορι θυμῷ εἴξας, of a lion, 24.42: freq. with collat. notion of *headstrong, arrogant*, of Achilles, 9.699; Thersites, 2. 276; the suitors, Od.1.106,144, al.; the Titans, Hes.*Th.*641, cf. *Op.*7; the Seven against Thebes, A.*Th.*124 (lyr.). 2. of animals and things, *stately, magnificent*, ἵππος Pi.*O.*9.23; *lavish*, μισθός *P.*3. 55; πλοῦτος ib.10.18; κόμπος *I.*1.43.

**ἀγήοχα**, pf. of ἄγω.

**ἀγήραντος**, ον, = sq., Simon.100.4, E.*Epigr.*2.1.

***ἀγήραος**, ον, Att. contr. **ἀγήρως, ων** (of which Hom. uses nom. dual ἀγήρω (v. infr.), nom. sg. and acc. pl. ἀγήρως Od.5.218, al.); acc. sg. ἀγήρων *h.Cer.*242; ἀγήρω Hes.*Th.*949, Jul.*Or.*4.142b: nom. pl. ἀγήρῳ Hes.*Th.*277; dat. ἀγήρῳς Ar.*Av.*689:—*ageless, undecaying*, ἀθάνατος καὶ ἀγήρως ἤματα πάντα Il.8.539; σὺ δ' ἀθάνατος καὶ ἀ. Od.5.218; ἀγήρω τ' ἀθανάτω τε Il.12.323, cf. Hes.*Th.*949; ἀπήμαντος καὶ ἀ. ib.955; ἄνοσοι καὶ ἀ. Pi.*Fr.*143; ἀ. χρόνῳ δυνάστας S.*Ant.*608 (lyr.). 2. of things, once in Hom., of the aegis, Il.2.447; κῦδος ἀ. Pi.*P.*2.52; χάριν τ' ἀγήρων ἕξομεν E.*Supp.*1178: in Prose, τὸν ἀγήρων ἔπαινον Th.2.43; ἀθάνατον καὶ ἀ. πάθος Pl.*Phlb.*15d, etc.

**ἀγηρασία**, ἡ, *eternal youth*, Sch.Il.11.1.

**ἀγήρατον**, τό, *pot-marjoram, Origanum Onites*, Dsc.4.58. 2. = θύμβρα, Ps.-Dsc.3.37.

***ἀγήρᾰτος** (A), ον, *ageless*, κλέος E.*IA*567 (lyr.), *IG*14.1930.3: also in Prose, Lys.2.79, X.*Mem.*4.3.13, Pl.*Ax.*370d, Arist.*Cael.* $270^{b}2$, Gal.12.201. [Later -ᾱτος, *Epigr.Gr.*35*a* (Athens), *IG*14.1188, Orac.ap.Ps.-Callisth.1.33.]

**ἀγήρατος** (B), ὁ, *stone* used by shoemakers to polish women's shoes, Gal.12.201, Asclep.ap.Aët.8.43.

**ἀγής** [ᾱ], ές, *guilty, accursed*, dub. in Hippon.1'. II. in good sense, *pure, holy*, of the sun, ἁγέα κύκλον Emp.47.

**'Αγήσανδρος**, ὁ, epith. of Pluto, = 'Αγησίλαος, Hsch.

**ἀγησί-λᾱος** [ᾱγ], ου, ὁ *leader of the people*, epith. of Hades, A.*Fr.* 406; Ion. ἡγησίλεως *AP*7.545 (Hegesipp.); Ep. ἡγεσίλαος Nic.*Fr.* 74.72; poet. also ἀγεσίλας, α, Call.*Lav.Pall.*130, *Epigr.Gr.*195 (Oaxos):—the form ἀγεσίλαος, cited in *EM*8.32 (misquoting Call. *Lav.Pall.*l.c.), etc., is corrupt. II. pr. n., esp. of the well-known Spartan king, 'Αγησίλαος X.*HG*3.3.4, etc.; 'Ηγησίλεως Id.*Vect.*3.7, D.19.290, cf. Hdt.7.204, 8.131; 'Αγησίλας, α, Paus.8. 18.8. **-χορος**, ον, *leading the chorus* or *dance*, προοίμια Pi.*P.* 1.4: fem. -χόρα, as pr. n., Alcm.23.77.

***ἀγητός**, ή, όν, (ἀγάομαι) *admirable, wonderful*, φυὴν καὶ εἶδος ἀγητὸν Ἕκτορος Il.22.370; elsewh. in Hom. of persons, c. acc. rei, δέμας καὶ εἶδος ἀ. 24.376; εἶδος ἀγητοί *wonderful* in form only, as a reproach, Il.5.787, 8.228; εἶδος ἀγητή *h.Ap.*198: later c. dat. rei, χρήμασιν ἀ. Sol.5.3:—of things, ῥόδων ἀ. ἔρνος *Anacreont.*53.36.

**'Αγήτωρ**, ὁ, *Leader*, epith. of Zeus at Sparta, X.*Lac.*13.2.

**ἄγι, -ιτε**, = ἄγε, ἄγετε, Alc.*Supp.*7.4,10, Sapph.*Supp.*19.6: perh. ἄγ' ἴτε, from which sg. was formed.

**ἁγι-άζω**, = ἁγίζω, Lxx *Ge.*2.3, al., Ph.2.238:—Pass., ἁγιασθήτω τὸ ὄνομά σου *Ev.Matt.*6.9. **-ασμα**, ατος, τό, = ἁγιαστήριον, Lxx *Am.* 7.13, al. II. *holiness*, ib.*Ps.*92(93).5. **-ασμός**, οῦ, ὁ, *consecration, sanctification*, Lxx *Jd.*17.3, al., 1*Ep.Thess.*4.7. **-αστήριον**, τό, *holy place, sanctuary*, Lxx *Le.*12.4, al. **-αστία**, ἡ, v.l. for ἁγιστεία, Lxx 4*Ma.*7.9. **-αφόρος**, ον, = ἱεραφόρος, *IG*3.162.

**ἀγίγαρτος**, ον, of grapes, etc., *without seed* or *stone*, Thphr.*CP* 5.5.1, Aët.9.30.

**ἁγίζω**, (ἅγιος) *hallow, make sacred*, esp. by burning a sacrifice, θεῷ βούθυτον ἑστίαν ἁγίζων S.*OC*1495 (lyr.); πόπανα ἥγιζεν ἐς σάκταν (for ἐς βωμόν) Ar.*Pl.*681:—Pass., βωμοὶ πατρὶ ἁγισθέντες Pi.*O.*3.19; θύματα ἐπὶ καθαρῷ πυρὶ -όμενα D.H.1.38:—Med., = ἅζομαι, Alcm.123.

**ἀγῑνέω**, lengthd. Ep. and Ion. (also later Dor., v. sub fin.) form of ἄγω, mostly used in pres. and impf. (with or without augm. in Hom.); inf. pres. ἀγινέμεναι Od.20.213: impf. ἀγίνεσκον Od.17.294 (ἠγίνεσκον Arat.111): fut. ἀγινήσω *h.Ap.*57,249, al.:—*lead, bring*, νύμφας .. ἠγίνεον ἀνὰ ἄστυ Il.18.493; μῆλον ἀ. Od.14.105; ἀ. αἶγας μνηστήρεσσι 22.198; ἀγίνεον ἄσπετον ὕλην Il.24.784; freq. of offerings, dedications, etc., δῶρα ἀγίνεον Hdt.3.89, cf. 92,97, etc., Hp.*Ep.*27, Herod. 4.87, Call.*Iamb.*1.251, *AP*6.75 (Paul. Sil.); πλοῦτον ἀ. εἰς ἀρετήν Crates Theb.10.8; ληιάδας ἀ. *lead captive*, A.R.1.613; ἄνθεα τοσσάπερ ὧραι ποικίλ' ἀγινεῦσι Call.*Ap.*82; τέτρατον ἦμαρ ἀ., of the moon, Arat.792; *keep, observe*, παιγνίην Herod.3.55:—Med., *cause to be brought*, ἐς τὸ ἱρὸν ἀγινεόμενος γυναῖκας Hdt.7.33:—Pass., Arr.*Ind.* 32.7; αἴκα τὰ πάθεα τᾶς ψυχᾶς ἐς τὸ μέτριον ἀγινῆται Hippod.ap.Stob. 4.1.94.

**ἁγιο-λόγος**, ον, *speaking holy things*, dub. in 1*Enoch*1.2. **-ποιέω**, *sanctify*, Phot.

***ἅγιος** [ᾰ], α, ον, *devoted to the gods*: I. in good sense, *sacred, holy*: 1. of things, esp. temples, 'Αφροδίτης ἱρὸν ἅ. Hdt. 2.41; ἱρὸν 'Ηρακλέος ἅ. ib.44, cf. Pl.*Criti.*116c, X.*HG*2.2.19; θηρίον Antiph.147.7; νηὸν ἐπὶ τῷ χάσματι Ἥρης ἅ. ἐστήσατο Luc.*Syr.D.*13: generally, θυσίαι, ξυμβόλαια, Isoc.10.63, Pl.*Lg.*729e (Sup.); μητρός .. ἐστι πατρὶς ἁγιώτερον Id.*Cri.*51a; ὅρκος ἅ. Arist.*Mir.*$834^{b}11$; ἅ., τό, *temple*, *OGI*56.59 (Canopus), Lxx *Ex.*26.33, al., cf. *Ep.Heb.*9.2; τὸ ἅ. τῶν ἁγίων *Holy of Holies*, Lxx l.c.; τὰ ἅ. τῶν ἁ. 3*Ki.*8.6, etc., cf. *Ep.Heb.*9.3. 2. of persons, *holy, pure*, Ar.*Av.*522 (anap.); λαὸς ἅ. Κυρίῳ Lxx *De.*7.6, al.; οἱ ἅ. *the Saints*, 1*Ep.Cor.*6.1, al.; πνεῦμα ἅ. *the Holy Spirit*, *Ev.Matt.*3.11, al. Adv. ἁγίως καὶ σεμνῶς ἔχειν Isoc. 11.25. II. in bad sense, *accursed, execrable*, Cratin.373, Eust. 1356.59.—Never in Hom., Hes., or Trag. (who use ἁγνός); rare in Att. (v. supr.). (Possibly cognate with Skt. *yájati* 'sacrifice'.)

**ἁγιότης**, ητος, ἡ, = ἁγιωσύνη, Lxx 2*Ma.*15.2, *Ep.Heb.*12.10. II. as title, *PGiss.*55.5 (vi A.D.).

**ἁγ-ισμός**, οῦ, ὁ, = ἐναγισμός, *offering to the dead*, D.S.4.39. **-ιστεία**, ἡ, *ritual, service*, τῶν θεῶν, in pl., Isoc.11.28, cf. Pl.*Ax.*371d, Arist. *Cael.*$268^{a}14$; later in sg., Str.9.3.7, J.*Ap.*1.7, Plu.*Rom.*22, Jul.*Or.* 5.178d. **-ίστευμα**, τό, *sanctuary*, Procop.*Aed.*1.4. **-ιστεύω**, *perform sacred rites*, Pl.*Lg.*759d: c. acc., ἱερουργίαν D.H.1.40:—Pass., ὅσα ἄλλα -εύεται Ph.2.231. 2. *to be holy, live purely*, ὅστις .. βιοτὰν ἁ. καὶ θιασεύεται ψυχάν E.*Ba.*74; *to be sacred*, Paus.6.20.2, cf. 8.13.1. II. Act., *purify*, φόνου χεῖρας Orac.ap.Paus.10.6.7. 2. *deem holy*:—Pass., of places, Str.9.3.1, D.H.1.40. **-ιστήριον**, τό, = περιρραντήριον, *Inscr.Perg.*255.9 (pl.). **-ιστός**, ή, όν, *hallowed*, *Et.Gud.* s.v. ἁγιστεία. ***-ιστύς**, ύος, ἡ, *ceremony*, Call.*Aet.*1.1.3.

**ἁγιώδως**, Adv. *in sacred manner*: Sup. -έστατα dub. in Ph.1.675.

***ἁγιωσύνη**, ἡ, *holiness, sanctity*, Lxx 2*Ma.*3.12, *Ep.Rom.*1.4, etc. II. as title, *PMeyer*24.2 (vi A.D.).

***ἀγκ-**, Poet. abbrev. for ἀνακ- in compds. of ἀνά.

***ἀγκάζομαι**, (ἀγκάς) Ep., *lift up in the arms*, νεκρὸν ἀπὸ χθονὸς ἀγκάζοντο Il.17.722; λίθον ἀγκάσσασθαι Call.*Hec.*21.1, cf. Nonn.*D.*7. 318.

***ἄγκᾰθεν**, Adv. *in the arms*, ἄ. λαβεῖν τι A.*Eu.*80. 2. *resting on the elbows*, A.*Ag.*3; also expl. as contr. for ἀνέκαθεν, = ἄνωθεν, *on the top*, cf. Sch. ad l.c., Hsch., *AB*337.

**ἀγκάλη** [ᾰ], ἡ, *bent arm*, mostly in pl., ἐν ἀγκάλαις A.*Ag.*723, *Supp.*481, E.*Alc.*351, al.; prov., ἐν ταῖς ἀ. περιφέρειν τινά X.*Cyr.*7.5. 50; without ἐν, ἀγκάλαις ἔχειν, περιφέρειν, E.*IT*289, *Or.*464; ἐπ' ἀγκάλαις λαβεῖν Id.*Ion*761, cf. *IT*1250; ἐς ἀ. *Ion* 1598; πρὸς ἀγκάλαις πεσεῖν ib.962; ὑπ' ἀγκάλαις σταθείς Id.*Andr.*747: rarely in sg., Corinn.19 (s.v.l.); φέρειν ἐν τῇ ἀ. Hdt.6.61, cf. X. l.c., Timocl.7. 4. 2. *bend of knee*, Cael.Aur.*TP*5.1.2. II. metaph., *anything closely enfolding*, κυμάτων ἐν ἀγκάλαις Archil.23; πετραία ἀ. A.*Pr.* 1019; πόντιαι ἀ. Id.*Ch.*587, cf. E.*Or.*1378; πελαγίοις ἐν ἀ. Nausicr. 1.3: of the air, γῆν .. ἔχονθ' ὑγραῖς ἐν ἀ. E.*Fr.*941. III. *bundle, sheaf*, *BGU*1180 (i B.C.), *PLond.*1.$131^{r}396$ (i A.D.), *POxy.*935.19 (iii A.D.).

**ἀγκᾰλῐδ-αγωγέω**, *carry a bundle*, Paus.Gr.*Fr.*90. **-ᾰγωγός**, όν, *carrying an armful* or *bundle*, of beasts of burden; **ἀγκαλιδη-φόρος**, **-φορέω** being used of men, Poll.2.139, 7.109.

**ἀγκαλίδη**, ἡ, = ἀγκαλίς, ἐν ἀγκαλίδῃσι γυναικός *Stud.Pont.*3.6 (Amisus).

***ἀγκᾰλ-ίζομαι**, *embrace*, ὅστις κακὸν ἀγκαλίζεται Semon.7.77; εἰς τρυφερὰς ἠγκαλίσασθε χέρας *AP*12.122 (Mel.), cf. Man.1.45; χεροῖν εἴδωλον ἠγκαλισμένος Lyc.142: ἀγκαλιζόμενος in pass. sense, Aesop. 366. **-ῖναι**, αἱ, = ἀγκάλαι (Arg.), Hsch. ***-ίς**, ἡ, in pl., = ἀγκάλαι, *arms*, Ep. dat. pl. ἀγκαλίδεσσιν Il.18.555, 22.503; ὑπ' ἀγκαλίσιν *IG* 9(1).882.13 (Corcyra). 2. *armful*, Ar.*Fr.*418, Nicostr.24, Ister 54 (s.v.l.), Ph.5.147C., Plu.*Rom.*8. II. = δρέπανον, Maced. word, J.*AJ*5.1.2, Hsch. ***-ισμα**, ατος, τό, *that which is embraced* or *taken in the arms*, Luc.*Am.*14: hence, *darling*, Lyc.308. II. *embrace*, metaph., ἀ. κλυσιδρομάδος αὔρας Tim.*Pers.*91. **-ισμός**, ὁ, *making* *into bundles*, *POxy.*1631.9 (iii A.D.). *-ος, ὁ, *armful, bundle*, *h.Merc.*82.

**ἀγκαλπίς**· κρημνός, οἱ δὲ βόθρον, Hsch.

**ἀγκάς** [ᾰς], Adv. *into* or *in the arms*, ἔχε δ' ἀ. ἄκοιτιν Il.14.353, cf. Theoc.8.55, A.R.1.276; ἀ. ἔμαρπτε Il.14.346; ἀ. ἐλάζετο θυγατέρα ἥν 5.371; τρόπιν ἀ. ἑλὼν νεός Od.7.252; ἀ. δ' ἀλλήλων λαβέτην (of wrestlers) Il.23.711.

**ἀγκή**, ἡ, = ἀγκάλη, Hsch.; metapl. dat. pl. ἀγκάσιν Opp.*H.*2.315.

**ἀγκηθής**· ἀβλαβής, Hsch. ***ἀγκής**· ἀντηχής, Hsch.

***ἀγκιστρ-εία**, ἡ, *angling*, Pl.*Lg.*823d. **-ευτικός**, ή, όν, *of* or *for angling*: τὸ -κόν, *angling*, Pl.*Sph.*220d; -κὴ τέχνη Gal.*Thras.* 30. **-εύω**, *angle for, entice*, τινά Aristaenet.1.5:—Med., Ph.1.344: metaph., ψυχάς 2.265; ἀπόλαυσιν 1.304. **-ιον**, τό, Dim. of ἄγκιστρον, Theoc.21.57, Bito51.1.

**ἀγκιστρό-δετος**, ον, *with a hook bound to it*, δόναξ *AP*6.27 (Theaet.). **-ειδής**, ές, *hook-shaped, barbed*, *Placit.*1.3.18, etc. Adv. -δῶς Erot. s.v. ἠγκίστρευται.

***ἄγκιστρον**, τό, (ἄγκος) *fish-hook*, Od.4.369, Hdt.2.70, etc.; *hook of a spindle*, Pl.*R.*616c; *surgical instrument*, Philum.*Ven.*2.6, Cael. Aur.*TP*5.1; generally, *hook*, D.C.60.35.

***ἀγκιστρόομαι**, Pass., *to be furnished with barbs*, Plu.*Crass.*25. II. *to be caught by a hook*, ἠγκιστρωμένος πόθῳ Lyc.67.

**ἀγκιστρο-πώλης**, ου, ὁ, *seller of fish-hooks*, Poll.7.198. **-φάγος**, ον, (φαγεῖν) *biting the hook*, Arist.*HA*621ᵇ1.

**ἀγκιστρ-ώδης**, ες, = ἀγκιστροειδής, Plb.34.3.5, D.S.5.34, Str.1.2. 16. **-ωτός**, ή, όν, *barbed*, βέλος Plb.6.23.10; ἐμβόλια Ph.*Bel.*95.45.

***ἀγκλάριον**, τό, perh. Dor. for ἀνακλήριον, *reapportionment*, *CIG* 2562.13 (Hierapytna).

**ἀγκλίνω**, and **ἄγκλιμα**, τό, poet. for ἀνακλ-.

**ἀγκλόν**· σκολιόν, Hsch.

***ἄγκοινα**, ἡ, (ἀγκον-yᾰ, cf. ἀγκών) poet. for ἀγκάλη, only in pl., Ζηνὸς.. ἐν ἀγκοίνῃσιν ἰαύεις Il.14.213, cf. Od.11.261, Hes.*Fr.*245, A.R. 2.954. 2. metaph., *anything enfolding*, ἐν χθονὸς ἀγκοίναις *AP*9.398 (Jul. Aegypt.), cf. Opp.*H.*3.34. II. *halyard*, *IG*2.794ᵇ20, al., prob. in Alc.18.9.

**ἀγκοινίζω**, = ἀγκαλίζω, dub. l. in Poll.3.155. **ἀγκόλαι**· ἀγκῶνες, Hsch.

**ἀγκομιδά**, v. ἀνακομιδή.

**ἀγκονίω**, v.l. for ἐγκ-, Ar.*Lys.*1311, as if from ἀνακονίω, = ἐγκονέω.

**ἀγκοπτήρ**· σφῦρα, Hsch.

***ἄγκος**, εος, τό, properly, *bend, hollow*: hence, *mountain glen*, Il. 20.490, Od.4.337, Hes.*Op.*389, Hdt.6.74, Theoc.8.33, etc.; Trag. only E.*Ba.*1051. (Cf. Skt. *áñcati* 'bend', Lat. *ancus, uncus*, etc.)

**ἀγκοτύλη**, ἡ, a game, Hsch. **ἀγκταλιάζει**· ἄγχει, Hsch. **ἄγκτειρα**, ἡ, fem. of sq., ποιναί *Orac.Chald.*265.

***ἀγκτήρ**, ῆρος, ὁ, (ἄγχω) *instrument for closing wounds*, Cels.5.26, Plu.2.468c, Heliod.ap.Orib.44.10.4, Gal.1.385. 2. part of the throat, Poll.2.134, Hsch. 3. in pl., *bonds*, Procl.*in Euc.*20.25F.: metaph., τῆς ὕλης Id.*in R.*2.150K., prob. *in Alc.*p.41C. 4. *bandage*, Heliod.ap.Orib.48.28.5. ***ἀγκτηριάζω**, *bind with an* ἀγκτήρ, Crito ap.Gal.13.878.

**ἀγκυλένδετος**, ον, *bound with thongs*, [Ἄρης] ἀ., i.e. javelin, Tim. *Pers.*23.

**ἀγκῠλέομαι**, *hurl like a javelin*, Ἔρως κεραυνὸν ἠγκυλημένος Satyr.1.

***ἀγκύλ-η** [ῠ], ἡ, (ἄγκος) properly, like ἀγκάλη, *bend of the arm* or *wrist*, ἀπ' ἀγκύλης ἱέναι, a phrase descriptive of the way in which the cottabus was thrown, B.*Fr.*13.2, cf. Hsch.; ἀπ' ἀγκύλης ἵησι λάταγας Cratin.273; wrongly expl. as *cup*, Ath.11.782d. 2. *bend of the knee, ham*, Philostr.*Im.*2.6, Sch.Il.23.726. 3. *joint bent and stiffened by disease*, Hp.*Liqu.*6, cf. Poll.4.196. II. *loop, noose*, πλεκτὰς ἀγκύλας E.*IT*1408; in the leash of a hound, X.*Cyn.*6.1; in bandages, Gal.18(1).790; in torsion-engines, Hero *Bel.*83.1. 2. *thong of a javelin*, by which it was hurled, Str.4.4.3; hence, *the javelin* itself, E.*Or.*1476, cf. Plu.*Phil.*6; δι' ἀγκυλῶν ἱππόται Them. *Or.*21.256d. 3. *bow-string*, ἀ. χρυσόστροφοι S.*OT*203. 4. ἀγκύλη τῆς ἐμβάδος sandal-*thong*, Alex.31. 5. *curtain-ring, hook*, Lxx *Ex.*38.18(36.34), al.; *hook* for a door, *IG*11(2).165.11, al. (Delos, iii B.C.). 6. *sides of the* κεραία, Poll.1.91. **-ητός**, ή, όν, verb. Adj. of ἀγκυλέομαι, *thrown from the bent arm*, of the cottabus, A.*Fr.*179. II. Subst., ἀγκυλητόν, τό, *javelin*, Id.*Fr.*16, *IG*2. 733*B*17. ***-ιδωτός**, όν, *having a loop for a handle* (ἀγκύλη II), Hp.ap.Gal.19.69. **-ίζομαι**, in wrestling, *clasp the adversary's neck*, dub. l. in Poll.1.176. **-ιον**, τό, Dim. of ἀγκύλη, *loop* in noose, Heracl.ap.Orib.48.2.1; *link of a chain*, *AB*329, Suid. 2. = ἀγκύλωσις, Antyll.ap.Orib.45.15.1. II. τὰ ἀγκύλια, = Lat. *ancilia*, Plu. *Num.*13. **-ίς**, ίδος, ἡ, *hook, barb*, Opp.*C.*1.155.

**ἀγκύλλω**, *bend back*, Aret.*SA*1.6, cf. Hsch.

***ἀγκῠλο-βλέφαρον**, τό, *adhesion of the eyelids*, Cels.7.7. ***-γλωσσον** πάθος, τό, *contraction of the tongue*, Orib.45.15 tit., Paul.Aeg.6. 29; and **-γλωσσος**, ὁ, *one who suffers from it*, Aët.8.38. **-γλώχιν**, ινος, ὁ, of a cock, *with hooked spurs*, Babr.17.3. **-δειρος**, ον, *crook-necked*, Opp.*H.*4.630.

**ἀγκῠλόδους**, οντος, ὁ, ἡ, *crook-toothed*, of a scimitar, Q.S.6.218; ἀ. χαλινοί, of anchors, Nonn.*D.*3.50. II. *barbed*, *AP*6.176 (Maced.).

***ἀγκυλοειδής**, ές, *winding*, τόποι, Suid. s.v. ἄγκη.

***ἀγκυλο-κοπέω**, *hamstring*, dub. in *PLond.*2.415.15. **-κυκλος**, ον, *curved in spires*, of a dragon's tail, Nonn.*D.*35.217. **-κωλος**, ον, *crook-limbed*, Κᾶρες Archestr.*Fr.*41 B. **-μαχία**, ἡ, *contest w. javelin*, *IPE*1².435 (Chersonesus). **-μήτης** (Boeot. ἀγκουλ-μείτας Corinn.*Supp.*1.13), ὁ, (μῆτις) *crooked of counsel*, epith. Κρόνος Il.2.205, Od.21.415, al., Hes.*Th.*18, etc.; of Prometheus, 546, *Op.*48. **-μητις**, ιος, ὁ, ἡ, = foreg., Nonn.*D.*21.255. **-ποι..** ὁ, ἡ, πουν, τό, gen. ποδος, *with bent legs*, δίφρος, = Lat. *sella curulis*, Plu.*Mar.*5.

***ἀγκύλος** [ῠ], η, ον, (ἄγκος) *crooked, curved*, τόξα Il.5.209, Od.2 264, etc.; ἅρμα Il.6.39; κάλαμος Theoc.21.47; of the eagle, ἀγκύλον κάρα *beaked*, Pi.*P.*1.8; ἀ. ἐκ τῶν ὀδόντων Ant.Lib.22.6; of greedy fingers, *hooked*, Ar.*Eq.*205; of the movement of a snake, ἀ. ἕρπει D.P.123. II. metaph., 1. of style, *intricate*, Luc.*Bis Acc.* 21; ἐριστικὸς καὶ ἀ. τὴν γλῶσσαν *catchy*, Alciphr.3.64; in good sense *terse*, D.H.*Th.*25 (Comp.). Adv. -λως ib.31; *intricately*, Procl.*in Prm.* p.525 S., Dam.*Pr.*187. 2. *wily, crafty*, Lyc.344; -ώτεραι ἐνέδραι Archig.ap.Orib.8.2.24.

**ἀγκῠλό-τοξος**, ον, *with crooked bow*, Παίονες Il.2.848, 10.428; Μήδειοι Pi.*P.*1.78. **-χείλης**, ου, ὁ, (χεῖλος) *with hooked beak*, αἰετός Od.19.538, *AP*6.229 (Crin.); αἰγυπιοί Il.16.428, Hes.*Sc.*405, Batr. 294. (Perh. -χήλης shd. always be read.) **-χήλης**, ου, ὁ, (χηλή) *with crooked claws*, v.l. in *Batr.*294, Ar.*Eq.*197, cf. Sch. (-χείλης codd.).

**ἀγκυλ-όω**, *crook, bend*, τὴν χεῖρα, as in throwing the cottabus, Pl.Com.47:—Pass., ὄνυχας ἠγκυλωμένος *with crooked* claws, Ar.*Av.* 1180. **-ωμα**, τό, *loop*, Gal.18(1).798. **-ωσις**, ἡ, as medic. term, *tongue-tie*, Antyll.ap.Orib.46.16.4; *stiffening of joints*, Paul. Aeg.4.55; *adhesion of the eyelids*, Gal.14.772. **-ωτός**, ή, όν, of javelins, *furnished with a thong*, στοχάσματα E.*Ba.*1205.

***ἄγκῡρα**, ἡ, *anchor*, Alc.18.9 (v. ἄγκοινα), Thgn.459; ἄ. βάλλεσθαι, καθιέναι, μεθιέναι, ἀφιέναι to cast *anchor*, Pi.*I.*6(5).13, Hdt.7.36, A.*Ch.* 662, X.*An.*3.5.10; ἄ. αἴρειν, αἴρεσθαι to weigh *anchor*, Plu.*Pomp.*50, 80; ἀνέλοιο *AP*10.1 (Leon.); τὰς νέας ἔχειν ἐπ' ἀγκυρέων Hdt.6.12; ὁρμίζειν Th.7.59; ἐπ' ἀγκυρέων ὁρμεῖν ride at *anchor*, Hdt.7.188; νηῦς μιῆς ἐπ' ἀγκύρης [οὐκ ἀσφ]αλὴς ὁρμεῦσα Herod.1.41; ἐπ' ἀγκύρας ἀποσαλεύειν D.50.22, cf. E.*Hel.*1071; prov., ἀγαθαὶ πέλοντ'.. δύ' ἄγκυραι 'tis good to have 'two strings to your bow', Pi.*O.*6.101; ἐπὶ δυοῖν ἀγκύραιν ὁρμεῖν αὐτοὺς ἐᾶτε D.56.44, cf. Plu.*Sol.*19; ἄ. δ' ἥ μου τὰς τύχας ὤχει μόνη E.*Hel.*277; ἐπὶ τῆς αὐτῆς (sc. ἀγκύρας) ὁρμεῖν τοῖς πολλοῖς, i.e. 'to be in the same boat' with the many, D.18.281; εἰσὶ μητρὶ παῖδες ἄγκυραι βίου S.*Fr.*685; οἴκων ἄ., of a son, E.*Hec.*80; ἱερὰ ἄ., last hope, Luc.*J.Tr.*51. II. *pruning-hook*, Thphr.*CP* 3.2.2. III. = αἰδοῖον, Epich.191.

**ἀγκῡρηβόλιον**, τό, = ἀγκυροβ-, Democr.148.

**ἀγκῡρίζω**, fut. Att. ιῶ, (ἄγκυρα) in wrestling, *hook* with the leg, *trip*, διαλαβὼν ἀγκυρίσας Ar.*Eq.*262; ἀγκυρίσας ἔρρηξεν Eup.262.

**ἀγκύριον**, τό, Dim. of ἄγκῡρα, Ph.*Bel.*100.24, 104.2, Arr. *Epict.Fr.*30, Demoph.*Sim.*45, Luc.*Cat.*1. II. **ἀγκύρια** (sc. πείσματα), τά, *anchor-cables*, D.S.14.73.

**ἄγκυρ-ις**· βοτάνη τις, Hsch. **-ισμα**, τό, *hook*, in wrestling, Schol.Ar.*Eq.*262, Hsch. **-ίτης** λίθος *anchor-stone*, Hsch. s.v. μασχάλην. **-ίττει**· μεταμέλεται (Cret.), Hsch.

***ἀγκῡρο-βολέω**, *secure by throwing an anchor*: *hook fast in, fasten securely*, ἠγκυροβόληται Hp.*Dent.*18. ***-βόλιον**, τό, *anchorage*, Str.3.4.7 (pl.), Plu.2.507b. ***-ειδής**, ές, *anchor-shaped*, Dsc.3. 158, Gal.2.766. Adv. -ειδῶς Erot. s.v. βυβδοειδέα τρόπον. **-μαχος**, ὁ, a kind of ship, Isid.*Etym.*19.1.16, *Gloss.* **-μήλη**, ἡ, *hooked probe*, Hp.ap.Erot., cf. Gal.19.60.

**ἀγκῡρουχία**, ἡ, (ἔχω) *a holding by the anchor*, ἐν ἀγκυρουχίαις A.*Supp.*766.

**ἀγκῡρωτός**, ή, όν, *bent like an anchor*, δοκίδες Ph.*Bel.*85.36.

**ἀγκωβόλος**· ἁλιεύς, Hsch.

***ἀγκών**, ῶνος, ὁ, *bend of the arm*, hence, *elbow*, ὀρθωθεὶς δ' ἐπ' ἀγκῶνος Il.10.80; ἦ, καὶ ἐπ' ἀγκῶνος κεφαλὴν σχέθεν Od.14.494; ἀγκῶνα τυχὼν μέσον Il.5.582, cf. 20.479; ἀγκῶνι νύττειν to nudge, Od.14.485, cf. Pl.*Riv.*132b; κροτεῖν τοῖς ἀγκῶσιν τὰς πλευράς D.54.9; prov., ἀγκῶνι ἀπομύττεσθαι Bion ap.D.L.4.46; ἐπ' ἀγκῶνος δειπνεῖν, of the attitude at meals, Luc.*Lex* 6. 2. *arm*, Νίκας ἐν ἀγκώνεσσι πίτνειν Pi.*N.*5.42; ἐς δ' ὑγρὸν ἀγκῶνα.. προσπτύσσεται S.*Ant.*1237, etc. 3. *bend* in animals' legs, X.*Cyn.*4.1. II. *any nook* or *bend*, as the *angle* of a wall, ἀγκὼν τείχεος Il.16.702, cf. Hdt.1.180; *bend, bay* of a river, Id.2.99; ἑσπεροι ἀγκῶνες S.*Aj.*805; *headlands which form a bay*, Str.12.8.19; ἀγκῶνες κιθάρας *ribs which support the horns* of the cithara, Semus 1, Hsch.; *ends* of stomach-bow, Hero *Bel.*78.4; *arms* of torsion-engine, Ph.*Bel.*53.40, al., Hero *Bel.*81.9; *cross-bar* of same, Bito 49.12; *arm* of throne or chair, Lxx 2*Ch.*9.18, Cael.Aur. *TP*2.1; perh. *clamp*, *PPetr.*3p.144. 2. kind of *vase*, Artem.1.74, cf. *Sammelb.*4292. III. prov., γλυκὺς ἀ. used κατ' ἀντίφρασιν of a difficulty, Pl.*Phdr.*257d, Clearch 6; expl. by Sch.Pl. l.c., Zen.2. 92, Ath.12.516a, from *a long bend* or *reach* in the Nile; but apptly. = παραγκάλισμα, *thing to be embraced, treasure*, Pl.Com.178; also = ἀβρότονον, Dsc.3.24. (For the Root v. ἄγκος.)

**ἀγκών-η**, ἡ, = ἄγκοινα, Sch.D.T.191.37 H. ***-ίζω**, *recline at table*, *Gloss.* II. Med., *pursue a sinuous course*, hence metaph., *use circumlocutions*, Com.*Adesp.*14.8 D. **-ιον**, τό, *elbow*, Gal.4. 452. ***-ίσκιον**, τό, Dim. of ἀγκών, Hero *Spir.*1.42. ***-ίσκος**, ὁ, = foreg., Hero *Spir.*1.42, Lxx *Ex.*26.17. **-ισμός**, οῦ, ὁ, *a bending, reach*, of an estuary, Eust.1712.29.

**ἀγκωνό-δεσμος**, *cubital*, *Gloss.* **-ειδής**, ές, *curve-shaped, curved*, Bito 58.9 (v.l.). ***-φόρος**, ὁ, *bearer of an* ἀγκών II.2, *IG*3.1280.

ἀγλαέθειρος, ον, *bright-haired*, *h.Pan.*5.

ἀγλα-ΐα, Ion. -ΐη, ἡ, (ἀγλαός) *splendour, beauty*, κῦδός τε καὶ ἀ. ὄνειαρ Od.15.78; ἀγλαΐηφι πεποιθώς Il.6.510; of Penelope, Od.18. 180; *splendour, magnificence*, S.*El.*211; ὡρῶν Jul.*Or.*4.148d; in bad sense, *pomp, show*, [κύνας] ἀγλαΐης ἕνεκεν κομέουσιν Od.17.310; in pl., *vanities*, 17.244, E.*El.*175. **2.** *joy, triumph*, Pi.*O.*13.14, etc.; pl., *festivities, merriment*, Hes.*Sc.*272,285. **3.** *adornment*, of a horse's *mane*, colours of oyster's *shell*, etc., X.*Eq.*5.8, Ael.*NA*10.13, A.R.4.1191. **4.** pr. n., Ἀγλαΐα, one of the Graces, who presided over victory in the games, Hes.*Th.*945, cf. B.3.6.—Mostly poet. -ΐζω, Hp.*Mul.*2.188, Ael., v. infr.: fut. Att. ἀγλαϊῶ (ἐπ-) Ar.*Ec.*575: aor. ἠγλάϊσα (Dor. ἀγλ-) Theoc.*Ep.*1.4, etc., (ἐπ-) Ar. Fr.682:—Pass., v. infr.:—*make splendid, glorify*, B.3.22, etc.; ἀθανάταις ἠγλάϊσεν χάρισιν *IG*12(3).1190.10 (Melos); θυσίαις τέμενος Syll.28, cf. Plu.2.965c, Ael.*NA*8.28. **2.** *give as an honour*, σοί, Ἴακχε, τάνδε μοῦσαν ἀγλαΐζομεν *Carm.Pop.*8, cf. Theoc. l. c. **II.** Ep. and Lyr. only Med. and Pass., *adorn oneself with* a thing, *take delight in*, σέ φημι διαμπερὲς ἀγλαϊεῖσθαι (sc. ἵπποις) Il.10.331 (the only form in Hom., even of compds.); ὅστις τοιούτοις θυμὸν ἀγλαΐζεται Simon.7.70; ἀ. μουσικᾶς ἐν ἀώτῳ Pi.*O.*1.14; Com., ἐλαίῳ ῥάφανος ἠγλαϊσμένη Ephipp.3.6 (cf. Eub.150). **III.** intr., ἀγλαΐζει· θάλλει, Hsch., cf. Antiph.301 codd.—Never in Trag. or Att. Prose. -ϊσμα, τό, *ornament, honour*, A.*Ag.*1312; of a child, μητρὸς ἀ. E.*Hel.*11, cf. 282; of the hair of Orestes placed on his father's tomb, A.*Ch.*193, S.*El.*908, cf. E.*El.*325; of a sarcophagus, *IG*12(8).600 (Thasos).—Poet. and late Prose; ἀ. φυτῶν, of the rose, Ach.Tat.2.1. -ϊσμός, ὁ, *adorning, ornament*, ῥημάτων Pl.*Ax.*369d. -ϊστός, ή, όν, *adorned*, Hsch.

ἀγλαό-βοτρυς, υ, gen. υος, *with splendid bunches*, Nonn.*D.* 18.4. -γυιος, ον, *beautiful-limbed*, Ἥβα Pi.*N.*7.4. -δενδρος, ον, *with beautiful trees*, Pi.*O.*9.20. -δωρος, ον, *bestowing splendid gifts*, Δημήτηρ *h.Cer.*54,192,492. -εργός, όν, (ἔργον) *ennobled by works*, Max.63. -θηλές· ἁπαλόν, Hsch. ⊛-θρονος, ον, *with splendid throne, bright-throned*, Μοῖσαι Pi.*O.*13.96, cf. *N.*10.1, B.16. 124. -θυμος, ον, *noble-hearted*, *AP*15.40.25 (Cometas). ⊛-καρπος, ον, (καρπός A) *bearing beautiful* or *goodly fruit*, of fruit-trees, ῥοιαί Od.7.115, 11.589; Σικελία Pi.*Fr.*106; εἰρήνη Epigr.ap.*SIG*274 (Delph., iv B.C.): of Demeter and the Nymphs, *givers of the fruits of the earth*, *h.Cer.*4,23. **II.** (καρπός B) *with fair wrists*, of Thetis, Pi.*N.*3.56 (v.l. ἀγλαόκολπος). -κοιτος· πάνυ τίμιος, Phot., Suid. -κουρος, ον, *rich in fair youths*, Κόρινθος Pi.*O.*13.5. -κωμος, ον, *giving splendour to the feast*, φωνή Pi.*O.*3.6. ⊛-μειδής, ές, *brightly smiling*, Ἔρως Eurytus (*PLG*3.639). -μητία· ἡ μεγάλη βουλή, *EM*11.30. -μητις, ιος, ὁ, ἡ, *of rare wisdom*, Tryph.183, Procl.*H.*5.10. -μορφέω, in Pass., *to be endowed with beauteous form*, -ουμένους τοὺς ἀστέρας ἱστάς *PLeid.W.*4.16. -μορφος, ον *of beauteous form*, *AP*9.524, Orph.*H.*14.5, al. -παις, ὁ, ἡ, *rich in fair children*, Opp.*H.*2.41, *Epigr.Gr.*896 (Syria). ⊛-πεπλος, ον, *beautifully veiled*, Q.S.11.240. -πηχυς, υ, gen. εος, *with beautiful arms*, Nonn.*D.*32.80. -πιστος, ον, *splendidly faithful*, Hsch. -ποιέω, *make famous*, Hermap.ap.Amm.Marc.17.4.19.

ἀγλαός [ἀγλᾰ-], ή, όν, also ός, όν Thgn.985, E.*Andr.*135:—*splendid, shining, bright*, epith. of beautiful objects, ἀ. ὕδωρ Il.2.307, etc.; γυῖα 19.385, cf. B.16.103; μηρία Hes.*Op.*337; ἥβης ἀ. ἄνθος Tyrt.10.28, cf. Thgn. l. c., B.5.154; then generally, *splendid, beautiful*, ἄποινα Il.1.23; δῶρα ib.213, etc.; ἔργα Od.10.223; ἄλσος Il.2. 506, cf. Pi.*N.*4.20, Simon.13, etc.; *noble, glorious*, ἀγλαόν [ἐστιν] ἀνδρὶ μάχεσθαι γῆς πέρι Callin.1.6. **II.** of men, either *beautiful* or *famous, noble*, Il.2.736,826, Hes.*Sc.*37, Pi.*O.*14.7, B.16.2, etc.: c. dat. rei, *famous for* a thing, κέρᾳ ἀγλαέ, sarcastically, Il.11.385.—Ep. and Lyr. word, twice in Trag. (lyr.) ἀγλαᾶς Θήβας S.*OT*152; Νηρῇδος ἀγλαὸν ἕδραν E. l. c.; also in later poetry, as Theoc.28.3. Adv. ἀγλαῶς Ar.*Lys.*640. (Perh. containing base γελα- in reduced form.)

ἀγλαό-τιμος, ον, *splendidly honoured* Orph.*H.*12.8, al. -τρίαινᾰ [ῐ], ὁ, acc. -αινᾰν, *he of the bright trident*, epith. of Poseidon, Pi.*O.*1.40. -φαντον, τό, = ἀγλαοφῶτις, *Cat.Cod.Astr.*8(3).154, 164. -φεγγής, ές, *splendidly shining*, Max.189. -φημος, ον, *of splendid fame*, Orph.*H.*31.4; Dor. -φᾱμος, pr. n. of Thracian mystic, Iamb.*VP*28.146, etc. -φοιτος, ον, *one who 'walks in beauty'*, Max.403. ⊛-φορτος, ον, *proud of one's burden*, Nonn.*D.* 7.253. -φωνος, ον, *with a splendid voice*, Procl.3.2. -φῶτις, ιδος, ἡ, *peony*, = γλυκυσίδη, Dsc.3.140, Plin.*HN*24.160, Ael.*NA*14. 24. -χαρτος, ον, *rejoicing in beauty*, *IG*12(1).783 (Rhodes).

ἀγλαρόν· μωρόν, Hsch. ἀγλασινόν· καλόν, Id. ἀγλαυκόν· ἀλυκόν, Id.

⊛ἄγλαυρος, ον, = ἀγλαός, Nic.*Th.*62,441. **II.** Ἄγλαυρος, ἡ, daughter of Cecrops, worshipped on the Acropolis at Athens, Hdt. 8.53.β', Paus.1.18.2.

ἀγλαφόρε· ἄσιτε (Cret.), Hsch.

⊛ἀγλαφύρως, Adv. *without polish, inelegantly*, Hegesand.22, cf. Eust.1295.15.

ἀγλαώψ, ῶπος, ὁ, ἡ, *bright-eyed, beaming*, πεύκη S.*OT*214 (lyr.).

⊛ἀγλευκής, ές, (γλεῦκος) *not sweet, sour*, X.*Hier.*1.21 (Comp.), cf. Rhinth.28; opp. γλυκύς, Arist.*Pr.*877ᵇ25; οἶνος Luc.*Lex.*6; heterocl. acc. ἀγλευκῆν, θάλασσαν Nic.*Al.*171: metaph., of persons, *sour, crabbed*, Epich.140; of the style of Thuc., *harsh*, Hermog.*Id.*2.12, cf. [Longin.]*Rh.*p.195 H.

⊛ἀγλευ(κι)τάς· ἄρτος ἄναλος, Hsch.

ἀγλίδια· σκόροδα, Hsch., *EM*11.41 (leg. ἀγλίθια).

ἀγλίη, ἡ, f. l. for αἰγίς, Gal.19.69.

ἀγλιθάριον, τό, Dim. of ἄγλις, Ruf.ap.Orib.8.39.10.

⊛ἄγλῑς, gen. ἄγλῑθος (ἀγλῖθος Choerob. *in Theod.*p.327 H., ἀγλῖθες Nic.*Th.*874), ἡ:—*clove* of garlic, Antyll.ap.Orib.8.16.3; = ῥάξ, Dsc. 2.152; mostly pl., *head* of garlic (cf. κεφαλή), made up of separate cloves, Ar.*Ach.*763, *V.*680, Hp.*Mul.*2.133, Call.*Fr.*140.

ἄγλισχρος, ον, *not sticky*, Hp.*Prorrh.*1.117, Thphr.*CP*6.11.16.

ἀγλίτης· οἰκέτης, *EM*11.45, *AB*338, cf. ἀγλεῖτις· οἰκέτις, prob. in Hsch.

ἄγλυ, Scyth. word = *swan*, Hsch.

ἀγλῠκής, ές, ἀγλευκής, Thphr.*CP*6.14.12 and 18.8.

⊛ἄγλῠφος, ον, *unhewn*, Sch.S.*OC*101.

ἀγλῶν· ἀγλαός, Hsch. ἀγλωσσεῖν· δυσφημεῖν, Id.

ἀγλωσσία, Att. -ττία, ἡ, *want of eloquence*, E.*Fr.*56, Antipho Soph.97.

ἄγλωσσος, Att. -ττος, ον, *without tongue*, of the crocodile, Arist. *PA*690ᵇ23, cf. Eub.107.1; of a flute, *without reed*, Poll.2.108. Adv. -τως Id.6.145. **II.** *lacking in eloquence*, Pi.*N.*8.24, Ar.*Fr.*734, D.Chr.12.55; *dumb*, *AP*7.191 (Arch.). **2.** = βάρβαρος, οὐθ' Ἑλλὰς οὔτ' ἄ. S.*Tr.*1060.

ἀγλ-ῶστα· ἔντριμμα γυναικεῖον, Hsch. -ωστῖναι· γογγυλίδες, Id.

⊛ἄγμα, τό, (ἄγνυμι) *fragment*, Plu.*Phil.*6; *fracture*, Pall. *in Hp.*12. 271 C. **II.** = κλέμμα, Hsch. **III.** *nasalized g*, Ion ap.Prisc. *Inst.*1.39.

ἀγμείονες· βουβῶνες, Hsch. ἀγμή· ἑστία, Id. ἀγμηρόν· ἥσυχον, Id. ἀγμικόν· ἄκρατον, Id.

ἀγμός, ὁ, (ἄγνυμι) *fracture* of a bone, περὶ ἀγμῶν, title of treatise by Hp., etc. **II.** *broken cliff, crag*, E.*IT*263; pl., Id.*Ba.*1094, Nic.*Al.*391, St.Byz. s. v. Ὀαξός.

ἀγναῖος· καθαρός, Hsch. ἀγναιώτης· ἐπὶ πολὺ κεκαυμένος, Id. ἀγνάκορος, ὁ, = ἀνάγυρος, Sch.Nic.*Th.*71 (fort. -κοπος). ἀ-γνα(μ)πτοπόλεμος, ον, *inflexible in war*, Hsch.

⊛ἄγναμπτος, ον, *unbending, inflexible, inexorable*, Ἔρωτες B.8.73, Orph.*L.*27; τὸ πρὸς ἡδονὰς ἄ. Plu.*Cat.Mi.*11, cf. *APl.*4.278 (Paul. Sil.); cf. ἄκναμπτος.

⊛ἄγναπτος, ον, of cloth, *not fulled* or *carded*, hence, *new*, χλαῖνα Pl. Com.18 D., cf. Plu.2.691d. **II.** *not cleansed, unwashed*, ib.169c.

⊛ἄγνᾰφος, ον, (γνάπτω) = foreg., *Ev.Matt.*9.16, *Marc.*2.21, *PLond.* 2.193ᵛ22 (ii A.D.).

⊛ἁγν-εία, ἡ, *purity, chastity*, λόγων ἔργων τε S.*OT*864 (lyr.), coupled with καθαρότης Hp.*Morb.Sacr.*1, cf. 1*Ep.Tim.*4.12; τῶν θεῶν Antipho 2.1.10; ἁγνείη δ' ἐστὶ φρονεῖν ὅσια *App.Anth.*4.18. **II.** *strict observance of religious duties*, Pl.*Lg.*909e (pl.), etc.; in pl., *purifications, ceremonies*, Isoc.11.21, J.*BJ prooem.*10, *BGU*1198.12, etc. ⊛-ευμα, τό, *chastity*, E.*Tr.*501. -ευτήριον, τό, *place of purification*, Chaerem.Hist.4, cf. *AB*267; *sacristy*, *POxy* 840.8. -ευτικός, ή, όν, *inclined to chastity*, opp. ἀφροδισιαστικός, Arist.*HA*488ᵇ5. **II.** Act., *purificatory*, τὸ ἁ. *sin-offering*, Ph.2.206; ἁ. ἡμέρα *BGU*993 (ii B.C.). -εύτρια, ἡ, *female purifier*, *Gloss.* ⊛-εύω, pf. ἥγνευκα D.l. citand., *consider as part of purity, make it a point of religion*, c. inf., ἁγνεύουσι ἔμψυχον μηδὲν κτείνειν Hdt.1.140: abs., *to be pure*, ὄρνιθος ὄρνις πῶς ἂν ἁγνεύοι φαγών; A.*Supp.*226, cf. Lys.6.51, Pl.*Lg.*837c, Alex.15.6: c. acc. rei, χεῖρας ἁ. E.*IT*1227; *keep oneself pure from*, τινός D.22.78, Phld.*Sto.Herc.*339.15, Luc.*Am.*5; also in Med., γυναικός *GDI*3636.43 (Cos). **2.** *perform religious ceremonies, officiate*, *BGU*1201.6 (ii B.C.), cf. 149.8 (ii/iii A.D.). **3.** Med., *purify*, τὸν νοῦν Phld.*Sto.Herc.*350.20. **II.** Act., = ἁγνίζω, *purify*, πόλιν Antipho 2.3.11:—Pass., *SIG*1078 (Cnidus): c. gen., *purify from*, ὁ παντὸς ἁγνεύων, of Epicurus, Phld.*Lib.*p.26 O.

ἀγνέω, Dor. = ἄγω, pf. ἀγνηκώς, *GDI*1413 (Aetol.), cf. Hsch.

ἁγνεών, ῶνος, ὁ, *place of purity*, κατ' ἀντίφρασιν, for *a brothel*, Clearch.6.

ἁγνιασμός, ὁ, = ἁγνισμός, v.l. in Lxx *Nu.*8.7.

⊛ἁγνίζω, fut. ιῶ (ἀφ-) Lxx *Nu.*8.6: pf. ἥγνικα 1*Ep.Pet.*1.22: (ἁγνός):—*wash off, cleanse away*, esp. by water (τὸ πῦρ καθαίρει.. τὸ ὕδωρ ἁγνίζει Plu.2.263e), λύμαθ' ἁγνίσας ἐμὰ S.*Aj.*655; τινὰ πηγαῖς E. *IT*1039. **2.** *cleanse, purify*, χέρας σὰς ἁγνίσας μιάσματος E.*HF* 1324, cf. Diph.126.1, Lxx *Ex.*19.10:—Med., *purify oneself*, *Ev.Jo.*3.55, Plu.2.1105b:—Pass., ἁγνίσθητι *Act.Ap.*21.24: ἀπὸ οἴνου Lxx *Nu.*6.3 (Pass.). **3.** esp. ἁ. τὸν θανόντα *purify* the dead *by fire*, S.*Ant.* 545:—Pass., σῶμαθ' ἡγνίσθη πυρί E.*Supp.*1211. **4.** *sacrifice*, E.*Fr.*314, *IT*705 (Pass.). **5.** *hallow, consecrate*, Aristonous 1.17 (Pass.). **6.** *burn up, consume*, S.*Fr.*116; ἐπαστράψας αἰθὴρ ἥγνισε ..ἱστορίαν *AP*7.49 (Bianor).

ἅγνινος, η, ον, *made of* ἄγνος, Plu.2.693f.

⊛ἅγν-ισμα, τό, *purification, expiation*, ματρῷον ἅ. φόνου, of Orestes, A.*Eu.*326 (lyr.), cf. Lxx *Nu.*19.9. ⊛-ισμός, ὁ, *purification, expiation*, ἁ. ποιεῖσθαι D.H.3.22; τοῖς ἁ. τοῖς πρὸ τῶν Θεσμοφορίων *SIG* 1219.19 (Gambreion); τῷ ὕδατι τοῦ ἁ. Lxx *Nu.*6.5. -ιστέος, α, ον, *to be purified*, E.*IT*1199. -ιστήριον, τό, *instrument of purification*, Hero *Spir.*2.32. -ιστής, οῦ, ὁ, *purifier*, *Gloss.* -ιστικός, ή, όν, = ἁγνευτικός II, Eust.43.6. -ίτης [ῑ], ου, ὁ, *purifier*, θεοὶ ἁ. Poll.1.24; πάγος Lyc.135. **II.** *one who requires purification*, Hsch., *AB*338, v.l. in Il.24.480 (Sch. T.).

ἁγνοδικεῖς· οἱ θεοί, Phot., *AB*338, Hsch. (-δοχεῖς). ἀγνόδικος· ἀγνοοῦσα τὸ δίκαιον, Hsch. (cod. -μοσ), Phot., *AB*338.

⊛ἀγνο-έω, Ep. ἀγνοι-, 3 sg. subj. ἀγνοιῇσι Od.24.218: impf. ἠγνόουν Isoc.7.21, etc.: fut. ἀγνοήσω B.*Fr.*12, Isoc.12.251, D.32.10,

54.31: aor. ἠγνόησα A.*Eu.*134, Th.2.49, etc.; Ep. ἠγνοίησα Il.2.807, Hes.*Th.*551, Ep. contr. 3 sg. ἀγνώσασκε Od.23.95: pf. ἠγνόηκα Pl.*Sph.*221d, Alex.20.4:—Pass., fut. (of med. form) ἀγνοήσομαι D.18.249; ἀγνοηθήσομαι v.l. in Luc.*J.Tr.*5: aor. ἠγνοήθην, v. infr.: pf. ἠγνόημαι Isoc.15.171, Pl.*Lg.*797a. (This Verb implies a form ἄ-γνοος, = ἀγνώς II):—*not to perceive* or *recognize*; Hom., almost always in aor., ἄνδρ' ἀγνοιήσασ' ὑλάει Od.20.15, cf. Th. l.c., Pl.*Phdr.*228a; mostly with neg., οὐκ ἠγνοίησεν *he perceived* or *knew well*, Il.2.807, etc.; μηδὲν ἀγνόει E.*Andr.*899.—Mostly c. acc., *to be ignorant of*, Hdt.4.156, S.*Tr.*78; πάντα Pl.*Smp.*216d; ἑαυτοὺς ἀ. *forget* their former selves, D.10.74; τὴν πόλιν ἀ. *not to discern* the temper of the city, Id.19.231; τὸν ξένον Philostr.*VA*2.26; *fail to understand*, τὸ ῥῆμα *Ev.Marc.*9.32; περί τινος Pl.*Phdr.*277d: c. gen. pers. and rel. clause, ἀγνοοῦντες ἀλλήλων ὅ τι λέγομεν Id.*Grg.*517c: dependent clauses in part., τίς..ἀ. τὸν ἐκεῖθεν πόλεμον δεῦρο ἥξοντα; D.1.15: with Conj., οὐδεὶς ἀ. ὅτι.. Id.21.156, etc.; ἀγνοῶν εἰ..X.*An.*6.5.12:—Pass., *not to be known, recognized*, Pl.*Euthphr.*4a, *Hp.Ma.*294d, etc.; ἀγνοούμενα ὅπῃ..ἀγαθὰ ἐστι Id.*R.*506a; ἠγνοῆσθαι ξύμπασιν ὅτι..Id.*Lg.*797a; ὑπελάμβανον ἀγνοήσεσθαι D.18.249; καιρὸν οὐ παρεθέντα οὐδ' ἀγνοηθέντα ib.303, cf. Isoc.15.171; τὰ ἠγνοημένα *unknown parts*, Arr.*An.*7.1.4. **II.** abs., *go wrong, make a false step*, first in Hp.*Art.*46, Antipho 5.44 (dub.l.), Isoc.8.39; part. ἀγνοῶν *ignorantly, by mistake*, X.*An.*7.3.38, Arist.*EN*1110$^b$27; ἀγνοήσαντες And.4.5: in moral sense, *to be ignorant of what is right, act amiss*, Plb.5.11.5, cf. *Ep.Heb.*5.2:—Med., *fail to recognize*, Gal.14.630. **-ημα**, τό, *fault of ignorance, oversight*, ψυχῆς Gorg.*Hel.*19, ἀ. ἕτερον προσαγνοεῖν Thphr.*HP*9.4.8, cf. D.S.1.1, Hipparch.1.3.11, Lxx *To.*3.3, *Ep.Heb.*9.7; in pl., opp. ἁμαρτήματα, *PTeb.*5.3 (ii B.C.). **II.** *ignorance*, περί τινος Str.7.2.4. **III.** *object of* ἄγνοια, Dam.*Pr.*7. **-ηματίζω**, *fail to observe*, Aq.*Ps.*118(119).10. **-ησις**, ἡ, *ignorance*, Phld.*D.*1.7. **-ητέον**, with neg., οὐκ ἀ. *one must not fail to remark*, Dsc.*Praef.*7, Ph.1.11, al. **⊛-ητικός**, ή, όν, *mistaken*, τὰ ἀ. πράττειν Arist.*EE*1246$^a$48. **-ητός**, ή, όν, *ignored*; τὸ -όν, *the object of ignorance*, Dam.*Pr.*6.

**⊛ἄγνοια**, ἡ, (v. γιγνώσκω) *want of perception, ignorance*, ἀγνοίᾳ A.*Ag.*1596; ἀγνοίας ὕπο *Supp.*499; ἣν ὑπ' ἀγνοίας ὁρᾷς whom seeing you *pretend not to know*, S.*Tr.*419; ἀγνοίᾳ ἐξαμαρτάνειν X.*Cyr.*3.1.38, cf. Th.8.92, Ar.*Av.*577, D.9.64, etc.; opp. ἐπιστήμη, Pl.*Tht.*199d, Arist.*APr.*66$^b$26; ἀ. κενότης ἐστὶ τῆς περὶ ψυχὴν ἕξεως Pl.*R.*585b; δι' ἄγνοιαν πράττειν, opp. ἀγνοῶν, Arist.*EN*1110$^b$25: in Logic, ἡ τοῦ ἐλέγχου ἀ. *ignoratio elenchi, ignorance* of the conditions of a valid proof, Arist.*SE*168$^a$18, al. **II.** *mistaken conduct, a mistake*, D.18.133, *Ep.*2.19, Plb.27.2.2. [In Poets sts. ἀγνοῖᾰ, S.*Tr.*350, *Ph.*129; old Att., acc. to Ael. Dion.*Fr.*11, cf. Moer.191; Ion. ἀγνοίη Phot.]

**ἀγνοιῆσι**, etc., v. ἀγνοέω.

**ἀγνό-κοκκος**, ὁ, = οἰσόκαρπος, Gal.14.552, Eust.824.36.

**ἀγνοούντως**, Adv. of ἀγνοέω, *ignorantly*, Arist.*Top.*114$^b$10.

**ἁγνο-πολέομαι**, *to be purified by sacrifices*, Phot. **-πόλος**, ον, ($q^{u}$el-, cf. τελέω) *making pure*, Δημήτηρ Orph.*H.*18.12, *A.*38. **-ρῦτος**, ον, *pure-flowing*, ποταμός A.*Pr.*434 (lyr.).

**⊛ἁγνός**, ή, όν, (cf. ἅγιος) *pure, chaste, holy*, Hom. (only in Od.), etc.: **I.** of places and things dedicated to gods, *hallowed*, ἑορτή Od.21.259; of frankincense, ἁγνὴ ὀδμή Xenoph.1.7; ἄλσος *h.Merc.*187; τέμενος Pi.*P.*4.204; ὕδωρ Id.*I.*6(5).74; πυρὸς ἁγνόταται παγαί Id.*P.*1.21; αἰθήρ A.*Pr.*282; φάος, λουτρόν, S.*El.*86, *Ant.*1201; θύματα Id.*Tr.*287, cf. Th.1.126, D.H.1.38; of food, Jul.*Or.*6.192c (Comp.); χρηστήρια E.*Ion*243, etc.; ἐν ἁγνῷ on *holy* ground, A.*Supp.*223, but χῶρον οὐχ ἁ. πατεῖν a spot not *lawful* to tread on, S.*OC*37. **2.** of divine persons, *chaste, pure*, Hom., mostly of Artemis, χρυσόθρονος Ἄ. ἁ. Od.5.123, 18.202, etc.; also ἁ. Περσεφόνεια 11.386, cf. *h.Cer.*337; of Demeter, *h.Cer.*203,439; Χάριτες Sapph.65; ἁ. θεαί, Demeter and Persephone, *IG*14.204, 4.31; Apollo, Pi.*P.*9.64; Zeus, A.*Supp.*653, S.*Ph.*1289: of the attributes of gods, θεῶν σέβας S.*OT*830. **II.** after Hom., of persons, *undefiled, chaste*, of maidens, Alc.55, Pi.*P.*4.103, A.*Fr.*242; ἁ. αὐδά, of a maiden's voice, *Ag.*245; of Hippolytus, E.*Hipp.*102: c. gen., λέχους ἁ. δέμας ib.1003; γάμων ἁ. Pl.*Lg.*840d, cf. Men.*Epit.*223; ἁ. ἀπ' ἀνδρὸς συνουσίας Jusj. ap.D.59.78. **2.** *pure from blood, guiltless*, ἁγνοὶ τοὐπὶ τήνδε τὴν κόρην S.*Ant.*889; ἁ. χεῖρας E.*Or.*1604; μητροκτόνος.. τόθ' ἁ. ὤν Id.*El.*975, cf. *IA*940; ὅθ' ἁ. ἦν when he had been *purified*, S.*Tr.*258: c. gen., ἁγνὰς χεῖρας αἵματος E.*Hipp.*316; φόνου Pl.*Lg.*759c; Δάματρος ἀκτᾶς δέμας ἁ. ἴσχειν *pure* from food, E.*Hipp.*138. **3.** generally, *pure, upright*, ἀέθλων ἁ. κρίσις Pi.*O.*3.21; ψυχῆς φιλία ἁ. X.*Smp.*8.15, etc. **III.** Adv. ἁγνῶς καὶ καθαρῶς *h.Ap.*121, Hes.*Op.*337; ἁ. ἔχειν X.*Mem.*3.8.10.

**ἄγνος**, ἡ, Att. ὁ, = λύγος, *chaste-tree*, the branches of which were strewed by matrons on their beds at the Thesmophoria, *Vitex Agnus-castus*, *h.Merc.*410, Chionid.2, cf. *Trag.Adesp.*396, Pl.*Phdr.*230b, Hp.*Intern.*30, Arist.*HA*627$^a$9, Nic.*Th.*71, Dsc.1.103. (Associated with the notion of chastity from the likeness of its name to ἁγνός.) **II.** ἄγνος, ὁ, name of *a fish*, = καλλιώνυμος Diph.Siph. ap.Ath.8.356a (sine acc. cod., ἀγνός Kaib.). **III.** a kind of *bird*, Sch.Pl.*Phdr.* l.c., Suid.

**ἁγνό-στομος**, ον, *with pure mouth*, Tz.*H.*6.33. **-σύνη**, ἡ, = ἁγνότης, *Eranos*13.87 (loc. incert.), Phld.*D.*3*Fr.*76. **-τελής**, ές, *worshipped in holy rites*, Θέμις Orph.*A.*551.

**ἁγνότης**, ητος, ἡ, (ἁγνός) *purity, chastity, integrity*, *IG*4.588.15 (Argos, ii A.D.), 2*Ep.Cor.*6.5.

**⊛ἄγνῡμι**, 3 dual ἄγνῡτον Hom., v. infr.: fut. ἄξω (κατ-) Il.8.403: ao ἔαξα Hom., (κατ-) Ar.*V.*1436, etc., ἦξα Il.23.392, (κατ-) Hp.*Epid* 26; imper. ἆξον Il.6.306; part. ἄξας 16.371, E.*Hel.*1598 (κατ-εάξαν Lys.3.42 codd., perh. to distinguish it from aor. 1 of ἄγω); inf. ἆ Il.21.178:—**Pass., pres.**, v. infr.: aor. 2 ἐάγην (ᾱ, exc. ἐάγη Il.1 559) Hom., etc.; Ep. 3 sing. ἄγη Il.3.367, 3 pl. ἄγεν 4.214: pf. Act. ( pass. sense) ἔᾱγα Hes.*Op.*534, Q.S.1.204; Ion. ἔηγα (κατ-) Hdt. 224, Hp.*Fract.*24: pf. Pass. κατ-έαγμαι Luc.*Tim.*10: (ϝ, cf. κανάξαι ᾱ by nature, ἆξον (Hdn.Gr.2.14), ἆξαι on analogy of contr. forms κατα-ϝάγνυμι):—*break, shiver*, εἴσω δ' ἀσπὶδ' ἔαξε Il.7.270; ἦξε θε ζυγόν 23.392; ἵπποι ἄξαντ' ἐν πρώτῳ ῥυμῷ λίπον ἅρματα 16.371 νῆας.. ἔαξαν κύματα Od.3.298; πρό τε κύματ' ἔαξεν *broke* the waves 5.385; ἄγνυτον ὕλην *crashed through* it, of wild boars, Il.12.148 ἄγνυσι κεραυνόν *APl.*4.250:—Pass., with pf. ἔαγα, *to be broken, shivered*, ἐν χείρεσσιν ἄγη ξίφος Il.3.367, cf. 16.801; ἐν καυλῷ ἐάγη δολιχὸν δόρυ 13.162; πάταγος.. ἀγνυμενάων (sc. of the trees) 16.769 νηῶν θ' ἅμα ἀγνυμενάων Od.10.123; τοῦ [ὀϊστοῦ] δ' ἐξελκομένοιο πάλιν ἄγεν ὀξέες ὄγκοι Il.4.214; ποταμὸς περὶ καμπὰς πολλὰς ἀγνύμενος *with a broken*, i.e. *winding, course*, Hdt.1.185: metaph., ἄγνυτο ἠχώ the sound *spread around*, Hes.*Sc.*279,348; κέλαδος ἀγνύμενος διὰ στομάτων, of the notes of song, *Lyr.Adesp.*93.—Act. never in Prose, Pass. once in Hdt., κατάγνυμι being in general use.

**ἄγνυον**, τό, doubtful word, perh. *water-wheel*, *PLond.*3.1177.149.

**ἀγνύς**, ῦθος (on the accent v. Hdn.Gr.2.763), ἡ, *loom-weight*, in pl., Plu.2.156b, cf. Poll.7.36.

**ἀγνώδης**, ες, f.l. for ἀκανθώδης, Thphr.*HP*3.18.4.

**ἀγνωμονεύω**, f.l. for -έω, Plu.2.484b (Pass.).

**ἀγνωμ-ονέω**, *to be* ἀγνώμων, *act without right feeling*, X.*HG*1.7.33; coupled with ἀδικεῖν, Zeno*Stoic.*1.69; ἀ. εἴς τινα *to act unfeelingly* or *unfairly towards* one, D.18.94, Men.*Sam.*292; πρός τινα Apollod. Com.7.6: with a neut. Adj., μὴ νῦν τὰ θνητὰ θνητὸς ὢν ἀγνωμόνει *Trag. Adesp.*112: abs., *disregard a summons, be contumacious*, *PStrassb.*41.16 (iii A.D.); ἀ. περί τινα, περί τι, Plu.*Alc.*19, *Cam.*28: c. acc., *treat unfairly*, τὴν πόλιν Him.*Or.*2.31:—Pass., *to be so treated*, Plu.2.484b; ἀγνωμονηθεὶς Id.*Cam.*18; ὑπὸ τοῦ πατρὸς *POxy.*237$^v$40 (ii A.D.). **2.** *act ill-advisedly*, Aq.1*Ki.*13.13. **-οσύνη**, ἡ, *want of acquaintance with* a thing, Pl.*Tht.*199d. **2.** *want of sense, folly*, Thgn.896, Democr.175; *senseless pride, arrogance*, Hdt.2.172, E.*Ba.*885 (lyr.); πρὸς ἀ. τραπέσθαι Hdt.4.93; ἀ. νωμοσύνῃ χρᾶσθαι Id.5.83; ὑπ' ἀγνωμοσύνης Id.9.3. **3.** *want of feeling, unkindness*, D.18.252; θεῶν ἀ. S.*Tr.*1266 (dub.); ἀ. τύχης, Lat. *iniquitas fortunae*, D.18.207. **4.** in pl., *misunderstandings*, X.*An.*2.5.6. **⊛-ων**, ον, gen. ονος, (γνώμη) *ill-judging, senseless*, Thgn.1260 codd. (s. v. l.), Pi.*O.*8.60, Pl.*Phdr.*275b; ὥσπερ κυνίδιον τοῖς εἴκουσιν ἀ. Phld.*Lib.*p.10O.; opp. μετὰ λογισμοῦ πράττειν, Men.617; *inconsiderate*, τὸ ἀ. καὶ θυμοειδὲς Hp.*Aër.*16. Adv. -όνως *senselessly*, X.*HG*6.3.11, etc.; ἀ. ἔχειν D.2.26. **2.** *headstrong, reckless*, (in Comp.) Hdt.9.41: Sup., X.*Mem.*1.2.26. **3.** *unfeeling, hard-hearted*, Φοίβῳ τε κἀμοὶ μὴ γένησθ' ἀγνώμονες S.*OC*86; of judges, X.*Mem.*2.8.5; joined with ἀχάριστος, Id.*Cyr.*8.3.49, cf. *Mem.*2.10.3, D.21.97; esp. *ignoring one's debts*, Ulp.ad D.2.26, Jul.*Or.*3.117e (Comp.); ἀ. περὶ τὰς ἀποδόσεις Luc.*Herm.*10. **4.** *unknowing, in ignorance*, ἀ. πλανᾶσθαι Hp.*Vict.*1.6. **II.** of things, *senseless, brute*, Aeschin.3.244; also φρονοῦσαν θνητὰ κοὐκ ἀγνώμονα (neut. pl.) S.*Tr.*473. **2.** *cruel*, πρᾶγμα ἀ. πάσχειν Parth.17.5. **III.** of horses, *without the teeth that tell the age* (γνώμονες) Poll.1.182. [ἀγν- only in Man.5.338.]

**ἀγνώριστος**, ον, *unascertained, unknown*, Thphr.*HP*1.2.3, cf. Poll.5.150, Hierocl.*Facet.*150; *not recognized*, Steph.*in Hp.*1.61 D.

**ἀγνώς**, ῶτος, ὁ, ἡ, (γνῶ-ναι) **I.** Pass., *unknown*, mostly of persons, ἀγνῶτες ἀλλήλοις Od.5.79; ἀγνὼς πρὸς ἀγνῶτ' εἶπε A.*Ch.*677, cf. *Supp.*993, S.*Ph.*1008; ἀ. πατρί *clam patre*, E.*Ion*14: in Prose, ἀ. τοῖς ἐν τῇ νήσῳ Th.1.137, cf. Pl.*R.*375e, etc. **b.** of things, *obscure, unintelligible*, ἀ. φωνὴ βάρβαρος A.*Ag.*1051, cf. S.*Ant.*1001; ἀ. δόκησις *dark, vague* suspicion, Id.*OT*681. **2.** *obscure, ignoble*, ἀ. ἀκλεής E.*IA*18; οὐκ ἀ. νίκαν a victory not *unknown to fame*, Pi.*I.*2.12; ἀ. διὰ νεότητα Jul.*Or.*3.116b. **II.** Act., *ignorant*, S.*OT*1133; ἀ. τί δύναται.. X.*Oec.*20.13. **III.** c. gen., where the sense fluctuates between Pass. and Act., [χθὼν] οὐκ ἀ. θηρῶν Pi.*P.*9.58, cf. *I.*2.30; ἀγνῶτες ἀλλήλων Th.3.53; ὁ ἀ. τῶν λόγων Arist.*SE*178$^a$26.

**ἀγνωσία**, ἡ, *ignorance*, Hp.*VM*9, Demetr.Lac.*Herc.*1055.15; συμφορᾶς ἀ. E.*Med.*1204; κέρδος ἐν κακοῖς ἀ. Id.*Fr.*205; διὰ τὴν ἀλλήλων ἀ. Th.8.66; opp. γνῶσις, Pl.*Sph.*267b: c. gen., θεοῦ Lxx *Wi.*13.1, 1*Ep.Cor.*15.34. **2.** *lack of acquaintance*, Luc.*Tim.*42. **II.** *being unknown, obscurity*, Pl.*Mx.*238d.

**ἀγνώσσω**, = ἀγνοέω, pres. only, mostly poet., Simm.1.12, Musae.249, D.P.173, Coluth.8, Nonn.*D.*1.425, etc.; in late Prose, Luc.*Ep.Sat.*25.

**ἀγνωστί**, Adv. *secretly, unperceived*, Ps.-Callisth.3.19.

**⊛ἄγνωστος**, ον, *unknown*, τινί Od.2.175; *unheard of, forgotten*, Mimn.5.7; ἀ. ἐς γῆν E.*IT*94; *unfamiliar*, Arist.*Top.*149$^a$5 (Comp.). **2.** *not to be known*, ἄγνωστόν τινα τεύχειν Od.13.191; πάντεσσι ib.397; ἀγνωστότατοι γλῶσσαν *most unintelligible* in tongue, Th.3.94. **3.** *not an object of knowledge, unknowable*, ἄλογα καὶ ἀ. Pl.*Tht.*202b; ἡ ὕλη ἀ. καθ' αὑτήν Arist.*Metaph.*1036$^a$9; in Comp., *harder to know*, ib.995$^a$2. Adv. -τως Procl.*in Alc.*p.52C. **4.** as the name of a divinity at Athens, νὴ τὸν Ἄγνωστον Ps.-Luc.*Philopatr.*9, cf. *Act.Ap.*17.23; in pl., θεῶν.. ὀνομαζομένων ἀ. Paus.1.1.4. **II.** Act., *not knowing, ignorant of*, ψευδέων Pi.*O.*6.67 (v.l. ἄγνωτον), cf. Luc.*Halc.*3. Adv. -τως *inconsiderately*, Phld.*Lib.*p.29O.

**ἰγνωτίδιον**, τό, = μύλλος, Dorio ap. Ath.3.118d.

**ἄγνωτος**, ον, = ἄγνωστος, γνωτὰ κοὐκ ἄ. μοι S.*OT*58; ἄγνωτα τοῖς ›μένοις Ar.*Ra*.926.

**ἀγξηραίνω**, v. ἀναξηραίνω.

**ἄγξις**, ἡ, (ἄγχω) *throttling*, *EM*194.50, *Gloss.*

**ἀγόγγυστος**, ον, *not murmuring*, in Adv. -τως, Sor.1.88.

**ἀγοήτευτος**, ον, *not to be bewitched* or *beguiled*, Plot.4.4.44. II. ct., *without guile*. Adv. -τως Cic.*Att*.12.3.1.

**ἀγόμφιος**, ον, *without grinders*, ἀ. αἰών *toothless* age, Diocl.Com. .

**ἀγόνᾰτος**, ον, (γόνυ) *without a knee*, Arist.*IA*700a3. II. of lants, *without knots* or *joints*, Id.*Fr*.195, Thphr.*HP*4.8.7.

**ἀγον-έω**, *to be unfruitful*, Thphr.*HP*9.18.3, Ph.2.402: metaph., υχὴ ἀ. τινῶν ib.435. **-ία**, ἡ, *sterility*, Arist.*GA*746b20, Dsc.2.179, 'lu.*Rom*.24 (pl.); opp εὐγονία, Iamb.*Comm.Math*.15. **-ος**, ον, γονή): I Pass., *unborn*, Il.3.40 (which Augustus translated *child-ess*, Suet.*Oct*.65), E.*Ph*.1598, Eub.107.11. 2. γόνος ἄ. *no longer son*, of a horse that mounts his dam, Opp.*C*.1.260. II. Act., *nfruitful*, *sterile*, of animals both male and female, Hp.*Aph*.5.59, *Art*.41 (Comp.), Arist.*GA*726a3 (Comp.), etc.; γαστήρ Ael.*NA*15.9; όκοισι ἀ. travail *without issue*, *bringing no children to the birth*, S.*OT* 27: metaph., ἄ. ποιητής Plu.2.348b. b. of flowers, *sterile*, or seeds, *infertile*, Thphr.*HP*1.13.4, 1.11.1; ὁμίχλη νεφέλη ἄ., i.e. not producing water, Arist.*Mete*.346b35, cf. Ar.Did.p.451.33 D. c. metaph., ἄ. ἡμέρα, ἔτος a day or year *unlucky for begetting children*, Hp.*Epid*.2.6.8 and 10 (of *odd* days and years); τὸ ἄ. τῆς ὕλης Plot.3.6.19, cf. 6.3.8. d. Astrol., *impeding generation*, ζῴδιον Vett.Val.10.11. 2. c. gen., *not productive of*, σοφίας Pl.*Tht*.150c, cf. 157c; γῆ θηρίων ἄ. *Mx*.237d. III. *childless*, γένος E.*HF*888, Hld.4.12. IV. **ἄγονον**, τό, = μυρσίνη ἀγρία, Ps.-Dsc.4.144; **ἄγονος**, = ἄγνος, Id.1.103, Sch.Nic.*Th*.71.

**ἄγοος**, ον, *unmourned*, A.*Th*.1068 (lyr.).

**✱ἀγορά** [ᾰγ], ᾶς, Ion. **ἀγορή**, ῆς, ἡ, (ἀγείρω):—*assembly*, esp. *of the People*, opp. the Council of Chiefs, Il.2.93, Od.2.69, etc.; τοῖσιν δ' οὔτ' ἀγοραὶ βουληφόροι (sc. Κυκλώπεσσι) Od.9.112; ὀρθῶν ἑσταότων ἀ. γένετ' οὐδέ τις ἔτλη ἕζεσθαι Il.18.246; ἀ. Πυλάτιδες, of the *Amphictyonic Council* at Pylae, S.*Tr*.638, cf. Ion Eleg.1.3; μακάρων ἀ. Pi.*I*.8(7).29, cf. *AB*210; ἀγορήνδε καλέσσασθαι, κηρύσσειν, Il.1.54, 2.51; ἀγορὴν ποιήσασθαι, θέσθαι, Il.8.489, Od.9.171; εἰς ἀ. ἰέναι, ἀγέρεσθαι, 8.12, Il.18.245; ἀγορήνδε καθέζεσθαι Od.1.372.—Not common in Prose, ἀγορὰν συνάγειν, συλλέγειν X.*An*.5.7.3; ποιῆσαι Aeschin.3.27; ἀγορὰς ποιεῖσθαι Hyp.*Fr*.150: of the assembly in Attic demes, D.44.36, *IG*2.585, al.; ἀ. συνέδριον φυλετῶν καὶ δημοτῶν *AB*327: in late Prose, ἀ. δικῶν προθεῖναι, καταστήσασθαι, = Lat. *conventus agere*, Luc.*Bis Acc*.4,12: *meeting for games*, Pi.*N*.3.14: metaph., μυρμήκων ἀ. Luc.*Icar*.19: prov., θεῶν ἀ. 'Babel', Suid., etc. II. *place of assembly*, τοὺς δ' εὗρ' εἰν ἀγορῇ Il.7.382; ἵνα σφ' ἀ. τε θέμις τε 11.807, cf. Od.6.266; pl., Od.8.16; οὔτε..εἰς ἀ. ἔρχεται οὔτε δίκας Thgn.268. 2. *market-place*, perh. not earlier than *Hom.Epigr*.14.5 πολλὰ μὲν εἰν ἀγορῇ πωλεύμενα, πολλὰ δ' ἀγυιαῖς; freq. in later authors, πρυμνοῖς ἀγορᾶς ἔπι Pi.*P*.5.93; θεοὶ..ἀγορᾶς ἐπίσκοποι A.*Th*.272; μέση Τραχινίων ἀ. S.*Tr*.424; ἀγορᾷ οὐδὲ ἄστει δέχεσθαι Th.6.44; ὀλιγάκις..ἀγορᾶς χραίνων κύκλον E.*Or*.919; οἱ ἐκ τῆς ἀ. *market* people, X.*An*.1.2.18; ἐξ ἀγορᾶς εἶ Ar.*Eq*.181, etc.; εἰς ἀ. ἐμβάλλειν to go into *the forum*, i.e. be a citizen, Lycurg.5; ἐν τῇ ἀ. ἐργάζεσθαι to trade in *the market*, D.57.31; εἰς τὴν ἀ. χειροτονεῖν (opp. ἐπὶ τὸν πόλεμον) 'for *the market*', Id.4.26; the Roman *Forum*, D.H.5.48. III. *business of the ἀγορά*: 1. *public speaking*, *gift of speaking*, mostly in pl., ἔσχ' ἀγοράων withheld him *from speaking*, Il.2.275; οἱ δ' ἀγορὰς ἀγόρευον ib.788, cf. Od.4.818; ᾠδὴν ἀντ' ἀγορῆς θέμενος Sol.1. 2. *market*, ἀγορὰν παρασκευάζειν Th.7.40, X.*HG*3.4.11; ἀ. παρέχειν Th.6.44, etc.; ἄγειν X.*An*.5.7.33, etc.; opp. ἀγορᾷ χρῆσθαι to have *supplies*, ib.7.6.24; τῆς ἀ. εἴργεσθαι Th.1.67, Plu.*Per*.29; ἀ. ἐλευθέρα, i.e. καθαρὰ τῶν ὠνίων πάντων, Arist.*Pol*.1331a31, cf. X.*Cyr*.1.2.3; opp. ἀ. ἀναγκαία Arist.*Pol*.1331b11; generally, *provisions*, *supplies*, *PPetr*.3p.131 (iii B.C.), *PSI*4.354 (iii B.C.), al.; in pl., Nic.Dam.p.6.17 D.; ἀγορὰς περικόπτειν cut off *supplies*, D.H.10.43. b. *market*, *sale*, ἀ. τῶν βιβλίων, τῶν παρθένων, Luc.*Ind*.19, Ael.*VH*4.1, cf. Nicoch.7. IV. as a mark of time, ἀ. πλήθουσα *the forenoon*, when the market-place was full, ἀγορῆς πληθυούσης Hdt.4.181; πληθούσης ἀγορᾶς X.*Mem*.1.1.10, cf. *SIG*695.38 (Magn. Mae.); περὶ or ἀμφὶ ἀ. πλήθουσαν X.*An*.2.1.7, 1.8.1; ἐν ἀ. πληθούσῃ Pl.*Grg*.469d, cf. Th.8.92; also ἀγορῆς πληθώρῃ Hdt.2.173, 7.223; poet., ἐν ἀ. πλήθοντος ὄχλου Pi.*P*.4.85; πρὶν ἀ. πεπληθέναι Pherecr.29: ἀγορῆς διάλυσις *the time just after mid-day*, when they went home from market, Hdt.3.104, cf. X.*Oec*.12.1. V. *market-day*, = Lat. *nundinae*, D.H.7.58.

**✱ἀγοράζω** [ᾰγ], fut. άσω Ar.*Lys*.633, ἀγορῶ Lxx *Ne*.10.31: aor. ἠγόρασα X.*HG*7.2.18, D.21.149, etc.: pf. ἠγόρακα Arist.*Oec*.1352b7, Plb.6.17.4:—Med., aor. ἠγορασάμην D.50.55: pf. ἠγόρασμαι (v. infr.):—Pass., aor. ἠγοράσθην Id.59.46: pf. ἠγόρασμαι Is.8.23, Men.828:—*frequent the* ἀγορά, αἱ γυναῖκες ἀ. καὶ καπηλεύουσι Hdt.2.35, 4.164, cf. Arist.*Ph*.196a5, *Com.Adesp*.710; *occupy the market-place*, Th.6.51. 2. *buy in the market*, πωλεῖν ἀ. Ar.*Ach*.625; ἐπιτήδεια ἀ. X.*An*.1.5.10; generally, *buy*, Ar.*Pl*.984, etc.; *farm* taxes or state-contracts, ὠνὴν ἀ. *PRev.Laws*41.22, al.; τὸν Σαίτην ἀγοράσας ib.60.23:—Med., *buy for oneself*, X.*An*.1.3.14:—Pass., διά τινος ἀ. D.50.25: pf. Pass. in med. sense, ἀντὶ τοῦ ἠγοράσθαι αὐτοῖς τὸν οἶνον Id.35.19. 3. *haunt the* ἀγορά, Corinn.34, Pi.*Fr*.103; οὐδ' ἀγοράσει γ' ἀγένειος οὐδεὶς ἐν ἀγορᾷ nor shall any boy *lounge in the* ἀγορά, Ar.*Eq*.1373. [-ᾱζω (i.e. -ᾴζω) in sense 1, Hdn.Gr.2.14.]

**✱ἀγοραῖος** [ᾰγ], ον, (fem. -αία epith. of Artemis and Athena, v. infr.):—*in*, *of*, or *belonging to the* ἀγορά, Ζεὺς Ἀ. as *guardian of popular assemblies*, Hdt.5.46, A.*Eu*.973 (lyr.), E.*Heracl*.70; Ἑρμῆς Ἀ. as *patron of traffic*, Ar.*Eq*.297, cf. *IPE*1$^2$.128 (Olbia), *IG*12(8).67 (Thasos), Paus.1.15.1; Ἄρτεμις Ἀ. at Olympia, Id.5.15.4; Ἀθηνᾶ Ἀ. at Sparta, Id.3.11.9; generally, θεοὶ ἀ. A.*Ag*.90. 2. of things, τὰ ἀ. *details of market-business*, Pl.*R*.425c. II. *frequenting the market*, ὁ ἀ. ὄχλος X.*HG*6.2.23; δήμου εἶδος Arist.*Pol*.1291b19, etc.; τὸ ἀ. πλῆθος..τὸ περὶ τὰς πράσεις καὶ τὰς ὠνὰς καὶ τὰς ἐμπορίας καὶ καπηλείας διατρῖβον ib.1291a4:—ἀγοραῖοι (with or without ἄνθρωποι), οἱ, *those who frequented the* ἀγορά, Hdt.1.93, 2.141; opp. ἔμποροι, X.*Vect*.3.13, but = *traders* (i.e. *sutlers*), Ael.*Tact*.2.2:—hence, *the common sort*, *low fellows*, Ar.*Ra*.1015, Pl.*Prt*.347c, Thphr.*Char*.6.2; of agitators, *Act.Ap*.17.5, Plu.*Aem*.38: Comp., *the baser sort*, Ptol.Euerg.1. Adv. -αίως, λέγειν D.H.*Rh*.10.11. 2. of things, *vulgar*, σκώμματα Ar.*Pax*750; τοὺς νοῦς ἀ. ἧττον..ποιῶ Id.*Fr*.471; ἀ. φιλία (opp. ἐλευθέριος) Arist.*EN*1162b26; *common*, ἄρτοι Lync.ap.Ath.3.109d. III. generally, *proper to the* ἀγορά, *skilled in*, *suited for forensic speaking*, Plu.*Per*.11, al.:—ἀγοραῖος (sc. ἡμέρα) *court-day*, *assize*, τὰς ἀ. ποιεῖσθαι Str.13.4.12; ἄγειν τὴν ἀ. Epist.Galb.ap.J.*AJ*14.10.21, cf. *Act.Ap*.19.38, *IGRom*.4.790. Adv. -ως *in forensic style*, Plu.*CG*4, *Ant*.24. 2. ἀγοραῖος, ὁ, = *tabellio*, *notary*, Aristid.*Or*.50(26).94, *Edict.Diocl*.7.41, *Gloss.*; also, *pleader*, *advocate*, in pl., Philostr.*VA*6.36. b. ἀγοραῖος, ἡ, *market day*, *IGRom*.4.1381 (Lydia). (The distn. ἀγόραιος *vulgar*, ἀγοραῖος *public speaker*, drawn by Ammon., etc., is prob. fictitious.)

**✱ἀγορᾱ-νομέω**, *to be* ἀγορανόμος, Alex.247, *IG*12(3).170 (Astypalaea); τῆς πόλεως *POxy*.910.2 (ii A.D.); at Rome, *to be aedile*, D.H.10.48, Plu.*Caes*.5, App.*BC*2.1, etc.: pf. -ηκα D.C.52.32. **-νομία**, ἡ, *office of* ἀγορανόμος, Arist.*Pol*.1331b9, *IG*4.203 (Corinth), *PGrenf*.1.10.7 (ii B.C.), etc. II. = Lat. *aedilitas*, Plb.10.4.1, D.H.5.18, App.*Pun*.112. **-νομικός**, ή, όν, *of* or *for the* ἀγορανόμος or *his office*, ἀ. ἄττα Pl.*R*.425d; νόμιμα Arist.*Pol*.1264a31; νόμος *Milet*.3.145 (200 B.C.); τιμαί *CIG*1716 (Delph.); στέφανος *POxy*.1252v17 (iii A.D.). II. = Lat. *aedilicius*, ἀρχαιρέσια Plu.*Pomp*.53; ἐξουσία D.H.6.95. **-νόμιον**, τό, *court* or *office of the* ἀγορανόμος, Pl.*Lg*.917e, *IG*2.192c11, 12(3).170, *PHib*.29.3 (iii B.C.), *AP*11.17 (Nicarch.). **-νόμιος**, ον, *of* or *in the forum*, περίπατος *IGRom*.4.504 (Perg.). **-νόμος**, ὁ, *clerk of the market*, who regulated buying and selling, Hp.*Epid*.4.24, Ar.*Ach*.723, al., Lys.22.16, Arist.*Pol*.1299b17, *IG*2.192c12, etc. 2. *public notary*, *PGrenf*.2.23a ii 2 (ii B.C.), *POxy*.99.2 (i A.D.), etc. II. = Lat. *aedilis*, D.H.7.14, *IG*14.719, etc.

**ἀγοράομαι**, almost always in Ep. forms, pres. ἀγοράασθε, impf. ἠγοράασθε, ἠγορόωντο (cf. Hdt.6.11), aor. 1 only 3 sing. ἀγορήσατο (v. infr.): 2 sg. impf. ἠγορῶ S.*Tr*.601; inf. ἀγορᾶσθαι Thgn.159:—*meet in assembly*, *sit in debate*, οἱ δὲ θεοὶ πὰρ Ζηνὶ καθήμενοι ἠγορόωντο Il.4.1. II. *speak in the assembly*, *harangue*, ὅ σφιν ἐϋφρονέων ἀγορήσατο Il.1.73, 9.95, cf. Od.7.185, Hdt. l. c.; παισὶν ἐοικότες ἀγοράασθε Il.2.337. 2. generally, *speak*, *utter*, εὐχωλαί..ἃς..κενεαυχέες ἠγοράασθε 8.230, μήποτε..ἀγορᾶσθαι ἔπος μέγα Thgn. l. c.: c. dat., *speak*, *talk with*, ἕως σὺ..ἠγορῶ ξέναις S. l. c. [ᾱγ- only in Il.2.337, metri grat.; otherwise ᾰγ-.]

**ἀγορ-ᾰσείω**, Desid. of ἀγοράζω, *wish to buy*, Sch.Ar.*Ra*.1068. **-ᾰσία**, ἡ, *purchase*, Telecl.51, Hyp.*Fr*.70, *Inscr.Magn*.116.20 (ii A.D.), D.L.2.78 (pl.), etc. **✱-ᾰσις**, εως, ἡ, = foreg., Pl.*Sph*.219d (pl.), cf. *Leg.Sacr*.2.69 (-ασσις, Tanagra), *PRyl*.2.45.5 (iii A.D.). **-ασμα**, τό, *that which is bought* or *sold*: mostly in pl., *wares*, *merchandise*, Aeschin.3.223, D.34.9, etc., cf. Alex.168. **-ασμός**, ὁ, *purchasing*, Phint.ap.Stob.4.23.61a, Vett.Val.180.11, al. II. *purchase*, Lxx *Ge*.42.19, al., *OGI*660.20 (Egypt, i A.D.) (pl.); freq. of auctions, ποιεῖσθαί τινος τὸν ἀ. *BGU*1128.9 (14 B.C.). **✱-αστής**, οῦ, ὁ, *the slave who had to buy* provisions for the house, *purveyor*, X.*Mem*.1.5.2:—generally, *purchaser*, μέτριος ἀ. Men.500, cf. Arist.*Oec*.1352b6, Dinon12, Ael.*VH*12.1, *POxy*.298.48 (i A.D.). **-αστικός**, ή, όν, *of* or *for traffic*, *commercial*, Pl.*Cra*.408a; ἡ -κή (sc. τέχνη) *traffic*, *commerce*, Id.*Sph*.223c; τὸ ἀ. δίκαιον *right of purchase*, *POxy*.1268.16 (iii A.D.), 1475.14 (iii A.D.). **✱-αστός**, ή, όν, *bought*, *paid for*, *PPetr*.3p.243 (iii B.C.), *BGU*802 iv 8 (i A.D.); δούλη *POxy*.95.14 (i A.D.), cf. Porph.Hist.20. **-άστρια**, ἡ, fem. of ἀγοραστής, *BGU*907.11 (ii A.D.), *PThead*.1.11 (iv A.D.). **-ατρός**, ὁ, = πυλαγόρας, *IG*2$^2$.1132.6, *Klio*14.287 (Delph., iii B.C.). **-ατυπεῖς**· ἄγαν θορυβεῖς, Hsch. **-ᾶχος**, ἡ, female official at Sparta, *IG*5(1).589.

**ἀγόρ-ευσις**, ἡ, *speech*, *oration*, *EM*13.51. **-ευτήριον**, τό, *place for speaking*, *IG*14.742 (Naples, i/ii A.D.). **-ευτής**, οῦ, ὁ, *speaker*, *POxy*.1590.1 (iv A.D.). **-εύω** (ἀγορά), impf. ἠγόρευον, Ep. ἀγόρευον Il.1.385: fut. -εύσω Hom., Alciphr.3.52, Philostr.*VA*4.45: aor. -ευσα Hom., D.H.1.65, Luc.*Pisc*.15: pf. -ευκα Lib.*Or*.37.4: 1 aor. Pass. -εύθην (προσ-) Str.3.3.5: in compds. these tenses and pf. Pass. -ευμαι are found in early Prose and Att. Inscrr., the simple vb. only in pres. and impf.:—*speak in the assembly*, *harangue*, freq. in Ep., ἀγορὰς ἀ. Il.2.788; ἐν Ἀργείοις ἔπεα πτερόεντ' ἀ. 23.535; ὡς Ἕκτωρ ἀγόρευε 8.542; τοῖσιν ἀ. *address* them, 1.571, al.; πρὸς ἀλλήλους ἔπεα 24.142; ὀνειδίζων ἀ. Od.18.380: in Att., of the crier's proclamation in the Ecclesia, τίς ἀγορεύειν βούλεται; who wishes *to address the house?* Ar.*Ach*.45, D.18.170, etc.; ἀ. ὡς..Il.1.109: c. inf., μή τι φόβονδ' ἀγόρευε *counsel* me not to flight, Il.5.252; ἀ. μὴ στρατεύεσθαι Hdt.7.10.α'. 2. generally, *speak*, *say*, τοιαῦτα πρὸς ἀλλήλους ἀγόρευον Il.5.274; κακόν τι ἀ. τινά Od.18.15;

κακῶς ἀ. τινά Arist.*Fr.*417; ἀ. ὡς.., ὅτι.., Hdt.3.156, Ar.*Pl.*102; οὐκ ἠγόρευον; *did I not say so?* Id.*Ach.*41, cf. S.*OC*838; *tell of, mention,* τι Od.2.318, 16.263, al.; ὑπὲρ τοῦ Διὸς ἀγορεύων *speaking* of Zeus, Pl.*Lg.*776e: metaph., δέρμα θηρὸς ἀ. χειρῶν ἔργον *tells a tale of..* Theoc.25.175. 3. *proclaim,* Il.1.385; πέμπων κήρυκα ἠγόρευέ σφι τάδε Hdt.6.97:—Pass., ὁ πολίτης..κακὸς ἀγορευέσθω Pl.*Lg.*917d:—aor. Med., ἀγορεύσασθαι ὡς..*to have it proclaimed* that.., Hdt.9.26:—ὁ νόμος ἀ. the law *declares,* Antipho3.3.7, Lys.9.9, Arist.*Rh.*1354[a]22; ἀ. μὴ ποιεῖν Ar.*Ra.*628; οὔνομα..ἧδ' ἀ. στήλη *IG*2.2753. 4. Pass., *to be delivered,* λόγον καλὸν ἐπὶ τοῖς..θαπτομένοις -εσθαι Th.2.35.

**ἀγορ-ηγός,** sc. ναῦς, ἡ, *ship which conveys provisions, EM*13.52. **-ῆθεν,** Adv. *from the assembly* or *market,* Il.2.264, al. **-ήιος,** = ἀγοραῖος, θεοὶ *IG*12(3).452 (Thera). **-ήνδε,** Adv. *to the assembly* or *market,* Il.1.54. **-ητής,** οῦ, ὁ, *speaker,* Ep. word, chiefly used of Nestor, λιγὺς Πυλίων ἀ. Il.1.248, al., cf. Ar.*Nu.*1057, Timo30.1. II. = ἀγορανόμος, or perh. *public auctioneer, OGI*262.20 (pl., Baetocaece). **-ητύς,** ύος, ἡ, *eloquence,* Od.8.168.—Ep. word. **-ῆφι,** Adv. *in the assembly,* Hes.*Th.*89.

**ἄγορος,** ὁ, = ἀγορά, used only by E. in lyr., generally in pl., as *IT* 1096, *El.*723, *Andr.*1037; sg. only *HF*412 ἄγορον ἁλίσας φίλων.

**ἀγορρίον·** ἐκκλησία, and **ἀγορρίς·** ἀγορά, ἄθροισις, Hsch.

**ἀγός** [ᾰ], οῦ, ὁ, (ἄγω) *leader, chief,* c. gen., Il.4.265, al., cf. Pi.*N.*1.51, A.*Supp.*248, 904 (lyr.), E.*Rh.*29 (lyr.), *AP*9.219 (Diod.).

*__ἄγος__ (A), [ᾰ], εος, τό, *any matter of religious awe*: I. *pollution, guilt,* ἐν τῷ ἄγεϊ ἐνέχεσθαι Hdt.6.56; ἀ. ἐκθύσασθαι 6.91; ἄ... κεκτήσεται θεῶν A.*Th.*1022; ἄ. αἱμάτων ἀρέσθαι Id.*Eu.*168, cf. *AP* 7.268 (Plato); ἄ. φυλάσσεσθαι A.*Supp.*375; φεύγειν S.*Ant.*256; ὅθεν τὸ ἄ. συνέβη τοῖς Συβαρίταις Arist.*Pol.*1303[a]30; ἄ. ἀφοσιώσασθαι Plu.*Cam.*18: in concrete sense, the *person* or *thing accursed,* S.*OT* 1426; ἄ. ἐλαύνειν, = ἀγηλατεῖν, Th.1.126. 2. *expiation, sacrifice,* S.*Ant.*775, *Fr.*689, prob. so in A.*Ch.*155. 3. ἄγεα· τεμένεα, and ἀγέεσσι· τεμένεσι, Hsch.; ἄγη· τὰ μυστήρια, *AB*212. (ἄγος (= τὸ καθαρόν, σέβασμα) postulated by Gramm. (cf. ἅγιος ἐκ τοῦ ἄγος γέγονεν *Et. Gud.*) is not found, unless ἄγος 3 be a dialectic form.)

**ἄγος** (B), εος, τό, (ἄγνυμι) *fragment,* Hsch., *EM*418.2.

**ἀγοσταί, ἀγοστέω,** variants for ἀκ- in Gramm., as *AB*213.

**ἀγοστός,** ὁ, *flat of the hand,* Hom. only in Il., in the phrase ὁ δ' ἐν κονίῃσι πεσὼν ἕλε γαῖαν ἀγοστῷ 11.425, al.; χειρὸς ἀ. A.R.3.120. II. *arm,* = ἀγκάλη, Theoc.17.129, *AP*7.464 (Antip.); pl., ib.5.254.15 (Paul. Sil.): metaph., [Ἀκαδημείας] ἐν ἀγοστῷ Simon. 150. III. *dirt, filth,* Sch.Il.6.506. (Perh. cognate with Skt. *hástas* 'hand'.)

**ἄγουρος,** ὁ, *youth,* Thracian word, Eust.1788.56.

*__ἄγρα,__ Ion. **ἄγρη,** ἡ, *hunting, the chase,* (never in Il.), ἄγρην ἐφέπειν Od.12.330; χαίρουσι δέ τ' ἀνέρες ἄγρῃ 22.306; ἐς ἄγρας ἰέναι E.*Supp.*885; ἄ. ἀνθρώπων Pl.*Lg.*823e; ἁλιαδᾶν ἔχων ἀΰπνους ἄγρας S.*Aj.* 880 (lyr.). 2. *way of catching,* Pi.*N.*3.81, Hdt.2.70. II. *quarry, prey,* Hes.*Th.*442; ἄγραν ὤλεσα A.*Eu.*148 (lyr.); εὔκερως ἄ. S.*Aj.* 64, cf. 407 (pl.); Μελέαγρε, μελέαν γάρ ποτ' ἀγρεύεις ἄ. E.*Fr.*517; *game,* Hdt.1.73, etc.; of fish, *draught, take, Ev.Luc.*5.9: metaph., δορὸς ἄγρα A.*Th.*322 (lyr.). III. Ἄγρα, ἡ, title of Artemis at Athens, Pl.*Phdr.*229c; τὰ ἐν Ἄγρας (sc. μυστήρια) Paus.Gr.*Fr.*13; τὰ πρὸς Ἄγραν *IG*2.315; μήτηρ ἐν Ἄγρας ib.273:—also **Ἄγραι,** αἱ, the precinct of Artemis Agra, Paus.1.19.6, St. Byz., *AB*334, etc. (With ἄγρα : ἄγρια cf. θήρα : θηρία.)

**ἄγρᾰδε,** Adv., poet. form of ἀγρόνδε, Call.*Fr.*26.

**ἀγραῖος,** α, ον, (ἄγρα) *of the chase,* epith. of Apollo, Paus.1.41.6; of Artemis, Paus.Gr.*Fr.*13; δαίμονες Opp.*H.*3.27.

**ἀγραμμ-ατία,** ἡ, *illiteracy,* Ph.1.502, Ael.*VH*8.6: pl., Phld.*Vit.* p.41 J. **-ατος,** ον, *illiterate,* X.*Mem.*4.2.20, Damox 2.12, Epicur. *Fr.*236, *AP*11.154 (Lucill.), cf. S.E.*M.*1.99; *unable to read* or *write,* Pl.*Ti.*23a. Adv. -τως Ph.1.195, Arr.*Epict.*2.9.10. II. = ἄγραπτος, ἔθη Pl.*Plt.*295a. III. of animals, *unable to utter articulate sounds,* Arist.*HA*488[a]33. 2. of sounds, *inarticulate,* Id.*Int.*16[a]29, D.L.3.107; *incapable of being written,* Porph.*Abst.*3.3, cf. Eustr. *in APo.*102.19; ᾠδὴ ἀ. *song without words,* Phld.*Po.*2*Fr.*47.22. *-ος, ον, *not on the line,* ἄγραμμα ἀφεῖται, of a throw of the dice, *counting nothing,* Hsch.

**ἀγράνδις,** = ἀγρόνδε, Dor. Adv. in Theognost.*Can.*163.33.

**ἄγραπτος,** ον, *unwritten,* ἄ. θεῶν νόμιμα S.*Ant.*454. II. ἄ. δίκη action *cancelled* in consequence of a special plea, Poll.8.57.

**ἀγρ-αυλέω,** *live in the open, out of doors,* Arist.*Mir.*831[a]29, Parth. 29.1, Plu.*Num.*4, Str.4.4.3; of shepherds, *Ev.Luc.*2.8. **-αυλής,** ές, *in the fields, out of doors,* κοίτη Nic.*Th.*78. **-αυλία,** ἡ, *service in the field,* D.H.6.44 (pl.), D.S.16.15 (pl.), etc. **-αυλος,** ον, (ἀγρός, αὐλή) *dwelling in the field,* of shepherds, Il.18.162, Hes.*Th.*26, A.R.4.317, Megasth.40; epith. of Pan, *AP*6.179 (Arch.); ἀ. ἀνήρ *a boor,* ib. 11.60 (Paul. Sil.). 2. of oxen, βοὸς ἀγραύλοιο Il.10.155, Od.12. 253; θὴρ S.*Ant.*349 (lyr.), E.*Ba.*1188 (lyr.), etc. 3. of things, *rustic,* πύλαι Id.*El.*342.

**ἀγραφ-ής,** ές, = ἄγραφος, δάνειον *BGU*895.31 (ii A.D.). **-ίου** γραφή an action against state-debtors, *who had got their debts cancelled* without paying, D.58.51, Arist.*Ath.*59.3, Lycurg.*Fr.*6, Poll. 8.54. **-ος,** ον, *unwritten,* μνήμη Th.2.43; ἄ. διαθῆκαι *nuncupatory* wills, Plu.*Cor.*9; ἄ. κληρονόμος Luc.*Tox.*23; ἄγραφα λέγειν to speak *without book,* Plu.*Dem.*8. Adv. -φως, κατὰ μνήμης σῴζεσθαι Procl. *in Prm.*p.553 S. II. ἄ. δίκαιον, *moral* or *equitable justice,* Arist. *EN*1162[b]22; ἄ. νόμοι or νόμιμα *unwritten laws*: 1. *laws of nature,* τοῖς ἀ. νομίμοις καὶ τοῖς ἀνθρωπίνοις ἤθεσι D.18.275, cf. Ar[ist.] *EN*1180[b]1. 2. *laws of custom,* Th.2.37; ἄ. νόμιμα Pl.*Lg.*793a, Arist.*Rh.*1373[b]5; ἄγραφα, τά, ib.1368[b]9; ἄ. ἀδίκημα a crime *not rec[og]nized by law,* Hsch. 3. *religious traditions,* as of the Eumolpida[e], Lys.6.10. III. *not registered,* ἄ. πόλεις (in a treaty) Th.1.4[..]; ἄ. γάμοι *without written contract, CPR*18.30 (ii A.D.). Adv. -ως ibi[d.], *POxy.*267.19 (i A.D.)); ἄ. συνουσίαι *not written down,* Phlp.*in Ph.*51 30; συναλλαγματογραφίαι *PTeb.*1.140; ἄγραφα καὶ ἄστατα neith[er] *catalogued* nor weighed, *IG*2.652*B*2; hence ἄγραφα, τά, *sundrie[s]* *PTeb.*112.104 (ii B.C.), al. 2. ἄ. μέταλλα mines *not registered,* b[ut] worked clandestinely, Suid. s.v. IV. *without inscription, I[G]* 2.754, al.—Prose word.

**ἄγρει,** v. sub ἀγρέω II.

*__ἀγρεῖος,__ α, ον, (ἀγρός) *of the field* or *country,* πλάτανος *AP*6.3[5] (Leon.). 2. *clownish, boorish,* Ar.*Nu.*655, *Th.*160.

*__ἀγρειοσύνη,__ ἡ, *clownishness*: or *a rude, vagrant life, AP*6.51.

**ἀγρεῖφνα,** ἡ, *harrow, AP*6.297 (Phanias); cf. ἀγρίφη.

*__ἀγρέμιον,__ τό, = ἄγρα II, *AP*6.224 (Theodorid.).

**ἀγρεμών,** όνος, ὁ, *hunter, EM*13.56; also glossed by κάμαξ, λαμπάς, δόρυ, Hsch.; = ἐπιμήνιος, A.*Fr.*141.

**ἀγρεσία,** Ion. -ίη, ἡ, = ἄγρα I, *AP*6.13 (Leon.).

**ἀγρεταί,** αἱ, (fem. pl. of ἀγρετός 'chosen', cf. ἀγρέω) priestesses of Athena at Cos, *B.Mus.Inscr.*968*A*, Hsch.

**ἀγρετεύω,** *hold office of* ἀγρέτας, *IG*5(1).1346 (Laconia, ii A.D.).

**ἀγρετήματα·** τὰ ἀγορευόμενα τῶν παρθένων (Lacon.), Hsch.

*__ἀγρέτης,__ ου, Dor. **-τας,** ὁ, = ἡγεμών, Hsch.; prob. for ἀγρόται, A. *Pers.*1002 Toup. II. **Ἀγρέτης,** ὁ, perh. from ἀγρός, *god of the fields,* title of Apollo at Chios, *GDI*5666.

*__ἄγρ-ευμα,__ τό, in pl., = τὰ ἐπὶ τῆς ἀγροικίας κτήματα, Sol.ap.*AB* 340. II. *that which is taken in hunting, prey,* E.*Ba.*1241: metaph., X.*Mem.*3.11.7; ἄ. ἀνθέων E.*Fr.*754. 2. *means of catching,* ἄ. θηρὸς A.*Ch.*998; ἐντὸς..μορσίμων ἀ., of the *net* thrown over Agamemnon, Id.*Ag.*1048, cf. *Eu.*460. *-εύς, έως, ὁ, *hunter,* epith. of Aristaeus, Pi.*P.*9.65; of Apollo, A.*Fr.*200, Herod.3.34; of Bacchus, E.*Ba.*1192 (lyr.); of Poseidon, Luc.*Pisc.*47; of Pan, Apollod.ap.Hsch. II. of an arrow, *AP*6.75 (Paul. Sil.). III. a kind of bird, Ael.*NA*8.24. (From ἀγρός, cf. οἰκεύς : οἶκος; the reference to hunting is secondary.) **-εύσιμος,** η, ον, *easy to catch,* Sch.S.*Ph.*863. **-ευσις,** εως, ἡ, *catching,* Hsch. **-ευτεῖ·** ὑβρίζει, Hsch. **-ευτήρ,** ῆρος, ὁ, = sq., Theoc.21.6, Call.*Dian.*218, *AP*7.578 (Agath.). II. as Adj., ἀ. κύνες Opp.*C.*3.456; ἀγρευτῆρι λίνῳ, i.e. with *fishing*-net, Man.5.279. **-ευτής,** οῦ, ὁ, *hunter,* epith. of Apollo as slayer of Python, S.*OC*1091 (lyr.), *PFlor.*297.19 (vi A.D.): metaph., of sleep, ἀ. πτηνοῦ φάσματος *AP*12.125 (Mel.). II. Adj., κύνες ἀ. *hounds,* Sol.23; ἀ. κάλαμοι a fowler's *trap of reeds, AP*7.171 (Mnasalc.), cf. 6.109 (Antip.). *-ευτικός, ή, όν, *of* or *skilled in hunting,* ἀγρευτικὸν [ἐστι] *useful for ensnaring* an enemy, X.*Eq.Mag.*4.12; ἀ. λίνος Sch.E.*Ba.*611. Adv. -κῶς Poll.5.9. **-ευτίς,** ίδος, ἡ, fem. of ἀγρευτής, prob. l. in Sch.Ar.*V.*367. **-ευτός,** όν, *caught,* Opp.*H.* 3.541. *-εύω, fut. εύσω Call.*Dian.*85: aor. ἤγρευσα E.*Ba.*1204:—Med., v. infr.:—Pass., aor. ἠγρεύθην *AP*, v. infr.: (ἀγρεύς):—*take by hunting* or *fishing, catch,* ἰχθῦς Hdt.2.95, cf. X.*Cyn.*12.6; ἄγραν ἠγρευκότες E.*Ba.*434; of war, φιλεῖ..ἄνδρας..ἀγρεύειν νέους S.*Fr.* 554:—also in Med., θύματ' ἠγρεύσασθε *ye caught* or *chose your* victim, E.*IT*1163; τί μοι ξίφος ἐκ χερὸς ἠγρεύσω; why *didst thou snatch..?* Id.*Andr.*842:—Pass., X.*An.*5.3.8, cf. Sphaer.*Stoic.*1.142; ἀγρευθεὶς ἤγρευσε *AP*9.94 (Isid.), 12.113 (Mel.). 2. metaph., *hunt after, thirst for,* αἷμα E.*Ba.*138; σὰν (sc. Ἀρετᾶς) ἀ. δύναμιν Arist.*Fr.*675. 11; ὕπνον *AP*7.196 (Mel.), cf. 12.125 (Mel.); but ἀγρεύειν τινὰ λόγῳ *to catch* by his words, *Ev.Marc.*12.13.

*__ἀγρέω,__ = αἱρέω, *take, seize,* freq. in Aeolic Inscrr. as *IG*12(2).6.33 (Pass., Lesbos); ἄγρει δ' οἶνον ἐρυθρόν Archil.4.3; τρόμος παῖσαν ἄγρει Sapph.2.14, cf. Thgn.294; ἀγρεῖ πόλιν *captures,* A.*Ag.*126 (lyr.); of fishing, *AP*6.304 (Phanias); in prescriptions, ἄγρει, *take!* Nic.*Th.*534, al. II. Hom. only in imper. ἄγρει, prop *take it!*, hence, *come on!* ἄγρει μάν οἱ ἔπορσον Ἀθηναίην Il.5.765, cf. A.R.1.487; pl., ἀγρεῖτε (ἄγρειτε *An.Ox.*1.71) Od.20.149. Cf. ἀργεῖτε.

**ἄγρηθεν,** Adv. *from the chase,* A.R.2.938. **ἀγρήθετο·** ἠθέλησεν, Hsch.

*__ἀγρηνόν,__ τό, *net,* Hsch.:—also, *net-like woollen robe* worn by Bacchanals and soothsayers, Id., Poll.4.116.

*__ἀγρία,__ ἡ, = ἄγρα II, *BGU*1123.9 (Aug.).

**ἀγρίαζε·** ἄγριος ἴσθι, Hsch.

**ἀγριαίνω,** fut. ανῶ Pl.*R.*501e: aor. ἠγρίανα D.C.44.47, Ael.*VH*2. 13:—Pass., D.H.9.32, Plu.*Ant.*58: fut. ἀγριανθήσομαι LXX *Da.*11.11: aor. ἠγριάνθην D.S.24.1.—In Att. the Pass. was supplied by ἀγριόω (q.v.), which was rare in Act.; but the compd. Pass. ἐξαγριαίνομαι occurs in Pl.*R.*336d, and the Act. ἐξαγριόω in Hdt 6.123, E.*Ph.*876, Pl.*Lg.*935a. 1. intr., *to be* or *become wild, to be angered, provoked,* Pl.*R.*493b, etc.; τινί *with* one, Id.*Smp.*173d; πρός τινα Porph.*Abst.* 3.12; of animals, Arist.*HA*608[b]31; of rivers and the like, *chafe,* πρὸς τὴν πλήμμυραν..ἀγριαίνων ὁ ποταμὸς Plu.*Caes.*38:—Pass., D.S. l.c.; of sores, *to be angry* or *inflamed,* Aret.*SD*2.11, cf. Antyll.ap. Orib.10.13.2. II. causal, *make angry, provoke,* D.C.44.47; of love, *irritate,* Ach.Tat.2.7:—Pass., *to be angered,* Plu. l.c., Hierocl. *in CA*10p.434 M.; ὑπὸ τῶν δημαγωγῶν D.H. l.c.

**ἀγρι-άνθρωπος,** ου, ὁ, *wild man, savage,* Ps.-Callisth.3.28. **-άπιος,** -ιδος, = ἀγριο-αππίδιον, *Gloss.*

**ἀγριάς,** άδος, ἡ, = fem. of ἄγριος, *wild,* A.R.1.28; νῆσσαι Arat.

; αἶγες Call.*Aet.*3.1.13; ἄμπελον ἀ. *AP*9.561 (Phil.), cf. Numen. Ath.371c. II. Ἀγριάδες, αἱ, *Nymphs*, Hsch.

ἀγριαχράς, ἡ, *wild pear*, Zopyr.ap.Orib.14.61.1.

ἀγριάω, *to be savage*, Opp.*C.*2.49, in Ep. form ἀγριόωντα.

ἀγρίδιον, τό, Dim. of ἀγρός, *Sammelb.*5230.29 (i A.D.), Arr.*Epict.* 0.9, al., M.Ant.4.3.

ἀγρι-ελαία, ἡ, *wild olive*, Hp.*Mul.*2.112, Dsc.1.105, etc. -ελάι-ς, *of wild olive*, ξύλα *IG*7.3073.189 (Lebad.). -έλαιος, ον, = foreg., ντάλη *AP*9.237 (Erycius). II. as Subst., = ἀγριελαία, Theoc. 8, Thphr.*HP*2.2.5, *Ep.Rom.*11.17, etc.

ἀγρ-ιεύς· ἀγροῖκος, Hsch. -ιεύω, *catch by hunting* or *fishing*, *Ryl.*98$^a$7 (ii A.D.). -ίζω, *inflame, irritate*, in Pass., dub. l. in p.*Mul.*2.154; Act., Sm.*Pr.*15.18; cf. ἀγγρίζω.

ἀγρικός, ή, όν, = ἄγριος, πήγανον *POxy.*1675.4 (iii A.D.).

ἀγριμαῖος, α, ον, *wild*; τὰ ἀ. *game*, Ptol.Euerg.6, *PLond.*3.1159.73 (i A.D.).

ἀγριμέλισσα, ἡ, *wasp*, metaph. of Hegesias, Hsch.; cf. ἀγριο-έλιττα.

ἄγρινοι· ἀγρονόμοι, Hsch.

ἀγριο-απίδιον, τό, *wild pear tree*, *Gp.*8.37.3. -βάλανος, ἡ, *evergreen oak*, *Quercus pseudo-coccifera*, Aq.Thd.*Is.*44.14. -βου-λος, ον, *wild of purpose*, Adam.1.18. -δαίτης, ου, ὁ, *eating wild fruits*, Orac.ap.Paus.8.42.6.

❋ἀγριόεις, εσσα, εν, = ἄγριος, Nic.*Al.*604. 2. *maddening*, ὀπώρη ib.30.

ἀγριό-θῡμος, ον, *wild of temper*, Orph.*H.*12.4. -κάναβος, ὁ, *hemp-mallow*, *Althaea cannabina*, Hsch. -κάρδαμον, τό, = ἰβηρίς, Gal.13.353. -καρδον, τό, = ἄκανθα Αἰγυπτία, *AB*1096. -κάρυον, τό, *cob-nut*, Hsch. -κινάρα, = ἄκανθα λευκή, Ps.-Dsc.3.12; = *carduus*, *Gloss.* -κοκκύμηλον, τό, = προῦμνον, Gal.6.619. -κολο-κύντη, = τολύπη 3, Phot. -κρόμμυον, τό, = βολβός, Sch.Ar.*Pl.* 283. -κύμῑνον, τό, *wild cumin*, Sch Nic.*Th.*709. -λάχᾰνα, ων, τά, *wild pot-herbs*, Sch.Theoc.4.52. ❋-λειχήν, ὁ, = ἄγριος λειχήν (3), Hsch. s.v. ἀγριοψωρία.

ἀγρίολον, τό, = ἱπποσέλινον Dsc.3.67.

ἀγριο-μᾰλάχη, ἡ, = ἀλθαία, Sch.Nic.*Th.*89. -μέλιττα, ἡ, *wasp*, *Gloss.* ❋-μορφος, ον, f.l. for σναγρ-, Orph.*A.*979. -μυρίκη [ῑ], ἡ, *tamarisk*, Lxx *Je.*17.6; Adj. -μυρίκινος, ξύλα *PHamb.*12.19 (iii A.D., ἀγρο- Pap.). -μύρμηξ, *weevil*, *Gloss.* -νους, ουν, *fierce*, *IG*12(7).115 (Amorgos). -πήγανον, τό, *Syrian rue*, Hsch., Aët.1. 295, al. -πηγός, ὁ, (πήγνυμι) = ἁμαξουργός, ἀγρίων ξύλων ἐργάτης, Sch.Ar.*Eq.*464. -ποιέω, *to make wild*, Sch.A.*Pers.*613. -ποιός, όν, *poet of savagery*, of Aeschylus in Ar.*Ra.*837. II. *making savage*, Sch.Nic.*Al.*30. -πρασον· *serpyllum* (sic), *Gloss.*

ἀγριορίγᾰνος, ὁ, *marjoram*, *Origanum viride*, Dsc.3.29.

ἀγριόρροδον, τό, = *saliuncula* (i.e. Κελτικὴ νάρδος), *Gloss.*

❋ἄγριος, α, ον, Od.9.119; also ος, ον (not in Trag. or Com.) Il.19.88, Phoc.3.6, Pl.*Lg.*824a, Theoc.22.36: Comp. -ώτερος Th.6.60: Sup. -ώτατος Pl.*R.*564a (ἀγρός): *living in the fields, wild, savage.* I. of animals, opp. τιθασός, ἥμερος, *wild*, βάλλειν ἄγρια πάντα Il.5.52; αἶξ, σῦς, 3.24, 9.539; even of flies, ἄ. φῦλα, μυίας 19.30; ἵπποι, ὄνοι, etc., Hdt.7.86, etc.; ἄ. τέρας, of a bull, E.*Hipp.*1214; ἄ. θηρία X.*An.* 1.2.7; of men, *living in a wild state*, Hdt.4.191. 2. of trees, opp. ἥμερος, *wild*, Pi.*Fr.*46, Hdt.4.21, etc.; μητρὸς ἀγρίας ἄπο ποτόν of the *wild* vine, A.*Pers.*614, cf. Arist.*Pr.*896$^a$8; ἄ. ἔλαιον S.*Tr.*1197; ὕλη Id.*OT*476, etc.; μέλι *Ev.Matt.*3.4. 3. of countries, *wild, uncultivated*, Pl.*Phd.*113b, *Lg.*905b. II. mostly of men, beasts, etc.: 1. in moral sense, *savage, fierce*, Il.8.96, Od.1.199, etc., cf. Ar.*Nu.*567; δεσπότης Pl.*R.*329c; ἄ. καὶ ἀπαίδευτος Id.*Grg.*510b; ἄγριε παῖ καὶ στυγνέ Theoc.23.19, cf. 2.54; ἄ. κυβευτής *a passionate gambler*, Men.965; esp. of παιδερασταί, Ar.*Nu.*349 (cf. Sch. ad loc.), Aeschin.1.52, Aen.Gaz.*Thphr.* p.14 B. 2. of temper, *wild, fierce*, θυμός, χόλος, Il.9.629, 4.23; λέων δ' ὥς, ἄγρια οἶδεν 24.41; ἄ. πτόλεμος, μῶλος, 17.737,398; ἄγριος ἄτη 19.88; ἄ. ὁδοί *cruel* ways or counsels, S.*Ant.*1274; ὀργή *OT*344 (Sup.); ἀγριώτατα ἤθεα Hdt.4.106; ἔρωτες Pl.*Phd.*81a; φιλία Id.*Lg.*837b, cf. *R.*572b, etc.; τὸ ἄ. *savageness*, Id.*Cra.*394e; ἐς τὸ -ώτερον *to harsher measures*, Th. l.c. 3. of things, circumstances, etc., *cruel, harsh*, δεσμά A.*Pr.* 177; νὺξ -ωτέρη *wild, stormy*, Hdt.8.13; δουλεία Pl.*R.*564a; σύντασις ἀ. a *violent* strain, Id.*Phlb.*46d; ἄ. βάρος, of strong, hot wine, Ar.*Fr.*351. b. ἀ. νόσος, prob., *malignant*, S.*Ph.*173,265; ἄ. ἕλκος Bion 1.16. III. Adv. -ίως, *savagely*, A.*Eu.*972, Ar.*V.*705; ἄγρια δερκομένω, παίσδων, Hes.*Sc.*236, Mosch 1.11. [ᾰ Hom.; ᾰ in trim., ᾱ in lyr. A. and S.; ᾱ E.; ῑ metri grat., where the ult. is long, Il.22.313 (nisi leg. ἀγρίοο).]

ἀγριο-σέλῑνον, τό, = ἀγρίολον, Dsc.3.67. ❋-σίκυον, τό, *squirting cucumber*, *Hippiatr.*22. -σταφίδες and -σταφύλιες (sic), *wild grapes*, Hsch. -σταφυλίτης οἶνος wine *made therefrom*, Dsc.5. 6. -συκῆ, ἡ, *wild fig*, Horap.2.77.

ἀγριό-της, ητος, ἡ, *savageness, wildness*, of animals, opp. ἡμερότης, X.*Mem.*2.2.7, cf. Isoc.12.163, Arist.*HA*588$^a$21; of plants, Thphr.*HP* 3.2.4; of untilled ground, ἀ. γῆς *Gp.*7.1.4; of diet, Hp.*VM*7 (as v.l. for θηριότητα), *Aër.*23. II. of men, in moral sense, *fierceness, cruelty*, Pl.*Smp.*197d, al., D.26.26 (pl.). -φαγρος, ὁ, *wild* φάγρος, Opp.*H.* 1.140. -φανής, ές, *appearing wild*, Corn.*ND*27. -φυλλον, τό, = πευκέδανος, Ps.-Dsc.3.78. -φυτα, τά, *wild herbs*, Sch.Nic.*Al.* 429. -φωνος, ον, *with rough voice* or *tongue*, like βαρβαρόφωνος, Od.8.294; Δᾶτις *App.Anth.*3.74.22. -χοιρος, ὁ, *wild swine*, Sch. Ar.*Pl.*304. -ψωρία, ἡ, (ψώρα) *inveterate itch*, Hsch.

❋ἀγριόω, aor. ἠγρίωσα E.*Or.*616, the act. tenses being mostly supplied by ἀγριαίνω, (ἄγριος):—*make wild* or *savage, provoke*, ἡ τῇ τεκούσῃ σ' ἠγρίωσε *against* thy mother, E. l.c. II. mostly in Pass., ἀγριοῦμαι Hp.*Aër.*4: impf. ἠγριούμην E.*El.*1031 codd.: aor. ἠγριώθην Plu.*Per.* 34: pf. ἠγρίωμαι S.*Ph.*1321, E.*IT*348, Ar.*Ra.*897:—*grow wild*; in pf. *to be wild*, properly of plants, countries, etc., νῆσος ἠγριωμένη τῇ ὕλῃ Thphr.*HP*5.8.2, cf. *CP*5.3.6; of men, *to be unkempt*, ὡς ἠγρίωσαι διὰ μακρᾶς ἀλουσίας E.*Or.*226, cf. 387. 2. in moral sense, *to be savage, cruel* ἠγρίωσαι S.*Ph.* l.c., cf. E.*El.* l.c., etc.; γλῶσσα.. ἠγρίωται, of Aeschylus, Ar. l.c.: metaph., ἠγριωμένον πέλαγος an *angry* sea, Plu.*Pyrrh.*15. 3. Medic., *become malignant*, of wounds, Hp. l.c.

Ἀγριππιασταί, οἱ, *worshippers of Agrippa*, guild at Sparta, *IG*5(1). 374.8.

ἄγριππος, ὁ, Lacon. name for the *wild olive*, Suid., etc.; prov., ἀκαρπότερος ἀγρίππου Zen.1.60; in Hsch. ἄγριφος.

ἀγρίς, ἡ, *Valonia oak*, opp. ἡμερίς, *EM*429.17.

ἀγρίτης, ου, ὁ, *countryman*, St. Byz. s.v. ἀγρός.

ἀγρίφη [ῐ], ἡ, *harrow, rake*, Hdn.Gr.1.345, Hsch.; cf. ἀγρεῖφνα.

ἀγριώδης, ες, *of wild nature*, Str.3.3.8.

❋Ἀγριώνιος, ὁ, epith. of Dionysus, transferred to Antony, Plu.*Ant.* 24. ❋Ἀγριώνια, τά, festival in honour of Dionysus, Id.2.291a, 299f, etc.

ἀγριωπός, όν, *wild-looking*, ὄμμα E.*HF*990, cf. *Ba.*542; τὸ ἀ. τοῦ προσώπου Plu.*Mar.*14, cf. Corn.*ND*6.

ἀγρο-βόας, ὁ, *rudely shouting*, Cratin.374. ❋-βότης, ου, Dor. -ας, α, ὁ, *feeding in the field, dwelling in the country*, S.*Ph.*214 (lyr.), E.*Cyc.*54 (lyr.). -γείτων, ονος, ὁ, *country neighbour*, Plu.*Cat. Ma.*25, *POxy.*1106.2 (vi A.D.); ἀ. τινός *having a field adjoining* his, J.*AJ*8.13.8. -δίαιτος, ον, *living in the country*, *Gloss.* -δότης, ου, ὁ, (ἄγρα) *giver of game*, δαίμονες *AP*6.27 (Theaet.).

ἀγρό-θεν, Adv. *from the country*, Od.13.268, 15.428, Epich.161, E.*Or.*866, Luc.*Macr.*22: also -θε, *AP*7.398 (Antip.). -θῐ, Adv. *in the country*, Call.*Cer.*136, Poll.9.12.

ἀγροικ-εύομαι, *to be stupid*, Phld.*Mus.*p.95 K., cf. *EM*14.2, Hsch. s.v. ἀγροιτιᾷ. -ηρός, ά, όν, *boorish*, ἀ. φύσις Anon.ap.St.Byz. s.v. ἀγρός. -ία, ἡ, *rusticity, boorishness*, Pl.*Grg.*461c, *R.*560d, al.; cf. Arist.*EN*1108$^a$26. II. *the country*, Herod.1.2, *Inscr.Magn.* 8, *SIG*344.100 (Teos), Muson.*Fr.*11p.60 H., Plu.2.519a, Longus 1.13, Aristid.*Or.*47(23).45; pl., Plu.2.311b. III. in pl., *country-houses*, D.S.20.8, Nymphod.12, M.Ant.4.3. -ίζομαι, *to be rude and boorish*, Pl.*Tht.*146a, Plu.*Sull.*6: aor. ἠγροικισάμην Aristid. 1.491 J. ❋-ικός, ή, όν, *rustic*, Cephalio6, Ath.11.477a, Sch. Nic.*Th.*78; ἀνδράποδα Just.*Nov.*7.6. Adv. -κῶς Alciphr.3.70.

ἀγροικοπυρρώνειος, ὁ, *rude, coarse Pyrrhonist*, Gal.8.711.

ἄγροικος, ον, (ἀγρός, οἰκέω) *dwelling in the fields*, ζῷα, opp. ὄρεια, Arist.*HA*488$^b$2; esp. of men, *countryman, rustic*, Ar.*Nu.*47; in Attica, οἱ ἄ., = γεωμόροι (q.v.), Arist.*Ath.*13.2, D.H.2.8: mostly with the collat. sense of *boorish, rude*, Ar.*Nu.*628,646, etc., cf. Thphr. *Char.*4; μέλος -ότερον Ar.*Ach.*674; ἄ. σοφία Pl.*Phdr.*229e, cf. Isoc.5. 82 (Comp.), Arist.*EN*1128$^a$9; of fortune, Apollod.Car.5.14; ἄ. Δημοσθένης, of Dinarchus, D.H.*Din.*8. Adv. -κως Ar.*V.*1320: Comp. -οτέρως Pl.*R.*361e, X.*Mem.*3.13.1; -ότερον Pl.*Phdr.*260d. II. *rustic*, βίος Ar.*Nu.*43. 2. of fruits, *common*, opp. γενναῖος, ὀπώρα Pl.*Lg.*844d. (ἀγροῖκος *dwelling in the country*, ἄγροικος *boorish*, acc. to Ammon.*Diff.*5, but this is very doubtful.)—Not found in early Ep. or Trag.

ἀγροικόσοφος, ον, *with rude mother-wit*, Ph.1.448; in bad sense, ib.577.

ἀγροικώδης, ες, *clownish, rude*, Sch.Il.23.476, Aristid.Quint.2.6.

ἀγροιώτης, ου, ὁ, = ἀγρότης 1, Hom. always in nom. pl., ἀνέρες ἀγροιῶται Il.11.549; βουκόλοι ἀ. Od.11.293; λαοὶ ἀ. Il.11.676; νήπιοι ἀ. Od.21.85; ποιμένες ἀ. Hes.*Sc.*39; sg., Ar.*Th.*58:—fem. ἀγροιῶτις, ἡ, (perh. as Adj., cf. II) Sapph.70. II. as Adj., *rustic*, Πρίηπος *AP*6.22 (Zon.), ὕλη 7.411 (Diosc.); *wild*, Numen.ap.Ath.371c.

ἀγρο-κήπιον, τό, Dim. of sq., Str.12.3.11. -κηπος, ὁ, *field kept as garden*, *IG*3.60*B*1.26. -κόμος, ὁ, *land-steward*, J.*AJ*5.9.2.

ἀγρο-ολέτειρα, ἡ, *waster of land*, Hsch.; epith. of Artemis, Suid.

ἀγρολικός, ή, όν, prob. by mistake for ἀρβυλικός (q.v.), *IG*11(2). 199*B*19 (Delos, iii B.C.).

ἀγρομενής, ές, *dwelling in the country*, Call.*Fr.anon.*142 (nisi leg. -μανής).

ἀγρόνδε, Adv., (ἀγρός) *to the country*, Od.15.370.

ἀγρονόμης, ου, Dor. -ας, = sq., μοῦσα *AP*7.196 (Mel.).

❋ἀγρο-νόμος, ον, (νέμομαι) *haunting the country*, Νύμφαι Od.6.106; θῆρες A.*Ag.*142 (lyr.), cf. Hp.*Vict.*2.49; βοτῆρες *Epic.Oxy.*1015. 7. 2. Subst. ἀγρονόμος, ὁ, (νέμω) a magistrate in charge of the country districts, Pl.*Lg.*760b, al., cf. Arist.*Pol.*1321$^b$30. II. ἀγρόνομος, ον, *affording open pasturage*, πλάκες, αὐλαί, S.*OT*1103, *Ant.*785 (both lyr.); ὕλη Opp.*H.*1.27. -πόνος, ὁ, *tiller of the soil*, Gloss.

❋ἀγρός, οῦ, ὁ, *field*, mostly in pl., *fields, lands*, Il.23.832, Od.4.757, Pi.*P.*4.149, etc.; opp. κῆποι, Theopomp.Hist.89; sg., *farm*, Od.24. 205; also in pl., X.*HG*2.4.1:—*tilled land*, opp. fallow, ἀγρὸς καὶ ἀργός, Ἀθηνᾶ 20.167 (Erythrae). 2. *country*, opp. town, Od.17. 182, E.*Supp.*884, etc.; ἀγρὸν τὰν πόλιν ποιεῖς Epich.169; ἀγρῷ *in the country*, Od.11.188; ἐπ' ἀγροῦ *in the country*, 1.190, 22.47; ἐπ' ἀγροῦ νόσφι πόληος 1.185; in pl., κατὰ πτόλιν ἠὲ κατ' ἀγρούς 17.18; ἐν οἴκοις ἢ 'ν ἀγροῖς S.*OT*112; ἐπ' ἀγρῶν ib.1049; ἀγροῖσι Id.*El.*313; τὸν ἐξ ἀγρῶν Id.*OT*1051; τὰ ἐξ ἀγρῶν Th.2.13, cf. 14; κατ' ἀγροὺς Cratin. 318, Pl.*Lg.*881c; οἰκεῖν ἐν ἀγρῷ Ar.*Fr.*387.2; τὰ ἐν ἀγρῷ γιγνόμενα *fruits*, X.*Mem*.2.9.4, cf. *An*.5.3.9 :—prov., οὐδὲν ἐξ ἀγροῦ λέγεις, ἀγροῦ πλέως, i.e. boorish, Suid., Hsch.—Rare in later Greek, *Ev.Marc*. 15.21, *PAmh*.2.134.5, *POxy*.967. [ᾰ by nature, so always in Com., exc. Ar.*Av* 579, Philem.116; ἀγρόθεν in Alc.Com.19 is paratrag.] (Cf. Skt. *ájras* ' plain ', prob. fr. *aj* ' drive ' (cf. ἄγω), i.e. *pasture*.)

**ἀγροτέκτων**, ὁ, = ἔποψ, Al.*Le*.11.19.

⊛**ἀγρό-τερος**, α, ον, (ἀγρός; properly opp. ὀρέσ-τερος) poet. for ἄγριος. in Hom. always of *wild* animals, ἡμίονοι, σύες, αἶγες, Il.2.852, 12.146, Od.17.295; ἀγροτέρης ἐλάφοιο Hes.*Sc*.407; φὴρ ἀ. Pi.*P*.3.4: abs., ἀγρότεροι Theoc.8.58; ἀ. καὶ νέποδες *AP*6.11 (Satyr.). 2. of *countrymen*, *AP*9.244 (Apollonid.), *APl*.4.235 (Id.). 3. of plants, *wild*, *AP*9.384.8, cf. Nic.*Th*.711, Coluth.111. II. (ἄγρα) *fond of the chase*, *huntress*, of the nymph Cyrene, Pi.*P*.9.6: metaph., μέριμνα ἀ. Id.*O*.2.60. 2. pr. n. Ἀγροτέρα, Artemis *the huntress*, Il.21.471, X.*Cyn*.6.13; worshipped at Agra in Attica, *IG*2.467, Paus.1.19.6; at Sparta and elsewhere, X.*HG*4.2.20, Ar.*Eq*.660, etc. -τήρ [ᾰ], ῆρος, ὁ, = ἀγρότης, E.*El*.463 (lyr.) :—fem. **ἀγρότειρα**, as Adj., *rustic*, ib.168 (lyr.). ⊛-**της**, ου, ὁ, (ἀγρός) poet. word, *countryman*, *rustic*, ἀ. ἀνήρ E.*Or*.1270, cf. *App.Anth*.4.20; πάροινος ἀ. ib.5.57. II. (ἄγρα) *hunter*, οἰωνοί . . οἷσί τε τέκνα ἀγρόται ἐξείλοντο Od.16.218, cf. Alcm.23.8; ἀγρότα Πάν, to whom δίκτυα ἀπ' ἀγρεσίης are offered, *AP*6.13 (Leon.):—fem. **ἀγρότις**, νύμφη A.R.2.509: ἀ. κούρα, i.e. Artemis, *AP*6.111 (Antip.); ἀ. αἰγανέη ib.57 (Paul. Sil.). III. for A.*Pers*.1002 v. ἀγρέτης.

**ἀγροῦαι**· ἀγροῖκοι, Hsch.

**ἄγροφον**· ὀρεινόν, Hp.ap.Gal.19.69, Suid.

**ἀγροφύλαξ** [ῠ], ὁ, *guardian of the country*, *APl*.4.243 (Antist.), *PRein*.48 (ii A.D.), *PLond*.403.11 (iv A.D.).

**ἄγρυκτος**, ον, (ἀ- priv., γρύζω) *not to be spoken of*, ἄγρυκτα παθεῖν Pherecr.157. **ἀγρυξία**, ἡ, *dead silence*, Pi.*Fr*.229.

⊛**ἀγρυπν-έω**, pf. ἠγρύπνηκα Hp.*Progn*.2 :—*lie awake*, *pass sleepless nights*, Thgn.471, Hp. l. c., Pl.*Lg*.695a, etc.; opp. καθεύδω, X.*Cyr*. 8.3.42; ἀγρυπνεῖν τὴν νύκτα *to pass a sleepless night*, Id.*HG*7.2.19, Men.113; οἱ -οῦντες *sufferers from insomnia*, Dsc.4.64. 2. metaph., *to be watchful*, Lxx *Wi*.6.15, *Ev.Marc*.13.33, *Ep.Eph*.6.18; ὑπὲρ τῶν ψυχῶν *Ep.Heb*.13.17; ἐπὶ τὰ κακά Lxx *Da*.9.14: c. inf., μηθέν σε ἐνοχλήσειν *PGrenf*.2.14a3. 3. c. acc., *lie awake and think of*, τινά *PMag.Par*.1.2966. -ητέον, *one must watch*, Eust.168.16. -ητήρ, ῆρος, ὁ, *watcher*, Man.1.81. -ητής, *excubitor*, *Gloss*. -ητικός, ή, όν, *wakeful*, D.S.33.21, Plu.*Cam*.27. II. *producing wakefulness*, *PLond*.1.96, *PMag.Par*.1.2943, Gal.10.930 :—-ητικόν, τό, *spell for this purpose*, *PMag.Lond*.121.374, *PMag.Leid.V*.11.26. -ία, Ion. -ίη, ἡ, *sleeplessness*, *wakefulness*, Hp.*Aph*.2.3, al., Pl.*Cri*.43b, etc.; in pl., Hp.*Acut*.42; ἀγρυπνίῃσιν εἴχετο Hdt.3.129, cf. *IG*4.952.50 (Epid.), Ar.*Lys*.27, Pl.*R*.460d. II. *time of watching*, Pl.*Ax*.368b; οἱ τῆς ἀ. ἄρχοντες Just.*Nov*.13*Pr*. III. of poetry, *product of sleepless nights*, Call.*Epigr*.29.4. [ῑ in Opp.*C*.3.511.] ⊛-ος, ον, *wakeful*, Hp.*Epid*.1.18, Pl.*R*.404a, Arist.*Pol*.1314b35, etc.: metaph., Ζηνὸς ἄ. βέλος A.*Pr*.360; ἠιόνες *AP*7.278 (Arch.):—τὸ ἄ. *vigilance*, Hp.*Aër*.24, Plu.2.355b. Adv. -νως *OGI* 194.23 (Egypt, i B.C.). II. Act., *banishing sleep*, *keeping awake*, νοήσεις Arist.*Pr*.917b1; μέριμναι *APl*.4.211 (Stat. Flacc.). [ἀγρῦπνος E.*Rh*.2 (lyr.), ἀγρῠπνος Theoc.24.106.] ⊛-ώδης, ες, *making sleepless*, Hp.*Prorrh*.1.10 as v.l.

**ἄγρωμα**, τό, perh. = *right of hunting*, *Annuario*3.195 (Gortyn).

**ἄγρωσσα**, ἡ, *huntress*, epith. of a hound, Simon.130.

⊛**ἀγρώσσω**, Ep. for ἀγρεύω, only in pres., *catch*, ἀγρώσσων ἰχθῦς Od.5.53; freq. in Opp., *H*.3.339,543, al., cf. Call.*Ap*.60, Lyc.598, etc.: abs., *go hunting*, Opp.*C*.1.129 :—Pass., Id.*H*.3.415, 4.565.

⊛**ἀγρ-ώστης**, ου, ὁ, = ἀγρότης, Subst. and Adj., S.*Fr*.94, E.*HF*377 (lyr.), *Rh*.287, *AP*6.37, Call.*Hec*.1.1.13, v.l. in Theoc.25.48. 2. *wild*, κήρυκες Babr.115.2. II. *hunter*, A.R.4.175. 2. a kind of *spider*, Nic.*Th*.734. -ωστῖνος, Syrac. for ἄγροικος, name of play by Epich.; ἀγρωστῖναι· νύμφαι ὄρειοι, Hsch. -ωστις, ιδος, Thphr.*HP*1.6.10, and εως, Arist.*HA*552a15, *PTeb*.104.26 (ii B.C.), ἡ, acc. ἄγρωστιν Plb.34.10.3, Str.4.1.7 :—*dog's-tooth grass*, *Cynodon Dactylon*, ἄ. μελιηδής Od.6.90; εἰλιτενὴς ἄ. Theoc.13.42, cf. Aeschrio6, D.S.1.43, Dsc.4.29. 2. ἄ. ἐν Κιλικίᾳ *Hordeum marinum*, Dsc.4.32; ἄ. ἐν Παρνασσῷ *grass of Parnassus*, *Parnassia palustris*, ib.31. -ωστήρ, ῆρος, ὁ, = -ώστης, S.*Ichn*.33 :—also -ώστωρ, ορος, ὁ, Nic.*Al*. 473. -ώτηρ, ὁ, fem. **ἀγρώτειρα**, = ἀγρότης, St. Byz. s. v. ἀγρός. -ώτης, ου, ὁ, *of the field*, *wild*, θῆρες E.*Ba*.564 (lyr.), *Rh*.266.

⊛**ἄγ-υια**, ᾶς, ἡ, *street*, *highway*, chiefly in pl., Il.5.642; σκιόωντό τε πᾶσαι ἀ. Od.2.388, etc.; of the paths of the sea, 11.12; ἀγυιαῖς *in the streets*, Hom.*Epigr*.14.5, cf. Pi.*P*.2.58, B.3.16, S.*OC*715, *Ant*.1136, E.*Ba*.87 (all lyr.): esp. in the phrase κνισᾶν ἀγυιάς Ar.*Eq*.1320, *Av*.1233, D.21.51 :—rare in Prose, X.*Cyr*.2.4.3, *PPetr*.3p.7 (iii B.C.), Lxx 3*Ma*.1.20, etc.; ἐν ἀγυιᾷ, of documents executed *in public* by a notary, *POxy*.722.12 (i A.D.), etc. 2. *collection of streets*, *city*, Pi.*O*.9.34, *N*.7.92; πολύπυρος ἀ. *Hymn.Is*.2. (Quasi-participial form from ἄγω, cf. ἄρπυια.) [ἀγυιάν Il.20.254 (Aristarch.), cf. Pi.*N*.7.92 codd. vett.; ἄγυια Ion. and old Att. acc. to Hdn.Gr.2.613, Eust.1631.29; ἀγυιά, incorrectly, *EM*14.21, etc.; ἀγυιάν freq. in codd., e. g. Pi.*O*.9.34, X. l. c.] -υιαῖος, α, ον, *with streets or highways*, γῆ S.*Fr*. 202. ⊛-υιάτης, ου, ὁ, = Ἀγυιεύς, voc. Ἀγυιᾶτα, A.*Ag*.1081. 2. in pl., *inhabitants of an* ἄγυια, *IG*9(2).241 (Phars.), cf. ἀγυιῆται· κωμῆται, Hsch., *EM*15.31. -υιᾶτις, ιδος, ἡ, fem. from foreg., *neighbour*, Pi.*P*.11.1. II. Adj. -ᾶτιδες, θεραπεῖαι worship *of Apollo Agyieus*, E.*Ion*186 (lyr.).

⊛**Ἀγυι-εύς**, έως, ὁ, a name of Apollo, as *guardian of the str*[eets] *and highways*, E.*Ph*.631, Orac.ap.D.21.52, *IG*3.159, al. [2.] *pointed pillar*, *set up as his statue* or *altar* at the street-door, Ar.*V*.8[75], Pherecr.87, Dieuchid.2; Ἀγυιεὺς βωμός S.*Fr*.370. ⊛-ηος, ὁ, sc. μ[ήν], name of month at Argos, *Mnemos*.44.221 (iii B.C.).

**ἀγυιό-πεζα** Κουρῆτις, ἡ, mystical name for Pythagorean tria[d], Nicom.ap.Phot.*Bibl*.143B. -πλαστέω, (πλάσσω) *to build in stre*[ets] *or rows*, Lyc.601.

**ἄγυιος**, ον, *without limbs*, *weak in limb*, Hp.*Mul*.1.25.

⊛**ἀγυμν-ασία**, ἡ, (γυμνάζω) *want of exercise* or *training*, Ar.*Ra*.108[8], Arist.*EN*1114a24 ⊛-αστία, ἡ, = foreg., Porph.*Abst*.1.35. ⊛-αστο[ς], ον, *unexercised*, *untrained*, ἵπποι X.*Cyr*.8.1.38, cf. Arist.*Pr*.886a23; τοῖς σώμασιν Plu.*Arat*.47: metaph., *undisciplined*, φαντασίαι *Stoic*. 39. 2. *unpractised*, τινός in a thing, E.*Ba*.491, X.*Cyr*.1.6.29, Pl. etc.; also εἴς or πρός τι Pl.*Lg*.731b, 816a; περί τι Plu.2.802d, Gal.[5.] 608; ἐν λόγοις Phld.*Rh*.1.189 S.: c. inf., Muson.*Fr*.6 p.23 H. [3.] *unharassed*, S.*Tr*.1083; οὐδ' ἀγύμναστον πλάνοις E.*Hel*.533; πόνοι[ς] οὐκ ἀγύμναστος φρένας Id.*Fr*.344. II. Adv. ἀγυμνάστως, ἔχει[ν] πρός τι X.*Mem*.2.1.6.

**ἀγύναιξ**, ὁ, (γυνή) *wifeless*, S.*Fr*.4 :—also **ἀγύναικος**, Phryn.Com. 19; **ἀγύναιος**, Lxx *Jb*.24.21, *PGnom*.79 (ii A.D.), D.C.56.1, Porph.*Abst*.4.17, Man.1.173; **ἀγύνης**, Poll.3.48; **ἄγυνος**, Ar.*Fr*.735.

**ἀγυρ-εῖ**· συναγκροτεῖ, Hsch. -ίζειν· συνάγειν, ἀγυρτάζειν, Id.

⊛**ἄγῠρ-ις** [ᾰ], ιος, ἡ, Aeol. for ἀγορά, *gathering*, *crowd*, ἀνδρῶν ἄγυριν Od.3.31; ἐν νεκύων ἀγύρει Il.16.661; ἐν νηῶν ἀ. 24.141; also in E.*IA*753 (lyr.); παμπληθὴς ἄ. Orac.ap.Phleg.*Macr*.4. 2. *gathering of herbs*, Orph.*L*.416. -ισμός, ὁ, *collection*, Suid. -μα, ατος, τό, *anything collected*, *AB*327. -μός, ὁ, = ἄγυρις, ἀγρίων ζῴων Babr.102.5, cf. *AB*331; = ἀγερμός (which is a v.l.), D.H.2.19, cf. *EM* 8.7. -τάζω, (ἀγύρτης) *collect by begging*, χρήματα Od.19.284. -τεία, ἡ, *begging*, *imposture*, Them.*Or*.5.70b; μαγγανεῖαι καὶ ἀ. Just.*Nov*.22.15. -τευτής, οῦ, ὁ, = ἀγύρτης, Tz.*H*.13 c.475 tit. -τεύω, *live by begging as a vagabond*, ἀπὸ μουσικῆς καὶ μαντικῆς Str.7*Fr*.18, cf. Sch.Luc.*Alex*.13. -τήρ, ῆρος, ὁ, = sq., Man. 4.221. ⊛-της, ου, ὁ, (ἀγείρω) prop. *collector*, esp. *begging priest* of Cybele, Μητρὸς ἀ. *AP*6.218 (Al.); Γάλλοις ἀ. Babr.141.1 :—then, 2. *vagabond*, E.*Rh*.503, 715, cf. Lysipp.6, Clearch.5; δόλιος ἀ., of Tiresias, S.*OT*388; ἀ. καὶ μάντεις Pl.*R*.364b. II. a throw of the dice, Eub.57.5. (On the accent cf. Hdn.Gr.1.77.) ⊛-τικός, ή, όν, *vagabond*, μάντις Plu.*Lyc*.9; *juggling*, πίνακες Id.*Comp.Aristid.Cat*.3; τὸ ἀ. γένος Id.2.407c; τὸ ἀ. *jugglery*, Str.10.3.23. Adv. -κῶς Hierocl.*in CA*26 p.479 M. -τός, ή, όν, *got by begging*, Hsch. -τρια, ἡ, fem. of ἀγυρτήρ, A.*Ag*.1273.

**ἄγυψος**, ον, *not clarified by gypsum*, οἶνος Alex.Trall.1.13.

**ἀγχ-**, Poet. abbrev. for ἀναχ- in compds. of ἀνά with words beginning with χ.

**ἀγχάζω**, Poet. for ἀναχάζω I. 2, *retire*, S.*Fr*.973.

**ἄγχαρμον**· ἀνωφερῆ τὴν αἰχμήν, Hsch.

⊛**ἄγχαυρος**, ον, (ἄγχι, αὔριον) *near the morning*, νύξ A.R.4.111.

**ἀγχέ-μαχος**, ον, *fighting hand to hand*, Il.13.5, Hes.*Sc*.25; τὰ ἀ. ὅπλα καλούμενα X.*Cyr*.1.2.13, cf. Arr.*Ind*.24.4; τεύχεσιν ἀ. *APl*.4.173 (Jul. Aegypt.). ⊛-μωλία, ἡ, (μῶλος, cf. ἀμφι-μωλέω) prob. = ἀγχιστεία, *GDI*4972 (Gortyn).

**ἀγχήρης**, ες, *neighbouring*, S.*Fr*.7, Orph.*A*.1072.

**ἄγχῐ**, Poet. Adv. of place, *near*, Il.5.185, Od.3.449, etc. :—freq. c. gen., which sts. precedes, Ἕκτορος ἄ. Il.8.117, cf. Od.4.370; but usu. follows, ἄ. νεῶν Il.10.161, etc.; ἄ. πελαγίας ἁλός A.*Pers*.467; ἄ. πλευμόνων Id.*Ch*.639; ἄ. γῆς S.*OC*399. 2. of Time, ἄ. γὰρ ἀμέρα Sapph.*Supp*.19.7. II. of resemblance, *like*, c. dat., Pi.*N*.6.9.—For Comp. and Sup. v. ἆσσον, ἄγχιστος.

**ἀγχί-ἄλος**, ον, also η, ον *h.Ap*.32, Androm.ap.Gal.14.42: (ἅλς):—poet. word, *near the sea*, of cities, Il.2.640; Ἐπίδαυρος Androm. l. c.; Κίρρας μυχοί B.4.14; of islands, *sea-girt*, as Peparethos, Lemnos, Salamis, *h.Ap*. l. c., A.*Pers*.887 (lyr.), S.*Aj*.135 (lyr.), *AP*9.288 (Gemin.); of the fountain Arethusa, ἀ. ὕδατα E.*IA*169 (lyr.), cf. A.R.2.160. ⊛-βαθής, ές, *deep inshore*, θάλασσα Od.5.413, cf. Pl.*Criti*.111a; τὰ ἀ. Arist.*Pr*.935a2, cf. Ph.*Bel*.95.20, Parth.26.2, Plu.2.667c; ἀκταί Arist.*HA*548b28; λιμήν Str.17.1.6, cf. 5.2.5, Dion.Byz.6, al. 2. of persons, *standing deep in water*, Nonn.*D*.10.166. -βασίη, = ἀμφισβήτησις, Heraclit.122. -βατέω, *stand by*, Hsch. II. Ion. for ἀμφισβητέω, Suid. -βάτης, ου, ὁ, *one that comes near*, Hsch. -βιον· μέγα· ἐγγὺς βοῆς, ἢ ἐπὶ τοῦ στενάξαι, Hsch., cf. *EM*15.36. -βλώς· ἄρτι παρών, Hsch., *EM*15.37. -γάμος, ον, *near marriage*, Parth.*Fr*.22, Nonn.*D*.5.572. -γείτων, ον, gen. ονος, *neighbouring*, A.*Pers*.886 (lyr.). -γυος, ον, (γύης) *neighbouring*, A.R.1.1222, D.P.215. II. *near land*, Nonn.*D*.3.44. -δίαι· ἐν θαλάσσῃ δίαι, Hsch. -δομος, ον, *dwelling near*, Νύμφαι B.12.89; μέλαθρα Coluth.247.

**ἀγχίζω**, Cret. aor. inf. ἀγχίξαι· ἐγγίσαι. Hsch.

⊛**ἀγχι-θάλασσος**, Att. -ττος, ον, *near the sea*, Poll.9.17. ⊛-θεος, ον, *near the gods*, i.e. akin to them, *godlike*, Od.5.35: as Subst., *demigod*, *IG*3.947, Luc.*Syr.D*.31. -θυρέω, *to be at the door*, *be close at hand*, Eust.1133.61. ⊛-θυρος, ον, *next door*, γείτονες Thgn.302, *IG*14.1389ii3; ἁ. ναίοισα Theoc.2.71; generally, *neighbouring*, Men.Prot.p.54 D., al. 2. *near the door*, of a statue, *Epigr.Gr*.906 (Gortyn). -κέλευθος, ον, *whose way is hard by*, Nonn.*D*.40.328; mostly = *near*, 5.476. -κρημνος, ον, *near the cliffs* or *coast*, Αἴγυπτος Pi.*Fr*.82. -κρηνος, ον, *from a neighbouring spring*, ὕδωρ *Arch.Anz*.26.333 (Panticapaeum).

**ἀγχιλά·** ἁλμυρά, θαλάσσια, ἄβρωτα, Hsch.

**ἀγχι-λεχής,** ές, *close to the bed*, Antim.66. **-λωψ,** ωπος, ὁ, *elling which obstructs the lachrymal duct*, Gal.19.438. **-μαστρον·** φίεσμα, Hsch. **-μᾰχητής,** οῦ, ὁ, = ἀγχέμαχος, only in pl., Il.2. 4, etc. **-μᾰχος,** ον, = ἀγχέμαχος, *EM*14.53, *AB*332. ⊛**-μολέω,** *me nigh*, Nonn.*D*.25.426. ⊛**-μολος,** ον, (μολεῖν) *coming near*; p. word, mostly used in neut. as Adv., *near, close at hand*, ἀγχίμολον οἱ ἦλθε Il.4.529, cf. Od.8.300, etc., Hes.*Sc*.325; ἐξ ἀγχιμόλοιο ών Il.24.352; ἀγχίμολον δὲ μετ' αὐτόν *close* behind him, Od.17.336: gen., ἔθεν ἀγχίμολοι cj. in Theoc.25.203.

**ἄγχιμος,** ον, (ἄγχι) = πλησίος, E.*Fr*.867.

**ἀγχί-μουσος,** ον, dub. in *Anacreont*.56.31. **-νεφής,** ές, *near he clouds*, σκόπελος *AP*6.219.14 (Antip.), Nonn.*D*.3.208, al.:—late Prose, ὄρη Men.Prot.p.48 D. ⊛**-νοια,** ἡ, (νοέω) *ready wit, sagacity, hrewdness*, Pl.*Chrm*.160a, Arist.*EN*1142$^{b}$6, *APo*.89$^{b}$10, Zeno *Stoic*. 1.56, Onos.*Praef*.9, D.S.1.65, etc.; ἀ. αὐλική Plb.15.34.4. **-νοος,** ον, contr. **-νους,** ουν, *ready of wit, shrewd*, Od.13.332, Pl.*Lg*.747b, *Stoic*.2.39, etc.; πρὸς τὰ συμβαίνοντα Arist.*HA*587$^{a}$12: Comp., Ptol. *Tetr*.57, S.E.*P*.2.41: Sup., ib.42. Adv. -νόως Aen.Tact.11.10; -νως Id.24.11, Arist.*VV*1250$^{a}$33, Andronic.Rhod.p.575 M.: Sup. -νούστατα Phlp.*in Ph*.483.1. **-πλοος,** ον, contr. **-πλους,** ουν, *near by sea*, πόρος *direct* voyage, E.*IT*1325. **-πολις,** poet. **-πτολις,** *near the city, dwelling hard by*, Παλλάς A.*Th*.501; Ἄρης S.*Ant*.970 (lyr.). II. *neighbouring*, of a city, Nonn.*D*.11.36. **-πορος,** ον, *passing near, always near*, κόλακες *AP*10.64 (Agath.); simply, *neighbouring*, Nonn.*D*.5.38, al. **-πους,** ὁ, ἡ, πουν, τό, *near with the foot, near*, Lyc.318.

**ἀγχίρροος,** ον, *flowing near*, A.R.2.367.

**ἀγχίσπορος,** ον, *near of kin*, οἱ θεῶν ἀγχίσποροι, οἱ Ζηνὸς ἐγγύς A.*Fr*.162; φύσιν αἰθέρος οὖσαν ἀ. Ph.2.374.

**ἀγχιστ-εία,** ἡ, (ἄγχιστος) *close kinship*, ἡ τοῦ γένους ἀ. Pl.*Lg*. 924d; ἀ. ὑπάρχει τινὶ πρός τινα Arist.*Rh*.1385$^{a}$3. 2. *rights of kin, right of inheritance*, Ar.*Av*.1661; προτέροις τοῖς ἄρρεσι τῶν θηλειῶν τὴν ἀ. πεποίηκε Is.7.20; νόθῳ μηδὲ νόθῃ εἶναι ἀ. Id.6.47, Lex ap.D.43.51; ταῖς ἀ. πρότεροι ὄντες τινός Is.7.44, cf. D.44. 2. 3. *exclusion by descent*, Lxx *Ne*.13.29. **-εῖα,** τά, = foreg., γένους κατ' ἀ. S.*Ant*.174. **-εύς,** έως, ὁ, mostly in pl. ἀγχιστεῖς, *next of kin*, of nations, Hdt.5.80:—*heir-at-law*, Lxx *Ru*.3.9 (with v.l. **-ευτής,** ib.4.1), Hierocl. *in CA*5 p.428 M.; συγγενὴς ἀ. Luc.*Tim*. 51. **-ευτικός,** ή, όν, *of the* ἀγχιστεύς, Asp. *in EN*77.14. **-εύω,** *to be next* or *near*, γῆ ἀγχιστεύουσα.. πόντῳ E.*Tr*.224 (lyr.). II. *to be next of kin, heir-at-law*, τινί Is.11.11: metaph., ἀ. ἀγοραίης ἐργασίης Hp.*Praec*.8. 2. c. acc., ἀ. τινά *do a kinsman's office* to a woman, i.e. *marry* her, Lxx *Ru*.3.13, 4.4; also κληρονομίαν ἀ. *enter upon..*, *Nu*.36.8. 3. Pass., *to be excluded by descent*, ἀπὸ τῆς ἱερατείας 2*Es*.2.62, *Ne*.7.64. **-ήρ,** ῆρος, ὁ, *one who brings near*, πάθους S.*Tr*.256. ⊛**-ικός,** ή, όν, *belonging to the* ἀγχιστεία, Ammon.*Diff*.5. ⊛**-ίνδην,** Adv. *within the near kin*, γαμεῖν Poll.6. 175, Lex ap.Hsch. **-ῖνος,** η, ον, Ep. Adj. *close, crowded, in heaps*, αἱ μέν τ' ἀ. ἐπ' ἀλλήλῃσι κέχυνται Il.5.141; τοὶ δ' ἀ. ἔπιπτον νεκροί 17.361, cf. Od.22.118. ⊛**-ος,** ον, Arc. **ἄσιστος** (v. sub fin.), Sup. of ἄγχι, *nearest*: as Adj. not in Ep.; *nearest* in place, A.*Ag*.256 (lyr.), S.*OT*919; γένει ἄ. πατρός E.*Tr*.48; τὸν ἄ. S.*El*.1105; *ever nigh*, Pi.*P*.9.64. II. Hom. has only neut. as Adv., ἄγχιστον *nearest*, Od.5.280; more commonly pl., ἄγχιστα ἐῴκει was *most nearly* like, Il.2.58, 14.474; ἄ. ἐοικώς Od.13.80; ἄ. ἔΐσκω 6.152, cf. Pi.*I*.2.10: freq. c. gen., Διὸς ἄ. *next to* Zeus, A.*Supp*.1035 (lyr.); ἄ. τοῦ βωμοῦ Hdt.9.81; ἄ. οἰκεῖν τινος Id.1.134, al., cf. Hp.*Mul*.2.181:—οἱ ἄ. those *next of kin*, Hdt.5.79; ἄ. ἦν αὐτῷ γένους Luc.*Cat*.17; also τοὶ 's ἄσιστα πόθικες *IG*5(2).159.17 (Tegea), cf. *Jahresh*.1.197 (Elis). 2. *nearest to what is right*, 'for choice', Hp.*Art*.14, cf. *Acut*.57. III. of Time, *most lately, but now*, ἄ...πόλεμος δέδηεν Il.20.18; ὁ ἄ. ἀποθανών he who died *last*, Hdt.2.143; τὰ ἄ. *most recently*, Antipho 2.1.6.

**ἀγχί-στροφος,** ον, *turning closely, quick-swooping*, ἰκτῖνος Thgn. 1261. 2. *quick-changing, changeable*, ἀγχίστροφα βουλεύεσθαι Hdt.7.13; ἀ. μεταβολή *sudden* change, Th.2.53; ἀστάθμητον πρᾶγμα εὐτυχία καὶ ἀ. D.H.4.23:—Rhet., τὸ ἀ. *rapidity of transition*, Longin. 27.3; ἁρμονία ἀ. περὶ τὰς πτώσεις a style *flexible* in the use of the cases, D.H.*Comp*.22. Adv. -φως Longin.22.1. **-τελής,** ές, *near its wane*, σελήνη Nonn.*D*.40.314. **-τέρμων,** ον, gen. ονος, (τέρμα) *near the border, neighbouring*, S.*Fr*.384, E.*Rh*.426; τινός Theodect.17, Lyc.1130.—Poet. (Dithyrambic acc. to Poll.6.113) and in X.*Hier*.10.7. **-τόκος,** ον, *near the birth*, ὠδῖνες pangs *of child-birth*, Pi.*Fr*.88.2, Nonn.*D*.24.197; of a woman, *AP*7.462 (Dionys.); νύμφαι Nonn.*D*.8.12. **-φανής,** ές, *appearing close at hand*, Nonn.*D*.2.97, al. **-φρων,** ονος, = ἀγχίνους, Ptol.*Tetr*. 160. **-φυτος,** ον, *growing hard by*, Nonn.*D*.3.152, 12.279.

**ἀγχίων,** ον, Comp. of ἄγχι, *nearer*, *EM*14.47.

**ἀγχοάδην·** ἀμβολάδην, Hsch.

**ἀγχό-θεν,** Adv. *from near at hand*, Hdt.4.31, Luc *Syr.D*.28. **-θι,** Poet. Adv. *near*, δειρῆς Il.14.412, cf. Od.13.103, A.R.1.37, etc.: abs., Theoc.22.40, *IG*9(2).645 (Thessal.).

**ἀγχ-όμορος,** ον, *neighbouring*, c. gen., dub. in Theoc.25.203.

**ἀγχον-άω,** (ἀγχόνη) *strangle*, Man.1.317, Suid. ⊛**-η,** ἡ, (ἄγχω) *strangling, hanging*, ἀγχόνης..τέρματα A.*Eu*.746; ἔργα κρείσσον' ἀγχόνης deeds too bad for *hanging*, S.*OT*1374; τάδ' ἀγχόνης πέλας 'tis nigh as bad as *hanging*, E.*Heracl*.246; ταῦτ' οὐχὶ.. ἀγχόνης ἔστ' ἄξια; Id.*Ba*.246; ταῦτα..οὐκ ἀ.; Ar.*Ach*.125; οἱ δ' ἀγχόνην ἥψαντο Semon.1.18: rare in Prose, ἀ. καὶ λύπη Aeschin.2.38:—in pl., ἐν ἀγχόναις θάνατον λαβεῖν E.*Hel*.200, cf. ib.299, *HF*154; αἱ ἀ. μάλιστα τοῖς νέοις Arist.*Pr*.954$^{b}$35. II. = μανδραγόρα, Ps.-Dsc. 4.75. **-ίζω,** *strangle*, Sch.E.*Hipp*.780 (Pass.). **-ιος,** α, ον, *fit for strangling*, βρόχος E.*Hel*.686; δεσμός Nonn.*D*.21.31, 34. 229. **-ιστής,** ὁ, *hangman*, *Gloss*.

**ἀγχόσε,** Adv. *coming near*, A.D.*Adv*.194.17.

**ἀγχοτάτω,** Adv., Sup. of ἀγχοῦ, *nearest, next*, c. gen., *h.Ap*.18, Hdt.2.169, E.*Fr*.620; ἀ. τινός, of likeness, Hdt.7.64 (v.l. -ότατα), 80, al.; τινί ib.91; οἱ ἀ. προσήκοντες the *nearest* of kin, 4.73.

**ἀγχότερος,** α, ον, Comp. of ἀγχοῦ, *nearer*, c. gen., Hdt.7.175. Adv. -οτέρω App.*BC*1.57.

**ἀγχοῦ,** = ἄγχι, *near*, freq. in Hom., usu. in phrase ἀγχοῦ δ' ἱσταμένη (or -ος) Il.2.172, al.; στεῦται δ' Ὀδυσῆος ἀκοῦσαι ἀ. Od.17.526, cf. 19.271; ἀ. καθῆσθαι Archil.*Supp*.3.3, cf. S.*Tr*.962: twice c. gen., Il.24.709, Od.6.5: c. dat., Pi.*N*.9.40, Hdt.3.85: in late Prose, λόγοι ἀ. τούτων Philostr.*VA*6.16.

**ἀγχούρης·** πένης, Hsch.

**ἄγχουρος** (A), ον, (ἄγχι, οὖρος Ion. for ὅρος) *neighbouring*, *AP*9. 235 (Crin.); *bordering on*, τινί Orph.*A*.124; τινός Lyc.418.

**ἄγχουρος** (B), ὁ, *gold*, from the name of the son of Midas, *AP*15. 25.7 codd. (Besant.), cf. Plu.2.306f.

⊛**ἀγχοῦρος,** *dawn*, Call.*Hec*.1.4.10; Cypr acc. to Hsch.

⊛**ἄγχουσα,** ἡ, *alkanet*, *Anchusa tinctoria*, Thphr.*HP*7.8.3, Dsc.4. 23; cf. ἔγχουσα.

**ἀγχουσίζομαι,** Med., *rouge*, Hsch.

**ἄγχραν·** μύωπα (Locr.), Hsch. **ἀγχράνασθαι** (for ἀναχρ-), *anoint* or *wash oneself*, Id.

**ἀγχύνωψ,** ωπος, ὁ, = φοῖνιξ, Dsc.4.43.

**ἄγχω,** fut. ἄγξω Ar.*Ec*.638, Luc.*D.Mort*.22.1: aor. 1 inf. ἄγξαι v.l. for ἄξαι Lxx 4*Ma*.9.17, (ἀπ-) Ar.*Pax*796:—**Med.** and **Pass.** (v. infr.) only in pres.:—*squeeze*, esp. the throat, ἄγχε μιν ἱμὰς ὑπὸ δειρήν Il.3.371; *embrace*, μὴ θέλουσαν *Anacreont*.57.22, cf. Herod.1.18; *hug*, in wrestling, Id.2.12, Luc.*Anach*.1, Paus.8.40.2, Philostr.*Im*. 1.6 (Pass.); *strangle, throttle*, τοὺς πατέρας ἦγχον νύκτωρ Ar.*V*.1039, cf. *Ec*.638, 640; τὸν Κέρβερον ἀπῆξας ἄγχων Id.*Ra*.468, cf. *Av*.1575; κἂν ταῦρον ἄγχοις Id.*Lys*.81, cf. Crates Com.29, D.54.20, Theoc.5. 106, *APl*.4.90; ἐν χαλινῷ τὰς σιαγόνας ἄ. Lxx *Ps*.31(32).9: metaph., of pressing creditors, Ar.*Eq*.775, Luc.*Symp*.32; ψυχὴ ὑπὸ τοῦ σώματος ἀγχομένη *Corp.Herm*.10.24, cf. 7.3; of a guilty conscience, τοῦτο.. ἄγχει, σιωπᾶν ποιεῖ D.19.208:—Med., *strangle oneself*, Hp. *Morb*.2.68:—Pass., Pi.*N*.1.46, D.47.59, Theoc.7.125; *to be drowned*, Hp.*Virg*.1.—Not in Trag.

**ἀγχώμᾰλος,** ον, (ὁμαλός) *nearly equal*, ἀγχώμαλοι ἐν χειροτονίᾳ Th. 3.49; ἀ. μάχη a *doubtful* battle, Id.4.134; τὴν νίκην ἐν ἀγχωμάλῳ καταλιπόντες J.*BJ*6.2.6; τὸ πλῆθος οὐκ ἀ. Plu.*Caes*.42, cf. D.H.5. 14:—neut. pl. as Adv., ἀγχώμαλα ναυμαχεῖν, Lat. *aequo Marte pugnare*, Th.7.71; ἀ. σφισι ἐγένετο Luc.*Herm*.12. Adv. -άλως Id *VH* 2.37, App.*Praef*.11.

⊛**ἄγω** [ᾰ], impf. ἦγον, Ep. and Ion. ἄγεσκον Hdt.1.148, A.R.1. 849: fut. ἄξω Il.1.139, etc.: thematic aor. imper. ἄξετε Il.3.105, inf. ἀξέμεναι, -έμεν, Il.23.50, 111: aor. 2 ἤγαγον Il.6.291, etc., opt. ἀγαγοίην Sapph.159: aor. 1 ἦξα rare, ἦξε Tim.*Pers*.165, part. ἄξας Batr. 119, inf. ἄξαι Antipho 5.46: pf. ἦχα *SIG*1 (Abu Simbel, vii/vi B.C.), Plb.3.111.3, (προ-) D.19.18, (συν-) X.*Mem*.4.2.8; ἀγήγοχα *OGI*219.15 (Sigeum, iii B.C.), etc., Dor. συν-αγάγοχα *Test.Epict*.3. 12; ἀγήοχα Lxx *To*.12.3, J.*BJ*1.30.1, Alex.*Fig*.1.11, etc. (also in compds., (εἰσ-) Ps.-Philipp. ap.D.18.39, (κατ-) Decr.ib.73); ἀγείοχα *PTeb*.5.193 (ii B.C.), etc.; ἀγέωχα (δι-) *CIG*4897*d* (Philae, i B.C.), *PTeb*.5.198 (ii B.C.), etc.: plpf. ἀγηόχει Plb.30.4.17:—**Med.,** fut. ἄξομαι Hom., Hdt., Trag.: them. aor. 1 ἄξοντο Il.8.545, imper. ἄξεσθε ib.505: also ἀξάμην (ἐσ-) Hdt.5.34, (προεσ-) 1.190, 8.20: aor. 2 ἠγαγόμην Hom., etc., 2 sg. ἀγάγαο *GDI*5088.8 (Cret.):—**Pass.,** fut. ἀχθήσομαι Pl.*Hp.Ma*.292a, (προσ-) Th.4.87, etc.; ἄξομαι in pass. sense, A.*Ag*.1632, Pl.*R*.458d, (προς-) Th.4.115, etc.: aor. 1 ἤχθην X.*An*.6.3.10, Ion. ἄχθην Hdt.6.30, part. ἀχθείς Hippon. 9: pf. ἦγμαι Hdt.2.158, D.13.15; also in med. sense, v. infr. B.2. I. *lead, carry, fetch, bring*, of living creatures, φέρω being used of things, δῶκε δ' ἄγειν ἑτάροισι..γυναῖκα, καὶ τρίποδα..φέρειν Il.23.512; βοῦν δ' ἀγέτην κεράων by the horns, Od.3.439; ἄ. εἰς or πρὸς τόπον, poet. also c. acc. loci, νόστοι δ' ἐκ πολέμων ἀπόνους (sc. ἄνδρας)..ἆγον οἴκους A.*Pers*.863 (lyr.); Ἅιδας..ἄγει τὰν Ἀχέροντος ἀκτάν S.*Ant*.811 (lyr.); ἄ. τινά τινι Od.14.386; ἵππους ὑφ' ἅρματ' ἄ. 3.476, cf. A.*Pr*.465. b. part. ἄγων *taking*, στῆσε δ' ἄγων Il.2.558, cf. Od.1.130, S.*OC*1342, etc. 2. *take with one*, ἑταίρους Od.10.405, cf. S.*OC*832, etc.; τι Il.15.531, Hdt.1.70; of a wife, A.*Pr*.559 (lyr.) (more usu. Med., q.v.). 3. *carry off* as captives or booty, Il.1.367, 9. 594, A.*Th*.340, etc.; ἄχθη ἀγόμενος παρὰ βασιλέα Hdt.6.30; ἀγόμενος, i.e. δοῦλος, Archil.155, cf. E.*Tr*.140, Pl.*Lg*.914e; Δίκην ἄγειν *to lead* Justice *forcibly away*, Hes.*Op*.220; ἡ ἐπιθυμία ἄγει Arist.*EN*1147$^{a}$ 34; of a fowler, φῦλον ὀρνίθων ἀμφιβαλὼν ἄγει S.*Ant*.343: esp. in phrase ἄ. καὶ φέρειν *harry, ravage* a country, first in Il.5.484 οἷόν κ' ἠὲ φέροιεν Ἀχαιοὶ ἤ κεν ἄγοιεν, cf. 23.512 sq.; freq. in Hdt. and Att. Prose:—in Pass., ἀγόμεθα, φερόμεθα E.*Tr*.1310, cf. Ar.*Nu*.241: more rarely reversed, φέρουσί τε καὶ ἄγουσι Hdt.1.88; ἔφερε καὶ ἦγε πάντας Id.3.39: c. acc. loci, φέρων καὶ ἄγων τὴν Βιθυνίδα X.*HG*3.2.2; ἦγον καὶ ἔκαον τὴν Β. ib.5; ἄ. alone, *ravage*, *IG*9(1).333 (Locr., v B.C.):—but φέρειν καὶ ἄγειν sts. means simply *bear and carry, bring together*, Pl.*Phdr*.279c; τὴν ποίησιν φέρειν τε καὶ ἄγειν, i.e. *bring it* *into* the state, Id.*Lg.*817a, cf. X.*Cyr.*3.3.2. **4.** ἄ. εἰς δίκην or δικαστήριον, ἐπὶ τοὺς δικαστάς *to carry* one before a court of justice, freq. in Att., πρὸς τὴν δίκην ἄ. E.*Fr.*1049; ὑπ' ἐπίγνωσιν ἀχθῆναι *PTeb.*28.11 (ii B.C.); simply ἄγειν Pl.*Grg.*527a, etc.; ἐπὶ θανάτῳ ἄ. X.*An.*1.6.10, etc.:—Pass., ἐπὶ βασιλεῖς ἀχθήσεσθε *Ev.Matt.*10.18, cf. *PTeb.*331.16 (ii A.D.); φόνου ἄγεσθαι Plu.2.309e. **b.** Pass., *to be confiscated*, τὰ κτήνη ἀχθήσεται πρὸς τὰ ἐκφόρια (to meet the rent) *PTeb.*27.75 (ii B.C.). **5.** of ships, *carry* as cargo, *import*, [οἶνον] νῆες ἄγουσι Il.9.72, etc.; ἵνα οἱ σὺν φόρτον ἄγοιμι (i.e. σύν οἱ) Od.14.296. **6.** *draw on, bring on*, πῆμα τόδ' ἤγαγον Οὐρανίωνες Il.24.547; Ἰλίῳ φθοράν A.*Ag.*406 (lyr.); τερμίαν ἁμέραν S.*Ant.*1330 (lyr.); ὕπνον Id.*Ph.*638; χαράν E.*Fr.*174; δάκρυ Id.*Alc.*1081. **7.** *bear up*, φελλοὶ δ' ὥς. ἄγουσι δίκτυον A.*Ch.*506. **8.** *carry far and wide, spread abroad*, κλέος Od.5.311. **9.** Medic., *remove*, φλέγμα Hp. *Nat.Hom.*6, cf. *Aph.*4.2; ἕλμινθα Dsc.1.16. **II.** *lead towards* a point, *lead on*, τὸν δ' ἄγε μοῖρα κακὴ θανάτοιο τέλοσδε Il.13.602; κῆρες ἄγον θανάτοιο 2.834; οἷ μ' ἀτιμίας ἄγεις S.*El.*1035: also c. inf., ἄγει θανεῖν *leads* to death, E.*Hec.*43: c. acc. cogn., ἄγομαι τάνδ' ἑτοίμαν ὁδὸν S.*Ant.*877 (lyr.); ὁδὸς ἄγει the road *leads*, Heraclit.71, S.*OT*734, *Tab.Heracl.*1.16, etc.: metaph., *tend*, ἐπὶ τὸ ἄκρον Pl.*Lg.*701e. **2.** *lead, guide*, esp. in war, λαόν Il.10.79; ἄ. στρατιάν, ναῦς, etc., Th.7.12, 8.59, etc., cf. X.*An.*4.8.12; hence abs., *march*, θᾶσσον ὁ Νικίας ἦγε Th.7.81, cf. X.*HG*4.2.19, etc.: simply, *go*, ἄγωμεν *Ev.Marc.*1.38; of the gods, etc., *guide*, Pi., Hdt., etc.; ἐπ' ἀρετὴν E.*Fr.*672; διὰ πόνων ἄγειν τινά Id.*IT*988. **3.** *manage*, νόῳ πλοῦτον Pi.*P.*6.47; πολιτείαν Th.1.127; τὴν σοφίαν *conduct* philosophical inquiry, Pl.*Tht.*172b; of reasoning, ἀγαγεῖν τοὺς λόγους Arist.*APr.*47ᵃ21; εἰς τὸ ἀδύνατον ἄ. ib.27ᵃ15 (v.l. ἀπάγοντας):—Pass., *to be led, guided*, λογισμῷ Pl.*R.*431c; ἡγούμενος τῶν ἡδονῶν ἀλλ' οὐκ ἀγόμενος ὑπ' αὐτῶν Isoc.9.45. **4.** *refer, attribute*, τι εἰς ἐθελοκάκησιν Plb.27.15.13; τι ἐς Διόνυσον Luc.*Syr.D.*33. **5.** *bring up, train, educate*, ἀγόμενοι ὀρθῶς Pl.*Lg.*782d; ἤχθη τὴν λεγομένην ἀγωγήν Plu.*Ages.*1; of animals, *train*, X.*Mem.*4.1.3. **6.** *reduce*, ἐς βραχὺ τὴν ἀρχὴν Hp. *VM*1; ἐς τὸ ἥμισυ Id.*Mul.*1.78; of propositions, εἰς ῥᾳδιεστέραν κατασκευήν Papp.1076.6. **III.** *draw out* in length, τεῖχος ἄ. *to draw a line of* wall, Th.6.99; μέλαθρον εἰς ὀρόφους *AP*9.649 (Maced.); ὄγμον ἄ. Theoc.10.2; ἄ. γραμμὰς *to draw* lines, Arist.*Top.*101ᵃ16; ἤχθωσαν κάθετοι *let* perpendiculars *be drawn*, *Mete.*373ᵃ11; ἄ. ἐπίπεδον *describe* a plane, Archim.*Sph.*1.7, etc.:—Pass., ἦκται ἡ διῶρυξ Hdt.2.158, cf. Th.6.100; κόλπου ἀγομένου τῆς γῆς, i.e. when the land forms a bight, Hdt.4.99. **IV.** *hold, celebrate*, Ἀπατούρια, ὁρτήν, Hdt.1.147,183 (more usu. ἀνάγειν); freq. in Att., ἄ. ἀγῶνα *IG*1.53.33; θυσίαν, θεωρίαν Isoc.19.10; κρεουργὸν ἦμαρ εὐθύμως ἄγειν A.*Ag.*1592; γάμους Men.*Sam.*336, cf. Lxx *To.*11.19 (Pass.); ἐκκλησίαν Plu.*Aem.*30:—Pass., ἀγοραῖοι ἄγονται *Act.Ap.*19.38. **2.** *keep, observe* a date, ἄ. τὴν ἡμέραν ταύτην πάντα τὸν χρόνον Th.5.54, cf. Men.521; κατὰ σελήνην τὰς ἡμέρας Ar.*Nu.*626; *reckon*, τοὺς ἐνιαυτοὺς καθ' ἥλιον Gem.8.6. **3.** *keep, observe*, ὀρθὰν ἄγεις ἐφημοσύναν Pi.*P.*6.20; σπονδὰς ἄ. πρός τινας Th.6.7; εἰρήνην Pl.*R.*465b, etc.: c. acc., as periphr. for a neut. Verb, σχολὴν ἄγειν, = σχολάζειν, E.*Med.*1238, Pl.*R.*376d; ἡσυχίαν ἄ., = ἡσυχάζειν, X.*An.*3.1.14; ἄ. ἀπαστίαν Ar. *Nu.*621; κρύψιν ἄ., of stars betw. setting and rising, Autol.2.9; *keep up, sustain, maintain*, νεῖκος Pi.*P.*9.31; γέλωτ' ἄγειν *to keep* laughing, S.*Aj.*382; ἄ. κτύπον E.*Or.*182 (lyr.); with predicate, *maintain*, ἐλευθέραν ἦγε τὴν Ἑλλάδα D.9.36. **4.** of Time, *pass*, ἀπήμαντον ἄγων βίοτον Pi.*O.*8.87; ποίας ἡμέρας δοκεῖς μ' ἄγειν; S.*El.*266; ὁ βίος ούμὸς ἑσπέραν ἄγει Alex.228, cf. ὥραν ἄγειν *to be ripe*, τῆς γαστρὸς ὥραν ἀγούσης Philostr.*VA*2.14; ὥραν ἦγε θανάτου Chor.p.38B.; τῆς ἡλικίας ἄγον τὸ ἄνθος Id.p.53B.; τέταρτον ἔτος ἄγων καὶ τριακοστόν Gal.*Lib. Propr.*1. **5.** of beliefs, *hold*, αἵρεσιν Plb.27.15.14. **V.** *hold account, treat*, ἄ. ἀρετὰν οὐκ αἴσχιον φυᾶς Pi.*I.*7(6).22; ἐν τιμῇ ἄγειν or ἄγεσθαι, ἐν οὐδεμιῇ μοίρῃ ἄ., περὶ πλείστου ἄ., Hdt.1.134, 2.172, 9.7, etc.; θεοὺς ἄ. *to believe in*, A.*Supp.*924; διὰ τιμῆς ἄ. τινά, etc., Luc. *Prom.Es*4, etc.; τὸ πρᾶγμ' ἄ... ὡς παρ' οὐδέν S.*Ant.*34; τὴν Ἀφροδίτην πρόσθ' ἄ. τοῦ Βακχίου E.*Ba.*225; τιμιώτερον ἄ. τινά Th.8.81; εὐεργεσίας εἰς ἀχαριστίαν καὶ προπηλακισμὸν ἄ. D.18.316:—with Adverbs, δυσφόρως τοὔνειδος ἦγον S.*OT*784; ἐντίμως ἄ. Pl.*R.*528c, etc.:—Pass., ἠγόμην δ' ἀνὴρ ἀστῶν μέγιστος S.*OT*775. **VI.** *draw down* in the scale, hence, *weigh*, ἄ. μνᾶν, τριακοσίους δαρεικούς, etc., *weigh* a mina, 300 darics, etc., D.22.76, 24.129, cf. Philippid.9.4, etc.; ἄ. πλέον Arist.*Pr.*931ᵇ15; ἄ. σταθμόν Plu.2.96b. **VII.** on ἄγε, ἄγετε, v. s. vocc.

**B.** Med. ἄγομαι, *carry away for oneself*, χρυσόν τε καὶ ἄργυρον οἴκαδ' ἄγεσθαι Od.10.35; *take with one*, 6.58, E.*Heracl.*808, etc.; of a ship's cargo, D.35.20: *take to oneself*, δῶρον Theoc.1.9, cf. 11; *take upon oneself*, ἄγεσθαι ἐς χεῖρας Hdt.1.126, 4.79. **2.** ἄγεσθαι γυναῖκα *take to oneself* a wife, Od.14.211; γυναῖκα ἄ. ἐς τὰ οἰκία Hdt.1.59, etc.; ἄγεσθαί τινα ἐς δῶμα Hes.*Th.*410; simply ἄ. *marry*, Hdt.2.47, etc.: pf. Pass. ἦγμαι is used in this med. sense, J.*AJ*14.12.1; of the father, *bring home* a wife *for his son*, Od.4.10, Hdt.1.34; of a brother, Od.15.238; of friends of the bridegroom and bride, Od.6.28, Hes.*Sc.*274: later in Pass. of the wife, *PGnom.*138 (ii A.D.). **3.** like Act., *bring*; διὰ στόμα ἄγεσθαι μῦθον *bring* through the mouth, i.e. *utter*, Il.14.91.

**ἀγωγαῖος**, ον, (ἀγωγή) *fit for leading by*, of a dog's collar or *leash*, *AP*6.35 (Leon.).

**ἀγωγεῖον**, τό, *pander's house*, Poll.9.48 (perh. f.l. for ἀσωτ-).

**ἀγωγεύς**, έως, ὁ, *haulier*, Hdt.2.175. **2.** *escort, guide*, *Milet.*3.152.16 (Methymna, ii B.C.). **3.** *prosecutor* (cf. ἄγω I. 4), Suid. **II.** *leading-rein, leash*, S.*Fr.*974, Stratt.52, X. 6.5. **III.** epith. of Zeus, *guide, director*, *Anecd.Stud.*1.265.

**ἀγωγή**, ἡ, (ἄγω) *carrying away*, Hdt.6.85, etc.; *freight, carria[ge]*, πρὸς τὰς ἀγωγὰς.. χρῆσθαι ὑποζυγίοις Pl.*R.*370e, cf. X.*Lac.*7.5, *PLo[nd.]*3.948.2 (iii A.D.). **b.** intr., τὴν ἀ. διὰ τάχους ἐποιεῖτο pursued [his] *voyage*, Th.4.29 (v.l.); *movement*, Pl.*R.*604b; ἀ. ἐπί τι *tendency* [to]wards.., Hp.*Epid.*1.1. **2.** *bringing to* or *in*, ὑμῶν ἡ ἐς τοὺς ὀλίγο[υς] ἀ. your *bringing* us *before* the council, Th.5.85. **3.** *forcible seizu[re], carrying off, abduction*, A.*Ag.*1263, S.*OC*662; ἀγωγὴν ποιήσασθαι *PT[eb.]*39.22 (ii B.C.), cf. 48.22. **4.** ὕδατος ἀγωγαί *aqueducts*, *IG*12(5).872 (Tenos), cf. D.H.3.67. **5.** *load*, *Ostr.*1168; *weight*, *AB*333. [**6.**] *winding up* of engine, Ph.*Bel.*57.13 (pl.). **7.** *drawing* of line[s], Procl. *in Euc.* pp.284, 376F. **8.** *evoking*, πνευμάτων Iamb.*Myst.*3.[..] (pl.). **b.** *spell for bringing* a person, usu. *love-charm*, *PMag.Par.*1.1390. **II.** *leading, guidance*, ἵππου X.*Eq.*6.4; ἡ τοῦ νόμου, το[ῦ] λογισμοῦ ἀ. Pl.*Lg.*645a, cf. *Plt.*274b. **2.** *leading* of an army, Id. *Lg.*746e (pl.); ἀ. στρατορχίας *conduct* of an expedition, Vett.Val.339.29; ἡ ἀ. τῶν πραγμάτων Plb.3.8.5. **3.** *direction, training*, παιδεία μέ[ν] ἐσθ' ἡ παίδων ὁλκή τε καὶ ἀ. πρὸς τὸν ὑπὸ τοῦ νόμου λόγον ὀρθὸν εἰρημένον Pl.*Lg.*659d, cf. 819a; ἀ. ὀρθῆς τυχεῖν πρὸς ἀρετήν Arist.*EN*1179ᵇ31; διὰ τὸ ἦθος καὶ τὴν ἀ. Id.*Pol.*1292ᵇ14, cf. Cleanth.*Stoic.*1.107: in pl., *systems of education*, Chrysipp. *Stoic.*3.173; esp. of the public education of the Spartan youth, Λακωνικὴ ἀ. Plb.1.32.1; Ἀγησίλαος ἤχθη τὴν λεγομένην ἀγωγὴν ἐν Λακεδαίμονι Plu.*Ages.*1; ἀ. στοιχειώδης elementary *course*, Apollon.Perg.*Con.*1 Praef.:—also of plants, *culture*, Thphr.*HP*1.3.2; of diseases, *treatment*, Gal.12.414, 15.436. **4.** *way* of life, *conduct*, Archyt ap.Stob.2.31.120 (pl.), *PTeb.*24.57 (ii B.C.), *OGI*223.15 (Erythrae, iii B.C.), Lxx *2Ma.*6.8, *2Ep.Tim.*3.10, M.Ant.1.6. **5.** *keeping, observance*, ἡμερῶν Aristox.*Rhyth.*2.37; μηνῶν Gem.8.48. **6.** generally, *method, construction* (of a law), Arist.*Rh.*1375ᵇ12; *style*, D.H.*Isoc.*20, al.; ἡ ἀ. τῶν διαλέκτων Str.14.1.41. **7.** *method of proof*, esp. of syllogistic reasoning, λόγοι τὰς ἀγωγὰς ὑγιεῖς ἔχοντες Chrysipp.*Stoic.*2.84, cf. Simp. *in Ph.*759.14; *line of argument*, Plu.2.106b. **8.** *school* of philosophers, Phld.*Sto.Herc.*339.12, *Acad.Ind.*p.68 M., S.E.*P.*1.145, etc. **9.** Milit., *manœuvre, movement*, Ascl.*Tact.*12.7 and 10; *order of march*, ib.11.8, cf. Ael.*Tact.*39.1. **10.** in Law, = Lat. *actio*, *Cod.Just.*4.24.1, al. **III.** *tempo*, in music, Pl.*R.*400c (pl.), Aristox.*Harm.* p.34 M., Aristid.Quint.1.19; *sequence*, of a melody, Aristox.*Harm.* p.29 M.; musical *style*, Str.14.1.41, Plu.2.1141c.

**ἀγωγικά**, τά, *expenses of transport*, *Cod.Just.*10.30.4.

**ἀγώγιμος**, ον, of things, *capable of being carried*, τρισσῶν ἁμαξῶν.. ἀ. βάρος *enough to load*, E.*Cyc.*385; τὰ ἀ. *things portable, wares*, Pl. *Prt.*313c, X.*An.*5.1.16, etc.; ἄλλο δὲ μηδὲν ἀ. ἄγεσθαι ἐν τῷ πλοίῳ D.35.20. **II.** of persons, *liable to seizure*, X.*HG*7.3.11, cf. D.23.11, Plu.*Sol.*13, *BGU*1116.27 (13 B.C.):—also of things, D.H.5.69. **2.** *easily led, pliable*, Plu.*Alc.*6. **III.** Act., ἀγώγιμον, τό, *love-charm, philtre*, Plu.2.1093d, cf. *PMag.Lond.*121.295: pl., *PMag.Par.*1.2231.

**ἀγώγιον**, τό, *load of a wagon*, X.*Cyr.*6.1.54, *PPetr.*3p.101 (iii B.C.), *PLond.*3.1166.13 (i A.D.). **II.** *carriage* of such a load, *PPetr.* l. c.

**ἀγωγός**, όν, *leading, guiding*, and as Subst., *guide*, Hdt.3.26; *escort*, Th.2.12, cf. 4.78; ἀ. ὕδατος *aqueduct*, *Mon.Anc.Gr.*19.5 (pl.); without ὕδατος, Just.*Nov.*128.16 (pl.): c. gen., δύναμις ἀνθρώπων ἀ. power *of leading* men, Plu.*Lyc.*5. **II.** *leading towards*, ἐπί τι Pl.*R.*525a, Phld.*D.*3.12; εἰς.. Plu.*Per.*1. **III.** *drawing, attracting*, δύναμις ἀ. τινος, of the magnet, Dsc.5.130. **2.** *drawing forth, eliciting*, χοαὶ νεκρῶν ἀγωγοί E.*Hec.*536; δακρύων ἀ. Id.*Tr.*1131; γυναικείων Hp.*Aph.*5.28; ἐμμήνων Dsc.1.16. **3.** abs., *attractive*, Plu.*Crass.*7; τὸ ἀ. *attractiveness*, Id.2.25b.

**ἀγωίλιον**, τό, = ἀωίλιον, *PSI*4.423.6, al. (iii B.C.).

**ἀγών** [ᾰ], ῶνος, ὁ, Aeol. **ἄγωνος**, ω, ὁ, Alc.121 (also E.ap.Sch.Il. *Oxy.*1087.60); Elean dat. pl. ἀγώνοιρ *GDI*1172.26: (ἄγω):—*gathering, assembly*, ἵζανεν εὐρὺν ἀ. Il.23.258; λῦτο δ' ἀ. 24.1, cf. Od.8.200; νεῶν ἐν ἀγῶνι Il.15.428, cf. Eust.1335.57: esp. *assembly met to see games*, freq. in Il.23; Ὑπερβορέων ἀ. Pi.*P.*10.30; κοινοὺς ἀ. θέντες A. *Ag.*845. **2.** *place of contest, lists, course*, βῆτην ἐς μέσσον ἀ. Il.23.685, cf. 531, Od.8.260, Hes.*Sc.*312, Pi.*P.*9.114, and esp. Th.5.50: prov., ἔξω ἀγῶνος out of the *lists* or *course*, i.e. *beside the mark*, Pi. *P.*1.44, Luc.*Anach.*21: pl., κατ' ἀγῶνας Od.8.259. **II.** *assembly* of the Greeks *at the national games*, ὁ ἐν Ὀλυμπίῃ ἀ. Hdt.6.127; ὁ Ὀλυμπικὸς ἀ. Ar.*Pl.*583; Ἑλλάδος πρόσχημ' ἀ. S.*El.*682, cf. 699:—hence, *contest for a prize* at the games, ἀ. γυμνικός, ἱππικός, μουσικός, Hdt.2.91, Pl.*Lg.*658a, Ar.*Pl.*1163, cf. Th.3.104; οἱ τῶν λαμπάδων ἀ. Arist.*Ath.*57.1; ἀ. τῶν ἀνδρῶν *contest* in which the chorus was composed of men, opp. to παίδων or ἀγενείων (q.v.), D.21.18, etc.; ἀ. στεφανηφόρος or στεφανίτης *contest* where the prize is a crown, Hdt.5.102, Arist.*Rh.*1357ᵃ19; ἀ. χάλκεος, where it is a shield of brass, Pi.*N.*10.22; ἀ. θεματικός *IG*14.739 (Naples); ἀργυρίτης δωρίτης Plu.2.820d:—hence many phrases, ἀγῶνα καταστῆσαι establish *a contest*, Isoc.4.1; τιθέναι Hdt.5.8; ποιεῖν Th.3.104; οὐ λόγων τοὺς ἀ. προθήσοντες Id.3.67; προηγόρευέ τε ἀγῶνας καὶ ἆθλα προυτίθει X. *Cyr.*8.2.26; προκαλούμενος ἑαυτὸν εἰς ἀ. Id.*Mem.*2.3.17; τοὺς ἀ. νικᾶν ib.3.7.1; ἐν τοῖς ἀγῶσι Isoc.15.301; of contests in general, εἰς ἀ. λόγων ἀφικέσθαι τινί Pl.*Prt.*335a; πρὸς τίν' ἀγῶνας τιθέμεσθ' ἀρετῆς; E. *Ion*863 (lyr.); ἀ. σοφίας Ar.*Ra.*883. **III.** generally, *struggle*, πολλοὺς ἀ. ἐξιών, of Hercules, S.*Tr.*159; ξιφηφόρος ἀ. A.*Ch.*584; εἰς ἀ. τῷδε συμπεσὼν μάχης S.*Tr.*20, etc.; ὁ Φίλιππος, πρὸς ὃν ἦν ἡμῖν ὁ ἀ. D.18.67; ποιέειν ἢ παθεῖν πρόκειται ἀ. Hdt.7.11; ἀληθείην ἀσκέειν ἀ.

ιστος ib.209 : pl., *πραγμάτων ἀγῶνας κεκτημένων* Epicur.*Sent.*21 ; ορος ἀ. Lys.7.2 ; *ὅπλων ἔκειτ' ἀ. πέρι* S.*Aj.*936 ; and without *περί*, ν *'Αχιλλείων ὅπλων ἀ.* ib.1240 ; *ψυχῆς ἀ. τὸν προκείμενον πέρι* uggle for life and death, E.*Or.*847, cf. *Ph.*1330 ; *πολλοὺς ἀ. δραμοῦνται περὶ σφέων αὐτῶν* Hdt.8.102 ; *λόγων γὰρ οὐ .. ἀγών, ἀλλὰ* s *ψυχῆς πέρι* S.*El.*1492, cf. infr. 5. **2.** *battle, action*, Th.2.89, c. **3.** *action at law, trial*, Antipho6.21, etc., cf. A.*Eu.*677, 744 ; *ἀγῶνα καθιστάναι ἀνθρώπους* Pl.*Ap.*24c, *R.*494e ; *περὶ τῆς ψυχῆς* *ἀγῶνα καταστῆσαί τινα* X.*Lac.*8.4. **4.** *speech* delivered in urt or before an assembly or ruler, *πρεσβευτικοὶ ἀ.* Plb.9.32.4; *τοὺς* ιφανεστάτους εἰρηκότος ἀ. τούς τε δικανικοὺς καὶ τοὺς δημηγορικοὺς .H.*Amm.*1.3, cf. *OGI*567 (Attalia, ii A. D.) ; *ἀ. ἐσχηματισμένοι* D.H. *h.*8.1, al. **b.** Rhet., *main argument* of a speech (opp. *προοίμιον*, ρίλογος), in pl., Syr. *in Hermog.*2.111, 170R., cf. *Proll.Hermog.*ap. Rh.4.12W. **5.** metaph., *οὐ λόγων ἔθ' ἀγών* now is not *the time for* vords, E.*Ph.*588 ; *οὐχ ἕδρας ἀ.* 'tis no *time for* sitting still, Id.*Or.* 291 ; *ἀ. πρόφασιν οὐ δέχεται the crisis* admits no dallying, Ar.*Fr.* 31, cf. Pl.*Cra.*421d, *Lg.*751d ; *μέγας ὁ ἀ...τὸ χρηστὸν ἢ κακὸν γενέσθαι the issue* is great.., Id.*R.*608b, cf. E.*Med.*235 ; *οὐ περί τινος ὁ ἀ. the question* is not about .., Th.3.44. **6.** *mental struggle, anxiety*, Th.7.71, Plb.4.56.4, *Ep.Col.*2.1 : in pl., *τρόμοι καὶ ἀ.* Plu. *Sol.*7. **b.** of speakers, *vehemence, power*, Longin.15.1, cf. 26. 3. **IV.** personified, *'Αγών, divinity of the contest*, Paus.5.26.3.

⊛**ἀγων-άρχης,** *ου, ὁ, judge of a contest*, S.*Aj.*572. **II.** (*ἀγών* = assembly) Boeotian magistrate, *IG*7.1817 (Thespiae), cf. Sch.Il. 24.1. ⊛**-ία,** *ἡ, contest, struggle for victory, ἀγὼν διὰ πάσης ἀγωνίης ἔχων* Hdt.2.91 ; *πολεμίων ἀ.* E.*Hec.*314, cf. *Tr.*1003 ; esp. in games, Pi.*O.*2.52, *P.*5.113 :—also in Prose, *ἐν δημοτικῇ ἀ.* X.*Cyr.*2.3.15 ; *ἅπασαν ἀ. ἐκτεῖναι* [D.]60.30, etc. **2.** *gymnastic exercise*, Hp.*Art.* 11, Pl.*Men.*94b, *Lg.*765c, etc. : generally, *exercise*, Id.*Grg.*456d sq., *R.*618b. **3.** of the mind, *agony, anguish, ἐν φόβῳ καὶ πολλῇ ἀ.* D.18.33, cf. Men.534.12 (pl.), Arist.*Pr.*869b6 ; *ἐν τοῖς τῆς ψυχῆς φόβοις, ἐλπίσιν, ἀγωνίαις* Id.*Spir.*483a5 ; cf. Chrysipp.*Stoic.*2.248, al., Phld.*Ir.*p.56 W. (pl.), Nic.Dam.*Vit.Caes.*9. **-ιάτης** [ᾱτ], *ου, ὁ, nervous person*, D.L.2.131. **-ιάω,** inf. *-ιᾶν* Pl.*Prt.*333e, part. *-ιῶν* Id.*Chrm.*162c, Isoc.4.91 : impf. *ἠγωνίων* Plb.1.10.6, etc. : fut. *-άσω* [ᾱ] Porph.*Abst.*1.54 : aor. *ἠγωνίᾱσα* Timocl.22.5, Phld.*Oec.*p.41 J., D.S. 14.60 : pf. *ἠγωνίᾱκα* (*ὑπερ-*) [D.]61.28 :—*contend eagerly, struggle*, D.21.61 ; *πρὸς ἀλλήλους* Isoc. l. c. **II.** *to be distressed* or *anxious, be in an agony, τετραχύνθαι τε καὶ ἀ.* Pl.*Prt.*333e ; *ἀγωνιῶντα καὶ τεθορυβημένον* Id.*Lys.*210e, cf. Arist.*Pr.*869b8, Men.*Her.*2, *PPetr.*3 p.151 ; *περί τινος* Arist.*Rh.*1367a15 : c. acc., Plb.1.20.6, al. ; *ἐπί τινι* Plu.*Caes.*46 ; *ἀ. μή..* Plb.3.9.2, etc. ; *ἀ. εἴ τι πείσεται* Nic.Dam.*Vit. Caes.*9. **-ίζομαι,** fut. *-ῐοῦμαι* E.*Heracl.*992, etc. (in pass. sense, v. infr. B) ; *-ίσομαι* only in late writers, as Porph.*Abst.*1.31 ; *-ισθήσομαι* Aristid.1.504J. : aor. *ἠγωνισάμην* E.*Supp.*427, etc. : pf. *ἠγώνισμαι* (in act. sense) Id.*Ion*939, Ar.*V.*993, Isoc.18.31 (Pass., v. infr. B) : aor. *ἠγωνίσθην* in pass. sense, infr. B : act. form *ἀγωνίσας* *IG*4. 429 (Sicyon) :—

**A.** *contend for a prize*, esp. in the public games, Hdt.2.160, al. ; *πρός τινα* Pl.*R.*579c, al. ; *περί τινος about* a thing, Hdt.8.26; *'Ολυμπίασιν* Pl.*Hp.Mi.*364a ; *περὶ πρωτείων* D.18.66 ; *ὑπὲρ τῆς ἐλευθερίας* Id.18.177 : freq. c. acc. cogn., *ἀ. στάδιον* Hdt.5.22 ; *τῶν ἀγώνων, οὓς περὶ τῆς ψυχῆς ἠγωνίζεσθε* D.18.262 ; *ἀγῶνα..τόνδ' ἠγωνίσω* thou *didst provoke* this contest, E.*Supp.*427, cf. *Ion*939 ; *ἠγωνίζου τι ἡμῖν;* Pl.*Ion*530a : metaph., *τὰ τῆς ψυχῆς 'Ολύμπια* Porph.*Abst.* l.c. **2.** *fight*, Hdt.1.76,82, al. ; *περὶ τῶν ἁπάντων* Th.6.16 ; *πρός τινα* Id.1.36, cf. 8.27 : c. acc. cogn., *μῶν τι κεδνὸν -ίζετο;* E.*Heracl.* 795 ; [*μάχην*] *-ίσαντο* E.*Supp.*637. **3.** *contend for the prize on the stage*, of the rhapsode, Hdt.5.67 ; of the playwright, Ar.*Ach.*140,419; of the actor, D.19.246, cf. 250, Arist.*Po.*1451a8 ; of the choragus, D. 21.66 : c. acc., *δράματα* *IG*12(7).226 (Amorgos) : generally, *contend for victory, καλῶς..ἠγώνισαι* Pl.*Smp.*194a, cf. *Mx.*235d ; *argue, ὅλῳ τῷ πράγματι* about the question as a whole, *Hp.Mi.*369c ; esp. *argue sophistically*, opp. *διαλέγομαι*, *Tht.*167e. **4.** of public speaking, X.*Mem.*3.7.4 ; *ἀ. πρὸς ἀπόδειξιν* Arist.*Fr.*133 (Theodect. ap.Rh.6.19W.). **II.** *contend in court*, as law term, Antipho 5.7 : c. acc. cogn., *ἀ. δίκην, γραφὴν fight* a cause *to the last*, Lys.3.20, D.23.100 ; *ἀ. ψευδομαρτυριῶν* (sc. *γραφήν*) Id.24.131 ; *ἀ. ἀγῶνα* And. 1.20, Lys.7.39 ; *ἀ. φόνον fight against* a charge of murder, E.*Andr.* 336 ; *αὐτοῖς ἀ. τοῖς πράγμασιν grapple with* the facts of the case, Arist. *Rh.*1404a5. **III.** generally, *struggle, exert oneself*, c. inf., Th. 4.87 ; *εὖ ἀ.* Lys.20.22, cf. Plu.*Phoc.*37.

**B.** Pass., *to be decided by contest, brought to issue*, mostly in pf., *πολλοὶ ἀγῶνες ἀγωνίδαται* Hdt.9.26 ; *τὰ ἠγωνισμένα points at issue*, E.*Supp.*465, D.24.145 : rarely in pres., *ὁ ἀγωνιζόμενος νόμος* the law *on trial*, D.24.28 ; or aor., *δεινὸς..κίνδυνος ὑπὲρ τῆς..ἐλευθερίας ἠγωνίσθη* Lys.2.34 ; *ἠγωνίσθη λαμπρῶς* (impers.) Plu.*Sert.*21 : fut. Med. in pass. sense, *ἀγωνιεῖται καὶ κριθήσεται τὸ πρᾶγμα shall be brought to issue* and determined, D.21.7. ⊛**-ικός,** *ή, όν*, v.l. for *ἀγωνιστικός*, D.H.*Rh.*6.6. **-ιος** (A), *ον, of* or *belonging to the contest, ἄεθλος ἀ. its* prize, Pi.*I.*5(4).7 ; *εὖχος* Id.*O.*10(11).63 ; *πούς* Simon.29 :— epith. of Hermes as *president of games*, Pi.*I.*1.60, cf. *IG*5(1).658 ; of Zeus as *decider of the contest*, S.*Tr.*26 :—*ἀ. θεοί*, in A.*Ag.*513, *Supp.*189,242, Pl.*Lg.*783a, either gods *in assembly*, or the gods *who presided over the great games* (Zeus, Poseidon, Apollo, and Hermes), = *ἀγοραῖοι θ.*, Eust.1335.58. **2.** *ἀγωνίῳ σχολᾷ* S. *Aj.*194, either *pause from battle*, or *strenuous rest* (oxymoron, cf. Sch.).

**ἀ-γώνιος** (B), *ον, without angle, ἀ. σχῆμα ὁ κύκλος* Arist.*Metaph.* 1020a35, cf. Thphr.*HP*3.14.2.

**ἀγών-ῐσις,** *ἡ, a contending for a prize*, Th.5.50. ⊛**-ισμα,** *τό, contest, conflict* : in pl., *deeds done in battle, brave deeds*, Hdt.8.76 ; *feats* of horsemanship, X.*Eq.Mag.*3.5 ; *ἀ. κατὰ τὰ ἆθλα* *CIG* 2741. **2.** in sg., *feat, achievement, ἀ. τινος a feather in* his *cap*, Th.8.12, cf. 17 : c. inf., Id.7.59,86 ; *ξυνέσεως ἀ. prize* of sagacity, Id.3.82 ; *ἀρᾶς ἀ. issue* of the curse, E.*Ph.*1355. **II.** *ἀ. ποιεῖσθαί τι* make it *an object to strive for*, Hdt.1.140 ; *οὐ μικρὸν τὸ ἀ. προστάττεις* Luc.*Im.*12. **III.** *that with which one contends, declamation, ἀ. ἐς τὸ παραχρῆμα* Th.1.22 ; of plays, Arist.*Po.*1451b 37. **IV.** in Law, *plea*, Antipho5.36, Lys.13.77. **-ισμός,** *ὁ, rivalry*, Th.7.70. **-ιστέον,** *one must contend*, X.*Cyr.*1.6.9, D.9.70. ⊛**-ιστήριος,** *α, ον*, also *ος, ον* (Poll.4.89), = *ἀγωνιστικός, κύβηλις* Anaxipp.6.6. **II.** ⊛**-ιστήριον,** *τό, place of assembly*, Aristid.1.108J. **-ιστής,** *οῦ, ὁ, combatant, ἀ. πικροί* E.*Ion*1257 :—esp. *competitor* in the games, Hdt.2.160, 5.22 ; generally, opp. *κριτής*, Isoc.2.13, Th.3.37, etc. :—as Adj., *ἀ. ἵπποι racehorses*, Plu.*Them.*25. **2.** *pleader, debater*, Pl.*Phdr.*269d, *Tht.* 164c. **3.** *actor*, Arist.*Pr.*918b28 ; *θεωροῖς εἴτ' ἀγωνισταῖς* Achae.3 ; *ἀ. τραγικῶν παθῶν* Timae.119. **II.** *master* in any art or science, Isoc.15.201,204 ; *ἄκρος ἀ.* [*τῆς γεωμετρίας*] [D.]61.44. **III.** c. gen., *one who struggles for* a thing, *champion, ἀ. τῆς ἀρετῆς, ἀληθείας*, Aeschin.3.180 (pl.), Plu.2.16c. ⊛**-ιστικός,** *ή, όν, fit for contest*, esp. in the games, *δύναμις ἀ.* Arist.*Rh.*1360b22 ; *ἀ. σώματος ἀρετή* ib.1361b21 ; *ἡ -κή* the art *of combat* or *contest*, Pl.*Sph.*225a sq. ; *τὸ ἀ.* ib.219c,e. **2.** *fit for contest* in speaking, *ἀ. λέξις debating* style, Arist.*Rh.*1413b9 ; *contentious, λόγοι* Id.*SE*165b11, al. ; *ἀ. διατριβαί* Id.*Top.*157a23 : Comp. *-ώτεραι, προτάσεις* Alex.Aphr.*in Top.*522.27. **3.** *masterly, striking, ἀ. προρρήματα* Hp.*Art.*58 ; *ἀ. τι ἔχουσα* having in it something *glorious*, ib.70 ; *πράξεις* Men.Rh. p.384S. **b.** Rhet., *striking, impressive*, Longin.23.1 ; *-κόν, τό*, Id.22.3 : Sup. *-ώτατος ἑαυτοῦ*, of Plato, Them.*Or.*34 p.448 D. **4.** Medic., '*heroic*', i.e. *copious, πόσεις* Philagr.ap.Orib.5.19. Adv. *-κῶς* Herod.ib.5.30.31, Gal.15.499 ; and so of '*heroic*' measures generally, *-κῶς θεραπεύειν* 18(1).61. **II.** of persons, *contentious, eager for applause*, Pl.*Men.*75c, Phld.*Oec.*p.65 J. **III.** Adv. *-κῶς contentiously*, Arist.*Top.*164b15 ; *ἀ. ἔχειν* to be *disposed to fight*, Plu. *Sull.*16 : Comp., *ἐπιστολὰς -ώτερον τοῦ δέοντος ἐπέστελλε* Philostr. *VS*2.33.3. **2.** *dramatically, ᾄδειν* Arist.*Pr.*918b21 ; opp. *καταστατικῶς*, Aps.p.266 H.

⊛**ἀγωνο-δίκης,** *ου, ὁ, judge of the contest*, Hsch. ⊛**-θεσία,** *ἡ, office of ἀγωνοθέτης, direction* or *exhibition of games*, *IG*2.379 (iii B. C.), Nic.Dam.*Vit.Caes.*9, Plu.*Ages.*21, etc. : pl., prob. in Phld.*Rh.*2. 27S. ⊛**-θετέω,** *exhibit games*, *GDI*1842 (Delph.), etc. ; *ἀ. Πύθια, 'Ολύμπια* *AP*12.255 (Strat.) ; *μίμοις ἀ.* Plu.2.621c : metaph., Th.3. 38. **2.** c. acc., *ἀ. τινάς embroil* them, Plb.9.34.3 ; *ἀ. στάσιν, πόλεμον*, etc., *stir up* faction, war, etc., Plu.*Cat.Mi.*45, J.*AJ*17.3.1. **II.** *preside at the games*, D.9.32, cf. Pl.*Smp.*184a. **-θετήρ,** *ῆρος, ὁ*, = sq., *IG*14.502 (Catana). ⊛**-θέτης,** *ου, ὁ, judge of the contests, president of the games*, or (later) *exhibitor of games*, Hdt.6.127, And.4.26, Decr. ap.D.18.84, *IG*2.314 (iii B. C.), etc. **2.** generally, *judge*, X.*An.* 3.1.21 ; *πολιτικῆς ἀρετῆς* Aeschin.3.180. ⊛**-θετικός,** *ή, όν, of* or *for the direction of the games, χρήματα* *CIG*2742 (Aphrodisias), *IG*5(1). 550 (Sparta) :—of a person, *CIG*6824 (Constantinople). **-θέτις,** *ιδος*, fem. of *ἀγωνοθέτης*, *IGRom.*4.1225 (Thyatira), 1238. **-θήκη,** *ἡ*, = *ἀγωνοθεσία*, S.*Fr.*975, criticized as irreg. by Poll.3.141. **-λογία,** *ἡ*, (*λέγω*) *laborious discussion*, Gal.1.79.

**ἄ-γωνος,** *ον*, = *ἀγώνιος, without angle*, Thphr.*HP*7.6.2 (Comp.).

**ἄγωνος,** *ὁ*, Aeol. and Elean for *ἀγών*, q. v.

**ἀγωνότριψ,** *ιβος, ὁ, frequenting declamations*, Phld.*Rh.*2.85 S.

**ἀδαγμός,** *ὁ*, v. sub *ὀδαγμός* ; cf. *ἀδακτῶ*.

**ἄδᾳδος,** *ον*, (*δαΐς, δᾷς*) *without resin*, Thphr.*HP*5.1.5.

**ἀδᾳδούχητος,** *ον*, (*δᾳδουχέω*) *not lighted by torches* : of marriage, *clandestine*, Apion ap.Eust.622.42.

**ἀδᾰ-ημονία,** Ep. *-ίη, ἡ, ignorance, unskilfulness in* doing, c. inf., Od.24.244 (v.l. **ἀδαημοσύνη**). **-ήμων,** *ον, unknowing, ignorant*, c. gen., *μάχης ἀδαήμονι φωτί* Il.5.634 ; *κακῶν ἀδαήμονες* Od.12.208 ; *ἀ. τῶν ἱρῶν τῶν ἐν 'Ελευσῖνι* Hdt.8.65, cf. Matro*Parod.Fr.*6, Hierocl.*in CA*4 p.425 M. : abs., Ps.-Phoc.86. **-ής,** *ές*, (**δάω δαῆναι*) = foreg., c. gen. pers., Hdt.9.46 : c. gen. rei, *τῆς θυσίης, τῶν χρησμῶν*, Id.2.49, 5.90, cf. X.*Cyr.*1.6.43 ; *βουνομίας -έστερος* Pi.*Pae.*4.27 ; *ὕπν' ὀδύνας ἀ.* S.*Ph.*827 (lyr.) : c. inf., *unknowing how to.., ἀ. δ' ἔχειν μυρίον ἄχθος* (sc. *κήρ*) ib.1167 (lyr.) ; *οὐκ ἀ.* *APl.*4.84 : abs., *ἀ. κόρη*, of a virgin, Paus.Dam.p.160D. **II.** *dark*, Parm.8.59. **-ητος,** *ον, unknown*, Hes.*Th.*655, *Hymn.Is.*157.

⊛**ἀδαίδαλτος,** *ον, not carved, plain*, Orph.*A.*403.

⊛**ἀδαίετος,** *ον*, (*δαίω* B) *undivided*, A.R.3.1033.

**ἀδάϊκτος,** *ον, undestroyed*, Q.S.1.196, 11.165.

**ἀδάϊος,** *ον*, Dor. for *ἀδήϊος*, Hsch.

**ἀδαῖος,** *ον*, (*ἄδην*) *producing surfeit*, Sophr.137.

**ἄδαιτος,** *ον*, (*δαίνυμαι*) *of which none might eat, θυσία* A.*Ag.*151.

⊛**ἀδαίτρευτος,** *ον, for which nothing has been slain, δεῖπνον* Nonn. *D.*17.51, 40.419.

**ἄδαιτρος,** *ον*, (*δαίω* B) *undivided*, Hsch.

**ἄδακρ-ῡς,** *υ*, gen. *υος, tearless, αἰών* Pi.*O.*2.66, E.*Alc.*1047, Clearch. 8 ; *ὑπὸ τροφῷ ἄ..* of a healthy child, Theoc.24.31. **II.** = *ἀδάκρυτος* II, E.*Med.*861 (lyr.) : *costing no tears, πόλεμος* D.S.15.72 ; *μάχη* Plu.*Ages.*33. **-ῡτί,** Adv. *tearlessly, without tears*, Isoc.14.47, Ph.

2.67, Plu.*Caes.*7, etc. ❄**-ῦτος,** ον, *without tears*: I. Act., *tearless*, ἀ. καὶ ἀπήμων Il.1.415, cf. Od.24.61; ἀδακρύτῳ ἔχεν ὄσσε 4.186; ἀστένακτος κἀ. S.*Tr.*1200; εὐνάζειν ἀ. βλεφάρων πόθον *so that they weep not*, ib.106 (lyr.):— Medic., ἀ. ὀφθαλμός *abnormally dry*, Aët. 7.91. 2. c. gen., *not weeping for*, τινός *Epigr.Gr.*241 a 13. II. Pass., *unwept*, S.*Ant.*881 (lyr.). 2. *costing no tears*, τρόπαια Plu. *Tim.*37.

**ἀδακτῶ·** κνήθομαι, Hsch.

**ἀδαλές·** ὑγιές, Hsch. [ᾰ, if from δαλέομαι, Dor. for δηλ-.]

**ἀδαμάντῐνος,** η, ον, *adamantine, of steel*, Pi.*P.*4.224, A.*Pr.*6,64, Aeschin.3.84; ἀ. κερκίδες, of the Μοῖραι, *Lyr.Adesp.*ap.Stob.1.5.11; αἱμασιή Eus.Myd.*Fr.*63. 2. metaph., *hard as adamant*, οὐδεὶς ἂν γένοιτο..οὕτως ἀ., ὃς ἄν.. Pl.*R.*360b; σιδηροῖς καὶ ἀ. λόγοις Id.*Grg.* 509a; δεσμοί Metrod.*Herc.*831.12; οὐκ ἀ. ἐστίν, of a girl, Theoc.3.39. Adv. -νως Pl.*R.*618e.

❄**ἀδᾰμαντό-δετος,** ον, *iron-bound*, λῦμαι A.*Pr.*148,426 (lyr.). **-πέδῐλος,** ον, *on a base of adamant*, κίονες Pi.*Fr.*88.5.

**ἀδάμ-ας,** αντος, ὁ, (δαμάω):—first in Hes. (in Hom. only as pr. n.), properly, *unconquerable*: I. Subst., *adamant*, i. e. the hardest metal, prob. *steel*, χλωρός, πολιός, Hes.*Sc.*231, *Th.*161: metaph., ἀδάμαντος ἔχον κρατερόφρονα θυμόν *Op.*147; of anything *fixed, unalterable*, ἔπος ἐρέω ἀδάμαντι πελάσσας Orac.ap.Hdt.7.141; ἀδάμαντος δῆσεν ἅλοις fixed them with nails *of adamant*, i. e. inevitably, Pi.*P.* 4.71, cf. *APl.*4.167 (Antip. Sid.); τὸν ἐν Ἅιδα κινήσαις ἀδάμαντα Theoc.2.34. 2. *diamond*, Thphr.*Lap.*19, Paus.8.18.6, *Peripl. M.Rubr.*56; prob. so meant in Pl.*Ti.*59b, *Plt.*303e, cf. Plin.*NH*37. 55. 3. metaph., ὁ πόνος ἀδάμαντος, of love, Alex.245.13. II. Adj., *unbreakable*, ἀνακτίτης Orph.*L.*192. **-αστί,** Adv. *unconquerably*, Suid. ❄**-αστος,** ον, (δαμάω) *unsubdued, inflexible*, of Hades, Il.9.158, cf. Phld.*D.*1.18: later in the proper sense, *untamed, unbroken*, πῶλος X.*Eq.*1.1, cf. Corn.*ND*20; ἀ. πᾶσιν Tim09.1. ❄**-ᾰτος,** ον, = ἀδάμαστος, *unconquered*, A.*Ch.*54, *Th.*233, S.*OT*205, etc.: of females, *unwedded*, S.*Aj.*450; *untamed*, μόσχος ἀ. πέσημα δίκε E. *Ph.*640.—Trag. word, always in lyr. (exc. S.*Aj.* l. c.); restored by Elmsl. for ἀδάμαντος or -αστος of codd. **-άτωρ,** ἡ, epith. of Hecate, *PMag.Par.*1.2717. **-νεῖς** (cod. -αῖς)· ἀκολαστaίνεις (cod. -αις), Hsch. **-νής,** ές, and **-νος,** ον, = ἀδάμαστος, Id. **-ος,** ον, = ἀδάμαστος, Ion Lyr.9.

**ἄδᾱν,** Aeol. for ἅδην, Alcm.76.

**ἀδάνειστος,** ον, *not pledged as security*, ἄλλου δανείου *BGU*741 (ii A. D.).

**ἀδαξάω,** or -έω, ἀδαξῆσαι, ἀδάξομαι, v. sub ὀδάξω.

**ἀδάπᾰνος,** ον, *without expense, costing nothing*, γλυκέα κἀδάπανα Ar.*Pax* 593, cf. Teles p.7.8 H., D.S.10*Fr.*12. Adv. ἀδαπάνως, τέρψαι φρένα E.*Or.*1176, cf. Phld.*Rh.*2.133 S. (prob.). II. of persons, *not spending*, ἀ. χρημάτων εἰς τὸ δέον Arist.*VV*1251$^b$7; ἀ. καταστῆσαι τὸ κοινόν *Michel* 1007.33 (Teos), cf. *Inscr.Prien.*111.133 (i B. C.).

**ἄδαπτον·** γυμνόν. ἄδερμον, Hsch.

**ἀδάρκη,** ἡ, or **ἀδάρκης,** ὁ, *salt efflorescence on the herbage of marshes*, Dsc.5.119, Democr.ap.Gal.13.105: **ἄδαρκος,** ὁ, Gal.12.370; Dim. **ἀδάρκιον,** τό, ibid.

**ἄδαρτος,** ον, (δέρω) *unflayed*: *not cudgelled*, Hsch., *Gloss.*

**ἄδασμος,** ον, *tribute-free*, A.*Fr.*63.

❄**ἄδαστος,** ον, (δάσασθαι) *undivided*, S.*Aj.*54; also **ἄδατος,** Hsch.

**ἀδαυῶς·** ἐγρηγόρως, Hsch.

**ἀδαχέω,** *scratch*, Ar.*Fr.*410.

❄**ἄδδαυον** (i. e. ἄζαυον)· ξηρόν (Lacon.), Hsch.

**ἄδδιξ,** ἴχος, ἡ, *measure of four* χοίνικες, Ar.*Fr.*709.

**ἄδε,** v. sub ἁνδάνω.

❄**ἀδεαλτόω** (sic), (ἀ-, δάλτος, = δέλτος) *erase, deface*, στάλαν *Michel* 1334 (Elis).

❄**ἀδεής** (A), Ep. **ἀδειής,** ές: voc. ἀδεές [ᾰ, i. e. ἀδϝεές]:—*fearless*, εἴ περ ἀδειής τ' ἐστί, of Hector, Il.7.117; κύον ἀδεές 8.423, Od.19. 91: c. gen., ἀ. θανάτου Pl.*R.*386b, cf. Arist.*EN*1115$^a$33; ἐν θαλάττῃ καὶ ἐν νόσοις ἀ. ὁ ἀνδρεῖος 1115$^b$1. 2. *without anxiety, secure*, τὸ ἀ. *security*, Th.3.37; ἀ. δέος δεδιέναι to fear *where no fear is*, Pl. *Smp.*198a. II. *causing no fear, not formidable*, πρὸς ἐχθρούς Th.1.36 (Comp.); οὐ γὰρ ἀδεὲς τοῦθ' ὑπολαμβάνω D.16.22. III. most common in Adv. ἀδεῶς *without fear* or *scruple, confidently*, Hdt.3.65, 9.109; ἀ. τινὰ ὠφελοῦμεν Th.2.40; ἀ. περί τινος ἀποφαίνεσθαι Pl.*La.*186d; ἀ. πολιτεύεσθαι Lys.24.25; ἀ. *bibit* Cic.*Att.*13. 52: Comp. -έστερον Th.4.92. 2. *with impunity*, μηνύειν Id.6. 27.

**ἀδε-ής** (B), ές, (δέομαι) *not in want*, τινός Max.Tyr.5.1, al. ❄**-ητος,** ον, (δέομαι) *not wanting a thing*, Antipho Soph. 10. II. *inexorable*, Ptol.*Tetr.*159; cf. ἀδεύητος.

**ἄδεια** (A), ἡ, (ἀδεής A) *freedom from fear*, Th.7.29; esp. *safe conduct, amnesty, indemnity*, ἀδείην διδόναι Hdt.2.121.ζ'; τοῖς ἄλλοις ἄ. ἐδώκατε οἰκεῖν τὴν σφετέραν Antipho 5.77; ἄ. εἶναι Hdt.8.120; ἐν ἀ. οὐ ποιεῖσθαι τὸ λέγειν to hold it not *safe*, Id.9.42; τὸ σῶμά τινος εἰς ἄ. καθιστάναι Lys.2.15; τῶν σωμάτων ἄ. ποιεῖν Th.3.58; πολλὴν ἄ. αὐτοῖς ἐψηφισμένοι ἔσεσθε ποιεῖν ὅτι ἂν βούλωνται Lys.22. 19; ἄ. τινι παρασκευάσαι Id.16.13, cf. D.13.17; παρέχειν Id.21.210; opp. ἄ. εὑρίσκεσθαι And.1.34, D.24.47; λαμβάνειν Id.18.286; ἀδείας τυγχάνειν 5.6; τοῦ μὴ πάσχειν ἄδειαν ἤγετε 19.149; μετὰ πάσης ἀδείας 18.305; μετ' ἀ. 22.25:—also γῆς ἄ. a *secure* dwelling-place, S.*OC*447:—*licence* to bring forward proposals or make charges, D.24.45, Plu.*Per.*31, etc. 2. Lit. Crit., *licence*, ἄ. ποιητική A.D. *Pron.*38.3, al., Him.*Or.*1.1; κωμική A.D.*Pron.*69.19.

**ἄδεια** (B), ἡ, (δέ μοι) *abundance, plenty*, Teles p.44.1 H.; κρ[...] Sch.Ar.*Nu.*386.

❄**Ἀδειγάνες,** οἱ, *name of certain Seleucian magistrates* in Plb.5. 10; prob. an Eastern word.

**ἀδειγμάτιστος,** ον, *without a sample*, or perh. *without an offic[ial] stamp*, *PHib.*98.17 (iii B. C.), *PSI*4.358.5 (iii B. C.).

**ἀδειής,** ές, Ep. for ἀδεής (A).

❄**ἄδεικτος,** ον, *not shown, invisible*, of God, Ph.1.197,618.

**ἄδειλος,** ον, *fearless*, Ps.-Callisth.1.6.

**ἀδείμαντος,** ον, (δειμαίνω) *fearless, dauntless*, Pi.*N.*10.17, etc[.]; ἦλθ' ἀ. ποδί E.*Rh.*697: c. gen., ἐμαυτῆς ἀ. *without fear for mysel[f]* A.*Pers.*162. Adv. -τως Id.*Ch.*771. 2. *where no fear is*, οἰκ[...] Luc.*Philops.*31.

**ἄδειμος,** ον, (δεῖμα) *fearless*, Hsch., Suid.

**ἀδεῖν,** Aeol. **ἀδ-,** v. sub ἁνδάνω.

**ἄδειος·** ἀκάθαρτος (Cypr.), Hsch.

**ἄδειπνος,** ον, *without the evening meal, supperless*, Hp.*Aph.*5.41, X.*An.*4.5.21, etc.

**ἀδεισία,** ἡ, = ἀφοβία, *EM*16.56.

**ἀδεισι-βόας,** ὁ, *not fearing the battle-cry*, B.5.155, 10.61. **-δαιμονία,** ἡ, *freedom from superstition*, Hp.*Decent.*5. **-δαίμων,** ον, *without superstition*, Adv. -μόνως D.S.38.7: Comp. -έστερον Sor.1. 80. **-θεος,** ον, *impious*, λογισμοί Orac.ap.Jul.*Ep.*88; ἄνδρες Procl.*H.*3.12.

**ἀδέκαστος,** ον, (δεκάζω) *unbribed, impartial*, Arist.*EN*1109$^b$8, Plu. *Cim.*10, Ael.*NA*17.16; διάνοια D.H.*Th.*34, etc. Adv. -τως, ἔχουσα φιλοσοφία Philostr.*VA*8.7.3, cf. Gal.11.417, Max.Tyr.6.6: Comp. -ότερον Luc.*Hist.Conscr.*47.

**ἀδεκάτευτος,** ον, *tithe-free*, Ar.*Eq.*301, *OGI*229.101 (Smyrna, iii B. C.).

**ἄδεκτος,** ον, (δέχομαι) *not receptive*, Thphr.*Metaph.*9: c. gen., *not capable of*, τῆς εὐδαιμονίας Hippod.ap.Stob.4.39.26; τοῦ μοιχεύειν Phld. *D.*3*Fr.*78; μεταβολῆς Plu.2.1025c, cf. Plot.3.6.13, Herm.ap.Stob. 3.11.31, Procl.*in Prm.*p.842 S., etc. II. Pass., *incomprehensible*, dub. l. in Ph.1.486. 2. *unacceptable*, δῶρα Zos.1.58.

**ἀδέλεσχος,** v. ἀδόλ-.

**ἀδελφεά, -εή, ἀδελφεός, -ειός,** v. sub ἀδελφή, ἀδελφός.

**ἀδελφεοκτόνος,** ον, Ion. for ἀδελφοκτόνος.

❄**ἀδελφ-ή,** ἡ, fem. of ἀδελφός, *sister*, Trag., E.*Fr.*866, etc.; ὁμοπατρία ἀ. Men.*Grg.*12, cf. *PTeb.*320.5 (ii A. D.): Ion. -εή, Hdt.2. 56, al.; Ep. -ειή, Q.S.1.30; Dor. -εά, Pi.*N.*7.4, and in lyr. passages of Trag., S.*OT*160, *OC*535. 2. *kinswoman*, Lxx *Jb.*42.11. 3. term of endearment, *Ca.*4.9, *To.*5.21; applied to a wife, *POxy.*744.1 (i B. C.), etc.:—as a title, Βερενίκη ἡ ἀ. καὶ γυνὴ αὐτοῦ (of a cousin) *OGI*60.3 (iii B. C.):—*sister* (as a fellow Christian), *Ep.Rom.*16.1, etc. **-ιδέος,** contr. -οῦς, ὁ, *nephew*, Alcm.56A, etc.; usu. *brother's son*, Hdt.1.65, 6.94, al., Th.2.101, etc.; also, *sister's son*, Hdt.4.147, Str.10.5.6, etc.:—also ❄**-ιδός,** *beloved one*, Lxx *Ca.*2.3, al. **-ιδῆ,** ἡ, Att. contr. for ἀδελφιδέη, *a brother's* or *sister's daughter, a niece*, Ar.*Nu.*47, Lys.3.6, Hp.*Epid.*6.2.19, etc. **-ιδῆς,** ὁ, and **-ίδισσα** (sic), ἡ, = foreg., *IGRom.*4.621 (Temenothyrae). **-ίδιον,** τό, Dim. of ἀδελφός, Ar.*Ra.*60, *PPar.*39.6 (ii B. C.). **-ίζω,** *adopt as a brother, call brother*, Hecat.8 J., Apolloph.4, Isoc.19.30:—Pass., *to be very like*, Hp.*Acut.*9, etc.; τινι Id.*Fract.*31, *Art.*45. **-ικός,** ή, όν, *brotherly* or *sisterly*, φιλία Arist.*EN*1161$^a$6; ἔρις Just.*Nov.*18.7; ἡ ὑμετέρα ἀ. παίδευσις *POxy.*1165.2 (vi A. D.). Adv. -κῶς Lxx 4*Ma.* 13.9, Ps.-Callisth.3.20. **-ιξις,** ἡ, *brotherhood, close connexion*, Hp. *Art.*57. ❄**-ιον,** τό, Dim. of ἀδελφός, Keil-Premerstein *Zweiter Bericht* 215 (Lydia, ii A. D.), *POxy.*1300.4 (v A. D.). ❄**-ίς,** ἡ, kind of date, Plin.*HN*13.45, *Gloss.* **-οδότης,** ου, ὁ, *bestowing brothers*, ἀστήρ Vett.Val.123.21. **-όθεν,** *germanitus*, *Gloss.*

**ἀδελφο-κτόνος,** ον, *murdering a brother* or *sister*, Hdt.3.65 (in Ion. form ἀδελφεοκτ-), Nic.Dam.p.142 D., Plu.2.256f, Ph.1.148. **-κτονέω,** *to be murderer of a brother* or *sister*, J.*BJ*2.11.4, Vett.Val.74. 28. **-κτονία,** ἡ, *murder of a brother* or *sister*, J.*BJ*1.31.2, Ph. 1.210, al. **-μιξία,** ἡ, *marriage of brother and sister*, Tz.*H.*1. 590. ❄**-παις,** παιδος, ὁ, ἡ, *brother's* or *sister's child*, D.H.4.64 (Cod. Vat.), cf. Just.*Nov.*127.1. **-ποιός,** όν, *adopting as a brother*, *EM* 255.1. **-πρεπῶς,** Adv. *as befits a brother*, Lxx 4*Ma.*10.12.

❄**ἀδελφός** [ᾰ], (ἀ- copul., δελφύς, Arist.*HA*510$^b$13; cf. ἀγάστωρ) properly, *son of the same mother*: I. as Subst., **ἀδελφός,** ὁ, voc. ἄδελφε; Ep., Ion., and Lyr. ἀδελφεός (gen. -ειοῦ in Hom. is for -εόο), Cret. ἀδελπιός, ἀδευπιός, *Leg.Gort.*2.21, *Mon.Ant.*18.319:—*brother*, Hom., etc.; ἀδελφοί *brother and sister*, E.*El.*536; so of the Ptolemies, θεοὶ ἀδελφοί Herod.1.30, *OGI*50.2 (iii B. C.), etc.; ἀπ' ἀμφοτέρων ἀδελφεός Hdt.7.97: prov., χαλεποὶ πόλεμοι ἀδελφῶν E.*Fr.*975: metaph., ἀ. γέγονα σειρήνων Lxx *Jb.*30.29. 2. *kinsman*, ib.*Ge.*13.8, al.; *tribesman*, *Ex.*2.11, al. 3. *colleague, associate*, *PTeb.*1.12, *IG*12 (9).906.19 (Chalcis); *member of a college*, ib.14.956. 4. term of address, used by kings, *OGI*138.3 (Philae), J.*AJ*13.2.2, etc.; generally, Lxx *Ju.*7.30; esp. in letters, *PPar.*48 (ii B. C.), etc.:—as a term of affection, applicable by wife to husband, Lxx *To.*10.12, *PLond.*1.42.1 (ii B. C.), etc. 5. *brother* (as a fellow Christian), *Ev.Matt.*12.50, *Act.Ap.*9.30, al.; of other religious communities, e. g. Serapeum, *PPar.*42.1 (ii B. C.), cf. *PTaur.*1.1.20. 6. metaph., of things, *fellow*, ἀνὴρ τῷ ἀ. προσκολληθήσεται, of Leviathan's scales, Lxx *Jb.*41.8. II. Adj., ἀδελφός, ή, όν, *brotherly* or *sisterly*, A.*Th.* 811, etc.; φύσιν ἀ. ἔχοντες, of Hephaistos and Athena, Pl.*Criti.* 109c. 2. generally, of anything double, *twin, in pairs*, X.*Mem.*

.19 :—also, *akin, cognate,* μαθήματα Archyt.1 ; ἀ. νόμοις Pl.*Lg.* ;a : mostly c. gen., ἀδελφὰ τῶνδε S.*Ant.*192 ; ἡ δὲ μωρία μάλιστ' τῆς πονηρίας ἔφυ Id.*Fr.*925 ; freq. in Pl., *Phd.*108b, *Cra.*418e, al., Hyp.*Epit.*35 : c. dat., ἀδελφὰ τούτοισι S.*OC*1262, cf. Pl.*Smp.*210b.

**ἀδελφότης**, ητος, ἡ, *brotherhood*, Lxx 1*Ma.*12.10, Vett.Val.2.28, Chr.38.15 : metaph., of men and animals, Iamb.*VP*24.108. II. *brotherhood*, 1*Ep.Pet.*2.17, 5.9. III. as form of address, ἡ σὴ *PGrenf.*2.89, *PAmh.*2.156 ; χάριν ἀπονέμομεν τῇ ἀ. τοῦ Καίσαρος en.Prot.p.16 D.

**ἀδέμνιος**, ον, *unwedded to* any one, τινός Opp.*C.*3.358.

**ἄδενδρος**, ον, *without trees*, Plb.3.55.9, D.H.1.37 :—poet. **ἀδέν-δρεος**, Opp.*C.*4.337.

**ἀδενοειδής**, ές, (ἀδήν) *glandular*, Herophil.ap.Gal.*UP*14.11 :—**ἀδενώδη** φύματα Plu.2.664f, cf. Gal.*UP*14.13, Sor.1.12.

**ἀδέξιος**, ον, *left-handed, awkward*, Arr.*Epict.*4.2.2, Luc.*Merc.Cond.* 4, *Sat.*4 : c. inf., Steph. *in Rh.*283.13.

**ἀδερκ-ής**, ές, *unseen, invisible*, *AP*11.372 (Agath.). **-τος**, ον, (δέρκομαι) *not seeing*, ἀδέρκτων ὀμμάτων τητώμενος *so that they see not*, S.*OC*1200. Adv. -τως *without looking*, ib.130.

**ἀδέρματος**, ον, *without skin*, Sch.Pi.*P.*4.398, cf. S.*Fr.*336. **ἄδερ-μος**, ον, = foreg., Hsch. s.v. ἄδαπτον.

**ἀδέσμ-ευτος**, ον, = sq., Sch.E.*Hec.*550. **-ιος**, ον, = sq., Nonn.*D.* 15.138. **-ος**, ον, *unfettered, unbound*, ἄ. φυλακή, Lat. *libera custodia*, '*parole*', Th.3.34, D.H.1.83, etc. ; βαλλάντια ἄ. *open* purses, Plu.2.503c ; δεσμὸν ἄδεσμον φυλλάδος, of suppliant's wreath, E. *Supp.*32 ; *unbandaged*, Gal.18(2).505.

⊛**ἀδέσποτος**, ον, *without master* or *owner*, ἀρετὴ ἀ. Pl.*R.*617e ; τὸ παρ' ἡμᾶς ἀ. Epicur.*Ep.*3p.65U. : of property, *POxy.*1188.15 (13 A.D.), cf. Str.17.1.12 : of freedmen, Myro Hist.2 ; οἰκήσεις Arist.*EN*1161ᵃ7, cf. E.*Hyps.Fr.*1.11 ; ἀ. καὶ αὐτοκρατεῖς, of the gods, Plu.2.426c ; ἀ. βίος Sallust.21. II. of rumours or writings, *anonymous*, Cic. *Fam.*15.17.3, D.H.11.50, Plu.*Cic.*15, etc. Adv. -τως J.*Ap.*1.16, Sch.Ar.*Ra.*1400. III. *ungovernable*, λύπη Democr.290.

**ἄδετος**, ον, (δέω) *unbound, loose*, Hp.*Art.*44 ; *not clamped together*, λίθοι *IG*7.3074 (Lebad.). 2. *free*, D.24.169, Aristaenet.1.20. 3. *unshod*, Philostr.*Ep.*37.

**ἀδετοχίτων**, gloss on ἀμιτροχίτων, *EM*83.53.

**ἀδεύητος**, ον, Ep. form of ἀδέητος, Hsch. : **ἀδεύητον**· χαλεπόν, ἢ οὗ οὐκ ἄν τις ἔτι δεηθείη, *EM*17.4.

**ἀδευκής**, ές, Hom. only in Od., ὀλέθρῳ ἀδευκεῖ 4.489 ; ἀδευκέα πότμον 10.245 ; φῆμιν ἀδευκέα 6.273, cf. A.R.2.267, etc. (Expl. by Scholl. either (cf. δεῦκος, q. v.) *not sweet*, i. e. *bitter, cruel*, or (cf. δεύκει) *unexpected*, cf. Apollon. *Lex.*, Hsch. :—ἀ. φωνή expl. as *not imitative*, opp. πολυδευκής, Ael.*NA*5.38.)

⊛**ἀδέψητος**, ον, (δεψέω) *untanned*, βοέη Od.20.2,142, cf. A.R.3.206, *AP*5.298 (Leon.).

**ἀδέω** [ᾰ], *to be sated with*, c. dat., only in aor. and pf., μὴ ξεῖνος .. δείπνῳ ἀδήσειε lest he *should be sated with* the repast, *feel loathing at* it, Od.1.134 (v.l. ἀηδήσειε) ; καμάτῳ ἀδηκότες ἠδὲ καὶ ὕπνῳ *sated with* toil and sleep, Il.10.98, cf. 312,399,471, Od.12.281 ; cf. ἄδην.

**ἀδῆ**· οὐρανός (Maced.), Hsch.

**ἀδήϊος**, contr. **ἀδῇος**, Dor. **ἀδάϊος**, ον, *unmolested, unravaged*, ἀδῇον .. σπαρτῶν ἀπ' ἀνδρῶν S.*OC*1533 : of persons, *not harmed*, A.R. 4.647.

**ἄδηκε**, v. ἀνδάνω.

**ἄδηκτος**, ον, (δάκνω) *not gnawed* or *worm-eaten*, Hes.*Op.*420 (Sup.) ; *not bitten*, Dsc.2.60, al. 2. metaph., *unmolested*, Phld. *D.*3*Fr.*81, Plu.2.864c. Adv. -τως ib.448a. 3. *unaffected, untouched*, by love, anger, etc., in Adv. -τως, Phld.*Mort.*34, Plu.*Pomp.* 2, M.Ant.11.18, Eun.*VS*p.495 B. II. Act., *not biting* or *pungent*, Hp.*Mul.*1.11, Dsc.1.30 : Comp. -ότερος *less stimulating*, Aret. *CA*1.10.

**ἀδηλ-έω**, (ἄδηλος) *to be in the dark about* a thing, *understand not*, σκοπὸς προσήκεις ὧν ἀδηλοῦμεν φράσαι S.*OC*35 :—Pass., *to be obscure*, Ph.2.42, al., S.E.*M.*11.233, cf. 7.393 ; *fail to appear*, ἐπιμήνια -εύμενα Hp.*Mul.*1.2. **-ητος**, ον, (δηλέομαι) *unhurt*, A.R.2.709 ; *invulnerable*, Nonn.*D.*47.617. II. Act., *not hurting*, δεσμός ib.41. 199. **-ία**, ἡ, = ἀδηλότης, A.D.*Pron.*25.18, v.l. in Corn.*ND*13 ; ἀ. τοῦ μέλλοντος Iamb.*Myst.*10.4, cf. *AP*10.96 (Pall.). **-οποιέω**, *make unseen*, Sm.*Jb.*9.5, Ps.-Alex.Aphr. *in SE*124.3. **-οποιός**, όν, *making unseen*, Sch.Il.2.455 ; φάρμακα Sch.E.*Med.*1201. ⊛**-ος**, ον, *unseen, invisible*, of a fish, ποιεῖν ἑαυτὸν ἄ. Arist.*HA*620ᵇ31 ; ἀ. χιτών, of the hyaloid membrane of the eye, [Gal.]14.712 ; *unknown, obscure*, Hes.*Op.*6 ; τὸν ἄ. ἄνδρα .. ἰχνεύειν S.*OT*475 ; ἐὰν δὲ .. ἄ. ὁ κτείνας ᾖ Pl.*Lg.*874a ; of troops, ἄ. τοῖς πολεμίοις X.*Cyr.*6.3.13 ; εἰς τὸ ἄ. ἀποκρύπτειν Id.*Eq.Mag.*5.7. II. mostly of things, ἄ. θάνατοι death *by an unknown hand*, S.*OT*496 ; ἄ. ἔχθρα *secret* enmity, Th. 8.108 ; ῥεῖ πᾶν ἄδηλον melts all *to nothing*, S.*Tr.*698 ; *inscrutable*, E.*Or.*1318. b. neut., ἄδηλόν [ἐστι] εἰ .. *it is uncertain whether* .., Pl.*Phdr.*232e, al. ; ἄ. μή .. Id.*Phd.*91d : abs., ἄ. ὂν Th.1.2 ; ἐν ἀδήλῳ εἶναι Antipho5.6 ; ἐν ἀδηλοτέρῳ εἶναι X.*HG*7.5.8 ; ἐξ ἀδήλου ἔρχεται [σελήνη] S.*Fr.*871.5 ; also ἄ. agreeing with the subject (like δίκαιός εἰμι), παῖδες ἄ. ὁποτέρων, = ἄδηλον ὁποτέρων παῖδές εἰσιν, Lys. 1.33 ; ἀδήλοις .. πῶς ἀποβήσεται, = ἃ ἄ. ἐστι πῶς ἀ., Arist.*EN*1112ᵇ9, cf. X.*Mem.*1.1.6. 2. *not evident to sense*, ὄψις τῶν ἀ. τὰ φαινόμενα Anaxag.21a, cf. Epicur.*Ep.*1p.6 U. ; opp. φανερόν, Phld.*Sign.*6, al. ; opp. ἐναργές, ib.14, cf. Diog.Oen.8. 3. *unintelligible*, φωνή 1*Ep. Cor.*14.8. 4. *unproved*, *Stoic.*2.89. III. Adv. -λως *secretly*, Th.1.92, etc. : Sup. -ότατα Id.7.50. **-ότης**, ητος, ἡ, *uncertainty*, Protag.4, Plb.5.2.3, Ph.1.277, Corn.*ND*13, etc. **-όφλεβος**, ον, *with inconspicuous veins*, Arist.*GA*727ᵃ24, *PA*667ᵃ31. ⊛**-όω**, *render invisible* :—Pass., *to be obliterated*, *Tab.Heracl.*1.57.

⊛**ἄδημα**, τό, = ψήφισμα, Hsch. (cod. ἀδήμας).

**ἀδημιούργητος**, ον, *not fashioned*, ἀ. πρὸς ἀνάστασιν *not made for* getting up again, of a fallen elephant, D.S.3.27.

**ἀδημοκράτητος**, ον, *not democratic*, D.C.43.45.

⊛**ἀδημονέω**, *to be sorely troubled* or *dismayed*, *be in anguish*, Hp.*Virg.* 1 ; ἀδημονῶν τε καὶ ἀπορῶν Pl.*Tht.*175d, cf. D.19.197 ; ἀδημονῆσαι τὰς ψυχάς X.*HG*4.4.3 : c. dat. rei, ἀδημονεῖ τῇ ἀτοπίᾳ τοῦ πάθους Pl.*Phdr.* 251d ; ὑπό τινος *to be puzzled* by .., Epicur.*Nat.*11.8 ; ἐπί τινι D.H. 3.70 ; χάριν τινός *POxy.*298.45 (i A.D.). (Eust., 833.15, derives it from ἀδήμων, which is found only as v.l. in Hp.*Epid.*1.18 (cf. Gal.17 (1).177), and is itself of doubtful derivation.) [ᾰδ- Nic.*Fr.*16.]

**ἀδημονία**, ἡ, *trouble, distress*, Epicur.*Fr.*483, *AP*12.226 (Strat.), Plu.*Num.*4 : pl., Ph.2.541.

**ἄδημος**, ον, = ἀπόδημος, S.*Fr.*639.

**ἀδημοσύνη**, ἡ, rarer form for ἀδημονία, Democr.212, X.ap.*AB*80.

⊛**ἀδήμων**, ον, gen. ονος, *sore troubled*. v. sub ἀδημονέω.

**ἄδην**, Ep. and Ion. **ἄδην**, Adv. *to one's fill*, ἔδμεναι ἄ. Il.5.203, al. ; ἐμπιμπλάμενοι σίτων ἄ. Pl.*Plt.*272c ; πιοῦσ' ἄ. χορεύω *Anacreont.*14. 30. 2. c. gen., οἵ μιν ἄ. ἐλόωσι .. πολέμοιο will drive him *to satiety* of war, Il.13.315 ; Τρῶας ἄ. ἐλάσαι πολέμοιο 19.423 ; ἔτι μέν φημι ἄ. ἐλάαν κακότητος Od.5.290 ; ἄ. ἔλειξεν αἵματος licked *his fill* of blood, A.*Ag.*828 ; καὶ τούτων μὲν ἄ. Pl.*Euthphr.*11e, cf. *R.*341c, etc. ; ἄ. ἔχειν τινός to have *enough of* a thing, be *weary of* it, Id.*Chrm.*153d, cf. E.*Ion*975 ; τοῦ φαγεῖν Arist.*Pr.*950ᵃ15 ; ἄ. ἔχουσιν οἱ λόγοι Pl.*R.* 541b : c. part., ἄ. εἶχον κτείνοντες Hdt.9.39. 3. *unceasingly*, A.R.2.82, cf. 4.1216. 4. = ἅλις, ἀ. ἐγένοντο μύκητες Call.*Fr.*47. [ᾰ, except in the phrase ἔδμεναι ἄδην ; v. sub ἀδέω.] (From sə-δην, cf. Lat. *sa-tis.*)

**ἀδήν** (ἀδ- Hdn.Gr.2.922), ένος, ἡ, *gland*, Hp.*Art.*11 ; later, ὁ, Gal. *UP*3.9, al., Alex.Aphr.*Pr.*2.12, Hdn.Gr. l.c. (ŋguen, cf. Lat. *inguen.*)

**ἀδηνής**, ές, (δῆνος) *ignorant, inexperienced*, Semon.7.53, cj. for ἀληνής, but expl. as '*without malice prepense*' by Hsch., *EM*17.11 : so in Adv. -έως *without malice*, διὰ τῆς πόλεως ἀ. γεγωνέοντες *GDI* 5653 (Chios) :—hence -εια, ἡ, *ignorance*, Hsch. (-είη).

**ἄδηρις**, ιος, ὁ, ἡ, *without strife*, *AP*7.440 (Leon.), Epigr. in *Rev.Phil.* 19.178 (Egypt).

**ἀδήρῖτος**, ον, *without strife* or *battle*, Il.17.42. 2. *uncontested, undisputed*, Plb.1.2.3, Orph.*A.*846. Adv. -τως Plb.3.93.1, D.S.4.14, Plu.*Caes.*3. II. *not to be striven against, unconquerable*, ἀνάγκης σθένος A.*Pr.*105.

⊛**Ἅιδης** or **ᾅδης**, ου, ὁ, Att. ; Ep. **Ἀΐδης**, αο and εω ; Dor. **Ἀΐδας**, α, used by Trag., in lyr. and anap. : gen. Ἄϊδος, dat. Ἄϊδι, Hom., Trag., v. infr. : (perh. ἀ- priv., ἰδεῖν) :—in Hom. only as pr. n. *Hades*, Ζεὺς καὶ ἐγώ, τρίτατος δ' Ἀΐδης Il.15.188, cf. Hes.*Th.*455 :—εἰν Ἀΐδαο δόμοισι in the *nether* world, Od.4.834 ; freq. εἰν, εἰς Ἀΐδαο (sc. δόμοις, δόμους), as Il.22.389, 21.48 ; εἰν Ἄϊδος Il.24.593 ; Trag. and Att. ἐν Ἅιδου, εἰς Ἅιδου (sc. οἴκῳ, οἶκον), S.*Aj.*865, Ar.*Ra.*69, etc. ; Ἄϊδόσδε, Adv. *to the nether world*, Il.7.330, etc. ; παρ' Ἅιδῃ, παρ' Ἅιδην, *OT*972, *OC* 1552 :—hence, 2. *place of departed spirits*, first in Il.23.244 εἰσόκεν αὐτὸς .. Ἄϊδι κεύθωμαι ; ἐπὶ τὸν ᾅδην Luc.*Cat.*14 ; εἰς ἀΐδην *AP*11.23 ; ἐν τῷ ᾅδῃ *Ev.Luc.*16.23. II. after Hom., *the grave, death*, ἀΐδαν λαγχάνειν, δέξασθαι, Pi.*P.*5.96, *I.*6(5).15 ; ᾅδης πόντιος *death* by sea, A.*Ag.*667, cf. E.*Alc.*13, *Hipp.*1047 ; ᾅδου πύλη, Astrol., region below the Horoscope, Vett.Val.179.13. 2. gen. ᾅδου with nouns in adjectival sense, *devilish*, θύουσαν ᾅ. μητέρ' A.*Ag.*1235 ; ᾅ. μάγειρος E.*Cyc.*397 ; *fatal, deadly*, δίκτυον, ξίφη ᾅ., A.*Ag.*1115, E.*Or.*1399. [ᾰ Hom. in all forms exc. ἄϊδος before vowels ; ἀΐδης Semon.7.117, prob. in S.*OC*1689.]

**ἀδήσω**, v. sub ἀνδάνω.

⊛**ἀδη-φάγέω** [ᾰδ], *to be greedy*, Hermipp.84 ; of horses, S.*Fr.*976, Isoc.6.55. **-φαγία**, ἡ, *gluttony*, Call.*Dian.*160 : pl., Arist.*Fr.*144, Opp.*H.*2.218 :—personified, Ἀδηφαγίας ἱερόν Polem.Hist.39. ⊛**-φάγος**, ον, (ἄδην) *gluttonous, greedy*, ἀνήρ Theoc.22.115 ; τὴν ἀ. νόσον S. *Ph.*313 ; ἀ. λύχνος, of a lamp *that burns much oil*, Alc.Com.21. 2. metaph., *devouring much money, costly*, τριήρεις Lys.*Fr.*39, cf. Philist.58 ; of racehorses, Pherecr.197, Ar.*Fr.*736.

**ἀδήωτος**, ον, *not ravaged*, X.*HG*3.1.5.

**ἀδιά-βᾰτος**, ον, *not to be passed*, ποταμός, νάπη, X.*An.*2.1.11, *HG*5. 4.44 ; ὄρη Them.*Or.*16.206d. II. Act., *not striding, closed*, σκέλη *AB*343. **-βεβαίωτος**, ον, *unconfirmed*, Ptol.*Geog.*2.1. **-βίβαστος**, ον, Gramm., *intransitive*, A.D.*Synt.*286.6. **-βλητος**, ον, *not listening to calumny*, ἡ τῶν ἀγαθῶν φιλία ἀ. ἐστι Arist.*EN*1157ᵃ 21 ; ἀνύποπτος καὶ ἀ. Plu.*Brut.*8. II. *unexceptionable* φιλοπονία ἕξις ἀ. πρὸς πόνον Pl.*Def.*412c ; τοῖς βίοις ἀ. Plu.2.4b ; τὰ πρὸς τοὺς ἄλλους ἀ. App.*Samn.*4.4. Adv. -τως Just.*Nov.*137.2. **-βολος**, ον, = foreg. I, *Stoic.*3.153. II. Pass., *unexceptionable*, *Mon.Ant.* 23.60 (Seleucia in Cilicia). **-γλυπτος**, ον, *not to be cut through*, *AB*344. **-γλυφος**, ον, *not hollowed out*, ὦτα Adam.2.29. ⊛**-γνωστος**, ον, *indistinguishable*, D.S.1.30 ; ἀ. τῷ χρώματι τοῦ ἐδάφους Antig.*Mir.*25(29) ; *hard to distinguish* or *understand*, ὀνόματα Aristid. Quint.1.5.

**ἀδι-άγωγος**, ον, *impossible to live with*, Ph.2.268 ; συνουσία 1.118.

⊛**ἀδιά-δοχος**, ον, *without successor, perpetual*, βουλή Sch.Aeschin. 3.2. **-δραστος**, ον, *inevitable*, Zeno*Stoic.*1.27, Ael.*Fr.*219. **-ζευκτος**, ον, *not disjoined, inseparable*, Corn.*ND*14, Iamb. *in Nic.*pp.15,

107 P.; ἕνωσις Procl.*in Prm.*p.521 S.; *indistinguishable*, Phld.*D.*1. 19. ⊛-θετος, ον, *not disposed* or *set in order*, Sch.Ar.*Nu.*1370, etc.; στίχοι ἀ. Sch.Il.22.487. 2. *having made no will, intestate*, Plu.*Cat.Ma.*9, D.Chr.54.4, *POxy.*105.6 (ii A.D.), al. b. *not disposed of by will*, *PGrenf.*1.17 (ii B.C.), *Sammelb.*4638.5.

⊛**ἀδιαίρετος**, ον, *undivided*, Arist.*Pol.*1265$^b$4; χώρα *SIG*141.10 (Corc. Nigr.), cf. *BGU*1119.9 (i B.C.), etc. 2. *indivisible*, like ἀμερής, Arist.*Ph.*231$^b$3, al.; Comp., *less divisible*, *Metaph.*1052$^a$21. Adv. -τως Phryn.146 (interp.). II. Act., *not having divided* joint property, ἀδελφοί Sor.2.1.

**ἀδιαίτητος**· ἀλλότριος, ἀήθης, Phot., Suid., *AB*341.

**ἀδια-κίνητος**, ον, *unmoved*, Phld.*Rh.*1.366 S. -**κλειστος**, ον, *not shut off*, τοῦ οὐρανοῦ τὸ -τον J.*BJ*5.5.4.

⊛**ἀδιᾱκόνητος**, ον, *not executed*, ἐκλιπεῖν ἀ. τὴν ἐπιστολήν J.*AJ*19. 1.1.

**ἀδιακόντιστος**, ον, *which no dart can pierce*, δέρμα prob. in Ael.*VH* 13.15 (interpol., codd. -κόνιστος, which Hsch. explains ἀναίσθητος, ἄτρωτος).

**ἀδιά-κοπος**, ον, *unbroken, uninterrupted*, χάρακες Aristeas 139; συνέχεια Herod.ap.Orib.7.8.4; λόγος Ph.1.81, cf. Porph.*Plot.*8. Adv. -πως Hero *Def.*37, Ulp. ad D.18.308, Steph.*in Hp.*1.149 D. -**κόρευτος**, ον, *undeflowered, virginal*, Sor.1.10. -**κόσμητος**, ον, *not set in order*, D.H.3.10; οὐσία *Stoic.*2.189, cf. Ph.2.505; of lands, *not disposed of, unassigned*, J.*AJ*5.1.23. -**κρισία**, ἡ, *want of discernment*, Suid. s.v. ἀκρισία. -**κρῐτος**, ον, *undistinguishable, mixed*, Hp.*Coac.*570; αἷμα Arist.*Somn.*458$^a$21 (Comp.); *not discriminated*, Dam.*Pr.*35. Adv. -τως *without distinction, in common*, Ph.*Fr.*105 H., Hierocl.*in CA*12 p.446 M., Iamb.*Myst.*4.1, Just.*Nov.* 89.7. b. *promiscuous*, ἐπιμιξίαι D.H.19.1. 2. *unintelligible*, Plb.15.12.9. 3. *undecided*, Luc.*J.Tr.*25, *OGI*509.8 (Aphrodisias). 4. Act., *not making due distinctions*, τὸ -τον Ph.2. 664. 5. Adv. -τως *without examination*, *POxy.*715.36 (ii A.D.). -**κωλύτως**, Adv. *without hindrance*, Herm.ap.Stob.1.49.68, *BGU*1048.19 (i A.D.). ⊛-**λειπτος**, ον, *unintermitting, incessant*, Ti. Locr.98e, *Ep.Rom.*9.2, Hierocl.p.19.55 A., Plu.2.121e, M.Ant.6.15. Adv. -τως Metrod.*Herc.*831.8, Polem.Hist.30, Plb.9.3.8, Posidon.25, Lxx 1 *Ma.*12.11, *Ep.Rom.*1.9, *PLond.*3.1166.6 (i A.D.). -**λεκτος**, ον, *without conversation*, βίος *solitary* life, Phryn.Com.18. -**ληπτεύω**, *to be lacking in comprehension, confused in mind*, Phld.*Rh.*2. 184 S. -**ληπτος**, ον, *indistinct, confused*, λόγος Metrod.*Herc.*831. 11, cf. 13; ἄδηλα καὶ ἀ. Phld.*Rh.*2.44 S.:—also of persons, *confused in mind*, ib.47 S., Id.*Po.*1676.3. Adv. -τως, opp. διειλημμένως, Id. *Mus.*p.32 K., al. -**ληψία**, *confusion, obscurity*, διανοημάτων Phld. *Rh.*2.190 S.: pl., ib.1.7 S.:—of persons, *failure to distinguish*, τινός ib.1.43 S.: abs., ib.1.204 S.

**ἀδιάλλακτος**, ον, *irreconcilable*, τὰ πρὸς ὑμᾶς ἀ. ὑπάρχει my relation to you *admits no reconciliation*, D.*Ep.*2.21, cf. 24.8, D.Chr.38.17, etc. Adv. -τως, ἔχειν πρός τινα D.H.6.56, cf. Plu.*Brut.*45.

**ἀδια-λόγιστος**, ον, *unreasoning*: c. gen., τοῦ συμφέροντος Phld.*Lib.* p.60 O. ⊛-**λῠτος**, ον, *undissolved*: *indissoluble*, Pl.*Phd.*80b; ἕνωσις Ph.2.635; σύμβασις Hierocl.p.17.23 A.:—*indestructible*, Epicur.*Fr.* 356 (nisi Hermarcho tribuendum); στερεὰ καὶ ἀ. Id.*Nat.*14.2. II. *irreconcilable*. Adv. -τως, πολεμεῖν πρός τινα Plb.18.37.4. III. -τον, τό, = ἡλιοτρόπιον, Ps.-Dsc.4.190. -**λώβητον**· ἀβλαβές, Hsch.

**ἀδι-αμάρτητος**, ον, *infallible*, Gem.17.24, cf. Gal.19.595.

**ἀδια-μέριστος**, ον, = ἀδιαίρετος, Sch.A.R.3.1033. -**μόρφωτος**, ον, *not fully formed*, Sor.1.101; σάρξ Sch.Orib.22.5.3. -**νέμητος**, ον, *not to be divided*, Longin.22.3. 2. *undivided*, Timae. 77. -**νοησία**, ἡ, *inconceivability*, Phld.*Sign.*38. -**νοητεύομαι**, *speak unintelligibly*, Sch.Ar.*Av.*1377. -**νόητος**, ον, *unintelligible*, -ητα σκώπτειν Did.ap.Sch.Ar.*V.*1309. Adv. -τως D.H. *Rh.*9.16. 2. *inconceivable*, Pl.*Sph.*238c, Epicur.*Fr.*606, cf. *Ep.* 2 p.43 U., Phld.*Sign.*12, al., Arr.*Epict.*2.20.18, S.E.*M.*8.389. II. Act., *not understanding, silly*, Arist.*Fr.*90; *unreflecting*, Phld.*Ir.* p.23 W.; τὸ ἀ. τοῦ πλήθους Id.*Rh.*2.40 S. Adv. -τως Pl.*Hp.Ma.* 301c.

**ἀδίαντος**, ον, (διαίνω) *unwetted*, ἀδιάντοισι παρειαῖς Simon.37.3; ἀ. ἐξ ἁλὸς B.16.122; *not bathed in sweat*, σθένος Pi.*N.*7.72. II. as Subst., ἀδίαντος, ὁ, *maidenhair, Adiantum Capillus-Veneris*, Orph. *A.*915: **ἀδίαντον**, τό, Theoc.13.41; ἀ. [τὸ μέλαν] Thphr.*HP*7.10.5: pl., Plu.2.614b. 2. ἀ. τὸ λευκόν, = τριχομανές, Thphr.*HP*7.14.1, Dsc.4.135.

**ἀδιά-ξεστος**, ον, *unpolished*, Gal.*UP*11.13. ⊛-**πάτητος**, ον, *untrodden*, πυρός *POxy.*1259.15 (iii A.D.). -**παυστος**, ον, *not to be stilled, incessant, violent*, Plb.4.39.10, Phalar.*Ep.*67.3. Adv. -τως Plb.1.57.1, Antyll.ap.Orib.4.11.14. -**πεπτος**, ον, *undigested*, Sch. Nic.*Al.*66. ⊛-**πλαστος**, ον, *as yet unformed*, Pl.*Ti.*91d, cf. Suid. s.v. φρῦνος. -**πνευστέω**, *not to evaporate*, [Gal.]10.528. -**πνευστία**, ἡ, *want of perspiration* or *suppressed perspiration*, Gal.10.763, Alex. Trall.*Febr.*1. ⊛-**πνευστος**, ον, (διαπνέω) *not ventilated*, Gal.10.745; *air-tight*, Asclep.ap.eund.13.159. II. Act., *without drawing breath*, Iamb.*VP*31.188. -**πόνητος**, ον, *undigested*, κρέα Ath.9. 402d. -**πόρευτος**, ον, *that cannot be traversed*, Simp.*in Cat.*470. 2. ⊛-**πταιστος**, ον, = ἀδιάπτωτος, Iamb.*Protr.*21.κδ', cf. Hierocl. *Prov.*p.463 B. -**πτωσία**, ἡ, *infallibility*, Hp.*Ep.*17, Iamb.*Protr.* 21.κ'. ⊛-**πτωτος**, ον, *infallible*, Hp.*Decent.*12, S.E.*M.*7.110; ἀρχὴ ἀ. τῇ πόλει *PRyl.*77.46 (ii A.D.). Adv. -τως Plb.6.26.4, cf. *Stoic.*3.69; *unerringly*, of archers, Hld.9.18. 2. *faultless*, of writers, Longin. 33.5; τὸ ἀ. *perfection* of style, Id.36.4; φράσις Diog.Bab.*Stoic.* 214; προφορά D.T.629.12. 3. Gramm., *not using cases at random*, A.D.*Pron.*109.23. b. *uninflected*, *EM*643.47.

**ἀδι-αρθρος**, ον, faulty form for sq., Thphr.*HP*3.10.5 (Comp.). -**άρθρωτος**, ον, *not jointed* or *articulated*, Arist.*HA*579$^a$24, al. 2. *confused*, λόγος Arr.*Epict.*1.17.1, Plu.2.378c. 2. *not distinctly conceived, unanalysed*, Phld.*D.*1.24 (Comp.); δόξα Alex.Aphr. *Metaph.*26.22. 3. of literary style, *disjointed*, ἀ. ἐν σχήματι Hermog.*Id.*2.11. III. *unorganized*, Arr.*Epict.*4.8.10. IV. Adv. -τως *without distinction*, Gal.16.240, cf. Alex.Aphr. *in Metaph.* 61.4, Plot.3.8.9.

⊛**ἀδια-ρίπιστος**, ον, *not scattered by the winds*, Hsch. s.v. ἀκρίπιστον. -**ρρευστος**, ον, *non-deliquescent*, φάρμακον Gal.12.840. -**ρρηκτος**, ον, *not torn in pieces*, gloss on ἄρρηκτος, *EM*149.12. -**ρροια**, ἡ, *constipation*, Hp.ap.Erot.48. -**σειστος**, ον, *not shaken about*, Gal.19. 81; gloss on ἀτίνακτος, Sch.Opp.*H.*4.415. -**σκέδαστος**, ον, *not scattered*, Sch.Ar.*Th.*1027. -**σκέπτως**, Adv. *inconsiderately*, Aen.Tact. 29.12 (prob. l.). -**σκευος**, ον, *unequipt*, ἵππος Anon.ap.Suid. -**σκοπος**, ον, *not perspicuous*, Sch.A.*Ch.*816. -**σπαστος**, ον, *not torn asunder, uninterrupted, unbroken*, X.*Ages.*1.4, Plb.1.34.5; *inseparable*, Dam.*Pr.*418, cf. Olymp.Alch.p.77 B. Adv. -τως Steph. *in Hp.* 1.65 D., Hsch. -**σταλτος**, ον, *not clearly unfolded*, Sch.Od.19. 560. -**στασία**, ἡ, *continuity*, Iamb. *in Nic.*p.57 P. -**στᾰτος**, ον, *continuous*, Antipho Soph.24; ἀγάπησις Andronic.Rhod. p.513 M. Adv. -τως *without intermission*, Ph.1.342, 501, etc. b. *without distinctions* or *intervals*, Plot.3.7.2, Dam.*Pr.*105, 370. 2. Gramm., of ι in diphthongs, *inseparable*, not forming a distinct syllable, A.D.*Pron.*86.21. Adv. -τως, σύλληψις συμφώνων μετὰ φωνήεντος .. ἀ. λεγομένη Sch.D.T.p.48 H. II. *without extension* or *dimension*, Plu.2.601c, Plot.1.5.7, Alex.Aphr. *in Top.*31.18. Adv. -τως Procl. *in Prm.*p.543 S., *Inst.*176. -**στικτος**, ον, *undistinguished, unvarying*, Ph.2.297. Adv., *Gloss.* ⊛-**στολος**, ον, Gramm., *not distinguished*, A.D.*Pron.*11.26. Adv. -λως, λ[έγο]ντας Phld.*Rh.*1.53 S., cf. Phoeb.*Fig.*1.3, Porph.*Abst.*2.37. -**στομος**, ον, (διὰ στόμα) *not currently named*, *PPar.*5.15 (ii B.C.), al. -**στρέπτως**, Adv. *without turning, continuously*, Hp.*Fract.*19. ⊛-**στροφος**, ον, *incapable of turning*: metaph., *rigid, inexorable*, νόμος Orph.*H.*64.9; *incontrovertible*, προλήψεις Procl.*Hyp.*5.20; of remedies, *infallible*, Aët.3.91, 109; Gramm., *strictly accurate*, S.E.*M.*1.187. II. *not distorted*, Arist.*Pr.*958$^a$12; κανών Plu.2.780b; θώρηξ Aret.*SD*1.12. Adv. -φως Gal.18(2).334. 2. metaph., *not perverted*, of persons, Ph.*Fr.*14 H., Lxx 3 *Ma.*3.3; ζῷα S.E.*P.*3.194. Adv. -φως *in the absence of perversion*, i.e. *by natural instinct*, Demetr.Lac.*Herc.*1012. 70; *straightforwardly*, ἀ. καὶ ἀπανούργως S.E.*M.*2.77. b. of judgements, etc., *unperverted*, κρίσεις D.H.*Th.*55; λόγοι, ἔννοιαι, Procl. *in Alc.*p.4 C., *Theol.Pl.*1.17. III. Adv. -φως *without molestation*, ἀ. καὶ ἀταράχως μεῖναι ἐν τοῖς ἰδίοις *PLond.*5.1674 (vi A.D.); ἀφίεσθαι ἀζημίως καὶ ἀ. *Cod.Just.*9.47.26.7. -**σφαλτος**, ον, *free from error*, μέθοδοι Hero *Geep.*164. Adv. -τως Ps.-Dioph.p.xxi H. -**σχιστος**, ον, *not cloven*, Arist.*HA*532$^b$13. ⊛-**σωστος**, ον, *not preserved*, βιβλίον Ptol.*Tetr.*47. -**τακτος**, ον, *disorganized*, ὄχλοι, πόλις, Artapan.ap.Alex.Polyh.14, D.H.3.10. Adv. -τως Simp.*in Cat.* 379.26. 2. *unclassified*, πρόσοδοι *BCH*6.14 (Delos, ii B.C.). ⊛-**τμητος**, ον, *not cut in pieces*, Aen.Tact.32.1. -**τρεπτος**, ον, *not to be turned aside*, c. gen., γνώμης Sch.Luc.*Herm.*53. II. *headstrong*, Lxx *Si.*26.10. Adv. -τως Lxx v.l. ibid., Jul.*Or.*6. 197b. -**τρεψία**, ἡ, *shamelessness*, Caligula ap.Suet.*Calig.* 29. -**τύπωτος**, ον, *unshapen*, D.S.1.10, Ocell.2.3, Ph.2.317, al.; ψυχή 1.50.

⊛**ἀδίαυλος**, ον, *with no way back, without return*, of the nether world, E.*Fr.*868; Φερσεφόνας ἀδίαυλον ὑπὸ .. δόμον *Epigr.Gr.*244.9 (Cyzicus).

**ἀδιά-φθαρτος**, ον, = ἀδιάφθορος 1, Pl.*Ap.*34b, *Lg.*951c, Ph.1. 408. II. = sq. II, Epicur.*Fr.*267, Gal.2.27. -**φθορος**, ον, *not affected by decay*, Antyll.ap.Orib.46.22.3; *uncorrupted, chaste*, Pl.*Phdr.*252d; ἀπ' ὀρθῆς .. καὶ ἀδιαφθόρου τῆς ψυχῆς D.18.298, cf. Men. 984, D.S.1.59, Plu.2.5e. Adv. -ρως, ἐρᾶσθαι Aeschin.1.137. 2. of judges, *incorruptible*, Pl.*Lg.*768b; of witnesses, Arist.*Rh.*1376$^a$ 17; of magistrates, Id.*Pol.*1286$^a$39 (Comp.), cf. *IG*2.240$^b$13. Sup. Adv. -ώτατα Pl. l.c. II. *imperishable*, Pl.*Phd.*106e. -**φορέω**, *to be indifferent*, κατά τι S.E.*P.*1.191; πρός τι M.Ant.11.16; ἀδιαφορεῖ impers., ἐάν .. ἐάν .. Ph.2.243: c. inf., A.D.*Pron.*45.22. 2. Gramm., *not to agree*, in case, gender, etc., ib.68.15, al. II. ἀ. τινός *not to differ from*, Ph.1.414. III. personal, *bring about no change*, Gal.1.194. IV. Math., *to be negligible*, Procl.*Hyp.* 3.31; ἀ. πρὸς αἴσθησιν *not to differ* appreciably, ib.3.15. V. of persons, *to be neglected, uncared for*, *PLond.*2.144 (i A.D.). -**φορητικός**, ή, όν, *like indifference*: τὸ ἀ. = ἀδιαφορία, Arr.*Epict.*2.1. 14. -**φόρητος**, ον, *not evaporating* or *perspiring*, Alex.Trall.2. II. *showing no difference*, Iamb.*in Nic.*p.76 P. -**φορία**, ἡ, *indifference*, Stoic, of the moral agent, Aristo *Stoic.*1.83, Chrysipp.ib.3.9, cf. Cic. *Acad.Pr.*2.42.130, S.E.*P.*1.152; *absence of difference*, Syr. *in Metaph.* 122.1, cf. sq. II. *neglect*, Hierocl. *in CA*7 p.430 M. III. *equivalence of signification*, Eust.150.25. ⊛-**φορος**, ον, *not different*, Arist.*Rh.*1373$^a$33; τοῖς ὁμοίοις καὶ ἀ. Id.*Cael.*310$^b$5; *indistinguishable*, ὅμοιον καὶ ἀ. Epicur.*Nat.*15 G. 2. in Logic, ἀδιάφορα, τά, *individual objects*, as having no *logical differentia*, ἀ. ὧν ἀδιαίρετον τὸ εἶδος Arist. *Metaph.*1016$^a$18; ἀ. εἴδει *Top.*121$^b$15; κατὰ τὸ εἶδος ib.103$^a$11. 3. *undiscriminating*, ὀνομασία Epicur.*Nat.*14.10. II. *indifferent*;

Stoic philosophy, τὰ ἀ. things *neither good nor bad*, Zeno *Stoic.* ,48, cf. Cic.*Fin.*3.16.53, Epict.*Ench.*32, etc., cf. S.E.*P.*3.177 sq.: ., Phld.*Rh.*1.129 S. Adv. -ρως, ἔχειν *to be indifferent*, of the moral nt, Aristo *Stoic.*1.79. **III.** in metre, *common*, Heph.4, cf. .Pi.p.15 Böckh. **IV.** of persons, *making no distinction*, πρὸς τα ξένον καὶ δημότην Dicaearch.1.14. **2.** *steadfast, unweary-*, Ant.Lib.41.2. **V.** Math., *negligible*, πρός τι Procl.*Hyp.*4.61; πρὸς αἴσθησιν *not differing* sensibly, Aristarch.Sam.4. Adv., Hip-ch.3.5.7. **VI.** Adv. -ρως *without discrimination*, D.H.*Dem.* , S.E.*P.*3.225. **-φρακτος**, ον, *with no divisions* or *joints*, Thphr. Pl.5.3, 8.5.2. Adv. -τως ib.6.5.3. **-χῦτος**, ον, (διαχέω) *not ftened by cooking*, Thphr.*CP*4.12.2; *not dissolved*, Dsc.5.79. **II.** t *diffuse* or *extravagant*, of persons, Hp.*Decent.*3:—of style, ngin.34.3. **-χώρητος**, ον, *without evacuation*, κοιλίη Hp.*Acut.* p.)38; *not passing through the bowels*, Sor.1.125. ***-χώριστος**, , *unseparated, undistinguished*, *EM*538.34, Suid. Adv. -τως Hsch. v. ἀδιασπάστως. **-ψευστος**, ον, *not deceitful*, D.S.5.37; of αταληπτικὴ φαντασία, Sphaer.*Stoic.*1.141, cf. M.Ant.4.49, Iamb. *rotr.*21. Adv. -τως S.E.*M.*7.191, Ruf.*Fr.*68.10.

**ἀδίδακτος**, ον, *untaught, ignorant*, Ps.-Phoc.89: c. gen., ἀ. ώτων *AP*5.121 (Diod.), cf. Hp.*Alim.*39. **2.** *unpractised, un-rained*, of a chorus, D.21.17. **II.** *untaught*, τοῖς ἀφ' αὑτοῦ αὶ ἀ. πάθεσι Plu.2.968c, cf. Luc.*Hist.Conscr.*34; *that cannot be aught*, Philostr.*VA*5.36. **2.** ἀ. δρᾶμα *not yet acted* (v. διδάσκω II) Ath.6.270a. **III.** Adv. -τως *without teaching*, Phld.*Rh.* 2.93 S, Juba 32, Plu.2.673f; οὐκ ἀ. οὐδὲ αὐτοφυῶς Ph.*Fr.*70 H.

**ἀδι-έγγυος**, ον, *not covered by security*, μέρος τῆς ὠνῆς *PRev.Laws* 17.3 (iii B.C.). **-έκβατος**, ον, = sq., ἕρκος Sch.Opp.*H.*4.117. **-έκδῦτος**, ον, *not to be escaped*, Apollon.*Lex.* s. v. νήδυμος. **-έξακτος**, ον, *not carried through, undone*, μηδὲν ἀ. ἀπολείποντες *OGI*335.34 (Perg.). **-εξέργαστος**, ον, *not wrought out*, τόπος Isoc.5.109. **-εξέταστος**, ον, *that will not stand examination*, λόγοι Lxx *Si.*21.18. **-εξήγητος**, ον, *indescribable*, πλῆθος Ph.1.407, prob. in *IG*5(1).1359 (Messenia, i B.C.):—*inexhaustible*, ταῖς ἡμετέραις ἐπιβολαῖς Dam.*Pr.*178. ***-εξίτητος**, ον, (διέξειμι) *that cannot be exhausted, infinite in extent* or *duration*, Arist.*Ph.*207$^b$29, cf. Alex.Aphr.*in Top.* 86.27, Plot.2.4.7, al.; αἰών Ph.1.554. **2.** *with no outlet*, ἄγυια Orib.9.20.3. **-εξόδευτος**, ον, *having no outlet*, λαβύρινθος Eust. 1688.37, cf. Sch.E.*Or.*25. **-έξοδος**, ον, *that cannot be gone through*, τὸ ἄπειρον Arist.*Ph.*204$^a$14. **2.** *having no outlet*, of places, App.*Mith.*100, Plu.2.957d. **II.** Act., *unable to get out*, *AP* 11.395 (Nicarch.), cf. Plu.2.679b, Ocell.1.15. **-έργαστος**, ον, *not wrought out, unfinished*, Isoc.12.268, Poll.6.143. Adv. -τως ib.144. **-ερεύνητος**, ον, *inscrutable*, Pl.*Ti.*25d. **2.** *uninvestigated*, Ph.1.470, etc. **II.** of persons, *not searched*, Plu.*Dio* 19. **-ευκρίνητος**, ον, *obscure, lacking in order*, of style, Hermog. *Id.*2.11; ὕλη Heraclit.*All.*48. **-εχής**, ές, = ἀζηχής, Sch.Opp.*H.* 3.129. ***-ήγητος**, ον, *indescribable*, X.*Cyr.*8.7.22, D.17.29, Cic.*Att.* 13.9.1. Adv. -τως *PMag.Lond.*125.13. **II.** *not related*, Hld. 5.16. **-ήθητος**, ον, *not filtered* or *strained*, πτισάνη ἀ. gruel *with the meal in it*, Hp.*Acut.*7.

**ἀδῐκαίαρχος**, ον, = ἄδικος ἄρχων Cic.*Att.*2.12 (with play on the name of the historian Dicaearchus).

**ἀδῐκαιοδότητος**, ον, *where no justice can be got*, Σικελία D.S.39. 20.

**ἀδίκαστος**, ον, *without judgement given*, Pl.*Ti.*51c; δίκη *IG*12(2). 530 (Eresos); *undecided*, Luc.*Bis Acc.*23. Adv. -τως *without judgement*, Aesop.223.

**ἀδίκευσις**, εως, ἡ, *wrongdoing*, = ἐνέργεια κατ' ἀδικίαν, *Stoic.*3. 25.

***ἀδῐκέω**, Aeol. -ήω Sapph.1.20, Dor. -ίω *Tab.Heracl.*1.138: Ion. impf. ἠδίκεον or -ευν Hdt.1.121:—Pass., fut. in med. form ἀδικήσομαι E.*IA*1436, Th.5.56, etc.; also ἀδικηθήσομαι Apollod.1.9.23, etc.:—*to be* ἄδικος, *do wrong* (defined by Arist.*Rh.*1368$^b$6 τὸ βλάπτειν ἑκόντα παρὰ τὸν νόμον, cf. ἀδίκημα), τῶν ἀδικησάντων τίσις ἔσσεται *those who have sinned*, *h.Cer.*367; freq. in Hdt. and Att.; τἀδικεῖν *wrongdoing*, S.*Ant.*1059; τὸ μὴ ἀδικεῖν *righteous dealing*, A.*Eu.*85,749:—in legal phrase, *do wrong in the eye of the law*, the particular case being added in part., as Σωκράτης ἀ... ποιῶν.. καὶ διδάσκων Pl.*Ap.*19b, cf. X.*Mem.*1.1.1: c. acc. cogn., ἀδικίαν, ἀδικήματα, etc., Pl.*R.*344c, 409a, cf. Arist.*Rh.*1389$^b$7; also ἀ. οὐδὲν ἄξιον δεσμοῦ Hdt.3.145; ἀ. πολλά, μεγάλα, etc., Pl.*Smp.*188a, al.; οὐδέν, μηδὲν ἀ. ib., al.:—ἀ. περὶ τὰ μυστήρια D.21.175, cf. *IG*2.811$^c$154; ἀ. εἰς πόλιν, κτῆμα, Lib. *Or.*15.39, 31.7:—in games or contests, *play foul*, Ar.*Nu.*25, Arist. *EN*1123$^b$32. **b.** in pres., *to be in the wrong*, εἰ μὴ ἀδικῶ γε *if I am not mistaken*, Pl.*Chrm.*156a. **II.** trans. c. acc. pers., *wrong, injure*, Archil.*Supp.*2.13, Sapph.1.20, Epich.286, Hdt.1.112, etc.:—*ruin*, of a girl, Men.*Georg.*30: c. dupl. acc., *wrong* one *in* a thing, Ar. *Pl.*460; ἃ πολλοὺς ὑμῶν ἠδίκηκεν D.21.129; μείζον' ἢ ἐλάττονα ἀ. τινά 20.124; ἀ. ἀδικίαν περί τινας Pl.*Lg.*854e:—Pass., *to be wronged, injured*, μὴ δῆτ' ἀδικηθῶ S.*OC*174; ἀ. εἴς τι E.*Med.*265; μέγιστα ἀ. Aeschin.3.84; οὔτ' ἀδικεῖ οὔτ' ἀδικεῖται Pl.*Smp.*196b, etc.; pres. ἀδικεῖται, -ούμενος used for the pf. ἠδίκηται, -ημένος (v. supr. 1), Antipho 4.4.9, Pl.*R.*359a: c. acc., *to be defrauded of*, μισθὸν ἀδικίας v.l. in 2*Ep.Pet.*2.13. **2.** *harm, injure*, ἀ. γῆν Th.2.71, etc.; ἵππον X.*Eq.*6.3; esp. in Medical sense, ἄνθρωπον Hp.*Nat.Hom.*9; νεφρούς Diph.Siph.ap.Ath.2.62f; τέμνειν καὶ θλᾶν καὶ ὁπωσοῦν ἄλλως ἀ. Gal. *UP*13.8, cf. Archig.ap.Philum.*Ven.*14.

**ἀδίκη**, ἡ, = ἀκαλήφη, Ps.-Dsc.4.93.

**ἀδίκ-ημα**, ατος, τό, (ἀδικέω) *wrong done*, Hdt.1.2,100, etc.: properly, *intentional wrong*, opp. ἁμάρτημα and ἀτύχημα, Arist.*EN* 1135$^b$20 sq., *Rh.*1374$^b$8; ἀ. ὥρισται τῷ ἑκουσίῳ Id.*EN*1135$^a$19: c. gen., *wrong done to*.., ἀ. τῶν νόμων D.21.225: also ἀ. πρός τινα Arist.*Rh.*1373$^b$21; ἀ. εἴς τι D.37.58; περί τι Plu.2.159c:—ἐν ἀδικήματι θέσθαι *to consider as a wrong*, Th.1.35; ἀ. θεῖναί τι D.14.37; ψηφίζεσθαί τι ἐν ἀ. εἶναι Hyp.*Eux.*26. **2.** *error of judgement*, dub. in Plb.9.26$^a$.7. **II.** *that which is got by wrong*, *ill gotten goods*, Pl.*R.*365e, *Lg.*906d. **-ητέον**, *one ought to do wrong*, Pl.*R.*365e; φαμὲν ἑκόντας ἀ. εἶναι Id.*Cri.*49a. **-ητής**, ὁ, *wronger, injurer*, Eust. 756.58. ***-ητικός**, ή, όν, *disposed to do wrong*, Plu.2.562d. Adv. -κῶς Stoic.ap.Stob.2.7.11$^m$. **-ήω**, v. ἀδικέω. ***-ία**, Ion. -ίη, ἡ, *wrongdoing, injustice*, ἀδικίης ἄρχειν Hdt.1.130, cf. 4.1, E.*Or.*28, Pl.*Grg.*477c, al.; τύχῃ μᾶλλον ἢ ἀδικίᾳ Antipho 6.1; *'foul'* in racing, Anon.*in SE*30.15. **II.** *wrongful act, offence*, Hdt.6.136; καταγνόντες αὐτῶν ἀδικίαν And.1.3:—in pl., Pl.*Phd.*82a, etc. **-ιον**, τό, = ἀδίκημα, Hdt.5.89, cf. *IG*7.235 (pl.) (Orop.); esp. -ίου γραφή suit for *malversation*, Arist.*Ath.*54.2, cf. Plu.*Per.*32; also, *damage*, *PTaur.*4.15 (iii B.C.), cf. *PFar.*14.44 (iii B.C.).

**ἀδῐκο-δοξέω**, *seek fame by unworthy means*, D.S.31.6. **-δοξία**, ἡ, *evil design*, Plb.22.17.7, *Fr.*95. **-κρισία**, ἡ, *unjust judgement*, Heph.Astr.3.34. **-μαχέω**, *fight unfairly*, esp. in the law-courts, Alciphr.3.29; dub. in Poll.3.154. **-μᾰχία**, ἡ, *unfair fighting*, Arist.*SE*171$^b$23, cf. Ascl.*in Metaph.*243.9. **-μαχος**, ον, of horses, *obstinate*, X.ap.*AB*344 (perh. fr. *Cyr.*2.2.26). **-μήχᾰνος**, ον, *plotting injustice*, Ar.*Fr.*697. **-πήμων**, ον, *unjustly harming*, *AB* 343. **-πρᾱγέω**, = ἀδικέω, *act wrongly*, Plu.2.501a, Ph.2. 329. **-πράγημα**, τό, *wrong action*, Stoic.ap.Stob.2.7.11$^e$, Phld. *Piet.*19 G. **-πρᾱγής**, Ion. -πρηγής, ές, *acting wrongly*, Perict.ap. Stob.4.28.19.

**ἄδῐκος**, ον, (δίκη) of persons, *wrongdoing, unrighteous, unjust*: ἄνθρωποι Hes.*Op.*260: Comp. -ώτερος ib.272; δίκαν ἐξ ἀδίκων ἀπαιτῶ A.*Ch.*398 (lyr.): Sup. -ώτατος S.*Tr.*1011 (lyr.): ἄ. εἴς τι *unjust in* a thing, ἔς τινα *towards* a person, Hdt.2.119; εἰς χρήματα X. *Cyr.*8.8.6; περί τινα ib.27; ἄ. [ἐν τῷ ἀστραγαλίζειν] one who *plays unfairly*, Pl.*Alc.*1.110b: c. inf., *so unjust as to*.., *Ep.Heb.*6.10. **2.** ἄ. ἵπποι *obstinate, unmanageable*, X.*Cyr.*2.2.26; ἄ. γνάθος the *hard* mouth of a horse, Id.*Eq.*3.5. **II.** of things, *unjust, unrighteous*, ἔργα Hes.*Op.*334, Hdt.1.5; ἔργματα Thgn.380, Sol.13.12; ἄδικα φρονέειν Thgn.395; ἄ. λόγος freq. in Ar.*Nu.*; ἄρχειν χειρῶν ἀ. *begin an assault*, Antipho 4.2.1, Lys.4.11, cf. X.*Cyr.*1.5.13, D.47.39; τὸ δίκαιον καὶ τὸ ἄ., τὰ δίκαια καὶ τὰ ἄ. *right and wrong*, Pl.*Grg.*460a, etc.; πλοῦτος ἄ. *ill-gotten, unrighteous*, Isoc.1.38; ζυγὸν ἄ. Lxx *Am.*8.5; νομὴ ἄ. οὐδὲν ἰσχύει *PTeb.*286.7 (ii A.D.); ἡ ἄ... συναγωγὴ ἀνδρὸς καὶ γυναικός the *unrighteous* union, Pl.*Tht.*150a; ἄ. δίκη *vexatious* suit, Cratin.19 D. **2.** of the punishment of wrongdoing, Ζεὺς νέμων ἄδικα κακοῖς A.*Supp.*404 (lyr.), cf. E.*Or.*647. **III.** ἄ. ἡμέρα, i.e. ἄνευ δικῶν, *a day on which the courts were shut*, Luc.*Lex.*9: δίκαιος ἄ. *who has not appeared in court*, Archipp.46. **IV.** Adv. -κως Sol.13.7, A.*Ag.*1546; τοὺς ἀ. θνήσκοντας S.*El.*113 (anap.); εἴτε ὦν δὴ δικαίως εἴτε ἀ. *jure an injuria*, Hdt.6.137; δικαίως καὶ ἀ. Pl. *Lg.*743b; οὐκ ἀ. *not without reason*, *h.Merc.*316, Simon.89.3, Pl.*Phd.* 72a.

**ἀδῐκό-τροπος**, ον, *of unjust disposition*, Crates Com.*Fr.inc.*7 M. **-χειρ**, χειρος, ὁ, ἡ, *with unrighteous hand*, S.*Fr.*977. **-χρήματος**, ον, *with ill-gotten wealth*, Crates Com.42.

**ἀδῐνός** [ᾰ], ή, όν, radic. sense, *close, thick*: hence in Hom., **1.** *crowded, thronging*, ἀ. κῆρ, like πυκιναὶ φρένες, in physical sense, Il.16.481, Od.19.516; of bees, flies, sheep, Il.2.87,469, Od.1. 92. **2.** *vehement, loud*, of sounds ἀ. γόος Il.18.316; Σειρῆνες ἀ. the *loud-voiced* Sirens, Od.23.326. Adv. -νῶς *frequently*, or *loudly, vehemently*, ἀ. ἀνενείκατο Il.19.314: neut. as Adv., ἀδινὸν γοόωσα Od.4.721; ἀ. μυκώμεναι 10.413: pl., ἀδινὰ στεναχίζων Il. 23.225; κλαῖ' ἀ. 24.510: Comp. ἀδινώτερον Od.16.216:—rare in Lyr. and Trag., ἀ. δάκος a *deep* bite, Pi.*P.*2.53; ἀ. δάκρυα *thick-falling* tears, S.*Tr.*848 (lyr.); βίοτος ἀ. *abundant*, Tim.*Pers.*29; and freq. in A.R., ἀ. ὕπνος, κῶμα *abundant, deep* sleep, 3.616,748; ἀ. εὐνή *frequent* wedded joys, 3.1206. (Aristarch. wrote ἀδ–, cf. ἁδρός.)

**ἄδιξις**, ἡ, *agreement* (Tarent.), Hsch. (ϝαδ-, cf. Hsch. s.v. γάδιξις.)

**ἀδι-όδευτος**, ον, *not to be travelled through*, δυσχωρίαι Them.*Or.*16. 206d, cf. Charito 7.3. **-οικησία**, ἡ, *want of management*, Vett.Val. 240.15. **-οίκητος**, ον, *unarranged*, D.24.28, cf. *IG*5(2).433 (Megalopolis, ii B.C.); *undigested*, Gal.19.217, *Hippiatr.*31:—of property, = ἐκτὸς μισθώσεως, *PPetr.*3p.198 (iii B.C.). **-οπος**, ον, *without commander*, of a ship, A.*Fr.*269. **-όρᾱτος**, ον, *not to be seen through*, Poll.5.150. **-οργάνωτος**, ον, *unorganized*, Iamb.*VP*17. 73. **-όρθωτος**, ον, *not corrected, not set right*, D.4.36:—of books, *unrevised*, Cic.*Att.*13.21a.1. **II.** *irremediable*, ὁρμή D.S.37.3; δουλεία App.*BC*3.90, cf. D.L.5.66; ἀδιόρθωτα ἀδικεῖν D.H.6.20. Adv. -τως D.S.29.25. **-οριστία**, ἡ, *indefiniteness*, Nicom.ap.Phot.*Bibl.* p.143 B. **-όριστος**, ον, in Logic, *indesignate*, Arist.*APr.*26$^b$23; *undefined*, ἀ. ἀπολέλοιπε τὴν ἀρετὴν τοῦ ποιητοῦ Phld.*Po.*1425.1, al.; *indefinite*, ἄδηλον καὶ ἀ. Arist.*PA*639$^a$22, cf. Dam.*Pr.*37, al. Adv. -τως Arist.*Ph.*184$^b$11, al.; *vaguely, loosely*, Anon.*in SE*62.31.

**ἀδιούνιος** ταῦρος· ὁ Ἀπόλλων ὑπὸ τῶν Κρητῶν, *AB*344, Phot.

**ἀδιπλ-ασίαστος**, ον, *not doubled*, of letters, Eust.781.15. Adv. -τως Id.870.63. **-αστος**, = foreg., Eust.763.25. **-ωτος**, ον, = foreg., Id.185.34.

**ἄδις**· ὡς Ἀπίων, ἀθρόοι· καὶ ἐσχάρα, Hsch. **ἄδισκον**· κυκεῶνα (Maced.), Id.

*__ἀδίστακτος__, ον, *undoubted, undisputed*, *PTeb.*124.26 (ii B.C., written -αστος), Phld.*Mus.*p.80 K. Adv. -τως *AP*12.151, Sch.A.R.2.62, Ptol.*Geog.*1.4. II. Act., *undoubting*: hence, *instinctive*, v.l. for ἀδίδακτος I (q.v.), Pall.*in Hp.*2.127 D. Adv. -τως *unhesitatingly*, Phld.*Rh.*1.133 S., Syr.*in Metaph.*73.18, Procl.*in Prm.*p.756 S.

**ἀδίστονον**· οἰκτρὸν στένοντα, Hsch., *EM*18.30.

**ἀδιύλιστος**, ον, (διυλίζω) *not strained* or *filtered*, Gal.13.285.

**ἀδίχαστος**, ον, (διχάζω) *not to be cut in two*, Nicom.*Ar.*1.9.

**ἀδιψ-έω**, *to be free from thirst*, Hp.*Coac.*599. -**ος**, ον, *not thirsty, not suffering from thirst*, Hp.*Epid.*3.17.ιε', E.*Cyc.*574, Arist.*PA*669ᵃ34, Clearch.74. Adv. -ψως Hp.*Epid.*3.13. II. Act., *quenching thirst*, Hp.*Acut.*15 (Sup.), 59, Diph.Siph.ap.Ath.2.69f. 2. *not causing thirst*, Xenocr.34. III. **ἄδιψον**, τό, = γλυκυρρίζα, Dsc.3.5; *adipsos*, a kind of *date*, gathered unripe, Plin.*HN*12.103.

**ἀδίωκτος**, ον, *not to be eliminated, irremovable*, Syn.Alch.p.63 B.

**ἀδιώμοτος**, ον, *not feeling bound by an oath*, Procop.*Arc.*5.

**ἀδμαίνειν**· ὑγιαίνειν, ζῆν, Hsch. **ἀδμενίδες**, αἱ, = δοῦλαι, *EM* 18.32. **ἀδμεύειν**, = ἀδμαίνειν, *EM*18.31, Suid. **ἀδμηλοῖ**· ἀφανίζει, Hsch.

**ἀδμ-ής**, ῆτος, ὁ, ἡ, poet. for ἀδάματος, (Hom. only in Od.), of maidens, *unwedded*, παρθένος ἀδμής 6.109, 228; ἀδμῆτας ἀδελφάς S.*OC*1056 (lyr.). 2. of animals, *unbroken*, ἡμίονοι.. ἀδμῆτες Od.4.637. 3. c. gen., ἀδμᾶτες νούσων *unsubdued by*.., B.*Fr.*19. -**ῆτις**, ιδος, ἡ, v.l. for ἀδμήτη in Il.23.655:—*virgin*, Benndorf-Niemann *Reise in Lykien* p.77. *-**ητος**, η, ον, poet. for ἀδάματος, in Hom. only in fem. and of cattle, *unbroken*, βοῦν ἦνιν.. ἀδμήτην, ἣν οὔ πω ὑπὸ ζυγὸν ἤγαγεν ἀνήρ Il.10.293, Od.3.383; ἵππον.. ἑξέτε' ἀδμήτην Il.23.266; ἡμίονον ib.655. 2. *unwedded*, of maidens. παρθένῳ ἀδμήτῃ *h.Ven.*82, cf. 133, A.*Supp.*149; of Artemis, τὰν αἰὲν ἀδμήταν S.*El.*1239 (lyr.); of Atalanta, τῆς πρόσθεν ἀ. Id.*OC*1321.

*__ἀδμολίη__, ἡ, *uncertainty*, Call.*Fr.*338 (-μωλ- Suid.). **ἀδμωλεί**· χωρὶς δόλου ἢ δουλείας, Suid. *__ἀδμωλή__, ἡ, = ἄγνοια, Hdn.Gr.1.324, cf. Hsch. **ἀδμωλῶ**· ἀκηδιῶ, Suid.:—also **ἀδμωλεῖν**· ἀγνοεῖν ἢ ἀγνωμονεῖν ἢ ἀκηδιᾶν, *EM*18.33.

**ἄδμωνες** or **ἄδμωες**, οἱ, a kind of *sea-fish*, Opp.*H.*3.371, 380.

**ἀδνός**, Cret. for ἁγνός, Hsch.

**Ἁιδοβάτης**, ου, ὁ, *one who has gone to the nether world*, prob. l. for ἀγδαβάται, A.*Pers.*924 (lyr.).

**ᾅδόθεν**, Adv. *from the nether world*, Hermesian.7.3.

**ἀδοιάστως**, (δοιάζω) *without doubt*, Anacr.95. [οἷ l. c.]

**ἀδοκεῖ**· ἀδοκήτως διακείμενος, Hsch.

**ἀδόκητος**, ον, *unexpected*, Hes. (v. infr.); τὰν ἀ. χάριν S.*OC*249 (lyr.); τὰ δοκηθέντ' οὐκ ἐτελέσθη, τῶν δ' ἀ. πόρον ηὗρε θεός E.*Med.*1418 (also in *Alc.*, *Ba.*, *Andr.*, *Hel.*, ad fin.); ξυμφορὰ ἀ. Th.7.29, etc.; τὸ ἀ. *surprise*, Id.4.36, al. II. ἀδόκητον καὶ δοκέοντα either *inglorious and glorious*, or *unexpecting and expectant*, Pi.*N.*7.31, cf. *Trag.Adesp.*482 (lyr.):—*unexpecting*, Memn.28.2, cf. Nonn.*D.*31.209. III. Adv. -τως Th.4.17, Phld.*Ir.*p.49 W.; ἀδόκητα, as Adv., Hes.*Fr.*79, E.*Ph.*311; ἀπὸ τοῦ ἀδοκήτου Th.6.47; ἐκ τοῦ ἀ. D.H.3.64.

**ἀδοκία**· ἀπροσδοκία, Hsch.

*__ἀδοκιμ-αστος__, ον, *not approved*, Lys.14.8, 15.11, Aeschin.3.15, etc.; πρᾶγμα D.H.11.57; τὸ ἀ. Onos.*Praef.*7. *-**ος**, ον, *not legal tender, not current*, of coin, Pl.*Lg.*742a; *not approved*, of horses, Arist.*Ath.*49.1. 2. *unsatisfactory, unconvincing*, of a statement, Ph.*Bel.*76.47, Alex.Aphr.*in Top.*576.14. 3. *disreputable*, λακίσματ' ἀδόκιμ' ὀλβίοις ἔχειν E.*Tr.*497; μοῦσα Pl.*Lg.*829d, cf. D.25.36, *Ep.Rom.*1.28. Adv. -μως Poll.5.160. 4. of persons, Pl.*R.*618b; *discredited, reprobate*, X.*Lac.*3.3, 2*Ep.Tim.*3.8, etc.

*__ἀδο-λεσχέω__ [ᾰ], *talk idly, prate*, Eup.353, Pl.*Phd.*70c, X.*Oec.*11.3, etc.; ἱκανῶς ἡμῖν ἠδολεσχήσθω ἐπὶ τοῦ πάροντος Epicur.*Nat.*28.13. II. generally, *talk*, Lxx *Ps.*68(69).12. III. *meditate*, ib.*Ge.*24.63, *Ps.*118(119).15, al. -**λέσχης**, ου, ὁ, *prater, idle talker*, esp. of reputed sophists: Σωκράτην, τὸν πτωχὸν ἀ. Eup.352, cf. Ar.*Nu.*1485; ἢ Πρόδικος ἢ τῶν ἀ. εἷς γέ τις Id.*Fr.*490; ἀ. τις σοφιστής Pl.*Plt.*299b, cf. *Tht.*195b, *R.*488e: generally, *talker, babbler*, Thphr.*Char.*3.2, Arist.*EN*1117ᵇ35, etc. II. in good sense, *subtle reasoner*, Pl.*Cra.*401b. [ᾰ- in Eup. and Ar. ll. c.; cf. ἀδέω, λέσχη.] *-**λεσχία** [ᾰ], ἡ, *prating, garrulity*, Ar.*Nu.*1480, Isoc.13.8, Pl.*Tht.*195c, Arist.*Rh.*1390ᵃ9, Thphr.*Char.*3: pl., Simp. *in Ph.*1141.8. II. *keenness, subtlety*, Pl.*Phdr.*269e. III. *conversation, talk*, Lxx 4*Ki.*9.11, *Ps.*54(55).2. -**λεσχικός** [ᾰ], ή, όν, *prating*, τὸ -κόν *garrulity*, Pl.*Sph.*225d, Procl.*in Prm.*p.501 S. -**λεσχος** [ᾰ], ον, = ἀδολέσχης, Cic.*Att.*16.11.2, *IG*14.1746 (ἀδελ- lapis); ἀ. καὶ λάλος Alciphr.3.66; τὸ ἀ. S.E.*M.*1.141: Comp. -ότερος Gal.5.315: Sup. -ότατος Plu.2.509a. Adv. -χως Phld.*Ir.*p.17 W., *Rh.*1.212 S. (Comp.).

**ἀδολίευτος**, ον, = sq., ἤθη Sch.Ar.*Pl.*1158. II. *not concealed*, ἄγκιστρον Sch.Opp.*H.*3.532.

**ἄδολος**, ον, *guileless, honest*, σοφία Pi.*O.*7.53; in Att. esp. of treaties, ἀ. εἰρήνα Ar.*Lys.*169; σπονδαὶ ἀ. καὶ ἀβλαβεῖς Th.5.18. Adv., freq. in the phrase ἀδόλως καὶ δικαίως *without fraud* or covin, Th.5.23, cf. *IG*1.42e; ἁπλόως καὶ ἀ. *GDI*5024 (Gort.): generally, πλουτεῖν ἀδόλως *Scol.*8; ἀδολώτερον λέγεσθαι, opp. πιστότερον, Antipho 3.3.4:—also, *genuinely, truly*, τεθνάκην ἀ. θέλω Sapph.*Supp.*23.1, cf. Theoc.29.32. II. *unadulterated, genuine*, χρίματος ἀδόλοισι παρηγορίαις A.*Ag.*95; στύραξ Dsc.1.66; χρυσός Eupolem.ap.Alex.Polyh.18; ἀργύριον Poll.3.86; σῖτος, πυρός, *PHib.*1.85, *PGrenf.*1.18; ἀ. παντός ib.2.29.14: metaph., αὔραις ἀδόλοις *pure*, E.*Supp.* (lyr.); τὸ λογικὸν ἀ. γάλα 1*Ep.Pet.*2.2. 2. *unpretentious*, *Pel.*3.

**ἄδον**, Ep. for ἔαδον, aor. 2 of ἁνδάνω.

*__ἀδόνητος__, ον, (δονέω) *unshaken*, *AP*5.267 (Paul. Sil.).

**ἀδονίς**, ἡ, poet. for ἀηδονίς, Mosch.3.46.

**ἀδοξάζω**, incorrectly formed, = ἀδοξέω II, Anon. *in Rh.*105 (Pass.).

**ἀδόξαστος**, ον, *unexpected*, S.*Fr.*223. 2. *not matter of opinion*, i.e. *certain*, Pl.*Phd.*84a. II. Stoic, *free from* δόξα, *not opinionated*, Aristo *Stoic.*1.78, Pers.ib.102; *refusing to form opinions*, Timo ap. Aristocl.ap.Eus.*PE*14.18. Adv. -τως, opp. δογματικῶς, S.E.*P.*1.15, etc.

**ἀδοξ-έω**, *to be held in no esteem, be in ill repute*, ἀδοξοῦντες, opp. οἱ δοκοῦντες, E.*Hec.*294, cf. D.19.103; opp. εὐδοκιμεῖν, Arist.*Rh.*1372ᵇ22. II. trans., *hold in no esteem, in contempt*, τινά J.*BJ*1.26.2, al., cf. Plu.*Luc.*14:—hence in Pass., αἱ βαναυσικαὶ [τέχναι] ἀδοξοῦνται πρὸς τῶν πόλεων X.*Oec.*4.2. -**ημα**, ατος, τό, *disgrace*, Plu.2.977e. -**ία**, ἡ, *ill repute*, Hp.*Lex*1, Th.1.76, Pl.*Phd.*82c, D.1.11, Phld.*Lib.*p.4 O., etc.; *obscurity*, Plu.*Agis*2. II. *contempt*, App.*Syr.*41. -**οποίητος**, ον, *not forming notions, unreasoning*, Plb.6.5.8. *-**ος**, ον, *without* δόξα, *inglorious*, πόλεμος D.5.5; *disreputable*, τέχνη X.*Smp.*4.56. 2. *obscure, ignoble*, πόλεις Isoc.12.253; ἀνώνυμοι καὶ ἀ. D.8.66, cf. Arist.*Rh.*1384ᵇ31; of eunuchs, *despised*, X.*Cyr.*7.5.61. Adv. -ξως Plu.*Thes.*35. II. = παράδοξος, *unexpected*, S.*Fr.*71; *improbable*, opp. ἔνδοξος, Arist.*Top.*159ᵃ39, etc.; τὰ -ότατα λέγειν ib.159ᵃ19.

**ἄδορος**, ον, (δέρω) = ἀνέκδαρτος, Suid. II. as Subst., **ἄδορος**, ὁ, = κώρυκος, *skin*, Antim.64.

**ἄδορπος**, ον, *without food, fasting*, Pi.*Pae.*6.128, Lyc.638.

**ἀδορυφόρητος**, ον, *without body-guard*, Arist.*Pol.*1315ᵇ28.

**ἄδος** (A), ὁ or τό, *satiety, loathing*, τάμνων δένδρεα μακρά, ἄδος τέ μιν ἵκετο θυμόν Il.11.88. (Cf. ἄδην.)

*__ἄδος__ (B), ὁ, *decree*, *SIG*45 (Halic.), *IG*12(8).263.8 (Thasos); cf. Hsch. s. v. ἄδημα. (Cf. ἁδεῖν, ἁνδάνω.)

*__ἆδος, ἀδοσύνη__, Dor. for ἦδος, ἡδοσύνη.

**ἄδοτος**, ον, *without gifts*, *h.Merc.*573.

**ἀδουλαγώγητος**, ον, *not enslaved*, ψυχή Vett.Val.220.20.

**ἀδούλ-ευτος**, ον, *one who has never been a slave*, Is.*Fr.*138, Arr. *Epict.*2.10.1. -**έω**, *have no slaves*, Str.15.1.59. -**ία**, ἡ, *being without slaves*, Arist.*Pol.*1323ᵃ6. -**ος**, ον, *unattended by slaves*, ἄδουλα δώμαθ' ἑστίας E.*Andr.*593: c. gen., τῶν τοιούτων ἄδουλος *unattended by*.., Ael.*NA*6.10. 2. *having no slaves, too poor to keep a slave*, Phryn.Com.18, Plu.2.831b. II. *impatient of slavery*, ἀδουλότερος τῶν λεόντων Ph.2.451. *-**ωτος**, ον, *unenslaved, unsubdued*, Pers.*Stoic.*1.99, D.S.1.53; ὑπό τινων Procl. *in Alc.*p.95 C.; ἀδούλωτοι ἡδονῇ Crates Theb.5.

**ἀδούπητος**, ον, *noiseless*, *AP*5.293.8 (Agath.).

*__ἀδουσιασάμενοι__· ὁμολογησάμενοι, and **ἀδούσιον**· ἀρεστόν, σύμφωνον, Hsch.

**Ἁιδοφοίτης**, ου, ὁ, = *frequenting Hades*, Ar.*Fr.*149.4, 6.

**ἀδραία**, Maced. for αἰθρία, Hsch. **ἀδρᾰκής**, ές, = ἀδερκής, Id.

*__ἀδράν-εια__, or -ία, ἡ, *listlessness, weakness*, Hdn.2.10.8, Just.*Nov.*102.3: Ep. ἀδρανίη, A.R.2.200, Call.*Fr.*520, *AP*6.296 (Leon.), etc. II. *non efficiency*, τοῦ μὴ ὄντος Simp.*in Cael.*136.30. [δρᾰ.] -**εος**, η, ον, = ἀδρανής, *AP*9.135. -**έω**, *to be weak*, of starlight, Arat.471, cf. Opp.*H.*1.296, Nonn.*D.*32.280. *-**ής**, ές, (δραίνω) *impotent, feeble*, *AP*9.359 (Posidipp.), Plu.2.373d, etc.; τὸ -έστατον ταῖς χερσίν Lxx *Wi.*13.19; τὴν χεῖρα ἀ. Philostr.*VA*3.39; -έστατοι ζῴων Babr.25.3; *non-efficient*, i.e. *unreal*, Simp.*in Ph.*533.19, 815.24; of nations, Arr.*Epict.*3.7.13: Comp., *less efficacious*, Dsc.3.110. 2. *deprived of its strength, useless*, of iron, Plu.*Lyc.*9, *Lys.*17. -**ίζομαι**, = ἀδρανέω, Sch.Arat.471, *Gloss.*

*__Ἀδράστεια__, Ion. **Ἀδρήστεια**, ἡ, (ἀ- priv., διδράσκω) title of Nemesis, A.*Pr.*936, cf. Pl.*R.*451a, etc. 2. fabulous plant, Ps.-Plu *Fluv.*18.13.

**ἄδραστος**, Ion. **ἄδρηστος**, ον, *not running away, not inclined to do so*, of slaves, Hdt.4.142, *PLond.*2.251.14 (iv A.D.): metaph., χαλκός D.Chr.37.10.—In Il. only as pr. n.

**ἄδρᾱτος**, ον, (δράω) *not done*, Hermipp.3 D. (ἄδραστα, Hsch., Phot.).

**ἀδράφαξυς** or **ἀδράφαξυς**, ἡ, v. ἀτράφαξυς.

**ἀδρέπᾰνος**, ον, *untouched by sickle*, S.*Fr.*978.

**ἀδρεπήβολος**, ον, (ἁδρός) τὸ περὶ τὰς νοήσεις ἀ. *the power of forming great conceptions*, Longin.8.1:—in bad sense, *ambitious*, Vett. Val.43.2.

**ἄδρεπτος**, ον, *unplucked*, A.*Supp.*663 (lyr.).

**ἀδρέω**, *to be full-grown, matured*, πυροὶ ἡδρηκότες Dsc.2.85:—Pass. forms ἀδρεῖτο, ἀδρώμενον (-ούμενον), Hsch.

**Ἀδρίας**, ου, Ion. **Ἀδρίης**, εω, ὁ, *the Adriatic*, Hdt.5.9, etc.:—Adj. **Ἀδρι-ανός**, ή, όν, A.*Fr.*71, also -**ηνός**, κῦμα τᾶς Ἀδριηνᾶς ἀκτᾶς E.*Hipp.*736 (lyr.): later, -**ακός**, νέκταρ, of Italian wine, called *Adriatic* because imported through Corcyra, *AP*6.257 (Antiphil.): -**ανικός**, ἀλεκτορίδες Arist.*GA*749ᵇ29: -**ατικός**, ὄρνιθες Chrysipp. Tyan.ap.Ath.7.285d:—also fem. -**άς**, άδος, ἅλμη D.P.92.

**ἄδρῑμυς**, υ, *not tart* or *pungent*, Luc.*Trag.*323.

**ἀδρό-βωλος**, ον, *in large pieces* or *masses*, of bdellium, Dsc.1.67. -**γραφία**, ἡ, *forcible writing*, Phld.*Rh.*1.165 S. (dub.). -**κέφαλος**, ον, *with large head*, Sor.2.63, Paul.Aeg.6.74; sens. obsc., Hierocl.

t.251. -μερής, ές, *of coarse, large grains*, opp. λεπτομερής, .5.26, Gal.8.336 (Sup.); *coarse*, of wine, Dsc.5.6: Comp. -έστεὄγκοι Ph.1.493. Adv. -ῶς Herasap.Gal.13.1045.

**ἀδρόμιος**, sc. μήν, month at Halos, *IG*9(2).109*a*6.

**ἀδρόμισθος**, ον, *with large prizes*, ἀγῶνες Scymn.353.

**ἄδρομος**, ον, *that will not gallop*, ἵπποι *Hippiatr.*105.

**ἀδρόομαι**, Pass., (ἁδρός) *grow stout*, Myro Hist.1.

**ἀδροπόρος**, ον, *with large pores*, Cass.*Pr.*48.

**ἁδρός**, ά, όν, *thick, stout, bulky*: I. of things, χιόνα ἁ. πίπτουν ἰδεῖν falling *thick*, Hdt.4.31; τῶν ἀνθράκων οἱ ἁδρότατοι the *most* ·id, Hp.*Mul.*2.133; κίονες ἁ. *large*, D.S.3.47; τοὺς ἁδροτάτους τῶν μβων Id.20.85:—*strong, violent*, πόλεμος Ar.*Ra.*1099; τὰ ἁδρότατα ν.. συμβάντων *Hell.Oxy.*4.1; ῥεύματα *full, swollen*, Arist.*Pr.*949$^b$ of raindrops, Id.*Mu.*394$^a$31 (Comp.); δῆγμα D.S.1.35; δωρεάς τε τιμὰς ἁ. δοῦναι *in abundance*, Id.19.86; κοιλότης *severe* deficiency, hld.*Oec.*p.71 J.:—of style, *powerful*, Longin.40.4 (Comp.), cf. hld.*Rh.*1.182 S.; ἁ. νοήματα dub. in D.H.*Comp.*4; ἀπειλή Phld. *Iom.*p.35 O.; τὸ ἁ. *the grand style*, opp. τὸ ἰσχνόν, Ps.-Plu.*Vit.Hom.* 2. Adv., Comp. ἁδροτέρως, διαιτᾶν live *more freely*, Hp.*Aph.*1.7; ἁ. αρμακεύειν ib.4.9; neut. as Adv., ἁδρὸν γελάσαι laugh *loud*, Antiph. 44; ἁδρότερον πιεῖν drink *more deeply*, Diph.5. II. of persons, *ine, well-grown*, ἐπεὰν τὸ παιδίον ἁ. γένηται Hdt.4.180; τῷ παιδί, ἐπὴν ἔῃ Hp.*Genit.*2; τῶν παίδων ὅσοι ἁ. Pl.*R.*466e; οἱ -ότεροι *the bestrown, the stronger*, Isoc.12.110; οἱ ἁ. *chiefs, princes*, Lxx 4*Ki.*10.6; also ἁ. τὴν ψυχήν Democh.3; ἡ κατὰ ψυχὴν ἁ. ὑπεροχή Procl.*in Alc.*p.94 C. 2. of animals, *fine, fat*, χοῖρος X.*Oec.*17.10; λύκος Babr.101; freq. in Com. of flesh, fish, etc., Antiph.20.5, 26.21, Alex. 170, etc. 3. of fruit or corn, *full-grown, ripe*, ὅκως εἴη καρπὸς ἁ. Hdt.1.17, cf. Arist.*Metaph.*1017$^b$8. b. ἁ. ῥίζα, = ἀριστολοχεία στρογγύλη, Ps.-Dsc.3.4. c. of an egg, *ready to be laid*, Arist. *HA*559$^b$11 (Comp.).—First in Hdt., never in Trag., rare in Att.; but the derivs. ἁδροτής, ἁδροσύνη occur in Ep. and ἁδρύνω in Trag.

**ἀδροσία**, ἡ, (δρόσος) *want of dew*, J.*AJ*2.5.5, Vett.Val.145.13: poet. -ίη *POxy.*1796.18 (sg. and pl.).

**ἁδροσύνη**, ἡ, (ἁδρός) = ἁδροτής, of ears of corn, Hes.*Op.*473.

※**ἁδρόσφαιρος**, ον, *in large balls*, μαλάβαθρον *Peripl.M.Rubr.*65.

※**ἁδροτής**, ῆτος, ἡ, *vigour, strength*, Epicur.*Ep.*1 p.31 U.; of plants, Thphr.*HP*7.4.11: metaph. of sound, *loudness*, Amarant.ap.Ath. 10.415a; of style or expression, *force*, Aristid.Quint.2.9. II. *abundance*, 2*Ep.Cor.*8.20. (In Hom. v.l. for ἀνδροτής, q.v.)

**ἁδρό-χωροι**· οἱ ἁδρὰς ἔχοντες χώρας, Hsch. ※-**χωρον**, τό, *full*, χῶρον, a wine-measure, *Ostr.*1600.

**ἁδρόω**, v. ἁδρόομαι.

**ἄδρυα**, τά, = ἀκρόδρυα, Ath.3.83a; Sicilian word, Hsch. II. *upright pieces* of a plough, Id. III. (ἀ- copul.) *canoes made of hollowed tree-trunks, dug-outs* (Cypr.), Id.

※**ἀδρυάς**, άδος, ἡ, (ἀ- copul., δρῦς) = Ἀμαδρυάς, in pl., Prop.1.20.12, *AP*9.664 (Paul. Sil.).

**ἀδρύμακτον**· καθαρόν, Hsch.; cf. δρυμάττω.

**ἁδρ-υνσις**, εως, ἡ, *coming to maturity*, Arist.*Metaph.*1065$^b$20, *Ph.*201$^a$19, Thphr.*CP*2.12.1:—written -υσις, Simp. *in Epict.* p.32 D. ※-**ύνω**, (ἁδρός) *ripen, mature*, S.*Fr.*979, X.*Mem.*4.3.8; ἁδρῦναι καὶ πέψαι τὸν καρπόν Thphr.*HP*3.1.3:—Pass., *grow ripe, ripen, come to maturity*, of fruit or corn, Hdt.1.193, Arist.*Ph.*230$^b$2; of embrya, Hp.*Septim.*1, *Oct.*12, cf. Arist.*HA*565$^b$13; of nestlings, 619$^b$30.

**ἄδρυπτος**, ον, (δρύπτω) *not scratching* or *tearing*, Nonn.*D.*11.137.

**ἀδρύφακτος**, ον, *unfenced*, ἀτείχιστος, ἀφύλακτος, ἄνευ δικαστηρίου, Hsch.: metaph., ἄπονος καὶ ἀταλαίπωρος, *AB*345.

**ἀδρώδης**, -φύτευμα, Ps.-Dsc.4.128.

**ἀδυβόας**, etc., Dor. for ἡδυ-.

**ἀδῠνᾰμ-έω**, *to want power, be incapable*, Lxx *Si.Prol.*, Simp.*in Cael.* 139.24: c. inf., *PLond.*2.361$^r$8 (i A. D.). ※-**ία**, Ion. -ίη, ἡ, *want of strength, debility*, Hp.*VM*10: pl., ib.19, Plu.2.791d; of medicine, *want of strength*, Thphr.*HP*9.18.4. 2. generally, *inability, incapacity*, Hdt.8.111, Arist.*Metaph.*1019$^b$15, etc.; ἡ τοῦ λέγειν ἁ. Antipho 5.2, cf. Pl.*Lg.*646b, etc.: pl., Lxx 3*Ma.*2.13: c. gen., ἁ. τοῦ ἀδικεῖν *for* wrongdoing, Pl.*R.*359b; τῶν πραγμάτων *for* political action, Arist.*Pol.*1314$^a$23; [ψυχῆς] *Stoic.*·.23: c. inf., Pl.*R.*532b. 3. *poverty, lack of resources*, X.*Oec.*20.22, D.19.186. ※-**ος**, ον, *weak*, of wine, Dsc.5.6:—*without potency*, Procl.*Inst.*80,149: -μον, τό, *absence of potency*, Olymp. *in Phd.*p.40 N.:—Astrol., of planets, Ptol. *Tetr.*53.

※**ἀδῠνᾰσία**, ἡ, = ἀδυναμία, Hdt.3.79, 7.172, Th.8.8: c. gen., ἀ. τοῦ λέγειν Id.7.8:—also **ἀδυναστία**, v.l. for -ασία in D.H.*Dem.*26, cf. *Gloss.* (**ἀδύναστος**, ib.), and **ἀδυνατία**, Dinol.9.

**ἀδῠναστί**, Adv. *impotently*, Suid.

**ἀδῠνᾰτ-έω**, of persons, *to be* ἀδύνατος, *lack strength*, Epich.266, Arist.*Somn.*454$^a$27: c. inf., *to be unable* to do, Hp.*de Arte*7, Pl.*R.* 366d, X.*Mem.*1.2.23, Arist.*EN*1165$^b$22, *Pol.*1287$^b$17, etc. II. of things, *to be impossible*, Lxx *Jb.*10.13, Phld.*Ir.*p.98 W., *Ev.Matt.*17. 20, *Ev.Luc.*1.37, Ps.-Callisth.3.26. -**ος**, ον, I. of persons, *unable* to do a thing, c. inf., Hdt.3.138, Epich.272, E.*HF*56, etc.; ἀ. εἰπεῖν Arist.*Rh.*1379$^a$2; ἀ. ὥστε.. Onos.1.13: Comp., τὸν δυνατώτερον τοῦ -ωτέρου [πλέον ἔχειν] Pl.*Grg.*483d: Sup. -ώτατος, λέγειν Eup.95. 2. abs., *without strength, powerless, weakly*, Hdt.5. 9, E.*Ion*596, *Andr.*746; οἱ ἀ. men *disabled for service*, whether as *invalids* or *paupers*, Lys.24 tit., Arist.*Ath.*49.4; ἐν τοῖς ἀ. μισθοφορεῖν Aeschin.1.103; ἀ. σώματι Lys.2.73; ἀ. χρήμασι *poor*, Th.7.28; εἴς τι Pl.*Hp.Mi.*366b; οἱ -ώτατοι persons *of no importance*, Phld.*Herc.* 1457.8; of ships, *disabled*, Hdt.6.16; τὸ ἀ. *want of strength*, Pl. *Hp.Ma.*296a; τὰ ἀ. *disabilities*, D.18.108. II. of things, *impossible*, E.*Or.*665, *Hel.*1043; ἐλπίδες *unrealizable*, Democr.58; τὸ ἀ. Arist.*Cael.*280$^b$12; ἡ εἰς τὸ ἀ. ἀπαγωγή *reductio ad impossibile*, *APr.*29$^b$5; ὁ διὰ τοῦ ἀ. συλλογισμός, ἡ διὰ τοῦ ἀ. δεῖξις, ib.34$^b$30, 45$^a$ 35; ἀδύνατα βούλομαι Lync.1.12:—ἀδύνατόν [ἐστι] c. inf., Hdt.1.32, al.; ἀδύνατά [ἐστι] Pi.*P.*2.81, Hdt.1.91, 6.106, Th.1.59; ἀ. ὑμῖν ὥστε.. Pl.*Prt.*338c; ὑμέας καταλελάβηκε ἀ. τι βοηθέειν Hdt.9.60; τὰ ἀ. καρτερεῖν E.*IA*1370; τολμᾶν ἀδύνατα Id.*Hel.*811; ἀδυνάτων ἐρᾶν Id.*HF*318, cf. Luc.*D.Deor.*8, etc.; prov., ἀδύνατα θηρᾷς Macar.1.26: Comp. -ώτερον, ἔτι.. εἰ οἷόν τε.. Pl.*Tht.*192b, cf. *Prm.*138d: Sup., ὃ δὴ πάντων -ώτατον Id.*Phlb.*15b. III. Adv. -τως *without power* or *skill, feebly*, ἀμύνεσθαι Antipho 4.3.3, cf. 3.3.4 (Comp.), Lys.12. 3:—ἀ. ἔχειν to be *unwell*, Pl.*Ax.*364b; to be *unable*, c. inf., Arist. *Rh.Al.*1435$^a$6; ἀ. ἔχει it is *impossible*, Epicur.*Ep.*2 p.49 U.; ἀ. λέγεται it is an *impossible* story, Phld.*Rh.*2.122 S.—Rare in poetry: Trag. only in E.

**ἀδυνατόω**, *debilitate*, in Pass., Erot. s.v. κατηπορήθη.

**ἀδυσκόλως**, Adv. *without complaint*, prob. in *Vit.Philonid.*p.13 C.

**ἀδυσώπητος**, ον, *not to be put out of countenance, inexorable*, Μοῖραι *JHS*32.274 (Pamphyl.), cf. Ph.2.543, Plu.2.64f. Adv. -τως, ἐνοχλεῖν ib.534b.

※**ἄδῠτος**, ον, (δύω) *not to be entered*, θησαυρός Pi.*P.*11.4; ἄ. ἐστιν ὁ τόπος Str.14.1.44. 2. *never setting*, of stars, Sch.Arat.632. II. mostly as Subst. (masc. in *h.Merc.*247, neut. in Hdt.5.72, E.*Ion*938), *innermost sanctuary* or *shrine*, Il.5.448,512, *h.Ap.*443; εὐώδεος ἐξ ἀ. Pi.*O.*7.32: metaph., ἐκ τοῦ ἀ. τῆς βίβλου Pl.*Tht.*162a; ἄ. θαλάσσης Opp.*H.*1.49, cf. *Hymn.Is.*152.

**ᾄδω**, Att. contr. for ἀείδω, q. v. **ἀδῶ**· ἀρέσκω, Hsch.

**ἀδώμητος**, ον, (δωμάω) *unbuilt*, Nonn.*D.*17.40.

**ἀδών** [ᾱ], όνος, ἡ, Dor. for ἀηδών, Mosch.3.9; cf. ἀδονίς.

**Ἄδων** [ᾰ], ωνος, ὁ, = Ἄδωνις, *AP*6.275 (Nossis), Theoc.15.149.

**Ἀδων-αία**, ἡ, epith. of Aphrodite, Orph.*A.*30; cf. Ἀδωνιάς. ※-**άρια**, τά, kind of *shoes* (prob. with play on ἀ- priv., Lat. *donarium, worthless gifts*), Procop.Gaz.*Ep.*146. -**ειος**, α, ον, *of Adonis*, κῆποι Suid. -**ηίς**· χελιδόνιον (prob. for -ών), ἡ θριδακίνη, Hsch. ※-**ια**, τά, *mourning for Adonis*, Cratin.15, Pherecr.170:—hence Ἀδωνιάζουσαι (from ※-**ιάζω**, *keep the Adonia*), title of Theoc. 15. -**ιακός**, ή, όν, *of* or *for Adonis*, κῆπος Arr.*Epict.*4.8.36. -**ιάς**, άδος, ἡ, = Ἀδωναία, Nonn.*D.*33.25. -**ιασμός**, οῦ, ὁ, *mourning for Adonis*, Ar.*Lys.*389. ※-**ιος**, ὁ, rare form of Ἄδωνις, Plu.2. 756c. II. as Adj., ος, ον, *of Adonis*:—hence Ἀδώνιον, τό, *a statue of him* borne in the Adonia, Suid. 2. (sub. μέτρον) a kind of *verse*, consisting of a dactyl and spondee, Sacerd.p.516 K. 3. = Ἄδωνις III, Plin.*HN*21.60. ※-**ις** [ᾰ], ιδος (also ιος Pherecr.198), ὁ, *Adonis*, ὦ τὸν Ἄδωνιν Sapph.63; Ἀδώνι' ἄγομεν καὶ τὸν Ἄ. κλάομεν Pherecr.170; ὤδωνις, i.e. ὁ Ἄ., Theoc.3.47:—hence, generally, *favourite, darling*, δεῖ Ἀδώνιδας αὐτοὺς ἀκούειν Luc.*Merc.Cond.*35, cf. Alciphr.1.39, *AP*5.112 (Marc.Arg.). 2. Ἀδώνιδος κῆποι cuttings planted in pots *for the Adonia*, Pl.*Phdr.*276b, Thphr.*HP*6.7.3, cf. Theoc.15.113: prov., of *any short-lived pleasure*, Sch.Pl. l. c. 3. αὐλὴ Ἀδώνιδος, at Rome, garden on the Palatine, Philostr.*VA*7. 32. II. kind of *flying-fish*, = ἐξώκοιτος, Clearch.73, Opp.*H.* 1.157, etc. III. *Adonis-flower, Anemone fulgens*, Aus.*Idyll.*6. 11. -**ίσιος**, sc. μήν, month at Seleucia, *Hemerolog.Flor.* -**ιών**, sc. μήν, month at Iasos, *JHS*9.342.

**ἀδώρ-ητος**, ον, = ἄδωρος, *h.Merc.*168; πρός τινος E.*Hec.*42; ἀ. λίθος of the philosopher's stone, Zos.Alch.p.114 B.: c. gen., πάντων ἀγαθῶν ἀ. *not endowed with*, Epicur.*Fr.*364. -**ία**, ἡ, *incorruptibility*, Poll.8.11.

**ἀδωρο-δόκητος**, ον, *incorruptible*, Aeschin.3.82, etc. Adv. -τως D.18.250, 19.·, *IG*2.114*A*5, Onos.1.8, D.S.30.20. -**δοκία**, ἡ, = ἀδωρία, D.C.*Fr.*40.1. -**δόκος**, ον, *incorruptible*, *AP*9.779. II. = ἀνάεδνος (q.v.), ὑμέναιοι Nonn.*D.*4.33, 34.176. -**ληπτος**, ον, = foreg., Hsch., Sch.Th.2.65.

**ἄδωρος**, ον, *taking no gifts, incorruptible*, c. gen., -ότατος χρημάτων Th.2.65. Adv. -ως Poll.8.11: Sup., D.C.72.10. b. *receiving no gifts*, Max.Tyr.11.8. 2. *unpaid*, πρέσβευσις *IG*7.2712 (Acraephia). II. *giving no gifts*, c. gen., ἄ. τινος *not giving* it, Pl.*Smp.* 197d; ἀ. ἐλαφαβολίαις by hunting *from which no gifts were offered*, S.*Aj.*177 (lyr.); *miserly*, Aret.*SD*1.5. III. ἄδωρα δῶρα gifts *that are no gifts*, like βίος ἀβίωτος, S.*Aj.*665.

※**ἀδωσι-δικία**, ἡ, *failure to give satisfaction*, *PLond.*2.357.7 (14 B. C.). -**δικος**, ον, ib.354.6 (10 B. C.).

※**ἀδώτης**, ου, ὁ, *non-giver*, coined as antithesis of δώτης, Hes.*Op.* 355. (Irregularly formed, cf. α I.)

**ἄεδν-ος**, ον, *undowered*, Hsch. II. (α III) = πολύφερνος, Id. -**ωτος**, ον, (ἑδνόω) *not accompanied by bridal gifts*, ἀλφή Lyc. 549.

※**ἀέθλ-ευμα**, -εύω, -έω, -ητήρ, -ητής, etc., Ep. and Ion. for ἀθλ-.

**ἀέθλιον**, Ep. and Ion. for ἆθλον, *prize*, Il.9.124, Od.8.108, *APl.*5. 374, *AP*9.637 (Damoch.). II. = ἆθλος, *contest*, Od.24.169, Call. *Del.*187.

**ἀέθλιος**, α, ον, *gaining the prize*, or *running for it*, ἵππος καλὴ καὶ ἀεθλίη a *race*-horse, Thgn.257; ἵππος ἀέθλιος Call.*Del.*113:—contr. ἆθλιος (q.v.) only in a restricted sense.

※**ἀεθλοθέτης**, ου, ὁ, = ἀθλοθέτης, *IG*3.1171.

**ἄεθλον**, τό, **ἄεθλος**, ὁ, Ep. and Ion. for ἆθλον, ἆθλος.

**ἀεθλο-νῑκία**, ἡ, *victory in the games*, Pi.*N*.3.7. ®**-σύνη**, ἡ, *contest, struggle*, *AP*5.293.18(Agath.). **-φορέω**, *win prize*, ἐκ διαύλου Call.*Sos*.42. **-φόρος**, ον, Ep. and Lyr. for ἀθλοφόρος.

®**ἀεί**, Adv. *ever, always*, Hom., etc.; with other specifications of time, ἐμμενὲς αἰεί Od.21.69; συνεχὲς αἰ. 9.74; ἀ. καθ' ἡμέραν, καθ' ἡμέραν ἀ., ἀ. καὶ καθ' ἡμέραν, ἀ. κατ' ἐνιαυτόν, ἀ. διὰ βίου, etc., Pl.*Phd.* 75d, etc.; ἀ. πανταχοῦ D.21.197, cf. Ar.*Eq*.568; διὰ παντὸς ἀ. *Pax* 397; ἐνδελεχῶς ἀ. Men.521; δεῦρ' ἀεί *until now*, E.*Or*.1663, Pl.*Lg.* 811c; αἰεί κοτε, ποτε *from of old*, Hdt.1.58, Th.6.82; αἰ. δήποτε 1.13; cf. εἰσαεί:—with the Art., ὁ ἀ. χρόνος *eternity*, Hdt.1.54, Pl.*Phd.* 103e, etc.; οἱ ἀ. ὄντες the *immortals*, X.*Cyr*.1.6.46, etc.:—but ὁ αἰ. βασιλεύων the king *for the time being*, Hdt.2.98; οἱ ἀ. δικάζοντες D. 21.223; ὁ αἰ. ἐντὸς γιγνόμενος *every one* as he got inside, Th.4.68; τὸν ἀ. προστυχόντα D.21.131; τοῖσι τούτων αἰ. ἐκγόνοισι to their descendants *for ever*, Hdt.1.105, cf. 3.83, etc.; in A.*Pr*.937, θῶπτε τὸν κρατοῦντ' ἀ., ἀεί is postponed metri gr.—Dialectic forms (cf. Hdn.Gr.1.497, *Et.Gud.z*): 1. **αἰεί**, Ep., Ion., Poet., and Early Att. (cf. Marcellin.*Vit.Thuc*.52); found (beside ἀεί) in Att. Inscrr. to 361 B.C. 2. **ἀεί** [ᾱ three times in Hom., ᾰ Att.] normal in Att. Inscrr. from 361 B.C. 3. **αἰέν**, Il.1.290, al. (ἀεν is v.l. in Il.11. 827), Pi.*N*.6.3, Sophr.90, A.*Pr*.428, *Ag*.891, S.*Aj*.682. 4. Dor. **αἰές**, Ar.*Lys*.1266, Bion *Fr*.1.1; also **ἀές**, *Tab.Heracl*.1.134. 5. Aeol. **αἶι(ν)**, **ἄι(ν)**, Hdn.Gr. l.c.; cf. *IG*9(2).461 (ἄϊν, Thess.), *SIG*58 (Milet.), and v. αἰπάρθενος, ἀείδασμος. 6. **αἰέ**, Hdn.Gr. l.c. 7. **ἀέ**, Pi.*P*.9.88, Pisand.11(ἀέ); cf. ἀέ-ναος. 8. Boeot. **ἡί**, Hdn. Gr. l.c. 9. Tarent. **αἰή**, ibid. II. τὸ ἀ. *eternity*, τὸ ἀ. τοῦτο οὐκ αἰώνιόν ἐστιν ἀλλὰ χρονικόν Procl.*Inst*.198. The statement of Harp. that ἀεί = ἕως in Att. is based on misinterpretation of such phrases as ἐς τόνδε αἰ. τὸν πόλεμον Th.1.18. (αἰϝεί *Epigr.Gr.*742, *GDI*60.31 (Cypr.), *IG*9(1).334.4 (Locr.), cf. Lat. *aevum*.)

**ἀει-βλαστής**, ές, *ever-budding*, Thphr.*CP*1.11.6. **-βλάστησις**, εως, ἡ, *perpetual budding*, ibid. ®**-βλύων**· ἐπιρρέων, Hsch. **-βολος**, ον, (βάλλω) *continually thrown*, σφαῖρα *AP*6.282(Theod.). **-βρυής**, ές, (βρύω) *ever-sprouting*, Nic.*Th*.848. **-γενεσία**, ἡ, *perpetual generation*, Jul.*Or*.6.185c, al., Iamb.ap.Stob.1.49.38, Procl.*in Cra.* p.24 P., etc. **-γενέτης**, only in Ep. form **αἰειγενέτης**, ου, ὁ, epith. of the gods, *everlasting*, used by Hom. only at the end of a line, θεῶν αἰειγενετάων Il.2.400, cf. 3.296. ®**-γενής**, ές, *eternal*, Hp.*Virg*.1, Pl.*Lg*.773e, *Smp*.206e, X.*Smp*.8.1; θεοί Antag.1.2. 2. *everlasting*, opp. ἀΐδιος, Plu.2.374d. ®**-γένητος**, ον, *eternally generated*, ψυχή Dam.*Pr*.410. II. = ἀειγενής, θεοί Procl.*in Ti*.3. 311 D. **-γεννητής**, οῦ, ὁ, *perpetual producer*, epith. of Apollo (τῷ τὸν αὐτὸν ἀεὶ γίγνεσθαι καὶ ἀεὶ γεννᾶν), Macr.*Sat*.1.17.35. **-γλεῦκος**, τό, *unfermented wine*, Plin.*HN*14.83. **-γνητος**, ον, = ἀειγενέτης, Orph.*A*.15. **-δάκρυτος**, *ever-lamented*, μνήμη *IG*2.3552b. **-δασμος**, ον, *subject to a perpetual charge*, γῆ *GDI*5661 (Chios, written αἰδ-); δασμὸς ἀ., Ἀθηνᾶ 20.169 (Chios).

**ἀ-ειδέλιος**, ον, = sq., *EM*21.33, Hsch. ®**-είδελος**, ον, (*ϝείδω) *unseen, dark*, Hes.*Fr*.112; *obscure*, Opp.*H*.1.86, etc. II. *not to be looked on, dazzling*, Nic.*Th*.20. **-ειδής**, ές, (εἶδος) *formless*, Arist.*Cael*.306$^{b}$17; *indistinct*, ὀσμαί Thphr.*Od*.1; f.l. for ἀιδής Pl. *Phd*.79a. 2. *unsightly*, χροιά *a bad* complexion, Hp.*Nat.Mul.* 41. **-ειδία**, ἡ, (ἀειδής 2) *deformity*, J.*BJ*7.5.5.

**ἀειδίνητος** [ῑ], ον, *ever-revolving*, ἄτρακτος, σφαῖρα, *AP*6.289 (Leon.), Nonn.*D*.6.87.

®**ἀείδιος**, ον, Adj. from ἀεί, *everlasting*, Hsch.

**ἀει-δουλεία** or **-δουλία**, ἡ, *perpetual slavery*, Poll.3.80, Hdn.*Epim.* 221. **-δράστεια**, ἡ, etym. of Ἀδράστεια, Corn.*ND*13.

®**ἀείδω**, Ion. and poet. form used by Hom., Pi., and sometimes in Trag. and Com. (even in trim., A.*Ag*.16, E.*Fr*.188; in tetram., Cratin. 305), also in Ion. Prose; contr. ᾄδω (also Anacr.45, Theoc.), Trag., Pl., etc.: impf. ἤειδον Od., Ep. ἄειδον Il., etc.; Trag. and Att. ᾖδον E.*Alc*.761, Th.2.21: fut. ἀείσομαι Od.22.352, Thgn.943, but ᾄσομαι *h.Hom*.6.2, 32.19, Thgn.243, and always in Att. (ᾄσεις, ᾄσουσιν in Ar. *Pax* 1297, Pl.*Lg*.666d are corrupt); rarely in act. form ἀείσω, Sapph. 11, Thgn.4, Ar.*Lys*.1243 (Lacon.), and late Poets, as Nonn.*D*.13.47 (in E.*HF*681 ἀείδω is restored by Elmsl.); still more rarely ᾄσω, Babr. 12.13, Men.Rh.p.381 S., Him.*Or*.1.6; Dor. ᾀσεῦμαι Theoc.3.38, ᾀσῶ Id.1.145: aor. ἤεισα Call.*Ep*.23.4, Opp.*C*.3.1, Ep. ἄεισα [ᾰ] Od.21. 411; ἄεισον E.*Tr*.513(lyr.); ἀείσατε Ar.*Th*.115(lyr.); ᾖσα Ar.*Nu.* 1371, Pl.*Ti*.21b:—Med., aor. ἀεισάμην (in act. sense) *PMag.Lond.* 47.43, imper. ἀείσεο *h.Hom*.17.1 (nisi leg. ἀείδεο):—**Pass.**, ἀείδομαι Pi., Hdt.: poet. impf. ἀείδετο Pi.: aor. ᾔσθην, v. infr. II. 1: pf. ᾖσμαι Pl.Com.69.11. (ἀϝείδω, cf. αὐδή, ὑδέω.) [ᾰ: but ᾱ metri gr. Od. 17.519, *h.Hom*.12.1, 27.1, *Il.Parv*.1, Thgn.4, Theoc.7.41, etc.]:—*sing*, Il.1.604, etc.: hence of all kinds of vocal sounds, *crow* as cocks, Pl.*Smp*.223c; *hoot* as owls, Arat.1000; *croak* as frogs, Arist. *Mir*.835$^{b}$3, Thphr.*Sign*.3.5, etc.; οἱ τέττιγες χαμόθεν ᾄσονται Stes. ap.Arist.*Rh*.1412$^{a}$23:—of other sounds, *twang*, of the bow-string, Od.21.411; *whistle*, of the wind through a tree, Mosch.*Fr*.1.8; *ring*, of a stone when struck, Theoc.7.26:—prov., πρὶν νενικηκέναι ᾄδειν '*to crow* too soon', Pl.*Tht*.164c.—Constr.: ἀ. τινί *sing to* one, Od.22.346; also, *vie with* one *in singing*, Theoc.8.6; ᾆ. πρὸς αὐλὸν ἢ λύραν *sing* to.., Arist.*Pr*.918$^{a}$23; ὑπ' αὐλοῖς Plu.2. 41c:—ἀείσας.. χαίρειν Δημοκλέα, poet. for εἰπών, *Epigr.Gr*.237.7 (Smyrna). II. trans., 1. c. acc. rei, *sing of, chant*, μῆνιν ἄειδε Il.1.1; παιήονα 1.473; κλέα ἀνδρῶν, νόστον, 9.189, Od.1.326; τὸν Βοιώτιον νόμον S.*Fr*.966: c. gen. (sc. μέλος), *sing* an air of.., Φρυνίχου Ar.*V*.269, cf. 1225: abs., ἀ. ἀμφί τινος *to sing* in one's praise, Od.8.266; ἀμφί τινα Terp.2, cf. E.*Tr*.513; εἴς τινα Ar. 1243: later, simply = καλεῖν, Ael.*NA*3.28:—Pass., of songs, *sung*, Hdt.4.35; τὰ λεχθέντα καὶ ᾀσθέντα Pl.*Lys*.205e; ᾆσμα κα ᾀσθέν, opp. λόγος καλῶς ῥηθείς, X.*Cyr*.3.3.55; ᾄδεται λόγος the st *runs*, Ph.1.189. 2. of persons, places, etc., *sing, praise, celebr* B.6.6, etc.:—Pass., ἀείδεται θρέψαισ' ἥρωας *is celebrated* as the nurs heroes, Pi.*P*.8.25, cf. 5.24. 3. Pass., *to be filled with song*, ἀ δετο πᾶν τέμενος.. θαλίαις Pi.*O*.10(11).76.

**ἀει-εστώ**, ἡ, *eternal being*, Antipho Soph.22. **-ζωής**, ές, *ev living*, Dam.*Pr*.161. **-ζωία**, ἡ, *everlasting life*, ibid. ®**-ζω** ον, Trag. contr. **-ζως**, ων, *ever-living, everlasting*, πῦρ ἀείζωον Herac 30, Nic.*Al*.174; ἀείζως γενεά S.*Fr*.740; ἀείζων πένθος ib.741; ἀεί θεός *CIG*4598 (Palaest.), *BGU*1247 (ii A.D.); οἱ ἀείζωοι *the immo tals*, Call.*Iamb*.1.265; ἀειζώου ψυχᾶς Melanipp.6, *IG*14.2241 (Italy metaph., ἄχθος ἀείζων A.*Supp*.988:—dist. fr. ἀΐδιος, *Corp.Her* 8.2. II. *evergreen*, πόα A.*Fr*.28, 29, cf. *Gp*.2.18.1: esp. **-ζωο** τό, *houseleek*, *Sempervivum*, Thphr.*HP*1.10.4, Dsc.4.88; ἀ. μέγ *S. arboreum*, ἀ. μικρόν *S. tectorum*, ib.89; ἀ. λεπτόφυλλον *ston crop*, *Sedum stellatum*, Ps.-Dsc.4.90. **-ζωτος**, ον, prob. *eve girded, aye ready*, *EM*22.20, sine expl. **-ζώων**, ουσα, ον, *eve living*, κεραυνός Cleanth.*Stoic*.1.122; ἱερά Call.*Del*.314. **-θαλής**, ές, *evergreen*, *AP*7.195 (Mel.), 12.256 (Mel.); δένδρα Chor.p.87 B. metaph., *ever-blooming*, Χάριτες Orph.*H*.60.5; νέος (of Γάμος personified) Men.Rh.p.404 S.; τὸ ἀ. τῶν φύλλων Dsc.4.88. **-θανής**, ές, *ever-dying*, *ever fearing death*, Man.1.166. **-θερής**, ές, (θέρω) *always warming*, Eratosth.16.8. II. *where it is always summer*, Μερόη Nonn.*D*.17.396.

**ἀειθέσσω**· ἀληθεύω, Cyr.

**ἀεί-θουρος**, ον, *ever-warlike*, Opp.*C*.2.189. **-θρύλητος**, ον, *ever talked of, celebrated*, Lyd.*Mag*.3.51. **-καρπος**, ον, *ever fruit-bearing*, Thphr.*CP*1.22.4.

®**ἀ-εικέλιος**, α, ον, Od.4.244, also ος, ον 19.341; poet. form of ἀεικής, 13.402, Il.14.84; contr. **αἰκέλιος** Thgn.1344, E.*Andr*.131 (lyr.):—of things, words, and actions; more rarely of persons, Od.6.242. Adv. **-ίως** Od.8.231, 16.109, B.3.45. ®**-εικής**, ές, (Att. αἰκής, q.v.) *unseemly, shameful*, ἀεικέα λοιγὸν ἀμύνειν Il.1.456, al.; ἀεικέα (εἵματα) ἕσσαι Od.24.250; δεσμός A.*Pr*.97, cf. 525; ἀεικεῖ σὺν στολᾷ S.*El*.191 (lyr.); **-έστερα** ἔπεα Hdt.7.13; οὐδὲν ἀ. παρέχεσθαι cause no *inconvenience*, Id.3.24; ἀεικέα μισθόν (v.l. ἀνεικέα, q.v.) *meagre*, Il.12.435; so οὐ.. ἀεικέα.. ἄποινα 24.594. Adv. ἀεικῶς Hsch.; Ion. **-έως** Simon.13; ἀεικές as Adv., Od.17.216. 2. οὐδὲν ἀεικές ἐστι, c. inf., it is nothing *strange* that.., Hdt.3.33, 6.98, A.*Pr*.1042. 3. *injurious, deadly*, ἰός Opp.*H*.2.422. **-εικία**, Ion. **-ίη** (Att. αἰκία, q.v.) [ῑ, whence in codd. often written **-είη**], ἡ, *outrage, injury*, πᾶσαν ἀεικίην ἄπεχε χροΐ (from Hector's body) Il.24.19: pl., μή τίς μοι ἀεικίας ἐνὶ οἴκῳ φαινέτω Od.20.308; ἀεικίῃ περιέπειν τινά Hdt.1.73, 115; ἀπαθὴς τῆς ἀ. Id.3.160. **-εικίζω** (Att. αἰκίζω, q.v.), fut. **-ιῶ** Il. (v. infr.), later Ep. also ἀεικίσσω Q.S.10.401: Ep. aor. ἀείκισσα Il.16.545:—**Med.**, Ep. aor. ἀεικισσάμην ib.559, 22.404:—**Pass.**, Ep. aor. inf. ἀεικισθήμεναι Od.18.222:—*treat unseemly, injure*, Hom. ll.cc.; οὐ γὰρ ἐγώ σ' ἔκπαγλον ἀεικιῶ *I will do* thee no great *dishonour*, Il.22.256, cf. 24.22 and 54, etc.:—Med. in act. sense, Il. ll.cc.

**ἀει-κινησία**, ἡ, *perpetual motion*, *Inscr.Perg*.333, [Gal.]19.376, Syr. *in Metaph*.37.13, Procl.*in Prm*.p.874 S. ®**-κίνητος**, ον, *in perpetual motion*, Pl.*Phdr*.245c, Philol.21, Ruf.*Anat*.27, Aen.Gaz.*Thphr.* p.46 B. Adv. **-τως** Arist.*Mu*.400$^{b}$31.

**ἀείκιον**· τὴν αἰκίαν, *EM*21.38.

®**ἀείκλαυτος**, ον, *filled with perpetual lamentation*, μέλαθρα prob. in Hymn.ap.Hippol.*Haer*.4.36.

**ἀει-κορσώσασθαι**· κεῖραι κεφαλήν, Hsch. **-κόρσωτοι**· ἄκαρποι Id.

**ἀεί-κωμος**, ον, *continually revelling*, Man.4.301. **-λάλος**, ον, *ever-babbling*, *AP*5.177 (Mel.). **-λαμπής**, ές, gloss on Ὄλυμπος, *ever-shining*, Stob.1.22.2.

**ἀείλη**· πνοή, Hsch.; cf. ἀέλλη.

**ἀείλλω**, *wheedle, cajole*, *EM*21.40, Hsch.; cf. ἀελλεῖ.

**ἀει-λογέω**, *to be always talking*, Hsch.; condemned by Phryn.*PS* p.35 B. **-λογία**, ἡ, *continual talking*:—as Att. law-term, τὴν ἀ. προτείνεσθαι or παρέχειν to court *continual inquiry* into one's conduct, D.19.2, 57.27.

**ἄειλος**, ον, (εἵλη) *unsunned*, πεδία A.*Fr*.334.

**ἀεί-μαργος**, ον, *ever-greedy*, Opp.*H*.2.213. **-μεριστός**, όν, *infinitely divisible*, Dam.*Pr*.178. **-μετάβλητος**, ον, *ever-changing*, ib. 405. **-μεταβόλος**, ον, = foreg., Procl.*in Ti*.1.125 D. **-μνημόνευτος**, ον, *ever-remembered*, J.*AJ*17.6.2, Ps.-Callisth.1.30. **-μνήμων**, ον, gen. ονος, *ever-remembering*, *of good memory*, Arist.*Phgn*.808$^{a}$ 37. ®**-μνηστος**, ον, *had in everlasting remembrance*, ἔργον A.*Pers.* 760; τάφος S.*Aj*.1166, E.*IA*1531 (lyr.), etc.; μετ' ἀ. μαρτυρίου Th. 1.33; τρόπαια Lys.2.25: Comp., Id.26.4; ἅπασι ἀ. ἡ ἁμαρτία Antipho 5.79; ἀρετή Isoc.9.4; χάριτες *PLips*.35.22 (iv A.D.). Adv. **-τως** Aeschin.2.180, *PLond*.3.854.12 (i A.D.). **-νάης**, ές, = sq., Nic.*Fr.* 78, in Ep. dat. pl. ἀειναέεσσι. **-ναος**, ον, = ἀέναος, q.v. ®**-ναῦται**, ῶν, οἱ, board of magistrates at Chalcis, *IG*12(9).909 (ἀε-), 923 (iii B.C.); also at Miletus, Plu.2.298c. (Cf. ναῦος; wrongly expl. by Plu. l.c. as *meeting on board ship*.)

**ἀεινεφεῖς**· τυφλώσεις, Hsch., cf. *EM*21.41.

**ἀείνως**, ων, Att. contr. for ἀείναος, v. ἀέναος.

**ἀει-παθής**, ές, *perpetually passive*, φύσις Crito ap.Stob.3.3.64, cf. Philol.21. **-πάθεια**· ἡ, *perpetual passivity*, Gal.1.317. **-παλής**, ές, *always beating*, καρδία *Hippiatr*.7. ®**-πάρθενος**, ἡ, *ever a virgin*, ɔph.96 (in Aeol. form ἀϊπ–); of the Vestals, αἱ ἱέρειαι αἱ ἀειπ. D.C. 5, cf. 59.3. **2.** in Pythag. language, of the number 7 (as ng neither factor nor multiple of any number up to 10), Ph.1.46; the Sabbath, ib.497. **–πλᾰνος,** ον, *ever-wandering*, χείλεα ηός Call.*Fr.anon.*2.

**ἄειρον** (ἐρῶ)· ἄρρητον, Hsch., *EM*21.43: also = ἀθώπευτον, ib.:— t **ἄειρος,** ον, (εἴρω) = ἄπειρος, Hsch., Suid.

**ἀεί-ροος,** ον, contr. **–ρους,** ουν, = sq., Aristeas 116, Suid. **–ρῦτος,** *ever-flowing*, κρήνη S.*OC*469.

**ἀείρω,** Ep., Ion., and poet.; **αἴρω** (once in Hom., v. infr.), Att. and rag. (exc. A.*Th.*759, *Pers.*660, both lyr.); Aeol. **ἀέρρω,** Alc.78: ıpf. ἤειρον (συν-) Il.10.499, Hdt.2.125, Ep. ἄειρον Il.19.386, Att. ıd Trag. ἦρον: fut. ἀρῶ [ᾱ], contr. for ἀερῶ (which is not found), A. *Pers.*795, E.*Heracl.*322, *Tr.*1148, prob. in Luc.*Hist.Conscr.*14: aor. 1 ειρα (συν-) Il.24.590, (παρ-) Archil.94, Herod.9.13, Ep. ἄειρα Il.23. 30; Aeol. imper. ἀέρρατε Sapph.91; subj. ἀέρσῃ Panyas.13.13; part. ἀείρας S.*Ant.*418; also ἄηρα *IG*12(3).449 (Thera); ἦρα Hdt. .59, A.*Ag.*47, Th.6.18, etc., 3 pl. ἤροσαν Lxx *Jo.*3.14, opt. ἄραις Herod.5.71, inf. ἆραι Call.*Cer.*35, part. ἄρας Th.2.12, etc., Cret. ἤραντας *GDI*5015 (Gort.) [ᾱ- in all moods]: pf. ἦρκα D.25.52, (ἀπ–) Th.8.100, plpf. ἤρκεσαν (ἀπ–) D.19.150:—**Med. ἀείρομαι** (ἀπ–) Il. 21.563, S.*Tr.*216 (lyr.); **αἴρομαι** E.*El.*360, Th.4.60: fut. ἀροῦμαι [ᾱ] E.*Hel.*1597: aor. 1 imper. ἄειραο A.R.4.746, inf. ἀείρασθαι (ἀντ–) Hdt.7.212, part. –άμενος Il.23.856, *IG*4.952.112 (Epid.); also ἠράμην [ᾱ- in all moods] Il.14.510, Od.4.107, E.*Heracl.*986, Ar. *Ra.*525, Pl.*R.*374e, etc., Dor. ἄρατο B.2.5: pf. ἦρμαι S.*El.*54:— Pass., E.*Alc.*450 (lyr.), Hp.*Mul.*2.174: fut. ἀρθήσομαι Ar.*Ach.*565: aor. ἠέρθην A.R.4.1651, (παρ–) Il.16.341, Ep. ἀέρθην Od.19.540, 3 pl. ἄερθεν Il.8.74, subj. ἀερθῶ E.*Andr.*848 (lyr.), part. ἀερθείς Od.8.375, Pi.*N.*7.75, A.*Ag.*1525 (lyr.), Hp.*Mul.*1.1, etc.; also ἤρθην Simon.111, A.*Th.*214 (lyr.), Th.4.42, etc., part. ἀρθείς Il.13.63, (ἐπ-) Hdt.1.90, etc.: pf. ἤερμαι A.R.2.171: Ep. plpf. 3 sg. ἄωρτο (for ἤορτο) Il.3.272, Theoc.24.43, ἔωρτο Hsch. [ἀείρω has ᾰ, exc. in late poetry, as Opp. *C.*1.347.] (ἀείρω = ἀ-ϝερ-yω, cf. αὐειρομέναι Alcm.23.63; αἴρω (once in Hom., Il.17.724 in part. αἴροντας) may = ϝαρ-yω for ϝr̥-yω from the reduced form of the root, but is more probably an analogical formation arising from the contracted forms. Fut. ἀροῦμαι [ᾰ] and aor. ἀρόμην, ἤρετο, etc., inf. ἀρέσθαι [ᾰ], belong to ἄρνυμαι, q.v.; ἠρᾰτο may have displaced ἤρετο in Hom., cf. Eust. ad Il.3.373. The sense *attach* found in compds. συν–, παρ-αείρω is prob. derived from the use v.1.)

**I.** Act., *lift, raise up*, νέκυν Il.17.724; ὑψόσ' ἀείρας [κυνέην] 10. 465; πίνακας παρέθηκεν ἀείρας Od.1.141; Εὐμάστας με ἄηρεν ἀπὸ χθονός *IG*12(3).449, inscr. on a stone (Thera); ἀπὸ γῆς αἴ. Pl.*Ti.*90a; ἱστία στεῖλαν ἀείραντες furled by *brailing them up*, Od.3.11; but ἀ. ἱστία *hoist* sail, A.R.2.1229; αἴ. κεραίας D.S.13.12; εὔμαριν ἀ. A.*Pers.* 660; κοῦφον αἴ. βῆμα *walk lightly, trip*, E.*Tr.*342; αἴ. σκέλη, of a horse, X.*Eq.*10.15, cf. Arist.*IA*710b20; ὀρθὸν αἴ. τὸ κάρα A.*Ch.*496; ὀφθαλμὸν ἄρας S.*Tr.*795; ἄρασα μύξας, of a deer, Id.*Fr.*89; ὀφρῦς αἴροντα Diph.85; αἴ. σημεῖον *make* a signal, X.*Cyr.*7.1.23; αἴ. μηχανήν, in the theatre, Antiph.191.15; so ἐπὶ τὰς μηχανὰς καταφεύγουσι θεοὺς αἴροντες Pl.*Cra.*425d; τεῖχος ἱκανὸν αἴ. Th.1.90, cf. 2. 75:—freq. in part., ἄρας ἔπαισε he *raised* [them] and struck, S.*OT* 1270; ἡ βουλὴ ἄρασα τὴν ἀφ' ἱερᾶς ἀφῆκεν Plu.*Cor.*32, cf. 1*Ep.Cor.* 6.15:—Pass., ἐς αἰθέρα δῖαν ἀέρθη Od.19.540, cf. Il.8.74; ὑψόσ' ἀερθείς Od.12.432; ἔμπνους ἀρθείς Antipho 2.1.9; φρυκτοὶ ἤροντο Th.2.94, cf. Aen.Tact.26.14; *mount up*, X.*HG*5.2.5; ἄνω ἀρθῆναι, of the sun, *to be high* in heaven, Hp.*Aër.*6; *to be seized, snatched up*, Ar.*Ach.*565. **2.** *take up*, in various uses: *draw* water, Ar.*Ra.* 1339; *gather* food, S.*Ph.*707; *pluck* herbs, *PMag.Par.*1.287, al. **3.** *take up and carry* or *bring*, ἐκ βελέων Σαρπηδόνα δῖον ἀείρας Il.16.678; νόσφιν ἀειράσας 24.583; ἄχθος ἀ. *convey*, of ships, Od.3.312; μῆλα ἐξ Ἰθάκης ἄειραν νηυσὶ *carried* them *off*, 21.18; μή μοι οἶνον ἄειρε *bring* me not wine, Il.6.264. **4.** *take up and bear*, as a burden, μόρον A.*Pers.*547; ἆθλον S.*Tr.*80; ἄλγος A.R.4.65. **b.** *wear* clothes, Lxx 1*Ki.*2.28, al. **5.** of armies or fleets, τὰς ναῦς αἴ. *get* the ships *under sail*, Th.1.52; esp. intr., *get under way, set out*, ἆραι τῷ στρατῷ Id.2.12: abs., ib.23:—Pass., ἀερθῆναι Hdt.9.52; ἀερθέντες ἐκ..1.165; ἀ. εἰς..1.170; ἐφ' ἡμετέρᾳ γᾷ ἀρθείς S.*Ant.*111 (lyr.); but ἀερθείς *carried too far*, Pi.*N.*7.75. **6.** *raise, levy*, λεκτὸν ἀροῦμεν στόλον A. *Pers.*795. **7.** *rear* a child, τοῖς τοκεῦσί σ' ἤειρα Herod.9.13. **II.** *raise up, exalt*, ἀπὸ σμικροῦ δ' ἂν ἄρειας μέγαν A.*Ch.*262, cf. 791; ὄλβον ὃν Δαρεῖος ἦρεν Id.*Pers.*164:—esp. of pride and passion, *exalt, excite*, ὑψοῦ αἴ. θυμόν *grow excited*, S.*OT*914; αἴ. θάρσος *pluck up* courage, E.*IA*1598:—Pass., *to be raised, increased*, ἡ δύναμις ἤρετο Th.1.118; ἤρετο τὸ ὕψος τοῦ τείχους μέγα Id.2.75; ἤρθη μέγας *rose* to greatness, D.2.8; οὐκ ἤρθη νοῦν ἐς ἀτασθαλίην Simon.111; ἀρθῆναι φόβῳ, δείμασι, A.*Th.*214, E.*Hec.*69: abs., ἀείρομαι S.*Tr.*216 (lyr.), cf. Ar.*Ec.* 1180. **2.** *raise by words*, hence, *praise, extol*, E.*Heracl.*322, etc.; αἴ. λόγῳ *to exaggerate*, D.21.71. **III.** *lift and take away, remove*, ἀπό με τιμᾶν ἦραν A.*Eu.*847; τινὰ ἐκ τῆς πόλεως Pl.*R.*578e; generally, *take away, put an end to*, κακά E.*El.*942; τραπέζας αἴ. *clear away* dinner, Men.273; ἀρθέντος τοῦ αἰτίου Arist.*Pr.*920b11; *deny* (opp. τίθημι *posit*), S.E.*P.*1.10; Delph. and Locr. pf. Pass. part. ἀρμένος *cancelled, null and void*, ὠνὰ ἀ. καὶ ἄκυρος *GDI*1746 (Delph.); ἀτελὴς καὶ ἀ. *IG*9(1).374 (Naupactus). **2.** *make away with, destroy*, *Ev.Matt.*24.39; ἆρον, ἆρον *away with him! Ev.Jo.*19.15; ἐκ τῶν ζώντων αἴ. *Tab.Defix.Aud.*1.18. **IV.** Med., *lift, take up for oneself* or *what is one's own*, [πέπλων] ἕν' ἀειραμένη Il.6.293; hence, *carry off, win*, πάντας ἀειράμενος πελέκεας 23.856; ἄρατο νίκαν B.2.5; ἠράμενοι νίκην Str.3.2.13. **2.** ὄγκον ἄρασθαι *to be puffed up*, S.*Aj.* 129; θαυμαστὸν ὄγκον ἀράμενοι τοῦ μύθου Pl.*Plt.*277b. **3.** *raise, lift*, τύπωμα ἠρμένοι χεροῖν S.*El.*54; κανοῦν αἴ. Ar.*Av.*850; βοῦς *IG*2². 1028.28, cf. Thphr.*Char.*27.5; ῥόθιον *raise* a surging cheer, Ar.*Eq.* 546; Σαμόσατα ἀράμενος μετέθηκεν Luc.*Hist.Conscr.*24; ἀείρεσθαι τὰ ἱστία *hoist* sail, Hdt.8.56, cf. 94. **4.** *raise, stir up*, νεῖκος ἀειράμενος Thgn.90, cf. E.*Heracl.*986, 991; *begin, undertake*, πόλεμον A. *Supp.*342, Hdt.7.132, Th.4.60, D.5.5 (Pass., πόλεμος αἴρεται Ar.*Av.* 1188); κίνδυνον Antipho 5.63; φυγὴν αἴρεσθαι *take to* flight, A.*Pers.* 481, E.*Rh.*54. **5.** *take upon oneself, undergo*, πόνον S.*Ant.*907; πένθος Id.*OT*1225; βάρος E.*Cyc.*473. **6.** abs., βαρὺς ἀ. slow to *undertake anything*, Hdt.4.150. **7.** *take away, remove*, E.*IT*1201; hence, *kill* or *destroy*, D.H.4.4, J.*AJ*19.1.3; πόλιν D.H.6.23. **V.** Pass., *to be suspended, hang*, [μάχαιρα] πὰρ ξίφεος μέγα κουλεὸν αἰὲν ἄωρτο Il.3.272, 19.253. **2.** Medic., *to be swollen*, [σπλὴν] ἀερθείς Hp.*Mul.*1.61; μαζοὶ ἀείρονται ib.2.174.

**ἀείς,** part. of ἄημι.

**ἀείσε,** late form for ἀεί, Steph. *in Hp.*1.129 D., al.

⊛**ἀει-σιτία,** Ion. –ίη, ἡ, *privilege of an* ἀείσιτος, Hp.*Ep.*27. ⊛**–σῖτος,** ον, *always fed*: *perpetual guest*, Epich.34; at Athens, of those maintained at public cost in the Prytaneum (in form ἀϊσ–), *IG*2².678.42, 3. 1019, al.

**ἀείσκωψ,** a kind of *owl* (cf. σκώψ), so called (acc. to Arist.) from not being migratory, perh. *Ephialtes scops*, Arist.*HA*617b32. (Pl. –σκῶπες, but ἀείσκωπες Eust.1524.6.)

**ἄεισμα,** τό, poet. and Ion. for ᾆσμα, Hdt.2.79, Eup.139, Call.*Ep.* 29.1.

**ἀείστροφος,** ον, *ever-turning*, Tz.*H.*10.568.

**ἀείτας,** α, ὁ, Boeot. for ἀετός, Lyc.461. **II.** v. sub ἀΐτας.

**ἀειτελής,** ές, *ever-perfect*, θεός Alcin.*Intr.*10.

**ἄειτον**· ταχύ, Hsch., *EM*21.42; cf. ἄελλον.

**ἀει-φᾰνής,** ές, *always above the horizon*, of stars, Nearch.ap.Arr. *Ind.*25.6, cf. Cleom.1.5. **2.** *ever-shining*, πῦρ, of the sun, D.P. 583; λύχνος Nonn.*D.*27.320. **–φεγγής,** ές, *ever-shining*, *Corp. Herm.*18.14. **–φόρος,** ον, = ἀειθαλής, dub. in S.*Fr.*580. **–φρουρος,** ον, *ever-watching*, i.e. *everlasting*, τῷ ἀ. μελιλώτῳ Cratin.98.7; οἴκησις ἀ., of the grave, S.*Ant.*892; πόνοι Opp.*H.*4.189. **–φῠγία,** ἡ, *exile for life*, φευγέτω ἀειφυγίαν Pl.*Lg.*877c, *IG*1.9, *SIG*194 (Amphipolis, iv B.C.); ἀειφυγίᾳ ζημιοῦν τινά D.21.43, etc. **–φύλακτος,** ον, gloss on ἀείφρουρος, Sch.Opp.*H.*4.189. **–φυλλία,** ἡ, *being non-deciduous*, Thphr.*CP*2.17.2. **–φυλλος,** ον, *not deciduous*, Arist. *GA*783b10, Thphr.*CP*1.10.7. **–χλωρος,** ον, *always green*, Euph. 133; used of κάππαρις, Dsc.2.173. **–χρόνιος,** ον, *everlasting*, *AP* 12.229 (Strat.). **–χρυσον,** τό, = ἀείζωον μέγα, Ps.Dsc.4.88.

⊛**ἀεκαζόμενος,** η, ον, particip. form, = ἀέκων, πόλλ' ἀ. Od.13.277, cf. *h.Cer.*30, Od.18.135. **ἀέκασσα**· ἄκουσα, Hsch. **ἀέκαστι,** Adv., etym. of ἀέκητι, A.D.*Conj.*233.26, *EM*19.33.

**ἀεκήλιος,** ον, for ἀεικέλιος, Il.18.77. (Derived from ἀ- priv., ἕκηλος by Hdn.Gr.2.106.)

⊛**ἀέκητῐ,** Ep. Adv. *against one's will*, c. gen., ἀ. σέθεν Od.3.213, 16.94; θεῶν ἀ., ἀ. θεῶν, Il.12.8, Od.4.504.

⊛**ἀεκούσιος,** ον (also α, ον Luc.*Syr.D.*18), Ion. and Ep. (also in anap., S.*Tr.*1263); Att. contr. **ἀκούσιος** [ᾱ], ον, also in Democr. 240:—*against the will, constrained*, of acts or their consequences, καὶ τῷ οὔ κως ἀεκ. ἐγίνετο τὸ ποιεύμενον Hdt.2.162; τλήσομαι..ἀεκούσια πολλὰ βίαια Thgn.1343; ἐς ἀ. ἀνάγκας πίπτειν Th.3.82; πόνοι Democr. l.c.; often in Att. of *involuntary* offences, ἀ. φόνος Antipho 3.2.6; πράκτορες τῶν ἀκουσίων ib., cf. Pl.*Lg.*733d, 864a, Arist.*EN*1109b35, al.; τὰ μὲν ἀ. ἁπλῆ, τὰ δὲ ἑκούσια διπλῆ *IG*1.1. Adv. –ίως D.21.43, Sever.ap.Eus.*PE*13.17. **II.** of persons, only in Adv. ἀκουσίως *involuntarily*, Th.2.8, Pl.*Ti.*62c; ἀ. ἀποθανεῖν, opp. ἑκουσίως ἀποκτείνειν, Antipho 1.5; ἀ. τινὶ ἀφῖχθαι to have come *as an unwelcome* guest, Th.3.31.

**ἀέκων,** Ep. and Ion.; Att. and Trag. contr. **ἄκων** [ᾱ], ουσα, ον (uncontr. form also in *IG*1.61 (law of Draco), A.*Supp.*39 (anap.), sts. found in codd. of Hdt., as 4.120, 164):—*involuntary, constrained*, of persons, ἀέκοντος ἐμεῖο Il.1.310; ἑκὼν ἀέκοντί γε θυμῷ 4.43; πόλλ' ἀέκων 11.557; opp. βουλόμενος, Hp.*VC*11; τὼ δ' οὐκ ἀέκοντε πετέσθην (v.l. ἄκοντε) Il.5.366, Od.3.484; κάρτα ἀ. Hdt.9.111; ἀέκουσι (v.l. ἀεκούσια) δάκρυα παραρρεῖ Hp.*Epid.*1.19: contr. first in *h.Cer.*413; ἄκοντος Διός *invito Jove*, A.*Pr.*771; repeated, ἄκοντά σ' ἄκων προσπασσαλεύσω ib.19, cf. 671; ἄ. ἀκούειν οὓς ἑκὼν εἶπεν λόγους S.*Fr.*929, cf. *Ant.*276; μηδένα τῶνδ' ἀέκοντα μένειν κατέρυκε Thgn.467. Adv. ἀκόντως *unwillingly*, ὁμολογεῖν Pl.*Prt.*333b, cf. *Hp.Mi.*374d; οὐκ ἀ. ἀλλὰ προθύμως ἐπείσθησαν X.*HG*4.8.5. **II.** Poet., like ἀκούσιος, of acts or their consequences, *involuntary*, κακὰ ἑκόντα κοὐκ ἄ. S.*OT* 1230; ἔργων ἀ. Id.*OC*240 (lyr.), cf. 977.

**ἀέλικτος,** ον, v.l. for τριέλικτος, Orac.ap.Hdt.6.77.

**ἀέλιοι** and **αἰέλιοι,** οἱ, *brothers-in-law*, whose wives are sisters, Hsch. (αἴλιοι), Eust.648.45, *EM*31.24; cf. εἰλίονες.

**ἀέλιος,** ὁ, Dor. for ἠέλιος, ἥλιος. [ᾱ, but ᾰ S.*Tr.*835.]

⊛**ἄελλα,** Ep. **ἀέλλη,** ης, Aeol. **αὔελλα** Alc.125 (αὐεοῦλλαι cod. Hsch.), ἡ, *stormy wind, whirlwind*, ἀργαλέων ἀνέμων ἀτάλαντοι ἀέλλῃ Il.13.795; ἄελλαι παντοίων ἀνέμων Od.5.292, 304; of dust, ὕψι δ' ἀέλλη σκίδνατο Il.16.374, cf. 13.334; in late Prose, Olymp. *in Mete.*13. 18. **2.** metaph., of any *whirling motion*, ὠκυδρόμοις ἀ., of an animal, E.*Ba.*873; ἄστρων ὑπ' ἀέλλαισι Id.*Hel.*1498.—Cf. ἀείλη.

**ἀελλαῖος,** α, ον, *storm-swift*, πελειάς S.*OC*1081 (lyr.). **ἀελλάς,** άδος, ἡ, = foreg., ἵπποι S.*OT*466 (lyr.); φωναί Id.*Fr.*688.

**ἀελλεῖ·** φιλεῖ, κολακεύει, Hsch.: but **ἀελλῶν·** στρέφων, ὀπτῶν, ποικίλ(λ)ων, Id. **ἀέλλεται·** πνεῖ, *EM*20.1.

**ἀελλήεις,** εσσα, εν, = ἀελλαῖος, Nonn.*D*.5.322, al.

**ἀελλής** κονίσαλος *eddying* dust, Il.3.13. (Perh. rather ἀελλῆς, contr. for -ήεις.)

**ἀελλησιθύμοις** (prob. -μυθοις)· ἀνυποστάτοις μετὰ παρρησίας, Hsch., *AB*348.

**ἀελλο-δρόμας,** α, *storm-swift*, πῶλος B.5.39. **-θριξ,** τριχος, ὁ, ἡ, *with hair floating in the wind*, S.*Fr*.292.

**ἀελλο-μάχος,** ον, *struggling with the storm*, *AP*7.586 (Jul. Aeg.). ⊛**-πος,** ποδος, ὁ, ἡ, for ἀελλόπους (like ἀρτίπος, Οἰδίπος, etc.):—*storm-footed, storm-swift*, Il.8.409, etc. (never in Od.); Ἅρπυια Euph.113; dat. pl. ἀελλοπόδεσσιν *h.Ven*.217: pl. ἀελλόποδες, -πόδων, Simon.7, Pi.*N*.1.6, etc.: once in Trag., E.*Hel*.1314.—Later ⊛**ἀελλοπόδης,** ου, of the hare, Opp.*C*.1.413.

**ἄελλον·** ταχύ, *EM*20.7.

**ἀελλός,** ὁ, a bird, Hsch.

⊛**Ἀελλώ,** όος, contr. οῦς, ἡ, (ἄελλα) *Storm-swift*, name of a Harpy, Hes.*Th*.267.

**ἀελλώδης,** ες, *storm-like, stormy*, Sch.Il.3.13, cf. Hsch.

**ἀέλον·** ἕωλον (Cret.), Hsch. **ἀελπάρεα·** δεινά, Id.

⊛**ἀελπ-ής,** ές, *unhoped for*, γαῖαν ἀελπέα δῶκεν ἰδέσθαι Od.5.408. **-τέω,** *have no hope, despair*, only in part., ἀελπτέοντες σόον εἶναι Il.7.310; ἀ. τοὺς Ἕλληνας ὑπερβαλέεσθαι Hdt.7.168. **-τία,** ἡ, *an unlooked for event*, ἐξ ἀελπτίης *unexpectedly*, Archil.54; *unexpected stroke*, Pi.*P*.12.31 [where ῑ]. ⊛**-τος,** ον, *unhoped for, unexpected*, *h.Cer*.219, Hes.*Fr*.96.57, B.3.29; ἐξ ἀέλπτου *beyond hope, unexpectedly*, in good sense, Hdt.1.111; ἐξ ἀέλπτων S.*Aj*.715 (lyr.); in bad sense, A.*Supp*.357,987 (prob. l.); πῆμ' ἄ., ἄ. κακόν, Id.*Pers*.265,1006; εἴπερ ὄψομαι τὰν ἄ. ἀμέραν E.*Supp*.784; ἄελπτα γὰρ λέγεις Id.*Hel*.585. **2.** *beyond hope, despaired of*, Archil.74, Hp.*Art*.42. **II.** Act., *hopeless, desperate*, *h.Ap*.91, A.*Supp*.907. **III.** Adv. -τως *beyond all hope*, in good sense, A.*Pers*.261, S.*El*.1263: neut. pl. as Adv., ἀ. φανείς E.*Ph*.311. [ᾱ Hes. l. c.]

⊛**ἄεμμα,** τό, Ep. for ἅμμα, *bow-string* or *bow*, Call.*Dian*.10, *Ap*.33.

**ἀέμπεδον·** βέβαιον, Hsch.

**ἀε-ναής,** ές, = sq., κελάδημα *IPE*1[2].519 (Chersonesus, ii A. D.). ⊛**-νᾱος** [ᾱ-], ον, (νάω A) ἀένναος Hdt., αἰέναος *IG*5(1).1119 (Geronthrae, iv B.C.); contr. **ἀείνως** Ar.*Ra*.146, gen. pl. ἀείνων Cratin.20 D.: Trag. only in lyr.:—*ever-flowing*, κρήνης τ' ἀενάου καὶ ἀπορρύτου Hes.*Op*.595; ἀ. λίμνη, ποταμός, Hdt.1.93,145, cf. Simon.120; ποταμοί A.*Supp*.553, E.*Ion* 1083, cf. 118; Ἀχέρων Theoc.15.102; ἀενάου πυρός Pi.*P*.1.6, cf. Call.*Ap*.83; βόρβορον καὶ σκῶρ ἀείνων Ar. l. c.; ἀέναοι νεφέλαι Id.*Nu*.275:—generally, *everlasting*, ἀρετᾶς..κόσμον ἀέναόν τε κλέος Simon.4.9; ἀ. τιμά, of Zeus, Pi.*O*.14.12; ἀ. κράτος E.*Or*.1299 (lyr.); ἀενάοις ἐν τραπέζαις, of public hospitality, Pi.*N*.11.8; γλῶτταν καλῶν λόγων ἀείνων Cratin. l. c.:—also in Prose, κλέος Heraclit.29; τροφή X.*Ages*.1.20; ἀεναώτερον..τὸν ὄλβον παρέχειν Id.*Cyr*.4.2.44; ἀέναον οὐσίαν πορίσαι Pl.*Lg*.966e; ἀ. ποταμῶν ἀμήχανα μεγέθη Id.*Phd*.111d, cf. Arist.*Mete*.349[b]9; θῖνες LXX *Ba*.5.7; ἀένναοι τῶν θεῶν πρόσοδοι Procl.*Inst*.152. Adv. ἀενάως Arist.*Oec*.1346[b]15. **-νάων,** ουσα, ον, = foreg., Od.13.109, Hes.*Op*.550, Antim.59.3.

**ἀέντιον·** Αἰγύπτιον σμυρνίον, Hsch.

**ἀεξί-βιος,** ον, *increasing while one lives* (?), πένθος *IG*14.2123. **-γυιος,** ον, *strengthening the limbs*, ἄεθλα Pi.*N*.4.73. **-κερως,** ων, gen. ω, *growing horns*, κριός *IG*14.1301. **-νοος,** ον, contr. **-νους,** ουν, *strengthening the mind*, Procl.*H*.3.16, Nonn.*D*.14.119. **-τοκος,** ον, *nourishing the fruit of the womb*, ib.5.614, al. **-τροφος,** ον, *fostering growth*, Orph.*H*.51.18. **-φυλλος,** ον, *nourishing leaves, leafy*, ἀκταί A.*Ag*.697. **-φῦτος,** ον, *nourishing plants*, Ἠώς *AP*9.363.5 (Mel.), cf. Nonn.*D*.7.304, al.

⊛ **ἀέξω,** poet. form of αὔξω (αὐξάνω), once in Hdt., twice in Trag. (lyr.); in early writers only in pres. and unaugm. impf.: in later Poets fut. ἀεξήσω Nonn.*D*.12.24, aor. ἠέξησα ib.8.104, *IG*4.787 (Troezen, iv A. D.): fut. Med. ἀεξήσομαι A.R.3.837: aor. Pass. ἀεξήθην *AP*9.631 (Agath.): plpf. ἠέξητο (ἀν-) Nonn.*D*.4.427: (ἀϝέξω, cf. Lat. *augeo*, Skt. *vakṣáyati*, etc.):—*increase, foster*, ἀνδρὶ δὲ κεκμηῶτι μένος μέγα οἶνος ἀέξει Il.6.261; θυμὸν ἀ. Il.17.226; πένθος ἀ. *cherish* woe, Od.17.489; υἱὸν ἀ. *rear* him *to man's estate*, 13.360; ἔργον ἀέξουσι.. θεοί they *bless* the work, 15.372. **2.** *exalt, glorify*, αὐτούς τ' ἀέξοι καὶ πόλιν Pi.*O*.8.88; τὸ πλῆθος ἀ. Hdt.3.80; *spread, diffuse*, [ἀγγελίαν] μῦθος ἀέξει S.*Aj*.226. **3.** ἀ. βούταν φόνον E.*Hipp*.537. **II.** Pass., *increase, grow*, Τηλέμαχος δὲ νέον μὲν ἀέξετο *was waxing tall*, Od.22.426; καλὰ μὲν ἠέξευ Call.*Jov*.55; οὐ..ποτ' ἀέξετο κῦμά γ' ἐν αὐτῷ no wave *rose high* thereon, Od.10.93; χόλος ..ἀνδρῶν ἐν στήθεσσιν ἠΰτε καπνὸς ἀ. *rises high*, Il.18.110; τόδε ἔργον ἀ. it *prospers*, Od.14.66; ἀέξετο ἱερὸν ἦμαρ *was getting on to noon*, Il.8.66; μηνὸς -ομένοιο Hes.*Op*.773; μῆτις ἀ. Emp.106; κέρδος ἀ. A.*Ch*.825 (cod. M), cf. *Supp*.856 (prob.). **III.** intr., = Pass., Q.S.1.116.

⊛**ἄεπτος,** ον, (ἕπομαι) v.l. for ἀέλπτοις in A.*Ag*.141 (Sch. Med. τοῖς ἕπεσθαι τοῖς γονεῦσι μὴ δυναμένοις). **II.** (ἔπος), = ἄρρητος, v.l. for ἄαπτος, q. v.

**ἀεργ-ηλός,** ή, όν, = ἀεργός, A.R.4.1186; ὕπνος *Lyr.Adesp*.92:—also **-ής,** ές, Nic.*Fr*.72.4. **-ία,** Ion. -ίη [ῐ], ἡ, *a not-working, idleness*, Od.24.251, Hes.*Op*.311, Bion *Fr*.14.6 (ubi vulg. ἀεργείᾳ). **2.** of a field, *a lying fallow* or *waste*, Orac.ap.Aeschin.3.108; of the bowels, *sluggishness*, Aret.*SD*1.15. **-ός,** όν, *not working, idle*, Il.9.320, Od.19.27, Hes.*Op*.303, Theoc.28.15, etc.; opp. ἐνεργός, Hp.*de Arte* [.]; c. gen., *not working out, not doing*, ἔργων αἰσχρῶν ἀπαθὴς καὶ Thgn.1177:—of things, *inert*, Aret.*SD*1.9. Adv. -γῶς *PFlor*.2[.] 5 (vi A. D.). **II.** Act., *debilitating*, μάλκαι Nic.*Th*.381 codd. Att. ἀργός, q. v.

**ἀέργυγον·** καθέδραν, οἱ δὲ τάγηνα, Hsch.

**ἀέρδην,** Adv. *lifting up*, A.*Ag*.234 (Att. ἄρδην).

**ἀερέθομαι,** see under Ion. form ἠερ-.

**ἀερήιον·** ἀμέτρητον, πολὺ ἀερῶδες, Hsch.

**Ἀερία,** ας, Ion. Ἠερίη, ης, ἡ, old name of Egypt, prob. from ἀή[ρ], *the misty land*, A.*Supp*.75, cf. A.R.4.267; also of Crete, Plin.*H*[*N*] 4.58. **II.** name of plant, *PMag.Par*.1.2363.

**ἀερίδες·** μέλισσαι, Hsch.

**ἀερ-ίζω,** (ἀήρ) *to be like air*, Secund.*Sent*.4; hence, **1.** *to b[e] thin as air*, Dsc.1.68.6. **2.** *to be light blue* (or perh. *grey, cloudy*) of μολύβδαινα, Id.5.85; of cataract, Dem.Ophth.ap.Aët.7.53; of [a] kind of jasper, Plin.*HN*37.115, *PMag.Leid.V*.6.28. **II.** '*trea[d] on air*', of boxers, Philostr.*Gym*.50. ⊛**-ικόν,** τό, *tax on lights*, Procop.*Arc*.21. ⊛**-ῐνος,** η, ον, *aerial, like air*, Arist.*Metaph*.1049[a]26, cf. *de An*.435[a]12. **2.** *light blue* (or *grey*), στολή LXX *Es*.8.15; ἐσθής Poll.4.119; κολλύριον Gal.12.78[.]. **3.** of the planet Jupiter, ὁ λεγόμενος Ζεὺς ἀ. Ps.-Callisth.1.4.

**ἀερίοικος,** ον, *dwelling in air*, Eub.139 (mock heroic).

⊛**ἀέριος** [ᾱ], α, ον, also ος, ον; Ion. ἠέριος, η, ον (q.v.): (ἀήρ):—*misty*, σκότον E.*Ph*.1534. **II.** *in the air, high in air*, κρότον ποδῶν Id.*Tr*.546; *of the air, aerial*, opp. χθόνιος, Id.*Fr*.27; πῦρ Hp.*Vict*.1.10; αἰτίαι ἀ., title of work by Democr.; opp. ὑπόγειος, *PMag.Par*.1.893; ἀ. φύσις Arist.*Mu*.392[b]14; ζῷα ib.398[b]33; γένος Pl.*Epin*.984e; τὰ ἀ. Luc.*Prom.Es* 6. Adv. -ως Iamb.*Myst*.1.9. **III.** *wide as air, infinite*, ἄμμου μέγεθος ἀ. D.S.1.33, cf. 5.42. **b.** *indefinite, vain, futile*, Phld.*Vit*.p.10 J., *Ir*.p.79 W.; ἐπιζήτησις Id.*Sign*.21.

⊛**ἀέριπον·** οὐ περιειργόμενον (i.e. ἄερκτον), Hsch.

⊛**ἀερίτης** λίθος, kind of *precious stone*, Ps.-Callisth.3.22.

**ἀερῖτις,** ἡ, = ἀναγαλλὶς ἡ κυανῆ, Ps.-Dsc.2.178.

⊛**ἄερκτος,** ον, (ἔργω, εἴργω) *unfenced, open*, Lys.7.28.

**ἀερο-βαθής,** ές, in neut. pl. -βαθῆ, τά, *depths of air*, 1 *Enoch* 17.3. **-βᾰτέω,** *walk the air*, of Socrates, Ar.*Nu*.225,1503, Pl.*Ap*.19c: aor. part. ἀεροβατήσας Ps.-Luc.*Philopatr*.12. **II.** *to be unduly puffed up*, Procop.*Arc*.13, cf. *Pers*.1.25. **-βάτης,** ου, ὁ, *one who walks the air*, Poet.ap.Plu.2.952f. **-βατικός,** ή, όν, *traversing air*, ζῷα prob. in Ath.3.99b. **-δονέομαι,** *to be whirled through air*, Sch.A.*Pr*.128. **-δόνητος,** ον, *air-tossed, soaring*, Ar.*Av*.1385. **-δρομέω,** *traverse the air*, Luc.*VH*1.10. **-δρόμος,** ον, *traversing the air*, *PMag.Par*.1.1359,1375. **-ειδής** [ᾰ], Ep. and Ion. ἠεροειδής, ές, *like the sky* or *air*, Pl.*Ti*.78c, Arist.*GC* 330[b]24, etc.:—*cloudy* in colour, Id.*Col*.794[a]4, cf. 797[a]7, *BGU*1207.6 (i B.C.).—For the Homeric usage of the word v. ἠεροειδής.

**ἀερόεις,** = ἠερόεις (q. v.), Τάρταρος *Tab.Defix*.108.3 (iii B.C.), cf. Hsch.

**ἀερό-θεν,** Adv. *out of the air, from on high*, Eust.1239.10. **-κόρδακες,** οἱ, and **-κώνωπες,** οἱ, fabulous creatures in Luc.*VH*1.16. **-λέσχης,** ου, ὁ, *man of big empty words*, Hsch. **-μαντεία,** ἡ, *divination by air*, Varr.ap.Serv. ad Virg.*Aen*.3.359. **-μαντις,** ὁ, *air-diviner*, Id.ap.Isid.*Etym*.8.9.13. **-μᾰχία,** ἡ, *air-battle*, Luc.*VH*1.18. **-μελι,** ιτος, τό, *oak-manna*, Amynt.ap.Ath.11.500d, cf. Gal.6.739. **-μετρέω,** *measure the air*; hence, *lose oneself in vague speculation*, X.*Oec*.11.3. **-μέτρητος,** ον, gloss on ἠεροειδής, Heracleon ap.*EM*421.49. **-μῐγής,** ές, *compounded of air*, Cleom.2.1, al., Corn.*ND*19, D.L.7.145, etc. **-μυθέω,** = μετεωρολογέω, περὶ σελήνης Ph.1.457:—from **-μυθος,** Id.2.268. **-νηχής,** ές, (νήχομαι) *floating in air*, οἰωνοί Ar.*Nu*.337. **-νομέω,** *to move in air*, Hld.10.30. **-νομικός,** ή, όν, *living in the air*, ζῷον prob. in Ath.3.99b.

**ἀερόομαι,** *turn into air*, Heraclit.*All*.22. **2.** *evaporate*, Gal.5.523.

**ἀερο-πετής,** ές, (πίπτω) *fallen from the sky*, Ph.Bybl.ap.Eus.*PE* 1.10, cf. Plb.36.10.2. **-πέτης,** ες, (πέτομαι) *flying in air*, σφήξ Horap.2.24, *PMag.Lond*.121.554. **-πλᾰνος,** ον, *wandering in air*, Hsch. s.v. ἠεροφοῖτις. **-πορέω,** *traverse the air*, Ph.2.116, 300. **-πόρος,** ον, *traversing the air*, Pl.*Ti*.40a, Ph.1.35, al. ⊛**-ριφής,** ές, *hurled through the air*, *PMag.Par*.1.2508. **-σκοπία,** ἡ, *divination by observing the heavens*, 1 *Enoch* 8.3, cf. Sch.Il.1.62 (as f.l. for ἱερο-). **-τεμις,** etym. of Ἄρτεμις, Porph.ap.Eus.*PE*3.11, Lyd.*Mens*.2.2. **-τόμα·** τὰ πετεινά, Cyr. **-τονος,** ον, *driven by air*, καταπάλτης Ph.*Bel*.77.13. **-φόβος,** ον, *afraid of the air*, Cael.Aur.*CP*3.12.108. **-φοίτητος,** ον, = sq., ἄνεμος *Hymn.Mag*.4.1; φοῖνιξ *PMag.Lond*.46.242. **-φοιτος,** ον, *roaming in air*, A.*Fr*.282:—also **-φοίτας,** ὁ, ἀστήρ Ion Eleg.10. **-φόρητος,** ον, *upborne by air*, Eub.104. **-φυής,** ές, *springing from air*, ῥίζωμα (i. e. γῆ), Secund.*Sent*.15. **-χροος,** -ους, = ἀέρινος 2, Dsc.5.75.

**ἀέροψ,** οπος, ὁ, Boeot. name for the bird μέροψ (q. v.), Sch.Ar.*Av*.1354.

**ἀέρρω,** Aeol. for ἀείρω, *lift, raise*, Sapph.91; *take away*, νόον Alc.78.

⊛**ἀερσί-λοφος,** ον, *high-crested*, A.R.2.1060; of places, Nonn.*D*.2.684, al. **-μαχος,** ον, *rousing the fight*, B.12.67. **-νοος,** ον, contr. **-νους,** ουν, *increasing intelligence*, Οὐρανίη Nonn.*D*.33.67. **II.** *cheering*, οἶνος prob. l. Ion Eleg.9; Βάκχος Orph.*Fr*.280.9. **-πέτης,** ες, (πέτομαι) = ἀερσιπότης, Q.S.3.211. **-πόδης,** ου, ὁ, = ἀερσίπους, Nonn.*D*.10.401. **-πόρος,** ον, *going on high*, Nonn.*D*.1.285. **-πότης,** ου,

-ποτάομαι) *high-soaring*, Hes.*Sc.*316, *AP*5.298 (Agath.). **-πότη-**, ον, = foreg., ἀράχνης Hes.*Op.*777; ἀτμός Nonn.*D.*2.483. **-πους**, ἡ, πουν, τό, *high-stepping*, ἵπποι ἀερσίποδες Il.18.532; contr. ἀρσί-ποδες *h.Ven.*211, *AP*7.717. **-φρων**, ονος, *uplifting, cheering the* heart, Διόνυσος *Ath.Mitt.*17.273 (Athens), cf. *EM*20.47.

**ἀερτάζω**, lengthd. Ep. form of ἀείρω, *lift up*, Call.*Fr.*19, etc.: pf. ἠέρταζον *AP*9.12 (Leon.), A.R.1.738, etc.: irreg. opt. ἀερτά-ζοιε Nonn.*D.*43.99:—also (from ⊛ἀερτάω) aor. 1 ἠέρτησε *AP*6.223 (Antip.): pf. Pass. ἠέρτημαι ib.5.229 (Paul. Sil.), Opp.*C.*2.99.

**ἀερώδης**, ες, *like air*, of the soul, Epicur.*Fr.*314; Astrol., of signs, *connected with the air*, Vett.Val.7.26; *light of texture*, Sch.E.*Or.* 1431. **2.** = ἀέρινος 2, τὴν χρόαν Dsc.5.152 (dub.). **3.** τὸ ἀ. *the airy nature*, *Placit.*2.11.2, al., cf. Arist.*Mu.*395$^{a}$20. **II.** *full of air*, Id.*PA*669$^{b}$2.

**ἀέρωσις**, ἡ, *rarefaction*, αἵματος Gal.10.742.

**ἀές**, Dor. for ἀεί. **ἄες**, Boeot. = ἄας (q.v.), Hsch.

**ἄεσα**, v. ἀέσκω.

**ἀεσίμαινα**· ἡ τοῖς πνεύμασι τῶν ἀνέμων μαινομένη, θαλάσσης δὲ τὸ ἐπίθετον, Hsch. **ἄεσις**· πόνος, βλάβη, Hsch., *EM*20.48.

**ἀεσι-φροσύνη**, ἡ, *folly*, in pl., Od.15.470, Hes.*Th.*502. **-φρων**, ον, gen. ονος, = φρεσὶν ἀασθείς, *damaged in mind, witless, silly*, Il.20.183, Od.21.302, Hes.*Op.*335 (more correctly ἀασίφρων Apollon.*Lex.*, Phot.).

**ἀέσκω**, Hdn.Gr.1.436, *EM*20.11: impf. Med. ἀέσκοντο Hsch.: aor. 1 ἄεσα, ἀέσαμεν, contr. ἄσαμεν, ἄεσαν, inf. ἀέσαι:—*sleep*, Od.19.342, 3.151,490, 15.40, A.R.4.884. (Etym. dub., but νύκτα ἀ. has been expl. as *pass, spend* the night, cf. Skt. *vásati.*) [ᾱ metri gr. or by contraction, ᾰ otherwise.]

**ἀέτειος** [ᾱ], ον, (ἀετός) *of the eagle*, πτερόν Suid.

**ἀετής**, ές, v. sub αὐετής.

**ἀετιδεύς** [ᾱ], έως, ὁ, *eaglet*, Ael.*Fr.*128, Aesop.5.

⊛**ἀετίτης** [ῑ] λίθος, ὁ, *eagle-stone*, said to be found in the eagle's nest, Ael.*NA*1.35, Philostr.*VA*2.14, Dsc.5.160.

**ἄετμα**· φλόξ, οἱ δὲ τὸ πνεῦμα, *EM*20.10; Hsch. gives **ἀετμόν** in the latter sense.

**ἀετογενής**, ές, prob. *bearing a mark in the shape of an eagle*, ἵππος *Hippiatr.*115.

⊛**ἀετός**, Ep., Lyr., Ion., and early Att. **αἰετός** (v. fin.), οῦ, ὁ, *eagle*, as a bird of omen, αἰ. τελειότατον πετεηνῶν Il.8.247, cf. 12.201, Od. 2.146 (cf. II): favourite of Zeus, ὅστε σοὶ αὐτῷ φίλτατος οἰωνῶν Il. 24.310, cf. Pi.*P.*1.6; Διὸς..πτηνὸς κύων, δαφοινὸς αἰ. A.*Pr.*1022, cf. *Ag.*136; ὁ σκηπτροβάμων αἰ., κύων Διός S.*Fr.*885:—prov., αἰετὸς ἐν ποτανοῖς Pi.*N.*3.80; αἰετὸς ἐν νεφέλαισι, of a thing quite out of reach, Ar.*Av.*987; ἀετὸν κάνθαρος μαιεύσομαι (v. μαιεύομαι):—the diff. kinds are distinguished by specific names, Arist.*HA*618$^{b}$18 sqq. **2.** *eagle as a standard*, of the Persians, X.*Cyr.*7.1.4; of the Romans, Plu.*Mar.*23, etc. **3.** the constellation *Aquila*, Arat.591, Ptol.*Tetr.* 27, etc. **II.** *omen*, Theoc.26.31. **III.** *eagle-ray, Myliobatis aquila*, Arist.*HA*540$^{b}$18. **IV.** in Architecture, *gable, pediment* (from its resemblance to outspread wings, Gal.18(1).519), Ar.*Av.* 1110, ubi v. Sch., *IG*1.322 ii 80, cf. Pi.*O.*13.21, *Fr.*53, E.*Fr.*764; ὑπὸ τὸν αὐτὸν ἀετὸν ὑπελθεῖν *come under the same roof*, *IG*14.644 (Bruttii, iii B.C.). **V.** name of *bandage*, Sor.*Fasc.*12.508 C. **VI.** *temporal vein* (Magna Graecia), Philistion ap.Ruf.*Onom.*201. **VII.** *iron part of spoke of wheel*, Poll.1.145, Hsch. **VIII.** Astrol. and Magic, fabulous plant growing in Libya, Pamphil.ap.Gal.11. 798, *Cat.Cod.Astr.*7.222. (αἰετός in early Att. Inscrr., *IG*1.322 ii 80, 2.1054.39; αἰητός Arat.522, v.l. in Pi.*P.*4.4; αἰβετός (i.e. αἰϝετός) Hsch.) [ᾱ always.]

⊛**ἀετοφόρος**, ὁ, *standard-bearer*, = Lat. *aquilifer*, Plu.*Caes.*52.

**ἀετώδης** [ᾱ], ες, *eagle-like*, ἀθληταί Philostr.*Gym.*37, cf. Ael.*NA* 4.27; -δες βλέπειν see *as clearly as an eagle*, Luc.*Icar.*14.

**ἀέτωμα** [ᾱ], τό, = ἀετός IV, *gable*, οἴκου Hp.*Art.*43; ἱεροῦ *IG*2$^{2}$. 1271.6., cf. Timae.50, J.*AJ*3.6.4: **αἴτωμα** (sic) *IG*3.162.

**ἀετώνυχον**, τό, = λιθόσπερμον, Dsc.3.141; = κῆμος, Ps.-Dsc.4.133: cf. **ἀετόνυχες**· βοτάνη, Hsch.

**ἀετώσιος**, ον, apptly. = ἐτώσιος, Ibyc.51, cf. Hsch., *EM*20.13.

**ἀέτωσις** [ᾱ], εως, ἡ, *arched roof* of χελώνη, Ath.Mech.13.3.

**ἀεφανέων**· λαμπρῶν, Hsch.

**ἀέχεια**, ἡ, *non-possession, privation*, Chrysipp.*Stoic.*2.51 (pl.).

⊛**ἀεχῆνες**· πένητες, Hsch.

**ἀέχοντο**· ὥρμων, Hsch.

**ἀϝάταται**, v. ἀτάω.

⊛**ἀϝλανέως**, = ἀδόλως, *GDI*1156 (Elis, v B.C.); cf. ἀλανές.

**ἄζα**, ἡ, *heat*, ἠελίου Opp.*C.*1.134, cf. 3.324. **2.** *dryness*, of the skin, χροός Nic.*Th.*304. **3.** metaph., *unsatisfied desire*, Call. in *PGen.*97 ii 7. **II.** *dirt, mould*, σάκος πεπαλαγμένον ἄζῃ Od. 22.184. **2.** *dry sediment*, Sch.Theoc.5.109. (Cf. Lat. *areo.*)

**ἀζαές** (cod. -ζαλές)· πολύπνουν, καὶ ὀλιγόπνουν, Hsch. ⊛**ἀζαθός**, Cypr. = ἀγαθός, ἰ(ν)τύχᾳ ἀζαθᾷ *Inscr.Cypr.*134 H., cf. 137. **ἀζαΐα**· φθονερά, Hsch.

⊛**ἀζαίνω**, (ἄζω) *dry, parch up*, aor. subj. ἀζήνῃ, -ήνῃσι Nic.*Th.*205, and v.l. in 368:—Pass., ἀζαίνεται (as v.l. for αὐαίνεται) ib.339: aor. ἀζάνθη Hsch.

**ἀζαλαί**· νέαι καὶ ἁπαλαί, Hsch.

**ἀζᾰλέος**, α, ον, *dry, parched*, οὖρος Il.20.491; ὕλη Od.9.234, etc.; βῶν ἀζαλέην *dry* bull's-hide, Il.7.239; ἀ. γῆρας *withered, sapless*, *IG* 14.1389 i 12, Plu.2.789c. **2.** metaph., *harsh, cruel*, *AP*5.237 (Maced.). **II.** Act., *parching, scorching*, Σείριος Hes.*Sc.*153, cf. A.R.4.679; of love, μανίαι Ibyc.1.9; of thirst, Nic.*Th.*339.—Poet. word. **III. ἀζαλέα**, ἡ, = ψίλωθρον, *Gloss.*

⊛**ἀζάλη**· νήνεμος, Hsch. **ἀζάλιον**· ξηρόν, ἢ ἄγαν ζέον, Phot.p.38 R.

**Ἀζᾶνες**, οἱ, title of play by Achaeus. **Ἀζανία**, ἡ, *land of* Ζάν or Ζεύς, i.e. Arcadia, St.Byz. **ἀζανίτης**, ὁ, horse-medicine, *Hippiatr.* 129.

**ἀζάνω**, = ἀζαίνω, *h.Ven.*270 (Pass.).

**ἀζάπα**· πτισάνη, Hsch. **ἀζατά**, ἡ, *drought*, *Inscr.Cypr.*59 H. **ἀζάτη**· ἐλευθερία, Hsch. (Cf. Zend *āzāta* 'free'.) **ἀζαυτός**· παλαιότης, καὶ κόνις, Id. **ἀζαχής**, ές, = σκληρός, χαλεπός: also = ἀδιάλειπτος (cf. ἀζηχής), Id. **ἀζεινοί** (cod. ἀζην-)· κύκνοι ταῖς πτέρυξιν ἀπολαμβάνοντες ἀέρα, Id. **ἀζείρει**· ξηραίνει, Id. (ἀζήρει Suid.). **ἀζειρός**, όν, (ζειρά) *not embroidered*, Hsch., *EM*22.56, Suid. **ἀζένα**· πώγωνα (Phryg.), Hsch. **ἄζενον**· γενειῶντα, Id. **ἀζέσιμοι**· ἀζεινοί, Id. **ἀζέσιος**, v. Ἀζόσιος. **ἄζεστος**, ον, (ζέω) *not coming to the boil*, Hp.*Morb.*3.17. ⊛**ἄζετον**· ἄπιστον (Sicel), Hsch. **ἀζετόω**, *detect*, in Pass., *GDI*2034 (Delph., ii A.D.).

⊛**ἄζευκτος**, ον, *unyoked*, D.H.2.31; ἄ. γάμου Sch.Ar.*Lys.*217: abs. in same sense, Sch.A.R.4.897.

**ἀζεχής**, ές, = ἀζαχής (cf. ἀζηχής), Hsch.

**ἀζηλία**, ἡ, *simplicity* of style, *freedom from mannerisms*, v.l. in Plu.*Lyc.*21.

⊛**ἀζηλοπραγμόνως**, Adv. *without jealousy, ungrudgingly*, *PLips.* 119$^{v}$ ii 5 (iii A.D.).

**ἄζηλος**, ον, *unenvied, unenviable, dreary*, γῆρας Semon.1.11; φρουρά A.*Pr.*143; θέα S.*El.*1455; βίος Id.*Tr.*284; ἔργον *sorry* deed, ib. 745; ἄζηλα πέλει all are *in ill plight*, Orac.ap.Hdt.7.140; πλοῦτος Plu. *Lyc.*10; ζῆλος ἀζήλων *not deserving of envy*, Phld.*Oec.*p.66 J. **II.** Act., *not envious*, Menetor ap.Ath.13.594c.

**ἀζηλο-τύπητος**, ον, *not likely to arouse jealousy*, Cic.*Att.*13.19.4; *not exposed to jealousy*, γῆρας Plu.2.787d. **-τῦπος**, ον, *free from envy*, Plu.*Comp.Lyc.Num.*3.

**ἀζήλωτος**, ον, *not to be envied*, Pl.*Grg.*469b: neut. pl. as Adv., -ωτα φιληθείς *AP*12.105 (Asclep.). Adv. -τως Poll.5.160. **2.** *not imitated*, ἀ. παραλιπεῖν τι J.*BJ*7.8.1.

⊛**ἀζήμιος**, ον, *free from further payment*, Hdt.6.92. **2.** *without loss, scot-free*, ἄπιθι ἀ. Id.1.212; ἀβλαβῆ παρεχέτω καὶ ἀζήμιον Pl.*Lg.* 865c; *unpunished*, E.*Med.*1050, Ar.*Ra.*408, Antipho 3.3.10, etc.; ὑπὸ θεῶν Pl.*R.*366a; *not liable to penalty*, ναῦς *IG*1.40; *not deserving punishment*, S.*El.*1102, etc.: c. gen., ἀσεβημάτων ἀ. Plb.2.60.5. Adv. -ίως *with impunity*, Philem.94.5: also, *without fraud, honestly*, J.*AJ* 15.4.4; ἐκδικεῖν *Cod.Just.*1.2.17. **II.** Act., *harmless*, of sour looks, Th.2.37; οὐκ ἀ. J.*AJ*15.5.1, cf. Ph.1.428, 2.246.

**ἀζημίωτος**, ον, *immune from penalties*, Secund.*Sent.*10.

**ἀζῆρις**, ἡ, *chariot-pole*, Hsch. (ἀζηλίς Poll.1.143).

**Ἀζησία**, ἡ, a name of Demeter, S.*Fr.*981, cf. Ἀζοσία.

**ἀζῆται**· οἱ ἐγγύτατοι τοῦ βασιλέως, Hsch.

**ἀζήτητος**, ον, *unexamined, untried*, Aeschin.3.22, Aristox.*Fr.Hist.* 15; *outside the scope of inquiry*, Thphr.*Metaph.*10. Adv. -τως, ἔχειν τῶν θείων Ph.1.96; τῆς αἰτίας Hierocl. *in CA* 10 p.437 M.

**ἀζητός**· σεβαστός, Suid.

**ἀζηχής**, ές, (prob. for ἀ-δια(σ)εχής, *continuous*, cf. ἀζαχής, ἀζε-χής) *unceasing*, ὀδύνη Il.15.25; ὀρυμαγδός 17.741: neut. as Adv., ἀζηχὲς φαγέμεν καὶ πιέμεν Od.18.3; [ὄϊες] ἀ. μεμακυῖαι Il.4.435. **II.** (ἄζα, cf. ἀζαλέος) *hard, seasoned*, κορύνη A.R.2.99; θυμός v.l. Il.15. 25.

**ἀζηώρα**· ταχέα, πυκνά, Hsch. **ἀζόκροτος**, v. αἰζ-.

**ἄζομαι**, only pres. and impf.; Act. only in part. ἄζοντα S.*OC* 134:—*stand in awe of*, esp. gods and one's parents, ἁζόμενοι..Ἀπόλ-λωνα Il.1.21; μήτ' οὖν μητέρ' ἐμὴν ἄζευ Od.17.401; followed by inf., χερσὶ δ' ἀνίπτοισιν Διὶ λείβειν.. ἅζομαι Il.6.267; ξείνους οὐχ ἅζεο.. ἐσθέμεναι Od.9.478; ἅ. μή Il.14.261; τίς δή κεν..ἅζοιτ' ἀθανάτους; Thgn.748, cf. Alcm.54: used by A. in lyr., τίς οὖν τάδ' οὐχ ἅζεται; *Eu.* 389; Παλλάδος δ' ὑπὸ πτεροῖς ὄντας ἅζεται πατήρ (sc. Ζεύς) *respects*.., ib.1002; ἅζονται γὰρ δαίμους Id.*Supp.*652; πλόκαμον οὐδάμ' ἅζε-ται ib.884 (all lyr.); θανεῖν οὐχ ἅζομαι *I fear* not to die.., E.*Or.* 1116. **2.** abs. in part., *reverently, in holy fear*, Od.9.200; ἀμφί σοι ἁζόμενος S.*OT*155. **3.** *to be angry*, E.*Fr.*348. (Cf. ἅγιος.)

**ἄζον**· μέλαν, ὑψηλόν, Hsch. **ἄζοξ**· ὕλη, Id.

**ἄζος**, ὁ, contr. from ἄοζος, *a servant*, Gloss.ap.Ath.6.267c.

**ἄζος**, η, ον, *dry*, v.l. in Sch.Theoc.5.109.

⊛**Ἀζόσιος**, ὁ, (sc. μήν) month at Epidaurus, *IG*4.1485.20, al. (Ἀζέ-σιος ib.51):—**Ἀζόσιοι** θεοί (= Δαμία and Αὐξησία), ib.1539.4; **Ἀζο-σία**, ἡ, ib.1062.12.

**ἀζῠγής**, ές, *not paired*, μόριον ἀ. ἑτέρῳ Gal.*UP*15.2, cf. 5.14.

⊛**ἄζῠγος**, ον, *unwedded*, κοίτη Luc.*Am.*44. **2.** = foreg., φλέψ the *vena azygos*, Gal.15.529: in pl., *not a pair*, σανδάλια Str.6.1.8.

**ἄζῡμος**, ον, *without process of fermentation*, Pl.*Ti.*74d:—of bread, *unleavened*, ἄρτος Hp.*Vict.*3.79, Trypho *Fr.*117; ἄρτους ἀ., ἄζυμα λά-γανα, Lxx *Ex.*29.2, *Le.*2.4: abs., ἄζυμα, τά, *Ex.*12.15; τὰ ἄ. *the feast of unleavened cakes*, *Ev.Marc.*14.1; ἡ ἑορτὴ τῶν ἀ. Lxx 2*Ch.*8.13, al., *Ev.Luc.*22.1.

⊛**ἄζυξ**, ῠγος, ὁ, ἡ, τό, (ζεύγνυμι) *unyoked, unpaired*, Archil.157; δάμα-λις D.H.1.40; *unmarried*, E.*Ba.*694; of Pallas, Id.*Tr.*536 (lyr.): c. gen., ἄ. λέκτρων, γάμων, εὐνῆς, Id.*Hipp.*546 (lyr.), *IA*805, *Med.* 673. **II.** *isolated*, ἄ. ὥσπερ ἐν πεττοῖς Arist.*Pol.*1253$^{a}$7, cf. *AP*9. 482.26 (Agath.); *single*, αὐλοί, opp. σύριγγες, Nonn.*D.*3.76: in pl., ἄζυγα *vowels*, opp. σύζυγα, ib.4.262.

**ἄζω**, v. sub ἅζομαι.

**ἄζω** (A), *dry up, parch*, ὁπότε χρόα Σείριος ἄζει Hes.*Sc.*397, cf. *Op.* 587, Alc.39.8, Nic.*Th.*779:—Pass., [αἴγειρος] ἀζομένη κεῖται lies *drying*, Il.4.487.

*ἄζω (B), *cry ἆ, groan, sigh*, S.*Fr.*980; so perh. in Med., εἴ τις.. ἄζηται κραδίην ἀκαχήμενος Hes.*Th.*99. 2. *breathe hard*, Nicoch. 19. (Perh. ἄζω (from the sound *ha!*) in this sense.)

**ἀζωΐα**, ἡ, *absence of life*, Porph.*Sent.*21,23, Procl.*in Prm.*p.646 S., Olymp.*in Grg.*p.356 J.

**ἀζωλεῖ**· ἀγανακτεῖ, Hsch.

**ἀζωνικός**, ή, όν, = sq., τάξις Procl.*in Ti.*3.127 D., Dam.*Pr.*131. Adv. -κῶς ibid.

**ἄζωνος**, ον, *confined to no zone* or *region*, opp. *local* deities, Serv. ad Virg.*Aen.*12.118, cf. Dam.*Pr.*96, al. (with secondary sense *not wearing a zone as a girdle*).

**ἄζωος**, ον, (ζωή) *without life*, Porph.*Sent.*20, Procl.*Inst.*188. II. (ζῷον) *without maggots*, of seeds, Thphr.*CP*4.15.3.

**ἄζωπες**· αἱ ξηραὶ ἐκ τῆς θεωρίας, Hsch. **ἄζωρος**· ὁ εὔκρατος οἶνος, Id. **ἄζως**, ων, = ἄζωος 1, Plot.3.4.1, 3.6.6, Syr.*in Metaph.*48.16, Procl.*in Prm.*p.543 S.

*ἄζωστος, ον, (ζώννυμι) *ungirt*, from haste, Hes.*Op.*345, Call.*Fr.* 225; *not girded*, Pl.*Lg.*954a; *unarmed*, *SIG*527.140 (Dreros, iii B.C.), Hsch.

**ἀζῶτες**· οἱ μὴ εἰς τὰ συνεστῶτα παρόντες, Hsch.

**ἄζωτος**, ον, = ἄζωστος, *EM*24.21. II. **ἄζωτον**· ἀβίωτον, Hsch.

**ἀηδ-έω**, *feel disgust at*, δείπνῳ ἀηδήσειεν v.l. for ἀδήσειεν in Od.1. 134, cf. **ἀηδῆσαι**· κοπιάσαι, καμεῖν, Hsch., cf. *EM*23.26. *-ής, ές, (ἦδος) *distasteful, nauseous*, of food, drugs, etc., Hp.*VM*10 (Comp.), *Acut.*23, Pl.*Lg.*660a, etc. 2. generally, *unpleasant*, οὐδέν οἱ ἀηδέστερον ἔσεσθαι Hdt.7.101, cf. Pl.*Lg.*893a, al.: freq. in Pl. of narration, ἀηδές or οὐκ ἀηδές ἐστι, *Ap.*33c, 41b, *Phd.*84d: Comp., Hdt. l. c.: Sup. -έστατος Pl.*Lg.*663c, *Phdr.*240b. II. of persons, *disagreeable, odious*, ἀπογηράσκων ἀ. γίγνεται Alex.278, cf. D.47.28, Arist. *EN*1108ᵃ30, Thphr.*Char.*20.1; τινί to one, Pl.*Phd.*91b, Phld.*Ir.* p.51 W. III. Adv. -δῶς *unpleasantly*, ζῆν Pl.*Prt.*351b; ἀ. ἔχειν τινί to be *on bad terms with one*, D.20.142, cf. 37.11; ἀ. διακεῖσθαι, διατεθῆναι, πρός τινα, Lys.16.2, Isoc 12.19. 2. *without pleasure to oneself, unwillingly*, πίνειν, ἀκούειν, X.*Cyr.*1.2.11, Isoc.12.62; οὐκ ἀ. Pl *Prt.*335c. *-ία, ἡ, *nauseousness*, of drugs, Hp.*Acut.*23. 2. *unpleasantness*, opp. ἡδονή, Phld.*Rh.*1.163 S.: pl., Id.*Oec.*p.64 J. II. mostly of persons, *unpleasantness, odiousness*, D.21.153, Aeschin.3. 72, Thphr.*Char.*20.1; τὴν σὴν ἀ. your *odious presence*, Aeschin.3. 164. 2. *disgust, dislike*, Pl.*Phdr.*240d, *Lg* 802d, etc.: pl., ἀ. καὶ βαρύτητες τῶν ἄλλων Isoc.12.31. *-ίζω, *disgust*, τὴν γεῦσιν S.E. *P.*1.92:—Pass., *to be disgusted*, Anon.*in Rh.*194.32; τινι Alex.Aphr. *Pr.*2.15; ἐπί τινι *PLond.*1.42 (ii B.C.). -ισμός, ὁ, *disgust*, opp. ἡδονή, S.E.*P.*1.87.

**ἀηδονία**, ἡ, *absence of pleasure*, D.L.2.89,90

**ἀηδ-ονιδεύς**, έως, ὁ, *young nightingale*, pl. -ῆες Theoc.15.121 (prob.). -όνιον, τό, Dim. of ἀηδών, prob. l. in D.Chr.66.11. *-όνιος, ον, *of a nightingale*, γόος, νόμος ἀ., A.*Fr.*291, Ar.*Ra.*684. 2. of sleep, *light*, Nicoch.4 D., cf. Nonn.*D.*5.411. -ονίς, ίδος, ἡ, = ἀηδών, *nightingale*, E.*Rh.*550 (lyr.), Call.*Lav.Pall.*94, Theoc.8.38; Μουσάων ἀηδονίς, of a poet, *AP*7.414 (Noss.); of a girl, *IG*14.1942.

**ἀήδονος**, ον, = ἀνήδονος, δαίμων Sch.E.*Hec.*685, cf. *Gloss.*

**ἀηδοποιός**, όν, *quarrelsome*, *Gloss.*

**ἀηδ-ώ**, = sq., gen. ἀηδοῦς S.*Aj.*628 (lyr.), voc. ἀηδοῖ Ar.*Av.*679 (lyr.): nom. pl. ἀηδοι Sapph.*Oxy.*1787.6.7. (Mytil acc. to Sch.S. l.c.) *-ών, όνος, ἡ (ὁ, v. infr.), (ἀείδω) *songstress*, i. e. *the nightingale*, Hes.*Op.*203, etc.; Πανδαρέου κούρη, χλωρηὶς ἀ., i. e. *living in the greenwood*, Od.19.518; χλωραύχην ἀ. Simon.73:—metaph., of a *poet*, B.3.98, cf. E.*Fr.*588 (lyr.), *AP*7.44 (Ion), Hermesian.7.49; also of the poet's song, τεαὶ ἀηδόνες thy *strains*, Call.*Ep.*2.5; ζωούσας ἔλιπες γὰρ ἀηδόνας *IG*14.2012. 2. metaph., *cicada*, *AP*7.190 (Anyte). II. *mouthpiece* of a flute, E.*Fr.*556; the *flute* itself, ib.931. 2. metaph., of *shuttle*, *AP*6.174 (Antip. Sid.).—Masc., only Ion l. c.; Ἀττικὸς ἀνὴρ τὸν αἶγα λέγει ὥσπερ καὶ τὸν ἀηδόνα Eust.376.24.

**ἀήθ-εια**, Ion. -ίη [ῑ metri gr.], ἡ, (ἀήθης) *unaccustomedness, novelty* of a situation, Batr.72, Pl.*Ti.*18c; ἀ. τινος *inexperience of* a thing, Th.4.55; ὑπὸ ἀηθείας from *inexperience*, Pl.*Tht.*175d; δι' ἀήθειαν (cod. ἀλήθ-) Aen.Tact.38.3. -έσσω, *to be unaccustomed*, c. gen., once in Hom., ἀήθεσσον γὰρ ἔτ' αὐτῶν Il.10.493; ἀηθέσσουσα δύης A.R.4. 38; λυγμοὶ ἀηθέσσοντες Nic.*Al.*378:—for A.R.1.1171 v. sq. -έω, *to be unaccustomed*, Hsch.: impf. ἀήθεον prob. l. A.R.1.1171 (codd. ἀήθεσον). -ης, ες, (ἦθος) *unwonted, strange*, ὄψις A.*Supp.*567; δώματα v.l. in S.*Fr.*583.10. Adv. -θως *unexpectedly*, Th.4.17. II. *unused to* a thing, c. gen., μάχης Th.4.34, cf. Pl.*Tht.*146b, al.; ἀ. τοῦ κατακούειν, τοῦ προπηλακίζεσθαι, D.1.23, 21.72. b. *strange in manner, unlike oneself*, prob. f.l. for ἀγηθής in S.*Tr.*869. 2. *without character*, τραγῳδία Arist.*Po.*1450ᵃ25, cf. 1460ᵃ11. -ία, ἡ, = ἀήθεια, E.*Hel.*418. -ίζομαι, *to be unaccustomed to* a thing, Posidon.26.

**ἄημα**, τό, *blast, wind*, A.*Ag.*1418, *Eu.*905, S.*Aj.*674, Call.*Aet.*3. 1.36.

*ἄημι, 3 sg. ἄησι Hes.*Op.*516, A.*Fr.*178 A., 3 dual ἄητον Il.9.5, 3 pl. ἀεῖσι Hes.*Th.*875; imper. 3 sg. ἀήτω A.R.4.768; inf. ἀῆναι Od.3. 183, Ep. ἀήμεναι ib.176; part. ἀείς, ἀέντος, etc., Emp.84.4, Il.5.526, al.: impf. 3 sg. ἄη Od.12.325, 14.458:—Pass., 3 sg. ἄηται, impf. ἄητο, part. ἀήμενος, v. infr. (ἄϝημι, cf. Skt. *vāti* 'blows', Lith. *vējas* 'wind'):—Ep. Verb, prop. *breathe hard*; hence, *blow*, of winds, τώ τε Θρῄκηθεν ἄητον Il.9.5, cf. Od.3.176,183, etc.; οἵ τε νέφεα.. σκιδνᾶσιν ἀέντες Il.5.526; ἀνέμων.. μένος ὑγρὸν ἀέντων Od.19.4[…] cf. Hes.*Th.*869,875:—Pass., *to be beaten by the wind*, ὑόμενος καὶ […]μενος Od.6.131; of sound, *to be carried by the wind*, A.R.2.81: m[…] freq. metaph., *toss, wave to and fro*, of the mind in doubt or fe[…] δίχα θυμὸς ἄητο Il.21.386; περὶ παίδων θυμὸς ἄηται A.R.3.688: also μαρτύρια ἄηται ἐπ' ἀνθρώπους *are wafted to and fro*, Pi.*I.*4(3). περί τ' ἀμφί τε κάλλος ἄητο beauty *breathed* all about her, *h.Cer.*27[…] ἀπὸ κρῆθεν τοῖον ἄητο Hes.*Sc.*8, cf. *Fr.*245. II. Act., *breathe*, […] πνευμόνων ὕπνον A.*Fr.*178 A.

*ἀήρ, ἀέρος, Hom. ἀήρ, ἠέρος; Ion. nom. ἠήρ Hp.*Aër.*6, al., Are[…] *CA*2.3; Aeol. αὔηρ Sch.Pi.*P.*2.52; Dor. ἀβήρ (i. e. ἀϝήρ) Hsch.:—fem. in Hom. and Hes. (exc. *Op.*549), Anaxag.ap.Thphr.*Sens.*30 from Hdt. downwds. masc. (Il.5.776, 8.50, *h.Cer.*383 cannot b[e] quoted for the masc. usage, since there πουλύς and βαθύς need not b[e] masc.):—in Hom. and Hes. always *mist, haze*, not (as Aristarch. *lower air* (opp. αἰθήρ, q. v.); [ἐλάτη] μακροτάτη πεφυυῖα δι' ἠέρος αἰθέρ[α] ἵκανεν Il.14.288, cf. Anaxag.1, Ar.*Nu.*264sq.; περὶ δ' ἠέρα πουλὺν ἔχευεν Il.5.776, cf. 3.381, 8.50; ἠέρα μὲν σκέδασεν καὶ ἀπῶσεν ὀμίχλην 17.649; τρὶς δ' ἠέρα τύψε βαθεῖαν 20.446; rare in Prose, Hp. l.c. 2. later, generally, *air*, Anaxim.1, Emp.17.18, S.*El.*87, Ar. *Av.*187,694, etc.; πρὸς τὸν ἀέρα διατρίβειν in *the open air*, Ar.*Nu.*198, cf. Telesp.11.3 H., Luc.*Anach.*24; τὸν ἀέρ' ἕλκειν καθαρόν Phillyl.20, cf. Philem.119; ἔσπασας τὸν ἀ. τὸν κοινόν Men.531.7; ἀέρα δέρειν 1 *Ep. Cor.*9.26; εἰς ἀέρα λαλεῖν ib.14.9:—in pl., Pl.*Phd.*98c,d; *climates*, Hp.*Aër.*tit., cf. Men.Rh.p.383 S.; of mephitic *exhalations*, Str.5. 4.5. 3. personified, ὦ δέσποτ' ἄναξ ἀμέτρητ' Ἀ. Ar.*Nu.*264; Ἀ. ὃν ἄν τις ὀνομάσειε καὶ Δία Philem.91.4, cf. Diph.126.6. II. *hot-air room* in baths, Gal.11.14. 2. *volume*, Hero *Stereom.*57, al. III. a pigment, *sky-blue* or *grey*, Id.*Aut.*28.3. [ᾱ, except in Arist.*Fr.* 642, Ps.-Phoc.[108].]

**ἄησις**, εως, ἡ, (ἄημι) = ἄημα, *blowing*, E.*Rh.*417, cf. *Fr.*781.46.

*ἀήσσητος, Att. ἀήττητος, ον, *unconquered, not beaten*, Th.6.70, Lys.33.7, D.18.247, *AP*7.741 (Crin.), etc.; esp. of the Stoic sage, Zeno *Stoic.*1.53, etc. 2. *unconquerable*, Pl.*R.*375b, Phld.*D.*3 *Fr.*88b.

**ἀήσυλος**, = αἴσυλος, *wicked*, ἔργα Il.5.876.

**ἀήσῠρος**, ον, (ἄημι) *light as air*, μύρμηκες A.*Pr.*452; ἀ. γόνυ κάμψει Call.*Fr.anon.*3; γυῖα Orph.*Fr.*18; *springing lightly*, πόρτις Tryph. 360; *blowing softly*, Βορέας A.R.2.1101.

**ἀητέομαι**, *fly*, Arat.523 (with play on αἰητός). *ἀήτη, ἡ, = sq., Hes.*Op.*645,675.

**ἀήτης**, ου, ὁ, (ἄω, ἄημι) *blast, gale*, ἀνέμοιο, Ζεφύροιο, ἀνέμων ἀῆται, Il.15.626, Od.4.567, Hes.*Op.*621: abs., *wind*, Tim.*Pers.*117, Theoc. 2.38.—Poet. word, οἱ ποιηταὶ τὰ πνεύματα ἀήτας καλοῦσι Pl.*Cra.* 410b.

**ἀητόρρους**, ουν, *creating* ἀῆται, coined by Pl.*Cra.*410b.

*ἄητος (A), ὁ, = ἀετός, the constellation *Aquila*, Arat.315.

*ἄητος (B), ον, only in phrase θάρσος ἄητον Il.21.395 (= θάρσος ἄατον Q.S.1.217); also **ἄητοι**· ἀκόρεστοι, ἄπληστοι, and **ἀήτους**· μεγάλας (A.*Fr.*3), Hsch. *ἄητος (C)· ὁ ἀκατάπαυστος, Hdn Gr.1.220; perh. *insatiate* (ἄω); cf αἴητος.

**ἄηχος**, ον, *without sound*, φωνή Aret.*SD*1.11, Sch E.*Ph* 960.

**ἀθάλαμευτος**, ον, *unwedded*, ἡλικίη *Epigr.Gr.*372.32 (Cotiaeum).

**ἀθαλάσσ-ευτος**, ον, = ἀθαλάσσωτος, Poll.1.121. *-ία, ἡ, *ignorance of the sea*, v.l. for sq. in Secund.*Sent.*16. -ος, Att. -ττος, ον, *without sea, far from it, inland*, Men.462.9. 2. = ἀθαλάσσωτος, βασιλεὺς Max.Tyr.1.3; ἔμπορος Secund.*Sent.*16. II. *not mixed with sea-water*, οἶνος Damocr.ap.Gal.14.134, Zopyr.ap.Orib.14.61.1, cf. Sor.1.95. -ωτος, Att. -ττωτος, ον, (θαλασσόω) *unused to the sea, a land-lubber*, Ar.*Ra.*204, Agath.1 *Praef.*

**ἄθαλδον**· ἐτύγχανον, τινὲς δὲ ἀθάδανον, Hsch.

*ἀθαλής or **ἀθαλλής**, ές, of the laurel, *not verdant, withered*, Plu. *Pomp.*31, Orac.ap.Ath.12.524b.

**ἀθαλπής**, ές, *without warmth*, Nonn.*D.*37.151, 40.286, etc. Adv. -πέως Hp.*Acut.*29.

**ἀθαμβ-ής**, ές, *fearless, unabashed*, ἔρος, ὕβρις, σῶμα, Ibyc.1.9, B.14. 58, Phryn.Trag.2; σκότου Plu.*Lyc.*16. -ητος, ον, *free from alarms*, *PMag.Par.*1.1064. -ία, Ion. -ίη, ἡ, *imperturbability*, Democr.215. -ος, ον, *imperturbable*, Id.216.

**Ἀθᾱνα, Ἀθᾶναι, Ἀθᾱναία**, Dor. for Ἀθην-, v. Ἀθήνη.

**ἀθᾰνᾰσία**, ἡ, *immortality*, Pl.*Phdr.*246a, Arist.*EN*1111ᵇ22, Epicur. *Ep.*3p.60 U., etc.; ὁ δὲ λιμὸς ἐστιν ἀθανασίας φάρμακον Antiph.86. 6. II. *elixir* or *antidote*, ἀ. Μιθριδάτου Gal.14.148, cf. 13. 203. 2. = ἀμβροσία, Luc.*D.Deor.*4.5.

**ἀθᾰνᾰτ-ίζω**, *make immortal*, τὴν φύσιν Arist.*Fr.*645, cf. Ph.2. 255, al.:—Pass., *to become* or *be immortal*, Plb.6.54.2, Ph.1.32, 37, al. 2. *regard as immortal*, ψυχάς J.*AJ*18.1.5. II. abs., *hold oneself immortal*, Γέται οἱ ἀθανατίζοντες Hdt.4.93sq., cf. 94; ἐφ' ὅσον ἐνδέχεται ἀ. *put off the mortal*, Arist.*EN*1177ᵇ33, cf. Philostr.*VA*8. 7. -ισμός, ὁ, *gift of immortality*, ὁ διὰ τῆς δόξης ἀ. D.S.1.1. *-ος, ον, also η, ον (so regularly in sense I. 1, poet. and Isoc.9.16):—*undying, immortal*, Hom., etc.; ἀ. πρόσωπον, of Aphrodite, Sapph.1.14:—hence ἀθάνατοι, οἱ, *the Immortals*, Hom., Pi.*Pae.*6.50, etc.; ἀθάναται ἅλιαι, i. e. the sea *goddesses*, Od.24.47: Comp. -ώτερος Pl.*Phd.* 99c. 2. *of immortal fame*, Tyrt.12.32. II. of things, etc., *everlasting, perpetual*, ἀ. κακόν Od.12.118; χάρις Hdt.7.178; ἀρετή, ἀρχά, S.*Ph.*1420, *OT*905 (lyr.); κλέος, μνήμη, B.12.65, Lys.2.81; συκοφάντης Hyp.*Lyc.*2; ἀ. ὁ θάνατος 'death *that cannot die*', Amph.8; of Nisus' purple locks, ἀ. θρίξ *on which life depended*, A.*Ch.*619. III.

ι. *the immortals*, a body of Persian troops in which vacancies were ..ed up by successors already appointed, Hdt.7.83,211; so ἀ. ἀνήρ ..e whose successor in case of death is appointed (as we say, *the ..g never dies*), ib.31; of a *standing* army, D.C.52.27. 2. *main..ined at a constant figure*, πρόβατα *PSI*4.377.5 (iii B.C.), *PThead*.30 (iii A.D.); αἶγες *PStrassb*.30.6 (iii A.D.); διὰ τὸ ἀθάνατον (sc. τὸ ..ιδίον) αὐτὴν ἐπιδεδέχθαι τροφεύειν *BGU*1106.25 (Aug.). IV. λυχνὶς στεφανωματική, Ps.-Dsc.3.100. V. Adv. ἀθανάτως, ..δειν *AP*9.570 (Philod.). [ᾰθ- always in the Adj. and all derivs., sub ἀ- 1 fin.] -όω, *make immortal*, Tz.*H*.6.740.

ἀθᾰνής, ές, *undying*, ψυχή Max.Tyr.16.2.

ἄθαπτος, ον, *unburied*, Il.22.386, MoschioTrag.6.32, etc.; ἄθατον ὠθεῖν, βάλλειν, ἐᾶν τινά, S.*Aj*.1307,1333, *Ant*.205. II. *unworthy of burial*, *AP*9.498.

ἀθαράπευτος, v. ἀθεράπ-.

❋ἀθάρη (not ἀθάρα, Moer.184, cf. Hdn.Gr.1.340), ἡ, *gruel* or *porridge*, Ar.*Pl*.673, Pherecr.108.3, Crates9, Nicoph.15, Anaxandr.41.42. [ἀθᾰρη ll. cc.: cf. ἀθήρα.]

❋ἀθαρής· ἄφθορος, of women, Hsch. ἀθάριοι· αἱ μὴ διαπεπαρθενευμέναι, τινὲς δέ, μὴ δεδεμέναι ἄρθρῳ, Id. ἀθαρσέω, *to be discouraged*, Procop.*Vand*.2.11 (s.v.l.).

ἀθαρσής, ές, *discouraged*, *downhearted*, Plu.*Cic*.35, Max.Tyr.25.4, Doroth. in *Cat.Cod.Astr*.2.195: τὸ ἀ. *want of courage*, Plu.*Nic*.4. Adv. -σῶς Id.*Pomp*.60, 2.150c (Comp.).

ἀθᾰρώδης, ες, *like* ἀθάρη, of the brain, Ruf.*Anat*.3.

ἀθαυμ-αστία, ἡ, *absence of wonder*, Str.1.3.21: c. gen., 1.3.16. -αστος, ον, *not wondering at* anything, πρός τι Zeno *Stoic*.1.57, M.Ant.1.15. Adv. -τως S.*Fr*.982; also ἀθαυμαστί Suid. II. *not wondered at* or *admired*, Luc.*Am*.13.

ἀθεάμων [ᾱμ], ον, gen. ονος, *not beholding*, καλλέων τοσούτων Men.Rh.p.383S. Adv. -όνως, i.q. ἀνεπιστημόνως, ἀπείρως, Poll.4.10:—also Subst. -οσύνη, ἡ, ib.9.

ἀθέᾱτος, ον, *unseen*, *invisible*, Luc.*Nav*.44, Plu.2.575b, Ael.*NA* 8.7. 2. *that may not be seen*, *secret*, Ps.-Phoc.100, Plu.*Num*.9, Luc.*D.Mar*.14.2; τὰ ἀ. J.*AJ*14.16.3, etc. II. Act., *not seeing*, *blind to*, τινός X.*Mem*.2.1.31, Arist.*Mu*.391ᵃ25, Plu.2.7c, Max.Tyr.3.10. Adv. -τως Poll.4.10.

❋ἀθεησίη, ἡ, Ion. Subst. *want of sight*, *blindness*, Aret.*CD*1.4.

ἀθεεί, Adv., (θεός) *without the aid of God*, mostly with neg., οὐκ ἀθεεί Od.18.353, Philostr.*VS*1.21.2, D.C.59.12, Plot.4.3.16, Nonn.*D*.7.178, etc.

ἀθεΐα, ἡ, = ἀθεότης, Ael.*Fr*.39, Sm.*Ho*.4.15, Sallust.18 (pl.), Hierocl. *in CA*1 p.418M.; v.l. for ἀθεσία, Lxx 1*Ma*.16.17.

ἀθείαστος, ον, *uninspired*, οὐκ ἀ. Plu.*Cor*.33.

ἀθειρής, ές, Ep. for ἀθερής, prob. in Thgn.733; also, = ἀκριβής, *EM* 24.58. Adv. ἀθειρέως ibid.

ἀθελβάζω, *filter*, Hsch., who also has ἀθελβεῖ· ἕλκει.

❋ἀθελγ-ής, ές, *unappeased*, Nonn.*D*.33.200. II. Act., *having no power to soothe*, 12.261, al. -ία, ἡ, *implacability*, *BGU*1024 (iv/v A.D.).

ἀθέλγω, = ἀμέλγω, Hsch.:—Pass., ἀθέλγεται *is drawn off* or *pressed out*, Hp.*Hum*.1 (expl. by Gal. ad loc. διηθεῖται, διεκλύεται).—For ἄθελξις v. ἄλθεξις.

ἀθέλδω, *filter*, in Pass., Diocl.Com.7.

ἀθέλ-εος, ον, (θέλω) = sq., dub. l. A.*Supp*.862 (lyr.). ❋-ητος, ον, *unwilling*, Hsch. Adv. -τως Aspas.ap.Ath.5.219d.

ἀθέλιμνος· κακός, Suid., cf. Hsch.

❋ἄθελκτος, ον, *implacable*, A.*Supp*.1055, Lyc.1335.

ἀθελξίνοος, ον, *not beguiling* or *seductive*, Μοῦσαι Auson.*Ep*.12.26.

ἀθεμείλιος, ον, *without foundation*, Ep. word implied by Hsch. ἀθέμηλος· οὐδὸν οὐκ ἔχουσα οὐδὲ θεμέλιον, and ἀθεμίλιος· ἀκροσφαλής, ψεύστης.

❋ἀθεμελίωτος, ον, = foreg., Hsch.; ἀ. οἰκία, of a ship, Secund.*Sent*. 17.

ἄθεμ-ις, ιτος, ὁ, ἡ, *lawless*, Pi.*P*.3.32, 4.109, E.*Ion*1093 (lyr.): Comp. -ίστερος Opp.*H*.1.756. -ιστέω, *do lawless deeds*, Hsch. -ιστία, ἡ, *lawlessness*, App.*BC*2.77 (pl.). -ίστιος, ον, *lawless*, *godless*, ἀνήρ Od.18.141; freq. in phrase ἀθεμίστια εἰδώς versed in *wickedness*, 9.428, etc.; ἀ. ἔργα Xenoph.12, Man.2.301. ❋-ιστος or ἀθέμιτος, ον, (the former in Poetry, the latter more correct in Prose) = foreg., Il.9.63; of the Cyclopes, Od.9.106; ἀθεμιστότεροι X.*Cyr*.8.8.5. Adv. -ίστως Phaënnis ap.Paus.10.15.3; -ίτως App.*Pun*.53. II. of things, *unlawful*, freq. in neut., ἀθέμιτα ἔρδειν Hdt.7.33; ποιεῖν X.*Mem*.1.1.9; εὔχεσθαι Id.*Cyr*.1.6.6; -ιστα δρᾶν S.*Fr*.742 (dub.), Din.*Fr*.89.4S.; κείνοις δ' οὐκ ἀθέμιστον *IG*14.1389 ii 29:—ἀ. εἰδωλολατρεῖαι 1*Ep.Pet*.4.3: c. dat., αἷς [θεαῖς] ἀ. νεκρὰ σώματα *PTaur*.1 ii 22 (ii B.C.).

ἀθεμιτο-γαμία, ἡ, *unlawful marriage*, Just.*Nov*.154.1:—Adj. -γαμος, ον, *Cat.Cod.Astr*.8(4).196 (Rhetor.). -μιξία, ἡ, = foreg., Tz. ad Lyc.1143. -ποιός, όν, *infanda faciens*, *Gloss*.

ἀθεμιτ-ουργία, ἡ, *doing of unlawful deeds*, *Cat.Cod.Astr*.2.178:—Adj. -ουργός, -όν, Hld.8.9.

ἀθεμιτο-φαγέω, *eat unlawful meats*, Vett.Val.184.6. -φάγος, ον, Ptol.*Tetr*.159.

❋ἄθεος (A), ον, *without God*, *denying the gods*, esp. those recognized by the state, Pl.*Ap*.26c, etc.: applied to Diagoras, Cic.*ND*1.23.63; παράδειγμα ἄ., opp. θεῖον, Pl.*Tht*.176e. 2. generally, *godless*, *ungodly*, Pi.*P*.4.162, A.*Eu*.151, S.*Tr*.1036: Comp. -ώτερος Lys. 6.32: Sup. -ώτατος X.*An*.2.5.39. 3. *abandoned of the gods*, S.*OT*661; μανίαι B.10.109. 4. *not derived from* the name of a *god*, ὀνόματα Clearch.6. II. Adv. -ως *by the anger of heaven* (cf. 1.3), ἀ. ἐφθαρμένη S.*OT*254, cf. *El*.1181: Sup. -ώτατα *in most unholy wise*, ib.124 (lyr.).

ἄθεος (B), ον, *without vision*, τινός Plot.5.3.17 (s.v.l.; ἀθέ(ατ)ος Volkmann). 2. *unseen*, Sch.Opp.*H*.1.10.

ἀθεότης, ητος, ἡ, *godlessness*, Pl.*Plt*.308e: in pl., Id.*Lg*.967c. II. *atheism*, Ph.1.360,368, etc., Plu.2.165c. 2. *neglect of the gods of the state*, D.C.67.14.

ἀθεραπ-εία, ἡ, = sq., *neglect of medical care*, Antipho 4.3.5. -ευσία, ἡ, *want of attendance*, c. gen., *neglect of* a thing, θεῶν ἀθεραπευσίαι Pl.*R*.443a; σώματος Thphr.*Char*.19.1, cf. Plb.3.60.3 (pl.). -ευτος, ον, *uncared for*, of things, X.*Mem*.2.4.3; of persons, D.H.3.22; of faults, *neglected*, *not treated*, Phld.*Lib*.p.39O.; τὸ ἀ. *neglect of one's personal appearance*, Luc.*Pisc*.12. II. *incurable*, πάθος *PGnom*.205 (ii A.D., in form ἀθαράπ-), cf. Luc.*Ocyp*.37, [Gal.]14.689; ταραχή Phld.*D*.1.15. Adv. -τως Ph.2.404. III. *not prepared* or *cured*, στέαρ Dsc.2.76.16.

ἀθερηίς, ίδος, ἡ, *prickly*, Nic.*Th*.849.

ἀθερής, ές, *reckless*, *impious*, Hsch., *EM*25.1; cf. sq.

ἀθερίζω, Hom. (only pres. and impf.): aor. 1 ἀθέριξα A.R.2.477, 488:—Med., aor. 1 ἀθερίσσατο D.P.997:—*make light of*, c. acc. pers., οὔποτέ μ' οἵγ' ἀθέριζον Il.1.261; οὔ.. τιν' ἀναίνομαι οὐδ' ἀ. Od. 8.212, cf. Man.6.217: abs., Od.23.174: also c. gen., A.R. ll. cc.

❋ἀθερίνη [ῐ], ἡ, kind of *smelt*, *Atherina hepsetus*, Arist.*HA*570ᵇ15, Call.*Fr*.38, Dorio ap.Ath.7.285a, etc.:—also ἀθερῖνος, ὁ, Arist.*HA* 610ᵇ6.

ἀθέριστος, ον, = ἀφρόντιστος, Zonar. 2. Act., χαλκὸς ἀ., i.e. ὁ ἀθερίζων καὶ οὐδενὸς ἔχων λόγον, A.*Fr*.128 (cod. -ιτον). II. (θερίζω) *not reaped*, Thphr.*HP*8.11.4, *PTeb*.72.372 (ii B.C.), *PFay*. 112.13 (i A.D.).

❋ἀθέρμ-αντος, ον, *not heated*; ἑστία A.*Ch*.629, either a *cold* hearth, or (as Sch.) a household *not heated by strife* or *passion*. -ος, ον, *without warmth*; τὸ ἄ. Pl.*Phd*.106a.

ἀθερολόγιον, τό, *surgical instrument for extracting splinters*, Heliod.(?) ap.Orib.46.11.30; cf. ἐθειρολόγος.

ἀθερώδης, ες, (ἀθήρ) *bearded like ears of corn*, Thphr.*HP*7.11.2. 2. = ἀθαρώδης, [Gal.]19.440.

ἀθέρωμα, τό, v. ἀθηρ-.

ἀθεσία, ἡ, *faithlessness*, *fickleness*, Plb.2.32.8, Lxx *Je*.20.8, al., *IPE*1².352.16 (Chersonesus, i B.C.), D.S.18.32: pl., ἀ. εἰς αὐτούς Plb.4.29.4.

ἀθεσμία, ἡ, *lawlessness*, *EM*25.7.

❋ἀθέσμιος, ον, *unlawful*, Suid.

ἀθεσμό-βιος, ον, *living a lawless life*, *lawless*, -βια φρονεῦντες Hp.*Ep*.17. -λεκτρος, ον, *joined in lawless love*, Lyc.1143.

❋ἄθεσμος, ον, = ἀθέσμιος, Lxx 3*Ma*.5.12, Ph.2.165, J.*BJ*7.8.1, Plu.*Caes*.10. Adv. -μως Lxx 3*Ma*.6.26 (v.l.), Hsch.

ἀθεσμοφάγος, ον, *eating unlawful meats*, Man.4.564.

❋ἄθεστος, ον, (θέσσασθαι) *not to be entreated*, *inexorable*, of the Erinyes, Hsch.

❋ἀθέσφᾰτος, ον, *beyond even a god's power to express*, *unutterable*: or *not according to a god's utterance*, *unblest*, *portentous*, *awful*, ὄμβρος, θάλασσα, νύξ, Il.3.4, Od.7.273, 11.373; *vast*, ἀ. οἶνος, σῖτος, Od.11.61, 13.244; βόες 20.211; of great beauty, ὕμνος Hes.*Op*.662; φρὴν ἱερὴ καὶ ἀ. Emp.134.4.—Once in Trag., ἀ. θέα E.*IA*232 (lyr.).

❋ἀθετ-έω, (ἄθετος) *set at naught* a treaty, promise, etc., πίστιν Plb. 8.36.5; θυσίαν Lxx 1*Ki*.2.17; διαθήκην *Ep.Gal*.3.15; θεόν 1*Ep.Thess*. 4.8; σύμφωνον *OGI*444.18 (Ilium); *deny*, *disprove*, τἀληθές Phld.*Rh*. 1.5S., cf. *Sign*.37 (Pass.):—Pass., *to be struck off a register*, *PTeb*.74.29 (ii B.C.); *to be rejected*, of a petition, *POxy*.1120.8 (iii A.D.):—Astrol., *cancel*, *render ineffectual*, Vett.Val.115.3, cf. 105.8 (Pass.). 2. c. dat., *refuse one's assent*, τοῖς ὑπὸ Τιμαίου εἰρημένοις Plb.12.14.6. 3. *deal treacherously with*, *break faith with*, τινά Plb.9.36.10, Lxx *Is*.1.2, *Ev.Marc*.6.26; εἴς τινα Lxx 3*Ki*.12.19; ἐν Ἰσραήλ 4*Ki*.1.1: abs., *IG*12(5).129 (Paros). II. Gramm., *reject as spurious*, D.H.*Din*.9, D.L.7.34, etc. III. abs., *to be unsuitable*, *unfit*, Diph. 1D. -ημα, τό, *a breach of faith*, *transgression*, D.H.4.27 (v.l.), Lxx 3*Ki*.8.50 (pl.); *cancellation*, *annulment* of grant, *PTeb*.124.9. -ήσιμος, ον, *to be cancelled*, *BGU*1028.17 (ii A.D.). -ησις, ἡ, *a setting aside*, *abolition*, ἁμαρτίας *Ep.Heb*.9.26, cf. S.E.*M*.8.142; '*annulling*' of a deed, *PLond*.2.142.24 (i A.D.). II. *rejection* (of a spurious passage), A.D.*Synt*.5.8, D.L.3.66; generally, *rejection*, opp. ἐποχή, Cic.*Att*.6.9.3. III. *breach of faith*, Vett.Val.191.24 (pl.). -ητέον, *one must set aside*, Plb.3.29.2. -ητος, ον, *cancelled*, ἡμισφαίριον Heph.Astr.2.11. ❋-ος, ον, (τίθημι) *without position* or *place*, μονὰς οὐσία ἄ., στιγμὴ δὲ οὐσία θετός Arist.*APo*.87ᵃ36, cf. *Metaph*.1016ᵇ25, 1084ᵇ27, Dam.*Pr*.22. 2. *not in its place*, i.e. *lying about*, πλίνθος, λίθος, *IG*1.322 i 10,22. 3. *not adopted*, Posidipp.39, Anon.Rhythm.*Oxy*.9 iv 16. II. *wasted*, *useless*, χρόνος Plb.18.9.10; *unfit*, *to be rejected*, πρός τι D.S.11.15: c. dat., ῥευματισμοῖς, σπληνικοῖς, Dsc.1.128, 2.70.6; of persons, *incompetent*, *PAmh*.2.64.12 (ii A.D.). Adv. -τως, = ἀθέσμως, *lawlessly*, *despotically*, A.*Pr*.150 (lyr.); *unsuitably*, ἔχειν πρός τι Plu.2.715b, Philum.*Ven*.2.3.

ἀθεωρ-ησία, ἡ, *want of observation*, D.S.1.37. -ητί, Adv. *without examination*, Hdn.Gr.2.934, Suid. -ητος, ον, *not seen*, *not to be seen*, Antipho Soph.67, D.S.2.35, Arist.*Mu*.399ᵇ22; ἄγνωστος καὶ ἀ. Procl. *in Prm*.p.799S. 2. *not scientifically considered*, διαφοραί Aristox.*Harm*.p.35M.; τὸ ἀ. M.Ant.1.9 (prob.); οὐκ ἀ. *not without considered meaning*, J.*BJ*5.5.4. II. Act., *not having observed, not conversant with*, τῶν ὑπαρχόντων Arist.*GC*316ᵃ8; πολιτικῶν πραγμάτων Phld.*Rh.*2.107 S.; *unable to perceive*, τῶν ἐναργειῶν Diogenian. Epicur. 3.25: abs., ἀ. ἐν λόγοις Plu.2.405a, cf. Gell.1.9. Adv. -τως Plu. *Num.*18. 2. *non-intellectual*, ἀρετή Hecato ap.D.L.7.90.

**ἀθήητος**, ον, Ion. for **ἀθέατος**, *that may not be beheld*, Nonn.*D.*5. 305, al.; *unseen*, ib.2.6.

**ἀθήλαστος**, ον, (θηλή) *not having suckled*, *EM*739.44.

**ἀθηλής**, ές, = foreg., μαζοί Nonn.*D.*48.365, cf. Tryph.34.

**ἄθηλος**, ον, *unsuckled*, Ar.*Lys.*881; *just weaned*, Semon.5.

**ἀθήλυντος**, ον, *not womanish*, Ptol.*Tetr.*69; Pythag., of odd numbers, *Theol.Ar.*53.20.

**ἄθηλυς**, υ, = foreg., Plu.2.285c, *Comp.Lyc.Num.*3.

*Ἀθῆναι, Dor. **Ἀθᾶναι**, ῶν, αἱ, *the city of Athens* (for the pl. cf. Θῆβαι, Μυκῆναι), Hom., etc.; (sg. Ἀθήνη Od.7.80, *IG*1.373¹⁰⁷):—Ἀθῆναι generally, = Ἀττική, of the whole country, Hdt.9.17. II. Advbs., **Ἀθήν-αζε**, *to Athens*, *IG*1.27a, Th.4.46, X.*Ath.*1.16: **-ηθεν**, *from Athens*, Lys.13.25, etc.; poet. **-όθεν**, *AP*7.369 (Antip.): *-**ησιν**, *at Athens*, *IG*1.59, D.18.66, etc.

*Ἀθήναια, τά, older name of the Παναθήναια, Paus.8.2.1: ephebic festival, *IG*3.1147.

**Ἀθην-αΐζω**, *to be wise as Athena*, Eust.1742.2. **-αϊκός**, ή, όν, *pertaining to Athena*, Dam.*Pr.*90, Procl.*in Alc.*p.43 C. Adv. **-κῶς** Id.*Theol.Plat.*5.33.

**Ἀθήν-αιον**, τό, (Ἀθηνᾶ) *the temple of Athena*, Hdt.5.95, etc. II. lecture-hall at Rome, D.C.73.17. **-αῖος**, α, ον, *Athenian*, Il.2. 551, etc. II. Dor. **Ἀθαναῖος**, sc. μήν, month in Locris, *IG*9(1). 385. **-αιότης**, τητος, ἡ, *quality of being Athenian*, Gal.19.431.

*Ἀθήνη, ἡ, *Athene*, Il.1.194, etc.; Παλλὰς Ἀ. ib.400, etc.:—also **Ἀθηναίη**, Παλλὰς Ἀ. ib.221,200, etc.:—Att. **Ἀθηναία**, A.*Eu.*288, Ar.*Eq.*763, *Pax* 271; Ἀ. Πολιάς *Av.*828, cf. X.*An.*7.3.39, and earlier Attic Inscrr.: contr. **Ἀθηνᾶ**, which in cent. iv superseded the fuller form: Dor. **Ἀθάνα** (this form and Ἀθηναία are the only ones used in Trag.); Ἀθαναία *IG*1.373¹⁰⁵, Theoc.15.80: Aeol. **Ἀθανάα** [νᾰ], Alc.9, Theoc.28.1 (also in some Attic Inscrr., as *IG*1.351; Ἀθηνάα ib.373¹²⁰). 2. Ἀθηνᾶς ψῆφος *casting vote*, i.e. that from that of A. given for Orestes, Philostr.*VS*2.3. 3. = Ἀθῆναι, q.v. 4. Pythag. name for 7 (cf. ἀειπάρθενος), TheoSm.p.103 H. 5. name of a plaster, Orib.*Fr.*88.

**Ἀθηνιάω**, *long to be at Athens*, Luc.*Pseudol.*24.

***ἀθήρ**, έρος, ὁ, *awn*, πυραμίνους ἀ. Hes.*Fr.*117; εἴσδυσις οὐδ' ἀθέρι prob. l. in *Lyr.Adesp.*2 B, cf. X.*Oec.*18.1, Arist.*HA*595ᵇ27:—in pl., *chaff*, Luc.*Anach.*31; χωρὶς δείσης καὶ ἀθέρος *POxy.*988 (iii A.D.). II. *barb* of a weapon, A.*Fr.*154, Hp.*Epid.*5.49, Plu.*Cat. Mi.*70. III. *spine* or *prickle* of a fish, prob. in Ath.7.303d.

**ἀθήρα** or **ἀθήρη**, ἡ, = ἀθάρη, Hellanic.192, Sophr.77, *PTeb.*131 (100 B.C.), Dsc.2.92, Eust.1675.60.—Egyptian, acc. to Plin.*HN*22. 121.

**ἀθήρ-ᾱτος**, ον, *not caught*, or *not to be caught*, Opp.*C.*1.514, Ael. *NA*1.4, Longus 2.4; τὰ ἀ. ἐκθηρᾶσθαι Max.Tyr.6.3. **-ευτος**, ον, *not hunted*, X.*Cyr.*1.4.16.

**ἀθηρηλοιγός**, ὁ, (ἀθήρ) *consumer of chaff*, i.e. *winnowing-fan*, Od. 11.128, 23.275.

**ἀθηρία**, ἡ, *want of game*, Ael.*NA*8.2. 2. *immunity from being hunted*, ib.14.1. 3. *want of experience in hunting*, ib.12.7.

**ἀθηρόβρωτος**, ον, (ἀθήρ) *devouring chaff*, ἀ. ὄργανον, i.e. a winnowing-fan, S.*Fr.*454.

**ἀθηρόλοον**· ἀθηρηλοιγόν, Hsch.

**ἀθηροπώλης**, ὁ, *seller of* ἀθάρη, *POxy.*1432.6 (iii A.D.).

**ἄθηρος**, ον, *without wild beasts* or *game*, χώρη Hdt.4.185; τὸ ἄθηρον ταῖς λίμναις ἔνεστι, = ἀθηρία 2, Plu.2.981c; ἄ. ἡμέρα a *blank* day, A. *Fr.*241. II. *repelling noxious animals*, κλάδος *Gp.*10.32, etc.

**ἀθηρ-ώδης**, ες, = ἀθερώδης, Hsch. s.v. ἔτνος. **-ωμα**, ατος, τό, *tumour full of gruel-like matter* (ἀθήρη), Gal.10.985, Heliod.ap.Orib. 45.5 tit. **-ωμάτιον**, τό, Dim. of foreg., ibid.1.

**ἀθησαύριστος**, ον, *not hoarded, not fit for hoarding*, Pl.*Lg.*844d; of food, *not fit for preserving*, *not keeping well*, Thphr.*HP*6.4. 11. II. Act., *not hoarding, prodigal*, Poll.3.117.

**ἀθήτευτος**, ον, *not serving for hire*, Hsch.

**ἀθίγγανος**· ὁ μὴ θέλων τινὶ προσεγγίσαι, *EM*25.28.

**ἀθῐγής**, ές, (θιγεῖν) *untouched*, Theopomp.Hist.76; of a virgin, *Epigr.Gr.*521 (Thessalonica). 2. *intangible*, S.E.*M.*9.281. II. Act., *not having touched*, νεκροῦ Porph.ap.Eus.*PE*5.10.

**ἄθικτος**, ον, *untouched*: mostly c. gen., *untouched by* a thing, ἀκτῖνος ἄ. S.*Tr.*686; ἄ. ἡγητῆρος Id.*OC*1521, etc.; κερδῶν ἄθικτον βουλευτήριον *untouched by* gain, i.e. incorruptible, A.*Eu.*704, cf. Plu.*Cim.*10: c. dat., νόσοις ἄ. A.*Supp.*561; ἄ. ὑπὸ τοῦ χρόνου Plu. *Per.*13. 2. *chaste, virgin*, κόραι Ion Trag.11; εὐνή E.*Hel.*795, cf. Arar.14; ἄ. ἄμματα παρθενίης *Epigr.Gr.*248.8 (Phryg.); ἄ. εἰς Κυθηρίην σφρηγίς Herod.1.55: of substances, ἄ. θεῖον, *virgin* sulphur, Ps.-Democr.Alch.p.45 B. 3. *not to be touched, holy*, τὸν ἄ. γᾶς ὀμφαλόν, of Delphi, S.*OT*897; ἄ. οὐδ' οἰκητὸς [ὁ χῶρος] Id. *OC*39; ἄθικτα *holy things*, A.*Ag.*371, S.*OT*891. 4. *not to be touched, abominable*, *EM*25.10. II. Act., *not touching*, c. gen., Call.*Dian.*201.

**ἀθίλοι**· κόγχου θαλασσίας εἶδος, Hsch.

**ἄθλαστος**, ον, *which cannot be crushed* or *dinted*, Arist.*Mete.*385ᵃ15, 386ᵃ18. 2. *unbruised*, of olives, *Gp.*9.29; **ἄθλαστον**, τό, of a food-stuff (?), *PFay.*333 (ii A.D.).

**ἀθλ-εύω**, Ep. and Ion. **ἀεθλεύω**: fut. -εύσω A.*Pr.*95 (anap.), Q. 4.113, Nonn.*D.*37.557:—*contend for a prize*, abs., ἀεθλεύειν προκαλ[ί]ζετο Il.4.389, cf. 23.274,737, Hes.*Th.*435; once in Hdt.5.22: cont[r.] ἀθλ-, once in Hom., ἀθλεύων πρὸ ἄνακτος *struggling* or *suffering f[or]* him, Il.24.734; once in Pl., ἐν ἀγῶνι ἀ. *Lg.*873e; but Trag. alway[s] use ἀθλέω, exc. A. l.c. *-**έω**, Ion. impf. ἀέθλεον Hdt.1.67, 7.21[2]: aor. ἤθλησα (v. infr.): pf. ἤθληκα Plu.*Demetr.*5:—Med., aor. ἐν[α]θλησάμην *AP*7.117 (Zenod.):—Pass., pf. κατήθλημαι Suid.: (ἆθλος, ἆθλον):—commoner form of foreg., used by Hom. only in aor. part., Λαομέδοντι.. ἀθλήσαντε *having contended with* him, Il.7.453; πολλά περ ἀθλήσαντα *having gone through* many *struggles*, 15.30; *contend in battle*, Hdt.7.212; πρός τινα 1.67; ἀ. ἄθλους, ἀ. κατὰ τὴν ἀγωνίαν Pl.*Ti.*19c and b, cf. *Lg.*830a; ἤθλησα κινδυνεύματα *have engaged in* perilous struggles, S.*OC*564; φαῦλον ἀθλήσας πόνον E.*Supp.* 317; ἀ. τῷ σώματι Aeschin.2.147. II. *to be an athlete, contend in* games, Simon.149, *CIG*2810b (Aphrodisias). III. *hold games*, ἐπ' Ἀρχεμόρῳ B.8.12. **-ημα**, τό, *contest, struggle*, Pl.*Lg.*833c, etc.: pl., *athletic exercises*, Arist.*Pr.*956ᵇ26, Phld.*Mus.*p.69 K. II. *implement of labour*, Theoc.21.9. **-ησις**, ἡ, *contest, combat*, esp. of athletes, Plb.5.64.6, *SIG*1073.24 (Olympia), *IG*14.1102: pl., Phld.*Mus.*p.14 K.; κατὰ τὴν ἄ. 'in the *athletic world*', *CPHerm.* 119ᵛiii 13 (iii A.D.); *training, practice*, D.S.3.33. 2. generally, *struggle, trial*, ἄ. ὑπομένειν *Ep.Heb.*10.32. **-ητέον**, *one must practise athletics*, Hermog.*Prog.*11. 2. glossed by ἀσκητέον, Erot. **-ητήρ**, ῆρος, ὁ, = ἀθλητής, Od.8.164, *IG*3.1171.3, *POxy.* 1015.8 (poet.). **-ητής**, contr. from ἀεθλητής, οῦ, ὁ:—*combatant, champion*; esp. in games, Pi.*N.*5.49, 10.51 (in form ἀεθλ-), cf. Pl.*R.* 410b, *IG*4.1508ᴮ (Epid.), etc.: of Christian martyrs, Epist.Gall.ap. Jul.454d, cf. *JRS* 10.53. 2. as Adj., ἀ. ἵππος a *race*-horse, Lys.19.63, Pl.*Prm.*137a. II. c. gen. rei, *practised in, master of*, πολέμου Pl.*R.*543b; τῶν καλῶν ἔργων D.25.97; βδελυρίας Theopomp.Hist.217; τῶν ἔργων (sc. τῶν πολεμικῶν) Arist.*Pol.*1321ᵃ26; τῆς ἀληθινῆς λέξεως D.H.*Dem.*18; πάσης ἀρετῆς D.S.9.1; οἵους ἡ γῆ τοὺς ἑαυτῆς ἀ. ἀποτελεῖ Philostr.*Im.*2.24. **-ητικός**, ή, όν, *of* or *for an athlete, athletic*, ἕξις Arist.*Pol.*1338ᵇ10; ἐνεργείαι prob. in Phld. *Mus.*p.14 K.; ἀ. ἀγῶνες Plu.2.724f; στέφανος *PRyl.*153.25 (ii A.D.). Adv. **-κῶς** Plu.2.192c, Aët.16.34.

**ἄθλητος**, ον, = ἄθλαστος, dub. l. Hierocl.p.25.3 A.

**ἀθλῐβής**, ές, *not pressed* or *hurt*, Nonn.*D.*9.31; *not pressed out*, ἰκμάδες 22.27. II. Act., *not pressing*, ib.37.220.

**ἄθλιβος**, ον, = ἀθλιβής 1, Gal.13.686.

**ἀθλιό-ομαι**, *to be made miserable*, Tz.*H.*3.364. **-ποιός**, όν, *creating misery*, Olymp.*in Alc.*p.224 C.

**ἄθλιος**, α, ον, also ος, ον E.*Alc.*1038, etc., Att. contr. from ἀέθλιος: (ἄεθλον, ἆθλον):—lit. *winning the prize* or *running for it* (this sense only in Ep. form ἀέθλιος, q.v.). II. metaph., *struggling, unhappy, wretched, miserable* (this sense only in Att. form ἄθλιος), freq. of persons, A.*Th.*922, etc.: Comp. -ιώτερος S.*OT*815,1204: Sup. -ιώτατος E.*Ph.*1679:—also of states of life, ἄ. γάμοι A.*Th.*779; βίος, τύχη, E.*Heracl.*878, *Hec.*425:—of that *which causes wretchedness*, ἆρ' ἄθλιον τοὔνειδος; S.*OC*753, cf. *El.*1140; πρόσοψις E.*Or.*952. Adv., τὸν ἀθλίως θανόντα S.*Ant.*26, cf. E.*HF*707, etc. 2. in moral sense, *pitiful, wretched*, Lys.32.13, D.10.43; τίς οὕτως ἄ. ὅστις ..; Id.21.66; καὶ γὰρ ἂν ἄ. ἦν, εἰ.. ib.191. 3. without any moral sense, *wretched, sorry*, θηρσὶν ἄθλιον βοράν E.*Ph.*1603; ἄ. ζωγράφος Plu.2.6f. Adv. -ίως καὶ κακῶς with *wretched* success, D.18.145; ζῆν ἀ. Philem.203.

**ἀθλιότης**, ητος, ἡ, *suffering, wretchedness*, Pl.*R.*545a, Clearch.25, Plu.2.112b, etc. 2. *degradation*, ἀ. βαθεῖα Phld.*Rh.*1.206 S.

**ἄθλιπτος**, ον, (θλίβω) = ἀθλιβής, Gal.9.373: metaph., *not oppressed*, βίος *PSI*1.65.4 (vi A.D.). Adv. -τως *without pressure* or *crushing*, Gal.18(2).794, Aët.9.28: metaph., ἐκπονεῖν Simp.*in Epict.*p.46 D.

***ἀθλο-θεσία**, ἡ, *office of* ἀθλοθέτης *IG*2².1368.131 (Athens, ii A.D.): —also **-θετία**, ἡ, Ar.*Fr.*739a. **-θετέω**, (τίθημι) *offer a prize, offer rewards*, Lxx 4*Ma.*17.12; τισί Clearch.18. II. *preside over, direct*, metaph., τὸν Ῥωμαϊκὸν ὄλεθρον Eun.*Hist.*p.264 D., cf. Hld.7. 12. **-θετήρ**, ῆρος, ὁ, = sq., *IG*5(1).456 (Sparta), 14.1815. *-**θέτης**, ου, ὁ, *one who awards the prize, the judge* or *steward* in the games, Pl. *Lg.*764d, Arist.*EN*1095ᵇ1, *IG*1.188, etc.

***ἆθλον**, τό, Att. contr. from Ep., Ion., Lyr. **ἄεθλον** (which alone is used by Hom. and Hdt., mostly also by Pi., once by S.*Tr.*506 (lyr.)):—*prize of contest*, Il.23.413,620, etc., Pi.*O.*9.108, al., A.*Supp.* 1033, E.*Hel.*43; τῶν Ἀθήνηθεν ἄ., inscr. on Attic prize amphorae, *CIG*776, etc.; ἄ. μουσικῆς *IG*2.814; in Prose, ἆθλα ἀρετῆς Th.2.46; ἁμαρτημάτων Lys.1.47. Phrases: ἄεθλα κεῖται or πρόκειται *prizes* are offered, Hdt.8.26, 9.101; ἆθλα προφαίνειν, προτιθέναι offer *prizes*, X.*Cyr.*2.1.23, *Hier.*9.4; τιθέναι Pl.*Lg.*834c; ἆθλα λαμβάνειν, φέρεσθαι to win *prizes*, Pl.*R.*613c, *Ion* 530a, etc.; ἆθλον νίκης λαμβάνειν *as the prize*, Arist.*Pol.*1296ᵃ30, cf. Th.6.80; ἀ. ποιεῖσθαι τὰ κοινά Th.3.82; τὰ ἆθλα ὑπὲρ ὧν ἐστιν ὁ πόλεμος D.2.28; ἆθλα πολέμου Id. 4.5; τῆς ἀρετῆς Id.20.107; βέλτιον τοῖς δούλοις ἀ. προκεῖσθαι τὴν ἐλευθερίαν Arist.*Pol.*1330ᵃ33. II. = ἆθλος, *contest*, only in pl., ζώνυνταί τε νέοι καὶ ἐπεντύνονται ἄεθλα Od.24.89, cf. Xenoph.2.5, Pi.*O.* 1.3: metaph., *conflict, struggle*, πολλῶν ἔλεξεν δυσοίστων πόνων ἆθλα S.*Ph.*508; ἄεθλ' ἀγώνων Id.*Tr.*506:—this usage is censured by Luc. *Sol.*2. III. in pl., *place of combat*, Pl.*Lg.*868a, 935b. IV. Astrol., = κλῆρος (q.v.), Manil.3.162.

***ἆθλος**, ὁ, contr. from Ep. and Ion. **ἄεθλος**, which alone is used by Hom. (except in Od.8.160), and mostly by Hdt. and Pi.:—*contest*

:her in war or sport, esp. *contest for a prize*, Hom.; νικῶν τοιῷδ' ἐπ' θλῳ (for the arms of Achilles) Od.11.548; ἄεθλος πρόκειται *a task set one*, Hdt.1.126; ἐμοὶ μὲν οὗτος ἄ. ὑποκείσεται Pi.*O*.1.84; ἄεθλον οτιθέναι to set it, Hdt.7.197; ἆθλοι Πυθικοί, Δελφικοί, S.*El*.49,682; *il*, Pi.*P*.4.165; of the labours of Heracles, D.S.4.11, etc.: metaph., *nflict, struggle, ordeal*, Alc.33, A.*Pr*.702,752, S.*Ant*.856. II. = ἆθλον I, Theoc.8.11 sqq.—On the proper difference of ἆθλον and θλος v. ἆθλον II. (For ἀϝ εθλος, ἄϝεθλον, as in *IG*5(2).75.)

**ᵜἀθλοσύνη**, ἡ, = ἆθλος, *AP*6.54 (Paul. Sil.).

**ἀθλοφόρος**, ον, Ep. and Lyr. **ἀεθλ-**, *bearing away the prize, victorious*, ἵππος Il.9.124, 22.22, Ibyc.2, cf. *Inscr.Olymp*.166; ἄνδρες Pi. O.7.7, cf. Hdt.1.31, etc.; of martyrs, *JRS*10.47. II. *prize-giving*, ἀγῶνες *IG*7.530.3 (Tanagra). III. ἀθλοφόρος, ἡ, title of priestess at Alexandria, ἀ. Βερενίκης *OGI*90.5 (Canopus), *PTeb*.176 (circ. 200 B.C.), etc.

**ἄθολ-ος**, ον, *not turbid, clear*, Luc.*Hist.Conscr*.51: Sup., Olymp. *in Mete*.271.22. **-ωτος**, ον, *untroubled*, of water, Hes.*Op*.595; of *pure* air, Luc.*Trag*.62: metaph., λόγος Them.*Or*.19.232d; ἀ. τὴν αἰδῶ φυλάττειν Just.*Nov*.78.2.1.

**ἄθορος**, ον, (θορεῖν) of male animals, *veneris expers*, Ant.Lib.13.7.

**ἀθορύβ-ητος**, ον, *undisturbed*: τὸ -ητότατον *tranquillity* of mind, X.*Ages*.6.7. **-ος**, ον, *without uproar*, Pl.*Lg*.640c; *unperturbed*, Polystr.p.29 W., prob. l. in Metrod.*Fr*.48 K.: Comp., Anon.*in SE* 15.19. Adv. -βως E.*Or*.630, Epicur.*Fr*.489, J.*BJ*2.12.6, Hierocl. *in CA* 12 p.447 M. II. *not causing confusion*, Ascl.*Tact*.12.10 (Comp.).

**ἄθουρος**, prob. f.l. for ἄθορος, *EM*25.12.

**ᵜἀθραγένη**, ἡ, *smoke-wood, Clematis Vitalba*, Thphr.*HP*5.9.6.

**ᵜἄθρακτος**, ον, (θράσσω) = ἀτάρακτος, Hsch.

**ἀθράνευτος**, ον, expl. by ἄστρωτος, prob. *uncushioned*, E.*Fr*.569, *AB*352.

**ἀθράσυντος**, ον, = ἄτολμος, Sch.A.*Ch*.629.

**ᵜἄθραυστος**, ον, *unbroken*, E.*Hec*.17, *IG*2.1054*d*14, Melinno ap.Stob. 3.7.12; of persons, Plb.2.22.5; μέρος τῆς δυνάμεως D.S.19.30. Adv. -τως *without breakage*, κάμπτειν *Gp*.10.19.2, etc. 2. *unbreakable*, Arist.*Mete*.385ᵃ14; *indestructible*, ἄτομος *Placit*.1.3.18.

**ᵜἄθρεπτος**, ον, *ill-nourished, underfed*, Ar.Byz.*Epit*.2.9.8; f.l. for ἄτρεπτος, *AP*5.177 (Mel.).

**ἀθρέω** (not ἀθρέω, Hdn.Gr.2.83): aor. opt. ἀθρήσειε, inf. ἀθρῆσαι, Il. 12.391, S.*OT*1305 (lyr.): aor. Med. ἀθρήσασθαι Timo 5.5:—*gaze at, observe*, ἵνα μή τις Ἀχαιῶν βλήμενον ἀθρήσειε Il. l.c., cf. 14.334; οὐδέ πῃ ἀθρῆσαι δυνάμην (sc. Σκύλλην) Od.12.232, cf. 19.478, E.*Hec*.679, *El*. 827; [οἱ μεθύοντες] ἀθρεῖν τὰ πόρρω οὐ δύνανται Arist.*Pr*.872ᵃ19. b. *inspect*, ἱερά *IG*12(1).694 (Rhodes). 2. abs. or with a Prep., *look earnestly, gaze*, ὅτ' ἐς πεδίον τὸ Τρωϊκὸν ἀθρήσειε Il.10.11; ἄθρει *observe, watch*, A.*Fr*.226; δεῦρ' ἄθρησον *look* hither, E.*Hipp*.300; λεύσσετ', ἀθρήσατε Id.*Andr*.1228; οὐ γὰρ ἴδοις ἂν ἀθρῶν *by observing*, S.*OC* 252; ἄθρει πᾶς κύκλῳ σκοπῶν Ar.*Av*.1196. II. later, of the mind, *look upon, observe*, θέλων ἄθρησον *view* kindly, Pi.*P*.2.70; πολλὰ πυθέσθαι, πολλὰ δ' ἀθρῆσαι S.*OT*1305, cf. *OC*1032; ἄθρησον αὐτὸ E.*Ba*. 1281; ἐς τοῦδ' ἀθρήσας θάνατον ἡγείσθω θεούς ib.1326, etc.:—foll. by interrog. or rel. clause, καὶ ταῦτ' ἄθρησον, εἰ.. *consider* this also, whether.., S.*Ant*.1077, cf. 1216: imper. freq. in Pl., as τόδε τοίνυν ἄθρει, πότερον.. *R*.394e; ἄθρει μὴ οὐ.. *Grg*.495b; ἄθρει ὅτι.. *R*. 583b; also ἀθρῶ *Prm*.144d, ἀθρῶν *Ti*.91e. 2. abs., ἄθρησον *consider*, E.*IA*1415. III. *perceive*, ἢ δοῦπον νέον οὔασιν ἠέ τιν' αὐγὴν ἀ. Nic.*Th*.165.

**ᵜἀθρήματα**, τά, *wedding-gifts*, Hsch.

**ἀθρήνητος**, ον, *unlamented*, gloss on νώνυμνος, Eust.928.63.

**ἀθρηνί**, Adv., (θρῆνος) *without mourning*, Hdn.*Epim*.255, Suid.

**ἀθρητέον**, *one must consider*, E.*Hipp*.379, X.*Smp*.8.39, Max.Tyr. 7.9.

**ἀθρίγγωτος**, ον, *without coping*, gloss on ἀγείσωτος, *EM*8.56.

**ἄθριξ**, τρῐχος, ὁ, ἡ, *without hair*, Matro *Fr*.4, Alex.Aphr.*Pr*.1.6.

**ἀθρῑπήδεστος**, ον, *not worm-eaten*, Thphr.*HP*5.1.2 (codd. ἀθριπηδέστατον); δέλτος Them.*Or*.23.293b.

**ᵜἀθροίζω**, Att. ἀθροίζω: aor. ἤθροισα E.*Ph*.495, etc.: pf. ἤθροικα Plu. *Caes*.20:—Pass., aor. ἠθροίσθην: pf. ἤθροισμαι: plpf. ἤθροιστο A.*Pers*. 414:—quadrisyll. ἀθροΐζω Archil.60,104, *APl*.4.308 (Eugen.); prob. in E.*IA*267 (lyr.), Ar.*Av*.253: (ἀθρόος):—*gather together, collect, muster*, ἀ. λαόν, etc., S.*OT*144, etc.; τὸ βαρβαρικὸν καὶ τὸ Ἑλληνικόν X. *An*.1.2.1; Τροίαν ἀ. *gather* the Trojans *together*, E *Hec*.1139; πνεῦμ' ἄθροισον *collect* breath, Id.*Ph*.851, cf. Arist.*GA*738ᵇ7; περιπλοκὰς λόγων ἀθροίσας *having strung together*, E.*Ph*.495: abs., *hoard* treasure, Arist.*Pol*.1314ᵇ10:—Med., *gather for oneself, collect round one*, E. *Heracl*.122, X.*Cyr*.3.1.19:—Pass., *to be gathered* or *crowded together*, εὖτε πρὸς ἄεθλα δῆμος ἠθροΐζετο Archil.104, cf. 60; ἐς τὴν ἀγορὴν ἀ. Hdt.5.101; ἀθροισθέντες *having rallied*, Th.1.50; τὸ δὲ.. ξύμπαν ἠθροίσθη δισχίλιοι but the whole *amounted collectively to*.., Id.5.6; ἐνταῦθα ἠθροίζοντο *they mustered in force* there, Id.6.44, etc.; *form a society*, Pl.*Prt*.322b; ἀθροισθέντες *having formed a party*, Arist.*Pol*.1304ᵇ33: of things, περὶ πολλῶν ἀθροισθέντων *taken in the aggregate*, Pl.*Tht*. 157b. 2. in Pass. of the mind, ἀθροίζεσθαι εἰς ἑαυτὸν *collect* oneself, Pl.*Phd*.83a, cf. 67c; φόβος ἤθροισται fear *has gathered strength*, X.*Cyr*.5.2.34.

**ᵜἄθροισις**, Att. **ἄθρ-**, εως, ἡ, *gathering, collecting*, στρατοῦ E.*Hec*. 314; χρημάτων Th.6.26; αἱ τῶν νεφῶν ἀ. Arist.*Mete*.340ᵃ31; λόγων Porph.*Abst*.1.29; κατ' ἄθροισιν λέγειν *collectively*, Hermog.*Id*.1.4.

**ἄθροισμα**, τό, *that which is gathered, a gathering*, ἀστῶν E.*Or*.874, cf. Lxx 1*Ma*.3.13; κυνῶν D.S.34.2.30. 2. *process of aggregation*, Pl.*Tht*.157b; *aggregate*, τέχνη ἄ. καταλήψεων Chrysipp.*Stoic*.2.23; ψυχὴ ἐννοιῶν καὶ προλήψεων ἄ. ib.2.228, cf. Gal.1.67; *compound*, Max. Tyr.40.5. II. in Epicur. philos., *assemblage of atoms*, Epicur. *Fr*.59, al.; esp. of the *human organism*, Id.*Ep*.1 p.19 U., al.

**ἀθροισμός**, ὁ, = ἄθροισις, Thphr.*CP*1.10.7, cf. Epicur.*Ep*.2 p.38 U., *Nat*.14.4, S.E.*P*.3.188; μισθοφόρων Max.Tyr.6.7; *condensation*, Thphr.*CP*5.2.1. **ἀθροιστέον**, *one must collect*, X.*Lac*.7.4.

**ἀθροιστικός**, ή, όν, *given to accumulation*, χρημάτων, Procl.*Par. Ptol*.246. II. Gramm., *collective*, ὀνόματα A.D.*Synt*.42.24; *copulative*, σύνδεσμοι Id.*Conj*.230.20, al.

**ἀθροοποσία**, ἡ, *copious drinking*, Herod.ap.Orib.5.30.23.

**ᵜἀθρόος**, α, ον, (ος, ον D.19.228, Arist.*PA*675ᵇ21, etc.), **ἀθρόος** in Hom. acc. to Aristarch.ap.Sch.Ven.Il.14.38 and Att. (also sometimes **ἄθρους**, ουν, as Ar.*Fr*.633, Hyp.*Eux*.32, D.27.35), poet. acc. pl. ἀθρόας *h.Merc*.106; dat. pl. ἀθροῖσιν *Epigr.Gr*.1034.26 (Callipolis):—but in later writers the spir. lenis prevailed: (ἀ- 11, θρόος):—*in crowds, heaps*, or *masses, crowded together*, Hom. only in pl., as Il.2.439, al.; ἀθρόοι.. ἅπαντες Od.3.34, etc.: sg. first in Pi.*P*.2.35; ἀθρόοι, of soldiers, *in close order*, Hdt.6.112, X.*An*.1.10.13, etc.; opp. ἀσύντακτοι, Id.*Cyr*.8.1.46; *in column*, ib.5.3.36; πολλαὶ κῶμαι ἀ. *close together*, Id.*An*.7.3.9. II. *together, in a body*, ἀθρόα πάντ' ἀπέτεισε he paid for all *at once*, Od.1.43; ἀ. πόλις the citizens *as a whole*, opp. καθ' ἕκαστον, Th.2.60, cf. 1.141; ἀ. δύναμις Id.2.39; ἀ. ἦν αὐτῷ τὸ στράτευμα was *assembled*, X.*Cyr*.3.3.22; τὸ ἀ. their *assembled force*, ib.4.2.20, cf. *An*.5.2.1; ἀθρόῳ στόματι with *one* voice, E.*Ba*.725; ἀ. δάκρυ *one flood of* tears, Id.*HF*489; ἀ. λόγος *a flood of* words, Pl.*R*. 344d; ἀθρόους κρίνειν to condemn *all by a single vote*, Id.*Ap*.32b; πολλοὺς ἀ. ὑμῶν D.21.131; ἄθρους ὤφθη was seen *with all his forces*, Plu. *Them*.12, cf. Id.*Sull*.12; ἀ. λεγόμενον used in a *collective* sense, opp. κατὰ μέρος, Pl.*Tht*.182a; ἀθρόας γινομένης μεταβολῆς taking place *all at once*, Arist.*Ph*.186ᵃ15; opp. ἐκ προσαγωγῆς, Id.*Pol*.1308ᵇ16; κατήριπεν ἀ. he fell *all at once*, Theoc.13.50, cf. 25.252; ἀθρόαι πέντε νύκτες five *whole* nights, Pi.*P*.4.130; κατάστασις ἀθρόα καὶ αἰσθητή Arist. *Rh*.1369ᵇ34; κάθαρσις ἀ., opp. κατ' ὀλίγον, Id.*HA*582ᵇ7; καταπιεῖν ἀθρόους τεμαχίτας *at a gulp*, Eub.9, cf. Plu.2.650c, etc.; ἀθρόον ἐκκαγχάζειν *burst out* laughing, Arist.*EN*1150ᵇ11, cf. Hp.*Ep*.17. 2. *continuous*, κίνησις Plot.3.7.8, cf. ib.1 (Comp.). 3. *sudden*, ἔφοδος Malch.p.412 D.; τῷ ἀ. μὴ καταπλαγῆναι Men.Prot.p.68 D.:—this sense may perh. be found in Plu.*Them*. l.c., *Sull*. l.c. 4. ἀθρόον, τό, = ἄθροισμα II, Epicur.*Ep*.1 p.16 U., *Fr*.314, Zeno Sidon.ap. Phld.*Herc*.1005.7. III. *complete, overwhelming*, ἀ. κακότης Pi.*P*. 2.35; *continuous, incessant*, πνεῦμα Arist.*Mete*.367ᵃ30; *concentrated*, of noise, D.H.*Comp*.22, etc. IV. Adv. ἀθρόον *all at once*; ἄθρουν *in one payment*, *PPetr*.2 p.27, cf. D.27.35; *generally*, εἰρῆσθαι Aret. *SA*1.6:—regul. Adv. ἀθρόως X.*Smp*.2.25, Arist.*HA*533ᵇ10, etc.; ἀ. λέγειν to speak *collectively* or *generally*, Aristid.*Rh*.2.547 S. 2. *suddenly*, ἀετὸς ἀ. φανείς Hsch.Mil.4.11, cf. 19 (perh. also in Arist.*HA* l.c.). V. Comp. ἀθροώτερος Th.6.34, etc.; ἀθρουστέρα Phylotim. ap.Ath.3.79b: Sup. ἀθρούστατος Plu.*Caes*.20.

**ἄθροος**, ον, *noiseless*, Hdn.Gr.1.126.

**ἀθροότης**, ητος, ἡ, (ἀθρόος) *a being massed together, collectivity*, κατὰ -ότητα, opp. κατὰ μέρη, Epicur.*Ep*.2 p.49 U.

**ἄθρυπτος**, ον, (θρύπτω) *unbroken, imperishable*, Plu.2.1055b; *tough*, of flesh, Herophil.ap.Gal.4.596. II. *not enervated*, *Carm.Aur*. 35; of language, *not affected*, λέξις ἀφελὴς καὶ ἄ. Plu.*Lyc*.21:—of a person, ἄ. εἰς γέλωτα *never breaking* into laughter, Id.*Per*.5; ὦτα ἄθρυπτα κολακείᾳ Id.2.38b. Adv. -τως Id.*Fab*.3.

**ἀθρυψία**, ἡ, *a simple way of life*, Plu.2.609c.

**ᵜἀθῡμ-έω**, *to be disheartened, despond*, ἐς νόσον πεσὼν ἀθυμεῖς A.*Pr*. 474; οἴμ' ὡς ἀθυμῶ S.*Aj*.587; ἀ. τινι *at* or *for* a thing, Id.*El*.769, etc.; ἐπί τινι Isoc.4.3; εἴς τι Pl.*Sph*.264b; πρὸς τὴν παροῦσαν ὄψιν Th.2.88; τὴν τελευτήν Id.5.91; τοῦτο, ὡς.. X.*Oec*.8.21; ἕνεκά τινος Id.*An*.5. 4.19:—*to be sore afraid* lest, ἀθυμῶ δ' εἰ φανήσομαι S.*Tr*.666; δεινῶς ἀθυμῶ μὴ βλέπων ὁ μάντις ᾖ Id.*OT*747. **-ητέον**, *one must lose heart*, X.*An*.3.2.23; οὐκ ἀ. τοῖς παροῦσι πράγμασιν D.4.2. **-ία**, Ion. **-ίη**, ἡ, *lack of spirit*, Hp.*Aër*.16; *faintheartedness, despondency*, Hdt.1.37, E.*HF*552; εἰς ἀ. καθιστάναι or ἐμβάλλειν τινά Pl.*Lg*.731a, Aeschin.3.177; ἀ. παρέχειν τινί X.*Cyr*.4.1.8; εἰς ἀ. καταστῆναι Lys.12.3; ἐν πάσῃ ἀ. εἶναι X.*HG*6.2.24; ἀθυμίαν ἔχειν S.*Ant*.237; ἀ. ἐμπίπτει τινί X.*Mem*.3.12.6: pl., ἀ. ἢ φέβοι Arist.*Pr*.954ᵃ23.

**ἀθυμί-αστος**, ον, *unconsecrated*, Procl.ad Hes.*Op*.746. **-ᾱτος**, ον, *which cannot exhale*, Arist.*Mete*.385ᵃ18.

**ἄθῡμος**, ον, *fainthearted, spiritless*, once in Hom., ἀσκελέες καὶ ἄ. Od.10.463; κακὸς καὶ ἄ. Hdt.7.11; οὐ τοῖς ἀ. ἡ τύχη ξυλλαμβάνει S.*Fr*. 927, cf. *OT*319; of nations, opp. ἔνθυμος, Arist.*Pol*.1327ᵇ28: Comp. -ότερος Men.405.2; ἄ. εἶναι πρός τι to have *little heart* for it, X.*An*.1. 4.9. Adv. ἀθύμως, ἔχειν πρός τι Id.*HG*4.5.4, cf. Isoc.3.58; ἀθύμως διάγειν X.*Cyr*.3.1.24; ἀθύμως πονεῖν to work *without spirit*, Id.*Oec*. 21.5; ὁδοὺς ἀ. τιθέντες *discouraging* their marches, A.*Eu*.770. 2. *without anger* or *passion*, Pl.*R*.411b, *Lg*.888a.

**ἀθυμόω**, *dishearten*, τινά Phld.*Lib*.p.70.

**ἀθυρεύεσθαι**· παίζειν, μιγνύειν, σκιρτᾶν, Hsch.

**ᵜἄθυρ-μα**, τό, (ἀθύρω) *plaything, toy*, Il.15.363, *h.Merc*.40: in pl., *beautiful objects, adornments*, Od.18.323, Sapph.*Supp*.20a.9; *delight, joy*, Ἀπολλώνιον ἄ., of a choral ode, Pi.*P*.5.23; ἀθύρματα Μουσᾶν, i.e. songs, B.*Fr*.33, cf. 8.87; ἀρηΐων ἀ. *pastimes* of Ares, i.e. battle, 17. 57; ἁβρὸν ἄ., of a pet dog, *IG*14.1647, cf. 12(5).677.10 (Syros):—rare in Trag. and Com., E.*Fr*.272, Cratin.145, *Com.Adesp*.839,

Alcid.ap.Arist.*Rh.*1406ᵃ9, ᵇ13; of a court-jester, ἄ. τοῦ βασιλέως J.*AJ*12.4.9, cf. Philostr.*VS*1.8.3. **-μάτιον**, τό, Dim. of foreg., Philox.3.23; *pet*, Luc.*D.Mar.*1.5.

**ἀθῠρο-γλωττία**, ἡ, *impudent loquacity*, Plb.8.10.1. **-γλωττος**, ον, *one that cannot keep his mouth shut, ceaseless babbler*, E.*Or.* 903 (-γλωσσος). **-νόμος**, ον, *making game of the laws*, Hsch.

**ἄθῠρος**, ον, (θύρα) *without door*, βούστασις *IG*11(2).287*A*161 (Delos, iii B.C.); οἶκος ib.2².1322 (iii/ii B.C.); νεώς Menodot.1; οἰκίαι Nic. Dam.p.148 D., cf. Plu.2.503c, Hdn.8.1.5, etc. II. metaph., *open, unchecked*, Adam.2.60; ῥῆτραι Nic.*Al.*132; γλῶττα Ph.1.678.

**ἀθῠρο-στομία**, ἡ, = ἀθυρογλωττία, Plu.2.11c, *AP*5.251 (Paul. Sil.). **-στομος**, ον, = ἀθυρόγλωττος, ἀ. Ἀχώ *ever-babbling* Echo, S.*Ph.*188 (lyr.).

**ἄθυρσις**, ἡ, *sport, festivity*, B.12.93.

**ἄθυρσος**, ον, *without thyrsus*, E.*Or.*1492 (lyr.).

**ἀθύρω** [ῡ], Ep. word, only pres. and impf., rare in Prose (v. infr.):—*play, sport*, of children, Il.15.364, Hp.*Ep.*17; νέος μὲν οὖν.. ἦλατ' ἀθύρων E.*Ion*53; τάχ' ἂν πρὸς ἀγκάλαισι..πηδῶν ἀθύροι Id.*Fr.* 323; σφαίρῃ A.R.4.950; of dancing, Pl.*Lg.*796b; playing on an instrument, κατὰ πηκτίδων *Anacreont.*41.11: c. acc. cogn., μοῦσαν ἀθύρων *singing sportive* songs, *h.Hom.*19.15:—Med., simply, *sing*, *h.Merc.*485. 2. metaph., ἀ. περὶ τὰ θειότατα τῶν πραγμάτων Procl.*in Prm.*p.863 S. II. c. acc., παῖς ἐὼν ἄθυρε μεγάλα ἔργα (of Achilles) *he did* them *in play*, Pi.*N.*3.44; ἔργα φωτῶν ἀ. *play* the deeds of men, of the comic Muse, *AP*9.505.8, cf. Him.*Or.*17.7. 2. *sing of*, ἀρετάν Pi.*I.*4(3).39. 3. *mock at*, Nonn.*D.*45.244.

**ἀθύρωτος** [ῠ], ον, = ἄθυρος, στόμα Ar.*Ra.*838 (v.l.), cf. Phryn. Com.82, *JHS*41.195 (Delos, ii B.C.).

**ἀθύσσει**· μιγνύει, ῥαπίζει, Hsch.

**ἄθυστος**, ον, = sq., ἱρά Semon.7.56.

**ἄθῠτος**, ον, *not offered*, i.e. *omitted*, ἱερά Lys.26.6. 2. *not successfully offered*, ἱερά Aeschin.3.131, 152: metaph., ἄ. παλλακῶν σπέρματα, of illegitimate children, Pl.*Lg.*841d, cf. Suid. s.v. ἄθυτοι γάμοι. 3. *not fit to be offered*, Lxx *Le.*19.7, cf. Philostr.*VA*8. 7.10. 4. of a god, *to whom no sacrifice is offered*, D.H.8.25. 5. *not fit for sacrifice*, opp. θύσιμος, Lib.*Decl.*13.63. 6. = ἄπυρος, Hsch. II. Act., *without sacrificing*, ἄθυτος ἀπελθεῖν X.*HG*3.2.22.

**ἀθώητος**· ἀζημίωτος, Hsch.

**ἀθῷος**, ον, (θωά, Ion. θωιή):—*scot-free*, E.*Ba.*672, etc.; ἐγὼ μὲν ἀ. ἅπασι D.18.125; ἀθῴους καθιστάναι τινάς to secure their *immunity*, Id.3.11; ἀθῷον ἀφιέναι Test.ap.eund.21.107; ἀ. ἀπαλλάττειν or -εσθαι to get off *scot-free*, Pl.*Sph.*254d, Lys.6.4; ἀπέρχεσθαι Archipp. 40; διαφυγεῖν Men.130. 2. c. gen., *free from* a thing, πληγῶν Ar. *Nu.*1413; ἀ. ἀδικημάτων *unpunished for* offences, Lycurg.79, cf. D.S.14.76. 3. *unharmed by*, ἀθῷος τῆς Φιλίππου..δυναστείας D.18.270. II. *not deserving punishment, guiltless*, ἀ. ὁ κτείνων Democr.257; ἀ. χερσί Lxx *Ps.*23(24).4; ἀ. ἀπὸ τοῦ αἵματος *Ev.Matt.* 27.24. III. Act., *causing no harm, harmless*, κίνδυνος D.*Prooem.* 26. (ἀθῷος distinguished by Gramm. from Ἄθωος, *of Mt. Athos*, A.*Ag.*285, cf. Hdn.Gr.1.128.)

**ἀθῳόω**, (ἀθῷος) *to hold guiltless*, ἀθῷον ἀθῳοῦν τινά Lxx *Na.*1.3, cf. Iamb.*Bab.*223; τινά τινος Ps.-Callisth.1.7:—fut. Pass. ἀθῳωθήσομαι Lxx *Pr.*6.29, al. 2. *avenge*, ἀπό τινος ib.*Je.*15.15. (Written ἀθο- before ω in codd. of Lxx.)

**ἀθώπευτος**, ον, *unflattered, without flattery*, τῆς ἐμῆς γλώσσης *from* my tongue, E.*Andr.*459. 2. *not open to flattery*, δίκαι Lyc.1399, cf. Nic.Dam.p.144 D. II. Act., *not flattering*, Telesp.44.8 H.; hence, *rough, rude*, θήρ *AP*6.168 (Paul.Sil.); συρίγματα, of the Python, *Pae.Delph.*20; ἀδροσίη *POxy.*1796.17. III. Adv. -τως *without flattery*, Them.*Or.*15.193d.

**ἀθωράκιστος** [ᾰκ], ον, *without breastplate* or *body-armour*, X.*Cyr.* 4.2.31, Plu.*Aem.*19.

**ἀθώρηκτος**, ον, = foreg., Nonn.*D.*35.162. II. *not drunken* (v. θωρήσσω II), Hp.*Steril.*220.

**Ἄθως** [ᾰ], ω, ὁ, acc. Ἄθω Aeschin.3.132, Theoc.7.77, etc., but in earlier writers Ἄθων, Hdt.6.44, 7.22, Th.5.3: Ep. gen. Ἀθόω Il. 14.229; later gen. Ἄθωος Str.*Fr.*33:—*mount Athos*, Ἄθως σκιάζει νῶτα Λημνίας βοός (prov. of those whose influence is felt at a distance, from the shadow cast by Athos) S.*Fr.*776.

**ἀθῴωσις**, ἡ, *acquittal*, Ctes.*Fr.*29.61.

**αἰ**, Dor. and Aeol. for εἰ, *if*, Epich.55,170, before a vowel αἰκ Id. 21, Sophr.25:—in Hom. only αἴ κε or κεν, *if only, so that*, always c. subj., exc. in or. obliq., as Il.7.387; Dor. αἴκα Epich.35, Theoc. 1.4, al. II. αἲ γάρ (with accent), Ep. for εἰ γάρ, *O that! would that!* c. opt., Il.7.132, al., cf. Hdt.1.27; once c. inf., αἲ γάρ..παῖδά τ' ἐμὴν ἐχέμεν καὶ ἐμὸς γαμβρὸς καλέεσθαι Od.7.311.—Cf. αἴθε.

**αἶ** or **αἶ** (authorities vary, cf. Hdn.Gr.1.496, Tz.ad Lyc.31), interj. of astonishment or grief:—αἶ τάλαν Ar.*Pl.*706, cf. *Mim.Oxy.*413.73: c. acc., αἶ τὸν Ἄδωνιν Bion 1.32; freq. doubled αἰαῖ (Hdn.Gr.2.933), Thgn.1341, B.5.153, A.*Th.*787, Alciphr.*Fr.*4: c. gen., αἰαῖ τόλμας E. *Hipp.*814 (lyr.), cf. A.*Ch.*1007, Alciphr.3.67, etc.: c. acc., αἰαῖ Ἄδωνιν Ar.*Lys.*393, cf. Bion 1.28; αἰαῖ πέτρον ἐκεῖνον *AP*7.554 (Phil.), cf. 9.424 (Duris Elait.). [αἰαῖ generally, sometimes αἰαῖ, as A.*Th.* l.c.]

**αἰ**, v. ἀεί.

**αἶα** (A), ἡ, Ep. form used for γαῖα metri gr., φυσίζοος αἶα Il.3.243, etc., cf. Emp.27, *Scol.*12, A.R.1.580, *Tab.Defix.*7; also in Trag., chiefly in lyr., A.*Pers.*59, S.*El.*95, also in trim., E.*Andr.*51: never in pl. II. Αἶα, ἡ, orig. name of Colchis, S.*Fr.*914: also part of Thessaly, ib.915.

**αἶα** (B)· ὑπὸ Κυρηναίων τηθὶς καὶ μαῖα, καὶ ἀδελφὴ Κρήτης· καὶ φυτι. ἔτι δὲ ὁ καρπὸς αὐτῷ ὁμώνυμος, *EM*27.24. (Possibly cogn. wi Lat. *avia*.)

**αἶα** (C), = ὄα, Ael.Dion.*Fr.*16.

**αἴαγμα**, τό, *wail*, E.*Alc.*873 (lyr.), etc.: **αἰαγμός**, οῦ, ὁ, Eust.1164.

**αἰάζω**, fut. -άξω E.*HF*1053 (cj. Herm.): aor. part. αἰάξας *Epig Gr.*233 (Chios):—*cry* αἰαῖ, *wail*, S.*Aj.*904, etc., Luc.*Salt.*45: c. acc. cogn., αὐδάν E.*IT*227, cf. Timo 66: c. acc., *bewail*, A.*Pers.*922, E.*Or.* 80, *AP*7.476 (Mel.), etc. 2. *groan*, ἐκπνεῖν καὶ αἰ. Arist.*HA* 536ᵇ22, cf. *GA*788ᵃ22.

**αἰαῖ**, v. sub αἶ.

**αἰακίς**, ἡ, = κύλιξ, Timach.ap.Ath.11.782f; **αἰακίξ**, Hsch., Suid.

**αἰακτός**, ή, όν, (αἰάζω) *lamentable*, πήματα A.*Th.*846 (lyr.), cf. Ar. *Ach.*1195 (paratrag.); *lamented*, θυγάτηρ *Epigr.Gr.*205 (Halic.). II. *wailing, miserable*, A.*Pers.*932, 1068 (both lyr.).

**αἰανής**, Ion. **αἰηνής**, ές, poet. word, δεῖπνον αἰηνές Archil.38; αἰανὴς κόρος, κέντρον, λιμός, Pi.*P.*1.83, 4.236, *I.*1.49: also in Trag. (not E.), Νυκτὸς αἰανῆ τέκνα A.*Eu.*416; νυκτὸς αἰ. κύκλος S.*Aj.*672; αἰ. νόσος A.*Eu.*479, 942 (lyr.); αἰ. βάγματα Id.*Pers.*636 (lyr.); αἰ. πάνδυρτον αὐδάν ib.941 (lyr.); Πέλοπος..ἱππεία, ὡς ἔμολες αἰ. τᾷδε γᾷ S.*El.*506; of Time, εἰς τὸν αἰ. χρόνον A.*Eu.*572, *IG*9(1).886.2 (Corcyra); *eternal*, θεός Lyc.928. Adv. αἰανῶς *for ever*, A.*Eu.*672:—**αἰανός**, Hsch., Suid. s.v. λεύκη ἡμέρα, and v.l. in A.*Eu.*416, 479, S.*Aj.*672, *El.*506, is dub. (Prob. fr. αἰεί, *everlasting, perpetual*, hence in bad sense, *wearisome, persistent*.)

**Αἰάντειος**, α, ον, *of Ajax*: τὸ Αἰ. *his tomb*, Philostr.*VA*4.13: τὰ Αἰ. (sc. ἱερά) *festivals in his honour*, Hsch.: prov., Αἰ. γέλως, *of insane* laughter, Zen.1.43. [Penult. short Pi.*O.*9.112.]

**Αἰαντίδης**, ου, ὁ, *son of Ajax*, patron.: hence, *one of the tribe* Αἰαντίς in Attica, [D.]60.31.

**αἰαντόν**· ἁμαρτία, Hsch.

**Αἴας**, αντος, ὁ, *Ajax*, masc. pr. n., borne by two heroes, the Greater, son of Telamon, the Less, son of Oïleus, Hom.:—nom. Αἶας Alcm.68; voc. Αἶαν Pi.*Fr.*184, Aeol. Αἶαν Alc.48A: pl. Αἴαντες, of tragedies named after Ajax, Arist.*Po.*1455ᵇ34. (S. derives it fancifully from αἰαῖ, *Aj.*430.)

**αἰαστής**, οῦ, ὁ, 'the mourner', of the plant ὑάκινθος, Nic.*Fr.*74. 32. **αἰαφοί**· αὐτοὶ ἀκούοντες, Hsch. **αἴαψ**· ματαίως, Id. (i.e. μάψ). **αἴαψος**· ὁ ποικίλος, Suid. **αἰβάνη**· θύρα, Hsch. (αἰβάλη Suid.).

**αἰβετός**, i.e. αἰϝετός, ὁ, dial. form of ἀετός, Hsch.

**αἰβοῖ**, *faugh!* exclam. of disgust, Ar.*Ach.*189, *V.*37; αἰβοιβοῖ, of laughter, Id.*Pax*1066.

**αἴγαγρος**, ὁ and ἡ, *the wild goat*, Babr.102.8, Opp.*C.*1.71.

**Αἰγᾶθεν**, Dor. for Αἰγῆθεν, Adv. *from* Αἰγαί (an island off Euboea), Pi.*N.*5.37.

**Αἰγαῖος**, α, ον, *Aegean*, πέλαγος A.*Ag.*659; ὄρος Αἰ. *mount Ida* in Crete, Hes.*Th.*484:—title of Poseidon, Pherecyd.115. II. Αἰγαῖος (sc. πόντος), ὁ, *the Aegaean*, Pl.*Eleg.*9.1, Arist.*Mete.*354ᵃ14, etc.

**Αἰγαίων**, ωνος, ὁ, *Aegaeon*, the name given by men to the hundred-armed son of Uranus and Gaia, called by gods Βριάρεως (q.v.), Il.1. 404. II. *the Aegaean sea*, πόντιόν τ' Αἰγαίων' E.*Alc.*595 (lyr.).

**αἰγᾰνέη**, ἡ, *hunting-spear, javelin*, Il.2.774, Od.4.626, *AP*6.57 (Paul. Sil.).

**αἰγάριον**, τό, Dim. of αἴξ, *Gloss.*

**ἀΐγδην**, Adv., (ἀΐσσω) *rushing swiftly, impetuously*, A.R.2.826.

**αἰγέα**, **αἰγέη**, ἡ, v. sub αἴγεος.

**Αἰγεῖον**, τό, *temple of Aegeus*, Din.*Fr.*3.1.

**αἴγειος**, α, ον, *of a goat*, αἴγειον κνῇ τυρόν Il.11.639, Hp.*Nat.Mul.* 38; ἀσκῷ ἐν αἰγείῳ in a *goat's* skin, Il.3.247; αἰγείη κυνέη a helmet *of goatskin*, Od.24.231; γάλα αἰ. Arist.*HA*522ᵃ23; κρέα αἰ. Hp.*Acut.* (*Sp.*)49.

**αἰγείρινος**, ον, *of the poplar*, Orib.*Syn.*5.16, Alex.Trall.8.1. **αἰγειρῖται** μύκητες mushrooms *produced from stump of poplar*, *Gp.*12. 41.1.

**αἴγειρος**, ἡ, *black poplar*, *Populus nigra*, μακεδνή, μακρή, Od.7.106, 10.510, cf. Il.4.482, S.*Fr.*23, etc.; αἰ. ὑδατοτρεφέες Od.17.208, cf. 9. 141, 5.64, 239, E.*Hipp.*210 (lyr.); named among ἄκαρπα in Arist.*Mu.* 401ᵃ4; καρποφόρος *Mir.*835ᵇ2: prov., αἰγείρου θέα, of a seat in the theatre which had no view of the stage, Cratin.339.

**αἰγειροφόρος**, ον, *poplar-bearing*, Max.Tyr.29.7.

**αἰγειρών**, ῶνος, ὁ, *poplar-grove*, Str.16.4.14.

**αἰγελάτης** [ᾰ], ου, ὁ, (ἐλαύνω) *goatherd*, Plu.*Pomp.*4, *APl.*4.229.

**αἴγεος**, α, ον, = αἴγειος, Od.9.196; διφθέραι Hdt.5.58. II. Subst., αἰγέη (sc. δορά), ἡ, *a goat's skin*, Hdt.4.189; τὴν αἰγέαν J.*AJ*1.18.6, cf. Lxx *Nu.*31.20; contr. αἰγῆ Hdn.Gr.1.310.

**αἴγερος**, ἡ, = αἴγειρος, *Com.Adesp.*1276.

**αἰγ-ήκης**, ες, *made of goatskin*, τύμπανον Procl.*Theol.Plat.*4.16 (nisi leg. αἰγήχης). **-ιάζω**, *to talk of goats*, Eup.2.

**αἰγιάλ-ειος**, α, ον, *frequenting the shore*, Aët.2.141, Ath.Med.ap. Orib.*Inc.*23.8. **-εύς**, ῆος, ὁ, = foreg., Nic.*Th.*786, Numen.ap.Ath.7. 313e:—pr. n., of the inhabitants of north coast of Peloponnese, Hdt. 5.68, 7.94; of the Argives, Theoc.25.174. **-ικός**, ή, όν, *for coastwise traffic*, sc. πλοῖα prob. l. in *PCair.Preis.*33.6 (iv A.D.). **-ίτης**, ου, ὁ, fem. -ῖτις, ιδος, ψῆφοι Str.4.1.7; Πάν *AP*10.10 (Arch. Jun.); γῆ *POxy.*918 (ii A.D.)

**αἰγιαλός**, ὁ, *sea-shore, beach*, Il.4.422, Od.22.385, Hdt.7.59, al., Th. 1.7 (pl.), X.*An.*6.4.4, Thphr.*HP*7.13.8 (pl.), etc.; distinguished from ἡ, Arist.*HA*547ᵃ10; also in E.(lyr.), *IT*425, *IA*210: αἰγιαλὸν ον τρέφει *a whole beach of voting-pebbles*, Ar.*V.*110: prov., αἰλῷ λαλεῖς, of deaf persons, Suid., Zen.1.38. (Prob. connected th αἰγίς II, αἴξ IV.)

**αἰγιαλοφύλαξ**, ὁ, *warden of the shore*, *PRyl.*81.3 (ii A.D.).

**αἰγιαλ-ώδης**, ες, *frequenting the shore*, ζῷα Arist.*HA*488ᵇ7. **-ώ-ς**, ὁ, *dweller on the shore*, Sch.Opp.*H.*3.375.

**αἰγιάς**, άδος, ἡ, = αἰγίς IV, Hsch.

**αἰγι-βάτης** [ᾰ], ου, ὁ, *goat-mounting*, epith. of he-goats, etc., Pi .201; of Pan, Theoc.*Ep.*5.6, *AP*6.31. **-βοσις**, εως, ἡ, *goat-pasture*, *AP*9.318 (Leon.). **-βότης**, ου, ὁ, *browsed by goats*, κόπελος *AP*6.334 (Leon.). **-βοτος**, ον, = foreg., Ἰθάκη Od.4.06, cf. 13.246, *AP*9.219 (Diod.). II. **-βότος**, ον, *feeding goats*, ιν Nonn.*D.*1.368, al.

**αἰγίδιον**, τό, Dim. of αἴξ, *kid*, Pherecr.25, Antiph.20.4, *IG*11(2).87*A*55 (Delos, iii B.C.), *PTeb.*404.9 (iii A.D.). II. *eye-salve*, Aët.7.103.

**αἰγίζω**, (αἰγίς) *rend asunder*, S.*Fr.*984.

**αἰγίθαλλος** or **αἰγίθᾱλος**, ὁ, *titmouse* (of various species), *parus*, Ar.*Av.*888, Alc.Com.3, cf. Arist.*HA*592ᵇ17, 616ᵇ3: prov., αἰγιθάλου τολμηρότερος, Apostol.1.76.

**αἴγιθος**, also **αἰγίοθος**, ὁ, an unknown bird, possibly *linnet*, Arist.*HA*609ᵃ31, 616ᵇ10, Call.*Fr.*321, Ael.*NA*5.48, etc.

**αἰγίκερας**, = αἰγόκερας, Hsch.

❋**αἰγί-κνημος**, ον, *goat-shanked*, *AP*6.167 (Agath.). ❋**-κορεῖς**, έων, οἱ, *goatherds*; name of one of the four Ionic tribes in Attica (cf. Hdt.5.66, who makes Αἰγικόρης son of Ion), E.*Ion*1581, Plu.*Sol.*23; also at Cyzicus, *IGRom.*4.144, cf. Αἰγικορὶς φυλή *Ath.Mitt.*9.27. (Expl. as *goatherds*, but this is doubtful.)

**αἰγικός**, ή, όν, = αἴγειος, *PGrenf.*2.51.15 (ii A.D.). 2. **-κόν**, τό, = ἄγρωστις, Ps.-Dsc.4.29.

**αἰγιλάδην**, = αἰγίλωψ I, dub. l. in Ps.-Dsc.4.137.

**αἰγίλιψ** [γῐ], ῐπος, ὁ, ἡ, (expl. by Gramm. from αἴξ, λείπω, cf. Sch. Il.9.15) *destitute even of goats*, hence, *steep, sheer*, πέτρη Il.9.15, al. (not in Od.), A.*Supp* 794 (lyr.), Lyc.1325; also in form **αἰγίλιπος**, Hsch. (Perh. cognate with Lith. *lipti* 'climb'.)

**αἴγῑλος**, ἡ, *a herb of which goats are fond*, = αἰγίλωψ I, Theoc.5.128, Babr.3.4.

**αἰγιλωπικός**, ή, όν, *for the treatment of* αἰγίλωψ III, καυτήρια Paul.Aeg.6.22.

**αἰγιλώπιον**, τό, = αἰγίλωψ III, Dsc.3.137.

**αἰγίλωψ** [ῐ], ωπος, poet. οπος Nic.*Th.*857, ὁ, *haver-grass*, *Aegilops ovata*, Thphr.*CP*5.15.5, Ph.*Bel.*89.3, Dsc.4.137. II. *Turkey oak*, *Quercus Cerris*, Thphr.*HP*3.8.2. III. *ulcer in the eye, lachrymal fistula*, Cels.7.7, Dsc.4.70, Gal.*UP*10.10. IV. a bulbous plant, Plin.*HN*19.95.

❋**Αἴγῑν-α**, ης, ἡ, *Aegina*, Il., etc.:—hence **-ήτης**, ου, ὁ, fem. **-ῆτις**, ιδος, *an Aeginetan*, ib., etc. ❋**-αῖος**, α, ον, *Aeginetan*, Cratin.165, al.; ὀβολὸς Αἰ., δραχμὴ Αἰ., etc., Th.5.47, etc.:—also **-ητικός**, ή, όν, Luc.*Tim.*57; ἔργα statues *of the Aeginetan School*, Paus.1.42.5.

**αἰγίνη**, ἡ, = περικλύμενον, Ps.-Dsc.4.14.

❋**αἰγῑ-νομεύς**, έως, ὁ, *goatherd*, *AP*9.318 (Leon.). **-νόμος**, ον, (νέμω) *feeding goats*: Subst., *goatherd*, *AP*6.221 (Leon.), cf. 9.744 (Leon.). II. αἰγίνομος, ον, Pass., *browsed by goats*, βοτανη ib.217 (Muc. Scaev.).

**αἴγινος** (A), ὁ, = κύνειον, Ps.-Dsc.4.78.

**αἴγινος** (B), = αἰγικός, *PFay.*222 (iii A.D.); δέρματα *PLond.*2.236.6 (iv A.D.).

**αἰγίοθος**, ὁ, v. sub αἴγιθος.

**αἰγιόνομοι**· ζῷα οὕτω καλούμενα, Hsch.

❋**αἰγίοχος**, ον, (Ϝέχω = *veho*) *aegis-bearing*, epith. of Zeus, Il.2.375, al., Alc.85, Emp.142, etc.

**Αἰγί-πᾶν**, ᾶνος, ὁ, *goat-Pan*, *goat-footed Pan*, Eratosth.*Catast.*27, Plu.2.311b. **-πλαγκτος**, ον, *wandered over by goats*:—pr. n., ὄρος Αἰγίπλαγκτον, a mountain near Megara, A.*Ag.*303. **-πόδης**, ου, ὁ, *goat-footed*, *h.Hom.*19.2,37; voc. αἰγιπόδη Πάν *AP*6.57 (Paul. Sil.). **-πους**, ποδος, ὁ, ἡ, πουν, τό, = foreg., Hdt.4.25.

**αἰγίποψ**· ἀετός (Maced.), *EM*28.19.

❋**αἰγίπῡρος**, ὁ, *rest-harrow*, *Ononis antiquorum*, Thphr.*HP*2.8.3, Theoc.4.25; αἰγίπυρον, τό, *IG*14.2508 (Nemausus).

❋**αἰγίς**, ίδος, ἡ, (αἴξ, cf. νεβρίς): I. *goatskin*, worn as a dress, Hdt.4.189, E.*Cyc.*360 (lyr.); hence, 2. esp. the skin shield of Zeus, Il.5.738, al.; lent by him to Athena, 2.447, al.; to Apollo, 15.318, al.; later, with fringe of snakes and Gorgon's head, the *aegis* of Athena, A.*Eu.*404, etc. 3. dress worn by priestess of Athena, Lycurg.*Fr.*23. 4. ornament worn on the breast, Poll.5.100. 5. *cuirass* (Lacon.), Nymphod.22. II. *rushing storm, hurricane*, terrible as the shaken aegis, A.*Ch.*593 (lyr.), Pherecr.117, Aristid.1.487J., Lib.*Or.*18.268. III. *heart-wood* of the Corsican pine, Thphr.*HP*3.9.3; in Arcadia also that of the silver-fir, ib.8; cf. Ἐφ. Ἀρχ. 1895.59 (Eleusis). IV. *speck in the eye*, Hp.*Coac.*214, *Prorrh.*2.20.

❋**αἰγίσκος**, ὁ, Dim. of αἴξ, *IG*11(2).287*A*19 (Delos, iii B.C.).

**αἰγλάεις**, contr. **αἰγλᾶς**, Dor. for αἰγλήεις.

**αἰγλάζω**, *to beam brightly*, Man.4.264.

❋**αἴγλη**, ἡ, *the light of the sun* or *moon*, Od.4.45, etc.:—of the radiance of Olympus, λευκὴ αἴ. 6.45, cf. S.*Ant.*610 (lyr.); εἰς αἴγλαν μολεῖν to come to *daylight*, i.e. to be born, Pi.*N.*1.35; φοιβὰν ὑπαὶ χειμῶνος αἴ., of *sunshine* on edge of storm-cloud, B.12.140; of *dream light* in sleep, S.*Ph.*831 (lyr.). 2. generally, *radiance, gleam*, ἀπὸ χαλκοῦ αἴ. Il.2.458; τὰς πυρφόρους Ἀρτέμιδος αἴ. the *gleam* of her torches, S.*OT*207 (lyr.); μέλαιναν αἴ., of dying embers, E.*Tr.*549 (lyr.). 3. metaph., *splendour, glory*, αἴ. ποδῶν, of swiftness, Pi.*O.*13.36; διόσδοτος αἴ. Id.*P.*8.96. II. of shining objects, as a *bracelet*, S.*Fr.*594; *fetter*, Epich.20.

❋**αἰγλήεις**, εσσα, εν, *dazzling, radiant*, in Hom. always αἰγλήεντος Ὀλύμπου Il.1.532, Od.20.103; Κλάρος αἰγλήεσσα *h.Ap.*40; πῶλοι αἰ. *h.Hom.*32.9: neut. as Adv., αἰγλῆεν στίλβουσι ib.31.11:—Dor. **αἰγλάεις**, contr. **αἰγλᾶς**, κῶας αἰγλᾶεν.. θυσάνῳ Pi.*P.*4.231; αἰγλᾶντα κόσμον ib.2.10; αἰγλᾶντα σώματα E.*Andr.*285 (lyr.).

❋**αἰγλήτης**, Dor. **-άτας**, ου, ὁ, *the radiant one*, epith. of Apollo, A.R.4.1716, *IG*12(3).259 (Anaphe), 412 (Thera).

**αἰγλο-βολέω**, Astrol., = ἀκτινοβολέω, Man.4.188. **-φάνής**, ές, *radiant*, *AP*12.5 (Strat.).

**αἰγο-βάτης**, ου, ὁ, = αἰγιβάτης, *AP*12.41 (Mel.). **-βόλος**, ὁ, *goat-slayer*, title of Dionysus, Paus.9.8.1. **-βοσκός**, ου, ὁ, *goat-herd*, Aesop.12b, *Gloss.* **-δίωξ**, ωκος, *pursuing goats*, Hdn.Gr.1.46. **δορος**, ον, (δορά) *of goatskin*, Opp.*H.*5.356. **-θήλας**, ὁ, *goatsucker, nightjar*, or *fern-owl*, *Caprimulgus europaeus*, Arist.*HA*618ᵇ2, Ael.*NA*3.39. **-θηρικός**, ή, όν, *belonging to ibex-hunting*, σοφία ib.14.16. **-κερας**, ατος, τό, = τῆλις, Hp.*Int.*30, Dsc.2.102, Gal.12.426. **-κερεύς**, έως, Ion. ῆος, ὁ, = -κέρως II, Arat.386, Q.S.1.356. **-κεριανός**, ὁ, *born under Capricorn*, *Cat.Cod.Astr.*8(4).191 (Rhetor.). ❋**-κερως**, gen. -κερω, dat. -κερῳ Man.1.106; acc. -κερων *Placit.*5.18.6, Luc.*Astr.*7; later gen. -κέρωτος Jul.*Or.*4.156a: (κέρας):—*goat-horned*, *APl.*4.234 (Phld.). II. Subst., *Capricorn*, Gem.*Calend.*7, Eudox.ap.Hipparch.1.2.20, Arat.286, *Placit.*l.c., Luc. l.c., *IG*14.1307.

**αἰγοκέφᾰλος**, ὁ, perh. *horned owl*, *Strix otus*, Arist.*HA*506ᵃ17.

❋**αἰγ-όλεθρος**, ὁ, *goat's-bane*, *Rhododendron ponticum*, Antig.*Mir.*17, Plin.*HN*21.74.

**αἰγο-μελής**, ές, *goat-limbed*, Orph.*H.*11.5. **-μορον**, τό, = κώνειον, Ps.-Dsc.4.78. ❋**-νομεύς**, έως, Ion. ῆος, ὁ, = αἰγινομεύς, *goatherd*, Nic.*Al.*39. **-νόμια**· αἰπόλια, Hsch. **-νόμιον**, τό, *herd of goats*, Id. s.v. αἰγοπόλιον, etc. **-νόμος**, ον, = αἰγινόμος, *AP*7.397 (Eryc.).

**αἰγ-όνυξ**, υχος, ὁ, ἡ, = αἰγῶνυξ, *APl.*4.258.

**αἰγό-πλαστος**, ον, *goat-shaped*, Ps.-Emp.*Sphaer.*140. **-πόδης**, ου, ὁ, = αἰγιπόδης, *APl.*1.15. **-πρόσωπος**, ον, *goat-faced*, Hdt.2.46; *stamped with a goat's face*, Aët.7.101. **-στασις**, ἡ, *goat-pen*, *Gloss.* **-τρῐχέω**, *have goat's hair*, Str.17.2.3. **-τριψ**, ιβος, ὁ, ἡ, (τρίβω) *trodden by goats*, ἀτραπαί D.H.20.11. **-φάγος**, ον, *goat-eating*, epith. of Zeus, Nic.*Fr.*99; of Hera at Sparta, Paus.3.15.7.

**αἰγ-όφθαλμος**, ὁ, *goat's-eye*, a precious stone, Plin.*HN*37.187.

**αἰγῠπιός**, ὁ, *vulture*, αἰ. γαμψώνυχες ἀγκυλοχεῖλαι Il.16.428, cf. 17.460, Od.16.217, Hes.*Sc.*405, Hdt.3.76, S.*Aj.*169, Arist.*HA*610ᵃ1, etc.:—αἰγυπιοὶ γῦπές τε Nic.*Th.*406, cf. Ael.*NA*2.46. (Both words seem to be generic terms, but αἰ. is an older word chiefly found in poetry.)

**αἰγυπτάριον**, τό, name of eye-salve, Aët.7.101.

**Αἰγύπτειος**, α, ον, = Αἰγύπτιος, prob. in A.*Supp.*817 (lyr.).

**αἰγύπτης**· σύντης, ὁ καλοβότης, Hsch.

**Αἰγυπτι-άζω**, *to be like an Egyptian*, i.e. *to be sly and crafty*, Cratin.378, cf. Ar.*Th.*922. 2. *speak Egyptian*, Luc.*Philops.*31. II. *to be like Egypt*, i.e. *be under water*, Philostr.*Im.*2.14. **-ακός**, ή, όν, *of* or *for the Egyptians*, Ath.4.150c, etc.: Αἰγυπτιακά, τά, title of works by Hellanicus and others, Id.15.679f, etc.; by Manetho, J.*Ap.*1.14. **-ασμός**, ὁ, *imitation of the Egyptians*, Eust. ad D.P.391.

❋**Αἰγύπτιος**, α, ον, *Egyptian*, Hom., etc.: Adv. -ίως *in Egyptian style*, D.C.48.30. 2. **αἰγυπτία**, ἡ, name of an ointment, Gal.13.643, etc. [In Hom. Αἰγυπτίη, Αἰγυπτίων, etc., are trisyll., Od.4.83, etc.]

**Αἰγυπτιόω**, *to make like an Egyptian*, i.e. *swarthy*, χρόαν *Com. Adesp.*9, Hsch.

**Αἰγυπτιστί**, Adv. *in the Egyptian tongue*, Hdt.2.46, J.*Ap.*1.14. II. *in Egyptian fashion*, i.e. *craftily*, Theoc.15.48.

**Αἰγυπτιώδης**, ες, *Egyptian-like*, Cratin.Jun.2.

**Αἰγυπτογενής**, ές, *of Egyptian race*, A.*Pers.*35.

**Αἴγυπτος**, ὁ, *the river Nile*, Od.4.477, al. 2. *King Aegyptus*, A.*Supp.*9, etc. II. ἡ, *Egypt*, Od.17.448, etc.; Αἴγυπτόνδε *to Egypt*, ib.426.

**αἰγωγαίαν**· ὀφθαλμός, Hsch.

**αἰγωλιός** or **αἰγώλιος**, ὁ, a small kind of *owl*, perh. *Strix flammea*, Arist.*HA*592ᵇ11, 609ᵃ27, Ant.Lib.19.3; f.l. αἰτώλιος, Arist.*HA*563ᵃ31.

❋**αἰγών**, ῶνος, ὁ, = μάνδρα, *Gloss.* II. **Αἰγών**, name of a month at Alexandria, Ptol.*Alm.*10.9.

**αἰγῶνυξ**, ῠχος, ὁ, ἡ, (ὄνυξ) *goat-hoofed*, *AP*6.35 (Leon.).

**αἰγωπόμματος**, ον, = sq., Phlp.*in GA*212.8.

❋**αἰγωπός**, όν, *goat-eyed*, of persons, Arist.*GA*779ᵇ1; also, *like those of a goat*, of eyes, ib., cf. *HA*492ᵃ3.

**αἰδάας**· δεσπότης, Hsch.

**αἰδάνης**· διατρίβων (Tarent.), Hsch.

**Ἀΐδας**, Dor. for Ἀΐδης, Ἅιδης, freq. in lyr. passages of Trag.

❋**αἰδ-έομαι**, and poet. **αἴδομαι** Hom., etc., Ep. imper. αἰδεῖο Il.24.503, Od.9.269; part. αἰδόμενος Hom. and Trag. (lyr.); imper. αἴδεο Il.21.74: impf. ᾐδοῦντο A.*Pers.*810, etc., αἰδέοντο Pi.*P.*9.41, poet. αἴδετο Il.21.468, *APl.*4.106: fut. αἰδέσομαι Il.22.124, Att., Ep. αἰδέσσομαι Od.14.388; αἰδεσθήσομαι D.C.45.44, Gal.1.62, (ἐπ-) E.*IA*

900: aor. Med. ᾐδεσάμην, Ep. αἰδ- Od.21.28, Att. (v. sub fin.), Ep. imper. αἴδεσσαι Il.9.640; aor. Pass. ᾐδέσθην Hom., etc., and in Prose, Ep. 3 pl. αἴδεσθεν Il.7.93; pf. ᾔδεσμαι (v. sub fin.): Act. only in καταιδέω, q. v.:—*to be ashamed*, c. inf., αἴδεσθεν μὲν ἀνήνασθαι δεῖσαν δ' ὑποδέχθαι Il.7.93; αἰδέομαι δὲ μίσγεσθ' ἀθανάτοισι 24.90; αἰ. γὰρ γυμνοῦσθαι Od.6.221: less freq. c. part., αἴδεσαι μὲν πατέρα προλείπων S.*Aj.*506, cf. Plu.*Aem.*35: c. dat., μὴ αἰδοῦ τῷ εὐκόλῳ Philostr.*Ep.* 19: abs., αἰδεσθεὶς *from a sense of shame*, Il.17.95. 2. mostly c. acc., *stand in awe of, fear*, esp. in moral sense, αἰδεῖο θεούς Il.24.503, Od.9.269; Τρῶας Il.6.442, cf. Od.2.65, etc.; ἀλλήλους αἰδεῖσθε *show a sense of regard* one for another, Il.5.530; οὐδὲ θεῶν ὄπιν αἰδέσατο Od.21.28; αἴδεσσαι μέλαθρον *respect* the house, Il.9.640; freq. of respect for suppliants, Il.22.124, cf. Hdt.7.141; ἐχθρὸν ὧδ' αἰδεῖ νέκυν; S.*Aj.*1356; τόνδ' ὅρκον αἰδεσθεὶς Id.*OT*647, cf. 1426:—in Pi.*P.*4.173 αἰδεσθέντες ἀλκάν *regarding* their reputation for valour, i.e. from *self-respect*, cf. ἑωυτὸν μάλιστα αἰδεῖσθαι Democr.264: abs., τὸ αἰδεῖσθαι *self-respect*, Id.179; in Prose, Δία αἰδεσθέντες Hdt.9.7.α'; φοβοῦμαί γε.. τοὺς μοχθηρούς (οὐ γὰρ δήποτε εἴποιμ' ἂν ὥς γε αἰδοῦμαι) Pl.*Lg.*886a, cf. *Euthphr.*12b, *Phdr.*254e; later αἰ. ἐπί τινι D.H.6.92; ὑπὲρ τῆς ἀνθρωπίνης φύσεως *have compassion upon, show mercy*, Plu.*Cim.*2. II. *respect* another's *misfortune, feel regard for* him, μηδέ τί μ' αἰδόμενος.. μηδ' ἐλεαίρων Od.3.96 (cf. I. 2); αἰ. τὴν τῶν μηδὲν ἀδικούντων εὐσέβειαν Antipho 2.4.11; esp. 2. as Att. law-term, *to be reconciled to* a person, of kinsmen who allow a homicide to return from exile, Lex ap.D.43.57; ἐὰν ἑλών τις ἀκουσίου φόνου.. αἰδέσηται καὶ ἀφῇ D.37.59, cf. 38.22; αἰδούμενος Pl.*Lg.*877a; ᾐδεσμένος D.23.77. 3. of the homicide, *obtain forgiveness*, D.23.72 codd. ⊛-έσιμος, ον, *exciting shame* or *respect, venerable*, M.Ant.1.9 (Sup.), Aristid.2.99 J. (Sup.), Hierocl. *in CA*13 p.448 M. (Comp.): c. dat., Aristid.*Or.*37(2).6; as honorary title, *PFlor.*15.6 (vi A.D.); τοῦ προσώπου τὸ αἰ. Luc.*Nigr.*26; *holy*, Paus.3.5.6. Adv. -μως *reverently*, Ael.*NA*2.25. -εσιμότης, ἡ, as title, *Your Reverence, Your Worship*, *POxy.*125 (vi A.D.), al. -εσις, ἡ, *forgiveness* (cf. αἰδέομαι II. 2), Arist.*Ath.*57.3, cf. D.21.43. -εστέον, *one must reverence*, Eust.1434.35. -εστικός, ή, όν, *modest, shamefaced*, τὸ αἰ. Sch.E.*Hipp.*345. -εστός, ή, όν, *revered, venerable*, Plu.2.67b.

⊛**ἀΐδηλος** [ῐ], Dor. **ἀΐδαλος**, ον, (ἀ- priv., ϝιδεῖν) *making unseen, annihilating, destructive*: in Hom., as epith. of Ares and Athena, Il.5.897,880; πῦρ ἀ. 2.455, al., Emp.109; ἠελίοιο ἔργ' ἀΐδηλα Parm.10.3; ἀΐδαλος τύχα *Epigr.Gr.*240.5 (Smyrna); ἄτη Opp.*H.*2.487; πότμος ib.1.150. Adv. -λως, = ὀλεθρίως, Il.21.220. II. Pass., *unseen, unknown, obscure*, v.l. in Il.2.318, cf. Hes.*Op.*756, A.R.1.102, al.; *unforeseen*, ib.298; *formless*, 4.681; *unsubstantial*, φρίκη Nic.*Th.*727; as epith. of Hades, *dark, gloomy*, S.*Aj.*608 (lyr.).

**αἰδη-μονικός**, ή, όν, *modest*, τὸ αἰ. Sch.E.*Hipp.*78. -μοσύνη, ἡ, *modesty*, *Stoic.*3.64, *IG*14.1637.

**αἰδήμων**, ον, gen. ονος, *bashful, modest*, Arist.*EN*1108a32, etc.: Comp. -έστερος X.*Lac.*2.10: Sup. αἰδημονέστατος Id.*An.*1.9.5. Adv. -μόνως Id.*Smp.*4.58, Arr.*Epict.*3.18.6, *PGen.*1.9. II. in bad sense, *ignominious, shameful*, θωή Max.576.

**ἀϊδής**, ές, (ἀ- priv., ϝιδεῖν) *unseen*, Hes.*Sc.*477, Pl.*Phd.*79a, al.; *secret*, γλῶσσα B.12.209. II. Act., *blind*, *IG*4.951.125 (Epid.), dub. in Thgn.1310.

**Ἀΐδης**, ὁ, poet. for Ἅιδης; v. sub ᾅδης.

**αἰδήσιμος**, ον, poet. for αἰδέσιμος, Orph.*A.*1346.

⊛**ἀΐδιος** [ᾰῐδ], ον, also η, ον Orph.*H.*10.21, al., (ἀεί):—*everlasting, eternal*, *h.Hom.*29.3, Hes.*Sc.*310; freq. in Prose, χρόνος Antipho 1.21; ἔχθρα Th.4.20; οἴκησις, of a tomb, X.*Ages.*11.16; ἡ ἀ. οὐσία *eternity*, Pl.*Ti.*37e; ἀ. στρατηγία, ἀρχή, βασιλεία, *perpetual*.., Arist.*Pol.*1285a7, 1317b41, 1301b27; ἀ. βασιλεῖς, γέροντες, ib.1284b33, 1306a17; τὰ ἀ., opp. τὰ γενητά and φθαρτά, Id.*Metaph.*1069a32, *EN* 1139b23, al.; ἐς ἀΐδιον *for ever*, Th.4.63; *ad infinitum*, Arist.*PA* 640a6; ἐξ ἀϊδίου Plot.2.1.3: Comp. -ώτερος Arist.*Cael.*284a17:—ἀ. is dist. fr. αἰώνιος as *everlasting* from *timeless*, Olymp.*in Mete.*146.16; but dist. fr. ἀείζωος as *eternal* (without beginning or end) from *everliving*, *Corp.Herm.*8.2. Adv. -ίως Sm.*Mi.*7.18, Iamb.*Comm.Math.*1, Hierocl.*in CA*1 p.419 M.

**ἀϊδιότης**, ητος, ἡ, *eternity*, Arist.*Cael.*284a1, *Ph.*252b3, Ph.1.3, al., Plot.3.7.5, Procl.*Inst.*55, etc.

**ἀϊδνός**, ή, όν, (ἀ- priv., ϝιδεῖν) poet. word, = ἀϊδής, *unseen, obscure*, Hes.*Th.*860, A.*Fr.*451 A; λιγνύς A.R.1.389; Νύξ *Lyr.Adesp.*92:—later **ἀϊδνήεις**, εσσα, εν, καπνός Euph.139: ⊛**ἀϊδνής**, ές, πηλός Call.*Fr.anon.*220 (as v.l.), cf. Opp.*H.*4.245 (perh. -νῆς, contr. fr. -νήεις).

**αἰδοιϊκός**, ή, όν, *of* or *belonging to the* αἰδοῖα, Antyll.ap.Orib.50.5.3, Paul.Aeg.3.59.

**αἰδοιολείκτης**, ὁ, = *cunnilingus*, Hsch. s.v. σκερός.

**αἰδοῖον**, τό, freq. in pl. αἰδοῖα, τά, *privy parts, pudenda*, both of men and women, Il.13.568, Hes.*Op.*733, Heraclit.15, Tyrt.10.25, Hp.*Aër.*9, Pl.*Ti.*91b, etc.: sg., Hdt.2.30,48, etc., freq. in Arist., *HA* 493a25, al. II. αἰ. θαλάσσιον, a sea animal, perh. *pennatula*, Nic.*Fr.*139, cf. Arist.*HA*532b23.

⊛**αἰδοῖος**, α, ον, (αἰδώς) *having a claim to regard, reverence*, or *compassion* (cf. αἰδώς), in Hom., Hes. only of persons, sts. of gods, θεῶν γένος Hes.*Th.*44, cf. *Op.*257, Il.18.394; more freq. of human beings, as kings, Il.4.402, members of family, esp. wife, 21.460, servants, ταμίη Od.1.139, women generally, παρθένος Il.2.514; then of the helpless or those needing protection, guests, Od.9.271, suppliants, 7.165: abs., αἰδοίοισιν ἔδωκα 15.373: Comp. -ότερος καὶ φίλτερος 11.360 (later -έστερος D.P.172):—after Hom. of things, ξείνων αἰ. λιμένες Emp.112.3: Sup. -ότατον, γέρας Pi.*P.*5.18; but -έστατος χρυσός *O.*3.42, cf. Alcm.74A. Adv. -ως, ἀπέπεμπον, of a guest, Od.19.243. II. Act., *bashful, shamefaced*, κακὸς δ' αἰ. ἀλήτης Od.578. 2. *showing reverence* or *compassion*, πνεῦμα A.*Supp.* (anap.); Ζεὺς Αἰ. the god *of mercy*, ib.192. 3. *claiming compassion*, λόγοι ib.455.—Poet.: used by Pl. in quotations.

**αἰδοιώδης**, ες, *like the* αἰδοῖα, Arist.*HA*541b8, Thphr.*HP*3.7.8.2.1.

**αἴδομαι**, poet. for αἰδέομαι.

**Ἄϊδος**, Ep. gen. of an obsol. nom. Ἄϊς, v. ᾅδης. II. Ἄιδος, ὁ, = ᾅδης, Antim.ap.Sch.Il.*Oxy.*1087.43.

**αἰδοσύνη**, ἡ, = αἰδημοσύνη, *AB*354, Phot.

**αἰδοφοίτης**, = ᾳδοφοίτης, Hsch.

**αἰδόφρων**, ον, gen. ονος, (φρήν) *regardful of mind, compassionate*, S.*OC*237 (lyr.); *respectful*, πρός τινα E.*Alc.*659.

⊛**ἀϊδρείη**, Ep. and Ion. -ίη [ῑη], ἡ, *want of knowledge, ignorance*, Od.12.41, Hdt.6.69; also in pl., Od.10.231, 11.272.

⊛**ἀϊδρήεις**, εσσα, εν, = sq., Nic.*Al.*415.

**ἄϊδρις**, ι, gen. ιος and εος, poet. Adj. *unknowing, ignorant*, Il.3.219, Pi.*P.*2.37; often c. gen., Od.10.282, Hes.*Sc.*410, A.*Ag.*1105, etc.; also **ἄϊδρος**, ον, Alc.*Oxy.*1789*Fr.*6, Ion Trag.54.

**ἀϊδροδίκης** [δῐ], ου, Dor. -δίκας, α, ὁ, *lawless*, ὕβρις Pi.*N.*1.63, cf. S.*Fr.*985.

**ἀΐδρυτος** or (more freq.) **ἀνίδρυτος**, ον, *unsettled, unstable*, δρόμοι ἀν. E.*IT*971; χρόνοι *irregular*, Ruf.*Interrog.*12; ἄοικοι καὶ ἀν. Plu.*TG* 9; νῆσος ἀν. *floating*, D.H.1.15; τὸ ἀν. τῆς γνώμης, τῆς οὐσίας, Ph.2.112, Dam.*Pr.*413. II. *with no fixed abode*, Τίμων ἦν ἀ. τις Ar.*Lys.*809 (lyr.); ἄσπειστος, ἀν. D.25.52; οἰκοῦσιν φεύγοντες, ἀ. κακὸν ἄλλοις Cratin.209 (expl. by ὃ οὐκ ἄν τις αὑτῷ ἱδρύσαιτο *EM*42.10).

**αἴδυλος**· θρασύς, Hsch.:—**αἰδύλος**, *EM*30.19.

**αἰδώ**, ἡ, = αἰδώς, Philet.9.

⊛**Ἀϊδωνεύς**, έως (έος *AP*7.480 (Leon.)), ὁ, lengthd. poet. form of Ἅιδης, twice in Hom., Il.5.190, 20.61, cf. Hes.*Th.*913, A.*Pers.*650 (lyr.); prob. scanned Αἰδωνεύς S.*OC*1560 (lyr.): gen. and dat. Ἀϊδονῆος, -ῆι in later poets, Q.S.6.490, Nonn.*D.*30.172; Αἰδωνῆος Mosch.4.86:—hence **Ἀϊδωναία**, ἡ, epith. of Hecate, *PMag.Par.*1.2855.

**ἀϊδώνια**· θανάσιμα, Hsch., *EM*30.20. **αἰδῷος**, = αἰδοῖος, *EM*29.25.

⊛**αἰδώς**, όος, contr. οῦς, ἡ (late nom. pl. αἰδοί Sch.E.*Hipp.*386), as a moral feeling, *reverence, awe, respect* for the feeling or opinion of others or for one's own conscience, and so *shame, self-respect* (in full ἑαυτοῦ αἰδώς Hierocl.*in CA*9 p.433 M.), *sense of honour*, αἰδῶ θέσθ' ἐνὶ θυμῷ Il.15.561; ἴσχε γὰρ αἰ. καὶ δέος ib.657, cf. Sapph.28, Democr.179, etc.; αἰ. σωφροσύνης πλεῖστον μετέχει, αἰσχύνης δὲ εὐψυχία Th.1.84, cf. E.*Supp.*911, Arist.*EN*1108a32, etc.; αἰδοῖ μειλιχίῃ Od.8.172; so ἀλλά με κωλύει αἴδως Alc.55 (Sapphus est versus); ἅμα κιθῶνι ἐκδυομένῳ συνεκδύεται καὶ τὴν αἰδῶ γυνή Hdt.1.8; δακρύων πένθιμον αἰδῶ tears of grief and *shame*, A.*Supp.*579; αἰ. τίς μ' ἔχει Pl.*Sph.*217d; αἰ. καὶ δίκη Id.*Prt.*322c; αἰδοῦς ἐμπίπλασθαι X.*Cyr.*1.4.4; *sobriety, moderation*, Pi.*O.*13.115; αἰδῶ λαβεῖν S.*Aj.*345. 2. *regard for others, respect, reverence*, αἰδοῦς οὐδεμιῆς ἔτυχον Thgn.1266, cf. E.*Heracl.*460; αἰ. τοκέων *respect for* them, Pi.*P.*4.218; τὴν ἐμὴν αἰδῶ *respect* for me, A.*Pers.*699; *regard* for friends, αἰδοῦς ἀχαλκεύτοισιν ἔζευκται πέδαις E.*Fr.*595; esp. *regard for the helpless, compassion*, αἰδοῦς κῦρσαι S.*OC*247; *forgiveness*, Antipho 1.26, Pl.*Lg.*867e (cf. αἰδέομαι II. 2). II. *that which causes shame* or *respect*, and so, 1. *shame, scandal*, αἰδώς, Ἀργεῖοι, κάκ' ἐλέγχεα Il.5.787, etc.; αἰδώς, ὦ Λύκιοι· πόσε φεύγετε; 16.422; αἰδὼς μὲν νῦν ἥδε.. 17.336. 2. = τὰ αἰδοῖα, Il.2.262, Arat.493, D.H.7.72. 3. *dignity, majesty*, αἰ. καὶ χάρις *h.Cer.*214. III. Αἰδώς personified, *Reverence*, Pi.*O.*7.44; *Mercy*, Ζηνὶ σύνθακος θρόνων Αἰ. S.*OC*1268, cf. Paus.1.17.1; παρθένος Αἰδοῦς Δίκη λέγεται Pl.*Lg.*943e.

⊛**αἰδῶσσα**· αἴθουσα, Hsch. **ἀϊδώτατον**· τειχίονα, Id.

**αἰεί**, Ion. and poet. for ἀεί, q.v. (For compds. omitted here v. sub ἀει-.)

**αἰει-γενέτης**, ὁ, poet. for ἀειγενέτης, Il.2.400, Od.2.432, al. -γενής, ές, = foreg., Opp.*C.*2.397.

**αἰέλιοι**, v. ἀέλιοι. **αἰέλουρος**, v. αἴλουρος. **αἰέν**, v. ἀεί.

⊛**αἰεν-αοιδός**, όν, *ever-singing*, Μοῦσα Alcm.1. ⊛-υπνος, ον, *giving eternal sleep*, epith. of Death, S.*OC*1578 (lyr.).

**αἰές**, Dor. for αἰέν, αἰεί.

**αἰετηδόν**, Adv. *like an eagle*, Apollon.*Lex.*68, Sch.Il.18.410.

**αἰετιαῖος**, α, ον, (ἀετός IV) *belonging to* or *placed in the pediment*, *IG*1.322 ii 73.

**αἰέτιον** χάριν ἐκτείσω, prov. of those who repay benefits quickly, Apostol.1.78.

**αἰετόεις**, εσσα, εν, *of eagle-kind*, Opp.*C.*3.117.

**αἰετός**, ὁ, v. sub ἀετός.

**αἰζήεις**, εσσα, εν, late form of αἰζηός, Theopomp.Col.ap.Ath.4.183b; αἰζῆεν Hsch.

**αἰζήϊος**, ὁ, lengthd. form of αἰζηός, Il.17.520, Od.12.83, Hes.*Sc.*408.

**ἀΐζηλος**, ον, = ἀΐδηλος, *unseen*, τὸν μὲν ἀΐζηλον θῆκεν θεός v.l. (prob. Aristarch.) in Il.2.318.

⊛**αἰζηός**, lengthd. **αἰζήϊος** (q.v.), ὁ, *in full bodily strength, vigorous*; in Hom. as Adj., ἀνέρι.. αἰζηῷ τε κρατερῷ τε Il.16.716, cf. 23.432; of a *stout, lusty* slave, τεσσερακονταέτης αἰ. Hes.*Op.*441, cf. *Th.*863:—freq. as Subst., Il.2.660, Od.12.440, Call.*Jov.*70, A.R.4.268, Nic.*Al.* 176, etc.; κταμένοις ἐπ' αἰζηοῖσι καυχᾶσθαι μέγα Cratin.95.

**αἰζόκροτος**· ξηρασία, Hsch., *EM*31.55: for ἀζο- (cf. ἄζα), Eust. 648.46.

**αἰηνής**, Ion. for αἰᾱνής, q.v.

**αἴητος**, prob. = ἄητος (q.v.), πέλωρ, of Hephaestus, Il.18.410.

**αἰητός**, ὁ, Dor. for ἀετός, αἰετός.

**αἰθᾰλέος** (better -άλεος, cf. *EM*262.4), α, ον, (αἰθάλη) *smoky*, A.R. 777. II. of ants, = αἰθαλόεις II. 2, Nic.*Th*.750.

**αἰθάλη**, ἡ, (αἴθω) = αἴθαλος, esp. *soot*, Hp.*Mul*.1.91, Lxx *Ex*.9.8, Sc.5.75, v.l. in Luc.*D.Deor*.15.1. II. *sublimed vapour*, Zos. Alch.p.250 B., al.

**ἀϊθᾰλής** [ᾰῐ-], ές, = ἀειθαλής, Orph.*H*.8.13.

**αἰθαλ-ίδας**· τὰ ἐν τῷ σίτῳ γινόμενα, ἢ τοὺς ἐν τῷ ὕδατι σταλαγμοὺς οὗ ἐλαίου, Hsch. **-ίων**, ωνος, prob. = αἰθαλόεις II. 2, τέττιγες Theoc.7.138. **-όεις**, όεσσα, όεν, contr. **αἰθᾰλοῦς**, οῦσσα, οῦν: (αἴθαλος) :—poet. Adj. *smoky, sooty*, μέλαθρον Il.2.415, cf. Theoc.13. 3; κόνις αἰ. *black* ashes *that are burnt out*, Il.18.23, Od.24.316. II. *burning, blazing*, κεραυνός Hes.*Th*.72, cf. E.*Ph*.183 (lyr.); φλόξ A. *Pr*.992. 2. *burnt-coloured*, i.e. *dark-brown*, Σάϊς Nic.*Th*.566; σώξ ib.716.

**αἰθᾰλοκομπία**, ἡ, *empty boasting*, that is nothing but smoke, Sch. Ar.*Eq*.696.

**⊛αἴθᾰλ-ος**, ὁ, *smoky flame, thick smoke*, Hp.*Mul*.1.91 (as v.l. for αἰθάλη), E.*Hec*.911 (lyr.), Semus 20, Lyc.55, etc. 2. grape grown in Egypt, Plin.*HN* 14.74. II. as Adj., αἴθαλος, ον, = αἰθαλόεις II. 2, Nic.*Th*.659. **⊛-όω**, *to soil with soot* or *smoke*, E.*El*.1140:— Pass., *burn to soot*, Dsc.1.66; poet., *to be laid waste by fire*, Lyc. 141. **-ώδης**, ες, *sooty, black*, Arist.*Mu*.395ᵃ26, Gal.9.470. **-ωσις**, εως, ἡ, in pl., *clouds of sooty smoke*, Max.Tyr.41.4 (pl.). **-ωτός**, ή, όν, *burnt to ashes*, Lyc.338.

**αἴθε**, Ep. for εἴθε, as αἰ for εἰ, in Hom. αἴθ' ὄφελες Il.1.415, al.

**ἀΐθεος**, Dor. for ἠΐθεος.

**αἰθερεμβᾰτέω**, *to walk in ether*. *APl*.4.328.

**αἰθεριβόσκας**, ὁ, *feeding on ether*, Cerc.1.3.

**⊛αἰθέριος**, α, ον, also ος, ον E.*Fr*.839.10, Arist.*Mu*.392ᵃ31:—*of αἰθήρ* or *the upper air*, hence, 1. *high in air, on high*, A.*Pr*.158 (anap.), *Th*.81, S.*OC*1082, etc.; αἰθερία ἀνέπτα flew up *into the air*, E.*Med*. 440, cf. *Andr*830; αἰ. γῆ, of the moon, Pythag.ap.Simp.*inCael*.511. 26: epith. of Zeus, Arist.*Mu*.401ᵃ17. 2. *ethereal, heavenly*, φύσις Parm.10.1; οἱ αἰ. Hierocl.*inCA*27p.484M.; γονή E.*Fr*. l.c. Adv. -ίως Iamb.*Myst*.1.9.—Trag. only in lyr.

**⊛αἰθερίτης** λίθος, a precious stone, Ps.-Callisth.1.4 (as v.l. for ἀέριvος).

**αἰθεριώδης**, ες, = αἰθερώδης, φύσις Heraclit.*All*.36.

**αἰθερο-βᾰτέω**, = αἰθερεμβατέω, of birds, Ph.1.506: metaph. of men, 2.242, al., cf. Ps.-Luc.*Philopatr*.25. **-δρόμος**, ον, *ether-skimming*, οἰωνοί Cines.ap.Ar.*Av*.1393; ὧραι *IG*12(5).891 (Tenos, perh. by Aratus), cf. 9(1).881.7 (Corcyra). **-ειδής**, ές, = αἰθερώδης, Plu.2.430e. **⊛-λαμπής**, ές, *shining in ether*, οὐρανός Man. 4.29. **-λόγος**, ον, *talking of ether and the like*, of Thales, Anaximen. ap.D.L.2.4: hence **-λογέω**, ib.2.5, cf. 8.50. **-ναία**, etym. of Ἀθηνᾶ, Corn.*ND*20. **-νόμος**, ον, (νέμομαι) = αἰθεροβόσκας, Hsch. **-νωμάω**, *to rule the sky*, Man.4.25.

**αἰθερόομαι**, *to be high in air*, Sch.Opp.*H*.1.201. **αἰθερόπλαγκτος**, ον, *roaming in ether*, Orph.*H*.6.1.

**αἰθερώδης**, ες, *like ether*, Plu.2.432f, Gal.*UP*10.4.

**Αἴθη**, v. αἰθός III.

**αἰθήεις**, εσσα, εν, (αἴθω) = αἰθαλόεις II.2, Nic.*Al*.394.

**⊛αἰθήρ**, έρος, in Hom. always ἡ; in Hes. and Att. Prose always ὁ; in Lyr. and Trag. mostly ὁ, as always in A., but ἡ Pi.*O*.1.6, B.8.35, S.*OT*867, and freq. in E.: (αἴθω):—in Hom., *ether, the heaven* (wrongly distinguished by Aristarch. from ἀήρ (q.v.) as *upper* from *lower air*); δι' ἠέρος αἰθέρ' ἵκανεν Il.14.288; [Ζεὺς] αἰθέρι ναίων 2.412, Hes.*Op*.18; νόμοι δι' αἰθέρα τεκνωθέντες S.*OT*867; αἰθὴρ μὲν ψυχὰς ὑπεδέξατο σώματα δὲ χθών *IG*1.442, cf. E.*Supp*.533; of the *sky*, both cloudless, νήνεμος αἰ. Il.8.556, and clouded, ἐν αἰθέρι καὶ νεφέλῃσι 15. 192, cf. 16.365; freq. in Trag., etc., A.*Pr*.1044, 1088, *Pers*.365, E. *Ba*.150; αἰ. ζοφερός, ἀχλυόεις, A.R.3.1265, 4.927; of the fumes of the Cyclops' mouth, E.*Cyc*.410. 2. *air*, Emp.100.5. 3. fifth element, Pl.*Epin*.981c, 984b, Arist.*Cael*.270ᵇ22; but equivalent to πῦρ, Anaxag.1, 15. b. = πῦρ τεχνικόν, Chrysipp.*Stoic*.2. 168, cf. Arist.*Mu*.392ᵃ5. 4. the divine element in the human soul, Philostr.*VA*3.34, cf. 42. II. *clime, region*, E.*Alc*.594 (lyr.).

**αἰθής**, ές, *burning*: αἰ. πέπλος the robe of Nessus, prov. of those who stir up στάσις, Cratin.88, cf. Zen.1.33. (Perh. rather αἰθῆς, contr. for -ήεις.)

**αἴθινος**, η, ον, *burning*, Hsch.; = αἶθοψ, καπνός *EM*33.11.

**Αἰθιοπίζω**, *to speak* or *be like an Ethiopian*, Hld.10.39.

**⊛Αἰθίοψ**, οπος, ὁ, fem. **⊛Αἰθιοπίς**, ίδος, ἡ (Αἰθίοψ as fem., A.*Fr*.328, 329): pl. Αἰθιοπῆες Il.1.423, whence nom. Αἰθιοπεύς Call.*Del*.208: (αἴθω, ὤψ):—properly, *Burnt-face*, i.e. *Ethiopian, negro*, Hom., etc.; prov., Αἰθίοπα σμήχειν 'to wash a blackamoor white', Luc.*Ind*. 28. 2. *a fish*, Agatharch.109. II. Adj., *Ethiopian*, Αἰθιοπὶς γλῶσσα Hdt.3.19; γῆ A.*Fr*.300, E.*Fr*.228.4: Subst. Αἰθιοπίς, ἡ, title of Epic poem in the Homeric cycle; also name of a plant, *silver sage, Salvia argentea*, Dsc.4.104:—also **Αἰθιόπιος**, α, ον, E.*Fr*.349: **Αἰθιοπικός**, ή, όν, Hdt., etc.; Αἰ. κύμινον, = ἄμι, Hp.*Morb*.3.17, Dsc. 3.62:—Subst. **⊛Αἰθιοπία**, ἡ, Hdt., etc. 2. *red-brown*, *AP*7.196 (Mel.), cf. Ach.Tat.4.5.

**αἰθόλιξ**, ικος, ἡ, *pustule, pimple*, Hp.*Liqu*.6:—Adj. **-κώδης** Gal. 19.71.

**αἶθος**, ὁ, *burning heat, fire*, E.*Rh*.990, cf. *Supp*.208 codd. (but cf. αἶθρος):—later also **αἶθος**, εος, τό, A.R.3.1304, Orph.*L*.174.

**⊛αἰθός**, ή, όν, *burnt*, Ar.*Th*.246. II. *shining*, ἀσπίς Pi.*P*.8.46; *red-brown*, ἀράχναι B.*Fr*.3.6, cf. Call.*Dian*.69, Nic.*Th*.288. III. pr. n. Αἴθη, name of a *bay* horse, Il.23.295.

**⊛αἴθουσα** (sc. στοά), ἡ, properly part. of αἴθω (q.v.), in the Homeric house, *portico, verandah, to catch the sun*, δόμον.. ξεστῇς αἰθούσῃσι τετυγμένον Il.6.243, cf. 20.11, A.R.3.39, 237: in Od. esp. of a *loggia* leading from αὐλή to πρόδομος, 3.399, al.; αἰ. ἐρίδουπος, echoing to the tramp of horses, 15.146. 2. = κώνειον, Ps.-Dsc.4.78. (αἴθουσσα Hdn.Gr.2.919, v.l. in Hom., which may point to αἰθοῦσσα = αἰθόεσσα.)

**⊛αἶθοψ**, οπος, (αἰθός, ὤψ) *fiery-looking*, in Hom. as epith. of metal, *flashing*, αἴθοπι χαλκῷ Il.4.495, etc.; and of wine, *sparkling* (or '*fiery*', cf. Epigr.ap.Luc.*Dips*.6), αἴθοπα οἶνον 4.259, etc.; once of smoke, *mixed with flame* (cf. αἴθαλος), Od.10.152; αἰ. φλογμός, λαμπάς, E. *Supp*.1019, *Ba*.594 (both lyr.). 2. *black*, Opp.*H*.1.133, etc.; αἴθοπι κισσῷ *App.Anth*.3.166 (Procl.). II. metaph.. *fiery, keen*, λιμός Hes.*Op*.363; μῶμος Tim.*Pers*.223; δίψη Nonn.*D*.15.7; βασκανίη *AP*5.217 (Agath.).

**αἴθρανος**, ὁ, *foot-warmer*, Suid., Eust 1571.25 (-κος codd.).

**αἰθρεῖ**· χειμάζει, Hsch., Suid.

**⊛αἴθρη**, ἡ, Hom. and Ar. ll. cc.: later **αἴθρα**, Antiph.52.14, etc.:— *clear sky*, ποίησον δ' αἴθρην Il.17.646; ἀλλὰ μάλ' αἴθρη πέπταται ἀνέφελος Od.6.44, cf. Ar.*Av*.778 (lyr.), Lyc.700, *AP*6.179 (Arch.), etc. II. *air*, as an element, *Orac.Chald*.169.

**⊛αἰθρη-γενής**, ές, (γενέσθαι) *born in clear sky*, Βορέας Il.15.171. **-γενέτης**, Od.5.296. **-εις**, εσσα, εν, = αἴθριος, Pherenic.ap.Sch.Pi.*O*. 3.28, Opp.*C*.4.73.

**⊛αἰθρ-ία**, Ion. -ίη, ἡ, = αἴθρη, first in Sol.13.22, then in Ion. Prose, Com., X., and Arist.: ἐξ αἰθρίης καὶ νηνεμίης Hdt.7.188; ἐξ αἰθρίας ἀστράψω Cratin.53, cf. Hdt.3.86, X.*HG*7.1.31; αἰθρίας οὔσης *in clear weather*, Arist.*Mete* 342ᵃ12; αἰθρίης or -ίας abs., Hdt.7.37, Ar.*Nu*. 371; τῆς αἰθρίας Arist.*Pr*.939ᵇ15. 2. esp. *the clear cold air* of night, Hdt.2.68, cf. Hp.*Aër*.8. [ῑ in penult. exc. in dact. and anap., Sol. l.c., Ar. l.c.] **-ιάζω**, *clear the sky*, ἀέρα Arist.*Pr*.941ᵃ4:—also = αἰθριάω, in pf. part. Pass. ᾐθριασμένα Hp.*Morb*.3.17. **-ίασις**, *exposure to air*, Olymp.Alch.p.87 B. **-ιάω**, *expose to the air, cool*, αἰθριήσας Hp.*Morb*.3.17; cf. αἰθριάζω. II. intr., *clear up*, of the sky, ὡς δ' ᾐθρίασε Babr.45.9.

**αἰθρίδιον**, τό, Dim. of αἴθριον, *PRyl*.312 (i A.D.).

**αἰθρινός**, ή, όν, = πρωϊνός, Hsch.

**⊛αἰθριο-κοιτέω**, *sleep in the open air*, Theoc.8.78, Antyll.ap.Orib.9. 3.8. **-ποιέω**, *clear the sky*, Gloss.

**⊛αἴθριος**, ον, *clear, bright*, of weather, αἰθρίου ἐόντος τοῦ ἠέρος Hdt. 2.25; αἰ. πάγος *clear* frost, S.*Fr*.149; f.l. in *Ant*.357. 2. epith. of Ζεύς, Heraclit.120, Theoc.4.43, cf. Arist.*Mu*.401ᵃ17, Thphr.*CP*5. 12.2; of winds *which cause a clear sky*, *h.Ap*.433, Arist *Mete*.364ᵇ 29; esp. of the North wind, ib.358ᵇ1. II. *kept in the open air*, στέφη Cratin.22. III. **αἴθριον**, τό, adaptation of Lat. *atrium* to a Greek sense, J.*AJ*3.6.2, Luc.*Anach*.2, *POxy*.268.22 (i A.D.), etc.

**αἰθρο-βάτης**, ου, ὁ, *walking through ether*, of Abaris, Porph.*VP* 29. II. *rope-dancer*, Man.4.278. **-βολέω**, Astrol., = ἀκτινοβολέω (q.v.), c. acc., ib.224. **-δόνητος**, ον, *whirling through ether*, ib. 298. **-πλᾰνής**, ές, *wandering in ether*, ἀστὴρ *a planet*, ib.586. **-πολεύω**, *roam through air*, Id.2.383:—also **-πολέω**, Max.483.

**αἶθρος**, ὁ, *the clear chill air* of morn, Od.14.318, cf. Alc.*Supp*.4. 14. II. = αἴθριον, *PLond*.3.1023.20 (v/vi A.D.).

**αἰθρότοκος**, ον, *born of air*, Man.4.339.

**⊛αἴθυγμα**, ατος, τό, (αἰθύσσω) *gleam, glamour*, ὅπλων Onos.28 (pl.); πυρός D.Chr.80.5, cf. Plu.2.966b: metaph., *spark*, αἰ. εὐνοίας, δόξης, Plb.4.35.7 (pl.), 20.5.4; μήτ' ἴχνος μήτ' αἰ. Phld.*Sign*.29; μηδενὸς εἰς τοὐναντίον μηδ' ἕως αἰθύγματος ἀνθέλκοντος ib.18.

**αἴθυια**, ἡ, diving-bird, prob. *shearwater*, Od.5.337, cf. Arist.*HA* 542ᵇ17, Call.*Del*.12, *AP*7.285 (Glauc.); ἰχθυβόλοι ib.6.23 (Zon.):— epith. of Athena, as protecting ships, Paus.1.5.3. II. metaph., *ship*, Lyc.230.

**αἰθυιόθρεπτος**, ον, *feeding with sea-birds*, Lyc.237.

**αἰθυκτήρ**, ῆρος, ὁ, *rushing violently*, of pigs, Opp.*C*.2.332; φύσαλοι αἰ. Id.*H*.1.368.

**⊛αἰθύσσω** (usu. in pres., impf. ᾔθυσσον Hsch., κατ-αίθυσσον Pi.*P*. 4.83): aor. παρ-αίθυξα Id.*O*.10(11).73, A.R.2.1253: (akin to αἴθω):— *set in rapid motion, stir up, kindle*, S.*Fr*.542, cf. Nonn.*D*.1.187, al.; κτύπον, νόον, ib.38.382, 48.689:—Pass., *quiver*, of leaves, Sapph.4, cf. Nonn.*D*.1.31. II. intr., Arat.1034.

**⊛αἴθω**, only pres. and impf., *light up, kindle*, Hdt.4.145, A.*Ag*.1435; θεοῖς ἱερά S.*Ph*.1033; λαμπάδας E.*Rh*.95; δάφναν Theoc.2.24, etc.; πυρά E.*Rh*.41, 78, 823: metaph., σέλας ὄμμασιν αἴθει *AP*12.93 (Rhian.); χόλον αἶθες ib.5.299 (Paul. Sil.). 2. rarely intr., *burn, blaze*, Pi.*O*.7.48; λαμπτῆρες οὐκέτ' ᾖθον S.*Aj*.286. 3. Pass., **αἴθομαι**, *burn, blaze*, Hom. always in part., πυρὸς μένος αἰθομένοιο Il. 6.182, cf. 8.563; αἰ. δαλὸς 13.320; δαΐδες Od.7.101, cf. Pi.*O*.1.1, *Pae*. 6.97, E.*Hipp*.1279, etc.; after Hom. in other moods, αἴθεται κάλλιστα [τὰ ὀστέα] Hdt.4.61; αἰθέσθω δὲ πῦρ E.*IA*1470; δώματ' αἴθεσθαι δοκῶν Id.*Ba*.624, cf. X.*An*.6.3.19: metaph., ἔρωτι αἴθεσθαι X.*Cyr*.5.1. 16, cf. *AP*12.83 (Mel.); αἴθετο.. ἔρως (Ep. impf.) *burnt fiercely*, A.R. 3.296. (Cf. Lat. *aestas, aestus*: the weak form of the root appears in ἰθαίνεσθαι, cf. Skt. *inddhé* 'kindles'.)

**⊛αἴθων**, ωνος, ὁ, ἡ, (αἴθω) *fiery, burning*, κεραυνός Pi.*O*.10(11).83; of *fiery* smoke, *P*.1.23. II. of burnished metal, *flashing, glitter-*

*ing*, σίδηρος Il.4.485, Od.1.184, S.*Aj.*147 (lyr.); χαλκός B.12.50; λέβητες, τρίποδες, Il.9.123, 24.233. III. of animals or birds, ἵπποι Il. 2.839; αἰετός 15.690; βόες Od.18.372; ἀλώπηξ Pi.*O.*11(10).20; δορά, of a boar, B.5.124; prob. of colour, *red-brown, tawny*, since *sleek, shining*, or *fiery, fierce* do not suit all cases (but αἴ. θῆρες *fierce*, Pl.*R.* 559d); pr. n. of horse, Il.8.185. IV. metaph. of men, *hot, fiery*, S.*Aj.*221 (lyr.), 1088, Hermipp.46; αἴθων λῆμα *fiery* in spirit, A.*Th.* 448; λιμὸς αἴθων prob. in Hes.*Op.*363, Epigr.ap.Aeschin.3.184, Call. *Cer.*68. (The forms αἴθονα, αἴθονος have been corrupted into αἴθοπα, αἴθοπος, Hes.*Op.* l.c., S.*Aj.*221.)

**αἰθωπός**, όν, *fiery*, Man.4.166.

**αἰκάλη**, ἡ, = ἀπάτη, Zonar.

**αἰκάλλω**, only pres. and impf., (αἰκάλος) *flatter, wheedle, fondle*, properly of dogs (cf. Phryn.*PS*p.36 B.), c. acc., E.*Andr.*630, cf. Pl.Com. 21 D.; τὸν δεσπότην ᾔκαλλε Ar.*Eq.*48; τὰ μὲν λόγι' αἰκάλλει με *flatter, please* me, ib.211; αἰκάλλει καρδίαν ἐμήν *it cheers* my heart, Id.*Th.*869; τοὺς περὶ τὴν αὐλήν Plb.5.36.1, cf. Axiop.3.4, Philostr.*VA*5.42:—Pass., ὑπό τινων Plb.15.25.31:—of a fox, σεσηρὸς αἰκάλλουσα *wagging the tail fawningly*, Babr.50.14.—Trag., Com., and later Prose.

**αἰκάλος**, ὁ, *flatterer*, Hsch.

**αἰκε, αἰκεν**, poet. and Dor. for ἐάν.

**αἰκείη**, Ion., = αἰκία, Herod.2.41.

**αἰκέλιος**, ον, poet. for ἀεικέλιος, Thgn.1344, E.*Andr.*131 (lyr.).

**ἀϊκή** [ᾰῑ], ἡ, (ἀΐσσω) *rapid motion, flight*, τόξων ἀϊκαί Il.15.709; ἐρετμῶν Opp.*H.*4.651.

**ἀϊκής** [ῐ], ές, poet. for ἀεικής. Adv. ἀϊκῶς Il.22.336:—in Trag. αἰκής, ές, αἰκὲς πῆμα A.*Pr.*472; θανάτους αἰκεῖς S.*El.*206 (lyr.). Adv. αἰκῶς S.*El.*102, 216 (both lyr.), Pl.Com.225.

**αἰκ-ία**, ἡ, Att. for Ion. ἀεικίη (q.v.), *insulting treatment, outrage*, A. *Pr.*179, S.*El.*515 (lyr.), *OC*748, etc. 2. *torture*, Plb.1.80.8, cf. 24.9. 13: pl., *torments*, A.*Pr.*93, S.*El.*486 (lyr.), And.1.138, etc. 3. in Prose usu. law-term, *assault*, αἰκίας δίκη Pl.*R.*425d, 464e; ἣν ὁ τῆς βλάβης ὑμῖν νόμος πάλαι, ἣν ὁ τῆς αἰ., ἣν ὁ τῆς ὕβρεως D.21.35, cf. Lys.*Fr.*44, etc. 4. generally, *suffering*, Th.7.75. [Prob. misspelt for -εια (which is freq. v.l.); - - - in Poets.] ⊛**-ίζω**, aor. ᾔκισα Herod.2.46: pf. αἴκικα· ὕβρικα, Hsch.:—*maltreat*, τινά S.*Aj.* 403, *Tr.*839; σῶμα Tim.*Pers.*189; of a storm, *mar, spoil*, πᾶσαν αἰκίζων φόβην ὕλης S.*Ant.*419:—Pass., *to be tortured*, rarely in pres. in A.*Pr.* 169, Pl.*Ax.*372a: pf. ᾔκισμαι D.S.18.47, Polyaen.8.6: more freq. in aor. 1, πρὸς κυνῶν ἐδεστὸν αἰκισθέντα S.*Ant.*206; ἐδέθη καὶ ᾐκίσθη Lys.6.27; τὰ σφέτερα αὐτῶν σώματα αἰκισθέντες And.1.138, cf. Isoc. 4.154; εἰς τὸ σῶμα αἰκισθῆναι πληγαῖς Arist.*Pol.*1311$^{b}$24. II. more freq. in Med. **αἰκίζομαι**, A.*Pr.*197, Isoc.4.123: impf. ᾐκιζόμην S.*Aj.* 300: fut. αἰκίσομαι *AP*12.80 (Mel.), Att. -ιοῦμαι (κατ-) E.*Andr.*829: aor. ᾐκισάμην S.*Aj.*111, *OT*1153, Isoc.5.103, X.*An.*3.4.5: pf. ᾔκισμαι E.*Med.*1130, plpf. ᾔκιστο Plu.*Caes.*29:—in same sense as Act., ll. cc.; *damage*, τὰ χωρία D.43.72: c. dupl. acc. pers. et rei, αἰκίζεσθαί τινα τὰ ἔσχατα X.*An.*3.1.18; αἰκίσασθαί τινας πᾶσαν αἰκίαν Plb. 24.9.13. **-ισμα**, ατος, τό, *outrage, torture*, A.*Pr.*989, Lys.6.26:—in pl. -ίσματα νεκρῶν *mutilated* corpses, E.*Ph.*1529. **-ισμός**, ὁ, = foreg., D.8.51, Ctes.*Fr.*29.58, etc.; πόλεως Lxx 2*Ma.*8.17. 2. Medic., *discomfort*, Antyll.ap.Orib.6.23.13; *wrench, shock*, αἰ. αἰφνίδιος Apollon.Cit.1. **-ιστικός**, ή, όν, *prone to outrage*, only in Adv. -κῶς Sch.Il.22.336, Poll.8.75, etc. **-ίστρια**, ἡ (as if from a masc. αἰκιστής), *she who tortures*, Suid.

**αἶκλοι**· αἱ γωνίαι τοῦ βέλους, Hsch.

**αἶκλον** or **ἄϊκλον**, τό, *the evening meal* at Sparta, Epich.37, Alcm. 71, Polem.Hist.86, cf. Ath.4.139b:—also **αἶκνον**, Hsch., Suid.

**ἀϊκτήρ** [ᾱ], ῆρος, ὁ, (ἀΐσσω) *swift-rushing, darting*, σκορπίος Opp. *H.*1.171; ἀστέρες Nonn.*D.*2.192.

**ἄϊκτος**, ον, (ἱκνέομαι) *unapproachable*, καὶ ὕψει καὶ ψαύσει Hp.*Vict.* 1.10 (sed leg. ἄθικτος), Hsch.

**αἴλινον**, τό, = λίνον, Ps.-Dsc.2.103.

⊛**αἴλινος**, ὁ, *cry of anguish, dirge*, αἴλινον αἴλινον εἰπέ A.*Ag.*121 (lyr.), cf. S.*Aj.*627 (lyr.), E.*Or.*1395; of an *epitaph*, *AP*6.348 (Diod.); said to be from αἶ Λίνον *ah me for Linos!* cf. Paus.9.29.8. 2. Adj., αἴλινος, ον, *mournful, plaintive*, αἰλίνοις κακοῖς E.*Hel.*171; βρέφος αἴ. *unhappy*, *IG*14.1502: neut. pl. αἴλινα as Adv., Call.*Ap.*20, Mosch.3.1: hence **αἰλινέω** *sing a dirge*, cj. in Dosiad.*Ara*15.

**αἶλος**, v. ἄλλος.

**αἰλούριος**, ὁ, ῥίζα τις, Hsch., *EM*34.9.

**αἰλουρίς**, ἡ, fem. of αἴλουρος I, *Gloss.*

**αἰλουρο-βοσκός**, ὁ, *keeper of sacred cats*, *PSI*4.440.2 (iii B.C.). **-πρόσωπος**, ον, *cat faced*, θεός *PMag.Par.*2.4.13 (ἐλ-).

**αἴλουρος**, Arist.*HA*540$^{a}$10, *Phgn.*811$^{b}$9, or **αἰέλουρος**, ὁ, ἡ, Hdt. and Comici ll. cc., S.*Ichn.*296:—*cat, Felis domesticus*, Hdt.2.66, Ar. *Ach.*879, Anaxandr.39.12, Timocl.1, Lxx *Ep.Je.*22, Plu.2.144c. II. = ἀναγαλλὶς ἡ κυανῆ, Ps.-Dsc.2.178; also αἰλούρου ὀφθαλμός, ὁ, ibid.

**αἰλουροτάφος**, ου, ὁ, *burier of cats*, Wilcken *Chr.*385 ii 25 (iii B.C.).

**αἰλουρόφθαλμος**, ον, *with cat-like eyes*, Heph.Astr.1.1.

⊛**αἷμα**, ατος, τό, *blood*, Il.1.303, etc.; φόνος αἵματος 16.162; ψυχῆς ἄκρατον αἷμα S.*El.*786: in pl., *streams of blood*, A.*Ag.*1293, S.*Ant.* 121, E.*El.*1172, *Alc.*496. 2. *of anything like blood*, Βακχίου Tim. *Fr.*7; αἷ. σταφυλῆς Lxx *Si.*39.26, cf. *App.Anth.*3.166 (Procl.). b. *dye* obtained from ἄγχουσα, *alkanet*, *PHolm.*15.25, *PLeid.X.*99. 3. with collat. meaning of *spirit, courage*, οὐκ ἔχων αἷμα *pale, spiritless*, Aeschin.3.160; τοὺς αἷμα φάσκοντας τὴν ψυχήν Arist.*de An.* 405$^{b}$4. II. *bloodshed, murder*, A.*Ch.*520, S.*OT*101; ὅμαιμον αἷ. a kinsman's *murder*, A.*Supp.*449; εἴργασται μητρῷον αἷ. E.*Or.* 285, cf. 406; αἷ. πράττειν ib.1139; αἷμα συγγενὲς κτείνας S.*Fr.*799; αἷμα τραγοκτόνον shedding of goat's *blood*, E.*Ba.*139; ἐφ' αἵμα[τι] φεύγειν to avoid trial for *murder* by going into exile, *SIG*58 (Milet., v B.C.), D.21.105; αἷμα συγγενὲς φεύγων E.*Supp.*148: pl. in this sense, A.*Ch.*66, 650, freq. in E., never in S.; αἵματα σύγγονα brothers' *corpses*, E.*Ph.*1502:—concrete, νεακόνητον αἷ. keen-edged *death*, i.e. a sword, S.*El.*1394 (expl. by μάχαιρα, Hsch.). III. *blood relationship, kin*, αἷ. τε καὶ γένος Od.8.583; αἵματός εἰς ἀγαθοῖο 4.611; οὐ σῆς ἐξ αἵματός εἰσι γενέθλης Il.19.111; τὸ αἷ. τινος his *blood* or *origin*, Pi.*N.*11.34; αἷ. ἐμφύλιον incestuous *kinship*, S.*OT*1406; τοὺς πρὸς αἵματος Id.*Aj.*1305, cf. Arist.*Pol.*1262$^{a}$11; μητρὸς τῆς ἐμῆς ἐν αἵματι *akin* to her *by blood*, A.*Eu.*606, cf. *Th.*141; ἀφ' αἵματος ὑμετέρου S.*OC*245. 2. concrete, of a person, ὦ Διὸς.. αἷμα *IG*14.1003.1, cf. 1389 ii 4, etc.

**αἱμαγμός**, οῦ, ὁ, *bloodshed*, in pl., Vett.Val.3.4, al.

**αἱμαγωγός**, όν, (ἄγω) *drawing off blood*, Sor.1.71: -γόν, τό, = γλυκυσίδη, Ps.-Dsc.3.140.

**αἱμακουρίαι**, ῶν, αἱ, (κορέννυμι) Boeot. for ἐναγίσματα, *offerings of blood* made to the dead, Pi.*O.*1.90, B.7.5 (prob. l.):—sg. in Plu.*Arist.* 21 (v.l. αἱμο-).

**αἱμακ-τικός**, ή, όν, *making bloody*, Sch.S.*Ant.*1003. **-τός**, ή, όν, *mingled with blood, of blood*, E.*IT*645 (lyr.).

**αἱμαλ-έος**, α, ον, *blood-red*, Tryph.70; *bloodstained*, *AP*6.129 (Leon.), Nonn.*D.*5.14. **-ώδης**, v.l. for αἱματ-, Hp.*Epid.*4.29 (Erot.).

**αἱμαλωπιάω**, *have the appearance of clotted blood*, Dsc.2.77.

**αἱμάλωψ**, ωπος, ὁ, *mass of blood*: *bloodshot place*, Hp.*Coac.*542, *Nat.Puer.*13, *POxy.*1088.13 (i A.D.); *blood-clot*, Aret.*SA*2.9. II. as Adj., *looking like clotted blood*, χυμὸς Id.*SD*2.1.

**αἵμαξις**, εως, ἡ, *letting of blood*, Aret.*CA*1.6.

**αἱμάρροια**, ἡ, = αἱμόρρ-, and **αἱμαροϊκός**, = αἱμορρ-, *BGU*1026 xxii 15 B (iv/v A.D.).

**αἱμάς**, άδος, ἡ, *gush, stream of blood*, S.*Ph.*695 (lyr.).

⊛**αἱμᾰσιά**, ἡ, *wall* of dry stones, αἱμασιάς τε λέγειν to lay *walls*, Od.18.359; αἱ. λέξοντες 24.224, cf. Hdt.2.69, Theoc.7.22; αἱ. ἐγγεγλυμμέναι τύποισι Hdt.2.138: of the walls of a city or fortress, Id.1. 180, 191, Th.4.43; αἱ. περιοικοδομῆσαι D.55.11; ἐφ' αἱμασιῇσιν ἥμενος Theoc.1.47, cf. *IG*12(3).248 (Anaphe).

**αἱμᾰσιολογέω**, *lay walls*, Theopomp.Com.73.

**αἱμᾰσιώδης**, ες, *like a* αἱμασιά, Pl.*Lg.*681a.

**αἱμάσσω**, Att. -ττω, D.H.2.74: fut. -άξω (v. infr.): aor. ᾕμαξα (v. infr.):—**Pass.**, aor. ᾑμάχθην E.*El.*574, αἱμάχθην S.*Aj.*909 (lyr.), part. A.*Pers.*595: pf. ᾕμαγμαι *SIG*1171 (Lebena):—*make bloody, stain with blood*, πεδίον Pi.*I.*8(7).50, cf. A.*Ag.*1589; ἑστίας θεῶν Id. *Th.*275; βωμόν Theoc.*Ep.*1, cf. Philostr.*VA*1.1; λίθους D.H. l.c.; κρᾶτ' ἐμὸν τόδ' αὐτίκα πέτρᾳ.. αἱμάξω πεσών S.*Ph.*1002; πότερος ἄρα πότερον αἱμάξει; *shall bring to a bloody end*, E.*Ph.*1289; πέσεα δᾶϊα.. αἱμάξετον ib.1299; αἱμάξεις..τὰς καλλιφθόγγους ᾠδάς Id.*Ion* 168: abs., τοῖς μὲν οὐχ ᾕμασσεν βέλος *drew* no *blood*, Id.*Ba.*761; οἰκέτῃ πλευράν Lxx *Si.*42.5:—Med., ᾑμάξαντο βραχίονας *AP*7.10:—Pass., *become bloody*, Hp.*Mul.*1.91; ᾑμαγμέναι σάρκες *SIG*1171:—*to be slain*, αὐτόχειρ αἱμάσσεται S.*Ant.*1175. 2. Medic., *draw blood*, as by cupping, Aret.*CA*1.4. II. intr., *to be bloody, blood-red*, Nic.*Al.*480, Opp.*H.*2.618.

**αἱματάω**, *to be bloodthirsty*, dub. l. Alcm.68.

**αἱμᾰτεκχυσία**, ἡ, *shedding of blood*, *Ep.Heb.*9.22.

⊛**αἱμάτη**, ἡ, = λεκάνη, Theognost.*Can.*5.32.

**αἱμᾰτηρός**, ά, όν (ός, όν E.*Or.*962):—*bloodstained*, χεῖρες S.*Ant.* 975 (lyr.); ξίφος E.*Ph.*625; ὄμμα *bloodshot*, Id.*IA*381; φλὸξ αἱματηρὰ κἀπὸ..δρυός, i.e. ἀφ' αἵματος καὶ δρυός, *fed by the blood of the victim* and the wood, S.*Tr.*766: esp. *bloody, murderous*, πνεῦμα A.*Eu.* 137; τεῦχος Id.*Ag.*815; θηγάναι Id.*Eu.*859; ὀμμάτων διαφθοραί S.*OC* 552; στόνος *caused by the blood-reeking wound*, Id.*Ph.*694 (lyr.). II. *of blood*, μένος A.*Ag.*1067; σταγόνες *gouts of blood*, E.*Ph.*1415; αἱ. ῥοῦς Hp.*Coac.*502; αἱ. φλέβες *conveying blood*, Philostr.*VA*8.7.

**αἱμᾰτηφόρος**, ον, *bringing blood*: *bloody*, μόρος A.*Th.*419 (lyr.).

⊛**αἱμᾰτία**, ἡ, *blood-broth*, eaten at Sparta, Poll.6.57.

**αἱμᾰτίζω**, *stain with blood*, αἱματίσαι πέδον γᾶς A.*Supp.*662. II. of insects, *draw blood, sting*, Arist.*HA*532$^{a}$13.

**αἱμᾰτικός**, ή, όν, *of the blood*, θερμότης Arist.*PA*697$^{a}$29; ὑγρότης Id.*GA*777$^{a}$7; τροφή, ὕλη, Id.*PA*652$^{a}$21, 665$^{b}$6; χυμός Gal.13. 332. II. = ἔναιμος, of animals *which have blood*, opp. ἄναιμος, Arist.*PA*665$^{b}$5, cf. *HA*489$^{a}$25; τὸ ἧπαρ -κώτατον *PA*673$^{b}$27.

**αἱμάτινος**, η, ον, *of blood, bloody*, στιγμή Arist.*HA*561$^{a}$11; δάκρυα Sch.E.*Hec.*241. 2. *red*, of glass, Plin.*HN*36.198.

**αἱμάτιον**, τό, Dim. of αἷμα, *a little blood*, Arr.*Epict.*1.9.33, Heliod.(?) ap.Orib.46.11.9, M.Ant.5.4. II. *blood-sauce*, a kind of γάρον, *Gp.*20.46.6. III. *black-pudding*, *SIG*1002.11 (Milet.), 1025.53 (Cos), Hsch.

**αἱμᾰτίς**, ίδος, ἡ, *blood-red cloak* (?), Arist.*Col.*797$^{a}$6: perh. f.l. for sq.

**αἱμᾰτίτης** [ῑτ], ου, ὁ, *blood-like*, λίθος αἱ. *haematite*, a red iron-ore, Dsc.5.126, cf. Athenod.Tars.4; εἰλεὸς αἱ., a disease, Hp.*Int.*46:—fem., αἱματῖτις φλέψ a vein *as conductor of blood*, Id.*Morb.Sacr.*15; αἱ. χορδή a *black*-pudding, Sophil.5; λίθος (cf. supr.), Thphr.*Lap.*37.

**αἱμᾰτο-δεκτικός**, ή, όν, = sq., ἀγγεῖον Sch.Ar.*Th.*754. **-δόχος**, ον, *holding blood*, Sch.Od.3.444. ⊛**-ειδής**, ές, *like blood, blood-red*, D.S.17.10.

⊛**αἱμᾰτόεις**, όεσσα, όεν, contr. **αἱματοῦς**, οῦσσα (S.*OT*1279 cj.), οῦν, = αἱματηρός, Il.5.82. 2. *blood-red*, or *of blood*, ψιάδες, σμῶδιξ, 16.

, 2.267. 3. *suffused with blood, flushed*, ῥέθος S.*Ant*.528; he petals of a rose, *AP*6.154 (Leon.). 4. *bloody, murderous*, ...εμος, etc., Il.9.650, etc.; ἔρις A.*Ag*.698 (lyr.); βλαχαί Id.*Th*. (lyr.).

**αἱμᾰτο-λοιχός**, όν, (λείχω) *licking blood*: ἔρως αἱ. *thirst for* ...*od*, A.*Ag*.1478 (lyr.). **-ποιέω**, *to make into blood*, Pall. *in Hp*.2. D. **-ποιητικός**, ή, όν, *blood-making*, δύναμις τοῦ ἥπατος Gal.16. 6:—also **-ποιός**, 7.213, Sch.E.*Hec*.90. **-ποσία** or **αἱμο-ποσία**, *drinking of blood*, Porph.ap.Stob.1.49.53. **-ποτέω**, *drink blood*, h.Ar.*Eq*.198. **-πώτης**, ου, ὁ, *blood-drinker, blood-sucker*, Ar.*Eq*. 8:—fem. **-πῶτις**, ιδος, Man.4.616. **-ρρόφος**, ον, *blood-drinking*, .*Eu*.193, Archipp.4 D.; τίσις S.*Fr*.743. **-ρρῦτος**, ον, *blood-reaming*, αἱ. ῥανίδες *a shower of blood*, E.*IA*1515 (lyr.). **-σπό-ητος**, ον, *splashed with blood*, S.*Fr*.817. ®**-στᾰγής**, ές, (στάζω) *ood-dripping, reeking with blood*, φόνος A.*Ag*.1309, cf. *Pers*.816, E. *upp*.812 (lyr.), Ar.*Ra*.471.

**αἱμᾰτουργός**, ή, όν, *murderous*, Ἄρεος δύναμις Porph.ap.Eus.*PE*3. 1.

**αἱμᾰτο-φλοιβοστάσιες**, αἱ, corrupt word, Hp.*Epid*.6.7.2, cf. Gal. 19.71. **-φυρτος**, ον, *blood-stained*, βέλη *AP*5.179 (Mel.); φόνος Phleg.*Mir*.3. **-χᾰρής**, ές, *delighting in blood*, Suid.

**αἱμᾰτ-όω**, *make bloody, stain with blood*, αἱμάτου θεᾶς βωμόν E. *Andr*.260; διὰ παρῇδος ὄνυχα.. αἱματοῦτε Id.*Supp*.77:—Pass., μηδὲν αἱματώμεθα A.*Ag*.1656; κρᾶτας αἱματούμενοι E.*Ph*.1149; ᾑματωμένη χεῖρας Id.*Ba*.1135, cf. Ar.*Ra*.476, Th.7.84, X.*Cyr*.1.4.10, etc. 2. *slay*, aor. αἱματῶσαι S.*Fr*.987. II. *turn into blood*, τὴν τροφήν Gal. 8.379:—Pass., Ruf.*Ren.Ves*.5.2, Gal.17(2).692. **-ώδης**, ες, *looking like blood*, διαχωρήματα Hp.*Prog*.11; φάρυγξ Th.2.49, cf. Arist. *Mete*.342$^{a}$36, Thphr.*HP*6.4.6, etc. 2. *of the nature of blood, bloody*, ὑγρότης Arist.*GA*726$^{b}$32, cf. *PA*665$^{b}$7 (Comp.), al.; διαχώρησις Diocl. *Fr*.147. ®**-ωπός**, όν, *bloody to behold, blood-stained*, κόραι, of the Furies, E.*Or*.256; δεργμάτων διαφθοραί Id.*Ph*.870. **-ωσις**, εως, ἡ, *changing into blood*, Gal.6.256, 8.350. **-ώψ**, ῶπος, ὁ, ἡ, = αἱματωπός, E.*HF*933 (cj. Pors.).

**αἱμηπότης**, ὁ, Ion. for αἱμοπότης, A.D.*Adv*.189.10.

**αἱμηρός**, ά, όν, = αἱματηρός, Man.1.338, of women, cf. Androm.ap. Gal.14.33, St. Byz. s.v. Ἐπίδαυρος; πρόσωπον αἱ. *flushed* with anger, Phld.*Ir*.p.5 W.

**αἱμίθεος**, Aeol. for ἡμί-, Alc.*Supp*.8.13. **αἰμίονος**, Aeol. for ἡμί-, Sapph.*Supp*.20.14. **αἴμισυς**, Aeol. for ἥμισυς, q.v.

**αἱμνίον**, τό, *basin for blood*, v.l. for ἀμνίον, Od.3.444.

**αἱμο-βᾰρής**, ές, *heavy with blood*, Opp.*H*.2.603. **-βᾰφής**, -ές, *bathed in blood*, S.*Aj*.219 (anap.), Nonn.*D*.2.52; τελαμῶνες Sor.1. 28. **-βόρος**, ον, *blood-sucking*, of certain insects, Arist.*HA*596$^{b}$13; γαστέρας αἱ., of serpents, *greedy of blood*, Theoc.24.18; ἔχιδνα *IG*4.620.4 (Argos); λύκος βλέπων -βόρον Alciphr.3.21. **-βότος**, ον, *feeding on blood*, Orac.ap.Porph.*Plot*.22. **-δαιτέω**, *to revel in blood*, Thphr.ap.Porph.*Abst*.2.8. **-διψος**, ον, *bloodthirsty*, Luc.*Ocyp*.97. **-δόχος**, ον, = αἱματοδόχος, *EM*84.41, Suid. s.v. αἱμνίον. **-δωρον**, τό, *herb-bane, Orobanche cruenta*, Thphr.*HP*8.8.5, Plin.*HN*19.176 (prob.). ®**-ειδής**, ές, = αἱματοειδής, Ph.2.244. **-κέρχνον**, τό, *cough with bloodspitting*, Hp.*Epid*.4.37. **-πότης**, = αἱματοπώτης, Vett.Val.78.6, Hsch. s.v. ἱεροπότης:—fem.®**-πότις**, ἡ, epith. of Hecate, *PMag.Par*.1.2864: of the Moon, *Hymn.Mag*.5.53. ®**-πτυϊκός**, ή, όν, *spitting blood*, Charixenes ap.Gal.13.50, Cael.Aur.*TP*3.2. 25, etc. **-πτυον**, τό, *bloodstained sputum*, Gal.14.444. **-πώτης**, ου, ὁ, = αἱματοπώτης, Lyc.1403. **-ροος**, ον, poet. for αἱμόρροος, Nic.*Th*.318. **-ρραγέω**, *have a haemorrhage, bleed violently*, ἐκ ῥινῶν Hp.*Acut*.67; αἱμορραγεῖ πλῆθος *there is a violent haemorrhage*, Id. *Aph*.4.27, cf. Sostrat.1, Zopyr.Hist.3:—impers. αἱμορραγεῖ Hp.*Aph*. 4.74; τούτοισιν αἱ. διὰ ῥινῶν Id.*Epid*.1.12. **-ρραγής**, ές, *bleeding violently*, S.*Ph*.825. **-ρραγία**, ἡ, *haemorrhage*, Hp.*Art*.69, *Aph*.7.21; any *violent bleeding*, ib.5.16; *nose-bleeding*, Gal.17(1).50, etc. **-ρραγικός**, ή, όν, *liable to* αἱμορραγία, Hp.*Prorrh*.1.135, etc. Adv. -κῶς, τελευτᾶν Gal.8.304. **-ρραγώδης**, ες, = foreg., σημεῖα *symptoms of haemorrhage*, Hp.*Prorrh*.1.130, Ruf.*Ren.Ves*.9. 2. **-ρραντος**, ον, (ῥαίνω) *blood-sprinkled*, θυσίαι E.*Alc*.134 (anap.), cf. *IT*225 (lyr.). **-ρροέω**, *to lose blood*, Hp.*Coac*.86, 110, Aristobul.32, etc.; *to have a* αἱμόρροια, Lxx *Le*.15.33, *Ev.Matt*.9.20. **-ρροια**, ἡ, *discharge of blood, bloody flux*, Hp.*Coac*.292, 301; αἱ. ἐκ ῥινῶν v.l. Id.*Aër*. 4. **-ρροϊδοκαύστης**, ου, ὁ, *forceps for applying caustics*, Paul.Aeg. 6.79. **-ρροϊκός**, ή, όν, *belonging to* αἱμόρροια, *indicating* or *causing it*, Hp.*Aph*.5.24, cf. *Coac*.300, etc. **-ρροΐς**, ΐδος, ἡ, mostly in pl., αἱμορροΐδες (sc. φλέβες) veins *liable to discharge blood*, esp. *haemorrhoids, piles*, Hp.*Aph*.3.30, etc. II. kind of *shell-fish*, perh. *Aporrhais pes-pelicani*, Arist.*HA*530$^{a}$19. III. female of αἱμόρροος II, Plin.*HN*20.210; poet., αἱμορροῒς θήλεια Nic.*Th*.315. **-ρροος**, ον, contr. **-ρρους**, ουν, *flowing with blood*, τρώματα Hp.*Art*.69; αἱ. φλέβες veins so large *as to cause a haemorrhage* if wounded, Id.*Fract*. 11, ubi v. Gal. 2. *suffering from haemorrhoids*, Hp.*Epid*.4.7. II. as Subst., a serpent, whose bite makes *blood flow* from all parts of the body, Philum.*Ven*.21, Nic.*Th*.282; cf. αἱμορροΐς III. **-ρρώδης**, ες, = αἱμορραγώδης, Hp.*Coac*.306. **-ρρυής**, ές, = αἱμόρρυτος, Phryn. *PSp*.26 B. **-ρρυσις**, εως, ἡ, = αἱμόρροια, Poll.4.186. ®**-ρρῠτος**, ον, (ῥέω) *dripping blood*, A.*Fr*.230:—poet. **-ρυτος**, νόσος *IG*12(5).310 (Paros). **-ρυγχιάω**, (ῥύγχος) *have a bloody snout*, Hermipp.80 (better taken as Subst. **-ίας**, ου, ὁ, reading -ίαν for -ιᾶν).

**αἱμός**, ὁ, = δρυμός, A.*Fr*.9 (pl.).

**αἱμο-σάτης**, ὁ, a Samian earth used in burnishing gold, interp. in Dsc.5.154. **-στᾰγής**, ές, = αἱματοσταγής, E.*Fr*.384. **-στασις**, εως, ἡ, *styptic*, Androm.ap.Gal.13.76: = σύμφυτον, prob. in Ps.-Dsc. 4.9. **-σταφίς**, ίδος, ἡ, = ῥοδοδάφνη, Dsc.4.81. **-φανής**, ές, *bloodshot*, of the eye, Aët.7.22. **-φόβος**, ον, *afraid of blood*, i.e. of bleeding, Gal.10.627. **-φόρυκτος**, ον, (φορύσσω) *defiled with blood*, κρέα Od.20.348; ῥεύματα Heraclit.*All*.42. ®**-φυρτος**, ον, = αἱματόφυρτος, Plb.15.14.2, Posidon.8. **-χᾰρής**, ές, = αἱματοχαρής, *Sammelb*.5829.4, Sch.E.*Hec*.24, *Or*.1563, Suid. s.v. αἱμωπούς. **-χροώδης**, ες, *blood-coloured*, Hp.*Epid*.4.52.

**αἱμόω**, = αἱματόω, in Pass., Hsch.

® **αἱμυλία**, ἡ, (αἱμύλος) *wheedling*, αἱ. καὶ χάρις Plu.*Num*.8, prob. in Phld.*Rh*.2.77 S.

**αἱμύλιος**, ον, = αἱμύλος, Od.1.56, *h.Merc*.317, Hes.*Th*.890, Thgn. 704; in good sense, *Eranos* 13.87.

**αἱμῠλο-μήτης**, ου, ὁ, *of winning wiles*, *h.Merc*.13. **-πλόκος**, ον, *weaving wiles*, Cratin.379a.

® **αἱμύλος** [ῠ], η, ον, also ος, ον *AP*7.643 (Crin.):—*wheedling, wily*, mostly of words, αἱμύλα κωτίλλουσα Hes.*Op*.374; μῦθος Pi.*N*.8.33, cf. Ar.*Eq*.687; also αἱ. μηχαναί A.*Pr*.208; μὴ κλωπὸς αἰνεῖ φωτὸς αἱμύλον δόρυ E.*Rh*.709; of persons, τὸν αἱμυλώτατον S.*Aj*.389 (lyr.), cf. Pl.*Phdr*.237b, Lyc.1124; of foxes, Ar.*Lys*.1268 (lyr.).

**αἱμῠλόφρων**, ον, gen. ονος, (φρήν) *wily-minded*, Cratin.379b.

**αἱμ-ωδέω** (more correct than αἱμωδιάω acc. to Phryn.*PSp*.14 B.), *to be set on edge*, of the teeth, Hp.*Hum*.9, Cratin.3 D., cf. Orion 617. 30. **-ώδης**, ες, *bloody, blood-red*, Luc.*D.Syr*.8. II. *having the teeth set on edge*, Gal.14.523. **-ωδία**, ἡ, *sensation of having the teeth set on edge*, caused by acid food or vomit, Hp.*Morb*.2.16, Arist. *Pr*.863$^{b}$11, Dsc.*Eup*.1.72 (pl.), Archig.ap.Gal.8.86. **-ωδιασμός**, ὁ, = foreg., Hsch. s.v. γομφιασμός. **-ωδιάω**, *have the teeth set on edge*, Hp.*Morb*.2.55, Diocl.*Fr*.43, Arist.*Pr*.886$^{b}$12, Lxx *Ez*.18.4 (Cod. A): c. acc., αἱ. τοὺς ὀδόντας Hp.*Morb*.2.73: metaph. of one *whose mouth waters*, ᾑμωδία Timocl.11.7. (In this group of words the termination may be connected with ὀδών.)

**αἵμων**, ονος, ὁ, dub. sens., perh. *eager*, Σκαμάνδριον αἵμονα θήρης Il. 5.49; expl. by Gramm. as = δαίμων, for δαήμων, *skilful*, cf. *EM*251. 13. II. (αἷμα) *bloody*, E.*Hec*.90, dub. l. in A.*Supp*.847 (lyr.).

**αἱμώνιος**, ον, *blood-red*, σῦκα Ath.3.76b.

**αἱμωπός**, όν, = αἱματωπός, *AP*6.35 (Leon.), S.E.*P*.1.44, Paul.Aeg. 3.41; *flushed*, Ph.2.585.

**αἰνᾰρέτης**, ου, ὁ, (αἰνός) *terribly brave*, voc. -έτη (v.l. -έτα) Il.16.31.

**Αἰνείας**, ου, ὁ, *Aeneas*, Ep. gen. Αἰνείᾱο, but in Il.5.534 Αἰνείω:—also **Αἰνέας**, Il.13.541 (disyll.), cf. S.*Fr*.373.1, etc.

® **αἰν-ελένη**, *Helen the direful* (cf. Αἰνόπαρις), *Epic.Alex.Adesp*.2. 11. **-επίκουρος**· ἐπὶ κακῷ βοηθῶν, Hsch. **-έσιμοι**· καθήκοντες, Id.

**αἴνεσις**, εως, ἡ, *praise*, Lxx *Ps*.72(73).28 (pl.), al., *Ep.Heb*.13.15.

**αἰνετ-ήριος**, α, ον, *laudatory*, Hdn.*Epim*.34. **-ής**, οῦ, ὁ, *one that praises*, opp. μωμητής, dub. in Hp.*de Arte* 8. ®**-ός**, ή, όν, *praiseworthy*, dub. in Antim.25 codd., Arist.*Rh*.1402$^{b}$11, *AP*7.429 (Alc.), Lxx *Le*.19.24.

® **αἰνέω** (cf. αἴνημι, αἰνίζομαι), impf. ᾔνουν E.*Hec*.1154, Ion. αἴνεον Hdt.3.73: fut. αἰνήσω Od.16.380, Thgn.1080, Pi.*N*.1.72; in Att. Poets always αἰνέσω, as in Pi.*N*.7.63, Semon.7.112: aor. ᾔνησα Hom., opt. αἰνήσειε Simon.57.1; Dor. αἴνησα Pi.*P*.3.13; in Att. always ᾔνεσα, Ion. αἴνεσα Hdt.5.113: pf. ᾔνεκα (ἐπ-) Isoc.12.207:—**Med.**, fut. αἰνέσομαι (only in compds. ἐπ-, παρ-):—**Pass.**, aor. part. αἰνεθείς Hdt.5.102: pf. ᾔνημαι (ἐπ-) Hp.*Acut*.51, Isoc.12.233.—Poet. and Ion. Verb, very rare in good Att. Prose (Pl.*R*.404d, *Lg*.952c), ἐπαινέω being used instead:—properly, *tell, speak of*, A.*Ag*.98, 1482 (both lyr.), *Ch*.192; σε κρηγύην αἰνεῖ *reports of* you as honest, Herod. 4.47. II. usu. *praise, approve*, opp. νεικέω, ψέγω, Il.10.249, Thgn. 612, etc.; ἀνδρὸς ἦν οὐδ' αἰνεῖν τοῖσι κακοῖσι θέμις Arist.*Fr*.673:—Pass., ὑπὸ Σιμωνίδεω αἰνεθείς Hdt.5.102; ἐπ' ἔργμασιν ἐσθλοῖς Theoc. 16.15. b. esp. in religious sense, *glorify* God, Lxx 1*Ch*.16.4, *Ev. Luc*.2.13, *PMag.Par*.1.1146, al.:—also c. dat., τῷ κυρίῳ, τῷ θεῷ, Lxx 1*Ch*.16.36, *Apoc*.19.5. 2. *approve, advise, recommend*, Od. 16.380, 403: c. inf., *recommend* to do a thing, euphem. for κελεύω, A.*Ch*.555, 715: c. part., αἰνεῖν ἰόντα *to commend* one's going, Id. *Pers*.643:—ὦ δεινὸν αἶνον αἰνέσας *giver of* dire counsel, S.*Ph*.1380:—c. acc. rei, *to be content with, acquiesce in*, γάμον Pi.*P*.3.13, cf. *N*.1.72, A.*Eu*.469, *Supp*.902, 1070 (lyr.), E.*Med*.1157; θῆσσαν τράπεζαν αἰνέσαι Id.*Alc*.2. 3. *praise*, with collateral sense, *decline courteously*, νῆ' ὀλίγην αἰνεῖν, μεγάλῃ δ' ἐνὶ φορτία θέσθαι Hes.*Op*.643 (cf. Plu. 2.22f), cf. S.*Fr*.109; but, *thank*, cj. in E.*Supp*.388. 4. abs., *approve*, ὁ δᾶμος αἰνεῖ *IG*9(1).119 (Locr.). III. *to promise* or *vow*, τινί τι or τινὶ ποιεῖν τι, S.*Ph*.1398, E.*Alc*.12.

**αἴνη**, ἡ, = αἶνος, *praise, fame*, ἐν αἴνῃ ἐών Hdt.3.74, 8.112.

**αἰνήθεστος**· οὐκ εὐλιτάνευτος, Hsch.; cf. θέσσασθαι.

**αἴνημι**, Aeol. for αἰνέω, Hes.*Op*.683.

**αἴνησις**, = αἴνεσις, Ph.2.245.

**αἰνητός**, ή, όν, = αἰνετός, *IG*4.1607 (Cleonae), Pi.*N*.8.39; αἰνητὸν πάντεσσιν ἐπιχθονίοις [Arist.]*Pepl*.14; παράκοιτις *IG*14.1363; στέμμα *Epigr.Gr*.247, al.

**αἴνιγμα**, ατος, τό, *dark saying, riddle*, Pi.*Fr*.177, A.*Pr*.610, etc., cf. Lxx *De*.28.37: freq. in pl., ἐξ αἰνιγμάτων *in riddles, darkly*, A.*Ag*. 1112, 1183; δι' αἰνιγμάτων Aeschin.3.121 (v.l.), etc.; ἐν αἰνίγματι 1*Ep.Cor*.13.12; αἱ. προβάλλειν, ξυντιθέναι, πλέκειν *to make* a riddle, Pl.*Chrm*.162b, *Ap*.27a, Plu.2.988a; opp. διειπεῖν, εἰδέναι, S.*OT* 393, 1525; μαθεῖν E.*Ph*.48. II. *taunt*, Aristaenet.1.27. III. *ambush* (Theban), Palaeph.4.

**αἰνιγμ-ατίας**, ου, ὁ, = αἰνιγματιστής, D.S.5.31. **-ατικός**, ή, όν, = -ώδης. Adv. -ῶς *in riddles, darkly*, Sch.E.*Hipp*.337. **-ατιστής**, οῦ, ὁ, *one who speaks riddles*, Lxx *Nu*.21.27. **-ατοποιός**, όν, *propounding riddles*, Eust.1074.60. ⊛**-ατώδης**, ες, *riddling, dark*, A.*Supp*.464; ῥηματίσκια, of the Heracliteans, Pl.*Tht*.180a; χρησμός D.S.32.10; of persons, Max.Tyr.38.4. Adv. -δῶς Arist.*Rh*.1441$^b$22, Pl.*Chrm*.164e (Comp.), etc.

**αἰνιγμός**, ὁ, *riddle*, mostly like αἴνιγμα in pl., δι' αἰνιγμῶν ἐρεῖν Ar.*Ra*.61, cf. Pl.*Ti*.72b, Aeschin.3.121; ἐν αἰνιγμοῖσι σημαίνειν τι E.*Rh*.754; ἐν αἰ. λαλεῖν Anaxil.22.23: sg., Callisth.ap.Ath.10.452a.

**αἰνίζομαι**, Dep. only pres., = αἰνέω, Il.13.374, Od.8.487:—Act. **αἰνίζω** in *AP*11.341 (Pall.).

**αἰνικ-τήρ**, ῆρος, ὁ, *one who speaks darkly*, αἰ. θεσφάτων S.*Fr*.771. **-τήριος**, ον, known from the Adv. -ίως *in riddles*, A.*Pr*.949. **-τής**, οῦ, ὁ, = αἰνικτήρ, of Heraclitus, Timo 43. **-τός**, ή, όν, *expressed in riddles, riddling*, S.*OT*439.

**αἴνιξις**, ἡ, *use of dark sayings*, δι' αἰνίξεως λέγεσθαι Plot.6.8.19.

**αἰνίσσομαι**, Att. -ττομαι: fut. -ίξομαι: aor. ᾐνιξάμην: (αἶνος):—*speak darkly* or *in riddles*, μῶν ᾐνιξάμην; S.*Aj*.1158; λόγοισι κρυπτοῖσιν αἰ. E.*Ion* 430; γνωρίμως αἰνίξομαι so as to be understood, Id.*El*.946: c. acc. cogn., λόγον.. αἰνίξατο Pi.*P*.8.40; αἰνίσσεσθαι ἔπεα *to speak riddling* verses, Hdt.5.56: c. acc. rei, *hint* a thing, *intimate, shadow forth*, Pl.*Ap*.21b, *Tht*.152c; τὸ δίκαιον ὃ εἴη *R*.332b; ὅτι.. *Phd*.69c; αἰ. εἰς.. *to refer as in a riddle to, to hint at*, εἰς Κλέωνα τοῦτ' αἰνίττεται Ar.*Pax* 47; τὴν Κυλλήνην.. εἰς τὴν χεῖρ' ὀρθῶς ᾐνίξατο *used the riddling word* Cyllene (cf. κυλλός).., Id.*Eq*.1085; so ᾐνίξαθ' ὁ Βάκις τοῦτο πρὸς τὸν ἀέρα Id.*Av*.970; αἰνιττόμενος εἰς ἐμέ Aeschin.2.108; αἰ. ὡς.. Ps.-Plu.*Vit.Hom*.4:—αἰ. τὸν ὠκεανὸν *form guesses about* it, Arist.*Mete*.347$^a$6. II. Act. in late Prose, Philostr.*VA*6.11. III. Pass., *to be spoken darkly*, aor. ᾐνίχθην Pl.*Grg*.495b: pf. ᾔνιγμαι Thgn.681, Ar.*Eq*.196, Arist.*Rh*.1405$^b$4.

**αἰνο-βάκχευτος**, ον, *raging direfully*, Lyc.792. **-βίας**, Ion. **-βίης**, ὁ, *terribly strong*, *AP*7.226 (Anacr.). ⊛**-γάμος**, ον, *fatally wedded*, E.*Hel*.1120 (lyr.), Orph.*A*.867, Man.3.148. **-γένεθλος**, ον, *born to ill luck*, Man.1.145. **-γένειος**, ου, *with dreadful jaws*, Call.*Del*.92. **-γίγας**, αντος, ὁ, *terrible giant*, Nonn.*D*.4.447. ⊛**-γόνος**, *child of praise*, Ph.Epic.ap.Eus.*PE*9.20. ⊛**-δακρυς**, ὁ, = foreg., *IG*12(7).115 (Amorgos). **-δότειραι** Ἐρινύες *giving terrible gifts*, Orph.*A*.352. **-δρυπτος**, ον, *terribly scarred*, term of abuse for a slave, Theoc.15.27 (v.l. αἰνόθρυπτε). ⊛**-δρυφής**, ές, *sadly torn*, in sign of mourning, Antim.[107].

**αἰνόθεν**, Adv. from αἰνός, only in the phrase αἰνόθεν αἰνῶς *horror of horrors*, Il.7.97.

**αἰνο-λαμπής**, ές, *horrid-gleaming*, A.*Ag*.389 (lyr.). **-λεκτρος**, ον, *fatally wedded*, ib.713 (lyr.), Lyc.820. II. *with a frightful bed*, of the cave of Echidna, Id.1354.

**αἰν-ολέτης**, ου, ὁ, *dire destroyer*, Orph.*A*.426.

**αἰνο-λεχής**, ές, = αἰνόλεκτρος, Orph.*A*.878. **-λέων**, οντος, ὁ, *dreadful lion*, Theoc.25.168. **-λῐνος**, ον, *unfortunate in life's thread* (i.e. dying young), *AP*7.527 (Theod.). **-λόγος**, ὁ, *terrible speaker*, *POxy*.465 (Astrol.). **-λῠκος**, ὁ, *a horrible wolf*, *AP*7.550 (Leon.). **-μᾰνής**, ές, *raving horribly*, Man.5.185, Nonn.*D*.20.152, etc. ⊛**-μορος**, ον, *doomed to a sad end*, Il.22.481, Od.9.53, Theoc.30.1; *come to a dreadful end*, A.*Th*.904 (lyr.). II. *of terrible doom*, ζόφος *h.Merc*.257; *deadly*, ὕδρος Q.S.9.395; σμύραιναι Marcell.Sid.14. ⊛**-πᾰθής**, ές, *suffering dire ills*, Od.18.201, A.R.4.1078, *AP*7.167 (Diosc. or Hecat.); πατρίς Anacr.36. **-πᾰρις**, ιδος, ὁ, like Δύσπαρις, *direful Paris, Paris the author of ill*, Alcm.40, E.*Hec*.945 (lyr.). **-πᾰτηρ**, ερος, ὁ, *unhappy father*, A.*Ch*.315. **-πέλωρος**, ον, *monstrous and terrible* δάκος Opp.*H*.5.303. **-πλήξ**, ῆγος, ὁ, ἡ, *with dire sting*, ἔχιδνα Nic.*Th*.517. **-ποιέω**, *sing praises*, Aq.*Ps*.80(81).2, al. **-ποτμος**, ον, = αἰνόμορος, Orph.*A*.1016.

**αἶνος**, ὁ, (αἰνέω) poet. and Ion. word, *tale, story*, Il.23.652, Od.14.508, A.*Supp*.534 (lyr.); αἰνεῖν αἶνον to tell *a tale*, Id.*Ag*.1483 (lyr.), S.*Ph*.1380: esp. *story with moral, fable*, Hes.*Op*.202, Archil.86, 89; ἄκουε δὴ τὸν αἶνον Call.*Iamb*.1.211: generally, *saying, proverb*, παλαιὸς αἰ. E.*Fr*.508, cf. Theoc.14.43; *riddle*, *Carm.Pop*.34. II. = Att. ἔπαινος, *praise*, Il.23.795, Od.21.110, Pi.*N*.1.6; ἐπιτύμβιος αἰ. A.*Ag*.1547, cf. 780, S.*OC*707 (all lyr.); ἄξιος αἴνου μεγάλου Hdt.7.107 (v.l. ἐπαίνου), cf. Lxx *Ps*.8.2, al., *Ev.Luc*.18.43. III. *decree, resolution*, τῶν Ἀχαιῶν *IG*4.926 (Epid.); κατ' αἶνον, opp. κατὰ ψήφισμα, *SIG*672.15 (Delph.), cf. *EM*36.16.

⊛**αἰνός**, ή, όν, poet., = δεινός, *dread, horrible*, freq. in Hom., of feelings, ἄχος, χόλος, τρόμος, κάματος, ὀϊζύς, Il.4.169, 22.94, 7.215, 10.312, Od.15.342; of states and actions, as δηϊοτής, πόλεμος, μόρος, Il.5.409, Od.8.519 (Sup.), Il.18.465; of persons, *dread, terrible*, esp. of Zeus, αἰνότατε Κρονίδη Il.4.25, etc.; σύ γ' αἰνοτάτη, of Pallas, 8.423; of monsters or animals, πέλωρα Od.10.219; ὄφις Hes.*Fr*.14; λίς Theoc.25.252. II. Adv. -νῶς *terribly*, i.e. strangely, *exceedingly*, Il.10.38; ἔοικέ τινι 3.158, Od.1.208; φιλέεσκε 1.264; ἐπὶ γόνυ κέκλιται A.*Pers*.930 (lyr.); φεύγειν τι Hdt.4.76; with Adj., αἰ. κακός *terribly* bad, Od.17.24; αἰ. πικρός Hdt.4.52; τῆς Σκυθικῆς αἰ. ἀξύλου ἐούσης ib.61:—neut. pl. αἰνά as Adv., Il.1.414: Sup. -ότατον 13.52.

**ἄϊνος** [ῑ], ον, (ἴς) *without fibres* or *veins*, Thphr.*HP*1.5.3, 8.3.1.

⊛**αἰνο-τάλᾱς**, αντος, ὁ, *most miserable*, Antim.[106] = Call.*Fr*.506. **-τίταν**, ὁ, *fearful Titan*, Hdn.Gr.1.13. **-τλητος**, ον, *terrible to bear*, ἀνίη Max.224. **-τόκεια**, ἡ, *unhappy in being a mother*, Mosch.4.27. **-τόκος**, ον, *unhappy in being a parent*, Opp.*H*.5.526, *IG*14.1858:—but **αἰνότοκος**· ὁ ἐπὶ κακῷ τεχθείς, Hsch. **-τύραννος**, ὁ, *dreadful tyrant*, *APl*.5.350. **-φρων**, gloss on ἀγανοφρ… Apollon.*Lex*. ⊛**-φυτα**, τά, *plants of praise*, Ph.Epic.ap.Eus… 9.20.

**αἴνυμαι**, poet. Verb, only in pres. and impf. without augm. *take*, αἴνυτο τεύχε' ἀπ' ὤμων Il.11.580, 13.550; ἀπὸ πασσάλου αἰνυ… τόξον Od.21.53; χεῖρας αἰνύμεναι *taking hold of*, 22.500: c. ge… partit., τυρῶν αἰνυμένους 9.225: metaph., ἀλλά μ' Ὀδυσσῆος πό… αἴνυται a longing *seizes* me for him, 14.144, cf. Hes.*Sc*.41; *enjo… feed on*, καρπόν Simon.5.17. (Root αἰ-, as in ἐξ-αι-τος.)

**αἴνω**, aor. inf. ἦναι Hp.ap.Gal.19.103 (glossed by κόψαι), Phot.:… *sift, winnow*, Pherecr.183, cf. Hdn.Gr.2.930; v. ἀνέω. (Possibly f… ϝαν-yω, cf. *vannus*.)

⊛**αἴξ**, αἰγός, ὁ, ἡ: dat. pl. αἴγεσιν Il.10.486, αἰγεσσιν Choerob.*Theod*.323; also Boeot. ἤγυς, = αἰγοῖς, *IG*7.3171:—*goat*, mostly fem… μηκάδας αἶγας Od.9.124; λεύκας αἶγος Sapph.7 (s.v.l.), cf. Ar.*Nu*.7… Pl.*Lg*.639a, etc., but masc. in Od.14.106, 530; also τῶν αἰγῶν τῶ… τραγῶν Hdt.3.112:—once in Trag., S.*Fr*.793 (anap.). 2. αἲ… ἄγριος wild *goat*, prob. *ibex* (cf. αἴγαγρος), ἰξαλο… ἰοβάς Od.14.50; ἰξαλο… Il.4.105; αἶγες ὀρεσκῷοι Od.9.155; ἀγρότεραι 17.295:—proverbs… αἲξ οὐρανία in Com. as a source of mysterious and suspected wealth… in allusion to the horn of Amalthea, Cratin.244; οὐράνιον αἶγα πλουτοφόρον *Com.Adesp*.8; αἲξ τὴν μάχαιραν (sc. ηὗρε), of those who 'ask for trouble', Zen.1.27; αἲξ οὔπω τέτοκεν 'don't count your chickens before they are hatched', 1.42; αἲξ Σκυρία· ἐπὶ τῶν τὰς εὐεργεσίας ἀνατρεπόντων· ἀνατρέπει γὰρ τὸ ἀγγεῖον ἀμελχθεῖσα Diogenian.2.33; αἲξ ἐς θάλασσαν· ἀτενὲς ὁρᾷς, ἐπὶ τῶν φιληδούντων 3.8; κἂν αἲξ δάκῃ ἄνδρα πονηρόν 5.87; οὐ δύναμαι τὴν αἶγα φέρειν, ἐπί μοι θέτε τὸν βοῦν Plu.2.830a; ἐλεύθεραι αἶγες ἀρότρων· ἐπὶ τῶν βάρους τινὸς ἀπηλλαγμένων Zen.3.69; κατ' αἶγας ἀγρίας, = ἐς κόρακας, Hsch., Diogenian.5.49; νοῦσος, αἶγας ἐς ἀγριάδας τὴν ἀποπεμπόμεθα Call.*Aet*.3.1.13; αἰγῶν ὀνόματα, of worthless objects, Suid. 3. *the star Capella*, Arat.157. II. a water-bird, apparently of the *goose* kind, Arist.*HA*593$^b$23. III. *fiery meteor*, Arist.*Mete*.341$^b$3. IV. in pl., *waves*, Artem.2.12. (Att. αἴξ, acc. to Hdn.Gr.1.937.)

**ἄϊξ**, ἄϊκος [ᾱῐ], ἡ, (ἀΐσσω) = ἀϊκή, ἀνέμων ἄϊκες A.R.4.820.

**ἀΐξασκε**, Ion. and Ep. aor. of ἀΐσσω, Il.

**αἰξωνεύομαι**, Dep., *to be slanderous*, like the people of the Attic deme *Aexone*, Harp. s.v. Αἰξωνή.

**αἰολάομαι**, Pass., (αἰόλος) *to be restless*, Hp.*Mul*.2.174$^b$ (with vv.ll.).

**αἰόλειος**· ὁ ποικίλος, *EM*33.32.

**Αἰολεύς**, έως, ὁ, *Aeolian*; pl. Αἰολέες Hdt.1.28, Att. Αἰολεῖς or -ῆς Th.7.57:—hence Adj. **Αἰολικός**, ή, όν, *of* or *like the Aeolians*, Theoc.1.56 (v.l.); of the Aeolic dialect, A.D.*Adv*.193.15, al.: Comp. -ώτερον 194.8; of Aeolic metre, Heph.7.5. Adv. -κῶς S.E.*M*.1.78:—**Αἰόλιος**, α, ον, *in the Aeolian mode*, νόμος Plu.2.1132d:—fem. **Αἰολίς**, ίδος, Hes.*Op*.636, Hdt., etc.; of the Aeolian mode, Pratin.5; of the Aeolic dialect, A.D.*Adv*.155.11: Subst., Αἰολίς, ἡ, Id.*Synt*.309.25: poet. fem. **Αἰοληΐς**, Pi.*O*.1.102.

**αἰολέω**, = ποικίλλω, Pl.*Cra*.409a.

**αἰόλησις**, εως, ἡ, *rapid motion*, Sch.Pi.*P*.4.412.

**αἰολίας**, ου, ὁ, *a speckled fish*, Epich.44, Pl.Com.173.13; as Adj., αἰολίην κορακῖνον Numen.ap.Ath.7.308e.

**αἰολίδας**· ποικίλους, ταχεῖς, Hsch.

**αἰολ-ίζω**, = αἰόλλω: metaph., *trick out with false words*, μηδ' αἰόλιζε ταῦτα S.*Fr*.912. II. (Αἰολεύς) *compose in the Aeolian mode*, αἰ. τῷ μέλει Pratin.*Fr*.5; *speak Aeolic*, Dicaearch.2.2, Str.8.1.2, Plu.*Cim*.1; αἰολίζεται τὰ Ἀλκαίου ποιήματα A.D.*Synt*.279.52. III. = ἀολλίζω, Menecl.8, cf. Hsch. **-ισμα**, τό, *varied tones*, λύρας S.*Ichn*.319. **-ιστί**, *in the Aeolic dialect*, Str.8.1.2.

**αἰόλλω**, only pres., *to shift rapidly to and fro*, ὡς δ' ὅτε γαστέρ' ἀνὴρ.. αἰόλλῃ Od.20.27. II. *variegate*, Nic.*Th*.155:—Pass., *shift colour*, ὄμφακες αἰόλλονται Hes.*Sc*.399.

**αἰολό-βουλος**, ον, *wily*, Opp.*C*.3.449, al. ⊛**-βρόντης**, ου, ὁ, *wielder of the flashing thunderbolt*, Ζεὺς αἰ. Pi.*O*.9.42. **-δακρυς**, *with glistening tears*, Nonn.*D*.26.79, 43.365. **-δείκτης**, ου, ὁ, *showing himself in various forms*, of Phoebus; voc. αἰολόδεικτα, cj. for -δικτε, Orph.*H*.8.12. **-δειρος**, ον, *with sheeny neck*, Ibyc.8, cf. Opp.*C*.2.317, Nonn.*D*.12.76, al. **-δωρος**, ον, *bestowing various gifts*, Epimenid.19. **-θώρηξ**, ηκος, ὁ, *with glancing breastplate*, Il.4.489, *Hymn.Mag*.2(2).16. **-μητις**, ιος, ὁ, ἡ, *full of various wiles*, like αἰολόβουλος, Hes.*Th*.511, A.*Supp*.1036 (lyr.); also **-μήτης**, ου, ὁ, Hes.*Fr*.7 (s.v.l.). **-μίτρης**, ου, ὁ, *with glittering girdle*, Il.5.707. II. *with variegated mitre* or *turban*, Theoc.17.19. **-μολπος**, ον, *of varied strain*, σῦριγξ Nonn.*D*.40.223. **-μορφος**, ον, *of changeful form*, Orph.*H*.4.7, etc. ⊛**-νωτος**, ον, *with spangled back*, Opp.*H*.1.125. **-πεπλος**, ον, *with spangled robe*, Nonn.*D*.7.173. **-πους**, = στικτόπους, Sch.Opp.*C*.1.306. ⊛**-πρυμνος**, ον, *with gleaming stern*, νῆες B.1.4. **-πτέρυξ**, υγος, ὁ, ἡ, *quick-fluttering*, Telest.1.12 (dub.). ⊛**-πωλος**, ον, *with quick-moving steeds*, Il.3.185, *h.Ven*.137, Theoc.22.34.

⊛**αἰόλος**, η, ον, (ος, ον Arist.*Pr*., v. infr.) *quick-moving, nimble*, πόδας αἰόλος ἵππος Il.19.404; αἰόλαι εὐλαί *wriggling* worms, 22.509; σφῆκες μέσον αἰ. 12.167; ὄφις ib.208; οἶστρος Od.22.300, cf. Achae.48. 2. as epith. of armour, *glittering*, τεύχεα Il.5.295; σάκος 7.222, 16.107; κνώδων S.*Aj*.1025:—generally, *changeful of hue, sheeny*, δράκων Id.*Tr*.11; αἰόλα νύξ *star-spangled* night, ib.94 (lyr.); αἰ. πυρὸς κάσις smoke *flushed by* fire-light, A.*Th*.494; κύων αἰ. *speckled*, Call.*Dian*.91, etc.; αἰόλα σάρξ *discoloured*, S.*Ph*.1157 (lyr.); ὀφθαλμοί Adam.1.8, cf. 11. II. metaph., 1. *chequered*, αἰόλ' ἀνθρώπων κακά A.*Supp*.328;

...ngeful, ἰαχή E.*Ion*499 (lyr.); χορεία Ar.*Ra.*248 (lyr.); νόμος ...lest.2; αἰόλα φωνέων Theoc.16.44; αἰόλοι ἡμέραι *changeable* days, ...ist.*Pr.*941ᵇ24. 2. *shifty, slippery*, ἔπος Sol.11.7; ψεῦδος Pi.*N.* ...5; κέρδεσσι B.14.57; μηχάνημα λυγκὸς αἰολώτερον *Trag.Adesp.* ...9.—Chiefly poet.

B. proparox. Αἴολος, ου, ὁ, the lord of the winds, properly *the* ...*apid* or *the Changeable*, Od., etc. 2. name of a kind of σκάρος, ...c.Thyat.ap.Ath.7.320c. 3. Pythag., = 4, or ἐνιαυτός, *Theol.* ...r.22.

**αἰολό-στομος**, ον, *shifting in speech*, of an oracle, A.*Pr.*661. **-φοι-...ος**, v.l. for -φυλος, *subject to changeful madness*, Sch.Opp.*H.*2. ...0. **-φῦλος**, ον, *of divers kinds*, Opp.*H.*1.617. **-φωνος**, ον, ...*ith changeful notes*, ἀηδών Opp.*H.*1.728. **-χαίτης**, ου, ὁ, *with* ...*arti-coloured hair*, Eust.1645.5. **-χρως**, ωτος, ὁ, ἡ, *spangled*, νύξ ...ritias 19.4 D.

**αἰον-άω**, *moisten, foment*, Hp.*Nat.Mul.*44: fut. αἰονήσω *BKT*3. ...o: aor. 1 ᾐόνησα A.*Fr.*425:—Med., Lyc.1425. **-ημα**, ατος, τό, ...*omentation*, D.C.55.17, *EM*348.27. **-ησις**, εως, ἡ, *fomenting*, Hp.*Liqu.*1, Poll.4.180, Gal.10.781.

⊛ **ἀΐος**, = αἰών, Stes.in Cod.Bodl.Auct.T.II(11)f.90.

**ἀϊπάρθενος**, v. ἀειπάρθενος.

**αἰπεινής**, ές, = sq., *Epigr.Gr.*1069 (ἐπ- lapis) (Syria).

**αἰπεινός**, ή, όν, (αἰπύς) poet. Adj. *high, lofty*, of cities on heights, Ἴλιον Il.9.419, al., cf. A.*Fr.*284, S.*Tr.*858 (lyr.), *Ph.*1000; αἰθήρ B. 8.34; of Delphi, μαντεῖα E.*Ion*739; of mountain-tops, κάρηνα Il.2. 869, Od.6.123. II. metaph., 1. αἰ. λόγοι *hasty, wicked* words, Pi.*N.*5.32. 2. *hard to reach*, σοφίαι μὲν αἰ. Id.*O.*9.108.

⊛ **αἰπήεις**, εσσα, εν, = foreg., Il.21.87, A.R.2.721, *AP*7.273(Leon.).

**αἰπολ-έω**, only in pres. and impf., *tend goats*, Eup.13, Theoc.8.85; ἠπόλει ταῖς αἰξίν Lys.*Fr.*25:—Pass., ἄνευ βοτῆρος αἰπολούμεναι a flock *tended* by no herdsman, A.*Eu.*196. **-ή**, sine expl., Suid. **-ικός**, ή, όν, *of* or *for goatherds*, θάημα Theoc.1.56; τρύπανον Call.*Fr.*412; σύριγγες *AP*12.128(Mel.), cf. 9.27(Muc. Scaev.). ⊛**-ιον**, τό, *herd of goats*, αἰπόλι' αἰγῶν Il.11.679, al., cf. Hdt.1.126, S.*Aj.*375 (lyr.), Lxx *Pr.*24.66(30.31). II. *goat-pasture*, *AP*9.101(Alph.). ⊛**-ος**, ὁ, *goatherd*, αἰπόλος αἰγῶν Od.20.173, cf. Hdt.2.46, Pl.*Lg.*639a, Lxx *Am.*7.14. II. αἰπόλος· κάπηλος (Cypr.), Hsch.

⊛ **αἶπος**, εος, τό, (αἰπύς) *height, steep*, A.*Ag.*285,309, etc.; πρὸς αἶπος ὁδοιπορῆσαι, ἰέναι to toil up *hill*, Hp.*Morb.*2.51,70; πρὸς αἶπος ἔρχεται, metaph. of a difficult task, E.*Alc.*500: hence αἶ. (v.l. ἆπος) ἐκβαλὼν ὁδοῦ, i.e. the *weariness* of the ascent (expl. by Hsch. as κάματος), Id. *Ph.*851 (unless ἐκβαλών = 'forgetting').

⊛ **αἰπός**, ή, όν, *high, lofty*, of cities, Il.13.625, al.; αἰπὰ ῥέεθρα streams *falling sheer down*, Il.8.369, Hes.*Oxy.*1358.2.23: αἰπόν, τό, dub. in *Ath.Mitt.*31.138 (Athens).

**αἰπύ-δμητος**, ον, (δέμω) *high-built*, Coluth.235, Nonn.*D.*4.13. ⊛**-κερως**, ων, gen. ω, = ὑψίκερως, *EM*37.38, Suid. **-λοφος**, ον, *high-crested*, Nonn.*D.*2.379, etc. **-μήτης**, ου, ὁ, *with high thoughts*, Θέμιδος αἰπυμῆτα παῖ A.*Pr.*18. **-νοος**, ον, = foreg., of Osiris, *Hymn.Is.*19. **-νωτος**, ον, *on a high mountain-ridge*, of Dodona, A.*Pr.*830. **-πλᾰνής**, ές, *high-roaming*, Man.4.249.

⊛ **αἰπύς**, εῖα, ύ, Ep. and Lyr. Adj., rare in Trag., *high and steep*, in Hom. mostly of cities on rocky heights, esp. of Troy, Od.3.485, al.; of hills, Il.2.603; later of the sky, αἰθήρ B.3.36; οὐρανός S.*Aj.*845; *on high*, ποδῶν αἰ. λωή Hes.*Th.*682; ἁψαμένη βρόχον αἰπὺν *hanging high*, Od.11.278. 2. metaph., *sheer, utter*, αἰ. ὄλεθρος freq. in Hom., death being regarded as *the plunge from a high precipice*; φόνος αἰ. Od.4.843; θάνατος Pi.*O.*10(11).42; σκότος *utter* darkness, Id. *Fr.*228; of passions, etc., αἰ. χόλος *towering* wrath, Il.15.223; δόλος αἰ. *h.Merc.*66, Hes.*Th.*589; αἰπυτάτη σοφίη *AP*11.354 (Agath.); *arduous*, πόνος Il.11.601, 16.651; αἰπύ οἱ ἐσσεῖται 'twill be *hard work* for him, 13.317.

⊛ **αἶρα**, ἡ, *hammer*, αἰράων ἔργα *smith's* work, Call.*Fr.*129. 2. = ἀξίνη, Hsch. II. *darnel, Lolium temulentum*, Thphr.*HP* 1.5.2: in pl., Ar.*Fr.*412, Pherecr.188, Arist.*Somn.*456ᵇ30, Herod. 6.100, etc.

**αἰρέσια**, τά, prob. *dues paid on discharge of cargoes*, *IG*11(2).203*A*30 (Delos, iii B.C.), al.

**αἱρεσι-αρχέω**, Astrol., *dominate the 'condition'*, Rhetor.in *Cat.Cod. Astr.*1.146. **-άρχης**, ου, ὁ, *leader of a school*, S.E.*P.*3.245; esp. of a medical school, *IG*14.1759, Gal.6.372; *heresiarch*, Just.*Nov.* 42.1.1 (pl.). II. Astrol., *dominating the 'condition'* (cf. αἵρεσις B. II. 4), Paul.Al.*R.*3.

**αἱρέσιμος**, ον, *that can be taken*, X.*Cyr.*5.2.4.

**αἱρεσιομάχος**, ον, *fighting for a sect*, Ph.2.84.

⊛ **αἵρεσις**, εως, ἡ, *taking*, esp. of a town, Hdt.4.1, etc.; ἡ βασιλέος αἵ. *the taking by* the king, Id.9.3; ἐλπίζων ταχίστην -σιν ἔσεσθαι Th. 2.75; αἵ. δυνάμεως *acquisition* of power, Pl.*Grg.*513a:—generally, *taking, receiving*, ἐπιγενημάτων *PTeb.*27.66 (ii B.C.).

B. (αἱρέομαι) *choice*, αἵρεσίν τ' ἐμοὶ δίδου A.*Pr.*779; τῶνδε.. αἵρεσιν παρδίδωμι Pi.*N.*10.82; foll. by relat., αἵ. διδόναι ὁκοτέρην.., εἰ.., etc., Hdt.1.11, cf. D.22.19; αἵ. προτιθέναι, προβάλλειν, Pl.*Tht.*196c, *Sph.*245b; εἰ νέμοι τις αἵρεσιν S.*Aj.*265; αἵρεσιν λαβεῖν D.36.11; ποιεῖσθαι Isoc.7.19; αἵ. γίγνεταί τινι Th.2.61; οὐκ ἔχει αἵρεσιν it admits no *choice*, Plu.2.708b. 2. *choice, election* of magistrates, Th.8.89, cf. Arist.*Pol.*1266ᵃ26, al.; αἱρέσει, opp. κλήρῳ, 1300ᵃ19, etc. 3. *inclination, choice*, πρός τινα Philipp.ap.D.18.166, Plb.2.61.9, etc., cf. *IG*2.591*b*; opp. φυγή, Epicur.*Ep.*3p.62U.; περὶ αἱρέσεων καὶ φυγῶν, title of treatise by Epicurus. II. *purpose, course of action* or *thought*, like προαίρεσις, Pl.*Phdr.*256c; ἡ αἵ. τῆς πρεσβείας Aeschin. 2.11; αἵ. Ἑλληνική *the study* of Greek literature, Plb.39.1.3:—*conduct*, *PTeb.*28.10 (ii B.C.). 2. *system of philosophic principles*, or *those who profess such principles, sect, school*, Plb.5.93.8, D.S.2.29, Polystr.p.20W., D.H.*Amm.*1.7, *Comp.*2, al., cf. Cic.*Fam.*15.16.3; κατὰ τῶν αἱ., title of treatise by Antipater of Tarsus; περὶ αἱρέσεων, title of Menippean satire by Varro, cf. *Fr.*164; αἵρεσις πρὸς Γοργιππίδην, title of work by Chrysippus, D.L.7.191; esp. *religious party* or *sect*, of the Essenes, J.*BJ*2.8.1; the Sadducees and Pharisees, *Act.Ap.*5.17, 15.5, 26.5; the Christians, ib.24.5,14, 28.22, generally, *faction, party*, App.*BC*5.2. 3. *corps* of epheboi, *OGI* 176 (Egypt). 4. Astrol., *'condition'*, Ptol.*Tetr.*21; ἡ ἡμερινὴ αἵ. Vett.Val.1.13. III. *proposed condition, proposal*, D.H.3. 10. 2. *commission*, ἡ ἐπὶ τοὺς νέους αἵ. Pl.*Ax.*367a; *embassy, mission*, *IG*4.937 (Epid.). 3. *freewill offering*, opp. *vow*, Lxx *Le.*22.18, al. 4. *bid* at auction, τὴν ἀμείνονα αἵ. διδόντι παραδοθῆναι *POxy.*716.22 (ii A.D.), cf. 1630.8 (iii A.D.).

**αἱρεσιώτης**, ου, ὁ, *member of a sect*, Porph.*Abst.*4.11 (v.l. αἱρετισταῖς):—fem. **-ῶτις**, πολιτεία Suid.

**αἱρετ-έος**, α, ον, *to be chosen*, ὠφελήματα, opp. αἱρετὰ ἀγαθά, Chrysipp.*Stoic.*3.22,61, al. II. αἱρετέον, *one must choose*, Pl.*Grg.* 499e, Phld.*Rh.*1.287S., etc. **-ής**, ὁ, (αἱρέω) *searcher of archives*, αἱ. ἡγεμονικῆς βιβλιοθήκης *POxy.*1654.7 (ii A.D.). II. (αἱρέομαι) *one who chooses*, ἀγαθῶν Vett.Val.55.17. 2. Astrol., = αἱρετιστής 4, Sch.Ptol.*Tetr.*96. **-ίζω**, fut. -ιῶ Lxx *Ge.*30.20, *choose*, τινά Com.ap.Phot.p.54 R., cf. Hp.*Ep.*17, Lxx *Ge.* l.c., Babr. 61.5; ᾑρέτικα ἐν αὐτῷ εἶναί μου υἱόν 1*Ch.*28.6; ᾑρέτικέ σε οἰκοδομῆσαι ib.10; αἱρετίσας πατήρ *adoptive* father, *IPE*2.299 (Panticap.): abs., αἱρετίσαντος τοῦ θεοῦ *IG*3.74:—Med., Lxx *Ps.*118(119).30, al., Aesop.53, Ctes.*Fr.*29.9. ⊛**-ικός**, ή, όν, (αἱρέω) *able to choose*, Pl.*Def.* 412a; *due to choice*, οἰκείωσις Hierocl.p.41.5A., Anon.*in Tht.*7. 40. 2. *factious*, *Ep.Tit.*3.10. 3. Astrol., *belonging to the 'condition'*, Paul.Al.*Q.*2. 4. Adv. -κῶς *from choice*, D.L.7.126, Hierocl. p.41.7A. **-ίς**, ίδος, ἡ, *one who chooses*, Lxx *Wi.*8.4. ⊛**-ιστής**, οῦ, ὁ, *one who chooses*, τινός Plb.22.6.11. 2. *partisan*, τῶν τρόπων τινός Philem.131, cf. Plb.1.79.9, etc.; *founder of a philosophical school*, D.L.9.6; τῶν λόγων *Vit.Philonid.*p.12C. 3. *sectarian*, J.*BJ*2.8.2, Iamb.*Protr.*21.κα'. 4. Astrol., *belonging to the 'condition'*, Jul.Laod.in *Cat.Cod.Astr.*5(1).183. **-ός**, ή, όν, *that may be taken* or *conquered*, δόλῳ Hdt.4.201; *to be understood*, Pl.*Phd.* 81b. II. (αἱρέομαι) *to be chosen, eligible*, opp. φευκτός, Pl.*Phlb.* 21d sq., Arist.*EN*1097ᵃ32, etc.: freq. in Comp. or Sup., Hdt.1.126, 156, al.; ζόης πονηρᾶς θάνατος αἱρετώτερος A.*Fr.*401. 2. *chosen, elected*, esp. opp. κληρωτός, Isoc.12.154, Pl.*Lg.*759b, Arist.*Pol.*1294ᵇ9, cf. Pl.*Lg.*915c, Aeschin.3.13; αἱ. βασιλῆς Pl.*Mx.*238d; τυραννὶς Arist.*Pol.*1285ᵃ31:—αἱ. ἄνδρες *commissioners*, Plu.*Lyc.*26; οἱ αἱ. X. *An.*1.3.21: = Lat. *optiones*, Lyd.*Mag.*1.46. 3. *that may be chosen*, opp. αἱρετέος (q.v.), Chrysipp.*Stoic.*3.22.

⊛ **αἱρέω**, impf. ᾕρεον Il.24.579, Ion. αἵρεον Hdt.6.31, but contr. ᾕρει even in Il.17.463, ᾕρευν Hes.*Sc.*302: fut. αἱρήσω Il.9.28, etc.: aor. 1 ᾕρησα late (ἀν-) Q.S.4.40, etc.: pf. ᾕρηκα A.*Ag.*267, Th.1.61, etc., Ion. ἀραίρηκα or αἵρηκα (ἀν-) Hdt.5.102: plpf. ἀραιρήκεε 3.39:—Med., fut. αἱρήσομαι Il.10.235, etc.: aor. 1 ᾑρησάμην Plb.38.13.7 s.v.l., Gal.19.53, etc.: pf. in med. sense ᾕρημαι Ar.*Av.*1577, X.*An.*5.6.12, D.2.15, etc.: 3 pl. plpf. ᾕρηντο Th.1.62:—Pass., fut. αἱρεθήσομαι Hdt. 2.13, Pl.*Mx.*234b; rarely ᾑρήσομαι Id.*Prt.*338c: aor. ᾑρέθην and pf. ᾕρημαι D.20.146, al.; pf. part. ἀραιρημένος Hdt.4.66: plpf. ᾕρητο X. *An.*3.2.1, ἀραίρητο Hdt.1.191, etc.—From √ἑλ-: fut. ἑλῶ only late (δι-) *Test.Epict.*6.18, (ἀν-) D.H.11.18, (καθ-) *APl.*4.334(Antiphil.): aor. 1 εἷλα (ἀν-) *Act.Ap.*2.23, (ἀν-) *Epigr.Gr.*314.24(Smyrna): elsewh. aor. 2 εἷλον Il.10.561, etc., Ep. ἕλον 17.321, Ion. ἕλεσκε 24.752:—Med., fut. ἑλοῦμαι D.H.4.75, (ἀφ-) Timostr.5, (δι-) D.H.4.60, (ἐξ-) Alciphr.1.9: aor. 1 εἱλάμην *Epigr.Gr.*314.5 (Smyrna), (ἀφ-) v.l. in Ath.12.546a, (δι-) *AP*9.56 (Phil.): elsewh. aor. 2 εἱλόμην Il.16.139, etc., 2 sg. ἥλεο Sapph.*Oxy.*1787.6.3:—Cret. forms αἰλεθῇ *Leg.Gort.* 2.21, ἀν-αιλῆθαι ib.7.10, al.:—the etym. is doubtful, and ἀγρέω (q.v.) prob. has a difft. root.

A. Act., *take with the hand, grasp, seize*, αἱ. τι ἐν χερσίν Od.4.66; αἱ. τινὰ χειρός *to take* one by the hand, Il.1.323; κόμης τινά ib.197; μ' ἑλὼν ἐπὶ μάστακα χερσίν Od.23.76: part. ἑλών adverbially, κατακτεῖναί μ' ἑλὼν S.*Ant.*497; ἄξω ἑλών Il.1.139, cf. Pi.*O.*7.1; but ἔνθεν ἑλών *having taken up* [the song], Od.8.500. 2. *take away*, ἀπ' ἀπήνης ᾕρεον ἄποινα Il.24.579. II. *take, get into one's power*, νῆας ib.13.42; esp. *take* a city, 2.37, S.*Ph.*347, etc.; *overpower, kill*, Il.4.457, etc.; ἕλοιμί κεν ἤ κε ἁλοίην 22.253:—freq. of passions, etc., *come upon, seize*, χόλος Il.18.322; ἵμερος 3.446; ὕπνος 10.193; λήθη 2.34, etc.: c. dupl.acc., τὸν δ' ἄτη φρένας εἷλε 16.805; of disease, Pl.*Tht.*142b. 2. *catch, take*, ζωὸν ἑλεῖν Il.21.102; *take in hunting*, Hes.*Sc.*302, Hdt. 1.36, etc.; *overtake*, in a race, Il.23.345; *get into one's power, entrap*, S.*OC*764, etc.; in good sense, *win over*, X.*Mem.*2.3.16, cf. 3.11.11, Pl.*Ly.*205e, etc. b. c. part., *catch, detect* one doing a thing, S. *Ant.*385,655; ἐπ' αὐτοφώρῳ ἑλεῖν E.*Ion*1214; φῶρα ἐπὶ κλοπῇ ἑλεῖν Pl.*Lg.*874b. 3. generally, *win, gain*, κῦδος Il.17.321; στεφάνους Pi.*P.*3.74, etc.; esp. in games, Ἴσθμι' ἑλὼν πύξ Simon.158; with double sense, *overcome* and *win*, ἑλέτην δίφρον τε καὶ ἀνέρε Il.11.328; ἕλεν Οἰνομάου βίαν παρθένον τε σύνευνον Pi.*O.*1.88, cf. S.*Tr.*353:—Pass., ἀγὼν ᾑρέθη the fight *was won*, S.*OC*1148. b. generally, *get, obtain*, Pl.*R.*359a, *Ti.*64b, etc. 4. as law-term, *convict*, τινά τινος Ar.*Nu.*591, Is.9.36, Aeschin.3.156; εἷλέ σ' ἡ Δίκη E.

*Heracl.*941, cf. *Supp.*608: c. part., αἱ. τινὰ κλέπτοντα *to convict* of theft, Ar.*Eq.*829, Pl.*Lg.*941d; ᾑρῆσθαι κλοπεύς (sc. ὤν) S.*Ant.*493, cf. 406. **b.** αἱ. δίκην, γραφὴν *get a verdict for conviction*, Antipho 2.1.5, etc.; also ἑλεῖν τινα *obtain a conviction against* one, Is.7.13; ἑλεῖν τὰ διαμαρτυρηθέντα *convict* the evidence of falsehood, Isoc.18.15. **c.** abs., *get a conviction*, οἱ ἑλόντες, opp. οἱ ἑαλωκότες, D.21.11; δολίοις ἕλε Κύπρις λόγοις Aphrodite *won her cause*.., E.*Andr.*289, cf. Pl.*Lg.*762b, etc. **d.** of a thing or circumstances which *convict*, τοῦτ' ἔστιν ὃ ἐμὲ αἱρεῖ Id.*Ap.*28a. **5.** ὁ λόγος αἱρέει reason or the reason of the thing *proves*, Hdt.2.33: c. acc. pers., reason *persuades* one, i.e. it *seems good* to one, Id.1.132, 7.41; ὡς ἐμὴ γνώμη αἱ. Hdt.2.43; ὅπῃ ὁ λόγος αἱ. βέλτιστ' ἂν ἔχειν Pl.*R.*604c, cf. *Lg.*663d: c. inf., *R.*440b; ὁ αἱρῶν λόγος Chrysipp.*Stoic.*3.92; αἱρεῖ alone, *proves*, Plu.2.651b. **b.** τὸ αἱροῦν the sum *due*, *PRyl.*167.25 (i A.D.); τὰ αἱροῦντα [τάλαντα] *PGrenf.*2.23.14 (ii B.C.), *PRyl.*88.19 (ii A.D.). **III.** *grasp with the mind, understand*, Pl.*Phlb.*17e, 20d, *Plt.*282d.

**B.** Med., with pf. ᾕρημαι (v. supr.), *take for oneself*, ἔγχος ἑλέσθαι *take one's* spear, Il.16.140, etc.; ἐκ γαίας λίθον A.*Fr.*199; δόρπον, δεῖπνον *take one's* supper, Il.7.370, 2.399; πιέειν δ' οὐκ εἶχεν ἑλέσθαι Od.11.584; Τρωσὶν.. ὅρκον ἑλ. *obtain* it from.., Il.22.119; and so in most senses of the Act., with the reflexive force added. **II.** *take to oneself, choose*, ἕταρον Il.10.235, cf. 9.139, Od.16.149, etc.; *prefer*, τι πρό τινος Hdt.1.87; τι ἀντί τινος X.*An.*1.7.3, D.2.15; τί τινος S.*Ph.*1101, cf. Theoc.11.49. **b.** c. inf., *prefer* to do, Hdt. 1.11, etc.; ἑλέσθαι μᾶλλον τεθνάναι X.*Mem.*1.2.16, cf. Pl.*Ap.*38e; μᾶλλον ἂν ἕλοιτό μ' ἢ τοὺς πάντας Ἀργείους λαβεῖν S.*Ph.*47: without μᾶλλον, Pi.*N.*10.59, Lys.2.62. **c.** αἱ. εἰ.. *to be content* if.., *AP* 12.68 (Mel.). **2.** αἱ. τά τινων *take* another's part, *join* their *party*, Th.3.63, etc.; αἱ. γνώμην *to adopt* an opinion, Hdt.4.137. **3.** *choose by vote, elect* to an office, αἱ. τινὰ δικαστήν, στρατηγόν, etc., Id.1.96, Eup.117, etc.; τινὰς ἀριστίνδην Lex ap.D.43.57; αἱ. τινὰ ἐπ' ἀρχήν Pl.*Men.*90b; αἱ. τινὰ ἄρχειν Id.*Ap.*28e, cf. Il.2.127.

**C.** Pass., *to be taken*, Hdt.1.185,191, 9.102; more commonly ἁλίσκομαι. **2.** v. supr. A. II.3. **II.** Pass. to med. sense, *to be chosen*, in pf. ᾕρημαι A.*Ag.*1209, etc.; Ion. ἀραίρημαι Hdt.7.118, 172,173, al.; στρατηγεῖν ᾑρημένος X.*Mem.*3.2.1; ἐπ' ἀρχῆς ᾑρῆσθαι ib.3.3.2; ἐπὶ τὴν τῶν παίδων ἀρχήν Pl.*Lg.*809a; τοῦ ἔτους.. ᾑρημένοι *elected* for the year.., *IGRom.*3.1422 (Bithyn.):—aor. ᾑρέθην is always so used, A.*Th.*505, Ar.*Av.*799, Th.7.31, etc.; pres. rarely, αἱροῦνται πρεσβευταί *are chosen*, Arist.*Pol.*1299$^a$19, cf. And.4.16.

**αἱρησιτείχης**, ους, ὁ, *taker of cities*, name of play by Diphilus.

**αἵρινος**, η, ον, *of darnel*, ἄλευρον Dsc.2.112, Archig.ap.Orib.8.46.3; ἄλητα Aret.*CA*2.6.

**αἰρο-λογέω**, *clear of darnel*, in Pass., *IG*5(2).514.15 (Lycosura, ii B.C.). **-πινον**, τό, *sieve* (ἐν ᾧ πυροὶ σήθονται ὑπὲρ τοῦ τὰς αἴρας διελθεῖν), Ar.*Fr.*480.

**ἄϊρος**, ὁ, only in phrase Ἶρος ἄϊρος *Irus, unhappy Irus*, Od. 18.73.

**αἴρω**, v. ἀείρω.

⊛ **αἰρώδης**, ες, *apt to be infested with darnel*, πυρός Thphr.*HP*8. 4.6.

⊛ **Αἶσα**, ἡ, like Μοῖρα, the divinity *who dispenses to every one his lot* or *destiny*, ἅσσα οἱ Αἶ. γιγνομένῳ ἐπένησε Il.20.127, cf. Od.7.197; Αἶ. φασγανουργός A.*Ch.*648 (lyr.). **II.** as Appellat., **1.** *decree, dispensation* of a god, τετιμῆσθαι Διὸς αἴσῃ Il.9.608; ὑπὲρ Διὸς αἶσαν 17.321, cf. 6.487; δαίμονος αἶσα κακή Od.11.61; τεὰν κατ' αἶσαν thanks to the *destiny decreed* by thee, Pi.*N.*3.16; θεοῦ αἶσα E.*Andr.* 1203 (lyr.):—κατ' αἶσαν *fitly, duly*, Il.10.445, etc.; κατ' αἶσαν, οὐδ' ὑπὲρ αἶσαν Il.6.333, cf. B.9.32; ἐν αἴσᾳ A.*Supp.*545 (lyr.); opp. παρ' αἶσαν Pi.*P.*8.13. **2.** *one's lot, destiny*, οὐ γάρ οἱ τῇδ' αἶσα.. ὀλέσθαι, ἀλλ' ἔτι οἱ μοῖρ' ἐστί.. Od.5.113: c. inf., ἔτι γάρ νύ μοι αἶσα βιῶναι 14. 359, cf. 13.306, al.; κακῇ αἴσῃ.. ἑλόμην by ill *luck*, Il.5.209; ἀσφαλεῖ σὺν αἴσᾳ B.12.66; τὸν αἶσ' ἄπλατος ἴσχει S.*Aj.*256 (lyr.), cf. *AP*7. 624 (Diod.). **3.** generally, *share in* a thing, ληΐδος, ἐλπίδος, αἶ., Od.5.40, 19.84; χθονός Pi.*P.*9.56; at a common meal (Argive), Hegesand.31; τῶ Διὸς τῶ Ϝοίνω αἶ. *Inscr.Cypr.*148; λαχεῖν αἶ. *IG*5 (2).40 (Tegea); for the prov. ἐν καρὸς αἴσῃ v.s. κάρ.—Ep., Lyr., and Trag., but only in lyr. in S. and E.

**αἴσακος**, ὁ, *branch of myrtle* or *laurel*, handed by one to another at table as a challenge to sing, Plu.2.615b, Hsch. **II.** = ἐριθακός, *EM*38.49.

**αἰσάλων**, ωνος, ὁ, a kind of hawk, prob. *merlin, Falco aesalon*, Arist.*HA*609$^b$8, Plin.*HN*10.205:—**αἰσάρων**, Hsch.

⊛ **αἰσθ-άνομαι** (cf. αἴσθομαι), Ion. 3 pl. opt. αἰσθανοίατο Ar.*Pax*209: impf. ᾐσθανόμην: fut. αἰσθήσομαι S.*Ph.*75, etc.; later αἰσθανθήσομαι Lxx *Is.*49.26; αἰσθηθήσομαι ib.33.11: aor. 2 ᾐσθόμην: pf. ᾔσθημαι: later, aor. 1 ᾐσθησάμην Sch.Arat.418; ᾐσθήθην Lxx *Jb.*40.18: (cf. ἀΐω):—*perceive, apprehend by the senses*, Alcmaeon 1$^a$, Hdt.3.87, Democr.11, etc.; τῇ ὄψει, τῇ ἁφῇ, τῇ ἀκοῇ Hp.*Off.*1; αἰ. τῇ ἀκοῇ, τῇ ὀσμῇ, Th.6.17, X.*Mem.*3.11.8; *see*, S.*Ph.*75, etc.; *hear*, βοήν Id.*Aj.* 1318, cf. *Ph.*252; οὐκ εἶδον αὐτόν, ᾐσθόμην δ' ἔτ' ὄντα νιν ib.445; τινὸς ὑποστενούσης αἰ. Id.*El.*79; βοῆς E.*Hipp.*603, etc. **2.** of mental perception, *perceive, understand*, τῇ γνώμῃ αἰσθέσθαι Hp.*Off.*1; τὸ πραχθέν Lys.9.4, cf. Th.3.36, etc.:—*hear, learn*, v. infr. II: abs., αἰσθάνει *you are right*, E.*Or.*752; ᾔσθημαι, in parenthesis, Id.*Hipp.* 1403. **II.** Construct. in both senses, c. gen., *take notice of, have perception of*, τῶν κακῶν E.*Tr.*638 s.v.l.; rarely περί τινος Th.1. 70; αἰ. ὑπό τινος *learn* from one, Id.5.2; διά τινος Pl.*Tht.*184e, al.: c. acc., S.*El.*89, *Ph.*252, E.*Hel.*653,764, etc.:—freq. with part. agreeing with subject, αἰσθάνομαι κάμνων Th.2.51; αἰσθώμεθα γελοῖοι ὄν[…] Pl.*Thg.*122c; agreeing with object, τυράννους ἐκπεσόντας ᾐσθό[…] A.*Pr.*957, cf. Th.1.47, etc.; ἤδη τινῶν ᾐσθόμην ἀχθομένων Lys.16.[…] cf. Pl.*Ap.*22c; ᾐσθόμην τεχνωμένου Ar.*V.*176: less freq. c. acc. [...] inf., Th.6.59; αἰ. ὅτι..: Id.5.2, Pl.*Ap.*21e, etc.; ᾔσθετο ὅτι τὸ στρ[…] τευμα ἦν.. X.*An.*1.2.21; αἰ. ὡς.. ib.3.1.40, etc.; οὕνεκα.. S.[…] 1477:—abs., αἰσθανόμενος *having full possession of one's facultie[s]* τῇ ἡλικίᾳ Th.5.26; *sensible, of keen perception*, καὶ μετρίως αἰσθ[…] νομένῳ φανερόν X.*Mem.*4.1.1, cf. Th.1.71, Pl.*R.*360d.—The Pas[s.] is supplied by αἴσθησιν παρέχω, cf. αἴσθησις I. **III.** *displa[y …] feeling*, Arist.*Po.*1454$^b$37. **-ημα**, ατος, τό, *object of sensation*, Aris[t.] *APo.*99$^b$37, *Metaph.*1010$^b$32, Plot.4.3.25 and 29; τὸ νοεῖν γέγονε[…] αἰσθήμασι μόνοις Phld.*D.*1.13, etc. **II.** *sense* or *perception of* [a] thing, κακῶν E.*IA*1243. **-ησίη**, ἡ, = sq., Aret.*SD*1.1. **-ησις**, εως, ἡ, *sense-perception, sensation*, Philol.13, Archyt.1, Arist.*APo.* 99$^b$35; τοῦ σώματος ἡ αἴ. Hp.*VM*9; πρὸς αἴσθησιν *perceptibly*, Ptol. *Alm.*1.10, etc.: in pl., *the senses*, Democr.9, al.; δι' ἑπτὰ σχημάτω[ν] αἱ αἰ. Hp.*Vict.*1.23, cf. Pl.*Tht.*156b, etc.: in sg. of the several senses, ἡ τοῦ ὁρᾶν αἴ. Id.*R.*507e; ἀπ' ὄψεως ἤ τινος ἄλλης αἰ. Id.*Phlb.*39b; *organ* or *seat of sensation*, X.*Mem.*1.4.6; πάσας τὰς αἰ. ἐν τῇ κεφαλῇ εἶναι Arist.*Fr.*95, cf. *Pr.*958$^b$16; αἴ. πημάτων *perception, sense of*.., E.*El.*290; esp. of *pain*, Vett.Val.113.10, al.; also of the mind, *perception, knowledge* of a thing, ἐν αἰ. γενέσθαι τινός Plu.*Luc.*11, etc.; αἴ. ἔχειν τινός, = αἰσθάνεσθαί τινος, have *a perception of* a thing, Pl.*Ap.* 40c; περὶ ὑμῶν *Tht.*192b; πᾶσαν αἴσθησιν αἰσθάνεσθαι *Phdr.*240d; λαμβάνειν Isoc.1.47; ἐν αἰ. εἶναι Plot.4.7.15:—also of things, αἴσθησιν ἔχειν give *a perception*, i.e. become *perceptible*, serving as Pass. to αἰσθάνομαι, Th.2.61; more freq. αἴσθησιν παρέχειν Id.3.22, X.*An.*4.6. 13, etc.; αἴ. ποιῆσαί τινι Antipho 5.44, cf. D.10.7; αἴ. παρέχειν τινός furnish *the means of observing*, Th.2.50; αἴ. ἐγένετο περί τινος D.48. 16. **II.** in object. sense, *impressions of sense*, Arist.*Metaph.*980$^a$22; *stage-effects*, *Po.*1454$^b$16; αἰσθήσεις θεῶν *visible appearances* of the gods, Pl.*Phd.*111b. **2.** *display of feeling*, Arist.*Rh.*1386$^a$32 (v.l.). **3.** in hunting, *scent*, X.*Cyn.*3.5 (pl.).—Confined to Prose in early writers, exc. E. l.c., Antiph.196.5. **-ητήριον**, τό, *organ of sense*, Hp. *Vict.*4.86, Arist.*de An.*421$^b$32, etc.; τὰ αἰ., opp. ἡ διάνοια, Epicur. *Ep.*1 p.12 U.; ἐπὰν ᾖ καθαρὰ τἀσθητήρια Macho 2; τὰ αἰ. *the faculties*, Lxx 4*Ma.*2.22, cf. *Ep.Heb.*5.14. **-ητής**, οῦ, ὁ, *one who perceives*, Pl.*Tht.*160d. **-ητικός**, ή, όν, *of* or *for sense-perception, sensitive, perceptive*, Pl.*Ti.*67a, etc.; ζῷα -κώτερα Thphr.*Sens.*29; αἰ. ἀναθυμίασις, of the soul, Zeno *Stoic.*1.39; τὸ αἰ. [τῆς ψυχῆς] Diog.Oen.*Fr.*39; ζωὴ αἰ. Arist.*EN*1098$^a$2; *quick*, γραῦς Alex.65. Adv. αἰσθητικῶς, ἔχειν to be *quick of perception*, Arist.*EE*1230$^b$37; κινεῖσθαι Arr.*Epict.*1.14. 7, S.E.*M.*7.356; αἰ. ἔχειν ἑαυτοῦ, c. part., to be *conscious* of oneself doing, Ael.*VH*14.23; αἰ. γιγνώσκειν Procl.*in Prm.*p.754 S. **II.** of things, *perceptible*, Plu.2.90b. **-ητός**, ή, όν, and ός, όν Pl.*Men.* 76d; *sensible, perceptible*, opp. νοητός, Id.*Plt.*285e, etc.; τὸ αἰ. *object of sensation* or *perception*, Id.*Ti.*37b, Arist.*de An.*431$^b$22, cf. *Metaph.* 999$^b$4. Adv. -τῶς Id.*Col.*793$^b$27, Posidon.95, Plu.2.953c; in act. sense, Ascl.*in Metaph.*277.13.

**αἴσθομαι**, sometimes in good Mss. as v.l. for αἰσθάνομαι, as Th.5. 26, Isoc.3.5, Pl.*R.*608a.

⊛ **ἀΐσθω**, (ἄημι) Ep. Verb, *breathe out*, θυμὸν ἄϊσθε *he was giving up the ghost*, Il.20.403, cf. 16.468.

⊛ **αἰσιμία**, ἡ, *due apportionment*, αἰσιμίαις πλούτου A.*Eu.*996.

**αἰσιμνάτας**, v. αἰσυμνήτης.

**αἴσιμος**, ον, also η, ον Od.23.14: (αἶσα):—Ep. Adj. *appointed by the will of the gods, destined*, αἴ. ἦμαρ the *fatal* day of death, Il.8.72, Bacis ap.Hdt.9.43, etc.; αἴσιμόν ἐστι Il.21.291. **II.** *agreeable to the decree of fate, meet, fitting*, αἴσιμα εἰπεῖν Od.22.46; αἴσιμα εἰδώς, opp. αἴσυλα ῥέζειν, 2.231; φρένας αἰσίμη *right*-minded, 23.14; αἴσιμα πίνειν to drink *in decent measure*, 21.294.

⊛ **αἰσιμῶ**, *expend*, Suid. **αἰσ⟨ιμ⟩ώματα**, *expenses*, Hsch.

**αἰσιομήτης**, ὁ, *of right counsel*, Zonar.

**αἰσιόομαι**, Med., *take as a good omen, think lucky*, Plu.2.774c, App.*BC*5.97: c. inf., *Mith.*20.

**αἰσιοποιέω**, *secundo*, and Pass., *prosperabitur*, *Gloss.*

⊛ **αἴσιος**, ον, also α, ον Pi.*N.*9.18, E.*Ion*421: (αἶσα):—poet. Adj. *auspicious, opportune*, ὁδοιπόρος Il.24.376, cf. A.*Ag.*104 (lyr.), S. *OC*34; ἡμέρα E. l.c.; αἴ. ἐν φιλότητι *IG*14.2068.9:—freq. of omens, αἰσία ὄρνις Pi. l.c., cf. S.*OT*52; ἀετός X.*Cyr.*2.4.19; ἄνεμος App.*Mith.*29; ὥρα Id.*Syr.*58 (Comp.). Adv. -ίως E.*Ion*410, Timae. 114. **II.** *meet, right*, αἴσιος ὁλκή, Lat. *justum pondus*, Nic.*Th.*93; αἴ. ἐμβολή Just.*Edict.*13.4.1.

**αἶσις**, ἡ, = κεῦσις, Hdn.*Epim.*37. **ἀϊσόμενος**· φραξάμενος, Hsch. **ἀΐσονες**· φραγμοί, Id.

**ἄϊσος**, ον, = ἄνισος, *unlike, unequal*, Pi.*I.*7(6).43.

⊛ **ἀΐσσω**, Hom., Hdt.; in Pi. and Trag. contr. **ᾄσσω**; Att. **ᾄττω**, or **ἄττω** (without ι subscr.) in Mss. of Pl., etc.: impf. ἤϊσσον Il.18. 506, Ion. ἀΐσσεσκον (παρ-) A.R.2.276, Att. ᾖσσον A.*Pr.*676, E.*Ph.* 1382: fut. ἀΐξω (ὑπ-) Il.21.126, Att. ᾄξω E.*Hec.*1106 (lyr.), Ar. *Nu.*1299: aor. ἤϊξα Hom., B.12.144, (δι-) Hdt.4.134; Dor. ᾇξα B.9.23 (prob.); Att. and Trag. ᾖξα A.*Pr.*837, S.*OC*890, etc., part. ᾄξαντες Is.4.10; Ion. ἀΐξασκον Il.23.369:—**Med.**, aor. ἀΐξασθαι Il.22. 195:—**Pass.**, Hom.: aor. ἠΐχθην, ἀΐχθην Il. (v. infr.).—Trag. use the uncontr. forms in lyr., S.*OC*1499, *Tr.*843, E.*Tr.*156,1086, *Supp.* 962; once in trim., E.*Hec.*31. Poet., chiefly Ep., Verb, rarely found in Prose:—of rapid motion, *shoot, dart, glance*, as light, αὐγή Il.18.212, etc.; νόος 15.80; διά μου κεφαλῆς ᾄσσουσ' ὀδύναι E.*Hipp.*

51:—of one *darting upon* his enemy, ἀΐσσειν ἔγχεϊ, φασγάνῳ, ποσί, Il.11.484, 5.81, 17.460, etc.; τοῖσιν (sc. σκήπτροισιν) 18.506; the *rapid flight* of birds, 23.868, etc.; ἤϊξεν πέτεσθαι 21.247; of ghosts *gliding about*, τοὶ δὲ σκιαὶ ἀΐσσουσιν Od.10.495; of javelins, Il. 657; of a tree, *shoot up*, Pi.*N*.8.40; of veins, etc., in the body, Hp.*Epid*.2.4.1, cf. *Morb*.4.54: c. acc. cogn., ἦξαν δράμημα E.*Ph.* 379; κέλευθον A.*Pr*.837: once in aor. Med., ἀντίον ἀΐξασθαι Il.22. 195: also in Pass., [ἔγχος] ὦσεν.. ἐτώσιον ἀϊχθῆναι Il.5.854; ἐς οὐρανὸν ἀϊχθήτην 24.97; ἐκ χειρῶν ἡνία ἠΐχθησαν *slipped* from his hands, 16.404; ἀμφὶ δὲ χαῖται ὤμοις ἀΐσσονται 6.510; κόμη δι' αὔρας.. ᾄσσεται S.*OC*1261; *shoot forth*, of limbs, Emp.29:—Act., *to be driven*, πνευμάτων ὑπὸ δυσχίμων ἄΐσσω E.*Supp*.962. 2. later, *turn eagerly to* a thing, *be eager after*, εἴς τι Id.*Ion*328; ἐπὶ τά τινος ᾄξαντες *making onslaught on* his property, Is.4.10; πρὸς τὰ πολιτικὰ ᾄ. Pl.*Alc*.1.118b, cf. Phld. *Mus*.p.12K., Plu.2.87d: c. inf., εἰπεῖν Pl.*Lg*.709a. II. trans., αὔραν.. ἀΐσσων *putting* the air *in motion* (with a fan), E.*Or*.1430; ἦξεν χέρα S.*Aj*.40. [ᾱ in Hom., save in the compd. ὑπαΐξει Il.21. 126, cf. A.R.3.1302; ᾰ Lyr., Trag. (exc. E.*Tr*.1086), Arat.334.]

**ἀϊστί**, Adv. of sq., Suid.

**ἄϊστος**, ον, (ἰδεῖν):—poet. Adj. *unseen*, καί κέ μ' ἄ. ἀπ' αἰθέρος ἔμβαλε πόντῳ Il.14.258; κεῖνον μὲν ἄ. ἐποίησαν περὶ πάντων Od.1.235; οἴχετ' ἄ., ἄπυστος ib.242; ὤλετ' ἄκλαυστος, ἄϊστος A.*Eu*.565; βωμοὶ δ' ἄϊστοι Id.*Pers*.811; ἐν ἀΐστοις τελέθων Id.*Ag*.466; ἀποτρέψειεν ἄϊστον ὕβριν (prolept.) Id.*Supp*.881; ἄ. ἀείραο A.R.4.746. Adv. ἀΐστως, θυμὸν ὀλέσσαν *utterly*, Man.3.263, cf. 28. II. Act., *unconscious of*, ἄτας ἐμᾶς ἄϊστος E.*Tr*.1314, cf. 1321.

**ἀϊστοσύνη**, ἡ, = ἀπώλεια, *EM*43.21; = *coniventia*, *Gloss.*

**ἀϊστόω**: fut. -ώσω Hdt.3.69: aor. ἠΐστωσα ib.127, contr. ἠστ- (v. infr.):—Med., aor. ἀϊστώσαντο Orph.*A*.473:—poet. Verb, not in Il., used by Hdt., and once in Pl., *make unseen*, *make away with*, *destroy*, ὥς ἔμ' ἀϊστώσειαν Od.20.79; πῦρ.. ἀϊστωσεν ὕλαν Pi.*P*.3.37; ἀϊστώσας γένος τὸ πᾶν A.*Pr*.234, cf. Pl.*Prt*.321a; πατρίδ' ἠστώσας δόρει S.*Aj*.515; κόρον ἀϊστώσας πυρί Id.*Fr*.536; τὰ πρὶν δὲ πελώρια.. ἀϊστοῖ A.*Pr*.151; ἀϊστώσει μιν Hdt.3.69; δύο ἡμέων ἠΐστωσε ib. 127:—Pass., οἱ δ' ἅμ' ἀϊστώθησαν ἀολλέες Od.10.259.

**ἀΐστωρ**, ορος, ὁ, ἡ, *unknowing*, *unaware*, ἀΐστωρ ὢν αὐτός Pl.*Lg*. 845b: c. gen., μάχης E.*Andr*.682.

**ἀϊστωτήριος**, ον, *destructive*, Lyc.71.

**αἰσῠητήρ**, ῆρος, ὁ, v.l. for αἰσυμνητήρ (q.v.), Il.24.347, expl. as ἐντρεχής, νεανίας, or νομεύς (Nic.); cf. pr. n. Αἰσυήτης in Il.

**αἰσῠλοεργός**, όν, = αἴσυλα ῥέζων, *ill-doing*, Max.368; read by Aristarch. in Il.5.403 for ὀβριμοεργός, cf. Clem.Al.*Protr*.2.33.

**αἴσῠλος**, ον, *unseemly, evil, godless*, αἴσυλα ῥέζων Il.5.403 (cf. αἰσιμος); μυθήσασθαι 20.202; οἶδε *h.Merc*.164, cf. *AP*7.624 (Diod.).

⊛**αἰσυμν-άω**, Dor. **αἰσιμνάω**, *rule over*, αἰσυμνᾷ χθονὸς E.*Med*.19; *preside over*, μολπῶν *SIG*57.1 (Miletus); generally, *rule*, οὐ δίκαια αἰ. Call.*Iamb*.1.162. 2. *hold office of* αἰσυμνήτης (q.v.), *GDI*3053 (Chalcedon), 5632 (Teos); at Naxos, *IG*12(9).223 (Eretria, iii B.C.). **-ητεία**, ἡ, *office of* αἰσυμνήτης II.1, = αἱρετὴ τυραννίς, Arist. *Pol*.1285b25, cf. D.L.1.100. **-ητήρ**, ῆρος, ὁ, *ruler*, *prince*, κούρῳ αἰ. Il.24.347 (v.l.). ⊛**-ήτης**, ου, ὁ, Dor. **αἰσιμνάτας**, *judge*, *umpire* at games, Od.8.258. 2. *overseer*, *bailiff*, Theoc.25.48. II. *ruler chosen* by the people, *elective monarch*, Arist.*Pol*.1285a31, 1295a 14, Arg.S.*OT*; compared with the Roman *dictator*, D.H.5.73. 2. title of magistrates in Greek cities, *IG*7.15 (Megara), *GDI*3045 (Chalcedon). 3. epith. of Dionysus in Achaia, Paus.7.21.6:—fem. ⊛**αἰσυμνῆτις**, ιδος, Suid. **-ητύς**, ύος, ἡ, *office of* αἰσυμνήτης, *Milet*.7.17. **-ιον**, τό, *council-chamber* at Megara, Paus.1.43.3.

**αἰσχεο-κερδής**, ές, = αἰσχροκερδής, Man.4.314; **-μυθος**, ον, **-ρήμων**, ονος, and **-φημος**, ον, *talking shameful things*, ib.57,445,592.

**αἶσχος**, εος, τό, *shame*, *disgrace*, Hom. (freq. in pl., as Il.3.242), Hes.*Op*.211, Sol.3, A.*Supp*.1008, etc. 2. in pl., *disgraceful deeds*, Od.1.229. II. *ugliness*, *deformity*, of mind or body, Pl.*Smp*. 201a, X.*Cyr*.2.2.29, etc.; αἰ. περὶ τὴν κάτηξιν Hp.*Art*.14; αἰ. ὀνόματος Arist.*Rh*.1405b8.

**αἰσχόω**, = αἰσχύνω, censured by Hdn.Gr.2.933, citing Eup.142; dub. in *Epigr.Gr*.336.

**αἰσχρήμων**, ον, gen. ονος, *shameful*, *base*, *APl*.1.15*(dub.); ἀσχήμων Porson.

**αἰσχρό-γελως**, ωτος, ὁ, ἡ, *shamefully ridiculous*, Man.4.283. **-διδάκτης**, ου, ὁ, *teacher of shameful things*, Man.4.307. **-επέω**, *use foul language*, Ephipp.23: c. acc., τὰς τέχνας Hp.*de Arte*1. **-επής**, ές, *foul-mouthed*, prob. in Ael.*Fr*.80. **-εργέω**, v. αἰσχρουργέω. **-κέρδεια**, ἡ, *sordid love of gain*, *base covetousness*, Hp.*Decent*.2, S.*Ant*. 1056, Lys.12.19, Pl.*Lg*.754e, Thphr.*Char*.30. **-κερδέω**, *to be sordid*, *greedy of gain*, Hyp.*Fr*.223. ⊛**-κερδής**, ές, *sordidly greedy of gain*, Hdt.1.187, E.*Andr*.451, And.4.32 (Sup.), cf. Pl.*R*.408c, Arist.*EN*1122a8, etc. Adv. -δῶς 1*Ep.Pet*.5.2. **-κερδία**, = αἰσχροκέρδεια, Diph.99, cf. Hdn.Gr.2.453. **-λογέω**, = αἰσχροεπέω, Pl. *R*.395e, Bryson ap.Arist.*Rh*.1405b10. **-λογία**, ἡ, *foul language*, *obscenity*, X.*Lac*.5.6, Arist.*EN*1128a23. 2. *abuse*, Plb.8.11.8, cf. *POxy*.410.77, *Ep.Col*.3.8, Phld.*Rh*.1.176S., etc. **-λόγος**, ον, *foul-mouthed*, and Adv. -γως, Poll.6.123, 8.80,81. **-λοιχός**, ὁ, *fellator*, Eust.518.52, Phot. s.v. λαπτώμενος. **-μητις**, ιος, ὁ, ἡ, *fostering* or *forming base designs*, A.*Ag*.222 (lyr.). **-μῡθέω**, = αἰσχροεπέω, of a delirious woman, Hp.*Epid*.3.17.ια'. **-πᾰθής**, ές, *submitting to foul usage*, Ph.2.268. **-ποιέω**, *act filthily*, Ath.8.342c; = λεσβιάζω, Sch.Ar.*Ra*.1308. II. trans., *degrade*, *dishonour*, τὰς τέχνας v.l. in Hp.*de Arte*1. **-ποιΐα**, ἡ, euphem. for *fellatio*, Sch.Ar.*Nub*.296. **-ποιός**, όν, *doing foully*, E.*Med*.1346; euphem. for *fellator*, Machoap.Ath.13.582d. ⊛**-πρᾱγέω**, = αἰσχροποιέω, Arist.*EN*1120a15. **-πρεπής**, ές, *of hideous appearance*, Sch.E. *Hipp*.75; f.l. for -επής, Ael.*Fr*.80. **-πρόσωπος**, ον, *of hideous countenance*, Suid. s.v. Φιλοκλῆς. **-ρρημονέω**, = αἰσχροεπέω, Charond. ap.Stob.4.2.24. **-ρρημοσύνη**, ἡ, = αἰσχρολογία, D.*Ep*.4.11, Phld. *Rh*.1.175S., Oenom.ap.Eus.*PE*5.32 (pl.). **-ρρήμων**, ον, = αἰσχρολόγος, Poll.8.80. Adv. -μόνως ib.81.

⊛**αἰσχρός**, ά, όν, also ός, όν *APl*.4.151: (αἶσχος):—in Hom., *causing shame*, *dishonouring*, *reproachful*, νείκεσσεν.. αἰσχροῖς ἐπέεσσιν Il.3. 38, etc. Adv. αἰσχρῶς, ἐνένισπεν 23.473. II. opp. καλός: 1. of outward appearance, *ugly*, *ill-favoured*, of Thersites, Il.2.216, cf. *h.Ap*.197, Hdt.1.196 (Comp.), etc.; *deformed*, Hp.*Art*.14 (Sup.); αἰσχρῶς χωλὸς *with an ugly* lameness, ib.63: but commonly, 2. in moral sense, *shameful*, *base*, Hdt.3.155, A.*Th*.685, etc.; αἰσχροῖς γὰρ αἰσχρὰ πράγματ' ἐκδιδάσκεται S.*El*.621; αἰσχρόν [ἐστι], c. inf., Il.2.298, S.*Aj*.473, etc.; αἰσχρόν, εἰ πύθοιτό τις ib.1159; ἐν αἰσχρῷ θέσθαι τι E.*Hec*.806; ἐπ' αἰσχροῖς on the ground of *base actions*, S. *Fr*.188, E.*Hipp*.511:—τὸ αἰ. as Subst., *dishonour*, S.*Ph*.476; τὸ ἐμὸν αἰ. my *disgrace*, And.2.9; τὸ καλὸν καὶ τὸ αἰ. virtue and *vice*, Arist.*Rh*. 1366a24, etc. Adv., *shamefully*, S.*El*.989, Pl.*Smp*.183d, etc.: Sup. αἴσχιστα A.*Pr*.959, S.*OT*367. 3. *ill-suited*, αἰ. ὁ καιρὸς D.18.178; αἰ. πρός τι *awkward* at it, X.*Mem*.3.8.7; αἰσχρὸν καὶ ἄτεχνον Hp. *Fract*.30. III. Regul. Comp. and Sup. -ότερος, -ότατος are late, Phld.*Rh*.2.58S. (prob.), Ath.13.587b: elsewh. αἰσχίων, αἴσχιστος (formed from a Root **αἰσχο-**), Il.21.437, 2.216; double Sup. αἰσχιστότατος Olymp.*in Alc*.p.124C. Adv., Sup. αἰσχίστως Mnasalc.ap. Ath.4.163a, Man.1.21.

⊛**αἰσχροσεμνία**, ἡ, *avoidance of obscenity*, Aus.*Idyll*.13.

**αἰσχρότης**, ητος, ἡ, *ugliness*, *deformity*, Pl.*Grg*.525a. II. *filthy conduct*, *Ep.Eph*.5.4; euphem. for *fellatio*, Sch.Ar.*Ra*.1308:—**αἰσχροσύνη**, ἡ, Tz.*H*.11.229.

⊛**αἰσχρ-ουργέω**, contr. for αἰσχροεργέω, *act obscenely*, esp. = *masturbari*, S.E.*P*.3.206:—Pass., τὰ -ούμενα D.L.*Prooem*.5. ⊛**-ουργία**, ἡ, *shameless conduct*, E.*Ba*.1062: pl., D.Chr.4.102. II. *obscenity*, Aeschin.2.99, cf. Plu.2.1044b. ⊛**-ουργός**, όν, *obscene*, Gal.12.249. Adv., Sup., D.C.79.3.

**Αἰσχύλειος**, α, ον, *of* or *like Aeschylus*, Sch.Il.19.87.

**αἰσχυνετάι** (-υντάδην Meinek.)· κατ' αἰσχύνην, Hsch.

**αἰσχύν-η** [ῡ], ἡ, *shame*, *dishonour*, ἐς αἰσχύνην φέρει Hdt.1.10, cf. 3.133; αἰσχύνην φέρει, ἔχει, S.*Tr*.66, E.*Andr*.244, etc.; αἰ. περιίσταταί με, συμβαίνει μοι, D.3.8, 18.85; αἰσχύνῃ πίπτειν S.*Tr*.597; περιπίπτειν X.*HG*7.3.9; αἰσχύνην περιάπτειν τῇ πόλει Pl.*Ap*.35a; αἰ. προσβάλλειν τινί Id.*Lg*.878c; ἐν αἰ. ποιεῖν τὴν πόλιν D.18.136; ἡ τῶν πραγμάτων αἰ. 1.27. 2. αἰ. γυναικῶν *dishonouring* of women, Isoc.4.114 (pl.), 12.259 (pl.); γράφεσθαί τινα γένους αἰσχύνης for *dishonour done* to his race, Pl.*Lg*.919e. 3. concrete, of a person, αἰ. φίλοις, πάτρᾳ, Thgn.1272, A.*Pers*.774; ἄνθρωπος αἰ. τῆς πόλεως γεγονώς Aeschin.3.241; of a decree, ib.105. II. *shame for* an ill deed, personified in A.*Th*.409; Αἰσχύνην οὐ νομίσασα θεόν *AP*7.450 (Diosc.). 2. like αἰδώς, *sense of shame*, *honour*, πᾶσαν αἰ. ἀφεὶς S.*Ph*.120; ἡ γὰρ αἰ. (πάρος) τοῦ ζῆν.. νομίζεται E.*Heracl*. 200; δι' αἰσχύνης ἔχειν τι *to be ashamed of*, Id.*IT*683; αἰσχύνην ἔχειν τινός *for* a thing, S.*El*.616; αἰ. ἐπί τινι Pl.*Smp*.178d; ὑπέρ τινος D.4.10; joined with δέος, S.*Aj*.1079; with ἔλεος and αἰδώς, Antipho 1.27:—rare in pl., πτήσσουσαν αἰσχύνῃσιν S.*Fr*.659.9; ἐν αἰσχύναις ἔχω I hold it *a shameful thing*, E.*Supp*.164. III. later = αἰδοῖον, Sch.Ar.*Eq*.365; cf. τὴν τοῦ σώματος αἰ. Alcid.ap Arist.*Rh*. 1406a29. **-ομένη**, ἡ, *sensitive plant*, *Mimosa asperata*, Apollod. ap.Plin.*HN*24.167. **-ομένως**, Adv. *modestly*, *shamefacedly*, D.H. 7.50. **-τέον**, *one must be ashamed*, X.*Cyr*.4.2.40. **-τηλία**, ἡ, *bashfulness*, Plu.2.66c. **-τηλός**, ή, όν, *bashful*, *modest*, Pl.*Chrm*. 160e, Arist.*EN*1128b20; τὸ αἰ. *modesty*, Pl.*Chrm*.158c. Adv. -λῶς Id.*Lg*.665e. II. of things, *shameful*, Arist.*Rh*.1384b18. **-τήρ**, ῆρος, ὁ, *dishonourer*, of Aegisthus, A.*Ch*.998. ⊛**-τηρός**, ά, όν, = αἰσχυντηλός, in Comp., Pl.*Grg*.487b. ⊛**-τικός**, ή, όν, *provocative of shame*, Arist.*Rh*.1384a9. **-τός**, ή, όν, *shameful*, Ps.-Phoc. 189.

**αἰσχύνω** [ῡ]: Ion. impf. αἰσχύνεσκε (κατ-) Q.S.14.531: fut. -ῠνῶ E. *Hipp*.719, Ion. -υνέω Hdt.9.53: aor. ᾔσχῡνα Il.23.571, Lys.1.4, etc.: pf. ᾔσχυγκα D.C.58.16:—**Pass.**, fut. αἰσχῠνοῦμαι A.*Ag*.856, Ar.*Fr*. 200, Pl.*Ti*.49d, etc., rarely αἰσχυνθήσομαι (v. sub fin.): aor. ᾐσχύνθην Hdt. and Att., poet. inf. αἰσχυνθήμεν Pi.*N*.9.27: pf. ᾔσχυμμαι (v. infr. B.1):—*make ugly*, *disfigure*, πρόσωπον, κόμην, Il.18.24,27, cf. S.*Ant*.529; αἰ. τὸν ἵππον *give* the horse *a bad form*, X.*Eq*.1.12. 2. mostly in moral sense, *dishonour*, *tarnish*, μηδὲ γένος πατέρων αἰσχυνέμεν Il.6.209, cf. 23.571; τὴν Σπάρτην Hdt.9.53; ξενίαν τράπεζαν A.*Ag*.401; τοὺς πρὸς αἵματος S.*Aj*.1305; τοὺς πατέρας Pl.*Mx*. 246d. b. esp. *dishonour* a woman, E.*El*.44, cf. Plu.*Marc*.19, etc.; εὐνήν A.*Ag*.1626; εἰς τὸ σῶμα αἰ. Arist.*Pol*.1311b7; abs., *Foed. Delph.Pell*.2 A 12. 3. *disdain*, ἐπιχώρια Pi.*P*.3.22.

B. Pass., *to be dishonoured*, νέκυς ᾐσχυμμένος, of Patroclus, Il. 18.180. II. *to be ashamed*, *feel shame*, abs., Od.7.305, 18.12, Hdt.1.10, E.*Hipp*.1291. 2. more commonly, *to be ashamed at* a thing, c. acc. rei, αἰσχυνόμενοι φάτιν ἀνδρῶν Od.21.323; τὴν δυσγένειαν τὴν ἐμὴν αἰ. S.*OT*1079: c. dat. rei, Ar.*Nu*.992, Lys.3.9, D.4. 42, etc.; αἰ. ἐπί τινι X.*Mem*.2.2.8; ἔν τινι Th.2.43; ὑπέρ τινος Lys.14. 39; περί τινος 33.6, etc. b. c. part., *to be ashamed at* doing a thing (which one does), A.*Pr*.642 (v.l.), S.*Ant*.540, Ar.*Fr*.200, Pl.*Grg*.

494e, etc. c. c. inf., *to be ashamed to* do a thing (and therefore not to do it), Hdt.1.82, A.*Ag*.856, *Ch*.917, Pl.*R*.414e, *Phdr*.257d, etc.; though this condition must not be pressed absolutely, cf. *Ap*. 22b. d. foll. by relat. clause, αἰσχύνεσθαι εἰ.. *to be ashamed* that.., S.*El*.254, And.4.42; ἐάν.. X.*Oec*.21.4; μή.. Pl.*Tht*.183e, cf. Macho ap.Ath.13.579f; ὅτι.. Lys.2.23. 3. c. acc. pers., *to feel shame before* one, E.*Ion*934,1074, Pherecr.23.6, Pl.*Smp*.216b; τοὺς γέροντας (at Sparta) Aeschin.1.180; ὅστις γὰρ αὐτὸς αὑτὸν οὐκ αἰσχύνεται, πῶς τόν γε μηδὲν εἰδότ' αἰσχυνθήσεται; Philem.229, cf. Gal. 5.26: c. acc. et inf., E.*Hel*.415; ᾐσχύνθημεν θεοὺς.. προδοῦναι αὐτόν X.*An*.2.3.22; αἰσχύνομαι ὑμᾶς λέγειν D.40.48; αἰ. πρός τινα Arist.*Rh*. 1383$^b$12.

**Αἰσώπειος**, α, ον, *of Aesop*, λόγοι D.L.5.80, Theon *Prog*.1, etc.; ἀθύρματα Him.*Or*.20.1; κύων Plu.2.157b; αἷμα, prov. of an indelible stain, Zen.1.47.

**Αἰσωποποίητος**, ον, *made by Aesop*, Quint.*Inst*.5.11 (prob.).

**®ἀΐτας** [ῑ], ὁ, Dor. word for *a beloved youth*, answering to εἰσπνήλας or εἴσπνηλος (the lover), Ar.*Fr*.738 (fort. Eratosth.), Theoc.12.14 (αἴτης, said to be a Thessalian word), cj. in 23.63; generally, *lover*, Χρύσας (sc. Ἀθανᾶς) δ' ἀΐτας Dosiad.*Ara* 5, cf. Lyc.461:—fem. **ἀΐτις** Hdn.Gr.1.105, 2.296, cf. Alcm.125.

**αἴτε**, Dor. and Aeol. for εἴτε.

**®αἰτ-έω** (Aeol. **αἴτημι** Pi.*Fr*.155, Theoc.28.5), Ion. impf. αἴτεον Hdt.: fut. αἰτήσω: aor. ᾔτησα: pf. ᾔτηκα 1*Ep.Jo*.5.15: plpf. ᾐτήκει Arr.*An*.6.15.5: pf. Pass. ᾔτημαι, etc.:—*ask, beg*, abs., Od.18.49, A.*Supp*.341. 2. mostly c. acc. rei, *ask for, demand*, Il.5.358, Od.17.365, etc.; ὁδὸν αἰ. *ask leave* to depart, Od.10.17; αἰ. τινί τι *to ask* something for one, 20.74, Hdt.5.17: c. acc. pers. et rei, *ask* a person *for* a thing, Il.22.295, Od.2.387, Hdt.3.1, etc.; δίκας αἰ. τινὰ φόνου *to demand* satisfaction from one for.., Hdt.8.114; αἰ. τι πρός τινος Thgn.556; παρά τινος X.*An*.1.3.16; τὰ αἰτήματα ἃ ᾐτήκαμεν παρ' αὐτοῦ 1*Ep.Jo*.5.15. 3. c. acc. pers. et inf., *ask* one *to* do, Od.3.173, S.*OC*1334, *Ant*.65, etc.; αἰ. παρά τινος δοῦναι Pl.*Erx*. 398e. 4. c. acc. only, *beg of*, D.L.6.49. 5. in Logic, *postulate, assume*, Arist.*APr*.41$^b$9 (Pass.), *Top*.163$^a$6, etc. II. Med., *ask for one's own use, claim*, Λύσανδρον ἄρχοντα Lys.12.59; freq. almost = the Act., and with the same construct., first in Hdt.1.90 (παρ-), 9. 34, A.*Pr*.822, etc.; αἰτεῖσθαί τινα ὅπως.. Antipho1.12 codd.; πάλαισμα μήποτε λῦσαι θεὸν αἰτοῦμαι S.*OT*880; freq. abs. in part., αἰτουμένῳ μοι δός A.*Ch*.480, cf. 2, *Th*.260, S.*Ph*.63; αἰτουμένη πού τευξεται Id.*Ant*.778; αἰτησάμενος ἐχρήσατο Lys.19.27; οὐ πῦρ γὰρ αἰτῶν, οὐδὲ λοπάδ' αἰτούμενος Men.476; αἰτεῖσθαι ὑπέρ τινος *to beg* for one, Lys. 14.22. III. Pass., of persons, *have a thing begged of* one, αἰτηθέντες χρήματα Hdt.8.111, cf. Th.2.97, etc.; αἰτεύμενος Theoc.14.63: c. inf., *to be asked to* do a thing, Pi.*I*.8(7).5. 2. of things, *to be asked*, τὸ αἰτεόμενον Hdt.8.112; ἵπποι ᾐτημένοι *borrowed* horses, Lys. 24.12. **-ημα**, ατος, τό, *request, demand*, Pl.*R*.566b, Lxx 1*Ki*.1.17, *Ev.Luc*.23.24, *PFlor*.296.16 (vi A.D.). II. in Logic and Math., *postulate, assumption*, Arist.*APo*.76$^b$23, Plu.*Demetr*.3, Luc.*Herm*. 74. **-ηματικός**, ή, όν, *disposed to ask*, Artem.4.2. **-ηματώδης**, ες, *question-begging*, Plu.2.694f. **-ήσιμος**, ον, *obtained by petition*, *Ath.Mitt*.44.25 (Samos, iii B.C.). **-ησις**, εως, ἡ, *request, demand*, Hdt.7.32, Antipho5.4, *POxy*.1024.20 (ii A.D.); ἡ ἐρώτησις ἀποκρίσεώς ἐστιν αἴ. Arist.*Int*.20$^b$22. **-ητέον**, verb. Adj. *one must ask*, X.*Eq.Mag*.5.11. **®-ητής**, οῦ, ὁ, *one that asks, petitioner*, *POxy*. 788 (i B.C.), D.C.*Fr*.66.2. **-ητικός**, ή, όν, *fond of asking*, τινός Arist.*EN*1120$^a$33. Adv. αἰτητικῶς, ἔχειν πρός τινα D.L.6.31. **-ητός**, όν, verb. Adj. *asked for*, ἀρχὴν δωρητόν, οὐκ αἰτητόν freely given, not *asked for*, S.*OT*384.

**®αἰτί-α**, ἡ, *responsibility*, mostly in bad sense, *guilt, blame*, or the imputation thereof, i.e. *accusation*, first in Pi.*O*.1.35 and Hdt., v. infr. (Hom. uses αἴτιος):—Phrases: αἰτίαν ἔχειν bear *responsibility for*, τινός A.*Eu*.579, S.*Ant*.1312; but usu. *to be accused*, τινός *of* a crime, φόνου Hdt.5.70: c. inf., Ar.*V*.506; foll. by ὡς.., Pl.*Ap*.38c; by ὡς c. part., Id.*Phdr*.249d; ὑπό τινος *by* some one, A.*Eu*.99, Pl. *R*.565b: reversely, αἰτία ἔχει τινά Hdt.5.70,71; αἰ. φεύγειν τινός S.*Ph*.1404; ἐν αἰτίᾳ εἶναι or γίγνεσθαι, Hp.*Art*.67, X.*Mem*.2.8.6; αἰτίαν ὑπέχειν lie under *a charge*, Pl.*Ap*.33b, X.*Cyr*.6.3.16; ὑπομεῖναι Aeschin.3.139; φέρεσθαι Th.2.60; λαβεῖν ἀπό τινος ib.18; αἰτίαις ἐνέχεσθαι Pl.*Cri*.52a; αἰτίαις περιπίπτειν Lys.7.1; εἰς αἰτίαν ἐμπίπτειν Pl.*Tht*.150a; αἰτίας τυγχάνειν D.*Ep*.2.2; ἐκτὸς αἰτίας κυρεῖν A. *Pr*.332; ἐν αἰτίῃ ἔχειν hold one *guilty*, Hdt.5.106; δι' αἰτίας ἔχειν Th. 2.60, etc.; ἐν αἰτίᾳ βάλλειν S.*OT*656; τὴν αἰτίαν ἐπιφέρειν τινί impute *the fault* to one, Hdt.1.26; αἰτίαν νέμειν τινί S.*Aj*.28; ἐπάγειν D.18.283; προσβάλλειν τινί Antipho3.2.4; ἀνατιθέναι, προστιθέναι, Hp.*VM*21, Ar.*Pax*640, etc.; ἀπολύειν τινὰ τῆς αἰτίης to acquit of *guilt*, Hdt.9.88, etc. 2. in forensic oratory, *invective* without proof (opp. ἔλεγχος), D.22.23, cf. 18.15. 3. in good sense, εἰ.. εὖ πράξαιμεν, αἰτία θεοῦ *the credit* is his, A.*Th*.4; δι' ὅντινα αἰτίαν ἔχουσιν Ἀθηναῖοι βελτίους γεγονέναι *are reputed* to have become better, Pl.*Grg*.503b, cf. *Alc*.1.119a, Arist.*Metaph*.984$^b$19; ὧν.. πέρι αἰτίαν ἔχεις διαφέρειν in which you *are reputed* to excel, Pl.*Tht*.169a; οἱ.. ἔχουσι ταύτην τὴν αἰ. who have this *reputation*, Id.*R*.435e, cf. And. 2.12; αἰτίαν λαμβάνειν Pl.*Lg*.624a. 4. *expostulation*, μὴ ἐπ' ἔχθρᾳ τὸ πλέον ἢ αἰτίᾳ Th.1.69. II. *cause*, δι' ἣν αἰτίην ἐπολέμησαν Hdt.*Prooem*., cf. Democr.83, Pl.*Ti*.68e, *Phd*.97a sq., etc.; on the four causes of Arist. v. *Ph*.194$^b$16, *Metaph*.983$^a$26:—αἰ. τοῦ γενέσθαι or γεγονέναι Pl.*Phd*.97a; τοῦ μεγίστου ἀγαθοῦ τῇ πόλει αἰτία ἡ κοινωνία Id.*R*.464b:—dat. αἰτίᾳ *for the sake of*, κοινοῦ τινος ἀγαθοῦ Th.4.87, cf. D.H.8.29:—αἴτιον (cf. αἴτιος II. 2) is used like αἰτία in the sense of *cause*, not in that of *accusation*. III. *occasion, motive*, αἰτίαν ἀοιδᾶν ῥοαῖσι Μοισᾶν ἐνέβαλε gave them *a theme* for song, Pi.*N*.7.11; αἰτίαν παρέχειν Luc.*Tyr*.13. IV. *head, category* under which a thing comes, D.23.75. V. *case in dispute*, ἡ αἰ. τοῦ ἀνθρώπου μετὰ τῆς γυναικός *Ev.Matt*.19.10. **-άζομαι**, only in Pass., *to be accused*, πόλις αἰτιάζεται X.*HG*1.6.5, cf. 12, Anon.*Oxy*.1012*Fr*.14; ᾐτιάζετο τινος *of* a thing, D.C.38.10. **-ᾱμα**, ατος, τό, *charge, accusation*, λαβεῖν ἐπ' αἰτιάματί τινα A.*Pr*.196, cf. 257, Th.5.72. **-άομαι**, used by Hom. only in Ep. forms, 3 pl. αἰτιόωνται, opt. αἰτιόῳο, -ῳτο, inf. αἰτιάασθαι, impf. ᾐτιάασθε, -όωντο: Aeol. impf. 2 sg. αἰτίαο *Lyr. Adesp*.66: fut. -άσομαι Ar.*Nub*.1433, Pl.*Phd*.85d: aor. ᾐτιασάμην E.*Fr*.254, Th.1.120, etc., Ion. -ησάμενος Hdt.4.94, -ήσασθαι Hp.*Art*.4: pf. ᾐτίαμαι D.19.215, Ion. -ίημαι Hp.*Ep*.17 (also in pass. sense, and aor. ᾐτιάθην always so, v. infr. 1. 1): (αἰτία):—*accuse, censure*, c. acc. pers., τάχα κεν καὶ ἀναίτιον αἰτιόῳτο Il.11.654, cf. Od. 20.135; ἀναίτιον αἰτιάασθαι Il.13.775; θεοὺς βροτοὶ αἰτιόωνται Od. 1.32, cf. E.*Fr*.254; καί μ' ᾐτιάασθε ἕκαστος Il.16.202, cf. S.*OT*608, Lys.7.38, etc.; αἰ. ὡς μιαρούς Pl.*R*.562d; αἰ. τινά τινος *to accuse of* a thing, Hdt.5.27, Pl.*R*.619c, D.21.104, etc.: c. inf., αἰ. τινὰ ποιεῖν τι *accuse* one of doing, Hdt.5.27, Pl.*Criti*.120c, X.*Mem*.1. 1.2; οὐ τὰ ὑμέτερα αἰτιασόμεθα μὴ οὐχ ἕτοιμα εἶναι Pl.*La*.189c; αἰ. τινὰ ὡς.. or ὅτι.., Th.1.120, X.*An*.3.1.7; αἰ. τινὰ περί τινος X.*HG*1.7.6: c. acc. cogn., αἰ. αἰτίαν κατά τινος *bring a charge* against one, Antipho6.27:—Pass., *to be accused*, aor. 1 ᾐτιάθην (always) Th.6.53, 8.68, X.*HG*.1.32: pf. ᾐτίαμαι Th.3.61: fut. αἰτιαθήσομαι D.C.37.56. b. in good sense, *give* one *the credit* of being, σὲ τὶς αἰτιᾶται νομοθέτην ἀγαθὸν γεγονέναι; Pl.*R*.599e, cf. 379c, *Cra*.396d. 2. c. acc. rei, *lay to* one's *charge, impute*, τοῦτο αἰ. X.*Cyr*.3.1.39; ταῦτα D.19.215: c. dupl. acc., τί ταῦτα τοὺς Λάκωνας αἰτιώμεθα; Ar.*Ach*.514. 3. *injure*, ὁπλὴν *Hippiatr*.105. II. *allege as the cause*, οὐ τὸ αἴτιον αἰ. not *to allege* the real cause, Pl.*R*. 329b; τίνα ἔχεις αἰτιάσασθαι.. τούτου κύριον; ib.508a; φωνάς τε.. καὶ ἄλλα μυρία αἰ. Id.*Phd*.98e; τἀναίτια Id.*Ti*.88a; ὧν τὴν πενίαν αἰτιάσαιτ' ἄν τις D.18.263; τὴν δίνην Arist.*Cael*.295$^a$32; τὸ αὐτόματον Id. *Ph*.196$^a$25. 2. c. inf., *allege*, τὸν λόγον αἰ. δυσχερῆ εἶναι Pl.*Prt*. 333d, cf. *Men*.93d; αἰ. τι αἴτιον εἶναι *Phlb*.22d, *Grg*.518d; ἰλίγγους ἐκ φιλοσοφίας ἐγγίγνεσθαι *allege by way of accusation* that.., Id.*R*. 407c; τῆς ἱερᾶς χώρας ᾐτιᾶτο εἶναι *he alleged* that it was part of.., D. 18.150, cf. 37.12. (Late in Act., *POxy*.1032.51 (ii A.D.).) **-ᾱσις**, εως, ἡ, *complaint, accusation*, Antipho5.25, Arist.*Po*.1455$^b$31, *PFlor*. 311.4 (v A.D.). **-ᾱτέον**, verb. Adj. *one must accuse, blame*, X.*Cyr*. 7.1.11, Str.1.2.30. II. *one must allege as the cause*, Pl.*R*.379c, *Ti*.57c, 87b, Arist.*Mete*.339$^a$32. **®-ᾱτικός**, ή, όν, *causal*, Sch.Il. 23.627. 2. Astrol., *noxious*, τόπος Vett.Val.208.10. II. ἡ αἰ. (sc. πτῶσις) *accusative case*, indicating the thing caused by the vb., *Stoic*.2.59, D.T.636.6, A.D.*Pron*.11.9, etc. Adv. -κῶς *in the accusative*, Sch.E.*Ph*.470. **®-ᾱτός**, ή, όν, verb. Adj. *produced by a cause, effected*, Arist.*APo*.76$^a$20; τὸ αἰ. *effect*, opp. τὸ αἴτιον *cause*, ib.98$^a$36, Plot.6.2.3: Comp. -ότερος Eustr.*in APo*.40.28.

**αἰτίζω**, Ep. form of αἰτέω (not in Il., once in Ar.); only pres. (exc. aor. part. αἰτίσσας in *AP*10.66 (Agath.)), *ask, beg*, c. acc. rei, σῖτον.. αἰτίζων κατὰ δῆμον Od.17.558, cf. 222; ἡνίκ' ἂν αἰτίζῃτ' ἄρτον Ar. *Pax*120 (hex.); generally, *ask*, φέρευ τέκος ὅσσ' ἐθέλημὸς αἰτίζεις Call.*Dian*.32. 2. c. acc. pers., *beg of*, αἰτίζειν.. πάντας ἐποιχόμενον μνηστῆρας Od.17.346. 3. abs., *beg*, αἰτίζων βόσκειν ἣν γαστέρα ib.228, cf. 4.651.

**αἰτιο-λογέω**, *inquire into causes, reason, account for*, ὑπὲρ τῶν μετεώρων Epicur.*Ep*.1 p.31 U., cf. Diocl.*Fr*.112, Plot.6.7.3, Plu.2.689b; τὸ ζητούμενον Aenesid.ap.S.E.*P*.1.181, cf. Demetr.Lac.1012.68:—Pass., ἐκ τοῦ συνδέσμου ᾐτιολογημένον ἐστίν the conjunction indicates that *the cause resides in*.., A.D.*Conj*.235.9. **-λογητέον**, verb. Adj. *one must investigate causes*, Epicur.*Ep*.1 p.29 U. **-λογία**, ἡ, *a giving the cause* of a thing, Democr.118, Aenesid.ap.S.E.*P*.1.181, Phld.*D*.1.10, A.D.*Conj*.231.16; ἡ (περὶ) τῶν μετεώρων αἰ. Epicur. *Ep*.2 p.42 U. **-λογικός**, ή, όν, *ready at giving the cause, inquiring into causes*, αἰτιολογικώτατος, of Aristotle, D.L.5.32; *causal*, τρόπος Epicur.*Nat*.144 G.:—Subst., τὸ -κόν *investigation of causes*, Str.2. 3.8. 2. Gramm., *causal*, σύνδεσμοι, σύνταξις, etc., A.D.*Conj*. 231.4, al., *Adv*.200.2. Adv. -κῶς Id.*Synt*.320.3.

**®αἴτι-ος**, α, ον, more rarely ος, ον Ar.*Pl*.547: (v. αἰτία):—*culpable, responsible*, ἐπεὶ οὔ τί μοι αἴτιοί εἰσιν Il.1.153, cf. B.10.34, Hdt.7.214: Comp. αἰτιώτερος Th.4.20: Sup., τοὺς αἰτιωτάτους *the most guilty*, Hdt.6.50; αἰ. τινος Id.3.52. 2. Subst., αἴτιος, ὁ, *the accused, the culprit*, A.*Ch*.70, etc.; οἱ αἰ. τοῦ πατρός *they who have sinned against* my father, ib.273:—c. gen. rei, οἱ αἰ. τοῦ φόνου ib.117, cf. S.*Ph*.590, Hdt.4.200. II. *responsible for*, c. gen. rei, Hdt.1.1, etc.; αἴτιός τινός τινι being *the cause of* a thing *to* a person, Lys.13.57, cf. D.23. 54, Isoc.8.100: c. inf., αἰ. τὸν ἠέρα ξηρὸν εἶναι Hdt.2.26; τοῦ μὴ φαλακροῦσθαι Id.3.12, etc.; αἰ. θανεῖν S.*Ant*.1173; αἰ. πεμφθῆναι ἄγγελον Antipho5.23, cf. Lys.13.82; αἴτιος τὸ σὲ ἀποκρίνασθαι Pl.*La*.190e: Comp., τοῦ.. ἐλευθέραν εἶναι.. αἰτιώτερον D.24.5, cf. 51.21: Sup. αἰτιώτατος, ἐν τῷ στενῷ ναυμαχῆσαι *mainly instrumental in causing* the sea-fight, Th.1.74; αἰ. τοῦ μὴ ἀποθανεῖν D.20.42; -ώτατόν τι καὶ τελέως δραστικόν Phld.*D*.1.23. 2. αἴτιον, τό, *cause*, Hp.*VM*6 (pl.), 21, Hdt.7.125, E.*IA*939, Th.4.26, etc.; τί ποτ' οὖν ἐστι τὸ αἴτιον τό.. μηδένα εἰπεῖν; D.8.56; freq. in Philos., τὸ δ' αἰ. τούτου εἶναι ὅτι.. Pl.*Phd*.110e, etc. **-ώδης**, ες, *resembling a cause, quasi-causal*, *Stoic*.2.119 (in Adv. -δῶς, sed leg. -ῶδες); *causal*, οὐσία ot.6.8.14; στοιχεῖα Simp.*inPh.*17.25; τὸ αἰτιῶδες *formal*, as p. to τὸ ὑλικόν, M.Ant.4.21, etc.; πρότασις αἰ. *giving the cause* the conclusion, Anon.*inSE*3.36. Adv. -δως *causally*, Dam.*Pr.* 6. II. Gramm., *causal*, ἀξίωμα Chrysipp.*Stoic.*2.70; σύνσμοι A.D.*Synt.*245.13, al. **-ωμα**, τό, = αἰτίαμα, *PFay.*111 (i A.D.), ct.*Ap.*25.7. **-ώνυμος**, ον, (ὄνομα) *named from a fault*, πάθος ch.S.*Aj.*205. **-ωσις**, ἡ, = αἰτίασις, Eust.1422.21.

**Αἰτναῖος**, α, ον, *of* or *belonging to Etna* (Αἴτνη), Pi.*P.*3.69, *O.*6.96, .*Pr.*367, etc.; *Sicilian*, πῶλος S.*OC*312; of a beetle, A.*Fr.*233, Ar. 'ax73, S.*Ichn.*300. II. αἰτναῖος, ὁ, *sea-fish*, Opp.*H.*1.512.

**αἰτρία**, for αἰθρία, barbarism in Ar.*Th.*1001.

**ἀΐττεσθαι**· δικάζειν ἢ δικάζεσθαι, Hsch. (Fort. ἄττεσθαι· διάζειν ἢ ιάζεσθαι.) **ἀΐτυρον**· ὕαλον, Id.

**Αἰτωλάρχης**, ὁ, *president of Aetolian League*, Phleg.*Mir.*2.

**Αἰτωλία**, ἡ, *Aetolia*, Th.3.96, etc.:—hence **Αἰτωλοί**, οἱ, *Aetolians*, Il.2.638, etc.: fem. **Αἰτωλίς**, χώρη Hdt.6.127: Adj. **Αἰτωλικός**, ή, όν, Th.4.30, etc.

**αἰτώλιος**, v. sub αἰγωλιός.

**αἴφνης**, Adv. *suddenly*, E.*IA*1581, Hp.*Int.*39 (**αἰφνηδίς**, Hdn. Gr.1.512; **-δόν**, Id.*Epim.*270). (Prob. cognate with αἶψα rather than with ἄφαρ, ἄφνω.)

⊛**αἰφνίδιος**, ον, *unforeseen, sudden*, A.*Pr.*680, Th.2.61, Arist.*EN* 1117$^{a}$18; ἀφικνοῦνται αἰφνίδιοι τοῖς Χίοις Th.8.14. Adv. -ίως Id.2. 53; also -ιον Plu.*Num.*15. **αἰφνιδιοτυχής**, ές, *profiting by strokes of good fortune*, Vett.Val.18.16.

**αἰχμάεις, αἰχμᾱτάς**, Dor. for αἰχμήεις, αἰχμητής.

**αἰχμάζω**, Ep. fut. -άσσω, *throw the spear*, αἰχμὰς αἰχμάσσουσι Il.4. 324; ἔνδον αἰχμάζειν *play the warrior* at home, A.*Pers.*756; αἰχμάσαι τάδε *to perform* these *feats of arms*, S.*Tr.*355; '*trail a pike*', Men. *Sam.*284. II. *arm with the spear*, πρὸς Ἀτρείδαισιν ᾔχμασας χέρα S.*Aj.*97: metaph. of general's speech, ἀ. τὴν διάνοιαν Onos.1. 13. III. *wound*, Nonn.*D.*35.178 s.v.l.

**αἰχμᾰλ-ωσία**, ἡ, *captivity*, D.S.20.61, Lxx *Am.*1.15, al., Plu. *Them.*31. II. *body of captives*, D.S.17.70, Lxx *Nu.*31. 12, al. **-ωτεύω**, = sq., Lxx *Ge.*34.29, al., *Ep.Eph.*4.8; *capture*, πλοῦτον Ps.-Callisth.3.20. **-ωτίζω**, *take prisoner*, D.S.14.37, Lxx 4*Ki.*24.14, al.:—more freq. in Med., αἰχμαλωτίζομαι J.*BJ*4.8.1: fut. -ίσομαι ib.2.4: aor. ᾐχμαλωτισάμην ib.1.22.1, D.S.13.24: pf. ᾐχμαλώτισμαι J.*BJ*4.9.8 (with v.l. -σάμενοι); also in pass. sense, *SIG*763 (Cyzicus). **-ωτικός**, ή, όν, *of* or *for a prisoner*, E.*Tr.* 871. **-ωτίς**, ίδος, ἡ, *captive*, S.*Aj.*1228, E.*Tr.*28, Lxx *Ge.*31. 26. 2. Adj. fem. of αἰχμάλωτος, τὰς αἰχμαλωτίδας χέρας S.*Aj.* 71. **-ωτισμός**, ὁ, = αἰχμαλωσία, Sch.Ar.*Nu.*186. **-ωτιστής**, *captivator*, *Gloss.* **-ωτος**, ον, *taken by the spear, captive, prisoner*, Pi.*Fr.*223, Hdt.6.79,134; freq. of women, A.*Ag.*1440, S.*Tr.*417:— αἰχμάλωτοι *prisoners of war*, And.4.22, Th.3.70; αἰ. λαμβάνειν, ἄγειν take *prisoner*, X.*Cyr.*3.1.37, 4.4.1; αἰ. γίγνεσθαι to be *taken*, ib.3.1.7; of things, αἰ. χρήματα A.*Eu.*400, cf. *Ag.*334, D.19.139; νῆες X.*HG* 2.3.8, *IG*2.789; τὰ αἰ. *booty*, X.*HG*4.1.26, *An.*4.1.13; αἰχμάλωτον, τό, = ἀνδράποδον, D.S.13.57. II. = αἰχμαλωτικός, δουλοσύνη αἰ. *such as awaits a captive*, Hdt.9.76; εὐνά A.*Th.*364 (lyr.); τύχη D.S.27.6, Lib.*Or.*59.157. III. αἰχμάλωτος, ὁ, name of plasters, Aët.15.20.

⊛**αἰχμ-ή**, ἡ, (Aeol. **αἴχμα** *AB*1095) *point of a spear*, πάροιθε δὲ λάμπετο δουρὸς αἰ. χαλκείη Il.6.320; αἰ. ἔγχεος 16.315. 2. generally, *point*, of arrows, τοξουλκὸς αἰ. A.*Pers.*239; ἀγκίστρου, κερδῶν, Opp.*H.* 1.216, *C.*2.451. II. *spear*, Il.12.45, etc.; δαμασίμβροτος αἰ. Pi.*O.* 9.79; πρὸς τὴν αἰχμὴν ἐτράπετο took to his *spear*, Hdt.3.78; αἰχμῇ εἷλε *with the spear*, i.e. in war, Id.5.94; otherwise rare in Prose, X.*Cyr.* 4.6.4. b. metaph. of the trident of Poseidon, A.*Pr.*925. 2. *body of spear-bearers*, Pi.*O.*7.19, E.*Heracl.*276. 3. *war, battle*, κακῶς ἡ αἰ. ἑστήκεε the *war* went ill, Hdt.7.152; παρμένοντας αἰχμᾷ standing their ground in *battle*, Pi.*P.*8.40; θηρῶν *with* wild beasts, E.*HF*158. 4. metaph. of plague, *sharpness*, βρωτῆρας αἰ. A.*Eu.* 803. III. *warlike spirit*, αἰ. νέων θάλλει Terp.6; θρέψε δ' αἰχμὰν Ἀμφιτρύωνος Pi.*N.*10.13; γυναικὸς αἰ. a woman's *temper*, A.*Ag.*483 (lyr.), cf. *Ch.*630 (lyr.; but perh. = *rule*, cf. *Pr.*406). (Cf. Lith. *jiešmas* 'spit'.) **-ήεις**, Dor. **-άεις**, εσσα, εν, *armed with the spear*, A.*Pers.* 137; *pointed*, σίδηρος Opp.*C.*3.321. **-ητά** [ᾰ], ὁ, Ep. collat. form of αἰχμητής, Il.5.197. **-ητήρ**, ῆρος, ὁ, = αἰχμητής, Opp.*C.*3.211, Q.S.8.85, Nonn.*D.*28.122; as Adj., αἰ. γάμος *prize of the spear*, ib.42. 501. **-ητήριος**, α, ον, *warlike*, Lyc.454. ⊛**-ητής**, οῦ, Dor. **-ᾱτάς**, ᾶ, ὁ, (αἰχμή) poet., *spearman, warrior*, esp. opp. to archers, Il.2.543, Od.2.19, al., Archil.119, cj. in Alcm.68, etc. II. In Pi. as Adj., 1. *pointed* (or *spear-wielding*), αἰ. κεραυνός *P.*1.5. 2. *warlike*, αἰ. θυμός *N.*9.37:—fem. **αἰχμητις** (sic), *EM*595.39.

**αἰχμό-δετος**, ον, (δέω) *bound in war*, = αἰχμάλωτος, S.*Fr.*47 (fort. -όλετος, cf. *EM*41.3). ⊛**-φόρος**, ον, *spearman*, Hdt.1.103,215. 2. esp., like δορυφόρος, of *body-guards*, Id.1.8, 7.40, B.10.89.

**αἶψα** (Boeot. ἦψα prob. in Corinn.*BKT*5(2).36), Adv. *quick, forthwith, on a sudden*, freq. in Hom. (also αἶψα μάλα, αἶψα δ' ἔπειτα, Il.4.70, Od.15.193), cf. Sapph.1.13, Thgn.663, Sol.2, Pi.*P.*4.133, Emp.35.14, A.*Supp.*481.—Poet., exc. in *Mon.Ant.*18.322 (Gortyn).

⊛**αἰψηροκέλευθος**, ον, *swift-speeding*, epith. of Boreas, Hes.*Th.*379, Poet.ap.Apollod.3.4.4.

**αἰψηρός**, ά, όν, (αἶψα) *quick, speedy, sudden*, αἰψηρὸς δὲ κόρος κρυεροῖο γόοιο satiety in grief *comes soon*, Od.4.103; λῦσεν δ' ἀγορὴν αἰψηρήν he dismissed the assembly *in haste*, Il.19.276, Od.2.257; Ζεφύρου αἰ. πνοαί Pi.*Parth.*2.17; πούς Lyc.515. Adv. -ῶς Aristarch. ap.Apollon.*Lex.* s.v. αἶψα.—Not in Trag.

⊛**ἀΐω** (A), Ep. and Lyr. word, freq. used by Trag. in lyr., cf. Hermipp.47.7 (anap.); once only in dialogue (S.*OC*304): only pres. and impf. (aor. ἐπ-ήϊσα Hdt.9.93):—*perceive* by the ear, *hear*, c. acc. rei, οὐκ ἀΐεις ἅ τέ φησι; Il.15.130, cf. 248; Νέστωρ δὲ πρῶτος κτύπον ἄϊε 10.532, cf. 21.388, Pi.*Pae.*6.8, A.*Ag.*55, *Supp.*59, E.*Med.*148, etc.: c. gen. rei, Sapph.1.6, S.*OC*304, *Ph.*1410: c. gen. pers., ἀΐει μου.. βασιλεύς A.*Pers.*633:—also, *perceive* by the eye, *see*, Od. 18.11, S.*OC*181:—generally, *perceive*, οὐκ ἀΐεις ὡς Τρῶες.. ἥαται ἄγχι νεῶν; Il.10.160. 2. c. gen., *listen to, give ear to*, δίκης Hes. *Op.*213 (dub. l.); *obey*, A.*Pers.*874, Ar.*Nu.*1166. (Cf. Skt. *āvis* 'clear', Lat. *au-dio.*) [Hom. uses ᾰ always in pres., ἄϊω; so A. *Pers.*633, S.*Ph.*1410; but ᾱΐεις, ᾱΐων A.*Supp.*59 (prob.), S.*OC*181, 304: impf. ᾱΐε Il.10.532, 21.388 (as always in Trag.), but ἄϊεν Il.11. 463, ἄϊον 18.222:—ι is always short, except ἀΐε in Hes.*Op.*213 (dub. l.), and perh. ἀϊόντεσσι Od.1.352.]

**ἀΐω** (B), [ᾱ], = ἄημι, *breathe*, (dub.) once in impf., ἐπεὶ φίλον ἄϊον ἦτορ when *I was breathing out* my life, Il.15.252.

**ἀϊών** [ᾱ], Dor. for ἠϊών.

⊛**αἰών**, ῶνος, ὁ, Ion. and Ep. also ἡ, as in Pi.*P.*4.186, E.*Ph.*1484: apocop. acc. αἰῶ, like Ποσειδῶ, restored by Ahrens (from *AB*363) in A.*Ch.*350: (properly αἰϝών, cf. *aevum*, v. αἰεί):—*period of existence* (τὸ τέλος τὸ περιέχον τὸν τῆς ἑκάστου ζωῆς χρόνον.. αἰὼν ἑκάστου κέκληται Arist.*Cael.*279$^{a}$25): I. *lifetime, life*, ψυχή τε καὶ αἰών Il.16.453; ἐκ δ' αἰ. πέφαται Il.19.27; μηδέ τοι αἰ. φθινέτω Od.5.160; λείπει τινά Il.5.685; ἀπ' αἰῶνος νέος ὤλεο (Zenod. νέον) 24.725; τελευτᾶν τὸν αἰῶνα Hdt.1.32, etc.; αἰῶνος στερεῖν τινά A.*Pr.*862; αἰῶνα διοιχνεῖν Id.*Eu.*315; συνδιατρίβειν Cratin.1; αἰ. Αἰακιδᾶν, periphr. for *the Aeacidae*, S.*Aj.*645 s.v.l.; ἀπέπνευσεν αἰῶνα E.*Fr.*801; ἐμὸν κατ' αἰῶνα A.*Th.*219. 2. *age, generation*, αἰ. ἐς τρίτον ib.744; ὁ μέλλων αἰών *posterity*, D.18.199, cf. Pl.*Ax.*370c. 3. *one's life, destiny, lot*, S.*Tr.*34, E.*Andr.*1215, *Fr.*30, etc. II. *long space of time, age*, αἰὼν γίγνεται 'tis *an age*, Men.536.5; esp. with Preps., ἀπ' αἰῶνος *of old*, Hes.*Th.*609, *Ev.Luc.*1.70; οἱ ἀπὸ τοῦ αἰ. Ῥωμαῖοι D.C. 63.20; δι' αἰῶνος *perpetually*, A.*Ch.*26, *Eu.*563; *all one's life long*, S. *El.*1024; δι' αἰῶνος μακροῦ, ἀπαύστου, A.*Supp.*582,574; τὸν δι' αἰ. χρόνον *for ever*, Id.*Ag.*554; εἰς ἅπαντα τὸν αἰ. Lycurg.106, Isoc.10. 62; εἰς τὸν αἰ. Lxx *Ge.*3.23, al., D.S.21.17, *Ev.Jo.*8.35, Ps.-Luc. *Philopatr.*17; εἰς αἰῶνα αἰῶνος Lxx *Ps.*131(132).14; ἐξ αἰῶνος καὶ ἕως αἰῶνος ib.*Je.*7.7; ἐπ' αἰ. ib.*Ex.*15.18; ἕως αἰῶνος ib.1*Ki.*1.22, al.:— without a Prep., τὸν ἅπαντα αἰ. Arist.*Cael.*279$^{a}$22; τὸν αἰῶνα Lycurg. 62, Epicur.*Ep.*1 p.8U.; *eternity*, opp. χρόνος, Pl.*Ti.*37d, cf. Metrod. *Fr.*37, Ph.1.496,619, Plot.3.7.5, etc.; τοὺς ὑπὲρ τοῦ αἰῶνος φόβους Epicur.*Sent.*20. 2. *space of time* clearly defined and marked out, *epoch, age*, ὁ αἰὼν οὗτος this present *world*, opp. ὁ μέλλων, *Ev. Matt.*13.22, cf. *Ep.Rom.*12.2; ὁ νῦν αἰ. 1*Ep.Tim.*6.17, 2*Ep.Tim.*4. 10:—hence in pl., *the ages*, i.e. *eternity*, Phld.*D.*3 *Fr.*84; εἰς πάντας τοὺς αἰ. Lxx *To.*13.4; εἰς τοὺς αἰ. ib.*Si.*45.24, al., *Ep.Rom.*1.25, etc.; εἰς τοὺς αἰ. τῶν αἰώνων Lxx 4*Ma.*18.24, *Ep.Phil.*4.20, etc.; ἀπὸ τῶν αἰ., πρὸ τῶν αἰ., *Ep.Eph.*3.9, 1*Cor.*2.7; τὰ τέλη τῶν αἰ. ib.10.11. 3. **Αἰών**, ὁ, personified, Αἰὼν Χρόνου παῖς E.*Heracl.*900 (lyr.), cf. *Corp. Herm.*11, etc.; as title of various divine beings, Dam.*Pr.*151, al.; esp. = Persian Zervan, Suid. s.v. Ἡραΐσκος. 4. Pythag., = 10, *Theol.Ar.*59.

B. *spinal marrow* (perh. regarded as seat of *life*), *h.Merc* 42, 119, Pi.*Fr.*111, Hp.*Epid.*7.122; perh. also Il.19.27.

**αἰωνίζω**, *to be eternal*, Phot., Suid.; *to be eternalized*, Dam.*Pr.*105.

⊛**αἰώνιος**, ον, also α, ον Pl.*Ti.*37d, *Ep.Heb.*9.12:—*lasting for an age* (αἰών II), *perpetual, eternal* (but dist. fr. ἀΐδιος, Plot.3.7.3), μέθη Pl.*R.* 363d; ἀνώλεθρον.. ἀλλ' οὐκ αἰώνιον Id.*Lg.*904a, cf. Epicur.*Sent.*28; αἰ. κατὰ ψυχὴν ὄχλησις Id.*Nat.*131 G.; κακά, δεινά, Phld.*Herc.*1251. 18, *D.*1.13; αἰ. ἀμοιβαῖς βασανισθησόμενοι ib.19; τοῦ αἰ. θεοῦ *Ep.Rom.* 16.26, Ti.Locr.96c; οὐ χρονίη μοῦνον.. ἀλλ' αἰωνίη Aret.*CA*1.5; αἰ. διαθήκη, νόμιμον, πρόσταγμα, Lxx *Ge.*9.16, *Ex.*27.21, *To.*1.6; ζωή *Ev.Matt.*25.46, Porph.*Abst.*4.20; κόλασις *Ev.Matt.* l.c., Olymp. *in Grg.*p.278 J.; πρὸ χρόνων αἰ. 2*Ep.Tim.*1.9: opp. πρόσκαιρος, 2*Ep.Cor.* 4.18. 2. *holding an office* or *title for life, perpetual*, γυμνασίαρχος *CPHerm.*62. 3. = Lat. *saecularis*, Phleg.*Macr.*4. 4. Adv. -ίως *eternally*, νοῦς ἀκίνητος αἰ. πάντα ὤν Procl.*Inst.*172, cf. Simp. *in Epict.*p.77 D.; *perpetually*, μισεῖν Sch.E.*Alc.*338. 5. αἰώνιον, τό, = ἀείζωον τὸ μέγα, Ps.-Dsc.4.88.

**αἰωνιότης**, ἡ, *perpetuitas*, *Gloss.*

**αἰώνισμα**, τό, *perpetual memorial*, *Ostr.*1148.

**αἰωνό-βῐος**, ον, *immortal*, title of Egyptian kings, Πτολεμαῖος *OGI*90.4 (Rosetta, ii B.C.), *PMag.Par.*1.154; of God, *PMag.Lond.* 46.176,482. **-πολοκράτωρ**, ορος, ὁ, *eternal ruler of the heavens*, *PMag.Berol.*1.201.

⊛**αἰωνόφθαλμος**, ον, *seeing with eternal eyes*, *PMag.Lond.*46.465.

⊛**αἰώρα**, ἡ, (ἀείρω) *swing, hammock, chariot on springs*, Pl.*Lg.* 789d. 2. *noose, halter*, S.*OT*1264 (in the form ἐώρα). II. *oscillatory movement, see-saw, pulsation*, Pl.*Phd.*111e, D.H.3.47, etc. 2. Medic., *passive exercise*, Plu.2.793b, Antyll.ap.Orib.6. 23, Sor.1.125: pl., *IG*4.955 (Epid., ii A.D.). III. metaph., αἰ. ψυχῆς *fluctuation* of mind, Metrod.*Herc.*831.8 (cf. Epicur.*Fr.*434).

⊛**αἰωρ-έω**: fut. Pass. -ηθήσομαι D.C.41.1, (ἀπ-) Hp.*Fract.*14, but -ήσομαι Aristid.2.289 J.: aor. ᾐωρήθην (v. infr.): pf. ᾐώρημαι Opp. *H.*3.532: (ἀείρω):—*lift up, raise*, ὑγρὸν νῶτον αἰωρεῖ, of the eagle *raising* his back and feathers, Pi.*P.*1.9; *swing* as in a hammock, αἰ. [γυναῖκα] ἐπὶ κλίνης φερομένην Hp.*Mul.*1.68, cf. Aret.*CA*1.4; τοὺς ὄφεις.. ὑπὲρ τῆς κεφαλῆς αἰωρῶν D.18.260. 2. *hang*, τινὰ ἐκ τοῦ ἀτράκτου Luc.*J.Conf.*4:—metaph., *ᾐώρει .. ἐλπίς, ὅτι τὸν χάρακα αἱρήσουσι excited* them *to think* that.., App.*BC*2.81, cf. Plu.*Brut.* 37.—Never in good Att. II. more freq. in Pass., *to be hung, hang*, δέρματα περὶ τοὺς ὤμους αἰωρεύμενα Hdt.7.92; αἰωρουμένων τῶν ὀστῶν *being raised, lifted*, Pl.*Phd.*98d; αἷμα ᾐωρεῖτο *spouted up*, Bion 1.25; ὁ ἥλιος ὑπὸ πνευμάτων αἰωρεῖται *is tossed, carried to and fro*, Diog.Oen.*Fr.*8. 2. *swing, float in air*, Pl.*La.*184a; *hover*, of birds, Arist.*Mir.*836$^a$12; of a dream, S.*El.*1390 (lyr.); *oscillate*, Pl. *Phd.*112b; of an army, αἰωρουμένης στρατιᾶς περὶ Μεσοποταμίαν Plu. *Ant.*28. b. *take passive exercise*, Gal.*Thras.*23. 3. metaph., *to be in suspense*, ἐν κινδύνῳ *to hang* in doubt and danger, Th.7.77; αἰ. ἐν ἄλλοις *depend* upon.., Pl.*Mx.*248a; αἰωρηθεὶς ὑπὲρ μεγάλων *playing for a* high *stake*, Hdt.8.100; αἰ. τὴν ψυχὴν X.*Cyn.*4.4; τὸ μὴ -ούμενον τῆς ψυχῆς Epicur.*Nat.*22G. 4. Pass., *to be held in suspense, threatened*, ἀπαιδίας πρὸς τιμωρίαν -ουμένης Chor.p.71.3B. ⊛**-ημα**, ατος, τό, *that which is hung up* or *hovers*, Lyc.1080. 2. *hanging cord, halter*, E.*Hel.*353 (lyr.); *hanging slings* or *chains*, Id.*Or.*984 (lyr.). **-ησις**, εως, ἡ, *oscillatory movement*, esp. Medic., of *passive exercise*, Pl.*Ti.*89a, cf. Gal.10.710; αἰ. δι' ὀχημάτων Poll.10.51. **-ητέον**, *one must take passive exercise*, Sor.1.109; ἐν φορείῳ Herod.Med.ap.Aët.9.13. **-ητός**, όν, *hanging*, *AP*5.203 (Mel.).

⊛**ἀκᾶ**, Dor. Adv. = ἀκήν, *softly, gently*, Pi.*P.*4.156; cf. ἦκα.

⊛**Ἀκᾰδήμεια** (the form is protected by metre in Alex.25,94, cf. Ar. *Nu.*1005, Epicr.11.11, St. Byz. s.v. Ἑκαδήμεια, Ath.10.419d), freq. written **-ία**, ἡ, *Academy*, a gymnasium in the suburbs of Athens, named from the hero Academus, ἐν δρόμοισιν Ἀκαδήμου θεοῦ Eup.32, cf. Pl.*Ly.*203a, etc., where Plato taught: hence, *the Platonic school of philosophy*, Ἀκ. παλαιά, μέση, νεωτέρα Phld.*Acad.Ind.*p.77M.: prov., **Ἀκαδημίηθεν** ἥκεις, of a philosopher, Apostol.2.1:—hence Adj. **Ἀκαδημεικός**, ή, όν, *Academic, of the school of Plato*, Phld. *Acad.Ind.*p.18M.: also **Ἀκαδημαϊκός**, Plu.2.1077c, Ath.11.509a, Luc.*Pisc.*43, Timo 35 codd., etc.; **Ἀκαδημιακός**, D.L.4.67, etc.; **Ἀκαδημικός**, Cic.*Att.*13.12.3 and 16.1; **Ἀκαδήμιος**, Philostr.*VA* 7.2 s.v.l.

**ἀκᾰθαίρετος**, ον, (καθαιρέω) *not to be put down*, Ph.1.39, al.; *not weakened*, Sor.1.21.

⊛**ἀκᾰθαρ-σία**, ἡ, *uncleanness, foulness*, of a wound or sore, Hp. *Fract.*31, cf. Pl.*Ti.*72c (pl.); ἀγγείων Hp.*Epid.*6.31. b. *dirt, filth*, *BGU*1117.27 (13 B.C.), etc. 2. in moral sense, *depravity*, D.21.119. 3. *ceremonial impurity*, Lxx *Le.*15.3, al. **-τίζομαι**, *to be ceremonially unclean*, v.l. ib.14.36. ⊛**-τος**, ον, (καθαίρω) *uncleansed, foul*, ἀήρ Hp.*Aër.*6; of the body, Arist.*Pr.*883$^b$27; ἕλκος Hp.*Fract.* 27; of a woman, *quae menstrua non habet*, Demad.*Fr.*4, Luc.*Lex.*19; of ceremonial impurity, Lxx *Le.*12.2, al., *IG*3.74.3. b. *unpurified*, Pl.*Lg.*866a, 868a. 2. *morally unclean, impure*, Pl.*Phd.*81b, D.19.199, etc.; ἀκάθαρτε *thou beast!* Bato 5; = μανιώδης, Achae.30; ἀ. πνεῦμα Lxx *Za.*13.2, *Ev.Matt.*12.43, cf. *PMag.Par.*1.1238. Adv. ἀκαθάρτως, ἔχειν Pl.*Ti.*92b. 3. of things, *not purged away, unpurged*, S.*OT*256, Pl.*Lg.*854b. b. *unpruned*, Thphr.*CP*1.15.1. c. *ceremonially unclean*, of food, Lxx *Le.*5.2, al., *Act.Ap.*10.14. d. *not sifted, containing impurities*, *PPetr.*2p.8 (iii B.C.). II. Act., *not fit for cleansing*, [φάρμακα] ἑλκέων ἀκαθαρτότερα Aret.*CD*1.8.

**ἀκᾰθεκτέομαι**, Pass., *to be unoccupied*, διάστημα -ούμενον ὑπὸ σώματος *Stoic.*2.163.

⊛**ἀκάθεκτος**, ον, *ungovernable*, Ps.-Phoc.193, Plu.*Nic.*8. Adv. -τως, λυττᾶν Ph.2.48; μαργαίνειν Sch.Opp.*H.*1.38.

**ἀκαθήκουσα** διαθήκη, = Lat. *inofficiosum testamentum*, Just.*Nov.* 38.3 (pl.), cf. *Gloss.*

⊛**ἀκᾰθ-οσίωτος**, ον, *unpurified*, Phot., Suid. ⊛**-υπερτέρητος**, ον, *unsurpassed*, Ptol.*Tetr.*157. **-υστέρητος**, ον, *lacking nothing*, βίος Vett.Val.67.18, cf. Ps.-Callisth.2.11. Adv. -τως *without delay*, *BGU* 1126.11 (i B.C.).

⊛**ἄκαινα**, ης, ἡ, (ἀκή A, ἀκίς) *spike, prick, goad*, A.R.3.1323, *AP*6.41 (Agath.). II. *ten-foot rod* used as a measure, ἄκαιναν ἀμφότερον κέντρον τε βοῶν καὶ μέτρον ἀρούρης Call.*Fr.*214, cf. Sch.A.R. l.c. 2. *square measure of 100 ft.*, in Egypt, Hero *Def.*130, cf. Sch. A.R. l.c., *POxy.*669.41 (? iii A.D.); in Bithynia, *BCH*27.318:—also ⊛**ἄκαινον**, τό, Olymp.*in Metaph.*43.1.

**ἀκαινοτόμητος**, ον, = *inlibatus*, *Gloss.*; *free from innovations*, Just. *Nov.*61.1.4.

**ἀκαιρ-εύομαι**, *behave unseasonably*, Ph.2.166, 280. **-έω**, *to be without an opportunity*, opp. εὐκαιρέω, D.S.10.7:—Med., impf. ἠκαιρεῖσθε *Ep.Phil.*4.10. 2. *talk nonsense*, Astramps.*Orac.*74.9. ⊛**-ία**, ἡ, *unfitness of times*, opp. ἐπικαιρία, Democr.26$^e$ (pl.); opp. εὐκαιρία, Pl.*Phd.*272a; opp. ἐγκαιρία, Id.*Plt.*305d; *time of trouble*, Lib.*Or.*59.38. 2. of bad seasons, *unseasonableness*, ἐνιαυτῶν πολλῶν ἀ. Pl.*Lg.*709a (pl.); τῶν πνευμάτων Arist.*Pr.*941$^b$25 (pl.). 3. *impropriety*, Pl.*Smp.*182a. 4. *bad taste* in writing, D.H.*Dem.* 7, al. 5. opp. καιρός, *want of opportunity*, τὴν ἀκαιρίαν τὴν ἐκείνου καιρὸν ὑμέτερον νομίσαντες D.1.24; *want of time*, Plu.2.130e. II. of persons, *tactlessness*, Thphr.*Char.*12. ⊛**-ιμος**, η, ον, *ill-timed*: prov., ὅ τι κ' ἐπ' ἀκαιρίμαν γλῶσσαν ἔλθῃ *quicquid in buccam venerit*, *Lyr.Adesp.*86A. **-ιος**, ον, poet. for ἄκαιρος, ἀ. ἥκεις, of *untimely* death, *IG*14.1363.11. Adv. -ίως *unseasonably*, *BGU*846.14 (ii A.D.).

**ἀκαιρό-γελως**, ωτος, *given to unseemly laughter*, Archig. (or Posidon.) ap.Aët.6.8. **-λογέω**, *prate unseasonably*, Sch.Pl. *Grg.*469a. **-λογία**, ἡ, Hsch. s.v. βαττολογία; prob. in D.H. *Lys.*4. **-λόγος**, ον, *unseasonable prater*, Ph.2.268, Eust.208.38. **-παρρησία**, ἡ, *ill-timed freedom of speech*, Eust.1069.10. **-παρρησιαστής**, οῦ, ὁ, *one who employs ill-timed freedom* [of] *speech*, Id.1857.2.

⊛**ἄκαιρος**, ον, *ill-timed, unseasonable*, ἐς ἄκαιρα πονεῖν Thgn.91[9]; οὐκ ἄκαιρα λέγειν A.*Pr.*1036; ἄ. κένωσις Hp.*VM*10; προθυμία Th.[4.]65; ἐλευθερία Pl.*R.*569c; ἔπαινος Id.*Phdr.*240e; ῥᾳθυμία D.18.4[?]; γέλως Men.*Mon.*88. Adv. -ρως A.*Ag.*808, *Ch.*624 (both lyr.), H[p.] *Acut.*17, al.: Comp. -οτέρως Id.*Epid.*1.19: neut. pl. as Adv., ἄκαι[ρα] ἀπώλλυτο E.*Hel.*1081. II. of persons, *importunate, troublesom[e]*, Thphr.*Char.*12; ἄ. καὶ λάλος Alciphr.3.62. 2. c. inf., *ill-suited* [to] do a thing, X.*Eq.Mag.*7.6 (Comp.). III. ἄκαιρον, τό, = μυρσίν[η] ἀγρία, Dsc.4.144.

**ἀκακαλίς**, ίδος, ἡ, *gall of the Oriental tamarisk*, Dsc.1.89. 2. = νάρκισσος, Eumach.ap.Ath.15.681e. 3. = ἄρκευθος, Ps.-Dsc.1.75.

**ἀκᾰκέμφατος**· κακῆς φήμης ἀπηλλαγμένος, *in no ill repute*, Hsch.

**ἀκάκης**, Dor. **ἀκάκας** [ᾰκᾰκ], ὁ, poet. form of ἄκακος, A.*Pers.*85[5] (lyr.); epith. of Hades, *IG*7.117.3 (Megara).

**ἀκᾰκήσιος**, ὁ, epith. of Hermes in Arcadia, = sq., Call.*Dian.*143, Paus.8.36.10.

**ἀκάκητᾰ** [ᾰκᾰκ], Ep. form, = ἄκακος, *guileless, gracious*, epith. of Hermes, Il.16.185, Od.24.10, Hes.*Fr.*23; of Prometheus, Id.*Th.* 614; of the poet's father, Orph.*L.*151. (Acc. ἀκακήτην in later poetry, *IPE*1$^2$.436 (Chersonesus, ii A.D.); ἀκάκητος Suid.)

⊛**ἀκακία** (A), ἡ, *shittah tree, Acacia arabica*, Dsc.1.101, Aret.*CD*2.6. II. = *Genista acanthoclada*, Dsc. l.c.

**ἀκᾰκία** (B), ἡ, (ἄκακος) *guilelessness*, D.59.81, Arist.*Rh.*1389$^b$9, Lxx *Jb.*2.3, etc.

**ἀκάκιστος**, ον, *not violent, gentle*, of remedies, Cass.Fel.76.

**ἀκᾰκο-ήθευτος**, ον, = sq., Eust.404.8. **-ήθης**, ες, *guileless*, Phot.; Medic., *benign*, μυρμηκιά Heliod.ap.Orib.45.14.44. Adv. -θως Iamb.*Protr.*21.ιθ'. **-παθέω**, *to be free from suffering*, *EM* 85.12. Adv. **-παθήτως** Apollon.*Mir.*35.

⊛**ἄκᾰκ-ος**, ον, *unknowing of ill, guileless*, A.*Pers.*663 (lyr.), Pl.*Ti.* 91d, *Ep.Rom.*16.18. 2. *innocent, simple* (cf. εὐήθης), D.47.46, 82; ἄ. ἀνθρώπων τρόπος Anaxil.33. Adv. -κως D.47.50. II. *unharmed*, Sapph.149. 2. *unadulterated*, *POxy.*142 (vi A.D.). **-ούργητος**, ον, *uncorrupted*, Harp. s.v. διασείστους; *undamaged*, φορτία σῶα καὶ ἀ. *PLond.*3.948.8 (iii A.D.). **-ούργως**, Adv., used to expl. εὐήθως, Sch.D.19.167. **-υντος**, ον, = sq., αἰτίας Hierocl.*in CA* 1 p.418M., cf. 3 p.424M. Adv. -τως Id.*Prov.*p.462B. **-ωτος**, ον, *unharmed*, Ph.1.490, D.C.77.15; ἀ. εὐχή *IG*14.2012*A*39 (Sulp.Max.). Astrol., *subject to no malignant influence, not 'afflicted'*, Vett.Val.111.24. II. *unsubdued*, M.Ant.5.18.

**ἀκᾰλανθίς**, ίδος, ἡ, = ἀκανθίς, Ar.*Pax*1079, Ant.Lib.9.3; epith. of Artemis, Ar.*Av.*872 (Lacon. **ἀκκαλανσίρ** (sic), Hsch.; **ἀκάλανθος**, *AB*370; **ἀκαλάνθεια**, *EM*44.26).

**ἀκᾰλαρ-ρείτης**, ου, ὁ, (ἀκαλός, ῥέω) *soft-flowing*, epith. of Ocean, Il.7.422, Od.19.434. **-ροος**, ον, = foreg., Orph.*A.*1187.

**ἀκᾰλήφη** (ἀκαλύφη Thphr.*HP*7.7.2 codd.), ἡ, *stinging-nettle*, Dsc.4.93, etc.: metaph., ἀπὸ τῆς ὀργῆς τὴν ἀ. ἀφελέσθαι Ar.*V.*884, cf. Anon.ap.Chrysipp.*Stoic.*3.178. II. *sea-anemone*, so called from its stinging properties, Eup.60, Pherecr.24, Ar.*Lys.*549 (cf. Sch.), Arist.*HA*531$^a$31, 588$^b$20, Plu.2.670d.

**ἀκαλλ-ής**, ές, *without charms*, γυνή Hp.*Ep.*15; σῶμα Luc.*Hist. Conscr.*48; γῆ αὐχμηρὰ καὶ ἀ. (v.l. ἀκαμής) Id.*Prom.*14; [ὕλη] ἀ. καὶ αἰσχρά Procl.*in Alc.*p.326C.: Comp., Olymp.*in Grg.* p.243J. ⊛**-ιέρητος**, ον, *not accepted* by gods, *ill-omened*, ἱερά Aeschin. 3.131, 152. **-ώπιστος**, ον, *unadorned*, Heraclit.92, Ph.1.1, Luc. *Pisc.*12, Gal.*Protr.*10, Max.Tyr.29.7.

**ἀκαλός**, ή, όν, (ἀκᾶ, ἀκήν) *peaceful, still*, ἀκαλὰ προρέων, of a river, Hes.*Fr.*218; ἄκαλα κλόνει Sapph.*Supp.*19, cf. Hsch., Eust.1009.30, *EM*44.29. Adv. -λῶς Eust.1871.54. **ἀκάλως**, Adv., (καλός) *unwell*, ἐὰν οὐκ ἀ. ἔχῃς, χαίρω *POxy.*1676.22 (iii A.D.).

**ἀκάλυπτος**, ον, *uncovered, unveiled*, S.*OT*1427, Arist.*HA*489$^b$5, 1*Enoch*9.5; ἐν ἀκαλύπτῳ..βίῳ, of one who has no house over his head, Men.404. Adv. -τως Lxx 3*Ma.*4.6.

**ἀκᾰλῠφής**, ές, = foreg., S.*Ph.*1327, Arist.*de An.*422$^a$1:—**-ος**, ον, Hippobot.ap.D.L.8.72.

**ἀκᾰμαντο-λόγχας**, α, ὁ, *unwearied at the spear*, Pi.*I.*7(6).10. **-μάχας**, α, ὁ, *unwearied in fight*, Id.*P.*4.171. **-πους**, ὁ, ἡ, πουν, τό, gen. ποδος, *untiring of foot*, ἵππος Id.*O.*3.3; βροντή, ἀπήνη, ib.4.1, 5.3. **-ρόας**, α, ὁ, *of untiring stream*, Ἀλφεός B.5.180. **-χάρμας**, α, ὁ, *unwearied in fight*, Pi.*Fr.*184, in voc. ἀκαμαντοχάρμᾰν Αἶαν.

**ἀκάμας** [ᾰκᾰ], αντος, ὁ, (κάμνω) *untiring*, ἠέλιος, Σπερχειός, etc., Il.18.239, 16.176, al. (not in Od.); ἵπποι Pi.*O.*1.87; Νότος, Βορέας S.*Tr.*112 (lyr.); χρόνος Critias 18; πόνοι *unceasing*, Arist.*Fr.*675; νόος Them.*Or.*6.79c.

⊛**ἀκάμᾰτος**, ον, also η, ον Hes.*Th.*747, B.5.25, S.*Ant.*339:—*without sense of toil*, hence, 1. *untiring, unresting*, in Hom. always epith. of fire, Il.5.4, Od.20.123, al.; ἄνεμοι Emp.111.3; σθένος A. *Pers.*901; ἅλς B.l.c.; ἀ. γῆ earth *that never rests* from tillage, or *inexhaustible*, S. l.c.:—neut. ἀκάματα as Adv., Id.*El.*164 (lyr.). 2. *not tired*, χείρ Hp.*Fract.*3; ὄμματα B.18.20. 3. metaph., δόξα 12.178; πρόνοια *Stoic.*1.125. II. Act., *not tiring*, Aret.*CD*2.13. Adv. -τως, in Comp., *less painfully*, Hp.*Mul.*1.1:—also -τεί Hsch. s.v. ἀκμητί. [ᾰκᾰμᾰτος S.*El.*164; but first syll. long in dactylic verse.]

**ἀκάμμυστος**, ον, *without winking*, Hsch. s.v. ἀσκαρδάμυκτος.

**ἄκαμνος**, ον, *unwearied*, prob. f.l. for ἀκάμας, *PMag.Berol.*2.91.

**ἀκαμπ-ής**, ές, = ἄκαμπτος, Thphr.*HP*3.10.4, Orph.*A.*173, etc.: metaph., θυμός ib.999, cf. Ph.1.528, Plu.2.959f. **-ία**, Ion. **-ίη**,

, = ἀκαμψία, Hp.*Art.*55. —ίας· ὁ εὐθὴς δρόμος, ἡ δρομεύς, Hsch., cf. Suid. —ιος, ον, = ἀκαμπής, S.*Fr.*968: — neut. —ιον, τό, in chariot- or horse-racing, *straight course*, *IG*2.966*A*43, *Delph.*3(2).38, al., cf. *CM*45.3. —τόπους, ὁ, ἡ, *with unbending foot*, ἐλέφαντες Nonn.*D.*5.148. —τος, ον, *unbent, rigid*, Hp.*Fract.*2 (Sup.), Pl.*Ti.*74b (Comp.), etc.; τὸ ἄ. *the part that will not bend*, Arist.*HA*493$^b$29. 2. metaph., *unbending, unflinching*, βουλαί Pi.*P.*4.72; ψυχὰν ἄ. Id.*I.*(3).53; ἀ. μένει A.*Ch.*455 (lyr.); τὸ πρὸς τοὺς πόνους, τὸ εἰς ἐπιείκειαν ἄ., Plu.*Lyc.*11, *Cat.Mi.*4. 3. *from which there is no return*, χῶρος ἐνέρων *AP*7.467 (Antip.); τρίβος *IG*12(7).449 (Amorgos).

**ἀκαμψία**, ἡ, *inflexibility*, Arist.*PA*654$^a$24.

**ἄκαν**, ανος, ὁ, = *thistle*, only in Lxx 4*Ki.*14.9.

**ἄκανθ-α** [ἄκ], ης, ἡ, (ἀκή A) *thorn, prickle*, Arist.*PA*655$^a$10, Thphr.*HP*6.1.3: hence, 1. *any thorny* or *prickly plant* (in Od.5.328 (pl.) prob. *Eryngium campestre*), S.*Fr.*718, Eub.107.19, Theoc.1.132, etc.: prov., οὐ γὰρ ἄκανθαι no *thistles*, i.e. 'an easy job', Ar.*Fr.*272,483:—special kinds: ἄ. Ἀραβική *smaller milk-thistle, Notobasis syriaca*, Dsc.3.13; ἄ. βασιλική *fish-thistle, Cnicus Acarna*, Thphr.*CP*1.10.5; ἄ. Ἰνδική, = *Balsamodendron Mukul*, Id.*HP*9.1.2; ἄ. λευκή *Acacia albida*, ib.4.2.8; = ἄ. βασιλική, Dsc.3.12; ἄ. λευκὴ τρίοζος, = *Euphorbia antiquorum*, Thphr.*HP*4.4.12; ἄ. ἀκανώδης (prob.) *corn-thistle, Carduus arvensis*, ib.10.6. 2. of other plants, e.g. *Spanish broom, Spartium junceum*, Str.3.5.10:— = ἀκακία, ἄ. Αἰγυπτία, Thphr.*HP*9.1.2, cf. *POxy.*1188.10 (13 A.D.), etc.; ἄ. μέλαινα *Acacia arabica*, Thphr.*HP*4.2.8, cf. Hdt.2.96, Thd.*Is.*41.19; ἄ. διψάς, = *Acacia tortilis*, Thphr.*HP*4.7.1. 3. central flowering-bud of χαμαιλέων λευκός, ib.9.12.1, Dsc.3.8. 4. = ἄκανθος, Ps.-Dsc.3.17. 5. in pl., *prickles* or *spines* of the hedgehog and of certain fish, Ion Trag.38, Arist.*HA*530$^b$8. 6. *backbone* or *spine* of fish, A.*Fr.*275, Ar.*V.*969, Alex.110.11, al.; of serpents, Hdt.2.75, Theoc.24.32, A.R.4.150; of men, Hdt.4.72, Hp.*Art.*14, E.*El.*492, Arist.*PA*654$^a$26, Gal.2.451, etc.; improperly used of mammalia, acc. to Arist.*APo.*98$^a$22; of *the spinous processes of the vertebrae*, Gal.2.758; χονδρώδεις ἄ. false ribs, Ruf.*Oss.*25. 7. metaph. in pl., *thorny* questions, Luc.*Hes.*5, Ath.3.97d. ⊛—έα, ἡ, = ἄκανθα Αἰγυπτία, *PLond.*2.214.13 (iii A.D.). —ές· ἀκανθῶδες, Hsch. ⊛—εών, ῶνος, ὁ, *thorny brake*, = *spinetum*, *Gloss.* —ήεις, εσσα, εν, *thorny, prickly*, Nic.*Th.*638. —ηλή, sine expl., Hdn.*Epim.*227. —ηρός, ά, όν, *with spines*, of certain fish, Arist.*HA*621$^b$16 (Comp.). ⊛—ίας, ου, ὁ, *prickly thing*, and so, 1. kind of *shark*, prob. *Squalus acanthias* L., Arist.*HA*565$^a$29, 621$^b$17. 2. kind of *grasshopper*, Ael.*NA*10.44. 3. = ἀσφάραγος, Poll.1.247, 6.54. —ικός, ή, όν, *spinous*, τὰ —κά Thphr.*HP*6.1.3, al.; φύσις ib.4.6. —ινος, η, ον, *of thorns*, στέφανος *Ev.Marc.*15.17, *Jo.*19.5. 2. metaph., *thorny*, ἐν ἀ. ἀταρποῖς *Anacreont.*53.12. II. *of shittah-wood*, ἱστός Hdt.2.96; ξύλα *PLond.*3.1177.191 (ii A.D.); τὰ ἀ. cloths *made of* ἀκάνθιον 2, Str.3.5.10. 2. ἀ. πάππος *thistle-down*, Dsc.4.81. ⊛—ιον, τό, Dim. of ἄκανθα, Arist.*HA*516$^b$19, Hp.*Mul.*1.36, *PStrassb.*29.37 (iii A.D.). 2. *cotton thistle, Onopordum illyricum*, Dsc.3.16. ⊛—ίς, ίδος, ἡ, a bird, *goldfinch, Fringilla carduelis*, or *linnet, Fr. linaria*, Arist.*HA*616$^b$31, Theoc.7.141. II. = ἠριγέρων, Call.ap.Plin.*HN*25.168: = ἄκανθα Ἀραβική, Ps.-Dsc.3.13: = ἀκάνθιον, ib.16. III. = κανθός, Gal.17(1).666. —ίων, ονος, ὁ, *hedgehog*, Gal.12.423.

⊛**ἀκανθο-βάτης**, ου, ὁ, *walking among thorns*, nickname of grammarians, *AP*11.322 (Antiphan.):—fem. —**βάτις**, ιδος, ib.7.198 (Leon.). —**βόλος**, ον, (βάλλω) *prickly*, χαίτη (of the plant ἔχις) Nic.*Th.*542; ῥάβδον Id.*Fr.*74.9. II. Subst. ἀ., ὁ, *surgical instrument for extracting a bone*, prob. f.l. for sq., Paul.Aeg.6.32. —**λάβος**, ὁ, *instrument for extracting thorns*, ibid.:—also —**λαβίς**, ἡ, *Gloss.* —**λόγος**, ον, *gathering thorns*, nickname of quibblers (cf. ἄκανθα 7), *AP*11.20 (Antip. Thess.), 347 (Phil.). —**νωτος**, ον, *prickle-backed*, Hsch.

**ἀκανθόομαι**, Pass., (ἄκανθα) *become prickly*, Thphr.*HP*7.6.2.

⊛**ἀκανθοπλήξ**, ῆγος, ὁ, ἡ, *wounded by the prickle* of a fish (cf. τρυγών), Ὀδυσσεὺς ἀ., name of play of Sophocles.

⊛**ἄκανθος**, ὁ, *bearsfoot, Acanthus mollis*, a plant imitated in Corinthian capitals, Arist.*Fr.*269 (prob.), cf. *IG*4.1484.243 (Epid.); ὑγρὸς ἄ. Theoc.1.55; ἄ. ἀγρία *Acanthus spinosus*, Dsc.3.17. II. *Acanthus*, = ἀκακία, Virg.*G.*2.119.

**ἀκανθο-στεφής**, ές, of a fish, *prickle-backed*, Arist.*Fr.*295. —**φάγος** [ᾰ], ον, *feeding on thistles*, Arist.*HA*592$^b$30. —**φορέω**, *bear thorns*, Dsc.3.18. —**φόρος**, ον, *producing thorns*, Thphr.*HP*3.18.2. 2. *prickly*, ἐχῖνος Nonn.*D.*13.421. —**φυέω**, *produce thorns*, (v.l. for —φορέω) Dsc.3.18. —**φυλλος**, ον, *with spinous leaves*, cj. in Thphr.*HP*1.10.4. —**χοιρος**, ὁ, *hedgehog*, Hsch. s.v. ἐχῖνος, Suid. s.v. χοιρογρύλλιος.

**ἀκανθ-υλλίς**, ίδος, ἡ, Dim. of ἀκανθίς (in form), prob. *goldfinch*, Eub.123 (dub.), Arist.*HA*593$^a$13, 616$^a$5, cf. *Edict.Diocl.*4.34. 2. = ἀσφάραγος, Apul.*Herb.*84. —**ώδης**, ες, *full of thorns, thorny*, χῶρος Hdt.1.126; τὸ ῥόδον Arist.*Pr.*907$^a$22, cf. Thphr.*HP*1.5.3, etc. 2. *prickly*, γλῶττα Arist.*HA*503$^a$2; τρίχες ib.490$^b$28; of the vertebrae, *spinous*, ib.516$^b$20: Comp., ib.516$^b$22. 3. metaph., λόγοι ἀ. *thorny* arguments, Luc.*D.Mort.*10.8; ἀ. βίος Suid. ⊛—**ών**, ῶνος, ὁ, = ἀκανθεών, *PFlor.*50.72 (iii A.D.), Hdn.Gr.1.29.

**ἀκᾰνίζω**, (ἄκανος) *to be thistle-headed*, Thphr.*HP*6.4.8.

**ἀκανικός**, ή, όν, *thistle-like*, Thphr.*HP*4.6.10.

**ἀκάνιον**, τό, Dim. of ἄκανος, Hsch.

**ἄκᾰνος**, ὁ, (ἀκή A, ἀκίς) *pine-thistle, Atractylis gummifera*, Thphr.*HP*1.10.6, al. 2. *thistle-head*, ib.6.4.3.

**ἀκᾰνώδης**, ες, *thistle-headed*; τὸ τῶν ἀ. γένος Thphr.*HP*1.10.6, cf. 6.4.3.

**ἀκαπήλευτος**, ον, = sq., Suid.

**ἀκάπηλος**, ον, *free from tricks of trade*, βίος Str.11.8.7.

⊛**ἀκάπν-ιστος**, ον, *unsmoked*, μέλι ἀ. honey *taken without smoking the bees*, Str.9.1.23. —**ος**, ον, *without smoke, free from it*, σκέπη Hp.*Acut.*65; *not smoking, making no smoke*, πῦρ Thphr.*Ign.*71; θυσία ἄ. an offering but *no burnt offering*, Luc.*Am.*4; so a poem is called Καλλιόπης ἄ. θύος *AP*6.321 (Leon.):—ἄκαπνα γὰρ αἰὲν ἀοιδοὶ θύομεν we sacrifice *without a fire of our own*, i.e. live at others' expense, Call.*Fr.*53P. II. = ἀκάπνιστος, Plin.*HN*11.45. III. ἄκαπνον, τό, = σάμψουχον, Ps.-Dsc.3.39. —**ωτος**, ον, *free from vapour*, E.*Fr.*781.54 (dub.).

**ἄκαρα**· τὰ σκέλη (Cret.), Hsch., *EM*45.16.

**ἀκαρᾰδόκητος**, ον, *unexpected*, Eust.1127.62.

⊛**ἀκάρδιος**, ον, *wanting the heart*, Polyaen.8.23.33, Plu.*Caes.*63: metaph., *spiritless, cowardly*, Chrysipp.*Stoic.*2.247,249; *heartless, weak*, Lxx *Je.*5.21; ἄφωνος καὶ ἀ. Procl.*in Cra.*p.41P. II. of wood, *without heart* or *pith, solid*, Thphr.*HP*3.12.1.

**ἀκάρηνος**, ον, *headless*, *APl.*4.116 (Euod.), *Epigr.Gr.*1013 (Memnon).

⊛**ἀκαρής**, ές, (κείρω) properly of hair, *too short to be cut*, hence generally, *small, tiny*, ἀκαρῆ τινα ἐνθυμήματα D.H.*Isoc.*20; ἐν ἀκαρεῖ χρόνῳ *Com.Adesp.*370 (and codd. in Ar.*Pl.*244). II. metaph., *within a hair's breadth of, all but*, στρουθὶς ἀκαρὴς νὴ Δί' εἶ Alex.144; ἀ. παραπόλωλας Men.835; ἀ. δέω φάσκειν Id.*Pk.*166; κατέπεσον ἀ. τῷ δέει *Com.Adesp.*581. III. freq. of Time, esp. neut. ἀκαρές, *moment*, ἐν ἀκαρεῖ χρόνου Ar.*Pl.*244 (ap.*EM*), Alciphr.3.56, Luc.*Tim.*3 (also ἐν ἀ. τοῦ χρόνου ib.23); ἐν ἀ. alone, Id.*Asin.*37, Plot.5.5.7; also ἀκαρῆ διαλιπών (sc. χρόνον) having waited *a moment*, Ar.*Nu.*496; ἀκαρὲς ὥρας *in a moment*, Plu.*Ant.*28; ἡμέρας μιᾶς ἀ. Id.2.938a; ἐπ' ἀκαρές Aret.*SD*2.2. 2. neut. pl. ἀκαρῆ, usu. with negs., not *a bit*, not *at all*, οὐκ ἀπολαύεις πλὴν τοῦθ' ὃ φέρεις ἀκαρῆ not *a bit*, not *at all*, Ar.*V.*701; οὐδ' ἀκαρῆ ib.541 (lyr.), D.50.56; ἀκαρῆ παντελῶς (v.l. ἀκαρεί) Xenarch.7.15; παρ' ἀκαρῆ within *a hair's breadth*, Pl.*Ax.*366c, Phld.*Rh.*2.28S. IV. τὸ ἀ. *ring on the little finger*, Poll.5.100, Hsch. V. Adv. ἀκαρῶς Sch.Ar.*Pl.*244 (—έως Hsch.); ἀκαρεί, *instantly*, Plu.*Sert.*16.

**ἀκαρί**, τό, kind of *mite*, bred in wax, Arist.*HA*557$^b$8.

⊛**ἀκαριαῖος**, α, ον, (ἀκαρής) *momentary, brief*, πλοῦς D.56.30, cf. Arist.*HA*590$^a$3, Phld.*Ir.*p.80W., etc.; τὸ ἀ. S.E.*P.*3.79; of a locus, ἀ. τόπος Aristox.*Harm.*p.55M. Adv. —ως Alciphr.1.39 (cj.).

**ἀκαρνάν**, ὁ, a fish, prob. = λάβραξ (cf. **ἀκάρναξ**· λάβραξ, Hsch.), Ath.8.356b.

**ἀκαρπ-έω**, *bear no fruit*, Thphr.*HP*3.3.4, etc. —**ία**, ἡ, *unfruitfulness, barrenness*, A.*Eu.*801, Hp.*Vict.*4.90, Arist.*Mir.*842$^a$22. —**ιστος**, ον, *where nothing is to be reaped, unfruitful*, of the sea, E.*Ph.*210 (lyr.). —**ος**, ον, *without fruit, barren*, E.*Fr.*898.8, Pl.*Ti.*91c; ἄ. ξύλον, = ἀκακία, Lxx *Is.*41.19: c. gen., λίμνη ἄ. ἰχθύων Paus.5.7.3. 2. metaph., *fruitless, unprofitable*, πόνος B.*Fr.*7.5; λόγοι Pl.*Phdr.*277a; τὰ ἄ. Arist.*EN*1125$^a$11. Adv. —πως S.*OT*254. II. Act., *making barren*, A.*Eu.*942, cf. Max.Tyr.5.4. —**ωτος**, ον, *not made fruitful, uncultivated*, Thphr.*CP*3.13.3. 2. metaph., χρησμὸς ἀ. *unfulfilled* oracle, A.*Eu.*714; νίκας ἀκάρπωτον χάριν because of some victory *which yielded her no tribute*, S.*Aj.*176.

**ἀκαρτέρητος**, ον, *insupportable*, κακόν Chrysipp.*Stoic.*3.131. Adv. —τως [Gal.]19.694. II. Act., *lacking in endurance*, Vett.Val.222.12.

**ἀκαρτέω**, = ἀκρατέω, γλώσσης Call.*Aet.*3.1.8.

**ἄκαρτος**, ον, (κείρω) *unshaven*, πώγωνες Ath.5.211e; ἀνθρωπάρια Ps.-Callisth.3.8.

⊛**ἀκαρφής**, ές, (κάρφω) *not dried* or *withered*, Nic.*Fr.*70.9.

⊛**ἀκασκᾶ**, Adv., (ἀκή B) *gently*, ἄ. προβῶντες Cratin.126; but ἀκασκᾷ Pi.*Fr.*28.

**ἀκασκαῖος**, α, ον, (ἀκή B) *gentle*, ἄγαλμα πλούτου A.*Ag.*741 (lyr.).

**ἄκαστος**, ὁ, = σφένδαμνος, Hsch.

**ἀκάτα**, corrupt in A.*Ag.*985; Ahrens' emend. (ψαμμὶς ἀκτά for ψαμμιὰς ἀκάτα) would suit the metre.

**ἀκατά-βλητος**, ον, *irrefragable*, λόγος Ar.*Nu.*1229. II. *not to be thrown down*, πύργοι Sch.E.*Hec.*1. —**βολέω**, *default* in payment, *GDI*1804 (Delph., ii B.C.). —**βολος**, ον, *unpaid, outstanding*, of arrears of taxation, *IG*5(1).1433 (Messene).

**ἀκατ-αγγείωτος**, ον, *not supplied with blood vessels*, δέρμα Antyll.(?) ap.Orib.45.17.8. —**άγγελτος**, ον, *unproclaimed*, πόλεμος D.H.1.58, Plu.*Num.*12, cf. App.*Hisp.*11.

⊛**ἀκατάγνωστος**, ον, *not to be condemned*, Lxx 2*Ma.*4.47, *Ep.Tit.*2.8, *CIG*1971 (Thessalonica), *IG*14.2139; σύμβιος Keil-Premerstein *Zweiter Bericht* 225 (iii A.D.). Adv. —τως *unexceptionably*, λογιστεύσας *IG*5(2).152 (Tegea, iii A.D.), cf. *POxy.*140.15 (vi A.D.).

**ἀκαταγώνιστος**, ον, *unconquerable*, D.S.17.26, Olymp.Hist.p.451 D., Procl.*in Cra.*p.112P.; epith. of the Stoic sage, *Stoic.*1.53.

**ἀκατα-δίκαστος**, ον, *indemnatus*, *Gloss.* —**δούλωτος**, ον, *not enslaved*, Sch.E.*Hec.*420,754. —**θύμιος**, ον, *disagreeable*, interp. in Artem.2.48, cf. Just.*Nov.*53.3.1, Eust.149.28, etc.

⊛**ἀκαταιτίᾰτος**, ον, *not to be accused*, J.*BJ*4.3.10, al.; *not to be accused, blameless*, ib.2.14.8.

**ἀκατα-κάλυπτος**, ον, *uncovered*, Lxx *Le.*13.45 (v.l.), Plb.15.27.2, 1*Ep.Cor.*11.5,13; ἀκαθαρσία Ph.1.72. —**καυστος**, ον, *not burnt*, Apollon.*Mir.*36:—also —**καυτος**, Dsc.5.102. —**κλαστος**, ον, *not* to be broken, stubborn, Sch.Od.10.329. -κόσμητος, ον, unarranged, Plu.2.424a. -κράτητος, ον, gloss on ἀάσχετος, EM1.31. -κρῖτος, ον, uncondemned, Act.Ap.16.37, 22.25.

**ἀκάτακτος**, ον, not to be broken, Arist.Mete.385a14; unbroken, Phld.Mort.39.

**ἀκατά-ληκτος**, ον, incessant, γένεσις Ocell.4.2, cf. Arr.Epict.1.17.3, Procl.in Prm.p.873S., etc. Adv. -τως Agathin.ap.Orib.10.7.26. II. acatalectic, in prosody, Heph.4, Aristid.Quint.1.23. -ληπτέω, not to understand, S.E.P.1.201, al. -ληπτος, ον, that cannot be reached or touched, Arist.Pr.921b23; τί ἐστι φίλος; ἄνθρωπος ἀ. Secund.Sent.11. Adv. -τως Sch.Il.17.75. II. not to be conquered, J.BJ3.7.7; defying suppression, τὸ ἀ. τῆς γοητείας Vett.Val.238.25. 2. Philos., incomprehensible, Phld.Acad.Ind.p.91 M., M.Ant.7.54, S.E.M.7.432; that cannot be grasped, πλῆθος, of the stars, Chrysipp.Stoic.2.168. 3. not comprehending or attaining conviction, φαντασία (opp. καταληπτική, q.v.) Chrysipp.Stoic.2.40, al.: c. gen., ἀ. τῶν ὁμοειδῶν Phld.Herc.1457.12. Adv. -τως, ἔχειν περί τινος Ph.1.78; prob. l. in Arr.Epict.2.23.46:—hence ⊕ἀκαταληψία, ἡ, inability to comprehend or attain conviction, Sceptic term, attrib. to Stoics by Galen, Stoic.1.17, but to Arcesilaus by Cic.Att.13.19.3, Numen.ap.Eus.PE14.7, S.E.P.1.1.

**ἀκατάλλακτος**, ον, irreconcilable, Zaleuc.ap.Stob.4.2.19, D.S.12.20. Adv. -τως, πολεμεῖν D.11.4; διακεῖσθαι πρός τινα Plb.11.29.13; ἔχειν Ph.1.507; μισεῖν ib.479.

**ἀκαταλληλ-ία**, ἡ, failure to conform with rules, inaccurate designation, PGnom.138 (ii A.D.). II. Gramm., false concord, A.D.Synt.167.1. -ος, ον, not fitting together, incongruous, τόποι Plb.6.42.3, cf. Arist.Mu.397b31, Arr.Epict.2.11.8; unsuitable, Ruf.Fr.63; inconsequent, Phld.Po.1676.8:—esp. Gramm., ungrammatical, ἐνθύμημα D.H.Dem.27; lacking in concord, A.D.Synt.30.5, al. Adv. -ως ungrammatically, λόγος -ως συντεταγμένος Diog.Bab.Stoic.3.214; -ως κείμενα A.D.Synt.89.18; generally, incongruously, Porph.Abst.2.40:—also in Law, not in conformity with regulations, χρηματίζειν, πρᾶξαι, PGnom.117,106 (ii A.D.).

⊕**Ἀκάταλλος**, ὁ, sc. μήν, month at Zelea, SIG279.23.

**ἀκατά-λῦτος**, ον, indissoluble, perpetual, κράτος, ζωή, D.H.10.31, Ep.Heb.7.16; βάσανος Lxx 4Ma.10.11; unimpaired, Jahresh.14 Beibl.135 (Cyme). -μάθητος, ον, not learnt or known, Hp.Acut.7, 51, Plot.3.9.3. ⊕-μακτος, ον, not softened by kneading, Sch.Ar.Lys.656. -μαρτύρητος, Astrol., not aspected by, not configurate with, Vett.Val.117.8. -μάχητος, ον, unconquerable, Lxx Wi.5.19, M.Ant.8.48, Men.Prot.p.4D., Ps.-Callisth.2.11. ⊕-μέμπτως, Adv. unexceptionably, IG12(7).231 (Amorgos). -μέτρητος, ον, unmeasured, Eratosth.ap.Str.2.1.21, Nicom.Ar.1.17. -μικτος, ον, not to be met with, rare, Gloss.

**ἀκατ-ανάγκαστος**, ον, not compulsory, Diogenian.Epicur.3.61, Porph.ap.Eus.PE5.10.

**ἀκατα-νέμητος**, ον, not pastured, PTeb.66.75 (ii B.C.). -νόητος, ον, inconceivable, Ps.-Luc.Philopatr.13, Hsch.s.v. δύσληπτα, gloss on ἀθέσφατος, Sch.Opp.H.4.520. Adv. -τως Suid.s.v. Νουμᾶς. -ξεστος, ον, not hewn, smooth, IG1.322, 7.3074 (Lebad.). -πάλαιστος, ον, unconquerable in wrestling, Sch.Pi.N.4.153, Gloss. ⊕-πάτητος, ον, v.l. for ἀκατάπαυστος (q.v.). ⊕-παυστος, ον, not to be set at rest, incessant, Plb.4.17.4, D.S.11.67, etc.; that cannot cease from, τινός 2Ep.Pet.2.14. Adv. -τως Sch.A.R.1.1001. II. not to be checked, irresistible, PMag.Par.1.2364. -πληκτος, ον, undaunted, Epicur.Fr.37, D.H.1.81, App.BC2.142. Adv. -τως Phld.Mort.39, D.H.1.57, App.BC1.110. -πληξία, ἡ, imperturbability, as the highest good, Nausiph.3; -πληξίαν ἔχειν πρὸς τὰ δεινά Phld.D.3Fr.81. -πόνητος, ον, inexhaustible, Philol.21, Theol.Ar.15. ⊕-ποτος, ον, not to be swallowed, Lxx Jb.20.18. -πράϋντος, ον, unappeasable, Sch.S.Tr.999, Gloss. -πτόητος, ον, not to be scared, Sch.Il.3.63. -πτωτος, ον, not liable to fall, Eustr.in EN311.18. -σβεστος, ον, unslaked, τίτανος Gal.12.471; unquenchable, ἐλλύχνια Apollon.Mir.36. -σειστος, ον, not to be shaken, Hsch. -σήμαντος, ον, unsealed, unwritten, ἀ. [ἔνταλμα] a commission by word of mouth, Hdn.3.11.9. -σκεύαστος, ον, not properly prepared, φάρμακον Thphr.HP9.16.6; unwrought, unformed, γῆ Lxx Ge.1.2; ἡ ἀ. chaos, 1Enoch21.1; unpolished, unartificial, ἁπλᾶ καὶ μονοειδῆ καὶ ἀ. Ps.-Plu.Vit.Hom.218. Adv. -τως D.H.Is.15. -σκευος, ον, lacking equipment, πλοῖα PEdgar8.4 (iii B.C.); of savage tribes, Theagen.17. II. in Lit. Crit., without artifice or elaboration, Phld.Rh.1.85., D.H.Th.27, Philostr.VA6.11; epith. of orator, Plu.2.835b. Adv. -ως Plb.6.4.7. III. uncivilized, βίος D.S.5.39. IV. disordered, v.l. for ἀπαρασκ., Aeschin.3.163. -σκήνωτος, ον, unsuitable for encampment, τόπος Onos.10.17. -σκοπος, ον, gloss on ἀνώϊστος, Sch.Opp.C.4.101. -σόφιστος, ον, not to be put down by fallacies, Ap.Ty.Ep.44. ⊕-στᾰσία, ἡ, instability, anarchy, confusion, Stoic.3.99, Plb.1.70.1, Nic.Dam.Vit.Caes.28, etc.: pl., Lxx Pr.26.28, D.H.6.31, 2Ep.Cor.6.5. II. unsteadiness, τοῦ σώματος Chrysipp.Stoic.3.121; ἀ. καὶ μανία Plb.7.4.8: pl., Man.5.57. -στᾰτέω, to be unstable, Arr.Epict.2.1.12, Heph.Astr.1.1:—Pass., Lxx To.1.15. ⊕-στᾰτος, ον, (καθίστημι) unstable, unsettled, καιροί Hp.Aph.3.8; πνεῦμα D.19.136, cf. Arist.Pr.941b29; disorderly, ὁρμαί Stoic.3.166; πολιτεία D.H.6.74:—of men, fickle, Plb.7.4.6; of fevers, irregular, Hp.Acut.(Sp.)20. Adv. -ως, ἔχειν Isoc.21.7. II. not making any deposit, οὖρον Hp.Prorrh.1.32.

**ἀκατ-αστέριστος**, ον, not arranged in constellations, οὐρανός Ach.Tat.Intr.Arat.40.

**ἀκατα-στόχαστος**, not conjectural, πράγματα Phld.Rh.2.274 (dub.), cf. Suid. -στρεπτος, ον, not to be overthrown, Sch.Pi.O.146. -στροφος, ον, never-ending, Favor.ap.Stob.4.15.29; of literary period, without conclusion, D.H.Comp.22. Adv. -φως i cessantly, Chrysipp.Stoic.2.273. -σχαστος, ον, without scar fication, Herod.in Rh.Mus.58.92. -σχεσία, ἡ, ungovernableness, Ptol.Tetr.170. -σχετος, ον, (κατέχω) not to be checked, ὁρμ Hipparch.ap.Stob.4.44.81, cf. Onos.1.3; δάκρυα D.S.17.38; of per sons, uncontrollable, Phld.Piet.86, Apollon.Mir.40, Plu.Mar.44. Adv. -τως D.S.17.34, Plu.Cam.37. -τακτος, ον, not reduce to order, Procl.in Prm.p.560S.; abstract, Ps.-Alex.Aphr.in SE38.13. II. unclassified, of sources of income, BCH6.14 (Delos, i B.C.). -τρητος, ον, not pierced, ὀστοῦν Gal.UP9.13. -τριπτος, ον, inexhaustible, Plb.3.89.9; not wearing out, Gal.UP1.15.

**ἀκατ-αύγαστος**, ον, not illuminated, Steph.in Hp.2.295 D.

**ἀκατά-φθορος**, unharmed, safe, SIG700.32 (ii B.C.). -φόρητος, ον, not to be borne, Hsch. s.v. ἀνάρσιος. -φρόνητος, ον, not to be despised, X.Ages.6.8, J.AJ9.11.2, Plu.2.483a, etc. Adv. -ως without negligence, PLond.1.113(4).15 (vi A.D.). ⊕-χρημάτιστος, not encumbered with debt, PTeb.318.1 (ii A.D.), PFlor.28b, Sammelb.364 (Alexandria), etc. -χρηστος, ον, unused, Eust.812.52, Gloss. -χώριστος, ον, undigested, ὕλη Arist.Pr.949b3. II. unregistered, Sammelb.5232.33. -ψευστος, not fabulous, θηρία Hdt.4.191; not belied, διάληψις Ath.Mitt.33.380 (Pergam.).

⊕**ἀκάτειος**, ον, prop. belonging to an ἄκατος, q.v.; esp. ἀ. ἱστός foremast, IG2.793, etc.; ἀ. κεραία yard belonging thereto, ib., cf. Poll.1.91. II. Subst. ἀκάτειον, τό, (sc. ἱστίον) small sail, opp. τὰ μεγάλα ἱστία, X.HG6.2.27, Epicr.10 (with play on ἄκατος II), cf. Luc.Lex.15, J.Tr.46, Hist.Conscr.45; ἄρασθαι τὸ ἀ., i.e. take to flight, prob. l. for ἀκάτιον in Epicur.Fr.163, cf. Ar.Lys.64.

**ἀκατ-έργαστος**, ον, not cultivated, γῆ PTeb.61b32 (ii B.C.); not worked up, Longin.15.5; of bread, not thoroughly baked, Gal.6.484. II. undigested, τροφή Arist.PA650a15, Diocl.Fr.43, etc.; indigestible, Xenocr.112, Gal.6.484. -εύναστος, ον, not put to bed, waking, Hsch., Suid., Phot. ⊕-ηγόρητος, ον, not accused, PTeb.5.47 (ii B.C.), Sammelb.343 (Alexandria), D.S.11.46, J.AJ17.11.3, BGU183.8 (i A.D.); blameless, Phalar.Ep.10. -ήχητος, ον, not encompassed by sound, Suid.

⊕**ἀκάτιον** [ᾰκᾰ], τό, Dim. of ἄκατος, light boat, used by pirates, Th.1.29, 4.67, Plb.1.73.2, etc. II. sort of woman's shoe, Ar.Fr.739b, Hsch. III. dwarf, Com.Adesp.923.

**ἀκατίς**, ίδος, millepede, Steph.in Hp.1.154 D.

**ἀκατ-ονόμαστος**, ον, nameless, ποιότης Epicur.Fr.314, cf. D.H.Comp.21, Archig.ap.Gal.8.592; θεός Ph.1.630, al. -όπτευτος, ον, not in aspect with, Paul.Al.O.2. -οπτος, ον, unobserved, Hld.6.14.

**ἄκᾰτος** [ᾰκ], ἡ (rarely ὁ, as Hdt.7.186):—light vessel, boat, Thgn.458, Pi.P.11.40, Hdt. l.c., Th.7.25, etc.; used in the mysteries, IG1.225c:—generally, ship, E.Hec.446, Or.342. II. boat-shaped cup, Theopomp.Com.3 (= Telest.6), Antiph.4.

**ἀκατούλωτος**, ον, not scarred over, Herod.Med.ap.Orib.10.11.3, Philum.Ven.10, Ruf.Fr.118.

**ἀκάττῡτος**, ον, not stitched, i.e. new, of shoes, Teles p.40 H.

**ἄκαυλος**, ον, without stalk, Dsc.1.8.2. II. of a feather, without shaft or stalk, Arist.PA682b18. III. Subst. ἄκαυλον, τό, = φυλλῖτις, Ps.-Dsc.3.107.

⊕**ἄκαυστ-ος**, ον, (καίω) unburnt, Hp.Haem.2, X.An.3.5.13. 2. incombustible, Arist.Mete.387a18, Thphr.Lap.4; unquenchable (v.l. for ἄσβεστος), πῦρ Lxx Jb.20.26. -όω, make fireproof, Zos.Alch.p.166B. -ωσις, ἡ, Id.p.217B.

**ἀκαυτ-ηρίαστος**, ον, not branded, of horses, Str.5.1.9. -ος, ον, = ἄκαυστος, Gal.12.212.

**ἀκάχημαι, ἀκαχήσω, ἀκάχησα**, etc., v. ἀχέω.

**ἀκᾰχίζω** [ᾰκ], only pres., trouble, grieve, τινά Od.16.432:—Med., μὴ.. λίην ἀκαχίζεο θυμῷ be not troubled, Il.6.486: c. part., μή τι θανὼν ἀκαχίζευ Od.11.486.

**ἀκαχμένος**, η, ον, Epic part. (cf. ἀκή A), sharp-edged, ἀ. ὀξέϊ χαλκῷ Il.15.482, Od.1.99, al.; πέλεκυν.. ἀμφοτέρωθεν ἀ. 5.235; φάσγανον 22.80. II. armed, c. dat., γένος σκυλάκων κυνόδουσιν ἀ. Opp.C.1.476, cf. 3.252.

**ἀκαχύνω**, = ἀχέω, inf. -έμεν Antim.80. **ἀκεᾶνες**· ἰχθύες (Ambrac.), Hsch.

**ἀκέᾰνος**, ὁ, kind of leguminous vegetable, Pherecr.188, cf. Ael.Dion.Fr.28.

**ἀκέαστος**, ον, = ἄκλαστος, Hsch.

**ἀκειόμενος**, v. sub ἀκέομαι.

**ἀκεῖον**· τὸ φάρμακον, Hsch., EM46.19.

**ἀκειρεκόμης**, Dor. -ας, ὁ, = ἀκερσεκόμης, of Apollo, Pi.P.3.14, I.1.7, Philostr.Ep.16; of Asclepius, IG3.171; of Avars, APl.4.72.

**ἀκέλευθος**, ον, pathless, Hsch.

**ἀκέλευμνον**· οὐ βεβηκὼς ἀσφαλῶς, οἱ δὲ τὸν σκληρὸν σίδηρον, Hsch.

**ἀκέλευστος**, ον, unbidden, A.Ag.731 (lyr.), S.Aj.1284, E.El.71, Pl.Lg.953d. Adv. -ως Suid. s. v. ἀπαγγέλτως.

**ἀκέλλεα(ν)**· ἔκλεψαν (Tarent.), Hsch.

**ἀκέλῡφος**, ον, without husk or capsule, of fruits, Thphr.CP1.17.8.

**ἀκενό-δοξος**, ον, without vain conceit, M.Ant.1.16. Adv. -ως Sch.Od.3.411:—hence -δοξία, ἡ, Zonar. ⊕-σπουδος, ον, shunning vain pursuits, Antip.Tars.Stoic.3.254, Cic.Fam.15.17.4, M.Ant.1.6.

**ἀκέντ-ητος**, ον, needing no spur, Pi.O.1.21, AP5.202 (Asclep.), Ael.NA15.24. 2. metaph., unpricked, by love, Chor.Zach.5. II.

…wless, of crystals, Plin.*HN*37.28. **-ριστος**, ον, = foreg. 1, …ch., *EM*432.11. **-ρος**, ον, *stingless*, κηφῆνες Pl.*R.*552c, 564b; *without spur*, of a cock, Clyt.1; *without thorns*, βάτος Ph.2.91. 2. *responding to the spur*, of horses, *Hippiatr.*105: metaph., of style, *pointless*, Longin.21.2. II. *not occupying a cardinal point*, Man. …108, Vett.Val.89.30. **-ρότης**, ἡ, *absence from a cardinal point*, …emoph.ap.Jul.Laod. in *Cat.Cod.Astr.*5(1).189 (pl.).

**ἀκέομαι** [ᾰ], Ion. imper. ἀκέο (for ἀκέεο) Hdt.3.40; Ep. part. ἀκειόμενος Il.16.29, Od.14.383, Pi.*P.*9.104: fut. ἀκέσομαι D.C.38.19, Ep. …κέσσομαι Musae.199, Att. ἀκοῦμαι (ἐξ–) Men.863: aor. ἠκεσάμην, …p. imper. ἄκεσσαι, etc.:—Pass., v. sub fin.: I. trans., *heal*, *cure*, c. acc. of thing healed, ἕλκος ἄκεσσαι Il.16.523; ἕλκε' ἀκειόμενοι 16.29; ψώρην ἀκέσασθαι Hdt.4.90; of part healed, τὰ ἔσω …κοῖσιν Hp.*Mochl.*25; ἄχος S.*Tr.*1035; βλέφαρον ἀκέσαιο τυφλόν …*Hec.*1067; τὸν Λητώ τε καὶ Ἄρτεμις . . ἀκέοντο Il.5.448, cf. 402: c. gen. morbi, νούσου . . μ' ἀκέσω βαρυαλγέος *Epigr.Gr.*803 (Delos), cf. Paus.8.18.8. 2. *stanch, quench*, πίον τ' ἀκέοντό τε δίψαν Il.22.2, cf. Pi.*P.*9.104. 3. generally, *mend, repair*, νῆας ἀκειόμενος Od.14.383; freq. of tailors or cobblers, Luc.*Fug.*33, *Nec.*17; of a spider *mending* its web, Arist.*HA*623ᵃ18. 4. metaph., *make amends for, repair*, ἁμαρτάδα Hdt.1.167; τὰ ἐπιφερόμενα Id.3.16, cf. E.*Med.*199; μήνιμα Antipho 4.3.7; ἀδίκημα Pl.*R.*364c; ἀπορίας X.*Mem.*2.7.1. II. intr. or abs., *apply a remedy, make amends*, ἀλλ' ἀκεώμεθα θᾶσσον· ἀκεσταί τοι φρένες ἐσθλῶν Il.13.115; ἀλλ' ἀκέσασθε, φίλοι Od.10.69, cf. S.*Ant.*1027, Hdt.3.40, Pl.*Phlb.*30b. III. Act., Hp.*Loc.Hom.* 10; ἀκέεται in pass. sense, Aret.*CA*1.1; ἀκεομένου τοῦ κακοῦ Id.*SD* 1.6: aor. ἀκεσθῆναι Paus.2.27.3.

**ἀκεόντως**, Adv. *noiselessly*, Hsch. **ἄκερα**· ἔνδυμά τι πολυτελές, Id.

**ἀκεραι-όομαι**, Pass., *to be* ἀκέραιος, Eust.277.16. ❋**-ος**, ον (fem. -αία Sch.Ar.*Pl.*593), Prose word (used by E., v. infr.) for poet. ἀκήρατος, *pure, unmixed*, ὕδωρ Arist.*HA*605ᵃ15; οἶνος Dsc.5.6; ἀργύριον Poll.3.86, etc.; *untouched*, γῆ, νομή, Pl.*Criti.*111b, Arist.*HA* 575ᵇ3; *unalloyed*, ἡδοναί Epicur.*Sent.*12. 2. of persons, *pure in blood*, E.*Ph.*943. II. *unharmed, unravaged*, ἀ. ἀπολαμβάνειν τὴν πόλιν Hdt.3.146; γῆ Th.2.18; χώρα D.1.28; δύναμις, of an army, *in full force*, Th.3.3; of troops, *fresh*, X.*An.*6.5.9, Plb.1.40.12, etc.; of property, *untouched*, οὐσία D.44.23; ἐάν τι ἀσινὲς καὶ ἀ. *IG*3.1418*f*; of a person, Persae.*Stoic.*1.99. 2. metaph., *pure, inviolate*, ἀκέραιον ὡς σῴσαιμι Μενέλεῳ λέχος E.*Hel.*48; [τέχνη] ἀβλαβὴς καὶ ἀ. Pl. *R.*342b; *complete, perfect*, φαντασίαι Phld.*D.*3.8; ἐλπίς Plb.6.9.3; ὁρμαί Id.1.45.2. 3. of persons, *uncontaminated, guileless*, E.*Or.*922; *incorruptible*, κριτής D.H.7.4: c. gen., ἀ. κακῶν ἠθῶν Pl.*R.*409a, cf. Men.*Epit.*489; *unprejudiced, with an open mind*, Plb.21.31.12. 4. ἐξ ἀκεραίου *anew*, Id.23.4.10; *while matters are undecided*, Id.6.24.9; ἀκέραιον ἐᾶν *leave alone*, Id.2.2.10; εἰς -ον ἀποκαθιστάναι, = Lat. *in integrum restituere*, *IG*14.951. Adv. -ως, of payment, *in full*, Cic. *Att.*15.21.2; *unreservedly*, Phld.*Lib.* p.57 O. **-οσύνη**, ἡ, *guilelessness, innocence*, Suid. **-ότης**, ητος, ἡ, *freshness*, of troops, Plb. 3.73.6, 6.40.9. 2. *integrity*, Just.*Edict.*7.8 *Intr.* **-οφανής**, v. ἀκραιφνής.

**ἀκέραστος**, ον, *unmixed, pure*, τόλμης ἀνδρείας Pl.*Plt.*310d. Adv. ἀκεράστως, πνέων, gloss on ἀκραής, Sch.Od.2.421. II. of vowel-sounds, *not coalescing*, D.H.*Comp.*22.

**ἀκέρᾱτος**, ον, (κέρας) *without horns*, Pl.*Plt.*265c sq., Arist.*HA* 501ᵃ14, al.

**ἀκέραυν-ος**, ον, = sq., of Capaneus, A.*Fr.*17. **-ωτος**, ον, *not struck by lightning*, Luc.*J.Tr.*25.

**ἀκέρδ-εια**, ἡ, *want of gain, loss*, Pi.*O.*1.53:—also -ία Procop.*Arc.* 13. **-ής**, ές, *bringing no gain, unprofitable*, χάρις S.*OC*1484, cf. Pl.*Cra.*417d, D.H.6.9, *AP*9.649 (Maced.). Adv. -δῶς *without profit*, Arist.*Pol.*1309ᵃ13, Plu.2.27d. II. *not greedy of gain*, φιλοτιμία Id.*Arist.*1. Adv. -ῶς Id.2.483e.

**ἀκέρκιστος**, ον, (κερκίζω) *unwoven*, *AP*7.472 (Leon.).

**ἄκερκος**, ον, *tailless*, Arist.*PA*689ᵇ6.

**ἀκερμ-ατία**, ἡ, (κέρμα) *want of money*, Ar.*Fr.*15 (unless as Verb -ιᾶν). **-ία**, ἡ, = foreg., Lyd.*Mag.*3.14.

❋**ἄκερος**, ον, = ἄκερως, Arist.*HA*499ᵇ16.

❋**ἀκερσεκόμης** (ἀκερσι- in Nonn. ll. cc. infr.), ου, ὁ, (Dor. voc. -κόμα Pi.*Pae.*9.45: dat. pl. -κόμοισιν Nonn.*D.*14.232), (κείρω, κόμη) *with unshorn hair*, i.e. *ever-young* (for Greek youths wore long hair till they reached manhood), of Phoebus, Il.20.39, *h.Ap.*134, etc. 2. *long-haired*, Nonn.*D.*10.29, al.; cf. ἀκειρεκόμης.

**ἀκερσίλα**· μυρσίνη (Sicel), Hsch. **ἀκερχές**· ἀπενθές, Id.

**ἄκερχνος**, ον, *without hoarseness*, Aret.*CA*1.10. II. Act., *curing hoarseness*, Id.*CD*1.8.

**ἄκερως**, ων, gen. ω, = ἀκέρατος, Pl.*Plt.*265b, Ael.*NA*2.53, Max.Tyr. 17.5.

**ἀκερωσύνη**, dub. in Suid. s.v. ἀκεραιοσύνη.

**ἀκέρωτος**, ον, (κέρας) *not horned*, *AP*6.258 (Adaeus).

❋**ἀκεσ-ίας**· ἰατρός, Phot. **-ίμβροτος** [ᾰ], ον, *healing mortals*, of Asclepius, Orph.*L.*8; ἀ. ἄνθος Poet. *de herb.*146. **-ιμος**, ον, (ἀκέομαι) *wholesome, healing*, Plu.2.956f. **-ιος**, ον, *healing*, epith. of Apollo, Paus.6.24.6. **-ίπονον**· θεραπευτικόν, Suid., Phot. **-ις**, εως, ἡ, *healing, cure*, Hdt.4.90,109, Hierocl. *in CA*25p.477 M.; τὸν εὐράμενον παυσινόσους ἀκέσεις *IG*3.900. 2. *mending, repair*, θυρᾶν *IG*4.1484 (Epid.); μηχανώματος *GDI*2502.62 (Delph.). II. name of *plaster*, Asclep.ap.Gal.13.442. **-μα**, τό, *remedy*, Il.15. 394 (v.l.), Pi.*P.*5.64, A.*Pr.*482, *IG*14.1750. **-μιος**, ον, *curable*, Hsch. **-μός**, ὁ, = ἄκεσις, Call.*Fr.anon.*227.

**ἀκεσσί-νοσος**, ον, *healing disease*, cj. in *AP*9.516 (Crin.). **-πονος**, ον, *assuaging pain* or *toil*, Nonn.*D.*7.86.

**ἀκεσ-τήρ**, ῆρος, ὁ, *healer*: Adj., ἀ. χαλινός rein *that tames the steed*, S.*OC*714 (lyr.). **-τήριον**, τό, *tailor's shop*, Lib.*Or.*11.254. **-τήριος**, ον, *medicinal, healing*, metaph., κακῶν φάρμακον App.*Pun.* 88. **-τής**, οῦ, ὁ, = ἀκεστήρ, Lyc.1052: Phrygian acc. to Sch.Ven. Il.22.2, Eust.1254.2, *EM*51.7. 2. ἀκεσταὶ ἱματίων ῥαγέντων *menders* of torn clothes, X.*Cyr.*1.6.16 (v.l. ἠπηταί), cf. Alciphr.3. 27. **-τίδες**, αἱ, *bars* in sublimating furnaces, Dsc.5.74. **-τικός**, ή, όν, *fitted for healing* or *mending*: ἡ -κή (sc. τέχνη) Democr.154, Pl.*Plt.*281b, Ael.*NA*6.57, Gal.*Thras.*30. **-τορία**, ἡ, *the healing art*, A.R.2.512, *APl.*4.272 (Leont.), Max.314. **-τορίς**, ίδος, ἡ, fem. of ἀκέστωρ, Hp.*Flat.*1. **-τός**, ή, όν, *curable*, Hp.*Art.*58; πρᾶγμα Antipho 5.91: metaph., ἀκεσταὶ φρένες ἐσθλῶν the hearts of the noble *admit treatment*, Il.13.115. **-τρα**, ἡ, *darning-needle*, Luc. *D.Mort.*4.1, *PLips.*28.6. **-τρια**, ἡ, *sempstress*, Antip.Tars.*Stoic.* 3.254, Luc.*Rh.Pr.*24; ἀ., ἡ, title of play by Antiphanes: in pl., title of mime by Sophron. **-τρίς**, ίδος, ἡ, fem. of ἀκεστήρ, *midwife*, Hp.*Carn.*19. **-τρον**, τό, *remedy*, S.*Ichn.*317, *Fr.*480. **-τωρ**, ορος, ὁ, *healer, saviour*, Φοῖβος E.*Andr.*900. **-φορία**, ἡ, *healing, salvation*, *AP*9.349 (Leon.), Max.167. **-φόρος**, ον, *bringing cure, healing*, c. gen. rei, E.*Ion*1005, Astyd.Trag.6. **-ώδῠνος**, ον, *allaying pain*, Paetus ap.Hp.*Ep.*2, *AP*9.815, *IG*14.1015, Men.Rh.p.443 S.

❋**ἀκεύει**· τηρεῖ (Cypr.), Hsch., dub. in *Leg.Gort.*2.17.

❋**ἀκέφᾰλος**, ον, *headless*: οἱ ἀ., fabulous creatures in Libya, Hdt.4. 191; ἀ. ταῦροι J.*BJ*4.8.4. 2. *without beginning*, λόγος, μῦθος, Pl.*Phdr.*264c, *Lg.*752a; *without peroration*, μῦθος Luc.*Scyth.*9; of verses *which lack the first mora*, Heph.6.2, al. cf. Ath.14.632d. Adv. -λως, ἐμβάλλειν τοῖς πράγμασι Hermog.*Inv.*2.7. 3. αἵρεσις ἀ. sect *with no known head*, Suid.; ἀ., οἱ, Just.*Nov.*109 *Praef.* II. = ἄτιμος, Artem.1.35; cf. Lat. *capite deminutus.*

**ἀκέω** (A), v. ἀκέομαι sub fin. **ἀκέω** (B), *to be silent* (cf. sq.), only opt. pres. ἀκέοις A.R.1.765.

❋**ἀκέων**, ουσα, participial form, *softly, silently*, fem. ἀκέουσα Il.1.565, Od.11.142: dual. ἀκέοντε 14.195; also indecl., ἀκέων δαίνυσθε 21.89, cf. *h.Ap.*404; Ἀθηναίη ἀκέων ἦν Il.4.22, 8.459.

**ἀκή** (A), ἡ, (cf. ἀκίς) *point*, Hsch., Suid. ❋**ἀκή** (B), ἡ, (cf. ἀκᾶ) *silence*, ἀκὴν ἔχεν Mosch.2.18; ἀκὴν ἦγες Hsch. ❋**ἀκή** (C), ἡ, (cf. ἀκέομαι) *healing*, Hp.*Mochl.*21, cf. *Hum.*1.

**ἀκήδ-εια**, ἡ, (κῆδος) *carelessness, indifference*, in pl., Emp.136, A.R.2.219: sg., 3.260, Diog.Oen.24. II. in pl., *anguish*, A.R. 3.298 (Sch. πολυκηδείαισι). **-εστος**, ον, *uncared for*, Il.6.60; esp. *unburied*, *AP*7.686 (Pall.); *unkempt*, κάρηνον Nonn.*D.*10. 272. Adv. -τως *without care for others, ruthlessly*, Il.22.465, 24.417, cf. *AP*9.375. **-ευτος**, ον, *unburied*, Plu.*Per.*28, J.*AJ*6.14.8. ❋**-έω**, fut. -ήσω cj. in S.*Ant.*414, cf. Q.S.10.29: aor. -ησα 12.376, ἀκήδεσα Il.14.427: (ἀκηδής):—*take no care for, no heed of*, c. gen., οὔ τίς εὖ ἀκήδεσεν Il. l.c.; οὐ μέν μευ ζώοντος ἀκήδεις, ἀλλὰ θανόντος 23.70; σαυτοῦ δ' ἀκήδει δυστυχοῦντος (imper.) A.*Pr.*508, cf. Mosch.4.81, Onos.33.3. 2. abs., *grow weary*, Q.S.10.16. (See also ἀφειδέω.) **-ής**, ές, I. Pass., *uncared for*: esp. *unburied*, ὄφρα μὲν Ἕκτωρ κεῖται ἀ. Il.24.554; ἢ αὔτως κεῖται ἀ. Od.20.130; σώματ' ἀκηδέα κεῖται Od.24.187, cf. 6.26, 19.18. Adv. -ῶς Suid. II. Act., *without care* or *sorrow*, Il.24.526, Hes.*Th.*489, *AP*11.42 (Crin.). 2. *careless, heedless*, τὸν δὲ γυναῖκες ἀκηδέες οὐ κομέουσιν Od.17.319, cf. Il.21.123: c. gen., *taking no thought for*, φίλων S.*Fr.* 208.10; παίδων Pl.*Lg.*913c. III. (κήδω *harm*) *harmless*, Opp.*H.* 1.611, 2.648, cf. Epic.ap.Suid. **-ία**, Ion. -ίη, ἡ, = ἀκήδεια: *indifference, torpor, apathy*, Hp.*Gland.*12, Cic.*Att.*12.45. 2. *weariness, exhaustion*, Luc.*Herm.*77, D.C.*Fr.*73; πνεύματος Lxx *Is.*61.3. 3. c. gen., *neglect, disregard*, τῆς παραφορῆς Aret.*CA*1.1. **-ιαστής**, Hsch. and Suid. s.v. ἀσηκόρος. **-ιάω**, *to be careless*, Zos.Alch. p.133 B. 2. *to be exhausted, weary*, Lxx *Ps.*60(61).2, etc.

**ἀκήλητος**, ον, *proof against enchantment*, Od.10.329 (dub. vers.), Pl.*Phdr.*259b; μανίας ἄνθος S.*Tr.*999 (lyr.); of the Dioscuri, Theoc. 22.169; ἀ. τὸ ἀπαθές Porph.ap.Eus.*PE*5.10.

**ἀκηλίδωτος** [ῐ], ον, *spotless*, ἔσοπτρον, ἐσθής, πέδιλα, Lxx *Wi.*7.26, Ph.1.156, Porph.*Abst.*2.46: metaph., βίος, ἀρετή, Lxx *Wi.*4.9, Ph.2. 235; σωτηρία Steph. *in Hp.*2.238D.

**ἄκημα**, τό, = ἄκεσμα, *cure, relief*, ὀδυνάων Il.15.394 codd., Max.142.

❋**ἀκήμων**· ἐκκεχυμένος, Hsch.

**ἀκήν** (cf. ἀκή B), acc. form as Adv., *softly, silently*, Hom. mostly in phrase ἀκὴν ἐγένοντο σιωπῇ Il.3.95, al.; also οἱ δ' ἄλλοι ἀκὴν ἴσαν 4.429.

**ἀκήνιον**· ἥσυχον, *EM*48.1.

**ἀκήπευτος**, ον, *not in a garden, wild*, γογγυλίδες Posidon.29, cf. Gal.12.509.

**ἀκηρ-ασία**, ἡ, *purity*, Hsch. (ἀκηρεσία in Ms.). **-άσιος**, ον, Ep. form of ἀκήρατος, *untouched*, ἀ. λειμῶνες *meadows not yet grazed* or *mown*, *h.Merc.*72; γυίων ἄνθος ἀ. *pure, fresh*, *AP*12.93 (Rhian.); σκῆπτρα ἀ. *inviolate*, *Epigr.Gr.*907 (Sinope). II. (κεράννυμι) *unmixed*, οἶνος Od.9.205. **-ᾰτος**, ον, (κηραίνω) *undefiled, pure*, ὕδωρ Il.24.303; *inviolate*, χεῦμα, ὄμβρος, S.*OC*471, 690 (lyr.); χρυσός *pure* gold, Archil.*Supp.*4, Alcm.23.54, Hdt.7.10.α', Simon.64, cf. Pl. *R.*503a, *Plt.*303e; φλόξ Secund.*Sent.*5; *untouched, unhurt*, οἶκος καὶ κλῆρος, κτήματα, Il.15.498, Od.17.532; ἀπαρτίη Hippon.26; σκάφος A.*Ag.*661; ἀνίαι *strong* reins, Pi.*P.*5.32; πλόκοι *unshorn* locks, E. *Ion*1266; λειμὼν *unmown* meadow, Id.*Hipp.*73; ἀ. ἐμπόριον *virgin* market, Hdt.4.152; ἀ. φιλία X.*Hier.*3.4; ἐπιστήμη, ἤθη, Pl.*Phdr.*247d,

*Lg.*735c; ἀ. φάρμακα spells *that have all their power*, A.R.4.157. 2. of persons, *undefiled*, a virgin, E.*Tr.*675, Pl.*Lg.*840d; ἀ. λέχος E.*Or.*575: c. dat., ἀκήρατος ἄλγεσι, τύχαις *untouched by* woes, etc., *Hipp.*1113, *HF*1314: c. gen., ἀ. κακῶν *without taint* of ill, *Hipp.*949; ἀ. ὠδίνων *free from* throes of child-birth, A.R.1.974, etc.: poet. Sup. ἀκηρότατος *AP*12.249 (Strat.). II. (κεράννυμι) *unmixed*, ποτόν A.*Pers.*614.

⊛**ἀκήριος** (A), ον, *unharmed by the* Κῆρες; generally, *unharmed*, Od. 12.98, 23.328, *h.Merc.*530, Nic.*Th.*190, Call.*Ap.*41, A.R.3.466; ψυχαὶ ἀκήριοι, = ἀθάνατοι, *free from power of the Fates*, Ps.-Phoc.99. II. *having no* κῆρ, i.e. *with no fortune attached to them*, ἡμέραι Hes.*Op.* 823. III. *harmless*, πάμπαν δ' ἄμωμος οὔτις οὐδ' ἀ. Semon.4, cf. Nic.*Th.*771.

**ἀκήριος** (B), ον, (κῆρ) *without heart*, i.e., I. *lifeless*, Hom. (not in Od.), ἀκήριον αἶψα τίθησι Il.11.392, cf. 21.466. II. *heartless, spiritless*, σέ που δέος ἴσχει ἀκήριον ib.5.812, cf. 13.224; ἥμενοι αὖθι ἕκαστοι ἀκήριοι 7.100; ἀκήριον ἠύτ' ὄνειρον A.R.2.197.

**ἄκηρος** (sc. ἔμπλαστρος), ἡ, name of *a plaster*, Gal.13.759.

**ἀκηρ-υκτεί** and **-υκτί**, Adv. *without flag of truce*, ἐπιμείγνυσθαι Th. 2.1; πολεμεῖν D.C.50.7. **-υκτος**, ον, *unannounced, unproclaimed*, ἀ. πόλεμος *sudden* war, Hdt.5.81; also a war *in which no herald was admitted, truceless*, X.*An.*3.3.5, Pl.*Lg.*626a, Aeschin.2.33; ἦν γὰρ ἄσπονδος καὶ ἀ. ὑμῖν πρὸς τοὺς θεατὰς πόλεμος D.18.262; ἀ. ἔχθρα Plu. *Per.*30. 2. *without flag of truce*, τὸ ἀ. τῆς ὁδοῦ App.*Mith.*104. Adv. **-τως**, ἐφοίτων Th.1.146; cf. foreg. II. *not proclaimed victor by heralds, inglorious*, E.*Heracl.*89, Aeschin.3.230. III. *with no tidings, not heard of*, S.*Tr.*45, Nonn.*D.*9.249. 2. *unheralded*, ἔρωτες ib.48.653.

⊛**ἀκήρωτος**, ον, (κηρόω) *unwaxed*, Luc.*Icar.*3, Polyaen.2.20.

**ἀκῆσκος**· τάλαρος, Hsch. **ἀκητόν**· κράτιστον, Id.

**ἀκηχέδαται, ἀκηχέμενος**, v. sub ἀχέω.

**ἀκηχεδών**, όνος, ὁ, = λύπη, Hsch. (pl.), cf. *EM*48.2.

**ἀκιβδήλευτος**, ον, = sq., Ph.1.565, etc.

**ἀκίβδηλος**, ον, *unadulterated, genuine*, Pl.*Lg.*916d, Arist.*Ath.*51. 1; χρυσός Hierocl. *in CA Praef.*p.417 M. 2. metaph., of men, *guileless, honest*, Hdt.9.7.ά. Adv. **-λως** Isoc.1.7.

**ἀκίδιον**, τό, Dim. of ἀκίς, *small barb*, *BCH*29.572.

⊛**ἀκιδνός** [ᾰ], ή, όν, Ep. and Ion., *weak, feeble*, Hom. only in Od., always in Comp., εἶδος ἀκιδνότερος 8.169, cf. 5.217, 18.130, cf. Nic. *Th.*224; later in Posit., δμωαί Man.2.178: Sup. **-ότατον**, βέλεμνον Nonn.*D.*7.270; *insipid*, ἔδεσμα Archestr.*Fr.*38 B. (s. v. l., καὶ κεδνόν Meineke, Brandt).—Ep. word, also in Hp., ἰατρός *Praec.*8: δύναμις *Nat.Puer.*30.

**ἀκιδοειδής**, ές, *barb-like*, of quadrilateral with re-entrant angle, Procl. *in Euc.*p.165 F. **ἀκιδόω**, (ἀκίς) *furnish with barb* or *point*, in Pass., βέλη ἠκιδωμένα *IG*2.807. **ἀκιδρός**· ἀσθενής, Cyr. **ἀκιδρωπάζω**· ἀμβλυωπῶ, Hsch.

**ἀκῐδ-ώδης**, ες, *pointed*, Thphr.*HP*4.12.2. ⊛**-ωτός**, ή, όν, = foreg., Paul.Aeg.6.88, Poll.1.97, 10.133, Hsch. II. **-ωτός**, ὁ, = παρωνυχία, Ps.-Dsc.4.54: **-ωτόν**, τό, = σέλινον ἄγριον, Id.2.175; = ποτίρριον, Dsc.3.15.

**ἀκίθᾰρις**, ι, *without the harp*, A.*Supp.*681 (lyr.).

**ἄκῖκυς**, υος, ὁ, ἡ, *powerless, feeble*, Od.9.515, 21.131, Theoc.*Ep.* 11. II. *weakening*, νοῦσος Orph.*L.*22.—Ep. word, also in A. *Pr.*548 (lyr.), and Ion. Prose, cf. Hp.*Morb.*4.43 (in sense 1).

**ἀκίναγμα** [ᾰκῐ], τό, = τίναγμα, χειρῶν ἠδὲ ποδῶν *Lyr.Adesp.*30B (= Call.*Fr.anon.*68): —also **ἀκιναγμός**, ὁ, Hsch.

⊛**ἀκινάκης**, ου, ὁ, Persian word, *short straight sword*, Hdt. (v. infr.), cf. X.*An.*1.2.27 (also acc. **-άκεα** Hdt.3.118; pl. **-άκεας** v.l. ib.128); ἀ. ἐπίχρυσος, a Persian *sword* kept in the Parthenon, *IG*1.170.17, cf. 2.646.11; νὴ τὸν ἀκινάκην, a Scythian oath, Luc.*Tox.*38, cf. *J.Tr.*42. [ăcīnăces in Hor.*Od.*1.27.5.]

**ἀκινδῡν-ί**, Adv. of sq., *without danger*, Suid. **-ος**, ον, *free from danger*, σιγᾶς ἀ. γέρας Simon.66; βίος Id.36, cf. E.*IA*17, Th.1.124; πυρετοί Hp.*Aph.*7.63; ἀρεταὶ ἀ. virtues *that court no danger*, i.e. *cheap, easy* virtues, Pi.*O.*6.9, cf. Th.3.40; ἀ. εἶναί τινι τὸν ἀγῶνα Hyp. *Lyc.*8: c. gen., *guaranteed against risk*, ἀ. παντὸς κινδύνου *IG*12(7). 67 (Amorgos), *PTeb.*105.18 (ii B.C.). II. Adv. **-νως** E.*Rh.* 588, Antipho 2.4.7, etc.; ἡ ἀ. δουλεία Th.6.80; τὸ ἀ. ἀπελθεῖν αὐτούς their departure *without danger* to us, Id.7.68: Comp. ἀκινδυνότερον *with less danger*, Pl.*Phd.*85d: Sup. ἀκινδυνότατα, ζῆν X.*Mem.*2.8. 6. **-ότης**, ητος, ἡ, *freedom from danger*, Gal.9.491. **-ώδης**, ες, *of no dangerous appearance*, f.l. in Hp.*Art.*65 (Comp.).

**ἀκιν-ήεις**, εσσα, εν, = ἀκίνητος, Nic.*Al.*436. **-ησία**, ἡ, *absence of motion*, Arist.*Ph.*202ᵃ5, al.; *stagnancy*, Hp.*Vict.*2.37; *incapacity to move*, Thphr.*Fr.*11; *failure of mobility*, Epicur.*Nat.*908.6; *pause, intermission*, of the pulse, Gal.8.510, Aret.*CA*2.3. **-ητέω**, *to be at rest* or *immovable*, Hp.*Mul.*1.11, cf. *Stoic.*2.161, Antyll.(?) ap.Orib.8.6.9, S.E.*M.*7.188; of bones, as opp. joints, Gal.19. 460. **-ητί** or **-τεί**, Adv. *immovably*, Poll.3.89, 9.115. **-ητίζω**, = ἀκινητέω, Arist.*HA*537ᵇ7, *Stoic.*2.161. **-ητίνδᾰ**, Adv., ἀ. παίζειν play the game 'who stirs first',—Poll.9.110. ⊛**-ητος**, ον, also η, ον Pi.*O.*9.33, *IG*14.1389 ii 14:—*unmoved, motionless*, Parm.8, Emp.17, etc.; of Delos, Orac.ap.Hdt.6.98, cf. Pi.*P.*4.57; ἐξ ἀκινήτου ποδός *without stirring* a step, S.*Tr.*875; τὰς κινήσεις ἀκίνητος Pl.*Ti.* 40b; τὸ πρῶτον κινοῦν ἀκίνητον αὐτό Arist.*Metaph.*1012ᵇ31; ὕλη ἀ. Stoic.ap.Plu.2.1054a; ἄστρα ἀ. *fixed* stars, Poll.4.156. 2. *idle, sluggish*, ἐπ' ἀκινήτοισι καθίζειν to sit *in idleness*, Hes.*Op.*750 (where others, to sit *on graves*, v. infr. II. 2); ἀ. φρένες a *sluggish* soul, Ar.*Ra.* 899; of the Boeotians, Alex.237; χώρα ἀ. *untilled*, Plu.2.38c. *unmoved, unaltered*, ἀ. νόμιμα Th.1.71, etc.; τοὺς νόμους ἐᾶν ἀ. Ar. *Pol.*1269ᵃ9, cf. Pl.*Lg.*736d, cf. X.*Lac.*14.1. II. *immovable, hard to move*, Pl.*Sph.*249a, Luc.*Im.*1 (in Comp.). Adv. **-τως**, ἔχ Isoc.13.12, cf. Pl.*Euthphr.*11d. b. of property, *realty*, Olym. Hist.p.458 D., *Cod.Just.*1.11.10.1, al. 2. *not to be stirred, inv late*, τάφος Hdt.1.187: esp. prov. of sacred things, κινεῖν τὰ ἀκίνη Id.6.134, cf. Pl.*Tht.*181a:—hence, *that must be kept secret*, τἀκίνη ἔπη S.*OC*624; τἀκίνητα φράσαι Id.*Ant.*1060. 3. of persons, etc *not to be shaken, steadfast*, ib.1027; νοῦς ἀκίνητος πειθοῖ Pl.*Ti.*51 ἕξις ἀ. ὑπὸ φόβου Id.*Def.*412a; πρὸς τὸ θεῖον Plu.2.165b. 4. *una terable*, κοινότητες Phld.*Sign.*25. 5. c. gen., *inseparable from* *PMag.Berol.*1.80,165. III. Adv. **-τως**, v. supr. II. 1.

**ἀκίνινος**, ον, *made of* ἄκινος, στέφανοι Ath.15.680d. **ἄκινος**, *wild basil, Calamintha graveolens*, Dsc.3.43:—also **ἄκονος**, ib.

**ἄκιος**, ον, (κίς) *not worm-eaten*, Sup. ἀκιώτατος Hes.*Op.*435.

**ἀκιρίς**· λύχνος, Hsch.

⊛**ἀκιρός**, όν (Aeol. **ἄκῖρος**, α, ον), *weak*, sc. γυνή, Theoc.28.15; πτέρυγες Nic.*Al.*559; v.l. Hes.*Op.*435 (Sup.), cf. *EM*48.50. Adv. ἀκιρῶς· εὐλαβῶς, ἀτρέμας, Hsch. II. ἀκιρός· ὁ βορρᾶς, Id.

⊛**ἀκίς**, ἴδος, ἡ, (cf. ἀκή A) *pointed object*; hence, *needle*, Hp.*Int.* 41; *splinter*, Id.*Epid.*5.46; πετροτόμος ἀ., of a chisel, *APl.*4.221 (Theaet.). 2. *barb* of an arrow or hook, βελῶν Plu.*Demetr.*20; ἀγκίστρου *AP*6.5 (Phil.). 3. *arrow, dart*, Ar.*Pax*443, Mnesim.7, Opp.*H.*5.151. 4. metaph., ἔρως . . ἡ φρενῶν ἀ. Tim.Com.2; πόθων ἀκίδες *stings* of desire, *AP*12.76 (Mel.): in pl., *sharp, acute pains*, Aret.*SD*2.4. II. surgical *bandage*, Gal.18(1).823.

⊛**ἀκίσκλη**, ης, ἡ, *chisel*, *BGU*1028.13 (ii A.D.).

**ἀκίχητος** [ῐ], ον, *not to be reached, unattainable*, ἀκίχητα διώκων Il. 17.75; μεταθεῖν Ael.*NA*4.52; *not to be overtaken, swift*, ἀκίχητος ἀίσσειν Nonn.*D.*45.236, cf. Tryph.333. II. *not to be reached by prayer, inexorable*, ἦθεα A.*Pr.*186.

**ἀκίων**, ονος, ὁ, ἡ, *not supported by pillars*, Hsch., *AB*391.

**ἄκκαθεν**· ἄναλθεν, Hsch. **ἀκκαῖον**· εὐκαταφρόνητον, Id.

⊛**ἀκκ-ίζομαι**, Dep. (Act. only Ael.*Ep.*9), fut. ἀκκιοῦμαι Men.*Epit.* 309:—*affect indifference*, Pi.*Fr.*203 (cj.). 2. *affect ignorance, dissemble*, οἶσθα, ἀλλ' ἀκκίζει Pl.*Grg.*497a, Cic.*Att.*2.19.5, Luc.*Merc. Cond.*14, Jul.*Or.*7.223b; τὰ κοινὰ ταυτὶ ἀκκιοῦμαι *I will dissemble* and talk commonplaces, Men. l.c. 3. esp. of women, *to be prudish, affect to be shocked*, Philippid.5, cf. Ael. l.c., Alciphr.1.39. **-ισμός**, ὁ, *prudery*, Philem.4.14, Luc.*Am.*4, Philostr.*Ep.*35, Hld.6.4. **-ιστικός**, ή, όν, *disposed to be coy*, Eust.1727.28.

**ἀκκιπήσιος**, ὁ, Lat. *acipenser, sturgeon*, Apion ap.Ath.7.294f.

**ἀκκόρ**, Lacon. for ἀσκός, Hsch. **ἀκκός**· παράμωρος, λέγεται δὲ παιδίοις ὡς μωρόis, Id.

**ἀκκώ**, ἡ, *bogey*, that nurses used to frighten children with, Plu. 2.1040b: acc. to others, *vain woman*, Zen.1.53.

**ἀκλάδας**· ἀμπέλους ἀκλαδεύτους (Aeol.), Hsch.

⊛**ἄκλαστος**, ον, *unbroken*, Thphr.*CP*1.15.17, *AP*9.322 (Leon.), Phld.*D.*1.17: metaph., of motion, *continuous* in space, ἡ κύκλῳ φορὰ μήκει ἄ. Arist.*Cael.*288ᵃ25; *unbent*, of a vein, Gal.5.659.

**ἀκλαυστεί** or **-τί**, **ἀκλαυτεί** or **-τί**, (κλαίω) Adv. of sq., *without weeping*, Call.*Dian.*267, A.D.*Adv.*133.19, Sor.1.79, Longus 1.5.

⊛**ἄκλαυστος** or **ἄκλαυτος** (the latter form has less Ms. authority), ον: (κλαίω): I. Pass., *unwept*, esp. *without funeral lamentation*, Il.22.386, Od.11.54, Sol.21; ὤλετ' ἄκλαυτος, ἄιστος A.*Eu.*565: c. gen., φίλων ἄκλαυτος S.*Ant.*847: in E.*Andr.*1235 Thetis says, ἐγὼ γάρ, ἣν ἄκλαυτα χρῆν τίκτειν τέκνα.., i.e. children *not liable to death*. II. Act., *unweeping, tearless*, οὐδὲ σέ φημι δὴν ἄκλαυτον ἔσεσθαι Od.4.494, cf. A.*Th.*696, E.*Alc.*173: in S.*El.*912, = χαίρων, *with impunity*.

⊛**ἀκλεής**, ές: acc. **-εᾶ** *Epigr.Gr.*850, **-εῆ** D.H.*Isoc.*5, Ep. ἀκλεέα Od. 4.728: dat. **-εῖ** Nonn.D.31.42:—Ep. **ἀκλειής**, A.R.3.932, Call.*Fr. anon.*365: nom. pl. ἀκλεέες (vulg. ἀκληεῖς) Il.12.318: (κλέος):—*without fame, inglorious*, Hom. ll. cc., Pi.*O.*12.15, Hdt.*prooem.*, E. *Hipp.*1028, Pl.*La.*179d, etc. Adv. ἀκλεῶς Hdt.5.77, Antipho 1.21; Ep. ἀκλεῶς Il.22.304: Comp. ἀκλεέστερον Jul.*Or.*1.28a: neut. as Adv., ἀκλεὲς αὔτως Il.7.100. 2. *ignominious*, ἀκλεεστάτῳ ὀλέθρῳ ἀπόλλυσθαι Lys.13.45.

**ἀκλεΐα**, Ion. **-ίη**, ἡ, *ingloriousness*, *AP*9.80 (Leon.).

**ἀκλειής**, ές, Ep. for ἀκλεής.

**ἄκλειστος**, ον, Ion. **ἀκλήιστος** Call.*Hec.*2, Att. contr. **ἄκληστος** E.*Andr.*593, Th.2.93: (κλείω):—*not closed* or *fastened*, ll. cc., X.*Cyr.* 7.5.25, Nic.Dam.p.72 D., etc.

**ἄκλεπτος**, ον, *not stealing, not deceiving*, S.*Fr.*690.

**ἀκληδονίστως**, gloss on ἀκλειῶς, *EM*49.11.

**ἀκλήης**, ές, v. sub ἀκλεής.

**ἀκληΐδας**· ἄζυγας, Hsch.

**ἀκλήιστος**, ον, v. ἄκλειστος.

**ἀκληρ-εί**· χωρὶς κλήρου, Zonar. **-έω**, *to be unfortunate*, Teles p.26H., D.S.3.13, al.: pf. ἠκλήρηκα Plb.1.7.4, D.S.27.16. ⊛**-ημα**, ατος, τό, *loss, mishap*, Dicaearch.1.25 (pl.), Telesp.25 H., Agatharch.24, M.Ant.10.33, etc. **-ία**, ἡ, *misfortune*, S.*Fr.*989, Antiph. 14, Plb.22.8.9, etc. ⊛**-ονόμητος**, ον, *without heirs*, *Berl.Sitzb.*1880. 649 (Anisa, i B.C.), *BGU*868.12 (ii A.D.), Eust.533.32:—also **-όνομος**, ον, *PLond.*3.905.12 (ii A.D.). **-ος**, ον, *without lot* or *portion, poor, needy*, Od.11.490, etc.: c. gen., *without lot* or *share in*, A.*Eu.*353, Is.3.32, etc. II. *unallotted, without owner*, *h.Ven.*123, E. *Tr.*32. **-ούχητος**, ον, *not having received a lot*, *OGI*229.102

myrna). -ωτεί or -ωτί, Adv. *without casting lots*, Lys.16.16, ist.*Ath*.30.5, *CIG*2880 (Miletus). -ωτος, ον, *without lot* or *rtion in* a thing, c. gen., χώρας ἀκλάρωτος Pi.*O*.7.59. 2. *without sting lots*, D.C.*Fr*.62. II. *not distributed in lots*, Plu.2.231e.

**ἄκληστος,** v. sub ἄκλειστος.

**ἀκλητ-ί,** Adv. *uncalled, unbidden*, Com.ap.Zen.2.46 [where . -ος, ον, *uncalled, unbidden*, Asius 1, A.*Pr*.1024, *Ch*.838, S.*Aj*. 9, Th.1.118, Pl.*Smp*.174b, Arist.*EN*1171b21.

**ἀκλῖνής,** ές, *bending to neither side, unswerving*, Pl.*Phd*.109a; πρὸς ) δίκαιον Nic.Dam.p.144 D.; *impartial*, ἀκοαί *POxy*.904.9 (v A.D.); *gular*, ἀκλινέων καλάμων *AP*10.11 (Satyr.), etc.: Math., *without clination*, of a perpendicular, Procl.*in Euc*.p.132 F.; *horizontal*, of plane, Papp.1048.2, Hero *Dioptr*.19: Music., *fixed*, of notes in scale, lyp.4: Medic., *persistent*, πυρετοί Herod.ap.Orib.6.20.24. Adv. -νῶς Ph.2.669; Ion. -νέως *AP*5.54 (Diosc.). 2. metaph., *steadfast, steady*, φιλία ib.12.158 (Mel.); ὁμολογία *Ep.Heb*.10.23; ψυχή uc.*Dem.Enc*.33; *unmoved, tranquil*, Nonn.*D*.35.11, al.

**ἀκλῐσία,** ἡ, *indeclinability*, A.D.*Pron*.12.4, etc.

**ἄκλῐτος,** ον, Gramm., *indeclinable*, D.T.641.23, A.D.*Synt*.30.10; Ael. Dion. wrote περὶ ἀκλίτων ῥημάτων. Adv. ἀκλίτως, ἔχειν Eust. 162.32. 2. Math., = ἀκλινής, Procl.*in Euc*.p.290 F. 3. *stable*, Iamb.*Myst*.1.15.

⊛**ἀκλόνητος,** ον, *unshaken, unmoved*, Suid., Phot.

⊛**ἄκλονος,** ον, of the pulse, *steady, regular*, Gal.9.347; of a limb, *free from jars*, 17(1).513; of a rider, *with a firm seat*, Palaeph.52.

⊛**ἀκλοπ-εία,** ἡ, *honest administration*, *BCH*32.204 (Alabanda). -ος, ον, *not guilty of peculation*, *Cat.Cod.Astr*.1.100 (v A.D.). II. *not furtively concealed*, ἄγκιστρον Opp.*H*.3.532.

**ἀκλῠδώνιστος,** ον, *not lashed by waves*; generally, *sheltered from*, λιμὴν ἀ. τῶν πνευμάτων Plb.10.10.4.

**ἄκλυστος,** ον, = foreg., Zeno *Stoic*.1.56, Lyc.736, Plu.*Mar*.15, Nonn.*D*.39.8, al.; λιμὴν ἄ. D.S.3.44; γῆ, *free from inundation*, Max. Tyr.414: fem., Αὖλιν ἀκλύσταν E.*IA*121.

**ἄκλῠτος,** ον, (κλύω) *unheard*, *IG*14.1389ii32; opp. κλυτός, Plu.2.722e (nisi leg. ἄκλυστος).

**ἄκλων,** ὁ, ἡ, *without branches*, Thphr.*HP*6.6.2.

**ἄκλωστος,** ον, (κλώθω) *unspun*, στήμονες Pl.Com.221.

**ἄκμα·** νηστεία, ἔνδεια, Hsch.; cf. ἄκμηνος.

⊛**ἀκμάδιον,** τό, kind of *surgical instrument*, *Hermes* 38.281 (s.v.l.); *conical crucible*, Ps.-Mos.Alch.p.39 B.

**ἀκμ-άζω,** (ἀκμή) *to be in full bloom, at the prime*: I. of persons, Hdt.2.134, Pl.*Prt*.335e; ἀ. σώματι, ῥώμῃ, X.*Mem*.4.4.23, Pl.*Plt*.310d, etc.; of cities and states, Hdt.3.57, 5.28; ἀ. τὸ σῶμα ἀπὸ τῶν λ′ ἐτῶν μέχρι τῶν ε′ καὶ λ′ Arist.*Rh*.1390b9; = τὰ τῶν νέων πράττειν Hyp.*Fr*. 122. 2. *flourish, abound in* a thing, πλούτῳ Hdt.1.29; παρασκευῇ πάσῃ Th.1.1; νεότητι Id.2.20; ναυσὶ καὶ χρήμασι Aeschin.3.163. 3. c. inf., *to be strong enough* to do, X.*An*.3.1.25. II. of things, ἀ. ὁ πυρετός, ἡ νόσος *is at its height*, Hp.*Aph*.2.29, *Epid*.1.25, Th.2.49; τοῦ πάθους ἀκμάζοντος Phld.*Lib*.p.31 O.; ἀ. ὁ πόλεμος Th.3.3; of corn, *to be ripe*, Id.2.19. 2. ἡνίκα.. ἀκμάζοι [ὁ θυμός] when passion *is at its height*, Pl.*Ti*.70d; ἀκμάζουσα ῥώμη Antipho 4.3.3; ἀκμάζει πάντα ἐπιμελείας δεόμενα require *the utmost* care, X.*Cyr*.4.2.40. 3. impers., c. inf., ἀκμάζει βρετέων ἔχεσθαι *'tis time* to.., A.*Th*.97 (lyr.); νῦν γὰρ ἀ. Πειθὼ.. ξυγκαταβῆναι now *'tis time* for her to.., Id.*Ch*. 726. ⊛-**αῖος,** α, ον, Aeol. **ἄκμαος** Jo.Gramm.*Comp*.2.14; *in full bloom, at prime, vigorous*, πῶλοι A.*Eu*.405; ἥβη Id.*Th*.11; ἀκμαῖος φύσιν *in the prime of* strength, Id.*Pers*.441; ἀ. τὴν ὀργήν Luc.*Tim*.3; κάλλει ἀκμαία *Epigr.Gr*.127; τὸ ἀκμαιότατον D.H.5.22; ἀκμαίων λέσχη at Chalcis, Plu.2.298d:—ἀ. πρὸς ἔρωτα *AP*7.221, cf. Luc.*D.Deor*.8.2, Ael.*NA*15.10. Adv. ἀκμαίως, ἔχειν κατὰ τὴν ἡλικίαν Plb.31.29.7: Comp. -ότερον *more vigorously*, Gal.4.525:—of things, *at the height*, ὁ ἀκμαιότατος καιρὸς τῆς ἡμέρας, i.e. noon, Plb.3.102.1; τὸ ἀ. τοῦ χειμῶνος Arr.*An*.4.7.1, etc. 2. Rhet., *belonging to the supreme effort, culmination of oratory*, ἔννοιαι, λόγος, Hermog.*Id*.1.7, *Inv*.4.4: Comp., *Id*.1.10. II. *in time, in season*, ἀ. καιρός *PTeb*.24.56 (ii B.C., Sup.); ἀ. ἡμέραι the *seasonable* days, Ath.5.180c, cf. *AP*10.2 (Antip.Sid.): neut. pl. as Adv., ἀκμαῖ' ἂν μόλοι S.*Aj*.921 (cj.). -**αστής,** οῦ, ὁ, = foreg. I.1, Hdn.1.17.11; ἀκμασταί, οἱ, gymnastic club at Thyatira, *IGRom*.4.1234, al. -**αστικός,** ή, όν, = ἀκμαῖος, Hp. *Sept*.28; ἀ. πυρετός Gal.10.615, of a continuous fever; ἀ. πρόσωπα persons *in their prime*, *Cat.Cod.Astr*.2.173. 2. = ἀκμαῖος I.2, σχήματα Hermog.*Id*.1.10.

⊛**ἀκμή,** ἡ, (cf. ἀκή A) *point, edge*: prov., ἐπὶ ξυροῦ ἀκμῆς on the razor's *edge* (v. sub ξυρόν); ἀ. φασγάνου, ὅπλων, Pi.*P*.9.81, Plb.15.16.3 (pl.); ὀδόντων Pi.*N*.4.63, etc.; λόγχης ἀκμή E.*Supp*.318; κερκίδων ἀκμαί S.*Ant*.976; ἀμφιδέξιοι ἀ. both *hands*, Id.*OT*1243; ποδοῖν ἀ. *feet*, ib.1034; ἔμπυροι ἀκμαί *pointed* flames, E.*Ph*.1255, cf. πυρὸς ἀκμαί Epicr.6 codd. II. *highest* or *culminating point* of anything, *flower, prime, zenith*, esp. of man's age, ἀκμὴ ἥβης S.*OT*741; ἐντῆδε τοῦ κάλλους ἀκμῇ Cratin.195; σώματός τε καὶ φρονήσεως Pl.*R*.461a; μέτριος χρόνος ἀκμῆς 460e; ὀξυτάτη δρόμου ἀ. ibid.; ἀ. βίου X.*Cyr*.7.2.20, etc.; ἐν ταύταις ταῖς ἀ. Isoc.7.37; ἐν ἀκμῇ εἶναι, of corn, to be *ripe*, Th.4.2; ἀκμὴν ἔχειν τῆς ἄνθης Pl.*Phdr*.230b; τοσοῦτον τῆς ἀ. ὑστερῶν Isoc. *Ep*.6.4; τῆς ἀ. λήγειν begin to decline, Pl.*Smp*.219a:—in various relations, ἀ. ἦρος spring-*prime*, Pi.*P*.4.64; ἀ. θέρους *mid*-summer, X. *HG*5.3.19; βραχεῖα ἀ. πληρώματος Th.7.14; ἀ. τοῦ ναυτικοῦ *flower* of their navy, Id.8.46; ἀ. τῆς δόξης Id.2.42; ἡ ἀ. τῆς Σπάρτης, τῶν νέων Demad.12; ἀ. νούσου *crisis* of disease, Hp.*Acut*.38:—generally, *strength, vigour*, ἐν χερὸς ἀκμᾷ Pi.*O*.2.63, cf. A.*Pers*.1060; ἀ. ποδῶν *swiftness*, Pi.*I*.8(7).41, cf. A.*Eu*.370; φρενῶν Pi.*N*.3.39; συμπεσεῖν ἀκμᾷ βαρύς cj. Id.*I*.4(3).51:—periphr. like βία, ἀκμὴ Θησειδᾶν S.*OC* 1066. 2. Rhet., ἀκμὴ λόγου *supreme effort, culmination, climax*, Hermog.*Inv*.4.4, *Id*.1.10; pl., ib.11, cf. Philostr.*VS*1.25.7. III. of Time, like καιρός, *the time*, i.e. *best, most fitting time*, freq. in Trag., ἡνίκ' ἂν δὴ πρὸς γάμων ἥκητ' ἀκμάς S.*OT*1492; ἔργων, λόγων, ἕδρας ἀκμή *time* for doing, speaking, sitting still, Id.*El*.22, *Ph*.12, *Aj*.811: c. inf., οὐκέτ' ἦν μέλλειν ἀ. A.*Pers*.407, cf. *Ag*.1353; ἀπηλλάχθαι δ' ἀ. S.*El*.1338; σοὶ.. ἀ. φιλοσοφεῖν Isoc.1.3; ὁ καιρὸς ἔστ' ἐπ' αὐτῆς τῆς ἀκμῆς Ar.*Pl*.256; ἐπ' ἀκμῆς εἶναι, c. inf., to be on *point* of doing, E.*Hel*. 897; εἰς ἀκμὴν ἐλθὼν φίλοις in *the nick of time*, E.*HF*532; ἐπ' αὐτὴν ἥκει τὴν ἀκμήν it is come to *the critical time*, D.4.41; ἀκμὴν εἴληφεν have reached a *critical moment*, Isoc.*Ep*.1.1, cf. Plu.*Sol*.12, 15, 2. 656f. IV. *eruption* on face, Cass.*Pr*.13, Aët.7.110, 8.13 (f.l. ἀκνάς, whence mod. *acne*). **ἄκμη,** v. ἄκμηνος.

⊛**ἀκμήν,** acc. of ἀκμή, used as Adv., *as yet, still*, A.*Fr*.451 G, Men. in *Cod.Vat.Gr*.122; un-Attic acc. to Phryn.100, but cf. Hyp.*Fr*.116; τὰ σκευοφόρα.. ἀκμὴν διέβαινε were *just* crossing the river, X.*An*.4.3. 26, cf. Plb.1.13.12, Theoc.4.60, *AP*7.141 (Antiphil.), Phld.*Ir*.p.29 W., *Ev.Matt*.15.16, etc.; νέος ἀ. Theoc.25.164; strengthd., ἀκμὴν ἔτι Plb.14.4.9, 15.6.6; ἔτι ἀ. Sor.1.26. II. = ἀκμαίως, Cratin. in *Cod.Vat.Gr*.122: perh., = *much*, *OGI*201.13 (Nubia).

**ἀκμηνός,** ή, όν, (ἀκμή) *full-grown*, θάμνος ἐλαίης Od.23.191; νυμφῶν ἃς ἀκμηνὰς καλοῦσιν Paus.5.15.6, cf. Jul.Laod. in *Cat.Cod.Astr*. 5(1).189.

⊛**ἄκμηνος,** ον, *fasting from* food, four times in Il.19.163, 207, 320, 346 (expl. by Sch. fr. Aeol. **ἄκμη,** = ἀσιτία); also in Lyc.672; σίτων Nic.*Th*.116; δόρποιο Call.*Fr.anon*.4.

⊛**ἀκμής,** ῆτος, ὁ, ἡ, also as neut., Paus.6.15.5: (κάμνω):—*untiring, unwearied*, Il.11.802, 15.697, S.*Ant*.353; πύλαι ἀ. Ὀλύμπου *AP*9.526 (Alph.):—also in late Prose, D.H.9.14, Paus. l.c., Plu.*Cim*.13, Onos.22.1.

**ἀκμητεί** and **-τί,** Adv. *without toil, easily*, J.*BJ*1.16.2, Lib.*Or*.59.71.

⊛**ἄκμητος,** ον, Lyr. **-ατος** S.*Ant*.609 Jebb, = ἀκμής, *unwearied*, ποσίν *h.Ap*.520, Onos.10.5. II. *not causing pain*, Nic.*Th*.737.

**ἀκμοθέτης,** ου, ὁ, (τίθημι) *anvil-block*, Poll.10.147. **-θετον,** τό, = foreg., Il.18.410, Od.8.274.

**ἀκμόνιον,** τό, Dim. of sq., Aesop.413.

⊛**ἄκμων,** ονος, ὁ, orig. prob. *meteoric stone, thunderbolt* (v. sub fin.), χάλκεος ἄ. οὐρανόθεν κατιών Hes.*Th*.722, cf. 724. II. *anvil*, Il.18.476, Od.8.274, Hdt.1.68: metaph., πρὸς ἄκμονι χάλκευε γλῶσσαν Pi.*P*.1.86; λόγχης ἄκμονες *very anvils* to bear blows (cf. Sch. ad loc.), A.*Pers*.51; ὑπομένειν πληγὰς ἄκμων Aristopho 4; Τιρύνθιος ἄ., i.e. Hercules, Call.*Dian*.146 (expl. by Sch. ὁ μὴ καμὼν ἐπὶ τοῖς ἄθλοις). 2. *pestle* (Cyprian), Hsch. 3. *head* of a battering-ram, Apollod.*Poliorc*.161.4. III. kind of *eagle*, Hsch. IV. kind of *wolf*, Opp.*C*.3.326. V. Pythag., = 6, *Theol.Ar*.37. (Cf. Skt. *áśman-* 'sling-stone', etc.)

**ἄκναμπτος, ἄκναπτος, ἄκνᾰφος,** = ἄγν-.

⊛**ἄκνημος,** ον, (κνήμη) *without calf*, of the leg, Plu.2.520c.

**ἄκνησ-μος,** ον, *without irritation* or *itching*, Hp.*Off*.18. **-τις,** ιος, ἡ, *spine* or *backbone* of animals, Od.10.161 (nisi leg. κατὰ κνῆστιν), A.R.4.1403; also τὸ μέσον τῆς ὀσφύος Poll.2.179. II. *stinging-nettle*, = ἀκαλήφη, Nic.*Th*.52 (other expl. ap. Sch. ad loc.). **-τον,** τό, = χαμελαία, Dsc.4.171.

**ἄκνῑσος,** ον, (κνῖσα) *without fat of sacrifices*, βωμός *AP*10.7 (Arch.); βωμοῖσι παρ' ἀκνίσοισι cj. Cobet in Luc.*J.Tr*.6. 2. *lacking in fats*, τροφή Thphr.*CP*2.4.6, cf. Plu.2.123b. 3. *without savoury odour*, Hp.*Morb*.2.54; ἔλαιον *not greasy*, Aret.*CA*1.6. Adv. -ως *without being smoked* or *burnt*, Gal.14.266.

**ἀκνίσωτος** [ῐ], ον, *without steam of sacrifice*, A.*Fr*.292.

**ἀκο-άζῃ·** ἀκούεις, Hsch. **-αστῆρες,** οἱ, board of officials at Metapontum, Id.

**ἀκοή,** ἡ, Ep. **ἀκουή**: (ἀκοϝ, cf. ἀκούω):—*hearing, sound heard*, ἕκαθεν δέ τε γίγνετ' ἀ. Il.16.634. 2. *thing heard, tidings*, μετὰ πατρὸς ἀκουὴν ἱκέσθαι, βῆναι, Od.2.308, 4.701; κατὰ τὴν Σόλωνος ἀκοήν according to Solon's *story*, Pl.*Ti*.21a; *report*, Pi.*P*.1.84, 90; ἀ. σοφοῖς *thing* for wise men *to listen to*, ib.9.78; ἀκοῇ ἱστορεῖν, παραλαβεῖν τι *by hearsay*, Hdt.2.29, 148; ἐπίστασθαι Antipho 5.67, Th. 4.126; ἐξ ἀκοῆς λέγειν Pl.*Phd*.61d; τὰς ἀ. τῶν προγεγενημένων *traditions*, Th.1.20; ἀκοαὶ.. λόγων Id.1.73; ἀκοὴν μαρτυρεῖν, προσάγειν, give, bring *hearsay evidence*, D.57.4; βαρὺν.. ἀκοῆς ψόφον *AP*6.220 (Diosc.); ἐκ γὰρ ἀκουῆς οἰκτίρω σε ib.7.220 (Agath.). II. *sense of hearing*, Hdt.1.38, etc.; joined with ὄψις, Pl.*Phd*.65b, etc.; οἷς ὦτα μέν ἐστιν, ἀκοαὶ δὲ οὐκ ἔνεισιν Ph.1.474. 2. *act of hearing*, ἐς ἀκοὰν ἐμήν to my *hearing*, my *ear*, A.*Pr*.689; γᾶρυν ἀραρεῖν ἀκοαῖσι Simon. 41; ὀξεῖαν ἀ... λόγοις διδούς S.*El*.30; ἀκοῇ κλύειν Id.*Ph*.1412; ἀκοαῖς δέχεσθαι, εἰς ἀκοὰς.. ἥκειν, E.*IT*1496, *Ph*.1480; δι' ἀκοῆς αἰσθάνεσθαι Pl.*Lg*.900a; ἀκοὴν ὑπειπών demanding *a hearing*, E.*HF*962; τοῖς ἀκροάμασι τὰς ἀ. ἀνατεθεικώς Plb.24.5.9. 3. *ear*, ὀππάτεσσι δ' οὐδεν ὄρημ', ἐπιρρόμβεισι δ' ἄκουαι Sapph.2.12, cf. A.R.4.17; ἀπεσθίει μου τὴν ἀ. Hermipp.52, cf. Pherecr.199; δυσὶν ἀκοαῖς κρίνειν with two *ears*, Arist.*Pol*.1287b27, cf. *Pr*.960a30, Call.*Fr*.106.5. III. *hearing, listening to*, ἀκοῆς ἄξιος Pl.*Tht*.142d; εἰς ἀκοὴν φωνῆς within *hearing* of.., D.S.19.41. IV. *obedience*, ἀ. ὑπὲρ θυσίαν ἀγαθή Lxx 1*Ki*.15.22. V. in pl., place where *supernatural voices are heard*, *IG*4. 955.10 (Epid.), Marin.*Procl*.32; αἱ ἀ. τοῦ θεοῦ Aristid.*Or*.47(23).13.

**ἀκοΐδιον,** τό, Dim. of ἀκοή II.3, *Gloss*. ⊛**ἀκοιλάντως,** Adv. *without deficiency, in full*, *PLond*.3.954.18 (iii A.D.), al.

**ἀκοίλιος**, *ον*, *without ducts*, Hp.*Loc.Hom.*4, Gal.5.617. 2. *without stomach*, Gal.5.384.

**ἄκοιλος**, *ον*, *not hollow*, Arist.*HA*515$^{a}$31, Gal.4.900.

**ἀκοίμητος**, *ον*, *sleepless*, *unresting*, of sea, A.*Pr.*139; Νύμφαι Theoc.13.44; πῦρ Plu.*Cam.*20, Ael.*NA*11.3; φέγγος Lxx *Wi.*7.10; ἀ. καὶ ἀπαραλόγιστος Arr.*Epict.*1.14.12, etc.; ἀ. δάκρυσι *IG*9(2).317.4 (Tricca). Adv. -τως, ἔχει πρὸς τὰ θεῖα Ph.*Fr.*101 H.

**ἀκοίμιστος**, *ον*, dub. in D.S.38/39.17; gloss on ἀκατεύναστος, Phot.

**ἀκοινονόητος**, *ον*, *lacking in 'savoir-faire'* (Lat. *sensus communis*), Cic.*Att.*6.3.7, cf. Gell.12.12, Juv.7.218. Adv. -τως Cic.*Att.*6.1.7 codd.

**ἄκοινος**, *ον*, *not common*, Them.*Or.*11.142a.

**ἀκοιν-ωνησία**, ἡ, *non-existence of community* of property, Arist.*Pol.*1236$^{b}$22. II. *unsociableness*, Stob.2.7.25. III. *lack of community*, *incompatibility*, Dam.*Pr.*221,423. ⊛**-ώνητος**, *ον*, *not shared with*, γάμοις ἀκοινώνητον εὐνάν bed *not shared in common with* other wives, E.*Andr.*470. 2. *not to be communicated*, ὄνομα Lxx *Wi.*14.21; *not to be shared*, *incommunicable*, Ph.2.201; τὸ ἴδιον καὶ ἀ. Alex.Aphr.*Pr.*2.72. II. Act., *having no share of* or *in*, c. gen., νόμων Pl.*Lg.*914c, cf. *Inscr.Prien.*114, D.S.20.15; τὸ ἀ. τῶν ἄρθρων absence of anything in common with the article, A.D.*Synt.*49.12: also c. dat., τὸ τοῖς κακοῖς -ότερον Arist.*Top.*117$^{b}$31: abs., *unsocial*, Pl.*Lg.*774a; *inhuman*, Cic.*Att.*6.3.7. Adv. -τως cj. ib.6.1.7, Jul.*Ep.*89.292d. **-ωνία**, ἡ, *unsociableness*, Pl.*Ep.*318e.

**ἀκοίτης**, *ου*, ὁ, (ἀ- copul., κοίτη, cf. Pl.*Cra.*405d) *bedfellow*, *husband*, Il.15.91, Od.5.120, Pi.*N.*5.28, S.*Tr.*525, E.*El.*166 (lyr.):—fem. **ἄκοιτις**, *ιος*, ἡ, *wife*, Il.3.138, B.5.169, A.*Pers.*684, etc.—Poet. words.

**ἄκοιτος**, *ον*, *unresting*, of Argus, B.18.23.

**ἀκολάκ-ευτος**, *ον*, *not liable to flattery*, οὐσία, τροφή, Pl.*Lg.*729a, Them.*Or.*6.97b; *not pampered*, σώματα Max.Tyr.23.1. II. Act., *not flattering*, λόγοι Id.31.6; θεραπεία Jul.*Or.*2.86b; ψῆφος Them.*Or.*2.27b. Adv. -τως Cic.*Att.*13.51.1, Ph.1.449. **-ος**, *ον*, = foreg. II, ψήφισμα D.L.2.141.

**ἀκολᾰσ-ία**, ἡ, *licentiousness*, *intemperance*, opp. σωφροσύνη, Hecat.144, Antipho 4.1.6, Th.3.37, Pl.*Grg.*505b, cf. Arist.*EN*1107$^{b}$6, etc.: pl., Lys.16.11, Pl.*Lg.*884. **-ταίνω**, fut. -ᾰνῶ Ar.*Av.*1227, *to be licentious*, Ar. l.c., Mnesim.4.19, Pl.*R.*555d, etc. ⊛**-τασμα**, τό, = ἀκολάστημα, restored by Dobree in Ar.*Lys.*398 (ἀκόλαστ' ᾄσματα codd.); ἀκολαστάσματα is prob. l. for -άματα in Anaxandr.73, Alciphr.1.38. **-τημα**, *ατος*, τό, *act of* ἀκολασία, Plu.*Crass.*32, M.Ant.11.20, Muson.*Fr.*4 p.14 H. **-τία**, ἡ, v.l. for ἀκολασία, Alex.36.6. **-τος**, *ον*, *undisciplined*, *unbridled*, δῆμος Hdt.3.81; ὄχλος E.*Hec.*607; στράτευμα X.*An.*2.6.10, cf. Ar.*Nu.*1348, Pl.*Prt.*341e, etc. 2. esp. *incontinent*, *licentious*, S.*Fr.*744; opp. σώφρων, Pl.*Grg.*507c, Arist.*EN*1117$^{b}$32, al.; περί τι Id.*HA*572$^{a}$12; πρός τι 582$^{a}$26. Adv. ἀκολάστως, ἔχειν Pl.*Grg.*493c: Comp. -οτέρως, ἔχειν πρός τι X.*Mem.*2.1.1, cf. Aen.Tact.26.2, dub. in Vett.Val.153.32, 271.12 (leg. ἀκοπιάστως). II. *unpunished*, c. gen., App.*Ill.*17.

**ἀκολλ-ητί**, Adv. of sq., *without adhering*, Herm.ap.Stob.1.49.68. **-ητος**, *ον*, *not cemented* or *glued*, λίθοι *BCH*35.43 (Delos); *not adhering*, δέρμα σώμασι Gal.11.125; *not united*, *healed up*, of wounds, Id.18(2).802. 2. *incapable of being compacted*, D.H.*Comp.*22. **-ος**, *ον*, *without glue*, *not adhesive*, Thphr.*CP*6.10.3.

**ἀκολλύβιστος**, *ον*, *without premium on exchange*, ἀργύριον *IG*12(5).817 (Tenos, ii B.C.).

**ἀκολόβωτος**, *ον*, *not curtailed*, Eust.727.39.

⊛**ἄκολος**, *ου*, ἡ, *bit*, *morsel*, Od.17.222, *AP*9.563 (Leon.), cf. 6.176 (Maced.), J.*BJ*5.10.3; Boeot. for ἔνθεσις, Stratt.47.7. (Perh. Phryg., cf. Inscr. Phryg. in *Jahresh.*8 *Beibl.*95 βεκος ακκαλος τι.)

⊛**ἀκολουθ-έω**, *follow* one, *go after* or *with* him, freq. of soldiers and slaves:—mostly c. dat. pers., Ar.*Pl.*19, etc.; ἀ. τῷ ἡγουμένῳ Pl.*R.*474c; with Preps., ἀ. μετά τινος Th.7.57, Pl.*La.*187e, Lys.2.27, etc.; τοῖς σώμασι μετ' ἐκείνων ἠκολούθουν, ταῖς δ' εὐνοίαις μεθ' ὑμῶν ἦσαν Isoc.14.15; ἀ. σύν τινι X.*An.*7.5.3; κατόπιν τινός Ar.*Pl.*13: rarely c. acc., Men.558: abs., Pl.*Plt.*277e, Thphr.*Char.*18.8, etc.; ἀ. ἐφ' ἁρπαγήν, of soldiers, Th.2.98; ἀκολουθῶν, ὁ, as Subst., = ἀκόλουθος I, Men.*Adul.Fr.*1. 2. of stars, *follow* in the diurnal rotation, Autol.2.2. II. metaph., *follow*, *be guided by*, τῇ γνώμῃ τινός Th.3.38; τοῖς πράγμασιν, τοῖς τοῦ πολέμου καιροῖς, D.4.39, 24.95; *obey*, τοῖς νόμοις And.4.19: c. acc. neut., ἀ. ἅπαντα *PLille* 1.26. 2. *follow the thread* of a discourse, Pl.*Phd.*107b, etc. 3. of things, *follow upon*, *to be consequent upon*, *consistent with*, εὐλογία..εὐηθείᾳ ἀ. Id.*R.*400e, cf. 398d; *follow analogy of*, Arist.*HA*499$^{a}$10, al. b. abs., *to be consequent*, ὡς γένους ὄντος τοῦ ἀεὶ ἀκολουθοῦντος *Top.*128$^{b}$4; as species to individual, *GA*768$^{b}$13. 4. abs., ἀκολουθεῖ *it follows*, Id.*Cat.*14$^{a}$31.—Not in Trag.: first in Hippon.55, with ᾱ (s.v.l.), elsewhere ᾰ; takes place of ἕπομαι in later Greek. **-ησις**, *εως*, ἡ, *following*, Arist.*Rh.*1410$^{a}$4. 2. *sequence in argument*, with reference to the *fallacia consequentis*, Id.*APr.*52$^{b}$29, *SE*181$^{a}$23. II. *obedience*, *conformity*, Pl.*Def.*412b. **-ητέον**, *one must follow*, abs., X.*Oec.*21.7; τῷ λόγῳ Pl.*R.*400d. **-ητικός**, ή, όν, *disposed to follow*, ταῖς ἐπιθυμίαις, τοῖς πάθεσι, Arist.*Rh.*1389$^{a}$5, *EN*1095$^{a}$4; τῷ αἱροῦντι λόγῳ Chrysipp.*Stoic.*3.93; τῷ ἄρχοντι *Stoic.*3.158. 2. *capable of following*, πόδες (in metre, opp. ἡγεμονικοί) Clearch.68. 3. *expressing consequence*, σύνδεσμος v.l. in Sch.D.T.p.62 H. **-ία**, ἡ, *following*, *attendance*, S.*Fr.*990, Pl.*Alc.*1.122c:—ἀ. πρὸς τὸ κενούμενον *filling up* a vacuum, Erasistr.(?) ap.Gal.*Nat.Fac.*1.16. 2. *sequence*, *succession*, τάξις καὶ ἀ. Chrysipp.*Stoic.*2.266, al.; *success*[ion] of philosophers, D.L.2.47; κατ' ἀκολουθίαν in *regular successi*[on], Hdn.7.5.2: Lit.Crit., *natural sequence* of words, D.H.*Comp.*22, Longin.22.1; *sequence* of argument, Phlp.*in Ph.*707.3; in rhyth[m], *orderly sequence*, D.H.*Comp.*25: Gramm., *agreement*, Id.*Amm.*2. *analogy*, A.D.*Pron.*2.24, al. II. *retinue*, *train*, D.S.27.6. II[I]. *conformity with*, τοῖς πράγμασι Pl.*Cra.*437c; φύσεως *Stoic.*3.4; κα[τ'] ἀκολουθίαν τῶν ἐτῶν *in conformity with* his age, *POxy.*1202.20 (A.D.): abs., *consistency*, *coherence*, Phld.*Sign.*37 (sg. and pl.). [2.] *obedience*, τοῖς θεοῖς M.Ant.3.9. IV. in Logic, *consequen*[ce], Ph.2.497, Chrysipp.*Stoic.*2.68, al.; ἐξ ἀκολουθίας Phld.*Ir.*p.9[…] W. **-ίσκος**, ὁ, Dim. of ἀκόλουθος, *foot-boy*, Ptol.Euerg.6. ⊛**-ος**, *ον*, (ἀ- copul., κέλευθος, cf. Pl.*Cra.*405d) *following*, *attending on*, mostly as Subst., *follower*, *attendant*, *IG*1.1, Ar.*Av.*73; ὅτοισι παῖ[ς] ἀ. ἐστιν Eup.159.3; freq. in Att. Prose, Antipho 2.1.4, Th.6.28, 7.75, Pl.*Smp.*203c, etc.; οἱ ἀ. *camp-followers*, X.*Cyr.*5.2.36: fem., Plu.*Caes.*10: metaph., Δίκα Εὐνομίας ἀ. B.14.55. 2. *following after*, c. gen., πλάτα..Νηρῄδων ἀ. S.*OC*719 (lyr.). 3. *following*, *consequent upon*, *in conformity with*, c. gen., τἀκόλουθα τῶν ῥακῶν Ar.*Ach.*438, cf. Pl.*Phd.*111c: mostly c. dat., Id *Lg.*716c, *Ti.*88d; ἀκόλουθα τούτοις πράττειν D.18.257; ἀ. τοῖς εἰρημένοις ἐστὶ τὸ διῃρῆσθαι Arist.*Pol.*1321$^{b}$3; *consistent*, οὐδὲν ἀ. αὑτῷ λέγει Demetr.*Eloc.*153; of persons, *conforming*, τῇ ὑμετέρᾳ βουλήσει *PTeb.*44.34 (ii B.C.): abs., *correspondent*, Lys.21.10; τἆλλα πάντα τὰ ἀ. Hyp.*Eux.*25; λόγους πράξεις ἀ. Epicur.*Sent.*25; *consistent with one another*, X.*An.*2.4.19. Adv. -θως *in accordance with*, τοῖς νόμοις D.44.67; ἀ. τῇ φύσει ζῆν Chrysipp.*Stoic.*3.4, cf. Phld.*Piet.*100, D.S.4.17: abs., *consistently*, Metrod.*Fr.*17, Aristid.2.28 J., Plot.4.3.20. 4. *in accordance with nature*, Zeno *Stoic.*1.55. 5. Gramm., *analogical*, A.D.*Pron.*11.21, al. Adv. -θως *analogically*, Id.*Synt.*159.6. 6. in Logic, *consequent*, περὶ ἀκολούθων, title of work by Chrysipp. *Stoic.*2.5, cf. 69; τοῦτο γὰρ ἀ. that *follows*, Phld.*Ir.*p.84 W.—Used once by S. l.c.; otherwise only in Com. and Prose.

**ἀκολουτέω**, for ἀκολουθέω, barbarism in Ar.*Th.*1198.

**ἄκολπος**, *ον*, *without sinus genitalis*, of the pipe-fish, Ael.*NA*15.16.

**ἀκόλυμβος**, *ον*, *unable to swim*, Batr.158, Str.6.2.9, Plu.2.599b.

**ἀκομιστ-ία**, Ep. -ίη [ῑ], ἡ, *lack of tending* or *care*, Od.21.284, Them.*Or.*22.274a, Max.Tyr.34.2. ⊛**-ος**, *ον*, *slovenly*, S.*Ichn.*143; *untended*, D.L.5.5, Nonn.*D.*40.174, al.

**ἀκόμμωτος**, *ον*, *unpainted*; metaph., *without meretricious ornament*, ὕμνος Them.*Or.*18.218b.

**ἄκομος**, *ον*, (κόμη) *without hair*, *bald*, Luc.*VH*1.23; of trees, *leafless*, Poll.1.236.

**ἀκόμπαστος**, *ον*, *unboastful*, A.*Th.*538, E.*Fr.*872:—**ἄκομπος**, A.*Th.*554, S.*Fr.*210.

**ἀκόμψευτος**, *ον*, *unadorned*, of style, D.H.*Comp.*22.

**ἄκομψος**, *ον*, *unadorned*, Archil.158, cf. Jul.*Caes.*317c; ἐγὼ δ' ἄκομψος '*rude* I am *in speech*', E.*Hipp.*986, cf. M.Ant.6.30, Chor. in *Jahrb.*9.176; οὐκ ἄ. Phlp.*in Ph.*528.19. Adv. -ψως Plu.2.4f.

⊛**ἀκονάω**, (ἀκόνη) *sharpen*, μαχαίρας Ar.*Fr.*684; λόγχην X.*Cyr.*6.2.33:—Med., ἀκονᾶσθαι μαχαίρας Id.*HG*7.5.20:—Pass., Arist.*Pr.*886$^{b}$10, Phld.*Sign.*34. 2. metaph., *spur*, *goad on*, D.25.46; *provoke*, γλῶσσαν ἠκονημένος *Trag.Adesp.*423, cf. X.*Oec.*21.3, Ph.1.469, al., Chor. in *Jahrb.*9.184; θυμὸν ἐπ' ἐλπίδι τινὸς ἀ. Demad.17:—Pass., Ph.2.178, al.

⊛**ἄκονδος** (leg. ἄκοννος)· ἄχαρις κονδάς (leg. κόννος), γὰρ ἡ χάρις, Hsch.

**ἀκόνδῠλος**, *ον*, *without knuckles*:—*without blows*, Luc.*Char.*2.

⊛**ἀκόν-η** [ᾰ], ἡ, *whetstone*, *hone*, λιθίνη Chilo 1, Hermipp.46, etc. 2. metaph., δόξαν ἔχω ἀκόνας λιγυρᾶς ἐπὶ γλώσσᾳ I feel the shrill note of a *whetstone* on my tongue, i.e. am roused to song, Pi.*O.*6.82; of persons, e.g. a trainer, ἀνδράσιν ἀεθληταῖσιν Ναξίαν ἀκόναν Pi.*I.*6(5).73; of Ἔρως, *AP*12.18 (Alph.), cf. Plu.2.838e. 3. part of tragus of ear, Poll.2.86. (Cf. Skt. *áśan-* 'stone'.) **-ησις**, *εως*, ἡ, *sharpening*, Hsch. and Suid. s.v. βρυγμός. ⊛**-ητής**, *οῦ*, ὁ, *one who sharpens*, σπάθης *Edict.Diocl.*7.33, cf. Hdn.Gr.1.73. ⊛**-ητί**· ἄνευ πόνου, *EM* 50.29. **-ητός**, ή, όν, = θηκτός, Sch.Opp.*H.*2.354. **-ήτως**· ἀκοπιάστως, Hsch.

**ἀκονίας**, *ου*, ὁ, a *fish*, Numen.ap.Ath.7.326a (s.v.l.).

**ἀκονίᾱτος**, *ον*, (κονιάω) *unplastered*, *not whitewashed*, Thphr.*HP*8.11.1, cf. Gal.13.356 (nisi leg. ἀκώνητος).

**ἀκόνιον**, τό, in Medicine, specific for eyes, prob. powdered *by rubbing on an* ἀκόνη, Dsc.1.98.

**ἀκονῑτί** or -εί (*SIG*36*B* (Olympia, v B.C.), D.19.77), Adv. of ἀκόνιτος, *without the dust of the arena*, i.e. *without struggle*, *without effort*, usu. of the conqueror, Th.4.73, X.*Ag.*6.3; of the loser, εἰ ταῦτα προεῖτο ἀ. D.18.200.

**ἀκονῑτικός**, ή, όν, *made of* ἀκόνιτον, X.*Cyn.*11.2.

⊛**ἀκόνῑτον**, τό, *leopard's bane*, *Aconitum Anthora*, Theopomp.Hist.177a, Thphr.*HP*9.16.4, Dsc.4.76, Gal.11.820:—also -ῑτος, ἡ, dub.l. in Nic.*Al.*42, cf. *AP*11.123 (Hedyl.), Euph.142. II. *wolf's bane*, *Aconitum Napellus*, Dsc.4.77.

**ἀκόνῑτος**, *ον*, (κονίω) *without dust*, *combat* or *struggle*, Q.S.4.319. II. f.l. for ἀκώνητος, Dsc.1.7; for κωνικός, Arist.*GA*739$^{b}$12.

**ἄκονος**, v. ἄκινος.

**ἀκοντί**, Adv. of ἄκων, *unwillingly*, Plu.*Fab.*5, Suid.

**ἀκοντ-ίας**, *ου*, ὁ, (ἄκων) *quick-darting serpent* (cf. ἀκοντίλος), Nic.*Th.*491, Philum.*Ven.*26, Luc.*Dips.*3. II. *meteor*, in pl., Plin.*HN*2.89. III. a plant, Hsch., *EM*50.53. ⊛**-ίζω**, Att. fut.

, (ἄκων) *hurl a javelin*, τινός *at* one, Αἴαντος . . ἀκόντισε φαίδιμος τωρ Il.14.402, cf. 8.118; also Αἴας . . ἐφ' Ἕκτορι . . ἵετ' ἀκοντίσ- . 16.359; ἀ. ἐς ὅμιλον, Od.22.263, Il.4.490; ἔς τινας Th. .o; εἰς τὸ φῶς ἐκ τοῦ σκότους X.*An*.7.4.18: c. dat., of the eapon, ἢ καὶ ἀκόντισε δουρί Il.5.533; ἀ. δουρὶ φαεινῷ ib.611, al.; χμαῖς Pi.*I*.1.24: also c. acc., ἀκόντισαν ὀξέα δοῦρα Od.22.265; οντίζουσι θαμειὰς αἰχμὰς ἐκ χειρῶν Il.12.44, cf. 14.422: abs., *use javelin*, τοξεύειν καὶ ἀ. Hdt.4.114, cf. Hp.*Aër*.17, Th.3.23, etc.:— ss., κῶλα . . ἐς πλευρὰ καὶ πρὸς ἧπαρ ἠκοντίζετο E.*IT*1370; ἀ. ἀπὸ ν ἵππων ὀρθός Pl.*Men*.93d. 2. after Hom., *hit* or *strike with velin*, or simply *aim at*, ἀ. τὸν σῦν Hdt.1.43, etc.:—Pass., *to be hit wounded*, E.*Ba*.1098, Antipho3.1.1, X.*HG*4.5.13. 3. *hurl, row*, ἑαυτούς, i.e. *leap overboard*, Ach.Tat.5.7; *jettison* cargo, Id. .2: metaph., τινὰς εἰς ἄπειρον χρόνον Olymp.Alch.p.75 B. 4. *hoot forth rays*, of moon, E.*Ion*1155:—Med., *flash*, Arist.*Mu*. 92$^b$3. 5. metaph., μῦθον Nonn.*D*.34.299; μερίμνας ἀνέμοισιν .12.258. II. intr., *dart* or *pierce*, metaph., of curses, εἴσω γῆς .*Or*.1241. **-ίλος**, ὁ, = ἀκοντίας, Hsch., *EM*50.52. ⊛**-ιον**, τό, Dim. of ἄκων (A), *javelin*, *h.Merc*.460, Hdt.1.34, Aen.Tact.29.6,8, l. 2. in pl., *javelin-exercise*, Pl.*Lg*.794c; also in sg., X.*Eq.Mag*. .21,25. **-ισία**, ἡ, = sq., *SIG*1060 (Tralles). **-ισις**, εως, ἡ, *hrowing the javelin*, X.*An*.1.9.5, Ascl.*Tact*.1.3. **-ισμα**, ατος, τό, *distance thrown with javelin*, ἐντὸς ἀκοντίσματος within *dart's throw*, X.*HG*4.4.16. II. *dart, javelin*, Str.4.6.7 (pl.), Plu.*Alex*.43, Arr.*Tact*.9.1. III. in pl., = the concrete ἀκοντισταί, Plu.*Pyrrh*. 21. **-ισμός**, ὁ, = ἀκόντισις, X.*Eq.Mag*.3.6, Str.11.5.1, Arr.*An*.1. 2.6; as a contest, *OGI*339 (Sestos); *emission* of liquids, [Gal.]19. 456, Sch.Il.17.297. 2. ἀκοντισμοὶ ἀστέρων, of *shooting* stars, Ptol. *Tetr*.102. ⊛**-ιστήρ**, ῆρος, ὁ, = -ιστής, E.*Ph*.142. II. as Adj., *darting, hurtling*, τρίαινα Opp.*H*.5.535: metaph., μαζοὶ ἀ. ἐρώτων Nonn. *D*.7.264:—also in pass. sense, θύρσος, λᾶας, 24.134, 30.230; ἀκοντιστῆρες μόλυβδοι, prob. *bullets*, Keil-Premerstein *Dritter Bericht* p. 89. **-ιστήριον**, τό, *engine for hurling projectiles*, τὰ τῶν μεγάλων λίθων ἀ. Agath.3.5. **-ιστής**, οῦ, ὁ, *darter, javelin-man*, Il.16.328, Od.18.262, Hdt.8.90, A.*Pers*.52, Th.3.97, Theoc.17.55, etc. **-ιστικός**, ή, όν, *skilled in throwing the dart*, X.*Cyr*.7.5.63: Sup., ib.6.2. 4; -κά, τά, *art of throwing the dart*, Pl.*Thg*.126b; -κή, ἡ, Ael.*Tact*. *Praef*., Arr.*Tact.Praef*. Adv. -κῶς Poll.3.151. **-ιστύς**, ύος, ἡ, = ἀκόντισις, *game of the dart*, ἀκοντιστὺν ἐσδύσεαι Il.23.622.

**ἀκοντο-βόλος**, ον, *dart-throwing*, A.R.2.1000: as Subst. in pl., Agath.3.20. ⊛**-δόκος**, ον, *receiving* (i.e. *hit by*) *the dart*, Simon. 106. **-φόρος**, ον, *bearing darts*, of persons or things, Nonn.*D*.20. 148, al.

**ἀκόντως**, Adv. of ἄκων (B), v. ἀέκων.

⊛**ἀκοός**, όν, = ἀκουστικός, Pl.Com.226.

⊛**ἀκοπ-ητί**, Adv. of ἄκοπος, f.l. for ἀκονιτί, Lib.*Decl*.29.6. **-ία**, ἡ, (ἄκοπος) *freedom from fatigue*, Cic.*Fam*.16.18.1. **-ίαστος**, ον, (κοπιάω) *not wearying*, ὁδός Arist.*Mu*.391$^a$12 (v.l. -ατος). II. *untiring, unwearied*, φῶς ἡλίου Herm.ap.Stob.1.49.44. Adv. -άστως Sch.S.*Aj*.852. **-ίατος**, ον, = foreg., πρόνοια *Stoic*.1.125, cf. *IG* 2.630b, Vett.Val.263.17, *PMag.Par*.1.1127; ἀ. πίστεις proofs which a writer *never tires of* repeating, Phld.*Mus*.p.40 K. Adv. -τως, ἀπολαύειν Id.*Piet*.15, Lxx *Wi*.16.20. ⊛**-ος**, ον, *unwearied*, Pl.*Lg*. 789d. Adv. -πως, διαπονεῖν Hp.*Vict*.3.70: Comp., ἡγούμενος -ωτέρως ἔσεσθαι τοῖς στρατιώταις prob. in *Hell.Oxy*.17.2. 2. *free from trouble*, Amips.28. 3. *unbruised*, of fruit, etc., *PHib*.49.9 (Sup., iii B.C.). II. Act., *not wearying*, ὄχησις Pl.*Ti*.89a; of a horse, *easy*, X.*Eq*.1.6 (Comp.); τοῖς τετράποσιν ἄκοπον τὸ ἑστάναι Arist.*PA*689$^b$17. 2. *removing weariness, refreshing*, Hp.*Aph*. 2.48, *Acut*.66, Pl.*Phdr*.227a, Agathin.ap.Orib.10.7.21 (Comp.):— ἄκοπον (sc. φάρμακον), τό, *application* (of various kinds) *for relief of* pain, etc., Dsc.1.1, Gal.13.1005, Luc.*Alex*.22, etc., cf. Antyll.ap. Orib.10.29; in Asclep.ap.Gal.13.343 also ἄκοπος, ἡ. 3. = ἀνάγυρος, Dsc.3.150, Sch.Nic.*Th*.71. III. (from κόπτω) *not worm-eaten*, Arist.*Pr*.909$^a$19. Adv. -πως, ἔχειν Thphr.*CP*4.16.2. 2. *not broken* or *ground, whole*, πέπερι Alex.Aphr.*Pr*.1.67; *not moth-eaten*, ἱμάτια Thphr.*HP*4.4.2. 3. *uncut*, χόρτος *PFlor*.232.11 (iii A.D.).

**ἀκόπρ-ιστος**, ον, (κοπρίζω) *not manured*, Thphr.*CP*4.12.3. ⊛**-ος**, ον, *with little excrement in the bowels*, Hp.*Acut*.62. II. = foreg., Thphr.*HP*8.6.4. **-ώδης**, ες, *producing little excrement*, of food, Hp.*Acut*.57 (Comp.).

**ἀκοράζεσθαι**· ἀκροᾶσθαι, Hsch. (i.e. ἀκοϝάζεσθαι). **ἀκοραῖος**· βλ βερός, ἀνωφελής, Id.

⊛**ἀκόρ-εστος**, ον, (κορέννυμι) = ἀκόρητος, *insatiate*, αὐάτα *Lyr.Adesp*. 123, Trag. in lyr. passages, A.*Ag*.1002, E.*Heracl*.927: c. gen., αἰχμᾶς ἀ. A.*Pers*.998, cf. Eus.Mynd.1. Adv. -τως, ὁπυίεσθαι *AP*10.56 (Pall.), cf. Eun.*VSp*.456 B.; ἀ. ὕδατος ἔχειν *Gp*.15.9.2, cf. Them.*Or*. 24.304d. 2. of things, *unceasing*, οἰζύς A.*Ag*.756; οἰμωγά S.*El*. 123; νείκη E.*Med*.638: Sup., γόοις A.*Pers*.545. II. Act., *not causing surfeit*, Id.*Ag*.1331; φιλία X.*Smp*.8.15 (Comp.). ⊛**-ετος**, ον, used in Trag. (metri gr.) for ἀκόρεστος, A.*Ag*.1117,1143, S.*El*. 122. **-ής**, ές, = ἀκόρεστος, οἰμωγής Them.*Or*.7.90d, cf. Hsch. (cod. ἀγκ-): Sup. -έστατος, of a person, S.*OC*120 (lyr.). **-ητος**, ον, *insatiate, unsated*, c. gen., πολέμου, μάχης, ἀπειλάων, Il.12.335, 20. 2, 14.479 (not in Od.), cf. Hes.*Sc*.346; προκάδων *h.Ven*.71. II. (κόρις) *undisturbed by bugs*, Ar.*Nu*.44 (wrongly expl. by Sch. and Phot.p.63 R. as *unswept*). ⊛**-ία**, ἡ, *not eating to satiety, moderation in eating*, Hp.*Epid*.6.4.18. II. ἀ. ποτοῦ *insatiable desire* of drink, Aret.*CD*2.2.

**ἀκορίτης** [ῑ] οἶνος, ὁ, *wine flavoured with* ἄκορον, Dsc.5.63.

**ἄκορνα**, ἡ, *fish thistle, Cnicus Acarna*, Thphr.*HP*1.10.6, 6.4.6.

**ἀκορνοί**· ἀττέλεβοι, Hsch.; cf. ὀκορνός.

**ἄκορον**, τό, *yellow flag, Iris Pseudacorus*, Dsc.1.2, Gal.11.819:—f.l. for ἄκκιρον, κόρκορον, Plin.*HN*15.27, 25.144, for ἄκαιρον, Dsc.4.144.

**ἄκορος**, ον, = ἀκόρεστος: *untiring, ceaseless*, εἰρεσία Pi.*P*.4.202.

**ἀκορραί**· ἄκανθαι, Hsch. ⊛**ἀκόρσωτον**· ἀκτένιστον, ἄκαρτον, ἀξύλιστον, Id.

**ἀκόρῠφ-ος**, ον, (κορυφή) *without top, without beginning*, D.H.*Comp*. 22. II. = sq., Hsch. **-ωτος**, ον, *not to be summed, countless*, Id. s.v. ἄκριτα.

**ἄκος**, εος, τό, (ἀκέομαι) *cure, remedy*, c. gen. rei, κακῶν Od.22.481, etc.; νυμφικῶν ἐδωλίων A.*Ch*.71; κύβους . . τερπνὸν ἀργίας ἄ. S.*Fr*. 479.4; κακὸν κακῷ διδοὺς ἄ. Id.*Aj*.363: abs., ἄ. εὑρεῖν Il.9.250; δίζησθαι, ἐξευρεῖν, ἐκπονεῖν, λαβεῖν, Hdt.1.94, 4.187, A.*Supp*.367, E.*Ba*. 327; ἄκη ποιεῖσθαι, c. dat., Pl.*Lg*.910a: in medical sense, Hp.*Acut*.1; by a medical metaph., ἄ. ἐντέμνειν, τέμνειν, A.*Ag*.17, E.*Andr*.121; ἄ. τομαῖον A.*Ch*.539: ἄ. [ἐστι], c. inf., ἄ. γὰρ οὐδὲν τόνδε θρηνεῖσθαι *it boots* not to . ., Id.*Pr*.43. 2. *means of obtaining* a thing, c. gen., σωτηρίας E.*Hel*.1055.

⊛**ἀκοσκίνευτος**, ον, *unwinnowed*, *PPetr*.3p.218 (iii B.C.).

⊛**ἀκοσμ-έω**, *to be disorderly, offend*, οἱ ἀκοσμοῦντες S.*Ant*.730, *Ph*. 387, Lys.14.13, D.24.92, Hyp.*Fr*.14, Arist.*Ath*.3.6; ἀ. περί τι *offend* in a point, Pl.*Lg*.764b. **-ήεις**, εσσα, εν, = ἄκοσμος, Nic.*Al*. 175. **-ητος**, ον, (κοσμέω) *unarranged*, Pl.*Grg*.506e, *Prt*.321c. Adv. -τως Id.*Lg*.781b. b. *not organized as a* κόσμος, ὕλη Plot.4.3. 9; σύγχυσις Dam.*Pr*.205. 2. of style, *unadorned*, D.H.*Th*.23, etc. 3. *unfurnished with*, χρήμασιν X.*Oec*.11.9. ⊛**-ία**, ἡ, *disorder*, Pl.*Grg*.508a, Ael.*Tact*.41.2; *extravagance, excess*, λόγων E.*IA*317:—in moral sense, *disorderliness* (with play on κόσμος II. 1), S.*Fr*.846: in pl., Pl.*Smp*.188b; αἱ ἀ. τοῦ πλήθους Phld.*Hom*. p.34 O. 2. *absence of* κόσμος, *chaos*, Dam.*Pr*.205. II. *abeyance of* κόσμοι, in Crete (κόσμος III), Arist.*Pol*.1272$^b$8. **-ιος**, ον, = ἀκοσμήεις, Sch.Nic.*Al*.175. ⊛**-ος**, ον, *disorderly*, φυγή A.*Pers*. 470; ἄ. καὶ ταραχώδης νυκτομαχία Plu.*Mar*.20:—in Hom. once, ἔπεα ἄκοσμά τε πολλά τε ᾔδη Il.2.213. Adv. -μως Hdt.7.220, A.*Pers*.374, etc. II. κόσμος ἄ. a world *that is no world*, *AP*7.561 (Jul.), but in 9.323 (Antip.) of an *inappropriate* ornament.

**ἀκοστ-άω** or **-έω**, (cf. sq.) only aor. part., ἵππος ἀκοστήσας ἐπὶ φάτνῃ horse *well-fed* at rack and manger, Il.6.506, 15.263; cf. ἀγοστέω. ⊛**-ή**, ἡ, *barley*, Nic.*Al*.106. (Cypr. acc. to Hsch., but Thess. for *grain* of all kinds acc. to Sch.Il.6.506.)

**ἀκόστιλα**· ἐλάχιστα, Hsch.

**ἄκοτος**, ον, *free from anger, cheerful*, Pi.*Pae*.1.3, cf. Hsch.

**ἀκουάζομαι**, *hear, listen to*, c. gen., ἀοιδοῦ Od.9.7, cf. 13.9; δαιτὸς ἀκουάζεσθον *ye are bidden to* the feast, like καλεῖσθαι, Il.4.343: Medic., of auscultation, ἀ. πρὸς τὰ πλευρά Hp.*Morb*.2.61:—Act., *h.Merc*.423.

**ἀκουή**, ἡ, Ep. for ἀκοή (q.v.).

**ἀκουόντως**, Adv. *as one that listens*, i.e. *with deference*, λέγειν Sch. Il.*Oxy*.1085.72.

**ἀκούρευτος**, ον, (κουρεύω) *unshaven, unshorn*, *EM*120.28, *Gloss*.

**ἄκουρος**, ον, (κοῦρος) *childless, without male heir*, Od.7.64. II. (κουρά) *unshaven*, Ar.*V*.476, Lyc.976, Str.10.3.6.

**ἀκουσείω** [ᾰ], Desiderat. of ἀκούω, *long to hear*, S.*Fr*.991; and in Hsch. the order of words requires ἀκουσείων for ἀκουστιῶν.

**ἀκουσ-ία** [ᾰκ], ἡ, *involuntary action*, S.*Fr*.746. **-ιάζομαι** [ᾰκ], in aor. 1 Pass., *sin through ignorance*, Lxx *Nu*.15.28.

**ἀκουσί-θεος** [ᾰ], ον, *heard of God*, *AP*6.249 (Antip. Thess.). **-μος** [ᾰ], η, ον, *fit to be heard*, S.*Fr*.745.

⊛**ἀκούσι-ος** [ᾱ], ον, Att. contr. for ἀεκούσιος. **-ότης** [ᾱ], ητος, ἡ, = ἀκουσία, Hsch. s.v. ἀέκητι, al.

**ἄκου-σις** [ᾰ], εως, ἡ, *hearing*, Arist.*de An*.426$^a$1, al., Phld.*Rh*.2. 60S. 2. in pl., = ἀκουσμάτια, Plot.4.1.12. ⊛**-σμα**, ατος, τό, *thing heard*, such as music, ἥδιστον ἄ. X.*Mem*.2.1.31, Men.660; ἀ. καὶ ὁράματα Arist.*Pol*.1336$^b$2, cf. *EN*1174$^b$28, Posidon.23, Plu.*Crass*.32. 2. *rumour, report*, S.*OC*518 (lyr.), Jul.*Or*.3.110d. 3. *oral instruction*, in the Pythag. school, Iamb.*VP*18.82. **-σματικός**, ή, όν, lit. *eager to hear*: οἱ ἀ. *probationers* in the school of Pythagoras, Iamb.*VP* 18.81, etc. **-σμάτιον**, τό, Dim. of ἄκουσμα, Ps.-Luc.*Philopatr*. 18. **-στέον**, *one must hear* or *hearken to*, c. gen. pers., E.*IA* 1010, X.*Smp*.3.9, etc. (also in pl. ἀκουστέα, Hdt.3.61; τῶν κρατούντων ἐστὶ πάντ' ἀκουστέα S.*El*.340): c. acc. rei, Pl.*R*.386a: abs., S.*OT* 1170. b. *one must understand*, τι διττῶς Str.9.5.12, cf. Gal. 15.484, Olymp.*in Mete*.337.14; *one must interpret*, ὀνείρους Artem. 1.3. **-στήριον**, τό, *lecture-hall*, Gal.*Libr.Propr*.2, Them.*Or*.2. 26c. 2. *assembly of hearers, audience*, Porph.*Plot*.15. **-στής**, οῦ, ὁ, *hearer, listener*, Men.988; τῶν ἀλλοτρίων κακῶν D.H.*Dem*. 45. 2. *auditor, disciple*, Scymn.20, Agathem.1.1, Phld.*Rh*.1. 95S., D.H.*Isoc*.1, etc. **-στικός**, ή, όν, *of* or *for hearing*, πάθος Epicur.*Ep*.1p.13U.; αἴσθησις ἀ. Plu.2.37f; δύναμις ἀ. Arr.*Epict*. 2.23.2; πόρος ἀ. orifice *of ear*, Gal.10.455; τὸ ἀ. *faculty of hearing*, Arist.*de An*.426$^a$7. 2. *ready to hear*, c. gen., Id.*EN*1103$^a$3, Arr. *Epict*.3.1.13. Adv. -κῶς Phld.*Mus*.p.107 K., S.E.*M*.7.355. 3. = ἀκουσματικός, Gell.1.9. 4. = sq., Sch.E.*Or*.1281. **-στός**, ή, όν, *heard, audible*, *h.Merc*.512, Hp.*Insomn*.86, Pl.*Ti*.33c, Phld.*Herc*. 698.20, etc.; opp. θεατός, Isoc.2.49. II. *that should be heard*, with neg., δεινόν, οὐκ ἀ. S.*OT*1312, cf. E.*Andr*.1084. **-τίζω**, *make to hear*, τινά τι or τινος Lxx *Ps*.50(51).8, *Si*.45.5.

⊛**ἀκούω**: Ep. impf. ἄκουον Il.12.442: fut. ἀκούσομαι (Act. ἀκούσω first in Hyp.*Epit.*34 s.v.l., then in Lyc.378,686, D.H.5.57, *Ev.Matt.*12.19, etc.: aor. ἤκουσα, Ep. ἄκουσα Il.24.223: pf. ἀκήκοα, Lacon. ἄκουκα Plu.*Lyc.*20, *Ages.*21; ἤκουκα is a late form, *POxy.*237 vii 23 (ii A.D.); later Ion. ἀκήκουκα Herod.5.49: plpf. ἀκηκόειν Hdt.2.52, 7.208; ἠκηκόειν X.*Oec.*15.7; old Att. ἠκηκόη Ar.*V.*800, *Pax*616, Pl.*Cra.*384b:—rare in **Med.**, pres. (v. infr. II. 2): Ep. impf. ἀκούετο Il.4.331: aor. ἠκουσάμην Mosch.3.119:—**Pass.**, fut. ἀκουσθήσομαι Pl.*R.*507d: aor. ἠκούσθην Th.3.38, Luc.*Somn.*5: pf. ἤκουσμαι D.H.*Rh.*11.10, Ps.-Luc.*Philopatr.*4; ἀκήκουσμαι is dub. in Luc.*Hist. Conscr.*49: plpf. ἤκουστο Anon.ap.Demetr.*Eloc.*217, (παρ–) J.*AJ*17.10.10. (ἀ-κοϝ–, cf. κοέω):—*hear*, Hom., etc.: prop. c. acc. of thing heard, gen. of person from whom it is heard, ταῦτα Καλυψοῦς ἤκουσα Od.12.389, cf. S.*OT*43, etc.; gen. pers. freq. omitted, πάντ' ἀκήκοας λόγον Id.*Aj.*480, etc.; or the acc. rei, ἄκουε τοῦ θανόντος Id.*El.*792, cf. 793:—also c. gen. rei, φθογγῆς, κτύπου, *hear* it, Od.12.198 (as v.l.), 21.237; λόγων S.*OC*1187; once in Hom. in Med., ἀκούετο λαὸς ἀϋτῆς Il.4.331. **b.** c. gen. objecti, *hear of, hear tell of*, ἀ. πατρός Od.4.114: freq. c. part., τεθνηῶτος (sc. πατρός) ἀκούσῃς 1.289, etc.; but εἰ.. πατρὸς νόστον ἀ. ib.287; ἀ. περί τινος Od.19.270, cf. E.*IT*964, Isoc.5.72, Pl.*R.*358d,e; τι περί τινος X.*An.*7.7.30. **c.** in Prose the pers. from whom thing is heard freq. takes Prep., ἀ. τι ἀπό, ἐκ, παρά, πρός τινος, first in Il.6.524, cf. Hdt.3.62, S.*OT*7,95, Th.1.125. **d.** less freq. c. dupl. gen. pers. et rei, *hear of* a thing *from* a person, as Od.17.115, D.18.9. **e.** with part. or inf. added, as εἰ πτώσσοντας ὑφ' Ἕκτορι πάντας ἀκούσαι *should he hear* that all are now crouching under Hector, Il.7.129, cf. Hdt.7.10.θ', X.*Cyr.*2.4.12, D.3.9; ἀ. αὐτὸν ὄλβιον εἶναι *to hear* [*generally*] that he is happy, Il.24.543, cf. X.*An.*2.5.13, etc.:—also ἀ. τινὰ ὅτι or ὡς, Ἀτρεΐδην ἀκούετε ὡς.. Od.3.193; τὸν Δαίδαλον οὐκ ἀκήκοας, ὅτι..; X.*Mem.*4.2.33; ἀ. οὕνεκα S.*OC*33. **f.** c. gen. et part., to express *what one actually hears* from a person, ταῦτ'.. ἤκουον σαφῶς Ὀδυσσέως λέγοντος S.*Ph.*595; ἀ. τινὸς λέγοντος, διαλεγομένου, Pl.*Prt.*320b, X.*Mem.*2.4.1: rarely c. acc. et part., S.*Ph.*614. **2.** *know by hearsay*, ἔξοιδ' ἀκούων S.*OT*105: pres. is used like a pf., νῆσός τις Συρίη κικλήσκεται, εἴ που ἀκούεις Od.15.403, cf. 3.193; in Prose, Pl.*Grg.*503c, Luc.*Gall.*13. **3.** abs., *hearken, give ear*, esp. in proclamations, ἀκούετε λεῴ *oyez! oyez!* Susar.1, etc.: for S.*OT*1386 v. πηγή 2. **4.** οἱ ἀκούοντες *readers of a book*, Plb.1.13.6, al. **II.** *listen to, give ear to*, c. gen., Il.1.381, etc.: metaph., Φωκυλίδου οὐκ ἀκούεις; Pl.*R.*407a: rarely c. dat., ἀ. ἀνέρι κηδομένῳ Il.16.515 (in S.*El.*227 τίνι is Eth. dat.): with gen. of part. after dat., ὅττι οἱ ὦκ' ἤκουσε.. θεὸς εὐξαμένοιο ib.531. **2.** *obey*, βασιλῆος, θεοῦ, Il.19.256, Od.7.11:—Med., Λεωφίλου δ' ἀκούεται [πάντα] Archil.64. **3.** *hear and understand*, κλύοντες οὐκ ἤκουον A.*Pr.*448, cf. *Ch.*5, Ar.*Ra.*1173; τὸ μὴ πάντας πάντων ἀκούειν S.E.*M.*1.37. **4.** *to be a pupil of*, c. gen., D.L.9.21. **III.** after Hom., serving as Pass. to λέγειν, *hear oneself called, be called*, like Lat. *audire*, εἴπερ ὄρθ' ἀκούεις, Ζεῦ S.*OT*903 (cf. A.*Ag.*161); freq. with εὖ and κακῶς, κακῶς ἀ. ὑπό τινος *to be ill spoken of by* one; πρός τινος Hdt.7.16.α'; περί τινος for a thing, Id.6.86.α'; ἄμεινον, ἄριστα ἀ., Hdt.2.173, 8.93, cf. S.*Ph.*1313, Antipho 5.75, etc. **2.** with nom. of subject, ἀκούειν κακός, καλός, S.*OC*988, Pl.*Ly.*207a; νῦν κόλακες καὶ θεοῖς ἐχθροὶ.. ἀκούουσι D.18.46, etc.; ἔχαιρε ἀκούων Αἰετὸς ὁ Πύρρος Ael.*NA*7.45; later in Pass. in this sense, Nonn.*D.*21.220, al. **3.** c. inf., ἤκουον εἶναι πρῶτοι *were said* to be first, Hdt.3.131; also ἀκούσομαι μὲν ὡς ἔφυν οἴκτου πλέως S.*Ph.*1074. **4.** c. acc. rei, ἀ. κακά *have* evil *spoken of* one, Ar.*Th.*388, cf. S.*Ph.*607; ἀ. λόγον ἐσλόν Pi.*I.*5(4).13; φήμας.. κακὰς ἤκουσεν E.*Hel.*615. **5.** οὕτως ἀ. *hear it* so *said*, i.e. *at first hearing*, ὡς οὕτω γ' ἀκοῦσαι Pl.*Euthphr.*3b; ὥς γε οὑτωσὶ ἀκοῦσαι Id.*Ly.*216a. **IV.** *understand, take* in a certain sense, Jul.*Or.*4.147a; esp. in Scholl., as Sch.E.*Or.*333; τι ἐπί τινος Sch.E.*Hipp.*73. **V.** Astrol., *aspect mutually*, of signs equidistant from an equinoctial sign, Doroth.189, Heph.Astr.2.2; also, = ὑπακούειν (q.v.), Id.1.9.

⊛ **ἄκρα**, Ion. **ἄκρη**, ἡ, (fem. of ἄκρος) *highest* or *farthest point*: **1.** *headland, cape*, Il.4.425, 14.36, Od.9.285, S.*Tr.*788, Pl.*Criti.*111a: metaph., ἄκρην πενίης οὐχ ὑπερεδράμομεν Thgn.619, cf. A.*Eu.*562; κάμπτειν Men.4. **2.** *hill-top, height*, Od.8.508, *Hymn.Is.*72 (pl.). **3.** of a wave, *crest*, οὐ γὰρ ὑπερθεῖν κύματος ἄκραν δυνάμεσθα E.*Fr.*230. **4.** Hom. only in phrase κατ' ἄκρης, νῦν ὤλετο πᾶσα κατ' ἄκρης Ἴλιος αἰπεινή *from top to bottom*, i.e. *utterly*, Il.13.772; κατ' ἄ. Ἴλιον ἑλέειν 15.557, cf. 24.728, Hdt.6.18, Th.4.112; κατ' ἄ. ἐξαιρεῖν Pl.*Lg.*909b; γῆν πατρῴαν.. πρῆσαι κατ' ἄ. *utterly*, S.*Ant.*201: metaph., κατ' ἄ. ὡς πορθούμεθα how *utterly*..! A.*Ch.*691, cf. S.*OC*1242, E.*IA*778; but ἔλατεν μέγα κῦμα κατ' ἄ. *from above*, Od.5.313. **5.** *citadel* built on a *steep* rock overhanging a town (usu. ἀκρόπολις), X.*An.*7.1.20, Hyp.*Lyc.Fr.*3, Luc.*Bis Acc.*13. **6.** *end, extremity*, Arist.*HA*512$^{a}$6, 518$^{a}$9: Math., of lines, Papp.682.14; of *the extremes* in a proportion, Id.70.6, Euc.6.16, etc.

⊛ **ἀκράαντος** [κρᾱ], ον, (κραιαίνω) = ἄκραντος, Il.2.138, Od.2.202.

**ἀκραγής**, ές, (κράζω) *not barking*, ἀκραγεῖς κύνες, of gryphons, A.*Pr.*803. Hsch. expl. ἀκραγές by δυσχερές, σκληρόν, ὀξύχολον, cf. ἄκραγγες (leg. ἀκραγές)· ἀκρόχολον *AB*369.

⊛ **ἀκράδαντος**, ον, (κραδαίνομαι) *unshaken*, Ph.2.136, etc. Adv. –τως 1.352, Nicom.*Harm.*4.

⊛ **ἀκρᾱής**, ές, (ἄκρος, ἄημι) *blowing strongly*, of winds, Od.2.421, 14.253, Hes.*Op.*594; *si* ἀκραὲς *erit* if a *brisk breeze* spring up, Cic.*Att.*10.17.9. Adv. **ἀκραεί**, πλεῖν sail *with fresh breeze*, Arr.*Ind.*24.1.

**ἀκραίνει**· ἀκρατεῖ, Hsch. :⊛**ἀκραινές**· ἀκρατές (cod. -ῶς· ἐγκρ-), Id.

⊛ **ἀκραῖος**, α, ον, = ἄκρος, Opp.*H.*2.395, *Tab.Defix.*18; ἀκραῖα, τά, *extremities*, Gal.7.416: Ion. **ἄκρεα**, τά, Hp.*Epid.*1.18, *Fract.*16, [...] 30. **II.** *dwelling on heights*, epith. of Hera, E.*Med.*1379, Apol[l.] 1.9.28; Aphrodite, Paus.1.1.3, 2.32.6; gods whose temples w[ere] ἐν ἀκροπόλει, Poll.9.40.

**ἀκραίπᾰλ-ος**, ον, *relieved of drunken nausea*, Arist.*Pr.*873$^{b}$11. [...] of wines, *not producing nausea*, Ath.1.32d. **3.** of herbs, *count[er]acting nausea*, Dsc.1.26. **–ωτος**, ον, = foreg. 3, Orib.*Eup.*1.12[...]

⊛ **ἀκραιφνής**, ές, derived by Sch.Th.1.52, etc., from ἀκεραιο-φανής, ἀκέραιος, *unmixed, pure*, κόρης ἀ. αἷμα E.*Hec.*537; ὕδωρ Ar.*Fr.*3[...] metaph., ἀρετή J.*AJProoem.*4; πενία ἀ. *sheer, utter* poverty, *AP*[...] 191 (Corn. Long.). Adv. –νῶς Ph.1.100; *honestly*, Hld.2.30: Su[p.] –έστατον (but may be Adj.) Ph.2.319. **II.** *untouched, inviola[te]*, E.*Alc.*1052; in Att. Prose only Th.1.19,52; freq. later, as D.H.[...] 14, Procop.*Aed.*1.10, al.; *innocent*, ψυχή Ph.1.515:—of troops, *fres[h]*, J.*AJ*18.10.7. **2.** c. gen., *untouched by*.., ἀ. τῶν κατηπειλη[μ]μένων S.*OC*1147; κόρους ἀκραιφνεῖς μυρρίνης *free from*.., Lysipp.9.

**ἀκραιφνότης**, τητος, ἡ, *purity*, Anon. *in Prm.*(*Rh.Mus.*47.614).

**ἀκραμύλα**· κοχλίας, Hsch.

**ἄκραντος**, ον, poet. Adj. (in Hom. ἀκράαντος, q.v.), *unfulfilled, fruitless, idle*, ἔπεα, ἐλπίδες, Pi.*O.*1.86, *P.*3.23; τέχναι A.*Ag.*249:—neut. pl. as Adv., *in vain*, Pi.*O.*2.87; ἄκραντα βάζω A.*Ch.*882; οὐδ' ἄκρανθ' ὡρμήσαμεν E.*Ba.*435, cf. 1231; ἄκραντ' ὀδύρῃ *Supp.*770. **2.** *ineffectual*, νύξ A.*Ch.*65.

**ἀκραξόνιον**, τό, (ἄξων) *end of the axle*, Poll.1.145, Sch.A.R.1.752.

**ἀκρᾱσία** (A), Ion. **–ησίη**, ἡ, (ἄκρᾱτος) *bad mixture, ill temperature*, opp. εὐκρασία, ἀ. ἀέρος an *unwholesome* climate, Thphr.*CP*3.2.5; διὰ τὴν ἀκρησίην, of meats, Hp.*VM*7; χυμῶν ἀκρησίαι ib.18.

**ἀκρᾰσ-ία** (B), Ion. **–σίη**, = ἀκράτεια, Archil.*Supp.*2.10, Democr.234, D.2.18, X.*Mem.*4.5.6, Isoc.15.221 (pl.), Arist.*EN*1145$^{a}$16, Men.544, *Ev.Matt.*23.25, etc.; βρώσιος *Dialex.*1.3. ⊛ **–ίων**, ωνος, ὁ, *incontinent person*, Cerc.4.1.

⊛ **ἀκράσπεδος**, ον, *without fringes*: metaph., of words, *without the article*, Plu.2.1010d (cj. Madvig).

**ἀκρατάριον**, τό, Dim. of ἄκρατον, = *mericulum*, *Gloss.*

**ἀκράτ-εια** [κρᾰ], ἡ, (ἀκρατής) *want of power, debility*, νεύρων Hp.*Aph.*5.16, *Liqu.*1. **II.** *incontinence, want of self-control*, opp. ἐγκράτεια, Pl.*R.*461b, *Lg.*734b, etc.; ἀ. ἡδονῶν τε καὶ ἐπιθυμιῶν ib.886a, etc., cf. Ph.2.406. **–εύομαι**, *to be incontinent*, Arist.*EN*1145$^{b}$22; τῶν ἀκρασιῶν ἣν οἱ μελαγχολικοὶ –εύονται 1152$^{a}$28: censured by Phryn.406, who quotes however Men.989:—Act. is cj. in Plu.ap.Stob.3.6.53. **–ευτικός**, ή, όν, *arising from incontinence*, ἀδικήματα Arist.*Rh.*1391$^{a}$19. **–έω**, *to be* ἀκρατής, Hp.*Mul.*1.25, Poll.2.154; Ep. part. –έοντι λογισμῷ Man.4.548. **–ής**, ές, (κράτος) *powerless, impotent*, γῆρας S.*OC*1236; παιδία Hp.*Aër.*10; of paralysed limbs, *IG*4.951.22 (Epid.), Aret.*SD*1.7. **2.** in Law, *invalid*, πρῆσις *GDI*5653 (Chios), cf. *IG*12(8).267.12 (Thasos). **II.** c. gen. rei, *not having power* or *command over* a thing, γλώσσης A.*Pr.*884; φωνῆς, παντὸς τοῦ σώματος, ἑωυτοῦ, Hp.*Morb.*1.3, *Art.*48, *Morb.*2.6; ὀργῆς Th.3.84; θυμοῦ Pl.*Lg.*869a; ἀ. τῶν χειρῶν, of persons *with* their hands *tied*, D.H.1.38; *intemperate in the use of* a thing, ἀφροδισίων, οἴνου, X.*Mem.*1.2.2, *Oec.*12.11; ἀ. κέρδους, τιμῆς *intemperate in pursuit of* them, Arist.*EN*1147$^{b}$33; with Preps., ἀ. πρὸς τὸν οἶνον Id.*HA*594$^{a}$10; περὶ τὰ πόματα Id.*PA*691$^{a}$3: c. inf., ἀ. εἴργεσθαί τινος *unable to* refrain from.., Pl.*Sph.*252c. Adv. –τῶς, Ion. –τέως, διακεῖσθαι Hp.*Acut.*(*Sp.*)55. **2.** abs. in moral sense, *without command over* oneself or one's passions, *incontinent*, Arist.*EN*1145$^{b}$11; ἀ. στόμα Ar.*Ra.*838; νηδύς Aristias 3. Adv. ἀκρατῶς, ἔχειν πρός τι Pl.*Lg.*710a. **3.** of things, *uncontrolled, immoderate*, δαπάνη *AP*9.367 (Luc.); οὖρον.. ἀκρατές *incontinence* of urine, Aret.*SA*1.6; cf. ἀκρᾰτί. **–ησία**, ἡ, *want of control, incontinence*, σπέρματος Sor.2.47. **–ητος**, ον, *unsubdued*, Arist.*Mete.*384$^{a}$33: *uncontrollable*, ἐπιθυμία Hdn.1.8.2. Adv. –τως Orib.*Syn.*7.47.3; ἐπτόηνται Iamb.*VP*20.94. **–ί**, Adv. = ἀκρατῶς, τὰ οὖρα ἐκχέειν Aret.*SD*1.7.

**ἀκρᾰτία**, Ion. **–τίη**, = ἀκράτεια, Pl.*Grg.*525a, dub. in Hp.*Coac.*166. **ἀκρᾱτία**, ἡ (sic), for ἀκρᾱσία, *absence of mixture*, Dam.*Pr.*155 (s.v.l.).

⊛ **ἀκρᾱτ-ίζομαι**, (ἄκρᾱτος) *drink neat wine*; hence, *breakfast*, because this consisted of *bread dipped in wine* (Ath.1.11c sq.), Ar.*Pl.*295, ubi v. Sch., Canthar.8: c. acc., ἀ. κοκκύμηλα *to breakfast on* plums, Ar.*Fr.*607; μικρόν Aristomen.14: metaph., c. gen., ἀμιγοῦς ἠκρατίσω σοφίας Ph.2.166:—later in Act. –ίζω, fut. –ιῶ, *entertain at breakfast*, τοὺς ἐφήβους *Inscr.Prien.*113.41: metaph., ποτιζέτω καὶ ἀκρατιζέτω ψυχάς Ph.1.103. **–ισμα**, ατος, τό, *a breakfast*, ἕως ἀκρατίσματος ὥρας Arist.*HA*564$^{a}$20, cf. *Inscr.Prien.*113.54, Ath.1.11d, Plu.2.726c. **–ισμός**, ὁ, *breakfasting*, Ath.1.11d, v.l. in Theoc.1.51 (ap.Sch.). **–ιστος**, ον, Theoc.1.51 codd. πρὶν ἢ ἀκράτιστον ἐπὶ ξηροῖσι καθίξῃ *having made a* dry *breakfast*, i.e. none at all; vv.ll. ἀκρατισμόν (Sch.), ἀνάριστον *dinnerless*.

**ἀκρᾱτο-κώθων**, ωνος, ὁ, *a hard toper*, Hyp.*Dem.Fr.*(a), Ath.6.246a. **–ποσία**, Ion. **ἀκρητοποσίη**, ἡ, *drinking of neat wine*, Hdt.6.84, Hp.*Aph.*6.31, Satyr.1, Plu.*Alex.*70. **–ποτέω**, *drink neat wine*, Arist.*Pr.*871$^{a}$28. **–πότης**, ου, Ion. **ἀκρητοπότης**, εω, ὁ, (πίνω) *drinker of neat wine*, Hdt.6.84, Ael.*VH*2.41; personified as name of hero, Polem.Hist.40. **–πώλιον**· *meritorium*, *Gloss.*

⊛ **ἄκρᾱτος**, Ion. **ἄκρητος**, ον: (κεράννυμι): **1.** of liquids, *unmixed, neat*, esp. of wine, Od.24.73; ἄκρητοι σπονδαί drink-offerings *of pure wine*, Il.2.341, 4.159; οἶνος πάνυ ἄ. very *strong*, X.*An.*4.5.27; οἶνος ἄκρητος wine *without water*, Hdt.1.207, etc.; ἄκρατος (without οἶνος) Ar.*Eq.*105, etc.; ὁ πολὺς ἄ. ὀλίγ' ἀναγκάζει φρονεῖν en.779, cf. Call.*Ep.*43, Phoen.3.3; ἄκρατον, τό, Arist.*Po.*1461$^{a}$15; λα Od.9.297; αἷμα A.*Ch.*578, etc. (without αἷμα Hp.*Epid.*1.26.α΄); μός Hp.*VM*14; ὑποχωρήσιες Id.*Aph.*7.6; διάρροια Th.2.49. Adv. -ως Hp.*Prorrh.*2.24 (-κρίτως Littré). **2.** of any objects, ἄ. σώματα *re, simple* bodies, Pl.*Ti.*57c; ἄ. χρῶμα Hp.*Acut.*42; ἄ. μέλαν *pure* ack, Thphr.*Col.*26; ἄ. νύξ Ael.*Fr.*262, cf. *NA*12.33; ἄ. σκότος Plu. *ic.*21; ἄ. σκιά Id.2.932b. **3.** of qualities, *pure, absolute*, ἄ. νοῦς .*Cyr.*8.7.20; πῶς . . ἡ ἄ. δικαιοσύνη πρὸς ἀδικίαν τὴν ἄ. ἔχει Pl.*R.*545a, f. 491e. Adv. -τως *Lg.*731d. **4.** of conditions or states, *pure, ntempered, absolute*, ἐλευθερία, ἡδονή, *R.*562d, *Lg.*793a; ὀλιγαρχία rist.*Pol.*1273$^{b}$37, etc.; παρρησία Demad.18; νόμων ἀποτομία *POxy.* 37 vii 40 (ii A. D.); ἄ. νόμος *absolute* law, Pl.*Lg.*723a; ἄ. ψεῦδος *sheer ie*, Id.*R.*382c. Adv. ἀκράτως *absolutely, entirely*, ἀ. μέλας, λευκός, Ael. *NA*16.11, Luc.*D.Mar.*1.3. **5.** of persons, *intemperate, violent*, ἄ. ὀργήν A.*Pr.*678; of sleep, ἄ. ἐλθέ come *with all thy power*, E.*Cyc.* 602. **6.** of feelings, ἄ. ὀργή Alcid.ap.Arist.*Rh.*1406$^{a}$10; ἵμερος S.*Fr.*941; ἄ. καῦμα *AP*9.71 (Antiphil.); φόβος *EM*621.13; τὸ τῆς δεισιδαιμονίας ἄ. J.*BJ*2.9.3, etc. **II.** Comp. ἀκρατέστερος, Ion. ἀκρητ- (as if fr. ἀκρατής) Hp.*VM*5, Hyp.*Dem.Fr.*(*b*), Arist.*Pr.*871$^{a}$16, Thphr. *Od.*24: Sup. ἀκρατέστατος Pl.*Phlb.*53a: but ἀκρατότερος Plu.2.677c.

**ἀκρᾰτόστομος,** *ον*, gloss on ἀθυρόγλωσσος, Sch.E.*Or.*903.

**ἀκρᾱτότης,** Ion. -ητότης, ητος, ἡ, *unmixed state*, οἴνου, μέλιτος Hp. *Acut.*56.

**ἀκρᾱτο-φόρος,** ὁ, and **-φόρον,** τό, *vessel for pure wine*, elsewh. ψυκτήρ, Cic.*Fin.*3.4.15, Poll.6.99, 10.70, J.*BJ*5.13.6.

**ἀκρᾰτόφρων,** *ονος, lacking in self-control*, gloss on χαλίφρων, Sch. Od.19.530.

**ἀκράτωρ** [ᾰ], *ορος*, ὁ, = ἀκρατής I, S.*Ph.*486, Ph.1.116, al. **II.** = ἀκρατής II, ἀ. ἑαυτοῦ Pl.*R.*579c, *Criti.*121a; γαστέρων Theopomp. Hist.39, cf. Ph.2.357, Ael.*Fr.*90.

**ἀκρᾱ-χολέω,** *to be passionate*, only in pres. part., Pl.*Lg.*731d. **-χολία,** Ion. **ἀκρηχολίη,** ἡ, *passionateness, burst of passion*, Hp.*Epid.*7. 11: later **ἀκροχολία,** Sopat.ap.Stob.4.5.56, Plu.2.454b. **-χολος** [ρᾱ], *ον, quick to anger, irascible*, Ar.*Eq.*41, Pl.*R.*411c, Phld.*Lib.* p.44 O., etc.; κύων ἀ. *ill-tempered* dog, Ar.*Fr.*594a; μέλισσα Epin. 1.7: Sup., ἀχέρδου τῆς ἀκραχολωτάτης, of a *spinous* pear. Pherecr. 164:—also **ἀκρόχολος,** *ον*, Arist.*EN*1126$^{a}$18, Ph.2.268, Plu.2.604b, etc. **II.** generally, *in passionate distress*, Theoc.24.61. (ἀκρᾱ- is confirmed by metre of Com., Ion. form ἀκρη-, and etym. (shortened fr. ἀκρᾱτ-); ἀκρο- is freq. v.l. in codd. of early authors, as Pl. l.c.)

**ἄκρεα,** v. ἀκραῖος. **II. ἀκρέα,** ἡ, *girl* (Maced.), Hsch.

⊛**ἀκρελεφάντινος,** *ον*, (ἄκρος, ἐλέφας) *with extremities of ivory*, ἱερόν (i.e. statue) *IGRom.*3.800 (Syllium).

**ἀκρεμονικός,** *ή, όν, branching*, Thphr.*HP*4.6.8.

⊛**ἀκρεμών,** *όνος*, ὁ (for the accent v. Hdn.Gr.1.33, -έμων in most codd.): (ἄκρος):—*bough, branch*, Thphr.*HP*1.1.9; οἱ ἀ. τῶν κλάδων Ael.*NA*4.38, cf. Simon.183, E.*Cyc.*455, Theoc.16.96, A.R.2.1101.

**ἀκρ-εσπέριος,** *ον*, = sq., *IG*12(7).123 (Amorgos). **-έσπερος,** *ον, on edge of evening* (ἄκρος II), hence, *at nightfall*, Nic.*Th.*25 (cf. Sch.), *AP*7.633 (Crin.); τὴν ἀκρέσπερον [νύκτα] Arist.*HA*619$^{b}$21, as cited by Ath.8.353b (ἀρχέσπερον codd. Ath., ἄχρις ἑσπερίου codd. Arist.):—neut. ἀκρέσπερον as Adv., Theoc.24.77; but, *on approach of evening*, Hp.*Epid.*7.23. **-εῶτις,** ἡ, Pythagorean word = ἑβδομάς, *Theol.Ar.*ap.Phot.p.144B. **-ήβης,** *ου*, ὁ, *youth in his prime*, *AP* 6.71 (Paul. Sil.), 12.124 (Artemo). ⊛**-ηβος,** *ον, in earliest youth*, Theoc.8.93.

**ἀκρήδεμνος,** *ον, without head-band*, Opp.*C.*1.497, Nonn.*D.*2.95.

**ἀκρηθής·** ἄψεκτος, Hsch. **ἀκρήμορον·** ἀστεργές, Id. **ἀκρήπεδος·** ἡ ἀγαθή (sc. γῆ), Id. **ἀκρής,** (κράζω) *dumb with astonishment*, Id. **ἀκρηστής·** δοῦλος, Id.; cf. ἄκριστιν. **ἀκρῆστις·** ῥάχις, καὶ ἄκρα, Id. **ἀκρηστόλουχος·** δοῦλος, Id.

**ἄκρητος, ἀκρητο-ποσίη, -πότης,** v. sub ἀκρατ-.

**ἀκρητόχολος,** *ον, accompanied by bilious vomiting*, of fever, Hp. *Fract.*43, *Art.*19. ⊛**ἀκρηχολία,** v. ἀκραχ-.

⊛**ἀκρία,** ἡ, *goddess of the citadel*, epith. of Athena, Hsch. **ἀκρίαι·** τὰ ἄκρα τῶν ὀρῶν, Id.

**ἄκρια,** τά, = ἄκρα, ἄκρια ῥινός Opp.*C.*2.552. **ἀκριάω,** *adjoin*, of land, *GDI*4999 (Gortyn, dub.).

⊛**ἀκρῑβ-άζω,** = ἀκριβόω, Aq.Thd.*Pr.*8.27, cf. Ps.-Callisth.3.20:—Pass., *to be proud*, Lxx *Si.*46.15; censured by Poll.5.152. **-ασμα,** τό, *commandment*, Aq.*De.*6.17. ⊛**-ασμός,** ὁ, *commandment*, Lxx 3*Ki.*11.34: pl., ἀ. καρδίας *searchings* of heart, ib.*Jd.*5.15 (cod. A); *portion, gift*, Aq.*Ge.*47.22. ⊛**-αστής,** *οῦ*, ὁ, *lawgiver*, Id.*Is.*33. 22; *inquirer*, Id.*Jd.*5.14. ⊛**-εια,** ἡ, *exactness, precision*, Hp.*VM* 12, Th.1.22, etc.; τῶν πραχθέντων Antipho 4.3.1, cf. Lys.17.6:—freq. with Preps. in adv. sense, δι' ἀκριβείας *with minuteness* or *precision*, Pl.*Tht.*184c, *Ti.*23d, etc.; διὰ πάσης ἀ. *Lg.*876c; εἰς τὴν ἀ. φιλοσοφεῖν *Grg.*487c; εἰς ἀ. Arist.*Pol.*1331$^{a}$2; πρὸς τὴν ἀ. Pl.*Lg.*769d, cf. Arist.*Resp.*478$^{b}$1:—ἡ ἀ. τοῦ ναυτικοῦ its *efficiency, rigid discipline*, Th.7.13; ἀ. νόμων *strictness, severity*, Isoc.7.40; περὶ τὸ διάφορον *strictness* in money matters, Plb.31.27.11: pl., *niceties*, Pl.*R.*504e, Is. 7.16. **2.** *parsimony, frugality*, Plu.*Per.*16; ὕδωρ δι' ἀκριβείας ἐστί τινι is *scarce*, Pl.*Lg.*844b. **-εύω,** *use accurately*, τὴν ἀντωνυμίαν Did.ap.Sch.Pi.*N.*4.3:—in Med., S.E.*M.*1.71:—Pass., ἐὰν μὴ ἀκριβεύσωμαι ὑφ' ὑμῶν unless *I receive precise instructions* from you, *PAmh.*2.154.7 (vi A. D.). ⊛**-ής,** *ές, exact, accurate, precise*, E.*El.*367, etc.; σημεῖον Th.1.10; δίαιτα Hp.*Aph.*1.4; τριταῖος *returning precisely* at its time, Id.*Epid.*1.24; γαλήνη *complete* calm, Jul. *Or.*1.25c. **II.** of persons, *precise, strict*, δικασταί Th.3.46; ἐπίσκοποι Pl.*Lg.*762d; δεινὸς καὶ ἀ. Lys.7.12; ἀ. τοῖς ὄμμασι *sharp-sighted*, Theoc.22.194; of arguments, Ar.*Nu.*130; ἀ. μουσική E. *Supp.*906, etc.; τὸ ἀ., = ἀκρίβεια, Hp.*VM*9; τὸ πάνυ ἀ. Th.6.18: freq. in Adv. -βῶς *to a nicety, precisely*, ἀ. εἰδέναι, ἐπίστασθαι, καθορᾶν, μαθεῖν, etc., Hdt.7.32, etc.; ἀ. οἶσθα A.*Pr.*330; opp. ἁπλῶς, Isoc.5. 46; opp. τύπῳ (*in outline, roughly*), Arist.*EN*1104$^{a}$2: Comp. -έστερον Pl.*R.*436c, *Act.Ap.*18.26: Sup. -έστατα Pl.*R.*484c; ἀ. καὶ μόλις *with greatest difficulty*, Plu.*Alex.*16:—also οὐκ εἰς ἀκριβὲς ἦλθες *at the right moment*, E.*Tr.*901. **2.** *in the strict sense of the word*, ὁ ἀ. ἰατρός Pl.*R.*342d; ὁ τῷ ἀ. λόγῳ ἰατρός ib.341c. **b.** *pure-bred, genuine*, Κόλχος Eun.*Hist.*p.263D. **c.** Astron., *true*, opp. φαινόμενος, Procl. *Hyp.*4.31. **3.** *parsimonious, stingy*, ἀ. τοὺς τρόπους Men.235. Adv. -βῶς, διαιτᾶσθαι And.4.32.—Rare exc. in Att., mostly Prose. (The sense points to ἄκρος as the first part of the word, but -ῑβης remains dub.)

**ἀκρῑβο-δίκαιος,** *ον, precise as to one's rights*, ἀ. ἐπὶ τὸ χεῖρον of one who strains the law, Arist.*EN*1138$^{a}$1; but in good sense, Ph.1.672, al. ⊛**-λογέομαι,** *to be exact* or *precise* in language, investigation, etc., abs., Pl.*R.*340e, *Cra.*415a: c. acc. rei, *weigh accurately*, Id.*R.* 403d; ταυτὶ πάνθ' ὑπὲρ τῆς ἀληθείας ἀκριβολογοῦμαι D.18.21; ἐμοῦ περὶ τούτων ἀκριβολογουμένου ib.240:—later in Act., D.H.*Dem.* 26, Alex.Aphr. *in Metaph.*479.15. **-λογητέον,** *one must require precision*, Arist.*Rh.*1404$^{a}$37, Antyll.ap.Orib.45.16.4. **-λογία,** ἡ, *exactness, precision* in speech, investigation, etc., Arist.*Rh.*1361$^{b}$34, *Metaph.*995$^{a}$15; περί τι Ph.1.251. **2.** *niggardliness*, Arist.*EN* 1122$^{b}$8. **-λόγος,** *ον, precise in argument*, in pl., Timo 25.2. **-ψηφία,** ἡ, *accurate computation*, Hero *Mens.*27.

⊛**ἀκρῑβ-όω,** fut. -ώσω, *make exact* or *accurate*, E.*Hipp.*469; ἀ. τάδε *to be perfect in* bearing these hardships, X.*Cyr.*2.3.13; *arrange precisely*, Ar.*Ec.*274:—Pass., *to be exact* or *perfect*, Ar.*Ra.*1483; ἠκριβῶσθαι πρὸς πᾶσαν ἀρετήν Arist.*Pol.*1279$^{b}$1.—Later in Med., J.*AJ*17.2.2, Eust.1799.33, etc. **2.** *investigate accurately, understand thoroughly*, οἱ τάδ' ἠκριβωκότες E.*Hec.*1192, cf. X.*Cyr.*2.2.9; τοὔνομά μου σὺ ἀκριβοῖς; *are you sure of . . ?* Pl.*Chrm.*156a; *inquire carefully of*, τὸν χρόνον *Ev.Matt.*2.7:—Pass., Vett.Val.265.3. **3.** *describe accurately*, τι Phld.*Lib.*p.47 O. **4.** abs., *to be exact*, ἡ φύσις οὐκ ἀκριβοῖ Arist.*GA*778$^{a}$6; [ὁ ἄνθρωπος] κατὰ τὴν ἁφὴν διαφερόντως ἀκριβοῖ Id.*de An.*421$^{a}$22; ἀ. περί τι *GA*780$^{b}$26. **-ωμα,** τό, *exact knowledge*, τὸ κατὰ μέρος ἀ. Epicur.*Ep.*1 p.3 U.; *precise account*, τινός ib.p.4 U. **2.** *consummate display of execution*, in music, Phld. *Mus.*p.90 K. (pl.). **-ωσις,** ἡ, *exact observance*, νόμου J.*AJ*17.2.4 (v.l. ἐξακρ-). **-ωτέον,** *one must examine* or *describe accurately*, Ph.1.357, al., Aët.16.65.

⊛**ἀκρίδιον,** τό, Dim. of ἀκρίς, in metaph. sense, *spikelet*, Dsc.2.94.

**ἀκρῐδο-θήρα,** ἡ, *locust-trap*, Theoc.1.52, Longus 1.10 (v.l. -θήκη *cage*). **-φάγος,** *ον, locust-eater*, D.S.3.29, cf. Str.16.4.12.

**ἀκρι⟨δ⟩ώδης,** *ες, like locusts*, Hsch. s.v. ὀκορνούς.

**ἀκρίζω,** (ἄκρος) *go on tiptoe*, E.*Fr.*570. **2.** = τὰ ἄκρα ἐσθίειν, Sch.Il.21.12.

**ἄκρῑθος,** *ον*, (κριθή) *not mixed with barley*, πυρός *POxy.*101 (ii A. D.), 1124.11 (i A. D.).

**ἀκρίνας·** γωνίας, καὶ καθαρός, ἁγνός, Hsch. **ἀκρινόμος,** ὁ, *forest-warden* (Lacon.), Id. **ἄκριον·** ποῖον (leg. ῥίον), Id.

⊛**ἄκρις,** *ιος*, ἡ, (ἄκρος) Ep.Noun, *hill-top, mountain peak*, Hom. only in Od., always in pl., ἄκριες ἠνεμόεσσαι windy *mountain tops*, Od. 9.400, cf. *h.Cer.*382; δι' ἄκριας through *hill-country*, Od.10.281:—sg., Περγαμίης ὑπὲρ ἄκριος *Epigr.Gr.*1035.8 (Pergam.).

⊛**ἀκρίς,** *ίδος*, ἡ, *grasshopper, locust, cricket*, Il.21.12, Ar.*Ach.*1116, Arist.*HA*555$^{b}$18, Thphr.*Fr.*174.3, Theoc.7.41, Lxx *Ex.*10.4, etc.:—sg., in collective sense, Men.Prot.p.108D.; πολλὴ ἀ. Heph.Astr. 1.21.

**ἀκρῐσία,** ἡ, (ἄκριτος) *want of distinctness and order, confusion*, X. *HG*7.5.27; ἀ. καὶ ταραχή Epicur.*Sent.*22. **II.** *want of judgement, bad judgement* or *choice*, Plb.2.35.3, *AP*7.629 (Antip.); περὶ τῶν φίλων Luc.*Tim.*8. **III.** *undecided character* of a disease, *not coming to a crisis*, Hp.*Epid.*1.8: pl., ἠέρος ἀ. *unsettled* climate, *POxy.*1796.22.

**ἄκριστιν·** κλέπτρια, ἀλετρίδα (Phryg.), Hsch. **ἀκρίστιος,** *ον, on top of the mast*, Id. **ἄκριστοι·** ἄκρα ὀρῶν, Id.

**ἀκρίσχιον,** τό, *end of the hip*, Heliod.ap.Orib.48.55.1, *SIG*1025. 53 (Cos).

⊛**ἀκριταγών·** πολύγωνον, Hsch.

**ἀκρῐτί** [τῑ], Adv. of ἄκριτος, Lys.*Fr.*88: **-τεί,** Aq.*Je.*17.11.

⊛**ἀκρῐτο-βάται·** ἀρχή τις παρὰ Ἐφεσίοις τῆς Ἀρτέμιδος θυσιῶν, Hsch. **-βουλος,** *ον, indiscreet of counsel*, Man.4.530. **-δακρυς,** *υ, shedding floods of tears*, Τάνταλος *AP*5.235 (Paul. Sil.). **-μῡθέω,** *babble*, Eust.349.17. **-μῡθία,** ἡ, *babbling*, Id.1878.4. **-μῡθος,** *ον, confusedly babbling*, Il.2.246, Ph.1.111. **II.** ὄνειροι ἀ. *hard of discernment*, Od.19.560.

**ἄκρῐτος,** *ον*, (κρίνω) *undistinguishable, confused*, ἄκριτα πόλλ' ἀγορεύειν Od.8.505; τύμβος ἄ. one *common undistinguished* grave, Il. 7.337; ἄ. πάγος *confused* mass, Hp.*Sept.*6, cf. Pl.*Grg.*465d, Philostr. *Gym.*26; ἄ. ἔρις καὶ ταραχή D.18.18; ἄ. καιροί Demad.34. **2.** *continual, unceasing*, μῦθοι Il.2.796; ἄχεα 3.412: neut. as Adv., πενθήμεναι ἄκριτον αἰεί Od.18.174, 19.120; δηρὸν καὶ ἄ. *h.Merc.*126; ὄρος ἄ. *continuous chain of* mountains, *AP*6.225 (Nicaen.). **3.** after Hom. in poets, *countless*, ἄστρων ὄχλος Critias 19; μυρία φῦλα καὶ ἄ. Opp.*H.*1.80; ἄ. πλήθει Babr.33.3. **II.** *undecided, doubtful*, νείκεα, ἄεθλος, Il.14.205, Hes.*Sc.*311; ἄ. τελευταί *which cannot be* predicted, B.9.45; ἀκρίτων ὄντων while the issue *is doubtful*, Th.4.20; *uncertain*, of weather-signs, Ὠρίων Arist.*Mete*.361ᵇ31; πυρετὸς ἄ. fever *that will not come to a crisis*, Hp.*Acut.*(*Sp.*)17. Adv. -τως Id. *Epid*.1.3; τὸ ἀκρίτως ξυνεχὲς τῆς ἁμίλλης *without decisive issue*, Th.7.71: neut. pl. as Adv., ἄκριτα δηρινθέντες Euph.94.?. 2. *unjudged, untried*, of persons and things, ἀκρίτους κτείνειν, ἀποκτεῖναι *without trial*, Hdt.3.80, Th.2.67, cf. Lys.19.7, D.17.3; ἄ. ἀποθανεῖν Antipho 5.48, cf. Th.8.48, etc.; πρᾶγμα ἄ. cause *not yet tried*, Isoc.19.2, cf. Pl.*Ti*.51c:—also, *subject to no judge*, πρύτανις A.*Supp*.371. Adv. ἀκρίτως, ἀποκτείνειν D.H.11.43, cf. Conon 28.1, Lxx 1 *Ma*.2.37. III. Act., *not giving judgement*, Hdt.8.124; *not capable of judging*, Parm.6.7, Plb.3.19.9, cf. Luc.*Am*.37; ἄκριτα μηχανώμενοι engaged in *rash* attempts, E.*Andr*.549; κατ' ἄκριτον *recklessly*, Phld.*Ir*.p.69 W. Adv. -τως *rashly, indiscreetly*, Plb.2.7.2, Epict.*Gnom*.65; *indiscriminately*, ἐκφέρειν Procl.*in Prm*.p.553 S. 2. *not exercising judgement, undiscriminating*, of fate, *AP*7.439 (Theodorid.), cf. 5.283 (Rufin.); ἄκριτε δαῖμον, of death, *Epigr.Gr*.204.3 (Cnid.).

**ἀκρῐτό-φυλλος**, ον, *of undistinguishable*, i.e. *closely blending, leafage*, ὄρος Il.2.868. **-φυρτος**, ον, *undistinguishably mixed*, A.*Th*.360. **-φωνος**, ον, gloss on βαρβαρόφωνος, Apollon.*Lex*., Hsch. **-χειρος**, ον, *with countless hands*, Emp.60.

**ἀκρο-άζομαι**, = ἀκροάομαι, Epich.109, f.l. in Men.150. **-ᾱμα**, ατος, τό, *anything heard*, esp. *with pleasure, piece read, recited, played* or *sung*, X.*Smp*.2.2, *Hier*.1.14; ἀ. καὶ δράματα Arist.*EN*1173ᵇ18; ἀ. καὶ πότοι Plb.31.25.4. II. pl. for concrete, *lecturers, singers*, or *players*, esp. during meals, Phylarch.62, *BCH*30.272 (Delph.), Plb.4.20.10, 16.21.12; so in Lat., *acroama* Cic.*Sest*.54.116, etc. **-ᾱματικός**, ή, όν, *designed for hearing only*, αἱ ἀ. διδασκαλίαι the *esoteric* doctrines of philosophers, delivered orally, Plu.*Alex*.7. 2. c. gen., *capable of attending to*, Asp.*in EN*27.14. ❋**-άομαι** [ᾰ Ar.*Ra*.315], fut. -άσομαι [ᾱ] Pl.*Ap*.37d, etc.: aor. ἠκροᾱσάμην Ar. l. c., etc.: pf. ἠκρόᾱμαι Arist.*HA*533ᵇ3: 2 sg. plpf. ἠκρόασο Antiph.93 ἠκρόασο· ἠκροῶ, wrongly, *AB* 8): aor. ἠκροάθην (in pass. sense) J.*AJ*17.5.2, Aristid.1.30 J.:—*hearken, listen to*: c. gen. pers., Antipho 5.4, Pl.*Grg*.499b: c. acc. rei, Th.6.89, etc.: c. gen. rei, Th.2.21, 6.17: c. gen. pers. et acc. rei, Pl.*Hp.Ma*.285d. 2. abs., *listen*, Hp.*Int*.35, Ar.*Lys*.503, Pherecr.154, Lys.19.3; ὁ ἀκροώμενος *hearer*, Eup.94.7; esp. of *those who hear lectures*, X.*Smp*.3.6; also, *reader*, Philostr.*VA*5.14: c. gen., ἀνὴρ Ἀριστοτέλους ἠκροαμένος Str.13.1.54, cf. Plu.*Caes*.3. II. *attend to, obey*, τινός Th.3.27, cf. Lys.20.9, Pl.*Grg*.488c: abs., ἐνδοιαστῶς ἀ. Th.6.10. ❋**-ᾱσις**, εως, ἡ, *hearing, hearkening* or *listening to*, Antipho 5.4, Th.1.21,22, etc.; ἀ. ποιεῖσθαί τινος, = ἀκροᾶσθαι, And.1.9; κλέπτειν τὴν ἀ. ὑμῶν to cheat you into *hearing*, Aeschin.3.35. 2. *obedience*, τῶν ἐν ἀρχῇ Th.2.37. II. *thing listened to, recitation, lecture*, Hp.*Praec*.12, Plb.32.2.5, *IG*2.466, etc.:—φυσικὴ ἀ., title of work by Arist. III. = ἀκροατήριον, Plu.2.58c. **-ᾱτέον**, *one must give heed to*, τῶν κρειττόνων Ar.*Av*.1228. ❋**-ᾱτήριον**, τό, *place of audience*, *Act.Ap*.25.23; *lecture-room*, Ph.1.528 (pl.), Plu.2.45f, etc. II. *audience*, Id.*Cat.Ma*.22. **-ᾱτής**, οῦ, ὁ, *hearer*, of persons who come to hear a public speaker, Th.3.38, Pl.*R*.536c, D.18.7, Men.286, etc.; *disciple, pupil*, Arist.*Pol*.1274ᵃ29, cf. *EN* 1095ᵃ2. II. *reader*, Plu.*Thes*.1, *Lys*.12. **-ᾱτικός**, ή, όν, *of* or *for hearing*; μισθὸς ἀ. *lecturer's* fee, Luc.*Enc.Dem*.25. Adv. -κῶς, ἔχειν to be *fond of hearing*, Ph.1.215. 2. = ἀκροαματικός, λόγοι Arist.*Fr*.662, Iamb.*Protr*.21.

❋**ἀκροαπίς**, *unable to articulate*, γλῶσσα dub. l. in Gal.19.73; cf. ἄκροπις.

**ἀκρο-βάζειν**· ἄκροις τοῖς ποσὶν ἐπιβαίνειν, Hsch. **-βαμονέω**, = ἀκροβατέω, *Hippiatr*.117. **-βαρέω**, *become top-heavy, lose balance by being overloaded at the extremity*, Apollod.*Poliorc*.164.3, 166.10. **-βασις**, ἡ, *foot* of table, *BCH*29.541 (Delos). **-βᾰτέω**, *walk on tiptoe, strut*, of ostriches, D.S.2.50; of haughty people, Ph.2.404. II. *climb aloft*, Polyaen.4.3.23. III. c. acc., ἀτραπόν *AP*9.13b. ❋**-βάτης**, ὁ, *acrobat*, *Inscr.Magn*.119; τῆς Ἀρτέμιδος *B.Mus.Inscr*.4.481*.459 (Ephesus). **-βᾰτικός**, ή, όν, *fit for mounting*, Vitr.10.1. ❋**-βᾰτος**, ον, *walking on tiptoe*, ἴχνεσιν ἀκροβάτοισιν Nonn.*D*.47.235. **-βᾰφής**, ές, *tinged at point* or *slightly*, *AP*6.66 (Paul. Sil.); *wetting feet* or *tip* of garment *only*, Nonn.*D*.1.65, 48.339. **-βελής**, ές, *with point at end*, *AP*6.62 (Phil.).

❋ **ἀκρ-οβελίς**, ίδος, ἡ, (ὀβελός) *point of dart*, Archipp.10. II. = εἶδος ἀκοντίου, Suid.

❋ **ἀκρο-βηματίζω**, = ἀκροβατέω, Hsch., Sch.Il.13.158. **-βλαστος**, ον, *with terminal growth*, Thphr.*HP*1.14.2. **-βολέω**, *throw*, κ̣αλαύροπα *AP*6.106 (Zon.). II. Astrol., = ἀκτινοβολέω, Man.4.354. **-βόλη**, ἡ, *skirmish*, *POxy*.1873.3 (v A.D.). II. in pl., αἱ τοῦ ἡλίου βολαί, Hsch. **-βολής**, ές, *skilful in hitting*, dub. l. in *APl*.4.213 (Mel. or Strat.). **-βολία**, ἡ, *slinging, skirmishing*, App.*BC*1.84, al. **-βολίζομαι**: aor. ἠκροβολισάμην Hdt.8.64, Th.3.73:—*throw from afar, fight with missiles*, as opp. to close combat, *skirmish*, πρός τινα Th.4.34: abs., Id.3.73, X.*Cyr*.8.8.22: metaph., ἀ. ἔπεσι Hdt.8.64, cf. Ph.1.134:—Act. only *AP*7.546, Hsch. **-βόλισις**, εως, ἡ, *skirmishing*, X.*An*.3.4.18, *Cyr*.6.2.15 (pl.). **-βόλισμα**, ατος, τό, = foreg., App.*Pun*.36 (pl.). ❋**-βολισμός**, οῦ, ὁ, = ἀκροβόλισις, Th.7.25, X.*HG*1.3.14, Aen.Tact.39.6, etc.; *discharge of weapons by light-armed troops*, Arr.*Tact*.15.4, 37.1. **-βολιστής**, οῦ, ὁ, = -βόλος II, X.*Cyr*.6.1.28. II. *mounted bowman* or *javelineer*, Ascl.*Tact*.7.1, Ael.*Tact*.2.13, Arr.*Tact*.4.5. **-βολιστικός**, ή, όν, *used as missiles*. -κά, τά, sc. ὅπλα, Ael. *Tact*.17. **-βολος**, ον, Pass., *struck from afar*, A.*Th*.158. **-βόλος**, ὁ, *one who throws from afar, skirmisher*, *IG*5(1).1426.10 (Messene, iv/iii B.C.), Hsch., Suid. **-βύθιον**, τό, *headland*, Di... Byz.30. **-βυστέω**, *to be uncircumcised*, Aq.Sm.Thd.*Le*.19. (nisi leg. -ιῶ, fut. of -βυστίζω). **-βυστία**, ἡ, *foreskin*, Lxx *Ge*.17.11, al., Ph.*Fr*.49 H., *Act.Ap*.11.3. II. *state of having the foreskin*, *uncircumcision*, *Ep.Rom*.2.25, etc. 2. collect., *the uncircumcised*, ib.2.26, 3.30, etc. (Prob. from ἄκρος and a Semitic root, cf. Ba... *buštu* 'pudenda', Heb. *bōsheth* 'shame': wrongly derived from ἄκρος, βύω by *EM*53.48.) **-βυστος**, ον, *uncircumcised*, Aq.*E*... 6.12, etc. **-γείσιον**, τό, *top of cornice*, *IG*2².463. **-γένειος**, ον, *with prominent chin*, Arist.*Phgn*.812ᵇ24. **-γωνιαῖος**, α, ον, *at the extreme angle*, ἀ. λίθος *corner foundation*-stone, Lxx *Is*.28.16, *Ep.Eph*.2.20. **-δάκτυλον**· *pollex*, *Gloss*. **-δετος**, ον, *bound at end* or *top*, *AP*6.5 (Phil.). ❋**-δίκαιος**, ον, = ἀκριβοδίκαιος, v.l. in Stob.2.7.25, Phot.

**ἀκρό-δρυα**, τά, prop. *fruits grown on upper branches of trees*, esp. *hard-shelled fruits*, opp. ὀπώρα, Hp.*Aff*.61, Arist.*HA*606ᵇ2, cf. *Gp*.10.74.2, Ath.2.52a; also, *fruits* generally, Glaucides ap.eund.3.81a, Arist.*Pr*.930ᵇ26, *PPetr*.3p.196 (iii B.C.), *PAvrom*.1 A 13 (i B.C.), Plu.*Alex*.23; μάζῃ καὶ τοῖς ἀ. ἀρκούμενοι Epicur.*Fr*.466. 2. *trees which produce such fruits*, Pl.*Criti*.115b, X.*Oec*.19.12, Thphr.*CP*6.11.2; φυτὰ ἀκροδρύων D.53.15:—*fruit-trees* in general (incl. vine and olive), Thphr.*HP*4.4.11. (Sg. in *AP*9.555 (Crin.), Ath.2.49e; cf. ἀκρόδρυον· πλῆρες μέτρον (Tarent.), Hsch.) **-ζεστος**, ον, (ζέω) *boiled* or *heated slightly*, Dsc.2.120. **-ζύγια**, τά, = ζεύγλη, Hsch., Poll.1.253. **-ζυμος**, ον, *slightly leavened*, Archig.ap.Gal.13.173, Isid.*Etym*.20.2.15. **-ζώνη**· *instita*, *Gloss*. **-θάλυπτος**, ον, *burnt at end*, Hsch.

**ἀκρόθεν**, Adv. *from the end* or *top*, Arist.*Phgn*.811ᵃ29, Nic.*Th*.337.

**ἀκρόθι**, Adv. *at the end*, c. gen., νυκτός Arat.308.

**ἀκρο-θῐγής**, ές, *touching on surface, touching the lips*, φίλημα *AP*12.68 (Mel.): metaph., ἀ. περὶ τὰς πράξεις Vett.Val.40.1. Adv. ἀκροθιγῶς, ἐμβάπτειν *just dip in, so that it is hardly wetted*, Dsc.2.83: metaph., ἀ. εἴρηται Marin.*Procl*.26, cf. Vett.Val.271.11, Men.Rh.p.417 S. **-θῑνιάζομαι**, *take the spoils, pick out for oneself*, E.*HF*476, cf. Dionys.Trag.1:—Act. in Hsch. ❋**-θίνιον** [θῐ], τό, E.*Ph*.282, Th.1.132, Pl.*Lg*.946b; mostly pl. -θίνια or -θῖνα, Pi.*N*.7.41, al.: sg.❋**-θις**, ἡ, acc. -θινα *GDI*2561 D 47 Rüsch (Delph., iv B.C.): (ἄκρος, θίς):—*topmost* or *best part of heap*; hence, *firstfruits of the field, booty*, etc., offered to the gods, Simon.109, Hdt.1.86,90, al., Pi. l. c., etc.; ἀ. τῆς Μαραθῶνι μάχης *Michel* 1117 (Delph.); ἀκρόθινα πολέμου, in Pi.*O*.2.4, of the Olympic games, *as founded from spoils taken in war*, cf. ib.10(11).57.—Properly neut. Adj., A.*Eu*.834 ἀκροθίνια θύη offerings *of firstfruits*. Post-Hom., rare in early Prose. ❋**-θώραξ**, ᾱκος, ὁ, ἡ, (θωρήσσω II) *slightly drunk*, = ἡμιμέθυσος, Hsch., cf. Arist.*Pr*.871ᵃ9, Plu.2.656c; πεπωκότ' ἤδη τ' ἀκροθώρακ' ὄντα Diph.46: Ion. -θώρηξ Hp.ap.Erot. s. v. θωρῆξαι. 2. *well drunken*, Ph.1.390. **-καρπος**, ον, *fruiting at top*, φοῖνιξ Thphr.*HP*1.14.2, al. **-κελαινιάω**, only used in Ep. part. ἀκροκελαινιόων *growing black on surface*, of swollen stream, Il.21.249; cf. Nonn.*D*.18.156. ❋**-κέραια**, τά, (κέρας) *ends of sail-yards* (cf. κέρας VIII), Poll.1.91:—also **-κερα**, Sch.A.R.1.566; ἀκρόκεροι κάλοι Phot. s. v. ἡνιόχους. **-κιόνιον**, τό, (κίων) *capital of a pillar*, Ph.2.147. **-κλαδος**, ὁ, gloss on ὕζος ἀκρότατος, Sch.Il.2.312. **-κνέφαιος**, ον, *at beginning of night, in twilight*, Hes.*Op*.567:—also **-κνεφής**, ές, *of morning twilight*, Luc.*Lex*.11, Id.*Rh.Pr*.17; cf. ἀκρόκνεφα· πρὸς ὄρθρον, Hsch. **-κόμης**, ὁ, = sq., Poll.2.28. ❋**-κομος**, ον, (κόμη) *with hair on crown*, epith. of Thracians, who either tied up their hair in a top-knot, or shaved all their head except crown, Il.4.533, Archil.*Supp*.1.4; *with hair at tip*, of goat's chin, Plb.34.10.9. II. *with leafy crown*, E.*Ph*.1516; esp. of palms, D.S.2.53, D.P.1010; ἀ. κυπάρισσοι *tapering* cypresses, Theoc.22.41. **-κονδύλιον**· *articulare*, *Gloss*. **-κόρινθος**, ὁ, *citadel of Corinth*, E.*Fr*.1084, X.*HG*4.4.4. **-κόρυμβοι**, πόδες, *extremities of* the feet, Poet.*de herb*.177:—also **-κόρυμβα**· τὰ ἀκροστόλια τῶν νεῶν, Hsch. **-κῡματόω**, (κῦμα) *float on topmost waves*, bombastic word ridiculed by Luc.*Lex*.15. **-κώλιον**, τό, mostly pl., *extremities of body*, esp. of animals, *snout, ears, trotters*, Hp.*Vict*.3.75, Pherecr.108.14, Telecl.48, Ar.*Fr*.4, Archipp.11, Arist.*Pr*.935ᵇ38, etc.: sg., Antiph.126, Alex.118, Eub.7. **-λειον**, τό, (λεία) = ἀκροθίνιον, Suid. ❋**-λῐθος**, ον, *with ends made of stone*; ξόανον ἀ. statue *with head, arms, and legs marble, rest wood*, *AP*12.40; ἄγαλμα *IG*4.558 (Argos). **-λῖνος**, ον, *at the edge of the net*, Opp.*C*.4.383. **-λῐπᾰρος** [λῐ], ον, *fat on the surface*, Alex.192. ❋**-λογέω**, *gather at top*, στάχυας *AP*9.89 (Phil.). **-λοφία**, ἡ, *mountain ridge, hilly country*, Aen.Tact.15.6 (pl.), Plb.2.27.5, Str.15.1.29 (pl.). ❋**-λοφίτης** [ῑ], ου, ὁ, *mountaineer*, *AP*6.221 (Leon.). **-λοφος**, ον, *high-crested, peaked*, πρῶνες Opp.*C*.1.418; πέτραι *AP*12.185 (Strat.):—Subst., *mountain crest*, Plu.*Publ*.22. **-λῡτέω** ζώνην, *play with the ends of* a belt, *as if untying it*, *AP*5.252 (Iren.). **-μαλλος**, ον, *very woolly*, Str.4.4.3. **-μᾰνής**, ές, *on the verge of madness, somewhat mad* (cf. ἀκράχολος, ἀκροθώραξ), οὐ φρενήρης ἀ. τε Hdt.5.42. **-μάσθιον**, τό, *teat*, *Gloss*. **-μέθῠσος**, ον, = ἀκροθώραξ, Sch.Ar.*Ach*.1132, *V*.1190. **-μέλας**, αινα, αν, *black at top*, πτερόν *PMag.Par*.1.800.10. **-μέτωπος**, dub. l. perh. for εὐρυ-, Nonn.*D*.26.310. **-μόλυβδος**, ον, *leaded at edge*, λίνον *AP*6.5 (Phil.); δίκτυον ib.30 (Maced.). **-μύλη**· ἡ γουνὶς μύλων ἢ μύλος αὐτός, Hsch.

ἀκρ-ομφάλιον, τό, *middle of navel*, Poll.2.169:—also -όμφαλον, Ruf.*Onom*.98.

ἄκρον, ου, τό, (neut. of ἄκρος) like ἄκρα, *highest* or *farthest* ...nt: 1. *mountain top, peak*, Γάργαρον ἄκρον Ἴδης Il.14.292; ...ον ὑπερβαλέειν Od.11.597; τὰ ἄκρα *heights*, Hdt.6.100, Pl.*Criti.* ...oe, etc. b. ἄκρα νάων ships' *tops*, Alc.*Supp*.12.9. 2. *head-* ...nd, cape, Σούνιον ἄκρον Ἀθηνέων Od.3.278. 3. *end, extremity*, τὰ τῆς θαλάσσης, [τοῦ ἀέρος], Pl.*Phd*.109d, e; ἄκρα χειρῶν *hands*, Luc. ...n.6; ἐξ ἄκρων at *the end*, Ar.*Fr*.29; ἐξ ἄκρου *Com.Adesp*.398; ἐπ' ...ροις Pl.*Sph*.220d:—*border, frontier*, Plb.1.42.2. II. metaph., ...ghest *pitch, height*, πανδοξίας ἄκρον Pi.*N*.1.11; εἰς ἄκρον ἀνδρείας ...έσθαι to *highest pitch*, Simon.58; εἰς ἄκρον ἁδύς *exceedingly*, Theoc. 4.61; ἐπ' ἄκρον ἀφικέσθαι, ἐλθεῖν, Pl.*Plt*.268e, *Ti*.20a; πρὸς ἄκρῳ ...ενέσθαι Id.*Phdr*.247b; ἄκρον ἔχων σοφίης *Epigr.Gr*.442 (Nabataea); ...κρον ἐρώτων εἰδότος, ἄκρα μάχας *AP*7.448 (Leon.):—ἄκρα, τά, *heights*, ...ighest point, οὔτοι ποθ' ἥξει (sic) τῶν ἄκρων ἄνευ πόνου S.*Fr*.397; ἄκρα ...ερέσθαι win *prize*, Theoc.12.31; ἄκρα φέροισ' ἀρετῆς ὑμῖν *Epigr.Gr.* ...24.2 (Samos). 2. of persons, Ἄργεος ἄκρα Πελασγοί *pride* of Ar-...os, Theoc.15.142. III. δρυὸς ἄκρα, = ἀκρόδρυα, ib.112. IV. ...n Logic of Arist. τὰ ἄκρα are *major and minor terms* of syllogism, opp. ...ο μέσον or middle, *APr*.$25^b36$, al. V. *extremes* in a proportion, ...d.*EN*$1133^b2$.

ἀκρό-νηον· τὸ τῆς νεὼς ἄκρον, Suid. -νιφής, ές, *snow-capped*, πάγος *Pae.Delph*.16. -νῠχῶς, Adv., (νύσσω) *touching at the edge*, συμβάλλοντα βλέφαρα Gal.14.701. -νύκτιος, ον, = sq., Ἄρης Man. 5.177. -νυκτος, ον, lit. *rising at sunset*: hence, *in opposition*, Ζεύς Vett.Val.168.13; ἀ. σχηματισμοί, προηγήσεις, Ptol.*Alm*.10.6, *Tetr.* 78:—as Subst., -νυκτος, ἡ, with or without φάσις, *opposition*, Ptol. *Alm*.10.7, *Tetr*.77. (Freq. written ἀκρων-.) -νυξ, -νυχος (Hdn. Gr.2.743), = ἀκρονυχία, *nightfall*, S.ap.Phot.p.68 R.

ἀκρ-ονῠχί [ῑ], Adv. *with tip of nail*, for ἀκρωνυχί, *AP*12.126 (Cod. Pal. ἀκρονυχῆ, from an Adj. -νυχής; but cf. αὐτονυχί).

ἀκρο-νῠχία, ἡ, *nightfall*, Suid., Tz.ad Hes.*Op*.565. ❀-νῠχος (A), ον, *at nightfall*, ἄνεμοι Arist.*Mete*.$367^b26$; ἀνατολαί Thphr.*Sign*.2; φάσεις Procl.*Hyp*.5.66; σφάζων ἀκρόνυχος Theoc.*Beren*.3, cf. Nic. *Th*.761:—neut. as Adv., Arist.*Pr*.$942^a23$. (Written ἀκρώνυχος in *PHib*.27 (iii B.C.).)

ἀκρ-όνῠχος (B), ον, = ἀκρώνυχος, *AP*6.103 (Phil.), Q.S.8.157.

ἀκρο-ξιφίς, ἡ, *sword-point*, Lyd.*Mag*.1.8. -ουλος, ον, = ἄκρουλος, ib.1.23. -πᾰγής, ές, *fastened at the extremity*, Jo.Gaz. 1.111. -παθος, ον, f.l. for ἀκρόπλοος, q.v. -παστος, ον, (πάσσω) *sprinkled on the surface*: *slightly salted*, Sopat.13, Xenocr. 76. -πᾰχής, ές, *thick at the end*, Moer.346. ❀-πενθής, ές, f.l. for ἁβρο-, A.*Pers*.135 (lyr.). -πηλος, ον, *muddy on the surface*, Plb.3.55.2.

ἄκροπις, *unable to articulate*, γλῶσσα Hp.*Epid*.7.43,46, cf. Gal. 19.73 (dub., v.l. ἀκροαπίς).

ἀκρό-πλοος, ον, contr. -πλους, ουν, *swimming at the top, skimming the surface*, φλέβια Hp.*Morb*.1.14, cf. Plu.2.591e; *buoyant*, ὑστέρη Aret.*SA*2.11; restored for ἀκρόπαθος in Hp.*Prorrh*.2.11:—*superficial*, Id.*Ep*.18 (Democr.). -ποδητί or -ῑτί [τῐ], Adv., (πούς) *on tiptoe*, Luc.*Prom*.1, *D.Mar*.14.3, al. -πόδιον, τό, Dim. of ἀκρόπους, Sor.1.101, Ptol.*Alm*.7.5. -πολεύω, *traverse the top*, Man.4.79.

❀ἀκρό-πολις, poet. ἀκρό-πτολις, εως, ἡ, *upper* or *higher city*; hence, *citadel, castle*, ἐς ἀκρόπολιν Od.8.494 (in Il. only *divisim*, ἄκρη πόλις, v. ἄκρος I.1), cf. Pi.*O*.7.49, A.*Th*.240, Hdt.1.84, etc.; as seat of tyranny, Ph.1.401,417. 2. esp. the *Acropolis* of Athens, *IG*1.58, al., And.1.76 (cf. Hdt.1.60, 8.51); which served as treasury, Th.2.13; hence ἀνενεχθῆναι εἰς ἀκρόπολιν, γεγράφθαι ἐν ἀκροπόλει to be entered as a state-debtor, D.58.19,48; freq. without Art., as And l.c., D.ll. cc.; at Erythrae, *IG*1.11. II. metaph., ἀ. καὶ πύργος ἐὼν δήμῳ, of a person, Thgn.233; ἀ. Ἑλλάνων, of Corinth, Simon.137; γῆν Δελφίδ' ..Φωκέων ἀκρόπτολιν E.*Or*.1094; *stronghold*, τῆς ψυχῆς, τοῦ σώματος, Pl.*R*.560b, Arist.*PA*$670^a26$, cf. Pl.*Ti*.70a; Pythag., of *seven*, *Theol. Ar*.44. ❀-πόλος, ον, (πολέω) *high-ranging, lofty*, ἐπ' ἀκροπόλοισιν ὄρεσσιν Il.5.523, cf. Od.19.205. II. Subst., ἀκροπόλοι, οἱ, *arctic* and *antarctic circles*, Olymp. in *Mete*.182.30. -πόρος, ον, *boring through, piercing with the point*, ὀβελοί Od.3.463. 2. proparox., ἀκρόπορος, ον, Pass., *with opening at end*, σῦριγξ Nonn.*D*.2.2. II. (πορεύομαι) *going on high*, ib.46.136. -πόρφυρος, ον, *with purple edge*, χιτῶνες Lyd.*Mag*.1.17. -ποσθία, Ion. -ίη, ἡ, *tip of foreskin*, Hp.*Aph*.6.19, Arist.*HA*$493^a29$:— -πόσθιον, τό, Poll.2.171, Ruf. *Onom*.102, Hsch. -πότης, ἡ, *a hard drinker*, Nonn.*D*.14. 108. -πουδί, Adv. = ἀκροποδητί, Hdn.Gr.1.512. -πους, ὁ, *extremity of leg*, i.e. *foot*, Ptol.*Alm*.7.5, al., Pall. in *Hp.Fract*.12.285 C.: pl., *PMag.Leid.W*.18.37; *trotters*, Aret.*CA*1.10. ❀-πρωρον, τό, *end of ship's prow*, Str.2.3.4. -πτερον, τό, *quill*, *AP*6.229 (Crin.); ἀκρόπτερα φωτῶν *flanking* men of a hunting-party, Opp.*C*.4. 127. -πτολις, ἡ, poet. for ἀκρόπολις, q.v. -πτυξ, χος, perh. *cloth, napkin*, Hierocl.*Facet*.71. -πῦρος, ον, *exceedingly hot*, κρύσταλλος Olymp.Alch.p.76 B. -ρρίνιον, τό, (ῥίς) *tip of the nose*, Poll.2.80. -ρρύμιον, τό, *fore-end of a pole*, Id.1.146.

❀ἄκρος, α, ον, (on the Root v. ἀκή A) *at the farthest point* or *end*, hence either *topmost, outermost*, or *inmost*. 1. *highest, topmost*, ἀκροτάτη κορυφῇ Il.1.499, al.; ἐν πόλει ἄκρῃ, = ἐν ἀκροπόλει, Il.6.88, cf. 257; ἄκρῳ Ὀλύμπῳ 13.523; ἀνὰ Γαργάρῳ ἄκρῳ 14.352; λάψοντες ..μέλαν ὕδωρ ἄκρον *at its surface*, 16.162; ἄκρον ῥινὸν *surface* of skin, Od.22.278; ἐπ' ἄκρων ὀρέων on mountain *tops*, S.*OT*1106: Sup. ἀκρότατος, ὕσδος Sapph.93.2; ὀρόφοισι Orac.ap.Hdt.7.140. 2. *outermost*, πεδίον ἐπ' ἄκρον to the *farthest edge* of the plain, S.*Ant.* 1197; κατ' ἄκρας σπιλάδος from the *surface* of a stone, Id.*Tr*.678; esp. of *extremities* of body, ἀ. χείρ, πόδες, ὦμος, *end* of hand, *ends* of feet, *tip* of shoulder, Il.5.336, 16.640, 17.599; ἄκρων χειρῶν καὶ ποδῶν Hdt.1.119, cf. Th.2.49, Pl.*La*.183b, *Ti*.76e; but τὸ ἀ. τῆς χειρός, τοῦ ποδός, *thumb, great toe*, Lxx *Ex*.29.20, *Le*.18.22; γλῶσσαν ἄκρον S.*Aj.* 238; πίτυν ἄκρας τῆς κόμης καθέλκων by the *top* of the crown, Cratin. 296:—ἐπ' ἄκρων [δακτύλων] on *tiptoe*, S.*Aj*.1230, ubi v. Sch.; comically, ἐπ' ἄκρων πυγιδίων on *tip-tail*, Ar.*Ach*.638; ἐν ἄκροισι βὰς ποσί E.*Ion*1166; παρ' ἄκρας τρίχας *Or*.128; ἀκροτάτοις χείλεσι *Epigr.Gr.* 547.8:—οὐκ ἀπ' ἄκρας φρενός not from the *outside* of the heart, i.e. from the inmost heart, A.*Ag*.805, cf. E.*Hec*.242; ἄκροισι λαίφους κρασπέδοις with *mere edges* of sail, i.e. under *close-reefed* sails, Id.*Med*.524, cf. Ar.*Ra*.999. b. Geom., of the *extremity* of a line, ἡ ἐπ' ἄκραν τὴν ἀποληφθεῖσαν ἀγομένη Apollon.Perg.*Con*.4.8: Math., of *extremes* in a proportion, Pl.*Ti*.36a, etc.; εἰς ἄκρον καὶ μέσον λόγον τέμνειν cut in *extreme* and mean ratio, Euc.6.30, cf. 5*Def*.17. c. in Tactics, ἄκροι, οἱ, *flank men*, Ascl.*Tact*.1.3, cf. 7.6. 3. *inmost*, μυελός E.*Hipp.* 255. II. of Time, ἄκρα σὺν ἑσπέρᾳ on the *edge* of evening, i.e. at *nightfall*, Pi.*P*.11.10, cf. ἄκρῃ νυκτί Arat.775; ἄκροι τοῦ ἔαρος at *beginning* of spring, *IPE*.1².352.29 (Cherson., ii B.C.); but usu. denoting completeness, ἄκρου τοῦ θέρεος at *mid-summer*, Hp.*Aph*.3.18; χειμῶνος ἄκρῳ Theoc.11.37; ἄκρας νυκτός at *dead* of night, S.*Aj*.285. III. of Degree, *highest* in its kind, *consummate*, 1. of persons, Hdt. 5.112, 6.122; τοξότης ἀ. A.*Ag*.628; θεσφάτων γνώμων ἀ. ib.1130; μάντις S.*El*.1499; ἰατροί Phld.*Lib*.p.67 O.; οἱ πάντῃ ἀ., οἱ ἀκρότατοι Pl.*Tht*.148c; of any extremes, opp. τὰ μεταξύ, τοῖς ἀ. τὰ ἀ. ἀποδιδόναι Id.*R*.478e, cf. *Phd*.90a; of classes in a state, Arist.*Pol*.$1296^b39$: in moral sense, both good and bad, ἐπιδικάζονται οἱ ἀ. τῆς μέσης χώρας Id.*EN*$1107^b31$; αἱ ἀ. [διαθέσεις] ib.$1108^b14$, cf. ἄκρον II.1:—c. acc. modi, ψυχὴν οὐκ ἀ. not *strong* of mind, Hdt.5.124; ἀ. τὰ πολέμια 7.111; ἀ. ὀργήν *quick* to anger, *passionate*, 1.73; Εὐρώπη ἀρετὴν ἄκρη 7.5: c. gen., οἱ ἀ. τῆς ποιήσεως Pl.*Tht*.152e; ἀ. εἰς φιλοσοφίαν *R*.499c; περὶ ὁπλομαχίαν *Lg*.833e. 2. of things, *highest, extreme*, συμφορά Alex.222.4 (cj. Dobree); νηστεία Diph.54: Sup., Pl.*Phlb*.45a. IV. as Subst., v. ἄκρα, ἄκρον. V. neut. as Adv., *on the top* or *surface*, ἄκρον ἐπὶ ῥηγμῖνος Il.20.229; ἄκρα δ' ἐπ' αὐτᾶς βαθμίδος *AP*7.428.3 (Mel.). 2. reg. Adv. ἄκρως, ἀνεστάλθαι to be turned up *at the point*, Hp.*Mochl*.24. b. *utterly, perfectly*, Pl.*R*.543a, Hegesand. 4; μόνος ἄκρως Euphro 1.5; σχῆμα ἀ. στρογγύλον *absolutely* round, Hero *Def*.76. c. *skilfully*, Phld.*Lib*.p.27 O.

ἀκρο-σᾰπής, ές, (σήπομαι) *slightly 'high'*, Hp *Alim*.41. -σίδηρος, ον, *pointed* or *tipped with iron*, *AP*6.95 (Antiphil.). ❀-σκιρία, ἡ, *hill-copse*, *Tab.Heracl*.1.65,71; cf. σκῦρος. -σοφος, ον, *high in wisdom*, Pi.*O*.11(10).19, *Lyr.Adesp*.93, D.H.*Dem*.51. -σπάθια, τά, gloss on ὑποχόνδρια, Suid. -σπελλος, ὁ, = αἰγίλωψ, Ps.-Dsc.4.137.

ἀκρόσσοσος, ον, *without fringes*, λέντια *Gp*.20.22.

ἀκρο-στήθιον, τό, *lower end of breast-bone*, Arist.*Phgn*.$810^b$ 17. ❀-στιχίς, ίδος, ἡ, *acrostic*, D.H.4.62, Cic.*Div*.2.54.111:—also -στιχα, τά, *AP*9.385 tit. ❀-στόλιον, τό, *terminal ornament* of ship (cf. ἄφλαστον), crowning either the stern-post, Ptol.*Alm.* 8.1; or more commonly, the stem-post, Callix.1, Plu.*Demetr*.43; taken as trophy, Str.3.4.3, D.S.18.75, Plu.*Alc*.32, App.*Mith*.25, Polyaen.4.6.9. -στόμιον, τό, *edge of the lips*, D.H.*Comp.* 14. II. = ἀκροφύσιον, Eust.1153.38. ❀-σφᾰλής, ές, (σφάλλω) *apt to trip, unsteady*, Plu.2.713b; ἀ. πρὸς ὑγίειαν *precarious* in health, Pl.*R*.404b; ἀ. οὐσίαι *insecure*, Phld.*Oec*.p.37 J.; ψυχὴ ἐν εὐτυχίᾳ ἀ. Max.Tyr.5.2. Adv. -ως, διακεῖσθαι Phld.*Oec*.p.40 J.; ἔχειν Plu. 2.682d. II. Act., *apt to throw down, slippery, dangerous*, Plb. 9.19.7. -σφυρα, τά, sort of *woman's shoes*, Hsch.:—also -σφύρια, τά, Herod.7.60, Poll.7.94. -σχῐδής, ές, *cloven at the end*, Thphr. *HP*3.11.1. -τελεύτιον, τό, *fag-end* of anything, esp. of verse or poem, Th.2.17, Phryn.Com.86: generally, τοῦ γήρως *Vit.Philonid.* p.8 C.:—*burden, chorus*, D.C.63.10. -τελής, ές, *pointed*, γένειον Hp.*Ep*.23 (Democr.). -τενής, ές, *stretching high*, Nonn.*D*.7.310.

❀ἀκρότης, ητος, ἡ, (ἄκρος) *highest pitch*, Hp.*VM*22. II. *extreme*, opp. μεσότης, Arist.*EN*$1107^a8$; ἀμφοτέρας παθεῖν τὰς ἀ. Diog.Oen. *Fr*.38: metaph., *excellence, perfection*, ἡ ἀνυπέρεκτος ἀ. Phld.*D*.3.5, cf. D.H.*Dem*.2, etc.; *summit*, Procl.*Inst*.147.

ἀκρότητος, ον, *not beaten down*, Hld.9.8. II. *not struck together* or *in unison*, μέλη πάραυλα κἀκρότητα κύμβαλα *Trag.Adesp*.93 = *Com.Adesp*.1254, cf. Phot. s.v. οὐκ ἀποψάλακτος.

ἀκρο-τομέω, *lop off* corn *by the ear*, X.*Oec*.18.2, cf. *PLond*.2.163. 21 (i A.D.); *saw off at end* σφῆνας Ph.*Bel*.67.21:—Pass., -τομηθεὶς τράχηλον Man.4.51: metaph., τῶν εὐγενεστάτων ἀνδρῶν ἀ. τὴν πατρίδα J.*BJ*2.10.1. -τομία· *rupes*, Gloss. -τομος, ον, (τέμνω) *cut off sharp, abrupt*, of precipice, Plb.9.27.4, Ph.1.82; ἡ ἀ. (sc. πέτρα) Lxx *Ps*.113(114).8, cf. *Jb*.28.9, *De*.8.15: of a stone, *sharp*, Thd.*Ex*.4.25; *smooth*, J.*AJ*3.3.2; of ends *sawn off*, τὰ τῶν σφηνῶν -τομα Ph.*Bel.* 67.23. -τονος, ον, *strained to the utmost, muscular*, Metrod. Sceps.14.

ἀκροτον· ἀδιαρρίπιστον, Hsch.

ἄκρουλος, ον, *curled at the tip*, τρίχες Arist.*Phgn*.$812^b33$.

ἀκροῦν· ὄρους κορυφή, and ἀκρουνοί· ὅροι (Maced.), Hsch.

ἄκρουρα· οὐραί, Hsch.

ἀκρουρᾰνία, ἡ, *heaven's citadel*, Luc.*Lex*.15.

❀ἀκρουροβόρη, ἡ, *swallowing the tip of her tail*, metaph. of the Moon, *Tab.Defix.Aud*.$41^A7$ (Megara, i/ii A.D.).

**ἄκρουρον·** ἄκρατον, Hsch.

**ἄκρουστος·** *impercussus, Gloss.*

**ἀκρουχέω,** (ἄκρον, ἔχω) *haunt the heights,* S.*Fr.*309.

**ἀκρο-φᾰής,** ές, = ἀκροφανής, Nonn.*D.*4.130, Jo.Gaz.1.331. **-φᾰληριάω,** *shine* or *be white at top,* only in Ep. part. ἀκροφαληριόωσα Nonn.*D.*2.462. **-φᾰνής,** ές, *just showing at the edge* or *tip,* Nonn. *D.*14.138, al.; of an island, *Peripl.M.Rubr.*42. **-φῠής,** ές, *grown high up on a tree,* Thphr.*HP*9.5.1. **-φύλαξ,** ἄκος, ὁ, *governor of a citadel,* Plb.5.50.10, *BCH*33.23 (Pontus, ii B.C.), *IG*5.3906. **-φυλλον,** τό, = βήχιον, Ps.-Dsc.3.112. **-φυλλος,** ον, *with leaves in a terminal crown,* Thphr.*HP*1.14.2. **-φύσιον,** τό, (φῦσα) *snout* or *pipe of pair of bellows,* S.*Fr.*992, Th.4.100; ῥήματα.. ἐπιδεικνύναι πάντ' ἀπ' ἀκροφυσίων fresh from *the bellows* (as we say, 'from the anvil'), Ar.*Fr.*699. II. *comet's tail,* D.C.78.30. **-χάλιξ,** ὁ, ἡ, = ἀκροθώραξ, A.R.4.432, D.P.948. **-χᾰνής,** ές, *yawning at top,* δέρμα *AP*6.57 (Paul. Sil.). **-χειρας·** τοὺς ὀξύχειρας, ἢ ἀνδ(ροφ)όνους, *EM*53.37, cf. Hsch.

**ἀκροχειρ-ία,** Ion. -ίη, ἡ, = -ισμός, Hp.*Vict.*2.64. **-ίζω,** *take hold of,* Aristaenet.1.4. II. more freq. in Med., *struggle at arm's length,* opp. συμπλέκεσθαι, *spar,* ἀ. τινι Pl.*Alc.*1.107e, cf. Arist.*EN* 1111ᵃ15, Posidon.24, Philostr.*Gym.*36. **-ιον,** τό, = ἀκρόχειρον, Sor.1.84. **-ίς·** τὸ ἄκρον τῆς χειρός, Suid. **-ισις,** εως, ἡ, = sq., Hp.*Vict.*3.78:—also **-ιξις,** v.l. ibid. and 2.64. ❋ **-ισμός,** ὁ, *wrestling with hands,* Luc.*Lex.*5, Gal.6.324: in pl., Hp.*Vict.*3.78. ❋ **-ον,** τό, = ἄκρα χείρ *hand,* Ptol.*Alm.*7.5, al., Gal.*UP*2.2; τὰ τῶν ἀγαλμάτων ἀ. *SIG*²754.6, cf. *Hymn.Id.Dact.*13.

**ἀκρο-χέριον·** *armilla,* Prisc.*Inst.*5.15. **-χερσίτης,** ου, ὁ, nickname of wrestler who broke his opponent's fingers, Paus 6.4.1. **-χηνίσκοι,** οἱ, *extremities of* ζεῦγλαι in chariot, Poll.1.146. **-χλίᾰρος** [ῐ], ον, *just warm, lukewarm,* Hp.*Acut.*58:—also **-χλίερος,** *Nat.Mul.*53, *Mul.*2.201. Adv. -χλιάρως *Mul.*2.204. **-χολέω, -χολία, -χολος,** v. sub ἀκραχ-. **χορδών,** όνος, ἡ, (χορδή) *wart with a thin neck,* Hp.*Aph.*3.26, Plu.*Fab.*1, Dsc.2.94, etc.; distinguished from μυρμήκια, τά, Paul.Aeg.4.15 (also **-δάνη** *Gloss.*, **-δόνη** Erot., Dim. **-δόνιον**) *Gloss.*: hence **-χορδονώδης,** ες, *troubled with warts,* D.C.*Fr.*47. **-χωλος·** ὁ πρὸς ὀλίγον χωλεύων, Suid. **-ψῑλος,** ον, *bare* or *smooth at top,* αἰδοῖον Hp.*Epid.*4.31. **-ψωλος,** ον, ψωλός *only at the end,* Suid. s.v. ψωλός.

**ἄκρυπτος,** ον, *unhidden,* E.*Andr.*834, Aen.Tact.39.6. Adv. -τως Phryn.*PS*p.11 B.

**ἀκρύσταλλος,** ον, *free from ice,* χώρη Hdt.2.22.

**ἀκρῶα·** σπλάγχνα, ἔντερα, Hsch.

❋ **ἀκρ-ωβέλια·** τὰ ἄκρα τοῦ ὀβελίσκου, Hsch. (cod. -σβ-). **-ωλένιον,** τό, *elbow* of a net, i.e. *outer angle* of mesh, X.*Cyn.*2.6, Poll.5.29. **-ωμία,** ἡ, *point of the shoulder, acromion process,* Hp.*Art.*14: in a horse, *withers,* X.*Eq.*1.11, cf. Arist.*HA*498ᵇ30:— **-ώμιον,** τό, Hp.*Art.*16, *Mochl.*5, Arist.*HA*500ᵃ16: **-ωμίς,** ἡ, Alciphr.*Fr.*5.4.

**ἄκρων,** ονος, ὁ, = ἀκροκώλιον, *Hippiatr.*7: - Dim. **ἀκρωνάριον,** ib. 64,129, cf. Sch.Luc.*Lex.*6.

**ἀκρωνία,** ἡ, prob. = ἀκρωτηριασμός, A.*Eu.*188; but expl. as ἄθροισμα by Hdn.Gr.1.294 ap.Sch. (reading κακῶν ἀ.), cf. *AB*372.

❋ **ἀκρωνῠχ-ία,** ἡ, (ὄνυξ) *tip of the nail;* hence, *ridge* or *top of a mountain,* = ἀκρώρεια, X.*An.*3.4.37, *HG*4.6.7, Plu.*Eum.*11. ❋ **-ος,** ον, (ὄνυξ) *with nails, claws, hoofs,* etc., χερὸς ἀκρώνυχα *tips of fingers, AP*12.82; ἴχνος ἀ. traces *of one walking on his toes,* Plu.2.317e, cf. 325b —**ἀκρῶνυξ,** Suid.

❋ **ἀκρώρ-εια,** ἡ, (ὄρος) *mountain ridge,* X.*HG*7.2.10, Theoc.25.31, Hp.*Ep.*10, Timae.94, Plb.24.6.5. ❋ **-εῖται,** οἱ, *inhabitants of mountain ridges,* Hdn.Gr.2.869.

**ἀκρωρία,** ἡ, (ὥρα) *daybreak,* Thphr.*Sign.*21.42.

**ἀκρώσσει·** ἀκροᾶται, ἑκὼν οὐχ ὑπακούει, προσποιεῖται, Hsch.

❋ **ἀκρωτερῆσαι·** κόψαι ἢ ἀχρειῶσαι, Hsch.

❋ **ἀκρωτηρι-άζω,** *cut off* ἀκρωτήρια, of ships, τὰς πρῴρας ἠκρωτηρίασαν *cut the beaks off* the prows, Hdt.3.59:—so in Med., τὰς τριήρεις ἀκρωτηριασάμενος X.*HG.*6.2.36:—Pass., Ath.12.535d. 2. of persons, *cut off hands and feet, mutilate,* Plb.5.54.10, etc.; ῥῖνα, πρόσωπον, Clearch. 8, Plu.*Alc.*18; χεῖρας σὺν αὐτοῖς τοῖς βραχίοσιν D.S.34.8; ὄργανον, of circumcision, Ph.2.211; μηδὲν ἀκρωτηριάσῃς ἐνθάδε, Inscr. on statue, *CIG*5855:—so in Med., μέλη Lxx 4*Ma.*10.20: metaph., ἠκρωτηριασμένοι τὰς πατρίδας D.18.296; ἀ. τὴν ἀρετήν τινος Max.Tyr. 5.8. 3. Medic., *amputate,* Heliod.ap.Orib.45.14.4. 4. metaph., *mutilate, maim,* τῇ συγκοπῇ τὸ μέγεθος Longin.39.4; πρᾶγμα *POxy.*237 vi 7 (ii A.D.); θείαν φύσιν Heraclit.*All.*26. II. intr., *form a promontory, jut out like one,* Plb.4.43.2, Str.2.1.40. **-ασις·** *truncatio, mutilatio, Gloss.* **-ασμα,** τό, *mutilation,* Hsch. s.v. τομία, Sch.A.R.4.477. **-ασμός,** ὁ, *amputation,* Dsc.*Ther.Praef.*, Heliod.ap.Orib.47.14tit., Philum.*Ven.*7.7, Leonid. ap.Aët.16.49.

**ἀκρωτήριον,** τό, (ἄκρος) *topmost* or *prominent part,* ἀ. τοῦ οὔρεος mountain *peak,* Hdt.7.217, cf. Pi.*O.*9.7; of a cup, *projecting part,* Arist.*Metaph.*1024ᵃ25. 2. *cape, promontory,* Hdt.4.43, Th.1.30. II. *end* or *extremity* of anything, ἀ. νεὼς *ornament of* ship's *stern* or *stem-post,* Hdt.8.121, cf. X.*HG*2.3.8, Polyaen.5.41, *Michel* 1116 (Delph.); ἀκρωτήρια πρύμνης *h.Hom.*33.10. 2. in pl., *extremities of body, hands and feet, fingers and toes,* Hp.*Aph.*7.1, *Acut.* 59, Th.2.49, Lys.6.26; τὰ ἀ. τῆς Νίκης her *wings,* D.24.121, cf. *IG*2.652 *A*23: sg., Arist.*GA*772ᵇ36. 3. in temples, etc., statues or ornaments placed on the angles of a pediment, Pl.*Criti.*116d, *SIG*80 (Olymp.), *IG*4.1484.102 (Epid.); generally, *pediment,* Plu.*Caes.*63.

**ἀκρωτηριώδης,** ες, *like an* ἀκρωτήριον, Sch.rec.A.*Pr.*726.

**ἀκτάζω,** (ἀκτή A) *banquet on the shore, enjoy oneself,* Plu.2.668b, prov. σήμερον ἀκτάσωμεν, cf. Hsch. s.v. ἀκτή. II. = ἀκταίνω, *EM*54.39: **ἀκταΐζω,** Hsch.

**ἀκταία,** ας, ἡ, *a Persian state robe,* Democr.Ephes.1. II. *marble mortar,* Clearch.65; cf. ἀκτίτης. III. *baneberry, Actaea spicata,* Plin.*HN*27.43.

❋ **ἀκταινόω,** *lift up, raise,* only aor. -ῶσαι Anacr.137, Pl.*Lg.*672e, Pl.Com.180, c. 19. (Derived fr. ἀκτή by Phryn.*PS*p.38 B.)

**ἀκταίνω,** = foreg., ἀκταίνειν στάσιν (γρ. βάσιν) *keep* my *stature erect,* A.*Eu.*36: metaph., ἀ. μένος *Trag.Adesp.*147; cf. ὑποακταίνομαι.

❋ **ἀκταῖος,** α, ον, (ἀκτή A) *on the shore or coast,* epith. of cities in Aeolis Th.4.52: 'Ακταία (sc. γῆ), ἡ, old name of Attica, = ἀκτή (A) I.2, Call.*Fr.*348, Paus.1.2.6. 2. *dwelling on the coast, belonging thereto,* ἰχθύες Hp.*Aff.*52; θεοί Orph.*A.*342; βάτραχοι Babr.25.6.

**ἀκτέα** (ἀκταία f.l. in Luc.*Trag.*71), contr. **ἀκτῆ,** ἡ, *elder tree, Sambucus nigra,* Emp.93, B.8.34, Hp.*Nat.Mul.*2 (ἀκτῆ), *Mul.*1.34 (ἀκτέα), Thphr.*HP*3.13.4, Dsc.4.173. 2. ἀ. ἕλειος, = χαμαιάκτη, *deadwort, Sambucus Ebulus,* ibid.

❋ **ἀκτέᾰνος,** ον, *without property, poor, BCH*15.430 (Stratonicea), Man.4.114, *AP*7.353 (Antip.).

**ἀκτεῖνος,** (ἀκτέα) *made of elder,* perh. to be read in Simon.155.6, Thphr.*HP*5.3.3.

**ἀκτένιστος,** ον, *uncombed,* κόμη S.*OC*1261, Sch.A.R.1.60.

**ἄκτενος·** ὀριός, ἀξίνης κρούσμα, Hsch.

❋ **ἀκτέον,** (ἄγω) *one must lead,* Pl.*R.*467e, etc.; *one must treat,* τινὰς τρυφερώτερον Sor.2.9; *one must bring,* εἰς ὑπόμνησιν Apollon.Cit. 3. 2. εἰρήνην ἀκτέον *one must keep* peace, And.3.40, D.8.5. II. *one must go, march,* X.*HG*6.4.5. III. Adj., **ἀκτέος,** α, ον, *to be drawn,* γραμμαί Gal.16.4-6; *to be led away,* ἐπὶ τὸ κολασθῆναι D.23 *Arg.*2.3.

**ἀκτέος,** ὁ, = ἀκτέα, Thphr.*HP*3.4.2.

**ἀκτερ-έϊστος,** ον, *unhallowed by funeral rites, AP*7.564. **-ής,** ές, = foreg., prob. in Hsch. **-ιστος,** ον, = foreg., S.*Ant.*1071, Lyc.1155.

❋ **ἀκτεροί·** ἄταφοι, αἱ κράνιοι ῥάβδοι, Hsch.

❋ **ἀκτή** (A), ἡ, *headland, foreland, promontory,* ἀ. προὔχουσα Od.24.82; ἀ. προβλῆτες 5.405, 10.89; opp. λιμήν, Il.12.284; often with epithets, denoting high rugged coast, τρηχεῖα, ὑψηλή, Od.5.425, Il.2.395; τρηχέα Hdt.7.33; στυφλοί A.*Pers.*303; ἀμφίκλυστος S.*Tr.*752; στόνῳ βρέμουσι δ' ἀντιπλῆγες ἀκταί Id.*Ant.*592:—usu. of sea-coast, χλωρὰ ἀ. ib.1132; ἀκταὶ ἔναλοι Tim.*Pers.*109; but also of *rugged banks* or *strand* of rivers, 'Ελώρου, Νείλου, Pi.*N.*9.40, *I.*2.42; Σιμόεντος A.*Ag.*697; 'Αχέροντος S.*Ant.*813.—Rare in early Prose, X.*An.* 6.2.1, Lycurg.17. 2. generally, *tract of land running out into the sea,* ἀ. διφάσιαι of the north and south coasts of Asia Minor, Hdt.4.38; of Africa, as jutting out from Asia, 4.41, cf. 177; of Cape Sepias, 7.183, al.; of Mt. Athos, Th.4.109; of Italy, Arist.*Pol.*1329ᵇ11; of the peninsula of the Piraeus, Hyp.*Fr.*185, Arist.*Ath.*42.3, Lycurg. 17 (also of Attica in general, E.*Hel.*1673, cf. Str.9.1.3); of the coast of Argolis, Plb.5.91.8, D.S.12.43: pl., ἀκτὰς τῆσδε γῆς S.*Fr.* 24. II. generally, *edge,* χώματος ἀ. of a sepulchral mound, A. *Ch.*722; βώμιος ἀ. of an altar, S.*OT*182 (lyr.). (As there is no trace of ϝ, the word is more probably connected with √*ak* 'pointed' than with ϝάγ-νυμι.)

**ἀκτή** (B), ἡ, poet. word for *corn,* Δημήτερος ἀκτή Il.13.322, 21.76, cf. E.*Hipp.*138 (lyr.), Epin.1.9; μυληφάτου ἀλφίτου ἀ. Od.2.355, cf. 14.429, Il.11.631:—in Hes. of *corn* generally, ὡσεὶ Δημήτερος ἀ., of standing crop, *Sc.*290, of unthreshed corn, *Op.*597, 805; of seed, οὐ σπόρον ὁλκοῖσιν Δηοῦς ἐνιβάλλομαι ἀ. A.R.3.413. (The connexion with ἄγνυμι is doubtful.)

**ἀκτῆ,** contr. for ἀκτέα, q.v.

**ἀκτημ-οσύνη,** ἡ, *poverty,* Crates Theb.ap.Epiph.*Haer.*3.2, Poll.3.111, 6.197. **-ων,** ον, gen. ονος, *without property, poor,* χρυσοῖο *in* gold, Il.9.126: abs., ἀ. πενίη Theoc.16.33; cf. Plu.*Sol.*14, Demoph. *Sent.*16, Alex.Aphr.*Pr.*1.89.

**ἀκτήν,** ῆνος, = ἀκτήμων, *EM*55.11.

**ἀκτηρίς,** ίδος, ἡ, *staff,* Achae.2. 2. *bar of wood* supporting chariot-pole, Poll.10.157.

**ἄκτητος,** ον, *not worth getting,* Pl.*Hp.Mi.*374e. II. *unobtainable,* prob. in Phld.*Herc.*1251.4.

**ἀκτινείδωλον,** τό, *ray-image, visual impression,* Hestiaeus ap. *Placit.*4.13.5.

**ἀκτίνη,** ἡ, = βούνιον, Ps.-Dsc.4.123.

**ἀκτῑνηδόν,** Adv. *like a ray,* Luc.*Salt.*18.

**ἀκτῑνο-βολέω,** *emit rays,* φέγγος ἀ. Ph.1.638:—Pass., *receive the rays of the sun,* Isid.Char.ap.Ath.3.94a. II. Astrol., of a planet, *aspect from the left* (opp. ἐφοράω, q.v.), Heph.Astr.1.16, Porph.*Intr.* p.189:—Pass., Vett.Val.116.22. **-βολία,** ἡ, *shooting of rays,* Plu. 2.761a. II. Astrol., *aspecting from the left,* Thessal. in *Cat. Cod.Astr.*8(3).138, Porph.*Intr.*p.18 :—also **ἀκτινηβολίη,** Man.1.322. ❋ **-βόλος,** ον, *sending forth rays,* δέσποτα *Sammelb.*4127 (Talmis). **-γρᾰφία,** ἡ, *treatise on radiation* (by Democritus), D.L. 9.48. **-ειδής,** ές, = ἀκτινώδης, στέφανοι Ph.2.559; τρίχες Horap. 1.17. Adv. -δῶς Gal.19.171, Steph.*in Hp.*1.144 D., al. ❋ **-κράτωρ,** *lord of the sun's rays, PMag.Berol.*1.202.

**ἀκτῖνος,** η, ον, (ἀκτή) *of elder-wood,* Thphr.*HP*5.3.3; cf. ἀκτεῖνος.

**ἀκτῑνο-φόρος,** ον, *bearing rays, Gloss.*:— as Subst., *rayed shell-fish,* Xenocr.85. **-χαῖτις,** ἡ, *with rays for hair, PMag.Par.*1.2286.

**ἀκτιν-ώδης**, ες, *like rays*, Philostr.*VA*3.46. **-ωτός**, ή, όν, *de-*ated *with rays*, Ph.2.560; φιάλη *Michel*815 (Delos, iv B.C.); of -wheels, *toothed*, Hero*Spir.*2.32.

**ἄκτιον**, τό, = ἀκτή (A), Ael.*NA*13.28. II. = βούνιον, Dsc.4.3.

**ἄκτιος**, ον, (ἀκτή A) *of the sea-shore*, of Pan as god of the coast, heoc.5.14; of Apollo, A.R.1.404.

**ἀκτίς** (nom. ἀκτίν Hdn.Gr.2.511), [ῑ], ῖνος, ἡ, *ray, beam*: Hom. nly dat. pl., ἀκτῖσιν Od.5.479, 19.441. ἀκτίνεσσιν 11.16, Il.10.547; ελίοιο ἀκτῖνες Mimn.11.6, cf. Emp.84, Ar.*Av.*1009, Arist.*Mete.* 74ᵇ4, etc.; sg., S.*Tr.*685, cf. ἀνὰ μέσσαν ἀκτῖνα, i.e. from south, S. *OC*1247; ἀκτῖνες μέσαι *noonday*, E.*Ion*1136; τὰ πρὸς ἀκτῖνα ἔθνη *peoples of the East*, Philostr.*VA*2.2:—of lightning, ἀκτῖνες στερο-πᾶς ἀπορηγνύμεναι Pi.*P.*4.198; ὦ Διὸς ἀκτίς, πεῖσον S.*Tr.*1086; πυρός Ἑοpat.13, Pl.*Ti.*78d; of the eyes, ἀκτῖνες προσώπου, Pi.*Fr.*123, cf. Ar.*V.*1032; visual *rays*, Hipparch.ap.*Placit.*4.13.9. 2. metaph., *brightness, splendour, glory*, ἀ. ἀγώνων, καλῶν ἐργμάτων, Pi.*P.*11.48, *I.*4(3).42; ἀκτῖνες ὄλβου *splendid* fortunes, Id.*P.*4.255. 3. *ray shot from the left by planet to planet* (opp. ὄψις, q.v.), Heph.Astr. 1.16, Porph.*Intr.*p.181; τὴν ἀ. ἐπιφέρων Vett.Val.136.19, cf. Ptol. *Tetr.*126. II. *spoke* of a wheel, *AP*9.418 (Antip.).

**ἄκτιστον**· *inconditum, Gloss.*: ἀποίητον, Hsch.

**⊕ἀκτίτης** [ῑ], ου, ὁ, (ἀκτή A) *dweller on coast*, *AP*6.304 (Phan.). II. ἀ. λίθος stone *from the Piraeus* (cf. ἀκτή (A) I.2), *IG*2.1054.16, al.; *from the Argolid*, S.*Fr.*68.

**⊕ἄκτῑτος**, ον, poet. for ἄκτιστος, *untilled*, *h.Ven.*123.

**ἄκτῠπος**, ον, *noiseless*, Eust.964.60. Adv. ἀκτυπί Adam.2.41.

**ἄκτωρ**, ορος, ὁ, (ἄγω) *leader*, A.*Pers.*557, *Eu.*399: as pr. n., Il., etc. II. *leash*, = ἀγωγεύς, Hsch.

**ἀκτ-ωρέω** and **-ωρία**, from **-ωρός**, ὁ, *coastguard*, Hsch.

**ἀκῠβέρνητος**, ον, *without steersman*, Ph.1.219, Plu.*Caes.*28, Luc. *J.Tr.*46: metaph., θυμός Ph.*Fr.*110 H., cf. 1.696; ἀμέλεια Onos.33.2.

**ἀκύβευτος**, ον, *risking nothing upon a die, cautious*, M.Ant.1.8.

**ἀκυητήριον** (sc. φάρμακον), τό, *drug to prevent conception*, Hsch.

**ἀκύθηρος**, ον, (Κυθήρη) like ἀναφρόδιτος, *without charms*, Cic.*Fam.* 7.32.2; τὸ ἀ. Eun.*VS*p.457.14 B.

**⊕ἄκῠθος**, ον, (cf. *EM*55.15) *unfruitful*, ὄϊες, opp. ὕπαρνοι, Call.*h.Ap.* 52: c. gen., τόκων Id.*Iamb.*1.242 (dub.). [ῠ in *Iamb.* s. v.l.]

**⊕ἀκυθῶν**· ἀγρυπνῶν, Hsch.

**ἀκύκητος**, ον, *untroubled*, διάνοιαι Phld.*D.*1.17.

**ἀκύκλιος**, ον, *one who has not gone the round* of studies, opp. ἐγκύκλιος, Pl.Com.227. **ἀκύκλωτος**, ον, *not surrounded*, Tz.*H.* 8.596. **ἀκυλαῖον**, τό, = ἄκυλος, Orac.ap.Eus.*PE*4.20. **ἀκυλεής**· ἀετός, Hsch.

**ἀκύλιστος**, ον, *not to be rolled about*: metaph., κραδίη ἀ. an *undaunted* heart, Timo 16. II. of Protagoras, οὐκ ἀ. not *without volubility* or *versatility*, Id.5.

**⊕ἄκῠλος**, ὁ (ἡ, Theoc.5.94), the *acorn* of *Quercus Ilex*, given to swine with βάλανος, Od.10.242, Pherecr.186, Arist.*HA*595ᵃ29, cf. Amphis 38, Thphr.*HP*3.16.3:—used in games, Poll.9.103. II. *ornament* or *jewel in form of acorn*, *IG*2.767 *b* 11:—neut., ἄκυλον, τό, Ἐφ. Ἀρχ.1895.70.

**⊕ἀκυλωτός**, ή, όν, *with acorn-shaped ornament*, φιάλαι Ἐφ.Ἀρχ. 1903.146 (dub.).

**⊕ἀκύμ-αντος** [ῡ], ον, *not washed by waves*, ψαμάθοις ἐπ' ἀκυμάντοις on sands *washed by no waves*, i.e. those of the stadium, E.*Hipp.*235, cf. 229; πλοῦς Them.*Or.*18.221b (Comp.); προσοχὴ σκάφους Iamb. *VP*3.16. II. *waveless, calm*, πέλαγος Luc.*D.Marin.*5.1; θάλαττα Max.Tyr.31.5. III. Act., *not raising waves*, ἐρετμοί, αὖραι, Nonn. *D.*2.14, 3.36. **⊕-ατος** [ῠ], ον, = foreg. 11, πορθμός *Trag.Adesp.* 336. **-ος**, ον, = foreg., τόπος Arist.*Pr.*931ᵇ31: metaph., ἀ. βίοτος E.*HF*698; ψυχή Plu.2.109cb; ἄφοβον καὶ ἀ. Epicur.*Fr.*413. **-ων** (A), [ῠ], ον, gen. ονος, (κῦμα) = ἀκύμαντος, Pi.*Fr.*235, A.*Ag.*566; θάλασσα Ar.*Fr.*708; ἀ. πομπὰ σιγώντων ἀνέμων E.*Fr.*773.39 (Pap.); γαλήνη Ph.1.680; ἀήρ Plu.2.722e; οὐρανός prob. in Plot.5.1.2: metaph., βίος Plu.2.8a. **⊕-ων** (B), [ῠ], ον, gen. ονος, (κυέω) *without fruit, barren*, of women, E.*Andr.*158; of the earth, Moschio Trag.8.

**ἄκυνον** (fort. ἄκυον)· ἄτοκον, Hsch. **ἀκυντόν**· ἀπρόσιτον, Id. **ἄκυον**· ἀτόκιον, Id. **ἄκυπρον** (Κύπρις)· ἀμιγῆ, παρθένιον, Id. **ἀκύρβιστος**, ον, prob. *without patches* or *insertions*, *BCH*35. 43 (Delos).

**ἀκῡρής**, ές, = ἀτυχής: hence **ἀκύρημα**· ἀτύχημα, and **ἄκυρμα**, τό, Hsch., *EM*55.5.

**ἀκῡρία** λέξεως, *impropriety* of language, Hermog.*Meth.*3.

**ἀκυρόεντα**· ἀνάρμοστα, ἄκυρα, Hsch.

**ἀκυρο-λέκτητος**, ον, *incorrectly used*, Eust.569.6 (ubi male ἀκυρο-). **-λεξία**, ἡ, = ἀκυρολογία, Suid. s.v. αὐθέντης, Eust. 1770. **⊕-λογέω**, *speak incorrectly*, Ph.1.216, *Lex.Vind.*3.19. **-λόγητος**, ον, Astrol., *not dominant*, ἀστέρες Vett.Val.203.7. **-λογία**, ἡ, *incorrect phraseology*, D.H.*Lys.*4 (nisi leg. ἀκαιρο-, q.v.). **ἄκυρον**, τό, = ἄλισμα, Ps.-Dsc.3.152.

**⊕ἄκῡρος**, ον, *without authority*, opp. κύριος, hence, I. of laws, sentences, etc., *invalid, unratified, obsolete*, ψήφισμα And.1.8; δίκη Pl.*Lg.*954e; συνθῆκαι Lys.18.15; ἄκυρον ποιεῖν, καταστῆσαι *set aside*, Pl.*Prt.*356d, Is.1.21, etc.; νόμοις ἀ. χρωμένη *not enforcing* the laws, Th.3.37. Adv. -ως Simp. *in Ph.*168.10. II. of persons, *having no right* or *power*, ἄ. ποιεῖν τινά X.*HG*5.3.24; καθιστάναι Lys. 9.19; τινός *over* a thing, Pl.*Tht.*169e; ἄ. πάντων . . γενήσεσθε D.19. 2: c. inf., Pl.*Lg.*929e. 2. of things, ἀκυροτέρα κρίσις *less trustworthy* decision, Pl.*Tht.*178d; ἄ. ἀμφορεύς voting urn *into which neutral votes were thrown*, Sch.Ar.*Eq.*1150, Poll.8.123; τὰ ἀκυρότερα *less important* parts of nature, Arist.*GA*778ᵃ1; of bodily members, *unimportant*, ἄ. μόριον Gal.16.540, cf. 18(1).33 (Comp.); *impotent*, Arist.*GA*772ᵇ28. III. of words and phrases, *used in improper sense*, Cic.*Fam.*16.17.1 (Comp.), Phlp.*in Ph.*717.12. Adv. -ρως Str.12.3.23, Phld.*Rh.*1.161 S., Hermog.*Meth.*3, cf. Dam.*Pr.*7,306.

**ἀκυρότης**, τητος, ἡ, *improper, illegitimate use*, οὐσίας Dam.*Pr.*306.

**ἀκῡρόω**, *cancel, set aside*, ψήφισμα, δόγμα, Din.1.63, D.S.16.24; ὀφειλήματα *SIG*742.30 (Pass., Ephesus), cf. Str.8.4.10 (Pass.), D.H.2.72, *BGU*1053 ii 14 (i B.C.). 2. *set at naught, treat as of no effect*, Lxx 1*Es.*6.32; λόγον θεοῦ *Ev.Matt.*15.6, cf. J.*AJ*18.8.8. b. *reject, deny the validity of*, Phld.*Sign.*3c. 3. metaph., *render powerless*, τῷ λογισμῷ τὸν τῶν παθῶν οἶστρον Lxx 4*Ma.*2.3. **-ωσία**, ἡ, *declaration of invalidity*, *BGU*944.20 (iv/v A.D.), *Gloss.* **⊕-ωσις**, εως, ἡ, *cancelling*, D.H.8.21; συγγραφῶν Phld.*Rh.*1.276 S., cf. *BGU* 1282.35 (i A.D.), *POxy.*266.107.5 (ii A.D.). **-ωτος**, ον, verb. Adj., *unconfirmed*, E.*Ion*801, *PRyl.*427 *Fr.*14.

**ἄκῠτος**, ον, (κύω) = ἄτοκος, *EM*54.5, Hsch.

**ἀκχαλίβαρ**· κράββατος (Lacon.), Hsch. **ἀκχημονικά**· καὶ κακοπαθήσεντα, Id.

**ἀκχός**· ὠμός, Hsch.

**ἀκωδώνιστος**, ον, *not tested*, Ar.*Lys.*485.

**ἀκωκή** [ᾰ], ἡ, (ἀκή A) *point* (Att. ἀκίς), δουρός, βέλεος, ἔγχεος, Il.10. 373, 13.251, 22.327, cf. Od.19.453, Theoc.22.195; of horns, quills, claws, teeth, Opp.*C.*2.160,604, 4.185, *H.*5.327:—also in late Prose, Arr.*Tact.*4.9 (pl.), Luc.*D.Mort.*27.4. 2. scorpion's *sting*, Orph. *L.*622; snake's *fangs*, ib.126 (pl.).

**ἀκώλιστος**, ον, *not divided into clauses* (κῶλα), D.H.*Comp.*23.

**ἄκωλος**, ον, *without limbs, mutilated*, Paus.1.24.3. II. *ill-jointed*, and so, *moving slowly*, gloss on ἄωροι πόδες, Sch.Od.12.89.

**ἀκώλῡτος**, ον, *unhindered*, Luc.*Tim.*18; τύχη, of death, *Epigr.Gr.* 149.8 (Rhenea), etc. Adv. -τως Pl.*Cra.*415d, Chrysipp.*Stoic.*2. 269, Str.17.1.25, *Act.Ap.*28.31, etc.; γλῶσσα ἀ. ῥέουσα Procop.*Ep.* 46; also ἀκωλυτί [Democr.] in Fabr.*Bibl.*4.338.

**ἀκώμαστος**, ον, *without revelry*, of persons, Lib.*Decl.*28.24.

**ἀκωμῴδητος**, ον, *not ridiculed*. Adv. -τως Luc.*VH*1.2.

**ἄκων** (A), [ᾰ], οντος, ὁ, (ἀκή A) *javelin, dart*, smaller and lighter than ἔγχος, Il.15.709, Od.14.531, al., Pi.*P.*9.20, E.*Ph.*1402, etc.; in later Prose, Eratosth.*Cat.*33, Aristid.*Or.*26(14).84, Artem.1.57, Ant.Lib. 41.5.

**ἄκων** (B), [ᾱ], ἄκουσα, ἆκον, Att. contr. for ἀέκων, q.v.

**⊕ἀκώνητος**, ον, *unpitched*, Dsc.1.7. **ἄκωνος**, ον, *without conical top*, πῖλος J.*AJ*3.7.3. **ἀκώπητος**, ον, *not having oars*: *unequipt*, *AB*373, Hsch. **ἄκωπος**, ον, *without oars*, *AP*9.88 (Phil.).

**ἄλαβα**, *ink*, Hsch., who also has ἀλάβη· λιγνύς, σποδός, καρκίνος, ὑπὸ δὲ Κυπρίων μαρίλη, and ἀ.· ἄνθρακες.

**ἀλαβ-αρχέω**, *to be* ἀλαβάρχης, J.*AJ*20.5.2. **-άρχης**, v. Ἀραβάρχης. **-αρχία** [ᾰλ], ἡ, *office of* ἀλαβάρχης, J.*AJ*20.7.3; also ἐξ ἀλαβαρχείης *AP*11.383 (Pall.).

**ἀλᾰβάστιον**, τό, Dim. of ἀλάβαστος, Eub.100. **ἀλαβαστῖτις**, v. ἀλαβαστρίτης. **⊕ἀλᾰβαστοθήκη**, ἡ, *case for alabaster ornaments*, Ἐφ.Ἀρχ.1903.443, D.19.237: generally, *small box* or *casket*, Ar.*Fr.* 548 (-στρο-), *PLond.*2.12 (-στρο-).

**⊕ἀλάβαστος** [ᾰλᾰ-] or **-στρος**, ὁ (ἡ, v.l. in *Ev.Marc.*14.3), *globular vase without handles for holding perfumes*, often made of alabaster, Hdt.3.20, Ar.*Ach.*1053, Crates Com.15.6, Alex.62,143, etc. (ἀλάβαστος (or -ον) is the earlier Att. form, *SIG*102, cf. Ael.Dion.*Fr.*31, Men.990: Dor. acc. pl. ἀλαβάστρως Call.*Lav.Pall.*15):—neut. **ἀλάβαστρον** *IG*2.745 *B*4, 11(2).161 *B*9 (Delos, iii B.C.), Lxx 4*Ki.*21.13 (cod. A), v.l. in *Ev.Marc.*14.3: pl. ἀλάβαστρα or -τα Theoc.15.114, *AP*9.153 (Agath.).

**ἀλᾰβ-αστρίνη** (sc. λιθοτομία), ἡ, *alabaster quarry*, *PThead.* 54. **⊕-άστρινος**, η, ον, *of alabaster*, ἔργα *PRyl.*92.1 (ii/iii A.D.). **-άστριον**, τό, *alabaster quarry*, *PThead.*36.3 (iv A.D.). **-αστρίτης** (sc. λίθος), ου, ὁ, *calcareous alabaster*, Thphr.*Lap.*65, cf. Str.12.8. 14, Zos.Alch.p.113 B.:—also **-αστῖτις**, ιδος, ἡ, πέτρα Callix.1. **-αστροειδής**, *like alabaster*, Zos.Alch.p.111 B. Adv. -δῶς, στίλβουσα Dsc.4.76. **-αστρος**, v. ἀλάβαστος. **-αστροφόρος**, ον, *carrying vases*, A.*Fr.*409. **-αστρών**, ῶνος, ὁ, *alabaster quarry*, *Sammelb.* 4639 (iii A.D.).

**ἀλάβη**, v. sub ἄλαβα.

**⊕ἀλάβης** or **ἀλλάβης**, ητος, ἡ, a Nile fish, Str.17.2.4, Ath.7.312b, *Gp.*20.7.1, *POxy.*1857.2 (vi A.D.); in Plin.*HN*5.51 *alabetes.*

**ἀλάβητοι**· θόρυβοι, and **ἀλαβυτῶ**· θορυβῶ, Hsch.

**⊕ἀλαβώδης**, ες, *sooty, murky*, πύργος Antim.Col.1.5, cf. Hsch.

**ἅλᾰδε** [ᾰλ], Adv., (ἅλς) *to* or *into the sea*, Il.1.308, Epicur.*Fr.*194, etc.; εἰς ἅλαδε Od.10.351. II. ἅλαδε μύσται, name of the second day of the Eleusinian mysteries, 16th Boedromion, Polyaen.3.11.2, cf. *IG*1.53 *a*35, 2.385 *d*20.

**ἀλάδρομος** [ᾰλ], ὁ, dithyrambic word coined by Ar.*Av.*1396, prob. from ἅλς (B), *race over the sea.*

**ἄλαζα**· αἰσχρά, Hsch.

**ἀλαζ-ονεία**, ἡ, *false pretension, imposture*, Pl.*Grg.*525a, D.22.47, etc., cf. Arist.*EN*1127ᵃ13, Thphr.*Char.*23; ὑπ' ἀλαζονείας Ar.*Ra.* 919: in pl., Id.*Eq.*290,903, Isoc.12.20; *boastfulness*, Procop.*Pers.* 1.11: metaph., ἀ. χορδῶν their *over-readiness* to sound, opp. ἐξάρνησις, Pl.*R.*531b. [That penult. is long appears from Ar. ll.cc., Men. 737.] **-όνευμα**, ατος, τό, *imposture, piece of humbug*, Aeschin.3.

238, cf. Aristid.27(16).29: in pl., *quackeries*, Ar.*Ach*.87, Aeschin.1.178. ⊛**–ονεύομαι**, fut. -εύσομαι D.36.41: (ἀλαζών):—*make false pretensions, brag*, Ar.*Ra*.280, Lys.*Fr*.73; of the Sophists, X.*Mem*.1.7.5, etc.; περί τινος Eup.146b, Isoc.12.74; ἐπί τινι Aristipp.ap.D.L.2.73. **2.** *feign*, Pl.*Hp.Mi*.371a; τὰ ἤθη ἀ. Arist.*Oec*.1344a19. **–ονίας**, ου, ὁ, *boaster, braggart*, Hdn.*Epim*.183. **–ονικός**, ή, όν, *disposed to make false pretensions, boastful, braggart*, Hp.*Medic*.4, X.*Mem*.1.2.5, Phld.*Rh*.2.149 S. (Sup.); -κόν, τό, Arist.*EN*1127b29. Adv. -κῶς Plu.*Mar*.9: Comp. -ώτερον Apollon.Cit.3: Sup. -ώτατα Men.Prot.p.118 D. **–ονοχαυνοφλύᾱρος**, ὁ, *swaggering empty babbler*, Archestr.*Fr*.59.12 B. **–οσύνη**, ἡ, = ἀλαζονεία, Aq.*Je*.49.16(29.17). ⊛**–ών** [ᾰλ], όνος, ὁ, ἡ, (ἄλη) prop. *wanderer about country, vagrant*, Alc.Com.31. **II.** *charlatan, quack*, esp. of Sophists, Cratin.380, Ar.*Nu*.102, Pl.*Chrm*.173c, al. **2.** *braggart, boaster*, X.*Cyr*.2.2.12, Arist.*EN*1127a21; title of play by Men. **3.** Adj., *boastful, pretentious*, Hdt.6.12; ἀ. λόγοι Pl.*R*.560c: Comp. -έστερος Suid. s.v. εἴρων: Sup., ἡδονὴ ἀλαζονίστατον *most shameless*, Pl.*Phlb*.65c. Adv. Sup. -έστατα, δρῶν Ael.*NA*4.29.

**ἀλάθεια, ἀλᾱθής**, Dor. for ἀλήθ–. **ἀλᾱθείς**, v. sub ἀλάομαι.

**ἀλάθητος** [λᾱ], ον, gloss on ἄληστος, Suid.: coupled with ἄλαστος, Sch.E.*Hec*.685. **2.** *not escaping detection*, Astramps.*Orac*.13.1.

**ἀλαίνω** [ᾰλ], = ἀλάομαι, *wander about*, A.*Ag*.82, E.*Tr*.1084, *El*.204,589, *Cyc*.79: c. acc., ἀ. πόδα δύστηνον Id.*Ph*.1536.—Always in lyr., exc. *Or*.532.

⊛**ἀλαιός**, όν, f.l. for ἀλεός, q.v. **ἀλακάτα**, ἡ, Dor. for ἠλακάτη:—Dim. **ἀλακάτιον**, τό, *POxy*.1740.8 (iii/iv A.D.).

**ἀλάκητον**· ἀψόφητον, Hsch. **ἀλακῶσαι**· ἀθροῖσαι, and συνάγεσθαι, Id. **ἀλαλά**, Dor. for ἀλαλή, q.v.

**ἀλᾰλ-ᾱγή**, ἡ, *shouting*, S.*Tr*.206. **–αγμα**, ατος, τό, = sq., Call.*Fr*.310, *Psalm.Solom*.17.8, Plu.*Mar*.45. ⊛**–αγμός**, ὁ, = ἀλαλαγή, Hdt.8.37, Plu.2.564b, Arr.*An*.5.10.4, Onos.29.1. **II.** generally, *loud noise*, τυμπάνων, αὐλοῦ, E.*Cyc*.65, *Hel*.1352 (lyr.). **–αγξ**· πλάνη, Hsch. **–άζω**, fut. -άξομαι v.l. in E.*Ba*.593, -άξω Lxx *Ez*.27.30: aor. ἠλάλαξα E.*HF*981, X. (v. infr.), poet. ἀλάλαξα Pi.*O*.7.37:—**Med.**, S.*Fr*.534, Arr.*An*.5.10.3: (formed from the cry ἀλαλαί):—*raise the war-cry*, τῷ Ἐνυαλίῳ ἠλάλαξαν (as v.l. for ἠλέλιξαν) X.*An*.5.2.14, cf. 6.5.27; Med., Arr. l.c.: c. acc. cogn., νίκην ἀλαλάζειν *shout the shout of* victory, S.*Ant*.133. **2.** generally, *cry, shout aloud*, Pi. l.c., E.*El*.855; esp. in orgiastic rites, A.*Fr*.57; of Bacchus and Bacchae, E.*Ba*.593 (in Med.), 1133, etc.; ὠλόλυξαν αἱ γυναῖκες, ἠλάλαξαν δὲ οἱ ἄνδρες Hld.3.5. **3.** rarely of a cry of pain or grief, ἠλάλαζε δυσθνήσκων φόνῳ E.*El*.843, Lxx *Je*.4.8, al., *Ev.Marc*.5.38, Plu.*Luc*.28. **II.** rarely also of other sounds than the voice, *sound loudly*, ψαλμὸς δ' ἀλαλάζει A.*Fr*.57; κύμβαλον ἀλαλάζον 1*Ep.Cor*.13.1.—Poet. word, used by X. and in late Prose.

**ἀλᾰλαί** or **ἀλαλαλαί** [ᾰλ], exclam. of joy, in formula ἀλαλαὶ ἰὴ παιών Ar.*Av*.1763, *Lys*.1291. **ἀλαλάξιος**, *god of the war-cry*, epith. of Ares, Corn.*ND*21; of Zeus, Call.*Aet*.3.1.60.

**ἀλᾰλᾱτός**, ὁ, Dor. for ἀλαλητός.

**ἀλᾰλάω**, (ἄλαλος) *make dumb*, in Pass., Aq.*Ps*.38(39).3; but **ἀλαλόω**, Pass., ib.30(31).19.

⊛**ἀλαλή** [ᾰλᾰ], Dor. **ἀλαλά**, ἡ, (ἀλαλαί) *loud cry*, μανίαι τ' ἀλαλαί τ' ὀρινομένων Pi.*Fr*.208; ἀλαλαὶ αἰαγμάτων (v.l. ἀλαλαγαί) E.*Ph*.337:—esp. *war-cry*, Pi.*N*.3.60; *battle*, Id.*I*.7(6).10: comically, ἀ. "μύρου χεῖτε" Phoen.3.3:—Ἀλαλά personified, κλῦθ', Ἀλαλά, πολέμου θύγατερ, Pi.*Fr*.78, cf. Plu.2.349c.

**ἀλάλημαι** [ᾰλᾰ], pf. of ἀλάομαι, only in pres. sense (part. ἀλαλήμενος with accent of pres., Od.14.122), *wander, roam about*, like a beggar, Hom. mostly in Od., 2.370, 15.10, etc.; of seamen, μαψιδίως ἀλάλησθε 3.72, cf. 313; of a departed spirit, ἀ. ἀν' εὐρυπυλὲς Ἄϊδος δῶ Il.23.74; of things, μυρία λυγρὰ κατ' ἀνθρώπους ἀλάληται Hes.*Op*.100:—once Trag., in plpf., ἀλάλητο E.*Andr*.306 (lyr.).

**ἀλάλητος** [λᾰ], ον, *unspeakable, unutterable*, v.l. in Thgn.422, cf. *AP*5.3 (Phld.), *Ep.Rom*.8.26. Adv. -τως, as expl. of ἀλόγως, Eust.723.30. **II.** ἀλάλητα· ξύλα ποταμόκλυστα, γομφώδη, Hsch.

**ἀλᾰλητός**, Dor. **–ᾱτός**, οῦ, ὁ, (ἀλαλαί) *shout of victory*, Il.16.78; *war-cry, battle-shout*, Hes.*Th*.686, Pi.*P*.1.72. **2.** generally, *loud shouting*, Il.2.149; *halloo*, in hunting, Nic.Dam.p.6 D. **3.** rarely, *cry of woe* or *wailing*, Il.21.10; com., τῶν δὲ πλακούντων.. ἦν ἀ. Telecl.1.13. **II.** rarely of other sounds, *loud noise*, αὐλῶν *AP*6.51.

**ἀλαλία**, ἡ, = πονηρία, ἀταξία, S.*Fr*.232.

**ἄλαλκε** [ᾰλα], 3 sg. aor. 2 (also 2 imper., Thgn.13), Il.23.185, Hes.*Th*.527, Pi.*N*.4.60 (augm. ἤλαλκε Hsch.); subj. (v. infr.); opt. ἀλάλκοις, -κοι, -κοιεν, Od.13.319, Il.21.138, 22.196; inf. ἀλαλκέμεναι Il.17.153, ἀλαλκεῖν (ἀλαλκέμεν Ar.Byz.) 19.30, *AP*7.8 (Antip.); part. ἀλαλκών Il.9.605, *AP*9.374:—*ward, keep off*, τί τινι something from a person, Il.19.30, etc.; less freq. τί τινος 21.539; ἀ. τί τινι κρατός Od.10.288.—Hence A.R.2.235 formed fut. ἀλαλκήσουσιν, Q.S.7.267 pres. ἀλάλκουσιν. (Cf. ἀλέξω.)

**Ἀλαλκ-ομενηΐς**, ΐδος, epith. of Athena, Il.4.8, 5.908: either from Boeot. town Alalcomenae or (as Aristarch.) from ἀλαλκεῖν, *Protectress*:—also **–ομένη** *BCH* 1.82 (Chios): masc. **–ομενεύς**, έως, of Zeus, *EM*56.10. **–ομένιος** or **–ειος**, ὁ, Boeot. month, answering to the Att. Μαιμακτηριών, *IG*7.2227, al., Plu.*Arist*.21. **–τήριον**, τό, (ἄλαλκε) *remedy*, Zonar.

⊛**ἄλᾰλος**, ον, *speechless, dumb*, prob. in A.*Fr*.60, Lxx *Ps*.37(38).13, *Ev.Marc*.9.17, etc.; κείμεσθα ἄ. *IG*14.1627: Comp. -ώτερος Sch.Pi.*N*.8.41.

**ἀλάλυγξ** [ᾰλᾰ], υγγος, ἡ, = λυγμός, *gulping, choking*, Nic.*Al*. cf. *AB*374.

**ἀλαλύκτημαι** [ᾰλᾰ], *to be in anguish, sore distressed*, pf. formed redupl. from ἀλυκτέω, οὐδέ μοι ἦτορ ἔμπεδον, ἀλλ' ἀ. Il.10.94.

**ἀλαλύσθαι**· φοβεῖσθαι, ⟨ἀ⟩λύειν, Hsch. **ἀλαμπάν**· τὸν ἥλι[ον] Id.

**ἀλάμπ-ετος**, ον, (λάμπω) *without light, darksome*, *h.Hom*.32.5; the nether world, S.*OC*1662 (v.l. ἀλύπητον), cf. *Epigr.Gr*.264 (dub.); ἀ. οὖδας Ἀΐδεω ib.149.3 (Rhenea, cf. ib.241.5 Smyrna); σκότ[ος] (metaph. of Heraclitus *AP*9.540. **–ής**, ές, = foreg., νύξ Simon.37.[…] *dull, not bright*, ὄψιες v.l. in Hp.*Prog*.2, πῦρ D.S.3.48; of colour, Aris[t.] *Col*.793a12; of sound, Orib.5[…].51.2; ἀ. ἡλίου *out of* sun's *light*, S.*Tr*.691; ὑπόγαιον J.*BJ*1.3.3; ἀλαμπέας Ἄϊδος εὐνάς *Epigr.Gr*.43 (Antioch.). **2.** metaph., *obscure*, ἀρετὴν.. ἀμαυρὰν καὶ ἀ. Plu.*Phoc*.1, cf. B.12.175. **–ία**, ἡ, Pythag. name for *one*, *Theol.Ar*.6.

⊛**ἀλανές**· ἀληθές, Hsch. Adv. ⊛**ἀλανέως**· ὁλοσχερῶς (Tarent.), Id. ἀϝλανέως, dub. sens., *GDI*1156.4 (Elis). **ἄλαξ**, v. ἄλξ.

**ἀλάομαι** [ᾰλ], Ep. 3 pl. ἀλόωνται, imper. ἀλόω (v. infr.), used by Hom. mostly in contr. forms ἀλᾶσθε, ἀλώμενος, impf. ἠλώμην, Ep. ἀλᾶτο: fut. ἀλήσομαι (ἀπ–) Hes.*Sc*.409 (v.l. ἀπαλήσατο): Ep. aor. ἀλήθην Od.14.120,362, Dor. part. ἀλᾱθείς A.*Supp*.870: pf. ἀλάλημαι (q.v.): (ἄλη):—*wander, roam*, οἷά τε ληιστῆρες.. τοί τ' ἀλόωνται ψυχὰς παρθέμενοι Od.3.73; ὅδε τις δύστηνος ἀλώμενος ἐνθάδ' ἱκάνει 6.206; μή πάθωμέν τι ἀλώμενοι Hdt.4.97; αἰσχρῶς ἀλῶμαι A.*Eu*.98; ἄσιτος νηλίπους τ' ἀ. S.*OC*349: esp. *to be outcast, banished*, ib.444, Th.2.102, Lys.6.30, D.19.310; ἐκ σέθεν by thee, S.*OC*1363:—freq. with Preps., ἀνὰ στρατὸν οἷοι ἀλᾶσθε Il.10.141; κὰπ πεδίον.. οἶος ἀλᾶτο 6.201; πολλὰ βροτῶν ἐπὶ ἄστε' ἀλώμενος Od.15.492; γῆς ἐπ' ἐσχάτοις ὅροις A.*Pr*.666; ἐπὶ ξένης χώρας S.*Tr*.300, cf. Isoc.4.168; οὕτω νῦν.. ἀλόω κατὰ πόντον Od.5.377, cf. A.*Supp*.870; νομάδεσσι γὰρ ἐν Σκύθαις ἀλᾶται Ar.*Av*.942: c. acc. loci, ἀ. γῆν *wander over* the land, S.*OC*1686; πορθμοὺς ἀ. μυρίους E.*Hel*.532; οὔρεα Theoc.13.66. **2.** c. gen., *wander away from, miss* a thing, εὐφροσύνας ἀλᾶται Pi.*O*.1.58; ψυχὴν ἀλᾶται τῆς πάροιθ' εὐπραξίας E.*Tr*.640. **II.** metaph., *wander in mind, be perplexed*, S.*Aj*.23.

**ἀλᾰός** [ᾰλ], όν, *not seeing, blind* (Cypr. for τυφλός, *AB*1095), Od.8.195, etc. (not in Il., Trag. only in lyr.); τὸ φωτῶν ἀ. γένος A.*Pr*.549, ἀλαοί, opp. δεδορκότες, *the dead*, Id.*Eu*.322; of eyes, S.*OC*149,244, E.*Ph*.1531; ἕλκος ἀ. *blinding* wound, i.e. *blindness*, S.*Ant*.974; ἐπ' ὀφθαλμῶν ἀ. νέφος A.R.2.259. **II.** *invisible, imperceptible* φθίσις ἀλαή prob. l. in Hp.*Loc.Hom*.10 (codd. ἄλλη, Gal. ἀλαΐα). (If from ἀ- priv., λάω A (q.v.), the accent is exceptional, but cf. Hdn.Gr.1.112.) [ᾰλᾰος Od. l.c., etc.; but μάντιος ἀλαοῦ init. vers. Od.10.493, 12.267.]

**ἀλᾰο-σκοπιά**, Ion. **–ιή**, ἡ, *blind man's watch*, i.e. *careless watch*, Il.10.515, 13.10, Od.8.285, Hes.*Th*.466. **–τόκος**, ον, *bringing forth young blind*, Suid. **ἀλᾰόω**, *blind*, ὀφθαλμοῦ ἀλαῶσαι *blind* him *of* his eye, Od.1.69, 9.516: c. acc., *AP*7.601 (Jul.).

**ἀλᾰπ-αδνός**, ή, όν, (ἀλαπάζω) *easily exhausted*, i.e. *powerless, feeble*, στίχες, σθένος, μῦθος, etc., Il.4.330, Od.18.373, *h.Merc*.334, cf. Hes.*Op*.437: Comp., ἀλαπαδνότεροι γὰρ ἔσεσθε Il.4.305. (ἀ- euph., cf. λαπαδνός.) **–αδνοσύνη**, ἡ, *feebleness*, Q.S.7.12. ⊛**–άζω** [ᾰλ], Ep. impf. ἀλάπαζον Il.11.503: fut. -άξω 2.367, A.*Ag*.130 (anap.): Ep. aor. ἀλάπαξα Il.11.750, Thgn.951:—Pass., Il.24.245:—*empty, drain, exhaust*, Od.17.424; ἀ. πόλιν *sack, plunder*, Il.2.367; of men, *overpower, destroy*, 5.166, 11.503, al.: metaph., [οἶνος] ἐκ κραδίης ἀνίας ἀνδρῶν ἀ. Panyas.14. (ἀ- euph., cf. λαπάσσω.)

⊛**ἄλαρα**· Ποντικὰ κάρυα, Hsch., *EM*57.53; also, *butt of spear-shaft*, Hsch., and **ἀλαρία**, ἡ, tree which furnished shafts for spears, *EM*57.54. **ἀλαρῦναι**· ῥυπᾶναι, Hsch.

⊛**ἅλας**, ᾰτος, τό, = ἅλς, *salt*, Arist.*Mir*.844b16, Lycon ap.Hdn.Gr.2.716, Lxx *Le*.2.13, al., *Ep.Col*.4.6, Gal.14.327; ἅ. ἀμμωνιακόν *POxy*.1222.2 (iv A.D.).

**ἀλασταίνω**· δυσπαθέω, Hsch.:—Pass., *EM*58.3 (codd. ἀλαιστάνομαι). **ἀλαστέω**, *to be full of wrath* or (more prob.) *to be distraught*, ἠλάστεον δὲ θεοί (as trisyll.) Il.15.21; ᾤμωξεν.. καὶ ἀλαστήσας ἔπος ηὔδα 12.163, cf. Call.*Del*.239, Musae.202, etc., cf. Gal.*Lex*. s.v. ἀλάστορες. (Only impf. and aor. part. in earlier Ep.; fut. -ήσω Q.S.5.584.)

**ἀλαστ-ορία**, ἡ, *vengeance of heaven*, J.*AJ*17.1.1. **–ορος**, ον, *under influence of an* ἀλάστωρ, A.*Fr*.294: *crying for vengeance*, ἀλαστόροισιν ὀμμάτων κύκλοις S.*Ant*.974 (lyr.). **II.** epith. of Zeus, *avenging*, Pherecyd.175 J.

**ἄλαστος**, ον, (cf. ἄληστος): (ἀ- priv., λαθεῖν, λήθομαι):—*not to be forgotten, insufferable*, πένθος, ἄχος, Il.24.105, Od.4.108, Hes.*Th*.467, cf. Alcm.23, A.*Pers*.990; ἔπαθον ἄλαστα S.*OC*538: Sup. **–ότατον**, πῆμα *IG*12(5).64 (Naxos); neut. as Adv., ἄλαστον ὀδύρομαι I wail *inconsolably*, Od.14.174, cf. B.3.34. **2.** of persons, as in Il.22.261, where Achilles calls Hector ἄλαστε *thou whom I will never forget nor forgive!*; *accursed wretch*, S.*OC*1482; πατρὸς.. ἄ. αἷμα ib.1672, cf. *Mim.Oxy*.413.60.—Poet. and late Prose, Demoph.*Sent*.13: used by Trag. only in lyr.

**ἀλάστωρ**, ορος, ὁ, ἡ, *avenging spirit* or *deity*, with or without δαίμων, freq. Trag., A.*Pers*.354, *Ag*.1501, 1508, cf. Men.8 D.; ἀ. θυμός S.*OC*788; ἐξ ἀλαστόρων νοσεῖν Id.*Tr*.1235; ἀλάστορας ἔχειν Hp.*Morb.Sacr*.1; ἀ. Πελοπιδῶν, prov. of utter ruin, Xenarch.1.3; generally, βουκόλων ἀ. herdsmen's *scourge*, of Nemean lion, S.*Tr*.1092: fem., of the Sphinx, Nicoch.18; Ζεὺς Ἀ. Orph.*H*.73. **II.** Pass., *he who does deeds which merit vengeance, wretch*, A.*Eu*.236, S.*Aj*.374; μιαροὶ.. καὶ λακες καὶ ἀ. D.18.296; βάρβαρόν τε..καὶ ἀ. τὸν Φίλιππον ἀποκαλῶν Id. .305; ἄνθρωπ' ἀλάστωρ Bato 2.5, cf. Men.7 D., *Pk.*408; Διονύσιος ἀ. τῆς Σικελίας ἀ. Clearch.10. (Connected with ἀλάομαι by Chrysipp.*Stoic.*2.47.)

**ἀλάτας, ἀλᾱτεία,** Dor. for ἀλήτης, ἀλητεία.

**ἁλ-ατίζω,** *sprinkle with salt,* [Gal.]14.576, Anon.*in Rh.*14.2.30 (Pass.). **-ατικόν,** *salarium,* Gloss. **-άτινος,** η, ον, (ἅλας) *made of salt,* Alex.Trall.12. ❋**-άτιον,** τό, Dim. of ἅλας, Aesop.322b, Aët. 109.

**ἅλατο,** Dor. 3 sg. aor. 1 of ἅλλομαι.

**ἁλᾰτοπωλία,** ἡ, *right of vending salt,* Arist.*Oec.*1346ᵇ21, *PFlor.*16. 3.

**ἀλατρίας·** ἁμαρτωλίας, Hsch. **ἀλαυρίδας·** σχίζας, Id.

**ἀλα-ῶπις,** ιδος, ἡ, pecul. fem. of sq., Emp.49. **-ωπός,** όν, lit. *blind-eyed*; hence, *dark,* ὀμίχλη Nonn.*D.*25.282. **-ωτύς,** ύος, ἡ, (ἀλαόω) *blinding,* ὀφθαλμοῦ Od.9.503.

**ἀλβάριος,** ὁ, *plasterer,* *IG*14.2271.

**ἀλγᾷ·** κρύπτει, Hsch. **ἀλγάς·** ἀλγηδόνας, Id. **ἀλγείη·** ἀρρωστία (Lacon.), Id.

**ἀλγεινός,** ή, όν, *painful, grievous,* A.*Pr.*199,240, S.*OT*1530, E.*Med.* 1037; τὰ μέλλοντα ἀ. Th.2.39, cf. ib.43 (Comp.). Adv. -νῶς S.*Ant.* 436, Pl.*Grg.*476c. II. rare in pass. sense, *feeling pain, suffering,* S.*OC*1664.—Comp. and Sup. in common use ἀλγίων, ἄλγιστος (q. v.), but ἀλγεινότερος, -ότατος, Th.2.43, Pl.*Grg.*477d, *Smp.*218a, Arist. *Pr.*890ᵃ37, and v.l. Isoc.14.48. Hom. form ἀλεγεινός, q.v.

**ἀλγεόθυμος·** ἀνώδυνος τῇ ψυχῇ, Hsch.

**ἀλγεσί-δωρος,** ον, *bringing pain,* Ἔρως Sapph.125; Ἔρις Opp.*H.* 2.668. ❋**-θῡμος,** ον, *grieving the heart,* Orph.*H.*65, cf. *PMag.Lond.* 121.355.

**ἀλγ-έω,** fut. -ήσω Od.12.27, (ἄλγος) *feel bodily pain, suffer,* ἀλγήσας *smarting with pain,* Il.2.269, etc.; *suffer, be ill,* Hdt.4.68; more fully, ἀλγήσας ὀδύνῃσι Il.12.206: suffering part in acc., ἄλγησον ἧπαρ A.*Eu.* 135; τὰς γνάθους ἀλγήσετε Ar.*Pax*237; τὸν δάκτυλον Pl.*R.*462d; τὰ ὄμματα ib.515e. 2. *suffer hardship,* ἢ ἁλὸς ἢ ἐπὶ γῆς ἀλγήσετε Od. l. c. II. *feel pain of mind, grieve,* ἀ. ψυχήν, φρένα, Hdt.3.43, E.*Or.*608, etc.; ἀ. τινί *to be pained at* a thing, Hdt.3.120, S.*OC*741, etc.; ἐπ' ἐξειργασμένοις Id.*Aj.*377, etc.; διά τι Hdt.4.68; περί τι or τινος, Th.2.65, E.*Andr.*240: c. gen., ἀλγεῖν χρὴ τύχης παλιγκότου A.*Ag.*571, cf. E.*Hec.*1256: c. acc., ἀλγῶ μὲν ἔργα A.*Ch.*1016; πρᾶξιν ἣν ἤλγησ' ἐγώ S.*Aj.*790: c. part., ἤλγησ' ἀκούσας Hdt.3.50, A.*Pers.* 844; ἀλγῶ κλύων S.*Ph.*86; ὁρῶν Eup.117.2: abs., τὸ ἀλγοῦν, opp. τὸ ἡδόμενον, Epicur.*Sent.*4. III. Pass., ὑποχόνδριον -ούμενον Hp. *Coac.*273; τὸν ἀλγούμενον ὀδόντα Dsc.*Eup.*1.66. ❋**-ηδών,** όνος, ἡ, *pain, suffering,* of body, Hdt.5.18, Hp.*Coac.*394, E.*Med.*24; ὀδύνη τις ἢ ἀ. Pl.*R.*413b: pl., *Prt.*354b. II. of mind, *pain, grief,* S.*OC*514, E.*Med.*56, Metrod.7: pl., Phld.*D.*1.16, etc. III. *cause of pain,* ἀλγηδόνες ὀμμάτων αἱ Περσίδες Alex.ap.Plu.*Alex.*21. Not in A., once in S. **-ημα,** τό, *pain felt* or *caused, suffering,* S. *Ph.*340, Hp.*VM*6, E.*Fr.*507, Plu.*Sull.*26, Plot.6.1.19; οὐκ ἔστι λύπης ἄ. μεῖζον Men.667. **-ηρός,** ά, όν, *painful,* Lxx *Je.*10.19, al. **-ησις,** εως, ἡ, *sense of pain,* S.*Ph.*792, Ar.*Th.*147: in later Prose, Iamb.*Protr.*21.κζ'; νεύρων Vett.Val.38.13. **-ητέον,** *one must grieve,* περί τινος Agath.1.13. **-ινόεις,** εσσα, εν, *painful, grievous,* Hes.*Th.*214,226, Mimn.11, Xenoph.2.4, A.R.4.64: in pass. sense, κρόταφος, τένων, Q.S.11.45,57. ❋**-ίων,** ον, **ἄλγιστος,** η, ον, irreg. Comp. and Sup. of ἀλγεινός, formed fr. Subst. ἄλγος (cf. καλλίων, αἰσχίων):—*more* or *most painful, grievous,* or *distressing*:—of Comp., Hom. has only neut. ἄλγιον, in signf. *so much the worse,* τῷ δ' ἄλγιον, αἴ κ' ἐθέλῃσιν..ἄμμι μάχεσθαι Il.18.278, cf. 306, Od.4.292: Sup. only in Il.23.655 ἥτ' ἀλγίστη δαμάσασθαι (of a mule).—Both are common in Trag., as ἀλγίων A.*Pr.*934, S.*Ant.*64; ἄλγιστος Id.*OT* 675, etc. [-ῑον Hom., -ῐον Trag.]

**ἄλγος,** εος, τό, (Cypr., = ὀδύνη, *AB*1095) *pain* of body, Il.5.394, S. *Ph.*734,1379; ἀ. καρδίης, ποδῶν, κεφαλᾶς, Hp.*Epid.*7.20, X.*Cyn.*3.3, *IG*4.953.52 (Epid.); in Hom. mostly in pl., *sufferings,* ἄλγεα τεύχει Il.1.110; ἄ. πάσχων 2.667, cf. Alc.95. 2. *pain of mind, grief,* freq. in pl., Il.1.2, 2.39, al.: sg., ἄλγος ἱκάνει θυμόν Il.3.97, cf. Od. 2.41, etc.; τὴν δ' ἅμα χάρμα καὶ ἄ. ἕλε φρένα 19.471; ἄ. ἀεικέλιον 14. 32; τὰ κύντατ' ἄλγη κακῶν E.*Supp.*807; ὑπ' ἄλγους *from pain,* A.*Eu.* 183; αἰσχύνας ἐμὰς ὑπ' ἀλγέων *from grief for* my shame, E.*Hel.*201; ἄ. καρδίας Lxx *Si.*26.6. II. later, *anything that causes pain,* Bion 2.11, *AP*9.390 (Menecr.), 5.166 (Asclep.); τοῦ ἄ. θιγεῖν Aret.*SD*2.9.

**ἀλγ-υνσις,** εως, ἡ, *causing of pain,* Phlp.*in de An.*17.33; δι' ἀλγύνσεως, opp. δι' ἡδύνσεως, Olymp.*in Grg.*p.531 J. **-υντήρ,** ῆρος, ὁ, *causing pain,* τινῶν Orac.ap.Zos.1.57. **-ύνω** [ῡ], Ion. impf. ἀλγύνεσκε Q.S.4.416: fut. -υνῶ S.*OT*332, etc.: aor. ἤλγῡνα Id.*Tr.*458, etc.:—Pass., with fut. Med. ἀλγυνοῦμαι (in pass. sense) Id.*Ant.*230, E.*Med.*622: aor. ἠλγύνθην, v. infr.—Rare exc. in Trag., Eup.90 (paratrag.), Democr.223, X.*Ap.*8, and later Prose, as Plu.2.82c:—*pain, grieve, distress,* τινά A.*Ch.*746, etc.:—Pass., *feel, suffer pain, be grieved* or *distressed* at a thing, τινί S.*Ant.*468; νόσοις X. l. c.; ἐπί τινι E.*Tr.*172; τι S.*Ph.*1021; εἰσιδοῦσά τ' ἠλγύνθην κέαρ A.*Pr.*247.

❋**ἀλδαίνω,** only pres. and impf., exc. Ep. aor. 3 sg. ἤλδᾰνε (v. infr.), ἀλδήσασκε Orph.*L.*370:—causal of ἀλδήσκω, *make to grow, nourish, strengthen,* μέλε' ἤλδανε ποιμένι λαῶν *she filled out* his limbs, Od.18.70, 24.368, cf. A.*Th.*12; θυμὸν ἀλδαίνουσαν ἐν εὐφροσύναις Id.*Pr.*539; *increase, multiply,* ὃς οὐκ ἐάσει γλῶσσαν..ἀλδαίνειν κακά Id.*Th.*557:—Pass., Aglaïas 12.

**ἄλδετα·** ἄτμητα, Hsch. (leg. ἄλαστα· ἄτλητα).

**ἀλδ-ή,** ἡ, *growth,* Hdn.Gr.1.311. **-ήεις,** εσσα, εν, *waxing, increasing,* Max.533. **-ήμιος,** *causing growth,* epith. of Zeus, Method.ap.*EM*58.20. **-ήσκω,** *grow,* ληΐου ἀλδήσκοντος Il.23.599, cf. Damocr.ap.Gal.14.101. II. trans. = ἀλδαίνω, Theoc.17.78, *Epigr.Gr.*511 (Epirus). **-ισκάνω,** = ἀλδήσκω, Hdn.Gr.2. 716. ❋**-ομαι,** v. ἀλδαίνω.

**ἀλέα** (A), [ᾰλ], Ion. ἀλέη, ἡ, (ἄλη, ἀλέομαι) *avoiding, escape,* ἐγγύθι μοι θάνατος.. οὐδ' ἀλέη Il.22.301 (not in Od.); οὐκ ἔστιν ἀ. οὐδὲ σκέπη Hp.*Aër.*19: c. gen., *shelter from* a thing, ὑετοῦ Hes.*Op.*545.—Ep. and Ion. word. ❋ **ἀλέα** (B), [ᾰλ], Ion. ἀλέη, ἡ, contr. ἀλῆ Androm.ap. Gal.14.33, cj. in Babr.18.11:—*warmth, heat,* of fire, Od.17.23 (not in Il.), Jul.*Mis.*341c; generally, *warmth,* or *warm spot,* ἐν ἀλέῃ γενέσθαι Hp.*VM*16, cf. Diocl.*Fr.*141; ἐσενεγκὼν ἐς ἀ. Hp.*Aër.*8; χρέεσθαι περιπάτοις ἐν ἀ. Id.*Vict.*3.68; ἐν ἀ. κατακείμενος Ar.*Ec.*541; ἀλέας καὶ ψύχους *in heat* and cold, Pl.*Erx.*401d, cf. Arist.*EN*1148ᵃ8; πνῖγος καὶ ἀ. Id.*Metaph.*1026ᵇ34; ἐν ταῖς ἀ. in the *hot season,* Id.*Pr.*939ᵇ9: later, *animal, bodily heat,* Plu.2.131d, Ael.*NA*3.20, Aristid.*Or.*48 (24).22; generally, *source of warmth,* τὸ ἔριον ἡμῖν κόσμος καὶ ἀ. Porph.*Abst.*1.21, etc.: in pl., *fomentations,* Alex.Trall.*Febr.*3.

**ἀλεάζω** (A), *to be warm,* Arist.*Pr.*863ᵇ22, *Resp.*472ᵇ4; trans., = θερμαίνω, Gal.19.73, Hsch.

**ἀλεάζω** (B)· κρύπτειν, ἢ προβάλλειν, καὶ εἴργειν, ἀφανίζειν, and **-άζων·** δικαζόμενος, Hsch. **ἀλεάζω·** ἀθροίζω, Id.; cf. ἀλής, ἀλία.

**ἀλεαί,** αἱ, = ἀλαί, *Inscr.Prien.*111 (i B. C.): sg., *SIG*827*D*iii 24 (Delph., ii A. D.).

❋**ἀλε-αίνω,** aor. -ᾱνα Ael.*VH*9.30, (ἀλέα B) *warm, make warm,* Hp. *Epid.*5.57, *Mul.*2.124:—Pass., Archil.ap.Plu.2.954f, etc. II. intr., *grow warm, be warm,* Ar.*Ec.*540, Arist.*PA*656ᵃ22, *Pr.*885ᵇ27; ἀ. πρὸς τὸ πῦρ καθημένη Men.832. **-αντικός,** ή, όν, *fit for warming,* S.E.*P.*3.179.

**ἀλέαντος,** ον, *not ground,* σίνηπι Phlp.*in GA*15.12.

**ἄλεαρ·** ἀλεωρίαν ἢ πολυωρίαν, Hsch.

**ἀλέασθαι, ἀλέασθε,** v. ἀλέομαι. **ἄλεατα,** v. ἀλείατα.

**ἀλεβεβᾶν·** ἐρευνᾶν, Hsch.

**ἀλεγεινός,** ή, όν, Ep. for ἀλγεινός, *causing pain, grievous,* αἰχμή, μάχη, Il.5.658, 18.248; εἰρεσίη Od.10.78; μεριμνάματα Pi.*Fr.*277: c. inf., *troublesome,* ἵπποι ἀλεγεινοὶ δαμήμεναι Il.10.402: neut. as Adv. -εινὸν ἀλαστήσασα Call.*Del.*239. Regul. Adv. -νῶς Q.S.3.557.

**ἀλεγίζω,** Ep. Verb, used only in pres. and impf.: (ἀλέγω):—*trouble oneself about* a thing, *care for, mind, heed,* in Hom. (only in Il.) always with neg., c. gen., τῶν οὔτι μετατρέπῃ οὐδ' ἀλεγίζεις Il.1. 160, al.; τῶν μὲν ἄρ' οὐκ ἀλέγιζε πατήρ 11.80, cf. Hes.*Th.*171: abs., ὁ δ' ἀφήμενος οὐκ ἀλεγίζει οὐδ' ὄθεται Il.15.106; in late Ep. c. acc., ἐγὼ δέ μιν οὐκ ἀλεγίζω Q.S.2.428; rare without neg., ὃς τρία μὲν τίκτει, δύο δ' ἐκλέπει, ἓν δ' ἀλεγίζει Musae.*Fr.*3 D.; ἡρώων ἀ. *IG*14.1389 i 42:—Pass., οὐκ ἀλεγιζόμενος f.l. in *AP*5.17 (Rufin.).—Poet. word, found in Aret.*CA*1.4.

❋**ἀλεγύνω,** Ep. Verb, Hom. only pres. and impf.: aor. ἀλέγῡνα A.R. 1.394, Med. ἀλεγύνατο Emp.137.4: (ἀλέγω):—*heed, care for,* Hom. (only Od.) always c. acc. δαῖτα or δαῖτας, ἄλλας δ' ἀλεγύνετε δαῖτας *find* your meals elsewhere, 1.374; δαῖτ' ἀλέγυνον, of invited guests, 13.23; but δαῖτας ἐΐσας..ἀλεγύνειν *prepare* a meal *for guests,* 11. 186; δολοφροσύνην ἀλεγύνων *h.Merc.*361; ἀγλαΐας ἀλέγυνε ib.476.

❋**ἀλέγω,** Ep. and Lyr., once in A. (lyr.), only pres., *have a care, mind, heed,* usu. neg.: 1. abs., οὐκ ἀ. *have no care,* Il.11.389, Od. 17.390; κύνες οὐκ ἀλέγουσαι Od.19.154: without neg., Λιταὶ ἀλέγουσι κιοῦσαι walk *with good heed,* Il.9.504. II. with a case, 1. c. gen., *heed, care for,* οὐδ' ἀλλήλων ἀλέγουσιν Od.9.115; οὐ γὰρ Κύκλωπες Διὸς.. ἀλέγουσιν ib.275, cf. Simon.37.10; βωμῶν ἀλέγοντες οὐδέν A.*Supp.*752; μακάρων οὐκ ἀλέγοντα θεῶν Call.*Aet.*3.1.65: without neg., ψυχῆς ἀ. ὕπερ A.R.2.634. 2. less freq. c. acc., *regard, respect,* θεῶν ὄπιν οὐκ ἀλέγοντες Il.16.388, Hes.*Op.*251; οἰωνοὺς R.A. 1.145: without neg., νηῶν ὄπλα..ἀλέγουσιν *take care of,* Od.6.268, cf. Pi.*O.*11(10).15, *I.*8(7).51. III. *count among,* Λύκαισον ἐν καμοῦσιν Alcm.32, cf. Pi.*O.*2.78 (Pass.); ἐν ἀθανάτοις ἀ. *IG*14.1389 ii 6. (Commonly deriv. from ἀ- copul., λέγω, *count with,* cf. III.)

**ἄλεε·** φύλασσε, Hsch. **ἀλεεῖ·** ἀδικεῖ, Id.

**ἀλεεινός,** ή, όν, (ἀλέα B) *lying open to the sun, warm, hot,* χώρη Hdt.2.25; νῆσοι Hp.*Vict.*2.37 (Comp.); opp. ψυχεινός, X.*Cyn.*10.6; χιτών Id.*Smp.*4.38; freq. in Arist., ἄνεμος, ὕδωρ, *Mete.*358ᵃ30 (Sup.), *HA*503ᵃ13 (Comp.). Adv. -νῶς Poll.5.111.

**ἀλεείνω** [ᾰ], Ep., only pres. and impf. (exc. aor. ἀλεεῖναι Man.6. 736): (ἀλέα A, ἄλη):—*avoid, shun,* mostly c. acc. rei, θυμὸν ὀπίζομαι ἠδ' ἀλεείνω Od.13.148, al.; κῆρ' ἀλεείνοντες Hes.*Fr.*96.83: abs., ὁ δὲ κερδοσύνῃ ἀλέεινε *evaded* [my question], Od.4.251: less freq. c. acc. pers., ἀλέεινε δ' ὑφορβόν 16.477, cf. *h.Merc.*239 codd.: c. inf., κτεῖναι μέν ῥ' ἀλέεινε Il.6.167; ἀλεξέμεναι ἀλέεινε 13.356, cf. Antim.53:—also in Luc.*Dem.Enc.*23. II. intr., *shrink,* ἄψ τ' ἀλέεινεν A.R.3.650.

**ἀλεεύς,** v. ἁλιεύς. **ἀλέη,** v. ἀλέα.

**ἀλεής,** ές, like ἀλεεινός, *in the warmth,* ὕπνος S.*Ph.*859 (lyr.) (codd., Sch.; ἀδεής cj. Reiske).

**ἄλεθρα** (cod. -αιθ-)· ἄλευρα, Hsch.

**ἀλεία,** ἡ, (ἄλη) *wandering about,* *AB*376, Hsch.

**ἀλεία,** ἡ, = ἁλιεία, v.l. in Arist.*Oec.*1346ᵇ20, cf. Hdn.3.1.5, etc. II. = ἀλεά (cf. ἀλεαί), *SIG*826*E*iv 28 (Delph., ii A. D.).

**ἀλείαντος,** ον, (λεαίνω) *unmasticated,* τροφή Arist.*PA*674ᵇ28.

❋**ἀλείατα,** τά, (ἀλέω A) *wheat-groats, coarse wheaten meal,* Od.20. 108:—ἄλεατα, *Milet.*3 p.163 No.31 (vi B. C.). [-ει- metri gr.]

❋**ἄλειμμ-α,** ατος, τό, (ἀλείφω) *anything used for anointing, unguent,* *fat*, *oil*, Pl.*Ti.*50e, Antiph.154, Arist.*Pr.*884ᵇ37, etc.: pl., Hices.ap. Ath.15.689c, Diocl.*Fr.*141. ⊛ **-άτιον**, τό, Dim. of foreg., Diog.ap. D.L.6.52. **-ατώδης**, ες, *unctuous*, Hp.*Steril.*235.

**ἀλεῖν·** οἰκεῖν, Hsch. (fort. νάειν). **ἀλεινόν·** ἀσθενές, λεπτόν, Id. **ἀλεῖον** ὕδωρ· ἀθροιστὸν καὶ συλλεκτόν, Id. ⊛ **ἀλεῖος·** πένης, Id. (i.e. Ἀλήιος).

**ἀλειπ-τέον**, *one must anoint*, Sor.2.16, Gal.6.229, *Gp.*16.4.1. **-τήρ**, ῆρος, ὁ, = ἀλείπτης, Man.4.178. ⊛ **-τήριον**, τό, *place for anointing* in gymnasia, or in Roman Thermae, used also as *sudatory*, Alex.101, Thphr.*Ign.*13, *IG*5(1).1390.108 (Andania, i B.C.), *CIG* 2782.25, al., Herod.Med.ap.Orib.10.10.1. II. *paint-brush* (Cypr.), Hsch. (-πήριον cod.). III. *unguent*, Erot. s.v. καμμάρω. ⊛ **-της**, ου, ὁ, *anointer*: hence (cf. ἀλείφω I) *trainer* in gymnasia, Arist.*EN* 1106ᵇ1, Plb.27.7.1, *Sammelb.*4224.7 (i B.C.), Plu.2.133b. 2. metaph., οἱ ἀθληταὶ τῆς ἀρετῆς μὴ ψεύσαντες τοὺς ἀλείπτας νόμους Ph. 2.409; *teacher*, τῶν πολιτικῶν Plu.*Per.*4; τῆς κακίας S.E.*M.*1. 298. 3. Lat. *aliptes*, *bath-attendant*, Juv.6.422. ⊛ **-τικός**, ή, όν, *of* or *for the* ἀλείπτης, *trained under him*, Plu.2.619a:—ἁ -κά (sc. τέχνα) *art of training*, Ti.Locr.104a; ἀ. συγγράμματα, treatises thereon, Iamb.*VP*5.25; ἀ. ἐπιμέλεια, kind of *massage*, Sor.2.38. Adv. -κῶς *like an* ἀλείπτης, Sch.Ar.*Eq.*492.

**ἀλειπτός** όν, *anointed*, *smeared*, Hdn.Gr.2.472: ἀλειπτά, τά, *ointments*, Hp.*Liqu.*7.

⊛ **ἄλειπτος** ον, (λείπω) *not left behind*, *unconquered*, πυθαυλης, περιοδονίκης, *IG*14.737,1102, cf. D.Chr.28.9, *PLond.*3.1178.54 (ii A.D.). Adv. -τως *perfectly*, Porph. *in Cat.*124.2.

**ἀλείπ-τρια**, ἡ, fem. of ἀλείπτης, Lys.*Fr.*88 S.; title of plays by Amphis, Antiph., etc. ⊛ **-τρον**, f.l. for ἐξάλειπτρον, q.v.

**ἀλείς**, εἶσα, έν, v. εἴλω.

⊛ **ἄλεισον** [ᾰ], τό, *cup*, *goblet*, = δέπας (Ath.11.783a), χρύσειον Il.11. 774, Od.3.50, al.; περιστείχοντος ἀλείσου Call.*Aet.*1.1.13:—masc. **ἄλεισος** Ar.*Fr.*623. II. *hip-socket*, Marsyas ap.Ath.11.479c.

**ἀλειτεία**, ἡ, = ἀλίτημα, Suid.

**ἀλείτης**, ου, ὁ, *sinner*, of Paris and suitors of Penelope, Il.3.28, Od.20.121:—ἀλείτης τινός *sinner against* one, A.R.1.1338:—fem. **ἀλεῖτις** Hdn.Gr.2.67; cf. ἀλιταίνω, ἀλοιτός.

⊛ **ἀλειτ-ουργησία**, ἡ, *exemption from* λειτουργίαι, late word for Att. ἀτέλεια, Str.13.1.27, *IGRom.*4.295 (Pergam.), *POxy.*1.140.10 (ii/iii A.D.), *Sammelb.*4224.15 (i B.C.), etc.; censured as εὐτελές by Poll.8.156:—also **-ουργία**, ἡ, Benndorf-Niemann *Reise in Lykien* p.78 (Sidyma). ⊛ **-ούργητος**, ον, *free from* λειτουργίαι, ἀ. πασᾶν τᾶν λειτουργιᾶν Decr.Byz.ap.D.18.91; πάσης ὑπουργίας Megasth.ap. D.S.2.40, cf. Din.*Fr.*89.5, *IG*2².682.17, *POxy.*62ᵛ (iii A.D.); ἀ. καὶ ἀνεπίσταθμος *IG*7.2413 (Thebes): metaph., ἡ θεία φύσις ἀ. διατηρείσθω Epicur.*Ep.*2 p.42 U.

⊛ **ἄλειφα**, τό, collat. form of sq., v.l. in Hes.*Th.*553, cf. *SIG*57.34 (Milet., vi/v B.C.), A.*Ag.*322, Call.*Fr.*12, Q.S.14.265.

⊛ **ἄλειφαρ**, ατος, τό, (ἀλείφω) *unguent*, *anointing-oil*, *oil*, *fat*, used in funeral sacrifices, Il.23.170, Od.3.408, etc.; ἄλειφαρ ἀπὸ κέδρου, ἀπὸ σιλλικυπρίων, *oil* of cedar, etc., Hdt.2.87,94; ἀ. ῥόδινον Hp.*Mul.*1. 74. II. *pitch* or *resin*, to seal wine-jars, Theoc.7.147.—Cf. foreg.

**ἀλειφάς**, άδος, ἡ, *blotting out*, *erasure*, πρᾶσιν καθαρὰν ἀπὸ ἀλειφάδος καὶ ἐπιγραφῆς *PRyl.*163.17 (ii A.D.).

**ἀλειφατίτης** ἄρτος, ὁ, bread *baked with oil*, Epich.52.

**ἀλειφεύς**, ὁ, = ἀλείπτης, *Inscr.Prien.*313.716.

**ἀλείφιον·** ᾧ χρῶνται οἱ ἀλεῖπται, Hsch.

**ἀλειφόβιος**, ον, *one that lives by anointing*, contemptuous word for ἀλείπτης, Ar.*Fr.*740. 2. generally, *poor*, Ph.2.537, Hsch.

⊛ **ἀλείφω**, Hdt.3.8, etc.: fut. -ψω Lxx *Ex.*40.15, (ἐξ-) E.*IA*1486, Pl.*R.*386c: aor. ἤλειψα Hom., Att., Ep. ἄλειψα Od.12.177: pf. ἀλήλιφα (ἀπ-) D.52.29:—**Med.**, fut. -ψομαι Th.4.68: aor. ἠλειψάμην Att., Ep. ἀλ- Il.14.171:—**Pass.**, fut. ἀλειφθήσομαι (ἐξ-) D.25.73: aor. 1 ἠλείφθην Hp.*Morb.*4.54, Pl.*Ly.*217c, etc.: aor. 2 ἐξ-ηλίφην v.l. in Pl.*Phdr.*258b, (ἀπ-) D.C.55.3: pf. ἀλήλιμμαι Th.4.68, (ἐξ-, ὑπ-) D.25.70, X.*Oec.*10.6 (-ει- is freq. found in pf. forms in codd.): (ἀ- euph., λιπ-, cf. λίπος):—*anoint the skin with oil*, as was done after bathing, Act. referring to another, Med. to oneself, λοῦσαι κέλετ' ἀμφί τ' ἀλεῖψαι Il.24.582; Hom. elsewh. always adds λίπα or λίπ' ἐλαίῳ (v. sub λίπα), πάντα λοέσσατο καὶ λίπ' ἄλειψεν Od.6.227; λοεσσαμένω καὶ ἀλειψαμένω λίπ' ἐλαίῳ Il.10.577, cf. 14.171, 18.350: later of *anointing for gymnastic exercises*, λίπα μετὰ τοῦ γυμνάζεσθαι ἠλείψαντο Th.1.6; generally, λίπα ἀλείφεσθαι Id.4.68; βακκάρι ῥῖνας Hippon.41; of *anointing* the sick, Men.*Georg.*60, cf. *Ep.Jac.*5. 14. 2. *supply oil* for gymnasts, ἀλειφούσης τῆς πόλεως *CIG* (add.) 1957g (Maced.); ἀ. πανήγυριν, ἔθνη, *Inscr.Magn.*163, *OGI*533.47 (Ancyra); οἱ -όμενοι *youths undergoing gymnastic training*, ib. 339.72 (Sestos), etc.; οἱ ἀ. ἐν τῷ γυμνασίῳ ib.764.5 (Pergam.), al.; ἀλείφεσθαι παρά τινι *to attend* a *gymnastic school*, Arr.*Epict.*1.2. 26. 3. *polish*, τράπεζαν Diph.74; δακτύλιον Thphr.*Char.*21; ἀγάλματα Artem.2.33. 4. metaph., *prepare as if for gymnastics*, *encourage*, *stimulate*, *instigate*, Demad.17, Pl.ap.D.L.4.6; ἐπὶ τὴν πολιτικὴν ἀγωνίαν Phld.*Rh.*2.59 S.; τινὰ ἐπὶ τὸν Κλώδιον App.*BC*2. 16, cf. Plu.*Them.*3; τινὰ κατά τινος Ph.1.549; τινὰ ἐπὶ φαρμακείαν App.*Mac.*11.7:—Pass., τοὺς -ομένους ἐπί τι Phld.*Rh.*2.158 S. II. *daub*, *plaster*, *besmear*, οὔατα ἀλεῖψαι *stop up* ears, Od.12.47,177,200; ἀ. αἵματι Hdt.3.8; μίλτῳ X.*Oec.*10.5; ψιμυθίῳ Pl.*Ly.*217d; κυανῷ Paus.5.11.5.

**ἄλειψις**, εως, ἡ, *anointing*, Hp.*Hum.*10, Arist.*GA*785ᵃ30, Thphr. *Sud.*39, etc.: pl., Perict.ap.Stob.4.28.19. 2. *method* or *custom* *of anointing*, Hdt.3.22. 3. *polishing*, ἀνδριάντων *BGU*362 vii (iii A.D.).

**ἀλείωτος**, ον, *not ground*, Gal.14.47.

**ἀλεκινός·** δυνατός, Cyr., Suid. (cf. ἀλικῖνος).

⊛ **ἀλεκτόρ-ειος**, ον, (ἀλέκτωρ) *of a fowl*, κόπρος Aët.2.118. **-ιδεύς**, έως, ὁ, *chicken*, Ael.*NA*7.47. ⊛ **-ιον**, τό, *poultry-yard*, *IGRom.* 4.921 (Cibyra). ⊛ **-ίς** [ᾰ], ίδος, ἡ, fem. of ἀλέκτωρ, *hen*, Hp.*Int.* 27, *Nat.Puer.*29 (pl.), Epich.152,172, Hecat.58 (pl.):—used by Trag. and Com. acc. to Phryn.207 as generic name, cf. Arist.*HA*544ᵃ32, 614ᵇ10, Diocl.*Fr.*141, Herod.6.100, etc.; Ἀδριαναὶ ἀ., a small kind, Arist.*HA*558ᵇ16. II. = θρὶξ ἡ ἀπὸ τῆς κεφαλῆς τρεφομένη, Hsch. cf. *EM*59.24. **-ίσκος**, ὁ, Dim. of ἀλέκτωρ, *cockerel*, Babr.5.1, Aesop.341.12: as ornament, ἀ. χαλκοῦς Roussel *Cultes Égyptiens* 230 (Delos). **-ον**, ου, τό, = ἀλέκτωρ, *PLond.*3.1259.25 (iv A.D.). **-οφωνία**, ἡ, *cock-crow*, i.e. third watch of night, Str. *Fr.*35, *Ev.Marc.*13.35.

**ἄλεκτος**, ον, *not to be told*, *indescribable*, Hp.*Ep.*13, Pherecr.157, Plb.30.22.12, App.*Hann.*40.

**ἄλεκτρος**, ον, *unwedded*, S.*Ant.*917, Heraclit.*All.*44; ἄλεκτρ' ἄνυμφα γάμων ἁμιλλήματα marriage *that is no marriage*, i.e. unhallowed marriage, S.*El.*492; ἄ. ζόα E.*Tr.*254 (lyr.); ἄλεκτρα γηράσκουσαν, as Adv., S.*El.*962.

**ἀλεκτρύαινα**, ἡ, fem. of ἀλεκτρυών, coined by Ar.*Nu.*666.

**ἀλεκτρυ-όνειος**, ον, *of a fowl*, κρέα Hp.*Int.*9. **-όνιον**, τό, Dim. of ἀλεκτρυών, Ephipp.15.8. **-ονίς**, = ἀλεκτορίς, Sch.Ar. *Nu.*226 (Suid. ἀλεκτορίς), cf. Gal.12.285. **-ονοπώλης**, ου, ὁ, *poulterer*, Poll.7.136. **-ονοτρόφος**, ὁ, *cock-feeder*, Aeschin.Socr. 14:—also **-οτρόφος** (sic), ὁ, *IG*5(1).771 (Sparta). ⊛ **-ονώδης**, ες, *like a cock*, πρὸς ἡδονάς, prob. for -νώδης, Eun.*Hist.*p.266 D. **-οπώλιον**, τό, *poultry-market*, Phryn.Com.13. ⊛ **-ών** [ᾰ], όνος, ὁ, *cock*, Thgn.864, etc., cf. Arist.*HA*536ᵃ28, etc.; ἤδη ἀ. ᾄδόντων *at cock-crow*, Pl.*Smp.*223c. 2. ἀ. Νομάς or Νομαδικός *guinea-fowl*, Luc. *Nav.*23. II. ἡ, *hen*, Ar.*Nu.*663, *Fr.*185, Pl.Com.19.20, Theopomp.Com.9, etc.

**ἀλέκτωρ** (A), [ᾰ], ορος, ὁ, poet. form of ἀλεκτρυών, *cock*, ἕως ἐβόησεν ἀ. Batr.192, cf. Pi.*O.*12.14, Simon.80 B, A.*Ag.*1671, *Eu.*861, Herod.4.12, etc.; later Prose, Arist.*Fr.*347, *PTeb.*140 (i B.C.), Lxx *Pr.*24.66 (30.31), *Ev.Matt.*26.34, al., *IG*3.77: metaph., of a trumpeter, κοινὸς Ἀθηναίων ἀ. Demad.*Fr.*4; of a flute, Ion Trag.39. 2. ἀλέκτορος λόφος *yellow rattle*, *Rhinanthus major*, Plin.*HN*27.40. II. *husband*, *consort*, Tz. *in Lyc.*1094, and so perh. in B.4.8, S.*Fr.*851. (Perh., like ἀκοίτης, ἄλοχος, from ἀ- copul., λέκτρον.)

**ἀλέκτωρ** (B), ορος, ἡ, (ἀ- priv., λέγω) = ἄλεκτρος, Ath.3.98b.

**ἀλέκω** [ᾰ], = ἀλέξω, *ward off*, ἀλέκοις πενίην, prob. for ἀλέγοις, *AP* 6.245 (Diod.):—for fut. ἀλέξω, etc., v. sub ἀλέξω.

**ἀλέλαιον**, τό, *salt in oil*, [Gal.]14.386.

⊛ **ἀλέματος, ἀλεμάτως**, Dor for ἠλεμ-.

**ἄλεν** and **ἀλέν**, v. εἴλω.

**ἀλεξαίθριος**, ον, *screening from chill air*, S.*Fr.*117.

**Ἀλεξανδρ-ίζω**, *to be on Alexander's side*, Apolloph.ap.Phylarch. 46. **-ιστής**, οῦ, ὁ, *partisan of Alexander*, Chares ap.Plu.*Alex.*24.

**Ἀλεξανδροκόλαξ**, ακος, ὁ, *flatterer of Alexander*, Chares ap.Ath.12. 538f.

⊛ **ἀλέξανδρος**, ον, *defending men*, πόλεμος Epigr.ap.D.S.11.14: fem., epith. of Hera, Menaechm.3. II. freq. as pr. n., esp. of Paris in Il., cf. A.*Ag.*61,363.

**Ἀλεξανδρώδης**, ες, *Alexander-like*, Men.924.

**ἀλεξ-άνεμος** [ᾰ], α, ὁ, *averting wind*, applied to Empedocles, Porph.*VP*29. **-άνεμος**, ον, = foreg., Od.14.529, Ph.1.666, Alciphr. 3.41:—also **-ήνεμος**, ον, Eust.1767.43. ⊛ **-ημα**, ατος, τό, *defence*, *guard*, *help*, A.*Pr.*479: c. gen., *remedy for*, ὀδύνης Hp.*Mul.*2.212; *protection* against, κρύους καὶ θάλπους Gal.*UP*12.3; ὑπονοίας Longin. 17.2; ἀ. πρός τι D.H.7.13, Paus.10.18.3. **-ήνωρ**, ορος, ὁ, *aiding man*, as name of physician, Paus.2.11.6 (in Dor. form -άνωρ). **-ησις**, εως, ἡ, *keeping off*, *defence*, πρὸς ἀ. τραπέσθαι Hdt.9.18. 2. *helping*, *assistance*, Hp.*Ep.*16. **-ήτειρα**, ἡ, *AP*9.764 (Paul. Sil.), Nonn.*D.*25.529: fem. of **-ητήρ**, ῆρος, ὁ, *one who keeps off*, ἀ. μάχης *stemmer* of battle, Il.20.396; λοιμοῦ ἀ. *a protector from* plague, A.R.2.519; κακῶν *IG*14.1003.25:—rare in Prose, ταῖς πατρίσιν ἀλεξητῆρες εἶναι X.*Oec.*4.3. II. as Adj., θυμὸς ἀ. Opp.*H.*4. 42. **-ητήριος**, α, ον, *able to keep off*, *defend*, or *help*, esp. as epith. of gods, Ζεὺς ἀ. A.*Th.*8; ξύλον ἀ. club *for defence*, E.*HF*470. 2. ἀλεξητήριον (sc. φάρμακον), τό, *remedy*, *medicine*, Hp.*Acut.*54; *protection*, X.*Eq.*5.6; ἀ. τῆς δηλήσεως *charm against*.., Thphr.*HP*7.13. 4; ἀ. νούσων Nic.*Th.*7, *IG*9(1).881.3 (Corcyra); ὄρη ἀ. ὑετῶν Aristid. *Or.*48(1).11. ⊛ **-ητικός**, ή, όν, *preventive*, ἀγαθά Alex.Aphr. *de An.* 162.16. **-ήτωρ**, ορος, ὁ, = ἀλεξητήρ, Ζεῦ ἀλεξῆτορ S.*OC*143, cf. Apollod.Hist.30.

⊛ **ἀλεξι-άρη** [ᾰ], ἡ, (ἀρή, Ἄρης) *she that guards from death and ruin*, Hes.*Op.*464; ἀ. ῥάμνος wand *that served as amulet*, Nic.*Th.*861:—masc. **ἀλεξιάρης** Hsch. **-βέλεμνος**, ον, *keeping off darts*, *AP*6.81 (Paul. Sil.). ⊛ **-γάμος**, ον, *shunning marriage*, Βάκχαι Nonn.*D.* 40.541. ⊛ **-κάκος**, ον, *keeping off ill* or *mischief*, μῆτις Il.10.20, cf. Hes.*Op.*123 (as v.l.), Ar.*V.*1043, Paus.8.41.8; ῥάμνος Euph.127; τὸ ἀ. τῆς ἐπιστήμης Hierocl. *in CA*12 p.447 M.: c. gen., δίψης ἀ. *AP*6. 170 (Thyill.): epith. of Heracles, Luc.*Alex.*4, etc.; of Hermes, Ar. *Pax*422; ὦ ἀλεξίκακε *save the mark!* Ar.*Nu.*1372; of Zeus, *Tab.Defix. Aud.*26.2 (Crete, iv/iii B.C.), Plu.2.1076b. **-κηπος**, ὁ, title of work on gardening by Nestor, *Gp.*12.16.1, 12.17.16. ⊛ **-λογος**, ον, moting or *supporting discourse*, γράμματα dub. in Critias 2.10, cf. 3382. **-μβροτος,** ον, *protecting mortals*, λόγχη Pi.*N.*8.30; ἀ. πομ- sacred processions *which shield men from ill*, Id.*P.*5.91. **-μορος,** *warding off death*, τρισσοὶ ἀ., i.e. Apollo, Artemis, Athena, S.*OT* 4.

**ἀλέξιον,** τό, = ἀλεξητήριον, Nic.*Th.*702 (v.l. ἀλέξιμον, cf. Phot.), 5, *Al.*4. ❀ **ἀλεξίπονος,** ον, *warding off pain*, S.(?)*Eleg.*7, *Carm. p.*47.10; σοφία Maced.*Pae.*10. **ἄλεξις,** εως, ἡ, *help*, *EM*59. . II. Κῷοι ἄλεξιν τὸν Ἡρακλέα νομίζουσιν Aristid.1.34J.

**ἀλεξι-φάρμᾰκος,** *acting as antidote*, μανίης *against* it, Hp.*Ep.* ). II. ἀλεξιφάρμακον, τό, *antidote*, Thphr.*HP*9.15.7; Ἀλεξι-ιφάρμακα, title of poem by Nic. 2. *charm*, *spell*, Ἐφέσια τοῖς αμοῦσιν..λέγων ἀ. Men.371. 3. generally, *remedy*, τινός *against* tning, Pl.*Lg.*957d, cf. Muson.*Fr.*17p.91H. **-χορος,** ον, *helping* r *favouring the chorus*, ἀοιδαί *IG*3.171^c17.

**ἀλέξω** [ᾰ], Ep. inf. ἀλεξέμεναι, -έμεν Hom., v. infr.: fut. ἀλεξήσω I.9.251: aor. opt. ἀλεξήσειε Od.3.346:—Med., fut. ἀλεξήσομαι Hdt. .81,108.—Besides these tenses (formed as if from ἀλεξέω), we find others formed from **ἀλέκω,** fut. ἀλέξω, aor. ἤλεξα (v. sub ἀπ-αλέξω):—Med., fut. ἀλέξομαι S.*OT*171,539, X.*An.*7.7.3: aor. ἀλέξασθαι Il., Hp.*Salubr.*1, Hdt.7.207, X.*An.*1.3.6, al.:—for aor. 2 ἄλαλκε, ἀλκαθεῖν, v. sub vocc. (Cf. Skt. *rákṣati* 'protect'):—*ward off*, *turn aside*, constructed like ἀμύνω:—c. acc. rei, Ζεὺς τό γ' ἀλεξήσειε Od.3.346: c. acc. rei et dat. pers., Δαναοῖσιν ἀλεξήσειν κακὸν ἦμαρ *will ward* it *off from* them, Il.9.251, cf. 20.315; ἀλλήλοις..ἀλεξέμεναι φόνον αἰπύν 17.365, etc.: c. dat. pers. only, *assist*, *defend*, ἀλεξέμεν ἀλλήλοισιν Il. 3.9, cf. 5.779, al., X.*Cyr.*4.3.2: abs., *lend aid*, Il.1.590:—Med., ἀλέξασθαι *keep off from oneself*, κύνας ἠδὲ καὶ ἄνδρας Il.13.475, cf. Hdt.7. 207; ἀλέξεσθαι περί τινι or τινος, A.R.4.551,1488: abs., *defend oneself*, Il.11.348, 15.565, Archil.66, Hdt.1.211, 2.63, al., Hp. l.c., S. *OT*539, X.*Cyr.*1.5.13: c. dat. instrum., οὐδ' ἔνι φροντίδος ἔγχος, ᾧ τις ἀλέξεται S.*OT*171. 2. in Med., also, *recompense*, *requite*, τοὺς εὖ καὶ κακῶς ποιοῦντας ἀλεξόμενος X.*An.*1.9.11.—Not in A. or E. (exc. ἀπ-).

❀ **ἀλέομαι** [ᾰλ], contr. **ἀλεῦμαι** Thgn.575, pres. part. ἀλευόμενοι Hes. *Op.*535 (v.l.), ἀλευμένη Semon.7.61: impf. ἀλέοντο (ἐξ-) Il.18.586:—chiefly used by Hom. in aor. ἀλευάμην, v. infr.; inf. ἀλέασθαι, -εύασθαι, Hes.*Op.*734,505; subj. ἀλεύεται Od.14.400; part. ἀλευάμενος 9. 277, Thgn.400. (Perh. from same Root as ἄλη, ἀλάομαι: ἀλεϝ- as aor. shows):—*avoid*, *shun*, c. acc. rei, ἔγχεα δ' ἀλλήλων ἀλεώμεθα Il. 6.226, cf. 13.184; ἐμὸν ἔγχος ἄλευαι 22.285; ἀλεύατο κῆρα μέλαιναν 3.360; Διὸς δ' ἀλεώμεθα μῆνιν 5.34; ὄφρα τὸ κῆτος..ἀλέαιτο 20.147; κακὸν..τό κεν οὔτις..ἀλέαιτο Od.20.368; μύθους μὲν ὑπερφιάλους ἀλέασθε 4.774: rarely c. acc. pers., θεοὺς ἢ δειδίμεν ἢ ἀλέασθαι 9.274: c. inf., *avoid* doing, λίθου δ' ἀλέασθαι ἐπαυρεῖν Il.23.340; ἀλεύεται (Ep. subj.) ἠπεροπεύειν Od.14.400. 2. abs., *flee for one's life*, τὸν μὲν ἀλευάμενον τὸν δὲ κτάμενον Il.5.28; οὔτε..φυγέειν δύνατ' οὔτ' ἀλέασθαι 13.436; μή πως..ἀλέηται Od.4.396.

❀ **ἀλεός,** όν, = ἀλεεινός, Hsch. II. = ἠλεός, Hdn.Gr.2.909, *EM* 59.45.

**ἀλεόσσω·** ματαΐζω, Hsch.; cf. ἀλεώσσω.

**ἁλεότης,** ητος, ἡ, (ἁλής) *assemblage*, Hp ap.Gal.19.75.

**ἀλεόφρων,** ον, gen. ονος, = Homer's φρένας ἠλεός, Hsch., *EM*59. 45.

**ἀλεπαδνόν·** ἄζευκτον, Hsch. **ἀλέπεσσι·** στέατι, Id.

**ἀλεπίδωτος,** ον, *without scales*, σελάχη Arist.*PA*$697^{a}7$: to be read for ἄλεπος, Ael.*NA*12.27, and prob. for ἀλέπιδος, Ph.2.352.

❀ **ἀλέπιστος,** ον, *not scaled*, *unscaled*, Archestr.*Fr.*45.8B. II. *unpeeled*, καρπός *Gp.*10.11.1; of flax, *not scutched*, Sch.Ar.*Lys.* 737.

**ἀλέρα,** dub. in Hdn.Gr.1.260. **ἀλέρον·** κόπρον, Hsch.

**ἄλ-εσις,** εως, ἡ, (ἀλέω) *grinding*, *Gp.*2.32.1. **-εσμα,** ατος, τό, *anything ground*, ἐλαιῶν *EM*216.22. **-εσμός,** ὁ, *grinding*, J.*AJ* 3.10.5. **-εσούριος,** ὁ, a fish, = καλλιώνυμος, *EM*59.52; also a shell-fish, Hsch. **-εστέον,** *one must grind*, Dsc.5.88: pl. -τέα Poll.1.226. ❀ **-εστρον,** τό, *cost of grinding*, *POxy.*739.6 (i A.D.).

❀ **ἀλέ-της,** ου, ὁ, *grinder*, ὄνος *GDI*4992 (Gortyn, v B.C.), cf. X.*An.* 1.5.5. **-τικός,** ή, όν, *for grinding*, [μηχανή] *PRyl.*321.5 (ii A.D.). ❀ **-τός,** ὁ, *grinding*, Plu.*Ant.*45; cf. ἀλητός. **-τρεύω,** fut. -εύσω, Lyc.159, strengthd. from ἀλέω, *grind*, Od.7.104, Hes.*Fr.* 264, A.R.4.1095, Babr.129. **-τρίβᾰνος** [ῑ], ὁ, (τρίβω) (Asiatic for δοῖδυξ, acc. to Crat.Mall.ap.Sch.Ar. l.c.), *pestle*, Ar.*Pax*259, al. ❀ **-τρίς,** ίδος, ἡ, *female slave who grinds corn*, γυνὴ ἀλετρίς Od. 20.105, cf. *Lyr.Adesp.*21, Call.*Del.*242, Ph.2.102, Zos.3.22. 2. at Athens, *one of the noble maidens who prepared meal* for offering-cakes, Ar.*Lys.*643, Eust.1885.9. **-τροπόδιον,** τό, i.e. ἀλεκτρο-, late name for the *constellation Orion*, interp. in Anon.*II Intr.Arat.*p.116 Maass. ❀ **-τών,** ῶνος, ὁ, = ἀλέτης, ἀ. ὄνος *upper millstone*, Alex. 13; also ἀλετών alone, Dieuchid.7.

**ἀλετώρια·** ἀσεβῆ, πονηρά, ἀθέμιστα, ἁμαρτήματα, Hsch.

**ἀλεύκαντος,** ον, *not growing white*, τρίχες *Cat.Cod.Astr.*8(3).157, cf. *Gloss.*

**ἀλεύρειν·** ἀφεστάναι, Hsch.

**ἀλεύρινος,** ον, *made of* ἄλευρον, ἄρτος, σταῖς, Dieuch.ap.Orib.4.5. 1,5.

**ἀλευρίτης** ἄρτος, ὁ, bread *of wheaten flour* (ἄλευρα), Diph.Siph.ap. Ath.3.115c, Philistion ib.d; πυροί Ath.Med.ap.Orib.1.2.2.

❀ **ἀλευροδοῦντες,** οἱ, kind of *wheaten cakes*, dub. in Anticl.20.

**ἀλευρό-κλεψ,** ὁ, *flour-thief*, Hdn.Gr.1.246. **-μαντεῖον,** τό, *divination from flour*, Oenom.ap.Eus.*PE*5.25. **-μαντις,** εως, ὁ, *one that divines from flour*, Hsch.; epith. of Apollo, Phot.

❀ **ἄλευρον** (A), [ᾰ], τό, mostly in pl. **ἄλευρα,** (ἀλέω A) = ἀλείατα, *wheat meal* (opp. ἄλφιτα *barley-meal*), Hdt.7.119; ἐκ μὲν τῶν κριθῶν ἄλφιτα σκευαζόμενοι, ἐκ δὲ τῶν πυρῶν ἄλευρα Pl.*R.*372b, cf. *Epin.*975b, X.*An.*1.5.6, Arist.*Pr.*$863^{b}2$: in sg., Ar.*Fr.*50, Sotad.Com.1.24, Arist.*Pr.*$927^{a}11$, Theoc.14.7. 2. generally, *meal*, ἄ. κρίθινον Dsc. 1.72; τήλινον 3.40, cf. 2.102; made from dried sorbs, 1.120.

**ἄλευρον** (B)· τάφος (Cypr.), Hsch.

**ἀλευρο-ποιέω,** *make into flour*, *POxy.*1454.9 (ii A.D.), *EM*62. 54. **-ποιΐα,** ἡ, Eust.1835.42.

**ἄλευρος,** ἡ, = ἄλευρον, *Et.Gud.z.*

**ἀλευρόττησις,** εως, ἡ, (cf. δια-ττάω) *flour-sieve*, Poll.6.74, *AB* 382. II. *flour sifted*, *fine flour*, Suid.

**ἀλευρώδης,** ες, *like flour*, Gal.12.212; ἄρτος Lyc.(?)ap.Orib.9. 26.8.

**ἄλευστος,** ον, (λεύσσω) *unseen*, Hsch.

**ἀλεύω,** used rarely by Trag. in lyr. passages as Act. of ἀλεύομαι (v. ἀλέομαι), *remove*, *keep far away*, imper. ἄλευ' ἆ Δᾶ A.*Pr.*567: fut. ἀλεύσω S.*Fr.*993: aor. imper., ἄλευσον ἀνδρῶν ὕβριν A.*Supp.*528, cf. *Th.*141; ἰὼ θεοὶ..κακὸν ἀλεύσατε ib.87.

**ἀλεφάτισον·** ἄλειψον, Hsch.

❀ **ἀλέω** (A), [ᾰ]: impf. ἤλουν Pherecr.10.1: aor. ἤλεσα Id.183, Hp.*Fist.* 7, *Steril.*230, etc.; Ep. ἄλεσσα (κατ-) Od.20.109: pf. ἀλήλεκα *AP*11. 251 (Nicarch.):—Pass., pf. ἀλήλεσμαι Hp.ap.Gal.19.76, Hdt.7.23; ἀλήλεμαι Th.4.26, Amph.9: aor. ἠλέσθην Dsc.1.120:—*grind*, *bruise*, Hom. only in compd. κατ-αλέω, q.v.; ἤλουν τὰ σιτία Pherecr. l.c.; βίος ἀληλεμένος *civilized* life, in which one uses *ground* corn and not raw fruits, Amph. l.c.; ἄλει, μύλα, ἄλει *grind*, mill, *grind! Carm. Pop.*43: metaph., ὀψὲ θεῶν ἀλέουσι μύλαι, ἀλέουσι δὲ λεπτά Poet.ap. S.E.*M.*1.287.

***ἀλέω** (B), only in Med. ἀλέομαι, q.v.

❀ **ἀλεωρή,** Att. -ρά, ἡ, (ἀλέομαι) *escape*, Il.24.216; ἀ. τινα εὑρέσθαι Hdt.9.6. 2. *place of shelter*, Opp.*H.*1.790. 3. c. gen., *defence* or *shelter from*, δηΐων ἀνδρῶν ἀ., of palisade, Il.12.57; of breastplate, 15.533; σκευὴν βελέων ἀ. (mock heroic) Ar.*V.*615; τὴν περὶ τὸ σῶμα ἀ. Arist.*PA*$687^{a}29$; of an animal's shell, etc., ib.$679^{b}28$, cf. *HA*$488^{b}$ 10; τῆς περὶ τοὺς ἱέρακας ἕνεκα ἀ. ib.$613^{b}11$; ἀ. παρέχειν, ποιεῖν, Hp. *Praec.*7, D.S.3.34.

**ἀλ⟨ε⟩ώσσω·** μωραίνω, Hsch.

❀ **ἄλη** [ᾰ], ἡ, *wandering* or *roaming* without home or hope of rest, Od.10.464, E.*Or.*56 (pl.); θεία ἄ., as etym. of ἀλήθεια, Pl.*Cra.*421b; in later Prose, Plu.*Mar.*45, Hld.7.6 (pl.), etc.; in pl., of the blood in fever, Hp.*Flat.*8. 2. *wandering of mind*, *distraction*, E.*Med.* 1285. II. Act., πνοαὶ βροτῶν ἄλαι winds *that keep* men *wandering*, A.*Ag.*194.

❀ **ἁλή,** ἡ, only pl. ἁλαί *salt-works*, ἁλαὶ τῶν ὀρυκτῶν ἁλῶν Str.12.3. 39; Ἅλυς..ὠνόμασται ἀπὸ τῶν ἁλῶν ἃς παραρρεῖ Id.12.3.12; ἁλάς, ἁλαῖς shd. be read for ἄλλας, ἄλλαις D.H.3.41, cf. 2.55, *PRyl.*92.22 (iii A.D.).

❀ **ἁληγός,** όν, *carrying salt*, Plu.2.685e.

**ἁληδόν·** ἀθρόως, ἐξαίφνης, Hsch.

❀ **ἀληθάργητος,** ον, *free from lethargy*, *energetic*, εὐεργέτης *CIG*2804 (Aphrod.); γυνή *JRS*2.92 (Antioch. Pisid.), cf. Hsch. s.v. ἀλήστων.

❀ **ἀλήθ-εια** [ᾰλ], ἡ, Dor. **ἀλάθεια** (also ἀλαθείᾱ B.12.204); ἀλάθεα Alc.57, Theoc.29.1 is neut. pl. of ἀλᾱθής; Ep. (and Early Att. acc. to Hdn.Gr.2.454) **ἀληθείᾱ**; Ion. **ἀληθείη**: I. *truth*, opp. *lie* or *mere appearance*: 1. in Hom. only opp. *a lie*, freq. in phrase ἀληθείην καταλέξαι Il.24.407, al.; ἀ. ἀποειπεῖν 23.361; παιδὸς πᾶσαν ἀ. μυθεῖσθαι to tell whole *truth* about the lad, Od.11.507; ἀλάθει' ἀτρεκής Pi.*N.*5.17, cf. B. l.c.; prov., οἶνος καὶ ἀ. '*in vino veritas*', Alc. l.c., etc.; ἁπλᾶ γάρ ἐστι τῆς ἀ. ἔπη A.*Fr.*176, cf. E.*Ph.*469; χρᾶσθαι τῇ ἀ. Hdt.1.116; εἰπεῖν τὴν ἀ. Id.6.69; ἡ ἀ. περί τινος Th.4.122, S. *Tr.*91; ἀ. ἔχειν to be *true*, Arist.*Pol.*$1281^{a}42$: pl., ταῖς ἀ. χρῆσθαι Isoc.9.5; τὰς ἀ. λέγειν Men.87,925; τὰς ἀ. ἀκοῦσαι τῶν γενομένων Alcid.*Od.*13:—Ἀλήθεια or περὶ Ἀληθείας, title of works by Protag., Pl.*Tht.*161c, *Cra.*391c; by Antipho Soph., *POxy.*1364, cf. Hermog. *Id.*2.11, etc. 2. after Hom. also *truth*, *reality*, opp. *appearance*, σὺν ἀλαθείᾳ καλῶν B.3.96; ἡ ἀ. τῶν πραχθέντων Antipho 2.4.1; τῶν ἔργων ἡ ἀ. Th.2.41; μιμήματα ἀληθείας Pl.*Plt.*300c:—in adverb. usages, τῇ ἀ. *in very truth*, Th.4.120, etc.; ταῖς ἀ. Isoc.15.283, cf. Philem.130, Plb.10.40.5, Babr.75.20; rarely (without the Art.) ἀληθείᾳ Pl.*Prt.*343d:—with Preps., ἐν τῇ ἀ. Pl.*La.*183d; ἐπὶ τῆς ἀληθείας καὶ τοῦ πράγματος *in truth and reality*, D.21.72; ἐπ' ἀληθείᾳ *for the sake of truth*, A.*Supp.*628, Ar.*Pl.*891; also, *according to truth and nature*, Theoc.7.44:—μετ' ἀληθείας X.*Mem.*2.1.27, D.2.4:—κατὰ τὴν ἀ. Isoc.1.2.46, etc.; κατ' ἀλήθειαν Arist.*Pol.*$1278^{b}33$, etc.:—ξὺν ἀληθείᾳ A.*Ag.*1567:—πρὸς ἀλήθειαν D.S.5.67, etc. 3. *real war*, opp. *exercise* or *parade*, Plb.10.20.4, al.; ἐπ' αὐτῆς τῆς ἀ. Id.1.21. 3. 4. *true event*, *realization* of dream or omen, Hdt.3.64, Damon ap.Sch.Ar.*Pl.*1003. II. of persons, *truthfulness*, *sincerity*, Hdt. 1.55; ἀλαθείᾳ φρενῶν A.*Ag.*1550, cf. Pl.*R.*331c, Arist.*EN*$1108^{a}$ 20. III. Ἀ. personified, Emp.1, Parm.1.29, etc. IV. *symbol of truth*, *jewel* worn by Egyptian high-priest, D.S.1.48,75, Ael. *VH*14.34: of the Thummim, Lxx *Le.*8.8. **-ευσις,** εως, ἡ, *possession of truth*, S.E.*M.*7.394. **-ευτής,** οῦ, ὁ, *truth-speaking person*, ἀ. λόγων Max.Tyr.21.6. **-ευτικός,** ή, όν, *truthful*, *frank*, *candid*, Arist.*EN*$1127^{a}24$, al.; τὸ ἀ. Hierocl. *in CA*2p.422M. Adv. -κῶς Eust.385.6, etc. **-εύω,** fut. -εύσω X.*Mem.*1.1.5, al.:—*speak truth*,

A.*Th.*562, Hp.*Prog.*15, Pl.*R.*589c; περί τι Id.*Tht.*202b: with neut. Adj., ἀ. πάντα *speak truth* in all things, Batr.14; πολλὰ ἀ. X.*An.*4.4.15; τὰς δέκα ἡμέρας ἠλήθευσε he *rightly foretold*.., ib.5.6.18; ἀ. τοὺς ἐπαίνους *prove* their praises *true*, Luc.*Ind.*20; τοὔνομα 'make good', Them.*Or.*1.4c. **2.** of things, *to be, prove true*, σημεῖα Hp.*Prog.*25:—Pass., *to be fulfilled*, of conditions, ἐπὶ τούτοις -ομένοις X.*Cyr.*4.6.10, freq. in Arist.:—Act. of reasoners, *arrive at truth*, Id.*Metaph.*1062$^{a}$25:—Pass., ὁ λόγος -εύεται *is in accordance with truth*, *Top.*132$^{b}$4, al.; ἀληθεύεσθαι κατά τινος *to be truly predicated of*.., ib.132$^{a}$31, al.: fut. Med. in same sense, *EN*1100$^{a}$35, al. ⊛**-ής** [ᾰ], Dor. **ἀλᾱθής**, ές, (λήθω, = λανθάνω: ἀληθὲς τὸ μὴ λήθῃ ὑποπῖπτον *EM*62.51):—*unconcealed*, so *true, real*, opp. *false, apparent*: **I.** Hom., opp. ψευδής, in phrases ἀληθέα μυθήσασθαι, εἰπεῖν, ἀγορεύειν, ἀληθὲς ἐνισπεῖν, Il.6.382, Od.13.254, 3.254,247, al.; in Hdt. and Att. τὸ ἀληθές, by Trag. crasis τἀληθές, Ion. τὠληθές (Hdt.6.68, 69), or τὰ ἀληθῆ, by crasis τἀληθῆ, etc.; ἀληθέϊ λόγῳ χρᾶσθαι Hdt.1.14, etc.; οἱ ἀληθέϊ λόγῳ βασιλέες 1.120; ἀληθεστάτη πρόφασις Th.1.23. **2.** of persons, etc., *truthful, honest* (not in Hom., v. infr.), ἀ. νόος Pi.*O.*2.92; κατήγορος A.*Th.*439; κριτής Th.3.56; οἶνος ἀ. '*in vino veritas*', Pl.*Smp.*217e; ὁ μέσος ἀ. τις Arist.*EN*1108$^{a}$20. **3.** of oracles, *true, unerring*, ἀλαθέα μαντίων θῶκον Pi.*P.*11.6, cf. S.*Ph.*993, E.*Ion*1537; of dreams, A.*Th.*710. **II.** of qualities or events, *true, real*, φίλος E.*Or.*424; ἀ. τὸ πραχθέν Antipho 1.6; *genuine*, ἀ. εἶναι δεῖ τὸ σεμνόν, οὐ κενόν Men.596. **2.** *realizing itself, coming to fulfilment*, ἀρά A.*Th.*944. **III.** Adv. ἀληθῶς, Ion. -θέως, *truly*, Simon.5.1, Hdt.1.11, al., A.*Supp.*315, etc. **b.** *actually, in reality*, γένος τόδε Ζηνός ἐστιν ἀ. ib.585; ἀ. οὐδὲν ἐξηκασμένα Id.*Ag.*1244, cf. Th.1.22, etc.; τὴν ἀ. μουσικήν (sc. οὖσαν) Antiph.209.6:—ὡς ἀ. *in the true way, really*, E.*Or.*739, Pl.*Phd.*63a, etc.; ἡ μὲν γὰρ ὡς ἀ. μήτηρ D.21.149: Comp. -εστέρως Pl.*R.*347e, -έστερον Antipho 3.3.4: Sup. -έστατα X.*Mem.*4.8.1. **2.** neut. as Adv., proparox. ἄληθες; *indeed? really?* ironically, S.*OT*350, *Ant.*758, E.*Cyc.*241, Ar.*Ra.*840, *Av.*174. **3.** τὸ ἀληθές *truly*, Ion. τὠληθές Herod.7.70. **B.** *not forgetting, careful*, γυνὴ χερνῆτις ἀ. Il.12.433, cf. Nonn.*D.*24.233:—the sense *honest* is post-Hom. **-ίζω**, *dye with genuine purple*, *PHolm.*18.6. **II.** Med. -ίζομαι, = ἀληθεύω, Hdt.1.136, 3.72, Plu.2.230b, Alciphr.3.39, 59. **-ικός**, ή, όν, = ἀληθινός, Ps.-Callisth.1.4.

**ἀληθινο-λογέω**, *speak truly*, Phld.*Rh.*1.286, 2.158S. (Pass.). **-λογία**, ἡ, *speaking truth*, Pl.ap.Poll.2.124, Plb.12.26$^{D}$.1.

**ἀληθινόν**· τὸ κοπανιστήριον, Hsch.

⊛**ἀληθινό-πινος** (-πειν- Pap.), ον, *with genuine patina*, ἐνώτια *CPR* 22.6 (ii A.D.). **-πόρφυρος**, ον, *of genuine purple*, *POxy.*114 (ii/iii A.D.).

⊛**ἀληθῑνός**, ή, όν, *agreeable to truth*: **1.** of persons, *truthful, trusty*, στράτευμα, φίλοι, X.*An.*1.9.17, D.9.12, cf. Posidipp.26. Adv. -νῶς, φιλεῖν X.*Smp.*9.5: Sup. -ώτατα Plb.39.37. **2.** of things, *true, genuine*, Pl.*R.*499c, Arist.*EN*1107$^{a}$31 (Comp.); esp. of purple, πορφυρίς X.*Oec.*10.3, cf. *Edict.Diocl.*24.6; ἰχθύς Amph.26; πέλαγος Men.65; λόγος Id.*Sam.*114; τὰ ἀ. *real objects*, opp. τὰ γεγραμμένα, Arist.*Pol.*1281$^{b}$12; of persons, ἐς ἀ. ἄνδρ' ἀποβῆναι to turn out a *genuine* man, Theoc.13.15: Astron., *true* (opp. φαινόμενος *apparent*), of risings and settings, Autol.1 *Def.*1, al. **II.** Adv. -νῶς *truly, really*, opp. γλίσχρως, Isoc.5.142; ζῶντα ἀ. *really* alive, Pl.*Ti.*19b; ἀ. γεγάμηκεν; Antiph.221. **2.** *honestly, straightforwardly*, *OGI* 223.17 (Erythrae).

**Ἀληθιών**, ῶνος, sc. μήν, month at Iasos, *Leipz.Stud.*7.397.

⊛**ἀληθο-επής**, ές, = ἀψευδής, Hsch. **-μαντις**, εως ὁ, ἡ, *prophet of truth*, A.*Ag.*1241, Ph.2.176. **-μῡθέω**, *speak truth*, Democr.225. **-μῡθος**, ον, *speaking truth*, Id.44.

**ἀληθ-ορκέω**, *swear truly*, Chrysipp.*Stoic.*2.63. **-οσύνη**, ἡ, poet. for ἀλήθεια, Thgn.1226. **-ότης**, ητος, ἡ, = ἀλήθεια, Ph.1.111, S.E.*M.*8.472. **-ουργής**, ές, *acting truly*, Heraclit.*All.*67 (Comp.).

**ἀλήθω** [ᾰ], = Att. ἀλέω (A), mostly pres. (and impf., Lxx *Nu.*11.8), Hp.*Vict.*1.20, Thphr.*CP*4.12.13, D.S.3.13, *AP*11.154 (Lucill.), *POxy.*908.26 (ii A.D.); prob. in Herod.2.20 (sens. obsc.): aor. part. Pass. ἀλησθέν *Gp.*9.19.7.

**Ἀλήιον πεδίον**, τό, (ἄλη) lit. *land of wandering*, in Lycia or Cilicia, κὰπ πεδίον τὸ Ἀλήιον οἶος ἀλᾶτο..πάτον ἀνθρώπων ἀλεείνων (with play on ἀλᾶτο, ἀλεείνων) Il.6.201, cf. Hdt.6.95.

**ἀλή'ιον**, τό, v. ἀλήσιον. **ἀλήιος**, ον, (λήιον) *without cornlands, poor in lands*, or (ληΐς) *without booty*, opp. πολυλήιος, Il.9.125, 267. **ἀληίς**· ἄκλοπος, ἀπόρθητος, Hsch. **ἄληκτος** (A), ον, (λήγω) *unceasing*, πένθος *IG*14.2126.6; δίψα Ph.1.381, al.; *interminable*, βυβλίον Demetr.Lac.*Herc.*1061.7. Adv. ἀλήκτως Ph.2.420; ἀ. ἔχειν τινός Eun.*VS*p.458.26B. **ἄληκτος** (B), ον, = ἄδαστος, Eust.64.40; cf. ἄλλ-. **ἀλήλεκα, -λεμαι** or **-λεσμαι**, v. ἀλέω (A). **ἀλήλῐφα, -λιμμαι**, v. ἀλείφω. **ἄλημα** [ᾰλ], ατος, τό, (ἀλέω A) *fine meal*: metaph., of a *fine-witted, wily knave*, as Ulysses, S.*Aj.*381,390 (lyr.), cf. *Ant.*320 (v.l.). **II.** (ἀλάομαι), = ὁδοιπορία, Hsch. **ἀλήμεναι, ἀλῆναι**, v. εἴλω.

**ἀλημ-οσύνη**, ἡ, (ἄλη) *wandering about*, Man.4.34, D.P.716: in pl., A.R.2.1260 codd., Man.6.226. ⊛**-ων** [ᾰ], ονος, ὁ, ἡ, (ἀλάομαι) *wanderer, rover*, ἀλήμονες ἄνδρες Od.19.74; of planets, *AP*9.25 (Leon.): abs., Od.17.376.—Ep. word.

**ἀλημώτων**· ἀφυλάκτων, Hsch. (leg. ἀλήμπτων· εὐφυλάκτων).

⊛**ἀληνής**· μαινόμενος, Hsch.; prob. l. in Semon.7.44.

**ἄληνον** ἔλαιον, *oil of almonds*, Aët.7.69.

⊛**ἀλήπεδον**, τό, = Ἀλήιον πεδίον, Lyc.681.

**ἀλήπορον**· λευκὸν τὸ ἄνθος, Hsch.

**ἄληπτος**, ον, *not to be laid hold of, hard to catch*, Plu.*Sert.*16, Poll 169, etc.; ἄ. τοῖς ἐχθροῖς J.*AJ*5.8.11: in Comp. ἀληπτότερος Th.1.82,143. **II.** *incomprehensible*, Phld.*Mus.*p.54K., Plu.*Nic.* al. **III.** in Stoic philos., ἄληπτα, τά, things *not to be ma matter of choice*, opp. ληπτά, *Stoic.*3.34.

**ἀλήπτωρ**· ἱερεύς, Hsch.

**ἁλής**, ές, Ion., = Att. ἀθρόος, *thronged, crowded, in a mass*, πολλ ἁλέα Hp.*Mul.*1.5, cf. Hdt.1.133; ὡς ἁλέες εἴησαν οἱ Ἕλληνες Hdt. 15, cf. 7.104, al.: sg. with collective nouns, ἁ. γενομένη πᾶσα ἡ Ἑλλ 7.157; ἁ. ἐὼν ὁ στρατός ib.236; ἁ. τροφή, αἷμα, Hp.*Vict.*2.45, *Mor* 2.4. Adv. -έως prob. in Hp.*Mul.*1.36: neut. pl. as Adv., ἐκχέουσιν τ οὖρον ἁλέα Aret.*SD*2.2. [ᾱ, Call.*Fr.*86; ἀλέα λέσχην is v.l. Hes.*Op* 493.] (*sm*-ϝαλής, cf. ϝαλῆναι.)

**ἀλησθύω** or **-ίω**, = ἀλυσθαίνω, Hp.*Mul.*2.124 codd. **ἀλήσθω** γῆ σπορίμη, κτηνοτρόφος, Hsch.

⊛**ἀλησία**, ἡ, = ἀσυλία, *EM*62.41: in pl., *truce*, Hsch. **ἀλήσιον** τό, (ἀλέω A) *meal*, Hsch.: Lacon. ἀλή'ιον *IG*5(1).1316 (Thalamae, B.C.).

**ἄλησις**, εως, ἡ, (ἀλάομαι) = ἄλη, of the course of the sun, Arat.319. **II.** (ἀλέω A) *grinding*, *Gp.*9.19.7.

**ἀλησμόνητος**, ον, *unforgotten*, *IG*3.3446.

**ἀλῄστευτος**, ον, *unpillaged*, J.*AJ*18.9.4, Arr.*Epict.*4.1.93.

**ἄληστος**, ον, = ἄλαστος (q.v.); *unforgettable*, κακά Ph.1.320. **II.** Act., *unforgetting*, μνήμη Id.1.619, al.

**ἀλητ-εία**, Dor. **ἀλᾱτεία**, ἡ, *wandering, roaming*; δυσπλάνοις ἀλατείαις A.*Pr.*900 (lyr.); ἀλατείᾳ βιότου ταλαίφρων E.*Hel.*523 (lyr.), cf. 934; in later Prose, Vett.Val.4.18, prob. in Ph.1.658. **-εύω**, Dor. ἀλατ-, fut. -σω E.*Heracl.*515:—*wander, roam*, mostly of beggars, Od.17.501, al., *AP*9.12 (Leon.); of hunters, Od.12.330; of exiles, E. l. c., *Hipp.*1048, Phalar.*Ep.*95; θνητὸν βίον ἀ. Ph.1.463. **-ήρ**, ῆρος, ὁ, name of a *dance* in Ithaca and at Sicyon, Aristox.Hist.*Fr.*50. ⊛**-ης** [ᾰ], ου, Dor. **ἀλάτας**, α, ὁ; voc. ἀλῆτα S.*OC*1096, Dor. ἀλᾶτα ib.165: (ἀλάομαι):—*wanderer, vagabond*, Hom. only in Od., always of beggars (17.420, al.); in Trag. also of exiles, A.*Ag.*1282, *Ch.*1042, S.*OC*50,746, E.*Heracl.*224, *Supp.*280 (lyr.):—τὸν μακρῶν ἀλάταν πόνων *one who has wandered* in long labour, S.*Aj.*888. **2.** as Adj., *vagrant, roving*, πόδ' ἀλάταν E.*El.*139 (anap.); βίος ἀλήτης Hdt.3.52; in later Prose, ἄνδρες D.Chr.1.9:—so also fem. **ἀλῆτις**, ιδος, D.P.490 (as v.l.); name of song in honour of Erigone, Ath.14.618e, Poll.4.55, Hsch. s.v.; cf. ἐώρα II. **-ικός**, ή, όν, *appropriate to a wanderer*, D.Chr.7.1.

**ἀλητοειδής**, ές, *like meal, meal-coloured*, Hp.*Coac.*590.

**ἄλητον**, τό, *meal*, Hp.*Art.*36, Philotim.ap.Orib.4.10.1; ἀ. κριθῆς Aret.*CA*1.1: pl., Sophr.39; ἀλήτων κἀλφίτων Rhinth.3.

**ἀλητός** (A), ὁ, poet. for ἀλετός, εἰς ἀ. ἐπράθη was sold *to grind* in the mill, Babr.29.1.

**ἀλητός** (B), ή, όν, Adj. *ground*, Archig.ap.Orib.8.1.33.

⊛**ἀλητύς**, ύος, ἡ, Ion. for ἄλη, Call.*Fr.*277, Man.3.379.

⊛**ἀλήτωρ**, ορος, ὁ, = ἱερεύς, Hsch. **ἄλθα**· θερμασία (i. e. ἀλέα) ἢ θεραπεία, Id.

**ἀλθαία**, ἡ, *marsh mallow, Althaea officinalis*, Thphr.*HP*9.15.5, Aret.*CA*1.6. **2.** = δενδρομαλάχη, Gal.12.67. **3.** = ὠκιμοειδές, Ps.-Dsc.4.28. (For **ἀλθαιᾶτις**, ἡ, *EM*63.12, ἀλθαία τις should be read.)

**ἀλθ-αίνω**, *heal*, Lyc.582, Timae.15: fut. ἀλθήσω Nic.*Th.*587: aor. ἤλθησα ib.496, *Al.*112: aor. 2 inf. ἀλθεῖν· ὑγιάζειν Hp.ap.Gal.19.76:—Pass., *become whole and sound*, pres., ἐπὴν τὸ ἕλκος ἀλθαίνηται Hp.*Morb.*2.33: Ep. impf. or aor. ἄλθετο χείρ Il.5.417; ἀλθομένη Q.S.9.475 (nisi leg. ἀλδομένη): fut. ἀλθήσομαι (ἀπ-) Il.8.405: aor. ἀλθεσθῆναι (συν-) Hp.*Art.*14:—later aor. Med. ἠλθησάμην Poet. *de herb.*44. **-εῖναι**· χαλεπῆναι, Hsch. **-εξις**, εως, ἡ, *healing, cure*, Hp.*Fract.*10, *Art.*34, cf. Aret.*CA*2.2:—fut. Med. **ἀλθέξομαι** (as if from *ἀλθέσσω) = ἀλθήσομαι, *SD*2.8. **-εστήρια**, τά, *remedies*, Nic.*Th.*493. **-εύς**, έως, ὁ, *healer, physician*, Hsch. ⊛**-ήεις**, εσσα, εν, *healing, wholesome*, Nic.*Th.*84,645. **-ήσκω** or **ἀλθίσκω**, = ἀλθαίνω, Hp.*Morb.*2.36. **-ίσκον**, τό, = ἀλθαία, Ps.-Dsc.3.146. ⊛**-ος**, εος, τό, *healing, medicine*, *EM*63.10, Hsch.

⊛**ἁλία** (A), Ion. **-ίη** [ᾱλ], ἡ, *assembly of people*, in Dor. states, answering to Att. ἐκκλησία, at Sparta, ἁ. συλλέγειν Hdt.7.134; at Byz., Decr.ap.D.18.90; at Corcyra, *IG*9(1).682; in Sicily and Magna Graecia, *IG*14.952 (Agrigentum), 612 (Rhegium), *Tab.Heracl.*1.118, 2.10; at Epidamnus and Tarentum, Arist.*Pol.*1301$^{b}$23 (prob. cj. for ἡλιαία). **II.** generally, *meeting, assembly*, ἁλίην ποιεῖσθαι Hdt.5.29,79; of the Persians, 1.125.

⊛**ἁλία** (B), [ᾰλ], ἡ, (ἅλς) *salt-cellar*, Archipp.13, Stratt.14; ἁλίην τρυπᾶν clear out *the salt-cellar*, mark of extreme poverty, Ap.Ty.*Ep.*7, cf. Call.*Ep.*48.1.

**ἁλιάδης**, ου, ὁ, (ἅλς) *seaman*, S.*Aj.*880 (lyr.). **II. Ἁλιάδαι**, οἱ, Dor. for Ἡλ-, religious association at Rhodes, *IG*12(1).155.

**ἁλιαδίτης**, ὁ, title of posting-official, = γραμματηφόρος τοῦ ὀξέως δρόμου, *PFlor.*39.16 (iv A.D.).

**ἁλι-άετος**, poet. **-αίετος**, ὁ, *sea-eagle*, prob. *osprey*, E.*Fr.*636, Ar.*Av.*891, Arist.*HA*619$^{a}$4. **-āής**, ές, (ἄημι) *blowing seaward*, Od.4.361.

⊛**ἁλιαία**, ἡ, = ἁλία (A), *IG*4.479 (Nemea), 497 (Mycenae); ἁ. τελεία *Mnemos.*44.221 (Argos, iii B.C.); at Epidamnus, Arist.*Pol.*1301$^{b}$23 (ἡλιαία codd.).

**Ἁλιαῖος**, sc. μήν, month at Dreros, *SIG*527.108.

ἁλι-ανθής, ές, prop. *sea-blooming*, hence = ἁλιπόρφυρος, *bright purple*, *AP*5.227 (Paul. Sil.), 7.705 (Antip.), cj. in Orph.*A*.586.

ἁλιαρός, όν, (ἅλς) *salted*, Eust.15c6.61.

ἁλιάς, άδος, ἡ, (ἅλς) *of or belonging to sea*: ἁλιάς (sc. κύμβα), ἡ, *fishing-boat* or *bark*, Arist.*HA*533b20, Moschio ap.Ath.5.208f, D.S.3.1.

ἅλιας, = ἅλις, Hippon.101. **ἁλιάς**· πρασιάς, πλινθείας, Hsch.

❋ **ἁλίασμα**, τό, (ἁλία A) *decree*, βουλᾶς *IG*14.256 (Gela).

❋ **ἁλίασσις**, ἡ, either *assembly* (cf. ἁλία A), or for ἀλ-λίασσις, = ἀναίασσις, *withdrawal* (cf. λιάζομαι), *IG*4.554 (Argos, v B.C.).

❋ **ἁλιαστάς**, ὁ, *member of the* ἁλία, at Tegea, *IG*5(2).6.24 (iv B.C.).

❋ **ἁλίαστος**, ον, (λιάζομαι) *not to be turned aside, unabating*, μάχη, ὅμαδος, γόος, Il.14.57, 12.471, 24.760; πόλεμον δ' ἀ. ἔγειρε 20.31; ἀ. ἀνίη Hes.*Th*.611: neut. as Adv., μηδ' ἁλίαστον ὀδύρεο Il.24.549, cf. φρὴν ἁλίαστος φρίσσει E.*Hec*.85. 2. = πολύς, κῦμα A.R.1.1326, acc. to Sch., cf. *EM*63.33. II. of persons, *undaunted*, E.*Or*.1479.—Ep. word, used twice by E. in lyr.

ἀλῐβάνωτος [ᾰν], ον, *not honoured with incense*, Pl.Com.113.

❋ **ἀλίβαπτος**, ον, *dipped in sea, drowned therein*, Nic.*Al*.618 [where ἀλῐ- metri gr.]. II. *a purple bird*, Alcm.126, Alc.122 (cod. Hsch. ἀλί-).

ἀλίβας, αντος, ὁ, *dead body, corpse*, ἔνεροι καὶ ἀλίβαντες Pl.*R*.387c, cf. *IPE*1².519 (Cherson.). 2. *dead river*, i.e. *Styx*, S.*Fr*.790 (cf. 994). 3. *dead wine*, i.e. *vinegar*, Hippon.102; ἔβηξαν οἶον (v.l. οἶνον) ἀλίβαντα (or ἁλίβ-, i.e. οἱ ἀλίβ-) πίνοντες Call.*Fr*.88; cf. *EM*63.52. (Ancient Gramm. derived the word fr. ἀ- priv., λιβάς and gave it the meaning *dry, withered*, cf. Did.ap.Sch.Ar.*Ra*.186, Corn.*ND*35, Plu.2.736a; the quantity of the first α is dub.)

ἀλίβατος, ον, Dor. for ἠλίβατος.

ἁλιβαφής, ές, = ἀλίβαπτος, πολύδονα σώμαθ' ἁλιβαφῆ restored in A.*Pers*.275 (lyr.) for ἁλίδονα σώματα πολυβαφῆ.

❋ **ἁλιβδύω** [ῡ], expl. by Gramm. as Aeol. for *ἁλιδύω, *sink* or *submerge in the sea*, νῆας ἀλιβδύουσι Call.*Fr*.269: *hide*, aor. ἀλιβδύσασα Lyc.351, cf. *EM*63.13, Hsch.

ἁλί-βρεκτος, ον, *washed by the sea*, *AP*7.501 (Pers.), Nonn.*D*.1.96. ❋-**βρομος**, ον, *murmuring like the sea*, ib.43.385. -**βροχος**, ον, = ἁλίβρεκτος, A.R.2.731. ❋-**βρωτος**, ον, *swallowed by the sea*, Lyc.760:—also ❋ἁλι-βρώς, Id.443. -**γδουπος**, ον, poet. for ἁλίδουπος, Opp.*H*.5.423, Nonn.*D*.1.266. -**γείτων**, ον, gen. ονος, *near the sea*, Hom.*Epigr*.4.6, Nonn.*D*.42.17. -**γενής**, ές, *sea-born*, of Aphrodite, Plu.2.685f.

❋ **ἀλίγκιος** [ᾰ], ον, *resembling, like*, ἀ. ἀστέρι καλῷ Il.6.401; ἀ. ἀθανάτοισιν Od.8.174; εἴδεα πᾶσιν ἀ., of paintings, Emp.23.5; σοὶ φυὰν ἀ. B.5.168; ὀνειράτων ἀ. μορφαῖσι A.*Pr*.449; ἀ. ἡρώεσσιν *IG*14.1356, cf. Arat.462, A.R.4.966, etc.:—but compd. ἐναλίγκιος is more freq.

ἀλιγύγλωσσος, ον, *with no clear voice*, Timo5.

ἁλιδῑνής, ές, *sea-tossed*, D.P.908. ❋**ἀλιδίως**· ἱκανῶς, μετρίως, Hsch.

ἁλι-δνοφεῖ· ἁλουργεῖ, Hsch. ❋-**δονος**, ον, = ἁλιδινής, σώματα A.*Pers*.275; cf. ἁλιβαφής. -**δουπος**, ον, *sea-resounding*, of Poseidon, Orph.*H*.17.4. -**δρομος**, ον, *running over the sea*, Nonn.*D*.43.281. ❋-**δροσος**, ον, dub. in *Lyr.Adesp.Oxy*.219.11.

❋ **ἁλιεία**, ἡ, *fishing*, Arist.*Pol*.1256a36, *Oec*.1346b20, Str.11.2.4 (pl.); later ἁλεία (q.v.).

❋ **Ἁλιεῖα**, τά, Dor. for Ἡλιεῖα, *festival of the Sun*, at Rhodes, *Com.Adesp*. (perh. Lysipp.) 336, cf. *SIG*1067.

ἁλι-ειδής, ές, *sea-coloured*, κίχλαι Numen.ap.Ath.7.305c. ❋-**εινή** ἐρέα *sea-blue* wool, *Edict.Diocl*.21.2. -**ειος**, α, ον, *fisher's*, τέχνη Alcid.*Od*.12. -**εργής**, ές, *working in sea, fishing*, Opp.*H*.4.635:—also -**εργός**, όν, Nonn.*D*.40.306. II. = ἁλουργής, *purple*, *EM*63.45. -**ερκής**, ές, *sea-fenced, sea-girt*, of Aegina, Pi.*O*.8.25; of the Isthmus, Id.*I*.1.9; ἁ. ὄχθαι Id.*P*.1.18.

ἀλιετρόν· ἁμαρτωλόν, Hsch.

ἁλί-ευμα, ατος, τό, *draught of fish*, Str.11.2.4. -**εύς** (later written ἁλεεύς Lxx *Is*.19.8, *Ev.Matt*.4.18, *PFlor*.127.15), ὁ, gen. έως, Ion. ῆος, and contr. ἁλιῶς Pherecr.200: acc. pl. ἁλιέας Antiph.190.17, Alex.155.1; gen. ἁλιέων Id.76.5: (ἅλς, ἅλιος A):—*one who has to do with the sea*, and so, 1. *fisher*, Od.12.251, 22.384, Hdt.3.42, S.*Fr*.115, Pl.*Ion*539e, etc.: ἀνὴρ ἁ. Hes.*Sc*.214. 2. *seaman, sailor*, Od.24.419; ἐρέτας ἁλιῆας rowers *on the sea*, 16.349; as Adj., ἁλιεὺς στρατός Opp.H.5.121. 3. a fish, = βάτραχος, Arist.*HA*620b12, Plu.2.978d, Paus.3.21.5. ❋-**ευτής**, οῦ, ὁ, = foreg.1, metaph., Πιερίδων Cerc.4.8. ❋-**ευτικός**, ή, όν, *of* or *for fishing*, ἁ. πλοῖον *fishing*-boat, X.*An*.7.1.20; ἁ. κάλαμος *fishing*-rod, Arist.*PA*693a23; ἁ. βίος *fisher's* life, Id.*Pol*.1256b2:—ἡ -κή (with or without τέχνη) *art of fishing*, Pl.*Ion*538d, *Sph*.220b; Ἁλιευτικά, τά, title of poem by Opp. on this subject; ἁλιευτικόν, τό, *the fishing population*, Arist.*Pol*.1291b22. ❋-**εύω**, (ἅλς) *fish*, *Ev.Jo*.21.3; *to be a fisher*, Plu.*Ant*.29; *fish for, catch*, σπάρους dub. l. in Epich.54; λίθους Luc.*Pisc*.47: abs., Luc.*Herm*.65, etc.: metaph. of avenger, ἁλιεύειν τινάς Lxx *Je*.16.16. II. only Med. occurs in Att., Pl.Com.44; Ἁλιευομένη, title of play by Antiph.:—also later, Posidon.68.

ἅλιζα· ἡ λεύκη τῶν δένδρων, i.e. *abele* (Maced.), Hsch.

❋ **ἁλίζω** (A), [ᾰ]: aor. ἥλῐσα E.*HF*412, Hdt.1.77, (συν-) X.*Cyr*.1.4.14:—Pass., aor. ἡλίσθην Emp.41, Hp. (v. infr.), Hdt.1.79: Ion. pf. part. ἁλισμένος Hdt.4.118, 7.172 (but ἡλ- Scriptor Ionicus ap. Stob.3.28.21): (ἀλής):—*gather together, assemble*, of military forces, Hdt.1.77,80, al.; *collect*, of fragments, ib.119, etc.; ἁ. εἰς ἓν E.*Heracl*.403:—Pass., *meet together*, Hdt.1.63,79, 7.172; *to be massed into a globe*, Emp. l.c.; *collect*, αἷμα ἁλισθὲν Hp.*Int*.47, cf. *Morb*.1.15; of moisture, etc., Arist.*Pr*.869a17, cf. 936b32; of rapid breathing, πνεῦμα ἁλίξεται Hp.*Coac*.333.—Not in A. or S.; rare in Prose, Act. in Pl.*Cra*.409a, App.*Fr*.1.4; Pass., X.*An*.2.4.3, 6.3.3, Arist.*Pr*.936b32: generally, compd. συναλίζω more freq.

ἁλίζω (B), [ᾰ], (ἅλς) *salt*, Pass., *to be salted*, Arist.*HA*570a1, *Pr*.927a36, Lxx *Le*.2.13:—Pass., *Ev.Matt*.5.13, Ph.*Bel*.86.29. II. *supply with salt* or *salt food*, Arist.*HA*574a9, al.:—Pass., of sheep, ib.596a24.

❋ **ἁλί-ζωνος**, ον, *sea-girt*, Call.*Sos*.24, *AP*7.218 (Antip.Sid.). -**ζωος**, ον, *living on* or *in the sea*, *AP*7.654 (Leon.), Pancrat.ap.Ath.7.321f.

ἀλίη· κάπρος (Maced.), Hsch. **ἁλίη**, ἡ, Ion. for ἁλία.

ἁλι-ηγής, ές, (ἄγνυμι) *broken on by the sea*, πέτρα Opp.*H*.3.460. -**ήμαθον**· παρὰ τὸν ἅλα καὶ τὴν ἄμαθον, Hsch. -**ήρης**, ες, (ἐρέσσω) *sweeping the sea*, κώπη E.*Hec*.455 (lyr.). -**ήτωρ**, ορος, ὁ, poet. for ἁλιεύς I, Hom.*Epigr*.16.1. -**ηχής**, ές, *resounding like the sea*, Musae.26.

ἁλίθιος, Dor. for ἠλίθιος.

ἀλιθοκόλλητος, ον, *not cemented*, οἶκοι Antyll.ap.Orib.9.13.5.

ἄλῐθος, ον, *without stones, not stony*, of lands, X.*An*.6.4.5. II. *without a stone* set in it, of a ring, Poll.7.179. III. *free from the stone*, as disease, Aret.*CD*2.3.

❋ **ἁλι-κάκαβον**, τό, *winter-cherry*, *Physalis Alkekengi*, Dsc.4.71, cf. *BGU*1120.37 (i B.C.):—also **ἁλικάκκαβα**, Hsch. 2. = στρύχνον ὑπνωτικόν, Dsc.4.72. 3. = δορύκνιον, Crateuas ap.Dsc.4.74.

Ἁλικαρνασσός, Ion. -**νησσός**, ἡ, *Halicarnassus*, Hdt.1.144, etc.:—Adj. **Ἁλικαρνασσεύς**, έως, Ion. -**νησσεύς**, έος, ὁ, *Halicarnassian*, Hdt. l.c., *SIG*45.2 (-σσ- expressed by T), etc.:—fem.❋-**νασσίς**, ίδος, ἡ, Aristodem.1.5. **Ἁλικαρνασσόθεν**, Adv. *from Halicarnassus*, Luc.*Dom*.20.

ἁλικία, ἡ, Dor. for ἡλικία. **ἁλικίανες** (leg. -κρατες)· θαλασσομιγεῖς, Hsch. **ἁλικίνος**· δυνατός, Id. (cf. ἀλεκινός).

ἁλίκλυστος, ον, *sea-washed, sea-beaten*, of coast, S.*Aj*.1219 (lyr.); ἁ. πὰρ χθονὶ Πειραέως *IG*3.1344; ἁ. δέμας *AP*9.228 (Apollonid.). 2. *high-surging*, πόντος Orph.*A*.333.

ἀλίκμητος, ον, *not winnowed*, ἄχυρα Aq. Sm. Thd.*Is*.30.24.

❋ **ἁλικνήμῑς**, ῑδος, ὁ, ἡ, ἀπήνη ἁ. *sea-borne* car, Nonn.*D*.43.199. **ἁλίκος**, α, ον, Dor. for ἡλίκος. ❋ **ἁλικός**, v. ἁλυκός:—hence **ἁλική**, ἡ, *salt-tax*, *PSI*4.388.1 (iii B.C.), *PTeb*.482 (ii B.C.): **ἁλικά**, τά, *charges for salt*, *PPetr*.3p.106 (iii B.C.).

ἁλί-κρᾱς, ᾱτος, ὁ, ἡ, *mixed with salt water*, Ael.Dion.*Fr*.32. -**κρείων**, οντος, ὁ, *lord of the sea*, Eust.57.27. ❋-**κρήπῑς**, ῖδος, ὁ, ἡ, *at the sea's edge*, Nonn.*D*.1.289. -**κρόκᾰλος**, ον, *shingly, pebbly*, Orph.*A*.335. ❋-**κτῠπος**, ον, *sea-smitten*, of ships, S.*Ant*.953 (lyr.), cf. *AP*6.23, Nonn.*D*.31.113; also ἁ. κῦμα *roaring on the sea*, E.*Hipp*.754 (lyr.). -**κύμων** [ῡ], ον, *surrounded by sea-waves*, *AP*9.429 (Crin.).

ἁλικύρκης, ὁ, a made dish, Hsch.

ἁλιμέδων, οντος, ὁ, = ποντομέδων, Ar.*Th*.323.

ἀλιμενία, ἡ, *want of harbours*, Hyp.*Fr*.156, Poll.1.101.

❋ **ἀλίμενος** [ῐ], ον, *harbourless*, A.*Supp*.768, E.*Hel*.1211, Th.4.8, etc. 2. metaph., *shelterless, inhospitable*, ὄρεα, ἄντλος, E.*Hel*.1132, *Hec*.1025; ἀλίμενον αἰθέρος αὔλακα Ar.*Av*.1400; καρδία E.*Cyc*.349.

❋ **ἀλῐμενότης**, ἡ, = ἀλιμενία, X.*HG*4.8.7, *Peripl.M.Eux*.37.

❋ **ἀλῐμενώτης** τόπος· μὴ ἔχων λιμένα, Suid., cf. Hsch.

ἀλίμικτος, v. ἀλίσμηκτος.

ἁλιμοκτόνον, = ποταμογείτων, Ps.-Dsc.4.100.

ἅλῐμος, ον, (ἅλς) *of* or *belonging to the sea*, ὄτοβος *Trag.Adesp*.247; τὰ ἅ. *seaside*, Lxx *Je*.17.6. II. as Subst., ἅλιμον, τό, *tree purslane*, *Atriplex Halimus*, Antiph.160, Thphr.*HP*4.16.5, Dsc.1.91 (ἅλιμος, ὁ, Ps.-Dsc. ibid.). (Sts. written ἄλιμον, cf. *AB*376.)

ἄλῑμος, ον, *banishing hunger*, τροφή, a food said to be prepared from asphodel and mallows, Herodor.1J., Hermipp.Hist.1.8, cf. Plu.2.157d, Porph.*Abst*.4.20.

❋ **ἁλῐ-μῡρήεις**, εσσα, εν, (μύρω) *flowing into the sea*, ποταμοί Il.21.190, Od.5.460, cf. A.R.2.936; cf. sq. ❋-**μῡρής**, ές, = foreg., Orph.*A*.344. 2. *salt-surging*, πόντος *Epigr.Gr*.256 (Cyprus); *of the flowing sea*, ἀφρός *APl*.4.180 (Democr.). II. = ἁλίκλυστος, πέτρη, αἰγιαλοί, A.R.1.913, Phanocl.1.17. ❋-**ναιέτης**, ου, *dwelling in the sea*, δελφῖνες B.16.97.

ἁλίνδα, mythical plant, Ps.-Plu.*Fluv*.14.2.

❋ **ἀλινδ-έω**, later **ἀλίνδω** [ᾰ], (pres. only in Pass.): aor. ἤλῐσα (ἐξ-) Ar.*Nu*.32, and pf. ἤλῑκα (ἐξ-) ib.33 (the simple forms only in Hsch., Suid.):—*make to roll*. II. Pass., mostly in part., *rolling in the dust*, like a horse, ἀλινδούμενος Plu.2.396e; ἀλινδόμενοι ψαμάθοισι Nic.*Th*.156; ἀλινδηθείς ib.204; ἠλινδημένος *rolled over, overturned*, Din.*Fr*.10; *to be twirled*, Call.*Iamb*.1.113. 2. generally, *roam about*, ἄλλην ἐξ ἄλλης εἰς χθόν' ἀλινδόμενος *AP*7.736 (Leon.); ἠλινδημένος ἐν αὐλαῖς σατραπικαῖς *having grovelled*, Plu.*Agis*3; *frequent*, περὶ τὴν Ἀκαδημίαν ἀ. Alciphr.3.14; of money-lenders, οἱ περὶ τὰς ψήφους -ούμενοι ib.1.26. 3. sens. obsc., μετά τινος Herod.5.30. -**ήθρα**, ἡ, *place for horses to roll in*, Phryn.*PS*p.5 B.: metaph., ἀλινδῆθραι ἐπῶν, of Euripides' tragedies, Ar.*Ra*904. -**ησις**, εως, ἡ, *rolling in dust*, exercise in which wrestlers rolled on the ground, Hp.*Vict*.2.64, 3.68, Ruf.ap.Orib.*Inc*.2.11.

ἀλινδόν· δρόμον, Hsch.

❋ **ἁλῐ-νήκτειρα**, ἡ, (νήχω) fem. as if fr. *ἁλινηκτήρ, *swimming in the sea*, *AP*6.190 (Gaet.). [ῑ metri gr.] -**νηχής**, ές, = foreg., ib.10.9; *of swimmers*, τέχνη ib.6.29 (Jul.).

**ἀλιννόν·** ἀμυδρόν (Cret.), Hsch. **ἀλινοί·** ἐπαφρόδιτοι, Id.

**ἄλῖνος,** *η, ον,* (ἅλς) *of salt,* χόνδροι Hdt.4.185; τοῖχοι ib.; οἰκίαι Str. 16.3.3. **ἄλῖνος,** *ον,* (λίνον) *without net,* ἄ. θήρα game *not caught with net, AP*9.244 (Apollonid.). ❋**ἄλινσις,** *εως, ἡ,* = ἄλειψις, τοῦ ἐργαστηρίου *IG*4.1484.39 (Epid.). **ἄλιντος·** ἅμιλλα, Hsch. ❋**ἀλίνω,** (ἀλέω A) = λεπτύνω, *pound,* S.*Fr.*995. II. ἀλινεῖν (leg. ἀλίνειν)· ἀλείφειν, and ἀλῖναι· ἐπαλεῖψαι, Hsch. (cf. ἄλινσις, Lat. *lino*).

**ἆλιξ,** Dor. for ἧλιξ. ❋**ἄλιξ,** *ἴκος, ὁ, groats of rice-wheat* (ζέα), Chrysipp.Tyan.ap.Ath.14.647d, cf. Plin.*HN*18.112. II. = Lat. *hallec, fish-sauce,* Dsc.4.148, *Gp.*20.46.2. **ἁλίξαντος,** *ον, worn by sea,* χοιράδες *AP*6.89 (Maec.); τύμβος *IG*9(1).878 (Corcyr.); ἁ. μόρος death *by being dashed on the beach, AP.*7.404 (Zon.).

❋**ἁλιονείκης** (sic) = ἁλειονίκης, *ὁ, victor in the* Ἁλιεῖα at Rhodes, *PLond.*3.1178.67 (ii A.D.), *Rev.Arch.*1915 ii 200 (Trajana Augusta).

**ἅλιος** (A), *α, ον,* also *ος, ον* S.*Aj.*357, E.*Heracl.*82(lyr.): (ἅλς):—*of the sea,* of sea-gods, nymphs, etc., θυγάτηρ ἁλίοιο γέροντος, i.e. of Nereus, Il.1.556, Hes.*Th.*1003, cf. Od.4.365, al.; θεαὶ ἅ. *sea*-goddesses, Nereids, Il.18.432; of Apollo, Arist.*Mir.*840ᵃ20; ἅ. ψάμαθοι *sea*-sand, Od.3.38; ἅ. πρών A. (only in lyr.) *Pers.*131,879; κῦμα Id. *Supp.*14; πρύμναι, πλάτα, νηῦς, Pi.*O.*9.72, S.*OC*716, Orph.*A.*236.

❋**ἅλιος** (B), *α, ον*: (perh. cf. ἠλίθιος):—mostly of things, *fruitless, idle,* ἔπος, μῦθος, Il.18.324, 5.715; πόνος 4.26; βέλος 5.18; ὅρκιον 4.158; in Od. only with ὁδός 2.273,318; of a person, Il.10.324: neut. as Adv., *in vain,* 13.505, cf. 4.179, S.*OC*1469: reg. Adv. -ίως Id.*Ph.* 840.—Ep. word, used by S. in lyr.

❋**ἅλιος** (C), *ὁ,* Dor. for ἥλιος. II. (ἁλίζω), Pythag. name for *nine, Theol.Ar.*57.

**ἁλιοτρεφής,** *ές, feeding in the sea, sea-reared,* φῶκαι Od.4.442.

❋**Ἁλιοτρόπιος,** sc. μήν, month at Epidamnus, *Inscr.Magn.*46.

**ἁλιόω,** poet. Verb, only fut. ἁλιώσω, aor. ἡλίωσα, Ep. ἁλίωσα: fut. Med. in act. sense, Max.582, in pass. sense, Id.512: (ἅλιος B):—*make fruitless, disappoint,* Διὸς νόον.. ἁλιῶσαι Od.5.104; οὐδ' ἁλίωσε βέλος nor *did he hurl* the spear *in vain,* Il.16.737; οὐχ ἡλίωσε τοὔπος *spake* not word *in vain,* S.*Tr.*258. 2. *destroy,* τὸ μέν τις οὐ.. ἁλιώσει Id.*OC*704.

**ἀλίπαντος,** *ον, without grease,* Paul.Aeg.4.4.

**ἀλῑπᾰρής,** *ές, not fit for a suppliant,* ἀ. θρίξ dub. l. in S.*El.*451; expl. by Sch. as αὐχμηρά, from ἀ- priv., λιπαρός.

❋**ἁλί-παστος,** *ον, sprinkled with salt,* Aristomen.6, Eub.7.10, Archestr.*Fr.*57.4 B. **-πεδον,** *τό, plain by the sea, sandy plain,* Thphr.*HP*7.15.2, Aristid.*Or.*17(15).16; of a plain in Attica near Piraeus, X.*HG*2.4.30. (ἀλ- Ar.*Fr.*233, acc. to Harp.)

**ἀλῑπής,** *ές,* (λίπος) *without fat, meagre, poor,* Hices.ap.Ath.7.315d; *without fatty substance,* Thphr.*HP*9.1.3, Str.4.4.1, Dsc.1.26: Medic., *not thick and fatty,* of lotions as opp. to salves, Gal.13.843; of perfumes, Thphr.*Od.*15 (Sup.); of bones, Gal.4.550; of persons, *skinny,* Aret.*CA*2.7. II. (λείπω, λιπεῖν) *unfailing,* προχοαί Poet.ap. Porph.*Antr.*8 (*PLG*3.684).

**ἁλί-πλαγκτος,** *ον, sea-roaming,* ὦ Πάν, Πὰν ἁλίπλαγκτε..φάνηθι S.*Aj.*695; Τρίτων *AP*6.65 (Paul. Sil.); ἔχις *IG*2.1660. ❋**-πλᾰνής,** *ές, sea-wandering,* νῆες *AP*11.390 (Lucill.). **-πλᾰνία,** *ἡ, wandering voyage, AP*6.38 (Phil.). **-πλᾰνος,** *ον,* = ἁλιπλανής, Opp. *C.*4.258. **-πλεύμων,** *ονος, ὁ,* = πλεύμων II, Marcell.Sid.27. **-πληκτος,** Dor. **-πλακτος,** *ον, sea-beaten,* of islands, Pi.*P.*4.14, v.l. in S. *Aj.*597 (lyr.). **-πλήξ,** *ῆγος, ὁ, ἡ,* = foreg., Call.*Del.*11, *AP*6.193 (Stat. Flacc.). ❋**-πλοος,** *ον,* contr. **-πλους,** *ουν, covered with water,* τείχεα Il.12.26. II. later Act., *sailing on the sea,* ναῦς Arion 1.17, cf. Apollod.Hist.209: as Subst., *seaman, fisher,* A.R.3.1329, Call.*Del.*15. 2. in form **ἁλίπλωος,** ἰχθύες Babr.61.4. **-πνοος,** *ον, redolent of sea,* ὀδμή Musae.265. ❋**-πόρος,** *ον, through which the sea flows,* διασφάξ Luc.*Trag.*24. **-πόρφῠρος,** *ον, of sea-purple, of true purple dye,* ἠλάκατα, φάρεα, Od.6.53, 13.108; οἶδμα Arion 1.18 codd.; ὄρνις Alcm.26.4; Νηρηΐδες Him.*Or.*16.2.

❋**ἄλιππα,** *τό,* Aeol., = ἄλειμμα, *EM*64.40.

**ἁλιπτοίητος,** *ον, driven by fear across the sea,* Nonn.*D.*8.58, cf. 13.119; perh. Act. in meaning, Ἐνυώ 39.85.

**ἄλιρ·** ὀξύβαφον, Hsch.

**ἁλιρ-ρᾰγής,** *ές,* (ῥήγνυμι) *against which the tide breaks,* σκόπελος *AP*7.383 (Phil.). **-ραίστης,** *ὁ,* (ῥαίω) *ravening in the sea,* δράκων Nic.*Th.*828. ❋**-ραντος,** *ον,* (ῥαίνω) *sea-surging,* πόντος *AP*9.333 (Mnas.) (s.v.l.); *washed by sea,* ἀκταί 14.72. **-ρηκτος,** *ον,* = ἁλιρραγής, δειράδες *AP*7.278 (Arch.). **-ρόθιος,** *α, ον, sea-beaten,* κόνις *AP*7.6 (Antip. Sid.); f.l. ib.624 (Diod., leg. ἁλὶ ῥοθίῃ). II. *roaring,* θάλασσα Orph.*A.*1296. **-ροθος,** *ον,* = foreg.; ἁ. πόροι pathways *of the roaring sea,* A.*Pers.*367, cf. S.*Aj.*412 (lyr.); ἁ. ἀκτή E.*Hipp.*1205, Mosch.2.132. **-ροιζος,** *ον,* = ἁλιρρόθιος, Nonn.*D.*13. 322, etc. **-ρῠτος,** *ον, washed by the sea, AP*12.55 (Artemo). II. ἁ. ἄλσος *surging sea's* domain, A.*Supp.*868 (lyr.).

**ἅλῐς** [ᾰ], Adv. *in crowds, in plenty,* hence, in a modified sense, *sufficiently, enough*: 1. Hom. mostly with Verbs, ἅ. πεποτήαται [μέλισσαι] Il.2.90; περὶ δὲ Τρῳαὶ ἅ. ἦσαν 3.384; κόπρος ἅ. κέχυτο Od. 17.298; ἅ. δέ οἱ ἦσαν ἄρουραι Il.14.122:—sts. *just enough, in moderation,* εἰ δ' ἅ. ἔλθοι Κύπρις E.*Med.*630; ἔφερε κακὸν ἅ. Id.*Alc.*907. 2. in Ep. freq. closely attached to Noun, χαλκόν τε χρυσόν τε ἅ. bronze and gold *in abundance,* Od.16.231, cf. Il.22.340; νῆα ἅ. χρυσοῦ καὶ χαλκοῦ νηησάσθω 9.137; ἅ. χέραδος 21.319; ἅ. δ' εὐῶδες ἔλαιον Od. 2.339:—rare in Trag. and Com., ἅ. βίοτον εὗρον E.*Med.*1107; λύπας ἅ. ἔχων (Elmsl. λύπης) Id.*Hel.*589; ἅ. ἐλαδίῳ διείς prob. in Sotad.Com.1.27; freq. in Alex. poetry, ἔχω οὐδ' ἅ. ὄξος Theoc.10. 13; ἅ. ὄλβος Call.*Jov.*84; ἄρτους ἅ. κατέθηκεν Id.*Hec.*35; ἱδρῶ A.R.2.87:—rare with Adj., ἅ. ἦσθ' ἀνάρσιος A.*Ag.*511. 3. ἅλ (sc. ἐστί) *'tis enough,* ἦ οὐχ ἅ. ὅττι..; is't not *enough* that..? I 5.349; ἦ οὐχ ἅ. ὡς..; 17.450, Od.2.312; ἅ. ἵν' ἐξήκεις δακρύων S.O 1515: abs., ἅλις *enough!* Id.*Aj.*1402:—in Trag. c. acc. et inf., Ἀρ γείοισι Καδμείους ἅ. ἐς χεῖρας ἐλθεῖν A.*Th.*679: c. dat., ἅ. δὲ κλάει τοὐμὸν ἦν ἐμοὶ κακόν E.*Alc.*1041. 4. like an Adj., as predicate, ἅ. γὰρ ἡ παροῦσα συμφορά ib.673, cf. *IT*1008, S.*Tr.*332. 5 ἅλις (sc. εἰμί) c. part., ἅ. νοσοῦσ' ἐγώ *enough* that I suffer, Id.*O* 1061; ἅ. ἐγὼ δυστυχῶν *Trag.Adesp.*76. 6. c. gen. rei, *enough of* a thing, ἅ. ἔχειν τῆς βορῆς Hdt.1.119, cf. 9.27; πημονῆς ἅ. γ' ὑπάρχει A.*Ag.*1656, cf. 1659; ἅ. [ἐστὶ] λελεγμένων Id.*Eu.*675; ἅ. λόγων S.*OC*1016; ἅ. ἀφύης μοι Ar.*Fr.*506; to conclude an argument, καὶ τούτων μὲν ἅ. Pl.*Plt.*287a; καὶ περὶ μὲν τούτων ἅ. Arist.*EN* 1096ᵃ3, etc.—Cf. ἅλιας. (ϝαλ-, cf. γάλι· ἱκανόν, Hsch.; cf. ἀλής.)

**ἁλίς,** *ίδος, ἡ,* (ἅλς) = ἁλμυρίς, Eust.706.56.

**ἀλίσβη,** *ἡ,* = ἀπάτη, Hsch.

**ἀλισγ-έω,** *pollute,* Lxx *Da.*1.8, al. **-ημα,** *ατος, τό, pollution, Act.Ap.*15.20.

**ἀλισθένειν·** ἀσθενεῖν, Hsch.

❋**ἁλίσκομαι** [ᾰλ], defect. Pass., Act. supplied by αἱρέω (ἁλίσκω Aq. *Ps.*21(22).14, cf. ἐλέφας μῦν οὐχ ἁλίσκει Zen.3.67): impf. ἡλισκόμην (never ἑαλ-) Hdt., etc.: fut. ἁλώσομαι Hdt., etc., later ἁλωθήσομαι Lxx *Ez.*21.24(19) cod. A: aor. (the only tense used by Hom.) ἥλων Od.22.230, always in Hdt., and sometimes in codd. of Att., as Pl. *Hp.Ma.*286a, Hyp.*Eux.*15, cf. X.*An.*4.4.21, but the common Att. form was ἑάλων *IG*2.38, etc., cf. Thom.Mag.146 [ᾱ, Ar.*V.*355, later ᾰ *AP*7.114 (D.L.), 11.155 (Lucill.); ᾰ in other moods, exc. part. ἁλόντε Il.5.487, inf., v. infr.]; subj. ἁλῶ, ῷς, ῷ A.*Th.*257, E.*Hipp.* 420, Ar.*Ach.*662, *V.*898, etc., Ion. ἁλώω Il.11.405, ἁλώῃ 14.81, Hdt. 4.127; opt. ἁλοίην Il.22.253, Antipho 5.59, etc., Ep. 3 sg. ἁλῴη (v.l. ἁλοίη, which is to be preferred) Il.17.506, Od.15.300; inf. ἁλῶναι [ᾰ] Il.21.281, [ᾱ] Hippon.74 s.v.l., Ep. ἁλώμεναι Il.21.495; part. ἁλούς Il.2.374, etc.; later, inf. ἁλωθῆναι v.l. in Lxx *Ez.*40.1, D.S.21.6: pf. ἥλωκα Hdt.1.83, Antiph.204.7, Xenarch.7.17, Hyp.*Phil.*11, D. 21.105; part. ἁλωκότα Pi.*P.*3.57; ἑάλωκα [ᾰλ] A.*Ag.*30, Hdt. 1. 191,209 codd., and Att., as Th.3.29, Pl.*Ap.*38d, D.19.179: plpf. ἡλώκειν Hdt.1.84, X.*An.*5.2.8.: (ϝαλ-, cf. ϝαλίσσκηται *IG*9(2). 1226 (Thess.), ϝαλόντοις ib.5(2).351.7 (Stymphalus)):—*to be taken, conquered, fall into an enemy's hand,* of persons and places, Il.2.374, etc.; ἁλώσεται (sc. ὁ Κρέων) S.*OC*1065; ἁλίσκεσθαι εἰς πολεμίους *to fall into the hands of* the enemy, Pl.*R.*468a, *IG*12(7).5 (Amorg.); ἐν τοιαύταις ξυμφοραῖς Pl.*Cri.*43c. 2. *to be caught, seized,* of persons and things, θανάτῳ ἁλῶναι *to be seized* by death, *die,* Il.21.281, Od.5.312; without θανάτῳ, Il.12.172, Od.18.265, etc.; ἄνδρ' ἐκ θανάτου κομίσαι ἤδη ἁλωκότα (sc. νόσῳ) Pi.*P.*3.57; γράμματα ἑάλωσαν εἰς Ἀθήνας letters *were seized and taken* to Athens, X.*HG*1.1.23; τοῖς αὑτῶν πτεροῖς ἁλισκόμεσθα, of eagle, i.e. by a feathered arrow, A.*Fr.*139:—*to be taken* or *caught* in hunting, Il.5.487, X.*An.*5.3. 10:—ἁ. ἀπάταις, μανίᾳ, S.*El.*125, *Aj.*216; ὑπ' ἔρωτος Pl.*Phdr.*252c; ὑπὸ νουσήματος τεταρταίου Hp.*Nat.Hom.*15; νοσήματι Arist.*Pr.*954ᵃ 35, etc.; μιᾷ νίκῃ ἁλίσκονται by one victory *they are ruined,* Th.1. 121: abs., *to be overcome,* A.*Eu.*67, S.*Aj.*648. 3. in good sense, *to be won, achieved,* S.*OT*542, E.*Alc.*786, X.*Cyn.*12.21. 4. c. gen., *succumb to,* τῆς ὥρας, τοῦ κάλλους, Ael.*VH*12.52, Ps.-Luc. *Charid.*9; κόρης Philostr.*Her.*8.2, prob. in Eun.*Hist.*p.238 D. 5. *to be established* by argument, *proved,* Phld.*Sign.*29,33. II. c. part., *to be caught* or *detected* doing a thing, οὔτε σὺ ἁλώσεαι ἀδικέων Hdt.1.112; ἐπιβουλεύων ἐμοὶ.. ἑάλωκε ib.209; ἐὰν ἁλῷς ἔτι τοῦτο πράττων Pl.*Ap.*29c; with Subst. or Adj., οὐ γὰρ δὴ φονεὺς ἁλώσομαι S.*OT*576; μοιχὸς γὰρ ἢν τύχῃς ἁλούς Ar.*Nu.*1079; ἁ. ἐν κακοῖσι S. *Ant.*496. 2. freq. as law-term, *to be convicted and condemned,* λιποταξίου γραφὴν ἡλωκέναι D.21.105, cf. Antipho 2.2.9, 2.3.6; ἁ. μιᾷ ψήφῳ And.4.9:—c. gen. criminis, ἁλῶναι ψευδομαρτυριῶν, ἀστρατείας, ἀσεβείας, etc. (sc. γραφήν), v. sub vocc.; ἁ. θανάτου *to be convicted of* a capital crime, Plu.2.552d; ἁλοῦσα δίκη *conviction,* Pl.*Lg.* 937d; of false evidence, ὁπόσων ἂν μαρτυρίαι ἁλῶσιν ibid.

**ἄλισμα,** *τό, water-plantain, Alisma Plantago,* Dsc.3.152.

**ἁλι-σμάρᾰγος,** *ον, sea-resounding,* Nonn.*D.*39.362. **-σμηκτος,** *ον, washed by the sea,* Lyc.994: Hsch. has ἁλίσμηκτα (cod. ἁλισίμικτα)· ἡλισμένα, Suid. ἁλίμικτον· πεπασμένον. ❋**-σμός,** *ὁ, sprinkling with salt,* Sor.1.82; = *salsura, Gloss.* **-σπαρτος,** *ον, sown* or *sprinkled with salt,* Eust.1827.61, Hsch., *EM*65.12. **-στέφανος,** *ον, sea-crowned, sea-girt,* πτολίεθρον *h.Ap.*410; νῆσος Alex. Lychn.ap.St.Byz. s.v. Ταπροβάνη, Nonn.*D.*40.521. **-στεφής,** *ές,* = foreg., Θάσος *Epigr.Gr.*208.16, cf. Orph.*A.*145, 186.

**ἀλιστία·** ἀναπέπλησται, Hsch.

**ἁλίστονος,** *ον, sea-resounding,* ῥαχίαι A.*Pr.*712. II. *groaning on the sea,* of fishers, Opp.*H.*4.149.

**ἄλιστος,** v. ἄλλιστος.

❋**ἁλιστός** [ᾰ], *ή, όν,* (ἁλίζω) *salted, pickled,* Str.4.4.3, Orib.*Fr.*58, Aët.9.38, *AP*9.377 (Pall.).

**ἀλίστρα,** *ἡ,* = ἀλινδήθρα, Poll.1.183, cf. Hsch. (cod. -τρία).

**ἁλίστρεπτος,** *ον, sea-tossed,* ναῦς *AP*9.84 (Antiphan.).

**ἁλίσχοινος,** *ον, ὁ,* = ὁλόσχοινος, Aët.2.214 (codd. -σχινος).

❋**ἀλῐταίνω** [ᾰλ], Ep. Verb, used by A. in lyr., chiefly in aor. 2 Act. and Med.:—Act., aor. 2 ἤλῐτον Il.9.375, Thgn.1170, A.*Eu.*269; subj. ἀλίτῃ Ps.-Phoc.208; opt. ἀλίτοιμι A.*Pr.*533; part. ἀλιτών *Eu.*316 (cj. Auratus): later Ep. aor. 1 ἀλίτησα Orph.*A.*644:—Med., ἀλιταίται Hes.*Op.*330: aor. ἀλίτοντο, ἀλίτωμαι, ἀλιτέσθαι Hom., v. infr.: articipial form ἀλιτήμενος:—*sin* or *offend against*, c. acc. pers., ἐκ ὰρ δή μ' ἀπάτησε καὶ ἤλιτεν Il.9.375; ὅτις σφ' ἀλίτηται ὀμόσσας 19. 65; Ἀθηναίην ἀλίτοντο Od.5.108; ἀθανάτους ἀλιτέσθαι 4.378, cf. Ies.*Sc.*80, Thgn. l. c.; ἀλιταίνητ' ὀρφανὰ τέκνα Hes.*Op.*330, cf. A. *Eu.*269, Ps.-Phoc. l. c. **2.** c. acc. rei, *transgress*, Διὸς δ' ἀλίτωμαι φετμάς Il.24.570; ὅρκον, σπονδάς, A.R.4.388, Opp.*H.*5.563. **3.** gen., *stray from*, ἀλίτησεν ἀταρποῦ Orph. l. c., cf. Call.*Dian.* 55. **4.** ἀλιτήμενος as Adj., = ἀλιτρός, θεοῖς ἀ. *sinful* in the yes of gods, Od.4.807.

⊛**ἀλιτάνευτος**, ον, *inexorable*, *PMag.Par.*1.1176, *Gloss.*; cf. ἀλλ-. Adv. -ως *AB*374, *EM*57.30.

⊛**ἁλῐ-τενής**, ές, *projecting into the sea*, πέτρα D.S.3.44, Longus 2.12; ἄκρα, χερρόνησος, Str.8.2.3, 7.3.19, cf. Posidon.66, Arr.*Ind.*21.9, Eun. *Hist.*p.241 D.; *ambulatio* ἁ. walk *by the shore*, Cic.*Att.*14.13.1. **II.** of ships, *of light draught*, Callix.1, Plu.*Them.*14. **III.** of the sea, *shallow*, Plb.4.39.3, App.*BC*2.84. **-τέρμων**, ον, gen. ονος, *bounded by sea*, *AP*9.672.

⊛**ἀλίτ-ημα**, ατος, τό, *sin*, *offence*, *AP*5.277 (Agath.), 9.643 (Id.) (both pl.). ⊛**-ήμερος**, ον, *missing the right day*, *untimely born*, like ἠλιτόμηνος, cj. Guyet in Hes.*Sc.*91 (for ἀλιτήμενον), cf. *EM*428. 10. **-ημοσύνη**, ἡ, = ἀλίτημα, Orph.*A.*1318 (pl.). **-ήμων**, ον, gen. ονος, (ἀλιτεῖν) = sq., Il.24.157,186, Call.*Dian.*123, A.R.4. 1057. ⊛**-ήριος**, ον, (ἀλιτεῖν) *sinning* or *offending against*, c. gen., τῶν ἀλιτηρίων..τῶν τῆς θεοῦ Ar.*Eq.*445; ἐναγεῖς καὶ ἀ. τῆς θεοῦ Th. 1.126; but κοινὸν ἀλιτήριον τῶν ὀλωλότων..ἁπάντων common *plague* of all, D.18.159; ἀλιτήριος Ἑλλάδος Aeschin.3.157, cf. Din.1.77. **2.** abs., *guilty*, D.19.197, Lys.13.79, And.1.130; Πρωταγόρας..ἀλιτήριος (i. e. ὁ ἀ.) Eup.146b, cf. 96, Men.563. **II.** = ἀλάστωρ, *avenging spirit*, Antipho 4.1.4, 4.2.8. **-ηριώδης**, ες, *abominable*, *accursed*, οἶστρος Pl.*Lg.*854b; στάσις Id.*R.*470d; γνώμη D.C.44.1. ⊛**-ηρός**, όν, = ἀλιτήριος: κἀξ ἀλῑτηροῦ φρενός is prob. f.l. for κἀλιτηρίου in S. *OC*371.

**ἀλίτης**, ου, ὁ, = ἀλείτης, Apollon.*Lex.*22.28, Orion 32.

**ἁλίτης** [ῑ], ου, ὁ, *salted*, ἄρτος Ludw.*Anecd.*175; = θαλάσσιος, Hdn. *Epim.*181; = ἁλιευτής, *Et.Gud.z.*

**ἀλιτό-καρπον**· ματαιότεκνον, Hsch. **-μηνος** [ᾱ], ον, = ἠλιτόμηνος, Suid., etc.; Pythag., = ὀκτάς, *Theol.Ar.*55.

**ἀλιτό-ξενος** [ᾰ], ον, *sinning against one's friend*, Pi.*O.*10(11). 6. **-φροσύνη**, ἡ, *wicked mind*, *AP*7.648.10 (Leon.).

**ἀλιτραί**· οἱ ἄδικα δικάζοντες, Hsch.

⊛**ἀλιτραίνω**, Ep. for ἀλιταίνω (when required by metre), abs., *sin*, *offend*, ὅστις ἀλιτραίνει or ὅς κεν ἀλιτραίνῃ Hes.*Op.*243 (cf. Aeschin. 2.158, 3.134); ἢν μὲν ἀλιτραίνῃς *AP*9.763 (Jul.); οὐδὲν ἀ. Tryph. 269.

**ἁλῐτρεφής**, ές, *sea-bred*, Q.S.3.272, Nonn.*D.*24.114.

**ἀλῐτρέω**, = ἀλιταίνω (q. v.), A.*Eu.*316 codd.

**ἀλῐτρία**, ἡ, *sinfulness*, *mischief*, S.*Fr.*48, Ar.*Ach.*907; but **ἀλίτρια**· ἡ ἁμαρτωλός, *Et.Gud.z.*

⊛**ἀλῑτρό-βιος**, ον, *living wickedly*, Nonn.*D.*12.72. **-νοος**, ον, *wicked-minded*, Maiist.56, Orac.ap.Eus.*PE*14.20, *Epigr.Gr.*1052 (Stratonicea).

⊛**ἀλῑτρός**, όν, = ἀλιτηρός, *sinful*, *wicked*, Il.8.361, Thgn.377, Sol.13. 27; also in late Prose, *PPar.*63.95 (ii B. C.): neut. pl., ἀλιτρά, τά, *sins*, Pi.*O.*2.59: as Subst., δαίμοσιν ἀλιτρός *sinner against* the gods, Il.23.595, cf. Theoc.10.17, Call.*Ap.*2, etc.; *knave*, Od.5.182; fem., ἀλιτρῆς ἀλώπεκος Semon.7.7.

⊛**ἀλῑτροσύνη**, ἡ, = ἀλιτρία, A.R.4.699 (pl.), *IG*14.1389 ii 19, *AP*7. 574 (Agath.), etc.

**ἁλί-τροφος**, ον, *sea-nurtured*, φῦλα, i. e. fishes, Opp.*H.*1.76, cf. Nonn.*D.*5.182, al. **-τροχος**, ον, *rushing through the sea*, Ibyc.50, in metapl. acc. sing. ἁλίτροχα. **-τρῡτος**, ον, *sea-beaten*, *sea-worn*, γέρων Theoc.1.45; κύμβη *AP*7.294 (Tull. Laur.). **-τῠπος**, ον, *sea-beaten*, ἁ. βάρη griefs *for sea-tossed corpses*, A.*Pers.*946 (lyr.): as Subst., *seaman*, *fisherman*, E.*Or.*373. **-τῡρος**, ὁ, *salted cheese*, v. l. in *AP*9.412 (Phld.).

⊛**ἀλίφατα**· ἄλφιτα ἢ ἄλευρα, Hsch.

**ἁλι-φθερόω**, *shipwreck*, and metaph., *ruin*, Sophr.35:—ἁλιφθερῶσαι· ἀφανίσαι, Hsch. **-φθορία**, ἡ, *disaster at sea*, *shipwreck*, *AP*9. 41 (Theon). **-φθόρος**, ον, *destroying on sea*: as Subst., *pirate*, *AP*7. 654 (Leon.). **-φιλεῖς**· πτωχοί, Hsch. **-φλοιος**, ὁ, ἡ, *sea-bark oak*, *Quercus Pseudosuber*, Thphr.*HP*3.8.5, Sch.Theoc.9.20 (**ἀλίφαλος**· δρῦς, Hsch., is f. l.). **-φροσύνη**, ἡ, = ἱκανὴ φρόνησις (from ἅλις, φρήν), Hsch.:—Adj. **ἁλίφρονες**, Naumach.ap.Stob.4.31.76.

**ἀλιχευτρίς**, ίδος, ἡ, dub. sens., *PFay.*331 (ii A. D.).

**ἁλί-χλαινος**, ον, *purple-clad*, Nonn.*D.*20.105.

**ἅλιψ** or **ἄλιψ**· πέτρα, Hsch.; cf. αἰγίλιψ, ἠλίβατος.

**ἀλκάζω**, *put forth strength* or *prowess*, *EM*56.11, 66.10:—Med., ἠλκάζοντο· ἠμύνοντο, Hsch. **ἀλκᾰθεῖν**, poet. aor. (accented as pres. by Gramm., Phot.p.76 R., *AB*383), *assist*, A.*Fr.*411, S.*Fr.*996.

⊛**ἀλκαία**, ἡ, *tail*, esp. of lion, Ael.*NA*5.39, Sch.A.R.4.1614; generally, Com. ib. cit., Call.*Fr.*317, Opp.*H.*5.264. **II.** *vervain mallow*, *Malva moschata*, Dsc.3.147:—also **ἀλκαῖον**, τό, Hsch.

**Ἀλκαϊκός**, ή, όν, *used by Alcaeus*, μέτρον Trypho *Trop.*3.

**ἀλκαῖος**, α, ον, (ἀλκή) *strong*, *mighty*, δόρυ E.*Hel.*1152 (lyr.).

⊛**ἄλκαρ**, τό, only nom. and acc.:—*safeguard*, *defence*, οὐδέ τί σε Τρώεσσιν ὀΐομαι ἄ. ἔσεσθαι Il.5.644; ἄ. Ἀχαιῶν 11.823; σᾶς δάμαρτος ἄ. E.*Tr.*590 (lyr.): c. gen. obj., γήραος ἄ. *defence against* old age, *h.Ap.*193; ἴδεος, ὑετοῦ ἄ., Call.*Fr.*124, A.R.2.1074: abs., *remedy*, Aret.*CA*1.1.—Ep. and Lyr. word, cf. Pi.*P.*10.52, Ps.-Phoc.128. Cf. ἀλέξω.

**ἀλκᾶς**, v. ἀλκήεις. **ἄλκασμα**, τό, in pl., *deeds of prowess*, S.*Ichn.* 247.

**ἀλκή**, ἡ, (cf. ἀλέξω) *strength* as displayed in action, *prowess*, *courage*, poet. word (also in Hdt., Th., and later Prose, Ti.Locr.103b, Arist.*EN*1115$^{b}$4, *Pol.*1338$^{a}$20, etc.), in Hom. joined with σθένος Il.17.212, Od.22.237; with μένος Il.9.706; with ἠνορέη Od.24.509; ἐπιειμένοι ἀλκήν Il.8.262; φρεσὶν εἱμένος ἀλκήν 20.381; δύεσθαι ἀλκήν 9.231:—later, χερὸς ἀλκᾷ Pi.*O.*10(11).100; θηρία ἐς ἀλκὴν ἄλκιμα Hdt. 3.110: generally, *force*, *might*, συνῆψαν ἀλκήν E.*Supp.*683; κατ' ἀλκήν, opp. κατὰ σύνεσιν, Arr.*Tact.*12.11: in pl., *feats of strength*, *bold deeds*, Pi.*N.*7.12, B.10.126, E.*Rh.*933, Hierocl.p.33.61 A. **II.** *strength to avert danger*, *defence*, *help*, Διὸς ἀ. Il.15.490, cf. 8.140; οὐδέ τις ἀ. Od.12.120, 22.305; ποῦ τις ἀ.; A.*Pr.*546; ἀ. βελέων S.*Ph.*1151; δορός E.*Ph.*1098: also ἀ. τινος *defence* or *aid against* thing, Hes.*Op.* 201, Pi.*N.*7.96, S.*OT*218; ἀλκὴν ποιεῖσθαι give *aid*, *OC*459; ἀ. τιθέναι make a *defence*, ib.1524; ἐς or πρὸς ἀ. τρέπεσθαι turn *and resist*, stand on *one's guard*, Hdt.2.45, 3.78, Th.2.84; στρέψας πρὸς ἀ. E. *Andr.*1149; ἐς ἀ. ἐλθεῖν Id.*Ph.*421; ἀλκῆς μεμνῆσθαι Hdt.9.70; ἐν οἷς ἔστιν ἀ. where they can *defend themselves*, Arist.*EN* l. c. **III.** *battle*, *fight*, A.*Th.*498,569,878 codd., E.*Med.*264.

**ἄλκη**, ἡ, *elk*, Paus.5.12.1.

⊛**ἀλκήεις**, εσσα, εν, Dor. contr. **ἀλκᾶς**, ᾶντος, *valiant*, *courageous*, *h.Hom.*28.3, Pi.*O.*9.72, *P.*5.71, A.R.1.71; of patients, Aret.*CA* 1.10, al.; *strong*, ὀϊστοί *AP*6.277 (Damag.); πίστις Man.4.48: Sup., Poet.ap.Parth.21.3.

⊛**ἀλκηστής**, οῦ, ὁ, = foreg., συνόδοντες Opp.*H.*1.170.

**ἀλκί** [ῐ], metapl. poet. dat. of ἀλκή, *might*, *strength*: λέων ὣς ἀλκὶ πεποιθώς Il.5.299, cf. Od.6.130, Thgn.949; of Hector, Il.18.158, cf. Nonn.*D.*39.34, etc.

**ἀλκιβιάδειον**, τό, = ἔχιον, Dsc.4.27: = ἄγχουσα, ib.24, Gal.13.149.

**ἀλκιβιάδες**, αἱ, sort of *shoes* (from Ἀλκιβιάδης), Ath.12.534c, Poll. 7.89.

**ἀλκίβιος**, ἡ, = ἔχις, *Cretan bugloss*, *Echium parviflorum*, used as an antidote to snake-bite, Sch.Nic.*Th.*541. (Ἀλκιβίου is pr. n. in Nic. l. c.)

**ἀλκίμαχος**, η, ον, *bravely fighting*, or *defender in fight*, of Athena, *AP*6.124 (Heges.).

**ἀλκῐμόβρῑθος**, ον, *mighty in weight*, *PMag.Par.*1.1364.

⊛**ἄλκῐμος**, ον, also η, ον S.*Aj.*401: (ἀλκή):—*stout*, *brave*, of men and things, Τρῶες, ἔγχος, δοῦρε, Il.11.483, 3.338, Od.22.125; ἦτορ Callin. 1.10; θυμός Tyrt.10.17; νέκυς Pi.*Pae.*6.98; δράκων Epich.60: Comp. -ώτερος Hdt.1.79,103, Arist.*HA*607$^{a}$11, etc.: Sup. -ώτατος E.*Ph.* 743, Plb.6.5.9; ἄ. τὰ πολεμικά Hdt.3.4; ἐς ἀλκὴν ἄλκιμα ib.110; ἄ. μάχη E.*Heracl.*683:—prov., πάλαι ποτ' ἦσαν ἄλκιμοι Μιλήσιοι 'times are changed', Anacr.85, Ar.*Pl.*1002, Philostr.*VS*1.22.4:—less common in Prose, Pl.*R.*614b (with play on Ἀλκίνου), Arist.*HA* 628$^{b}$6. **II.** *fortifying*, ὕδωρ Plu.2.669b s. v. l.; *giving succour*, *PMag.Leid.W.*14.10.

**ἀλκίφρων**, ον, gen. ονος, (φρήν) *stout-hearted*, λαός A.*Pers.*92 (lyr.).

**ἀλκμαῖος**· νεανίσκος, Hsch.

**Ἀλκμανικός**, ή, όν, *used by Alcman*, σχῆμα Hdn.*Fig.*p.101 S., Lesb.Gramm.5.

**ἀλκμαρές**· ἰσχυρόν, Hsch.

**ἀλκ-τήρ**, ῆρος, ὁ, *one who wards off*, *protector from* a thing, c. gen., ἀρῆς, κυνῶν καὶ ἀνδρῶν, Il.18.100, Od.14.531; νούσων Pi.*P.*3.7. **-τήριος**, ον, *helping*, *healing*, ὕδωρ Nonn.*D.*45.348:—neut. ⊛**-τήριον**, τό, *remedy*, *antidote*, τινός *against* a thing, Nic.*Th.*528, etc.; so prob. E. *Fr.*697 (cod. ἀρκτήρια).

⊛**ἀλκυόνειον** (-ιον Dsc.5.118), τό, *bastard-sponge*, a zoophite, so called because like *the halcyon's nest*, Hp.*Mul.*1.106, Antyll.ap.Orib. 10.21.2.

**ἀλκυόνειος**, α, ον, *of the* ἀλκυών, ἀ. ἡμέραι, = ἀλκυονίδες, Arist.*HA* 542$^{b}$6, cf. Ael.*NA*1.36.

**ἀλκυονίς**, ίδος, ἡ, = ἀλκυών, A.R.1.1085, *Epigr.Gr.*205 (Halicarn.), 241.8 (Smyrna). **II.** Adj. **ἀλκῠονίδες**, αἱ, with or without ἡμέραι, *winter days during which the halcyon builds, and the sea is calm*, hence prov. of undisturbed tranquillity, Ar.*Av.*1594, cf. Arist.*HA* 542$^{b}$15, Philoch.180, Luc.*Halc.*2, Suid.; placed in spring by Ps.-Democr.ap.Gem.*Calend.*9: sg. in Alciphr.1.1.

**ἀλκυών**, όνος, ἡ, mythical bird, identified with the *kingfisher*, *Alcedo ispida*, Il.9.563, Alcm.26, Simon.12, Ar.*Av.*251, Arist.*HA*542$^{b}$ 4, Theoc.7.57. (Freq. written ἁλ- by false etymology from ἅλς, κυέω: ἁλκυδών Hdn.Gr.2.285.)

⊛**ἀλλά**, Conj., orig. neut. pl. of ἄλλος, *otherwise*: used adversatively to limit or oppose words, sentences, or clauses, stronger than δέ: **I.** in simple oppositions, *but*, **1.** after neg. clauses, οὐ κακός, ἀλλ' ἀγαθός Thgn.212; οὐδὲ μὲν Ἕκτωρ μίμνεν, ἀλλ'..ἐφορμᾶται Il.15.690, etc. **b.** after a simple neg., ἦ παραφρονεῖς; οὔκ, ἀλλ' ὕπνος μ' ἔχει Ar.*V.*9, etc. **c.** freq. after οὐ μόνον, μὴ μόνον, with or without καί, οὐ μόνον ἅπαξ, ἀ. πολλάκις Pl.*Phdr.*228a, cf. Th. 3.59, X.*Mem.*1.4.13, etc.; without μόνον, οὐχ ἑσπέρας, ἀλλὰ καὶ μεσημβρίας E.*Fr.*1006: also after οὐχ (or μὴ) ὅτι, οὐχ (or μὴ) ὅπως, either, *not only.. but..*, μὴ ὅτι ἰδιώτην τινά, ἀλλὰ τὸν μέγαν βασιλέα Pl.*Ap.*40d; μὴ ὅτι κατὰ τὸ σῶμα, ἀλλὰ καὶ κατὰ τὴν ψυχήν Id.*Smp.* 207e; or, *not only not .. but..*, οὐχ ὅπως κωλυταὶ..γενήσεσθε, ἀλλὰ καὶ..περιόψεσθε Th.1.35; οὐχ ὅτι ὠργίζοντο, ἀλλ' ἐζήλουν D.19.265; the neg. form is ἀλλ' οὐδέ, μὴ ὅτι ὑπὲρ ἄλλου, ἀλλ' οὐδὲ ὑπὲρ ἐμαυτοῦ δίκην εἴρηκα Is.10.1, etc. 2. in the apodosis of hypothetical sentences, *still, at least*, εἴπερ γάρ τε.. ἀλλά τε Il.1.82, etc.: in Prose, esp. ἀλλ' οὖν..γε or ἀλλά..γε, εἰ καὶ σμικρά, ἀ. οὖν ἴση γε ἡ χάρις Hdt.3.140; εἰ μή (sc. δρῶ), ἀλλ' ἀκούω γε, Pl.*Grg*.470d, cf. Isoc.3.15, al.; εἰ μηδέν ἐστι τελευτήσαντι, ἀλλ' οὖν τοῦτόν γε τὸν χρόνον ἧττον ἀηδὴς ἔσομαι Pl.*Phd*.91b (in later Gk. ἀλλά γε may be in juxtaposition, εἰ ἄλλοις οὐκ εἰμὶ ἀπόστολος, ἀλλά γε ὑμῖν εἰμί 1*Ep.Cor*.9.2, and ἀ. γε δή is found with vv.ll. in Pl.*Phdr*.262a); εἰ καὶ μετέχουσι .. ἀλλ' οὐ.. Arist.*Pol*.1282ᵃ11:—less freq. after Conjunctions of Time, as ἐπεὶ δή Od.14.151; ἐπεί S.*OC*241. b. after Hom., ἀ. is used elliptically, esp. with Advbs. of Time, ὦ θεοὶ πατρῷοι, συγγένεσθέ γ' ἀ. νῦν (sc. εἰ μὴ πρότερον, ἀ. νῦν γε) S.*El*.411, cf. *Ant*.552, E.*Heracl*.565; ἀ. τῷ χρόνῳ Id.*Med*.912; ἐὰν οὖν ἀ. νῦν γ' ἔτι, i.e. ἐὰν οὖν [μὴ ἄλλοτε], ἀ. νῦν γε.. if then now *at least* ye still.., D.3.33, cf. Lys.10.15:—without an Adv. of Time, *at least*, ἢ δ' ἀ. πρός σε μικρὸν εἰπάτω μόνον Ar.*Pax* 660, cf. S.*OC*1276, E.*HF* 331. 3. sts. = ἀλλ' ἤ (q.v.), *except, but*, οὔτι μοι αἴτιος ἄλλος, ἀ... τοκῆε no one else, *but*.., Od.8.312; οὐδέ τις ἄλλη φαίνετο γαιάων, ἀ. οὐρανὸς ἠδὲ θάλασσα 12.404; ἔπαισεν οὔτις ἀ. ἐγώ S.*OT*1331; ἡδέα ..οὐκ ἔστιν ἀ. τούτοις Arist.*EN*1176ᵃ22, cf. 1152ᵇ30: cf. reverse process in our word *but* = *be out, except*:—sts. with force of ἤ after comparatives, τάφον, οὐκ ἐν ᾧ κεῖνται μᾶλλον, ἀ. ἐν ᾧ ἡ δόξα κτλ. not that in which they are lying, *but* far more.., Th.2.43; οὐχ ὅπλων τὸ πλέον, ἀ. δαπάνης Id.1.83. 4. with neg. after an affirmative word or clause, to be rendered simply by *not*, ἀγαθῶν, ἀ. οὐχὶ κακῶν αἴτιον Lys.14.16; τῶν σπουδαίων, ἀ. μὴ τῶν φαύλων Isoc.1.2; ἐκεῖθεν, ἀ. οὐκ ἐνθένδε ἡρπάσθη Pl.*Phdr*.229d:—after a question, τί δεῖ ἐμβαλεῖν λόγον περὶ τούτου, ἀ. οὐχὶ προειπεῖν; X.*Cyr*.2.2.19, cf. Isoc.15.229, etc. b. without neg., μικρὸς μὲν ἔην δέμας, ἀ. μαχητής Il.5.801. II. to oppose whole sentences, *but, yet*: 1. freq. in transitions, as Il.1.135,140, etc.; ἀ. καὶ ὥς.. 1.116; ἀ. οὐδ' ὥς.. Od.1.6:—after Hom. in answers and objections, *nay but*.., *well but*.., freq. with negs., esp. in making and answering objections, Ar.*Ach*.402,407; also in affirmative answers, Pl.*Prt*.330b, *Grg*.449a, etc.:—repeated in a succession of questions or objections, πότερον ἤτουν σέ τι..; ἀ. ἀπῄτουν; ἀ. περὶ παιδικῶν μαχόμενος; ἀ. μεθύων ἐπαρῴνησα; X.*An*.5.8.4, cf. Pl.*Thg*.123e, Isoc.17.47; ἀ. μήν.., answered by ἀ., Arist.*Pol*.1287ᵃ23:—in vehement answers Pl. often uses νὴ τοὺς θεοὺς ἀ..., μὰ Δί' ἀ..., *Grg*.481c, *Phlb*.36a, cf. *Alc*.1.110b,c:—at beginning of speech, to introduce a general objection, Od.4.472, cf. X.*Smp*.1, Men.*Georg*.22. 2. with imper. or subj., to remonstrate, encourage, persuade, etc., freq. in Hom., ἀ. ἄγε, ἴθι, Il.1.210, 11.611; ἀ. ἴομεν 6.526; ἀ. πίθεσθε 1.259; after voc., ὦ Φίντις, ἀ. ζεῦξον Pi.*O*.6.22, cf. Tyrt.10.15, etc.; answered by a second ἀ., ἀ. περιμένετε. ἀ. περιμενοῦμεν Pl.*R*.327b; ἀλλ' ἕρπεθ' ὡς τάχιστα S.*OC*1643, cf. *Ant*.1029, etc. 3. to break off a subject abruptly, ἀ. τά γε Ζεὺς οἶδεν Od.15.523; ἀ. ταῦτα μὲν τί δεῖ λέγειν; S.*Ph*.11, cf. *Tr*.467, etc. 4. in resuming an address after parenthesis, Pi.*O*.2.12, 4.7. 5. in elliptical phrases, οὐ μὴν ἀ., οὐ μέντοι ἀ... *it is not* [*so*], *but*.., ὁ ἵππος πίπτει καὶ μικροῦ αὐτὸν ἐξετραχήλισεν· οὐ μὴν [ἐξετραχήλισεν] ἀ. ἐπέμεινεν ὁ Κῦρος it did not however [throw him], *but*.., X.*Cyr*.1.4.8; οὐ μέντοι ἀ. Pl.*Smp*.173b; οὐ γὰρ ἀ. Ar.*Ra*.58,498:—after δέ, ὑμεῖς δέ μ' ἀ. παιδὶ συμφονεύσατε E.*Hec*.391. III. when joined with other Particles, each retains proper force, as, 1. ἀλλ' ἄρα, used by Hom. in transitions, Il.6.418, 12.320, etc.; later, to introduce an objection, Pl.*Ap*.25a; in questions, ἀλλ' ἄρα..; Id.*R*.381b. 2. ἀλλ' οὖν, concessive, *at all events*, Ar.*Ra*.1298; τοὺς πρώτους χρόνους ἀ. οὖν προσεποιοῦνθ' ὑμῖν εἶναι φίλοι Aeschin.3.86; *well then*, Pl.*Prt*.310a; *but then, however*, with γε following, Hdt.3.140, S.*Ant*.84, E.*Cyc*.652, Isoc.3.18, etc.; ἀλλ' οὖν γε in apodosi, v. supr. 1.2. 3. ἀλλὰ γάρ, freq. with words between, *but really, certainly*, as ἀλλὰ γὰρ Κρέοντα λεύσσω.., παύσω γόους, but this is irreg. for ἀλλά, Κρέοντα γὰρ λεύσσω, παύσω γόους, E.*Ph*.1308, cf. S.*Ant*.148; for the reg. order cf. S.*Ph*.81, E.*Heracl*.480, *Med*.1067; freq. elliptical, the Verb being understood, Hdt.8.8, A.*Pr*.941, S.*Ant*.155: in Hom. only with negs., ἀλλ' οὐ γάρ Il.7.242, Od.14.355, al., cf. S.*OT*1409; ἀ. γὰρ δή, ἀ. γάρ τοι, S.*Aj*.167, *Ph*.81. 4. ἀ. εἰ.. *quid si*..? Il.16.559. 5. ἀ. ἤ in questions, chiefly of surprise or remonstrance, A.*Ch*.220, S.*El*.879, Ar.*Ach*.1111; ἀλλ' ἤ, τὸ λεγόμενον, κατόπιν ἑορτῆς ἥκομεν; Pl.*Grg*.447a, cf. *Prt*.309c. 6. ἀ. followed by strengthening Particle, ἀλλ' ἤτοι μὲν ταῦτα θεῶν ἐν γούνασι κεῖται Il.17.514; esp. c. imper., 1.211, al.; ἀλλά τοι Od.15.518, A.*Pers*.795, etc.; ἀ. μέντοι, with or without γε, Pl.*Smp*.214e, *Hp.Ma*.287d, al.; ἀ. μήν, v. μήν; ἀ. δή, mostly with words between, S.*Aj*.1271, *OC*586, Isoc.4.109, etc.; without intervening words, Pl.*Ap*.37c, al.; ἀ. δῆτα Id.*Hp.Ma*.285c; ἀ. μὲν δὴ καὶ αὐτός Id.*Tht*.143b, cf. S.*El*.103. IV. = *et quidem*, Olymp. *in Mete*.1.13, al.

**ἀλλάγ-δην**, Adv. *alternately*, Doroth.65, Hdn.Gr.1.508. **-ή** [ᾰγ], ἡ (ἀλλάσσω) *change*, A.*Ag*.482, etc.; ἀλλαγᾷ βίου S.*OT*1206; ἡ κατὰ τόπον ἀ. Arist.*Spir*.485ᵃ22; ἀ. θεῶν Plu.2.166d. II. *exchange, barter, buying and selling*, Pl.*R*.371b, Arist.*EN*1133ᵃ19, *Pol*.1257ᵃ13; pl., διὰ τὰς ἀ. *for purposes of exchange*, ib.1280ᵃ35. 2. *agio*, whether premium or discount, *Peripl.M.Rubr*.49, *PEleph*.14.10 (iii B.C.), *PTeb*.99.2 (ii B.C.), *BGU*1194.17 (i B.C.), etc. III. later, *change of post-horses, stage*, Eust.531.21, cf. *POxy*.1863.5, etc. ❋**-μα**, ατος, τό, *that which is given* or *taken in exchange*, καινῆς διαίτης Hp.*VM*3. 2. *reward, price* of a thing, *AP*12.132 (Mel.), Lxx *De*.23.18(19). 3. *change, vicissitude*, Lxx *Si*.2.4. ❋**-μός**, ὁ, = foreg., Man.4.189.

**ἀλλάθαρον**· ἀλμύρον (Cret.), Hsch.

**ἀλλαθεάς**, άδος, ἡ, at Delphi, *funeral ceremony*, in pl., τὰ ἐς τὸ ταφὰν καὶ ἀ. *GDI*1796, cf. 1731, 1775.

**ἀλλακ-τέον**, *one must change*, Plu.2.53b, Sor.2.11. ❋**-τικός**, ή, όν, *of* or *for exchange*: ἡ -κή or τὸ -κόν *the business of exchange*, Pl.*Sph*.223c; κοινωνία ἀ. Arist.*EN*1132ᵇ31. Adv. -κῶς *in exchange*, Sch.E.*Hec*.1159. **-τός**, ή, όν, *equivalent*, πρός τι Phld.*Oec*.pp.47, 55 J.: -τόν, τό, = ἀνάφορον, Arg. Ar.*Ra*.

❋**ἀλλαμπᾶν**· τὸν ἥλιον, οἱ δὲ ἐπιχειρίδιον (leg. -χωρ-) δαίμονα, Hsch.

**ἀλλανής** (-ῆς cod.)· ἀσφαλής (Lacon.), Id.

❋**ἀλλάντιον**, τό, in later Gk., Dim. of ἀλλᾶς, Moer.12.

**ἀλλαντο-ειδής**, ές, *sausage-shaped*, ἀ. ὑμήν the *allantoid* membrane of the foetus, Gal.*UP*15.5, Aët.16.2. **-ποιός**, ὁ, *maker of sausages*, Hsch. Mil.7 A3, D.L.2.60. **-πωλέω**, *deal in sausages*, Ar.*Eq*.1242. **-πώλης**, ου, ὁ, *sausage-seller*, Ar.*Eq*.143, al., Procop.*Pers*.1.26 (pl.).

**ἀλλάξ**, Adv. = ἐνηλλαγμένως, Hsch.

**ἀλλάξιμα** (sc. ἱμάτια), *changes of raiment*, *POxy*.1728.2 (iii A.D.), *Gloss*.

**ἄλλαξις**, εως, ἡ, *exchange, barter*, Arist.*MM*1194ᵃ24.

**ἀλλᾶς**, ᾶντος, ὁ, *force-meat, sausage* or *black-pudding*, Hippon.48, Ar.*Eq*.161, Crates Com.17, etc.

❋**ἀλλάσσω**, later Att. -ττω Pl.*Prm*.139a: impf. ἤλλαττον Men.*Epit*.466: fut. -άξω Thgn.21: aor. ἤλλαξα E.*Alc*.661: pf. ἤλλᾰχα (ἀπ-) X.*Mem*.3.13.6, (δι-) Dionys.Com.2.10:—Med., fut. ἀλλάξομαι Luc.*Tyr*.7, (ἀντ-) E.*Hel*.1088: aor. ἠλλαξάμην Id.*El*.103, Antipho 5.79, Th.8.82, etc.: pf. (in med. sense) ἤλλαγμαι (ἐν-) S.*Aj*.208:—**Pass.**, fut. ἀλλαχθήσομαι Trag. and Com., (ἀπ-) E.*Med*.878, Ar.*Av*.940; ἀλλαγήσομαι in early Prose, (ἀπ-) Hdt.2.120, (ἐξαπ-) Th.4.28: aor. ἠλλάχθην and ἠλλάγην, former more freq. in S. and E., latter in Prose: pf. ἤλλαγμαι Antiph.176, *AP*9.67, al.: plpf. ἤλλακτο Hdt.2.26. (More common in compds., esp. in later Gk.): (ἄλλος) :—*make other than it is, change, alter*, τόπον Parm.8.41; μορφήν Emp.137; χροιάν E.*Med*.1168; ἤλλαττε χρώματ' Men.*Epit*.466; τὸ ἑαυτοῦ εἶδος εἰς πολλὰς μορφάς Pl.*R*.380d; χώραν Id.*Prm*.139a. II. ἀ. τί τινος *give in exchange, barter* one thing *for* another, τῆς σῆς λατρείας τὴν ἐμὴν δυσπραξίαν.. οὐκ ἂν ἀλλάξαιμ' ἐγώ A.*Pr*.967; τι ἀντί τινος E.*Alc*.661:—Med., τὴν παραυτίκα ἐλπίδα.. οὐδενὸς ἂν ἠλλάξαντο Th.8.82. 2. *repay, requite*, φόνον φονεῦσιν E.*El*.89. 3. *leave, quit*, οὐράνιον φῶς S.*Ant*.944, cf. E.*IT*193. 4. Med., ἔξω τρίβου ἀλλάσσεσθαι ἴχνος *move one's position*, Id.*El*.103. III. *take* one thing *in exchange for* another, κίκιον τοὐσθλοῦ παρεόντος Thgn.21; πόνῳ πόνον ἀ. *to exchange* one suffering *with* another (nisi leg. πόνου), *Trag.Adesp*.7.3; ἠλλαττόμεσθ' ἂν δάκρυα δόντες χρυσίον *should take in exchange*, Philem.73: ἀ. θνητὸν εἶδος *assume* it, E.*Ba*.53, cf. 1331:—more freq. in Med., τί τινος one thing *for* another, εὐδαιμονίας κακοδαιμονίαν Antipho 5.79, cf. Pl.*Lg*.733b; τὰ οἰκήϊα κακὰ ἀλλάξασθαι τοῖσι πλησίοισι *exchange* them with them, Hdt.7.152: hence, *buy*, τι ἀντ' ἀργυρίου Pl.*R*.371c; διά τινος ὠνῆς ἢ καὶ πράσεως ἀλλάττεσθαί τί τινι Id.*Lg*.915d, e; τοῦ παντὸς ἀ. *prize above* all things, Ph.*Bel*.56.30. 2. *take a new position*, i.e. *go to* a place, ἀ. Ἀΐδα θαλάμους E.*Hec*.483; πόλιν ἐκ πόλεως Pl.*Plt*.289e. IV. abs., *have dealings*, as buyer or seller, in Med., πρός τινα Pl.*Lg*.915e. 2. *alternate*, Emp.17.6; σκῆπτρ' ἔχειν ἐνιαυτὸν ἀλλάσσοντε to enjoy power *in turn*, E.*Ph*.74, cf. Pl.*Ti*.42c:—Pass., ἀρεταὶ.. ἀλλασσόμεναι *in turns*, Pi.*N*.11.38, cf. Arist.*Pr*.940ᵃ15. V. Pass., *to be reconciled*, S.*Fr*.997.

**ἀλλαττόλογος**, ον, *complicated*, μῦθος *POxy*.1381.180 (ii A.D.).

**ἀλλαχ-ῆ**, Delph. -χᾷ *GDI*2085, Adv., (ἄλλος) *elsewhere, in another place*, ἄλλος ἀ. one *here*, another *there*, X.*An*.7.3.47; ἄλλοτε ἀ. now *here*, now *there*, Id.*Mem*.1.4.12; = ἄλλοσε, ἀπιὼν ἀ. Ar.*Av*.1020, cf. *PLips*.104 (i B.C.). **-όθεν**, Adv. *from another place*, Lxx 4*Ma*.1.7, *Ev.Jo*.10.1, Plu.2.1129e; *from another source*, δηλοῦσθαι Antipho 3.4.3. ❋**-όθι**, Adv. *elsewhere*, A.D.*Synt*.333.26, Plu.2.20d, *AP*9.378 (Pall.), Jul.*Or*.1.5c. ❋**-όσε**, Adv. *elsewhither*, v.l. in X.*Cyr*.7.4.7, Simp. *in Ph*.1164.38. **-οῦ**, Adv. *elsewhere*, S.*OC*43, X.*HG*2.3.20; ἄγωμεν ἀ. *Ev.Marc*.1.38, cf. Arr.*Epict*.3.26.4.—These forms are censured by Moer.11 as less Att. than ἄλλοθεν, ἄλλοθι, ἄλλοσε.

**ἄλλεγον, ἀλλέξαι**, v. sub ἀναλέγω.

**ἀλλεπαλληλία**, ἡ, *accumulation*, Eust.12.3. **ἀλλεπάλληλος**, ον, *one upon another, successive*, ῥανίδες *EM*702.20; νῆσσαι Sch.Arat.982; *cumulative*, σύνθεσις (as in συν-ομ-ήλικες) *EM*291.37; τὸ ἀ. *accumulation*, Paus.9.39.4; *alternating, varying*, δρόμοι Vett.Val.331.22; *constantly changing*, ἀποτελέσματα 243.29. Adv. -ως *in varied style*, 272.23:—also, *in layers*, of stones, Arg.E.*Ph*.:—perh. to be written divisim ἄλλ' ἐπ., Alciphr.*Fr*.6.11.

**ἄλλῃ**, Dor. ἄλλᾳ or ἀλλᾷ (as A.D.*Adv*.175.13), Delph. and Megar. ἀλλεῖ *GDI*1830, 3052 (Chalcedon), Adv., properly dat. fem. of ἄλλος: I. of Place, 1. *elsewhere*, Il.13.49, S.*Ph*.23, etc.; τῇ ἄ. Hdt.2.36, 4.28: c. gen. loci, ἄλλος ἄ. τῆς πόλεως one *in one part of* the city, one *in another*, Th.2.4; ἄ. τῆς κεφαλῆς Hp.*VC*8; ἄλλοτε ἄ. X.*HG*1.5.20; ἄ. καὶ ἄ. *here* and *there*, prob. l. Id.*An*.5.2.29. 2. *to another place, elsewhither*, Il.5.187, Od.18.288; ἔρχεται ἄ., i.e. is *lost* Il.1.120; ἄλλοι ἄ. Hdt.1.46, cf. 7.25; οὔτ' ἐπὶ θήρην ἰοῦσαι οὔτ' ἄ. οὐδαμῇ Id.4.114. II. of Manner, *otherwise*, Il.15.51, etc.; τῇ τε ἄ. πολλαχῇ καὶ.. Hdt.6.21; ἄ. γέ πῃ Pl.*Smp*.189c; ἄ. πως X.*Cyr*.1.1.1.

**ἀλλ' ἤ**, ἤ, = ἀλλά 1.3, *except, but*, after negs., esp. οὐδείς or μηδείς, which are often joined with ἄλλος or ἕτερος, as οὐδεὶς ἀλλ' ἢ ἐκείνη no one *except* her, Hdt.9.109, cf. Th.3.71, al.; μηδὲν ἄλλο δοκεῖν εἶναι ἀληθὲς ἀλλ' ἢ τὸ σωματοειδές Pl.*Phd*.81b, cf. *R*.429b, etc.; ἀργύριον ν οὐκ ἔχω ἀλλ' ἢ μικρόν τι X.*An*.7.7.53:—after questions implying neg., Pl.*Phdr*.258e:—in Ar.*Ach*.1111,1112 ἀλλ' ἦ (bis) is prob. l. for ἀλλ' ἤ (bis). (This form seems to arise from a confusion of οὐδὲν ἄλλο ἢ *other than, except*, cf. Hdt.1.49, 9.8, ἄλλο γε ἢ ὅτι.. *except that*.., and οὐδὲν ἄλλο..ἀλλά.)

**ἀλλ' ἦ**, in questions, v. ἀλλά III. 5.

**ἀλληγορ-έω**, (ἀγορεύω) *interpret allegorically*, Ἕλληνες Κρόνον ἀλληγοροῦσι τὸν χρόνον Plu.2.363d, cf. 996b, Heraclit.*All*.1:—Pass., *to be spoken allegorically*, *Ep.Gal*.4.24; ἀλληγορεῖται ὁ Ἀπόλλων εἰς τὸν Ἥλιον, Sch.S.*Aj*.186. 2. abs., *speak figuratively* or *metaphorically*, Demetr.*Eloc*.151,285; *speak allegorically*, J.*AJProoem*.4. **-ητής**, οῦ, ὁ, *allegorical expounder*, Eust.123.32. **-ία**, ἡ, *allegory, veiled language*, Cic.*Att*.2.20.3(pl.):—*allegorical exposition* of mythical legends, Plu.2.19e; κατ' ἀλληγορίαν Longin.9.7. II. *figurative, metaphorical language*, Demetr.*Eloc*.99, Cic.*Orat*.27.94, Quint.*Inst*.8.6.44; χρῆσθαι μεταφοραῖς ἢ -γορίαις Phld.*Rh*.1.174S., cf. 164S. **-ικός**, ή, όν, *figurative*, Demetr.*Eloc*.282; ἀ. στόμφος Longin.32.7. Adv. -κῶς Cleanth.*Stoic*.1.118, Demetr.*Eloc*.243. **-ος**, ον, *allegorical*, *Et.Gud*.515.42. Adv. -ως *allegorically*, Anon. (fort. Tz.) ap.Sch.A.*Pr*.428.

**ἄλληκτος** (A), ον, poet. for ἄληκτος (A), *unceasing, ceaseless*, νότος Od.12.325; ὀδύναι S.*Tr*.985 (lyr.); *implacable*, θυμός Il.9.636: neut. as Adv., ἄλληκτον, ἄλληκτα, Man.3.252,206.—So Ἀλληκτώ is restored for Ἀληκτώ (the Fury) in Luc.*Trag*.6.

**ἄλληκτος** (B), ον, = ἄληκτος (B), *AB*202:—Adv. -τί, Hsch.

**ἀλληλ-ανάδοχος**, ον, *giving mutual security*, *PLond*.3.994.7 (vi A. D.), *PHamb*.23.7 (vi A. D.). **-ανεμία**, ἡ, *constant change of wind*, ἀ. ἐπισφαλὴς ταῖς βοτάναις Lyd.*Ost*.31.

**ἀλληλάξαι**· ἀλλήλους ἐλάσαι, Hsch.

❋**ἀλληλ-εγγύη**, ἡ, *mutual security*, ἐξ -ύης *PFlor*.368.10 (i A. D.), *POxy*.918 ii 15 (ii A. D.), etc.; τὸ τῆς ἀ. δίκαιον *PCair*.67126.18. **-έγγυοι**, α, *mutual sureties*, *BGU*1001 (i B. C.), 1106.41 (i B. C.): sg., Hsch. Adv. -ως Just.*Edict*.9.3, *Nov*.99.

**ἀλληλίζω**, *lie together*, sens. obsc., *AB*383:—also ἀλληλίζειν· ἄλλως καὶ ἄλλως λέγειν, and ἀλληλίζεσθαι· τὸ ἀλλήλους ἐπιχειρῆσαι, Hsch.

**ἀλληλο-βόρος**, ον, in pl., *devouring one another*, Hsch. s. v. ἀλληλοδωδόται. **-γραφία**, ἡ, *writing of amoebaean poems*, Eust. 55.39.

**ἀλληλ-οδωδόται**, *devouring one another*, dub. in Hsch.

**ἀλληλο-κληρονομία**, ἡ, *mutual inheritance*, Suid. s. v. ῥευξωρία. **-κτονέω**, *slay each other*, Hp.*Ep*.17, Arist.*Fr*.344, Ph.2.38. **-κτονία**, ἡ, *mutual slaughter*, D.H.1.87, Ph.2.567. **-κτόνος**, ον, of things, *producing mutual slaughter*, δαῖτες Moschio Trag.6; ζῆλος D.H.2.24. **-μανδάτορες**, οἱ, *mandatories of each other*, *PHamb*.23.7 (vi A. D.). **-μᾰχία**, ἡ, *mutual fight*, Sch.Il.3.443. ❋**-μῑσέω**, *hate one another*, *PMag.Lond*.46.108. **-πάθεια**, ἡ, Astrol., *subjection to mutual influence*, Vett.Val.5.13. **-τῠπέω**, *impinge mutually*, Alex.Aphr.*in Metaph*.36.22. **-τῠπία**, ἡ, *mutual impact*, of atoms, *Placit*.1.12.6: pl., Ph.2.489.

**ἀλληλ-ουχέω**, *hold together*, intr., Ph.1.464, 2.417:—Pass., Nicom. *Ar*.1.2; -ούμενος κόσμος Iamb.*in Nic*.p.7.13 P., cf. Simp.*in Ph*.711.16, Syrian.*in Metaph*.150.1, Dam.*Pr*.206. **-ουχία**, ἡ, *holding together, conjunction*, Longin.36.4; *coherence*, Epicur.*Nat*.2.993.5; *continuity*, opp. παράθεσις, *Theol.Ar*.4; τάξις καὶ ἀ. Procl.*Inst*.97, cf. Dam.*Pr*. 85; κόσμου Iamb.*Protr*.21.ιζ'; *close texture, consistency*, Gal.14.12; κτηδόνων Dsc.5.127; *mutual support*, of words in composition, D.H. *Comp*.23. **-οῦχοι**, α, *holding together*, ἄτομοι Epicur.*Ep*.2 p.44 U.; φύσεις Id.*Nat*.2.9; ἐγκεντρίσεις Jul.*Ep*.180.

**ἀλληλο-φᾰγέω**, *eat one another*, Arist.*HA*591ᵃ17. **-φᾰγία**, ἡ, *an eating one another*, Hdt.3.25, Pl.*Epin*.975a, Athenio 1, etc. **-φάγοι**, α, *eating each other*, Arist.*HA*593ᵇ27, Orac.ap.Paus.8.42.6; ἡ ἀ. ἀνομία S.E.*M*.2.32; ἀ. δίκαι Telecl.2. **-φθονία**, ἡ, *mutual envy*, D.H.4.26. **-φθορία**, ἡ, *mutual slaughter*, Pl.*Prt*.321a (pl.), D.H.5.66 (pl.). **-φθόρος**, ον, *destroying one another*, Max.Tyr. 41.5. **-φῐλέω**, *love one another*, *PMag.Lond*.46.107. **-φῐλοι**, α, *fond of each other*, *Gp*.20.6.1. **-φονία**, Dor. ἀλλᾱλ-, ἡ, *mutual slaughter*, Pi.O.2.42, Philipp.Perg. in *IG*4.1153 (Epid.), Them. *Or*.6.74b, Herm.ap.Stob.1.49.44. ❋**-φόνος**, Dor. ἀλλᾱλ-, α, *murdering one another*, λόγχαι Pi.*Fr*.163; χεῖρες, μανίαι, A.*Th*.931, *Ag*.1576; ἀδελφοί X.*Hier*.3.8. **-φυής**, ές, in pl., *grown out of one another*, f.l. for ὁλοφυής, *Placit*.5.19.5.

**ἀλλήλων**, Aeol. and Dor. **ἀλλάλων**, gen. pl., dual ἀλλήλοιν, Ep. ἀλλήλοιϊν Il.10.65, fem. -αιν X.*Mem*.2.3.18 codd.: dat. ἀλλήλοις, αις, οις, dual ἀλλήλοιν: acc. ἀλλήλους, ας, α, dual ἀλλήλω (fem.) X.*Mem*. 2.3.18, cf. Lxx *Ge*.15.10,al.: the dual is rare in Prose: sg., κεράμῳ ἁρμόττοντι πρὸς ἄλληλον *IG*2.1054.59: (redupl. from ἄλλος):—*of one another, to one another, one another*; hence, *mutually, reciprocally*, used of all three persons, Il.4.62, Od.1.209, etc.: freq. with Preps., ἐν ἀλλάλοισι among *one another*, Pi.*P*.4.223, etc.; τούτω.. ἐν ἀλλήλαισι A.*Pers*.188; πρὸς ἀλλήλους, εἰς ἄλληλα, Id.*Pr*.491,1085; ἐπὶ, πρὸς ἀλλήλοις, Od.22.389, A.*Pers*.506, *Ag*.654; ἐξ ἀλλήλων X.*Mem*. 4.4.23; κύκλῳ καὶ ἐξ ἀλλήλων δείκνυσθαι Arist.*APr*.57ᵇ18; παρ' ἀλλήλους, -α, Pl.*Grg*.472c, *Phdr*.264b; ἡ δι' ἀλλήλων δεῖξις *reciprocal proof*, Arist.*APr*.59ᵃ32, cf. D.L.9.89, etc.; μετ' ἀλλήλων Arist.*Pr*. 953ᵇ32; πρὸς αὑτὰ καὶ πρὸς ἄλληλα Pl.*Grg*.451c; ὑπ' ἀλλήλων A.*Th*. 821. (Wrongly interpreted by Gramm. as = ἑαυτούς, -ῶν, Il.12.105, Th.2.70, E.*Fr*.1124.)

**ἄλλην**, acc. fem. of ἄλλος, used (sc. ὁδόν) as Adv., *elsewhither*, ἄ. καὶ ἄ. διώκειν X.*Cyr*.4.1.15, cf. Aen.Tact.26.3: also of Time, ἄ. καὶ ἄ. ἀποβλέπειν εἴς τινα *again and again*, Pl.*Euthd*.273b.

**ἄλληνˑ** λάχανον (Ital.), Hsch.

**ἀλλήναλλος**, ον, *this way and that, irregular*, κίνησις Theo Sm. p.151 H. Adv. -ως Eustr.*in APo*.149.29.

**ἀλλῆσαι**· ἀναστρέψαι, Hsch. (fort. ἀλλῦσαι).

**ἄλλιξ**, ῑκος, ἡ, *man's upper garment*, Euph.144, Call.*Fr*.149; *purple cloak* (Thessal.), *EM*68.33.

❋**ἄλλιστος**, ον, Ep. for ἄλιστος, (λίσσομαι) *inexorable*, Ἀΐδης *AP*7. 643 (Crin.), *IG*14.1909.3.

**ἀλλιτάνευτος**, Ep. for ἀλιτάνευτος, *inexorable*, *AP*7.483.

**ἄλλῐτος**, ον, = foreg., αἶσα *Epic.Alex.Adesp*.6.5; ἄλλιτα κωκύοντες shrieking *unanswered prayers*, *App.Anth*.4.54.7.

**ἀλλο-γενής**, ές, *of another race*, *OGI*598, Lxx *Ge*.17.27,al., *Ev.Luc*. 17.18, Agath.4.5, Ps.-Callisth.3.26. **-γλωσσία**, ἡ, *use of a strange tongue, difference of tongue*, J.*AJ*1.5.1. **-γλωσσος**, ον, *using a strange tongue*, Hdt.2.154, *SIG*1.4 (Abu Simbel, vi B. C.), *IG*12(3). 328.20 (Thera, iii B. C.), Lxx *Ba*.4.15. **-γνοέω**, (γνο-, γνῶναι) *take one for another*, ἀλλογνώσας Κροῖσον Hdt.1.85. II. *to be deranged*, Hp.ap.Gal.19.75. **-γνώμων**, ονος, *fickle*, Ptol.*Tetr*.183; *holding strange opinions*, Agath.4.26. **-γνώς**, ῶτος, ὁ, ἡ, *unknown, strange*, Emp.126. **-γνωτος**, ον, = foreg., δῆμος Od.2. 366. ❋**-δαπός**, ή, όν, (perh. ἀλλοδ-, cf. Lat. *aliud*, -απος = -*ᵘq*ᵘ*os*, cf. Lat. *long-inquus*) *belonging to another people* or *land, foreign*, Il. 16.550, Od.17.485, Sapph.92, Pi.*N*.1.22, A.*Th*.1082, X.*Cyr*.8.7. 14, etc.; ἐν ἀλλοδαπῇ *in foreign parts*, *Sammelb*.4284.7 (iii A. D.):—later **-δᾰπής**, ές, *EM*68.2, cf. Ps.-Callisth.2.21. **-δημία**, Dor. **-δαμία**, ἡ, = ἀποδημία, *stay in foreign land*, Hp.*Int*.48; ἐν ἀλλοδημίᾳ *abroad*, Pl.*Lg*.954e; καταστρέφειν ἐπ' ἀλλοδημί⟨ας⟩ Phld.*Mort*.26: pl., Iamb.*VP*35.252. II. concrete, *foreign people*, στείχειν ἐπ' ἀλλοδαμίαν B.17.37, cf. Poll.9.21. **-δημος**, ον, *foreign*, Id.3.54. **-δοξέω**, *mistake one thing for another*, Pl.*Tht*.189d, 190d. **-δοξία**, ἡ, *mistaking of one thing for another*, ib.189b. II. *revolutionary spirit*, D.C.79.5. **-δοξος**, ον, *holding a different opinion, belonging to a different school*, Phld.*Herc*.19.2. **-εθνής**, ές, *of foreign nation*, D.S.2.37, Nic.Dam.p.94 D., J.*AJ*15.11.5; *with foreign foe*, πόλεμος D.H.5.5, cf. Lxx 3*Ma*.4.6. **-εθνία**, ἡ, *difference of nation*, Str.12. 1.2. **-ειδής**, ές, *of different form*, τοὔνεκ' ἄρ' ἀλλοειδέα (trisyll., but perh. ἀλλοϝιδέα) φαινέσκετο πάντα ἄνακτι Od.13.194, cf. Plu. *Strom*.2, Plot.6.8.18. Adv. -εῶς, f.l. for στυλοειδῶς, Epicur.*Ep*.2 p.47 U.

**ἄλλοθεν**, Adv. *from another place*, ἄ. ἄλλος one *from one place*, another *from another*, Il.2.75, etc., cf. Alc.86, Emp.23, Thgn.518, A. *Ag*.92,595, etc.; ἄ. εἰλήλουθε he came *from abroad*, Od.3.318; ποθεν ἄλλοθεν 7.52; in Att., ἄ. ὁθενοῦν or ὁποθενοῦν *from* what *other place* soever, Pl.*Lg*.738c, *Grg*.512a; οὐδαμόθεν ἄ. Id.*Phlb*.30a: c. gen. loci, ἄ. τῶν Ἑλλήνων Id.*Lg*.707e.

❋**ἄλλοθι**, Adv. *elsewhere, in another place*, esp. *in a strange* or *foreign land*, Od.14.130, al. (not in Il.): c. gen., ἄ. γαίης *in another* or *strange* land, Od.2.131; but ἄ. πάτρης *elsewhere than* in one's native land, i.e. *away from* home, 17.318; ἄ. που or πῃ some*where else*, Pl.*Phd*. 91e (v.l.), *Sph*.243b; ἄ. οὐδαμοῦ, πολλαχοῦ, X.*Mem*.1.4.8, Pl.*Smp*. 209e; ἄ. ἐν οἷς.., as if ἐν ἄλλοις ἔργοις, Id.*La*.181e; ἄ. καὶ ἄ. *to different points* (cf. ἄλλος II.3), Arist.*Mete*.370ᵇ11. II. *in other ways, from other causes*, Th.1.16; ἄ. οὐδαμοῦ *in no other way*, Pl.*Prt*.324e, *Smp*.184e, etc. III. with Verbs of motion, Antipho 1.4, X.*HG* 2.2.2, D.34.37.

**ἀλλό-θροος**, ον, contr. **-θρους**, ουν (as always in Trag.) *speaking a strange tongue*, ἐπ' ἀλλοθρόους ἀνθρώπους, κατ' ἀλλοθρόους ἀνθρ., Od. 1.183, 3.302, 15.453: generally, *foreign*, στρατός Hdt.1.78; Αἴγυπτος Id.3.11; πόλις A.*Ag*.1200; *strange, alien*, γνώμη S.*Tr*.844.—Not in Att. Prose.

**ἀλλοινία**, ἡ, *drinking several wines, mixing liquors*, Plu.2.661c(pl.).

**ἀλλοιό-μορος**, ον, *unfortunate*, *PMag.Par*.1.1409. **-μορφος**, ον, *strangely formed*, ἄνθρωπος Hanno *Peripl*.7; θεωρία Onos.10. 28. **-προσωπέω**, *to be separated from another planet by a distance differing from that between their two domiciles*, Vett.Val.65.8.

❋**ἀλλοῖος**, α, ον, (ἄλλος) *of another sort* or *kind, different*, Il.4.258, 5.638 (v.l.), Od.16.181, etc.; ἄλλοτε ἀλλοῖος Pi.*I*.4(3).5, cf. *P*.3. 104, Diog.Apoll.2: prov., ἢν πολλὰ βάλλῃς, ἄλλοτ' ἀλλοῖον βαλεῖς 'every bullet has its billet', *Com.Adesp*.448; ἀλλοῖα φρονεῖν Emp. 108; ἀλλοῖόν τι, euphem. for κακόν τι, *other than good*, Hdt.5.40; εἴ τι γένοιτο ἀ. Arcesil.ap.D.L.4.44; ἄν.. [ὁ λόγος] ἀλλοιότερος φανῇ D. *Prooem*.32.4, cf. Alex.Aphr.*Pr*.1.99:—foll. by ἤ.., Hdt.2.35, Pl.*Ap*. 20c, etc.; or by gen., Id.*Lg*.836b:—Comp. ἀλλοιότερος Hdt.7.212, Th.4.106, D.l.c., Arist.*Cael*.280ᵃ12; ἀλλοιέστερος Epich.186, cf. Sch.Od.2.190. 2. *containing* or *subject to diversity*, Porph.*Sent*. 20,21. II. Adv. -ως *otherwise*, Pl.*Ly*.212d: Comp. -ότερον X. *Mem*.4.8.2; -οτέρως *worse*, Charis.80.17.

**ἀλλοιό-στροφος**, ον, *of irregular strophes*, i.e. not consisting of alternate strophe and antistrophe, Heph.*Poëm*.5. **-σχήμων**, ον, *of varying form*, κόσμοι Epicur.*Fr*.82, cf. S.E.*M*.7.206. **-της**, ητος, ἡ, *difference, alteration*, Hp.*Flat*.2, Pl.*Ti*.82b. **-τροπέω**, *change colour*, Hp.*Int*.37:—Med. -έομαι *vary*, Gal.19.75. **-τροπος**, prob. l. for ἀλλότροπος, Linus ap.Stob.1.10.5; gloss on αἰλότροπος, Hsch. **-φανής**, ές, gloss on ἀλλοίους, Hsch.; on ἀείδελον, *EM*21. 28. **-χροος**, ον, contr. **-χρους**, ουν, (χρόα) *of varying colour*, S.E. *M*.7.206.

❋**ἀλλοι-όω**, (ἀλλοῖος) *change, alter*, φύσιν Hp.*Praec*.9; τροφὴν ἐς τὸ γάλα Id.*Gland.*16, Pl.*R.*381a, etc. **2.** *represent as* ἀλλοῖος (q.v.), Plot.3.6.3. **II.** Pass., fut. -ωθήσομαι Gal.*UP*8.6, etc., but -ώσομαι ib.10.1:—*become different, be changed*, Hp.*Vict.*1.4, etc.; ἀλλοιοῦσθαι τὴν γνώμην Th.2.59; τῇ ὄψει X.*Cyn.*9.4; ἀλλοίωσιν ἀλλοιοῦσθαι *undergo an alteration*, Pl.*Tht.*181d; rare in Poetry, ὅλοιντ' ἰδοῦσαι τούσδ' ἂν ἠλλοιωμένους E.*Supp.*944. **2.** *to be estranged*, D.C.37.11. **3.** *to be changed for the worse*, X.*Cyr.*3.3.9, Euphro 10, Lxx *La.*4.1. **4.** *to be confused in mind*, ὑπὸ τῆς μέθης Plb. 8.27.5. **5.** *disguise oneself*, Lxx 3*Ki.*14.2. **-ώδης**, ες, *strange, altered in appearance*, τὰς ὄψιας Aret.*SD*1.6; *strange in manner*, Vett. Val.18.5. **-ωμα**, ατος, τό, = -ωσις Damox.2. **-ωπός**, όν, *of different shapes*, Emp.21. **-ωσις**, εως, ἡ, *difference*, Pl.*R.*454c; *alteration*, Arist.*Ph.*226ᵃ26, Aristox.*Harm.*p.74 M.: pl., Thphr.*CP* 4.5.5; cf. ἀλλοιόω II.1. **2.** *confusion of mind*, Plb.3.81.5. **3.** Gramm., *varied construction*, Ps.-Plu.*Vit.Hom.*41,48. **-ωτικός**, ή, όν, *transformative*, Arist.*Sens.*441ᵇ21, *Ph.*257ᵃ24; δύναμις, of digestion, Gal.*UP*4.7; *alterative*, φάρμακον ὅτι περ ἂν ἀ. ᾖ τῆς φύσεως Id.11.380. **-ωτός**, ή, όν, *subject to change*, Arist.*Ph.*201ᵃ12, cf. *Placit.*1.9.2, etc.

**ἀλλο-κοτία**, ἡ, *absurdity*, Simp.*in Ph.*1142.31, *in Epict.*p.72 D. **-κοτος**, ον, *of unusual nature* or *form, strange, portentous*, Hp.*Fract.*1, Ar.*V.*71, Crates Com.43, etc.; ἀ. πρᾶγμα *unwelcome, against the grain*, Th.3.49; ἀ. ὄνομα *strange, uncouth* word, Pl.*Tht.*182a: c. gen., ἀλλοκότῳ γνώμᾳ τῶν πάρος with purpose *utterly different from..*, S.*Ph.* 1191; of persons, Pl.*Euthd.*306e, etc.: Comp. and Sup. -ώτερος, -ώτατος Pl.Com.28. Adv. -τως Pherecr.201, Pl.*Ly.*216a (v.l.). (κότος = ὀργή, i.e. *temper*, Phryn.*PS*p.23 B.)

***ἅλλομαι**, *h.Cer.*175, etc.: impf. ἡλλόμην X.*Cyr.*1.4.11, etc.: fut. ἁλοῦμαι (ὑπερ-) X.*Eq.*8.4, Dor. ἁλεῦμαι Theoc.3.25, 5.144: aor. 1 ἡλάμην Batr.225, E.*Ion*1402, Ar.*Ra.*243, no subj. or opt., part. ἁλάμενος [1st syll. long] *Av.*1395, inf. ἅλασθαι Ael.*Ep.*16, (καθ-) v.l. Luc. *D.Mort.*14.5: aor. 2 ἡλόμην, rare in ind., v.l. X.*HG*4.4.11, (ἐξ-) S.*OT*1311, (ἐν-) v.l. A.*Pers.*516, subj. ἅληται [ᾰ] Il.21.536, opt. ἁλοίμην X.*Mem.*1.3.9 (cf. εἰσ-), inf. ἁλέσθαι Opp.*C.*1.83, etc., part. ἁλόμενος [ᾰ] A.*Eu.*368 (lyr.), X.*An.*4.2.17, etc.; to aor. 2 also belong Ep. 2 and 3 sg. ἆλσο, ἆλτο, subj. ἅλεται Il.11.192, part. ἅλμενος only in compds., but ἅλμενος Opp.*H.*5.666: (*sal-*, cf. Lat. *sal-io*):—*spring, leap*, prop. of living beings, μὴ .. ἐς τεῖχος ἅληται Il.21.536; ἐπεί κ' .. εἰς ἵππους ἅλεται 11.192; εἰς ἅλα ἆλτο 1.532 (but ἥλατο πόντον Call.*Dian.*195); ἐξ ὀχέων .. ἆλτο χαμᾶζε Il.6.103; ἆλτο κατ' Οὐλύμπου 18.616:—ἅλλεσθαι ἐπί τινι *leap upon* or *against*, 21.174, Od.22.80; ἐπὶ στίχας Il.20.353: c. inf., ἆλτο θέειν, πέτεσθαι, *h.Cer.* 389, *Ap.*448: abs., of horse, X.*Eq.*8.4. **2.** c. acc., *leap over*, βόθρον Ael.*NA*6.6; τάφρον Opp.*C.*1.83. **3.** of things, ἆλτο ὀϊστός Il.4.125; of sound, ἀπὸ λείων ἠχὼ ἀλλομένη Pl.*Phdr.*255c; of parts of body, *twitch, quiver, throb*, ἅλλεται ὀφθαλμός Theoc.3.37, cf. Arist. *HA*604ᵃ27, *PRyl.*1.28.

**ἀλλο-μορφέω**, *disguise oneself*, Ps.-Callisth.1.3; *change one's shape*, Sm.*Ez.*31.15. ***-μορφος**, ον, *of strange shape*, τέρατα, σώματα Hp.*Morb.*4.93.

**ἀλλόμος**· τυφλός, Hsch.; i.e. ἀλαό[λαο]ς.

**ἀλλο-πάθεια**, ἡ, *subjection to external influences*, D.S.26.1. **-παθής**, ές, properly, *subject to external influence*, hence in Gramm. of Pronouns, *non-reflexive*, A.D.*Pron.*44.17, *Synt.*175.13, *EM*496. 45. **2.** Adv. -θῶς, of Verbs, *transitively*, Eust.920.27. **-πειρίους**· ἀλλοφύλους, Hsch. ***-πίας**, Ep. -ίης, ὁ, a fish, Numen.ap.Ath. 7.326a. **-ποιός**, ά, όν, *producing otherness*, Procl.*in Prm.* p.569 S. ***-πολία**, ἡ, = ἀλλοδημία, *Leg.Gort.*6.47: hence ***-πολιᾶται**, οἱ, *GDI*4954 (Cret.). **-πρόσαλλος**, ὁ, i.e. ἄλλοτε πρὸς ἄλλον, *leaning first to one side, then to the other, fickle*, epith. of Ares, Il.5.831,889, cf. Eun.*VS*p.496 B.; πλοῦτος *AP*15.12, cf. 1.34 (Agath.); τὸ ἀ. *respect of persons*, *Corp.Herm.*18.4. **2.** simply, *transferred*, ἀ. ἀρωγή, coupled with ἑτεραλκέα νίκην, Tryph.565; *deceitful*, Nonn.*D.*46.4, al.; *changeful, successive*, of waves, etc. (cf. ἀλλεπάλληλος), ib.3.24, al., cf. Man.5.68.

***ἄλλος**, η, ο, Cypr. αἶλος *Inscr.Cypr.*135 H. (Idalion): (from ἀλyος, cf. Lat. *alius*):—*another*, i.e. *one besides* what has been mentioned, either Adj. or Pron.: when Adj., its Subst. is either in the same case, or in gen., Ζεῦ ἄλλοι τε θεοί Il.6.476; θεῶν ἄ. 16.446:—ἄ. μέν .. ἄ. δέ .. *one .. another ..*, more rarely *the one .. the other ..* (of *two* persons, etc.), Il.22.493, etc.; τὰ μέν .. ἄλλα δέ .. Il.6.147, and Att.; ἕτερον μέν .. ἄλλον δέ .. Il.9.313; ἄλλο μέν .. ἑτέρου δέ .. Hdt.1.32; θάτερον .. τὸ δ' ἄλλο E.*IT*962. **II.** with τις, *any other*, οὐδέ τις ἄ. ἔγνω ἀλλ' ἄρα Κασσάνδρη Il.24.697; ἄ. τις Hdt. 3.85; οὐδεὶς ἄ. no *other*, ibid.; ἄλλα πολλά Il.9.639; πολλὰ καὶ ἄλλα Th.3.56; for εἴ τις ἄλλος Id.6.32, etc., and εἴ τις καὶ ἄ. X.*An.*1.4. 15, etc., v. εἰ. **2.** freq. with another of its own cases or derived Adverbs, ἄ. ἄλλα λέγει *one man* says *one thing, one another*, X.*An.*2.1.15; ἄ. ἄλλῳ ἔλεγεν Pl.*Smp.*22cc; ἄ. ἄλλῃ ἐτράπετο X.*An.* 4.8.19; v. ἄλλοθεν, ἄλλοσε, ἄλλοτε; also with Verb in pl., παραλαμβάνων ἄ. ἄλλον ἐπ' ἄλλου, τὸν δ' ἐπ' ἄλλου χρείᾳ .. ἐθέμεθα πόλιν ὄνομα Pl.*R.*369c, cf. X.*Cyr.*2.1.4, etc.: pl., ἄλλοι when the several parties are pl., λείπουσι τὸν λόφον .. ἄλλοι ἄλλοθεν X.*An.*1.10. 13. **3.** ἄ. καὶ ἄ., *one and then another, one or two*, X.*An.*1.5. 12; ἄλλο καὶ ἄλλο *one thing after another*, Id.*Cyr.*4.1.15; πρὸς ἄλλῳ καὶ ἄλλῳ σημείῳ to *different* points, Euc.1.7. **4.** repeated for emphasis, ἄ. ἄ. τρόπος *quite another* sort, E.*Ph.*132. **5.** οὐδ' ἄ. for οὐδέτερος, Theoc.6.45. **6.** with Art., ὁ ἄλλος, *the rest, all besides*; in pl., οἱ ἄλλοι (Ion. contr. ὧλλοι) *all the others, the rest*, freq. from Hom. downwards (ἄλλοι in same signf., Il.2.1); τὰ ἄλλ[α], contr. τἆλλα, *all else*, τἆλλα πλὴν ὁ χρυσός *Scol.*1 (Pytherm.); Att. freq. as Adv., *for the rest*, esp. in amendments to decrees, τ[ὰ] μὲν ἄλλα καθάπερ ὁ δεῖνα κτλ. *IG*1².27a70, etc.: of Time, = τὸν ἄλλ[ον] χρόνον, X.*HG*3.2.2; ὁ ἄ. χρόνος, = ὁ λοιπὸς χρόνος, of the future, Ly. 14.4 (but also of the past, D.20.16); τῇ ἄλλῃ ἡμέρᾳ, τῷ ἄλλῳ ἔτε[ι] *next* day, *next* year, X.*HG*1.1.13, 1.2.1; οἵ τε ἄλλοι καί .. *all other[s]* and especially .., γυναῖκας ἄλλας τε πολλὰς καὶ δὴ καὶ βασιλέος θυγατέρ[α] Hdt.1.1, etc.; ἄλλα τε δὴ εἶπε, καί .. Pl.*Tht.*142c; (v. ἄλλως I):—τ[ὸ] ἄλλο is much less freq. than τὰ ἄλλα. **7.** with Numerals, *ye[t] still, further*, τρίτον ἄ. γένος Hes.*Op.*143; πέμπτος ποταμὸς ἄ. *yet* [a] fifth river, Hdt.4.54, cf. A.*Th.*486, S.*Ant.*1295, etc. **8.** in enu[-] merations, *as well, besides*, ἅμα τῇγε καὶ ἀμφίπολοι κίον ἄλλαι wit[h] her their mistress came attendants *also*, Od.6.84; μήτηρ ἠδὲ πατὴ[ρ] ἠδ' ἄλλοι πάντες ἑταῖροι 9.367; οὐ γὰρ ἦν χόρτος οὐδὲ ἄ. δένδρον οὐδέν there was no grass nor any tree *at all*, X.*An.*1.5.5; πολιτῶν καὶ τῶν ἄλλων ξένων Pl.*Grg.*473d; προσοφλὼν οὐ τὴν ἐπωβελίαν μόνον ἀλλὰ καὶ ἄλλην ὕβριν *besides*, Aeschin.1.163:—pleonastic, παρ' ἀγγέλων ἄλλων ἀκούειν S.*OT*7, cf. X.*Cyr.*1.6.2; ἰδὼν ἐς πλησίον ἄλλον Il.4. 81; γυναικῶν τῶν ἄλλων μία E.*Med.*945; μόνη τῶν ἄλλων ἐπιστημῶν Pl.*Chrm.*166e; with Comp., freq. in Hom., οὔτις σεῖο νεώτερος ἄ. Ἀχαιῶν Il.15.569, cf. 22.106, al.; with Sup., ὀϊζυρώτατος ἄλλων Od. 5.105. **III.** less freq., = ἀλλοῖος, *of other sort, different*, Il.13.64, 21.22; ἄ. γέγονεν Pl.*Phdr.*241a. **2.** in this sense, c. gen., ἄλλα τῶν δικαίων *other than* just, X.*Mem.*4.4.25:—followed by ἤ.., with preceding neg., οὐδὲ ἄλλο.., οὐδὲν ἄλλο (or ἄλλο οὐδέν).., ἤ.. nothing *else* than.., Hdt.1.49, 7.168, Th.4.14; οὐδὲν ἄλλο γ' ἢ πτήξας A.*Pers.*209; ἃ μηδὲν ἄλλο ἢ διανοεῖταί τις which one *only* thinks, Pl. *Tht.*195e:—more freq. in questions, τίς ἄλλος ἢ 'γώ..; A.*Pr.*440; τί δ' ἄλλο γ' ἢ πόνοι..; Id.*Th.*852: ellipt., τί ἄλλο (sc. πάσχω) ἢ ἱπποκένταυρος γίγνομαι; X.*Cyr.*4.3.20; τί ἄλλο (sc. ἐποίησαν) ἢ ἐπεβούλευσαν; Th.3.39:—followed by πλήν, S.*Aj.*125, Ar.*Ach.*39; by Preps., πρό.. Hdt.3.85; ἀντί.. A.*Pr.*467; παρά.. Pl.*Phd.*80b, etc.: with neg., sts. followed by ἀλλά, Il.18.403, 21.275:—see also ἄλλο τι. **3.** *other than what is, untrue, unreal*, Od.4.348. **4.** *other than right, wrong, bad*, ἄλλου τινὸς ἡττῆσθαι yield to some *unworthy* motive, D. 21.218, cf. Plu.2.187d, etc.; cf. ἄλλως.

***ἄλλος**, Aeol., = ἠλέος, dub. in Sapph.110.

***ἄλλοσε**, Adv. *elsewhither*, Od.23.184; ἄλλος ἄ. A.*Pers.*359; ἄ.. ὄμμα θατέρᾳ δὲ νοῦν ἔχοντα S.*Tr.*272; *to foreign lands*, ἄ. ἐκπέμπειν to export, X.*HG*6.1.11; ἄ. οὐδαμόσε *to* no *other place*, Pl.*Cri.*52b; ἄ. πολλαχόσε *to* many *other places*, Id.*Mx.*241e; ποῖ ἄ.; *to* what *other place?* Id.*Phd.*82a; ἄ. ποι *to* some *other place*, Id.*Tht.*202e: c. gen., ἄ. ποι τῆς Σικελίας *to* some *other part* of Sicily, Th.7.51; ἄ. τοῦ σώματος Pl.*Lg.*841a:—by attraction, = ἀλλαχοῦ, ἄλλοσε ὅποι ἂν ἀφίκῃ Id. *Cri.*45b.

**ἄλλοτε**, Aeol. ἄλλοτα Alc.47, Dor. ἄλλοκα Theoc.1.37, Adv. *at another time*, freq. repeated, ἄ. μέν .. ἄ. δέ .. *at one time .. at another ..*, Il.23.368, etc.; also ὅτε μέν.., ἄ. δέ.. Il.11.65; ἄ. μέν.., ἄ. δ' αὖτε Od.16.209, Hes.*Fr.*14; τότ' ἄλλος, ἄλλοθ' ἅτερος S.*El.*739; ποτὲ μὲν κακόν, ἄ. ἐπ' ἐσθλὸν ἕρπει Id.*Ant.*367; ἄ. μέν.., τότε δέ X.*An.*4.1.17: sts. the former ἄλλοτε is omitted, φοιτῶν ἐναργὴς ταῦρος, ἄ. αἰόλος δράκων S.*Tr.*11; κεῖμαι δ' ἐπ' ἀκταῖς, ἄ. ἐν πόντου σάλῳ E.*Hec.*28; ἄ. μέν.. ἐν πυμάτῳ S.*OC*1674:—ἄ. καὶ ἄ. *now and then*, X.*An.*2.4.26: freq. with ἄλλος, etc., πρὸς ἄλλοτ' ἄλλον *sometimes* to this man, *sometimes* that, A.*Pr.*278, etc.; ἄλλως ἄ. *Th.*1077.

**ἀλλοτέρμων**, ονος, (τέρμα) *foreign*, γῆ Ezek.*Exag.*58.

**ἀλλότης**, ητος, ἡ, *otherness*, Simp.*in Ph.*862.13.

**ἄλλο τι**, *anything else*, in interrog. sentences, mostly foll. by ἤ, ἤ σοι ἄλλο τι φαίνεται.. ἢ λόγος; Pl.*Phdr.*258a, cf. *Phd.*64c:—hence freq. (esp. in Pl.) elliptical, implying an affirm. answer, ἄλλο τι ἢ πεινήσουσι; (i.e. ἄλλο τι πείσονται ἢ πεινήσουσι;) *will* they *not* be starved? Hdt.2.14, cf. 1.109; ἄλλο τι ἢ ἠρέμα ἐπανασκεψόμεθα; *shall we not* calmly reconsider? (i.e. let us do so) Pl.*Tht.*154e, cf. *Phd.* 70c, *Meno*82d, *Grg.*481c, etc.; ἄλλο τι ἢ καταγελῴης ἄν; Id.*Alc.*1. 116d:—with other words interposed, σκόπει εἰ ἄλλο τι λέγεις ἢ τόδε Id.*Smp.*200d, cf. *Phd.*106a, *Sph.*228a, etc.:—ἄλλο τι πλήν..; Id.*Sph.* 228a:—but often ἄλλο τι with or without οὖν stands alone, ἄλλο τι οὖν.. ἔλεγες; *did not* you say? Id.*Grg.*495c, cf. 470b, *Phd.*79b, *Tht.* 165e, *R.*337c, etc. **2.** rarely without a question, ἀπόγνοια τοῦ ἄλλο τι ἢ κρατεῖν τῆς γῆς Th.3.85.

***ἀλλοτριάζω**, *to be ill-disposed*, Plb.15.22.1: c. gen., *towards..*, τοῦ βασιλέως ib.25.34.

**ἀλλοτριό-γνωμος**, ον, *thinking of other things, absent*, Cratin. 154. **-επίσκοπος**, ὁ, *busybody in other men's matters*, 1*Ep.Pet.* 4.15. **-λογέω**, *speak irrelevantly*, Aristox.*Harm.*p.32 M., Str.1.4. 1. **-λογία**, ἡ, *unorthodox views*, Phld.*Acad.Ind.*p.67 M. **-μορφοδίαιτος**, ον, *ever changing in form*, epith. of nature, Orph.*H.*10. 23. **-νομέω**, *assign* things *to their wrong place*, opp. διανέμειν ἐπὶ τὰ αὑτῶν ἕκαστα, Pl.*Tht.*195a. **II.** *adopt foreign customs*, D.C.52.36. ***-πραγέω**, *meddle with other folk's business*: *excite commotions*, Plb.5.41.8; opp. αὐτοπραγέω, Procl. *in R.*2.149 K. **-πραγία**, ἡ, *meddling with other folk's business*, Plu.2.57d, Procl. *in R.*1.216 K. **-πραγμονέω**, = -πραγέω, Simp. *in Epict.*pp. 51,113 D. **-πραγμοσύνη**, ἡ, *meddlesomeness*, Pl.*R.*444b, Procl. *in Alc.*p.14 C. **-πράγμων**, ον, *meddlesome*, *AB*81.

***ἀλλότριος**, Aeol. ἀλλότερρος *EM*520.24, α, ον, (ἄλλος) *of* or *belonging to another*, βίοτος, νηῦς, ἄχεα, Od.1.160, 9.535, Il.20.298; γυνὴ *another man's* wife, A.*Ag.*448 (lyr.); ἀλλοτρίων χαρίσασθαι to e bountiful *of what is another's*, Od.17.452; γναθμοῖσι γελοίων ἀλ-οτρίοισιν with faces *unlike their own*, of a *forced, unnatural* laugh, ).20.347; ἀ. ὄμμασιν εἶρπον by the help of *another's* eyes, S.*OC* 46 (lyr.); οὐκ ἀ. ἄτην not *inflicted by other hands*, Id.*Ant.*1259; but .. φόνος murder *of a stranger* (cf. II. 1), Pl.*Euthphr.*4b: prov., ἀ. ἀμᾶν ·έρος reap *where one has not sown*, Ar.*Eq.*392, cf. Hes.*Th.*599; ἀλ-λοτριωτάτοις τοῖς σώμασιν χρῆσθαι deal with one's body *as if it belonged to another*, Th.1.70; τὰ ἀλλότρια, contr. τἀλλότρια, *what belongs to others, not one's own*, τὰ. ἀποστερεῖν, δειπνεῖν, X.*Ages.*4.1, Theopomp. Com.34. II. opp. οἰκεῖος, *foreign, strange*, 1. of persons, ἀ. φώς *stranger*, Od.18.219, cf. Ar.*Ra.*481; almost = *enemy*, Il.5.214, Od.16.102; οὐδέ τις ἀλλοτρίων no *stranger*, Hdt.3.155; εἴτε ἀ. εἴτε οἰκεῖος ὁ τεθνεώς Pl.*Euthphr* 4b; ἀ. τῆς πόλεως Lys.28.6; οὐδείς ἐστί μοι ἀ., ἂν ᾖ χρηστός Men.602; ἀλλοτριώτερος τῶν παίδων *less near* than thy children, Hdt.3.119; ἀλλοτριώτερος, opp. οἰκειότερος, Arist.*EN* 1162ᵃ3: c. dat., ἀλλότριοι ὑμῖν ὄντες Isoc.14.51. b. *hostile, unfavourably disposed*, c. gen., ἀ. Ῥωμαίων Plb.28.4.4; -ώτατος μοναρχίας D.S.16.65; ἀλλότρια φρονῶν τοῦ βασιλέως Plb.36.15.7, cf. *OGI*90.19 (Rosetta). c. *disinclined*, πρὸς τὰς κακοπαθείας Plb.36.15.2. 2. of things, *alien, strange*, τροφή Pl.*R.*491d (Comp.), etc.; εἴ τι πρότερον γέγονεν ἀ. *estrangement*, Decr.ap.D.18.185; ἡ ἀ. *alien country, enemy's country*, Lys.2.6, Isoc.10.50, cf. Hdt.8.73: c. gen., *alien from*, ἐπιτηδεύματα δημοκρατίας ἀ. Lys.31.34; οὐδὲν ἀ. ποιῶν τοῦ τρόπου Decr.ap.D.18.182. b. Medic., *abnormal*, Sor.2.5, Gal.14.780; ἀ. σάρκες *superfluous* fat, Pl.*R.*556d. c. *foreign to the purpose*, λόγοι Arist.*EE*1218ᵇ23: Comp., Id.*EN*1159ᵇ24: Sup., Id.*Cat.*15ᵇ29, cf. Polystr.p.17 W. d. Astrol., = ἀπόστροφος, *POxy.*464.6. III. Adv. ἀλλοτρίως, διακεῖσθαι πρὸς ἀλλήλας to be *unfavourably* disposed towards.., Lys.33.1, cf. Isoc.12.159; ἀ. ἔχειν πρός.. Id.5.80: Comp. -ιώτερον *less favourably*, D.18.9. 2. *strangely, marvellously*, *Epigr.Gr.*989.2. 3. *in a manner foreign to*, c. gen., Pers.*Stoic.*1.100. [-ὄτρ- only in Men.557 s. v. l.]

**ἀλλοτριότης**, ητος, ἡ, *derivativeness*, opp. οἰκειότης, *Plt.*261a; *estrangement*, Arist.*Pol.*1311ᵇ15; τινὸς πρός τινα Pl.*Ep.*318d, cf. Decr.ap.D.18.165, Plb.38.12.3. 2. *unattractiveness*, of style, Phld. *Po.*994.6,37. II. *qualitative difference*, Epicur.*Nat.*11.12.

**ἀλλοτριο-φᾰγέω**, *eat another's bread*, Eust.1404.9. **-φαγία**, ἡ, ib.13. **-φάγος**, ον, *eating another's bread*, S.*Fr.*329, Eust.1404.13. **-φρονέω**, *to be estranged, ill-disposed*, D.S.17.4. **-χρως**, ωτος, ὁ, ἡ, *changing colour*, *AP*11.7 (Nic.). **-χωρος**, ον, *of strange land*, J.*AJ*3.12.3, 8.7.5.

**ἀλλοτριόω**, *estrange from*: c. gen., *deprive*, τῶν σωμάτων τὴν πόλιν οὐκ ἀλλοτριοῦντες Th.3.65; τοὺς ἠλλοτριωκότας ἑαυτοὺς ἀπὸ τῆς λῃτουργίας those who have *withdrawn* themselves from.., D.51.17. 2. c. dat. pers., *make hostile to* another, τὴν χώραν τοῖς πολεμίοις X.*Cyr.*6.1.16:—Pass., *become estranged, be made enemy*, τινί Th.8.73; πρὸς τὴν αἵρεσιν *Vit.Philonid.*p.12 C.; πρός τι *to be prejudiced* against thing, D.H.*Th.*27; ἀπό τινος *disguise oneself from*, Lxx *Ge.*42.7; πρὸς τὰ καίοντα *to be inaccessible* to cautery, Antyll.ap.Orib.10.22.4. 3. *to be unnatural, have a strange taste*, τροφὴν -ιοῦσαν ἔκπτυε Phld.*Lib.*p.9 O. 4. Pass., *to be alienated from one's natural condition*, Pl.*Ti.*64e. 5. Pass., also of things, *to be alienated, fall into other hands*, ἀλλοτριοῦται ἡ ἀρχή Hdt.1.120, cf. D.18.88.

⊛**ἀλλοτρίωσις**, εως, ἡ, *estrangement*, Phld.*D.*3*Fr.*1; *aversion*, πρὸς πόνον Gal.5.459; τινὸς *from* one, App.*BC*5.78; τινὸς εἴς τινα 3.13; opp. οἰκείωσις, Porph.*Abst.*3.19; τῆς ξυμμαχίας οὐχ ὁμοία ἡ ἀ. Th.1.35:—Medic., *loss of substance, mortification*, Aët.13.3.

**ἀλλο-τροπῆσαι**· μεταθεῖναι, Hsch. **-τροπος**, ον, *strange*, φαντασίαι Linus ap.Stob.1.10.5; ἄσματα Iamb.*VP*25.114. Adv. -τρόπως Sch.E.*Hec.*299. **-τύπωτος**, ον, *differently formed*, Man.4.75. ⊛**-φᾰνής**, ές, *appearing otherwise*, Nonn.*D.*14.156, Jo.Gaz.2.225, etc. **-φασ(σ)ις**· θόρυβος ταραχώδης, Hsch., *AB*386. **-φάσσω**, *to be delirious*, Hp.*Prog.*20, al., cf. Gal.18(2).249, prob. l. in Aret.*SA*2.4.—Ionic word, cf. Xenocrit.ap.Erot.*Fr.*1, Eust.1324.10. **-φᾰτος**, ον, (v. φόνος) *slain by others*, *AB*386, Hsch. II. (φαίνομαι) = ἀλλοφανής, Nic.*Th.*148. **-φέρμονες**· ἀλλαχοῦ τραφέντες, Hsch.

**ἄλλοφος**, ον, Ep. for ἄλοφος, *without a crest*, Il.10.258, *AP*6.163 (Mel.).

**ἀλλο-φρήτωρ**, ορος, ὁ, *one of another* φρατρία, *IG*14.759 (Naples). **-φρονέω**, (ἀλλόφρων) Ep. and Ion., *think of other things, give no heed*, ἀλλ' ἥμην ἀλλοφρονέων Od.10.374; of one in a swoon, *to be senseless*, κὰδ δ' ἀλλοφρονέοντα.. εἶσαν Il.23.698; κεῖτ' ἀλλοφρονέων Theoc.22.129, cf. Arist.*Metaph.*1009ᵇ30; ὑπὸ τούτων ἀλλοφρονῆσαι *were seized with frenzy* by reason of the thunder, etc., Hdt.5.85; ἀλύει καὶ ἀ. ὑπὸ τῆς ὀδύνης Hp.*Morb.*2.16, cf. *Mul.*1.41. II. *to be of another mind, have other views*, v.l. in Hdt.7.205. **-φροσύνη**, ἡ, *absence or derangement of mind*, Poll.8.163. **-φρων**, ονος, ὁ, ἡ, *thinking differently*, Man.4.563. ⊛**-φυής**, ές, *changed in shape*, Nonn.*D.*4.419, al. 2. *of strange, abnormal shape*, ib.2.148, al. **-φῡλέω**, *adopt foreign customs or religions*, Lxx 4*Ma.*18.5. **-φῡλία**, ἡ, *foreign matter*, Epicur.*Ep.*2 p.48 U. **-φῡλισμός**, ὁ, *adoption of foreign customs*, Lxx 2*Ma.*4.13. **-φῡλος**, ον, (φυλή) *of another tribe, foreign*, Hp.*Aër.*12; freq. in Lxx of Philistines, *Jd.*14.1, al.; in Egypt, *settled in another nome*, *BGU*419.2 (iii A.D.); ἐς ἀλλόφυλον ..χθόνα A.*Eu.*851; ἄνθρωποι Th.1.102, Pl.*Lg.*629d; ζῷα *alien to man, wild*, D.S.3.18, Porph.*Abst.*1.10; πόλεμος ἀ. war *with foreigners*, Plu.*Cam.*23; opp. ὁμόφυλος, Epicur.*Sent.*39; ἀ. πρός τι Dam.*Pr.*308; μᾶζαν ἐπ' ἀ. *alien, not one's own*, Eup.159.12. **-φωνία**, ἡ, *confusion of tongues*, J.*AJ*1.4.3. **-φωνος**, ον, *speaking a foreign tongue*, Lxx *Ez.*3.6, Hsch. s.v. ἀλλόθροος. **-χροέω**, *to change colour*, Arist.*Pr.*880ᵃ25, Them.*Or.*4.56a, 19.228c. **-χροια**, ἡ, *change of colour*, Adam.2.36. **-χροος**, ον, contr. **-χρους**, ουν, *changed in colour*, E.*Hipp.*174 (lyr.):—also ⊛**-χρως**, ωτος, ὁ, ἡ, *looking strange* or *foreign*, Id.*Ph.*138, *Andr.*879.

**ἄλλῠδις**, Adv., (ἄλλος) Ep. for ἄλλοσε, *elsewhither*, in Hom. only with ἄλλος, ἄ. ἄλλος one *hither*, another *thither*, Il.11.486, Od.5.71, cf. A.R.2.980, etc.; τρέπεται χρὼς ἄ. ἄλλῃ his colour changes *now one way, now another*, Il.13.279; imitated from Hom. by Eup.159.11; later by itself, *AP*15.24.1 (Simm.).

**ἀλλύεσκε, ἀλλύουσα** [ῡ], Ep. for ἀνέλυε, ἀναλύουσα.

**ἄλλυι**, Aeol., = ἄλλῃ, Hdn.Gr.1.507, prob. in Alc.89:—also **ἄλλῠς** (dub.), *AB*1316.

**ἀλλύτας**, v. sub ἀναλύτης.

**ἄλλῠτος**, ον, = ἄλυτος, Μοιράων νῆμα Phanocl.2.

**ἀλλώνιος**, Aeol., = ἀλλοῖος, Sch.D.T.p.542 H., Eust.1214.28.

⊛**ἄλλως**, Dor. ἀλλῶς, A.D.*Adv.*175.13, Adv. of ἄλλος, *otherwise*, Il.19.401, etc.: freq. with other Advbs., ἄ. πως *in* some *other way*, ἄ. οὐδαμῶς in no *other wise*, Pl.*R.*343b, 526a, etc.; πως ἄ. X.*Mem.*2.6.39; ἄ. καὶ ἄ. Hierocl. *in CA*23 p.468 M. 2. καὶ ἄλλως and *besides* (cf. ἄλλος II. 8), ἀγήνωρ ἐστὶ καὶ ἄλλως Il.9.699; a woman is described as very tall καὶ ἄ. εὐειδής Hdt.1.60, etc.; ἀρίστου καὶ ἄ. φρονιμωτάτου Pl.*Phd.*118: so ἄ. δέ.. Hdt.6.105, Ar.*Av.*1476; ἄλλως τε S.*OT*1114, Hdt.8.142. b. *at all events, any how*, εἴ πέρ γε καὶ ἄ. ἐθέλει.. Hdt.7.16.γ'; ἄλλως alone, εἰ ἄ. βούλοιτο Id.8.30; ἐπείπερ ἄλλως.. εἰς Ἄργος κίεις A.*Ch.*680. 3. freq. in phrase ἄλλως τε καί.. *both otherwise and..*, i.e. *especially, above all*, A.*Eu.*473, Th.1.70, etc.; strengthd., ἄ. τε πάντως καί.. A.*Pr.*636, *Eu.*726; freq. followed by ἤν, εἰ, ἐπειδή, *especially* if.., Hp.*VC* 21, Th.1.81, 2.3; by part., Id.4.104, 7.80 —without καί, ἄ. τε ἐάν X.*Mem.*1.2.59; ἄλλως τε ἐπειδή Isoc.2.51, Pl.*Men.*85e, etc. II. *otherwise than* something implied, *differently*, τοῦτ' οὐκ ἔστιν ἄ. εἶπαι to deny it, Hdt.6.124; οὐκ ἄ. λέγω I say no *otherwise*. i.e. I say *so*, E.*Hec.*302: hence, 2. *far otherwise*, i.e. *better*, οὐδέ κεν ἄλλως οὐδὲ θεὸς τεύξειε Od.8.176, cf. Il.14.53. 3. more freq., *otherwise than should be, at random, without aim or purpose*, Od.14.124, Hdt.3.16, 4.77, etc.:—*in vain*, Il.23.144; freq. in Trag. and Com., ἀλλ' ἄ. πονεῖ S.*OT*1151, cf. 333, E.*Med.*1030, Ar.*Eq.*11; with Subst., εἴδωλον ἄ. *mere* image, S.*Ph.*947; ἀριθμὸν ἄ. E.*Tr.*476; παρὰ καιρὸν ἄ. Id.*IA* 800; ἀριθμός, πρόβατ' ἄ. Ar.*Nu.*1203; ὄχλος ἄ. καὶ βασκανία D.19.24, cf. Th.8.78; τὴν ἄ., sc. ἄγουσαν ὁδόν, *in vain*, λέγειν D.3.21; ψηφίζεσθαι 19.181, cf. Philem.51, etc.; also, *in no particular way*, i.e. *concerning indifferent matters*, οἱ ἀγῶνες οὐδέποτε τὴν ἄ., ἀλλ' ἀεὶ τὴν περὶ αὐτοῦ Pl.*Tht.*172e; τὴν ἄ. θεωρεῖν Pl.*Lg.*650a; τήν γε ἄλλως *otherwise*, i.e. *generally*, D.C.38.24, 42.50:—*for nothing*, Hdt.3.139: —*otherwise than right, wrongly*, D.*Ep.*1.12, etc.

**ἅλμα**, τό, (ἅλλομαι) *spring, leap*, poet. for Prose πήδημα, Od.8.103, 128; ἅ. πέτρας, πετραῖον *leap* or *fall from* rock, E.*HF*1148, *Ion* 1268; κρημνῶν ἅ. *Epigr.Gr.*225 (Ephesus); οἰκεῖον.. ἅ. ἐπὶ ξίφος E.*Hel.*96; κυνῆς ἅ. *the leap* of the lot from the helmet, S.*Aj.*1287; κοῦφον ἅλμα ποδῶν Ἀχιλῆ E.*El.*439; *track* of a comet, Arist.*Mete.*343ᵇ23. 2. *jumping*, as an athletic contest, Simon.153:—in pl., *jumping-ground*, τῶν ἁ. τὴν σκάψιν καὶ ὁμάλιξιν *BCH*23.566 (Delph., iii B.C.). II. Medic., *pulsation, palpitation*, of the embryo, Hp.*Alim.*42; of the heart, Id.*Cord.*4; f.l. in Pl.*Ti.*70d.

⊛**ἄλμα**, τό, (ἄλδω) = ἄλσος, Lyc.319, Epic.ap.Did. ad D.13.32.

**ἁλμ-αία**, ἡ, = ἅλμη, *brine*, Ar.*Fr.*706, Nic.*Fr.*70.18: in pl., Dsc.2.174. **-αιοπώλης**· *salgamarius* (sic), Gloss. **-άς**, άδος, ἡ, *salted, steeped in brine*, ἐλάα Ar.*Fr.*141: Subst., *salted olive*, ἐς τὰς ἁ. (sc. ἐλάας) Hermipp.81, cf. Eup.255, Ar.*Fr.*393, Apollon.ap.Gal.12.999. **-ατίας**, ου, ὁ, *person of tripping gait*, Adam.2.52. **-ατισταί**· *salitores*, Gloss. **-ατύραι**· τὰ παραθαλάσσια χωρία, Hsch. **-άω**, *become mildewed*, cj. in Thphr.*HP*7.5.4, 8.10.1, *CP*6.10.5. **-εῖον**· ἀνδρεῖον, Hsch. **-ευσις**, εως, ἡ, *pickling*, Dsc.3.77 (pl.). **-ευτής**, οῦ, ὁ, *seller of pickled fruit*, Id.1.29. **-εύω**, (ἅλμη) *steep in brine, pickle*, Id.2.111 (Pass.). **-η**, ἡ, (ἅλς) *sea-water, brine*, Od.5.53, Pi.*P.*2.80, etc.; *spray that has dried on the skin*, Od.6.219; *salt incrustation* on soil, Hdt.2.12, Thphr.*CP*6.10.4. 2. after Hom., *brine*, i.e. *the sea*, Arion 1.3, Pi.*P.*4.39, A.*Pers.*397, Tim.*Pers.*96, etc. 3. *salt-water, brine* used for pickling, Hdt.2.77, Ar.*V.*1515, *Fr.*416; ἡ Θασία ἅ. Cratin.6; ἐν ἅλμῃ ἕψειν [τὸν ἰχθύν] Antiph.222, cf.Eub.44; καταπνίγειν Sotad.Com.1.21, etc.: prov., πρὶν τοὺς ἰχθῦς ἑλεῖν σὺ τὴν ἅλμην κυκᾷς 'first catch your hare, then cook it', Phot. s.v. πρίν. II. *saltness*, esp. as a bad quality in soil, X.*Oec.*20.12, cf. Thphr.*CP*6.10.4. 2. *salt soil*, *PLond.*2.267.95, al. (i/ii A.D.). **-ήεις**, εσσα, εν, *salt, briny*, πόρος ἁ., i.e. *the sea*, A.*Supp.*844 (lyr.) codd. (-ιόεις Herm.). **-ια**, τά, *salted provisions*, Men.462.5. **-ίζομαι**, *to be made salt*, ὑπὸ θαλάσσης Sch.Il.2.538, cf. Zos.Alch.p.248 B.

**ἁλμο-ποσία**, ἡ, *drinking of brine*, Afric.*Cest.*2 (pl.). **-πότις**, ιδος, ἡ, *drinking brine*, Menipp.ap.Ath.1.32e.

**ἁλμῡρίδιον**, τό, Dim. of ἁλμυρίς I. 3a, Plin.*HN*19.142.

**ἁλμῡρίζω**, *to be saltish*, Arist.*HA*613ᵃ3; πρὸς τὴν γεῦσιν Dsc.2.129.

**ἁλμῡρίς**, ίδος, ἡ, *anything salt*, and so, 1. *salt humour*, Hp.*Epid.*3.13; *salt scum*, Arist.*Mete.*357ᵇ4. 2. *salt soil* or *land*, Thphr.*CP*2.5.4, Lxx *Jb.*39.6, *PPetr.*3 p.237, etc.; in Attica, = ἁλίπεδον, *IG*2.1059, Hsch.: pl., Ἁλμυρίδες, Ar.*Fr.*132. 3. kind of κράμβη, *Brassica cretica*, Eudem.ap.Ath.9.369e, *POxy*.736.73 (i B.C.): pl., Diocl.*Fr*.138, Plu.2.801a. b. = ἅλιμον, Aët.1.21. II. *saltness*, D.S.3.39. **ἁλμυρῖτις** γῆ, = foreg. I. 2, Zopyr.ap.Orib. 14.62.1.

**ἁλμυρόγεως**, ων, (γῆ) *with salt soil*, πεδιάς Ph.2.111.

⊛**ἁλμυρ-ός**, ά, όν, (ἅλμη) *salt, briny*, Hom. only in Od., and always in phrase ἁ. ὕδωρ *salt sea*-water, 4.511, etc.; πόντος Hes.*Th*.107, Alc.26; θάλασσα Sapph.*Supp*.25.10; καθ' ἁ. ἅλα Epich.53, E.*Tr*.76; βένθεα Pi.*O*.7.57; ποταμός, of the Hellespont, Hdt.7.35. 2. in Prose, of taste, *salt*, γίνεται τὸ στόμα ἁ. Hp.*Acut*.(*Sp*.)44; ὄψα ἁ. X.*Cyr*.6.2.31, cf. Hp.*Vict*.1.56; αἷμα Pl.*Ti*.84a s.v.l.; of drinking-water, *brackish*, Th.4.26; of soil, Thphr.*CP*6.10.1, Lxx *Je*.17.6; opp. μῶρος (insipid), *Com.Adesp*.596. 3. metaph., *bitter, distasteful*, γειτόνημα Alcm.116, cf. Pl.*Lg*.705a; ἀκοή *Phdr*.243d; λόγοι Ath.3. 121e; ἁλμυρὰ κλαίειν weep *bitterly*, Theoc.23.34; ἁλμυρὸν καταπτύσαι Cerc.19.37. b. *piquant*, ἁ. καὶ δριμύ Plu.2.685e. **-ότης**, ητος, ἡ, *saltness*, Arist.*Mete*.356$^b$4. **-όω**, *make salt*, θάλασσαν Olymp.*in Mete*.152.9. ⊛**-ώδης**, ες, *saltish*, ῥεῦμα Hp.*Epid*.1.26.ε'; πτύαλον Id.*Coac*.238, cf. X.*Oec*.20.12 (Comp.); of soil, *impregnated with salt*, Thphr.*HP*8.7.6; *hoary*, χνοῦς Id.*CP*.6.10.7.

**ἄλξ**· πῆχυς (Athaman.), Hsch. (cod. ἄλαξ). **ἄλξεων**· τειχέων, Id. **ἀλξίας**· πράξεις, καὶ ἐκλήψεις, Id.

**ἀλοατός**, ὁ, *threshing-floor*, X.*Oec*.18.5 (v.l. -ητός).

⊛**ἀλοάω**, Ep. **ἀλοιάω** Theoc.10.48: Ep. impf. ἀλοία Il.9.568: fut. -ήσω Lxx *Je*.5.17, Dor. ἀλοιησέω Tyrt. in *Berl.Sitzb*.1918.728: aor. ἠλόησα Ar.*Ra*.149, Herod.2.34 (ἀλοιήσῃ ib.51), part. ἀλοάσας [ᾰσ] Pherecr.65; Ep. ἠλοίησα (ἀπ-) Il.4.522, (συν-) Theoc.22.128:— Pass., fut. -ηθήσομαι Lxx *Je*.28(51).33: aor. ἠλοήθην Thphr.*CP*4.6.5, Plb.10.12.9, Plu.2.327a: pf. ἠλόημαι Thphr.*CP*4.12.9 (Cod.Urb.):— poet. aor. part. ἀλοίσας (as if from ἀλοίω, cf. Eust.775.8, Hdn.*Epim*. 277) dub. l. in Epigr.ap.D.L.7.31; ἀλοϝάω dub. in *Glotta*4.202 (archaic Apulian vase):—*tread, thresh*, Pl.*Thg*.124a, X.*Oec*.18.2, Lxx *De*.25.4. 2. *thresh, smite*, γῆν χερσὶν ἀλοία Il.9.568, cf. Epigr. l.c.; μηρόν Plu.*TG*2; *cudgel, thrash*, *Glotta* l.c., S.*Fr*.20 (dub.), Ar. *Ra*.149, Herod.2.34; ῥοπάλῳ τινά Babr.98.15. 3. *crush, smash*, σκεύη Id.129.16; *destroy*, πόλεις Lxx *Je*.5.17. II. *drive round and round*, like cattle treading out corn, Ar.*Th*.2 (acc. to Sch.).

**ἄλοβος**, ον, *with lobe wanting*, of livers of victims, ἄ. ἱερά X.*HG*3. 4.15, Plu.*Ages*.9, Arr.*An*.7.18.4.

**ἀλογεύομαι**, *speak casually*, Cic.*Att*.6.4.3.

**ἀλόγευτος**, ον, *not collected*, *PLond*.2.354.22 (i B.C.).

⊛**ἀλογ-έω**, *pay no regard to* thing, εἰ δέ μοι οὐκ ἐπέεσσ' ἐπιπείσεται, ἀλλ' ἀλογήσει Il.15.162: c. gen., δίκης Democr.174; πάσης συμβουλίης Hdt.3.125; τῶν ἐντολέων Id.8.46: abs., ib.116: c. acc., Procop. *Pers*.1.4, al.; *insult*, *PTeb*.138 (ii B.C.):—Pass., *to feel slighted*, Cic. *Att*.12.3.3. 2. *to be unreasonable*, Phld.*Ir*.p.34 W. II. Pass., *to be disregarded*, D.L.1.32; *commit an indiscretion, be misled*, διά τινος *miscalculate*, Plb.8.36.4, cf. 28.9.8. 2. *to be out of one's senses*, Luc.*Ocyp*.143; ἠλογημένη 'nonplussed', Alciphr.2.1; ἡ. ψυχή Hierocl.*in CA*12p.446M. 3. Gramm., *to be irregularly formed*, A.D.*Adv*.162.18, al., *EM*405.34, etc. **-ημα**, ατος, τό, *miscalculation, error*, Plb.12.20.2: in pl., 9.16.5, al. **-ητέον**, *one must take no heed of*, τινός Ph.1.312. ⊛**-ητος**, ον, gloss on ἀλόγιστος, Sch.E.*Or*.1156. **-ί**, = ἀλογιστί, Lib.*Decl*.16.31 (s.v.l.). **-ία**, Ion. **-ίη**, ἡ, *want of respect* or *regard*, ἀλογίην εἶχον τοῦ χρηστηρίου took *no heed* of it, Hdt.4.150; ἐν ἀλογίῃ ἔχειν or ποιεῖσθαί τι 6.75, 7. 226:—in 2.141 ἐν ἀλογίῃσι ἔχειν παραχρησάμενον τῶν Αἰγυπτίων, gen. is anacoluthon (as if ἀλογίην ἔχειν τῶν Αἰγ.); ἀλογίης ἐγκυρῆσαι is *to be disregarded*, 7.208 codd.:—this sense is Ion. and late Prose, ἐν ἀλογίᾳ ποιεῖσθαί τι Procop.*Pers*.1.2, al. 2. Att., *want of reason, absurdity*, opp. λόγος, Pl.*Tht*.207c, cf. 199d, *Phd*.67e, D.23.168; πολλὴ ἁ. τῆς διανοίας Th.5.111; concrete, *the irrational part of the soul*, Porph.*Abst*.1.42. 3. *confusion, disorder*, Plb.15.14.2; τύχη ἐν ἀλογίᾳ κειμένη Plot.6.8.17:—*speechlessness, amazement*, Plb. 36.7.4. 4. *indecision, doubt*, Paus.7.17.6. 5. Rhythm., *irrationality*, relation of time-elements which cannot be expressed by a simple ratio, Aristox.*Rhyth*.2.20. **-ίζομαι**, Dep., *to be irrational*, Eust.1656.43, etc.:—Act. only as f.l. for ἀλογέω, Procop. *Goth*.4.20. **-ίου** δίκη prosecution of a public official *for not having his accounts passed*, Eup.349.

**ἀλογίστ-ευτος**, ον, *unheeded, unprovided for*, τῇ προνοίᾳ Hierocl. *Prov*.p.466B. **-έω**, *lose one's senses, rave*, Plu.2.656d, Longin.10. 3, Vett.Val.130.30. **-ί**, Adv. *thoughtlessly*, Harp., *AB*380. **-ία**, Ion. **-ίη**, ἡ, *thoughtlessness*, Democr.289, Plb.5.15.3, Chrysipp.*Stoic*. 3.129, Phld.*Ir*.p.93 W., Plu.2.466c. ⊛**-ος**, ον, *inconsiderate, thoughtless*, τόλμα Th.3.82; ὀργή Men.574; of persons, Phld.*Ir*.p.97 W. Adv. -τως *thoughtlessly*, Lys.7.12, Isoc.2.29; δαπανᾶν ἀ. βίον Men. 623, etc. 2. *irrational*, Pl.*Ap*.37c; opp. λογιστικός, *R*.439d, al.; *foolish, unthinking*, Phld.*Ir*.p.97 W.; πλοῦτος ἀ. προσλαβὼν ἐξουσίαν Men.665; τὸ ἀ. *unreason*, i.e. *chance*, Th.5.99. Adv. -τως Id.3.45, Pl.*Prt*.324b, al. II. *incalculable*, S.*OC*1675 (lyr.); *indefinite, indeterminate*, φορά Procl.*in Prm*.p.547 S. 2. *not to be accounted, vile*, E.*Or*.1156, Men.75.

**ἀλογο-γράφητος**, ον, *undescribed*, Eust.888.49. **-ειδής**, ές, = ἀλογώδης, *irrational*, ἀ. τὴν ψυχήν Dam.*Pr*.401. **-θέτητος**, ον, *of which no account is given*, Gloss. **-μυΐα**, ἡ, *horse-fly*, Anon. *in Rh*. 125.10.

⊛**ἀλογόομαι**, *to be rendered irrational*, Plot.5.3.10 (prob. l.); [φύσις] ἠλογωμένη *non-rational*, Procl.*in Prm*.p.617 S.

**ἀλογο-πάθεια**, *irrational affection*, Plot.4.4.28 (pl.). **-πρεπῶς** *unreasonably*, Eustr.*in EN*275.8.

⊛**ἄλογος**, ον, *without* λόγος, hence, I. *speechless*, Pl.*Lg*.696e. Adv. -ως *without speech*, S.*OC*131, Isoc.3.9:—ἄ. ἡμέρα, = Lat. *dies nefastus, on which no business may be done*, Luc.*Lex*.9. b. *lacking in eloquence*, Lxx *Ex*.6.12. 2. *inexpressive*, Pl.*Tht*.203a; *unutterable*, = ἄρρητος, S.*Fr*.262. II. *unreasoning*, ἡδονή, ὄχλος, etc., Pl.*R*.591c, *Ti*.42d, etc.; τὰ ἄλογα *brutes, animals*, Democr.164, Pl.*Prt*.321b, X.*Hier*.7.3; esp. in late Greek, ἄλογον, τό, = *horse*, *POxy*. 138.29 (610 A.D.), *PGen*.14 (late). 2. *not according to reason, irrational*, ἄ. δόξα, opp. ἡ μετὰ λόγου δ., Pl.*Tht*.201c; ἀλόγῳ πάθει τὴν ἄ. συνασκεῖν αἴσθησιν, *instinctive* feeling, in appreciating works of art, D.H.*Lys*.11; ἄ. πάθος Id.*Comp*.23. 3. *contrary to reason, absurd*, Th.6.85, Pl.*Tht*.203d; *unaccountable, unintelligible*, Lys.26. 19; *unfit, unsuited to its end*, Th.1.32; *groundless*, Plb.3.15.9; ἀηδία *PRyl*.144.15 (38 A.D.). Adv. most freq. in this sense, Pl.*R*. 439d, etc.; οὐκ ἀ. οὐδ' ἀκαίρως Isoc.15.10: Sup. -ώτατα Phld.*Ir*. p.44 W. III. *without reckoning*: 1. *not reckoned upon, unexpected*, Th.6.46 (Comp.). 2. *not counted, null and void*, ἡμέραι Lxx *Nu*.6.12. 3. Act., *not having paid one's reckoning*, of an ἐρανιστής, *EM*70.31. IV. of magnitudes, *incommensurable*, περὶ ἀλόγων γραμμῶν, title of work by Democr., cf. Arist.*APo*. 76$^b$9, *LI*968$^b$18, Euc.10.*Def*.10, etc. 2. in Rhythm, *irrational*, of feet or syllables whose time-relations cannot be expressed by a simple ratio, χορεῖος Aristox.*Rhyth*.2.20; ἄλογοι, sc. συλλαβαί, D.H. *Comp*.20:—in Music, ἄ. διαστήματα Plu.2.1145d:—of the pulse, *unrhythmical*, Herophil. ap.Ruf.*Syn.Puls*.4.3.

**ἀλογχεῖν**· Ἀλόγχους μιμεῖσθαι, ὅ ἐστι ἔθνος Θρᾳκῶν, Hsch.

**ἄλογχος** (A), ον, *without lances* or *weapons*, ἄ. ἀνθέων στρατός Chaerem.10. II. of a spear, *without a head*, Hsch., *EM*70.36.

**ἄλογχος** (B), ον, (λογχή, = λῆξις) *unlucky*, opp. εὔλογχος (q.v.), sc. ἡμέρα, prob. l. in Democr.ap.Gem.*Calend*.8.

**ἀλογώδης**, ες, *irrational*, v.l. Arist.*Spir*.481$^b$27 (Comp.); τὰ -έστερα ψυχῶν γένη Procl.*in Cra*.p.69 P.

**ἀλόη**, ἡ, *bitter aloes, Aloe vera*, Dsc.3.22, Plu.2.141f, etc. 2. = ἀγάλλοχον, Lxx *Ca*.4.15 (in Heb. form **ἀλώθ**), *Ev.Jo*.19.39. 3. ἀ. γαλλική, = γεντιανή, Ps.-Dsc.3.3. 4. ἀ. ἡπατῖτις, *hepatic aloes, Aloe Perryi*, *Gp*.6.6.2.

**ἀλοηδάριον**, τό, *purgative prepared from aloes*, Aët.3.100, al.

**ἀλό-ησις**, εως, ἡ, (ἀλοάω) *threshing*, Gloss.:—**ἀλοίησις**, *EM*74. 22. **-ησμός** (written -ωεισ-), ὁ, *threshing*, *PLond*.1.113(3).8 (vi A.D.), *BGU*340 (vi A.D.). **-ητέα**, *one must thresh*, Poll.1. 226. **-ητής**, οῦ, ὁ, *thresher*, *PLond*.1.131$^r$619 (i A.D.). **-ητός**, ὁ, *threshing*, Ael.*NA*6.43; *threshing-time*, Lxx *Le*.26.5, *BGU*1031.11 (ii A.D.): perh. *payment for threshing*, *PTeb*.48.17 (ii B.C.). ⊛**-ητρα**, τά, *payment for threshing*, *PFlor*.379.18 (ii A.D., prob. in *BGU*698.27 (ii A.D.).

**ἀλόθεν**, Adv., (ἅλς) *from the sea*, ἐξ ἀλόθεν Il.21.335.

**ἁλοθήκη**, ἡ, *salt-box*, Hdn.Gr.2.418.

**ἀλοί**· πηλοί, Hsch. **ἀλοιάω**, Ep. for ἀλοάω.

**ἀλοιδόρ-ητος**, ον, *unreviled*, Plu.2.757a. 2. *irreproachable*, *IG*14.2139, 12(7).395 (Amorgos), Plu.2.89a. II. *not reviling*: neut. pl. as Adv., ἄκομπ' ἀλοιδόρητα διαβεβλημένοι S.*Fr*.210.8. ⊛**-ος**, ον, = foreg. II, A.*Ag*.412.

⊛**ἀλοιητήρ**, ῆρος, ὁ, (ἀλοιάω) *thresher, grinder*, as Adj., σίδηρος Nonn. *D*.17.237; ἀ. ὀδόντες *grinders*, *AP*11.379 (Agath.): metaph., λιμός Orac.ap.Jul.*Mis*.370a.

⊛**ἀλοιμός**, οῦ, ὁ, *polishing* or *plastering*, of wall-decoration, S.*Fr*.69, cf. *IG*2$^2$.463.85.

**ἀλοιτ-εύειν**· ἀλιτήριος εἶναι, *EM*69.52. **-ήεσσαν**· κοινήν, ἄνανδρον, Hsch.

⊛**ἀλοιτηρός**, v. sub ἀλιτηρός.

⊛**ἀλοίτης**, ου, ὁ, = ἀλείτης, *avenger*, Emp.10:—fem. **Ἀλοῖτις**, ιδος, ἡ, of Athena, Lyc.936: but ἀλοῖτις, ἡ, = γεντιανή, Ps.-Dsc.3.3; = μανδραγόρα ἄρρεν, Id.4.75. **ἀλοιτός**, ὁ, (ἀλιτεῖν) = ἀλείτης, Lyc.136: fem. ἀλοιταί· κοιναί, ἁμαρτωλαί, ποιναί (cf. ἀλοίτης), Hsch.

**ἀλοιφ-αῖος**, α, ον, *for anointing*, Lyc.579. **-άω**, *daub with pitch*, κιβωτόν Aq.*Ge*.6.14. **-εῖον**, τό, *anointing-room*, Eust.764.14. ⊛**-ή**, ἡ, (ἀλείφω) *anything with which one can smear* or *anoint*; esp. *hog's lard, grease*, either in carcase, Il.9.208, or when melted for use, 17. 390. 2. *unguent*, Od.6.220, 18.179. 3. *paint, varnish*, etc., Pl.*Criti*.116b, cf. *IG*2$^2$.463.85, Lxx *Mi*.7.11, etc.; νεώς Polyaen. 5.34. II. *anointing, laying on* of unguents or paint, ἀ. μύρων Pl.*Alc*.1.122c. III. *erasure*, Lxx *Ex*.17.14, Plu.2.611a.

**ἀλοίω**, v. sub ἀλοάω.

⊛**ἀλοκίζω**, (ἄλοξ) prop. *trace furrows*: hence, *write, draw*, with play on words, Ar.*V*.850:—Pass., pf. part. ἠλοκισμένος *scratched, torn*, Lyc.119,381.

**ἄλοξ**, οκος, ἡ, = αὖλαξ (q.v.).

**ἀλοπευει**, v. ἀλωπ-.

**ἁλο-πήγιον**, τό, *salt-works, salt-pit*, Str.7.4.7, al., Plu.*Rom*. 25 (pl.). **-πηγός**, όν, *one who prepares salt*, Nic.*Al*.519.

**ἀλόπιστος**, ον, *not barked* or *peeled*, Thphr.*HP*5.1.2.

**ἄλοπος**, ον, (λέπω) *not scutched*, ἀμοργίς Ar.*Lys*.736: neut. pl., ἄλοπα, τά, *PTeb*.120.16 (i B.C.).

**ἁλο-πώλης**, ου, ὁ, *dealer in salt*, *PTeb*.1.120, *PFay*.23.12 (ii A.D.), etc.:—fem. **-πῶλις**, *IG*2.3932. **-πώλια**, τά, *salt-stores*, *BGU*9 (iii A.D.).

**ἀλορόα**· ἄρουρα, καὶ γεωργία παρὰ θάλασσαν, Hsch.

**ἅλος**, Dor. for ἧλος.

**ἁλοσ-άνθινος**, η, ον, *prepared with efflorescence of salt*, οἶνος Dsc.5.6 tit. **-ανθον**, τό, *efflorescence of salt*, Gal.12.374. **-άχνη**, ἡ, lit. *sea-foam*, a zoophyte of the class ἀλκυόνεια, Arist.*HA*616$^a$20, Thphr. *Od*.35.

**Ἁλοσύδνη**, ἡ, epith. of Thetis, Il.20.207; νέποδες καλῆς ἁλοσύδνης, of seals, Od.4.404 (expl. by Gramm. as 'child of the sea'); of Nereids, A.R.4.1599; cf. ὑδατοσύδνη. (Perh. containing the root of ὕδωρ.)

**ἁλο-τρίβανος**, (τρίβω) *pestle to pound salt*, Eust.183.10. **-τριψ**, ῖβος, ὁ, = foreg., *AP*6.306 (Aristo). **-τροφέω**, *feed with salt*, Sch.Il.13.493.

**ἄλουα**· κῆποι (Cypr.), Hsch.

**ἁλούργ-ημα**, ατος, τό, *purple clothing*, Vett.Val.263.16, Lib.*Decl*.12.27 (pl.). **-ής**, ές, (ἅλς, ἔργον) lit. *wrought in* or *by the sea*, always in sense *sea-purple*, i.e. *genuine purple dye*, opp. imitations, ἐμβαίνονθ' ἁλουργέσιν on *cloths of purple*, A.*Ag*.946; μίτρα ἁ. Pherecr.100; στρώμαθ' ἁ. Anaxandr.41.7; γῆ Pl.*Phd*.110c; τὸ ἁ. Arist.*Col*.792$^a$7:—less freq. **ἁλουργός**, όν (also ά, όν Phylarch.41), ἔρια Pl.*R*.429d; χιτωνίσκος *IG*2.754.12,14, etc. (but χ. ἁλουργής ib.21); στολαί Phylarch. l.c.; στρωμναί Plu.*Lyc*.12, *AB*81:—also **ἁλουργοῦς**, οῦν, *IG*2.757, v.l. in Arist.*Sens*.442$^a$24, Ion. **ἁλοργοῦς** *GDI*5702.23 (Samos). **-ία**, Ion. **ἁλοργίη**, ἡ, *purple-dyeing*, *GDI*5633 (Teos). 2. *purple clothing*, Philostr.*VA*4.21. **-ίδιον**, τό, Dim. of ἁλουργίς, Antiph.310 (also attrib. to Ar., *Fr*.741: vv. ll. ἁλουργαῖον, ἁλουργιαῖον). **-ικός**, ή, όν, = ἁλουργής, *AB*379, Phot. **-ίς**, ίδος, ἡ, *purple robe*, Ar.*Eq*.967, *IG*2.754, Chamaeleon ap.Ath.9.374a. II. as Adj., ἐσθὴς ἁ. f. l. in Luc.*Nav*.22.

**ἁλουργο-πώλης**, ου, ὁ, *dealer in purple*, Arist.*Mech*.849$^b$34. **-πωλική** (τέχνη), ἡ, *trade of an* ἁλουργοπώλης, Is.*Fr*.38.

❀ **ἁλουργός**, όν, v. sub ἁλουργής.

**ἀλουσία**, ἡ, *being unwashed*, Hp.*de Arte* 5; ἠγρίωσαι διὰ μακρᾶς ἀλουσίας E.*Or*.226, cf. Alex.197: pl., ἀλουσίῃσι..συμπεπτωκώς Hdt.3.52, cf. Hp.*Morb*.2.71.

**ἀλουτ-έω**, *go without bathing*, Hp.*Salubr*.4, al., Arr.*Epict*.3.22.73, etc. **-ία**, ἡ, = ἀλουσία, Eup.251. **-ιάω**, Sch.Ar.*Nu*.442. **-ος** (ἄλουστος *Gloss*.), ον, *unwashen*, Hdt.2.64, Semon.7.5, E.*El*.1107, Ar.*Av*.1554.

**ἁλοφόρος**, ὁ, *one who conveys salt*, *Jahresh*.7 *Beibl*.44, cf. ib.18 *Beibl*.287 (Ephesus, i B.C.).

**ἄλοφος**, v. ἄλλοφος.

**ἀλόχευτος**, ον, *born not in the natural way*, of Athena, Coluth.183. 2. *unborn*, Nonn.*D*.8.27. II. *without birth-pangs*, αὖλαξ κόσμου ib.24.269, cf. 41.53.

❀ **ἄλοχος** [ᾰ], ον, ἡ, (ἀ- copul., λέχος) poet., *partner of one's bed, wife*, Il.1.114, Od.3.403, al., A.*Pers*.63, S.*OT*181, E.*Fr*.543, etc., cf. Arist.*Pol*.1253$^b$7; ἄλοχον εἰς δόμους ἄγειν Theodect.13. 2. *leman, concubine*, Il.9.336, Od.4.623. II. (ἀ- priv.) *unwedded*, ἁ. οὖσα τὴν λοχείαν εἴληχε, of Artemis, Pl.*Tht*.149b, cf. Porph. ad Il.11.155.

**ἀλόω**, Ep. imper. of ἀλάομαι, Od.5.377.

❀ **ἄλπνιστος**, η, ον, Sup. of ἄλπνος (only in compd. ἔπαλπνος, q.v.), *sweetest, loveliest*, Pi.*I*.5(4).12; cf. **ἀλπαλέον** (cod. -αῖον)· ἀγαπητόν, Hsch. (Cf. ἔλπω (Fέλπω), Lat. *volup*.)

❀ **ἅλς** (A), ἁλός [ᾰ], ὁ: dat. pl. ἅλασιν (v. infr.):—*salt*, πάσσε δ' ἁλὸς θείοιο Il.9.214, cf. Od.17.455; ἁλὸς μέταλλον a *salt*-mine, Hdt.4.185; ἁλὸς χόνδροι lumps of *rock-salt*, ib.181: sg. also Ar.*Ach*.835, Philyll.28, Axionic.8: more freq. in pl., Od.11.123, Hdt.4.53, al., etc.:—prov. phrases: οὐ σύ γ' ἂν..σῷ ἐπιστάτῃ οὐδ' ἅλα δοίης Od.17.455; φῄς μοι πάντα δόμεν· τάχα δ'..οὐδ' ἅλα δοίης Theoc.27.61; ἅλας συναναλῶσαι, i.e. to be bound by ties of hospitality, Arist.*EN*1156$^b$27; τῶν ἁλῶν συγκατεδηδοκέναι μέδιμνον to have eaten a bushel of *salt* together, i.e. to be old friends, *Com.Adesp*.176; οἱ περὶ ἅλα καὶ κύαμον, of friends, Plu.2.684e, cf. Arist.*EE*1238$^a$3; ὅρκον μέγαν, ἅλας τε καὶ τράπεζαν Archil.96; ποῦ ἅλες; ποῦ τράπεζαι; D.19.189; τοὺς ἅλας παραβαίνειν ib.191; τοὺς τῆς πόλεως ἅλας περὶ πλείονος ποιήσασθαι τῆς ξενικῆς τραπέζης Aeschin.3.224; ἁλῶν δὲ φόρτος ἔνθεν ἦλθεν, ἔνθ' ἔβη 'light come, light go', Zen.2.20; ἅλασιν ὕει, of great abundance, Suid. 2. in pl. of medical preparations, Dsc.5.109. II. *brine*, Call.*Fr*.50. III. ἁ. ἀμμωνιακός *rock-salt*, *PLond*.1.78.90. 2. ἁ. Ἰνδικός *sugar*, Archig.ap.Paul.Aeg.2.53. IV. ἅλες, οἱ, metaph., like Lat. *sales*, *wit*, possible but unlikely in Pl.*Smp*.177b, *Ep.Col*.4.6; certain in Plu.2.854c; ἅλες called "χάριτες" ib.685a. (Cf. sq.)

**ἅλς** (B), ἁλός [ᾰ], ἡ (ἁλὸς πολιοῖο Il.20.229), *sea* (generally of shallow water near shore), εἰς ἅλα δῖαν Il.1.141; χεῖρας νιψάμενος πολιῆς ἁλός *in sea-water*, Od.2.261; ἢ ἁλὸς ἢ ἐπὶ γῆς 12.27: sts. pleonast. πόντος ἁλός Il.21.59, Thgn.10; ἁλὸς πελάγη or πέλαγος, Od.5.335, *h.Ap*.73, E.*Tr*.88; πελαγίαν ἅλα A.*Pers*.427; παρ' ἁλμυρὰν ἅλα E.*Ba*.17; in pl. (with a pun on ἅλς A), Ar.*Ach*.760.—Poet. word: nom. only Emp.56. (Cf. Lat. *sal*: both masc. and fem. are from the same root.)

**ἀλσείαν**· πορείαν, Hsch.

❀ **Ἀλσεῖος**, ὁ, sc. μήν, month at Cos, *SIG*1023.25.

❀ **ἀλσηίς**, ἡ, (ἄλσος) *of the grove*, νύμφαι A.R.1.1066.

**ἀλσίνη**, ἡ, *lich-wort, Parietaria lusitanica*, Thphr.*HP*9.13.3, Dsc.4.86.

**ἄλσις**, εως, ἡ, (ἅλλομαι) *leaping*, Hp.*Morb.Sacr*.17, Arist.*EN*1174$^a$31, Antyll.ap.Orib.6.31.5, etc.

**ἄλσις**, εως, ἡ, (ἀλδαίνω) *growth*, Did. ad D.13.32, Apollon.*Lex*. s. v. ἀλδαίνει, etc.

**ἄλσο**, v. sub ἅλλομαι.

**ἀλσο-κομέω**, *to be keeper of a grove* or *precinct*:—also **-κομία**, ἡ; **-κομικός**, ή, όν, (-κομική, ἡ, sc. τέχνη). Adv. **-κῶς** Poll.7.141:— **-κόμος**, ὁ, ib.140. **-ποιία**, ἡ, *planting of groves*, ibid.

❀ **ἄλσος**, εος, τό, *grove*, Il.20.8, Od.10.350: pl., Phanocl.1.3, Theoc.1.117, etc. II. esp. *sacred grove*, Od.6.291, Hes.*Sc*.99, Hdt.5.119, Pl.*Lg*.761c, etc.:—hence, *any hallowed precinct*, even without trees, Il.2.506, Sch.Pi.*O*.3.31, cf. B.3.19, S.*Ant*.844; Μαραθώνιον ἄ., of the field of battle, viewed as a holy place, A.*Eleg*.4: metaph., πόντιον ἄ. the ocean-*plain*, B.16.85, A.*Pers*.111. (Perh. for ἄλτ-ιος (cf. Ἄλτις), i.e. *alq-ios*, cf. Goth. *alhs* 'temple'.)

**ἀλσ-ώδης**, ες, *woodland*, κρῆναι E.*IA*141 (lyr.); τόποι Nic.Thyat. ap.Ath.11.503c, Dsc.4.86. II. *growing in woods*, of plants, Thphr.*HP*3.2.4, Lxx 4*Ki*.16.4, Hecat.Abd.ap.J.*Ap*.1.22, Plu.2.648c. **-ωμα**, τό, = ἄλσος, Aq. 4*Ki*.23.4. **-ών**, ῶνος, ὁ, = foreg., ib.17.16.

**ἀλτεῖ**· ἀπορεῖ, Hsch. (leg. ἀλύει). **ἀλτηρεία**· ἀφὴ τῆς χειρός, Id.

**ἁλ-τῆρες**, ων, οἱ (sg., Philostr.*Gym*.55), (ἅλλομαι) *weights held in the hand* to give an impetus *in leaping*, Crates Com.11, Arist.*IA*705$^a$16, *Pr*.881$^b$5, etc. **-τηρία**, ἡ, *use of* ἁλτῆρες, Artemid.1.57. **-τηροβολία**, ἡ, = foreg., Iamb.*VP*21.97. **-τικός**, ή, όν, *good at leaping*, X.*Cyr*.8.4.20; τὰ ἁ. μόρια parts *used in leaping*, Arist.*PA*683$^b$3; ἁ. ὄρχησις, of the Salii, Plu.*Num*.13.

**Ἄλτις**, ιος, ἡ, *sacred precinct of Zeus at Olympia*, Pi.*O*.10(11).50, X.*HG*7.4.29, etc.: Elean for ἄλσος, Paus.5.10.1.

**ἀλτο**· πολύ, ἐλαφρόν, Hsch. **ἀλτὸς καὶ** ❀**ἀλτρός**· μισθός, Id. **ἄλυγος**· ἄνευ μάστιγος, Id. **ἀλύδαινος**· ὁ κακὸς ἄνεμος, Suid. **ἀλύδοιμος**, ον, = πικρός, Sophr.139. **ἀλύζα**· ἄλυπον, Hsch. ❀ **ἀλύζω**, fut. ἀλύξω, = ἀλύω, Gal.19.76. **ἀλύη**, ἡ, *socket for* ἐχέτλη, q.v., Eratosth.ap.*EM*173.24; dub. l. Phld.*Mort*. p.318 M. **ἁλυκᾶτος**, η, ον, *pickled*, κεστρεῖς Xenocr.149.

**ἁλυκεία**, ἡ, *salting*, Ptol.*Tetr*.181.

**ἀλύκη** [ῠ], ἡ, = ἄλυσις, ἀλυσμός, Hp.*Aph*.7.56, al.

**ἁλῠκ-ίς**, ίδος, ἡ, (ἅλς) *salt-spring*, Str.4.1.6. II. *saltness*, Plu.2.897a. ❀ **-ός**, ή, όν, *salt*, Hp.*Acut*.42, *Aër*.1, Ar.*Lys*.403, Lxx *Ge*.14.3; *brackish*, Thphr.*HP*4.3.5. **-όσμυρνα**, ἡ, a kind of *myrrh*, *Hippiatr*.52. **-ότης**, ητος, ἡ, *saltness*, Arist.*Fr*.217, Thphr.*CP*2.5.4, Mnesith.ap.Ath.3.92b. ❀ **-ρός**, ά, όν, *lukewarm*, Epic.ap.*EM* 71.31, Nic.*Al*.386 (Comp.); cf. ἀλυκτρόν.

**ἀλυκτάζω**, (v. ἀλύω) only impf., *wander distraught*, B.10.93; *to be distressed*, Hdt.9.70:—also ❀**ἀλυκτέω**, *to be in distress, anguish*, Hp.*Mul*.1.5, cf. Erot., *EM*71.38, Hsch., Suid.: aor. part. ἀλυκτήσας in act. sense, = θορυβήσας, Hsch., *EM*71.39; cf. ἀλαλύκτημαι.

❀ **ἀλυκτέω**· ὑλακτέω (Cret.), Hsch., cf. *EM*71.33.

❀ **ἀλυκτοπέδαι**, αἱ, *bonds*, in pl., Hes.*Th*.521, A.R.2.1249: sg., *AP*5.229 (Paul. Sil.), etc. (ἀλυκτο- prob. = *unbreakable*, cf. Skt. *rujáti* 'break', but taken by late Poets as = ἀλυτο- *indissoluble*, cf. Paul. Sil. l. c., *AP*9.641 (Agath.), Nonn.*D*.21.56.)

❀ **ἀλυκτός**, όν, *to be shunned*, φόνοι *Epigr.Gr*.793 (Phryg.):—wrongly expl. by ἄφυκτος, Suid., Zonar.

**ἀλυκτοσύνη**, ἡ, = ἔκκλισις, Suid. 2. = ἀκοσμία, Hsch.

**ἀλυκτρόν**· εὔδινον, Hsch. **ἀλύνει**· φύει, Id.

**ἁλῠκώδης**, ες, *like salt, saltish*, γλῶσσα Hp.*Acut*.(*Sp*.)2; φλοιός Thphr.*HP*9.11.2 (ubi ἁλικώδης).

**ἀλύμαντος** [ῠ], ον, *unhurt, unimpaired*, Plu.2.5e, Porph.ap.Eus. *PE*11.28.

**ἄλυξις**, εως, ἡ, (ἀλύσκω) *escape*, A.*Ag*.1299, Q.S.12.212.

**ἀλῡπ-έω**, *to be free from pain*, imper. ἀλύπει *IG*14.1030, etc.; prob. l. in Phld.*Rh*.1.373S. **-ητος**, ον, *not pained* or *grieved*, S.*Tr*.168. II. Act., *not causing pain*, S.*OC*1662 (but v. sub ἀλάμπετος): so Adv. **-τως** Pl.*Lg*.958e. **-ία**, ἡ, *freedom from pain* or *grief*, Antipho Soph.ap.Plu.2.833c, Pl.*Ax*.371d, Men.549, Arist.*Rh*.1365$^b$13, Epicur.*Fr*.120, Sotad.5.10, etc. II. *digestibility*, Thphr. *HP*2.4.2. **-ιάς**, ἡ, = sq. III, Paul.Aeg.7.4, Alex.Trall.1.15. ❀ **-ος**, ον, *without pain*, freq. in Trag. (not A.), E.*IA*163, etc.: c. gen., ἄ. γήρως *without pains* of age, S.*OC*1519; ἄ. ἄτης *El*.1002; βίος E.*Ba*.1004; ἀρχή S.*OT*593; τὸ ἄ. Pl.*R*.585a: Comp. -ότερος ib.581e: Sup. -ότατος *Lg*.848e. Adv. ἀλύπως, ζῆν, διατελεῖν live *free from pain and sorrow*, Id.*Prt*.358b, *Phlb*.43d, cf. Men.549; ἀποθανεῖν Id.14: Sup. ἀλυπότατα Lys.24.10. II. Act., *causing no pain* or *grief*, Hp.*Art*.39 (Sup.), Pl.*Plt*.272a, etc.; ἄ. οἶνος *harmless*, Hermipp.82.5, cf. E.*Ba*.423; ἄ. ἄνθος ἀνίας *setting free from the pain* of sorrow of wine, S.*Fr*.172; ἀλυπότατος κλιντήρ, of a hospice, *Epigr.Gr*.450 (Batanaea); σωλῆνες -ότατοι μετὰ ἁλῶν *cause least pain*, i.e. *are least indigestible*, Xenocr.57, cf. Mnesith.ap.Ath.3.92c; πεσσὸς -ότατος Aët.16.36. Adv. ἀλύπως, τοῖς ἄλλοις ζῆν live *without offence* to others, Isoc.12.5. III. **ἄλυπον**, τό, *herb terrible, Globularia Alypum*, Plin.*HN*27.22, Dsc.4.178.

**ἄλῠρος**, ον, *without the lyre, unaccompanied by it*, ὕμνοι ἄ., i.e. *wild* dirges (accompanied by flute, not lyre), E.*Alc*.447; ἄ. ἔλεγος *Hel*.185; μέλος Poet.ap.Arist.*Rh*.1408$^a$7; Ἄϊδος μοῖρ' ἄ., of death, S.*OC*1223 (lyr.); ἄ. φθόγγοι *sad* talk, Alexis 162.6 anap.); ἄ. μαθήματα ποιητῶν Pl.*Lg*.810b.

**ἄλυς**, υος, ὁ, (ἀλύω) *agitation*, Hp.*Ep*.1, Gal.9.613; χειρῶν Adam.2.21. II. *ennui, boredom*, Zeno *Stoic*.1.58, Plu.*Eum*.11, Diog.Oen.*Fr*.24; ἄ. ναυτιώδης Plu.*Pyrrh*.13.

**ἁλῠσηδόν**, Adv. *in chains*, Man.4.486.

❀ **ἀλυσθαίνω**, (ἀλύω) = ἀδημονέω, Nic.*Th*.427, *EM*70.45, prob. in Hp.*Morb*.2.54,58,67; cf. ἀλυσταίνω.

**ἀλυσθένεια**, ἡ, = ἀσθένεια, *EM*70.45.

**ἀλῠσίδετος**, ον, *bound with chains*, Hsch.

⊛ **ἀλῠσίδιον** or -είδιον, τό, Dim. of ἅλυσις, Hero *Spir.*1.38, Ph.2.152, *POxy.*496.3 (ii A. D.), *AB*380.

⊛**ἀλῠσιδωτός**, ή, όν, *wrought in chain fashion*, ἁ. θώραξ Plb.6.23.15 (pl.), D.S.5.30, etc.; opp. λινοθώραξ, στάδιος θώραξ, Str.3.3.6, Sch. A.R.3.1226.

⊛**ἀλῠσιον**, τό, Dim. of sq., Men.258, Philippid.33, *PHib.*1.121.3 (iii B.C.), *PMeyer* 22.6 (iii/iv A.D.).

⊛**ἅλῠσις** (on the breathing v. Hdn.Gr.1.539), εως, ή, *chain*, χαλκέῃ ἁλύσι δεδεμένη ἄγκυρα Hdt.9.74, cf. Th.2.76, etc.; ἐν ἁλύσει μιᾷ δεδεμένους D.Chr.30.17, cf. *Ep.Eph.*6.20; πέτραν ἁλύσεσι χρυσέαισι φερομέναν E.*Or.*982:—as a woman's ornament, Ar.*Fr.*320.12, Nicostr. 33; σφραγῖδε. . ἁλύσεις χρυσᾶς ἔχουσαι *IG*2.652*B*35. 2. collectively, *chains, bondage*, Plb.21.3.3. 3. *link* in chain armour, Arr. *Tact.*3.5.

**ἄλῠσις**, εως, ή, (ἀλύω) *distress, anguish*, Dsc.5.2; gloss on ἀλυσμός, Gal.19.75.

**ἀλῠσι-τέλεια**, ή, *damage, prejudice*, Plb.4.47.1. -**τελής**, ές, *unprofitable*, Pl.*Cra.*417d, X.*Oec.*14.5, Polystr.p.18 W.; of a person, ἁ. τῇ πόλει Bato 2.9: Sup. -έστατος Aeschin.1.105. Adv. -λῶς X. *Mem.*1.7.2, Hierocl.*in CA* 12 p.447 M., etc. II. Medic., *unfavourable*, of symptoms, Hp.*Prog.*14.

**ἀλυσκάζω**, strengthd. for ἀλύσκω (from which it borrows obl. tenses); irreg. opt. ἀλυσκάζειε Nonn.*D.*42.135, al.:—*shun, avoid*, c. acc., ὕβριν ἀλυσκάζειν Od.17.581: abs., *skulk*, Il.5.253, 6.443, Orph.*A.*437; dub. in Hes.*Fr.*96.94.—Ep. word, used by Cratin. 137. ⊛**ἀλύσκω**, Od.22.363: fut. ἀλύξω Il.10.371, A.*Pers.*94, S.*Ant.* 488, etc.; ἀλύξομαι v.l. in Hes.*Op.*363: aor. ἤλυξα, poet. ἄλυξα, v. infr.:—Med. in compd. ἐξαλύσκω.—Ep. Verb used by A. and S., both in lyr. and dialogue (also in late Prose, Philostr.*Her.*7):—*flee from, shun*, c. acc., Il.10.371, Od.12.335, Hes. l.c., Pi.*P.*8.16, A. *Pr.*587, etc.: rarely c. gen., S.*Ant.*488, *El.*627: abs., *escape*, ὅθεν οὔπως ἦεν ἀλύξαι Od.22.460; προτὶ ἄστυ ἀλύξαι Il.10.348; ἄλυξεν ἐν Γερήνῳ *he escaped* by staying in Gerenus, Hes.*Fr.*16. II. = ἀλύω, *wander restlessly*, A.R.4.57.

**ἀλυσμ-ός**, ὁ, (ἀλύω) *anguish, disquiet*: esp. *tossing about*, of sick persons, Hp.*Prog.*3, al. -**ώδης**, ες, *uneasy, troubled*, Hp.*Coac.*296.

**ἀλυσπαθείη**· κακοπαθείᾳ, Hsch. (leg. δυσπ-).

**ἄλυσσον**, τό, (λύσσα) *madwort, Farsetia clypeata*, Dsc.3.91 (ἀλύσσιον Ps.-Dsc. l. c.), cf. Plu.2.648a. 2. *Galen's madwort, Sideritis romana*, Ruf.*Fr.*76.10; cf. sq.

**ἄλυσσος**, ον, *curing madness*, βοτάνη (= foreg. 2) Asclep.ap.Gal. 14.168; πηγὴ ἄ. well (in Arcadia) *curing hydrophobia*, Paus.8.19.3.

**ἀλύσσω**, fut.-ξω, v. infr., (ἀλύω) *to be uneasy, restless*, pres. only Il. 22.70 ἁ. περὶ θυμῷ: fut., ἀλύξει τε καὶ ῥίψει ἑαυτὴν *will be restless*. . , Hp. *Mul.*1.2: plpf. Pass., κραδίη ἀλάλυκτο φόβῳ *was disquieted*, Q.S.14.24.

**ἀλυστ-άζω**· ἀλύω, Hsch., *EM*71.54. -**αίνω**· ἀλυσθαίνω, Hsch., *EM*70.46 (-ιαιν-). -**ινόν**· δεινόν, Hsch., *EM*70.46 (-τηνόν). -**ον**· [σ]τρυβλίον, Hsch. -**ονέω**, = ἀλυσθαίνω, dub. in Cerc.19.89.

⊛**ἀλυτ-αρχέω**, *hold office of* ἀλυτάρχης, *Inscr.Olymp.*468, *BCH*28.82 (Tralles). ⊛-**άρχης**, ὁ, *chief of police at* Olympic games, Luc.*Herm.* 40, *Inscr.Olymp.*240; ἁ. τῶν μεγάλων Ὀλυμπίων *BCH*28.81 (Tralles), cf. *Cod.Theod.*15.9.2 (Antioch.). -**αρχία**, ή, *office of* ἀλυτάρχης, *Cod.Just.*1 36.1; cf. ἀλύτης.

⊛**ἀλύταται**· παρατηρεῖ, Hsch.

⊛**ἀλύτης**, ου, ὁ, *police-officer* at Olympic games (and elsewhere), *Inscr.Olymp.*483, *EM*72.14.

**ἀλυτίς**, ή, = *pediculus*, Apul.*Herb.*81.

**ἄλυτον**· χλιαρόν, Hsch. (cf. ἀλυκρός, ἀλυκτρόν).

⊛**ἄλῠτος**, ον, poet. ἄλλυτος Phanocl.2.1, *AP*6.30 (Maced.), *not to be loosed or broken, indissoluble*, πέδαι, δεσμοί, Il.13.37, Od.8.275, A.*Pr.* 55; ἀδάμας *AP*12.93 (Rhian.); Μοιράων νῆμα Phanocl. l. c., cf. *Epigr. Gr.*520 (Thessalonica); πτολέμοιο πεῖραρ Il.13.360; κύκλος (of the wheel of the ἴϋγξ) Pi.*P.*4.215; *irremediable*, S.*El.*230 (lyr.): of substances, *insoluble*, Arist.*Mete.*384ᵇ7. Adv. -τως Pl.*Ti.*60c. 2. of arguments or evidence, *not to be confuted, irrefutable*, Arist.*Rh.*1357ᵇ 17, 1403ᵃ14; συλλογισμός Arist.*APr.*70ᵃ29. II. *undissolved*, Pl. *Ti.*60e.

**ἄλυτρον**, τό, perh. for ἅλοιτρον = ἀλόητρον, *threshing implement*, *PAmh.*2.143.14 (iv A.D.).

**ἀλύτρωτος**, ον, *not redeemed*, Sm.*Le.*25.23.

⊛ **ἀλυχή**, ή, = ἀλυσμός, Gal.19.76, cf. Hsch., who also has **ἄλυχα**· ἀδημονία; cf. ἀλύκη.

**ἄλῠχνος**, ον, *without lamp* or *light*, E.*Fr.*411, D.L.1.81.

⊛ **ἀλύω**, Att. ἀλύω acc. to Suid., cf. Eust.1636.28, Aeol. **ἀλυίω** *EM* 254.16; only pres. and impf.; Poet. (rare in Com.) and late Prose:—*to be deeply stirred, excited*: 1. from grief, *to be distraught, beside oneself*, ἡ δ' ἀλύουσ' ἀπεβήσετο Il.5.352; δινεύεσκ' ἀλύων παρὰ θῖνα 24. 12; ἀλύων *in mad passion*, Od.9.398; ἐᾶτέ μ' ὧδ' ἀλύειν S.*El.*135; τί χρῆμ' ἀλύω; E.*Or.*277, etc. 2. from perplexity or despair, *to be at a loss, perplexed*, ἀλύει δ' ἐπὶ παντὶ S.*Ph.*174; ἀλύοντα χειμερίῳ λύπᾳ ib.1194; ἐν πόνοις ἀλύουσαν Id.*OT*695; οἱ μὲν εὐποροῦμεν οἱ δ' ἀλύομεν *are at our wit's end*, Alex.116.13; ἄλλως ἀλύει *is wasting her pains*, Men.*Epit.*342; ψυχὴ ἁ. διὰ τὴν ἀπορίαν Plu.*Brut.*15. 3. *to be weary, ennuyé*, ἐπὶ τῶν συμποσίων Metrod.*Herc.*831.13, cf. Plu.2. 965a, Ael.*VH*14.12. 4. *to be fretful, restless*, Hp.*Epid.*1.26.α', Men.*Epit.Fr.*4, Gal.18(1).167. 5. *struggle, kick*, τῶν σκελῶν ἀλυόντων Hld.10.30. 6. from joy or exultation (rarely), *to be beside oneself*, Od.18.333, A.*Th.*391, cf. Jac.*AP*p.760. II. later, *wander, roam about*, Plb.26.1.1, Luc.*DMar.*13.1, Plu.*TG*21; *lounge idly*, Babr.9.[11]. III. trans., μετὰ φρεσὶν ἄχθος ἀλύει Opp.*H.* 4.195. [ῠ Hom., except at the end of the verse, Od.9.398, as A.R. 3.866; ἀλῡοντες in 4th foot, Emp.145, Opp.*H.*4.195; ῡ always in Trag.]

⊛ **ἄλφα**, τό, indecl. (pl. τὰ ἄ. Arist.*Metaph.*1087ᵃ8), v. Α α init. cf. Aen.Tact.31.18, Callias ap.Ath.10.453d, Pl.*Cra.*431e; ἐπίστατα δ' οὐδ' ἄλφα συλλαβὴν γνῶναι Herod.3.22. 2. Ꞁ-*square*, Eustr. *in EN*74.2. 3. Phoenician for βοὸς κεφαλή, Hsch. 4. metaph., τὸ ἄλφα καὶ τὸ ὦ the *first* and last, *Apoc.*1.8, al.

⊛ **ἀλφάβητος**, ὁ, *alphabet*, *AB*181, Sch.D.T.p.320 H.

**ἀλφαδεῖ**· εὑρίσκει, καὶ ἀλφαίνει, and **ἀλφαίει**· τὸ αὐτὸ δηλοῖ, Hsch.

**ἀλφάδιον**· ἐχθρόν, Hsch. 2. Dim. of ἄλφα, *carpenter's square*, Eustr.*in EN*322.18.

**ἀλφάνω** [ᾰν] (ἀλφαίνω *EM*72.39, Aët.13.133), Hom. only in aor. 2 ἦλφον, cf. *IG*1.53*a*15, Plu.2.668c: pres., E.*Med.*297, *Fr.*326 (nowhere else in Trag.), Ar.*Fr.*324, Eup.258, Men.362:—*bring in, yield, fetch*, ἵνα μοι βίοτον πολὺν ἄλφοι Od.17.250; ὁ δ' ὑμῖν μυρίον ὦνον ἄλφοι 15.452, cf. 20.383; ἑκατόμβοιον δέ τοι ἦλφον Il.21.79; ὁπόσην ἂν ἄλφῃ μίσθωσιν τὸ τέμενος *IG* l. c., cf. Plu. l. c.: metaph., φθόνον ἀλφάνειν *to incur* envy, E.*Med.*297. II. = ἐναλλάσσω, *change*, Aët. l. c. (cf. Skt. *arghás* 'price').

**ἀλφάριον**, τό, Dim. of ἄλφα, *plumb-line, level*, Theo Sm. *in Ptol.* p.228 H.

**ἀλφεσίβοιος**, α, ον, *bringing in oxen*, παρθένοι ἀ. maidens *who yield their parents many oxen as presents from their suitors*, i.e. *much-courted*, Il.18.593, *h.Ven.*119; ὕδωρ ἀ., of the Nile, water *that yields fat oxen* (by enriching pastures), A.*Supp.*855 (lyr.); Πειρήνης ἀ. ὕδωρ Alex.Aet.3.8: pr. n. Ἀλφεσίβοια used at beginning of trim., S. *Fr.*880.

**ἀλφ-ή**, ή, *produce, gain*, Lyc.549, 1394. -**ησις**, εως, ή, *Gloss.* ⊛-**ηστής**, οῦ, ὁ, Hom. only in Od., in phrase ἀνέρες ἀλφησταί, lit. *earners* (ἀλφάνω), i.e. *enterprising* men, Od.1.349, cf. Hes. *Op.*82; esp. of *traders* or *seafarers*, Od.13.261, *h.Ap.*458; ἑκὰς ἀνδρῶν ἀλφηστάων, of the Phaeacians, Od.6.8.—Ep. word, twice in Trag. (lyr.), A.*Th.*770, S.*Ph.*709. II. kind of *fish* that went in pairs, *Labrus cinaedus*, Epich.44, Numen.ap.Ath.7.320e: metaph., of *lewd men*, Sophr.63. -**ηστικός**, ὁ, = ἀλφηστής II, Arist.*Fr.*307, Diocl. *Fr.*135.

⊛ **ἄλφι**, τό, poet. indecl. abbrev. of ἄλφιτον, ἄλφι καὶ ὕδωρ *h.Cer.*208, cf. Str.8.5.3, *EM*769.39.

**ἀλφινία**, ή, = λεύκη (Perrhaeb.), Hsch.

**ἀλφίσκω**, f.l. in Od.22.57 ap. *EM*758.47.

**ἀλφιτ-ἄμοιβός**, ὁ, *dealer in* ἄλφιτα, Ar.*Av.*491, al. -**εία**, ή, *preparing of* ἄλφιτα, Hyp.*Fr.*225 (ἀλφίτια codd. Poll.), Poll.7. 18. -**εῖον**, τό, *mill for grinding* ἄλφιτα, Poll.3.78, 7.19, *AB* 261. -**εύς**, έως, ὁ, *barley-miller*, Hyp.*Fr.*224. -**εύω**, *grind barley*, Hippon.46. -**ηδόν**, Adv. *like* ἄλφιτα, Dsc.*Eup.*2.51. II. of fractures, *where bone is comminuted*, Gal.10.424, Paul.Aeg. 6.89. -**ηρός**, ά, όν, *of or belonging to* ἄλφιτα, ἀγγεῖον ἀ. *meal*-tub, Antiph.63 (-τήριον Poll.10.179). 2. ἀλφιτηρὸν ἐργαλεῖα κινεῦσι 'a living wage for the worker', Herod.7.73. ⊛-**ισμός**, ὁ, *mixing with barley-groats*, οἴνου *BCH*6.26 (Delos, ii B.C.).

**ἀλφῐτο-ειδής**, ές, *like* ἄλφιτα, Poet. *de herb.*77. -**μαντις**, εως, ὁ, ή, *one that divines from barley-meal*, Iamb.*Myst.*3.17, Phryn.*PS* p.91 B., Poll.7.188, Hsch.

⊛ **ἄλφῐτον**, τό, *barley-groats*, sg. in Hom. only in phrase ἀλφίτου ἀκτή Il.11.631, Od.2.355, 14.429, and Medic., Gal.6.507: elsewh. in pl. ἄλφιτα, opp. ἀλείατα, q.v., ἄ. μυελὸν ἀνδρῶν Od.2.290, al., Hdt.7. 119, freq. in Att.; used to sprinkle over roast meat, Il.18.560, cf. Od. 14.77; esp. over sacrificial victims, Od.14.429: ἐπ' ἀλφίτου πίνειν to drink wine with *barley-groats* in it, Epin.1:—of this was made a kind of *barley-water*, πιεῖν ἄλφιτα Hp.*Epid.*5.10; also, *poultices*, Dsc.4.87: also used as *hair-powder* by κανηφόροι, Hermipp.26. II. generally, *meal, groats*, ἄ. πύρινα Hp.*Acut.*(*Sp.*)53; ἄ. φακῶν καὶ ὀρόβων Id. *Int.*23; even λίθοιο ἄλφιτα Orph.*L.*212. III. metaph., *one's daily bread*, 'bread and cheese', Ar.*Pl.*219, *Nu.*106, etc.

**ἀλφῐτο-ποιέω**, Suid. s.v. τηλία. -**ποιία**, ή, = ἀλφιτεία, X.*Mem.* 2.7.6. -**ποιός**, ὁ, ή, *preparer of* ἄλφιτα, Oenom.ap.Eus.*PE*5. 34. -**πώλης**, ου, ὁ, *seller of* ἄλφιτα, Nicoph.19:—fem. -**πωλις**, D.L.6.9, 7.168; as Adj., ἀ. στοά *flour*-market at Athens, Ar.*Ec.* 682. -**πωλήτρια**, ή, pecul. fem. of ἀλφιτοπώλης, Poll.6.37. -**πωλικός**, ή, όν, *of the meal-sellers*, πλατεῖα *AB*275. -**σῑτέω**, *eat barley-bread*, X.*Cyr.*6.2.28. -**σκόπος**, ὁ, = ἀλφιτόμαντις, Hsch. (-σκόπαι cod.). ⊛-**φάγος** [ᾰ], ον, *eating barley-bread*, Ael.*NA* 17.31. -**χρως**, ωτος, ὁ, ή, *of the colour of barley-meal*, κεφαλὴ ἀ. *powdered*, i.e. *mangy* head, Ar.*Fr.*533.

**Ἀλφῐτώ**, οῦς, ή, *bugbear* with which nurses frightened children, Chrysipp.*Stoic.*3.77.

**Ἀλφιῷος**, ὁ, sc. μήν, name of month at Elis, *GDI*1168.

**ἀλφο-ειδής**, ές, = ἀλφώδης, Philum.*Ven.*23.2. -**πρόσωπος**, ον, *white-faced*, and -**ρυγχος**, ον, *with white snout*, *Hippiatr.*13.

**ἀλφός**, ὁ, *dull-white leprosy*, esp. on the face, Hes.*Fr.*29, Thphr. *Char.*19.2, Lxx *Le.*13.39, etc.: pl. in Hp.*Aph.*3.20, Pl.*Ti.*85a. (Cf. Lat. *albus*.)

**ἀλφώδης**, ες, *leprous*, Gal.6.243, Vett.Val.13.2.

**ἀλχηρής**· ὕπνος· ἀηδής, οὐκ ἔχων χαράς, Hsch.

**Ἁλῶα** or **Ἀλῷα**, ων, τά, (ἅλως) festival of Demeter as inventress of agriculture, *harvest home*, *IG*2.834*b*ii8, D.59.116, Philoch.161, Luc.

.*Meretr.*7.4. **ἁλωαῖος,** *α, ον,* (ἅλως) *belonging to the threshing-floor*: Ἁλωαίη, epith. of Demeter, Orph.*H.*41.5. **Ἁλωάς,** *άδος,* or **Ἁλωίς,** *ίδος, ἡ,* = Ἁλωαία, Theoc.7.155.

**ἀλώβητος,** *ον, unblemished,* φύσις Ph.1.451; *intact,* ἀ. καὶ ἀκέραιος Them *Or.*3.43c, cf. Zos.2.5; *sound* in limb, Gal.13.1026.

**ἁλώδης,** *ες, like salt,* Plu.2.627f. **ἁλωεινός,** *ή, όν,* (ἅλως) *of* or *used in a threshing-floor,* ἵπποι *AP*9.301 (Secund.). **ἀλωεύς,** *έως,* Ep. ῆος, ὁ, *one who works in an* ἀλωή, *husbandman,* A.R.3.1401, Arat. 1045, etc.: in Hom. only as pr. n.

⊛**ἀλωή** [ᾰ], Dor. **ἀλωά,** *ἡ,* (ἀλέω A, cf. Att. ἅλως) poet.: I. *threshing-floor,* ἱερὰς κατ' ἀλωάς Il.5.499; μεγάλην κατ' ἀλωήν, ἐϋκτιμένῃ ἐν ἀλωῇ, 13.588, 20.496, cf. Hes.*Op.*597. II. more commonly, *any prepared ground* (cf. Sch.Od.1.193), *garden, orchard, vineyard,* etc., Il.5.90, Od.6.293, etc.: Ποσειδάωνος ἀ., i.e. sea, Opp. *H.*1.797. III. *halo,* of sun or moon, Arat.811, 875.

**Ἁλωιάς,** *ἡ, of the threshing-floor,* Δηώ Nonn.*D.*30.68.

**ἁλώιος,** *α, ον,* = ἁλωεινός, Nic.*Th.*113. **Ἁλωίς,** v. Ἁλωάς.

**ἁλωίτης** [ῑ], *ου, ὁ,* = ἁλωεύς, dub. l. *AP*6.98 (Zon.).

**ἄλωμα,** *τό,* Boeot. = ἀνάλωμα, *SIG*1185 (Tanagra), *IG*7.2426 (Thebes).

**ἁλώμεναι,** Ep. for ἁλῶναι, v. sub ἁλίσκομαι.

**ἅλων,** *ωνος, ἡ,* = ἅλως (usu. in sense I), rare in nom., Thphr.*Sign.* 31 (pl., in sense II. 1), Lxx *Ho.*9.2, *BGU*651.5 (ii A.D.); more freq. in oblique cases, *BCH*39.55 (Arcad., iv B.C., in sense of *plantation* (?)), *PLille* 3.3, Arist.*Vent.*973$^{a}$14, Lxx *Ge.*50.10, etc.

**ἁλωνάκη·** ἀνάλωμα (Chalcis), Hsch.

**ἁλωνεύομαι,** *work on a threshing-floor,* App.*Mac.*13.

**ἁλώνης,** *ου, ὁ, contractor for salt-works, Inscr.Prien.*111.

**ἁλώνητος,** *ον, bought with salt,* ἁ. δουλάρια worthless slaves from Thrace, because Thracians *sold men for salt,* Zen.2.12.

⊛**ἁλων-ία,** *ἡ,* = ἅλως, *threshing-floor,* Ath.12.524a, *CPR*73.20 (ii A.D.), Sch.Nic.*Th.*541:—written **ἁλωνεία,** *ἡ,* Sch.Il.5.499, *BGU* 663 (iii A.D.). II. *grain on threshing-floor, PRyl.*442.4 (iii A.D.), *POxy.*1107.3 (v/vi A.D.). III. = ἅλως II. 2, Sch.Nic. *Th.*166. **-ίζω·** ἁλωνεύομαι, Hsch. **-ικός,** *ή, όν, for a threshing-floor,* ὑποζύγια prob. in *PStrassb.*93.5 (ii B.C.); κόσκινον *Edict.Diocl.* 15.56. **-ιον,** *τό,* Dim. of ἅλων, *Gp.*12.2.2, Hdn.Gr.2.763, *Gloss.*

**ἁλωνο-ειδής,** *ές, shaped like a threshing-floor,* χώρα Hero *Mens.* 56. **-τρῐβέω,** = ἁλωνεύομαι, Suid. s.v. ἁλωνία. II. *beat on a threshing-floor,* Longus 3.29. **-φυλακία,** *ἡ, office of guard of a threshing-floor, PRyl.*90.39 (iii A.D.). ⊛**-φύλαξ,** *ακος, ὁ, guard of a threshing-floor, POxy.*1465.8 (i B.C.).

⊛**ἀλωόφυτος,** *ον, grown in a vineyard,* οἶνος Nonn.*D.*13.267.

**ἀλωπέκ-ειος,** *α, ον,* Ion. **-εος,** *η, ον, of a fox,* στέαρ Gal.14.331; λίπος Philum.ap.Orib.45.29.36. II. ἀλωπεκέη, Att contr. -κῆ (sc. δορά), *fox-skin,* Hdt.7.75: prov., ὅπου ἡ λεοντῆ μὴ ἐφικνεῖται, προσραπτέον ἐκεῖ τὴν ἀλωπεκῆν Plu.*Lys.*7. **-εως,** *ὁ,* name of a vine, and of the wine made therefrom, Hsch.; cf. ἀλωπεκίς III. **-ία,** *ἡ,* disease, like *mange in foxes,* in which hair falls off, dub. in S.*Fr.*419, cf. Gal.12.381: pl., *bald patches* on the head, Arist.*Pr.*893$^{b}$38. II. *fox-earth,* Hsch., *EM*75.6. **-ίας,** *ου, ὁ, branded with a fox,* Luc. *Pisc.*47. II. *thresher shark,* Lat. *Squalus vulpes,* Arist.*Fr.*310, Mnesim.4.49, Diph.Siph.ap.Ath.8.356c. **-ίασις,** *εως, ἡ,* = ἀλωπεκία I, Gal.6.244. **-ιδεύς,** *έως, ὁ, fox-cub,* Ar.*Pax* 1067, Ael.*NA* 7.47. 2. = ἀλωπεκίς, *Epic.Alex.Adesp.*2.9. **-ίζω,** *play the fox,* οὐκ ἔστιν ἀλωπεκίζειν Ar.*V.*1241; ἄλλοις ἀλωπέκιζε τοῖς ἀπειρήτοις Babr.95.64: prov., ἀ. πρὸς ἑτέραν ἀλώπεκα 'Greek meets Greek', Zen.1.70. II. trans., *overreach,* Hsch. **-ιον,** *τό,* Dim. of ἀλώπηξ, *little fox,* Ar.*Eq.*1076, 1079. **-ίς,** *ίδος, ἡ, mongrel between fox and dog,* = κυναλώπηξ, X.*Cyn.*3.1. II. *fox-skin cap,* X.*An.* 7.4.4. III. kind of *grape,* so called from its colour, Plin *HN* 14.42. **-οειδής,** *ές, like fox,* Gal 4.604. **-ουρος,** *ὁ, beard-grass, Polypogon monspeliensis,* Thphr.*HP*7.11.2. **-ώδης,** *ες, fox-like, sly,* Hsch., *EM*75.5.

**ἀλωπεύει** (cod. ἀλοπ-)· ἀνιχνεύει, Hsch.; cf. ἀλωπός.

**ἀλώπηξ** [ᾰ], *εκος* (also ἀλώπηκος Anan.5), *ἡ*; dat. pl., ἀλώπεξι Lxx 3*Ki.*21.10, Ep. ἀλωπήκεσσι Opp.*C.*1.433:—*fox, Canis vulpes* (smaller Egyptian species Arist.*HA*606$^{a}$24, *C. niloticus*), Archil.86.2, 89.5, Semon.7.7, Hdt.2.67, etc.: of sly persons, ἀλώπεκος ἴχνεσι βαίνειν Sol.11.5; μῆτιν ἀ. *a very fox* for craft, Pi.*I.*4(3).65: prov., τὴν..Ἀρχιλόχου ἀλώπεκα ἑλκτέον ἐξόπισθεν we must trail Archilochus' *fox-skin* behind, i.e. deceive by false appearances, Pl.*R.*365c; πολλῆς αὐτῆς τῆς ἀ. ἐπιχέαντες Eun *Hist.*p.249 D.; ἡ ἀ. τὸν βοῦν ἐλαύνει 'sleight masters might', Diogenian.2.73; πεινῶσαν ἀ. ὕπνος ἐπέρχεται 'qui dort dîne', Id.7.91; ἡ κέρκος τῇ ἀλώπεκι μαρτυρεῖ 'ex pede Herculem', Id.5.15; ἀλλ' οὐκ αὖθις ἀ. (sc. πάγαις ἁλώσεται) 'a burnt child dreads the fire', Id.2.15. II. a large *bat, Sciurus* or *Pteromys volans,* Arist.*HA*490$^{a}$7. III. = ἀλωπεκίας II, ib.566$^{a}$ 31. IV. in pl., *muscles of the loins, psoas-muscles,* Clearch.92, Ruf.*Onom.*189. V. = ἀλωπεκία I, *mange,* Herod.7.72, Call.*Dian.* 79: in pl., *bald patches,* Hp.*Aff.*35. VI. kind of *dance,* dub. in S.*Fr.*419 (prob. in sense V), cf. Hsch. s.v. ὄρχησις.

⊛**ἀλωπός,** *ὁ,* = ἀλώπηξ, Hdn.Gr.1.189:—fem. **ἀλωπά,** *ἡ,* Hsch. II. as Adj., = ἀλωπεκώδης, S.*Fr.*263. **ἀλωπόχροος,** *ον,* contr. **-χρους,** *ουν, fox-coloured,* f.l. for ἀλφιτόχρους, *AB*381, Eust.1968.39.

⊛**ἁλωρῆται,** *οἱ, watchers of salt,* Suid., *EM*74.28.

⊛**ἅλως** [ᾰ], *ἡ,* gen. ἅλω Hp.*VM*13, X.*Oec.*18.8, ἅλωος *AP*6.258 (Adaeus); dat. ἅλῳ Arist.*Ph.*198$^{b}$22; acc. ἅλω A.*Th.*489, *IG*2.834*b* ii 21, ἅλων Nic.*Th.*166, ἅλωα Call.*Fr.*51: pl., nom. ἅλῳ Arist.*Mete.* 344$^{b}$2, ἅλωες Ach.Tat.*Intr.Arat.*32, ἅλως D.42.6, Thphr.*Sign.*22; acc. ἅλως Arist.*Mir.*835$^{b}$9, etc.: (v. sub ἀλέω A):—*threshing-floor,* Hp. l.c., X. l.c., etc.; *grain on the floor, PRyl.*122.10 (ii A.D.):—hence, from round shape, II. *disk* of sun or moon, or shield, A. l.c.: later, *halo,* Arist.*Mete.*344$^{b}$2, Epicur.*Ep.*2 p.51 U., Gal.5.640, etc. 2. *serpent's coil,* Nic.*Th.*166. 3. *bird's nest,* Ael.*NA* 3.16. 4. *ciliary body of the eye,* Poll.2.71. 5 *circular piazza* at Delphi, *GDI*2101, 2642.

⊛**ἁλ-ώσῐμος,** *ον,* (ἁλῶναι) *easy to take* or *conquer,* of places and persons, Hdt.3.153, E.*Hel.*1622, Th.4.9: metaph., *easily beguiled,* X. *Mem.*3.11.11. 2. of the mind, *easy to apprehend,* S.*Ph.*863 (lyr.). 3. *capable of solution,* ἀπόκρισις Aristid.2.275 J. II. (ἅλωσις) *of* or *belonging to capture* or *conquest,* παιὰν ἁ. song of triumph *on taking city,* A.*Th.*635; βάξις ἁ. tidings *of capture, Ag.*10. **-ωσις,** *εως,* Ion. *ιος, ἡ, capture,* Pi.*O.*10(11).42, Hdt.1.5, 3.156, A.*Ag.*589, etc.; δαΐων ἅ. *conquest* by enemy, Id.*Th.*119: *means of conquest,* S. *Ph.*61. 2. *taking, catching* of birds and fish, Arist.*HA*593$^{a}$20, 600$^{a}$3 (pl.); ἑαλωκότες ἰσχυρὰν ἅλωσιν taken *without power to escape,* Plu.*Num.*15. II. law-term, *conviction,* Pl.*Lg.*9.0a, D.C.*Fr.*97.3.

**ἅλωσος,** dub. sens., Hdn.Gr.1.213.

**ἄλωστοι·** ἄρραφοι, Hsch.

**Ἁλώτια,** *τά,* festival at Tegea, Paus.8.47.4.

**ἁλωτός,** *ή, όν, liable to capture* or *conquest,* Th.6.77, Philostr.*Im.*1. 4; ἡδονῇ ἁλωτὸν ἄνθρωπος Ph.2.381. 2. *captured,* Philostr.*VA* 2.10. II. *attainable,* S.*OT*111, Men.13.

⊛**ἀλώφητος,** *ον,* (λωφάω) *unremitting,* Plu.*Fab.*23, *AP*5.254.12 (Paul. S.l.).

**ἀλωφούς·** λευκούς, Hsch.

**ἄμ,** for ἀνά, before words beginning with β, π, φ, μ, e.g. ἂμ βωμοῖσι, ἂμ μέσον, ἂμ πεδίον, ἂμ πέλαγος, ἂμ φυτά; also compds., as ἀμπαύω:—mostly Dor., as in Pi., but also in Hom., sts. in Trag.

⊛**ἅμᾰ** [ᾰμ], Dor. **ἁμᾶ,** q.v.: (v. sub fin.): A. Adv. *at once, at the same time,* mostly of Time, freq. added to τε.. καί, ἅμ' οἰμωγή τε καὶ εὐχωλή Il.8.64; ἅ. τ' ὠκύμορος καὶ ὀϊζυρός 1.417; σέ θ' ἅ. κλαίω καὶ ἐμέ 24.773; σαυτόν θ' ἅ. κἀμέ S.*Ph.*772, cf. 119; ἄνους τε καὶ γέρων ἅ. *Ant.*281:—with καί only, ἅ. πρόσσω καὶ ὀπίσσω Il.3.109; with τε.. τε, χειρῶν τε βίης θ' ἅ. ἔργον ἔφαινον Hes.*Th.*677. 2. ἅ. μέν.. ἅ. δέ.., *partly..partly..*, Pl.*Phd.*115d, X *HG*3.1.3:—ἅ. τε.. καὶ ἅ. Pl. *Grg.*497a; ἅμ' ἡδέως ἔμοιγε κἀλγεινῶς ἅμα S.*Ant.*436. 3. in Prose ἅ. δέ.. καί.., ἅ. τε.. καί.., ἅ... καί.. may often be translated by *no sooner..than..*, ἅ. δὲ ταῦτα ἔλεγε καὶ ἀπεδείκνυε Hdt.1.112; ταῦτά τε ἅμα ἠγόρευε καὶ πέμπει 8.5; ἅ. ἀκηκόαμέν τε καὶ τριηράρχους καθίσταμεν D.4.36; ἅ. διαλλάττονται καὶ τῆς ἔχθρας ἐπιλανθάνονται Isoc.4.157. b. ἅ. μῦθος ἔην, τετέλεστο δὲ ἔργον 'no sooner said than done', Il.19.242; ἅ. ἔπος τε καὶ ἔργον ἐμήδετο *h.Merc.*46; ταῦτα εἶπε καὶ ἅ. ἔπος τε καὶ ἔργον ἐποίεε Hdt.3.134, cf 9.92: prov., ἅμ' ἔπος ἅμ' ἔργον Diogenian.1.36. c. with part. and finite Verb in same sense, βρίζων ἅ... ἐξήμελξας εὐτραφὲς γάλα A.*Ch.*897; ἅ. εἰπὼν ἀνέστη *as soon as* he had done speaking, he stood up, X.*An.*3.1.47; τῆς ἀγγελίας ἅ. ῥηθείσης ἐπεβοήθουν *as soon as* news was brought they assisted, Th.2.5; ἅ. γιγνόμενοι λαμβάνομεν Pl.*Phd.*76c; ἡμῖν ἅ. ἀναπαυομένοις ὁ παῖς ἀναγνώσεται *Tht.*143b. 4. ἅ. μέν.. ἔτι δέ.. X.*Cyr.*1.4.3; ἅ. μέν.. πρὸς δέ.. Hdt.8.51. II. *together, at once, both,* without direct ref. to time, ἅ. πάντες or πάντες ἅ. Il.1.495, al.; ἅ. ἄμφω *h.Cer.*15; ἅ. κρατερὸς καὶ ἀμύμων Od.3.111, etc.: of Place, Arist.*Metaph.*1028$^{b}$27. III. with σύν or μετά, E.*Ion* 717, Pl.*Criti.*110a. IV. abs. with Verb, *at one and the same time,* αἱ πᾶσαι [νῆες] ἅ. ἐγίγνοντο ἐν ἑνὶ θέρει σ' καὶ ν' Th.3.17, cf. οὐχ ἅ. ἡ κτῆσις παραγίγνεται D.23.113.

B. Prep. with dat. (freq. with part. added), *at the same time with, together with,* ἅμ' ἠοῖ φαινομένηφι *at* dawn, Il.9.682, al.; ἅ. ἕῳ, ἅ. ἕῳ γιγνομένῃ, Th.1.48, 4.32; ἅμ' ἠελίῳ ἀνιόντι or καταδύντι *at* sunrise or sunset, Il.18.136, 210, al.; ἅμ' ἡμέρῃ διαφωσκούσῃ Hdt.3.86, al.; ἅμ' ἡμέρᾳ E.*El.*78, Th.2.94, etc., Att.; ἅμ' ἦρι ἀρχομένῳ or ἅ. ἦρι *at* beginning of spring, Th.5.20, 2.2, etc.; ἅ. κήδεϊ κεκάρθαι τὰς κεφαλάς *during the time of..*, Hdt.2.36; ἅ. τειχισμῷ Th.7.20; ἅμα τῷ διαυγάζειν Plb.3.104.5 (without Art. ἅμα εὑρεθῆναι Ps.-Plu.*Fluv.*23. 2). 2. generally, *together with,* ἅ. τινὶ στείχειν Il.16.257; ὀπάσσαι 24.461, al.; Ἑλένην καὶ κτήμαθ' ἅμ' αὐτῇ 3.458; ἅ. πνοιῇς ἀνέμοιο *keeping pace with* the wind, Od.1.98; repeated, ἅμ' αὐτῷ.. ἅμ' ἕποντο 11.371; οἱ ἅ. Θόαντι Hdt.6.138, cf. Th.7.57. II. rarely c. gen., Herod.4.95, *POxy.*903 (iv A.D.), Pythag.*Sim.*28, Olymp.Hist. p.453 D.; dub. in Thphr.*Char.*6.9.

C. Conj., *as soon as,* ἅ. ἂν ἡβήσῃ τις τῶν ὀρφανῶν Pl.*Lg.*928c, cf. Lex ap.D.46.20; ἅ. κα διεξέλθῃ ὁ χρόνος *GDI*2160 (Delph., ii B.C.). (Root *sm-*, cf. A α II.)

⊛**ἁμᾶ,** Dor. for ἅμα, Pi.*O.*2.21, *IG*5(1), Ar.*Lys.*1318, Call.*Lav.Pall.* 75, Theoc.9.4. (ἁμᾷ Hdn.Gr.1.489; ἅμᾳ Thphr.*Metaph.*6, al. (cod. opt.).)

**ἁμαδέον,** *τό,* kind of *fig,* Cretan, Hermonax ap.Ath.3.76f.

**ἁμάδις,** Adv. = ἅμα, Theognost.*Can.*163.22; in form ἁμάδιος, *Et. Gen.*

**ἁμάδρυα·** κοκκύμηλα (Sicyon.), Phot.p.85 R., Hsch.

**Ἁμαδρυάδες,** *αἱ,* (δρῦς) Nymphs whose life depended on that of trees to which they were attached, Pl.*Epigr.*14, Pherenicus ap.Ath. 3.78b: sg., Ἁμαδρυάς A.R.2.477, Ant.Lib.30.4.

**ἀμαζακάραν·** πολεμεῖν (Persian), Hsch.

**ἀμαζανίδες·** μηλέαι, Hsch.

**Ἀμαζονομαχία,** *ἡ, battle with Amazons,* Sch.Il.2.219.

⊛**'Αμαζών, όνος, ἡ,** mostly pl., *the Amazons,* Il.3.189, etc.; ὁ τῶν 'A. τροχίσκος, a famous remedy, Asclep.ap.Gal.12.152, etc.:—also **'Αμαζονίδες, αἱ,** Pi.*O.*13.87, Call.*Dian.*237. II. epith. of Artemis, Paus.4.31.8:—Adj. **'Αμαζ-ονικός, ή, όν,** Plu.*Pomp.*35, Paus. 1.41.7:—κά, τά, title of Epic by Onasus, Sch.A.R.1.1236, Sch. Theoc.13.46:—also **-όνιος, ον,** Nonn.*D.*37.17; epith. of Apollo in Laconia, Paus.3.25.3. (Commonly derived from μαζός, from the fable that they got rid of the right breast, that it might not interfere with the use of the bow.) III. (ἀ- priv., μᾶζα) *poor, starveling,* ἄνδρες Call.*Fr.*523.

**ἀμᾰθ-αίνω,** (ἀμαθής) *to be untaught, ignorant,* only pres.; abs., Pl.*R.*535e, Ph.1.498, Aristid.34(50).44, Plot.4.4.24; ἀ. τι or εἴς τι *to be ignorant in* a thing, Pl.*Lg.*689c,d. **-εί,** Adv. of ἀμαθής, Suid.

**ἀμαθεῖν·** θερίζειν, Hsch. **ἀμαθηίς,** suggested for ψαμαθηίς (v. ἄμαθος) by Sch.Nic.*Th.*887.

⊛**ἀμαθ-ής, ές,** (μαθεῖν) *ignorant, stupid,* Hdt.1.33, Democr.169, etc.; ἔθνεα ἀμαθέστατα Hdt.4.46; ἀνὴρ πένης, εἰ καὶ γένοιτο μὴ ἀ. E. *Supp.*421, al., Ar.*Nu.*135; ἀ. καὶ βδελυρός Id.*Eq.*193; ἀμαθεστάτους πάντων ἀνθρώπων And.2.2; ἀ. τὴν [ἐκείνων] ἀμαθίαν Pl.*Ap.*22e; opp. δεξιός, Th.3.82; of animals, such as wild boars, *unmanageable,* θυμώδη καὶ ἀ. Arist.*HA*488$^{b}$14: c. gen. rei, *without knowledge of* a thing, *unlearned in* it, -έστερος τοῦ καλοῦ E.*Or.*417; λῃστείας Th. 4.41, cf. 3.37; ἀ. περί τινος Pl.*Erx.*394e; τι *La.*194d; πρός τι *Lg.* 679d. Adv. -θῶς *ignorantly, through ignorance,* ἥμαρτον E.*Ph.*874: Comp. -έστερον, τῶν νόμων ὑπεροψίας παιδεύεσθαι to be educated *with too little learning* to despise the laws, Th.1.84; -έστερόν πως εἰπὲ καὶ σαφέστερον *less learnedly,* Ar.*Ra.*1445. b. of moral defects, *unfeeling, inhuman,* ἀ. τις εἶ θεός E.*HF*347. 2. of things, ἀ. παρρησία *boorish* freedom of speech, E.*Or.*905; ἀ. ῥώμη *brute* force, Id.*Fr.*732; ἀ. δύναμις Plu.*Demetr.*42; ἀ. φρόνημα *barbarous* pride, E.*Heracl.*459. II. *not heard of, unknown,* ἀ. ἔρρει E.*Ion* 916. Adv. ἀμαθῶς, χωρῆσαι, of events, to take *an unforeseen course,* Th.1.140. **-ητος, ον,** = ἀμαθής, Phryn.Com.8; ἀ. γραμμάτων Procop.*Arc.*6. **-ία, ἡ,** *ignorance, stupidity,* Heraclit.95, 109, Hp.*Art.*67 (v.l. -είην), S.*Fr.*924, E.*Ph.*584, etc.; opp. δεξιότης, Th.3.37; ἀ. τινός Democr.83, X.*Mem.*4.2.22; περὶ τὰ μέγιστα Pl. *Lg.*688c. 2. *boorishness, lack of culture,* X.*Ath.*1.5, E.*Cyc.*173, Isoc.15.248. 3. *wilful blindness, sin, IG*4.951.39 (Epid.), cf. E. *Ba.*490. 4. *discourtesy,* Id.*Med.*224; *perversity,* Id.*HF*1254.

**ἀμᾰθῖτις, ιδος, ἡ,** (ἄμαθος) *dwelling in sand,* ἀ. κόγχοι *sand*-snails, Epich.42. ⊛**ἄμᾰθος** [ᾰμ], ἡ, Ep. form of ἄμμος, *sand,* Il.5.587, A.R.4.1239, etc.: pl., *links, dunes* by the sea, *h.Ap.*439; generally, *sandy soil,* Nic.*Th.*262. (Dist. by Gramm., e.g. Sch.Il.9.384, from ψάμμος (q.v.) as *dust* from sea-sand, but prob. wrongly:—ἄμ- is for ἅμ-, i.e. σάμ-, cf. *sand.*)

**ἀμᾰθύνω,** (ἄμαθος) Ep., only pres., impf., and (in Q.S.14.645) aor.:—*level with the dust, utterly destroy,* πόλιν Il.9.593; [ἄνδρα] μέγα φωνοῦντα A.*Eu.*937 (lyr.); ἀ. ἐν φλογὶ σάρκα Theoc.2.26:—Pass., Q.S.2.334. 2. *scatter like sand, h.Merc.*140.

**ἀμᾰθώδης, ες,** *sandy,* ποταμός Str.8.3.14.

**ἀμαίευτος, ον,** *not yet delivered,* Nonn.*D.*1.5; γαστήρ 41.133. II. *without aid of midwife,* λοχείη Opp.*C.*1.40.

**ἀμαιμάκετος, η, ον,** also ος, ον Hes.*Sc.*207:—*irresistible,* old Ep. word, also in Lyr. and Trag. (lyr.); of Chimaera, Il.6.179, 16.329; of fire vomited by her, Hes.*Th.*319; of fire generally, S.*OT*177; θάλασσα, πόντος, Hes.*Sc.*207, Pi.*P.*1.14; of ship's mast, proof against any strain, Od.14.311; of the trident, Pi.*I.*8(7).37; ἀ. μένος, κινηθμός, *P.*3.33, 4.208; νεῖκος *stubborn,* B.10.64; of the Furies, S.*OC*127; ἀ. βυθοῖς in *unfathomable* depths, *IG*3.900. [Usu. derived fr. ἀ- intens., μαιμάω, i.e. *furious*; but apptly. connected with ἄμαχος by Poets.]

**ἀμάκιον·** ἄβαξ (Lacon.), Hsch.

**ἁμάκις·** ἅπαξ (Cret.), Hsch. (-κι- = -$q^{u}$i-, cf. ἀμάτις, πολλάκις).

**ἀμακρῶτις,** = ἀμπελόπρασον, Ps.-Dsc.2.150.

**ἄμαλα·** τὴν ναῦν ἀπὸ τοῦ ἀμᾶν τὴν ἅλα, Hsch. (A.*Fr.*214); ἁμάδα· τὴν ναῦν, *EM*75.22: hence ἐπ' ἄμαλα restored by Herm., A.*Supp.* 842,847, where ἐπαμίδα cod. Med.

**ἀμαλακ-ία, ἡ,** v.l. for sq., Lyd.*Mens.*4.71. **-ιστία, ἡ,** *incapability of being softened, hardness,* etym. of 'Αμάλθεια, D.S.4.35. ⊛**-τος, ον,** (μαλάσσω) *that cannot be softened, intractable,* of materials, Arist. *Mete.*385$^{a}$13; ἄτηκτα καὶ ἀ. 388$^{b}$25. 2. *unmitigated,* τὸ ψυχρόν Plu.2.953e: metaph. of expression, *harsh,* Longin.15.5. II. *unfeeling,* Sch.S.*Aj.*776.

**ἀμᾰλάπτω,** = ἀμαλδύνω, *destroy, efface,* aor. ἠμάλαψα S.*Fr.*465, Lyc.34:—Pass., ἀμαλαπτομέναν prob. in A.*Pr.*899 (Weil).

**ἀμαλαυρεῖ·** μαραίνει, Hsch.

**ἀμαλδύνω,** (ἀμαλός) Ep. (not in Od.) and Ion. word, properly, *soften, mitigate,* ἐλπωρὴ ἀμαλδύνει κακότητα Q.S.1.73, cf. 13.401; but in early Ep. *crush, destroy,* τεῖχος ἀμαλδῦναι Il.12.18; *bring low,* συμφορὰ ἐσθλὸν ἀμαλδύνει B.13.3; *put an end to,* τὴν διὰ τοῦ ὀμφαλοῦ πνοήν Hp.*Nat.Puer.*17; *use up, squander,* χρήματα Theoc.16.59; *weaken,* ὀφθαλμούς *Cat.Cod.Astr.*2.174:—Pass., ὥς κεν..τεῖχος ἀμαλδύνηται Il.7.463; ἀμαλδυνθήσομαι Ar.*Pax*380; ὄμματα ἀ. Hp.*Mul.* 2.201; ἀ. ἡ δίοδος τῆς γονῆς Id.*Genit.*2; ἀμαλδυνθεῖσα χρόνῳ περικαλλέα μορφήν *AP*6.18 (Jul.); *neglect, waste,* Democr.202. 2. metaph., *conceal, disguise,* εἶδος *h.Cer.*94, cf. A.R.1.834; *efface,* στίβον Id.4.112.

**ἀμάλη** [ᾰμᾰ], ἡ, = ἄμαλλα, Semus 19, Philostr.Jun.*Im.*10.

**ἀμαλητόμος, ον,** (τέμνω) *reaper,* Opp.*C.*1.522.

**ἀμάλθακτος, ον,** (μαλθάσσω) *unmitigated,* Aret.*CA*2.11; *inexorabl[e],* φρένες *AP*5.233 (Paul. Sil.); ἐπιθυμία Olymp.*in Alc.*p.66 C.

**'Αμάλθ-εια,** Ion. **-είη** or **-ῐη, ἡ,** goat *Amaltheia,* which suckle[d] Zeus, Call.*Fr.*49: from her horn flowed whatever its possesso[r] wished, hence κέρας 'Αμαλθείας horn *of plenty,* Anacr.8, Phoc.7, Ar. *Fr.*39 D.; applied to parks, etc., Duris 41, D.S.3.68, etc.; title o[f] book, Gell.*Praef.*6:—also⊛**-εῖον, τό,** country-house of Atticus i[n] Epirus, Cic.*Att.*1.16, cf. 18.

**ἀμαλθεύω,** = τρέφω, S.*Fr.*95; cf. foreg.

**ἀμαλίζω·** πνίγω, in impf., Hsch.

**'Αμάλιος, ὁ,** sc. μήν, month at Delphi, *GDI*1694, al.

**ἀμαλκιεῖν·** τὸ μὴ ῥιγοῦν, *EM*76.5.

⊛**ἄμαλλ-α** [ᾰμ], ἡ, (ἀμάω A) *bundle of ears of corn, sheaf,* S.*Fr.*607, Plu. *Publ.*8. 2. poet. for *corn,* Q.S.11.156,171, etc. ⊛**-εῖον, τό,** *sheaf-band,* Call.Com.3 D. **-εύω,** *bind into sheaves* or *bundles, EM*76.6. **-ιον, τό,** = ἀμαλλεῖον, Hsch., Eust.1162.29.

**ἀμαλλο-δετήρ, ῆρος, ὁ,** (δέω) *binder of sheaves,* Il.18.553, Aret.*SD* 2.13. **-δέτης, ου, ὁ,** = foreg., Theoc.10.44, *AP*10.16 (Theaet.).

**ἄμαλλος** (A), ον, *without fleece* or *nap,* Eust.1057.1[illegible].

⊛**ἄμαλλος** (B)· πέρδιξ (Polyrrhenian), Hsch.:—also ἄμαλλοι· φυτὰ σικύων ἢ τῶν ὁμοίων, Id.

**ἀμαλλο-τόκεια, ἡ,** *producer of sheaves,* Jo.Gaz.2.31; pecul. fem. of, **-τόκος, ον,** *sheaf-producing,* Nonn.*D.*7.84; πεδία *Hymn.Is.* 3. **-φόρος, ον,** *bringing sheaves,* Euph.103, Porph.*Abst.*2.19; of Demeter, Nonn.*D.*17.153, Eust.1162.27; cf. ἀμιλλοφόρος.

⊛**ἀμα-λογεῖ** (prob. for ὁμο-)· *effutat, Gloss.* **-λογία·** ἀβδηριτισμός, *Gloss.,* v.l. for ὁμολογία in Alciphr.2.3. **-λόγος·** φλύαρος, *Gloss.*

⊛**ἀμᾰλ-ός** [ᾰμ], ή, όν, *soft, weak,* in Hom. of young animals, Il.22. 310, Od.20.14; γέρων E.*Heracl.*75; παῖς Call.*Fr.*49 P.: irreg. Comp. -έστερος, ὄψις -εστέρα Adam.2.2. (Perh. cognate with Skt. *mṛdús* 'soft', Lat. *mollis.*) **-όω·** ἀμαλδύνω, Hsch.

**'Αμαλώιος, ὁ,** sc. μήν, month at Cyme in Aeolis, *BCH*12.362.

**ἁμαλῶς,** Adv. ὁμαλῶς (in the sense of ὁμοίως), v.l. in Hp.*Morb.* 1.8, 2.8, *Int.*30, cf. Gal.19.76.

⊛**ἁμάμαξῠς** [ᾰμᾰ], ἡ, gen. υος or (in Sapph.) υδος, *vine trained on two poles,* Epich.24, Sapph.150, Matro *Conv* 114.

**ἁμᾰμηλίς, ίδος, ἡ,** = ἐπιμηλίς, *medlar, Mespilus germanica,* Hp. *Mul.*1.44, Aristomen.11, cf. Ath.14.650c.

⊛**ἀμαμιθάδες, αἱ,** *mince-meat,* Phot.p.86 R. **ἀμαμίξαι·** ἀποπνῖξαι, Hsch. (Cf. ἀμαλίζω, ἀμμιάξαι.) **ἀμάναν·** ἅμαξαν, Id. **ἀμανδαλοῖ·** ἀφανίζει, Id. **ἀμάνδᾰλος,** = ἀφανής, as if ἀμάλδανος fr. ἀμαλδύνω, Alc.123.

⊛**ἀμᾱνῖται** [ᾰμ], ῶν, οἱ, *'champignons',* a kind of fungus, Nic.*Fr.*79, Gal.6.656, Eust.290.3, etc. **ἀμάνορες·** δοθιῆνες (Elean), Hsch.

**ἀμάντευτος, ον,** *not to be foretold* or *conjectured,* τύχη Max.Tyr.11. 6. 2. *lacking in oracles,* Philostr.*Im.*1.4. 3. Act., *not divining,* τοῦ μέλλοντος Charito 2.2: hence, of dogs with bad noses, Poll. 5.63. **ἄμαντις, ι,** *not divining,* ἀ. μαντική Oenom.ap.Eus.*PE*5.21.

⊛**ἄμαξα** [ᾰ], Att. **ἅμαξα, ἡ,** (v. ἄξων) prop. *frame-work, 'châssis'* of a four-wheeled wagon (ἀπήνη), opp. πείρινς (body), Il.24.263 sqq., cf. Od.6.37, al.:—also, of the whole *wagon,* ib.260, cf. Hes.*Op.*453, Hdt.1.31, Th.1.93, etc.; of the *wagons* of the Scythians, Hdt.4.114, 121; βοῦς ὑφ' ἁμάξης *draught*-oxen, X.*An.*6.4.22,25. 2. c. gen., *wagon-load,* πετρῶν, σίτου, X.*An.*4.7.10, *Cyr.*2.4.18; ἐλλεβόρου Pl. *Euthd.*299b; τρισσῶν ἁμαξῶν βάρος E.*Cyc.*385, cf. 473. 3. prov., ἡ ἅμαξα τὸν βοῦν (sc. ἕλκει) 'the cart before the horse', Luc.*D.Mort* 6.2; ἐξ ἁμάξης ὑβρίζειν, of abusive ribaldry, such as was allowed to the women as they were taken *in wagons* to the Eleusinian mysteries, Sch.D.18.122, cf. Ar.*Pl.*1014, Men.396; βοᾷς.. ὥσπερ ἐξ ἁμάξης D. l. c. II. *carriage of a plough,* Hes.*Op.*426,453. III. = Ἄρκτος, *the Great Bear,* Il.18.487, Od.5.273, Call.*Iamb.*1.119, etc. IV. metaph., of a *ship,* A.*Fr.*451 B. V. = ἁμαξιτός, *AP* 7.479 (Theodorid.).

**ἁμαξ-αία,** = ἅμαξα, A.D.*Adv.*160.6, Hdn.Gr.1.281. **-αῖος, α, ον,** *of* or *like a wagon,* ἁ. ἄρκτος (cf. ἅμαξα III), Arat.93, cf. Nonn.*D.*1.251.

**ἁμαξακάρινον** (? -κάρριον)· ἅμαξα, Hsch.

**ἁμαξ-άρχης, ου, ὁ,** prob. *official of the imperial transport service, BCH*33.67 (Caesarea Cappad.). **-εία, ἡ,** *loading of wagons,* Suid.; *haulage* (in form -ήα), *IG*4.823 (Troezen). ⊛**-εύς, έως, ὁ,** *wagoner,* D. Chr.64.23: βοῦς ἁ. *draught*-ox, Plu.*Dio*38, Philostr.*Gym.*43. **-εύω,** *traverse with a wagon*:—Pass., *to be traversed by wagon-roads,* of country, Hdt.2.108. 2. metaph., ἁ. βίοτον *drag on a weary life, AP*9.574. II. intr., *to be a wagoner,* Plu.*Eum.*1; *travel in a wagon, AP*7.478 (Leon.); *live in wagons,* of Scythians, Philostr. *VA*7.26. **-ηγός, ὁ,** = Βοώτης, Eust.1535.29. **-ηδόνια, τά,** *axle-pins,* Sch.E.*Hipp.*1235. **-ηλατέω,** *drive a wagon,* Hsch. s. v. ἀμπρεύειν. ⊛**-ηλάτης, ου, ὁ,** *wagoner, Ostr.Strassb.*671 (ii A.D.): written **-ολάτης** ib.738. **-ήλᾰτος, ον,** *traversed by wagons*: ἡ ἁ. (sc. ὁδός) *carriage-road,* Aen.Tact.16.14, Poll.9.37, cf. Str.6.3.7. ⊛**-ήποδες, οἱ,** *axle-blocks,* Poll.1.253, cf. Ath.Mech.16.9: sg., -ήπους *IG*2. 834c. **-ήρης, ες,** (*ἄρω) *of* or *on a carriage,* θρόνος, = δίφρος, A.*Ag.* 1054; τρίβος *high*-road, E.*Or.*1251. ⊛**-ιαῖος, α, ον,** *large enough to load a wagon,* λίθος X.*HG*2.4.27, Arist.*Mir.*838$^{b}$1, D.55.20, Diph. 38, cf. *IG*2$^{2}$.463.45, 'Εφ.'Αρχ.1895.59: metaph., ἁ. ῥῆμα of big words, *Com.Adesp.*836; ἁ. χρήματα money *in cart-loads,* ib.835. ⊛**-ικός, ή, όν,** *for wagon,* Thphr.*HP*5.7.6. **-ιον, τό,** = sq., Arist.*MA*701$^{b}$4, Plu.*Dio*9. ⊛**-ίς, ίδος, ἡ,** Dim. of ἅμαξα, *little wagon,* Hdt.3.113; *go-cart,* as child's toy, or *cake* of that shape, Ar.*Nu.*864. 2. = ἁμάμαξυς, Hsch. ⊛**-ίτης** [ῑ], ου, ὁ, *of* or *for wagon,* φόρτος *AP*

306 (Antiphil.). -ῖτις, ἡ, = ἄγρωστις, Ps.-Dsc.4.29. -ἰτός, όν, Ep. and Lyr. ἀμ-, (ἄμαξα, εἶμι ibo) *traversed by wagons*, ἁ. ὁδός *carriage-road, high-road, highway*, Pi.*N*.6.54, X.*An*.1.2.21; without ὁδός, as Subst., Il.22.146, *h.Cer*.177, Thgn.599, Hdt.7.200, *IG*4.926 (Epid.), *Tab.Heracl*.1.60; ἐν τριπλαῖς ἁ. in a place where three *ways meet*, S.*OT*716, etc. 2. metaph., πειθοῦς ἁ. Emp.133; μακρά μοι νεῖσθαι κατ' ἀμαξιτόν Pi.*P*.4.247.

ἁμαξό-βιος, ον, *living in wagons*, as nomad tribes do, Porph.*Abst*. 3.15. -ειδῶς, Adv. *like a wagon*, Eust.1156.15.

ἁμάξοικος, ον, *dwelling in a wagon*, Str.7.3.2, 11.2.1.

ἁμαξο-κυλιστής, οῦ, ὁ, (κυλίνδω) *down-roller* (i.e. *destroyer*) *of wagons*: in pl., name of a Megarian family, Plu.2.304e. -πηγέω, *build wagons*, Nic.Dam.p.28D., Poll.7.115. -πηγία, ἡ, *wagon-building*, Thphr.*HP*5.7.6. -πηγός, όν, *cartwright*, *PLond.ined*. 2383A (ii B.C.), Plu.*Per*.12. -πληθής, ές, (πλῆθος) *large enough to fill a wagon*, λᾶας E.*Ph*.1158; λίθος Aen.Tact.32.5; ὄστρεια Luc. *VH*1.41. -ποδες, οἱ, = ἁμαξήποδες, Vitr.10.14.1. -ποιός, ὁ, = -πηγός (quod fort. leg.), Heraclid.*Pol*.36. -τροχιά, ἡ, (τροχός) *track of a wain* or *car*, Call.Com.10.

ἁμαξ-ουργία, ἡ, = ἁμαξοπηγία, Thphr.*HP*3.10.1. -ουργός, όν, = ἁμαξοπηγός, ἐξ ἁμαξουργοῦ λέγειν talk *cartwrights' slang*, Ar.*Eq*. 464.

ἁμαξοφόρητος, ον, *carried in wagons*, οἶκος, of the Scythians, Pi. *Fr*.104.

ἆμαρ, ατος, τό, Dor. for ἦμαρ.

ἀμάρα [ἄμᾰ], Ion. ἀμάρη, ἡ, *trench, conduit, channel*, for watering meadows, χερσὶ μάκελλαν ἔχων, ἀμάρης ἐξ ἔχματα βάλλων Il.21.259; κρηναῖαι ἀμάραι A.R.3.1392; βάλλεις εἰς ἀμάραν με Theoc.27.53, cf. Sapph.151, Call.*Cer*.30, *PFlor*.50.106. 2. *hollow* of ear, *EM*77. 23 (pl.).

*ἀμᾱράκινος, η, ον, *made of amaracus*, μύρον Antiph.106; ἔλαιον *Edict.Diocl.Delph*.16. ἀμᾱρακόεις, εσσα, εν, *like amaracus*, Nic. *Th*.503.

ἀμάρᾰκον [ᾰμᾰ], τό, and ἀμάρᾰκος, ὁ, *marjoram*, *Origanum Majorana*, Pherecr.131.3 (gender uncertain); masc. in Chaerem.14.16; Thphr. has both, *HP*6.1.1 (-ος), 1.9.4 (-ον), cf. Nic.*Th*.575, *APl*.4. 188 (Nicias). II. = σάμψουχον, Dsc.3.39, Gal.11.823.

ἀμαρανθίς, ἡ, = ὠκιμοειδές, Ps.-Dsc.4.28.

*ἀμᾰράντινος, η, ον, *of amaranth*, i.e. *unfading*, στέφανος Philostr. *Her*.19.14. 2. *unfading, imperishable*, στέφανος 1*Ep.Pet*.5.4.

*ἀμάραντος [ᾰμᾰ], ον, (μαραίνω) *unfading*, λειμών Luc.*Dom*.9: metaph., σοφία Lxx *Wi*.6.12; κληρονομία 1*Ep.Pet*.1.4, cf. *CIG*2942c (Tralles); πνεῦμα prob. in *IPE*2.286 (Panticapaeum): neut. pl. as Adv., Philostr.*Im*.1.9. II. Subst. ἀμάραντον, τό (but in Lat. *amarantus*), *never-fading flower*, *IG*14.607e (Carales), Poll.1.229; = ἑλίχρυσον, Dsc.4.57; = κενταύρειον μικρόν, Ps.-Dsc.3.7; = χρυσοκόμη, Id.4.55.

*ἀμαράσαι· αἱ σῦς, οἱ δὲ κύνες, Hsch.; cf. μαράσαι. ἄμαργος, ον, = ἄπληστος, Id. s. v. ἄβαρτος. ἀμαρεῖν· ἀκολουθεῖν, πείθεσθαι, ἁμαρτάνειν, Id.

ἀμάρ-ευμα, ατος, τό, *foul water carried off by drain* (ἀθροίσματα βορβόρου), Hsch. -εύω, (ἀμάρα) *flow off*, Aristaenet.1.17.

*ἀμαρήιος, ον, *from a conduit*, ὕδωρ Nonn.*D*.47.183.

ἀμαρησκαπτήρ, ῆρος, ὁ, *digger of trenches*, Man.4.252.

ἀμαρθρῖτις, ιδος, ἡ, *gout in all limbs at once*, Cael.Aur.*TP*5.2.

*'Αμάριος, fem. 'Αμαρία, epith. of Zeus and Athena in Achaea, *SIG*490 (Orchomenus in Arcadia, iii B.C.), cf. *Sammelb*.357 (Egypt): —'Αμάριον, τό, precinct at Aegium in which the Achaean League met, prob. l. in Str.8.7.3 and 5 (but 'Ομάριον Plb.5.93.10, hence 'Αμάριος prob. = 'Ομάριος, 'Ομαγύριος (cf. ἁμαρεῖν, ἁμαρτῇ), and is not connected with ἀμάρα = ἡμέρα).

*ἁμαρτάνω [ᾰμ.. ᾰν]: fut. ἁμαρτήσομαι Od.9.512, Th.4.55, etc.; later -ήσω *Ev.Matt*.18.21, D.C.59.20, Gal.7.653, (δι-) Hp.*Praec*.9, (ἐξ-) Id.*Acut.*(*Sp*.)13: aor. 2 ἥμαρτον Thgn., Pi., Att.: Ep. ἤμβροτον, but only ind.; Aeol. 3 sg. ἄμβροτε Sapph.*Supp*.1.5, inf. ἀμβρότην *IG*12(2).1.15 (Mytilene); opt. ἀμάρτοιν (for ἁμάρτοιμι) Cratin.55 (dub.): aor. 1 ἡμάρτησα Emp.115.4 (dub.), *AP*7.339 (Pall. or Luc.), D.S.2.14: pf. ἡμάρτηκα Hdt.9.79, Ar.*Pl*.961, etc., Att.:—Pass., aor. ἡμαρτήθην Th.2.65, X.*Vect*.4.37: pf. ἡμάρτημαι S.*OC*439, Antipho 5.77, etc.: plpf. ἡμάρτητο Th.7.18, Lys.31.20:—*miss the mark*, esp. of spear thrown, abs., Il.5.287, etc.; ἔρριψεν, οὐδ' ἥμαρτε A. *Fr*.80: c. gen., φωτὸς ἁ. Il.10.372; also τῶν μεγάλων ψυχῶν ἱεὶς οὐκ ἂν ἁμάρτοις S.*Aj*.155; ἁ. τῆς ὁδοῦ *miss* road, Ar.*Pl*.961; τοῦ σκοποῦ Antipho 3.4.5. 2. generally, *fail of one's purpose, go wrong*, abs., Od.21.155, A.*Ag*.1194, etc.: c. gen., οὔ τι νοήματος ἤμβροτεν ἐσθλοῦ Od.7.292; μύθων ἡμάρτανε *failed of good* speech, 11.511; γνώμης, ἐλπίδων, βουλήσεως ἁ., Hdt.1.207, E.*Med*.498, Th. 1.33,92; ἁ. τοῦ χρησμοῦ *mistake* it, Hdt.1.71: c. acc., ἁ. τὸ ἀληθές Hdt.7.139 (codd., τἀληθέος Schäfer). 3. *fail of having, be deprived of*, mostly c. gen., χειρῶν ἐξ 'Οδυσῆος ἁμαρτήσεσθαι ὀπωπῆς *that I should lose* my sight by Ulysses' hands, Od.9.512; τοῦ ῥυσίου θ' ἥμαρτε A.*Ag*.535; ἁ. πιστῆς ἀλόχου E.*Alc*.879, cf. 144:—once with neut. Adj., οὐ γὰρ εἰκὸς.. ἐμὲ ὑμῶν ἁμαρτεῖν τοῦτό γ' 'tis not seemly *that I should ask* this of you *in vain*, S.*Ph*.231:—rare in Prose, ἡμάρτομεν τῆς Βοιωτίης Hdt.9.7.β', cf. Th.7.50; δυοῖν κακοῖν οὐκ ἦν ἁμαρτεῖν (i.e. either one or the other) And.1.20, cf. S.*El*. 1320:—so μηδὲ δυοῖν φθάσαι ἁμάρτωσιν, ἢ.. ἢ.. *fail* to be beforehand in one of two things, Th.1.33. 4. rarely, *fail to do, neglect*, φίλων ἡμάρτανε δώρων Il.24.68; ξυμμαχίας ἁμαρτών A.*Ag*.213. II. abs., *do wrong, err, sin*, Il.9.501, Semon.7.111, A.*Pr*.262, S.*El*.1207, etc.; ἄκοντες ἡμαρτάνομεν Pl.*R*.336e, cf. 340e, etc.:—c. part., ἥμαρτε χρηστὰ μωμένη S.*Tr*.1136; πρόθυμος ὢν ἥμαρτες E.*Or*.1630, cf. Antipho 2.2.1: c. dat. rei, ἁ. ῥήματι Pl.*Grg*.489b; ἐν λόγοις Id.*R*.396a; τοιαῦθ' ἁμαρτάνουσιν ἐν λόγοις ἔπη S.*Aj*.1096:—with cognate acc., ἁμαρτίαν ἁ. S.*Ph*.1249, E.*Hipp*.320: with neut. Adj. or Pron., αὐτὸς ἐγὼ τόδε γ' ἤμβροτον I *erred* in this, Od.22.154; πόλλ' ἁμαρτών A. *Supp*.915; ἀνθρώπινα X.*Cyr*.3.1.40: in Prose more freq. ἁ. περί τινος or τι *do wrong in* a matter, Pl.*Lg*.891e, *Phdr*.242e; ἐπί τινι Antipho 5.91 (codd.); ἁ. εἴς τινα *sin* against.., Hdt.1.138, S.*OC*968; ἐπὶ τὴν ἔλλειψιν, ἐπὶ τὸ πλεῖον, Arist.*EN*1126$^b$1, 1118$^b$16; περί τινα Antipho 3.2.7; τινί Lxx *Jd*.10.10. 2. Pass., ἡμαρτήθη ὁ ἐς Σικελίαν πλοῦς Th.2.65, etc.: in pf. part., τὰμὰ δ' ἡμαρτημένα my plans *are frustrate*, S.*OT*621; τῶν περὶ τὰ τοιαῦτα ἐς τὰ θεῖα ἁμαρτανομένων Pl.*Lg*.759c; ἀπειρίᾳ αὐτὸ μᾶλλον ἢ ἀδικίᾳ ἡμαρτῆσθαι Antipho 5. 5:—τὰ ἡμαρτημένα, τὰ ἁμαρτηθέντα, S.*OC*439, 1269, X.*An*.5.8. 20. 3. ἁμαρτανόμενος, as Adj., *wrong, mistaken*, Pl.*Phlb*.37d, al.; αἱ ἡμαρτημέναι πολιτεῖαι Id.*R*.449a, Arist.*Pol*.1275$^b$1, 1301$^a$36; and of persons, ἡμαρτημένοι *mistaken*, Id.*EN*1125$^a$19.

ἁμαρτάς, άδος, ἡ, Ion. and later Gk. for ἁμαρτία, Hdt.1.91, 119, al., Hp.*Acut*.39, A.*Fr*.451C, S.*Fr*.699, Phld.*Sto*.339.15, Eus.Mynd *Fr*. 31, Olymp.*in Mete*.146.7; copyist's *error*, Str.13.1.54; *sin*, in religious sense, J.*AJ*3.9.3, al.

ἁμαρτέω, = ὁμαρτέω, *attend, accompany*, c. dat., B.17.46, E.*Fr*.682, prob. l. in Herod.4.95.

ἁμαρτῆ or ἁμαρτῇ (-τῄ Aristarch.) [ᾰμ], Adv. *together, at same time, at once*, Il.5.656, Od.22.81, Sol.33.4. ἁμαρτήδην, Adv. = foreg., Sch.Il.21.162, Hsch.

*ἁμάρτ-ημα, ατος, τό, *failure, fault*, S.*Ant*.1261 (lyr.); freq. in Att. Prose, Antipho 3.3.8, Th.2.65, etc.; midway between ἀδίκημα and ἀτύχημα, Arist.*EN*1135$^b$18, *Rh*.1374$^b$7; *sinful action*, opp. κατόρθωμα, Zeno *Stoic*.1.54, cf. *PTeb*.5.3, etc.; τὸ περὶ τὴν τέχνην λεγόμενον ἁ. Pl.*Plt*.296b, cf. *Ap*.22d; εἴς τινα Id.*Lg*.729e; περὶ τὸ σῶμα Id.*Grg*.479a. -ημον (sic, prob. neut. of Adj. -ήμων *sinful*), Pl. (Com.?) ap.Phot.p.88R. -ητικός, ή, όν, *prone to err*, Arist.*EN* 1104$^b$33; περὶ τοὺς πλησίον M.Ant.11.18. *-ία, ἡ, *a failure, fault*, τῶνδ' ἁ. δόμων A.*Ag*.1197, etc.; οὐ τῇ ἑαυτοῦ ἁμαρτίᾳ χρῆσθαι Antipho 4.3.4; ἁ. δόξης *error* of judgement, Th.1.32. 2. in Philos. and Religion, *guilt, sin*, Pl.*Lg*.660c, al., Arist.*EN*1148$^a$3, al., Lxx *Ge*.18.20, al., *Ev.Jo*.8.46, al.

ἁμαρτί-γαμος, ον, *failing of marriage*, Nonn.*D*.48.94. -νοος, ον, *erring in mind, distraught*, Hes.*Th*.511, Sol.22.2, A.*Supp*.542 (lyr.), Rhian.1.1.

ἁμάρτιον, τό, = ἁμάρτημα, in pl., A.*Pers*.676, *Ag*.537.

ἁμαρτο-επής, ές, (ἔπος) *erring in words, speaking at random*, Il.13. 824; οἶνος ἁ. wine *that makes men talk at random*, Poet.ap.Clem.Al. *Paed*.2.2.28. -λόγος, ον, *speaking faultily*, Ath.4.165b.

ἀμαρτ-ύρητος [ῠ], ον, *needing no witness*, E.*HF*290, Antiph.311. Adv. -τί *without witnesses*, *POxy*.1852.10 (vi A.D.). -ῡρος, ον, *without witness, unattested*, Th.2.41, D.20.149, *PFlor*.59.13 (iii A.D.); ἀμαρτύρων ἐόντων Herod.2.85; ἁ. οὐδὲν ἀείδω Call.*Fr*.442; *unsupported by evidence*, δίκη Procop.*Arc*.16, etc. Adv. -ρως Antipho Soph.93$^b$, D.30.21, cf. Sch.Il.*Oxy*.21.203. -υς, υ, = foreg., Agatho ap.Phot.p.87R.

ἁμαρτωλ-ή, ἡ, = ἁμαρτία, Thgn.327, Rhian.1.12; ἁ. διαίτης Aret. *CD*1.6. -ία, ἡ, = foreg., Hp.*Epid*.2.1.8, Eup.199, Ar.*Pax*415. *-ός, όν, *erroneous*, ἁμαρτωλότερον Arist.*EN*1109$^a$33; *erring*, ἐν πᾶσιν Plu. 2.25c. 2. *of bad character*, δοῦλοι Phld.*Ir*.p.73W.: c. gen., *sinning against*, θεῶν *Michel*547.31 (Telmessus):—ἁμαρτωλὴ γέρων, barbarism in Ar.*Th*.1111. Adv. -ῶς Eup.24D. II. Subst. ἁμαρτωλός, ὁ, *sinner*, Lxx *Ge*.13.13, al., *Ev.Luc*.18.13, al.

ἀμᾰρυγή [Att. ῡ, Ep. ῠ], ἡ, *sparkling, twinkling, glancing*, of objects in motion, as of the eye, *h.Merc*.45; of stars, A.R.2.42; of the sun, Procop.*Vand*.2.14; of any quick motion, ἵππων ἁ. Ar.*Av*.925:—also ἀμάρυγξ, γγος, ἡ, Hdn.Gr.2.743: ἀμάρυξις, εως, ἡ, Sch.A.R. 3.1018.

ἀμαρυγκυσία· βοστρυχία, Hsch.

ἀμάρυγμα, Aeol. -υχμα, ατος, τό, *sparkle, twinkle*, ἁ. λάμπρον προσώπω *flashing, radiant glance*, Sapph.*Supp*.5.18, cf. A.R.3.288; of changing colour, and light, *AP*5.258 (Paul. Sil.); διδύμης ἁ. χροιῆς, of gems, Tryph.71, etc.; of any quick, light motion, Χαρίτων ἀμαρύγματ' ἔχουσα with *the flashing steps* of Graces, Hes.*Fr*.21, 94; of wrestling, ἁ. πάλας B.8.36; ἁ. χείλεος *quivering* of the lip, Theoc. 23.7: metaph., τῶν πισύρων ἀρετῶν ἀμαρύγματα *AP*7.343.

ἀμαρύκαρ· ἀπ' ἀρχῆς, Hsch. ἀμαρύς· ἄπλετος, πολύς, Id.

ἀμᾰρύσσω [ᾰμ], Ep., only pres. and impf., *sparkle, twinkle, glance*, of the eye, ἐκ δέ οἱ ὄσσων πῦρ ἀμάρυσσεν Hes.*Th*.827; πυκνὸν or πύκν' ἀμαρύσσων *darting* quick *glances*, *h.Merc*.278; φολίδων στικτοῖσι τύποις ἀμάρυσσεν ὄφιος Nonn.*D*.18.79:—Med., of light, colour, etc., A.R. 4.178, 1146; ἀμαρύσσεται ἄνθεσι λειμών *AP*9.668 (Marian.), cf. Nonn. *D*.5.77, al. II. Act., *shoot forth, dart*, πῦρ *h.Merc*.415, Q.S.8. 29. 2. *dazzle*, Nonn.*D*.5.485.

ἀμαρύττα· τοὺς ὀφθαλμούς, Hsch.

ἀμάσητος, ον, (μασάομαι) *unchewed*, Lxx *Jb*.20.18, Archig.ap. Orib.8.46.11, Philum.*Ven*.3.3.

ἀμαστίγωτος, ον, *unscourged*, Ach.Tat.5.18, Procop.*Arc*.17.

*ἀμάστικτος, ον, = foreg., Sch.Pi.*O*.1.32.

ἀμάστρευτος, ον, (μαστρός) *unexamined*, *IG*5(2).357.38 (Stymphalus, iii B.C.).

**ἀμασῡκάς**, άδος, ἡ, = sq., Hsch.

**ἀμάσῡκον**, τό, with or without μῆλον, *fruit-tree flowering at the same time as the fig*, Paus.Gr.*Fr.*42.

**ἀμάτα**, Adv., (perh. ἀ- priv., μάτην) = ἀδόλως, *SIG*421*A*5,26 (Aetolia, iii B.C.): but perh. ἅματα, cf. ἦμαρ.

**ἀμᾰταιότης**, ητος, ἡ, = ἕξις ἀναφέρουσα τὰς φαντασίας ἐπὶ τὸν ὀρθὸν λόγον, *Stoic.*2.39.

**ἀματίζει**· ἀναφυρᾷ, Hsch. **ἀμάτις**· ἅπαξ (Tarent.), Id.; cf. ἀμάκις.

**ἁμα-τροχάω**, (τρέχω) *run together, run along with*, only Ep. part. ἁματροχόων (al. ἅμα τρ.) Od.15.451:—also -έω, Hsch. **-τροχιά**, ἡ, *driving side by side*, ἁματροχιὰς ἀλεείνων Il.23.422; of stars, *common motion*, -τροχιῇ πεφόρηται Man.4.108. 2. by error for ἁρματροχιά, *track of wheels*, Call.*Fr.*135, Nic.*Th.*263, *Hippiatr.*87.

**ἀμάτωρ**, Dor. for ἀμήτωρ.

**ἀμαυρ-ία** [ᾰμ], *caligo*, *Gloss.*, cf. *PMag.Rain.*1.38. **-ίσκω**, = ἀμαυρόω, Democr.177. **-όβῐος**, ον, *living in darkness*, ἄνδρες Ar. *Av.*685. **-ός** [ᾰμ], ά, όν (ός, όν Pl.Com.1 D.), *dark*, i.e., 1. *hardly seen, dim, faint*, εἴδωλον ἀ. *shadowy* spectre, Od.4.824; νέκυες Sapph.68; ἴχνος *faint* footstep, of an old man, E.*HF*124, cf. X.*Cyn.* 6.21; of the sun, ἀχλυώδης καὶ ἀμαυρότερος *obscure, glimmering*, Arist. *Mete.*367ᵃ21; of a comet's tail, ib.343ᵇ12, cf. Theoc.22.21. 2. *having no light*, νύξ Luc.*Am.*32; ὄψις X.*Cyn.*5.26:—hence, *blind, sightless*, of man, S.*OC*1018; ἕπεο..ἀμαυρῷ κώλῳ ib.182; ψαύσας ἀμαυραῖς χερσίν ib.1639; ἀμαυρά or ἀμαυρῶς βλέπειν *dimly*, Hp.*Acut.* (*Sp.*)55, *AP*12.254 (Strat.), cf. *IG*14.2111. 3. of sound, *dim, faint*, Arist.*Aud.*802ᵃ19. II. metaph. 1. *dim, faint, uncertain*, κληδών A.*Ch.*853; σθένος E.*HF*231; δόξα, ἡδοναί, ἐλπίς, Plu.*Lyc.*4, 2.125c, Arr.ap.Suid.; ζῷα -ότερα creatures *of obscure kind*, Arist.*HA*608ᵃ11; ἐντομαὶ -ότεραι *less conspicuous* notches, Thphr. *HP*6.2.5, cf. 6.7.1. 2. *obscure, mean, unknown*, -οτέρη γενεή Hes.*Op.*284; τυχηρὸν..τιθεῖσ' ἀμαυρόν A.*Ag.*466, cf. E.*Andr.*204; ἀ. ἀσθενής τε Pl.Com. l.c. Adv. -ρῶς *obscurely*, opp. ἀκριβῶς, Arist. *Cael.*279ᵃ29. 3. *gloomy, troubled*, φρήν A.*Ag.*546, *Ch.* 157. III. Act., *enfeebling* (or perh. *baffling, obscure*), νοῦσος *AP*7.78 (Dionys.): Subst. ἀμαυρά, ἡ (sc. τελετή), = ἀμαύρωσις 1. 3, *PMag.Leid.W.*6.21. **-ότης**, ητος, ἡ, *dimness*, αἰσθήσεων Gal.11.282; *obscurity*, Epist.Maximini ap.Eus.*HE*9.7, cf. Eust. 1585.47. **-οφᾰνής**, (φαίνομαι) *dimly gleaming*, of the moon, *Stoic.*2. 198. **-όω**, Sol. and X., v. infr.: fut. -ώσω Simon.4.5: aor. ἀμαύρωσα Pi.*P.*12.13, ἠμαύρωσα *AP*9.24, Plb.6.15.7, etc.: pf. ἠμαύρωκα Str.8. 1.1:—Med., aor. opt. ἀμαυρώσαιτο Aristaenet.1.16:—Pass., Philist. ap.Phot.p.88 R.: pf. ἠμαύρωμαι Plu.*Per.*11: aor. ἀμαυρώθην (without augm.) Hdt.9.10:—*make dim, faint*, or *obscure*, ἡ σελήνη ἀ. τὰ ἴχνη X.*Cyn.*5.4: ἄστρα ἠμαύρωσε ἥλιος *AP*9.24 (Leon.):—Pass., *become dark* or *dim*, ὁ ἥλιος ἀμαυρώθη Hdt. l.c.; ὄμμα -ούμενον Hp.*Prorrh.* 1.46; φορτί' ἀμαυρωθείη *perished utterly*, Hes.*Op.*693; τὸ θερμὸν μικρὸν ὂν ἐν μεγάλοις ἀ. Arist.*PA*667ᵃ19. 2. *render invisible*, *PMag. Berol.*1.102. 3. *blind*, ὄμματα *Tab.Defix.Aud.*241.13 (Carthage, ii/iii A.D.), etc. II. metaph. in same sense, εὐνομία..ὕβριν ἀ. Sol.4.35; ἐντάφιον..οὔτ' εὐρὼς οὔτ'..ἀμαυρώσει χρόνος Simon.4.5, cf. Call.*Iamb.*1.429; χρόνος δ' ἀμαυροῖ πάντα S.*Fr.*954, cf. Str. l.c.; τίς ἄρα σάν..ἀμαυροῖ ζόαν; E.*Hipp.*816; πολλοί γε..τῷ θράσει τὰς συμφορὰς ζητοῦσ' ἀμαυροῦν Id.*Fr.*416; ἀ. δόξαν Plb.20.4.3; τὰς ἄλλας κακίας Plu.*Crass.*2; οἶκον -ώσας ὤλετο *IG*12(7).107 (Amorgos); *deface* a tomb, ib.12(9).1129.22 (Chalcis):—*weaken, impair*, πόνος πόνον ἀ. Hp.*Aph.*2.46, cf. *Aër.*23, Aret.*CD*2.6; ἡ νεαρὴ [τροφὴ] ἠμαύρωσε τὴν παλαιήν ib.13:—Pass., Thphr.*HP*9.14.3; ἡ ἡδονὴ -οῦται Arist.*EN*1175ᵃ10; ἠμαυρωμένος τὸ ἀξίωμα, τῇ δόξῃ, Plu.*Per.*11, *Cor.* 31; *to be dazzled*, περὶ τὸν χρυσόν Onos.1.8. **-ωμα**, ατος, τό, *obscuration*, of sun, Plu.*Caes.*69. 2. *dimness* of sight, Mnesith.ap. Orib.4.4.2. **-ωσις**, εως, ἡ, *darkening*, ὀμμάτων ἀ. *becoming dull* of sight, Hp.*Coac.*221: later, *complete hindrance to sight without any visible cause*, Gal.14.776. 2. *dulling*, as of mind in old age, Arist. *de An.*408ᵇ20, cf. Diog.Oen.*Fr.*70 (pl.). 3. *spell which renders invisible*, *PMag.Berol.*1.222ᵃ,247. II. *lowering, detraction*, Plu.2.149a. III. = κώνειον, Ps.-Dsc.4.78. IV. Astrol., name for eighth τόπος of the δωδεκάτωρος, *Cat.Cod.Astr.*8(4).161.

**ἀμάχαιρος**, ον, *without knife*, Pherecr.82.

**ἀμᾰχ-εί**, Adv. of ἄμαχος, *without stroke of sword, without resistance*, Th.1.143, X.*An.*1.7.9, etc.: *without question, undoubtedly*, prob. l. for ἀμελεί, Plu.2.433c:—written ἀμαχί, Phot.p.88 R. **-ετος**, ον, poet. for ἀμάχητος, A.*Th.*85 (lyr.), S.*Fr.*813. **-ητί**, Adv. of sq., *without battle, without stroke of sword*, Il.21.437, Hdt.1.174 (freq. written -τεί in codd., X.*Cyr.*4.2.28, etc.). **-ητος**, ον, *not to be fought with, unconquerable*, S.*Ph.*198 (lyr.). II. *not having fought, not having been in battle*, X.*Cyr.*6.4.14; ἀ. ὄλεθρος destruction *without fighting*, Lys.*Fr.*71. **-ος**, ον, *without battle*: hence, I. *with whom no one fights, unconquerable*, of persons, Hdt.5.3, A.*Pers.*856 (lyr.), Ar.*Lys.*253,1014 (lyr.); χεῖρες Pi.*I.*6(5).41; δύναμις Pl.*Mx.* 240d, Isoc.5.139: c. inf., πολύποδες..πᾶν ὅτι οὖν φαγεῖν ἄ. Ael.*VH*1.1, etc.: of places, *impregnable*, Hdt.1.84: of things, *irresistible*, κακόν Pi.*P.*2.76; κῦμα θαλάσσης A.*Pers.*90: of feelings, ἄλγος Id.*Ag.*733; φθόνος E.*Rh.*456; ἄ. πρᾶγμα, of a woman whose beauty is *irresistible*, X.*Cyr.*6.1.36; ἄ. φιλοφροσύνη Plu.2.667d; ἄ. κάλλος Aristaenet.1. 24; ἄ. τρυφή Ael.*NA*16.23:—ἄμαχόν [ἐστι] c. inf., like ἀμήχανον, *'tis impossible* to do.., Pi.*O.*13.13. Adv. -ως *irresistibly*, Luc.*Merc. Cond.*3; *incontestably*, S.E.*M.*8.266. II. Act., *not having fought, taking no part in the battle*, X.*Cyr.*4.1.16; ἄ. διάγειν to remain *without fighting*, Id.*HG*4.4.9: ἄμαχον, τό, *non-combatants*, Ael.*Tact.* 2, cf. D.C.53.12; ἄ. νίκη *gained without fighting*, Eun.*VS* p.4[illegible] B. 2. *disinclined to fight, not contentious*, *1 Ep.Ti.*3.3, *Ep.Tit.*3. cf. *Inscr.Cos* 325; ἄ. ἐβίωσα *Epigr.Gr.*387.6 (Apamea Cibotus).

**ἀμαχητηρία**· εἶδος ἀκάνθης, Hsch.

**ἀμάω** (A), Od.9.135, etc.; Ep. pres. part. ἀμάων A.R.3.118[illegible] dat. pl. ἀμώντεσσι Theoc.10.16: impf. ἤμων Il.18.551: fut. ἀμήσω He[s.] *Op.*480, Hdt.6.28: aor. ἤμησα Hes.*Th.*181, A.*Ag.*1044, Ep. ἄμησ[α] (δι-) Il.3.359:—Med., Hes.*Op.*778, E.*Fr.*419: fut. ἀμήσομαι S.*F[r.]* 625 (v. infr. 3), A.R.1.688:—Pass., aor. part. ἀμηθείς Nic.*Al.*216 pf. ἤμημαι (ἐξ-) S.*Aj.*1179. Simple Verb takes augm. in Hom., bu[t] not compds., v. Il.3.359, 24.165, Od.5.482. [Hom. has ᾱ in simple Verb, ᾰ in compds., Trag. always ᾰ; later, ᾱ Theoc.10.16,50, A.R. 1.1183, etc., ᾰ Theoc.11.73, Call.*Cer.*137, etc.]:—orig., *reap corn*, abs., ἤμων ὀξείας δρεπάνας ἐν χερσὶν ἔχοντες Il.18.551; γυμνὸν ἀμάειν Hes.*Op.*392; θερίζειν καὶ ἀ. *PHib.*1.47.12 (iii B.C.); ἥμενος ἀμήσεις Hes.*Op.*480: metaph., ἤμησαν καλῶς they *reaped* abundantly, A.*Ag.* 1044: c. acc., μάλα κεν βαθὺ λήϊον..εἰς ὥρας ἀμῷεν Od.9.135, cf. Thgn. 107; ὡς ἀμήσων τὸν σῖτον Hdt.6.28, cf. 4.199; τἀλλότριον ἀμῶν θέρος Ar.*Eq.*392. b. metaph., ἐλευθερίαν ἀμάμεθα Plu.2.210b. 2. generally, *cut*, λαχνήεντ' ὄροφον λειμωνόθεν ἀμήσαντες Il.24.451; θαλλὸν ἀμάσας Theoc.11.73:—Med., σχοῖνον ἀμησάμενος *AP*4.1. 26 (Mel.); στάχυν ἀμήσονται A.R.1.688, cf. Call.*Di.*164; ἀμῶνται Q.S.14.199. 3. *mow down* in battle, A.R.3.1187,1382, *AP*9. 362.25: fut. Med. ἀμάσεται is cited from S.(*Fr.*625) in this sense by Hsch.

**ἀμάω** (B), mostly Ep. in Med., *draw, gather* (cf. ἐξ-, ἐπ-, κατ-αμάομαι), ταλάροισιν ἀμησάμενοι [γάλα] Od.9.247, cf. A.R.3.859; ἀλλότριον κάματον σφετέρην ἐς γαστέρ' ἀμῶνται Hes.*Th.*599; ἀμήσατο γαῖαν ἀμφ' αὐτοῖς A.R.1.1305: metaph., ἀρετήν Jul.*Or.*5.169b:—Act., χερσὶν ἀμήσας κρατὸς ὕπερθε κόνιν, of a mourner, *pouring* dust on his head, *AP*7.241 (Antip.).—Poet. and later Prose. (Cf. Lith. *sémti* 'draw (water)'.)

**ἀμβ-**, Ep. Ion., and poet. for ἀναβ- at the beginning of words. Only the most important of such forms will be found in their place: for the rest v. sub ἀναβ-.

**ἀμβαδέως**, Adv. *thoughtlessly*, Hsch.

**ἀμβαδόν**, = ἀναβαδόν, Opp.*C.*3.500.

**ἄμβαξ**, ακος, = ἄμβη, Orib.49.24.2.

**ἄμβαρ**, αρος, τό, *ambergris*, Aët.16.130,142.

**ἄμβασε**, Dor. for ἀνέβησε: **ἄμβᾰσις, ἀμβάτης, ἔμβᾰτος**, poet. for ἀναβ-: **ἀμβᾶτε**, Dor. for ἀναβῆτε.

**ἀμβές**· δύσκολον, ἢ ἀβλαβές, Hsch.

**ἄμβη**, ἡ, Ion. for ἄμβων, *raised edge* or *protuberance*, Hp.*Art.*7, cf. 80, Gal.18(1).340; *rim* of felloe of wheel, Democr.29.

**ἄμβῐξ**, ῐκος, ὁ, *spouted cup*, Ath.11.480d:—also ἔμβῑκος, ὁ, Posidon. 25, *CIG*3071.7 (Teos), Hsch., etc. 2. *cap of still*, Dsc.5.95. 3. *alembic*, Zos.Alch.p.141 B.

**ἀμβλακ-εῖν, -ημα, -ίσκω**, older and Dor. forms of ἀμπλ-.

**ἀμβλήδην**, Adv., poet. for ἀναβλήδην (q.v.):—*with sudden bursts*, ἀ. γοόωσα Il.22.476.

**ἀμβλίσκω**, Pl.*Tht.*149d: **ἀμβλισκάνω**, Max.Tyr.16.4, Poll.3.49; cf. ἀμβλύσκω:—also **ἀμβλόω** J.*Ap.*2.24, **ἀμβλώω** Max.172, -ώεσθαι 197, and in comp. ἐξ-αμβλόω (q.v.): fut. ἀμβλώσω *Gp.*14.14, (ἐξ-) Ael.*NA*13.27: aor. ἤμβλωσα Hp.*Mul.*1.25, Ael.*VH*13.6, (ἐξ-) Pl. *Tht.*150e: pf. (ἐξ-)ήμβλωκα, (ἐξ-)ήμβλωμαι, Ar.*Nu.*137,139: (ἀμβλύς):—*cause to miscarry*, S.*Fr.*132, Pl.*Tht.*149d. 2. of the woman, *bring on miscarriage*, Muson.*Fr.*15A p.77 H., Plu.*Lyc.*3, Ael.*VH*13.6. 3. intr., *miscarry*, Procop.*Pers.*2.22. II. ἀμβλόω, usu. in Pass. ἀμβλόομαι, *to be abortive*, κἂν..τὸ γινόμενον ἀμβλωθῇ Arist.*GA*773ᵃ1: also of eyes of vines, ἀμβλοῦνται *they go 'blind'*, Thphr.*HP*4.14.6; rare in Act., Ph.2.580: metaph., ἀμβλώσαντες καὶ ἐπιφράξαντες ἀργὸν τὸ μεγαλοφυὲς κατέλιπον 1.637.

**ἀμβλουχία**, ἡ, = ἄμβλωσις, S.*Fr.*1000.

**ἀμβλῠ-γώνιος**, ον, *obtuse-angled*, τρίγωνα Euc.1.28, al.; κωνοειδές, κῶνος, Archim.*Con.Sph.Praef.*: Subst. -γώνιον, τό, *obtuse angle*, Plb. 34.6.7. **-δερκής**, ές, *dull of sight*, Nicom.Trag.ap.Phot.p.89 R. **-ηκοΐα**, ἡ, *hardness of hearing*, Alex.Aphr.*in Top.*327.15.

**ἀμβλ-υνσις**, εως, ἡ, *blunting, dulling*, νοήσεων Phlp. *in de An.*164. 10. **-υντέον**, *one must deaden, counteract*, Dsc.*Ther.Praef.* **-υντήρ**, ῆρος, ὁ, *causing dimness of sight*, in pl., Poet. *de herb.*65. **-υντικός**, ή, όν, *apt to dull*, ὄψεως Diph.Siph.ap.Ath.2.64b, cf. Dsc.1.69, Antyll. ap.Orib.10.24. **-ύνω** [ῡ], fut. -ῠνῶ (ἀπ-) A.*Th.*715: aor. ἤμβλῡνα *AP*6.67 (Jul.):—Pass., fut. -υνθήσομαι (ἀπ-) A.*Pr.*866, but -υνοῦμαι (in pass. sense) Hp.*Aph.*1.9: aor. ἠμβλύνθην Lxx *Ge.*27.1, *AP*6.65 (Paul. Sil.), etc.: pf. ἤμβλυμμαι, 3 sg. ἤμβλυνται S.E.*M.*7.183, pl. -υνται (ἀπ-) Hom.*Epigr.*12; ἀπήμβλυνται is 3 sg. in Herod.*Fr.*10.4:—*blunt, dull, take the edge off*, properly of a sharp instrument, and metaph., *make dim, dull*, μερίμνας Emp.2, cf. 110.7; τὸ ψυχρὸν..τοὺς χυμοὺς ἀ. Arist.*Sens.*443ᵇ15; ὄμματος αὐγὴν ἀμβλύνας *AP*6.67 (Jul.); τὸ ἄλγος Aret.*CA*1.10; ἄκρατον *take away strength of* wine, Plu.2. 656a; οὐ γὰρ ἀοιδὰς ἀμβλύνειν αἰὼν..δύναται *AP*7.225; θυμὸν ἀ. Phld.*Mus.*p.76 K. II. Pass., *become blunt* or *dull, lose edge*, of the teeth, Arist.*PA*661ᵇ22, cf. *GA*789ᵃ9; of eyesight, ἠμβλύνθησαν οἱ ὀφθαλμοὶ τοῦ ὁρᾶν Lxx *Ge.*27.1. 2. *become obtuse*, γωνία Papp.118.6. 3. metaph., ὀργὴ γέροντος ὥστε μαλθακὴ κοπὶς.. ἀμβλύνεται S.*Fr.*894, cf. Pl.*R.*490b; of an oracle, *lose its edge* or *force*, A.*Th.*844; ἡ νοῦσος ἀμβλύνεται Hp.*Aph.*1.9; of the mind, *to be disheartened*, Th.2.87: c. gen., ἀμβλύνεσθαι ἐρωῆς Opp.*H.*2.338.

**ἀμβλυό-εις,** *εσσα, εν, dull, dark,* ὀμίχλη Man.4.156. **-χρους,** *ον, faint,* ἥλιος Lyd.*Ost.*9$^{c}$ (vv. ll. ἀμβλυώχρους, -ωχρος).

**ἀμβλ-ύς,** *εῖα, ύ, blunt, dulled, with edge* or *point taken off,* properly of a sharp instrument, opp. ὀξύς, Pl.*Ly.*215e, *Tht.*165d; ἀ. γωνία *obtuse* angle, Id.*Ti.*55a; ἀμβλεῖα, ἡ, sc. γωνία, Arist.*Mech.*855$^{a}$10, etc.; ἀ. πλευρά side *adjacent to such angle,* Hero *Geom.*12.35, etc. **2.** of light, *dim, faint,* ὄρθρος Ion ap.Phot.p.89 R. **3.** metaph., *dim, faint,* of sight, ἀμβλὺ ὁρᾶν, -ύτερον βλέπειν, Pl.*Tht.*174e, Arist.*PA* 656$^{b}$36, al.; of hearing, τῆς ἀκοῆς οὔσης -υτέρας αἰσθήσεως ἢ τῆς ὄψεως *Pr.*886$^{b}$32; of the feelings or mind, ἀμβλυτέρᾳ τῇ ὀργῇ *less keen,* Th. 3.38: ἀμβλύτερον ποιεῖν τι *less vigorous,* Id.2.65. Adv. ἀμβλέως Archig.ap.Orib.8.2: Comp., v. supr. **b.** *dull, monotonous,* τὦμβλὺ τῆς ζόης Herod.3.52. **c.** of persons, in A.*Eu.*238, of Orestes purified, *having lost the edge* of guilt: mostly, *dull, spiritless, having lost keenness of feeling,* E.*Fr.*821; ἀμβλύτερος τὴν φύσιν *duller,* X.*Mem.*3.9.3; ἀ. εἴς, περί, or πρός τι *dull* or *sluggish* in a thing, Plu. *Cat.Ma.*24, *Alc.*30, D.S.11.43 (Comp.): abs., Th.2.40. Adv., Comp. -υτέρως J.*AJ*19.2.5. **II.** Act., *making dull, darkening,* of a cloud, *AP*7.367 (Antip.). **-ύσκω,** dub. form of ἀμβλίσκω, S.*Fr.*132, Procop. *Arc.*17, *Hippiatr.*15. **-υσμός,** ὁ, = ἀμβλωσμός, Pall. *in Hp.*2. 5 D. **-υστονέω,** v. ἀναβλ-. **-ύτης,** ητος, ἡ, *bluntness* of teeth, Arist.*GA*789$^{a}$11; *dullness,* τῆς διανοίας, τῆς ὄψεως, Plu.2.42c, 1110d; *sluggishness,* Aret.*CA*1.5 (pl.), cf. Plu.*Galb.*18; σπερμάτων, of seeds which *fail to germinate,* Max.Tyr.16.4. **2.** *obtuseness,* σχήματος Them.*in Ph.*173.7.

**ἀμβλυ-φαέω,** = ἀμβλυώσσω, S.*Fr.*647. **-χειλής,** *ές, with rounded rim,* of cupping-glass, Antyll.ap.Orib.7.16.15. **-ωγμός,** ὁ, (ἀμβλυώσσω) *dull* or *dim sight,* Hp.*Prog.*24. **-ωπέω,** *to be dim-sighted,* Hp.*Prog.*7, X.*Cyn.*5.27 codd., Men.908, Lxx 3*Ki.*12.24, Sor.1.82, Plu.2.53f, etc.; un-Attic acc. to Harp., etc. **-ωπής,** *ές,* in Comp. -έστερον Suid. **II.** Act., *weakening sight,* Dsc.2.141. **-ωπία,** ἡ, *dim sightedness,* Hp.*Aph.*3.33 (pl.), Pl.*Hp.Mi.*374d, etc. **-ωπισμός,** ὁ, = ἀμβλυωγμός, Archig. or Posidon.ap.Aët.6.7. **-ωπός,** *όν, dim-sighted,* E.*Fr.*1096, Arist.*Fr.*588 (Comp.), *Epigr.Gr.*459 (Trachonitis); of stars, *dim,* ἀμβλυωπότερα Hp.*Morb.Sacr.*13. **II.** Act., = ἀμβλυωπής II, Dsc.2.107. **-ωσμός,** ὁ, v.l. for -ωγμός in Hp.*Prorrh.*1.18. ⊛**-ώσσω,** Att. **-ττω,** only in pres.: (ἀμβλύς):—*to be short-sighted, have weak sight,* Hp.*Prorrh.*2.42, etc., Pl.*R.*508c, al., *Hp.Mi.*374d; ἀ. πρὸς τὸ φῶς *to be dazzled* by it, Luc. *Cont.*1, cf. Jul.*Or.*5.163a; ἀ. τὰ τηλικαῦτα Luc.*Tim.*27; τὸ τοῦ γήρως ἀμβλυῶττον Plu.2.13e.

**ἀμβλ-ωθρίδιον,** τό, **I.** (sc. παιδίον) *abortive child,* ἀ. καὶ ἐκτρώματα Ph.1.59, cf. Hsch., Harp. **II.** Act. (sc. φάρμακον), *drug to cause abortion,* Poll.2.7.—Prop. neut. from **ἀμβλωθρίδιος,** *ον, causing abortion,* Aret.*CA*2.11:—also **ἀμβλώθριον,** τό, Sch.Ar.*Nu.* 137 (s.v.l.). **-ωμα,** ατος, τό, (ἀμβλίσκω) *abortion,* Antipho Soph. 148, Aret.*CA*1.6. **-ῶνες·** χαλβάνη, Διονύσιος, Hsch. **-ωπής,** *ές, abortive,* of the flowers of the vine, Thphr.*CP*3.15.2. **-ωπός,** *όν,* = foreg., *bedimmed, dark,* βίος A.*Eu.*955; ἀχλύς Critias 6, cf. Pl.Com.23 D. **-ώσιμος,** *ον, belonging to abortion,* Max.275. **-ωσις,** εως, ἡ, *abortion,* Lys.*Fr.*8; ἄμβλωσιν ποιεῖσθαι Arist.*Pol.*1335$^{b}$25; ἄ. γίγνεται τοῦ κυήματος Id.*GA*773$^{a}$1, cf. Ph.2.319, Procop.*Arc.*10 (pl.). **II.** *abortion of* buds in vines and trees, Thphr.*CP*5.9. 13. **-ώσκω,** = ἀμβλίσκω I. 2. **-ωσμός,** οῦ, ὁ, = ἄμβλωμα, Aret.*CD*2.11, Man.4.413. **-ώσσω,** = ἀμβλυώσσω, Nic.*Th.*33. **2.** = ἀμβλίσκω, Hsch. **-ωτήριον,** τό, *instrument for causing abortion,* Orib.*Inc.*6.19 (Gal. or Ruf.). **-ωτικός,** *ή, όν, producing abortion,* φάρμακα Gal.17(1).799. **-ώψ,** ῶπος, ὁ, ἡ, = ἀμβλωπός, αὐγαί E.*Rh.* 737, cf. S.*Fr.*1001, Ion Trag.ap.Phot.p.89 R., Pl.Com.23 D.

**ἀμβόαμα, ἀμβοάω,** poet. for ἀναβόαμα, ἀναβοάω.

**ἀμβοειδής,** *ές, like an* ἄμβων, *protuberant,* Heliod.ap.Orib.49.8.7.

**ἀμβολά,** ἡ, poet. for ἀναβολή. **ἄμβολα,** τά, *middle of ship's yard,* Poll.1.91.

**ἀμβολ-άδην** [ᾰδ], Adv., poet. for ἀναβολάδην: (ἀναβολή):—*bubbling up,* ὡς δὲ λέβης ζεῖ ἔνδον..πάντοθεν ἀ. Il.21.364, cf. Hdt.4.181: metaph., *by jets,* i.e. *capriciously, AP*10.70 (Maced.). **II.** *like an* ἀναβολή or *prelude, h.Merc.*426, Pi.*N.*10.31. **-αδίς,** Adv., poet. for ἀναβολαδίς, either *in turns,* or *with uplifted arms,* τετυπόντες Call. *Dian.*61. **-άς,** άδος, ἡ, for ἀναβολάς, ἀ. γῆ earth *thrown up,* X.*Cyr.* 7.5.12.

**ἀμβολι-εργός,** *όν,* poet. for ἀναβολ-, (ἀναβάλλω B. II) *putting off work, dilatory,* ἀνήρ Hes.*Op.*413; τινός or ἔν τινι *in* a thing, Plu.2. 548d, 118c. **-η,** ἡ, poet. for ἀναβολή, *delay,* A.R.3.144: c. gen., 4.396, Nonn.*D.*38.12, al. ⊛**-μος,** *ον,* = ἀναβ-, *surging up,* ἅλμα Tim. *Pers.*74. **II.** *adjourned,* ἁλιαία *Mnemos.*44.221 (Argos, iii B.C.).

**Ἀμβολογήρα,** ἡ, *she that puts off old age, youth-prolonging,* Spartan title of Aphrodite, Paus.3.18.1. **ἄμβος·** ἡ ἐπίγειος πλάστη, Hsch.

**Ἀμβούλιος,** (perh. connected with βουλή) title of Zeus, Athena, and the Dioscuri at Sparta, Paus.3.13.4.

**Ἀμβρακίδες,** αἱ, *Ambracian women's shoes,* Poll.7.94.

**ἀμβρίζειν·** θεραπεύειν ἐν τοῖς ἱεροῖς, Hsch.

**ἀμβροσί-α,** Ion. **-ίη,** ἡ, *immortality,* rare in general sense, σώματος ἀ. *Epigr.Gr.*338 (Cyzicus); usu. *elixir of life,* as used by gods for food, Od.5.93, etc.; as perfume, 4.445; as unguent, Il.14.170, cf. 16.680; as pasture for horses, 5.777; coupled with νέκταρ (q.v.), the two distinguished as food and drink, Od.5.93 (later reversed, ἀ. being drunk, Sapph.51, Ar.*Eq.*1095, Anaxandr.57), cf. Pi.*O.*1.62, *P.*9.63, Arist.*Metaph.*1000$^{a}$12, A.R.4.871, Theoc.15.108; βολβοφακῆ δ' ἴσον ἀμβροσίῃ ψύχους κρυοέντος Chrysipp.*Stoic.*3.178; allegorically expl. as vapour, Democr.25. **2.** in religious rites, *mixture of water, oil, and various fruits,* Anticl.13. **3.** Medic., name for antidote, Zopyr.ap.Cels.5.23, Gal.14.149; also of an external emollient, Aët.14.2. **4.** *ambrose, Ambrosia maritima,* Dsc.3.114. **b.** Corinthian, = κρίνον, Nic.*Fr.*126. **c.** = ἀείζωον μέγα, Dsc.4. 88. **d.** vine whose grapes were eaten, Plin.*HN*14.40. **B.** Ἀμβροσία, ἡ, *a festival* of Bacchus, *EM*564.13. **-οδμος,** *ον, smelling of ambrosia,* Philox.2.43. **-ος,** *α, ον,* also *ος, ον* E.*Med.*983 (lyr.):—*immortal, divine,* rarely of persons, νύμφη *h.Merc.*230:—in Ep., epith. of everything *belonging to gods,* as hair, Il.1.529, etc.; robes, sandals, etc., 5.338, 21.507, 24.341, al.; anointing oil, 14.172, 23. 187; voice and song, *h.Hom.*27.18, Hes.*Th.*69; fodder and mangers of horses, Il.5.369, 8.434; of night and sleep, as *divine* gifts, Od. 4.429, etc.; ὕδωρ Hom.*Epigr.*1.4; κρῆναι E.*Hipp.*748:—of things *divinely excellent* or *beautiful,* κάλλος Od.18.193; of verses, Pi.*P.*4. 299; Ἀφροδίτας ἀ. φιλοτάτων Id.*N.*8.1. **-ώδης,** *ες, ambrosial, fragrant,* φυτά *Corp.Herm.*18.11 (Sup.).

⊛**ἀμβρότιγνον·** ἄκοιρον, Hsch. **ἀμβροτίξας·** ἀπαρξάμενος, Id.

⊛**ἀμβροτόπωλος,** *ον, with immortal steeds,* Παλλάς E.*Tr.*536.

⊛**ἄμβροτος,** *ον,* also *η, ον* Pi.*Fr.*75.17, Tim.*Fr.*7: (v. βροτός):—poet. Adj. *immortal, divine,* of persons as well as things, θεὸς ἄ. Il. 20.358, Od.24.445, Pi.*N.*10.7; θεά A.*Eu.*259 (lyr.); ἄμβροτε Φάμα, of an oracle, S.*OT*158 (lyr.). **2.** epith. of all *belonging to the gods,* αἷμα Il.5.339; ἵπποι 16.381; τεύχεα 17.194, κρήδεμνον Od.5. 347; ἱστός 10.222; νύξ 11.330:—also Pythag., = *five, Theol.Ar.*32.

⊛**ἄμβρυττοι,** kind of *shell-fish* (cf. βρύττοι), Hsch. **ἀμβρυχαί·** αἱ τῶν χειρῶν ἐμβολαί, Id.

**ἄμβυξ,** ὕκος, ὁ, perh. = ἄμβιξ, Hdn.Gr.1.44, al.

⊛**ἄμβων,** *ωνος, ὁ,* Att. for Ion. **ἄμβη,** acc. to Gal.18(1).340, but Rhodian acc. to Bacchius ap.Apollon.Cit.1.7:—*crest* of a hill, A.*Fr.* 103; ἐπ' οὔρεος ἀμβώνεσσιν Call.*Aet.*3.1.34. **2.** *rim* or *edge* of a cup (esp. of one that curves inwards), Eup.52, Ephipp.3.16, Critias 34 D., Plu.*Lyc.*9. **b.** (from similarity of shape), *rim of joint-socket,* Gal.*UP*1.15, al., cf. 18(1).340. **3.** = γυναικεῖον αἰδοῖον, Eust.1539.33 (so perh. in Eup. l. c.). **4.** in Cos, *steps, rungs* of ladder, Apollon.Cit.1.7. **5.** *pulpit,* title of poem by Paul. Sil., cf. *JHS*28.195 (Aspendus).

**ἀμβώσας,** Ion. for ἀναβοήσας, v. sub ἀναβοάω.

**ἁμέ** or **ἀμέ,** Dor. for ἡμᾶς, Ar.*Ach.*759, *Lys.*95, Decr.Byz.ap.D. 18.90.

**ἀμέγαρτος,** *ον,* poet. Adj., (ἀ- priv., μεγαίρω) *unenviable:* **1.** mostly of things or conditions, *sad, melancholy,* πόνος Il.2.420; ἀνέμων..ἀϋτμή Od.11.400; μάχη Hes.*Th.*666; ἀμέγαρτα κακῶν E. *Hec.*192; πάθος Ar.*Th.*1049 (lyr.), cf. A.*Pr.*403. **2.** *undesirable,* κρέα *AP*11.60 (Paul. Sil.); ἄγρη, of fish which follow a wreck, Opp. *H.*4.412. **3.** of persons, *unhappy, miserable,* ἀμέγαρτε συβῶτα *wretched* swineherd! Od.17.219; ἀμεγάρτων φῦλ' ἀνθρώπων *h.Merc.* 542; ἀ. ποίμνα A.*Supp.*642 (lyr.).

**ἀμεγέθης,** *ες, without magnitude, unextended,* Arist.*Metaph.*1075$^{b}$ 29, Plot.6.5.12, etc. Adv. -θῶς *non-spatially,* Syrian.*in Metaph.* 85.15; *non-quantitatively,* Porph.*Sent.*34. **2.** *lacking in size,* σύγκριμα τῶν μαστῶν Sor.1.88: metaph., *without dignity,* σύνθεσις D.H.*Comp.*18, Longin.34.4; of writers, 40.2.

**ἀμέθεκτος,** *ον, imparticipable,* Alex.Aphr.*in Metaph.*637.12, Simp.*in de An.*218.5, Procl.*Inst.*23, al.; αἰτίαι Chrysipp.(?)*Stoic.*2.308. Adv. -τως Ascl.*in Metaph.*115.36.

**ἀμέθελκτος,** *ον, free from distraction,* dub. in Ph.2.427. Adv. -τως Id.1.559.

**ἀμεθεξία,** ἡ, *non-participation,* τινός Corn.*ND*35, Procl.*in Prm.* p.559 S.

⊛**ἀμεθίστατος,** *ον,* incorrect for ἀμετάστατος, *PAmh.*2.85.

⊛**ἀμεθόδευτος,** *ον, not to be cajoled, led astray,* κριτής Herm.ap.Stob.1. 49.44. **2.** *unscientific,* ἰατρός Alex.Trall.*Febr.*5.

**ἀμέθοδος,** *ον, not in logical* (i.e. *syllogistic*) *form,* λόγοι Chrysipp. *Stoic.*2.83, cf. Phld.*Rh.*1.132 S. Adv. -ως, περαίνειν Chrysipp.*Stoic.* 2.87. **2.** *without plan* or *system,* Longin.2.2, S.E.*P.*2.21; esp. Medic., *non-'methodic',* αἵρεσις Gal.10.51. Adv. -ως, δημιουργῆσαι Phld.*Rh.*1.127 S., cf. S.E.*M.*8.300, Alex.Aphr.*in Metaph.*50.7.

**ἀμέθῠσον,** τό, = ἀμέθυστος II. 1, Dsc.1.123 (s.v.l.). **II.** = ἀμέθυστος II. 2, Thphr.*Lap.*30, Hld.5.13; ἀμέθυσος, ἡ, v.l. in J.*AJ*3.7.5; cf. Hsch.

**ἀμεθύστινος,** *η, ον, of amethyst,* βωμοί Luc.*VH*2.11.

**ἀμέθυστος,** *ον,* (μεθύω) *not drunken, without drunkenness,* Plu.2. 464c: Comp., *Gp.*7.34.2. **II.** *not intoxicating,* perh. so used in Nonn.*D.*19.133: as Subst., ἀμέθυστον, τό, *remedy against drunkenness,* Archig.ap.Gal.12.572, Dsc.*Eup.*1.24; also ἀμέθυστος, ἡ, Plu. 2.15b, Ath.1.34c:—hence, such things as were supposed to act as remedies, viz., **1.** kind of *herb,* Plu.2.647b; = σέλινον ἄγριον, Ps.-Dsc.2.175. **2.** *amethyst,* Lxx *Ex.*28.19, *Apoc.*21.20, D.P. 1122, *AP*5.204, 9.748 (Pl. Jun.):—also **ἀμέθυστον,** τό, *IG*11(2). 287*B*22 (Delos, iii B.C.). **3.** **ἀμέθυστον,** τό, kind of *grape,* Colum.3.2.24.

**ἀμεῖ,** Delph., = ἅμα, *GDI*2561*D*47.

**ἀμείβοντες,** οἱ, v. sq. A. II.

⊛**ἀμείβω** [ᾰ], Il., Trag.: Ep. impf. ἄμειβον Il.14.381: fut. -ψω A.*Pr.* 23: aor. ἤμειψα, Ep. ἄμειψα [ᾰ] *h.Cer.*275, A.R.3.280; Dor. ἀμ- [ᾱ] Pi.*P.*5.38; Trag.:—**Med.,** impf. ἠμειβόμην, Ep. ἀμ- Il.3.171, etc.: fut. ἀμείψομαι E.*Supp.*517: aor. ἠμειψάμην, Ep. and Ion. ἀμ- Il.4.403, Hdt.1.37, al.:—**Pass.,** fut. ἀμειφθήσεται Hsch.: aor. ἠμείφθην *AP*7.589 (Agath.), 638 (Crin.), etc. (in med. sense, Pi.*P*.4.102, Theoc.7.27): pf. ἤμειπται Gal.1.210: Ep. plpf. ἄμειπτο Nonn.*D*.44.241.—Verb and compds. are almost exclus. poet. and Ion., but used once or twice in Pl. and X., and late Prose.

**A.** Act., *change, exchange*, (not Od.), ἔντε' ἄμειβεν Il.17.192, etc.: τί τινος, as γόνυ γουνὸς ἀμείβων *changing* one knee for other, i.e. walking slowly, ib.11.547, etc.:—so either, **1.** *give in exchange*, ὃς πρὸς Τυδεΐδην Διομήδεα τεύχε' ἄμειβε χρύσεα χαλκείων ib. 6.235: c. acc., δάμαρτ' ἀμείψας E.*Alc*.46: or more freq., **2.** *take in exchange*, τι ἀντί τινος Pi.*P*.4.17, E.*Hel*.1382; πόσιν ἀντὶ σᾶς ἀμεῖψαι ψυχᾶς *redeem* at that price, Id.*Alc*.462, etc.; μορφὴν ἀ. ἐκ θεοῦ βροτησίαν Id.*Ba*.4; ἀ. τὰν ἐμὰν [φυλακάν] Id.*Rh*.527; τιμὰν πρὸς ἀνθρώπων ἀμείψω Ibyc.24, cf. A.*Ch*.1019 (anap.) (prob.). **3.** in Att. often of Place, *change* it, so *pass, cross*, πορθμόν, πόρον, Id.*Pers*.69, E.*IA*144, etc.:—hence, **b.** either *pass out of* a house, *leave* it, ἀ. στέγας, δώματα, S.*Ph*.1262, E.*El*.750; or *pass into, enter* it, ἀ. θύρας Hdt.5.72, cf. A.*Ch*.571: generally, πόλιν ἐκ πόλεως ἀ. Pl.*Sph*.224b, cf. *Prm*.138d; v. infr. B.II.2. **4.** *change, alter*, χρῶτα βαφῇ A.*Pers*.317; χροιᾶς ἄνθος Id.*Pr*.23; ἐς κακοχυμίην ἤμειψε τὰ σπλάγχνα Aret.*SD*2.13: abs., πολλὰ ἀ. *change* colour, Jul.*Caes*.309a; so Med., χροιῆς ἄνθος ἀμειβομένης Sol.27.6. **5.** causal, *make* others *change*, τεύχε' ἄμειβον Il.14.381; *pass on, hand on from one to another*, τέκνα..διαδοχαῖς ἀμείβουσαι χεροῖν E.*Hec*.1159. **b.** *shift, dislodge*, κακὸν κακῷ Aret.*SD*2.1. **6.** rarely like Med. B.I.3, *repay, return*, ἀ. χάριν A.*Ag*.729, cf. *Ch*.793. **II.** intr. in part., ἀμείβοντες, οἱ, *the interchangers*, i.e. *rafters that meet and cross each other*, Il.23.712, cf. Theo Sm.p.122 H., Nonn.*D*.37.588; ἐν ἀμείβοντι, = ἀμοιβάδις, Pi.*N*.11.42:—so prob. ἀμείβει καινὸν ἐκ καινῶν τόδε *succeeds*, E.*Or*.1503.

**B.** Med., *change one with another, do in turn* or *alternately*, abs., ἀμειβόμενοι φυλακὰς ἔχον Il.9.471; ἄειδον ἀμειβόμεναι ὀπὶ καλῇ 1.604; ὀρχείσθην..ἀμειβομένω Od.8.379; ἀμειβόμενοι κατὰ οἴκους at every house *in turn*, 1.375, 2.140; ἄρουραι ἀμειβόμεναι *ploughed and fallow in turn*, Pi.*N*.6.9; so ἀμειβόμεναι ὁπλαῖς *alternating, crosswise*, of the motion of the legs in horses or oxen, Id.*P*.4.226; ἄλλα ἄλλοθεν ἀμείβεται now *comes* one thing, now another *in turn*, E.*Hipp*.1108; ἀμείβεται μιάσματα Id.*Med*.1267: c. part., θρῴσκων ἄλλοτ' ἐπ' ἄλλον ἀμείβεται leaps *in turn*.., Il.15.684:—ἀ. στενότητι *vary* in narrowness, X.*Cyn*.9.14. **2.** of dialogue, ἀμείβεσθαι ἐπέεσσι *answer one another*, Od.3.148, etc.; in part., ἀμειβόμενος προσέειπε, προσηύδα, Il.3.437, 17.33; ἀ. πρός τινα Hdt.8.60 codd.; πρός τι ib.58, E.*Tr*.903: c. acc. pers. et dat. rei, ἀ. τινα μύθῳ, μύθοις, Od.12.278, 2.83; ἀ. τινα alone, *answer* one, *reply to* him, Il.1.172, etc.; τὸν λόγοις ἀμείφθη Pi.*P*.4.102, cf. Theoc.7.27; ἀμείβετο τοῖσδε in these words, Hdt.1.35, al.:—later c. acc. rei, τούτοις ἀμείβου..εὐμαθές τι A.*Eu*.442; ἔπος πρὸς ἔπος 586; μὴ σφριγῶντ' ἀμείψῃ μῦθον E.*Supp*.478; ταῦτα ἀμείψατο Hdt.1.37: c. dupl. acc., ταῦτα τοὺς φίλους ἀμείψατο Id.2.173, cf.3.52, A.*Supp*.195; ἕν μ' ἄμειψαι μοῦνον S.*OC*991; τὸν δὲ..μῆτιν..ἀμείβετο *gave* him counsel *in reply*, Pi.*P*.9.39:—also late Prose, Luc.*Alex*.19. **3.** *repay, requite*, c. acc. pers. et dat. rei, δώροισιν ἀ. τινα Od.24.285; χρηστοῖσι Hdt.1.41, cf. 4.97; ὁμοίοις D.20.6; ἀμείβομαί σε τῷ φυγεῖν τὴν οἰκίαν *Com.Adesp*.371: c. acc. pers. only, τὸν ἄδικον ἀ. S.*Fr*.12; τοὺς μὲν ἐκόλαζε, τοὺς δὲ ἠμείβετο D.C.74.8: c. acc. et dat. rei, ἀ. εὐεργεσίας χάρισιν X.*Mem*.4.3.15: c. acc. rei only, χάριν φιλότητος S.*El*.134; βροτῶν ἀσυνεσίας E.*Ph*.1727; τὴν προϋπαρχὴν Arist.*EN*1165a5: rarely c. dat. pers., πολλοῖσι γὰρ κέρδη πονηρὰ ζημίαν ἠμείψατο E.*Cyc*.312: rarely also c. gen. rei compensatae, ἀ. τινα τῆς δικαιοσύνης Luc.*Somn*.15:—mostly, *return good for good*; but also, *bad for good*, φθόνον ἀμειβόμενον τὰ καλὰ ἔργα Pi.*P*.7.17; *bad for bad*, ἀμείψεται φόνον φόνος E.*El*.1093; κακὸν κακῷ Aret.*SD*2.13. **4.** *purchase*, λύχνον Lib.*Or*.45.10. **II.** *get in exchange*, [οὗτοι] νιν (sc. Καρθαίαν) Βαβυλῶνος ἀμείψομαι Pi.*Pae*.4.16; θητικοῦ ἀντὶ τέλους ἱππάδ' ἀμειψάμενος Epigr.ap.Arist.*Ath*.7.4; λῴους φρένας τῶν νῦν παρουσῶν S.*Tr*.737. **2.** like Act., *change* a place, *pass* either *out* or *in*, ψυχὴ..ἀμείψεται ἕρκος ὀδόντων Il.9.409; and reversely of things swallowed, φάρμακα..ἀ. ἕρκ. ὀδ. Od.10.328; ἀμειβόμεναι μέγαν οὐδὸν.., ἡ μὲν ἔσω..ἡ δὲ θύραζε Hes.*Th*.749; πατρίδ' ἀμειψάμενος Sol.2; ποταμόν Simon.94; πρόθυρα A.*Ch*.965; πύλας E.*Alc*.752; γῆν οὐρανοῦ ἀ. *change* earth for heaven, Plu.2.607e; ὑπὲρ οὐδὸν ἀμειβόμενον Theoc.2.104; ἄλλην ἐξ ἄλλης πόλεως ἀμειβόμενος Pl.*Ap*.37d; ἕτερα δ' ἕτερος ἀμείβεται πήματα *passes through* them, E.*Or*.979. **3.** *exchange*, τὶ πρὸς νόμισμα Plu.*Aem*.23. **III.** *surpass, outdo*, μελισσᾶν πόνον Pi.*P*.6.54. **IV.** χεροῖν πίτυλον, ὃς αἰὲν δι' Ἀχέροντ' ἀ. θεωρίδα *convoys, accompanies* it, A.*Th*.856.

**ἀμειβώ**, οῦς, ἡ, = ἀμοιβή, Eust.1471.30.

⊛**ἀμειδ-ής**, ές, *not smiling, gloomy*, Plu.2.477e, Orph.*A*.1079, Opp.*C*.2.459. **–ητος**, ον, = foreg., Lxx *Wi*.17.4; νύξ A.R.2.908; βέρεθρον Orph.*A*.975; Τάρταρος *IG*14.769 (Naples). **–ίᾱτος**, ον, = foreg., D.Chr.4.92 (v.l. –ίαστος).

**ἀμειλέοις**· ἀθλίοις, Hsch.

⊛**ἀμείλ-ικτος**, ον, (μειλίσσω) *unsoftened, harsh, cruel*, of words, Il.11.137, 21.98; ἀρά Max.Tyr.12.6; of fetters, Hes.*Th*.659; μίτοι, of the thread of Clotho, *IG*12(7).301 (Amorgos); τὸ ἀ. Hierocl. *in CA* 13 p.448 M. **II.** of persons, = sq., A.R.3.337, Mosch.4.26. Adv. –τως, ἔχειν τινί Ph.2.298, cf. Syrian. *in Metaph*.42.3; μοίρας ἀτυχούσης ἀμειλίκτως, of *pitiless* fate, App.*BC*4.54. ⊛**–ῐχος**, ον, *implacable, relentless*, Ἀΐδης Il.9.158; ἦτορ ib.572; βία Sol.32; στρατός (of rain), κότος, Pi.*P*.6.12, 8.8:—a form **ἀμειλίχιος** occurs in Adv. –ίως *Epigr.Gr*.313 (Smyrna). **II.** of things, *unmitigated*, πόι[…] A.*Ch*.623; ἀμείλιχα σάρκες ἔχουσιν *IG*14.2461 (Massilia).

⊛**ἀμείνασις**· ἡ δύοσμον (Perga), *EM*83.50, cf. Hsch.

⊛**ἀμείνων**, ον, gen. ονος, irreg. Comp. of ἀγαθός, *better*: **I.** […] persons, *stouter, stronger, braver*, freq. Hom., etc.: μέγ' ἀ. Il.2[…] 158; πολλὸν ἀ. Hes.*Op*.19: c. acc. vel inf., ἀμείνων παντοίας ἀρετά[…] ἠμὲν πόδας ἠδὲ μάχεσθαι Il.15.641, cf. Hes.*Op*.445, A.*Fr*.337, etc. οἱ ἀμείνονες *the better sort*, Pl.*Lg*.627a. **II.** of things, ὀμίχλη[…] νυκτὸς ἀμείνω Il.3.11; esp. from Hom. downwds., ἄμεινόν [ἐστι] '*t*[…] *better*, either c. inf., ἐπεὶ πείθεσθαι ἄ. Il.1.274, cf. S.*El*.1238, etc.; o[…] ἄμεινόν ἐστι or γίγνεταί τινι c. part., εἴ σφι ἄμεινον γίγνεται τιμωρέουσ[…] if *it is good* for them to assist, Hdt.7.169, cf. Th.1.118, 6.9: abs., […] τό γ' ἄ. Il.1.116; βουλοίμην..εἴ τι ἄ. καὶ ὑμῖν καὶ ἐμοί Pl.*Ap*.19a[…] freq. with neg., οὐ γὰρ ἄ. 'twere *better* not, Hes.*Op*.750, Hdt.1.[…] 187; εἰρήσεται γάρ, εἴτ' ἄ. εἴτε μή D.21.198. **2.** neut. as Adv., ἄ. πρήσσειν to fare *better*, Hdt.4.156 sq., etc.; συνήνεικε[…] Ἀθηναίοις ἐπὶ τὸ ἄ. Decr.ap.And.1.77, cf. Orac.ap.D.43.86; τὰ ἀμείνω φρονέειν choose the *better part*, Hdt.7.145; τοῖσι τὰ ἀ. ἑάνδανε Id.9.19. **III.** Adv. ἀμεινόνως Ar.*Fr*.340. **IV.** new Comp. ἀμεινότερος, α, ον, formed from ἀμείνων, Mimn.14.9, Poet.ap.Phld.*Rh*.2.61 S.

⊛**ἀμειξία**, ἡ, *interruption of communications*, *PLond*.2.301.20, *PTeb*.72.45 (ii B.C.); cf. ἀμιξία.

**ἀμειπτικός**, ή, όν, *of* or *for exchange*, τράπεζα *IG*5(1).18 (Sparta, i A.D.); –κή, ἡ, *business of exchange*, *OGI*484 (Pergam.). **II.** *in requital*, χάρις Sch.Pi.*P*.2.33.

**ἀμείρω**, = ἀμέρδω, *bereave*, c. gen. rei, Pi.*P*.6.26.

**ἀμεῖς**· εὑρήσεις, Hsch.

**ἀμειψι-κοσμίη**, ἡ, = μετακόσμησις, Democr.138. **–ρρυσμέω**, (ῥυσμός = ῥυθμός) *change form*, Id.139. **–ρρυσμία**, ἡ, *change of form*, περὶ –ιῶν, title of work by Democr.ap.D.L.9.47.

⊛**ἄμειψις**, εως, ἡ, (ἀμείβω) *exchange, interchange*, Plb.10.1.5; ἐν ἀμείψει τῶν τάξεων Plu.*Arist*.16; ὀνομάτων Anon. *in SE*46.25: *succession*, τῶν γενῶν Plu.*Sull*.7; *change*, τῆς χρόας Id.2.978d. **II.** *requiting, repaying*, [τῶν εὐεργετημάτων] *Inscr.Prien*.105.18. **2.** *repartee*, Plu.2.803c.

**ἀμείψιχρον**· μεταβάλλοντα.., Hsch. (fort. –χρουν *changing colour*).

**ἀμείωτος**, ον, *not to be diminished*, σιτωνία Ph.2.66; *incapable of diminution*, ἀναυξὲς καὶ ἀ. Simp. *in Cael*.109.22. Adv. –τως Olymp. *in Alc*.p.111 C.

**ἀμέλαθρος**, ον, *houseless*, Man.4.113.

**ἀμέλατον**· τὸ ἴσον, Hsch.

**ἀμέλγω** [ᾰ], fut. –ξω Theoc.23.25, *milk*, with acc. of animals milked, μῆλα..ὅσσ' ἤμελγε Od.9.238; ἤμελγεν ὄϊς καὶ μηκάδας αἶγας ib.244; βόας Theoc.4.3: metaph., ἀμέλγεις τοὺς ξένους *you drain* them *of all they have*, Ar.*Eq*.326: prov., ἀ. τὸν τράγον, of wasted labour, Plb.33.21.1, Luc.*Demon*.28:—Med., ἀ. χροὸς αἷμα Nic.*Al*.506: metaph., ἐκ Σαπφοῦς τόδ' ἀμελγόμενος μέλι τοι φέρω *Lyr.Adesp*.62. **2.** *suck up* moisture, of the sun, Nonn.*D*.2.500. **II.** c. acc., of milk, ἀ. γάλα Hdt.4.2:—Pass., ὄϊες..ἀμελγόμεναι γάλα λευκόν *milch*-ewes, Il.4.434; γάλα πολὺ ἀ. Arist.*HA*523a7, cf. 522a15; νέκταρ ἀμέλγονται Ion Eleg.1:—Med., *let suck*, Opp.*C*.1.437. **2.** metaph., *squeeze out like milk, press out*, ἐκ βοτρύων ξανθὸν ἄμελξε γάνος *AP*9.645 (Maced.); δάκρυ ἠλέκτροιο D.P.293. **III.** *drink*, αὐτὸ λαβὼν ποτὶ χεῖλος ἀμέλξω Theoc.23.25, cf. Bion 1.48, Nonn.*D*.12.321:—Med., ib.12.320, al. (ἀ- euph., cf. *mulgeo, milk*.)

**ἀμέλδειν**· τήκειν, Hsch.

**ἀμέλει**, properly imper. of ἀμελέω (cf. ἀμέλησον Luc.*DMort*.5.2), *never mind, do not trouble yourself*, esp. to begin an answer, Ar.*Nu*.877, Lib.*Decl*.20.18:—hence, **II.** as Adv., *doubtless, by all means, of course*, Ar.*Ach*.368, *Nu*.488, al., Pl.*Phd*.82a, al., X.*Mem*.1.4.7, Men.*Sam*.8; freq. ironically, as Ar.*Ra*.532; freq. in Thphr.*Char*. to introduce a subject, 13.1, al., or a further point, 2.9, al. **2.** *for instance*, Thphr.*Char*.6.3, Luc.*DDeor*.25.1, etc. **3.** *at any rate*, Luc.*Nigr*.26, *Gp*.10.2.3. **4.** *and indeed*, Phld.*Ir*.p.16 W., Str.1.2.34, D.H.*Rh*.2.2, J.*AJ*7.4.1; *and so*, Polyaen.2.22.3, 7.6.4. **5.** *actually*, to give emphasis, Agath.2.3, al. **ἀμέλεια**, ἡ, *indifference, negligence*, Th.1.122, 5.38, etc.; θεῶν *towards* the gods, Pl.*Lg*.905b, cf. ib.903a: also in pl., *negligences*, Id.*R*.443a, Arist.*Rh*.1370a15.

**ἀμελεϊστί**, prob. f.l. for ἀμελλητί, Suid.

**ἀμελετ-ησία**, ἡ, *want of practice, negligence*, Pl.*Tht*.153b; μνήμης Id.*Phdr*.275a, cf. Eus.Mynd.*Fr*.33, Ph.1.548, etc. **–ητος**, ον, *unpractised, unprepared*, περί τινος Pl.*Smp*.172a: c. inf., ἀ. ἐν ταῖς ἡδοναῖς καρτερεῖν Id.*Lg*.635c, cf. Procop.*Goth*.1.9; τινός, πρός τι, Luc.*Cont*.7, *Tox*.29, Arist.*SE*175a26: abs. of horses, *untrained*, X.*Eq.Mag*.1.19, al. Adv. –τως, ἔχειν τινός Jul.*Or*.1.2d. Adv. –τως, ἔχειν to be *unprepared*, Pl.*Smp*.173c.

**ἀμελ-έω** [ᾰ], aor. ἠμέλησα, Ep. ἀμ- Il., v. infr.: pf. ἠμέληκα X.*Cyr*.1.6.43: (ἀμελής):—*have no care for, be neglectful of*, in Hom. always c. neg. (not in Od.), οὐδ' ὣς Μενελάου ἐφημοσύνης ἀμέλησεν Il.17.697; οὐκ ἀμέλησε κασιγνήτοιο πεσόντος 8.330; οὐκ ἀμέλησε Πατρόκλοιο πεσόντος *he lost* not *sight* of Patroclus [in order to *plunder* him], 17.9:—after Hom., with and without neg., εἰ τούτων ἀμελήσει Hdt.2.121.γ', cf. Ar.*Nu*.989, Th.3.40, Pl.*Lg*.900b, al.; δόξης ἀμελῆσαι D.18.227; ἀμελήσας ὑμῶν 21.167; (τούτῳ is f.l. for τούτου in Lycurg.15); οὐκ ἐμοῦ τοῦ νομοθέτου ἀμελήσων ἀλλ' εἰς τὸν Κρόνον αὐτόν Luc.*Sat*.10. **2.** abs., *to be careless, negligent*, Hes.*Op*.400, eq. in Att., Isoc.9.78, etc.; τὸ μὴ ἀμελεῖν μάθε A.*Eu.*86; πῶς ἐπὶ τοῖς …ιμένοις ἀμελεῖν καλόν; S.*El.*237. 3. c. acc. rei, Hdt.7.163: acc. pers. et part., *overlook*: hence, *allow, suffer*, παῖδας ἐκτεκνουμένος λάθρᾳ θνήσκοντας ἀμελεῖ *lets* them die, E.*Ion* 439: c. gen., τοῦ …γίζεσθαι X.*Mem.*2.3.9. 4. c. inf., *neglect* to do, Hdt.2.66, Pl. *Phd.*98d, *Lg.*944d, al. II. Pass., *to be slighted, overlooked*, E.*IA* 994, Th.1.68; ἐκφεύγει τἀμελούμενον S.*OT* 111; οὐδ' ἐκεῖνά μοι ἀμελεῖται X.*Oec.*12.2; οἱ ἠμελημένοι ἄνθρωποι Th.2.49. III. pf. part. Pass. in med. sense, *careless*, Max.Tyr.8.7, 21.9. Adv. ἠμελημένως *carelessly*, X.*An.*1.7.19. IV. ἀμέλει, v. sub voc. **-ής** (A), [ᾰ], ές, (μέλει) *careless, negligent*, Ar.*Lys.*882, X.*Mem.*2.6.19; φιλοπότης τε κἀμελής Eup.208; ἀργὸς.. καὶ ἀ. Pl.*R.*421d, etc. Adv. **-λῶς** *carelessly*, Th.6.100: Comp. **-έστερον** Id.2.11; **-εστέρως** Aen.Tact. 26.8. 2. c. gen., *careless of*.., Pl.*Sph.*225d, etc.; περί τινα Isoc. 19.32. Adv., ἐάν τις γονέων **-έστερον** ἔχῃ τοῦ δέοντος Pl.*Lg.*932a; ἀμελῶς ἔχειν πρός τι X.*Oec.*2.7; περὶ θεούς Id.*Cyr.*1.2.7. 3. c. inf., οὐκ ἀ. ποιεῖν not *negligent* in doing, Plu.2.64f. II. Pass., *uncared for, unheeded*, οὐδενὶ τούτων ἀ. X.*HG*6.5.41, cf. D.50.15; οὐκ ἀμελὲς γεγένηταί μοι, c. inf., I have taken *pains* to.., Luc.*Dips.*9. **ής** (B), ές, (μέλος) *unmelodious*, φωνή Poll.2.117. **-ητέον**, *one must neglect*, τινός Isoc.9.7: also in pl., ἀμελητέα ἐστί τινος Arr.*An.*1.24.1. II. ἀμελητέος, α, ον, *to be neglected*, Luc.*Tim.*9, Arr.*An.*1.7.4. ***-ητής**, οῦ, ὁ, *one who neglects*, Gal.3.827. **-ητικός**, ή, όν, *carelessly written*, ἦτα, of a musical note, Alyp.1, al., Gaud.*Harm.*23. **-ητος**, ον, *not to be cared for, unworthy of care*, πόλλ' ἀμέλητα μέλει Thgn.422. Adv. ***ἀμελητί** *heedlessly*, Luc.*Tim.*12. **-ία**, ἡ, poet. for ἀμέλεια, E.*IA* 850, *Fr.*187:—also in Inscrr. and Papyri, *OGI* 383 (Nimrud Dagh), *PTeb.*61ª176 (ii B.C.). **-ίου** δίκη action for *negligence*, Hsch.

**ἀμελκ-τέον**, *one must milk*, *Gp.*18.3.9. **-τήρ**, ῆρος, ὁ, *milking-pail*, Hsch. s. v. ἀρακτήρ. **-τός**, όν, *milked*, or *to be milked*, Hdn. Gr.2.901.

**ἀμέλλ-ητος**, ον, *without delay* or *hesitation*, Luc.*Nigr.*27. Adv. **-τως** Plb.16.34.12, al.:—also **-ητί** Ph.1.172, J.*AJ*19.6.3, Them. *Or.*16.208c, Iamb.*VP*3.14.

**ἄμελξις**, εως, ἡ, (ἀμέλγω) *milking*, Pi.*Fr.*106, Lxx *Jb.*20.17.

**ἀμελῴδητος**, ον, *unmelodic*, διαστήματα Aristox.*Harm.*p.25 M.

***ἄμεμπτος**, ον, *blameless, without reproach*, E.*IA* 1158, *Cyc.*342; ἀμέμπτους ὑμᾶς ἐδείξατε D.18.216; ἄ. χρόνου in regard of time, A.*Pers.* 692; ἄ. τἆλλα Men.521; πρός τι A.*Supp.*629 (dub.); ἄ. ὑπὸ τῶν φίλων X.*Ag.*6.8; ἄ. ἐκείνῃ *without blame* to her, Plu.*Sull.*35: Comp. **-ότερος** *less blameworthy*, Plu.*Ages.*5. 2. of things, *perfect in its kind*, δεῖπνον X.*Smp.*2.2; δίκη Pl.*Lg.*945d; ἄ. πάντα ἔχειν X.*Mem.*3.10.2. Adv. **-τως** *irreproachably*, A.*Supp.*269, S.*Ph.*1465, X.*Cyr.*7.3.10, *Stoic.*3.64. II. Act., *not blaming, well content*, ἄμεμπτόν τινα ποιεῖν or ποιεῖσθαι, X.*Cyr.*4.5.52, 8.4.28. Adv. **-τως**, δέχεσθαί τινα ib.4.2.37.

***ἀμεμφ-ής**, ές, mostly in pass. sense, = ἄμεμπτος I, *IG*12(3).1075 (Melos), Pi.*O.*6.46, A.*Pers.*168, *Supp.*581; in epitaph, Εὔκλειαν ἀ. Ἀρχ. Ἐφ.1910.66 (Piraeus):—poet. and late Prose, Plu.*Cim.*2, Jul. *Or.*2.99a. II. Act., = ἄμεμπτος II, Plu.2.610e; ἀ. τῶν ἀμελειῶν Id.*Aem.*3. Adv. **-φῶς**, Ion. **-φέως** Orph.*H.*43.11. **-ία**, ἡ, *freedom from blame*, διαλλακτῆρι δ' οὐκ ἀ. φίλοις mediator has no *freedom from blame* on the part of his friends, A.*Th.*909; ἀμεμφίας χάριν for *avoidance of censure*, S.*Fr.*283. (ἀμεμφεία shd. perh. be written in both passages.)

***ἀμεμψι-μοίρητος**, ον, *unexceptionable*, *OGI* 323 (Pergam.), *PPar.* 63.8 (ii B.C.). Adv. **-τως** *without cause of complaint*, *BGU* 251 (i A.D.). **-μοιρος**, ον, *not complaining of one's lot*, Teles p.56.2 H., M.Ant.5.5.

**ἄμεναι** [ᾰ], Ep. pres. inf. from ἄω (q.v.), Il.21.70.

***ἀμενην-ός** [ᾰ], όν, also ή, όν Opp.*H.*2.58: (ἀ- priv., μένος):—poet. Adj., in Hom. chiefly of ghosts or shades, *fleeting*, νεκύων ἀ. κάρηνα Od.10.521, al.; of dreams, 19.562; of one wounded, ἀ. ἔα χαλκοῖο τυπῇσι Il.5.887; Πυγμαῖοι Hes.*Oxy.*1358.18; rare in Trag. (alw. lyr.), ἀ. ἀνήρ, of Ajax, S.*Aj.*890; νεκύων ἀ. ἄγαλμα E.*Tr.*193. 2. of men in general, *fleeting, feeble*, φῦλ' ἀ. ἀνθρώπων *h.Cer.*352; σκιοειδέα φῦλ' ἀ. Ar.*Av.*686. 3. in physical sense, *feeble, weak*, ἰσχνοῖσι καὶ ἀμενηνοῖσι Hp.*Prorrh.*2.30; ἀ. φωνή Arist.*Pr.*899ª30; οἱ ἄκεντροι σφῆκες.. ἀμενηνότεροι Id.*HA*628ᵇ4, cf. Ti.Locr.100c; ὕδωρ **-ότατον** πάντων Arr.*Ind.*6.3; ἀ. κλῆμα, φύλλον, Thphr.*CP*3.14.5, *HP*3.9.1; σπερμάτιον 4.12.2 (Comp.); πῦρ Ph.2.564; *faint, shadowy*, ὄναρ Them.*Or.*21.263c:—neut. as Adv., *feebly, faintly*, ἀμενηνὸν φθέγγεσθαι Arist.*Pr.*899ª31; ὁρᾶν Philostr.Jun.*Im.*17; ἀμενηνὰ φαείνειν Arat.905. Regul. Adv. **-νῶς** Agathem.ap.Gal.8.938. II. (as if from ἀ- priv., μένω) *not permanent*, κατηγορίαι Simp.*in Ph.*832. 12. **-όω**, *weaken, deaden the force of*, ἀμενήνωσεν δέ οἱ αἰχμὴν Il.13. 562.

***ἀμενής**, ές, = ἀμενηνός, E.*Supp.*1116 (lyr.).

**ἀμενητά**· ὑμένα, Hsch. **ἀμενητί**, Adv. *without remaining*, Suid.

***ἀμένητος**, ον, = ἀμενηνός, Hdn.Gr.2.684.

**ἀμενθήριστος**, ον, *not careful*, Timo 59 (codd. ἀπενθ-).

**ἀμεργόν**· ἡ εἱμαρμένη (Cret.), Hsch.

***ἀμέργω** [ᾰ], fut. **-ξω** (v. infr.), *pluck* or *pull*, ἄνθε' ἀμέργοισαν παῖδα Sapph.121; πετάλων ἄπο.. χερὶ καρπὸν ἀμέρξων E.*HF* 397 (lyr.), cf. A.R.1.882; ἀ. τὰς ἐλάας *Com.Adesp.*437 (*squeeze out* juice, acc. to Eust.318.11):—Med., ἀμερξάμεναι.. δρυὸς ἄγρια φύλλα Theoc.26.3, cf. A.R.4.1144, Nic.*Th.*864, etc.

***ἀμέρδω** [ᾰ], fut. **-σω** Orph.*L.*169: aor. ἤμερσα, poet. ἄμ- (v. infr.):—Pass., aor. ἠμέρθην (v. infr.).—Ep., rarely in Trag., never in Att. Prose:—*deprive, bereave* one *of* something properly belonging to one, c. acc. pers. et gen. rei, ὀφθαλμῶν μὲν ἄμερσε Od.8.64 (v.l.); εὖτ' ἂν δὴ Κύκνον γλυκερῆς αἰῶνος ἀμέρσῃς Hes.*Sc.*331, cf. Simon.117; εἰ μὴ στάσις.. σ' ἄμερσε πάτρας Pi.*O.*12.16: also c. dupl. acc. pers. et rei, τιμὴν ἤμερσεν Ὀλύμπια δώματ' ἔχοντας *h.Cer.*312: also c. acc. et dat., ὀφθαλμῶν σέλας ἤμερσε βροτοῖσιν Man.6.550:—Pass., *to be bereft of*, φίλης αἰῶνος ἀμερθῇς Il.22.58; οὐδέ τι δαιτὸς ἀμέρδεαι Od.21.290; τὸ ἧπαρ τῆς ἐκροῆς ἀμερθέν Aret.*CA*2.6, cf. Hierocl. *in CA*24 p.470 M.: rarely c. acc. rei, ἂν.. καρπὸν ἀμερθῶσι Thphr.*HP*9.8.2. 2. c. acc. pers. only, *bereave of natural rights*, τὸν ὁμοῖον ἀμέρσαι Il.16.53; ὄσσε δ' ἄμερδεν αὐγὴ χαλκείη *blinded* the eyes, ib.13.340, cf. Hes.*Th.*698; ἔντεα πατρὸς καλά, τὰ.. καπνὸς ἀμέρδει *robs of their lustre, tarnishes*, Od.19.18. 3. Act. in pass. sense, *lose*, βίον E.*Hec.*1029 (lyr.). II. later, = ἀμέργω, *pluck*, λειμώνιον ἄνθος ἀμέρσας (cj. Scalig.) *AP*7.657 (Leon.). (ἀ- euph., cf. μέρδει.)

**ἀμέρ-εια**, ἡ, *being without parts*, Porph.*Sent.*34, Procl.*Inst.*86, al., Dam.*Pr.*60; τοῦ νοῦ Hero *Def.*136.25. **-ής**, ές, *without parts, indivisible*, Pl.*Tht.*205e, *Prm.*138a, Arist.*Ph.*231ᵇ3, etc.; τὸ ἀ. Hp. *Virg.*1; introduced into Latin by Cic., Plu.*Cic.*40. Adv. **-ρῶς** Alex. Aphr.*in Metaph.*714.25; ἀ. καὶ ἀδιαστάτως Porph.*Sent.*33. 2. τὰ ἀ. in Logic, *summa genera*, Arist.*APo.*100ᵇ2. 3. *impartial*, κρίσεις Luc.*Cal.*8. **-ιαῖος**, α, ον, *momentary*, φρόνησις Chrysipp.*Stoic.*3.50.

***ἀμεριμν-έω**, *to be care-free*, Iamb.*VP*5.21. (ἀμεριμνάω, only Moer. 79.) **-ία**, ἡ, *freedom from care*, Plu.2.830a, Secund.*Sent.*8ᵇ; ἀ. τῆς δεσποτείας Hdn.2.4.6. 2. as law-term, *guarantee, release*, *IG*14.956; τινός *PLips.*59; *receipt*, Just.*Nov.*128. II. personified, Σεβαστῶν Ἀ., = *Securitas Augustorum*, *CIG*2778 (Aphrodisias). **-ικός**, ή, όν, = ἀμέριμνος I, c. gen. obj., ἐμοῦ *PFay.*130 (iii A.D.). ***-ος**, ον, *free from care, unconcerned*, Men.1083; βίος *AP*9.359 (Posidipp. or Pl.Com.); ἀ. ὕπνον εὕδεις *Eranos* 13.87. Adv. **-νως** Vett.Val.355.6, Hdn.4.5.7, *IG*14.1839: Comp. **-ότερον**, ἔχειν *PLips.*105 (i A.D.). II. Pass., *uncared for*, S.*Aj.*1207. III. οἰνοχοεῖ κρήνης ἐξ ἀμεριμνοτέρης, either *causing less care*, i.e. *more easily attained*, of the fount of inspiration, or possibly *less celebrated*, *AP*11.24 (Antip.). IV. ἀμέριμνον, τό, = ἀείζωον μέγα, Plin.*HN* 25.160.

***ἀμέριστος**, ον, *undivided, indivisible*, Pl.*Tht.*205c, *Ti.*35a, Dam.ap. Simp.*in Ph.*625.4, Procl.*Theol.Plat.*1.4: Comp., Id.*Inst.*62. Adv. **-τως** Iamb.*Myst.*1.9, Jul.*Or.*4.157a, Syrian.*in Metaph.*107.6. II. Astrol., in act. sense, *not imparting*, ἀστέρες ἀ. τῶν ἰδίων ἀγαθῶν Vett.Val.64.3.

**ἀμέρμερα**· πολλά (Lacon.), Hsch.

**ἀμερμηρεί**, Adv. *carelessly*, Suid., Eust.1416.10.

**ἀμερνός**· ἄπειρος, Hsch.

**ἀμερο-κοίτης**, **-κοιτος**, Dor. for ἡμερό-.

**ἀμερσί-γᾰμος**, ον, *robbing of wedlock*, Nonn.*D.*7.226. **-νη**, ἡ, = ἑλξίνη, Dsc.4.39. **-νοος**, ον, *depriving of mind, maddening*, Nonn.*D.*1.388, prob. in Ps.-Dsc 4.78. **ἄμερσις**, εως, ἡ, *deprivation*, Eust.1585.46. **ἀμερσίφρων**, ον, = ἀμερσίνοος, Hsch.

**ἀμερφές**· αἰσχρόν, Hsch. **ἀμέσαι**· ἀμαυρῶσαι, Id. (leg. ἀμέρσαι).

**ἀμεσολάβητος**, ον, *not seized by the middle*, i.e. *not thrown*, of a victorious wrestler, *BCH*16.445 (Phaselis), *LW*3.363 (Mylasa): metaph., φῶς ἀ. παρέχων, of the sun, Jul.*Or.*4.153c.

**ἄμεσος**, ον, *immediate*: ἄμεσα καὶ ἀναπόδεικτα, of propositions *that cannot be proved syllogistically by means of a middle term*, Arist.*APr.* 68ᵇ30, *APo.*72ᵇ19, etc.; τὰ ἄ. τῶν ἐναντίων *direct* opposites, Plot.6.3. 20. Adv. ἀμέσως *immediately*, Olymp.*in Phlb.*p.256 S., Alex.Aphr.*in Metaph.*162.19, Procl.*Inst.*30, dub. in Phld.*Herc.*1251.3. **ἀμεσότης**, τητος, ἡ, *immediacy*, Eustr.*in APo.*176.4. **ἀμέσω**· ὠμοπλάται, Hsch. (cf. Lat. *umerus*, Goth. *ams*-).

***ἀμετά-βᾰτος**, ον, *not changing place, stationary*, ἥλιος Cleom.2.1; οὐρανός Simp.*in Ph.*611.5. Adv. **-τως** *without transition*, ἀκινήτως καὶ ἀ. Procl.*Inst.*52, cf. Simp.*in Ph.*1162.6. 2. Gramm., *intransitive*, ῥῆμα A.D.*Pron.*44.12, al. Adv. **-τως** *intransitively*, Sch.Ar.*Pl.* 158. II. Pass., *incapable of being traversed*, i.e. *unextended*, Epicur. *Ep.*1 p.18 U. **-βλησία**, ἡ, *unchangeableness*, Arist.*Ph.*230ª10, Thphr.*CP*6.19.3. ***-βλητος**, ον, hyperdor. **-ατος** Philol.21, *unchangeable*, κόσμος l.c., cf. Arist.*Metaph.*1019ª27; ἄτομα καὶ ἀ. Epicur.*Ep.*1 p.7 U.; ἀ. εἰς ἄλλα Ti.Locr.98c. 2. *unchanged*, J.*AJ* 15.7.5; τὸ ἀμετάβλητον Plu.2.1011a: Gramm., *not inflected*, A.D. *Synt.*322.26; of food, *not transformed* by digestion, Gal.6.575, cf. Thphr.*CP*6.10.2. Adv. **-τως** Iamb.*Protr.*21.κϛ', Hierocl. *in CA* 1 p.420 M.; and **-τί**, gloss on ἀσπερχές, Sch.Il.16.61. ***-βολος**, ον, = foreg., Plu.*Mar.*42. 2. Music, *without modulation*, σύστημα Aristid.Quint.1.8, Bacch.*Harm.*74; ἁρμονία Plu.2.437d **-γνωστος**, ον, *unalterable, implacable*, μῖσος J.*AJ*16.10.1. 2. *not to be repented of*, ἡδονή Max.Tyr.1.4. **-δόξαστος**, ον, *unshakeable in one's convictions*, Phld.*Herc.*1003. Adv. **-τως** ibid. **-δοσία**, ἡ, *the habit of not giving, avarice*, Sch.Od.17.407. **-δοτος**, ον, *not imparting, sharing*, τινός Sch.E.*Hipp.*145: abs., *niggardly*, βίος Nic.Dam.p.144ᵇ 28 D.; of persons, opp. κοινωνητικοί, Epict.*Sent.*6. Adv. **-ως**, ζῆν live *without giving to any one*, Plu.2.525d. II. Pass., *not imparted, secret*, ὑφήγησις Vett.Val.331.6, cf. *PMag.Par.*1.256. **-θετος**, ον, *unalterable, immutable*, κατάληψις, of knowledge, Zeno *Stoic.*1.20; of fate, Chrysipp.ib.2.264, cf. Plb.30.17.2; ἀκίνητα καὶ ἀ. *OGI* 331 (Pergam.), etc. Adv. **-τως**, διακεῖσθαι D.S.1.83, cf. Ascl.*in Metaph.* 22.6. 2. Gramm., *not inflected*, A.D.*Synt.*322.1. **-κίνητος**, ον, *not to be moved from place to place, immovable*, Pl.*Ep.*343a, Arist. *Ph.*212ª15; of persons, D.H.8.74. Adv. **-τως**, ἔχειν stand *unmoved*,

Arist.EN1105ᵃ33, cf. Jul.Mis.348d, al. **-κλαστος**, ον, not to be broken, inflexible, τὸ ἀ. τῆς γνώμης X.Ep.1.2. *-**κλητος**, ον, irrevocable, uncontrollable, ὁρμή Plb.36.15.7; ὀργή Hld.2.10 (v.l. -βλητος). **-κλιτος**, ον, inflexible, steadfast, Sch.A.Th.312, cf. ib.Pr.34. *-**ληπτος**, ον, not to be substituted, A.D.Pron.8.19, 46.28.

**ἀμετ-άλλακτος**, ον, unchanging, J.AJ18.1.6, Dam.Pr.370.

**ἀμετα-μέλητος**, ον, not to be repented of or regretted, ἡδονή Pl.Ti. 59d; τὸ πεπραγμένον αὐτοῖς ἀ. γίγνεται Id.Lg.866e; ἀμεταμέλητον ἐστί τί τινι one has nothing to repent of, Plb.21.11.11. 2. having no opportunity of repentance, Just.Nov.129.3. II. of persons, unrepentant, feeling no remorse, ἀ. ἀνίατος Arist.EN1150ᵃ22, 1166ᵃ29. Adv. -τως Them.Or.19.231a, Inscr.Prien.114. *-**μίσθωτος**, ον, not sublet, PTeb.372 (ii A.D.). **-νόητος**, ον, = ἀμεταμέλητος I, Luc.Abd.11, Plot.6.7.26, Vett.Val.263.16, al. II. Act., unrepentant, Ep.Rom.2.5, Arr.Epict.Fr.25. Adv. -τως PStrassb.29 (iii A.D.). **-πειστος**, ον, not to be moved by persuasion, inexorable, Arist.APo.72ᵇ3; ἀ. ὑπὸ λόγου Id.Top.130ᵇ16; of necessity, Id. Metaph.1015ᵃ32. Adv. -τως Epicur.Fr.222, Phld.Herc.1003. II. of things, unchangeable, steadfast, συμμαχία D.S.37.20. **-πλαστος**, ον, not to be remoulded or altered, Diog.ap.Stob.App.p.42G. **-ποίητος**, ον, indigestible, Xenocr.42. **-πταιστος**, ον, infallible, πρόρρησις Gal.17(1).863. **-πτωσία**, ἡ, unchangeableness, Arr.Epict.3.2.8, Hierocl.p.48.7A. **-πτωτος**, ον, unchanging, unchangeable, λόγοι μόνιμοι καὶ ἀ. Pl.Ti.29b; ἐπιστήμη Arist.Top.139ᵇ33; ἡ ἀρετή Id.MM 1209ᵇ13, Stoic.1.50, etc.; κατάληψις ἀ. ὑπὸ λόγου Zenoib.1.20; πίστεις Phld.Rh.1.378S. (Sup.). b. not losing its power, of medicine, Gal.12.422. II. of persons, Plu.2.659f. Adv. -τως Id.Dio 14, cf. Phld.Rh.1.158S., Polystr.p.29W. **-στατος**, ον, unchangeable, unchanging, ἴτω ἀ. μέχρι θανάτου Pl.R.361c; of ideas, ib.378e; τὸ ἀμετάστατον uniformity, Plu.2.135b. Adv. -τως Procl.in Ti.3.22D., etc. **-στρεπτος**, ον, not to be diverted, Max.Tyr.11.5, cf. POxy. 705.62. Adv. **-στρεπτί** [ῐ] or -εί without turning round, straight forward, φεύγειν X.Smp.4.50, Pl.Lg.854c, cf. R.620e, Ph.1.517, M.Ant.8.5 (v.l. -τρεπτί), etc. **-στροφος**, ον, not to be turned round, unalterable, Pl.R.620e, Lg.960c. **-τρεπτος**, ον, = foreg., Plu.Thes.17, Iamb.Myst.6.6, Herm.ap.Stob.1.4.7ᵇ. Adv. -τως, gloss on ἀσκελές, Sch.Od.4.543; also -τρεπτί v.l. in M.Ant.8.5. **-τρεψία**, ἡ, = sq., Ptol.Tetr.16. **-τροπία**, ἡ, immovableness, Sch.A.R. 4.1082. *-**τροπος**, ον, = ἀμετάτρεπτος, Orph.H.59.17; δόγμα Μοιρῶν IG12(7).393 (Amorgos). **-φόρητος**, ον, irremovable, Phlp.in Cat.32.21. **-φραστος**, ον, untranslatable, Phot. s.v. πύππαξ, Sch.Il.9.607, Hsch. s.v. θρίττε. **-χείριστος**, ον, not handselled, new, Ar.Fr.710. II. difficult to handle, intractable, Gloss., Hsch.

**ἀμετέναι**· ἀποδοῦναι, Hsch.

**ἀμέτ-οιστος**, ον, which cannot be alienated or secularized, πρόσοδοι OGI332.19 (Pergam.). **-ουσίαστον**· ἀμέτοχον, Hsch. *-**οχος**, ον, having no share of, free from, ἐγκλημάτων interp. in Th.1.39; ἀγαθῶν Epicur.Fr.364; ἀρετῆς, κακίας Stoic.3.90, cf. S.E.M.7.93; Αἰὼν μεταβολῆς ἀ. SIG1125.11 (Eleusis), cf. Ph.1.17, Hierocl.p.33.7A., Alex. Aphr.in Metaph.644.12, Dsc.5.87; ἀ. ὕλης οὐσία Plot.3.5.2; πολλὰ ἑνὸς ἀ. Procl.in Prm.p.559S.; without gen., Phld.Ir.p.63W.

**ἀμετρ-ητος**, ον, also η, ον Pi.I.1.37:—immeasurable, immense, πένθος, πόνος, Od.19.512, 23.249; ἅλς Pi. l. c.; ἀήρ Ar.Nu.264; ταραχαί Phld.Herc.1251.18; inexhaustible, στόμα Μούσης AP7.75 (Antip.), cf. Pyth.Sim.1. Adv. -τως, χρῆσθαι τῇ τιμῇ J.AJ11.6.12. 2. unnumbered, countless, ἐρετμοί E.El.433. 3. not measured, πλευρόν Str.2.1.23, cf. 29. **-ί**, Adv. of ἄμετρος, μέτρῳ ὕδωρ πίνοντες, ἀ. δὲ μᾶζαν ἔδοντες Zen.5.19. *-**ία**, ἡ, excess, disproportion, opp. συμμετρία, Pl.Ti.87d, cf. R.486d, Heraclit.All.8, Alex.Aphr.Pr.1. 112, etc. b. want of moderation, Arist.VV1251ᵇ15. 2. infinity, countless number, κακῶν Pl.Ax.367a (in pl.). **-ιος**, α, ον, unreasonable, οὐκ ἀ. Inscr.Prien.113.32.

**ἀμετρο-βαθής**, ές, immensely deep, Opp.H.1.85. **-βιος**, ον, of immensely long life, ἐλέφαντες Man.1.53; κόρακες prob. l. in Epigr. ap. Philostr.Her.19.17. **-δικος**, ον, breaking bounds of justice, διχοστασίαι B.10.68. **-επής**, ές, unbridled of tongue, Il.2.212, Ph. 1.616. **-επία**, ἡ, garrulity, in pl., Gal.18(1).253. **-κάκος**, ον, immeasurably bad, Eun.Hist.p.255D. *-**παθής**, ές, excessive in emotion, Alcin.Intr.30. **-πότης**, ου, ὁ, drinking to excess, AP 9.644 (Agath.), Zen.5.19.

**ἄμετρος**, ον, without or beyond measure, immense, κακόν Simon. 37.16 codd.; opp. μετρητός, Pl.Lg.820c. Adv. -τρως Id.Phd.86c, etc.; neut. pl. as Adv., Babr.11.10. 2. immoderate, in moral sense, Pl.Lg.690e, etc. Adv. -τρως X.Cyr.1.6.34. 3. neverceasing, τέττιγες Simon.174. 4. disproportionate, Pl.Ti.87e: Sup. -ότατος most unequal, Cleom.1.7. II. without metre, prosaic, opp. ἔμμετρος, Arist.Po.1451ᵇ1, D.H.Comp.3, etc. Adv. -τρως unmetrically, Critias 4; not in metre, Poll.1.19. III. ἄμετρος, = βάτος, Dsc.4.37.

*__ἀμεύομαι__, Dor. = ἀμείβομαι, only fut. and aor. 1, surpass, outstrip, ἀμεύσασθ' ἀντίους Pi.P.1.45; ἀμεύσεσθε Τίσανδρον Id.Fr.23. 2. pass over, ὕδατα Euph.119. II. purchase (?), GDI4964 (Gortyn).

**ἀμευσιεπής**, ές, surpassing words, φροντίς Pi.Fr.24.

**ἀμεύσιμος**, ον, (ἀμεύομαι) passable, A.R.4.297.

**ἀμευσίπορος**, ον, path-shifting, τρίοδος Pi.P.11.38.

*__ἄμη__, ἡ, shovel, Ar.Av.1145, Pax 426, X.Cyr.6.2.34; hod, IG1.225e, cf. Suid. 2. water-bucket, pail, ἄμαις καὶ σκάφαις ἀρύσασθαι, prov. of great abundance, Plu.2.963c. 3. spade, Gp.2.23.5. 4. Ion. for ἄμης, Silen.ap.Ath.14.644f. 5. hobble for young goat, Hsch.

**ἀμῆ**, Adv., (properly ἀμῇ, dat. fem. of ἀμός = τις) in a certain way, Hp.ap.Gal.19.78: elsewh. in the phrase ἀμῇ γέ πῃ somehow or other, Ar.Ach.608, Pl.Prt.331d, R.474c, etc.

**ἀμήκωα**· δεινά (Tarent.), Hsch.

**ἀμήν**, Hebr. Adv. verily, of a truth, so be it, Lxx 1Ch.16.36; at beginning of sentence, Ev.Matt.5.18, al.; doubled, Ev.Jo.1.51, al.; τὸ ἀ. 1Ep.Cor.14.16.

**ἀμήνας**· ἐκπιάξας, ἀμύξας, Hp.ap.Gal.19.78.

**ἄμηνις**, ιος, ὁ, ἡ, = sq., J.AJ19.4.6.

*__ἀμήνῑτος__, ον, (μηνίω) not angry, Hdt.9.94; βάξις A.Supp.975; χειμὼν Ἀχαιῶν οὐκ ἀμήνιτος θεοῖς Id.Ag.649. Adv. -τως ib.1036.

**ἀμήν-ῠτος**, ον, not denounced, Hld.8.13, cf. Theognost.Can.83. Adv. -υτί unannounced, without warning, Steph. in Hp.1.100 D., al., prob. in A.D.Adv.161.8.

**ἄμηροι**, = ὅμηροι, EM83.19, Hsch.; cf. Ἀμάριος. **ἄμηρον**· νέον, EM83.18. **ἀμήρυνος**, v.l. for sq. ap.Sch.A.R.2.221.

**ἀμήρῠτος**, ον, not to be wound up, i.e. tedious, γῆρας A.R.2.221; λόγοι Com.Adesp.837; μάθησις Phld.Herc.873.8; ἥλιοι Anon.ap. Stob.3.28.21.

**ἄμης**, ητος, ὁ, kind of milk cake, Ar.Pl.999, Antiph.89, Men.491, Clearch.65, Ph.1.390. II. kind of oven, Dieuch.ap.Orib.4.5.2.

**ἀμ-ητήρ** [ᾰ, but ᾱ metri gr.], ῆρος, ὁ, (ἀμάω A) reaper, Il.11.67, Theoc.7.29: Adj., ἀμητῆρι τύπῳ in form like a sickle, Nonn.D.26. 302:—fem. **-ήτειρα** EM83.2. **-ητήριον**, τό, sickle, Max.Tyr.30. 7. **-ητής**, ὁ, reaper, Porph.ad Il.19.222. **-ητικός**, ή, όν, of or for reaping, δρέπανον ἀ. reaping-hook, Ael.HA17.37.

**ἀμητίσκος**, ὁ, Dim. of ἄμης, Telecl.1.12, cf. Pherecr.130.7 codd. Ath. *__ἄμητος__ [ᾱ], ὁ, (ἀμάω A) reaping, harvesting, Il.19.223. 2. harvest, harvest-time, Hes.Op.384, 575, Hdt.2.14, 4.42, Hp.Epid.6.8.19, Thphr.HP3.4.4, A.R.3.418, etc. II. crop, harvest gathered in, or field when reaped, D.P.194, Arat.1097: with another Subst., ληΐοιο ἀμήτοιο Opp.C.1.527: metaph., of a beard, AP11.368 (Jul.). (Gramm. distinguish ἄμητος (I) from ἀμητός (II), the latter being regarded as Adj. (sc. σῖτος), cf. Hdn.Gr.1.220, but Ammon. reverses the distinction.) **ἀμητρίς**, ίδος, ἡ, fem. of ἀμητήρ, dub. l. in Poll.1.122.

**ἀμητύς**, ύος, ἡ = ἄμητος I, Hymn.Is.85.

*__ἀμήτωρ__, ορος, motherless, Hdt.4.154, E.Ion 109, Id.ap.Phot.p.91R.; of Melchizedek, Ep.Hebr.7.3; of the number 7, Hierocl.in CA20 p.465M., cf. Ph.1.24; but ἡ μονὰς ἀ. Gal.9.934. II. that is no mother, unmotherly, μήτηρ ἀμήτωρ S.El.1154; of dam mounted by her foal, Opp.C.1.261; childless, Epigr.Gr.365 (Cotiaeum).

**ἀμηχαν-άω**, = sq., Opp.H.3.328, AP9.591, etc., in Ep. forms ἀμηχανόωσιν, -όων. *-**έω**, fut. -ήσω Th.7.48: impf. ἠμηχάνουν Pl.Com. 45:—to be ἀμήχανος, to be at a loss for, or in want of, χρήματος οὐδενός Hdt.1.35, cf. A.R.4.692; ἀ. περί τινος about thing, E.IT734: c. acc., τέρμα A.Ag.1177, etc.; ταῦτα E.Heracl.492: c. dat., ἀ. θεσφάτοισι A.Ag.1113:—freq. foll. by relative clause, ἀ. πότερον.. ἤ.. S.Ph. 337; ἀ. ὅπᾳ τράπωμαι, ὅποι τράποιντο, A.Ag.1530, Pers.458: abs., A. Supp.379, S.El.1174, E.Andr.983, Epicur.Fr.203, etc. 2. c. inf., not to know how to do, ὅσσαν συμβαλεῖν ἀμηχανῶ Neophr. 1; χρόνος.. ὃν λανθάνειν ἀ. know not how to escape, Antiph.254. 3. ἀμηχανῶν βιοτεύειν live without the necessaries of life, X.Cyr.2.1.19; to be reduced to great straits, τὰ μὲν ἀπορεῖν, τὰ δ' ἔτι ἀμηχανήσειν Th.7. 48. 4. to be at a loss, amazed, perplexed, ἀ. κιόντων at their coming, A.R.4.692; so prob. ἀ. κακότητι 2.410. **-ής**, ές, poet. for ἀμήχανος, h.Merc.447, in gen. pl. -έων (but perh. fem. of -ος). **-ητος**, ον, = ἀμήχανος II, X.ap.Suid., f. l. in J.AJ1.19.8. *-**ία**, Ion. -ίη, ἡ, want of means or resources, helplessness, ἀμηχανίη δ' ἔχε θυμόν Od.9.295; πενίην μητέρ' ἀμηχανίης Thgn.385, cf. 619 (pl.), Alc.92, Hdt.8.111, etc.; ὑπ' ἀμηχανίας Ar.Av.475. II. of things, hardship, trouble, χειμῶνος ἀμηχανίη Hes.Op.496.

**ἀμηχᾰνο-εργός**, όν, unfit for work, Hes.Fr.198. **-ποιέομαι**, go awkwardly to work, μηχανοποιέοντα ἀ. Hp.Fract.30.

**ἀμήχᾰνος**, Dor. ἀμάχανος, ον, without means or resources, helpless, Od.19.363; πενία ἀ. B.1.61; πόριμον αὐτῷ τῇ πόλει δ' ἀ. Ar.Ra.1429; ἀ. καὶ ἄτεχνος Pl.Plt.274c; of animals, opp. εὐμήχανος, Arist.HA 614ᵇ34: hence, 2. incapable, awkward, ἀφραδέες καὶ ἀ. h.Ap. 192, cf. Theoc.1.85; τὸν ἀ. ὀρθοῦν A.Th.227; ἀ. γυνή E.Hipp.643; ἀ. εἴς τι awkward at thing, Id.Med.408. Adv., ἀμηχάνως ἔχειν, = ἀμηχανεῖν, A.Ch.407, E., etc. 3. c. inf., at a loss how to do, unable to do, τὸ δὲ βίᾳ πολιτῶν δρᾶν ἔφυν ἀ. S.Ant.79; -ώτατος δ' τι χρὴ λέγειν πορίσασθαι [D.]60.12, etc. II. more freq. in pass. sense, allowing of no means: 1. impracticable, unmanageable, c. inf., ἀμήχανός ἐσσι πιθέσθαι Il.13.726. b. of things, hard, impossible, τοῦτό μ' ἄνωγας ἀμήχανον ἄλλο τελέσσαι ib.14.262; τοῦτο δ' ἀ. εὑρεῖν Pi.O.7.25, cf. Hdt.1.48; ὁδὸς ἀ. εἰσελθεῖν road hard or impossible to enter on, X.An.1.2.21; ἀ. ἐστὶ γενέσθαι Emp.12, cf. Hdt. 1.48, 204, S.Ant.175, etc.: abs., ἀμήχανα impossibilities, ἀμηχάνων ἐρᾷν ib.90, cf. 92; δεινὸς.. εὑρεῖν κἀξ ἀ. πόρον A.Pr.59, cf. Ar.Eq.759: Sup., Them. in Ph.91.12. 2. against whom or which nothing can be done, irresistible, freq. in Hom. of Zeus, Hera, Achilles; ἀ. ἐσσι, ἀ. ἔπλευ, Il.10.167, 16.29; Ἔρος.. ἀ. ὄρπετον Sapph.40. b. of things, ἀ. ἔργα mischief without help or remedy, Il.8.130; δόλος Hes.Th. 589; κήδεα Archil.66; δύαι A.Eu.561 (lyr.); ἄλγος, νόσοι, S.El.140 (lyr.), Ant.363 (lyr.); συμφορά Simon.5.11, cf. E.Med.392; κακόν ib.447: Comp. -ώτερα, ἀγλαΐα Them.Or.4.51c. c. esp. of dreams, inexplicable, not to be interpreted, Od.19.560. 3. extraordinary, ormous, ποταμῶν ἀ. μεγέθη Pl.*Phd.*111d; ἡδοναί Id.*Phlb.*46e; ἀμή-χανον εὐδαιμονίας *an inconceivable amount* of happiness, Id.*Ap.*41c: ...eq. c. acc., ἀ. τὸ μέγεθος, τὸ κάλλος, τὸ πλῆθος, etc., i.e. *inconceivable* point of size, etc., Id.*R.*584b, 615a, X.*Cyr.*7.5.38: c. dat., ἀ. πλήθει ... καὶ ἀτοπίᾳ Pl.*Phdr.*229d (nisi leg. ἀμηχάνων πλήθη τε καὶ ἀτοπίαι, here ἀ. = *monsters*): abs., *infinitely great*, δύναμις Plot.5.3.16. b. ...eq. in Pl. with οἷος, ὅσος, ἀμήχανον ὅσον χρόνον *Phd.*95c; ἀμηχάνῳ ...σῳ πλέονι by *it is impossible to say* how much more, *R.*588a; ἀμή-...ανόν τι οἷον *Chrm.*155d. Adv., ἀμηχάνως ὡς εὖ *R.*527e; ἀ. γε ὡς σφόδρα *Phdr.*263d.

**ἀμηῷος**, ον, *with the dawn*, Orph.*A.*484.

**ἄμι** (ἄμμι Eudem.ap.Gal.14.185), -εως (or -ιος *PTeb.*, v. infr.), τό, *ajowan, Carum copticum*, *PTeb.*55.5 (ii B.C.), Plin.*HN*20.163, Dsc. 3.62, etc. 2. ἄ. ἄγριον, = δρακοντία μεγάλη, Ps.-Dsc.2.166.

**ἀμία** (A), ἡ, kind of *tunny*, which ascends rivers, perh. *bonito*, Sotad.Com.1.26, Archipp.20, Arist.*HA*506$^b$13, *Fr.*308:—also **ἀμίας**, ου, ὁ, Matro*Conv.*61:—gender indeterminate, Epich.59, cf.124, Arist. *HA*488$^a$7, al.

**ἀμία** (B)· φυλακία, Hsch.

**ἀμίαντος**, ον, *undefiled, pure*, ὕδωρ Thgn.447; φάος Pi.*Fr.*142; αἰθήρ B.3.86; A.*Pers.*578 calls the sea ἡ ἀμίαντος; ἀ. τοῦ ἀνοσίου πέρι *free from stain* of ungodliness, Pl.*Lg.*777d; περὶ τῶν ὁσιωτάτων Epicur.*Nat.*15.34; γάμοι οἱ ἀ. *Epigr.Gr.*204.13 (Cnidos), cf. *Ep.Hebr.* 13.4; τόπος Lxx 2*Ma.*15.34; κληρονομία 1*Ep.Pet.*1.4. 2. *not to be defiled*, D.H.2.75. II. ὁ ἀ. λίθος *asbestos*, Arist.*Fr.*495, Dsc. 5.138, Plin.*HN*36.139.

**ἀμίας**, ου, ὁ, v. ἀμία (A).

**ἀμῑγής**, ές, (μίγνυμι) *unmixed, pure*, ἡδοναί Arist.*EN*1173$^a$23; ἀ. καὶ καθαρός, of νοῦς, Id.*Metaph.*989$^b$15; τὰ ἐλάχιστα καὶ ἀ. πέρατα τῶν μηκῶν, of geometrical points, Epicur.*Ep.*1 p.17 U.: c. gen., εἰλικρινῶς Ἕλληνες καὶ ἀ. βαρβάρων Pl.*Mx.*245d; ἀ. πρὸς ἄλληλα Id.*Plt.*265e; ἀ. τινί Aret.*CD*2.3, Jul.*Or.*2.70b. Adv. -γῶς Iamb.*Myst.*1.9, Herm. ap.Stob.1.49.68; also -γί Hdn.*Epim.*254. II. *virgin*, Sch.E. *Or.*108. III. ἀ. βίβλοι rolls *containing a single author*, opp. συμμιγεῖς, Tz.*Proll.Ar.*

**ἀμιδάναι**· κρύψαι, Hsch.

**ἀμίδιον**, τό, Dim. of ἀμίς, Aeschin.Socr.43, S.E.*M.*1.234.

**ἀμιέρα**· ἀμμώδη, ἔρημα, Hsch. **ἀμιερεῖ**· δείξει, Id.

**ἄμιθα**, kind of *cake*, perh. = ἄμης, Anacr.139, *PHamb.*90.18 (iii A.D.).

**ἀμίθιος**· μωλῶν, Hsch.

**ἀμιθρέω, ἀμιθρός**, Ep. and Ion. metath. for ἀριθμέω, ἀριθμός, Nicoch.5 D., Call.*Cer.*86, *Fr.*339, Phoen.1.9, Herod.6.6, Simon.228.

**ἀμικτίσας**· αἰτήσας, χωρισάμενος, Hsch.

**ἀμικτομίαινον**, = ἄγνος, Ps.-Dsc.1.103.

**ἄμικτος**, ον, *unmingled, that will not mingle*, Emp.35.8; ἄ. βοή cries *that will not blend* or *harmonize*, A.*Ag.*321; ὡς ἄμικτον ἀνθρώποις ἐρᾶν λεόντων Babr.98.19. Adv. -τως, Sup. -τότατα Pl.*Phlb.*59c. II. *unmixed, pure*, βίος, ἡδονή, ib.50e, 61b:—ἀ. τινι *unmixed with* a thing, Id.*Plt.*310d; ἄμικτα κατὰ στίχον, of poems, *uniform* in metre e.g. of the Epic hexameter, Heph.*Poëm.*2. III. of persons, *not mingling with others, unsociable, savage*, of Centaurs and Cyclopes, S.*Tr.*1095, E.*Cyc.*429; δράκαινα Anaxil.22.3; τὸ ἄ., = ἀμιξία II, Hp. *Aër.*23; ἄ. πατήρ *morose*, E.*Fr.*500; φίλοις ἄ. καὶ πάσῃ πόλει ib.425; of laws and customs, ἄ. νόμιμα τοῖς ἄλλοις Th.1.77; πρὸς ἀλλήλω Pl. *Sph.*254d; ἄ. τινα ἑαυτοῖς καταστῆσαι *refuse to admit* him *to* their *society*, D.25.63. b. *not mixing the breed*, Pl.*Plt.*276a; ἄ. θυραίω ἀνδρὸς *not having intercourse with*.., Phint.ap.Stob.4.23.61. 2. of places, *uncivilized*, ἄ. αἶα *inhospitable* land, E.*IT*402; τόπος Isoc. 9.67. (Better written ἄμεικτος.)

**ἄμιλλα**, ης, ἡ, *contest for superiority, conflict*, τῶν νεῶν ἄμιλλαν.. ἰδέσθαι Hdt.7.44; ἄ. ἵππων *horse-race*, ib.196, cf. Pi.*O.*5.6, *I.*5(4).6; ῥιμφαρμάτοις ἁμίλλαις in *racing* of swift chariots, S.*OC*1063, cf. *El.* 861; ἄ. ἀγαθῶν ἀνδρῶν *contest* of brave men, D.20.108; μειρακίων Ar. *Eq.*556; χορῶν Pl.*Lg.*834e; of boat-*races*, *IG*2$^2$.1028.20, Pl.Com. 183. 2. c. gen. rei, ἰσχύος *trial* of strength, Pi.*N.*9.12 (pl.); πτερύγων ἁμίλλαις A.*Pr.*129; ποδοῖν, λόγων, φρονήματος, E.*IA*212, *Med.* 546, *Andr.*214; ἀρετῆς Pl.*Lg.*731b: c. gen. obj., ἄ. λέκτρων *contest for* marriage, E.*Hipp.*1141; ἔρωτος Gorg.*Hel.*5: abs., *eager desire*, Herod.6.68 (s.v.l.):—also ἄ. περί τινος Isoc.10.15; freq. in Poets with Adj., ἄ. φιλόπλουτος, πολύτεκνος *striving after* wealth or children, E. *IT*411, *Med.*557: with gen. in adjectival sense, ἄ. αἵματος, = αἱματόεσσα, Id.*Hel.*1155:—phrases: ἅμιλλαν τιθέναι, προτιθέναι *propose contest*, Id.*Andr.*1020, *Med.* l.c.; ἄ. ποιεῖσθαι *contend* eagerly, ὅκως.. Hdt.8.10; ἄ. ἐποιοῦντο they had a *race*, Th.6.32; ἄ. ποιεῖσθαι πρὸς ἀλλήλους Pl.*Lg.*830d; εἰς ἄ. ἔρχεσθαι, ἐξελθεῖν, E.*Tr.*621, *Hec.*226; πρὸς ἄ. ἐλθεῖν Id.*Med.*1083; ἄ. γίγνεται ὅπως.. *struggle* arises, Th.8.6.

**ἀμίλλακαν**· οἶνον (Theban), Hsch.

**ἁμιλλ-άομαι**: fut. -ήσομαι Ar.*Pax*950, Pl.*R.*349c: aor. ἡμιλλήθην E. (v. infr.), Th.6.31; later ἡμιλλησάμην Plu.*Arat.*3, Luc.*Par.*51, Aristid.1.127, 149 J., etc.: pf. ἡμίλλημαι E. (v. infr. II. 1):—*compete, vie, contend*, Ar. l.c., etc.; πρὸς ἀλλήλους Th. l.c.: c. dat. pers., Hdt.4. 71, E.*Andr.*127, etc.; πρός τινα Id.*HF*960: c. dat. rei, *contend in* or *with* a thing, ἁμιλληθεὶς λόγῳ Id.*Supp.*195, cf. *HF*1255; βίῳ *Hipp.*426; ἵπποις, τόξοις, etc., And.4.27, Pl.*R.*328a, cf. *Lg.*834a; περί τινος *about* or *for* a thing, Luc.*Charid.*20; περί τινι Pi.*N.*10.31; ἐπί or πρός τι, Pl.*Lg.*830e, 968b; ὑπέρ τινος Plb.5.86.8: ἀ. ὡς.. or ὅπως.., Pl.*R.* 349c, X.*HG*7.2.14: c. acc. cogn., ἀ. στάδιον Pl.*Lg.*833a. 2. in pass. sense, πόλλ' ἁμιλληθέντα *made subjects of contest*, E.*Fr.*812. 2. II. without idea of rivalry, *strive, hasten eagerly*, ἐπὶ τὸ ἄκρον X.*An.*3.4.44; πρός τι *to obtain* a thing, Pl.*R.*490a, Arist.*EN*1162$^b$8, al.; δεῦρ' ἁμιλλᾶται ποδί E.*Or.*456; σὲ τὴν ὄρεγμα δεινὸν ἡμιλλημένην Id.*Hel.*546: metaph., c. acc. cogn., ποῖον ἁμιλλᾶθῶ γόον; how shall I groan loud enough? ib.165; τόνδ' ἁμιλλῶμαι λόγον *Hec.*271. III. Hsch. has Act., ἁμιλλᾶν· ἐρίζειν, καὶ εἰς τάχος γράφειν. **-ημα**, ατος, τό, *conflict, struggle*, S.*El.*493; καθ' ἁμιλλάματα πρᾶτος *CIG* 5149*b* (Cyrene). **-ητέον**, *one must vie*, πρός τι Isoc.7.73; Socr.*Ep.* 31; τινί Isoc.*Ep.*7.7. **-ητήρ**, ῆρος, *racing*, τρόχους ἁμιλλητῆρας ἡλίου S.*Ant.*1065. **-ητήριος**, α, ον, *of contest*, ἵππος Philostr.*VA* 2.11, *Gym.*26; ἅρμα Aristid.*Or.*37(2).15; ἀγῶνες Men.Prot.p.1 D.:— τὸ ἁ. *place of contest*, Suid. **-ητικός**, ή, όν, *of* or *for contest*, Pl.*Sph.* 225a.

**ἄμιλλος**, ὁ, = ἅμιλλα, Doroth.ap.Phot.p.92 R. **ἁμιλλοφόρος**, Ar.*Fr.*42 D., perh. f.l. for -ότερος (cf. ἁμιλλότεροι· ἐπὶ πλέον ἐρίζοντες, Hsch.); sed potius leg. ἀμαλλοφόρος.

**ἀμίλλυκα**· δρέπανον (Elean), Hsch.

**ἀμίλτωτος**, ον, *not painted red*, λύχνος *PMag.Par.*1.2372, *PMag. Berol.*1.377, etc.

**ἀμιμητόβιοι**, οἱ, *the 'Inimitables'*, name of club, Plu.*Ant.*28.

**ἀμίμητος** [ῐ], ον, *inimitable*, χάριτες *AP*5.107 (Crin.); τινί *in* thing, Plu.*Per.*13, etc. Adv. -τως, *of inferior imitation*, opp. μιμητικῶς, Arist.*Po.*1460$^b$32; *superlatively*, Plu.*Nic.*1. II. *not imitated*, Id.2.53d.

**ἀμιναῖος** or **ἀμμιναῖος** οἶνος, an Italian wine, Dsc.5.19, *Gp.*4.1.3; made from the grape of that name, Gal.12.922:—hence **ἀμμινίζοντες** οἶνοι *Gp.*8.22.1.

**ἀμῖξαι**· οὐρῆσαι ἢ ἠχῆσαι ἢ ὀμίξαι, Hsch., *EM*83.36.

**ἀμιξία**, Ion. -ίη, ἡ, *a being* ἄμικτος, and so, I. *purity*, Thphr. *CP*4.16.2. II. of persons, *want of intercourse*, ἀλλήλων Th. 1.3; πρὸς ἅπαντας Luc.*Tim.*42; *unsocialleness*, Isoc.6.67; ἀμιξίη χρημάτων *want of* commercial *dealings*, Hdt.2.136; cf. ἀμειξία. 2. *abstinence from sexual intercourse*, Aristaenet.2.3.

**ἄμιξος**, ον, = ἄμικτος, πυρός *PLond.*2.256(a)11.

**ἄμιππος**, ον, *keeping up with horses*, i.e. *fleet as horse*, S.*Ant.* 985 (lyr.). II. ἅμιπποι, οἱ, *infantry mixed with cavalry*, Th.5. 57, X.*HG*7.5.23 (cj.), Arist.*Ath.*49.1, cf. Aristarch.ad Hdt.1.215 in *PAmh.*2.12. 2. *pair of horses* ridden by a postillion, Suid.

**ἀμίς**, ίδος, ἡ, *chamber-pot*, Hp.*Loc.Hom.*47, Ar.*V.*935, *Th.*633, etc., f.l. in A.*Supp.*842; prov., σιτία εἰς ἀμίδα μὴ ἐμβάλλειν 'cast not pearls before swine', Plu.2.12f; ἐς τὴν ἀμίδα ἐνουρεῖν 'to be suitably treated' (in contempt), Luc.*Merc.Cond.*4. (ἀμ- Ar.*Fr.*41 D.)

**ἀμίσαλλος**, ον, *unsociable*, expl. as = ἀμίσγαλλος, γέροντες Epic. ap.*Et.Gen.*

**ἀμίσαρος**· ἀκόρεστος, Hsch.

**ἀμισγής**, ές, poet. for ἀμιγής, Nic.*Al.*105.

**ἀμῑσής**, ές, *not hateful, agreeable*, Ph.2.70, Plu.2.10a: Comp. -έστερος *less troublesome*, X.*Eq.*8.9. Adv. -σῶς Ph.2.57.

**ἀμισθ-ί**, Adv. of ἄμισθος, *without reward* or *hire*, Archil.41, E.*Tr.* 409, D.24.99; *rent-free*, *SIG*344 (Teos); χρημάτων καὶ δόξης ἀ. *without reward* of money or honour, Plu.*Arist.*3; ἀ. ἐπαινεθέντες *only paid with* praise, Brut.*Ep.*38; ἀ. θεάσασθαι *without paying*, Plu.*CG* 12. [ῐ Archil. l.c.] **-ία**, ἡ, *non-receipt of pay*, App.*Hann.*17; of *free teaching*, Olymp.*in Alc.*p.140 C. **-ος**, ον, *without hire* or *pay*, opp. ἔμμισθος: hence, 1. Pass., *unpaid, unhired*, ἀοιδή A. *Ag.*979, cf. S.*Fr.*829, etc.; λύπη, ἄ. ξυνέμπορος A.*Ch.*733. Adv. -θως, Cret. -τως *GDI*5125 (Oaxos). 2. Act., *without paying*, Luc.*DMeretr.*12.1. **-ωτος**, ον, *not let, bringing no return*, οἶκος D. 30.6, cf. *BCH*35.14 (Delos). II. *unhired*, D.S.18.21.

**ἀμιστύλλευτος**, ον, = sq., metaph., θεοί Dam.*Pr.*182; κραδίη Procl. *H.*7.11.

**ἀμίστυλλος**, ον, *not cut into small pieces*, Call.*Aet.Fr.*7.35 P.

**ἄμισχος**, ον, *without stalk*, Thphr.*HP*1.10.7, 3.7.5.

**ἄμιτρα**· μικρά (Cret.), Hsch.

**ἄμιτρος**, ον, *without head-band* or *girdle*, παῖδες ἄ. girls *who have not yet put on the woman's girdle*, i.e. *unmarriageable*, Call.*Dian.*14.

**ἀμιτροχίτωνες**, οἱ, *wearing no* μίτρη (q.v.) *with the* χιτών, epith. of Lycian warriors, Il.16.419; of women, Nonn.*D.*48.507.

**ἀμίτρωτος**, ον, *not bound with a head-band*, Nonn.*D.*35.220.

**ἀμιχθαλόεις**, εσσα, εν, = ἄμικτος III, *inhospitable*, epith. of Lemnos in Il.24.753, *h.Ap.*36: otherwise expl. as *smoky*, from the volcano Mosychlos, cf. ὀμίχλη. (Cypr. acc. to Sch. Il. l.c.)

**ἀμμ-**, poet. for ἀναμ-, e.g. **ἄμμιγα, ἀμμίγνυμι**, = ἀναμ-, Tim. *Pers.*37, B.*Fr.*16, etc.

**ἅμμα**, ατος, τό, (ἅπτω) *anything tied* or *made to tie*: hence, 1. *knot*, Hp.*Fist.*4; ἅ. λύειν, ἀπάπτειν Hdt.4.98; ἅ. ποιεῖσθαι X.*Eq.* 5.1. 2. *noose, halter*, E.*Hipp.*781. 3. *cord*, Id.*Ba.*696, cf. Hp.*Steril.*244, etc.; ἅ. παρθενίας maiden *girdle*, *AP*7.182 (Mel.), cf. 164 (Antip.), imitated in *Epigr.Gr.*248.8 (Philomelium). 4. *link* of chain, Them.*Or.*2.32d. 5. in pl., *clinches* in wrestling, Gal. 6.143, cf. Plu.*Fab.*23; of the *wrestler's arms*, Id.*Alc.*2. 6. *measure of length* (like our *chain*), = 40 πήχεις, Hero *Geom.*23.14, al., *POxy.*669 (iii A.D.). II. *that which kindles*, Ph.2.504.

**ἀμμά**, ἡ, *mother*, *EM*84.24; *foster-mother, nurse*, *SIG*$^2$868 (Calymna):—also **ἀμμάς**, ἡ, *EM*84.26, *BGU*449 (iii A.D.); epith. of Rhea and Demeter, Hsch.

**ἀμμαλλῆς**· ἀνοστία, Hsch. **Ἀμμαλῶ**· ἑορτὴ ἀγομένη Διί, Id. **ἀμμαμηθάδης**, = ἀμαμινθάδες (q.v.), Id. **ἀμμάξαι**· αἰωρῆσαι καὶ κρεμάσαι, ἢ ἀποπῆξαι, Id.

**ἀμματ-ίζω**, (ἅμμα) *tie, bind*, in Pass., Orib.49.21.4 (prob. Heliod.),

Heliod.ib.48.28.4, Apollod.*Poliorc.*180.13. **-ιον,** *τό,* Dim. of ἅμμα I.1, Gal.14.794. **-ισμός,** *ὁ, tieing, knotting,* Heliod.ap.Orib. 48.43.1, cf. 48.28.5.

⊛**ἀμμεδαπάν·** *τὴν ἐγχώριον,* Hsch.

**ἀμμεμίξεται, ἀμμένω,** poet. for *ἀναμεμίξεται, ἀναμένω.* **ἄμμες,** Aeol. and Ep. for *ἡμεῖς*: acc. *ἄμμε*: gen. *ἀμμέων*: dat. *ἄμμι(ν)* Hom., etc.; *ἄμμεσιν,* Alc.100. **ἀμμέσον,** poet. for *ἀνὰ μέσον,* Hes. **ἀμμέτερος** and **ἄμμος,** = *ἡμέτερος,* Alc.105 A, B.

**ἄμμι,** v. *ἄμι.* II. v. *ἄμμες.*

⊛**ἀμμία,** Ion. **-ίη,** *ἡ, mother* or *nurse,* Herod.1.7, *EM*84.26.

**ἀμμιάξαι·** *ἀποπνίξαι,* Hsch.

⊛**ἄμμινος,** *η, ον,* = *ψάμμινος, sandy, νῆσοι Peripl.M.Rubr.*4.

**ἀμμιρός·** *πεπληρωμένος,* Hsch. **ἀμμισκόμιστον·** *συγκομιστὸν ἄρτον,* Id. ⊛**ἀμμίτης** (sc. *λίθος*), *ὁ,* also ⊛**ἀμμῖτις,** *ἡ, sandstone,* Plin. *HN*37.168.

**ἀμμο-βάτης,** *ὁ,* = *ἀμμοδύτης,* Ael.*NA*6.51. ⊛**-γειος,** *α, ον, in sandy soil, ἀγκυροβόλια Peripl.M.Rubr.*24. **-δρομος,** *ὁ, sandy place for racing, AB*208. ⊛**-δύτης,** *ὁ, sand-burrower,* a kind of *serpent,* Philum.*Ven.*22.1.; *διψάς* Str.17.1.21. **-δύτωρ,** *ορος,* (prob. for *-δυότας* codd.) *burrowing in sand, πάγουρος AP*6.196 (Stat. Flacc.). [ῠ, but cf. *χηραμοδύτης, σισυρνοδύτης.*] **-κονία,** *ἡ, sand mixed with lime, cement,* Str.5.4.6, cf. *Gp.*2.27.4. **-κοπρηγὸν** *πλοῖον* ship *carrying sand and manure, Sammelb.*423. **-νιτρον,** *τό, potash mixed with sand,* fused together to produce glass, Plin.*HN*36.194. **-πλῠσία,** *ἡ, sand-washing* for gold, Zos.Alch. p.240 B. **-πλυτα,** *τά, results of such washing,* Anon.Alch.p.37 B.

⊛**ἀμμορία** (A), Ion. **-ίη,** *ἡ,* poet. for **ἀμορία** (not in use), *Ζεὺς οἶδε μοῖράν τ' ἀμμορίην τ' ἀνθρώπων* what is man's fate and *what is not,* or their good fortune and their *bad,* Od.20.76, cf. *AP*9.284 (Crin.).

⊛**ἀμμορία** (B), Ion. **-ίη,** *ἡ,* = *δμορία,* Epigr.ap.D.7.40.

**ἄμμορος,** *ον,* poet. for *ἄμοιρος* (q. v.), *without share of, without lot in,* c. gen., *ἄμμορος.. λοετρῶν Ὠκεανοῖο* Il.18.489, Od.5.275; *καλῶν* Pi.*O.*1.84; *πάντων* S.*Ph.*182 (lyr.); *τέκνων ἄ. bereft of* children, E. *Hec.*421; *οὐκ ἄ. ἀμφὶ πάλᾳ κυναγέτας* Pi.*N.*6.14; *ἄ. ἐσθλῆς ἐλπίδος IG* 14.1942.11. 2. later, simply, *free from, without, ἄ. κακότητος* Q.S.1.430. II. abs., *ill-fated,* Il.6.408, 24.773. (*ἀ-* priv., *smor-,* cf. *κάσμορος.*)

**ἄμμος** (A), or **ἅμμος** (cf. *ὕφ-αμμος*), *ἡ, sand,* Pl.*Phd.*110a, etc. II. *sandy ground, racecourse,* X.*Mem* 3.3.6. (Related to *ἄμαθος* as *ψάμμος* to *ψάμαθος.*)

**ἄμμος** (B), Aeol. = *ἁμός* (A), q. v.

**ἀμμο-σκοπία,** *ἡ, divination by sand,* title of Orphic work, prob. in Suid. s. v. *Ὀρφεύς.* **-τροφος,** *ον, growing in sand, AP*4.1.20 (Mel.).

**Ἀμμοῦς,** epith. of Zeus, Arist.*Fr.*530.

**ἀμμο-φᾰνής,** *ές, sandy, χθὼν Epigr.Gr.*430 (Egypt). **-χρῡσος,** *ὁ,* gem resembling *sand veined with gold,* Plin.*HN*37.188. **-χωσία,** *ἡ, sand-bath,* Herod.Med.ap.Orib.10.8 tit., Antyll.ap.Aët.3.9. ⊛**-χωστος,** *ον, sanded up* or *over,* Eust.690.5.

**ἀμμωδέω,** suggested as error for *αἱμωδέω,* Hermog.*Meth.*3.

**ἀμμώδης,** *ες, sandy, gravelly,* Arist.*HA*547$^{b}$14, 569$^{a}$29, Thphr. *CP*2.4.1, D.S.17.50, etc.; *οὖρον* Hp.*Coac.*478.

**Ἄμμων,** *ωνος, ὁ,* the Libyan *Zeus, Ζεὺς Ἄ.* Pi.*P.*4.16: said to be Egyptian, Hdt.2.42; *Ἄμμωνος ⟨κέρας⟩,* = *κορωνόπους,* Ps.-Dsc.2.130, etc.:—fem. Adj. **Ἀμμωνίς,** *ίδος, Libyan, Ἀ. ἕδρα* seat *of Ammon,* i. e. Libya, E.*Alc.*114, *El.*734: Subst. *Ἀ., ἡ,* name of state-trireme, Din.*Fr.*14.2:—also **Ἀμμωνιάς,** *άδος,* Phot. s. v. *Πάραλος*: **Ἀμμωνιακός,** *ή, όν, ἀπάτη AP*7.687 (Pall.), esp. *Ἀ. ἅλας* kind of *rock-salt,* Dinon 15, cf. Dsc.5.109, *Gp.*6.6.1, *PMag.Lond.*46.397:—⊛**-κή,** *ἡ, Ferula marmarica,* Ps.-Dsc.3.84:—**-κόν,** *τό, gum-ammoniacum,* Dsc.3.48.

**ἀμμωχεῖν·** *ἀργεῖν,* Hsch.

⊛**ἄμνᾱμος,** *ὁ, descendant,* Lyc.144, 872, etc.:—also ⊛**ἀμνάμων** (A), *ονος, ὁ,* Poll.3.19, cf. *EM*84.43.

**ἀμνάμων** (B), Dor. for *ἀμνήμων.*

⊛**ἀμνάς,** *άδος, ἡ,* fem. of *ἀμνός, lamb,* Lxx *Ge.*21.28, al., J.*AJ*7.7.3.

**ἀμνάσει, ἀμνάσειε,** Dor. for *ἀναμνήσ-.* **ἀμναστέω, ἄμναστος,** Dor. for *ἀμνηστ-.*

**ἀμνεῖος,** *α, ον, of lamb, ἀ. χλαῖνα lambskin* cloak, Theoc.24.62:—also **ἀμναῖος,** *PRev.Laws*97.7 (iii B.C.). II. **ἀμνειός** or **ἄμνιος** (sc. *χιτών, ὑμήν*), *ὁ, inner membrane* surrounding the foetus, Sor.1.58, Gal.*UP*15.4: also in neut. form **ἀμνεῖον,** *τό, Hippiatr.*14; cf. *ἀμνίον.* **ἀμνεύς,** *έως, ὁ, south-east wind,* Arist.*Vent.*973$^{b}$7.

⊛**ἀμνή,** Dor. **ἀμνά,** *ἡ,* fem. of *ἀμνός, ewe-lamb, GDI*3639 (Cos), 4990.11 (Gortyn), Orph.*A.*319.

**ἀμνημόνευτος,** *ον, unmentioned,* Plb.2.35.4, Plu.*Cam.*29; *τὸ μετὰ τὴν ζωὴν ἀ.* Phld.*Mort.*36; *impossible to be remembered,* Gal.8.856; *ἐξ ἀ. χρόνου POxy.*1915 (vi A.D.); *unheeded,* E.*IT*1419. II. Act., = *ἀμνήμων, unmindful,* D.L.1.86, Numen.ap.Eus.*PE*14.7.

**ἀμνημονέω,** A.*Eu.*24, etc.: fut. *-ήσω* Isoc.12.253: aor. *ἠμνημόνησα* Id.5.72, X.*Smp.*8.1, etc.:—*to be unmindful,* abs., A. l. c., E.*Or.*216: c. acc., *forget,* D.6.12, 7.19, Aeschin.3.221: also c. gen., D.18.285: freq. in sense, *make no mention of,* E.*IT*361, Th.3.40, Lys.31.25; *ἀ. τι περί τινος* Th.5.18; Pass., Max.Tyr.8.5:—dependent clauses either in partic., *ἀμνημονεῖς σαυτὸν δρῶντα; do you forget* your doing? Pl. *Tht.*207d; or in relative clause with *ὅτι..,* Id.*R.*474d. ⊛**ἀμνημοσύνη,** *ἡ, forgetfulness,* E.*Ion* 1100 (lyr.).

**ἀμνημοῦντες·** *ἀθυμοῦντες,* Phot.p.93 R. (*-ύονες* Hsch.).

⊛**ἀμνήμων,** Dor. **ἀμνάμων,** *ον,* gen. *ονος, unmindful, forgetful,* Pi.*I.*7(6).17, S.*Fr.*920, Pl.*Ti.*88b; *τινός of* a person or thing, *θεῶν* A.*Th.* 606, cf. E.*HF*1397, Antipho 2.1.7; *unmindful of kindness, ungra[teful],* Arist.*EN*1167$^{b}$27. 2. Pass., *forgotten, not mentioned,* E.[*I*]64. II. *Ἀμνήμονες, οἱ,* council of 60 at Cnidus, Plu.2.292a.

**ἀμνησία,** *ἡ,* = *λήθη, forgetfulness,* Lxx *Wi.*14.26, *Si.*11.25. *decree of amnesty, POxy.*1668.18 (iii A.D.).

⊛**ἀμνησι-κᾰκέω,** *forgive and forget, bestow amnesty on, τινός* N[ic.] Dam.*Vit.Caes.*29:—Pass., *enjoy an amnesty,* D.S.18.56. **-κάκ[ητ]ος,** *ον, not maliciously remembered, ἀμνησικάκητον ποιεῖσθαι τὴν ἁμα[ρ]τίαν* Plb.39.7.5. **-κᾰκία,** *ἡ, forgivingness,* Lxx 3*Ma.*3.21. **-κᾰκο[ς],** *ον, forgiving,* Nic.Dam.p.110 D. Adv. *-κῶς* D.S.31.8.

⊛**ἀμνήστευτος,** *ἡ, unwooed; not sought in lawful wedlock* (but a concubine), E.*Fr.*815: neut. pl. as Adv., *without honourable wooing,* Ps.-Phoc.198.

**ἀμνηστ-έω,** Dor. **ἀμναστέω,** = *ἀμνημονέω,* only pres., *to be un[]mindful, forget,* S.*El.*482 (lyr.), Arat.847:—Pass., *to be forgotten,* Th.1.20. **-ία,** Ion. **-ίη,** *ἡ, forgetfulness, εἶναι ἐν ἀ.* Pl.*Mx.*239e; *ἀ. ἔχειν τινός* Heraclit.*Ep.*2, cf. Lxx *Wi.*19.4, Plu.2.612d, etc. 2. esp. *amnesty, τῶν προγεγενημένων ἐγκλημάτων SIG*633.36 (Milet., ii B.C.), cf. Str.7.2.1, Nic.Dam.*Vit.Caes.*28, Ph.2.75, Plu.*Cic.*42, *Ant.*14. II. *failure to mention* thing, *passing* it *over* Corn.*Rh.* p.371 H. ⊛**-ος,** *ον, forgotten,* Theoc.16.42, Lyc.1230. 2. Act., *forgetful,* Phryn.*PS*p.20 B.

**Ἀμνιάς,** *ἡ,* epith. of Eileithyia, Ruf.*Onom.*229; cf. sq.

**ἀμνίον** (not so well *ἄμνιον*), *τό, bowl in which the blood of victims was caught,* Od.3.444. 2. *inner membrane round the foetus,* Emp.71; cf. *ἀμνειός.* II. Dim. of *ἀμνός,* Hermipp.3 (*Ἄμνιος* as pr. n. wrongly *Et.Gen.*).

⊛**ἀμνίς,** *ίδος, ἡ,* = *ἀμνή,* Theoc.5.3.

**ἀμνόα·** *πρόβατον, οἱ δὲ ἀμνός,* Hsch.

⊛**ἀμνο-κόπος·** *ποιμήν,* Hsch. **-κῶν,** *ὁ,* (*κοέω*) *sheep-minded,* i.e. *simpleton,* Ar.*Eq.*264.

⊛**ἀμνός,** *ὁ, lamb,* S.*Fr.*751, Ar.*Av.*1559; *ἀμνοὶ τοὺς τρόπους lambs* in temper, Id.*Pax*935: metaph., *ὁ ἀ. τοῦ θεοῦ Ev.Jo.*1.36: fem. (cf. *ἀμνή, ἀμνίς*), Theoc.5.144, 149, *AP*5.205.—Oblique cases usu. formed from *ἀρήν,* q. v. (For *ἀβνός,* i. e. *ag$^{w}$nos,* cf. Lat. *agnus.*)

**ἀμνοφόρος,** *ον,* f.l. for *μαννοφόρος,* Theoc.11.41.

**ἀμογ-ητί,** Adv. of sq., *without toil* or *effort,* Il.11.637, Call.*Dian.* 25, D.H.*Dem.*8, Luc.*Nav.*21, Plot.6.2.21, etc. **-ητος,** *ον,* (*μογέω*) *untiring, h.Hom.*8.3. **-ῳ·** *ἀκοπιάστῳ,* Hsch.

**ἁμόθεν,** Ion. **ἀμόθεν,** Adv.: (*ἁμός*):—*from some place or other, τῶν ἁμόθεν γε, θεά,.. εἰπὲ καὶ ἡμῖν* Od.1.10; *ἁ. γέ ποθεν from some quarter or other,* Pl.*Grg.*492d, *Lg.*798b; *ἁ.* alone, Opp.*C.*1.401.

**ἁμόθι** (cf. *ἅμα*), *together, in common,* Decr.Laced.ap.Th.5.77 (codd. *ἀμοθεί,* expl. by Hdn.Gr.2.464 as *without strife,* cf. *μόθος*).

**ἁμοῖ,** Adv., (*ἁμός* B) *somewhither, ἁμοιγέποι AB* 04.

**ἀμοιβ-άδιος,** *α, ον,* = *ἀμοιβαῖος,* Opp.*C.*4.349, Q.S.5.65, *AP*12.238 (Strat.). **-ᾰδίς,** Adv., (*ἀμοιβή*) *by turns, alternately, ἀ. ἄλλοθεν ἄλλος* one after another, Theoc.1.34; *ἀ. ἀνέρος ἀνὴρ ἑζόμενος* A.R.4.199, cf. Nonn.*D.*24.227:—also **-αδόν,** Parm.1.19, A.R.2.1226, Ti. Locr.68e, Them.*Or.*17.215b, Agath.2.21. II. *in turn, again, Epigr.Gr.*998.9. ⊛**-άζω,** *exchange, τὰς ἐμπορίας* Men.Prot. p.22 D. **-αῖος,** *ον,* also *α, ον, giving like for like, retributive, δεῖπνα* Pi.*O.*1.39; *retributive, νέμεσις, φόνος, AP*10.123 (Aesop.), Opp.*C.*2.485. Adv. *-ως alternately,* Luc.*Am.*9. II. *interchanging, reciprocal,* Emp.30.3; *ἀ. βιβλία interchanged* letters, Hdt.6.4; *ἀ. χάρις exchange of* favours, A.R.3.82 (but *ἀ. εὐνή ambiguous* (half-human, half-animal), 2.1241):—*τὰ ἀ. dialogue* in Trag., Pl.*R.*394b; of the responsion of choric odes, Plu.*Pomp.*48; *ἀ. ἀοιδά* Theoc.8.31, cf. Il. 1.604; *answering as in dialogue,* Sch.Ar.*Pl.*253, 487. **-άς,** *άδος, ἡ,* pecul. fem. of foreg., *χλαῖναν.. ἥ οἱ παρεκέσκετ' ἀμοιβάς* which lay beside him *as change of raiment,* Od.14.521; *in succession, μάχαιρα* Nonn.*D.*28.135. **-εύς,** *έως, ὁ, exchanger, γηπέδων* Lyc. 617. ⊛**-ή,** *ἡ,* (*ἀμείβω*) *requital, recompense,* Hom. only in Od.; *σοὶ δ' ἄξιον ἔστιν ἀμοιβῆς* Od.1.318; *ἄλλοισι δίδου χαρίεσσαν ἀ... ἑκατόμβης* 3.58; *εὖ ἔρδοντι κακὴν ἀπέδωκας ἀ.* Thgn.1263, cf. E.*Or.* 467; *γλυκεῖαν μόχθων ἀ.* Pi.*N.*5.48; *ἀγαναῖς ἀ. τινὰ τίνεσθαι* to requite him *by like return,* Id.*P.*2.24; *χαρίεσσα ἀμοιϝά GDI*3119c (Corinth); *οἵας ἀ. ἐξ Ἰάσονος κυρεῖ* E.*Med.*23; *ἀμοιβαὶ τῶν θυσιῶν* Pl.*Smp.*202e; *retribution, ἔργων ἀντ' ἀδίκων χαλεπὴν ἐπέθηκεν ἀ.* Hes.*Op.*334: pl., *αἰωνίαις ἀ. βασανισθησόμενοι* Phld.*D.*1.19. 2. *repayment, compensation, τείσουσι βοῶν ἐπιεικέ' ἀ.* Od.12.382. 3. *that which is given in exchange, τῷ σκυτοτόμῳ ἀντὶ τῶν ὑποδημάτων ἀ. γίνεται κατ' ἀξίαν* Arist.*EN*1163$^{b}$35; *τὴν ἀ. ποιητέον κατὰ τὴν προαίρεσιν* 1164$^{b}$1; *δέκα μνῶν ἀ.* Plu.*Lyc.*9. 4. *answer, ἀσχήμων ἐν τῇ ἀ.* Hdt.7. 160. II. *change, exchange, τὰς ἀ. ποιεῖσθαι* Str.11.4.4; of money, Plu.*Luc.*2. III. *change, alternation, κακῶν* E.*El.*1147; *ἑορτῶν* Pl.*Lg.*653d. 2. *transformation,* D.L.9.8. **-ήδην,** A.R.2.1071, Orph.*L.*691. **-ηδίς,** Adv., (*ἀμοιβή*) *alternately, in succession,* Il.18.506, Od.18.310, *h.Cer.*326. **-ηδόν,** Hp.*Ep.*17; read by Aristarch. in Il.18.506. **-ιμαῖος,** *α, ον,* in neut. sg., *requital, reward, IGRom.*4.1348 (Lydia). ⊛**-ός,** *ὁ, one who exchanges, ἀμοιβοί soldiers that relieve others,* Il.13.793. II. Adj. *in requital* or *exchange for, νέκυν νεκρῶν ἀ. ἀντιδούς* S.*Ant.*1067; *ἀ. ἑῆς θρέψε διδασκαλίης AP*7.341 (Procl.). 2. *alternating, κληῖδες,* of Day and Night, Parm.1.14.

**ἀμοιμός,** = *ἀμοιβός,* Theognost.*Can.*65.2.

**ἄμοινα,** *ἡ,* dub. sens., *IG*5(2).4.22 (Tegea, iv B.C.).

**ἄμοιος·** *κακός* (Sicel), Hsch.; cf. *σμοῖος.*

**ἀμοιρ-έω,** *have no lot* or *share in, ὑγροῦ Placit.*1.3.1, cf. Phld.*Rh.*1.

S., Ph.2.9, Plu.*Alex.*23, etc.; *get no benefit from*, c. gen., Jul.Laod. Cat.Cod.Astr.4.104: also in Pass., c. gen., Steph. *in Hp.*1.222. **-ημα**, τό, *loss, want*, Hsch. (cod. ἀμύρ-). **-ία**, ἡ, = foreg., Ael.*NA*6.65. **-ος**, ον, (cf. ἄμμορος) *without lot* or *share in* thing, ...νός A.*Th.*733, *Eu.*353, etc.; mostly of those *bereft of* some good, τῶν καλῶν καὶ ἀγαθῶν ἄ. Pl.*Smp.*202d; τῆς τοῦ θείου συνουσίας Id.*Phd.* 83e; τῆς ἀρετῆς Arist.*EN*1102ᵇ12:—rarely, *freed from* some evil, ἄ. ...βρεως, μεταβολῆς, Pl.*Smp.*181c, *Plt.*269e; τοῦ γήρως Isoc.9.71. 2. abs., *portionless*, E.*Ph.*610, Pl.*Smp.*197d:—of things, ἄχωρα καὶ ἄ. *Tab. Defix.*96.18, 97.30. 3. *exempt from fate*, *Trag.Adesp.*248. II. c. gen. pers., τῶν κάτωθεν θεῶν *having no portion with* them, S.*Ant.* 1071.

**ἀμοίχευτος**, ον, *not born in adultery*, παῖδες Ps.-Callisth.1.21 (cod. Leid.).

**ἀμολγ-άδες** βόες, *milch-kine*, S.*Ichn.*5. **-άζει**· μεσημβρίζει, Hsch. **-αῖος**, α, ον, (ἀμέλγω) *made with milk*, μᾶζα ἀ. Hes.*Op.* 590; also expl. as = ἀκμαία (from ἀμολγός, Achaean for ἀκμή), bread *of the best flour*, Ath.3.115a, cf. Eust.1018.21. 2. *full of milk*, μαστός *AP*7.657 (Leon.). **-εύς**, έως, ὁ, *milk-pail*, Theoc.8.87, *AP*9.224 (Crin.). **-ή**, ἡ, *milking*, Hdn.Gr.1.310: but **ἀμόλγη**, ἡ, = ἀμόργη, *Gloss.* *-ιον, τό, *milk-pail*, Theoc.25.106; also ἀμολγαῖον, Sch.Luc.*Hes.*4.

*ἀμολγός, ὁ, Hom. always in the phrase νυκτὸς ἀμολγῷ, usu. of *dead* of night, Il.11.173, 15.324, cf. *h.Merc.*7; also of evening twilight, Il.22.317 (when Venus is seen), and morning twilight, ib.28 (when Sirius rises in autumn); ἱερᾶς νυκτὸς ἀμολγὸν A.*Fr.*69; ἀμολγός alone, Orph.*H.*34.12, f.l. in E.*Fr.*781.6:—as Adj., νύξ ib.104. (Derived by Eust.1018.21 from ἀμολγός, Achaean for ἀκμή, but more prob. = *milking-time*.)

*ἀμόλυντος, ον, (μολύνω) *undefiled*, Lxx *Wi.*7.22, X.Eph.2.9, Muson.*Fr.*18Bp.105 H., Arr.*Epict.*4.11.8; παρθένος *IG*14.264 (Agrigentum). II. Act., *not leaving any stain*, κινεῖν μέχρι ἀμολύντου Crito ap.Gal.12.487, cf. Antyll.ap.Orib.9.24.4, Olymp.*in Mete.*307.1.

**ἀμόμηλις**· ἄπιος, ἀχράς, Hsch.

**ἀμόμφητος**, f.l. in A.*Ch.*510. **ἄμομφος**, ον, (μομφή) *blameless*, A.*Eu.*475; πρὸς ὑμῶν ib.678. II. Act., *having nothing to complain of*, cj. Robortellus for ἄμορφος, ib.413.

**ἀμονάδιστος**, ον, *not reduced to a unit*, Dam.*Pr.*117.

*ἀμόρα, ἡ, *sweet cake*, Philet.ap.Ath.14.646d.

**ἀμορβ-αῖος**, ον, epith. of χαράδραι, Nic.*Th.*28,489, expl. by Sch. as *rustic, pastoral*, or *dark*. **-άς**, άδος, ἡ, fem. of ἀμορβός: ἀμορβάδες Νύμφαι in A.R.3.881 (acc. to Sch.) *rural* or *attendant* Nymphs. **-εύς**, έως, ὁ, = ἀμορβός, Opp.*C.*3.295. *-εύω, *follow, attend*, c. dat., Nic.*Fr.*90:—Med., *let follow, make follow*, Id.*Th.* 349:—ἀμορβέω, Antim.23. **-ίτης**, ὁ, Sicel for ἀμόρα, Ath.14. 646f; cf. ἀμοργίτης. *-ός, ὁ, *follower, attendant*, Call.*Dian.*45: esp. *herdsman, shepherd*, Id.*Hec.*6, Nic.*Th.*49, Opp.*C.*1.132. II. as Adj., *dark*, Sch.Nic.*Th.*28; ἀπὸ ἀμορβῷ is v.l. for ἀμολγῷ, Hom.

**ἀμόργεια**· χρώματος εἶδος, ἀπὸ νήσου Ἀμοργοῦντος, Suid.

**ἀμοργεύς**, έως, ὁ, *one who presses olives*, Poll.1.222.

**ἀμόργη**, ἡ, (ἀμέργω) *watery part which runs out when olives are pressed*, Hp.*Aph.*7.45, Thphr.*CP*6.8.3, Dsc.1.102. 2. kind of *dye* (as expl. of ἀμόργινος, q.v.), Sch.Ar.*Lys.*150. II. = ἀμοργίς, Sch.Aeschin.1.97.

*ἀμόργης, ου, ὁ, = foreg. I. 1, Arist.*Col.*796ᵃ27.

**ἀμοργίδιον**, τό, Dim. of ἀμοργίς, dub. l. in Paus.Gr.*Fr.*47 (leg. ἀμόργινα).

**ἀμόργινος**, ον, *made of* ἀμοργίς, χιτώνια Ar.*Lys.*150, Pl.*Ep.*363a; χιτών Antiph.153, *IG*2.754.10; κάλυμμα Clearch.25; τὰ ἀ. (sc. ἱμάτια) Eup.241, Aeschin.1.97:—also expl. as pr. n., *made in Amorgos*, Poll.7.74; or *purple*, St.Byz. s. v. Ἀμοργός, *EM*129.15, cf. 86.16, Sch.Ar.*Lys.*150.

**Ἀμόργιον**, τό, = Ἀμοργός, Charax 44.

**ἀμοργίς**, ίδος, ἡ, *stalks of mallow* (*Malva silvestris*), used like hemp or flax, ἄλοπος ἀ. Ar.*Lys.*735: acc. ἀμοργιν, v.l. ἀμοργίδα, ib.737. (Perh. from the pr. n. Ἀμοργός as place of growth.) II. proparox. ἄμοργις, εως, ἡ, = ἀμόργη, Hdn.Gr.1.87.

**ἀμοργίτας** (i.e. ἀμορϝ-, cf ἀμορβίτης)· πλακοῦντας, Hsch. **ἄμοργμα**· σύλλεγμα, ἄρτυμα, Id.

**ἀμοργός** (A), ὁ, (ἀμέργω) *one who squeezes* or *drains*, ἀμοργοί, πόλεως ὄλεθροι Cratin.214. 2. ἀνέμων λαμπτῆρας ἀμοργούς lanterns *which protect* [the light] *from* winds, Emp.84. II. proparox. ἄμοργος (v.l. ἄμεργος), = ἀμόργη, Ph.*Bel.*86.34, al.

**ἀμοργός** (B), ὁ, = ἀμοργίς, Cratin.96, cf. Paus.Gr.*Fr.*47, Harp.

**Ἀμοργός**, ὁ, *the island of Amorgos*, Heraclid.*Pol.*47, etc.:—Adj. **Ἀμόργιος**, *IG*1.244, 2.17, etc.:—also **Ἀμοργῖνος**, Suid. s. v. Σιμωνίδης Κρίνεω; **Ἀμοργίτης**, Nic.Dam.p.37 D.

**Ἀμοργοῦς**, οῦντος, ὁ, = foreg., Suid. s. v. ἀμόργεια, q. v.

**ἀμορία**, ἡ, v. ἀμμορία.

*ἀμορίτης, ὁ, ἄρτος, = ἀμόρα, Lxx 1*Ch.*16.3.

**ἀμόρξαι**, = ὀμόρξαι, Hsch.

**ἄμορος**, ον, = ἄμοιρος, c. gen., τέκνων E.*Med.*1395; ὠδίνων *AP*7. 465 (Heraclit.). II. abs., *unlucky, wretched*, cj. Pors. for ἄμοιρος in S.*OT*248.

**ἀμόρρωτον**· ἀθάνατον, Hsch.

*ἀμορφ-ία, ἡ, *formlessness*, Thphr.*Metaph.*33; ὕλης Herm.ap.Stob. 1.11.2, cf. Plot.6.7.20. II. *unshapeliness, unsightliness*, E.*Or.* 391, Arist.*Ph.*190ᵇ15. **-ος**, ον, *misshapen, unsightly*, γυνή Hdt. 1.196; γῆρας Thgn.1021; στολήν γ' ἄμορφον ἀμφὶ σῶμ' ἔχεις E.*Hel.* 554: metaph., μῦθος Pl.*Lg.*752a: Sup. ἀμορφέστατος (as if from ἀμορφής) Hdt. l.c.: regul. Comp. -ότερος X.*Smp.*8.17: Sup. -ότατος Plu.*Mar.*2, etc. Adv. -φως *uglily*, Luc.*Am.*41. II. *without form, shapeless*, Pl.*Ti.*51a: c. gen., ἄ. ἐκείνων ἁπασῶν τῶν ἰδεῶν *without partaking of* their *form*, ib.50d; ἡ ὕλη τὸ ἄ. ἔχει πρὶν λαβεῖν τὴν μορφήν Arist.*Ph.*191ᵃ10. III. metaph., *degrading*, Pl.*Lg.* 855c. **-όω**, *disfigure*, πρόσωπον δάκρυσι Sch.Il.2.269. **-ύνω**, = foreg., Antim.72. **-ωτος**, ον, *not formed, unwrought*, S.*Fr.*249; *without form*, θεός Procl.*in R.*1.40 K.; ἀ. καὶ ἀσχημάτιστος ὕλα Ti. Locr.94a, cf. Plot.6.7.3; *unfigured* of stars in no constellation, Ptol. *Alm.*7.5. Adv. ἀμορφώτως Procl.*in Prm.*p.780 S.

**ἀμός** (A) or **ἀμός** [ᾰ], ἡ, όν, Aeol. ἄμμος Alc.105A, *Milet.*3 No. 152.35, = ἡμέτερος (cf. ὑμός for ὑμέτερος, σφός for σφέτερος), A.D.*Pron.* 111.18), freq. used for ἐμός, Il.8.178, Od.11.166, etc.; esp. in Dor., Pi.*P.*3.41, 4.27, Theoc.5.108; Lacon., Ar.*Lys.*1181; Cretan, *GDI* 4952*D*23, etc.; Sicilian, *IG*14.952 (Agrigentum); also Trag., A.*Th.* 417, *Ch.*428, S.*El.*279, *Ph.*1314, etc. (Written ἀμός when = ἐμός by Demetr. ad Il.6.414; but the distn. is not observed.)

*ἀμός (B), [ᾰ], old word equiv. to τις, only in Adv. forms ἀμοῦ, ἀμῆ, ἀμοῖ, ἀμῶς, ἀμόθεν, ἀμόθι, and in compds. as οὐδαμός, Hdn.Gr.1. 169. (*sm*-, cf. Goth. *sums* (*some one*), *suman* (*sometime, once*).)

**ἆμος**, Dor. for ἦμος, *as, when*, Theoc.4.61, etc.

**ἀμόσχευτος**, ον, (μόσχος A) *without branches*, Nonn.*D.*22.21.

**ἀμοτον**, Adv. *insatiably, incessantly*, in Hom. always with Verbs expressing passion, desire, etc., esp. ἄ. μεμαώς full of *insatiate* longing, Il.4.440, al.; ἄ. κλαίω τεθνηότα I weep *continually*, 19.300; ἄ. κεχολωμένος *implacably* angered, 23.567; μάχης ἄ. μενεαίνων Hes.*Sc.* 361; ἡμίονοι ἄ. τανύοντο they struggled *restlessly* forwards, Od.6.83: later, *vehemently, violently*, λὶς ἄ. κεραΐζει Theoc.25.202; but στῆ δ' ἄ. stood *unwaveringly*, A.R.2.78:—later regul. Adv. -τως Sch.Il.4. 410. II. later, Adj. **ἄμοτος**, ον, *furious, savage*, κακόν prob. in Simon.37.16; θήρ Theoc.25.242; πῦρ Mosch.4.104.—Poet. word.

**ἀμοῦ**, Adv. of ἀμός (B), *somewhere*, ἀμοῦ γέ που somewhere or other (Bekk. for ἄλλου γέ που), Lys.24.20; ἄλλοθι μηδὲ ἀμοῦ no-*where* else *at all*, *IG*2.11.

**ἀμουργός**, όν, v.l. for ἀμοργός (A) I. 2.

*ἀμουσ-ία, ἡ, *want of education, taste* or *refinement, rudeness*, E.*Fr.* 1020, etc., cf. Chor.*Zach.Dial.*2; joined with ἀπειροκαλία, Pl.*R.* 403c. II. *want of harmony*, E.*HF*676. **-ολογία**, ἡ, *inelegance of language*, Ath.4.164f (pl.). **-ος**, ον, *without song*, of fishes, Emp. 74; but usu. *without the Muses*, i. e. *without taste* or *refinement, rude*, E.*Ion*526, Ar.*V.*1074; ἄ. καὶ ἀφιλόσοφος Pl.*Sph.*259e; ἄ. ἡδονή, ἁμαρτήματα, *gross* pleasure, faults, Pl.*Phdr.*240b, *Lg.*863c; ἄ. ἐστι, c. inf., it is *incongruous*, Ar.*Th.*159; τῶν Λειβηθρίων ἀμουσότερος, prov. for lowest degree of mental cultivation, Zen.1.79: Sup., γλῶττα -οτάτη Agath.2.28. Adv. -ως Pl.*Hp.Ma.*292c. II. of persons, *unmusical*, Id.*Sph.*253b, al. 2. of sounds, *unmusical, discordant*, ἄμουσ' ὑλακτεῖν E.*Alc.*760; ἀμουσόταται ᾠδαί *Ph.*807, etc. Adv. -ως Jul.*Or.*8.247d. **-ωτος**, ον, = ἄμουσος, S.*Fr.*819.

**ἄμουχα**· καθαρεύουσα (Lacon.), Hsch.; cf. ἀμυσχρός.

**ἀμοχθ-εί** or **-ί** [ῑ], Adv. *without toil*, A.*Pr.*210, E.*Ba.*194. *-ητος, ον, = sq., Opp.*C.*1.456. Adv. -τως Babr.9.2. **-ος**, ον, *free from toil and trouble*, of persons, S.*Fr.*410; ἄ. βίος *Tr.*147. Adv. ἀμόχθως Man.2.173, al. 2. *shrinking from toil*, καρδία Pi.*N.*10.30, E.*Fr.* 240. 3. *not tired*, X.*Mem.*2.1.33.

**ἀμόω**, in aor. part. ἀμώσας, *hang* (Tarent.), Hsch. **ἀμόωλον**, *clean vessel*, Id. **ἀμόωμφος**· ἄπιστος, Id.

**ἀμπ-**, poet., esp. Ep., Lyr., abbrev. for ἀναπ-, under which will be found words beginning with ἀμπ-.

**ἀμπαδίην**· ἀμφαδίην, Hsch. **ἀμπάζονται**· ἀναπαύονται, Id. *ἄμπαιδες, v. ἀμφίπαις.

*ἀμπαίνεθαι, v. ἀναφαίνομαι.

*ἀμπαιστήρ, ῆρος, ὁ, *door-knocker*, *IG*4.1484.79 (Epid.).

*ἀμπαλίνορρος, ον, strengthd. for παλίνορρος, Philetaer.11 (cj. Meineke).

*ἄμπαλος, poet. for ἀνάπαλος, *fresh casting of lots*, ἄμπαλον θέμεν Pi.*O.*7.61, cf. Eust.64.43, 1434.28; κατ' ἄνπαλον μισθούντω let *by repeated auction*, *SIG*546.15 (Aetol., iii B.C.).

**ἀμπανάμενος**, v. ἀναφαίνομαι.

*ἄμπανσις, *ἀμπαντός, *ἀμπαντύς, v. ἀμφ-.

**ἀμπάξαι**· παῦσαι (Lacon.), Hsch.; cf. ἀμπάζονται.

**ἄμπαυμα**, ἀμπαύω, etc., v. ἀναπ-.

**ἀμπεδίον**, **ἀμπεδιήρεις**, **ἀμπέλαγος**, should be written divisim ἀμ πεδίον, i. e. ἀνὰ πεδίον, etc.

**ἄμπειρα**, = ἀνάπειρα (q. v.). **ἄμπειρος**· ἔμπειρος, Hsch.

**ἀμπείρω**, poet. for ἀναπείρω.

**ἀμπελ-άνθη**, ἡ, = οἰνάνθη, Luc.*VH*2.5. **-εία**, ἡ, *vineyard*, *IPE* 1².418 (Cherson.). **-ειος**, ον, *of vine* or *vineyard*, Suid. *-εών, ῶνος, ὁ, poet. for ἀμπελών, Theoc.25.157. *-ικός, ἡ, όν, *of the vine*, v. l. in Hp.*Acut.*(*Sp.*)5, cf. M.Ant.8.46; χωρίον *IG*7.2808 (Hyettus); ἀμπελικά, τά, *tax on vineyards*, *PPetr.*3 p.242, cf. Vett.Val.76.10; also -κή, ἡ, *PPetr.*3 p.289. Adv. -κῶς Arr.*Epict.*2.20.18. *-ινος, ον, also η, ον, = foreg., καρπός Hdt.1.212; οἶνος ἀ. *grape*-wine, opp. οἶνος κρίθινος, etc., Id.2.37,60; φύλλα Arist.*PA*668ᵃ23; ἀ. βακτηρία *vine*-stick, Plb.29.27.5. II. metaph., γραῦς ἀμπελίνη *anus vinosa*, *AP*7.384 (Marc.Arg.). *-ιον, τό, Dim. of ἄμπελος, Ar.*Ach.* 512, *Pax*596, Hp.*Nat.Mul.*109. **-ιος**, ον, = ἀμπέλειος, μέθυσμα Ph. 1.680; ποτόν Ach.Tat.2.2. **-ίς**, ίδος, ἡ, Dim. of ἄμπελος, *young vine, vine-plant*, Ar.*Ach.*995. II. = ἀμπελίων, Id.*Av.*304, cf. Poll.6.

52. III. kind of *sea-plant*, Dionys.*Av*.2.7. -ιτικός, ή, όν, *planted with vines*, γῆ *PTeb*.5.17 (ii B.C.). -ῖτις, ιδος, ἡ, *of* or *for vines*, ἀ. γῆ *vine*-land, *OGI*90.15 (Rosetta), cf. *Mélanges Holleaux* 105. II. ἀ. γῆ, a bituminous earth (cf. Plin.*HN*35.194) *used to cure* φθειρίασις *in vines*, Posidon.64; as a cosmetic, Dsc.5.160. ⊛-ίων, ωνος, ὁ, kind of *singing bird*, Dionys.*Av*.3.2.

**ἀμπελο-γενής**, ές, *of vine kind*, Arist.*Ph*.199ᵇ12. **-δεσμος**, ὁ, Sicilian plant used *for tying up vines*, *esparto*, *Lygeum Spartum*, Plin.*HN*17.209. ⊛**-εις**, εσσα, εν, but fem. εις Il.2.561:—*rich in vines*, *vine-clad*, of countries, Il.l.c., 3.184, 9.152, Thgn.784, Pi.*Pae*. 2.25, etc. 2. *of the vine*, ἀ. βάκτρον *vine*-stick, Nonn.*D*.14.102; ἀ. καυλία *vine*-shoots, Nic.*Al*.142. **-εργός**, ὁ, = ἀμπελουργός, *AP* 6.56 (Maced.). **-καρπον**, τό, = ἀπαρίνη, Dsc.3.90. **-κλημα**· *vitis*, and **-κλημία**· *vitis vineae*, *Gloss*. **-μιξία**, ἡ, *intercourse with vines*, Luc.*VH*1.9. **-ποιία**, ἡ, = ἀμπελουργία, Eust.1619. 59. **-πρασον**, τό, *wild leek*, *Allium Ampeloprasum*, Dsc.2.150, Did.ap.Ath.9.371f.

⊛**ἄμπελος**, ἡ, any climbing plant with tendrils, esp. *grape-vine*, *Vitis vinifera* (ἄ. οἰνοφόρος Dsc.4.181; ἄ. τῆς Ἴδης is a variety, *V. v. apyrena*, *grape-currant*, Thphr.*HP*3.17.4), Hom. (not in Il. exc. in Adj. ἀμπελόεις), etc.; πυροὶ καὶ κριθαὶ καὶ ἄμπελοι Od.9.110, cf. 133, Alc.44, Hdt. 4.195, etc.; ἄ. καὶ ἐλάαν καὶ τὰ ἄλλα ἀκρόδρυα Thphr.*HP*4.4.11; ἄ. τὴν περὶ τὸ ἱερὸν κόπτοντες, in collective sense (cf. ἵππος, ἡ), Th.4.90; of wine, ἀμπέλου δρόσος Pi.*O*.7.2; ἀμπέλου παῖς Id.*N*.9.52. 2. ἄ. ἀγρία *wild vine*, *Vitis silvestris*, Dsc.4.181, 5.2, Plin.*HN*23.19:—also = ἄ. λευκή, Thphr.9.14.1, 9.20.3, Gal.14.186. 3. ἄ. λευκή *bryony*, *Bryonia cretica*, Dsc.4.182, Gal.11.826 (but λευκὴ ἄ. white *grape*, Thphr.*CP*1.20.5). 4. ἄ μέλαινα *black bryony*, *Tamus communis*, Dsc.4.183, Gal.11.827. 5. ἄ. ποντία *wrack*, *Fucus volubilis*, Thphr.*HP*4.6.9. II. *vineyard*, Ael.*NA*11.32. III. *engine for protecting besiegers*, *mantlet*, Apollod.*Poliorc*.141.7. IV. measure of length, = 20 παλαισταί, Hero*Def*.131. V. = αἰγιαλός (Cyren.), Hsch.

**ἀμπελο-στᾰτέω**, *plant vines*, *GDI*3632 (Cos), Poll.7.141. **-τέμνω** (sic), *prune vines*, *PLond*.1.131.375 (i A.D.). ⊛**-τόμον** δρέπανον *pruning-hook for vines*, Hsch. s. v. βίσβη. **-τρόφος**, ον, *nurturing vines*, B.6.5.

**ἀμπελουργ-εῖον**, τό, *vineyard*, Aeschin.2.156 (v.l. ἀμπελῶνι), Suid. s. v. ἀμπέλειος. **-έω**, fut. -ήσω Philostr.*Im*.2.17: *work in* or *cultivate vineyard*, esp. *dress* or *strip vines*, Ar.*Fr*.43 D., Thphr.*CP*3.7.5, Plu.*Phil*.4, Luc.*VH*1.39:—Pass., ἄμπελος ἀμπελουργουμένη Thphr. *CP*3.14.1. 2. metaph., *strip*, *plunder*, πόλιν D.ap.Aeschin.3. 166. **-ημα**, τό, *vine-dresser's work*, Poll.7.140 (pl.). **-ία**, ἡ, *vine-dressing*, Thphr.*CP*3.14.2, Luc.*Salt*.40: in pl., *vineyards*, Lib. *Or*.11.234, Poll.1.228. **-ικός**, Dor. -ωργικός, ή, όν, *of* or *for culture of vines*, [γᾶ] *Tab.Heracl*.2.43; ἡ -κή (sc. τέχνη), *vine-dressing*, Pl.*R*.333d, Ph.1.329. Adv. -κῶς Poll.7.141. ⊛**-ός**, ὁ, *vine-dresser*, Ar.*Pax*190, Hp.*Epid*.4.25, *IG*2.1055, Thphr *CP*2.4.8, *PPetr*.3p.59; title of plays by Amphis and Alexis; cf. ἀμπελοεργός.

**ἀμπελο-φάγος** [ᾰ], ον, *eating* or *gnawing vines*, ἶπες Str.13.1. 64. **-φόρος**, ον, *bearing vines*, Thphr.*CP*2.4.4, *PTeb*.82, Poll. 1.228. **-φύλαξ**· *custos vineae*, *Gloss*. **-φυλλον**, τό, *vine-leaf*, Hsch. s. v. Κλαρία; = *pampinus*, *Gloss*. ⊛**-φῠτος**, ον, *planted with vines*, *growing vines*, D.S.1.36, Str.5.3.1, Ph.2.371. **-φύτωρ**, ορος, ὁ, *vine-planter*, of Bacchus, *AP*6.44 (Leon.). [ῡ metri gr., as in πτεροφύτωρ.]

**ἀμπελ-ώδης**, ες, *rich in vines*, Poll.1.228, Hsch. s. v. οἰνάδες. **-ών**, ῶνος, ὁ, *vineyard*, Aeschin.2.156 (v.l.), Thphr.*HP*9.10.2, Lxx *Ge*.9. 20, al., *PHib*.151 (iii B.C.), *PTeb*.5.99 (ii B.C.), D.S.4.6, Plu.*Mar*.21, etc.; cf. ἀμπελεών:—Dim. ⊛-ωνίδιον, τό, *PSI*4.375.7 (iii B.C.).

**ἀμπερέως**· διαμπάξ, Hsch. **ἀμπέσαι**· ἀμφιέσαι (Lacon.), Id.

**ἀμπέτιξ**, Adv., (cf. ἀμπί) *round*, dub. l. in *CIG*2554 (Cret.).

**ἀμπεχές**· ἔνδυμα, Hsch.

**ἀμπέχογκος**, = γνάφαλλον, Ps.-Dsc.3.117.

⊛**ἀμπεχόνη**, ἡ, (ἀμπέχω) *fine shawl* worn by women and effeminate men, Pherecr.108.28. 2. *clothing*, X.*Mem*.1.2.5, etc.; in pl., *modes of dress*, Pl.*R*.425b:—Dim. **-όνιον**, *AB*388, Hsch.

**ἀμπέχονον**, τό, = ἀμπεχόνη, Ar.*Fr*.320.7, *IG*2.754, Theoc.15.21.

**ἀμπ-έχω** (dissimil. fr. ἀμφέχω), Semon.12 (dub.), A.*Pers*.848, S. (v. infr.), later **ἀμφέχω** *AP*7.693 (Apollonid.), *IG*12(3).220 (Thera), Aret.*CA*1.4, etc.; Med., ἀμφέχετο A.R.1.324; also **ἀμπ-ίσχω** E. *Hipp*.192, *Supp*.165: Ep. impf. ἄμπεχον Od.6.225 (late ἄμφεχον Q.S. 3.6, 5.106): fut. ἀμφέξω E.*Cyc*.344: aor. 2 ἤμπεσχον Ar.*Lys*.1156, etc.:—Med., ἀμπέχομαι Ar. (v. infr. II.2); ἀμπίσχομαι E.*Hel*.422, 3 pl. ἀμπισχνοῦνται Ar.*Av*.1090: impf. ἠμπειχόμην Pl.*Phd*.87b, Ep. ἀμφεχόμην A.R.1.324: fut. ἀμφέξομαι Pherecr.7 D., Philetaer.19: aor. 2 ἠμπεσχόμην E.*Med*.1159, Ar.*Th*.165, 2 sg. subj. ἀμπίσχῃ E.*IA* 1439, part. ἀμπισχόμενος Ar.*V*.1150.—The aor. forms, ἀμπισχεῖν, ἀμπισχών, are sts. falsely written (as if pres.) ἀμπίσχειν, ἀμπίσχων: I. *surround*, *cover*, *enclose*, ἅλμη οἱ νῶτα ἄμπεχεν Od.6.225; κυνῆ πρόσωπα Θεσσαλίς νιν ἀμπέχει S.*OC*314, cf. A. l. c.: metaph., ἀ. τινὰ σμικρότητι *invest* one with.., Pl.*Prt*.320e: abs., σκότος ἀμπίσχων *surrounding* darkness, E.*Hipp*.192; κρυπτὸν ἀμπισχὼν δόρυ, of the wooden horse, Id.*Tr*.12; τὰ ἀμπέχοντα ὑμένια Aret.*SA*2. 2. 2. *embrace*, γόνυ σὸν ἀμπίσχειν χερί E.*Supp*.165. II. *put round*, esp. *put* clothes and the like *on* another, c. dupl. acc., κρίβανόν μ' ἀμπίσχετε Ar.*V*.1153, cf. *Ra*.1063, *Lys*.1156: with prep., τοίχοισιν δ' ἔπι ἤμπισχεν.. ὑφάσματα *put them* all over.., E.*Ion*1159: metaph., ἡ βασιλικὴ τέχνη δούλους καὶ ἐλευθέρους ἀμπίσχουσα Pl.*Plt*. 311c. 2. Med., *put round oneself*, *put on*, πέπλους E.*Med*.1159; *wear*, τὸ τῆς γυναικὸς ἀμπέχει χιτώνιον Ar.*Ec*.374; λευκὸν ἀμπέχει; do you *wear* a white cloak? Id.*Ach*.1023; χλαίνας οὐκ ἀμπισχνοῦνται Id.*Av*.1090; καλῶς ἠμπίσχετο *was* well *dressed*, Id.*Th*.165; ἐν ἀριστερὰ ἀ. Id.*Av*.1567; ἀμπεχόμενοι *with their cloaks on*, opp. γυμνοί (cf. γυμνός 1.5), Pl.*Grg*.523c, Arist.*Pr*.867ᵃ19; ἄνω τοῦ γόνατος ἀ. *wear a tunic* not reaching to the knee, Philetaer. l. c.; περιττῶς ἀ. *to be* gorgeously *dressed*, Plu.*Demetr*.41: c. dat., *clothe* or *cover oneself with* (v. ἔκβολος), E.*Hel*.422.

**ἀμπήδησε**, poet. for ἀνεπήδησε.

**ἀμπί**, said to be Aeol. for ἀμφί, Hdn.Gr.2.376, but prob. coined to expl. forms such as ἀμπέχω, which are due to dissimilation.

**ἀμπίθυρον** (cod. -ουρον)· πυλῶνα (Tarent.), Hsch. **ἀμπιστᾶσθαι**· ἐξετάζειν, and **ἀμπιστάτηρ**· ἐξεταστής, Id. **ἀμπιτίαρ**· παρατατταομένη, Id.

**ἀμπλᾰκ-εῖν**, inf. of aor. ἤμπλακον (ἤμβλακον Archil.73, Ibyc.24), part. ἀμπλ- and ἀπλ-ακών (v. infr.): pf. Pass. ἠμπλάκημαι A.*Supp*. 916:—pres. only later **ἀμπλακίσκω**, Dor. **ἀμβλακίσκω** Theag.ap. Stob.3.1.117: Dor. impf. ἀμβλάκισκον Phint.ap.eund.4.23.61 (ἀμβλακεύω is v.l. for βλακεύω in Hp.*Art*.17; cf. βλάξ): I. c. gen., *miss*, *fail* or *come short of*, ἀνορίας οὐκ ἀμπλακών Pi.*O*.8.67, cf. S.*Ant*. 554, 1234. 2. *lose*, *be bereft of*, εἰ τοῦδ' ἤμπλακον (sc. παιδός) ib. 910; νόστου Simon.119; ἀρίστης ἀπλακὼν ἀλόχου E.*Alc*.242; λέκτρων ἀπλακών Id.*IA*124. II. abs., *do amiss*, *sin*, *err*, παρ θεοῖς Ibyc. 24, cf. Archil.73, E.*Hipp*.892, *Andr*.948, etc.: c. neut. pron., ὡς τάδ' ἤμπλακον when *I committed* these *sins*, A.*Ag*.1212:—Pass., τί δ' ἠμπλάκηται τῶνδέ μοι; Id.*Supp*.916.—Not in Hom. **-ημα**, τό, *error*, *fault*, A.*Pr*.112, 388, S.*Ant*.51, etc.—Poet. and late Prose, Plu. 2.226e, Thd.*Da*.6.4:—metri gr., ἀπλάκημα A.*Eu*.934. **-ητος**, v. ἀναμπλάκητος. **-ία**, and ἀμβλ- (v. infr.), ἡ, = ἀμπλάκημα, Thgn.204, Emp.115, Hp.*Ep*.22; ἀμπλακίαισι φρενῶν Pi.*P*.3.13; τίνος ἀμπλακίας ποινὰς ὀλέκει; A.*Pr*.564; ἀμπλακίαισι τῶν πάροιθεν E. *Hipp*.835, cf. A.R.4.1082, Rhian.1.20. **-ιον**, τό, = ἀμπλακία, Pi.*P*.11.26. **-ίσκω**, v. ἀμπλακεῖν. ⊛**-ιῶτις**, ἡ, = ἱερὰ νόσος, Poet.*de herb*.174.

**ἀμπν-είω**, Ep. for ἀναπνέω. **-ευμα**, **-οά**, poet. for ἀνάπνευμα, ἀναπνοή. **-υε**, v. ἀναπνέω.

⊛**ἄμπνῡτο**, Ep. aor. Med., Pass. **ἀμπνύνθη** (better ἀμπνύθη), *recover consciousness* after a swoon, Il.5.697, 22.475, al. (ἀνα-, πνῦ-, cf. πέπνυμαι. Not connected with ἀνα-πνέω, q. v.)

**ἀμποίχοιτις**· ἐν Συρακούσαις ἀρχή, Hsch.

**ἄμποτε**, i. e. ἂν ποτε, with opt., *o that!* Sch. rec. A.*Pr*.971.

⊛**ἄμποχος**, ὁ, = ἀνάδοχος, *guarantor*, *Not.Scav*.1912.452 (Sicily, i B.C.).

**ἀμπρακόν**· μακρόθεν, Hsch.

**ἀμπρ-ευτής**, οῦ, ὁ, *hauling*, ὄνος S.*Fr*.820. **-εύω**, *draw along*, *drag*, E.ap.Phot.p.95 R.; αἰχμάλωτον ἤμπρευσαν Lyc.1298; ἄνδρα.. ἀμπρεύοντες Call.*Fr*.234: metaph., λυπρὸν βίον ἀμπρεύσει *will drag on* a wretched life, Lyc.975, cf. 635.

**ἀμπρόν** (on the accent v. *Et.Gen*., Hsch.), τό, *rope for drawing loads*, Ἐφ.Ἀρχ.1895.59 (v B.C.), *IG*2.678*B* (iv B.C.), cf. Sch.Ar.*Lys*. 289.

⊛**ἀμπτᾶσα**, **ἀμπταίην**, v. ἀναπέτομαι.

⊛**ἀμπῠκ-άζω**, *bind front hair*, κισσῷ καὶ στεφάνοισιν ἀμπυκασθεὶς *AP* 13.6 (Phalaec.). **-τήρ**, ῆρος, ὁ, *horse's bridle*, A.*Th*.461. **-τήριον**, τό, = foreg., S.*OC*1069. ⊛**-ωμα**, τό, = sq., Id.*Fr*.1002 (pl.).

⊛**ἄμπυξ**, ῠκος, ὁ (ἡ, S., E., v. infr.):—*woman's diadem*, *frontlet*, Il.22.469, A.*Supp*.431 (lyr., with play on 1.2), E.*Hec*.465, Theoc. 1.33. 2. *horse's headband* (Thess. acc. to Sch.Pi.*O*.5.15), Q.S. 4.511. II. *rim of wheel*, S.*Ph*.680 (lyr.).

**ἀμπώλημα** (Dor. for ἀναπ-), τό, *indemnification*, *Tab.Heracl*.1. 110, 155.

**ἀμπωτίζω**, *ebb and flow*, of the sea, Ph.1.298:—Med., Eust.688.52.

⊛**ἄμπωτις**, ἡ, gen. εως, Ion. ιος, for ἀνάπωτις (ἀναπίνομαι), v. infr.:—*being sucked back*, i. e. of sea, *ebb*, opp., πλημμυρίς or ῥαχία (Ion. ῥηχίη), Hdt.2.11, 7.198, 8.129, Arist.*Mete*.366ᵃ19, *Iacit*.3.17, Agatharch. 32, etc.: in pl., *ebb and flow*, *tides*, Arist.*Mu*.396ᵃ26, *Peripl.M.Rubr*. 45, App.*Hisp*.1, Hdn.3.14.6.—The full form **ἀνάπωτις** only Pi.*O*. 9.52, Scymn.110, and later Prose, Plb.10.14.2 (s. v. l.), Arr.*Ind*.22.8: gen. **-πώτιδος**, Agatharch.101. 2. *retiring of a stream*, Call.*Del*. 130. 3. metaph., τῆς ἀδολεσχίας ὥσπερ ἄμπωτιν λαβούσης Plu. 2.502d. II. *return of humours* inward from surface of body, ἄ. τῶν χυμῶν Hp.*Hum*.1, cf. Erot.*Fr*.8; of blood in the lungs, Gal. *UP*6.10.

**ἀμύαλος**, ον, for ἀμύελος, *without marrow*, *Tab.Defix.Aud*.162.19, cf. 168.31.

**ἀμυγδᾰλ-έα**, contr. -ῆ, ἡ, *almond-tree*, *Prunus Amygdalus*, Eup. 70, Thphr.*HP*1.6.3, Dsc.1.123. **-έλαιον**, τό, = ἔλαιον ἀμυγδάλινον, [Gal.]14.519. **-εος**, α, ον, v.l. for ἀμυγδαλόεις in Nic.*Th*.891 (ap. Ath.14.649d). ⊛**-η**, ἡ, *almond*, Phryn.Com.68, Hp.*Vict*.2.55, Thphr.*HP*1.11.3, Dsc.1.123, Ath.2.52c. II *kernel of peach-stone*, *Gp*.10.14.1. **-ινος**, η, ον, *of almonds*, χρῖμα X.*An*.4.4.13; ἔλαιον Thphr.*Od*.14. **-ιον**, τό, Dim. of ἀμυγδάλη, Hp.*Morb*.2.64. **-ιος**, α, ον, *almond-shaped*, ὠτάρια *BGU*781 iii 16 (i A.D.). **-ίς**, ίδος, ἡ, = ἀμυγδάλη, Philox.3.20, Plu.2.624d. **-ίτης** [ῑ], ου, ὁ, = τιθύμαλλος χαρακίας, Dsc.4.164, Plin.*HN*26.70.

**ἀμυγδαλο-ειδής**, ές, *like the almond* or *almond-tree*, Dsc.4. 164. **-εις**, εσσα, εν, *like an almond*, Nic.*Th*.891. **-κατάκτης**, ου, ὁ, *almond-cracker*, Ath.2.53b.

**ἀμύγδαλ-ον**, τό, = ἀμυγδάλη, Hp.*Morb.*3.15, Hermipp.63, Arist. 4614ᵇ15, Dsc.1.123, etc.; = ἀμυγδαλῆ, Lxx *Ec.*12.5. **-ος**, ἡ, = υγδαλῆ, Luc.*Apol.*5, Hsch. s.v. καρύα. **-ώδης**, ες, *like an nond*, σχήματι Thphr.*HP*4.2.5.

**ἄμυγ-μα**, ατος, τό, (ἀμύσσω) *scratching, tearing*, πολιᾶς ἄ. χαίτας *Aj.*634; ὀνύχων ἀμύγματα E.*Andr.*827. **-μός**, ὁ, = foreg., cj. A.*Ch.*24.

**ἀμυγνόν**, v. ἀμυσχρός.

**ἄμῡδις** [ᾰ], Aeol. = ἅμα, Sch.D.T.p.281 H.: I. of Time, *together, the same time*, Od.12.415, Hes.*Sc.*345, etc. II. more freq. of lace, *all together*, ἄ. κικλήσκετο Il.10.300; ἄ. στήσασα (v.l. καλέσασα) ούς 20.114, cf. 13.336; ὀστέα..πάντ' ἄ. 12.385; ἄ. φλόγ' ἔβαλλον rew burning embers *together*, 23.217; freq. in late Ep., A.R.1.961, rat.581, etc.

**ἀμυδρ-ήεις**, εσσα, εν, = sq., Nic.*Th.*274. ***-ός**, ά, όν, *dim, faint, bscure*: 1. of impressions on the eye, ἀ. χοιράς a rock *dimly een through water*, Archil.129; ἀ. γράμματα *scarce legible* letters, Th.6.54; ἀ. φέγγος, χρῶμα, Arist.*Mete.*343ᵇ13, 372ᵃ2; ἀ. τὰ εἴδη τῶν χθύων, σκιᾶς μᾶλλον ἢ ἰχθῦς εἰκάσεις (in a painting) Paus.10.28.1. Adv. ἀμυδρῶς, βλέπειν, ὁρᾶν, Arist.*HA*537ᵇ11, 556ᵇ19; ἀ. μιμεῖσθαί τι represent its form *obscurely*, ib.502ᵇ9; ἀ. ἔχειν to be *ill-defined*, *PA* 668ᵃ3. 2. generally, *faint, weak*, σφυγμὸς ἀ. τὸν τόνον Aret.*CA*2.3, cf. *SD*1.12; τυπαί Nic.*Th.*358 (Comp.). 3. of impressions on the mind, *vague*, ἀ. εἶδος Pl.*Ti.*49a; ἀ. πρὸς ἀλήθειαν *faint* in comparison with truth, Id.*R.*597a; δι' ἀμυδρῶν ὀργάνων by *imperfect* organs, Id. *Phdr.*250b, cf. *Tht.*195a; μαντεῖα ἀμυδρότερα τοῦ τι σαφὲς σημαίνειν *too obscure*.., Id.*Ti.*72b; ἀ. ἐλπίς Plu.*Alc.*38; ἀ. λόγος [Longin.] *Rh.*p.195 H.; -ότερα σχήματα Aps.p.327 H.; συναίσθησις Dam.*Pr.*81 (Sup.), etc. Adv. -ῶς καὶ οὐθὲν σαφῶς Arist.*Metaph.*985ᵃ13, cf. 988ᵃ 23; *faintly*, of one near death, Max.Tyr.16.2: Comp. ἀμυδρότερον Pl. *Sph.*250e, Plu.2.1025d. **-ότης**, ητος, ἡ, *dimness*, αἰσθήσεων Ph.2. 432; *faintness*, of the pulse, Gal.9.15; *indistinctness*, opp. τρανότης, Plot.1.4.3. **-όω**, *make indistinct*, Procl.*Inst.*143:—Pass., Ph.1.273, Olymp. *in Mete.*211.11; *become indistinct* or *feeble*, ib.150.4. **-ωσις**, εως, ἡ, *making indistinct* or *feeble*, Anon. *in Cat.*26.9: metaph., Dam. *Pr.*423.

**ἀμύελος**, ον, *without marrow*, Arist.*PA*655ᵃ35, Gal.*UP*1.15.

**ἀμυ-ησία**, ἡ, *a being uninitiated*, *AB*406, Hsch. s.v. ἀνοργίας. **-ητος**, ον, *uninitiated, profane*, And.1.12, Lys.6.51; ἀ. καὶ ἀτέλεστος Pl.*Phd.*69c: c. gen., ἀ. Ἀφροδίτης *not admitted into mysteries of* Aphrodite, Aristaenet.1.14; ὠδίνων, of Artemis, Orph.*H.*36.4. 2. μυήσεις ἀ. *no true* initiations, Ph.1.156. II. *not closed, open*, Philostr.*Gym.*29 codd.; with play on both meanings, *leaky*, Pl.*Grg.* 493a,b.

**ἀμύθητος** [ῡ], ον, *unspeakable*, esp. *unspeakably great, untold*, χρήματα D.4.34; κακὰ καὶ πράγματ' ἀ. παρέχων 21.17; ἀ. πλῆθος μυῶν Arist.*HA*580ᵇ16; ἀμύθητον ὅσον διαφέρει Id.*Pol.*1263ᵃ40, cf. Phld. *Mort.*29; ἀμύθητα περὶ ἕκαστα παρατιθεὶς Id.*Herc.*1005.7.

**ἄμῡθος**, ον, *without mythic tales*, ποίησις Plu.2.16c.

**ἀμυκάλαι**· αἱ ἀκίδες τῶν βελῶν, παρὰ τὸ ἀμύσσειν, Hsch. **ἀμύκαρις**· πλῆθος, ἄθροισμα, πλούσιον, πολύ, Id.

**ἀμύκητος** [ῡ], ον, of places, *where no herds low*, *AP*9.150 (Antip.).

**Ἀμύκλαι**, ῶν, αἱ, *Amyclae* in Laconia, famous for worship of Apollo, Il., etc.:—***Ἀμυκλ-αῖος**, or **-αεύς**, έως, ὁ, *Amyclean*, X.*HG* 4.5.11, Arist.*Fr.*532:—**-αῖον**, τό, *temple of Amyclean Apollo*, ἐν Ἀ. Foed.ap.Th.5.18 and 23; ἐν τῷ Ἀ. Str.6.3.2; of Artemis, Call.*Aet.* 1.1.24. Adv. **-ᾶθεν** *from Amyclae*, Pi.*N.*11.34. **Ἀμύκλαι**, αἱ, sort of *shoes*, named after *Amyclae*, Theoc.10.35:—also **-ᾶδες**, αἱ, Ar.*Fr.*44 D., Phryn.Com.5 D., cf. Poll.7.88, Hsch. **Ἀμυκλαΐζω**, *speak in the Amyclean* (i.e. *Laconian*) *dialect*, Theoc.12.13.

**ἀμυκλίς**· γλυκύς, ἡδύς, Hsch. **ἀμύκταν**· γλυκύν, οἱ δὲ ἄμικτον, Id.

**ἀμυκτέον**, *one must scarify*, Menem.ap.Orib.7.22.6, Archig.ap. Aët.6.27.

**ἀμύκτηρ**, ηρος, ὁ, ἡ, *without nose*, Str.15.1.57.

**ἀμυκτικός**, ή, όν, *fit for tearing, lacerating*, Plu.2.642c. Adv. -κῶς Sch.Nic.*Th.*131. II. Medic., of remedies, *irritant*, Sor.2.12, al., Dsc.1.174 (Sup.).

**ἀμυλᾶτον**, τό, = ἄμυλος II, Sch.Ar.*Pax*1195.

**ἀμυλιδωτόν**, τό, kind of *tunic*, Hermipp.2 D.

**ἀμύλιον**, τό, Dim. of ἄμυλος II, *cake*, Plu.2.466d, Aq.*Ex.*16.31 (cod. A); of ἄμυλος III, *starch*, Hp.*Mul.*2.197, Arist.*Pr.*879ᵃ10, Dieuch. ap. Orib.4.7.24.

***ἄμῠλος**, ον, *not ground at the mill*: hence, *of the finest meal*, ἄρτος Poll.6.72; cf. foreg. II. as Subst., ἄμυλος, ὁ, *cake of fine meal*, Ar.*Ach.*1092, *Pax*1195, cf. Stratt 2 D., Theoc.9.21, Telecl.32:—also ἄμυλον, τό, Ath.14.647f. III. ἄμυλον, τό, *starch*, Dsc.2.101, Plin.*HN*18.76, *SIG*1171.11 (Lebena), *POxy.*1088 i 5, etc.

**ἄμυμος**, ον, = sq., Cyr., prob. in Hsch.

***ἀμύμων** [ῡ], ον, gen. ονος: dat. pl. ἀμύμωσιν *Epigr.Gr.*451 (Trachonitis), dub. l. in *IG*14.1424: (cf. μῦμαρ· αἶσχος, ψόγος, Hsch.):—*blameless, noble, excellent*, οἶκος ὅδ' ἀφνειὸς καὶ ἀ. Od.1.232; ἅμα κρατερὸς καὶ ἀ. ib. 3.111; in Hom. an honorary epithet or title even of Aegisthus, ib.1.29:—never of gods, for Aesculapius is ἀ. *as a physician*, Il.4.194; of a mortal nymph, 14.144. II. of things, ὃς δ' ἂν ἀ. αὐτὸς ἔῃ καὶ ἀμύμονα εἰδῇ Od.19.332; θεῶν ὑπ' ἀμύμονι πομπῇ Il.6.171; μῆτις 10.19; ὀρχηθμός 13.637; νῆσος Od.12.261; ἕρκος 22.442.—Freq. in Hom.; twice in Hes. (*Th.*264,654); once in Pi.*O.*10(11).27; not in B. or Trag.; found in Comic parodies, as Hermipp.82.

**ἄμῡνα**, ης, ἡ, *warding off an attack, self-defence*, Theopomp.Com. 3 D., Ps.-Phoc.32, Ph.2.31, App.*Pun.*73, etc.: c. gen. obj., ἐχθρῶν Lxx *Wi.*5.17, Ph.1.322. II. *vengeance, requital*, Ps.-Phoc.77, Phld.*Ir.*p.66 W., Nic.Dam.p.104 D., Plot.4.4.17, etc.

**ἀμῡν-άθω**, pres. assumed by Gramm., cf. Hdn.Gr.1.440, 2.782, as lengthd. form of ἀμύνω: but forms so accented in codd. are best taken to belong to aor. ἠμύναθον and written ἀμυναθεῖν (so Hsch.), -θοῦ, cf. ἀλκαθεῖν:—*defend, assist*, c. dat. pers., εἰ σοῖς φίλοις ἀμυναθεῖν χρῄζεις E.*Andr.*1079, cf. *IA*910; ἀμυνάθετέ μοι Ar.*Nu.*1323: abs., ἄξιαι δ' ἀμυναθεῖν [αἱ ξυμφοραί] S.*OC*1015:—Med., *ward off from oneself, repel*, τόνδ' ἀμυναθοῦ ψόγον A.*Eu.*438; *take vengeance on*, μὴ ..ἀμυνάθοιτό σε E.*Andr.*721. **-ανδρος**, *warding off enemies*, S.*Fr.* 1003. Adv. -ρως A.*Fr.*451 D. **-ητί**, Adv. *in self-defence*, A.D. *Adv.*161.8 (dub.).

**Ἀμυνίας** [ῠ], ου, ὁ, (ἀμύνω) masc. pr. n. II. Appellat., ὁ θυμὸς εὐθὺς ἦν ἀ. *on its guard*, Ar.*Eq.*570.

**ἀμύν-τειρα**, ἡ, fem. of ἀμυντήρ, = *cultrix*, *Gloss.* **-τέον**, verb. Adj. of ἀμύνω, *one must assist*, c. dat. pers., X.*Cyr.*8.6.6: also pl., ἀμυντέ' ἐστὶ τοῖς κοσμουμένοις S.*Ant.*677. II. *one must repel*, Ar. *Lys.*661. **-τήρ**, ῆρος, ὁ, lit. *defender*: ἀμυντῆρες, οἱ, *brow-tines* of stag's antlers, Arist.*HA*611ᵇ5. **-τήριος**, ον, *defensive*, ὅπλα (i.e. *weapons* in general) Pl.*Lg.*944d, cf. D.S.3.54, D.H.5.46, Str.7.3.17, 17.1.54; τέχναι Pl.*Lg.*920e: c. gen., φάρμακον ἀ. γήρως *antidote for* .., Ael.*NA*6.51; πόαι τῶν δηγμάτων ἀ. 12.32. II. Subst. ***-τήριον**, τό, *means of protection*, Pl.*Plt.*279c sq.; *defence, bulwark*, Plb.18. 41ᵃ.2; *weapon*, Plu.2.714f; ἀ. τοῦ κακοῦ *antidote for*.., Ael.*NA*3.41; ἀ. ἐξ ἀπόρων *way of escape* from.., ib.3.22. ***-της**, ὁ, *defender*, Phot. p.96 R., cf. Hdn.Gr.1.78. **-τικός**, ή, όν, *prompt to repel affront* or *attack*, Arist.*EN*1126ᵃ7; of animals, opp. φυλακτικά, *HA*488ᵇ8; τὸ ἀ. ὄργανον *PA*683ᵃ21; αἱ ἀ. ὁρμαί Plu.2.457c. Adv. -κῶς Procl. *in Prm.*p.555 S., Simp. *in Epict.*p.41 D. 2. *fit for keeping off*: ἡ -τικὴ χειμώνων Pl.*Plt.*280e. **-τρόν**, τό, *reward for defence*, A.*Fr.* 451 E. ***-τωρ**, ορος, ὁ, poet. word, *defender, helper*, Il.13.384 (as v.l.), Od.2.326, etc. 2. *repeller*, δυσφροσυνάων Simon.86. 3. *avenger*, πατρός E.*Or.*1588.

***ἀμύνω** [ῡ], Ep. impf. ἄμῡνον Il.15.731: fut. ἀμῠνῶ, Ion. -ῠνέω Hdt. 9.60, 3 pl. -εῦσι ib.6: aor. 1 ἤμῡνα, Ep. ἄμυνα [ᾰμ] Il.17.615: aor. 2, v. ἀμυνάθω:—Med., Ep. impf. ἀμυνόμην ib.13.514: fut. ἀμυνοῦμαι: aor. 1 ἠμυνάμην: aor. 2, v. ἀμυνάθω:—Pass. rare (v. infr. c):—*keep off, ward off*, Hom., mostly in Il.—Construction: 1. c. acc. of the person or thing *to be kept off*, c. dat. pers. *for* or *from whom* danger averted, Δαναοῖσιν λοιγὸν ἄμυνον *ward off* ruin *from* the Danai, Il. 1.456, cf. 341, Od.8.525:—dat. freq. omitted, ὅς λοιγὸν ἀμύνει Il.5. 603; ἀ. τὸν βάρβαρον Pl.*Lg.*692e, cf. *AB*79. b. c. dat. only, *defend, aid, succour*, ἀ. ὤρεσσι, σοῖσιν ἔτῃσι, Il.5.486, 6.262, cf. Od.11.500, Hdt.8.87, 9.6, etc.; τοιαῦτ' ἀμύνεθ' Ἡρακλεῖ such *aid ye give* to H., E.*HF*219; ἀ. τῇ πόλει, τῷ δήμῳ, Ar.*Eq.*577,790; τῷ νόμῳ E.*Or.*523, Th.3.67:—with inf. added, τοῖς μὲν οὐκ ἠμύνατε σωθῆναι so that they might be saved, Th.6.80. 2. c. acc. et gen., Τρῶας ἄμυνε νεῶν *he kept* the Trojans *off from* the ships, Il.15.731, cf. 4.11, 12.402. b. c. gen. only, ἀ. νηῶν *defend* the ships, ib.13.109. 3. abs., *succour*, χεῖρες ἀμύνειν hands *to aid*, ib.814; ἀμύνειν εἰσὶ καὶ ἄλλοι ib.312; ὦ ξυνδικασταί..ἀμύνατε *help!* Ar.*V.*197; τὰ ἀμύνοντα *means of defence*, Hdt.3.155: c. dat. modi, σθένει ἀ. *defend* with might, Il.13.678. 4. with Preps., once in Hom. with περί, ἀμυνέμεναι περὶ Πατρόκλοιο (cf. B.I.3) ib.17.182; in Prose, ἀ. ὑπὲρ τῆς Ἑλλάδος Pl.*Lg.*692d; ἀ. πρὸ πάντων Plb.6.6.8. II. less freq. like B.II, *requite, repay*, ἔργ' ἀμύνουσιν κακά S.*Ph.*602; ἀμύνειν.. τοῖσδε τοῖς λόγοις τάδε Id.*OC* 1128.

B. Med., *keep* or *ward off from oneself, guard* or *defend oneself against*, freq. with collat. notion of *requital, revenge*: 1. c. acc. rei, ἀμύνετο νηλεὲς ἦμαρ Il.13.514; ἀμύνεσθαι μόρον A.*Ag.*1381; τὸ δυστυχὲς γὰρ ηὑγένει' ἀμύνεται E.*Heracl.*303, cf. S.*Fr.*1004. b. c. acc. pers., ἀ. τὴν Δαρείου στρατιήν Hdt.3.158; ἐκεῖνον ἠμύναντο S.*Fr.* 589. 2. that from which danger is warded off in gen., as in Act. I. 2, ἀμυνόμενοι σφῶν αὐτῶν Il.12.155; νηῶν ἠμύνοντο ib.170. 3. with Preps., ἀμύνεσθαι περὶ πάτρης ib.243; περὶ τῶν οἰκείων Th.2.39; ὑπέρ τινος X.*Cyn.*9.9. 4. abs., *defend oneself, act in self-defence*, ἀμύνεσθαι φίλον ἔστω Il.16.556; ἢν συλλαμβανόμενος ἀμύνηται Hdt.1.80, cf. 4. 174, al.; ἀλλ' ἀμύνου Ar.*Eq.*244; τοῦ ἄρξαντος καὶ οὐ τοῦ ἀμυνομένου Antipho 4.4.8; οὐδ' ἀμυνόμενος ἀλλ' ὑπάρχων Isoc.16.44, cf. Pl.*Grg.* 456e; κακῶς πάσχοντα ἀ. ἀντιδρῶντα κακῶς Pl.*Cri.*49d; ἂν ᾖ χαρίεις, ἀ. εὖ δρῶν Arist.*EN*1162ᵇ10. II. after Hom., ἀ. τινά *avenge oneself on* an enemy: hence, *requite, repay*, Ar.*Nu.*1428, etc.: freq. c. dat. instr., ἔργοις πεπονθὼς ῥήμασίν σ' ἀμύνομαι S.*OC*873; ἀ. τινὰ σιδήρῳ Antipho 4.2.2; τοῖς ὁμοίοις, ἀρετῇ, Th.1.42, 4.63; ὠμότητα ὠμότητι D.S.14.53; ἀ. τινὰς ὑπέρ τινος to punish *for* a thing, Th.5.69; good sense, Simon.229; ἀ. ὁμοίως εὖ παθόντα, ὥσπερ κακῶς Socr.ap. Arist.*Rh.*1398ᵃ25: abs., *retaliate*, c. dat. instr., ταῖς ναυσίν Th.1.142; ἀ. ὧν ἔπαθον 1.96.

C. very rarely Pass., ἀμύνονται ἆται *are warded off*, Pi.*P.*11.54; ἀμυνέσθω *let him be driven away*, Pl.*Lg.*845c.

**ἀμύξ**, Adv., (ἀμύσσω) *scratching, tearing*, ἀ. ἐμφῦσα Nic.*Th.* 131. 2. = μόλις, Euph.146.

**ἄμυξ**· ἀμυχή Hsch. (dub.).

**ἀμύξανος**· ἀνόσιος, Hsch.

***ἄμυξις**, εως, ἡ, (ἀμύσσω) *tearing, rending, mangling*, Orph.*A.*24, Ach.Tat.8.4; *scarification*, Antyll.ap.Orib.7.16.1; *irritation*, Cass. *Pr.*62.

**ἄμυος**, ον, *not showing muscle*, σκέλος Hp.*Art.*52, cf. Orib.*Syn.* 5.44.20.

**ἀμύριστος** [ῠ], ον, *not steeped in unguents*, στέμματα *Epigr.Gr.* 418 (Cyrene). 2. metaph., *rude, rough*, ἀμύριστα φθεγγομένη Heraclit.92.

**ἀμυροιραῖνος**· ὁ μὴ μυσαττόμενος τὸ ῥαίνεσθαι, Hsch.

**ἄμυρον**, τό, = ἀτρακτυλίς, Ps.-Dsc.3.93.

***ἄμυρος**, ον, (ἀ- intens., μύρω) *watery*, τόποι S.*Fr.*512, but perh. (ἀ- priv., μύρον) *not perfumed*, of byres.

**ἀμυρτόν**· ἱμάτιον (Cret.), Hsch. **ἄμυς**· ὁμοῦ σὺν αὐτῷ (Lacon.), Id.

**ἀμύς**, ύδος, ἡ, = χελώνη λιμναία, Archig.ap.Gal.12.575.

**ἀμύσακτος**, ον, (μυσάττω) *without pollution*, *AB*321.

**ἀμύσκαρον**, v. ἀμυσχρός.

**ἄμυσσος**· κῆτος (Lacon.), Hsch.

***ἀμύσσω**, Att. -ττω, Phld.*Lib.*p.57 O.: Ep. impf. ἄμυσσον Il.19. 284: fut. -ξω Il.1.243, Aeschin.*Ep.*12.10: aor. ἤμυξα Nonn.*D.*40. 161, poet. ἄμ- B.16.19, *AP*7.218 (Antip.):—**Med.**, pres., Hp.*Mul.* 1.78: aor. part. ἀμυξάμενος (κατ-) *AP*7.491 (Mnasalc.):—**Pass.**, fut. ἀμυχθήσομαι Aq 2*Ki.*6.19: aor. part. ἀμυχθέν *AP*11.382 (Agath.), Ath.10.433d:—*scratch, tear, lacerate*, χερσὶ δ' ἄμυσσεν στήθεα Il.19. 284; *tear in pieces, mangle*, Hdt.3.76,108; ἀ. τοῖς ὄνυξιν, of the eagle, Arist.*HA*619ᵃ23:—esp. of any slight surface-wound, from whatever cause, *prick* as a thorn, Longus 1.14; *sting* as a fly, Luc *Musc.Enc* 6: abs., *scratch*, ἀμφοτέραισιν ἀ. Theoc.22.96; *sting*, Hp.*Mul.*1.78. II. metaph., σὺ δ' ἔνδοθι θυμὸν ἀμύξεις χωόμενος *thou wilt tear* thy heart with rage, Il.1.243, cf. Call.*Aet.*3.1.10; καρδίαν ἄμυξεν ἄλγος B.16. 19, cf. 17.11, A.*Pers.*161; φρὴν ἀμύσσεται φόβῳ ib.116; ὑπόμνημα δ' τὴν γνώμην ἀμύξει Aeschin. l.c., cf. Phld. l.c., Jul.*Or.*2.96a. (For ἀμύχ-yω, cf. ἀμυχή.)

**ἀμυστηρίαστος**, ον, *not initiated*, Sch.Theoc.3.51, *PLeid.W.*9.38.

**ἀμυστ-ί** [ῑ], Adv., (μύω) *without closing the mouth*, i.e. *at one draught*, ἀμυστὶ πιεῖν prob. in Hp.*Int.*12, cf. Pherecr.202, *Anacreont.* 8, Luc.*Lex.*8. **-ία**· μέτρον τι, Hsch. **-ίζω**, *drink at one draught*, ἠμύστισα E.*Cyc.*565: pres., Plu.2.650c. ***-ις**, ιος and ιδος (Alc. *Supp.*4.20), ἡ, *long draught*, ἄμυστιν προπιεῖν, πίνειν Anacr.63; ἑλκύσαι E.*Cyc.*417; χανδὸν ἄμυστιν οἰνοποτεῖν Call.*Aet.*1.1.11: metaph., ἄμυστιν ὥσπερ κύλικα πίνει τὸν βίον Epich.34. 2. *deep drinking, tippling*, E.*Rh.*438, cf. Sch. II. *large cup*, used by Thracians, ἄμυστιν ἐκλάπτειν Ar.*Ach.*1229, Amips.22, cf. Ath.11.783d.

**ἀμύσχεσθαι**· τὸ ξέειν τὰς σάρκας τοῖς ὄνυξιν, Hsch. **ἀμυσχῆναι**· καθᾶραι, ἁγνίσαι, Id.

**ἀμυσχρός**, ά, όν, (μύσος) *undefiled*, Parth.*Fr.*2, prob. l. in S.*Fr.* 1005, cf. Hsch., *EM*87.26 (ἀμυχρόν Phot.p.97 R.; ἀμυχνόν, ἀμυγνόν, ἀμύσκαρον are also cited by Suid.).

***ἀμῠχ-ή**, ἡ, (ἀμύσσω) *scratch, skin-wound*, Hp.*Epid.*7.32; ἀμυχὰς καταμύξαντες Phryn.Com.3; of *marks of strangling*, D.47.59. 2. Medic., *scarification*, Antyll.ap.Orib.7.18.3, Gal.10.964. II. = ἄμυξις, in sign of sorrow, ἀμυχὰς κοπτομένων ἀφεῖλεν Plu.*Sol.* 21. III. metaph., ἀ. καὶ ἑλκώσεις ἐν ταῖς φιλίαις Iamb.*VP*33. 231. **-ηδόν**, Adv., = ἀμύξ: hence, *slightly*, *EM*88.5. **-ιαῖος**, α, ον, *scratched slightly*: metaph., *superficial*, Pl.*Ax.*366a. **-μός**, ὁ, = ἄμυξις; ἀ. ξιφέων sword-*wound*, Theoc.24.126. **-νός**, **-ρος**, v. sub ἀμυσχρός. **-ούσης**· στυφούσης ἐπὶ πλέον, Hsch. **-ώδης**, ες, *chapped*, ἐξανθίσματα Hp.*Coac.*435.

**ἀμύω** (cf. ἠμύω), *sink down, fall*, [φύλλα] ἀμύοντα χαμᾶζε Hes.*Fr.* 96.86. **ἀμύωτος**, ον, dub. sens. in *GDI*4979 (Gortyn).

**ἀμφ-**, poet. for ἀναφ- (cf. ἀμπ-), but more commonly for ἀμφί before vowels.

**ἀμφάγαμαι**, *stand round and admire*: aor. -αγάσαντο Q.S.7.722.

**ἀμφᾰγᾰπάζω**, used by Hom. only in impf. ἀμφαγάπαζον, pres. part. Med. -όμενος; by later Ep. only in pres., impf., cf. *IG*12(9). 289.14 (Eretria, ii/i B.C., prob. l.):—*embrace with love, greet warmly*, Od.14.381, Canthar.2D. (2 sg. impf. -ηγάπαζες), A.R.3.258, etc.; so Med., Il.16.192, *h.Cer.*290.

**ἀμφᾰγᾰπάω**, Ep. = foreg., aor. ἀμφαγάπησε *h.Cer.*439; ἐὸν κακὸν ἀμφαγαπῶντες (i.e. Pandora) Hes.*Op.*58; ἀμφαγαπᾷ Orac.ap.D.S.8 *Fr.*21.

**ἀμφαγείρομαι**, Med., *gather round*, Hom. only in aor. 2, θεαὶ δέ μιν ἀμφαγέροντο Il.18.37, cf. A.R.4.1527: in later Ep. pres. ἀμφαγέρομαι Theoc.17.94, Opp.*H.*3.231, 4.114.

****ἀμφαγνοέω**, pres. assumed by Gramm. for deriv. of ἠμφηγνόουν, but v. ἀμφιγνοέω.

**ἀμφάγνυμαι**, *to be broken around*, πέλαγος ἕρκεσιν ἀ. prob. l. in J. *BJ*4.10.5.

**ἀμφ-άδην**, Adv., = ἀμφαδόν, Archil.66. ***-άδιος**, α, ον, (poet. for ἀναφάδιος which does not occur, v. sq.):—*public*, γάμος Od.6. 288. II. acc. fem. ἀμφαδίην as Adv., = ἀμφαδόν, *publicly, openly*, Il.13.356, Thgn.90, etc. ***-ᾰδόν**, Adv., poet. for ἀναφαδόν = ἀναφανδόν (ἀμφανδόν), *publicly, openly, without disguise*, opp. λάθρη, βαλέειν Il.7.243; opp. κρυφηδόν, Od.14.330; opp δόλῳ, κτείνειν 1.296; ἀ. πάντ' ἀγορεύειν Il.9.370; ὡς ἀ. πέπραγα πανταχῇ καλῶς Ion Trag.ap. Phot.p.98 R.—Prop. neut. of Adj. **ἀμφαδός**, ή, όν, which occurs in Od.19.391 μὴ ἀμφαδὰ ἔργα γένοιτο *discovered, known*, cf. A.R.3.615.

***ἀμφαεικής**· κύκλῳ σειομένης, Hsch.

**ἀμφαής**, shortened fr. ἀμφιφαής, Hsch.

**ἀμφαίνω**, poet. for ἀναφαίνω.

**ἀμφαΐσσομαι**, Pass., *rush on from all sides*, ἀμφὶ δέ τ' ἀΐσσονται [κύνες] Il.11.417; *float around*, ἀμφὶ δὲ χαῖται ὤμοις ἀΐσσοντο 6.510.

**ἀμφαιωρέω**, *cause to float around*, prob. for ἀμφαιρέω, Aret.*CA*1.

**ἀμφάκανθος**, ον, (ἄκανθα) *surrounded with prickles*, ἀ. δέμας, of hedgehog, Ion Trag.38.

**ἀμφάκης** [ᾱ], ες, Dor. for ἀμφήκης. ***ἀμφακλῆς**· ἀξίνη, Hsch.

**ἀμφᾰλᾰλάζω**, *shout around*, Nonn.*D.*40.98.

**ἀμφᾰλάλημαι**, *wander round about*, Opp.*C.*3.423.

**ἀμφαλλάξ**, Adv. strengthd. for ἀλλάξ, *alternately, reciprocally*, Ath. Mech.22.1, Ps.-Hes.ap.Ath.3.116c, *AP*12.238 (Strat.).

***ἀμφαλλάσσω**, *change entirely*, Opp.*C.*3.13.

**ἀμφανδόν**, Adv., poet. for ἀναφανδόν, prob. in Pi.*P.*9.41.

**ἀμφανέειν**, poet. for ἀναφανεῖν, inf. fut. of ἀναφαίνω, *h.Merc.*16.

***ἀμ-φανσις**, εως, ἡ, Cret. for ἀνάφανσις, *adoption*, *Leg.Gort* 10. 33. **-φαντός**, *adopted*, ib.50, al. **-φαντύς**, ύος, ἡ, = ἄμφανσις, ib.11.21.

***ἀμφάνω**, dub. sens., *GDI*5024.58 (Cret.), Hsch.

**ἀμφαξονέω**, (ἄξων) *go unsteadily, totter*: metaph. from wheels loose on axles, Paus.Gr.*Fr.*50.

**ἀμφᾰρᾰβέω**, Ep., *rattle* or *ring around*, τεύχεα ἀμφαράβησε Il.21. 408:—**ἀμφᾰρᾰβίζω**, in Ep. impf. ἀμφαράβιζεν Hes.*Sc.*64.

**ἀμφαρής**· πωρουμένη, κατολιγωρουμένη, Hsch.: also glossed by γυμνός (i.e. ἀφαρής) and ἐπιφανής (i.e. ἀμφιφαής), Id.

**ἀμφᾰρίστερος**, ον, *with two left hands*, i.e. *utterly awkward* or *clumsy* (cf. ἀμφιδέξιος), Ar.*Fr.*512: hence, *luckless*, Hsch., Eust. 1228.44.

**ἀ(μ)φαρμένη**· δίκελλα, Hsch.

**ἀμφᾰσίη**, ἡ, Ep. for ἀφασία, *speechlessness* caused by fear, amazement, or rage, δὴν δέ μιν ἀμφασίη ἐπέων λάβε Il.17.695, Od.4.704, cf. A.R.3.284, Bion *Fr.*13.1.

**ἄμφασμα**, τό, *cake* soaked in wine and honey (Syrac.), Hsch.

**ἀμφαυγεῖ**· ἀντιλάμπει, Hsch.

**ἄμφαυξις**, εως, ἡ, (αὔξειν) *callus* or *overgrowth* on the scar of a removed branch (cf. ἀμφιφύα), Thphr.*HP*3.7.1.

***ἀμφαϋτέω**, *ring around*, κόρυθες δ' ἀμφ' αὖον ἀΰτευν Il.12.160.

***ἀμφαφάω**, *touch* or *feel all round*, κοῖλον λόχον ἀμφαφόωσα Od.4. 277; καί κ' ἀλαὸς . . διακρίνειε τὸ σῆμα ἀμφαφόων *by feeling* it, 8.196; *handle*, τόξον ἐΰξοον ἀμφαφόωντας 19.586; 2 sg. ἀμφαφάεις Orph.*L.* 528; Ep. impf. ἀμφαφάασκε Mosch.2.95:—also Med. like Act., τὸν μὲν . . χείρεσιν ἀμφαφόωντο Od.15.461, cf. 19.475; τόξον οἶδα . . ἀμφαφάασθαι (Ep. inf.) 8.215. 2. of persons, μαλακώτερος ἀμφαφάασθαι easier *to deal with*, Il.22.373.—Ep. Verb used by Aret. in forms -όωσι *SD*2.4, *CA*1.1; -όωντα ib.2.4; cf. ἀμφαφᾷς· ψηλαφᾷς, Hsch.

***ἀμφεικάς**, άδος, ἡ (sc. ἡμέρα), *day next after the twentieth, twenty-first*, *Test.Epict.*3.1, cf. *GDI*3720 (Cos), Hsch. s. v. ἀμφ' εἰκάς.

**ἀμφεκτέον**· περιβλητέον, Hsch. **ἀμφεκτήρ**· χιτὼν διπλοῦς, Id. **ἀμφελαΐς**· μᾶζα ἐλαίου πλήρης, Id.

**ἀμφελελίζω**, *shake all round*, γαῖαν Orph.*Fr.*285.6; οὐρανόν Nonn. *D.*13.361; *brandish*, 42.318:—Pass., *swing* or *wave to and fro*, Q.S. 11.465. **ἀμφελικτός**, όν, poet. for ἀμφιελ-, *coiled round*, E.*HF* 398. **ἀμφελίσσω**, poet. and Ion. for ἀμφιελ-, *wrap, fold about*, ἀμφελίξαντες χέρας Id.*Andr.*425; *enwrap*, Aret.*CA*2.4:—Med., τέκνοισιν γνάθους ἀμφελίξασθαι *close their* jaws *upon* the children, Pi.*N.* 1.43.

**ἀμφέλκω**, *draw around*: Med., ἀμφέλκεσθαί τι *draw* a thing *round one*, i.e. *be surrounded by* it, D.P.268.

**ἀμφελόνη**· *amictus*, *Gloss.*

**ἀμφελυτρ-όω**, *wrap round*, Lyc.75. ***-ωσις**, εως, ἡ, *wrapper, coating*, Id.845.

**ἀμφεμμένος**, poet. pf. part. of ἀμφιέννυμι. **ἀμφενέπω**, strengthd. for ἐνέπω, v.l. in Nic.*Th.*627.

**ἀμφέπω**, v. ἀμφιέπω.

**ἀμφερείδω**, *fix around*, ζυγόν τινι Lyc.504.

**ἀμφερέφω**, *cover up*, *AP*11.37 (Antip.).

**ἀμφερκής**, ές, *fenced round*, πίθος Achae.36.

**ἀμφερυθαίνω**, *redden, make red all over*, Q.S.1.60.

**ἀμφέρχομαι**, *surround*, Hom. only aor. 2, c. acc., με κουράων ἀμφήλυθε θῆλυς ἀϋτή Od.6.122; με κνίσης ἀμφήλυθεν ἡδὺς ἀϋτμή 12. 369. II. intr., *pass, elapse*, of time, αἱ φωνίοι πεντεκαίδεκ' ἀμέρανς ἀμφεληλεύθεν (pf. inf.) ὁ ἄρχων τᾶς δίκας *GDI*4999 (Gortyn).

**ἀμφέρω**, v. ἀναφέρω.

**ἀμφεωρία**· περισσευομένη, Hsch.

**ἀμφεώτας**· ὁ Κρητικὸς χιτών, Hsch.

**ἀμφηγερέθομαι**, Ep. = ἀμφαγείρομαι, ἀμφὶ δ' . . ἠγερέθοντο Od.17. 34.

***ἀμφήκης**, ες, (ἀκή A) *two-edged*, φάσγανον, ξίφος, Il.10.256, Od.16. 80, B.10.87, etc.; κέντρον, δόρυ, A.*Pr.*692 (lyr.), *Ag.*1149; ἔγχος, γένυς, S.*Aj.*286, *El.*485; of lightning, *forked*, πυρὸς ἀ. βόστρυχος A. *Pr.*1044; κεραυνός Cleanth.1.10. II. metaph., ἀ. γλῶττα tongue *that will cut both ways*, i.e. maintain either right or wrong, Ar.*Nu.* 1160 (parod.); of an oracle, *ambiguous*, ἀ. καὶ διπρόσωπος Luc.*J.Tr.* 43.

***ἀμφημερινὸς** πυρετός, *quotidian fever*, opp. τριταῖος and τεταρταῖος, Hp.*Epid.*1.6, Pl.*Ti.*86a: neut. as Adv., -νὸν πυρεταίνειν Aret. *SD*1.2:—also **-ήμερος** (sc. πυρετός), S.*Fr.*507.

**ἄμφην**, Aeol. for αὐχήν, q.v. **ἀμφήν**· αὐλήν, Hsch.

**ἀμφηρεφής**, ές, (ἐρέφω) *covered on both sides, close-covered*, epith. of Apollo's quiver, Il.1.45: in late Prose, ἄντρον Agath.1.10, cf. 3.5; στάδιον ἀ. ὕλαις Zos.2.50.

**ἀμφήρης**, ες, (ἀραρίσκω) *fitted* or *joined on both sides*; ξύλα ἀ. wood of the funeral pyre *regularly piled all round*, E.*HF*243; ἀ. σκηναὶ wellings *well secured*, Id.*Ion* 1128. II. (ἐρέσσω) *with oars on both sides*, Hsch.; ἀ. δόρυ *sculling*-boat, E.*Cyc.* 15.

**ἀμφηρικός**, ή, όν, = ἀμφήρης II: ἀκάτιον ἀ. *sculling*-boat, Th.4.67.

**ἀμφήριστος**, ον, (ἐρίζω) *contested on both sides, disputed, doubtful*, ἀμφήριστον ἔθηκεν, i.e. made it a dead-heat, Il.23.382; γένος ἀ. Call. *Iov.*5; νεῖκος A.R.3.627; ἐλπίδες Plb.5.85.6; ἐς ἀμφήριστον ἐλθεῖν τινι App.*Pun.*51; *evenly matched*, πόλεις Str.8.4.8, cf. Q.S.5.310, Luc.*Eun.*4, etc.; of stars, *of doubtful position*, Serap. in *Cat.Cod. Astr.*1.100.

**ἄμφης·** ἀμφίας, Hsch.

***ἀμφί**, Prep. with gen., dat., acc.: (cf. Skt. *abhitas* 'on both sides', Lat. *ambi-*):—radic. sense, *on both sides*; chiefly Poet. and Ion. Prose, replaced by περί in later Gk.

A. c. GEN. (Poet., Hdt., X.): I. causal, *about, for the sake of*, ἀ. πίδακος μάχεσθαι fight *for the possession of* a spring, Il.16.825; ἀ. γυναικός Pi.*P.*9.105, A.*Ag.*62; ἀ. λέκτρων E.*Andr.*123: like πρός, in entreaties, πρὸς Ζηνός.. Φοίβου τ' ἀ. *for* Phoebus' *sake*, A.R.2. 216. 2. *about, concerning*, once in Hom., ἀμφ' Ἄρεος φιλότητος ἀείδειν sing *of* love, Od.8.267; ἀμφὶ τιμῆς *h.Merc.*172 (cf. c. 4); once in Hdt., ἀμφὶ κρίσιος (as v.l. for κρίσι) μνηστήρων τοσαῦτα ἐγένετο 6.131; more freq. in poets, ἀ. δαιμόνων Pi.*O.*1.35, cf. A.*Th.*1017, E.*Supp.*642, etc.; prob. l. in S.*Ph.*554. II. of Place, *about, around*, post-Hom., ἀ. ταύτης τῆς πόλιος Hdt.8.104; τὸν ἀ. Λίμνας τρόχον E.*Hipp.*1133.

B. c. DAT. (Poet., Ion. and later Prose): I. of Place, *on both sides of*, ἀμφ' ὀχέεσσι Il.5.723; ἀ. κεφαλῇ, ὤμοισιν, στήθεσσι, ποσσί, *about* the head, etc., ib.24.163, 3.328, Od.16.174, Il.13.36; ἀ. δέρᾳ Sapph.*Supp.*23.16; ἀμφί οἱ *around* him, Il.12.396; μοι ἀμφ' αὐτῷ *around* me, 9.470; likewise ἀμφὶ περὶ στήθεσσι Od.11.609:—*all round*, κρέα ἀμφ' ὀβελοῖσι μεμύκει *round*, i.e. *upon*, spits, ib.12.395; πεπαρμένη ἀμφ' ὀνύχεσσι Hes.*Op.*250. 2. more generally, *at, by*, ἀ. πύλῃσι μάχεσθαι *at* the gates, Il.12.175; ἀμφὶ [κόρυθι] διατρυφέν smashed *on* the helmet, 3.362; ἀ. πυρί *on* the fire, 18.344; ἀμφ' ἐμοί *clinging to* me, Od.11.423; esp. of falling *over* one, Il.4.493; of a guardian, *over*, φύλακα ἀ. σοι λείψω S.*Aj.*562; ἀ. γούνασι πίπτειν E.*Alc.*947. II. of Time, ἁλίῳ ἀ. ἑνί *in compass of* one day, Pi. *O.*13.37. III. generally, of connexion or association, without distinct notion of place, ἀ. νεκροῖσιν *as concerning* the dead, Il.7. 408; freq. in Pi., ὅσσα δ' ἀμφ' ἀέθλοις *as far as concerns* games, *N.*2. 17; ἐπ' ἔργοισιν ἀ. τε βουλαῖς *in* deeds and counsels, Id.*P.*5.119; *in virtue of*, ἀμφὶ σοφίᾳ 1.12; ἐμᾷ ἀ. μαχανᾷ 8.34; ἀμφ' ἀρετᾷ 1.80, cf. *O.*8.42; σέο ἀμφὶ τρόπῳ *N.*1.29; ἀ. ἰατορίᾳ *in respect of* healing, B.1. 39. IV. causal, *about, for the sake of*, ἀμφ' Ἑλένῃ μάχεσθαι Il.3. 70; ἀ. γυναικὶ ἄλγεα πάσχειν ib.157, cf. Luc.*DDeor.*20.14; ἀ. τοῖσδε καλχαίνων τέκνοις E.*Heracl.*40, cf. *Rh.*457 (lyr.); ἀ. δώλῳ μωλίειν *Leg.Gort.*1.17; *concerning*, Od.1.48; εἰπὼν ἀμφ' Ὀδυσῆϊ 14.364; ἀρνεύμενον ἀ. βόεσσι *h.Merc.*390; ἀ. Τειρεσίαο βουλαῖς Pi.*I.*7(6).8; ἔξετ' ἀμφ' ἐμοὶ τροφήν S.*OC*1614, cf. *El.*1144; ἔρις ἀ. μουσικῇ Hdt. 6.129; ἀ. σοι A.*Ag* 890; ἀ. τῷ θανάτῳ αὐτῆς λόγος λέγεται *about* her death it is reported, Hdt.3.32, cf. S.*Aj.*303; ἀ. βοῶν ἀγέλαις δόμον αὔξειν B.9.44. 2. of impulses, ἀ. τάρβει, ἀ. φόβῳ *for* very fear, A.*Ch.*547, E.*Or.*825; ἀ. θυμῷ S.*Fr.*565; ἀμφ' ὀδύνῃ A.R.2.96. V. like ἐπί, *added to*, πόνος ἀ. πόνῳ Simon.39.

C. c. ACC., most freq. in Prose (twice only in Th.): I. of Place, *about, around*, mostly with a sense of motion, ἀ. μιν φᾶρος βάλον Il.24.588, cf. Od.10.365; ἀ. βωμίαν ἔπτηξε παστάδα E.*HF* 984. 2. generally, *by, on*, ἀμφ' ἅλα *by* the sea, Il.1.409; ἀ. ῥέεθρα *somewhere by* the banks, 2.461; ἀ. περὶ κρήνην *somewhere about* the fountain, 2.305; ἀ. ἄστυ *all about in* the city, 11.706; Τάρταρον ἀ. μέγαν *somewhere* in Tartarus, *h.Ap.*336, cf. A.*Pr.*1029; ἀ. Εὔβοιαν B.9.34; ἀ. Θρῄκην E.*Andr.*215; ἀ. ψάμαθον *somewhere on* the sand, S.*Aj.*1064; ἀ. βωμόν *at* the altar, E.*IT*705; περὶ πίδακας ἀ. Theoc. 7.142; of motion, *to the neighbourhood of*, ἦλθες ἀ. Δωδώνην A.*Pr.* 830. 3. of persons grouped *about* one, οἱ ἀ. Πρίαμον Priam *and his train*, Il.3.146, cf. 2.417,445; οἱ ἀ. Ξέρξεα his *army*, Hdt.8. 25; but οἱ ἀ. Κορινθίους, οἱ ἀ. Μεγαρέας καὶ Φλειασίους the Corinthians, Megarians, etc., and those *next* them, Id.9.69: hence Att., οἱ ἀ. Πρωταγόραν the *school of* Protagoras or even Protagoras himself, Pl. *Tht.*170c; οἱ ἀ. Εὐθύφρονα Euthyphro's *friends*, *Cra.*399e, cf. Th.8. 65; of a single person, perh. Pl.*Hp.Ma.*281c; so in later Prose, as Luc.*VH*2.18. 4. τὰ ἀ. τι that which *concerns* a thing, τὰ ἀ. τὸ ἄριστον Th.7.40; τὰ ἀ. τὴν δίαιταν domestic arrangements, X.*Cyr.*8. 2.6. 5. causal, *about, for the sake of*, κλαίειν ἀ. τινα weep *about* or *for* one, Il.18.339; μνήσασθαι ἀ. τινα make mention *of* one, *h.Hom.* 7.1, cf. Terp.2, Ar.*Nu.*595; κελαδέοντι φᾶμαι ἀ. Κινύραν Pi.*P.*2.15, cf. *I.*7(6).9, A.*Th* 843; ἀ. νιν γηθόμενος S.*Tr.*937. 6. ἀ. τι ἔχειν to be occupied *about* a thing, ἀ. λιτάν' ἔξομεν A.*Th.*101; ἀ. δεῖπνον εἶχεν X.*Cyr.*5.5.44, cf. 5.2.26; εἶναι ἀμφί τι 7.1.1; ἀ. τὰν δ[ί]ασιν *Leg. Gort.*5.46. II. of Time, *throughout, for*, τὸν λοιπὸν ἀ. βίοτον, τὸν ὅλον ἀ. χρόνον, Pi.*O.*1.97, 2.30; *about, at the time of, during*, ἀ. Πλειάδων δύσιν A.*Ag.*826; ἀ. τὸν χειμῶνα X.*Cyr.*8.6.22, etc. 2. of Number, ἀ. τὰς δώδεκα μυριάδας *about* 120,000, ib.1.2.15.

D. POSITION. In poets ἀμφί sts. follows its case, οἵ δέ μιν ἀμφί Od.23.46, cf. 10.218, B.17.53; φρένας ἀ. Hes.*Th.*554, Mimn.1.7; but never suffers anastrophe, Hdn.Gr.1.480.

E. WITHOUT CASE, as Adv., *about, around, on both* or *all sides*, freq. in Ep., ῥῆξεν δέ οἱ ἀ. χιτῶνα Il.13.439; ἀ. δὲ λειμών *around* is meadow, Od.6.292; so ἀ. περὶ Il.21.10, etc.

F. IN COMPOS.: I. *on both sides*, ἀμφίστομος, ἀμφίαλος. 2. *on all sides*, ἀμφιβάλλω I.3, ἀμφιλαμβάνω, ἀμφιλαφής. II. causal, *for the sake of*, ἀμφιμάχομαι, ἀμφιτρομέω.

***ἀμφιάζω**, Plu.*CG*2 (v.l.): fut. -άσω Alciphr.3.42: aor. ἠμφίασα *AP*7.368 (Eryc.), *OGI*200.24 (Axum), Polyaen.1.27.2 (v.l.), (μετ-) Philostr.*Her.Prooem.*2: pf. ἠμφίακα (συν-) Clearch.25:—Med., fut. -άσομαι (μετ-) Luc.*Herm.*86 codd.: aor. ἠμφιασάμην Apollod. 2.1.2, etc.: pf. ἠμφίασμαι in med. sense (μετ-) D.S.16.11 (v.l.):—ἀμφιέζω is a common v.l.: (perh. from ἀμφί, as ἀντιάζω from ἀντί):—later word for ἀμφιέννυμι, *clothe*, τινά Plu. l.c.; ἱματίοις τινά Alciphr. l.c.: metaph., of the grave, ὀστέα ἠμφίασεν *AP*l.c.; σοφίαν ἀσαφείᾳ Them.*Or.*13.235a:—Med., *put on*, ἀμφιάσασθαί τι Lxx *Jb.*40.5, Apollod. l.c.

**ἀμφιαλής**, ές, (ἅλς B) *sea-girt*, Δῆλος Maiist 6.

***ἀμφίᾰλος**, ον, = foreg., freq. of Ithaca in Od., as 1.386,395: of Lemnos, S.*Ph.*146; with ref. to Corinth, *of two seas*, ἀ. Ποτειδᾶνος τεθμοί, of Isthmian games, Pi.*O.*13.40. 2. *living amid seas*, ζῷον Plu.2.667e. 3. ἡ ἀ. (sc. ὁδός) dub. l. in X.*HG*4.2.13.

**ἀμφιάνακτες**, ων, οἱ, nickname of *dithyrambic poets*, because their odes often began thus—ἀμφί μοι αὖθις ἄνακτα or ἀμφί μοι αὖτε, ἄναξ, Sch.Ar.*Nu.*595. **ἀμφιανακτίζω**, *sing dithyrambic hymns*, Cratin. 67, Ar.*Fr.*59, cf. foreg.

***Ἀμφιάραος**, ου (also Ἀμφιάρης Pi.*N.*9.24, -ηος *O.*6.13), Att. Ἀμφιάρεως (choriamb. in S.*OC*1313), ω, *Amphiaraus*, Argive hero and seer, A., etc.; prob. also called Ἄμφις A.*Fr.*410:— hence **Ἀμφιαρᾷον**, τό, *sanctuary of A.*, esp. at Oropus, and ***Ἀμφιαράϊα**, τά, *festival of A.* held there, *IG*7.48, al., cf. Did.ap.Sch.Pi.*O.*7.153, Str. 9.1.22, etc. ***Ἀμφιάρειον**, τό, cj. in Pi.*I.*7(6).33; cf. Ἀμφιερα[ϊ]στής.

**ἀμφίας**, ὁ, a bad Sicilian wine, Nicostr.Com.18, Sosicr.Com.7; cf. ἄμφης.

**ἀμφίασ-ις**, εως, ἡ, (ἀμφιάζω) *garment*, Lxx *Jb.*22.6, al. ***-μα**, ατος, τό, *garment*, Ctes.*Fr.*29.10, Luc.*Cyn.*17. ***-μός**, ὁ, = ἀμφίασις, D.H.8.62 (pl.).

**ἀμφῐάχυῖα**, irreg. part., perh. for ἀμφι-ϝάχυῖα (cf. ἰάχω = ϝιϝάχω), *flying about and shrieking*, of a bird, Il.2.316; later ἀμφ-ιάχω as pres., μέγα ἀμφιάχων Orph.*A.*819: impf. ἀμφίαχε λαός Q.S.4.147; trans., βοὴ ἀμφίαχεν ἄστυ 13.460.

**ἀμφιβαίνω**, fut. -βήσομαι, etc.:—*go about* or *around*, ἠέλιος μέσον οὐρανὸν ἀμφιβεβήκει sun *in his course had reached* mid-heaven, Il 8. 68. 2. *bestride*, ἀμφ' ἑνὶ δούρατι βαῖνε *he bestrode* a beam, Od.5. 371, ἵππον ἀ. Call.*Del.*113; ἀ. θηλείαις, of a cock, Babr.5.8: esp., 3. *bestride* a fallen friend, *so as to protect* him, ἀμφὶ κασιγνήτῳ βεβαὼς Il. 14.477: hence, b. of tutelary deities, *guard, protect*, Χρύσην ἀμφιβέβηκας ib.1.37; δαίμονες ἀμφιβάντες πόλιν A.*Th.*175:—so, of a wild beast, *guard* its young, Opp.*C.*3.218; or its prey, X.*Cyn.*10. 13. II. *surround, encompass*, c. acc., νεφέλη σκόπελον ἀμφιβέβηκε Od.12.74; σὲ πόνος φρένας ἀμφιβέβηκεν Il.6.355, cf. Od.8.541; ταραγμὸν ἀμφιβάντ' εἶχον μάχης E.*Ph.*1406; ὦ μοῖρα.. οἷά με.. ἀμφιβᾶσ' ἔχεις Id.*Andr.*1082: c. dat., Τρώων νέφος ἀμφιβέβηκε νηυσίν Il.16.66; ἀ. ἀμφί τι, of a slit bandage which *embraces* a tender part without pressing on it, Hp.*Art.*33. 2. metaph., τόδε μοι θράσος ἀμφιβαίνει E.*Supp.*609; ἀμφιβᾶσα φλὸξ οἴνου, metaph. from flame *spreading round* a vessel on the fire, *Alc.*758.

***Ἀμφίβαιος**, ὁ, epith. of Poseidon at Cyrene, = ἀμφίγαιος, γαιήοχος, Tz. ad Lyc.749.

***ἀμφιβάλλω**, fut. -βαλῶ, etc.:—Med., Ep. fut. ἀμφιβαλεῦμαι Od. 22.103:—*throw* or *put round*, used by Hom. mostly in tmesi: I. of clothes, etc., *put them on* a person, c. dupl. acc. pers. et rei, ἀμφὶ δέ με χλαῖναν.. βάλεν ἠδὲ χιτῶνα Od.10.365, cf. 451; ἀμφὶ δέ μιν ῥάκος ..βάλεν 13.434: c. dat. pers., ἀμφὶ δέ μοι ῥάκος.. βάλον v.l. in 14. 342; ἀμφὶ δ' Ἀθήνη ὤμοις.. βάλ' αἰγίδα Il.18.204; στολὴν.. ἀμφέβαλλε σῷ κάρᾳ E.*HF*465; γῆρας κόμαις Pi.*P.*5.32:—Med., *put round one-self*, δὸς δὲ ῥάκος ἀμφιβαλέσθαι Od.6.178, cf. 22.103, etc.; ἄγραν.. ἀ. πλοκάμοις E.*Ba.*104. b. metaph. and half metaph., τῷ δ' ἐγὼ ἀμφιβαλὼν θάλαμον δέμον I built chamber *over* him, Od.23.192; ζυγὸν Ἑλλάδι ἀ. A.*Pers.*50, cf. 72; ἀνδράσι κρατὴρ ὕπνον ἀμφιβάλλῃ E.*Ba.* 385; ἐξ ὅτου λευκὴν ἐκ μελαίνης ἀμφιβάλλομαι τρίχα since *I have put on* white hair, S.*Ant.*1093; ἀ. νέφος θανάτου Simon.99. c. Act. in med. sense, κρατερὸν μένος ἀμφιβαλόντες [ἑαυτοῖς] 'girding themselves with strength', Il.17.742; δουλοσύναν ἀμφιβαλοῦσα κάρᾳ [ἐμαυτῆς] E.*Andr.*110: reversely, Med. for Act., ἀμφιβάλλεσθαι Ἀΐδαν ἐπί τινι 1191:—Pass., ὕμνος ἀμφιβάλλεται σοφῶν μητίεσσι song *is cast* (*like a net*) *over* the minds of poets, Pi.*O.*1.8. 2. *throw* the arms *round*, so as to embrace, c. dat. pers., ἀμφ' Ὀδυσῆϊ.. χεῖρε βαλόντε Od.21.223; ἀμφὶ δὲ χεῖρας δειρῇ βάλλ' Ὀδυσῆϊ 23.208; ἀμφὶ δὲ παιδὶ.. βάλε πήχεε 24.347; but ἀμφὶ δὲ χεῖρας βάλλομεν, of *seizing* or *taking prisoner*, 4.454; also ἀμφὶ δὲ χεῖρα.. βάλεν ἔγχεϊ *grasped* it, 21.433; ἀμφὶ δὲ.. βάλε γούνασι χεῖρας, as a suppliant, 7. 142. 3. c. acc. pers., *encompass, embrace*, ἀμφιβαλόντε ἀλλήλους Il. 23.97; ἀ. τινὰ χερσί E.*Ba.*1363; ἀ. μαστὸν ὠλέναισι *Ph.*306; ἀ. μέλη *Supp.*70. 4. *encompass, beset*, δυσμενὴς ὅρι' ἀμφιβάλλει B.17.6; πόλιν φόνῳ E.*Andr.*799, cf. *Trag.Adesp.*127.6 (lyr.); ἀ. φῦλον ὀρνίθων *surround* them *with nets*, S.*Ant.*344; *strike* or *hit on all sides*, τινὰ βέλεσι E.*HF*422. b. abs., *fish* (cf. ἀμφιβληστρον), *Ev.Marc.*1.16, cf. *PFlor.*2.119.3 (ii A.D.). c. metaph., ἀμφὶ κτύπος οὔατα βάλλει Il.10.535 (unless ἀ. be Adv.). II. *force, move round*, τὸ ἄρθρον v.l. for ἀμφισφάλλω (q.v.), Hp.*Art.*2. III. *doubt*, περί τινος Plb. 39.5.2: also folld. by inf., Hld.5.17; by ὡς.. Ael.*NA*9.33; by ὅτι.. Hermog.*Id.*2.10; περί τινος Id.*Meth.*23. IV. intr., ἀ. εἰς τόπον *go into another* place, E.*Cyc.*60. 2. *to be doubtful* or *in dispute*,

Arist.*EE*1243a12,25; ἀμφιβάλλειν εἴωθε τὰ φίλτρα *are uncertain* in their action, Alciphr.1.37:—Pass., *to be in dispute*, Simp.*in Ph.*21.11. V. Med., *change*, μορφήν Opp.*C.*3.16.

⊛**ἀμφιβαρής**, gloss on ἀμφικέλεμνον, Hsch., Phot.

**ἀμφίβᾰσις**, εως, ἡ, *defence of* fallen comrade, δεῖσε δ' ὅ γ' ἀμφίβασιν.. Τρώων Il.5.623.

**ἀμφιβάσκω**, = ἀμφιβαίνω, Sapph.*Supp.*10.7. **ἀμφιβατεῖν**· ἀμφισβητεῖν, Hsch.

**ἀμφίβιος**, ον, *living a double life*, esp. *amphibious*, νομή, of frogs, Batr.59; ἀ. στόμα Pl.*Epigr.*2, cf. *Ax.*368b; θήρ Man.4.23; of plants, Thphr.*HP*1.4.3; ἀμφίβιον, τό, = ἀλόη, Ps.-Dsc.3.22:—said by Thphr. (*Fr.*171.12) to have been first used by Democr. 2. metaph., of the soul, *denizen of two worlds*, Plot.4.8.4; of man, Hierocl.*in CA*23p.468M.; ὁ κατὰ τὴν ζωὴν κόσμος ἐστὶν οἷον ἀμφίβιον Dam.*Pr.*81, cf. 85; φύσις ἀ. ib.399, cf. 400; of the moon, ἄστρον ἀ. πρὸς νύκτα καὶ ἡμέραν Max.Tyr.40.4; of Tiresias (who lived both as man and as woman), Luc.*Astr.*11.

**ἀμφίβλημα**, ατος, τό, *something thrown round*, *enclosure*, E.*Hel.*70. II. *garment*, *cloak*, πέπλους τε τοὺς πρὶν λαμπρά τ' ἀμφιβλήματα ib.423; πάνοπλα ἀ. *coats* of panoply, Id.*Ph.*779; *coverlet*, Aret.*SD*2.6.

**ἀμφιβληστρ-ευτική** (sc. τέχνη), ἡ, *net-fishery*, Poll.7.139. **-εύω**, *catch with a net*, Aq.*Is.*51.20 (Pass.). **-ικός**, ή, όν, *serving for a net*, Pl.*Sph.*235b. **-οειδής**, ές, *net-like*, χιτών prob. *the retina*, Gal.*UP*3.6, 10.2, cf. Ruf.*Onom.*153, Poll.2.71. ⊛**-ον**, τό, *anything thrown round*: 1. *casting-net*, Hes.*Sc.*215, Hdt.1.141, 2.95; ἀμφιβλήστρῳ περιβάλλεσθαι Men.27, cf. Stratt.7, Epil.1, Ph.*Bel.*95, *Ev.Matt.*4.18. b. metaph., of *the garment thrown like a net over* Agamemnon, A.*Ag.*1382, *Ch.*492; of the shirt of Nessus, Ἐρινύων ὑφαντὸν ἀ. S.*Tr.*1052; ἀμφίβληστρα σώματος ῥάκη rags *thrown around* body, E.*Hel.*1079. 2. *fetter*, *bond*, A.*Pr.*81. 3. of *encircling* walls, ἀμφίβληστρα τοίχων E.*IT*96.

⊛**ἀμφίβλητος**, ον, *put* or *thrown round*, ῥάκη E.*Fr.*697.

**ἀμφιβο-άομαι**, Pass., *to be celebrated*, *PCair.*67120F39 (vi A.D.). ⊛**-ητος**, ον, *sounding round*, *resounding*, Call.*Del.*303; κτύπος Nonn.*D.*45.44. 2. *noised abroad*, *far-famed*, *AP*9.241 (Antip.), cf. Nonn.*D.*26.141.

⊛**ἀμφιβολ-εύς**, έως, ὁ, (ἀμφιβάλλω) *fisherman*, Lxx *Is.*19.8. **-έω**, *to be in doubt*, Greg.Cor. in Rh.7.1339W. **-ή**, ἡ, *cast* as of a net, λίνοιο ἀ. *fishing-net*, Opp.*H.*4.149. **-ητικός**, ή, όν, *ambiguous*, φωνή Olymp.*in Cat.*86.39. **-ία**, Ion. **-ίη**, ἡ, *state of being attacked on both sides*, ἀμφιβολίῃ ἔχεσθαι Hdt.5.74. II. *ambiguity*, Arist.*Po.*1461a25, *SE*165b26, cf. Epicur.*Nat.*28.5, D.H.*Rh.*8.16, Ael.*Tact.*47(51).1, A.D.*Synt.*311.10, etc.; *double entente*, Cic.*Fam.*7.32.2, cf. Philostr.*VS*2.25.1; ἀ. ἀναιρεῖν remove *doubt*, Plu.2.1050a; *uncertainty of mind*, App.*Pun.*42. ⊛**-ος**, ον, *put round*, *encompassing*, σπάργανα E.*Ion*1490; ὄρη Opp.*C.*2.133: Subst. -βολον, τό, κλωστοῦ -βόλοις λίνοιο E.*Tr.*537, cf. *AP*6.296 (Leon.). II. *struck* or *attacked on both* or *all sides*, A.*Th.*298; ἀ. εἶναι to be *between two fires*, Th.4.32,36; ἀ. γεγονέναι ὑπὸ τῶν πολεμίων Plu.*Cam.*34, cf. Ph.*Bel.*86.13. 2. Act., *hitting at both ends*, *double-pointed*, κάμακες *AP*6.131 (Leon.). III. *doubtful*, *ambiguous*, Pl.*Cra.*437a, X.*Mem.*1.2.35, etc.; τἀγαθὰ ἐς ἀμφίβολον ἀσφαλῶς ἔθεντο prudently accounted their good fortune as *doubtful*, Th.4.18; ἐς ἀ. θέσθαι call *in question*, Plu.2.756c; τὰ ἅπαξ κεκριμένα ἀ. ποιῆσαι *OGI*664 (Egypt, i A.D.); ἀ. νόμος Arist.*Rh.*1375b11; τὸ ἀ. *Top.*162a29; ἀμφίβολα λέγειν *Rh.*1407a37; δηλώσεις ἀ. Epicur.*Ep.*1p.27U.; συλλογισμοί, λέξεις, Chrysipp.*Stoic.*2.67,107; διάλεκτοι, prob. *contradictory*, ib.56,58; οἰνάριον ἀ. *doubtful* whether it is wine or vinegar, Polioch.2.8; ἐν ἀμφιβόλῳ εἶναι to be *doubtful*, Luc.*D.Mort.*1.1; κατὰ δύο ἀμφίβολα Olymp.*in Mete.*22.27. Adv., οὐκ ἀμφιβόλως A.*Th.*863; ἀ. ἔχειν D.H.*Rh.*10.5; δέξασθαι Arr.*Tact.*31.1. IV. of persons, *in doubt*, *wavering*, *uncertain*, Luc.*DDeor.*20.11, D.C.37.36, etc.; also ἀ. βίος, of a turncoat, Luc.*Pseudol.*16; ἄνθρωπος, of a eunuch, Lib.*Eth.*26.3.

**ἀμφιβόσκομαι**, Dep., *eat all about*, Luc.*Trag.*303.

**ἀμφίβουλος**, ον, *double-minded*: c. inf., *half-minded* to do, A.*Eu.*733 (cj. Turneb.).

**ἀμφιβράγχια**, τά, *parts about the tonsils*, Hp.*Int.*53.

**ἀμφίβρᾰχυς**, εια, υ, *short at both ends*: ὁ ἀ., the metrical foot ⏑ – ⏑, e.g. ἄμεινον, D.H.*Comp.*17, Heph.3.2.

**ἀμφίβροτος**, η, ον, also ος, ον, *covering the whole man*, Hom. always ἀμφιβρότη ἀσπίς Il.2.389; ἀ. χθών, of body as *surrounding* soul, Emp.148; ἀ. κώδεια (ἡ γὰρ κεφαλὴ συνέχει πᾶν τὸ σῶμα Sch.) Nic.*Al.*216.

**ἀμφίβροχος**, ον, *thoroughly soaked*, *AP*7.27 (Antip.).

**ἀμφιβώμιος**, ον, *at the altar*, E.*Tr.*562.

⊛**ἀμφίβωτος**, ον, contr. from ἀμφιβόητος, Ion Trag.35.

**ἀμφιγάνυμαι**, = ἀμφιγηθέω, Q.S.1.62.

**ἀμφίγειος**, ον, *with land on both sides*, θάλασσα Phot., Suid. s.v. πορθμός.

**ἀμφιγενής**, ές, *of doubtful gender*, Eust.668.48.

**ἀμφίγενυς**, υ, gen. υος, *two-edged*, of an axe, Hsch.

**ἀμφιγηθέω**, *rejoice throughout*, *h.Ap.*273.

**ἀμφίγλωσσος**, ον, *ambiguous*, Eust.489.19, al.

**ἀμφιγνοέω**: impf. ἠμφεγνόουν Pl.*Sph.*236c, X.*An.*2.5.33: aor. ἠμφεγνόησα Pl.*Plt.*291b, *Sph.*228e (ἀμφαγνοέω v.l. in X.*An.* l.c., and Procop.*Goth.*2.16):—*to be doubtful* or *mistaken about* a thing, τι Pl.*Sph.*228e; περί τινος Isoc.2.28; ἐπί τινος πότερον.. Pl.*Grg.*466c; ὑπέρ τινος Procop. l.c.; ἠμφεγνόουν ὅ τι ἐποίουν *they knew not wh*[at] they were about, X.*An.* l.c.; οὐκ ἀμφιγνοῶ σε γεγονότα συστρατιώτ[ην] *I am* not *mistaken in thinking*.., Plu.*Pomp.*79:—Pass., ἀμφιγνοηθ[είς] *unrecognized*, X.*HG*6.5.26; but ἀμφιγνοούμενόν ἐστι *is in dispu*[te], Arr.*Tact.*6.2, cf. Plot.4.4.12.

**ἀμφίγνοια**, ἡ, *doubt*, Sch.S.*Aj.*23. **ἀμφιγνωμονέω**, *to be* [of] *doubtful mind*, Doroth.ap.*EM*87.48, Sch.Pl.*Grg.*466c.

**ἀμφιγόητος**, ον, *bewailed all round*, Κωκυτοῦ ὕδωρ *AP*7.700 (Diod.).

**ἀμφίγονος**, ον, *stepchild*, Hsch., *EM*87.50.

⊛**Ἀμφιγυήεις**, ὁ, epith. of Hephaestus, *with both feet crooked*, *lame*, Il.1.607, etc.

**ἀμφιγυιόω**, *mutilate*, or *impale*, Hsch., cf. *EM*89.17.

⊛**ἀμφίγῠος**, ον, in Hom. always epith. of ἔγχος, either (γυῖον) *with a limb at each end*, *double-pointed*, or (γύης) *bending both ways*, *elastic*, Il.13.147, Od.24.527; ἀ. δούρασιν A.R.3.135; prob. (from γυῖον) *stout rivals*, S.*Tr.*504 (lyr.).

⊛**ἀμφιδαής**, *two-edged knife*, Suid.

**ἀμφιδαίω**, *kindle around*:—only intr. in pf. and plpf., *burn*, *blaze around*, ἀϋτή τε πτόλεμός τε ἄστυ τόδ' ἀμφιδέδηε Il.6.329; ἀμφὶ μάχη τ' ἐνοπή τε δεδήει τεῖχος 12.35; of dust, κόνις σφ' ἀμφιδεδήει Hes.*Sc.*62.

**ἀμφιδάκνω**, *bite all round*: hence, *grip close*, *APl.*4.118 (Paul.Sil.).

**ἀμφιδάκρῡτος**, ον, *all-tearful*, πόθος E.*Ph.*330.

**ἀμφιδαρκανές**· ὁμαλόν, Hsch.

**ἀμφίδᾰσυς**, εια, υ, *shaggy* or *fringed all round*, epith. of the Aegis, which was hung with θύσανοι, Il.15.309; also of the head of Marsyas, Simon.177.

**ἀμφίδαφος**, prob. = ἀμφιτάπης, *POxy.*298.9 (i A.D.).

**ἀμφιδέα**, ας, ἡ, *anything that binds* or *is bound around*, *bracelet* or *anklet*, mostly pl., Hdt.2.69, Ar.*Fr.*320.11, *IG*2.652*A*18, cf. 660.11, Aristaenet.1.19, Lib.*Or.*31.12. 2. *iron rings*, by which folding-doors were secured in hinges, Lys.*Fr.*37, *IG*2.834*b*ii99: sg. -δῆ *IG* 11(2).147.7 (Delos, iv B.C.). 3. τὰ ἀμφίδεα, *rim* of the *os uteri*, Hp.*Mul.*1.57, cf. Gal.19.78:—sg. **-δήιον** Ruf.*Onom.*195, **-διον** Erot.

**ἀμφιδεής**, ές, *afraid on all sides*, Hsch., Phot., Suid.

⊛**ἀμφιδεΐδιον**, τό, Dim. of ἀμφιδέα, *door-ring*, prob. in *BCH*10.463 (Delos, iv B.C.).

**ἀμφιδείκελος**, *visible from all sides*, Suid.

**ἀμφιδεκάτη**, ἡ, Arc. for the *21st of the month*, Hsch. (dub.):—also **ἀμφιδεκατία**, ἡ, *IG*5(1).363 (Sparta); cf. ἀμφεικάς.

**ἀμφιδέμω**, *build round about*, in aor. 1 Med. ἀμφεδείμαντο J.*BJ* 5.5.1.

⊛**ἀμφιδέξιος**, ον, *ambidextrous* (cf. ἀμφαρίστερος), Hp.*Aph.*7.43 (wrongly expl. by Glaucias ap.Erot., S.E.*M.*7.50), Arist.*EN*1134b34; = περιδέξιος, Hippon.83. Adv. -ίως, παίζειν Polem.Hist.45. 2. *ready to take with either hand*, i.e. *taking either of two things*, *indifferent*, *Trag.Adesp.*355 (= *Com.Adesp.*360); so ἀμφιδεξίως ἔχει it is *indifferent*, A.*Fr.*266. 3. *two-edged*, σίδηρος E.*Hipp.*780. b. metaph., *double-meaning*, *ambiguous*, χρηστήριον Hdt.5.92.ε', cf. Luc.*JTr.*43. 4. *on either hand*, *with both hands*, ἀ. ἀκμαῖς with *both* hands *at once*, S.*OT*1243; ἐρείσατ'.. πλευρὸν ἀμφιδέξιον ἐμφύντε τῷ φύσαντι *OC*1112. 5. ἀμφιδέξια, τά, *bracelets*, Hsch.: sg. ἀμφίδεξιν (sic) *IG*2.238*a*.

**ἀμφιδεξιότης**, ητος, ἡ, *ambidextrousness*, *dexterity*, Eust.957.30.

**ἀμφιδέραιον**, τό, *necklace*, Lib.*Decl.*46.17, Hsch.: pl. **ἀμφιδέρρεα**, *AB*388.

**ἀμφιδέρκομαι**, Dep., *look upon*, *behold*, *AP*15.22 (Simm.).

⊛**ἀμφιδὲσφάγανον** (sic)· σκολοπένδρα, Hsch.

**ἀμφι-δέτης**, ου, ὁ, (δέω A) *yoke* for oxen, Artem.2.24. 2. *necklace*, Procop.Gaz.*Ecphr.*164.21 (pl.). ⊛**-δετος**, ον, *bound* or *set all round*, *AP*6.103 (Phil.). **-δέω**, *bind round*, A.R.2.64:—Med. in Hsch.

**ἀμφίδηλος**, ον, gloss on ἀμφιδείκελος, Suid.

⊛**ἀμφιδήμα**, ἡ, *foot-wear*, *GDI*4992,5000 (Gortyn).

**ἀμφιδηριάομαι**, Dep., *fight about*, γυναικὸς εἵνεκα Semon.7.118: c. dat., Lyc.1437.

**ἀμφιδήρῑτος**, ον, *disputed*, *doubtful*, νίκη Th.4.134, Plb.4.33.8; μάχη Id.35.2.14.

**ἀμφιδήτιοι**, prob. = ἀμφιδέαι, Democr.130.

**ἀμφιδιαίνω**, *moisten all round*, ἱδρῶτι κόμην *AP*9.653 (Agath.).

**ἀμφιδῑν-έομαι**, Pass., *to be put round in a circle*, Hom. in pf. only, ᾧ πέρι χεῦμα φαεινοῦ κασσιτέροιο ἀμφιδεδίνηται *round* whose edge a stream of tin *is rolled*, Il.23.562; κολεὸν ἀμφιδεδίνηται [ἄορ] scabbard *is fitted close round* it, Od.8.405; of persons, *to be dizzy*, σκοτάδεις ἀμφιδινεύμενοι Aret.*SD*2.3. ⊛**-δινεύω**, *whirl around*, πυρήια A.R.1.1184 (tm.).

**ἀμφιδιόρθωσις**, εως, ἡ, *guarding oneself both before and after* saying something which may seem too bold, Alex.*Fig.*1.5.

**ἀμφιδοκεύω**, *lie in wait for*, τινά Bion *Fr.*9.6; *guard*, Orph.*A.*925.

**ἀμφίδομος**, ον, *built around*, Opp.*H.*2.351.

**ἀμφιδονέω**, *whirl round*, *agitate violently*, Ζέφυρος δένδρεα ἀμφιδονεῖ *AP*9.668 (Marian.), cf. 5.121 (Diod.).

**ἀμφι-δοξέω**, *to be doubtful*, τὸ ἀμφιδοξεῖν *room for doubt*, Arist.*Rh.*1356a8; ἀ. περί τινος Plb.32.16.5. II. c. acc., *doubt about*, Arist.*SE*176b15:—Pass., *to be doubtful*, τἀληθὲς ἀμφιδοξεῖται ib.176b20; ἀποφάσεις Plb.36.0.2; ἐλπίδες D.S.19.96, cf. Plu.*Thes.*23. ⊛**-δοξος**, ον, of persons, *with doubtful mind*, Ps.-E.*Fr.*1132.52; πρὸς τὸ θεῖον Plu.2.434d; περί τινος ib.11d. 2. of a witness, *of doubtful* *edibility*, Arist.*Rh.Al.*1431ᵇ23. II. of things, *ambiguous*, *doubtful*, ἐν ἀμφιδόξῳ Thphr.*CP*1.22.2; ἀ. νίκη, ἐλπίδες Plb.11.1.8, 5.1.12; of oracles, Luc.*JConf.*14 (v.l.), *causing doubt*, ποῖαι Onos. 5. Adv. -δόξως Gal.1.273, al. 2. in Prosody, *of doubtful quantity*, Lat. *anceps*, Sch.Heph.1.4.

**ἀμφίδορος**, ον, *quite flaved*, *AP*5.165 (Phalaec.).

**ἀμφίδουλος**, ον, *slave both by father and mother*, Eub.2 D., Eust. 445.5.

**ἀμφίδοχμος**, ον, (δοχμή) *as large as can be grasped*, λίθος ἀ. X.*Eq.* 4.4, cf. Poll.1.200, Hsch.

**ἀμφιδρανές**, (δρᾶνος) *embroidered on both sides*, ἱμάτιον Hsch., Phot.p.100R.

***ἀμφι-δρόμια**, ων, τά, Att. festival at the naming of a child, so called because the parents' friends *carried it round the hearth*, Ar.*Lys.*757, Ephipp.3, Lys.*Fr.*22: on fifth day after birth, Sch.Pl.*Tht.*160e; tenth, acc. to Sch.Ar.*Lys.* l.c.:—hence -**δρομέω**, *AB*207. -**δρομος**, ον, *running both ways*, οἱ κατὰ τὸν πορθμὸν τόποι ἀ. ὄντες *subject to a constant ebb and flow*, Plb.34.2.5; πορθμός with harbour *on both sides*, Pl.Com.24 D. 2. *encompassing, enclosing*, S.*Aj.*352; ἄρκυς ἱστάναι ἀ. X.*Cyn.*6.5 (dub.). II. pr. n. Ἀμφίδρομος, divinity connected with ἀμφιδρόμια, A.*Fr.*222.

**ἀμφι-δρύπτομαι**, *be torn all round*, Q.S.4.396. -**δρυπτος**, ον, = ἀμφιδρυφής, *AP*6.84 (Paul.Sil.), 9.323 (Antip. (Sid.)).

**ἀμφίδρυς**· *femella*, i.e. *oak-wood handle*, *Gloss.*

**ἀμφιδρυτί**· δένδρον ἀκῆς, Hsch.

**ἀμφι-δρυφής**, ές, (δρύπτω) *torn on both sides*, ἄλοχος ἀ. a wife who *has torn both cheeks*, in grief, Il.2.700, Orac.ap.Hdt.6.77. -**δρυφος**, ον, = foreg., παρειαί Il.11.393.

***ἀμφίδυμος**, ον, *two-fold, double*, λιμένες ἀ. Od.4.847; ἀκταί A.R. 1.940; πλάστιγγες Opp.*H.*2.179; ἰσθμός Str.6.1.5; *of double nature*, Opp.*C.*3.483; *with two barbs*, ἄκοντες 1.92. (The termin. -δυμος recurs in δίδυμος, τρίδυμος.)

**ἀμφίδυσις**, ἡ, *double cup*, like δέπας ἀμφικύπελλον, Anaxandr.74.

**ἀμφιδύω**, *put on*, τινί τι Sch.Ar.*Th.*1053:—Med., *put on oneself*, ἀμφιδύσεται χροΐ [πέπλον] S.*Tr.*605.

**ἀμφιέζω**, freq. as v.l. for ἀμφιάζω, cf. *An.Ox.*2.338.

**ἀμφιεκτ⟨ήρ⟩**· χιτὼν διπλοῦς, Hsch.

**ἀμφίεκτον**, τό, measure between ἡμίεκτον and ἀμφορεύς, dub. in Them.*Or.*8.113d.

**ἀμφιελικτός**, όν, *revolving*, of stars, Arat.378; *winding*, περίπλοος D.P.466. **ἀμφιέλισσα**, ἡ, (ἑλίσσω) Ep. Adj., only fem., in Hom. always of ships, Il.2.165, al., either *curved at both ends* (or *on both sides*), or *wheeling either way, handy*; in late Ep., *twisting, doubling*, ἱμάσθλη ἀ. Nonn.*D.*48.328; μίτρη Jo.Gaz.1.319; *wavering, doubtful*, ἀοιδή Tryph.667.

**ἀμφιελίσσω**, *wind round*, Arat.996, Orph.*Fr.*115.

**ἀμφιελόν**· ἄφθονον, Hsch.

***ἀμφιέννυμι** Pl.*Prt.*321a; -ύω Plu.*Per.*9: fut. ἀμφιέσω Od.5.167, Att. ἀμφιῶ (ἀπ-) Men.339, (προσ-) Ar.*Eq.*891: aor. ἠμφίεσα Od.18. 361 (opt. -έσαιμι), X.*Cyr.*1.3.17:—Med., ib.8.2.21: fut. -έσομαι ib. 4.3.20, Pl.*R.*457a: aor. ἠμφιεσάμην App.*BC*2.122, Ep. ἀμφιέσαντο Od.23.142:—Pass., aor. part. ἀμφιεσθείς Hdn.1.10.5: pf. ἠμφίεσμαι Ar.*V.*1172, etc.; poet. part. ἀμφιειμένος *Epigr.Gr.*1035.25:—*put round* or *on*, ἀμφὶ δὲ καλὰ λέπαδν' ἕσαν Il.19.393: but mostly c. dupl. acc. pers. et rei, ἐμὲ χλαῖνάν τε χιτῶνά τε εἵματα.. ἀμφιέσασα Od.15.369; in tmesi, ἀμφὶ δέ με χλαῖνάν τε χιτῶνά τε εἵματα ἕσσεν 10. 542; ἀμφὶ δέ μιν μέγα δέρμα.. ἕσσ' ἐλάφοιο 13.436, cf. Ar.*Pl.*936, Pl. *Smp.*219b, X.*Cyr.*1.3.17, etc.:—Pass., ἠμφιεσμένος τι *clothed in*.., *wearing*, Ar.*V.*1172, *Th.*92, *Ec.*879, etc.; τροφαλὶς σκῖρον ἠμφιεσμένη *with* a rind *on*, Eup.277. 2. rarely c. dat. rei, ἀ. τινά τινι *clothe* one *in* or *with*, θριξὶ καὶ δέρμασι Pl.*Prt.*321a: metaph., πονηρὰ χρηστοῖς ἀ. λόγοις *cloak*.., D.H.6.16. II. Med., *put on oneself, dress oneself in*, ἀμφιέσαντο χιτῶνας Od.23.142; ἀμφὶ δ' ἄρα.. ἑανὸν ἕσαθ' Il.14. 178; ἀμφὶ δ' ἄρα.. νεφέλην ὤμοισι ἕσαντο *they put* cloud *round* their shoulders, 20.150; γυίοις ἀμφιέσαντο κόνιν A.*Eleg.*3; λευκὴν ἀμφιέσασθε κόμην *AP*12.93; ἀρετὴν ἀντὶ ἱματίων ἀ. Pl.*R.*457a: abs., οὐ γὰρ παρέχεις ἀμφιέσασθαι τῷ πατρί Ar.*Fr.*17 D.

**ἀμφιέπω**, poet. also **ἀμφέπω** (the only form in Trag.): impf. or aor. ἀμφίεπον and ἄμφεπον, both in Hom. (v. infr.): poet. Verb only in the tenses cited, and once or twice in Med.: (ἕπω):—*go about, be all round*, γάστρην τρίποδος πῦρ ἄμφεπε Il.18.348, Od.8.437; πρύμνην πῦρ ἄμφεπε Il.16.124; ἕρσ' ἀμφέπει the dew (of milk and honey, metaph. of song) *crowns* [the bowl], Pi.*N.*3.78. 2. *beset, press hard*, Il.11.483; so perh. in Od.3.118 (v. infr. II.2). II. *to be busy about, look after*, ἀμφίεπον τάφον Ἕκτορος Il.24.804, cf. 5.667; ἀμφὶ βοὸς ἕπετον κρέα *dressed* the meat, 11.776; βοῦς, οἶν ἀ., Od.8.61, Il.24.622:—*do honour* or *reverence to*, Δάματρα Pi.*O.*6.95; *tend* or *heal* sick, *P.*3.51; ἀ. σκῆπτρον *sway* the sceptre, *O.*1.12, cf. S.*El.*651; esp. *guard, protect*, Pi.*P.*5.68, prob. in E.*Med.*480, etc.; Βακχεῦ.. ὃς ἀμφέπεις Ἰταλίαν S.*Ant.*1118; μαντεῖον E.*IT*1248; simply, *frequent*, χῶρον Simon.58:—ἀ. κῆδος *cherish* an alliance, E.*Ph.*340; ἀ. μόχθον *go through* toil and trouble, Pi.*P.*4.268; σύμπειρον ἀγωνίᾳ θυμὸν ἀ. *foster* spirit in contests, *N.*7.10; ἀ. ὄλβον *enjoy* happiness, *I.*4(3).59; ἀ. παννυχίδας Critias 1.8. 2. abs., in part., *with good heed, carefully*, ἵππους ἀμφιέποντες ζεύγνυσαν Il.19.392; στίχας ἵστατον ἀμφιέποντες ib.2.525; κακὰ ῥάπτομεν ἀμφιέποντες Od.3.118; ὁ ἀμφέπων δαίμων the fortune *that attends one*, Pi.*P.*3.108. 3. Med., *crowd about*, ἀμφὶ δ' ἄρ' αὐτὸν Τρῶες ἕποντ' Il.11.473 codd.; *accompany round about*, τινί Q.S.1.47.

**Ἀμφιεραϊστής**, οῦ, ὁ, *worshipper of Amphiaraus*, *IG*2².1322 (iii/ii B.C.). **Ἀμφιεράια**, τά, *festival of A.*, *IG*3.1171.

**ἀμφίεργος**, ον, *worked* or *prepared in two ways*, ἡμιβρεχῆ καὶ ἡμίεφθον ἣν καλοῦσί τινες ἀ. Thphr.*CP*3.23.1.

**ἀμφιέρχομαι**, v. ἀμφέρχομαι.

**ἀμφί-εσις**, εως, ἡ, *clothing*, Sch.Od.9.51, Simp.*in Cat.*401.21. ***-εσμα**, ατος, τό, *garment*: pl., *wraps, clothes*, Hp.*Mul.*2.133, Pl.*Grg.* 523d, *R.*381a; in anatomy, of membranes, Gal.2.554, al. ***-εσμός**, ὁ, *clothing*, D.H.8.62 (v.l. -ασμός). -**εστρίς**, ίδος, ἡ, *cloak, wrap*, Poll.6.10, 7.61.

**ἀμφι-ετεί**, Adv., (ἔτος) *year by year*, prob. in *SIG*963.7 (Amorgos, iv B.C.), cf. Suid., Eust.1385.1. -**ετες**, Adv. = foreg., Moer. 45. -**ετέω**, *offer yearly sacrifices*. *EM*90.26. ***-ετηρίς**, ίδος, ἡ, *yearly festival*, *SIG*1109.69 (Athens, ii A.D.), Suid. -**έτηρος**, ον, *celebrated in yearly festivals*, epith. of Dionysus, Orph.*H.*52. 10. ***-ετής**, ές, = foreg., Call.*Del.*278, Orph.*Fr.*232. -**ετίδαι**, οἱ, Com. name for stupid persons, Men.13 D. -**ετίζομαι**, Pass., *return yearly*, of festivals, Hsch., *EM*90.27:—also -**ετηρίζομαι**, Cratin.2 D.

**ἀμφιζάνω**, *sit on*, c. dat., χιτῶνι ἀμφίζανε τέφρη ashes *settled upon* the tunic, Il.18.25.

**ἀμφίζευκτος**, ον, *joined from both sides*, A.*Pers.*130.

**ἀμφιζέω**, *boil* or *bubble around*, Q.S.6.104.

**ἀμφίζωστος**, ον, *girt around*, Nonn.*D.*32.159.

**ἀμφιήκης**, ες, (ἀκή A) = ἀμφήκης, Hsch.

**ἀμφιθάλαμος**, ου, prob. f.l. for ἀντι-, *corresponding chamber*, Vitr. 6.7.2.

***ἀμφιθάλασσος**, Att. -ττος, ον, *with sea on both sides, sea-girt*, of Rhodes, Pi.*O.*7.33; of Attica, X.*Vect.*1.7, cf. Str.9.1.2.

**ἀμφι-θαλεύς**, έος, ὁ, = παῖς ἀμφιθαλής, hence, in religious ceremonies, *acolyte*, τῶν μεγάλων Ἀντωνίων *BCH*10.415 (Thyatira):—hence -**θαλεύω**, τὰ μεγάλα Ἀσκληπιεῖα ib.11.98 (ibid.). ***-θαλής**, ές, (θαλεῖν) lit. *blooming on both sides*, of children *who have both parents alive*, Il.22.496, Pl.*Lg.*927d, Call.*Iamb.*3.1.2, *SIG*589.19 (Magn. Mae.), etc. 2. *flourishing on all sides*, χωρίον Poll.1.209: metaph., *all-abounding*, of gods, A.*Ch.*394; Ἔρως Ar.*Av.*1737 (cf. Sch.); of a man, πόσις ἀ. *IG*14.1863: metaph., ἀμφιθαλὴς κακοῖς *abounding in*.., A.*Ag.*1144. II. of things, *complete*, ἀλήθεια Pl.*Ax.* 37cd. ***-θάλλω**, pf. (with pres. sense) ἀμφιτέθηλα, *to be in full bloom*, *AP*9.231 (Antip.), 12.96.

**ἀμφιθάλπω**, *warm on both sides, cherish*, Luc.*Trag.*28.

**ἀμφιθέατρος**, ον, *having seats for spectators all round*, of the Roman *circus*, ἀ. ἱππόδρομος D.H.4.44: also στοά Id.3.68; στάδιον *IGRom.*4.861 (Laodicea ad Lycum): esp. neut. as Subst., -**θέατρον**, τό, *amphitheatre*, *IGRom.*1.1024.27 (Berenice, i B.C.), Str.14.1.43, J.*AJ*15.8.1, Arr.*Epict.*1.25.27, Procop.*Goth.*3.23, etc.

***ἀμφίθετος**, ον, in Il.23.270, 616 ἀ. φιάλη, acc. to Aristarch., a cup *that will stand on both ends*; acc. to others, *with handles on both sides, that may be taken up by both sides*, cf. Ath.11.501a sq., Eust.1299. 55, Hsch.

**ἀμφιθέω**, generally pres., *run round about*, ἀμφιθέουσι μητέρας Od. 10.413: c. dat., νόος δέ οἱ αἴσιμος ἀμφιθέει right mind *surrounds* him, Mosch.2.107: impf. ἀμφιθέεσκεν Q.S.5.371.

***ἀμφι-θηγής**, ές, *sharpened on both sides, two-edged*, ξίφος S.*Ant.* 1309 (lyr.). ***-θηκτος**, ον, = foreg., *AP*6.94 (Phil.).

**ἀμφί-θλασις**, εως, ἡ, *pressure all round*, Aret.*CA*1.6. -**θλασμα**, Ion. -**φλασμα**, ατος, τό, *bruise* of the flesh *round* a spot, Hp.*Art.* 50. -**θλάω**, Ion. -**φλάω**, *crush, contuse round*: in Pass., σὰρξ περὶ ὀστέον Id.*Fract.*11, *Art.*50; of fruit, μήλων σάρκες ἀμφιθλασθεῖσαι Aret.*CD*2.6.

**ἀμφιθνήσκω**, of flesh, *mortify round* a wound, v.l. in Hp.*Fract.* 33; later, *die around*, τισί Q.S.6.440.

**ἀμφιθοάζω**, *rush around*, οὐρανόν Man.4.84.

**ἀμφίθρεπτος**, ον, *clotted round* a wound, αἷμα S.*Tr.*572.

**ἀμφιθρύπτομαι**, *to be broken up*, dub. l. Aret.*SD*2.4.

**ἀμφιθρῴσκω**, in aor. part. ἀμφιθορόντες, *leap around*, Eumel.9 (= A.R.3.1373).

**ἀμφίθυρος**, ον, *with a door on both sides, with double entrance*, οἶκος S.*Ph.*159; οἰκία Lys.12.15; Boeot. **ἀμφιθιουρος**, ὁ, as Subst., *IG*7.2876 (Coronea). II. Subst. ἀμφίθυρον, τό, *hall*, Theoc.14.42.

**ἀμφιθύσανος**, ον, *fringed all about*, πρόσλημμα *GDI*5702 (Samos).

**ἀμφιίζομαι**, *sit upon*, δίφρον Hp.*Mul.*2.114.

**ἀμφιίστημι**, v. ἀμφίστημι.

**ἀμφικαθίζομαι** (v.l. -έζ-), *take a sitz-bath*, Hp.*Mul.*1.13. II. causal, *cause to be seated upon a* πυελός, ib.2.134.

**ἀμφικάθημαι**, Pass., *sit all round*, Orac.ap.Eus.*PE*4.23.

**ἀμφικαίνυμαι**, in plpf. Pass. ἀμφεκέκαστο, *to be adorned with*, τεύχεσι Q.S.10.179, cf. 188.

**ἀμφικᾰλύπτω**, fut. -ψω A.R.2.583: aor. -ψα, v. infr. I. c. acc., *enwrap, enfold*, of garments, Il.2.262; of a coffin, ἀ. ὀστέα 23.91; ἐπὴν πόλις ἀμφικαλύψῃ δουράτεον μέγαν ἵππον *received within* it, Od.8.511, cf. 4.618; ἔρως φρένας ἀμφεκάλυψε *love enfolded* my senses, Il.3.442; θάνατος δέ μιν ἀμφεκάλυψε 5.68, cf. 12.116; θανάτου δὲ μέλαν νέφος ἀμφεκάλυψε 16.350; ἀμφὶ δὲ ὄσσε κελαινὴ νὺξ ἐκάλυψε 11.356; [ὕπνος] βλέφαρ' ἀμφικαλύψας Od.5.493; of a wave, *overwhelm*, A.R. l.c.:—in Pass., ἀμφικεκαλύφθαι ἀμφιέσμασι Hp.*Mul.*2.133. II ἀ. τί τινι *put round* any one *as a veil, cover*, or *shelter*, ἀ. σάκος τινί Il.8.331; νέφος τινί 14.343; νύκτα μάχῃ ἀ. *throw the mantle* of night over the battle, 5.506; ὄρος πόλει ἀ. *overshadow* a city with a mountain, Od.

8.569. III. after Hom., ἀ. τινά τινι *surround* one *with*, φύλλοις κνήμας Batr.161, cf. Opp.*H*.1.746:—Pass., ἀμφεκαλύφθη κρᾶτα λέοντος χάσματι *he had* his head *covered with* lion's jaws, E.*HF*361. 2. *guard*, μαχαίριον δακτύλῳ Hp.*Mul*.1.70.

***ἀμφικάρηνος**, ον, *two-headed*, Nic.*Th*.373; in *Al*.417 v.l. for ἀμφίκρηνα, q.v. **ἀμφικάρής**, ές, = foreg., Id.*Th*.812.

**ἀμφίκαρπος**, ον, *fruiting both above and below ground, amphicarpic*, Thphr.*HP*1.6.12.

**ἀμφίκαρτος**, ον, *shorn all round*, Herod.8.24.

**ἀμφίκαυστις** or **-καυτις**, εως, ἡ: (καίω):—*ripe barley*, Ael.Dion. *Fr*.184, Hsch.s.v. καῦστις. II. Com., *pudenda*, Cratin.381. III. epith. of Demeter, Hsch. l.c.

**ἀμφικεάζω**, *cleave asunder*, in Ep. aor. part. -κεάσσας Od.14.12.

**ἀμφίκειμαι**, Pass., *lie round* or *upon*, τινι Pi.*Fr*.92; ἐπ' ἀλλήλοισιν ἀμφικείμενοι *locked in* each other's *arms*, S.*OC*1620; ἐπ' ὀλέθρῳ.. ἀμφικεῖσθαι μόρον slaughter *is heaped on* slaughter, *Ant*.1292 (lyr.).

**ἀμφικείρω**, aor. 2 Pass. -εκάρην, *shear all round*, *AP*9.56 (Phil.).

**ἀμφι-κελεμνίς**, *hanging evenly on both shoulders*, Hsch., Theognost. *Can*.163.16. ***-κέλεμνον·** ἀμφιβαρές, or, *chair carried by two men*, Hsch.; *satyric dance*, *EM*91.1.

**ἀμφίκερως**, ων, gen. ω, *two-horned*, Man.1.306, 4.274.

**ἀμφίκεστον·** περιτμητὸν ἢ περιγραφόμενον, Hsch. (Fort. -ξεστον.)

**ἀμφικεύθω**, *cover all round*, Hsch.

***ἀμφικέφᾰλος**, ον, *two-headed*, Eub.107.10 (in poet. form ἀμφικέφαλλος); of the ἀμφίσβαινα, Gal.14.243; σκέλους τὸ ἀ., i.e. the thigh-bone, Arist.*HA*494ᵃ5. II. of a couch, *having two places for the head*, i.e. *two ends*, κλίνη *IG*1.277*d* (-κνέφαλλος wrongly cited by Poll.10.36).

**ἀμφικίων** [κῐ], ον, gen. ονος, *with pillars all round*, S.*Ant*.285.

***ἀμφίκλαστος**, ον, *broken* (cf. ἀμφιρρώξ), *AP*6.223.

**ἀμφίκλαυτος**, ον, *mourned around*, Opp.*H*.4.257.

***ἀμφικλάω**, *break all in pieces*, Q.S.8.345; τρόμος ἀ. γυῖα 12.399.

**ἀμφικλῐνής**, ές, *unsteady, uncertain*, χαρά Ph.2.548. Adv. -νῶς, ἔχειν *to be in doubt*, 2.171.

**ἀμφι-κλύζω**, *wash* or *flood around*, Orph.*A*.271. **-κλυστος**, ον, *washed on both sides by waves*, ἀκτή, of a promontory, S.*Tr*.752, cf. 780; ἠιών Str.11.4.2; χῶμα App.*BC*5.72.

**ἀμφικνέφαλλος**, ον, *with cushions at both ends*. v. ἀμφικέφαλος II.

**ἀμφικνεφής**, ές, *wrapped in darkness*, βυθός *Orac.Chald*.242.

**ἀμφίκοιλος**, ον, *hollowed on both sides*, Suid. II. *doubly concave*, of a curvilinear angle, Procl.*in Euc.Def*.8 p.127 F., al.

**ἀμφίκοιτος·** ὁ τάπης, *coverlet*, Suid.

**ἀμφίκολλος**, ον, *glued on both sides*:—κλίνη ἀ. couch *with two ends fixed on*, Pl.Com.34.

**ἀμφικομέω**, *tend on all sides* or *carefully*, *AP*7.141 (Antiphil.).

***ἀμφίκομος**, ον, *with hair all round*, *AP*9.516 (Crin.). 2. *thick-leafed*, θάμνῳ ὑπ' ἀμφικόμῳ Il.17.677, cf. Archestr.*Fr*.9.

**ἀμφίκοπος**, ον, (κόπτω) *two-edged*, Eust.1531.34.

**ἀμφίκορος**, ὁ, *middle of three brothers*, Hsch., Suid.

**ἀμφίκουρος**, ον, *lopped of its branches*, κορμός S.*Fr*.821. 2. *shorn on both sides*, Hsch., Phot.p.102 R. II. *seized by men on either side*, Suid.

***ἀμφίκρᾱνος**, ον, = ἀμφικάρηνος, E.*HF*1274; ῥάβδος, of Hermes' wand, S.*Fr*.701. II. *surrounding the head*, in Ion. form -κρηνος, *AP*6.90 (Phil.), prob. l. in Nic.*Al*.417.

**ἀμφικρατέω**, *occupy*, Antioch.Astr. in *Cat.Cod.Astr*.1.112.

**ἀμφικρέμαμαι**, Pass., *hang round*, φρένας ἀμφικρέμανται ἐλπίδες Pi.*I*.2.43, cf. *O*.7.24. **ἀμφικρεμής**, ές, *overhanging*, σκόπελος *AP*9.90 (Alph.). 2. *hanging round shoulder*, φαρέτρη *APl*.4.212 (Alph.); χλαμύς *App.Anth*.3.166 (Procl.). **ἀμφίκρημνος**, ον, *with cliffs all round*, ἄγκος E.*Ba*.1051. II. metaph., ἀπάτη ἀ. deceit *which is always on the edge of the precipice*, Ps.-Luc.*Philopatr*.16.

**ἀμφίκρηνος**, ον, Ion. for ἀμφίκρανος, q.v.

***ἀμφίκροτος**, ον, *struck with both hands*, ψαλμοί *IG*3.82.

**ἀμφικρύπτω**, *cover* or *hide on every side*, τοῖον νέφος ἀμφί σε κρύπτει E.*Hec*.907.

**ἀμφι-κτίονες** or **-κτύονες**, ων, οἱ, (v. κτίζω) *they that dwell round* or *near, next neighbours*, Hdt.8.104, Pi.*P*.4.66, 10.8, *N*.6.39; cf. sq. (Accented -κτιών or -κτυών by Hdn.Gr.2.724, 1.22, and some codd.)

***'Αμφικτύον-ες**, ων, οἱ, *Amphictyons*, deputies of states associated in an ἀμφικτυονία, e.g. at Onchestos, Str.9.2.33; Calauria, 8.6.14; Delos, Ath.6.234e; esp. at Delphi, D.5.14, al., Aeschin.2.115, etc.; 'Αμφικτίονες *IG*2.545.16, al., and this form seems to preserve the etym., v. foreg.: sg. in Lib.*Decl*.17.10, al. **-εύω**, *to be a member of the Amphictyonic Council*, *IG*7.106 (Megara), *SIG*158 (Delos):—Pass., *to be subject to the Amphictyony*, *Gött.Gel.Anz*.1913.175. **-ία** or **-εία**, ἡ, *Amphictyonic League*, D.5.19, 11.4, cf. Did.*in D*.4.6; τὸ δίκαιον τῆς 'Α. *IG*4.589 (Argos); of the League of Calauria, Str.8.6.14:—τῆς τῶν Λοκρῶν 'Α. τὸ τρίτον μέρος a third share in *the representation* of Locri *in the Amphictyony*, *Klio*16.163. ***-ικός**, ή, όν, *belonging to the Amphictyons* or *their League*, 'Α. δίκαι trials *in their court*, D.18.322; ἱερά offerings *made at their meeting*, Lexap.eund. 23.37; πόλεμος D.18.143; τὰ χρήματα τὰ 'Α. *IG*2.545.6; 'Α. ἔγκλημα *IG*12(5).526.4 (Ceos, iii B.C.). **-ίς**, ίδος, ἡ, fem. of foreg.; 'Α. (sc. πόλις), ἡ, *city* or *state in the Amphictyonic League*, Aeschin.2.116. II. name of Demeter at Anthela, Hdt.7.200.

**ἀμφι-κύβωται·** πρόχοι· ἢ ἀπὸ ⟨τῆς⟩ τοῦ ὅλου περιφερείας ἢ ἀπὸ τῆς τῶν ὤτων, Hsch.:—also -κ[τ]υπος, ον, *EM*543.7: **-κυφος**, ον, κεραμίδες *BCH*28.159 (Delos, ii B.C.).

**ἀμφικῡκάω**, *mix up*, Nic.*Th*.602.

**ἀμφικυκλόομαι**, Pass., *encircle, surround*, ἀμφὶ δὲ κυκλοῦντο νῆσ[ον] A.*Pers*.458.—Act. in Agath.3.6.

**ἀμφικῠλίνδω**, aor. -εκύλῖσα, *roll about, round*, or *on*, φασγάνῳ ἀ[μ]φικυλίσαις Pi.*N*.8.23.

**ἀμφικύμων**, ον, gen. ονος, = ἀμφίκλυστος, B.15.16.

**ἀμφικῠνέω**, *deosculari*, Q.S.7.328, in aor. ἀμφικύσαι.

**ἀμφικύπελλος**, ον, in Hom. always δέπας ἀ. *double cup*, such a[s] forms a κύπελλον both at top and bottom, Il.1.584, al.: ἀμφικύπελλ[οι] are compared with the cell of a honeycomb, as possessing ἀμφίστομ[οι] θυρίδες, Arist.*HA*624ᵃ9; but acc. to Aristarch., *two-handled*, cf. Ath. 11.783b (post 11.466c).

**ἀμφι-κυρτέω**, *to be gibbous*, σελήνης -ούσης Olymp.*in Mete*.226.6. **-κυρτόομαι**, Pass., *to be gibbous*, of the moon, Man.6.57 (tm.). **-κυρτος**, ον, *convex on each side*, like the moon in he[r] second or third quarter, *gibbous*, Arist.*Cael*.291ᵇ20, Thphr.*Sign*.56, Plu.2.381d. 2. *doubly convex*, of a curvilinear angle, opp. ἀμφίκοιλος, Procl.*in Euc.Def*.5 p.127 F., al.; γραμμαί Gal.2.673; λεπίδες Ph.*Bel*.70.23.

**ἀμφιλαγχάνω**, *exchange*, τόπους Ptol.*Tetr*.179.

***ἀμφίλᾰλος**, ον, *talking in two languages, in broken Greek*, Ar.*Ra*.979.

**ἀμφιλαμβάνω**, *grip, clasp*, Hp.*Art*.37, Aret.*SD*2.13.

**ἀμφιλασθείς·** περιελασθείς, Hsch.

**ἀμφι-λάφεια** or **-ία**, ἡ, *wealth, abundance*, Cic.*QF*2.14.3, *Gp*.2.8.1, Hsch., *AB*389. ***-λᾰφής**, ές, (prob. from √λαφ-, cf. εἴ-ληφ-α; so) *taking in on all sides, wide-spreading*, of large trees, Hdt.4.172; πλάτανος.. ἀ. τε καὶ ὑψηλή Pl.*Phdr*.230b. 2. *thickly grown, thick*, ἀ. ἄλσος δένδρεσιν Call.*Cer*.27, cf. Ael.*NA*7.6; also of hair, Philostr. Jun.*Im*.8, etc.; ἀ. φολίδεσσι δράκων Nonn.*D*.5.153. 3. generally, *abundant, enormous*, δύναμις Pi.*O*.9.82; βρονταί, χιών, Hdt.4.28,50; δόσις ἀ. a *bounteous* gift, A.*Ag*.1015; γόος ἀ. *loud* wail, *Ch*.331; πήματα Id.*Fr*.149A; κατάλυσις Jul.*Ep*.36. Adv. -φῶς *copiously*, Plu. *Eum*.6; ἀ. ἔχειν, c. gen., Alciphr.3.60. 4. *bulky, huge*, ἐλέφαντες Hdt.3.114; ἵππος A.R.4.1366; νῆσος ib.983; παστάς Theoc.24.46; χορός Call.*Dian*.3, etc. b. (as if Passive, *held on all sides*), *palpable*, Dam.*Pr*.12, 111. 5. rarely of persons, ἀ. τέχνῃ *great* in art, Call.*Ap*.42; ἀ. τὴν διάνοιαν Dam.ap.Suid.—Not in Hom. or in Early Prose.

**ἀμφιλαχαίνω**, *dig, hoe round*, φυτὸν ἀμφελάχαινεν Od.24.242.

**ἀμφιλάων·** περικυκλούντων, Hsch.

**ἀμφιλέγω**, Dor. ἀμφιλλ-, *dispute about*, τι X.*An*.1.5.11; χώρας ἃς ἀμφέλλεγον *IG*4.926 (Epid.):—Pass., τὰ ἀμφιλλεγόμενα *GDI*5149 (Cret.). 2. foll. by μή.., *dispute, question* that a thing is, X.*Ap*. 12: abs., *dispute*, αἴ κ' ἀμφιλλέγωντι τοὶ ταγοί *GDI*2561 *A*42.

***ἀμφιλειπής**, ές, *incomplete at both ends*, of the *metrum Choerileum*, [⏑] – ⏑ – – | – ⏑ ⏑ – ⏑ ⏑ – ‖ ⏑ – ⏑ – [–] Sch.Metr.Pi.*N*.11, Mar.Vict. 2559.

**ἀμφιλείπω**, *forsake utterly*, Q.S.12.106.

**ἀμφίλεκτος**, ον, *spoken both ways*: hence, *doubtful*, ἀ. ὢν κράτει *questioned* in his title to rule, A.*Ag*.1585; *involving dispute*, ἔρις E. *Ph*.500. Adv. -τως A.*Th*.800. 2. *double*, πήματα Id.*Ag*.881.

**ἀμφίλῐνος**, ον, *bound with flaxen thongs*, κρούπαλα S.*Fr*.44 (apptly. λῖν-, but the line is corrupt).

**ἀμφιλίτην·** τὸν λιτανευτήν, Hsch.

**ἀμφιλιχή·** περιμάχητον, Hsch.

**ἀμφιλιχμάζω**, *lick all round*, Opp.*H*.4.115, 321 (tm.).

**ἀμφι-λογέομαι**, Dep., *dispute, doubt*, περί τινος Plu.*Lys*.22.—Act. in J.*AJ*18.1.4, Hsch. **-λογία**, Ep. ἀμφιλλ-, ἡ, *dispute, doubt*, Hes.*Th*.229; ἀ. ἔχειν, διαλύειν, Plu.*Comp.Arist.Cat*.4, *Ages*.28, cf. App.*Hann*.46. ***-λογος**, ον, *disputed, disputable*, ἀγαθά X.*Mem*. 4.2.34; τὰ ἀ. *disputed points*, Th.4.118, 5.79; ὀφείλημα Arist.*EN* 1162ᵇ28; εἴ τι ἀμφίλογον πρὸς ἀλλήλους γίγνοιτο. δίκῃ διακριθῆναι X. *HG*5.2.10. 2. *uncertain, wavering*, neut. pl. ἀμφίλογα as Adv., E.*IT*655 (lyr.). Regul. Adv. -ως A.*Pers*.904. II. Act., *disputatious, jarring*, νείκη S.*Ant*.111; ὀργαί E.*Med*.637 (lyr.).

**ἀμφίλοξος**, ον, *slanting both ways*, ἀμφίλοξα μαντεύεσθαι *utter ambiguous oracles*, Ps.-Luc.*Philopatr*.5, cf. 16.

**ἀμφίλοφος**, ον, *encompassing the neck*, ζυγόν S.*Ant*.351 (dub.).

**ἀμφιλύκη** νύξ, ἡ, = λυκόφως, *half-light, morning twilight*, Il.7.433; without νύξ, A.R.2.671, Opp.*C*.1.135, *AP*5.280 (Paul. Sil.), Lyd.*Ost*. 65. (No masc. is found.)

**ἀμφίμακρος**, ον, *long at both ends*:—ὁ ἀ. metrical foot *amphimacer*, – ⏑ – (as Οἰδίπους), also called *creticus*, Heph.3.2, Quint.*Inst*.9.4.81, etc.

**ἀμφίμαλλος**, ον, *woolly on both sides*, Pherecr.1 D., Ael.*VH*3.40, Poll.7.57.

**ἀμφιμάντορα·** δύσμορον, κακοθάνατον, Hsch.

***ἀμφιμάομαι**, only in aor.; imper. ἀμφιμάσασθε, *wipe all round*, τραπέζας Od.20.152; ind. ἀμφεμάσαντο Q.S.9.428.

**ἀμφιμάρπτω**, only in pf. -μέμαρπα (-μέμαρφα Q.S.3.614), *grasp all round, handle*, A.R.3.147, Opp.*H*.5.636.

**ἀμφίμαστα**, τά, *cakes of flour and honey* (Lacon.), Hsch.; cf. ἀμφίπαστον.

**ἀμφιμάσχᾰλος**, ον, *with two arm-holes*, ἀ. χιτών Ar.*Eq*.882, cf. Pl.Com.229, Luc.*Lex*.10.

**ἀμφιμάτορες**, Dor. for ἀμφιμήτορες.

**ἀμφι-μάχητος**, ον, *fought for*, *AP*7.705 (Antip.). **-μάχομαι** [ᾰ], Ep. Verb, only pres. and impf., *fight round*: 1. c. acc., *assail, besiege*, Ἴλιον ἀμφεμάχοντο Il.6.461; Τρώων πόλιν 9.412; στρατόν

.73. 2. c. gen., *fight for*, as for a prize, of defenders and assailants, τείχεος ἀμφεμάχοντο 15.391; νέκυος δὲ δὴ ἀ. 18.20; χώρας *IG*527.151 (Dreros, iii B.C.).

**ἀμφιμέλας**, -μέλαινα, -μέλᾰν, *black all round*: Hom. always epith. φρένες (best written divisim, as by Alex. critics), *darkened on ther side*, of strong emotions, as anger, Il.1.103, 17.83, Od.4.661; ourage, Il.17.499,573: prob. metaph. from an angry sea. 2. enerally, ἀ. κόνις *coal-black* dust, *AP*7.738 (Theodorid.).

**ἀμφιμέλει**, *to be a care to*, σοι ἀμφιμέμηλε θράσος Q.S.5.190.

**ἀμφιμερίζομαι**, Pass., *to be completely parted*, *AP*9.662 (Agath.).

**ἀμφιμήκης** ἀριθμός *containing length of both kinds*, i.e. sum of *odd nd even*, Iamb.*inNic*.p.12.21 P.

**ἀμφίμηλον**, τό, *probe with two ends*, Antyll.ap.Orib.7.14.5.

⊛**ἀμφι-μήτορες**, οἱ, αἱ, (μήτηρ) *brothers* or *sisters by different mothers* but the same father, A.*Fr*.76, E.*Andr*.466 (lyr.): sg. in Hsch.; cf. ἀμφιπάτορες. **-μήτριος**, ον, (μήτρα) *round the womb*, *concerning it*, σημεῖον Hp.*Epid*.7.19 acc. to Gal.19.78 (dub.). 2. ἀμφιμήτρια, τά, *ship's bilge*, = ἐγκοίλια, Artem.4.30, Poll.1.87. II. (μήτηρ) *by different mother*, Lyc.19.

**ἀμφι-μῐγής**, ές, *well mixed*, Hsch. **-μίγνυμι**, *mix up well*, aor. 2 Pass. ἀμφιμιγεῖσα Orph.*Fr*.238.12.

**ἀμφίμῐτος**, ον, *with double woof* (cf. *dimity*), Poll.7.57, 10.38.

⊛**ἀμφιμῡκάομαι**, properly of cattle, *low all around*: metaph., δάπεδον δ' ἅπαν ἀμφιμέμῡκε floor *echoed* to song [of Circe], Od.10.227.

**ἀμφι-μωλέω**, *sue at law concerning*, ἐλευθέρῳ *Leg.Gort*.1.2, cf.9.19:—hence **-μωλος**, ον, *subject of legal process*, 10.27.

**ἀμφινάω**, *flow round about*, ὕδατος ἀμφιναέντος Emp.84.

**ἀμφι-νεικής**, ές, *contested on all sides*, *eagerly wooed*, of Helen, A.*Ag*.686; of Deïanira, S.*Tr*.104 (lyr.). **-νείκητος**, ον, = foreg., ὄμμα νύμφας ib.527 (lyr.).

**ἀμφινέμομαι**, Med., *dwell round*, c. acc. loci, Ὑάμπολιν ἀμφενέμοντο Il.2.521; Ὄλυμπον ἀ., of gods, 18.186; Ἰθάκην Od.19.132; of constellations, δύ' Ἰχθύες ἀμφινέμονται Ἵππον Arat.282: abs., D.P.127, al.: metaph., σὲ ὄλβος ἀ. *encompasses* thee, Pi.*P*.5.14.

**ἀμφινεύω**, *nod this way and that*, *AP*9.709 (Phil.).

**ἀμφι-νοέω**, *think both ways*, *be in doubt*, ἀμφινοῶ τόδε, πῶς εἰδὼς ἀντιλογήσω S.*Ant*.376. **-νοος**, ον, *looking at both sides*, Δημόκριτος Timo46.

**ἀμφινωμάω**, *surround*, A.*Fr*.304.8. 2. *distribute*, *turn over* or *peer round*, ἀμφὶ ἓ νωμήσας *h.Cer*.373.

**ἀμφι-νωτίζοντα**· προσπελάζοντα, προσφερόμενον, Hsch. **-νωτις**, ἡ, kind of χιτών, *EM*93.16. **-νωτοι** χιτῶνες, = foreg., Hsch. (prob.).

**ἀμφι-ξέω**, *smooth all round*, κορμὸν.. ἀμφέξεσα χαλκῷ Od.23.196. **-ξοος**, ον, contr. **-ξους**, *polishing all round*, σκέπαρνον *AP*6.205 (Leon.).

⊛**ἀμφίον**, ου, τό, = ἀμφίεσμα, S.*Fr*.420 (anap.), D.H.4.76, Sch.Arat.1073 (pl.): ἀμφία καὶ οἰκήσεις *IG*3.60. (From ἀμφί, as ἀντίος from ἀντί; ἄμφιον acc. to Sch.D.T.p.196 H.)

**ἀμφιορκία**, ἡ, *oath taken by each party* in a lawsuit, Hsch.; also by heliasts, Poll.8.122, *AB*184.

**ἀμφιπᾰγής**, ές, (πήγνυμι) *set all round*, τινί *with*.., Nonn.*D*.5.362.

⊛**ἀμφιπαίω**, *spike*, *transfix*, περὶ σκόλοπας τοὺς ὀπτίλλους *IG*4.951.92 (Epid.).

**ἀμφίπαλτος**, ον, *tossed about*, *re-echoing*, αὐδή *AP*15.27.10 (Besant.).

**ἀμφιπᾰλύνω**, *sprinkle all over*, A.R.3.1247.

**ἀμφιπαρίσταμαι**, *stand about and beside*, Epic.ap.Afric.*Cest.Oxy*.412.42.

**ἀμφίπαστον**· ἀλφίτοις ἀναδεδευμένοις ἐλαίῳ, Hsch.; cf. ἀμφίμαστα.

**ἀμφιπᾰτάσσω**, *strike on* or *from all sides*, *AP*9.643.

⊛**ἀμφιπάτορες** [ᾰ], οἱ, αἱ, *brothers* or *sisters by different fathers* but the same mother, Suid.; cf. ἀμφιμήτορες.

**ἀμφιπεδάω**, *fetter all round*, Opp.*H*.2.34.

**ἀμφίπεδος**, ον, *surrounded by a plain*, Pi.*P*.9.55.

**ἀμφιπέλεκκον**, τό, *double axe*, wrongly read in Il.13.612, cf. Hsch.

**ἀμφιπέλομαι**, *hover*, *float around*, of music, ἥτις ἀκουόντεσσι νεωτάτη ἀμφιπέληται Od.1.352; *encompass*, *Sammelb*.5829.16.

**ἀμφιπένομαι**, Ep. only pres. and impf., = πένομαι ἀμφί τινα, *to be busied about*, *take charge of*, c. acc. pers., οἵ μευ πατέρ' ἀμφεπένοντο Od.15.467; of people *tending* a wounded man, Il.4.220, 16.28, Od.19.455: c. acc. rei, δῶρα Il.19.278; τάφον, στόλον, δόρπον, A.R.2.925, 1199, 4.883; ταῦρον Id.3.271. b. τὸν οὐ κύνες ἀμφεπένοντο dogs *made* not *a meal of* him, Il.23.184, cf. 21.203; λέων.. ὅν τ' ἐν ὄρεσσιν ἀνέρες ἀμφιπένονται *hem in*, A.R.2.27.

**ἀμφιπερι-ΐσταμαι**, Pass., *stand around*, Q.S.3.201. **-κτίονες**, ων, οἱ, *dwellers all around*, Callin.1.2, Thgn.1058, Q.S.6.224.

**ἀμφιπέριξ**, Adv. *all around*, ὁ ἀ. χῶρος Hp.*Mul*.2.175.

**ἀμφιπερι-πλάσσω**, aor. -έπλασα, *spread all round*, of a drug, Hp.*Steril*.22. **-πλέγδην**, Adv. *twined round*, *AP*5.275 (Agath.), prob. in Jo.Gaz.1.6; ἀ. πεπεδημένος Nonn.*D*.36.360. **-πλέκομαι**, *to be folded about*, Orph.*L*.80. **-πτώσσω**, *tremble all about*, Q.S.12.472. **-σκαίρω**, *skip all about*, Opp.*H*.1.190. **-στείνομαι**, Pass., (στεινός, στενός) *to be pressed*, *crowded on all sides*, Call.*Del*.179. **-στέφομαι**, Pass., *to be put round as a crown*, ἀλλ' οὔ οἱ χάρις ἀμφιπεριστέφεται ἐπέεσσι grace *crowns* not his words, Od.8.175. **-στρωφάω**, Frequent. of -στρέφω, *keep turning about all ways*, Ἕκτωρ δ' ἀμφιπεριστρώφα καλλίτριχας ἵππους Il.8.348:—Pass., Q.S.13.11. **-σφίγγω**, *bind all round*, Nonn.*D*.48.338. **-τρομέω**, *tremble all over*, Opp.*H*.4.193. **-τρύζω**, *chirp*, *twitter round about*, *AP*5.236 (Agath.). **-φθῐνύθω** [ῠ], *decay*, *die all around*, *h.Ven*.271. **-φρίσσω**, *bristle all round*, *all over*, Opp.*H*.4.54.

**ἀμφιπετάννυμι**, *spread round*, aor. part. ἀμφιπετάσσας Orph.*L*.643.

**ἀμφιπέτομαι**, *fly around*, c. acc., Opp.*H*.2.448.

**ἀμφιπήγνῠμαι**, Pass., *to be fixed around*, aor. 2 ἀμφιπαγῆναι Opp.*H*.1.297; *to be pierced by*, ὀδύνῃσι 241.

**ἀμφιπήρους**· τυφλούς, ἢ μηδὲν λέγοντας, Hsch.

⊛**ἀμφιπιάζω**, Dor. for -πιέζω, *squeeze all round*, *hug closely*, [τὰν χίμαρον] χαλαῖς ἀμφεπίαξε λύκος Theoc.*Ep*.6.4.

⊛**ἀμφιπίπτω**, poet. **-πίτνω**, *fall upon and embrace*, *embrace eagerly*, c. acc., φίλον πόσιν ἀμφιπεσοῦσα Od.8.523, cf. Parth.15.2; ἀμφιπίτνουσα τὸ σὸν γόνυ E.*Supp*.278: c. dat., οὔτ' ἀμφιπίπτων στόμασιν *embracing* so as to kiss, S.*Tr*.938; *fall over*, προβάτοις Parth.8.4: metaph., *take to one's heart*, ἔθνος Λοκρῶν ἀμφέπεσον Pi.*O*.10(11).98.

**ἀμφιπλάσσω**, *spread around*, [ἔμπλαστρον] μήλῃ Hp.*Steril*.221.

**ἀμφι-πλεκής**, ές, = sq., Orph.*A*.607. **-πλεκτος**, ον, *intertwined*, S.*Tr*.520 (lyr.). ⊛**-πλέκω**, aor. 2 part. Pass. -πλακεῖσα Orph.*A*.881:—*twine round*, κείσθω δόρυ μοι μίτον ἀμφιπλέκειν ἀράχναις E.*Fr*.369 (lyr.); αὔραν ἀμφιπλέκειν καλάμοις, of musician, Telest.2.4; *embrace*, Opp.*H*.4.158; so in Pass., Orph. l.c.

**ἀμφί-πλευρος**, ον, *with traverses on both sides*, θυρίδες Ph.*Bel*.81.30. **-πλέω**, impf. ἀμφέπλεον, = περιπλέω, Hsch. **-πλη**· ἐμπλεκόμια, Id. **-πληκτος**, Dor. **-πλακτος**, ον, *beaten on both sides*, ἰσθμοί, Id. II. Act., *dashing on both sides*, ῥόθια S.*Ph*.688 (lyr.). ⊛**-πλήξ**, ῆγος, ὁ, ἡ, *striking with both sides*, φάσγανον Id.*Tr*.930: metaph., of a father's and mother's curse, ἀρά *OT*417.

**ἀμφι-πλίξ**, Adv. *astride*: hence, *gripping with coils*, of serpents, S.*Fr*.596. **-πλίσσω**, *straddle*, Poll.2.172.

**ἀμφίπλους**, ουν, *which may be sailed round*, γῆ, of islands, Poll.9.18.

**ἀμφιπλύνω**, *wash all over*, Hp.*Mul*.2.133, 144.

**ἀμφίποκος**, ον, = ἀμφίμαλλος, Hsch.

**ἀμφιπολ-εῖον**, τό, *chamber of the* ἀμφίπολος 1.3, *IG*4.39 (Aegina, v B.C.). ⊛**-εύω**, Ep. Verb (used by Hdt.) mostly in pres.: aor., Ἐφ. Ἀρχ.1910.397 (Ambracia):—*serve as an attendant*, *tend*, *care for* (not in Il.), βίον, ὄρχατον, ἵππους, Od.18.254, 24.244, *h.Merc*.568; of temple-slaves, *serve*, *have the care of*, ἀμφιπολεύουσαν ἱρὸν Διός Hdt.2.56; of the departed soul, Ὀσίριδος θῶκον *Epigr.Gr*.414 (Alexandria); ψυχὴ σκῆπτρον Ῥαδαμάνθυος ἀ. *IG*14.1389i47. 2. abs., [τὰς κούρας] ἔδοσαν.. Ἐρινύσιν ἀμφιπολεύειν Od.20.78, cf. Hes.*Op*.803; *hold the yearly office of* ἀμφίπολος, *IG*12(9).906 (Chalcis). 3. c. dat., *minister to*, as priest, Q.S.13.270; Ἀρτέμιτι Ἐφ.Ἀρχ. l.c.; Διί *IG*14.574 (Centuripa); θεῷ Αὐγούστῳ ib.601 (Malta). 4. *traverse*, *go about*, ἥλιος μέγαν οὐρανὸν ἀ. Emp.41; δόμον Man.6.273, cf. 3.36, al. ⊛**-έω**, later form of ἀμφιπολεύω, mostly in pres. (aor. 1, Pi.*N*.8.6):—*attend constantly*, ἤδη με γηραιὸν μέρος ἁλικίας ἀ. Id.*P*.4.158. 2. *attend on*, *watch*, *guard*, Ἱμέραν Id.*O*.12.2, cf. Theoc.1.124; λέκτρον Pi.*N*.8.6; *busy oneself with*, μυρία φρενί B.*Fr*.7.3. 3. *tend*, *treat gently*, τρώμαν ἕλκεος Pi.*P*.4.271. II. c. dat., *roam with*, *accompany*, θεαῖς S.*OC*680 (lyr.). **-πολῆσι**· περιπορείαις, *EM*91.7. **-ία** or **-εία**, ἡ, *office of* ἀμφίπολος, D.S.16.70.

**ἀμφίπολις**, poet. **ἀμφίπτολις**, ὁ, ἡ, *encompassing city*, ἀνάγκη ἀμφίπτολις A.*Ch*.75 (lyr.). II. Subst. ἀ., ἡ, *city encompassed by a river*, as pr. n., Th.4.102, etc.

⊛**ἀμφίπολος**, ον, (πέλω, πολέω) *busied about*, *busy*, epith. of Κύπρις, S.*Tr*.860:—in Hom. and Hdt. only as fem. Subst., *handmaid*, *waiting-woman*, Od.1.331, 6.199, etc.; λάβετ' ἀμφίπολοι γραίας ἀμενοῦς E.*Supp*.1115:—with other Substs., ἀ. ταμίη, γραῦς, Il.24.302, Od.1.191. b. later, *handmaid of gods*, *priestess*, θεᾶς E.*IT*1114; Διός *IG*14.2111. 2. masc., *attendant*, *follower*, Pi.*O*.6.32. 3. masc., *priest*, *sacrist*, E.*Fr*.982; ὁ τῶν θεῶν ἀ. Phld.*D*.1.13, cf. Plu.*Comp.Demetr.Ant*.3, *IG*9(1).683 (Corcyra). 4. ἀ. Διὸς Ὀλυμπίου, title of magistrate at Syracuse, D.S.16.70. II. in pass. sense, *frequented*, τύμβος Pi.*O*.1.93.

⊛**ἀμφιπονέομαι**, (πονέω) *attend to*, *provide for*, τάδε δ' ἀμφιπονησόμεθ' Il.23.159; κείνου κεφαλὴν.. Ἥφαιστος.. ἀμφεπονήθη, of funeral fire, Archil.120. II. Pass., τὰ ἀμφιπονεόμενα *neighbouring parts affected*, Hp.*Mul*.2.135.

**ἀμφιπορφύρεος**, α, ον, *edged with purple*, πέπλων prob. in E.*Or*.1457 (lyr.) (-πόρφυρος Sch. ad loc.).

**ἀμφιποτάομαι**, *fly round and round*, of a bird, ἀμφεποτᾶτο Il.2.315, cf. Sapph.*Supp*.14.4, Q.S.5.12.

**ἄμφιπποι**, ων, οἱ, *cavalry who went into action with a spare horse*, Ael.*Tact*.2.4, Arr.*Tact*.2.3, prob. l. in D.S.19.29. **ἀμφιπποτοξόται**, οἱ, ἄμφιπποι *armed with bows*, prob. l. in D.S.19.29 (codd. ἀφ-, ἐφ-), Plu.2.197d.

**ἀμφιπρόστῡλος**, ον, *having a portico on either front*, Vitr.3.2.1.

**ἀμφιπρόσωπος**, ον, *double-faced*, Emp.61; epith. of Janus, = Lat. *bifrons*, Plu.*Num*.19; epith. of Hecate, Orac.Chald.ap.Procl.*in Ti*.2.246 D. 2. *on two fronts*, μάχη Onos.10.2.

**ἀμφί-πρυμνος**, ον, *with two sterns*, i.e. *with rudder behind and before*, ναῦς S.*Fr*.131, cf. *Milet*.7 p.60, D.C.74.11, Agath.3.21: metaph., *two-edged*, λόγῳ E.ap.Phot.p.103 R. **-πρῳρος**, ον, *with two prows*, Gal.14.243.

**ἀμφιπτολεμοπηδησίστρᾰτος**, ον, Com. name in Eup.393.

**ἀμφίπτολις**, poet. for ἀμφίπολις.

**ἀμφι-πτύσσομαι**, Med., *embrace*, Opp.*H*.4.289 (tm.). **-πτῠχή**, ἡ, *folding round*, *embrace*, σώματος δὸς ἀμφιπτυχάς E.*Ion*519.

***ἀμφίπῠλος**, *ον*, *with two entrances*, μέλαθρα E.*Med.*135 (lyr.).

**ἀμφίπῠρος**, *ον*, (πῦρ) *with fire at each end*, of the double-pointed thunderbolt, E.*Ion* 212; βροντά Id.*Hipp.*559; δειράδες Παρνασοῦ.. ἵνα Βάκχιος ἀμφιπύρους ἀνέχων πεύκας..πηδᾷ *with twin fires*, of two peaks of Parnassus, Id.*Ion*716; of Artemis as *bearing a torch in either hand*, S.*Tr.*214 (lyr.). **II.** *with fire all round*, τρίποδες Id. *Aj.*1405.

**ἀμφιρίοστον**· ἐξ ἀμφοτέρων ἐρετός, Hsch.

**ἀμφιριφές** (cod. -ρεφ-), *hurled from either side*, Hsch. **ἀμφιρόν**· ἀμφορέα, Id.

**ἀμφιρρεπής**, ές, (ῥέπω) *inclining both ways*, Eustr.*inEN*119.29, Sch.E.*Or.*633; τὸ ἀ. *ambiguity*, Eust.1394.57, cf. Sch.E.*Or.*866. Adv. -πῶς, ἔχειν Eust.200.11.

**ἀμφιρρήγνῡμι**, *rend all in pieces*, aor. 2 Pass. ἀμφιραγείς Q.S.1.39.

**ἀμφιρρηδής**, = περιρρηδής, *Lex.Rhet.*ap.Eust.1920.33.

**ἀμφίρροπος**, *ον*, *doubtful*, νίκη Polyaen.2.1.23; ἔννοιαι Agath. 4.2. **II.** *precipitous on both sides*, κρημνοί Malch.p.415 D.

**ἀμφιρρώξ**, ῶγος, ὁ, ἡ, *jagged*, πέτραι A.R.1.995. **2.** *broken*, κλωβοί *AP*6.109.

**ἀμφίρῠτος**, η, ον, also ος, ον S.*Aj.*134, (ῥέω) *flowed around, sea-girt*, Od. always fem. ἀμφιρύτη of islands, as 1.50; ἐν Κέῳ ἀμφιρύτᾳ Pi.*I.*1.8; τῆς ἀμφιρύτου Σαλαμῖνος S. l. c.:—**ἀμφίρρυτος**, *ον*, Hes.*Th.* 983, Orac.ap.Hdt.4.163,164.

**ἀμφιρῶτις**· περιβόητος, Hsch.

**ἀμφίς**, Ep. word, once in Pi. (v.infr.), Trag. only E.*Hyps.* (v. infr.), prop. = ἀμφί, but mostly as Adv.: **I.** *on both sides*, ἀ. ἀρωγοί helpers *on either hand, to either party*, Il.18.502, cf. 519; ἁμαρτῇ δούρασιν ἀ. βάλεν threw with spears *from both hands* at once, 21.162; σεῖον ζυγὸν ἀ. ἔχοντες having it *on both sides*, Od.3.486. **2.** generally, *round about*, ἀ. ἐόντες Il.24.488; ἀ. ἰδών having looked *about*, Hes.*Op.*701 (cf. infr. B. 1); δεσμοὶ..ἀ. ἔχοιεν may bonds *encompass*, Od.8.340; σιδηρέῳ ἄξονι ἀ. *at each end*, Il.5.723; and so (rather than *between*) 3.115, 7.342; μολπὴ ἀ. ἔχει δώματα *fills* the house, Xenoph. 1.12. **II.** *apart, asunder*, γαῖαν καὶ οὐρανὸν ἀ. ἔχειν Od.1.54; ἀ. ἐέργειν to keep *apart*, Il.13.706; ἀ. ἀγῆναι snap *in twain*, 11.559; τόξων ἀϊκὰς ἀ. μένον 15.709; ἀ. φράζεσθαι think *separately*, each for himself, i.e. *to be divided*, 2.13; ἀ. φρονέοντε 13.345; ἀ. ἕκαστα εἴρεσθαι to ask each *by itself*, i.e. one after another, Od.19.46 codd.; ἀ. ἔμμεναι to be *absent*, Orac.ap.Hdt.1.85.

**B.** less freq as Prep., like ἀμφί: **I.** c. gen. (which it may either precede or follow), *around*, ἅρματος ἀ. ἰδεῖν look *all round* his chariot, Il.2.384. **b.** *concerning*, ἀ. ἀληθείης Parm.8.51; ἀέθλοις..ἐσθᾶτος ἀ. Pi.*P.*4.253. **2.** *apart from, far from*, ἀ. ἐκείνων εἶναι Od.14.352; Διὸς ἀ. ἥσθην Il.8.444; ἀ. φυλόπιδος Od.16.267; ἀ. ὁδοῦ *aside from, out of* road, Il.23.393; πάτρας ἀ. *far from* her fatherland, E. *Hyps.Fr.*3 iii 30. **II.** c. acc., *about, around*, always after its case, Κρόνον ἀ. Il.14.274; Ποσιδήϊον ἀ. Od.6.266, cf. 9.399.

***ἀμφισαλεύομαι**, Pass., *toss about*, *AP*5.54 (Diosc.).

**ἀμφίσβαινα**, ης, ἡ, (βαίνω) kind of *serpent, supposed to go either forwards or backwards*, A.*Ag.*1233, Ar.*Fr.*18 D.; ἀ. ἀμφίκρηνος, δίστομος, Nic.*Th.*372, Nonn.*D.*5.146. **II.** ἀ. φλέβες veins connecting the breast and generative organs, Pall.*inHp.*2.103 D.

**ἀμφισ-βᾰσίη**, ἡ, Ion. for ἀμφισβήτησις, ἐς -βασίας ἀπικνέεσθαί τινι come to *controversy* with one, Hdt.4.14; ἐγένετο λόγων ἀ. Id.8.81, cf. *Inscr.Prien.*37.129. **-βᾰτέω**, Ion. for ἀμφισβητέω, q.v. **-βᾰτος**, *ον*, = ἀμφισβήτητος, Hellanic.193 J. **-βητέω**, impf. ἠμφεσβήτουν: fut. -ήσω: aor. ἠμφεσβήτησα:—Pass., fut. of med. form -ήσομαι Pl. *Tht.*171b: aor. ἠμφεσβητήθην Id.*Plt.*276b, al., Is.8.44:—Ion. **ἀμφισβᾰτέω** twice in Hdt. (v. infr.), *SIG*279.18 (Zelea): impf. ἀμφεσβάτει *Inscr.Prien.*37.99; also Aeol. pf. part. Pass. ἀμφισβατημένος *IG*12(2).6.25 (Mytilene): (v. βαίνω):—lit. *go asunder, stand apart*: hence, *disagree with*, ὁ ἕτερος τῶν λόγων τῷ πρότερον λεχθέντι -βατέων Hdt.9.74. **b.** abs., *disagree, dispute, wrangle*, Id.4.14, etc.: περί τινος And.1.27, Isoc.4.19, Pl.*Prt.*337a; ὑπέρ τινος Antipho3.4.3; πρός τινα 3.1.1; οἱ ἀμφισβητοῦντες *the parties*, in a law-suit, Arist.*Rh.*1354$^{a}$31. **2.** c. dat. pers., *dispute* or *argue with* a person, Pl.*Phdr.*263a, al.; τινὶ περί τινος Id.*Plt.*268a. **3.** c. gen. rei, *dispute for* or *about* a thing, τοῦ σίτου τοῦ ἡμετέρου D.32.9; *lay claim to*, τῆς ἡγεμονίας Isoc.4.20; τῶν οὐδὲν ὑμῖν προσηκόντων Epist. Phil.ap.D.12.23; τῆς ἀρχῆς D.39.19; τῆς πολιτείας Arist.*Pol.*1280$^{a}$6, cf. 1283$^{a}$11; τρία τὰ ἀμφισβητοῦντα τῆς ἰσότητος three things *which claim* equal shares in.., 1294$^{a}$19; τῆς μεσότητος ἀ. τὰ ἄκρα *EN*1125$^{b}$18:—also ἀ. πρός τι *make a claim* with reference to a standard, *Pol.* 1283$^{a}$24. **b.** Att. law-term. *lay claim to* property of deceased or guardianship of heiress, χρημάτων Isoc.19.3; κλήρου D.3.5, 44.38; κληρονομίας Is.3.1: abs., 3.61, 6.3; τινὶ περὶ τῶν πατρῴων 3.61; πρὸς διαθήκην in defiance of a will, Isoc.19.1. **4.** c. acc. rei, *dispute* point, *be at issue upon* it, ἃ ἐν τουτὶ ἀμφισβητοῦμεν Pl.*Grg.*472d; οὐκ ἀληθῆ ἀ. *Mx.*242d; cf. ἀμφισβητητέον. **5.** c. acc. et inf., *argue, maintain that*.., ἀ. εἶναί τι Id.*Grg.*452c, cf. D.27.62, etc.; but ἀ. ὅτι ἐστί τι *dispute* the fact that.., Pl.*Smp.*215b: with neg., *argue* or *maintain* that it is not, τὸ μὴ οὐχὶ ἡδέα εἶναι τὰ ἡδέα λόγος οὐδεὶς ἀ. *Phlb.*13a; ἠμφεσβήτει μὴ ἀληθῆ λέγειν ἐμέ D.19.19; ἀ. ὡς οὐκ ἀληθῆ λέγει τις Pl.*R.*476d, al.; οὐδεὶς ἀ. περὶ τούτων, ὡς οὐ.. Arist.*Pol.*1287$^{b}$17; σὺ δὲ ἀμφισβητῶν ἀνὴρ εἶναι Aeschin.2.148. **II.** Pass., *to be the subject of dispute, to be in question*, ἀμφισβητεῖταί τι Pl.*R.*581e, etc.: impers., ἀμφισβητεῖται περί τι *Sph.*225b; περί τινος *R.*457e; ἠμφεσβητήθη μηδεμίαν εἶναι τέχνην *Plt.*276b; ὁ πολίτης ἀ. *is a debatable term*, Arist.*Pol.*1275$^{a}$2; τὰ ἀμφισβητούμενα, = ἀμφισβητήματα, Th. 6.10, 7.18, Isoc.4.19, Pl.*Lg.*641e, etc. **-βήτημα**, ατος, τό, *poi in dispute, question*, Id.*Tht.*158b, Arist.*Pol.*1275$^{b}$37, etc. **2.** *poi maintained in argument*, Pl.*Phlb.*11b. **-βητηματικός**, ή, όν, sq.; τὰ -κά Aps.p.236 H. **-βητήσιμος**, *ον*, *disputable*, Antipl 3.1.1, etc.; χώρα ἀ. *debatable* ground, X.*HG*3.5.3, D.7.43, *Hell.Ox* 13.3, Theopomp.ap.Phot.p.104 R.; τὰ ἀ. *disputed property*, Pl.*Lg.* 954c; ἀ. ἀγαθά Arist.*Rh.*1362$^{b}$29; *doubtful*, Pl.*Smp.*175e; ἀ. ἐσ πότερον.. Arist.*Metaph.*996$^{b}$27; οὐκέτ' ἐν -ησίμῳ τὰ πράγματα ἦν D. 18.139. **-βήτησις**, εως, ἡ, *dispute, controversy*, ἀ. γίγνεται, ἔστ περί τινος, Pl.*Phlb.*15a, *R.*533d; ἀ. Δελφῶν πρὸς Ἀμφισσεῖς ὑπὲρ τῶ ὅρων *CIG*1711 (Delph., i A.D.); ἀμφισβήτησιν ὑπολείπειν leave *roon for dispute*, Antipho5.16; ἀμφισβήτησιν ἔχει it admits of *question* Arist.*EN*1100$^{a}$18, etc.; ἀ. ἔσται, τίνας ἄρχειν δεῖ *Pol.*1283$^{b}$3; ἀμφισβητήσεις [εἰσίν], c. acc. et inf., *Rh.*1417$^{a}$8: ἐξ ὧν ἡ πόλις συνέστηκεν, ἐν τούτοις ποιεῖσθαι τὴν ἀ. make a *claim*, *Pol.*1283$^{a}$15, etc. **2.** as Att. law-term, *claim* to an inheritance, ἀ. ποιεῖσθαι Lys.17.5, cf. Is. 6.4, D.48.26. **-βητητέον**, verb. Adj. *one must argue against*, τοῖς εἰρημένοις Arist.*EN*1113$^{b}$17; cf. ἀμφισβητέω 1.4. **-βητητικός**, ή, όν, *fond of disputing, disputatious, contentious*, οἱ περὶ λόγους ἀ. Pl.*Plt.* 306a:—ἡ -κή (sc. τέχνη) *art of disputing*, *Sph.*226a; τὸ -κόν *argumentation*, ib.225b. **-βήτητος**, *ον*, *disputed, debatable*, γῆ Th. 6.6. **-βητος**, *ον*, = foreg., Antag.1.1.

**ἀμφίσγονοι**, = ἑτερόγονοι, Hsch.; = ἑτερομήτορες, *EM*87.57.

***ἀμφισκέπαρνος**, *ον*, *dressed on both sides*, λίθοι *Milet.*7 p.56; ἱερόν *Rev.Phil.*43.200 (Didyma).

**ἀμφίσκιος**, *ον*, (σκιά) *throwing shadow both ways*, sometimes north, sometimes south, of those who live within the tropics, Posidon.70, Cleom.1.7, Ach.Tat.*Intr.Arat.*31. **II.** *shady all round*, πέτρη Opp. *H.*1.789.

**ἀμφίσκω**· ἀμπίσχω, Hsch.

**ἀμφίσκωμοι**, *living around in villages*, Hsch.

**ἀμφι-σμίλη**, ἡ, and **-σμιλον**, τό, prob. ff. ll. for -μηλον (q.v.), Gal. 2.574,581.

**ἀμφισπάω**, *draw about*, Sch.E.*Or.*1457.

**ἀμφίσπορα**, τά, *boundary lands of which the sowing is disputed* (in Latin form), *CIL*3.586 (Lamia, ii A.D.).

**ἀμφιστέλλομαι**, Med., *fold round oneself, deck oneself in*, ξυστίδα ἀμφιστειλαμένη Theoc.2.74.

**ἀμφιστένω**, *roar around*, of the sea, Q.S.9.440; *echo*, of mountains, Id.5.646, 14.82.

**ἀμφιστερῆ**· καταρχὴ τῶν θυσιῶν (Lacon.), Hsch.

**ἀμφίστερνος**, *ον*, *double-breasted*, Emp.61.

**ἀμφι-στεφᾰνόομαι**, Pass., ἀμφὶ δ' ὅμιλος..ἐστεφάνωτο the assembly *stood all round*, *h.Ven.*120. **-στεφής**, ές, *placed round like a crown*, Il.11.40 (v.l.). **II.** *brim-full*, κρατήρ Hsch., Suid. s.v. ἐπιστεφής.

**ἀμφίστημι**, *place round*: in this sense only poet. in Pass. ἀμφίσταμαι, with intr. aor. ἀμφέστην, Ep. 3 pl. ἀμφέσταν, and 3 pl. pf. ἀμφεστᾶσι, *stand around*, abs., φίλοι δ' ἀμφέσταν ἑταῖροι Il.18.233; κλαίων δ' ἀμφίσταθ' ὅμιλος 24.712: c. acc., ἀμφὶ δέ σ' ἔστησαν Od. 24.58; πεδίον ἀμφεστᾶσι πᾶν S.*OC*1312, cf. *Aj.*724: c. dat., ἀμφίσταμαι τραπέζαις *El.*192. **II.** Med., *investigate*, *Tab.Heracl.*1.125; cf. ἀμπιστατήρ.

**ἀμφίστομος**, *ον*, *with double mouth*, of the ichneumon, Eub.107.15; ὄρυγμα ἀ. *tunnel*, Hdt.3.60; σπήλαιον Apollod.2.5.1; λαβὰς ἀ. handles *on both sides of bowl* (ἑκατέρωθεν τοῦ στόματος Sch.), S.*OC* 473; ἀ. θυρίδες, of honeycombs, Arist.*HA*624$^{a}$8; of fistulae, Meges ap.Orib.44.24.11. **2.** *two-edged*, ξίφη D.S.5.33; ἕκτορες anchors *with two flukes*, Luc.*Lex* 15. **3.** of a body of soldiers, *facing both ways*, δύναμις, τάξις, Plb.2.28.6, 29.4, cf. Ascl.*Tact.*3.5, Onos.21.2; φάλαγξ Ael.*Tact.*37.1, Arr.*Tact.*29.1. Adv. -μως *with* λοχαγοί *in front and rear*, Ascl.*Tact.*11.3, Ael.*Tact.*37.2, Arr.*Tact.*29.2. **4.** *pointed at both ends*, ἄκοντες Tim.*Pers.*176.

**ἀμφιστρᾰτάομαι**, Dep., *beleaguer, besiege*, Ep. impf. ἀμφεστρατόωντο πόλιν Il.11.713.

**ἀμφι-στρεφής**, ές, *turning all ways*, of a dragon's three heads, Il. 11.40 (v.l. ἀμφιστεφέες):—also **-στραφής**, Diotog.ap.Stob.4.7.62.

**ἀμφιστρόγγῠλος**, *ον*, *quite round*, Luc.*Hipp.*6.

**ἀμφι-στροφή**, ἡ, *wheeling round*, Hsch. **-στροφος**, *ον*, *turning to and fro, quick-turning*, βᾶρις ἀ. A.*Supp.*882 (Sch. expl. by ἀμφιέλισσα). **2.** **Ἀμφίστροφον**, τό, at Delos, possibly a *domed building*, *IG*11(2).142.38 (iv B.C.), al.

**ἀμφίσφαιρα**, τά, (cf. σφαιρωτήρ) *buttoned boots*, Herod.7.59, Hsch.

**ἀμφι-σφάλλω**, *treat* a dislocated joint *by circumduction*, Hp.*Art.* 2:—Pass., Id.*Mochl.*5. **-σφαλσις**, εως, ἡ, *circumduction*, *Art.*71.

**ἀμφίσφῠρα**, τά, kind of *shoes*, Poll.7.94 (prob. f.l. for ἀμφίσφαιρα).

**ἀμφίσωπος**, *ον*, = περίωπος, A.*Fr.*41.

**ἀμφιτᾰλαντεύω**, *cause to weigh evenly on both sides*, Nonn.*D.*1.183, cf. 6.110.

**ἀμφιτάμνω**, Ion. for ἀμφιτέμνω.

**ἀμφιτανύω**, = ἀμφιτείνω, *h.Merc.*49 (tm.).

**ἀμφιτάπης** [ᾰ], ητος, ὁ, *rug* or *carpet with pile on both sides*, Alex. 93, Diph.51; but also ἀμφιτάπητες ψιλαί *CIG*3071 (Teos):—also **ἀμφίταπις**, ιδος, ἡ, Ael.Dion.*Fr.*304, Lycon ap.D.L.5.72; and **ἀμφίταπος**, ὁ, *PEdgar*29.4 (iii B.C.), Lxx *Pr.*7.16, Callix.2.

**ἀμφιτᾰράσσομαι**, Pass., *to be troubled all round*, ἁλὸς ἀμφιταρασσομένας ὀρυμαγδός Simon.51.

**ἀμφιτείνομαι**, Pass., *to be spread round* or *over*, ἀμφιταθείς Opp. *H.*1.163.

**ἀμφιτειχής**, ές, *encompassing the walls*, λεώς A.*Th*.291.

**ἀμφιτέμνω**, Ion. **-τάμνω**, *cut off on all sides, intercept and surround*, tmesi, τάμνοντ' ἀμφὶ βοῶν ἀγέλας Il.18.528; *clear away*, κόνιν, ... *AP*7.281 (Heraclid. Sinop.), *IG*4.823.49 (Troezen); *pare all round*, ὀνύχων ἀκίδα *AP*5.227 (Paul. Sil.).

**ἀμφίτερμος**, ον, *bounded on all sides, hedged about*, Hsch. Adv. -μως S.*Fr*.123.

**ἀμφιτεύχω**, *make* or *work round about*, plpf. Pass., Τηθὺς δ' ἀμφιέτυκτο, of sea round shield of Achilles, Q.S.5.14.

***ἀμφιτίθημι** [τῐ], 3 sg. ἀμφιτιθεῖ Xenoph.1.2, imper. ἀμφιτίθει Thgn.847: aor. ind. ἀμφέθηκα, other moods supplied by aor. 2: (v. -ίθημι):—*put round*, Hom. mostly in tmesi, ἀμφὶ δέ οἱ κυνέην κεφαλῆφιν ἔθηκεν Il.10.261, cf. Od.13.431; τοῖς ἀδίκοις ἀμφιτίθησι πέδας Sol.4.34; κἄνπερ κόσμον ἀμφιθῇ χροΐ E.*Med*.787, cf. *El*.512; ἀμφιθεῖναι σῇ δέρῃ θέλω χέρας *Or*.1043; also στέφανον ἀμφὶ κάρα.. ἀμφιθεῖναι Id.*IA*1531:—c. acc. rei only, ζεύγλην δύσλοφον ἀμφιτίθει Thgn. l.c., cf. Theoc.15.40; δεσμὸν ἀμφέθηκεν πέδῃς Semon.7.116 (Lyc.1344, τραχήλῳ ζεῦγλαν ἀμφιθεὶς πέδαις, is corrupt):—Med., *put round oneself, put on*, ὁ δ' ἀμφέθετο ξίφος Od.21.431; ἀμφέθετο στεφάνους κρατὸς ἐπὶ σφετέρου Epigr.ap.Ath.1.19b:—Pass., *to be put on*, κυνέη ἀμφιτεθεῖσα Il.10.271. 2. rarely c. dat. rei, *cover* with a thing, ἀμφιθεὶς κάρα πέπλοις E.*Hec*.432.

**ἀμφιτιμάομαι**, *to be disputed*, of an assessment or estimate, *BCH* 37.184 (Clazomenae, iii B.C.).

**ἀμφιτῐνάσσω**, *shake around*, δικλίδας ἀμφετίναξε.. προσώποις *swung round* the door in my face, *AP*5.255 (Paul. Sil.).

**ἀμφιτιττῠβίζω**, *twitter* or *chirp around*, Ar.*Av*.235.

**ἀμφίτομος**, ον, *cutting on both sides, two-edged*, βέλεμνον A.*Ag*. 1496; λόγχαι, ξίφη, E.*Hipp*.1375, *El*.164; βουπλήξ Q.S.11.190.

**ἀμφί-τορνος**, ον, *well-rounded*, ἀσπίς E.*Tr*.1156. **-τόρνωτος**, η, ον, = foreg., Lyc.704.

**ἀμφίτοροι**· ἄλφιτα ἐλαίῳ δεδευμένα (Lacon.), Hsch.

**ἀμφιτράχηλος** [ᾰ], ον, *round the neck*, Sch.S.*Ant*.351.

**ἀμφιτρέμω**, *tremble round* one, ἀμφὶ δ' ἄρ' ἀμβρόσιος ἑανὸς τρέμε Il. 21.507.

**ἀμφιτρέχω**, *run round, surround*, αὐλὴν ἕρκος ἀμφιδέδρομεν Archil. 40; σέλας δ' ἀμφέδραμεν Pi.*P*.3.39; θείη δ' ἀμφιδέδρομεν χάρις Semon. 7.89.

**ἀμφι-τρής**, ῆτος, ὁ, ἡ, (τετραίνω) = sq.; ἀμφιτρής (sc. πέτρα) rock *pierced through*, cave *with double entrance*, E.*Cyc*.707: also neut., ἀμφιτρῆς αὔλιον S.*Ph*.19. **-τρητος**, ον, *pierced through*, *AP*6.233 (Maec.).

**Ἀμφιτρίτη** [τρῑ], ἡ, *Amphitrite*, Poseidon's wife, Hom., etc. 2. poet., *sea*, *Hymn.Is*.145, D.P.53, Opp.*H*.1.423: pl., D.P.99. 3. Pythag., = 6, *Theol.Ar*.38 (as if from ἀμφίς, τριάς).

**ἀμφίτριψ**, ιβος, ὁ, (τρίβω) *rubbed all round*: metaph., like περίτριμμα, *practised knave*, Archil.124, cf. Hsch.

**ἀμφιτρομέω**, *tremble for*, τοῦ δ' ἀ. καὶ δείδια Od.4.820.

**ἀμφιτροχόω**, *run round, encompass*, ἀμφιτροχώσας Apollod.1.9. 12, prob. from a poet.

**ἀμφιτρυχῆ**· κατερρωγότα, Hsch., Phot., Suid.

**ἀμφιτύπος**, ον, (τύπτω) *pointed at both ends*, βουπλήξ Q.S.1.159.

**ἀμφι-φαείνω**, *beam around*, αἴγλη δέ μιν ἀ. h.*Ap*.202. ***-φαής**, ές, (φάος) *everywhere visible*, Arist.*Mu*.395ᵇ14; Ἑκάτη *visible from all sides*, Dam.*Pr*.122, cf. *Orac.Chald*.62.

**ἀμφίφᾰλος** κυνέη helmet *with double* φάλος, Il.5.743, 11.41, Q.S. 3.334.

***ἀμφιφᾰνής**, ές, (φαίνομαι) *visible all round, seen by all, known to all*, E.*Andr*.834 (lyr.), *IG*3.1324, *Orac.Chald*.300. 2. of stars, *seen twice in a night*, when they set after and rise before the sun, Gem.14.11, Arr.ap.Stob.1.28.2.

**ἀμφιφέρομαι**, Pass., *to be borne round, revolve*, in impf., Q.S.5.10.

**ἀμφί-φλασμα**, **-φλάω**, v. -θλασμα, -θλάω.

**ἀμφιφοβέομαι**, Pass., *fear, tremble*, or *quake all round*, ἕταροι δέ μιν ἀμφεφόβηθεν Il.16.290 (al. ἀμφὶ φόβ-), cf. Q.S.2.546, 11.117.

***ἀμφιφορεύς**, gen. έως, Ep. ῆος, ὁ: (φέρω, φορέω):—*large jar* or *pitcher with two handles*, of gold, Il.23.92, Od.24.74; of stone, 13.105; for wine, 2.290, etc.; for oil, Simon.155.4: used as *cinerary urn*, Il. l.c. II. = μετρητής, Theopomp.Hist.374. (The later form was ἀμφορεύς, q.v.)

**ἀμφιφορίτης** [ῑ], ὁ, v. ἀμφορίτης.

**ἀμφιφράζομαι**, Med., *consider on all sides, consider well*, ἀμφὶ μάλα φράζεσθε, φίλοι Il.18.254.

**ἀμφιφύα**, ἡ, (φύω) = ἄμφαυξις, Thphr.*HP*3.7.1.

**ἀμφιφῶν**, ῶντος, ὁ, properly part. of *ἀμφιφάω, cake offered to Munychian Artemis *by double light*, i.e. either *surrounded by lighted tapers*, or *offered when sun and moon were both visible*, Pherecr.156, Philem.67, cf. Poll.6.75, *EM*94.55.

**ἀμφίχαιτος**, ον, *with foliage all round*, D.S.2.53.

**ἀμφιχᾰνής**, ές, *gaping wide*, Abyden.1.

**ἀμφιχᾰράσσω**, *scratch, incise around*, γράμματα σκήπτρῳ *PMag. Par*.1.2845; *lance all round*, ῥίζην (sc. ὀδόντος) Marcell.Sid.89; of stars, *mark the course of*, κύκλον Man.2.66.

***ἀμφιχάσκω**, impf., v. infr.: aor. ἀμφέχᾰνον:—*gape round, gape for*, c. acc., ἐμὲ μὲν Κὴρ ἀμφέχανε Il.23.79; μαστὸν ἀμφέχασκ' ἐμόν, of an infant, A.*Ch*.545; ἀμφιχανὼν λόγχαις ἑπτάπυλον στόμα, of the Argive army round Thebes, S.*Ant*.118; ἀγκίστρου.. πλάνον ἀμφιχανοῦσα, of a fish, *AP*7.702 (Apollonid.): rarely c. dat., Opp.*H*.3.178.

**ἀμφιχέω**, *pour around, pour* or *spread over*, ἀμφὶ δ' ἄρ' ἑρμίσιν χέε δέσματα Od.8.278. II. mostly Pass., *to be poured* or *shed around*, πάρος κόνιν ἀμφιχυθῆναι Il.23.764: c. acc., θείη δέ μιν ἀμφέχυτ' ὀμφή ib.2.41; τὴν ἄχος ἀμφεχύθη Od.4.716; ἀμφιχυθὲν γῆρας Mimn.5; ἀμφὶ δὲ σποδὸν κάρᾳ κεχύμεθα *we have* ashes *poured over* our head, E. *Supp*.826. 2. of persons, *embrace*, ἀμφιχυθεὶς πατέρα Od.16.214, cf. 22.498.

**ἀμφιχορεύω**, *dance around*, abs., Critias 19 (anap.), *AP*9.83 (Phil.): c. dat., Opp.*C*.1.27.

**ἀμφιχρίομαι**, Med., *anoint oneself all over*, ἀμφὶ δ' ἐλαίῳ χρίσομαι Od.6.219.

**ἀμφίχρῡσος**, ον, *gilded all over*, φάσγανον E.*Hec*.543.

**ἀμφίχῠτος**, ον, *poured around*; *thrown up around*, τεῖχος ἀ., i.e. an *earthen* wall, Il.20.145, cf. Hellanic.26 J.

***ἀμφίχωλος**, ον, *lame in both feet*, *AP*6.203.

**ἀμφοδ-άρχης**, ου, ὁ, (ἄμφοδον II) *officer commanding troops levied in a ward*, Ph.*Bel*.93.8: also a civil official, *OGI*483.82 (Pergam.), Wilcken *Chrest*.61 (i A.D.). **-αρχία**, ἡ, *quarter under the direction of an ἀ.*, *CPR*8.7 (iii A.D.).

**ἀμφοδέω**, *miss, fail to meet*, *Rev.Egypt*.1.208, Hsch. s.v. ἀβροτάξομεν; cf. ἀντ-, δι-, παρ-αμφοδέω.

**ἀμφοδικός**, ή, όν, *of, belonging to streets*, κέλευθοι Man.4.252.

***ἀμφόδιον**, τό, Dim. of sq., Luc.*Rh.Pr*.24, *EM*557.46 (as v.l.).

***ἄμφοδον**, τό, *street*, Ar.*Fr*.327, *OGI*483.80 (Pergam.), *Ev.Marc*.11. 4, Cleom.2.1; *compitum*, *Gloss*. II. *block of houses surrounded by streets*, Hyp.*Fr*.137, *PMag.Par*.1.349: prov., οὐ θύρα ἀλλ' ἀμφόδῳ διέψευσται Plb.39.3.2: hence, *ward, quarter of a town*, Lxx *Je*.17. 27, *SIG*961.1 (Smyrna), Ph.*Bel*.92.42, *BGU*496 (ii A.D.), etc.:—also **ἄμφοδος**, ἡ, Gal.*UP*16.1, Sm.*Am*.5.16, Procop.*Aed*.2.3.

***ἀμφόδων**, = ἀμφώδων, Hp.*Art*.8.

**ἄμφ-οισμα**, ατος, τό, (ἀμφι-φέρω) *revolving figure*, Papp.682.8, 11:—hence **-οιστικός**, ή, όν, *described by revolution*, 682.8, 15.

**ἀμφόνη**· ἀκρατής, ἁμαρτωλός, μὴ δυναμένη νηστεῦσαι, Hsch.

**ἀμφορεᾱ-φορέω**, *carry water-pitchers*, Ar.*Fr*.299. **-φόρος**, ου, ὁ, *water-carrier*, Eup.187, Men.431, *IG*2.768.

**ἀμφορ-είδιον** (not -ίδιον), τό, Dim. of ἀμφορεύς, Ar.*Pax* 202, al. **-είω**· φορτίῳ, Hsch. (ἀμφορεῖ· τῷ φορείῳ, Ruhnken). ***-εύς**, έως, ὁ: acc. ἀμφορέα Ar.*Fr*.299: dual ἀμφορῆ Telecl.2 D.: pl. ἀμφορῆς Ar.*Nu*.1203:—*jar* with narrow neck (στενόστομον τὸ τεῦχος Id.*Fr*. 108), Hdt.4.163, Ar.*Nu*.1203, etc.; used for various purposes, esp. for keeping wine in, *Pl*.807, *Fr*.299; or milk, E.*Cyc*.327; for pickles, X. *An*.5.4.28. 2. ornament in shape of vase, ὅρμος -έων *IG*11(2).161*B* 38 (Delos, iii B.C.), cf. *SIG*²588.199 (ib., ii B.C.). II. liquid measure, = μετρητής (Philyll.7, Moer.45, etc.), 1½ Roman *amphorae* or nearly 9 gallons, Hdt.1.51, *IG*3.38, D.43.8, etc. (Shortened form of ἀμφιφορεύς, q.v., from *having two handles*.) **-ίζω**, dub. sens. in Eust.1924. 13. **-ικός**, ή, όν, *like an amphora*, κάδοι Sch.Ar.*Av*.1032. **-ίξ**, Adv. *like an amphora* (?), Eust.1924.13. **-ιον**, τό, Dim. of ἀμφορεύς, *Gloss*. ***-ίσκος**, ὁ, Dim. of ἀμφορεύς, D.22.76; ἀ. Πανώνιος *IG*2. 818. ***-ίτης** [ῑ] ἀγών, ὁ, race *run by bearers of amphorae*, and *of which an amphora was prize*, Call.*Fr*.80 (ap.Sch.Pi.*O*.7.156); ἀμφιφορίτης *EM*95.3. II. *kept in* ἀμφορεῖς, [ἔλαιον] *PSI*5.535.31 (iii B.C.).

**ἀμφοτερ-άκις**, Adv. *in both ways*, Arist.*Mech*.855ᵇ32, *Pr*.902ᵇ 31. **-η**, Adv. *in both ways*, Hdt.7.10.β'; *by both branches*, of a river, 1.75: Argive **-εῖ** *Mnemos*.47.160 (v B.C.). **-ήκης**, ες, *two-edged*, Epic.Anon.in *PHib*.8. **-ίζω**, *to be in both ways*, ἀ. τῇ χρείᾳ, of figs, *to be good to eat either* fresh or dried, Jul.*Ep*.180.

**ἀμφοτερό-βλεπτος**, ον, *looking on both sides, circumspect*, Timo 59. **-γλωσσος**, ον, *speaking both ways, double-tongued*, of Zeno the inventor of dialectic, Id.45, cf. Eust.1440.35. **-γνώμων**, ονος, *of two opinions*, βουλή Sch.E.*Hec*.219. **-δέξιος**, ον, = ἀμφιδέξιος, Lxx *Jd*.3. 15, Aristaenet.1.8, Gal.18(1).147. **-δύναμος**, ον, *with power for good or ill*, of Zeus, Eust.1363.29. **-πλοος**, ον, contr. **-πλους**, ουν, *navigable on both sides*, γῆ Poll.9.18. 2. τὸ ἀ. (sc. ἀργύριον or δάνειον) *money lent on bottomry*, when the lender bore the risk *of the outward and homeward voyage*, ἐδάνεισα Φορμίωνι κ' μνᾶς ἀμφοτερόπλουν εἰς τὸν Πόντον D.34.6, etc.; ἀ. κέρδος Ael.*Ep*.18; opp. ἑτερόπλουν, q.v.

***ἀμφότερος** (Locr. ἀμφόταρος *IG*9(1).334.39), α, ον, (ἄμφω) rare in sg., *either*, i.e. *both of two* (opp. ἑκάτερος *each one* of two), ἀμφοτέρας κοινὸν αἴας common to *either* land, A.*Pers*.131; ποίημα ἢ πάθος ἢ ἀμφότερον or *partaking of both*, Pl.*Sph*.248d; τὸ ἀμφότερον ἑκατέρῳ οὐχ ἕπεται Id.*Hp.Ma*.302e. 2. Hom. has sg. only neut. ἀμφότερον as Adv., foll. by τε.. καί; ἀ. βασιλεύς τ' ἀγαθὸς κρατερός τ' αἰχμητής *both together*, prince as well as warrior, ib.3.179; ἀ. γενεῇ τε καὶ οὕνεκα.. Il.4.60; foll. by τε.. δέ.., Pi.*P*.4.79: also neut. pl., ἀμφότερα μένειν πέμπειν τε A.*Eu*.480; φιλοχρήματος καὶ φιλότιμος, ἤτοι τὰ ἕτερα τούτων ἢ ἀ. Pl.*Phd*.68c; ἀ. ἄριστος καὶ στρατηγὸς καὶ ῥαψῳδός *Ion* 541b; by τε.. καί.., Pi.*O*. 1.104. 3. dual in Hom., as ἀ. Αἴαντε Il.12.265, al., less freq. in later writers, X.*An*.1.1.1, Pl.*Prm*.143c, Isoc.4.134, etc.; but pl. is much more freq., and is found with a dual Noun, χεῖρε πετάσσας ἀμφοτέρας Il.21.115.—Phrases: κατ' ἀμφότερα *on both sides*, Hdt.7. 10.β', Pl.*Prm*.159a; ἐπ' ἀμφότερα *towards both sides, both ways*, Hdt. 3.87, al., Th.1.83, al.; ἀμφότερα, abs., *on both sides*, ib.13, al.; ἀπ' ἀμφοτέρων *from* or *on both sides*, Ξέρξεω ἀπ' ἀ. ἀδελφεός Hdt.7.97; παρ' ἀμφοτέρων D.S.16.7, al.; μετ' ἀμφοτέροισι *one with another* (s.v.l.), Theoc.12.12; ἀμφοτέροις βλέπειν (sc. ὄμμασι) Call.*Epigr*.32. 6; ἀμφοτέραις, Ep. -ῃσι (sc. χερσί) Od.10.264; ἐπ' ἀμφοτέροις βεβακώς (sc. ποσί) Theoc.14.66. II. later, of more than two, *all together*, *Act.Ap*.19.16, *PLond*.2.336.13 (ii A.D.).

**ἀμφοτερότης**, ητος, ἡ, *duality*, etym. of Ἀμφιτρίτη, Sch.Opp.*H.* 1.385.

**ἀμφοτερόχωλος**, ον, = ἀμφίχωλος, Apollon.*Lex.* s.v. ἀμφιγυήεις.

®**ἀμφοτέρ-ωθεν** (also **-θε** Orph.*Fr.*168.14, Androm.ap.Gal.14.39), Adv. *from* or *on both sides*, Il.5.726, Hdt.2.29, Pi.*P.*1.6; of combatants, Th.5.16: c. gen., ἀ. τῆς κεφαλῆς Hp.*VC*1; τῆς ὁδοῦ X.*HG*5.2.6. 2. *from both ends*, Od.10.167. **-ωθι**, Adv. *in both ways*, X.*Mem.*3.4.12. **-ως**, Adv. *in both ways*, Pl.*Prm.*159a, *Grg.*469a, etc. **-ωσε**, Adv. *to both sides*, γεγωνέμεν ἀ. Il.8.223, 11.6.

**ἀμφουδίς**, Adv., only Od.17.237 ἀμφουδὶς ἀείρας lifting *by the middle.* (Prob. Adv. from ἀμφί; cf. ἄλλυδις.)

®**ἀμφούριον**, τό, (οὖρος = ὅρος) *acknowledgement paid to neighbours on sale of a plot of land*, *PHal.*1.253 (iii B.C.).

**ἀμφύσκη**· τῇ χειρὶ κυρτωθείσῃ, ἔνιοι δὲ τὸ λεῖκνον, Hsch.

®**ἄμφω**, τώ, τά, τώ, also οἱ, αἱ, τά; gen. ἀμφοῖν S.*Ph.*25, etc., dat. ἀμφοῖν *Aj.*1264, etc.:—*both*, of individuals, Il.1.363; of armies or nations, 2.124:—Hom. uses only nom. and acc.: from Hom. downwards freq. with pl. Noun or Verb, Il.2.767, 7.255, etc.; ἐξ ἀμφοῖν, = ἐξ ἀλλήλοιν, S.*OC*1425: sts. indecl., *h.Cer.*15, Arist.*Top.*118$^{a}$28, Theoc.17.26, A.R.1.165. (For the root cf. ἀμφί.)

**ἀμφώβολος**, ὁ, (ὀβολός) *javelin* or *spit with double point*, E.*Andr.* 1133. 2. as Adj., in neut. pl., *roasted on the spit*, of victims sacrificed in divination, S.*Fr.*1006 (expl. as διὰ σπλάγχνων μαντεῖαι by Eust.1405.30, Hsch.).

®**ἀμφώδων**, οντος, ὁ, ἡ, (ὀδούς) *with incisor-teeth in both jaws*, opp. ruminants, Arist.*HA*501$^{a}$11, cf. *PA*675$^{a}$5, *HA*495$^{b}$31, al. II. Subst., *ass*, Lyc.1401. (Freq. written ἀμφόδων; cf. ἀμφόδους.)

**ἀμφώης**, ες, (οὖς) = ἄμφωτος, Theoc.1.28.

**ἀμφωλένιον**, τό, (ὠλένη) *bracelet*, Aristaenet.1.25.

**ἄμφωμος**, ον, *round* or *on the shoulders*, Hsch. **ἀμφωμοσία**, ἡ, = ἀμφιορκία, Id. **ἀμφώνυξ**, v. ἀμφώτιξ. **ἄμφωξις**, v. ἄμφωτις. **ἀμφώτας**· χιτών τις, *EM*93.15: **ἄμφωτος**, Hsch. ®**ἀμφώτιξ ἢ ἀμφώνυξ**· γαστρίμαργος, ἀκρατής, Id.

®**ἄμφωτις**, ιδος, or **ἀμφωτίς**, ίδος, ἡ, (οὖς) *two-handled pail*, Philet. ap.Ath.11.783d: written **ἄμφωξις** in Hsch., *EM*94.7. II. *covering for the ears*, A.*Fr.*102; worn by boxers, Plu.2.38b, 706c, cf. Paus.Gr.*Fr.*52.

**ἄμφωτος**, ον, (οὖς) *two-eared*, *two-handled*, Od.22.10: neut. as Subst., *jar*, Hierocl.*Facet.*35.

**ἄμωκος**, ον, *without mockery*, *serious*, Iamb.*VP*23.105.

**ἀμωλεί**, *without dispute*, *GDI*4992 (Gortyn).

®**ἀμώμητος**, ον, *blameless*, Il.12.109, Archil.6.2, Pi.*P.*2.73, etc.; *faultless*, ποιημάτιον, λόγοι, D.S.33.5,7; of victims, *unblemished*, Aristeas 93, cf. Ph.*Fr.*69 H.; ἄσπιλοι καὶ ἀ. 2*Ep.Pet.*3.14, cf. Eus. Mynd.*Fr.*21; in epitaphs, *CIG*4642 (Palestine), *IG*14.1937 (Ravenna). Adv. -τως Hdt.3.82.

**ἀμωμίς**, ίδος, ἡ, plant used for adulterating *amomum*, Dsc.1.15, cf. Plin.*HN*12.49, *Edict.Diocl.Troez.*21.

**ἀμωμίτης** [ῑ], ου, ὁ, *like amomum*, kind of λίβανος, Dsc.1.68.

®**ἄμωμον**, τό, Indian spice-plant, prob. *Nepaul cardamom*, *Amomum subulatum*, Arist.*Fr.*110, Thphr.*HP*9.7.2, Dsc.1.15.

®**ἄμωμος**, ον, *blameless*, Semon.4; νόμος Hdt.2.177; *without blemish*, εἶδος ἄ. Hes.*Th.*259; κάλλει A.*Pers.*185; in epitaphs, *CIG*1974 (Thessalonica), al. 2. *unblemished*, of victims, etc., Lxx *Ex.*29.1, al., 1*Ep.Pet.*1.19, Ph.1.171, al. 3. *unimpaired*, *perfect*, ὑγίεια *IG*5(1).1119 (Geronthrae, iv B.C.).

**ἀμωμότης**, ητος, ἡ, *blamelessness*, Sm.*Ps.*25.1.

**Ἀμών**, ῶνος, ὁ, sc. μήν, month at Amphissa, *GDI*1684, 1922.

**ἀμώνα**, Aeol. for ἀνεμώνη, Hsch.

**ἀμωρέα**, ἡ, kind of *radish*, Thphr.*HP*7.4.2. **ἀμωρεύουσιν**· ἰχθυοφοροῦσιν, *EM*117.26. **ἄμωρος**, kind of *cake*, Hsch.

**ἁμῶς** or **ἀμῶς**, Adv. from obsol. ἁμός = τίς, only in form ἁμωσγέπως *in some way or other*, Ar.*Th.*429, Lys.13.7, Pl.*Prt.*323c, Epicur. *Fr.*607, etc. (Cf. ἁμός B.)

**ἀμώσας**· κρεμάσας (Tarent.), Hsch. **ἄμωτον**, τό, = καστάνειον, Ageloch.ap.Ath.2.54d; prob. cj. for μότα, Dsc.1.106.

**ἄν** (A), [ᾰ], Ep., Lyr., Ion., Arc., Att.; also **κε(ν)** Ep., Aeol., Thess., **κᾱ** Dor., Boeot., El.; the two combined in Ep. (infr. D.II.2) and Arc., εἰκ ἄν *IG*5(2).6.2,15 (iv B.C.):—modal Particle used with Verbs to indicate that the action is limited by circumstances or defined by conditions. In Hom. κε is four times as common as ἄν, in Lyr. about equally common. No clear distinction can be traced, but κε as an enclitic is somewhat less emphatic; ἄν is preferred by Hom. in negative clauses, κε(ν) with the relative.

**A.** In Simple Sentences, and in the Apodosis of Compound Sentences; here ἄν belongs to the Verb, and denotes that the assertion made by the Verb is dependent on a condition, expressed or implied: thus ἦλθεν *he came*, ἦλθεν ἄν *he would have come* (under conditions, which may or may not be defined), and so *he might have come*; ἔλθοι *may he come*, ἔλθοι ἄν *he would come* (under certain conditions), and so *he might come*.

**I.** WITH INDICATIVE: **1.** with historical tenses, generally impf. and aor., less freq. plpf., never pf., v. infr., **a.** most freq. in apodosis of conditional sentences, with protasis implying nonfulfilment of a past or present condition, and apod. expressing what *would be* or *would have been* the case if the condition *were* or *had been* fulfilled. The impf. with ἄν refers to continued action, in Hom. always in past time, exc. perh. καί κε θάμ' ἐνθάδ' ἐόντες ἐμισγόμεθ' Od.4.178; later also in pres. time, first in Thgn.905; πολὺ ἂν θαυμαστότερον ἦν, εἰ ἐτιμῶντο it *would be* far more strange if they were honoure[d] Pl.*R.*489a; οὐκ ἂν νήσων ἐκράτει, εἰ μή τι καὶ ναυτικὸν εἶχεν he *wou[ld]* not *have* been master of islands if he had not had also some nav[al] power, Th.1.9. The aor. strictly refers only to past time, Pi.*N.*1.24, etc.; εἰ τότε ταύτην ἔσχε τὴν γνώμην, οὐδὲν ἂν ὧν νυνὶ πεποίηκ[εν] ἔπραξεν if he had then come to this opinion, he *would have* accomplished nothing of what he has now done, D.4.5, al., but is use[d] idiomatically with Verbs of saying, answering, etc., as we say *should have* said, εἰ μὴ πατὴρ ἦσθ', εἶπον ἄν σ' οὐκ εὖ φρονεῖν S.*Ant.*755, cf. Pl.*Smp.*199d, *Euthphr.*12d, etc.: the plpf. refers to complete[d] actions, as ὃ εἰ ἀπεκρίνω, ἱκανῶς ἂν ἤδη παρὰ σοῦ τὴν ὁσιότητα ἐμεμαθήκη I *should have* already learnt.., ib.14c; εἰ ὁ ἀνὴρ ἀπέθανεν, δικαίως ἂν ἐτεθνήκει Antipho 4.2.3. **b.** the protasis is freq. understood: ὑπό κεν ταλασίφρονά περ δέος εἷλεν fear *would have* seized even the stout-hearted (had he heard the sound), Il.4.421; τὸ γὰρ ἔρυμα τῷ στρατοπέδῳ οὐκ ἂν ἐτειχίσαντο they *would* not *have* built the wall (if they had not won a battle), Th.1.11; πολλοῦ γὰρ ἂν ἦν ἄξια for (if that were so) they *would be* worth much, Pl.*R.*374d; οὐ γὰρ ἦν ὅ τι ἂν ἐποιεῖτε for there was nothing which you *could have* done, i.e. *would have* done (if you had tried), D.18.43. **c.** with no definite protasis understood, to express what *would have been likely to happen*, or *might have happened* in past time: ἢ γάρ μιν ζωόν γε κιχήσεαι, ἤ κεν Ὀρέστης κτεῖνεν ὑποφθάμενος for either you will find him alive, or else Orestes *may* already *have* killed him before you, Od.4.546; ὃ θεασάμενος πᾶς ἄν τις ἀνὴρ ἠράσθη δάϊος εἶναι every man who saw this (the 'Seven against Thebes') *would have* longed to be a warrior, Ar. *Ra.*1022; esp. with τάχα, q.v., ἀλλ' ἦλθε μὲν δὴ τοῦτο τοὔνειδος τάχ' ἂν ὀργῇ βιασθὲν μᾶλλον ἢ γνώμῃ φρενῶν, i.e. it *might* perhaps *have* come, S.*OT*523; τάχα ἂν δὲ καὶ ἄλλως πως ἐσπλεύσαντες (sc. διέβησαν) and they *might* also perhaps *have* crossed by sea (to Sicily) in some other way, Th.6.2, cf. Pl.*Phdr.*265b. **d.** ἄν is freq. omitted in apodosi with Verbs expressing obligation, propriety, or possibility, as ἔδει, ἐχρῆν, εἰκὸς ἦν, etc., and sts. for rhetorical effect, εἰ μὴ..ἤσμεν, φόβον παρέσχεν it *had* caused (for it *would have* caused) fear, E.*Hec.*1113. This use becomes more common in later Gk. **2.** with fut. ind.: **a.** frequently in Ep., usu. with κεν, rarely ἄν, Il.9.167, 22.66, indicating a limitation or condition, ὁ δέ κεν κεχολώσεται ὅν κεν ἵκωμαι and he *will likely be* angry to whomsoever I shall come, ib.1.139; καί κέ τις ὧδ' ἐρέει and in that case men will say, 4.176; ἐγὼ δέ κέ τοι καταλέξω Od.3.80; so in Lyr., μαθὼν δέ τις ἂν ἐρεῖ Pi.*N.*7.68, cf. *I.*6(5).59. **b.** rarely in codd. of Att. Prose writers, σαφὲς ἂν καταστήσετε Th.1.140; οὐχ ἥκει, οὐδ' ἂν ἥξει δεῦρο Pl.*R.*615d, cf. *Ap.*29c, X.*An.*2.5.13; dub. in Hp.*Mul.*2.174: in later Prose, Philostr.*VA*2.21, S.E.*M.*9.225: also in Poetry, E.*El.*484, Ar.*Av.*1313; οὐκ ἂν προδώσω Herod.6.36 (corr. -δοίην):—for ἄν with fut. inf. and part. v. infr.

**II.** WITH SUBJUNCTIVE, only in Ep., the meaning being the same as with the fut. ind. (I.2a), freq. with 1st pers., as εἰ δέ κε μὴ δώῃσιν, ἐγὼ δέ κεν αὐτὸς ἕλωμαι in that case *I will* take her myself, Il.1.324; πείθευ, ἐγὼ δέ κέ τοι εἰδέω χάριν obey and *if so* I will be grateful, 14.235 (the subj. is always introduced by δέ in this usage); also with other persons, giving emphasis to the future, οὐκ ἄν τοι χραίσμῃ κίθαρις 3.54, al.

**III.** WITH OPTATIVE (never fut., rarely pf. πῶς ἂν λελήθοι [με]; X.*Smp.*3.6): **a.** in apodosis of conditional sentences, after protasis in opt. with εἰ or some other conditional or relative word, expressing a fut. condition: ἀλλ' εἴ μοί τι πίθοιο, τό κεν πολὺ κέρδιον εἴη Il.7.28; οὐ πολλὴ ἂν ἀλογία εἴη, εἰ φοβοῖτο τὸν θάνατον; Pl.*Phd.*68b:—in Hom. pres. and aor. opt. with κε or ἄν are sts. used like impf. and aor. ind. with ἄν in Attic, with either regular ind. or another opt. in the protasis: καί νύ κεν ἔνθ' ἀπόλοιτο..εἰ μὴ..νόησε κτλ., i.e. he *would have* perished, had she not perceived, etc., Il.5.311, cf. 5.388, 17.70; εἰ νῦν ἐπὶ ἄλλῳ ἀεθλεύοιμεν, ἦ τ' ἂν ἐγὼ..κλισίηνδε φεροίμην if we were now contending in another's honour, I *should* now carry.., ib.23.274: so rarely in Trag., οὐδ' ἂν σὺ φαίης, εἴ σε μὴ κνίζοι λέχος (for εἰ μὴ ἔκνιζε) E.*Med.*568. **b.** with protasis in pres. or fut., the opt. with ἄν in apodosi takes a simply future sense: φρούριον δ' εἰ ποιήσονται, τῆς μὲν γῆς βλάπτοιεν ἄν τι μέρος they *might perhaps* damage, Th.1.142, cf. 2.60, Pl.*Ap.*25b, *R.*333e; ἢν οὖν μάθῃς ..οὐκ ἂν ἀποδοίην Ar.*Nu.*116, cf. D.1.26, al. **c.** with protasis understood: φεύγωμεν· ἔτι γάρ κεν ἀλύξαιμεν κακὸν ἦμαρ Od.10.269; οὔτε ἐσθίουσι πλείω ἢ δύνανται φέρειν· διαρραγεῖεν γὰρ ἄν for (if they should do so) they *would* burst, X.*Cyr.*8.2.21; τὸν δ' οὔ κε δύ' ἀνέρε ..ἀπ' οὔδεος ὀχλίσσειαν two men *could* not heave the stone from the ground, i.e. *would* not, if they should try, Il.12.447; οὐδ' ἂν δικαίως ἐς κακὸν πέσοιμί τι S.*Ant.*240, cf. D.2.8: in Hom. sts. with ref. to past time, Τυδεΐδην οὐκ ἂν γνοίης ποτέροισι μετείη Il.5.85. **d.** with no definite protasis implied, in potential sense: ἡδέως δ' ἂν ἐροίμην Λεπτίνην but I *would* gladly ask Leptines, D.20.129; βουλοίμην ἄν I *should* like, Lat. *velim* (but ἐβουλόμην ἄν I *should* wish, if it were of any avail, *vellem*); ποῖ οὖν τραποίμεθ' ἄν; which way then *can* we turn? Pl.*Euthd.*290a; οὐκ ἂν μεθείμην τοῦ θρόνου I *will* not give up the throne, Ar.*Ra.*830; idiomatically, referring to the past, αὗται δὲ οὐκ ἂν πολλαὶ εἶεν but these *would* not (on investigation) prove to be many, Th.1.9; εἴησαν δ' ἂν οὗτοι Κρῆτες these *would* be (i.e. *would have* been) Cretans, Hdt.1.2: used in order to soften assertions by giving them a less positive form, as οὐκ ἂν οὖν πάνυ γέ τι σπουδαῖον εἴη ἡ δικαιοσύνη, i.e. it *would* not *prove to be*, etc. (for, it *is* not, etc.), Pl.*R.*

33e. e. in questions, expressing a wish: τίς ἂν θεῶν.. δοίη; S.*OC* 100, cf. A.*Ag*.1448; πῶς ἂν θάνοιμι; S.*Aj*.389: hence (with no question) as a mild command, exhortation, or entreaty, τλαίης κεν Μενελάῳ ἐπιπροέμεν ταχὺν ἰόν Il.4.94; σὺ μὲν κομίζοις ἂν σεαυτὸν ᾗ θέλεις you *may* take yourself off (milder than κόμιζε σεαυτόν), S.*Ant*.444; χωροῖς ἂν εἴσω you *may* go in, *El*.1491; κλύοις ἂν ἤδη, Φοῖβε hear me now, Phoebus, ib.637; φράζοις ἄν, λέγοις ἄν, Pl.*Phlb*.23c, 48b. f. in a protasis which is also an apodosis: εἴπερ ἄλλῳ τῳ ἀνθρώπων πειθοίμην ἄν, καὶ σοὶ πείθομαι if I *would* trust any (other) man (if he gave me his word), I trust you, Id.*Prt*.329b; εἰ μὴ ποιήσαιτ' ἂν τοῦτο if you *would* not do this (if you could), D.4.18, cf. X.*Mem*.1.5.3, Plot.6.4.16. g. rarely omitted with opt. in apodosis: ῥεῖα θεός γ' ἐθέλων καὶ τηλόθεν ἄνδρα σαώσαι Od.3.231, cf. 14.123, Il.5.303; also in Trag., θᾶσσον ἢ λέγοι τις E.*Hipp*.1186; τεὰν δύνασιν τίς.. κατάσχοι; S.*Ant*.605. h. ἄν c. fut. opt. is prob. always corrupt (cf. I.2b), as τὸν αὐτὸν ἂν ἐπαινέσοι (ἐπαινέσαι Bekk.) Pl.*Lg*.719e; εἰδὼς ὅτι οὐδέν' ἂν καταλήψοιτο (οὐδένα Bekk.) Lys.1.22.

IV. WITH INF. and PART. (sts. ADJ. equivalent to part., τῶν δυνατῶν ἂν κρῖναι Pl.*R*.577b) representing ind. or opt.: 1. pres. inf. or part.: a. representing impf. ind., οἴεσθε τὸν πατέρα.. οὐκ ἂν φυλάττειν; do you think he *would* not *have* kept them safe? (οὐκ ἂν ἐφύλαττεν), D.49.35; ἀδυνάτων ἂν ὄντων [ὑμῶν] ἐπιβοηθεῖν when you *would have* been unable, Th.1.73, cf. 4.40. b. representing pres. opt., πόλλ' ἂν ἔχων (representing ἔχοιμ' ἄν) ἕτερ' εἰπεῖν παραλείπω D. 18.258, cf. X.*An*.2.3.18: with Art., τὸ ἐθέλειν ἂν ἰέναι ἄκλητος ἐπὶ δεῖπνον Pl.*Smp*.174b. 2. aor. inf. or part.: a. representing aor. ind., οὐκ ἂν ἡγεῖσθ' αὐτὸν κἂν ἐπιδραμεῖν; do you not think he *would* even *have* run thither? (καὶ ἐπέδραμεν ἄν), D.27.56; ἴσμεν ὑμᾶς ἀναγκασθέντας ἂν we know you *would have* been compelled, Th.1.76, cf. 3.89; ῥᾳδίως ἂν ἀφεθεὶς when he *might* easily *have* been acquitted, X.*Mem*.4.4.4. b. representing aor. opt., οὐδ' ἂν κρατῆσαι αὐτοὺς τῆς γῆς ἡγοῦμαι I think they *would* not even be masters of the land (οὐδ' ἂν κρατήσειαν), Th.6.37, cf. 2.20; ὁρῶν ῥᾳδίως ἂν αὐτὸ ληφθέν (ληφθείη ἄν) Id.7.42; οὔτε ὄντα οὔτε ἂν γενόμενα, i.e. things which are not and never *could* happen (ἃ οὔτε ἂν γένοιτο), Id.6.38. 3. pf. inf. or part. representing: a. plpf. ind., πάντα ταῦθ' ὑπὸ τῶν βαρβάρων ἂν ἑαλωκέναι (φήσειεν ἄν) he *would* say that all these *would have* been destroyed by the barbarians (ἑαλώκη ἄν), D.19.312. b. pf. opt., οὐκ ἂν ἡγοῦμαι αὐτοὺς δίκην ἀξίαν δεδωκέναι, εἰ.. καταψηφίσαισθε I do not believe they *would* (then) have suffered (δεδωκότες ἂν εἶεν) punishment enough, etc., Lys.27.9. 4. fut. inf. or part., never in Ep., and prob. always corrupt in Att., νομίζων μέγιστον ἂν σφᾶς ὠφελήσειν (leg. -ῆσαι) Th.5.82, cf. 6.66, 8.25, 71; part. is still more exceptional, ὡς ἐμοῦ οὐκ ἂν ποιήσοντος ἄλλα Pl.*Ap*.30c (codd.), cf. D.19.342 (v.l.); both are found in later Gk., νομίσαντες ἂν οἰκήσειν οὕτως ἄριστα Plb.8.30.8, cf. Plu.*Marc*.15, Arr.*An*.2.2.3; with part., Epicur. *Nat*.14.1, Luc.*Asin*.26, Lib.*Or*.62.21, dub. l. in Arr.*An*.6.6.5.

B. IN DEPENDENT CLAUSES. I. In the protasis of conditional sentences with εἰ, regularly with the subjunctive. In Attic εἰ ἄν is contracted into ἐάν, ἤν, or ἄν (ᾱ) (q.v.): Hom. has generally εἴ κε (or αἴ κε), sts. ἤν, once εἰ δ' ἄν Il.3.288, twice εἴπερ ἄν 5.224, 232. The protasis expresses either future condition (with apod. of fut. time) or general condition (with apod. of repeated action): εἰ δέ κεν ὣς ἔρξῃς καί τοι πείθωνται Ἀχαιοί, γνώσῃ ἔπειθ' ὅς.. if thus thou shalt do.., ib.2.364; ἢν ἐγγὺς ἔλθῃ θάνατος, οὐδεὶς βούλεται θνήσκειν if death (ever) come near.., E.*Alc*.671. 2. in relative or temporal clauses with a conditional force; here ἄν coalesces with ὅτε, ὁπότε, ἐπεί, ἐπειδή, cf. ὅταν, ὁπόταν, ἐπήν or ἐπάν (Ion. ἐπεάν), ἐπειδάν: Hom. has ὅτε κε (sts. ὅτ' ἄν), ὁππότε κε (sts. ὁπότ' ἄν or ὁππότ' ἄν), ἐπεί κε (ἐπεὶ ἄν Il.6.412), ἐπήν, εὖτ' ἄν; v. also εἰσόκε (εἰς ὅ κε):—τάων ἥν κ' ἐθέλωμι φίλην ποιήσομ' ἄκοιτιν whomsoever of these I *may* wish.., Il.9.397; ὅταν δὴ μὴ σθένω, πεπαύσομαι when I shall have no strength.., S.*Ant*.91; ἐχθρὸς γάρ μοι κεῖνος.. ὅς χ' ἕτερον μὲν κεύθῃ ἐνὶ φρεσίν, ἄλλο δὲ εἴπῃ who*ever* conceals one thing in his mind and speaks another, Il.9.312, cf. D.4.6, Th.1.21.—Hom. uses subj. in both the above constructions (1 and 2) without ἄν; also Trag. and Com., S.*Aj*.496, Ar.*Eq*.805; μέχρι and πρίν occasionally take subj. without ἄν in prose, e.g. Th.1.137, 4.16 (μέχρι οὗ), Pl.*Phd*.62c, Aeschin.3.60. 3. in final clauses introduced by relative Advbs., as ὡς, ὅπως (of Manner), ἵνα (of Place), ὄφρα, ἕως, etc. (of Time), freq. in Ep., σαώτερος ὥς κε νέηαι Il.1.32; ὄφρα κεν εὕδῃ Od.3.359; ὅπως ἂν εἰδῇ.. φράσω A.*Pr*.824; ὅπως ἂν φαίνηται κάλλιστος Pl.*Smp*.198e; μηχανητέον ὅπως ἂν διαφύγῃ *Grg*. 481a (where ὅπως with fut. ind. is the regular constr.); also after ὡς in Hdt., Trag., X.*An*.2.5.16, al., once in Th.6.91 (but fut. ind. is regular in Att.); ἵνα final does not take ἄν or κε exc. ἵνα εἰδότες ἤ κε θάνωμεν ἤ κεν.. φύγοιμεν Od.12.156 (ἵνα = *where* in S.*OC*405). Μή, = *lest*, takes ἄν only with opt. in apodosis, as S.*Tr*.631, Th.2.93.

II. in Ep. sts. with OPTATIVE as with subj. (always κε(ν), exc. εἴ περ ἂν αὐταὶ Μοῦσαι ἀείδοιεν Il.2.597), εἴ κεν Ἄρης οἴχοιτο Od.8.353; ὥς κε.. δοίη ᾧ κ' ἐθέλοι that he *might* give her to whomsoever he *might* please, ib.2.54: so in Hdt. in final clauses, 1.75, 99:—in Od.23.135 ὥς κέν τις φαίη, κέν belongs to Verb in apod., as in ὡς δ' ἂν ἥδιστα ταῦτα φαίνοιτο X.*Cyr*.7.5.81. 2. rarely in *oratio obliqua*, where a relat. or temp. word retains an ἄν which it would have with subj. in direct form, S.*Tr*.687, X.*Mem*.1.2.6, Isoc.17.15; ἐπειδὰν δοκιμασθείην D.30.6:—similarly after a preceding opt., οὐκ ἀποκρίναιο ἕως ἄν.. σκέψαιο Pl.*Phd*.101d.

III. rarely with εἰ and INDICATIVE in protasis, only in Ep.: 1. with fut. ind. as with subj.: αἴ κεν Ἰλίου πεφιδήσεται Il.15.213:—so with relat., οἵ κέ με τιμήσουσι 1.175. 2. with εἰ and a past tense of ind., once in Hom., εἰ δέ κ' ἔτι προτέρω γένετο δρόμος Il.23.526; so Ζεὺς γάρ κ' ἔθηκε νῆσον εἴ κ' ἐβούλετο Orac.ap.Hdt.1.174, cf. Ar.*Lys*. 1099 (cod. R), A.R.1.197.

IV. in later Greek, ἄν with relative words is used with INDICATIVE in all tenses, as ὅπου ἂν εἰσεπορεύετο *Ev.Marc*.6.56; ὅσ' ἂν πάσχετε *PFay*.136 (iv A.D.); ἔνθ' ἂν πέφυκεν ἡ δλότης εἶναι Phlp. *in Ph*.436.19; cf. ἐάν, ὅταν.

C. with impf. and more rarely aor. ind. in ITERATIVE construction, to express elliptically *a condition fulfilled whenever an opportunity offered*; freq. in Hdt. (not in Pi. or A.), κλαίεσκε ἂν καὶ ὀδυρέσκετο she *would* (i.e. *used to*) weep and lament, 3.119; εἶτα πῦρ ἂν οὐ παρῆν S.*Ph*.295; εἴ τινες ἴδοιεν.., ἀνεθάρσησαν ἄν whenever they saw it, on each occasion, Th.7.71; διηρώτων ἂν αὐτοὺς τί λέγοιεν Pl.*Ap*.22b: inf. representing impf. of this constr., ἀκούω Λακεδαιμονίους τότε ἐμβαλόντας ἄν.. ἀναχωρεῖν, i.e. I hear they *used to* retire (ἀνεχώρουν ἄν), D.9.48.

D. GENERAL REMARKS: I. POSITION OF ἄν. 1. in A, when ἄν does not coalesce with the relat. word (as in ἐάν, ὅταν), it follows directly or is separated only by other particles, as μέν, δέ, τε, γάρ, καί, νυ, περ, etc.; as εἰ μέν κεν.. εἰ δέ κε Il.3.281–4; rarely by τις, as ὅποι τις ἄν, οἶμαι, προσθῇ D.2.14:—in Hom. and Hes. two such Particles may precede κε, as εἴ περ γάρ κεν Od.8.355, cf. Il.2.123; εἰ γάρ τίς κε, ὃς μὲν γάρ κε, Hes.*Op*.280, 357; rarely in Prose, ὅποι μὲν γὰρ ἄν D.4.45; ὁπότερος οὖν ἄν Ar.*Ra*.1420: also ὁπόσῳ πλέον ἄν Pl.*Lg*.647e, cf. 850a; ὅπου τὸ πάλαι λεγόμενον ἂν γίγνηται 739c. 2. in apodosis, ἄν may stand either next to its Verb (before or after it), or after some other emphatic word, esp. an interrog., a negative (e.g. οὐδ' ἂν εἷς, οὐκ ἂν ἔτι, etc.), or an important Adjective or Adverb; also after a participle which represents the protasis, λέγοντος ἄν τινος πιστεῦσαι οἴεσθε; do you think they *would have* believed it if any one had told them? (εἴ τις ἔλεγεν, ἐπίστευσαν ἄν), D.6.20. 3. ἄν is freq. separated from its inf. by such Verbs as οἴομαι, δοκέω, φημί, οἶδα, etc., οὐκ ἂν οἴει..; freq. in Pl., *Grg*.486d, al.; καὶ νῦν ἡδέως ἄν μοι δοκῶ κοινωνῆσαι I think that I *should*, X.*Cyr*.8.7.25; οὕτω γὰρ ἄν μοι δοκεῖ ἥ τε πόλις ἄριστα διοικεῖσθαι Aeschin.3.2; ἃ μήτε προῄδει μηδεὶς μήτ' ἂν ᾠήθη τήμερον ῥηθῆναι (where ἄν belongs to ῥηθῆναι) D. 18.225:—in the phrase οὐκ οἶδ' ἂν εἰ, or οὐκ ἂν οἶδ' εἰ, ἄν belongs not to οἶδα, but to the Verb which follows, οὐκ οἶδ' ἂν εἰ πείσαιμι, for οὐκ οἶδα εἰ πείσαιμι ἄν, E.*Med*.941, cf. *Alc*.48; οὐκ ἂν οἶδ' εἰ δυναίμην Pl. *Ti*.26b; οὐκ οἶδ' ἂν εἰ ἐκτησάμην X.*Cyr*.5.4.12. 4. ἄν never begins a sentence, or even a clause after a comma, but may stand first after a parenthetic clause, ἀλλ', ὦ μέλ', ἄν μοι σιτίων διπλῶν ἔδει Ar.*Pax* 137. II. REPETITION OF ἄν:—in apodosis ἄν may be used twice or even three times with the same Verb, either to make the condition felt throughout a long sentence, or to emphasize certain words, ὥστ' ἄν, εἰ σθένος λάβοιμι, δηλώσαιμ' ἂν S.*El*.333, cf. *Ant*.69, A.*Ag*. 340, Th.1.76 (fin.), 2.41, Pl.*Ap*.31a, Lys.20.15; ἀφανεῖς ἂν ὄντες οὐκ ἂν ὑμνήθημεν ἄν E.*Tr*.1244, cf. S.*Fr*.739; attached to a parenthetical phrase, ἔδρασ' ἄν, εὖ τοῦτ' ἴσθ' ἄν, εἰ.. Id.*OT*1438. 2. ἄν is coupled with κε(ν) a few times in Hom., as Il.11.187, 202, Od.5.361, al.; cf. ἦν περ γάρ κ' ἐθέλωσιν v.l. ib.18.318. III. ELLIPSIS OF VERB:—sts. the Verb to which ἄν belongs must be supplied, in Hom. only εἰμί, as τά τ' ἔλδεται ὅς κ' ἐπιδευὴς (sc. ᾖ) Il.5. 481; ἀλλ' οὐκ ἂν πρὸ τοῦ (sc. ἔρρεγκον) Ar.*Nu*.5; τί δ' ἂν δοκεῖ σοι Πρίαμος (sc. πρᾶξαι), εἰ τάδ' ἤνυσεν; A.*Ag*.935:—so in phrases like πῶς γὰρ ἄν; and πῶς οὐκ ἄν (sc. εἴη); also in ὥσπερ ἂν εἰ (or ὡσπερανεί), as φοβούμενος ὥσπερ ἂν εἰ παῖς (i.e. ὥσπερ ἂν ἐφοβήθη εἰ παῖς ἦν) Pl.*Grg*.479a; so τοσοῦτον ἐφρόνησαν, ὅσον περ ἂν (sc. ἐφρόνησαν) εἰ.. Isoc.10.48:—so also when κἂν εἰ (= καὶ ἂν εἰ) has either no Verb in the apod. or one to which κἄν cannot belong, Pl.*R*.477a, *Men*.72c; cf. κἄν:—so the Verb of a protasis containing ἄν may be understood, ὅποι τις ἂν προσθῇ, κἂν μικρὰν δύναμιν (i.e. καὶ ἐὰν προσθῇ) D.2.14; ὡς ἐμοῦ οὖν ἰόντος ὅπῃ ἂν καὶ ὑμεῖς (sc. ἴητε) X.*An*.1.3.6. IV. ELLIPSIS OF ἄν:—when an apodosis consists of several co-ordinate clauses, ἄν is generally used only in the first and understood in the others: πείθοι' ἂν εἰ πείθοι'· ἀπειθοίης δ' ἴσως A.*Ag*.1049: even when the construction is continued in a new sentence, Pl.*R*.352e, cf. 439b codd.: but ἄν is repeated for the sake of clearness or emphasis, ib. 398a, cf. D.19.156 (where an opt. is implied with the third ὡς): rarely expressed with the second of two co-ordinate Verbs and understood with the first, τοῦτον ἄν.. θαρσοίην ἐγὼ καλῶς μὲν ἄρχειν, εὖ δ' ἂν ἄρχεσθαι θέλειν (i.e. καλῶς μὲν ἂν ἄρχοι, εὖ δ' ἂν θέλοι ἄρχεσθαι) S.*Ant*.669.

**ἄν** (B), [ᾱ], Att., = ἐάν, ἤν, Th.4.46 codd., al.; freq. in Pl., ἂν σωφρονῇ *Phd*.61b; ἂν θεὸς θέλῃ ib.80d, cf. D.4.50; ἄν τ'.. ἄν τε Arist. *Ath*.48.4: not common in earlier Att. Inscrr., *IG*1.2a5, 2.179b49, al.: but freq. later, *SIG*1044.27 (iv/iii B.C.), *PPetr*.2 p.47 (iii B.C.), *PPar*.32.19 (ii B.C.), *PTeb*.110.8 (i B.C.), *Ev.Jo*.20.23, etc.

**ἄν**, by crasis for ἃ ἄν, S.*OT*281, 580, etc.

**ἄν** or **ἀν**, Ep. form of ἀνά, q.v.

**ἄν**, shortened from ἄνα, v. sub ἀνά G.

**ἀν-**, negat. Prefix, of which ἀ- privativum (q.v.) is a shortened form.

**ἀνά** [ᾰνᾰ], Aeol., Thess., Arc., Cypr. ὀν, Prep. governing gen., dat., and acc. By apocope ἀνά becomes ἄν before dentals, as ἂν τὸν ὀδελόν; ἄγ before gutturals, as ἄγ γύαλα; ἄμ before labials, as ἂμ βωμοῖσι, ἂμ πέτραις, etc.; ἀμπεπλεγμένας *IG*5(2).514.10 (Arc.).

A. WITH GEN., three times in Od., in phrase ἀνὰ νηὸς βαίνειν go *on board* ship, 2.416, 9.177, 15.284; ἂν τοῦ τοίχου, τᾶς ὁδοῦ, τοῦ ῥοειδίου, *IG*14.352 i 40, ii 15, 83 (Halaesa).

B. WITH DAT., *on, upon*, without any notion of motion, Ep., Lyr., and Trag. (only lyr.), ἀνὰ σκήπτρῳ *upon* the sceptre, Il.1.15, Pi.*P.* 1.6; ἂμ βωμοῖσι Il.8.441; ἀνὰ σκολόπεσσι 18.177; ἀνὰ Γαργάρῳ ἄκρῳ 15.152; ἀνὰ ὤμῳ *upon* the shoulder, Od.11.128; ἀν ἵπποις, i.e. *in* a chariot, Pi.*O.*1.41; ἀμ πέτραις A.*Supp.*351 (lyr.); ἀνά τε ναυσὶν καὶ σὺν ὅπλοις E.*IA*754; ἀγ Κόσσῳ *GDI*1365 (Epirus).

C. WITH ACCUS., the comm. usage, implying *motion upwards*: I. of Place, *up, from bottom to top, up along*, κίον' ἂν' ὑψηλὴν ἐρύσαι Od.22.176; ἀνὰ μέλαθρον *up to*, ib.239; [φλέψ] ἀνὰ νῶτα θέουσα διαμπερὲς αὐχέν' ἱκάνει Il.13.547; ἀνὰ τὸν ποταμόν Hdt.2.96; ἂν ῥόον *up*-stream, *GDI*5016.11 (Gortyn); κρῆς ἂν τὸν ὀδελὸν ἐμπεπαρμένον Ar.*Ach.*796 (Megarian); simply, *along*, ἂν τὼς ὅρως *Tab.Heracl.*2.32. 2. *up and down, throughout*, ἀνὰ δῶμα Il.1.570; ἀνὰ στρατόν, ἄστυ, ὅμιλον, ib.384, Od.8.173, etc.; ἀγ γύαλα A.*Supp.*550 (lyr.); ἀνὰ πᾶσαν τὴν Μηδικήν, ἀνὰ τὴν Ἑλλάδα, Hdt.1.96, 2.135, etc.; ὂν τὸ μέσσον Alc.18.3; ἀνὰ τὸ σκοτεινόν *in* the darkness, Th.3.22. 3. metaph., ἀνὰ θυμὸν φρονέειν, ἀνὰ στόμα ἔχειν, to have *continually in* the mind, *in* the mouth, Il.2.36, 250; ἀν' Αἰγυπτίους ἄνδρας *among* them, Od.14.286; ἀνὰ πρώτους εἶναι to be *among* the first, Hdt.9.86. II. of Time, *throughout*, ἀνὰ νύκτα *all* night *through*, Il.14.80; ἀνὰ τὰς προτέρας ἡμέρας Hdt.7.223; ἀνὰ τὸν πόλεμον 8.123; ἀνὰ χρόνον *in course of* time, 1.173, 2.151, 5.27; ἀνὰ μέσσαν ἀκτῖνα (i.e. *in* the south) S.*OC*1247. 2. *distributively*, ἀνὰ πᾶσαν ἡμέραν day *by* day, Hdt.2.37, 130, etc.; ἀνὰ πᾶν ἔτος 1.136, etc.; ἀνὰ πάντα ἔτεα 8.65: also ἀνὰ πρεσβύτατα *in order of* age, *Test.Epict.*4.28. III. distributively with Numerals, κρέα εἴκοσιν ἀν' ἡμιωβολιαῖα 20 pieces of meat *at* half an obol *each*, Ar.*Ra.*554; τῶν ἀν' ὀκτὼ τὠβολοῦ that sell 8 *for* the obol, Timocl.18; ἀνὰ πέντε παρασάγγας τῆς ἡμέρας [they marched] *at the rate of* 5 parasangs a day, X.*An.*4.6.4; ἔστησαν ἀνὰ ἑκατὸν μάλιστα ὥσπερ χοροί they stood *in bodies of* about 100 men *each*, ib.5.4.12; κλισίας ἀνὰ πεντήκοντα companies *at the rate of* 50 *in each*, *Ev.Luc.*9.14; ἔλαβον ἀνὰ δηνάριον a denarius *apiece*, *Ev. Matt.*20.10; in doctor's prescriptions, ἀνὰ ὀβολὼ β' Sor.1.63, etc.: also ἀνὰ δύο ἥμισυ ζῳδίων *amounting to* $2\frac{1}{2}$ signs, Autol.1.10; *multiplied by*, *PPetr.*3 p.198. IV. Phrases: ἀνὰ κράτος *up to* the full strength, i.e. *vigorously*, ἀνὰ κράτος φεύγειν, ἀπομάχεσθαι, X.*Cyr.*4.2.30, 5.3.12; ἀνὰ τὸν αὐτὸν λόγον and ἀνὰ λόγον *proportionately*, Pl.*Phd.*110d; esp. in math. sense, Id.*Ti.*37a, Arist.*APo.*85ᵃ38, etc.; ἀνὰ μέσον *in* the midst, Antiph.13, Men.531.19; ἀνὰ μέρος *by turns*, Arist.*Pol.*1287ᵃ17.

D. WITH NOM. of Numerals, etc., distributively, *Apoc.*21.21, v.l. in Sor.1.11, 12, cf. Orib.*Fr.*50, 54.

E. WITHOUT CASE as Adv., *thereupon*, Hom. and other Poets:—and with the notion of *spreading all over* a space, *throughout, all over*, μέλανες δ' ἀνὰ βότρυες ἦσαν *all over* there were clusters, Il.18.562, cf. Od.24.343:—but ἀνά often looks like an Adv. in Hom., where really it is only parted from its Verb by tmesis, ἀνὰ δ' ἔσχετο; ἀνὰ δ' ὦρτο (for ἀνῶρτο δέ); ἀνὰ τεύχε' ἀείρας (for τεύχεα ἀναείρας), etc.

F. IN COMPOS. 1. as in C. I, *up to, upwards, up*, opp. κατά, as ἀνα-βαίνω, -βλέπω, ἀν-αιρέω, -ίστημι: poet. sts. doubled, ἀν' ὀρσοθύρην ἀναβαίνειν Od.22.132. 2. hence flows the sense of *increase* or *strengthening*, as in ἀνακρίνω; though it cannot always be translated, as in Homer's ἀνείρομαι:—in this case opp. ὑπό. 3. from the notion *throughout* (E), comes that of *repetition* and *improvement*, as in ἀνα-βλαστάνω, -βιόω, -γεννάω. 4. the notion of *back, backwards*, in ἀναχωρέω, ἀνανεύω, etc., seems to come from such phrases as ἀνὰ ῥόον *up*, i.e. *against*, the stream.

G. ἄνα, written with anastr. as Adv., *up! arise!* ἀλλ' ἄνα Il.6.331, Od.18.13:—in this sense the ult. is never elided; cf. ἀλλ' ἄνα, εἰ μέμονάς γε Il.9.247; ἀλλ' ἄνα ἐξ ἑδράνων S.*Aj.*194. 2. apocop. ἂν after ὤρνυτο, ὦρτο, *and up stood..arose*, Il.3.268, 23.837, etc. 3. when used as Prep. ἀνά never suffers anastrophe.

***ἄνα** (A), [ἄνᾰ], voc. of ἄναξ, *king*, only in the phrases ὦ ἄνα, contr. ὦνα, and Ζεῦ ἄνα, and always as address to gods: fem., = ὦ ἄνασσα, Pi.*P.*12.3: ult. elided only in *h.Ap.*526 codd.—Ep., Lyr., and occasionally Trag., as S.*OC*1485 (lyr.).

***ἄνα** (B), ἡ, = ἄνυσις, Alcm.23.83, Call.*Jov.*90; cf. ἄνη.

***ἀνάατος**, = ἄνατος, *IG*5(2).357.177 (Stymphalus, iii B.C.); ἀνάατορ ἤστω *Michel*1334 (Elis, iv B.C.).

**ἀνα-βάδην** [βᾰ], Adv., (ἀναβαίνω) lit. *going up*, but usu. *with one's feet up, lying down*, Ar.*Pl.*1123, D.Chr.62.6, Plu.2.336c, cf. Ath.12.528f, Poll.3.90; so prob. in Ar.*Ach.*399, 410, but expl. by a Sch. as *upstairs*. **-βάδισις**, εως, ἡ, *retrogression*, Antyll.ap.Orib.6.22.9. **-βᾰδόν**, Adv. *by mounting*, ἀ. τὴν ὀχείαν ποιεῖσθαι Arist.*HA* 579ᵃ19.

**ἀναβαθ-μίς**, ίδος, ἡ, *step, stair*, Lxx *Ex.*20.26. ***-μός**, ὁ, *flight of steps, stair*, Hdt.2.125, Arist.*Oec.*1347ᵃ5, D.C.65.21; δι' ἀναβαθμῶν *by degrees*, Ph.2.557. **-ρα**, ἡ, = sq., αἱ ἀ. αἱ στοϊκαί *CIG*4436b (Soli). II. *flight of steps*, Str.7.2.3. III. *going up, ascent*, ᾠδὴ τῶν ἀ. Lxx *Ps.*118(119) tit., al. ***-ρον**, τό, *raised seat* or *chair*, *CIG*2924 (Tralles).

***ἀναβαίνω**, impf. ἀνέβαινον: fut. -βήσομαι: (for aor. 1 v. infr. B): aor. 2 ἀνέβην, imper. ἀνάβηθι, -βῶ, -βῆναι, -βάς: pf. -βέβηκα:—Med., aor. 1 -εβησάμην, Ep. 3 sg. -εβήσετο, v. infr. B:—Pass., v. infr. II. 2:—*go up, mount*, c. acc. loci, οὐρανόν, ὑπερῷα ἀ. *go up to* heaven, *to* the upper rooms, Il.1.497, Od.18.302; φάτις ἀνθρώπους ἀναβαίνει *goes up among*, ib.6.29; more freq. with Prep., ἀ. ἐς ἐλάτην, ἐς δίφρον, Il.14.287, 16.657; rarely with ἀνά repeated, ἀν' ὀρσοθύρην ἀ. Od.22.132; after Hom., most freq. with ἐπί, ἀ. ἐπὶ τὰ ὑψηλότατα τῶν ὀρέων Hdt.1.131: c. dat., νεκροῖς ἀ. *to trample on* the dead, Il.10.493: metaph., ἐπειδὴ ἐνταῦθα ἀναβεβήκαμεν τοῦ λόγου Pl.*R.*445c. II. Special usages: 1. *mount* a ship, *go on board*, in Hom. mostly abs.; ἐς Τροίην ἀ. *embark* for Troy, Od.1.210; ἀπὸ Κρήτης ἀ. 14.252; ἐπὶ τὰς ναῦς Th.4.44, etc.: metaph., ἀναβάσομαι στόλον I *will mount* a prow, Pi.*P.*2.62. 2. *mount* on horseback (cf. ἀναβάτης), ἀ. ἐφ' ἵππον X.*Cyr.*4.1.7, cf. 7.1.3: abs. ἀναβεβηκώς *mounted*; ἀναβάντες (abs.) ἐφ' ἵππων ἐλάσαι 3.3.27; ἀ. ἐπὶ τροχόν *mount* on the wheel of torture, Antipho 5.40. b. c. acc., ἀ. ἵππον *mount* a horse, Theopomp.Hist.2:—Pass., [ἵππος] ὁ μήπω ἀναβαινόμενος that *has* not yet *been mounted*, X.*Eq.*1.1; ἀναβαθείς *when mounted*, ib.3.4; ἐν ἵππῳ ἀναβεβαμένῳ Id.*Eq.Mag.* 3.4, cf. 1.4. 3. of land-journeys, *go up* from the coast into Central Asia, Hdt.5.100, X.*An.*1.1.2; ἀ. παρὰ βασιλέα Pl.*Alc.*1.123b. b. *go up* to a temple, *PPar.*47.19, *Ev.Luc.*18.10; to a town, *Ev.Matt.*20.18, al., cf. *PLond.*3.1170ᵇ.46 (iii A.D.), etc.; in curses, ἀ. παρὰ Δάματρα πεπρημένος *GDI*3536.19 (Cnidus), cf. *SIG* 1180.9 (ibid.). c. *ascend* to heaven, *Ascens.Is.*2.16. 4. of rivers in flood, *rise*, Hdt.2.13; ἀ. ἐς τὰς ἀρούρας *overflow* the fields, Id.1.193. 5. of plants, *shoot up*, ἐπὶ δένδρα X.*Oec.*19.18; *climb* on sticks, Thphr.*HP*8.3.2; generally, *shoot, spring up*, *Ev.Matt.*13.7; of hair, X.*Smp.*4.23. 6. in Att., ἀ. ἐπὶ τὸ βῆμα, or ἀ. alone, *mount the tribune, rise to speak*, D.18.66, 21.205, *Prooem.*56; ἀ. εἰς τὸ πλῆθος, εἰς or ἐπὶ τὸ δικαστήριον *come before* the people, *before* the court, Pl.*Ap.*31c, 40b, *Grg.*486b; ἀ. ἐπὶ τὸν ὀκρίβαντα *mount* the stage, Id.*Smp.*194b: abs., ἀνάβαινε Ar.*Eq.*149; ἀνάβηθι Id.*V.*963; of witnesses in court, Lys.1.29. 7. of the male, *mount, cover*, ἀ. τὰς θηλέας Hdt.1.192, cf. Ar.*Fr.*329; ἀ. ἐπὶ Ph.1.651, cf. Moer.3:—Pass., *Milet.*3.31(a).6 (vi B.C.). 8. of age, δύο ἀναβεβηκὼς ἔτη τῆς ἡλικίας τῆς ἐμῆς two years *older*.., Ach.Tat.1.7. 9. *ascend to higher knowledge*, ἡ ἀναβεβηκυῖα ἐπιστήμη Simp. *in Ph.*15.34, cf. 9.30; τὰ ἀναβεβηκότα *generalities*, Sor.2.5. 10. c. acc., *surpass*, κάλλει τὴν πᾶσαν διακόσμησιν Lyd.*Ost.*22. III. of things and events, *come to an end, turn out*, Hdt.7.10.θ'; ἀπό τινος ἀ. *result from*, X.*Ath.*2.17. b. ἀ. ἐπὶ καρδίαν *enter* into one's heart, of thoughts, Lxx 4*Ki.*12.4, *Je.*3.16, 1*Ep.Cor.*2.9, cf. *Ev.Luc.*24.38. 2. *come to, pass over to*, ἐς Λεωνίδην ἀνέβαινεν ἡ βασιληΐη Hdt.7.205, cf. 1.109. IV. *return to the beginning*, of discourse, Democr.144ᵃ; *go back*, ἀναβήσεται ἐπὶ τὰς κτίσεις τῶν προγόνων Hermog.*Inv.*2.2.

B. aor. ἀνέβησα in causal sense, *make to go up*, esp. *put on shipboard*, Il.1.143, Pi.*P.*4.191; so in aor. Med., νῶ ἀναβησάμενοι *having taken* us *on board* with them, Od.15.475: rare in Prose, ἄνδρας ἐπὶ καμήλους ἀνέβησε *he mounted* men on camels, Hdt.1.80.

***ἀναβακχεύω**, *rouse to Bacchic frenzy, madden*, E.*HF*1086, cf. *Or.* 337. II. intr., *break forth in Bacchic frenzy*, Id.*Ba.*864, Plu.*Crass.* 33, Lib.*Or.*40.23.

***ἀναβαλλαγόρας**· φάρμακόν τι καὶ λίθος ἐν Σάμῳ, Hsch. **ἀναβαλλίδες**· ταινίαι ἢ σφαῖραι, *EM*95.43, cf. Hdn.Gr.1.91.

***ἀναβάλλω**, *throw up*, χοῦν ἐξ ὀρύγματος Th.4.90, cf. X.*Cyr.*7.5.10, *Ostr.*1399 (i A.D.); τάφρος ἀναβεβλημένη *foss and dyke*, X.*An.*5.2.5. 2. ἀ. τινὰ ἐπὶ τὸν ἵππον *put on* horseback, *mount* him, Id.*An.* 4.4.4, *Eq.*6.12; of the horse, ἀ. τὸν ἀναβάτην *unseat* his rider, ib.8.7. 3. ἀ. τὰ ὄμματα *cast up* one's eyes, so as to show the whites, Arist.*Pr.*876ᵃ31; τὰ λευκά Alex.222.9, Ctes.*Fr.*20. 4. *cause to spring up*, κρήνην Str.8.6.2. 5. *lay* bricks, *SIG*²587.59, cf. Hyp.*Fr.*103. 6. *lift, remove* a tumour, Antyll.(?)ap.Orib.45.17.6. 7. Pass., *to be lifted up*, in prayer, εὔχονται σπλάγχνοισι κακῶς ἀναβαλλομένοισι AristeasEpic.1. II. *put back, put off*, μηκέτι νῦν ἀνάβαλλε.. ἄεθλον Od.19.584 (the only place in which Hom. uses the Act.); ἀ. τινά *put off* [with excuses], D.8.52; ἀ. τὰ πράγματα 4.14; *distract* one's attention, Philostr.*Im.*2.24:—Pass., ἀνεβλήθη ἡ ἐκκλησία it *was adjourned*, Th.5.45; ὥστε.. εἰς τοὺς παῖδας ἀναβληθήσεσθαι τὰς τιμωρίας *will be put off* to the time of the sons, Isoc.11.25; ὑμεναίους οὐκ ἀναβαλλομένους Call.*Aet.*3.1.43; cf. infr. B. II. 2. pf. part. Pass. ἀναβεβλημένος *slow, measured*, αὔλημα D.Chr.1.1, cf. Hld.2.8: so in Adv. -μένως *slowly*, D.H.*Dem.*54. b. of style, *diffuse*, τὸ ὕπτιον καὶ ἀ. Hermog.*Id.*2.11; λέξις ἀ., opp. συνεστραμμένη, Aristid. *Rh.*2 p.540 S. III. like B. III, *put on*, ἀ. τὸ Κρητικόν (a short cloak) Eup.311 (s.v.l.). IV. *run* a risk (prob. metaph. from dice), ἐγώ σφε θάψω κἀνὰ κίνδυνον βαλῶ A.*Th.*1033.

B. more freq. in Med., *strike up, begin to play* or *sing* (cf. ἀναβολή II), ἀνεβάλλετο καλὸν ἀείδειν Od.1.155, 8.266, Theoc.6.20: abs., ἀναβάλεο Pi.*N.*7.77; ἀναβαλοῦ Ar.*Pax*1269: c. acc., εὐχὴν ἀ. τῷ Ἔρωτι Philostr.*Im.*1.29. II. *put off, delay* a thing *in which oneself is concerned* (v. supr. II), μηδ' ἔτι δηρὸν ἀμβαλλώμεθα ἔργον Il.2.436, cf. Hes. *Op.*410, Pi.*O.*1.80, *N.*9.29, Hdt.3.85; τὸ μέν τι νυνὶ μὴ λάβῃς, τὸ δ' ἀναβαλοῦ Ar.*Nu.*1139; εἰσαῦθις ἀναβεβλήμεθα *Ec.*983; εἰς τὴν ὑστεραίαν ἀναβαλέσθαι [τὴν δίαιταν] *to adjourn* till the morrow, D.21.84, cf. Pl.*Mx.*234b; ἀ. τινας *Act.Ap.*24.22: abs., *defer payment*, Isoc.3.33: c. fut. inf., ἀ. κυρώσειν ἐς τέταρτον μῆνα Hdt.6.86.β'; ἀ. ἐς τρίτην ἡμέρην ἀποκρινέεσθαι 5.49; ἀ. ποιήσειν τὰ δέοντα D.3.9: c. aor. inf., ἀ. ὑποκρίνασθαι Hdt.9.8; οὐκέτι ἀνεβάλλοντο μὴ τὸ πᾶν οὐ μηχανήσασθαι 6.88. 2. *throw off oneself* on another, *refer* a thing to him, τί ἐπί τινα Luc.*Pisc.*15. III. *throw one's cloak up* or *back, throw it over the shoulder*, so as to let it hang in folds, ἀναβάλλεσθαι χλαῖναν Ar.*V.* 1132: so also ἀναβάλλεσθαι alone, Id.*Ec.*97; ἀ. ἐπιδέξια Pl.*Tht.*175e,

Ar.Av.1568; εἴσω τὴν χεῖρα ἔχοντα ἀναβεβλημένον with one's cloak thrown up or back, D.19.255; ἀναβεβλ. ἄνω τοῦ γόνατος Thphr. Char.4.4; cf. ἀναβολή I.2. IV. = supr. A.IV, ἀναβάλλεσθαι μάχας risk battles, Hdt.5.49. V. to be wroth, Lxx Ps.77(78).21.

**ἀναβαπτίζω**, sink, ναῦς cj. in Plu.Marc.15.

**ἀναβάπτω**, stain, dye, τὰς κεφαλάς Thphr.HP3.13.6.

**ἀναβάσιον**, τό, = ἵππουρις, Dsc.4.46 (v.l. ἀνάβασις, and so Ps.-Dsc. c.).

⊛**ἀνάβᾰσις**, poet. **ἄμβασις**, εως, ἡ, (ἀναβαίνω) going up, mounting, esp. on horseback, X.Eq.3.11; way of mounting, ib.7.4. b. concrete, πᾶσα ἅμβατις, = πάντες ἀναβάται, all the horsemen, S.OC 1070. c. ascension, εἰς τὸν ἕβδομον οὐρανόν Ascens.Is.10.21. d. ascent of soul to God, Hierocl. in CA26 p.481 M. 2. expedition up from the coast, esp. into Central Asia, as that of the younger Cyrus related by X. 3. rising of a river, Heph.Astr.1.23; esp. inundation of the Nile, D.S.1.34, Placit.4.1, POxy.483; δικαία ἀ. normal rise, OGI666 (i A.D.): pl., Str.16.1.24, Plu.2.368b. 4. Medic., increasing period of a disease, before the crisis (ἀκμή), Gal.9.556,al. 5. leaves of tree, Lxx Ez.47.12. II. way up, ascent of a tower, mountain, etc., Hdt.1.181,7.223, Men.Sam.20, etc.; ἡ ἀ. τῶν Ἐπιπολῶν Th.7.42; ἀναβῆναι ἐκείνην τὴν ἀ. to make that ascent, Pl.R. 519d, cf. 515e. 2. stairs, Lxx 1Ch.26.16,al. III. metaph., progress, Artem.4.28; of numbers, progression, Id.2.70. IV. = ἵππουρις; cf. ἀναβάσιον. ⊛**ἀναβασμός**, ὁ, = ἀναβαθμός, Ar.Fr.46 D. (pl.), Michel 1512 (Piraeus, iv B.C.), cf. Paus.10.5.2: metaph., progress, in learning, Plot.6.7.36 (pl.), cf. Them.Or.13.177c. (Written ἀναβαζμός SIG²587.308.)

**ἀναβασσαρέω**, = ἀναβακχεύω II, ἀνὰ δηὖτε βασσαρήσω Anacr.63.

**ἀναβαστ-άζω**, raise or lift up, carry, J.AJ19.3.1, Luc.Anach. 24. **-αξις**, ἡ, gloss on ἀνακωχή, Gal.19.79.

**ἀναβᾰτ-έον**, one must ascend, metaph., ἐπὶ τὰ καλὰ ἐπιτηδεύματα Them.Or.13.177b; ἐπὶ τὸ θεῖον Porph.Marc.27. **-ήριον** (sc. ἱερόν), τό, sacrifice for fair voyage, Plu.2.984b. II. step-ladder, Gp.9.17.8 (pl.). **-ης**, poet. **ἀμβάτης**, ου, ὁ, one who mounts, one mounted, of Pentheus in the tree, E.Ba.1107; esp. horseman, rider, X.HG5.3.1, Pl.Criti.119b, etc. II. stallion, Hsch. III. firebrand(?), Sch.Ar.Ach.321. **-ικός**, ή, όν, skilled in mounting, ready at mounting, ἀναβατικώτεροι ἐπὶ τοὺς ἵππους X.Mem.3.3.5. 2. Pass., fit to be ridden, κτήνη J.AJ15.6.3; ὄνοι Hsch. s.v. ἀστράβη. 3. of the sign Capricornus, affording an ascent for souls, Porph.Antr. 22. II. of fever, gradually increasing in heat (cf. ἀνάβασις I.4), Gal.7.337. III. of irrigation-works, for raising water (?), ὕδρευμα PFlor.50.15,al. **-ός**, Ep. **ἀμβατός**, όν, to be mounted or scaled, easy to be scaled, Il.6.434, Od.11.316, Pi.P.10.27.

**ἀναβεβλημένως**, v. ἀναβάλλω A.II.2.

⊛**ἀναβέβρῦχε**, pf. with no pres. in use, ἀναβέβρυχεν ὕδωρ the water gushed or bubbled up, Il.17.54 (Zenod. ἀναβέβροχεν).

⊛**ἀναβήσσω**, to cough up, expectorate, Hp.Prog.15.

⊛**ἀναβῐβ-άζω**, fut. -βιβάσω Ph.Bel.97.43 (s.v.l.): aor. -εβίβασα:— Med., fut. -βιβάσομαι, Att. -βιβῶμαι Amips.30, Aeschin.2.14: aor. -εβιβασάμην: (v. βιβάζω):—causal of ἀναβαίνω, make to go up, cause to mount, ἐπὶ τὴν πυρήν, ἐπὶ πύργον, Hdt.1.86,3.75, X.Cyr.6.1.53; ἐπὶ τὸν τροχόν, of torture, And.1.43; κατὰ τὸ ἀκρότατον X.HG4.5.3: metaph., uplift, ἐπὶ μετεωροτέραν ἐπίνοιαν Corn.ND28. II. Special usages: 1. ἀ. τινὰ ἐφ' ἵππον mount one on horseback, Hdt.1.63,4.72, X.Eq.6.12; ἐπ' ἅρμα Hdt.4.180; ἐπὶ τὰ ὀχήματα X.Cyr.4.2.28. 2. ἀ. ναῦν draw a ship up on land, Id.HG1.1.2. 3. Med., ἀναβιβάζεσθαί τινας ἐπὶ τὰς ναῦς have them put on board ship, embark for sea, Th.7.33: abs., ἀναβιβασάμενοι ib.35, cf. X.HG3.4.10. 4. at Athens, bring up to the bar of a court of justice as a witness, Is.9.30:—so in Med., Lys. 12.24, Pl.Ap.18d; bring forward a fellow-prosecutor, Hyp.Eux. 13; but usu. of a culprit, bring up his wife and children to raise compassion, And.1.148, Pl.Ap.34c, Lys.18.24,20.34, Hyp.Eux.41, Aeschin.3.7, cf. 2.146: so Act., Hyp.Phil.9. 5. ἀ. ἐπὶ τὴν σκηνήν bring upon the stage, Plb.23.10.16, 29.19.2. 6. ἀ. τὰς τιμὰς raise the prices, D.S.5.10, cf. POxy.513.27. 7. promote, advance, στρατιώτην Ph.Bel.97.43: c. acc. cogn., ἀ. χώραν advance a step, 94. 25:—Pass., ἀναβιβάζεσθαι εἰς τιμήν ascend to honour, Plu.Cat.Ma. 16. 8. Gramm., ἀ. τὸν τόνον throw back the accent, A.D.Pron. 49.15, al.; of postpositions, Id.Synt.308.10. 9. ἀ. τοὺς φθόγγους lower, moderate them, Plu.TG2. 10. Astron., ὁ ἀναβιβάζων σύνδεσμος ascending node, Ptol.Alm.4.9, etc.; without σύνδεσμος, Procl.Hyp.5.105. ⊛**-ασμός**, ὁ, the throwing back the accent, A.D. Conj.233.30. 2. Arith., sum total, Hero Geom.4.13. 3. Medic., aggravation, of headache, Steph. in Hp.1.223 D. ⊛**-αστέον**, one must cause to mount, τοὺς ἱππέας X.Eq.Mag.1.2; ἐπὶ τοὺς ἵππους ἀ. ὡς νεωτάτους Pl.R.467e.

**ἀναβῐβρώσκω**, aor. -έβρωσα, gnaw through, Nic.Th.134: aor. Pass. ἀναβρωθῆναι to be corroded, ὑφ' ἁλὸς Philostr.Im.2.17; to be eroded, of ulcers, Gal.8.392.

**ἀναβιοτή**, ἡ, coming to life again, Sch.E.Or.1691.

**ἀναβῐ-όω**, ἀναβιοῖ Arist.Mir.832$^b$6 (but ἀναβιώσκομαι (q.v.) is the common pres.): aor. 2 ἀνεβίων (v. infr.), ἀνεβίουν Luc.Hist.Conscr. 40; later aor. 1 ἀνεβίωσα Arist.HA587$^a$24, Thphr.HP4.14.12: also aor. Med. ἀναβιώσασθαι Lib.Or.12.50: pf. ἀναβεβίωκα E.ap. Phot.p.107 R., Luc.Nec.1:—come to life again, ἀναβιοίην νῦν πάλιν Ar.Ra.177; ἐπειδὴ ἀνεβίω And.1.125; ἀναβιοὺς ἔλεγεν Pl.R.614b:— also Med., ἀναβιοῦσθαι Plu.2.377b. **-ωσις**, εως, ἡ, return to life, Lxx 2Ma.7.9, Plu.Luc.18, App.Gall.1.3, etc. ⊛**-ώσκομαι**, as Pass., = ἀναβιόω (q.v.), Pl.Phd.71e, al., Aristid.Or.20(21).19, Hierocl. in CA26 p.479 M.: pf. inf. -βεβιῶσθαι Sannyr.3 D.: aor. part. -βιωθεῖσα Philostr.VA4.45. II. causal of ἀναβιόω, bring back to life, ἀποκτεινύντων καὶ ἀναβιωσκομένων Pl.Cri.48c: aor. inf. ἀναβιώσασθαι Phd.89b: fut. ἀναβιώσῃ τὴν μυῖαν Ael.NA2.29: later in Act., ἀναβιώσκω Them.Or.8.115c, Sch.E.Alc.1; Act. ἀναβιώσκω (= ἀναβιόω) only interpol. in Polyaen.6.38.2.

⊛**ἀναβλαστ-άνω**, fut. -βλαστήσω v.l. in Hdt.3.62: aor. -έβλαστον Id. (v. infr.), -εβλάστησα Eun. (v. infr.):—shoot up, of plants, Pl. Lg.835d, Plu.2.366b; of monstrous births, ib.991a; shoot afresh, Thphr.HP4.14.13:—of a city, [αἱ Συρήκουσαι] ἀνά τ' ἔδραμον καὶ ἀνέβλαστον Hdt.7.156; of misfortunes, spring up, ἔδει..κακὰ ἀναβλαστεῖν Id.5.92.δ', cf. 3.62; ἡ ἀναβλαστάνουσα καθ' ἡμέραν τιμή Plu.2. 769a. II. trans., put forth, τῆς ψυχῆς ἔρνη διττὰ ἀναβλαστούσης Ph. 1.304, cf. 1.118; ἔρις πολέμους -ησε Eun.Hist.p.255 D. **-έω**, = foreg., Emp.146.3. **-ησις**, εως, ἡ, up-shooting, Thphr.HP8.1.6; κεράτων J.AJ10.11.7; τῶν γηγενῶν Agath.2.5 (pl.).

**ἀνάβλεμμα**, ατος, τό, looking up, of dogs, X.Cyn.4.4, Poll.2.56.

⊛**ἀναβλέπω**, fut. -βλέψω Hdt.2.111, -βλέψομαι E.HF563: aor. -έβλεψα Hdt.l.c., etc.:—look up, Ar.Nu.346; πρὸς τὸ φῶς Pl.R.515c; εἰς τὸν οὐρανόν Ax.370b: esp. as a mark of confidence, ἀ. ὀρθοῖς ὄμμασιν X.HG7.1.30; ἀ. πρός τινα ἐκ τοῦ ἴσου look him in the face, Cyr.1.4.12. 2. c. acc., look up at, φῶς ἀναβλέψεσθε E. l. c.: c. dat., ἀελίου ἀ. λαμπάσι Ion 1467; τοῖς κερτομοῦσι γοργὸν ὣς ἀναβλέπει Supp.322 codd. 3. c. acc. cogn., ἀ. φλόγα cast up a glance of fire, Id. Ion 1263. II. recover one's sight, Hdt.2.111, Pl.Phdr. 243b, Ev.Jo.9.11; πάλιν ἀ. Ar.Pl.95,117. 2. open one's eyes, Pl. R.621b, X.Cyr.8.3.29. III. metaph., revive, ᾧ δῶμ' ἀνέβλεψ' E. Ba.1308.

**ἀνάβλεψις**, εως, ἡ, looking up, seeing, Arist.Ph.247$^b$8. II. recovery of sight, Lxx Is.61.1, cf. Ev.Luc.4.18.

**ἀναβλ-ήδην**, = ἀμβλήδην (q.v.), afresh, Arat.1070, Max.287. ⊛**-ησις**, εως, ἡ, putting off, delay, κακοῦ Il.2.380; λύσιος 24.655; θανάτοιο Call.Ap.45: abs., AP12.184 (Strat.). **-ητικῶς**, gloss on ἀμβολάδην, ἀμβλήδην, Eust.1241.36, 1282.1.

⊛**ἀνα-βλύες**· πηγαί, Hsch. ⊛**-βλύζω**, poet. ἀμβλ-, AP9.374, Orph.A.1130: fut. -βλύσω prob. in Ezech.Exag.137: aor. ἀνέβλυσα Arist.Mu.400$^a$32, Q.S.10.108 (tm.): inf. ἀναβλῦσαι (leg. -βλύσαι) Plu.Sull.6:—spout up, ἔλαιον Arist.Mir.841$^a$17; ἄκρητον AP7.31 (Diosc.) codd.; ἐέρσην Nonn.D.9.58, al. 2. intr., gush forth, Arist.Mu. l.c., IG14.889 (Sinuessa), Heliod.ap.Orib.46.11.9, etc.; Νεῖλος ἀναβλύζων Theoc.17.80.

**ἀνάβλυσις**, εως, ἡ, gushing up, πηγῶν Arist.Mu.396$^a$22, cf. Aët. 16.21. **ἀναβλύσσω**, = ἀναβλύζω, Aq., Sm.Pr.18.4.

**ἀναβλυστάνω**, = ἀναβλύζω, Str.Chr.16.22, Procop.Aed.2.3, al.:— also ⊛**ἀναβλυσθαίνω**, Sch.Pl.Ti.22e: **ἀμβλυσθονῆσαι** or **-τονῆσαι**, Eup.105, cf. Eust.1095.8, EM200.52.

**ἀναβλύω**, Ep. impf. ἀναβλύεσκε A.R.3.223, = ἀναβλύζω, boil over, Hp.Mul.1.78; gush out, Plb.34.9.7, Str.3.5.7, Nonn.D.48.878 [κρήνη] ἀναβλύεσκε γάλακτι A.R. l.c.: c. acc. cogn., spout out, ἀνέβλυον ἰκμάδα, ὕδωρ, Nonn.D.9.31, 6.255:—spurt foam from the mouth, Hp.Morb.Sacr.7.

**ἀναβό-ᾱμα**, poet. ἀμβ-, τό, = ἀναβόησις, A.Ch.34. **-άω**, fut. -ήσομαι E.IA465, Dor. -άσομαι Ar.Pl.639: aor. ἀνεβόησα Th.1.53, Ion. ἀνέβωσα Hdt.1.10, al., part. ἀμβώσας 1.8, 3.38:—cry, shout aloud, esp. in sign of grief or astonishment, ἀμβώσας μέγα Hdt. ll. cc., cf. Antipho 5.69, E.Ba.1079; οἰκτρὸν ἀνεβόασεν Hcl.184; of the war-cry, X.Cyr.7.1.38; ἀ. "παρεῖναι τοὺς πρώτους" call out 'let the front rank pass', HG4.2.22. 2. c. acc., τάδ' ἀναβοάσας E.Ba. 525; ἄχη ἀ. bewail, lament, A.Pers.572; Πανὸς ἀναβοᾷ γάμους E. Hel.190. 3. c. acc. pers., call on, συμμάχους ib.1592; Ἀσκληπιόν Ar.Pl.639. 4. cry up, extol, Alex.98.12. **-ησις**, εως, ἡ, shouting, calling, D.H.9.10; invocation, Sch.S.OT80; ἄσημος ἀ. Paul. Aeg.3.13.

**ἀναβοθρεύω**, dig up, force up, AB389, Suid., Hsch.

**ἀναβολ-άδην**, Adv. bubbling up, ἀ. ζέοντα ὕδατα Polem.Hist.83 (cf. ἀμβ-). **-άδιον**, τό, Dim. of ἀναβολή I.2, mantle, Aq.Is.61.3, POxy.109, Isid.Etym.19.25.7:—also **-αιον**, τό, Sm.Is.3.22, Edict. Diocl.26.78,93. **-άς**, άδος, ἡ, v. sub ἀμβολάς. ⊛**-εύς**, έως, ὁ, groom who helps one to mount, App.Pun.106, Plu.CG7. 2. stirrup, Eust.1406.5, Suid. II. lever, instrument for lifting, Heliod.ap. Orib.46.11.26, cf. Paul.Aeg.6.88. ⊛**-ή**, poet. **ἀμβολή**, ἡ: (ἀναβάλλω): I. of things: 1. that which is thrown up, mound of earth, bank, X.An.5.2.5, D.S.17.95; ἀ. χωμάτων casting up of dykes, Arch.Pap.6.132 (Denderah); διωρύγων PAmh.2.91.11 (pl.). 2. that which is thrown back over the shoulder, mantle, Pl.Prt.342c, PPetr.3p.48 (iii B.C.), Lxx Ne.5.13, al.; of the toga, Nic.Dam. p.119 D.: also, fashion of wearing a cloak, Luc.Somn.6. II. of actions, 1. striking up, prelude on the lyre preliminary to singing, ὁπόταν προοιμίων ἀμβολὰς τεύχῃς ἐλελιζομένα, addressed to the lyre, Pi.P.1.4; esp. of dithyramb, Eup.5 D.: hence, rambling dithyrambic ode, Ar.Av.1385, cf. Pax 830, Arist.Rh.1409$^b$25; cf. ἀναβάλλω B.I. 2. putting off, delaying, οὐκέτι ἐς ἀναβολὰς ἐποιεῦντο τὴν ἀποχώρησιν Hdt.8.21; ὅ τι μέλλετε..μὴ ἐς ἀ. πράσσετε Th.7.15; οὐκ ἐς ἀμβολάς without delay, E.Heracl.270; ἐς μηδεμίαν ἀ. PAmh. 2.34$^d$.5; ἐν ταῖς ἀ. τῶν κακῶν ἔνεστ' ἄκη E.HF93; ἐπὶ ἀναβολῇ πρᾶσιν, ὠνὴν ποιεῖσθαι sell, buy on credit, Pl.Lg.915e; ἀναβολήν τινος ποιεῖσθαι Th.2.42; ποιεῖν Pl.Smp.201d; εἰς τὸ γῆρας ἀναβολὰς ποιεῖν Men. 235.8; δακρύοις..ἐμποιεῖν ἀ. τῷ πάθει Id.599; ἀναβολὰν λαβόντες ἔτη τρία *IG*9(2).205.22 (Thess.). **b.** *deferred payment*, εὐχρηστήσας σῖτον ἐπ' ἀναβολῇ Ἀρχ.Ἐφ.1912.60 (Gonni). **3.** ἀ. δίκης ἐπὶ τὸν βασιλέα *reference, appeal*, Str.13.1.55. **4.** *lifting*, hence, *removal*, of tumours, Antyll.ap.Orib.45.2.6. **III.** intr., *going up, ascent, way up*, ἀ. τῶν Ἄλπεων Plb.3.39.9, etc.; τὴν ἀ. ποιεῖσθαι 50.3. **2.** *bubbling up*, πομφολύγων Arist.*Pr.*936ᵇ1, Thphr.*Ign.*16; of the Nile, *sources*, ἀμβολαί *CIG*4924 (Philae). ⊛**–ικός**, ή, όν, *filled by a machine*, λάκκος *PLond.*1695.7 (vi A.D.). **II.** *delayed, deferred*, of payments, *OGI*669.21 (i A.D.): **–κόν**, τό, *deferment of payments*, *PAmh.* 2.131; but λίνον ἀ., perh. = linen *for cloaks*, *PThead.Inv.*15. Adv. **–κῶς**, = ἀναβλητικῶς (q.v.), Eust.1241.38. ⊛**–ιμος**, ον, *to be delayed*, δίκαι Hsch. **–ιον**, τό, dub. in *PFay.Ostr.*49.

**ἀναβορβορύζω**, *grumble loudly*, Ar.*Ec.*433.

**ἀναβουλεύομαι**, Dep., *change one's opinion*, Eust.1385.59.

⊛**ἀναβρ-άζω**, intr., *boil* or *foam up*, v.l. for –βρύσσω, Procop *Goth.* 3.35: also trans., Aët.1.226. **–ασις**, εως, ἡ, *boiling up, bubbling up*, e.g. of water, v.l. in Str.3.1.9. **–ασμός**, ὁ, prop. *boiling up*; hence ἀ. γῆς kind of *earthquake*, Suid. s.v. ἐκτιναγμός: metaph., '*réchauffé*', *rehash*, Olymp. *in Mete.*230.11. **–άσσω**, Att. **–άττω**, aor. subj. ἀναβράσῃ Dsc.5.14, *boil well, seethe*, ἀναβράττω κίχλας Ar. *Pax* 1197; κρέα ἀνέβραττεν ὀρνίθεια *Ra.*510: abs., ἀναβράττετ', ἐξοπτᾶτε *Ach.*1005, cf. Dsc.l.c.: metaph., ζωὴν..ζέουσάν τε καὶ ἀναβράττουσαν Dam.*Pr.*86. **2.** *throw up*, τὰ ἐν τοῖς λίκνοις ἀναβραττόμενα Arist.*Mete.*368ᵇ29; esp. of the sea, ἅλμη ἀναβρασθεῖσα spray *dashed up*, A.R.2.566, cf. Lxx *Wi.*10.19. **II.** intr., *jump*, of chariot, ib.*Na.*3.2. **–αστος**, ον, *boiled*, κρέα Ar.*Ra.*553, Aristomen.8; κίχλαι Pherecr.130.10, cf. 108.23; ὕδωρ Dsc.3.83.

*ἀναβράχω, v. sub ἀνέβραχε.

**ἀναβρέχομαι**, Pass., *become wet again*, v.l. Arist.*Pr.*927ᵇ6.

**ἀναβρομέω**, *boil up*, of soup, Ath.3.126d. **2.** *roar aloud*, Nonn. *D.*45.330.

**ἀναβροντάω**, *thunder aloud*, of Odysseus speaking, Tryph.118.

**ἀναβρόξειε, ἀναβροχέν**, v. βρόχω.

**ἀναβροχ-ισμός**, ὁ, *extraction of eye-lashes by a loop*, an operation for trichiasis, Paul.Aeg.6.13, cf. Gal.15.918:—**–ίζω**, 14.784.

**ἀναβρυάζω**, *neigh aloud*, of horses, ἀνεβρύαξαν Ar.*Eq.*602.

**ἀναβρῡχάομαι**, Dep., *roar aloud*, Pl.*Phd.*117d; ἀ. ἐλεεινὸν καὶ θρηνῶδες Philostr.*VA*5.42.

⊛***ἀναβρύχω**, v. ἀναβέβρυχε, Eust.1095.6.

⊛**ἀναβρύω**, = ἀναβλύω, Ael.*VH*3.43, f.l. in Ph.1.477: c. acc., ἄνθεα Nonn.*D.*7.346.

**ἀνάβρ-ωσις**, εως, ἡ, *corrosion* or *erosion*, Sor.2.40, Gal.1.154,239, Antyll.(?)ap.Orib.44.32.11. **–ώσκων**· κατεσθίων, Hsch. **–ωτικός**, ή, όν, *corrosive*, Alex.Aphr.*Pr.*1.92.

⊛**ἀναβῶνες**· βαθμοῦ εἶδος, Hsch. (cod. –ῶδες); cf. ἄμβων.

**ἀναγαγγανεύουσιν**· ἀναβοῶσιν, Hsch.

**ἀνάγαιον**· ἀνὰ τὴν γῆν, Hsch. **II. ἀνάγαιον**, τό, = ἀνώγεων, v.l. in *Ev.Marc.*14.15, *Ev.Luc.*22.12.

**ἀναγαλλίς**, ίδος, ἡ (also ὁ, Hsch.), *pimpernel, Anagallis arvensis*, and *A. caerulea*, Dsc.2.178, Longus 3.12, etc. **II.** ἀ. ἔνυδρος, = σίον, Ps.-Dsc.2.127.

**ἀναγαργαρ-ίζω**, *gargle*, χλιαροῖσιν Hp.*Morb.*2.26,27, *Aff.*4:— so also in Med., *Mul.*2.185, *IG*4.955.30 (Epid.), Archig.ap.Gal.12. 976 (Pass.). (–γαργαλ– is v.l. in codd. of Hp.) **–ισμα**, ατος, τό, *gargle*, Dsc.1.128, Archig.ap.Orib.8.1.39. **–ισμός**, ὁ, *gargling*, Hp. *Int.*38. **–ιστέον**, *one must gargle*, Philum.ap.Aët.8.48. **–ιστον**, τό, *gargle*, Hp.*Morb.*2.26.

**ἀναγγείωτος**, ον, *without blood-vessels*, μέρη Orib.45.17.5.

⊛**ἀναγγελία**, ἡ, *proclamation*, *SIG*598.11, *OGI*332.44 (Elaea).

**ἀναγγέλλω**, (v. ἀγγέλλω) *carry back tidings of, report*, τι A.*Pr.*661; πάντ' ἀναγγεῖλαι φίλοις E.*IT*761; τῷ Βρασίδᾳ τὴν ξυνθήκην Th.4.122, etc.; τι τῷ δήμῳ Arist.*EN*1113ᵃ9; ἐν ἁλίᾳ, of valuers, *Tab.Heracl.*1. 118; τι πρός τινα Plb.1.67.11: c. part., *tell of* person doing, X.*Ages.* 5.6:—Pass., ὡς ἀνηγγέλθη τεθνεώς Plu.*Per.*18. **II.** *proclaim*, τοὺς στεφάνους *OGI*6 (Scepsis), *SIG*412.13 (Delph.):—Pass., of rewards, ἀνηγγέλθαι αὐτῷ ἀργύριον Aen.Tact.10.15.

**ἀνάγγελμα**, τό, *proclamation*, *IPE*1².352.49 (Cherson.).

**ἀνάγγελος**, ον, *from which no messenger returns*, μάχη *AP*7.244 (Gaet.). **II.** = μυρσίνη ἀγρία, Ps.-Dsc.4.144.

**ἀναγγ-ελτικός**, ή, όν, *capable of expressing*, δυνάμεις τινὸς ἀ. Anon. *in Prm.*(*Rh.Mus.*47.613). **–ελτος**, ον, *unannounced, secret*, Hld. ap.Hsch. s.v. ἀνάπαυστα.

⊛**ἀνάγειον**, τό, = ἀνάγαιον, Petersen-Luschan *Reise in Lykien* p.36 (Myra).

**ἀναγείρω**, *reassemble*, v.l. Q.S.2.577.

**ἀναγελάω**, *laugh loud*, X.*Cyr.*5.1.9, Plu.*Arat.*6, Philostr.*VA*5.7; ἐπί τινι *at* one, X.*Cyr.*6.1.34.

⊛**ἀναγενν-άω**, *beget anew, regenerate*, 1 *Ep.Pet.*1.3, cf. 23:—Pass., prob. in *Corp.Herm.*13.1. **2.** metaph., *arouse afresh*, ἀ. πάλιν κακά Phld.*Ir.*p.18 W. **–ησις**, εως, ἡ, *regeneration*, κόσμου Ph.2. 489. **–ητικός**, ή, όν, *able to produce*, εἰδώλων Iamb.*Myst.*3.28 (dub. l.).

**ἀναγεπόπτης**, ὁ, perh. *uplifting to full vision*, *PMag.Lond.*121. 355.

**ἀναγέτρια**, ἡ, = μαῖα (Tarent.), Hsch.; cf. ἀγέτρια.

⊛**ἀναγεύω**, *give* one *a taste*, πρώτους ἠξίωσ' ἀναγεῦσ' ὑμᾶς Ar.*Nu.*523.

**ἀναγηρύομαι**, Dep., *cry aloud*, Ael.*NA*5.34.

**ἀνᾰγής**, ές, (ἄγος) = ἐναγής, *wretch*, Herod.2.70, Hsch. (who also glosses it by καθαρός).

⊛**ἀναγιγνώσκω**, later **ἀναγῑνώσκω**: **I.** Ep. only in aor. 2 ἀ[νέ]γνων, **1.** *know well, know certainly*, οὐ γάρ πώ τις ἑὸν γόνον αὐ[τὸς] ἀνέγνω Od.1.216, cf. 21.205, Il.13.734. **b.** *perceive*, Theoc.2[…] 23. **2.** *know again, recognize*, Od.4.250; once in Hdt., *acknowledg[e as] own*, ἀναγνῶναι τοὺς συγγενέας Hdt.2.91, cf. Pi.*I.*2.23: aor. Pass. on[ce] in E., εἰ μὲν γὰρ ἔζη πόσις, ἀνεγνώσθημεν ἂν *Hel.*290. **II.** aft[er] Hom., fut. ἀναγνώσομαι dub. in *GDI*5075: aor. 2 ἀνέγνων, Cret. 3 p[l.] subj. –γνῶντι *GDI*5040.43: pf. ἀνέγνωκα:—Pass., fut. –γνωσθ[ή]σομαι Lys.17.9: aor. ἀνεγνώσθην Pl.*Prm.*127d: pf. ἀνέγνωσμαι Iso[c.] 15.67, etc.:—of written characters, *know* them *again*, and so, *rea[d]* first in Pi.*O.*10(11).1, cf. Ar.*Eq.*118, 1065, Th.3.49, And.1.47, et[c.] (never in Trag.); ἀναγνώσεται (sc. ὁ γραμματεύς) D.20.27, etc. λαβὼν ἀνάγνωθι τὸ ψήφισμα Id.18.118; λέγε..καὶ ἀνάγνωθι Id.19.70 τὴν διαμαρτυρίαν ἀναγνώτω Id.44.45; ἀ. πρὸς ἐμαυτόν Ar.*Ra.*52: abs. οἱ ἀναγιγνώσκοντες *students*, Plu.*Alex.*1, Marin.*Procl.*15; ἀ. παρ[ά] τινι Ἀριστοτέλους τὰ περὶ ψυχῆς *attend lectures on A.*, ib.12:—Pass., τὰ βιβλία τὰ ἀνεγνωσμένα books *read aloud*, hence, *published*, opp. τὰ ἀνέκδοτα, Lycon ap.D.L.5.73. **III.** Ion. usage, causal, mostly in aor. ἀνέγνωσα, *induce* one to do a thing, τούτους..ἀναγνώσας ἕπεσθαι Hdt.5.106, cf. 1.87, 4.158, 6.83, al.; inf. is omitted, ὡς ἀνέγνωσε when *he had persuaded* him, Id.1.68: once in pres., ἀναγιγνώσκεις στρατεύεσθαι βασιλέα Id.7.10; *persuade, convince*, ὅτι.. Hp.*Art.* 1:—aor. Pass., ἀνεγνώσθην *to be persuaded* to do a thing, c. inf., Hdt.7.7 and 236: without inf., ὑπὸ τῆς γυναικὸς ἀναγνωσθείς 4.154; χρήμασι ἀ. 6.50: plpf. Pass., ὡς οὗτοι..οἱ ἀνεγνωσμένοι ἦσαν 8.110: rare in Att., ὑπὸ τῶν κυρίων ἀναγιγνωσκόμενον Antipho 2.2.7.

⊛**ἀναγκ-άζω**, fut. –άσω E.*Andr.*337, Th.5.35 (later 2 pl. –ᾶτε *Arch. Pap.*6.286): pf. ἠνάγκακα Pl.*Hipparch.*232b: plpf. –ειν D.33.28: (ἀνάγκη):—*force, compel*, mostly c. acc. pers. et inf., ἀ. τινὰ κτείνειν, πόλισμα, συνθήκας ποιεῖσθαι, etc., Hdt.1.11, 98, 6.42; δρᾶν, λέγειν, etc., S.*El.*256, *OC*979, etc.: so in Pass., ἠναγκάζοντο ἀμύνεσθαι Hdt.5.101: without inf., κἄμ' ἀναγκάζεις τάδε (sc. δρᾶν) S. *Ph.*1368, cf. *OT*280; ἀναγκάζεσθαί τι *to be forced* [to do] a thing, Pl. *Phdr.*242a, 254b, cf. X.*Mem.*4.5.4; ἀ. τινὰ ἐς τὸ πολεμεῖν Th.1.23; ἐς τὸ ἔργον Id.2.75. **2.** c. acc. pers. only, *constrain* a person, τὸ συνδρῶν σ' ἀναγκάσει χρέος E.*Andr.*337; esp. by argument, opp. ῥητορικῶς ἐλέγχειν, Pl.*Grg.*472b; δεινοῖς ἠναγκάσθην *I was constrained, tortured*, S.*El.*221, cf. X.*Hier.*9.2; ἠναγκασμένος, ἀναγκασθεὶς *under compulsion*, Th.6.22, 8.99; ὑπὸ δεσμῶν ἀναγκασθεὶς And.1. 2; φανεροὶ ἦσαν ἀναγκασθησόμενοι D.18.19. **3.** c. acc. rei only, *carry through by force*, πόλις ἀναγκάζει τάδε E.*IT*595, cf. X.*Mem.*4.5.5, Arist.*Rh.*1392ᵃ27; ἠναγκασμένα λάχανα *forced* vegetables, Philostr. *VA*1.21. **4.** c. acc. rei et inf., *contend that* a thing *is necessarily* so and so, μὴ ἀνάγκαζε ὃ μὴ καλόν ἐστιν αἰσχρὸν εἶναι Pl.*Smp.*202b, cf. *Cra.*432c, *Tht.*196b: foll. by Conj., οἱ λόγοι ἀναγκάσειαν ἂν ὅτι ἀθάνατον ψυχή *R.*611b. **5.** abs., *apply compulsion*, Arist.*Pol.* 1304ᵇ9 (ἀναγκάζω is a gloss in Pl.*Tht.*153c.). **6.** in surgery, *use force* to reduce dislocations, etc., Hp.*Art.*3,5, al. **–αίη**, ἡ, Ep. and Ion. for ἀνάγκη, Il.6.85, Tyrt.6, Sol.36.8, Hdt.1.11, etc. **–αίνισμα**· ἀνακίνημα, Hsch. **–αῖον**, τό, *place of constraint, prison*, X.*HG*5. 4.8 and 14, cf. Harp., who adds Καλλισθένης δὲ ἀνώγεων εἶπεν, ὃ δεῖ μᾶλλον λέγεσθαι: but correct reading is prob. ἀνάκαιον (preserved in Suid. and *AB*98, as used by Boeotians), or Ἀνάκειον, q.v., as in D.45.80, cf. *EM*98.32. **II.** = αἰδοῖον, Artem.1.45, Eust.1968.39, *Cat.Cod.Astr.*8(4).133 (pl.). **III.** *privy, Gloss.* **IV.** = sq., Plaut.*Rud.*363. **–αιοπότης**, ου, ὁ, kind of *cup*, *SIG*²588.209 (Delos). ⊛**–αῖος**, α, ον, in Att. also ος, ον Th.1.2, Pl.*R.*554a, etc.: *of, with*, or *by force*: **I.** Act., *constraining, applying force*, μῦθος ἀ. a word *of force*, Od.17.399; χρειὼ ἀ. *urgent* necessity, Il.8.57; ἦμαρ ἀ. day *of constraint*, i.e. life *of slavery*, 16.836; ἀ. τύχη a doom *imposed by fate*, or *fateful* chance, S.*Aj.*485, cf. 803 (but, *fatal* chance, Id.*El.*48); πᾶν γὰρ ἀ. χρῆμ' ἀνιηρὸν ἔφυ Thgn.472, cf. 297, E.*Or.*230; τῆς ἀρχῆς τῷ ἀ. παροξυνομένους by the *compulsory nature* of our rule, Th.5.99; δεσμὸς ἀ. Theoc.24.33; ἐξ ἀναγκαίου under *stress of circumstances*, Th.7.60. **2.** *forcible, cogent*, πειθώ Pl.*Sph.*265d; ἀποδείξεις *Ti.*40e; διαλλακτὰς πολὺ τῶν ἐμῶν λόγων ἀναγκαιοτέρους Th.4. 60; τὰ –ότερα τῶν ἀντιγράφων the *more authoritative* copies, Sch.S. *OC*390. **II.** Pass., *constrained, forced*, twice in Od., πολεμισταὶ ἀ. soldiers *perforce*, Od.24.499; so δμῶες ἀ. ib.210 (where however Eust. expl. it χρειώδεις *trusty, serviceable*, v. infr. 6). **2.** *necessary* (physically or morally), οὐκ ἀ. *unnecessary* (on its diff. senses in philosophy v. Arist.*Metaph.*1015ᵃ20 ff.), ἀ. [ἐστί] *it is necessary to..*, S.*Ph.*1317, etc.; γίνεταί μοι ἀναγκαιότατον, c. inf., Hdt.3.65; ἀ. κακόν *a necessary* evil, Men.651, cf. Hybreas ap.Str.14.2.24: also c. inf., ἔνιαι τῶν ἀποκρίσεων ἀναγκαῖαι διὰ μακρῶν τοὺς λόγους ποιεῖσθαι Pl.*Grg.* 449b; ὁδὸν ἀναγκαιοτάτην εἶναι τρέπεσθαι *Sph.*242b; [μαθήματα] ἀναγκαῖα προμεμαθηκέναι *necessary* for us to have learnt them before, *Lg.*643c. **3.** τὰ ἀ. *necessaries of life*, Antipho 4.1.2, Pl.*Lg.*848a; τὰ ἀ. τοῦ βίου Isoc.4.40; ἀ. τροφή Th.1.2. **b.** τὰ ἀ. *things necessary to be done*, X.*Mem.*1.1.6; τὰ ἐκ θεοῦ ἀ. the *appointed order of things*, *HG* 1.7.33; θεῶν ἀναγκαῖον τόδε E.*Hec.*584 codd.: τὸ ἀ., = ἀνάγκη, Arist. *Ph.*200ᵃ31. **4.** *indispensable*, i.e. *a bare minimum*, freq. in Sup., τὸ ἀναγκαιότατον ὕψος *the least* height *that was absolutely necessary*, Th.1.90; ἡ ἀναγκαιοτάτη πόλις *the least that could be called* a city, Pl.*R.*369d; ἐκ τεττάρων ἀναγκαιοτάτων συγκεῖσθαι πόλιν Arist.*Pol.* 1291ᵃ12; αὐτὰ τἀναγκαιόταθ' εἰπεῖν give *a bare outline* of the facts, D.18.126, cf. 168; ἡ ἀ. συγγένεια *the most distant degree* of kinship *recognized by law*, 44.26: less freq. in Posit., οὐδὲ τἀναγκαῖα ἐξικέσθαι Th.1.70: hence, *scanty, makeshift*, παρασκευή 6.37. **5.** of persons, nnected by necessary or natural ties, i.e. related by blood, Antipho 4, Pl.R.574b; ἀ. δόμοις E.Alc.533; οἱ ἀ. kinsfolk, X.An.2.4.1; φίλοι E.Andr.671; συγγενεῖς καὶ ἀ. ἄνθρωποι D.19.290; τοὺς συγγενεῖς αὐτοῦ καὶ ἀ. φίλους Act.Ap.10.24, cf. PFlor.2.142.2 (iii D.). 6. Astrol., efficacious, Vett.Val.63.1 (Comp.): ἀ. γραμμή ne of fate, Cat.Cod.Astr.7.238. 7. costly, ὄξος POxy.1870 (v D.); ἐσθής Suid. s.v. βεστιάριον. III. Adv. -ως of necessity, perforce, ἀ. ἔχει it must be so, Hdt.1.89, A.Ch.239, S.Tr.723, Pl. Phd.91e, etc.; ἀ. ἔχει μοι ποιέειν ταῦτα Hdt.8.140.α', al.; ἀ. φέρειν, pp. ἀνδρείως, Th.2.64; as best might be, Pl.Ti.69d. 2. γελοίως αἱ ἀ. λέγειν in a narrow sense (cf. II. 4, but prob. with play on III. 1), d.R.527a; πτωχῶς μέν, ἀλλ' ἀ. Babr.55.2:—Sup. ἀναγκαιότατα, λέγεις Pl.Phlb.40c. 3. strictly, κελεύειν OGI669.41 (i A.D.). IV. αἱ ἀ. τόποι privy parts, Vett.Val.113.9. V. ἀναγκαῖον, τό, v. sub v. -αιότης, ητος, ἡ, blood-relationship, Lys.32.5 (pl.), Plb.18. 51.10, D.H.2.10. II. later, necessity, S.E.P.2.205. -αιώδης, ες, = ἀναγκαῖος II. 4, in Comp., τὰ -έστερα τῶν λόγων Sch.E.Ph. 494. -ασμα, ατος, τό, compulsion, J.AJ19.2.5. -αστέος, α, ον, to be compelled, ἀ. ἄρχειν Pl.R.539e. II. ἀναγκαστέον one must compel, ib.377d, X.Hier.8.6, etc. -αστήρ, ῆρος, ὁ, one that constrains, ἀ. ἄτρακτοι the constraining spindles of Fate, IG 2(7).447 (Amorgos). -αστήριος, α, ον, = sq., ἀ. δικαιοσύνης D.H. 2.75. -αστικός, ή, όν, compulsory, coercive, opp. συμβουλευτικός, of law, Pl.Lg.930b; ὁ νόμος ἀ. ἔχει δύναμιν Arist.EN1180a21. 2. cogent, σημείωσις Phld.Sign.4, al.; λόγοι Id.Rh.1.247S., al. Adv. -κῶς Ascl.in Metaph.371.8, S.E.P.1.193. 3. Astrol., having the fixity of law, Vett.Val.19.34, al. -αστός, ή, όν, forced, constrained, Hdt.6.58; ἀ. στρατεύοντες Th.7.58, cf. 8.24; ἀ. τροφή Aristid.Or.47 (23).59. Adv. -τῶς Pl.Ax.366a; opp. ἑκουσίως, 1Ep.Pet.5.2.

**ἀνάγκη**, Ion. and Ep. **ἀναγκαίη**, ἡ, force, constraint, necessity, κρατερὴ δ' ἐπικείσετ' ἀ. Il.6.458; ἀναγκαίη γὰρ ἐπείγει ib.85; ἀναγκαίῃ πολεμίζειν 4.300; τίς τοι ἀνάγκη πτώσσειν; 5.633: οἶσιν ἀ. (sc. φυλάσσειν) 10.418, al.: but in Hom. usu. in dat. as Adv., ἀνάγκῃ perforce, of necessity, ἀείδειν Od.1.154; φεύγειν Il.11.150: in act. sense, forcibly, by force, ἴσχειν, ἄγειν, Od.4.557, 22.353; μνήσασθαι 7.217: strengthd. by καί, 10.434; ὑπ' ἀνάγκης 19.156; opp. ἑκόντες, Pl.Phdr.231a; ὑπ' ἀναγκαίης Hdt.7.172, al.; ἐξ ἀνάγκης S.Ph.73, Th.3.40, etc.; δι' ἀνάγκης Pl.Ti.47e; σὺν ἀνάγκᾳ Pi.P.1.51; πρὸς ἀνάγκαν A.Pers.569 codd. (lyr.), cf. Epict.Ench.29.2; κατ' ἀνάγκην X.Cyr.4.3.7: ἀνάγκη ἐστί, c. inf., it must be that.., is necessary that.., cf. Il. supr. cit.; πᾶσα ἀ. ἐστὶ ὦσαι Hdt.2.22; τρέφειν τοὺς τοκέας τοῖσι μὲν παισὶν οὐδεμία ἀ., τῇσι δὲ θυγατράσι πᾶσα ἀ. ib.35: c. dat. pers., ἀ. μοι σχεθεῖν A.Pr.16, cf. Pers.293:—in Trag. freq. in answers and arguments, πολλή γ' ἀνάγκη, πολλὴ 'στ' ἀνάγκη, or πολλή μ' ἀνάγκη, with which an inf. may always be supplied, E.Med.1013, Hec.396, S.Tr.295; so πᾶσ' ἀνάγκη El.1497, cf. Pl.R.441d; ἀνάγκη μεγάλη [ἐστί] ib.485e, Is.3.6, D.28.9; ἐν ἀνάγκῃ ἐστί Lys.6.8: later ἀνάγκην ἔχω, c. inf., Ev.Luc. 14.18. 2. necessity in the philosophical sense, Arist.APo.94b37, Metaph.1026b28, Ph.199b34; logical necessity, Metaph.1064b33: in pl., laws of nature, τίσιν ἀνάγκαις ἕκαστα γίγνεται τῶν οὐρανίων X. Mem.1.1.11, cf. Hp.Aër.21. b. natural need, γαστρὸς ἀνάγκαις A.Ag.726, cf. Ar.Nu.1075, X.Cyn.7.1; ὑπ' ἀ. τῆς ἐμφύτου Pl.R.458d; ἐρωτικαῖς ἀ. ib., etc. c. ἡ ἀ. τοῦ τόπου the lie of the ground as a necessary condition, PLille4.14. d. ἀνάγκη δαιμόνων, αἱ ἐκ θεῶν ἀνάγκαι, fate, destiny, E.Ph.1000, 1763: freq. personified in Poets, Parm.8.30, Emp.116, A.Pr.105, S.Fr.256; Ἀνάγκᾳ δ' οὐδὲ θεοὶ μάχονται Simon.5.21. 3. compulsion exerted by a superior, ἀ. προστιθέναι, ἐπιτιθέναι, X.Hier.9.4, Lac.10.7. b. violence, punishment, esp. of torture, mostly pl., ἐς ἀνάγκας ἄγεσθαι Hdt.1.116, cf. Antipho 6.25, Herod.5.5; προσάγειν τινὶ τὰς ἀνάγκας Th.1.99; τὰ πρὸς ἀνάγκας ὄργανα instruments of torture, Plb.15.28.2: later in sg., ἡ ἀ. τῶν βασάνων Plu.2.305e; πρὸς ἀνάγκην under torture, Id.Publ.17: metaph., Hp.de Arte13; δολοποιὸς ἀ., i.e. the stratagem of Nessus, S.Tr.832; βρόχων πλεκταῖς ἀνάγκαις Xenarch.1.9. c. duress, 'force majeure', ὅρκους οὓς ποιέονται ἐν ἀνάγκῃ ὄντες Democr.239; stress of circumstances, ἀκούσιοι ἀ. Th.3.82. d. treatment by mechanical force, τῶν ἀναγκῶν τινὰ προσφέρειν Hp.Fract.15, cf. Art.73. 4. bodily pain, anguish, κατ' ἀνάγκην ἕρπειν painfully, S.Ph.206 (lyr.); ὑπ' ἀνάγκης βοᾷν ib.215; ὠδίνων ἀνάγκαι E.Ba.89 (lyr.): generally, distress, ἐν ἀνάγκαις γλυκὺ γίνεται καὶ τὸ σκληρόν Simon.226; freq. in Lxx, Jb.15.24, al.; ἡ ἐνεστῶσα ἀ. 1Ep.Cor.7.26: esp. in pl., IG12 (7).386.23 (Amorgos, iii B.C.), D.S.4.43, 2Ep.Cor.6.4, etc. II. tie of blood, kindred, Lys.32.5. III. = ἡ δικαστικὴ κλεψύδρα, Hsch.

**ἀναγκό-δακρυς**, υ, shedding forced tears, A.Fr.172A. -θέτησις, εως, ἡ, compulsion, coined by Oenom.ap.Eus.PE6.7 as a parody on νομοθέτησις. -μόναρχος· ὁ τύραννος, Hsch. -πέδη, ἡ, fetter, PMag. Par.1.2131. -σῖτος, ον, eating perforce, i.e. getting what one can, epith. of parasites, Crates Com.44, Nicostr.Com.32. -τροφέω, (τρέφω) eat perforce: hence, eat by regimen, not after one's own appetite, like athletes, Epict.Ench.29.2. ※-φαγέω, = ἀναγκοτροφέω, Arr. Epict.3.15.3, Philostr.VS2.17: metaph., stomach, ἀ. τὰ πράγματα Theopomp.Hist.282, Philostr.Gym.44. -φαγία, ἡ, strict diet, of athletes, Arist.Pol.1339a6, Them.Or.15.185d. -φορέω, bear on compulsion, apptly. f.l. for -φαγ-, ἀ. τὰ δεινά D.H.10.16.

**ἀνάγκῠλος**, ον, without thong (ἀγκύλη), of a javelin, D.S.3.8.

**ἀναγλῠκαίνω**, sweeten:—Pass., become sweet, Thphr.CP3.22.3.

**ἀνάγλ-υπτος**, ον, = ἀνάγλυφος, γρῦπες SIG996.10 (Smyrna), cf. Plin.HN33.139, Mart.4.39.8. -υφή, ἡ, work in low relief, Aristeas 58, Str.17.1.28. 2. scooped out cavity, καλάμου Herophil. ap.Gal.2.731. -υφος, ον, wrought in low relief, ἀνδριάντες Ps.-Callisth.3.28; ἱστορίαι AP3 tit.: ἀνάγλυφα, τά, Lxx 3Ki.6.18. ※-ύφω, aor. -έγλυψα, carve in relief, Keil-Premerstein Dritter Bericht No.37 (Lydia, i A.D.), J.AJ12.2.9, Gal.UP16.11: plpf. Pass. ἀναγέγλυπτο J.AJ12.2.10.

**ἀναγνάμπτω**, bend back, αἰχμὴ ἀνεγνάμφθη the spear-point was bent back, Il.3.348, 7.259, etc. 2. undo, loose, δεσμὸν μὲν ἀνέγναμψαν θεοὶ αὐτοί Od.14.348.

**ἀναγν-εία**, ἡ, (ἁγνεύω) abominable wickedness, Lxx 2 Ma.4. 13. ※-ιστος, ον, unpurified, unexpiated, Orph.A.1231. ※-ος, ον, unclean, unholy, defiled, A.Ag.220, Ch.994, S.OT823; ἄ. καὶ μιαρός Antipho 2.1.10; ἀ. ἁγνεία Ph.1.156. Adv. -νως Id.1.2, Poll. 1.32.

※**ἀνάγνωμα**, v. ἀνάγνωσμα.

**ἀναγνωρ-ίζω**, recognize, Pl.Plt.258a, Prm.127a, al.:—Med., Apollod. 3.5.5: Pass., Lxx Ge.45.1. 2. in a tragedy, recognize or come to the knowledge of a person or thing, so as to produce a dénouement, Arist.Po.1452a36, al. b. reveal oneself, make oneself known, ib. 1452b5, al. c. causal, cause to recognize, reveal oneself to, D.S.4. 59. 3. recognize a rule in a new instance, Arist.APr.67a24. -ισις, εως, ἡ, recognition, Pl.Tht.193c. 2. in Tragedy, recognition, as leading to the dénouement (cf. foreg. 2), Arist.Po.1452a29, 1454b 19. -ισμα, ατος, τό, = foreg., Hp.Flat.14:—pl. -ίσματα, τά, tokens of recognition, Lat. crepundia, Charis.p.55 K. -ισμός, ὁ, = ἀναγνώρισις, Arist.Po.1452a16, Men.Epit.581, Hld.7.7. -ιστικός, ή, όν, contributing to recognition, Sch.Luc.Laps.5.

**ἀναγν-ωσείω**, Desiderat. of ἀναγιγνώσκω, wish to read, Gloss. -ωσις, εως, ἡ, recognition, Hdt.1.116. 2. reading, Pl.Euthd.279e, Arist.Po.1462a17 (prob. l.), Rh.1414a18, etc.: pl., Aristeas 283. b. reading aloud, Hp.Vict.2.61, Sor.1.49, Act.Ap.13.15, SIG959.8 (Chios), D.T.642.11: in pl., public readings, Pl.Lg.810e; -ώσεις τῷ θεῷ ποιούμενος BCH31.351 (Delos). II. Gramm., in textual criticism, reading, ἡ Ἀριστάρχειος ἀ. A.D.Synt.164.2. III. = πραγματεία, Olymp.in Mete.3.34. IV. persuasion, Suid. (misunderstanding Hdt.1.116). -ωσμα, ατος, τό, reading, in concrete, of a book, etc., read, D.H.1.8, Luc.VH1.2, Plu.2.328d, Orib.Fr.67 (pl.). II. = ἀνάγνωσις II, A.D.Synt.122.8, al. -ωστέον, one must read, Ph.1.200, D.T.642.12, Gal.18(2).235, Sch.E.Andr. 1044. -ωστήριον, τό, lectern, reading-desk, Hsch. ※-ώστης, ου, ὁ, reader, slave trained to read, Cic.Att.1.12, Phld.Rh.1.199S., Corn.Nep.Att.13, Plu.Crass.2. II. secretary, τῆς πόλεως Inscr. Prien.111.194; γερουσίας Inscr.Cos238. -ωστικός, ή, όν, capable of reading, a good reader, Arr.Epict.2.18.2; fond of reading, Plu.2. 514a. 2. suitable for reading, Arist.Rh.1413b12, cf. PGrenf.1.14. 12. -ωστος, f.l. for ἄγνωστος in Call.Fr.422 as cited by Eust. 743.7, comparing ἀνάεδνος.

※**ἀνᾰγόρ-ευσις**, εως, ἡ, public proclamation, Decr.ap.D.18.118; freq. in Inscrr., as GDI3502.4 (Cnidus): = Lat. renuntiatio, Plu.Marc. 4, etc. -ευτος, ον, not to be spoken or told, Sch.S.Tr.1093. -εύω, Aeschin.3.3: impf. ἀνηγόρευον ib.122: fut. -εύσω Plu.Galb.21: aor. -ηγόρευσα Docum.ap.D.18.54, IG7.4148, Plb.18.29.4:—Pass., aor. -ηγορεύθην X.Cyn.1.14, Plu.2.176e: pf. -ηγόρευμαι Id.Mar.45:—fut., aor., and pf. in classic authors are mostly supplied by ἀνερῶ, ἀνεῖπον, ἀνείρηκα, also aor. Pass. ἀνερρήθην Aeschin.3.45:—proclaim publicly, ib.122, etc.; ἀ. κήρυγμα make public proclamation, Plb.l.c.; ἀ. τινὰ αὐτοκράτορα Plu.Galb.2:—Pass., to be proclaimed, ἀναγορευέσθω νικηφόρος Pl.Lg.730d, cf. D.18.319, Aeschin.3.45: = Lat. renuntiari, ὕπατος ἀνηγορευμένος Plu.Mar.45, cf. 2.470d. 2. designate, ἀ. τινὰς τῶν δήμων call after their demes, Arist.Ath.21.4:—Pass., φιλοπάτωρ -ευθῆναι X. l.c.

**ἀναγραμματ-ίζω**, write the letters of a name in direct and then in reverse order, PMag.Leid.W.3.21 (Pass.), al. II. transpose the letters of one word so as to form another, Eust.46.2, 488.12 (Pass.); e.g. Ἥρα ἀήρ, ἀρετὴ ἐρατή, Ἀρσινόη ἴον Ἥρας, Πτολεμαῖος ἀπὸ μέλιτος. -ισμός, ὁ, transposition of this kind, Artem.4.23, Sch.Lyc. p.5 S., Eust.45 fin.

**ἀναγραπτ-έον**, one must inscribe, εὐεργέτην ἀ. τινά Luc.DMort. 30.2; generally, one must count among, Ph.1.299. -ος, ον, recorded, εὐεργεσία Th.1.129, Procop.Gaz.Ep.16; registered, εἴς τινας Procop.Vand.2.6. 2. rendered famous, immortalized, Him.Or. 15.5. II. marked with, c. dat., βασιλείῳ συμβόλῳ, γράμμασιν ἱεροῖς, Hld.4.8, 8.11; painted, in a picture, Chor. in Philol.54.111.

※**ἀναγρᾰφ-εύς**, έως, ὁ, recorder, esp. as title of commissioners appointed to codify laws, IG1.61, cf. Lys.30.2,25. II. registrar of decrees, IG2.192c, cf. 191. III. plan, pattern, design, IG2.1054b 33, Ph.Bel.52.42. ※-εύω, hold office of ἀναγραφεύς, IG14.757 (Naples). ※-ή, ἡ, inscribing, registering, of properties, contracts, etc., Pl.Lg.850a; συναλλαγμάτων Arist.Pol.1322b34; of names of public benefactors, etc., X.Vect.3.11; στήλης IG2.14c, cf. 227, etc. 2. ἀ. τῶν νόμων codification, Lys.30.25. 3. Medic., prescription, formula, Hp.Decent.10; formula for a magic ink, PMag. Leid.V.12.16. 4. record, description, Plb.3.33.17, Plu.Per.2, etc. 5. treatise, Hero Bel.73.5: composition, τῶν διαλόγων Phld. Acad.Ind.p.4 M. II. register, esp. in pl., public records, GDI1743. 10 (Delph.), Plb.12.11.4, etc.: also ἀ. ἀρχόντων, φιλοσόφων, D.L.1. 22,42; σταθμῶν Str.15.1.11; copy of decree, SIG622A8 (Delph., ii B.C.). 2. the Sacred Scriptures, Ph.1.694. -ιον, τό, list, index, PAmh.2.62. ※-ω, contr. ἀγγράφω IG7.8, Tab.Heracl.1.126: (v. γράφω):—engrave and set up publicly, of treaties, laws, and public acts, τὰς ξυνθήκας ἐν στήλῃ λιθίνῃ Th.5.47; τὸν Δράκοντος νόμον *IG*1. 61, cf. And.1.82; ἀ. τι ἐς στήλην, εἰς λεύκωμα, etc., Lycurg.117, Lex ap. D.24.23; ἀναγραψάτωσαν τὸ ψήφισμα *IG*7.303.44; ἀγγραψάτω ib.7.8; *register*, τὰ συμβόλαια καὶ τὰς κρίσεις πρὸς ἀρχήν τινα Arist. *Pol.*1321$^b$34 (Pass.):—Med., ἀναγρψάσθαι συνθήκας *have* them *registered*, App.*Mith.*70. 2. of a person, *register* or *record* his name, στηλίτην ἀ. τινά Isoc.16.9:—Pass., *to be inscribed* or *entered in a public register*, ἀναγραφῆναι πατρόθεν Hdt.6.14, cf. 8.90; ἀναγράφεσθαι εὐεργέτης *to be registered* as a benefactor, as was the custom of the Persians, 8.85, cf. Th.1.129: hence generally, μέγιστος εὐεργέτης παρ' ἐμοὶ ἀναγεγράψῃ Pl.*Grg.*506c, cf. Lys.20.19, X.*Vect.*3.11: also, *to be registered* as a state-debtor, Lys.9.7:—generally, Ἄρθμιον.. ἐχθρὸν αὐτῶν ἀνέγραψαν D.9.43; ἐν τοῖς φίλοις -γεγράφθαι D.C.38.44; Εὐβούλου κούρα ἀνεγραφόμαν *became his adopted* daughter, *Epigr.Gr.*205 (Halicarn.):—Med., τὴν εὐεργεσίαν ἀνεγραψάμην εἰς ἐμαυτόν *Corp.Herm.* 1.30. 3. c. acc. rei, ἀ. στήλην *set up* a pillar *with an inscription on it*, Lys.30.21. b. Pass., *to be registered*, of a deed, *PRyl.*65.4 (i B.C.). II. of an author, *write out, place on record*, ὅσα ἀμφω ξυνέγραψαν, ταῦτα ἐγὼ ἀναγράφω Arr.*An.Praef.*1; *describe*, X.*Ep.*1.6, Arr.*Tact.*1.2, Philostr.*VA*5.37, Eun.*VSp.*476B. (Pass.); *compose*, Epicur.*Nat.*28.5; of the mind, *depict, imagine*, Philostr.*VA*6.19, 7.14. 2. *record*, πράξεις Plb.1.1.1, cf. D.L.1.40, Longin.13.3, etc.; *commemorate*, τινά Porph.*VP*2. 3. *describe* lines and figures mathematically, ἀ. ἀπό.. upon a base, Pl.*Men.*83b (Med.), cf. Euc. 1.47, etc.; ἀ. τὰς τῆς γῆς περιόδους Arist.*Mete.*350$^a$17; also of lines used as bases, αἱ ἴσαι αὐτοῖς τετράγωνα -ουσαι Euc.10 *Def.*4:—Pass., τὸ τετράγωνον τὸ ἀναγραφησόμενον ἀπό.. that *can be described* upon.., Id.2.14. 4. *reduce to a formula* or *prescription*, δυνάμεις ἀναγεγραμμέναι Hp.*Decent.*9. III. *entitle*, Λούκουλλος ἀναγέγραπται τὸ βιβλίον Plu.*Luc.*42. IV. *fill up outlines*, opp. περιγράφω, Arist. *EN*1098$^a$22, cf. Philostr.*Im.*2.17, Alex.Aphr.*in Top.*444.6.

*ἀναγρετόν· ἀνυπόστροφον, Hsch.

**ἀναγρία**, ἡ, (ἄγρα) *time when hunting was forbidden, close season*, X.*Cyn.*5.34.

**ἄναγρον** ἢ ἄνιγρον· ἐναγές, Hsch.

**ἀναγρύζω**, strengthd. for γρύζω, *to mutter, grunt*, ἢν ἀναγρύζῃ Ar. *Nu.*945: c. neg., σὲ δὲ χρὴ σιγᾶν μηδ' ἀ. Crates Com.1 D., cf. X.*Oec.* 2.11.

**ἀναγυμν-όω**, *strip naked, unveil*, metaph. in Pass., Dam.*Pr.* 404. **-ωσις**, εως, ἡ, *stripping*, Simp.*in Ph.*226.27.

**ἀνάγυρος**, ὁ, *Anagyris foetida, stinking bean-trefoil*, Ar.*Lys.*68:—also **ἀνάγυρις**, ιος (-εως Gal.16.143), ἡ, Dsc.3.150: prov., μὴ κινεῖν τὸν ἀ. 'let sleeping dogs lie', Lib.*Ep.*78; ὁ ἀ. κεκινῆσθαι δοκεῖ 'the fat is in the fire', Ar. l. c., cf. Sch. ad loc.—From it the Att. deme **Ἀναγυρ-οῦς** took its name, Adv. **-ουντόθεν** *from Anagyrus*, Ar.*Lys.* 67 (also **-οῦντάδε** *to A.*, **-οῦντι** *at A.*, St.Byz.); Adj. **-άσιος**, ὁ, *man of this deme*, Ar.*Fr.*6 D., Pl.*Thg.*127e, etc. [ῡ, Ar.*Fr.*6 D.]

**ἀναγχ-ιππέω**, *to be forced to serve as knight*, Eup.394:—Subst. **-ιπποι**, οἱ, Phot.p.109 R.

***ἀναγχίστευτος**, ον, *without heirs*, *CR*11.137 (Phryg.).

***ἀνάγχω**, *hang up, choke, strangle*, Nic.*Th.*475.

***ἀνάγω**, fut. ἀνάξω Hdt.7.10.θ', etc.: aor. 2 ἀνήγαγον, etc.: (v. ἄγω):—opp. κατάγω, I. *lead up* from a lower place to a higher, ἐς Ὄλυμπον Thgn.1347, E.*Ba.*289; πρὸς τὸ ὄρος X.*An.*3.4.28; ἱερὸν ἀ. ξόανον, of the Trojan horse, E.*Tr.*525; ὁ πέπλος ἀνάγεται εἰς τὴν ἀκρόπολιν Pl.*Euthphr.*6c. 2. *lead up to the high sea, carry by sea*, λαὸν ἀνήγαγεν ἐνθάδ' ἀείρας Il.9.338; γυναῖκ' εὐειδέ' ἀνῆγες ἐξ Ἀπίης γαίης 3.48, cf. 6.292; στρατὸν ἐπὶ τὴν Ἑλλάδα Hdt.7.10.θ': but freq. = simple ἄγω, *conduct, carry to* a place, Il.8.203, Od.3.272; ἀ. ναῦν *put* a ship *to sea*, Hdt.6.12, 7.100, etc.; ἀνάγειν abs. in the same sense, Id.3.41, 8.76, cf. D.23.169:—but this is more common in Med., v. infr. B. I. 3. *take up* from the coast into the interior, Od.14.272; esp. from Asia Minor into Central Asia, ἀ. παρὰ or ὡς βασιλέα Hdt. 6.119, X.*HG*1.4.6, *An.*2.6.1, etc.; from Piraeus to Athens, Id. *HG*2.4.8. 4. *bring up*, esp. from the dead, ἀ. εἰς φάος Hes.*Th.* 626; εἰς φῶς Pl.*R.*521c, S.*Fr.*557 (Pass.); τῶν φθιμένων ἀ. A.*Ag.* 1023, cf. E.*Alc.*985; κλίνει κἀνάγει πάλιν lays low and *brings up* again, S.*Aj.*131; ἐκ λεχέων ἀ. φάμαν παλαιάν *waken up, revive, renew*, Pi.*I.*4(3).22. 5. ἀ. χορόν *conduct* the choir, Hes.*Sc.*280, E.*Tr.*326, Th.3.104; ἀ. θυσίαν, ὀρτὴν *celebrate*.., Hdt.2.48, 60, al., cf. *Act.Ap.* 7.41; *sacrifice*, ταύρους *OGI*764.47 (ii B.C.). 6. *lift up, raise*, κάρα S.*Ph.*866; τὸ ὄμμα ἀ. ἄνω Pl.*R.*533d; ἀ. τὰς ὀφρῦς, = ἀνασπᾶν, Plu. 2.975c; ἂν πυκτεύοντες ἀνάγωσιν ἑαυτούς Id.2.541b. 7. ἀ. παιᾶνα *lift up* a paean, S.*Tr.*210; ἄναγε πολύδακρυν ἀδονάν, of a song of lamentation, E.*El.*126; κωκυτόν *Ph.*135. 8. ἀ. εἰς τιμὴν *raise* to honour, Plu.*Num.*16; τίμιον ἀ. τινά E.*HF*1333; *elevate*, οἱ εἰς φιλοσοφίαν ἀνάγοντες [ἀστρονομίαν] Pl.*R.*529a. 9. in various senses, φάρμακα ἀνάγοντα *expectorants*, Hp.*Morb.*3.15; ἀ. ὀδόντας *cut* teeth, Id.*Aph.*3.25; ἀ. πλῆθος αἵματος *bring up* blood, Plu.*Cleom.*30; ἀ. μηρυκισμόν *chew* the cud, Lxx *Le.*11.3, al.; τὸν Νεῖλον ἀναγέτω *bring* the Nile *up* [over its banks], Luc.*DDeor.*3; ἀ. φάλαγγα *deploy*, Plu. *Crass.*23: Geom., *draw* a line, Arist.*Metaph.*1051$^a$25; ἀ. τεταγμένως *erect* as an ordinate, Apollon.Perg.*Con.*2.49; in building, *carry* a line of works to a point, Plu.*Nic.*18: ἀ. ὕδωρ *distil*, Syn.Alch. p.66 B. 10. μύρια τάλαντ' εἰς τὴν ἀκρόπολιν ἀνήγαγον, i.e. *paid* them *into* the treasury there, D.3.24. 11. *bring up* a prisoner for examination, X.*HG*3.3.11, *OGI*483.185 (Pergam.), Plb.40.4.2, *Act. Ap.*12.4. 12. *train, rear*, θετὸν υἱόν *AP*9.254 (Phil.):—Pass., εἰς μέτρα ἥβης ἀνηγόμην *IG*12(7).449 (Amorgos); of plants, ἀ. ἀμπελῶνας S.(?)*Fr.*1010. II. *bring back*, ἀνήγαγον αὖθις Ἄργος ἐς ἱππόβοτον Il.15.29, cf. Od.24.401, Pi.*P.*5.3, etc. 2. τὸν λόγον ἐπ' ἀρχὴν ἀ. *carry back, refer* to its principles, Pl.*Lg.*626d; εἰς ἄλλας ἀρχὰς Arist. *EN*1113$^b$20; εἰς αὐτὸν τὴν ἀρχὴν 1113$^a$6, cf. *GA*778$^b$1, al.; εἰς γνωριμώτερον *Metaph.*1030$^b$20; generally, *refer*, πάντα τοῖς λογισμοῖς εἰς ἀσφάλειαν Plu.*Brut.*12; εἰς κοινὸν ὄνομα A.D.*Synt.*266.13; freq. in Pass., ἀνάγομαι εἴς τι Procl.*Inst.*21; ὑπό τι Olymp.*in Mete.*326.33; ἀπό, ἔκ τινος *to be derived from*, A.D.*Adv.*121.25, *Synt.*23.26; ἀ. ἀπό, ἐξ.. *derive one's subsistence from*.., Vett.Val.10.15, 73.11. 3. ἀ. τι εἰς τὸν δῆμον, Arist.*Pol.*1292$^a$25; of persons, ἀ. τινὰ ἐπὶ τὴν συγγραφὴν *refer* him to the contract, D.56.31. 4. *reduce* syllogism to another figure, Arist.*APr.*29$^b$1; *reduce* an argument to syllogism, ib.46$^b$ 40, al. 5. in Law, *return* a slave sold with an undisclosed defect, εἰς πρατῆρα Pl.*Lg.*916c, cf. Hyp.*Ath.*15. 6. *refer a claimant*, πράτορι ἢ εἰς πόλιν ἔνδικον *Milet.*3 No.140.42: abs., ὁ ἔχων ἀναγέτω *Foed.Delph.Pell.*2$^A$15; ἀ. ὅθεν εἴληφας D.45.81. 7. *rebuild*, Plu.*Publ.*15, *Cam.*32. 8. *restore to its original shape*, Parth.*Ep. Dedic.*; τάφρον *PHal.*1.5. 9. *reckon, calculate*, ἀ. τὰς ἡμέρας πρὸς τὸ μαντεῖον Plu.*Cim.*18; χρόνον ἐκ τῶν Ὀλυμπιονικῶν *Num.*1. 10. intr. (sc. ἑαυτόν), *withdraw*, X.*Cyr.*7.1.45, etc.; ἐπὶ πόδα ἀ. *retreat* facing enemy, 3.3.69; ἀ. ἐπὶ σκέλος Ar.*Av.*383: metaph., ἄναγε εἰς τοὐπίσω, perh. nautical, *put back again*, Pl.*R.*528a.

B. Med. and Pass., *put out to sea, set sail* (v. supr. I. 2), Il.1.478, Hdt.3.137, etc.: fut. ἀνάξεσθαι Th.6.30, etc.; ἀναχθέντες Hdt.3.138, 4.152, cf. A.*Ag.*626. 2. metaph., *put to sea*, i.e. *make ready, prepare oneself*, ὡς ἐρωτήσων Pl.*Chrm.*155d, cf. *Erx.*392d. 3. in thought, *ascend* to higher unity, Dam.*Pr.*117.

**ἀναγ-ωγεύς**, έως, ὁ, *one that brings up from below*, ψυχῶν ἀ. Procl. *H.*1.34. II. *strap for holding a shield*, Eust.995.26: in pl., *straps which keep up the sandal* round the foot, Ael.*VH*9.11, Ath.12. 543f. ***-ωγή**, ἡ, *leading up*, esp. *taking a ship into the high sea, putting to sea*, ἀ. γίγνεται Th.6.30, X.*HG*1.6.28. b. *bringing upstream*, of a ship, *OGI*56.51 (Egypt, iii B.C.). 2. *bringing up* from the stomach or lungs, πτυάλου ἀ. *expectoration*, Hp.*Acut.*54, cf. 58; σιτίων ἀπέπτων ἀ. *vomiting*, *Epid.*1.5; φάρμακα τῆς ἀ. *expectorants*, *Morb.*3.15; αἵματος Erasistr.ap.Gal.*Libr.Propr.*1, Plb.2.70.6 3. *bringing up, rearing*, φυτῶν Thphr.*CP*3.7.4. 4. *lifting up of the soul* to God, Iamb.*Myst.*3.7; ἡ πρὸς τὸ πρῶτον ἀ. Porph.*Sent.*30, cf. Eun. *VSp.*482B. 5. *evocation*, Σεμέλης Plu.2.293d. 6. *sublimation*, αἰθαλῶν Zos.Alch.p.141 B.; *distillation*, ὕδατος ibid. II. *referring* to a principle, Arist.*Metaph.*1005$^a$1; of phenomena to a cause, 1027$^b$14: generally, ἀ. πρός τι ποιεῖσθαι Epicur.*Sent.*23; ἐπὶ τὸ κοινωνικὸν τέλος M.Ant.12.20. 2. *resolution* of definitions into syllogisms, Arist.*APo.*90$^a$37. 3. *reference* to a principle, Id. *Metaph.*1027$^b$14. 4. *return* of a defective slave to vendor (cf. ἀνάγω A. II. 5), ἀ. ἔστω Pl.*Lg.*916a; ἀναγωγὴν ποιεῖσθαι ib. b; ἀναγωγῆς τυχεῖν ib. a, cf. Hyp.*Ath.*15. 5. *reference of a claimant* to a third party, *Foed.Delph.Pell.*2$^A$17. 6. *delivery, payment*, γενημάτων *PTeb.*24.56 (ii B.C.); φόρων Philostr.*VS*2.12.2 codd. 7. ἀναγωγαί, αἱ, = sq., Ath.9.395a. **-ώγια** (sc. ἱερά), τά, *offerings made on embarkation*, a feast of Aphrodite at Eryx, Ael.*VH*1.15. **-ωγία**, ἡ, (ἀ- priv., ἀγωγή) *want of discipline, dissoluteness, corruption*, Plb.7. 10.5, D.Chr.51.7, Eun.*Hist.*p.244 D. 2. *lack of breeding, vulgarity*, Plu.2.1065c, Demetr.*Eloc.*171; *unpleasantness*, E.*Ep.*5.2. **-ώγιος**, ον, *raising the mind to heavenly things, mystical*, κέντρα, πῦρ, Procl.*H.* 2.5, 4.2. II. ἀναγώγιον, τό, *reward for restoration of a fugitive slave*, σώματος *Milet.*3 No.150.97. **-ωγός**, όν, *bringing up, eliciting*, πτυάλου Hp.*Acut.*58. 2. *raising or conveying up*, ἡ διὰ τοῦ πυρὸς προσαγωγὴ τῶν θυσιῶν ἀ. ἐπὶ τὸ οὐράνιον πῦρ Iamb.*Myst.*5.11. b. *uplifting the soul, elevating*, θεός Jul.*Or.*5.173c, cf. Iamb.*Myst.*2.6, Syrian.*in Metaph.*14.36, Procl.*Inst.*158; σωτηρία Dam.*Isid.*232; ἀ. τοῦ τρίτου εἰς τὸ πρῶτον Id.*Pr.*75.

**ἀν-άγωγος**, ον, *ill-bred*, Timo 51 (Sup.), Plu.2.147f; καύχησις Phld.*Vit.*p.27 J.; ἀ. καὶ ἀπαίδευτος τρόπος D.S.34/5.2.35; *tasteless*, σκώμματα Longin.34.2; ῥητορικὴ D.H.*Orat.Vett.*1; *unlearned*, Plb. 12.25.6; *dissolute*, περὶ τὰς ἡδονάς Plu.2.14cb; of horses and dogs, *ill-broken, unmanageable*, X.*Mem.*3.3.4, 4.1.3, prob. l. in Arist.*Ath.* 49.1. Adv. -γως Macho ap.Ath.13.580e, Lxx 2 *Ma.*12.14 (Comp.); *inerudite et* ἀ. Tiro ap.Gell.6.3.12.

**ἀναγων-ίατος**, ον, *free from anxiety*, *PTeb.*58.51 (ii B.C.). ***-ιστος**, ον, *without contest* or *conflict*, ἀ. ἀπιέναι Th.4.92 (v.l.); *never having contended for a prize*, X.*Cyr.*1.5.10; ἀ. περὶ τῆς ἀρετῆς *failing* in the race of virtue, Pl.*Lg.*845c.

**ἀναδαιμονίζειν**· τὸ ἐκ δευτέρου κληροῦσθαι, Hsch.

***ἀναδαίομαι**, v. ἀναδατέομαι.

**ἀναδαίω**, poet. ἀνδαίω, *light up*, φλογὸς μέγαν πώγωνα A.*Ag.*305: —Pass., metaph., ἀνεδαίετο κερτομίῃ A.R.4.1726.

**ἀναδάκνω**, *stimulate*, of salt applied to roots, Thphr.*CP*3.17.4; ἀ. τὴν κατάποσιν Xenocr.25: generally, *irritate*, Ruf.ap.Orib.8.39.3, *Hippiatr.*33; ἀ. σφοδρῶς Dsc.5.136.

**ἀναδαρδαίνω**, aor. ἀνεδάρδανα, = ἀναμολύνω, Hsch.

**ἀναδάσασθαι**, aor. inf. of ἀναδατέομαι.

**ἀναδάσ-ιμος**, ον, *to be distributed afresh*, Sch.Ven.Il.1.300. **-μός**, ὁ, *redistribution, partition* of land among colonists, Hdt.4.159, 163; as a revolutionary measure, freq. coupled with χρεῶν ἀποκοπαί, Pl.*R.* 566a, D.17.15, Jusj.ap.eund.24.149, *SIG*526.22 (Itanos). **-τος**, ον, *divided anew, redistributed*, ἀ. γῆν ποιεῖν Pl.*Lg.*843b; ἀ. ποιεῖν τὴν χώραν Arist.*Pol.*1307$^a$2; τὰς οὐσίας ἀ. ποιεῖν 1305$^a$5, cf. 1309$^a$ 15. II. later, ἀ. ποιεῖν τι *undo, rescind*, *OGI*669.20 (Egypt, i A.D.), uc.*Abd.*11. III. Adv. -τως· ἀνωμάλως ἔχων τις τοῦ σώματος, sch.

**ἀναδατέομαι**, *divide anew, redistribute*, ὁ δῆμος τὴν γῆν ἐπενόει ναδάσασθαι Th.5.4 :—Pass., ἀναδαίομαι *to be distributed*, Orac.ap. Hdt.4.159 : aor. -δασθείς Plu.*Agis*8.

**ἀνά-δειγμα**, ατος, τό, *image for show*, Hsch. **2.** *mouthpiece worn by public criers* to serve the purpose of a speaking-trumpet, Epigr.ap.Poll.4.92, Hsch. **-δείκνῡμι**, also -ύω Plu.2.417e : on. aor. -έδεξα Hdt. (v. infr.): pf. -δέδειχα Plb.21.21.3 : (v. δείκνυμι) :—*lift up and show, exhibit, display*, πύλας ἀναδεικνύναι *display by opening* gates, i.e. *throw wide* the gates, S.*El.*1458 ; μυστοδόκος δόμος ἀναδείκνυται Ar.*Nu.*304 ; ἀναδέξαι ἀσπίδα *hold* up shield *as signal*, Hdt.6.115,121 sq.; ἀνέδεξε σημήιον τοῖς ἄλλοις ἀνάγεσθαι *made signal* for them to put to sea, Id.7.128 ; [Μίλητος] Θαλῆν ἀ., on a statue, Epigr.ap.D.L.1.34. **II.** *notify*, esp. *proclaim* any one as elected to office, αὐτὸν ἀναδεδειχὼς βασιλέα Plb.4.48.3 ; ἀ. τινὰ μέγιστον *make* him the greatest man, 22.4.3 ; ἀνέδειξεν ἑτέρους ἑβδομήκοντα *Ev. Luc.*10.1 :—Pass., ἀναδεδεῖχθαι τὸ ἱερὸν ἄσυλον *SIG*630.23 (Delph., ii B.C.). **2.** *dedicate*, τῷ Διὶ ταῦρον *SIG*589.6 (Magn. Mae., ii B.C.); τὴν Πιερίδα ταῖς θεαῖς Str.9.2.25; θέατρον Plu. *Pomp.*52; ἱερά *AP*9.340. **3.** ἀ. πόλεμον *declare* war, *SIG*742.12 (Ephesus, i B.C.). **-δειξις**, εως, ἡ, *showing forth*: esp. *public proclamation* or *appointment* to an office, ἡ τῶν ὑπάτων ἀ. Plu.*Mar.*8 ; τῶν συναρχόντων ἡ ἀναγόρευσις καὶ ἀ. *CG*12 : abs., ἡ ἀ. *the election*, *Cat.Mi.*44, 46. **2.** ἡ ἀ. τοῦ διαδήματος *ceremony* of coronation, Plb.15.25.11 (pl.); *dedication* of temple, Str.8.6.23. **3.** *declaration*, χρόνων Lxx *Si.*43.6. **II.** (from Pass.) *manifestation*, of Osiris, D.S.1. 85, but rather from Act. in ἡ ἀ. αὐτοῦ πρὸς τὸν Ἰσραήλ *Ev.Luc.*1.80.

**ἀναδείπνια**, τά, *second supper*, or *second course at supper*, ascribed to Lycians by Eust.1141.14.

**ἀναδέκ-ομαι**, Ion. for ἀναδέχομαι. **-τέον**, *one must take back*, Hyp.*Ath.*15. **-τικός**, ή, όν, *fitted for receiving*, S.E.*M.*7.355.

**ἀνάδελφος**, ον, *without brother* or *sister*, E.*Or.*310, Ph.2.291, Vett. Val.15.6, etc.

**ἀνάδεμα**, poet. **ἄνδεμα**, ατος, τό, = ἀνάδημα, *IG*5(1).1390.22 (Andania, i B.C.), *AP*7.423 (Antip.).

**ἀναδέμω**, *block by building up*, πύλας Aen.Tact.23.4. **II.** Med., *build up again*, J.*BJ*2.20.6 ; simply, *build up*, Ph.1.317,324.

**ἀναδενδρ-αδικός**, ή, όν, *for* ἀναδενδράδες, ἀμπελών *PSI*6.697 (ii A.D.), prob. in *BGU*1279 (iii B.C.). **-άς**, άδος, ἡ, *vine that grows up trees*, Pherecr.109, D.53.15, Thphr.*CP*1.10.4, 3.10.8, Chrysipp. *Stoic.*3.180, Aesop.33. **2.** = σκιάς, Hsch. **-ίτης** [ῑ] οἶνος, ὁ, wine *from the* ἀναδενδράς, Plb.34.11.1 :—fem. -ῖτις ἄμπελος *Gp.*5. 51.1. **-ομαλάχη**, ἡ, *hollyhock*, *Alcea rosea*, Gal.10.960, Orib.14. 38.13, cf. 15.1.4.

**ἀναδέξαι**, v. ἀναδείκνυμι.

**ἀναδέρκομαι**, Dep., *look up*, aor. 2 Act. ἀνέδρακεν ὀφθαλμοῖσιν, of one who recovers from fainting, Il.14.436, cf. A.R.3.1010.

**ἀναδέρω**, poet. **ἀνδ-**, *strip a scab off*, ψήκτρῃ *Hippiatr.*68 ; *expose, lay bare*, in dissection, Gal.2.719 ; *strip off*, τὸν φλοιόν *Gp.*10.18.10 ; ἀνδέροντι πόδας *strip skin off* the feet, Pi.*Fr.*203 :—Pass., ἀναδαρέντα μέρεα Aret.*CD*2.13 ; ἀναδέρεται ἡ ἕλκωσις Antyll.ap.Aët.9.40. **2.** metaph., *lay bare, expose*, ἀνά (τε) δέρετον τά τε παλαιὰ καὶ τὰ καινά Ar.*Ra.*1106 (al. δέρεσθον), cf. Luc.*Pseudol.*20 :—Med., ἠρώτα δ' ὑπὲρ αὐτῶν οὐδέν, ὡς μὴ ἀναδέροιτο Philostr.*VS*1.25.3.

**ἀνάδεσ-ις**, εως, ἡ, *binding on*, στεφάνων Plu.*Sert.*22. **2.** *binding up*, or *decking*, κόμης Luc.*JTr.*33. **-μεύω**, *tie up, suspend*, ἔκ τινος D.S.18.42, cf. Mnesith.Cyz.ap.Orib.*Inc.*15.16 :—also **-μέω**, κλήματα πρὸς χάρακας *Gp.*4.7.3, cf. Sch.A.*Pers.*191 : metaph., of religious scruples or *taboos*, Lyd.*Ost.*16. **-μη**, ἡ, *band for women's hair, snood*, πλεκτὴ ἀ. Il.22.469, cf. *AP*5.275 (Agath.), E.*Med.*978 Porson. **-μος**, ὁ, = foreg., *APl.*4.134 (Mel.); *bandage* for female breast, Heliod.ap.Orib.48.50 tit.

**ἀνάδετος**, ον, *binding up* hair, μίτραι E.*Hec.*923. **2.** in pass. sense, πῶλον Χαρίτων μίτραις ἀνάδετον Him.*Ecl.*13.36.

**ἀναδεύω**, *soak, steep*, Thphr.*HP*9.13.3 : metaph., ἤθεσι ἀ. τοὺς νόμους *imbue* them with moral principle, Plu.*Comp.Lyc.Num.*4, cf. Max.Tyr.10.6 : fut. ἀναδεύσομαι in pass. sense, Gal.10.867 **2.** *mix into a paste*, οἴνῳ καὶ μέλιτι Phylarch.26, cf. Plu.2.997a.

**ἀναδέχομαι**, fut. -δέξομαι : aor. ἀνεδεξάμην, Ep. aor. ἀνεδέγμην (v. infr.): pf. Pass. ἀναδέδεγμαι :—*take up, catch, receive*, σάκει δ' ἀνεδέξατο πολλά (sc. δόρατα) Il.5.619 ; ἀ. πληγὰς εἰς τὸ σῶμα Plu. *Tim.*4 ; βέλη τῷ σώματι *Marc.*10. **2.** *receive, entertain* as a guest, *Act.Ap.*28.7. **II.** *take upon oneself, submit to*, ἀνεδέγμεθ' ὀϊζύν Od.17.563, cf. Archil.60 ; ἁμαρτήματα D.19.36 ; πόλεμον Plb.1.88. 12 ; ἀπέχθειαν Plu.*Eum.*6 ; ἅ τι ἐφ' ἑαυτόν D.22.64, cf. Din.1.3 : abs., *acknowledge* one's evidence, of an absent witness, D.46.7. **2.** *accept, receive*, ἀγγελίαν Pi.*P.*2.41 (al. -δέξατ'); λουτρὰ . . μητρὸς ἀνεδέξω πάρα E.*IT*818 ; χορηγίας, ἡγεμονίαν, Plu.*Arist.*1,23 ; τὸν κλῆρον *Cic.*43 ; τῶν σωμάτων τὰ μανὰ ἀ. θερμότητα *Cat.Mi.*61 (dub.); *accept* a statement, Them.*in Ph.*77.8. **3.** *admit of*, κλίσιν, ἀριθμόν A.D. *Pron.*29.9, al. ; σχέσιν πρός τι Procl.*Inst.*122. **4.** *undertake* to say or do, c. fut. inf., Hdt.5.91, X.*Cyr.*6.1.17, etc. : c. aor. inf., Plu. *Arist.*14. **b.** *undertake*, c. acc., S.*Ichn.*157 ; ὅσα ὑπισχνεῖτο καὶ ἀνεδέχετο D.35.7 ; *take upon oneself*, αἰτίαν Pl.*Hp.Mi.*365d ; πρεσβείας, κινδύνους, *OGI*339.20 (Sestos, ii B.C.), 441.9 (Stratonicea, i B.C.). **5.** *give security to one*, τινί Th.8.81 ; τινί τι Plb.11.25.9 ; *go bail for*, τινά Thphr.*Char.*12.4 ; τινὰ τῶν χρημάτων Plb.5.16.8 ; ἀ. τοὺς δανειστάς *undertake to satisfy* them, Plu.*Caes.*11 ; ἀ. τὴν πίστιν ὑπέρ τινος Id.*Phoc.*14 : abs., *Leg.Gort.*9.24,41. **6.** *take back*, D.59.58. **7.** *experience, suffer*, πάθος, ταραχάς, Phld.*Ir.*p.82 W., *D.*1.13 ; σῆψιν Aët.13.3. **III.** *wait for*, Plb.1.52.8.

**ἀναδέω**, poet. **ἀνδέω**, Att. contr. part. ἀναδῶν (infr. I. 2): fut. -δήσω : aor. ἀνέδησα (v. infr.) : pf. ἀναδέδεκα Nic.Dam.p.113 D. :—Med. and Pass., Att. contr. ἀναδοῦνται, ἀναδούμενος (infr. I. 2, III):—Pass., pf. -δέδεμαι :—*bind, tie up, wreath*, δάφνᾳ κόμας ἀναδήσαντες Pi.*P.*10.40 ; στέφανοι ἀνέδησαν ἔθειραν *I.*5(4).9 :—Med., ἀναδέεσθαι τὰς κεφαλὰς μίτρῃσι *bind their* heads.., Hdt.1.195 ; ἀνδησάμενος κόμαν *having wreathed one's* hair, Pi.*N.*11.28, cf. *I.*1.28 :—so in Pass., μίτρᾳ ἀναδεδεμένος τὴν κόμην Luc.*DDeor.*18.1 ; κρωβύλον ἀναδεῖσθαι τῶν τριχῶν *bind one's* hair into a knot, Th.1.6 ; στέμμ' ἀναδησάμενος *having bound his brows* with the fillet, *Epigr.Gr.*873.4 (Cyrene) ; τίς τοσάσδε.. ἀνεδήσατο νίκας; who *has won* so many *crowns of* victory? Simon.10 : metaph., τὴν ἀρχήν App.*BC*1.84 ; κλέος, κράτος, Procop.*Vand.*2.27, *Pers.*1.14 ; ἆθλον Chor.*Zach.*6.9. **2.** c. acc. pers., *crown*, τινὰ στεφάνοις Pi.*P.*2.6 ; λήροις (Com. for στεφάνοις) ἀναδῶν τοὺς νικῶντας Ar.*Pl.*589 ; ἀ. τινὰ εὐαγγέλια *crown* him for good tidings, 764 ; τὸν ἡνίοχον Th.5.50 :—metaph. in Pass., τροφῇ τε καὶ τοῖς ἄλλοις πᾶσιν, ὅσων βίος δεῖται, ἀναδοῦνται *are well furnished with*.., Pl.*R.*465d. **II.** ἀναδῆσαι τὴν πατριὴν ἐς ἑκκαιδέκατον θεὸν *trace* one's family to a god in the sixteenth generation, Hdt.2. 143. **III.** Med., *fasten by a rope to oneself*, ὤνευον ἀναδούμενοι τοὺς σταυρούς Th.7.25 ; esp. of a ship, ἀναδούμενος ἕλκειν *take in tow*, 1.50, 2.90, etc. : metaph., ἀναδεῖσθαί τινας *attach* them *to oneself*, Aristid. *Or.*46(3).25, Ael.*VH*4.9, Luc.*Im.*1 ; ἀπὸ τῶν ὤτων τινὰ ἀναδησάμενος Id.*Scyth.*11 ; ἀναδεῖσθαί τι ἔκ τινος *make dependent* upon.., Plu.2.222e; ἐκ τοῦ φιλοκάλου μάλιστα τῆς ψυχῆς ἀναδούμενος τὴν πίστιν 343a :—Pass., ἀναδεδέσθαι ἔκ τινος, εἰς τὴν ὀροφήν, Id.*Dio* 26, *Eum.*11.

**ἀνάδηγμα**, ατος, τό, *bite*, κωνώπων Hp.*Epid.*2.3.1.

**ἀνάδηλος**, ον, *evident*, Phld.*Rh.*2.246 S.

**ἀνάδημα**, poet. **ἄνδημα**, ατος τό, = ἀνάδεσμη, Pi.*Fr.*179, E.*Hipp.* 83, *El.*882, *IG*2.758*B* ; ἀ. χρυσοῦν Pl.Com.178 ; βασιλέων ἀ. Aristid. *Or.*19(41).4.

**ἀνάδηξις**, εως, ἡ, lit. *biting*: hence in Thphr.*CP*3.17.5 of *the stimulating effect* of certain manures.

**ἀνάδησις**, εως, ἡ, = ἀνάδεσις, Paul.Aeg.3.59.

**ἀνα-δῐδακτέον**, *one must teach otherwise* or *better*, Ph.1.162. **-δῐδάσκω**, *teach otherwise* or *better*, ἀ. ὡς.. Hdt.4.95 ; τινά τι Luc.*Pseudol.* 13 ; simply, *instruct, inform*, Th.1.32, al., Ar.*Pl.*563, etc. :—Pass., *to be better instructed*, ὅτι.. Pl.*Hp.Ma.*301e ; *learn better things, change one's mind*, Hdt.8.63 (dub.) ; *learn anew* or *from the beginning*, J.*AJ* 2.9.1. **II.** ἀ. δρᾶμα *produce* play *a second time*, *Vit.Aesch.*, Arg. 1 Ar.*Ra.*, Philostr.*VA*6.11. **2.** *explain*, ἐν οὐκ ἀναδιδάσκει σε τῶν λογίων Ar.*Eq.*1045.

**ἀναδιδράσκω**, *run away again*, Plb.29.19.1 (dub.).

**ἀναδίδωμι**, poet. **ἀνδ-** : fut. -δώσω, etc. :—*give up, hold up and give*, φιάλαν Pi.*I.*6(5).39, X.*Smp.*2.8. **2.** *deliver*, ἐπιστολάς Plb. 29.10.7, D.S.11.45, cf. *IG*14.830 ; ψήφισμα *OGI*437.78 (Pergam., i B.C.). **II.** *give forth, send up*, esp. of the earth, *yield*, καρπόν Plu.*Cam.*15, cf. Hp.*Aër.*12, E.*Fr.*484.4 ; ὡραῖα Th.3.58. **2.** *send up*, Φερσεφόνα.. ἀνδιδοῖ ψυχὰς πάλιν Pi.*Fr.*133.3. **3.** of a river, ἀ. θρόμβους ἀσφάλτου Hdt.1.179 ; of a volcano, ἀ. πῦρ καὶ καπνόν Th.3. 88, etc. ; ἀ. εὐωδίαν Plu.2.645f, cf. Thphr.*Sud.*10. **4.** intr., of springs, fire, etc., *burst, issue forth*, Hdt.7.26, Arist.*Mete.*351ᵃ15 (also Pass., τὰ ἐν ἄντροις ἀναδιδόμενα ὕδατα Porph.*Antr.*6). **5.** *send up to* higher authority, *present* by name, *PFay.*26.13 (ii A.D.), etc. **b.** Math., in Pass., *to be given*, of elements in calculation, Vett.Val.21.1. **III.** *deal round, distribute, impart*, διαβούλιον τοῖς φίλοις Plb.5.58.2 ; of one person, τὴν πρᾶξίν τινι 8.17.2 ; τοῖς λόχοις τὰς ψήφους D.H.10.57, cf. Plu.*TG*11, etc. ; ἀ. φήμην *spread* it, Id.*Aem.*25 :—Pass., ἀνεδίδοντο χρυσοῖ στέφανοι Posidon.17. **2.** Medic., *distribute* food, juices, etc., throughout the body, Philotim. ap.Orib.2.69.9, al. : esp. in Pass., Dieuch.ib.4.7.1, Phld.*D.*3.14 ; πέττεσθαί τε καὶ ἀναδίδοσθαι Gal.15.457, cf. 6.650, Porph.*Abst.*1. 47. **IV.** Med., *sell*, Arist.*Fr.*558 (prob. f.l. for ἀποδόσθαι). **V.** in Gramm., ἀ. τὸν τόνον *throw back* accent, *EM*739.22, Sch.Ven.Il.5. 182. **VI.** intr., *go backwards, retrograde* (cf. ἐπιδίδωμι), Arist. *Rh.*1390ᵇ28.

**ἀναδῐκ-άζω**, *decide again, hear on appeal*, τὰ γνωσθέντα Ph.1.299 : abs., *reverse a decision*, *AP*5.221 (Agath.). **II.** Med., *renew an action after a previous judgement had been cancelled*, Is.*Fr.*145. **-εῖν**, defect. aor., *throw back*, Ep. 3 sg. ἄνδικε *AB*394. **-έω**, *appeal for rehearing of a case*, *PLille*29.4. **-ία**, ἡ, *renewal of an action*, Lys. *Fr.*298 S. **-ος** (Arc. **ὄνδικος** *IG*5(2).343*B*2), ον, *tried over again*, δίκαι ἀ. γίγνονται And.1.88, Pl.*Lg.*937d, cf. D.40.39, etc. ; ψῆφον ἀ. καθιστάναι render *subject to appeal*, Id.24.191.

**ἀναδῑν-εύω**, *whirl about*, Opp.*H.*3.296. **-έω**, intr., of the eyes, *roll*, Hp.*Mul.*1.36 :—also **ἀναδινίω**· περιπατῶ, and **ἄνδινος**· περίπατος, Hsch.

**ἀναδιπλασι-άζω**, *reduplicate*, Choerob.*in Theod.*p.75 H. : Rhet., *repeat*, Anon.*Fig.*p.160 S. **-ασμός**, ὁ, *reduplication*, *EM*45.45, 55.26.

**ἀναδιπλ-όω**, *double, fold*, Sor.1.84 :—Pass., *to be made double*, φάλαγξ βραχυτέρα ἐγίγνετο ἀναδιπλουμένη *being made twice as* deep, X.*Cyr.*7.5.5. **2.** Gramm., of a word or syllable, *reduplicate*, Phryn.*PSp.*32 B. :—Pass., Trypho *Fr.*21, cf. *EM*98.38. **3.** Rhet., *repeat*, Phoeb.*Fig.*2.4. **-ωσις**, εως, ἡ, *convolution*, τοῦ ἐντέρου Arist. *HA*508ᵇ13, *PA*675ᵇ2. **2.** *repetition, duplication*, Ph.2.56, Phlp.*in*

*Mete.*103.37; esp. in Rhet. (cf. ἐπαναδίπλωσις), Demetr.*Eloc.*66, al., Alex.*Fig.*2.2, etc. 3. Medic., *double infection*, in malarial fevers, etc., Gal.7.369, al., cf. Alex.Trall.*Febr.*2. 4. Gramm., *reduplication*, Trypho *Fr.*12.

⊕**ἀναδῑφάω,** *grope after*, Cratin.2.

**ἀναδιχότομος** φάσις *last quarter* of the moon, *Cat.Cod.Astr.*8(4).205.

**ἀναδοιδῡκίζω,** *stir up*, *EM*96.7, Hsch.

**ἀνάδομα,** ατος, τό, *product of digestion*, cj. in Plu.2.384a (pl.).

**ἀνα-δομέω,** *rebuild*, Agath.2.17:—Med., 5.9:—Pass., 2.15. **-δομή,** ἡ, *rebuilding*, Suid., Zonar.

**ἀναδονέω,** *stir up*, *agitate*, Ph.1.659; ἀνὰ βάρβιτον δονήσω *Anacreont.*58.1.

**ἀναδορά,** ἡ, *excoriation*, Aret.*SD*2.3,9, Orib.*Fr.*3

⊕**ἀνά-δοσις,** εως, ἡ, (ἀναδίδωμι intr.) *sprouting*, of plants, Thphr.*CP* 2.1.4; *bursting*, *issuing forth*, of fire, wind, water, Arist.*Mu.*395$^{a}$9, D.S.2.12, J.*BJ*7.6.3; *exhalation*, Plu.2.31e. 2. *sending up*, *presentation* of names, ἀναδόσεις λειτουργῶν *POxy.*82.2 (iii A.D.). II. (trans.) *distribution*, Posidon.17; τῶν ὄντων J.*Ap.*2.39. 2. of food, *distribution*, *assimilation*, Plb.3.57.8, Phld.*D.*3.13 (sg. and pl.), Plu.2.654a, Gal.*Nat.Fac.*1.2, Jul.*Ep.*180; πέψις καὶ ἀ. Muson.*Fr.*18 B p.103 H., Porph.*Abst.*1.45: metaph., *digestion* of knowledge, Plu.*Per.*2. III. Gramm., ἀ. τόνου *throwing back* of the accent, *EM* 549.30. **-δοτικός,** ή, όν, *causing to spring up*, σπερμάτων Corn.*ND*28. 2. Medic., *digestive*, Gal.6.416. **-δοτος,** ον, *given up* or *to be given up*, Th.3.52.

**ἀναδουλόω,** *reduce to slavery again*, App.*BC*4.29.

**ἀναδοχ-εύς,** = ἀνάδοχος II, Hsch. **-ή,** ἡ, *series*, *succession*, πόνων S.*Tr.*825 (lyr.). 2. *reception*, τινῶν A.D.*Synt.*144.10. II. *surety*, Plb.5.27.4: Cret. **ἀνδοκά** *Leg.Gort.*9.34: so prob. **ἀνδοκεία** *IG*14.422 (pl.), 423 (Tauromenium). **-ος,** ον, *taking upon oneself*, *giving security for*, πρὸς τὴν ἀδελφὴν ἀ. τῶν χρημάτων Men.516. II. as Subst., *security*, *surety*, D.H.6.84, Plu.*Dio*18; τῆς φιλίας Κύπρις ἀ. *PGrenf.*1.1; περί, ὑπέρ τινος, Phalar.*Ep.*22,38.

**ἀναδρᾰμ-εῖν,** aor. 2 inf. of ἀνατρέχω. **-ητέον,** *one must run back*: metaph., *have recourse*, ἐπὶ τὴν τῶν ὅλων θεωρίαν Procl.*in Ti.*1.103 D.

**ἀναδράω,** aor. inf. -δρᾶσαι, = ἀναπρᾶξαι, Hsch.

**ἀναδρέπω,** *break off*, *pluck*, Nonn.*D.*9.120:—Med., *cull*, ῥητορικοὺς λόγους ἀναδρέψασθαι Them.*Or.*27.332d.

**ἀναδρομ-ή,** ἡ, *running up*: hence, *sprouting*, *impulse*, Thphr.*CP*4.5.1; *shooting up*, of plant, Hermog.*Prog.*7; *bud*, *burgeon*, E.*Fr.*766, 855: metaph., *ascent*, of the soul, Procl.*Inst.*209; εἰς θεόν, εἰς τὸν ὄντως ἑαυτόν, Porph.*Marc.*7, *Abst.*1.29. b. *climbing up*, of a tree, Agatharch.51. 2. Rhet., *returning* to a point, Corn.*Rh.*p.376 H. 3. *place of refuge*, Poet.ap.Plb.*Fr.*102. 4. *running back*, *retreat*, J.*BJ*5.2.2. b. *reflux*, γυναικείων Hp.*Liqu.*6. 5. *sudden throb* of pain, Id.*Coac.*308, 310; = πνῖξις, Steph.*in Hp.*1.316 D. ⊕**-ος,** ον, *running up*, of a fish entering a river from the sea, Alex.Trall.1.15.

**ἀναδρύγματα·** θύματα, Hsch. **ἀναδρύψει·** ἀναξ[ηρ]ανεῖ, Id.

**ἀναδύνω,** *come to the top of the water*, Batr.90, Arist.*Fr.*335; of rivers which have disappeared into the earth, *emerge*, Id.*Mete.*356$^{a}$25.

**ἀναδύομαι,** Ep. 3 sg. ἀνδύεται [ῠ] Il.13.225: fut. -δύσομαι [ῡ]: aor. ἀνεδῡσάμην, Ep. 3 sg. -ατο or -ετο: aor. intr. ἀνέδῡν, subj. ἀναδύῃ or opt. ἀναδύη [ῡ] Od.9.377: pf. ἀναδέδῡκα: (v. δύω):—*come up*, *rise*, esp. from the sea, c. gen., ἀνέδυ πολιῆς ἁλὸς ἠΰτ' ὀμίχλη Il.1.359; ἀνεδύσατο λίμνης Od.5.337: c. acc., ἀνεδύσετο κῦμα θαλάσσης Il.1.496: abs., εἴπερ ἀναδύσει πάλιν Ar.*Ra.*1460; Ἀφροδίτη ἀναδυομένη, a famous picture by Apelles, Str.14.2.19, Plin.*HN*35.91, cf. *AP*12.207 (Strat.). II. *shrink back*, *withdraw*, Od.9.377; ἀναδῦναι ἂψ λαῶν ἐς ὅμιλον Il.7.217; *hesitate*, *shirk*, ἕτοιμός εἰμ' ἔγωγε, κοὐκ ἀναδύομαι, δάκνειν Ar.*Ra.*860, cf. Lys.16.15, X.*Smp.*5.2, D.8.50, 19.210, Men.*Epit.*205; of rivers, *fail*, Plu.*Thes.*15. 2. rarely c. acc., *draw back from*, *shun*, ἀνδύεται πόλεμον Il.13.225, cf. D.H.5.52; ἀναδύεσθαι τὰ ὡμολογημένα *back out of* one's admissions, Pl.*Tht.*145c.

**ἀνάδῠσις,** εως, ἡ, *drawing back*, *retreat*, Pl.*Euthd.*302e, Jul.*Or.*5.175b: c. gen., *shirking*, τῆς στρατείας Plu.*Cim.*18. 2. *emergence* from underground, J.*BJ*7.2.2; of land from water, Lxx *Wi.*19.7; of bird from lake, Sch.Od.5.337.

**ἀναδυσμός,** ὁ, = foreg. 2, Sch.Od.5.337.

**ἀνιδωδωναῖος,** title of Zeus, wrong expl. of Il.16.233, Cleanth. ap.Plu.2.31e.

**ἀνάεδνος,** ἡ, *without bride-price*, Il.9.146, 13.366; also of the husband, *bringing no gifts*, Nonn.*D.*4.43, 48.633. (Prob. misspelt for ἀν-έϝεδνος.)

⊕**ἀναείρω,** *lift up*, of a wrestler, ἤ μ' ἀνάειρ', ἢ ἐγὼ σέ Il.23.724; ἀνάειρε δύω χρυσοῖο τάλαντα *took* them, *carried* them *off*, ib.614,778; ἀθανάτοισι φίλας ἀνὰ χεῖρας ἀείραι 7.130:—Med., *lift up in one's arms*, *carry off*, A.R.4.94:—Pass., *arise*, ἀνηέρθησαν ἄελλαι A.R.1.1078; of a ship, *leave the stocks*, Orph.*A.*268.

**ἀνάελπτος,** ον, = ἄελπτος, *unlooked for*, ἀνάελπτα παθόντες Hes.*Th.*660. (Prob. misspelt for ἀν-έϝελπτος.)

⊕**ἀναέξω,** *enlarge*, *increase*, Q.S.1.460; *make grow*, ἄνθος Coluth.247:—Pass., *grow*, Nonn.*D.*38.184, al.; *grow into*, *be changed into*, λαῖφος ἀνηέξητο καλύπτρη ib.44.243.

⊕**ἀναερτ-άζω,** = sq., Nonn.*D.*9.55, al. **-άω,** *hang up*, *dedicate*, *AP*6.195 (Arch.), Antip.Sid.*Oxy.*662.53.

**ἀναζάω,** inf. -ζῆν, *return to life*, *be alive again*, *Ev.Luc.*15.24 a 32, Sotion p.183 W.: in Ep. form **-ζώω** Nic.*Fr.*70.5.

⊕**ἀνα-ζεμα,** ατος, τό, *boiling* or *bubbling up*, Sch.Ar.*Av.*1243. **-ζ σις,** εως, ἡ, *boiling up*, of fire, Arist.*Mir.*833$^{a}$22, Sch.Il.*Oxy.*221 x. 18. **-ζεσμός,** ὁ, *irritation*, τῶν οὐλῶν Aët.9.43.

**ἀνα-ζεύγνῡμι** and **-ζευγνύω,** *yoke* or *harness again*, ἀναζευγνύν τὸν στρατόν *move off* the army, Hdt.9.41; ἀ. τὸ στρατόπεδον *break u* the camp, ib.58; ἀ. πρὸς τὸν Ἰσθμὸν τὰς νῆας *withdraw..*, Id.8.60 α'. 2. abs., *break up*, *shift one's quarters*, mostly in part., ἀναζεύξα ἤλαυνε Th.8.108, cf. X.*An.*3.4.37, Ph.*Bel.*103.15: ἀ. ἐκ τῆς Ἀραβία Plu.*Pomp.*42; ἀ. διὰ Συρίας *march through..*, Id.*Ant.*84; ἐπὶ τὰ πράξεις *Chron.Lind.*D.43. 3. *repel*, [ὕβριν] *Inscr.Cos*350. **-ζευξις,** εως, ἡ, *breaking up one's quarters*, *marching forth*, Plu.*Ages.*22; *return home*, Id.*Cor.*31.

**ἀναζέω,** fut. -ζέσω, *boil up*, *bubble up*, ἐκ γῆς S.*Tr.*702; λέγεται ἀναζέσαι πῦρ Arist.*Mir.*833$^{a}$19; of a lake, ib.837$^{b}$9; of bile in the mouth, Aret.*SD*1.15. 2. ἀ. εὐλὰς ἀγεννῶν βασιλέων *boil*, *swarm with* worms, metaph., of Alexander's empire, Plu.2.337a; εὐλαὶ ἀναζέουσιν Id.*Art.*16. b. of sores or boils, *break out*, Lxx *Ex.*9.9. 3. metaph., of passion, *boil over*, Arist.*Pr.*947$^{b}$32, Plu.2.728b; ἀναζείουσα βαρὺν χόλον *boil* with rage, A.R.4.391; ἀνέζεσεν αἷμα Pherecr.18 D.; ἀνέζει ἡ καρδία Them.*Or.*13.172d. II. causal, *make to boil*, Hp.*Acut.*21; ἀναζείουσιν ἀϋτμήν *AP*9.626 (Marian.).

**ἀνάζησις,** εως, ἡ, *living again*, *Theol.Ar.*40.

**ἀναζητ-έω,** *investigate*, τὰς αἰτίας Pl.*Lg.*693a; τὰ ὑπὸ γῆς *Ap.*18b:—Pass., Hdt.1.137, Ar.*Lys.*26, Th.2.8. II. *search out*, *discover*, τὰ παραλελειμμένα ὑπὸ τῶν προτέρων ἀρχείων *OGI*267 (Pergam., iii B.C.); *search for*, μαστροπούς Ph.1.40 **-ησις,** εως, ἡ, *investigation*, Pl.*Criti.*110a: *search for*, τινός Memn.41; *inspection*, ὑδάτων, in pl., Just.*Nov.*26.4 *Intr.* **-ητέον,** *one must search for*, σημεῖον S.E.*M.*8.248.

⊕**ἀναζῠγή,** ἡ, = ἀνάζευξις, Plb.3.44.13, Lxx *Ex.*40.38, etc.

**ἀναζῠγόω,** *push back the bolt* (ζύγωθρον), *unbolt*, τὴν θύραν ἀναζυγώσας Ar.*Fr.*654; *open*, *unfasten* a casket, Hsch.

**ἀναζῡμ-όω,** *raise as by leaven*, *loosen*, χιὼν ἀ. καὶ μανοῖ τὴν γῆν Thphr.*CP*3.23.4, cf. Gal.11.435:—Pass., *ferment*, D.S.1.7. **-ωσις,** εως, ἡ, *fermentation*, γῆς ὑπὸ χιόνος Thphr.*Ign.*18.

**ἀνάζω,** Tarent. for ἀνάσσω, Heraclid.ap.Eust.1654.27.

**ἀναζωγρᾰφ-έω,** *paint completely*, *delineate*, Str.8.3.30; *picture to oneself*, Ph.2.59, Arr.*Epict.*2.18.16, S.E.*M.*7.222:—Pass., *to be painted on*, ἀσπίδες αἷς οὐδὲν ἀνεζωγράφητο μίμημα Ph.2.591; *to be represented*, Diog.Oen.7. **-ημα,** ατος, τό, *memory-image*, Peripatetic word, Alex.Aphr. *de An.*60.6, al. **-ησις,** εως, ἡ, Chrysipp.*Stoic.*2.9, Posidon.ap.Gal.5.474.

⊕**ἀναζωγρ-έω,** *recall to life*, of those in imminent danger of death, Nonn.*D.*13.119, al.: metaph. of poetical works, *rescue from oblivion*, *AP*7.594 (Jul.). 2. *restore to life*, Ὑάκινθον ἀνεζώγρησεν Ἀπόλλων Nonn.*D.*19.102. **-ησις,** εως, ἡ, *restoration to life*, Agath.1.13.

⊕**ἀναζώννῡμι** or **-ύω,** fut. -ζώσω, *gird up again*, *recall to service*, metaph., τινὰ ἐπὶ τοὺς λόγους Them.*Or.*18.224a; τὸ ἕκτον βιβλίον πρὸς τὴν ἀΐδιαν κίνησιν Simp.*in Ph.*1118.6:—Med., ἀ. τὰς ὀσφύας *gird up one's loins*, 1*Ep.Pet.*1.13; ἀ. πέπλους Nonn.*D.*19.73; ἀνεζωσμένοι, Lat. *alte praecincti*, Polycr.ap.Ath.4.139d:—Pass., *to be held in check*, of passions, Ph.1.117. 2. Med., c. acc., πόλεμον *embark on*, Eust.Epiph.p.361 D.

**ἀναζωόω,** *recall to life*, οἱ τοῦ θεοῦ λόγοι ἀ. τὴν ψυχήν Ph.1.643, cf. Sch.E.*Med.*9, Aq.*Ho.*6.2, Sm.*Ps.*29(30).4, al.

⊕**ἀναζωπῠρ-έω,** *rekindle*, *light up again*, in tmesi, ἀν' αὖ σὺ ζωπυρεῖς νείκη νέα E.*El.*1121; θερμῷ τὸ θερμὸν ἀ. Arist.*Spir.*484$^{a}$7; τὴν ὅλην φύσιν Jul.*Or.*4.151c; τὸ χάρισμα τοῦ θεοῦ 2*Ep.Ti.*1.6:—Pass., *to be rekindled*, Pl.*R.*527d, X.*HG*5.4.46 (metaph.); *to be excited*, Iamb.*VP*25.112. II. intr. in Act., Plu.*Pomp.*41, etc. **-ησις,** εως, ἡ, *restoration of strength*, J.*AJ*12.8.1; *regeneration* by heat, of metals, Syn.Alch.p.54 B. **-όω,** = -έω, Olymp. *in Mete.*282.4. **-ωσις,** εως, ἡ, = -ησις, Zos.Alch.p.211 B.

**ἀναζώστρα,** ἡ, (ζώννυμι) kind of *bandage*, Gal.18(1).774.

**ἀνα-ζώω,** v. ἀναζάω. **-ζώωσις,** εως, ἡ, *recalling to life*, Eustr. *in EN*71.25, Sch.E.*Or.*288.

**ἀναθάλλω,** aor. ἀνέθηλα Ael.*VH*5.4, *NA*2.25: aor. 2 ἀνέθαλον *Ep.Phil.*4.10:—*shoot up again*, *sprout afresh*, Ael. ll. cc.:—fut. Pass. in act. sense, ἀναθαλήσεται στάχυς *AP*7.281 (Heracl.): metaph., ἡ σὰρξ ἀ. Lxx *Ps.*27.7. II. trans., *make to flourish*, *revive*, Lxx *Si.*11.22, 50.10, *Ep.Phil.* l. c.

**ἀνα-θάλπω,** *warm again*, *cherish*, *Anacreont.*31.21, J.*AJ*17.6.5, Plu.2.60cb. **-θαλψις,** εως, ἡ, *heat*, τῆς γῆς Olymp. *in Phd.*p.201 N.

**ἀναθαρσ-έω,** Att. **-θαρρέω,** *regain courage*, Ar.*Eq.*806, Th.6.63, 7.71; τινί *at* a thing, Id.6.31; πρὸς ἄλλην αὖθις πεῖραν Plu.*Alex.*31. **-ησις,** Att. **-θάρρησις,** εως, ἡ, *recovery of courage*, Onos.14.1, Eust.1267.22.

**ἀναθαρσύνω,** Att. **-θαρρύνω,** *fill with fresh courage*, X.*Cyr.*5.4.23. 2. intr., = foreg., Plu.*Luc.*14.

**ἀναθαυμάζω,** strengthd. for θαυμάζω, v.l. in D.C.43.13.

**ἀναθεάομαι,** *contemplate again*, Plu.2.586a, Them.*Or.*23.290c.

⊕**ἀνάθεμα,** poet. **ἄνθεμα,** ατος, τό, (ἀνατίθημι) properly, like ἀνάθημα, *anything dedicated*, Theoc.*Ep.*13.2, *AP*6.162 (Mel.), *CIG*2693*d* (Mylasa), al., Phld.*Mus.*p.85 K. 2. *anything devoted to evil*, *an accursed thing*, Lxx *Le.*27.28, *De.*7.26, 13.17, al.; of persons, *Ep.Rom.*9.3, 1*Ep.Cor.*12.3, etc. II. *curse*, *Tab.Defix.Aud.*41 B (Megara, i/ii A.D.), cf. sq.

**ἀναθεματιαῖος**, gloss on ἀνθεμόεις, Sch.Ven.Il.23.885.

**ἀναθεμᾰ-τίζω**, *devote to evil*, Lxx*Nu.*21.2, *Jo.*6.20, al., *Tab.Defix.* *ud.*41 A, *Cod.Just.*1.1.5.3; ἀναθέματι ἀ. Lxx*De.*13.15; but ἀναθέματι ἀ. ἑαυτούς *bind* themselves *by a curse*, c. inf., *Act.Ap.*23.14:—Pass., *to be devoted to evil*, Lxx*Nu.*18.14. II. intr., *curse and swear*, *Ev.Marc.*14.71. **-τικός**, ή, όν, = ἀναθηματικός, πίνακες Roussel *Cultes Égyptiens* 222 (Delos, ii B.C.), D.S.31.8. **-τισμός**, ὁ, *a cursing*, Just.*Nov.*42.1.1: pl., *Cod.Just.*1.3.38, Just.*Nov.*146.1.2.

**ἀναθεραπεύω**, *rear with care*, τοὺς βλαστούς Thphr.*HP*4.13.3.

**ἀναθερίζω**, *reap again*, τὴν κριθοφόρον γῆν Ph.2.390; *glean*, Hsch. s.v. ἀνεκαλαμήσατο.

**ἀναθερμ-αίνω**, *warm up*, *heat again*, *AP*11.55:—Pass., *become warm again*, Hp.*Epid.*1.2, cf. 26.β′, Arist.*HA*569$^{b}$11: πυρετὸς -όμενος Hp.*Prog.*17. **-ανσις**, εως, ἡ, *warming again*, Antyll.ap.Orib.6.10.19.

**ἀνάθεσις**, εως, ἡ, *setting up in public*, *dedicating* of gifts in temples, ἀ. σκευῆς, τρίποδος, Lys.21.2 and 4, cf. Ph.1.592 (pl.); εἰς ἀνάθεσιν τοῖς θεοῖς as *an offering*, *OGI*214.14 (Branchidae). II. *putting off*, *adjournment*, Poll.9.137; τοῦ γάμου Ant.Lib.34.1. III. *laying on*, *imposition*, ἄχθεος Aret.*SA*2.2.

**ἀναθετέον**, (ἀνατίθημι) *one must put off*, Pl.*Lg.*935e; ἀ. τὴν ἄμυναν εἰς τὸν χρόνον Plu.2.817c. II. *one must ascribe*, τί τινι Pl.*Mx* 240e.

**ἀναθέω**, *run up*, ἐπὶ δένδρα Ael.*NA*5.54, etc.: c. acc., τὰ ἀνάντη ib.13.14. 2. of plants, *shoot up*, ib.2.36; τὸ ὀμιχλῶδες..ἀναθέον εἰς ὕψος Gal.18(2).178. II. *run up*, *rise*, Pl.*Ti.*60c.

⊛**ἀναθεωρ-έω**, *examine carefully*, Thphr.*HP*8.6.2, D.S.12.15 (Pass.); *consider a second time*, Thphr.*HP*1.5.1. ⊛**-ησις**, εως, ἡ, *close examination*, D.S.13.35, Plu.2.19e; κατὰ τὴν ἀ. on *further reflection*, Longin.23.2. II. *attention attracted* by an event, *magnam* ἀ. *res habet* Cic.*Att.*14.5.1, cf. ib.9.19.1, 14.6.2.

⊛**ἀναθήκη**· ἀνάθεσις, Hsch.

**ἀναθηλάζω**, *suck up* water, of a tree, Ph.Byz.*Mir.*1.5; τὸ πύον Aët.15.18.

⊛**ἀναθηλέω**, *sprout afresh*, οὐδ' ἀναθηλήσει Il.1.236.

**ἀνάθημα**, ατος, τό, (ἀνατίθημι) *that which is set up*: hence, like ἄγαλμα, *votive offering set up* in a temple, Hdt.1.14,92, S.*Ant.*286, etc.; ἀ. ἐκ λειτουργιῶν Lys.26.4. 2. used by Hom. only in first sense of ἄγαλμα, *delight*, *ornament*, μολπή τ' ὀρχηστύς τε· τὰ γάρ τ' ἀναθήματα δαιτός Od.1.152, cf. 21.430, *IG*14.1390; τοῖς τεκοῦσιν ἀνάθημα βιότου, of children, E.*Fr.*518, cf. Pl.*Hp.Mi.*364b; to help deserving poverty is βασιλικοῦ πλούτου ἀ. καὶ κατασκεύασμα λαμπρότατον D.H.19.14. 3. of a slave in a temple, ἀ. πόλεως *devoted to* this service by the city, E.*Ion* 310.—Cf. ἀνάθεμα.

**ἀναθηματικός**, ή, όν, *consisting of votive offerings*, τιμαί Plb.27.18.2.

**ἀνά-θλασις**, εως, ἡ, = ἔκθλιψις, Erot. **-θλάω**, *crush in pieces*, in aor. ἀνέθλασσα v.l. in Q.S.8.94.

**ἀνα-θλίβω** [ῑ], *force up*, ἐκ τῶν φαρύγγων τοὺς ἀκόλους J.*BJ*5.10.3; μαστὸς ἀ. χεύματα Ναϊάδος *AP*9.668 (Marian.); [ὕδατα] εἰς κρήνην Str.3.5.7:—Pass., 16.2.13, *AP*7.23 (Antip.Sid.), Aret.*SA*1.8. 2. simply, *press*, βυβλίδιον *AP*12.208; of *reducing* a rupture, Archig.ap.Aët.9.28. **-θλιψις**, εως, ἡ, *reduction* of rupture, Orib.*Fr.*85.

**ἄναθλος**, ον, *unathletic*, Luc.*Cal.*12.

**ἀναθολ-όω**, *make turbid*, ᾠά Arist.*GA*753$^{a}$30:—Pass., ἀναθολοῦται τὸ ὕδωρ *HA*592$^{a}$8, cf. Procop.*Aed.*1.5; of urine, Gal.6.252. 2. metaph., ἀ. τινὰ ἐπί τινα *trouble* his mind *with suspicion* against.., Philostr.*VS*2.1.11:—Pass., *to be troubled*, ὑπὸ τῆς ἀνίας ἀνεθολοῦθ' ἡ καρδία Pherecr.116. **-ωσις**, εως, ἡ, *making turbid*, ἀ. ὀπῶν *thick mixture* of the juices of herbs, Pl.*Lg.*824; *a stirring up*, χολῆς *Stoic.*3.56.

**ἀναθορεῖν**, aor. 2 inf. of ἀναθρῴσκω.

**ἀναθόρνῠμαι**, = ἀναθρῴσκω, Ael.*NA*1.30, 12.18:—act. form ἀναθορνύω in D.C.63.28.

**ἀναθορῠβέω**, *cry out loudly*, commonly in applause, ἀ. ὡς εὖ λέγοι Pl.*Prt.*334c, cf. X.*An.*5.1.3; ὡς εὖ εἰπόντος τινὸς ἀ. ib.6.1.30, cf. Pl.*Smp.*198a: abs., *Euthd.*276b.

**ἀνά-θρεμμα**, ατος, τό, *nursling*, λεαίνας Theoc.23.19. **-θρεπτέον**, *one must feed up*, ὄρνεα *Gp.*14.19.1; *one must restore nutrition*, Philum.ap.Orib.45.29.12. ⊛**-θρεπτικός**, ή, όν, *of* or *for feeding up*, Gal.*Thras.*30. **-θρεπτος**, ον, *foster child*, of a slave, Lat. *verna*, App.*BC*4.43. ⊛**-θρεψις**, εως, ἡ, *renewal*, *restoration* in physiological sense, αἱ ἀ. σφαλεραί Hp.*Aph.*1.3.

**ἀναθρέω**, *look up at*, *view narrowly*, E.*Hec.*808; ἀ. ὃ ὄπωπεν Pl.*Cra.*399c:—Pass., τὰ ἔργα ἐκ τῶν λόγων ἀναθρούμενα *compared with*.., Th.4.87.

**ἀναθρηνέω**, *lift up one's voice in wailing*, D.C.74.13, Sch.E.*Or.*1335.

**ἀνάθρησις**, εως, ἡ, *close observation*, Timo 61.

**ἀνάθριξ**· *licinus*, *reburrus*, *Gloss.*

**ἀναθρύπτομαι**, *indulge in affectation*, pf. inf. Pass. ἀνατεθρύφθαι Poll.6.185.

⊛**ἀναθρῴσκω**, poet. and Ion. **ἀνθρ-**: aor. 2 -θορεῖν X.*Lac.*2.3: aor. 1 subj. ἀναθρώξωσι Opp.*H.*3.293:—*spring up*, ὕψι δ' ἀναθρῴσκων πέτεται Il.13.140; of blood, Emp.100.8; of men, ὃς δ' ἀμβώσας μέγα ἀναθρῴσκει Hdt.7.18, cf. *AP*9.774 (Glauc.); ἀναθρῴσκει ἐπὶ τὸν ἵππον Hdt.3.64.

**ἀναθυάω**, *to be again at heat*, of swine, Arist.*HA*546$^{a}$28, 573$^{b}$8; prov., γραῦς ἀναθυᾷ Diogenian.4.10, cf. Phot.p.118 R., and prob. in Pherecr.35.

**ἀναθυμί-αμα**, ατος, τό, *result of exhalation*, Chrysipp.*Stoic.*2.196, cj. in Zeno ib.1.35. **-ασις**, εως, ἡ, *rising in vapour*, *exhalation*, Arist.*Mete.*365$^{b}$22, cf. Thphr.*Fr.*33, Petron.47, Plu.2.365e, Hdn.3.14.8: pl., Corn.*ND*7, Porph.*Abst.*1.47; of sacrifices, Jul.*Caes.*333d. 2. of the soul, Heraclit.12. 3. of bodily processes, ἡ ἐκ τῶν χυμῶν ἀ. Gal.*UP*11.14, cf. 6.17. **-άω**, *vaporize*, Thphr.*Ign.*38:—Pass., *steam up*, *rise in fume* or *vapour*, ἀναθυμιωμένης διὰ τῶν φλεβῶν τῆς τροφῆς Arist.*PA*652$^{b}$36, cf. 653$^{a}$4; of fire, Id.*Mete.*341$^{a}$7; of the earth, *send forth vapour*, ib.360$^{b}$32; οἶνος ἀναθυμιαθεὶς Plu.2.432e; of smoke, Luc.*VH*1.23: metaph., μῖσος ἀναθυμιᾶται Plb.15.25.24; of the soul, ψυχαὶ ἀπὸ τῶν ὑγρῶν -ῶνται Heraclit.12. II. Med., *draw up vapour*, οἱ ἡρακλειτίζοντές φασιν ἐκ τῆς θαλάττης τὸν ἥλιον ἀ. Arist.*Pr.*934$^{b}$36.

**ἀναθυράζω**, only aor. ἀνεθύραξεν· ἀνεθυμώθη, Hsch.

**ἀναθυρόω**, *dress* vertical joints of masonry so that only their edges are in contact, *IG*7.3073.121,142 (Lebad.).

**ἀναθύω** (A), *dart up*, *burst forth*, ὕδωρ Call.*Cer.*30.

**ἀναθύω** (B), *sacrifice again*, in Pass., D.C.37.46. 2. *dedicate*, *IG*5(2).554,555 (Melpea). 3. ἀναθύοντες· ἀναιροῦντες, παραβαίνοντες, Hsch.

**ἀναθωΰξας**· ἀναβοήσας, Hsch.

⊛**ἀναίδεια**, Ep. and Ion. **ἀναιδείη**; Att. also **ἀναιδείᾱ** Ar.*Fr.*226, poet. **ἀναιδία** Hdn.Gr.2.453:—*shamelessness*, ἀναιδείην ἐπιειμένε Il.1.149; ἀναιδείης ἐπιβῆναι Od.22.424; ἡ γαστὴρ φρένας παρήγαγεν εἰς ἀναιδείην Archil.78; ἀναιδείῃ διαχρεώμενοι Hdt.7.210, cf. 6.129; ἀναιδείας πλέα S.*El.*607; μετ' ἀναιδείας, = ἀναιδῶς, Pl.*Phdr.*254d; εἰς τοῦθ' ἧκεν ἀναιδείας D.18.22. II. in the Areopagus, λίθος ἀναιδείας was the stone of *unforgivingness*, on which stood an accuser who demanded the full penalty of the law against one accused of homicide (v. αἰδέομαι II.3), Paus.1.28.5; cf. ὕβρις.

**ἀναίδεστον**· ἄμοιρον, ἄτιμον, Hsch.

**ἀναιδεύομαι**, *behave impudently*, Ar.*Eq.*397 codd., Phld.*Rh.*1.251 S.

**ἀναιδήμων**, ον, *shameless*: in Adv. -μόνως Gal.17(1).895.

⊛**ἀναίδην**, faulty form for ἀνέδην (q.v.), Procop.*Arc.*22.

⊛**ἀναιδής**, ές, (αἰδώς) *shameless*, of Agamemnon, ὦ μέγ' ἀναιδές Il.1.158; of Penelope's suitors, Od.1.254, al.; ὦ θρέμμ' ἀναιδές S.*El.*622. 2. c. gen., Κυδοιμὸν ἀναιδέα δηϊοτῆτος *ruthless* in havoc, Il.5.593. II. of things, as, in Od.11.598, the stone of Sisyphus is called λᾶας ἀναιδής *the reckless*, *ruthless* stone, cf. Il.4.521, 13.139; πότμος ἀ. Pi.*O.*10(11).105; ἐλπὶς ἀ. *greedy*, Id.*N.*11.45; ἃ πέπονθ' ἀναιδῆ the *shame* that I have suffered, S.*OC*516; λόγοι τῶν ἀναιδῶν ἀναιδέστεροι Ar.*Eq.*385: τὸ ἀναιδές = ἀναίδεια, βλέφαρα πρὸς τἀνειδὲς ἀγαγών E.*IA*379; ἔνθα τἀνειδὲς κρατεῖ Diph.111b; εἰς ἀναιδὲς..δός μοι σεαυτόν S.*Ph.*83; ἐπὶ τὸ ἀναιδέστερον τραπέσθαι Hdt.7.39. III. Adv. -δῶς S.*OT*354, E.*Alc.*694, Ar.*Th.*525, etc.: Sup. -έστατα Heraclit.15.

**ἀναίδητος**, ον, = foreg., A.R.3.92, 4.360.

**ἀναιδίζομαι**, v.l. for ἀναιδεύομαι, Ar.*Eq.*397 ap.*AB.*

**ἀναιδομάχας**, ὁ, *ruthless in fight*, κάπρος B.5.105.

**ἀναιή**· τροφός, τιθήνη, Hsch. (leg. ἀμμίη).

**ἀναιθύσσω**, *stir up*, *rouse*, S.*Fr.*542 (dub.); φλόγα E.*Tr.*344.

**ἀναίθω**, *light up*, *set on fire*, E.*Cyc.*331; τὸν Ἅλιον αὐτόν Mosch.1.23:—Pass., *to be inflamed*, Opp.*C.*2.188: metaph. of anger, Max.Tyr.24.9. II. *blaze up*, ἀνῇθον..λαμπτῆρες A.*Ch.*536 (Sch.).

**ἀναίκλεια**· ἄδειπνα, Hsch.

**ἀναίλιπος** (cod. -λειπως)· ἀνυπόδητος, Hsch.; cf. νήλιπος.

**ἀναιμακτί**, Adv. of sq., *without bloodshed*, Them.*Or.*7.90a, Hsch.

⊛**ἀναίμακτος**, ον, *bloodless*, *unstained with blood*, ἀ. φυγαί A.*Supp.*196; χρώς E.*Ph.*264; βωμός Pyth.ap.D.L.8.22; ἀ. κεν ἰαύοις Nic.*Th.*90; ἀρχή, νίκη, Them.*Or.*5.66d, 2.37c, cf. Antyll.ap.Orib.44.23.32.

**ἀναίμᾰτος**, ον, = ἄναιμος, A.*Eu.*302, Aenigm.ap.Ath.2.63b.

**ἀναιμία**, ἡ, *want of blood*, Arist.*PA*652$^{b}$26.

**ἀναιμόδιτον**, τό, = ἀνδράχνη, Hsch.

**ἀναιμορράγητος**, ον, *without haemorrhage*, Antyll.ap.Orib.45.24.15, Leonid.ap.Aët.15.5.

⊛**ἄναιμος**, ον, (αἷμα), opp. ἔναιμος, *bloodless*, of parts of the body, Pl.*Ti.*70c, *Prt.*321b, Arist.*HA*495$^{a}$4: Comp., 520$^{b}$33, al. II. of animals, Id.*PA*678$^{a}$33, al. 2. generally, of colour, νᾶπυ ἀναιμότερον κεχρωσμένον Aët.1.298. 3. metaph., χλωρὰ καὶ ἄ. τὰ πράγματα Gorg.*Fr.*16. III. *shedding no blood*, πολλοὺς δὲ βροντῆς πνεῦμ' ἄ. ὤλεσεν E.*Fr.*982; ἀ. νίκη D.C.68.19.

**ἀναιμόσαρκος**, ον, *with bloodless flesh*, of the cicada, *Anacreont.*43.17.

**ἀναιμότης**, ητος, ἡ, = ἀναιμία, Arist.*PA*676$^{a}$31.

**ἀναιμόχρους**, ουν, *of bloodless complexion*, Gal.14.326.

**ἀναίμων**, ον, = ἄναιμος, *bloodless*, epith. of the gods, Il.5.342; of cuttlefish, Ion Trag.36; of wine, Plu.2.692e.

⊛**ἀναιμωτί**, Adv. *without shedding blood*, οὐ γὰρ ἀναιμωτί γ' ἐμάχοντο Il.17.363, cf. Od.18.149, Ph.1.323, al., Gal.2.604, Them.*Or.*16.213a.

⊛**ἀναίνομαι**, impf. ἠναινόμην, Ep. ἀναινόμην, late also ἀνῃνόμην Agath.1.13: aor. ἀνηνάμην Alciphr.3.37, subj. ἀνήνηται, inf. ἀνήνασθαι: 1. c. acc., *refuse* or *reject with contempt*, *spurn*, σὲ δ' ἀναίνεται ἠδὲ σὰ δῶρα Il.9.679; ὃς δέ κ' ἀνήνηται [σφέας] ib.510; τῶν ἄλλων οὔτινα ἀναίνομαι *on* no one of the rest *do I turn my back*, Od.8.212; and without a notion of contempt, πρὶν μὲν ἀναίνετο ἔργον ἀεικές *refused*, *declined to do* it, ib.3.265; χαλεπόν κεν ἀνήνασθαι δόσιν εἴη 'twould be hard *to refuse* a gift, ib.4.651; ὡς μηδὲν ἀναίνοιντο ἔργον X.*Cyr.*2.1.31. 2. *renounce*, *disown*, φάος..οὐκ ἠναίνετο A.*Ag.*300;

οὐδ' οἷόν τ' ἀνήνασθαι πόσιν E.*Med.*237; of sexual favours, φιλότητα καὶ εὐνήν Hom.*Epigr.*12.2; ἀναίνεται δὲ λέκτρα E.*Hipp.*14, cf. *El.* 311, Pl.Com.181, Men.446; ἡμᾶς..ἀναίνοιτ' ἂν ἡ τοῦ διαλέγεσθαι δύναμις Pl.*Phlb.*57e; εἰ..ἀναίνει Φορμίωνα κηδεστήν D.36.31. II. c. inf., *refuse, decline* to do, ἠναίνετο λοιγὸν ἀμῦναι Il.18.450; ἔζεσθαι μὲν ἀνήνατο 23.204; and with pleon. neg., ἀναίνετο μηδὲν ἑλέσθαι he *declined* to take anything, 18.500; οὐκ ἀναίνομαι θανεῖν A.*Ag.*1652, cf. *Supp.*801; εἰ..ἀναίνεται εἰ ἐγὼ ἔσομαι υἱὸς Μενεκλέους *repudiates the prospect of* my being.., Is.2.27. III. abs., *refuse*, αἴδεσθεν μὲν ἀνήνασθαι Il.7.93; *deny*, οὐδ' αὐτὸς ἀ. 9.116; ἐπειδὴ πάμπαν ἀναίνεαι Od.14.149; ἀναινόμενος ταῦτα D.61.48. IV. c. part., *disown* doing or having done, νικώμενος λόγοισιν οὐκ ἀναίνομαι *I am not ashamed*, A.*Ag.*583; ἀναίνομαι τὸ γῆρας ὑμῶν εἰσορῶν *I am ashamed* to look on your old age, E.*Ba.*251; θανοῦσα δ' οὐκ ἀναίνομαι *IA* 1503, cf. *HF* 1124.—Chiefly poet., once in Pl.

**ἀναίρ-εμα**, ατος, τό, = ἐλώριον, Sch.A.R.2.264. **-εσις**, εως, ἡ, *taking up* or *away*, esp. of dead bodies for burial, ὀστέων E.*Or.*404; νεκρῶν Th.3.109, 113; οἳ ἂν μὴ εὑρεθῶσιν ἐς ἀναίρεσιν 2.34, cf. Antipho 5.68, Lys.2.7; ἀναίρεσιν δοῦναι E.*Supp.*18; in a sea-fight, νεκρῶν ἢ ναυαγίων ἀ. Th.7.72; τῶν ναυαγῶν X.*HG*1.7.5. 2. *taking up*, ἀ. καὶ θέσις ὅπλων Pl.*Lg.*814a, cf. Antipho 3.3.6. 3. *undertaking*, ἔργων Pl.*Lg.*847b. II. *destruction*, X.*HG*6.3.5; τειχῶν καὶ πόλεων D.19.141; φθορὰ ἡ κατ' ἀναίρεσιν *Stoic.*3.266. 2. *slaying, putting to death*, Lxx *Nu.*11.15, J.*AJ*5.2.11, Plu.2.1051d; *banishment*, Hp.*Decent.*2. 3. *repeal*, δογμάτων Plu.*Cic.*34; *quashing* of indictment, Hermog.*Stat.*3. 4. *direct confutation* of arguments, opp. διαίρεσις (confutation by drawing a distinction), Arist.*SE* 183ᵃ10; *destruction* (by argument), τινός Phld.*Sign.*12. 5. Astrol., = ἀκτινοβολία, Thrasyll.ap.Porph.*in Ptol.*189. **-ετέον**, *one must take up* or *take away*, Dsc.5.99; *one must put to death, kill*, Ph.2.313, Porph.*Abst.*3.26. **-ετήριος**, α, ον, = ἀναιρετικός, Tz. ad Hes.*Op.* 142. **-έτης**, ου, ὁ, *destroyer, murderer*, Sch.Ar.*Pl.*1147. II. Astrol., *Anareta*, a planet *cutting short* human life, Balbill. in *Cat. Cod.Astr.*8(4).236. **-ετικός**, ή, όν, *destructive*, Arist.*Rh.*1386ᵃ6; ἀ. τινος Ph.*Fr.*103 H.; ἀ. ἀλλήλων mutually *destructive*, Plu.2.427e, Iamb.*Myst.*5.11; of plants, *poisonous*, Gal.14.57, Dsc.1.129; φάρμακα Men.Prot.p.47 D. Adv. **-κῶς** *negatively* D.L.9.75. 2. Astrol., *having the nature of* ἀναιρέτης II, Ptol.*Tetr.*127. **-έτις**, -έτιδος, ἡ, fem. of ἀναιρέτης II, *Cat.Cod.Astr.*8(4).235.

**ἀν-αίρετος**, ον, (αἱρέομαι) *incapable of choosing*, Timo 72. II. Pass., opp. αἱρετός, Simp.*in Epict.*p.14 D., al.

***ἀναιρέω**, pf. ἀνήρηκα (ἀνειρ- dub. in *Com.Adesp.*18.6 D.): (v. αἱρέω):—*take up*, ἀνελόντες ἀπὸ χθονὸς *having raised* the victim from the ground, so as to cut its throat (cf. αὐερύω), Od.3.453. 2. *take up and carry off, bear away*, esp. prizes, ἄεθλια Il.23.736, cf. 551; στεφανηφόρους ἀγῶνας ἀναραιρηκότα Hdt.5.102; Ὀλύμπια ἀναραιρηκὼς 6.36, cf. B.I.1. 3. simply, *take up*, παῖδα Pi.*P.*9.61; τὰ ὀστᾶ Th.1. 126. 4. *take up* bodies for burial, ἀνελόντες καὶ κατακλαύσαντες Ar. *V.*386, cf. X.*An.*6.4.9; more common in Med., v. infr. B.I.3. II. *make away with, destroy*, of men, *kill*, Hdt.4.66; πολλοὺς ἀναιρῶν A.*Ch.*990; σὲ μὲν ἡμετέρα ψῆφος ἀ. E.*Andr.*517; θανάτοις ἀ. Pl.*Lg.* 870d; ἐκ πολιτείας τοιαῦτα θηρία ἀ. Din.3.19, etc. 2. of things, *abrogate, annul*, ὅρους ἀνεῖλον πολλαχῇ πεπηγότας Sol.36.4; νόμον Aeschin.3.39; διαθήκας Is.1.14; στήλας And.1.103; ἀταξίαν D.3.35, etc.; ἐκ μέσου ἀ. βλασφημίας Id.10.36; τηλικαύτην ἀνελόντας μαρτυρίαν Id.28.5; *abolish*, τὰς τῶν παρανόμων γραφάς Arist.*Ath.*29.4:— Pass., ἀνῄρηνται ὀλιγαρχίαι X.*Cyr.*1.1.1. 3. *destroy* an argument, *confute* it, Arist.; esp. *confute directly*, opp. διαιρέω (v. ἀναίρεσις II.4), Arist.*SE* 176ᵇ36, al.; ἀ. ἑαυτὸν *confute* oneself, Olymp.*in Mete.*25. 14. 4. in argument, *do away with*, τὰς ὑποθέσεις Pl.*R.*533c; *deny*, opp. τιθέναι, S.E.*P.*1.192, al. III. *appoint, ordain*, of oracle's answer to inquiry, ὁ θεὸς αὐτοῖς ἀ. παραδοῦναι Th.1.25; οὓς ἂν ὁ θεὸς ἀνέλῃ Pl.*Lg.*865d, cf. 642d; ἀνεῖλεν θεοῖς οἷς ἔδει θύειν X.*An.*3.1.6: also c. acc. et inf., ἣν τὸ χρηστήριον ἀνέλῃ μιν βασιλέα εἶναι Hdt.1. 13, etc.: abs., *answer, give a response*, ἀνεῖλε τὸ χρηστήριον ibid.; ἀ. τι περί τινος *give an oracle* about a thing, Pl.*Lg.*914a; μαντείας ἀ. D. *Ep.*1.16:—Pass., Id.21.51.

B. Med., *take up for oneself, take up, pick up*, οὐλοχύτας ἀνέλοντο Il.1.449; ἀσπίδα, ἔγχος, 11.32, 13.296; κυνέην Hdt.1.84; δίκτυα Arist. *HA* 602ᵇ9; *achieve, win*, ἀ. τὴν Ὀλυμπιάδα, τὴν νίκην, Hdt.6.70, 103, D.H.5.47; generally, ἀ. ἐπιφροσύνας *take* thought, Od.19.22; εὐδαιμονίαν Pi.*N.*7.56, cf. Thgn.281; in bad sense, ὄνειδος σπαργάνων ἀ. S.*OT* 1035; εἴ σ' ἀνελοίμην if *I should take* thee *into my service*, Od.18. 357; σῖτα ἀ. *get* forage, Hdt.4.128; ποινὴν τῆς Αἰσώπου ψυχῆς ἀ. *exact* vengeance for.., Id.2.134. 2. *take up and carry off, snatch*, κούρας ἀνέλοντο θύελλαι Od.20.66; ἀναιρούμενος οἴκαδε φέρειν Pl.*Lg.* 914b; ἀνείλατο (for the form cf. Hsch.) δαίμων *Epigr.Gr.*404.1. 3. *take up for burial* (cf. A.I.4), Hdt 4.14, Th.4.97, etc.; πατέρων ἀρίστων σώμαθ' ὧν ἀνειλόμην E.*Supp.*1167; τὰ ὀστέα Hdt.2.41; of the ashes of the dead, πυρὸς ἀ. ἄθλιον βάρος S.*El.*1140; of one still living, E.*Hel.* 1616, X.*HG*6.4.13; τοὺς ναυαγοὺς ib.1.7.4, cf. 11; τοὺς δέκα στρατηγοὺς τοὺς οὐκ ἀνελομένους τοὺς ἐκ τῆς ναυμαχίας Pl.*Ap.*32b:—Pass., ἀναιρεθέντων τῶν νεκρῶν..ὑγιὴς ἀνῃρέθη Id.*R.*614b, al. 4. *take up in one's arms*, Il.16.8: hence, *take up* new-born children, *own* them, Plu.*Ant.*36, cf. Ar.*Nu.*531; *take up* an exposed child, Men. *Sam.*159, cf. *BGU* 1110, etc. 5. *conceive in the womb*, c. acc., Hdt. 2.108, 6.69. 6. *take up* money at interest, D.50.17. 7. *take up* a lease, *Michel* 1359 (Chios). cf. *BCH* 27.204. 8. *withdraw* money from a bank, etc., αὐτὸς ἀνελέσθω *IG* 5(2).159. II. *take upon oneself, undertake*, πόνους Hdt.6.108; πόλεμόν τινι war *again*[st] one, Id.5.36; πολέμους ἀναιρούμεσθα E.*Supp.*492, cf. D.1.7; ἀ. ἔχθ[ρας] Pl.*Phdr.*233c, D.6.20; ἀ. δημόσιον ἔργον *undertake, contract for* [the] *execution of* a work, Pl.*Lg.*921d, cf. a, b, D.53.21. 2. *accept* [as] *one's own, adopt*, γνώμην Hdt.7.16.α'; τὰ οὐνόματα τὰ ἀπὸ τῶν βα[ρ]βάρων ἥκοντα 2.52; ἀ. φιλοψυχίην *entertain* a love for life, 6.29. II[I.] *rescind, cancel*, συγγραφήν, συνθήκας, etc., D.34.31, 48.46, *IG* 7.317 (Orchom. Boeot., iii B.C.).

**ἄναιρον**· ὄνειρον (Cret.), Hsch.; cf. ὄναρ.

**ἀναίρω**, *raise, lift up*, Aen.Tact.23.4:—Med., Ἕως γὰρ λευκὸν ὄμ[μα] ἀναίρεται E.*El.*102:—Pass., ἀναρθείς, of Ganymede, *AP* 12.67.

**ἀναισθής**, ές, = ἀναίσθητος, Max.Tyr.17.5, 37.5.

***ἀναισθ-ησία**, ἡ, *lack of sensation*, Pl.*Ti.*74e, Epicur.*Fr.*495; μετ' ἀναισθησίας *without the aid of sense-perception*, Pl.*Ti.*52b; *unconsciousness*, *Ax.*365d; *insensibility* to pleasure or pain, Arist.*EN* 1109ᵃ4, 1119ᵃ7; *insensibility* under surgical treatment, Dsc.5.140. 2. *mental obtuseness*, D.22.64. 3. *stupor*, Aret.*SA* 1.5. **-ησιολογία**, ἡ, *insensibility-theory*, Phld.*D.*1.24. **-ητεύομαι**, = sq., condemned by Phryn.329. **-ητέω**, *lack perception*, D.18.221; ἀ. ταλαιπωρίας *to be without sense of* weariness, J.*AJ* 11.5.8; συμφορῶν ἀ. *BJ* 4.3.10: abs., Epicur.*Ep.*1p.21U., Sor.2.49, prob. in Porph.*Abst.*1.39. *** -ητος**, ον, *without sense* or *feeling*, Thrasymach. 1, Pl.*Ti.*75e; ἀ. τινός *without sense of* a thing, Id.*Lg.*843a; ἀ. καὶ νεκρός Men.705; ἀ. ψαύσιος καὶ τρώσιος Aret.*SD*2.12; ἀ. ἡ ἁφή *the sense* of touch *is lost*, ib.1.7. Adv. ἀναισθήτως, πάντων ἔχειν Hp. *Epid.*3.17.ιε'; ἀ. ἔχειν to be *insensible* or *indifferent*, Isoc.12.112, cf. Th.1.82; ἀ. διακεῖσθαι Arist.*EE* 1231ᵃ1. 2. *without perception* or *common sense, wanting tact, stupid*, Th.6.86; οἱ ἀ. Θηβαῖοι *those blockheads*.., D.18.43, cf. Phld.*Rh.*1.215S.: τὸ ἀναίσθητον, = ἀναισθησία, Th.1.69. Adv. -ως Phld.*Rh.*1.227S. II. Pass., *unfelt*, θάνατος Th.2.43. 2. *not perceptible by sense*, ἀόρατον καὶ ἄλλως ἀ. Pl.*Ti.*52a, cf. Phld.*Piet.*20, etc.; ἐν ἀ. χρόνῳ in an *unappreciable* time, Arist.*Ph.*222ᵇ15, cf. *Po.*1450ᵇ39.

**ἀν-αίσιμος**, ον, *unseemly*, δῆρις Emp.27a.

***ἀναισιμ-όω**, impf. ἀναισίμουν (v.infr.): aor. subj. ἀναισιμώσωσι (v. infr.): pf. ἀνῃσίμωκα v.l. in X.*Cyr.*2.2.15:—Pass., aor. ἀναισιμώθην: pf. ἀναισίμωμαι:—*use up, use, spend, consume*, τὸν χοῦν.. ἀναισίμου *he used up* the earth, Hdt.1.185; ἵνα μὴ τὸν σῖτον ἀναισιμώσωσι 3.150:—Pass., οἶνος ἀναισιμοῦται 2.60; εὐζώνῳ ἀνδρὶ πέντε ἡμέραι ἀναισιμοῦνται 1.72, cf. 2.11, 5.53: often ἀ. ἔς τι *to be used* for a purpose, or *spent* upon a thing, τεσσεράκοντα καὶ ἑκατὸν τάλαντα ἐς τὴν ἵππον ἀναισιμοῦτο 3.90; ὅσα ἐς συρμαίην ἀναισιμώθη 2.125; ταλάντων χιλιάδες ἀναρίθμητοι ἀναισίμωνται (sc. ἐς τὴν πυραμίδα) ib.134; also κοῦ ταῦτα ἀναισιμοῦται; where (i.e. how) *are these disposed of?* 3.6; δεῖ ἔτι φράσαι ἵνα ἡ γῆ ἀναισιμώθη 1.179. (ἀνα-, αἴσιμος, q.v.; Ion. (and v.l. in X.*Cyr.*2.2.15); κατ- in Com., otherwise not found in Att., who use ἀναλίσκω, δαπανάω.) *** -ωμα**, ατος, τό, = Att. δαπάνη, *that which is used up*, τὰ ἀναισιμώματα τῇ στρατιῇ the war-*expenses*, Hdt.5.31.

**ἀν-αίσιος**, ον, *ill-omened, unfortunate*, Lyd.*Mag.*3.45.

***ἀναΐσσω** [ᾰνᾰ], Att. contr. **ἀνᾴσσω**, used also by Pi.:—*start up*, μὴ πρὶν ἀναΐξειαν Ἀρήϊοι υἷες Ἀχαιῶν Il.4.114; ὅτε δὴ..ἀναΐξειεν Ὀδυσσεύς whenever *he rose to speak*, 3.216; of a spring, *gush forth*, 22.148: so in later Poets, μυελὸς στέρνων ἐντὸς ἀνᾴσσων *springing fresh* within the breast, A.*Ag.*77 cj. Herm., cf. *Pers.*96 cj. Brunck; ὀρθοὶ ἀνῇξαν πάντες E.*Hel.*1600; βωμὸς ἀνᾴσσων an altar *rising up*, Pi.*O.*13.107.—Rare in Prose, ἀναΐσσει νόσημα Hp.*Prog.*19; ἀναΐξας, of a hare, X.*Cyn.*6.17. 2. c. acc., ἀναΐξας.. ἅρμα καὶ ἵππους *having leapt upon* it, Il.24.440. 3. Act., *cause to start up*, ἀνήϊξεν δὲ φέβεσθαι Opp.*C.*1.107.

**ἀναισχής**, ές, = ἀναίσχυντος, *AB* 207.

**ἀναισχυντ-έω**, *to be* ἀναίσχυντος, *to be shameless, behave impudently*, Ar.*Lys.*460, Th.1.37, And.2.4; πρός τινα X.*Smp.*8.33: also c. part., ἀναισχυντεῖ ποιῶν *he is impudent enough* to do, Ar.*Th.*708; ἀ. διαλεγόμενος Pl.*Cri.*53c: c. acc. cogn., ποῖα..ἀναισχυντοῦσιν Arist. *Rh.*1383ᵇ12. 2. trans., *treat shamelessly*, and Pass., *to be so treated*, ὁ ἀναισχυντῶν πρὸς τὸν ἀναισχυντούμενον ib.1412ᵃ6. **-ημα**, ατος, τό, *impudent act* or *speech*, Hyp.*Fr.*226, Gal.*UP*10.9. **-ία**, ἡ, *shamelessness, impudence*, Ar.*Th.*702, D.20.166, etc.; ὑπ' ἀναισχυντίας Pl.*Smp.*192a.

**ἀναισχυντο-γράφος**, ὁ, *obscene writer*, Timae.141. **-ποιός**, όν, *doing shameless deeds*, Procop.*Arc.*9.

**ἀναίσχυντος**, ον, *shameless, impudent*, Alc.*Supp.*21.5, E.*IA* 327, etc., Ar.*Pax* 182, And.4.17, Pl.*Lg.*671c (Comp.), *Ap.*17b (Sup.), etc.:—τὸ ἀναίσχυντον, = ἀναισχυντία, E.*IA* 1144. Adv. -τως Pl.*Ap.* 31b: Sup. ἀναισχυντότατα ἀνθρώπων D.27.18. II. of things, *shameful, abominable*, βορά E.*Cyc.*416; θῆκαι Th.2.52.

**ἀναίτητος**, ον, *unasked*, Pi.*Fr.*169.7 (fem. -τήτη); *unclaimed*, γῆ *Sammelb.*4298.3.

**ἀναιτιάτος**, ον, *unblamed*, Ion Trag.ap.Phot.p.113R.

**ἀναιτιολόγητος**, ον, *for which no cause can be assigned*, Dsc.*Ther. Praef.*, Alex.Aphr.*Pr.*1.52, Ptol.*Tetr.*111.

**ἀναίτιος**, ον, also α, ον Hdt.9.110, A.*Ch.*873:—in the best authors, only of persons, *not being the fault* or *cause of* a thing, *guiltless*, ἀναίτιον αἰτιάασθαι Il.13.775, cf. Od.20.135, etc.; αἰτία ἑλομένου, θεὸς ἀ. Pl.*R.*617e; ἀναίτιος ἀθανάτοις *guiltless* before the gods, Hes.*Op.*827, cf. E.*Med.*730; ἀ. παρά τινι X.*Cyr.*1.6.10; ἀ. αἷμα ἐκχέαι *SIG* 1181. 6. 2. c. gen. rei, *guiltless of* a thing, Hdt.1.129, 7.233, etc; φόνου, κακῶν, A.*Ag.*1505, *Ch.*873; κακίας Pl.*Ti.*42d; ἀφροσύνης X.*Cyr.*1.

10: οὐκ ἀναίτιόν ἐστι, c. inf., *it is blamable* to do, ib.5.5.22. II. *not being the cause*, τὸ ἀ. τιθέναι ὡς αἴτιον Arist.*APr.*65$^{b}$16, cf. *Rh.* 1401$^{b}$30; *having no cause, unjustifiable*, κολάσεις Phld.*Ir.*p.52 W. Adv. -ως *not in the form of a cause*, ἀ. τὴν αἰτίαν ἔχειν Plot.6.7.2; *without assigning any reason*, ὁλοσχερῶς καὶ ἀ. λεκτέον Simp.*in Cael.*665.11. III. *uncaused*, Plot.3.1.1, Phlp.*in Ph.*277.1: Sup., Sch.E.*Hipp.*672. Adv. -ως *without a cause*, Gal.10.36, S.E.*P.*3.67, Simp.*in Ph.*641.10; ἀ. γίγνεσθαι Alex.Aphr.*in Metaph.*309.15.

**ἄναιτος**, v. ἄνατος.

**ἀναιχμάλωτος**, ον, *not made captive*, Hsch. s. v. ἀπόρθητοι.

***ἀναιωρέω**, *lift up*, ἑαυτὸν..ἐς ἠέρα..ἀνῃώρησε Coluth.155: plpf. Pass. ἀνῃώρητο Nonn.*D.*16.342.

**ἀνάκα**, dub. in *IG*5(2).p.xxv.72 (Arc. = ἡνίκα).

**ἀνακαγχάζω**, *burst out laughing*, Hp.*Ep.*17; μέγα πάνυ ἀνακαγχάσας Pl.*Euthd.*300d; ἀνεκάγχασε μάλα σαρδάνιον *R.*337a.

***ἀνακαθ-αίρω**, *clear out, clear completely*, τοὺς πόρους the ducts, Anaxipp.1.16; *cleanse* ulcer, Paul.Aeg.4.41; τάφρους D.H.8.13; *clear* streets, *OGI*483.79 (Pergam.); τράφως καὶ ῥόως..ἀγκοθαρίοντι (= ἀνακαθαροῦσι) *Tab.Heracl.*1.132; *prune*, Thphr.*HP*1.3.3; *clear* ground for foundations, *SIG*$^{2}$587.46 (Eleusis, iv B.C.), *BCH*29.468 (Delos, iii B.C.), *IG*12(2).11.3 (Mytilene):—Med., ἀνακαθηράμενον τὸ χωρίον *Ath.Mitt.*31.134 (Athens, iv B.C.), *IG*2.1054.8 (iv B.C.):—Pass., ib.7.3073.64 (Lebad.); of a mine, *to be cleared out*, Arist.*Mir.* 834$^{a}$27; οἰκόπεδα D.H.14.2; of the air, *become quite clear*, Plu.*Flam.* 8. II. Med., *clear* or *sweep away*, τὸ βάρβαρον ἀνακαθαίρεσθαι ἐκ τῆς θαλάσσης Pl.*Mx.*241d (so Act. in D.H.1.12); τὰ πρὸ ποδῶν Plb. 10.30.8; τὴν παραλίαν ἀ. Plu.*Alex.*17. 2. *extract*, μεταλλεῖα Pl.*Lg.* 678d. 3. ἀνακαθαίρεσθαι λόγον *clear up* or *enucleate* a subject, μέθης πέρι, σμικροῦ πράγματος, παμμήκη λόγον -όμενος ib.642a. 4. Medic., *cleanse thoroughly*, Hp.*Aph.*5.8: metaph., *purify*, τῆς κακίας γῆν καὶ θάλατταν Jul.*ad Them.*254a. **-αρμα**, ατος, τό, (in pl.) *rubbish, lumber*, dub. in Hsch. s. v. ὀξυθύμια. ***-αρσις**, εως, ἡ, *clearing away*, of rubbish, Plb.5.100.6; λίθων Ph.*Bel.*100.41; *cleaning*, of sewers, D.H.3.67; of streets, etc., *OGI*483.51 (Pergam.); of ground for foundations, *SIG*$^{2}$587.19. 2. Medic., *cleansing*, Gal.8.327. 3. *end of an eclipse*, opp. ἔμπτωσις, Heph.Astr.1.21. II. *clearing up an obscure passage, explanation*, Suid. **-αρτικός**, ή, όν, *promoting vomiting*, Dsc.1.71. II. *for cleansing*, Meges ap.Orib.44. 24.7, cf. Paul.Aeg.4.41.

**ἀνακάθημαι**, *sit upright*, Luc.*Ocyp.*112.

**ἀνακαθίζω**, *set up*: whence Med., *sit up*, εἰς τὴν κλίνην Pl.*Phd.* 60b. II. intr., *sit up*, Hp.*Prog.*3, Aen.Tact.27.8; δὶς ἑπτὰ [μηνῶν] -ει [τὰ βρέφη] *Theol.Ar.*48; of a hare listening, X.*Cyn.*5.7.

**ἀνακαθίννυμαι**, = ἀνακάθημαι, Aret.*SA*1.10.

***ἀνακαιν-ίζω**, *renew*, τὸν πόλεμον Plu.*Marc.*6, cf. App.*Mith.*37; οἶκον Hsch.Mil.4.33; *revive* legend, Str.2.1.9: metaph., ἀ. εἰς μετάνοιαν *Ep.Hebr.*6.6:—Pass., τῆς ἔχθρας ἀνακεκαινισμένης Isoc.7.8; ὑποθέσεις Just.*Nov.*111.1. **-ισις**, εως, ἡ, *a making new, renewal*, Suid.

**ἀνακαινουργέω**, = ἀνακαινίζω, prob. l. in *AP*14.60.

**ἀνακαιν-όω**, in Pass., *to be renewed*, 2*Ep.Cor.*4.16, *Col.*3.10:—in Med., *renew*, Heliod.*in EN*221.13. **-ωσις**, εως, ἡ, = ἀνακαίνισις, *Ep.Rom.*12.2, *Tit.*3.5.

**ἀνάκαιον**, τό, v. ἀναγκαῖον.

**ἀνακαίω**, Att. -κάω, aor. ἀνέκαυσα E.*Cyc.*383:—*kindle, light up*, ἢ οἱ πῦρ ἀνέκαιε Od.7.13, Hdt.4.145, etc.:—Med., *light oneself* a fire, Id.1.202, 8.19: metaph., *kindle*, ὄρεξιν Plu.2.1089a; μάχην Porph. *Chr.*23. 2. Pass., *fire up* with anger, Hdt.5.19; στάσις ἀ. D.H. 9.27.

**ἀνακαλαμάομαι**, = ἀναθερίζω, in aor. 1 -ησάμην, Hsch.

***ἀνακᾰλέω**, poet. ἀγκ-, *call up* or *back*, esp. of magical invocations: —in Med., *call up the dead*, A.*Pers.*621, E.*Hel.*966; χαλκοῦ πατάγοις τὸ φῶς [τῆς σελήνης] Plu.*Aem.*17. II. *call again and again*; and so: 1. *invoke again and again, appeal to*, θεούς Hdt.9.90, E. *Ph.*608, al.; τὰς ἐπωνυμίας τοῦ θεοῦ ἀνακαλῶν Pl.*R.*394a; τοὺς προγόνους D.25.97, etc.:—so in Med., τὸν αὑτῆς δαίμον' ἀνακαλουμένη S.*Tr.* 910; *invoke again*, κεκλημένους μὲν ἀνακαλούμεθ' αὖ θεούς E.*Supp.* 626: c. inf., ἀνακαλοῦμαι ξυμμάχους ἐλθεῖν [ἀράς] S.*OC*1376, cf. E. *Tr.*469. 2. *summon, cite*, Hdt.3.127, And.1.45; *cite* before a court, Lys.15.5:—Med., *call to oneself, send for, summon*, Hdt.2.121.α', Arist.*Ath.*8.2; εἰς τοὺς μυρίους ἀ. X.*HG*7.4.33. 3. *call* by a name, Δαναούς Th.1.3; ὀνομαστὶ ἀ. 7.70; ἐξ ὀνόματος ἀ. D.H.8.65; with the Art., ἀνακαλοῦντες τὸν προδότην X.*An.*6.6.7, cf. *Cyr.*3.3.4; ἀνακαλοῦντες ταῦτα τὰ ὀνόματα ἑαυτούς Pl.*R.*471d:—Pass., Ἀργεῖος ἀνακαλούμενος *proclaimed* an Argive, S.*El.*693; so prob. τῷ Λημνίῳ τῷδ' ἀνακαλουμένῳ πυρί yon fire *famed as* Lemnian, Id.*Ph.*800. 4. *call on, call to*, esp. for encouragement, ἀλλήλους X.*Cyr.*7.1.35, etc.: —Med., *rally*, ὥσπερ πεφευγότας Pl.*Phd.*89a; εἴ τις κύνας ἐν θήρᾳ -οῖτο X.*Cyr.*1.6.19; simply, *call to*, Th.7.73: c. acc. cogn., τίνα στοναχὰν..ἀγκαλέσωμαι; E.*Ph.*1490; ἀνακαλεῖς με τίνα βοάν; with what cry *dost thou call upon me*? Id.*HF*910. III. *call back, recall*, mostly in Med., αἷμα τίς ἂν πάλιν ἀγκαλέσαιτ' ἐπαείδων A.*Ag.* 1021, etc.; *recall* a general from his command, Th.1.131; *call back* from battle, ἀνακαλεῖσθαι τῇ σάλπιγγι *sound a retreat*, X.*An.*4.4.22; *call* dogs *to heel*, Pl.*R.*440d (Pass.). 2. *restore to health*, Dsc.2. 34. 3. in Med., *recall, recollect oneself*, Hp.*Epid.*1.26.α', cf. Gal. 17(1).259; so ἀ. τὸν νόον ἐξ ἀγνοίας Ti.Locr.104c; ἀνάνηφε καὶ ἀνακαλοῦ σεαυτόν M.Ant.6.31: hence, *recall, make good*, τὰ ἁμαρτήματα Lys.6.49; ἐν ὀλίγῳ πάντα D.C.73.10.

**ἀνακαλλύνω**, *sweep up*, Phryn.Com.2 D.

**ἀνακαλπάζω**, *trot, gallop* (?), A.*Fr.*145 A, S.*Fr.*1007, Ar.*Fr.*48 D., Pl.Com.25 D.; prob. in Ar.*Th.*1174.

***ἀνακᾰλυπτήρια**, τά, *festival of unveiling*, when the bride first took off her maiden veil, and received presents from the bridegroom, Poll.3.36, cf. Timae.149, Hsch. s. v. sq. II. *the presents themselves*, subject of a speech attributed to Lysias, Theon *Prog.*2: in sg., Plu. *Tim.*8. III. *revelations*, Ph.1.358.

**ἀνακάλυπτρα**, τά, = ἀνακαλυπτήρια II. D.S.5.2.

**ἀνακᾰλύπτω**, Dor. ἀγκ-, *uncover*, *IG*4.952.62 (Epid.); *reveal*, τι πρός τινα Plb.4.85.6; τινά, i. e. his character, Philoch.20; ἀ. λόγους *use open* speech, E.*IA*1146; ἀ. κάρα *unveil oneself*, *Or.*294: so in Med., *unveil oneself*, X.*HG*5.4.6. II. *remove a covering*, βλεφάρων μὴ ἀνακαλυφθέντων Arist.*Sens.*444$^{b}$25, cf. 2*Ep.Cor.*3.14.

**ἀνακαμπ-ή**, ἡ, *bend* at the end of a rod, Bito50.10; of a tube, Hero *Spir.*1.8, 2.33. **-τέον**, *one must return*, Sor.1.98, Philum.ap.Orib. 45.29.19. **-τικός**, ή, όν, *returning*, διαυλωνισμός Eust.1107.63. **-τω**, *bend convexly*, Arist.*Mete.*385$^{b}$33 (Pass.); *bend back*, τῷ δ' οὐ πάλιν θυμὸς ἀνεκάμπτετ' B.16.82. II. *make to return*, Antiph.12. 2. mostly intr., *bend back, return*, ταύτῃ λῆγον ἀ. ἐς τὰ εἴρηται τὸ ὄρος Hdt.2.8; ἡ περιφορὰ ἐπ' ἀρχὴν ἀ. Arist.*de An.*407$^{a}$30, cf. Pl.*Phd.*72b; πάλιν ἀ. Arist.*GC*337$^{a}$6, Men.*Sam.*341, etc. b. *walk up and down*, Str.3.4.16, Plu.2.796d, D.L.2.139. c. in Logic, of the terms of a proposition, *to be converted*, Arist.*APo.*72$^{b}$36, *de An.*407$^{a}$28. d. ἀνακάμπτων, name of a *throw of the dice*, Eub.57.

**ἀνακάμψερως**, ωτος, ὁ, *a herb* the touch of which was said *to bring back love*, *Sedum Anacampseros*, Plu.2.939d, cf. Plin.*HN*24. 167. (Hsch. writes it paroxyt.)

**ἀνακαμψίπνοος** ἄνεμος *a returning wind*, a kind of *whirlwind*, Arist.*Mu.*394$^{b}$36.

**ἀνάκαμψις**, εως, ἡ, *a bending back*, Hp.*Oss.*15, Arist.*Mete.*386$^{a}$5.

**ἀνάκανδα**· ἐν ὑπερῴῳ (Lacon.), Hsch.

**ἀνάκανθος**, ον, *without a spine*, of certain fish, Hdt.4.53; κοχλίας Aenigm.ap.Ath.2.63b. 2. of plants, *without thorns*, Thphr.*HP* 3.12.9.

**ἀνακάπτω**, *gulp down*, Hdt.2.93, Ar.*Av.*579, Arist.*HA*541$^{a}$13, al.

**ἀνάκαρ**, Adv., (κάρα) *up to* or *towards the head, upwards*, Hp.ap. Gal.19.79. ***ἀνακάς**, Adv. = ἄνωθεν, Hsch.

**ἀνάκαυσις**, εως, ἡ, *setting on fire, kindling*, λύχνων J.*Ap.*2.39, cf. Plu.2.248d (dub.), Anon.*Incred.*8.

**ἀνακαχλ-άζω**, *boil up, burst forth*, Opp.*C.*1.275. **-ασις**, εως, ἡ, *a bursting forth*, Sch.A.*Pr.*367.

**ἀνάκαψις**, εως, ἡ, *gulping down*, Arist.*GA*756$^{b}$4.

**ἀνακέαται**, Ion. for ἀνάκεινται.

***Ἀνάκεια**, ων, τά, *festival of the Dioscuri*, Lys.*Fr.*75.3, Poll.1.37; v. Ἄνακες.

***ἀνάκειμαι**, poet. ἄγκ-, serving as Pass. to ἀνατίθημι, *to be laid up* as a votive offering in the temple, *to be dedicated*, κρητῆρές οἱ..ἐξ χρύσεοι ἀνακέαται Hdt.1.14; ἀ. ἐν ἱρῷ Id.2.135; πρὸς τοῖς ἱεροῖς Lys.10.28: metaph., αἶνος Ὀλυμπιονίκαις ἄγκειται Pi.*O.*11(10).8, cf.13.36; λόγος τῷ θεῷ ἀ. Pl.*Smp.*197e; ἐν οὐρανῷ παράδειγμα ἀ. *R.*592b. b. *to be set up* as a statue in public, Σόλων ἀνάκειται παράδειγμα D.19.251, cf. *IG*14.1389 i 8; χρύσεοί κ' ἀνεκείμεθα Theoc.10.33, cf. Lycurg. 51. 2. *to be ascribed* or *offered*, αἱ πράξεις ἀ. τινι Plu.*Lyc.*1; ἡ ἡγεμονία ἀ. τινι Id.*Arist.*15; ἐς τοὺς ἀστέρας τοὺς ἑπτὰ..τὰς ἡμέρας ἀνακεῖσθαι D.C.37.18, cf. Polem.*Cyn.*15. II. πᾶν or πάντα ἀνάκειται ἔς τινα everything *is referred to* a person, *depends on* his will, Hdt.1.97, 3.31: so c. dat. pers., πάντων ἀνακειμένων τοῖς Ἀθηναίοις ἐς τὰς ναῦς since *they had* their whole fortunes *depending* on their ships, Th.7.71; ἐπὶ σοὶ τάδε πάντ' ἀνάκειται Ar.*Av.*638; ἅπαντα..ἐπὶ τῇ τύχῃ μᾶλλον ἀ. ἢ τῇ προνοίᾳ Antipho 5.6; of persons, σοὶ ἀνακείμεσθα E.*Ba.*934; εἰς θάνατον ἦν ἀνακείμενα τοῖς ἀλογήσασι the death penalty *was reserved* for.., J.*AJ*17.6.5; λιμὸς εἰς ὑστάτην ἀνακείμενος ἀναισχυντίαν 18.1.1. 2. *to be put aside*, ταῦτα ἀνακείσθω Them.*in Ph.*29.20. III. *lie at table, recline*, S.*Fr.*756, Philippid.30, Arist. *Cat.*6$^{b}$12, *Fr.*607, Diph.40 Mein. (om. Kock), Plb.13.6.8, *Ev.Matt.* 9.10, al.; cf. Phryn.191.

***Ἀνάκειον**, τό, (Ἄνακες) *temple of the* Ἄνακες or *Dioscuri*, And.1. 45, Th.8.93, D.45.80 (cf. *AB*212), *IG*4.1028.4 (Epid., ii B.C.); ἐν τῷ Ϝανακείῳ ib.9(1).129 (Elatea, v B.C.); cf. ἀναγκαῖον.

**ἀνακείρω**, *shear* or *cut off, rip up*, Str.16.4.15, [Gal.]14.790, Aët. 13.4.

**ἀνακεκαλυμμένως**, Adv. pf. Pass., *openly*, Hsch.

**ἀνακέκλομαι**, poet. for ἀνακαλέω, *call out*, *h.Hom.*19.5.

**ἀνακέλᾰδος**, ὁ, *loud shout* or *din*, dub. l. in E.*Or.*185, where Sch. uses the Verb **ἀνακελαδέω**.

**ἀνᾰκέομαι**, *repair*, τοῖχον *IG*11.203*A*56 (Delos, iii B.C.); cf. ἐνακέομαι; *make good*, Ael.*NA*5.19; τάχ' ἄν τι καὶ ἐξαμάρτοις, ὃ μὴ δυνηθήσῃ -σασθαι D.C.52.37.

**ἀνακεραμόω**, *re-tile*, *IG*11.287*A*72,112 (Delos, iii B.C.).

**ἀνακεράννῡμι** and -ύω, *mix up* or *again*, ἀνὰ κρητῆρα κέρασσεν Od. 3.390; οἶνον ἀνεκεράννυ γλυκύτατον Ar.*Ra.*511: metaph., τὴν πόλιν αὐτὴν πρὸς αὑτὴν ἀ. ταῖς οἰκειότησιν Plu.*Cat.Mi.*25; κοινωνίαις πολέμων -ασθέντες D.H.1.60:—Pass., πολλῷ τῷ θνητῷ ἀνακεραννυμένη Pl.*Criti.*121a: aor. -εκράθην Id.*Ti.*87a, part. -κρᾱθείς Plu.*Rom.*29.

**Ἄνᾰκες**, ων, οἱ, *the Dioscuri, Pollux and Castor*, σωτήροιν Ἀνάκοιν τε Διοσκούροιν *IG*3.195, cf. 1.34.8, 2.699.3c, etc., Plu.*Thes.*33, Cic. *ND*3.21: old pl. of ἄναξ; cf. Ἀνάκειον, -εια.

***ἀν-άκεστος**, ον, = ἀνήκεστος, Hp.ap.Erot. (ἀνηκ- in *Acut.*39).

❋ἀνακεφαλαι-όομαι, *sum up the argument*, of an orator, D.H.*Lys.* 9; ἀ. πρὸς ἀνάμνησιν Arist.*Fr.*133:—Pass., *to be summed up*, ἐν τῷ λόγῳ τούτῳ *Ep.Rom.*13.9. -ωσις, εως, ἡ, *a summary*, D.H. 1.90. -ωτικός, ή, όν, *fit for summing up*: τὸ ἀ., = foreg., Id. *Lys.*19. Adv. -κῶς *summarily*, Eust.1579.8, etc.

ἀνακηδής, -ές, = ἀκηδής, Democr.174,254.

ἀνακηκίω, *spout up, gush forth*, ἀνεκήκιεν αἷμα Il.7.262; ἀνακηκίει ἱδρώς 13.705; πέτρης *from..*, A.R.3.227. 2. rare in Prose, *bubble up, throb violently*, Pl.*Phdr.*251b. II. causal, *make to spout out*, freq. in later Ep., A.R.4.600, Nonn.*D.*12.359, Tryph.322. [ῐ Ep., cf. κηκίω.]

ἀνακήρ-υκτος, ον, = ἀκήρυκτος, dub. in Poll.8.139. ❋-υξις, εως, ἡ, *proclamation*, Poll.8.130, Just.*Nov.*6.1.9. ❋-ύσσω, Att. -ττω, *proclaim by voice of herald, publish abroad*, φόνον τὸν Λαΐειον S.*OT*450:—Pass., μὴ ἀνακηρυχθῇ ἡ βδελυρία εἰς πόλιν Aeschin.1.160. 2. c. acc. pers., *proclaim* as conqueror, τοὺς νικῶντας Ar.*Pl.* 585:—Pass., ἀνακηρυχθῆναι Hdt.6.103, cf. Th.5.50; of slaves, ἀνεκαρύχθησαν ἐπ' ἐλευθερίᾳ *GDI*3600 (Calymna). 3. *extol, sing praises of*, τινά Jul.*Or.*1.46a. II. *put up to auction*, Hdt.1.196. III. *offer by voice of herald*, ἀ. σῶστρά τινος X.*Mem.*2.10.2.

ἀνᾰκής, ές, = ἀνήκεστος, Eup.21. II. Subst., an Indian bird, Hsch. ἀνακῆσαι· ἡσυχάσαι, Id.

ἀνακίδνᾰμαι, *spread upwards*, Ἄραψ ἀτμὸς ἐς Ὄλυμπον ἀνακίδναται *Pae.Delph.*11.

ἀνακίδωτος, ον, (ἀκίς) *pointless*, Hdn.Gr.1.222.

ἀνακινδῡνεύω, *run a further risk*, D.C.41.25, 42.1 (Pass.); generally, *run risks*, c. inf., Hdt.8.100: c. dat., ἀ. ναυμαχίῃσι ib.68.α′: c. part., ἀ. συμβάλλοντα Id.9.26.

ἀνακῑν-έω (once -άω, imper. ἀνακείνα *PHolm.*20.19), *sway* or *swing to and fro*, Hdt.4.94, cf. Hp.*VC*21. II. *stir up, awaken*, νόσον ἀ. S.*Tr.*1259; of cocks or quails, *stir them up* (to fight), Pl.*Lg.* 789c; ἀ. πόλεμον Plu.*Luc.*5; ὑπολείμματα στάσεων *Pomp.*16:—Pass., δόξαι ἀνακεκίνηνται Pl.*Men.*85c, cf. Pherecyd.102 J. III. *uproot*, τὰς κρηπῖδας Agath.2.1: metaph., τὰ καθεστῶτα Id.4.27. -ημα, ατος, τό, *swinging of the arms* as an exercise, Hp.*Vict.*2.64. -ησις, εως, ἡ, *swinging to and fro* of the arms as preparatory exercise of pugilists: metaph., *preparation, prelude*, Pl.*Lg.*722d. II. *stirring up, excitement*, φρενῶν S.*OT*727; ἀλογίας Porph.*Abst.*1.41.

❋Ἀνάκιον, τό, = Ἀνάκειον, *IG*2.660: ❋Ἀνάκια, τά, *festival of Dioscuri*, ib.570.

❋ἀνακίρνᾰμαι, *mix*, ἀνακίρναται ποτόν S.*Fr.*255.8: metaph., φιλίας..ἀνακίρνασθαι *mix the bowl of* friendship, E.*Hipp.*254. II. as Pass., ἀὴρ ἡλίου ἀκτῖσιν ἀνακιρνάμενος *tempered by..*, Pl.*Ax.*371d; *mingle with*, Iamb.*in Nic.*p.73 P.:—Act., ἀνακίρνησιν Ph.1.284, part. -κιρνάς 1.153:—Pass., ἀνακιρνᾶται Id.*Fr.*74 H. (s. v. l.), cf. Alex. Trall.1.13.

ϝανακισία, name of a tribe at Mantinea, *IG*5(2).271.19.

ἀνακκάζω, Locr. for ἀναγκ-, *Jahresh.*14.168 (Tolophon, iii B.C.).

❋ἀνακλάζω, aor. 2 ἀνέκλᾰγον E.*IA*1062, Call.*Hec.*1.1.10: aor. 1 ἀνέκλαγξα Ael.*NA*12.33:—*cry aloud, scream out*, E. l. c.; of a dog, *bark, bay*, X.*Cyr.*1.4.15; of geese, *cackle*, Ael. l. c.

ἀνακλαίω, Att. -κλάω, fut. -κλαύσομαι Telecl.1 D.:—*weep aloud, burst into tears*, ἀνακλαύσας μέγα Hdt.3.14, cf. 66, D.C.*Fr.*18.10. 2. c. acc., *weep for*, κακὰ μέζω ἢ ὥστε ἀνακλαίειν Hdt.3.14: so in Med., ὑμῖν τάδ'..ἀνακλαίομαι S.*Ph.*939; τὰς παρούσας ἀτυχίας ἀνακλαύσασθαι πρὸς ὑμᾶς Antipho 2.4.1.

ἀνάκλᾰ-σις, εως, ἡ, (ἀνακλάω) *a bending back, flexure*, Hp.*Fract.*2; of swords, D.S.5.30; *curve*, of the lines of a ship, Callix.1. II. *reflection* of light or *reverberation* of sound, Arist.*APo.*98a29, *Sens.* 437b10, al., *Stoic.*2.199; so of the wind, Arist.*Pr.*945a7; of water, ἀ. ποιεῖσθαι have its course *turned*, Plb.4.43.9; ἀ. τῆς σαρκὸς ποιεῖσθαι make it *elastic*, Arist.*Pr.*966b17. -σμός, ὁ, = foreg. I, Heliod. ap.Orib.46.12.1. II. in metre, *overlapping*, cf. ἀνακλάω II. 2, Sch. Heph.12. -στος, ον, *bent back, reflected*: metaph., of participles derived from Nouns or Adjectives, Plu.2.1011d.

ἀνα-κλαυθμός or -κλαυσμός (so codd. l. citand.), ὁ, = sq., D.H. 6.46. -κλαυσις, εως, ἡ, (κλαίω) *lamentation*, Id.9.33 (pl.).

ἀνακλάω, *bend back*, ξύλα Hp.*Fract.*13; ἀνακλάσας δέρην E.*Or.* 1471 (lyr.); ταὼς ἀ. οὐρὰν D.Chr.12.2; ἀ. τὴν γλῶσσαν πρὸς τὸν οὐρανόν Aret.*CA*1.7; to a wrestler, ἀνάκλα *POxy.*466.29 (ii A.D.):—Pass., πίοιμι τὸν τράχηλον ἀνακεκλασμένη *with* my neck *bent back*, Theopomp.Com.54, cf. D.Chr.5.25 (Act.); but in Medic., τὴν κεφαλὴν ἀνακεκλασμένην μεσσηγὺ τῶν ὠμοπλατέων κέεσθαι Aret.*SA*1.6; ἀνακεκλασμένοι *with eyelids slightly open*, Hp.*Coac.*64. 2. *break short off*, or more prob., *fend off*, μηχανὰς βρόχους περιβάλλοντες ἀ. Th. 2.76; prob. in D.C.66.4. 3. metaph., ἀ. ἐπ' ἄλλα τὴν διάνοιαν Plu. 2.359a. II. of light, *reflect*, ib.696a, al.:—Pass., Arist.*Mete.*340a 28, al.; τοσοῦτον ἀνακλασθῆναι τῶν ἀδυνάτων εἶναί φασιν *that* [the rays] *should be* so much *reflected*, ib.343b7; of sound, *to be reverberated*, Thphr.*Sens.*53; of a ball, *rebound*, Arist.*Ph.*255b27. 2. ἀνακλώμενος, in metre, of the *overlapping* of Ionic feet, μέτρον ἀνακλώμενον Heph.12, cf. Sch. ad loc.

ἀνάκλεις, ειδος, ἡ, *picklock*, Poll.7.107.

❋ἀνακλέπτω, *steal*, prob. l. in *h.Merc.*515, cf. *GDI*1586 (Dodona), Theoc.5.9:—Pass., *steal away, retire*, Hsch.

ἀνάκλημα, ατος, τό, = ἀνάκλασις, τοῦ ῥυθμοῦ Jul.*Ep.*186.

ἀνακλήρωσις, εως, ἡ, *re-allotment*, Sch.Pi.*O.*7.110.

ἀνάκλη-σις, εως, ἡ, (ἀνακαλέω) *calling on, invocation*, θεῶν Th.7.71; *salutation, address*, Plu.2.35a. 2. *calling aloud*, οἱ βάτραχοι ..ἀνακλήσεσι χρῶνται ib.982e; ζητεῖν τινα μετ' ἀνακλήσεως Nymph. 9. II. *recalling*, ἀ. θέρμης ποιέεσθαι Aret.*CD*2.7, cf. *SD*2.1; metaph., ἀπὸ τῶν αἰσθητῶν ἐπὶ τὰ νοητά Porph.*Marc.*10. 2. [re]*storation, revival*, Aret.*SA*1.6, cf. *SD*1.7. 3. *retreat*, ἀ. σάλπιγγι σημαίνειν Plu.*Fab.*12, cf. *Alex.*32, Onos.10.2. -τέον, *one must revive, restore*, Aët.16.36, Orib.*Fr.*56. -τήρια, τά, *a festival* [on] *a king's proclamation*, Plb.18.55.3, 28.12.8. -τικός, ή, όν, [fit] *for exhorting*, πρὸς ὁμόνοιαν Plu.*Lyc.*4. II. *fit for recalling*; τ[ὸ] ἀνακλητικὸν σημαίνειν, σαλπίγξαι sound *a retreat*, D.H.8.65, *A.* 11.136 (Lucill.): metaph., ἐκδίδωσι τὸ ἀ. τῷ Ἀττίδι Jul.*Or.*5.169[c]. Adv. -κῶς Sch.E.*Ph.*818. ❋-τος, ον, *called back to service*, La[t.] *evocatus*, D.C.45.12; οἱ ἀ. Id.55.24, 78.5.

ἀνάκλιθρον, τό, gloss on *fulcrum*; of the back of Cassiepeia's chair, Ptol.*Alm.*7.5.

❋ἀνάκλῐμα, ατος, τό, *slope, ascent*, τῆς γῆς Apollod.*Poliorc.*173.11.

ἀνακλῐνοπάλη, ἡ, Mart.14.201 (f. l. for ἐπι-).

ἀνακλιν-τήρ, ῆρος, ὁ, *neighbour at dinner*, πρῶτος ἦν ἀ. Δαρείου Ps.-Callisth.2.13. ❋-τήριον, τό, *head-rest* of a couch, Erot. s. v. ἀνακλισμοῦ:—also ❋-τρον, τό, Poll.6.9; condemned by Phryn.130.

ἀνα-κλίνω, poet. ἀγκλ-, (v. κλίνω) *lean* one thing *upon* another, [τόξον] ποτὶ γαίῃ ἀγκλίνας *having laid* it on the ground, Il.4.113; Ἔρως ἀνακλίνας τοῦ τόξου τὸν πῆχυν Philostr.*Im.*2.1; ἀ. ἑαυτοὺς ἐπὶ τὸ ἐναντίον, of sailors struggling against the wind, Arist.*Mech.* 851b13; *cause to recline* at table, Plb.31.4.5, *Ev.Luc.*12.37:— mostly in Pass., *lie, sink*, or *lean back, recline*, ἀνακλινθεὶς πέσεν ὕπτιος Od. 9.371; of persons asleep, 18.189; of rowers, 13.78; of the elephant, Arist.*HA*498a11; to be *strung*, of strings of lyre, Philostr.*Im.*1.10. 2. Pass., of ground, *lie sloping upwards*, *Gp.*2.3.1. II. *push* or *put back*, and so, *open*, θύρην ἀγκλίνας Od.22.156; so of the door of Olympus, ἠμὲν ἀνακλῖναι πυκινὸν νέφος ἠδ' ἐπιθεῖναι Il.5.751, cf. Call.*Ap.*6; τὴν θύρην τὴν καταπηκτὴν ἀ., i. e. the trap-door, Hdt. 5.16. III. *throw* the head *back*, and so, *lift up*, τὴν τῆς ψυχῆς αὐγήν Pl.*R.*540a. IV. *overthrow*, of earthquake, compared to battering-ram, Paus.7.24.10. ❋-κλίσις, εως, ἡ, *lying* or *leaning back, position in bed*, Hp.*Coac.*487, Arist.*Cat.*6b11. 2. *bending back*, in tetanus, Aret.*SA*1.6. II. *back to lean against*, θρόνοι..ἀνακλίσεις ἔχοντες.. *IG*2.676, cf. 2.701 ii (iii) 45, cf. Ath.5.192f; βάθρον ἀνάκλισιν ἔχον *IG* 4.39 (Aegina); *bench, seat*, *JHS*12.232, cf. *IG*1.277 *d.* -κλισμός, ὁ, *back of a chair* or *couch*, Hp.*Art.*7, Erot. s. v. ἕδος. -κλῐτος, ον, *for reclining*, δίφρος Hp.*Superf.*8, Aret.*CA*1.4; θρόνος, = ἀνακλιντήριον, Plu.*Rom.*26; τὰ ἀνάκλιτα Ps.-Callisth.3.22.

ἀνακλονέω, *toss up and down*, Opp.*H.*3.478.

❋ἀνακλύζω, fut. -ύσω, *wash up against*, A.R.2.551. 2. abs., *boil as with waves*, Plu.2.590f:—causal, *stir up*, χερσὶ θαλάσσιον ὕδωρ Sch.Nic.*Al.*165. 3. Med., *rinse* the mouth, Dsc.*Eup.*1.66.

ἀνακλώθω, of the Fates, *undo the thread* of one's life, *change* one's *destiny*, Luc.*Hist.Conscr.*38; Μοιρῶν νῆμ' ἀνέκλωσαν [αἱ Μοῦσαι] *IG* 14.1188.

ἀνακμ-άζω, *break out afresh with renewed vigour*, of στάσις, J.*BJ* 5.1.1. -αστικός, ή, όν, = ἀνηβητήριος, Sch.E.*Andr.*552.

ἀνακναδάλλω, *excite by scratching*, of quails, Poll.7.136, 9.108, Hsch.

ἀνακνάπτω, *make* old clothes *fresh by fulling*: metaph., ἀ. τὰς ἀλλοτρίας ἐπινοίας *vamp* them *up as new*, Lysipp.4.

ἀνακνάω, *scratch*, Paul.Aeg.4.25 (in Med.), cf. Phryn.*PS*p.12 B.

ἀνακνίδεσι· τῇ ὀσφύϊ, Hsch.

ἀνακνισόω, *perfume thoroughly, fill with vapour*, Tryph.349.

ἀνακογχίζω, dub. in Hp.*Mochl.*2.

ἀνακογχῠλ-ιάζω, (κόγχη) *break open* the capsule covering the seal of a will, διαθήκην Ar.*V.*589 (with *double entente*), cf. Aristid.*Or.* 51(27).9. 2. = ἀναγαργαρίζω (sc. ὕδατι), Pl.*Smp.*185d (but ἀνακογχυλίσαι, Hsch.). -ιασμός, ὁ, *gargling*, Ath.5.187a, Antyll. ap.Orib.5.28.3; and -ιαστόν (sc. φάρμακον), τό, *gargle*, Pl.Com. 196. -ίζω, = -ιάζω, Eup.275, Ruf.ap.Aët.2.92, Poll.6.25, Gal.11. 769. -ισμα, ατος, τό, *gargle*, Orib.*Eup.*4.69. -ισμός, ὁ, = -ιασμός, Aret.*CA*1.7, Orib.*Fr.*74.

ἀνακοιλιασμός, ὁ, in pl., *purgative*, Cael.Aur.*TP*2.14.

ἀνακοινέω, = sq., only in Med. imper. ἀνακοινέο (for -έεο) Thgn.73.

ἀνακοιν-όω, *communicate, impart*, τινί τι, v.l. in Pl.*Cra.*383a. 2. ἀ. τινί *communicate with, take counsel with*, Ar.*Lys.*1177; ἀ. τοῖς μάντεσι Pl.*Lg.*913b; ἀ. τισὶν ὑπέρ τινος Arist.*Mir.*843b20. II. Med., with plpf. Pass. ἀνεκεκοίνωντο X.*An.*5.6.36:—properly, *communicate* what is *one's own* to another, so of a river, ἀνακοινοῦται τῷ Ἴστρῳ τὸ ὕδωρ Hdt.4.48; ἀ. τὸ ὕδωρ πρὸς τὴν πηγήν Paus.5.7.3, cf. 8.28.3. 2. much like Act., *impart*, τῷ θεῷ περί τινος X.*An.* 3.1.5, cf. 5.6.36, etc.; ἀνακοινοῦσθαί τινι *consult* one, Pl.*Prt.*314b; τοῖς συμμάχοις X.*HG*6.3.8; πρὸς τοὺς οἰκέτας ἀνακοινοῦσθαι περὶ τῶν μεγίστων Thphr.*Char.*4.2: abs., βουλομένους ἀνακοινοῦσθαί τε καὶ ἐς λόγον ἐλθεῖν Ar.*Nu.*470, cf. Pl.*Prt.*349a. -ωσις, εως, ἡ, *communication*, Sch.Ar.*Pl.*39. -ωτέος, α, ον, Sch.E.*Hipp.*295.

ἀνακοιρᾰνέω, *rule* or *command* in a place, Posidipp.ap.Ath.7. 318d.

ἀνακοιτάζομαι, *deflower* a maiden, Sch.Opp.*H.*1.390.

ἀνακολλ-άω, *glue on* or *to, glue together*, τρίχας Dsc.2.133:—Pass., χιτὼν ἐφ' ἑαυτὸν ἀνακεκολλημένος Lyd.*Mag.*2.13. -ημα, ατος, τό, *adhesive plaster*, Dsc.2.135, Aët.7.70. -ησις, εως, ἡ, *sticking up* or *out* of in-growing eyelashes *with an adhesive*, Gal.6.627, Dsc. 1.71. ❋-ητικός, ή, όν, *of* or *for glueing*, Id.2.133; of a plaster, Heras ap.Gal.13.782.

**ἀνακολούθητος**, ον, prob. f.l. for -ουθος, D.H.*Th.*49.

**ἀνακολουθ-ία**, ἡ, Rhet., *inconsequence*, esp. employed with humorous effect, Demetr.*Eloc.*153; generally, Demetr.Lac.*Herc.*1012.63, Corn.*Rh.*p.368 H., Diogenian.Epicur.3.26. **-ος**, ον, *inconsequent*, Epicur.*Ep.*2 p.41 U.; μετάβασις ἀ. Aët.6.22; *inconsistent*, οἷς ἑαυτοῦ λόγοις Muson.*Fr.*10 p.56 H.; v.l. in Arr.*Epict.*1.7.18. 2. Gramm., *anomalous*, of inflexions, A.D.*Pron.*66.1, al.; also of changed constructions, ἀ. σχῆμα, σχηματισμοί, D.H.*Th.*41,42. Adv. -θως Id.*Rh.*8.13, Sch.Il.2.469, *EM*722.2.

**ἀνακολπ-άζω**, (κόλπος) *tuck up one's gown, gird oneself up*, Ar.*Th.* 174; but cf. ἀνακαλπάζω. **-όω**, = foreg., *EM*410.20:—Pass., *form a bay*, Anon.*Geog.Comp.*40.

**✱ἀνακολυμβάω**, *come up after diving*: trans., *bring up from the bottom*, Thphr.*HP*4.6.5:—Pass., Hsch.

**ἀνακομάω**, *get hair again*, Luc.*DMeretr.*12.5.

**✱ἀνακομβόομαι**, *gird oneself up* for action, *Gp.*10.83.1.

**✱ἀνακομ-ιδή**, Dor. **ἀγκομιδά** *IG*4.742.17, ἡ:—*a carrying away again, recovery*, ἡ τῶν πλοίων ἀ. Decr.ap.D.18.75. 2. *recovery*, ἐκ τῶν νούσων Hp.*VM*21. 3. *return*, Arist.*HA*597^b9, *SIG*615.14 (Delph., ii B.C.), Onos.11.3. 4. *bringing up*, τῶν ἐπιτηδείων Str.3.3.1. **-ίζω**, poet. **ἀγκομ-**, *carry up*, X.*HG*2.3.20:—Pass., Din.1.68; esp. *to be carried up-stream*, or *up the country*, Hdt.2.115. II. *bring back, recover*, οἰκέτην v.l. in X.*Mem.* 2.10.1:—Med. (with pf. Pass., Id.*An.*4.7.1 and 17), *bring* or *take back* or *away with one*, Hdt.5.85, Th.6.7:—Pass., *to be brought back*, Hdt.3.129, etc.; and of persons, *return, come* or *go back*, Id.2. 107, Th.2.31; *get safe away, escape*, Plb.1.38.5: so in Med., ἑαυτὸν ἀνακομίζεσθαι ἐκ τῆς Φιλίππου συνηθείας *withdraw from..*, Plu.*Arat.* 51. 2. τὸ Μηδείας ἔπος ἀγκομίσαι *bring back safe*, i.e. *redeem, fulfil*, Pi.*P.*4.9 (prob.):—Med., ἀ. τύχαν δαιμόνων *bring it back upon oneself*, E.*Hipp.*831 (lyr.). III. *restore to health, strengthen*, Hp.*Fract.*7, cf. Gal.1.405 (Pass.): metaph., πεπονηκυῖαν ἐξ ἀρχῆς ἀνακεκομίσθαι τὴν οἰκουμένην Aristid.*Or.*26(14).98. **-ιστέον**, *one must restore to health*, Paul.Aeg.3.39. 2. of Pass., *one must return*, Ach.Tat.5.11.

**ἀνάκομμα**, ατος, τό, (ἀνακόπτω) *check*, φλεγμονῶν, ὀδυνῶν Aët.12.20.

**ἀνακονεῖν**, v. ἀνακωνῆν.

**ἀνᾰκοντίζω**, intr., *dart* or *shoot up*, αἷμα δ' ἀνηκόντιζε Il.5.113; so of water, Hdt.4.181. 2. causal, θαλασσίους αὔρας Callistr.*Stat.*14.

**ἀνα-κοπή**, ἡ, *resistance, check* due to collision, Epicur.*Ep.*1 p.7 U. (pl.), Phld.*D.*1.14 (pl.), Plu.2.76f, cf. 1128c. II. *recoil* of the waves, Id.*Pyrrh.*15, cf. J.*BJ*1.21.6; in a tidal river, Str.3.5.9. III. *back-water*, Plu.*Alex.*44. IV. *clashing* of vowels in hiatus, etc., D.H.*Comp.*22, cf. *Dem.*38. **-κοπτέον**, *one must remove, eliminate*, Paul.Aeg.6.90. **✱-κόπτω**, *drive back, push back*, θυρέων δ' ἀνέκοπτεν ὀχῆας Od.21.47. 2. *beat back* an assailant, Th.4.12, cf. Plu.*Caes.* 38. 3. ἀ. ναῦν *check* a ship's course, v.l. in Thphr.*Char.*25.2. 4. *return* food, διὰ ῥινῶν, εἰς τὰς ῥῖνας, Herod.Med. in *Rh.Mus.*58.86,90 and 96, cf. Aret.*SA*1.6. II. *knock out*, τὰς ὄψεις ἀνακοπεὶς Philostr. *Her.Prooem.*2. 2. *cut from below*, Hld.9.18. 3. *beat up* eggs, Sor.1.222, *PMag.Lond.*121.180. III. *check, stop*, ἦχον D.H.*Comp.* 22; προσδοκίαν Phld.*Piet.*25; ἀοιδὴν Coluth.125:—Pass., *to be stopped, restrained*, τῆς ὁρμῆς Luc.*Alex.*57, cf. *PFlor.*36.3; *stop short* in a speech, Luc.*Nigr.*35. IV. Medic., *take effect*, ἀνακόπτει γὰρ οὕτως ἡ ὠφέλεια Herod.Med. in *Rh.Mus.*58.92 (fort. διακ., cf. *SIG*1170.16).

**ἀνακορέω**, *sweep again* or *out*, Pherecr.5 D.

**ἀνακός**, ὁ, = ἄναξ, Hdn.Gr.1.150, 2.647, cf. Ael.Dion.*Fr.*56.

**✱ἀνακοσμέω**, *adorn anew, restore*, *IGRom.*4.468.14 (Pergam.), v.l. in Aristid.*Or.*26(14).98.

**ἀνάκουστος**, ον, *not hearing, deaf*, cj. in Ph.2.417.

**✱ἀνακουφ-ίζω**, *lift* or *raise up*, S.*Fr.*23; ἀ. δέμας E.*Or.*218; ἑαυτὸν εἰς ἀνάβασιν, of a horseman mounting, X.*Eq.*7.2; of the ship of state, ἀ. κάρα βυθῶν S.*OT*23; ὁ ἀὴρ ἀ. τὸν ἀσκόν Arist.*Pr.*939^a35:—Pass., *feel lightened* or *lifted up*, ἀνεκουφίσθην δέμας E.*Hipp.*1392; *to be relieved in mind*, X.*HG*5.2.28. **-ισις**, εως, ἡ, *relief*, κακῶν S.*OT* 218. **✱-ισμα**, ατος, τό, *a relief*, Hp.*Vict.*2.64.

**ἀνάκοψις**, εως, ἡ, *interval*, τῶν παροξυσμῶν Herod.Med. in *Rh.Mus.* 58.91.

**ἀνα-κραγγαίνω**· ἀνακράζω, Hsch.:—also **-κραγγάνω**, Phot.p.114 R.

**✱ἀνακρᾰδεύω**, *brandish*, Hsch.

**✱ἀνακρᾰζω**, fut. -κράξομαι or fut. pf. -κεκράξομαι Lxx *Jl.*3(4).16: aor. ἀνέκρᾰγον; late ἀνέκραξα ib.*Jd.*7.20, *BGU*1201.11, *Ev.Marc.*1. 23, al.:—*cry out, lift up the voice, shout*, ἐπεὶ..ἀνέκραγον Od.14.467; εἴ τι πέραν ἀερθεὶς ἀνέκραγον if I *raised my voice* too high, Pi.*N.*7.76; ἐξ ἑνὸς στόματος ἅπαντες ἀνέκραγον Ar.*Eq.*670, cf. *V.*1311, etc.; οὐκ ἀνέκραγεν, of a dying man, Antipho 5.44; πρῶτος ἐπὶ τοῦ βήματος ἀνέκραγεν Arist.*Ath.*28.3: foll. by a relat., ἀνέκραγον ὡς εὖ λέγοι Ar. *Ec.*431, cf. X.*An.*5.1.14; τηλικαῦτ' ἀνεκράγετε, ὥς.. D.21.215: c. inf., ἀνακραγόντων βάλλειν.. Plu.*Phoc.*34. 2. rarely of animals, ἂν γλαὺξ ἀνακράγῃ Men.534.11.

**ἀνάκρᾱσις**, εως, ἡ, *mixing with others*, Plu.*Alex.*47, etc.

**ἀνακρατέω**, *hold up, support*, Sor.1.114.

**ἀνακραυγ-άζω**, *cry aloud*, Arr.*Epict.*2.19.15. **-ασμα**, ατος, τό, *loud outcry*, Epicur.*Fr.*414 (pl.).

**ἀνακρέκομαι**, *begin to play*, ἐς σὲ ἅπας ὄρνις ἀνακρέκεται each bird *tunes its voice* for thee, *AP*9.562 (Crin.).

**ἀνακρεμ-άννῡμι**, poet. **ἀγκρ-**:—Pass., -κρέμᾰμαι:—*hang up on* a thing, πασσάλῳ ἀγκρεμάσασα Od.1.440; τὰς πέδας ἀνεκρέμασαν ἐς τὴν ἀκρόπολιν, as a votive offering, Hdt.5.77; τὰ ὅπλα πρὸς τὸ Ἀθήναιον ib.95; ἀ. τινά *crucify*, Id.9.120; βροχὸν ἑαυτῷ περιθεὶς ἀνεκρέμασε D.S.2.6; *suspend* a wounded limb in a sling, Hp.*Art.*22:—Pass., ἀνακρεμαμένου τοῦ νέκυος *being hung up*, Hdt.2.121.γ'; τούτου..τοῦ ἀνακρεμασθέντος Id.9.122, cf. 7.194. II. *make dependent* ἀ. ἐξ ἀλλήλων τὴν δύναμιν Pl.*Ion*536a; ἀνακρεμάσας [ὑμᾶς] ἀπὸ τῶν ἐλπίδων Aeschin.3.100; ἀ. τὴν πίστιν εἴς τινα Plb.8.19.3. **-ασμός**, ὁ, *hanging up*, *AB*447. **✱-αστήρ**, ῆρος, ὁ, = κρεμαστήρ, Sor.ap. Orib.54.31.20.

**Ἀνακρεόντειος**, α, ον, *of Anacreon*, μέτρον Heph.15.22, cf. Sch. Heph.p.118 C.

**ἀνακρήμνημι**, = ἀνακρεμάννυμι, *shore up*, J.*BJ*5.11.4; *undermine*, ὑπονόμοις τὸ τεῖχος App.*Mith.*75:—also **ἀνακρημνάω**, prob. in J.*BJ*2. 17.8, *AJ*7.10.2.

**ἀνακρῑβής**, ές, *inaccurate*, Eust.878.37, al.

**✱ἀνακρίνω**, *examine closely, interrogate*, esp. judicially, Παυσανίαν Th.1.95, cf. Antipho 2.1.9, Pl.*Smp.*201e; ἀ. τινὰ πόθεν ζῇ Diph.32.3; *sound* a person, Lxx 1 *Ki.*20.12. 2. *inquire into*, ἀ. τοὺς ἐργασαμένους Antipho 2.3.2; τὴν [αἰτίαν] Phld.*Po.*994 *Fr.*21, cf. *Lib.* p.21 O.:—Med., ἀ. ποινὰ τίς ἔσται what remedy there shall be, Pi.*P.* 4.63. II. *examine* magistrates so as to prove their qualification, D.57.66 and 70. 2. of the magistrates, *examine* persons concerned in a suit, so as to prepare the matter for trial, And.1.101, Is.5.32; ὁ ἄρχων ἀνέκρινε πᾶσιν ὑμῖν καὶ ἀνακρίνας εἰσήγαγεν εἰς τὸ δικαστήριον D.48.31, cf. Arist.*Ath.*56.6:—Pass., ἀνεκρίθησαν αἱ ἀμφισβητήσεις D.48.23:—Med., οὐκ ἀνεκρίνατο ταύτην [τὴν γραφήν] *he did* not *have* it *examined*, of the prosecutor, Id.21.103, cf. 53. 17. 3. generally, *examine*, μάρτυρας *SIG*953.46 (Calymna); τινά 1 *Cor.*9.3:—Med., *Michel*409.9 (Cos). 4. *select*, Ps.-Callisth.3. 26. III. in Med., abs., ἀνακρίνεσθαι πρὸς ἑωυτούς *dispute, wrangle* one with another, Hdt.9.56.

**ἀνάκρισις**, poet. **ἄγκρ-**, εως, ἡ, (ἀνακρίνω II. 1) *examination* of the qualifications of magistrates, Poll.8.85. II. (ἀνακρίνω II. 2) *previous examination* of parties concerned in a suit, *preparation* of the matter for trial, X.*Smp.*5.2, etc., cf. *PSI*4.392 (iii B.C.), *OGI*374 (pl.), *Act.Ap.*25.26; of the magistrate, ἀνάκρισιν διδόναι, παραδιδόναι, Pl.*Chrm.*176c, *Lg.*855e; of the parties, εἰς ἀνάκρισιν ἥκειν Is.6.13, etc.; μηδ' εἰς ἄγκρισιν ἐλθεῖν, i.e. should not even *begin proceedings* (where however the Sch. explains ἐς ἄγκρισιν by ἐς μάχην, cf. ἀνακρίνω III), A.*Eu.*364; οὐδ' ἀ. μοι δώσεις you will not allow me *the first forms of law*, Pl.*Chrm.* l.c. III. generally, *inquiry, examination*, Id.*Phdr.*277e. IV. *preliminary examination* of a slave before sale, *POxy.*1463.12, etc. V. *examination, testing* of magical ingredients, etc., *PMag.Par.*1.1992, 2007. VI. *quarrel, dispute*, Hdt.8.69; *disputation*, Phld.*Acad.Ind.*p.72 M.

**ἀνακριτήρ**, Dor. **ἀνκριτήρ**, ῆρος, ὁ, *examining magistrate*, *GDI* 3055.1 (Chalcedon) (pl.).

**ἀνακρίτως**, Adv. *with a second* κρίσις, *relapse*, Pall. *in Hp.*2.181 D.

**ἀνακροτᾰλίζω**, = ἀνακροτέω, Hippoloch.ap.Ath.4.129c.

**✱ἀνακροτέω**, *lift up and strike together*, τὼ χεῖρ' ἀνεκρότησ' ὑφ' ἡδονῆς Ar.*Pl.*739; ἀνακροτήσας τὰς χεῖρας Aeschin.2.226; ταῖς χερσὶν ὑφ' ἡδονῆς Plu.*Mar.*44: abs., οἱ δ' ἀνεκρότησαν *applauded vehemently*, Ar.*Eq.*651, *V.*1314, cf. J.*AJ*12.4.9, Alciphr.1.39: aor. part. ἀνακορτήσασα cj. in Hexam.ap.Diogenian.3.67.

**ἀνάκρου-μα**, ατος, τό, = -κρουσις II, Corn.*Rh.*p.353 H. **-σία**· παιδιᾶς εἶδος ἐπὶ σφαίρας, Hsch. **-σις**, εως, ἡ, *pushing back*, esp. *pushing* a ship *back, backing water*, Th.7.36; ἡ πάλιν ἀ. ib.62; of a horse, with the bit, Plu.2.549c: metaph., *reaction* against depression, -σεις τοῦ φρονήματος ib.78a; *return*, τῆς παλινδρομίας Iamb.*in Nic.*p.76 P. II. in Music, *first beginning of a tune*, Str.9.3. 10. **-στέον**, *one must check*, X.*Eq.*10.12. II. ἀ. τὸν λόγον *put back* for a fresh start, Dam.*Pr.*85. **-στικός**, ή, όν, *capable of reacting*, πληγή Plu.2.936f. **✱-ω**, poet. **ἀγκρ-**, *push back* a gate-pin, βάλανον Aen.Tact.18.6; *stop short, check*, ἵππον χαλινῷ X.*Eq.* 11.3; *back* horses, τὸ ζεῦγος Plu.*Alc.*2:—Pass., Them. *in Ph.*130. 25. 2. ἀπὸ χερσοῦ νῆα..ἀνακρούεσκον *thrust* her *off* from shore, A.R.4.1650; *throw up*, δίσκον Philostr.*Her.*2.5. II. in Med., ἀνακρούεσθαι πρύμνην *put* one's ship *astern*, by backing water, Ar.*V.* 399, cf. D.S.11.18; or ἀνακρούεσθαι alone, Th.7.38,40; [ἐπὶ] πρύμνην ἀ. Hdt.8.84; but νῆας ἀ., simply *row back*, Tryph.523: metaph., τὸν λόγον πάλιν ἀ. *put back* and make a fresh start, Pl.*Phlb.*13d; παῦε.. μικρὸν ἀνακρουόμενος Luc.*Nigr.*8; ὥσπερ ἁρμονίαν ἐκλελυμένην ἀ. αὖθις ἐπὶ σώφρονα νόμον καὶ βίον Plu.*Cleom.*16. 2. in Music, *strike up*, Theoc.4.31: hence, *begin* a speech, Plb.4.22.11. III. ἀνακρούειν χεροῖν, = ἀνακροτεῖν, Autocr.1.

**✱ἀνακρύπτω**, only in aor. 2 ἀνέκρυφε Nonn.*D.*6.87.

**ἀνακρωτηρίαστος**, ον, *unmutilated*, Eust.31.41, Sch.Th.3.34.

**ἀνακτάομαι**, fut. -ήσομαι: pf. ἀνέκτημαι S.*Fr.*358:—*regain for oneself, recover*, τυραννίδα, ἀρχήν ἀ. ὀπίσω, Hdt.1.61, 3.73; Ἄργος ἐς ἑωυτοὺς ἀ. ὀπίσω 6.83; δῶμα πατρός A.*Ch.*237; ἀ. ταῖς πόλεσι τὴν ἐλευθερίαν D.S.16.14; *repair, retrieve*, ἐλαττώσεις Plb.10.33.4. 2. *refresh, revive*, σώματα, ψυχάς, Id.3.60.7, 87.3; τοὺς κεκμηκότας ὑπὸ τραυμάτων D.H.2.42; γλήχων.. λειποθυμοῦντας -κτᾶται Dsc.3.31; ἀ. ἑαυτόν J.*AJ*9.6.4, Arr.*Epict.*3.25.4, etc. 3. *reinstate*, τοὺς ἐπταικότας D.C.44.47; *restore*, ναούς Id.53.2; θυσίας *IG*2.628. II. c. acc. pers., *win* a person *over, gain* his *favour* or *friendship*, τὸν θεόν Hdt.1.50, X.*Cyr.*1.3.9, Men.*Pk.*123, etc.; παμπόλλους φίλους X.*Cyr.*2.2.10. (Act. dub., v. sub ἀνακτίζω.)

**ἀνακτένισμα**, ατος, τό, *carding, screening, sifting*, Gloss.

**ἀνακτέον**, (ἀνάγω) *one must bring up*, φλέγμα διὰ τοῦ στόματος

Hp.*Dent*.25. II. *one must refer*, εἰς τὴν ὕλην τὰς αἰτίας Arist.*GA* 778b1. III. *one must reduce, bring back*, εἰς τὴν παλαιὰν ἀταξίαν Plu.*Nob*.3.

*__ἀνά-κτησις__, εως, ἡ, *regaining*, ἀγαθῶν Hierocl.*in CA* 24 p.474 M., Herm.ap.Stob.1.41.44, Dam.*Pr*.75; ἀρουρῶν *PTeb*.378.12; *a recovery* of strength, etc., Thphr.*Fr*.166, Porph.*Marc*.4, f.l. in Hp.*VM* 4. **-κτητέος**, α, ον, *able to be recovered*, Philostr.*VA* 2.7. 2. ἀνακτητέον *one must recover, recruit*, Antyll.ap.Orib.7.12.5. *__-κτητικός__, ή, όν, *recuperative*: ἀνακτητικόν· γλήχων, Hsch. (cf. ἀνακτάομαι I. 2).

**ἀνα-κτίζω**, *rebuild*, Str.9.2.5, D.Chr.2.79: fut. ἀνακτίσσω, prob. l. for ἀνακτήσουσι in *App.Anth*.6.75:—Pass., *CIG* 8646 (vi A. D.), al. **-κτίσις**, εως, ἡ, *rebuilding*, J.*AJ* 15.11.6. **-κτιστής**, οῦ, ὁ, *refounder*, Sch.Theoc.5.72.

*__ἀνακτίτης__, ου, ὁ, a precious stone, Orph.*L*.194.

**ἀνακτόρεος**, α, ον, = ἀνακτόριος, *of the emperor*, ἐχθρός *APl*.5.350.

*__ἀνακτορία__, ἡ, (ἀνάκτωρ) *lordship, rule*, A.R.1.839; *management* of horses, *h.Ap*.234.

**ἀνακτόριος**, α, ον, *belonging to a lord* or *king, royal*, ὕες Od.15.397. II. ἀνακτόριον, τό, = ἀνάκτορον, Hsch., Suid., v.l. in Hdt. 9.65. 2. = ξιφίον, Ps.-Dsc.4.20. III. -ιος, ὁ, = ἀρτεμισία, Id.3.113.

**ἀνάκτορον**, τό, *king's dwelling, palace*, in pl., *AP* 9.657 (Marian.): mostly of the dwelling of gods, *temple, shrine*, Δήμητρος ἀ. ib.147 (Antag.); Θέτιδος εἰς ἀ. E.*Andr*.43: pl., ib.117, al., S.*Fr*.757; τὸ ἐν Ἐλευσῖνι ἀ. Hdt.9.65, cf. Hegesand.8, Posidon.41, Chor.p.86.24 B.

**ἀνακτός**, ή, όν, *drawn from a spring*, ὕδωρ *Stad*.26, cf. 75.

**Ἀνακτοτελέσται**, ῶν, οἱ, (τελέω) *presidents of the mysteries of the Corybantes* (cf. Paus.10.38.7), prob. in Hsch. (-τελευταί cod.).

*__ἀνάκτωρ__, ορος, ὁ, = ἄναξ, of gods, A.*Ch*.357, E.*IT* 1414: pl., Cerc. 4.36, cf. Ptol.*Tetr*.122.

**ἀνακυΐσκω**, *impregnate again*, Arist.*HA* 573b18.

**ἀνακυκάω**, *stir up and mix, mix up*, Θασίαν (sc. ἅλμην), φάρμακα, Ar.*Ach*.671, *Pl*.302, cf. Thphr.*CP* 6.1.5: metaph., τὸν λογισμόν Ph. 1.690.

**ἀνακυκλεύω**, *reverse*, App.*BC* 4.103.

**ἀνακυκλ-έω**, *turn round again*, ἀνακύκλει δέμας E.*Or*.231; *revolve in one's mind*, πρὸς ἐμαυτόν Luc.*Nigr*.6; *repeat*, τοὺς αὐτοὺς λόγους Plu.*Dem*.29, cf. Phld.*Mus*.p.40 K., Herm.*in Phdr*.p.191 A.:—Pass., *to be renewed*, πόλεμος ἐφ' ἑαυτὸν -ούμενος Procop.*Arc*.11. II. intr. in Act., *come round in a circle*, Arist.*GC* 338a4; αἱ αὐταὶ δόξαι ἀ. ἐν τοῖς ἀνθρώποις Id.*Mete*.339b29:—so in Pass., ἀ. πρὸς αὑτήν Pl.*Ti*. 37a; αἱ τύχαι πολλάκις ἀ. περὶ τοὺς αὐτούς Arist.*EN* 1100b3. **-ησις**, εως, ἡ, *a coming round again, circuit, revolution*, Pl.*Plt*.269e, cf. Plu. *Sol*.4. 2. in Metric, *recurrence* of form, strophic arrangement, Heph.17.4, *Poëm*.3.2. **-ητέον**, *one must employ a cycle of treatment*, Orib.ap.Aët.11.11. **-ικός**, ή, όν, *easy to turn round*, of a verse that will read either backwards or forwards, ἀναστρέφον ἢ ἀνακυκλικόν *AP* 6.323 tit. **-ισμός**, ὁ, *circuit, revolution*, ἐνιαυτοῦ μεγάλου D.S.12.36. **-όω**, = ἀνακυκλέω, v.l. in *AP* 9.342 (Parmen.), in Pass.—The Act. perh. in Jul.*Ep*.180 p.394c (ἀνακυκλούσης). **-ωμα**, ατος, τό, *cycle, revolution*, μηνιαῖον ἀ., of the moon, Secund.*Sent*. 6. **-ωσις**, εως, ἡ, = ἀνακύκλησις, Ptol.*Tetr*.87; *wheeling about*, ἱππικοῦ τάγματος Hdn.4.2.9; ἀ. τῶν πολιτειῶν *cycle* of constitutions, Plb.6.9.10.

*__ἀνακυλίνδω__, '*reflect*', t.t. in dissection, Gal.2.730.

**ἀνακυλίω** [ῑ], *roll up*, λίθους Luc.*Luct*.8, cf. D.H.*Comp*.20; *overturn*, ἁμάξας Plu.2.304f: metaph., χιλιοταλάντους ἀνακυλίων οὐσίας Alex.116.7; *roll away* or *back*, ἀνακεκύλισται ὁ λίθος *Ev.Marc*.16.4.

**ἀνακυμβαλιάζω**, (κύμβαλον), only in Il.16.379 δίφροι ἀνακυμβαλίαζον the chariots *fell rattling over*.

**ἀνακυντεῖν**· ῥέγχειν, Hsch.

**ἀνακυπόω**, *overturn, turn upside down*, Lyc.137, Nic.*Th*.705.

*__ἀνακύπτω__, fut. -κύψομαι Ar.*Av*.146, Pl.*Euthd*.302a; -ψω Luc. *DMar*.3.1: aor. ἀνέκυψα Hdt.5.91, etc.: pf. ἀνακέκῡφα E.*Cyc*.212, X. *Eq*.7.10:—*lift up the head*, Thphr.*Char*.11.3; ἀνακεκυφὼς *with the head high*, of a horse, X.l.c.; κἀγκύψας (for καὶ ἀνακύψας) ἔχε and keep *your head up*, Ar.*Th*.236; ἐν ὀροφῇ ποικίλματα θεώμενος ἀνακύπτων *throwing his head back*, Pl.*R*.529b; ἀνακύψατε καὶ ἐπάρατε τὰς κεφαλὰς *Ev.Luc*.21.28; esp. in drinking, Arist.*HA* 613a13, cf. E. l.c.; ἐπικύπτειν καὶ ἀ. Gal.6.146. II. *come up out of the water, pop up*, Ar.*Ra*.1068; ἐκ τῆς θαλάσσης εἰς τὸν ἐνθάδε τόπον Pl.*Phd*. 109d; ἀ. μέχρι τοῦ αὐχένος, opp. καταδῦναι, Id.*Tht*.171d, cf. *Phdr*. 249c. b. metaph., *emerge, crop up*, ὅτι ἐξ αὐτῶν καλόν τι ἀνακύψοιτο Id.*Euthd*.302a; αἱ -κύπτουσαι χρεῖαι Ascl.*Tact*.11.7, cf. Ath.1.25e, *Cod.Just*.1.2.17. c. of persons, *rise out of difficulties, breathe again*, Hdt.5.91, X.*Oec*.11.5; τὰ τῶν Καρχηδονίων ἀνέκυψε Plb.1.55. 1, cf. D.Chr.13.35; ἀπὸ τῶν μυχῶν τοῦ σώματος Porph.*Marc*.6.

**ἀνακυρίωσις**, εως, ἡ, *authoritative demeanour*, Hp.*Decent*.12.

**ἀνακυρτᾶσαι**· ἀνασκιρτῆσαι, ἀναπηδῆσαι, Hsch.

**ἀνάκυρτος**, ον, *curved upwards* or *backwards*, *Gloss*.

**ἀνακωδωνίζω**, *try by the sound, ring*, Ar.*Fr*.303.

**ἀνακωκύω** [ῠ], *wail aloud*, κἀνακωκύσας λιγὺ A.*Pers*.468, cf. S.*Ant*. 1227; κἀνακωκύει..ὀξὺν φθόγγον *utters a loud* shrill wailing cry, ib. 423.

**ἀνάκωλος**, ον, *docked, curtailed*, ἀ. χιτωνίσκος a '*cutty* sark', *short* frock, Plu.2.261f, *SIG* 1179.8 (Cnidus); of a camel, *short-legged*, D.S. 2.54.

**ἀνάκωμα**, ατος, τό, f.l. for ἀνακώναμα (?), [Philol.]ap.Stob.1.20.2.

**ἀνακωμῳδέω**, *to bring on the stage, satirize*, dub. in Plu.2.10c.

**ἀνακωνῆν**· ἀναστρέφειν, Hsch. (ἀνακονεῖν cod.); cf. κωνᾶν.

**ἀνακῶς**, Adv. *carefully*, ἀνακῶς ἔχειν τινός look *well* to a thing, gi*ve* *good heed* to it, Hdt.1.24, 8.109, Th.8.102, Plu.*Thes*.33; ἀ. θερ*α*πεύειν Hp.*Carn*.19; τὰς (τῆς Pierson) θύρας ἀ. ἔχων Pl.Com.202.- Dor. acc. to Erot. s.v., but found in Ion. and Early Att. (Connecte*d* with ἄναξ by Plu. l.c., cf. *AB* 391, Phot.p.113 R.)

**ἀνακωχέω**· ἀναχωρέω, Hsch. II. v. ἀνοκωχεύω.

**ἀνακωχή, ἀνακωχεύω**, v. ἀνοκωχή:—also **ἀνακωχάζω**, *bring to stop*, ναῦν Dam.*Isid*.272.

**ἀναλάζομαι**, *take again*, μορφήν Mosch.2.163.

**ἀναλάκατα**· οὐ πρὸς ἠλακάτην ἐργαζόμενος, Hsch.

**ἀναλακεῖν**, *cry aloud*, Sch.A.*Ch*.33.

**ἀναλακτίζω**, *kick upwards*, Antyll.ap.Orib.6.31.2.

*__ἀν-ἀλαλάζω__, *raise a war-cry*, ἀνηλάλαζον [οἱ στρατιῶται] X.*An*.4. 3.19; στρατὸς δ' ἀνηλάλαξε E.*Ph*.1395: generally, *cry aloud*, Id. *Supp*.719.

*__ἀναλαμβάνω__, fut. -λήψομαι: Ion. pf.inf. Pass. -λελάμφθαι or -λελάφθαι Hp.*Off*.11, part. -λελαμμένος Id.*Art*.11:—*take up, take into one's hands*, τὸ παιδίον Hdt.1.111; τὰ τόξα, τὰ ὅπλα, etc., 3.78, 9.46; *take on board ship*, 1.166, Th.7.25, etc.; *take up into heaven*, in Pass., Lxx 4*Ki*.2.9, *Act.Ap*.1.11: and generally, *take with one*, esp. of troops, supplies, etc., Hdt.9.51, Th.5.64, 8.27, etc.; part. ἀναλαβών often = *with*, ἄνδρας ἀναλαβὼν ἡγήσομαι X.*An*.7.3.36, cf. Th.5.7. b. *suspend* in a sling, Hp.*Art*.22. c. metaph., *take up*, for the purpose of examining, Pl.*Ap*.22b, *Men*.87e, al. 2. *receive*, φιλοφρόνως ἀ. Id. *Ep*.329d, etc.; of women, ἀ. τὴν γονήν *conceive*, Plu.2.495e. 3. *take upon oneself, assume*, τὴν προξενίαν Th.6.89; τὴν ἀρχὴν *Inscr. Prien*.123; κόσμον, of a king, *OGI* 383.135; ἐσθῆτα Plu.*Arist*.21; πρόσωπον, σχῆμα, Luc.*Nigr*.11, *Somn*.13. 4. in Med., *undertake, engage in*, ἀναλαβέσθαι κίνδυνον Hdt.3.69:—also Act., ἀντὶ τῆς φιλίας τὸν πόλεμον ἀναλαβεῖν Philipp.ap.D.18.78. 5. *take up, adopt*, Arist.*Fr*.76:—Pass., Aeschin.1.52, cf. Epicur.*Fr*.172. 6. of money, *confiscate*, in Pass., *OGI* 338.24 (Pergam.), *PSI* 1.104.10 (late ii A. D.); κλῆρος ἀνειλημμένος εἰς τὸ βασιλικόν *PTeb*.61b74 (ii B. C.), etc., Plu.2.484a, D.L.7.181. 7. *learn by rote*, Arr.*Epict*. 2.16.5, Plu.*Ages*.20, Alex.Aphr.*in Top*.494.31. 8. *include*, τῷ νόμῳ *OGI* 629 (Palmyra). 9. Medic., *make up* ingredients, κηρῷ καὶ νάρδῳ Aret.*CA* 1.1, cf. 2.3 (Pass.); so in Magic, ἀ. οἴνῳ καὶ μέλιτι, ὄξει, *PMag.Par*.1.1316, 2690. 10. *raise, erect* a wall, *IG* 2.1054.9. 11. abs., *lift up* one's voice, Lxx *Nu*.14.1. II. *get back, regain, recover*, τὴν ἀρχήν Hdt.3.73, X.*HG* 3.5.10; ἀ. ἐπιστήμην Pl.*Men*.85d; οὐδ' ἀφέντι λίθον δυνατὸν ἀναλαβεῖν Arist.*EN* 1114a18. 2. *retrieve, make good*, τὴν αἰτίην Hdt.7.231; ἁμαρτίαν S.*Ph*.1249, E.*Ion* 426; τὴν ἀρχαίαν ἀρετήν X.*Mem*.3.5.14; ταῦτα ἀ. καὶ μεταγιγνώσκειν D. 21.109. 3. *restore, repair*, τὴν προτέρην κακότητα Hdt.8.109: abs., Id.5.121; ἀ. τὴν πόλιν ἐκ τῆς πρόσθεν ἀθυμίας X.*HG* 6.5.21; ἀ. ἑαυτόν *recover* oneself, *regain strength*, Th.6.26, Pl.Com.10 D., Men.*Sam*. 243; *collect* oneself, Isoc.5.22: abs., Pl.*R*.467b, D.18.163, Hp.*Mul*. 2.118. 4. *take up again, resume*, in narrative or argument, τὸν λόγον Hdt.5.62, Pl.*R*.544b, al.; πολλάκις ἀ. Id.*Phd*.95e; ἀναλαβεῖν διεξιόντα *repeat* in detail, Id.*Euthd*.275c; at Rome, ἀ. θυσίας, = *instaurare sacra*, Plu.*Cor*.25; ἀ. τῇ μνήμῃ *recollect*, Pl.*Plt*.294d; without τῇ μνήμῃ, Plu.*Lyc*.21; but ἀ. μνήμην *recover* a memory, Arist. *Mem*.451a22; πρὸς ἑαυτὸν ἀ. *run over* in one's mind, Pl.*Ti*.26a. 5. *receive back* into a family, Luc.*Abd*.9, al. III. *pull up short*, of a horse, X.*Eq*.3.5; *check*, οἷόνπερ ἵππον τὸν λόγον ἀ. Pl.*Lg*.701c; τὴν ὁρμὴν τῆς νεώς Plb.16.3.4; ἀ. τὰς κύνας *call* them *back*, X.*Cyn*.7. 10. IV. *win over*, Ar.*Eq*.682, Din.1.28, Plu.*Brut*.24, al.; ἀ. τὸν ἀκροατήν Arist.*Rh*.1354b32. V. ἀγορὰν στοαῖς ἀνειλημμένην διτταῖς, perh. on a terrace *supported* by two colonnades, Dicaearch. 59.23; cf. ἀνάλημμα II.

**ἀναλάμπω**, *flame up, take fire*, X.*Cyr*.5.1.16; *shine out*, of the sun, Thphr.*CP* 4.13.6: metaph., ἀκτῖνες ἀρετῆς ἀ. Ph.1.335; *flame up*, of envy, Jul.*ad Ath*.274d. II. metaph., *break out*, as war, Plu.*Sull*.6, cf. 7. 2. of a person, *come to oneself again, revive*, Id.*Brut*.15, cf. 2.694f; *blaze up* with enthusiasm, Philostr.*VA* 5. 30. III. trans., *cause to shine*, φῶς Plu.*Alex*.30; λιθοκαλλέα μορφήν, of a sculptor, *App.Anth*.2.534 (Halic.). 2. *illuminate*, τὸ ζοφερόν Heraclit.*Ep*.6.3.

**ἀνάλαμψις**, εως, ἡ, *shining forth*, τοῦ νοητοῦ φωτός Ph.1.7; ἀ. εὐμενεῖς ἔχειν Plu.2.419f.

**ἀναλγής**, ές, = ἀνάλγητος, πρὸς τὸ αἰσχρόν Plu.2.528d: of a mortified state of body, Hp.*Art*.69; *painless*, θάνατος Plu.*Sol*.27.

**ἀναλγησία**, ἡ, *want of feeling, insensibility*, Democr.193, D.18.35, Arist.*EN* 1100b32, Ph.2.318.

**ἀνάλγητος**, ον, *without pain*, and so: I. of persons, *insensible to pain* or *danger*, Meliss.ap.Arist.*Xen*.974a19, cf. *EN* 1115b26. 2. *unfeeling, hard-hearted, ruthless*, S.*Aj*.946 (lyr.); -ότερος εἶναι to feel *less resentment*, Th.3.40: c. gen., ἀ. γενέσθαι τινός to be *insensible to*, Plu.*Aem*.35. Adv. -τως *unfeelingly*, S.*Aj*.1333; *callously*, ἀ. ἀκούειν Plu.2.46c. II. of things, *not painful*, ἀνάλγητα (sc. πράγματα) *a lot free from pain*, S.*Tr*.126. 2. *cruel*, πάθος E.*Hipp*.1386 (lyr.).

*__ἀναλδής__, ές, (ἀλδαίνω) *not thriving, feeble*, καρποί Hp.*Aër*.15; *barren*, Ar.*V*.1045 (anap.); ἄρουραι ἀναλδέα φυλλιόωσαι *without fruiting*, Arat.333.

**ἀναλδήσκω**, *grow up*, A.R.3.1363; *spring up afresh*, Opp.*C*.2.397.

*__ἀναλεαίνω__, *bruise, crush, pound fine*, v.l. in Dsc.5.74.

*__ἀναλέγω__, Ep. impf. ἄλλεγον (v. infr.): fut. -λέξω Ar.*Av*.591: Ep. aor. inf. ἀλλέξαι:—Med., v. infr.:—*pick up, gather up*, ὀστέα ἀλλέξαι

.21.321; ὀστέα..ἄλλεγον ἐς φιάλην 23.253; ἀνά τ' ἔντεα καλὰ λέγοντες 1.755; ἐκ βίβλων ἀ. *collect* materials from books, *IG*3.716:—Med., *ick up for oneself*, τοὺς στατῆρας Hdt.3.130; [σκώληκας] ἀ. τῇ γλώττῃ, of the woodpecker, Arist.*HA*614ᵇ1; ἀ. πνεῦμα *collect one's* breath, *P*12.132 (Mel.); *select* or *take up* a theme for discussion, Ps.-Alex. phr. *in SE*17.15. II. in Med., *reckon up*, τὸν χρόνον Plu.*Lyc.*1:—Pass. (with fut. ἀναλέξομαι Them.*in Ph.*132.7), ὅ σοι τιμὴν οἴσει εἰς ὃν ἔπειτα χρόνον ἀναλεγόμενον *being recounted*, X.*An.*2.1.17. III. in Med., *read through*, τὸ περὶ ψυχῆς γράμμ' ἀναλεξάμενος Call.*Epigr.* 5; συχνὰς ἀναλεξάμενος γραφάς D.H.1.89; ἐκ γραμμάτων ἀ. τι Plu. 2.582a:—Pass., Σιμφοῦς -ομένης ib.711d. 2. Med., *recover*, ἀπὸ τῆς καταπλήξεως dub. in D.S.32.6.

**ἀναλεῖ·** σχολάζει (Tarent.), Hsch.

**ἀναλει-όω**, *grind, rub down again*, Pelag.Alch.p.255 B. **-ωσις,** εως, ἡ, Id.p.254 B.

**ἀν-άλειπτος**, ον, *unanointed*, Antyll.ap.Aët.3.9:—also **-άλειφος,** ον, Them.*Or.*20.235d, Archig.ap.Aët.3.194.

**ἀναλείφω**, *smear on, apply* a drug, Orib.*Fr.*117.

**ἀναλείχω**, *lick up*, τὸ αἷμα Hdt.1.74.

**ἀν-αλειψία**, ἡ, *neglect of anointing*, Sm.*Ps.*108.24, prob. l. for **ἀναλειφίη** in Hp.*Vict.*2.57. II. *lack of oil*, *CPR*57.16 (iii A.D.).

**ἀνα-λεκτέον**, *one must collect*, Agath.*Praef.*p.139 D., Eust.1039. 47. ***-λέκτης**, ου, ὁ, Lat. *-lecta, slave who picked up broken meats*, Mart.7.20. ***-λεκτος**, ον, *select, choice*, γυναῖκες ἀ. τὸ κάλλος Socr. *Ep.*9. **-lectris**, **-idos**, dub. in Ov.*AA*3.273 (v. ἀναληπτρίς).

**ἀν-αλήθης**, ες, *untrue, false*, Plb.12.26ᵈ6, Plu.*Comp.Alc.Cor.*2. Adv. -θως M.Ant.2.16. II. of styles, *affected*, D.H.*Dem.*4 (Comp.), Longin.3.4.

***ἀνά-λημμα**, ατος, τό, *that which is used for repairing* or *supporting*; *sling* for a wounded limb, Hp.*Off.*23. II. any high *erection* or *embankment*, esp. of *substructures* or *retaining-walls*, *SIG*²587.20, *SIG*290 (Delph.), 813 *A* 5 (Delph.), *IG*11.163 *A* 38 (Delos), cf. 165.33, D.S.17.71: pl., Id.20.36, D.H.3.69, *IG*4.203.21; τὸ ἀ. τῆς πόλεως Δαυίδ Lxx 2 *Ch.*32.5; ἀ. ὑψηλὸν περιβόλου ἱεροῦ ib.*Si.*50.2. III. *sun-dial*, *CIG*2681, Vitr.9.7.7. IV. = μέρος τι τοῦ ἥπατος, Hsch. **-ληπτέον**, *one must take up* a question, Pl.*Phlb.*33c; *recall*, εἰς μνήμην Id.*Lg.*864b; ἀ. ἑαυτούς they *must recover* themselves, Plu.2.136a, cf. Sor.2.59:—Adj. -τέος Plu.2.1116e. **-ληπτήρ**, ῆρος, ὁ, *bucket*, J.*AJ*3.3.7; *ladle* or *bowl*, Lxx 2 *Ch.*4.16. **-ληπτικός**, ή, όν, *restorative*, κύκλος, of medical treatment, Sor.2.88, cf. Gal.1.301. Adv. -κῶς Id.14.672. ***-ληπτρίς**, ίδος, ἡ, *suspensory bandage*, Gal.18(1).323; *analemptris*, = στρόφιον, prob.l. in Ov.*AA*3. 273. **-λῆσαι·** ἀνατρέψαι, Hsch. (fort. -λῦσαι). ***-ληψις**, later **-λημψις**, hyperdor. **-λαψις** Ti.Locr.100c, εως, ἡ:—*taking up*, e.g. *suspension* in a sling, *fixing* a bandage, Hp.*Art.*22, *Off.*9; *looping* or *tying up* of vines, *POxy.*1692.20 (ii A.D.), cf. 1631.13 (iii A.D.). 2. *receiving back* into a family, Luc.*Abd.*5. 3. *acquirement* of knowledge, etc., Phld.*Rh.*1.31 S., al., Ti.Locr. l.c., S.E.*P.*1.73, D.S.1.1; ἱερῶν Plu.2.351e. 4. *assumption* of an office, dub. in *Inscr. Prien.*123; διαδήματος *OGI*383.102. 5. Pass., *being taken up* or *away*, *Psalm.Solom.*4.20; *ascension*, *Ev.Luc.*9.51. 6. *reception, entertainment*, *SIG*888.36 (Thrace). 7. *assimilation*, τροφῆς Menon *Iatr.*25.48. II. *recovery*, μνήμης Arist.*Mem.*451ᵃ20; *means of regaining*, Plu.*Publ.*9. 2. *making good, making amends*, Th. 5.65; *refreshing* of soldiers after hard work, Plb.3.87.1, cf. Luc. *Par.*40; ἀνάληψιν ποιεῖν Demetr.Com.Nov.1.10:—*recovery* from illness, Hp.*Aph.*4.27, Pl.*Ti.*83e. 3. *repair*, Str.13.1.38, *PSI*1.83. 11 (iii A.D.). 4. *repetition*, [Longin.]*Rh.*p.200 H.

**ἀναλθ-ής**, ές, *not to be healed*, ἑλκύδριον Hp.*Art.*63, cf. Arctin.*Iliup.* 5, Aret.*SD*1.7, Q.S.3.84. 2. *not healing, powerless to heal*, φάρμακα Bion *Fr.*13.4. 3. *deadly, inflicting incurable wounds*, Opp. *C.*2.424. **-ητος**, ον, = foreg., *incurable*, Nonn.*D.*35.296.

**ἀν-αλίγκιος**, ον, *unlike*, Hsch.

**ἀναλικμάω**, *winnow out*, of grain, v.l. in Pl.*Ti.*52e.

**ἀνάλιος**, ον, Dor. for ἀνήλιος.

**ἀνάλιπος** [ᾰλ], ον, Dor. for ἀνήλιπος, *barefoot*, f.l. in Theoc.4.56.

***ἀνᾱλίσκω** E.*IT*337, Ar.*Th.*1131, Th.7.48:—also **ἀνᾱλόω** Hp.*VM* 10, A.*Th.*813, E.*Med.*325, Ar.*Pl.*248, Arar.10, Th.2.24, al., Democr. 280, X.*Hier.*11.1: impf. ἀνήλισκον Pl.*R.*552b, X.*Cyr.*1.2.16, ἀνάλισκον App.*BC*3.58, ἀνάλουν Ar.*Fr.*220.2, Th.8.45: fut. ἀνᾱλώσω E. *Cyc.*308, Pl.*R.*568d: aor. ἀνήλωσα S.*Aj.*1049, Lys.19.18, etc., ἀνάλωσα [ᾱ] E.*El.*681 (s.v.l.) and later: pf. ἀνήλωκα Lys.26.3, etc., and ἀνάλωκα [ᾱ] Th.2.64 codd. and later:—Pass., fut. ἀναλωθήσομαι E. *Hipp.*506, D.22.19, wrongly ἀνηλωθήσομαι *PRev.Laws*51.17 (iii B.C.), ἀναλώσομαι Gal.15.129: aor. ἀνηλώθην and ἀνᾱλώθην: pf. ἀνήλωμαι and ἀνάλωμαι:—in Attic Inscrr. both forms are found in cent. v, ἀναλίσκω only from cent. iv onwards. The augmented forms are sts. wrongly used, ἀνηλοῦντι *POxy.*1143 (i A.D.), ἀνηλώση *PStrassb.*92. 17 (iii B.C.); cf. ἀνήλωμα: ἀνάλωσα is found at Amorgos, *IG*12(7).22. 16, and at Delos, ib.11(2).161 *A* 114:—*use up, spend*, Ar.*Pl.*381: abs., ib.248; τὰ ἀναλωθέντα ἀποδοῦναι Th.1.117; ἀ. εἴς τι *spend upon* a thing, Id.7.83, Ar.*Fr.*220, Pl.*Phd.*78a, *R.*561a, al.; πρός τι D.3.19; ὑπὲρ φιλοτιμίας Id.18.66: c. dat., Ἰσοκράτει ἀργύριον ἀ. *spend* money in paying him, Id.35.40:—Pass., τἀνηλωμένα *the monies expended* Id.18.113; τοῦτο γὰρ μόνον οὐκ ἔστι τἀνάλωμ' ἀναλωθὲν λαβεῖν E.*Supp.* 776. 2. metaph., ἀνήλωσας λόγον *hast wasted* words, S.*Aj.*1049, cf. E.*Med.*325; χρόνον καὶ πόνον ἐπί τινι Pl.*R.*369e; σώματα καὶ πόνους πολέμῳ Th.2.64; τὴν τῶν προγόνων δόξαν Pl.*Mx.*247b; ἀ. ὕπνον *waste time in* sleep, Pi.*P.*9.27; λόγῳ ἀ. τὸν χρόνον τῆς ἡμέρας *diem eximere dicendo*, Plu.*Aem.*30. 3. *consume*, σιτία Hp.*VM*10; κρέα Paus.10.4.10; of animals, in Pass., *to be eaten*, Pl.*Prt.*321b:—Pass., *to be expended*, εἰς τὴν πιμελὴν in forming fat, Arist.*GA*727ᵇ1, al. II. of persons, *kill, destroy*, τοὺς ἀναλωθέντας A.*Ag.*570, cf. S.*OT*1174, *Fr.*892, E.*El.*681, Th.8.65:—Med., *kill oneself*, Id.3.81:—Pass., *to be consumed, perish*, Pl.*Plt.*272d; *to be disposed of, got rid of*, ib.289c. (ἀνά, ἁλίσκομαι.)

**ἀνάλιστος**, ον, *unsalted*: *silly*, Timo 35.

**ἀναλιχμάομαι**, = ἀναλείχω, Philostr.*VA*5.42: aor. ἀνελιχμήσαντο J.*AJ*8.15.6.

**ἀναλκάταλλα·** ἄνοσον κάτω, Hsch.

**ἀνάλκ-εια**, ἡ, *want of strength, feebleness, cowardice*, ἀναλκείῃσι δαμέντες Il.6.74, 17.320:—also in sg., ὤ μοι ἀναλκείης Thgn.891. **-ής**, ές, = sq., Hp.*Aër.*16, Arist.*Phgn.*809ᵃ39 (Comp.). **-ιμος**, ον, = sq., *POxy.*79. ***-ις**, ιδος, ὁ, ἡ: acc. -ιδα Il.8.153, etc., but -ιν Od.3.375, A.*Ag.*1224: (ἀλκή):—*without strength, impotent, feeble*, of unwarlike men, ἀπτόλεμος καὶ ἄ. Il.2.201, cf. 9.35; κακὸν καὶ ἀνάλκιδα 8.153, 14. 126; of the suitors, Od.4.334; of Aegisthus, 3.310, cf. A.*Ag.*1224; of Aphrodite, Il.5.331; also ἄ. θυμός 16.656; φύζα 15.62; ὁ πάντ' ἄ. S.*El.*301, cf. Hdt.2.102.

**ἀνάλλακτος**, ον, *unchangeable*, Orph.*Fr.*248.8.

**ἀναλληγόρητος**, ον, *without allegory*, Eust.83.23, 549.29.

***ἀναλλοίωτος**, ον, *unchangeable*, Arist.*Metaph.*1073ᵃ11, *Cael.*270ᵃ 14; ἀ. τὴν φωνήν D.L.4.17; κάλλος Ph.1.649; of undigested food, Gal.6.575; ἀ. ὕλη *Stoic.*2.114; *not permitting change*, Thphr.*CP*6. 10.1.

**ἀνάλλομαι**, *leap, spring up*, Ar.*Ach.*669; ἐπὶ ὄχθους X.*Eq.Mag.*8.3.

***ἄναλλος**, ον, *topsy-turvy*, Eust.1000.31.

**ἄναλμ-ος**, ον, *not salted*, X.*Oec.*20.12. ***-υρος**, ον, = foreg., Diosc.Gloss.ap.Gal.19.79.

**ἀναλογάδην**, Adv., (ἀνάλογος) *proportionately*, Hsch.

**ἀναλογεῖον**, τό, gloss on ἀναγνωστήριον, Hsch.; *manuale lectorium*, *Gloss.*, cf. Poll.10.60, Hdn.Gr.2.457.

**ἀναλογ-έω**, *to be analogous*, σπλάγχνον οὐκ ἔχει ἀναλογοῦν Arist. *Fr.*334: c. dat., Phld.*Sign.*37, Ph.1.278, etc.; ὁ τεχνίτης ὁ -ῶν τῷ Φειδίᾳ Gal.*Nat.Fac.*2.3: c. acc., ἀ. τὴν ἐπιμέλειαν *to be capable of performing* a service, *PAmh.*64.13; ἀ. τοῖς τᾶς ἀξίας βάσμοις *to keep up to* the degrees of his rank, *IG*12(2).243.17 (Mytilene), cf. *CIG*3486 (Thyatira), J.*AJ*4.8.4, Ath.3.80c, etc. 2. Math., *to be proportionate*, Cleom.1.7. **-ή**, ἡ, *account, bill*, *Sammelb.*4425.3.1 (ii A.D.). **-ητέον**, *one must sum up*, dub. in Arist.*Rh.Al.*1443ᵇ15 (fort. leg. ἀναλογιστέον). **-ητικός**, ή, όν, *proportional*, dub. in D.L.1.17. II. of the *analogical* school of grammarians, A.D. *Conj.*241.14. ***-ία**, ἡ, (λόγος) *mathematical proportion*, Pl.*Ti.* 31c, 32c; ἡ ἀ. ἰσότης ἐστὶ λόγων Arist.*EN*1131ᵃ31; of progressions, ἀ. γεωμετρική ib.ᵇ13; ἀριθμητική ib.1106ᵃ36, cf. Ael.*Tact.*10.3; ἁρμονική Thrasyll.ap.Theon.Sm.p.85 H., Nicom.*Ar.*2.22; κατὰ τὴν ἀ. *comparing the ratios*, Arist.*Pol.*1282ᵇ40; τὸ κατ' ἀ. ἴσον ib.1301ᵃ27; ὑπὲρ τὴν ἀ. τινός *out of proportion*, Olymp.*in Mete.*89.22. 2. *proportion* generally, Arist.*Pol.*1296ᵇ25, cf. Epicur.*Nat.*11.7,10. II. *analogy*, Arist.*HA*486ᵇ19, Epicur.*Fr.*212, etc. 2. esp. *grammatical analogy*, Gell.2.25, A.D.*Synt.*36.23, etc. III. *relation*, ἀ. ἔχειν stand *in relation with*, πρός τι Phld.*Lib.*p.38 O., cf. p.51 O. IV. *correspondence, resemblance*, ὁμοιότης ἢ ἀ. [τινί] Id.*Sign.*37, cf. *Fr.*3; κατ' -ίαν, opp. διαφοράν, Id.*D.*1.22. **-ίζομαι**, *reckon up, sum up*, τὰ ὡμολογημένα Pl.*Prt.*332d, cf. *R.*330e: abs., ἐκ τῶν προειρημένων ἀ. ib.524d; τὰ δεινά X.*Mem.*2.1.4, cf. *Ep.Heb.*12.3; τὰ γεγονότα καὶ τὰ παρόντα πρὸς τὰ μέλλοντα ἀ. *calculate* the past and the present *in comparison with* the future, Pl.*Tht.*186a; ἀ. τι πρός τι Arist.*Pol.* 1320ᵇ20; ἐκ τούτων ἀ. *make calculations* from.., Id.*Cael.*293ᵃ33; *infer*, Epicur.*Nat.*14.4, Phld.*D.*1.13, Diog.Oen.*Fr.*38. 2. *calculate, consider*, Th.5.7, Lys.14.47. 3. foll. by a Conjunction, ἀ. ὡς.. *calculate* or *reflect* that, Th.8.83, X.*HG*2.4.23, etc.; *take into account*, Phld.*Herc.*1251.5. 4. *recapitulate*, Hyp.*Phil.*4. **-ικός**, ή, όν, *based on mathematical ratios*, Plu.2.1144f, cf. Iamb.*in Nic.*p.100 P. ἡ -κὴ τέχνη the art *of applying analogy*, S.E.*M.*1.199; οἱ -κοί *the analogical school of grammarians*, Suid. s.v. Ἀτρείδης, Eust.802. 38. **-ισμα**, ατος, τό, *a result of reasoning*, τὰ περὶ τούτων ἀ. Pl.*Tht.*186c. **-ισμός**, ὁ, *reconsideration*, Th.3.36; *reckoning, calculation*, 8.84; *course* or *line of reasoning*, X.*HG*5.1.19; ἐν τῷ πρὸς αὑτὸν ἀ. Men.447; opp. ἐπιλογισμός, *Stoic.*2.89. 2. κατὰ τὸν ἀ. according to *proportionate reckoning*, Docum.ap.D.18.106; δι' ἀναλογισμοῦ S.E.*P.*1.147. **-ιστέον**, v. ἀναλογητέον. ***-ιστικός**, ή, όν, *judging by analogy, analogical*, S.E.*M.*11.250; ἡ -κὴ τέχνη ib. 1.214. 2. of knowledge, etc., *reflective*, Phld.*Herc.*1003. Adv. -κῶς ibid. II. *teaching analogy*, γραμματικοί S.E.*M.*2.59; αἵρεσις -κή, of the Rational or Dogmatic school of physicians, opp. ἐπιλογιστική (the Empirics), Gal.1.65; *analogisticus sermo* Id.*Subf.Emp.*8 p.52 Bonnet. Adv. -κῶς S.E.*M.*3.40, Gal.18(2).346.

**ἀνάλογος**, ον, *according to a due* λόγος, *proportionate, conformable*, Pl.*Ti.*69b, cf. Ti.Locr.103d; but ἐὰν τέσσαρα ἀνάλογα ᾖ *in arithmetical progression*, Ascl.*Tact.*3.1: neut. ἀνάλογον freq. in Arist. in adverbial sense, *in proportion*, *EN*1158ᵃ35, etc.; freq. as Adj., τὸ ἀνάλογον λέγω, ὅταν.. *Po.*1457ᵇ16; παρὰ τὸ ἀ. *EN*1131ᵇ11, al., etc.; but ἐκ τοῦ ἀνάλογον *Rh.*1399ᵃ33, 1405ᵃ11, al.; μεταφοραὶ αἱ ἀνάλογον (sc. οὖσαι) ib.1408ᵃ8; τὰ τούτοις ἀνάλογον *HA*487ᵃ5, etc.; ἀ. οἰκοδόμοι (as a predicate) *EN*1103ᵇ9, cf. *Rh.*1364ᵇ11, al.:—so that it is plain that ἀνάλογον is merely equiv. to ἀνὰ λόγον, as it is written in Pl.*Ti.*37a; cf. λόγος:—the regul. Adv. ἀναλόγως Hp.*Ep.*27, Lxx

*Wi.*13.5, S.E.*P.*1.88, Alex.Aphr. *in Metaph.*156.5. II. *well-proportioned, suitable,* σχῆμα Philostr.*Im.*1.10 (Sup.). III. *equivalent to, resembling,* λυπηρὸν ἢ ἀ. λυπηρῷ Phld.*Ir.*p.76 W., cf. *Sign.* 2,37.

**ἀναλογούντως,** Adv. pres. part., = ἀναλόγως, c. dat., *CIG*2766 (Aphrodisias); *fittingly, BGU*248.21 (i A. D.).

**ἀναλογχόω,** *embroider with points,* Lyd.*Mag.*2.4 (Pass.).

**ἀναλοκίζω,** *rend, lacerate,* S.*Fr.*376 (Pass.).

**ἄνᾰλος,** *ον,* (ἅλς A) *without salt, not salted,* Arist.*Pr.*927$^{a}$35, Gal. 10.401. 2. of salt itself, salt *which is no salt, Ev.Marc.*9.50.

**ἀνᾱλόω,** v. ἀναλίσκω.

**ἄναλτος** (A), *ον, not to be filled, insatiate,* βόσκειν ἣν γαστέρ' ἄναλτον Od.17.228, 18.364, cf. Cratin.382. (ἀ- priv., *ἀλ-τός, cf. Lat. *alo,* etc.)

**ἄναλτος** (B), *ον,* (ἅλς A) *not salted,* Hp.*Morb.*2.54, Timocl.14.7, Din.*Fr.*89.7, Dsc.*Eup.*2.51.

*ἀναλύζω, lit. *hiccough*: hence, *sob aloud,* Luc.*Somn.*4 (ἀνολύζων codd.), Q.S.14.281 (vulg. ἀνωλύζεσκε). 2. ἀναλύζων· ἀνανύττων (sic), Hsch.; ἀναλύζουσα· στενάζουσα, λυγκαίνουσα, Suid.

***ἀνάλῠ-σις,** *εως, ἡ,* (ἀναλύω) *loosing, releasing,* κακῶν *from* evils, S.*El.*142 (lyr.); ὅρκων Timae.23. 2. *dissolving,* Arist.*Mu.*394$^{b}$17, Plu.2.915c (pl.); σώματος, of death, Secund.*Sent.*19. 3. *resolution* of a problem *by the analysis of its conditions,* opp. σύνθεσις, Arist.*EN*1112$^{b}$23; esp. in Math., Phld.*Acad.Ind.*17, Papp.634.11, Procl.*in Euc.*p.43 F. 4. in the Logic of Arist., *reduction* of the imperfect figures into the perfect one, *APr.*51$^{a}$18, al., Chrysipp. *Stoic.*2.7. 5. *solution* of a problem, etc., Plu.*Rom.*12. II. (from Pass.) *retrogression,* Id.2.76d; *retirement, departure,* J.*AJ*19.4.1; *death* (cf. ἀναλύω III), 2*Ep.Ti.*4.6. **-τέον,** *one must dissolve, PHolm.*24.23. **-τήρ,** *ῆρος, ὁ, deliverer,* A.*Ch.*160 (lyr.). **-της,** *ου, ὁ, deliverer,* esp. from a magic spell, Magn.4. ***-τικός,** *ή, όν, analytical,* ἐπιστήμη Arist.*Rh.*1359$^{b}$10; θεωρία, of mathematical analysis, Papp.410.28; συλλογισμός Arr.*Epict.*2.3.4; τὰ ἀναλυτικά *principles of analysis,* ἀπαιδευσίᾳ τῶν ἀ. Arist.*Metaph.*1005$^{b}$4; title of A.'s treatises on this subject; so *-κή, ἡ,* Ammon.*in APr.*7.34. Adv. *-κῶς* Arist.*APo.*84$^{a}$8. 2. *dissolvent,* τῆς διακρίσεως Dam.*Pr.*161. **-τος,** *ον, dissoluble,* Plot.4.7.2.

***ἀν-αλύω** (A), *cause to wander, unsettle,* βασιλέα Philostr.*VA*5.35.

***ἀνα-λύω** (B), Ep. **ἀλλύω** (**ἀνλύω** *Hymn.Is.*145): (v. λύω for the tenses and prosody: Hom. has ἀλλύουσα, ἀλλύεσκε with ῡ):—*unloose, undo,* of Penelope's web, νύκτας δ' ἀλλύεσκεν Od.2.105; ἀλλύουσαν..ἀγλαὸν ἱστόν ib.109, etc.; ἀνά τε πρυμνήσια λῦσαι ib. 9.178, etc. 2. *unloose, set free,* ἐμὲ δ' ἐκ δεσμῶν ἀνέλυσαν ib. 12.200 (never in Il.), cf. Ant.Lib.22.4; ὀφθαλμόν, φωνάν Pi.*N.*10.90; τινὰ καταδίκης Ael.*VH*5.18. 3. Medic., *relax,* in Pass., Arist.*GA*728$^{a}$15, Men.213, Dsc.5.3. II. *undo* in various senses: 1. *unloose,* ζώνην Call.*Del.*237; in Med., *unwind* a cocoon, Arist.*HA*551$^{b}$14. 2. Astrol., *nullify,* of planetary influence, Ptol.*Tetr.*133 (Pass.). 3. *dissolve* matter *into its elements,* ἐς αὐτὰ ταῦτα Ti.Locr.102d:—Pass., of snow, *melt,* Plu.2.898a. b. *resolve into its elements,* οὐ καλὸν ἁρμονίην ἀναλυέμεν ἀνθρώποιο Ps.-Phoc.102:—*investigate analytically,* διάγραμμα Arist.*EN*1112$^{b}$20, Plu.2.792d, etc.:—Pass., Archim.*Sph.Cyl.*1.4; ὁ -όμενος τόπος the treasury *of analysis,* Papp.634.2; ἀναλύοντες καὶ ἀναλυόμενοι Dam.*Pr.*2; ἀ. τοὺς μύθους ἐς λόγους πιθανούς Jul.*Or.*2.74d. 4. in the Logic of Arist., *reduce* a syllogism, *APr.*47$^{a}$4, al.; cf. ἀνάλυσις I. 4. 5. *reduce,* σχοινία εἰς ὀργυιάς Hero *Geom.*5.8. 6. Gramm., *resolve,* κτητικὰ εἰς γενικάς A.D.*Synt.*292.17. 7. *do away, cancel,* μόρσιμ' ἀ. Ζεὺς οὐ τολμᾷ Pi *Pae.*6.94, cf. D.21.218, Plu.*Sol.*25, etc.: mostly in Med., *cancel faults,* πάντα ταῦτα X.*HG*7.5.18; ἁμαρτίας D.14.34; ἀλλύοιτό κα τὸ χρέος *discharge* the debt, prob. in *GDI*1151 (Olymp.). 8. *suspend,* τὰ περὶ κυνηγέσιον X.*Cyn.*5.34. 9. *solve the problem* of a thing, τὸν Ἰνδὸν ἀ. *trace* its *source,* Plu.2.133c. 10. *release from a spell,* Luc.*Vit.Auct.*25, cf. Hsch.:—Pass., Men.*Her.Fr.*6. 11. *relieve,* Ptol.*Tetr.*133 (Pass.). III. intr., *loose from moorings, weigh anchor,* and so, *depart, go away,* Plb.3.69.14, Babr.42.8, etc.: metaph., of death, ἐς θεοὺς ἀνέλυσα *Epigr.Gr.*340.7 (Macestus): abs., *die, Ep.Phil.*1.23, *IG*14.1794; ἀ. ἐκ τοῦ ζῆν Diog.Oen.2. 2. *return, Ev.Luc.*12.36; ἐξ ᾅδου Lxx *Wi.*2.1.

***ἀναλφάβητος,** *ον, not knowing one's a b c,* Nicoch.2 D.

**ἀνάλφιτος,** *ον, without barley-meal,* Philyll.1 D.

***ἀνάλ-ωμα** [ᾱλ], *ατος, τό,* ἀνήλωμα freq. in Pap. and Inscrr. as *IG*2$^{2}$.1228.12, 12(5).1061.17 (iii B. C.), Wilcken *Chrest.*30 i 1 (ca. 200 B. C.):—*expense, cost,* A.*Supp.*476; opp. λῆμμα, Lys.32.20, Pl.*Lg.*920c: in pl., *expenses,* Th.7.28, D.21.106, etc.; οὐσίαν, ἧς αἱ πρόσοδοι λύουσι τἀναλώματα Diph.32.5; ἐκ τῶν ἰδίων ἀναλωμάτων καθοπλίζειν at their own private *costs,* Decr.ap.D.18.116, cf. *IG*7.3073, etc.: metaph., σκαιόν γε τἀνάλωμα τῆς γλώσσης τόδε E.*Supp.*547. 2. *exhalation,* Plu.2.384a codd. **-ωμάτιον,** *τό,* Dim. of foreg., *slight loss,* Ph.*Bel.*67.28. 2. *trifling expenditure, PFlor.*131.3 (iii A. D.). ***-ωσις,** *εως, ἡ, outlay, expenditure,* Thgn.903, Th.6.31, Pl.*Cri.*48c, etc. II. *wasting, consumption,* ἐγκεφάλου Hp.*Epid.*6.3.1. **-ωτέος,** *α, ον, to be spent,* Pl.*Lg.*847e. **-ωτής,** *οῦ, ὁ, spender, waster,* Id.*R.*552b, c. **-ωτικός,** *ή, όν, expensive, spendthrift,* ἡδοναί, ἐπιθυμίαι, ib.558d, 559c; *consuming,* c. gen., Ph.2.151, Iamb.*Myst.*2.5.

***ἀν-άλωτος** [ᾰλ], *ον,* (ἀ- priv., ἁλίσκομαι) *not to be taken, impregnable,* of strong places or forts, Hdt.1.84, 8.51; οὐδὲν ἀ. ἀρετῇ Chor. in *Rev.Phil.*1.70: *not taken, holding out,* Th.4.70. 2. metaph., *unassailable, convincing,* αἰσθήσεις Pl.*Tht.*179c; of persons, ἀ. ὑ[πὸ] χρημάτων *incorruptible,* X.*Ages.*8.8: c. gen., τῶν Ἀφροδίτης παθ[ῶν] Men.Rh.p.416 S. 3. of things, *unattainable,* [D.]61.37.

**ἀναλωφάω,** *to be relieved again, have a respite from suffering,* Are[t.] *CA*2.11.

**ἀναμαιμάω,** *rage through,* ὡς δ' ἀναμαιμάει βαθέ' ἄγκεα θεσπιδαὲ[ς] πῦρ Il.20.490.

**ἀναμᾰλάσσω,** *soften thoroughly,* Hp.*Mul.*2.205, Gal.12.419.

**ἀναμανθάνω,** *inquire closely,* Hdt.9.101; *learn afresh,* Hsch. simply, *learn,* D.S.34.17, Ph.1.406.

**ἀναμαντεύομαι,** *take the auspices a second time,* D.C.37.25. 2. *unmake a prophecy,* Phryn.*PS*p.45 B.

**ἀναμάξευτος,** *ον, impassable for wagons,* Hdt.2.108.

**ἀνάμαξις,** *εως, ἡ, impression,* τοῦ εἴδους Alex.Aphr. *de An.*137.25.

***ἀναμαρμαίρω,** *move quickly,* of a smith's bellows, A.R.3.1300.

**ἀναμαρτ-ής,** *ές, unerring,* Hsch. s. v. νημερτής. **-ησία,** *ἡ, faultlessness, innocence,* App.*Pun.*52. **-ητος,** *ον, making no mistake, unerring,* X.*Cyr.*8.7.22, Pl.*R.*339b. 2. in moral sense, *blameless,* Hp.*Fract.*16 (Comp.), cf. Antipho 3.2.10, Men.*Epit.*487, Phld.*Sto.Herc.*339.17; *sinless, Ev.Jo.*8.7, cf. Aristeas 252, Muson.*Fr.*2 p.6 H.; ἀ. πολιτεία a *faultless* form of government, Arist.*Pol.*1275$^{b}$2; ἀ. πρός τινα *having done no wrong to* a person, Hdt.1.117; τινί 5.39; ἀ. τινός *guiltless of* a thing, 1.155: τὸ -ητότατον, = ἀναμαρτησία, X.*Ages.*6.7, cf. Pl.*R.*477e; πρὸς τὸ ἀ. *to preserve from error,* Arist.*EN*1155$^{a}$13. Adv. -τως *without fail, unerringly,* X.*Mem.*2.8.5; *without making a mistake,* Ps.-Alex.Aphr. *in SE*15.33; *inoffensively,* [D.]61.21. II. of things, *not done by fault, done unavoidably,* συμφορά Antipho 3.2.11. 2. *unfailing,* Dion.Byz.17.

**ἀναμᾱρυκ-άομαι,** v. ἀναμηρ-:—also **-ίζω,** Jul.*Gal.*314d.

**ἀναμᾰσάομαι,** *chew over again, ruminate,* Ar.*V.*783.

**ἀνα-μάσσω,** Att. **-ττω,** fut. *-ξω* (v. infr.): (v. μάσσω):—*rub* or *wipe off,* ἔργον, ὃ σῇ κεφαλῇ ἀναμάξεις a deed (as if a stain), which thou *wilt wipe off* with or on thine own head (since it was believed that the pollution of murder was avoided by wiping the weapon on the victim's head), Od.19.92; τὰ μὲν ἐμῇ κεφαλῇ ἀναμάξας φέρω Hdt.1.155:—Med., ἀσέβειαν δημοσίᾳ -ξασθαι Paus.10.33.2; ἀναματτομένη τῷ προσώπῳ τοῦ αἵματος *having* [some of] the blood *wiped on her* face, Plu.*Ant.*77; τὸ ἑτέρου κακόν Ph.2.379; ψυχὴ ἀ. πάθος J.*AJ*16.8.5; τοσαύτας ἀναμεμαγμένος κηλῖδας Porph.*Chr.*88. II. Med., *knead one's bread,* Ar.*Nu.*676 codd., cf. *AB*391. 2. *receive an impression,* Ti.Locr.94a; of the eyes, ἀ. τοὺς τύπους τῶν δρωμένων Arr.*Epict.*2.23.3; ἡ ψυχὴ ἀναμάττεσθαι δύναται τοὺς τῶν αἰσθητῶν τύπους Plot.4.3.26; ἀ. τὸ εἶδος Alex.Aphr. *de An.*137.1. 3. *obtain an impression of,* τὴν ψυχήν τινος διὰ τῶν λόγων Eun.*Hist.* p.266 D. 4. *refurbish,* τὴν μνήμην Max.Tyr.8.2.

***ἀναμαστεύω·** ἀναζητῶ, Hsch.; *make a search* (for fugitives), Men.Prot.p.131 D.

***ἀναμασχᾰλιστήρ,** *ῆρος, ὁ,* (μασχάλη) *shoulder-strap,* an article of female dress, Philippid.1.

***ἀναμάχομαι,** *renew the fight, retrieve a defeat,* Hdt.5.121, 8.109, Th.7.61, Jul.*Or.*1.24c. II. metaph., ἀ. τὸν λόγον *fight* the argument *over again,* Pl.*Hp.Ma.*286d, cf. *Phd.*89c. 2. *make good* a loss, ἀ. τὰ ἁμαρτανόμενα Thphr.*CP*3.2.5, cf. Plu.*Arat.*28; περιπέτειαν Plb.1.55.5; ἡ φύσις τὴν φθορὰν ἀ. nature *makes good* the waste, Arist.*GA*755$^{a}$31; ἀ. ταῖς μὴ ἀνελευθέροις συστολαῖς Phld.*Oec.*p.71 J.; *recover,* Id.*Mort.*37; τὴν νίκην Memn.58; *counteract,* Aret.*CD*2.6.

**ἀνάμβᾰτος,** *ον,* of a horse, *that one cannot mount, unbroken,* X.*Cyr.*4.5.46.

***ἀναμείγνῡμι,** later **-μίγνυμι** and **-ύω,** poet. **ἀμμείγνυμι** B.*Fr.*16: poet. aor. part. ἀμμείξας Il.24.529; cf. ἀναμίσγω:—*mix up, mix together,* ἀνὰ δὲ κρῖ λευκὸν ἔμειξαν Od.4.41; πάντα τὰ κρέα Hdt.4.26; κἀμοὶ..μἀναμείγνυσθαι (i.e. μὴ ἀναμ-) τύχας τὰς σάς E.*Supp.*591; θεὰς ἀνθρώποις *h.Ven.*52. II. often in Pass., *to be mixed* with, Διονυσίοισι δώροις B. l.c.; πάντες ἀναμεμειγμένοι S.*El.*715; τοῖσ. πολλὰ ἔθνεα ἀναμεμίχαται Hdt.1.146; Κάδμου παισὶν ἀναμεμειγμέναι E.*Ba.*37; πάντες ἀλλήλοις Arist.*Pol.*1319$^{b}$25; ἐν μέσοις τοῖς Ἕλλησιν X.*An.*4.8.8, cf. Pl.*Phlb.*48a. 2. *join company,* ὡς δὲ ἀνεμείχθημεν D.54.8; *have social intercourse,* Plu.*Num.*20.

**ἀναμέλγω,** *drain sap from,* ἀνὰ φυλλάδ' ἀμέλξαι Nic.*Al.*428.

**ἀναμελετάω,** *con over,* παράγγελμα πρὸς ἑαυτόν S.E.*M.*11.122.

**ἀν-άμελκτος,** *ον, unmilked,* Sch.Theoc.1.6; cf. ἀνήμελκτος.

**ἀναμέλπω,** *raise a strain,* c. acc. cogn., ἀοιδάν Theoc.17.113; ἁρμονίαν Ph.1.312; οἰκτρὸν μέλος Ps.-Callisth.1.46:—Med., *raise a strain, Pae.Delph.*13:—Pass., Phld.*Mus.*p.85 K., Plu.*Daed.*6. II. trans., *praise in song, Anacreont.*36.2.

**ἀναμεμιγμένως,** *promiscuously,* Hsch. s.v. ἀναμίξ, Sch.S.*Tr.*519.

**ἀναμενετέον,** *one must await,* τινά Ach.Tat.5.11.

**ἀναμένω,** poet. **ἀμμένω,** Aeol. **ὀμμένω** Alc.41:—*wait for, await,* ἀνέμεινα..Ἠῶ δῖαν Od.19.342; νύκτα, τὸν ἥλιον, Hdt.7.42,54; τέλος δίκης A.*Eu.*243; freq. in E., and Att. Prose:—οὐδὲ..ἐπιθυμίαν ἀναμένεις *dost* not *wait for* desire to arise, X.*Mem.*2.1.30, cf. *Smp.*4.41; ἀ. τινά Hdt.9.57; *face* an enemy *in battle,* Pi.*P.*6.31: c. acc. et inf., οὐκ ἀ. τοὺς Ἕλληνας μάχης ἄρξαι Hdt.8.15; ἀ. φῦναι τὰς τρίχας Id.5.35; ἀ. ἡμέραν γενέσθαι Th.4.135, cf. 120: foll. by relat. clauses, ἀ. ἕως ἄν.. Pl.*Ly.*209a; ἀ. αὐτοὺς ἔστ' ἐμφάγοιέν τι X.*Cyr.*8.1.44; ποῖ χρῆν ἀναμεῖναι; i.e. ἐς τίνα χρόνον; Ar.*Lys.*526: abs., *wait, stay,* Ἑρμῆς..οὐκέτ' ἀμμένει S.*El.*1397, cf. 1389, *Tr.*528, Ar.*Ra.*175: c. part., πεινῶν ἀ. Id.*V.*777. 2. *put off, delay,* X.*Cyr.*1.6.10: c. inf., D.19.224.

**ἀναμερ-ίζω**, *distribute, distinguish*, πρόσωπα A.D.*Synt.*114.3, al. **-ῐσις**, εως, ἡ, *distribution*, Lyd.*Mens.*4.67. ※**-ισμός**, ὁ, *redistribution*, Sch.rec.Pi.*O.*7.110.

**ἀνάμεσος**, ον, *in the midst, in the heart of a country*, πόλεις ἀνάμεσοι Hdt.2.108; simply, *in the midst, between*, *PLond.*2.267.189; χρόνος ἀ. ἡμέρας καὶ νυκτός Eudox.*Ars* 16; τὴν ἀνάμεσον ἀλλήλων χώραν Ph.Byz.*Mir.*1.2.

**ἀνάμεστ-ος**, ον (fem. -τη Eup.16 codd.), *filled full*, τινός *of* a thing, Ar.*Nu.*984, Eup. l.c., Philum.ap.Aët.5.125, Phld.*Piet.*74, Man.4.82, Eun.*VS* p.454 B.; ἔχθρας πρὸς τὸν δῆμον ἀνάμεστος D.25.32; βίος ἀ. ἰλύος Epict.*Gnom.*1. **-όω**, *fill up, fill full*, Ar.*Ra.*1084 (Pass.).

**ἀναμεταξύ**, Adv. *between, intermediate*, Arist.*Ph.*243$^a$15: of Time, *in the meanwhile*, Nic.Dam.p.63 D., Dexipp.p.196 D.: Prep. c. gen., Aq., Sm.3*Ki.*20.3.

**ἀναμετρ-έω**, *measure back again, re-measure the road, retrace one's steps*, ὄφρ'.. ἀναμετρήσαιμι Χάρυβδιν Od.12.428; ἀ. σαυτὸν ἀπιών *measure yourself off!* Ar.*Av.*1020; πόνοισι πόνους ἀ., i.e. undergo a succession of labours, *IG*3.1374. 2. *enumerate*, Hp.*Ep.*27:—in Med., *recapitulate*, E.*Or.*14. II. *measure over again*, τὸ ὕδωρ Hp.*Aër.*8. 2. *measure carefully*, ἀ. ὅσῳ ἐλάσσων ὁ χῶρος γέγονε Hdt.2.109; ἀ. τὸ ὅλον Arist.*Ph.*221$^a$3; τινί τι one thing by another, Pl.*R.*531a:—also in Med., ἀ. γῆν Ar.*Nu.*203; ἀνεμετρησάμην φρένας τὰς σάς *took the measure of*.., E.*Ion* 1271; γνώμης πονηροῖς κανόσιν ἀναμετρούμενος τὸ σῶφρον Id.*El.*52:—Pass., ἀ. τινί *to be measured by*, Pl.*Ti.*39d. 3. *measure out*, θουμόφυλον ἀ. δάκρυ E.*IT*346. **-ησις**, εως, ἡ, *measurement*, τῆς γῆς Str.1.1.20, cf. *POxy.*918 xi 14 (ii A.D.); τῶν θείων περιόδων Iamb.*Myst.*9.4. 2. *estimate*, τῆς εὐδαιμονίας πρὸς ἀργύριον ἀ. ποιεῖσθαι Plu.*Sol.*27, cf. Hierocl.*in CA* 19 p.461 M. **-ητέον**, *one must measure*, Iamb.*Protr.*5. ※**-ητής**, οῦ, ὁ, *official in charge of land-survey*, Wilcken *Chrest.*229.3 (iv A.D.). **-ικῶς**, Adv. *by measurement*, f.l. in Gem.17.5.

**ἀναμηλόω**, *examine with a probe*, *h.Merc.*41 (Ruhnken), Hsch.

**ἀναμηρυκ-άομαι** or ἀναμᾱρ-, *chew the cud*, Ath.9.390f, Luc.*Gall.*8. **-ησις**, εως, ἡ, *rumination*, Aristeas 154.

**ἀναμηρύομαι**, *wind up, draw back*, as a thread, Plu.2.978d.

※**ἀνά-μῖγα**, poet. ἄμμῖγα, Adv. = ἀναμίξ, *promiscuously, confusedly*, A.*Th.*239, S.*Tr.*839 (lyr.), *IG*5(1).726; τινί *with*.., A.R.1.573, *AP*7.12; also τινός ib.22. **-μιγδα**, = ἀναμίξ, S.*Tr.*519 (lyr.). ※**-μίγδην**, Nic.*Th.*912. **-μῖγή**, ἡ, *mixture*, Sch.A.*Th.*330. **-μικτέον**, *one must mix*, Orib.*Syn.*1.33.2.

**ἀν-αμίλλητος**, ον, *undisputed*, Hsch. (ἀναμήλλικτον cod.), Suid.

**ἀναμιμέομαι**, *imitate*, Plu.2.303a.

※**ἀναμιμνήσκω**, fut. ἀναμνήσω, poet. ἀμμνήσω: Aeol. aor. Act. ὀμναῖσαι Sapph.*Supp.*23.10: aor. inf. Pass. ὀμνάσθην Theoc.29.26:—*remind* one *of* a thing, c. dupl. acc., ταῦτά μ' ἀνέμνησας Od.3.211. cf. Hdt.6.140, S.*OT*1133, Th.6.6: but also c. gen. rei, μή μ' ἀναμνήσῃς κακῶν E.*Alc.*1045, cf. Pl.*Mx.*246a: c. acc. pers. only, Sapph. l.c. 2. c. acc. pers. et inf., *remind* one to do, Pi.*P.*4.54. 3. c. acc. rei only, *recall to memory, make mention of*, Antipho 2.4.11, D.18.213. 4. foll. by Conj., ἀ. ὅτι.. Th.2.89, etc.; ὡς εἶχε τὰ πράγματ' ἀναμνῆσαι D.18.17. 5. ἀναμιμνήσκων, ὁ, *remembrancer*, Lxx 2*Ki.*20.24, al. II. Pass., *remember, recall to mind*, τινός Hdt.2.151, Th.2.54, etc.; less freq. τι, Ar.*Ra.*661, Pl.*Phd.*72e, X.*An.*7.1.26; περί τι Pl.*R.*329a: foll. by a relat., ἀναμνησθέντας οἷα ἐπάσχετε Hdt.5.109: abs., Id.3.51, Ar.*Ec.*552. 2. ἀ. νοσήματος have a *relapse*, Gal.17(2).423.

**ἀναμίμνω**, poet. for ἀναμένω, c. acc., Il.11.171: abs., 16.363.

**ἀναμινυρίζω**, *sing languishingly*, Protagorid.2.

※**ἀνα-μίξ**, Adv. *promiscuously, pell-mell*, Hdt.1.103, Hellanic.71(a)J., Th.3.107: c. dat., γυναῖκες ἀ. ἀνδράσιν Str.3.3.7, cf. 4.6.3, Jul.*Gal.*100c. **-μιξις**, εως, ἡ, *mingling, admixture*, Thphr.*CP*4.15.4, Plu.*Num.*17, Gal.2.850. ※**-μίσγω**, poet. and Ion. for ἀναμείγνυμι, ἀνέμισγε δὲ σίτῳ φάρμακα Od.10.235; αἷμα δακρύοισι Tim.*Fr.*7:—Med., *have intercourse with*, τινί Hdt.1.199:—Pass., γέλως ἀνεμίσγετο λύπῃ Call.*Aet.Fr.*7.3 P.

**ἀναμισθαρνέω**, *serve again for pay*, *Com.Adesp.*11.

※**ἀναμισθ-όομαι**, Dor. ἀμμ-, Pass., *to be let anew*, *Tab.Heracl.*1.111. **-ωσις**, εως, ἡ, *renewal of lease, re-letting*, ἱερῶν *LW*483 (Caria), *BGU*1122.32 (13 B.C.).

**ἄναμμα**, ατος, τό, (ἀνάπτω) *ignited mass*, πυρὸς ἄ. Epicur.*Ep.*1 p.28 U. (cj.); ἄ. νοερὸν ἐκ θαλάττης, of the sun, Heraclit.ap.*Placit.*2.20.16, cf. Zeno *Stoic.*1.35, Cleanth.ib.112.

**ἀνάμματος**, ον, (ἅμμα) *without knots*, X.*Cyn.*2.4, Hsch.

**ἀναμνημονεύω**, *remember*, Anon.*in Rh.*116.30.

※**ἀνάμνη-σις**, εως, ἡ, (ἀναμιμνήσκω) *calling to mind, reminiscence*, Pl.*Phd.*72e, 92d, *Phlb.*34c (pl.), Arist.*Mem.*451$^a$21; ἀ. τινος λαβεῖν *recall* it *to memory*, *IG*2.628.20; ἀναμνήσεις θυσιῶν *reminders to the gods* of sacrifices offered, Lys.2.39. 2. *memorial sacrifice*, Lxx *Nu.*10.10, cf. *Ev.Luc.*22.19. 3. παλίνδρομος ἀ., of the moon, Secund.*Sent.*6. **-στέον**, *one must remember*, Gal.10.214, Eust.357.16. ※**-στικός**, ή, όν, *able to recall to mind readily*, opp. μνημονικός (*of retentive memory*), Arist.*Mem.*449$^b$7, 453$^a$5. II. *indicative of the past*, σημεῖα Gal.1.313. **-στός**, όν, *that which one can recollect*, Pl.*Men.*87b.

**ἀναμολεῖν, ἀνέμολον**, aor. 2 with no pres. in use (cf. βλώσκω), *go through*, ἀνὰ δὲ κέλαδος ἔμολε πόλιν E.*Hec.*928.

**ἀναμολύνω**, strengthd. for μολύνω, Pherecr.173, cf. Plu.2.580f.

**ἀναμονή**, ἡ, *patient abiding, endurance*, Sm.*Ps.*38(39).8; *waiting, delay*, Iamb.*VP*31.197, Ps.-Callisth.1.5, Sch.E.*Or.*1101.

**ἀναμορμύρω**, *roar loudly, boil up*, πᾶσ' ἀναμορμύρεσκε, of Charybdis, Od.12.238, cf. Jul.*Or.*2.60d.

**ἀναμορφ-όω**, *transform*, εἴς τι Philostr.Jun.*Im.*4. **-ωσις**, εως, ἡ, *forming anew*, Suid. s.v. καινουργισμός. **-ωτής**, οῦ, ὁ, Hsch. s.v. εἰδοποιός.

※**ἀναμοχλεύω**, *raise by a lever*, ἀ. πύλας *force open* the gates, E.*Med.*1317; τὴν Ὄσσαν Luc.*Cont.*4: metaph. of dislocated limbs, Gal.18(1).403.

**ἀναμπέχονος**, ον, *without upper garment*, of a woman, Euph.53, Pythaen.6.

**ἀναμπλάκητος**, ον, *unerring, unfailing*, Κῆρες ἀνᾰπλάκητοι S.*OT*472 (lyr.). 2. of a man, *without crime* or *error*, A.*Ag.*345, S.*Tr.*120.

※**ἀνάμπυξ**, ῠκος, ὁ, ἡ, *without head-band* or *fillet*, Call.*Cer.*124.

**ἀναμυλλᾶναι**· ἀνανεῦσαι, ἀρνήσασθαι, Hsch.

**ἀναμυρησάμενος** (-μοιρ- Cyr.Dresd.)· χρηματισάμενος, Hsch.

**ἀναμυχθίζομαι**, *moan loudly*, A.*Pr.*743.

**ἀναμύω**, *open* the eyes, opp. συμμύω, *AB*391, Hsch.

**ἀναμφήριστος**, ον, = ἀναμφίβολος, Hsch.

※**ἀναμφίβολος**, ον, *unambiguous*, σύντομα καὶ ἀ. Ascl.*Tact.*12.11; ἀ. νίκη v.l. in D.H.3.57; φύσις Gal.17(1).370(358). Adv. -λως M.Ant.1.8, Luc.*Anach.*24.

**ἀναμφιδόξως**, Adv. *incontrovertibly*, Plu.2.441f.

**ἀναμφίλεκτος**, ον, = sq., τιμή D.H.9.44; πίστις Longin.7.4. Adv. -τως *PPar.*15.3.56 (ii B.C.), S.E.*M.*7.5, Luc.*Rh.Pr.*15.

※**ἀναμφίλογος**, ον, *undisputed, undoubted*, X.*Mem.*4.2.34, *Smp.*3.4 (Sup.); νίκη D.H.3.57. Adv. -γως *without dispute, willingly*, X.*Cyr.*8.1.44; *unquestionably, indisputably*, Id.*Ages.*2.12, D.H.3.41, Luc.*Herm.*36.

※**ἀναμφισβήτητος**, ον (Comp. written ἀναμφισβητότερον Dam.*Pr.*136; cf. ἀναφίσβητ' *IG*12(9).1273 iii 7), *undisputed, indisputable*, ἀρχή Diog.Apoll.1; τεκμήρια Th.1.132; ἀριστεῖα Lys.2.43; ἀ. ἡ κρίσις Arist.*Pol.*1283$^b$5; ἀ. καὶ φανερὰ ἡ ὑπεροχή ib.1332$^b$20; ἀ. χώρα a place *about which there is no dispute*, i.e. *well-known*, X.*Cyr.*8.5.6. II. Act., of persons, *without dispute* or *controversy*, ἀ. διετελέσαμεν Is.8.44. Adv. -τως Antipho 5.16, Pl.*Euthd.*305d, al.

※**ἀναμφόδαρχος**, ον, *not registered under an ἀμφόδαρχος* (q.v.), *POxy.*257.22.

**ἀναμωκάομαι**, *mock*, Sch.Ar.*Ra.*1323.

**ἀνανάγκαστος**, ον, *unconstrained*, Arr.*Epict.*1.6.40, al. Adv. -τως Id.3.24.39.

**ἄνανδες**· ἄνωθεν (Cypr.), Cyr.Dresd.; but **ἀνανδές**· οὐκ εὐάρεστον, ἡ ἀληθές, Hsch.

**ἀνανδρ-ία** (in codd. sts. wrongly -εία, and in later Ion. -ηΐη), ἡ, *want of manhood*, Hp.*Aër.*16, E.*Med.*466, Pl.*Phdr.*254c, etc.; of eunuchs, Luc.*Syr.D.*26. 2. *unmanliness, cowardice*, A.*Pers.*755, E.*Or.*1031, Th.1.83, And.1.56, etc.; ἀνανδρίᾳ χερῶν E.*Supp.*314. II. *unmarried womanhood*, Plu.2.302f. ※**-ιεῖς**, οἱ, *impotent persons*, dub. l. in Hp.*Aër.*22; cf. ἀναριεῖς. **-όομαι**, *become impotent*, Hp.*Aër.*22. **-ος**, ον, (ἀνήρ): I. = ἄνευ ἀνδρός, *husbandless*, of virgins and widows, A.*Supp.*287, *Pers.*289 (lyr.), S.*OT*1506, etc., and in Prose, as Hp.*Mul.*1.4, Pl.*Lg.*930c. 2. = ἄνευ ἀνδρῶν, *without men*, χρήματα ἄνανδρα A.*Pers.*166; πόλις S.*OC*939; ἄνανδρον τάξιν ἠρήμου (a prolepsis, = ὥστε εἶναι ἄνανδρον) A.*Pers.*298. II. *wanting in manhood, cowardly*, Hdt.4.142, Pl.*Grg.*522e, al.; τὸ ἄ., = ἀνανδρία, Th.3.82. 2. of things, *unworthy of a man*, δίαιτα Pl.*Phdr.*239d. 3. Adv. -δρως, opp. ἀνδρικῶς, Antipho 2.1.8, Pl.*Tht.*177b. **-ωτος**, *widowed*, εὐναί S.*Tr.*110 (lyr.).

※**ἀνανεάζω**, *become young* or *new again*, Ar.*Ra.*592, Lxx 4*Ma.*7.14, Sm.*Jb.*29.20, Phryn.*PS* p.59 B., Suid. s.v. ἀνηβᾶν; ἐκ τῶν νόσων Corn.*ND*33.

※**ἀνανέμω**, poet. ἀννέμω, *distribute*: hence, *count up*, in Med., ἀνανεμέεται (Ion. fut.) τὰς μητέρας Hdt.1.173. 2. *read, con over*, Epich.224, Theoc.18.48.

**ἀνανέομαι**, *mount up*, οὐδ' ὅπῃ [ἠέλιος] ἀννεῖται Od.10.192.

※**ἀνανε-όω**, fut. -ώσομαι Plb.22.7.1, al.: aor. ἀνενεωσάμην Th.5.43,46, poet. inf. ἀννεώσασθαι, v. infr.:—*renew*, τὸν ὅρκον Th.5.18; τὴν προξενίαν ib.43; τὰς σπονδάς ib.80; φιλίαν Id.7.33, D.23.121; ὁμόνοιάν τινι Philipp.ap.D.18.167; συμμαχίαν Plb. l.c., al. II. κἀννεώσασθαι λόγους *revive* them, prob. for καὶ νεώσασθαι, S.*Tr.*396, cf. E.*Hel.*722, Plb.5.36.7.—Act. freq. in Lxx, *Jb.*33.24, al., *IG*14.1078$^a$, *Delph.*3(1) No.60, cf. *SIG*478.503 (iii B.C.), Dam.*Pr.*391:—Pass., *Ep.Eph.*4.23.

**ἀνανέσαι**· καταστῆσαι (Cret.), Hsch.

**ἀνάνετος**, ον, *not relaxed*, διάθεσις *Stoic.*2.129, cf. 3.141; *not capable of diminution*, Porph.*Intr.*20.4.

※**ἀνά-νευσις**, εως, ἡ, (νέομαι) *return, revival*, Lxx *Ps.*72(73).4, cf. Andronic.Rhod.p.571 M., Hsch. II. *upward inclination*, Dam.*Pr.*56. III. *upward motion*, Ath.Mech.26.2. **-νευστικῶς**, Adv. *showing a disposition to refuse*, Arr.*Epict.*1.14.7. ※**-νεύω**, fut. -νεύσομαι Pl.*R.*350e, -νεύσω Luc.*Sat.*1: aor. ἀνένευσα, etc.:—*throw the head back* in token of denial, *make signs of refusal*, opp. κατανεύω, ἐπινεύω, ὣς ἔφατ' εὐχομένη, ἀνένευε δὲ Παλλὰς Ἀθήνη Il.6.311; ἀνένευε καρήατι 22.205; ὀφρύσι Od.9.468, cf. Hdt.5.51, Ar.*Lys.*126, Pl.*R.* l.c., etc. 2. c. acc. rei, *deny, refuse*, ἕτερον μὲν ἔδωκε πατήρ, ἕτερον δ' ἀνένευσε Il.16.250: c. fut. inf., σόον δ' ἀνένευσε μάχης ἐξ ἀπονέεσθαι 16.252:—Pass., ἀνανενευμένη *rejected*, Ph.1.146. 3. later, c. gen. rei, *look up from*, Alciphr.3.53; *go back from*, ἀπὸ τοῦ ψεύδους Arr.*Epict.*2.26.3. II. generally, *throw the head up*: hence ἀνανενευκώς upright, [τὰς σαρίσας] ἀ. φέρουσι Plb.18.13.3, cf. 1.23.5. 2. Astron., tilt back, of the pole, opp. κατανεύω, Eudox.Ars6.

ἀνανέω, come to the surface, Ael.NA5.22.

*ἀνανέ-ωσις, εως, ἡ, renewal, ξυμμαχίας Th.6.82; ἀγώνων CIG2932 (Tralles); ὑποθήκης POxy.274.20 (i A.D.); of a term of office, PTeb. 5.186 (ii B.C.) (pl.). II. revival of a suspended ceremony or office, OGI764.25 (Pergam., ii B.C.), POxy.1252ʳ16 (iii A.D.). 2. recalling to memory, D.S.5.67. *-ωτής, οῦ, ὁ, restorer, CIG2804 (Aphrodisias), Ephes.2 No.46. -ωτικός, ή, όν, renewing, reviving, τινός J.AJ11.4.7.

ἀνανῆσαι· σφάξαι, Hsch. (fort. ἀμῆσαι).

*ἀνανήφω, become sober again, come to one's senses, Arist.Mir.847ᵇ9; ἐκ μέθης D.H.4.35, cf. Lync.ap.Ath.3.109e; ἐκ τοῦ οἴνου Nic.Dam. p.7 D.; return to sobriety of mind, 2 Ep.Ti.2.26; recover from a swoon, Charito 3.1, D.Chr.4.77. 2. trans., make sober again, Luc.BisAcc.17.

ἀνανήχομαι, = ἀνανέω, swim, Arist.Resp.475ᵇ1 (s.v.l.); rise to the surface, Plu.2.985b: metaph., revive, recover, Ael.NA8.4; ὥσπερ ἐκ κλύδωνος Ph.1.260; ἐκ νόσου λοιμώδους Paus.7.17.1. 2. swim upstream, Opp.H.1.120:—Act. form ἀνανήξας· διαπλεύσας, Hsch.; cf. ἀνήξεις· κολυμβήσεις (fort. ἀννήξεις· ἀνακ.), Id.

ἀνανθέω, blossom again, continue blossoming, Thphr.CP3.24.3, Lib.Or.18.90, IGRom.4.1540.25 (Erythrae).

ἀνανθής, ές, flowerless, Pl.Smp.196a, Thphr.HP1.14.3, CP3.19.1, Plu.2.684c; οὐδεὶς χρόνος ἀ. Thphr. HP6.8.4.

ἀνάνθρωπος, ον, inhuman, savage, POxy.1681.6 (iii A.D.).

ἀνάνιος, ον, without pain: Act., not giving pain, Hsch., EM.97.43. Adv. -ως ib.44. Cf. ἀνήνιος.

ἀνανίσσομαι, = ἀνανέομαι, Opp.H.5.410.

ἀνανοέω, call to mind, v.l. in X.Eph.1.11.

ἀνανομή, ἡ, redistribution, Eur.Fr.748.

ἀνανοσέω, relapse, ἐς στάσιν J.BJ5.6.1.

ἀνανοστέω, return to the path, S.Ichn.160.

ἄναντα, Adv. up-hill, opp. κάταντα (q.v.), Il.23.116.

ἀναντᾰγώνιστος, ον, without a struggle, Th.4.92; ἀ. εὔνοια unchallenged, i.e. unalloyed goodwill, Id.2.45; ἀ. γέρας ἔλαχεν without having to strive for it, Ph.1.646. Adv. -τως Plu.2.1128b. II. irresistible, Ph.1.454, al., Plu.Phoc.14; ἐρώτημα Polem.Call.50. III. without a rival, incomparable, Ph.2.6, al.

ἀνανταλλακτος, ον, not to be exchanged, Gloss.

ἀνανταπό-δοσις, εως, ἡ, suppressed apodosis in a conditional sentence, Anon.Fig p.157 S. -δοτος, ον, without apodosis: τὸ ἀ. hypothetical proposition wanting the consequent clause, Sch.Ar.Pl.469.

ἀνάντης, ες, (ἀνά, ἄντην) up-hill, steep, opp. κατάντης, χωρίον Hdt. 2.29; πεδία Hp.Aër.19; ὁδός, ἀνάβασις, Pl.R.364d, 515e; πρὸς ἄναντες ἐλαύνειν, opp. κατὰ πρανοῦς, X.Eq.3.7, cf. Pl.Phdr.247b; πρὸς τὸ ἄ. τῶν πολιτειῶν in the ascending scale of our constitutions, Id.R.568c; πρὸς ὑψηλὰ καὶ ἀνάντη Id.Lg.732c.

ἀναντί-βλεπτος, ον, what one dares not face, Plu.2.67b: metaph., irrefragable, διαίρεσις Procl.in Alc.p.201 C. -θετος, ον, not to be contradicted, Olymp.in Phlb.p.247 S.; αἵρεσις Simp.in Epict.p.7 D., al. II. without contrary or opposite, Dam.Pr.26, Anon.in Cat.23.21. -λεκτος, ον, undisputed, PHib.95.13; incontestable, Cic.QF 2.8.1, Luc.Eun.13; not to be opposed δεήσεις J.AJ19.1.4. Adv. -τως Aen.Tact.31.9, Str.13.3.6, Luc.Cal.6. -ληπτος, ον, insensible to, ἀλγηδόνων Dsc.Eup.1.12. -ρρητος, ον, not to be opposed, Plb.6.7.7, 28.13.4; undeniable, Act.Ap.19.36; λόγοι S.E.M.8.160. Adv. -τως without opposition, by consent, Plb.22.8.11; incontrovertibly, OGI335.138 (Pergam.), Aët.15.15; without gainsaying, Act.Ap.10.29. -τῠπος, ον, giving no resistance, S.E.M.9.411. -φωνησία, ἡ, not answering, Cic.Att.15.13.2. -φώνητος, ον, unanswered, ib.6.1.23, PRyl.78.30 (ii A.D.).

ἀναντλέω, draw up or out, ποταμοὺς ἀ. κοχλίαις Str.3.2.9: metaph., exhaust, go patiently through, πόνους D.H.8.51; συμφοράς D.Chr.12.51.

ἄναντος, ον, not winnowed or bruised, dub. in S.Fr.294.

*ἄναξ [ᾰ], ἄνακτος (cf. Ἄνακες), ὁ, rarely fem. ὦ ἄνα for ἄνασσα, Pi.P.12.4, cf. A.Fr.342: (ϝάναξ IG4.236 (Corinth), etc., cf. ϝάνακες 4.564 (Argos)):—lord, master, 1. of the gods, esp. Apollo, ἄγουσι δὲ δῶρα Ἄνακτι Il.1.390, al.; ὁ Πύθιος ἄναξ A.Ag.509; ἄναξ Ἄπολλον ib.513, Eu.85, etc.; ὦναξ Ἄπ. S.OT80; ὦναξ without Ἀπόλλον, Hdt.1.159, 4.150, al.; of Zeus, Hom. only in voc., Ζεῦ ἄνα Il.3.351, 16.233; Ζεὺς ἄναξ A.Pers.762; ἄναξ ἀνάκτων.. Ζεῦ Id.Supp.524; μὰ τὸν Δία τὸν Ἄνακτα D.35.40; Poseidon, A.Th.130; ὦ δέσποτ' ἄναξ, of Ἀήρ, Ar.Nu.264; of Apollo Ἀγυιεύς, Id.V.875; ὦναξ δέσποτα, of Πλοῦτος, Id.Pl.748; esp. of the Dioscuri, cf. Ἄνακες, Ἄνακοι; of all the gods, πάντων ἀνάκτων.. κοινοβωμίαν A.Supp.222, cf. Pi.O.10(11).49.—The irreg. voc. ἄνα (q.v.) is never addressed save to gods; ὦναξ is freq. in Trag. and Com. II. of the Homeric heroes, esp. of Agamemnon, as general-in-chief ἄναξ ἀνδρῶν Ἀ. Il.1.442, al. (so Euphetes 15.532, while Ortilochos is called πολέεσσ' ἄνδρεσσιν ἄνακτα 5.546):—also as a title of rank, e.g. of Teiresias, Od.11.144, 151, S.OT284; of the sons or brothers of kings (υἱεῖς τοῦ βασιλέως καὶ οἱ ἀδελφοὶ καλοῦνται ἄνακτες Arist.Fr.526, cf. Isoc.9.72, Clearch.25, and so of Creon, S.OT85, cf. 911), and esp. of kings, as Xerxes, A.Pers.5, Darius, ib.787, cf. Ag.42, E.Ph.17, Or.349, etc.; βασιλῆι ἄνακτι lord king, Od.20.194; of the emperors, ἄνακτες IG14.2012 A 2, 4.1475 (Epid.). III. master of the house, οἴκοιο ἄναξ Od.1.397; ἀμφὶ ἄνακτα κύνες 10.216; as denoting the relation of master to slave, freq. in Od.; ἄναξ, θεοὺς γὰρ δεσπότας καλεῖν χρεών E.Hipp.88; of the Cyclops, as owner of flocks, Od.9.440. IV. metaph., κώπης, ναῶν ἄνακτες lords of the oar, of ships A.Pers.378, 383; πύλης ἄ. θυρωρέ, of a porter, S.Fr.775; ἄ. ὅπλων E.IA1260; ψευδῶν Id.Andr.447; ὑφήνης Pl.Com.122; κέντρων, of planets holding cardinal points, Man.1.66.—Poet. word.

Ἀναξαγόρειος, α, ον, of Anaxagoras, διάκοσμος Satyr.Vit.Eur.Fr.37; τὸ Ἀ. the saying of A., Plu.2.679a; οἱ Ἀ. Pl.Cra.409b.

ἀνα-ξαίνω, tear open, ἀ. λύπην Babr.12.24, Antyll.ap.Orib.44.23.4, Them.Or.7.98c; τὰ -οντα φάρμακα Phld.Ir.p.60 W. (dub.):—Pass., of evils, break out afresh, Plb.27.7.6; εἰς κάκωσιν ἀ. Plu.2.610d, cf. Dem.17: but ἀναξανθεῖσαι τοὺς στομάχους, of those whose appetite is stimulated afresh, Alciphr.Fr.6.18. -ξασμός, ὁ, laceration, Archig. ap.Gal.12.406.

ἀναξέω, hew smooth, polish, IG7.3073.123 (Lebad.); part. contr. ἀναξῶν ib.2².463.72:—Pass., λίθου ἀνεξεσμένου J.AJ13.6.6.

ἀναξηρ-αίνω, fut. -ᾰνῶ: aor. ἀνεξήρᾱνα, Ion. -ηνα, Ep. subj. ἀγξηράνῃ:—dry up, ὡς δ' ὅτ' ὀπωρινὸς Βορέης.. ἀλωὴν αἶψ' ἀγξηράνῃ Il.21.347; τὰ ὑποζύγια ἀρδόμενα ἀνεξήρηνε [τὴν λίμνην] Hdt.7.109:—Pass., Hp.Aër.8, Phylarch.50, Ph.2.511, etc. 2. metaph., consume, exhaust, οἶκον ἀ. ὀδόντες Call.Cer.114. II. dry again, after bathing, in Pass., Hp.Acut.65. -ανσις, εως, ἡ, drying up, Thphr.HP3.1.2. -αντικός, ή, όν, fit for drying, Dsc.1.7, Crito ap.Gal.12.488, Plu.2.624d. -ᾰσία, ἡ, = ἀναξήρανσις, Thphr.Fr.171.12. -ασμός, ὁ, drying up, Sor.2.10, Leonid.ap.Aët.16.44, Herod.Med.in Rh.Mus.58.90.

ἀναξία (A), ἡ, (ἀνάσσω) command, behest, Pi.N.8.10 (pl.). 2. = βασιλεία, A.Fr.283.

ἀναξία (B), ἡ, lack of value: inferiority, Pl.Prt.356a (s.v.l.).

ἀναξί-αλος, ὁ, lord of the sea, epith. of Poseidon, B.19.8. -βρένται, α, ὁ, lord of the thunder, epith. of Zeus, Id.16.66; cf. ἀργιβρένταs, βρένται. -δώρα, ἡ, = ἡ ἀνάγουσα δῶρα, of Demeter, S.Fr.1010; cf. ἀνησιδώρα. -μολπος, ἡ, queen of song, epith. of Urania, B.6.10.

ἀναξιό-λογος, ον, inconsiderable, D.S.31.9. -πάθεια, ἡ, unworthy treatment, or rather, just indignation thereat, J.AJ15.2.7, Hp.Ep.17. -πᾰθέω, to be indignant at unworthy treatment, Str.8.4.7 (v.l.), D.H.4.11, J.AJ15.3.2. -πιστος, ον, unworthy of credit, Eudem.ap.Simp.in Ph.115.35, Alex.Aphr.in Metaph.317.15.

ἀνάξιος (A), ον, also α, ον freq. in Att.: I. of persons, unworthy, not deemed or held worthy; ἀνάξιον σοῦ too good for thee, S.Ph.1009: also c. inf., ἀ. γὰρ πᾶσίν ἐστε δυστυχεῖν undeserving in the eyes of all to suffer, S.OC1446; νικᾶν Pl.Prt.356a. 2. abs., worthless, despicable, Hdt.7.9, S.Ph.439, etc.; ἀπερεί τις ἔποικος ἀναξία Id.El.189 (lyr.). Adv. -ίως Id.Aj.1392, etc. 3. undeserving of evil, Id.Ant.694, E.Heracl.526, Th.3.59. II. of things, undeserved, ἀνάξια σφέων αὐτῶν πεπονθότες Hdt.1.73, cf. 114, Lys.21.25, Pl.Cri.53e: also abs., ἀνάξια παθεῖν E.IA852, al., Pl.Tht.184a. Adv. -ίως ἐφθάρησαν ἀ. ἑωυτῶν Hdt.7.10.ε'. 2. unworthy, πολλὰ καὶ ἀ. ἐμοῦ Pl.Ap.38e. 3. worthless, τὸ ἀ. ἀκερδὲς Id.Hipparch.231e.

ἀνάξιος (B), ον, (ἄναξ) kingly, royal, Sch.Il.23.630.

ἄναξις, εως, ἡ, bringing up, raising up, Psalm.Solom.18.6.

ἀναξιφόρμιγξ, ιγγος, ὁ, ἡ, ruling the lyre, ἀναξιφόρμιγγες ὕμνοι Pi.O.2.1.

ἀναξῡνόω, (ξυνός) v.l. for ἀνακοινόομαι in X.HG1.1.30 (ap.Suid.).

ἀναξῠράω, shave again, τὸν τόπον Cleopatra ap.Gal.12.404.

*ἀναξυρίδες, ίδων, αἱ, trousers worn by eastern nations, Hdt.5.49, 7.61, X.An.1.5.8; by the Scythians, Hdt.1.71, cf. Hp.Aër.22; by the Sacae, Hdt.3.87, etc.: sg., Luc.Hist.Conscr.19, Philostr.VA 1.25. II. sg. ἀναξυρίς, ἡ, = ὀξαλίς, Dsc.2.114, Sch.Nic.Th.838. (Derived from ἀνασύρεσθαι by Eust.22.8, but really Persian. Wrongly expl. as a head-covering by Poll.7.58.)

ἀνάξυστον, = γναφάλλιον, Ps.-Dsc.3.117.

ἀναξύω [ῡ], scrape up or off, τὰ ἐν τῇ γῇ ὄντα [σημεῖα] ἀναξῦσαι Antipho 5.45:—Pass., ἀναξυομένης τῆς γῆς being scraped up by fishermen dredging, Arist.HA569ᵇ7, cf. 603ᵃ23; ἀναξυσθέντες having the surface scraped off, Plu.Publ.15; to be scraped down, Orib.Fr.99.

ἀναοίγω, poet. for ἀνοίγω, Il.24.455.

ἀναπαιδεύω, educate afresh, S.Fr.487, Ar.Eq.1099.

ἀνα-παιστικός, ή, όν, anapaestic, D.H.Comp.25, Heph.8, Demetr. Eloc.189, etc. -παιστος, ον, (cf. sq.) hammered, forged, κλεὶς IG2.678B64, al., 11.161A94 (Delos, iii B.C.). II. struck back, rebounding:—as Subst., anapaest (i.e. a dactyl reversed), D.H.Comp.25, Heph.8, etc.; ἀ. ἀπὸ μείζονος dactyl, Aristid.Quint.1.15. 2. anapaestic verse, Arist.Po.1452ᵇ23, D.H.1.25, etc.: in pl., of the Comic parabasis, Ar.Eq.504, Pax735, al.; ἀνάπαιστοι σύμπτυκτοι Pherecr.79, cf. Sch.metr.Pi.O.4.1; ἀνάπαιστόν τι something in anapaestic metre, Aeschin.1.158: ἀνάπαιστα, τά, anapaestic verses, Alciphr.3.43; esp. of ribald or satirical songs, D.C.66.8, Plu.Per.33. -παιστρίς, ίδος, ἡ, smiter, i.e. smith's hammer, Hsch.

ἀναπαίτητος, ον, not reclaimable, χρήματα Ἀρχ.Δελτ.6.100 (Methymna, ii B.C.).

ἀναπαίω, drive back, in Pass., Eust.587.18: metaph., ῥυθμοὶ ἔμμετροί τε καὶ ἀναπαίοντες, = ἀνάπαιστοι, Philostr.VS2.20.3.

ἀναπᾰλαίω, retrieve by contest, τὰ σφάλματα J.BJ4.1.6. II. ἀ. τὰς ὑποσχέσεις retract, Sch.Od.8.567.

ἀναπαλεύω, overthrow, cancel, μέρισιν PLond.2.394.12 (late).

ἀναπάλη [πᾰ], ἡ, name of a dance, Ath.14.631b. II. ἀναπάλαι χειρῶν, a form of exercise, Ruf.Ren.Ves.2.33.

*ἀνάπᾰλιν, Adv. back again, ἰέναι Pl.Plt.269d, cf. Phdr.264a, al.; ἐπὶ τὸ πέρας ἢ ἀ. Arist.EN1095ᵇ1; ἀ. στραφῆναι Id.Cael.285ᵃ8, tc. II. *over again*, = ἔμπαλιν, Pl.*Tht.*192d. III. *contrariwise, n the opposite side*, Hp.*Coac.*321; ἀ. πορεύεσθαι proceed *in reverse*, .e. *wrong order*, Pl.*Ti.*82c; ἀ. τιθέναι Arist.*APr.*$37^{b}11$, etc.; ἀ. στιν ἡμῖν ἢ τοῖς ἄλλοις *in the opposite way to*.., Thphr.*HP*8.3.5; τοῖς τολλοῖς.. καὶ τοῖς ἀ. (i.e. τοῖς ὀλίγοις) Teles p.15.9 H. IV. in proportion, *inversely*; ὁ ἀ. λόγος the *inverse* ratio Euc.5*Def.*13.; ἀ. ἔχειν Arist.*Cael.*$273^{b}32$. 2. *conversely*, *An.Ox.*4.325.

**ἀναπαλινδρομέω**, *to be brought back again to the same spot*, of a bandage, Hp.*Fract.*4.

**ἀναπάλλακτος**, ον, *irremovable*, αἰσχύνη Jul. *ad Them.*265d.

***ἀναπαλλοτρίωτος**, ον, *inalienable*, ἀγροί *TAM*261 *b*15 (Lycia).

***ἀναπάλλω**, poet. ἀμπάλλω, Ep. aor. part. ἀμπεπαλών:—*swing to and fro*, ἀμπεπαλὼν προΐει δολιχόσκιον ἔγχος Il.3.355, etc.; ἀμπάλλειν κῶλα, i.e. *dance*, Ar.*Ra.*1358; ἀνέπηλεν ἐπὶ θήρᾳ.. μαινάδας *urged* them *on*, E.*Ba.*1190; κλήρους εἰς ἄγγος ἐμβαλοῦσαι ἀνέπηλαν Ant.Lib.10.3:—Med., αἰ.. αἰθέρα ἀμπάλλεσθε *agitate* it *as you fly*, E.*Or.*322:—Pass., *dart, spring* or *bound up*, ὡς δ' ὅθ' ὑπὸ φρικὸς.. ἀναπάλλεται ἰχθύς.. ὣς πληγεὶς ἀνέπαλτο Il.23.692, cf. Eun.*Hist.*p.239D., Agath.3.16, 4.18:—Il. l. c. proves that the sync. aor. ἀνέπαλτο (also found in Il.8.85, 20.424, cf. ἀνὰ δ' ἔπαλτ' ὀρθῷ ποδί Pi.*O.*13.72, and metaph., νεῖκος ἀνέπαλτο B.10.65) must be referred to this Verb (cf. ἔκπαλτο, ἐνέπαλτο, κατέπαλτο); but part. ἀνεπάλμενος is formed from ἀνεφάλλομαι in A.R.2.825; those who, like Heyne, refer it to ἀνεφάλλομαι, write it ἀνεπᾶλτο (cf. ἐπᾶλτο):—aor. Med. ἀνεπήλατο Mosch.2.109: aor. part. Pass. ἀναπαλείς Str.8.6.21. II. ἀναπάλλων (sc. σεισμός), ὁ, an earthquake *with an upward movement*, Arist. *Mu.*$396^{a}8$.

***ἀνάπᾰλος**, v. ἄμπαλος: κατ' ἄμπαλον μισθοῦν by *auction*, *IG*9(2).205.15 (Thess.). II. a word coined to expl. ἀναπάλη, Ath.14.631d.

**ἀνάπαλσις**, εως, ἡ, *a flinging up*, Arist.*Mu.*$396^{a}9$.

**ἀναπάντητος**, ον, *where one meets no one*, Cic.*Att.*9.1.3.

**ἀνα-παντοῦσιν**· ἀνακύπτουσιν, Hsch. **-παππλον**· ἀνοίμωξον, Id.

**ἀναπαρθένευσις**, εως, ἡ, *restoration of virginity*, Sch.A.*Ch.*71.

***ἀναπαρίάζω**, *break treaties like the Parians*, prov. in Ephor.107.

**ἀναπάρτιστος**, ον, *incomplete*, of verbal expression, *Stoic.*2.58.

**ἀνάπας**, ασα, αν, = ἅπας, *AP*7.343 (Reiske ἅμα πάσῃς).

**ἀναπάσσω**, *scatter* or *shed upon*, χάριν τινί Pi.*O.*10(11).94.

**ἀναπατάσσω**, *strike*, κεφαλὴν ἀνεπάταξε Men.*Epit.*468. 2. ἀνεπάταξεν· ἐξ ὕπνου ἀνέβλεψε, Hsch. II. *strike up*, ἀναπατάξασθαι· ἀνακρούσασθαι ᾆσμα, Id.

**ἀναπᾰτέω**, *go up, go back*, *AB*397; of horses, *jib, shy*, *Hippiatr.*26.

**ἀνά-παυλα**, ης, ἡ, *repose, rest*, ὕπνον κἀνάπαυλαν ἤγαγεν S.*Ph.*638; κατ' ἀναπαύλας διῃρημένοι divided into *reliefs*, of workmen, Th.2.75. 2. c. gen. rei, *rest from* a thing, κακῶν S.*El.*873, cf. *Ph.*878; πόνων Th.2.38; τῆς σπουδῆς Pl.*Phlb.*30e. II. *resting-place*, E.*Hipp.*1137, Pl.*Lg.*722c; *inn*, Ar.*Ra.*113; ἀνάπαυλαι κατὰ τὴν ὁδόν Pl.*Lg.*625b; εἰς ἀναπαύλας ἐκ κακῶν (where there is a play upon the first sense) Ar.*Ra.*185, cf. 195. **-παύλησις**, εως, ἡ, = foreg., κακοῦ Orac.ap.Phleg.*Mir.*2:—also ***-παυλις** (sic), Hsch.

***ἀνά-παυμα**, poet. ἄμπ-, ατος, τό, *repose, rest*, μερμηράων Hes. *Th.*55; κακῶν ἄμπαυμα μεριμνέων Thgn.343; μόχθων *Lyr.Oxy.*9iii4; πλάτας E.*Hyps.Fr.*3iii14. 2. *resting-place*, *APl.*4.228 (Anyte); of a tomb, *CIG*4623 (Syria), cf. *Epigr.Gr.*453.3. II. *fallow land*, *PTeb.*115.3 (ii B.C.), *PFay.*112.4 (i A.D.). 2. *the state of such land*, ἐν ἀναπαύματι or ἀναπαύμασι *PTeb.*$61^{a}385$ (ii B.C.), *PLond.*3.1223.8 (ii A.D.), *BGU*1092.16 (iv A.D.). **-παυματικός**, ή, όν, *of* or *for fallow land*, Wilcken *Chrest.*377.11, al., *BGU*860.11 (iii A.D.). **-παύσιμος**, ον, *of* or *for rest*, Eust.1260.53, al. ***-παυσις**, poet. ἄμπ-, εως, ἡ, *repose, rest*, Mimn.12.2, Pi.*N.*7.52, Hp.*VM* 11, X.*Lac.*12.6: esp. *relaxation, recreation*, Pl.*Ti.*59c, X.*Cyr.*7.5.47. 2. c. gen. rei, *rest from* a thing, κακῶν Th.4.20; πολέμου X.*Hier.*2.11; κακῶν Epicur.*Ep.*3p.61 U.; λειτουργίας *PFlor.*57.56. 3. Rhet., *cadence* of a period, Hermog.*Id.*1.1, al. ***-παυστήριος** or **-παυτήριος**, Ion. ἀμπ-, ον, *of* or *for resting*, θῶκοι Hdt.1.181. II. Subst. ἀναπαυτήριον, τό, *time of rest*, οἱ θεοὶ τὴν νύκτα διδόασιν, κάλλιστον ἀ. X.*Mem.*4.3.3. 2. *place of rest*, Luc.*Am.*18. 3. *sound of trumpet for a halt*, opp. τὸ ἀνακλητικόν, Poll.4.86. III. ἀναπαυστηρία, ἡ, *prop* for head of torsion-engine, Ph.*Bel.*76.17, cf. Hero *Bel.*89.6. **-παυστόν**· τὸ μηκώνιον, Hsch. **-παυτικός**, ή, όν, *giving rest*, Ptol.*Tetr.*20. ***-παύω**, poet. and Ion. ἀμπ-, fut. Med. ἀναπαύσομαι: aor. ἀνεπαυσάμην Att. and Hellenistic (but ἀνεπαύθημεν Lxx *La.*5.5): later, aor. Pass. ἀναπάη *IG*14.158: fut. Pass. ἀναπαήσομαι v.l. *Apoc.*14.13, al.: pres. Med. ἀναπάεται *IG*14.1717, cf. *PTeb.*264:—*make to cease, stop* or *hinder from* a thing, χειμῶνος.. ὅς ῥά τε ἔργων ἀνθρώπους ἀνέπαυσεν Il.17.550; ἀ. τινὰ τοῦ πλάνου *give* him *rest* from wandering, S.*OC*1113; τοὺς λειτουργοῦντας ἀ. (sc. τῶν ἀναλωμάτων) *to relieve* them from.., D.42.25, cf. 42. 2. c. acc. only, *put an end to*, βοήν S.*Tr.*1262; more freq. *rest, make to halt*, ἀ. στράτευμα X.*Cyr.*7.1.4; κατὰ μέρος τοὺς ναύτας ἀ. Id.*HG*6.2.29; κάματον ἵππων ἀ. A.*Fr.*192 (lyr.); σῶμα E.*Hipp.*1353; εἴδωλον ἀ. ἐπὶ ἅμαξαν *lay* it *in a reposing posture*, Ael.*VH*12.64, cf. *NA*7.29: abs., ἀνάπαυσον *give me rest*, Luc.*Tyr.*21. 3. *bring to a close*, τὸν λόγον Hermog.*Id.*1.8. 4. rarely intr. in sense of Med., *take rest*, ἀναπαύοντες ἐν τῷ μέρει Th.4.11; ἡσυχίαν εἶχε καὶ ἀνέπαυεν X.*HG* 5.1.21. 5. of land, *cause to lie fallow*, *PSI*400.10 (iii B.C.), *PTeb.* 105.3 (ii B.C.). II. in Med. and Pass., *take rest*, ἀναπαύου κακῶν *take rest from*.., Cratin.297; ἀπὸ ναυμαχίας ἀ. *rest* after a sea-fight, Th.7.73; ἐκ μακρᾶς ὁδοῦ Pl.*Criti.*106a; ἀπ' ἄγρας κεκμακὼς ἀμπαύεται [Πάν] Theoc.1.17; esp. of troops, *halt, rest*, X.*Cyr.*2.4.3, etc.; ἀναπεπ. τῶν εἰσφορῶν *to be relieved from*.., Isoc.8.20. 2. abs., *take one's rest, sleep*, Hdt.1.12, 2.95, al., E.*Hipp.*211, v.l. in Ar.*Pl.*695, cf. Lys.13.12, etc. b. of land, *lie fallow*, Pi.*N.*6.11. c. of the dead, ἀμπ. σὺν φιλίῃ ξυνῶς ἀλόχῳ *Epigr.Gr.*520.5 (Thessalonica); ὧδε ἀναπάεται *IG*14.1717, cf. Call.*Epigr.*15.1; ἀ. τοῦ βίου Heraclit. *All.*68, Hdn.3.15.2; ἀ. alone, *die*, Id.1.4.7, cf. Plu.2.110f; ἀ. τὸν βίον *POxy.*1121.12 (iii A.D.). d. *regain strength*, dub. l. in X.*Cyr.* 6.1.11. 3. *rest* or *settle* upon an object, τὸ τοῦ Θεοῦ πνεῦμα ἐφ' ὑμᾶς ἀναπαύεται 1*Ep.Petr.*4.14, cf. Lxx *Is.*11.2; of shadows, Iamb.*Comm. Math.*8.

**ἀναπαφλάζω**, *boil* or *bubble up*, Hsch.

***ἀναπείθω** (Arc. ἀμπ- *SIG*306.59), *persuade, convince*, X.*Mem.*1.2.52, al.:—Pass., Th.1.84. 2. *persuade, move* to do a thing, c. acc. pers. et inf., Hdt.1.124, 156, etc.; foll. by Conj., ἀ. ὡς χρή.. Id.1.123; ἀ. λόγῳ ὅκως.. 1.37: c. dupl. acc., ἀ. τινά τι *persuade* one *of* a thing, Ar.*Nu.*77, cf. *AP*9.438 (Phil.). 3. *seduce, mislead*, τινά Hdt.3.148, 5.66, etc.; ἀ. χρήμασι, δώροις, *bribe*, Ar.*Pax*622, X.*Cyr.*1.5.3; χρυσίον διδοὺς ἀναπείσεις ὅπως.. Ar.*Eq.*473, cf. *PMagd.*14.3, *Act.Ap.*18.13:—Pass., ἀναπεπεισμένος *bribed*, Ar.*V.*101.

**ἀναπεινάω**, *to be hungry again*, Lync.ap.Ath.3.109e.

**ἀνά-πειρα**, ἡ, *trial, proof*, πλοίων Plb.25.4.8, cf. Callix.1. II. in pl., *exercises*, -ρας ποιῶν τοῖς πληρώμασι Plb.1.59.12. III. ἀνάπειρα· ῥυθμὸς αὐλητικός, Hsch. **-πειράομαι**, *try* or *attempt again*: generally, *make a trial, essay*, τοῖς σκάφεσι Plb.25.4.9; ἀναπειρᾶσθαι ναῦν *make trial of* a new ship, *prove* her, D.51.5; also of the ship herself, πάντες ἑωρᾶθ' ὑμεῖς ἀναπειρωμένην τὴν ναῦν ibid.; esp. as a naval term, *manœuvre, exercise*, Hdt.6.12, Th.7.7, 12, 51.

**ἀναπείρω**, poet. ἀμπ-, *pierce through, fix on a spit*, σπλάγχνα δ' ἄρ' ἀμπείραντες Il.2.426; ἵν' ἀναπείρω τὰς κίχλας Ar.*Ach.*1007; ὅταν ἐπὶ τὸν ὀβελίσκον ἀναπαρῇ Arist.*Mir.*$835^{a}18$. II. *impale*, ἐπὶ ξύλου ἀ. Hdt.4.103:—Pass.. ἀποθανεῖν ἀναπαρείς Id.4.94; μή.. τὸν πόδ' ἀναπαρῶ Macho ap.Ath.8.349c. III. *pierce upwards*, opp. καταπείρω, Antyll.ap.Orib.7.10.1.

**ἀναπειστήριος**, α, ον, *persuasive*, χαύνωσις Ar.*Nu.*875.

***ἀναπελάσας**· ἀναρρωσθείς, Hsch. (cf. ὀλιγ-ηπελίη).

**ἀναπελεκάω**, *dress* stone, *IG*7.4255.19 (Oropus).

**ἀναπεμπάζομαι**, *count again, count over*, Pl.*Ly.*222e; *think over, ponder over*, Id.*Lg.*724b, Plu.2.605a, Ath.6.263b, al.; ἀ. ὅκωσπερ ὄναρ τὴν νοῦσον Aret.*CA*2.3, etc.:—Act. later in same sense, Lyc.9, 1470, *AP*11.382.12 (Agath.), Hld.3.5, etc.

***ἀναπέμπω**, poet. ἀμπ-, *send up*, κάτωθεν A.*Ch.*382 (lyr.), cf. Ar.*Th.*585; Ἀφαίστοιο κρουνοὺς ἀ. *sends forth*.., Pi.*P.*1.26; χθὼν ἠρινὰ φύλλ' ἀ. ib.9.46; παντοῖα φύματα Pl.*Ti.*85c:—Med., *send up from oneself*, X.*An.*1.1.5. 2. *send up* to higher ground, εἰς τὰς ἄκρας Id.*Cyr.*7.5.34; esp. from the coast inland, into Central Asia, ἀ. ὡς βασιλέα Th.2.67, cf. Isoc.8.98; to the metropolis, εἰς τὴν Ῥώμην Plb.1.7.12, etc. 3. *remit, refer* to higher authority, *PHib.*1.57 (iii B.C.), *PTeb.*7.7 (ii B.C.); ψήφισμα πρὸς βασιλέα *OGI*329.51; τινὰ πρός τινα *Ev.Luc.*23.7; τινά τινι *Ep.Philem.*12; of a higher authority *referring* to delegates, *BGU*613.4 (ii A.D.), cf. 19120, *PLond.*2.196.11 (ii A.D.); *refer* to a book, Gal.18(2).663, etc. 4. *trace up* one's pedigree, γένος εἴς τινα D.S.4.83. 5. *transmit*, in Pass., τῶν κατ' ὄψιν ἀναπεμπομένων Epicur.*Nat.*11.7; αἰσθήσεων ἀναπεμπομένων Plot.4.4.42. II. *send back*, Pi.*I.*7(6).10: metaph., *send back* in discussion to something previously said, Alex.Aphr.*in Top.*445.15. 2. *refer*, τὰ εἰς τὸ θεῖον -όμενα *OGI*194, cf. D.S.4.43; *ascribe*, τι ἐπί τι Dam.*Pr.*37; τί τινι *Corp.Herm.*18.12. 3. *throw back* the accent, of enclitics, Hdn.*Gr.*2.828.

**ἀναπεπταμένος**, η, ον, pf. part. Pass. of ἀναπετάννυμι, q. v. Adv. -νως *explicitly*, Plot.5.1.8.

**ἀναπεπτωκότως**, Adv. pf. part. of ἀναπίπτω, *despondingly*, Poll.3.123.

**ἀναπέσσω**, Att. -ττω, *digest again*, f.l. in Arist.*HA*$565^{b}23$.

***ἀναπετάννυμι** or -ύω X.*An.*7.1.17 (cf. ἀναπίτνημι), poet. ἀμπ-; ἀναπετάω Luc.*Cal.*21: fut. -πετάσω, Att. -πετῶ Men.*Fr.*3 D.:—*spread out, unfold*, ἀνὰ θ' ἱστία λευκὰ πέτασσαν Il.1.480, etc.; ἀ. βόστρυχον E.*Hipp.*202; τὰν ἐπ' ὄσσοις ὀμπέτασον χάριν *unfold, display*, Sapph.29; φάος ἀμπετάσας *having shed* light *abroad*, E.*IA*34; ἀναπετάσαι τὰς πύλας *throw wide* the gates, Hdt.3.146, cf. X.*An.* l.c.:—Pass., ἀναπεπταμέναι σανίδες, θύραι, Il.12.122, Pi.*N.*9.2; βλέφαρα ἀναπετάννυται X.*Mem.*1.4.6; ἀλώπηξ ἀναπιτναμένη a fox *sprawling on its back* to await the eagle's swoop, Pi.*I.*4(3).47: in pf. Pass., *to be open, lie open*, οἰκία πρὸς μεσημβρίαν -πέπταται *lies open* to the south, X.*Oec.*9.4; αὐλὼν ἀναπέπταται πρὸς τὴν θάλατταν Plu. *Fab.*6; freq. in pf. part., *open*, ἐν πελάγει ἀ. ναυμαχήσεις Hdt.8.60.α'; ἀ. ὄμματα X.*Mem.*2.1.22; ἀ. πρὸς τὸ φῶς τὴν εἴσοδον ἔχουσα, of the cave, Pl.*R.*514a; δίαιτα ἀ. *in the open air*, Plu.*Per.*34: metaph., ἀ. παρρησία *open, barefaced* impudence, Pl.*Phdr.*240e; ὄμμα ἀ. *impudent, brazen*, Zeno *Stoic.*1.58; ἀ. τῇ ψυχῇ δέξασθαί τι Luc.*Nigr.*4.

**ἀνα-πέτεια**, ἡ, *expansion, dilatation*, πόρων Gal.6.848, cf. Alex. Aphr.*Pr.*1.90. **-πετής**, ές, (πετάννυμι) *expanded, wide open*, ἀδένες Hp.*Gland.*9; ὀφθαλμοί Aret.*SA*1.6. II. (πέτομαι), A.*Supp.*782 (in form ἀμπ-).

**ἀναπέτομαι**, poet. ἀμπέταμαι *IG*14.1934*f*, late **ἀναπετάομαι** v.l. in *Gp.*2.5.12: fut. -πτήσομαι: aor. ἀνεπτόμην or ἀνεπτάμην, in Trag. also ἀνέπτην, 3 pl. ἀνέπτησαν Ant.Lib.14.4:—*fly up, fly away*, ἢν.. ἀναπτῆσθε ἐς τὸν οὐρανόν Hdt.4.132, cf. 5.55; οἰχήσονται ἀναπτόμενοι Antipho *Fr.*58; αἰθερία δ' ἀνέπτα E.*Med.*440; ἀν' ὑγρὸν ἀμπταίην αἰθέρα Id.*Ion* 796; ἀναπέτομαι δὴ πρὸς Ὄλυμπον Anacr.24 = Ar.*Av.* 1372, cf. 35, *Lys.* 774; εἰ..πτηνὸς γενόμενος ἀνάπτοιτο Pl.*Phd.* 109e; εἰς τὸν οὐρανὸν ἀναπτήσῃ Id.*Lg.* 905a, cf. Aeschin.3.209; *hurry off*, Luc.*Alex.* 30: metaph., ἀμπτάμενα φροῦδα πάντα κεῖται E.*Andr.* 1219. 2. metaph., *to be on the wing*, περιχαρὴς δ' ἀνεπτάμαν S.*Aj.* 693; ἀνέπταν φόβῳ Id.*Ant.* 1307.—Cf. ἀνίπταμαι.

**ἀνάπευσις**, εως, ἡ, (ἀναπυνθάνομαι) *inquiry*, Charito 3.4.

**ἀναπεφλασμένως**, Adv. pf. part. Pass. of ἀναφλάω, q.v.

**ἀναπηγάζει**· ἀναδίδωσιν, Hsch.

**ἀναπηγνῦμι**, *transfix, fix on a spit*, λαγῴ' ἀναπηγνύασι Ar.*Ec.* 843. 2. *impale, crucify*, τινὰ ἐπὶ τοῦ ξύλου Alex.222; τὸ σῶμα διὰ τριῶν σταυρῶν Plu.*Art.* 17. 3. intr. pf. ἀναπέπηγα *project sharply*, of headlands, Philostr.*VA* 3.23.

*__ἀναπηδ-άω__, poet. ἀμπ-, fut. -ήσομαι Luc.*Asin.* 53:—*leap up, start up*, esp. in haste or fear, ἐκ λόχου ἀμπήδησε Il.11.379; ἐκ τοῦ θρόνου Hdt.3.155; ἀναπηδῶσιν πάντες ἐπ' ἔργον *jump up* from bed, Ar.*Av.* 490, cf. X.*Cyr.* 1.4.2; ἀ. πρὸς τὸν πάππον *jump up on* his *knees*, ib.1.3.9; *start up* to speak, ἀ. ἐν δήμῳ Cratin.356, cf. Ar.*Ec.* 428; ἐπὶ τὸ βῆμα Aeschin.3.173, cf. 1.71. 2. of water, *spring*, Arist.*HA* 596$^b$18. 3. Medic., *swell up*, Hp.*Gland.* 2. —**ημα**, ατος, τό, *outburst*, αἵματος Eust.680.23. —**ησις**, εως, ἡ, *leaping up*, ἐκ τῆς κλίνης Hp.*Morb.Sacr.* 1. 2. ἀ. τῆς καρδίας *palpitation* of the heart, opp. σφύξις, Arist.*Resp.* 480$^a$13.

**ἀναπηλέω**, aor. part. -ήσας dub. sens. in *h.Merc.* 41.

**ἀναπηνίζομαι**, *unwind, reel off*, of the thread of a silk-worm's cocoon, Arist.*HA* 551$^b$14; τὸ τῆς πέρκης κύημα ἀ. οἱ ἁλιεῖς ib.568$^a$24.

**ἀναπηρ-ία**, ἡ, *lameness, mutilation*, Cratin.168, Arist.*Rh.* 1386$^a$11; of the crocodile's tongue, *stunted development*, Id.*PA* 660$^b$26. —**όβιος**, ον, *with maimed life*, Phryn.Com.4 D. —**όομαι**, Pass., *to be maimed*, Pl.*Plt.* 310e, Arist.*Pr.* 960$^b$37:—Act., prob. l. in Plu.2.373d. —**ος**, ον, *maimed, mutilated*, Hermipp.35, Lys.24.13, Pl.*Cri.* 53a, etc.; ψυχὴ ἀ. πρὸς ἀλήθειαν Id.*R.* 535d; ἀνάπηρα θύειν Id.*Alc.* 2.149a, cf. Arist.*PA* 773$^a$13, al. Adv. -ρως Zonar. (Sts. spelt ἀνάπειρος in codd., Lxx *To.* 14.2, *Ev.Luc.* 14.13,21, cf. Phryn.*PS* p.13 B.)

*__ἀναπηρτισμένως__, *incompletely*, Chrysipp.*Stoic.* 2.107.

**ἀναπιδάω**, = διαπιδάω, prob. in Alex.Aphr.*in Mete.* 56.7.

*__ἀναπῑδύω__, *spring up, ooze out*, Thphr.*CP* 6.4.1. 2. of ground, *send forth water*, Plu.*Aem.* 14.

**ἀνα-πιέζω**, aor. Pass. ἀνεπιέχθην, *press back*, Hp.*Art.* 41. II. *force upwards*, Hero *Spir.* 1.10. III. *apply, press upon*, Androm. ap.Gal.12.945, cf. Asclep.ib.986. —**πίεσις**, εως, ἡ, *pressure*, Glaucias ap.Erot. s.v. ἀνοκώχησις. —**πίεσμα**, ατος, τό, a kind of *trap-door* on the stage, Poll.4.127,132. *—**πιεσμός**, ὁ, = foreg., πρὸς τόπον Hero *Spir.* 1.28. 2. *reduction* of hernia, Heliod.(?) ap.Orib. 50.42.6.

*__ἀναπίμπλημι__, 3 sg. -πιμπλᾷ Arist.*Pr.* 967$^b$4:—*fill up*, πίθον Epigr. ap.Luc.*Dips.* 6: but mostly, 2. metaph., *accomplish* what is destined, as always in Hom., πότμον ἀναπλήσαντες *having filled up the full measure* of their fate, Il.11.263; αἴ κε θάνῃς καὶ μοῖραν ἀναπλήσῃς βιότοιο 4.170; ἀναπλῆσαι οἶτον, κακά, ἄλγεα, κήδεα, ib.8.465, 15.132, Od.5.302, 13.307 (v.l.), cf. Hdt.5.4, 6.12, 9.87, etc. II. c. gen. rei, *fill full of* a thing, καὶ ξυντυχών σ' Ὑπέρβολος δικῶν ἀναπλήσει Ar.*Ach.* 847, cf. *Nu.* 1023, Pl.*Phlb.* 42a, D.20.28. 2. freq. with a notion of *defiling, infecting*, ὡς πλείστους ἀναπλῆσαι αἰτιῶν Pl.*Ap.* 32c:—so in Pass., *to be infected with disease*, Th.2.51; ἀ. τῆς τούτου [τοῦ σώματος] φύσεως Pl.*Phd.* 67a, cf. Iamb.*Myst.* 5.15.

**ἀναπίμπρημι**, *blow, swell up*, in Pass., Nic.*Th.* 179: aor. ἀνεπρήσθην Hp.*Nat.Mul.* 41.

**ἀναπίνω** [ῐ], *drink up, suck in like a sponge*, Hp.*VM* 22; *absorb again*, of suppurations which do not come to a head, Id.*Art.* 40; of extravasated blood, ib.50, cf. Gal.7.694.

**ἀναπιπράσκω**, *sell again*, Poll.7.12:—Pass. in aor. 1 part. ἀναπραθείσης *IPE* 1$^2$.32 *A* 53.

*__ἀναπίπτω__, poet. ἀμπ-, *fall back*, A.*Ag.* 1599, E.*Cyc.* 410; *lay oneself back*, like rowers, Cratin.345, X.*Oec.* 8.8; ἀ. ὑπτία Pl.*Phdr.* 254b, cf. e; of riders, ὑπτίους ἀναπεπτωκότας ἐλαύνειν X.*Eq.Mag.* 3.14. 2. metaph., *fall back, give ground*, Th.1.70; *flag, lose heart*, D.19.224; ταῖς σπουδαῖς (vulg. σπονδ-) ἀναπεπτωκέναι D.H.5.53. b. pf. part. ἀναπεπτωκώς *lifeless*, of style, σχῆμα ἀ. Aristid.*Rh.* 2 p.518 S., al. 3. of a plan, *to be given up*, ἀνεπεπτώκει τὰ τῆς ἐξόδου D.21.163. 4. ἀ. ἀπ' οἴκων *to be banished* from one's house, Poet.ap.Athenag.*pro Christo* 22. 5. *recline* at meals, like ἀνάκειμαι, Alex.293, *Com. Adesp.* 638, *PPar.* 51.4, *Ev.Marc.* 6.40, Luc.*Asin.* 23. b. *take to one's bed* in sickness, *PMag.Leid.V.* 11.1. 6. *recoil*, of the arms of torsion-engines, Hero *Bel.* 100.2.

**ἀναπισσόω**, *cover over again with pitch*, *Gp.* 6.8.3.

**ἀναπίτνημι**, poet. for ἀναπετάννυμι, inf. -πιτνάμεν Pi.*O.* 6.27.

**ἀναπιτ-ύζω**, *cause to spirt out*, Hero *Aut.* 13.1. —**υσμός**, ὁ, *spirting out*, ib.4.3; cf. ἀναπυτίζω.

**ἀναπλάκητος**, ον, = ἀναμπλάκητος, q.v.

*__ἀνά-πλασις__, εως, ἡ, *remodelling, new formation*, σαρκῶν Hp.*Off.* 24; *adjustment*, ib.15; simply, *modelling, shaping*, Hp.*Hebd.*ap.Ph. 1.29. —**πλασμα**, ατος, τό, *shape, form, model*, τὰ ἀ. τῶν σωμάτων D.S.2.56. II. *representation, imagination*, Str.11.14.12; ἀ. τῆς διανοίας S.E.*M.* 8.354. 2. *correlative term*, Ascl.*in Metaph.* 331.30. —**πλασμός**, ὁ, = ἀνάπλασις, ἀ. ἐκ ματαίων ἐλπίδων *building of castles in the air*, Plu.2.113d. II. = ἀνάπλασμα II; ἀ. διανοίας Metrod.*Herc.* 831.4, S.E.*M.* 7.223, Mich.*in PN* 9.21. —**πλάσσω**, Att. -ττω, *form anew, remodel, restore* a broken nose, Hp.*Mochl.* 2; *rebuild*, οἰκίδια *PHal.* 1.183 (iii B.C.): metaph., ἀ. ταύτας [τὰς ἑταίρας] Alex.98.5:—Med., ἀναπλάσασθαι οἰκίην *rebuild one's* house, Hdt.8.109. 2. simply, *model, mould, fashion*, τῆς Αἰδοῦς..τἄγαλμ' ἀ. Ar.*Nu.* 995, cf. *AP* 7.410 (Diosc.), al.; τὰ μέλη τοῦ παιδός Pl.*Alc.* 1.121d: metaph., τοῖς ψηφίσμασιν ἀ. [Ἀλέξανδρον] Demad.11; *make up*, τροχίσκους Dsc.1.8, al. 3. metaph., ἀ. διπλάσια τῆς ἀληθείας κακὰ *invent, imagine* them, Philem.160, cf. Plb.3.94.2, D.H.1.53; πολλοὺς θεοὺς Ph.2.262; αἰτίας Procop.*Arc.* 15; ἐπιστολὴν ib.12, Philostr.*VA* 7.35: abs., *imagine vainly*, Metrod.*Herc.* 831.14, cf. 17, Phld.*D.* 1.17:—also in Med., *AP* 9.710 (Diosc.). 4. *compose*, λόγους D.H.*Dem.* 46. II. *plaster up*, ὑπὸ τοῖς ὄνυξι κηρὸν ἀναπεπλασμένος Ar.*V.* 108. —**πλαστέον**, *one must make up into shapes*, Dsc.5.88. —**πλαστικός**, ή, όν, *imaginative*, Porph.*Sent.* 38, Procl. *in Ti.* 1.320 D. —**πλαστος**, ον, *that may be moulded, plastic*, Gal. 18(1).670.

**ἀναπλατύνομαι** [ῠ], *to be spread wide*, Plu.*Daed.* 4.

**ἀναπλείω**, Ep. for ἀναπλέω III, Nic.*Th.* 308.

*__ἀναπλέκω__, *enwreath, entwine*, ὅρμοισι χέρας Pi.*O.* 2.74; ἀ. τὰς τρίχας Poll.2.35:—Pass., *IG* 5(1).1390.22 (Andania, i B.C., in form ἀμπλ-), ib.5(2).514.10 (Lycosura):—Med., *braid one's hair*, Luc.*Nav.* 3. 2. metaph., ἀ. ῥυθμόν *AP* 11.64 (Agath.). 3. ἀναπεπλεγμένοι *closely engaged*, Plu.*Brut.* 17.

**ἀνάπλεος**, α, ον, Att. masc. and neut. **ἀνάπλεως**, ων, but fem. ἀνάπλεα Pl.*Phd.* 83d:—pl., nom. masc. and fem. ἀνάπλεῳ Pl.*Tht.* 196e, Eub.98.8, neut. ἀνάπλεα Arist.*de An.* 423$^a$27: acc. masc. ἀνάπλεως Pl.*R.* 516e:—*quite full of* a thing, πτερῶν λέγουσι ἀνάπλεον εἶναι τὸν ἠέρα Hdt.4.31; ἀ. ψιμυθίου Ar.*Ec.* 1072, cf. Eub. l.c.; σκότους ἀ. οἱ ὀφθαλμοί Pl.*R.* 516e, etc. II. *infected*, τοῦ σώματος ἀναπλέα [ἡ ψυχή] *with* the body, Id.*Phd.* 83d; αὐτὸ τὸ καλὸν μὴ ἀ. σαρκῶν Id.*Smp.* 211e; ἀ. ἐσμεν τοῦ μὴ καθαρῶς διαλέγεσθαι Id.*Tht.* 196e.

*__ἀνάπλευσις__, εως, ἡ, *separation, splitting off*, ὀστέου Hp.*Coac.* 234. II. *mounting, rising*, of food in vomiting, Archig.ap.Orib. 8.1.20.

**ἀναπλέω**, Ion. -πλώω, Ep. -πλείω (q.v.), *sail upwards, go upstream*, στεινωπὸν ἀνεπλέομεν we *sailed up* the strait, Od.12.234, cf. Hdt.2.97, 4.89; *sail up* the Hellespont, X.*HG* 4.8.36:—Pass., ἀναπλεῖται ἐκ θαλάττης ὁ Πάδος Plb.2.16.10. 2. *put out to sea*, ἐς Τροίην νήεσσιν ἀναπλεύσεσθαι Il.11.22, cf. And.1.76, Decr.ap.D.18.184; ἀ. ἐπὶ τρόπαιον *IG* 2.471.28. 3. *float up, rise to the surface*, ναυάγιον ἀ. Arist.*Pr.* 932$^a$1. 4. *overflow*, Ael.*NA* 10.19. II. *sail back*, Hdt.1.78; of fish, *swim back*, Id.2.93. 2. metaph. of food, *return from the stomach*, for rumination, Ael.*NA* 2.54. III. *become loose, split off*, of bone-splinters, Hp.*Fract.* 24; ὀδόντες ἀναπλέουσι the teeth *fall out*, Id.*Epid.* 4.19, cf. ἀναπλείω; of chalk-stones, *come away*, Orib.*Syn.* 9.58.2.

**ἀνάπλεως**, v. ἀνάπλεος.

**ἀναπλήθω**, poet. for ἀναπίμπλημι, Q.S.11.312. 2. intr., *to be full*, Id.13.22.

**ἀναπλημμυρέω**, *overflow*, Philostr.*Im.* 1.31.

**ἀναπλημμύρω**, *make overflow*, ἀνεπλήμμυρε θάλασσαν Q.S.14.635.

*__ἀναπληρ-όω__, *fill up* a void, Pl.*Ti.* 81b, cf. 78d; τὸ κεχηνὸς τῆς ἑρμηνείας, τοῦ ῥυθμοῦ, A.D.*Synt.* 266.22, Luc.*Tim.* 1:—Pass., *to be filled up*, Arist.*Cael.* 306$^b$4. 2. *make up, supply*, εἴ τι ἐξέλιπον ἀ. Pl.*Smp.* 188e; τὴν ἔνδειαν Arist.*Pol.* 1318$^b$22; τοὺς..ἀμόρφους ἀναπληροῖ ἡ τοῦ λέγειν πιθανότης *compensates* them, Id.*Fr.* 101:—Med., δώματ' ἀ. *fill their* houses, E.*Hel.* 907. 3. *fill up* the numbers of a body, τὴν βουλήν Plu.*Publ.* 11, cf. X.*Vect.* 4.24; ἀ. τὴν συνηγορίαν *fill* the place of advocate (left vacant by another), Plu.*Crass.* 3, cf. 1*Ep. Cor.* 14.16. 4. *pay in full*, τὰς ὠνάς, of tax-farmers, *PPar.* 62.5.3 (ii B.C.):—in Med., *get paid, receive*, ἕως ἀνεπληρώσατο τὴν προῖκα D.27.13. 5. *use expletive particles*, Demetr.*Eloc.* 58. 6. *fulfil*, ἀναπληροῦται ἡ προφητεία *Ev.Matt.* 13.14; of a task, *perform*, *PPetr.* 3 p.104. II. Pass., *to be restored to its former size* or *state*, ἀνεπληρώθη ὁ ἥλιος, after an eclipse, Th.2.28; ἀναπληρουμένης τῆς φύσεως *being in process of restoration*, Arist.*EN* 1153$^a$2, cf. *HA* 548$^b$18. —**ωμα**, ατος, τό, *filling*, Id.*Mir.* 833$^b$4; ἐρημίας Phalar.*Ep.* 98; λόγων Ph.2.166. —**ωσις**, εως, ἡ, *filling up, means of filling up*, τῆς ἐνδείας Arist.*EN* 1118$^b$18; τοῦ λείποντος A.D.*Synt.* 250.18; τῶν κενουμένων τάξεων Ph.2.382. 2. *satisfying*, τῆς ἐπιθυμίας Arist.*Pol.* 1267$^b$4; *satisfaction* of the wants and appetites, Id.*EN* 1173$^b$8. 3. *restoration*, τῆς κατὰ τὴν φύσιν αὐταρκείας Id.*Pol.* 1257$^a$30, cf. Plu.*Demetr.* 45. 4. *fulfilment*, τοῦ ῥήματος τοῦ Κυρίου Lxx 1*Es.* 1.54. II. (from Pass.) *becoming full, overflowing*, of the Nile, Thales ap.Ath.*Epit.* ad fin. lib. ii (vol. i p.278 Schw.). —**ωτέον**, *one must fill up, supply*, Plu.*Cim.* 2, *Gp.* 9.11.3.

**ἀναπληρωτικός**, ή, όν, *filling up*, Asp.*in EN* 24.3; δύναμις Dsc.5.75; φάρμακα Gal.14.763.

**ἀναπλιστικός**, ή, όν, (ἀναπίμπλημι) *fit for filling up*, and so, *that which takes the shape of the vessel which it fills, fluid*, Arist.*PA* 649$^b$16, cf. *GC* 329$^b$34, *Pr.* 939$^a$31.

**ἀναπλίσσω** πόδεσσι *trot*, prob. in Arat.1108.

**ἀναπλοκή**, ἡ, (ἀναπλέκω) *a braiding*, χαίτης Philostr.*VA* 6.10. II. in Music, *progression* of notes ascending in the scale, opp. καταπλοκή, Ptol.*Harm.* 2.12.

**ἀνάπλοος**, contr. -πλους, ὁ, (ἀναπλέω) *sailing up-stream*, Hdt.2.4 and 8; ὁ ἀ. ἐκ τῆς θαλάττης, of a *canal* from the sea to an inland harbour, Pl.*Criti.* 115d, cf. 117e. 2. *putting out* to sea, Plb.1.53.13, etc. II. *sailing back, return*, Thphr.*HP* 4.7.3, cf. Str.1.3.15.

**ἀν-απλόω,** *unfold, open,* ταρσὸν ἀναπλώσας Mosch.2.60; τὰς θύρας Babr.74.3:—Pass., of pods or flowers, Dsc.2.159,4.113. 2. *cause to expand,* τῷ -οῦν τὰ σώματα τὴν θερμότητα Anon.*in Cat.*49.26. II. *explain, unravel,* Anon.*in Tht.*23.6, *Corp.Herm.*1.16, Procl.*inEuc.*p.4F.; ἀπορίαν Simp.*in Ph.*441.11. III. *simplify,* μέχρι τοῦ ἑνός Dam.*Pr.*5:—so in Pass., of compounds, *to be resolved into simple elements,* Ph.1.433 (s.v.l.): pf. part. Pass. ἀνηπλωμένος *open, shallow,* λοπάδας *PHolm.*11.17. Adv. -ως, q.v.

**ἀνάπλῠσις,** εως, ἡ, *washing* or *rinsing out,* Arist.*Insomn.*460ᵃ17.

**ἀνάπλωσις,** εως, ἡ, *unfolding; explanation,* Erot.*Praef.*p.9N., Alex.Aphr.*in Metaph.*467.8. II. *unfolding, evolution,* ἡ τῶν λόγων ἐξέλιξις καὶ ἀ. Plot.5.7.3; opp. συνείλησις, Iamb.*Comm. Math.*12. III. *simplification,* Dam.*Pr.*26,70.

**ἀναπλώω,** Ion. for ἀναπλέω.

**ἀνά-πνευμα,** poet. ἄμπν-, ατος, τό, *resting-place,* Pi.*N.*1.1. **-πνευσις,** εως, ἡ, *recovery of breath*: *respite from,* ὀλίγη δέ τ' ἀνάπνευσις πολέμοιο Il.11.801, 16.43. II. *breathing in,* ὕδατος, of fishes, Pl. *Ti.*92b; *inhalation,* opp. ἔκπνευσις, Arist.*HA*492ᵇ8. **-πνευστικός,** ή, όν, *of* or *for respiration,* ὁ ἀ. τόπος the *respiratory* region, Id.*Sens.* 445ᵃ27, Thphr.*Sud.*38; τὰ μὴ ἀ. [ζῷα] Arist.*Spir.*482ᵃ8; ἀ. δύναμις the power *of breathing,* M.Ant.6.15; τὰ -κά *respiratory organs,* Alex.Aphr.*Pr.*1.119. **-πνευστος,** ον, poet. for ἄπνευστος, *without drawing breath, breathless,* Hes.*Th.*797 codd. II. ἀναπνευστός, όν, Pass., *capable of being breathed,* ὁ ἀήρ Arist.*Top.*135ᵃ33. **-πνεύω,** = sq., Hsch.

***ἀναπνέω,** Ep. impf. ἀμπνείεσκον A.R.3.231: Ep. aor. imper. ἄμπνυε (v. infr.):—*take breath,* στῆθι καὶ ἄμπνυε Il.22.222: more commonly c. gen., *enjoy a respite, recover from,* ἀνέπνευσαν κακότητος 11.382; ὥς κε..ἀναπνεύσωσι πόνοιο 15.235; τῆς νόσου S.*Aj.*274; ἀ. ἐκ τῆς ναυηγίης Hdt.8.12; ἐκ καμάτων *IG*14.14 (Syrac.); ἀνέπνευσα ἐκ σέθεν by thy help I *recovered,* S.*OT*1221: c. part., ἀ. τειρόμενοι Il. 16.42; ἐς τεῖχος ἀλέντες 21.534: abs., *revive,* X.*An.*4.1.22, D.18. 195. 2. πυρεῖα ἀ. *revive, burn up again,* Thphr.*HP*5.9.6. II. *draw breath,* ἀ. πάντα καὶ ἐκπνεῖ Emp.100, cf. Pl.*Phd.*112b, etc.; ἀ. πυκνά Hp.*Mul.*2.203; *gather breath* before a race, Pi.*N.*8.19: metaph., ἀ. οὐχ ἅπαντες ἐπὶ ἴσα ib.7.5. 2. c. acc., *draw breath from, inhale,* τὴν οἰκείαν ἀρχήν Dam.*Pr.*8:—Pass., τὸν ἀναπνεόμενον ἀέρα Corn.*ND*32. III. *breathe forth, send forth,* c. acc. cogn., ἀμπνεῦσαι καπνόν Pi.*O.*8.36; πυρὸς σέλας ἀμπνείεσκον A.R.3.231; ἀ. ὑάκινθον *breathe* hyacinth, Pherecr.131.2: abs., *exhale an odour,* Thphr.*Od.*69: impers., ἡδὺ ἀναπνεῖ τῶν φυτῶν Philostr.*Her.Prooem.* 2: metaph., ἀ. χρησμούς Id.*VS*1.18.3. 2. of vapour, αὐτμὴ ἀ. μυχοῖο A.R.2.737. IV. causal, ἀ. τὸν ἵππον *breathe* the horse, Hld.8.14.

**ἀναπνοείτης,** ου, ὁ, *one who restores breath* to an athlete after a contest, *BMus.Inscr.*1109 (ii A.D.) (dub. sens.).

***ἀνα-πνοή,** poet. ἀμπν-, ἡ, *recovery of breath,* μόχθων ἀμπνοά *rest from* toils, Pi.*O.*8.7, cf. E.*IT*92, etc.; ἀμπνοὰν ἔστᾱσαν they recovered *breath,* took *fresh courage,* Pi.*P.*4.199; ἀ. διδόναι, παρέχειν, E.*Andr.*1137, Pl.*Ti.*70d; λαμβάνειν Id.*Phdr.*251e; ἀναπνοὴν ἔχει.. εἰπεῖν has *breath enough* to say, Men.536.6. II. *respiration, breathing,* Pi.*P.*3.57, Ar.*Nu.*627, Pl.*Ti.*33c, etc.; including εἰσπνοή and ἐκπνοή, Arist.*Resp.*471ᵃ7; ἀμπνοὰς ἔχειν, = ἀναπνεῖν, *breathe, live,* S.*Aj.*416; τὴν ἀ. ἀπολαβεῖν τινος *strangle,* Plu.*Rom.*27; ὑπὸ τὴν ἀ. in a *breath,* Plb.10.47.9. 2. = εἰσπνοή, *inspiration,* opp. ἐκπνοή, Pl.*Ti.*78e, 79e, cf. Arist.*Resp.*480ᵇ10. III. *exhalation,* Thphr. *HP*6.2.4. IV. *breathing organ,* of the nose and mouth, D.S.2.12, Luc.*Nigr.*32. 2. *air hole, vent,* Pl.*Ti.*85a, 91b, Plu.*Aem.*14.—Only sg. in Pi.; only pl. in Trag. **-πνοια,** ἡ, = foreg. II. 1, Ti. Locr.101d, Arist.*Pr.*962ᵃ26. ***-πνοϊκός,** ή, όν, *affecting respiration,* νόσος Ptol.*Tetr.*87.

**ἀναπό-βλητος,** ον, *not capable of being lost,* ἀγαθά S.E.*P.*3.238, cf. Cleanth.*Stoic.*1.129, Alex.Aphr.*Quaest.*121.16. **-γρᾰφος,** ον, *not registered* in the custom-house books, *contraband,* Poll.9.31; ἀ. μέταλλα *unregistered* mines, Hyp.*Eux.*34; *not registered* in the census, *PLond.*2.260.29 (i A.D.); πρόβατα ἀ. *BGU*338 ii 6 (ii A.D.). **-δεικτος,** ον, *not proved, undemonstrated,* Lycurg.129, Arist.*EN*1143ᵇ12. Adv. -τως *without proof,* Plu.*CG*10. II. of first principles, *indemonstrable,* Pl.*Def.*415b, Arist.*APr.*53ᵇ2, 57ᵇ33, al.; ἀ. συλλογισμοί, of syllogisms, Chrysipp.*Stoic.*2.79, al. Adv. -τως S.E.*P.*1.173, Gal.17(2).160. 2. *incapable of proof,* Plu.*Cor.* 20. III. Act., *furnishing no proof,* *PPar.*15.3.62, cf. *Stoic.*2.90. **-δεκτος,** ον, *not to be received,* Sch.E.*Ph.*527. **-δέχομαι,** *take responsibility for,* θυσίαν *Inscr.Magn.*61.56 (dub.). **-δήμητος,** ον, *untravelled,* Ph.2.11.

***ἀναποδ-ίζω,** (πούς) *make to step back, call back and question, cross-examine,* ἐπειρωτῶν τε καὶ ἀ. τὸν κήρυκα Hdt.5.92.ζ'; πολλάκις ἀνεπόδιζον τὸν γραμματέα Aeschin.3.192, cf. Luc.*Abd.*17:—Pass., Antipho Soph.18. 2. οὐδαμῇ ἄλλῃ ἀνεπόδισε ἑωυτόν in no other passage *did* he *correct* himself, *retract* what he before said, Hdt.2.116. 3. *deduct for retrograde motion,* Vett.Val.25.26. II. intr., *step back, return,* ἐπὶ τὴν μονάδα Pythag.ap.Stob.1.10.12 (corr. Heeren), Lxx *Si.*46.4, Luc.*Nec.*7; εἰς τοὐπίσω Hdn.5.6.7; ἀ. πρὸς.. *revert,* Chor. in *Rh.Mus.*49.492; κύκλον ἀ. *recur* in a cycle, Hippod. ap.Stob.4.34.71; of the *retrograde* motion of the planets, Theo Sm. p.147H., Procl.*Hyp.*5.72, etc.: metaph. of festivals which *fall late* in the calendar, Gem.8.19. **-ισμός,** ὁ, *going back,* εἰς μονάδα, opp. προποδισμὸς ἀπὸ μονάδος, Moderat.ap.Stob.1 *Coroll.*8; of the *retrograde* motion of planets, Vett.Val.226.1, Nicom.*Ar.*1.5; in pl., opp. προποδισμοί, Alex.Aphr.*in Metaph.*440.7; generally, *reversal* of planet's motion, Theo Sm.p.148H. II. *calling back, recall,* Lxx *Wi.*2.5. **-ιστής,** οῦ, ὁ, *one who drives back,* Eust.717.16. ***-ιστικός,** ή, όν, *in retardation,* Vett.Val.182.31; -κοὶ ἀστέρες *Cat.Cod. Astr.*1.133.23.

**ἀν-απόδοτος,** ον, *not given back, not returned,* ἀ. δόσις ἢ δωρεά Arist. *Top.*125ᵃ18; ἀργύριον ἀ. δόντα *not to be repaid,* *CIG*(add.)4278*k* (Xanthus), cf. 4300o (Limyra), *PTeb.*105.20 (ii B.C.), *PRyl.*171.16 (i A.D.); σῖτον *Inscr.Prien.*108.58. II. τὸ ἀ., = ἀνανταπόδοτον, Sch.Ar.*Av.*7, cf. Simp.*in Ph.*45.11.

***ἀνα-ποδόω,** = ἀναποδίζω II, ἀ. ἐπὶ τὴν μονάδα Plu.2.876f. II. ἀναποδόομαι *grow fresh feet,* of scorpions, Lyd.*Mag.*1.42.

**ἀναπό-δραστος,** ον, *unavoidable, not to be escaped,* Arist.*Mu.*401ᵇ13, Plu.2.166e, Alex.Aphr.*Fat.*166.3; τὸ ἀ. Plot.4.3.13. 2. Act., *unable to run away,* *AB*392, Alb.*Intr.*6. **-θετος,** ον, *not stored up,* Hsch.

**ἀνα-ποιέω,** *make up, prepare* a medicine, Hp.*Nat.Mul.*36; *mix up, stir up,* *PHolm.*25.22, al.; μετ' ἐλαίου Bilabel Ὀψαρτ.p.11. II. *make fresh, vamp up,* τὰ ἱμάτια Sch.Ar.*Pl.*1063. **-ποίητος,** ον, *made up, wrought up,* ἔκ τινος Ammon.*Diff.*123.

**ἀναποικίλλω,** *variegate,* Sch.Pi.*O.*11(10).113 Böckh.

**ἀν-άποινος,** ον, *without ransom,* only once in neut. (as Adv., acc. to Aristarch.) ἀνάποινον Il.1.99.

**ἀναποκλύζω,** *wash out again,* θαλάσσῃ *PHolm.*20.6.

**ἀναπόκρῐτος,** ον, *unanswered,* ἀ. ἀποστέλλειν πρέσβεις Plb.4.34.1, cf. Zeno *Stoic.*1.64; ἀ. ἀπελθεῖν Plb.22.10.13. Adv. ἀναποκρίτως, εἰπών Antipho 3.3.2. 2. Act., *not answering,* οἰμωγή Plb.8.23.6.

**ἀναπολάζω,** *roll about,* of an engine on shipboard, Ath.Mech.32.7.

**ἀναπο-λαυστία,** ἡ, *non-enjoyment,* Phld.*D.*1.16. **-λαυστος,** ον, *not to be enjoyed,* Plu.2.829d, 1104f. 2. Act., *not enjoying,* Phld.*Mort.*13; ἡδονῶν Heph.Astr.1.1, Hsch.

**ἀναπολεμ-έω,** *renew the war,* Str.17.3.15, *Mon.Anc.Gr.*15.8. **-ησις,** εως, ἡ, Str.11.8.3.

**ἀναπολεύω,** *move upwards in an orbit,* opp. καταπολεύω, *PMag. Par.*1.702.

**ἀναπολ-έω,** poet. ἀμπ-, properly, *turn up* the ground *again* (τρὶς ἀροτριᾶν τὴν γῆν, Hsch. s.v. ὡραπολεῖν): hence, *go over again, repeat,* ταὐτὰ τρὶς τετράκι τ' ἀμπολεῖν Pi.*N.*7.104; δὶς ταὐτὰ βούλει καὶ τρὶς ἀναπολεῖν μ' ἔπη; S.*Ph.*1238; ὅταν [ψυχὴ] αὖθις ταύτην ἀναπολήσῃ [μνήμην] Pl.*Phlb.*34b, cf. Vett.Val.242.20:—aor. 1 Pass., J.*AJ*13.5.8. **-ησις,** εως, ἡ, *repetition,* A.D.*Synt.*29.10, al., Plot.2.9.12; *reconsideration, recalling to mind,* Id.4.6.3, Hierocl.*in CA*19 p.461M. **-ητέον,** *one must recall to mind,* M.Ant.4.32. **-ίζω,** = ἀναπολέω, of a field, Pi.*P.*6.3.

**ἀναπο-λόγητος,** ον, *inexcusable,* Plb.12.21.10, *Ep.Rom.*1.20, 2.1; *undefended,* τινὰ ἐᾶσαι D.Chr.2.39, cf. Eun.*VS*p.489B.; *without making a defence,* D.H.7.46. **-λῠτος,** ον, *not able to get loose, sessile,* Arist.*HA*599ᵃ15. Adv. -τως Gal.12.8. **-μικτος,** ον, f.l. for ἀνεπι-, Thphr.*CP*6.8.4.

***ἀνα-πομπή,** ἡ, (ἀναπέμπω) *sending up,* e.g. to the metropolis, Plb.30.9.10. 2. ἀ. θησαυρῶν *digging up* of treasures, Luc.*Alex.* 5. II. *restoration,* ἐπὶ τοὺς πεπρακότας Ph.2.290. 2. *reference, reduction,* ἐπὶ γένος S.E.*M.*10.274; *reference* to a book, Jul.Laod. in *Cat.Cod.Astr.*8(4).246. 3. *delegation* of jurisdiction, *PTeb.*489 (ii A.D.), *BGU*1911 (ii A.D.). ***-πόμπιμος,** ον, *sent back,* Luc.*Luct.* 10, D.C.62.2; of slaves, τοῖς κυρίοις -ους ποιεῖν D.S.14.96. 2. of trials, *referred* to a higher court, Luc.*Eun.*12, D.C.52.33, etc. ***-πομπός,** ὁ, *one that sends up* or *back,* epith. of Hades, as *sending up* the shade of Darius, A.*Pers.*650. II. *distributor* of bread to soldiers, *POxy.*1115.2 (iii A.D.).

**ἀναπόνιπτος,** ον, *unwashen,* Ar.*Eq.*357, Phryn.Com.3D. II. = *not to be washed out,* Suid.

***ἀναπορεύομαι,** *proceed up-stream,* D.C.75.9.

***ἀναπό-ρριφος,** ον, (ἀπορρίπτω) *not liable to be rejected, free from blemish,* *PLond.*2.282.13 (i A.D.), etc. **-σβεστος,** ον, *inextinguishable,* Hecat.Abd.14.

**ἀνάποσις,** εως, ἡ, *swallowing up* of rivers, Olymp.*in Mete.*218.12, al.

**ἀναπό-σπαστος,** ον, *inseparable,* τοῦ ἑνός Dam.*Pr.*113. Adv. -τως Simp.*in Epict.*p.6D. **-στᾰτος,** ον, *unable to escape from,* θανάτου *Epigr.Gr.*526 (Beroe): abs., *without means of escape,* *POxy.*1469.5 (iii A.D.). 2. δεσπότης ἀ. *from whom there is no escape,* Plu.2.166e (codd.). 3. *inseparable,* Porph.*Sent.*40. **-στολος,** ον, *without permit,* ἐξὸν ἐκπλεῖν ἀ. *PGnom.*165 (ii A.D.). **-στρεπτος,** ον, *not to be turned away,* Sm.*Jb.*9.13. **-τέλεστος,** ον, *unfinished,* Eust.922.19. **-τευκτος,** ον, *unerring in its aim,* ὄρεξις Arr.*Epict.* 2.8.29; of persons, 1.4.11, al. Adv., Comp. -ότερον 4.6.26.

**ἀναποτικός,** ή, όν, *absorbent,* Ptol.*Tetr.*18.

**ἀναποτισμός,** ὁ, *watering,* dub. in *PLond.*3.1177.187 (ii A.D.).

**ἀναπό-τμητος,** ον, *not to be cut off* or *severed,* Arr.*Epict.*1.1. 24. **-τριπτος,** ον, gloss on ἀλίαστος, Sch.Il.*Oxy.*1086.74 (fort. -τρεπτος).

**ἀναπούλωτος,** ον, *not scarred over,* Gal.19.446.

**ἀναποφέρω,** *bring back again,* in aor. 1 Med. ἀναπηνεγκάμην *PCair. Preis.*32.12 (ii A.D.).

**ἀνάπραξις,** εως, ἡ, *exaction* of a debt or penalty, δανείων D.H.6.1; τοῦ ἀργυρίου *IG*9(1).694.10 (Corcyra).

**ἀνάπρᾱσις,** εως, ἡ, *retail dealing,* Poll.7.12.

***ἀναπράσσω,** Att. -πράττω, contr. ἀμπρ-, *exact, levy* money or debts, Th.8.107, Lys.16.6; ἀ. τό τε κεφάλαιον καὶ τὸν τόκον *IG*9(1).

694.58 (Corcyra); *demand back*, of loans already repaid, *OGI*669.20 (so in Med., of interest already paid, Plu.2.295d); ἀ. ὑπόσχεσιν *exact the fulfilment of* a promise, Th.2.95, cf. Ar.*Av*.1621; *distrain upon*, τὰ ἐμφανέα *SIG*554.16 (Thermon):—Med., *exact for oneself*, δίκας D.H.6.19.

**ἀναπρεσβεύω**, *send up ambassadors*, J.*AJ*18.2.4.

**ἀναπρήθω**, *let burst forth*, δάκρυ' ἀναπρήσας Il.9.433, Od.2.81.

**ἀνάπρῖσις**, εως, ἡ, *sawing off*, Hp.*Ep*.22.

**ἀνάπταιστος**, ον, = ἄπταιστος, Suid.

**ἀναπτέον**, *one must attach*, τὸν λόγον ἀπὸ τῶν φανερωτέρων Str.1.3.10.

**ἀναπτεροποιέω**, *represent as winged*, τὸν Ἔρωτα Men.Rh.p.337S.

**ἀναπτεροφορέομαι**, *fly upwards*, Ph.*Fr*.59H.

**ἀναπτερ-όω**, prop. *raise its feathers*, of a bird: hence metaph., *raise, set up*, ὀρθίους ἐθείρας ἀνεπτέρωκα E.*Hel*.633. 2. metaph., *set on the wing, put on the tiptoe* of expectation, *excite*, ἀναπτερώσας αὐτὴν οἴχεαι Hdt.2.115, cf. Pl.*Phdr*.255c; μῶν τι.. ἄγγελμ' ἀνεπτέρωκε Δαναΐδῶν πόλιν; E.*Or*.876; φόβος μ' ἀναπτεροῖ Id.*Supp*.89, cf. S.*Fr*.355; ἀ. τινὰ χρηστοῖς λόγοις Ar.*Av*.1449, cf. Men.*Epit*.510:—Pass., *to be in a state of eager expectation*, ἀνεπτερώθης A.*Ch*.228; ἀ. τὴν ψυχήν Cratin.384; ἀνεπτέρωμαι κλύων Ar.*Av*.434; ἀνεπτερωμένων τῶν Λακεδαιμονίων X.*HG*3.4.2; ἀνεπτερωμένος θεᾶσθαι Id.*Smp*.9.5; ἀναπτερωθεὶς ὑπό τινων ὡς.. *being irritated* by the remark of some, that.., Id.*HG*3.1.14. II. *furnish with new wings*, Ar.*Lys*.669:—Pass., *get new wings*, Pl.*Phdr*.249d. **-ωσις**, εως, ἡ, *clamour*, λόγοι ἀναπτερώσεως *clamorous* words, Lxx *Si*.31.1, cf. *Pr*.7.11. **-ωτός**, όν, *excitable, fickle*, χρῆμα ἡ νίκη Men.Prot.p.10D.

**ἀναπτερῠγίζω**, *raise the wings and fly away*, Ael.*NA*4.30: metaph., Phld.*Vit*.p.21J.

**ἀναπτερύσσομαι**, *to be furnished with wings*, Sch.Ar.*Eq*.1341.

**ἀνα-πτησίκερως**, ὁ, = ἰκτῖνος, Phot.p.119R. **-πτησις**, εως, ἡ, *upward flight*, Hierocl.*in CA*26p.478M.

**ἀναπτοέω**, poet. -πτοιέω, *scare exceedingly*, Mosch.2.23, Opp.*C*.1.107, etc.:—Pass., *to be scared*, Plu.*Pel*.16; *to be in great excitement*, Id.2.261a, etc.

**ἄναπτος**, ον, (ἀ- priv., ἅπτομαι) *not to be touched, impalpable*, Arist.*de An*.424ᵃ12. II. ἀναπτός, όν, (ἀνάπτω) *fastened on*, φᾶρος Eust.1774.15.

**ἀνά-πτυκτος**, ον, *that may be opened*, Arist.*PA*683ᵇ15. **-πτυξις**, εως, ἡ, *opening, gaping*, τοῦ στόματος ib.692ᵃ29. 2. *explanation*, Id.*Rh.Al*.1435ᵇ18, cf. Plu.2.382d, Ath.1.1a.

**ἀνάπτῠσις**, εως, ἡ, *expectoration*, Gal.15.480, Herod.Med. in *Rh.Mus*.58.93; αἵματος Alex.Trall.5.5; of fistulae, *opening out*, Antyll. ap.Orib.44.23.6.

***ἀνα-πτύσσω**, pf. inf. Pass. ἀνεπτύχθαι E.*El*.357: aor. Pass. ἀνεπτύχθην Hp.*Judic*.3, but -επτύγην *Int*.48:—*unfold* the rolls on which books were written, *open for reading*, ἀ. τὸ βιβλίον Hdt.1.125, cf. 48; δέλτων ἀναπτύσσοιμι γῆρυν E.*Fr*.370: also ἀ. πύλας, κύτος, *undo, open*, E.*IT*1286, *Ion* 39; χλαμύδα Plu.*Demetr*.42; even χεῖλος Opp.*H*.3.247; ἀναπτύξας χέρας with arms *outspread*, E.*Hipp*.1190; σεισμοὶ -ξαντες τὴν ἁρμονίαν τῶν ὀρῶν Philostr.*Im*.2.17:—Med., *fold up*, Arist.*PA*664ᵇ27, al. b. *cut open*, of freshly killed animals, Pherecyd.97J., Philum.*Ven*.17.3, *PMag.Leid.V*.10.1, etc. c. *ruminate, chew*, Opp.*H*.1.137. 2. *unfold, disclose*, πᾶν ἀ. πάθος A.*Pers*.254,294; πάντ' ἀναπτύσσει χρόνος S.*Fr*.301; ἀ. πρὸς φῶς Id.*El*.639, cf. E.*HF*1256; φρένα πρός τινα Id.*Tr*.662: in later Prose, Porph.*Antr*.4. II. as military term, τὴν φάλαγγα ἀ. *fold back* the phalanx, i.e. *deepen* it by countermarching from front to rear, X.*Cyr*.7.5.3; conversely, τὸ κέρας ἀ. *open out* the wing, i.e. *extend* the line by countermarching from rear to front, X.*An*.1.10.9, cf. Plu.*Pel*.23, Arr.*Tact*.9.5. **-πτυχή**, ἡ, = ἀνάπτυξις, ἰὼ.. αἰθέρος ἀμπτυχαί oh *wide expanse* of heaven! E.*Ion* 1445; νυκτός τε πηγὰς οὐρανοῦ τ' ἀναπτυχάς S.*Fr*.956; ἡλίου ἀναπτυχαί the sun's *unclouded orb*, E.*Hipp*.601; ἀ. ἐλεύθεροι (sc. ὀμμάτων) *El*.868. **-πτῠχος**, ον, = ἀνάπτυκτος, Arist.*HA*528ᵃ14.

**ἀναπτύω**, *spit up* or *out*, αἷμα Hp.*Aph*.5.13; σίαλον Plb.12.13.11: abs., *sputter*, ξηρὰ δ' ἀναπτύει [ῡ] Nic.*Al*.211; μυδῶσα κηκὶς.. ἔτυφε κἀνέπτυε S.*Ant*.1009:—Pass., Gal.16.210.

***ἀνάπτω**, *make fast on* or *to*, Hom. (only Od.), ἐκ δ' αὐτοῦ [ἱστοῦ] πείρατ' ἀνῆπτον Od.12.179, cf. 51,162; πρυμνήσι' ἀνάψαι 9.137: c. dat., γαίῃ A.R.2.177; ἀ. τι πρός τι E.*HF*1012:—Med., ἐκ τοῦδ' ἀναψόμεσθα πρυμνήτην κάλων to him will we *moor* our bark, i.e. he shall be our protector, Id.*Med*.770, etc.; θεοῖσι κῆδος ἀνάψασθαι *form a close connexion* with.., Id.*Tr*.845; χάριτας ἔς τινα ἀ. *confer* favours on.., Id.*Ph*.569; also, *fasten to oneself*, ἐπιστολὴν ἐκ τῶν δακτύλων ἀ. Din.1.36; *take in tow*, ναῦν D.S.13.19, Plu.*Cam*.8; τὸ κράτος Ph.1.474:—Pass., *to be fastened* or *fasten oneself on to, cling to*, c. gen., πέπλων E.*HF*629: c. dat., κίοσιν ib.1038 (prob., lyr.); *have* a thing *fastened* on one, περιβόλαι' ἀνήμμεθα ib.549. 2. *hang up* in a temple, *offer up*, like ἀνατίθημι, πολλὰ δ' ἀγάλματ' ἀνῆψεν Od.3.274, cf. Arist.*Fr*.572, Lyc.853, Philostr.*VA*1.11, Tryph.256. 3. metaph., *fasten upon, attach to*, μῶμον ἀνάψαι Od.2.86; αἷμα ἀ. τινί a charge of bloodshed, dub. in E.*Andr*.1196, cf. Ps.-Phoc.70, etc.; κήδε' ἀνῆπταί τινι A.R.2.245; *ascribe, refer to*, τοὺς λόγους εἰς ἀριθμοὺς ἀ. Arist.*Metaph*.1078ᵇ22; ἀρχήν, αἰτίαν ἀ. εἰς τὸν Πύθιον Plu.*Lyc*.6, etc.; χάριν ἀ. τινί *ascribe* a favour to him, Id.*Ant*.46; τὴν χάριν εἰς Καίσαρα πάντων ἀνῆπτεν Id.*Brut*.6; τοῖς ἐκ τοῦ θεοῦ τὴν εὐδαιμονίαν ἀνάψασι Porph.*Abst*.2.3:—Med., *attach oneself*, πρὸς πολλούς Phld.*Herc*.1457.8. II. *light up, kindle*, λύχνα Hdt.2.133; πῦρ E.*Or*.1137; φῶς Pl.*Ti*.39b; πυρὶ ἀ. δόμους E.*Or*.1594: metaph., νέφος ο.. μωγῆς ὡς τάχ' ἀνάψει Id.*Med*.107:—Pass., *to be kindled*, Zeno *Sto*.. 1.31, etc. 2. *inflame with anger*, Lib.*Or*.68.35:—Pass., ib.33.1.., Ps.-Callisth.3.22; *excite* emotionally, Phld.*Po*.1425.20. 3. intr.. *to be lighted* up, Arist.*Mir*.841ᵃ32.

**ἀνάπτωσις**, εως, ἡ, *falling back*: metaph., *slackness*, Eust.1406.8.. of machines, *recoil*, Ph.*Bel*.68.45, Hero *Bel*.82.13; of style, *lifeless*ness, Eust. ad D.P.69. 2. *reclining at meals*, Aristeas 187,203.. generally, *lying down*, in pl., Onos.10.11.

**ἀνάπτωτος**, ον, *flat*, of style, v.l. in Eust. ad D.P.69.

**ἀναπυνθάνομαι**, *inquire closely into*, τὰς πάτρας αὐτῶν ἀνεπύθετο.. Hdt.6.128; ἀνεπυνθάνετο τὸν ποιήσαντα Id.8.90; ἀναπυθώμεθα τούσδε.. τίνες ποτὲ καὶ πόθεν ἔμολον Ar.*Av*.403. 2. abs., ἀναπυνθανόμενος εὑρίσκω discover *by inquiry*, Hdt.5.57; also, *learn by inquiry*, ἀ. ταῦτα.. πραττόμενα X.*An*.5.7.1 codd.; ἀ. περί τινος Pl.*Hp.Mi*.363b; ἀ. τι.. τινος *ask of* a person, Ar.*Pax* 693.

**ἀναπυρέττω**, *suffer from recurrence of fever*, Gal.16.649.

**ἀναπυρίζω**, in aor. part. ἀμπυρίξας, *kindle*, of fire, *Lyr.Alex.Adesp*.31.

**ἀναπῠρόω**, *set on fire*, Arist.*Mu*.395ᵃ22 (Pass.): intr., metaph., *break out afresh*, πάθη.. πάλιν ἀναπυρώσαντα Gal.16.742.

**ἀναπυρσεύω**, *make glaring*, τὴν βαφὴν τὴν πορφύρας Poll.1.49.

**ἀνάπυστος**, ον, *well-known, notorious*, Od.11.274, Hdt 6.64,66, etc.

**ἀναπῡτ-ίζω**, *spit up, spout up*, Hero *Spir*.1.28. **-ισμός**, ὁ, Id.*Aut*.4.3 (but see ἀνα-πιτύζω, -υσμός).

***ἀναπωλέω**, *put up for sale again*, *PPetr*.3p.109 (Pass.); *sell again*, Poll.7.12:—Pass., prob. in *CIG*2266.11 (Delos).

***ἀναπωμάζω**, (πῶμα) *lift up the cover*, Hero *Spir*.1 *Praef*., Crito ap. Gal.12.732.

**ἀνάπωσις**, εως, ἡ, *a drinking up*, Erot. s.v. ἄμπωτις (οἷον ἀ. τις οὖσα) s.v.l. Cf. ἀνάποσις.

**ἀνάπωτις**, v. ἄμπωτις:—Adj. **ἀναπωτικός**, ή, όν, Eust.1719.44.

**ἄναρ**· ὄναρ (Cret.), Phot.p.119R., Hsch.

**ἀναρ-**: when ἀνά is compd. with words beginning with ρ, the ρ is usually doubled, as in ἀναρριπτέω, etc., though in Poets and Ion. Greek it is sometimes single, as in sq.

**ἀναραγαθῆσαι**· ἀναψοφῆσαι, ἀναπηδῆσαι, Hsch.

**ἀνάρακτος**· δημόσιος, Hsch.

**ἀναράομαι**, *recall a curse*, Callisth.ap.Suid., Poll.5.130.

***ἄναρβηλα**· τὰ μὴ ἐξεσμένα, ἄρβηλοι γὰρ τὰ δέρματα, Hsch.

**ἀνάρβῠλος**, ον, *without shoes, unshod*, E.*Fr*.530.7.

***ἀναργῠρ-ία**, ἡ, *want of cash*, Stratt.8D.; ἡ τῆς ἀ. παραγραφή *non numeratae pecuniae*, *Cod.Just*.4.21.16; ἡ τῆς προικὸς ἀ. Just.*Nov*.100 *Pr*.: pl., ibid. **-ος**, ον, *without silver*: *without money*, Lys.*Fr*.35, Pl.*Lg*.679b. II. *not bought with silver*: *incorruptible*, Poll.6.191.

**ἀναρθρ-ία**, ἡ, *want of vigour*, Arist.*Pr*.894ᵇ21. ***-ος**, ον, *not differentiated* or *articulated*, Pl.*Ti*.75a, Arist.*HA*583ᵇ10, al. 2. *without strength, nerveless*, S.*Tr*.1103, E.*Or*.228. 3. *without visible joints*, like fat men, Hp.*Aër*.19. II. of sound, *inarticulate*, ψόφοι Thphr.*Sens*.41; ᾠδαί D.S.3.17; ἀλαλαγμός Plu.*Mar*.19, cf. *Caes*.63; φθογγή Id.2.613e, etc.; φθέγματα *Epigr.Gr*.1003 (Memnon). Adv. -ρως *confusedly*, Plu.2.611b. III. *avoiding the use of the article*, ἁρμονία D.H.*Comp*.22.

**ἀνᾰριθμ-έομαι**, Med., *reckon up, enumerate*, D.19.18. II. *reconsider*, Pl.*Ax*.372a:—Act., D.C.36.25. **-ησις**, εως, ἡ, *numbering*, Gal.17(1).314, Simp.*in Ph*.714.28. **-ητος**, ον, *not to be counted, countless*, Pi.*O*.7.25, Hdt.1.126, 7.190,211, al.; of time, *immeasurable*, S.*Aj*.646. 2. *unregarded*, E.*Ion* 837, *Hel*.1679. **-ιος**, ον, = ἀνάρσιος, and ἀναρίθμιον· ἐχθρόν (opp. ἐναρίθμια· φίλα, συνήθη), Hsch. **-ος** [ᾰρ], poet. **ἀνήριθμος**, ον, *without number, countless*, Sapph.*Supp*.20.10, Pi.*I*.5(4).50; κυμάτων ἀ. γέλασμα A.*Pr*.90; πλῆθος ἀνάριθμοι Id.*Pers*.40: c. gen., ἀ. ὧδε θρήνων *without count* or *measure* in lamentations, S.*El*.232; μηνῶν ἀ. (Herm. for μήλων) *without count* of months, Id.*Aj*.604 (lyr.); ὧν πόλις ἀνάριθμος ὄλλυται by [the loss of] *countless hosts* of them.., Id.*OT*179; χρόνον.. ἡμερῶν ἀνήριθμον Id.*Tr*.247. II. *without number*, i.e. *having no assigned number*, Plot.6.6.11. 2. *not numerable*, Dam.*Pr*.117. [ἀνᾰρῐθμος Sapph. l.c., A.*Pers*.40 (lyr.); ἀνᾱρῑθμος in E.*Ba*.1335 (iamb.). S. has ἀνάρῖθμος in lyr., *OT*167,179, *El*.232. S. also uses ἀνήρῐθμος in lyr., *Aj*.604: Theoc. has ἀνάριθμος 15.45, but ἀνᾰριθμος 16.90.]

***ἀνᾰριστ-έω**, *take no breakfast*, v.l. in Hp.*Acut*.28. **-ητος**, ον, *not having breakfasted*, Eup.68, Ar.*Fr*.454, Gal.15.562. **-ία**, ἡ, *want of breakfast*, Hp.*Vict*.3.75 (pl.); prob. for **ἀναρίστησις**, ib.4.90. **-ος**, ον, = ἀναρίστητος, Id.*VM*11, Plb.3.72.3; *dinnerless*, X.*An*.1.10.19. Theoc.15.147.

***ἀνᾰρίτης** [ῑ], ου, ὁ, = νηρείτης, Ibyc.22, Epich.42, cf. 114, Herod.11 (ἀνηρ-). (ῑ not ει acc. to Hdn.Gr.2.475.)

**ἄναρκτος**, ον, (ἄρχω) *not governed* or *subject*, Th.5.99; *not submitting to be governed*, βίος A.*Eu*.526 (where Wieseler metri gr. ἀνάρχετος, on analogy of ἀπεύχετος), S.*Fr*.30.

**ἄναρμενος**, ον, *unequipped*, *AP*11.29 (Autom.).

**ἀναρμόδιος**, ον, *unfit*, Zos.1.29, Men.Prot.p.110D., David *in Porph*.132.23. Adv. -ίως *AB*363.

**ἄναρμος**, ον, *without joints*, of atoms, Gal.1.416, cf. Heraclid.Pont. ap.eund.19.244; ὄγκοι S.E.*M*.10.318. 2. *loose*, of the groin, prob. l. in Philostr.*Gym*.48.

**ἀναρμοστ-έω**, *not to fit* or *suit*, τινί Pl.*R*.462a; πρὸς ἄλληλα Id.*Sph*.253a; of musical instruments, *to be out of tune*, Id.*Grg*.

82b (cj.). **-ία**, ἡ, *discord*, of musical sounds, Id.*Phd.*93c, e, al.: metaph., Dam.*Pr.*341. **-ος**, ον, *not fitting*, of dress, X.*Mem.*3.10.13; of sound, *out of tune*, Pl.*Ti.*80a; opp. εὐάρμοστος, *Tht.*178d: metaph. of the soul, *Phd.*93c, cf. *Smp.*206c; ἀ. τινί 206d; *incongruous*, μεταβολὴ ἀ. τοῖς θεοῖς Iamb.*Myst.*3.27. Adv. **-τως** Pl.*R.*790b. II. of persons, *impracticable*, Hdt.3.80, Ar.*Nu.*908. 2. *unfitted, unprepared*, πρός τι Th.7.67.

**ἀναροδανισθῆναι**· ἀναβληθῆναι, Hsch.

**ἀναροιβδέω**, v. sub ἀναρρ–.

**ἀναρός**· ἄγγελος (Tarent.), Hsch. (leg. ἄγγαρος).

***ἀναροτρίαστος**, ον, *unploughed*, γῆ *EM*175.36.

**ἀναρπ-άγδην**, Adv. *snatching up violently*, A.R.4.579,1232. **-αγή**, ἡ, *recapture*, E.*Hel.*50 (pl.). ***-άζω**, fut. -άσω (v. infr. III) and -άξω, more freq. in Med. form -άσομαι (v. infr. III): aor. -ήρπασα and -ξα, in Hom. as suits the metre: aor. 2 Pass. ἀνηρπάγην D.S.4.75, Plu.*Pyrrh.*7:—*snatch up*, ἀνὰ δ' ἥρπασε Παλλὰς Ἀθήνη (sc. τὸ ἔγχος) Il.22.276, cf. Pi.*P.*4.34; ἀ. τὰ ὅπλα X.*An.*7.1.15; of the sun *causing* the earth's moisture *to evaporate*, Hp.*Aër.*8, cf. Plu.2.658b, Aristid.*Or.*36(48).60. II. *snatch away, carry off*, ὅτε μιν.. ἀνήρπασε Φοῖβος Il.9.564, cf. 16.437, Od.4.515, 5.419; of slave-dealers, ἀλλά μ' ἀνήρπαξαν Τάφιοι *kidnapped* me, 15.427, cf. X.*An.*1.3.14, Aristid.1.161 J., etc.; ἀνήρπασέν ποτε.. Κέφαλον ἐς θεοὺς Ἕως E.*Hipp.*454; ἀ. τοῖς ὄνυξιν, of an eagle, Ar.*V.*17, cf. Epicr.2.10:—Pass., φροῦδος ἀναρπασθεὶς S.*El.*848 (lyr.), etc.; ὑπὸ τῆς εἱμαρμένης *IG*12(7).51 (Amorgos): in Prose, *to be carried off to prison*, δεῖ με ἀνηρπάσθαι D.21.120,124, cf. 10.18. 2. in good sense, *rescue*, Plu.*Pyrrh.*16:—Pass., ib.7. III. *take by storm, ravage*, σὺ.. ἀναρπάσεις δόμους; E.*Ion* 1303; of persons, ἀναρπασόμενος τοὺς Φωκέας *take* them *by storm* or *at once*, Hdt.8.28, cf. 9.59:—Pass., ἀνήρπασται πόλις E.*Ph.*1079, *Hel.*751, D.9.47; ἐκ μέσης τῆς Ἑλλάδος Aeschin.3.133. IV. *carry off, steal*, πολλοὺς καὶ πολλὰ χρήματα ἔχομεν ἀνηρπακότες X.*An.*1.3.14; τρία τάλαντα ἀνηρπάκασι D.27.29; of regraters, *buy up unfairly*, ἀ. σῖτον Lys.22.15. **-άξανδρος**, f.l. for ἁρπάξανδρος, q.v. **-αστέον**, *one must wipe off*, τοὺς ἱδρῶτας Herod.Med. in *Rh.Mus.*58.92. **-αστός**, όν, also ή, όν E.*Hec.*207 (lyr.):—*snatched up, carried off*, ἀ. γίγνεσθαι to be *carried off*, l.c., Pl.*Phdr.*229c. 2. *carried up the country*, i.e. into Central Asia, ἀ. γίγνεσθαι πρὸς βασιλέα v.l. in X.*Mem.*4.2.33. II. of things, ἀ. ποιεῖν τὸν βίον to give up his substance *as plunder*, Plb.9.26.7, cf. Hdn.7.3.3.

**ἀναρραγής**, ές, = ἄρρηκτος, Sch.A.*Pr.*6 (s. v. l.).

**ἀναρραΐζω**, *recover from a bad illness*, Poll.3.108, Hsch.

**ἀναρραίνω**, *send gushing forth*, πέτρα κρουνὸν ἀ. Arist.*Mir.*$841^a22$.

**ἀνα-ρράπτω**, *lift up by sewing*, βλέφαρα Gal.*Thras.*23. **-ρράσσω**, *shake up* ingredients, *Hippiatr.*128. **-ρραφή**, ἡ, *lifting by sewing up*, of the eyelid, Leonid.ap.Aët.7.71. **-ραφικός**, ή, όν, *used in* ἀναρραφή, σμιλίον ibid.

***ἀναρραψῳδέω**, *begin singing*, προοίμιον Luc.*JTr.*14.

**ἀναρρέζω**, only aor. 1 ἀνέρεξα· ἔπραξα, Hsch.

**ἀναρρέπω**, *fly up*, of scales, *Theol.Ar.*29.

**ἀναρρέω**, *flow, stream back*, Pl.*Ti.*78d; of blood, *IG*12(7).115 (Amorgos); of smoke, Philostr.*Im.*2.27.

**ἀναρρήγνυμι** (-ύω App.*BC*4.115), *break up*, μή οἱ ὕπερθε γαῖαν ἀναρρήξειε Ποσειδάων Il.20.63; ἀ. αὔλακας Hdt.2.14; ἀ. τάφου διά a grave, E.*Tr.*1153. 2. *break through, break open*, τεῖχος ἀναρρήξας Il.7.461; οἴκων μυχοὺς E.*Hec.*1040; ὑπόνομον Plb.5.71.9; ἐργαστήρια Plu.*Pel.*12:—Pass., νῆες ἀναρραγεῖσαι τὰς παρεξειρεσίας Th.7.34. 3. *tear open* a carcase, of lions, Il.18.582; of hounds, X.*Cyn.*7.9; of Ajax, δίχα ἀνερρήγνυ *was cleaving* them *asunder*, S.*Aj.*236. II. *make to break forth*, λόγον Pi.*Fr.*180; ἔπη Ar.*Eq.*626; νεῖκος Theoc.22.172; πόλιν *make* it *break out, excite greatly*, Plu.*Flam.*10, *Mar.*35:—Pass., with pf. ἀνέρρωγα, *burst forth, break*, of sores, Hp.*Fract.*11; of floods, Arist.*Mete.*$368^a26$; of volcanoes, Id.*Mir.*$846^a9$: metaph., of words, ἀνέρρωγεν τὸ φρόνημα Pherecr.10 D.; of persons, ἀναρρήγνυσθαι πρὸς ὀργήν, εἰς ἅπαν τόλμης, Plu.*Brut.*18, *Cic.*19. III. intr., *break* or *burst forth*, δέδοιχ' ὅπως μὴ.. ἀναρρήξει κακά S.*OT*1075: esp. in pf. part. ἀνερρωγώς, of the mouth of carnivorous animals, *with a wide gape*, στόμα ἔχειν ἀνερρωγὸς Arist.*HA*$502^a6$, *PA*$696^b34$; of the animals themselves, τὰ καρχαρόδοντα πάντα ἀνερρωγότα ib.$662^a27$, cf. 30.—Pres. **ἀναρρήττω**, D.S.17.58.

**ἀναρρηθῆναι**, aor. inf. Pass. of ἀνειπεῖν, q.v.

**ἀνάρρημα**, ατος, τό, *proclamation*, Phryn.*PS*p.39 B.

**ἀνάρρηξις**, εως, ἡ, (ἀναρρήγνυμι) *breaking up*, νεῶν Plu.*Ant.*66 (pl.): αἱμάτων ἀ. *haemorrhage* from lungs, Hp.*Prorrh.*2.7.

**ἀνάρρησις**, εως, ἡ, *public proclamation*, ἡ ἀ. τοῦ στεφάνου Aeschin.3.32, D.18.58.

**ἀναρριζόω**, *root, implant in*, θαλάσσῃ dub. in Nonn.*D.*18.36.

**ἀνάρρινον**, τό, = κάρδαμον, *nose-smart*, Arist.*Pr.*$925^a30$, Speus.ap.Ath.9.369b, prob. in Nic.*Fr.*84. II. = ἀντίρρινον, Dsc.4.130 (prob.), Gal.11.834. III. *sternutative*, Hp.ap.Gal.19.79.

**ἀναρριπίζω**, *rekindle*, τὸ θερμὸν Arist.*Fr.*233, cf. D.H.1.59: metaph., στάσιν Id.7.15, cf. Ph.2.377; ἐπιθυμίαν Alciphr.1.35; *fan*, Antiph.202.16:—Pass., ἀνὴρ ἀναρριπίζεται Pherecr.4 D.; πόλεμος ἀ. Jul.*Or.*1.13b. 2. *scatter to the winds*, νίκης ἐλπίδα Nonn.*D.*25.307.

***ἀναρρίπτω** (also **-ριπτέω** Od.13.78, Hdt.7.50, Th.4.95, etc.), *throw up*, ἀ. ἅλα πηδῷ, i.e. row with might and main, Od.7.328; without πηδῷ, οἱ δ' ἅλα πάντες ἀνέρριψαν 10.130; of a boar *tossing* a dog, X.*Cyn.*10.9; ἀ. τὴν κόνιν, of the bison, Arist.*HA*$630^b5$; ἀ. ὑπὲρ τὴν κεφαλὴν Plu.*Aem.*20. II. ἀ. κίνδυνον, metaph. from dicing, *stand the hazard of* a thing, *run* a risk, Hdt.7.50, Th.4.85,95; τὸν περὶ ὀστράκου κίνδυνον Plu.*Nic.*11; τὸν ὑπὲρ τῆς ἡγεμονίας καὶ τοῦ σώματος κίνδυνον Id.*Dem.*20; διὰ μιᾶς μάχης τὸν περὶ τῆς πατρίδος κύβον ἀ. Id.*Brut.*40: with κίνδυνον omitted, ἐς ἅπαν τὸ ὑπάρχον ἀναρρίπτειν *throw for* one's all, *stake* one's all, Th.5.103; ἀ. μάχην *risk* a battle, Plu.*Caes.*40, etc.; also πρὸς ἕνα κίνδυνον τὸ πᾶν ἀ. Id.*Arat.*5:—Pass., ἀνερρίφθω κύβος *jacta sit alea*, Men.65, cf. Ar.*Fr.*673, Plu.*Caes.*32. III. *set in motion, stir up*, στάσιν D.H.10.17 codd. (prob. -ερρίπιζον).

***ἀναρριχ-άομαι**, impf. ἀνερριχώμην Ar.*Pax*70, Aristaenet.1.20: fut. -ήσομαι Poll.5.82: aor. ἀνερριχησάμην D.C.43.21:—in Suid. and *EM* the augm. tenses are written ἀνηρρ-, cf. ἀρριχάομαι:—*clamber up with the hands and feet, scramble up*, ἀ. ὥσπερ οἱ πίθηκοι ἐπ' ἄκρα τὰ δένδρα Hellanic.197 J.; ἀ. εἰς οὐρανὸν Ar.l.c.; also in late Prose, Philostr.*Im.*2.28, Ael.*NA*7.24, 10.29, Aristaenet.1.3, Lib.*Or.*18.238, etc.: rarely c. acc., τοὺς ἀναβασμοὺς τοῖς γόνασιν ἀ. D.C. l.c.; τὸν τοῖχον Aristaenet.1.20 (s. v. l., ⟨πρὸς⟩ add. Pierson):—ridiculed as obsolete by Luc.*Lex.*8. **-ησις**, εως, ἡ, *clambering, swarming up*, ἐπὶ τοὺς οἴκους Arist.*Fr.*84.

**ἀνάρριψις**, εως, ἡ, *throwing up*, πετρῶν, of a volcano, Plu.2.398e, v.l. ib.951c.

**ἀναρροή**, ἡ, = ἀνάρροια, κυμάτων Nicoch.6 D. (ἀναρρόη acc. to Hdn. Gr.1.305.)

**ἀναρροθιάζω**, *dash up*, of the sea, dub. cj. in Eup.324.

**ἀνάρροια**, ἡ, *back flow, reflux*, Arist.*Mir.*$843^a27$, Plu.2.929e (of the moon's reflected light); θαλάσσης Thphr.*Metaph.*29.

***ἀναρροιβδ-έω**, poet. ἀναροιβδέω, *swallow back, suck down again*, Χάρυβδις ἀναρροιβδεῖ μέλαν ὕδωρ Od.12.104; τρὶς δ' ἀναροιβδεῖ ib.105, cf. 236:—Pass., Gal.*Sect.Intr.*9; but in S.*Fr.*440, *throw up*, as expl. by Phot.p.120 R., cf. Paul.Aeg.3.10. (The spelling ἀναρρυβδ– has Ms. authority in Hom. and is supported by the assonance with Χάρυβδις, Od. ll. cc.; cf. καταρυβδήσας Hsch.) **-ησις**, εως, ἡ, *a sucking down*, Str.1.2.36.

***ἀναρροιζέω**, *rush up, rush back*, Plu.2.979e. II. *hurtle in air*, of arrows, Nonn.*D.*29.289. III. trans., *discharge*, οἱ καταπέλται τὰς λόγχας ἀ. J.*BJ*3.7.9.

**ἀναρροπ-ία**, ἡ, *motion upwards*, Hp.*Hum.*1, cf. *Epid.*2.1.6; *elevation*, Gal.10.318. **-ος**, ον, *tilted up*, like one side of a balance, σχήματα Hp.*Mochl.*35; κατάκλισις Gal.18(2).60, cf. Antyll.ap.Orib.6.1.2; of the motion of humours, *with an upward tendency*, Id.ap. eund.5.28.3. Adv. **-πως** Pall.*in Hp.Fract.*12.282 C. II. *retrograde*, ἀνάρροπον τιθέναι τὴν τῶν Ἀβάρων κατάβασιν Men.Prot.p.68 D.

**ἀνάρρους**, ου, ὁ, *upward flow*, opp κατάρρους, τοῦ αἵματος Hp.*Ulc.*24.

**ἀναρροφ-έω**, = ἀναρροιβδέω, Cratin.7 D., Arist.*Mete.*$356^b13$, *Placit.*3.5.2, Luc.*VH*1.30; *gulp down*, D.C.71.10. **-ημα**, ατος, τό, *noise of gulping*, Hsch. s. v. ἀναροιβδεῖ (pl.). **-ησις**, εως, ἡ, *sucking up* through a tube, Sch.Opp.*H.*4.462.

**ἀναρροχθέω**, *retire with a roar*, of waves, Orph.*A.*706.

**ἀναρρυβδέω**, v. ἀναρροιβδέω.

**ἀναρρυθμίζω**, *reduce to order*, Philostr.*VA*2.22.

**ἀνά-ρρυμα**, ατος, τό, *victim*, Sch.Pl.*Ti.*21b:—also **ἀνάρυμα**, *AB* 417. **-ρρυσις**, εως, ἡ, *rescuing*, Phot.*Bibl.*p.2 B. (prob.); αἰχμαλώτων Just.*Nov.*7.8, cf. 115.3.13: pl., ibid. 2. name of *second day of festival* Ἀπατούρια, Ar.*Pax*890, ubi v. Sch., cf. *AB*417.

**ἀναρρύττειν**· διδάσκειν, ἀναδιδάσκειν, Hsch.

**ἀναρρύω**, (ῥύω, ἐρύω) *draw* the victim's head *back* so as to cut the throat, like Homer's αὐερύω: hence, *sacrifice*, Epich.139, Pi.*O.*13.81, Eup.395. 2. Med., aor. ἀνερρυσάμην, *draw back, rescue*, ψυχὴν ἀ. παθέων *from*.., Hp.*Ep.*23; ἀ. πόλεις Iamb.*VP*7.33; ἀ. ἧτταν *repair* a defeat, D.H.5.46 codd.:—Pass., ἀνερρύσθησαν Just.*Nov.*115.3.13.

**ἀναρρώννυμι**, aor. ἀνέρρωσα, *strengthen afresh*, Plu.2.694d, etc.:—Pass., *regain strength*, ἀναρρωσθέντες Th.7.46, Plu.2.75c, etc. 2. intr. in Act., τὴν γονὴν ἀναρρώννυσι Pherecyd.33 J.; νοσήσας ἀνέρρωσε Plu.*Pomp.*57, cf. 2.182b.

**ἀναρρώομαι**, *rush back*, ἀναρρώσασθαι ὀπίσσω Orph.*A.*1257.

**ἀνάρρωσις**, εως, ἡ, *recovery*, τῶν κεκμηκότων Simp. *in Ph.*5.1, cf. Philum.ap.Aët.5.123, Hsch. s. v. ἀναστατηρίαι.

***ἀνάρσιος**, ον, also α, ον S.*Tr.*641 (lyr.): (ἄρσιος):—*incongruous*: hence, I. of persons, *hostile, implacable*, δυσμενέες καὶ ἀνάρσιοι Il.24.365, Od.14.85; ὅσ' ἀνάρσιοι ἄνδρες ἐδηλήσαντ' ἐπὶ χέρσου ib.10.459, 11.401, etc.; ἦσθ' ἀνάρσιος (vulg. ἦλθες), of Apollo, A.*Ag.*511; ἀνάρσιοι *enemies*, S.*Tr.*853 (lyr.); ἀ. καναχά, opp. θεία μοῦσα, ib. 641 (lyr.), cf. Theoc.17.101. II. of events, *untoward, strange*, ἀ. πρήγματα πεπονθέναι Hdt.1.114, cf. 9.37; οὐδὲν ἀ. πρῆγμα συνηνείχθη 3.10, 5.89,90; δεινόν τε καὶ ἀ. ἐποιέετο [τὸ πρῆγμα] 9.110.—Ep., Ion., and (rarely) Trag.

***ἀναρτ-άω**, *hang to* or *upon*, ὀνάρταις (Aeol. pres. part.) χέρρας ὐμ ἐμμάτων Alc.*Supp.*4.21; λαιμὸν ἀ. μελάθρῳ A.R.3.789; *hang up*, ἑαυτόν Plu.2.841a; τὸ ζῆν ib.314b:—but mostly, 2. metaph., *attach to, make dependent upon*, δήμῳ.. μήτε πᾶν ἀναρτήσῃς κράτος E.*Fr.*626.1; ἀ. ἑαυτὸν εἰς δῆμον D.*Ep.*3.23; ἐς θεοὺς ἀ. τι *leave* it *depending upon* them, E.*Ph.*705; Rhet., ἀ. τι τῇ ὑποστάσει Aristid.*Rh.*1 p.480 S. 3. *keep in suspense*, Alciphr.1.22; *uplift*, ταῖς ὑποσχέσεσι Lib.*Decl.*33.26. 4. *suspend*, i.e. *withhold*, c. dat., τὸ σιτηρέσιόν τινι Just.*Nov.*88.2.1. II. Pass., *to be hung up*, παραδείγματα ἀνηρτημένους as examples, Pl.*Grg.*525c. 2. *depend upon*, ἔκ τινος Id.*Ion* 533e: metaph., ἐλπίσιν ἐξ ἐλπίδων ἀναρτωμένους *clinging to* one hope after another, D.19.18; ἀνηρτῆσθαι εἰς.. *to be referred* or *refer-*

*able to*.., τὰ ἁμαρτήματα..εἰς θεὸν ἀνηρτημένα τιμωρόν Pl.*Lg*.729e; τὰ ἄλλα πάντα εἰς τὴν ψυχὴν ἀ. Id.*Men*.88e; ὅτῳ ἀνδρὶ εἰς ἑαυτὸν ἀνήρτηται πάντα Id.*Mx*.247e; ἀνηρτημένοι ταῖς ὄψεσιν πρός τινα *hanging on* one with their eyes, Plu.*Oth*.3; ταῖς ἐπιθυμίαις εἴς τι Id.2.989d; ἀνηρτημένοι ταῖς ψυχαῖς *in suspense*, D.S.33.5. III. Med., also with pf. Pass., = Act., D.H.11.46: hence, *attach to oneself, make dependent upon one*, τινά X.*Cyr*.1.4.1; *subdue*, ib.1.1.5. -έομαι, Ion. Verb, used only in pf. Pass. (cf. ἀρτέομαι), *to be ready, prepared* to do, c. inf., ἀναρτημένου σεῦ χρηστὰ ἔργα ποιέειν Hdt.1.90; ἀναρτημένος ἔρδειν τινὰ κακῶς 6.88; ἀνάρτημαι ἐπ' αὐτοὺς στρατεύεσθαι 7.8.γ'. -ησις, εως, ἡ, *suspension*, Thphr.*Lass*.10, Sor.2.85; *crucifixion*, Suid.: metaph., ἡ κατὰ τὴν ὑπόστασιν ἀ. Aristid.*Rh*.1 p.480 S.; ἡ εἰς νοῦν ἀ. Procl.*Inst*.202. 2. metaph., *suspension*, = *withholding*, χορηγίας ἄρτων Just.*Nov*.88 tit.

ἀνάρτιος, ον, *uneven, odd*, Pl.*Phd*.104e, al. 2. *at odds with one, hostile*, Plu.2.1030a.

ἀνάρτῡτος, ον, *unseasoned*, of food, Phld.*Mus*.p.53 K., Diogenian. 2.12, Sm.*Jb*.6.6; ἀ. βίος cj. Coraës in Ath.12.511d.

ἀναρυγή, corrupt for ἀνορυγή (q. v.), *PRyl*.95.8.

ἀνάρῠσις, εως, ἡ, *drawing of water*, Plu.2.951c (pl.).

ἀναρυστῆρα· ἐν ᾧ ὁ οἶνος ἀνιμᾶται, Hsch.

ἀνᾰρύτω [ῠ], aor. 1 ἀνήρυσα Hsch., *draw as from a well*, Plu.2.949f: metaph., ἀ. θριάμβους Cratin.36.

*ἀναρχᾱΐζω, *bring back to old ways*, πόλιν *AP*7.707 (Diosc.).

ἀνάρχετος, v. ἄναρκτος.

*ἀναρχ-ία, ἡ, *lack of a leader*, ἀναρχίης ἐούσης since there was *no commander*, Hdt.9.23; οὐκ ἐρεῖτ' ἀ. A.*Supp*.906. II. *lawlessness, anarchy*, δημόθρους ἀναρχία Id.*Ag*.883, cf. Th.6.72; ἀ. καὶ ἀνομία Pl.*R*.575a; opp. ἐλευθερία, 560e; ἀ. καὶ ἀταξία Arist.*Pol*.1302b29; ἀ. δούλων καὶ γυναικῶν their *independence*, ib.1319b28. III. at Athens, *a year during which there was no archon*, X.*HG*2.3.1, Arist.*Ath*.13.1. IV. *not holding office*, Arr.*Epict*.3.20.17. -ος, ον, *without head* or *chief*, Il.2.703; ναυτικὸν στράτευμ' ἄ. E.*IA*914, cf. *Hec*.607; ἄ. ζῷα, opp. τὰ ὑφ' ἡγεμόνα ὄντα, Arist.*HA*488a11: τὸ ἄ., = ἀναρχία, A.*Eu*.696. 2. ἔτος ἄ. a year *without any regular magistrates*, *GDI*5635 (Teos). II. Act., *holding no office* or *magistracy*, prob. l. Arr.*Epict*.4.6.3. b. *not qualified to hold office*, Max.Tyr. 21.5 (Sup., s. v. l.). III. *without beginning*, Parm.8.27, Ocell. 1.2, S.E.*M*.7.312; κύκλος ἄ. καὶ ἀτελεύτητος Procl.*Inst*.146; ἄ. δίκη *PLips*.33 ii 5 (iv A. D.). b. *without first principles*, S.E.*M*.1.180.

*ἀνασαβρῶσαι· εἰς ὀροφὴν ἐμπλῆξαι, Hsch.

ἀνασᾰλεύω, *shake up, stir up*, Luc.*Astr*.29; τὴν ὀσφῦν Alciphr.1.39.

*ἀνασάξιμον, τό, *a mine that is reopened and worked*, after having been closed, *IG*2.780, 1078b.

ἀνάσαρξ, κος, Adj., in sense of ἀνὰ σάρκα, τοὺς ἀνάσαρκας ὕδρωπας Gal.14.275.

ἀνασάττω, *load up, pile up*, pf. part. Pass. ἀνασεσαγμένος Plb.12. 25h.2; cf. ἀνασάσσει· *luxatur*, *Gloss.Philox*.

ἀνασβέννῡμι, *quench, damp*, ὁρμάς Plu.2.917d.

*ἀνασειράζω, *draw back with a hawser*, A.R.1.391: metaph., *hold in check*, φλόγα v.l. in Ar.*Fr*.561; τὴν ὄρεξιν *AP*9.687. 2. *draw off the right road*, E.*Hipp*.237; *draw away*, c. gen., τινὰ χάρμης Nonn. *D*.39.355.

ἀνασεισίφαλλος, ον, *phallum agitans*, Hippon.111.

ἀνά-σεισις, εως, ἡ, *shaking up and down*, esp. for the purpose of threatening, ὅπλων Dexipp.p.182 D.; χειρός Lib.*Or*.18.189. -σεισμα, ατος, τό, = foreg., D.H.14.9. -σεισμός, ὁ, *threatening gestures*, Id.6.62. -σειστικός, ή, όν, *exciting*, τοῦ ὄχλου Eust.211.7. *-σείω, poet. ἀνασσείω, Ep. impf. ἀνασσείασκε *h.Ap*.403:—*shake back*, ἀνασείοντά τε κόμας E.*Ba*.240; *swing to and fro, brandish*, αἰγίδα Hes.*Sc*.344; ἀ. τὰς χεῖρας *wave* the hands, Th.4.38; ἀ. φοινικίδας Lys.6.51. 2. *brandish at* one, *threaten with*, εἰσαγγελίαν D.25.47; βοὴν Ar.*Ach*.347 (παρὰ προσδοκίαν). 3. *shake out*, ὑδρίαν *IG*2.104a36 (iv B. C.); πάντα κάλων *shake out* every reef, Ph.1.327, al.; ἀ. τὰ ἱστία Philostr.*VA*6.12, cf. *VS*2.32; πάσας τὰς ἡνίας Poll.1.214; τὴν χλαμύδα Philostr.*Im*.1.6. II. *stir up*, τὰ πλήθη Phld.*Rh*.2.290 S., cf. D.H.8.81, D.S.13.91, *Ev.Marc*.15.11, *Ev.Luc*. 23.5:—Pass., *to be incited, encouraged*, c. inf., *PTeb*.28.20 (ii B. C.).

*ἀνασεύομαι, Pass., only aor., αἷμα..ἀνέσσυτο the blood *sprang forth, spouted up*, Il.11.458.

ἀνασηκόω, *make up what is wanting by adding weight, compensate for*, τὴν μεταβολὴν Hp.*Acut*.29, cf. Ar.*Fr*.743; αἱ γενέσεις ἀ. τὰς φθοράς Arist.ap.Stob.1.34.2 (where in *Mu*.397b3 codd. give ἐπαναστέλλουσι).

ἀνάσηψις, εως, ἡ, *wasting disease*, *Mon.Ant*.24.167.

ἀνασθμαίνω, *breathe with difficulty*, Q.S.4.244, cf. Opp.*H*.5.212 (where it may be trans.).

ἀνασιλλιάομαι, *wear the hair bristling up*, Hsch.

ἀνασιλλοκομάω, = foreg., dub. l. Plu.*Crass*.24.

*ἀνάσιλλος (cf. Hdn.Gr.2.446) or -σιλος, ον, *with hair brushed up* on the forehead as the Parthians wore it, τῷ ἀνασίλλῳ κομᾶν Plu. *Crass*.24; restored by Sylburg in Arist.*Phgn*.809b24, 812b35, cf. *PGrenf*.1.10.11 (iii B. C.).

ἀνασῑμαίνομαι, = ἀνασιμόω, Poll.2.73.

*ἀνά-σῑμος, ον, *snub-nosed*, Ar.*Ec*.940. 2. generally, *turned up at end*, ὀδόντες ἀ., of the elephant's tusks, Arist.*HA*501b33; ἀ. πλοῖα Id.*Pr*.932a18; of a horse's neck, *curved up*, Simon *Eq*.6. -σῑμόω, *turn up the nose, sniff*, esp. of male animals following the females, Hsch.

ἀνασίνδης· ἀναπήδησις, Hsch.

ἀνασίτησις, εως, ἡ, *loading with wheat*, πλοίων *PTeb*.486 (ii A. D.).

ἀνασκαίρω, Ep impf. -εσκαίρεσκε, *hop* or *skip up*, Q.S.8.321.

ἀνασκᾰλεύω, *scrape up*, Hsch., Zen.1.27:—Med., *clean out* the ears, Pl.Com.148. II. metaph., *ransack*, τὴν ὅλην οἰκουμένην *PMag.Par*.1.186.

ἀνασκάλλω, *dig up*, in Pass., f. l. for foreg., Pl.Com.148.

*ἀνα-σκάπτω, *dig up*, πλοῦτον Str.9.3.8; τύπον Plu.*Thes*.36; ὅλην πόλιν *Pomp*.62:—Pass., Arist.*Mir*.835b22, Plu.2.924c. 2. *extirpate*, of plants, Thphr.*HP*3.18.5 (prob. l.); *raze to the ground*, of buildings, Plb.16.1.6, *IG*12(2).526a4 (Eresus). 3. metaph. of ulcers with 'undermined edges', βεβρωμένα καὶ ἀνεσκαμμένα Archig. ap.Aët.16.106(96). *-σκᾰφή, ἡ, *digging up*, Str.9.3.8.

ἀνασκεδάννῡμι or -ύω, *dissipate*, χροιήν Hp.*Liqu*.1; *scatter abroad*, Plu.*Pyrrh*.22:—Pass., v. l. in Polyaen.1.40.2.

ἀνα-σκεπτέον, *one must consider*, Thphr.*CP*6.13.2. -σκέπτομαι, = ἀνασκοπέω, Plu.2.438d, Gal.8.352.

*ἀνασκευ-άζω, *pack up the baggage* (τὰ σκεύη), and so, *carry away, remove*, τὴν ἀγορὰν εἴσω X.*An*.6.2.8, etc.; ἀ. τοὺς Ἀθηναίους ἐκ θαλάττης *divert* them from naval enterprise, Philostr.*VS*1.17.3, cf.1.25.7:—in Med., *break up camp, march away*, Th.1.18; κατεσκευάζετο καὶ πάλιν ἀ. X.*Cyr*.8.5.2, etc. 2. *dismantle* a place, Th.4.116:—in Med., *dismantle one's* house or city, Id.1.18. 3. *waste, ravage*, X.*Cyr*.6.2.25 (Pass.); ἀ. τὰς συνθήκας *break* them, Plb.9.31.6:—in Med., τάφον Plu.2.578f. 4. Pass., *to be bankrupt*, τῆς τραπέζης ἀνασκευασθείσης D.33.9, cf. 49.68; οἱ ἀνεσκευασμένοι τῶν τραπεζιτῶν *broken* bankers, ibid.: metaph., ἀνεσκευάσμεθα E.*El*.602. 5. of logicians, *demolish* opponent's arguments, definitions, etc., opp. κατασκευάζειν, Arist.*APr*.43a2, cf. *Rh*.1401b4, Str.1.2.18, Polystr. p.24 W. 6. *reverse* a decision or judgement, Vett.Val.283.23 (Pass.): metaph., ἀ. ψυχάς *disturb*, opp. οἰκοδομέω, *Act.Ap*.15.24, cf. 9.31. 7. Medic., *remove*, νόσον Sor.2.8. II. *build again, remodel*, Str.16.1.5:—also in Med., *build*, οἴκους J.*BJ*6.5.2. -ασμός, ὁ, *upsetting, reversal*, πραγμάτων Vett.Val.228.27 (pl.). -αστέον, *one must demolish*, Theon *Prog*.5, Aphth.*Prog*.5. -αστικός, ή, όν, *destructive*, in Logic, ἀ. τόποι Arist.*Top*.152b37. Adv. -κῶς *destructively, by way of refutation*, Id.*APr*.52a38. 2. c. gen., *destructive of*, ἀλλήλων S.E.*M*.8.196. II. *restorative, curative*, Sor.2.50, Dsc. 1.33. Adv. -κῶς Herod.Med.ap.Orib.5.30.17. -ή, ἡ, opp. κατασκευή, *pulling down*: *suppression* of desires, Arr.*Epict*.4.1.175. 2. *refutation* of arguments, S.E.*M*.6.4, cf. Quint.*Inst*.2.4.18, Hermog. *Prog*.5; ὁ κατ' -ὴν τρόπος *negative* mood, proof by *denial* or *argument from non-existence*, Phld.*Sign*.31, al.; *removal, cure*, πυρετῶν Dsc. 3.137; ἰσχιάδος Archig.ap.Aët.12.1. 3. *subversion*, πραγμάτων Vett.Val.2.7, al. (pl.).

ἀνασκηθής, ές, *not free from blemish*, *IG*5(2).3.6 (Tegea, iv B. C.).

ἀνασκ-ησία, ἡ, *want of practice* or *exercise*, Eus.Mynd.39, Muson. *Fr*.4 p.15 H., Poll.1.159. -ητος, ον, *unpractised, unexercised*, X. *Cyr*.8.8.24, Plb.1.61.4, Onos.10.3, Plu.*Cam*.18, etc. Adv. -τως Id. 2.112e.

ἀνασκίδνημι, = ἀνασκεδάννυμι, Ph.1.262, al.

ἀνασκινδᾰλεύω or -ῠλεύω, = Att. ἀνασχινδυλεύω, Hsch., *EM*100. 51, Phryn.*PS*p.48 B.

*ἀνασκιρτάω, *leap, skip* with joy, D.S.19.55; but of wounded horses, ὑπ' ὀδύνης Plu.*Crass*.25; ἀνεσκιρτηκότες τὴν ὄψιν, of athletes, Philostr.*Gym*.39: pf. part. Pass. ἀνεσκιρτημένος Eup.22.

ἀνασκολοπ-ίζω:—Pass., with fut. Med. -σκολοπιοῦμαι (in pass. sense) Hdt.3.132, 4.43, but Pass. -σκολοπισθήσομαι Luc.*Prom*.7: aor. -εσκολοπίσθην ib.2,10: pf. -εσκολόπισμαι Id.*Peregr*.13:—*fix on a pole* or *stake, impale*, Hdt.1.128, 3.159, al.; in 9.78 it is used convertibly with ἀνασταυρόω, as in Ph.1.237,687, Luc.*Peregr*.11. -ισις, εως, ἡ, *impaling*, Sch.A.*Pr*.7, Eust.1136.54.

ἀνασκολύπτω· ἀποσκολύπτω, Hsch.

ἀνα-σκοπέω, c. fut. -σκέψομαι, aor. ἀνεσκεψάμην: (cf. ἀνασκέπτομαι):—*look at narrowly, examine well*, πάντ' ἀνασκόπει καλῶς Ar.*Th*.666, cf. Th.1.132, etc.:—also in Med., ἀνασκοπουμένοις Ar. *Ec*.827. II. *look back at, reckon up*, X.*Vect*.5.11 (nisi leg. ἐπανα-). -σκοπή, ἡ, *consideration*, Timo 61.

ἀνασκυζάω, *to be at heat again*, *Com.Adesp*.930.

ἀνασμύχω, *consume as by fire*, of disease, Aret.*SD*1.1.

*ἀνασοβέω, *scare and make to start up*: generally, *rouse*, ἄγραν Pl. *Ly*.206a; τοὺς ἀκροωμένους Plu.2.44d; τινὰ πρὸς ὀργήν Chor.p.206 B.:—Pass., ἀνασεσοβημένος τὴν κόμην *with ruffled* hair, Luc.*Tim*.54; κόμη ἀνασεσοβημένη Id.*JTr*.30.

ἀνασπάζουσιν· ἀνασπαράσσουσιν, Hsch.

ἀνασπᾰράσσω, *tear up*, ῥίζας E.*Ba*.1104.

ἀνασπάς· (φυ)τὸν ἀνεσπασμένον, Hsch. (ἀνασπάσιον· ἀ. cod.; cf. παρασπάς).

*ἀνά-σπασις, εως, ἡ, *drawing back*, Hp.*Art*.48; *tearing up*, τῆς γῆς Thphr.*CP*5.4.7; ἀ. θυρῶν *breaking open*, *Cat.Cod.Astr*.1.97. -σπασμα, ατος, τό, *uprooted plant*, σελίνου Eust.679.34. -σπαστήριος, ον, *fitted for drawing up*: τὸ ἀ., a machine *for raising* a portcullis, App *BC*4.78. *-σπαστός, όν, *drawn up*, Ar.*V*.382: but mostly, *dragged up the country*, of tribes compelled to emigrate into Central Asia, ἀνασπαστοὺς ποιῆσαι τοὺς Παίονας ἐς τὴν Ἀσίην Hdt.5.12; τούτους ἐξ Αἰγύπτου ἀ. ἐποίησαν παρὰ βασιλέα Id.4.204, cf. 6.9, 32; τοὺς ἀ. κατοικίζειν Id.3.93; εὐθὺς ἀ. *removing* hastily, Plb.2.53.5. 2. of a door or gate, *drawn back, opened* from inside, S. *Ant*.1186. II. as Subst., οἱ ἀ. (sc. ἱμάντες) *latchets*, Ath.12.

3f. ※-σπάω, poet. ἀνσπ-, *draw, pull up*, σπυρίδα Hdt.5.16, 4.154; βύβλον ἐκ τῶν ἑλέων Id.2.92:—Pass., *BGU*1041.8 (iii D.). b. *draw* a ship *up* on land, Pi.*P*.4.27, Hdt.7.188, Th.4. 2. *draw, suck up greedily*, ὅταν αἷμ' ἀνασπάσῃ κόνις A.*Eu*.647; ὑγρὸν Hp.*VM*22; ἀ. ποτόν, τροφήν, Arist.*HA*495ᵃ26, *PA*661ᵃ19; ὕδωρ ἀ. *draw* water, Th.4.97. 3. *draw back*, τὴν χεῖρα Ar. *Pl*.691:—so in Med., ἐκ χροὸς ἔγχος ἀνεσπάσατ' Il.13.574. 4. *tear up, pull down*, τὰ ἀγάλματα ἐκ τῶν βάθρων Hdt.5.86; τὴν σκηνὴν Id.7.119; τὸ σταύρωμα Th.6.100; τύμβους E.*Med*.1381, cf. *Ba*.949; δένδρα Arist.*HA*497ᵇ29, al.; τὰς σανίδας τῆς γεφύρας Plb.2.5.5; πυλίδας Id.5.39.4, etc. 5. metaph., ἀνασπᾶν λόγους, in S.*Aj*.302, *draw forth* words, *utter wild, incoherent* words; ἀνασπῶντ' αὐτοπρέμνοις τοῖς λόγοισιν Ar.*Ra*.903:—the phrase may be expl. from Pl.*Tht*.180a (ὥσπερ ἐκ φαρέτρας ῥηματίσκια.. ἀνασπῶντες) and Men.429 (πόθεν.. τούτους ἀνεσπάκασιν οὗτοι τοὺς λόγους;); so ἀ. γνωμίδιον Ar.*Fr*. 49D. 6. τὰς ὀφρῦς ἀνασπᾶν *pucker* the eyebrows, and so put on a grave important air, τὰς ὀφρῦς ἀνεσπακὼς ὥσπερ τι δεινὸν ἀγγελῶν Id. *Ach*.1069, cf. Alex.16, D.19.314; ἔβλεψε νᾶπυ καὶ τὰ μέτωπ' ἀνέσπασεν Ar.*Eq*.631; μέχρι νεφέων τὴν ὀφρὺν ἀ. Philem.174, cf. X.*Smp*. 3.10; οἱ τὰς ὀφρῦς ἀνεσπασμένοι πρὸς τὸν κρόταφον Arist.*Phgn*.812ᵇ 27. II. *retract*, ὁ στόμαχος αὐτὸς ἑαυτὸν ἀ. Hp.*Superf*.22, *Steril*. 217. III. *carry away from home*, Luc.*Tox*.28 codd.

**ἄνασπις**, ιδος, ὁ, ἡ, *without a shield*, Nonn.D.30.18, 36.262.

※**ἀνασπογγίζω**, *sponge clean, sponge well*, τὸ ἕλκος Hp.*Ulc*.4; *soak up* drugs, ἀνασπογγίσας εἰρίῳ.. πρόσθες Id.*Nat.Mul*.32, cf. 74.

※**ἄνασσα** (ϝάνασσα *Inscr.Cypr*.101 H., al.), ἡ, fem. of ἄναξ, *queen, lady*, addressed to goddesses, Od.3.380, 6.175; esp. in Att. to Athena, A.*Eu*.228, 235, 443, etc. 2. to a mortal, Od.6.149, etc.—Common in Poetry from Pi. downwds.; rare in Prose, as Isoc.9.72, Arist. *Fr*.526: c. dat., ἐνέροισιν A.R.3.862. 3. generally, like ἄναξ IV, ἄνασσα πράγους καὶ βουλεύματος *authoress* of this deed, E.*Fr*.704; ὀργίων Ar.*Ra*.387. II. as Adj., *royal*, ἀ. βουλή, of the Roman Senate, *IG*14.1389 i 34.

**ἀνασσείασκε**, v. ἀνασείω.

**ἀνάσσυτος**, ον, (ἀνασεύω) *rushing upwards*, of air, Hp.*Mul*.2.124, cf. Hsch.

※**ἀνάσσω** [ᾰ], impf. ἤνασσον Od.11.276, Dor. ἄνασσον [ᾱ] Pi.*O*.6.34, Ep. ἄνασσον [ᾰ] Il.1.252, Aeol. 3 sg. ἐάνασσε Alc.64: fut. ἀνάξω Il.20.180: Ep. aor. ἄναξα Hes.*Th*.837:—rare in Med. and Pass., v. infr.: (ϝανάσσω, cf. ἄναξ):—poet. Verb, mostly pres., *to be lord, master*, of gods and human rulers: in Hom. mostly c. dat., νήσοισι καὶ Ἄργεϊ *to be lord, hold sway in*.., Il.2.108; κτήμασι, κτεάτεσσι, Od.1.117, 4.93: also c. gen., Ἀργείων, πεδίοιο ἀ. *to be lord of*.., Il.10. 33, Od.4.602, cf. Pi. l.c., E.*Andr*.22, etc.: with dat. pers. added, ἐλπόμενον Τρώεσσι ἀνάξειν.. τιμῆς τῆς Πριάμου *to be master of* Priam's sovereignty among the Trojans, Il.20.180; γῆς ἀνάσσει βαρβάροισι βάρβαρος E.*IT*31; πάντων μὲν κρατέειν ἐθέλειν, πάντεσσι δ' ἀνάσσειν, πᾶσι δὲ σημαίνειν Il.1.288: with Prep., μετ' ἀθανάτοισι ib.4. 61, cf. 23.471; ἐν Βουδείῳ 16.572; ἐν Φαίηξι Od.7.62; παρὰ τὸν Ἀχέροντα S.*El*.184; ὑπὸ γαίας ib.841: with neut. Adj., Ζεῦ πάντ' ἀνάσσων Id.*OT*904: in Hom. freq. with ἶφι, Τενέδοιό τε ἶφι ἀνάσσεις Il.1.38, al.: abs., τῶν ἀνασσόντων *the kings*, S.*Ph*.6:—Med. once in Hom., τρὶς ἀνάξασθαι γένε' ἀνδρῶν *to have been king* for three generations, Od.3.245:—Pass., *to be ruled*, ἀνάσσονται δ' ἐμοὶ αὐτῷ 4.177. II. in Trag. sts. metaph. of things, κώπης ἀνάσσων E.*Fr*.705; ὄχων ἀνάσσουσ' *Hel*.1040; στρατηγίας *IT*17; πηδήματος ἀνάσσων *lord of* the leap, dub. in A.*Pers*.96; ἃ τῶν νυκτιπόλων ἐφόδων ἀνάσσεις, of Persephone, E.*Ion* 1049 (lyr.):—Pass., παρ' ὅτῳ σκῆπτρον ἀνάσσεται *is held as lord*, S.*Ph*.140 (lyr.).

**ἀν-άσσω**, Att. for ἀναΐσσω.

**ἀνασταδόν**, Adv., (ἀνίστημι) *standing up*, Il.9.671, 23.469.

**ἀνασταλάω**, *make trickle forth*, Opp.*C*.4.324.

**ἀνάσταλ-σις**, εως, ἡ, *reduction of diet*, prob. for ἀνάστασις in Herod.Med.ap.Aët.5.129 (pl.). **–τικός**, ή, όν, *fitted for checking*, λύπης Ael.*VH*7.3; θεραπεία Gal.12.664.

**ἀνασταλύζω**, *sob*, Anacr.43.4. (Etym. dub.; cf. ἀσταλύζω.)

※**ἀνάσταμα**, ατος, τό, dub. sens. in *PPetr*.3 p.291.

**ἀναστάς**, f.l. for παστάς in A.R.1.789.

※**ἀνά-στᾰσις**, εως, Ion. ιος, ἡ, I. Act., (ἀνίστημι) *making to stand* or *rise up, raising up* the dead, ἀνδρὸς δ' ἐπειδὰν αἷμ' ἀνασπάσῃ κόνις.. οὔτις ἔστ' ἀ. A.*Eum*.648; ἔλαβον.. ἐξ ἀναστάσεως τοὺς νεκροὺς αὐτῶν *Ep.Heb*.11.35. 2. *making to rise and leave their place, removal*, as of suppliants, ἀ. ἐκ τοῦ ἱεροῦ Th.1.133; ἀ. τῆς Ἰωνίας *removal* of the Greeks from Ionia [for safety], Hdt.9.106: mostly in bad sense, *desolation*, ἅλωσιν Ἰλίου τ' ἀνάστασιν A.*Ag*.589; πόλεων ἀ. Id.*Pers*. 107, cf. E.*Tr*.364; τῆς πατρίδος D.1.5; *disturbance*, Hp.*Decent*.3 (pl.). 3. *setting up, erection*, τειχῶν D.20.72; τροπαίου Plu. 2.873a; εἰκόνος *GDI*3505.20 (Cnidus), cf. *IPE*1².34.8 (Olbia), Arr. *An*.4.11.2; οἰκοδομημάτων Luc.*Phal*.1.3 (pl.). II. (ἀνίσταμαι) *standing* or *rising up*, πόδες ἀναστάσεως χάριν Arist.*Spir*.485ᵃ18, cf. Id.*Fr*.156. 2. *rising and moving off, removal*, στρατεύματος Th. 7.75, cf. 2.14. 3. *rising up*, ἐξ ὕπνου S.*Ph*.276. b. esp. for the stool, dub. in Hp.*Epid*.6.7.1: hence, *motions*, Id.*Coac*.605, Dieuch. ap.Orib.4.6.2. c. *rising again* after a fall, *Ev.Luc*.2.34. d. *rising from the dead*, Τυνδάρεω Luc.*Salt*.45; εἰς ἀνάστασιν [fort. βλέποντες] *IGRom*.4.743 (Eumeneia, iii A.D.): freq. in N.T., *Ev.Matt*. 22.23, al.; ἀ. νεκρῶν *Act.Ap*.23.6; ἀ. ζωῆς, κρίσεως *Ev.Jo*.5.29; ἀπὸ σώματος ἀ. Plot.3.6.6. **–στᾰτέω**, *carry off*, or perh. *seduce*, *POxy*.1836 (vi A.D.). **–στάτήρ**, ῆρος, ὁ, *destroyer*, A.*Th*.1020, *Ch*.303. **–στᾰτήρια**, τά, *sacrifice on one's recovery*, Hsch. (cod. -ιαι). **–στάτης**, ου, ὁ, = ἀναστατήρ, A.*Ag*.1227. ※**–στᾰτος**, ον, (ἀνίσταμαι) *made to rise up and depart, driven from one's house and home*, ἀ. ποιεῖν τινας, ἀ. γίγνεσθαι, Hdt.1.76, 177, 7.118, Isoc.4.108, S.*OC*429, *Tr*.39. 2. of cities, *ruined, laid waste*, Hdt.1.155, 178, And.1.108, etc.; ἀ. δορὶ χώρα S.*Tr*.240; δόμους τιθέναι ἀ. Id.*Ant*. 673; ἀ. ποιεῖν τὰ χωρία Th.8.24; οἴκους ἀ. γεγενημένους Isoc.6.66, cf. Alex.1D., Men.*Inc*.2.30 Körte. 3. of arguments, *upset*, Pl. *Sph*.252a. 4. c. gen., *driven from, deprived of* a thing, Χαρίτων Plu.2.613b. 5. *unstable*, Olymp.*in Mete*.141.28. II. Subst. ἀνάστᾰτος, ὁ, a kind of *light bread* at Athens, prob. in Ath.3.114a, Paus.Gr.*Fr*.94.

**ἀναστᾰτ-όω**, *unsettle, upset*, [τὴν γῆν] LXX *Da*.7.23; τὴν οἰκουμένην *Act.Ap*.17.6, cf. 21.38, *PMag.Par*.1.2244; of the mind, *Ep. Gal*.5.12; ἀναστατοῖ με he *upsets* me, *POxy*.119.10 (ii/iii A.D.); *destroy*, Asp.*in EN*61.28; *drive out*, *BGU*1079.20 (i A.D.):—Pass., ἀναστατωθῆναι Harp. s. v. ἀνεσκευάσατο: ἀναστατοῦ ἐς τὰ ὄρη Aq.*Ps*. 10(11).1. **–ωσις**, εως, ἡ, *unsettling*, Heph.Astr.2.32, Eust.81. 41. 2. *destruction*, Poll.3.91.

**ἀνασταυρ-ίζω**, *impale*, Ctes.*Fr*.29.59 (Pass.). **–όω**, = foreg., Hdt.3.125, 6.30, al.; identical with ἀνασκολοπίζω, 9.78:—Pass., Th. 1.110, Pl.*Grg*.473c. II. in Rom. times, *affix to a cross, crucify*, Plb. 1.11.5, al., Plu.*Fab*.6, al. 2. *crucify afresh*, *Ep.Hebr*.6.6. **–ωσις**, εως, ἡ, *crucifixion*, X.Eph.4.2.

**ἀναστᾰχύω**, (στάχυς) *shoot up with ears*, A.R.4.271, Procl.*H*.5.10: metaph., κατὰ ὦλκας ἀ. Γίγαντες A.R.3.1054; trans., *cause to spring up*, φυταλιὴν δρακόντων Nonn.*D*.25.199.

**ἀναστείβω**, *tread under foot*, *AP*7.544.

**ἀν-άστειος**, ον, *lacking in wit*, Aristod.ap.Ath.13.585b.

**ἀνάστειρος**, ον, (στεῖρα) *with a high prow*, ναῦς Plb.16.3.8.

※**ἀναστείχω**, *go up*, ἐπὶ γαῖαν Opp.*H*.1.422; *ascend*, κολώνην ib.4.65.

**ἀναστέλλω**, *send up, raise*, νέφεα Arat.417:—Med., *gird* or *tuck up* one's clothes, νεβρίδας ἀνεστείλαντο E.*Ba*.696; ἀναστέλλεσθ' ἄνω τὰ χιτώνια Ar.*Ec*.268: abs., ἀναστειλαμένη Artem.4.44:—Pass., ἀνεσταλμένῳ τῷ χιτῶνι with one's frock *girt up*, Plu.2.178c. II. *draw back*, e. g. the flesh in a surgical operation, Hp.*VC*14; *push back* or *up*, τὰς ῥίζας [τῶν ὄρχεων] Arist.*HA*632ᵃ17:—Pass., *to be turned up*, of the foot, Hp.*Mochl*.24. 2. *open*, στόμια μεμυκότα Ph.1.278, al. 3. *repulse, check* an assault, E.*IT*1378, Th.6.70, X.*An*. 5.4.23: generally, οἱ ἄνεμοι ἀ. τὰ νέφη Arist.*Pr*.943ᵃ35, cf. Epicur. *Ep*.2 p.51 U.; φόβος ἀ. τινά Ael.*NA*5.54: Medic., *check* a discharge, etc., Leonid.ap.Aët.16.40, cf. Sor.2.9:—Med., *suppress one's inclinations, dissemble*, Plb.9.22.9:—Pass., Th.3.98, Phld.*Ir*.p.82 W.: c. gen., ἀ. τοῦ.. *to be restrained from*.., Ael.*NA*8.10; ἀνεστάλησαν τὴν ὁρμὴν *VH*6.14. 4. *remove, make away with*, γῆν D.S.17.82; τὰ ἐμποδών Ph.1.407. 5. *lay aside*, Dam.*Pr*.400. III. in Med., *renounce, refuse*, ἀναστέλλεσθαι τροφὴν Ael.*NA*11.14.

**ἀνα-στενάζω**, = ἀναστένω, Hdt.1.86, 6.80, *Ev.Marc*.8.12: c. acc. cogn., τοιά μοι ἀ. ἐχθοδοπά such bitter words *didst* thou *groan forth*, S.*Aj*.930. II. c. acc. pers., *groan for, lament*, A.*Ch*.335, E. *HF*118 (lyr.). **–στενᾰχίζω**, *groan oft and loudly, wail aloud*, Il.10. 9. **–στενάχω**, c. acc. pers., *groan aloud over, bemoan, bewail aloud*, ib.23.211:—so in Med., 18.315, 355. **–στένω**, *groan aloud*, A.*Ag*.546, 1286, S.*Tr*.939. II. *bemoan*, c. acc., Archil. 9.8, E.*IT*551.

**ἀναστέριστος**, ον, *not marked by stars*, of positions in the heavens, Hipparch.1.7.21, 1.8.1.

**ἀνάστερος**, ον, poet. for ἄναστρος, Arat.349, Man.4.528.

**ἀναστέφω**, *crown, wreath*, τὸν σὸν κρᾶτα E.*Fr*.243; ἀ. στεφάνοισι ib.362.48; στόρνῃσιν Call.*Hec*.1.1.15:—Pass., ἀνέστεμμαι κάρα φύλλοις I *have* my head *wreathed* with leaves, E.*Hipp*.806; but also δάφνας κλῶνας ἀναστέφεται *Epigr.Gr*.786.

**ἀναστηλ-όω**, *set up* as or *on a monument*, Lyc.883, Plu.2. 1033e. **–ωσις**, εως, ἡ, *setting up of a monument*, Ptol.Heph.ap. Phot.*Bibl*.p.147 B.

※**ἀνάστημα**, ατος, τό, (ἀνίσταμαι) *height*, Thphr.*HP*9.9.5; of animals, D.S.5.17 (pl.); τὸ τῆς ἡλικίας ἀ. J.*AJ*2.9.6; ἀ. βασιλικὸν royal *majesty*, D.S.19.92; ἀ. τραγικὸν D.Chr.18.7 (prob. l.); ἡ ψυχὴ γαῦρόν τι ἀ. λαμβάνουσα Longin.7.2 (prob.). 2. *protuberance, prominence*, Simp.*in Cael*.480.15. 3. *high ground*, in pl., Str.2.3.2, D.S. 2.14, etc. 4. *erection, building*, Epict.*Gnom*.62 (pl.): metaph., *structure*, φιλοσοφίας Phld.*Herc*.1457.10. 5. *eruption*, φλυκταινῶν Lyd.*Ost*.35:—also ἀνάστεμα, LXX *Ju*.9.10, al.

**ἀναστηρίζω**, aor. 1 -ξα, *set up firmly*, *AP*7.321.

**ἀναστησείω**, Desiderat. of ἀνίσταμαι, Agath.3.4.

**ἀναστίδωνος**· ἀνατεταμένος, Hsch.

**ἀναστοιχει-όω**, *resolve* matter *into its elements*, Chrysipp.*Stoic*.2. 188, cf. Ph.1.501, 477 (Pass.), Gal.1.508. **–ωσις**, εως, ἡ, *dissolution*, Alex.Aphr.*Pr*.1.79, Lyd.*Mens*.4.26, cf. 40; of the body, Gal. 7.251. **–ωτικός**, ή, όν, *dissolvent*, Steph.*in Hp*.1.132 D.

**ἀναστολή**, ἡ, *putting back*, τῆς κόμης Plu.*Pomp*.2. 2. *opening up* of a fistula, Heliod.ap.Orib.44.23.60.

※**ἀναστομ-όω**, *furnish with a mouth, open up*; τάφρον *clear out* a trench, X.*Cyr*.7.5.15; τὰς Νείλου διώρυγας Plb.5.62.4, cf. S.E.*M*.5. 59; ταῦτα τῶν ἡδυσμάτων ἀ. τὰς αἰσθητήρια Diph.18.6: ἀ. μήτραν Dsc.1. 19:—Med., φάρυγος ἀναστόμου τὸ χεῖλος *open* your gullet *wide*, E. *Cyc*.357:—Pass., τραυλὴ μέν ἐστιν, ἀλλ' ἀνεστομωμένη *with mouth wide-opened, loud-talking*, Call.Com.19; also, *to be opened, dilated*, ἀ. οἱ πόροι Arist.*HA*581ᵇ19, *GA*751ᵃ2; ἰχῶρες ἀναστομωθείσης τῆς σαρκὸς ἐξέρρεον Memn.2. **2.** of one sea *opening* into another, κατὰ στενοπόρους αὐχένας ἀνεστομωμένος Arist.*Mu*.393ᵃ22; ὁ Ἀράβιος κόλπος ἀνεστόμωται εἰς τὸν..Ὠκεανόν D.S.3.38, cf. Ph.2.475, Hld.1.29. **-ωσις**, εως, ἡ, *outlet, opening*, Plu.2.590f, Gal.11.750; *inosculation*, Id.*UP*6.17. **2.** *patency*, Cels.4.5, Gal.7.31. **3.** *opening up* or *keeping open*, ἕλκους Ruf.*Fr*.118, cf. Procl.*in Alc*.p.119 C. (pl.); αἱμορροΐδων Dsc.1.58; τὰ εἰς ἀ. βρώματα *appetizing* foods (cf. ἀναστομόω 1), Ath.4.132f; ἀ. καὶ δῆξις, of manures, Thphr.*CP*3.17.6. **-ωτέον**, *one must open*, of piles, Gal.17(2).287. **-ωτήριος**, ον, *proper for opening*, τῆς ὑστέρης Hp.*Nat.Mul*.109. **-ωτικός**, ή, όν, = foreg., Dsc.1.4, Antyll.ap.Orib.10.25.2. **-ωτός**, όν, of an abscess, prob. f.l. for ἀστόμωτος, Gal.18(2).795.

**ἀνα-στονᾰχέω**, = ἀναστένω, Orph.*A*.1287:—also **-στοναχίζω**, Q.S.2.634 (s.v.l.).

***ἀναστοφάγος**, ον, *not eating the* ναστός (q.v.), Orac.ap.Paus.8.42.6.

**ἀναστράπτω**, *lighten*, Ph.2.204.

**ἀναστρᾰτεύω**, *enlist again*, App.*BC*3.66:—Med., *serve again*, of soldiers, D.C.41.35.

**ἀναστρᾰτοπεδ-εία**, ἡ, *decamping*, Plb.6.40.1. **-εύω**, *move camp*, Id.1.24.4, D.H.5.34, etc.:—Med., J.*AJ*14.15.14, D.C.49.11.

**ἀνά-στρεμμα**, ατος, τό, f.l. for ἀνάβλεμμα in X.*Cyn*.4.4. **-στρεπτέον**, *one must invert*, τι Isoc.5.132. **2.** *one must write with anastrophe*, Hdn.Gr.1.481, etc.

***ἀναστρέφω**, poet. **ἀνστρέφω**, pf. ἀνέστροφα v.l. in Theognet.1.8, 3 pl. ἀνέστροφαν Cerc.*Fr*.17.30:—*turn upside down*, μήπως.. δίφρους ἀνστρέψειαν *might upset* them, Il.23.436; ὁ θεὸς πάντ' ἀ. πάλιν E.*Supp*.331; ἀ. γένος Ar.*Av*.1240; τὴν ζοήν Cerc. l.c.; ἀ. καρδίαν *upset* the stomach, i.e. cause sickness, Th.2.49; *reverse*, A.*Pers*.333, Ar.*Pl*.779:—Pass., fut. ἀναστραφήσεσθαι τὰ τῆς Ἑλλάδος πράγματα Isoc.5.64: pf. ἀνεστράφθαι τῆς πολιτείας Id.6.66 codd.; ὅρος ἀνεστραμμένον ἐν τῇ ζητήσει *turned up* by digging, Hdt.6.47, cf. X.*Oec*.16.12. **2.** *invert* order of words or statements, Demetr.*Eloc*.11, al., Hermog.*Id*.1.11:—also in Pass., with ref. to ἐπαναστροφή (q.v.), ib.12. **3.** = ἀρνεῖσθαι, S.*Fr*.1012. **II.** *turn back*, *Com.Adesp*.22.73 D.; *bring back*, τινὰ ἐξ Ἅιδου S.*Ph*.449, cf. E.*Hipp*.1228; ἀ. δίκην τινί Id.*Ba*.793; ὄμμ' ἀ. κύκλῳ *to roll* it *about*, Id.*Hel*.1557. **2.** intr., *turn back, retire*, Hdt.1.80, etc.; esp. in part., ἀναστρέψας ἀπήλαυνεν X.*An*.1.4.5, etc.; but also, *rally*, of troops, Th.4.43, X.*HG*6.2.21, cf. B.III.1:—ἀναστρέφον, τό, v. ἀνακυκλικός. **III.** in Gramm., *write with anastrophe*, as πέρι for περί, Hdn.Gr.2.52,66:—Pass., 1.481, al. **2.** Math., ἀναστρέψαντι *convertendo*, Euc.5.19 *Cor*.; so in Logic, οἱ ἀντιστρέφοντες οὐχ οἱ ἀναστρέφοντες ἀλλήλοις λόγοι συναληθεύονται Gal.11.465.

**B.** Pass., v. supr. A. I. **II.** *dwell in* a place, ἀλλά τιν' ἄλλην γαῖαν ἀναστρέφομαι *go to* a place *and dwell there*, Od.13.326, cf. Call.*Lav.Pall*.76, *Aet*.1.1.6 (so ἀναστρέφειν πόδα ἐν γῇ E.*Hipp*.1176); ἀναστρέφεσθαι ἐν Ἄργει Id.*Tr*.993; ἐν φανερῷ, ἐν μέσῳ, *go about* in public, X.*HG*6.4.16, Pl.*R*.558a; ἀ. ταύτῃ Th.8.94; ἐν εὐφροσύναις X.*Ag*.9.4; ἐν τοῖς ἤθεσι Pl.*Lg*.865e; ἀ. ἐν ξυμμαχίᾳ *continue in* an alliance, X.*HG*7.3.2; ἀ. ἐν γεωργίᾳ *to be engaged in*.., Id.*Oec*.5.13; ἐπὶ κυνηγεσίαις Plb.32.15.9; ἀ. ἔν τινι *dwell upon*, in writing, Apollon.Cit.2: generally, *conduct oneself, behave*, ὡς δεσπότης X.*An*.2.5.14; οὑτωσί Arist.*EN*1103ᵇ20; θρασέως, ἀχαρίστως καὶ ἀσεβῶς εἴς τινα, Plb.1.9.7, 27.17.10; ἐν ταῖς ἀρχαῖς ὁσίως *IG*12(7).233 (Amorgos); ὡς τὰ παιδία Epict.*Ench*.29.3; πῶς δεῖ ἐν οἴκῳ θεοῦ ἀ. 1*Ep.Ti*.3.15. **2.** *revolve*, like the sun in the heavens, X.*Mem*.4.3.8. **III.** of soldiers, *face about, rally*, Id.*An*.1.10.12, *HG*6.2.20, etc. **2.** *to be reversed* or *inverted*, ἐμοὶ τοῦτ' ἀνέστραπται Id.*Hier*.4.5, cf. *Cyr*.8.8.13, Arist.*Mech*.854ᵃ10. **3.** *return*, Pl.*Plt*.271a; *retreat*, Arist.*HA*621ᵇ34.

**ἀναστρολόγητος**, ον, *ignorant of astronomy*, Str.2.1.19.

***ἄναστρος**, ον, *carrying no planet*, σφαῖρα Thphr.*Fr*.31,32, cf. Eratosth.*Cat*.22; without σφαῖρα, Jul.*Or*.4.148a; *starless*, νύξ ib.153c.

**ἀναστροφάδην**, Adv. *reversely*, Hsch.

***ἀνα-στροφή**, ἡ, *turning upside down, upsetting, overthrow*, E.*Fr*.301 (pl.); μοῖραν εἰς ἀ. δίδωσι, = ἀναστρέφει, Id.*Andr*.1007; *disorder, confusion*, Posidipp.26.22. **2.** *turning back, return*, S.*Ant*.226; πολλὰς ἀ. ποιούμενος, of a hunter, making many *casts backward*, X.*Cyn*.6.25; *wheeling round*, of a horse, Id.*Eq.Mag*.3.14; of soldiers in battle, whether to flee or rally, Id.*Cyr*.5.4.8; μηκέτι δοῦναι αὐτοῖς ἀ. *time to rally*, Id.*HG*4.3.6, cf. *Ages*.2.3; esp. of the *reversal* of a wheeling movement, Ascl.*Tact*.10.6, Ael.*Tact*.25.7, Arr.*Tact*.21.4; of a ship, Th.2.89; ἐξ ἀ. *turning back*, Plb.4.54.4; κατ' ἀναστροφὴν *conversely*, S.E.*M*.7.430. **3.** in Gramm., *throwing back of the accent*, as in Prepositions after their case, A.D.*Synt*.308.15, etc. **4.** Rhet., = ἐπαναστροφή, *repetition* of words which close one sentence at the beginning of another, Hermog.*Id*.1.12, etc. **b.** *inversion* of the natural order, A.D.*Synt*.71.18, Phoeb.*Fig*.1.4, etc.; τῆς τάξεως Theon *Prog*.4. **5.** Math., *conversion* of a ratio, ἀ. λόγου Euc.5 *Def*.16; κατ' ἀναστροφὴν Papp.1002.25. **II.** *dwelling in* a place, Plu.2.216a. **2.** *abode, haunt*, δαιμόνων ἀναστροφή A.*Eu*.23. **3.** *mode of life, behaviour*, Plb.4.82.1, D.L.9.64; -φὴν ποιεῖσθαι *IG*2.477*b*12, cf. *SIG*491.5, Lxx *To*.4.14, *Ep.Gal*.1.13, *Ep.Eph*.4.22, al.; ἀ. πολιτική *PGiss*.40ii29 (iii A.D.); ἐξημερωμένης -φῆς civilized *life*, Phld.*Sto.Herc*.339.19. **4.** *delay, respite, time for doing* a thing, Plb.1.66.3, al., D.S.10.5. **5.** *occupation, concern*, περί τι τὰν ἀ. ἔχειν Archyt.1, cf. Phld.*Po*.5.1425.6. **6.** *return, way back*, Arist.*HA*631ᵃ26, cf. *Pr*.940ᵇ23. **7.** *recourse*, ἀ. λαμβάνειν πρός τι Plu.2.112c. **-στροφία**, Ep. -ίη, ἡ, = foreg., Man.4.312. **-στρόφιος**, ον, *converse*, of mathematical proportions, Papp.210.15, al. **-στρόφισμα**, ατος, τό, *hinge*, καλυπτῆρας ἐξ ἀ. *hinged* lid *IG*7.3498 (Oropus). **-στροφος**, ον, = ἀναστρόφιος, Papp.828.15 (s.v.l.). **-στρόφως**, Adv. *conversely, vice versa*, *Stoic*.2.71, Iamb.*VP*26.118.

**ἀναστρώννυμι**, *spread with coverings*, Lyd.*Mag*.1.18 (Pass.).

**ἀναστρωπή**, ἡ, word coined by Pl.*Cra*.409c, to explain ἀστραπή (ὅτι τὰ ὦπα ἀναστρέφει).

**ἀναστρωφάω**, Frequentat. of ἀναστρέφω, τόξον ἐνώμα πάντῃ ἀναστρωφῶν *turning* it *constantly*, Od.21.394:—Med., *wander about*, S.*Fr*.945; ἀ. ἐν ἀφθόνοισι *live* in the midst of plenty, E.*Fr*.1063.5. **II.** intr. in Act., *retire, desist from*, ὀχῆς Arat.1069.

**ἀναστῠφελίζω**, = στυφελίζω, Nonn.*D*.1.181, Hsch.

**ἀναστύφω** [ῡ], = στύφω, aor. inf. ἀναστῦψαι S.*Fr*.421.

**ἀνασύν-ταξις**, εως, ἡ, *reassessment of war-tax levied on property*, Poll.6.179, Suid. **-τάσσω**, *reassess war-tax*, Hyp.*Fr*.151.

**ἀνασυρίζω**, *hiss shrilly*, Orph.*A*.995 (tm.).

**ἀνασυρτόλις**, εως, ἡ, *lewd woman*, Hippon.110.

***ἀνασύρω** [ῡ], *pull up*, δοκόν Procop.*Goth*.4.11; another's clothes, D.L.2.116; *expose to view*, τὴν ἀκρασίαν Clearch.14:—Med., *pull up one's clothes, expose one's person*, Hdt.2.60, Thphr.*Char*.11.2, D.S.1.85, etc.; ἀνασυράμεναι τοὺς χιτωνίσκους Plu.2.248b: pf. part. Pass. as Adj., ἀνασεσυρμένος *obscene*, Anacr.ap.Phot.p.123 R.; *lacking in decency*, Thphr.*Char*.6.2. **2.** in Pass. also, of Alexander's hair, *to be curly*, Ael.*VH*12.14. **II.** Med., *plunder, ravage*, Plu.2.330d, cf. Hsch.

**ἀνασφᾰδάζω**, *struggle violently*, Hsch.

**ἀνα-σφάλλω**, fut. -σφαλῶ J.*AJ*17.6.5 (v.l. -σφῆλαι), intr., *rise from a fall* or *illness, recover*, συμπτώματος ἀνασφῆλαι Pl.*Ax*.364c; ἐκ τῆς νόσου Nic.Dam.p.98 D., cf. Babr.75.9; νόσου καὶ πόνων Id.78.3, cf. D.Chr.34.5; ἐκ κακῶν Luc.*Abd*.32: abs., J. l.c. **-σφαλσις**, εως, ἡ, *recovery*, Vett.Val.285.20.

**ἀνασφηνόω**, *tighten with wedges*, Apollod.*Poliorc*.159.6.

**ἀνασφίγγω**, *bind tight up*, ἵππον χαλινῷ Nonn.*D*.42.51: aor. 1 part. -σφίξας *IG*12(2).11 (Mytilene).

**ἀνασφοδάξαι**· ἀναπηδῆσαι, ἐξελάσαι, Hsch. (-ῆξαι cod.).

**ἀνάσφορον**, τό, = πτερίς, Ps.-Dsc.4.184.

**ἀνα-σχεθέειν**, -θεῖν, inf. of the poet. aor. 2 of ἀνέχω. **-σχεσις**, εως, ἡ, (ἀνέχομαι) *holding up, lifting up*, προβοσκίδος, of an elephant, Plu.2.972b. **2.** *holding in suspense*, τῶν δεινῶν Id.*Num*.13. **3.** ἀ. ἡλίου *rising* of the sun, Arist.*Mu*.393ᵇ2 (pl.). **-σχετικός**, ή, όν, *enduring, patient*, Plu.2.31a. **-σχετός**, Ep. **ἀνσχετός**, όν, *endurable*, Thgn.119: mostly with negat., οὐ γὰρ ἔτ' ἀνσχετὰ ἔργα τετεύχαται Od.2.63; πεσεῖν..πτώματ' οὐκ ἀ. A.*Pr*.919; θρέμματ' οὐκ ἀ. Id.*Th*.182; so with a question expecting a negative answer, S.*Ph*.987: οὐκ ἀ. [ἐστι], c. acc. et inf., Hdt.1.207, cf. 3.81, 8.142; ζῆν γὰρ κακῶς κλύουσαν οὐκ ἀ. S.*Tr*.721, cf. *OC*1652; οὐκ ἀ. ποιεῖσθαί τι Hdt.7.163: abs., οὐκέτι ἀ. ἐποιοῦντο Th.1.118.

**ἀνα-σχίζω**, *rip up*, τοῦ λαγοῦ τὴν γαστέρα Hdt.1.123, cf. 124, 3.35; τὰς κυούσας Arist.*EN*1148ᵇ20; δερμα ὀνύχεσσι Theoc.25.277, cf. *IG*4.952.32 (Epid.); *plough up*, νῶτον γᾶς Pi.*P*.4.228 (tm.):—Pass., τρίβος -όμενος track *opened up*, Plu.2.161f. **-σχινδῠλεύω**, = ἀνασκολοπίζω, Pl.*R*.362a; cf. ἀνασκινδυλεύω. **-σχισις**, εως, ἡ, *ripping open*, Gal.14.675.

***ἀνασῴζω**, fut. -σώσω: pf. ἀνασέσωικεν *IG*12(5).1061.9 (Ceos, iii B.C.): aor. ἀνέσωισε ib.1004.5 (Ios, iv/iii B.C.), cf. *OGI*56.11:—*recover what is lost, rescue*, ἀπὸ φόνου ἔρρυτο κἀνέσωσέ μ' S.*OT*1351 (lyr.); ἀ. φίλον ἀλλοιωθέντα Arist.*EN*1165ᵇ22:—more freq. in Med., ἀνασῴζεσθαί τινα φόνου *rescue* from death, S.*El*.1133; ἀνασωσάμενός μοι δὸς.. Σάμον Hdt.3.140:—but Hdt. commonly uses the Med. in the proper sense, ἀ. τὴν ἀρχὴν *recover* it *for oneself*, 1.82,166, etc.; in 3.65 he joins Act. and Med., μὴ ἀνασωσαμένοισι δὲ τὴν ἀρχὴν μηδ' ἐπιχειρήσασι ἀνασῴζειν:—Pass., *to be restored, recover*, Pl.*Phlb*.32e; *return safe*, εἰς Κατάνην Lys.20.24; ἀνασωθῆναι ἐς τὰς πατρίδας, of exiles, X.*HG*4.8.28; ἐκ φυγῆς Plb.18.27.2, al. **2.** *preserve in mind, remember*, Hdt.6.65.

**ἀνασωρεύω**, *heap up*, in Pass., Plb.8.33.5.

**ἀνά-σωσμα**, ατος, τό, *preservation*, Tz. ad Lyc.1297. ***-σωσμός**, ὁ, = foreg., Aq.*Ge*.45.7.

***ἀνασωφρονίζω**, *reduce to sobriety*, in Pass., Hsch. s.v. ἄμπνυτο.

**ἀνασώχω**, = σώχω, Sch.Nic.*Th*.695.

**ἀνατάκται**, οἱ, *assessors*, title of financial board at Miletus, *OGI*213 (ca. 300 B.C.), *SIG*577.19, etc.

**ἀνατᾰνύω**, poet. ἀντ-, = ἀνατείνω, Call.*Jov*.30, *IG*14.1015, *APl*.4.101:—Med., ἀνὰ χεῖρα τανύσσατο A.R.1.344.

**ἀνάταξις**, εως, ἡ, *financial estimate, assessment*, *SIG*577.21.

***ἀνατᾰράσσω**, Att. -ττω, *stir up* the mud, Arist.*HA*620ᵇ16:—Pass., οὖρα ἀνατεταραγμένα *thick* urine, Hp.*Aph*.4.70, cf. *Epid*.1.26.δ'. **II.** *rouse to frenzy*, S.*Tr*.218; *confound*, Pl.*Phd*.88c:—Pass., ἀνατεταραγμένος πορεύεσθαι march *in disorder*, X.*An*.1.7.20.

***ἀνάτᾰσις**, εως, ἡ, (ἀνατείνω) *extension*, εἰς ὕψος Plb.5.44.3, etc. **b.** abs., *height*, J.*BJ*6.9.1; ἀ. ὀρῶν Phlp.*in Mete*.37.10. **2.** *stretching out*, Hp.*Art*.11; ἀκοντίων Onos.17: metaph., *threats* of violence, Plb.4.17, *Fr*.108 (pl.); μετὰ ἀ. καὶ ἀπειλῆς Epict.*Fr*.25, cf. D.S.38.8. **3.** *intensity, inflexibility*, τοῦ φρονήματος Plu.*Mar*.6; *intensity* of passion, Phld.*Lib*.p.29 O.: abs., *courage, steadfastness*, prob. in D.Chr.34.40. **4.** *endurance of hunger, fasting*, Sor.1.49, Plu.2.62a. **5.** ἀ. τῆς βοῆς *straining*, Sch.E.*Or*.149; κατ' ἀνάτασιν of the *acute accent*, D.T.620.1. **6.** metaph., *straining, effort*, Phld.*Rh*.

.31 S., al.; ἡ πρὸς τὸ ἓν διαγνώσεως ἀ. Dam.*Pr.*27, cf. Procl.*Inst.*21, al.: c. gen., τιμῆς Procop.Gaz.*Pan.*496.4.

**ἀνατάσσω,** Att. **–τάττω,** aor. 2 Pass. ἀνετάγην, *countermand* expenditure, D.C.78.18 (Pass.):—Med., *go regularly through again, rehearse*, Plu.2.968c; *set in order*, διήγησιν *Ev.Luc.*1.1.

**ἀνατᾰτικός,** ή, όν, *threatening*, Plb.5.43.5, D.S.5.31. Adv. **–κῶς** Plb.4.4.7.

***ἀνατείνω,** poet. **ἀντ–,** *lift up*, χεῖρας ἀ., in swearing, Pi *O.*7.65; also in prayer, Id *I.*6(5).41; εὐξόμεθ'.. ἀνατείνοντες τὼ χεῖρ' Ar.*Av.*623; as token of assent in voting, X.*An.*5.6.33, etc. **2.** *stretch forth*, so as to threaten, τὴν μάχαιραν ἀνατεταμένος X.*Cyr.*4.1.3:—Med. (with aor. 1 Pass.), οὐδὲ Πολυδεύκεος βία χεῖρας ἀντείναιτ' ἂν ἐναντίον αὐτῷ Simon.8; οὐδὲν ἂν ὑμῖν εἶχε ἀνατείνασθαι φοβερόν *hold out* any alarming *threat*, D.19.153: abs., *threaten*, Plb.5.55.1: c. dat., 4.82.8: c. fut. inf., 4.18.10. **3.** *hold up, offer* as a prize, Pi.*N.*8.25 (Pass.). **4.** *present* a document to a magistrate, *BGU*613.3 (ii A.D.). **5.** *lift up, exalt*, κῦδός τινος Pi.*N.*8.34; ἀνατείνασθαι ἀρχήν *strain* or *augment* its *force*, Plu.*Cleom.*10. **6.** *lift up*, κάρα Pi.*N.*1.43; ἑαυτόν Ael.*NA*3.21; ἀ. τὰς ὀφρῦς *pucker*, Luc.*Tim.*54. **7.** of sound, *strain* to a high pitch, Arist.*Pr.*920$^{b}$20 (Pass.). **8.** metaph., *excite*, τινά Plu.2.60c:—Pass., Phld.*Lib.*p.44 O.; of the soul, etc., εἰς ἀμέθεκτον αἰτίαν Procl.*Inst.*100, cf. 23. **II.** *spread out, expand*, e.g. a line of battle, τὰ κέρατα X.*Cyr.*7.1.6, cf. ib.23; ἀετὸς ἐπὶ δόρατος ἀνατεταμένος *spread* eagle, ib.4; ἀ. ἱστία πρὸς ζυγόν Pi.*N.*5.51:—Pass., *to be distended upwards*, Ti.Locr.102a; *extend*, εἰς ὕψος Plb.9.21.10. **III.** *hold out, persevere*, esp. in abstinence from food, Sor.1.56, Arr.*Epict.*2.17.9. **IV.** intr., *reach up, stretch up*, πέδιλα ἐς γόνυ ἀνατείνοντα Hdt.7.67. **2.** *extend, stretch out*, ὄρος.. ἀ. ἐς τὴν Οἴτην Hdt.7.176, cf. 8.107, Arist.*HA*524$^{b}$19, Epicur.*Nat.*11.5, *Inscr.Prien.*37.160, 42.69: metaph. in Pass., πρὸς ἄφρονας ταῦτ' ἀ. these things only *reach* or *affect* foolish people, Phld.*Herc.*1251.12.

**ἀνατειχ-ίζω,** *rebuild*, τείχη X.*HG*4.4.18:—in Med., *build up*, τὸ ταπεινότατον J.*BJ*5.5.1. **–ισμός,** ὁ, *rebuilding of walls*, X.*HG*4.8.9.

**ἀνατέλλω,** poet. **ἀντ–,** aor. ἀνέτειλα: pf. part. ἀνατεταλκώς Plb.9.15.10:—*make to rise up*, τοῖσιν δ' (sc. ἵπποις) ἀμβροσίην ἀνέτειλε νέμεσθαι Il.5.777; Αἴγυπτος.. Δήμητρος ἀντέλλει στάχυν A.*Fr.*300, cf. Lxx *Ge.*3.18; ὕδωρ ἀ. *make* water *gush forth*, Pi.*I.*6(5).75; τὸν ἥλιον *Ev.Matt.*5.45:—so in Pass., φλὸξ ἀνατελλομένα a flame *mounting up*, Pi.*I.*4(3).83. **2.** *bring forth, give birth to*, ἄντειλας Διόνυσον ib.7(6).5; ἰούλους A.R.2.44: of events, μυρί' ἀπ' αἰσχρῶν ἀνατέλλοντα S.*Ph.*1139. **II.** intr., *rise, appear above the horizon*, of any heavenly body, as sun and moon, Hdt.2.142, S.*OC*1246, Ar.*Nu.*754; πρὸς ἠῶ τε καὶ ἥλιον ἀνατέλλοντα Hdt.1.204, 4.40; also of constellations, A.R.3.959; ἠὼς ἀντ. Id.2.1007; dist. from ἐπιτέλλω (q.v.), Ptol.*Alm.*8.4; cf. ἀνατολή. **b.** = ἐπιτέλλω, of the Pleiades, Theoc.13.25. **2.** of a river, *take its rise*, ἐκ ταύτης [τῆς λίμνης] Hdt.4.52, cf. Ael.*NA*14.16, etc. **b.** of persons, *originate*, ἐξ Ἰούδα ἀνατέταλκεν ὁ κύριος *Ep.Heb.*7.14. **3.** *grow*, of hair, ταρφὺς ἀντέλλουσα θρίξ A.*Th.*535; of teeth, Arist.*HA*501$^{b}$29; *spring up*, of plants, Thphr.*HP*3.1.6, al.; cf. ἀνατολή II. **4.** of mountains, *rise*, A.R.1.501; but, *appear on the horizon*, ib.601. **5.** *rise up*, ἀνέτειλε σωτήρ prob. in *Epigr.Gr.*978 (Philae).

***ἀνατέμνω,** *cut up, cut open*, νεκρόν Hdt.2.87, cf. Luc.*Prom.*21. **2.** *dissect*, Hp.*Ep.*17, Arist.*Spir.*478$^{a}$21. **3.** *open up, clear*, ὁδούς, αὔλακας, Ph.1.16,20; ὁδὸν καινήν *OGI*701 (Egypt). **II.** *cut off*, κλήματα Aeschin.3.166; γεισηπόδισμα *IG*2$^{2}$.463.63.

***ἀνατεταμένον,** τό, = ἑλξίνη, Ps.-Dsc.4.39.

**ἀνατεταμένως,** Adv. pf. part. Pass. of ἀνατείνω, *stretched* or *strained to the utmost* Sch.Ar.*Ra.*1282.

**ἀνα-τήκω,** *melt*: metaph., *relax*, τὸ σῶμα ἡδοναῖς Plu.2.136b:—Pass., of snow, *thaw*, Plb.2.16.9. **–τηξις,** εως, ἡ, *melting, thawing*, Id.9.43.5.

**ἀνᾱτί** [ῐ], Adv. of ἄνατος, *without harm, with impunity*, A.*Eu.*59, S.*Ant.*485, E.*Med.*1357, Pl.*Lg.*871e, prob. in Th.8.67, cf. Is.*Fr.*2, D.S.20.58, etc. (Spelling ἀνατεί attested by Hdn.*Epim.*256.)

***ἀνατίθημι,** pf. ἀνατέθηκα *SIG*1018.9 (Pergam.), etc.:—*lay upon*, once in Hom., ἐλεγχείην ἀναθήσει μοι Il.22.100; ἀ. ἄχθος *lay on* as a burden, Ar.*Eq.*1056 (hex.), cf. X.*An.*3.1.30; κινδύνους ἰδιώταις ἀ. Hyp.*Eux.*9: in good sense, ἀ. κῦδός τινι Pi.*O.*5.8. **b.** Med., *put on board ship*, *IG*5(1).1421 (Cyparissia). **2.** in Prose, *refer, attribute*, a thing to a person, μεγάλα οἱ χρήματα ἀ. Hdt.2.135; οὐ γὰρ ἄν οἱ πυραμίδα ἀνέθεσαν ποιήσασθαι would not *have attributed* to her the erection of the pyramid, ib.134; Φοίβῳ τήνδ' ἀναθήσω πρᾶξιν E.*El.*1296; εἰ μή, ὅταν.. εὖ πράξητε, ἐμοὶ ἀναθήσετε *will give* me *the credit of* it, Th.2.64; οὐ τῷ συμβούλῳ τὴν τοῦ κατορθοῦν.. ἀνέθηκε δύναμιν D.18.290; ἀ. τινὶ τὴν αἰτίαν τινός Isoc.1.37, Aeschin.2.10; also, *compare*, τινὰ εἴς τι Eun.*Hist.*p.261 D. **b.** ἀ. τινὶ ἅπαντα πράγματα *lay* them *upon* him, *entrust* them to him, Ar.*Nu.*1453, Th.8.82. **II.** *set up as a votive gift, dedicate*, τινί τι Hes.*Op.*658, Pi.*O.*3.30, Hdt.2.159, 7.54, Ar.*Pl.*1089, etc.; Ῥήνειαν ἀνέθηκε τῷ Ἀπόλλωνι Th.1.13; ἀνάθημα ἀνατιθέναι Hdt.1.53, 2.182; ἀ. τι ἐς Δελφούς Id.1.92, 2.135, 182, Pl.*Phdr.*235d, etc.; less freq. ἐν Δελφοῖς Theopomp.Com.1 D., Plu.*Sol.*25; *dedicate* a book, Id.*Sull.*6; ἀ. τινά *set up a statue of*.., *SIG*420 (Delos, iii B.C.); incorrectly of burial, *OGI*602 (Jaffa):—Pass., ἀνατεθῆναι Ar.*Eq.*849; cf. ἀνάκειμαι. **2.** *set up, erect*, [στήλην] παρὰ βωμόν, νεών, Plb.5.93.10, Plu.*Publ.*14: metaph., *dedicate*, μακραγορίαν λύρᾳ Pi.*P.*8.29; ἀ. τὰς ἀκοὰς τοῖς ἀκροάμασι *give* them *up* to, Plb.23.5.9. **3.** *set up and leave* in a place, ἀ. τινὰ ἐπὶ κρημνόν Ar.*Pl.*69; ἀ. ζῶντα (on a cross) Plb.1.86.6. **III.** *put back*, τί γὰρ παρ' ἦμαρ ἡμέρα τέρπειν ἔχει, προσθεῖσα κἀναθεῖσα τοῦ γε κατθανεῖν; pushing us forward or *moving* us *back* on the verge of death, S.*Aj.*476; cf. B. II. 2.

**B.** Med., *put upon for oneself*, ἀναθέσθαι τὰ σκεύη ἐπὶ τὰ ὑποζύγια X.*An.*2.2.4; *pack* on one's cart, Lys.7.19; τοῖς ὤμοις ἀ. τινά *put on one's* shoulders, Plu.2.983b; freq. like Act., ἀ. τινὰ ἐφ' ἵππον Id.*Art.*11, etc. **2.** *impart, communicate* something *one's own*, τινί τι *Act.Ap.*25.14, *Ep.Gal.*2.2, Plu.2.772d. **3.** *remit, refer*, ἀ. περί τινος εἰς σύγκλητον *refer* the consideration of it to the Senate, Plb.21.46.11, cf. App.*Samn.*4. **II.** *place differently, change about*, e.g. the men on a draught board, ἀνὰ πάντα τιθεσθαι v.l. in Orac.ap.Hdt.8.77. **2.** *take back a move* at πεττοί, Pl.*Hipparch.*229e: hence metaph., *retract one's opinion*, X.*Mem.*1.2.44, cf. 2.4.4; freq. in Pl., ἀνατίθεσθαι ὅ τι δοκεῖ Pl.*Grg.*462a, cf. *Prt.*354e, *Chrm.*164d; οὐκ ἀνατίθεμαι μὴ οὐ.. *retract and say* this is not so, Id.*Phd.*87a; οὐκ ἀ. μὴ οὐ καλῶς λέγεσθαι Id.*Men.*89d; ἀνατιθέμενος τὸ διημαρτημένον Luc.*Pseudol.*29.

**ἀνατίκτω,** *bring forth again*, Ael.*NA*1.17, Hsch.

**ἀνατῑμάω,** *raise in price*, Hdt.9.33; ἀ. ἑαυτόν D.C.38.5:—Med., Poll.3.125.

**ἀνα-τῑναγμός,** ὁ, *shaking violently*, Lxx *Na.*2.10(11). **–τῑνάσσω,** fut. –ξω, *shake up and down, brandish*, θύρσον E.*Ba.*80 (lyr., tm.): also of the wind *shaking about* a sail, Id.*Or.*341 (tm.), cf. Gal.14.638.

**ἀνατιταίνω,** *brandish*, τόξα Musae.17 (tm.), cf. Opp.*H.*2.90.

**ἀνατιτήσαντες·** πληρώσαντες, Hsch.

**ἀνα-τιτραίνω,** = sq., of trepanning, Aët.15.15. **–τιτράω,** *bore through, bore*, Dsc.1.66 (Pass.), Trypho *Fr.*112 V. (Pass.); part. ἀνατιτράς, –άντος, Gal.*UP*16.11, etc., Orib.46.11.10.

**ἀνά-τλημα,** ατος, τό, *sufferance*, Suid. **–τλῆναι,** inf. of ἀνέτλην, aor. with no pres.: fut. ἀνατλήσομαι: also aor. 1 ἀνέτλησα Orac. ap.Lact.*Inst.*4:—*bear up against, endure*, κήδε' ἀνέτλης Od.14.47; ὀϊζύος ἣν ἀνέτλημεν 3.104; φάρμακ' ἀνέτλη, i.e. *resisted* the strength of the magic drink, 10.327; πολύθρηνον αἰῶνα.. ἀνατλᾶσα A.*Ag.*716; πατέρα.. οὐκ ἀνέτλατε S.*OC*239, etc.; πόλλ' ἀνατλάς Ar.*Pax*1035; τὴν εἱμαρμένην Pl.*Tht.*169c; τὰ προσήκοντα πάθη Id.*Grg.*525a: c. part., ἀνέτλην μογέουσα *IG*14.1960.

**ἄνατλος·** ἀκρατής, Hsch.

**ἀνα-τμήγω,** = ἀνατέμνω, aor. 2 part. Pass. ἀνατμηγείς Marcell.Sid.85. **–τμητικός,** ή, όν, *fit for cutting up*, Sm.*Ps.*54(55).22.

**ἀν-ατμίζομαι,** Pass., *evaporate*, Democr.ap.Ath.*Epit.*lib. ii 89 (vol. i p.281 Schw.).

**ἀνατοιχάσαι·** περὶ τοῖχον περιπατῆσαι, Hsch.

**ἀνατοιχέω,** (τοῖχος) *roll from side to side*, esp. of sailors in a storm: metaph., Arr.*Epict.*3.12.7; διατοιχέω is preferred by Phryn.139, Poll.1.114.

***ἀνατοκισμός,** ὁ, *compound interest*, Cic.*Att.*5.21.11, *CIL*10.3334.30 (Puteoli, iii A.D.).

**ἀνατολάς,** Adv. *eastwards*, Lxx *Nu.*10.5 (dub.).

***ἀνατολή,** poet. **ἀντ–,** (ἀνατέλλω) *rising* above the horizon, of any heavenly body, e.g. the sun, freq. in pl., ἀντολαὶ ἠελίοιο Od.12.4, E.*Ph.*504:—also in sg., ἀπ' ἀνατολᾶς ἁλίου ἄχρι δύσεως *IG*4.606; δύσεώς τε καὶ ἀνατολῆς ἡλίου καὶ τῶν ἄλλων ἄστρων Pl.*Plt.*269a, cf. *Lg.*807e; dist. from ἐπιτολή (q.v.), Gem.13.3. **2.** = ἐπιτολή, A.*Pr.*457, *Ag.*7; περὶ Ὠρίωνος ἀνατολήν Arist.*Mete.*361$^{b}$23; ἀπὸ Πλειάδος ἀ. Id.*HA*599$^{b}$11. **3.** *the quarter of sunrise, east*, opp. δύσις, freq. in pl., ἀπὸ ἡλίου ἀνατολέων Hdt.4.8; ἡλίου πρὸς ἀντολάς A.*Pr.*707; without ἡλίου, πρὸς ἀνατολάς Thphr.*HP*9.15.2, *Mon.Anc.Gr.*14.12; πρὸς τὰς ἀ. Plb.2.14.4; ἀπὸ ἀνατολῶν Lxx *Nu.*23.7, *Ev.Matt.*2.1, etc. **b.** the *ascendant*, i.e. the point where the eastern horizon cuts the zodiac, Ptol.*Tetr.*20. **c.** phase of new moon when 15° distant from sun, *Cat.Cod.Astr.*8(4).204, Paul.Al.*G.*3. **4.** in pl., *sources* of a river, Plb.2.17.4. **II.** *growing*, of the teeth, Arist.*HA*501$^{b}$28; of the white at the root of the nails, Poll.2.146: pl., ἀγρὸς ἀνατολὰς καὶ βλάστας ἔχει Ph.1.68, cf. Lxx *Je.*23.5, al.

**ἀνατολικός,** ή, όν, *eastern*, ἡμισφαίριον Str.2.3.2; στοά J.*AJ*20.9.7, al.; θάλασσα Epicur.*Fr.*346b: Comp., Str.2.1.27, Marin.*Procl.*36: Sup., Marcian.*Peripl.*1.6, al. **2.** ἀνατολικοί, οἱ, = *Orientales*, title of a *numerus*, *PFlor.*278 v 1 (iii A.D.). **3.** ἀ. χρόνος time occupied *in rising*, Gem.7.18, Ptol.*Alm.*2.11; ἀ. φάσεις Ptol.*Tetr.*99; but ἀ. σελήνη *waxing moon*, Xenocr.ap.Orib.2.58.77, Ptol.*Tetr.*116. **II.** Subst. ἀνατολικόν, τό, = κλύμενον, of a flower *opening at sunrise*, Ps.-Dsc.4.13.

**ἀνατόλιος,** poet. **ἀντ–,** η, ον, = foreg., ἄρουρα Nonn.*D.*25.98.

**ἀνατολμάω,** *regain one's courage*, Plu.*Luc.*31, *Ant.*50; f.l. in E.*Alc.*277.

***ἀνα-τομή,** ἡ, *dissection*, αἱ ἀ., title of a treatise freq. cited by Arist., as *HA*509$^{b}$22, al., cf. Thphr.*HP*1.1.4; ἡ τἀνθρωπίνου σκήνους ἀ. Longin.32.5, cf. Chrysipp.*Stoic.*2.246 (pl.). **II.** in a logical sense, ἀ. καὶ διαιρέσεις Arist.*APo.*98$^{a}$2. **–τομικός,** ή, όν, *relating to anatomy*, ἀ. ἐγχείρησις, title of work by Galen; *skilled in anatomy*, ἄνδρες Gal.4.555. Adv. **-κῶς** Id.18(2).927.

**ἀνάτονος,** ον, (ἀνατείνω) *stretching upwards*, Vitr.10.10.6.

**ἄνᾱτος,** ον, (ἄτη) *unharmed*, B.*Fr.*19 (cj.); Λοξίου κότῳ A.*Ag.*1211; κακῶν ἄνατος *harmed by no* ills, S.*OC*786, where the Laur. Ms. ἄναιτος. **II.** Act., *not harming, harmless*, A.*Supp.*356, 359, 410. **2.** *immune from punishment*, Ἀρχ.Ἐφ.1920.76 (Crete, vi/v B.C.). Adv. **–τως** *with impunity*, *IG*9(1).333 (Locr.). (Contr. fr. ἀνάατος, q.v.)

**ἀνα-τρεπτέον**, *one must overthrow, refute*, Luc.*Herm*.49, Gal.4.620. 2. *one must go back, return*, Orib.*Fr*.142. **-τρεπτικός**, ή, όν, *turning upside down, upsetting*, ἐπιτήδευμα..πόλεως ὥσπερ νεὼς ἀ. Pl.*R*.389d; στομάχου Dsc.2.70; of the pulse (dub. sens.), Gal. 8.928, cf. 644; οἱ ἀ. διάλογοι Plato's *refutative* dialogues, as 'Euthydemus' and 'Gorgias', Thrasyll.ap.D.L.3.59, cf. Hermog.*Meth*. 10. ***-τρέπω**, poet. ἀντρ-, Aeol. aor. ὀνέτροπε Alc.*Supp*.25.7: pf. -τέτροφα S.*Tr*.1009, And.1.131, later -τέτρᾰφα Din.1.30 codd., v.l. in D.18.296, Aeschin.1.190, 3.158: aor. 2 Med. ἀνετράπετο in pass. sense, Il.6.64, 14.447 (only here in Hom.), Pl.*Cra*.395d, Theoc. 8.90: aor. 2 Pass., Alex.76.3, etc.:—*overturn, upset*, Act., Archil.56. 3, Alc. l. c.; τράπεζαν D.19.198, cf. Sch. ad eund.24.136; in Hom. ἀνετράπετο, = ὕπτιος ἔπεσεν, Il.6.64; ἀνατετραμμένος Ar.*Ra*.543; freq. of ships, Pl.*Lg*.906e, Arist.*Rh*.1398ᵇ7, etc.; ἂν ἀνατραπῇ γὰρ πλοῖον Alex. l. c.; τὴν σωφροσύνην, τὸν βίον ἅπαντα And.1.131, cf. Plu. *Pomp*.46. b. Medic., *upset*, στόμαχον Gal.12.911: so abs., *create nausea*, Aristaenet.1.12. 2. *overthrow, ruin*, πρόρριζον ἀνατρέψαι τινά Hdt.1.32, cf. 8.62; μὴ..δαίμων..ἀντρέψῃ ποδὶ ὄλβον A.*Pers*. 163; λακπάτητον ἀ. χαράν S.*Ant*.1275; πλοῦτον And.1.131; πόλιν Ar.*V*.671; πολιτείαν, οἰκίαν, Pl.*Lg*.709a, *R*.471b; τὰ τῶν Ἑλλήνων D.18.143:—Pass., ἤρυξε πόλιν μἀνατραπῆναι A.*Th*.1082; ὁ βίος ἀνατετραμμένος ἂν εἴη Pl.*Grg*.481c, etc. 3. *upset* in argument, *refute*, Ar.*Nu*.901; ἀ. πρόβλημα Alex.Aphr.*in Top*.514.28. II. Pass., *to be upset, disheartened*, ἀνετράπετο φρένα λύπᾳ Theoc.8.90; ταῖς ψυχαῖς ἀ. Plb.21.25.8. 2. c. acc., *to be checked in, diverted from*, ὁρμήν J.*BJ*2.15.6; τὴν φιλαργυρίαν 2.14.6. 3. *to be turned back*, εἰς χώραν Herm.ap.Stob.1.49.68. 4. *to be made null and void*, Just. *Nov*.2.2 *Intr*. III. *stir up, arouse*, ἀνατέτροφας ὅ τι καὶ μύσῃ S.*Tr*. 1009:—Pass., of the sea in a storm, Arist.*HA*620ᵃ4, etc. IV. intr. in Act., *slip, trip up*, Plu.2.631c; of a ship, *capsize*, D.Chr.34.32.

**ἀνατρέφω**, *bring up, cherish, educate*, A.*Eu*.523, *Ev.Luc*.4.16, al.; ἀ. τὸ φρόνημα *raise* the spirit, X.*Cyr*.5.2.34:—Med., ἀναθρέψασθαι υἱόν *have* him *educated*, Hdn.1.2.1; ἀ. λειμὼν κάλλεα Nic.*Fr*.74.58:—Pass., *grow up*, ἀνατραφῆναι ἐν.. Plu.*Cam*.34, etc.; τῇ Ἑλλάδι φωνῇ Ael.*NA*11.25; ἀνέτραφες in *AP*5.156 (Mel.) = ἀνετράφης. 2. *feed up*, opp. ἰσχναίνω, Hp.*Art*.33,50: metaph., ἀ. μονῳδίαις Ar.*Ra*. 944:—Pass., ἀνατρέφεσθαι ἐκ νόσου *convalesce*, Hp.*VM*14; of fish after milting, Arist.*HA*608ᵃ2.

**ἀνατρέχω**, fut. -δραμοῦμαι Luc.*Ind*.4, poet. 3 sg. -δράμεται *AP*9. 575 (Phil.): aor. -έδραμον (v. infr.); aor. subj. Med. ἀναδράμηται Hp.*Ep*.19 (*Hermes* 53.69):—*run back*, ὁ μὲν αὖθις ἀνέδραμε Il.16.813, cf. 11.354; ἀνά τ' ἔδραμ' ὀπίσσω 5.599; *return*, of the sea, Plu.2.915a; εἰς τὰς ἐξ ἀρχῆς τάξεις Plb.2.67.6; εἰς τὴν ἑαυτοῦ φύσιν Plu.*Pel*.31; εἰς τὴν προϋπάρχουσαν φιλίαν D.S.20.59; of property, *revert*, ἐπί τινα Just.*Nov*.7.4; in writing, *recur* to a point, ἐπί τι Plb.5.40.4: abs., ἀ. τοῖς χρόνοις 1.12.6, al. 2. c. acc., *retrace, traverse*, κῦδος ἀνέδραμον ὕμνῳ Pi.*O*.8.54, cf. Semon.10; *undo*, ἁμαρτίαν Men.15D.; ἀ. τὴν τῆς φύσεως ἐλάττωσιν *make amends for*, Plu.2.2c, cf. Luc.*Ind*. 4. 3. *revert*, ἐπὶ τοὺς λόγους, τὴν ὕλην, Plot.5.8.1; *return* to source, of light, 4.5.7; *run back* to (logically), ἐπὶ τὴν κοινοτάτην αἰτίαν Phld. *D*.1.16, cf. Plot.6.1.30. 4. *have recourse to*, ἐπί.. Luc.*Abd*.11, al., Eun.*Hist*.p.251 D. II. *jump up and run, start up*, of men, ἀναδραμὼν ἔθεε Hdt.3.36; ἐκ τῆς κοίτης, ἐκ τοῦ θρόνου, Id.7.15,212; πρὸς τὰ μετέωρα Th.3.89, cf. X.*HG*4.4.4. 2. of things, ἐγκέφαλος δὲ.. ἀνέδραμεν ἐξ ὠτειλῆς the brains *spurted up* from the wound, Il.17.297; σμώδιγγες..ἀνέδραμον weals *started up* under the blow, 23.717; *slip up*, Gal.18(1).829; *run* or *spread over*, τὸ πάθος ἀ. ἐπὶ τὴν χεῖρα Plu. 2.978c; ἔρευθος ἀ. Call.*Lav.Pall*.27. 3. *run up, shoot up*, of plants, ὁ δ' ἀνέδραμεν ἔρνεϊ ἶσος Il.18.56, cf. Hdt.8.55: hence, of cities and peoples, *shoot up, rise quickly*, ἀνά τ' ἔδραμον καὶ εὐθενήθησαν Hdt.1. 66, cf. 7.156; ἀ. εἰς ἀξίωμα Plu.*Publ*.21; ἀ. τοῖς βίοις, ταῖς ἐλπίσι, D.S.5.12, 18.20; ἀ. ἡ πολυτέλεια *increased*, Plu.*Mar*.34. 4. λίσση δ' ἀναδέδρομε πέτρη the rock *ran sheer up*, Od.5.412. 5. metaph., *soar aloft*, of digression to a nobler theme, ἀνέδραμε πρὸς τὴν ἐν οὐρανῷ λύραν Anon. *in SE*40.23.

**ἀνάτρεψις**, εως, ἡ, *turning upside down*, Arist.*Mete*.368ᵃ32. 2. *refutation*, Phld.*Sign*.11.

**ἀνά-τρησις**, εως, ἡ, (ἀνατιτράω) *perforation*, Ph.*Bel*.57.16; *trepanning*, Plu.*Cat.Ma*.9, Leonid.ap.Aët.15.12. 2. *hole bored*, Plu.2. 968b. **-τρητος**, ον, *bored through*, ἐμβάδες Suid.

**ἀνατριαινόω**, (τρίαινα) *shake as with a trident*, Amphis 14.8.

**ἀνατριακοσιολόγιστος**, ον, *reckoned at* 300 *a head*, *Michel*731.20 (Ilium).

**ἀνα-τρῐβή**, ἡ, *education*, τὰ τῆς ἀ., opp. τὰ τοῦ βίου, Ps.-Ptol.*Centil*. 224. **-τρίβω** [ῑ], *rub, chafe*, τὸν ὦμον Hp.*Art*.9:—Med., Id.*Vict*. 3.83; *massage oneself*, Aristid.*Or*.47(23).18, cf. 50, al.:—Pass., sens. obsc., Ar.*Ach*.1149. 2. *rub clean*, κύνας X.*Cyn*.6.26. 3. Med., ἐλαίῳ ὕδωρ συμμείξας ἀ. *rub oneself down*, Arist.*Pr*.881ᵃ5. 4. Pass., *to be worn away*, Hdt.3.113.

***ἀνατρίζω**, *chirp aloud*, of cranes, Q.S.13.107 (al. -τρύζω).

**ἀνάτριμμα**, ατος, τό, = -τριψις, Aët.8.62.

**ἀνατριπλόω**, *repeat a third time*, Syr.*in Metaph*.61.8 (Pass.).

**ἀνα-τριπτέον**, *one must chafe*, Archig.ap.Orib.44.26.9. **-τριπτος**, ον, *rubbed up*: ἀ. ἱμάτια cloths *with rough, raised pile*, like plush or velvet, Dsc.3.33.

**ἀνα-τριχόομαι**, Pass., *have one's hair grow again*, Suid. **-τρῐχος**, ον, (θρίξ) *with hair bristling backwards*, Porph.ap.Eus.*PE*3. 13. **-τριχοφυέω**, *grow fresh hair*, Cleopatra ap.Gal.12.405.

**ἀνάτριψις**, εως, ἡ, *chafing, friction*, Hp.*Art*.9, Gal.6.92.

**ἀνατροπ-εύς**, έως, ὁ, *overturner, destroyer*, τοῦ οἴκου Antipho 2.2.2; τῆς νεότητος Plu.2.5b; *subverter*, τῶν ἐν ἀνθρώποις νομιζομένων D.Chr. 37.32. **-ή**, ἡ, *capsizing*, [τοῦ πλοίου] Arist.*Metaph*.1013ᵇ14. 2. *overthrow, ruin*, ἀνατροπαὶ δωμάτων, οἴκων, A.*Eu*.355, Pl.*Prt*.325c; ἀ. βίων Clearch.10. 3. *pouring out*, of drink, Lxx *Ha*.2.15. 4. *upsetting*, στομάχου Sor.1.27, Asclep.Jun.ap.Gal.13.140; ἀ. ναυτιώδεις Plu.2.442f. 5. *refutation*, Str.2.1.22, Hermog.*Prog*.5. 6. *annulment*, Just.*Nov*.2.2 *Intr*.; *undoing*, ἐπ' -ῇ τῆς νοήσεως τοῦ θεοῦ Phld.*D*.3.7. 7. *raising* of body, Cass.Fel.82. **-ιάζω**, *turn back*, *AB*312. **-ος**, ον, dub. l. in *App.Anth*.4.104.15.

**ἀνατροφ-εύς**, έως, ὁ, *nurturer*, Ps.-Callisth.1.13. **-ή**, ἡ, *education*, Aphth.*Prog*.8; *rearing, nurture*, D.H.*Rh*.5.3, Plu.2.608c, Arr.*Cyn*. 29, Artem.1.16, etc. II. *feeding, diet*, ἡ ἐκ ζῴων ἀ. Porph.*Abst*.3. 17. III. of plants and trees, *cultivation*, *Gp*.4.12.11, 9.14.5.

**ἀνατροχ-άζω**, = ἀνατρέχω, κοχλιοειδῶς Ph.Byz.*Mir*.1.4. **-ασμός**, ὁ, *running backwards*, Antyll.ap Orib.6.22.8.

**ἀνατρῡγάω**, *glean grapes off again*, τοὺς ἀμπελῶνας Ph.2.390.

**ἀνατρύζω**, v. ἀνατρίζω.

**ἀναττικός**, όν, *alien to the Attic dialect*, Phryn.ap.St.Byz. s.v. Ἀθῆναι.

**ἀνατῠλίσσω**, Att. -ττω, *unroll*, βιβλία Luc.*Ind*.16: metaph., ἀ. τοὺς λόγους πρὸς ἑαυτόν Id.*Nigr*.7.

**ἀνατυπ-όω**, *describe, represent*, Philostr.*VA*1.19, cf. *Her*.2.19 (Pass.):—Med., *form an image of* a thing, *imagine*, Plu.2.329b, 331d; *represent* in writing, εἰς ἐπιστολάς Philostr.*VA*1.32. II. *remodel, transform*, τὴν ἀνθρωπίνην περὶ τοῦ δαιμονίου δόξαν D.Chr. 12.26, cf. Antim.81. **-τομαι**, Med., strengthd. for τύπτω, τὴν κεφαλήν J.*AJ*17.7.1. ***-ωμα**, ατος, τό, *mental image*, *Stoic*.1. 214. **-ωσις**, εως, ἡ, = τύπωσις, Hsch. **-ωτικός**, ή, όν, *representing*, Simp. *in Epict*. p.20D.

**ἀνατυρβάζω**, *stir up, confound*, Ar.*Eq*.310.

**ἀνανγητος**, ον, *rayless, sunless*, Ἅιδης A.*Pr*.1028.

**ἀναυδάω**, *uplift the voice*, *PMag.Par*.1.2532.

**ἀναυδ-ής**, ές, *speechless*, Epicr.11.20. II. = sq., Hsch. **-ητος**, Dor. -ᾱτος, ον, *not to be spoken, unutterable*: hence, *horrible*, ἀναυδάτῳ μένει A.*Th*.897 (lyr.); ἄφατον ἀναύδητον λόγον E.*Ion*783. 2. *unspoken, impossible*, οὐδὲν ἀναύδατον φατίσαιμ' ἄν S.*Aj*.715 (lyr.). II. *speechless*, Id.*Tr*.968 (cj.). **-ία**, ἡ, *speechlessness*, Hp.*Coac*.353, *Mul*.2.126; *lethargy*, Antigen.ap.Cael.Aur.*AP*2.10. ***-ος**, ον, *speechless*, Od.5.456, 10.378, Hes.*Th*.797, etc.; *silent*, ἄ. ἄγγελος, of dust, A.*Th*.82 (lyr.), etc.:—properly, *unable to articulate*, whereas ἄφωνος is *voiceless*, Hp.*Epid*.3.17.γ', but of fishes, A.*Pers*.577; *without speaking*, S.*OC*1274,1404, Plu.*Pomp*.74, etc. Adv. -δως Hp. *Prorrh*.1.90, J.*AJ*16.11.4. 2. *preventing speech, silencing*, χαλινῶν ἄ. μένος A.*Ag*.238 (lyr.). II. *unspeakable, horrible*, ἔργον S. *Aj*.947.

***ἀναυλεί**, Adv., (ναῦλον) *without passage-money*, Suid.

***ἄναυλος** (A), ον, *without the flute*, κῶμος -ότατος a procession *unaccompanied by flutes*, i.e. *joyless*, E.*Ph*.791; ἔρωτες Plu.2.406a: neut. pl. as Adv., ἄναυλα ὀρχεῖσθαι Babr.9.9; θύειν Plu.2.277f. 2. *unmusical*, μέλη βοῶν ἄναυλα (as Bgk. for ἄναυδα) S.*Fr*.699. II. *unskilled in flute-playing*, Luc.*Halc*.7.

***ἄναυλος** (B), ον, (αὐλίον) *weary of its stall*, χοῖρος dub. in Herod. 8.7.

**ἀναυλόχητος**, ον, *not brought to haven*, Lyc.745.

**ἀναυμάχ-ητος**, ον, *without sea-fight*, ὄλεθρος ἀ. loss *of a fleet without striking a blow*, Lys.ap.D.H.*Lys*.14. ***-ίου**, sc. γραφή, *indictment* of a trierarch *for keeping his ship out of action*, ἀ. ὀφλεῖν And. 1.74.

**ἀναυξ-άνω**, *increase*, in Pass., *PBaden*39 iii 16 (ii A. D.). **-ής**, ές, *not increasing*, Thphr.*CP*4.6.3. II. intr., *not waxing* or *growing*, Hp.*Art*.53, *Mochl*.24, al., Arist.*HA*569ᵃ30, *Cael*.270ᵃ13. **-ησία**, ἡ, Gramm., *omission of the augment*, Greg.Cor.180. **-ητος**, ον, = ἀναυξής, Arist.*Cael*.270ᵃ25, Sor.1.47 (Comp.), Aq.*Je*.22.30; μορφαὶ ἀ. πυρός dub.l. in Theodect.17. 2. *without augment*, Eust.19.29. Adv. -τως Greg.Cor.180. **-ία**, Ion. -ίη, ἡ, *defect in growth*, Hp.*Art*.52 (v.l. ἀναυξήσιος); written -εια in Ath.Med.ap.Orib.*Inc*. 21.1. **-ος**, ον, = ἀναυξής 1, Plu.2.981f.

**ἄναυος**, ον, etym. of Att. ἄνεως, A.D.*Adv*.155.4, cf. Eust.387.44.

**ἄναυρος**, ον, *without air, windless, still*, Hsch.

**Ἄναυρος**, ὁ, river in Thessaly, Hes.*Sc*.477, etc. II. as Appellat., ἄναυρος, ὁ, *mountain-torrent*, Mosch.2.31, Nic.*Al*.235, Lyc.1424, *IG* 14.1089, etc. (Orig. pr. n., cf. Ἀχελῷος of any river.)

**ἄναυς**, gen. ἄ ᾱος, ὁ, ἡ, only A.*Pers*.680 in nom. pl., νᾶες ἄναες ships *that are ships no more*.

**ἄ-ναυτα**· ἠπειρωτικά, Hsch. II. ἄν-αυτα· παραχρῆμα (Tarent.), Id. (cf. πάραυτα).

**ἀναϋτέω** [ῠ], *shout aloud*, Opp.*C*.4.301: c. acc., κρυπτὸν ἀνηΰτησεν ἔπος Nonn.*D*.10.288, cf. Coluth.85.

**ἀναυτούργητος**, ον, *not to be cultivated* by the lessor *in person*, *PTeb*.378.29 (iii A. D.).

**ἄναυχην**, ενος, ὁ, ἡ, *without neck* or *throat*, Emp.57.

**ἀναΰω** (αὔω B), = ἀναϋτέω, aor. ἀνήυσα, Dor. ἀνᾱ́ϋσα Theoc.4.37, A.R.4.75.

**ἀναφαία**· ἡ θερμοποτις παρὰ Κρησίν, Ath.11.783f.

***ἀναφαίνω**, poet. ἀμφ-: fut. -φᾰνῶ, but -φᾱνῶ E.*Ba*.528 codd. (-φαίνω Herm.): aor. ἀνέφηνα, Hellenistic -έφᾶνα: pf. -πέφηνα late, Ps.-Luc.*Philopatr*.3:—*cause to give light, make to blaze up*, ξύλα, δαΐδας Od.18.310. 2. *bring to light, produce*, ὕφιας Hdt.4.

.05. b. *show forth, make known, display*, θεοπροπίας, ἀρετήν, ἐπεσ-.ολίας, Il.1.87, 20.411, Od.4.159; πραπίδων καρπόν Pi.*Fr.*211; κανέ-.ηνεν οὐ δεδειγμένα S.*Fr.*432.7; ἀ. θυσίας E.*IT*466; ὀργάν Id.*Ba.* 38; ἄστρα X.*Mem.*4.3.4; ἡμέρα καὶ ἡλίῳ..χάριν οἶδα ὅτι μοι Κλεινίαν . Id.*Smp.*4.12: rarely of sound, βοὰν ἀμφ. *send forth a loud* cry, A. *Supp.*829; ἀ. μελέων νόμους Ar.*Av.*745:—in Med., νίκαν ἀνεφάνατο Pi.*I.*4(3).71. 3. *proclaim, declare*, βασιλέα ἀ. τινά Id.*P.*4.62; νι-.κάσαις ἀνέφανε Κυράναν ib.9.73, cf. *N.*9.12: c. part., τοὺς πολίτας .γαθοὺς ὄντας ἀ. Pl.*Criti.*108c: c. inf., ἀναφαίνω σε τόδε..ὀνομάζειν *proclaim that* they call thee by this name, E.*Ba.*528:—Med., in Dor. form ἀμφ-, *adopt* as one's son, *Leg.Gort.*10.34, al. b. of things, *appoint, institute*, ὃς τελετὰς ἀνέφηνε καὶ ὄργια *IG*3.713, cf. *Marm.Par.*28; νῆσον ἀ. τινὶ οἰκεῖν Philostr.*Her.*19.16. 4. ἀνα-φάναντες τὴν Κύπρον *having sighted..*, *Act.Ap.*21.3. II. Pass., fut. ἀναφᾰνήσομαι Ar.*Eq.*950, Pl.*Prm.*132a, al.; but also -φανοῦ-μαι Id.*Plt.*289c: pf. ἀναπέφασμαι, but -πέφηνα Hdt. (v. infr.), etc.: aor. ἀνεφάνην Ar.*V.*124:—*to be shown forth, appear plainly*, ἀναφαίνεται ἀστήρ Il.11.62; ἀ. αἰπὺς ὄλεθρος ib.174; τῇ δεκάτῃ..ἀνε-φαίνετο πατρὶς ἄρουρα Od.10.29; τὸ Δέλτα ἐστὶ νεωστὶ ἀναπεφηνός Hdt.2.15, cf. S.*OC*1222 (lyr.), etc.; ἀ. ὁ βλάπτων A.*Ch.*328. b. *reappear*, Hdt.4.195; of rivers which flow underground, Id.6.76, 7. 30; simply, *spring up*, ib.198. 2. ἀναφανῆναι μούναρχος *to be declared* king, Id.3.82; στρατηγὸς ἀ. Pl.*Ion*541e; κλέπτης τις ὁ δίκαιος ..ἀναπέφανται *proved to be..*, Id.*R.*334a, cf. *Smp.*185a; ἀ. λογογρά-φος ἐκ τριηράρχου from a sea-captain *to come out* a romancer, Aeschin. 3.173:—also c. part., ἀναπέφανται ὢν ἀγαθός Pl.*R.*350c; ἀναφαίνεσθαι ἔχων, σεσωσμένοι, *to be seen* or *found to* have, *to be plainly* in safety, etc., Id.*Sph.*233c, X.*Cyr.*3.2.15, etc. III. the Act. intr. in later Greek, ἀνέφαινεν ἕσπερος Musae.111 (v.l.), cf. Hld.5.22:—ἀναφῆναι is prob. f.l. for ἀναφανῆναι in Hdt.1.165.

***ἀναφαίρετος**, ον, *not to be taken away*, Men.*Mon.*2, D.H.8.74, D. Chr.31.22; χάρις *POxy.*273.15 (i A.D.); ὠφέλεια Just.*Nov.*68*Pr.*; *inseparable*, opp. *accidental*, *Stoic.*2.214 (? Diog.Bab.); *not diminished by subtraction*, *Theol.Ar.*30. Adv. -ως *PFlor.*47a4 (iii A.D.), Just. *Nov.*2.3 *Intr.*

***ἀναφάλακρος**, ον, *forehead-bald*, *PPetr.*3p.9, Procl.*Par.Ptol.*203, *BGU*998, al.

***ἀναφαλαντ-ιαῖος**, = foreg., dub. in Antioch.Astr. in *Cat.Cod.Astr.* 7.112.8. **-ίας**, ου, ὁ, = foreg., Luc.*Tim.*47, al., *Cat.Cod.Astr.*8(2). 58.27, etc.:—also **-ανθίας**, Phryn.*PSp.*124B. (cod.). **-ίασις**, εως, ἡ, *forehead-baldness*, Arist.*HA*518ᵃ28. ***-ος**, ον, *forehead-bald*, Lxx *Le.*13.41, freq. in Pap., *PPar.*5.1.5 (ii B.C.), etc.:—**-ανθος**, *PPetr.*1p.54 (iii B.C.), etc. **-ωμα**, ατος, τό, *forehead-baldness*, Lxx *Le.*13.42.

**ἀναφαν-δά**, Adv. *visibly, openly, before the eyes of all*, opp. κρύβδην, Od.3.221, 11.455: as neut. Adj., A.R.4.84. **-δόν**, Adv. = foreg., Il.16.178, Hdt.2.35,46, Pl.*Prt.*348e, etc.: poet. **ἀμφανδόν** Pi.*P.*9. 41. ***-σις**, εως, ἡ, *appearance*, Anon.in Ptol.*Tetr.*5. II. v. ἄμφανσις.

**ἀναφέγγει**, gloss on ἀναμαιμάει, Hsch.

***ἀναφέρω**, poet. **ἀμφ-**, fut. ἀνοίσω: aor. ἀνήνεγκα, Ion. ἀνήνεικα, also inf. ἀνοῖσαι Hdt.1.157: I. *bring, carry up*, [Κέρβερον] ἐξ Ἀΐδαο Od.11.625; ἐκ τῆς ἰλύος ψῆγμα ἀ. χρυσοῦ Hdt.4.195, cf. 3.102 (as v.l. for -φορέω); ἀ. τινὰ εἰς Ὄλυμπον, εἰς θεούς, X.*Smp.*8.30 (Pass.), Plu. *Rom.*28, etc.; in histor. writers, *carry up the country*, esp. into Central Asia, Hdt.6.30; *raise up*, εἰς τὸ ἄνω Hp.*Art.*37; ἀ. πόδα *lift* it, E.*Ph.*1410:—Med., *carry up* to a place of safety, *take with one*, Hdt.3.148; *remove one's goods*, 8.32,36, etc. b. esp. *carry up to the Acropolis, put by*, of treasure, And.3.7, X.*Vect.*5.12, Aeschin.2. 174, etc. 2. *bring up, pour forth*, of tears, ἑτοιμότερα γέλωτος ἀ. λίβη A.*Ch.*447; αἵματος πλῆθος ἀ. *spit up*, Plu.*Cleom.*15; ἀ. φωνάς, στεναγμούς, Id.2.433c, *Alex.*52:—Med., ἀνενείκασθαι, abs., *fetch up a deep-drawn breath, heave a deep sigh*, μνησάμενος δ' ἀδινῶς ἀνενείκατο Il.19.314; ἀνενεικάμενόν τε καὶ ἀναστενάξαντα Hdt.1.86 (where others, *having recovered himself, come to himself*, v. infr. II. 7): in Alex. Poets, *utter*, ἀνενείκατο μῦθον, φωνήν, A.R.3.463,635. 3. *uphold, take upon one*, ἄχθος A.*Ch.*841; κινδύνους Th.3.38; διαβολάς, πόλεμον, etc., Plb.1.36.3, 4.45.9, etc.; πολλῶν ἀ. ἁμαρτίας Lxx *Is.* 53.12, *Ep.Heb.*9.28. 4. *offer* in sacrifice, ib.7.27, 13.15, etc.: abs., *make expiation* or *compensation*, *GDI*3537, al. (Cnidus). 5. *raise up, yield*, ἀρχαῖαι ἀρεταὶ ἀμφέροντ' ἀνδρῶν σθένος Pi.*N.*11. 38. 6. intr., *lead up*, of a road, ἁμαξιτὸς εἰς τὸν Πειραιᾶ ἀ. X.*HG* 2.4.10, cf. Plb.8.29.1, *Inscr.Prien.*37.161. II. *bring* or *carry back*, εἰς τοὔπισθεν ἀ. πόδα E.*Ph.*1410: freq. in Prose, ἀ. τὰς κώπας *recover* the oars (after pulling them through the water), Th.2.84; ἡ εἰρεσία ἀναφέρεται Plu.*Demetr.*53, *Ant.*26. 2. *bring back* tidings, *report*, παρά τινα Hdt.1.47; ἔς τινα Id.1.91, Th.5.28, etc.; τὰ ἐκ τῆς ἐκκλη-σίας ἀνενεγκόντες Decr.ap.D.18.75:—Pass., Hdt.1.141, al. 3. *bring back from exile*, Th.5.16. 4. *carry back, trace* one's family to an ancestor, τὸ Ἡρακλέους γένος εἰς Περσέα ἀναφέρεται Pl.*Alc.*1. 120e; without γένος, ἀ. εἰς Ἡρακλέα Id.*Tht.*175a. 5. *refer* a matter to another, βουλεύματα ἐς τὸ κοινόν Hdt.3.80; ἐς ἀφανὲς τὸν μῦθον ἀ. Id.2.23; ἁμαρτίαν εἴς τινα ἀ. *ascribe* E.*Or.*76, *Ba.*29, etc.; τῆς κηλῖδος εἰς ὑμᾶς -ομένης Antipho 3.3.11; τὴν αἰτίαν εἴς τινα Lys.22.8; rarely ἀ. τί τινι E.*Or.*432, Lys.12.81; τι ἐπί τινα D.18.224, Aeschin. 3.215; τι ἐπί τι Pl.*Phd.*76d; τι πρός τι Arist.*EN*1101ᵇ19 (Pass.), al.; ποῖ δίκην ἀνοίσομεν; to whom *shall* we *refer* the judgement? E. *Ion*253; τὴν ἀπόδοσιν εἴς τινα D.34.46:—Pass., *to be attributed* (of authorship), εἰς Μητρόδωρον Phld.*Herc.*1005.8; *to be traced to, derived from*, ἐπί τι ib.1251.11. 6. Pass., *refer to*, of a statement, πρός τι Ps.-Alex.Aphr.*in SE*127.8. b. without acc., ἀ. εἴς τινα *refer* or *appeal* to another, *make reference* to him, Hdt.3.71, Pl.*Ap.*20e; ἔς τινα περί τινος Hdt.1.157, 7.149; ἀ. πρός τι *refer* to something as to a standard, Hp.*VM*9; ἐκεῖσε ἀ. Pl.*R.*484c, cf. *Phdr.*237d. c. *report*, μέτρα καὶ γειτνίας καὶ ἀξίας *PTeb.*14.11 (ii B.C.), etc.:—Pass., ib.10.3 (ii B.C.): abs., *make a report*, τινί *PRyl.*233.8 (ii A.D.), *PFay.* 129.8 (iii A.D.). 7. *bring back, restore*, πόλιν ἐκ πονηρῶν πραγμάτων Th.8.97; ἀ. ἑαυτόν Ael.*NA*13.12:—Pass., *come to oneself, recover*, μόγις δὴ τότε ἀνενειχθεὶς εἶπε (v. supr. I. 2) Hdt.1.116; ἄφωνος ἐγένετο, ἔπειτα πάλιν ἀνηνέχθη Theopomp.Com.66:—so, b. intr. in Act., *come to oneself, recover*, τῷ πόματι ἀνέφερον (sc. ἑαυτούς) Hdt.3.22, cf. Hp.*Aph.*2.43, D.16.31; ἐκ τραύματος D.H.4.67; ἐξ ὕπνων Plu. *Cam.*23; ἀνέφερέ τις ἐλπὶς ἀμυδρά *revived*, Id.*Alc.*38; ἐκ τοσούτων κυμάτων ἀνενεγκών Eun.*Hist.*p.227D. 8. *bring into account*, εἰς τὸ κοινόν D.41.8, cf. 11, Philonid.1D.; πρὸς ἣν [ἀρχὴν] αἱ πρόσοδοι ἀναφέρονται Arist.*Pol.*1321ᵇ32. 9. *pay over*, εἰς τὸ βασιλικόν *PHib.*50.2, cf. 42.5. 10. *call to mind, consider*, Pl.*Lg.*829e: also c. gen., App.*Pun.*93,112. 11. *repeat*, Pl.*Ti.*26a. 12. *recall a likeness*, ἀ. πρὸς ἀνδριάντα τὴν ὁμοιότητα τῆς ἰδέας Plu.*Brut.*1, cf. 2.53d.

**ἀνα-φεύγω**, *flee up*, X.*An.*6.4.24, Plu.*Crass.*29, al.: c. acc., *fly to*, Philostr.*VA*1.24. 2. *escape*, X.*HG*6.5.40, cf. 2.3.50: metaph., *retreat*, εἰς τὴν ἀνείδεον φύσιν Plot.6.7.28. 3. of a rumour, *to be lost* in tracing, Plu.*Aem.*25. **-φευκτικός**, ή, όν, *given to flight*, Str.15.1.29. **-φευξις**, εως, ἡ, *fleeing away*, D.C.75.6.

**ἀναφήριτον**· ἄμαχον, Hsch.

**ἀναφής**, ές, (ἁφή) *impalpable*, Pl.*Phdr.*247c, Epicur.*Ep.*1 p.6 U., Plu.2.721c, etc.; ἀρεταί Ph.1.689. Adv. -φῶς Iamb.*Myst.*3.31, 5.4, Procl.*in Cra.*p.37 P., Dam.*Pr.*339. II. of wine, *tasteless, insipid*, Plu.2.650b (al. ἀβαφής).

**ἀνα-φθέγγομαι**, *call out aloud*, Ph.1.74, al., Plu.*Thes.*24, *Caes.*46, etc.: c. acc., Plb.18.5.6; λόγιον Ph.2.177. **-φθεγμα**, ατος, τό, *utterance*, Phld.*D.*3.14 (pl.), Ph.1.661. **-φθεγξις**, εως, ἡ, *mode of utterance*, λύπη καὶ φόβος ἰδίας ἀναφθέγξεις ἔχουσιν ib.618, cf. Diog. Oen.10.

***ἀναφθείρομαι**, Pass., κατὰ τί δεῦρ' ἀνεφθάρης; *by what ill luck came* you hither? Ar.*Av.*916, cf. Cratin.13D.; cf. φθείρω. II. *to be frustrated*, *PTeb.*24.32.

**ἀναφλᾶ**· λάχανον φέρει ἄνθος, ὡς ἡ μαλάχη καὶ τὸ ἄνηθον, Hsch.

**ἀνα-φλασμός**, ὁ, *masturbation*, Eup.61. ***-φλάω**, *masturbari*, Luc.*Peregr.*17: pf. part. Pass. -πεφλασμένος Ar.*Lys.*1099

**ἀναφλεγμαίνω**, *inflame*, Plu.*Ant.*82, cf. Gal.18(1).73.

**ἀνα-φλέγω**, *light up, rekindle*, E.*Tr.*320 (lyr.). II. *inflame*, ἐπιθυμίαν Ph.2.48; ἔρωτα Plu.*Alc.*17:—Pass., *to be inflamed with anger*, Pl.*Ep.*349a; ἐξ ὑποψίας Conon 23.1; *to be inflamed*, Ἔρωτος τραῦμα *AP*12.80 (Mel.); *to be excited*, ὑπ' ὀργῆς Plu.2.798f; ὑπὸ λιμοῦ Ael.*NA*15.2; ἀ. τὴν ψυχήν Plu.*Dio*4; δίψος ἀναφλέγεται Id.*Ant.*47, etc.; διανοίας ὑπὸ φιλοτιμίας ἀναφλεγομένης Jul.*Or.*2.83c. **-φλεξις**, εως, ἡ, *lighting up*, Plu.*Lys.*12.

**ἀναφλογίζω**, = ἀναφλέγω, Call.*Epigr.inc.*2, *AP*12.127 (Mel.).

**ἀναφλύω**, *bubble, boil up*, ἀνὰ δ' ἔφλυε καλὰ ῥέεθρα Il.21.361: also in Prose, *PHolm.*25.26.

**ἀναφοβέω**, *frighten away*, Ar.*V.*670.

**ἀναφοιβάσας**· ἀνακαθάρας, Hsch.

**ἀναφοινίσσω**, in Pass., *blush, redden*, Lib.*Ep.*225.

**ἀναφοιτάω**, *go back*, Nic.*Th.*138.

***ἀναφορ-ά**, ἡ, (ἀναφέρομαι) *coming up, rising*, ἀ. ποιεῖσθαι *rise*, Arist.*HA*622ᵇ7; of vapours or exhalations, *Placit.*3.7.4, *Theol.Ar.* 31, cf. Orib.9.16.3, etc. 2. Astron., *ascent* of a sign measured in degrees of the equator, Ptol.*Tetr.*134. b. Astrol., = ἐπα-ναφορά, τόπος next to a κέντρον, Vett.Val.19.18. c. *ascendant*, *Cat.Cod.Astr.*8(3).100; opp. ἀπόκλιμα, Serapion in *Cat.Cod.Astr.* 1.99, S.E.*M.*5.20, etc. d. *rising* of a sign, Ach.Tat.*Intr.Arat.* 39. II. (ἀναφέρω) *carrying back, reference* of a thing *to a standard*, διὰ τὸ γίνεσθαι ἐπαίνους δι' ἀναφορᾶς Arist.*EN*1101ᵇ20; in Law, *recourse*, ἐκείνοις εἶναι εἰς τοὺς ἔχοντας ἀναφοράν D.24.13: abs., Thphr. *Char.*8.5 (pl.), *IG*5(1).1390.111 (Andania, i B.C.); ἡ ἀ. ἐστι πρός τι Arist.*Cat.*5ᵇ20, al.; ἀ. ἔχειν πρός or ἐπί τι to be *referable* to.., Epicur. *Fr.*409, Plb.4.28.3, Plu.2.290e, al.; ἀ. τινος γίγνεται πρός or ἐπί τι, Plb.1.3.4, Plu.2.1071a; ἐπ' ἀναφορᾷ τῇ πρὸς τὸν δῆμον *BCH*46.312 (Teos); ἀ. ἔχειν ἐπί τι, of writings, *refer to*, Alex.Aphr.*in Mete.*4.1; τούτων εἰς Κυναίγειρον ποιήσασθαι τὴν ἀναφοράν *assign to, give credit for* .., Polem.*Call.*23. 2. *way of retreat*, ὑπέλιπε ἑαυτῷ ἀναφοράν D.18. 219; νῦν δὲ αὐτοῖς μὲν κατέλιπον τὴν εἰς τὸ ἀφανὲς ἀναφοράν Aeschin. 2.104, cf. Plb.15.8.13, etc. 3. *means of repairing* a fault, defeat, etc., ἀλλ' ἔστιν ἡμῖν ἀ. τῆς ξυμφορᾶς E.*Or.*414; ἀ. ἁμαρτήματος ἔχειν *way to atone for..*, Plu.*Phoc.*2; ἀ. ἔχειν *means of recovery*, Id.*Fab.* 14. 4. *offering*, Lxx *Ps.*50(51).21; ἡ ἀ. τοῦ πνεύματος τοῦ λεκτικοῦ *PMag.Par.*2.281. 5. *report*, *PLond.*1.17.34 (ii B.C.), etc. 6. *petition*, *PRyl.*119.28 (i A.D.). 7. *payment on account, instalment*, *OGI*225 (Milet.), *PEleph.*14.26 (iii B.C.), *PRev.Laws*16.10 (iii B.C.), etc. 8. Rhet., *repetition* of a word, Longin.20.1, Demetr.*Eloc.* 141. 9. *office of* ἀναφορεύς, Lxx *Nu.*4.6,10. 10. Medic., = ἀνάδοσις, opp. πέψις, Aret.*SD*2.7. III. *ceiling* of a wine-press, *Gp.*6.1.3. ***-εύς**, ὁ, *bearer, bearing-pole*, Lxx *Ex.*25.12(13) sq., al. II. = τελαμών, Eust.243.31. ***-έω**, = ἀναφέρω I, but used in a frequentat. sense, Hdt.3.102,111, Th.4.115. **-ητικός**, ή, όν, = sq. II, of consumption with empyema, Cael.Aur.*TP*2.18. ***-ικός**, ή, όν, *standing in relation*: in Gramm., *relative*. Adv. -κῶς *relatively*, A.D.*Pron.*5.20, al., D.T.636.12; *with a reference*, Stob.2.6.6, Gal.

18(1).504. II. Medic., *bringing up blood, phlegm*, Dsc.2.171, cf. *Eup.*2.39, Androm.ap.Gal.13.31. III. ἀναφορικόν, τό, treatise by Hypsicles *on the ascension* of stars; ἀ. πραγματεῖαι Ptol.*Alm.* 8.6. **-ιον**, τό, Dim. of ἀναφορά, *petition, proposal*, etc., *BGU* 1123.3, *POxy.*294.13, etc.

**ἀναφορμίζομαι**, *play a prelude*, Apollon.*Lex.* s. v. ἀνεβάλλετο.

**ἀνάφορον**, τό, = ἀναφορεύς 1, Ar.*Ra.*8, *Ec.*833, *Fr.*559, cf. Phryn. *PS*p.15B.

**ἀναφορύσσω**, Ion. for ἀναφυράω, Hp.*Mul.*1.53, 2.205, al.

**ἀναφράζω**, *relate, describe*, Eun.*Hist.*p.223D.; Med., *to be aware of*, οὐλὴν ἀμφράσσαιτο Od.19.391.

**ἀναφράσσω** or **-φράγνῦμι**, *barricade again, block up*, τὰς παρόδους dub. l. in Str.4.3.5, cf. J.*AJ*15.7.10:—Pass., Lxx *Ne.*4.7; λιμένες ἀνεφράγνυντο Them.*Or.*7.91d. II. *remove barriers*, Hsch.

❋**ἀναφρίζω**, *cover with foam*, Phryn.*PS*p.46B.

**ἀναφρίσσω**, *bristle up*, ἀκάνθαις *with..*, Opp.*H.*4.599; of hair, Poll.2.25.

**ἀναφροδῑ-σία**, ἡ, *want of power to inspire love, lack of charm*, Philostr.*VA*8.7, Jul.*Mis.*367b. II. *insensibility to love*, Gell. 19.9.9. **-τος**, ον, *without* Ἀφροδίτη, *not enjoying her favours*, Plu. 2.751e, etc.; ἀ. εἰς τὰ ἐρωτικά *unlucky* in.., Luc.*DDeor.*15.2; *loveless*, μίξεις D.Chr.7.133. 2. *insensible to love*, Plu.2.57d, Jul.*Mis.* 347c. 3. *without charms*, Plu.*Ant.*4, Gell.1.5.3, etc.

**ἀνα-φρονέω**, *come back to one's senses*, X.*An.*4.8.21, D.C.60.14; ἀναφρονέων· ἀναλογιζόμενος, Hsch. **-φροντίζω**, *think over*, c. inf., ἀ. γάμον σχεθέμεν *meditate how* to get, Pi.*O.*1.69.

**ἄναφρος**, ον, *without froth*, διαχωρήματα Hp.*Hum.*4; αἷμα Aret. *SA*2.2.

**ἀναφρύγω** [ῡ], aor. 2 inf. Pass. -φρυγῆναι, *dry up*, Lyd.*Ost.*14.

**ἀναφῠγή**, ἡ, (ἀναφεύγω) *escape, release from*, ἀναφυγὰς κακῶν A.*Ch.* 943. II. *place of retreat*, Plu.*Aem.*16. III. *withdrawal, retraction*, μήτρας Sor.2.26.

**ἀναφύησις**, εως, ἡ, *springing up, growth*, Sor.1.87.

**ἀναφῠλάσσω**, *guard*, prob. in *Epic.Alex.Adesp.*9.2.19.

❋**ἀνάφυξις**, εως, ἡ, = ἀναφυγή, ἀ. κακῶν Pl.*Lg.*713e.

**ἀνα-φῡράω**, *mix up well*, Hp.*Mul.*2.157, Thphr.*Od.*25; τέφραν μετ' οἴνου ἀ. *IG*14.966.8. **-φύρω** [ῡ], *mix up, confound*, τινάς τισι Them.*Or.*21.260c:—Pass., ἀναμὶξ ἦν πάντα ὁμοίως ἀναπεφυρμένα Hdt.1.103, cf. Epicur.*Fr.*250, Metrod.1. 2. *defile*, μάστιξι καὶ αἵματι ἀναπεφυρμένος Hdt.3.157, cf. E.*Ba.*742.

❋**ἀναφῡσ-άω**, *blow away*, κέλυφος Hp.*Mul.*1.78; *blow up* or *forth, eject*, ἀποσπάσματα ἀ., of volcanoes, Pl.*Phd.*113b:—Pass., *to be blown upwards*, Arist.*Mete.*367$^{a}$16. 2. abs., of the elephant going through water, μυκτῆρι ἀ. *blows upward*, Id.*HA*497$^{b}$30; of whales, Id.*PA*669$^{a}$7; of Tritons, Philostr.*Im.*1.25. 3. *spray, sprinkle*, οἴνῳ καὶ ἐλαίῳ *Hippiatr.*10. II. metaph. in Pass., *to be puffed up, arrogant*, X.*Cyr.*7.2.23, *HG*7.1.24. III. *blow the flute*, Ath.8.351e; κύκνοι -ῶντες ἡδύ Philostr.*Im.*1.11. **-ημα**, ατος, τό, *upward blast, eruption* of wind or fire, as in volcanoes, Arist.*Mete.* 367$^{a}$15, *Mu.*395$^{a}$8, cf. Plb.34.11.17, Ps.-Luc.*Philopatr.*3. II. Medic., *powder for inflation*, *Hippiatr.*98. ❋**-ησις**, εως, ἡ, *upward blast*, of volcanoes, Arist.*Mu.*395$^{b}$21, Plb.34.11.17. II. *prelude* in flute-playing, Hsch. s. v. γρόνθων, Eust.1406.50. III. *blowing* a powder *into* the nostrils, *Hippiatr.*98. ❋**-ητός**, ή, όν, *blown up, into*, or *upon*, Eust.1139.58. **-ιάω**, *fetch a deep-drawn breath, blow*, of a dolphin, Hes.*Sc.*211; ἀ. ἆσθμα A.R.2.431.

**ἀνάφῠσις**, εως, ἡ, *growing again*, κεράτων Ael.*NA*12.18.

**ἀναφύσσω**, *draw water*: aor. ἀνήφῠσα Nonn.*D.*43.31.

**ἀναφῠτεύω**, *plant* or *sow again*, Arist.*Mir.*838$^{b}$29.

❋**ἀναφύω**, aor. Pass. ἀνεφύην Lxx 1*Ki.*5.6, part. -φυείς Chor. in *Rev. Phil.*1.75:—*produce again*, ὅμοια κέρατα Arist.*HA*611$^{b}$1; πτιλὰ νεαρά Ael.*NA*12.4; generally, *let grow*, πώγωνα Theoc.10.40; *foster*, ὄφιν A.R.2.1209; πλῆθος συκοφαντῶν, ἐπιθυμίας, Plu.*Arist.*26, *Arat.*49, etc. 2. abs., *produce* vegetation, Arist.*Fr.*252. II. Pass., with aor. 2 -έφυν and pf. -πέφυκα, *grow up*, Pherecyd.22(a)J., Hdt. 4.58, Pl.*Plt.*272a, etc.; ἢν γὰρ ἀποθάνῃ εἷς τις πονηρός, δύ' ἀνέφυσαν ῥήτορες Pl.Com.186; ἀναφύονταί τινι διαβολαί, δίκαι, Plu.*Thes.*17, *Per.*37. 2. *grow again*, of the hair, Hdt.5.35. 3. metaph., *recover, make a fresh start*, Aeschin.2.177. III. intr. in pres. -φύει, Phlp.*in de An.*195.12.

❋**ἀναφων-έω**, *call aloud, shout*, Plb.3.33.4, Lxx 1*Ch.*15.28, al., *Ev. Luc.*1.42; *exercise the voice*, Aret.*CD*1.3: esp. *practise the voice* by declaiming, Plu.2.130c; τὰ πρός τι ἀναπεφωνημένα *declamations upon..*, ib.30e. 2. *proclaim*, βασιλέα Id.*Demetr.*18: c. dat., *decree*, τοῦ ἀναπεφωνημένου Νουμηνίῳ στεφάνου *PFay.*14.2. 3. ἀ. τὴν ἐλευθερίαν *claim* liberty, Artem.1.58, cf. Plu.*Cic.*27. 4. of poetic *utterance*, Arist.*Mu.*400$^{a}$18, Plu.*Cor.*32; of any *utterance*, c. acc., Epicur.*Ep.*1p.24U., cf. p.27U. 5. *invoke*, in Pass., Dam. *Pr.*125 (quater). **-ή**, ἡ, *crying aloud*, Anon.*in Rh.*190.22. **-ημα**, ατος, τό, *acclamation, salutation*, Plu.*Pomp.*13, etc. 2. *exclamation*, Id.*Mar.*19. 3. *interjection*, Heph.*Poëm.*5.3. **-ησις**, εως, ἡ, *vocal exercise*, Sor.1.49, Plu.2.1071c, Aret.*CD*2.7,13. II. *ejaculation*, Plu.*Brut.*24; *utterance*, τὰς πρώτας τῶν ὀνομάτων ἀ. Demetr.Lac.*Herc.*1012.70; τὴν τῆς τέχνης ἀ. *appellation*, Phld.*Rh.*1. 75S. III. αἱ ἀ., title of work by Epicurus, Id.*Ir.*p.89W. **-ητής**, οῦ, ὁ, = *nomenclator*, Lyd.*Mag.*3.8. ❋**-ητικῶς**, Adv. *as an exclamation*, Eust.1044.53.

❋**ἀναχάζω**, *make to recoil, force back*, found only in poet. aor. 1, οὐδ' ἀνέχασσαν prob. in Pi.*N.*10.69. II. mostly as Pass., **ἀναχάζομαι**, Ep. aor. ἀνεχασσάμην:—*draw back*, freq. in Il. of warriors, ἀλλ' ἀναχασσάμενος λίθον εἵλετο 7.264, cf. 15.728, 16.819, 17.47, etc.; ἀναχασσάμενος νῆχον πάλιν *giving way to* the wave, Od.7.280: c. gen. ἀ. ἠπείροιο *draw back from..*, A.R.4.1241; ἐπὶ πόδα ἀναχάζεσθαι *retire* slowly, of soldiers, X.*Cyr.*7.1.34:—Act. in sense of Pass., Id. *An.*4.1.16.

**ἀναχαίνω**, v. ἀναχάσκω.

❋**ἀναχαιτ-ίζω**, (χαίτη) of a horse, *throw the mane back, rear up*, ἀ. φόβῳ E.*Rh.*786; κόμην ἀ. Hld.2.36: metaph. of men, *become restive*, S.*Fr.*179, Plu.*Demetr.*34; θάλαττα ἀναχαιτίζουσα a *turbulent* sea, Philostr.*Im.*2.17. 2. c. acc., *throw* a rider, φυλάσσων μὴ ἀναχαιτίσειέ νιν, of a branch, E.*Ba.*1072: metaph., *overthrow, upset*, ἔσφηλε κἀνεχαίτισεν Id.*Hipp.*1232, cf. Tim.*Pers.*18; ἀνεχαίτισε καὶ διέλυσε D.2.9; ἀνακεχαίτικεν [ἡμᾶς], of wine, Anaxandr.3; βίος -ισμένος Epicur.*Sent.Vat.*57. 3. c. gen., ἀ. τῶν πραγμάτων *shake off the yoke of, retire from* business, Plu.*Ant.*21; ἀ. ἐκ.. 2.611f (cj.). b. *lose, be disappointed of*, ἑνὸς δὲ..οὐκ ἀνεχαιτίσθην τῆς φιλίας one [sage] did not *disappoint* me, Harp.Astr. in *Cat.Cod.Astr.* 8(3).136.9 (s.v.l.). II. *hold back by the hair*: hence generally, *check*, τοῦ δρόμου τὸ ῥόθιον Luc.*Lex.*15, cf. Procop.*Goth.*4.18; *restrain*, ἐπιδρομάς Id.*Aed.*2.11; πόλεμον Memn.51; ἀ. [τὸ θυμικὸν] τῆς ἀλόγου ὁρμῆς Alex.Aphr.*in Top.*372.17. **-ισις**, εως, ἡ, *restraint*, Jo.Sic. in Rh.6.235W.; τῆς τάσεως τῆς φωνῆς Anon.*in Rh.* 197.20. **-ισμα**, ατος, τό, = foreg., dub. l. in Plu.2.611f:—also **-ισμός**, ὁ, = foreg., Lyd.*Mag.*2.15, 3.52.

**ἀναχᾰλ-ασμός**, ὁ, *relaxation*, πνεύματος *Placit.*5.24.4, cf. *Stoic.*2. 215. **-αστικός**, ή, όν, *relaxing*, ὑστέρας Dsc.1.128. **-άω**, poet. **ἀγχ-**, *relax*, in Pass., *Placit.*5.26.1, Plb.6.23.11, cf. Gal.19.537, Aspasia ap.Aët.16.22. 2. *ease*, [νῆα] ἀγχαλάσας A.R.2.585.

**ἀναχαλινόω**, gloss on ἀναχαιτίζω, Hsch., Suid.

**ἀναχαλκεύω**, *forge anew*, τὰς πύλας Ps.-Callisth.3.29.

**ἀναχάρ-ᾰγή**, ἡ, *scraping up*, Apollod.*Poliorc.*47.27. **-αξις**, εως, ἡ, = foreg., τῆς λεπίδος Plu.2.979c. **-άσσω**, Att. **-ττω**, *scrape up*, ib.913e; ἀὴρ ἀναχαράσσει ἰόν air *causes the roughness of* rust, ib.396a, cf. 454c.

❋**ἀναχάσκω**, only pres. and impf., Ar.*Av.*502, *Fr.*68, Luc.*VH*2.1; poet. ἄγχασκε Pherecr.196:—other tenses from pres. *ἀναχαίνω, fut. -χᾰνοῦμαι Hp.*Superf.*29: aor. 2 ἀνέχᾰνον: pf. ἀνακέχηνα:—*open the mouth, gape wide*, ἀναχανὼν μέγα Ar.*Eq.*641; στόμα ἀνακεχηνός Hp.*Nat.Mul.*45.

**ἀναχαυνόω**· ἀναλύω, Suid. 2. Pass., *to be puffed up*, Arist.*VV* 1251$^{b}$18.

**ἀναχειοῖ**· οἰκειοῦται, Hsch.

**ἀναχειρίζομαι**, *delay, hinder*, D.C.38.13.

**ἀναχελύσσομαι**, *cough up*, Hp.ap.Sch.Nic.*Al.*81; expl. as = ἀναπνεῖ, Erot.

❋**ἀναχέω**, *pour forth*, ποταμούς Ph.1.50; *cause to overflow*, θάλασσαν Opp.*H.*2.33:—Pass., *to be poured out*, Anacr.42; of floods, Max. Tyr. 8.7; *to be spread over a wide space*, Arist.*Pr.*944$^{a}$27, *Mu.*393$^{a}$20, Arr.*An.*6.18.5: metaph., of a rumour, Plu.*Aem.*24. 2. metaph., *relax*, ἡ χάρις ἀναχεῖ τὴν ψυχήν Ph.1.104; ἡ γνῶσις ἀναχεῖται εἰς ἀγνωσίαν *is dissipated, dissolved*, Dam.*Fr.*29. 3. Med., aor. ἀναχέασθαι *anoint oneself*, Gal.*Thras.*46. II. = ἀναχώννυμι, Orph.*A.*568 (tm.), cf. 724.

**ἀναχλαινόω**, *clothe with a mantle*, Nonn.*D.*11.232.

**ἀναχλιαίνω**, *warm up*, Hp.*Nat.Mul.* 56, Arist.*Pr.*889$^{a}$8:—Pass., ib.930$^{b}$18.

**ἀναχλίζω**, *warm up*: metaph., *refurbish*, cj. in Phlp.*in de An.* 455.29 (codd. ἂν χλίζεσθαι).

**ἀναχνοαίνομαι**, (χνοῦς) *get the first down*, Ar.*Ach.*791.

**ἀναχοή**, ἡ, (ἀναχέω) *eruption*, Αἴτνης Longin.35.4; ἀναχοαί· πόροι, Hsch.

**ἀναχορεύω**, *begin a choral dance*, Ar.*Th.*994: and c. acc. cogn., ἀ. θίασον, ὄργια, E.*Ph.*1756, *Ba.*482, al. 2. *celebrate in the chorus*, Βάκχιον ib.1153. 3. οὐκ ἄν με..ἀνεχόρευ' Ἐρινύσι *would* not *have scared* me *away by a band* of Furies, Id.*Or.*582. II. intr., *dance for joy*, ἀνεχόρευσεν αἰθήρ Id.*Ion* 1079.

**ἀναχόω**, ἀναχώννυμι, Luc.*Lex.*2 (in dat. pl. of part. ἀναχοῦσι).

**ἀναχράομαι**, *use up*, and so, *make away with, destroy*, v.l. in Th.3. 81, cf. D.C.51.8; οἱ ἑαυτοὺς -χρώμενοι 58.16. 2. *use*, *IG*5(1).1390. 60 (Andania, i B.C.).

**ἀναχρέμ-πτομαι**, *cough up*, D.L.2.75:—Act. in Suid., Zonar. **-ψις**, εως, ἡ, *coughing up*, Hp.*Prorrh.*1.6, Aret.*SA*2.2, etc.

**ἀναχρίω**, *anoint*, Dsc.*Eup.*1.35.

**ἀναχρον-ίζομαι**, Pass., *to be an anachronism*, Sch.E.*Hipp.*231, *Ph.*854, Eust.1404.29:—Act. c. part., *to be late in doing*, ἀ. πέμποντες ἐπιστόλια *PTeb.*413.14 (ii/iii A.D.). **-ισμός**, ὁ, *anachronism*, Sch. A.*Pr.*846. 2. *exchange of the quantity* of two syllables, Eust. 1704.8.

**ἀνα-χρῡσόω**, *regild*, *Ostr.*156, al. **-χρώννῡμι**, *colour anew, discolour*, Plu.2.930f:—Pass., v.l. in Thphr.*Sud.*12: metaph., *to be defiled with*, πολλαῖς γυναιξίν Eust.122.26. **-χρωσις**, εως, ἡ, *discolouring*; *taint, infection*, Plu.2.53c.

**ἀνάχυλις**, εως, ἡ, = σύμφυτον, Ps.-Dsc.4.9 (dub., cf. ἀνάχυσις III).

**ἀνάχῠμα**, ατος, τό, *expanse*, ἀ. αἰθέριον Nicom.*Harm.*3. II. = ἀνάχυσις II, Str.*Chr.*7.45.

**ἀναχύρωτος** [ῠ], ον, *without chaff* or *husks*, Ar.*Fr.*56.

**ἀνάχῠσις**, εως, ἡ, (ἀναχέω) *expansion, effusion*, χολῆς Aret.*SD*1.15; ἰκτεριώδης Sor.1.48, cf. Ruf.*Fr.*79.9; πύου Erasistr.ap.Gal.8.318;

ὧν εἰδῶν εἰς τὸ ὄν Simp. *in Ph.* 503.32: metaph., ἀ. ψυχῆς *exhilaration*, Ph.2.187. b. *exhalation*, τοῦ ὠκεανοῦ (causing fogs) Prisc. p.341 D. 2. ἡ τῆς ἀσωτίας ἀ. *excess* of profligacy, 1*Ep.Pet.* 4.4; τοῦ ἀλόγου πάθους Ph.1.695; of enthusiasm, Metrod.*Herc.* 831.13. II. *expanse* of water, e.g. *estuary*, Str.3.1.9: pl., ἀ. θαλάττης *inundations*, Max.Tyr.38.3; ἀνάχυσιν λαμβανούσης τῆς θαλάσσης Ocell.3.4. III. an expectorant, = σύμφυτον, Ps.-Dsc.4.9.

**ἀνά-χωμα**, ατος, τό, *dike, dam*, Aristeas 301, Harp. s.v. ἄνδηρα; cf. ἀνάχωσμα. **-χωματίζω**, *throw up a mound*, Eust.652.30. **-χωμᾰτισμός**, ὁ, *the throwing up a mound*, Sch.A.*Pers.* 646, *BGU* 199, etc.

**ἀναχών-ευσις**, εως, ἡ, *melting down*, εἰκόνων *Ephes.* 2 No.23. **-εύω**, *smelt over again*, Str.9.1.23, cf. *PHolm.* 2.8, *PLeid.X.* 6.

**ἀνα-χώννῡμι**, *heap up into a mound*, κόνιν *AP* 7.537 (Phan.):—in Pass., v.l. Th.2.102 (for ἂν κεχῶσθαι); ἀ. ὁδόν *raise* a road *by throwing down rubbish*, D.55.28, cf. *PPetr.* 2 p.43 (Pass., iii B.C.), 3 p.111; τάφους Luc.*Tox.* 43. ⊛**-χωσις**, εως, ἡ, *raising of an embankment*, *PSI* 5.488.13 (iii B.C.).

⊛**ἀναχωρ-έω**, Locr., Cret. ἀνχ-, *go back*, πόλινδε ἂψ ἀναχωρήσουσιν Il.10.210, cf. Od.17.461. b. *walk backwards*, of oxen feeding, Hdt.4.183. 2. in Il., mostly, *retire, withdraw* from battle, ἀλλά σ' ἔγωγ' ἀναχωρήσαντα κελεύω ἐς πληθὺν ἰέναι Il.17.30; τόφρ' ἀναχωρείτω 11.189, cf. 4.305, 20.335, etc.: in Prose, μάχης οὔσης εἰς τοὐπίσω ἀ. Lys.14.6; φυγῇ ἀ. Pl.*Smp.* 221a; generally, *retire, withdraw*, μεγάροιο μυχόνδε Od.22.270; ὀπίσω ἀ. Hdt.5.94, etc.; ἐς τοὔπισθεν Ar.*Pl.* 1208; ἀνεκεχωρήκεσαν *they had retired* or *returned*, Th.8.15, cf. *IG* 9(1).334 (Locr.): with Preps. denoting motion to or from, ἐς τὴν ἀκρόπολιν Hdt.3.143; ἐπ' οἴκου Th.1.30; ὑπὸ Βοιωτῶν ἐς Ἀθήνας *were forced* by them *to retire to*.., Hdt.5.61; ἀπὸ Pl.*Smp.* l.c. II. *come back* or *revert to the rightful heir*, ἡ βασιληΐη ἀνεχώρησε ἐς τὸν παῖδα Hdt.7.4; ἡ ποινὴ ἀ. εἰς ἡμᾶς Antipho 2.1.3, cf. *Leg.Gort.* 11.10. III. metaph., *withdraw, retire*, ἐξ αἰσθήσεων Pl.*Phd.* 83a; ἀ. ἐκ τῶν πραγμάτων *retire from* public life, *from* the world, Plb.29.25.5, cf. Cic.*Att.* 9.4.2, *Ev.Matt.* 2.14, al.: abs., *withdraw, retire*, Pl.*Smp.* 175a, cf. Ar.*Nu.* 524; ἀνακεχωρηκυῖα χώρα *inland* spot, Thphr.*HP* 9.7.4; ἀ. ἀπὸ θαλάσσης Plb.2.11.16; ἀνακεχωρηκὸς ῥῆμα, ὄνομα *obsolete*, D.H.*Rh.* 10.7; *recondite*, ἱστορία Phld.*Rh.* 1.157 S. IV. = συγχωρέω, πάντες ἀνεχώρησαν συμπεραίνεσθαι τὸ μίασμα Procop.*Arc.* 10. 2. *strike, refuse to work*, *PTeb.* 26.18, 41.4, al.; ἀνακεχωρηκότα σώματα ib.56. **-ημα**, ατος, τό, *withdrawal, reflux*, θαλάσσης Arist.*Mu.* 396$^a$18. ⊛**-ησις**, εως, Ion. ιος, ἡ, *retiring, retreat*, Hdt.9.22, Th.1.12, al.; ἀ. ποιεῖσθαι, of a river, D.S.1.10; of waves, ἐπιδρομαὶ καὶ -σεις Arist.*Mu.* 400$^a$27; τοῦ ποταμοῦ *PPetr.* 2 p.45 (iii B.C.). II. *place* or *means of retreat*, Th.1.90, D.19.41. III. *return*, Pl.*Phlb.* 32b. IV. *absence*, τὰ ὄντα ἐν -ήσει *BGU* 447.6 (ii A.D.), cf. *PTeb.* 353.6 (ii A.D.); *retirement*, μετὰ φίλων -ιν εὔσχολον Phld.*Oec.* p.64 J. **-ητέον**, *one must withdraw*, Pl.*Cri.* 51b. ⊛**-ητής**, οῦ, ὁ, *one who has retired from the world, anchoret*, Just.*Nov.* 5.3 (pl.), *Rev.Épigr.* 1.159 (Egypt, vi A.D.). **-ητικός**, ή, όν, *disposed to retire*; τὸ ἀ. Arr.*Epict.* 2.1.10. **-ίζω**, *make to go back* or *retire*, X.*Cyr.* 7.1.41, *An.* 5.2.10; ἀγχωρίξαντες (Dor.) τὸν ὅρον *having drawn* it *back*, *Tab.Heracl.* 1.56, 59.

**ἀνάχωσμα**, ατος, τό, *silted mound*, Sch.Ar.*Eq.* 527.

**ἀναψᾰθάλλω**, *touch up, work up*, Phryn.*PS* p.12 B., cf. Hsch.

**ἀναψᾰλάσσω**, *tear up, open*, Lyc.343.

**ἀνα-ψάω**, *wipe up*, σταγόνας ἐρίῳ Ctes.*Fr.* 57.28; δάκρυον Dsc.4.64. 2. *clean out*, φρέαρ *PLond.* 1.131$^r$631:—Pass., aor. ἀνεψήσθην *BGU* 530.17 (i A.D.). **-ψησις**, εως, ἡ, *cleaning out*, φρέατος *PLond.* 3.1177.329 (ii A.D.). ⊛**-ψησμός**, ὁ, = foreg., λάκκου ib.1.131$^r$621 (i A.D.).

**ἀναψηλᾰφ-άω**, *retry*, in Law, Just.*Nov.* 82.11.1:—Pass., ib.113.1 *Intr.* **-ησις**, εως, ἡ, *close search*, τροφῆς Eust.254.31; *re-examination, retrial*, *Cod.Just.* 7.62.35, cf. 12.37.19, Just.*Nov.* 82.12, al.

⊛**ἀναψηφίζω**, *put to the vote again*, Th.6.14; *propose to repeal*, *SIG* 194 (Amphipolis), cf. D.C.39.39:—Med., *vote anew*, Pherecr.47. II. *reckon backwards*, εἰς τοὐπίσω Porph.*Plot.* 2.

**ἄναψις**, εως, ἡ, (ἀνάπτω) *lighting up, kindling*, D.H.2.66; of stars, ἀ. καὶ σβέσις Epicur.*Ep.* 2 p.39 U.

**ἀναψοφέω**, *make a noise*, Hsch. s.v. ἀναρραθαγῆσαι.

**ἀνα-ψυκτήρ**, ῆρος, ὁ, *refresher*, πόνων *from labours*, E.*Fr.* 146. ⊛**-ψυξις**, εως, ἡ, *cooling*, Posidon.72; *exposure*, ἕλκεος Hp.*Fract.* 25. 2. *drying up*, Str.10.2.19. 3. *relief, respite*, Lxx *Ex.* 8.15; κακῶν Jul. *ad Them.* 258c; καιροὶ -εως *Act.Ap.* 3.20. **-ψῡχή**, ἡ, *coolness*, Pl.*Lg.* 919a. 2. *relief, respite*, Id.*Smp.* 176a, *PLond.* 1.42.19 (ii B.C.); κακῶν *from* misery, E.*Supp.* 615; πόνων Id.*Ion* 1604. 3. *ventilation*, Pl.*Ti.* 84d, Arist.*Fr.* 219. ⊛**-ψύχω** [ῡ], Ep. impf. -εσκον Orph.*L.* 562:—*cool, refresh*, ἀήτας Ὠκεανὸς ἀνίησιν ἀναψύχειν ἀνθρώπους Od.4.568; ἀνέψυχον φίλον ἦτορ *were reviving* their spirit, Il.13.84; ἕλκος ἀναψύχοντα 5.795; ἀ. φίλα γούνατα Hes.*Op.* 608; ἀ. βάσιν *cool* the feet *in water*, E.*IA* 421:—Pass., *to be revived, refreshed*, ἀνέψυχθεν φίλον ἦτορ Il.10.575; of the body, Pl.*Ti.* 78e, cf. 70d; ὥστ' ἀνεψύχης [ῠ] Amips.13. 2. ναῦς ἀ. *let* the ships *rest and get dry*, Hdt.7.59, X.*HG* 1.5.10; ἀ. τὸν ἱδρῶτα *let it dry off*, Plu.*Sull.* 29; ἀ. τὰς αὐλαίας *dry* them, Id.*Them.* 30:—Pass., *to be dried up*, Str.10.2.19. 3. metaph., c. gen., ἀ. πόνων τινά *give* him *relief from* toil, E.*Hel.* 1094; πολέων.. μεριμνέων Call.*Hec.* 1.1.7; ἀ. κακότητος ψυχάς Orph.*Fr.* 230: abs., 2*Ep.Ti.* 1.16. 4. Medic., *expose* to air, κατὰ τὸ ἕλκος ἐῶσιν ἀνεψῦχθαι Hp.*Fract.* 25; cf. ἀναψύχειν· γυμνοῦν, Erot. II. the Act. is also used intr., *become cool, recover, revive*, Diph.81, *AP* 12.132 (Mel.), Opp.*H.* 5.623; εὗρεν.. δρόμων ἀναψύχουσαν [τὴν ἔλαφον] Babr.95.57; *take relaxation*, *POxy.* 1296.7 (iii A.D.).

**ἄνδα**· αὕτη (Cypr.), Hsch.

⊛**ἀνδαβάτης**, ου, ὁ, *gladiator*, Lyd.*Mag.* 1.46.

**ἄνδαιτος**, ον, = ἀνάδαστος, *SIG* 141.11 (Issa).

**ἀνδαίω**, poet. for ἀναδαίω.

⊛**ἁνδάνω** [δᾰ], impf. ἥνδανον, Ep. ἑήνδανον, in Ion. Prose ἑάνδανον Hdt.9.5 and 19 (in 7.172, 8.29, codd. give ἥνδανον): fut. ἁδήσω Id.5.39: pf. ἅδηκα Hippon.100, Locr. ϝεϝάδηκα (v. infr. II); ἔαδα A.R.1.867; part. ἑαδώς Il.9.173: aor. ἕαδον Hdt.4.201, 6.106, cf. *SIG* 57.40; Ep. εὔαδον (i.e. ἔϝαδον) Il.14.340, Od.16.28; ἅδον [ᾰ] Il.13.748; 3 sg. subj. ἅδῃ Hdt.1.133, opt. ἅδοι Od.20.327, inf. ἁδεῖν Il.3.173, S.*Ant.* 89: later, aor. 1 ἧσα Plut.2.3.7:—*please, delight, gratify*, mostly Ion. and poet., used like ἥδομαι, except as to construction: mostly c. dat. pers., Od.2.114, Pi.*P.* 1.29, Hdt.5.39: also c. dupl. dat., Ἀγαμέμνονι ἥνδανε θυμῷ Il.1.24, cf. Od.16.28; εἴ σφωϊν κραδίῃ ἅδοι 20.327; Πηνελοπείῃ ἥνδανε μύθοισι *pleased* her *with* words, 16.398:—in ἁδόντα δ' εἴη με τοῖς ἀγαθοῖς ὁμιλεῖν the dat. belongs both to the part. and to the inf., Pi.*P.* 2.96: abs., τοῖσι δὲ πᾶσιν ἑαδότα μῦθον ἔειπε Il.9.173, Od.18.422: c. acc., v. dub. in Thgn.26, E.*Or.* 1607, both prob. corrupt readings. II. in Hdt. ἁνδάνει expresses *the opinion* of a body of people, οὔ σφι ἥνδανε ταῦτα 7.172, cf. 9.5; τοῖσι τὰ ἀμείνω ἑάνδανε 9.19: c. inf., τοῖσι μὲν ἕαδε βοηθέειν Ἀθηναίοισι 6.106, cf. 4.145, 153, 201; so ἐπεί νύ τοι εὔαδεν οὕτως (sc. ποιεῖν) Il.17.647, cf. Od.2.114:—τὰ ϝεϝαδηκότα *quae placuerunt*, *IG* 9(1).334 (Locr.). III. Med., ἦν ἁνδάνηται Hp.*Mul.* 2.150; cf. τιμὴ δαίμοσιν ἁνδάνεται *AP* 10.7 (Arch.). (Cf. Skt. *svádati*, Lat. *suādeo, suāvis*, O.E. *swēte*, etc.)

**ἄνδας**· βορέας (Tyrrhen.), Hsch.

**ἀνδειράδες**, αἱ, = ἄνδηρα, *AB* 394, cf. Hsch.

⊛**ἄνδεμα, ἀνδεσμός, ἀνδέχομαι, ἀνδέω, ἄνδημα**, poet. for ἀναδ-.

⊛**ἄνδεργμα**· ὁ ἐπὶ τῆς τραγικῆς σκηνῆς παραγόμενος παράκοτος, Hsch.

**ἀνδηρευτής**, οῦ, ὁ, *workman employed on dikes*, *PRyl.* 157.15 (ii A.D.), *PFlor.* 369.9 (ii A.D.).

**ἄνδηρον**, τό, *raised bank* by the side of a river or ditch, *dike*, Mosch.4.102: mostly in pl., ἄνδηρα, τά, Hyp.*Fr.* 113, Lyc.629; Πακτωλοῦ χρυσέοισιν ἐπ' ἀνδήροισι Call.*Fr.* 45 P., cf. *Fr.anon.* 110; τετμῆσθαι καθάπερ ἀνδήροις καὶ ὀχετοῖς Plu.2.650c, cf. Luc.*Lex.* 2. 2. *border, edge*, of the sea, dub. in B.1.54 (p.439 J.); ἀ. θαλάσσης Opp.*H.* 4.319. 3. *border* for plants or flowers, Thphr.*CP* 3.15.4, Theoc.5.93, *AP* 12.197 (Strat.), Nic.*Th.* 576. 4. = στῆθος χειρός, Poll.2.144.

⊛**ἀνδίκα**· ὁ βόλος (ἀνδικλόβολος cod.), δίκη ἡ ἐξ ὑπαρχῆς δικαζομένη παρὰ Ταραντίνοις (i.e. ἀνδίκα = ἀναδίκη), Hsch.

**ἀνδικε**· ἀνάρριψον, Hsch.; cf. ἔδικον.

⊛**ἀνδίκτης**, ου, ὁ, for ἀναδίκτης (ἀναδικεῖν), *catch of a mousetrap*, Call.*Fr.* 233.

**ἄνδινος**· περίπατος, Hsch. (ἀνδινός· περὶ παντός cod.).

**ἄνδιχα**, Adv., (ἀνά, δίχα) *asunder, in twain*, ἡ δ' [κεφαλὴ] ἄνδιχα πᾶσα κεάσθη Il.16.412; ἄνδιχα πάντα δάσασθαι 18.511; opp. ἀμμίγδην, Nic.*Th.* 912; *far away*, A.R.4.31. 2. as Prep., c. gen., *apart from*, A.R.1.908, 2.927; ἀλλήλων *AP* 5.4 (Stat. Flacc.):—hence

⊛**ἀνδιχάζω**, *to be divided in opinion*, of judges, *IG* 9(1).333 (Locr.).

**ἀνδοκάδην**· ἐκ διαδοχῆς, Hsch.

**ἀνδοκ-εία**, ἡ, = ἀναδοχή II, ἐν ἀνδοκείᾳ Ζωτικοῦ *guaranteed by* Zoticus, *IG* 14.423 ii 19: pl., ib.422 iii (Tauromenium). **-εύς**· ἀνάδοχος, Hsch. **-ιάρχης**, ου, ὁ, *officer in charge of* ἀνδοκεῖαι, *IG* 14.2417.1.

**ἀνδραγαθ-έω**, pf. ἠνδραγάθηκα D.S.11.25: aor. -ησα Plb.6.39.2: (ἀνήρ, ἀγαθός):—later form of ἀνδραγαθίζομαι, *behave in a manly, upright manner*, Id.1.45.3, al., *SIG* 785.14 (Chios), *BGU* 1207.11 (i B.C.), Onos.34.2:—Pass., ἠνδραγαθημένα, opp. ἡμαρτημένα, Plu.*Fab.* 20. **-ημα**, ατος, τό, *brave, manly deed*, Str.1.2.8, Plu.*Sert.* 10, *IG* 14.951, Jul.*Caes.* 329c, etc. **-ησις**, εως, ἡ, = sq., Lxx 1 *Ma.* 5.56. ⊛**-ία**, Ion. -ίη, ἡ, *bravery, manly virtue*, Hdt.1.99, 136, al., Th.2.42; *the character of an upright man*, Ar.*Pl.* 191, Phryn.Com.1; ἀνδραγαθίας ἕνεκα στεφανοῦσθαι Hyp.*Lyc.* 6. **-ίζομαι**, aor. ἀνδραγαθίσασθαι App.*BC* 5.101:—*act uprightly*, εἴ τις ἀπραγμοσύνῃ -ίζεται if any one thinks to sit at home and *play the honest man*, Th.2.63; ἐκ τοῦ ἀκινδύνου ἀ. Id.3.40, cf. Arist.*VV* 1250$^b$4. **-ικός**, ή, όν, *befitting a good man*, Hp.*Art.* 78 (Comp.).

**ἀνδρ-άγρια**, τά, *spoils of a slain enemy*, Il.14.509. **-αγχος**, ὁ, *throttler of men*: *executioner*, Eust.1833.54, 1858.57: ἄνδραχοι· δήμιος Hsch. ⊛**-άδελφος**, ὁ, *husband's brother, brother-in-law*, Suid.:—fem. ⊛**-αδέλφη**, ἡ, *husband's sister*, Eust.392.2. **-ᾰκάς** (A), Adv. *man by man*, Od.13.14, Cratin.19, cf. Plu.2.151e; ἀ. καθήμενος *apart*, A.*Ag.* 1595, cf. Hsch. (-κάς perh. cognate with Skt. -*śás* in *dviśás* 'two by two', etc.) ⊛**-ᾰκάς** (B), άδος, ἡ, *a man's portion*, Nic.*Th.* 643. **-αλογία**, ἡ, v. ἀνδρολογία.

**ἀνδραπόδ-εσσι**, v. ἀνδράποδον. **-ητοι**· οἱ σὺν ἀνδραπόδοις ἀποδημοῦντες, Hsch. **-ίζω**, pres. Act. first in Alciphr.3.40: Att. fut. -ιῶ X.*HG* 2.2.20: aor. ἠνδραπόδισα Hdt., Th.:—Med., fut. ἀνδραποδιεῦμαι in pass. sense, Hdt.6.17:—Pass., fut. ἀνδραποδισθήσομαι X.*HG* 2.2.14: aor. ἠνδραποδίσθην Lys.2.57: pf. ἠνδραπόδισμαι Isoc.17.14, part. ἀνδραποδισμένος Hdt.6.119: (ἀνδράποδον):—Prose Verb, *enslave*, esp. of conquerors, *sell the free men* of a conquered place *into slavery*, Hdt.1.151, Th.1.98; παῖδας καὶ γυναῖκας Id.3.36; πόλιν 6.62:—Pass., *to be sold into slavery*, Hdt.6.106, 119, 8.29, X.*HG* 1.6.14, etc.; πόλις ὑπὸ τῶν βαρβάρων ἠνδραποδίσθη Lys. l.c.:—Med. also in act. sense, Hdt.1.76, al., Th.4.48, And.3.22, etc. II. less freq. of individuals, *kidnap*, Pl.*Grg.* 508e, X.*Mem.* 4.2.14, *Smp.* 4.36. III. metaph., -ίζοντες ἀπὸ τοῦ φρονεῖν τοὺς νέους Alciphr.3.40. **-ιον**, τό, Dim. of ἀνδράποδον, Hyp.*Fr.*227, Diph.80, *POxy.*1102.15 (ii A.D.). **-ισις**, εως, ἡ, = sq., X.*Ap.*25. **-ισμός**, ὁ, *selling into slavery, enslaving*, Th.2.68, Isoc.4.100, etc.; πατρίδος D.1.5. **II.** of individuals, *kidnapping*, whether of free men or other people's slaves, ὑπόδικος -ισμοῦ liable to action *for kidnapping*, Pl.*Lg.*879a, 955a. **-ιστήριος**, α, ον, *fitted for enslaving*, Tz.ad Lyc.784. **-ιστής**, οῦ, ὁ, *slave-dealer* or *kidnapper*, Ar.*Eq.*1030, *Pl.*521, Lys.10.10, etc., cf. Poll.3.78; coupled with ἱερόσυλοι, τοιχωρύχοι, etc., Pl.*R.*344b: metaph., ἀ. ἑαυτοῦ *one who sells* his own *independence*, X.*Mem.*1.2.6. **-ιστικός**, ή, όν, = -ιστήριος: ἡ -κή (sc. τέχνη) *man-stealing, kidnapping*, Pl.*Sph.*222c. Adv., Sup. -ιστικώτατα Eup.396.

**ἀνδρᾰποδο-κάπηλος**, ὁ, *slave-dealer*, Is.*Fr.*53 S., Luc.*Ind.*24, Gal. *UP*1.9. **-κλέπτης**, ου, ὁ, *slave-stealer*, Men.23 D. **-κλόπος**, ὁ, = foreg., *Fr.*1011.

**✱ἀνδράποδον** [δρᾰ], τό, *one taken in war and sold as a slave*, whether originally slave or free, *captive*, Hdt.3.125, 129, 5.31, etc.: orig. dist. from δοῦλος, ὅσοι δὲ ἦσαν ξεῖνοί τε καὶ δοῦλοι.. ἐν ἀνδραπόδων λόγῳ ποιεύμενος εἶχε Id.3.125; τὰ ἀ. πάντα, καὶ δοῦλα καὶ ἐλεύθερα Th.8.28; τὰ ἀ. τὰ δοῦλα πάντα ἀπέδοτο X.*HG*1.6.15. **II.** *low fellow*, 'creature', Pl.*Grg.*483b, *Thg.*130b, X.*Mem.*4.2.39, D.Chr.31.109; of a female slave, Pherecr.16 D. **III.** as a playful mode of address, Arr.*Epict.*1.4.14, al.—Hom., Il.7.475, has Ep. dat. pl. ἀνδραπόδεσσι (as if from ἀνδράπους), where Aristarch. proposed to read ἀνδραπόδοισι; but it is almost certain that the word was post-Homeric, and the line was rejected on that account by Zenod. and Ar. Byz. (Orig. pl.; formed on the analogy of τετράποδα, cf. τετραπόδων πάντων καὶ ἀνδραπόδων *Foed.Delph.Pell.*1 *B*7. Sg. in X.*Ath.*1.18, etc.)

**ἀνδραποδ-ώδης**, ες, *slavish, servile, abject*, opp. ἐλευθέριος, Arist. *EN*1128$^{a}$21; ἀρετή Pl.*Phd.*69b; ἄγροικος καὶ ἀνελεύθερος..ἀ. τε Id. *Lg.*880a, cf. X.*Mem.*4.2.22; θηριώδης καὶ ἀ. Pl.*R.*430b, cf. Arist. *EN*1118$^{a}$25; τεχνιτεῖαι Epicur.*Ep.*2 p.40 U.; ἀ. θρὶξ *short coarse hair like that of slaves*, hence metaph., ἔτι τὴν ἀ. τρίχα ἔχοντες ἐν τῇ ψυχῇ Pl.*Alc.*1.120b. Adv. -δῶς Id.*Smp.*215e. **-ωδία**, ἡ, *servility*, Arist.*Pol.*1336$^{b}$12, Plu.2.7b. **-ώνης**, ου, ὁ, *slave-dealer*, Ar.*Fr.*312. **-ωνία**, Ion. -ίη, ἡ, *tax on sale of slaves*, *SIG*4.8 (Cyzicus).

**ἀνδράριον**, τό, Dim. of ἀνήρ, *manikin, pitiful fellow*, Ar.*Ach.*517.

**ἀνδράφαξυς**, v. ἀτράφαξυς. **ἀνδραφάσσειν·** κατ' ἄνδρα ἐφάπτεσθαι, Hsch.

**ἀνδραφόνος**, ὁ, = ἀνδροφόνος, Lex Sol.ap.Phot.p.126 R.

**ἀνδραφυστεῖν·** φεύγειν, ἢ ἐπὶ φόνῳ διώκειν, Hsch.

**ἀνδραχθής**, ές, *loading a man, as much as a man can carry*, χερμάδια Od.10.121; βώλακες A.R.3.1334; γόγγροι Eudox.ap.Ath.7.288c.

**ἀνδράχλη**, ἡ, said to be Att. form for ἀνδράχνη (1), Hellad.ap.Phot. *Bibl.*p.533 B., S.*Fr.*823, but in this passage, as in Thphr.*HP*1.5.2, 1.9.3, = *Arbutus Andrachne*. **II.** *warming-pan* or *brazier*, Eust.1571.25, Poet.ap.Suid. **ἄνδραχλος**, ἡ, = ἀνδράχνη, *EM*102.36, v.l. in Thphr.*HP*4.15.2. **ἀνδράχνη**, ἡ, *purslane, Portulaca oleracea*, Id.*CP*1.10.4, al., Dsc.2.124, Luc.*Trag.*151, prob.l. in Pl. Com.44; ἀ. κηπαία Dsc.4.168. **2.** ἀ. ἀγρία, = πεπλίς, Dsc.4.168; but = *Sedum stellatum, stonecrop*, ib.90; also = τηλέφιον, Ps.-Dsc.2.186, Gal.19.146. **3.** ἀ. θαλασσία, = πεπλίς, Ps.-Dsc.4.168. **ἄνδραχνος**, ἡ, = ἀνδράχλη, Paus.9.22.2 and 28.1.

**ἀνδρεάστρια**, v. ἀνδρεράστρια.

**✱ἀνδρεία**, ἡ, Ion. -ηίη (Hdt.7.99), generally written **ἀνδρία** in the Mss., in agreement with the opinion of A.D.*Adv.*136.8, refuted by Orus ap.*EM*461.53:—ἀνδρεία is required by the metre in Ar.*Nu.*510, and *may* always stand in the few poet. passages where it occurs (Simon.58, A.*Th.*52, S.*El.*983, E.*Tr.*674): ἀνδρία is required in E. *HF*475 μέγα φρονῶν ἐπ' ἀνδρίᾳ (s.v.l., εὐανδρίᾳ Elmsley): ἀνδρεία is also confirmed by the Ion. form ἀνδρηίη:—*manliness, manly spirit*, opp. δειλία, ll. cc., cf. Arist.*Rh.*1366$^{b}$11, *EN*1115$^{a}$6; also of women, S.*El.*983, Arist.*Pol.*1260$^{a}$22; ἀνδρεία ἡ περὶ τὰς ναυτιλίας Str.3.1.8:—in pl., *brave deeds*, Pl.*Lg.*922a; ironically, αἱ διὰ τῶν λόγων ἀνδρεῖαι D.*Prooem.*45. **II.** in bad sense, *hardihood, insolence*, D. Chr.12.13. **III.** = ἡ τῶν ἀνδρῶν ἡλικία, Antipho Soph.67$^{a}$. **IV.** *membrum virile*, Artem.1.45. **V.** *skill*, Lxx *Ec.*4.4.

**ἀνδρ-είκελον**, τό, *image of a man*, App.*BC*2.147, *APl.*4.221 (Theaet.). **II.** *flesh-coloured pigment*, Pl.*R.*501b, *Cra.*424e, X.*Oec.*10.5, Arist.*GA*725$^{a}$26, Thphr.*Lap.*51. **-είκελος**, ον, *like a man*, εἴδωλα D.H.1.38; διατύπωσις Plu.*Alex.*72.

**ἀνδρειόθυμος**, gloss on ψυχικός, Suid.

**✱ἀνδρεῖος**, α, ον, Ion. -ήιος, η, ον (codd. of Hdt. have the common form in the Comp. and Sup. ἀνδρειότερος, -ότατος, 1.79, 123), Delph. ἀνδρέος *GDI*1724, al.:—*of* or *for a man*, στέγη dub. in A.*Fr.*124; θαἰμάτια Ar.*Ec.*75; opp. γυναικεῖος, Id.*Th.*154, Archipp.6 D., Pl.*R.*451c, X. *Mem.*2.7.5; πέπλοι Theoc.28.10 (where ἀνδρέïοι); αὐλός (v. αὐλός) Hdt.1.17; ἀ. ἀγορά the *men's* market, *CIG*3657 (Cyzicus); ἀνδρεῖος (sc. σύλλογος) *Test.Epict.*1.22, 2.29; ἀνδρεῖα ἠμπίσχετο *vestem virilem*, D.L.3.46; ἀ. ἱμάτιον, = *toga virilis*, Plu.*Brut.*14. **II.** *manly, masculine, courageous*, ῥώμη Hdt.7.153, etc.; even of women, Arist.*Pol.*1277$^{b}$22, *Po.*1454$^{a}$23; and in bad sense, *stubborn*, ἀναίσχυντος καὶ ἀ. τὰ τοιαῦτα Luc.*Ind.*3: neut., τὸ ἀνδρεῖον, = ἀνδρεία, Th.2.39; καὶ τοῦτ' ἐμοὶ τἀνδρεῖον ἡ προμηθία E.*Supp.*510; ἔβησαν εἰς τἀνδρεῖον Id.*Andr.*683. Adv. -ως Ar.*Pax*498, al.: Sup. -ότατα Pl.*Plt.*262a. **2.** of animals, Arist.*HA*488$^{b}$17, cf. Pl.*La.*196d, e. **3.** of things, *strong, vigorous*, λαφυγμός Eup.148; θήρατρον Ael.*VH* 1.1. **III. ἀνδρεῖα**, τά, the public meals of the Cretans, also the older name for the Spartan φειδίτια or φιλίτια (q.v.), Alcm.22, Arist. *Pol.*1272$^{a}$3, Plu.*Lyc.*12, Str.10.4.18 (v.l. ἄνδρια):—also **ἀνδρήιον**, τό, Cretan for *the public hall*, *GDI*4992 a ii 9, cf. 5040.38, al. **IV.** ἀνδρεῖον, τό, = σίνηπι ἄγριον, Ps.-Dsc.2.154.

**ἀνδρειότης**, ητος, ἡ, = ἀνδρεία, X.*An.*6.5.14, Ti.Locr.103d.

**ἀνδρει-όω**, *fill with courage*, τὰ σπλάγχνα Lxx 4*Ma.*15.23:—Pass., *become a man*, Procl.*Par.Ptol.*89. **✱-φόντης**, ου, ὁ, *man-slaying*, epith. of Ἐνυάλιος, Il.2.651, etc.; but the metre requires ἀδρι-φόντης, cf. ἀνδρότης. **-ωμα**, ατος, τό, *manly effort*, Metrod.*Herc.*831.12. **-ών**, ῶνος, ὁ, poet. for ἀνδρεών, ἀνδρών, *AP*9.322 (Leon.).

**ἀνδρεράστια**, v.l. for sq. in Poll.3.70, cf. Phryn.*PS*p.34 B.

**ἀνδρεράστρια**, ἡ, *woman that is fond of men*, Ar.*Th.*392 (ἀνδρεάστρια cod. R).

**ἀνδρεύομαι**, = ἀνδρίζομαι, *EM*599.17.

**ἀνδρεφόνος**, Dor. for ἀνδροφόνος, Hdn.Gr.2.418.

**✱ἀνδρεών**, = ἀνδρών, Hdt.1.34, al., *IG*14.291 (Segesta).

**ἀνδρηλᾰτ-έω**, *banish from house and home*, ἐκ γῆς τῆσδε A.*Ag.*1419, cf. *Eu.*221; ἐκ πόλεώς τε καὶ δόμων *Ag.*1586, cf. S.*OT*100, Pl.*R.*565e, etc.:—Pass., D.C.47.19. **-ης** [ᾰ], ου, ὁ, *he that drives one from his home*, dub. l. in A.*Th.*637, cf. Hsch.

**ἀνδρία**, v. ἀνδρεία. **II. ἄνδρια**, τά, v. ἀνδρεῖος III.

**ἀνδριαντ-άριον**, τό, Dim. of ἀνδριάς, *POxy.*1459.58 (iii A.D.), Sch. Luc.*Lex.*3. **✱-ίδιον**, τό, = foreg., *SIG*$^{2}$588.167, al. (Delos). **-ιον**, τό, = foreg., *IG*11.161*B*119 (Delos, iii B.C.), *GDI*5063 (Itanos). **✱-ίσκος**, ὁ, = foreg., *statuette*, *IG*2$^{2}$.47.5, 20 (iv B.C.), 11.161*B*17, 60 (Delos, iii B.C.), *GDI*5702 (Samos); *puppet*, Plu.*Thes.*2c.

**ἀνδριαντο-γλύφος**, ὁ, *carver of statues*, Tz.ad Lyc.615. **-ειδής**, ές, *like a statue*, Aethlius 1. **-εργάτης**, ου, ὁ, = ἀνδριαντοποιός, Tz. *H.*10.268. **-θήκη**, ἡ, *niche for a statue*, *CIG*2749.1 (Aphrodisias). **-πλάστης**, ου, ὁ, *modeller of statues*, *Cat.Cod.Astr.*8(4).213 (Rhetor.), Eust.206.37. **-πλαστική** (sc. τέχνη), ἡ, *art of modelling*, S.E.*M.*11.188. **-ποιέω**, *make statues*, X.*Mem.*3.1.2. **-ποιΐα**, ἡ, *the sculptor's art, statuary*, Pl.*Grg.*450c, X.*Mem.*1.4.3. **-ποιϊκή** (sc. τέχνη), ἡ, = foreg., Arist.*Ph.*195$^{a}$6, *Metaph.*1013$^{b}$6 (v.l. -ποιητική, which is found in Id.*PA*640$^{a}$30, Ocell.2.3). **-ποιός**, ὁ, *sculptor*, Pi.*N.*5.1, Pl.*R.*540c, etc.; *statuary* in bronze (cf. ἀνδριάς), opp. λιθουργός, Arist.*EN*1041$^{a}$11.

**ἀνδριαντ-ουργία**, ἡ, *sculpture*, Tz.*H.*8.348. **✱-ουργός**, ὁ, (ἔργον) = ἀνδριαντοποιός, Gal.19.162.

**✱ἀνδριάς**, ὁ, gen. ἄντος (Att. ᾶντος, acc. to Hdn.Gr.1.51): (ἀνήρ):—*image of a man, statue*, Pi.*P.*5.40, Hdt.1.183, 2.91, Ar.*Pax*1183, Th.1.134, etc.; ἀνδριάντας καὶ ἄλλα ζῷα λίθινά τε καὶ ξύλινα Pl.*R.*515a; ἀνδριάντας γράφειν paint statues, ib.420c; esp. of portrait-statues, ἀ. εἰκονικός Plu.*Lys.*1; ἀ. ὁλοσώματος *IG*12(7).240 (Amorgos); ἀ. ἔφιππος *SIG*730.26 (Olbia); of female figures, Ath.10.425f, etc.; of men, opp. ἀγάλματα of the gods, Gorg.*Hel.*18, Plb.21.29.9; rarely of gods, *GDI*5421 (Delos): prov., λάλος, οὐκ ἀ. Luc.*Vit.Auct.*3; ἀπαθὴς ὡς ἀ. Arr.*Epict.*3.2.4; ἀνδριάντος γυμνότερος D.Chr.34.3: ironically, τὸν καλὸν ἀ., a mother's term of endearment, D.18.129; μακρὸν ἀ. παίζειν, a kind of game, Thphr.*Char.*27.12.

**✱ἀνδρίζω**, *make a man of, make manly*, τοὺς γεωργοῦντας X.*Oec.*5.4. **II.** mostly in Pass. or Med., *come to manhood*, Ar.*Fr.*744, Hyp.*Fr.*228, Luc.*Anach.*15. **2.** *play the man*, X.*An.*4.3.34, Pl. *Tht.*151d, Arist.*EN*1115$^{b}$4, Lxx *Jo.*1.6, al., 1*Ep.Cor.*16.13; *dress like a man*, Philostr.*Im.*1.2. **3.** sens. obsc., D.C.79.5; of a eunuch, ἀ. ἐπὶ γυναῖκα Philostr.*VA*1.37, cf. *Ep.*54, Ach.Tat.4.1.

**✱ἀνδρικός**, ή, όν, *masculine, manly*, Pl.*R.*474e, etc.; [δίαιτα] σώφρων καὶ ἀ. Id.*Ep.*359a; νοσήματα Hp.*Mul.*1.62; ἀ. ἱδρώς the sweat *of manly toil*, Ar.*Ach.*693; σφηκὸς ἀνδρικώτερον Id.*V.*1090, cf. 1077; ἐσθής D.C.45.2; τὸ τῆς χρόας ἀ. Arist.*Fr.*542: Comp., Anaxandr.1 D. c. inf., πίνειν καὶ φαγεῖν μὲν ἀνδρικοὶ *like men* to eat and drink, Eub.12. Adv. -κῶς *like a man*, Ar.*Eq.*599, *V.*153, al.: Comp. -ώτερον Id.*Pax* 515: Sup. -ώτατα Id.*Eq.*81; opp. ἀνάνδρως, Pl.*Tht.*177b. **2.** of things, *large*, Eub.56. **II.** *composed of men*, χορός X.*HG*6.4.16, Lys.21.1.

**Ἀνδρίνεια**, τά, festival at Phigalea (prob. from the founder's name), *IG*5(2).422 (ii/i B.C.).

**ἀνδρίον**, τό, Dim. of ἀνήρ, *manikin*, Ar.*Pax*51; *pitiful fellow*, E. ap.Phot.p.127 R., Theoc.5.40, cf. Eup.316.

**ἀνδρίς**, ίδος, ἡ, fem. of ἀνήρ, *woman*, Sm.*Ge.*2.23.

**ἄνδρ-ισμα**, ατος, τό, *genuine, straightforward dealing*, in pl. (opp. εἰρωνεύματα), Max.Tyr.38.4. **✱-ισμός**, ὁ, = ἀνδρεία, Poll.3.120. **-ιστέον**, *one must play the man*, Pl.*Phd.*90e. **-ιστί** [ῑ], Adv. *like a man, like men*, Ar.*Ec.*149, cf. Crates Com.3 D., Theoc.18.23; *with a male voice*, εἰπεῖν τι D.Chr.33.38.

**✱ἀνδρο-βάμων** [βᾰ], ονος, ὁ, *foot-path* or *sidewalk*, *IGRom.*1.980. **-βαρής**, ές, = ἀνδραχθής, Eust.1651.9. **-βασμός**, ὁ, *foot-path*, ὁδὸς ἀ. *GDI*5690 (Erythrae), cf. Hsch. **-βατέω**, = Lat. *paedico*, *AP*5.207 (Mel.). **-βάτης**, ου, ὁ, = *paedicator*, Hsch. s.v. παιδοπίπας. **-βῐος**, ον, *living like a man*, Anon.ap.Suid. s.v. θρύπτεται. **-βόρος**, ον, *man-devouring*, *AP*7.206 (Damoch.), Q.S.6.247. **-βουλος**, ον, *of manly counsel, man-minded*, like ἀνδρόφρων, A.*Ag.*11, cf. Phryn.*PS* p.31 B.: opp. γυναικόβουλος. **-βρώς**, ῶτος, ὁ, ἡ, *man-eating, cannibal*, γνάθος E.*Cyc.*93; χαρμοναί Id.*HF*384; ἡδοναί *Fr.*537. **-γαμος**, ὁ, = κίναιδος, *Cat.Cod.Astr.*2.175. **-γένεια**, ἡ, (γένος), κατ' ἀνδρογενείην of descent by *the man's side*, Hp.*Ep.*27; πρεσβύτατος κατ' ἀ. *SIG*1044.20 (Halic.), cf. 1106.25 (Cos). **-γίγας**, αντος, ὁ, *giant-man*, Call.*Cer.*35. **-γόνος**, ον, *begetting men*, ἡμέρα ἀ.

day *favourable for begetting* (or *for the birth of*) *male children*, Hes. Op.783,788. **-γύνης** [ῠ], ου, ὁ, = ἀνδρόγυνος, prob. in Sch.T.Il.13. 291. II. Adj., *common to men and women*, λουτρὰ ἀ. baths *used by both at once*, AP9.783. **-γῠνία**, ἡ, Pythag., = πεντάς, i.e. odd and even (3+2), *Theol.Ar.*32. **-γῠνος**, ὁ, *man-woman, hermaphrodite*, Pl.*Smp.*189e. 2. *womanish man, effeminate person*, Hp.*Vict.*1.28, Hdt.4.67, Aeschin.2.127, Plu.2.219f, cf. Lxx*Pr.*18.8; ἀνδρογύνων ἄθυρμα Eup.3D. 3. = *pathicus, cinaedus*, AP6.254 (Myrin.), cf. Lib.*Decl.*12.42. b. of women, *Sapphic*, ἀ. ἔρωτες Luc. *Am.*28, cf. Artem.2.12. **-δάϊκτος** [δᾰ], ον, *man-slaying, murderous*, A.*Ch.*860, cf. *Fr.*132. ***-δάμας** [δᾰ], αντος, ὁ, ἡ, *man-taming*, φόβος, ῥιπὰ οἴνου, Pi.*N.*3.39, *Fr.*166; *man-slaying*, of Eriphyle, Id. *N.*9.16 (ubi al. ἀνδροδάμαν τ' pro -δάμαντ'). II. *arsenical pyrites*, Ps.-Democr.Alch.p.45B. **-δμής**· ὕπανδρος γυνή, Hsch. **-δομος**, ὁ, = ἀνδρών, Eust.1573.29, Hsch. **-ελής**, ές, (ἑλεῖν) *subduing men*, ἀνίη *Epigr.Gr.*1034.32 (Callipolis). **-θέα**, ἡ, *man-goddess*, i.e. Athena, AP15.22 (Simm.).

**ἀνδρόθεν**, Adv. *from a man*, ἀ. ἐκκέχυθ' ἵππος, of a Centaur, *APl.* 4.115.

**ἀνδρό-θηλυς**, υδος, ὁ, ἡ, = ἀνδρόγυνος I, Philostr.*VS*1.8. **-θνής**, ῆτος, ὁ, ἡ, *murderous*, φθοραί A.*Ag.*814. **-κάπηλος**, ὁ, *slave-dealer*, Gal.6.530, Orib.14.48.1. **-κάπραινα**, ἡ, *lewd woman, wanton*, Pherecr.17D.

**ἀνδροκ-άς**, = ἀνδρακάς (B), Hsch.: **-άδες**· πόα τις, Id.

**ἀνδρό-κλας**, α, ὁ, *weakening men*, of the climacterical year, i.e. the 63rd, Firm.4.20.3:—also **-κλάστης**, ου, ὁ, prob. in Critodem.ap. Vett.Val.237.7. **-κμής**, ῆτος, ὁ, ἡ, *man-wearying*, λοιγός, μόχθοι, A.*Supp.*678, *Eu.*248; *man-slaying*, πέλεκυς Id.*Ch.*889; ἀνδροκμῆτας προσφέρων ἀγωνίας E.*Supp.*525. **-κμητος**, ον, *wrought by men's hands*, τύμβος Il.11.371. **-κόβᾱλος**, ὁ, *rogue*, Hsch., Suid. **-κογχυλευτής**, οῦ, ὁ, v. ἀνδροπορφυρεύς. **-κοιτέω**, *sleep with a man*, *BGU* 1058.30 (i B.C.), Aët.1.142. **-κόνος**, ον, = ἀνδροκτόνος (q.v.), *AB* 394, Hsch. **-κόρινθος**, ὁ, *a Man-Corinth*, in allusion to the lewdness of the men of Heraclea and the women of Corinth, Stratonic.ap.Ath. 8.351c. **-κτᾰσία**, ἡ, (κτείνω) *slaughter of men* in battle, mostly in pl., παύσασθαι..Ἄρην ἀνδροκτασιάων Il.5.909; μάχας τ' ἀνδροκτασίας τε 7.237, etc.: personified, Hes.*Th.*228: in sg., ἀνδροκτασίης ὕπο λυγρῆς by reason of sad *homicide*, Il.23.86, cf. Hes.*Oxy.*1359.1.17, A.*Th.*693 (lyr.). **-κτάστης**, ὁ, prob. f. l. for -κλάστης, Vett. Val.237.7. **-κτονεῖον**, τό, *slaughter-house of men*, Phryn.*PS* p.49B. **-κτονέω**, *slay men, commit homicide*, A.*Eu.*602. ***-κτόνος**, ον, (κτείνω) *man-slaying, murdering*, Hdt.4.110, S.*Fr.*187, E. *Cyc.*22. **-λαλος**, ον, *gossiping about men*, Thphr.*Char.*28.3 (dub.l.).

***ἀνδρ-ολέτειρα**, ἡ, *murderess*, A.*Ag.*1465: as Adj., Id.*Th.*314 (lyr.).

**ἀνδρο-λήμη**, ἡ, (λῆμα) = ἀνδρόβουλος, Hsch. ***-ληπτέω**, *seize men*, Ἀρχ.Ἐφ.1918.132. **-ληψία**, ἡ, *seizure of foreigners* in reprisal for the murder of a citizen abroad, Lex ap.D.23.82, 51.13, *Ath.Mitt.*32.245 (Pergam.). **-λήψιον**, τό, *right of seizure*, D. 23.83, cf. 6.217; generally, *seizure, arrest*, App.*BC*4.6, Philostr. *Ep.*50. **-λογεῖον**, τό, v. ἀνδρολογία. **-λογέω**, *enlist soldiers*, Alciphr.1.11:—Pass., Luc.*Tox.*58. **-λογία**, ἡ: κατ' ἀνδρολογίαν, κατ' ἀνδραλογίαν, κατ' ἀνδρολογεῖον, ff.ll. in Lxx 2*Ma.*12.43 for κατ' ἄνδρα λογείαν. **-μανέω**, *lust after men*, Eustr. *in EN*274.6. **-μανής**, ές, *mad after men, lustful*, Plu.*Comp.Lyc.Num.*3, *AB*394. **-μάχος** [ᾰ], ον, *fighting with men*, χεῖρες AP7.241 (Antip. Sid.): fem. ἀνδρομάχη, ἄλοχος ib.11.378 (Pall.).

**Ἀνδρομέδα**, ας, ἡ, *Andromeda*, Pherecyd.12J., etc. II. *the constellation Andromeda*, Eudox.ap.Hipparch.1.2.13, Arat.189, etc.

***ἀνδρόμεος**, α, ον, (ἀνήρ) *human*, κρέα, αἷμα, χρὼς ἀ., Od.9.297, 22. 19, Il.20.100; ψωμοὶ ἀ. gobbets *of man's flesh*, Od.9.374; ὅμιλος ἀ. throng *of men*, Il.11.538; ἀ. κεφαλή Emp.134; αὐδή, ἐνοπή, A.R.1. 258, 4.581. II. ἀνδρόμεον· ἱμάτιον (Cret.), Hsch. (-μεο- cognate with Skt. -*máya*- in *hiraṇ-máya*- 'golden', etc.)

**ἀνδρο-μήκης**, ες, *of a man's height*, σταύρωμα X.*HG*3.2.3; φοῖνιξ Thphr.*HP*2.6.7; ὕψος, βάθος, Plb.8.5.6, 10.46.3; θυρεοί Onos.20.1; πυρός Sosith.2.18. **-μηκιαῖος**, ον, = foreg., *POxy.*896 (iv A.D.).

***ἀνδρομητὸν** (i.e. ἀνα-δρ., cf. ἀνέδραμον) ἐγχειρίδιον a dagger *with a blade slipping back into the haft*, used for stage-murders, Hsch.

**ἀνδρόμορφος**, ον, *of man's form* or *figure*, Apollod.1.6.3, cf. Eust. 1571.45.

**ἄνδρομος**, ον, = ἀνδρώδης, Hdn.Gr.1.171.

**ἀνδρο-νομέομαι**, *to be imperious*, dub. in M.Ant.10.19 codd. **-παις**, αιδος, ὁ, *man-boy*, i.e. *boy with a man's mind*, of Parthenopaeus, A. *Th.*533; of Troilus, S.*Fr.*619, cf. Ar.*Fr.*53D. **-πλήθεια**, ἡ, *multitude of men*, ἀ. στρατοῦ A.*Pers.*235. **-ποιός**, όν, *making manly*, Plu.2.334f. **-πορνος**, ὁ, *cinaedus*, Theopomp.Hist.17. **-πορφυρεύς**· ἀνδροκογχυλευτής, ἀναλέγων τὰς κόγχλους, Hsch. **-πρόσωπος**, ον, = sq., Hsch. **-πρῳρος**, ον, (πρῷρα) *with man's face*, Emp. 61. **-σάθων**, ὁ, (σάθη) obscene epith. of Priapus, Phot.p.127R., Eust.1968.43, *AB*394 (prob.l. for -σάνθων), Suid.:—also **-σάθης**, ὁ, *AB* l.c., Hsch.

**ἀνδρόσαιμον**, τό, (αἷμα) a kind of *St. John's wort, Hypericum perfoliatum*, Dsc.3.156, Gal.11.829. 2. = ὑπερικόν, Dsc.3.154. 3. = ἄσκυρον, ib.155.

**ἀνδρόσακες**, ους, τό, *sea-navel, Acetabularia mediterranea*, Dsc.3. 133.

**ἀνδρό-σῖνις**, ιος, ὁ, ἡ, *hurtful to men*, *APl.*4.266. **-στροφος**, ον, *after the manner of men*, ἔργα Man.4.358.

**ἀνδροσύνη**, ἡ, = ἀνδρεία, Orac.ap.D.S.7.12.

**ἀνδρο-σφᾰγεῖον**, τό, *slaughter-house of men*, A.*Ag.*1092 (Dobree, for ἀνδρὸς σφαγεῖον). **-σφιγξ**, ιγγος, ὁ, *sphinx with the bust of a man*, not (as usually) of a woman, Hdt.2.175. **-σώτειρα**, ἡ, *saviour of men*, title of Isis, *POxy.*1380.55 (Pap. ἀνδρασ-).

***ἀνδροτής**, ῆτος, ἡ, *manhood*, Il.16.857, 24.6 (with first syll. shortened; v.l. ἀδροτῆτα). II. = ἀνδρεία, Phintys ap.Stob.4. 23.61.

**ἀνδρο-τομέω**, *castrate*, τὸν πατέρα S.E.*M.*1.289. **-τῠχής**, ές, *getting a man* or *husband*, ἀ. βίοτος *wedded* life, A.*Eu.*959 (lyr.). **-φᾰγέω**, *eat men*, v.l. for ἀνθρωποφ-, Hdt.4.106. **-φάγος**, ον, *eating men*, Κύκλωψ Od.10.200; οἱ Ἀ., a people north of the Scythians, Hdt.4.18, 106, cf. Palaeph.7. **-φθόρος**, ον, *man-destroying, murderous*, μοῖρα Pi.*Fr.*177; ἔχιδνα S.*Ph.*266. II. proparox., ἀνδρόφθορον αἷμα the blood *of a slain man*, Id.*Ant.*1022. **-φονεύς**, έως, ὁ, = ἀνδροφόνος, Man.2.302. **-φονέω**, *slay men*, ἥβηδὸν ἀ. Str.4.6.8: c. acc., Hp.*Ep.*17:—Pass., Ph.2.314. **-φονία**, ἡ, *slaying of men*, Arist.*EN*1107$^a$12, Epicur.*Fr.*237 (pl.), D.H.4.24 (pl.), Plu.*Rom.* 22. ***-φόνος**, ον, *man-slaying*, Homeric epith. of Hector, Il.24. 724, etc.; of Achilles, χεῖρες ἀ. 18.317; *homicide*, Pl.*Phd.*114a; generally, *murderous*, ἀ. τὴν φύσιν Theopomp.Hist.217:—rarely exc. of *slaughter in battle*, but in Od.1.261 φάρμακον ἀ. a *murderous* drug:—epith. of αἷμα, Orph.*H.*65.4. 2. of women, *murdering their husbands*, Pi.*P.*4.252. II. as law-term, *one convicted of manslaughter, homicide*, Lys.10.7, D.23.29, cf. ib.216:—hence as a term of abuse, τοὺς ἀ. ἰχθυοπώλας Ath.6.228c, cf. Amphis 30. III. ἀ. Κῶνος, a landmark at Athens, *IG*3.61*A* ii 15. **-φόντης**, ου, ὁ, = ἀνδρειφόντης, A.*Th.*572. **-φρων**, ονος, ὁ, ἡ, *man-minded*, like ἀνδρόβουλος, γυνή S.*Fr.*943. **-φυής**, ές, *of human shape*, Emp.61, Nonn.*D.*36.94. **-φυκτίς**, ίδος, ἡ, a kind of *mollusc*, Epich.42.

***ἀνδρ-όω**, *change into a man*, Lyc.176,943. II. *rear up into manhood*, AP7.419 (Mel.), Plu.2.490a:—Pass., *become a man, reach manhood*, Hdt.1.123, 2.32, Hp.*Art.*58, E.*HF*42, Ant.Lib.13.3, etc.: metaph., διθύραμβοι ἠνδρωμένοι Macho ap.Ath.8.341c: also in Med., = συγγενέσθαι, Hsch. III. in Pass., also of a woman, *virum experta sum*, ἠνδρώθησαν D.C.*Fr.*87.3; ἠνδρωμέναι Id.67.3. **-ύνω**, = foreg., Ps.-Callisth.1.13 (Pass.). **-ώδης**, ες, *manly*, -έστεροι ἄνδρες Emp.67, cf. Isoc.5.76 (Comp.); ἀ. τὴν φύσιν Arist.*EN*1171$^b$6; -έστεροι τὰ ἤθη Id.*Rh.*1391$^a$22; ἀ. ῥυθμοί, σχήματα, D.H.*Dem.*43, al.; λόγοι Plu.2.110d; δίαιτα Hierocl.*in CA*17 p.458M.: Sup., J.*BJ*7. 8.6. Adv. **-δῶς**, διακεῖσθαι Isoc.12.31: Sup. -δέστατα X.*Mem.*4.8. 1. ***-ών**, ῶνος, ὁ, *men's apartment* in a house, *banqueting-hall*, Hdt. (v. infr.), etc.; εὐτράπεζοι, εὔξενοι, A.*Ag.*244, *Ch.*712, cf. E.*HF*954, X.*Smp.*1.4, etc.; Ion. -εών (q.v.); Ep. -ειών (q.v.). **-ώνιον**, τό, Dim. of foreg., *IG*11(2).287*A* 147,154 (Delos, iii B.C.). **-ωνῖτις**, ιδος, ἡ, = ἀνδρών, opp. γυναικωνῖτις, Lys.1.9, X.*Oec.*9.6, *IG*11(2).158 *A*18 (Delos, iii B.C.): as Adj., ἀ. ἑστία Ph.1.312, al. II. among the Romans, *passage between two courts of a house*, Vitr.6.7.5. **-ωνῦμικόν** (sc. ὄνομα), τό, *name transferred* from an animal *to a man*, e.g. Σκύμνος, Πῶλος, Sch.Il.18.319. ***-ωνύμιον** [ῠ], τό, *proper name*, Theognost.*Can.*9, Sch.Ar.*V.*1239. **-ῷος**, α, ον, late form of ἀνδρεῖος, Muson.*Fr.*3p.17H., Gal.2.888, Sch.Ar.*Ra.*47, Aspasia ap. Aët.16.18; distinguished by Sch.Lib.*Or.*64.54 ἀνδρεῖα ἐσθήματα ἤτοι ἀνδράσι πρέποντα· ἀνδρῷα δὲ οἰκήματα τὰ ἐμπεριέχοντα ἄνδρας.

**ἀ-νέαστος**, ον, of land, *unploughed*, Str.11.4.3.

***ἀνέβρᾰχε**, (v. *βράχω), 3 sg. aor. 2, with no pres., τὰ δ' ἀνέβραχε but it [the armour] *clashed* or *rang loudly*, Il.19.13; τὰ δ' ἀνέβραχεν [the door] *creaked* or *grated loudly*, Od.21.48; of water, *gushed roaring forth*, A.R.1.1147.

**ἀνεγγάρευτος**, ον, = ἀναγγ., *free from obligation to serve as* ἄγγαρος. *Sammelb.*4226 (ii A.D.).

**ἀνέγγραφος**, ον, *of which no written evidence exists*, ἀδικήματα *IG* 5(2).357.162 (Stymphalus, iii B.C.), cf. Sch.Pl.*Ap.*19b, Suid.

**ἀνέγγυος**, ον, *not vouched for, not accredited*, ὧραι ἀ., of uncertain weather, Anacr.113; of an illegitimate child, νόθος καὶ ἀ. Pl.*R.*461b; γάμοι *unhallowed*, E.ap.Phot.p.128R.; of a woman, *unbetrothed, unwedded*, Plu.*Caes.*14, *Comp.Rom.Thes.*6, D.C.59.12, etc.; ἀ. ποιεῖν τὰς μίξεις D.H.2.24.

***ἀνεγ-είρω**, *wake up, rouse*, ἐξ ὕπνου Il.10.138; ἐκ λεχέων Od.4.730; τὴν ἀηδόνα Ar.*Av.*208:—Pass., E.*HF*1055; ἀνηγέρθη X.*An.*3.1.12, AP11.257 (Lucill.): poet. aor. Med. ἀνεγρόμην A.R.1.522; ἀναέγρετο Maiist.31. II. metaph., *wake up, raise*, κῶμον Pi.*I.*8(7).2; μολπὴν Ar.*Ra.*370:—Pass., ἀνεγειρομένα φάμα Pi.*I.*4(3).23. 2. metaph. also, *rouse, encourage*, ἀνέγειρα δ' ἑταίρους μειλιχίοις ἐπέεσσι Od.10. 172; *stir, rouse the spirit of*, θυμοειδῆ ἵππον X.*Eq.*9.6:—Med., *take heart*, Ph.2.120. III. of buildings, *raise*, δόμον AP9.693a, cf. Lib.*Or.*11.56; ἀπὸ θεμελίων *OGI*422 (Judaea). **-έρμων**, ον, gen. ονος, *wakeful*, κύνες AP9.558 (Eryc.). ***-ερσις**, εως, ἡ, *raising up*, Plu.2.156b. 2. *waking up*, ib.378f. **-ερτος**, ον, *not broken by waking*, ἀ. ὕπνος Arist.*GA*779$^a$3, *EE*1216$^a$3.

**ἀνεγκάλυπτος**, ον, *uncovered*, Hsch.

**ἀνεγκαρτέρητος**, ον, *not to be endured*, κακὸν διὰ τὴν πολυχρονιότητα Phld.*Herc.*1251.4: v. ἀνεκκ-.

***ἀνεγκέφαλος**, ον, *without brain*, Gal.5.314.

**ἀνεγκλη-σία**, ἡ, γραφὴ ἀνεγκλησίας deed *of indemnity*, *PLips.*29.13 (iii A.D.), etc. **-τί** [ῐ], Adv. of sq., Pl.Com.231: -τεὶ Isoc.15. 28. **-τος**, ον, *without reproach, blameless*, X.*HG*6.1.13, D.*Ep.*2. 14; διαφυλάττειν τοὺς πολίτας ἀ. Arist.*Rh.*1360$^a$16; ἀ. ἑαυτὸν παρέχειν *IG*2$^2$.1271, cf. *CIG*2270.7 (Delos). Adv. -τως D.17.2, *SIG*436.

6 (Delph., iii B.C.), *PIand.*33.14 (ii A.D.). **II.** *giving no ground for dispute*, ἀ. τὰς οὐσίας πρὸς ἀλλήλους κατασκευάζεσθαι Pl.*Lg.*737a. Adv. -τως, ἔχειν Arist.*Pol.*1321ᵇ22. **III.** Act. in Adv. -τως *uncomplainingly*, Plu.2.102e.

**ἀνέγκλῐτος**, ον, *unchanging*, Plu.2.393a, cf. *Per.*15. **II.** Gramm., *not enclitic*, A.D.*Synt.*136.7, al. **III.** Math., *not inclined*, i.e. at right angles, Ptol.*Alm.*1.16.

**ἀνεγκόπτως**, Adv. *without hesitation*, of speech, Aët.8.38.

**ἀνεγκωμίαστος**, ον, *not praised*, Isoc.9.73, J.*AJ*4.6.13.

**ἄνεγμα**· αἴνιγμα (Tarent.), Hsch.

**ἀνέγρομαι**, late poet. form for ἀνεγείρομαι, formed from the aor. ἀνηγρόμην, Opp.*H.*2.204, Q.S.5.610.

**ἀνεγχώρητος**, ον, *impossible*, Sch.Hermog. in Rh.7.135 W.

**ἀνεδάφιστος** [δᾰ], ον, *not levelled*, γῆ Arist.*Pr.*934ᵇ22.

**ἀνέδην**, Adv., (ἀνίημι) *let loose, freely, without restraint*, Pl.*Prt.*342c, S.*Ph.*1153 (lyr.); ἀ. φεύγειν flee *pell-mell*, A.*Supp.*14; τῆς πομπείας τῆς ἀ. γεγενημένης D.18.11; ἀ. βακχεύειν *AP*6.172; ἀ. καὶ ὡς ἔτυχε Ael.*NA*2.9. **2.** *licentiously, violently*, Plb.15.20.3. **II.** *without more ado, simply, absolutely*, Pl.*Grg.*494e; *straightforwardly*, ἀ. ἐρωτᾶν Ps.-Alex.Aphr.*in SE*101.22.

**ἀνέδραστος**, ον, *without firm foundation*, βάσις, of a rhetorical period, D.H.*Comp.*22; δρόμος *IG*7.2543 (Thebes); of a bandage, *liable to slip*, Gal.18(2).379; *unsteady*, ib.819, cf. Plu.2.654a, Procl. *in Prm.*p.794 S., *in Ti.*3.122 D. Adv. -τως, gloss on ἀνέδην, Sch. Philum.ap.Orib.45.29.14.

**ἀνέεδνος**, ον, v. ἀνάεδνος.

***ἀνέζω**, pres. not found, *set upon*, ἐς δίφρον ἀνέσαντες Il.13.657; εἰς εὐνὴν ἀνέσαιμι 14.209, cf. 1.310 (tm.); *restore to one's place*, οὐκ οἶδ' ἤ κέν μ' ἀνέσει θεὸς Od.18.265:—Pass., *sit upright*, ἀνὰ δ' ἕζετο σιγῇ A.R.1.1170, 4.1332.

**ἀνεθέλητος**, ον, *unwished for, unwelcome*, ἐπὶ συμφορὴν ἐνέπεσε ἀνεθέλητον Hdt.7.88; ἀ. γίνεταί τι ib.133.

**ἀνεθ-ίζομαι**, *become used to* a thing, D.L.2.96. **-ιστέον**, *one must accustom*, Dam.*Pr.*3.

❊**ἀνέθιστος**, ον, *unaccustomed*, πόνοι Hp.*Vict.*2.66; ἱερά D.H.2.73.

❊**ἀνείδεος**, ον, (εἶδος) *formless*, ὕλη *Placit.*1.2.3, cf. Ph.1.417, al., Plot.1.8.3, al., Ael.*NA*2.56; ὕλη *without specific difference*, Dam.*Pr.*425; of persons, μικρά τις καὶ ἀνείδεος Aen.Gaz.*Thphr.*p.62 B.

**ἀνειδωλόπληκτος**, ον, *not afflicted by ghosts*, *PMag.Par.*1.1063.

**ἀνειδωλοποι-έω**, *represent in imagery*, of poets, Plu.2.1113a; *form a mental image of, imagine*, τὰ μὴ ὄντα ὡς ὄντα Ph.2.59, cf. S.E.*P.*3.155:—Med., *Placit.*5.2.3:—Pass., τὰ ἀνειδωλοποιούμενα μέτρα patterns *conceived in the mind*, Longin.14.1. **-ησις**, εως, ἡ, S.E. *P.*3.189.

**ἀνεικάζομαι**, Med., *represent satirically*, Cratin.63 (dub.).

**ἀνεικαιότης**, ητος, ἡ, *levelheadedness, discretion*, Chrysipp.*Stoic.*2.40, Arr.*Epict.*3.2.2, D.L.7.46.

**ἀνείκαστος**, ον, *unattainable by conjecture, immense*, βοή Lxx 3*Ma.*1.28; πλῆθος Ps.-Callisth.3.20; *incomparable*, στρατιώτης Polem. *Call.*50; f.l. for ἀνήκεστος, D.8.46. **II.** *incapable of artistic representation*, D.Chr.12.59.

**ἀνεικής**, ές, *uncontested*, v.l. for ἀεικής, Il.12.435.

**ἀνεικία**, ἡ, Pythag., = πεντάς, as reconciling the feud of odd and even (3 + 2), *Theol.Ar.*27, al.; cf. ἀνικία. **2.** also = ἐννεάς, ib.57.

**ἀνεικόνιστος**, ον, *not registered with personal description*, *BGU* 258.9 (ii A.D.).

**ἄνεικος**, ον, *without demur*, φόρον ἄ. τελεῖν *CIG*2693e11 (Cyzicus).

**ἀνειλείθυια**, ἡ, *without the aid of Eileithyia*, ἀ. ὠδίνων λοχιᾶν *never having invoked her aid* in childbirth, E.*Ion*453, cf. Eust.1861.44.

**ἀνειλ-έω**, *roll up* or *crowd together*, πολεμίους Philostr.*VA*2.11:—Pass., *crowd* or *throng together*, ἀνειληθέντες εἴς τι χωρίον Th.7.81; αἱ μέλιτται.. αὐτοῦ ἀνειλοῦνται Arist.*HA*627ᵇ12; of wind *pent in the bowels*, v.l. in Hp.*Prog.*11; πνεῦμα -ούμενον Epicur.*Ep.*2 p.46 U.; of sound, Arist.*Aud.*804ᵃ20; ἀνειλεῖται ἡ γλῶσσα *is kept within bounds*, Plu.2.503c. **II.** *unroll*, ib.109d. **-ημα**, ατος, τό, *rolling up*: in pl., *flatulent colic*, Hp.*VM*22. **II.** *scroll*, Aristeas 177 (pl.). ❊**-ησις**, εως, ἡ, = foreg., Hp.*Epid.*3.8. **2.** *penning up, confinement*, πνεύματος Epicur.*Ep.*2 p.44 U. **3.** *twisting of the body*, in gymnastic exercises, Aret.*CD*1.2, 2.13.

**ἀνειλιγμένως**, Adv. pf. part. Pass. of ἀνελίσσω, *explicitly*, opp. συνεσπειραμένως, Herm.*in Phdr.*p.137 A., cf. Phlp.*in Ph.*20.5; [ψυχὴ μετέχει θεοῦ] ἀ. Anon.*Incred.*21.

**ἀνείλιξις**, εως, ἡ, *reversal of motion*, Pl.*Plt.*270d, 286b.

**ἀνειλίσσω**, v. ἀνελίσσω.

❊**ἀνείλλω** or **ἀνείλω**, = ἀνειλέω:—in Pass., *shrink up* or *back*, Pl. *Smp.*206d.

**ἀνειλυσπᾶσθαι**· ἀναρ(ρ)ιχᾶσθαι, Hsch.

**ἀνείλυστος**, ον, *accompanied with gripes*, στρόφοι Aret.*SD*2.3.

**ἀνειμάρθαι**, pf. inf. Pass., = οὐχ εἱμάρθαι *not to be decreed by fate*, dub. in *Placit.*1.27.4 (ἀνειμαρτά Diels).

**ἀνείμασθος**· ἄφθορος, ἄπληστος, Hsch.

**ἀνειμένως**, Adv. pf. part. Pass. of ἀνίημι, *at ease, carelessly*, ἀργῶς καὶ ἀ. X.*Mem.*2.4.7; ἀ. διαιτᾶσθαι *without restraint, freely*, Th.2.39; πίνειν X.*Cyr.*4.5.8; ζῆν Arist.*EN*1114ᵃ5; ἀ. ποιεῖσθαι τοὺς λόγους *frankly*, Isoc.8.41; κατηγορίαν τινὸς ποιήσασθαι ἀ. *openly*, Aristid.2.116 J.; *in a milder form*, Dsc.2.153, 5.159. **2.** *without accent*, opp. περισπωμένως, ὀξυτόνως, Anon.*in SE*8.23.

❊**ἄνειμι**, in Att. serving as fut. to ἀνέρχομαι, and ἀνῄειν, Ep. ἀνήϊον, as impf.:—*go up*, ἅμ' ἠελίῳ ἀνιόντι at sun-*rise*, Il.18.136, cf. Hdt.3.85; ἀνήϊον ἐς περιωπήν *I went up a hill*, Od.10.146, cf. Pl.*R.*614d γῆ δ' ἄνεισ' εἰς αἰθέρα E.*Fr.*687; ἱδρὼς ἀνῄει χρωτί *came up* upon the skin, S.*Tr.*767: metaph., *reach, attain to*, εἰς προβλήματα Pl.*R.*531c Medic., ἐπὶ τὰς ϛ' *raised the dose* to six cotylae, Ruf.ap.Aët.5.84. **2.** *sail up*, i.e. *out to sea*, ἐκ Τροίης ἀνιόντα θοῇ σὺν νηΐ Od.10.332; πόντον ἀνήϊον A.R.4.238. **3.** *go up inland* (v. supr. 1), esp. *go up* into Central Asia, ἡ ἀγγελίη ἀνῄιε παρὰ τὸν βασιλέα Hdt.5.108; ἐκ Πειραιῶς Pl.*R.*439e, etc.; εἰς ἄστυ Φαληρόθεν Id.*Smp.*172a. **4.** *come forth*, Ael.*NA*11.33. **5.** *to be promoted*, εἰς Ἄρειον πάγον Hyp.*Fr.*138, Lex ap.D.24.22. **6.** ἀνιόντα καὶ κατιόντα πρόσωπα *ascendants* and descendants, Just.*Nov.*117.7, 118*Pr.* **II.** *approach*, esp. as a suppliant, ἄνεισι παῖς ἐς πατρὸς ἑταίρους Il.22.492, 499. **III.** *go back, return*, freq. in Od., ἐξ Αἰθιόπων ἀνιών 5.282; ἀ. ἐπὶ τὸν πρότερον λόγον Hdt.1.140, cf. 7.239; θαλάσσης ἐς τέκνα Pl.Com.173.11; without Prep., πάλιν δὲ τῶνδ' ἄνειμί σοι γένος *genus repetam*, E. *Heracl.*209.

❊**ἀνείμων**, ον, gen. ονος, (εἷμα) *without clothing, unclad*, Od.3.348.

**ἀνεινῶς**· οἰκτρῶς, Hsch.

❊**ἀνεῖπον**, aor. with no pres. in use, ἀναγορεύω being used instead; imper. ἀνειπάτω *IG*2².1186.19, but -έτω ib.1247.13:—*announce, proclaim*, esp. by herald, ἀ. τινά *proclaim* conqueror, Pi.*P.*1.32, 10.9; στέφανον *IG*12(5).129.33 (Paros), cf. Docum.ap.D.18.55; τῷ ἀπειθοῦντι πάντα τὰ χαλεπὰ ἀνεῖπεν X.*Cyr.*4.2.35; τὸν νόμον ἄνειπε Herod.2.42: c. acc. et inf., *make proclamation that*.., τοὺς γεωργοὺς ἀπιέναι Ar.*Pax* 550; κήρυγμα τόδε ἀνειπών.. τὸν μὲν βουλόμενον.. μένειν κτλ. Th.4.105; also εἴ τις εἴη.. ἐκφαίνεσθαι X.*Cyr.*4.5.56: abs., *proclaim, give notice*, in law-courts, theatres, etc., ἀνεῖπεν ὁ κῆρυξ, εἴ τις βούλεται.. ξυμμαχεῖν, τίθεσθαι τὰ ὅπλα Th.2.2, cf. Pl.*R.*580b, etc.; ὁ δ' ἀνεῖπεν, εἴσαγ', ὦ Θέογνι, τὸν χορόν Ar.*Ach.*11; ἐν τῷ βουλευτηρίῳ ἀ. Docum.ap.D. l.c. supr.: simply, *say aloud*, τῷ δὲ ἀνεῖπεν ἔνδοθεν, "εἰς κόρακας" Luc.*Alex.*46.—Pass., aor. ἀνερρήθην, ἀναρρηθεὶς ἡγεμών X.*HG*1.4.20, etc.; ἀναρρηθέντος ἐν τῷ θεάτρῳ τοῦ στεφάνου D.18.83, cf. ib.149; τὸν ἐν τῇ ἐκκλησίᾳ στέφανον ἀναρρηθέντα Aeschin.3.47: fut. ἀναρρηθήσεται ib.147: pf. imper. ἀνειρήσθω *let the proclamation be taken as made*, Pl.*R.*580c. **II.** *call upon, invoke*, θεούς Plu.*Comp.Rom.Thes.*6.

**ἀνείργω**, *keep back, restrain*, used by Hom. always in Ep. impf., Τρώων ἀνέεργε φάλαγγας Il.3.77; μάχην ἀνέεργον ὀπίσσω 17.752; so ἀ. τὸν θυμόν Pl.*Lg.*731d; τοὺς στρατιώτας X.*HG*7.1.31; ταῖς τιμωρίαις τοὺς ἁμαρτάνοντας D.H.*Is.*8; τινὰς ἀπὸ πράξεως Porph.*Abst.*1.7: c. acc. et inf., ἀ. μὴ διασκίδνασθαι τὴν ἀγέλην Luc.*DDeor.*20.5:—f.l. in X.*Cyr.*5.4.45 (leg. ἀνειρμένοις). **II.** *force back*, D.H.3.32.

**ἀνειρεσίαν**· οὐσίαν πολλήν, Hsch. **ἀνείρετον**· ἀπαραίτητον, Id.

**ἄνειρξις**, εως, ἡ, *restraint*, Plu.2.584e.

**ἀνείρομαι**, used by Hom. only in pres., whereas Att. prefer ἀνερωτάω: but Trag. (in lyr.) use aor. ἀνηρόμην S.*Aj.*314, inf. ἀνερέσθαι Id.*OT*1304; Pl.*Men.*85c has fut. ἀνερήσομαι, and Hsch. gives ἀνηρήμεθα· ἠρωτήθημεν: **1.** c. acc. pers., *inquire of, question*, ὅτε κεν δή σ' αὐτὸς ἀνείρηται ἐπέεσσι Od.4.420; so μή μ' ἀνέρῃ τίς εἰμι S.*OC*210, cf. *Aj.*314, Pl.*Ap.*20a, etc. **2.** c. acc. rei, *ask about*, τί,νδε τε γαῖαν ἀνείρεαι Od.13.238: in Prose also περί τινος Pl.*Men.*74c. **3.** c. dupl. acc., ὅ μ' ἀνείρεαι what thou *inquirest of* me, Il.3.177; ἀνήρετ'.. Χαιρεφῶντα Σωκράτης ψύλλαν ὁπόσους ἅλλοιτο.. πόδας Ar. *Nu.*145, cf. Pl.*Smp.*173b, etc.

**ἀνειρύω**, poet. and Ion. for ἀνερύω.

**ἀνείρω**, (v. εἴρω) *fasten on* or *to, string*, ἀνείρας [τὰ ὦτα] περὶ τὸν χαλινόν Hdt.3.118; ἀ. τὰ κρέα *fasten upon* a spit, Pl.Com.201; ἐνώτια ἀργυρᾶ ἀνειρμένα *IG*11(2).161 B61 (Delos); ἀ. στεφάνους *twine* or *wreathe* them, Ar.*Ach.*1006; τρίχας βελόνῃ D.C.51.14.

**ἀνεῖσαι**· ἐρευνῆσαι, ζητῆσαι, Hsch.

❊**ἀνείσακτος**, ον, *not initiated*, = ἀμύητος, Iamb.*VP*17.75; applied by Stoics to their opponents, *Stoic.*2.250.

**ἀνεισοδίαστος**, ον, ἔσται δὲ ἄπρατον καὶ ἀ. dub.l. in *IGRom.*4.1475 (Smyrna; prob. ἀνεξ- *inalienable*).

**ἀνείσοδος**, ον, *without entrance* or *access*, Plu.*Dio* 7, *Pyrrh.*29.

**ἀνείσπρακτος**, ον, *free from pecuniary liability*, *BGU*1133.13 (i B.C.), *POxy.*270, 286.

**ἀνεισφορ-ία**, ἡ, *exemption from taxation*, *SIG*612 B3 (Delph., ii B.C.), *Jahresh.*14 *Beibl.*126 (Tralles), Plu.*Eum.*4, *IPE*2.36.2, *BGU* 1074.4 (quoting Hadrian's decree), etc. **-ος**, ον, *exempt from taxation*, τῶν εἰς τὰ στρατιωτικὰ ἀναλισκομένων D.H.5.22, cf. Plu. *Cam.*2, *IG*14.951, J.*AJ*13.6.7.

❊**ἀνέκαθεν**, before a cons. -θε (Hdt.6.128 codd.), Adv. of Place (cf. ἀνεκάς), *from above*, A.*Ch.*427, *Eu.*369 (lyr.); τἀνέκαθεν ῥεῖ ἐκ.. Hdt.4.57; cf. ἄγκαθεν. **II.** of Time, *from the first*, ἐόντες ἀ. Πύλιοι being Pylians *by origin*, Id.5.65, cf. 7.221; more often with the Art., γεγονότες τὸ ἀ. ἀπὸ Αἰγύπτου 2.43, cf. 6.128; γένος ἐόντες τὰ ἀ. Γεφυραῖοι 5.55, cf. 1.170, 6.35; τὰ ἀ. λαμπροί of *ancestral* renown, 6.125; πόλις ἀ. συγγενὶς *OGI*566 (Lycia). **2.** ἀ. κατηγορεῖν narrate *from the beginning*, Plb.2.35.10, 5.16.6.

**ἀνεκαιρεν**· ἀνεβάλλετο, ἀνήρχετο, ἀνεφέρετο, Hsch.

**ἀνεκάς**, Adv. *upwards*, ὅταν.. μοῖρα πέμπῃ ἀ. ὄλβον Pi.*O.*2.22; ἀσπίδα φέρειν.. ἀ. ἐς τὸν οὐρανόν Ar.*V.*18, cf. *Fr.*188; [τρέπειν] τὸν αὐχέν' ἐκ γῆς ἀ. Crates Com.10; ἀ. δ' ἐπήρω τὸ σκέλος Eup.50, cf. Pherecr.169 (Valck.); εἰς τὸ ἀ. Hp.*Mul.*1.1. (Plu.*Thes.*33 wrongly derives the name of the Ἄνακες from this word, τὸ γὰρ ἄνω τοὺς Ἀττικοὺς ἀνέκας (sic) ὀνομάζειν καὶ ἀνέκαθεν τὸ ἄνωθεν, cf. *Num.*13: but -κάς perh. as in ἀνδρα-κάς (A) (q.v.), ἑ-κάς: ἀνεκάς does not contain ἑκάς; ἀνεκάς· ψιλῶς, Phot.p.129.13 R., i.e. not ἀνηκάς.)

**ἀνεκβάλλω**, *draw out*, σκόλοπας καὶ ἀκίδας, of a plaster, Gal.14.242.

**ἀνέκ-βᾰτος**, ον, *without outlet*, χαράδρα Th.3.98; "Αϊδος εὐνή Opp.H.4.392. 2. *not 'coming off'*, ὄνειρος, opp. ἀποβαίνειν, Cat.Cod.Astr.5(3).89.31. **-βίαστος**, ον, *not to be overpowered*, Chrysipp.Stoic.2.64, v.l. in Gell.1.2.7. **-δαρτος**, ον, *not skinned*, and Adv. **ἀνεκδαρτί**, both in Suid. **-δήμητος**, ον, *unpropitious for a journey*, ἡμέρα Plu.2.269e. **-διήγητος**, ον, *indescribable, ineffable*, 2Ep.Cor.9.15, Hsch., v.l. in Aristeas 99. **-δίκητος**, ον, *unavenged*, J.AJ20.3.1; *unpunished*, PGoodsp.15.5; βλασφημίαι Just.Nov.77.1.1, cf.137Pr. **-δοτος**, Arc. **ἀνέσδοτος** SIG306.5 (Tegea, iv B.C.), ον, *not given in marriage, unaffianced*, of a girl, Lys.13.45, D.45.74, Is.6.14; ἀ. ἔνδον καταγηράσκειν Hyp.Lyc.13. II. *unpublished*, D.S.1.4, Cic.Att.14.17.6; of a *secret* remedy, ἀ. δύναμις Philum.Ven.10.9. **-δρομος**, ον, *inevitable*, θῶμιγξ AP9.343 (Arch.). **-δυτος**, ον, *not to be escaped from*, to interpr. νήδυμος, Eust.1580.13. ⊛**-θέρμαντος**, ον, *not warmed* or *to be warmed*, Gal.7.189, Orib.ap.Phot.Bibl.p.175B. Adv. **-τως** Antyll.ap.Orib.9.25.27. **-θῦτος**, ον, *not to be removed by sacrifice*, μιάσματα Corn.ND9 (codd. ἀνέκπλυτα). **-καρτέρητος**, ον, *unendurable*, κακόν Phld.D.1.12. (Less usual spelling of ἀνεγκ-, cf. ἀνέκκλητος 2.) **-κλησίαστος**, ον, *not used for assemblies of the people*, θέατρον Posidon.41. **-κλητος**, ον, *unchallenged*, of a περιοδονίκης (q.v.), IG14.1102,1104. 2. = ἀνέγκλητος. Adv. **-τως** GDI1723, 1729 (Delph.). **-κλῖτος**, ον, *not to be evaded*, Hsch. s.v. ἀλίαστος, Sch.Il.2.797. Adv. **-τως** *unavoidably*, ibid. **-κόπως**, Adv. *without excision* (but prob. ἀνεκκόπτως), Heliod.ap.Orib.50.9.5. **-κρῖτος**, ον, *not emptied*, γαστήρ Poet. de herb.137. **-λάλητος**, ον, *unutterable, ineffable*, 1Ep.Pet.1.8, Eun.VS p.486B., Ar.Byz.Epit.26.10, Jul.Or.5.158d. 2. *not capable of expression* or *calculation*, δύναμις Dsc.Eup.Praef.; ἰδιότης Heliod.ap.Sch.Orib.45.2. **-λειπτος**, ον, *incessant, uninterrupted*, Hyp.Epit.20 (dub.), D.S.4.84, PLond.3.1166.7 (i A.D.); *infinite*, of divisions of space, S.E.M.10.141; *unfailing*, Lxx Wi.7.14, Ev.Luc.12.33, D.S.1.36, Procl.Inst.84. Adv. **-τως** D.S.18.50, Hero ap.Procl.Hyp.4.75. 2. ἀ. μᾶζα, in Alchemy, of the asem alloy, PHolm.2.17, PLeid.X.7 and 39. **-λεκτος**, ον, *not carefully chosen*, ὀνόματα D.H.Comp.3. **-λητ[..]**· ἐξαίρεσιν ποιεῖσθαι (Rhod.), Hsch. **-λῐπής**, ές, = ἀνέκλειπτος, Lxx Wi.7.14, 8.18. **-λόγιστος**, neut. pl. as Adv., **-ιστα** *without reckoning*, BGU183.24 (i A.D.): regul. Adv. **-τως**, πίνειν Pherecr.143.1. ⊛**-λῦτος**, ον, *indissoluble*, Just.Nov.39 Pr. **-νιπτος**, ον, *indelible*, Poll.1.44. **-πίμπλημι**, *fill up* or *again*, f.l. in X.An.3.4.22. **-πληκτος**, ον, *undaunted, intrepid*, Pl.Tht.165b, Hyp.Fr.117; ὑπὸ κακῶν Pl.R.61(a:—τὸ -ότατον X.Ages.6.7. Adv. **-τως** Plu.2.260c, Hierocl. in CA10p.434M. II. Act., *making no impression*, λέξις Plu.2.7a. **-πληξία**, ἡ, *imperturbability*, Pl.Def.412c. **-πλήρωτος**, ον, *incapable of fulfilment*, τἀγαθὸν ⟨οὐκ⟩ -τον Phld.D.1.12. **-πλῦτος**, ον, *indelible*, Pl.Ti.26c, Poll.1.44. **-ποίητος**, ον, *not alienated*, of property, πράγματα Just.Nov.22.20.2, cf. 22.39. **-πραξία**, ἡ, *non-effect*, Sch.A.Th.843. **-πύητος**, ον, *not suppurating*, Hp.Aph.5.20, Ruf.ap.Orib.7.26.21; δακρυώδης καὶ ἀ. exuding serum *instead of pus*, Hp.Fract.25. **-πύρωτος**, *not set on fire*, Olymp. in Mete.12.25. **-πυστος**, ον, *not found out by inquiry*, J.AJ17.11.2.

⊛**ἀνεκτέος**, α, ον, *to be borne*, ἀνεκτέα (sc. ἐστι τάδε) S.OC883; ἀνεκτέα τάδε (restored for ἀνεκτά) Ar.Lys.477: **ἀνεκτέον**, Clearch.4.

**ἀνεκτικός**, ή, όν, (ἀνέχομαι) *enduring, patient*, τῶν ἰδιωτῶν M.Ant.1.9; τινός Arr.Epict.2.22.36. Adv. **-κῶς** Hierocl. in CA12p.447M.

**ἀνέκτιτος**, ον, *unpaid*, χρέος D.Chr.12.43.

**ἀνέκτομος**, ον, *not castrated, entire*, prob. in Philotim.ap.Orib.2.69.3.

⊛**ἀνεκτός**, όν, later ή, όν IGRom.4.293 ii 4 (Pergam.), D.L.2.36: Aeol. **ὄνεκτος** Alc.Supp.27.9:—*bearable, sufferable, tolerable*, mostly with a neg. (like ἀνασχετός), λοίγια ἔργα.. οὐδ' ἔτ' ἀνεκτά Il.1.573; χρειὼ.. οὐκέτ' ἀνεκτός 10.118, Thgn.1195, etc.: so mostly in Att., οὐκ ἀνεκτόν A.Ag.1364; οὐκ ἀνεκτὰ S.Ant.282, etc.; or with a question, ἦ ταῦτα δῆτ' ἀνεκτά; Id.OT429; ταυτὶ δῆτ' ἀνέκτ' ἀκούειν; Ar.Th.563:—οὐκ ἀνεκτόν [ἐστι] foll. by inf., with or without μὴ οὐ, Pl.Tht.154c, 181b; τὸ μὲν οὐκ ἀ. ἐμοὶ.. γίγνεσθαι Id.Lg.861d. 2. without a neg., τὸ μὲν καὶ ἀνεκτὸν ἔχει κακόν *that can be endured*, Od.20.83; ἀ. χοῦτος ἦν ὅμως ἐμοί Pherecr.145.13; ἀνεκτὰ παθεῖν Th.7.77; μέχρι τοῦδε ἀνεκτοὶ οἱ ἔπαινοι ἐς ὅσον.. Id.2.35; παντὶ τρόπῳ ὅστις καὶ ὁπωσοῦν ἀνεκτός in any *tolerable* manner whatsoever, Id.8.90; ἀ. τι λέγειν Isoc.8.65; συμβίωσιν -όν Phld.Ir.p.78W.; ἀνεκτότερα *more tolerable*, Cic.Att.12.45.2; ἀνεκτότερον ἔσται τινί Ev.Matt.10.15, 11.22, etc.: Sup., Phld.Rh.2.226S. b. of persons, μόγις ἀνεκτοί Lys.22.20, cf. D.Ep.3.13. II. Adv. **-τῶς**, in Hom. always οὐκέτ' ἀνεκτῶς, Od.9.350, etc.; οὐκ ἀνεκτῶς ἔχει *it is not to be borne*, X.HG7.3.1: without neg., Phld.D.3 Fr.2, Oec.p.31J.

**ἀνεκτότης**, ητος, ἡ, *endurableness*, Gloss.

**ἀνέκ-τριπτος**, ον, *indelible*, Poll.1.44. **-φαντος** (v.l. -φατος), ον, *not to be revealed* or *uttered*, i.e. *mystical, obscure*, Procl. in Prm.p.549S., in Ti.3.169D. Adv. **-τως** Id. in Prm.p.589S., cf. Eust.382.9. **-φευκτος**, ον, *not to be escaped, inevitable*, D.S.20.54, Plu.2.166e, Corn.ND13, Phld.Ir.p.79W. ⊛**-φοίτητος**, ον, *not proceeding* or *emanating*: hence, *inseparable from*.., τὰ μέρη τῶν ὅλων Procl. in Ti.1.16D., in Prm.p.634S.; τοῦ ὅλου Dam.Pr.289; τοῦ ἑνός ib.59; ἀπὸ [τῆς οὐσίας] ib.66; ἑαυτῆς Eustr. in EN40.8. **-φορος**, ον, *not to be brought to light*, Iamb.VP32.226, Poll.5.147. 2. Medic., ἀνέκφορα πάντα γίγνεται there is a general *stoppage* (of intestinal obstruction), Archig.ap.Aët.9.28. ⊛**-φραστος**, ον, *inexpressible, unutterable*, Procl. in Prm.p.549S. 2. *not visiting*, τῶν ἐκεῖ Syrian. in Metaph.109.25. **-φώνητος**, ον: in Gramm., ἀνεκφώνητα *unpronounced letters*, as ι subscriptum, EM203.7. **-χύμωτος**, ον, *not drained of juices*, Gal.13.194.

**ἀνέλαιος**, ον, *without oil*, Thphr.CP2.3.8; *without olives*, Str.17.1.35.

**ἀνέλατος**, ον, = ἀνήλατος, Olymp. in Mete.326.38.

**ἀνελάττωτος**, ον, *undiminished*, Procl. in Alc.p.16C. Adv. **-τως** Id.Inst.27.

**ἀνέλεγ-κτος**, ον, *not cross-questioned, safe from being questioned*, Th.5.85; ἡ γλῶττα ἀ. ἡμῖν ἔσται, ἡ δὲ φρὴν οὐκ ἀ. Pl.Tht.154d, cf. Phlb.41b. 2. *not refuted*, ἐὰν τινὰ ἀ. Id.Grg.467a; ἵνα μοι καὶ ἀ. ἡ μαντεία γένοιτο *irrefutable*, Id.Ap.22a, cf. Ti.29b. Adv. **-τως**, λεγόμενον *without refutation* or *reply*, Plu.CG10. 3. of persons also, *without trial*, ἀ. διαφυγεῖν Th.6.53. **-ξία**, ἡ, *irrefutableness*, Stoic.2.39. **-χω**, *convince, convict utterly*, E.Ion1470.

**ἀνελεήμων**, ον, gen. ονος, *merciless, without mercy*, Arist.Rh.Al.1442$^{a}$13, Ep.Rom.1.31, Cat.Cod.Astr.2.173:—also **ἀνηλεήμων**, Nicoch.20; and in AB400 **ἀνελήμων**. Adv. ἀνελεημόνως, ἀπολέσθαι Antipho 1.25, Lxx Jb.6.21.

**ἀνελεής**, ές, = sq. Adv. **-ῶς** *mercilessly*, PLips.39.12 (iv A.D.).

**ἀνελέητος**, ον, *without pity*, Arist.Phgn.808$^{b}$1; εἰς ἀδελφόν Lib.Decl.47.32.

**ἀνελελίζω**, *shake and rouse*, Opp.C.4.302.

**ἀνέλεος**, ον, *unmerciful*, Ep.Jac.2.13.

**ἀνελευθερ-ία**, ἡ, *illiberality of mind, servility*, joined with κολακεία, Pl.Smp.183b, R.590b, etc. 2. esp. in money matters, *stinginess*, X.Cyr.8.4.32, Arist.EN1107$^{b}$10, 1121$^{b}$13, etc. **-ιος**, ον, = ἀνελεύθερος, Asp. in EN101.14. **-ιότης**, ητος, ἡ, = ἀνελευθερία, Arist.MM1192$^{a}$8. **-ος**, ον, *not free*, σωμα, of a slave, Pherecr.8D.; *slavish*, of a shameful death, A.Ag.1494 (lyr.); ἀτιμίαι Arist.Pol.1336$^{b}$12. 2. of actions, *servile, mean*, ἀ. εἶναι νομίζω κακηγορίας δικάζεσθαι Lys.10.2, cf. Pl.Tht.182c; ἀ. ἐργασίαι Arist.EN1121$^{b}$33; παιδιαί Pol.1336$^{a}$29. 3. esp. in money matters, *niggardly*, Ar.Pl.591, Arist.EN1107$^{b}$13, 1122$^{a}$5, etc. 4. *rude, unpolished*, διάλεκτος Ar.Fr.685. 5. of animals, *mean, treacherous*, ζῷα ἀ. καὶ ἐπίβουλα, οἷον οἱ ὄφεις Arist.HA488$^{b}$16. II. Adv. **-ρως** *meanly*, προσαιτεῖν X.Ap.9; ζῆν Alex.265.7.

**ἀνέλ-ιγμα**, ατος, τό, *anything rolled up*, ἀ. χαίτης *a ringlet*, AP6.210 (Philet.), cf. 7.485 (Diosc.). **-ικτος**, ον, *without turns or twists*, Aret.CD1.4, Gal.UP5.3. **-ιξις**, εως, ἡ, *unfolding*: hence, *evolution* in dancing, Plu.Thes.21. 2. *unfolding* in growth, Simp. in Ph.632.31. 3. logical *unfolding, exposition*, αἱ -ξεις τῶν λόγων Procl. in Prm.p.542S., cf. Syrian. in Metaph.97.4, Prisc.Lyd.34.23; ἡ μαθηματικὴ ἐπιστήμη γνῶσίς ἐστι.. διεξόδοις τισὶ χρωμένη καὶ ἀνελίξεσιν Iamb.Comm.Math.1. **-ίσσω**, Att. **ἀνελίττω**, Ep. and Ion. **ἀνειλίσσω**: (v. ἑλίσσω):—*unroll*, ἀγαλίδα Pherecyd.148J.: but mostly, *unroll* a book, Arist.Pr.914$^{a}$26 (Pass.); *read, interpret* it, X.Mem.1.6.14; λόγον Pl.Phlb.15e. 2. *unravel, 'explicate'*, τὸ συνεσπειραμένον τῆς νοερᾶς ἐπιβολῆς Procl. in Euc.p.4F., cf. Prisc.Lyd.34.23; ἀνειλιγμένος ὁρισμός *explicit* definition, Simp. in Ph.276.28. 3. *cause to move backward*, πόδα E.Or.171. II. *roll back*, i.e. *counteract*, ἀνελίττουσαι σφαῖραι Arist.Metaph.1074$^{a}$2, cf. Simp. in Cael.32.17, al., Procl.Hyp.4.98, Theo Sm.p.180H.: metaph., ὅπως ἂν στρέφῃ καὶ ἀνελίττῃ τὸν βίον ὁ θεός Plu.Num.14:—Med., *reverse the direction of motion*, Arist.GA741$^{b}$21:—Pass., *to be counteracted*, Id.Metaph.1074$^{a}$7; μίαν δ' ἀνελίσσετ' ἀμοιβήν Opp.H.1.420; γλῶσσ' ἀνελισσομένη *moving glibly*, Ar.Ra.827. III. intr., πνεύματ' ἀνειλίσσοντα Nic.Al.596.

**ἀνελκής**, ές, *free from ulceration*, Hp.Off.18.

**ἀνελκόομαι**, Pass., *suppurate afresh*, Hp.Mul.2.122, Morb.1.21, Cass.Pr.9.

**ἄνελκτος**, ον, *inextensible*, Arist.Mete.385$^{a}$16, 386$^{b}$14.

**ἀνελκτός**, όν, *up-drawn*, ἀ. ὀφρύσι, prob. of Pericles, Cratin.355.

**ἀνέλκυστος**, ον, *incapable of being pulled*, ὑπὸ φαντασίας Chrysipp.Stoic.2.40.

**ἀνέλκω**, *draw up*, τάλαντα.. ἀνέλκει *holds* them *up* (in weighing), Il.12.434; ἀνελκύσαι νηῦς *haul* them *up high and dry*, Hdt.7.59, Th.6.44; νῆες ἀνελκυσμέναι Hdt.9.98; δοκοὺς ἀ. Th.2.76; *haul up* a sail, Epicr.10. 2. *drag up, drag out*, ἀνελκύσαι εἰς τὸ φῶς Ar.Pax307; κατ' ἀνελκύσας ἐρωτᾷ *having dragged* him *into open court*, Id.Ach.687; τὰ παιδάρι' εὐθὺς ἀνέλκει *drags* them *into the witness-box*, Id.V.568:—Med., ἀνέλκεσθαι τρίχας *tear one's own* hair, Il.22.77:—Pass., κύνα χερσὶν ἀνελκόμενον D.P.790. II. *draw back*, ὁ δὲ τόξου πῆχυν ἀνέλκεν (in act to shoot) Il.11.375, cf. Od.21.128:—Med., ἔγχος ἀνελκόμενον *drawing back* his spear [out of the corpse], ib.22.97; τόξον ἀνέλκεται τοξευτής Arat.305:—Pass., pf. part. ἀνειλκυσμένος Procl.Hyp.7.39.

**ἀνέλκωσις**, εως, ἡ, (ἀνελκόομαι) *suppuration*, Cass.Pr.9.

**ἀνέλκωτος**, ον, *without ulcers*, Dsc.2.32, Aret.SD1.12; καρκινώματα, = κρυπτά, Leonid.ap.Aët.16.42, cf. 15.14, Aret.SD2.11.

**ἀνέλλειπτος**, ον, *unfailing*, πρὸς τὰς ὑπηρεσίας Inscr.Prien.113.90 (i B.C.). Adv. **-ως** *ceaselessly*, IG14.2498 (Nemausus).

**ἀνέλλην**, ηνος, ὁ, ἡ, *un-Greek, outlandish*, ὅμιλον ἀνέλληνα στόλον A.Supp.234 (ἀνελληνόστολον Bothe).

**ἀνελλήνιστος**, ον, *not Grecian*, S.E.M.1.181, Phryn.300, EM777.53.

**ἀνελλῐπής**, ές, *unfailing, unceasing*, ἀ. παρασχεῖν τὴν ἀγοράν *SIG* 799.17 (Cyzicus), cf. Ael.*VH*1.33; of rivers, Poll.3.103. Adv. –πῶς Plu.2.495c, S.E.*M*.8.439, *CIG*(add.)2775*b*(Aphrodisias). II. *not lacking*, τινός *OGI*194: abs., *lacking nothing*, Plot.5.8.7. Adv. = ἀπερίττως, σημαίνειν mean *exactly*, Alex.Aphr.*in Top*.43.3.—Also spelt **ἀνελλειπής** Eutoc.*in Archim*.3.114.16 H., Ammon. *in APr*.32.22.

**ἀνελλίπους**, *lame*, Hsch.

**ἄνελπις**, ιδος, ὁ, ἡ, *without hope*, σωτηρίας E.*IT*487.

**ἀνελπιστ-έω**, *despair*, Suid. **–ία**, ἡ, *hopelessness*, Ascl.*Tact*. 5.2, Sch.Th.2.51; *non-expectation*, Onos.10.20. **–ος**, ον, *unhoped for*, Heraclit.18; φυγή A.*Supp*.330; θαῦμα S.*Tr*.673; ἔργον Th.6.33; τύχη E.*Hel*.412; τὸ ἀ. τοῦ βεβαίου *the hopelessness* of attaining any certainty, Th.3.83; τὰ ἀ. Arist.*Rh*.1383ᵃ8; οὐκ ἀ. μοι γέγονεν τὸ γεγονός Pl.*Ap*.36a. Adv. –τως *unexpectedly*, γέγονεν ἀ. μέγας Decr.ap.D.18.182, cf. Plu.*Pel*.4. II. Act., 1. of persons, *having no hope, hopeless*, Hp.*Aph*.7.47, *Prog*.19; ἀ. δὲ θανόντες Theoc. 4.42: c. inf., ἀ. σωθήσεσθαι Th.8.1; ἀ. ἐπιγενέσθαι ἄν τινα σφίσι πολέμιον *not expecting that*.., Id.3.30; ἀ. τοῦ ἑλεῖν X.*Cyn*.7.9; ἀ. ἔς τινα Th.6.17; ἀ. καταστῆσαί τινι ὡς.. Id.3.46. Adv. –τως, ἔχει he is *in despair*, Pl.*Phlb*.36b. 2. of things or conditions, *leaving no hope, desperate*, βίοτος S.*El*.186 (lyr.), Th.5.102; πρὸς τὸ ἀ. τραπόμενοι Id. 2.51; ἀ. οὐδέν [ἐστι], c. acc. et inf., it is nowise *unreasonable to expect that*.., And.4.24: Comp., τὰ ἐκ τῆς γῆς ἀνελπιστότερα ὄντα Th.7.4. Adv. –τως, νουσέειν Aret.*CA*2.5.

**ἀνέλυτρος**, ον, *unsharded*, of bees, wasps, etc., opp. κολεόπτερα (beetles), Arist.*HA*490ᵃ15, 532ᵃ24, al.

**ἀνεμαφέτης**, ου, ὁ, *wind-releaser*, *PMag.Par*.1.1363.

**ἀνέμβᾰτος**, ον, *inaccessible*, Eratosth.*Fr*.16.14, D.H.1.3; ἀ. δρυμῶνα Babr.45.11; of a river, σκαφέεσσιν ἀ. *AP*9.641 (Agath.): metaph., ἡ οὐσία τῶν πραγμάτων ἀ. Ocell.1.15; βελέεσσιν ἀ. *AP*5.233.3 (Paul. Sil.). 2. *not to be trodden*, of a spot struck by a thunderbolt, Plu. *Pyrrh*.29. 3. Act., *not going to* or *visiting*, *AP*9.287 (Apollonid.).

**ἀνεμέσητος**, ον, (νέμεσις) *not incurring the wrath of God*, Pl.*Cra*. 401a: εἰ -ητον εἰπεῖν Id.*Smp*.195a; also, *not liable to blame*, ἀ. [ἐστι] ..τινί, c. inf., Id.*Tht*.175e, Aeschin.3.66, Epicur.*Fr*.161, etc. Adv. –τως Pl.*Lg*.684e.

**ἀν-έμετος** or **–ήμετος**, ον, *without vomiting*, Hp.*Prorrh*.1.85, *Epid*. 2.3.1. Adv. –τως *Coac*.546.

**ἀνεμέω**, *vomit up*, Hp.*Prorrh*.1.31, Arist.*HA*594ᵃ29, al.: metaph., Chrysipp.*Stoic*.2.243.

**ἀνέμητος**, ον, *not distributed*, οὐσία Aeschin.1.102, D.44.10; *undivided*, Max.Tyr.35.7. 2. Act., *having no share*, Plu.*Cat.Mi*.26.

**ἀνεμ-ία**, ἡ, (ἄνεμος) = ἐμπνευμάτωσις, *flatulence*, Hp.*Epid*.2.5.5. **–ιαῖος**, ον, *windy*, ᾠὸν ἀνεμιαῖον a *wind-egg*, Arar.6, *Com.Adesp*.5 D., Ath.2.57e; ἄγονα καὶ ἀ. ἔκγονα ψυχῆς Them.*Or*.32.356a. 2. metaph., *empty, vain*, γόνιμον ἢ ἀ. Pl.*Tht*.151e; ἀ. τε καὶ ψεῦδος ib. 161a; ἀ. ἐλπίς Alciphr.1.21. **–ίζομαι**, Pass., *to be driven with the wind*, *Ep.Jac*.1.6, Sch.Od.12.336: Act. in Hsch. s.v. ἀναψῦξαι. **–ιος**, ον, f.l. for ἀνεμιαῖος in Ph.1.96, cf. Hsch.

**ἀνεμό-δαρτος**, ον, *stripped by the wind*, Eust.1095.12. **–δρομος**, ον, *running with the wind, swift as the wind*, Luc.*VH*1.13. **–εις** [ᾰ], v. ἠνεμόεις. **–επάκτης**, ου, ὁ, *wind-bringer*, *PMag.Par*.1. 1360. **–ζάλη** [ζᾰ], ἡ, *strong surging sea*, Sch.Od.5.1 (pl.), Id.E. *Ph*.1154. **–κοῖται**, οἱ, *wind-lullers*, sorcerers at Corinth, Eust. 1645.42, Hsch. ⊛**–μαχία**, ἡ, *meeting of contrary winds*, Lyd.*Mens*. 4.13. **–ομαι**, Pass., *to be filled with wind*, Pl.*Ti*.83d; ἠνεμωμένος τὴν τρίχα with hair *floating in the wind*, Callistr.*Stat*.14; ἠνεμωμένη πτεροῖς Lyc.1119: of the sea, *to be raised by the wind*, *AP*13.12 (Hegesipp.). II. *to be inflated, swollen*, Hp.*Nat.Mul*.64: metaph., ἠνεμῶσθαι περί τι *to be eager* for.., Ael.*NA*11.7. **–ποιός**, *wind-creating*, *PMag.Lond*.121.776. **–πους**, ουν, gen. οδος, *with feet swift as the wind*, *EM*20.6.

⊛ **ἄνεμος** [ᾰ], ὁ, *wind*, πέτετο πνοιῇς ἀνέμοιο Il.12.207; ἀνέμων ἀτάλαντοι ἀέλλῃ 13.795; ὦρσεν..ἀνέμοιο θύελλαν 12.253; ἀνέμοιο.. δεινὸς ἀήτης 15.626, cf. 14.254; ἀνέμων ἀμέγαρτον ἀϋτμήν Od.11.407, etc.; ἀνέμων πνεύματα Hdt.7.16.α', E.*HF*102; ῥιπαί S.*Ant*.137, 930 (both lyr.); ἀήματα A.*Eu*.905; αὖραι E.*Med*.838; πνοιαί Ar.*Av*.1396; ἀνέμων φθόγγος Simon.37.10; ἀνέμου κατιόντος μεγάλου *a gale* having come on, Th.2.25; ἀνέμου ἐξαίφνης ἀσελγοῦς γενομένου Eup.320; ἄνεμος κατὰ βορέαν ἑστηκώς *the wind* being set in the north, Th.6.104; ἀνέμοις φέρεσθαι παραδιδόναι τι cast a thing *to the winds*, E.*Tr*.419, cf. A.R.1.1334; κατ' ἄνεμον στῆναι stand *to leeward*, Arist.*HA*541ᵃ26, cf. Plu.2.972a; κατ' ἄνεμον καὶ ῥοῦν νήχεσθαι ib.979c: metaph., ἄνεμος..ἄνθρωπος 'unstable as the wind', Eup.376; φέρειν τιν' ἄρας (sic l.) ἄ. *a very wind* to carry off, Antiph.195.5 (Lobeck); ἀνέμους θηρᾶν ἐν δικτύοις try to catch *the wind*, and ἀνέμῳ διαλέγεσθαι talk *to the wind*, Zen.1.38; ἀνέμους γεωργεῖν 'plough the sands', ib.100. 2. *cardinal point, quarter*, ἐκ τῶν τεσσάρων ἀ. Lxx *Za*.2.6, *Annales du Service* 19.40 (Theadelphia, 93 B.C.), *Ev.Matt*.24.31, al., Vett.Val. 140.6, *PFlor*.50.104: sg., ib.20.19 (ii A.D.); τὸ κατ' ἄνεμον *aspect*, *POxy*.100.10 (ii A.D.). II. *wind* in the body, Hp.*Mul*.2.179, al. (From ἀνε- 'blow, breathe', cf. Skt. *áni-ti* 'breathes', Goth. *uzanan* 'expire', etc.)

**ἀνεμο-σκεπής**, ές, *sheltering one from the wind*, χλαῖναι Il.16. 224. **–στροφος**, ον, *whirling with wind*, θύελλα prob. for –τρόπῳ in *Anacreont*.36.14. ⊛ **–συρις**, ιδος, ἡ, a kind of *fan*: hence, *fan-shaped whirlwind*, Olymp. *in Mete*.200.19. **–σφάραγος** [φᾰ], ον, *echoing to the wind*, κόλποι Pi.*P*.9.5. **–τραφής**, ές, = sq., Eust.1095.12. ⊛ **–τρεφής**, ές, *fed by the wind*, κῦμα ἀ. Il.15.625; ἔγχος ἀ. a spear from a tree *reared by the wind*, i.e. *made tough and strong by battling with the wind*, 11.256 (v.l. ἀνεμοτρεπές or –στρεφές *turned*, i.e. *shaken by the wind*), cf. Philostr.*Im*.2.3.

⊛**ἀνεμούριον**, τό, (οὖρος) *windmill*, Hero *Spir*.1.43.

**ἀνεμο-φθορία**, ἡ, *blasting, blight*, Lxx *De*.28.22, *IG*12(9).955.7, 1179.25 (Euboea). ⊛**–φθορος**, ον, *blasted by the wind*, Lxx *Ho*.8. 7, Ph.2.431. **–φοιτος**, ον, v. sub ἠνεμ–. ⊛**–φόρητος**, ον, *carried by the wind*, of rumours, Cic.*Att*.13.37.4; of delicate vessels, Luc.*Lex*.7; dub. sens. in *Sammelb*.4324.8(–φόρετος), 14.

**ἀνέμ-πληκτος**, ον, *intrepid*, Sch.E.*Or*.1479. Adv. –τως Plu.*Galb*. 23 (nisi legendum ἀνεκπλήκτως). **–πληστος**, ον, *of which one cannot have one's fill*, θέαμα v.l. in Them.*Or*.2.40b. **–πόδιστος**, ον, *unhindered*, ἐνέργεια Arist.*EN*1153ᵃ15; βίος *Pol*.1295ᵃ37. Adv. –τως D.S.1.36, *PFlor*.370.17 (ii A.D.), Jul.*Or*.6.193d. 2. *not obscured, clear*, Procl.*Hyp*.4.92. Adv. –τως ib.88. II. Act., *offering no impediment*, πρός τι Arist.*PA*663ᵇ11. **–πόλητος**, ον, *unsold*, Sch.S.*Ant*.1036. **–πτωτος**, ον, *not falling into*, εἰς λύπας Pl. *Def*.412c: abs., D.L.7.117. **–υμάχθη**· ὑπείδετο, Hsch. **–φάνιστος**, ον, *without formal notification*, δωρεαί, opp. ἐμφανεῖς, Just.*Nov*.162. 1. **–φαντος**, ον, *not expressive* or *indicative*, ὕβρεως κτλ. Plu.2. 45c; πλήθους Procl. *in Prm*.p.630S. ⊛**–φᾰτος**, ον, v.l. for foreg., Procl.*in Prm*. l. c., cf. eund. *in Ti*.3.1 and 12 D.; *without a tinge of*, Elias *in Cat*.20.26: abs., *lacking in expression*, πλοκή, of melody without rhythm, Aristid.Quint.1.13; λέξις Aristid.*Rh*.2 p.434 S. Adv. –τως Hermog.*Id*.2.10, 11, Aristid.*Rh*.2 pp.434, 450 S.

**ἀνεμ-ώδης**, ες, *windy*, Σκῦρος S.*Fr*.553; χώρα Hp.*Aër*.24, cf. Nic. *Th*.96; ἀκρωτήριον Plu.2.967b; ἔτος ἀ. Arist.*Mete*.360ᵇ5; κύματα ἀ. *bringing wind*, Id.*Pr*.932ᵇ29; σημεῖον ἀ. a sign *of wind*, Thphr.*Sign*. 18. 2. metaph., *vain, idle*, Hsch. s.v. κραπαταλίας. **–ώκης**, ες, *swift as the wind*, νεφέλα E.*Ph*.163 (lyr.); δῖναι Ar.*Av*.697; κόρα *Lyr.Adesp*.106. **–ώλιος**, ον, *windy*, Hom., but only metaph., ἀνεμώλια βάζειν talk *words of wind*, Il.4.355, Od.11.464; οἱ δ' αὖτ' ἀνεμώλιοι are *like the winds*, i.e. *empty boasters*, Il.20.123; τί νυ τόξον ἔχεις ἀνεμώλιον αὔτως; why bear thy bow *in vain?* 21.474; δίκη ἀ., of a trial, Maiist.38; ἔπεσεν.. ἀνεμώλιον αὔτως Theoc.25.239; εἶπε δ' ὕδωρ πίνειν, ἀνεμώλιος *the empty fool!* *AP*11.61 (Maced.); ἀ. ἀσπίδα θεῖναι make it *powerless*, i.e. *harmless*, Orph.*L*.512.—Ep. and Ion. word, used by Luc.*Astr*.2. (From ἄνεμος, with Aeol. ending –ώνιος, by dissimilation –ώλιος, Eust.1214.27; cf. μετα-μώνιος.)

**ἀνεμ-ώνη**, ἡ, *poppy anemone*, *Anemone coronaria*, Cratin.98, Pherecr.108.25, Theoc.5.92, Thphr.*HP*7.10.2; ἀ. ἥμερος Dsc.2. 176. 2. ἀ. ἀγρία *scarlet wind-flower*, *Anemone fulgens*, ibid.; also called ἀ. φοινικῆ Crateuas *Fr*.4; ἀ. λειμωνία Thphr.*HP*6.8.1. 3. ἀ. ὀρεία, *mountain wind-flower*, *Anemone blanda*, ibid.; αἷμα ῥόδον τίκτει, τὰ δὲ δάκρυα τὰν ἀ. Bion 1.66. II. metaph., ἀνεμῶναι λόγων *flowers* of speech (with suggestion of *emptiness*), Luc.*Lex*. 23. **–ωνίς**, ίδος, ἡ, = ἀνεμώνη ἥμερος, Nic.*Fr*.74.64, Nonn.*D*.42. 323.

**ἀνεμώτας**, α, ὁ, *ass sacrificed to the winds* at Tarentum, Hsch.

⊛**Ἀνεμῶτις**, ιδος, ἡ, *she that stills the wind*, Ἀθηνᾶ Paus.4.35.8.

⊛ **ἀνεν-δεής**, ές, *in want of naught*, Plu.2.1068c, *AP*10.115; sup., Plot.6.9.6, Dam.*Pr*.13; πάντων ἀ. βίος Hdn.8.7.5; τὸ ἀνενδεὲς τῆς τροφῆς *IG*5(2).268.17 (Mantinea, Aug.). Adv. –εῶς *faultlessly, unexceptionably*, D.H.*Rh*.1.5, D.Chr.12.34; ἀ. ἐκτελέσας *CIG*3989 (Laodicea Combusta), cf. 4085 (Pessinus), *SIG*888.21 (Maced.), *PLond*. 3.974 i 4 (iv A.D.). 2. *completely*, Iamb.*Comm.Math*.10. 3. *with no need of*, βοηθείας Jul.*Mis*.341c. **–δεκτος**, ον, *inadmissible, impossible*, *Ev.Luc*.17.1, Artem.2.70. **–δετος**, ον, *not bound up with*, νοῦς ἀ. σώματι Ph.1.71. ⊛**–δοίαστος**, ον, *unhesitating*, Ph.1. 440, 2.36; *indubitable*, Id.1.302, al., Luc.*Herm*.67; *unambiguous*, Anon. *in SE*61.15; Gramm., *unquestionably correct*, ἀ. καὶ ὑγιές A.D. *Synt*.21.1. Adv. –τως 218.19; *without doubt*, Ph.2.319; *unhesitatingly, unequivocally*, 1.351, *POxy*.138.25 (610 A.D.). **–δοτος**, ον, *unyielding, rigid*, τόνος κλίνης Antyll.ap.Orib.9.14.5; *not giving way*, Ph.1.154, al.: metaph., προθυμία Hierocl.p.57.3 A., Orib.*Fr*.55; πάθος Herod.Med.in *Rh.Mus*.58.89. Adv. –τως, διαθλεῖν Ph.2.66, cf. Eustr.*in EN*297.23. **–δῦτος**, ον, *not put on*, Hsch. s. v. ἄφαροι.

**ἀνένεικα**, Ion. aor. Act. of ἀναφέρω.

**ἀνενεκτέον**, (ἀναφέρω) *one must refer*, Plot.4.4.38, Dam.*Pr*.277.

**ἀνενεργ-ής**, ές, *inefficacious*, Thphr.*HP*9.17.1, Dsc.2.111. **–ησία**, ἡ, *want of exercise*, Sor.1.106; *inactivity*, Alex.Aphr. *de An*.74.27; as criticism of Sceptics by Stoics, *Stoic*.2.36. **–ητος**, ον, *inefficacious, inactive*, Ruf.*Anat*.30, S.E.*M*.7.30, cf. Alex.Aphr. *de An*.39.8, Hierocl.*in CA* 21 p.466 M.; οὐσία Plot.6.8.21. 2. *not possessing an* ἐνέργεια, of the Good, Plot. 5.6.6. 3. *not actualized* or *realized*, Procl. *in R*.2.160 K., *in Prm*.p.600 S., *in Ti*.3.32 D. **–ος**, ον, = ἀνενεργής, Serapion in *Cat.Cod.Astr*.8(4).228 (Comp.).

**ἀνενεύει**· ἀρνεῖται, ἀπὸ τοῦ ἄνω νεύειν, ἢ ἀπαρνεῖται, Hsch.

⊛**ἀνενεχύραστος**, ον, *not liable to distraint*, *CPR*1.15 (i A.D.), etc.

**ἀνενήνοθεν**· ἀνῆγεν ἢ ἀνέβη, Hsch.; cf. ἐνήνοθε.

**ἀνεν-θουσίαστος**, ον, *unimpassioned*, ἡδοναί Plu.2.751b; βίος ἀ. εἰς τιμήν ib.1098d. Adv. –τως ib.346b. **–θύμητος**, ον, *failing to consider*, τοῦ θνητοῦ Phld.*Mort*.38. **–νόητος**, ον, *without conception of*, τινός Plb.2.35.6, Phld.*Herc*.862.9, D.S.1.8, Plot.6.7.29, Procl.*in Prm*.p.484 S.; foll. by indirect qn., Alex.Aphr. *de An*. 175.14. Adv. –τως *without the use of concepts*, Eustr.*in EN*40.7; *without discursive thought*, i.e. by intuition, Porph.*Sent*.10. II. *inconceivable*, Cleom.2.1; ἐννοεῖν τὰ –τα Dam.*Pr*.7. **–όχλητος**, ον, *undisturbed*, Hdn.5.7.2, Hld.5.19; of a sepulchre, *CIG*2845.9

Aphrodisias), *BGU*935.3 (iii/iv A. D.). Adv. -τως Ruf. and Aspasia ap.Aët.16.50, Sch.E.*Or.*630, Simp.*in Ph.*1176.24. ⊛-τᾰτος, ον, *without tension* or *force*, Theopomp.Com.71 ; *without over-exertion*, Antyll.ap.Orib.6.21.5. -τᾰφιάστως, Adv. *without burial*, Eust.1278.60. -τευκτος, ον, *unsociable*, ἤθη Plu.2.10a. 2. *inaccessible to persuasion* or *influence*, δικαιοσύνη ib.355a, etc. -τονον· ἱμάτιον (Lacon.), Hsch. -τρέπτως, *without doubt*, *An.Ox.*2.341. -τρεχής, ές, *ill-adapted, inappropriate*, Hierocl.p.50.22 A. ⊛ -τροπος, ον, *not heeding* or *respecting* a thing, Hsch.; δαίμων *Eranos*13.87 (inc. loc.).

**ἀνεξ-άκουστος** [ᾰκ], ον, *unheard of*, Sch.S.*Aj.*318. -**άλειπτος** [ᾰλ], ον, *indelible*, Isoc.5.71, Plu.2.1b, *PHolm.*22.43, cf. 1.12. Adv. -τως Hsch. -**άλλακτος**, ον, *unchangeable*, Procl. *in Ti.*1.238D., Id. *in Prm.*p.599 S. ⊛-**αλλοτρίωτος**, ον, *unalienated*, *BGU*1151.43 (i B.C.), *PLond.*2.360.9, etc., cf. *Ath.Mitt.*3.58 (Lydia). -**ᾰπᾰτησία**, ἡ, *freedom from deception* or *mistake*, Arr.*Epict.*3.2.2. -**ᾰπάτητος**, ον, *infallible, not to be deceived*, Arist.*Top.*132ᵃ32 ; πρός τι in a thing, Id.*Pol.*1338ᵃ42, cf. Hierocl. *in CA*23p.470M., al. Adv. -τως Ph.1.483, Poll.8.11. -**ᾰρίθμητος**, ον, *not to be counted or told*, Id.3.88, 4.162. ⊛-**έλεγκτος**, ον, *incapable of disproof* or *criticism*, Th.1.21 ; τὸν λόγον ἀ. ποιεῖν Arist.*SE*176ᵇ24 ; ἀ. μᾶλλον ἢ πιθανήν *difficult to disprove* rather than credible, D.S.1.40, etc.; ἀ. ἔχει τὸ ἀνδρεῖον leaves their courage *without any real test* or *proof*, Th.4.126 ; *unrefuted*, Gal.15.547. Adv. -τως X.*Oec.*10.8, prob. in S.E.*M.*7.191. 2. of persons, *not to be convicted*, Antipho 2.1.10 : of conduct, etc., *blameless, unexceptionable*, X.*Cyn.*13.7, D.25.39, Plu.*Pel.*4. -**έλευστος**, ον, = ἀνεξίτητος, Hsch. -**έλικτος**, ον, *whose development cannot be fully exhausted*, ταῖς ἡμετέραις ἐπιβολαῖς Dam.*Pr.*177. Adv. -τως dub. l. S.E.*M.*7.191. -**εράω**, = ἀναπτύω, Sch.Opp.*H.*1.137. -**έργαστος**, ον, *not worked out, unfinished*, Luc. *Fug.*21, Gal.*Nat.Fac.*2.3. -**ερεύνητος** (Hellenistic ἀνεξεραύν-), ον, *not to be searched out*, Heraclit.18, *Ep.Rom.*11.33, D.C.69.14. ⊛-**έταστος**, ον, *not searched out, not inquired into* or *examined*, D.4.36, 21.218, Aeschin.3.22. II. *without inquiry* or *investigation*, ὁ ἀ. βίος οὐ βιωτὸς ἀνθρώπῳ Pl.*Ap.*38a. Adv. -τως Ph.1.550, Plu.2.94d, etc. -**εύρετος**, ον, *not to be found out*, ἀριθμός Th.3.87, cf. Hellanic.194 J., Arist.*Mu.*392ᵃ17, Plu.2.964a. -**ήγητος**, ον, *not to be told*, μυστήρια Hsch. s.v. σεμνά. 2. *unexplained*, Gal.*UP*2.7, Simp. *in Ph.*241.21, Sch.Pi.*N.*9.95. 3. *unspeakable, ineffable*, πέλαγος κάλλους Them.*Or.*13.177d.

⊛**ἀνεξία**, ἡ, *endurance, resignation*, Sicilian word, Cic.*Att.*5.11.5.

**ἀνεξῐκᾰκ-έω**, *to be long-suffering*, Charito 8.4. -**ία**, ἡ, *forbearance*, Plu.2.90e, Luc.*Par.*53, Hld.10.12 ; ἀ. πόνων *patient endurance under*.., Hdn.3.8.8, cf. Eun.*Hist.*p.258D. -**ος**, ον, *enduring pain* or *evil*, Herod.Med.ap.Orib.5.30.7, Luc.*Jud.Voc.*9, Vett.Val.38.21, Gal.5.38, Them.*Or.*15.190a (Sup.), Aret.*SA*2.6 (Comp.) ; *forbearing, long-suffering*, 2*Ep.Ti.*2.24. Adv. -κως Luc.*Asin.*2.

**ἀνεξίκμαστος**, ον, *not dried up*, Arist.*Pr.*928ᵃ29, cf. Gal.8.367.

**ἀνεξῐκώμη**, ἡ, expl. by Hsch. as ἧς οὐκ ἂν ἀνάσχοιτο ὅλη κώμη, Cratin.383, but rather ἡ ὅλην κώμην ἀνέχουσα.

⊛**ἀνεξ-ίλαστος** [ῐ], ον, *implacable*, Ptol.*Tetr.*162, Harp. s.v. ἀνίδρυτος. -**ινάσκετο**· ἐξαινίσκετο, ἀνεξηραίνετο, Hsch. -**ιόομαι**, (ἰός) *to be reduced to a metallic state*, Zos.Alch.p.153 B. -**ίτηλος** [ῑ], ον, *indelible*, βαφή Poll.1.44. -**ίτητος** [ῐ], ον, *with no outlet*: *inevitable*, Hsch. -**ιχνίαστος**, ον, *unsearchable, inscrutable*, Lxx *Jb.*5.9, *Ep.Rom.*11.33, *Ep.Eph.*3.8. -**όδευτος**, ον, *with no issue* or *outlet*, ἀ. ἐς φέος τρίβοι *IGRom.*4.743 (Eumeneia). ⊛-**οδίαστος**, ον, *not to be alienated*, *CIG*2050 (Philippopolis), cf. *BCH*27.318, prob. in *IGRom.*4.1475 (Smyrna). ⊛-**οδος**, ον, *with no outlet, not to be got out of, impassable*, Ἀχέρων Theoc.12.19; δυσχωρίαι D.H.3.59 ; λαβύρινθος *AP*12.93 (Rhian.). 2. ἡμέρα ἀ. *unfit for an expedition*, Plu.2.269e. II. of persons, conditions, etc., *not coming into public, unsocial*, ib.242e, 426b, etc.; βίος 1098d; διάνοια 610a; λόγοι ἀ. *without practical result*, 1034b. -**οιστος**, ον, *not to be expressed, ineffable*, ib.728d, Gorg.(?)ap.S.E.*M.*7.82, Jul.*Or.*5.158d. -**ούσιος**, ον, *without power*, Gloss.

**ἀνεορτ-άζω**, *instaurare ludos*, D.C.*Fr.*51 (Pass.). -**αστος**, ον, *without holidays* or *festive joy*, βίος Democr.230, cf. Plu.2.1102b. -**ος**, ον, *without festival*, Alciphr.3.49 ; ἑορταὶ ἀ. festivals *unkept*, D.H.8.25, but, *impious* festivals, Ph.2.320 : c. gen., ἀ. ἱερῶν *without share in festal* rites, E.*El.*310.

**ἀνεοστᾰσίη**, ἡ, = ἐνεοστασίη, Hsch.

⊛**ἀνεπ-άγγελτος**, ον, *not announced*, πόλεμος ἀ. a war *begun without formal declaration*, Plb.4.16.4. 2. *uninvited*, ἀ. φοιτᾶν ἐπὶ δεῖπνον Cratin.44. -**αίσθητος**, ον, *unperceived, imperceptible*, Ti.Locr. 100b, Plu.2.1062b, Luc.*Sat.*33. Adv. -τως Simp. *in Cat.*309.3. 2. Act., *not perceiving*, τινός Plb.28.1.6, Longin.4.1, *OGI*194 (Egypt). Adv. -τως Ph.*Fr.*70 H., *Hippiatr.*38, Syrian. *in Metaph.*100.38, Simp. *in Ph.*1198.39. -**άϊστος**, ον, *inaudible*, Agathocl.2. -**αίσχυντος**, ον, *having no cause for shame*, 2*Ep.Ti.*2.15 ; μηδὲ -τον ἡγοῦ *J.AJ* 18.7.1. -**αιτίᾱτος**, ον, *unimpeached*, ib.4.8.38. -**ακτος**, ον, *not brought in* or *home*, Ph.1.139. -**άλλακτος**, ον, *not alternating*, ἀ. ζῷα animals in which the upper and lower teeth *do not lock into one another*, but meet flat, opp. καρχαρόδοντα, Arist.*HA* 501ᵃ17.

**ἀνέπαλτο, ἀνεπάλμενος**, v. sub ἀναπάλλω.

**ἀνεπ-άνακτος**, ον, *not to be brought back*, ἀ. ἐκβάλλεσθαι Ph.1.139, cf. 2.338 (dub.). -**ανόρθωτος**, ον, *irreparable*, ἀτύχημα J.*AJ*16.11.3 ; *incorrigible*, Iamb.*VP*22.102 ; *uncorrected*, Plu.2.49b, Arr.*Epict.* 3.1.11. II. *not to be amended, perfect*, Ph.2.614. -**αύξητος**, ον, Gramm., *unaugmented*, *An.Ox.*4.180.

⊛ **ἀνέπᾰφος**, ον, *untouched, unharmed*, ἀ. παρέχειν τι D.35.24, cf. Syngr.ib.11 ; ἀ. σώματα *not liable to seizure*, Men.*Perinth.*8 ; ἐλευθέρα ἔστω καὶ ἀ. *GDI*1532, cf. Thphr.*Fr.*97.2, *IG*2.584c, *BGU*193.19 (ii A. D.) ; ὑποθήκη *PHamb.*28.8 (ii B. C.) ; *unencumbered*, οἰκία *PThead.*1.12 (iv A. D.) : c. gen., *unharmed by*, ὕβρεως M.Ant.3.4. Adv. -φως Suid.

**ἀνεπαφρο-δῑσία**, ἡ, = ἀναφροδισία, *BGU*1197.14 (12 B. C.). -**δῑτος**, ον, = ἀναφρόδιτος, X.*Smp.*8.15, *Com.Adesp.*123, Alciphr.3.60.

**ἀνεπαχθής**, ές, *not burdensome, without offence*, Plu.*Cat.Mi.*8, *Pomp.*1 ; σκώμματα Luc.*Ep.Sat.*34. II. Adv. -θῶς, προσομιλεῖν Th.2.37 ; λέγειν Luc.*Sol.*5. 2. *not taking offence*, ἀνεπαχθῶς φέρειν Plu.2.102e. 3. *without discomfort*, Jul.*Or.*6.191d.

**ἀνεπείγομαι**, dub. l. in Man.5.97.

**ἀνεπ-είσακτος**, ον, *not adventitious, native, instinctive*, Sch.Opp. *H.*1.705. -**έκτᾰτος**, ον, *not lengthened*, A.D.*Synt.*110.14, al.; of declensions, *parisyllabic*, D.T.632.10. -**έλευστος**, ον, *not coming back*, Sch.S.*El.*182. -**εξέργαστος**, ον, *not wrought out, imperfect*, Simp. *in de An.*4.13, Eust.499.2. -**εξήγητος**, ον, *unexplained*, ἀ. καταλιπεῖν Gal.15.14 (al. ἀνεπιζήτητος). -**έρειστος**, ον, *not supported*, Iamb.*Comm.Math.*8. -**ερώτητος**, ον, *not asked for* or *arranged for*, τὸ μὴ προσήκειν ἀ. τρέχειν τόκον Just.*Nov.*136.4. ⊛-**ηρέαστος**, ον, *free from injury* or *insult, unmolested*, D.S.31.8, Memn.2.3, J.*AJ*14.10.6, *PFlor.*91.17 (ii A. D.), cf. *BGU*1022.24 : Medic., *uninjured*, Archig.ap.Orib.8.1.6, Id.ap.Aët.8.73. Adv. -τως J.*AJ* 16.2.5.

**ἀνεπής**, ές, *without a word, speechless*, Hsch.

**ἀνεπι-βάρητος**, ον, *unburdened*, πόλις *IGRom.*4.219 (Ilium), cf. *IG* 7.2711, *SIG*799.16 (Cyzicus), *Ath.Mitt.*33.382 (Pergam.). -**βᾰσία**, ἡ, (ἀ- priv.) *prohibition of traffic* or *intercourse*, *IG*4.752.6 (Troezen), Heraclit.*Ep.*9.8. -**βᾰτος**, ον, *not to be climbed*, γυμνῷ ποδί Str. 12.3.11 ; *inaccessible*, Plu.2.228b. ⊛-**βλητος**, ον, *inattentive, heedless*, prob. l. Phld.*D.*1.14, *Mus.*p.80 K. -**βούλευτος**, ον, *without plots*, and so, 1. Act., *not plotting*, τὸ ἀ. πρὸς ἀλλήλους *the absence of intrigue*, Th.3.37 ; *not insidious*, λόγος Aristid.*Rh.*2 p.445 S. 2. Pass., *not plotted against, not liable to attack*, ἀ. φθόνῳ *Com.Adesp.*1212, cf. Plb.7.8.4, Agatharch.42, Ael.*NA*9.59, etc. Adv. -τως Ph.2.645, Suid. s.v. Ξάνθος. -**βουλος**, ον, *not exposed to treachery*, *PSI*1.96.3 (v A. D.). Adv. -λως *without treachery*, Eust.905.57. -**γνώμων**, ον, gen. ονος, *ignorant, unconscious*, τινός Porph.*Abst.*1.45. -**γνωστος**, ον, *not distinctly known*, Herm.ap. Stob.1.41.44 ; τὸ ἀ. τῆς συμβολῆς J.*AJ*12.2.11 :— Act., *not knowing distinctly*, τινός Simp. *in de An.*299.37. Adv. -τως *not noticeably*, Plb.18.18.16. ⊛-**γρᾰφος**, Dor. -γροφος *Tab.Heracl.*1.84, ον, *without title* or *inscription*, χιτωνίσκιον ἀ. (for the names of those who offered vestments were embroidered upon them) *IG*2.754.28, al., ib. 7.303.102 (Oropus), etc. : μέσσοροι *Tab.Heracl.* l. c. 2. *unregistered*: hence, *free of charge*, of a harvest, γένημα ἀ. *PGnom.*234 (ii A. D.), cf. Plb.8.31.6, D.S.1.64, etc. : metaph., *without distinguishing marks*, Luc.*Nec.*15 ; *unmarked*, *Cat.*25. ⊛-**δάνειστος** [δᾰ], ον, *on which no money has been borrowed, not mortgaged*, *IG*12(7).515 (Amorgos), *BGU*193.19 (ii A. D.), Sch.Luc.*JTr.*48. -**δεής**, ές, = ἀνενδεής, v. l. in Pl.*Lg.*947e, cf. Chrysipp.*Stoic.*3.16 ; ἀ. τινος Ph.1.334, al., Luc.*DMort.*26.2. -**δείκνῡμι**, *make clear, show*, Gal. 1.172.

**ἀνεπί-δεικτος**, ον, *not able to be shown*, Herophil.ap.S.E.*M.*11.50. 2. *not exhibited*, *IG*7.3073.172 (Lebad.). 3. *unsupported by proof*, αἰτία Gorg.*Pal.*4. -**δεκτος**, ον, *not accepting* or *admitting*, νόμων Phld.*Rh.*1.383 S.; κακοῦ S.E.*M.*9.33, cf. D.L.3.77, Alex. Aphr. *in Metaph.*393.13, Id. *in Top.*210.16. ⊛-**δετος**, ον, *not bandaged*, Hp.*Fract.*20 ; *not requiring a bandage*, of plasters, Dsc.5.85, Damocr.ap.Gal.13.915. -**δηκτος**, ον, f.l. for -δετος, Dsc.5.85. -**δηλος**, ον, *not manifest* or *observable*, Ptol.*Harm.*1.4. -**δῐκος**, ον, *without the process of* ἐπιδικασία, by which claims to inheritance or guardianship were enforced, ἀ. ἔχειν τὰ πατρῷα Is.3.59 ; παραλαμβάνειν ἀ. τὴν ἀγχιστείαν Id.8.34 (cj.) ; ἀ. ἔχειν κλῆρον D.46.22, cf. Poll.3.33. -**δόκητος**, ον, *unexpected*, Simon.62. -**δοτος**, ον, *not growing* or *sprouting*, Thphr.*HP*7.4.8, *CP*4.6.3. -**είκεια**, ἡ, *unfairness, unkindness*, D.29.3. -**εικής**, ές, *unreasonable, unfair*, Th.3.66, Ar.*Fr.*50 D., Phld.*Ir.*p.57 W., Alex.Aphr. *in Top.*208.9 : neut. as Adv., *without consideration*, *PGiss.*39.3 (ca. 200 B. C.) : regul. Adv. -κῶς Arr.*An.*7.29.1, Poll.8.13. -**ζητησία**, ἡ, *absence of inquiry*, Andronic.Rhod.p.572 M. -**ζήτητος**, ον, *leaving nothing to be desired*, *IPE*1².39.8 (Olbia). 2. v. l. for ἀνεπεξήγητος, *uninvestigated*, Gal.15.14. -**θετος**, ον, *admitting no addition*, Dicaearch. 59.7. -**θεώρητος**, ον, Astrol., *not overlooked* or *controlled*, Gal.19.548. -**θόλωτος**, ον, *untroubled, unpolluted*, S.E.*M.*1.303, Procl. *in Alc.*p.251 C. -**θύμητος** [ῡ], ον, *without desire*, opp. ἐπιθυμητικός, Stob.2.6.14, Chaerem.Hist.4. -**καλύπτως**, Adv. *openly*, v. l. in D.S.2.21. -**καυτος**, ον, *free from sunburn*, πρόσωπα Dsc.2.50. -**κέλευστος**, ον, *not under orders*, φύσις, metaph. of untilled land, Ph.2.207. Adv. -τως 1.115. -**κηρύκευτος** [ρῡ], ον, = ἀκήρυκτος, Hsch.; πολέμιοι Procop.*Aed.*4.1. -**κινδύνως** [ῡ], Adv. *without danger*, ib.5.3. -**κλήρωτος**, ον, *not assigned by lot*, *IG*2.789a28, al. -**κλητος**, ον, *free from blame, unimpeachable*, X.*Cyr.*2.1.22 ; πίστις J.*AJ*18.9.4 : Comp. -ότερος X.*Ages.*1.5. Adv. -τως D.C.39.22. II. *without preferring any charge*. Adv. -τως Th.1.92. -**κλῖτος**, ον, *unwavering*, Simp. *in Cat.*201.31. -**κλυστος**, ον, *not liable to inundation*, τεῖχος J.*AJ*2.10.2. **-κόητα**· ἀσύνετα, Hsch. (-νόητα cod.). **-κοινώνητος**, ον, *not social* or *gregarious*, Eust.73.38. **-κόρριστος**, ον, *not insulted*, *EM*103.35, cf. Hsch. **-κούρητος**, ον, *without succour*, Philem.213.2, Onos.3.2. **-κράτητος** [ρᾰ], ον, *without dominant planet*, γένεσις Vett.Val.151.5. **-κρῐσία**, ἡ, *inability to form a judgement*, S.E.*M*.11.182. **-κρῐτος**, ον, *not decided*, *indeterminate*, πράγματα Aristocl.ap.Eus.*PE*14.18, cf. S.E.*P*.1.98, etc. Adv. -τως Id.*M*.11.230. 2. *indistinct*, *indeterminate*, φαντασία Plot.3.6.4. 3. Medic., *untested*, *untried*, ἡ διαφωνία ἡ ἀ., t.t. of the Empirics, Gal.1.78. 4. *not officially examined*, *POxy*.257.23 (ii A.D.), etc.; of a question, etc., *unexamined*, Simp.*in Ph*.1148.29. **-κρυπτος**, ον, *unconcealed*, M.Ant.1.14. ⊛**-κώλῡτος**, ον, *unhindered*, J.*AJ*18.6.4, Onos.35.2. Adv. -τως *without let or hindrance*, *IPE*2.52 (Panticapaeum); *without restraint*, D.S.17.116, Decr.ap.J.*AJ*19.5.3, Alciphr.3.8. **-λειπτος**, ον, *unfailing*, Alex.Aphr.*in Mete*.89.13, Them.*in Ph*.81.27. **-ληπτος**, ον, *not open to attack*, τοῖς ἐχθροῖς Th.5.17; *not censured*, *blameless*, βίος v.l. in E.*Or*.922, X.*Cyr*.1.2.15; *perfect*, τέχνη Ph.1.15; ἀνεπιληπτότερον *less open to criticism*, Pl.*Phlb*.43c; ἐξουσία ἀ. *not subject to control*, D.H.2.14; *unassailable*, *not subject to cancellation*, συγγραφαί *PTaur*.1.7.15. Adv. -τως X.*An*.7.6.37, Ph.2.2, al. ⊛**-ληστος**, ον, *not to be forgotten*, Aristaenet.2.13, Hsch. s.v. ἀλαστοῖς. Adv. -τως Sch.Od.14.174. **-λόγιστος**, ον, *unable to consider*, c. gen., τῶν ἐναργειῶν Diogenian.Epicur.3.25; *inconsiderate*, *thoughtless*, Epicur.*Sent.Vat*.63, Sor.1.48; τῶν παθῶν Phld.*Ir*.p.24 W., Mitteis *Chr*.361 (iv A.D.). Adv. -τως Pl.*Ax*.365d, 369e:—Subst. **-ιστία**, ἡ, Sch.Od.15.225:—Verb **-ιστέω**, Phld.*Ir*.p.19 W. (Pass.). ⊛**-λυτος**, ον, *unbandaged*, Crito ap.Gal.13.708. II. *unsolved*, Olymp.*in Cat*.111.15. **-μέλητος**, ον, *uncared for*, Sch.A.R.1.1175, *Gp*.12.29.1. **-μικτος**, ον, *unmixed with*, τῷ ἔξω Arist.*Spir*.483$^{b}$1; *pure from*, ῥυπαρίας Dsc.5.126, cf. *Eup. Praef*., Eustr.*in EN*294.12: abs., σπέρματα J.*AJ*4.8.20, cf. Max.Tyr.40.6. II. *avoiding contact*, Epicur.*Sent*.39; *not mixing* with others, *unsocial*, βίος ἀ. ὁμιλίαις Plu.2.438c; δίαιτα ἀ. Id.*Rom*.3; τὸ ἀ., = ἀνεπιμιξία, Str.8.1.2: of a country, *unfrequented*, *unvisited*, ξενικαῖς δυνάμεσι D.S.5.21, cf. Plu.2.604b; ψυχὴ ἀ. πάθεσι ib.989c; ποιῆσαί τι ἀ. ἑαυτῷ to make it *alien from* oneself, D.S.5.17, cf. Phld.*Rh*.1.121 S. **-μιξία**, ἡ, *want of intercourse* or *traffic*, Plb.16.29.12, App.*Mith*.93. **-μονος**, ον, *not enduring long*, Plu.2.7b, Vett.Val.40.22. **-μώμητος**, ον, = ἀμώμητος, Sch.Od.13.42:—also **-μωμος**, ον, Phot. **-νοησία**, ἡ, *inconceivability*, S.E.*M*.3.57. **-νόητος**, ον, *unintelligible*, σημεῖα τοῖς ἄλλοις ἀ. D.S.19.94; *inconceivable*, *unthinkable*, S.E.*P*.2.104, Dam.*Pr*.22. Adv. -τως *inconceivably*, Procl.*in Prm*.p.864 S., Id.*in Ti*.1.3 D. 2. Act., *having no experience of*, τινός D.S.2.59. 3. = *sine adinventione*, Just.*Nov*.59.7. ⊛**-ξεστος**, ον, *not polished*, *not finished*, δόμος Hes.*Op*.746, Them.*Or*.26.388b. **-πλαστος**, ον, *not plastered over*: metaph., *unaffected*, D.L.2.117. **-πλεκτος**, ον, *without connexion with others*, *isolated*, Str.2.5.8, al. **-πληκτος**, ον, *not liable to be reproved*, Eup.397; βίος E.*Or*.922, Men.*Epit*.489. Adv. -τως Hsch., f.l. in Ph.2.454. 2. in bad sense, *not reproved*, *licentious*, τροφῇ ἀ. τραφῆναι Pl.*Lg*.695b, cf. Eus.Mynd.62. II. Act., *not reproving* or *blaming*, τὸ ἀ. *abstinence from blame* or *criticism*, M.Ant.1.10. **-πληξία**, ἡ, *impunity*, *licentiousness*, Pl.*Lg*.695b. **-πρόσθητος**, ον, *not occultable*, Procl.*Hyp*.5.12, cf. Eustr.*in APo*.192.33: metaph., τῷ ἀσωμάτῳ τὸ ἔνογκον -θητον the material *forms no obstacle to* the incorporeal, Porph.*Sent*.27. Adv. -τως Eust.1138.59. **-ρρεκτος**, ον, (ῥέζω) *not dedicated*, χυτρόποδες Hes.*Op*.748. **-ρρήτως**, Adv. *without demur* or *subterfuge*, *PAmh*.2.147.11 (iv/v A.D.). ⊛**-σήμαντος**, ον, *undistinguished*, κατὰ τὴν ἐσθῆτα Plb.5.81.3; *unrecorded*, *unnoticed*, ἀ. τινα or τι παραλιπεῖν Id.11.2.1, D.S.11.59, cf. Phld.*Sign*.34. Adv. -τως *without notice*, Aps.p.259 H. II. *without an attack of* ἐπισημασία (q.v.), Gal.14.277. III. Act., *not conferring distinction*, σοφοῖς ἀνδράσι Darius ap.D.L.9.14. **-σκεπτεί**, Adv. of sq., Diog.Oen.24. **-σκεπτος**, ον, *inattentive*, *inconsiderate*, πρᾶγμα Ph.5.143 C.; ἀλογία Porph.*Abst*.1.43; ὁρμή Procop.*Goth*.4.32. Adv. -τως Hdt.2.45; ἀ. ἔχειν τινός to give *no consideration* to.., Arist.*GA*778$^{b}$10. II. Pass., *not examined*, *unregarded*, X.*Mem*.2.4.3; *unobserved*, Anon.*in SE*12.27. **-σκευος**, ον, *without equipment*, *IG*2.789$^{b}$27, al. **-σκεψία**, ἡ, *disregard*, Arist.*APo*.79$^{a}$6. **-σκίαστος**, ον, *not in the shade*, Alex.Aphr.*in Mete*.19.15. **-σκόπητος**, ον, *unregarded*, Eustr.*in APo*.202.19. **-σκοπος**, ον, gloss on ἀνεπιστάρητος, Hsch. **-σκότητος**, ον, *not obscured* or *overclouded*, Gal.*UP*10.2, Ptol.*Tetr*.100, Heph.Astr.1.25; and so prob. Procl.*Par.Ptol*.144 (-ιστος codd.). **-σταθμεία**, ἡ, *exemption from billeting*, *IGRom*.4.295, *Sammelb*.4224.15. ⊛**-στάθμευτος**, ον, *exempt from billeting*, Plb.15.24.2:—also **-σταθμος**, ον, *OGI*262.13 (Baetocaece), *PTeb*.5.168 (ii B.C.). **-στᾰσία**, ἡ, *inattention*, *thoughtlessness*, Pl.*Ax*.365d; *distraction*, *insensateness* (of passion), Phld.*Ir*.p.33 W.; *want of reflection*, Simp.*in Cael*.163.35, al. **-στάτητος**, ον, *without inspector*, *without tutelary genius*, Max.Tyr.14.8, cf. Hsch. **-στᾰτος**, ον, (ἐφίστημι) *inattentive*, Plb.5.34.4, Phld.*Ir*.p.44 W.; τινός *to* a thing, Porph.*Abst*.1.9. Adv. -τως Plb.1.4.4, Longin.33.4, Herod.Med.ap.Orib.10.5.11; *without a check*, Plb.10.47.9, etc. 2. Pass., *not attended to*, *unregarded*, Ptol.*Alm*.10.6, cf. Simp.*in Cael*.163.35. Adv. -τως Porph.*in Cat*.65.22. 3. *without guidance*, ὀχεῖαι Ph.2.309. 4. *ill-considered*, Alex.Aphr.*in Mete*.9.2, Simp.*in Cael*.157.11. Adv. -τως ib.89.12. **-στημονέω**, *to be ignorant*, *EM*23.24. **-στημονικός**, ή, όν, *non-scientific*, πρᾶξις Arist.*EE*1220$^{b}$25. **-στημοσύνη**, ἡ, *want of knowledge*, *ignorance*, *unskilfulness*, Th.5.7; of bees, Arist.*HA*626$^{b}$4; τινός Pl.*R*.560b: *want of science*, opp. ἐπιστήμη, ib.350a, al., Plot.6.1.10: pl., X.*Oec*.20.21; of κακία, Chrysipp.*Stoic*.3.60. **-στήμων**, Dor. **-άμων** Archyt.3, ον, gen. ονος, *ignorant*, *unskilful*, Hdt.9.62, Th.7.67, etc.; νῆες ἀνεπιστήμονες ships *with unskilful crews*, opp. ἔμπειροι, Id.2.89: so μηδὲν ἀ. ἐᾶν leave no part *untrained*, Pl.*Lg*.795c; ἀ. τινός or περί τινος *unskilled in* a thing, Hp.*VM*1, Pl.*Prt*.350b, *Tht*.202c: c. inf., *not knowing how* to do a thing, X.*Mem*.2.3.7: foll. by relat., ἀ. ὅτι.. *not knowing* that.., Th.5.111; ἀ. ὅπῃ τράπωνται Id.3.112. Adv. -μόνως Pl.*Lg*.636e, X.*Cyn*.3.11, etc. II. *without knowledge*, *unintelligent*, Pl.*R*.350b, etc.; ἡ δ' ἑτέρη [γνώμη] ἀνεπιστημονεστέρη μέν ἐστι τῆς ἑτέρης *less intelligent*, Hdt.2.21. **-στητος**, ον, *not the object of knowledge*, Eustr.*in APo*.45.9. **-στρεπτέω**, *to be indifferent*, *pay no heed*, D.L.6.91, Arr.*Epict*.2.5.9, Vett.Val.43.27, Artem.3.42, *POxy*.486.10 (ii A.D.). **-στρεπτος**, ον, prop. *without turning round*: hence metaph., *indifferent*, *heedless*, πάντων Phld.*Herc*.1251.17, cf. Artem.2.37. Adv. -τως Arr.*Epict*.2.9.4, *PMag.Par*.1.45: also -τεί or -τί Ph.1.90 (-τί), Plu.2.46e, 418b, *PMag.Lond*.121.439. **-στρεφής**, ές, = foreg., ἀ. τινος *careless of*, *Placit*.1.7.7; *inexorable*, τὸ ἀ. τῆς δίκης Corn.*ND*21. ⊛**-στρεψία**, ἡ, *want of regard*, *heedlessness*, Arr.*Epict*.2.1.14. **-στρόφητος**, ον, = sq., *PTeb*.27.168 (ii B.C.). ⊛**-στροφος**, ον, = ἀνεπίστρεπτος, αὐχήν Ar.Byz.*Epit*.100.10; ἀ. πρός τι Simp.*in de An*.79.5; τινός Eustr.*in EN*110.2; ἀ. τι ἔχειν to be *inattentive to*, Sophon.*in de An*.20.34. Adv. -φως dub. in Hdn.7.10.4; ἀ. κρέμασθαι, of a bat, Trypho *Trop*.1.4. 2. *not capable of inversion*, Procl.*Inst*.44. **-σφᾰλής**, ές, = ἀσφαλής, Them.*Or*.15.190a, Ps.-Alex.Aphr.*in SE*40.18, 41.3. **-σχετος**, ον, *not to be stopped*, ὁρμή J.*Vit*.51; φορή Aret.*SD*2.5; δακρύων ἀ. πηγαί Aristaenet.2.5; of persons, Ph.2.268. Adv. -τως Id.1.296, Plu.*Ages*.27. ⊛**-τακτος**, ον, *subject to no control*, τῆς ἀ. πᾶσιν ἐς τὴν δίαιταν ἐξουσίας Th.7.69, cf. Plu.2.987b. Adv. -τως *without orders* or *command*, J.*AJ*19.2.2, D.L.5.20. **-τᾰτος**, ον, *not to be extended farther*, S.E.*M*.10.272. 2. *not capable of* τὸ μᾶλλον, opp. ἀνάνετος, διαφορά Porph.*Intr*.20.4; ἕξεις *in Cat*.138.5. Adv. -τως *without augmentation* or *intensification*, Procl.*Inst*.52; *without stress*, opp. μετ' ἐπιτάσεως, Ammon.*in Interp*.11.26 (misplaced). **-τάττω**, *enjoin*, Eustr.*in EN*370.24. **-τετελεσμένος**, η, ον, *not properly executed* (incorrect form), *Sammelb*.4512.79. **-τευκτος**, *not hitting the mark*, *vain*, Sch.E.*Ph*.1387: c. gen., ἀ. ἀγαθῶν βίος Vett.Val.177.14, cf. Ptol.*Tetr*.157. Adv. -τως Heph.Astr.3.20. **-τευξία**, ἡ, *failure to attain*, Id.2.30. **-τέχνητος**, ον, *without design*. Adv. -τως *Placit*.4.11.3. **-τήδειος**, ον (α, ον *Gp*.5.26.3), Ion. **-εος**, η, ον:—*unserviceable*, *unfit*, of persons and things, X.*HG*1.6.4, etc.; πρός τι Pl.*Sph*.219a; in a positively bad sense, *mischievous*, *prejudicial*, Hdt.1.175, Th.3.71; γνῶναί τι ἀ. περί τινος And.2.28; of bad omens, X.*HG*1.4.12; of food, Hp.*Acut*.17 (Comp.), *VM*20: c. inf., *unfitted to*.., Lys.31.2. Adv. -ως, πράττειν fare *ill*, opp. εὖ πράττειν, ib.5; ἀ. ἔχειν Plu.2.819a: Comp. -ότερον Pl.*Lg*.813b. 2. *unkind*, *unfriendly*, X.*HG*7.4.6; ἄλλους τινὰς ἀ. ἀνήλωσαν, i.e. political *opponents*, Th.8.65; στῆλαι ἀ. *IG*2$^{2}$.43 *A* 34. **-τηδειότης**, ητος, ἡ, *unfitness*, *inconvenience*, *inaptitude*, Ph.1.191, 521, M.Ant.5.5, Procl.*Inst*.143. **-τήδευτος**, ον, *made without care* or *design*, *artless*, D.H.*Comp*.22, cf. 25, Onos.10.3, Luc.*Hist.Conscr*.44. Adv. -τως Phld.*Rh*.1.156 S., D.H.*Lys*.8, Luc.*Pisc*.12. II. *unpractised*, *untried*, οὐδὲν ἀμίμητον οὐδ' ἀ. Plu.*Alc*.23. Adv. -τως, γλώττης οὐκ ἀ. εἶχεν Philostr.*VA*7.27. **-τίμητος** [τῑ], ον, *not to be censured*, Arist.*EN*1154$^{b}$4, etc.; τινός *for* a thing, D.61.54; *uncriticized*, Isoc.12.245. 2. *unpunished*, Plb.35.2.8, Onos.*Praef*.6, Ph.1.219. II. *not estimated* or *rated*, *IG*2$^{2}$.1241.14, cf. 2.1059.7. **-τμητος**, ον, *subject to no deduction* or *restriction*, μισθώσεις, ἀπολογία, Hsch. **-τρέπτως**, Adv. *without permission*, Lxx 3 *Ma*.1.20. **-τρόπευτος**, ον, *without guardian*, Ph.1.219: metaph., ib.696, cf. Gal.*Nat.Fac*.2.3:—also **-τροπος**, ον, Phryn.*PS*p.12 B. **-φανής**, ές, *undistinguished*, *obscure*, J.*AJ*17.10.7: Comp., Ptol.*Tetr*.168. ⊛**-φαντος**, ον, *without ostentation*, Ph.2.76, Vett.Val.16.21; *insignificant*, ἀποτελέσεις Paul.Al.*F*.1. Adv. -τως M.Ant.1.9. **-φᾰτος**, ον, *unexpected*, Ph.2.533 (v.l. for -φαντος), Hsch. Adv. -τως Ph.2.521, Suid. **-φθόνητος**, ον, *unenvied*, *EM*81.25. **-φθονος**, ον, *without reproach*, ἔγχος S.*Tr*.1033 (lyr.); ἀ. ἐστι πᾶσιν it is *no reproach to* any one, Th.6.83, cf. Pl.*R*.612b, Epicur.*Fr*.161; οὕτω γάρ μοι..ἀνεπιφθονώτατον εἰπεῖν *least invidious*, D.18.321; *ungrudging*, ἔπαινος Onos.*Praef*.10. Adv. [τὴν ἀρχὴν] ἀνεπιφθόνως κατεστήσατο *so as not to create odium*, Th.6.54, cf. Plu.*Cam*.1; ἀ. εἰπεῖν Isoc.15.8. **-φραστος**, ον, *unthought of*, δύαι Semon.1.21. **-χάδην**· οὐκέτι χωροῦν, Hsch. **-χαρής**, ές, *lacking in refinement*, Vett.Val.75.23. ⊛**-χείρητος**, ον, *unassailable*, Plu.*Caes*.25; = ἀνεπιβούλευτος, Hsch. 2. *unattempted*, Plu.2.1075d.

**ἀνεπ-όπτευτος**, ον, *not admitted among the* ἐπόπται, Hyp.*Fr*.174, cf. Poll.8.124. **-οπτος**, ον, *not to be discerned* or *distinguished*, Id.5.150. **-οργίζομαι**, *to be roused by anger*, Phld.*Lib*.p.41 O. **-όψιος**, ον, *not in sight*, Suid.

**ἀνέραμαι**, aor. ἀνηράσθην, *love again*, *love anew*, c. gen., And.1.127, and perh. X.*Mem*.3.5.7 (cj.).

**ἀνεραστ-ία**, ἡ, *ignorance of love*, Them.*Or*.13.163d. **-ος**, ον, *loveless*, ἔρωτες D.Chr.7.133, cf. Plu.2.406a, etc.; ἀ. κοινωνία, ὁμιλία, ib.752c, 756e; τὸ ἀ. ἑτέρων *want of love for*.., ib.634b; βίος *AP*12.18 (Alph.). 2. *not loved*, Luc.*DMort*.6.3. 3. *unlovely*, Chor.

n *Rh.Mus.*49.498. II. Act., *not loving*, Hld.3.9, Aristaenet.1.10; *unloving, cruel, harsh*, Call.*Epigr.*34.4 (Sup.), Luc.*DDeor.*14.1; ἀνέραστα ποιεῖν Plu.2.61a.

**ἀνεργ-άζομαι,** *knead, work up*, Orib.9.39.2. **-ασία,** ἡ, *unemployment, idleness*, in pl., Artem.1.67, 2.28 (v.l. ἀνεργίας). ※**-αστος,** ον, *not thoroughly wrought, imperfect*, Arist.*Metaph.*1048b4; λίθος ἀ. *unwrought*, D.S.14.18; γῆ ἀ. *untilled*, dub. l. in Luc.*Prom.*11; σῖτος ἀ. *raw*, J.*BJ*5.10.2: of a subject, *not thoroughly handled* or *treated*, Plb.10.43.1. **-εια,** ἡ, *cessation from work, holiday*, J.*BJ*4.9.12 (dub.). **-ία,** ἡ, = ἀεργία, v. l. for ἀνεργασία, Artem.2.28. **-ος,** ον, *not done*, ἔργα ἄ., Lat. *facta infecta*, E.*Hel.*363. 2. = ἀνέργαστος, δέρμα *Edict.Diocl.*8.13, al. 3. *inactive*, opp. ἐνεργός, v.l. in J.*AJ* 16.2.4.

**ἀνέργω,** v. ἀνείργω.

**ἀνερεθίζω,** *provoke, stir up, excite*, J.*AJ*19.7.1, Plu.*Thes.*6:—Pass., *to be in a state of excitement*, Th.2.21, X.*An.*6.6.9, Plu.*Pyrrh.*11; εἴς τι Dam.*Pr.*150.

**ἀνερείδω,** *prop up, rest* a thing *on*, τὸ πρόσωπον τῇ χειρί dub. in Aristaenet.1.22.

※**ἀνέρεικτος** or **-ικτος,** ον, *not bruised, unground*, Hp.*Aff.*52.

***ἀνερείπομαι,** Ep. Dep., used by Hom. only in 3 pl. aor., *snatch up and carry off*, ἀνηρείψαντο, of the gods, Il.20.234, cf. Pi.*Pae.*6.136, A.R.2.503; of the Harpies, Od.1.241, etc.; of storms, 4.727; so παῖδα..'Αφροδίτη ὦρτ' ἀνερειψαμένη Hes.*Th.*990; τὴν 'Αργὼ οὐρανὸς ἀνηρείψατο Them.*Or.*27.333a:—later, *take upon oneself*, πόνον Orph.*A.*290. (The true spelling is prob. ἀνηρεψ-, which has Ms. authority in Hes. l.c. and A.R.1.214; cf. ἀ[ν]ᾱρέψατο Pi.*Pae.* l.c., and ἀνερεψάμενοι, Hsch.: v. ἅρπυια.)

**ἀνερέπτομαι,** Pass., στόμαχος ἀνερεπτόμενος the stomach *drawn up spasmodically* so as to cause vomiting, dub. l. in Nic.*Al.*256, cf. *AB*401.

※**ἀνερεύγω,** *throw up, disgorge*, ἀνήρῠγεν ἀτμόν (aor. 2) Nonn.*D.*1.239; ἰωήν ib.485:—Pass., *discharge itself*, of a river, Arist.*Mu.*392b16, A.R.2.744.

**ἀνερευθής,** ές, of cancerous ulcers, *pallid*, Archig.ap.Aët.16.106 (bis), but prob. f.l. for ἐν-.

※**ἀνερευν-άω,** *search out, examine, investigate*, λόγους Pl.*Phd.*63a; ἔγγραφα *POxy.*1468.18 (iii A.D.):—in Med., Pl.*Lg.*816c, J.*AJ*19.1.15:—Pass., *BJ*2.8.6. **-ησις,** εως, ἡ, *a searching out*, Tz. ad Lyc. 11. ※**-ητος,** ον, *not investigated*, Pl.*Hp.Ma.*298c; ἀ. παραλιπεῖν τι Arist.*EN*1181b12. 2. *that cannot be searched* or *found out*, v.l. in Pl.*Cra.*421d; ἀνερεύνητα δυσθυμεῖσθαι harass oneself about *inscrutable things*, f.l. in E.*Ion* 255.

※**ἀνερίθευτος** [ῑ], ον, *unbribed, uncorrupted*, *GDI*3585 (Calymna), *Michel* 473 (Mylasa); *not honeycombed by intrigues*, ἡγεμονία Ph.2.555, cf. 538.

**ἀνερίναστος** [ῑ], ον, *not ripened by caprification*, of figs, Thphr.*HP* 2.8.3, *CP*2.9.12, Suid.; cf. ἀνηρίναστος.

**ἀνερίνεος,** ον, = foreg., Hermipp.59 (s. v.l.).

**ἀνερκής,** ές, *unprotected*, Q.S.3.494.

**ἀνερμάτιστος,** ον, *without ballast*, ὥσπερ τὰ ἀ. πλοῖα Pl.*Tht.*144a; *unstable*, Olymp.*in Mete.*147.4, cf. Gal.*UP*2.14. 2. metaph., ἀ. τράπεζα an *empty* table, Plu.2.704b; *unstable*, εἶδος Dam.*Pr.*413; also of persons, *without ballast*, Ph.2.451, Plu.2.501d, Plot.1.8.8; ἀ. ἐαθέντα τὰ μεγάλα Longin.2.2.

**ἀνερμήνευτος,** ον, *with none to interpret*, E.*Hyps.Fr.*1 iv 18. II. *inexplicable, indescribable*, τῷ πέλας S.E.*M.*7.65; ὀδύνη Aristaenet. 2.5.

**ἀνερπύζω,** = sq., Opp.*H.*1.289, Dionys.*Av.*1.31.

※**ἀνέρπω,** *creep upwards*, E.*Ph.*1178: aor. ἀνείρπῠσα Ar.*Pax* 585, Luc.*Nec.*22, etc.; of ivy, E.*Fr.*88; *spring up*, of water, Call.*Ap.*110; ἀ. πρὸς τὸ μετεωρότερον Arist.*PA* 688a10; ἐς τὰς ῥῖνας Hp.*Vict.*3.76.

**ἀνέρρω,** *go quite away, take oneself off*, Eup.221 (in aor. ἀνήρρησα).

**ἀνερυγγάνω·** ἀνερεύγω, Suid.

**ἀνερυθρίαστος,** ον, *unblushing*, Ph.2.664.

**ἀνερυθριάω,** *begin to blush, blush up*, Pl.*Chrm.*158c, X.*Smp.*3.12.

**ἀνερύω,** Ion. and Dor. **ἀνειρύω** [ῠ], *draw up*, ἀνά θ' ἱστία λεύκ' ἐρύσαντες Od.9.77, 12.402; ἀνειρύσαι νῆας, = ἀνελκύσαι, Hdt.9.96, cf. A.R.2.586; ἀ. πέπλως Theoc.14.35:—Med., ἐκ νούσου ἀνειρύσω *AP* 6.300 (Leon.).

※**ἀνέρχομαι,** (cf. ἄνειμι): aor. -ήλυθον or -ῆλθον:—*go up*, ἀνελθὼν ἐς σκοπιήν Od.10.97; εἰς τὴν ἀκρόπολιν X.*HG*2.4.39; ἐπὶ τὴν σκηνήν Arr.*Epict.*3.22.26; ἐπὶ βῆμα Hdn.1.5.2: abs., *mount the tribune*, Plu. *Aem.*31; *go up from* the coast inland, Od.19.190; *come up from* the nether world, ἀ. ἐξ 'Αΐδεω Thgn.703; κἀξ ῞Αιδου θανὼν πρὸς φῶς ἀ. S.*Ph.*625; ἐξ ῞Αιδου εἰς θεούς Pl.*R.*521c. 2. of trees, *grow up, shoot up*, Od.6.163, 167; of the sun, *rise*, A.*Ag.*658; ἀ. ὠκεανοῖο A.R.3.1230; of water, *rise*, Arist.*Mete.*358b32, Heph.Astr.1.23: metaph., ὄλβος ἀ. E.*Or.*810. 3. *go up to* a first principle, in argument, ἐπ' ἀρχὴν ἀνελθόντες σκοπεῖν Pl.*R.*511d. II. *go* or *come back, return*, ἂψ or αὖθις ἀ. Il.4.392, Od.1.317. 2. *come back to* a point, *recur to* it *and say*, ἄνελθέ μοι πάλιν τί.. E.*Ph.*1207, cf. *Ion* 933; πάλιν ἐπ' ἀρχὴν ἀ. v.l. in Pl.*Ti.*69a. 3. νόμος..εἴς σ' ἀνελθὼν εἰ διαφθαρήσεται *being brought home to* you, E.*Hec.*802. [In Il.4.392, A.R.1.821, ἀνερχομένῳ is corrupt.] III. trans., *traverse*, νειόν Call.*Aet.Fr.*7.4 P.

**ἀνερῶ,** Att. fut. of ἀναγορεύω; v. ἀνεῖπον.

**ἀνερωτ-άω,** *question*, c. acc. pers., καί μιν ἀνηρώτων Od.4.251, cf. Pl.*R.*454c; ἐμαυτὸν ὑπέρ τινος Id.*Ap.*22d: τινὰ περί τινος Hdt.9.89:—Pass., Pl.*Grg.*455d. 2. c. acc. rei, *inquire into*, τὰς δόξας Id.*Men.*84d, al. 3. c. dupl. acc., *question* a person *about* a thing, E.*IT*664, Ar.*Pl.*499, Pl.*Tht.*143d. **-ητέον,** *one must interrogate*, Id.*Phlb.*63c. **-ίζω,** = ἀνερωτάω, Telecl.52.

**ἀνεσθίω,** *eat away*, of ulcers, etc., in Pass., Hp.*Epid.*4.1, Aret.*SD* 1.13. **ἀνεσθίων·** μηκέτι ἐσθιομένων, Hsch.

**ἀνεσία,** ἡ, = ἄνεσις, Cratin.20.

**ἀνέσιμος,** ον, (ἀνίημι) *given up to idleness*, ἀ. ἡμέρα *a holiday*, Sch. Th.7.73; *loose*, Sch.Lyc.18.

※**ἄνεσις,** gen. εως, Ion. ιος, ἡ: (ἀνίημι):—*loosening, relaxing*, τῶν χορδῶν of the strings, opp. ἐπίτασις, Pl.*R.*349e; coupled with χάλασις, ib.590b; τῆς αἰσθήσεως..δεσμὸν τὸν ὕπνον εἶναί φαμεν, τὴν δέ.. ἄνεσιν ἐγρήγορσιν Arist.*Somn.Vig.*454b27; ἀέρος Thphr.*CP*2.1.6; πάγων ἄ., i.e. a *thaw*, Plu.*Sert.*17; of the *ebb*-tide, Str.7.2.1. 2. metaph., *remission, abatement*, κακῶν Hdt.5.28; opp. θλῖψις, 2*Ep. Cor.*8.13, al.; λύπης, μοχθηρίας, etc., Plu.2.102b, etc.; τὴν ἡδονὴν ἄνεσιν λαμβάνειν Phld.*D.*3*Fr.*1; ἄ. φόρων, τελῶν, *remission* of tribute, taxes, Plu.*Sert.*6, *IG*7.2227 (Thisbe), etc.; κολάσεως Plot.4.3.24; of fevers, opp. παροξυσμός, Gal.7.427. 3. *relaxation, recreation*, opp. σπουδή, Pl.*Lg.*724a, Arist.*Rh.*1371b34, cf. Cleanth.*Stoic.*1.122; ἄ. καὶ σχολή Plb.1.66.10; ψυχῆς Mnesith.Ath.ap.Ath.11.484a. 4. *solution*, Dsc.5.96. 5. = τὸ τελευταῖον τῆς παρακμῆς Archig.ap. Gal.7.424. II. *indulgence, licence*, ἡδονῶν Pl.*R.*561a; ἡ τῶν γυναικῶν παρ' ὑμῖν ἄ. Id.*Lg.*637c, cf. Arist.*Pol.*1270a1; δούλων ib.1313b35; *relaxation of custody*, *Act.Ap.*24.23. III. of musical pitch, Aristid.Quint.1.5; of an unaccented syll., Phld.*Po.*2.18.

**ἀνέσπερον·** ἀσκότεινον, Hsch.

※**ἀνέσσῠτο,** 3 sg. Ep. aor. Pass. of ἀνασεύω, Il.11.458.

**ἀνεσταλμένως,** Adv. pf. part. Pass. of ἀναστέλλω, *tucked up*, gloss on ἐπιστολάδην, Sch.Hes.*Sc.*287.

※**ἀνέστιος,** ον, *without hearth and home, homeless*, Il.9.63; ἄπαις τε κἀγύναιξ κἀνέστιος S.*Fr.*4, cf. Ar.*Eq.*1266; ἄοικος καὶ ἀ. Luc.*Sacr.* 11, cf. Eus.Mynd.59: metaph., ψυχή Max.Tyr.14.8; *savage*, ἄγρη Opp.*H.*2.417.

**ἀνεστραμμένως,** Adv. pf. part. Pass. of ἀναστρέφω, *inversely*, *EM* 584.20; *perversely*, *PTeb.*25.16 (ii B.C.).

**ἀνέσχεθε, ἀνεσχέθομεν,** v. sub ἀνέχω.

**ἀνετάζω,** *inquire of*, ἀλλήλους τὴν αἰτίαν Lxx *Su.*14 (Thd.), *Jd.*6.29 (cod. A). II. *examine* documents, *POxy.*34 i 13; *examine by torture*, τινά *Act.Ap.*22.24, cf. 29.

**ἀνέταιρος,** ον, *without friends* or *fellows*, Plu.2.807a.

**ἀνετέον,** (ἀνίημι) *one must relax*, Pl.*Sph.*254b: c. gen., τῆς ἀκριβεστέρας οἰκονομίας Phld.*Oec.*p.73 J.; *one must loosen*, Gal.17(1).434; *one must let slip*, Pl.*Smp.*217c, *Plt.*291c. 2. *one must permit*, Sor.1.108. 3. *one must dilute*, Orib.*Fr.*54.

**ἀνετεροίωτος,** ον, *unchangeable*, Arist.*Mu.*392a32; *unaltered*, Phld. *Po.*994.3, S.E.*M.*8.455; *undifferentiated*, Dam.*Pr.*68, Procl.*in Prm.* p.926 S.

**ἀνετικός,** ή, όν, *relaxing*, Antyll.ap.Orib.6.21.30, cf. Crito ap.Gal. 13.1041. Adv. -κῶς Stob.2.6.6.

**ἀνέτοιμος,** ον, *unready, not ready*, Plb.12.20.6, D.S.12.41, J.*Vit.* 22; εἴς τι *APl.*4.242 (Eryc.). Adv. -ως, ἔχειν πρός τι App.*Mith.* 12. 2. *out of reach, unattainable*, ἀνέτοιμα διώκειν Hes.*Fr.*219.

※**ἄνετος,** ον, (ἀνίημι) *relaxed, slack*, ἡνίαι γαστρός Philostr.*VA*6.11; of the hair, Luc.*Alex.*13; τὸ ἄ. τῆς κόμης Philostr.*VA*1.32:—of bodily parts, *relaxed*, Arist.*GA*738a2. Adv. ἀνετῶς (sic Hsch.) S.*Fr.*641, Ps.-Alex.Aphr.*in SE*121.32, dub. in Call.*Aet.*3.1.39. 2. *set free from labour*, esp. of men and animals dedicated to a god, Hyp.*Fr.* 72; θηρία Philostr.*Im.*1.28, cf. App.*BC*1.110; of land, *consecrated and lying untilled*, Ael.*NA*11.2, Poll.1.10. 3. metaph., τὴν τῶν μειρακίων ὁρμὴν ἄνετον εἴασαν νέμεσθαι f.l. for ἄφ- in Plu.2.12a; *uncontrolled, licentious*, ἐξουσία Hdn.2.4.4; *intemperate*, ἁμάρτημ' ἄνετον Phld.*Lib.*p.6 O.

**ἀνετῠμολόγητος,** ον, *of unknown derivation*, S.E.*M.*1.245.

**ἀνέτῠμος,** ον, = foreg., S.E.*M.*1.245. Adv. -μως ib.244.

※**ἄνευ,** Megarian and Hellenistic **ἄνις** (q.v.); ἄνευν *IG*4.1484.58 (Epid.); ἄνευς *GDI*1157 (Olymp.):—Prep. (never used in compos.) c. gen. (c. acc. only *GDI* l.c.), *without*, opp. σύν, ἄνευ ἕθεν οὐδὲ σὺν αὐτῷ Il.17.407; ἄ. κέντροιο *without* the goad, 23.387; μόνος ἄ. τινός Ar.*Lys.*143, Pl.*Smp.*217a; in pregnant sense, ἄ. θεῶν, mostly with neg., οὔτι ἄ. θεοῦ ἥδε γε βουλή Od.2.372; οὔ τοι ἄ. θεοῦ ἔπτατο.. ὄρνις 15.531; οὐκ ἄ. θεῶν τινος A.*Pers.*164; μηδὲ θύεσθαι μέν τιν' ἰδίᾳ ἄ. τοῦ ἄρχοντος Aen.Tact.10.4; also without neg., ἄ. ἐμέθεν *without* my knowledge and will, Il.15.213; ἄ. πολιτᾶν *without* their consent, A.*Ch.*431; ἄ. τοῦ κραίνοντος S.*OC*926; ἄ. τοῦ ὑγιεινοῦ *without reference to* health, Pl.*Grg.*518d, cf. 519a; οὐκ ἐνδέχεται ζῆν ἄ. κακοῦ τινος Diph.32.12, etc. II. *away from, far from*, ἄ. δηΐων Il.13.556; ἄ. ὄψου ποιεῖν τινας ἑστιωμένους Pl.*R.*372c, cf. *Hp.Ma.*290e. III. in Prose, *except, besides*, πάντα ἄ. χρυσοῦ Id.*Criti.*112c; ἄ. τοῦ καλὴν δόξαν ἐνεγκεῖν *praeterquam quod attulerit*.., D.18.89; καὶ ἄ. τοῦ λαμβάνειν even *without* it, X.*Cyr.*5.4.28.—In early writers it rarely follows its case, ὑφηγητοῦ δ' ἄ. S.*OC*502; ὧν ἄ. X.*Cyr.*6.1.14; freq. in later Prose, as always in Arist., *Metaph.*1071a2, al., cf. Plu.2.47c, etc. (Cf. Goth. *inu*, OHG. *āno* 'without'; perh. akin to neg. pref. ἀ-.)

**ἀνευάζω,** fut. -άξω Nonn.*D.*1.20:—*utter cries of* εὖα, D.P.579, *AP* 9.139 (Claud.). II. c. acc. pers., *honour with such cries*, Lyc.207, Arr.*An.*5.2.7.

**ἀνευ-δοκησία,** ἡ, *discredit*, Phld.*Ir.*p.80 W. **-δόκητος,** ον, discredited, ib.p.53W. -ένδοτος, ον, f.l. for εὐένδοτος, Ph.2.269. -ήκοος, ον, disobedient, PGen.50.12.

**ἄνευθε**, before a vowel -θεν: (ἄνευ):—Ep. and Lyr. word: 1. Prep. c. gen., like ἄνευ, without, οἷος ἄνευθ' ἄλλων Il.22.39; μούνω ἄνευθ' ἄλλων Od.16.239; ἄ. πόνου 7.192; ἄ. θεοῦ, = ἄνευ θεοῦ, Il.5.185, cf. Pi.O.9.103 (v.l.). 2. away from, ἄνευθεν ἄγων πατρός τε φίλων τε Il.21.78.—Hom. always puts it before its case, though sts. parted from it, as ἄ. δέ σε μέγα νῶϊν ib.22.88; later it freq. follows, as πατρὸς ἄνευθεν A.R.4.746. II. Adv. far away, distant, αἱ δέ τ' ἄνευθε [νῆσοι] Od.9.26; τοὶ δ' ἄλλοι ἄνευθεν καίοντ' Il.23.241; ἐγγύθι μοι θάνατος κακὸς οὐδ' ἔτ' ἄνευθεν 22.300; οὐδέ.. ἄνευθ' ἔσαν ἀλλὰ μάλ' ἐγγύς 23.378; ἄ. λείπειν leave far away, Pi.P.1.10:—often with part., ἄ. ἐών Il.2.27, cf. 4.277.

**ἀνεύθετος**, ον, inconvenient, λιμὴν ἀ. πρὸς παραχειμασίαν Act.Ap.27.12.

**ἀνεύθῡνος**, ον, not accountable, irresponsible, opp. ὑπεύθυνος, τῇ [μουναρχίῃ] ἔξεστι ἀνευθύνῳ ποιέειν τὰ βούλεται Hdt.3.80, cf. Arist. Pol.1271ᵃ5; ὑπεύθυνον τὴν παραίνεσιν ἔχοντας πρὸς ἀνεύθυνον τὴν ὑμετέραν ἀκρόασιν Th.3.43; free from liability or censure, POxy.906.8 (ii/iii A.D.), Lib.Or.59.100; not open to objection, of a statement, Alex.Aphr. in Top.425.5. 2. guiltless, innocent, Luc.Abd.22: c. gen., ἀ. ἁμαρτήματος Id.Nigr.9; irreproachable, ἀ. τὸ ἰσχίον, of athletes, Philostr.Gym.48. Adv. -νως Poll.3.139, Just.Nov.8.12 Intr.—In Att., ἀνυπεύθυνος was more common.

**ἀνεύθυντος**, ον, which cannot be straightened, Arist.Mete.386ᵃ8.

**ἀνευθύνω**, straighten, in Pass., Gal.18(1).776.

**ἄνευκτος**, ον, not wishing, not praying, εὐχομένοις καὶ ἀνεύκτοις AP 10.108.

**ἀνευλᾰβής**, ές, irreverent, impious, Aq.Is.57.11.

**ἀνευνοησία**, ἡ, malevolence, Vett.Val.37.19.

**ἀνευόδωτος**, ον, that does not prosper, Aq., Sm.Je.22.30.

**ἀνευπρεπής**, ές, unseemly:—in Adv. -πῶς Hsch. s. v. σχέδιον.

**ἀνεύρ-εσις**, εως, ἡ, discovery, E.Ion 569, v.l. in D.H.11.27, cf. Ph.1.285, Plu.Thes.12, etc. -ετέον, one must find out, Pl.Plt. 294d. ⊛-ετής, οῦ, ὁ, inspector, τῶν χωρίων τῶν δημοσίων SIG279.3 (Zeleia).

**ἀνεύρετος**, ον, undiscovered, Pl.Lg.874a, D.S.5.20, Plu.2.700d, POxy.472.14 (ii A.D.), etc.

**ἀνεύρ-ημα**, ατος, τό, invention, discovery, Paus.5.9.2. -ίσκω, fut. -ευρήσω: aor. -εῦρον, later -ευράμην A.R.4.1133:—Pass., aor. -ευρέθην:—find out, discover, Hdt.1.67, 2.54, etc.; ἀγαθὰ ἀ. λογιζόμενος Id.7.8.γ'; ἀ. φόνον A.Ag.1094; σὸν χρέος ἀνευρίσκειν πότερον .. E.IT883; ἀ. τὴν αἰτίαν Pl.Phd.100b; τὴν τοῦ θεοῦ φύσιν Phdr. 252e, etc.:—Med., win, gain, ἱερὸν χῶρον ἀνευρομένην Epigr.Gr. 259:—Pass., to be found out or discovered, ὡς ὕστερον ἀνευρέθη Th. 1.128: c. part., ἀνεύρηται ὁμοῖα παρεχομένη Hdt.4.44. II. think out, invent, μόνος ἀνευρηκὼς τέχνην Antiph.113, cf. Timocl.37, Pl. Phdr.273c; ἀ. πρόφασίν τινα Philem.88.10, etc.

**ἄνευρος**, ον, without sinews, Hp.Mochl.41. 2. nerveless, slack, S.Ichn.143, Theopomp.Com.71, Arist.HA538ᵇ7 (Comp.), al.; νεῦρα ἄνευρα Phld.Ir.p.69 W.

**ἀνεύρ-υνσις**, εως, ἡ, dilatation, Gal.1.402; ἀρτηρίας Antyll.ap. Orib.45.24.2. -ύνω [ῡ], dilate, Hp.Superf.29, Placit.5.16.2; ἡ ῥὶς τοὺς μυκτῆρας ἀνευρύνετο Philostr.Her.19.9; -υσμένον στόμα ἀγγείου Aët.8.69; esp. of arterial aneurism, Antyll.ap.Orib.45.24.1; ἀ. πάλιν ὁ Ὠκεανὸς broadens out, Arist.Mu.393ᵇ6: metaph., νοῦς ἀ. τὰς δυνάμεις Ph.1.249, cf. Dam.Pr.74 (Pass.). -υσμα, ατος, τό, aneurism, Ruf. ap.Aët.14.51, Antyll.ap.Orib.45.24.1, Gal.7.725, 10.335. -υσματώδης, ες, like an aneurism, Aët.15.10, Paul.Aeg.6.38. -υσμός, ὁ, dilatation, ἀρτηρίας Antyll.ap.Orib.45.24.2; μήτρας Dsc.1.13.

**ἀνευφημέω**, shout εὐφήμει or εὐφημεῖτε: hence, as this was mainly done on sorrowful occasions, cry aloud, shriek, ἅπας δ' ἀνηυφήμησεν (so Brunck for ἀνευφώνησεν) οἰμωγῇ λεώς S.Tr.783, cf. E.Or.1335, Pl.Phd.60a. 2. proclaim, c. acc. et inf., Alex.Aphr. in Metaph. 767.30, cf. Simp. in Ph.1360.20: c. dupl. acc., Dam.Pr.58. II. later, receive or honour with auspicious cries, τινὰ ὡς εὐεργέτην J.BJ 4.2.5, cf. 2.21.4, Hdn.6.4.1.

**ἀνευφρ-αίνομαι**, f.l. for ἐν-, Ph.2.476. -ανσία, ἡ, joylessness, Cat.Cod.Astr.2.161. -αντος, ον, joyless, ἀπόλαυσις Secund.Sent. 9, cf. Annales du Service 22.9 (Egypt, i A.D.), Ptol.Tetr.158, Suid.

**ἀνευφρόσυνος**, ον, joyless, θήρη Sch.Opp.H.4.533.

**ἀνεύχομαι**, unsay a prayer, Pl.Alc.2.142d, 148b.

⊛**ἀνεφάλλομαι**, leap up at, used only in part. ἀνεπάλμενος, v. ἀναπάλλω.

⊛**ἀνέφαπτος**, ον, not to be claimed as a slave (cf. ἀνέπαφος), GDI 1684 sqq. (Delph.).

**ἀνέφεδρος**, ον, without drawing a bye, ἀ. νικᾶν SIG1070.6 (Olymp.), IG5(1).680, al. (Sparta).

**ἀνεφέλκομαι**, Med., draw up for oneself, ἐξ ἁλὸς ἰχθὺν Man.5.279.

**ἀνέφελος**, ον, unclouded, cloudless, αἴθρη Od.6.45; ἀὴρ Arist.Mu. 394ᵃ23; νὺξ Plu.Arat.21, etc.: metaph., not to be veiled or hidden, κακόν S.El.1246 (lyr.). (ἀνν. is v.l. in Arat.415, etc.; Eust.945.4 has also the form ἀνεφής, ές.)

**ἄνεφθος**, ον, unboiled, Antyll.ap.Orib.9.24.3, Gal.6.354: Comp., Paul.Aeg.1.74, Gp.10.67.1. 2. ἄ. πλίνθος unbaked, Agath.2.16.

⊛**ἀνέφικτος**, ον, out of reach, unattainable, Ph.1.228, al., Phld.Rh. 1.27 S., Plu.2.54d, Luc.Herm.67, Jul.Or.2.82d.

**ἀνεφόδευτος**, ον, undetected, unexamined, Phld.Lib.p.39 O.

**ἀνέφοδος**, ον, not liable to invasion, Lyd.Mag.3.32.

**ἀνεφριτικὰ** συμπτώματα not-nephritic, Gal.17(1).136.

⊛**ἀνεχέγγυος**, ον, unwarranted, διὰ τὸ τὴν γνώμην ἀνεχέγγυον γεγενῆσθαι because they had no sure confidence in themselves, Th.4.55.

⊛**ἀνέχραζεν**· ἀνέχριμπτεν, ἀνῄρει δ' ἀνεκούφιζεν, Hsch.

⊛**ἀνέχω**, impf. ἀνεῖχον: also ἀνίσχω, impf. ἀνῖσχον: fut. ἀνέξω Archil. 82, Luc.Hist.Conscr.4 (s. v. l.), also ἀνασχήσω Hdt.5.106, 7.14, E.IA 732: aor. ἀνέσχον Il.17.310, etc.; poet. ἀνέσχεθον ib.10.461, E. Med.1027, Ep. inf. ἀνσχεθέειν Od.5.320: pf. ἀνέσχηκα S.E.M.7.190, Phalar.Ep.105:—Med. **ἀνέχομαι**: impf. ἠνειχόμην (with double augm.) A.Ag.905, S.Ph.411, Th.1.77, etc.: fut. ἀνέξομαι Il.5.895, S.El.1028, D.18.160, etc.; also ἀνασχήσομαι A.Th.252, Ar.Ach.299, Ep. inf. ἀνσχήσεσθαι Il.5.104: aor. ἀνεσχόμην 18.430, A.Ch.747 codd., E.Hipp.687 (where ἠνέσχου is contra metr.); more freq. with double augm. ἠνεσχόμην Hdt.5.48, A.Ag.1274; and Att., as Ar.Nu. 1363, Th.3.28, Lys.3.3, etc.; sync. ἠνσχόμην S.Ant.467; 2 sg. imper. ἄνσχεο (v. infr. C. II):—Pass., D.H.3.55, Lxx 4 Ma.1.35.

A. trans., hold up, lift up, χεῖρας ἀνέσχον held up their hands in fight (v. infr. C. I), Od.18.89 (later of pugilists, hold up the hands in token of defeat, Theoc.22.129):—freq. lift up the hands in prayer, θεοῖσι δὲ χεῖρας ἀνέσχον Il.3.318, cf. 1.450, Archil.82, etc.; so ἀνακτι εὐχὰς ἀ. offer prayers, perhaps with uplifted hands, S.El.636; ἄνεχε χέρας, ἄνεχε λόγον E.El.592; also ἀ. τὴν χεῖρα offer the hand (to shake), Theopomp.Com.82 (dub.). 2. lift up as an offering, τά γ' Ἀθηναίῃ ληΐτιδι.. ὑψόσ' ἀνέσχεθε χειρί Il.10.461; as a testimony, σκῆπτρον ἀ. πᾶσι θεοῖσι 7.412; μαζὸν ἀ., of Hecuba entreating her son Hector, 22.80; κενεὰς.. ἀνέσχε γλήνας A.R.2.254; ἄκουε δ' ἀν' οὖς ἔχων A.Fr.126. 3. ἀ. φλόγα hold up a torch, esp. at weddings, E.IA732: hence the phrase ἄνεχε, πάρεχε (sc. τὸ φῶς) hold up, pass on the light in procession, Id.Tr.308, Cyc.203, cf. Ar.V.1326; also ἀ. φάος σωτήριον E.Med.482; τὸ σημεῖον τοῦ πυρὸς Th.4.111. 4. lift up, exalt, τὰ κείνων Pi.P.2.89. 5. hold up, prop, sustain, οὐρανὸν καὶ γῆν, of Atlas, Paus.5.11.5; κίων ἀ. τὴν στέγην Oenom.ap.Eus.PE 5.34:—Pass., γέφυρα σκάφαις ἀνεχομένη D.H.3.55:—but more freq., b. metaph., uphold, maintain, εὐδικίας Od.19.111; πολέμους Th.1.141; ὄργια ἀ. keep up the revels, Ar.Th.948; Βάκχης ἀνέχων λέκτρ' Ἀγαμέμνων remaining constant to, E.Hec.121 (v. infr. B. 3); οἰνῶπ' ἀνέχουσα κισσόν keeping constant to, haunting the ivy, S. OC674 (s. v. l.); βαρὺν ἀνὰ θυμὸν ἔχοισα keeping up his anger, Theoc. 1.96. 6. put forth, δάφνα ἀ. πτόρθους E.Hec.459 (lyr.). II. hold back, check, ἄνεχ' ἵππους Il.23.426; ἀ. τὰ ὅπλα διὰ τῶν ἀνακλητικῶν D.H.9.21; ἀ. Σικελίαν μὴ ὑπ' αὐτοὺς εἶναι keep it from being.., Th.6.86; ἑαυτὸν ἀπό τινος Plu.2.514a:—Pass., ἀνέχεται τὰ πάθη ὑπὸ τοῦ λογισμοῦ Lxx 4 Ma.1.35.

B. intr., rise up, emerge, ἀνσχεθέειν.. ὑπὸ κύματος ὁρμῆς Od.5. 320; of a diver, Hdt.8.8; σκόπελοι ἐν τῷ Νείλῳ ὀξέες ἀ. Id.2.29; ἀ. ἐς ἀέρα A.R.3.1383. b. esp. in form ἀνίσχω, of the sun, πρὸς ἥλιον ἀνίσχοντα Hdt.3.98, etc.; so λαμπὰς ἀνίσχει A.Ag.93 (lyr.); ἅμ' ἡλίῳ ἀνίσχοντι X.Cyn.6.13, cf. Eub.119.9. c. of events, arise, happen, Hdt.5.106, 7.14. d. appear, show oneself, θᾶλπτον ὄμμα.. φήμης ἀνασχόν S.Tr.204; turn out, prove to be, μελοποιὸς ἢ τραγῳδὸς ἄριστος Eun.Hist.p.209 D. e. stand up, κίονες περὶ τοίχοις A.R. 3.217. 2. come forth, αἰχμὴ παρὰ.. ὦμον ἀνέσχεν Il.17.310, cf. Plu. Caes.44; of a headland, jut out into the sea, Hdt.7.123, Th.1.46, etc.; ἀ. πρὸς τὸ Σικελικὸν πέλαγος Id.4.53, cf. D.23.166; ἐς τὸν πόντον [τὴν ἄκρην] ἀνέχοντα jutting out with its headland into the sea, Hdt. 4.99 (dub. l.); reversely, κοιλάδες ἐς μεσόγαιαν ἐκ θαλάσσης ἀ. Str. 3.2.4. 3. hold on, keep doing, c. part., ἀ. διασκοπῶν Th.7.48; σε.. στέρξας ἀνέχει is constant in his love for thee, S.Aj.212 (lyr., cf. supr. A. I. 5b): c. dat., τελεταῖς practise regularly, Eun.Hist.p.249 D.: abs., wait, ταύτῃ ἀνέχειν Th.8.94, cf. 2.18. 4. hold up, cease, Ζεὺς οὐθ' ὕων πάντεσσ' ἁνδάνει οὔτ' ἀνέχων Thgn.26, cf. X.HG1.6.28; dub. l. in Hp.Epid.5.20. 5. c. gen., cease from, οὐδὲ.. καμάτων ἀνέχουσι γυναῖκες S.OT174; τοῦ πολέμου App.Pun.75; τοῦ φονεύειν Plu.Alex. 33.—Hom. uses no tense intr. exc. aor.

C. Med., hold up what is one's own, ὁ δ' ἀνέσχετο μείλινον ἔγχος Il.5.655; δοῦρατ' ἀνασχόμενοι 11.594, etc.: hence ἀνασχόμενος is often used abs. (sc. ἔγχος, ξίφος, etc.), πλῆξεν ἀ. 3.362; κόψε δ' ἀ. Od.14.425; πὺξ μάλ' ἀνασχομένω πεπληγέμεν Il.23.660; also ἄντα δ' ἀνασχομένω χερσὶ ib.686. II. hold oneself up, bear up, οὐδέ σ' οἴω δηρὸν ἔτ' ἀνσχήσεσθαι ib.5.285, cf. Od.11.375: aor. imper. ἀνάσχεο, = τέτλαθι, be of good courage, Il.1.586; ἄνσχεο be patient, 23.587; ἀνὰ δ' ἔχευ is prob. l. for ἀνὰ δ' εὖ in Archil.6.2: in pres. part., ἀνεχόμενοι φέρουσι τὸν χειμῶνα they bear with patience, Hdt.4.28; Stoic motto ἀνέχου καὶ ἀπέχου Gell.17.19. 2. c. acc., τοσσάδ' ἐνὶ φρεσὶν ᾗσιν ἀνέσχετο κήδεα Il.18.430; ἢ δὴ πολλὰ κάκ' ἄνσχεο σὸν κατὰ θυμόν 24.518; τὴν δουλοσύνην οὐκ ἀ. Hdt.1.169; τὰ πρὶν κακὰ ἠνειχόμεσθα A.Ag.905, etc.; χαλκὸν ἀνασχέσθαι Il.4.511, etc.: c. acc. pers., οὐ γὰρ ξείνους.. ἀνέχονται they do not suffer or bear with strangers, Od.7.32, cf. 17.13; τῶν ἵππων οὔτι ἀνεχομένων τὰς καμήλους Hdt.7. 87; τούτους ἀνάσχου δεσπότας E.Alc.304, cf. Eup.6 D.: c. acc. rei et gen. pers., οὐδεὶς ἂν αὐτοῦ ἀγελαστὶ ἠνέσχετο ταῦτα τὰ ἔπη Ath.5. 188c, cf. Ar.Lys.507. 3. c. gen., dub. in Hom., δουλοσύνης ἀνέχεσθαι v.l. in Od.22.423; so ἅπαντος ἀνδρὸς ἀ. Pl.Prt.323a, cf. D.19. 16; to be content with, τοῦ ἐν σώματι κάλλους Plot.5.9.2. 4. the dependent clause is mostly (always in Hom.) in part., οὐ μάν σε.. ἀνέξομαι ἄλγε' ἔχοντα I will not suffer thee to have.., Il.5.895; οὐ γὰρ ἀεργὸν [ὄντα] ἀνέξομαι I will not suffer one [to be].., Od.19.27; εἰ τὸν.. θανόντ' ἄθαπτον ἠνσχόμην νέκυν S.Ant.467; οὐκ ἀνέξεται τίκτοντας ἄλλους E.Andr.712; καὶ γάρ κ'.. ἀνεχοίμην ἥμενος for I would *be content* to sit.., Od.4.595; σοῦ κλύων ἀνέξεται A.*Pers*.838, cf. S. *El*.1028, *Ph*.411; ἀνάσχεσθε σιγῶσαι Id.*Fr*.679; also οὐ σῖγ' ἀνέξει; Id.*Aj*.75: freq. in Prose, Hdt.1.80,206, 5.19, al., Th.2.74, etc.; ἄποτος ἀ. Arist.*HA* 596ᵃ2; also ἀ. τοῦ ἄλλα λέγοντος Pl.*R*.564d; ἀ. τῶν οἰκείων ἀμελουμένων Id.*Ap*.31b; οὐδ' ἂν ἠνέσχεσθε εἴ τις.. D. 21.170:—also in Act., ἀνέσχηκα Phalar.*Ep*.105. 5. rarely c. inf., *suffer*, οὐκ ἀνέξομαι τὸ μὴ οὐ.. A.*Eu*.914; κοκκύζειν τὸν ἀλεκτρυόν' οὐκ ἀνέχονται Cratin.311; ἀνακεκλίσθαι οὐκ ἀ. Aret.*SA*1.9; ἀ. πάντα ὑπομένειν Alciphr.3.34; σὺν ἄλλοις βιοῦν οὐκ ἀ. Ael.*NA*6.30. b. *dare to* do, ἀνέσχοντο τὸν ἐπιόντα δέξασθαι Hdt.7.139. c. οὐκ ἀ., c. inf., *refuse* to do.., *POxy*.903.36, al. III. rarely, *hold on by one another, hang together*, ἀνά τ' ἀλλήλῃσιν ἔχονται Od.24.8.

ἀνεψαινυγμένως· ἐσπουδασμένως, Hsch.

ἀνέψ-ᾰνος, ον, (ἕψω) *bad for cooking*, ὕδατα Hp.*Aër*.7. -ητος, ον, *unboiled*, Dsc.1.102, Alex.Aphr.*in Mete*.190.34, Tim.*Lex*. s. v. κερασβόλον:—later form ἀνέψετος *PMag.Par*.1.53. II. *undigested*, δόρπος Sch.Nic.*Al*.66.

ἀνεψι-ά, ἡ, fem. of ἀνεψιός, X.*Mem*.2.7.2, Isoc.19.8, etc. -ἀδῆ, ἡ, *first cousin's daughter*, Ar.*Fr*.745. -ἀδης, ου, ὁ, = sq., *Sammelb*.176, Iamb.*Protr*.21.κζ', Poll.3.28. *-ᾰδοῦς, οῦ, ὁ, *first cousin's son*, Pherecr.203, Hermipp.86, D.44.26, Is.11.12; also, of *second cousins*, acc. to Poll.3.28, but this rests on a misinterpretation of D. 45.54. *-ός, ὁ, *first cousin*, or generally, *cousin*, Il.9.464, Hdt.5. 30, 7.82, A.*Pr*.856, *Com.Adesp*.58 D., etc., v. esp. And.1.47; ἀ. πρὸς πατρός Is.11.2; ἐκ πατρός Theoc.22.170: comically, ἐγχέλεων ἀ. Stratt.39. [ἀνεψιοῦ κταμένοιο Il.15.554, = ἀνεψιόο κτ., cf. Q.S.3. 295.] (Cf. Skt. *napāt* 'grandson', Lat. *nepos*, etc.) *-ότης, ητος, ἡ, *relationship of cousins*, esp. in phrase ἐντὸς ἀνεψιότητος Pl.*Lg*. 871b, Lex ap. D.43.57.

ἀνέψω, *boil again*, Arg.E.*Med*. (in aor. part. ἀνεψήσασα); ἔλαιον ἀνεψήσασθαι f.l. in Carm.Pop.ap.Sch.Ar.*Eq*.725.

ἀνέω [ᾱ], = πτίσσω, Ar.*Fr*.694 (v.l. αἰνεῖθ'), Ath.10.455e, Paus. Gr.*Fr*.21, prob. in Poll.7.24 (ἀλεῖν codd.). Cf. αἴνω, ἀφάνέω.

*ἄνεω, Adv. *without a sound, in silence*, δὴν δ' ἄ. ἦσαν Il.9.30,695; τίπτ' ἄ. ἐγένεσθε; 2.323; οἱ δ' ἄ. ἐγένοντο 3.84, Od.7.144, 10.71; ἅπαντες ἧσθ' ἄ. 2.240.—In all the places cited it is joined with a pl. Verb, and is commonly written ἄνεῳ (as if nom. pl. from ἄνεως).

ἀνέῳγα, ἀνέῳγον, v. ἀνοίγνυμι.

ἀνεῳγότως, Adv. pf. part. of ἀνέῳγώς (from ἀνοίγω), *openly*, *Gloss*.

ἀνέωνται, v. ἀνίημι sub init.

*ἄνη, ἡ, (ἄνω) *fulfilment*, A.*Th*.713, Call.*Jov*.90.

ἀνηβ-άσκω, = sq., D.H.*Rh*.2.6 (censured by Thom.Mag.p.171 R.), *POxy*.1381.197. -άω, *grow young again*, Hes.*Op*.132 (prob.), A.*Supp*.606 (Tyrwh. ἀνηβῆσαί με for ἂν ἡβήσαιμι), E.*Ion* 1465, Pl. *Lg*.666b; δὶς ἀ. Thgn.1009; πάλιν X.*Cyr*.4.6.7; μόνος ὁ νοῦς παλαιούμενος ἀνηβᾷ Plu.2.5e. II. *grow up, attain to* ἥβη, Call.*Jov*. 56. -ητήριος, α, ον, *making young again*, ἀ. ῥώμη the *returning* strength *of youth*, E.*Andr*.552. *-ος, ον, *not yet come to man's estate*, opp. ἔφηβος, παῖς Heraclit.117, cf. *Leg.Gort*.11.19, Lys.14.25, Theoc.8.3; οἱ ἄ. *pueri*, *CIG* 2034 (Byzantium), cf. *SIG* 1028.32 (Cos); ἄνηβοι καὶ ἄγονοι ἐκ γενετῆς *impotent*, Arist.*HA* 581ᵇ22; of a girl, Pl.*Lg*.833c. -ότης, ητος, ἡ, *childhood, minority*, Just.*Nov*.159 *Pr*.

ἀνηγεμόνευτος, ον, *without leader, unguided*, ψυχή Ph.1.337, cf. 696, Luc.*Icar*.9; φυρμός M.Ant.12.14.

ἀνηγέομαι, Dor. ἀνᾱγ-, *relate, rehearse*, Pi.*N*.10.19, cf. *I*.6(5).56, Hdt.5.4. 2. intr., ἀ. πρόσφορος ἐν Μοισᾶν δίφρῳ *advance* worthily in the Muses' car, Pi.*O*.9.80.

ἀνήδομαι, *renounce one's enjoyment of* a thing, *no longer enjoy* it, ἃ τόθ' ἥσθην, ταῦτα νῦν ἀ. Hermipp.77.

ἀνήδονος, ον, *disagreeable*, J.*AJ*17.3.1, Them.*Or*.26.319d. II. *without pleasure*, Plot.4.8.8.

ἀνήδυντος, ον, *not sweetened* or *seasoned*, Hp.*Int*.21, al., Arist.*Pr*. 925ᵇ18, etc. 2. metaph., Id.*Pol*.1340ᵇ16; ἀ. βραχυλογία Plu.*Phoc*. 5; ὕπνος Them.*Or*.18.218b; so, *unpleasant*, Hegesand.26; γυνή, φωνή, Plu.2.142b, 405d; ἦθος ἀ. πρὸς χάριν ib.799d.

ἀνήδυστος, ον, v.l. for foreg., Plu.*Phoc*.5.

ἀνήη, v. ἀνίημι. ἀνηθείη· ὁμιλία, Hsch.

ἀνηθέλαιον, τό, *oil of dill*, Gal.19.666, Orib.*Fr*.1.

ἀνηθίκευτος, ον, *without characteristic*, Sch.Lyc.14.

ἀνήθ-ινος, η, ον, *made of dill*, στέφανος (in form ἀνήτ-) Theoc. 7.63; οἶνος Dsc.5.65; μύρον Id.1.51, cf. Aret.*CA*1.2; cf. ἀνήτινος, ἀννήθιον. -ίτης [ῑ] οἶνος wine *flavoured with dill-seed*, *Gp*.8. 3. -οειδής, ές, *like dill*, Dsc.4.164.

ἄνηθον or ἄννηθον, τό, Aeol. ἄνητον Alc.36, Sapph.78,128, also Anacr.ap.Poll.6.107. ἄννητον Thphr.*HP*9.7.3:—*dill, Anethum graveolens*, Ar.*Nu*.982, *Th*.486, Thphr.*HP*1.11.2, Alex.127.5, Theoc.15. 119, *Ev.Matt*.23.23, Dsc.3.58, *SIG* 1170.26 (ii A.D.), Bilabel Ὀψαρτ. p.10. (ἀνν- in Ar. ll.cc. Not to be confused with ἄννησον, q.v.)

*ἀνηθοποίητος, ον, *not giving exact delineation of character*, D.H. *Lys*.8, Longin.34.3. 2. *unprincipled*, Cic.*Att*.10.10.5.

ἀνήιον, v. ἄνειμι (εἶμι).

*ἀνήκεστος, ον, (ἀκέομαι) *incurable, desperate, fatal*, ἄλγος, χόλος, Il. 5.394, 15.217; ἀ. πάθος ἔρδειν τινά Hdt.1.137; ἀ. λώβην λωβᾶσθαί τινα Id.3.154; λυμαίνεσθαί τινα λύμῃσι ἀ. Id.6.12, cf. A.*Ch*.516, etc.; κακόν, κακά, συμφοραί, Hes.*Th*.612, Archil.9.5, Th.5.111; μίασμα.. ἀ. τρέφειν keep it *till it is past cure*, S.*OT*98; ἁμαρτάδες Hp.*Acut*.39; ἔργον Antipho 5.91; πονηρία X.*Mem*.3.5.18; ἀνήκεστα ποιεῖν τινα *ruin utterly*, Id.*An*.2.5.5; ἀνήκεστα πάσχειν to be *utterly ruined*, Th. 3.39; ἀ. τι παθεῖν D.54.5; ἀ. τι βουλεῦσαι περί τινος Th.1.132; ἀπάντων τῶν ἀνηκέστων αἴτιον D.21.70, etc. 2. of persons, ἀ. πλεονέκται X.*Oec*.14.8; χρήσασθαί τινι τῶν ἐχθρῶν ὡς ἀνηκέστῳ Plu.*Per*. 39; ἀ. εἴς τι J.*AJ*18.6.10: Comp. -έστερος f.l. in Antipho 5.91: Sup., Ph.2.316. II. Act., *damaging beyond remedy, pernicious*, πῦρ S. *El*.888; χαρά Id.*Aj*.52. III. Adv. ἀνηκέστως, διατιθέναι treat *cruelly*, Hdt.3.155, cf. 8.28; ἀ. ἔχειν Aret.*SD*1.5, App.*BC*2.123.

ἀνηκής, ές, (ἄκος) = foreg., S.*Fr*.49.

ἀνηκίδωτος, ον, (ἀκιδωτός) *without point*, A.*Fr*.279; opp. ἠκιδωμένος, βέλη *IG*2.807b138.

ἀνηκο-έω, *to be deaf*, Hdn.*Epim*.188. -ΐα, ἡ, *not hearing*, Plu. 2.38b, Hierocl.*in CA*25 p.477 M. 2. *ignorance*, Plu.2.676f. 3. *disobedience*, Steph.*in Rh*.288.36. -ος, ον, *without hearing*, Arist. *Pr*.903ᵇ38; of the dead, Mosch.3.103; πέτραι Lyc.1451. 2. c. gen., *not hearing* a thing, *never having heard* or *learnt* it, Pl.*Phdr*. 261b, X.*Mem*.2.1.31: hence, *ignorant of* it, παιδείας Aeschin.1.141; *with no ear for*, τῶν Διονυσίου ῥυθμῶν Philostr.*VS*1.22.3; *not attending the lectures of*.., c. gen., ib.2.2. Adv. ἀνηκόως, ἔχειν ἀστρολογίας Plu.2.145c; ἔς τι Paus.10.17.13. b. c. acc. rei, ἀνήκοος εἶναι ἔνια γεγενημένα (where ἀ. εἶναι = ἀγνοεῖν) Pl.*Alc*.2.141d. c. abs., σκαιὸς καὶ ἀ. *ignorant, untaught*, D.19.312, cf. Sallust.5. 3. *not willing to hear, not listening*, Call.*Del*.116; τὸ ἀ. *disobedience*, D.H. 6.35. II. *unheard*, Philostr.*Her*.12.3; *without result*, ἀ. τέθνται Alciphr.3.35.

ἀνηκουστ-έω, *to be unwilling to hear, disobey*, c. gen., οὐδ' ἄρα πατρὸς ἀνηκούστησε Il.15.236; τῶν πατρὸς λόγων A.*Pr*.40; τῶν νόμων Th.1.84: c. dat., ἀ. τοῖσι στρατηγοῖσι Hdt.6.14: also abs., 1.115, Aen.Tact.10.3. -ία, Ion. -ίη, ἡ, *want of hearing, deafness*, Hp. *Morb*.3.4. 2. *disobedience*, Pl.*Lg*.671b. -ος, ον, *not to be heard, inaudible*, Arist.*de An*.421ᵇ5. 2. *unheard of*, ἤκουσ' ἀνήκουστα.. ὥστε φρῖξαι S.*El*.1407, cf. E.*Hipp*.363 (lyr.). 3. of prayers, *not to be granted*, Antipho 1.22. II. Act., *not willing to hear*: τὸ ἀ. *disobedience*, X.*Cyn*.3.8.

ἀνήκω, *to have come up to* a point, *reach up to*, of persons and things, ἐς μέτρον τινὸς ἀ. Hdt.2.127; αἱμασιὴν ὕψος ἀνήκουσαν ἀνδρὶ ἐς τὸν ὀμφαλόν Id.7.60; ἐς τὰ μέγιστα ἀ. ἀρετῆς πέρι 5.49; χρήμασι ἀ. ἐς τὰ πρῶτα 7.134; φρενῶν ἐς τὰ ἐμεωυτοῦ πρῶτα οὔκω ἀ. *have* not yet *reached* the highest point I aim at, ib.13; οὐκ ἐς τοσοῦτο εὐηθίης ἀ. ib.16.γ', cf. 9.γ'; πρόσω ἀρετῆς ἀ. ib.237; ἀ. εἰς τὸ ὀξύ to *rise to* a point, Ael.*NA*1.55; τοῦτο μὲν ἐς οὐδὲν ἀ. *amounts to* nothing, Hdt. 2.104; μεῖζον ἀ. ἢ κατ' ἐμὰν ῥώμαν the matter *has gone* too *far*.., S. *Tr*.1018; αἱ πολλαὶ [ζημίαι].. ἐς τὸν θάνατον ἀ. *have gone as far as*.., Th.3.45. 2. ἀ. ἐς σὲ ἔχειν it *has come to* you to have, *has become* yours to have, Hdt.6.109. 3. ἀ. εἴς τι *refer to* or *be connected with* .., D.60.6, Arist.*EN*1167ᵇ4 (v.l.); τὰ εἰς ἀργυρίου λόγον ἀ. ἀδικήματα which *involve* a money consideration, Din.1.60; so ὁ φόνος ἀνήκει εἴς τινα Antipho 3.3.7; ἀ. πρός τι Plb.2.15.4, Callix.2, etc. II. *belong, appertain*, Lxx 1*Ma*.10.42, al.; τὰ εἰς τιμὴν καὶ δόξαν ἀνήκοντα *OGI* 763.36 (Pergam.); τὰ ἐκείνοις -οντα ib.532 (Paphlag.); τὰ ἀ. τῇ πόλει *Inscr.Magn*.53.65 (iii B.C.); τὰ ἀ. τοῖς ἱεροῖς *PTeb*.6.42 (ii B.C.). 2. abs., *to be fit* or *proper*, *Ep.Eph*.5.4, *Ep.Col*.3.18; τὸ ἀνῆκον, = τὸ προσῆκον, *Ep.Philem*.8. III. *come back*, εἰς τοὺς πρώτους πάλιν ἀ. λόγους Pl.*Tht*.196b.

*ἀνηλακάτος, ον, *unable to spin*, γυνή Matro *Parod.Fr*.5.

ἀνήλᾰτος, ον, *not malleable*, Arist.*Mete*.385ᵃ16: metaph., *stubborn*, Anacr.140. 2. *not struck with a hammer*, Lxx *Jb*.41.15.

*ἀνηλεγής, ές, *unconcerned, reckless*, πόλεμος Q.S.2.75: neut. in Hsch. Adv. -έως Q.S.2.414.

ἀνηλε-ήμων, v. sub ἀνελεήμων. -ής, ές, = ἀνελεής, *without pity, unmerciful*, Men.*Epit*.478, Call.*Del*.106, Parth.14.2, App.*Mith*.38; poet. acc. ἀνηλέα (as if from ἀνηλής) *Epigr.Gr*.418 (Cyrene); gen. ἀνηλέος Man.1.263; ἀνηλής is dub. in Alcm.81, cf. *An.Ox*.1.60. Adv. -εῶς Hp.*Aff*.40, And.4.39. *-ητος, ον, *unpitied*, Lycurg.148 (ἀνελ- codd.). II. *unmerciful*, Aeschin.2.163, Eub.1 D. Adv. -τως Pl.*Lg*.697d, Ar.*Fr*.51 D.

*ἀνήλειπτος, ον, *unanointed*, should be read for ἀνείληπτος in Antyll.ap.Orib.10.13.19:—also ἀνήλειφος (so codd.) or ἀνήλῐφος, ον, D.C.56.30, Philagr.ap.Orib.5.19.10, Hp.*Ep*.17.

ἀνηλειψία, ἡ, *being unanointed, uncleanliness*, Hp.*Vict*.2.57, Plb. 3.87.2.

ἀνηλής, v. ἀνηλεής.

ἀνηλιάζω, *place in the sun*, f.l. in Protagorid.4.

ἀνήλῐκος, ον, *not yet arrived at man's estate*, Ps.-Callisth.1.38, Suid. s.v. ἄνηβος.

ἀνηλιοδείκτης, ου, ὁ, dub. sens. in *PMag.Par*.1.1374.

*ἀνήλιος, Dor. -άλιος, ον, *without sun, unsunned, sunless*, of the nether world, A.*Th*.859 (lyr.); μυχοί, δνόφοι, Id.*Pr*.453, *Ch*.51 (lyr.); φυλλάς S.*OC*676 (lyr.); λιβάς E.*Andr*.534 (lyr.).

*ἀνηλιποκαιβλεπέλαιος (fort. -καλιπ-), ον, *barefoot and unanointed* (?), Epigr.ap.Hegesand.1.

*ἀνήλῐπος, Dor. ἀνάλ-, ον, *barefoot*, v.l. for νήλιπος, Theoc.4.56.

ἀνηλῐφής, ές, = ἀνήλειπτος, Suid.: ἀνήλῐφος, ον, v. ἀνήλειπτος.

ἀνήλῠσις, εως, ἡ, *going up*: *return*, Hsch.

ἀνήλ-ωμα, ατος, τό, = ἀνάλωμα, *PTeb*.212 (ii B.C.), *PHal*.15.7 (iii B.C.), *BGU*1117.15 (i B.C.), *IG*2.595, etc. -ωτικός, ή, όν, = ἀναλ-, *PLond*.2.265.10 (i A.D.); ἀ. μέτρον *PPetr*.3 p.317.

*ἀνήλωτος, ον, *not nailed*, Suid. s.v. ἀγόμφωτος.

ἀνήμελκτος, ον, *unmilked*, Od.9.439.

ἀνήμερ-ος, ον, *not tame, wild, savage*, of persons, πολιήτας Anacr. 1.7; ἀνήμεροι γάρ, οὐδὲ πρόσπλατοι ξένοις A.*Pr*.716, cf. Carneisc.

*Herc.*1027.16, 2*Ep.Ti.*3.3, Arr.*Epict.*1.3.7; of a country, A.*Eu.*14; ἐκβολή E.*Hec.*1078; βίος Plu.2.86d; διάθεσις Phld.*Ir.*p.57 W., cf. p.85: Sup., Clearch.37. Adv. -ρως, ἀ. τισὶ χρήσασθαι D.S.13. 23. **-ότης**, ητος, ἡ, *wildness, savageness*, Phld.*Oec.*p.68 J., *Gloss.*

**ἀνημερ-όω**, *to clear of wild beasts*, ἀ. κνωδάλων ὁδόν S.*Fr.*905. ❋**-ωτος**, ον, *untilled*, γῆ ib.825, Cratin.26 D.

**ἀνήμετος**, ον, v. ἀνέμετος.

**ἀνήμυκτος**, ον, (ἀμύσσω) *not torn* or *lacerated*, Hsch.

**ἀνήνασθαι, ἀνήνατο**, v. ἀναίνομαι.

**ἀνηνεμ-έω**, f.l. for νην-, Str.7.3.18. **-ία**, ἡ, = νηνεμία, *AP*9.544 (Adaeus); noted as an archaic form by Luc.*Pseudol.*29. **-ος**, ον, *without wind*, ἀνήνεμος χειμώνων *without the blast* of storms, S. *OC*677 (lyr.); *gentle*, τυφών Olymp.*in Mete.*201.22.

**ἀνήνιος** (A), ον, *unbridled*, *EM*107.20.

**ἀνήνιος** (B), ον, = ἀνάνιος (q.v.), *without pain*, Hp.ap.Gal.19.81.

**ἀνήνοθε**, Ep. pf. used like an aor.: αἷμ' ἔτι θερμὸν ἀνήνοθεν ἐξ ὠτειλῆς blood *gushed forth from* the wound, Il.11.266; κνίση μὲν ἀνήνοθεν the savour *mounted up*, Od.17.270 (ἐνήνοθε Aristarch.).

**ἀνήνυστος**, ον, (ἀνύω) *of none effect, ineffectual*, ἀνηνύστῳ ἐπὶ ἔργῳ Od.16.111, cf. A.R.4.1307; κάματοι Opp.*C.*4.196. 2. *impossible of fulfilment*, Emp.12.

❋**ἀνήνῠτος**, ον, = ἀνήνυστος, ἀ. πόνος, εὐχαί, Pl.*Lg.*735b, 936c; ἀ. ἔργον πράττειν, of Penelope's web, Id.*Phd.*84a, cf. E.*Hel.*1285. Adv., ταῦτ' ἀνηνύτως ἔχει S.*Fr.*557.4. 2. *endless, never-ending*, οἶτος Id.*El.*167, cf. Plb.9.24.4; κακόν Pl.*Grg.*507e; κακοπαθία Phld. *Herc.*1251.17; βυθός, etc., Ph.1.85, etc.: neut. pl. as Adv., ἀνήνυτα μοχθοῦσιν Epicur.*Fr.*470.

**ἀνήνωρ**, ορος, ὁ, *unmanly*, Od.10.301; ἀνὴρ ἀνήνωρ a man *of no manhood*, Hes.*Op.*751. II. *childless*, Hsch.

**ἀνήξεις**· κολυμβήσεις, Hsch.; cf. ἀνανήχομαι.

❋**ἀνηπελίη**· ἀσθένεια, Hsch.; cf. εὐηπελίη.

**ἀνηπλωμένως**, Adv. pf. part. Pass. of ἀναπλόω, *at length, in detail*, opp. συνῃρημένως, τὸν λόγον παραδίδωσι Simp.*in Ph.*1215.20; ἀ. καὶ ἀφηγηματικῶς Aps.p.243 H.

**ἀνήπυστος**, ον, (ἠπύω) *unheard of*, dub. in Zonar.

**ἀνηπύω**, *sound*, αὐλοῦ ἦχον ἀνηπύοντος Mosch.2.98. 2. c. acc., *sing aloud*, ὑμέναιον A.R.4.1197.

❋**ἀνήρ**, ὁ, ἀνδρός, ἀνδρί, ἄνδρα, voc. ἄνερ: pl. ἄνδρες, -δρῶν, -δράσι [ᾰ], -δρας: Aeol. dat. pl. ἄνδρεσι Alc.*Supp.*14.8: late nom. sg. ἄνδρας *Cat.Cod.Astr.*7.109.7: in Att. the Art. often forms a crasis with the Noun, ἁνήρ for ὁ ἀνήρ, τἀνδρός, τἀνδρί for τοῦ ἀνδρός, etc., ἅνδρες for οἱ ἄνδρες; the Ion. crasis is ὡνήρ, ὦνδρες, Hdt.4.161,134: Ep. also ἀνέρα, ἀνέρος, ἀνέρι, dual ἀνέρε, pl. ἀνέρες, ἀνέρας, ἄνδρεσσι. [Ep. Poets mostly use ᾱ in arsi, ᾰ in thesi; but in trisyll. forms with stem ἀνέρ- always ᾱ; so also Trag. in lyr., S.*Tr.*1011, *OT*869. But in Trag. senarians ᾰ always.] (ἀ- in nom. by analogy; cf. Skt. *nar*- from I.-E. *ner-*, *nr̥-* from *nr̥-*, Gk. ἀνδρ- from *n̥r-*):—*man*, opp. *woman* (ἄνθρωπος being *man* as opp. to *beast*), Il.17.435, Od.21.323; τῶν ἀνδρῶν ἄπαις without *male* children, Pl.*Lg.*877e; in Hom. mostly of princes, leaders, etc., but also of *free* men; ἀ. δήμου *one* of the people, Il.2.198, cf. Od.17.352; with a qualifying word to indicate rank, ἀ. βουληφόρος Il.2.61; ἀ. βασιλεύς Od.24.253; ἡγήτορες ἄ. Il.11.687. II. *man*, opp. *god*, πατὴρ ἀνδρῶν τε θεῶν τε ib.1.544, al.; Διὸς ἄγγελοι ἠδὲ καὶ ἀνδρῶν ib.334, cf. 403, Hdt.5.63, etc.: most common in pl., yet sts. in sg., e.g. Il.18.432:—freq. with a Noun added, βροτοί, θνητοὶ ἄ., Od.5.197, 10.306; ἄ. ἡμίθεοι Il.12.23; ἄ. ἥρωες ib.5.746:—also of *men*, opp. *monsters*, Od.21.303:—of *men* in societies and cities, οὔτε παρ' ἀνδράσιν οὔτ' ἐν ναυσὶ κοίλαις Pi.*O.* 6.10; and so prob., ἄλλοτε μέν τ' ἐπὶ Κύνθου ἐβήσαο.., ἄλλοτε δ' ἂν νήσους τε καὶ ἀνέρας.. *h.Ap.*142. III. *man*, opp. *youth*, unless the context determines the meaning, as in οὔ πως ἔστι νεωτέρῳ ἀνδρὶ μάχεσθαι ἄνδρα γέροντα Od.18.53; but ἀ. alone always means *a man in the prime of life*, esp. *warrior*, ἀ. ἕλεν ἄνδρα Il.15.328; so ἀ. ἀντ' ἀνδρὸς ἐλύθησαν Th.2.103; the several ages are given as παῖς, μειράκιον, ἀ., πρεσβύτης X.*Smp.*4.17; εἰς ἄνδρας ἐγγράφεσθαι, συντελεῖν, D.19.230, Isoc.12.212; εἰς ἄνδρας ἀναβῆναι *BMus.Inscr.*898; in Inscrr. relating to contests, opp. παῖδες, *IG*2².1138.10, etc. IV. *man* emphatically, *man indeed*, ἀνέρες ἔστε, φίλοι Il.5.529; freq. in Hdt., πολλοὶ μὲν ἄνθρωποι, ὀλίγοι δὲ ἄνδρες 7.210; πρόσθεν οὐκ ἀ. ὅδ' ἦν; S.*Aj.*77; ἄνδρα γίγνεσθαί σε χρή E.*El.*693; ἀ. γεγένησαι δι' ἐμέ Ar.*Eq.*1255; ὁ μαθὼν ἀ. ἔσει Id.*Nu.*823; ἄνδρας ἡγοῦνται μόνους τοὺς πλεῖστα δυναμένους καταφαγεῖν Id.*Ach.*77; εἰ ἄνδρες εἶεν οἱ στρατηγοί Th.4.27; οὐκέτι ἀ. ἀλλὰ σκευοφόρος X.*Cyr.*4.2.25; τὸν Λυκομήδην.. μόνον ἄνδρα ἡγοῦντο Id.*HG*7.1.24; οὐκ ἐν ἀνδράσι not *like a man*, E.*Alc.*723, cf. 732; ἀνδρὸς τὰ προσπίπτοντα γενναίως φέρειν 'tis *the part of a man*.., Men.771, etc. V. *husband*, Il.19. 291, Od.24.196, Hdt.1.146, etc.; εἰς ἀνδρὸς ὥραν ἡκούσης τῆς κόρης Pl. *Criti.*113d; so ἐξοικιεῖν εἰς ἀνδρὸς [οἶκον] θυγατέρα Luc.*Lex.*11:—also of *a paramour*, opp. πόσις, S.*Tr.*551, cf. E.*Hipp.*491, Theoc.15.131; ἀ. ἁπασῶν τῶν γυναικῶν ἐστι νῦν Pherecr.155; αἰγῶν ἄνερ Theoc.8. 49. VI. Special usages: 1. joined with titles, professions, etc., ἰητρὸς ἀ. Il.11.514; ἀ. μάντις, ἀ. στρατηγός, Hdt.6.83,92 (dub.); ἀ. νομεύς S.*OT*1118; ἄνδρες λοχῖται, λῃσταί, ἀπιστῆρες, ib.751,842, *Aj.*565; esp. in disparagement, κλῶπες ἄ. E.*Rh.*645; ἀ. δημότης S. *Ant.*690; with names of nations, as Φοίνικες ἄ. Hdt.4.42; ἀ. Θρῄξ E. *Hec.*19, al.; esp. in addresses, ἄ. ἔφοροι Hdt.9.9; ἄ. πολῖται S.*OT* 513; ἄ. δικασταί D.21.1, etc.; ὦ ἄνδρες *gentlemen* of the jury, Antipho 1.1, Lys.1.1, etc.; ὦ ἄ. Ἀθηναῖοι Id.6.8, etc.: hence in Comedy, ἄ. ἰχθύες Archipp.29; ἄ. θεοί Luc.*JTr.*15; ὦ ἄ. κύνες Ath.4.160b. 2. ὁ ἀνήρ, by crasis Att. ἁνήρ, Ion. ὡνήρ, is freq. used emphatically for αὐτός, ἐκεῖνος Ar.*V.*269, prob. in Pl.*Sph.*216b, etc.: sts. so in oblique cases without the Art., S.*Tr.*55, 109, 293, etc.; but not in Prose. 3. ἀ. ὅδε, ὅδ' ἀ., in Trag., = ἐγώ, S.*Aj.*78, E.*Alc.*690, etc. 4. πᾶς ἀ. every *man*, every *one*, freq. in Pl.*Lg.*736c, al., cf. E.*Or.* 1523. 5. *a man, any man*, εἶτ' ἄνδρα τῶν αὐτοῦ τι χρὴ προϊέναι; Ar.*Nu.*1214; οὐ πρέπει νοῦν ἔχοντι ἀνδρί Pl.*Phd.*114d, etc.; οὐ παντὸς ἀνδρὸς.. ἔσθ' ὁ πλοῦς 'tis not *every one* that can go, Nicol.Com. 1.26. 6. ὦ δαιμόνι' ἀνδρῶν Eup.316; and often with a Sup., ὦ φίλτατ' ἀνδρῶν Phryn.Com.80, etc. 7. κατ' ἄνδρα *viritim*, Isoc. 12.180, *POxy.*1047 iii 11, *BGU*145.5, etc.; so τοὺς κατ' ἄνδρα *individuals*, opp. κοινῇ τὴν πόλιν, D.Chr.32.6. 8. In LXX, ἀνήρ = ἕκαστος, ὥστε μοι ἀνὴρ ἐνώτιον *Jd.*8.24; ἀ. τῷ ἀδελφῷ αὐτοῦ προσκολληθήσεται '*each to his fellow*', of leviathan's scales, *Jb.*41.8; also ἀ. εἷς 4*Ki.*6.2; with negs., ἀ. μὴ ἐπισκεπήτω ib.10.19; ἀνὴρ ἀνήρ *any one*, *Le.*15.2. 9. ἄνδρας γράφειν· τὸ ἐν διδασκάλου τὰ παιδία ὀνόματα γράφειν, Hsch. VII. *male animal*, Arist.*HA*637ᵇ15.

**ἀνηρέμητος**, ον, *restless*, Corn.*ND*26, S.E.*M.*3.5. Adv. -τως 10.223.

**ἀνηρεοί**, οἱ, *rings through which cables were passed*, Hsch.

**ἀνήρεστον**· οὐκ ἀρεστόν, Hsch. (prob.).

**ἀνηρεφής**, ές, *not covered*, A.R.2.1171.

**ἀνηρήμεθα**, v. ἀνείρομαι.

**ἀνήρης**, ες, = ἀνδρώδης, dub. in A.*Fr.*218.

**ἀνηρίθευτος**, ον, = ἀνερίθευτος (q.v.), *GDI*5653*B* (Chios, v B.C.).

**ἀνήριθμος**, v. ἀνάριθμος. **ἀνηρίναστος**, ον, = ἀνερίναστος, Hsch. **ἀνήριστα**· ἀνέριστα, ἄπλαστα, Id.

**ἀνηρός**, ά, όν, = ἀνιαρός, ὀρθόπνοια Ph.Tars.ap.Gal.13.267; but ἀνηρόν· ἀβλαπτον, *EM*108.22.

**ἀνήροτος**, ον, *unploughed*, γύαι A.*Pr.*708; *without tillage*, ἀνήροτα πάντα φύονται Od.9.109: neut. pl. as Adv., λειμῶνες ἀνήροτα πορφύρουσι Opp.*C.*1.462: metaph., γυνή ἀ. Luc.*Lex.*19.

**ἀνηρτημένως**, Adv. pf. part. Pass. of ἀναρτάω, *disconnectedly, incoherently*, Herm.*in Phdr.*p.177 A.

**ἀνησιδώρα**, ἡ, *sending up gifts*, epith. of Earth, *Ath.Mitt.*37.288 (ii A.D.), cf. Sch.Ar.*Av.*971; of Demeter, S.*Fr.*826, Alciphr.1.3, Paus.1.31.4, Plu.2.745a; ἑστία ἀ., of Rome, ib.317a.

❋**ἀνήσσητος**, Dor. **ἀνήσσᾱτος**, ον, *unconquered*, Theoc.6.46.

**ἄνησσον**, τό, v. ἄννησον.

**ἀνηστις**, ιδος, ἡ, = νῆστις, A.*Fr.*258 A, Cratin.45.

**ἄνηστος**, ον, (νέω) *unspun*, σίππιον *POxy.*1288.34.

**ἀνήσυχος**· *inquietus*, *Gloss.*

**ἀνήτινος**, η, ον, Dor. for ἀνήθ-: **ἄνητον** or **ἄννητον**, v. ἄνηθον.

**ἀνήφαιστος**, ον, ἀ. πῦρ fire *that is no fire*, i.e. discord, E.*Or.*621.

**ἀνηχέω**, *raise a shout*, Sch.E.*Or.*1335.

❋**ἀνθαιρ-έομαι**, *choose* one person or thing *instead of* another, τὸ δ' εὐσεβὲς τῆς δυσσεβείας ἀνθελοῦ E.*Cyc.*311; ἄλλους ἀ. ἀντὶ τούτων *CIG* 2715.11 (Stratonicea); στρατηγοὺς ἔπαυσαν.. καὶ ἄλλους ἀνθείλοντο Th.6.103, cf. X.*HG*6.2.13, Pl.*Lg.*765d; τὰν εὔδοξον ἀ. φάμαν *prefer, choose rather*, E.*Hipp.*773 (lyr.). II. *dispute, lay claim to*, οὐδεὶς στέφανον ἀνθαιρήσεται Id.*Hec.*660. **-εσις**, εως, ἡ, *choice of* one *to succeed* another, *CIG*2715.12. ❋**-ετιστής**, οῦ, ὁ, of planets, *belonging to the opposite 'condition'*, Jul.Laod. in *Cat.Cod.Astr.*5(1).183.21, cf. 192.36.

**ἀνθάλιον**, τό, = μαλιναθάλλη, Plin.*HN*21.88,175.

**ἀνθᾰλίσκομαι**, *to be captured in turn*, i.e. after one has captured others, οὐ τἂν ἑλόντες αὖθις ἀνθαλοῖεν ἄν A.*Ag.*340; *to be convicted in turn*, ἀντικατηγορήθη καὶ ἀνθεάλω D.C.36.40.

**ἀνθᾰμαρτάνω** [ᾰν], *err in retaliation*, Agath.4.4.

**ἀνθᾰμιλλ-άομαι** (ἀντ- Hsch.), *vie one with another, be rivals*, Pl. *Lg.*731a; *race*, of triremes, X.*HG*6.2.28:—Act., part. ἀνθαμιλλεῦντες Hp.*Ep.*17. **-ος**, ον, *vying with, rivalling*, E.*Ion*606.

❋**ἀνθάπτομαι**, Ion. ἀντ-, *lay hold of in return*, οἱ Πέρσαι.. ἅπτοντο αὐτοῦ·.. οἱ δὲ ἀντάπτοντο Hdt.3.137, cf. E.*Hec.*275: but mostly, II. simply, *lay hold of, grapple with, engage in*, c. gen., ἀ. τοῦ πολέμου Hdt.7.138; ἀ. τῶν πραγμάτων Th.8.97; ἀ. τῆς λογιστικῆς Pl.*R.*525c: generally, *reach, attain*, τερμόνων E.*Med.*1182 (dub.). 2. *lay hold of, seize, attack*, esp. of pain, grief, etc., πλευμόνων S.*Tr.*778, cf. Ar. *Ra.*474; φρενῶν, καρδίας, E.*Med.*55,1360; περὶ τῆς μισθοφορᾶς.. μαλακωτέρως ἀνθήπτετο (sc. Τισσαφέρνους) *attacked* him, Th.8.50 (unless abs., 'was less firm in his *counter-grip*').

**ἀνθάριον**, τό, *pimple, eruption*, = ἐρύθημα, Hsch.

**ἀνθαρμόζω**, *fit* one thing *to* another, χειρὶ χεῖρα Sch.Pi.*P.*4.65.

**ἀνθάρπαγμα**, ατος, τό, *a thing seized by way of reprisal* or *pledge*, Eust.877.37.

**Ἄνθεια**, ἡ, epith. of Hera at Argos, Paus.2.22.1, *EM*108.47; at Miletus, in dat., Ἥρῃ Ἀνθέῃ *Milet.*3 No.31(a).5 (vi B.C.); of the Ὧραι, Hsch.; also of Aphrodite at Cnossus, Id.

**ἀνθεινός**, ή, όν, = ἀνθινός, D.S.4.4, Ael.*NA*2.11.

**ἄνθειον**, τό, *flower, blossom*, dub. in Ar.*Ach.*869 (Boeot.).

**ἀνθεκτέον**, *one must cleave to*, τούτου ἀ. τοῖς ἐπιμεληταῖς Pl.*R.*424b; ἀ. τῆς μέσης ἕξεως Arist.*EN*1126ᵇ9: so in pl., ἀνθεκτέα ἐστὶ τῆς θαλάσσης Th.1.93.

**ἀνθεκτικός**, ή, όν, *clinging to, attached to*, τινός Arr.*Epict.*4.11.3.

**ἀνθελετός**, ή, όν, *preferred*, Poet.*de herb.*194.

**ἀνθελιγμός**, ὁ, *counter-winding*, *Placit.*3.15.5 (pl.) (ἀντ- codd.).

**ἀνθέλιξ**, ικος, ἡ, *the interior curvature of the ear*, the exterior being ἕλιξ, Ruf.*Onom.*44.

**ἀνθέλκω**, aor. inf. -ελκύσαι Herm.*in Phdr.*p.170 A.:—*draw* or *pull against*, Th.4.14; ἀ. ἀλλήλαις *pull against* one another, Pl.*Lg.*644e;

. τὴν ψυχὴν *draw it in a contrary direction*, Id.*R*.439b; φιλανθρώπως ιὰς ἀ. D.S.30.8: metaph., of *resistance* of facts *to* suggested inference, εἰς τοὐναντίον μηδενὸς -κοντος Phld.*Sign*.17, cf. 18; ἀ. τινὰ πρὸς αὐτὰς ἑκάστῃ Luc.*Demon*.63:—Pass., Pl.*Ax*.372, D.H.3.30.

**ἄνθεμα**, ατος, τό, v. ἀνάθεμα. II. name of *dance*, in Ath.14.629e, unless this be neut. pl. of ἄνθεμον.

**ἀνθεμίζομαι**, in A.*Supp*.73 γοεδνὰ ἀνθεμίζεσθαι, i.e. (says the Sch.) τὸ ἄνθος τῶν γόων ἀποδρέπεσθαι; cf. ἀπανθίζω.

**❀ἀνθέμ-ιον**, τό, = ἄνθος, f.l. for ἄνθεμον in Thphr.*HP*1.13.3, al., cf. *AP*4.1.36 (Mel.), *PMag.Leid.V*.13.9. 2. *honeysuckle pattern* on Ionic columns, *IG*1.322; so ἀ. ἐστιγμένοι tattooed with a similar pattern, of the Mossynoeci, X.*An*.5.4.32: pl., *artificial flowers*, *IG*11.161*B*50 (Delos, iii B.C.). 3. of gold, *the purest quality*, Lxx *Ec*.12.6. ❀-ίς, ίδος, ἡ, = ἄνθος, J.*AJ* 2.2.10, *AP*6.267 (Diotim.). 2. *camomile*, Nic.*Fr*.74.37; ἀ. λευκή *Matricaria Chamomilla*, *wild c.*, ἀ. μελίνη *Anthemis tinctoria*, *dyer's c.*, ibid.; ἀ. πορφυρᾶ *A. rosea*, ibid., Dsc.3.137. b. = ἀνθυλλίς, Ps.-Dsc.3.136; = ἀργεμώνη, Id.2.177; = ἀμάρακον, Id.3.138:—also **ἀνθεμίσιον**, τό, Alex.Trall.9.1. **-οειδής**, ές, = ἀνθεμώδης, Orph.*H*.43.4. **-όεις**, εσσα, εν, also εις as fem., Il.2.695, Hes.*Fr*.16:—*flowery*, of places, ἐν λειμῶνι Σκαμανδρίῳ ἀνθεμόεντι Il.2.467, cf. 695, B.12.88; ἐπ' ἀνθεμόεντι Ἕβρῳ on the *flowery* banks of Hebrus, 15.5. II. of works in metal, *adorned with flowers*, λέβητ' ἄπυρον.. ἀ. Il.23.885; ἐν ἀ. λέβητι Od.3.440; κρητῆρα πανάργυρον ἀ. 24.275; *embroidered*, κύπασσις *AP*6.272 (Pers.). (ἀνθεμεῦντας ps.-Ion. form in Anacr.62.)

**❀ἄνθεμον**, τό, = ἄνθος, Sapph.85, Semon.7.66, Pi.*N*.7.79, Cratin.98, Ar.*Ach*.992, *Tab.Heracl*.1.96; ἄνθεμα χρυσοῦ golden *flowers*, Pi.*O*.2.72; ἄνθεμ' ὀρειχάλκου *h.Hom*.6.9; ἄνθεμα κοτταβείων *IG*11.164 *B*25 (Delos, iii B.C.). 2. name of a *plant*, ἄ. ἀφύλλανθες *Matricaria Chamomilla* var. *eradiata*, and ἄ. φυλλῶδες *Anthemis chia*, Thphr.*HP*7.8.3. 3. v. ἄνθεμα II. 4. pl., name of *cake*, Poll.6.76, Hsch.

**ἀνθεμό-ρρυτος**, ον, *flowing from flowers*, ἀ. γάνος μελίσσης, i.e. honey, E.*IT*634. **-στρωτος**, ον, *strewn with flowers*, Id.ap.Phot. p.138 R.

**ἀνθεμουργός**, όν, *working in flowers*, ἡ ἀ., i.e. *the bee*, A.*Pers*.612.

**Ἀνθεμουσία**· τάγμα τι παρὰ Μακεδόσιν ἐξ Ἀνθεμοῦντος πόλεως Μακεδονίας, Hsch.

**ἀνθεμοφόρον**, τό, = βούνιον, Ps.-Dsc.4.123.

**ἀνθεμ-ώδης**, ες, *flowery, blooming*, μελίλωτος Sapph.*Supp*.25.14; Νεῖλος B.18.39; ἔαρ A.*Pr*.455; Τμῶλος E.*Ba*.462; λειμών Ar.*Ra*.450. ❀-ωτός, ή, όν, *adorned with flowers* or *with flower-patterns*, καλυπτήρ *IG*2.807*b*107.

**ἄνθεξις**, εως, ἡ, *clinging to*, ἀλλήλων Pl.*Ep*.323b (pl.).

**ἄνθεο**, Ep. aor. 2 imper. Med. of ἀνατίθημι.

**ἀνθερεών**, ῶνος, ὁ, *chin*, δεξιτερῇ δ' ἄρ' ὑπ' ἀνθερεῶνος ἑλοῦσα, in token of supplication, Il.1.501; παρὰ νείατον ἀνθερεῶνα, i.e. just under the *chin*, 5.293, cf. Hp.*Oss*.18, Nic.*Th*.444. 2. later, *neck, throat*, Euph.92.1 (pl.): sg., *AP*9.129 (Nestor), Q.S.1.110: sg. in both senses, Ruf.*Onom*.47,48. 3. *mouth*, Nonn.*D*.3.247, 25.476.

**❀ἀνθέρ-ῑκος**, ὁ, *flowering stem of asphodel*, Thphr.*HP*7.13.2, cf. Hp. *Coac*.491, Hellanic.67 J., Longus 1.10; and so prob. ἐξ ἀνθερίκων in Hdt.4.190, which others refer to ἀνθέριξ. 2. *flower-head of asphodel*, Dsc.2.169. 3. *the plant* itself, *asphodel*, Cratin.325, Eup. 14.5. II. = ἀνθέριξ I, Sch.Arat.1060. **-ῑκώδης**, ες, *like asphodel*, καυλὸς Thphr.*HP*9.10.1. ❀-ιξ, ῐκος, ὁ, = ἀθήρ, *beard* of an ear of corn, *the ear* itself, Il.20.227, Hes.*Fr*.117, *AP*12.121 (Rhian.). II. = ἀνθέρικος I. 1 (q.v.), *stalk of asphodel*, v.l. in Theoc.1.52. **-ίσκος**, ὁ, = ἀνθέρικος, dub. in *AB*403.

**ἄνθεσαν**, Ep. 3 pl. aor. 2 Act. of ἀνατίθημι.

**ἀνθεσι-ουργός**, όν, *creating flowers*, Orph.*Fr*.197. **-πότᾰτος**, ον, *fluttering round flowers*, μέλεα Antiph.209. **-χρως**, ωτος, ὁ, ἡ, *variegated*, πέρκη Matro *Conv*.51.

**❀Ἀνθεσ-τήρια**, τά, *Feast of Flowers*, i.e. three days' festival of Dionysus at Athens, in the month Anthesterion, Apollod.*Fr*.28; also in Ionic cities, *SIG*38.32 (Teos), *CIG*3655 (Cyzicus). (Deriv. from ἀνα-θέσσασθαι is dub.; from ἀνθεῖν acc. to Ister 28.) ❀-τηριάδας· τὰς ἐχούσας ὥραν γάμου (Rhod.), Hsch. **-τηριών**, ῶνος, ὁ, the month *Anthesterion*, eighth of the Attic year, answering to the end of February and the beginning of March, in which the Anthesteria were celebrated, Th.2.15, etc.; also in Ionic cities, as Tenos, *IG*12(5).872.48.

**ἀνθεστιάω**, *entertain in return* or *mutually*, Plu.*Ant*.27, cf. 32 (Pass.), Luc.*Am*.9.

**Ἀνθεσ-φόρια**, τά, a festival in honour of Persephone, who was carried off while *gathering flowers*, Poll.1.37. **-φόρος**, ον, *bearing flowers, flowery*, μῖλαξ E.*Ba*.703; λείμακες ἀνθεσφόροι Id.*IA* 1544. II. ἀνθεσφόροι, αἱ, *women celebrating the Anthesphoria*, Poll.4.78.

**ἄνθεται**· ἐλεύθεροι (Tarent.), Hsch.

**ἄνθετο**, Ep. 3 sg. aor. 2 Med. of ἀνατίθημι.

**❀ἀνθέω**, *blossom, bloom*, of the youthful beard, πρὶν.. ὑπὸ κροτάφοισιν ἰούλους ἀνθῆσαι Od.11.320 (the only place in Hom.), cf. Orph.*L*.255; of persons, τυτθὸν δ' ἀνθήσαντας ὑπὸ κροτάφοισιν ἴουλον *with* the young down *just showing*, *IG*5(1).1355 (Geraneia), cf. *APl*.5.381. 2. of flowers and plants, first in Hes.*Op*.582, Alc.39; στάχυς S.*Fr*.395; *flourish*, ἀ. κυπάρισσοι Theoc.27.46: c. dat., ἄνθεσιν *h.Ap*.139; ῥόδοις Pi.*I*.4(3).18: metaph., ἀνθοῦν πέλαγος Αἰγαῖον νεκροῖς A.*Ag*.659; ἀφρὸς ἤνσει (Lacon.) dub.l. in Ar.*Lys*.1257. II. metaph., 1. *bloom, be brilliant, shine* with colour, etc., ἤνθει φοινικίσι.. ἡ στρατιὰ X.*Cyr*.6.4.1; of linen garments, Plu.2.352d. 2. *to be in bloom, blooming*, Ἥβας καρπὸν ἀνθήσαντα Pi.*P*.9.110; ἀνθοῦσαν ἀκμὴν ἔχων Isoc.5.10; ἐν ὥρᾳ ἀνθεῖν *to be in the bloom* of youth, Pl.*R*.475a; τὰ σὰ λήγει ὥρας, σὺ δ' ἄρχῃ ἀνθεῖν Id.*Alc*.1.131e, cf. ib.c. 3. *flourish* in wealth and prosperity, λαοὶ Hes.*Op*.227; ἀνθεύσης Ἐρετρίης Hdt. 6.127, cf. Th.1.19, etc.; ὄλβος σμικρὸν ἀνθήσας χρόνον E.*El*.944; ἀνθοῦσα ἐφ' ὥρᾳ πολιτεία Plu.*Per*.16; ἀνθούσης τῆς νέας Ἀκαδημίας Id. *Luc*.42; τὸ ἀνθοῦν τῆς δυνάμεως the *flower* of the force, Id.*Cor*.39: c. dat., ἀ. τῆς Ἀσίας ἀνδράσι *flourish, abound* in men, Hdt.4.1. b. of persons, *flourish, be popular*, οὕτως ἤνθησεν ἐκεῖνος Ar.*Eq*.530, cf. *Nu*.897,962; πραπίδεσσι, δόξῃ ἀ., Pi.*O*.11(10).10, Plu.*Dem*.5; Ἕκτορος ἤνθει δόρυ E.*Hec*.1210; σφόδρα γε ἤνθησεν ἐπὶ ταῖς ἐλπίσιν D.2.10; ἀ. πρὸς δόξαν, πρὸς χάριν, Plu.*Sert*.18, *Phoc*.3. 4. *to be at the height* or *pitch*, ἀνθεῖ πάθος τινί A.*Ch*.1009 (lyr.); of a disease, ἤνθηκεν S.*Tr*.1089, cf. Hp.*Epid*.1.25; ὕβρις ἐν νέοις ἀνθεῖ S.*Fr*.786; σκωμμάτων ἀνθούντων when they *were in full swing*, Plu.*Ant*.32. 5. c. gen., *swarm with*, φθειρῶν ἤνθησεν Paus.9.33.6.

**ἀνθεών**, ῶνος, ὁ, *flower-bed* or *garden*, *OGI*365 (Amasia):—also **ἀνθών**, *Gloss*.

**❀ἄνθη**, ἡ, *full bloom* of a flower or plant, ἀκμὴν ἔχει τῆς ἄνθης Pl. *Phdr*.230b, cf. Porph.ap.Eus.*PE*3.10: a special Att. form, Moer.4, Thom.Mag.p.10 R. 2. *blossom* or *bloom*, Nic.*Th*.625, Ael.*NA* 12.4.

**ἀνθηδών**, όνος, ἡ, *the flowery one*, i.e. *the bee*, Democr.ap.Gal.14.91, Ael.*NA*15.1, *EM*108.43. II. *eastern thorn*, *Crataegus orientalis*, Thphr.*HP*3.12.5:—hence **ἀνθηδονοειδής**, ές, as epith. of *Crataegus monogyna*, *hawthorn*, ibid.

**❀ἀνθήεις**, εσσα, εν, *bright coloured*, βασιλίσκος Marcell.Sid.26; σάλπη Id.30; κίσσος Ruf.ap.Gal.12.425.

**❀ἀνθηλᾶς**, ὁ, prob. *flower-merchant*, *PLond*.2.387.21 (vi/vii A.D.).

**❀ἀνθήλη**, ἡ, *the silky flower-tufts* of the reed, Thphr.*HP*4.10., Dsc. 1.85, cj. for ἀνθίνη in Phan.Hist.25:—ἀνθήλη· πώγων, Hsch. (cf. ἀνθήλη πυρός Id.).

**ἀνθήλιον**, τό, f.l. for ἀνθύλλιον, Dsc.3.156, 4.121; = κανθήλιον, Charax 21:—ἀνθήλια· περιδέρματα, Hsch. (-ηλά· περίδερμα cod.).

**ἀνθήλιος**, ον, = ἀντήλιος, q.v.

**ἄνθημα** (A), ατος, τό, = ἐξάνθημα, Hsch. II. = ἄνθος, κρίνου Sch. Nic.*Al*.406.

**ἄνθημα** (B), ατος, τό, poet. for ἀνάθημα, *offering*, *IG*12(5).911.21 (Tenos).

**ἀνθήμερον**, Adv. *to-day*, prob. in S.*Fr*.168; cf. ἀντί A.II, ἀνταλλές.

**ἀνθήμων**, ον, gen. ονος, = ἀνθηρός, κυτίνοιο.. καρπόν Nic.*Al*.610.

**ἀνθηρο-γρᾰφέω**, *write in a florid style*, Eust.991.8:—Pass., *to be embellished*, Cic.*Att*.2.6.1. **-ποίκῐλος**, ον, *brocaded with flowers, flowered*, Ph.1.666.

**❀ἀνθηρός**, ά, όν, *flowery, blooming*, ἔαρ Chaerem.9; λειμών, δάπεδον, Ar.*Av*.1093, *Ra*.352; χώρα Str.17.3.12 (Comp.); πρόσοψις, διάθεσις, D.S.5.3,19; τὰ ἀ. *flowery meads*, Plu.2.770b; but also, *flowering plants*, ib.765d. II. metaph., *fresh, young*, χλόη E.*Cyc*.541; of music, etc., *fresh, new*, X.*Cyr*.1.6.38; of persons, Plu.*Pomp*.69; ἱλαρὸς καὶ ἀ. 2.50b; cf. ἄνθος II.1 fin. 2. τᾶς μανίας ἀνθηρὸν μένος rage *bursting* (as it were) *into flower*, i.e. *exuberant*, S.*Ant*.960. 3. *bright-coloured, brilliant*, τοῦ χαλκοῦ τὸ ἀ. Plu.2.395b; of colours, τὸ ἀ. τῶν χρωμάτων Luc.*Nigr*.13, cf. Plu.2.79d, etc. 4. *brilliant, splendid*, δειπνάριον Diph.64; ἐδωδή Ph.1.679 (Comp.) (s.v.l.); βίος Max.Tyr.21.1; θεωρία Iamb. *in Nic*.p.35 P.; of personal appearance, dress, etc., ἀνθηρὸς εἱμάτων στολῇ E.*IA*73. Adv. -ῶς Sch.Opp.*H*.1. 459. 5. of style, *flowery, florid*, ἀ. *genus dicendi* Quint.*Inst*.12.10. 58, cf. Plu.2.648b; of music, ἀ. καὶ μαλακὴ ἁρμονία (metaph. of policy), Id.*Per*.15; ἂν ἀ. ᾖ τὸ πρᾶγμα, ἔστω καὶ ἡ λέξις τοιαύτη Hermog.*Prog*. 10. Adv. "ἀνθηρῶς", an exclamation of applause, Plu.2.46a: Comp. ἀνθηρότερον, λέγειν Isoc.13.18. III. ἀνθηρός, ὁ, = ἄλιμον, Ps.-Dsc.1.91. 2. ἀνθηρά, ἡ, name of a *lip-salve*, Plin.*HN*24.69, Gal.13.839; also of a *plaster*, Cels.6.11, Sor.ap.Gal.12.957.

**ἀνθηρότης**, ητος, ἡ, *brilliancy*, Sch.Pi.*O*.9.72.

**ἄνθησις**, εως, ἡ, *flowering*, Thphr.*CP*4.10.1, Plu.2.647f.

**ἀνθησσάομαι**, *give way* or *yield in turn*, τινί Th.4.19, D.C.49.44.

**ἀνθησῠχάζω**, *to be quiet in turn*, App.*BC*2.93.

**ἀνθητικός**, ή, όν, = ἀνθικός, τὰ ἀ. *flowering plants*, Thphr.*HP*1.14.3.

**ἀνθηφόρος**, ἡ, = ἀνθοφόρος II; ἀ. καὶ ἀρχιέρεια *CIG*2821, 2822 (Aphrodisias); but ἀρχιέρεια ἀ. *Rev.Ét.Gr*.19p.137.

**ἀνθίας**, ου, ὁ, a kind of *sea-fish*, *Labrus* or *Serranus anthias* (Adams), Anan.5.1, Epich.58, Diph.64; = αὐλωπίας, Arist.*HA*570b 19.

**ἀνθιερόω**, *consecrate in return*, Epicur.*Fr*.141.

**ἀνθ-ίζω**, *strew* or *deck with flowers*, E.*Ion*890; κεφαλὴν ῥόδοις Philostr.*Im*.1.15 (but σκευὴ ἠνθισμένη *adorned, embroidered with flowers*, ibid.): metaph., ἀ. τὴν λέξιν D.H.*Isoc*.13:—Med., *gather, cull flowers*, App.*BC*4.105. 2. *colour, dye, stain*, [πορφύρα] ἀ. τὴν χεῖρα Arist. *HA*547a18:—Pass., ἠνθισμένοι φαρμάκοισι Hdt.1.98; οὐ γάρ σε μή.. γνῶσ'.. ὧδ' ἠνθισμένον thus *disguised* or with *silvered* hair, S.*El*.43; κρέα πυρὸς ἀκμαῖς ἠνθισμένα meat *browned* at the fire, Epicr.6; οἶνος ἠνθισμένος wine *flavoured with flowers*, Gal.19.81. 3. ἀνθίζουσα, ἡ, a *plaster*, Id.13.856. **-ικός**, ή, όν, *flowering*, τὰ ἀ., opp. τὰ φρυγανικά, Thphr.*HP*6.6.2. **-ιμος**, η, ον, = sq., μελίσσης ἄ. εἶδαρ Orph.*L*.735. **-ινος**, η, ον, *of* or *like flowers, blooming, fresh*, like ἀνθηρός: in Od.9.84 the esculent lotus is called ἄνθινον εἶδαρ, where prob. *vegetable* as opp. to *animal* food is all that is meant; ἄ. κυκεών a drink *flavoured with flowers*, Hp.*Int*.12; ἄ. ἔλαιον oil *of lilies*, Id.

*Mul.*1.35; ἄ. μέλι Arist.*Mir.*831$^{b}$18; ἄ. οἶνος Gal.19.81; τριμμάτιον Sotad.Com.1.17; στέφανος *SIG*1017.12 (Sinope); εὐωδία Plu.2.645e. II. *flowered, bright-coloured*, of women's dress, ἐσθῆτες, στολή, Str.3.3.7, Plu.2.304d; τὰ ἄνθινα (sc. ἱμάτια) *gay-coloured dresses* worn by the ἑταῖραι at Athens, Phylarch.45; forbidden at religious festivals, *IG*11.1300 (Delos), ib.5(2).514.6 (Lycosura, ii B.C.); also of dresses worn at the Anthesteria by the Satyrs: hence τὴν φιλοσοφίαν ἄνθινα ἐνέδυσεν he clothed philosophy *in motley*, of Bion, who delivered his precepts in sarcastic verses, like those used in the satyric drama, Eratosth.ap.D.L.4.52, cf. Thphr.ap.Demetr. Lac.*Herc.*1055.15, Str.1.2.2. (On the accent v. Hdn.Gr.1.182.)

**ἄνθιον,** τό, in Orphic phraseology, *spring*, Orph.*Fr.*33.

**ἀνθιππ-άρχης,** ου, ὁ, *deputy-master of the horse*, Lyd.*Mag.*1.38. **-ἄσία,** ἡ, *sham fight of horse*, X.*Eq.Mag.*1.20, *IG*2.1291, cf. 1305*b*. **-εύω,** *ride against*, ἀλλήλοις, of cavalry, X.*Eq.*8.12.

**ἀνθισμός,** ὁ, *lustre*, of dyes, *PHolm.*18.25.

**ἀνθ-ιστάω,** later form of ἀνθίστημι, dub. in Hermog.*Stat.*2:—also **-ιστάνω,** *PPetr.*2 p.120. ⊛**-ίστημι,** *set against*, Th.4.115; esp. in battle, πελταστικὴν τῇ τοῦ παγκρατίου μάχῃ Pl.*Lg.*834a; ἀ. τροπαῖον *set up* a trophy *in opposition*, Th.1.54,105; *weigh against*, Ar.*Ra.*1389; ἀ. τινὸς τὴν ὁλκὴν *outweigh* him, Lxx *Si.*8.2. 2. *match with, compare*, ἀντιστῆσαι καὶ παραβαλεῖν Plu.*Thes.*1. II. Hom. uses only Pass., with intr. aor. 2 ἀντέστην: aor. 1 Pass. ἀντεστάθην Hdt.5.72: pf. ἀνθέστηκα *Ep.Rom.*9.19; Att. contr. part. ἀνθεστώς Th.6.70: fut. ἀντιστήσομαι Hdt.8.75, S.*OC*645:—*stand against*, esp. in battle, *withstand*, Ἥρῃ δ' ἀντέστη.. Ἄρτεμις Il.20.70, cf. 72, Hdt.6.117, al.; τοὺς ἀνθισταμένους τοῖς ὑμετέροις βουλήμασι D.18.49; πρὸς τὴν ἀνάγκην οὐδ' Ἄρης ἀ. S.*Fr.*256, cf. Th.1.93, X.*Smp.*5.1: rarely c. gen., δέος.. σοὶ φρενῶν ἀνθίσταται A.*Pers.*703 (ἀνθάπτεται Wakef.), cf. Q.S.1.520. 2. of things, *turn out unfavourably* to one, ἀντιστάντος αὐτῷ τοῦ πράγματος Th.5.4, cf. 38; ἂν τὰ παρ' ὑμῶν τῶν ἀκουόντων ἀντιστῇ D.19.340. 3. abs., *make a stand*, ἀλλ' ἔτ' ἄρ' ἀνθίσταντο Il.16.305; *resist, fight on*, Hdt.5.72, etc.; ὑπέρ τινος S.*Aj.*1231, *Ant.*518.

⊛**ἀνθο-βἄφής,** ές, *bright-coloured*, στρωμνή Antyll.ap.Orib.9.14.7, cf. Ph.2.274; ἐσθής S.E.*P.*1.148; πέδιλα Luc.*Am.*41; γῆ *IG*7.1802. **-βἄφία,** ἡ, *dyeing in bright colours*, Plu.*Fr.*16 p.113B. **-βάφος** [ᾰ], ὁ, *dyer in bright colours*, Id.2.830e, Man.2.326. **-βολέω,** *bestrew with flowers*, χαίτην *AP*5.146 (Mel.); as a mark of honour, ὥσπερ ἀθλητὴν ἀ. Plu.*Caes.*30:—Pass., Id.*Pomp.*57. II. *put forth flowers*, *Gp.*10.2.10. **-βόλησις,** εως, ἡ, *putting forth of flowers*, ib.59.3. **-βολος,** ον, *garlanded with flowers*, θρίξ *AP*9.270 (Marc. Arg.), but codd. have ἀνθοβόλον, i.e. *shedding flowers*. **-βοσκός,** όν, *nourishing, growing flowers*, or perh. *feeding on flowers*, S.*Fr.*31. **-γρἄφέω,** *paint in bright colours*, Ph.1.33. **-δίαιτος,** ον, *living on flowers*, μέλισσα *AP*5.162 (Mel.). **-δόκος,** ον, *holding flowers*, τάλαρος Mosch.2.34. **-κάρηνος,** ον, *crowned with flowers*, Opp.*C.*4.235. ⊛**-κομέω,** *produce flowers*, of the earth, βοτάνας ἀ. *AP*7.321. ⊛**-κόμος,** ον, *decked with flowers, flowery*, λειμῶνες ib.10.6 (Satyr.). 2. *parti-coloured*, οἰωνοί Opp.*C.*2.190. **-κρᾰτέω,** *govern flowers*, Luc.*Pseudol.*24. **-κροκος,** ον, (κρέκω) *worked with flowers*, πῆναι E.*Hec.*471 (lyr.).

**ἀνθ-ολκή,** ἡ, *pulling in the contrary direction, retraction*, Aret.*CA*1.4; *revulsion* in venesection, Antyll.ap.Orib.7.11.1; *means of drawing back*, D.C.35.5; *counterpoise*, τοῦ βλάπτοντος ἀ. Plu.2.20c; *resistance, countercheck*, ἀνθολκαὶ καὶ διατριβαί Id.*Luc.*11. **-ολκός,** όν, = ἀντίρροπος, ἀ. καὶ κωλυσιεργά Iamb.*Protr.*21.κβ'.

**ἀνθο-λογέω,** *gather flowers*, Plu.2.917f: c. acc., Hp.*Ep.*16, Porph. *Abst.*2.6:—Med., of bees, *gather honey from flowers*, Arist.*HA*628$^{b}$32:—Pass., *Gp.*11.26.2. **-λογία,** ἡ, *flower-gathering*, Luc.*Pisc.*6. **-λογικά,** τά, *books on floristics*, Plin.*HN*21.13. **-λόγιον,** τό, *collection of extracts*, ἐπιγραμμάτων Suid. s.v. Διογενειανός, cf. eund. s.vv. Ὠρίων, Ὦρος. **-λόγος,** ον, *flower-gathering*, *AP*12.249 (Strat.): c. gen., *culling the flower of*, κάλλευς ib.95 (Mel.).

**ἀνθομῑλέω,** *associate, deal with one another*, Hp.*Ep.*17 (but f.l. for ἀνθαμιλλεῦντες).

**ἀνθομοιόω,** *compare*, τὸν νόμον τῇ φύσει Philostr.*Dial.*2:—Pass., *to be compared in turn*, πρὸς ἄλληλα Iamb.*in Nic.*p.12 P.

**ἀνθόμοιος,** ον, *like*, ὕδωρ μέλιτος Ps.-Callisth.2.42.

**ἀνθομολογ-έομαι,** *make a mutual agreement* or *covenant*, πρός τινα D.33.8 (s.v.l.), Plb.5.105.2; ὑπέρ τινος 15.19.9; τινί *PTeb.*21.6 (ii B.C.); περί τινος ib.410.14 (16 A.D.). II. *confess freely and openly*, τὰς ἀρετάς τινος D.S.1.70; ἁμαρτίας J.*AJ*8.10.3; τὸν τοῦ βασιλέως θάνατον Plb.15.25.4: abs., 30.8.7. 2. *admit, signify*, πρός τινα μηδὲν ἑωρακέναι 29.17.1; ὡς.. Plu.*Brut.*16. 3. *assent, agree*, τοῖς εἰρημένοις Plb.28.4.4. 4. *return thanks* to God, Lxx *Ps.*78(79).13, *Ev.Luc.*2.38; χάριν ἀ. *return* thanks, Plu.*Aem.*11:—Act., -λογέω *admit a claim*, is late, *PGrenf.*2.71 ii 14 (iii A.D.). **-ησις,** εως, ἡ, *mutual agreement*, Plb.31.24.12, 36.4.4. 2. *confession, admission, testimony*, S.E.*M.*7.184, 8.453. **-ία,** ἡ, = foreg., *Gloss.*

**ἀνθο-νομέω,** *feed on flowers*, A.*Supp.*44. **-νόμος,** ον, *browsing on flowers*, ib.539.

**ἀνθοπλ-ίζω,** *arm against*, ἱππεῦσι δ' ἱππῆς ἦσαν ἀνθωπλισμένοι E.*Supp.*666; ἀνθώπλισται πρὸς τὰ πολέμια πλοῖα X.*Oec.*8.12:—Med., *arm oneself*, Id.*HG*6.5.7. **-ῐσις,** εως, ἡ, *counter-arming, hostile armament*, Sch.Th.1.141. **-ίτης** [ῑ], ου, ὁ, *one armed in like manner*, Lyc.64.

**ἀνθο-πλοκία,** ἡ, *plaiting of flowers*, Jul.Laod. in *Cat.Cod.Astr.*5(1).189.9. **-πλόκος,** ὁ, *one who plaits flowers*, Rhetor.ib.8(4).209.9. **-πωλεῖν·** οἰνοπωλεῖν, φαρμακοπωλεῖν, Hsch. **-πώλης,** ου, ὁ, *flower-seller*, Rhetor. in *Cat.Cod.Astr.*8(4).211.

**ἀνθορ-ίζω,** *make a counter-definition*, in Med., Sch.D.21.28, *PLond.*2.355.4 (i A.D.); *define* terms *by* their *mutual relations*, Elias *in Cat.*138.9. **-ισμός,** ὁ, *counter-definition*, Hermog.*Stat.*4, *Inv.*3.14, cf. Sch.D.21.28; *alternative definition*, Elias *in Cat.*205.25.

**ἀνθορμέω,** *lie at anchor opposite*, τινί Th.7.19; ἀ. ἀλλήλοις, of two hostile squadrons before fighting, 2.86; ἀ. πρός τινα 7.34.

**ἄνθορος,** Dor. **ἄντ-,** ὁ, *corresponding boundary-stone*, *Tab.Heracl.*1.60.

⊛**ἄνθος** (A), ους, τό: gen. pl. ἀνθέων, freq. used for ἀνθῶν, S.*El.*896, Hermipp.5,6, Eub.105, Aristag.3; but ἀνθῶν Pherecr.46, Pl.*Criti.*115a, X.*Cyn.*5.5:—*blossom, flower*, πέτονται ἐπ' ἄνθεσιν εἰαρινοῖσιν Il.2.89; ὑακινθίνῳ ἄνθει ὁμοίας Od.6.231; βρύει ἄνθεϊ λευκῷ Il.17.56; τέρεν' ἄνθεα ποίης Od.9.449; ἐπ' ἄνθεσιν ἵζειν Ar.*Eq.*403; δένδρα καὶ ἄνθη καὶ καρπούς Pl.*Phd.*110d; ἡ κατ' ἄνθη δίαιτα Id.*Smp.*196a; ἄνθεα τεθρίππων *the chaplets of flowers* which graced them, Pi.*O.*2.50, cf. 7.80; [Δάφνιν] φέρβον μαλακοῖς ἄνθεσσι μέλισσαι, i.e. with honey, Theoc.7.81. 2. generally, *anything thrown out upon the surface, eruption*, προσώπου Hp.*Coac.*416; cf. ἐξανθέω: *froth* or *scum*, ἄ. οἴνου Gal.11.628, *Gp.*6.3.9, 7.15.6; ἄνθη χαλκοῦ, = χάλκανθος, Nic.*Th.*257; ἄ. χαλκοῦ, v. χαλκός; ἄ. χρυσοῦ, = ἀδάμας, Poll.7.99. 3. in pl., *embroidered flowers* on garments, Hermipp.5,6, Pl.*R.*557c, Cypr. *Fr.*4. II. metaph., *bloom, flower* of life, ἥβης ἄ. Il.13.484, Pi.*P.*4.158, A.*Supp.*663; ἥβης ἄνθεσι Sol.25; κουρήιον ἄ. *h.Cer.*108; ὥρας ἄ. X.*Smp.*8.14; παῖς καλὸν ἄ. ἔχων Thgn.994; χροιᾶς ἀμείψεις ἄ. *the bloom* of complexion, A.*Pr.*23; τὸ τοῦ σώματος ἄ. its *youthful bloom*, Pl.*Smp.*183e; ὅταν [τὰ πρόσωπα] τὸ ἄ. προλίπῃ Id.*R.*601b; also, *the flower* of an army and the like, ἄ. Ἄργους A.*Ag.*197; ἄ. Περσίδος αἴας Id.*Pers.*59, cf. 252, 925, E.*HF*876 (lyr.); ὅ τι ἦν αὐτῶν ἄ. ἀπολώλει Th.4.133; ἄνθεα ὕμνων νεωτέρων *the choice flowers* of new songs, Pi.*O.*9.48; τὸ σὸν.. ἄ., παντέχνου πυρὸς σέλας thy *pride* or *honour*, A.*Pr.*7; τὰ ἄνθη *flowers* or *choice passages, elegant extracts*, *APl.*4.274, Cic.*Att.*16.11.1. 2. like ἀκμή, *the bloom*, i.e. *height* of anything, bad as well as good, δηξίθυμον ἔρωτος ἄ. A.*Ag.*743; ἀκήλητον μανίας ἄ. S.*Tr.*999; ἀ. τοῦ νοῦ Procl.*in Alc.*p.248 C., Dam.*Pr.*70; τῆς οὐσίας Procl.*in Ti.*1.412 D.; τῆς ψυχῆς ib.472 D. III. *brightness, brilliancy*, as of gold, Thgn.452; χαλκήϊον ἄ. Orph.*Fr.*174; of dyes, *lustre*, *PHolm.*17.37; freq. of purple, in sg., Pl.*R.*429d, Arist.*HA*547$^{a}$7, J.*AJ*3.6.1; ἁλὸς ἄνθεα *AP*6.206 (Antip. Sid.); of *bright colours* generally, περιβόλαια παντὸς ἄνθους D.H.7.72; ἄ. θαλάσσιον seaweed *dye*, Ps.-Democr.Alch.p.42 B. IV. ἄ. πεδινόν, = ἀνθεμίς, Ps.-Dsc.3.136.

**ἄνθος** (B), ὁ, a kind of *bird*, perh. *the yellow wagtail*, Arist.*HA*592$^{b}$25, 609$^{b}$14, Ael.*NA*5.48.

⊛**ἀνθοσμ-ίας,** ου, ὁ, *redolent of flowers*, almost always of wine, οἶνος ἀ. *with a fine bouquet*, Hp.*Steril.*235, Ar.*Pl.*807, *Ra.*1150, Pherecr.108.30; also ἀ. (sc. οἶνος) X.*HG*6.2.6, Luc.*Sat.*22:—in Id.*Lex.*2 ἀ. λειμῶνες, as a pedantic phrase:—also **-ιος,** ον, Sch.Ar.*Ra.*1150.

**ἀνθοσύνη,** ἡ, *bloom, luxuriant growth*, τεκέων *AP*5.275 (Agath.); ὑλαίη ib.11.365 (Id.).

**ἀνθο-τρόφος,** ον, = ἀνθοβοσκός, γαῖα Aristonous 1.21. **-φορέω,** *gather honey from flowers*, of bees, Arist.*HA*625$^{b}$19. II. *produce flowers*, *AP*10.16 (Theaet.). III. *to be an* ἀνθοφόρος II, *IG*12(8).553 (Thasos) (-ίσασα lapis). **-φόρος,** ον, *bearing flowers, flowery*, ἄλσος Ar.*Ra.*445, *AP*12.256 (Mel.); opp. κάρπιμος, Thphr.*CP*1.5.5. II. ἀνθοφόρος, ἡ, *flower-bearer*, title of a priestess of Demeter and Kore, *IG*12(8).526 (Thasos), cf. 609 (ibid.) **-φυής,** ές, *parti-coloured*, πτέρυξ, of a parrot, *AP*9.562 (Crin.). II. *producing flowers*, βῶλος *IG*12(9).954.13 (Chalcis).

**ἀνθρᾰκ-άριος·** *carbonarius*, *Gloss.* **-εία,** ἡ, *making of charcoal*, Thphr.*HP*3.8.7. ⊛**-εύς,** έως, ὁ, *charcoal-maker*, Aesop.59, Cic.*Att.*15.5.1 (cj.), Them.*Or.*21.245a, App.*BC*4.40:—also **-ευτής,** οῦ, ὁ, And.*Fr.*4, Ael.*NA*1.8. **-ευτός,** ή, όν, *which can be carbonized*, Arist.*Mete.*387$^{b}$19. **-εύω,** *make charcoal*, Thphr.*HP*9.3.1, cf. Poll.7.146; τὰ ἀνθρακευόμενα *charcoal*, Antig.*Mir.*136. 2. *burn to a cinder*, ἀ. τινὰ πυρί Ar.*Lys.*340. ⊛**-ηρός,** ά, όν, *belonging to charcoal*, Alex.208, *SIG*975.40 (Delos, iii B.C.). **-ιά,** ᾶς, Ep. **-ιή,** ῆς, ἡ, *burning charcoal, hot embers*, ἀνθρακιὴν στορέσαι Il.9.213; ὑποθεῖναι Hp.*Nat.Mul.*61; ἀνθρακιᾶς ἄπο a broil hot from *the embers*, E.*Cyc.*358, cf. *AP*6.105 (Apollonid.); ἐπ' ἀνθρακιᾶς ὀπτῆσαι Cratin.143; σου τῆς ἀνθρακιᾶς ἀπολαύει warms himself at your *fire*, Ar.*Eq.*780: metaph. of lovers, τιθέναι τινὰ ὑπὸ ἀνθρακιῇ or ἀνθρακιὴν *AP*12.17, 166 (Asclep.); Κύπριδος ἀ. ib.5.210 (Posidipp.). 2. *black sooty ashes*, ib.11.66 (Antiphil.). **-ίας,** ου, ὁ, *burnt to a cinder*, Luc.*Icar.*13, cf. *DMort.*20.4, al. ⊛**-ίδες,** αἱ, *small fish for frying*, Philyll.13.3. **-ίζω,** *make charcoal of, roast* or *toast*, Ar.*Pax*1136; *carbonize*, *PHolm.*6.4. ⊛**-ινος,** η, ον, *of the nature of*, or *made of, a carbuncle*, Lxx *Es.*1.7. 2. ἀνθρακίνου βαφή *blue* dye (*woad*), *PHolm.*18.35. **-ιον,** τό, Dim. of ἄνθραξ, a stone of which mirrors were made, Thphr.*Lap.*33. II. Dim. of ἄνθραξ II.1, *IG*11.161*B*82 (Delos, iii B.C.); of ἄνθραξ II.2, Cass.Fel.22. III. *brazier*, Alex.134. ⊛**-ίτης** [ῑ], ου, ὁ, name of a *gem*, Plin.*HN*36.148. II. fem. ⊛**-ῖτις,** ιδος, a kind of *coal*, ib.37.99. **-οβότανον,** *betony*, *Gloss.* **-οειδής,** ές, *like*, or *of the colour of, coal*, Ph.1.383. **-οθήκη,** ἡ, *coal-cellar*, *Gloss.* **-οκαύστης,** ου, ὁ, = ἀνθρακεύς, Sch.Ar.*Ach.*326. **-όομαι,** Pass., *to be burnt to cinders* or *ashes*, κεραυνῷ Ζηνὸς ἠνθρακωμένος A.*Pr.*374, cf. E.*Cyc.*614, Thphr.*Lap.*12. II. *form a malignant ulcer* (cf. ἀνθράκωσις), Aët.7.2. **-οπώλης,** ου, ὁ, *coal-merchant*, Philyll.

14. **-ώδης**, ες, = ἀνθρακοειδής, Hp.*Mul.*11, Arist.*Sens.*437ᵇ17, Diog.Oen.8. **-ωμα**, ατος, τό, *heap of charcoal, coal-fire*, Dsc.*Eup.*1.45. **-ών**, ῶνος, ὁ, *coal-store*, Hdn.Gr.1.30, 2.860. **-ωσις**, εως, ἡ, *malignant ulcer*, commonly in the eye, Paul.Aeg.3.22. 2. *carbuncle*, Gal.14.777. II. *carbonization, charring*, Dsc.*Eup.*1.49.

***ἄνθραξ**, ᾰκος, ὁ, *charcoal*, Sotad.Com.1.12: mostly in pl. ἄνθρακες Ar.*Ach.*34,332, *Nu.*97; ἄ. Παρνήθιοι Id.*Ach.*348; ὀπτωμέναις κόγχαισιν ἐπὶ τῶν ἀ. Id.*Fr.*68; ἄνθρακας ἡμμένους Th.4.100, etc.; their vapour produced stupor, Arist.*Sens.*444ᵇ31: prov., ἄνθρακας κατεσθίειν, of a glutton, Euphro 10.14, cf. Ion Trag.29. 2. *coal*, οἷς καὶ οἱ χαλκεῖς χρῶνται Thphr.*Lap.*16, *PHolm.*2.33; ἐπὶ ἀνθράκων μαλακῶν on a slow *fire*, Xenocr.16. II. a precious stone of dark-red colour, including the *carbuncle, ruby*, and *garnet* (Adams), Arist.*Mete.*387ᵇ18, Lxx *Ex.*28.18, Phylarch.41, etc. 2. hence, *carbuncle, malignant pustule* (acc. to some, *small-pox*), Hp.*Epid.*3.7, Gal.7.719, al. III. = ἰσάτις, *woad*, *PHolm.*18.34, al.

**ἀνθρεῖ**· κρύπτει, Hsch.

**ἀνθρηδών**, όνος, ἡ, *hornet*, D.S.17.75, Hsch.

**ἀνθρηκόν**, τό, = ἀνθρίσκος (?), Phot.p.140R.

**ἀνθρήν-η**, ἡ, *hornet, wasp*, Ar.*Nu.*947; in Arist. the name seems to be given to several diff. species, *HA*628ᵇ32, al. **-ιον**, τό, *wasp's nest*, Ar.*V.*1080,1107; Μουσῶν ἀνθρήνιον, of Sophocles, Philostr.Jun.*Im.*13 (= *Com.Adesp.*22). **-ιώδης**, ες, *honeycombed*, ἀ. καὶ πολύπορος Plu.2.916e. **-οειδής**, ές, *like an ἀνθρήνη*, Thphr.*HP*7.13.3.

***ἄνθρυσκον**, τό, *chervil, Scandix australis*, Sapph.*Supp.*25.13, Cratin.98.6, Pherecr.109 (ἔνθ–), Thphr.*HP*7.7.1 (ἔνθ–):—in Hsch. **ἀνθρίσκιον**, τό; in Poll.6.106 **ἀνθρίσκος**, ὁ.

**ἀνθρωπ-άρεσκος** [ᾰρ], ὁ, *man-pleaser*, Lxx *Ps.*52(53).6, *Ep.Eph.*6.6, *Ep.Col.*3.22. **-άριον**, τό, Dim. of ἄνθρωπος, *manikin*, Eup.26D., Ar.*Pl.*416, Demad.51 (of Demosthenes), Arr.*Epict.*1.3.5. **-έη**, contr. **-ῆ** (sc. δορά), ἡ, *man's skin*, like ἀλωπεκῆ, λεοντῆ, etc., Hdt.5.25 codd., Poll.2.5. **-ειος**, α, ον, Ion. **-ήϊος**, η, ον, (ος, ον Luc.*Asin.*46):—*human*, opp. θεῖος, Heraclit.78; τὰ -ήϊα Democr.37; ἀνθρωπηΐη φωνή Hdt.2.55; ἡ ἀ. φύσις Id.3.65, al.; ἀ. σῶμα Canthar.3D.; ἀ. τι παθεῖν *IG*5(1).1208.52 (Gythium); ἀ. πήματα *such as man is subject to*, A.*Pers.*706; ἀ. ψόγος reproach *of men*, Id.*Ag.*937; τέχνη ἀ. Th.2.47; ἀνθρωπήϊα πρήγματα *human* affairs, Hdt.1.32, cf. Pl.*Prm.*134e; τὰ ἀ. A.*Fr.*159, Pl.*Phd.*89e; ἅπαντα τἀ. S.*Aj.*132, Antiph.240b, etc.; τὸ ἀ. *mankind, human nature*, πέφυκε τὸ ἀ. ἄρχειν τοῦ εἴκοντος Th.4.61, cf. 5.105. 2. *human, suited to man, within man's powers*, ἡ ἀ. εὐδαιμονίη Hdt.1.5; ἀδύνατον καὶ οὐκ ἀ. not *for man to attempt*, Pl.*Prt.*344c; ὅσα γε τἀ. *in all human probability*, Id.*Cri.*47a; κατὰ τὸ ἀ. (v.l. -πινον) Th.1.22. 3. *human*, opp. *mythical*, ἡ ἀ. λεγομένη γενεή Hdt.3.122. 4. ἀνθρωπείους ἡμέρας· τὰς ἀποφράδας (Rhod.), Hsch. II. Adv. -ως *by human means, in all human probability*, Th.5.103; ἀ. φράζειν to speak *as befits a man*, Ar.*Ra.*1058.—Said to be the correct Attic form by Moer.26. ***-εύομαι**, *act as a human being*, as opp. both to gods and beasts, Arist.*EN*1178ᵇ7; ψυχὴ ἀνθρωπευομένη a *human* soul, Herm.ap.Stob.1.41.68. **-ήϊος**, η, ον, v. ἀνθρώπειος. **-ίζω**, *act like a man, play the man*, Archyt.ap.D.L.3.22; opp. κυνάω, Luc.*Demon.*21: so in Med., Ar.*Fr.*37. II. Pass., *become man*, Alex.Aphr.*in Top.*137.27, Simp.*in Ph.*1138.28:—so in Act., *AP*1.105. **-ικός**, ή, όν, *human*, ἔργα Philol.11, cf. Pl.*Sph.*268d; ἡ ἀ. ἀρετή *EN*1102ᵇ12, cf. 1178ᵃ21, al.: ἀνθρωπικόν [ἐστι], c. inf., *it is like a man, suited to man's nature*, ib.1163ᵇ24, al.: Comp. -ώτεροι, οἱ, the *commoner specimens of humanity*, Plot.2.9.9; ἀ. μῦθος a play *dealing with human characters*, Ar.*Fr.*3D.; παρασκευή Phryn.*PS*p.135B. Adv. -κῶς Luc.*Zeux.*4, Plu.2.999b, Porph.*Abst.*3.4. ***-ινος**, η, ον, also ος, ον Pl.*Lg.*737b:—*of, from*, or *belonging to man, human*, ἀ. βίος Philol.11, cf. Hdt.7.46; ἅπαν τὸ ἀ. all *mankind*, Id.1.86; τὸ ἀ. γένος (v.l. φῦλον) Antipho 4.1.2, Pl.*Phd.*82b; ἀ. κίνδυνοι, opp. θεῖοι, And.1.139; ἀ. δίκη Lys.6.20; ἀ. τεκμήρια, opp. omens, Antipho 5.81; τἀνθρώπινα *human affairs*, Pl.*Tht.*170b, Arist.*EN*1102ᵇ3 (v.l. -ικά); ἀνθρώπινόν τι παθεῖν die, *IG*5(2).266.20 (Mantinea, I B.C.), cf. *PPetr.*1p.33 (iii B.C.), *PRyl.*153.39 (ii A.D.); so ἐάν τι τῶν ἀ. περί τινα γένηται Epicur.*Fr.*217. 2. *human, suited to man*, ἀνθρωπίνη δόξα *fallible, human* understanding, Pl.*Sph.*229a; οὐχ ἀ. ἀμαθία *superhuman, monstrous* folly, Id.*Lg.*737b, etc.; ἀ. καὶ μετρία σκῆψις D.21.41; οὐ χρὴ ἀνθρώπινα φρονεῖν ἄνθρωπον ὄντα Arist.*EN*1177ᵇ32; ἀ. νοῦς Men.482; ἀ. τὸ γεγενημένον X.*Cyr.*5.4.19. 3. ἀνθρώπινα, τά, *secular revenues*, *SIG*527.133; *secular rites*, opp. θῖνα, *Leg.Gort.*10.43. II. Adv. ἀνθρωπίνως, ἁμαρτάνειν commit *human*, i.e. *venial*, errors, Th.3.40; ἀνθρωπινώτερον *more within the range of human faculty*, Pl.*Cra.*392b, D.18.252; ἀνθρωπίνως ἐκλογίζεσθαι, i.e. *with fellow-feeling*, And.2.6; *humanely, gently*, D.23.70; ἀ. χρὴ τὰς τύχας φέρειν *with moderation*, Men.816; εὐτυχίαν D.S.1.60.—Of the three forms, ἀνθρώπειος is used exclusively in Trag. and generally in Th. (but cf. 1.22); ἀνθρώπινος prevails in Comedy and in Prose from Pl. downwds. (though he uses ἀνθρώπειος no less frequently); ἀνθρωπικός is freq. in Arist. **-ιον**, τό, = sq., E.*Cyc.*185, Anaxandr.34; *paltry fellow*, ὦ πόνηρ' ἀνθρώπια Ar.*Pax*263, cf. X.*Mem.*2.3.16, *Cyr.*5.1.14, D.18.242. **-ίσκος**, ὁ, Dim. of ἄνθρωπος, *manikin*, E.*Cyc.*316, Pl.*R.*495c; with a shade of contempt, Id.*Phdr.*243a, cf. Luc.*Pisc.*17; ἰδιώτας ἀ. κωμῳδῶν Ar.*Pax*751. **-ισμός**, ὁ, *humanity*, Aristipp.ap.D.L.2.70. **-ιστί** [τῖ], *in the language of men*, S.*Fr.*827, cf. Sch.Od.6.125, Ps.-Callisth.3.17.

**ἀνθρωπο-βορέω**, *practise cannibalism*, Chrysipp.*Stoic.*3.186. **-βορία**, ἡ, *cannibalism*, Zeno *Stoic.*1.59 (pl.). **-βόρος**, ον, *man-eating*, Ph.2.423. **-γλωσσος**, Att. **-ττος**, ον, *speaking man's language*, of the parrot, Arist.*HA*597ᵇ27. **-γνάφεῖον**, τό, *a place for fulling men*, comic name for a bath, ap.Clem.Al.*Paed.*3.9. **-γονέω**, *beget, produce men*, Ph.2.494. **-γονία**, ἡ, *begetting of men*, title of play by Antiphanes, *POxy.*427; *origin of man*, J.*Ap.*1.8. **-γράφος** [ᾰ], ὁ, *painter of men*, Plin.*HN*35.113. **-δαίμων**, ονος, ὁ, ἡ, *man-god*, i.e. *deified man*, E.*Rh.*971; *semi-devil*, Procop.*Arc.*12. ***-δηκτος**, ον, *bitten by a man*, Dsc.1.125, Antig.ap. Philum.*Ven.*5.1. **-ειδής**, ές, *like a man, in human shape*, τύπος Hdt.2.86; θεὸν ἀ. οὐδένα γενέσθαι ib.142; θηρίον Phryn.*PS*p.6B.; θεοί Arist.*Metaph.*997ᵇ10, Phld.*Piet.*15, al.; πίθηκοι Arist.*HA*502ᵃ24; of zodiacal signs, Ptol.*Tetr.*145. Adv. -δῶς D.L.10.139. **-είκελος**, ον, *like a man*, Hsch.*Prooem.* ***-θεν**· *humanitus*, *Gloss.* **-θηρία**, ἡ, *hunting of men*, Pl.*Sph.*223b. **-θῡμος**, ον, *bold as a man*, opp. θυμολέων, Plu.2.988d. **-θῠσία**, ἡ, *human sacrifice*, ib.857a, al.: in pl., ib.417c, Str.4.4.5, Pallasap.Porph.*Abst.*2.56. **-θῠτέω**, *offer human sacrifices*, Ph.2.28, Porph.*Abst.*2.27. **-κομικός**, ή, όν, *belonging to the care* or *government of men*: ἡ -κή (sc. τέχνη) *politics*, Them.*Or.*15.186d:- also **-κόμος**, ον, Anon. in Rh.3.607W. **-κτονέω**, v.l. for ἀνθρωποσφαγέω, E.*Hec.*260; *offer human sacrifice*, Phylarch.63:—Subst. **-κτονία**, ἡ, Porph.*Abst.*2.55, Hld.10.7. **-κτόνος**, ον, *murdering men, homicide*, E.*IT*389, 1*Ep.Jo.*3.15, *Ev.Jo.*8.44. II. proparox., ἀνθρωπόκτονος βορά feeding *on slaughtered men*, E.*Cyc.*127. **-λάτρης**, ου, ὁ, *man-worshipper*, Νεστόριος ὁ ἀ. *Cod.Just.*1.1.5.

***ἀνθρωπ-όλεθρος**, ον, *plague of men, murderous*, Suid.

**ἀνθρωπό-λιχνος**, ον, *greedy of human flesh*, μυῖα Herm.ap.Stob.1.41.68. **-λογέω**, *describe* or *represent in the form of man*, Ph.1.282:—Pass., ib.181. **-λόγος**, ον, *speaking of man*, i.e. *fond of personal conversation*, Arist.*EN*1125ᵃ5. **-μάγειρος** [ᾰγ], ὁ, *one who cooks human flesh*, Luc.*Asin.*6. **-μῖμος**, ον, *imitating men*, Ps.-Plu.*Fluv.*14.3. **-μορφος**, ον, *of human form*, θεός Epicur.*Fr.*353, cf. Str.17.1.28, Ph.1.15, Corn.*ND*27, Procop.*Arc.*18; ζῴδια Ptol.*Tetr.*79,181. **-νομικός**, ή, όν, *feeding men*: ἡ -κή (sc. τέχνη) Pl.*Plt.*266e. **-νοος**, ον, contr. **-νους**, ουν, *with human understanding, intelligent*, πίθηκοι Ael.*NA*16.10: Sup. -νούστατος Str.15.1.29.

**ἀνθρωπόομαι**, *to have the concept* or *idea of a man*, Plu.2.1120d.

**ἀνθρωπο-πάθεια** [ᾰθ], ἡ, *humanity*, Alciphr.2.1. **-πᾰθέω**, *to have human feelings*, ἄνθρωπος ὢν ἀ. Ph.1.134. **-πᾰθής**, ές, *with human feelings*, ib.182, al. Adv. -θῶς, λέγεσθαι, of the gods, Hermog.*Id.*2.10. **-πλάστης**, ου, ὁ, *fashioner of men*, Ph.1.652. **-ποιέω**, *make, form man* or *men*, Simp.*in Cat.*333.6. **-ποιΐα**, ἡ, *making of man* or *men*, Luc.*Prom.*5,17. **-ποιός**, όν, *making men*, of a portrait-sculptor, opp. θεοποιός, Id.*Philops.*18,20; γυνὴ -ποιὸν ὑπούργημα Secund.*Sent.*8; ἀ. χώρα Simp.*in Epict.*p.64D. **-πολις**, εως, ἡ, *city of men*, title of Menippean satire by Varro. **-ρραίστης**, ου, ὁ, (ῥαίω) *man-destroyer*, *Drawcansir*, a comedy of Strattis. II. title of Dionysus at Tenedos, Ael.*NA*12.34.

***ἄνθρωπος**, ὁ, Att. crasis ἅνθρωπος, Ion. ὥνθρωπος, for ὁ ἄνθρ-:—*man*, both as a generic term and of individuals, Hom. etc., opp. *gods*, ἀθανάτων τε θεῶν χαμαὶ ἐρχομένων τ' ἀνθρώπων Il.5.442, etc.; πρὸς ἠοίων ἢ ἑσπερίων ἀνθρώπων *the men* of the east or of the west, Od.8.29; even of the dead in the Isles of the Blest, ib.4.565; κόμπος οὐ κατ' ἄνθρωπον A.*Th.*425, cf. S.*Aj.*761. 2. Pl. uses it both with and without the Art. to denote *man* generically, ὁ ἄ. θείας μετέσχε μοίρας *Prt.*322a; οὗτος.. εὐδαιμονέστατος γίγνεται ἄ. *R.*619b, al.; ὁ ἄ. *the ideal man, humanity*, ἀπώλεσας τὸν ἄ., οὐκ ἐπληρώσας τὴν ἐπαγγελίαν Arr.*Epict.*2.9.3. 3. in pl., *mankind*, ἀνθρώπων.. ἀνδρῶν ἠδὲ γυναικῶν Il.9.134; ἐν τῷ μακρῷ.. ἀνθρώπων χρόνῳ S.*Ph.*306; ἐξ ἀνθρώπων γίγνεσθαι depart *this life*, Paus.4.26.5, cf. Philostr.*VA*8.31. b. joined with a Sup. to increase its force, δεινότατον τῶν ἐν ἀνθρώποις ἁπάντων D.53.2; ὁ ἄριστος ἐν ἀνθρώποις ὄρτυξ the best quail *in the world*, Pl.*Ly.*211e; freq. without a Prep., μάλιστα, ἥκιστα ἀνθρώπων, most or least *of all*, Hdt.1.60, Pl.*Lg.*629a, *Prt.*361e; ἄριστά γ' ἀ., ὀρθότατα ἀ., Id.*Tht.*148b, 195b, etc. c. τὰ ἐξ ἀνθρώπων πράγματα 'all the trouble in the world', ib.170e; γραφὰς τὰς ἐξ ἀνθρώπων ἐγράφετο Lys.13.73; αἱ ἐξ ἀνθρώπων πληγαί Aeschin.1.59; πάντα τὰ ἐξ ἀνθρώπων κακὰ ἔλεγε D.C.57.23. 4. joined with another Subst., like ἀνήρ, ἄ. ὁδίτης Il.16.263; πολίτας ἀ. D.22.54; with names of nations, πόλις Μερόπων ἀνθρώπων *h.Ap.*42; in Att. freq. in a contemptuous sense, ἄ. ὑπογραμματεύς, ἄ. γόης, ἄ. συκοφάντης, Lys.30.28, Aeschin.2.153,183; ἄ. ἀλαζών X.*Mem.*1.7.2; ἄ. ὑφάντης Pl.*Phd.*87b; Μενίππου, Καρός τινος ἀνθρώπου D.21.175; ἄ. βασιλεύς *Ev.Matt.*22.2. 5. ἄνθρωπος or ὁ ἄνθρωπος alone, *the man, the fellow*, Pl.*Prt.*314e, *Phd.*117e; ὡς ἀστεῖος ὁ ἄ., with slight irony, ib.116d, al.; with a sense of pity, D.21.91. 6. in the voc. freq. in a contemptuous sense, as when addressed to slaves, etc., ἄνθρωπε or ὤνθρωπε *sirrah! you sir!* Hdt.3.63, 8.125, and freq. in Pl., but in Trag. only S.*Aj.*791,1154; simply, *brother*, *POxy.*215.1, Diog.Oen.2. 7. *slave*, ἂν ἄ. ᾖ Philem.22; ἄ. ἐμός Gal.14.649; ὁ ἄ. τῆς ἁμαρτίας or ἀνομίας 2*Ep.Thess.*2.3; ἄ. τοῦ Θεοῦ 1*Ep.Tim.*6.11; but τιθέναι τινὰ ἐν ἀνθρώποις make *a man of*, of a freed slave, Herod.5.15. 8. ἄ. ἄ. *any one*, Hebraism in Lxx *Le.*17.3 (cf. ἀνήρ VI.8); ἄ. like Germ. *man* 'one', 1*Ep.Cor.*4.1, al. 9. Medic., name of a *plaster*, ἡ διὰ σάνδυκος ἄ. καλουμένη Aët.15.43. II. as fem., *woman*, Pi.*P.*4.98, Hdt.1.60, Isoc.18.52, Arist.*EN*1148ᵇ20; contemptuously, of female slaves, Antipho 1.17, Is.6.20, etc.; with a sense of pity, D.19.197.—Prop. opp. θηρίον, cf. ἀνήρ; but opp. γυνή, Aeschin.3.137; ἀπὸ ἀνθρώπου ἕως γυναικός LXX 1Es.9.40, etc.

**ἀνθρωποσφᾰγέω**, *slay men*, E.*Hec*.260.

**ἀνθρωπότης**, ητος, ἡ, *abstract humanity*, Ph.1.206, S.E.*M*.7.273, Vett.Val.346.29, Plot.6.1.10, Dam.*Pr*.58.

**ἀνθρωπο-τρόφος**, ον, *nourishing men*, Hsch. **-φᾰγέω**, *eat human flesh*, Hdt.4.106, Porph.*Abst*.2.57; of carnivora, Arist.*HA* 594ᵃ29. **-φᾰγία**, ἡ, *cannibalism*, Arist.*Pol*.1338ᵇ20, Phld.*Sto. Herc*.339.14, Porph.*Abst*.2.57: in pl., Plu.*Luc*.11. **-φᾰγικῶς**, Adv. *like cannibals*, Eust.634.59. **-φάγος** [ᾰ], ον, *man-eating*, Antiph.68.12, Arist.*HA*501ᵇ1, Heraclit.*Incred*.31:—esp. of *cannibal* tribes, Str.4.5.4, etc. **-φθόρος**, ον, *destroying men*, gloss on βροτολοιγός, Sch.Il.5.31. **-φυής**, ές, *of man's nature*, οὐκ ἀνθρωποφυέας ἐνόμισαν τοὺς θεούς Hdt.1.131; Κένταυροι D.S.4.69. **-χειρον**, τό, *herb of mercury* (= πενταδάκτυλον, ἑρμοδάκτυλον, Ps.-Dsc.), *Cat. Cod.Astr*.8(3).162:—also **-χειρ**, ὁ, ib.7.234.

**ἀνθρωπώ**, ἡ, Lacon. for ἄνθρωπος II, Hsch.

**Ἀνθρωφηρακλῆς**, -έος, ὁ, title of play by Pherecrates, Phot. p.145 R.

**ἀνθυβρ-ίζω**, *abuse one another, abuse in turn*, E.*Ph*.620 (Pass.), Plu. *Per*.26, Luc.*DMeretr*.33, etc. **-ισις**, εως, ἡ, *counter-abuse*, Mich. *in EN*54.9.

***ἀνθυλακτέω**, *bark* or *bay in answer*, Ael.*HA*4.19.

**ἀνθύλλιον**, τό, Dim. of ἄνθος, M.Ant.4.20, Dsc.2.183. II. = sq. 1, Plin.*HN*26.84, cf. 21.175. III. = μυοσωτίς, Ps.-Dsc.4.86.

**ἀνθυλλίς**, ίδος, ἡ, a plant, *Cressa cretica*, Dsc.3.136. 2. *herb ivie, Ajuga Iva*, ibid., Plin.*HN*26.84.

**ἄνθυλλον**, τό, = foreg. 1, Ps.-Dsc.3.136, Plin.*HN*21.175.

**ἀνθυπ-άγω** [ᾰγ], *bring to trial* or *indict in turn*, Th.3.70. 2. *rejoin, reply*, A.D.*Pron*.53.21, al.: Pass., τὸ -αγόμενον, -αχθησόμενον, Id.*Synt*.118.1, 121.22. b. *substitute*, ib.129, etc. 3. *lead under in turn*, αἰχμαλώτους ὑπὸ τὸ ζυγόν D.C.*Fr*.36.22; but in Med., *bring over*, τινὰς ἐς εὔνοιαν ib.35.10. 4. *withdraw in turn*, ἀνθυπῆγε Μαρδόνιος Aristid.1.146 J. **-ᾰγωγή**, ἡ, *reply*, A.D.*Synt*.19.12, al. **-ᾰκούω**, *listen to in turn*, τινός Nicol.*Prog*.6.10 in Rh.1. 314 W. II. *correspond, answer to*, Iamb.*in Nic*.p.21 P. **-αλλᾰγή**, ἡ, Rhet., *substitution of one case for another*, Demetr.*Eloc*.60, A.D.*Synt*.201.27, al. ***-αλλάσσω**, Att. -ττω, *substitute*, esp. in Rhet., *substitute one case for another*, Demetr.*Eloc*.59, cf. A.D.*Synt*. 232.2; of *interchange* of moods, in Pass., ib.211.19:—Med., *receive in exchange*, θνητὸν ἀθανάτου βίον Ph.2.440. **-αντάω**, *meet, reply to objections*, πρός τινα Longin.18.1. **-άρχω**, *to be set over against*, of ἀντίστοιχα, Stoic.ap.Plu.2.960b.

**ἀνθῠπᾰτ-εία**, ἡ, *proconsulate*, *CIG* (add.)3841*f* (Aezani), *BCH* 11.110 (Epist. Hadriani), Hdn.7.5.2, Just.*Nov*.8.1: pl., ib.26.5 *Intr*. **-εύω**, *to be proconsul*, Plu.*Comp.Dem.Cic*.3, *Act.Ap*.18. 12, Hdn.7.5.2. **-ιανός**, = *proconsularis*, Just.*Nov*.30.1. **-ικός**, ή, όν, *proconsular*, ἐξουσία D.C.58.7. 2. ἀ. δεκαδαρχία the body of military tribunes *which took the place of the consulate*, Plu.2. 277f. **-ος**, ὁ, *proconsul*, Lat. *pro consule*, Plb.28.5.6, *Act.Ap*.13. 7, etc., freq. in Inscrr. as *SIG*684.3, and Pap. as *Sammelb*.3924.32 (i A.D.); στρατηγὸς ἀ. *SIG*704*K*, etc. II. as Adj., *proconsular*, ἐξουσία D.H.9.16; ἀρχή Id.11.62.

**ἀνθυπ-είκω**, *yield in turn* or *mutually*, τινί Plu.*Cor*.18, D.C.45. 8. **-ειξις**, εως, ἡ, *a mutual yielding*, Plu.*Sol*.4.

**ἀνθυπερβάλλω**, *surpass in turn*, J.*AJ*16.7.2.

**ἀνθυπερηφανέω**, *to be haughty in return*, August.ap.Suet.*vit. Horat*.

**ἀνθυπέρχομαι**, *insinuate oneself into, creep upon in turn*, τινά Anon. *Prog*. in Rh.1.601 W. II. Gramm., *take the place of*, A.D.*Synt*. 95.9, 112.6.

***ἀνθυπηρετέω**, *serve in turn*, τινί Arist.*EN*1133ᵃ4, 1170ᵇ25.

**ἀνθυπισχνέομαι**, *promise in return*, Sch.Ar.*Eq*.694.

**ἀνθυπο-βάλλω**, *bring objections in turn, retort*, Aeschin.3.209. II. *substitute fraudulently*, Ph.2.630. **-δεικτος**, ον, *brought forward as an instance in opposition*, Phld.*D*.1.16. **-κρίνομαι** [ῑ], Ion. ἀντυπ-, *answer in return*, Hdt.6.86.γ'. II. *put on* or *pretend in turn*, ὀργήν Luc.*Dom*.30. **-λείπω**, *leave on the other side*, f.l. in Ph.2.505 (Pass.). **-λογέω**, *compensate*, *Gloss*. **-λογίζομαι**, *charge against, deduct*, *PPetr*.3p.149. **-λογισμός**, ὁ, *compensation*, *Gloss*.

**ἀνθυπ-όμνῡμι**, *make a counter-affidavit*, in Med., D.48.25, 58. 43. **-οπτεύω**, *suspect mutually*, ἀλλήλους D.C.45.8: abs., Aen. Tact.24.11 (cj.):—Pass., ἀνθυποπτεύεται..πλέον ἔξειν *he is met by the suspicion* that.., Th.3.43. **-ορύσσω**, *make countermines*, Aen. Tact.37.5, Polyaen.6.17. **-όρυξις**, εως, ἡ, *countermining*, Ph. *Bel*.100.22 (pl.).

**ἀνθυπό-στᾰσις**, εως, ἡ, *convertibility of substance*, Dam.*Pr*. 158. **-στρέφω**, *recur*, of an illness, Poll.3.107; *return*, Olymp. *in Mete*.148.1, Pall.*in Hp.Fract*.12.276 C.; *turn round upon*, Ps.-Callisth.2.29; *turn back*, ib.31, al. **-στροφή**, ἡ, *return*, of a clyster, Sever.*Clyst*.25. **-στροφέω**, = ἀνθυποστρέφω, Steph. *in Hp*.2.279 D. **-τείνομαι**, *maintain by way of rejoinder*, Ulp. ad D.23.88. **-τίθημι**, *interpose to counteract*, πρός.. Aristeas 239. **-τῑμάομαι**, *reply to the* ὑποτίμησις (q.v.), Poll.8.150. **-τίμησις** [τῐ], εως, ἡ, *reply to* ὑποτίμησις, Rh.5.7 W.

**ἀνθυπουργ-έω**, Ion. ἀντυποργέω, *return a kindness*, ἀ. τινὶ τοῦτο τὸ ἂν δεηθῇ Hdt.3.133; χάριν S.*Fr*.339; αἰσχρά τινι E.*Hipp*.999; τι καθ' αὑτὸν Corn.*ND*15. **-ία**, ἡ, *service done in return*, Anon. *in Rh*.109.1. **-ησις**, εως, ἡ, *returning of a kindness*, Hsch.

***ἀνθυπο-φαίνω**, *reveal in turn*, *CIG*4958 (Egypt). **-φέρω**, *reply, rejoin*, opp. πυνθάνομαι, D.H.*Dem*.54, cf. Hermog.*Inv*.4.14, S.E.*M*. 7.44. II. *use* a word or phrase *in reply* to a question, in Pass., A.D.*Pron*.24.17, *Synt*.73.6. III. *cause to retrogress*, Plu.2.76d:—Pass., ib.939a. **-φορά**, ἡ, *reply*, opp. πεῦσις, D.H.*Dem*.54; esp. *reply to a supposed objection*, Quint.*Inst*.9.3.87, Hermog.*Inv*.3.4, Ulp. ad D.3.10. II. *reply*, A.D.*Synt*.72.26. **-χωρέω**, *give place in turn*, τινί Dam.*Pr*.303, Steph. *in Hp*.2.279 D. **-χώρησις**, εως, ἡ, *retiring in turn*, εἰς τὸ ἐκτός Plu.2.903d.

**ἀνθυφαιρ-εσις**, εως, ἡ, = ἀνταναίρεσις I, Alex.Aphr.*in Top*.545. 16. **-έω**, *take away again* or *in turn*, Iamb. *in Nic*.p.28 P., Porph. *in Ptol*.194:—Pass., LXX *Le*.27.18, *PLond.ined*.2361ᵛ (iii B.C.), D.C. 48.33, Procl.*Hyp*.4.12. 2. ἀ. μισθοῦ *deduct* on account of wages, *IG*4.1508*A*8 (Epid.).

**ἀνθυφίστᾰμαι**, Pass., with aor. 2 ἀνθυπέστην, *undertake for* another, ἀνθυποστῆναι (sc. χορηγός) *undertake to serve* as choragus *in rivalry with* another, D.21.68:—later in Act., *imply reciprocally*, Dam.*Pr*.72.

**ἀνθώδης**, ες, *flowerlike*, Thphr.*HP*1.13.1. II. *full of flowers*, τόπος Sch.Nic.*Th*.438.

**ἀνθωρο-σκοπέω**, *to be in a diametric aspect with the horoscope*, Ptol. *Tetr*.200, Vett.Val.135.3. **-σκόπος**, name of the *seventh* τόπος *in an* ἀποτελεσματογραφία, Paul.Al.*M*.2.

**ἀνία**, Ion. ἀνίη, Aeol. ὀνία, ἡ, *grief, sorrow, distress, trouble*, Hes. *Th*.611, Sapph.1.3 (pl.), Thgn.76, etc.; ὑπὸ τῆς ἀνίας ἀνεθολοῦθ' ἡ καρδία Pherecr.116; εἰς ἀνίαν ἔρχεταί τινι is like to be *a mischief* to him, S.*Aj*.1138, cf. Pl.*Grg*.477d, *Prt*.355a, al.: in pl., ὀνίαισι Sapph. l.c.; ἀντ' ἀνιῶν ἀνίαι Thgn.344; ἐμοὶ λιπὼν ἀνίας S.*Aj*.973, cf. 1005, *Ph*.1115, Pl.*Prt*.353e. 2. concrete, δαιτὸς ἀνίη *the killjoy* of our feast, Od.17.446; ἄπρηκτος ἀνίη inevitable *bane*, of Scylla, 12.223; ἀνίη καὶ πολὺς ὕπνος *an annoyance*, 15.394. [In Hom. and S. always ῑ, also E.*IT*1031 (s.v.l.). Other Poets made the ι long or short as the verse required, though the Homeric quantity prevailed in Ep.]

***ἀνιάζω**, only pres. and impf. (exc. aor. ἠνίασα *AP*11.254 (Lucill.)): Ion. impf. ἀνιάζεσκον A.R.3.1138:—Ep. Verb, *grieve, distress*, like ἀνιάω, c. acc. pers., ὅς κεν τοῦτον ἀνιάζῃ Od.19.323; ἀλλ' ὅτε δή ῥ' ἀνίαζον..'Αχαιούς Il.23.721 (v.l. 'Αχαιοί). II. intr., *to be grieved* or *distressed*, θυμῷ ἀνιάζων *grieving* at heart, Od.22.87; ἀλλ' ὅτε δή ῥ' ἀνίαζε *was grieving, growing weary*, 4.460, cf. A.R.4.1347; κτεάτεσσιν ὑπερφιάλως ἀνιάζει he *grieves for* his goods, Il.18.300; ἐπὶ παιδὶ Arat.196. [ῑ metri gr. in Hom. and other Ep.]

**ἀνιακκάς**, apptly. the name of a *tune*, Eub.46.

**ἀνιάομαι**, *cure again, repair*, τὸ παρεὸν τρωμα ἀνιεῦνται (which in sense at least is an Ion. fut.) dub. in Hdt.7.236 (leg. ἀκεῦνται).

***ἀνιᾰρίζω**, Dor. for ἀνιερίζω, *dedicate*, *IG*14.644 (Bruttii).

**ἀνιᾱρός**, ά, όν, Ion. and Ep. ἀνιηρός, ή, όν:—*grievous, troublesome, annoying*, of persons, πτωχὸν ἀνιηρόν Od.17.220; ἐχθροῖς ἀνιαροί Ar. *Pl*.561, cf. Lys.25.20 (Sup.):—of animals, σχέτλια καὶ ἀ. Hdt.3.108. Adv. ἀνιαρῶς, λέγειν S.*Ant*.316. 2. mostly of things, *painful, grievous*, πτωχεύειν πάντων ἔστ' ἀνιηρότατον Tyrt.10.4, cf. Thgn.124; πόλλ' ἀνιηρὰ παθὼν Id.276; πᾶν γὰρ ἀναγκαῖον χρῆμ' ἀ. ἔφυ Id.472 (= Even.8); opp. ἡδύ, E.*Med*.1095 (lyr.), cf. Pl.*Prt*.355e; τοῖς γεγενημένοις ἀνιαροῖς D.18.291: Comp. ἀνιαρότερος Lys.10.28; irreg. Comp. ἀνιηρέστερος Od.2.190: Sup. -ότατος Pl.*Grg*.477d. II. Pass., *grieved, distressed*, X.*Cyr*.1.4.14. Adv. -ρῶς *wretchedly*, ζῆν Id.*Mem*. 1.6.4; ἔχειν Sor.1.53. [ῑ Hom. and S., ῐ Eleg., E., Com.]

***ἀνίᾱτος** [ῐ], Ion. -ίητος, ον, *incurable*, Hp.*Aph*.7.87; ἕλκος, τραῦμα, Pl.*Lg*.877a, 878c: also in moral sense, πράγματα ib.660c; ἀ. καὶ ἀνήκεστα κακά Aeschin.3.156; ἀνελευθερία ἀ. ἐστιν Arist.*EN*1121ᵇ 13. 2. of persons, *incurable, incorrigible*, Pl.*R*.410a, *Grg*.526b; ἀ. κατὰ τὴν μοχθηρίαν Arist.*EN*1165ᵇ18, al. Adv. ἀνιάτως, ἔχειν *to be incurable*, Pl.*Phd*.113e, D.18.324; οἱ ἀ. κακοί Arist.*EN*1137ᵃ 29. II. Act., ἀ. μετάνοια *unavailing* repentance, Antipho 2.4.12.

**ἀνιάτρευτος**, ον, = foreg., Suid. s.v. βρίω.

**ἀνιᾱτρεύω**, *heal again*, Tz.*H*.6.665.

**ἀνιᾱτρολόγητος**, ον, *uninstructed in medical science*, Vitr.1.1.13.

**ἀνίᾱτρος**, Ion. -ίητρος, ὁ, *no-physician*, Hp.*Praec*.7, Arist.*Ph*. 191ᵇ6, Plot.6.7.37, Alex.Aphr.*in Top*.33.2: Adj., *unworthy of a physician*, ἀ. τι ἔχειν Antyll.ap.Orib.10.23.24.

**ἀνίαχος**, f.l. for ἄϊαχος (q.v.) in Hom. and Q.S.

***ἀνῐάχω** [ᾰχ], *cry aloud*, A.R.2.270, 3.253, Nonn.*D*.15.417. 2. c. acc., *proclaim loudly*, *APl*.4.296 (Antip.); ἔπος Nonn.*D*.44.190.

**ἀνιάω** [ᾰν], S.*Aj*.266, etc.: 3 sg. impf. ἠνία ib.273, Pl.*Grg*.502a: fut. ἀνιάσω [ᾱσ] X.*An*.3.3.19, Ep. ἀνιήσω Hom.: aor. ἠνίασα And.1. 50, etc.; Dor. ἀνίασα Theoc.2.23: pf. ἠνίακα Hld.7.22:—Pass., ἀνιῶμαι Od.15.335, etc., Ion. 3 pl. opt. ἀνιῴατο Hdt.4.130: 3 pl. impf. ἠνιῶντο X.*Cyr*.6.3.10: fut. ἀνιάσομαι Ar.*Fr*.488.11, X.*Mem*.1.1.8 (ἀνιαθήσομαι only in Gal.*Anim.Pass*.9); Ep. 2 sg. ἀνιήσεαι Thgn.991: aor. ἠνιάθην X.*HG*6.4.20; Ion. -ήθην Il.2.291: pf. ἠνίημαι Mosch. 4.3: the aor. Med. ἀνιάσασθαι is v.l. for ἀνᾶσθαι in Gal.*UP*6.16 (ἀνία). [ῑ always in Hom. and S.; ῐ in Thgn. and late Poets; ῑ in Ar. l.c., etc.]:—commoner form of the Ep. ἀνιάζω, *grieve, distress*, c. acc. pers., ἀνιήσει..υἷας 'Αχαιῶν Od.2.115, cf. 20.178; μηδὲ φίλους ἀνία Thgn.1032; φίλους ἀνιῶν S.*Aj*.266: c. acc. rei, ἀνιᾷ μου τὰ ὦτα Pl.*Grg*.485b: c. dupl. acc., ὁ δρῶν σ' ἀνιᾷ τὰς φρένας S.*Ant*.319: c. acc. pers. et neut. Adj., τί ταῦτ' ἀνιᾷς με; ib.550; παῦρ' ἀνιάσας, πόλλ' εὐφράνας (sc. ὑμᾶς) Ar.*Pax*764; ἠνίασά σε οὐδὲν πώποτε And. 1.50:—Pass., *to be grieved, distressed*, c. dat. pers. vel rei, ἀνιᾶται παρεόντι he *is vexed* by one's presence, Od.15.335; ἀ. ὀρυμαγδῷ 1.133;

τύν σοι. . παθόντι κακῶς ἀνιώμεθα Thgn.655; πάσχων ἀνιήσεαι Id.991; ἀ. ὑπομιμνήσκων Lys.12.43; δαπανῶντα ἀνιᾶσθαι X.*Cyr.*8.3.44; περί τινος Ar.*Lys.*593: c. neut. Adj., τοῦτ' ἀνιῶμαι πάλαι I *have* long *been vexed at* this, S.*Ph.*906; πολλὰ μὲν αὐτοὺς ἀνιωμένους, πολλὰ δὲ ἀνιῶντας τοὺς οἰκέτας X.*Oec.*3.2: abs., οὐδ' ἂν ἀνιῷτο Thgn.1205: esp. in aor. part. Pass. ἀνιηθεὶς *disheartened*, Od.3.117, Il.2.291.

**ἀνιγροδέτης**· βυρσοδέψης, Hsch. **ἄνιγρον**, v. ἄναγρον.

⊕**ἀνιγρός**, ά, όν, = ἀνιαρός I, Nic.*Th.*8, Call.*Iamb.*1.164 (prob.), Opp. *H.*3.188; νοῦσος Call.*Aet.*3.1.14; cf. ἀνιγρόν· ἀκάθαρτον, φαῦλον, κακόν, δυσώδες, ἀσεβές, Hsch.; ἀ. ἀντίπαλοι *AP*7.561 (Jul. Aegypt.); δαίμων *IG*14.2123.

**ἀνιδεῖν**, aor. inf., *look up*, dub. in A.*Ch.*808.

**ἀνῐδ-ῑτί**, Adv., (ἰδίω) *without sweat* or *toil*, Pl.*Lg.*718e. **-ίω**, *perspire so that the sweat stands on the surface* Id.*Ti.*74c (prob.).

**ἄνιδρος**, ον, v. ἀνίδρως.

**ἀνῑδρόω**, *get into a sweat*, Hp.*Coac.*24.

**ἀνίδρ-ῠτος** (v. ἀΐδρυτος), ον, Ph.2.451, Dam.*Pr.*413. **-ύω**, *set up*, e. g. a statue, D.C.77.14.

**ἀνίδρ-ως** [ῑ], ων, *without perspiration*, Ruf.*Ren.Ves.*6.2, Aret.*SD* 1.16, 2.7; and so, with v.l. ἄνιδρος, in Hp.*Acut.*(*Sp.*)17. **-ωσις**, εως, ἡ, *sweating*, Id.*Epid.*7.105. **-ωτί**, Adv. *without sweat*, Id.*Prorrh.* 1.61, X.*Cyr.*2.1.29: metaph., *without toil* or *trouble*, Il.15.228; *lazily, slowly*, X.*Cyr.*2.2.30, *Oec.*21.3. **-ωτος**, ον, *without having sweated* or *exercised oneself*, ἀ. γενόμενοι εἰσίοιεν Id.*Cyr.*2.1.29· *not accompanied by perspirations*, ἴκτεροι Hp.*Judic.*9.

**ἀνῐέρ-ειος**, ον, = ᾧ ἱερεῖα μὴ θύεται, *AB*405, Suid. **-εύω**, = ἀνιερόω, τέμενος Men.Eph.1. **-ος**, ον, *unholy, unhallowed*, A.*Ag.* 220,769, *Supp.*757; ἀνίεροι ἀθύτων πελάνων *unhallowed because of* the unoffered sacrifices, E.*Hipp.*146 (all lyr. passages); of a child *born out of wedlock*, Pl.*R.*461b. II. *receiving no victims*, Ἄρης E.*Fr.*992 (lyr.). ⊕**-όω**, *dedicate, devote*, Arist.*Oec.*1346b5; τινί τι Plu.*Cor.*3:—Pass., *PTeb.*6o.10 (ii B.C.), *BGU*1202.5 (i B.C.), etc.: used of persons involving the wrath of the gods upon themselves or others in case of breach of faith, *SIG*1179 (Cnidus). **-ωσις**, εως, ἡ, *consecration*, ἱερῶν D.H.5.35, cf. *SIG*563.9,16 (Teos), *IG*9(1).278 (Locr., ii B.C.); *dedication* of a manumitted slave, Boeot. ἀνιάρωσις *IG*7.3315 (Chaeronea). **-ωτέον**, *one must consecrate*, Ph. 1.184. **-ωστί**, Adv. of ἀνίερος, Heraclit.14.

⊕**ἀνίημι**, ης (ἀνιεῖς, as if from ἀνιέω, dub. in Il.5.880), ησι: impf. ἀνίην, Hom. and Att. 2 and 3 sg. εις, ει, Ion. 3 sg. ἀνίη *SIG*1 (Abu Simbel, vi B.C.), Iterat. ἀνίεσκε Hes.*Th.*157; also ἠνίει Hp.*Epid.* 46; 1 sg. ἀνίειν Luc.*Cat.*4: fut. ἀνήσω: pf. ἀνεῖκα: aor. 1 ἀνῆκα; Ion. ἀνέηκα:—the Homeric forms ἀνέσει Od.18.265, aor. opt. ἀνέσαιμι 14.209, part. ἀνέσαντες 13.657 should be referred to ἀνέζω, but ἄνεσαν Il.21.537 is from ἀνίημι: aor. 2, 3 pl. ἀνεῖσαν Th.5.32, imper. ἄνες A.*Ch.*489, S.*Ant.*1101, E.*Hel.*442, subj. ἀνῇς A.*Eu.*183, Ep. 3 sg. subj. ἀνήῃ Il.2.34, opt. ἀνείη, inf. ἀνεῖναι, part. ἀνείς:—Pass., ἀνίεμαι: pf. ἀνεῖμαι Hdt.2.65, A.*Th.*413, 3 pl. pf. ἀνέωνται Hdt.2.165 (v.l. ἀνέονται), inf. ἀνέωσθαι (sic) *Tab.Heracl.*1.153: aor. part. ἀνεθείς Pl.*R.*410e: fut. ἀνεθήσομαι Th.8.63. [ᾰνῑ- Ep., ᾰνῐ- Att.: but even Hom. has ἀνίει, ἀνιέμενος, and we find ἀνῑησιν in Pl.Com.153 (anap.).]:—*send up* or *forth*, Ζεφύροιο. . ἀήτας Ὠκεανὸς ἀνίησιν Od.4.568; of Charybdis, τρὶς μὲν γάρ τ' ἀνίησιν. . τρὶς δ' ἀναροιβδεῖ 12.105; ἀφρὸν ἀ. *spew up, vomit*, A.*Eu.*183; στ[ρ]όγγυλας [αἵματος] ἀ. S.*OT*1277; of the earth, καρπὸν ἀ. *make* corn or fruit *spring up*, *h.Cer.*333; κνώδαλα A. *Supp.*266; also of the gods, ἀ. ἄροτον γῆς S.*OT*270, etc.; so of females, *produce*, ib.1405:—in Pass., σπαρτῶν ἀπ' ἀνδρῶν ῥίζωμ' ἀνεῖται A.*Th.*413: then in various relations, συὸς χρῆμα ἀ. S.*Fr.*401; κρήνην E.*Ba.*766; of a forest, πῦρ καὶ φλόγα Th.2.77; πνεῦμ' ἀνεὶς ἐκ πνευμόνων E.*Or.*277:—*send up* from the grave or nether world, A.*Pers.*650, Ar.*Ra.*1462, Phryn.Com.1 D., Pl.*Cra.*403e, etc.:—Pass., ἐκ γῆς κάτωθεν ἀνίεται ὁ πλοῦτος ibid.; of fruit, Thphr.*CP*5.1. 5. 2. *let come up, give access to*, τινά X.*HG*2.4.11; εἰς τὸ πεδίον ib. 7.2.12. II. *let go*, from Hom. downwds. a very common sense, ἐμὲ δὲ γλυκὺς ὕπνος ἀνῆκεν, i.e. *left* me, Il.2.71, etc., cf. Pl.*Prt.*310d: —Pass., ἀνίεσθαι *wake up*, D.S.17.56; *set free*, ἐκ στέγης ἀ. S.*Ant.* 1101; *let go unpunished*, ἄνδρα τὴν ὀλιγαρχίαν λυμαινόμενον X.*HG*2. 3.51, cf. Lys.13.93; ἄνετέ μ' ἄνετε *leave* me *alone, forbear*, S.*El.* 229 (lyr.); of a state of mind, ἐμὲ δ' οὐδ' ὣς θυμὸς ἀνίει. . ὀδύνη Il. 15.24; ὅταν μ' ἀνῇ νόσος μανίας E.*Or.*227; ὥς μιν ὁ οἶνος ἀνῆκε Hdt.1. 213, etc.; ἀ. ἵππον *to let* him *go* (by slackening the rein), S.*El.*721; ἵππους εἰς τάχος ἀ. X.*Eq.Mag.*3.2; τῷ δήμῳ τὰς ἡνίας ἀ. Plu.*Per.* 11. b. *loosen, unfasten*, δεσμόν Od.8.359 (v.l. δεσμῶν); δεσμά τ' ἀνεῖσαι Call.*Hec.*1.2.13: hence, *open*, πύλας ἄνεσαν Il.21.537; ἀ. θύρετρα E.*Ba.*448; ἀ. σήμαντρα *break* the seal, Id.*IA*325:—Pass., πύλαι ἀνειμέναι D.H.10.14. 2. ἀ. τινί *let loose at* one, *slip at*, ἀ. τὰς κύνας X.*Cyn.*7.7: hence ἄφρονα τοῦτον ἀνέντες Il.5.761, cf. 880: c. acc. et inf., Διομήδεα μαργαίνειν ἀνέηκεν ib.882: generally, *set on* or *urge* to do a thing, c. inf., Μοῦσ' ἄρ' ἀοιδὸν ἀνῆκεν ἀειδέμεναι Od.8.73, cf. 17.425, Il.2.276, 5.422: freq. c. acc. pers. only, *let loose, excite*, as οὐδέ κε Τηλέμαχον. . ὧδ' ἀνιείης Od.2.185; μέγας δέ σε θυμὸς ἀνῆκεν Il.7.25; τοῖσιν μὲν Θρασυμήδεα δῖον ἀνῆκεν *urged* Thrasymedes *to* their *aid*, 17.705:—so in Pass., ἅπας κίνδυνος ἀνεῖται σοφίας Ar.*Nu.*955. 3. ἀ. τινὰ πρός τι *to let go for* any purpose, τὸν λεὼν ἀνεῖναι πρὸς ἔργα τε καὶ θυσίας Hdt.2.129; ἐς παιγνίην ἑωυτὸν ἀ. ib. 173; τὰ μικρὰ εἰς τύχην ἀνείς E.*Fr.*974 (v.l. ἀφείς); τὰ σώματα ἐπὶ ῥᾳδιουργίαν X.*Cyr.*7.5.75; ἐὰν δ' ἀνῇς, ὑβριστὸν χρῆμα κἀκόλαστον [γυνή] if you *leave* her *free*, Pl.Com.98. 4. *let, allow*, c. acc. et inf., ἀνεῖναι αὐτοὺς ὅ τι βούλονται ποιεῖν Pl.*La.*179a; ἀ. τρίχας αὔξεσθαι Hdt.2.36, cf. 4.175: with inf. omitted, ἀνεῖσα πένθει κόμαν E. *Ph.*323; ἀ. στολίδος κροκόεσσαν τρυφάν ib.1491; κόμας Plu.*Lys.*1: c. dat. pers. et inf., ἀνεὶς αὐτῷ θηρᾶν *having given* him *leave* to hunt, X.*Cyr.*1.6.3. 5. Med., *loosen, undo*, c. acc., κόλπον ἀνιεμένη *baring her* breast, Il.22.80; αἶγας ἀνιέμενοι *stripping* or *flaying* goats, Od.2.300; so ἀνεῖτο λαγόνας E.*El.*826; so in Act., ἀνιέναι· δέρειν, Hsch. 6. *let go free, leave untilled*, of ground dedicated to a god, τέμενος ἀνῆκεν ἅπαν Th.4.116; ἀργὸν παντάπασι τὸ χωρίον ἀνιέντες τῷ θεῷ Plu.*Publ.*8; generally, τὴν χώραν ἀ. μηλόβοτον Isoc.14.31; ἀρούρας ἀσπόρους ἀ. Thphr.*HP*8.11.9; στέλεχος ἀνειμένον *allowed to run wild*, Lxx *Ge.*49.21:—but this sense mostly in Pass., *devote oneself, give oneself up*, ἐς τὸ ἐλεύθερον Hdt.7.103; esp. of animals dedicated to a god, which are *let range at large* (cf. ἄνετος), ἀνεῖται τὰ θηρία Id.2.65; of a person *devoted to* the gods, νῦν δ' οὗτος ἀνεῖται στυγερῷ δαίμονι S.*Aj.*1214; of places, etc., θεοῖσιν ἀ. δένδρεα Call. *Cer.*47; ἄλσος ἀνειμένον a *consecrated* grove, cj. in Pl.*Lg.*761c; of land, ἀ. εἰς νομάς *PTeb.*60.8, 72.36 (ii B.C.): hence metaph., ἀνειμένος εἴς τι *devoted to* a thing, *wholly engaged in* it, e. g. ἐς τὸν πόλεμον Hdt.2.167; ἀνέωνται ἐς τὸ μάχιμον they *are given up* to military service, ib.165; ἐς τὸ κέρδος λῆμ' ἀνειμένον *given up* to. ., E.*Heracl.* 3: hence pf. part. Pass. ἀνειμένος as Adj., *going free, left to one's own will and pleasure, at large*, S.*Ant.*579, *El.*516; ἀ. τι χρῆμα πρεσβυτῶν γένος καὶ δυσφύλακτον E.*Andr.*727; πέπλοι ἀνειμένοι *let hang loose*, ib.598; τὸ εἰς ἀδικίαν καὶ πλεονεξίαν -μένον *unrestrained propensity to*. ., Plu.*Num.*16; σώματα πρὸς πᾶσαν ἐπιθυμίαν ἀνειμένα Id. *Lyc.*10. 7. *slacken, relax*, opp. ἐπιτείνω or ἐντείνω, of a bow or stringed instrument, *unstring*, as Hdt.3.22, cf. Pl.*R.*442a, *Ly.*209b, X.*Mem.*3.10.7, etc.; esp. of musical scales, ἁρμονίαι ἀνειμέναι, opp. σύντονοι, Arist.*Pol.*1342b22, al.; ἀνειμένα Ἰαστὶ μοῦσα Pratin.Lyr.5: metaph., ὀργῆς ὀλίγον τὸν κόλλοπ' ἀ. Ar.*V.*574, cf. Pherecr.145.4, Pl.*R.*410e; πολιτεῖαι ἀνειμέναι καὶ μαλακαί Arist.*Pol.*1290a28; τοῖς γηράσκουσι ἀνίεται ἡ συντονία *GA*787b13; ἀνειμένη τάσις the *grave* accent, Sch.D.T.p.130 H.; οἱ πάγοι τὰς φλόγας ἀ. *temper*, Arist. *Mu.*397b2: hence, b. *remit, neglect, give up*, στέρνων ἀραγμούς S.*OC*1608; φυλακὰς ἀνῆκα E.*Supp.*1042; φυλακήν, ἄσκησιν, etc., Th.4.27, X.*Cyr.*7.5.70, etc.; ἀ. θάνατόν τινι *to remit* sentence of death to one, let one live, E.*Andr.*531; ἔχθρας, κολάσεις τισί Plu.2.536a; ἀ. τὰ χρέα, τὰς καταδίκας, Id.*Sol.*15, D.C.64.8, cf. 72.2; ἄνες λόγον speak *more mildly*, E.*Hel.*442; so ἀ. τινὸς ἔχθραν Th.3.10; ἀ. ἀρχήν, πόλεμον, etc., Id.1.76, 7.18, etc.:—Pass., *to be treated remissly*, ἀνεθήσεται τὰ πράγματα Id.8.63; ὁ νόμος ἀνεῖται *has become effete, powerless*, E.*Or.*941: freq. in pf. part. ἀνειμένος as an Adj., ἐν τῷ ἀνειμένῳ τῆς γνώμης when their minds are *not strung up for action*, Th.5. 9; ἀνειμένῃ τῇ διαίτῃ *relaxed, unconstrained*, of the Athenians, Id.1. 6; δίαιτα λίαν ἀ., of the Ephors, Arist.*Pol.*1270b32; ἀ. ἡδοναί *dissolute*, Pl.*R.*573a; ἄνανδρος καὶ λίαν ἀ. ib.549d; ἀ. χείλεα *parched*, Theoc.22. 63; of climate, ἀ. καὶ μαλακός Thphr.*CP*5.4.4; ὀσμὴ μαλακὴ καὶ ἀ. 5.7. 1: Comp. ἀνειμενώτερος Iamb.*VP*15.67:—but, 8. the sense of *relaxation* occurs also as an intr. usage of the Act., *slacken, abate*, of the wind, ἐπειδὰν πνεῦμ' ἀνῇ S.*Ph.*639, cf. Hdt.2.113, 4.152; ἕως ἀνῇ τὸ πῆμα S.*Ph.*764, cf. Hdt.1.94; ἐμφῦσα οὐκ ἀνίει, of a viper, having fastened on him she *does* not *let go*, Id.3.109: esp. in phrase οὐδὲν ἀνιέναι not to *give way* at all, X.*HG*2.3.46, cf. *Cyr.*1.4.22; τὰς τιμὰς ἀνεικέναι ἤκουον that prices *had fallen*, D.56.25, cf. Arist.*Rh.*1390a 15; σιδήρια ἀ. ἐν τοῖς μαλακοῖς *lose* their *edge*, Thphr.*HP*5.5.1. b. c. part., *give up* or *cease* doing, ὕων οὐκ ἀνίει [ὁ θεός] Hdt.4.28, cf. 125, 2.121.β', E.*IT*318, etc. c. c. gen., *cease from* a thing, μωρίας Id. *Med.*457; τῆς ὀργῆς Ar.*Ra.*700, D.21.186; φιλονικίας Th.5.32; ἀνῆκε τοῦ ἐξελθεῖν *forbore to* come forth, Lxx 1*Ki.*23.13. 9. *dilute, dissolve*, διά τινος or τινί, Gal.13.520, al., *Gp.*4.7.3, cf. Arr.*An.*7.20. 5 (Phryn.19 says that διίημι is more correct in this sense); διυγραινομένων καὶ ἀνιεμένων Thphr.*Vent.*58.

**ἀνίηρ**· βοτάνη τις, Hsch.

**ἀνιηρός**, ή, όν, Ion. for ἀνιαρός.

**ἀνίκα** [ῑ], Dor. for ἡνίκα.

**ἀνίκᾰνος** [ῐ], ον, *insufficient, incapable*, Babr.92 *Subscr.*, Hld.2. 30. 2. *dissatisfied with everything*, Arr.*Epict.*4.1.106.

**ἀνῑκεί** or **ἀνῑκί**, Adv. *without victory*, D.C.61.21.

**ἀνῐκέτευτος**, ον, *without prayer, not entreating*, E.*IA*1003.

⊕**ἀνίκητος** [ῑ], Dor. **-ᾱτος**, ον, *unconquered, unconquerable*, Hes. *Th.*489, Tyrt.11.1, Thgn.491, Pi.*P.*4.91, S.*Ant.*781, *Ph.*78, E.*Andr.* 997, etc. Adv. -τως Phld.*Ir.*p.67 W., Hsch. s. v. ἀτρώτως.—Poet., but used by Gorg.*Fr.*11, Pl.*R.*375b, X.*Cyn.*1.17, and in later Prose, Lxx 2*Ma.*11.13, Plu.*Alex.*14, etc.; λευκὴ ἀ., name of a *plaster*, Crito ap.Gal.12.487. II. ἀνίκητον, τό, = ἄνηθον, Plin.*HN*20.186, Ps.-Dsc.3.58. 2. = σμῖλαξ τραχεῖα, Id.4.142.

**ἀνῑκία**, ἡ, *non-victory*, Pythag. term, f.l. for ἀδικία, Arist.*Metaph.* 990a24, cf. Alex.Aphr.ad loc.

**ἀνικμ-άζω**, *draw up*, Sch.Nic.*Al.*524:—Pass., *evaporate*, Dsc.4. 64:—hence **-αστέον**, Philum.*Ven.*16.6.

⊕**ἀνίκμαντος**, ον, *unmoistened*, Lyc.988.

**ἀνικμάω**, *winnow, sift out*, in Pass., Pl.*Ti.*53a (ἀνικλ- Hsch.); cf. ἰκμάω, ἀπικμάω.

**ἄνικμος**, ον, *without moisture*, Arist.*Pr.*906b19, Plu.2.951b; *sapless*, Thphr.*CP*6.20.2.

**ἀνίκω**, *attain to*, εἰς δόξαν *SIG*560.16.

⊕**ἀνίλαστος** [ῐ], ον, *unappeased, merciless*, Plu.2.170c.

**ἀνίλεως** [ῐ], ων, Att. for ἀνίλαος (not in use), *unmerciful*, *Ep.Jac.* 2.13 (s. v. l.), Hdn.*Epim.*257.

**ἀνίλλω**, = ἀνείλλω, Phryn.*PS* p.31 B., Olymp.*in Phlb.* p.240 S. :—Pass., *shrink back*, of the soul, Plot.1.6.2, cf. Porph.*Plot.*14.

**ἀνίλλωμα**, ατος, τό, = ἀνάβλεμμα, Poll.2.54.

**ἀνιλυσπάομαι**, Dep., *wind one's way* or *struggle upwards*, Hsch.; wrongly written ἀνειλ-.

⊛**ἀνῑμ-άω**, used by early writers only in pres. and impf. (aor. ἀνίμησα Hierocl.p.63.19 A., Plu.*Phoc.*18), *draw up, raise* water by means of leather straps (ἱμάντες), ἀπὸ τροχιλιᾶς Thphr.*HP*4.3.5, cf. Hierocl. l.c.; generally, *draw out* or *up*, ἀλλήλους δόρασι ἀνίμων X.*An.*4.2.8, cf. *Eq.*7.2; κάδον Sor.1.93 :—Pass., aor. ἀνῑμήθην App.*Mith.*32, D.L.1.116, Antig.*Mir.*157 : pf. ἀνίμημαι Luc.*Pisc.*50 :—freq. used by later writers in Med., ἀνιμῶμαι Id.*Alex.*14; τῇ προβολῇ φόρτον, of an elephant, Aret.*SD*2.13; of the sun causing evaporation, *Stoic.*1.35, 2.197, *Gp.*1.13.1 : fut. -ήσομαι Longus 1.12 : aor. -ησάμην Plu.2.773d, Luc.*VH*2.42, etc. II. seemingly intr. (sc. ἑαυτόν), *get up*, X.*Eq.*7.1. ⊛-ησις, εως, ἡ, *drawing up*, of water, Simp.*in Ph.*571.6, Suid.

**ἄνῐος**, ον, = ἀνιαρός, A.*Pers.*256,1055,1061; ἄνιος· ἀνατεπείς (sic), Hsch.

**ἀνιοχίων**, Dor. (Lacon.) for ἡνιοχέων, *IG*5(1).213.

**ἀνιππεύω**, *ride on high*, -οντος ἡλίου E.*Ion*41.

**ἀνιππία**, ἡ, *tax paid in lieu of service in cavalry*, *PSI*4.388.36 (ii B.C.), *PPetr.*2 p.129 (iii B.C.), *PTeb.*99.56 (ii B.C.).

⊛**ἄνιππος**, ον, *without horse, not serving on horseback*, ἱππόται καὶ ἄνιπποι Hdt.1.215, S.*OC*899; *without a horse to ride on*, Ar.*Nu.*125, Plb.10.40.10; *unable to ride*, Plu.2.100a. 2. of countries, *unsuited for horses*, ἄ. καὶ ἀναμάξευτος Hdt.2.108, cf. Aen.Tact.8.4, D.H.2.13.

**ἀνίπταμαι**, = ἀναπέτομαι, Max.Tyr.22.6.

**ἀνιπτόπους**, ὁ, ἡ, gen. ποδος, *with unwashen feet*, epith. of the Σελλοί, Dodonaean priests of Zeus, Il.16.235, cf. *BCH*7.276 (Lydia); applied to parasites by Eub.139; to the Great Bear, as *metuens aequore tingi*, by Nonn.*D.*40.285.

**ἄνιπτος**, ον, *unwashen*, χερσὶ δ' ἀνίπτοισιν (v.l. -ησιν) Διὶ λείβειν.. ἅζομαι Il.6.266, cf. Hes.*Op.*725, *Ev.Matt.*15.20 : prov., ἀ. ποσί, i.e. *unprepared*, Luc.*Pseudol.*4. 2. *not to be washed out*, αἷμα A.*Ag.*1459.

⊛**ἄνις**, = ἄνευ, Megarian in Ar.*Ach.*798,834, cf. *IG*14.432 (Tauromenium); also in late Poets, Lyc.350, Nic.*Al.*419, *Epigr.Gr.*418.3.

**ἀνῐσ-άζω**, *equalize*, Hp.*Vict.*3.85, Arist.*IA*708$^b$14, *Cael.*293$^a$2 :—Pass., ib.297$^b$12. -άκις [ᾰκ], Adv. *an unequal number of times*, Theo Sm.p.26 H., al., Nicom.*Ar.*2.17. -άριθμος [ᾰρ], ον, *unequal*, ἐτῶν ὅρον X.*Ep.*3.

**ἀνῑσάριον** σπέρμα *aniseed*, Damocr.ap.Gal.14.97,124.

**ἀνῐσασμός**, ὁ, *equalization*, Eust.42.6.

**ἀνῑσᾶτον**, τό, *decoction of aniseed*, Alex.Trall.8.2: also ἀννησᾶτον Orib.5.33.10 (interpol.).

**ἀνῐσεπίπεδος**, ον, *having unequal plane faces*, of certain solid numbers, e.g. βωμίσκος (q.v.), Iamb.*in Nic.*p.93 P.

**ἀνῐσήλικος**, ον, *unequal in age*, Procl.*in Prm.*pp.945,949 S.

**ἀνῑσίτης**, ου, ὁ, *flavoured with aniseed*, οἶνος *Gp.*8.4 tit.

**ἀνῐσο-βᾰρής**, ές, *unequal in weight*, Simp.*in Cael.*225.34, Alex. Aphr.*in Top.*166.24, 173.18. -γώνιος, ον, *having unequal angles*, Iamb.*in Nic.*p.93 P. -διάστᾰτος, ον, *having their three dimensions unequal*, ibid. -δρομος, ον, *of unequal course*, περίοδοι τῶν ἑπτὰ ἀστέρων Ph.1.143. -δύνᾰμος [ῠ], ον, *of unequal strength*, Sch.Heph. p.103 C. -ειδής, ές, *of uneven form*, Porph.*VP*50. -κρᾰτέω, *to be unequal in strength*, S.E.*M.*10.28. -λαμπής, ές, *shining unequally*, κύκλος *PMag.Par.*1.1132. -μετρος, ον, *not commensurate with*, τινι Aret.*SD*2.2. -μήκης, ες, *of unequal length*, Gal.13.545.

**ἄνῑσον**, τό, v. ἄννησον.

**ἀνῐσο-πᾰχέω**, *to be of unequal thickness*, Hero *Stereom.*2.59.4. -πᾰχής, ές, *of unequal thickness*, Gal.13.545. -πλᾰτής, ές, *of unequal breadth*, Euc.*Opt.*6. -πλευρος, ον, *scalene*, τρίγωνον Ti.Locr.98a, Theo Sm.p.113 H. -πληθής, ές, *unequal in number*, ἀ. γωνίας ἔχειν, of polygons, Papp.308.6. -ρροπος, ον, *unequally balanced, unfair*, Plu.*Nob.*6, Phlp.*in Ph.*677.25.

⊛**ἄνῐσος**, ον (η, ον Aesar.ap.Stob.1.49.27), *unequal, uneven*, Hp.*Fract.*37, Pl.*Ti.*36d, etc.; τὸ ἄ. *inequality*, Arist.*EN*1129$^b$1, etc.; ἄ. πολιτεία, of an oligarchy, Aeschin.1.30: so of persons, οἱ ἄ. Arist.*Pol.*1280$^a$13; ἄ. κατά τι ib.23; but also, *not content with equality* or *justice, unjust*, Id.*EN*1129$^a$33, 1129$^b$10; *unfair*, χεῖρες *AP*9.263 (Antiphil.). Adv. *unequally*, Hp.*Art.*61; *unfairly*, ἀ. σχεῖν πρός τινας D.24.168; ἀ. νενεμῆσθαι τὰς ἀρχάς Arist.*Pol.*1282$^b$24.

⊛**ἀνῐσο-σθενής**, ές, *of unequal strength*, Gal.5.415. -σκελής, ές, *with uneven legs*, Sch.D.P.175; *with tails of unequal length*, of a bandage, Heliod.ap.Orib.48.63 tit. -στροφος, ον, *revolving unevenly*, Tz.*H.*10.563. -τᾰχής, ές, *unequally rapid*, παλμοί Ph.2.637; φορά Theo Sm.p.189 H. Adv. -ῶς Alex.Aphr.*in Mete.*39.17, Them.*in Ph.*133.11, Procl.*Hyp.*2.14.

**ἀνῐσότης**, ητος, ἡ, *inequality*, Pl.*Phd.*74c, al., Arist.*Pol.*1302$^a$26, etc.: pl., Procl.*Hyp.*5.3.

**ἀνῐσο-τοιχέω**, *to be out of trim, lean over to one side*, metaph. from a ship, Simp.*in Epict.*p.108 D. ⊛-τονος, *unequally stretched*, βρόχος Heliod.ap.Orib.44.14.2; *not in unison*, Ptol.*Harm.*2.2. -υψής, ές, *of unequal height*, Apollod.*Poliorc.*142.5, Hero *Dioptr.*12. -φυές· ἀνόμοιον, Hsch. -χρονος, ον, *of unequal duration*, Herodic.ap. Orib.8.4.6; in Metric, *composed of unequal times*, Aristid.Quint.1.24.

**ἀνῐσόω**, *equalize, balance*, Pl.*Plt.*289e; ὁ σίδηρος τοὺς ἀσθενεῖς ἀ. τοῖς ἰσχυροῖς *puts* them *on a par with*.., X.*Cyr.*7.5.65; of *giving* late-comers *an equal share of* wine, *AB*80, Hsch. (cf. ἀνίσωμα):—Pass., *to be equal in* a thing, πλήθεϊ ἀνισωθῆναι Hdt.7.103: Med., *make oneself equal, contend with*, ζυγαίναις Opp.*H.*5.37. II. *make smooth, level*, στενωπούς J.*BJ*5.5.1: Pass., ibid. B. (ἄνισος) *make unequal*, Phlp.*in Ph.*364.16 (Pass.), Dam.*Pr.*401 (Pass.), Elias *in Cat.*200.22.

⊛**ἀνίστημι**, A. causal in pres. ἀνίστημι (later **ἀνιστάω** S.E.*M.*9.61): impf. ἀνίστην: fut. ἀναστήσω, poet. ἀνστήσω: aor. 1 ἀνέστησα, Ep. ἄνστησα, Aeol. 3 pl. ὄστασαν Hsch.: pf. ἀνέστακα LXX 1 *Ki.*15.12, Arr.*Epict.*1.4.30: also in aor. 1 Med. ἀνεστησάμην (v. infr. I. 5, III. 6). I. *make to stand up, raise up*, γέροντα δὲ χειρὸς ἀνίστη *he raised* the old man *up* by his hand, Il.24.515, cf. Od.14.319; τί μ' αὖ.. ἐξ ἕδρας ἀνίστατε; S.*Aj.*788; ἀ. τινὰ ἐκ τῆς κλίνης Pl.*Prt.*317e; ὀρθὸν ἀ. τινά X.*Mem.*1.4.11; ἀπὸ τοῦ καθαρμοῦ τινα D.18.259. 2. *raise from sleep, wake up*, Il.10.32, etc.; εἰς ἐκκλησίαν ἀ. τινά Ar.*Ec.*740; ἀ. τινὰ ὠμόϋπνον Eup.305: metaph., ἀ. νόσον S.*Tr.*979. 3. *raise from the dead*, οὐδέ μιν ἀνστήσεις Il.24.551, cf. A.*Ag.*1361, S.*El.*139; from misery or misfortune, Id.*Ph.*666, Aeschin.1.67. 4. *produce* a witness, etc. (cf. III. 6), προφήτην ὑμῖν ἀ. ὁ Θεός *Act.Ap.*3.22, al. 5. after Hom., also of things, *set up, build*, στήλας v.l. in Hdt.2.102; πύργους X.*Cyr.*7.5.12, etc.; τρόπαια Διί E.*Ph.*572; ἀνδριάντα ἐς Δελφούς Philipp.ap.D.12.21; so ἀ. τινὰ χρυσοῦν, χαλκοῦν (in pure Attic ἱστάναι), *set up a* golden, brazen *statue* of him, Plu.2.170e, *Brut.*1 (Pass., v. infr. B):—so in aor. 1 Med., ἀναστήσασθαι πόλιν *build oneself* a city, Hdt.1.165; ἀνεστήσαντο δὲ βωμούς *they set them up* altars, Call.*Dian.*199. b. *build up again, restore*, τείχη D.20.68: metaph., θεῶν τιμάς E.*HF*852. 6. *put up for sale*, Hdt.1.196. II. *rouse to action, stir up*, ἀλλ' ἴθι νῦν Αἴαντα.. ἄνστησον Il.10.176, cf. 179, 15.64, etc.: c. dat. pers., *raise up against* another, τούτῳ δὲ πρόμον ἄλλον ἀναστήσουσιν ib.7.116 (v. infr. B. I. 5): *rouse to arms, raise* troops, Th.2.68,96; ἀ. πόλεμον ἐπί τινα Plu.*Cor.*21; ἀναστήσας ἦγε στρατόν he *called up* his troops and marched them, Th.4.93, cf. 112, etc. III. *make* people *rise, break up* an assembly *by force*, Il.1.191; but ἐκκλησίαν ἀναστῆσαι *adjourn* it, X.*HG*2.4.42. 2. *make* people *emigrate, transplant* (cf. infr. B. II. 2), ἔνθεν ἀναστήσας ἄγε Od.6.7; ἀνίστασαν τοὺς δήμους Hdt.9.73; Αἰγινήτας ἐξ Αἰγίνης Th.2.27; even γαῖαν ἀναστήσειν A.R.1.1349; οἴκους Plu.*Publ.*21; also ἀ. τινὰ ἐκ τῆς ἐργασίας D.18.129. 3. *make* suppliants *rise and leave sanctuary*, Hdt.5.71, Th.1.137, S.*OC*276, etc.: also ἀ. στρατόπεδον ἐκ χώρας *make* an army *decamp*, Plb.29.27.10; τὰ πράγματα ἀνίστησί τινα Plu.*Alc.*31. 4. ἀ. ἐπὶ τὸ βῆμα *make to ascend* the tribune, Id.2.784c, cf. *Cam.*32. 5. of sportsmen, *put up* game, X.*An.*1.5.3, cf. *Cyr.*2.4.20 (Pass.), *Cyn.*6.23, D.Chr.2.2. 6. μάρτυρα ἀναστήσασθαί τινα *call* him *as one's* witness, Pl.*Lg.*937a.

B. intr. in pres. and impf. ἀνίσταμαι, -μην, in fut. ἀναστήσομαι, in aor. 2 ἀνέστην (but ἀναστῶ, for ἀναστήσω, Crates Com.4 D.), imper. ἄστηθι (for ἄν-στηθι) Herod.8.1, part. ἀστάς *IG*4.951.112 (Epid.): pf. ἀνέστηκα, Att. plpf. ἀνεστήκη; also pf. ἀνεστέασι Hdt.3.62: aor. Pass. ἀνεστάθην, Aeol. part. ὀσταθείς Hsch.:—*stand up, rise*, esp. to speak, τοῖσι δ' ἀνέστη Il.1.68,101, etc.; ἐν μέσσοισι 19.77: in Att. c. fut. part., ἀ. λέξων, κατηγορήσων, etc.: so c. inf., ἀνέστη μαντεύεσθαι Od.20.380: in part., ἀναστὰς εἶπε E.*Or.*885; παραινέσεις ἐποιοῦντο ἐν σφίσιν αὐτοῖς ἀνιστάμενοι Th.8.76; also, *rise from one's seat* as a mark of respect, θεοὶ δ' ἅμα πάντες ἀνέσταν Il.1.533; ἀπὸ βωμοῦ (cf. A. III. 3) Aeschin.1.84. 2. *rise from bed* or *sleep*, ἐξ εὐνῆς ἀνστᾶσα Il.14.336, cf. A.*Eu.*124; εὐνῆθεν Od.20.124; ὄρθρου ἀ. Hes.*Op.*577; ὀψὲ Ar.*V.*217; οὐδ' ἀνιστάμην ἐκ κλίνης, of a sick person, And.1.64: abs., *rise from sleep*, Hdt.1.31. 3. *rise from the dead*, Il.21.56, cf. 15.287, Hdt.3.62, A.*Ag.*569; παρὰ τῶν πλειόνων Ar.*Ec.*1073. 4. *rise from* an illness, *recover*, ἐκ τῆς νούσου Hdt.1.22, cf. Pl.*La.*195c: abs., Th.2.49. 5. *rise* as a champion, Il.23.709; θανάτων χώρᾳ πύργος ἀνέστα [Oedipus] S.*OT*1201: hence c. dat., *stand up* [to fight against..], Ἀγκαῖον.., ὅς μοι ἀνέστη Il.23.635; μή τίς τοι.. ἄλλος ἀναστῇ Od.18.334; Τυφῶνα θοῦρον πᾶσιν ὃς ἀνέστη θεοῖς A.*Pr.*354 codd.; v. supr. A. II. 6. *rise up, rear itself*, πύργοι E.*Ph.*824 (lyr.), cf. Plb.16.1.5; of statues, etc., *to be set up*, Plu.2.91a, 198f: metaph., μή τι ἐξ αὐτῶν ἀναστῇ κακόν Pi.*P.*4.155; πόλεμος D.H.3.23; θορύβου ἀναστάντος App.*BC*1.56. 7. *to be set up*, βασιλεύς as king, Hdt.3.66 codd. 8. of a river, *rise*, ἐξ ὀρέων Plu.*Pomp.*34. 9. pf. part., γῆ γηλόφοισιν ἀνεστηκυῖα Arr.*Ind.*4.7: metaph., *lofty*, ἀ. τὴν ψυχὴν γενόμενος Eun.*Hist.*p.233 D. II. *rise to go, set out, go away*, εἰς Ἄργος E.*Heracl.*59, cf. Th.1.87, 7.49,50; ἀνίστατο εἰς οἴκημά τι ὡς λουσόμενος Pl.*Phd.*116a. 2. *to be compelled to migrate* (supr. A. III. 2), ἐξ Ἄρνης ἀναστάντες ὑπὸ Θεσσαλῶν Th.1.12, cf. 8: of a country, *to be depopulated*, χώρα ἀνεστηκυῖα Hdt.5.29; πόλις.. πᾶσ' ἀνέστηκεν δορὶ E.*Hec.*494; ἡσυχάσασα ἡ Ἑλλὰς καὶ οὐκέτι ἀνισταμένη no longer *subject to migration*, Th.1.12; τὴν ἀσφάλειαν.. περιείδετ' ἀνασταθεῖσαν D.19.84. 3. of a law-court, *rise*, Id.21.221. 4. *cease*, οὐκ ἀνέστη ἕως ἐνίκησε σκορπίσαι *Psalm.Solom.*4.13.

**ἀνιστορ-έω**, *make inquiry into, ask about*, ἄρνησις οὐκ ἔνεστιν ὧν ἀνιστορεῖς S.*OT*578: c. acc. pers. et rei, *ask* a person *about* a thing, πεύσει γὰρ οὐδὲν ὧν (= ἐκείνων ἃ) ἀνιστορεῖς ἐμέ A.*Pr.*963, cf. S.*OC*991, *Ph.*253; σε.. ἀνιστορῶ E.*Supp.*110; ἀ. τινὰ περί τινος Id.*Hipp.*92; *investigate*, τι Thphr.*CP*1.5.5. -ησία, ἡ, *ignorance of history*, Cic.*Att.*6.1.17. ⊛-ητος, ον, *ignorant of history, uninformed*, περί ινος Plb.12.3.2; τινός Phld.*Rh.*1.188S., Arr.*Epict.*1.6.23, cf. D. Chr.12.59. Adv. -τως, ἔχειν τινός Plu.*Demetr.*1. II. *uninvestigated*, Ph.*Bel.*78.36; *unrecorded*, Phld.*Mus.*p.28K., Plu.2.731c; χώρα, ἰδέαι ὀρνέων, Agatharch.58,84.

**ἀνίστωρ**, ορος, ὁ, ἡ, late form for ἀΐστωρ, Tz.*H.*3.272.

**ἀνίσχαλος**· ἄτοκος, ἀνήμελκτος, ἀθήλαστος, *EM*110.32, cf. Hsch. s.v. σχαλίσαι (-αδον *EM*739.43, Suid.).

**ἀνισχάνω**, like ἀνίσχω, poet. for ἀνέχω, Orph.*A.*445.

**ἀνίσχιος**, ον, *without prominent haunches*, Arist.*HA*499$^{b}$1.

**ἀνίσχ-ῡρος**, ον, *not strong, without strength*, Str.2.1.36, v.l. in D.H.4.54, Sch.Theoc.14.15: Comp., ῥῖγος -ότερον Hp.*Flat.*8; *invalid*, of a document, ἄκυρος καὶ ἀ. *PSI*183.9 (v A.D.), Just.*Nov.*72.5. **-ῡρότης**, ητος, ἡ, *want of strength*, *Gloss.* ⊛**-υς**, υ, gen. υος, *without strength*, Lxx*Is.*40.30.

**ἀνίσχω**, v. sub ἀνέχω.

⊛**ἀνίσωμα**, ατος, τό, = ἐπίστιος, ἡ, prob. in Ath.10.447a; cf. ἀνισόω.

**ἀνίσωσις** [ῐ], εως, ἡ, *equalization*, Th.8.87, Pl.*Lg.*740e. II. (ἀ- priv.) *inequality*, Mich.*in EN*15.22.

**ἀνῐσωτέον**, *one must make equal*, Aristid.1.423J.

**ἀνῐτέον**, verb. Adj. of ἄνειμι, *one must return*, ὅθεν ἐξέβημεν D.H.*Lys.*13.

**ἀνῑΰζω**, *squeal*, of swine, Q.S.11.177.

**ἄνιχθυς**, υ, gen. υος, *without fish*, λίμνη Str.16.1.21.

**ἀνίχν-ευσις**, εως, ἡ, *tracing out, investigation*, Eust.1437.16. **-ευτος**, ον, *not tracked*, Luc.*Am.*35; βυθοί Ps.-Callisth.2.38. **-εύω**, (ἀνά, ἰχνεύω) *track*, as a hound, Il.22.192, cf. Arist.*HA*624$^{a}$28 (of bees), *AP*5.301 (Agath.), Porph.*Sent.*43, Jul.*Or.*6.183b: generally, *trace out, search out*, Plu.*Caes.*69; χέρσον ἀ. Lyc.824:—also **ἀνιχνεῖν**, *Epigr.Gr.*270.

**ἀνίψᾰλος**, ον, (ἵπτομαι) *unhurt*, Stes.76 (v.l. ἀνίψανον).

**ἀνίωτος** [ῑ], ον, (ἰόω) *not liable to rust*, Arist.*Mir.*833$^{b}$31, *PLeid.X.*36B.

**ἀννεῖται**, Ep. for ἀνανεῖται, from ἀνανέομαι.

**ἀννέφελος**, Ep. for ἀνέφελος.

**ἀννήθιον**, τό, = neut. of ἀνήθινος, *POxy.*1923.13 (v/vi A.D.).

**ἀννησοειδής**, ές, *like* ἄννησον: neut., = κώνειον, Hsch., Sch.Nic.*Al.*186.

⊛**ἄννησον** or **ἄνησσον** (*PSI*4.422.28 (iii B.C.), Dsc.3.56), τό, *anise, Pimpinella Anisum*, Hdt.4.71, Hp.*Acut.*23, Thphr.*HP*1.11.2, 1.12.1 (prob.), Alex.127.7, Nic.*Th.*650, Phaenias ap.Ath.9.371d, *POxy.*1088.67 (i A.D.), Bilabel Ὀψαρτ.p.10.—ἄννισον, ἄνισον, and ἄνησον are variants in codd.

**Ἀννιβαϊκός**, ή, όν, *of* or *for Hannibal*, Plb.2.71.9, D.S.2.5.

**Ἀννιβίζω**, *side with Hannibal*, Plu.*Marc.*10.

⊛**ἀννίς**· μητρὸς ἢ πατρὸς μήτηρ, Hsch.

**ἄννῑσον**, τό, v. ἄννησον.

**ἀννωδέως**· τρυφερῶς, σοβαρῶς, Hsch. **ἄννωμα**· θρυπτόμενα, (Tarent.), Id.

⊛**ἀννων-αρχέω**, *to be curator annonae*, *IGRom.*3.1412. **-εακὸν** φρόντισμα, = *cura annonae*, Lyd.*Mag.*3.38. ⊛**-έπαρχος**, ὁ, *praefectus annonae*, *PFlor.*75.20 (iv A.D.). **-εύομαι**, Pass., *to have as an allowance* (*annona*), ἀ. καθ' ἑκάστην ἡμέραν ἄρτους μβ' *OGI*200.20 (Axum). ⊛**-η**, ἡ, = Lat. *annona*, *CIG*4447 (Syria), *OGI*200.16 (Axum), *POxy.*1192.4 (iii A.D.), al. ⊛**-ιακός**, ή, όν, *belonging to the annona*, εἴδη *PFlor.*377.15 (vi A.D.). ⊛**-ικός**, ή, όν, *concerning the annona*, *PLips.*6 ii 11.

**ἀνόδευτος**, ον, *impassable*, Aq.*Je.*18.15; πεζῇ φήσαντος ἀνόδευτα εἶναι στρατοπέδοις Str.16.4.23, cf. App.*BC*4.106. II. *trackless*, χεῦμα Hedyl.ap.Str.14.6.3; ἐρημίαι Lyd.*Mag.*1.50.

**ἀνοδηγέω**, *guide back*, dub. l. in Babr.95.55.

**ἀνοδία**, ἡ, *a road that is no road*, ὁδὸν ἢ κυριώτερον εἰπεῖν ἀνοδίαν Ph.2.156, al.; ἐρήμην ἀνοδίαν ἑαυτοῖς συντεμεῖν Porph.*Chr.*1; mostly in dat. ἀνοδίᾳ, ἀνοδίαις, *through places with no roads*, Plb.5.13.6, 4.57.8, D.S.19.5, Plu.2.508d, cf. *Mar.*37. II. *ascent*, ἀνοδίαι καὶ στάσεις τοῦ ἡλίου Vett.Val.343.18.

**ἄνοδμος**, ον, *without smell, having no smell*, Hp.*Acut.*63 (vv. ll. ἄνοσμος, ἄοσμος), Arist.*Pr.*873$^{a}$2.

**ἀνόδοντος**, ον, = ἀνόδων, Pherecr.74,82.

**ἄνοδος** (A), ον, *having no way* or *road, impassable*, ὁδοὶ ἄ. E.*IT* 889 (lyr.); opp. εὔοδος, X.*An.*4.8.10.

⊛**ἄνοδος** (B), ἡ, *way up*, e.g. to the Acropolis at Athens, Hdt.8.53; τὴν ἄ. οἰκοδομήσασα *CIG*1948 (incert. loc.): metaph., ἡ εἰς τὸν νοητὸν τόπον τῆς ψυχῆς ἄ. Pl.*R.*517b, cf. Phld.*D.*1.6. b. *journey inland*, esp. into Central Asia, like ἀνάβασις, τριῶν μηνῶν ἄ. Hdt.5.50; ἄ. παρὰ βασιλέα ib.51, cf. X.*An.*2.1.1. 2. *rising*, τοῦ ὑγροῦ Arist.*Mete.*355$^{a}$6; *rising* of a star, κατηλυσίη τ' ἄνοδός τε Arat.536; *slope of a hill*, Plb.5.24.4. II. the first (or second) day of the Thesmophoria, Alciphr.3.39, cf. Sch.Ar.*Th.*86, Hsch. III. *ascent* of the soul to its original source, Hierocl.*in CA*24p.471M. IV. Math., *increasing progression*, *Theol.Ar.*58.

**ἀνόδων**, οντος, ὁ, ἡ, *toothless*, Arist.*PA*674$^{b}$20, *Fr.*294.

**ἀνοδύρομαι** [ῡ], *break into wailing*, E.*Hyps.Fr.*1 iv 7, X.*Cyr.*5.1.6, Plu.2.123c.

⊛**ἀνόδυρτος**, ον, *not mourning*, *Trag.Adesp.*303.

⊛**ἀνόζεστα**· τὰ μὴ ἐζεσμένα, Hsch. (fort. ἀπόζεστα).

**ἄνοζος**, ον, *with no*, or *very few, branches*, Thphr.*HP*1.8.1, etc.: Comp. -ότερος ib.3.13.3:—also **ἄοζος**, ον, ib.1.5.4, al.

**ἀνό-ημα**, ατος, τό, *a foolish act*, f. l. for ἀνόμημα, *Stoic.*3.136. **-ήμων**, ον, gen. ονος, *without understanding*, Od.2.270, 17.273, Democr.197, al. **-ησία**, ἡ, *want of understanding*, Suid. s. v. ἀβέλτερος. 2. opp. νόησις, *un-knowing*, i.e. mystical vision, θεωρεῖται ἀνοησίᾳ κρείττονι νοήσεως Porph.*Sent.*25. 3. *mindlessness*, ib.44. ⊛**-ηταίνω**, *to be devoid of intelligence*, Pl.*Phlb.*12d, Henioch.5, Plot.5.5.1; opp. νοεῖν, 2.9.1:—also **-ητεύω**, Sch.Ar.*Nu.*1480. **-ητία**, ἡ, Att. for ἀνοησία, Ar.*Fr.*746, cf. Moer.28. ⊛**-ητος**, ον, *not thought on, unheard of*, ἄφραστ' ἠδ' ἀνόητα *h.Merc.*80. 2. *not within the province of thought*, νοήματα ὄντα ἀνόητα εἶναι Pl.*Prm.*132c; *not the object of thought, unthinkable*, Plot.5.3.6 and 10. Adv. -τως *without discursive thought*, of vision, βλέψαι ἀ. Id.6.7.16. II. Act., *not understanding, unintelligent, senseless, silly*, Hdt.1.87, 8.24; ὦ ἀνόητοι oh *fools!* Ar.*Lys.*572; ὠνόητε Id.*V.*252; opp. προνοητικός, X.*Mem.*1.3.9: Comp. -ότερος Luc.*Peregr.*33; τὸ ἀ., opp. τὸ νοῦν ἔχον, Pl.*Ti.*30b; τῷ θνητῷ καὶ ἀ. Id.*Phd.*80b; τὸ ἀ. [τῆς ψυχῆς] Id.*R.*605b, etc.:—of animals, τὸ τῶν προβάτων ἦθος εὔηθες καὶ ἀ. Arist.*HA*610$^{b}$23, cf. 622$^{a}$3. b. c. gen., *not understanding*, θεοῦ Max.Tyr.41.5; τῆς φωνῆς Luc.*Asin.*44, cf. Ecphant.ap.Stob.4.7.64. 2. of acts, thoughts, etc., ἀ. γνῶμαι S.*Aj.*162 (lyr.); δόξαι Pl.*Phlb.*12d; εὐχειρίη Hp.*Art.*35; ἀ. καὶ κενόν Ar.*Ra.*530; οἴνου..καὶ τῶν ἄλλων ἀνοήτων and all other *follies*, Id.*Nu.*417. b. *without mind*, ἀνόητα καὶ ἄνευ ζωῆς Plot.5.5.1. III. Adv. -τως Ar.*Lys.*518, Pl.*R.*336e, etc.; ἀ. διακεῖσθαι Lys.10.4: Sup. -ότατα D.C.44.35:—also **-ητεί**, *AB*1327, *An.Ox.*2.313.

**ἀνόθευτος**, ον, *pure, genuine*, χρυσίον Ps.-Plu.*Fluv.*7.4: metaph., μαρτυρία D.S.1.72; βίος Ph.2.267; φίλος Gal.14.7. II. *free from adultery*, γάμος Arist.*Mir.*846$^{a}$30, Ps.-Plu.*Fluv.*5.2.

**ἀνόθηρον**· νωθρόν, Hsch.

**ἄνοθος**, ον, = ἀνόθευτος, *pure, genuine, unadulterated*, εὔνοια Ph.1.454; κάλλος 2.156. Adv. -θως ib.216, al., Hsch.

⊛**ἄνοια**, Ep. **ἀνοίη** Thgn.453, ἡ:—*the character of an* ἄνοος, *want of understanding, folly*, ἀνοίῃ *in folly*, Hdt.6.69; ὑπ' ἀνοίας A.*Pr.*1079, Philem.143; νεότητι καὶ ἀνοίᾳ Pl.*Lg.*716a; ἄ. λόγου S.*Ant.*603; τὴν ἄ. εὖ φέρειν E.*Hipp.*398; πολλῇ ἀνοίᾳ χρῆσθαι to be *a* great *fool*, Antipho 3.3.2; πολλὴ ἄ. [ἐστι] πολεμῆσαι Th.2.61; ἄνοιαν ὀφλισκάνειν to be thought *a fool*, D.1.26; δύο ἀνοίας γένη, τὸ μὲν μανίαν, τὸ δ' ἀμαθίαν Pl.*Ti.*86b; but opp. μανία, Id.*R.*382c, e, etc.: pl., *follies*, Isoc.8.7. [In Trag. sts. paroxyt. ἀνοίᾱ (cf. ἀγνοίᾱ), cf. A.*Th.*402, S.*Fr.*583.5, E.*Andr.*519.]

**ἀνοιγ-εύς**, έως, ὁ, *opener*, Dam.*Pr.*125 ter. ⊛**-μα**, ατος, τό, *opening, door*, Lxx 3*Ki.*14.6 (cod. Alex.); *valve*, Zos.Alch.p.225B., etc. II. ἄ. σφαίρας, used of the *diameter* of a sphere, *IGRom.*4.503.12 (Pergam.). ⊛**-νῡμι** Lys.12.10; **ἀνοίγω** Pi.*P.*5.88, Hdt.3.37,117, and Att. as *IG*1.32 (συν-), al.: later **ἀνοιγνύω** Demetr.*Eloc.*122, Paus.8.41.4: impf. ἀνέῳγον Il.16.221, al., Hdt.1.187, etc.; also ἀνῷγον Il.14.168; rarely ἤνοιγον X.*HG*1.1.2 and 6.21; Ion. and Ep. ἀναοίγεσκον Il.24.455; late ἀνεῴγνυον App.*BC*4.81, etc.: fut. ἀνοίξω Ar.*Pax*179: aor. ἀνέῳξα Id.*V.*768, Th.2.2, Hp.*Vict.*2.56, part. ἀνεῴξας *CIG* (add.) 4300*d* (Antiphellus); also ἤνοιξα X.*HG*1.5.13 and in late Prose; Ion. ἄνοιξα Hdt.1.68 (best codd. ἄνῷξα), 4.143, 9.118; poet. ἀνῷξα Theoc.14.15, κἀνῷξε Phld.*Acad.Ind.*p.103M.: pf. ἀνέῳχα D.42.30, Men.229; ἀνέῳγα Aristaenet.2.22 (v. infr.): plpf. ἀνεῴγει Pherecr.86 (Pors.):—**Pass., ἀνοίγνῠμαι** E.*Ion*923, Ar.*Eq.*1326: late fut. ἀνοιχθήσομαι Lxx*Is.*60.11, Epict.*Ench.*33.13 (v.l.); ἀνοιγήσομαι Lxx*Ne.*7.3, *PMag.Par.*1.358; ἀνεῴξομαι X.*HG*5.1.14: pf. ἀνέῳγμαι E.*Hipp.*56, Th.2.4, etc.; ἀνῷγμαι Theoc.14.47; later ἤνοιγμαι (δι-) best reading in Hp.*Epid.*7.80, cf. J.*Ap.*2.9; plpf. ἀνέῳκτο X.*HG*5.1.14 (pf. 2 ἀνέῳγα is used in pass. sense in Hp.*Morb.*4.39, *Cord.*7, and later Prose, as Plu.2.693d, *Ev.Jo.*1.51, 2*Ep.Cor.*6.11, Luc.*Nav.*4 (though he condemns it *Soloec.*8); but in Att., only Din.*Fr.*81): aor. ἀνεῴχθην E.*Ion*1563, subj. ἀνοιχθῇ D.44.37, opt. ἀνοιχθείην Pl.*Phd.*59d, part. ἀνοιχθείς Th.4.130, Pl.*Smp.*216d; later ἠνοίχθην Paus.2.35.7, Lxx*Ps.*105(106).17; and aor. 2 ἠνοίγην *Ev.Marc.*7.35, Luc.*Am.*14, etc.—In late Gr., very irreg. forms occur, ἠνέῳξα Lxx*Ge.*8.6; ἠνέωχα *PMag.Par.*1.2261; ἠνέῳγμαι *Apoc.*10.8, Hld.9.9; ἠνεῴχθην Lxx*Ge.*7.11; also aor. 1 inf. ἀνωῖξαι Q.S.12.331; ἀνωΐχθην Nonn.*D.*7.317:—*open*, of doors, etc., ἀναοίγεσκον μεγάλην κληῗδα *they tried to put back* the bolt *so as to open* [the door], Il.24.455, cf. 14.168; πύλας ἀνοῖξαι A.*Ag.*604; θύραν Ar.*V.*768; also without θύραν, ἐπειδὴ αὐτῷ ἀνέῳξέ τις Pl.*Prt.*310b, cf. 314d; χηλοῦ δ' ἀπὸ πῶμ' ἀνέῳγε *took off* the cover *and opened* it, Il.16.221; φωριαμῶν ἐπιθήματα κάλ' ἀνέῳγεν 24.228; so ἀ. σορόν, θήκας, Hdt.1.68,187; κιβωτόν Lys.12.10; ἀ. σήμαντρα, σημεῖα, διαθήκην, *open* seals, etc., X.*Lac.*6.4, D.42.30, Plu.*Caes.*68; and metaph., καθαρὰν ἀνοίξαντι κλῇδα φρενῶν E.*Med.*660; ἀ. βίβλινον (sc. οἶνον) *tap* it, Theoc.14.15; γῆρυν ἀνοίξας, for στόμα, Tryph.477; ἀ. φιλήματα kiss *with open mouths*, Ach.Tat.2.37. b. *throw open* for use, γυμνάσιον *OGI*529.11; κἀνῷξε σχολὰς *opened* school, Phld.*Acad.Ind.*p.103M.; εἰ ἀνοίξω ἐργαστήριον; shall I *open* a shop? Astramps.*Orac.*43p.5H. 2. metaph., *lay open, unfold, disclose*, ὄνομα A.*Supp.*322; ἔργ' ἀναιδῆ S.*OC*515, cf. E.*IA*326; λανθάνουσαν ἀτυχίαν Men.674. 3. as nautical term, abs., *get into the open sea, get clear of land*, X.*HG*1.1.2, 5.13, 6.21; but ἁλὸς κέλευθον ἀ. Pi.*P.*5.88 is *to open* or *first show* the way over the sea. II. Pass., *to be open, stand open, lie open*, ὄπισθε τῆς ἀνοιγομένης θύρης Hdt.1.9; ἀνεῳγμένην καταλαμβάνειν τὴν θύραν Pl.*Smp.*174e; ἀνεῳγμένας πύλας Ἅιδου E.*Hipp.*56; δικαστήρια ἀνοίγεται Pl.*R.*405a; παρέξει τἀμπόρι' ἀνεῳγμένα Ar.*Av.*1523; ἀνέῳκται τὸ δεσμωτήριον D.24.208; λέων τὰ ἐντὸς ἀνοιχθείς *cut open*, Arist.*HA*497$^{b}$17; κόλποι δι' ἀλλήλων ἀνοιγόμενοι *opening* one into another, Plu.*Crass.*4: metaph., θησαυρὸς ὡς ἀνοίγνυται κακῶν E.*Ion*923.

**ἀνοιδ-αίνω,** *blow up, inflate,* Poll.4.179: aor. inf. ἀνοιδῆναι Q.S. 14.470. II. intr., = ἀνοιδέω, Nic.*Fr.*68.7. **-ανσις,** εως, ἡ, = ἀνοίδησις, *dilatation,* opp. συστολή, Plot.4.5.7 (pl.). **-έω,** Ep. **-είω** Nic.*Th.*355: fut. -ήσω: aor. ἀνῴδησα E.*Hipp.*1210, Pl.*Ti.*84e: pf. ἀνῴδηκα Hp.*Acut.*10:—*swell up,* Hp. l.c.; of a wave, E. l.c., cf. Alciphr.1.10; of wind in the body, Pl. l.c.; of figs ripening, Nic. l.c.; τὰ στέρνα ἀνῴδει Aeschin.*Ep.*1.2; τὸ κάλυμμα ἀνῳδηκός *swollen out, inflated,* Arist.*HA*625$^{a}$2, cf. *GA*728$^{b}$28. 2. metaph., θυμὸς ἀνοιδέει Hdt.7.39; ὀργαῖς..-ούσαις Phld.*Ir.*p.63 W.; of anger, ἀνοιδήσας ὁ βασιλεὺς Philostr.*VA*7.33 (so in Med., θυμὸν ἀνοιδήσαντο they *swelled* with rage, Q.S.9.345); ἀνοιδούσης τῆς νόσου Philostr.*VA*4.4. **-ησις,** εως, ἡ, *swelling, intumescence,* τῶν μαστῶν Arist.*HA*574$^{b}$16, al.: θαλάσσης Id.*Mu.*399$^{a}$27 (pl.). **-ίσκω,** *make to swell,* σῖτον Thphr. *CP*4.13.7:—Pass., = ἀνοιδέω, Hp.*Acut.*10.

**ἀνοίκ-ειος,** ον, *not of the family,* S.E.*P.*1.67: Comp. -ότερος *less closely related,* Phlp.*in Ph.*256.14. II. *unfitting, unseasonable,* Cic.*Att.*16.11.4, D.S.3.56, Plu.2.102a: c. gen., *foreign to, incongruous with,* Epicur.*Ep.*3p.60 U., Plb.6.10.1, 24.5.13, D.S.12.21: c. dat., *dissimilar to,* Plb.5.96.8; *alien from,* κενοδοξίᾳ Porph.*Antr.*4 (Sup.): abs., Phld.*Po.*1676.9, Id.*D.*3.8 (Comp.). Adv. -ως, ῥηθῆναι Simp.*in Ph.*350.27. III. Astrol., *not in its domicile,* Vett.Val. 50.2. Adv. -ως Id.44.5. **-ειότης,** ητος, ἡ, *ineptitude,* Eustr.*in EN*364.18. 2. *incongruity,* Iamb.*Myst.*1.4. **-είωτος,** ον, *not to be adapted, alien,* ἀλλήλοις M.Ant.12.30. **-ῆ·** παρὰ τὸ εἰκὸς εἰρημένον, *EM*110.55, cf. Hsch. s.v. ἀνοκηδεολόγον. **-ητος,** ον, = ἀοίκητος, Hdt.4.31. **-ίζω,** *remove up the country,* ἀ. τὴν Σπάρτην, i.e. *break it up* as a city, Arist.*Rh.Al.*1423$^{a}$7; ἀ. τινὰς ἐς τὴν Περσίδα Paus.1.25.5, cf. Str.13.3.3; ἀ. [τέττιγας] φθόνου ἐς δένδρα *remove* them *out of* envy's *way,* dub. in Philostr.*VA*7.11 (leg. ἀπ-):—Pass. and Med., *shift one's dwelling up the country, migrate inland* or *to higher ground,* αὐτοὶ δ' ἀνῳκίσανθ' ὅπως ἀνωτάτω Ar.*Pax*207, cf. *Av.* 1351, Str.9.2.17, App.*Pun.*84; and of cities, *to be built inland* or *away from the coast,* Th.1.7: generally, *migrate,* ἀνοικίσασθαι εἰς Ὄλυνθον Id.1.58, cf. 8.31. II. *resettle, colonize afresh,* Paus.2.1.2, Memn. 60 (Med.); *rebuild,* Aps.pp.239, 245 H.:—Pass., *to be repeopled,* Plu. *Luc.*29. **-ισις,** εως, ἡ, *shifting* people *upward and inland,* App. *Pun.*84. **-ισμός,** ὁ, = foreg., Str.9.2.17, prob. in Ph.2.526. II. *rebuilding, restoration,* πόλεων Hdn.3.6.9.

**ἀνοικο-δεσπότητος,** ον, Astrol., *without a dominant planet,* Vett. Val.134.17, 151.5. ❋**-δομέω,** *build up,* τὰ χείλεα τοῦ ποταμοῦ.. ἀνοικοδόμησε πλίνθοισι Hdt.1.186. 2. *wall up,* λαύρας καιναῖς πλίνθοισιν ἀ. Ar.*Pax*100; θύραν Lycurg.128; πύλας dub.l. in D.S.11. 21 (in this sense ἀποικ- is a freq. v.l.). II. *build again, rebuild,* πόλιν καὶ τείχη Th.1.89, cf. Jusj.ap.Lycurg.81, X.*HG*4.4.19, etc.; ἀ. χώραν *occupy again with buildings,* D.S.15.66:—Pass., metaph., *to be exalted,* Lxx *Ma.*3.15. **-δομή,** ἡ, *rebuilding, restoration,* *PLond.*2.216.18 (i A.D.), *PAmh.*93.19 (ii A.D.); Dor. **-μά** *IG*12(1).9 (Rhodes). **-δόμησις,** εως, ἡ, = foreg., Arist.*Ath.*23.4. **-δομία,** ἡ, *building up,* *IG*4.823.6 (Troezen), Sch.Th.8.90. **-νόμητος,** ον, *not set in order, unarranged,* Macho ap.Ath.8.341b, Longin.33. 5. II. Act., *managing badly,* Plu.2.517e, v.l. in Gell.12.12.4.

**ἄνοικος,** ον, *houseless, homeless,* ἄ. ποιέειν τινά Hdt.3.145; cf. ἄοικος.

**ἀνοικτεί** or **-τί,** Adv. = ἀνοίκτως, Hdn.*Epim.*257.

**ἀνοικτέον,** *one must open,* E.*Ion*1387.

**ἀνοικτές·** ἀταλαιπώρητον, Hsch.

**ἀνοίκ-της,** ου, ὁ, *one who opens,* A.D.*Synt.*324.6. **-τικός,** ή, όν, *fit for opening,* Lyd.*Mens.*4.64: -κόν *means of opening* the mouth, Orib.*Fr.*48.

**ἀνοικτίρμων,** ον, gen. ονος, *pitiless, merciless,* S.*Fr.*659.8, *AP*7. 303 (Antip. Sid.).

**ἀνοίκτιστος,** ον, *unmourned,* σῶμα [Arist.]*Pepl.*28. II. Act., *pitiless,* Περσεφόνης θάλαμοι *IG*2.3765 (*Supp.*p.283). Adv. -τως Antipho 1.25.

**ἀνοικτός,** ή, όν, *capable of being opened,* Babr.59.11, Luc.*VH*1.24.

**ἄνοικτος,** ον, *pitiless, ruthless,* E.*Tr.*787, Ar.*Th.*1022. Adv. -τως *without pity, without being pitied,* S.*OT*180, E.*Tr.*756: also ἀνοίκτρως Ant.Lib.39 (s.v.l.).

**ἀνοιμ-ώζω,** *wail aloud,* A.*Pers.*465, Th.3.113, Telecl.1 D. **-ωκτί** [ῑ], Adv. *without need to wail, with impunity,* S.*Aj.*1227; *without wailing,* Philostr.Jun.*Im.*10. **-ωκτος,** ον, *unmourned, unlamented,* A.*Ch.*433, 511.

**ἄνοινος,** ον, = ἄοινος, Hdn.*Epim.*216.

❋**ἄνοιξις,** εως, ἡ, *opening,* πυλῶν Th.4.67, 68; πόρων Thphr.*Od.* 13; χειλῶν Plu.2.738c, cf. *PMag.Lond.*46.274 (iv A.D.): pl., Porph. *Antr.*27; ἄ. τοῦ στόματος, Hebraism for παρρησία, Lxx *Ez.*29.21, 2 *Ep.Cor.*6.11, *Ep.Eph.*6.19, etc.

**ἄνοισ-ις,** εως, ἡ, (ἀναφέρω, ἀνοίσω) *bringing back,* Suid. **-τέος,** α, ον, *to be referred,* E.*Fr.*970. II. ἀνοιστέον *one must carry back* or *report,* S.*Ant.*272, E.*HF*1221:—*one must refer,* τι πρός τι Plu. *Phoc.*5; ἐπί τι Thphr.*CP*4.11.8. **-τός,** ή, όν, *brought back,* ἀ. ἔς τινα *referred to* some one *for decision,* Hdt.6.66 (v.l. ἀνωΐστου).

**ἀνοιστρέω,** *goad to madness,* E.*Ba.*979; ἔρωτι καρδίην ἀνοιστρηθείς Herod.1.57.

**ἀνοίσω,** v. ἀναφέρω. **ἄνοιτο,** v. ἄνω.

**ἀνόκαιον·** ὑπερῷον, γράφεται καὶ ἀνώγεων, Hsch.

**ἀνοκηδεολόγον,** v. ἀνοικῆ.

**ἀνόκνως,** Adv. = ἀόκνως, *POxy.*743.39 (i B.C.), *PFay.*130.14 (iii A.D.).

**ἀνοκωχεύω,** Ion. **ἀνακ-,** *hold back, stay, hinder,* ἀ. τὰς νέας *keep* the[m] *riding at anchor,* Hdt.6.116 (cf. Hsch. s.v. ἀνακ-), etc.: metaph., [of] a chariot, *hold* it *in, keep* it *back,* S.*El.*732; also ἀ. πόλεμον D.H.9. 16. 2. ἀ. τὸν τόνον τῶν ὅπλων *keep up* the tension of the ropes, *keep* them *taut,* Hdt.7.36. 3. *keep afloat,* Arist.*Cael.*313$^{a}$23. II. also intr. (sc. ἑαυτόν), *keep still,* Hdt.9.13; *hold back,* of ships, D.S. 11.18.—The form **ἀνακωχέω** *support, relieve strain upon,* is found in Hp.*Art.*9, 38, *Mochl.*2.

**ἀνοκωχή,** ἡ, redupl. form = ἀνοχή (cf. ὄκωχα pf. of ἔχω), *stay, cessation,* κακῶν Th.4.117; ἀ. νομῆς *a stay* in the spreading of the ulcer, Aret.*SD*2.9, cf. 1.8. 2. esp. *cessation of arms, truce,* δι' ἀνοκωχῆς γίγνεσθαί τινι to be at *truce* with one, Th.1.40; ἀ. ἐστί τινι πρός τινα one party has *a truce* with another, Id.5.32. II. *hindrance,* τριβὴ καὶ ἀ. τῶν Ἑλλήνων Id.8.87. (Archaic word used by Th. acc. to D.H.*Amm.*2.3. Mss. generally have the corrupt form ἀνακωχή, which gave rise to a deriv. παρὰ τὸ ἄνω τὰς ἀκωκὰς ἔχειν *EM*96.52: but Hsch. gives the correct form. Ammon.*Diff.*19 attempts to distinguish the forms.)

**ἀνοκώχησις,** εως, ἡ, glossed by σύμπτωσις, Bacch.ap.Erot. s.v. (ἀνακ- codd.).

❋**ἀνολβ-έω,** *to be ἄνολβος,* Epic.*Oxy.*1794.13. **-ία,** Ion. **-ίη,** ἡ, *the state of an ἄνολβος, misery,* Hes.*Op.*319 [ῑ]. ❋**-ιος,** ον, = sq., v.l. in Hdt.1.32. ❋**-ος,** ον, poet. Adj. *unblest, wretched, luckless,* ἦμαρ Orac.ap.Hdt.1.85; γαῖα, ὄμμα, E.*Hel.*247, *IA*354; ὤμοι ἐμῶν ἄνολβα βουλευμάτων, for ἐμὰ..βουλεύματα, S.*Ant.*1265: of persons, Thgn.288 (Comp.), A.*Eu.*551, S.*Aj.*1156, etc. 2. *without means, poor,* Arat.1073.

**ἀνόλεθρος,** ον, *not ruined, having escaped ruin,* Il.13.761.

❋**ἀνολισθάνω,** aor. -ώλισθον, *slip* or *glide back, return,* ἔς τινα Call. *Fr.*96.

**ἀνολκή,** ἡ, *hauling up,* λίθων Th.4.112; ἀ. καὶ καθολκή Aen.Tact. 10.12.

**ἀνολολύζω,** *cry aloud, shout aloud,* ἀνωλόλυξα χαρᾶς ὕπο A.*Ag.* 587, cf. Simon.148.2, S.*Tr.*205, E.*Med.*1173, etc. 2. c. acc., *bewail loudly,* S.*El.*750: but c. acc. cogn., βοὴν ἀ. E.*Tr.*1000. II. causal, *excite by Bacchic cries,* πρώτας δὲ Θήβας..ἀνωλόλυξα Id.*Ba.*24.

**ἀνολοφύρομαι** [ῡ], *bewail aloud,* Th.8.81, X.*Cyr.*7.3.14, J.*AJ*2. 6.4: c. part., ἀ. ποθῶν.. Pl.*Prt.*327d.

**ἀνολόφυρτον·** ἀδάκρυτον, Hsch. (ἀνωλόφυκτον cod.).

**Ἀνολυμπιάς,** άδος, ἡ, *an Olympiad omitted in the list,* Paus.6.22.3.

**ἄνομαι,** v. ἄνω.

**ἀνομαλ-ίζω,** *restore to equality, equalize,* Pass., pf. inf. ἀνωμαλίσθαι Arist.*Rh.*1412$^{a}$16: fut., cj. in *Pol.*1265$^{a}$40; cf. sq. **-ωσις,** εως, ἡ, *restoration of equality, equalization,* ib.1274$^{b}$9.

**ἀνομβρ-έω,** *gush out with water,* πηγή Ph.2.91: metaph., ὥσπερ ἀπὸ γῆς τῆς αἰσθήσεως -ησάντων παθῶν 1.575: c. acc., *pour forth,* ὕδωρ 2.115: metaph., Lxx *Si.*18.29, al., Ph.1.477. **-ήεις,** εσσα, εν, *rainy,* Nic.*Al.*288. **-ία,** ἡ, *want of rain,* Arist.*HA*606$^{b}$20, D.S.1.29, J.*AJ*8.13.2, Ph.2.383: metaph., [τὴν παίδευσιν] οὔτε ὄμβρος οὔτε ἀ. ἀφαιρεῖται Antipho Soph.60. **-ος,** ον, *without rain,* of countries, Hdt.2.22, 4.185. 2. ἄ. ῥοαί streams *not fed by showers,* E.*Ba.*406.

**ἀνομέω,** *to be ἄνομος, act lawlessly,* περὶ τὸ ἱρόν Hdt.1.144. 2. Pass., *to be unlawfully used,* *POxy.*1465.9 (i B.C.).

**ἀνομήλῐκος,** ον, *of unlike age,* Procl.*in Prm.*p.949 S.

**ἀνόμ-ημα,** ατος, τό, *transgression of the law,* Lys.ap.Phot.p.143 R., Lxx *Le.*20.14, al., *Stoic.*3.136, D.S.17.5. ❋**-ία,** Ion. **-ίη,** ἡ, *lawlessness, lawless conduct,* opp. δικαιοσύνη, Hdt.1.96, 97; ἀ. νόμων κρατεῖ E.*IA*1095 (lyr.); ἀ. ἀμύνειν Antipho 4.1.7; ἀ. ὀφλισκάνειν E. *Ion*443; ἀντὶ αὐτονομίας..εἰς ἀνομίας ἐμπίπτειν Isoc.6.64, cf. Plu.2. 755b; ζῆν ἐν πάσῃ ἀναρχίᾳ καὶ ἀ. Pl.*R.*575a. 2. *the negation of law,* opp. νόμος, D.24.152.

**ἀνομίλητος** [ῑ], ον, *having no communion with others, unsociable,* Pl.*Lg.*951a, Plu.2.50b, etc. 2. c. gen., ἀ. παιδείας *uneducated,* Pl. *Ep.*332c: abs., Luc.*Merc.Cond.*14: c. dat., ἀ. τοῖς ἔργοις τῆς τέχνης Gal.15.159, 18(1).287.

❋**ἀνόμιμος,** ον, v.l. for ἄνομος, Pl.*Min.*314d.

**ἀνόμιστος,** ον, *not customary,* Orac.ap.Phleg.*Mir.*10.

**ἀνόμιχλος,** ον, *without mist,* ἀήρ Arist.*Mu.*394$^{a}$23.

**ἀνόμμᾰτος,** ον, *eyeless, sightless,* S.*Ph.*856 (lyr.), Orph.*Fr.*82.

**ἀνομο-γένεια,** ἡ, *difference in kind,* Epicur.*Fr.*36. **-γενής,** ές, *of different kind,* ibid. (prob.), Chrysipp.*Stoic.*2.81, Arr.*Epict.*1.20.2, Alex.Aphr.*in Top.*116.10, al., S.E.*M.*8.229.

**ἀνομο-ειδής,** ές, *differing in species,* Plot.4.3.2, Iamb.*Myst.*1.19, Dam.*Pr.*34; v.l. for ἀνόμοιο-, Arist.*EN*1163$^{b}$32. Adv. -ειδῶς Dam. *Pr.*37.

**ἀνομόζηλος,** ον, *having a different bent,* S.E.*M.*7.56.

**ἀνομοθέτητος,** ον, *unregulated by law,* Pl.*Lg.*781a, 785a, Arist. *Pol.*1269$^{b}$19; ἄγραφον καὶ ἀ. φύσεως δίκαιον D.H.7.41.

**ἀνομοιο-βᾰρής,** ές, *of unevenly distributed weight,* Arist.*Cael.*273$^{b}$ 23. **-γενής,** ές, *of different kind,* Ph.2.307. Adv. -νῶς *in a different gender,* Sch.rec.S.*Ant.*74. **-γώνιος,** ον, *with dissimilar angles,* Papp.216.20. **-ειδής,** ές, *of unlike kind, heterogeneous,* φιλίαι Arist.*EN*1163$^{b}$32, cf. Dam.*Pr.*440:—hence Subst. **-είδεια,** ἡ, A.D.*Pron.*101.22. **-κατάληκτος,** ον, *with different terminations,* Id.*Synt.*167.25. **-μερής,** ές, *consisting of unlike parts, not homogeneous,* esp. of organs, opp. tissues, Arist.*HA*486$^{a}$7, *Mete.*388$^{a}$18, *GA*722$^{b}$31, Thphr.*Fr.*22, Gal.6.844, al. 2. in Metric, [συστήματα] κατὰ περικοπὴν ἀνομοιομερῆ Heph.*Poëm.*4. **-ποιός,** όν, *causing* nlikeness, Dam.*Pr.*342. **-πτωτος**, ον, *with unlike inflexions*, ust.1228.62. Adv. -τως Id.631.27.

**ἀνόμοιος**, ον, Pl.*Phlb.*13e, etc., also α, ον Isoc.12.225, etc.:—*unke, dissimilar*, Pi.*N.*8.28; ἀ. τινι *unlike* it, Pl.*Grg.*513b, al.; ἐξ νομοίων ἡ πόλις is composed of *dissimilar elements*, Arist.*Pol.*1277ᵃ . Adv. -ως Th.1.84, Pl.*R.*388c, al.; ἀ. ἔχειν X.*An.*7.7.49. 2. f number, = ἑτερομήκης, *Theol.Ar.*9,58.

**ἀνομοιό-στροφος**, ον, *consisting of unequal strophes*, Heph.*Poëm.* .3. **-σχήμων**, ον, gen. ονος, *of unlike form*, Gal.18(1).774, Procl. *nst.*210, Phlp.*in Ph.*677.2.

**ἀνομοιότης**, ητος, ἡ, *unlikeness, dissimilarity*, Pl.*Prm.*159e, *Plt.* 273d, Thphr.*CP*1.2.2, Hierocl.*in CA*26p.481 M.: in pl., Pl.*Plt.*294, Arist.*Po.*1448ᵃ10.

**ἀνομοιό-τροπος**, ον, *differing in modality* (including quantity and quality), πρότασις Eustr.*in APo.*52.17. **-φυλος**, ον, *of different kind*, Sm.*Le.*19.19. **-χρονος**, ον, in Metric, *of dissimilar quantity*, Eust.13.7. **-χρους**, ουν, *of different colour*, Alex.Aphr.*de An.* 146.8.

**ἀνομοι-όω**, (ἀνόμοιος) *make unlike* or *dissimilar*, Pl.*R.*546b, *Prm.* 148b:—Pass. (c. fut. Med., Porph.*Abst.*1.37), *to be* or *become so*, Pl. *Tht.*166b, al. II. (ἀνά, ὁμοιόω) *make even again*, *PHal.*1.100 (iii B.C.). **-ώδης**, ες, *unlike*, Procl.*Inst.*203. **-ωσις**, εως, ἡ, *a making unlike, dissimilarity*, Pl.*Tht.*166c.

**ἀνομολογ-έομαι**, *agree upon* a thing, *come to an understanding*, περί τινος Pl.*R.*442e; πρὸς ἀλλήλους ib.348b; πρός τι with a view to.., Id.*Tht.*164c; τινί *with* a person, Plu.2.1070d (Act. in codd.): abs., *admit*, Muson.*Fr.*17p.92 H., *Sammelb.*4638.14. 2. *recapitulate, sum up* one's conclusions, τὰ εἰρημένα Pl.*Smp.*200e. 3. *pay money by note of hand* or *order*, Lys.ap.Phot.p.143 R., *IG*1.188.34:—hence Subst. **ἀνομολόγημα**, ατος, τό, *promissory note*, ib.17. II. Act., in later Prose, ἀ. τινί Plu.2.1070d codd.; D.18.86 uses the pf. in pass. sense, ἀνωμολόγημαι..τὰ ἄριστα πράττειν *I am allowed by all* to have done what is best, cf. ib.266, 60.4, and late Prose, Ph.1.161, al.: aor. part. Pass. -ηθείς 2.520. **-τέον**, *one must admit*, τοῦτο περὶ αὐτῶν Pl.*R.*459e, cf. *Lg.*737c. **-ητος**, ον, *agreed on again, under a renewed bill for both the principal debt and the unpaid interest*, *AB*211. II. (ἀ- priv.) *inconsistent*, τὸ ἀ. Ptol.*Tetr.*47. **-ία**, ἡ, *verbal agreement*, Hsch. II. (ἀνομόλογος) *disagreement*, Str.2.3.3, Plu.*Comp.Nic.Crass.*1. 2. *failure to lead a consistent life*, title of treatise by Chrysipp., *Stoic.*3.94, cf. Posidon. ib.112; generally, *inconsistency*, Hierocl.p.56A. **-ος**, ον, *not agreeing, incongruous*, S.E.*M.*8.331, cf. Harp. s.v. ἀσυνθετώτατον, Apollon.Cit.3: c. dat., Alex.Aphr.*in Top.*548.17. Adv. -γως Porph. *Abst.*2.40. **-ούμενος**, η, ον, *not agreeing, inconsistent*, ἵνα μὴ ἀ. ᾖ ὁ λόγος Pl.*Grg.*495a; ἀ. τοῖς προειρημένοις Arist.*APr.*48ᵃ21, cf. Chrysipp.*Stoic.*3.125. 2. *not admitted, not granted*, τὰ ἀνομολογούμενα συνάγειν Arist.*Rh.*1396ᵇ28, cf. 1400ᵃ15:—Adj., compd. of ἀ- priv. and ὁμολογούμενος; for a Verb ἀνομολογέομαι, *disagree with*, does not occur. Adv. -νως Gal.5.470.

**ἄνομος**, ον, *lawless, impious*, τράπεζα Hdt.1.162; of persons, S. *OC*142, al.; στρατός *Tr.*1096; Ἐχίονος γόνος E.*Ba.*995; of things, θυσία A.*Ag.*151; πάθη E.*Or.*1455; μοναρχία Pl.*Plt.*302e: τὰ ἄνομα *lawless acts*, Hdt.1.8: Comp. -ώτερος Pl.*Hp.Ma.*285a. Adv. -μως E.*Med.*1000, Antipho 4.1.2, Th.4.92. 2. c. gen., ἀ. θεοῦ, i.e. *without* (*the Mosaic*) *Law* and therefore without God, 1*Ep.Cor.*9.21. Adv. ἀνόμως, = χωρὶς νόμου, *Ep.Rom.*2.12. 3. *illegal*, κατοχή *POxy.* 237 vii 11 (ii A.D.). II. (νόμος II) *unmusical*, νόμος ἄ. A.*Ag.*1142 (lyr.).

**ἀνομό-σημος**, ον, *contradictory*, *PHib.*31.4.15. **-ούσιος**, ον, *differing in* οὐσία, Ps.-Alex.Aphr.*in SE*12.17. **-τᾰγής**, ές, *of a different order*, Dam.*Pr.*119; *not co-ordinated*, of lines of vision, prob. l. in Gal.*UP*10.12; cf. ὁμοταγής. **-ῦλος** [ῡ], ον, *differing in substance*, Phlp.*in de An.*526.18.

**ἀνονδόκως**· ἄνωθεν, Hsch. (fort. ἀνοκόνδως, cf. ἀνάκανδα).

**ἀνονείδιστος**, ον, *irreproachable*, Nic.Dam.p.119 D.

**ἀνόνητος**, Dor. -ᾱτος, ον, *unprofitable*, περισσὰ κἀνόνητα σώματα S.*Aj.*758; ὦ πολλὰ λέξας..κἀνόνητ' ἔπη v.l. ib.1272; ἀ. γάμος E.*Or.* 1501 (lyr.), cf. *Hel.*886; ἀ. γίγνεσθαι D.9.40, cf. Plu.2.248a; τινί Arist.*EN*1095ᵃ9, cf. *Pol.*1334ᵇ40; ἄργυρον εἰς ἀνόνατα ῥέοντα Cerc.4. 4:—neut. pl. ἀνόνητα is freq. in E. as Adv., *in vain*, as *Hec.*766, *Alc.*412 (lyr.), al.; ἀνόνητα πονεῖν Pl.*R.*486c: regul. Adv. -τως Pall. *in Hp.*2.147 D, Sch.E.*Or.*1501: Comp., ibid. II. Act., c. gen., τῶν ἀγαθῶν ἀ. τινα ποιῆσαι *deprive of all benefit from..*, D.18.141, cf. 19.315, Plu.2.800d, Nic.Dam.p.13 D.

**ἀνονόμαστος**, ον, faulty form for ἀνωνόμαστος, Gal.7.425, Hdn. *Epim.*203, Suid.

**ἀνόξυντος**, ον, *not to be written with the acute accent*, Eust.930.57.

**ἄνοος**, ον, contr. ἄνους, ουν, *without understanding, silly*, κραδίη Il.21.441; ψυχή Pl.*Ti.*44a, etc.; of persons, S.*Ant.*99; ἄνοος τε καὶ γέρων ἅμα ib.281; πλοῦτος ἄ. wealth *without wit*, *AP*9.43 (Parmen.): Comp. ἀνούστερος A.*Pr.*987: Sup. ἀνούστατος Pherecr.19 D. Adv., Comp. ἀνουστέρως S.*Fr.*589.1.

**ἀνοπαῖα**, only in Od.1.320 ὄρνις δ' ὣς ἀνοπαῖα διέπτατο, where it is variously written and explained: 1. acc. to Hdn.Gr.2.133, it is an Adv. (compd. of ἀνά, *ὄπτομαι), she flew away *unseen, unnoticed*; or, acc. to Eust., = ἄνω, ἀνωφερές, *up into the air*, cf. καρπαλίμως ἀνόπαιον Emp.51, and Ἀνόπαια, the name of the pass above Thermopylae (Hdt.7.216). 2. acc. to Aristarch., ἀνόπαια or πανόπαια, a kind of *eagle*, cf. Hebr. *'ănāphā* 'heron'. 3. acc. to Gramm. in *An.Ox.*1.83, ἀν' ὀπαῖα (= ἀνὰ ὀπήν) *up by the hole in the roof, up the smoke-vent.*

**ἀνόπιν**, Adv. *backwards*, Hsch.; *farther back*, in a book, etc., Eust.1031.46.

**ἄνοπλος**, ον, *without the* ὅπλον or *large shield*, of the Persians, who bore only γέρρα, Hdt.9.62: generally, *unarmed*, Pl.*Euthd.*299b, Onos.42.17; τὸ ἄ., opp. τὸ ὁπλιτικόν, of citizens *not entrusted with arms*, Arist.*Pol.*1289ᵇ32:—of ships, *unarmed*, Plb.2.12.3. (On the form v. ἄοπλος.)

**ἄνοπτος**, ον, *unseen*, Suid.

**ἄνορ**· νοῦς, Scythian word, Hsch., cf. Hdn.*Epim.*240.

**ἀνόρᾱτος**, ον, v.l. for ἀόρ- in Pl.*Ti.*51a, Polycharm.1.

**ἀνοργάζω**, lit. *knead up*: in Pass., ἀνωργασμένον σῶμα *relaxed*, Hp.*Int.*21. II. *toss, dandle*, παιδία Hsch. (nisi ad ἀνορταλίζειν spectat).

**ἀνόργᾰνος**, ον, *without instruments*, Plu.*Per.*16; βίος Porph.*Abst.* 1.6; κίνησις ἀ. movement *without limbs for the purpose*, of serpents, Plu.2.381b.

**ἀνόργητος**, ον, Hellenistic for ἄνοργος, Moer.12, cf. Sch.Pi.*P.* 10.33.

**ἀνοργία**, ἡ, = ἀμυησία, Hsch., Suid.

**ἀνοργίαστος**, ον, *not celebrated with orgies*, ἱερά Ar.*Lys.*898; τελεταί, i.e. *no true* mysteries, Ph.1.156. 2. of a god or person *in whose honour no orgies are held*, Pl.*Epin.*985d. II. *uninitiated*, Ph.2.268; ἀμύητος καὶ ἀ. τῶν ἱερῶν Them.*Or.*13.166c.

**ἄνοργος**, ον, *not wrathful*, Cratin.385.

**ἀνορέα**, ἡ, more common in Ion. form ἠνορέη (q. v.), Pi.*O.*8.67, al., Theoc.29.19.

**ἀνορ-έγω**, *hand up*, of the elephant's use of his trunk, Arist.*HA* 497ᵇ28. **-εκτέω**, *have no appetite*, Antyll.ap.Orib.5.29.8, Sor.2. 43. **-εκτος**, ον, *without appetite for*, ἀπολαύσεως Arist.*VV*1250ᵇ9; ἡδονῆς Andronic.Rhod.p.576 M.; περὶ τὰς ἀπολαύσεις Arist.*VV*1250ᵃ 8: abs., Sor.1.24, Plu.2.46ca, etc. Adv. ἀνορέκτως, ἔχειν Gal.10. 576. II. Pass., *not desired*, of food, Plu.2.664a. **-εξία**, ἡ, *want of desire* or *appetite*, Ti.Locr.102e, Aret.*CA*2.3.

**ἀνόρεος** [ᾰ], α, ον, (ἀνήρ) = ἀνδρεῖος, πόλεμος S.*Fr.*436.

**ἀνορθιάζω**, *call out, shout aloud*, And.1.29. II. *prick up*, τὰ ὦτα Ph.2.188, al.:—Pass., ἐγήγερται καὶ ἀνωρθίασται 1.381.

**ἄνορθος**, ον, (ἀ- priv.) perh. *sloping*, ἄ. εἰς τὸ εἴσω *IG*2².463.60; prob. corrupt in Herophil.ap.Gal.2.571.

**ἀνορθ-όω**, aor. ἀνώρθωσα E.*Alc.*1138, Isoc.5.64, etc.: plpf. with double augm. ἠνωρθώκει v.l. in Lib.*Ep.*1039: the double augm. is common in the compd. ἐπανορθόω:—*set up again, restore, rebuild*, τὸν νηόν Hdt.1.19; τὸ τεῖχος 7.208; τὸ στρατόπεδον Th.6.88, etc.; τὸ σῶμά τινος E.*Ba.*364:—Med., ἀνορθοῦσθαι τὰ πίπτοντα τῶν οἰκοδομημάτων *have* them *rebuilt*, Arist.*Pol.*1322ᵇ20. 2. *restore to health* or *well-being*, πόλιν S.*OT*46; τινά Pl.*Lg.*919d. 3. *set straight again, set right, correct*, τινά E.*Supp.*1228; τὰ ἀλλότρια κακά Pl.*R.* 346e. **-ωσις**, εως, ἡ, *restoration*, τειχῶν *PRyl.*157.13 (ii A.D.); = ἐπανόρθωσις, Ph.*Fr.*54 H.; f.l. in Plb.15.20.5, Corn.*ND*16.

**ἀνορίνω**, Aeol. impf. ὀννώριν⟨ν⟩ε, *stir up, arouse*, (sc. παφλάσμους) Alc.*Supp.*25.8.

**ἄνορκος**, ον, *bound by no oath*, Poll.1.39.

**ἀνορμ-άομαι**, Pass., *start up, try eagerly to do* a thing, c. acc. cogn., στόλον Opp.*H.*3.105.—Hsch. has the Act. in neut. signf., and so Ruf.ap.Orib.45.30.40, *mount*, of a disease. **-ητικῶς**, Adv. *with an upward rush*, Sch.Opp.*H.*5.210. **-ητος**, ον, *impetuous*, Erot. s.v. ἀνάσσυτος.

**ἀνορμίζω**, *take* [ships] *from* their *moorings*, ἐς τὸ πέλαγος τὰς ναῦς D.C.48.48:—Med., *put to sea*, Id.42.7: Pass., *anchor above*, ὑπὲρ τόπον Id.71.2.

**ἄνορμος**, ον, *without harbour*, πέτραι Anon.ap.Suid. s.v. λισσάδας πέτρας: metaph., ὑμέναιον ὃν δόμοις ἄνορμον εἰσέπλευσας S.*OT*423.

**ἀνόρνῡμι**, fut. -όρσω, *rouse, stir up*, ἀνὰ μὲν φόρμιγγ', ἀνὰ δ' αὐλὸν ὄρσομεν Pi.*N.*9.8; τινά A.R.4.1352:—Pass., ἂν δ' ἄρα Τυδεΐδης ὦρτο (Ep. aor.) *up he started*, Il.23.812, cf. Od.8.3; ἀνὰ δ' ὤρνυτ' Ἰήσων A.R.1.349.

**ἀνορούω**, poet. Verb, used by Hom. only in aor. 1 (X.*Eq.*3.7, 8.5 has pres. inf. and part.):—*start up, leap up*, abs., Il.9.193, Od.3. 149, Sapph.*Supp.*20a.11, etc.; ἐκ δὲ θρόνων ἀνόρουσαν Od.22.23; ἐξ ὕπνοιο μάλα κραιπνῶς ἀ. Il.10.162, etc.; ἐς δίφρον δ' ἀ. 11.273; so Ἠέλιος δ' ἀνόρουσε..οὐρανὸν ἐς.. Helios *went swiftly up* the sky, Od. 3.1; τοῖσι δὲ Νέστωρ ἡδυεπὴς ἀ. Il.1.248; ἀνορούσαις (Aeol. part.) Pi. *O.*7.37.

**ἀνόροφος**, ον, *roofless*, πέτρα E.*Ba.*38.

**ἀνορροπύγιος** [ῡ], ον, *without rump*, καρκίνος Arist.*HA*525ᵇ31; πτῆσις ἀ. *without help from the tail* or *rump*, of insects, ib.532ᵃ24.

**ἀνορτᾰλίζω**, *clap the wings and crow*, like a cock, Ar.*Eq.*1344.

**ἀνόρυκτος**, ον, *not obtained by digging*, ἅλες Orib.*Eup.*4.24.

**ἀνορύσσω**, Att. -ττω, pf. Pass. ἀνορώρυγμαι Men.468:—*dig up* what has been buried, τὰ ὀστέα Hdt.2.41, Lycurg.113; ὑδρίας Ar. *Av.*602; τινά Id.*Pax*372, Plu.*Ages.*20; χρυσόν Luc.*Cont.*11. 2. ἀ. τάφον *dig up, break open, destroy* it, Hdt.1.68, Isoc.16.26.

**ἀνορχέομαι**, *leap up and dance*, E.*Supp.*719; of the soul, Ph.1.379.

**ἄνορχος**, ον, *without testicles*, i.e. *castrated*, Hp.*Vict.*2.49. II. *without stones*, φοίνικες Arist.*Fr.*267.

**ἀνοσάμικτον**· ὀλιγόρρυτον ὕδωρ, Hsch.

**ἀνοσήλευτος**, ον, *untended*, S.*Fr.*264.

**ἀνόσητος**, ον, *without sickness*, S.*Fr.*1014, *Pland.*13.11 (iv A.D.).

*ἀνοσία, ἡ, (ἀ- priv., νόσος) *freedom from sickness*, Poll.3.107. II. (ἀ- priv., ὅσιος) ἀνοσίja ϝοι γένοιτυ *may he be accursed*, *Inscr.Cypr.* 135.29 H. (perh. neut. pl. ἀνόσιja); cf. sq.

ἀνόσιος, ον, more rarely α, ον E.*Tr.*1316 (lyr.), Aeschin.2.157 (dub.), and later:—*unholy, profane*, opp. ἄδικος, as ὅσιος to δίκαιος (v. ὅσιος I.1), of persons, A.*Th.*611, S.*OT*353, etc.; ἀ. ὁ θεομισής Pl. *Euthphr.*7a; ἄδικος καὶ ἀ. Id.*Grg.*505b. 2. of things, ἔργον, μόρος, στόμα, etc., Hdt.2.114, 3.65, S.*OC*981, etc.; αὐδῶν ἀνόσι' οὐδὲ ῥητά μοι Id.*OT*1289; ἀνόσια πάσχειν Antipho 2.4.7; ἀσεβὲς μηδὲν μηδὲ ἀ. X.*Cyr.*8.7.22; οὐ μόνον ἄνομον ἀλλὰ καὶ ἀ. Id.*Lac.*8.5; ἀ. νέκυς a corpse *with all the rites unpaid*, S.*Ant.*1071; ἀ. τι γεγένηται ἐμοῦ παρόντος the holy rites have been *profaned*, Antipho 5.84. II. Adv. -ίως *in unholy wise*, S.*Ph.*257; κάτω γῆς ἀ. οἰκῶν *without funeral rites*, or *through an unholy deed*, E.*El.*677.

*ἀνοσιότης, ητος, ἡ, *unholiness, wickedness*, v.l. in Pl.*Euthphr.*5d; ἀ. καὶ δεινότης τῶν πεπραγμένων Isoc.12.121.

ἀνοσιουργ-έω, *act impiously, wickedly*, Pl.*Lg.*905b, Ph.2.128, D.C.56.5, 77.12. -ημα, ατος, τό, *impious act*, Ph.2.313, Porph. *Chr.*58. *-ία, ἡ, *impiety, wickedness*, Pl.*Ep.*335b, Plu.*Arat.*54, D.C.71.30. -ός, όν, *acting impiously*, Pl.*Ep.*352c, Arist.*EN*1166ᵇ5, Ph.2.313.

*ἄνοσμος, ον, = ἄνοδμος, *without smell*, v.l. in Hp.*Acut.*63, cf. Arist. *HA*634ᵇ19, etc.; ἴχνη ἄνοσμα footsteps *that leave no scent*, Poll.5.12:—but ἄοσμος (q.v.) was preferred.

ἄνοσος, Ion. and Ep. ἄνουσος, ον, *without sickness, healthy, sound*, of persons, ἀσκηθέες καὶ ἄ. Od.14.255; ἄ. καὶ ἀγήραοι Pi.*Fr.*143, cf. Pl.*Ti.*33a; ἄπηρος, ἄ. Hdt.1.32; λῷστον δὲ τὸ ζῆν ἄ. S.*Fr.*356. Adv. ἀνόσως, διάγειν Hp.*Epid.*1.1; ζῆν Ph.1.267; ἄ. ᾤχετ' ἐς ἡμιθέους *IG* 5(2).472.13 (Megalopolis, ii/iii A.D.). 2. c. gen., ἄ. κακῶν *untouched by* ill, E.*IA*982; ἄ. πρὸς τὰ ἄλλα ἀρρωστήματα, τῶν ἄλλων ἀρρωστημάτων, Arist.*HA*604ᵃ12,22. 3. of a season, *free from sickness*, ἔτος ἄ. ἐς τὰς ἄλλας ἀσθενείας Th.2.49; ἕξις, λόγος ἄ., Plu.*Cic.*8, 2.7b. II. of things, *not causing disease, harmless*, E.*Ion* 1201.

*ἀνόστεος, ον, *boneless*, of the polypus, Hes.*Op.*524 (Lacon. acc. to Clitarch.ap.Procl. ad loc.) cf. Hp.*Epid.*2.2.19; ἀ. ἡ καρδία Arist.*PA* 666ᵇ17; τὰ περὶ τὴν κοιλίαν ib.655ᵃ2; φυὴ μελέων Opp.*H.*1.639.

*ἀνόστ-ητος, ον, *unreturning*, Orph.*A.*1269. II. *whence none return*, χῶρος ἐνέρων *AP*7.467 (Antip. Sid.), cf. Opp.*H.*3.586, etc. -ιμος, ον, *not returning*, κεῖνον ἀ. ἔθηκεν *cut off* his *return*, Od.4.182. 2. *not to be retraced*, κέλευθος E.*HF*431 (lyr.). II. (νόστος II) *giving a low yield*, of corn, Thphr.*CP*3.21.1 (Sup.); *not nutritious*, Sor.1.91. *-ος, ον, *unreturning, without return*, πάντας ὄλεσαν καὶ ἔθηκαν ἀνόστους Od.24.528; πάντες ἐγένοντο ἄ. Arist.*Fr.* 145: Sup., ἡβάσεις ἥβαν ἀνοστοτάταν *never, never to return*, *AP*7.482. II. = foreg. II, Thphr.*CP*4.13.2 (Comp.).

ἀνόστρᾰκος, ον, *with no shell*, ᾠά Sch.Nic.*Al.*295.

ἀνόσφιστος, ον, *not stolen*, Eust.1768.54.

ἀνόσφρ-αντος, ον, *that cannot be smelt*, Arist.*deAn.*421ᵇ6:—also -ητος, ον, Alex.Aphr.*de An.*52.15.

ἀνοσχήν· ἄνανδρος, Hsch.

ἀνότιστος, ον, *free from moisture, dry*, τόποι Dsc.1 *Praef.*9; κονιορτός Archig.ap.Orib.8.2.6.

ἄνοτος, ον, *without the south wind*, Hsch. s.v. βορεασμοί.

ἀνοτοτύζω, *break out into wailing*, A.*Ag.*1074, E.*Hel.*371 (lyr.).

ἀνοτότυκτον· ἀθρήνητον, Hsch. (ἀνότευκτον cod.).

ἄνου· ἄνω (Ion.), Hsch.

*ἀνούᾰτος, ον, *without ear*: *without handle*, Theoc.*Ep.*4.3.

Ἀνουβ-ιακός, ή, όν, *of Anubis*, epith. of a kind of thread, *PMag. Par.*1.1083. -ιάς, άδος, ἡ, a plant, perh. = στάχυς, ib.901. -ιδεῖον, τό, *sanctuary of A.*, Roussel *Cultes Égyptiens* 224 (Delos, ii B.C.):—also -ιεῖον, τό, ib.229,231 (ii B.C.).

ἀνουθέτητος, ον, *unwarned, unadmonished*, Isoc.2.4, D.*Ep.*3.11. 2. *that will not be warned*, Men.*Mon.*49, Plu.2.283f.

*ἀνούλεγοι· ἀνώλεθροι, Hsch.

ἄνουλος, ον, in Comp. -ότερον *less wavy*, cj. in Thphr.*HP*3.11.3.

ἄνουροι· ἄβρεκτοι, ὑψηλοί, Hsch.

ἄνους, ουν, contr. for ἄνοος.

ἀνουσίαστος, ον, = ἀνούσιος, opp. οὐσιώδης, *Corp.Herm.*2.5. II. *without the use of an* οὐσία (q.v.), *PMag.Par.*1.2441.

ἀνούσιος, ον, *without substance*, οὐδὲ ἄρα ἡ ἑτερότης ἀ. Dam.*Pr.* 192; ἀ. καὶ νεκροί Procl. *in Alc.*p.271 C., cf. Olymp. *in Alc.*p.92 C.; δύναμις, of God, opp. οὐσιώδης, Procl.*Inst.*121. Adv. -ίως Syrian. *in Metaph.*114.29. II. in Alchemy, *not affecting substance, superficial in action*, σώματα Zos.Alch.p.160 B., al.

ἀνουσιότης, ητος, ἡ, *unsubstantiality*, Simp. *in de An.*247.9.

ἀνουσίωσις, εως, ἡ, *conferring of non-existence*, Simp. *in Ph.*433.18.

ἄνουσος, ον, Ion. for ἄνοσος.

ἀνούτ-ᾰτος, ον, *unwounded* by stroke of sword, ἄβλητος καὶ ἀ. Il.4.540, cf. A.R.2.75. II. *invulnerable*, Nonn.*D.*16.157, al. III. *where no wounds are inflicted*, ἀγῶνες ib.37.774. -ητί [ῑ], Adv. *without inflicting a wound*, οὐδ' ἄρα οἵ τις ἀνουτητί γε παρέστη Il.22.371. II. *without receiving a wound*, Q.S.3.445. -ητος, ον, = ἀνούτατος, Nic.*Th.*719. II. *invulnerable*, Nonn.*D.*16.382, etc.

ἀνοῦχι, prob. some kind of *brushwood*, *PPetr.*3 p.101.

ἀνοφθαλμίᾱτος, ον, *free from ophthalmia*, Dsc.*Eup.*1.29.

ἀνόφθαλμος, ον, *without eyes*, Tz.*H.*3.219.

ἀνοφρυάζομαι, *arch one's eyebrows*: metaph., *to be supercilious*, *Com.Adesp.*842.

ἀνοχεύς, έως, ὁ, *suspensory membrane*, in pl., Aret.*SA*2.6,11.

ἀνόχευτος, ον, *non-copulating*, Arist.*HA*546ᵇ16, al.

ἀνοχέω, *raise up*, Olymp. *in Mete.*24.13.

ἀνοχή, ἡ, *holding back, stopping*, esp. of hostilities: hence mostly in pl., *armistice, truce*, X.*Mem.*4.4.17; ἀνοχὰς ποιεῖσθαι Decr.ap.D.18.164; διδόναι D.H.8.68; σπείσασθαι Plu.*Pel.*29; αἱ Καλλισθένους ἀ. Aeschin.2.31; αἱ ἑξαετεῖς ἀ. D.H.3.59; cf. ἀνοκωχή. 2. *time, opportunity*, οὐκ ἔδωκεν αὐτοῖς ἀνοχὴν ἐμβατεῦσαι Lxx 1 *Ma.*12.25; ἡμερῶν ἀ. *delay* of some days, *POxy.*1068.15 (iii A.D.). 3. pl. ἀνοχαί, = Lat. *feriae*, D.C.39.30. 4. ἀνοχαὶ δικῶν, = Lat. *iustitium*, Id.55.26. II. (ἀνέχομαι) *long-suffering, forbearance*, *Ep.Rom.*2.4, 3.26. 2. ἀνοχὴν ἀναπαύλης διδόναι *permission* to rest, Hdn.3.6.10. 3. *relief from* disease, Philum.ap.Orib.*Syn.*8.3.4. III. = ἀνατολή, Poll.4.157, Hsch.

*ἀνοχ[ικ]ός· ἀνατολικός, Hsch. II. Adv. -κῶς *connectedly*, Simp. *in de An.*285.19.

ἀνοχλ-έω, = ἀνοχλίζω, S.E.*M.*10.83. -ησία, ἡ, = ἀοχλησία, Luc.*Am.*27, D.L.2.87, Gal.6.18. -ητικός, ή, όν, *heaving upwards*. Adv. -κῶς S.E.*M.*10.83. -ίζω, *heave up*, A.R.1.1167, Opp.*H.*5.128, Hsch. 2. *heave out of the way*, A.R.3.1298. -ος, ον, *not in the way, not an impediment*, Arist.*PA*663ᵇ20 (Sup.).

ἀνοχμάζω, *hoist, lift up*, *AP*9.204 (Agath.).

ἄνοχον, τό, *evacuation of the bowels*, Thphr.*HP*3.18.13. ἄνοχος, ον, of weather, *tolerable*, *Cat.Cod.Astr.*7.184.35.

ἀνοχῠρόομαι, *fortify*, dub. in Polyaen.4.11.2.

*ἀνόχῠρος, ον, v. sub ἀνώχυρος.

ἀνοψία, ἡ, *want of fish* (ὄψον) *to eat with bread*, ἔφερον δεινῶς τὴν ἀ. Antiph.190.8; ἀνοψίαν ὑποφέρειν Plu.2.237f. II. Ion. ἀνοψίη, ἡ, = τὸ μὴ βλέπειν, Hsch. (ἀνοψοφίην cod.).

ἄνοψος, ον, (ὄψον) *without relish*, Plu.2.123b.

*ἄν-περ, = ἐάνπερ, ἤνπερ, v. ἐάν. -ποτε, = εἴθε, Sch.E.*Or.*1580.

ἀνρεία, ἡ, coined by Pl.*Cra.*413e as etym. of ἀνδρεία.

ἀνσατήρ· βουβών (Lacon.), Hsch. *ἄνσατον· ἅψασθαι, συνάψαι (Cret.), Id. ἀνσερίσασθαι· τὸ μόνον πρὸς τὸ πῦρ στῆναι (Lacon.), Id.

ἀνσπάω, poet. for ἀνασπάω.

ἄνστα, ἀνστάς, ἀνστήμεναι, ἀνστήσεις, ἀνστήσων, ἀνστήτην, poet. forms, v. ἀνίστημι. ἀνσχεθέειν, ἄνσχεο, poet. forms, v. ἀνέχω. ἀνσχετός, v. ἀνασχετός.

ἄντα, Ep. Adv. *over against, face to face*, in Hom. mostly in the phrases, ἄ. μάχεσθαι fight *man to man*, Il.19.163; ἄ. ἰδεῖν look *before one*, ib.13.184, cf. E.*Alc.*877 (lyr.); θεοῖς ἄ. ἐῴκει he was like the gods *to look at*, Il.24.630; εἴδεται ἄ. πελιδνή Nic.*Th.*238; ἄ. τιτύσκεσθαι aim *straight at them*, Od.22.266, cf. Pi.*N.*6.27; ἄ. πρός τινος *Epigr. Gr.*223.4 (Milet.). II. as Prep. with gen., like ἀντί, *over against*, Ἤλιδος ἄ. Il.2.626; ἄ. παρειάων σχομένη κρήδεμνα.. *before* her cheeks, Od.1.334; ἄντ' ὀφθαλμοῖιν 4.115; also of persons, ἄ. σέθεν *before* thee, *to* thy *face*, ib.160, cf. 22.232; so in Il.21.331, with a notion of comparison, *confronted with* thee; ἔρπει ἄ. τῷ σιδάρῳ τὸ καλῶς κιθαρίσδεν *rivals* it, Alcm.35. 2. in hostile sense, *against*, Διὸς ἄ. πολεμίζειν Il.8.428; Διὸς ἄ... ἔγχος ἀείραι ib.424; εἴ κέ μεν ἄ. στήῃς 17.29; Αἴαντος στήμεναι ἄ. ib.166.

ἄνται· ἄνεμοι, and ἀντάς· πνοάς, Hsch. (leg. ἆηται, ἀήτας).

ἀντᾰγανακτέω, *to be indignant in turn*, Oenom.ap.Eus.*PE*6.7.

ἀντᾰγαπάω, *love in turn* or *return*, in Pass., Ph.2.8, Them.*Or.*4.55d.

ἀντᾰγείρω, *rival as a collector, beggar*, Celsus ap.Orig.*Cels.*6.42.

ἀνταγλαΐζομαι, *shine brightly*, Ps.-Callisth.2.26.

ἀντᾰγοράζω, *buy with money received in payment* for something else, πωλεῖν τι καὶ ἀ. σῖτον X.*An.*1.5.5; τὰ ἀνταγορασθέντα D.35.24.

ἀντᾰγορεύω, *speak against, reply*, ἀντᾰγόρευσεν Pi.*P.*4.156. II. *gainsay, contradict*, τοῖς ἄρχουσιν Ar.*Ra.*1072.

*ἀντᾰγωνία, ἡ, *adversity*, dub. in *IG*14.1977 (pl.).

ἀντᾰγων-ίζομαι, I. *struggle against, prove a match for*, τινί, esp. in war, Hdt.5.109, Th.6.72, X.*Cyr.*1.6.8, etc.; ἀ. ταῖς παρασκευαῖς τινός D.43.81; πρὸς τοὺς βαρβάρους *Inscr.Prien.*17.15, cf. *Ep.Hebr.*12.4. 2. generally, *struggle, vie with*, τινί Th.3.38; περί τινος And.4.2; οἱ ἀνταγωνιζόμενοί τι *the parties in a lawsuit*, X. *Cyr.*8.2.27; [οἱ ἐλευθέριοι] οὐκ ἀ. περὶ τῶν χρημάτων Arist.*Rh.* 1366ᵇ8. 3. *act a part in rivalry with*, τινί Plu.*Dem.*29. II. as Pass., *to be set against*, τινί X.*Oec.*10.12. -ιστέω, *oppose, be a rival*, Arist.*Rh.*1416ᵇ14. *-ιστής, οῦ, ὁ, *opponent, competitor, rival*, *Dialex.*2.7, X.*Cyr.*1.6.8, 3.3.36, Alex.272; τινί τινος X.*Hier.* 4.6, etc.; ἀ. ἔρωτος *a rival* in love, E.*Tr.*1006, cf. Pl.*R.*554e, al.; χαλεποὶ ἀ. τοῖς βαρβάροις Isoc.4.75; ἀ. τῆς παιδείας *opponents* of their system of education, Arist.*Pol.*1338ᵇ37; ἀ. ἔχειν τινὰ ταῖς ἐπιβολαῖς Plb.2.45.5. -ιστος, ον, in Poll.3.141, is interpreted, *contending as an adversary*:—but ἀνταγωνίστως (Id.1.157) is f.l. for ἀναντ- in Lib.*Decl.*15.21.

ἀντᾰδικ-έω, *injure in return, retaliate upon*, ἀλλήλους Pl.*Tht.*173a, cf. *Cri.*49b,c, Max.Tyr.18.5. -ητέον, *one must retaliate*, ibid.

ἀντᾴδω, *sing in answer*, esp. of the partridge, *answer* when another calls, ἀ. ὡς μαχούμενος Arist.*HA*614ᵃ11, cf. *Mir.*845ᵇ25, Ael.*NA*4.16; ἀ. Μούσαις Luc.*Pisc.*6; τοῖς φθεγγομένοις Plu.2.794c; *cry out at one*, ἐγὼ δ', ἣν τοῦτο δρᾷς, ἀντᾴσομαι Ar.*Ec.*887:—Pass., στροφὴ ἀντᾳσθῆναι Poll.4.112.

ἀνταείρω, = ἀνταίρω, only in Med., ἀνταείρεσθαι χεῖράς τινι *raise one's* hands *against* one, *make war upon* him, Hdt.3.144, 7.101; or without τινί, 6.44, 7.212; also πόλεμον βασιλεῖ ἀ. 8.140.α'.

ἀντάεις, Dor. for ἀντήεις.

**ἄνταθλος**, ον, *contending against, rivalling*, τινός AP12.68 (Mel.).

**ἀνταιδέομαι**, Med., *respect in return*, αἰδουμένας ἀ. X.Cyr.8.1.28.

**ἀνταῖος**, α, ον, (ἄντα) *set over against, right opposite*, ἀνταία πληγή wound *in front, right in the breast*, S.El.195, E.Andr.844; ἀνταίαν παισεν (sc. πληγήν) S.Ant.1308. 2. *opposed to, hostile, hateful*, κνώδαλον ἀ. βροτοῖσιν A.Ch.588 (lyr.); πομπά E.IA1323 (lyr.), cf. S.Fr.72,334; θεός ib.335; τἀνταῖα θεῶν their *hostile purposes*, A.Pers.604. II. *besought with prayers*, epith. of Hecate, etc., A.R.1.1141, cf. Orph.H.41.1; ἀνταία· ..ἱκέσιος, A.(Fr.223)ap.Hsch.; ἀνταῖος Ζεύς Sch.Il.22.113.

*ἀνταίρω, Ion. ἀνταείρω (q.v.), *raise against*, χεῖρας τινι AP7.139 (so in Med., Th.3.32, 1.53); πόλεμόν τινι Plb.15.7.8; πρὸς Ἔρωτα μάχην AP12.147 (Mel.); *raise in reply*, λαμπτῆρας Aen.Tact.26.13:—Med., ὅπλα ἀνταιρόμενοι Th.1.53, cf. 3.32. II. intr., *rise up* or *rebel against, withstand*, ἀνταραί τινι Pl.Euthd.272a, D.2.24; πρός τι or τινα, Id.6.5, Plu.Pyrrh.15, D.H.6.48:—so in Med., τινί Luc.Herm.33, JTr.34. 2. of a cliff, *rise opposite to* or *in the same parallel with*, τοῖς κατὰ Μερόην τόποις Str.2.1.2, cf. 20; πρὸς τὴν Λιβύην Plu.Aem.6.

**ἀνταισχύνομαι** [ῡ], *to be ashamed in turn*, Ach.Tat.8.4.

**ἀνταιτέω**, *demand in return*, Th.4.19, Lib.Or.54.75; σμικρὰ τῆς ἀμνηστίας τὴν βουλήν App.BC3.35. II. *contest with*, τινὶ τὴν ὑπατείαν D.C.40.53.

**ἀνταιτιάομαι**, *make a countercharge*, D.C.Fr.99.

**ἀνταιωρέομαι**, *rise over against*, Plot.6.5.11.

*ἀντᾰκαῖος, ὁ, a sort of *sturgeon*, Hdt.4.53, Lync.1.9, Ael.NA14.23. 2. Adj., τάριχος ἀν καῖον Antiph.186.

**ἀντακάς**· σήμερον, and **ἀντακές**· σημεῖον (sic), Hsch.; cf. ἀνταλλές.

**ἀντᾰκολουθ-έω**, *to be reciprocally implied*, of the virtues, Chrysipp.Stoic.3.72, cf. S.E.P.1.68 (abs.); ἀ. ἀλλήλαις αἱ εὐφυΐαι Anon.in Tht.11.16; οὐδὲ ἀ. ἀλλήλαις [ἀκμὴ καὶ λαμπρότης] Hermog.Id.1.10, cf. Them.in Ph.150.29. **-ησις**, εως, ἡ, *reciprocal implication*, of the virtues, Stoic.3.76, Procl.in Alc.p.319C. **-ία**, ἡ, = foreg., Stoic.2.121; *correspondence*, Iamb.in Nic.p.39P. **-ος**, ον, *reciprocally implied*, τὸ ἀ. ἀλλήλαις Eustr.in EN311.15: abs., *corresponding*, ἕξις dub. in Phld.Rh.1.27S. (cf. Supp.15).

**ἀντᾰκοντίζω**, *hurl against in return*, λίθον D.C.59.28.

**ἀντᾰκούω**, fut. -ούσομαι S.Aj.1141, *hear in turn*, ἀντὶ τῶν εἰρημένων ἴσ' ἀντάκουσον Id.OT544; ἅ. γ' εἶπας ἀντήκουσας E.Heracl.1014 (cj.); κἀμοῦ νῦν ἀντάκουσον Id.Supp.569; ἀντακούσει τοῦτον ὡς τεθάψεται S.Aj.1141: abs., *listen in return*, ἀ. ἐν μέρει A.Eu.198, cf. Crates Com.5D.: also in Prose, X.An.2.5.16, Lib.Decl.5.89.

**ἀντακροάομαι**, *hear in turn*, Ar.Lys.527.

**ἀντακρωτήριον**, τό, *opposite headland*, Str.6.1.1.

**ἀντᾰλαζονεύομαι**, *boast in reply*, Eust.590.11.

**ἀντᾰλᾰλάζω**, *return a shout*, of friendly armies, Plu.Pyrrh.32, Flam.4; of an echo, A.Pers.390.

**ἀνταλλάγ-ή**, ἡ, *exchanging, exchange, barter*, Gloss., Simp.in Ph.1350.32. **-μα**, ατος, τό, *that which is given* or *taken in exchange*, φίλου *for* a friend, E.Or.1157, cf. Lxx Jb.28.15, al.; τῆς ψυχῆς Ev.Matt.16.26, cf. Ph.Fr.110H. **-ος**, ον, *exchanged for another*, Men.16,254,513.

**ἀνταλλα-κτέον**, *one must give in exchange*, τινός *for* a thing, D.19.223. **-κτης**, ου, ὁ, *one who requites*, τῶν κακῶν Phld.Mort.17 (pl.). **-κτος**, ον, *taken as equivalent*, πρός τι Porph.Abst.1.51. **-σσω**, Att. -ττω, *exchange* one thing *with* another, δάκρυα δ' ἀνταλλάσσετε τοῖς τῆσδε μέλεσι E.Tr.351; τὴν ἀξίωσιν τῶν ὀνομάτων ἐς τὰ ἔργα ἀ. they *changed* the signification of the names in relation to things, Th.3.82; τὴν ψυχὴν τοῦ χρυσίου Poll.3.113. II. more freq. in Med., *take in exchange*, ἄνδρα A.Ch.133; ἀνταλλάσσεσθαί τί τινος *take* one thing *in exchange for* another, E.Hel.1088, etc.; τι ἀντί τινος D.16.5; ἀνταλλάσσεσθαι τῇ διανοίᾳ *interchange* in thought, Pl.Tht.189c; θάνατον ἀνταλλάξεται *shall receive* death *in exchange*, i.e. as a punishment, E.Ph.1633:—so in Pass., ἀντηλλαγμένου τοῦ ἑκατέρων τρόπου *having made an interchange* of each other's custom, i.e. having each adopted the way of the other, Th.4.14. 2. *give in exchange*, μηδεμιᾶς χάριτος μηδ' ὠφελίας τὴν εἰς τοὺς Ἕλληνας εὔνοιαν D.6.10.

**ἀνταλλές**· ταύτης τῆς ἡμέρας, Hsch.; cf. ἀντακάς, ἀντακές.

*ἄνταλλος, ον, *exchanged*, Sch.D.T.p.343H.

*ἀντᾰμείβομαι, *exchange* one thing *with* another, ὅταν δελφῖσι θῆρες ἀνταμείψωνται νομόν Archil.74.7. II. c. acc. pers., *repay, requite, punish*, ἀνταμείβεσθαί τινα κακοῖς Id.65; κακαῖσι ποιναῖς A.Pr.225; παθὼν κακῶς κακοῖσιν ἀντημείβετο Id.Th.1054; ἀνταμειψόμεσθά σ' ὥσπερ εἰκὸς ἀντὶ τῶνδε Ar.Th.723. III. *answer again*, τοῖσδε Hdt.9.79; πρὸς τοὺς φίλους οἷ' ἀνταμείβει ῥήματ' S.OC814; τινὰ οὐδέν ib.1273; also ὑμᾶς..τοῖσδ' ἀνταμείβομαι λόγοις E.Andr.154.

*ἀντάμειψις [ᾰμ], εως, ἡ, *exchanging, requital*, v.l. in Lxx Ps.118(119).112, Hsch.

**ἀνταμελέω**, in fut. Pass. ἀνταμεληθήσομαι, *neglect in turn*, Ph.2.275.

**ἀνταμιλλᾶσθαι**· ἀντερίζειν, Hsch.

**ἀντᾰμοιβαῖος**, sc. πούς, the foot ◡ ◡ – – ◡, Diom.1.481K.

**ἀντᾰμοιβή**, ἡ, *interchange*, πυρὸς ἀ. τὰ πάντα καὶ πῦρ ἁπάντων Heraclit.90. 2. *repayment, requital*, εὐεργεσίας Charito 5.2.

*ἀντᾰμοιβός, όν, v. ἀντημοιβός.

**ἀντᾰμύνομαι** [ῡ], Med., *defend oneself against another, resist*, Th.4.19. II. *requite*, ἐχθρὸν κακοῖς S.Ant.643; οἱ ἀνταμυνόμενοι Th.3.84.

**ἀνταμφοδέω**, (ἄμφοδον) *miss* a person *in the street* going to meet him, BGU1030.5 (iii A.D.).

**ἀνταναβῐβάζω**, *make go up in turn*, X.HG3.2.15.

**ἀνταναβοάω**, *cry out in answer* or *opposition*, App.BC2.131.

**ἀνταναγιγνώσκω**, *read and compare*, Cratin.386; νόμους D.20 Arg. ii 8, cf. PPetr.3p.50 (iii B.C.).

**ἀντανάγω** [ᾰγ], *lead up against*, esp. ἀ. νέας *put* ships *to sea against*, Hdt.6.14, cf. Th.7.37: also ἀ. ναυσὶν ἓξ καὶ ὀγδοήκοντα ib.52: more freq. abs. in same sense, whether in Act., as Id.8.38, X.HG2.1.23, or in Med., as Th.4.13, X.HG1.1.5:—Pass., ναυσὶν ἀνταναχθεὶς D.S.13.71:—generally, *attack*, ἀντανήγετο πρὸς τὸ μειράκιον Pl.Erx.398e. 2. *raise in opposition*, [ὄρος] τῇ Οἴτῃ Philostr.VA4.23. 3. *bring up instead*, AP9.285 (Phil.).

**ἀνταναίρ-εσις**, εως, ἡ, *corresponding diminution*, Arist.Top.158$^b$33. II. *alternate removal*, Eust.1397.44. III. *cancellation*, Simp.in Ph.1237.23. *-ετέος, α, ον, *to be struck off*, PTeb.61(b).220 (ii B.C.). **-ετικός**, ή, όν, *cancelling opposite sides of an account, striking a balance*: metaph., εὐλογιστία ἐστὶν ἐπιστήμη -κή Stoic.3.64. *-έω, *strike out of an account*, D.18.231:—Pass., *to be cancelled correspondingly*, Arist.Metaph.1040$^a$22, Demad.59; *to be struck off*, PTeb.60.111, al. (ii B.C.). 2. *kill in return*, Ph.2.321 (Pass.). 3. *set off against, deduct*, Sammelb.4369(a).10, al. (iii B.C.), PRyl.154.33 (i A.D., Pass.); prob. l. for ἀνταναίρειν (= ἀνθυφελεῖν), Ar.Fr.12D. 4. Med., *resume*, ἀποβεβληκὼς τὴν ἁλουργίδα οὐκέτι ἀντανείλετο Agath.4.29.

**ἀντανά-κλᾰσις**, εως, ἡ, *reflection of light*, Placit.4.14.3, cf. Vett.Val.1.14, Ath.Med.ap.Orib.9.12.1 (pl.); also, of sound, *echo*, Plu.2.502d. 2. *bending back*, ἀγκίστρου Sch.Opp.H.1.216. II. *use of a word in an altered sense*, Lat. *contraria significatio*, Quint.Inst.9.3.68, Sch.A.R.1.746. **-κλασμός**, ὁ, *reflexive sense*, of words, A.D.Pron.43.12. **-κλαστος**, ον, *reciprocal*, προσηγορία Priscian.Inst.11.1. **-κλάω**, *reflect*, φῶς v.l. in Plu.2.696a:—Pass., ἀντανακλᾶται ἀκτὶς S.E.M.5.82; ὀφθαλμοὶ ἀλλήλοις ἀντανακλώμενοι *reflected* one in another, Ach.Tat.1.9. 2. of sound, in Pass., *to be reflected* or *echoed*, Lxx Wi.17.19, Placit.4.20.2. 3. *bend back*, τὸν ἀγκῶνα Heliod.ap.Orib.49.13.8. 4. Gramm., in Pass., *to be reflexive*, of pronouns, A.D.Synt.175.12, cf. Pron.28.3, al. 5. *cause to revert*, in writing, εἴς τι πάλιν ἀ. τὸ πέρας CPHerm.18.11. **-κοπή**, ἡ, *recoil*, κυμάτων Arist.Mu.396$^a$19. **-κόπτω**, *throw back again*, Phryn.PS p.61B. **-κράζω**, *cry out in turn* or *reply*, App.Mith.26. **-λαμβάνω**, *take over instead*, Ptol.Phas.p.11H.

**ἀντανᾱλίσκω**, *destroy in return*, E.Or.1165.

**ἀντανά-λῠσις**, εως, ἡ, *counteraction, incongruity of position*, Vett.Val.186.28, Antioch.Astr. in Cat.Cod.Astr.8(3).107. **-λύω**, Astrol., *counteract*, Vett.Val.289.17 (Pass.). **-μένω**, *wait instead of* taking active measures, c. inf., Th.3.12. **-παύομαι**, Med., *rest correspondingly*, Polyaen.1.14. **-πίμπλημι**, *fill in return*, v.l. in X.HG2.4.12. **-πλέκω**, *plait in rivalry with*, ἄνθεα τοῖς Μελεαγρείοις στεφάνοις AP4.2 (Phil.). **-πληρόω**, *fill up*, τὴν θέσιν τοῦ ὀνόματος A.D.Synt.14.1; τὰ ὑστερήματα τῶν θλίψεων τοῦ Χριστοῦ Ep.Col.1.24; ἀ. πρὸς τὸν εὐπορώτατον ἀεὶ τοὺς ἀπορωτάτους *put in* the poorest *so as to balance* the richest, D.14.17. **-πλήρωσις**, εως, ἡ, *filling up again*, Epicur.Ep.1p.11U.

**ἀντανα-σηκόω**, *compensate*, IG14.956A19. **-τρέχω**, *return*, of the foreskin, Paul.Aeg.6.60. **-φέρω**, *bring back in turn*, ἀ. τὴν πίστιν Plu.2.2cc. II. abs., *make compensation*, τῇ λοιπῇ δόξῃ πρὸς τὴν δυσφημίαν Them.Or.7.99c. **-χωρέω**, *give ground in turn*, Aristid.Or.23(42).47.

**ἄντανδρος**, ον, *instead of a man, as a substitute*, ἀντί τινος Luc.DMort.16.2, etc.

**ἀντάνειμι**, (εἶμι *ibo*) *rise so as to balance*, τινί Th.2.75.

**ἀντανεμία**, ἡ, *contrary wind*, Simp.in de An.60.32.

**ἀνταν-έχω**, *hold up in turn* or *in reply*, πυρσούς Polyaen.6.19.2, cf. 1.40.3, Men.Prot.p.72D. **-ισόω**, *make equal, adjust, compensate*, Lib.Or.59.161 (dub.):—Pass., Them.in Ph.137.21. **-ίστημι**, *set up against* or *in rivalry*, λόγον Plu.2.40e; τρόπαιον D.C.42.48; τί τινι Plu.2.348d. II. Pass., with aor. 2 Act., *rise up against*, τινὶ ἐς χεῖρας S.Tr.441, cf. Plu.Sull.7; *rise one against another*, Id.2.723b. **-ίσωμα** [ῐ], ατος, τό, *an equivalent*, J.AJ18.9.7. **-ίσωσις** [ῐσ], εως, ἡ, *balancing, equalizing*, Boethus ap.Porph.ap.Eus.PE11.28, David Proll.214.11, Simp.in Cael.458.2.

**ἀντᾰνοίγω**, *open against*, ἀ. ὄμματα κεραυνοῖς *face* them, Longin.34.4.

**ἀντάντάν**· ἐπίβουλον, ἀντίδικον, Hsch.

**ἀντᾰνύω**, v. ἀνατανύω.

**ἄνταξ**· ἐν μέρει, Hsch. (cf. ὑπαντάξ).

*ἀντάξιος, α, ον, also ος, ον Theoc.17.114:—*worth just as much as*, c. gen., ψυχῆς ἀ. *worth* life *itself*, Il.9.401; πολλῶν ἀ. ἄλλων 11.514; ἕκαστος δέκα ἀνδρῶν ἀ. *worth as much as* ten, Hdt.7.103, cf. 2.148, Pl.Lg.73cd, X.Mem.2.10.3 etc.; *worthy of*, τέχνας Theoc. l.c. 2. abs., *worth as much, worth no less*, Il.1.136.

**ἀνταξιόω**, *demand as an equivalent* or *in turn*, Th.6.16: c. dupl. acc., ἀνταξιῶσαι δωρεὰν αὐτόν Macho ap.Ath.13.579a.

**ἀνταπαιτέω**, *demand in return*, Th.3.58, 5.17, Plu.Sol.3:—Pass., *to be called on for* a thing *in turn*, λόγον Id.Cat.Mi.53.

*ἀνταπᾰμείβομαι, Med., *obey in turn*, ῥήτραις Tyrt.4.6.

**ἀντᾰπᾰτάω**, *deceive in turn*, τινά J.AJ5.8.11.

**ἀντᾰπειλέω**, *threaten in turn*, τινί Ph.2.469, cf. Them.Or.7.95b.

**ἀνταπερύκω** [ῠ], *keep off in turn*, AP15.14 (Theoph.).

**ἀνταπέχω**, *receive in return*, χάριτάς τινος Anatolian Studies p.343.

**ἀνταπο-δείκνῡμι** or **-ύω**, *prove in return* or *answer*, X.*Smp.*2.22; τὸ ἀντικείμενον Arist.*Rh.*1403ᵃ7. 2. *appoint instead*, D.C.40.43. ®**-δίδωμι**, *give back, repay, tender in repayment* or *requital*, Batr.186; ἀ. τὸ ὅμοιον, τὸ ἴσον, Hdt.1.18, Th.1.43; χάριν Pherecr.2 D.; τὴν ἴσην Arist.*Rh.*1379ᵇ7; ἀ. τροφεῖα Lys.6.49; ἀρετήν Th.4.19; ὕβριν Plu.2.825c; τὰ αὐτὰ ἀ. *react* in the same way, Pl.*Ti.*7 e; of counter-arguments, Id.*Prm.*128d: abs., *pay back*, Th.3.40, Arist.*Rh.*1367ᵃ21. 2. *take vengeance*, Lxx *De.*32.35, al., *Ep.Rom.*12.19. II. *assign as a balance*, ἐναντίαν γένεσιν Pl.*Phd.*71e. 2. *make convertible*, τὴν μεταφορὰν τὴν ἐκ τοῦ ἀνάλογον Arist.*Rh.*1407ᵃ15:—Pass., Demetr.*Eloc.*79. b. Gramm., *make to correspond*, of correlatives (e.g. τοιοῦτος, οἷος), in Pass., A.D.*Conj.*254.19, *Synt.*54.5, al.; so of μέν..δέ, Arist.*Rh.*1407ᵃ23, Demetr.*Eloc.*53, cf. Hermog.*Id.*1.4, al. 3. intr., *answer to, correspond with*, εἰ μὴ ἀνταποδιδοίη τὰ ἕτερα τοῖς ἑτέροις Pl.*Phd.*72a, cf. b; οὐκ ἀνταποδίδωσι τὸ ὅμοιον *there is* no similar *correspondent*, Arist.*Mete.*347ᵇ32, cf. *IA* 707ᵇ16, Ps.-Alex.Aphr.*in SE*192.14. 4. *give back words, exchange* 'tu quoque's', Pl.*Phdr.*236c. III. *deliver in turn*, τὸ σύνθημα X.*Cyr.*3.3.58 (Pass.); *explain in turn*, Pl.*Ti.*87c. IV. *give back* a sound, of an echo, Plu.*Sull.*19; of troops, κραυγὴν ἀ. Id.*Tim.*27. **-δομα**, ατος, τό, *repayment, requital*, whether of good or evil, Lxx *Si.*12.2, 14.6, al., *Ev.Luc.*14.12, *Ep.Rom.*11.9. ®**-δοσις**, εως, ἡ, *giving back in turn*, opp. ἀποδοχή, Th.4.81; *rendering, requiting, repayment*, Arist.*EN*1133ᵃ3, 1163ᵃ11, al.; χάριτος Men.*Mon.*330, D.S.20.100; τῶν εὐεργεσιῶν Phld.*Piet.*14; *retribution*, Lxx *Is.*61.2, 63.4, al.; *reprisals*, γίγνεται ἀ. ἔκ τινος Plb.5.30.6; *reward*, Lxx *Ps.*18(19).11, *Ep.Col.*3.24. II. *turning back, opposite direction* or *course*, of a current, ἀ. ποιεῖσθαι Plb.4.43.5, etc., cf. Plu.2.13 b. 2. *responsive sound*, Arist.*Aud.*803ᵃ31. III. *alternation*, e.g. of action and reaction, περιόδων πρὸς ἀλλήλας Hp.*Aph.*1.12; *reaction*, prob. in Epicur.*Ep.*2 p.48 U., cf. Thphr.*Vent.*10. 2. Rhet., *parallelism* or *opposition of clauses* in a periodic sentence, Demetr.*Eloc.*23, cf. 250; in a simile, *correspondence with* the object of comparison, Quint.*Inst.*8.3.77. b. Gramm., *correlativity* of words such as τοιοῦτος, οἷος, A.D.*Synt.*54.1. c. *answering clause*, Hermog.*Id.*1.11, 2.1; v.l. in A.D.*Synt.*20.6. 3. *capping verses*, as a subject of competition, *Michel*913 (Teos). **-δοτέον**, *one must repay*, τὴν ἀξίαν ὧν ἔπαθεν Arist.*EN*1163ᵃ2; τιμήν 1163ᵇ14; χάριν 1164ᵇ26; τὰς εὐεργεσίας ib.31. II. ἀ. ἐξὸν τινὶ *one must make* it *correspond to..*, Pl.*Phlb.*40d. **-δοτικός**, ή, όν, = ἀμοιβαῖος, Sch.Opp.*H.*2.255. II. Gramm., *belonging to* or *marking* ἀνταπόδοσις, Plb.Rh.p.107 S.; of pronouns, *correlative*, A.D.*Adj.*158.24, *Conj.*237.9, al. Adv. **-κῶς** Sch.A.R.1.5. **-δύομαι** [ῡ], *strip, prepare for a contest with*, τινί Philostr.*Im.*2.19. **-θνήσκω**, *die* or *am killed in requital*, ἀνταποθανεῖν τὸν ἀποκτείναντα Antipho 5.10; τοῦ ἐμψύχου δόγματος ὃ ἀνεῖλε Ph.1.04.

®**ἀντάποινα**, f.l. for ἀντίποινα, S.*Ph.*316, E.*HF*755; also in *POxy.*1381.234.

**ἀνταπο-κατάστᾰσις**, εως, ἡ, *renewal by substitution*, *Corp.Herm.*11.2. 2. of planets, *the opposite position to* ἀποκατάστασις, Doroth.ap.*Cat.Cod.Astr.*2.196.19. **-καταστατικός**, ή, όν, Astrol., *opposite to the position of* ἀποκατάστασις, σελήνη Max.*Epit.*p.80 L. **-κρίνομαι** [ῑ], Med., *answer again*, Lxx *Jb.*16.8, *Ev.Luc.*14.6; *argue against*, τινί *Ep.Rom.*9.20. II. *correspond to*, Nicom.*Ar.*1.8.10, 11. **-κρῐσις**, εως, ἡ, *correspondence* (cf. foreg. II), ib.8, Iamb.*in Nic.*p.36 P. **-κτείνω**, *kill in return*, Hdt.7.136, A.*Ch.*121, E.*Hec.*262, Ar.*Ach.*326, X.*HG*2.4.27, etc. **-λαμβάνω**, *receive* or *accept in return*, ἑστίασιν Pl.*Ti.*27b; χάριν D.20.46.

**ἀνταπόλλῡμι**, *destroy in return*, E.*Ion*1328, Pl.*Cri.*51a. II. Pass. and Med., with pf. 2 Act., *perish in turn*, αὐτὸς ἀνταπωλόμην E.*Hel.*106, cf. *IT*715; ὑπὲρ ἀνδρὸς ἑκάστου δέκα ἀνταπόλλυσθαι Hdt.3.14.

**ἀνταπο-λογέομαι**, *speak for the defence* or *in reply*, Is.5.17, D.C.50.. **-παίζω**, *lose what one has won at play*, ἀστραγάλους Menecr.1 D. **-παλσις**, εως, ἡ, *rebounding, revulsion*, Cass.*Pr.*26. **-πέρδω**, Lat. *oppedere*, πρὸς τὰς βροντὰς Ar.*Nu.*293.

**ἀνταπορέω**, *raise questions in turn*, S.E.*M.*1.231.

®**ἀνταπο-στέλλω**, *send in exchange*, ὁμήρους Plb.21.43.22; *send backwards and forwards*, πρέσβεις D.C.50.2, cf. Aen.Tact.31.9 (Pass.); *refer* one *back again*, ἐπί τι S.E.*M.*8.86; of an echo, τὰς ἀνακλάσεις ἀ. Plu.2.248c. **-στρέφω**, *turn back again*, Tz.*H.*5.903. **-στροφή**, ἡ, *turning away from one another*, of places which face opposite ways, Str.6.1.5. **-ταφρεύω**, *cut off in turn by trenches*, App.*BC* 2.61. **-τειχίζω**, *wall off, fortify on the other side*, D.C.43.7. **-τίνω** [ῑ], *requite, repay*, *AP*9.223 (Bianor), Orph.*Fr.*32d, c. **-τος**· συνδεδεμένος, Hsch. ®**-φαίνω**, *show on the other hand*, Th.3.38, 67. **-φέρω**, *catch in turn*, of a ball, Poll.9.107.

**ἀντάποχον**, τό, *counter-receipt*, *POxy.*1542.1 (iv A.D.), *BGU*974.10 (iv A.D.).

**ἀντάπτομαι**, Ion. for ἀνθάπτομαι.

**ἀνταπ-ωθέω**, *repel in turn*, Arist.*Pr.*936ᵇ35:—Pass., Id.*Somn.Vig.*457ᵇ23. **-ωσις**, εως, ἡ, *mutual repulsion*, *Placit.*2.23.2.

**ἀνταρ**· ἀετός (Etruscan), Hsch. 2. = δίασμα, Euph.147.

**ἀντάρης**, ου, ὁ, *the star α Scorpii*, Heph.Astr.1.3, Ptol.*Calend.*p.214 W., Id.*Alm.*8.1.

**ἀντᾰριθμ-έω**, *count against one another*, Paus.10.20.1. **-ητέον**, ἑκάστῳ σταγόνι τοὺς ἴσους [ὀδόντας] Poll.2.93.

®**ἀνταρκέω**, *hold out against*, τοῖς παροῦσιν Th.7.15; πρός τι Plu.*Cleom.*30. II. abs., *hold out, persist*, Ar.*Eq.*540, Isoc.6.79, 19.26: c. part., τρέφουσα..ἀντήρκεσεν D.C.68.25.

**ἀνταρκτικός**, ή, όν, *antarctic*, πόλος Arist.*Mu.*392ᵃ4; κύκλος Gem.5.16; without κύκλος, ib.39; ζώνη *Placit.*3.14.1.

®**ἀντ-αρσία**, ἡ, *insurrection*, Lyd.*Ost.*33, *Cat.Cod.Astr.*7.171. ®**-αρσις**, εως, ἡ, = foreg., Sm.4*Ki.*11.14. **-αρτης**· τύραννος, ἐπιβαίνων βασιλεῖ, Hsch.

**ἄνταρχος**, ὁ, *pro-magistrate*, *Gloss.*

**ἀντάρχων**, οντος, ὁ, *vice-president*, τοῦ ἀγῶνος *IG*2².1077, cf. ib.12(2).35e (Mytil.); *pro-magistrate*, *SIG*785.17 (Chios), *POxy.*907.21 (iii A.D.); ἀ. τῶν στρατηγῶν *AJA*18.329 (Sardes, i B.C.).

**ἀντασπάζομαι**, *welcome, greet in turn*, X.*Cyr.*1.3.3; *return greeting*, Hierocl.*Facet.*7; *receive kindly*, X.*Cyr.*5.5.42, Pl.Com.12 D., Plu.*Tim.*38.

**ἀνταστράπτω**, *lighten against*, ἀστραπαῖς D.C.59.28.

**ἀντάτας**, α, ὁ, (ἄτη) *surety*, *GDI*5015.23 (Gortyn).

**ἀντατιμάζω**, *requite with dishonour*, prob. cj. in S.*Aj.*1339.

**ἀνταυγ-άζω**, = ἀνταυγέω, πρὸς ἥλιον Hld.1.2, cf. 9.14. II. trans., *expose to the light, illuminate*, ἡλίῳ βίον ἀ. Ph.2.260. **-ασία**, ἡ, *reflection of light*, *Gloss.*:—also **-εια** or **-ία**, ἡ, *Placit.*2.20.12, X.*Cyn.*5.18, Plu.2.921b, Ps.-Hp.*Hebd.*1.52; ἡλίου Onos.29.2; τῆς χιόνος *from* the snow, D.S.17.82; *shining in one's face*, ἡλίου Ascl.*Tact.*12.10. **-έω**, *reflect light*, Hp.*Carn.*17, Arist.*Pr.*932ᵃ27, Chaerem.14; πρὸς Ὄλυμπον Emp.44; φάσγανον ἀνταυγεῖ φόνον *flashes back* murder, E.*Or.*1519; *gleam, glitter*, Eub.56. **-ής**, ές, *reflecting light, sparkling*, κάλλος Sannyr.1 D.; κέραι Ar.*Th.*902; χιών D.S.17.82: pr. n. Ἀνταύγης, of the sun, Orph.*Fr.*237.

**ἀνταυδάω**, *address face to face*, τινά S.*El.*1478.

®**ἀνταυλέω**, *play on the flute against*, τινί Agath.4.23.

**ἀνταΰω**, *sound in turn, answer*, οἱ ἀντάϋσε [ῡ] βροντᾶς φθέγμα Pi.*P.*4.197, cf. Opp.*C.*2.78.

**ἀνταφαιρ-έω**, *take away in return*, in Med., Antipho 4.1.7:—Act., intr., *diminish in turn*, Aristid.*Or.*23(42).50, cf. 2.309 J. II. *subtract from the opposite side*, and **-εσις**, εως, ἡ, *subtraction from the opposite side*, Nicom.*Ar.*1.13.

**ἀνταφεστιάω**, *feast in return*, Pl.*Ti.*17b.

**ἀνταφίημι** [φῑ], *let go in turn*, δάκρυ ἀ. *let* the tear *fall in turn*, E.*IA*478. II. *send back*, σφαῖραν Poll.9.107.

**ἀντάω**, Ep. impf. ἤντεον Il.7.423: I. c. dat. pers., *come opposite to, meet face to face, meet with*, ἥ οἱ ἔπειτ' ἤντησ' ib.6.399; ἤντεον ἀλλήλοισιν 7.423; so also in Trag., ἀνέμοις ἀ. A.*Supp.*36; πατρί S.*Tr.*902, etc. II. = ἀντιάω, c. gen., 1. c. gen. pers., *meet* in battle, εἴ κεν πάντων ἀντήσομεν Od.16.254, cf. Il.16.423: also without any hostile sense, σπέρμα μὲν ἄντασ' Ἐρεχθειδᾶν by lineage *she reached, went up to* the Erechtheidae, S.*Ant.*982. 2. c. gen. rei, *meet with, take part in, partake in* or *of*, μάχης, δαίτης, Il.7.158, Od.3.44; κατάλεξον ὅπως ἤντησας ὀπωπῆς how thou *hast gained* sight of him, ib.17.44, cf. 3.97; so ἀ. ξεινίων Hdt.2.119; ἀλώσιος Pi.*O.*10(11).42; ἀ. τινὸς ὑπό τινος *meet with* such and such treatment from another, Hdt.1.114; σφῷν..θεοὺς ἀρῶμαι μή ποτ' ἀντῆσαι κακῶν S.*OC*1445. III. c. acc., ἥν νιν πομπαῖς ἀντήσῃς E.*IA*150 (s.v.l.).—The simple Verb never in Com. or Att. Prose; but cf. ἀπαντάω.

**ἀντεγγράφω** [ᾰφ], *insert* one name *instead of* another, Arist.*Ath.*36.2, D.25.73 (Pass.).

**ἀντεγείρω**, *raise* or *build instead*, D.C.69.12; *build in opposition*, τί τινι App.*Pun.*114.

**ἀντεγκᾰλέω**, *make a counter-claim*, D.40.14. 2. *bring a counter-charge*, τινί Isoc.17.12, D.H.8.64, Plu.*Ant.*55, etc.; ἀλλήλοις δώρων Hermog.*Stat.*3.

**ἀντέγκειμαι**, Pass., *to be urgent on the other side*, Eun.*VS* p.470 B. II. *to be inserted in place of* another letter (as θ for ε), Eust.1863.56.

®**ἀντέγκλημα**, ατος, τό, *counter-claim* or *-charge*, Hermog.*Stat.*2, cf. 11: pl., Corn.*Rh.*p.387 H.

**ἀντεγκληματικός**, ή, όν, *of* or *for a counter-accusation*, ἀντίθεσις Hermog.*Stat.*6, 12; τὸ -κόν Antipho 4.2 Arg.; τὰ -κά Aps.p.235 H. Adv. **-κῶς** Sch.A.R.1.834.

**ἀντεγχειρίζω**, *entrust to* another *instead*, τινὶ δίκας D.C.60.24.

**ἀντεγχέω**, *pour in instead*, Gal.18(1).282.

**ἀντεικ-άζω**, fut. -άσομαι Pl.*Men.*80c: aor. -ήκασα Ar.*V.*1311, subj. -εικάσω Pl. l.c.:—*compare in return*, τινά τινι Ar. l.c.: c. acc., Pl. l.c.:—hence **-ασία**, ἡ, Sch.Ven.Il.8.560.

**ἀντειλέω**, *unwind in opposite direction*, Orib.49.22.18 (Pass.).

**ἀντεῖν**· ὁ ἐναντίος τῇ ἀγωγῇ, Hsch.

**ἀντείνω**, poet. for ἀνατείνω.

**ἀντεῖπον**, aor. 2 without any pres. (cf. ἀντερῶ, ἀντιλέγω, ἀνταγορεύω), *speak against* or *in answer, gainsay*, c. dat., S.*OC*999, etc.; ἀ. τινὶ δεομένῳ Th.1.136: abs., οὐδὲν ἀντειπεῖν ἔχω A.*Pr.*51; ἀ. πρός τινα or τι, Th.3.61, X.*HG*3.3.3; *oppose*, Pl.*Thg.*131a; ἀ. ὑπέρ τινος *speak* in one's defence, Ar.*Th.*545: c. acc. cogn., ἀ. ἔπος *utter* a word *of contradiction*, E.*IA*1391; δύο λόγω περὶ τῶν αὐτῶν ἀντειπεῖν *speak on both sides of* a question, Isoc.10.1; τούτῳ ἂν δίκαιον λόγον ἀντείποιμι Pl.*Ap.*28b. 2. κακῶς ἀ. τινά *malign* him *in turn*, S.*Ant.*1053.

**ἀντείρομαι**, Ion. aor. -ειρόμην, Att. -ηρόμην:—*ask in turn*, Hdt.1.129, 3.23, X.*Cyr.*2.2.22: in part., Plu.2.739b.

®**ἀντεισ-άγω** [ᾰγ], *introduce, import instead*, D.9.39 (Pass.), Pl.*Ax.*369e, Men.402.16, etc. II. *bring in to office*, etc., *in turn*, ἀλλήλους εἰς ἐπαρχίας κτλ. Plu.*Caes.*14. III. *restore*, Gal.6.75, al. ®**-ἀγωγή**, ἡ, *compensatory antithesis* (as οἰκτρόν..σεμνὸν δέ), Alex.*Fig.*1.25, Zonae.*Fig.*20. **-ακτέον**, v.l. for ἀντεισενεκτέον,

v. 2. *one must restore*, Gal.1.393. **-βάλλω**, intr., *make an* road *in reprisal*, D.C.48.21. **-δύνω** [ῡ], *enter instead*, εἰς τοὺς ρους Eust.1111.45. **-ειμι**, (εἶμι *ibo*) *enter in turn* or *in return*, mp.*inPh.*573.4. **-ενεκτέον,** *one must introduce instead*, Hermog. *tat.*3. **-έρχομαι,** *enter in turn* or *instead*, Aristid.*Or.*37(2).27, eroSpir.2.36, Them.*inPh.*113.26. **-κρίνομαι** [ῑ], *to be introduced* place of, Hero *Spir.*1.3. ⊛**-οδιάζω,** *bring in, introduce in turn*, ch.D.T.p.72 H. **-φέρω,** *contribute in return*, τὰς εἰσφοράς Ar. ys.654 : metaph., οὐδὲ τυχόντα ἔρανον ἀλλήλαις Gal.*UP*8.7. II. όμον ἀ. *substitute a new* law *for* an old one, D.20.97 ; καινὰ δαιμόνια D.C.52.36. III. *introduce as a counter measure*, Onos.42. 2. **-φορά,** ἡ, *contribution in return*, *Milet.*3 No.147.22 (iii B.C.).

**ἀντεκ-βάλλομαι,** *to be produced in an opposite direction*, *Theol. Ar.*26 ; ἀλλήλοις *to be correspondingly projected*, Anon.*in EN*224. 24. **-δικος,** ὁ, *deputy defensor*, *POxy.*1987 (vi A.D.), cf. *PLond.*5. 1709.80 (vi A.D.). **-θέω,** *rush out on the other side from*, Arr.*An.* 1.21.3. **-θλίβω** [ῑ], *squeeze out in turn*, Hp.*Loc.Hom.*9. **-καίω,** *kindle in turn*, metaph. of passion, J.*AJ*15.7.3 (Pass.). **-κλέπτω,** *steal away in return*, Ar.*Ach.*527. **-κομίζω,** *carry out* or *away in return*, in fut. ἀντεκκομιεῖ, Hsch. **-κόπτω,** *knock out in return*, ὀφθαλμόν D.24.140 ; εἴ τις τὸν ὀφθαλμὸν ἐξέκοψέ τινος, ἀντεκκοπῆναι Arist.*MM*1194a38, cf. D.S.12.17. **-κρίνω** [ῑ], *excrete in turn*, Gal. 4.517 (Pass.). **-πέμπω,** *send out in turn*, X.*HG*4.8.25 ; *expel, discharge in turn*, of respiration, Gal.5.710. **-πλέω,** *sail out against*, τινί Th.4.13 : abs., Plu.*Lys.*10. **-πλήσσω,** *frighten in return*, Ael. *NA*12.15, Aristid.1.130 J. **-πνέω,** *breathe out in turn*, Gal.*Nat. Fac.*3.13, al. **-ρέω,** *flow out in turn*, ib.1.13, *UP*6.11. **-τᾰσις·** ἀνταπόδοσις, Hsch. **-τάσσω** (sc. στρατόν), *draw up troops in opposition*, App.*BC*4.108. **-τείνω,** *stretch out in rivalry*, ἀ. αὑτόν τινι *match* oneself *with* another, Ar.*Ra.*1042 ; τῇ ἐκείνου δεινότητι τὸν ἐκείνου πλοῦτον Philostr.*VS*1.21.4. **-τίθημι,** *set forth* or *state instead*, Plu.*Arat.*1 ; *publish a counter-edict*, Id.*CG*12. II. *contrast with*, S.E.*M.*1.251. **-τίνω** [ῑ], *repay*, Ph.2.78, al. **-τῑσις,** εως, ἡ, *retribution*, Id.1.159 ; *requital*, Sch.Pi.*P.*1.112. ⊛**-τιστος,** ον, (ἐκτίνω) *punished in turn*, Sch.Il.24.213. **-τρέφω,** *to maintain in return*.— in Pass., ἀντεκτρέφεσθαι ὑπὸ τῶν ἐκγόνων Arist.*HA*615b25. 2. *train as a rival*, βότρυν βότρυϊ Lync.ap.Ath.14.654a. **-τρέχω,** *sally out against*, X.*HG*4.3.17, *Ages.*2.10. **-φέρω,** *bring out against, oppose*, τί τινι Plu.2.72e. **-φύομαι,** *grow out, issue opposite*, Gal. 5.537.

**ἀντελαττόομαι,** *to be worsted in turn*, D.C.44.27.

**ἀντελαύνω,** intr., *sail against*, τριήρει with a trireme, Plu.*Nic.*24.

**ἀντελιγμός,** ὁ, Ion. for ἀνθελ- (q.v.).

**ἀντελ-λογέω,** *deduct*, *POxy.*1578.11 (iii A.D.). **-λογισμός,** ὁ, *compensation*, *Gloss.* **-λογος,** ὁ, = foreg. : metaph., ἐν ἀντελλόγῳ σταθμᾶσθαι Eust.997.54.

**ἀντελπίζω,** *hope instead* or *in turn*, ἄλλα Th.1.70 ; ἕτερον πλοῦτον Lib.*Decl.*26.28.

**ἀντεμ-βαίνω,** *fit into each other*, of hinge-joints (γίγγλυμοι), Gal. 2.737 :—also **-βᾰσις,** εως, ἡ, ibid. ⊛**-βάλλω,** *put in instead*, τῇ γῇ παγκαρπίαν Thphr.*HP*9.8.7 ; *substitute*, Dsc.2.49. 2. intr., *make an inroad in turn*, X.*HG*3.5.4, Plb.5.96.3 ; *attack in turn*, Plu.*Phil.* 18. **-βᾰσις,** v. sub ἀντεμβαίνω. **-βῐβάζω,** *put on board instead*, Th.7.13, cf. D.4.37. **-βοάω,** *shout at* a person *in answer*, *AB*85, Eust.855.21. **-βοή,** ἡ, *answering cry*, Anon. in Rh.3. 580 W. **-βολή,** ἡ, *pipe made of pieces fitted into each other*, *BGU*1117.16 (13 B.C.), cf. 1116.12. 2. = ἀντέμβασις, Hsch. s.v. ἐπαλλάξαντες, Suid. s.v. γίγγλυμοι. 3. *substitute*, κίκεως *PHolm.* 10.11. ⊛**-βριάζειν·** ἀντεξετάζειν, Hsch. **-βροχή,** ἡ, *remedy for external application*, Orib.*Fr.*90. **-μάσασθαι,** *requite an injury*, dub. word in E.*Fr.*611 (= Eup.458). **-παίζω,** *mock at in return*, τινί Sch.Ar.*Pax*1112. **-πείρω,** in Pass., *resist and become fixed*, of barbs, Paul.Aeg.6.88. **-πήγνῠμαι,** aor. 2 -ενεπάγην, Pass., *to be plunged in in revenge*, τισί Ar.*Ach.*230. **-πίπλημι,** *fill in turn*, ἀντενέπλησαν τὴν ὁδόν X.*HG*2.4.12 ; *fill in return, by way of compensation*, τί τινος Id.*An.*4.5.28 :—Pass., *to be filled with in exchange*, τινός Pl.*Lg.*705b. **-πίπρημι,** *set on fire in return*, ἀντενεπίμπρᾰσαν τὰ ἱρά Hdt.5.102. **-πίπτω,** *fall into the place of*, Phlp. *inPh.*547.19; *attack in return*, Agath.5.19. **-πλέκομαι,** Pass., *to be entwined together*, ἀλλήλαις Dsc.4.75, cf. Poll.1.184 ; of *crossed* or *reversed* bandaging, Sor.*Fasc.*12.513 C. :—*return* one's *embraces* or *salutation*, J.*AJ*16.2.5. **-πλοκή,** ἡ, *mutual entwining*, αἱ ἐν ταῖς ἀτόμοις ἀ. M.Ant.7.50 ; *crossing* of veins, Gal.*in Pl.Ti.*7 ; *complication, confusion*, M.Ant.6.10. **-φαίνω,** *oppose by a counter-statement*, ἀ. ταῖς ἀποφάσεσιν Plb.18.28.12. ⊛**-φᾰνίζω,** = foreg., Hsch. **-φᾰσις,** εως, ἡ, *difference of appearance*, Str.2.4.8 ; also pl., ibid. ; *opposition, antithesis*, S.E.*M.*1.57 ; *distinction*, Hdn.Gr.1.941, A.D.*Adv.*159. 19. **-φράττω,** *obstruct*, Simp.*in Cael.*441.7. **-φύομαι,** *to be inserted opposite*, Gal.4.384.

**ἀντεν-αντίωσις,** εως, ἡ, Rhet., *positive statement made in a negative form*, as οὐκ ἐλάχιστα for μέγιστα, Alex.*Fig.*2.23, Zonae.*Fig.* 22. **-δείκνῠμαι,** *give contrary indications*, of symptoms, Gal.10. 626. **-δειξις,** εως, ἡ, *counter-indication*, Steph.*in Hp.*2.282 D. **-δίδωμι,** *give way in turn*, of sawyers, ὁ μὲν ἕλκει, ὁ δ' ἀντενέδωκε Ar. *V.*694 (Dobree, for ἀντανέδωκε). **-δύομαι** [ῠ], *put on instead*, Plu. 2.139c. **-έδρα,** ἡ, *counter-ambuscade*, Plb.1.57.3. **-εδρεύω,** *lay a counter-ambuscade*, Hp.*Ep.*17, D.C.41.51. **-εργέω,** *to be efficacious against*, θανασίμοις Dsc.1.115. **-έχῠρον,** τό, *counter-pledge*, Sch.A.R.1.1355 :—hence **-εχῠράζομαι,** *take a counter-pledge*, Hsch. s.v. ῥυσιάζει. **-θεσις,** εως, ἡ, *insertion instead*, Eust. 1679.12. **-ίστημι,** *insert instead*, prob. rest. in *IGRom.*4.293 i 37 (Pergam., ii B.C., Pass.). **-οικίζω,** *introduce as inhabitants instead* :—Pass., αἱ ψυχαὶ ἁγνοῖς πάλιν ἀ. σώμασιν J.*BJ*3.8.5. **-τίθημι,** *insert in turn* or *instead*, Nicom.*Ar.*2.27.

**ἀντεξ-άγω** [ᾰγ], *export in return*, X.*Vect.*3.2. 2. *evict in return*, *BGU*1273.34 (iii B.C. ; written ἀντιεξ-). II. *lead out against*, τὰ στρατόπεδα Plb.2.18.6, cf. D.H.8.65, Plu.*Publ.*9 ; v.l. for προσήγαγε, D.S.13.66 :—abs., *march out against*, τινί Plb.3.66.11. **-αίρω,** *raise to an equal height*, λόγοις ἔργα Philostr.*VS*1.19.1. **-αιτέω,** *demand in return*, Plu.*Alex.*11. ⊛**-ανίστᾰμαι,** Pass., with aor. 2 Act., *rise up against*, πρός τι Hld.7.19. **-ᾰπᾰτάω,** *deceive in return*, D.C.58.18. **-αρμα,** ατος, τό, (ἀντεξαίρω) *southerly elevation* (i.e. *latitude*), *corresponding to* a northerly one, *Theol.Ar.*25. **-ειμι,** (εἶμι *ibo*) *go out against*, X.*HG*4.5.10, Plb.1.24.10. **-ελαύνω,** *charge against, attack*, Plu.*Phil.*18, al., D.C.47.43. **-έρχομαι,** = ἀντέξειμι, X.*HG*7.2.12, *Cyr.*6.3.13. **-ετάζω,** *try* one *by the standard of another*, Aeschin.1.8,37, Arr.*Epict.*2.18.21 ; τι πρός τι Plu. *Caes.*3, cf. Gal.18(1).229 ; τινὰ ἀλλήλοις Them.*in Ph.*52.20 ; *compare*, λόγους Luc.*Herm.*30, cf. Aps.p.247 H., etc. :—Pass., *to be measured* or *compared*, παρά or πρός τι, Plu.*Tim.*36, 2.65b ; τινί Ph. 2.45, al., D.Chr.31.126 :—Med., *measure one's strength against* another, τινί Luc.*DMort.*12.2 : esp. *dispute with* him *at law*, like ἀντιδικέω, ib.29.1 : metaph., ἀ. τῇ νόσῳ Id.*Abd.*16. **-έτᾰσις,** εως, ἡ, *comparison*, A.D.*Synt.*161.10, Aps.p.248 H., al. 2. *term of comparison*, of an integer compared with the sum of the preceding integers, *Theol.Ar.*10. **-εταστέον,** *one must compare*, Max.Tyr.30. 6. **-εταστικός,** ή, όν, *comparative*, Aphth.*Prog.*10. Adv. -κῶς Men. Rh.p.403 S. **-ήγησις,** εως, ἡ, *counter-explanation*, αἱ πρὸς Ἰόβαν ἀ., title of work by Didymus, Ath.14.634c. **-ηγητής,** οῦ, ὁ, *deputy*-ἐξηγητής *BGU*362 xv 10 (iii A.D.), *PMeyer*6.9 (ii A.D.), *PRyl.*397.1 (iii A.D.). **-ιππεύω,** *ride out against*, Plu.*Pomp.*7. ⊛**-ῐσάζω,** *make equal, compare*, Sch.Od.11.308. **-ίστᾰμαι,** Pass., with aor. 2 Act., *yield to an attack, retire from the contest*, Plu.2.946d. **-οδος,** ἡ, a *military movement*, τὰς δι' ἀλλήλων ἀ. καὶ εἰσόδους Onos.10. 2. **-ορμάω,** *sail* or *march out against*, D.C.48.47, 63.24. **-όρμησις,** εως, ἡ, *sailing against*, v.l. in Th.2.91 ; *countercharge*, Plu.*Pomp.* 69. **-ωσις,** εως, ἡ, *counter-thrust*, Epicur.*Ep.*2 p.4 U.

**ἀντεπ-άγω** [ᾰγ], *lead against* : abs. (sc. στρατόν or the like), *advance against, advance to meet an enemy*, Th.4.124, Plb.12.18.11, etc. II. *inflict in return*, ποινήν τινι Aristaenet.2.9. III. *introduce as a counter-measure*, ἀλεξήματα Onos.30. **-ακτέον,** *one must march against*, πρός τινα Id.21.6. **-ᾴδω,** *use charms against*, Plot. 4.4.43. **-αινέω,** *praise in return*, X.*Cyr.*8.3.49. II. Pass., ἀ. τινι *to be extolled in comparison with*, Luc.*Pr.Im.*19. **-ανάγομαι** [ᾰγ], *put to sea against*, πρός τινα Th.4.25. **-αρχος,** ὁ, *subpraefectus*, *Gloss.* **-αφίημι** [φῐ], *let go, let slip against*, τινί Luc.*Zeux.*9. **-ειμι,** (εἶμι *ibo*) *rush upon, meet an advancing enemy*, Th.4.33,96, etc. ; τινί Id.7.6, cf. Lib.*Decl.*37.15, Onos.8.2 ; πρός τι Id.21.8. **-εισάγομαι** [ᾰγ], *to be carried in* or *enter instead*, Ti.Locr.102a ; f.l. for sq., *Placit.* 4.22.1. **-είσειμι,** (εἶμι *ibo*) *enter in turn*, εἰς τὰ ἀραιώματα ibid. **-είσοδος,** ἡ, *entrance in return*, ἀ. παρέχειν ibid. **-εισφέρομαι,** *come in instead*, ib.2. **-έκτᾰσις,** εως, ἡ, *stretching in the opposite direction*, Hsch. s.v. τόξου πῆχυν. **-εκτείνω,** *stretch in the contrary direction*, Gal.18(1).213. **-ελαύνω,** *rush to meet, attack one*, App.*Pun.*26. **-εξάγω** [ᾰγ], intr., *sail* or *march out against*, Th.8. 104, Luc.*Bacch.*3 : c. acc., στρατιάν, δύναμιν, J.*AJ*6.9.1, 8.14.4 :—also in Med., D.C.50.31. **-έξειμι,** (εἶμι *ibo*) *march out to meet* an enemy, πρός τινα Th.7.37 : abs., X.*Cyr.*3.3.30, etc. **-εξελαύνω,** foreg., Th. 4.72. **-εξέρχομαι,** = ἀντεπέξειμι, ib.131, Aristid.1.149 J. **-έξοδος,** ἡ, *sally in turn*, D.C.47.37. **-ερείδομαι·** *obnitor*, *Gloss.* **-έρχομαι,** *march against in return*, Aristid.1.150 J., cf. D.C.36.51. **-ερωτάω·** *restipulor*, *Gloss.* II. *ask a question in turn*, *PLond.*1.118(1).70 (vi A.D.). **-ερώτησις,** εως, ἡ, *restipulatio*, *Gloss.* **-ηχέω,** *clamour against* one, Luc.*Cat.*19.

**ἀντεπι-βουλεύω,** *form counter-designs*, Th.1.33, 3.12, etc. **-γράφω** [ᾰ], *write* something *instead*, καλὰ ἐπιγράμματα ἀνελὼν ἀσεβῆ ἀ. D.22. 72 :—Med., -εσθαι ἐπὶ τὸ νίκημα *put their own* names *instead of the other party to* the victory, i.e. *claim* it, Plb.18.34.2. **-δείκνῡμι,** *exhibit in turn*, Pl.*Tht.*162b : c. part., *contrast*, ἀ. ἑαυτὸν ποιοῦντά τι X.*Ages.* 1.12 :—Med., *exhibit oneself in competition*, Plu.2.674b : also c. acc. rei, ἀ. τι καλόν τινι *display a* fine *sight in rivalry with*, Id.*Ant.*23 ; also τι πρός τι Id.*Alex.*21. **-θεσις,** εως, ἡ, *mutual attack, contention*, Ph. 1.7, al. **-θύω,** *offer sacrifice as substitute*, *BCH*15.207. **-θῡμέω,** *desire* a thing *in rivalry with*, τινός And.4.28 :—Pass., ἐπιθυμῶν ξυνεῖναι καὶ ἀντεπιθυμεῖσθαι τῆς ξυνουσίας and *have one's* company *desired in turn*, X.*Mem.*2.6.28. **-κᾰλέω,** *accuse in return*, ἀ. ὅτι.. App. *BC*5.59. **-κειμαι,** *to be placed upon*, Gal.12.604. **-κηρύσσω,** *put a price on* one's *head in return*, χρήματά τινι Poll.4.93. **-κουρέω,** *help in return*, τινί X.*HG*4.6.3. **-κράτεια** [ρᾰ], ἡ, *alternate mastery*, νείκους καὶ φιλίας *Placit.*2.4.8. **-κρᾰτέω,** *get the upper hand in turn*, Str.16.1.19, D.C.44.27. **-λαμβάνομαι,** *lay hold on the other side*, Luc.*Symp.*43. **-μελέομαι** or **-μέλομαι,** *attend* or *give heed in turn*, v.l. X.*Cyr.*5.1.18 ; τινός *to* one, Id.*An.*3.1.16. **-μέλλω,** v.l. for ἀντιμέλλω (q.v.). **-μετρέω,** *measure to in return*, Poll.5. 142. **-νοέω,** *devise in turn*, Ael.*NA*6.23, J.*AJ*10.8.1 : c. inf., App.*BC*4.109. **-πλέω,** *sail against in turn*, Th.1.54 and prob. in 1.50, Poll.1.124. **-ρρέω,** *admit a counter-fluxion*, Hp.*Loc.Hom.* 29. **-ρρημα,** ατος, τό, *counter*-ἐπίρρημα, Heph.*Poëm.*8.2, Poll.4.112 ;

v. ἐπίρρημα. **-σκώπτω,** *mock in return,* τινά Plb.18.7.5. **-σπάω,** gloss on ἀνθέλκω, Hsch.:—Med., Ph.1.247; *absorb* nutriment, Gal.17(2).312. **-σταλμα,** ατος, τό, *return furnished in reply, CPR*20i20 (iii A.D.). **-σταλτικός,** ή, όν, *of* or *for replying to a letter*: -κή (sc. τέχνη), ἡ, *art of writing replies, Epist.Charact.*19. ⊛**-στάτης** [ᾰ], ου, ὁ, *vice-president,* τοῦ Μουσείου *Recueil de Travaux* 37.94 (Denderah). **-στέλλω,** *write an answer, CPR*20ii5 (iii A.D.): c. inf., J.*AJ*15.6.2, al.; οὐδέν Luc.*Sat.*19:—Pass., τὰ ἀντεπεσταλμένα Paus.4.22.6, etc. **-στρᾰτεύω,** *take the field against,* X.*HG*4.8.33. **-στρέφω,** *turn against, retort,* Plu.2.810e; *turn round and back,* of a needle, Gal.10.418. **-στροφή,** ἡ, *turning back upon,* χειρὸς ἐπὶ τὸν ὦμον *Placit.*4.14.3; κατ' ἀ. Ruf.ap.Orib.49.35.4. **-τάσσω,** *order in turn,* τινὶ ποιεῖν τι Th.1.135; τινί τι Pl.*Ti.*20b. **-τείνω,** *excite by contrast,* τὴν φαντασίαν Plu.2.933c. **-τειχίζω,** *raise a counter-work*: metaph., Λυκείῳ τὴν Ἰταλίαν ἀ. Him.*Or.*7.13: so as Dep. with pf. Pass., *establish a fort in the enemy's country,* Th.1.142. **-τίθημι,** *put on in exchange,* D.C.58.7 (Pass.). **2.** ἀ. ἐπιστολὴν πρός τινα *give* a letter *in answer,* Th.1.129, Is.*Fr.*49, cf. J.*AJ*17.5.1. **II.** Med., *make a counter-attack, throw oneself upon,* D.S.36.4, Ph.1.661; simply, *attack,* 2.111:—Act. in same sense, ἀλλήλοισιν *make* mutual *plots,* Hp.*Ep.*17. **-τρέχω·** ἀντεφοδεύω, Suid.; *turn and attack,* of animals at bay, Ph.2.354. **-τροπος,** *sub-procurator, Ephes.*2 No.28, cf. *CIL*3.14195$^4$, al.; ἀπὸ τῶν ἀ.· *a ramulariis, Gloss.* **-φέρω,** *lay, inflict in turn upon,* κακὰ πόλεσι Ph.1.407; ἀντεποισόμεθα· ἀντεπενέγκω.., Hsch. (-επονησ- cod.). **2.** Pass., *rush upon in turn,* Ti.Locr.102a. **-χειρέω,** *make a counter-attack,* Str.5.2.2, cf. Max. Tyr.18.9; τινί Plu.*Them.*31. **II.** *make attempts to prove the contrary,* Arist.*Top.*160b10; τὰ ἀντεπιχειρούμενα *controversial efforts to prove* or *disprove,* S.E.*M.*9.191. **-χείρησις,** εως, ἡ, *a counter-attack,* D.H.9.14.

**ἀντεπόπτευσις,** v.l. ἀντεμπότευσις, εως, ἡ, Lat. *compensatio, reputatio, Gloss.*

**ἀντέρᾰμαι,** aor. -ηράσθην, *to be a rival in love,* τινί τινος Luc.*Musc. Enc.*10.

**ἀντερᾰνίζω,** *contribute one's share in turn*:—Pass., *to be repaid,* ὕμμασιν ἀλλοτρίοις *AP*9.12 (Leon.).

⊛**ἀντεραστής,** οῦ, ὁ, *rival in love,* τινός Ar.*Eq.*733; generally, *rival,* Pl.*R.*521b, Arist.*Rh.*1388a14:—fem. **ἀντεράστρια,** *Gloss.*

**ἀντεράω,** *love in return,* τῶν ἀντερώντων ἱμέρῳ πεπληγμένος A.*Ag.*544; ἐρῶν ἀντερᾶται X.*Smp.*8.3, cf. Bion *Fr.*8.1; ἀντερᾶν τινός Luc. *DMar.*1.5; ἀντερᾶσθαι ὑπό τινος Plu.*Dio* 16. **II.** *rival in love,* τινί Id.2.972d; ἀ. τινί τινος *rival* one *in love for..,* E.*Rh.*184: abs., τὸ ἀντερᾶν *jealous love,* Plu.*Lyc.*18.

**ἀντεργάζομαι,** *retaliate,* τὰ αὐτά τινας ἀ. D.C.*Fr.*36.21.

**ἀντεργολᾰβέω,** *compete with,* τι *in* a thing, Posidipp.3.1.

**ἀντερεθίζω,** *provoke in turn,* τινὰ πρὸς μάχην Eust.848.17.

⊛**ἀντερεί-δω,** *set firmly against,* χειρὶ χεῖρ' ἀντερείσαις *clasping* hand in hand, Pi.*P.*4.37; but ἄκναμπτον Ἥρᾳ μένος ἀν[τ]ερείδων Id.*Pae.*6.87; ἀντέρειδε τοῖς Ἐρεχθείδαις δόρυ E.*Supp.*702; ἀ. ξύλα [τῷ πύργῳ] *set* wooden stays or props *against* it, X.*HG*5.2.5; ἀ. βάσιν *plant* it *firm,* S.*Ph.*1403; λίθοι οἱ -οντες τὰς περιφερεῖς στέγας *springers* of a vault, Demetr.*Eloc.*13. **II.** intr., *stand firm, resist pressure, offer resistance,* opp. ὑπείκω, X.*Cyr.*8.8.16, cf. *Cyn.*10.16, Pl.*Ti.*45c, Arist. *MA*698b18, Epicur.*Fr.*76 bis; *exert counter-pressure,* θέναρι ἀ. Hp. *Fract.*14; τὸ ὠθούμενον ἀ. ὅθεν ὠθεῖται *offers resistance* in the direction from which the pressure comes, Arist.*Mech.*858a26; πρός or περί τι, Plu.2.924d, 923e. **2.** metaph., *exert mutual pressure,* of contending politicians, Phld.*Rh.*2.51 S. (dub.); simply, *argue against,* Sor.2.57. **-σις,** εως, ἡ, *thrusting against, resistance,* Hp.*Art.*50; esp. *the fulcrum* or *resistance* used in reducing a dislocation, ib. 2; of joints, Arist.*IA*705a14; λάμπειν ἀντερείσει τοῦ αἰθέρος *by* its *resistance,* Plu.*Lys.*12; *forward pressure,* Ael.*Tact.*18.8; *repulsion,* Plu.2.396a, cf. Ph.1.153, Plot.4.3.26 (pl.). **II.** Rhet., *buttressing, mutual support,* of clauses in a period, Demetr.*Eloc.*12. **-σμα,** ατος, τό, *prop,* Hsch. s.v. στῆλαι. **-στικός,** ή, όν, *of* or *for resistance,* ἕξις Metop.ap.Stob.3.1.115, Hierocl.p.23A.; κίνησις Simp. *in Ph.*1 46.12.

**ἀντερέσσω,** Att. **-ττω,** *row against,* πρὸς αὐτὸν τὸν ἄνεμον D.C.48.48.

**ἀντερίζω,** *strive against, contend,* ταύροις Philostr.*Her.*12b, cf. Hsch.

**ἀντερύομαι** [ῠ], *make equal in weight with, value equally with,* c. gen., χρυσοῦ τε καὶ ἀργύρου ἀντερύσασθαι Thgn.77:—Act., -ερύω *pull in the opposite direction,* Ep. impf. -ερύεσκε Nonn.*D.*46.214.

⊛**ἀντερῶ,** fut. without any pres. in use: pf. ἀντείρηκα S.*Ant.*47 (cf. ἀντεῖπον): —*speak against, gainsay,* S. l.c.; τεθνάναι δ' οὐκέτ' ἀ. θεοῖς A.*Ag.*539; τι πρός τινα Ar.*Nu.*1079; πρός τι *Ach.*701; τινί Pl.*R.*580a:—Pass., οὐδὲν ἀντειρήσεται no *denial shall be given,* S.*Tr.*1184; τὰ -ημένα Gal.5.477.

⊛**ἀντέρως,** ωτος, ὁ, *return-love, love-for-love,* Pl.*Phdr.*255d, Ach.Tat. 1.9, Them.*Or.*24.305a. **II.** *Anteros,* personified as *a god who avenged slighted love,* Paus.1.30.1, etc.:—but also (as it seems) *a god who struggled against* Ἔρως, Id.6.23.5. **III.** name of a *gem,* Plin. *HN*37.123 (pl.).

**ἀντερωτάω,** *question in turn,* ἐρωτώμενος ἀντερωτᾷς; Pl.*Euthd.*295b, cf. Aeschin.3.226, Aen.Tact.24.16, Plu.*Cor.*18.

**ἀντέσο·** ἀντί⟨α⟩σον, ἄντικρυς ἐλθέ, Hsch.

**ἀντεστραμμένως,** Adv. pf. part. Pass. of ἀντιστρέφω (q.v.).

**ἀντεταγών,** part. (cf. τεταγών), *holding aloft,* prob. in A.R.2.119.

**ἀντεταιῶς·** ἀναγεγραμμένως, Hsch. (Perh. ἀντ' ἔτεος ἀναγεγραμμένως (Dor. acc. pl.), = *enrolled in the same year.*)

**ἀντετοῦς·** τοῦ αὐτοῦ ἔτους (Lacon.), Hsch.

**ἀντευ-δοκιμέω,** *rival in distinction,* Lyd.*Mens.*1.28 (Pass.). **-εργετέω,** *return a kindness,* X.*Mem.*2.6.4; ἀ. τοὺς εὖ ποιήσαντας Arist. *Rh.Al.*1422a32. ⊛**-εργέτημα,** ατος, τό, *kindness returned,* Hsch. s.v. ἀνθυπούργησον. **-εργέτης,** ου, ὁ, *one who returns kindnesses,* Asp.*in EN*113.14, Sch.A.R.2.321. **-εργετικός,** ή, όν, *disposed to return kindnesses,* Arist.*EN*1124b11. **-κρατος** ζώνη *south temperate* zone, Cleom.1.2, *Stoic.*2.195. **-νοέω,** *wish well in return,* τινί X.*Cyr.*8.3.49 (divisim). **-πάσχω** and ⊛**-ποιέω** are by recent edd. written divisim ἀντ' εὖ π. (v. Pl.*Grg.*520e, X.*An.*5.5.21, D.20.124), on the ground that εὖ never enters into direct composition with Verbs, v. εὖ fin.; but ἀντευποιεῖν is read in Arist.*EN*1179a28, *Rh.*1374a24. **-ποιΐα,** ἡ, *requital of benefits,* Mich.*in EN*465.27. **-φρασμα,** ατος, τό, *the opposite of joy,* Agatho 30. **-χαριστητέον,** *one must give thanks in turn,* Porph.*Abst.*2.37.

**ἀντεφ-εστιάω,** *entertain in return,* Ph.2.139, Philostr.*VS*2.5.3, Ael.*NA*9.45, 15.7; as f.l. for ἀνταφ-, Pl.*Ti.*17b. **-ευρίσκω,** *find out against,* J.*AJ*10.8.1. **-ήδομαι,** aor. inf. -ησθῆναι, *exult over in turn,* Ph.2.313. **-ίστημι,** *appoint against* one, στρατηγούς τισι Aristid.1.173J. **-οδεύω,** *go forth to meet,* Suid. **-οδιάζομαι,** Pass., *to be furnished instead of provisions*: metaph. in J.*AJ*15.9.1. **-οράω,** *check, verify, SIG*1023.89 (Cos). **-ορμάω,** *rush against, attack,* Hld.8.16: abs., Ph.2.122. **-ορμέω,** *anchor over against* the enemy, Plu.*Alc.*36. ⊛**-όρμησις,** εως, ἡ, *rushing against, attack,* Ph.2.31, Hld. l.c.

**ἀντέχω** or **ἀντίσχω,** fut. ἀνθέξω; part. ἀντισχήσων (in sense II) Lib. *Ep.*33.2: aor. ἀντέσχον:—*hold against,* c. acc. et gen., χεῖρ' ἀ. κρατός *hold* one's hand *against* one's head so as to shade the eyes, S.*OC*1651: c. dat., ὄμμασι δ' ἀντίσχοις (-έχοις codd.) τάνδ' αἴγλαν *may'st* thou *keep* this sunlight *upon* his eyes, Id.*Ph.*830 (lyr.); τοὺς χαλινοὺς τῶν ἵππων Hdn.5.6.7. **II.** c. dat., *hold out against, withstand,* Ἁρπάγῳ Hdt.1.175, cf. 8.68.β'; τοῖς δικαίοις S.*Fr.*78; τῇ ταλαιπωρίᾳ Th.2.49; πρός τινα Id.6.22; πρὸς τοὺς καμάτους Hdn.3.6.10, etc.: c. acc., *endure,* ἀντέχομεν καμάτους *AP*9.299 (Phil.); but in Th.8.63 ἀ. τὰ τοῦ πολέμου rather belongs to the next signf., *hold out* as regards the war; so πολλὰ ἀ. ib.86. **2.** *hold out, endure,* c. part., ἡ Ἄζωτος ..ἐπὶ πλεῖστον χρόνον πολιορκουμένη ἀντέσχε Hdt.2.157, cf. 5.115, Th.2.70; μηκέτι ἀντέχωσι τῷ πόνῳ διϊστάμενοι Pl.*Ti.*81d; πολλάκις γιγνομένην ψυχὴν ἀντέχειν *last* through several states of existence, Id.*Phd.*88a. **3.** abs., *hold out, stand one's ground,* Hdt.8.16, A. *Pers.*413, etc.; πῶς δύσμορος ἀντέχει; S.*Ph.*176 (lyr.); νόσημα ἀντίσχει τὸν αἰῶνα πάντα Hp.*Fract.*11; ἔστ' ἂν αἰὼν ἀντέχῃ E.*Alc.*337; βραχὺν χρόνον D.2.10; ἀ. ἐπὶ πολύ, ἐπὶ πλέον, Th.1.7, 65; ἀ. ἐλπίσιν in hope, D.S.2.26; ἀ. περί τινος X.*HG*2.2.16: peculiarly, ἀ. μὴ ὑπακοῦσαι I *hold out against.., refuse..,* Plu.2.708a. **b.** of the rivers drunk by the Persian army, *hold out, suffice,* Hdt.7.196, cf. A.*Pers.*413 (in full ἀ. ῥέεθρον Hdt.7.58; ἀ. ὕδωρ παρέχων ib.108); so ἀντέχει ὁ σῖτος Th.1.65. **4.** *extend, reach,* ἐς ὅσον ἡ ἐπιστήμη ἀ. Id. 6.69; *prevail,* διὰ τὴν λῃστείαν ἐπὶ πολὺ ἀντίσχουσαν 1.7. **III.** Med., *hold before one against* something, c. acc. et gen., ἀντίσχεσθε τραπέζας ἰῶν *hold out* the tables *against* the arrows, Od.22.74. **2.** c. gen. only, *hold on by, cling to,* ἐκείνου τῆς χειρός Hdt.2.121.ε'; πέπλων E.*Tr.*750, cf. *Ion* 1404; τῶν θυρῶν Ar.*Lys.*161: metaph., ἀ. τῶν ὄχθων *cling to* the banks, *keep close to* them, Hdt.9.56; ἀ. Ἡρακλέος *cleave to* Hercules, i.e. *worship* him *above all,* Pi.*N.*1.33; ἀ. τῆς ἀρετῆς, Lat. *adhaerere virtuti,* Hdt.1.134; ἀ. τοῦ πολέμου Id.7.53; τοῦ κέρδους S.*Fr.*354; τῆς θαλάσσης Th.1.13; σωτηρίας Lys.33.6; τῆς ἀληθείας Pl.*Phlb.*58e, cf. *R.*600d, al.; τῶν παραδεδομένων μύθων Arist.*Po.*1451b24; τῆς ἐλευθερίας Decr.ap.D.18.185; τῶν δικαίων *POxy.*1203.30 (i A.D.). **b.** c. gen. pers., *care for, support,* 1*Ep. Thess.*5.14. **3.** abs., αὐτὸς ἀντέχου S.*Ph.*893, cf. Ar.*Ach.*1121. **4.** c. dupl. gen. pers. et rei, ἀνθέξεταί σου τῶν πατρῴων χρημάτων *will lay claim to* the property *from* you, *dispute* it *with* you, Ar.*Av.*1658. **5.** *resist,* Pl.*R.*574b; φονεῦσαι τοὺς ἀντεχομένους D.S.4.49. **6.** *adhere,* Arist.*HA*583a18: Medic., of constipation, γαστὴρ ἀντίσχετο Hp.*Epid.*4.20; γαστρὸς ἀντεχομένης ib.17.

**ἄντη,** ἡ, (ἄντομαι II) *prayer*—a word preserved by Hsch. (ἄντησι (cod. ἀντήσει)· λιτανείαις, ἀντήσεσι), and restored by Herm. for λιταῖς (metri gr.) in S.*El.*139 (dub.).

**ἀντῆ·** δῶρον ἱκέσιον, Hsch.

⊛**ἀντήδην,** Adv. *in supplication,* Hsch. (-δης cod.).

**ἀντήεις,** Dor. **-άεις,** εσσα, εν, (ἄντα) *hostile,* Pi.*P.*9.93.

**ἀντήλιος,** ον, (ἀντί, ἥλιος) *opposite the sun,* i.e. *looking east,* S.*Aj.*805, E.*Ion* 1550; δαίμονες ἀντήλιοι statues of gods *which stood in the sun* before the house-door, A.*Ag.*519, cf. E.*Fr.*538. **2.** of the moon, *reflecting the sun's rays, AB*403 (ἀνθ-), cf. Suid.: hence metaph., *imitation, reflection,* Theopomp.Hist.367 (ἀνθ-). **II.** ἀντήλια, τά, = παρήλια, *parhelia,* Suid., cf. Men.511. **2.** *screens* or *parasols,* Eust.1281.3; also, *blinkers* on horses' bridles, Poll.10.54 (ἀνθ-), Eust.1562.39.—The Ion. form ἀντήλιος is always used in Trag.; ἀνθήλιος first in Theopomp. l.c., cf. Ph.1.656, *Placit.*3.6.

⊛**ἀντημοιβός,** όν, Ep. for ἀνταμοιβός, *corresponding,* Call.*Del.*52.

**ἄντην,** Ep. Adv., (ἀντί) *against, over against,* οὔ μιν ἔγωγε φεύξομαι.. ἀλλὰ μάλ' ἄ. στήσομαι I will *confront* him, Il.18.307, cf. 11.590; ὁμοιωθήμεναι ἄ. match himself *openly against* me, 1.187, Od.3.120; so πειρηθήμεναι ἄ. 8.213; more rarely with Verbs of motion, μηδ' ἔα ἄ. ἔρχεσθαι *straightforwards,* opp. πάλιν τρέπε, Il.8.399; also βαλλομένων *in front*, 12.152; οὐδέ τις ἔτλη ἄ. εἰσιδέειν look him *in face*, 19.15, cf. 24.223; ἄ. λοέσσομαι will bathe *before all, openly*, Il.6.221, cf. 8.158; ἀγαπαζέμεν ἄ. greet *in the face of all*, Il.24.464; ἱκεσέ τ' ἄ. 10.158; ὅς μ' εἴρεαι ἄ. 15.247:—θεῷ ἐναλίγκιος ἄ. like a god *presence*, Od.2.5, 4.310; χελιδόνι εἰκέλη ἄ. 22.240; cf. ἄντα. II. Prep. c. gen., only in late Ep., as Nic.*Th.*474, Opp.*C.*3.210.

**ἀντήνωρ,** ορος, ὁ, ἡ, (ἀνήρ) *instead of a man*, σποδὸς ἀ. dust *for men*, A.*Ag.*442.—In Il. as pr. n.

**ἀντηρετέω,** *row against* or *on the opposite side to* another, *EM*112. 50.

**ἀντηρέτης,** ου, ὁ, (ἐρέτης) properly, *one who rows against* another, cf. *AB*411: generally, *opponent, adversary*, A.*Th.*284, 595; ἀ. δορός τινι ib.997 (lyr.).

**ἀντήρης,** Dor. **-άρης,** ες, poet. Adj. *set over against, opposite*, λαβεῖν τινὰ ἀντήρη meet *face to face* in battle, E.*Ph.*754, cf. 1367; ἀντήρεις στέρνων πληγάς blows *on the breast*, S.*El.*89: c. gen., Φοινίκας ἀ. χώρα *over against, facing* it, E.*Tr.*221 (lyr.): c. dat., ἀ. τινί *opposite to* a thing, Id.*IA*224; ἀ. ὄψεσι, of the bat, *hostile to*, S.*Fr.*747 (lyr.).

**ἀντηρίδιον,** τό, Dim. of ἀντηρίς, *stanchion* supporting the base of a torsion-engine, Hero *Bel.*89.4. 2. *support, base*, *Milet.*7 p.60 (ii B.C.), Haussoullier *Cinquantenaire de l'École Pratique des Hautes Études* p.89 (ii B.C.).

**ἀντήριος·** στήμων, καὶ κανὼν ὁ προσκείμενος τῇ θύρᾳ, Hsch.

**⊛ἀντηρίς,** ίδος, ἡ, *prop, stay, support*, E.*Fr.*1111: pl., Plb.8.4.6; *stanchion* or *strut* in torsion-engines, Ph.*Bel.*76.16, Hero *Bel.*101.9; ἀρκύων X.*Cyn.*10.7; in Th.7.36 ἀντηρίδες are *stay-beams* fixed inside a ship's bow, and projecting beyond it, so as to support and strengthen the ἐπωτίδες. II. = θυρίς, *window*, Suid.:—and in E.*Rh.*785 it must mean *nostrils*, if it be the right reading. [ῐδος E. ll.cc.: hence ἀντήρειδες in Apollod.*Poliorc.*178.4, Hero *Bel.*101.9, is wrong; so -είδιον ib.89.4 is f.l. for -ίδιον as Inscrr. show.] (-ηρῐδ- = -ερῐδ-, weak form of stem of ἐρείδω (cf. ἔρις).)

**ἄντησις,** εως, ἡ, *entreaty, prayer*, Hsch.

**ἄντηστις,** εως, ἡ, *confronting*, κατ' ἄντηστιν θεμένη Od.20.387.

**ἀντηχ-έω,** Dor. **-ᾱχέω** Theoc.*Ep.*4.11 (Scal.):—*sing in answer*, παιᾶνα θεῷ E.*Alc.*423; ἀντάχησ' ἂν ὕμνον ἀρσένων γέννᾳ would *have sung* a song *in answer to*.., Id.*Med.*426. II. abs., *sound responsively*, of a musical string, Arist.*Pr.*919b16; of bronze vessels, Aen.Tact. 37.7, Plb.22.11.12; *resound*, Hp.*Morb.*4.56, cf. *Carn.*18, Luc.*VH*1.38; *echo*, φωναῖς ἀ. Plu.2.414c. III. *shout in opposition*, Id.*Mar.*19, cf. J.*BJ*2.19.8, Them.*Or.*21.255d. 2. *contradict*, Plu.2.925e, cf. 1000c. **-ημα,** ατος, τό, *echo*, Sch.Philostr.*Her.*19.12. **-ησις,** εως, ἡ, *a re-echoing*, Plu.2.589d. **-ος,** ον, *sounding in response*, ἁρμονία Ph.1.312, 2.485.

**⊛ἀντί,** Prep. governing gen.:—orig. sense, *over against*. (Cf. Skt. *ánti* 'opposite', 'facing', Lat. *ante*, etc.)

A. Usage: I. of Place, *opposite, over against*, formerly quoted from several places of Hom., as Il.21.481 ἀντὶ ἐμεῖο (where now ἀντί' ἐμεῖο, i.e. ἀντία); Τρώων ἄνθ' ἑκατόν (i.e. ἄντα) 8.233; so ἄντ' Αἴαντος (i.e. ἄντα) 15.415, cf. Od.4.115, Hes.*Op.*727; but ἀντί is so used in X.*An.*4.7.6, *IG*2.835c–l68; αἱ ὀπαὶ αἱ γιγνόμεναι ἀ. τόρμων mortises *facing* tenons, Hero *Bel.*97.5; ἀντὶ μαιτύρων *in the presence of* witnesses, *Leg.Gort.*1.40; ἀντὶ τῆς ὄψεως ἡμῶν Eudox.*Ars*18. II. of Time, ἀντὶ νυκτός *the same* night, *SIG*1025.43 (Cos); ἀντὶ Ϝέτεος *GDI*2561*A*45 (Delph.); ἀντ' ἐνιαυτοῦ *IG*5(2).266.8 (Mantinea, i B.C.); ἀνθ' ἡμέρας· δι' ὅλης τῆς ἡμέρας, Hsch.; cf. ἀντετοῦς. III. *instead, in the place of*, Ἕκτορος ἀντὶ πεφάσθαι Il.24.254; ἀντὶ γάμοιο τάφον Od.20.307; so later πολέμιος ἀντὶ φίλου καταστῆναι Hdt.1.87; ἀντὶ ἡμέρης νὺξ ἐγένετο Id.7.37; ἀντὶ φωτῶν σποδός A.*Ag.*434; τὸν πόλεμον ἀντ' εἰρήνης μεταλαμβάνειν Th.1.120, cf. 4.20, 7.75; βασιλεύειν ἀντί τινος X.*An.*1.1.4; also ἀντὶ ἄρχεσθαι ὑπ' ἄλλων ἄρχειν ἁπάντων Hdt.1.210, cf. 6.32, 7.170 (where the usual constr. would be ἀντὶ τοῦ ἄρχεσθαι, cf. Th.7.28, X.*Cyr.*6.2.19, etc.); ὀργίλοι ἀντὶ θυμοειδοῦς γεγένηνται Pl.*R.*411c: sts. used elliptically, ἦ 'τολμήσατ' ἀντ' ἐμοῦ δοῦναί τινι; i.e. ἀντὶ τοῦ ἐμοὶ δοῦναι, S.*Ph.*369, cf. *OC*448, Ar.*Av.*58. 2. in Hom. often to denote equivalence, ἀντί νυ πολλῶν λαῶν ἐστιν ἀνήρ he is *as good as* many men, Il.9.116; ἀντὶ κασιγνήτου ξεῖνος..τέτυκται a guest is *as much as* a brother, Od.8.546; ἀντί τοί εἰμ' ἱκέταο I am *as* a suppliant, Il.21.75, cf. 8.163; so later τοῦτό σφι ἀντὶ λουτροῦ ἐστί serves *as* a bath, Hdt.4.75; ὑπάρχειν ἀντὶ τῶν ἔνδον to be *as hostages for*.., Th.2.5; δουλεύειν ἀντὶ ἀργυρωνήτων *just like* bought slaves, D.17.3; ἀντὶ [πλεύμονος] βράγχια Arist.*PA*669a4. 3. to denote exchange, *at the price of, in return for*, σοὶ δὲ θεοὶ τῶνδ' ἀντὶ χάριν..δοῖεν Il.23.650; νῆσον ἀντὶ χρημάτων παρέλαβον *for* money paid, Hdt.3.59; ἀντ' ἀργυρίου ἀλλάξασθαι Pl.*R.*371d; ἀμείβειν τι ἀντί τινος Pi.*P.*4.17, cf. E.*Or.*646, 651; ἀντὶ ποίας εὐεργεσίας; Lys.6.40, etc.; τί δ' ἐστὶν ἀνθ' οὗ..; S.*Ant.*237; ὄνειδος ἀνθ' ὅτου Id.*OC*967; δοίην ἀντ' ἀνιῶν ἀνίας grief *for* grief, Thgn.344; ἀντ' ἀγαθῶν ἀγαθοῖσι βρύοις A.*Supp.*966:—hence ἀνθ' ὧν *wherefore*, A.*Pr.*31, S.*OT*264, Th.6.83, *Ev.Luc.*12.3; ἀντὶ τούτου *therefore*, *Ep.Eph.*5.31; but ἀνθ' ὧν also for ἀντὶ τούτων ὅτι.., *because*, S.*Ant.*1068, Ar.*Pl.*434; ἀντὶ τοῦ; *wherefore? why?* S.*OT*1021; also ἀνθ' ὧν ὅτι ἦτε.. *instead of being as you were*.., Lxx *De.*28.62. 4. *for the sake of*, Pl.*Mx.*237a, Arist.*EN*1110a21; with Verbs of entreaty, like πρός c. gen., ἀντὶ παίδων ἱκετεύομέν σε S.*OC*1326. 5. to mark comparison, ἓν ἀνθ' ἑνός one *set against* the other, *compared with* it, Pl.*R.*331b, *Lg.*705b; χάριν ἀντὶ χάριτος, i.e. ever-increasing grace, *Ev.Jo.*1.16; *in preference to*, ἀφνεὸν βούλεται ἀντ' ἀγαθοῦ Thgn.188; ἀντὶ αὐλοῦ καὶ ἀντὶ κιθάρας ὁ ἦχος ἀκούεται Demetr.*Eloc.*71; αἱρεῖσθαί τι ἀντί τινος Isoc.9.3, D.1.1, cf. X.*Lac.*9.1: even after Comparatives, πλέον ἀντὶ σοῦ S.*Tr.*577; μείζον' ὅστις ἀντὶ τῆς αὑτοῦ πάτρας φίλον νομίζει Id.*Ant.*182; so (esp. after a neg.) ἄλλος ἀντ' ἐμοῦ A.*Pr.*467, S.*Aj.*444, Ar.*Nu.*653; δόξαν ἀντὶ τοῦ ζῆν ἠγαπηκώς Plu.*Alex.*42.

B. Position: ἀντί rarely follows its case, as in Il.23.650, A.*Ag.*1277, *IG*5(1).1119 (Geronthrae, iv B.C.), *AP*7.715 (Leon.); but the Gramm. hold that it never suffers anastrophe.

C. in Compos. it signifies, 1. *over against, opposite*, as ἀντιβαίνω, ἀντίπορος. 2. *against, in opposition to*, as ἀντιλέγω, ἀντίβιος. 3. *one against another, mutually*, as ἀντιδεξιόομαι. 4. *in return*, as ἀντιβοηθέω. 5. *instead of*, as ἀντιβασιλεύς, ἀνθύπατος. 6. *equal to, like*, as ἀντίθεος, ἀντίπαις, ἀντίδουλος. 7. *corresponding, counter*, as ἀντίφορτος, ἀντίτυπος.

**ἀντία,** v. sub ἀντίος.

**ἀντιάζω,** impf. ἀντίαζον Hdt.1.166 (but ὑπ-ηντίαζον 4.121), ἠντίαζον (ὑπ-) X.*An.*6.5.27, etc.: fut. ἀντιάσω [ᾰ]; Dor. -άξω (v. infr.): aor. ἠντίᾰσα Hdt.4.80, 9.6; but these two tenses belong also to ἀντιάω: (ἀντί):—*meet face to face*: I. c. acc. pers., *encounter*, whether as friend or foe, τὸν ἐπιόντα Id.4.118, cf. 2.141, 4.80, etc.; ἀ. [τινὰ] ἐς τόπον Hdt.1.166, cf. 9.6; πατέρ' ἀντιάσασα πρὸς..πόρθμευμα A.*Ag.*1557: abs., κόρος..βαρὺς ἀντιάσαι Pi.*N.*10.20; μολπὰ πρὸς κάλαμον ἀντιάξει song *shall answer to* the pipe, Id.*O.*10(11).84. 2. *approach as suppliants*, ἀ. τινὰ δώροισι Hdt.1.105: hence simply, *entreat, supplicate*, Ἄρεα ἀντιάζω S.*OT*192; καί σ' ἀντιάζω πρὸς..Διός Id.*Aj.*492, cf. E.*Andr.*572, etc.; freq. with acc. omitted, ἀλλ' ἀντιάζω S.*El.*1009, cf. *Ph.*809, E.*Alc.*400; βᾶθι καὶ ἀντίασον γονάτων *entreat* [her] by her knees, Id.*Supp.*272. II. = ἀντιάω II, ἀντάω, c. dat. pers. et acc. rei, ὅταν θεοὶ..Γιγάντεσσιν μάχαν ἀντιάζωσιν *in* fight, Pi.*N.*1.68.—This Verb is never used in correct Att. Prose.

**ἀντιάνειρᾰ,** ἡ, (ἀντί, ἀνήρ), fem. form of a masc. in -άνωρ or -ήνωρ: in Il. always as epith. of the Amazons, *a match for men*, 3.189, 6.186, etc.; so of Athena, Coluth.170. II. in Pi.*O.*12.16 στάσις ἀντιάνειρα faction *wherein man is set against man*.

**ἀντιάς,** άδος, ἡ, *tonsil*, mostly in pl., Hp.*Morb.*2.11 and 30: esp. when inflamed, Cels.7.12, Gal.7.263; cf. παρίσθμια.

**ἀντιαττικιστής,** οῦ, ὁ, *Anti-Atticist*, title of grammatical work, *AB*77.

**⊛ἀντιᾰχάτης** [ᾱτ], ου, ὁ, a stone *like an agate*, dub. in Orph.*L.*637 (Abel).

**ἀντ-ῐᾰχέω,** *cry* or *call against*, Theoc.*Ep.*4.11 codd. (ἀνταχεῦσι Scal.), A.R.2.828. **-ῐάχω** [ᾰ], = foreg., Orph.*A.*828; ἀμοιβήδην ἀντίαχεν A.R.4.76.

**ἀντιάω,** Hom. uses pres. only in the Ep. forms ἀντιόω, inf. ἀντιάαν, 3 pl. imper. ἀντιοώντων, part. ἀντιόων, όωσα, όωντες; but ἀντιόω, which is pres. in Il.1.31, 23.643, serves as fut. in 13.752: fut. ἀντιάσω [ᾰ] Od.22.28, Thgn. (v. infr.): aor. ἠντίᾰσα Hom. (these two tenses in form belong to ἀντιάζω; but such instances as belong in sense to ἀντιάω are given here):—**Med.**, once in Hom. (v. infr.), A.R.1.470, 2.24: (ἀντί, ἀντίος):—Ep. Verb: I. *go for the purpose of meeting* or *receiving*: 1. c. gen. rei, *go in quest of*, when an aim or purpose is implied, πολέμοιο μενοίνα ἀντιάαν Il.13.215; ὄφρα πόνοιο..ἀντιάσητον 12.356; οὐκέτ' ἀέθλων ἄλλων ἀντιάσεις Od.22.28, al.: metaph. of an arrow, *hit*, ἀλλά κεν ἢ στέρνων ἢ νηδύος ἀντιάσειε Il.13.290:—often of the gods, *come* (as it were) *to meet* an offering, and so, in past tenses, *to have received, accepted* it, ἀντιόων ταύρων τε καὶ ἀρνειῶν ἑκατόμβης Od.1.25; ἀρνῶν κνίσης αἰγῶν τε τελείων..ἀντιάσας Il.1.67; generally, *partake of, enjoy*, αἲ γὰρ..ὀνήσιος ἀντιάσειεν Od.21.402; so ἔργων ἀντιάσεις χαλεπῶν Thgn.1308; οὔτε του τάφου ἀντιάσας οὔτε γόων S.*El.*869: abs., ἀντιάσαις *having obtained* [his wishes], Pi.*I.*6(5).15:—once in Med., ἀντιάασθε, θεοί, γάμου Il.24.62. 2. more rarely c. gen. pers., *match* or *measure oneself with*, ἡμεῖς δ' εἰμὲν τοῖοι οἳ ἂν σέθεν ἀντιάσαιμεν ib.7.231; δηίων ἀντιάσειν Thgn.552. b. rarely, *come to aid*, οὗ παιδὸς τεθνηότος ἀντιόωσα Od.24.56. II. c. dat. pers., *meet with, encounter*, as by chance, μηδ' ἀντιάσειας ἐκείνῳ ib.18.147; δυστήνων δέ τε παῖδες ἐμῷ μένει ἀντιόωσιν Il.6.127. 2. c. gen., *encounter*, ψύχεος Emp.65. III. abs. in aor. part., ἀλλά τιν' ὔμμ' ὀΐω δόμεναι θεὸν ἀντιάσαντα *having haply met* you, Il.10.551, cf. Od.6.193, 13.312, 17.442. IV. c. acc. rei, only in ἐμὸν λέχος ἀντιόωσα, euphem. for *sharing* it, only in Il.1.31. V. *approach as a suppliant, supplicate*, like ἀντιάζω I.2, only in later Ep., c. gen. pers., A.R.1.703: also c. acc. pers., Id.3.694: c. acc. rei, ib.717. VI. ἀντιόωσα σελήνη dub. in Orph.*Fr.*168.16.

**ἀντιβάδην** [ᾰ], Adv. *going against, opposite*, ἀ. ὠθεῖν Plu.2.381a.

**ἀντιβᾰδίζω,** *go against, the contrary way*, Phot. s.v. ῥαβάττειν.

**ἀντιβαιβάζω·** *obvagio*, *Gloss.*

**ἀντιβαίνω,** fut. -βήσομαι, *go against, withstand, resist*, c. dat., Hdt.5.40, A.*Pr.*236, Decr. ap. D.18.186, etc.; πλευραῖσιν ἀντιβᾶσα *having set her foot against*.., E.*Ba.*1126: abs., ἀντιβὰς ἐλᾶν row *with foot planted against* the stretcher, Ar.*Ra.*202. 2. abs., Hdt.3.72, 8.3, E.*IA*1016, etc.; βιασθεὶς πολλὰ κἀντιβάς *reluctant*, S.*El.*575; εἰ..μὴ περὶ σοῦ μάχομαι μόνος ἀντιβεβηκώς Ar.*Eq.*767 (ἀμφι- Dawes); ἀ. πρὸς τἀριστερὰ μόνον Pl.*Lg.*634a.

**ἀντι-βάκχειος** (sc. πούς), ὁ, the foot – – ᴗ, Diom.1.513 K., al.:—also **-βακχος,** ὁ, Ter.Maur.1411.

**ἀντιβάλανος·** ἡ κικκίς, Hsch.

**⊛ἀντιβάλλω,** *throw against* or *in turn*, Th.7.25 (the acc. pers. being understood); βέλος Plb.6.22.4: c. dat., ἀ. ἀκοντίοις Plu.*Nic.*25; ἀ.

τῷ κωρύκῳ *practise by striking against* the sack, in the gymnasium, Luc.*Lex.*5; *put back* a protruding bone, Pall.*in Hp.Fract.*12.285 C. II. *put one against the other, compare, collate,* of Mss., Str.13.1.54, 17.1.5, *POxy.*1479 (i B.C., Pass.); *match, compare with,* λέοντι τίς αἰετὸν ἀντιβάλλοιτο; Opp.*C.*1.68; λόγους ἀ. πρὸς ἀλλήλους *exchange* words in conversation, *Ev.Luc.*24.17; πρὸς ἑαυτὸν ἀ. τὸ γεγονός *weigh* with oneself, Lxx 2*Ma.*11.13. III. in Med., *change,* μορφήν dub. l. Opp.*C.*3.16.

**ἀντιβάλμους·** ἀντιστρόφους, Hsch.

**ἀντιβαρνικί,** τό, *cassia,* Hsch.

**ἀντιβᾰσῐλεύς,** έως, ὁ, = Lat. *interrex,* D.H.9.69.

**ἀντιβᾰσῐλεύω,** *reign as a rival king,* τισί J.*BJ*4.7.1.

**ἀντίβᾰσις,** εως, ἡ, *resistance,* Ph.*Bel.*73.14, Plu.*Caes.*38, etc.; πρός τι Id.2.584f; ἡ κατ' ἀντίβασιν ἁφή S.E.*M.*10.2; opp. ἐπέρεισις, Sor.2.10, cf. Antyll.ap.Orib.9.23.11. 2. *ground of opposition* (?), διαφόρου τετευχότα -σεως Phld.*Sign.*27. II. in the ballista, *counter-prop,* Vitr.10.11.9.

**ἀντιβαστάζω,** *support, prop,* Eust.1933.37.

**ἀντιβάτης** [ᾰ], ου, ὁ, *bolt of a door,* Sch.Ar.*V.*202.

**ἀντιβᾰτικός,** ή, όν, *contrary, opposite,* φορά Plu.*Phoc.*2. II. of contact, *firm, thorough,* -κωτέρα ἡ κατὰ τὴν κίνησιν τοῦ οὐρανίου σώματος ἁφή Simp.*in Cael.*140.19, cf. 9; *resistent,* Hierocl. p.23 A., Alex.Aphr.*Quaest.*62.4, Olymp.*in Mete.*18.30; of the pulse, Gal.8.949, cf. 644. Adv. -κῶς ib.668: Comp., κλίνης -κώτερον ἐστρωμένης Sor.2.61.

**ἀντιβῐάζομαι,** *use force against, AP*12.183 (Strat.): abs., Ph.1.295, al.:—Pass., ῥώμῃ -βιασθέντες κραταιοτέρᾳ 2.423.

**ἀντιβιβλίον,** τό, *counter-account, PFlor.*388.48 (i A.D.); *counter-summons,* Just.*Nov.*53.3.2 (ἀντιβίβλῳ codd.).

**ἀντιβῐβρώσκω,** fut. Pass. -βρωθήσομαι, *eat in turn,* Ath.7.343c.

⊛**ἀντιβίην** [βῐ], Adv., (βία) *against, face to face,* ἐριζέμεναι βασιλῆϊ ἀντιβίην Il.1.278; Ἕκτορι πειρηθῆναι ἀ. 21.226, cf. 5.220, Orph.*L.*26.

⊛**ἀντίβῐος,** α, ον, also ος, ον: (βία):—*opposing force to force*: as Adj. in Hom. only in the phrase ἀντιβίοις ἐπέεσσι with *wrangling* words, Il.1.304, Od.18.415, etc.; ἀ. ὅμιλος *hostile,* Tryph.624. b. Subst., *enemy,* Jul.*Caes.*319b (anap.), Nonn.*D.*2.508, al., Opp.*H.*5.114. 2. as Adv., ἀντίβιον, = ἀντιβίην, ἀ. μαχέσασθαι Il.3.20; Μενελάῳ ἀντίβιον.. πολεμίζειν ib.435; εἰ μὲν ἀντίβιον.. πειρηθείης 11.386.

**ἀντιβλάπτω,** *harm in return,* Arist.*EN*1138a8, Ph.2.371.

**ἀντιβλασφημέω,** *retaliate with abuse* Sch.Aristid p.673 D.

**ἀντι-βλεπτέον,** *one must look in the face,* μοι πρός τι Luc.*Dem. Enc.*17. ⊛**-βλέπω,** fut. -βλέψομαι D.25.98:—*look straight at, look in the face,* c. dat. pers., τῷ ἐμῷ πατρὶ οὐδ' ἀντιβλέπειν δύναμαι X.*HG*5.4.27; τοῖς φίλοις *Com.Adesp.*22.41 D.; εἰς or πρὸς τὸν ἥλιον, X.*Mem.*4.7.7, Thphr.*Sens.*18: metaph., πρὸς δωρεὰς βασιλέων Plu.*Comp.Dem. Cic.*3: c. acc., ἀντιβλέπειν ἐκεῖνον οὐ δυνήσομαι Men.586: abs., part., ἀντιβλέπουσαι.. αἱ αἶγες *facing one another,* Arist.*HA*611a5. **-βλεψις,** εως, ἡ, *looking in the face, look,* X.*Hier.*1.35, Plu.2.681b.

**ἀντίβλημα,** ατος, τό, *stone inserted in vacant space* in masonry, *POxy.*498.16 (ii A.D.).

**ἀντιβοάω,** *return a cry,* of an echo, Bion 1.38; *call aloud in answer,* J.*BJ*3.5.4: c. acc., ἰήϊον ἀντεβόησαν prob. in Euph.80; ἴακχον θρήνοις Him.*Ecl.*2.4.

**ἀντιβοηθέω,** *help in turn,* τινί Th.6.18, 7.58, Pl.*R.*559e, X.*HG*7.4.2.

**ἀντίβοιος,** ον, (βοῦς) *worth an ox* or *in place of an ox,* of offerings, S.*Fr.*405.

**ἀντιβολεύς·** *dictator. Gloss.*

**ἀντιβολέω,** impf. ἠντιβόλουν Ar.*Eq.*667 codd., Lys.1.25: fut. ἀντιβολήσω Od. (v. infr.), Lys.14.16: aor. in Hom., ἀντεβόλησα; with double augm., ἠντεβόλησα Ar.*Fr.*38:—*meet,* esp. in battle, c. dat. pers., Il.16.847, al.: abs., 11.365, al. 2. rarely c. dat. rei, *to be present at,* φόνῳ ἀνδρῶν ἀντεβόλησας Od.11.416; τάφῳ ἀνδρῶν ἀ. 24.87; cf. ἀβολέω. 3. c. gen. rei, *partake of, have one's share of,* μάχης καυστείρης ἀντιβολῆσαι Il.4.342; οὐ γάρ τευ ἐπητύος ἀντιβολήσεις Od.21.306; σὺ δέ κεν τάφου ἀντιβολήσαις 4.547; γάμου ἀ. Hes.*Op.*784, cf. Pi.*O.*13.30; even πυκινοῦ νόου ἀ. Timo 59.1. 4. rarely of the thing, *fall to one's lot,* c. gen. pers., στυγερὸς γάμος ἀντιβολήσει.. ἐμέθεν Od.18.272. 5. c. acc. pers., *meet as a suppliant, entreat, supplicate,* freq. in Com., Ar.*Nu.*110, *Pl.*444: c. acc. et inf., Id.*Eq.*667, *Ach.*147, D.21.188: abs., περὶ τῶν ἀντιβολούντων those who *supplicate,* Ar.*V.*559; freq. in parenthesis, εἴπ', ἀντιβολῶ, Id.*Eq.*109, cf. *Pl.*103 (freq. also ἀντιβολῶ σε Pl.Com.43.5, 173.3; also in Lys.1.25, 29, X.*Ath.*1.18):—Pass., *to be supplicated,* ἀντιβοληθείς Ar.*V.*560. II. causal, *cause to meet,* τινά τινι *IG*14.2431 (Fréjus).

**ἀντιβολ-ή,** ἡ, *confronting, comparing, collation,* ἀντιγράφων Str.17.1.5; *opposition,* ἐξ ἀντιβολῆς παραβάλλειν Hsch. s.v. παραβλήδην. II. *discussion,* A.D.*Conj.*213.20. III. *substitute, PHolm.*10.14. **-ήρ·** στρωτὴρ μικρός (Lacon.), Hsch. **-ησις,** εως, ἡ, = sq., Pl.*Ap.*37a, *Smp.*183a. **-ία,** ἡ, *an entreaty, prayer,* Eup.317, Th.7.75. **-ον,** τό, = ἀντίγραφον, Sch.Il.18.490, Sch.Od.12.556.

**ἀντιβομβέω,** *return a humming sound,* Ach.Tat.3.2, cf. Eust.1885.19.

**ἀντιβόρειον,** τό, name of a *sundial,* Vitr.9.8.1.

**ἀντιβουλεύομαι,** Med., *give contrary advice,* Polyaen.1.30.4.

**ἀντιβρᾰδύνω** [ῡ], *delay in turn,* Sch.Th.3.10.

**ἀντιβρίθω** [ρῑ], *press down in the opposite scale,* Ph.2.170.

**ἀντιβροντάω,** *rival in thundering,* τινί Luc.*Tim.*2; βρονταῖς ἀ. D.C.59.28.

**ἀντιγᾰμέω,** *marry in turn,* Eust.1796.53.

**ἀντιγέγωνα,** pf. in pres. sense, *return a cry, AP*9.177.

**ἀντιγενεηλογέω,** Ion. form, *give a different pedigree,* Hdt.2.143.

**ἀντιγένεσις,** εως, ἡ, Astrol., *recasting of nativity in a later yea[r]* Vett.Val.213.20, al.

**ἀντιγεννάω,** *generate in rivalry,* Lync.ap.Ath.7.285f; or *in retur[n]* τοὺς γονεῖς Ph.1.89.

**ἀντιγεοῦχος,** ὁ, *land-agent, BGU*303.4 (vi A.D.), *POxy.*943.8 ( A.D.).

**ἀντιγεραίρω,** *honour in turn,* App.*BC*2.140.

**ἀντιγηροτροφέω,** *support in old age in turn,* Lesb.Rh.2.10.

**ἀντιγλαυκισμός,** ὁ, *substitute for blue dye, PLeid.X.*100.

**ἀντιγνωμονέω,** *to be of a different opinion,* τινί D.C.46.44; ἀ. μ[ὴ] οὐκ εἶναί τι *think* that a thing is *otherwise,* X.*Cyr.*4.3.8.

**ἀντι-γόνιον·** βοτάνη, καὶ ἄνθος, Hsch. **-γόνιος·** βόλος τις οὕτω[ς] ἐκαλεῖτο, Id. **-γονον** ἀκακία, Id.

⊛**Ἀντίγονος,** ὁ, name of several Macedonian kings:—hence ⊛**Ἀντιγόνειος,** α, ον, *of Antigonus,* Polyaen.4.9.1; **Ἀντιγόνεια,** τά, name of a *festival in his honour,* Plb.28.19.3, *IG*11.154*A*42 (Delos, ii B.C.): also **Ἀντιγονικός,** ή, όν, Plu.*Arat.*54:— fem. **Ἀντιγονίς,** ίδος, a kind of *cup named from him,* Polem.Hist.57, Plu.*Aem.*33:—**Ἀντιγονίζω,** *to be on Antigonus' side, of his party,* Polyaen.4.6.13, D.T.638.16.

**ἀντίγραμμα,** ατος, τό, *duplicate letter,* Luc.*Herm.*40; = ἀντίγραφον, Gal.17.59.

**ἀντιγρᾰφ-εία,** ἡ, *office of* ἀντιγραφεύς, *PPetr.*3p.162, *PTeb.*5.85 (ii B.C., pl.), cf. *Inscr.Prien.*108.222 (ii B.C.; -ία lapis). ⊛**-εῖον,** τό, *office whence* ἀντίγραφα *were issued, Jahresh.*7 *Beibl.*44 (Ephesus), cf. ib.18 *Beibl.*286. ⊛**-εύς,** έως, ὁ, *checking-* or *copying-clerk,* a public officer, Aeschin.3.25, cf. *IG*2.408, al., cf. 575 (of a deme), *SIG*364.22 (Ephesus), etc., Plb.6.56.13, *PRev.Laws* 12.1; ἀ. τῶν εἰσενεγκόντων *one who keeps a check upon* their *accounts,* D.22.70. ⊛**-ή,** ἡ, *a reply in writing,* such as Caesar's *Anticato* in reply to Cicero's *Cato,* Plu.*Caes.*3, cf. *Sol.*1, Id.2.1059b, Herm.*in Phdr.*p.189 A. II. as law-term, *answer put in by the defendant, plea,* D.45.46 (where a specimen is found); sts. of *the plaintiff's plea, indictment,* Pl.*Ap.*27c, Hyp.*Eux.*31:– sts. ἀντιγραφή was used indifferently of both parties, cf. Harp.:—in Ar.*Nu.*471, generally, *counter-pleas,* cf. Poll.8.58. III. *transcribing,* D.H.4.62. 2. = ἀντίγραφον, Plu.2.577e. IV. *rescript, imperial decree, OGI*262.27. **-ικός,** ή, όν, τὸ ἀ. κεφάλαιον *concerning the indictment,* Sch.Aristid p.441 D. ⊛**-ος,** ον, *copied, in duplicate,* στῆλαι, διαθῆκαι, etc., D.20.36, 45.10, etc. II. as Subst., ἀντίγραφον, τό, *transcript, copy,* Decr.ap.And.1.79, Lys.32.7, D.25.47, Arist.*Pol.*1309a11; esp. of *copies* of a book, Ἀττικιανὰ ἀντίγραφα *copies* of an edition issued by Atticus, Harp. s.v. Ἀργᾶς, al.; *certified copy* of official document, *CIR*1.4 (i A.D.); εἰκόνος ἀ. *copy* of a picture, Luc.*Zeux.*3 (but -φος Jac.). ⊛**-ω,** *write against* or *in answer, write back,* v.l. in Th.1.129 (Pass.), Phld.*Ir.*p.86 W., Plu.*Luc.*21, D.Chr.2.18, *PFlor.*278 ii 30 (iii A.D.), etc.; ἀ. τῇ γραφῇ *vie in description* with painting, Longus *Prooem.* II. Med., with pf. Pass. (Aeschin.1.154, D.45.45), as law-term, *put in as an* ἀντιγραφή, *plead against,* τι περί τινος Is.11.17, cf. D.48.31; also ἀ. τινί, c. inf., *plead against* another *that* such is the case, Lys.23.5, D.44.39:—also, *bring a counter-accusation,* Poll.8.58, cf. Aeschin.1.119, 154; later in Act., *plead in answer to* a charge, -γράψαι ὡς οὐκ ἔπραξεν D.S.1.75. 2. *keep a counter-reckoning* of money paid or received (cf. ἀντιγραφεύς), Arist.*Ath.*54.3; simply, *check* accounts, *PTeb.*89.13 (ii B.C.). 3. *issue a rescript, SIG*888.8. III. Pass., aor. ἀντιγραφῆναι *to be copied,* εἰς στήλας *Milet.*3.148.93. **-γραψις,** εως, ἡ, *putting in of an* ἀντιγραφή, v.l. in Lys.23.10.

⊛**ἀντιγυμνᾰσιαρχέω,** *to be deputy-gymnasiarch, AJA*19.324 (Locr.).

**ἀντιγώνιος,** ον, *marking opposite angles,* of stars in a quadrilateral, Hipparch.3.4.3, Ptol.*Alm.*7.1.

**ἀντιδάκνω,** fut. -δήξομαι Muson.*Fr.*10p.55 H.: the aor. ἀντέδακα dub. in Luc.*Ocyp.*27:—*bite in turn,* Hdt.4.168, Ael.*NA*4.19, Muson. l.c.

**ἀντιδάκτῠλος,** ὁ, *thumb,* Aq.*Ex.*29.20. II. in Metric, *dactyl reversed, anapaest,* Diom.1.478 K., Choerob.*in Heph.*p.215 C.

**ἀντιδᾰνειστέον,** *one must lend in return,* τῷ δανείσαντι Arist.*EN*1165a8.

**ἀντιδᾰπᾰνάω** or **-αομαι,** *spend in turn upon,* τοὺς δαπανωμένους Lib.*Ep.*843 (dub. l.).

**ἀντίδειξις,** εως, ἡ, *refutation, Corp.Herm.*16.1.

**ἀντίδειπνος,** ον, *taking anothers place at dinner,* Luc.*Gall.*9.

**ἀντιδεξιόομαι,** *give the right hand in turn, return one's salute,* τινά X.*Cyr.*4.2.19, D.Chr.38.47, Luc.*Laps.*13.

**ἀντιδέομαι,** *entreat in return,* Pl.*La.*186d.

**ἀντιδέρκομαι,** = ἀντιβλέπω, c. acc., E.*HF*163.

⊛**ἀντιδέχομαι,** *receive in return,* A.*Ch.*916; ἀμοιβὰς κακάς *Cat.Cod. Astr.*2.211; ἔδωκα κἀντεδεξάμην E.*IA*1222.

**ἀντιδέω,** *fetter in turn,* Diog.Oen.39.

**ἀντιδημᾰγωγέω,** *practise counter-demagogy,* πρὸς τὴν Κίμωνος εὐπορίαν Arist.*Ath.*27.3, cf. Plu.*CG*8.

**ἀντιδημηγορέω,** *harangue in opposition to,* τινί Eust.1029.1.

**ἀντιδημιουργέομαι,** Med., *manufacture in competition,* πρός τι Lync.ap.Ath.11.469b.

**ἀντιδια-βαίνω,** *cross over in turn,* X.*Ages.*1.8, dub.l. J.*AJ*13.1.3. **-βάλλω,** *to attack in return,* τὸν διαβάλλοντα Arist.*Rh.*1416a26. **-γράφω** [ᾰφ], *pay in money instead of kind, PPetr.*2 p.102

ii B.C., Pass.) :—Med., *Inscr.Magn.*103.68 (ii B.C.) :—hence ※γρᾰ-ή, ἡ, *Ostr.*1509, al. (ii B.C.). -ζεύγνῡμαι, *pair off with*, in ichotomy, S.E.*M.*11.15 ; *to be subjoined in turn*, A.D.*Synt.*126.10.

※ἀντιδιαίρ-εσις, εως, ἡ, in Logic, *division by dichotomy*, Plot.4.4.8, 6.3.10, D.L.7.61, Iamb.*Myst.*1.15. II. in Surgery, *counter-incision*, Paul.Aeg.4.48. -έω, *distinguish logically*, βαρβάρους πρὸς Ἕλληνας Str.14.2.28, cf. Demetr.Lac.*Herc.*1012.68, Phld.*Oec.*p.35 J.; τὸ σύνθετον τῷ ἁπλῷ Plot.6.2.10, cf. Iamb.*Comm.Math.*4 :— Pass., *to be opposed as the members of a natural classification*, Arist.*Cat.*14$^b$34, *Top.*142$^a$36, cf. Iamb.*Myst.*9.7. II. Med., τροφὴν τοῖς νεύροις, perh. *distribute*, TheoGymn.ap.Gal.6.208.

ἀντιδιάκειμαι, *to be different*, of mixed stuffs, Aq.*De.*22.11.

ἀντιδιάκονος [ᾱ], ον, *serving in return*, τοῖς ἄλλοις Str.16.4.26.

ἀντιδιακοσμέω, *arrange* or *array in opposition*, of troops, App.*BC*2.75.

ἀντιδιαλέγομαι, *reply to, answer in discussion*, in Pass., περὶ τῶν ἀντιδιαλεγομένων τοῖς διαλεκτικοῖς, title of work by Chrysipp., D.L.7.202.

ἀντιδιαλλάσσομαι, Med., *exchange* prisoners, τινά τινος D.H.19.13. II. of historians, *differ* in an account, πρός τι Id.1.84.

ἀντιδια-λογίζομαι, *set off in compensation*, *Gloss.* -νυκτερεύω, *bivouac opposite to*, τινί App.*BC*4.130. -πλέκω, *retort*, ἀντιδιαπλέκει ὡς.. Aeschin.3.28, cf. *AB*406. -σταλτικός, ἡ, όν, *distinctive*, A.D.*Pron.*24.12, *Synt.*97.17. Adv. -κῶς Id.*Pron.*40.4. -στᾰτέω, *be at variance*, ἀλλήλοις Ammon.*Diff.*35. -στέλλω, *distinguish, discriminate*, Str.10.2.17 ; ἁπλᾶ καὶ σύνθετα Plot.6.1.29 ; τι ἀπό τινος Longin.*Proll.Heph.*p.83C.:—Med., *controvert*, Sor.2.54. II. *contrast, oppose*, τί τινι S.E.*P.*1.9 ; τινὰς πρός τινας D.H.*Th.*32 ; τι πρός τι Alex.Aphr.*in Metaph.*400.17 :—Pass., A.D.*Synt.*14.24. -στολή, ἡ, *opposition, distinction*, Id.*Pron.*23.14, *Synt.*15.17, al., Alex.Aphr.*in Metaph.*11.12, etc. II. Medic., *counter-dilatation*, ἀρτηριῶν πρὸς καρδίαν Gal.8.760. -ταξις, εως, ἡ, *comparison of arguments* for and against a thesis, Iamb.*Comm.Math.*35. -τάσσομαι, Med., *oppose*, τινὶ πρὸς τὰ ὅλα Arr.*Epict.*3.24.24 ; τινὶ περί τινος S.E.*M.*7.150 : abs., ib.8.126. -τίθημι, *retaliate upon* a person, D.S.34.12 ; κακῶς παθόντα ἀ. Eust.546.28 .—Med., *offer resistance*, πρὸς τὴν πειθώ Longin.17.1 ; τοὺς ἀντιδιατιθεμένους *opponents*, 2*Ep.Ti.*2.25.

ἀντιδῐδάσκᾰλοι, οἱ, *poets who are rivals in dramatic* or *lyric contests*, Sch.Pi.*N.*4.60.

ἀντιδῐδάσκω, *inform, instruct in turn* or *on the other side*, App.*BC*5.19, *AP*6.236(Phil.). II. of dramatists, etc., *contend for the prize*, Ar.*V.*1410, cf. Satyr.*Vit.Eur.Fr.*38.19, D.Chr.37.40.

ἀντιδίδωμι, *give in return, repay*, τινί τι Hdt.1.70, 3.135, A.*Ch.*94, etc. ; πόνον, οὐ χάριν, ἀντιδῶσιν ἔχειν S.*OC*232, cf. A.*Ch.*498, *Eu.*264 ; νέκυν νεκρῶν ἀμοιβὸν ἀ. S.*Ant.*1067 ; ἀ. χάριν E.*HF*1337, cf. Th.1.41, 3.63 ; τιμωρίαν Id.2.53 ; λαμβάνων ἀντεδίδου X.*Cyr.*8.6.23 :—Pass., ἔλεος πρός τινα δίκαιος ἀντιδίδοσθαι Th.3.40. 2. *give for* or *instead of*, τί τινος E.*Alc.*340, *IT*28 ; τι ἀντί τινος Ar.*Pax*1251. II. at Athens, ἀ. [τὴν οὐσίαν] *offer to change fortunes with* one (cf. ἀντίδοσις II), Lys.24.9, D.20.130 ; ἀ. τριηραρχίαν Id.21.78 ; *accept such an offer*, Id.28.17. III. *give as an antidote*, Damocr.ap.Gal.14.90.

ἀντιδιέξειμι, (εἶμι *ibo*) *go through, recount in turn*, ὀνόματα Aeschin.1.155.

ἀντιδιεξέρχομαι, *go through in opposition*, ἀ. λόγῳ Pl.*Tht.*167d.

ἀντιδιεσταλμένως, Adv. pf. part. Pass. of ἀντιδιαστέλλω, *as distinguished from, opposed to*, Iamb.*in Nic.*p.12 P.

ἀντιδιηγέομαι, *introduce a counter narration*, Corn.*Rh.*p.364 H. b. *relate in turn*, X.Eph.5.1.

ἀντιδιήγησις, εως, ἡ, *counter-narration*, Fortunat.*Rh.*2.19.

ἀντιδιΐστημι, = ἀντιδιαστέλλω, Dam.*Pr.*67, Hsch., Suid. s. v. ἀντιδιαστέλλεται.

ἀντιδῐκ-άζομαι, *implead one another*, Lys.*Fr.*300S. -ᾰσία, ἡ, *litigation*, Aq.*Pr.*20.3. -έω, impf. ἠντιδίκουν Lys.6.12, but ἠντεδίκουν (acc. to the best MSS.) D.39.37, 40.18 : aor. ἠντεδίκησα Id.47.28 :—*to be an* ἀντίδικος, *dispute, go to law*, περί τινος X.*Mem.*4.4.8 ; οἱ ἀντιδικοῦντες ἑκάτεροι *the parties to a suit*, Pl.*Lg.*948d : abs., of the defendant, ἀντιδικῶν Ar.*Nu.*776 ; ἀ. πρός τι or πρός τινα *to urge one's suit against..*, D.28.17, 41.10, Is.11.9 ; *join issue*, ἠντιδίκει ἢ μήν.., c. acc. et inf., Lys. l. c. ; *oppose, rebut*, διαβολαῖς D.41.13 ; ἀλλήλοις prob. in Thugen.1 D. II. Pass., *to be an object of dispute*, Phot.p.147 R. -ησις, εως, ἡ, = sq., *Gloss.* -ία, ἡ, *litigation, contention*, πρός τινα ὑπέρ τινος Plu.2.483b ; ὁ ἐξ -ίας *the opponent in a process*, Mitteis*Chr.*88.14 (ii A.D.) ; Astrol., opp. συναφεῖαι, συνάψεις, Ptol.*Tetr.*191. -ος, ον, *opponent* or *adversary in a suit*, Aeschin.2.165, cf. Pl.*Phdr.*273c : fem., ἡ ἀ. *POxy.*37 i 8 (i A.D.) : properly, *the defendant*, Antipho 1.2 ; but also, *the plaintiff*, Lys.7.13 ; ἀ. πρός τινα Antipho 1.5 : —generally, *opponent, adversary*, A.*Ag.*41 ; ἀληθινῶν ἀ. [Heraclit.]133, cf. 1*Ep.Pet.*5.8, Phld.*Ir.*p.65 W.

ἀντιδικτάτωρ, ορος, ὁ, = Lat. *pro dictatore*, Lyd.*Mag.*1.38.

ἀντιδιορίζω, *define in turn, give a counter-definition*, Gal.18(2).837.

ἀντιδιορύσσω, Att. -ττω, *countermine*, Str.12.8.11.

※ἀντιδίσκωσις, εως, ἡ, *doubling of the sun's disk*, Lyd.*Ost.*9c.

ἀντιδοκέω, *think oneself equal to*, κύμασιν Lxx 2 *Ma.*9.8.

ἀντιδόκιον, τό, Archit., *course supporting beams*, ἀ. λίθινον *Milet.*3 p.172 (iii B.C.).

※ἀντιδομή, ἡ, (δέμω) *opposed* or *substituted building*, Aen.Tact.23.5.

ἀντι-δοξάζω, *to be of a contrary opinion*, Pl.*Tht.*170d, Epicur.*Nat.*14.8, Phld.*Sign.*19, cf. 31, D.L.9.18. -δοξέω, = foreg., τινί or πρός τινα, Plb.2.56.1, 16.14.4 ; τινὶ περί τινος D.S.2.29 : abs., Boeth.*Stoic.*3.267. -δοξος, ον, *of a different opinion* or *sect*, Luc.*Herm.*17, Aristaenet.1.10 ; μάχη φορᾶς ἀ. Luc.*Par.*29.

ἀντίδορος, ον, (δορά) *instead of skin*, κάρυον χλωρῆς ἀντίδορον λεπίδος *with a green husk as integument*, *AP*6.22 (Zon.).

ἀντί-δοσις, εως, ἡ, (ἀντιδίδωμι) *giving in return, exchange*, Arist.*EN*1133$^a$6, Call.*Fr.*221 ; φορτίων D.S.2.54 ; αἰχμαλώτων 12.63 ; καρπῶν D.Chr.38.22 ; κακῶν App.*BC*1.3 ; ἡ εἰς τὴν σιωπὴν ἀ. Ael.*NA*5.9 :—*repayment, requital*, ὕβρεως Orac.ap.Luc.*Alex.*50 ; ἀντίδοσιν τινος *in return for..*, *IG*3.172. II. at Athens, *a form by which a citizen charged with a* λειτουργία or εἰσφορά *might call upon any other citizen*, whom he thought richer than himself, *either to exchange properties, or to submit to the charge himself*, Lys.3.20, etc., cf. Cratin.14 D. ; καλεῖσθαί τινα εἰς ἀ. τριηραρχίας ἢ χορηγίας X.*Oec.*7.3 ; καταστὰς (sc. χορηγὸς) ἐξ ἀντιδόσεως D.21.156 ; ποιεῖσθαι ἀ. τινι Id.4.36 ; ἀ. ἐπ' ἐμὲ παρεσκεύασαν 28.17 ; cf. Isoc.15, D.42. ※-δοτος, ον, (ἀντιδίδωμι) *given in lieu of*, πυρὸς *AP*9.165 (Pall.). II. *given as a remedy for*, κακῶν φάρμακον ἀ. ib.10.118. 2. as Subst., ἀντίδοτος (sc. δόσις), ἡ, *an antidote, remedy*, *AP*12.13 (Strat.), Gal.14.1, etc. : in other places the gender is uncertain, Plu.2.42d, 54e, etc. :—hence Dim. ἀντιδότιον, τό, Archig.ap.Philum.*Ven.*14.7.

ἀντιδουλεύω, *serve in turn*, τοῖς τεκοῦσι γὰρ δύστηνος ὅστις μὴ ἀντιδουλεύει τέκνων E.*Supp.*362.

ἀντίδουλος, ον, *instead of a slave*, neut. pl. as Adv., ταύρων γονὰς δοὺς ἀντίδουλα A.*Fr.*194. II. of persons, *being as a slave, treated as a slave*, Id.*Ch.*135.

ἀντίδουπος, ον, *re-echoing*, ᾄδειν A.*Pers.*121 (lyr.) ; βοᾶν ἀντίδουπό τινι ib.1040, parodied by Pl.Com.27 D.

ἀντιδράσσομαι, Att. -ττομαι, *lay hold of*, καρδίας Them.*Or.*32.357b.

ἀντί-δρᾱσις, εως, ἡ, *retaliation*, Anon.*in Rh.*91.30. -δράω, fut. -δράσω [ᾱ], *act against, retaliate*, παθὼν μὲν ἀντέδρων S.*OC*271, cf. 953, E.*Andr.*438, Antipho 4.2.2, etc. ; πρὸς τὰς πράξεις ἀ. S.*OC*959 .—Pass., Iamb.*Myst.*3.29. II. c. acc. pers., *repay, requite*, ἀ. τινὰ κακῶς S.*OC*1191, cf. Pl.*Cri.*49d ; γενναῖα γὰρ παθόντες ὑμᾶς ἀντιδρᾶν ὀφείλομεν E.*Supp.*1179.

ἀντιδρομέω, *run in a contrary direction*, Luc.*Astr.*12.

ἀντιδύνᾰμος [ῠ], ον, = ἀντίβιος, Sch.Opp.*H.*5.267.

ἀντιδύνω [ῡ], *set opposite to*, *Intr.Arat.*p.328 Maass.

ἀντιδυσχεραίνω, *to be angry in turn*, τοῖς δυσχεραίνουσιν M.Ant.6.26.

※ἀντι-δωρεά, ἡ, *a return-gift, recompense*, Arist.*EN*1123$^a$3. -δωρέομαι, *present in return*, ἀ. τινά τινι one *with* a thing, Hdt.2.30 ; τινί τι a thing *to* one, θεοὶ δέ σοι ἐσθλῶν ἀμοιβὰς ἀντιδωρησαίατο E.*Hel.*159, cf. Pl.*Euthphr.*14e ; *offer instead* τούτου ἐφιέμενος ἀ. ἄλλο Arist.*EN*1159$^b$14. -δωρον, τό, *return-gift*, Men.Prot.p.20 D., Just.*Nov.*120.11, v.l. for ἀντίδουλα in A.*Fr.*194.

ἀντιζεύγνῡμι, *annex*, e. g. a word in the corresponding clause of a sentence, D.H.*Amm.*2.11.

ἀντι-ζηλία, ἡ, *rivalry*, Vett.Val.39.27, Heph.Astr.2.28. -ζηλος, ὁ, ἡ, *rival, adversary*, Lxx *Le.*18.18, *Si.*26.6 : as Adj., *controversial, in rivalry*, παράδοσις Vett.Val.198.11 : Astrol., ὁ διάμετρος ἀ. Porph. in Ptol.*Tetr.*186. -ζηλόω, in Pass., *to be emulous of, rival*, Vett.Val.47.15.

ἀντιζητέω, *seek one who is seeking us*, X.*Oec.*8.23.

ἀντίζομαι, Ion. for ἀνθίζομαι.

ἀντιζῠγ-ής, ές, = διάμετρος, Petos.ap.Vett.Val.128.25. -ία, ἡ, *equivalence*, *Theol.Ar.*57. II. *diametrical opposition*, Vett.Val.123.26. ※-ος, ον, *put in the opposite scale* : hence, *balancing, correspondent*, Arist.*PA*666$^a$27, Plu.2.723c ; ζῴδια Anon.*II Intr. Arat.*p.128 Maass. II. ἀντίζυγα, τά, *vertical cross-pieces*, in building, *IG*1$^2$.463. -όω, *insert cross-pieces*, ibid. II. *counterbalance*, πρός τι Eust.60.29.

ἀντιζωγρέω, *save alive in turn*, Babr.107.16.

ἀντιθάλπω, *warm mutually*, ἀλλήλους J.*BJ*4.4.6.

ἀντιθᾰνᾰτάω, *devise death in turn*, Eust.1029.40.

ἀντιθάπτω, *bury opposite* :—Pass., aor. ἀντετάφην *IG*14.1721.

※ἀντίθεμα, ατος, τό, = ἀντίθημα, *IG*4.823.69, Haussoullier *Milet* p.163.

※ἀντίθεος, η, ον, *equal to the gods, godlike* (cf. S.E.*M.*7.6) : Homeric epith. of heroes, Il.5.663, etc. ; of nations, ib.12.408, Od.6.241 ; of women, only ib.11.117 ; applied even to Polyphemus and the suitors, ib.1.70, 14.18 ; ἥρωες ἀ. B.10.79. II. *contrary to God*, Ph.1.566, al. 2. Subst. ἀντίθεος, ὁ, *hostile deity*, Hld.4.7, Iamb.*Myst.*3.31, *PMag.Lond.*121.635 (unless Adj., *disguised as a god*).

ἀντιθερᾰπεύω, *take care of in turn*, γονέας X.*Cyr.*8.3.49. 2. *court in return*, in Pass., J.*AJ*17.2.4, Max.Tyr.20.6.

ἀντιθερμαίνω, *warm in turn*, Alex.Aphr.*Pr.*1.115, Gal.1.656.

ἀντιθέσιον, τό, = ξάνθιον, Dsc.4.136.

※ἀντί-θεσις, εως, ἡ, *opposition*, Pl.*Sph.*257e, 258b ; ἀντίθεσιν ἔχειν πρός τι *correspond to..*, Arist.*HA*502$^a$25 ; *resistance*, *AP*12.200 (Strat.). 2. in Logic, *opposition* of propositions, in pl., Arist.*Int.*19$^b$20, *Top.*113$^b$15, *Metaph.*1054$^a$23. b. *substitution of the contradictory*, as 'not-man' for 'man', ἡ σὺν -θέσει ἀντιστροφή, conversion *by negation*, e.g. 'man is an animal ∴ what is not an animal cannot be a man', Anon.*in SE*15.23, al. 3. Rhet., *antithesis*, Isoc.12.2, Arist.*Rh.*1410$^a$22 ; in forensic oratory, *counter-proposition*, Hermog.*Id.*1.4, al. 4. Gramm., *change* or *transposition* of a letter, Hdn.Gr.2.945, Diom.1.442 K. -θετέον, *one must oppose*, πρός τι ὅτι.. Arist.*Pol.*1286$^b$2. -θετικός, ἡ, όν, *setting in opposition, contrasting*, ἀ. δύναμις φαινομένων τε καὶ νοουμένων S.E.*P.*1.8 ;

*antithetical*, Eust.1325.19; ἀντιθετικά, τά, D.21 Arg.ii 9; ἀ. στάσις Hermog.*Stat.*4, al. II. *contrasted, correspondent*, of poems in which a number of κῶλα are repeated in reversed order, Heph. *Poëm.*4.6. **-θετος**, ον, *opposed, antithetic*, ἀ. εἰπὼν οὐδέν Timocl. 127; φύσιν ἔχειν ἀ. πρός τι Plu.2.672c; ἀρεταῖς κακίαι ἀ. S.E.*M.*9.156, cf. Plot.2.5.2, Phld.*Ir.*p.87 W.: c. gen., *inconsistent with*, *PTeb.*24.63. Adv. **-τως**, συζυγεῖν Plu.2.1022e, cf. Demetr.*Eloc.*24; ἀ. ἔχειν, of bones in arm, Heliod.ap.Orib.44.23.27: ἀ. ἀντικεῖσθαι, of ὑγίεια and νόσος, opp. ἀντιφατικῶς, Alex.Aphr. *in Top.*580.1. 2. = διάμετρος, Vett.Val.340.23. 3. ἀ. ψῆφος *blackball*, *GDI*4p.1204 (Itanos). 4. ἀντίθετον, τό, *antithesis*, Ar.*Fr.*326, Arist.*Rh.Al.*1435b26, Aeschin. 2.4.

***ἀντιθέω**, fut. -θεύσομαι Hdt.5.22:—*run against* another, *compete in a race*, l.c. II. *run contrary ways*, *AP*9.822.

**ἀντιθήγω**, *whet against* another, ὀδόντας ἐπί τινα Luc.*Par.*51.

**ἀντίθημα**, ατος, τό, *revetment* of wall, *IG*1.321, cf. 11.203*A*45 (Delos).

**ἀντιθλίβω** [λῑ], *press against, counteract*, ἀλλήλους Archyt.ap. Stob.2.13.120:—Pass., ἀντιθλίβεται τὸ θλῖβον crushing *produces counter-crushing*, Arist.*GA*768b20.

**ἀντιθνήσκω**, *die in turn* or *for* another, *EM*114.14.

**ἀντιθρηνέω**, *wail in return*, τινί *An.Ox.*3.180.

***ἀντίθροος**, ον, *echoing, resounding*, Coluth.118, *APl.*4.153 (Satyr.).

**ἀντιθρῴσκω**, *leap to meet*, Emp.105.1.

**ἀντιθῡμόομαι**, *show anger in turn*, Ael.*NA*17.13 codd. (ἀντιφιλοτιμ– Hercher).

***ἀντίθῠρος**, ον, (θύρα) *opposite the door*, κατ' ἀντίθυρον κλισίης *opposite the door* of the house, Od.16.159, as the Sch.; or it may be a neut. Subst. ἀντίθυρον *the part facing the door, vestibule*, as it is in βᾶτε κατ' ἀντιθύρων S.*El.*1433, ubi v. Herm.: in Luc.*Symp.*8, *the side of a room facing the door*, cf. *Alex.*16, *Dom.*26.

**ἀντιθύω**, *sacrifice in turn*, Philox.10 (Pass.).

**ἀντικαθαιρέω**, *pull down* or *destroy in turn*, D.C.46.34.

**ἀντικαθεύδω**, *sleep again* or *instead*, *AP*11.366 (Maced.).

**ἀντικάθημαι**, Ion. **ἀντικάτ–**, properly pf. of ἀντικαθίζομαι, but used as pres.:—*to be set over against*, τινί Archyt.ap.Stob.4.1.138. 2. mostly of armies or fleets, *lie over against*, so as to watch each other, ἡμέραι σφι ἀντικατημένοισι ἐγεγόνεσαν ὀκτώ Hdt.9.39, cf. 41, Th.5.6, X.*Eq.Mag.*8.12, etc.: metaph., λόγος ἀ. τινι S.E.*M.*1.145.

**ἀντικαθίζομαι**, Ion. **ἀντικατ–**, fut. -εδοῦμαι: aor. -εζόμην:—Med., *sit* or *lie over against*, of armies or fleets watching one another, Hdt. 4.3, 5.1, Th.1.30, 4.124. II. Act., *place* or *settle instead of* another, Lxx 4*Ki.*17.26.

***ἀντικαθίστημι**, Ion. **ἀντικατ–**, fut. -καταστήσω:—*replace, substitute*, ἄλλα Hdt.9.93; μὴ ἐλάσσω ἀντικαταστῆσαι πάλιν *replace* an equal quantity of gold, Th.2.13; ἄλλους ἀ. *set up* others *in their stead*, Arist.*Mir.*838a3. 2. *set against, oppose*, τινὰ πρός τινα Th. 4.93; *establish as a counterpart*, τινά τινι Pl.*R.*591a. 3. *set up* or *bring back again*, ἀ. ἐπὶ τὸ θαρρεῖν Th.2.65; *rally*, τοὺς θορυβηθέντας D.H.6.11. II. Pass., with aor. 2 and pf. Act.; also aor. 1 κατεστάθην X.*An.*3.1.38:—*to be put in another's place, reign in his stead*, Hdt.2.37, X.l.c. 2. *to be pitted against* another, *opposed*, abs., Th.1.71, 3.47, etc.; τινί X.*Eq.Mag.*7.5. b. in lawsuits, *to be confronted with*, τινί, πρός τινα, *POxy.*97.9 (ii A.D.), *BGU*168.11 (ii A.D.).

**ἀντίκαινον**· ἰσόκαινον, Hsch.

**ἀντικαίω**, Att. -κάω, *set on fire in turn*, Pl.*Ti.*65e.

**ἀντικᾰκουργέω**, *damage in return*, τινά Pl.*Cri.*49c, 54c.

**ἀντικᾰκόω**, = foreg., J.*BJ*3.7.30.

**ἀντικᾰλέω**, *invite in turn*, X.*Smp.*1.15 (in fut. Pass. -κληθήσομαι), cf. *Ev.Luc.*14.12.

**ἀντικαλλωπίζομαι**, *adorn oneself in rivalry with*, πρὸς τὴν πολυτέλειαν εὐτελείᾳ Plu.2.406d.

**ἀντικάνθαρον**, = ἡμεροκαλλές, Ps.-Dsc.3.122. II. perh. *cost of carriage*, Just.*Edict.*13.15.

**ἀντικάρδιον**, τό, in Poll.2.165, *pit of the stomach*: but Ruf.*Onom.* 68 makes it *the depression in the throat above the clavicle*, = σφαγή, λαυκανίη, cf. Hsch. (ἀντικαραῶν cod.).

**ἀντικαρτερέω**, *hold out against*, πρός τι D.C.39.41.

**ἀντικαταβάλλω**, in Med., *repay, render*, τὴν προσήκουσαν χάριν Lib.*Decl.*43.3.

**ἀντικατάγω** [ᾰγ], *bring in instead*:—Pass., ἀντικαταχθῆμέν τινι *come into the place of* another, Ti.Locr.101d.

**ἀντικατα-δύνω** [ῡ], *set over against*, of stars setting at sunrise, Hipparch.2.2.11, al., TheoSm.p.137 H. **-δύομαι**, *stoop down in turn* or *in opposition*, Ach.Tat.6.18. **-δῠσις**, εως, ἡ, *setting in the opposite quarter*, in pl., Hipparch.2.1.14, 2.2.1. **-θνήσκω**, aor. 2 -έθανον, *die* or *be slain in turn*, τοὺς κτανόντας ἀντικατθανεῖν A.*Ch.* 144. **-κλείω**, in Pass., *to be enclosed in turn*, Ruf.*Oss.*38. **-λαμβάνω**, *take possession of in turn*, Ti.Locr.102d. II. = ἀντιλαγχάνω, δίκην Pl.Com.9 D. III. *occupy in opposition*, λόφον D.C.36.47, cf. 42.31. **-λέγω**, *enroll instead*, soldiers or senators, Id.40.65, 54.14. **-λείπω**, *leave in one's stead*, Pl.*R.*540b, Pyth.*Sim.*36.

**ἀντικατ-αλλᾰγή**, ἡ, *exchange*, τινὸς πρός τι Plu.2.49d, cf. *PFlor.* 47.15 (iii A.D.); *requital*, Sch.Opp.*H.*2.687. **-άλλαγμα**, ατος, τό, *satisfaction*, J.*AJ*15.9.2, Onos.34.4 (pl.). **-αλλακτέον**, *one must exchange*, τινά τινων Arr.*Epict.*4.3 tit. ***-άλλαξις**, εως, ἡ, *profits of commerce*, D.L.7.99, *BGU*1210.177 (ii A.D., pl.). **-αλλάσσομαι**, Att. **-ττομαι**, Med., *exchange* one thing *for* another: 1. *give* one thing *for* another, τὴν ἰδίαν ψυχὴν ἀντὶ τῆς κοινῆς σωτηρίας Lycurg.88; τὸ ζῆν ὑπὲρ ἄλλου οὐδενός Isoc.5.135. 2. *receive* one thing *in exchange for* another, τι ἀντί τινος Id.6.109, Aeschin.3.92, D.Chr.40. 30. 3. *set off* or *balance* one thing *against* another, εὐεργεσίας κρίσεως Din.1.14; ἀ. τι πρὸς τὴν περὶ τὰ θεῖα φιλοσοφίαν *afford* some *compensation for*.., Arist.*PA*645a3; ἀ. ἀδικοῦντα, εἰ βλαβερόν, ἀλλὰ καλό *submit in justification a balance* in case of injury.., Id.*Rh.*1416 11. 4. *interchange*, Id.*EN*1157a12. II. Pass., ἀντικαταλλαγῆναι (sc. τῇ τύχῃ) *to be reconciled*, Plb.15.20.5: abs., *come to an agreement*, περὶ οὗ ἀντικατηλλάγη *PFlor.*47.13. III. Act., *come to an agreement*, ὁμολογῶμεν ἀντικατηλλαχέναι πρὸς ἀλλήλους ib.3 (iii A.D.).

**ἀντικατα-μετρέω**, *assign* land *in compensation* or *exchange*, *PTeb.* 61b111, 72.39 (ii B.C., Pass.). **-μύω** [ῡ], *shut one's eyes in turn*, Poll.9.113. **-πλήσσω**, *frighten in turn*, App.*BC*3.91, Onos.29. 2. **-ρρέω**, *flow down, drip in turn*, Olymp. *in Mete.*80.36, al., Steph. *in Hp.*1.130 D., al.; *run back again*, Gal.8.285. **-σκευάζω**, *establish instead*, D.H.1.5. 2. 'paint in the opposite colours', πολλὰ τῶν ἀδίκων J.*AJ*16.7.1. 3. *prepare in opposition*, D.C.49.37, 77. 15. ***-στᾰσις**, εως, ἡ, *being confronted with one another*, Plb.4. 47.4; *opposition*, J.*AJ*16.2.5; λόγοι ἐξ ἀντικαταστάσεως γενόμενοι Decr.ib.14.10.21, cf. *SIG*785.7 (Chios). **-στρᾰτοπεδεύω**, *to encamp opposite*, D.H.8.84. **-σχεσις**, εως, ἡ, *holding in by force*, τοῦ πνεύματος Arist.*Pr.*961b22. **-τᾰσις**, εως, ἡ, *counter-extension*, Hp.*Art.*72. II. *confronting*, πρός τινα *BGU*1138.3 (i B.C.), *POxy.*260.10 (i A.D.). **-τείνω**, *make counter-extension*, Hp.*Fract.* 14, *Art.*3. II. metaph., ἂν ἀντικατατείναντες λέγωμεν αὐτῷ λόγον παρὰ λόγον if we speak *setting* speech *directly* in contrast with speech *against* him, Pl.*R.*348a, cf. Plu.2.669e. **-τρέχω**, aor. -έδρᾰμον, *overrun in turn*, D.C.60.9. **-φέρομαι**, *to be carried down again*, Gal.17(2).57. **-φρονέω**, *despise in turn*, τινός D.C.54.33. **-φῠτεύω**, *plant instead*, ἕτερα ἀντὶ τῶν ἐκλειπόντων [δένδρων] *BGU*1120. 33 (i B.C.). **-χωρισμός**, ὁ, *replacement*, Antyll.ap.Orib.6.10.14.

**ἀντικατ-έχω**, *hold fast on the other side*, Hp.*Art.*74. 2. Astrol., *occupy incongruous position*, τοὺς οἴκους ἢ τὰ ὑψώματα *Cat.Cod.Astr.* 8(3).115. ***-ηγορέω**, *accuse in turn, recriminate upon*, τινός Gorg. *Pal.*27, Lys.6.42, Aeschin.1.178:—in Pass., D.C.36.40. II. Pass., in Logic, *to be convertible*, ἀ. τοῦ πράγματος Arist.*Top.*102a 19, al.; *reciprocate*, of cause and effect, Id.*APo.*73a16, cf. 78a 28. **-ηγορητικός**, ή, όν, *contradictory*, sermo (i.e. λόγος) Gal. *Subf.Emp.*12 p.65 Bonnet. **-ηγορία**, ἡ, *countercharge*, Quint. *Inst.*3.10.4. **-ημαι**, **ἀντικατίζομαι**, **ἀντικατίστημι**, Ion. for ἀντικάθ–. **-ολισθαίνω**, *slip down correspondingly*, Paul.Aeg.6.65.

**ἀντικάτων**, ωνος, ὁ, *Anticato*, name of a book written by Caesar in reply to the *Cato* of Cicero, Plu.*Caes.*54, App.*BC*2.99.

***ἀντίκειμαι**, 3 pl. ἀντικέαται Archyt.ap.Stob.2.2.4, used as Pass. of ἀντιτίθημι:—*to be set over against, correspond with*, τιμὰ ἀγαθοῖσιν ἀ. *is held out to* them *as a fitting reward*, Pi.*I.*7(6).26:—ἀντικείμενος, ὁ, name of a *bandage*, Sor.*Fasc.*12.515 C. II. *to be opposite to*, of places, τινός Hp.*Aër.*4; τινί Str.2.5.15; of things, *to be opposite* or *opposed*, πρὸς ἄλληλα Pl.*Sph.*258b; ἀ. κατὰ διάμετρον in a circle, Arist.*Cael.*277a23, al. Adv. **-μένως**, συνέστηκεν *PA*654a11. 2. *to be opposed*, in various ways, *Cat.*11b17, *Metaph.*1055a38, al.; in Logic, αἱ -κειμέναι προτάσεις *APr.*63b24, al. Adv. **ἀντικειμένως** *Metaph.*1054b15, etc.; propositions are *opposed* either contradictorily (ἀντιφατικῶς) or contrarily (ἐναντίως), *Int.*17b16; ἀντικείμενα defined as ὧν τὸ ἕτερον τοῦ ἑτέρου ἀποφάσει πλεονάζει *Stoic.*2.70, cf. 82, al. 3. Rhet., ἀντικειμένη [λέξις] *antithetical*, Arist.*Rh.*1409b 35; ἀντικειμένως εἰπεῖν ib.1401a5, cf. 1410b29; ἀντικείμενα κῶλα Demetr.*Eloc.*22. III. *resist, be adverse*, ἀντικείσομαι τοῖς ἀντικειμένοις σοι Lxx *Ex.*23.22, cf. *Is.*66.6, al., *Ev.Luc.*13.17, al.; *to be hurtful*, τοῖς σώμασι Procop.Gaz.*Ep.*27.

**ἀντικέλευθος**, ον, *pursuing an opposite path*, φάος Man.4.74; simply, *opposite*, τοῖχος Nonn.*D.*8.191: c. gen., Καρκίνος ἀ. Αἰγοκερῆος 2.658. II. *opposing, hostile*, αἰχμή 2.459, cf. 23.35, al.

**ἀντικελεύω**, *bid, command in turn*, Th.1.128: Pass., *to be bidden* to do a thing *in turn*, ib.139.

**ἀντίκεντρον**, τό, *that which acts as a goad*, A.*Eu.*136, 466.

**ἀντικέφᾰλον**, τό, *back of the head*, Lyd.*Mens.*4.54, *Hippiatr.* 115. II. as Adj., κροκοδείλους -κεφάλους αὑτοῖς *back to back*, *PMag.Par.*1.2954.

**ἀντικηδεύω**, *mind, tend instead of* another, τινός E.*Ion* 734:—also **ἀντικήδομαι**, Poll.5.142.

**ἀντικῆρυξ**, υκος, ὁ, *deputy-herald*, *IG*3.1295.

**ἀντικηρύσσω**, *proclaim in answer to*, οὐδὲν ἀντεκήρυξεν λόγοις E. *Supp.*673; *in opposition to*, τινί Lib.*Decl.*39.45.

**ἀντικῑν-έω**, *move in opposition*, Arist.*Mem.*453a26, cf. Ph.2.22:—Med. or Pass., ἀνάγκη τὸ κινοῦν ἀντικινεῖσθαι must *suffer a counter-movement*, Arist.*Ph.*257b23, cf. *GA*768b10, *Cael.*272b4. II. in Pass. also, *make counter-movements*, πρὸς πᾶν Plb.2.66.3; σφοδρότερον -ηθῆναι *retaliate* more ruthlessly, Chor.p.226 B. **-ησις**, εως, ἡ, *contrary motion*, *Corp.Herm.*2.6, Simp. *in Ph.*677.20, Id. *in Cael.*366. 8, 395.29. **-ητος**, ον, *moved in return*, Phlp. *in Ph.*355.15.

**ἀντικῐχάνω** [χᾱ], *encounter*, only aor. Med. ἀντικ[ι]χομένην *BGU* 1024 vii 20 (iv/v A.D.).

**ἀντικλάζω**, *sound by striking against*, κραυγὴ.. πέτραισιν ἀντέκλαγξ' *is echoed* by them, E.*Andr.*1145. 2. c. acc. cogn., ἀ. ἀλλήλαις μέλος *sing against* one another, Id.*Ba.*1057.

**ἀντικλαίω**, Att. -κλάω, *weep in return*, Hdt.3.14 (v.l. ἀνέκλαιον), Eust.37.14.

**ἀντικλάω**, *bend back*, Sch.Opp.*H.*1.152.

**ἀντικλείομαι**, *to be enclosed*, εἰς τὴν κοιλότητα Ruf.*Oss.*32.

**ἀντίκλεις**, ειδος, ἡ, *false key*, Poll.10.22, Palch. in *Cat.Cod.Astr.* 97.13:—also **-κλειθρον**, τό, *Gloss.*

**ἀντίκλησις**, εως, ἡ, *calling upon, summoning in return*, Jul.*Ep.*192.

**ἀντικλίνω** [ῑ], *turn* or *bend again*, Musae.107.

**ἀντίκλῐσις**, εως, ἡ, *alternative inflexion*, Sch.Opp.*H.*1.59.

**ἀντικνημιάζω**, *strike on the shin*, S.E.*M.*1.217 (s. v. l.).

**ἀντικνήμιον**, τό, *part of the leg in front of the* κνήμη (τῆς κνήμης ὁ πρόσθεν Arist.*HA*494ᵃ6; but τὸ ὄπισθεν Sch.Ar.*Pl.*784), *shin*, Hippon.49, Hp.*Fract.*18, Ar.*Ach.*219, *Eq.*907.

**ἀντίκοιλον**, τό, *hollow of the instep*, dub. l. in Polem.*Phgn.*85.

**ἀντικολάζω**, *punish in return*, Luc.*Tyr.*12 (Pass.).

**ἀντικολᾰκεύω**, *flatter in turn*, Plu.*Alc.*24.

**ἀντικομίζω**, *bring back as an answer*, λόγον Plu.*Lys.*26:—Med., *receive in exchange*, J.*BJ*2.8.4, App.*BC*4.70.

**ἀντικομπάζω**, *boast in opposition*, τινί Plu.*Ant.*62.

**ἀντικοντόω**, *support with a pole* or *stick*, ξύλῳ ἀ. τῷ σώματι Hp.*Mochl.*20 (ἀντικονταίνουσι prob. l. for -κοταίνουσι Erot., -κοτέουσι or -κοντέουσι codd.).—But -όω is confirmed by **ἀντικόντωσις**, εως, ἡ, *the support of a stick* to a lame man, Id.*Art.*52, 58.

**ἀντι-κοπή**, ἡ, *beating back, hindrance, check*, Epicur.*Ep.*1 p.10 U.; *resistance*, Id.*Nat.Herc.*908.4; προσκρούσει καὶ ἀ. Plu.2.77a; *clashing*, of streams meeting, Str.5.2.5. **-κοπτικός**, ή, όν, *resisting, repellent*, S.E.*M.*10.137. **-κόπτω**, *cut down mutually*, ἀλλήλους D.C.43.37 (nisi leg. ἀνακ-). II. *beat back, resist*, 1. in a physical sense, c. acc., ὁκόταν νέφεα.. ἀντικόψῃ πνεῦμα ἐναντίον Hp.*Aër.* 8: abs., ὅταν πνεῦμα ἀντικόπτῃ νότιον Arist.*HA*599ᵃ1, cf. *PA*642ᵇ1; *check growth*, ὅταν ἀντικόψῃ ὁ χειμών Thphr.*CP*1.12.6, cf. Epicur. *Ep.*1 p.11 U., al.:—in Pass., *meet with resistance*, Id.*Nat.Herc.*908.2; ἀ. ἀλλήλοις, of winds, Thphr.*Vent.*53. 2. of persons, ὁ δὲ Θηραμένης ἀντέκοπτε λέγων.. X.*HG*2.3.15, cf. Aristid.*Or.*43(1).10: c. dat., Phld.*Vit.*pp 9, 25 J. 3. of things, ἤν τι ἀντικόψῃ *if there be any hindrance*, X.*HG*2.3.31; ἡ πυκνότης ἀ. πρὸς τοῦτο *militates against* this, Demetr.Lac.*Herc.*1055.18.

**ἀντικορύσσομαι**, Med., *take arms against*, ἀνέμοις *AP*7.668 (Leon.), Ath.15.701b.

**ἀντικοσμ-έω**, *arrange in turn*, Plu.2.813d. 2. *adorn in turn*, ib.828a:—Pass., Aristid.*Or.*25(43).33:—Subst. **-ησις**, εως, ἡ, Suid. **-ήτης**, ου, ὁ, *deputy-κοσμητής* (signf. 1. 2), *IG*3.1120, al.:—hence **-ητεύω**, *discharge this office*, ib.1126.

**ἀντικοτ-έω**· *obstrigillo, obtrecto, officio*, *Gloss.*:—also **-ησις**· *offensio*, ib.

**ἀντίκοψις**, εως, ἡ, *opposition*, ἀνέμων Thphr.*Vent.*55.

**ἀντικράζω**, pf. ἀντικέκραγα, *to shout in return*, πολλὰ βλάσφημά τισι J.*BJ*6.2.3.

**ἀντικρατέω**, *hold, have instead of something else*, *AP*11.298.

**ἀντικρίνω** [ῑν], *judge in turn*, τινά Aristid.*Or.*34(50).40; *compare, match*, τί τινι Ael.*NA*5.56, al.:—Pass., πρός τι 2.43, al.:—Med., *contend against*, Lxx *Jb.*9.32, 11.3.

**ἀντίκριος**, ὁ, *counter-ram*, Aen.Tact.22.7.

**ἀντίκρῐσις**, εως, ἡ, = ἀπόκρισις, Anaxil.41, Poll.4.113.

**ἀντί-κρουσις**, εως, ἡ, *abrupt close*, in a rhetorical period, Arist. *Rh.*1409ᵇ22; *hindrance, check*, Plu.2.721b; dub. sens. in Aeschin. 1.168, perh. *repartee*. **-κρουσμός**· *offensio*, *Gloss.* **-κρουστία**, ἡ, dub. sens. in Phld.*Po.*1677.23. **-κρούω**, *strike* or *clash against, come into collision*, 1. in a physical sense, ὀλίγα.. τὰ ἀντικρούοντα αὐτοῖς Arist.*Cael.*313ᵇ2: abs., Id.*PA*642ᵃ36, al., cf. Pl. *Lg.*857c; ἀσπὶς ἀσπίδι Lib.*Decl.*37.8. 2. in a general sense, αὐτοῖς.. τοῦτο ἀντεκεκρούκει *had been a hindrance to* them, *had counteracted* them, Th.6.46; ἀ. τοῖς λογισμοῖς J.*AJ*2.4.3; ἀ. ταῖς συμβουλίαις Plu.*Ages.*7; ἀ. πρός τι Id.*Cat.Ma.*24: abs., *prove a hindrance, offer resistance*, ἀντέκρουσέ τι καὶ γέγον' οἷον οὐκ ἔδει D.18.198; ἐὰν ἀντικρούσῃ τις Arist.*Rh.*1379ᵃ12; ἀντέκρουον αἱ γυναῖκες *Pol.*1270ᵃ7.

**ἀντικρύ**, Adv. = ἄντην, *over against, right opposite*, θεοῖς ἀντικρὺ μάχεσθαι Il.5.130: c. gen., Ἕκτορος ἀντικρύ ib.8.301. II. = ἄντῐκρυς, *straight on, right on*, ἀντικρὺ δόρυ χάλκεον ἐξεπέρησεν Od.10.162; ἀντικρὺ μεμαώς Il.13.137: mostly followed by a Prep., ἀντικρὺ δ' ἀν' ὀδόντας 5.74; ἀντικρὺ δι' ὤμου 4.481, cf. Od.22.16; ἀντικρὺ κατὰ μέσσον *right* in the middle, Il.16.285; once in X., ἀντικρὺ διάττων *Cyr.*7.1.30; cf. καταντῑκρύ. 2. *outright, utterly, quite*, ἀντικρὺ δ' ἀπόφημι Il.7.362; ἀντικρὺ δ' ἀπάραξε 16.116; ἀντικρὺ μακάρεσσιν ἔϊκτο A.R.4.1612, etc. (Cf. ἄντικρυς sub fin.) [ῡ generally, but ῠ Il.5.130, 819; ῐ by nature (cf. καταντῐκρύ Ar.*Ec.*87), ῑ by position in Ep.]

**ἄντῐκρῠς**, Adv. *straight on, right on*, ἄντικρυς ἰὼν παρεκαθέζετο ἐκ δεξιᾶς he came *straight up* and.., Pl.*Euthd.*273b, cf. Ar.*Lys.*1068, Th.2.4; also εἰς τὸ ἀ. πορεύεσθαι Pl.*Smp.*223b. 2. *outright, openly, without disguise*, ὅπως ἄ. τάδ' αἰνέσω A.*Ch.*192; ὁ χρησμὸς ἄ. λέγει Ar. *Eq.*128; εὔχονταί γε πλουτεῖν ἄ. Id.*Pl.*134; ἄ. ἔφη χρῆναι πλεῖν Th. 6.49; ἀ ἠδικοῦντο οὐ δηλοῦντες ἄντικρυς Id.5.30; οὐδὲν ἢ ἄ. δουλείαν *downright* slavery, Id.1.122; ἡ ἄ. ἐλευθερία Id.8.64; οὐκ ἄ. *not at all*, οὐ διοίσοντ' ἄ. τῶν Ἡρακλειδῶν Ar.*Pl.*384. 3. sts. of Time, *straightway*, συλλαβόντες ἄγουσιν ἄ. ὡς ἀποκτενοῦντες Lys.13.78, cf. Men.*Pk.*38, Pl.*Ax.*367a. II. later, = ἀντικρύ, *opposite*, ἄ. εἶναι *to oppose*, Arist.*EE*1243ᵃ37; ἄ. ἐπιέναι *against*, D.H.3.24; καταστῆναι Plu.*Sol.*27; κατακλιθῆναί τινος Lxx 3*Ma.*5.16; ἐν τῇ ἄ. πυλαΐδι *CIG* (add.)4224e (Cragus): c. gen., ἄ. Χίου *Act.Ap.*20.15, cf. *PTeb.*395.4 (ii A.D.), etc.—Gramm. distinguish ἀντικρύ, = ἐξ ἐναντίας, and ἄντικρυς, = φανερῶς, διαρρήδην, cf. *AB*408, but ἀντικρύ (q. v.) has both senses in Hom. (-κρυ(ς) prob. akin to κέρας, κάρα.)

**ἀντικρύσιον**, dub. sens., Theognost.*Can.*125.2 (from ἄντικρυς).

**ἀντίκτησις**, εως, ἡ, *acquisition of* one thing *for* another, ἀδελφοῦ ἀ. οὐκ ἔστιν Plu.2.481e.

**ἀντικτόνος**, ον, (κτείνω) *in requital for murder*, ἀντικτόνοις ποιναῖσι.. πατρός A.*Eu.*464.

**ἀντικτῠπέω**, aor. ἀντέκτυπον, *ring in response*, *AP*14.10.3; *clash against*, τινί *APl.*4.221 (Theaet.): abs., Procop.*Goth.*2.23.

**ἀντικῡδαίνω**, *praise in turn*, Them.*Or.*4.57d.

**ἀντικῡμαίνομαι**, Pass., *boil with conflicting waves, dash hither and thither*, Plu.2.897c; of wind in a cul-de-sac, *surge back*, Orib.9. 20.3.

**ἀντικῡματόω**, *surge against*, Procop.*Aed.*4.8.

**ἀντικύπριος**, sc. πούς, the foot – ᴗ – – ᴗ, Diom.1.482 K.

**ἀντικύπτω**, *occur, crop up*, τὰς ἀντικυπτούσας χρείας Ascl.*Tact.*12. 10 (fort. ἀνα-).

**ἀντικυρία**, ἡ, *hellebore*, Suid.:—also **ἀντικύρικον**· ὁ ἐλλέβορος, Hsch. (From the place-name Ἀντικύρα.)

**ἀντικύρω** [ῠ], aor. ἀντέκυρσα, *hit upon, encounter, meet*, τινί Pi. *O.*12.12, S.*OC*99, etc.: abs., Id.*Ph.*545.

**ἀντικύων**· ἀλώπηξ, Hsch.

**ἀντικωλύω**, *hinder by resisting*, Hp.*Loc.Hom.*10:—hence **-ῡτέον**, Gal.18(2).390.

**ἀντικωμάζω**, *celebrate by a festival in turn*, Sch.Pi.*P.*9.156.

**ἀντικωμῳδέω**, *ridicule in turn*, Plu.*Flam.*9, Max.Tyr.9.3.

**ἀντικωπηλάτης**, ου, ὁ, = ἀντηρέτης, Sch.A.*Th.*283.

**ἀντιλᾰβ-εύς**, έως, ὁ, = πόρπαξ, Hsch. **-ή**, ἡ, *thing to hold by, handle*, ὅπως ἄν.. μὴ ἔχοι ἀντιλαβὴν ἡ χείρ Th.7.65; of a shield, οὔτε πόρπακας οὔτ' ἀντιλαβὰς ἔχει Str.3.3.6. 2. *grip*, of a dog, Ael.*NA*8. 1. 3. metaph., πολλὰς.. ἔχει ὑποψίας καὶ ἀντιλαβάς gives many *handles against* one, *points of attack*, Pl.*Phd.*84c; so ἀ. διδόναι D.H. *Rh.*8.15; παρέχεσθαι Luc.*Tim.*29. 4. Gramm., in dramatic dialogue, *division of a line between two speakers*, Hsch. 5. *apprehension*, Dam.*Pr.*6.

**ἀντιλαγχάνω**, pf. -είληχα D.40.3:—as law-term, *move for a rehearing of a suit*, when the case had gone by default, ἀ. δίαιταν Id. 21.86; ἀ. τὴν μὴ οὖσαν (sc. δίαιταν) ib.90, cf. Poll.8.61, Hsch.; τὴν ἔρημον (sc. δίκην) ἀ. D.32.27. II. *enter an exceptive plea*, οἱ νόμοι διδόασι τὰς παραγραφὰς ἀντιλαγχάνειν Id.37.33. III. *bring counteraction*, Procop.*Arc.*17.

**ἀντιλάζομαι** or **-ῠμαι**, poet. and Dor. Prose for ἀντιλαμβάνομαι, *take hold of, hold by*, c. gen., E.*IA*1227; πραγμάτων Theag.ap.Stob. 3.1.67, cf. Archyt.ib.117; *take a share of, partake in*, πόνων E.*Or.* 452, etc. 2. c. acc., *to receive in turn, to be repaid*, ἀντιλάζυται.. τοιάδ' ἂν τοκεῦσι δῷ Id.*Supp.*363. (-λάζυμαι l.c., *Or.*753, *IA*1109; -λάζομαι ib.1227, *Or.*452 (-λάζου); both forms in codd. *Med.*1216.)

**ἀντιλακτίζω**, *kick against*, τινί Ar.*Pax*613; τῷ νῷ Phld.*Rh.Supp.* p.52 S. 2. *kick back in return*, ὄνον Plu.2.10c.

**ἀντιλᾰκωνίζω**, *answer in Laconian fashion*, Eust.1642.51.

**ἀντι-λᾰλέω**, *speak against* one, dub. in Men.*Epit.*529, Sm.*Ps.*138 (139).20. **-λᾰλος**, dub. in *Epic.Alex.Adesp.*9 ix 15.

**ἀντιλαμβάνω**, *receive instead of*, χρυσοῦ δώματα πλήρη τᾶς ἥβας ἀ. E.*HF*646 (lyr.); mostly without a gen., οὔτε κακοὺς εὖ δρῶν εὖ πάλιν ἀντιλάβοις *receive in turn*, Thgn.108; κἂν.. ᾖ σώφρων.. σώφρον' ἀντιλήψεται E.*Andr.*741; ἡδονὴν δόντας.. κακίαν.. ἀ. Th.3.58; ἔρανον Arist.*Pol.*1330ᵇ40; ἀ. ἄλλην [χώραν] *seize in return, get instead*, Th.1.143; ἀ. ἄλλους τινάς X.*Cyr.*5.3.12, cf. 8.7.16; χάριτα *AP*6. 191 (Longus). II. mostly in Med., with pf. Pass. -είλημμαι Lys.28.15, Pl.*Prm.*130e: c. gen., *lay hold of*, σαπροῦ πείσματος ἀντελάβου Thgn.1362; ἄκρου τοῦ στύρακος ἀ. Pl.*La.*184a, cf. *Prt.* 317d, al.; τῇ ἀριστερᾷ ἀ. τοῦ τρίβωνος ib.335d; φιλίου χωρίου ἀ. *gain* or *reach* it, Th.7.77, cf. Ar.*Th.*242: abs., -όμενος Th.3.22. b. metaph. c. gen., *lay hold of*, τῆς σωτηρίας, τῆς ἐλευθερίας, τοῦ ἀσφαλοῦς, Id.2.61, 62, 3.22; *lay claim to*, τοῦ θρόνου Ar.*Ra.*777, 787; τοῦ πατρικοῦ μέρους *BGU*648.10 (ii A.D.). 2. *help, take part with, assist*, οὐκ ἀντιλήψεσθ'; E.*Tr.*464; of persons, ἀ. Ἑλλήνων *to take* their *part*, D.S.11.13; ἀ. τῶν ἀσθενούντων *Act.Ap.*20.35, etc.: abs., Th.7.70:—also in Pass., ἀντειλημμένη *having received help*, *BGU*1105.21 (Aug.), al. 3. *take part* or *share in* a thing, *take in hand*, τῶν πραγμάτων X.*Cyr.*2.3.6, D.1.20, etc.; τοῦ πολέμου Isoc.6.101; τῆς θαλάττης Plb.1.39.14; τῆς Ἀφροδίτης Alex.219.15; τῆς παιδείας Pl.*R.*534d; ἀ. τοῦ λόγου *seize on* the conversation (to the interruption of the rest), ib.336b: abs., ἀρχόμενοι πάντες ὀξύτερον ἀ. Th.2.8, cf. 8. 106. 4. *take hold of for the purpose of finding fault, reprehend, attack*, ἡμῶν Pl.*Sph.*239d, cf. *R.*497d, etc.; τοῦδε ἀντιλαβώμεθα *let us attack* the question, Id.*Tht.*169d; ἀ. ὡς ἀδύνατον.. *to object* that.., Id.*Sph.*251b: abs., Id.*Grg.*506a. 5. *take fast hold of*, i.e. *captivate*, ὁ λόγος ἀντιλαμβάνεταί μου Id.*Phd.*88d, cf. *Prm.*130e, Luc.*Nigr.*19. 6. of plants, *take hold*, Thphr.*HP*4.1.5; of scions, *unite*, *CP*1.6.4. 7. *grasp with the mind, perceive, apprehend*, Pl.*Ax.* 370a; noted as an obsol. word for συνίημι by Luc.*Sol.*7:— so of the senses, ἀ. κατὰ τὴν ἀκοήν, ὀσφρήσει, S.E.*P.*1.50, 64, cf. Phot.p.148 R., Alex.Aphr.*in Top.*103.1, al. III. in Med. also, *hold back*, ἵππου τῷ χαλινῷ X.*Eq.*10.15, cf. Arist.*MM*1188ᵇ6; *interrupt*, *Aud.*802ᵇ 26. IV. Act. in sense of Med., Alex.Aphr.*Pr.*1.38.

**ἀντι-λάμπω**, inf. -λάμπην Sapph.*Supp.*3.6:—*light up in turn*, οἱ δ' ἀντέλαμψαν (sc. οἱ φύλακες) A.*Ag.*294. II. intr., *reflect light, shine*, X.*Cyn.*5.18: πρὸς τὴν σελήνην Plu.*Arat.*21; of the rainbow, Anaxag. 19. 2. *shine opposite to* or *in the face of*, ὁ ἥλιος ἀ. τινί Plu.*Mar.* 26, etc., cf. Arr.*Tact.*27.4: metaph., *dazzle*, τῷ ἀκροάτῃ λέξις ἀ. Plu.

2.41c. III. *vie in brilliance with*, τινί Philostr.*Ep.*32. -**λαμψις**, εως, ἡ, *reflection of light*, Plu.2.930d, 93 b.

**ἀντιλαοί·** τῶν ἄρτων κλάσματα, Hsch.

***ἀντιλέγω**, Hdt., Com., and Att. Prose (cf. ἀνταγορεύω): fut. ἀντιλέξω E.*Hipp.*993, Ar.*Ra.*998, Lys.8.10 (but the common fut. is ἀντερῶ): aor. ἀντέλεξα S.*OT*409, Ar.*Nu.*1040 (but the aor. commonly used is ἀντεῖπον): pf. ἀντείρηκα: fut. Pass. ἀντειρήσομαι:—*speak against, gainsay, contradict*, τινί Th.5.30, Pl.*Smp.*216b, X.*Mem.*4.6.13, etc.; περί τινος Th.8.53, X.*Mem.*4.4.8; ὑπὲρ τῶν δικαίων ib.3.5.12: πρός τι 1.2.17; πρὸς πάντα τὰ δίκαια Ar.*Nu.*888:—often folld. by a dependent clause, ἀ. ὡς.. *declare in opposition* or *answer* that.., χρησμοῖσι οὐκ ἔχω ἀντιλέγειν ὡς οὐκ εἰσὶ ἀληθέες Hdt.8.77, cf. Ar.*Eq.*980, Th.8.24, X.*An.*2.3.25, etc.; οὐ τοῦτό γ' ἀντιλέγουσιν, ὡς οὐ.. Arist.*Pol.*1287$^{b}$23; also ἀ. ὑπέρ τινος ὡς.. Th.8.45: so c. inf., ἀ. ποιήσειν ταῦτα, ἤν.. *to reply* that they will.., if.., Id.1.28; ἀ. μὴ κτεῖναι Μυτιληναίους Id.3.41; ἀ. τὸ μὴ οὐ ἀξιοῦσθαί τινα X.*Cyr.*2.2.20. 2. c. acc. rei, ἴσ' ἀντιλέξαι S.*OT*409; ἀ. τὸν ἐναντίον λόγον Lys.8.11; μῦθον ἀ. τινί *tell* one tale *in reply to* another, Ar.*Lys.*806; ἀντιλέγομεν πρᾶγμά τι Men.*Epit.*8:—Pass., *to be disputed, questioned*, X.*HG*6.5.37; of a place, ὑπό τινος ἀντιλεγόμενον *counter-claimed*, ib.3.2.30; ἀντιλέγεσθαι μικρὸν πρός τινα περί τινος D.27.15; τὰ ἀντιλεγόμενα *points in dispute*, Aeschin.2.44; πρὸς τὰ ἀντειρημένα κτλ., title of work by Chrysippus, *Stoic.*2.8; τόπος ἀντιλλεγόμενος (sic) *IG*5(2).443.15 (Megalopolis, ii B.C.): abs., -λέγεται περί τινος Str.8.6.6; of the genuineness of literary works, *to be disputed*, Plu.2.839c. 3. abs., *speak in opposition*, Hdt.9.42, E.*Hipp.*993, Ar.*Ra.*1076, etc.; ὁ ἀντιλέγων *the opponent*, Pl.*Prt.*335a; οἱ ἀντιλέγοντες Th.8.53; λαὸς ἀπειθῶν καὶ -λέγων Lxx *Is.*65.2.

**ἀντιλειτουργέω**, *render service in return*, *PPar.*63.183 (ii B.C.).

**ἀντι-λεκτέον**, *one must gainsay*, οὐδὲν ἀ. E.*Heracl.*975, cf. Hp.*Ep.*27:—Adj. -**τέος**, α, ον, Luc.*Anach.*17. -**λεκτος**, ον, *questionable, to be disputed*, ὅρος οὐκ ἀ. Th.4.92. -**λεξις**, εως, ἡ, *answer*, Hp.*Decent.*12. 2. *dialogue*, ἀντιλέξεις τῶν ὑποκριτῶν, opp. μονῳδίαι, Philostr.*VA*6.11. 3. *contradiction*, J.*AJ*18.1.3.

**ἀντιλεσχαίνω**, *chatter against*, Perict.ap.Stob.4.25.50.

**ἀντιλέων**, οντος, ὁ, *lion-like*, formed like ἀντίθεος, Ar.*Eq.*1044; where, however, it is in fact a pr. n.

**ἀντιλημματίζω**, *set off in accounts, deduct*, *POxy.*1577.11 (iii A.D.), cf. 1578.17 (iii A.D., Pass.).

**ἀντιλήμ-πτωρ, -ψις**, v. ἀντιλή-πτωρ, -ψις.

**ἀντίληξις**, εως, ἡ, *motion for a new trial*, D.29.38; cf. ἀντιλαγχάνω.

**ἀντι-ληπτέον**, *one must take part in* a matter: abs., Ar.*Pax*485; τῶν πραγμάτων αὐτοῖς ἀ. D.1.2, cf. 14. II. *one must hold back*, ἀ. τοῦ ἵππου τῷ χαλινῷ X.*Eq.*8.8. III. Adj. -**ληπτέος**, α, ον, ὁ λόγος Plu.*Nob.*3. ***-ληπτικός**, ή, όν, Dor. -**λαπτ-**, *able to apprehend*, λόγων Ti.Locr.100c; χρωμάτων Phld.*Herc.*19.18; δύναμις ἀ. πληγῆς ἀέρος Plu.2.98b; ἀ. δύναμις, of the soul, Aristo *Stoic.*1.86, cf. *Stoic.*2.230; *assisting* a scion *to unite*, γλισχρότης Thphr.*CP*1.6.4; of the hand, *prehensile*, Gal.*UP*2.6. Adv. -**κῶς**, ἔχειν to be *aware, apprehend*, Hierocl.p.19A. 2. *taking hold of*, i.e. *impressing itself upon* the senses, φωνή Thphr.*Fr.*89.3, cf. Cass.*Pr.*35 (Comp.); τὸ ἀ. Iamb.*Comm.Math.*8. II. *able to check*, Pl.*Def.*416a. 2. abs., *self-controlled*, Ptol.*Tetr.*188. -**ληπτός**, ή, όν, *which can be apprehended*, τῇ ἁφῇ Alex.Aphr.*in Mete.*201.4; τῇ ὄψει Phlp.*in Ph.*417.16; τὰ -ληπτά *objects of sense-perception*, Plot.4.5.8. **λήπτωρ**, later -**λήμπτωρ**, ορος, ὁ, *helper, protector*, Lxx *2Ki.*22.3, *BGU*1130.17 (i B.C.), Eustr.*in APo.*93.19; θεοὶ ἀ. *UPZ*14.18 (ii B.C.). -**ληψις**, later -**λημψις**, εως, ἡ, *receiving in turn* or *exchange*, Th.1.120; *counter-claim*, X.*HG*3.5.5. II. (from Med.) *laying hold of in turn, reciprocation*, Democr.ap.Arist.*Fr.*208; of cultivated plants, *giving a return*, Thphr.*CP*3.6.6; of a vine *laying hold* by its tendrils, ib.2.18.2. b. *taking in hand*, τοῦ λ(ε)ιτουργήματος *POxy.*900.13 (iv A.D.). 2. = ἀντιλαβή, *hold, support*, X.*Eq.*5.7; of a bandage, Hp.*Off.*9; ἀντίληψιν βοηθείας ἔχειν D.S.1.30; ἀ. διδόναι τινί give one *a handle*, Plu.2.966e; ἀ. παρέχειν Luc.*Anach.*2. 3. *defence, succour*, *UPZ*42.38 (ii B.C.), *PAmh.*35.58 (ii B.C.), *BGU*1187.27 (i B.C.), Lxx *Ps.*21(22).20, al., *1Ep.Cor.*12.28, Iamb.*Myst.*7.3. 4. *claim to* a thing, X.*HG*3.5.5. 5. *objection*, Pl.*Phd.*87a, *Sph.*241b, *Hp.Ma.*287a, Plu.*Alex.*18, Iamb.*Myst.*1.1, al.: in forensic oratory, *plea of justification*, Hermog.*Stat.*2, al., Syrian.*in Hermog.*2p.79R.; *discussion*, θεολογικὴ ἀ. Iamb.*Myst.*1.8. 6. *grasping with the mind, apprehension*, Epicur.*Fr.*250, *Stoic.*2.206, Diog.Oen.4; φυσικὴν -ψιν ποιεῖσθαί τινος D.S.3.15; οὐκ ἐπιστρέφει τὴν ἀ. does not attract the *attention*, [Longin.]*Rh.*p.190H.; of sensuous *perception*, *Stoic.*2.230, Ti.Locr.100b, Anon.*in Tht.*59.48, Phld.*Herc.*1003, Alex.Aphr.*in Top.*91.5; ποιοτήτων Plu.2.625b, cf. Metrod.1. 7. of disease, *seizure, attack*, τῶν ἀκρωτηρίων Th.2.49.

**ἀντιλῐτανεύω**, *entreat in return*, Plu.2.1117c.

**ἀντι-λόβιον**, τό, *upper edge of the ear*, opp. προλόβιον, Gal.14.701, Poll.2.86. -**λοβίς**, ίδος, ἡ, = foreg., Ruf.*Onom.*44.

**ἀντιλογ-έω**, = ἀντιλέγω, *deny*, S.*Ant.*377 (lyr.). 2. = ἀντιλέγω 3, Ar.*Nu.*321, al.:—in Med., Democr.85, Antipho Soph.98. -**ητικός**, ή, όν, = ἀντιλογικός, Gal.7.281, Hsch. ***-ία**, ἡ, *contradiction, controversy*, ἀ. χρησμῶν πέρι λέγειν Hdt.8.77; ἡμέας.. ἐς ἀ. παρέξομεν will offer ourselves to *argue the point*, Id.9.87; ἐδόκεον ἀντιλογίης κυρήσειν expected to be allowed *to argue it*, ib.88; εἰς -ίαν κατέστησαν Lys.*Fr.*75.1; -ίας ἅπτεσθαι Pl.*R.*454b; ἐς -ίαν τινὶ γενέσθαι Th.1.73; ἀ. καὶ λοιδορία D.40.32; ἀντιλογίαν ἔχει it is open to *contradiction*, Arist.*Rh.*1418$^{b}$25, cf. 1414$^{b}$3: in pl., *opposing arguments*, Ar.*Ra.*775; δι' ἀντιλογιῶν καταλλαγῆναι Th.4.59; ἀ. πρός τινα X.*HG*6.3.20; -ίαν ἐλθεῖν Th.1.31; ἀντιλογίαν ἐν αὑτῷ ἔχειν to have *grounds f[or] defence* in itself, Id.2.87; ἄνευ -ίας without *dispute*, *BGU*1133.[…] (Aug.), etc. 2. later, *quarrel, dispute*, *PPetr.*2p.56 (iii B.C.), *PGren[f.]*1.38.8 (ii/i B.C.), *Ep.Hebr.*12.3, etc. 3. *right, claim*, τοῦ αὐτοῦ λάκκο[υ] *POxy.*1892 (vi A.D.). ***-ίζομαι**, *count up* or *calculate on the othe[r] hand*, Antipho 2.2.8; ἀ. ὅτι.. X.*HG*1.5.24. (Act. dub. in Phld.*D*[…]1.21 (ἀντιλογικῶν Diels).) -**ικός**, ή, όν, *given to contradiction, disputatious*, Ar.*Nu.*1173, Isoc.15.48, Ph.1.412, Sor.1.14, Pl.*Tht.*197a, al.: ἡ -κή (sc. τέχνη) *the art of disputation*, Id.*R.*454a, *Phdr.*261d; τὸ -κόν Id.*Sph.*225b: οἱ -κοί *persons skilled in this art*, Id.*Ly.*216a, *Phd.*101e; of arguments, οἱ περὶ τοὺς ἀντιλογικοὺς λόγους διατρίψαντες ib.90c: (λόγοι) -κοί, οἱ, title of work by Protagoras, D.L.3.37. Adv. -κῶς *in the manner of such disputants*, Pl.*Tht.*164c. -**ισμός**, ὁ, *countercharge*, Philostr.*VS*2.1.4. -**ος**, ον, *contradictory, reverse*, τύχαι E.*Hel.*1142 (lyr.); φιλονεικίαι love *of contradiction*, Simp.*in Ph.*1135.28, cf. Epicur.*Nat.*28*Fr.*8.

**ἀντιλοιδορέω**, *rail at* or *abuse in turn*, *PPetr.*3p.48 (iii B.C.), Plu.2.88f (Pass.), *1Ep.Pet.*2.23:—Med., c. acc. rei, Luc.*Symp.*40.

**ἀντίλοξος**, η, ον (or ος, ον), name of a *bandage*, Sor.*Fasc.*12.512, cf. 516C.

**ἀντιλοχέω**, *lay counter-ambush*, Ph.1.664 (s.v.l.).

**ἀντιλῡπ-έω**, *vex in return*, Plu.*Demetr.*22, Luc.*DMeretr.*3.3, 12.5. -**ησις**, εως, ἡ, *vexing in return*, Arist.*de An.*403$^{a}$3, Plu.2.442b.

**ἀντίλῡρος**, ον, *responsive to the lyre* or *like that of the lyre* (Sch.), καναχά, of the flute, S.*Tr.*643.

**ἀντίλῠτρ-ον**, τό, *ransom*, *1Ep.Ti.*2.6. 2. *antidote, remedy*, Orph.*L.*593. -**ωτέον**, *one must ransom in return*, Arist.*EN*1164$^{b}$35.

**ἀντιλωβάω**, *maltreat in return*, Eust.757.59 (Pass.).

**ἀντιμαίνομαι**, pf. part. ἀντιμεμηνώς, *to be filled with passion for a lover in return*, Luc.*DMeretr.*12.2. 2. *rage against*, βρονταῖς Διός *APl.*1.30 (Gem.).

**ἀντιμανθάνω**, *learn in turn* or *instead*, Ar.*V.*1453.

**ἀντιμαντεύομαι**, *divine, predict in reply*, Them.*Or.*13.163a.

**ἀντιμαρτ-ῠρέω**, *appear as witness against*, Ar.*Fr.*437; *contradict*, τινί Plu.2.418a; opp. συμφωνεῖν, Polystr.p.10W.; esp. in Epicurus' Logic, *disprove* by fact or experience, *Ep.*1p.10U., al.; so ἀ. πρὸς τὴν αἴσθησιν Plu.2.447c: abs., Id.*Alc.*21, cf. Gal.4.735: c. acc., ἀ. τὰ εἰρημένα Plot.6.4.4:—Pass., *to be disproved, invalidated*, Epicur.*Ep.*1p.11U., al. -**ύρησις** [ῠ], εως, ἡ, *counter evidence*, Id.*Fr.*247: in pl., Id.*Nat.*28*Fr.*7, Plu.2.1121e. -**ύρομαι** [ῡ], *protest on the other hand*, Luc.*Symp.*47.

**ἀντιμᾰχ-έω**, *resist by force of arms*, D.S.22.7. 2. as law-term, *resist, demur*, *AB*184. -**ησις**, εως, ἡ, *conflict, struggle*, ἐπ' ἀλλήλοις D.H.8.58. -**ητύς**, ύος, ἡ, = foreg., Eratosth.31 (v.l. -ησύς). -**ομαι**, *fight against* one, Th.4.68: abs., D.S.22.10. -**ος**, ον, *capable of meeting in war*, τινί App.*Hisp.*9.

**ἀντιμεγᾰλοφρονέω**, *vie in pride* or *boasting with*, τινί Eust.676.5.

**ἀντιμεθέλκω**, *drag different ways, distract*, τὰ -οντα πράγματα Ph.1.231, cf. *APl.*4.136 (Antiphil.), 139 (Jul. Aegypt.), in Pass.; τῇ καὶ τῇ *AP*10.74 (Paul. Sil.).

**ἀντιμέθεξις**, εως, ἡ, *reciprocal participation*, Simp.*in Ph.*101.18.

**ἀντιμεθίστημι**, *move from one side to the other, revolutionize*, ψηφίσματα καὶ νόμον Ar.*Th.*362. II. Pass., with aor. 2 and pf. Act., *exchange places*, ἀ. ἀλλήλοις τό τε ὕδωρ καὶ ὁ ἀήρ Arist.*Ph.*209$^{b}$25, cf. 211$^{b}$27, *Mete.*366$^{b}$20; ἀλλήλαις Jul.*Or.*8.241a. 2. *make countermoves*, Luc.*Dem.Enc.*37.

**ἀντιμειρᾰκιεύομαι**, *behave petulantly in return*, πρός τινα Plu.*Sull.*6.

**ἀντιμελίζω**, *compete in music with*, τινί *AP*5.221 (Agath.).

**ἀντιμέλλω**, *wait and watch against* one, ἀντιμελλῆσαι Th.3.12 (Sch. for ἀντεπι-).

**ἀντιμέμφομαι**, *blame in turn, retort upon* one, ἀ. ὅτι.. Hdt.2.133.

***ἀντιμερίζομαι**, *impart in turn*, χάριν *AP*6.209 (Antip. Thess.). 2. *distinguish*, Hsch.

**ἀντιμερίτης**, ου, ὁ, *rival claimant*, τινῶν Jul.*Gal.*148c.

***ἀντιμεσουρᾰν-έω**, *to be in the opposite meridian*, as the sun at midnight, Plu.2.284e, Ptol.*Tetr.*33, Vett.Val.116.5, al., Man.4.613. -**ημα**, ατος, τό, *opposite meridian*, S.E.*M.*5.12, Ptol.*Tetr.*201; name of the *fourth* τόπος in a '*nativity*', Paul.Al.*L.*3. -**ησις**, εως, ἡ, *occupation of the opposite meridian*, Heph.Astr.1.2.

**ἀντιμετα-βαίνω**, *pass over in turn*, ἐπί τι Alex.Trall.5.6. -**βάλλω**, *meet one change with another*, Hp.*Acut.*26. ***-βᾰσις**, εως, ἡ, *rowing up stream*, πρὸς τὸ ῥεῦμα τοῦ ποταμοῦ Plu.2.319c. -**βᾰτικός**, ή, όν, *resilient*, Sor.2.31. -**βολή**, ἡ, *transposition*, as a figure of speech, as in 'non ut edam vivo sed ut vivam edo', Quint.*Inst.*9.3.85, cf. Alex.*Fig.*2.22, Phoeb.*Fig.*2.4.

**ἀντιμετ-άγω** [ᾰγ], *countermarch*, λόχον Onos.33.6; *press in contrary direction*, Heliod.ap.Orib.49.8.20. -**ᾰγωγή**, ἡ, *counter-extension*, τοῦ σώματος ib.9.3.

**ἀντιμετά-δοσις**, εως, ἡ, *mutual contribution*, Dam.*Pr.*17. -**θεσις**, εως, ἡ, *interchange*, προσώπων Longin.26.1; of meanings, Alex.*Fig.*2.22. -**κλίνω** [ῑ], *turn aside* or *the opposite way*, Ph.1.678. -**λαμβάνω**, *assume in turn* or *in exchange*, πρόσωπον Plu.2.785c; τὸν τόπον τινός Ascl.*Tact.*10.15; ὥσπερ ἐκ κληρονομίας τὸ μῖσος J.*AJ*16.3.1. 2. *receive back in return*, Phld.*Oec.*p.65J., cf. *Piet.*113. 3. *take arguments in reverse order*, Dam.*Pr.*350. II. Gramm., *use* a form *in place of* another, A.D.*Adv.*130.14:—Pass., 154.22, al.; also, *to be changed*, εἰς.. 130.11. -**ληπτέον**, *one must use instead, substitute*, λέξεις ἀντὶ λέξεων Phld.*Rh.*1.159S. -**ληψις**, εως, ἡ, *partaking* f the opposite, Plu.2.438d (fort. ἀντίληψις); ἀ. τῶν βίων experience of divers kinds of life, ib.4 6c. 2. double reflex movement, Heliod.ap. Orib.8.28.28,29. 3. Gramm., interchange of forms, A.D.Adv. 155.1.

**ἀντιμεταλλακτέον**, one must substitute, Thphr.Metaph.16 codd.

**ἀντιμεταλλεύω**, countermine, Ph.Bel.99.13, Plb.1.42.12; τοῖς πολεμίοις 16.31.8.

**ἀντιμετα-ρρέω**, flow off in turn or back, Placit.4.22.2, but ἀντιμετερᾷ (cj Bernardakis) is prob. **-σπάω**, draw off in a different direction, εἰς φροντίδας J.AJ13.5.3. **-στᾰσις**, εως, ἡ, counter-change, reciprocal replacement, Arist.Ph.208ᵇ2; reverse movement, εἰς τὸ ἀντίπαλον D.H.3.19, Simp.in Ph.1352.14. **-ταξις**, εως, ἡ, interchange of gender, D.H.Amm.2.10. **-τάσσω**, change the order of battle so as to meet the enemy, in Med., D.H.3.25. **-τίθεμαι**, to be changed, replaced, J.AJ16.7.6, cf. Numen.ap.Eus.PE14.5. **-χωρέω**, go away to the other side, ταῖς ἐλπίσι make room for new hope, J.AJ 15.2.2. **-χώρησις**, εως, ἡ, interchange, of letters, etc., Eust.1618.36.

**ἀντιμετειλέομαι**, to be unrolled in reverse direction, of cables, Orib. 49.22.14.

**ἀντιμέτ-ειμι**, (εἶμι ibo) compete with others: οἱ ἀντιμετιόντες rival competitors, Plu.Comp.Arist.Cat.2. **-εράω**, v. ἀντιμεταρρέω.

**ἀντιμετέχω**, participate reciprocally, Dam.Pr.14,33,65.

**ἀντιμετρ-έω**, measure out in turn, give one thing as compensation for another, τί τινι Luc.Am.19:—Pass., ἀντιμετρηθήσεται ὑμῖν it shall be measured in turn, Ev.Matt.7.2, Ev.Luc.6.38. II. Astrol., correspond in ascension, Cat.Cod.Astr.8(4).187. **-ησις**, εως, ἡ, reciprocal measurement, Simp.in Ph.733.29.

**ἀντιμέτωπος**, ον, front to front, face to face, X.HG4.3.19, Ages.2.12, Hld.9.16.

**ἀντίμηνα**· κατὰ μῆνα, Hsch.

**ἀντιμηνίω**, rage, be wrathful against, Ael.Fr.205.

**ἀντιμηνύω**, testify in return, BMus.Inscr.4.481*.388 (Ephesus, ii A.D.).

**ἀντιμηχᾰν-άομαι**, contrive against or in opposition, ἄλλα ἀ. Hdt.8.52, cf. E.Ba.291; σβεστήρια κωλύματα Th.7.53: abs., Arist.HA613ᵇ27; πρός τι X.HG5.3.16. **-ημα**, ατος, τό, counter-engine or device, μηχανήμασιν ἀ. εὐτρεπίζειν Polyaen.4.2.20, cf. Ath.Mech.9.1.

**ἀντιμῑμ-έομαι**, abs., follow an example, App.BC5.41,94. **-ησις**, εως, ἡ, close imitation of a person in a thing, c. dupl. gen., Th.7.67. **-ος**, ον, closely imitating, ἠχή, of an echo, Callistr.Stat.9; τινός Alcid.ap.Arist.Rh.1406ᵃ29; of man as a microcosm, ἀ. τῆς οὐρανίου τάξεως Ruf.Anat.1; ἀ. οὐρανοῦ ποταμός Hld.9.9, cf. Ph.2.164, Sthenidas ap.Stob.4.7.63: c. dat., ὀφθαλμὸν ἀ. ἡλίου τροχῷ Ar.Th.17. II. = μανδραγόρας, Dsc.4.75; = ὠκιμοειδές, Ps.-Dsc.4.28.

**ἀντιμῑσέω**, hate in return, Ar.Lys.818.

⊛**ἀντιμισθ-ία**, ἡ, requital, recompense, Ep.Rom.1.27, 2Ep.Cor.6.13. **-ιον**, τό, reward, Ps.-Callisth.3.26. **-ος**, ον, as a reward, in compensation, μνήμην ἀντίμισθον ηὗρετ' ἐν λιταῖς A.Supp.270. **-ωτός**, όν, hired as a substitute, Hsch.

**ἀντιμίσιον**, τό, (mensa) table in a court of justice, Suid.

⊛**ἀντιμνηστεύω**, rival in love, D.S.8.19.

**ἀντιμοιρ-εί**, Adv. in proportionate shares, D.36.8. **-έω**, receive a proportionate share, Poll.4.176. **-ία**, ἡ, compensation, v.l. for ἀντιμοιρεί, D.36.8. ⊛**-ος**, ον, prob. for ἰσοτίμοιρος, A.Ch.319.

**ἀντιμολεῖν**, (v. βλώσκω) go to meet, Apollon.Lex. s.v. ἀντιβολῆσαι.

⊛**ἀντίμολπος**, ον, sounding instead of, ἀ. ὀλολυγῆς κωκυτός a shriek of far other note than the cry of joy, E.Med.1176; ὕπνου τόδ' ἀντίμολπον..ἄκος song, sleep's substitute, A.Ag.17.

**ἀντίμορος**, ον, corresponding, of stones in a building, IG1.322.

⊛**ἀντίμορφος**, ον, formed after, corresponding to a thing, Luc.Am.44. Adv. -φως, τινί Plu.Crass.32.

**ἀντιμῡκάομαι**, low in answer, τινί D.H.1.39. 2. roar against, ἀλλήλοις, of sea and lake, Procop.Aed.4.8.

**ἀντιμυκτηρίζω**, answer mockery, gladio Cic.Fam.15.19.4.

⊛**ἀντιμῶλος**, ὁ, Cret., = ἀντίδικος, Leg.Gort.6.25.

**ἀντιναυπηγέω**, build ships against, Th.7.36,62 (Pass., as v.l.).

⊛**ἀντινέμομαι**, bestow in return, τὰν αὐτὰν χάριν Epigr.Gr.205.

**ἀντινεοποιός**, ὁ, deputy-νεοποιός, Rev.Ét.Gr.19.251 (Aphrodisias).

**ἀντινήχομαι**, swim against, πρὸς κῦμα Plu.2.979b.

**ἀντινῑκάω**, conquer in turn, A.Ch.499, cf. D.C.48.21.

**Ἀντινόεια**, τά, festival in honour of Antinous at Athens and Eleusis, IG3.1129,1147 (ii A.D.).

**ἀντινομ-έω**, disobey, θεοῖς Philostr.VA6.20 (fort. ἀντινομ⟨οθετ⟩εῖν). **-ία**, ἡ, conflict of laws, Quint.Inst.7.1.15, Hermog.Stat.2, D.22 Arg.ii 12; ἐν ἀντινομίᾳ γίγνεσθαι to be in a strait between two laws, Plu.Caes.13; ambiguity in the law, Id.2.742a. **-ίζομαι**, Pass., νόμοι ἀντινομιζόμενοί τινος, prob. laws enacted against one, Archyt.ap.Stob.4.1.132. **-ικός**, ή, όν, relating to ambiguity in the laws, Plu.2.741d. Adv. -κῶς by citing a contrary law, D.22 Arg.ii 24.

**ἀντινομοθετέω**, make laws in rivalry with, τινί Plu.2.1044c, etc.

**ἀντίνοος**, ον, opposite in character, resisting, τινί Hp.Epid.6.5.4.

**ἀντινουθετέω**, warn in return, Plu.2.72e.

**ἀντίνωτος**, ον, in pl., back to back, D.S.2.54, Ael.Tact.37.1, Arr.Tact.29.1.

**ἀντιξενίζω**, entertain in return, ξενισθεὶς μὴ -ίσαι Phld.Vit.p.30 J., cf. Eust.1961.37.

**ἀντιξηραίνω**, prob. f.l. for ἀνα-, Gal.18(2).804.

**ἀντι-ξοέω**, set oneself against, oppose, Pi.O.13.34. ⊛**-ξοος**, ον, contr. **-ξους**, ουν:—Ion. word, opposed to, adverse, ἐλπόμενοι οὐδέν σφι φανήσεσθαι ἀντίξοον Hdt.7.218, cf. 6.50; τὸ..τοῖσι Σκύθῃσι ἀ. 4.129; στρατὸν..ἀ. Πέρσῃσι 6.7:—abs., ἐν μυρίῃσι γνώμῃσι μίαν οὐκ ἔχω ἀντίξοον 8.119; δοῦρα ἀ. γόμφοις A.R.2.79; τὸ ἀντίξοον opposition, Hdt.1.174; τὸ ἀ. συμφέρον Heraclit.8; of diseases and remedies, Aret.SA2.4, CA2.1. Adv. ἀντιξόως in hostile spirit, Philostr.VA7.6. II. τὸ ἀ. the opposite side of the compass, Placit.2.12.1. (Prob. from ξέω 'hew'.)

**ἀντιξύω** [ῡ], scrape in turn, ἀ. τὸν ξύοντα 'claw me, claw thee', Sophr.149, Aristid.2.84 J.

⊛**ἀντίον**, as Adv., = ἄντην, v. ἀντίος. **ἀντίον**, τό, a part of the loom, Ar.Th.822, cf. Poll.7.36,10.125. 2. generally, loom, ἀντίον ὑφαινόντων Lxx 2Ki.21.19, al.

**ἀντιόομαι**, fut. -ώσομαι Hdt.7.9.γ',102, al.: aor. Pass. ἠντιώθην, Ion. ἀντ- Id.4.126, 7.9.α', al.:—resist, oppose, τινί Id.1.76, A.Supp.389, etc.; τινὶ ἐς μάχην Hdt.7.102: abs., οἱ ἀντιούμενοι, = οἱ ἐναντίοι, Id.1.207, 4.1. 2. in Id.9.7.β' (dub.), c. acc., τὸν Πέρσην ἀντιώσεσθαι ἐς τὴν Βοιωτίην that ye would meet him in Boeotia. (ἐναντ- is used in pure Att., ἀ. in Aen.Tact.36.7. The Homeric forms ἀντιόω, ἀντιόωσι, etc., belong to ἀντιάω.)

⊛**ἀντίος**, ία, ίον, (ἀντί) set against, and so, I. in local sense, face to face, opposite, ἀντίοι ἔσταν ἅπαντες Il.1.535; ἀντίος ἦλθε θεῶν went to meet them, 6.54; ἡ δ' οὐκ ἀθρῆσαι δύνατ' ἀντίη though she faced him, Od.19.478; esp. in battle, Il.11.216, etc.: ἐχώρεον..οἱ Πέρσαι ἀντίοι Hdt.9.62; ἐκ τοῦ ἀντίου προσφέρεσθαι X.Cyr.1.4.8; ἀντίος ἐλαύνειν ibid.; ἐκ τῆς ἀντίης προσπλέειν Hdt.8.6; κατ' ἀντίον Hp.VC11:—freq. c. gen., which often precedes, Ἀγαμέμνονος ἀντίος ἐλθών Il.11.231, cf. 5.301, 7.98; but also follows, ἀ. ἦλθεν ἄνακτος Od.16.14, cf. Il.17.31, etc.: less freq. in Hom. c. dat., ὅς ῥά οἱ ἀ. ἦλθε 15.584, cf. 7.20; but mostly so after Hom., ἀντίαι ἵζοντο τοῖσι Πέρσῃσι Hdt.5.18, cf. Pi.N.10.79, E.Supp.667, X.An.1.8.17, etc.; ἀ. ἐς .. h.Merc.345; = διάμετρος, Man.3.339. b. direct, opp. πλάγιος, Antyll.ap.Orib.44.23.9, cf. Heliod.ib.28. 2. opposite, contrary, τὸν ἀ. τοῖσδε λόγον A.Ag.499; τούτοις ἀντία opinions opposed to these, E.Supp.466; ἄδεια μὲν ἀντία δ' οἴσω with pleasure [I speak], though I shall offer reproof, S.Tr.122; οἱ ἀντίοι, = οἱ ἐναντίοι, Pi.P.1.45 (so later, PTeb.43.21 (ii B.C.)); εἰς τὸ ἀντίον X.Eq.12.12; also λόγοι ἀντίοι ἢ οὓς ἤκουον words the very reverse of those I have heard, Id.An.6.6.34. II. as Adv. in neut. ἀντία and ἀντίον, against, over against, abs., ἀντίον ἷζεν Od.14.79, cf. 17.334, etc.: more freq. like a Prep. c. gen., ἀντί' ἐμεῖο στήσεσθαι Il.21.481; ἀντία δεσποίνης φάσθαι before her, Od.15.377; so ἀντία σευ in thy presence, Hdt.7.209, cf. 1.133; ἀντίον τοῦ μεγάρου facing it, Id.5.77; τὰς καμήλους ἔταξε ἀντία τῆς ἵππου Id.1.80, cf. 3.160, al.; τἀνδρὸς ἀντίον μολεῖν S.Tr.785: so, 2. against, ὅς τις σέθεν ἀντίον εἴπῃ Il.1.230; ἀντίον αὐτῶν φωνὴν ἱέναι Hdt.2.2; ἐρίζειν ἀντία τοῖς ἀγαθοῖς Pi.P.4.285: c. dat., ἱέναι ἀντία τοῖσι Πέρσῃσι ἐς μάχην Hdt.7.236; ὕδωρ καπνῷ φέρειν ἀντίον Pi.N.1.25. 3. in the phrase τὸν δ' ἀντίον ηὔδα answered, Od.15.48, etc. (more freq. in Od. than Il.). 4. ἀντία εἶναι to be present, help, of a god, Milet.7 p.64 (ii/iii A.D.).—The word is almost confined to Poets and Ion. Prose; in Att. Prose ἐναντίος is preferred, though X. uses ἀντίος.

**ἀντιο-στᾰτέω**, = ἀνθίσταμαι, to be contrary, of a wind, S.Ph.640. **-τόμον**, τό, tonsillotome, Gal.14.785, Hermes 38.281. **-φρων**· ἐναντίον φρονῶν, Hsch. **-χεῖ**· ἐναντιοῦται, Id.

⊛**Ἀντιόχειος**, α, ον, of Antiochus, τέτραχμον IG11.203 B40,46 (iii B.C.).

**ἀντιοχεύομαι**, Pass., contrario more futuo, AP11.284 (Pall.).

**ἀντιόω, ἀντιόωσα**, etc., v. sub ἀντιάω.

**ἀντιπᾰγές**· ἐναντίως συνεστηκός, EM114.10.

**ἀντιπαγκρᾰτιάζω**, contend in the παγκράτιον, Sch.Philostr.Im.2.6.

**ἀντιπάθ-εια** [ᾰθ], ἡ, suffering instead, λυπεῖ τὸν στερόμενον τῶν ἀγαθῶν ἢ ἀ. κακῶν Pl.Ax.370a. II. opposition, contrast, τῆς γῆς πρὸς τὴν αἰθέρα Plu.2.952d. III. counteraction, antipathy, S.E.P.1.43, Archig.ap.Philum.Ven.14.4, Sor.2.42. IV. in Metric, of opposed rhythms, ἡ κατ' ἀντιπάθειαν μεῖξις Heph.14, cf. Aristid.Quint.1.28. V. contrary affection, Str.3.5.7; περὶ συμπαθειῶν καὶ ἀντιπαθειῶν, title of work by Bolus, Suid. s.v. Βῶλος, etc. **-έω**, have an aversion, Alex.Aphr.Pr.Prooem. 2. to be opposed, reversed in metric, as iambus or trochee, Sch.Heph.p.115 C. II. to be affected, ὑπὸ τῶν ἔξωθεν A.D.Synt.291.14. 2. to be affected in a contrary manner, τινί Plb.34.9.5, cf. Str.3.5.7. **-ής**, ές, in return for suffering, A.Eu.782; felt mutually, ἡδονή Luc.Am.27. 2. of opposite feelings or properties, δύναμις Plu.2.664c; φύσιν ἔχειν ἀ. πρός τι ib.940a. Adv. -θῶς Gp.5.11.4, Alex.Trall.8.2. 3. in Metric, of opposed rhythms, Sch.Heph.p.122 C., al. II. Subst. ἀντιπαθές, τό, remedy for suffering, Plu.Ant.45, cf. ἀντίτομον· φάρμακον ἀντιπαθές, Hsch.; λίθος ἀντιπαθὴς καλούμενος Ps.-Plu.Fluv.21.5:—name of a black kind of coral, Dsc.5.122. **-ητικός**, ή, όν, opposed to passivity, Sch.Opp.H.1.653. **-ιον**, τό, = ἀντιπαθής II, Hsch. s.v. μῶλυ.

**ἀντιπαιανίζω**, v. ἀντιπαιωνίζω.

**ἀντιπαιδεύω**, teach as a rival master, τινί Suid. s.v. Γενέθλιος.

**ἀντιπαιδονόμος**, ὁ, deputy-παιδονόμος, IG12(2).259 (Mytil.).

**ἀντιπαίζω**, play one with another, X.Cyn.5.4, Pl.Erx.395b.

**ἀντίπαις**, αιδος, ὁ, ἡ, like a child, γραῦς A.Eu.38; little more than a child, θυγατρὸς ἀντίπαιδος E.Andr.326; ἡλικία Luc.Am.2. II. instead of a boy, i.e. no longer a boy, S.Fr.564 (s.v.l.). 2. Subst., a mere boy, Plb.15.33.12, 27.15.4, D.H.4.3, Plu.Aem.22, Luc.Somn.16, Ant.Lib.13.5.

**ἀντιπαίω**, *strike against, resist*, τὸ ἀντιπαῖον Hp.*VM*22, cf. Arist. *Pr.*902$^b$13: metaph., πρός τι Plb.18.46.15; τινί Iamb *in Nic.* p.22 P.:—Pass., ib.p.24 P.

**ἀντιπαιωνίζω** or **-ᾱνίζω**, *sing the battle song against*, ἀλλήλοις Max. Tyr.32.2, cf. Aen.Tact.27.4 (-παιαν-).

**ἀντιπᾰλαιστής**, οῦ, ὁ, *antagonist in wrestling*, Ael.*VH*4.15.

**ἀντιπᾰλαίω**, *wrestle against*, *POxy.*1099, Sch.Ar.*Ach.*570, Eustr. *in EN*117.34.

**ἀντιπάλλομαι**, *rebound*, Cass.*Pr.*26, Eust.948.12.

**ἀντίπᾰλος**, ον, (πάλη) properly, *wrestling against*: hence, *antagonist, rival*, κράτος ἀ. A.*Pr.*528 (lyr.); ἀ. θεοῖς E.*Ba.*544 (lyr.): c. gen., μένος γήραος ἀντίπαλον Pi.*O.*8.71; γοητείας φάρμακον ἀ. *AP*10.50 (Pall.):—Subst. ἀντίπαλος, ὁ, *antagonist, rival, adversary*, Pi.*N.*11. 26, S.*Ant.*126 (lyr.): mostly in pl., Hdt.7.236, Ar.*Ra.*365,1027, Pl. *Alc.*1.119e, al.; cf. φθόνος πρὸς τὸ ἀ. Th.2.45, etc.; ὁ δ' ἦλθεν ἐπὶ τἀντίπαλον E.*Ba.*278 (dub.). 2. of things, *nearly matched, nearly balanced*, ἀπὸ ἀ. παρασκευῆς Th.1.91; ἀ. τριήρης *equally large*, Id.4. 120; ἀ. τινι Id.1.11, Pl.*Mx.*240a; γνῶμαι μάλιστα ἀ. πρὸς ἀλλήλας Th.3.49; ἀ. δέος fear *caused by the balance of the power of the parties, mutual* fear, ib.11; ἀ. ποιναί *adequate* punishment, E.*IT*446; ἤθεα ἀ. [τῇ πόλει] habits *corresponding to*.., Th.2.61; ὑμεναίων γόος ἀ. E. *Alc.*922; ἀντίπαλόν τι τῆς ναυμαχίας a point *where* the action *was evenly balanced*, Th.7.71, cf. 38, Lys.2.38; ἀντίπαλα καταστῆσαι bring to *a state of balance*, Th.4.117; εἰς ἀ. καταστῆναι to be in *such state*, Id.7.13. Adv. -λως Id.8.87: also neut. pl., ναυμαχήσαντες ἀντίπαλα Id.7.34. II. τὸν ἀμὸν ἀ. *him who fights for* me, my *champion*, A.*Th.*417 (lyr.).

***ἀντιπαρα-βαίνω**, *transgress*, *PLips.*298 (iii A.D.). **-βάλλω**, *place side by side* so as *to compare* or *contrast*, τι πρός τι Pl.*Ap.*41b; λόγον παρὰ λόγον *Hp.Mi.*369c, cf. Isoc.5.142; τί τινι Arist.*Fr.*91; βίον τινὸς καί τινος Plu.*TG*1:—Pass., c. dat., *measure oneself against, rival*, App.*BC*2.15. II. *contribute instead*, X.*Lac.*5. 3. **-βλητέον**, *one must compare*, prob. for -τόν in *An.Ox.*3. 216. **-βολή**, ἡ, *reply by comparison* or *contrast*, Arist.*Rh.*1414$^b$10, 1419$^b$34, Plu.2.40f, Longin.*Fr.*11, Ruf.ap.Orib.49.30.9.

**ἀντιπαρ-αγγελία**, ἡ, *competition for a public office*, Plu.*Arat.* 35. **-αγγέλλω**, *give orders, command in turn*, X.*HG*4.2.19, D.C. 65.1. II. *compete for a public office*, Plu.*Caes.*7; δημαρχίαν Id. *Mar.*29; τινί *with* one, Id.*Cat.Mi.*49.

**ἀντιπαρα-γρᾰφή**, ἡ, *counter-παραγραφή, perscriptio, replicatio*, *Gloss.* **-γράφω** [ᾰφ], *add* or *insert on the other side*, Ptol.*Geog.* 8.1.3:—Med., as law-term, *reply to a* παραγραφή, *remancipo*, *Gloss.*

**ἀντιπαρ-άγω** [ᾰγ], *shift in order to meet attacks*, τοὺς σάκκους J.*BJ* 3.7.20:—Pass., *to be shifted in the other direction*, Paul.Aeg.6.3. 2. Pass., *to be produced correspondingly*, Plot.2.4.11. 3. *adduce, allege on the other side*, Plu.2.719c: abs., *argue on the other side*, Phld. *Rh.*2.267 S., cf. *Vit.*p.4 J. II. more freq. intr., *lead an army against, advance to meet the enemy*, X.*Cyr.*1.6.43. 2. *march parallel with, skirt*, ταῖς ὑπωρείαις Plb.1.77.2, cf. 3.53.4. **-ἀγωγή**, ἡ, *flank march*, Id.9.3.10 (pl.), 11.18.2, Plu.*Pyrrh.*21. 2. metaph., *machinations*, *UPZ*20.44 (ii B.C.). II. in pl., *hostility*, πρός τινα Plb.10.37.2, al.

**ἀντιπαρα-δέχομαι**, *admit instead* or *in place of*, A.D.*Synt.*108. 13. 2. *receive in turn*, *BGU*977.15 (ii A.D.); dub. sens. in Ph.2. 508. **-δίδωμι**, *deliver up in turn*, τὴν ἀρχήν τινι J.*AJ*15.3.1, cf. *PFlor.*384.74 (V A.D.). ***-δοσις**, εως, ἡ, *mutual accommodation*, of heavenly bodies, Vett.Val.162.31. ***-θεσις**, εως, ἡ, *comparison, contrast*, J.*Ap.*2.33, A.D.*Synt.*49.21, al., Herm. *in Phdr.*p.183 A. **-θέω**, *outflank*, X.*An.*4.8.17. II. *run parallel to* a thing, Plot.6.5.11.

**ἀντιπαρ-αινέω**, *advise contrariwise*, c. inf., D.C.65.11. **-αιτέομαι**, *deprecate in answer*, A.D.*Synt.*296.18.

**ἀντιπαρα-κᾰλέω**, *summon in turn* or *contrariwise*, ἐπὶ ἀληθεστέραν γε σωτηρίαν Th.6.86, cf. X.*Cyr.*2.2.24, Pl.*Grg.*526e; ὑπέρ τινος *change one's attitude and petition*, J.*BJ*1.25.5. ***-κειμαι**, *lie just opposite*, τινί Plb.3.37.7. 2. Gramm., *correspond with, to be correlative to*, τινί A.D.*Adv.*155.1, al.; *to be opposed*, *Synt.*118.23. **-κελεύομαι**, *exhort in turn* or *contrariwise*, τοῖς πρεσβυτέροις μὴ καταισχυνθῆναι Th.6.13, cf. X.*Cyr.*3.3.42 and 59. **-κλησις**, εως, ἡ, *mutual exhortation*, Plb.11.12.2.

**ἀντιπαρα[κρ]ισις**, εως, ἡ, *comparison*, Diog.Oen.38 (dub. rest.).

**ἀντιπαραλαμβάνω**, *compare by contrasting*, Gal.14.221. II. Astrol., *take* a function *in exchange*, Vett.Val.174.7.

**ἀντιπαραλλάσσω**, *pass from side to side*, χεῖρας περὶ τὸ στέρνον Sor. 1.103.

**ἀντιπαράλληλος**, sc. πούς, = διτρόχαιος, Sch.Heph.p.219 C.

**ἀντιπαρα-λῡπέω**, *annoy in turn*, Th.4.80. **-πέμπομαι**, ἀ. τῇ μνήμῃ *to be cheered on one's way* [to death] by the remembrance, Plu. 2.1099d. **-πήγνῡμι**, *set up as a standard of comparison* or *reference*, A.D.*Synt.*37.22 (Pass.). **-πλέω**, *sail along on the other side*, Th.2.83. **-πορεύομαι**, *march on the flank*, ταῖς χώραις Plb. 5.7.11. **-σκευάζομαι**, Med., *prepare oneself in turn, arm on both sides*, Th.1.80, D.10.29, etc.; ἀ. ἀλλήλοις ὡς ἐς μάχην Th.7.3. II. later, in Act., *instigate in return*, τινὰ ἐναντιωθῆναί σφισι D.C.38. 14. **-σκευή**, ἡ, *hostile preparation*, Th.1.141. **-στᾰσις**, εως, ἡ, as a figure of speech, *counter-objection, rejoinder, retort*, Hermog. *Stat.*3, al., Aps.p.270 H., Olymp. *in Cat.*78.26, Alex.Aphr. *in Metaph.* 518.28; *indirect reply*, Procl. *in Alc.*p.303 C.:—Adj. **-στᾰτικός**, ή, όν, Hermog.*Inv.*3.6. Adv. **-κῶς** ibid., Eust.704.36. **-στρᾰτοπεδεύω**, *encamp opposite*, D.H.8.25. **-ταξις**, εως, ἡ, *hostile demonstration*, ἀντιπαρατάξεις κατὰ τὴν ἀγοράν Id.6.22; ἀ. τῆς γνώμης *stubborn determination to resist*, J.*AJ*18.8.5. **-τάσσομαι**, Att. **-ττομαι**, Med. and Pass., *stand in array against*, ἀλλήλοις Th.6.98, cf. X.*HG*1.3.5; ἀντιπαρατεταγμένους πρὸς τὴν τούτων ἀσέλγειαν Aeschin.3.257: metaph., *hold one's ground against*, Epicur.*Fr.*138: abs., *stand in hostile array*, Th.1.63; ἀπὸ τοῦ ἀντιπαραταχθέντος in *hostile array*, Id.5.9; in a Com. metaph., ἡ δημιουργὸς ἀντιπαρατεταγμένη κρεάδι' ὀπτᾷ Men.518.12; λίαν -τεταγμένοι, of a *hostile* audience, Corn.*Rh.*p.360 H.: c. acc., ἀντιπαρετάξαντο φάλαγγα X.*An.*4.8. 9. II. Act., = Med., is dub. l. in Plb.9.26.4. **-τείνω**, *stretch side by side* so as *to compare or contrast*, ἄλλον [λόγον] πρὸς αὐτὸν ἀ. Pl.*Phdr.*257c. 2. intr., *extend beside*, Anon.*Geog.Comp.*7; and Pass. in same sense, ib.21. **-τίθημι**, *contrast and compare*, τὰς ἄλλας νύκτας ταύτῃ ἀ. Pl.*Ap.*40d, cf. Men.325.15, Phld.*Po.*2.28, *Hom.*p.12 O., Jul.*Gal.*99d. **-χωρέω**, *yield, give up in turn*, τινὰ ἀλλήλοις Phlp. *in Ph.*553.20; *give place in turn*, ἀλλήλοις Gal.19.474: Astrol., *yield to adverse influence*, Vett.Val.125.10; *return a pledge*, *BGU*1158.6 (i B.C.). **-χώρησις**, εως, ἡ, *making way for each other*, Simp. *in Cael.*459.16; *mutual concession*, Eust.445.11: Astrol., *yielding to adverse influence*, Vett.Val.274.19.

**ἀντιπάρ-ειμι**, (εἶμι *ibo*) *march on opposite sides of* a river or entrenchments, X.*An.*4.3.17, *HG*5.4.38. **-εισᾰγωγή**, ἡ, *introduction of a second* soul, Plot.2.9.5 (as v.l.). **-έκτᾰσις**, εως, ἡ, *interpenetration* of two or more bodies in κρᾶσις, Chrysipp.*Stoic.*2.153. **-εκτείνομαι**, *to be reciprocally interpenetrated*, τὰ ἀλλήλοις δι' ὅλων -όμενα Id.ib.154:—also Act., [αἱ ψυχαὶ] δι' ὅλων τῶν σωμάτων -ουσιν Id.ib. 153. 2. Act., *extend in line with*, τῷ τείχει τὸ ἱππικόν J.*BJ*3.7. 24. 3. Pass., *extend in the contrary direction*, Iamb. *in Nic.* p.13 P. **-εξάγω** [ᾰγ], *lead on against* the enemy, τὴν δύναμιν, τὸν ἵππον, Plu.*Luc.*27, *Pyrrh.*16: metaph., *cite* an authority *in contradiction of* another, Gal.8.715; *incite to rivalry*, Them.*Or.*22.275d. 2. *bring into action as an enemy*, τὸν θεόν J.*AJ*18.8.1. 3. (sc. στρατόν) *march against*, Philipp.ap.D.18.39: metaph., *adduce arguments against*, [τοῖς ποιηταῖς] D.Chr.7.98, cf. Ael.*VH*4.9, S.E.*M.*7.166. b. *march parallel with*, τινί Plu.*Aem.*30, cf. Arr.*An.*5.17.1: c. acc., τὴν δύναμιν Plu.*Luc.*27. II. *compare*, ἑαυτὸν πρός τινα Id.2. 47cb. **-εξᾰγωγή**, ἡ, *a means of attack in controversy*, πρός τινα S.E.*M.*7.150. **-έξειμι**, (εἶμι *ibo*) *proceed in a parallel direction*, J.*AJ*2.9.4, Plu.2.195c. II. *make hostile demonstrations*, Id.*Cic.* 43. **-εξέρχομαι**, = foreg., D.C.47.46. **-εξετάζω**, *compare*, τοὺς βίους τῶν πόλεων ἀλλήλοις D.H.3.11; βύβλον βίβλῳ Id.*Th.* 16. **-έρχομαι**, *pass by on the opposite side*, *Ev.Luc.*10.31: c. acc. loci, *AP*12.8 (Strat.). II. *come up and help*, as *against* an enemy, Lxx *Wi.*16.10. III. *enter in place of*, Diog.Oen.29. IV. *penetrate*, Chrysipp.*Stoic.*2.248. **-έχω**, *furnish* or *supply in turn*, Th. 6.21:—also in Med., X.*Hier.*7.12; *supply mutual need*, τοὐλλιπὲς ἀλλήλοις *AP*9.12 (Leon.). 2. *cause in return*, τοὺς ἀντιπαρέχοντας πράγματα D.21.123. **-ηγορέω**, *persuade, comfort in turn*, Plu.2. 118a. **-ήκω**, = ἀντιπαρεκτείνομαι, Chrysipp.*Stoic.*2.153,230; *stretch parallel to*, c. dat., Arist.*Mu.*393$^a$31, Str.2.5.28; *outflank*, τῷ στρατεύματι Paus.8.10.6. **-ιππεύω**, *bring their cavalry against*, Arr. *An.*5.16.3. ***-ίστημι**, Rhet., *retort*, τινί τι Aps.p.270 H., Ps.-Alex. Aphr. *in SE*102.15 (-ιστῶντος):—Pass., νόμος -ίσταται νόμῳ Aps. p.271 H.; *correspond*, Ptol.*Geog.*8.1.14. **-οδεύω**, *meet on a march*, ἀλλήλοις App.*Pun.*107. **-ονομάζομαι**, *to be opposite in expression*, Iamb. *in Nic.*p.29 P.

**ἀντιπαρρησιάζομαι**, *speak freely in turn*, Plu.2.72e.

**ἀντιπαρ-ῳδέω**, *write a parody against*, Str.9.1.10:—Subst. **-ῴδησις**, εως, ἡ, Steph. *in Rh.*319.19. **-ωνῠμέομαι**, Pass., *to be opposite in name* or *expression*, Nicom.*Ar.*1.8:—Act. in same sense, Iamb. *in Nic.* p.18 P., al.:—Subst. **-ωνῠμία**, ἡ, ib.p.13 P., al.; and Adj. **-ώνῠμος**, ον, Nicom.*Ar.*2.3.

**ἀντιπάσχω**, *suffer in turn*, κακὰ ἀ. *suffer* evil *for* evil, Antipho 4.2.3; δεσμοὺς X.*Hier.*7.12; τί ἂν δράσειαν αὐτούς, ὅ τι οὐκ ἂν μεῖζον ἀντιπάθοιεν; Th.6.35; δρῶν ἀντιπάσχω χρηστά I *receive* good *for* good done, S.*Ph.*584; καλὸν τὸ εὖ ποιεῖν μὴ ἵνα ἀντιπάθῃ Arist.*EN*1163$^a$1; ἀ. ἀντί τινος Th.3.61: abs., *suffer for* one's acts, X.*An.*2.5.17. b. *to be affected in a contrary manner*, ἡ ψυχὴ τοῖς σώμασιν ὡς ἀσώματος ἀντιπέπονθε Sallust.8; opp. συντρέχειν, Alex.Aphr. *in Top.*437.16. 2. τὸ ἀντιπεπονθός *requital*, Arist.*EN*1132$^b$21 (Pythag.); of persons, εὔνοιαν ἐν ἀντιπεπονθόσι φιλίαν εἶναι ib.1155$^b$33. 3. *to be in the same proportion*, πρός τι Id.*Mech.*850$^b$2. 4. *to be reciprocally proportional*, Euc.6.14, al.; -πεπονθότα σχήματα figures *having* the sides about the equal angles *reciprocally proportional*, Id.6 *Def.*2, cf. Hero *Deff.* 118. Adv. **-πεπονθότως** *reciprocally*, Archim.*Aequil.*1.6,7, al., cf. Iamb. *in Nic.*p.11 P. II. *counteract*, δυσουρίαις, θανασίμοις φαρμάκοις, Dsc.3.62,64. III. *to be of opposite nature to*, τινί Thphr.*Lap.* 14. IV. Gramm., ἀντιπεπονθώς *reflexive*, κατηγορήματα *Stoic.*2. 59. V. *to be adversely affected*, Agathin.ap.Orib.10.7.11, Archig. ap.eund.8.2.15.

**ἀντιπᾰτᾰγέω**, *rattle so as to drown* another sound, ψόφῳ Th.3.22; τοῖς ὅπλοις Dam.*Isid.*63.

**ἀντιπᾰτάσσω**· *repercutio*, *Gloss.*

**ἀντιπᾰτέω**, *trample upon in turn*, Sch.Ar.*Pl.*973.

**ἀντιπατρίς**, ίδος, ἡ, name of a kind of *silver vessel*, *IG*11.110, al. (Delos, iii B.C.). (Prob. from pr. n. Ἀντίπατρος.)

**ἀντιπειστικός**, ή, όν, *availing to persuade to the contrary*, *An.Bachm.* 2.291.

*ἀντιπελαργ-έω, *cherish in turn*, Iamb.*VP*5.24, Zen.1.94; *cherish in place of* another, of a sister acting as parent, Aristaenet.1.25:—Subst.*-ωσις, εως, ἡ, *Com.Adesp.*939.

ἀντι-πέμπω, *send back an answer*, Hdt.2.114; πέμψασιν ἀντέπεμψεν S.*OT*306:—Pass., Hdt.6.4. **2.** *send back* sound, *echo*, Arr.*An.*6.3.3. **3.** *send in requital* or *repayment*, οἰκούρια S.*Tr.*542; τινὶ θηρίον Philem.47. **II.** *send against*, στρατιάν τινι Th.6.99. **III.** *send in the place of* another, στρατηγοὺς ἐπὶ τὰς ναῦς Id.8.54. **-πεμψις**, εως, ἡ, *sending back* of sound, *echo*, Arr.*An.*6.3.3.

**ἀντιπενθής**, ές, *causing grief in turn*, A.*Eu.*782.

**ἀντιπεπόνθησις**, εως, ἡ, *reciprocal proportion*, Nicom.*Ar.*1.7, Iamb.*Comm.Math.*7.

**ἀντιπέρᾱ**, Adv. for ἀντιπέρᾱν, Plb.1.17.4 (dub.): c. gen., ἀ. τῆς Γαλιλαίας *Ev.Luc.*8.26: proparox. in Hsch.

**ἀντιπεραίνομαι**, *accomplish in turn*, τὸ δρᾶν καὶ τὸ παθεῖν, sens. obsc., *AP*12.238 (Strat.).

**ἀντιπέρ-αιος**, α, ον, *lying over against*, ἀντιπέραι' ἐνέμοντο *the lands lying over against*, Il.2.635:—in late Ep. also fem. ἀντιπεραιά A.R.2.351, D.P.962, Nonn.*D.*24.148:—also **ἀντιπεραῖτις**, ιδος, ἡ, Tz.*H.*1.896. **-αλαχεῖν**· ἀντιτρέφειν, Hsch. *-ᾱν, Ion. -ην, Adv. = ἀντιπέρᾱς, v.l. in X.*HG*6.2.9, cf. A.R.2.177, al.; also κατ' ἀντιπέραν, c. gen., Plb.9.41.11. **II.** Adj., Ἀσίδα τ' ἀντιπέρην τε Asia and *the opposite coast*, Mosch.2.9. **-ᾱς**, Adv. *over against, on the other side*, c. gen., Th.2.66, etc.; εἰς τὸ ἀ. X.*Cyn.*9.3: abs., ἡ ἀ. Θρᾴκη Th.1.100, cf. 4.92. **-ηθεν** (-θε Man.6.579), Adv. *from the opposite side*, A.R.1.613, *AP*9.551 (Antiphil.): c. gen., A.R.2.1030.

*ἀντιπερι-άγω [ᾰγ], *bring round*, τὸν δὲ [σκορπίον] τὸ κέντρον ἐπαίροντα ἀντιπεριάγειν Arist.*Mir.*844$^{b}$27; of the *corvus* employed on the Roman ships, Plb.1.22.8; τὸν αὐχένα τοῦ ἵππου Ph.1.311. **-άγωγή**, ἡ, *contrary revolution*, Ptol.*Alm.*5.2, Procl.*Hyp.*4.34. **2.** in midwifery, *rotatory movement* used in extracting the afterbirth, Sor.1.73. **-βάλλω**, *put round in the other direction*, e.g. a bandage, Hp.*Fract.*11. **2.** *embrace in return*, Ach.Tat.5.8:—Pass., *to be clothed about*, θανάτῳ Lxx *Si.*23.12. **-ειλέομαι**, *to be rolled in the contrary direction*, Orib.49.22.24. **-ειμι**, (εἶμι *ibo*) *come round as in a cycle*, Aret.*SA*2.2. **-έλκω**, *draw round to the other side*, S.E.*M.*7.189. **-ηχέω**, *echo around*, Plu.2.502d. **-ίστημι**, *oppose by surrounding, compress*, Arist.*Mete.*382$^{b}$10, 347$^{b}$6:—Pass., with intr. tenses in Act., *to be compressed*, ib.348$^{b}$6, al. **2.** Pass., *to be replaced by another substance*, ib.382$^{a}$14; ἀ. ἀλλήλοις *change places with*, Id.*Resp.*472$^{b}$16, cf. Gal.17(2).292. **3.** Pass., *to be opposed*, in general sense, Iamb.*in Nic.*p.19 P.; of the shadow of the earth, TheoSm. p.121 H. **II.** *bring all round*, φόβους ἀ. τινὶ Plb.4.50.1; εὐδαιμονίαν τισὶ Lib.*Decl.*43.6. **-λαμβάνω**, *embrace in turn*, X.*Smp.*9.4. **-πλέω**, *sail round on the other side*, Str.1.1.8. *-ποιέομαι, *express reciprocal action*, of certain verbs, A.D.*Synt.*429.3. **-ποιητικός**, ἡ, όν, *expressive of a claim*, *An.Bachm.*2.291. **-σπασμα**, ατος, τό, as military term, *diversion*, ἀ. ποιεῖν τινὶ Plb.3.106.6. **-σπασμός**, ὁ, = foreg., D.S.14.49. **-σπαστός**, ή, όν, *drawn through*, of cautery, Paul.Aeg.6.42. **-σπάω**, *draw off, divert*, D.S.3.37; esp. as military term, Plb.2.24.8, etc.:—Pass., Arist.*PA*670$^{b}$10. **2.** *divert, distract*, ἑαυτὸν ἄβακι Iamb.*VP*5.24. **-στάσις**, εως, ἡ, *surrounding so as to compress*, Arist.*Somn.Vig.*457$^{b}$2, 458$^{a}$27, *Pr.*867$^{b}$32, 962$^{a}$2. **2.** *reciprocal replacement, interchange*, Id.*Ph.*215$^{a}$15, 267$^{a}$16 (v. Simp. ad loc.), *Mete.*348$^{b}$2, Thphr.*Ign.*18, *Sud.*23. **3.** *alternation*, Nicom.*Ar.*1.8 and 13. **-στροφή**, ἡ, *turning round to the other side*, *Placit.*4.14.2. **-σχίζομαι**, *to be broken up and return*, of sputum, Steph.*in Hp.*1.174 D. **-φορά**, *contrary revolution*, Procl.*in Ti.*1.76 D., al., Simp.*in Cael.*473.19: pl., Procl.*in Prm.*p.571 S. **-χωρέω**, *move round in turn* or *in opposition*, Plu.*Ages.*39. **-ψύχω** [ῡ], *cool* or *chill in turn*, Plu.2.691f. *-ωθέω, *push* or *press back any surrounding body*, ib.1005f:—hence Subst. **-ωσις**, εως, ἡ, ibid.

**ἀντιπέσσομαι**, Att. -ττομαι, Pass., of food, *to be quite digested*, Arist.*Pr.*884$^{a}$2.

**ἀντίπετρος**, ον, *like stone, rocky*, S.*OC*192 codd. (lyr.). **II.** in Theoc.*Syrinx* 2 (acc. to Sch.), *exchanged for a stone*, of Zeus in his infancy.

**ἀντιπήγνῡμι**, in pf. -πέπηγα, *to be fixed opposite*, ἀλλήλοις, of crocodile's teeth, Tim.Gaz.in *An.Ox.*4.264.

*ἀντίπηξ, ηγος, ἡ, (πήγνυμι) *wheeled cradle* or *perambulator* for infants, κοίλης ἐν ἀντίπηγος εὐτρόχῳ κύκλῳ E.*Ion* 19; κύτος ἑλικτὸν ἀντίπηγος ib.40. (Mytil., = κιβωτός, acc. to Eust.1056.46.)

**ἀντιπηρ-όομαι**, Pass., *to be blinded in return*, Ph.2.332. **-ωσις**· *talio*, *Gloss.*

**ἀντιπίνω** [πῐ], *drink to, to pledge in turn*, Sch.Opp.*H.*3.226.

**ἀντιπίπτω**, *collide*, Arist.*Pr.*915$^{b}$18; *fall upon*, ταῖς σπείραις Plb.3.19.5. **2.** *resist*, ἀντιπῖπτον *resisting body*, Arist.*Pr.*961$^{b}$3; ἀ. τινὶ *Act.Ap.*7.51; μηδὲν ἀντιπεσόντα without *demur*, *UPZ*36.21 (ii B.C.); τῆς φράσεως οὐκ -ούσης A.D.*Adv.*123.5; εἰ μηδὲν -πίπτει *POxy.*1473.20 (iii A.D.), cf. Aët.16.73; ἀντιπῖπτον an *objection*, Phlp.*in Mete.*58.3; ἡ τοῦ ἀντιπίπτοντος λύσις Aps.p.238 H. **3.** of circumstances, *to be adverse*, τινὶ Plb.16.2.1, etc.: abs., τῆς τύχης -ούσης ib.28.2; of contrary winds, 4.44.9; *tell against, conflict with* (fact or theory), Phld.*Sign.*8, al. **II.** *to fall in a contrary direction*, αἱ σκιαὶ Str.2.1.19.

**ἀντιπιστεύω**, *trust in return*, Charito 2.11.

**ἀντιπιφάσκω**· ἀνταποδίδωμι, Hsch.

**ἀντιπλᾰγιάζομαι**, *to be placed athwart*, of bars in lattice-work, Lyd.*Mag.*3.37.

*ἀντιπλάδη, ἡ, *substance* or *process for protecting walls from damp*, *Ath.Mitt.*26.110.

**ἀντίπλαστος**, ον, lit. *similarly formed*; generally, *like*, νόμος S.*Fr.*284.

**ἀντιπλέκω**, *intertwine*, in Pass., Gal.18(2).748; of crossed or reversed bandaging, Sor.*Fasc.*12.513 C.

**ἀντιπλεονεκτέω**, *have equal precedence* or *privilege*, ἐν τῷ οὐρανῷ τό τε μέσον αὐτοῦ καὶ τὸ πέριξ Simp.*in Cael.*515.5; *have respective advantages over each other*, Id.*in Cat.*335.1, Elias *in Cat.*98.1:—hence **-ησις**, εως, ἡ, Simp.*in Cat.*341.2.

**ἀντίπλευρος**, ον, *with its side opposite, parallel*, κῆπος Εὐβοίας S.*Fr.*24.4; ἀ. παριππεύειν Hld.10.29.

**ἀντιπλέω**, *sail against* an enemy, v.l. in Th.1.50 and 54; ἀ. ἀνέμοισιν Ps.-Phoc.113.

**ἀντιπληκτίζω**, *struggle with*, πρός τινα Tz. ad Lyc.930.

**ἀντιπλήξ**, ῆγος, ὁ, ἡ, *beaten by the waves*, ἀκταὶ S.*Ant.*592 (lyr.).

**ἀντιπληρόω**, *fill in turn* or *against*, τὰς ναῦς *man* them *against* the enemy, Th.7.69, etc.:—Med., ἀ. φιλοτησίαν πρός τινα *fill one's* cup in his honour, *pledge* him, Aristid.2.115 J. **II.** *fill up by new members*, ἀ. τάξεις ἐκ πολιτῶν X.*Cyr.*2.2.26; *replenish after exhaustion*, Thphr.*CP*1.13.3.

**ἀντιπλήσσω**, *strike in turn*, in Pass., Arist.*EN*1132$^{b}$29, *MM*1194$^{a}$33.

**ἀντίπλοια**, ἡ, *sailing close to the wind*: metaph. of a mixed constitution, dub. l. in Plb.6.10.7 (fort. -πνοια).

**ἀντί-πνευσις**, εως, ἡ, *opposite current of air*, Orib.9.20.3. **-πνέω**, of winds, *blow against*, πρός τι Arist.*Pr.*940$^{b}$34; ἀλλήλοις Thphr.*Vent.*53: impers., ἀντιπνεῖ, διὰ τὸ ἀντιπνεῖν Arist.*Mete.*370$^{b}$22. **2.** *to be adverse* or *contrary*, Ph.1.593, Plu.*Cic.*32, Luc.*Nav.*7: metaph. of fortune, Plb.25.3.9, Clitomachus ap.Stob.4.41.29: c. dat., Luc.*Tox.*7. **3.** trans., πνεῦμα ταῖς ναυσὶ Plu.2.309b. **-πνοή**, ἡ, = sq., Sch.A.R.4.820. **-πνοια**, ἡ, *conflicting wind*, τῷ βορέᾳ Thphr.*Vent.*28. **2.** *contrary wind*, Ph.1.352, Hdn.5.4.11. **-πνοος**, ον, contr. **-πνους**, ουν, *caused by adverse winds*, ἀντιπνόους . . ἀπλοίας A.*Ag.*147 (lyr.); στάσις ἀ. Id.*Pr.*1087 (lyr.). Adv. **-νόως** Tz. ad Lyc.739.

**ἀντίποδες**, οἱ, v. ἀντίπους.

**ἀντιποθέω**, *long for in turn*, X.*Mem.*2.6.28 (Pass.).

*ἀντιποι-έω, *do in return*, ταῦτα Pl.*Cri.*50e; ἀντ' εὖ ποιεῖν Id.*Grg.*520e; οἱ μὴ ἀντιποιοῦντες εὖ Arist.*Rh.*1397$^{b}$7; κακῶς μὲν πάσχοντας, ἀντιποιεῖν δὲ οὐ δυναμένους X.*An.*3.3.12, cf. ib.7; ἀ. κακῶς τὸν ἄρξαντα Muson.*Fr.*10p.56 H.; ἀ. τὸ αὐτὸ Arist.*EN*1138$^{a}$22:—Pass., *to have done to one in turn*, Lxx *Le.*24.19. **II.** Med. (aor. Pass. in Luc.*DMort.*29.2), c. gen., *exert oneself about* a thing, *seek after* it, ἀ. τῶν σπουδαίων Isoc.1.2; *lay claim to*, τῆς πόλεως Th.4.122; ἀρετῆς Isoc.6.7; τῆς τέχνης, τῶν νικητηρίων, Pl.*Men.*90d, *Phlb.*23a; τοῦ πρωτεύειν D.10.52; τῆς θαλάττης Antiph.190.11; τῶν ἐν τῇ Ἑλλάδι πραγμάτων D.Chr.11.62; οἱ Δωριεῖς ἀντιποιοῦνται τῆς τραγῳδίας Arist.*Po.*1448$^{a}$30: also c. inf., ἀ. ἐπίστασθαί τι *lay claim to* knowing . ., Pl.*Men.*91c, cf. *Hp.Mi.*363a: c. acc., τὴν κληρονομίαν *Michel* 546.16 (Cappad., i B.C.). **2.** *contend with* one *for* a thing, ἀ. τινὶ τῆς ἀρχῆς X.*An.*2.1.11, 2.3.23; more rarely τινὶ περί τινος ib.5.2.11; τινὸς πρός τινα Arr.*Epict.*1.29.9. **3.** abs., *set up opposition*, Pl.*Prt.*336c, Arist.*Pol.*1314$^{a}$12; *maintain resistance*, Plb.2.9.5, 21.25.6. **-ησις**, εως, ἡ, *laying claim to*, τινός D.H.11.30, cf. S.E.*M.*6.27, *PLond.*2.251.25 (iv A.D.).

**ἀντίποινα**, τά, *requital, retribution*, ἀντίποιν' ὡς τίνῃς ματροφόνου δύας prob. in A.*Eu.*268; ἀντίποινά τινος πράσσειν, λαμβάνειν, to exact *retribution for* . ., Id.*Pers.*476, S.*El.*592; ἀντίποιν' ἐμοῦ παθεῖν suffer *retribution for* me, Id.*Ph.*316, cf. Nech. in *Cat.Cod.Astr.*7.145.—In codd. sts. written ἀντάποινα, q.v. Later in sg., as Lib.*Decl.*43.69.

**ἀντίποινος**, ον, *for recompense*, Lyc.271. **2.** *in substitution*, Id.1201.

**ἀντιπολεμέω**, *wage war against*, Th.3.39: c. dat., Pl.*Criti.*112e, X.*Cyr.*7.2.24: c. acc., Lxx *Is.*41.12:—Pass., *to be warred against*, D.C.38.40.

**ἀντιπολέμιος**, ον, *warring against*, οἱ ἀντιπολέμιοι *enemies*, Th.3.90 codd. (but -πόλεμοι Poll.1.150); in Hdt.4.134, 140, codd. vary between ἀντιπόλεμοι and -μιοι; but in 7.236, 8.68.β' ἀντιπόλεμοι occurs without v.l., and is the only form cited by Hsch., cf. Onos.10.9, al.

**ἀντιπολίζω**, *build up as an opposing city*, ἑαυτόν J.*BJ*5.2.4.

**ἀντιπολιορκέω**, *besiege in turn*, τόπον Th.7.28; τινά Plu.*Marc.*7:—Pass., J.*BJ*3.7.19.

**ἀντίπολις**, εως, ἡ, *rival city*, τινὶ Str.3.5.3, v.l. in D.S.11.81.

**ἀντιπολῑτ-εία**, ἡ, *political opposition*, τινὶ πρός τινα Plb.20.5.5, cf. Plu.*Caes.*11. **II.** in pl., *opposite parties*, Plb.11.25.5. **-εύομαι**, *to be a political opponent*, Arist.*Pol.*1274$^{a}$14; οἱ -όμενοι *the opposite party*, Din.1.97: in sg., *political opponent*, Cic.*Att.*7.8.5: metaph., ὁ φθόνος ταῖς πράξεσιν ἀ. Aristonym.ap.Stob.3.38.36; ἀ. τινι Plu.*Them.*19, *Per.*8.

**ἀντιπονέομαι**, *exert oneself in opposition*, App.*BC*5.33.

**ἀντίπονον**, τό, *return for labour, wages*, Iamb.*VP*5.22.

**ἀντιπορεία**, ἡ, *marching against*, Ascl.*Tact.*10.2, Ael.*Tact.*25.1.

**ἀντιπορεῖν**, aor. with no pres. in use, *give instead*, *APl.*5.341.

**ἀντιπορεύομαι**, *march to meet* another, X.*HG*7.3.5.

**ἀντιπορθέω**, *ravage in return*, E.*Tr.*359, Lyc.1398.

**ἀντίπορθμος**, ον, *over the straits*, ἠπείροιν δυοῖν πεδία plains *on opposite sides of the straits*, E.*Ion* 1585; Πελοπίας χθονὸς ἐν ἀντιπόρθμοις *in the parts opposite* Peloponnesus, Id.*Fr.*515, cf. Arist.*Mu.*$392^{b}23$, Lyc.1071: c. dat., Str.8.6.21.

**ἀντιπορνόβοσκος**, ὁ, title of a comedy by Dioxippus, Ath.3.100e.

**ἀντίπορος**, ον, = ἀντίπορθμος, *on the opposite coast*, ἐς ἀ. γείτονα χώραν, i.e. Europe, as separated by a strait from Asia, A.*Pers.*66, cf. *Supp.*544, E.*Med.*210; Ἄρτεμιν Χαλκίδος ἀντίπορον, i.e. her temple at Aulis *over against* Chalcis in Euboea, Id.*IA*1494 (all lyr. passages):—in X.*An.*4.2.18 τὸν ἀ. λόφον τῷ μαστῷ, simply, *over against, opposite to.*

**ἀντίπορπος**, ἡ, *seton* for keeping incision open, *Hippiatr.*24,26.

***ἀντίπους**, ὁ, ἡ, πουν, τό, gen. οδος, *with the feet opposite*, στὰς ἀ., of one *at the Antipodes*, Pl.*Ti.*63a; so ἀ. ἔσται πορευόμενος ἕκαστος αὐτὸς αὑτῷ Arist.*Cael.*$308^{b}20$, cf. Eratosth.16.19; οἱ ἀ. *the Antipodes*, Str. 1.1.13, Cleom.1.2, Cic.*Acad.Pr.*2.39.123, Plu.2.869c.

**ἀντι-πρακτικός**, ή, όν, *counteracting*, M.Ant.2.1: Comp. -ώτερος Xenocr.ap.Orib.2.58.72. **-πραξις**, εως, ἡ, *counteraction, resistance*, Plb.6.17.8, D.H.11.53, Plu.*Publ.*11, Demetr.Lac.*Herc.*1012.71.

***ἀντίπρᾱσις**, εως, ἡ, *contract of sale executed by the purchaser*, *PLond. ined.*2227 (iv A.D.).

**ἀντιπράσσω**, Att. -ττω, Ion. **-πρήσσω**, *act against, seek to counteract*, τινί X.*Ath.*2.17, Alex.264 (Med.); πρός τι Arist.*Pol.*$1320^{a}6$, etc. 2. abs., *act in opposition*, D.32.14; ὁ ἀντιπρήσσων, = ἀντιστασιώτης, Hdt.1.92; ἀ. τι *oppose* in any way, X.*HG*2.3.14; ἐάν τε ἀντιπράττῃ τις ἐάν τε μὴ συμπράττῃ Arist.*Rh.*$1379^{a}13$; *conflict with, tell against* a theory, Demetr.Lac.*Herc.*1055.20:—Med., X. *Hier.*2.17.

**ἀντιπρεσβεύ-ομαι**, Med., *send counter-ambassadors*, Th.6.75, Luc. *Peregr.*16: c. dat., Paus.7.9.5:—Act. in Aristid.1.372 J., App.*Mith.* 87. **-τής**, οῦ, ὁ, = Lat. *pro legato*, *Gloss.*

**ἀντιπρίασθαι** [ρῐ], aor., *buy in return*, *SIG*$^{2}$861 (Delph.).

**ἀντιπρο-αίρεσις**, εως, ἡ, *mutual preference*, πρὸς ἀλλήλους Arist.*EE* $1236^{b}3$. **-βάλλομαι**, *propose instead of* another, τὸν ἕτερον Pl.*Lg.* 755d:—Act., Gal.19.64. ***-βολή**, ἡ, *proposing instead of* another, Pl.*Lg.*755e, 756a (cj.). **-εῖδον**, aor. 2, *recognize before meeting*, ἀλλήλους Ph.2.544. **-ειμι**, (εἶμι *ibo*) *come forward against* or *to meet*, τινί Th.6.66: abs., App.*Pun.*107. **-ηγέομαι**, *precede instead of following*, *EM*462.35, Hdn.Gr.2.394. **-θῡμέομαι**, *to be hostilely disposed*, Aen.Tact.11.1.

**ἀντίπροικα**, Adv. *for next to nothing, cheaply*, X.*Ages.*1.18, Poll. 7.10.

**ἀντιπροικῷον**, τό, *compensation*, *PFlor.*294.74 (vi A.D.).

**ἀντιπρο-ΐσχομαι**, *hold out before one, present*, as weapons, ἡ λύπη ἀ. τὰ ἄμαχα κέντρα τῆς φύσεως Them.*Or.*32.357b:—Hsch. has the Act. ἀντιπροΐσχειν· ἀντιδοῦναι. **-κᾰλέομαι**, Med., *retort a legal challenge* (πρόκλησις), D.37.43; *challenge in turn*, c. acc. et inf., D.H. 15.8. **-καταληπτέον**, *one must reply to an anticipation*, Arist.*Rh.Al.* $1433^{b}1$. **-κλησις**, εως, ἡ, *retorting of a* πρόκλησις, Hsch. ***-πίνω** [πῐ], *drink in turn*, αἷμα ἀλλήλοις J.*BJ*5.10.4. II. *present in return* (cf. προπίνω I.2), ἀοιδάς Dionys.Eleg.1; τὰ ὅμοια Ath.4.128a.

**ἀντιπροσ-ᾰγορεύω**, *return salute*, Plu.*Crass.*3 (in aor. -ευσα):—but in earlier Prose, aor. 2 ἀντιπροσεῖπον Thphr.*Char.*15.3:—Pass., ἀντιπροσερρήθην X.*Mem.*3.13.1. **-άγω** [ᾰγ], *adduce on the other side*, τι πρός τινα Phld.*Rh.*1.377 S. **-αμάομαι**, Med., *heap in turn*, ἀ. τὴν γῆν *scrape up new* soil *upon*, X.*Oec.*17.13. **-βάλλομαι**, Pass., *to be impinged upon in return*, Hierocl.p.23 A. **-ειμι**, (εἶμι *ibo*) *march against*, X.*Cyr.*3.3.24. **-εῖπον**, v. ἀντιπροσαγορεύω. **-ελαύνω**, intr., *charge against*, of cavalry, D.C.46.37. **-έρχομαι**, *come to meet*, τινί Id.60.6. **-κᾰλέομαι**, Med., *summon in turn*, D.47. 45. **-κρίνω** [ρῑ], *join instead*, Alex.Aphr.*de An.*134.32:—Pass., *to be added to in exchange*, c. dat., Id. *in Sens.*57.2. **-κῠνέω**, *fall down and worship in turn*, Plu.2.1117c. **-οψις**, εως, ἡ, *appearing instead*, glossed by ὁμηρεία, Suid., Zonar. **-φέρω**, *bring near in turn*, λύχνον τινί X.*Smp.*5.9. **-φθέγγομαι**, *accost in return*, Ph. 1.36. ***-ωπος**, ον, *with the face towards, facing*, τοῖς πολεμίοις X. *Cyr.*7.1.25, cf. Aen.Tact.22.11; *face to face*, ἀντιπρόσωποι μαχόμενοι X.*HG*6.5.26; φιλήματα *AP*12.251 (Strat.); of images, *reflected*, Thphr.*Sens.*52,53; of winds, *blowing in a contrary direction*, *Placit.* 4.1.1. Adv. -πως Arist.*Mir.*$835^{b}11$, Steph. *in Hp.*1.95 D., al. II. Subst. -ωπον, τό, *prow*, Artem.2.23, 4.24.

**ἀντιπρό-τᾰσις**, εως, ἡ, *counter-proposition*, Hermog.*Inv* 3.4, Steph. *in Int.*24.1. **-τείνω**, *hold out in turn*, τὴν δεξιάν X.*HG*4.1.31; ἱκετηρίας D.H.8.19 codd. 2. *propose in turn*, D.C.48.11 (Med.). 3. *adduce on the other side*, Gal.10.112. **-τίθημι**, *publish, post up in opposition*, γράμματα D.C.65.1. **-φέρω**, in Med., *adduce in reply*, Demetr.Lac.*Herc.*1012.49.

**ἀντίπρῳρος**, ον, *with the prow towards*, ἀ. τοῖσι βαρβάροισι γενόμενοι Hdt.8.11; τοὺς ἔσπλους ταῖς ναυσὶν ἀντιπρῴροις κλῄειν Th.4.8; [ἐμβολαῖς] μὴ ἀντιπρῴροις χρῆσθαι not to charge *prow to prow*, Id.7.36; τὸ ἀ. ξυγκροῦσαι ibid.; ἀ. ἐμβάλλεσθαι ib.34; τῶν πολεμίων ἀ. ἐφορμούντων Id.8.75; of ships, *ready for action*, ib.53; ἀ. καταστῆσαι τὰς τριήρεις X.*HG*6.2.28; τὸ στράτευμα ἀ. ὥσπερ τριήρη προσῆγε ib.7.5. 23. 2. *face to face*, τάδ' ἀντίπρῳρα..βλέπειν πάρεστ' S.*Tr.*223 (lyr.); κατ' ἀντίπρῳρα ναυστάθμων *in front of* them, E.*Rh.*136 (lyr.); ὀργῆς ἀντιπρῴρου κυλινδουμένης Plu. *de Ira Fr.*27 B.

**ἀντιπταίω**, *obstruct, stand in the way*, πρός τι Onos.17.

***ἀντί-πτωμα**, ατος, τό, *stumble against*, Lxx *Si.*34(31).29; *accident*, Ptol. *Tetr.*116, Paul.Al.*N.*3b. **-πτωσις**, εως, ἡ, *opposition, resistance*, Hp.*Decent.*3 (pl.). II. Gramm., *interchange of cases*, Priscian. *Inst.*17.155, Sch.Ar.*V.*135. **-πτωτικός**, ή, όν, *of* or *belonging to* ἀντίπτωσις II, Anon.*Fig.*p.151 S. Adv. -κῶς *with such interchange*, Eust.29.39.

**ἀντίπῡγος**, ον, *rump to rump*, Arist.*HA*$540^{a}14$, $542^{a}16$. 2. c. gen., *turned away from*, λιμὴν ἀ. λιμένος Scyl.46, cf. 108.

**ἀντιπυκτεύω**, *wrestle against*, τῷ ἔρωτι Sch.S.*Tr.*441.

**ἀντίπῠλος**, ον, *with the gates opposite*, ἀλλήλῃσι Hdt.2.148.

**ἀντίπυργος**, ον, *like a tower* or *fort*, E.*Ba.*1097. II. Subst. ἀ., ὁ, *repository, cupboard*, ἀ. ξύλινοι Lib.*Or.*11.254.

**ἀντιπυργόω**, *build a tower over against*, c. acc. cogn., πόλιν τήνδ' ἀντεπύργωσαν *reared up* this *rival* city, i.e. the Areopagus as a rival to the Acropolis, A.*Eu.*688.

**ἀντιπυρσεύω**, (πυρσός) *return signals*, Plb.8.28.3, 10.46.1.

**ἀντιρρέπω**, *counterpoise, balance*, A.*Ag.*574; τινί Hp.*Art.*4: metaph., *vacillate*, ὥσπερ ἐπὶ πλάστιγγος Ph.2.170, etc.

**ἀντιρρέω**, *flow* or (of wind) *blow contrariwise*, Poll.1.111.

**ἀντιρρήγνῡμι**, *break opposite ways*, Plu.2.1005b.

**ἀντί-ρρησις**, εως, ἡ, *gainsaying, altercation*, ἀ. γίγνεταί τινι πρός τινα περί τινος Plb.2.7.7; *controversy*, Gal.*Phil.Hist.*24 D.; *refutation of*, D.S.1.38, J.*Ap.*2.1, Hermog.*Id.*1.8, Gal.1.131; *counter-statement*, *POxy.*68.11 (ii A.D.); *reply*, Phld.*Rh.*1.384 S., al., *Sign.*7, cf. 11. **-ρρητέον**, *one must speak against*, Pl.*Plt.*297b. **-ρρητικός**, ή, όν, *controversial*, λόγος S.E.*P.*1.21. Adv. -κῶς, ἔχειν πρός τινας Steph. *in Hp.*1.72 D.

***ἀντιρρητορεύω**, *speak against, dispute with*, τινί Max.Tyr.9.3.

**ἀντίρρῑνον**, τό, *calf's snout*, *Antirrhinum Orontium*, Thphr.*HP* 9.19.2 (codd. -ριζον, cf. Hsch.), Dsc.4.130.

**ἀντίρροια**, ἡ, *back current*, Thphr.*Vent.*53.

**ἀντιρροπ-ή**, ἡ, *counterpoise*, Hp.*Art.*38,39 (v.l. -ίη, as in Gal.18 (1).481). **-ία**, ἡ, in pl., τύχης ἀ. *vicissitudes* of fortune, Agath. *Praef.*p.134 D.

**ἀντίρροπος**, ον, like ἰσόρροπος, *counterpoising, compensating for*, τινός D.1.10; ἄγειν..λύπης ἀ. ἄχθος to balance the *counterpoising* weight of sorrow, S.*El.*120 (lyr.); Θεανοῖ..ἀ. *balancing* her, *weighing as much as*.., Antiph.26.24; κτῆμα πόνοις ἀ. Max.Tyr.6.6; ῥώμη πρὸς κίνδυνον ἀ. Pl.*Def.*412a. Adv. ἀντιρρόπως, πράττειν τινί *so as to balance* his power, X.*HG*5.1.36: also neut. pl. as Adv., ψυχὰς δ' ἀντίρροπα θέντες *as a counterpoise*, *IG*1.442. 2. like ἀντίζυγος, *equivalent to*, c. dat., X.*Oec.*3.15.

**ἀντίρρους**, ουν, *flowing directly opposite to*, Νείλῳ Str.11.2.2.

**ἀντίρρωται**· ἀποπέμπεται, Hsch.

**ἀντίς**, (ἀντί) *opposite*, c. gen., *POxy.*941.4 (vi A.D.).

**ἀντῐσάζω**, *to be equal with, compensate*, c. gen., Sch.E.*Alc.*859.

**ἀντισέβομαι**, *revere in turn*, Epicur.*Fr.*141.

**ἀντισεμνύνομαι** [ῡ], Med., *meet pride with pride*, Arist.*Pol.*$1314^{a}$ 7. II. Act., *extol in return*, Eust.1563.40.

**ἀντίσηκ-ος**, ον, *compensating, equivalent*, χάρις Eust.1075.8. **-όω**, *counterbalance, compensate for*, c. dat. rei, ὡς τοῖσδε (sc. κακοῖς) δὶς ἀντισηκῶσαι A.*Pers.*437: c. gen., ἀντισηκώσας δέ σε φθείρει θεῶν τις τῆς πάροιθ' εὐπραξίας some god ruins thee, *making compensation for, balancing*, thy former happiness, E.*Hec.*57, cf. D.S.31.12: c. acc., τιμαῖς ἀντισηκώσω χάριν I *will compensate* the favour by honours, Luc.*Trag.*243; *support by way of compensation*, τινά Hp.*Acut.*29, cf. *Art.*6:—Pass., ἡ ὠφέλεια πολλαῖς ὀδύναις -οῦται Simp. *in Epict.* p.27 D. **-ωμα**, ατος, τό, *equipoise, compensation*, *PSI*238.10 (vi/vii A.D.), Eust.546.24. **-ωσις**, εως, Ion. ιος, ἡ, = foreg., ἀ. γίνεται Hdt.4.50; *equivalence*, Plot.1.4.14.

**ἀντισημαίνω**, *give a countersign*, J.*AJ*19.1.10. II. *give hostile signs*, τοῖς βαρβάροις ἀντεσήμαινε τὰ ἐκ τοῦ θεοῦ Paus.10.23.1.

**ἀντισήπω**, *make to putrefy in turn*, Gal.11.608.

**Ἀντισθέν-ειοι**, οἱ, *followers of Antisthenes*, Arist.*Metaph.*$1043^{b}24$; ὁ Ἀ. Ἡρακλῆς, referring to a book *by A.*, Plu.2.536b. **-ισμός**, ὁ, *a way of life according to the teaching of Antisthenes*, Jul.*Or.*6.187c.

**ἀντίσιγμα**, ατος, τό, *sigma reversed*, as a critical mark, D.L.3.66, Sch.Od.5.247. 2. *symbol for ps*, Priscian.*Inst.*1.42.

**ἀντισῑωπάω**, *to be silent in turn*, Ar.*Lys.*528.

**ἀντισκαιωρέω**, *lay snares for*, τινά Tz.*H.*3.256.

**ἀντισκευάζομαι**, Med., *furnish for oneself in opposition*, τὸν οἶκον X.*Ages.*8.6:—Pass., Ph.*Bel.*92.11.

***ἀντίσκηνος**, ον, *opposite the stage-buildings*, prob. sc. στοά, *Ephes.* 2.41 (iii A.D.).

**ἀντίσκιος**, ον, *throwing a shadow the opposite way*, Ach.Tat.*Intr. Arat.*31, Vett.Val.142.28, Jul.*Or.*4.147c; ζόφον..ἀ. Ἠοῦς Nonn.*D.* 7.311.

**ἀντισκόροδον**, τό, = σκόροδον τὸ Κύπριον, Plin.*HN*19.112.

**ἀντισκοτ-έω**, *obstruct*, τῷ δικαίῳ S.E.*M.*2.78. **-ησις**, εως, ἡ, *obstruction*, *Gloss.*

**ἀντισκώπτω**, *mock in return*, Plu.*Tim.*15, *Ant.*24:—Pass., *take a gibe in return for one's own*, ἡδέως D.C.66.11.

**ἀντῐσόομαι**, Pass., *oppose on equal terms*, Th.3.11.

**ἀντισοφ-ίζομαι**, *use counter-devices*, πρός τι Arist.*Pol.*$1297^{a}36$: abs., Ph.1.364. **-ιστεύω**, = foreg., τῷ θείῳ λόγῳ Id.1.449, cf. Numen.ap.Eus.*PE*14.8. **-ιστής**, οῦ, ὁ, *one who seeks to refute*, c. gen., μαγγανείας Luc.*Alex.*43, cf. *Cal.*16.

**ἀντί-σπασις**, εως, ἡ, *revulsion*, esp. of bodily humours, Hp.*Hum.*1, *Vict.*2.56, Gal.10.315, etc. **-σπασμα**, ατος, τό, in war, *distraction, diversion*, Plb.2.18.3, D.S.20.86, J.*AJ*19.1.10; ἀ. τῆς φυγῆς Ph.1. 549. II. *cause of dissension*, J.*AJ*17.2.4. **-σπασμός**, ὁ, *convulsion*, Ar.*Lys.*967. II. *counter-movement* (ebb and flow), of the sea, *Placit.*3.17.7. **-σπαστέον**, *one must draw off by another out-*

*let*, Hp.*Vict*.4.90, Gal.16.153. **-σπαστικός**, ή, όν, *able to draw back, retractile*, Arist.*HA*638$^a$31. II. *revulsive*, βοηθήματα Gal. 17(1).907. Adv. -κῶς Id.11.305. III. in Metric, *antispastic*, Heph.10, al. **-σπαστος**, ον, *drawn in the contrary direction*, νεφέλαι πνεύμασιν ἀ. Orph.*H*.21.5. 2. *spasmodic, convulsive*, ὀστέων ἀδαγμὸς ἀ. S.*Tr*.770. II. ἀντίσπαστος (sc. πούς), ὁ, in Prosody, *antispast*, a foot made up of an iambus and trochee, ⏑ – – ⏑, Heph. 3, Aristid.Quint.1.22. 2. = ἀντίφθογγος, ἀντίσπαστα μέλη Phryn. Trag.11 ; ἀντίσπαστα ἐφυμνεῖ πηκτίδος συγχορδίᾳ S.*Fr*.412 (unless '*doubly twanged*', of an instrument with two registers). III. ἀντίσπαστον· φιλήματος ὄνομα, Hsch. IV. Subst. -σπαστος, ὁ, *tackle, pulley-rope*, Ath.Mech.9.13, al. ※**-σπάω**, *draw the contrary way, hold back*, ἀ. ὁρμώμενον A.*Pr*.339 ; τοὺς μὲν τείνειν τοὺς δ' ἀ. Ar. *Pax*493, cf. Luc.*Cat*.4 ; opp. σπάω, Arist.*HA*542$^a$15, al.:—Pass., *suffer a check*, Id.*Rh*.1409$^b$21 ; *to be drawn in a contrary direction*, Epicur.*Ep*.2 p.53 U., Ph.2.171 : metaph., περίοδοι -σπώμεναι *dragging*, Phld.*Rh*.2.95 S. 2. *draw to itself*, X.*Cyn*.5.1 ; εἰς αὐτό Arist. *Pr*.929$^a$39 :—Med., *draw over to one's own side*, Plb.22.10.14. II. intr., = ἀντέχομαι, *seize*, c. gen., A.R.2.598.

**ἀντισπεύδω**, *oppose eagerly, contend against*, πρός τινα Antipho 1.7 ; τοῖς ἐπιθυμήμασί τινος D.C.59.13.

**ἀντισπόδιον**, τό, (σποδός) *substitute for* [mineral] *ashes, vegetable ashes*, Orib.15.1.27(36), Gal.12.234 :—also **ἀντίσποδον**, Dsc.1.109, 5.75.

**ἀντισπουδάζω**, = ἀντισπεύδω, τινί D.C.40.55.

**ἀντισπουδία**, ἡ, *opposite exertion*, Oenom ap.Eus.*PE*5.24.

**ἀντιστᾰδιαῖος**, α, ον, *a furlong long*, i. e. *enormous*, Sch.Od.12.90.

**ἀντισταθμ-άω**, = ἀντισηκόω, Sm.*Jb*.28.19 :—in Med., Eust.1875. 8. **-ησις**, εως, ἡ, = ἀντισήκωσις, Id.1625.27, Sch.Od.4.612. **-ίζω**, = ἀντισηκόω, Incert.*Jb*.28.19. **-ος**, ον, (σταθμός) *counterpoising, balancing*, τινί Pl.*Sph*.229c ; χρυσὸν ἀ. τῆς κεφαλῆς οὐκ ἐδέξαντο D.S. 5.29 : metaph., *in compensation for*, ὡς πατὴρ ἀ. τοῦ θηρὸς ἐκθύσειε τὴν αὐτοῦ κόρην S.*El*.571.

**ἀντιστᾰσ-ιάζω**, *form a party against*, τινί X.*An*.4.1.27 ; οἱ ἀντιστασιάζοντες, = οἱ ἀντιστασιῶται, Id.*Cyr*.7.4.3 ; ἀ. πρὸς πάντα *to offer opposition to*.., D.C.37.54. **-ιαστής**, οῦ, ὁ, = ἀντιστασιώτης, J. *BJ*1.7.5, D.C.73.4, *Fr*.84.1. **-ιμος**, ον, *sloping*, Anon.Alch. p.26 B. **-ιος**, ον, *of equal weight* : metaph., λόγοι Max.Tyr.4. 1 ; τὸ ἀ. Id.39.1. **-ις**, εως, ἡ, *counter-faction*, στάσις καὶ ἀ. καὶ μάχη Pl.*R*.560a. II. *opposition*, αἰώνιος Ph.1.577 ; ἐπὶ τῇ ἀρχῇ J.*AJ* 17.11.2 ; τύχης Plu.*Aem*.36 ; ἐξ ἀ. ἀγωνίζεσθαι *in pitched battle*, Hdn. 5.4.4 ; ἴσην ἀ. ἔχειν *weigh* equally, Arist.*Mu*.397$^a$1. III. *counterplea, set-off*, e.g. benefit conferred *balanced against* injury done, Hermog.*Stat*.2, cf. 6 (pl.), Arg.Lycurg. **-ιώτης**, ου, ὁ, *one of the opposite faction* or *party*, Hdt.1.92, 4.164, X.*An*.1.1.10, Aen.Tact. 11.7, etc.

**ἀντιστᾰτέον**, *one must check*, ταῖς κενώσεσι Philum.ap.Aët.9.6.

**ἀντιστᾰτ-έω**, = ἀνθίσταμαι, *resist, oppose*, esp. as a political partisan, Hdt.3.52 ; τινί Pl.*Grg*.513c, J.*AJ*18.9.2, cf. Ph.1.205, al. ; πρός τι Plu.2.802b ; trans., τῷ φόβῳ τὸ κλέος Lib.*Vit*.1.7. **-ης** [ᾰ], ου, ὁ, *opponent, adversary*, A.*Th*.518, Plu.2.1084b. II. *vertical beam* in plinth of torsion-engine, Hero *Bel*.91.11. **-ικός**, ή, όν, *of* or *for a counter-plea* (cf. ἀντίστασις III), Hermog.*Stat*.5,10.

**ἀντίστερνον**, τό, *the part of the spine opposite the breast*, Sor.2.63 (pl.), Ruf.*Anat*.25.

※**ἀντιστήκω**, = ἀνθίσταμαι, Hsch. s.v. ἀντεξάγω.

**ἀντιστήρ-ιγμα**, ατος, τό, *a prop* or *support*, Hp.*Art*.9,16 : metaph., *support, stay*, Lxx *Ps*.17(18).18. **-ιγμός**, ὁ, *blocking the way, resistance*, ἀνακοπαὶ καὶ -μοί D.H.*Dem*.38 ; -μοὶ γραμμάτων Id.*Comp*. 16. **-ίζω**, *press against*, Hp.*Art*.47 ; *offer resistance*, Democr.9, Arist.*Pr*.940$^a$11.

**ἀντιστίλβω**, *shine by reflection*, Zen.3.8.

**ἀντιστοιχ-είωσις**, εως, ἡ, *change of a letter*, e.g. φιτρῶν for φυτρῶν, Sch.Il.12.29. **-έω**, *stand opposite in rows* or *pairs*, χοροὶ ἀντιστοιχοῦντες ἀλλήλοις X.*An*.5.4.12 ; ἀ. τινί *stand vis-a-vis to* a partner in a dance, Id.*Smp*.2.20. II. of letters, *correspond*, ἀ. τὰ δασέα τοῖς ψιλοῖς *EM*443.17. **-ία**, ἡ, *standing opposite in pairs*, τῶν ποδῶν Arist.*Pr*.894$^a$19 ; πραγμάτων Plu.2.474a. II. of letters, *correspondence*, of the relation of tenuis, media, and aspirate to each other, Ascl.Myrl.ap.Ath.11.501b. ※**-ος**, ον, *ranged opposite in rows* or *pairs*, Arist.*IA*708$^b$8, al. 2. *standing over against*, σκιὰ ἀντίστοιχος ὥς E.*Andr*.745 ; ἀντίστοιχα λέγων .. τούτοισι *corresponding with*, D.H.*Rh*.9.7. II. of letters, *corresponding*, as tenuis, media, and aspirate, A.D.*Synt*.55.14, cf. *Fr*.7 b, D.T.631.27 ; also of vowels, Hdn.*Epim*.2 ; κατ' ἀντίστοιχον Lyd.*Mag*.1.7.

**ἀντίστομος**, ον, *drawn up face to face*, διφαλαγγία Ascl.*Tact*.11.3, cf. Ael.*Tact*.37.3, Arr.*Tact*.29.2, Hsch.

**ἀντιστορέννῡμι**, aor. 1 inf. ἀντιστρῶσαι, *lay paving instead*, *SIG*$^2$ 587.48 (Eleusis).

**ἀντιστοχαστικός**, ή, όν, *conjecturing in turn*, Sch.D.8.17.

**ἀντιστρᾰτεύομαι**, *take the field, make war against*, τινί X.*Cyr*.8.8. 26 :—later in Act., D.S.22.15, J.*AJ*2.10.1 (abs.) : metaph., Ἔρωτες ἀ. τοῖς ὑπερηφανοῦσι Aristaenet.2.1.

**ἀντιστρᾰτηγ-έω**, *act against as general* or (generally) *make war against*, τινί D.H.11.37 ; τοῖς ἐπιχειρήμασί τινων J.*Vit*.55, cf. Max. Tyr.41.3. **-ησις**, εως, ἡ, *hostile manœuvre*, Onos.32.9.

※**ἀντιστράτηγος** [ρᾰ], ὁ, *enemy's general*, Th.7.86, D.H.6.5, Plu. *Sert*.12. II. at Rome, *acting commander* or *governor*, either *pro consule*, Plb.28.3.1, or *pro praetore*, D.C.41.43. 2. *propraetor*, i.e. *governor* of a province with rank of *pro praetore*, *IG*12(5).722 (Andros, ii B.C.). 3. *lieutenant* of a commander, Lat. *legatus pro praetore*, *OGI* ii p.551 (Bargylia, ii B.C.), Plb.3.106.2, 15.4.4, Plu. *Comp.Lys.Sull*.4, etc. ; in full, πρεσβευτὴς καὶ ἀ. J.*AJ*14.12.13 ; ἀντιταμίας καὶ ἀ. proquaestor *pro praetore*, *OGI*448 (i B.C.) ; πρεσβευτὴς Σεβαστοῦ ἀ., = Lat. *legatus Augusti pro praetore*, *IGRom*.3.186 (Ancyra, ii A.D.), etc.

**ἀντιστρᾰτιώτης**, ου, ὁ, *soldier of the enemy*, Gal.19.180, Chor. in Lib.4.522 Reiske.

**ἀντιστρᾰτοπεδ-εία**, ἡ, = sq., Plb.3.101.8. **-ευσις**, εως, ἡ, *an encamping opposite, the position of two armies in sight of one another*, D.C.78.26. **-εύω**, *encamp over against*, τινί Isoc.6.80, Plb.1.74. 13, Onos.10.19, etc. II. more freq. in Med., τινί Hdt.1.76 : abs., Th.1.30 : so pf. Pass., Id.4.124, X.*HG*7.4.13.

**ἀντιστρεπτ-έος**, α, ον, in Logic, *to be converted*, Arist.*APr*.51$^a$ 23. II. *one must reverse*, τὴν δόξαν Plot.5.5.11. **-ος**, ον, *that can be turned about* : τὰ ἀ. *machines that move on a pivot* or *swivel*, D.S.20.91.

※**ἀντιστρέφω**, pf. -έστροφα, *turn to the opposite side* :—Pass., *to be turned in the opposite direction*, μόχλος ἀντεστραμμένος *reversed* lever, Ph.*Bel*.59.25 ; *turn and look at*, Aristaenet.1.4 : also c. acc., οὐδ' ἀ. ὃ λέγουσιν *cast a glance at*, Phld.*Rh*.1.245 S. Adv. ἀντεστραμμένως Arist.*IA*712$^a$4. 2. intr., *wheel about, face about*, X. *Ages*.1.16. II. *retort* an argument, τοὺς λόγους Arist.*Top*.163$^a$30, cf. *APr*.59$^b$1 ; αἰτίας Procop.*Pers*.1.16. III. *correspond*, ἀλλήλοις Anon. *in Tht*.19.47. IV. in Logic, *to be convertible*, Arist. *Cat*.14$^b$11, al. ; τὰ γένη κατὰ τῶν εἰδῶν κατηγορεῖται, τὰ δὲ εἴδη κατὰ τῶν γενῶν οὐκ ἀντιστρέφει *are* not *conversely predicable* of genera, ib. 2$^b$21 : impers., ἀντιστρέφει *the relation is reciprocal*, Id.*GC*337$^b$23, cf. *deAn*.423$^a$21, *Pr*.883$^b$8 ; περὶ ἀντιστρεφόντων λόγων καὶ συνημμένων *complementary* propositions, title of work by Chrysipp. ; so of metaphors, Anon.*Fig*.p.228 S. 2. most freq. in the doctrine of syllogism, of reduction by *conversion* of one of the premisses, Arist. *APr*.50$^b$25 ; either of the terms, τὸ B τῷ A ἀντιστρέφει the term B *is convertible with* A, ib.67$^b$30, al. ; τὸ Γ πρὸς τὸ A ἀ. ib.38 ; ἀ. τὸ καθόλου τῷ κατὰ μέρος ib.31$^a$27, al. ; or of the propositions, ib.25$^a$8, al. ; ἀ. καθόλου *to be* simply *convertible*, ib.28 ; ἀ. ἐπὶ μέρους, ἐν μέρει, κατὰ μέρος, ib.29$^a$15, 25$^a$8,10. 3. in Pass., of propositions, *to be converted* or *changed into their opposites*, Id.*APr*.45$^b$6, *APo*.80$^b$25, al. 4. *to be interdependent, have a reciprocal nexus*, τὰ μὲν οὖν ἀ. . καὶ ποιητικὰ ἀλλήλων καὶ παθητικὰ ὑπ' ἀλλήλων Id.*GC*328$^a$19 : hence of cyclical argument, ἐν μόνοις τοῖς ἀ. κύκλῳ καὶ δι' ἀλλήλων (sc. αἱ ἀποδείξεις) Id. *APr*.58$^a$13, cf. *APo*.95$^b$40, *GC*337$^b$23. 5. generally, *to be suited conversely* for one or another purpose, ὁ τόπος ἀντιστρέφει πρὸς τὸ ἀνασκευάζειν καὶ κατασκευάζειν Id.*Top*.109$^b$25 ; ἀ. πρὸς ἄμφω ib.112$^a$ 27, al. V. pf. part. Pass., *conversely opposed*, of concavities, *facing one another*, ἀντεστραμμένα πρὸς ἄλληλα Id.*HA*498$^a$8 ; but, *back to back*, Plb.6.32.6. 2. in Logic, *converted*, συλλογισμὸς -μμένος Arist.*APr*.44$^a$31 ; πρότασις ib.58$^a$1 ; ἀ. τῇ πάχνῃ ὁ εὐρώς its *converse*, Id.*GA*784$^b$16 ; ἡ ἀ. πρόσθεσις Id.*Ph*.207$^a$23. 3. Adv. ἀντεστραμμένως *inversely*, ib.206$^b$5 ; *conversely*, *PA*684$^b$35, *IA*712$^a$4, al. : in Logic, *opposedly*, Id.*Int*.22$^a$34. VI. of lyrics, *possess strophe and antistrophe*, Aristid.Quint.1.29, Sch.Ar.*Ach*.1037, Sch.Heph. p.167 C. VII. of grammatical construction, *to be inverted*, A.D. *Synt*.180.16, al.

※**ἀντιστροφ-ή**, ἡ, *a turning about* : I. in choruses and dances, *strophic correspondence*, D.H.*Comp*.25 ; in later writers, = ἀντίστροφος, ἡ (q.v.), Sch.Ar.*Nu*.595, al. II. Rhet., *repetition of closing words in successive members*, Phld.*Rh*.1.195 S., Hermog.*Id*.1.12, cf. 2.1, Eust.945.60 ; ἀ. τὸ ἐναντίον τῆς ἐπαναφορᾶς Alex.*Fig*.2.4. 2. *inversion*, of construction, e.g. ἠχῶν ἔπεσα for πεσὼν ἤχησα Phoeb. *Fig*.1.5. 3. Gramm., *inversion of letters* (e.g. ἀκήν, ἧκα), *EM* 424.8. III. *inversion*, κατὰ τὴν ἀ. τῆς ἀναλογίας in *inverse ratio*, Arist.*Ph*.266$^b$18 :—in Logic, *conversion of terms* of a proposition, Id.*APr*.25$^a$40 ; ἀ. δέχεσθαι to be *convertible*, ib.50$^b$32. b. Math., τῶν θεωρημάτων ἡ ἀ. Procl. *in Euc*.p.251 F., cf. Apollon.Perg.*Con*.2. 49 ; ἀ. προηγουμένη complete *conversion*, Procl. *in Euc*.p.253 F ; ἀ. ἀξιωμάτων *Stoic*.2.64 ; generally, κατ' -φήν *conversely*, Metrod.*Herc*. 831.14. 2. *retortion* of an argument, Arist.*APr*.61$^a$22. 3. *change* of a proposition *into its opposite*, ib.38$^a$3, 39$^a$28. ※**-ος**, ον, *turned so as to face one another* : hence, *correlative, co-ordinate, counterpart*, Pl.*Tht*.158c, etc. ; τινί *to* a thing, Id.*Grg*.464b, *R*.605a ; ἡ ῥητορική ἐστιν ἀ. τῇ διαλεκτικῇ Arist.*Rh*.1354$^a$1, *Pol*.1293$^a$33, etc. ; ἰατρικὴ ἀ. δικαιοσύνῃ Aristid.2.37 J. ; also τινός *the correlative* or *counterpart of*.., Pl.*R*.530d, *Grg*.465d, Isoc.5.61, etc. ; ἀ. . . ὥσπερ Arist.*Pol*.1292$^b$7. Adv. -φως *in a manner corresponding*, τινί Pl.*R*. 539d ; ἡ γλῶττα ὥσπερ -φως ἔχουσα τῷ μυκτῆρι *being the counterpart of*.., Arist.*PA*661$^a$27 ; συμβαίνει δ' ἀντιστρόφως the result follows *by a reversible proof*, Id.*Ph*.265$^b$8. 2. in Logic, *converse*, λόγος Phld.*Rh*.1.179 S. Adv. -φως Id.*Sign*.6 : also in Math., *converse*, θεώρημα Papp.970.20 ; τὰ ἀ. *the converse proposition*, Apollon.Perg.*Con*. 4.55. Adv. -φως *conversely*, ib.1.38, Max.Tyr.34.4. 3. *contrary, opposed*, τινός D.Chr.4.87 ; πρός τι Luc.*Merc.Cond*.31. Adv. -φως *in the opposite way*, Phld.*Lib*.p.31 O., Ps.-Luc.*Philopatr*.18. II. *that can be retorted*, D.H.*Rh*.9.5 (as v.l., cf. ἀγχι-). III. ἐξ ἀντιστρόφου *by an inverted construction* (cf. ἀντιστροφή II.2), Hdn.*Fig*. p.102 S. IV. in lyrics, *antistrophic*, Arist.*Pr*.918$^b$27, etc. : esp. Subst. ἀντίστροφος (sc. ᾠδή), ἡ, *antistrophe*, Id.*Rh*.1409$^a$26, D.H. *Comp*.19, etc. ; also of members in a rhet. period, ἐν στροφῇ καὶ ἀντιστρόφῳ Hermog.*Id.*1.11. V. f.l. for ἀμφίστροφος, *wheeling both ways*, A.*Supp.*882 codd. VI. *retorting* a charge, Procop.*Arc.* 17. VII. ἀντίστροφος, ἡ, = ἀπόστροφος Sch.Ar.*Pl.*3. 2. ἀντίστροφοι, name for the *two upper ribs*, Poll.2.182. VIII. Adv. -φως *crosswise*, τὰς χεῖρας ἀλλήλαις ἐπιβάλλειν Gal.*UP*5.14; *inversely*, Herod.Med.ap.Orib.10.5.4, cf. Diogenian.3.30.

*ἀντισύγκλητος, ἡ, *counter-senate*, name given by Marius to his body-guard, Plu.*Mar.*35, *Sull.*8.

**ἀντισυγκρίνω** [ρῑ], *compare* one *with* another, Nicom.*Ar.*1.13:—Pass., ib.20, Charito6.1.

**ἀντισυζῠγία**, ἡ, = συζυγία, of signs rising and setting at the same point of the horizon, Gem.2.1.

**ἀντισυλλογίζομαι**, *answer by syllogism*, Arist.*Rh.*1402ᵃ31, al.

**ἀντισυμβολ-έω**, *give a counter-receipt*, *PFay.*73.1 (ii/iii A.D.), al. **-ον**, τό, *counter-receipt*, ib.73, al., *PGrenf.*2.23, *PLond.*1.15.3.

**ἀντισυμβουλεύω**, *give contrary advice*, Stob.2.6.2.

**ἀντισυμμᾰχέομαι**, Pass., *to be helped in return*, ὑπό τινος Longin. 17.1.

**ἀντισυμποσιάζω**, *write a Symposium in rivalry of* Plato, Luc. *Lex.*1.

**ἀντισυν-ᾰλείφω**, *anoint in return*, τὸν συναλείψαντα Phld.*Vit.* p.30 J. **-αντάω**, *meet face to face*, *AP*12.227. **-άπτω**, *meet in opposite directions*, dub. in Gal.18(2).727.

**ἀντισῡριγγιακός**, ἡ, όν, *protecting against fistula*, κολλύριον Aët. 15.13.

**ἀντισφαιρίζω**, *play at ball against*, οἱ ἀντισφαιριοῦντες *parties about to play in a match*, X.*Lac.*9.5.

**ἀντισφάττω**, *slaughter in turn*, D.C.45.47 (in aor. 2 Pass.).

**ἀντισφήν**, ῆνος, ὁ, *counter-wedge* which drives out another, Ph.*Bel.* 67.32.

**ἀντισφίγγω**, ἔνθεν καὶ ἔνθεν ἀ. *form an obstacle by tension*, Hp.*Art.*3.

**ἀντισφράγισμα**, ατος, τό, *sealed copy*, *SIG*785.12 (Chios).

**ἀντισχηματ-ίζω**, *meet one figure by another*, D.H.*Rh.*9.14. **-ισμός**, ὁ, *the use of such figures in turn*, ibid.

**ἀντισχῡρίζομαι**, Med., *to be stiff in maintaining a contrary opinion*, Th.3.44; πρός τι Plu.2.535e.

**ἀντίσχῡρος**, ον, *strong to resist*, Hsch.

**ἀντισχύω**, fut. -ύσω [ῡ], *repel by force*, Lxx *Wi.*7.30, D.C.48.11.

**ἀντίσχω**, = ἀντέχω (q.v.), Hp.*Fract.*11, S.*Ph.*830 (lyr.), Th.1.7 [codd. often confuse -ίσχων, -ισχών].

**ἀντισῴζω**, *preserve in turn*, Anon.ap.Suid. s.v. δυσκλεές, Aristid. 1.418 J.

**ἀντίσωσις** [ῐσ], εως, ἡ, *equalization*, Iamb.*Protr.*21.ιθ'.

**ἀντί-ταγμα**, ατος, τό, *opposing force*, D.S.11.67, Plu.*Cleom.*23; of a person, 'a political force', *Nic.*2, *Luc.*38. **-τακτέον**, (ἀντιτάσσω) *one must array against*, τι πρός τι Id.2.127f. 2. (from Pass.) *one must make resistance*, πρός τινα Arist.*Top.*134ᵃ4. **-τακτικός**, ή, όν, *fit for resistance*, πρός τι Plu.2.759e. **-τακτος**, ον, *contrary*, *opposed*, τῶν πραγμάτων ἐχόντων τι -ον Hierocl.p.60A.

**ἀντιτᾰλαντεύω**, = ἀντισηκόω, *APl.*4.221 (Theaet.); *put into the opposite scale*, Lib.*Decl.*43 *Intr.*2.

**ἀντιτάλαντον**· ἀντίσταθμον, ἴσον, Hsch.

**ἀντιτᾰμίας**, ου, ὁ, = Lat. *pro quaestore*, *SIG*745 (Rhodes, i B.C.), J. *AJ*14.12.13, D.C.41.43, etc., prob. in *IG*14.356 (Halaesa); cf. ἀντιστράτηγος.

**ἀντίταξις**, εως, ἡ, *a setting in array against*, ἡ σφετέρα ἀ. τῶν τριήρων their ships *ranged for battle*, Th.7.17; ἀ. ποιεῖσθαι πρός τινα, = ἀντιτάσσεσθαι, Id.5.8, cf. Phld.*Piet.*12; *contest*, of bulls fighting, Hierocl. p.11 A. 2. generally, *opposition*, D.H.10.57, Plu.2.663b, Andronic. Rhod.p.572 M.

**ἀντιτᾰράττω**, *stir up in opposition*, Max.Tyr.14.7.

**ἀντίτᾰσις**, εως, ἡ, (ἀντιτείνω) *stretching the contrary way*, e.g. in the setting of a dislocated limb, Hp.*Art.*75. 2. *opposition*, *resistance*, πᾶσαν ἀ. ἀντιτείνειν Pl.*Lg.*781c.

*ἀντιτάσσω, Att. -ττω, *set opposite to*, *range in battle against*, τὸ ἄριστον ἀ. Πέρσῃσι Hdt.5.110; τίν' ἀντιτάξεις τῷδε; A.*Th.*395, cf. 408, etc.; ἀ. τὸν νόμον πρὸς τὴν ἀναίδειαν *set* the law *in opposition to* their impudence, Aeschin.3.16, cf. Isoc.9.61, etc.:—so in Med., πρὸς τὸ ἐμπειρότερον αὐτῶν τὸ τολμηρότερον ἀντιτάξασθε Th.2.87; τῶν Ἑλλήνων τινὰ ἀρετὴν τῇ Ξέρξου δυνάμει ἀντιτάξασθαι Id.3.56. II. Med., *set oneself against*, *meet face to face*, ἀντιτάξομαι κτενῶν σε E.*Ph.*622, cf. Th.4.55, etc.; περὶ τῶν πρωτείων ἡμῖν ἀντιτάξασθαι D.3.27:—Pass., *to be drawn out in array against*, τινί Hdt.4.134, X.*HG*3.1.6; πρὸς τὸ διπλήσιον Hdt.7.103; πόλιν -ομένην πρὸς πόλιν X.*Cyr.*3.1.18, etc.; κατά τινας Id.*HG*4.2.18; τὸ ἀντιτετάχθαι ἀλλήλοις τῇ γνώμῃ Th.3.83: abs., dub. in E.*Supp.*1144. 2. generally, *oppose*, *resist*, Plb.31. 25.8, *Act.Ap.*18.6, *Ep.Rom.*13.2, etc. 3. *set against*, *compare*, Lxx *Pr.*3.15 (Pass.).

**ἀντιταφρεύω**, *dig a trench in opposition*, Ph.*Bel.*93.26.

**ἀντιτείνω**, fut. -τενῶ Pl.*R.*604a (v.l.):—*stretch*, *strain back*, εἰς τοὔπισθεν τὰ σπαρτία Arist.*Pr.*888ᵃ20; τὰς ἡνίας Plu.2.13d. 2. *stretch out* or *offer in return*, νῆπι' ἀντὶ νηπίων E.*Med.*891. II. intr., *act* or *strive against*, *resist*, ἐπιβουλίᾳ Pi.*N.*4.37; τινί Hdt.7.161, Pl.*R.*547b, etc.; παντὶ λόγῳ Id.*Phd.*91c; πρός τι *Phdr.*256a, Arist. *EN*1126ᵇ15 (πρός = *with respect to*): abs., Hdt.7.219, S.*Ant.*714, etc.; οὐκ ἀντέτεινον, ἀλλ' εἶκον Hdt.8.3; ὑπείκει καὶ οὐκ ἀ. Pl.*Lg.*727d; δύο ἄνδρες ἀντιτείνοντες *pulling one against the other*, Hp.*Fract.*15. 2. of countries and places, *lie over against*, τινι Plu.*Them.*8.

**ἀντιτειχ-ίζω**, *erect counter-fortifications*, πρὸς τὰς μηχανάς J.*AJ*14. 16.2; trans., *fortify instead*, τὸ καταρριφθὲν τοῖς σώμασι Id.*BJ*5.8.2; metaph., τῷ τέλει τῆς ἡδονῆς Ph.1.426 (Pass.). **-ισμα**, ατος, τό, *counter-fortification*, Th.2.77, Ath.13.602d (pl.).

**ἀντιτέμνω**, *cut against*, i.e. *as a remedy* or *antidote*, φάρμακα.. ἀντιτεμὼν βροτοῖσι E.*Alc.*972 (lyr.).

**ἀντιτέρπω**, *delight in return*, Plu.2.334a (Pass.).

**ἀντιτεταγμένως**, Adv. pf. part. Pass. of ἀντιτάσσω, *in the opposite sense*, τῷ ποιεῖν Plot.5.3.15.

**ἀντίτευχος**, (gend. uncertain), name of a *throw at dice*, Eub.57.3.

**ἀντιτεύχω**, *make in opposition*, ἀντιτέτυκτο Antim.35 codd.

**ἀντιτεχν-άζω**, *use art in turn*, D.H.*Rh.*9.5:—also in Med., πρός τι J.*AJ*1.19.8. **-άομαι**, *contrive in opposition*, *counter-plan*, τάδε Hdt.5.70; τινί Max.Tyr.32.9: abs., Plu.*Sert.*18; πρός τι J.*AJ*14. 16.2. **-έω**, *to be a rival in art*, Sch.Ar.*V.*1402. **-ησις**, εως, ἡ, *counter-manœuvring*, *emulation*, Th.7.70, D.H.14.10. **-ίτης**, ου, ὁ, *professional rival*, Gal.5.655. *-ος, ον, *rival in an art* or *craft*, Ar.*Ra.* 816, Pl.*R.*493a, etc.; οὐκ ἐκείνῳ οὐδὲ τοῖς ποιήμασιν αὐτοῦ Id.*Phd.* 60d, cf. *Lg.*817b; ἀ. καὶ ὁμότεχνος τοῖς ποιηταῖς D.Chr.12.46: c. gen., τῆς μαγγανείας αὐτοῦ Luc.*Alex.*43.

**ἀντιτηρέω**, *maintain in turn*, Arr.*Epict.*2.20.14.

**ἀντιτίθημι** (pres. part. -τιθοῦντας Ps.-Callisth.1.29), *set against* or *so as to oppose*, θαλασσαίαισι δίναις ἀντιθέντα μένος στάλας Simon.57 (dub.). b. *set against so as to balance*, *contrast*, or *compare*, τὠυτὸ ἀντιθήσω ἐκείνῳ Hdt.1.207, cf. 8.66; δύο γὰρ ἀντίθες δυοῖν E.*Or.*551: also c. gen., ἀ. τὴν Ἀθηναίων ἐκ πολλοῦ ἐμπειρίαν τῆς σφετέρας ἐξ ὀλίγου μελέτης Th.2.85, cf. 3.56: with a Prep., ἀ. τι πρός τι D.21.175:—Pass., *to be contrasted*, τινί or πρός τι, Pl.*Sph.*257d, 258e. 2. ἀ. τινί τινα *match* one *against* the other *in battle*, ἴσους ἴσοισι.. ἀντιθεὶς E.*Ph.* 750, cf. Ar.*Eq.*353:—Pass., *to be matched* one *against* another, of counteracting tendencies, Hdt.4.50; of opposing motives, Id.8. 83. 3. *retort*, *rejoin*, ἀντίθες παρρησίᾳ ὅπως.. E.*El.*1049; ἀντιθεῖσ' ἀμείψομαι Id.*Tr.*917; ἀ. ὅτι.. Th.6.18. 4. intr., *oppose*, *resist*, πρὸς τὸν Δία Arr.*Epict.*3.24.24, etc. II. *place* or *deposit in return*, ἀντιθέντας ἐν ναοῖς ἢ χαλκὸν ἢ.. E.*Hipp.*620, cf. X.*Mem.*3.14.1; ἀ. τί τινος *give* one thing *for* another, τὴν ἐνθάδ' Αὖλιν ἀντιθεῖσα τῆς ἐκεῖ E. *IT*358.

*ἀντιτῑμ-άω, *honour in return*, τινά X.*HG*3.1.13; τινὰ πᾶσι τοῖς καλοῖς Id.*Cyr.*5.2.11, etc.:—fut. Med. in pass. sense, Id.*Oec.*9.11. II. Med. as law-term, *make a counter-estimate of damages*, c. gen. pretii, Pl.*Ap.*36b, D.24.138. **-ημα**, ατος, τό, glossed by **-ησις**, εως, ἡ, Hsch.

**ἀντίτῑμος**, ον, *of equal worth*, Ἀθηνᾶ 20p.163 (Chios), and **ἀντίτῑμα**· τὰ ἄποινα, τὰ ἀντέκτιτα, Hsch.

*ἀντιτῑμωρ-έομαι, *avenge oneself on*, τινά E.*IT*357, Th.3.82, Plb.1. 81.9: abs., *revenge oneself*, *take vengeance*, Ar.*Pax*134, 626:—a fut. Pass. occurs in Sch.Lyc.1337. **-ημα**, ατος, τό, and **-ία**, ἡ, *vengeance*, *revenge*, ib.1297. **-ησις**, εως, ἡ, = foreg., Gal.6.138, al. **-ητέον**, dub. in Gal.*UP*2.8 codd. (misquoting Hp.*Acut.*37. β'). **-ητος**, η, ον, gloss on ἄντιτος, Eust.1346.3, Hsch.

**ἀντιτίνω**, fut. -τείσω, *suffer punishment for* a thing, τι Thgn.741: abs., S.*Aj.*1086: generally, *repay*, χάριτάς τινι Eust.142.15. II. Med., *exact* or *inflict in turn*, ἐμῆς ἀγωγῆς ἀντιτείσασθαι φόνον *exact* death *as a punishment for*.., A.*Ag.*1263; πόσιν δίκην (codd. δίκῃ) τῶνδ' ἀντιτείσασθαι κακῶν *exact* a penalty from him *for* these evil deeds, E.*Med.*261, cf. Lyc.1367. [On the quantity v. τίνω.]

**ἀντίτιτος**, v. ἄντιτος.

**ἀντιτιτρώσκω**, *wound in turn*, Sch.E.*Hipp.*507: plpf. Pass. ἀντετέτρωτο Hld.7.27.

**ἀντίτοιχος**, ον, *striking full on the bulwarks*, ἀκτίς Tim.*Pers.*12.

**ἀντιτολμ-άω**, *dare to stand against* another, abs., Th.2.89; πρὸς τολμηρούς Id.7.21. **-ος**, ον, *boldly attacking*, A.*Eu.*553 (lyr.).

**ἀντίτομος**, ον, (ἀντιτέμνω) *cut as a remedy for* an evil:—Subst. ἀντίτομον, τό, *remedy*, *antidote*, *h.Cer.*229, Hsch.; ἀντίτομα ὀδυνᾶν *antidotes for* pains, Pi.*P.*4.221. II. *having opposite curvatures for cutting*, Paul.Aeg.6.30.

**ἀντιτονέομαι** or **-όομαι**, Pass., *to have a different accent from*, τινί Eust.1025.4.

**ἀντίτονος**, ον, (ἀντιτείνω) *strained against*, *resisting*, Pl.*Ti.*62c; of a bow, *APl.*4.211.4 (Stat. Flacc.). 2. Subst. ἀντίτονα, τά, *guy-ropes* securing torsion-engines, Plu.*Marc.*15, Ph.*Bel.*99.47.

**ἀντιτοξεύω**, *shoot arrows in return*, X.*An.*3.3.15, Philostr.*Im.*1.6.

*ἀντιτορ-έω, (cf. τετορεῖν) *bore right through*, c. gen., δόρυ χροὸς ἀντετόρησεν Il.5.337: c. acc., πυκινὸν δόμον ἀντιτορήσας *having broken it open*, ib.10.267, cf. *h.Merc.*178. **-ησις**, εως, ἡ, *piercing*, Eust. 672.30.

*ἄντῑτος (by haplology for ἀντίτιτος, which occurs in Hsch.), ον, = παλίντιτος, *requited*, *revenged*, ἄ. ἔργα the work *of revenge*, Od.17. 51, 60; ἄ. ἔργα παιδὸς *revenge for* her son, Il.24.213, cf. Call.*Iamb.* 1.160.

**ἀντιτρᾰγος**, ὁ, (cf. τράγος) *the eminence of the external ear*, Aret. *CD*1.2, Poll.2.85, Ruf.ap.Orib.25.1.7.

**ἀντιτρᾱχύνομαι** [ῡ], Pass., *to be exasperated in turn*, πρός τινα Eust.467.9.

*ἀντιτρέφω, *sustain*, *maintain in turn*, X.*Cyr.*8.3.38.

**ἀντιτρίβω** [ρῑ], *rub in return*, Plot.6.1.20 (Pass.).

**ἀντιτρῡπάω**, gloss on ἀντετόρησεν, Sch.Opp.*H*3.556.

**ἀντιτυγχάνω**, aor. -έτυχον, *meet with in return*, τινός Simon.128, Thgn.1334; ἀ. ἐπικουρίας ἀπό τινος Th.6.87; ἀ. μάχας *fall into* quarrel, Pi.*N.*7.42; κρείττονος Prov.ap.Plb.15.16.6; ἀ. χοιράδος *hit* *upon* a rock, Opp.*H*.4.480; πλείστων ἀ. ἀέθλων *IG*4.682 (Hermione). II. ὁ ἀντιτυγχάνων *any chance person*, *GDI*1918, al. (Delph.). 2. ἁ βωλὰ ἀντιτυχόνσα the council *for the time being*, *IG*4.554 (Argos); οἱ ἔφοροι..ἀεὶ οἱ ἀντιτυγχάνοντες ib.5(1).1146 (Gythium, i B.C.), cf. 7.3080 (Lebad.), 5(2).266 (Mantinea, i B.C.), *Delph*.3(1).294 v 5.

**ἀντιτυμπᾰνίζω**, *beat drums in rivalry with*, βρονταῖς prob. cj. in Anon.Vat.42.

**ἀντιτῠπ-έω**, *strike against*, esp. of a hard body, τινί Arist.*Mete*. 370$^{b}$18; *resist*, τὰ ἁπτὰ ἀ. τὴν ἁφήν Phld.*Sign*.18; πεδίου μὴ ἀντιτυποῦντος τῇ ὁπλῇ Luc.*Dom*.10; προσάλληλα Ach.Tat.2.38: abs., Hp.*Mul*.2.177; τὸ εἶκον καὶ μὴ ἀντιτυποῦν Pl.*Cra*.420d:—also in Med., Hp.*Mul*.1.61. **-ής**, ές, *resisting*, *repellent*, Hdn.6.7.7; συγκρίσεις Epicur.*Nat*.2.9; of αἴσθησις, *Stoic*.2.115. 2. metaph., *hard*, Alex.Aphr.*de An*.125.9; ἀ. καὶ στερρὸν ὁ πόνος Ph.2.162. II. of sounds, *clashing*, *dissonant*, D.H.*Comp*.22, al. **-ησις**, εως, ἡ, *collision*, Olymp.*in Mete*.204.19. ❋**-ία**, ἡ, *resistance of a hard body*, Phld.*Sign*.34, *Mus*.p.30 K., S.E.*P*.3.39, Aret.*SD*1.14, *Corp.Herm*. 2.6, Plot.2.6.2, Plu.2.599d (pl.); *repercussion*, Cass.*Pr*.26. 2. of light, *reflection*, Plot.4.4.29. 3. *surface* of a solid, *Theol.Ar*.18, Iamb.*Comm.Math*.8. ❋**-ος**, ον, rarely η, ον, v. infr. II. 1 a: (τύπτω): —*repelled* by a hard body, τύπος ἀ. *blow and counter-blow*, of the hammer and anvil, Orac.ap.Hdt.1.67, cf. 68; of sound, *echoed*, *echoing*, στόνος S.*Ph*.694 (lyr.), 1460 (lyr.), cf. *APl*.4.154 (Luc. or Arch.); κατὰ τὸ ἀ. by *repercussion*, of an echo, Luc.*Dom*.3; of light, *reflected*, ἀκτῖνες Tryph.519, cf. *AP*9.822. 2. *corresponding*, as the stamp to the die, ἅγια ἀ. τῶν ἀληθινῶν *figuring* or *representing* the true, *Ep.Hebr*.9.24, cf. 1*Ep.Pet*.3.21; ἀ. τοῖς δακρύοις χάριτα *IG*14.1320; *resembling*, c. dat., Nonn.*D*.26.327; μίμημα ib.8.23: hence, *feigned*, *counterfeit*, 1.422, al. b. *corresponding*, φιλότης *mutual* affection, 13.552. c. Subst. ἀντίτυπος, ὁ, or ἀντίτυπον, τό, *image*, Ἄμμωνος κεραοῦ χάλκεον ἀ. *Epigr.Gr*.835 (Berytus); ἀντίτυπον, τό, = ἀντίγραφον, *reproduction*, *copy*, *POxy*.1470.6 (iv A.D.): metaph., *antitype*, Plot.2.9.6. II. Act., *repelling*, as a hard body does: hence, 1. *firm*, *resistent*, χωρίον Hp.*Art*.43; *rigid*, *inelastic*, *AP*9.739 (Jul. Aegypt.); -ώτερα ὄντα, of a horse's fetlocks, X.*Eq*.1.4; ἀντιτύπᾳ δ' ἐπὶ γᾷ πέσε S.*Ant*.134; οἱ ἐν ἀντιτύποις περίπατοι walking on *hard ground*, Arist.*Pr*.885$^{a}$36; ἀντιτυπώτατον εἶδος, expl. of σκληρόν, *most resistent*, Pl.*Ti*.62c. b. metaph., *stubborn*, *obstinate*, ἄνθρωποι Id.*Tht*.156a; μάχη ἀ. X.*Ages*.6.2; *harsh-sounding*, ἁρμονίαι D.H.*Comp*.22, cf. 16; ἀ. ἀκοῦσαι Ael.*NA*12.15; of colour, *glaring*, Plu.*Dem*.22. 2. *opposed to*, ἦθος δόλιον πίστιος ἀντίτυπον *the reverse of*.., Thgn.1244; ἀ. Διός *the adversary* of Zeus, A.*Th*.521 (lyr.); *adverse*, of events, X.*HG*6.3.11: simply, ἀ. τινι *opposite*, *over against*, Plb.6.31.8. **-όω**, *express as by a figure*, χρώμασι..χάριν *AP*1.36 (Agath.).

**ἀντιτύπτω**, fut. -τήσω Ph.*Bel*.85.10, *beat in turn*, Ar.*Nu*.1424, Antipho 4.4.3; τυπτόμενον ἀντιτύπτειν Pl.*Cri*.51a.

**ἀντιτύπωσις** [ῠ], εως, ἡ, *an image impressed*, *impression*, Orib.45.3.3.

**ἀντιτῠραννέω**, *set up a counter-tyranny*, Lyd.*Mag*.2.1.

**ἀντιτυφλόω**, *blind in return*, Mich.*in EN*31.27.

**ἀντιτωθάζω**, *ridicule in turn*, Conon 49.3.

**ἀντιφαίνω**, *reflect light*, Thphr.*Sens*.26:—Pass., ἀντιφαίνομαι, aor. ἀντεφάνην, *appear face to face*, Hes.*Cat.Oxy*.1359 i 5.

**ἀντιφάνεια** [φᾰ], ἡ, *reflection*, Damian.*Opt*.12.

❋**ἀντιφάρα**, ἡ, (φάρω, Dor. for φέρω) *dispute*, *EM*114.19, Hsch.; so ἀντιφαρές· ἐναντίον, Id.

**ἀντιφάρμᾰκον**, τό, *antidote*, Arist.*Mir*.837$^{a}$18, Ceb.26, Ath.3.84f, Ruf.*Fr*.58.1, Apollon.ap.Philum.*Ven*.33.6, Dsc.1.125:—Adj. **-κός**, ή, ἀ. ῥίζα D.S.17.90.

❋**ἀντί-φᾰσις**, εως, ἡ, (ἀντίφημι) in Logic, *contradiction* of propositions, Arist.*Int*.17$^{a}$33, *APo*.72$^{a}$12, *Metaph*.1011$^{b}$23, 1055$^{b}$1, al.; ἐξ ἀντιφάσεως *per contra*, Porph.*Chr*.58; ἐξ ἀντιφάσεως συλλογισμός, e.g. 'either there is day or there is not day', Chrysipp.*Stoic*.2.87; ἡ κατ' ἀντίφασιν ἐρώτησις, e.g. 'Does A possess B or not?', Ps.-Alex.Aphr.*in SE*81.35, cf. 103.16. II. *contradictory proposition*, Arist.*Int*.22$^{a}$39, *APr*.34$^{b}$29, al. **-φάσκω**, *contradict*, ἑαυτῷ Olymp.*in Mete*.181.11; *to be in contradiction*, Simp.*in Ph*.1155.28; τὰ ἀντιφάσκοντα *contradictories*, Id.*in Cat*.44.21, cf. 19.21; ὁ ἀντιφάσκων *the opponent* in argument, Phld.*Po*.2.54. ❋**-φᾰτικός**, ή, όν, in Logic, *contradictory*, only in Adv. -κῶς Arist.*Int*.17$^{b}$17, 22$^{a}$34.

**ἀντιφερίζω**, *set oneself against*, *measure oneself with*, οὔ τις σοίγε.. δύνατ' ἀντιφερίζειν Il.21.357; κακὸν ἐσλῷ Hes.*Th*.609; ὅτι μοι μένος ἀντιφερίζεις Il.21.488; σὺ Θεμιστοκλεῖ ἀντιφερίζεις; Ar.*Eq*.813, cf. 818; ἀ. πὰρ σοφόν Pi.*P*.9.50.

**ἀντίφερνος**, ον, (φερνή) *instead of a dower*, ἀ. φθορά A.*Ag*.406 (lyr.). II. ἀντίφερνα, τά, = *donatio propter nuptias*, *Cod.Just*.5.3.20.

❋**ἀντιφέρω**, *set against*, Pl.*Erx*.395b; ἀ. πόλεμον ἐπί τινι *AP*7.438 (Damag.): used by Hom. only in Med. or Pass., *set oneself against*, *fight against* another, ἀντεφέροντο μάχῃ Il.5.701; ἀργαλέος γὰρ Ὀλύμπιος ἀντιφέρεσθαι hard *to oppose*, 1.589, cf. Od.16.238: c. acc. cogn., μένος ἀ. τινί *match oneself with* another in strength, Il.21.482; τίς Ὁμηρείοις ἀντιφέροιτο λόγοις; *AP*9.625 (Maced.). II. Pass., *to be borne in a contrary direction to*, τῷ οὐρανῷ Arist.*Cael*.291$^{b}$2, cf. *Ph*.215$^{a}$30; τῷ παντὶ τὴν φοράν Theo Sm.p.134 H.

**ἀντιφεύγω**, *flee* or *go into exile in turn*, ἀντί τινος E.*El*.1091.

**ἀντίφημι**, *say 'no'*, *contradict*, abs., Pl.*Grg*.501c, Arist.*APr*.65$^{b}$1; ἀ. τινί *contradict* a thing, Id.*Insomn*.462$^{a}$7; πρός τι ib.460$^{b}$19.

**ἀντι-φθέγγομαι**, *return a sound*, *echo*, *repeat*, E.*Hipp*.1216; τὸ ἀκουσθέν Arist.*GA*781$^{a}$26. II. *speak against*, *contradict*, J.*AJ*18.7.2, Luc.*Salt*.23, *Pisc*.31, S.E.*M*.7.332, al. III. *answer*, Pi.*O*.6.61. IV. *raise a shout in reply*, D.S.17.33. **-φθεγμα**, ατος, τό, *echo*, Sch.rec.S.*El*.109. **-φθογγος**, ον, *of answering sound*, *concordant*, c. gen., Pi.*Fr*.125; *imitative*, *AP*7.191 (Arch.).

**ἀντιφῐλ-έω**, *love in return*, Pl.*Ly*.212d, Theoc.12.16, 28.6, Arist.*EN*1157$^{b}$30:—Pass., Pl.*Ly*.212c, X.*Mem*.2.6.28, Arist.*EN*1159$^{a}$30, al. II. *kiss in return*, *AP*5.284 (Agath.). **-ησις**, εως, ἡ, *return of affection*, Arist.*EN*1155$^{b}$28. **-ία**, ἡ, *mutual affection*, Id.*EE*1236$^{b}$2.

**ἀντιφῐλο-δοξέω**, *vie in ambition*, πρός τινα Plb.1.40.11. **-νεικέω**, *strive jealously against*, πρὸς πάντα Id.3.103.7; τῇ συγκλήτῳ 32.3.16: abs., J.*AJ*2.9.1. **-σοφέω**, *hold contrary tenets*, τῇ στοᾷ Luc.*Bis Acc*.21; τῷ τυράννῳ Lxx 4*Ma*.8.15. **-τῑμέομαι**, Pass., *to be moved by jealousy against*, πρὸς τὴν βουλήν D.H.6.96, cf. Plu.*Per*.14; τῇ ἀρετῇ Max.Tyr.14.7: plpf. ἀντεπεφιλοτίμητο D.C.59.19; in good sense, *show public spirit in return*, D.Chr.32.95. 2. Medic., *set up a vicious circle with*, ταῖς νόσοις Sever.*Clyst*.4. ❋**-φρονέομαι**, *receive kindly in turn*, J.*AJ*14.11.5; also, *rival*, Plu.*Sert*.20.

**ἀντιφλέγω**, *light up again* or *to meet* one, αὐτῷ ὅλον ὀφθαλμὸν ἀντέφλεξε Μήνα Pi.*O*.3.20.

**ἀντιφλῠᾱρέω**, *talk nonsense against*, τοῖς φλυαροῦσιν ἀ. Gal.8.696, 9.923.

**ἀντιφοβέω**, *frighten in turn*, Ael.*NA*12.15.

**ἀντιφολκός**· μέρος τῆς πολεμικῆς νεώς, Hsch.

**ἀντιφον-εύω**, *murder in return*, Sch.E.*Or*.415. **-ος**, ον, *in revenge for blood*, ποινὰς ἀντιφόνους ἄτας A.*Eu*.982; δώσουσ' ἀντιφόνους δίκας S.*El*.248; ἀντίφονον κορέσαι στόμα Id.*Ph*.1156. II. θάνατοι ἀ. deaths *by mutual slaughter*, A.*Th*.893.—Trag. word, but only in lyric passages.

**ἀντιφορά**, ἡ, *contrary motion*, Simp.*in Cael*.156.20.

**ἀντιφορικῶς**, as Adv., = ἀντιφραστικῶς, Sch.Th.3.15.

**ἀντιφορτ-ίζω**, *take in a return-cargo*, Str.5.3.5, *Peripl.M.Rubr*.32; but the Med. is more usual in same sense, D.35.25 and 37: so metaph., Hp.*Ep*.17; τίμημα ἀ. τοῦ ἔργου Procop.*Arc*.20. II. in Med. also, *import in exchange for* exports, X.*Vect*.3.2; *take as return-freight*, ἀργύριον Arist.*Mir*.844$^{a}$18. 2. Pass., χρήματα.. ἀντιφορτισθέντα goods *received in exchange for the cargo*, Syngr.ap.D.35.11, cf. ib.24. **-ος**, ὁ, *return-freight*, Arg. 1 Ar.*Ach*. II. Subst. ἀντίφορτον, τό, *load which balances* another, *BGU*248.27 (i A.D.).

**ἀντίφραγμα**, ατος, τό, *counter-fence*, *bulwark*, πρός τι Plu.2.558d.

**ἀντιφράζω**, *translate*, Gal.11.793. II. *express by antithesis* or *negation*, Trypho *Trop*.2.15 (Pass.).

**ἀντίφραξις**, εως, ἡ, (ἀντιφράσσω) *barricading*, γῆς ἀ. *the interposition* of the earth, so as to cause a lunar eclipse, Arist.*APo*.90$^{a}$16, cf. *Mete*.367$^{b}$21; so ἥλιον ἐκλείπειν σελήνης ἀντιφράξει Id.*Fr*.210, cf. Plu.2.169a. II. Pythag. name for *seventeenth day of the month*, ib.367f.

**ἀντίφρᾰσις**, εως, ἡ, (ἀντιφράζω) Rhet. and Gramm., *antiphrasis*, i.e. the use of words of good sense in place of those of a contrary sense, Εὐμενίδες for Ἐρινύες, πόντος εὔξεινος for ἄξεινος, Ath.3.90b; or οὐδ' ἄρα..γήθησεν for ἐλυπήθη, Trypho *Trop*.2.15; κατ' ἀντίφρασιν Corn.*ND*4, Erot. s.v. ἀσήμοις, Herm.*in Phdr*.p.176 A., Porph.*Chr*.87. II. *expression by means of negation*, Anon.*Fig*.p.212 S.

**ἀντιφράσσω**, Att. **-ττω**, *barricade*, *block*, τὴν ὁδόν τισι Plu.2.548d:—Pass., *to be screened*, ἀντιπεφραγμένος λαμπτήρ *lantern*, Philist.15; τόπος ὑπὸ τῆς γῆς -φραττόμενος Plu.*Nic*.23. II. c. dat., *stand in the way of*, τῷ ἀέρι Arist.*Juv*.470$^{a}$13, cf. *Pr*.929$^{a}$38; esp. of a body intercepting the sun's light, ὅσοις ἀντιφράττει ἡ γῆ ὥστε μὴ ὁρᾶσθαι ὑπὸ τοῦ ἡλίου.. Id.*Mete*.345$^{a}$29: c. acc., ἕκαστον ἀντιφράττειν αὐτήν (sc. τὴν σελήνην) Id.*Cael*.293$^{b}$25: abs., X.*Smp*.5.6, Thphr.*Ign*.49; ἡ γῆ ἀ. Arist.*APo*.87$^{b}$40; ἡ θάλαττα ἀ. Id.*Mete*.368$^{b}$10; κωλύει τὸ ἀλλότριον καὶ ἀ. Id.*de An*.429$^{a}$20. 2. Pass., *to be placed as an obstacle*, τινὸς ἀντιφραχθέντος περὶ τὴν ἀναπνοήν Pl.*Ti*.66e.

**ἀντιφραστικῶς**, Adv. *by way of* ἀντίφρασις, Eust.399.38.

**ἀντιφρίσσω**, *bristle up in self-defence*, Arist.*HA*630$^{a}$2.

**ἀντίφρουρος**· τὴν ἴσην ἔχων φρουράν, Hsch.

**ἀντιφῠλ-ᾰκή**, ἡ, *a watching against* one another, πρὸς ἀλλήλους Th.2.84: pl., D.C.77.2, Luc.*Hist.Conscr*.28. **-άσσω**, Att. **-ττω**, *watch in turn*, Pl.*Lg*.705e:—Med., *to be on one's guard in turn*, X.*An*.2.5.3, cf. Plu.*Demetr*.36.

**ἀντιφῡσάω**, *blow against*, Antyll.ap.Orib.9.23.11.

**ἀντιφῠτεύω**, *implant in turn*: metaph., ἔρις ἔριν ἀ. Ps.-Phoc.78.

**ἀντιφύω**, in pf. part. ἀντιπεφυκότων, *to be of contrary nature*, Hsch.

❋**ἀντιφων-έω**, *sound in answer*, *reply*, *rejoin*, abs., A.*Eu*.303, S.*Ant*.271, etc.; esp. *answer in a loud voice*, Plu.*Mar*.19, etc. 2. c. acc. cogn., ἀ. ἔπος *utter* a word *in reply*, S.*Aj*.773; πόλλ' ἀ. Id.*El*.1501; ἀ. Ἔρωτας, of a lute, *sound* love strains *in reply*, *Anacreont*.23.9. 3. c. acc. pers., *reply to*, *answer*, μή μ' ἀντιφώνει μηδέν S.*Ph*.1065. 4. *answer by letter*, τινί Plb.8.16.11, *POxy*.805 (i B.C.), al.: abs., Plb.8.17.8:—Pass., *to be received in answer*, ἐκ Ῥώμης Id.15.18.6, cf. J.*AJ*14.10.26; but -πεφωνημένα ἐκ τῶν δημοσίων δέλτων ἀντίγραφα copies *taken from*.., *OGI*453.26 (M. Antonius). 5. *controvert*, *disagree with*, τινί S.E.*M*.7.327; *to be discordant with*, -φωνοῦντος τοῦ νῦν βίου τῷ βιβλίῳ Luc.*Apol*.4. II. legal t. t., = *constituere*, Anon.*de Actionibus* in *Zeitschr.d.Savigny-Stiftung* 1893 p.92. ❋**-ησις**, εως, ἡ, *answer by letter*, *POxy*.294.12 (i A.D.), *BGU*1204.4 (i B.C.). ❋**-ητής**, οῦ, ὁ, *one who answers for*, *is responsible for* another, *POxy*.136.39 (vi A.D.). **-ος**, ον, (φωνή) *sounding in answer*, *concordant*, as in the octave, ὀξύτητα βαρύτητι σύμφωνον καὶ ἀ. Pl.*Lg*.812d: abs., ἁρμονίαι Ph.2.485. 2. *responsive to*, c. gen., στεναγμάτων E.*Supp*.800 (lyr.). II. *discordant, contradictory*, Plu.2.361a, *Corp.Herm*.16. 1: c. gen., τῶν γενησομένων Plu.2.412b. III. as Subst., ἀντίφωνον, τό, *concord in the octave*, τὸ ἀ. σύμφωνόν ἐστι διὰ πασῶν Arist. *Pr*.918$^b$30, 921$^a$8.

**ἀντιφωτ-ίζομαι**, *to be directly exposed to light*, -ομένου ὄμματος Dam. *Pr*.29. **-ισμός**, ὁ, *reflection of light*, Plu.2.625e; πρὸς τὴν σελήνην Id.*Nic*.21.

**ἀντιχαίνω**· *rehisco*, Gloss.

**ἀντιχαίρω**, *rejoice in turn* or *answer*, Νίκα ἀντιχαρεῖσα Θήβᾳ S.*Ant*. 149.

⁎**ἀντιχᾰλεπαίνω**, *to be embittered against*, D.H.17.5, Plu.2.468b.

**ἀντιχάλημα** (leg. -χέλυσμα)· μέρος τι τῆς μακρᾶς νεώς, Hsch.

**ἀντιχαλκεύω**, *forge against*, in Med., πρὸς τὰς μαχαίρας κράνη ὁλοσίδηρα Polyaen.8.7.2.

**ἀντι-χᾰρίζομαι**, *show kindness in return*, τινί Hdt.7.114, X.*Cyr*.4.1. 20, Ph.2.26, etc. **-χᾰρις**, ιτος, ἡ, *acknowledgement of a favour*, Heliod. *in EN*95.18, Lib.*Decl*.43.29.

**ἀντιχασμάομαι**, *yawn in answer to*, τοῖς χασμωμένοις Arist.*Pr*.886$^a$ 24, 887$^a$4.

**ἀντίχειρ** (sc. δάκτυλος, which is supplied in Heliod.ap.Orib.48. 54.1, S.E.*M*.1.137, *Gp*.4.12.13), ὁ, *thumb*, as being *opposite to* the fingers, Sor.1.103, Dsc.5.79, Plu.2.761c, etc. II. *responsive to the touch*, βόμβοι κυμβάλων Diog.Trag.1.4 (Casaubon). III. Subst. (sc. σωλήν), *inverse tube* of alembic, Zos.Alch.p.225B.

**ἀντίχειρον**, τό, *thumb-breadth*, Hero *Geom*.4.11; also ὁ ἀντίχειρος δάκτυλος *thumb*, Antyll.ap.Orib.7.9.8.

**ἀντιχειροτον-έω**, *vote against*, abs., Th.6.13,24, Ar.*Ec*.423; ἀ. ὡς.. D.59.5; τινί Max.Tyr.17.5. **-ία**, ἡ, *contrary vote*, Poll.2.150.

**ἀντίχθων** (sc. γῆ), ονος, ἡ, *opposite* or *counter-earth*, in the Pythag. system, Arist.*Cael*.293$^a$24, *Metaph*.986$^a$12, *Placit*.2.7.7. 2. *southern hemisphere*, Cic.*Tusc*.1.28.68; ἀ. ζώνη Jul.*Or*.5.173c: in pl., *people of the southern hemisphere*, Ach.Tat.*Intr.Arat*.30, Plin.*HN*6.81.

**ἀντίχορδος**, ον, *concordant*, Hsch.: but, II. metaph., *in reply* or *opposition to*, τοῖς πεφιλοσοφημένοις Plu.2.663f.

**ἀντιχορεύω**, *dance in harmony*, Nonn.*D*.22.44.

**ἀντιχορηγ-έω**, *to be a rival choragus*, And.4.42; ἀ. τινί *rival* him *in the choragia*, D.21.62. II. *furnish in return*, J.*BJ*2.20.8 (Pass.). **-ος**, ὁ, *rival choragus*, And.4.20, D.21.59.

**ἀντιχόρια**, τά, *odes sung alternately by two semichori*, Poll.4.107.

**ἀντιχόρτοις**· συνόροις, Hsch.

**ἀντι-χράω**, (χράω B) *to be sufficient*, only in aor. 1, ὁ ποταμὸς οὐκ ἀντέχρησε τῇ στρατιῇ πινόμενος Hdt.7.127, cf. 187. **-χρημᾰτίζομαι**, *transact business instead of* another, *PFlor*.382.59 (iii A.D.). ⁎**-χρησις**, εως, ἡ, *substitution of usufruct for interest*, *Dig*.20.1.11.1.

**ἀντίχριστος**, ὁ, *Antichrist*, 1*Ep.Jo*.2.18,22, etc.

**ἀντιχρον-ία**, ἡ, *use of one tense for another*, Sch.E.*Or*.82. **-ισμός**, ὁ, = foreg., ib.48, Hdn. in *An.Ox*.3.274.

**ἀντιχρώζω**, *colour, tinge in turn*, [Lib.] *Descr*.30.13.

**ἀντιχώννῡμι**, *raise an embankment against*, πόλει Amynt.ap.Ath. 12.529e.

**ἀντιχωρέω**, *move in opposite direction*, dub. l. in Porph.*Sent*.11.

**ἀντι-ψάλλω**, *play a stringed instrument in accompaniment* of song, ἀ. ἐλέγοις φόρμιγγα Ar.*Av*.218. ⁎**-ψαλμος**, ον, *responsive, harmonious*, ᾠδάς E.*IT*179 (lyr.).

**ἀντιψαύω**, = ἀνθάπτομαι, Sch.E.*Hec*.275.

**ἀντιψέγω**, *blame in turn*, Sch.A.*Eu*.416.

**ἀντιψηλᾰφάω**· *obtrecto*, Gloss.

**ἀντιψηφ-ίζομαι**, *vote against*, πρός τι Plu.*Lys*.27; τὸ ἀληθὲς τῷ λόγῳ ἀ. Lib.*Or*.64.37. **-ος**, ον, *voting against*, τῷ θεῷ Pl.*Alc*.2. 150b.

⁎**ἀντίψῡχος**, ον, *given for life*, Luc.*Lex*.10. 2. ἀ. ἀποθανεῖν *giving one's own life for another's*, D.C.59.8. 3. name for οἱ Μέμνονος ὄρνιθες, Hsch.

**ἀντιψύχω** [ῡ], *cool, chill in turn*, Alex.Aphr.*Pr*.1.113.

**ἀντιψωμίζω**, *feed with dainty morsels in rivalry*, Arg.1 Ar.*Eq*.

⁎**ἀντλ-έω**, (ἄντλος) *bale out bilge-water, bale the ship*, Thgn.673, Alc. 19. 2. generally, *draw water*, ἀντλέει καὶ ἐγχέει Hdt.6.119, *Ev. Jo*.2.8, etc.; οἷον ἐκ κρήνης ἐπ' ὀχετοὺς ἀ. *draw* as from a well, *and pour into*.., Pl.*Ti*.79a; διὰ χώνης τοῖσι βουλομένοις πιεῖν Pherecr. 108.31: prov. of labour in vain, ἠθμῷ ἀντλεῖν *draw water* in a sieve, Arist.*Oec*.1344$^b$25; εἰς τετρημένον πίθον ἀ. X.*Oec*.7.40; but ἐκ πίθω ἀ., of one who has abundance in store, Theoc.10.13; ἕτοιμον ἀ. Herod.4.14. II. metaph., *drain dry*, i.e., 1. *use the utmost, make the most of*, τὰν ἔμπρακτον ἄντλει μαχανάν Pi.*P*.3.62: but more commonly, 2. of toil, suffering, etc., *drain to the dregs*, τὴν παροῦσαν ἀντλήσω τύχην A.*Pr*.377; τλημόνως ἤντλουν κακά Id.*Ch*. 748; λυπρὸν ἀντλήσει βίον E.*Hipp*.898; δέκα ἀντλήσας ἔτη v.l. Id. *Tr*.433. 3. *squander*, πατρῴαν κτῆσιν ἀντλεῖν S.*El*.1291. III. Pass., ἀντλούμενος ὄλβῳ *flooded with*, Man.4.92. **-ημα**, ατος, τό, *bucket for drawing water*, Plu.2.974e, Sch.Ar.*Ra*.1332, *Ev.Jo*.4. 11. **-ησις**, εως, ἡ, *drawing up* or *emptying*, Ruf.ap.Orib.5.3.1, *POxy*.971 (i/ii A.D.), Ael.*VH*1.24. ⁎**-ησμός**, ὁ, = foreg., *PFlor*.16. 21 (iii A.D.). **-ητήρ**, ῆρος, ὁ, *one who draws water*, Poll.10.31; ληνῶν Man.4.257. 2. = κάδος ναυτικός, Hsch. II. *ladle*, Ath.10. 424a. **-ητήριος**, α, ον, *of* or *for drawing up*: τὸ ἀ. (sc. ἀγγεῖον) *bucket*, D.C.50.34. **-ητής**, οῦ, ὁ, = ἀντλητήρ 1, *PLond*.1.131$^r$311 (i A.D.), al., Ptol.*Tetr*.179. **-ητικός**, ή, όν, *for irrigation*, ἄξων *POxy*.137.20 (vi A.D.); *suitable for irrigation*, κτήματα *PFlor*.148. 3 (iii A.D.). ⁎**-ητός**, όν, *irrigated*, *PAmh*.2.96.3, *PFlor*.369.6 (ii A.D.). ⁎**-ήτρια**, ἡ, *she who draws up*, priestess at the Thesmophoria, Sch.Luc.*DDeor*.2.1. **-ία**, ἡ, = ἄντλος, i.e., 1. *hold of a ship*, S.*Ph*.482; τὴν ἀντλίαν φυλάξω Ar.*Eq*.434; δεῖπνον.. ἐξ ἀντλίας ἥκοντα, i.e. the coarse food used by seamen, Dionys.Com.2. 41. 2. *bilge-water, filth*, Ar.*Pax*17. 3. *reservoir*, *BGU*1120. 26 (i B.C.), *PRyl*.92.5 (ii/iii A.D.). 4. = καδίσκος, Hsch.

⁎**ἀντλιαντλητήρ**, ῆρος, ὁ, *bucket*, Men 30.

**ἀντλίον**, τό, = foreg., Ar.*Fr*.470, Epil.5.

⁎**ἄντλος**, ὁ, in Poll.1.92 also ἄντλον, τό:—in Hom., *hold of a ship*, Od.12.411, 15.479. 2. *bilge-water*, πόλις.. ἄντλον οὐκ ἐδέξατο let in no *water*, metaph. for 'let no enemy come in', A.*Th*.796; ἄντλον εἴργειν ναός pump out *water* from a ship, E.*Tr*.691; εἰς ἄντλον ἐμβαίνειν πόδα, metaph. for getting into a difficulty, Id.*Heracl*.168. 3. a *flood* of water, Pi.*O*.9.53; ἀλίμενον ὥς τις εἰς ἄντλον πεσών E.*Hec*. 1025 (lyr.); ἐν ἄντλῳ τιθέναι *scuttle, sink*, metaph., ὕβριν Pi.*P*.8. 12. II. *bucket*, Man.6.424. III. *heap of corn*, threshed but not yet cleansed, Nic.*Th*.114,546, Q.S.1.352, *AP*6.258 (Adaeus).

**ἀντοδυνάω**, *hurt in return*, Sch.Theoc.3.13.

**ἀντοδύρομαι** [ῠ], *lament in return*, App.*BC*1.10.

**ἀντοικέω**, *to be ἄντοικος* (q.v.): – Pass., ἡ ἀντοικουμένη, Ptol.*Geog*. 1.8.1, cf. Ach.Tat.*Intr.Arat*.30, Olymp. *in Grg*.p.541 J.

**ἀντοικοδομ-έω**, *build* or *fortify against*, Plb.1.42.12, D.S.16.49; τινά App.*BC*2.61:—Med., Arr.*An*.1.21.4: metaph., ἀ. τινι διατριβήν Ael.*VH*4.9. **-ητέον**, *one must build against*, Ph.*Bel*.92.22. ⁎**-ή**, ἡ, = sq., *IG*12(1).420 (Thera). **-ία**, ἡ, *building against*, ib.11.165. 15 (Delos, iii B.C.), Plb.1.48.1.

⁎**ἄντοικος**, ον, *living on the same side of the equator, but under the opposite meridian*, Gem.16.1, Cleom.1.2.

**ἀντοικτίζω**, *pity in return*, Th.3.40.

**ἀντοικτίρω**, = foreg., τινά E.*Ion*312.

**ἀντοίομαι**, aor. ἀντῳήθην, *to be of contrary opinion*, Pl.*Tht*.178c.

**ἀντολ-ή**, ἡ, poet. for ἀνατολή, q.v. ⁎**-ίη**, ἡ, collat. poet. form of ἀνατολή, Androm.ap.Gal.14.37, *APl*.4.61 (Crin., pl.), *Epigr.Gr*. 441 (Trachonitis), al.; personified, *PMag.Berol*.2.9.3. 2. as Adj., *eastern*, ἐν ἀντολίῃ.. ἀρούρῃ Nonn.*D*.25.98. **-ίηθε**, Adv. for ἀνατολίηθε, *from the east*, Opp.*C*.2.123; -θεν ib.1.43, Man.2.11, 3. 49. **-ίηνδε**, *towards the east*, D.P.260.

**ἀντολοφύρομαι** [ῠ], *bewail in turn*, J.*BJ*4.5.1.

**ἄντομαι**, only pres. and impf.: (ἀντί, ἄντα):—poet. Verb (Hom. only in Il.), = ἀντάω, *meet*, Il.2.595, al.; esp. in battle, c. dat., ἀλλήλοισιν ἄντεσθ' ἐν πολέμῳ 15.698, cf. 16.788; ἀργύρῳ ἀντομένη.. ἐτράπετ' αἰχμή 11.237; so χαλεπῇ ἤντ. θευμορίῃ Call.*Ep*.32: abs., διπλόος ἤντετο θώρηξ the breastplate *opposed* or *stopped* (the dart), Il.4. 133. 2. *meet with favour, greet*, Pi.*P*.2.71. II. c. acc. pers., = ἀντιάζω I. 2, *approach with prayers, entreat*, πρός σε.. ἄντομαι Διός E. *Alc*.1098; πρός σε γενειάδος.. ἄντομαι Id.*Supp*.279 (lyr.); πρός σ' ὅ τι σοι φίλον ἐκ σέθεν ἄντομαι S.*OC*250; ἀ. Ἑρμῆν Ar.*Th*.977; ἀ. ὑπέρ τινος *beg* in another's behalf, S.*OC*243 (lyr.): abs., ἔλθετον, ἀντόμεθ' Ar.*Th*.1155 (lyr.).

⁎**ἀντόμνῡμι**, *swear in turn, swear on the other part*, in a treaty, c. fut. inf., X.*HG*3.4.6, *Ages*.1.10. II. as Att. law-term, *make an affidavit*, both of the accuser and the defendant (cf. ἀντωμοσία), Antipho 1.18, Is.9.1, D.43.3, etc.:—in Med., Is.5.16.

⁎**ἄντομος**, ὁ, dialectic form of ἀνάτομος, *stake* or *pale*, cf. ἄντομοι· σκόλοπες (Sicel), Hsch.: hence collectively, *paling, boundary-fence*, *Tab.Heracl*.1.15, al.; also, *road adjoining such a fence*, ib.2.13, al.

**ἀντομῶσαι**· παρακαλέσαι, Hsch. **ἀντοναί**· αἱ τῶν χειρῶν φοραί, Id.

**ἀντονειδίζω**, *upbraid in return*, τινί Eust.1042.46.

**ἀντονίνημι** [νῐ], fut. -ονήσω, *serve mutually*, dub. in Lib.*Or*.5.53 codd.

**ἀντονομ-άζω**, *name instead, call by a new name*, c. dupl. acc., Th. 6.4. 2. ὁ -άζων ὅρος plea *of avoidance and confession*, Arg.Lycurg., cf. Hermog.*Stat*.4. 3. *nominate instead*, Pass., *POxy*.1405.17 (iii A.D.). II. *use* ἀντονομασίαι or *rhetorical figures*, Ar.*Th*.55. 2. *use the pronoun*, Eust.103.23; ἀ. τινά A.D.*Synt*.192.21:—Pass., ib. 98.11. III. Arith., in Pass., *to be of a contrary denomination*, Nicom.*Ar*.1.23. **-ασία**, ἡ, *use of an epithet, patronymic*, or *appellative for a proper name*, and vice versa, Tryph.*Trop*.2.17, Ps.-Plu.*Vita Hom*.24; ἀ. καὶ μετάληψις Demetr.Lac.*Herc*.1014.19,20. 2. *nomination of his successor by retiring official*, *POxy*.1642.15 (iii A.D.). II. Gramm., = ἀντωνυμία, *pronoun*, or *the use of it*, D.H.*Comp*.2, A.D. *Pron*.4.18. III. Arith., *contrary denomination*, Nicom.*Ar*.1. 23. **-αστικός**, ή, όν, *pronominal*, cj. for ἀντωνυμικός (q.v.), D.H. *Amm*.2.12.

**ἀντόπτρα**, ἡ, name of a *surgical instrument*, *Hermes*38.281.

**ἀντοργίζομαι**, *to be angry in turn*, M.Ant.6.26, Gal.19.211.

**ἀντορέγω**, *stretch out, present in turn*, Them.*Or*.11.153a.

**ἀντορθιάζω**, *rise up in opposition*, Hierocl.p.17A.

**ἄντορος**, ὁ, dialectic form of ἄνθ-ορος, *opposite boundary, counter-fence*, *Tab.Heracl*.1.60, al.

⁎**ἀντορύσσω**, *dig a countermine*, Hdt.4.200, Aen.Tact.37.7: metaph., ἀ. ὀφθαλμούς Paus.3.14.10.

**ἀντορχέομαι**, *imitate one's dancing*, Arist.*HA*597$^b$24, cf. Metrod. Sceps.13.

**ἄντος**· εὖρος, οἱ δὲ Εὐριπίδης, Hsch.

**ἀντοφείλω**, *owe a good turn, to be indebted*, Th.2.40.

**ἀντοφθαλμ-έω**, *look in the face, meet face to face*, ἀ. κατὰ πρόσωπον

Ib.18.46.12: hence, *defy, withstand*, τινί and πρός τινα, Id.1.17.3, 24.1, etc., cf. Lxx *Wi.*12.14; ἀ. τῷ ἀνέμῳ, of a ship, *Act.Ap.*27.15; ἀθέσι Longin.34.4. -ησις, εως, ἡ, *looking straight in the face*: hence, *straightforward dealing*, ἀ. πεποίηται πρὸς τοὺς πολίτας *IG*5(1).1114.17. -ος, ον, *looking in the face*, Hsch. s. v. ἀντωπόν.

**ἀντόφρυς**, name of a *plant*, Hsch.

**ἀντοχέομαι**, *drive* or *ride against*, f.l. in Mosch.2.119.

**ἀντοχεύς**· πόρπαξ ἀσπίδος, Hsch.

**ἀντοχή**, ἡ, *adhesion*, Orib.45.2.6, Gal.19.440. II. *attachment*, c. gen., ἑαυτῶν, of rings, Alex.Aphr.*Pr.*2.67: metaph., Procl. *in Ti.* 1.75 D.

**ἀντοχῡρόω**, *fortify in turn*, τὸ καταρριφθέν J.*BJ*3.7.23.

**ἀντραῖος**, α, ον, *haunting caves* or *grots*, E.*Fr.*13.

**ἀντρέπω**, poet. for ἀνατρέπω.

**ἀ(ν)τρέσας**· ἀναφοβηθείς, Hsch.

**ἀντρηΐς**, ΐδος, ἡ, *cave-dwelling*, Antip.Sid.*Oxy.*662.50.

**ἀντριάς**, άδος, ἡ, = fem. of ἀντραῖος, Νύμφαι ἀ. *grot*-Nymphs, *AP*6.224 (Theodorid.), cf. Phryn.*PS*p.27 B.

**ἀντρίτης**, ου, ὁ, = ἀντραῖος, coined by St.Byz. s. v. Ἄντρον.

**ἀντρο-δίαιτος** [ῐ], ον, *living in caves*, Orph.*H.*32.3; of Pan, ib.11.5. -ειδής, ές, *like caves*, Epicur.*Ep.*2 p.48 U., *Placit.*3.15.11.

**ἄντροθε**, *from a cave*, Pi.*P.*4.102.

***ἄντρον**, τό, poet. word, *cave*, Hom. only in Od., as 9.216, al., cf. Hes.*Th.*483, Pi.*P.*1.17, etc.; of a lion, A.*Eu.*193; of a serpent, E.*Ph.*232. II. *inner chamber, closet*, Lxx 3*Ki.*16.18.

***ἀντρο-φυής**, ές, *born in caves*, ἀνθίαι Opp.*H.*3.212. -χαρής, ές, *cave-haunting*, epith. of nymphs and Pan, Orph.*H.*11.12, 51.5.

**ἀντρώδης**, ες, *full of caves*, πέτρα X.*An.*4.3.11; τόπος Arist.*Pr.*932ᵃ2; ὑπώρειαι Ph.*Fr.*36 H.; τὰ ἀ. Corn.*ND*28. 2. *like a cave*, οἰκίαι Philostr.*VS*2.23.3.

**ἀντύα**· τὸ ὑποπόδιον, Hsch.

**ἀντῠγωτός**, όν, *wearing a frontlet*, Hsch.

**ἀντυκάρτερα**· ἀντίσχυρα (Lacon.), Hsch.

**ἄντυξ**, ῠγος, ἡ, *edge* or *rim of anything round* or *curved*; and so, I. in Hom. (only in Il.): 1. *rim* of round shield, Il.6.118, al., E.*Rh.*373 (lyr.). 2. *rail* round front of chariot, ἐξ ἄντυγος ἡνία τείνας 5.262, 322; δοιαὶ δὲ περίδρομοι ἄντυγές εἰσι 5.728; καὶ ἄντυγες αἱ περὶ δίφρον 11.535: in pl. also S.*Aj.*1030, Pl.*Tht.*207a: in sg., μάρπτει δὲ . . ἡνίας ἀπ' ἄντυγος E.*Hipp.*1188. II. post-Hom.: 1. pl., *the chariot* itself, S.*El.*746, E.*Ph.*1193: sg., κατ' ἄντυγα Νυκτὸς ὀπαδοί Theoc.2.166, cf. Jul.*Or.*3.122b. 2. *bridge of the lyre*, E.*Hipp.*1135 (lyr.). 3. *orbit* of a planet, *h.Hom.*8.8, Procl.*H.*2.17; *vault* of heaven, ἄ. οὐρανίη *AP*9.806, cf. 11.292 (Pall.); ἄ. αἰθερίη *IGRom.*4.607; *orb, circle* of the world, Nonn.*D.*38.108; ἄ. ἡμίτομος . . σελήνας the *disk* of the half-moon, Mosch.2.88. 4. in Nonnus, of the *curve* of the body, ἄ. μαζοῦ, μηρῶν, *D.*1.348, 15.228, so perh. in Herod.8.29. 5. *outermost tier*, in a theatre, ἡ ἐσχάτη ἄ. τοῦ θεάτρου Eun.*VS*p.489 B.—Poet. word, used by Pl. l.c., Luc.*DDeor.*25.2, in signf. I.2, cf. also II.5.

**ἀντυποκρίνομαι, ἀντυπουργέω**, Ion. for ἀνθυπ-.

**ἄντυπος**· ἴσος, ὅμοιος, ἢ ἐναντίος, Hsch.

**ἀντ-ῳδή**, ἡ, in Comic Parabasis, *lyric passage responding to* ᾠδή, ἀ. καὶ ἀντιστροφή Sch.Ar.*V.*1091, *Nu.*298. -ῳδός, όν, *singing in answer, responsive*, ἠχὼ λόγων ἀντῳδός Ar.*Th.*1059; ἀ. Πανὶ κρέκων κέλαδον *AP*7.196 (Mel.); μέλος ἀ. ἠχεῖν, of birds, Ael.*NA*4.16.

**ἀντωθ-έω**, *push in the contrary direction*, Hp.*Fract.*39, cf. Ph.2.354:—Pass., τὸ ὠθοῦν ἀντωθεῖται Arist.*GA*768ᵇ19, cf. *Mech.*851ᵃ3:—Med., *push one against another*, Theopomp.Hist.283. -ησις, εως, ἡ, *counter-thrust*, Gal.18(1).324, Phlp. *in Ph.*646.19; prob. cj. for ἀντίθεσις in Paul.Aeg.6.117.

**ἄντωμος**, ον, *shoulder to shoulder*: ἄντωμοι, οἱ, = ἄντοικοι (q. v.), Cleom.1.2.

**ἀντωμοσία**, ἡ, (ἀντόμνυμι) *oath* or *affidavit* made by the prosecutor, Pl.*Ap.*19b, Lys.23.13; also, by the defendant, Is.3.6, cf. Harp. s. v., Poll.8.55.

**ἀντωνέομαι**, *buy instead*, X.*Oec.*20.26, Men.438.3: metaph., κλέος ἀείμνηστον ἀ. Jul.*Or.*1.42b. 2. *bid against*, ἐπεὶ οὐδεὶς ἀντεωνεῖτο And.1.134; ἀ. ἀλλήλοις Lys.22.9; ὁ ἀντωνούμενος *rival bidder*, D.18.239.

**ἀντωνῠμ-έω**, *have an opposite denomination*, Theol.Ar.41. -ία, ἡ, *pronoun*, D.H.*Comp.*6, Plu.2.1009c, etc.; περὶ ἀντωνυμίας, title of work by A.D. II. *interchange of names*, Dam.*Pr.*73. *-ικός, ή, όν, *pronominal*, D.H.*Amm.*2.12. Adv. -κῶς *like a pronoun*, A.D.*Synt.*156.7, al.

**ἀντ-ωπέω**, = ἀντοφθαλμέω, Hld.1.21, Heph.Astr.1.24; πρὸς τὸ ἕν Dam.*Pr.*118. -ώπιος, ον, = ἀντωπός, A.R.4.729, Man.4.336, Nonn.*D.*5.485, al.: c. gen., 5.78: c. dat., 33.184. -ῶπις, ιδος, = fem. of sq., ib.6.75. -ωπός, όν, (ὤψ) *with the eyes front, facing*, ἀντωπὰ βλέφαρα E.*IA*564; ἀντωπὸς βλέψαι *AP*12.196 (Strat.); τῆς ὄψεως ἀντωπὰ *front parts* of the face, Luc.*Im.*6; *opposite*, *AP*10.14 (Agath.); *full in the face*, βέλος *APl.*4.134 (Mel.); of an eagle, ἀ. ἁλίῳ Ecphant.ap.Stob.4.7.64. 2. *like*, Opp.*H.*5.7.

**ἀντωρύνομαι** [ῡ], *roar against* or *at*, Sch.Luc.*Par.*51.

**ἄντωσις**, εως, ἡ, *pushing against* or *back*, Arist.*Resp.*480ᵃ14.

**ἀντωφέλ-εια**, ἡ, *benefit in return*, Mich. *in EN*469.18. -έω, *assist* or *benefit in turn*, τινά X.*Mem.*2.10.3:—Pass., *derive profit in turn*, ib.2.8.3, *Cyr.*1.6.11.

***ἀνυβριστί**, Adv. of sq. II, Anacr.63.

***ἀνύβριστος**, ον, *not insulted*, *PRyl.*117.26 (iii A. D.); τελευτή Plu.*Pel.*9, cf. *Luc.*18. Adv. -τως Ps.-Phoc.157. II. Act., *not insulting, decorous*, παιδιαί Plu.*Sert.*26; σκῶμμα Id.2.46c; τὸ ἀ. τοῦ βίου 92d: Sup., D.Chr.3.98. Adv. -τως Democr.73.

**ἀνῠγίαστος**, ον, = ἀναλθής, *incurable*, Hsch. s. v. ἀναλθές.

**ἀνῠγιής**, ές, *unhealthy*, *Gloss.*

**ἀνυγρ-αίνω**, *moisten*, Hp.*Int.*51, Thphr.*CP*2.6.1. 2. metaph., *melt, soften*, τὰ ἤθη Plu.2.156d:—Pass., ib.566a. -ασμός, ὁ, *moistening*, Archig.ap.Orib.8.2.6.

**ἀνύδᾰτος** [ῠ], ον, *without water*, Man.1.144.

**ἀνυδρ-εύομαι**, *draw up from a well*, τὸν κάδον Pherecr.76. -ευτος, ον, *unwatered*, Thphr.*HP*7.4.6. -ία, ἡ, *want of water, drought*, Hp.*Aër.*12, Th.3.88, *PPetr.*2 p.22; *lack of irrigation*, *PLond. ined.*2179 (iii A. D.). -ις, ἡ, fem. of sq., κώμη *PThead.*20.5 (iv A. D.). -ος, ον, (ὕδωρ) *waterless*, of arid countries, Hes.*Fr.*24, Hdt.4.185; γῆ Hp.*Aër.*1; δάπεδα Trag.ap.Phot.p.151 R.; esp. *without spring-water*, Hdt.2.7 codd., cf. 149, 3.5; ἡ ἄνυδρος (sc. γῆ) Id.3.4 and 9, Arist.*Fr.*103, Lxx *Is.*44.3; of seasons, Hp.*Aph.*3.14; θέρος Id.*Aër.*10; in E.*Tr.*1085 (lyr.), of a corpse, *deprived of funeral lustrations; unwatered*, σμύρνα Id.*Ion*89 (anap.). II. ἄνυδρον, τό, = στρύχνον μανικόν, Dsc.4.73.

**ἀνύλακτος** [ῠ], ον, *without barking*, Suid. s. v. μαιουμᾶς.

**ἄνῡλος**, ον, (ὕλη) *treeless*, τόποι Thphr.*CP*1.5.2 (v.l. ἄϋλος). 2. *immaterial*, Ascl. *in Metaph.*26.4.

**ἀνῠμέναιος**, ον, *without the nuptial song, unwedded*, S.*Ant.*876, 917, E.*Hec.*416, Men.548, etc.; μοῖρα ἀ. S.*OC*1221 (lyr.): neut. pl. as Adv., Id.*El.*962, E.*Ph.*347 (lyr.). Adv. -ως Sch.ad loc.

**ἀνῠμεναιόω**, *celebrate with nuptial ode*, γάμους S.*Fr.*725.

**ἀνυμνέω**, *proclaim by an oracle*, δίκαν E.*El.*1190 (lyr.). II. *celebrate in song*, γάμον D.H.*Rh.*2.1, cf. Jul.*Or.*5.172d, Chor.p.127 B., Procop. Gaz.*Ep.*52, Ps.-Luc.*Philopatr.*4 (Pass.): -είω Orac. in *App.Anth.*6.261.18, Nonn.*D.*24.328. III. *declaim*, Eun.*VS*p.468 B. IV. c. dupl. acc., *proclaim as*, ὅπερ ὂν -οῦμεν Dam.*Pr.*48, cf. 58:—Pass., ib.34.

**ἀνύμφευτος**, ον, *unwedded*, S.*El.*165 (lyr.); ματρὸς ἔχοντες ἀ. γονάν born *of an ill marriage*, Id.*Ant.*980, v. Sch.: transf. of things, κάρηνον (of Zeus), Nonn.*D.*46.48, cf. 20.155, al.

***ἀνυμφής**, ές, acc. sg. ἀνυμφέα cj. for ἄνυμφο[ν], *Milet.*6.46 (*Mnemos.*50.255).

***ἄνυμφος**, ον, *not bridal*, ἄ. τροφή S.*El.*1183 (lyr.); νύμφη ἄ. a bride that is no bride, *unhappy* bride, E.*Hec.*612, cf. *Hipp.*547 (lyr.), Men.548. II. *without bride* or *mistress*, μέλαθρα E.*Hel.*1125 (lyr.), cf. *Sammelb.*4301.

**ἀνύξιον**· ἄβρωτον, Euclid.ap.Hsch.

***ἀνῠόδρομος**, ον, *swiftly-running, fleet*, Sapph.71.

**ἀνυπαίτιος**, ον, *blameless*, Ph.1.4, al., Hld.9.11; ἡ κατ' ὀρθὸν λόγον ἀ. διοίκησις Boeth.*Stoic.*3.266. Adv. -ίως Ph.1.206.

**ἀνυπάκουστος**, ον, *not suited for hearing*, i. e. *for declamation*, λέξις Phld.*Rh.*1.198 S.

**ἀν-ύπαρκτος**, ον, *non-existent, unreal*, Epicur.*Fr.*27, Zeno *Stoic.*1.19, Phld.*Mus.*p.65 K., Ph.2.307, Plu.2.1124a, *PGiss.*7.8 (ii A. D.), etc. -υπαρξία, ἡ, *non-existence, nonentity*, Phld.*Mort.*28, Antip.*Stoic.*3.252, S.E.*P.*1.21, Plot.5.5.2. 2. *absence of predication*, ἡ ἀπόφασις said to be ἀναίρεσις (τῆς φάσεως) καὶ ἀ. Alex.Aphr. *in Top.*409.19.

**ἀνυπείκαστον**, sine expl., Hsch.

***ἀνύπ-εικτος**, ον, *unyielding, hard*, Suid. *-εξαιρέτως, Adv. *without exception*, M.Ant.8.41.

**ἀνυπέρ-αρτος**, ον, *not ostentatious*, ἐν δαπάναις καὶ παρασκευαῖς ἀ. Andronic.Rhod.p.576 M. -βᾰτος, ον, *impassable*, κρημνοί D.Chr.64.21. 2. *not to be overcome, unsurpassable*, S.E.*M.*9.153; ἀηδία Phld.*Vit.*p.12 J. 3. Act., *not transgressing the bounds*, διάθεσις ἀ. τῶν κατ' ὀρθὸν λόγον D.L.7.93. Adv. -τως *without omission*, of numerical progression, Nicom.*Ar.*2.23; *unfailingly*, Gal.19.544. *-βλητος, ον, *not to be surpassed* or *outdone*, φιλία X.*Cyr.*8.7.15; ἀρετή Isoc.4.71; φιλοτιμία D.2.18; εὔνοια Lycurg.101; ἄνθρωπος ἀ. εἰς πονηρίαν Antiph.168.5; τάχη Epicur.*Ep.*1 p.10 U. Adv. -τως Arist.*Rh.*1370ᵇ31, Pyth.*Sim.*144. 2. *persistent, obstinate*, of disease, Gal.13.61. -εκτος, ον, *unsurpassable*, ἀκρότης Phld.*D.*3.5.

***ἀνυπερθε-σία**, ἡ, *immediateness, haste*, Aq.*Ps.*7.7 (pl.). -τέω, *do immediately, to be hasty*, ib.77(78).21. -τος, ον, *immediate*, Ph.2.58, al., Dsc.*Ther.Praef.* Adv. -τως *forthwith, without delay*, *BGU*1167.51 (i B. C.), Lxx 3*Ma.*5.20, *IG*3.77, Ph.1.599, etc. II. *unsurpassed by*, c. dat., Democr.275; *incomparable*, [Philol.]21.

**ἀνυπέροχος**, ον, *without superiority on either side*, Eust.832.3.

***ἀνυπ-εύθῡνος**, ον, *not liable to a* εὔθυνα, *not accountable*, of persons, esp. magistrates or statesmen, Ar.*V.*587, Pl.*Lg.*761e; ἀ. ἄρχειν ib.875b, cf. Arist.*Pol.*1295ᵃ20; = Lat. *dictator*, Plu.*Fab.*3. Adv. -νως Andronic.Rhod.p.574 M., D.S.1.70. 2. of things, *beyond human control* or *criticism*, τὰ τῆς τέχνης ἀ. Hp.*Praec.*7; ἀνάγκη Epicur.*Ep.*3 p.65 U.; ἐξουσία ἀ. *unchartered* freedom, Phld.*Herc.*1251.3. II. *that will not bear investigation*, ἔργα Ph.2.266. -ήκοος, ον, *not obeying*, τοῦ λόγου Pl.*Ti.*91b, cf. 73a. -ηλῐφής, ές, *EM*61.6, or -ήλῐφος, ον, Phryn.*PS*p.34 B., *not anointed with pitch*.

***ἀνύπηνος** [ῠ], ον, *beardless*, Eust.1353.47, Hsch.

**ἀνυπηρε-σία**, ἡ, *unserviceableness*, Simp. *in Epict.*p.49 D. -τητος, hyperdor. -τᾶτος, ον, *without attendance*, Euryph.ap.Stob.4.39.27.

**ἀνυπόγρᾰφος**, ον, *without subscription, unsigned*, *PFlor.*16.38 (iii A. D.).

**ἀνυπο-δεσία, -δετέω, -δετος**, = ἀνυποδησία, -δητέω, -δητος, found in codd. and Inscrr., as -δετος *IG*5(1).1390.15 (Andania, i B.C.), but condemned by Phryn.409, Id.*PS*p.27B., etc. -δήματος, ον, = ἀνυπόδητος, *AB*82. -δησία, ἡ, *a going barefoot*, Pl.*Lg.*633c, X.*Lac.*2.3. -δητέω, *go barefoot*, Arist.*Fr.*74, Luc.*Cyn.*1. -δητος, ον, *unshod, barefoot*, as the philosophers and Spartans, Epich.108, Lys.32.16, Pl.*Phdr.*229a, *Smp.*173b, Ar.*Nu.*103, etc.; ἀ. ὄρθρου περιπατεῖν Aristopho 10.8. 2. *having the feet unprotected*, Pl.*Prt.* 321c.

***ἀνυπό-δῐκος**, ον, *not liable to action*, Plu.*Cat.Mi.*11; ἀ. πάσας δίκας καὶ ζαμίας *GDI*1685, al. (Delph.), cf. 5170 (Cret.). -ζωστος, ον, of ships, *without* ὑπόζωμα (q.v.), *IG*2.789*b*79,83. *-θετος, ον, *not hypothetical, unconditioned, absolute*, ἀρχή Pl.*R.*510b, cf. Phld. *D.*1.19; τὸ ἀ. Pl.*R.*511b, al. Adv. -τως *not hypothetically*, Plu.2. 399b. II. *without foundation*, ib.358f.

**ἀνύπ-οιστος**, ον, *insupportable*, Timae.60, D.H.7.15, J.*AJ*19.2.2, Eus.Mynd.54; *irresistible*, φάλαγξ Ascl.*Tact.*5.1. Adv. -τως Poll.3. 130. II. Act., *impatient*, Ptol.*Tetr.*159. -οιστότης· *intolerabilitas*, *Gloss.*

***ἀνυπό-κρῐτος**, ον, *without dissimulation*, Lxx *Wi.*5.18, *Ep.Rom.* 12.9, *Ep.Jac.*3.17. Adv. -τως M.Ant.8.5. II. *undramatic*, Demetr.*Eloc.*194. III. in punctuation, of a stop in a simple sentence, opp. ἐνυπόκριτος (q.v.), Sch.D.T.p.24H. *-ληπτος, ον, perh. f.l. for ἀνυπόδητος, Anon.*in Rh.*82.38. -λογος, ον, *subject to no claim* or *charge*, *POxy.*7116 (iv A.D.): c. gen., ἀ. παντὸς κινδύνου *BGU*1119.7 (i B.C.). II. *without deduction*, φόρος *CIG*2693*e* (Mylasa). -μενετέος, α, ον, *not to be sustained*, Stob.2.6.6:—also -μενετός, ή, όν, ibid. -μένητος, ον, = ἀνυπομόνητος, Phld.*Mus.* p.91K. *-μνηστος, ον, dub. sens. in Id.*Piet.*98. -μόνητος, ον, *unbearable*, κακόν Chrysipp.*Stoic.*3.131; ἀ. θεάσασθαι Arist.*Mir.* 843ᵃ15, cf. D.S.3.29, D.H.6.51, Crates *Ep.*29, etc. Adv. -τως Hsch. s.v. ἀστέκτως. II. Act., *not enduring*, Procl.*Par.Ptol.*224. -νόητος, ον, *unsuspected*, πρός τι *in* a thing, D.61.11; ἄνθρωποι Plb.13. 6.8. 2. *unexpected*, ἐλπίς Id.2.57.6. Adv. -τως Id.1.84.9. II. Act., *unsuspecting*, τοῦ μέλλοντος Id.4.10.7, cf. Phld.*Mort.*13, cf. 39. Adv. -τως *unsuspiciously*, Plb.5.39.2. -παστος, ον, of a stone, *with nothing spread below it*, *IG*7.3073.164 (Lebad.).

***ἀνύποπτος**, ον, *without suspicion*, i.e., 1. Pass., *unsuspected*, Th.3.43 (Comp.), X.*Cyr.*5.3.11; λεηλασίαι *unexpected*, Arr.*Tact.*17. 5. Adv. -τως *unsuspectedly*, Aen.Tact.10.20, al., Men.666. 2. *free from risk*, κίνησις Sor.1.55; θάνατος Phld.*Sto.Herc.*339.4. 3. Act., *unsuspecting*, πράξεως Plb.8.27.2, Plu.*Brut.*8. Adv. -τως Th. 1.146; ἀ. ἔχειν Arist.*Top.*156ᵇ18; *unhesitatingly*, Plu.2.614b.

**ἀνυπό-πτωτος**, ον, (ὑποπίπτω) *not coming under the cognizance of*, τῇ αἰσθήσει S.E.*M.*7.345, etc. 2. = ἀμετάπτωτος, Herill.*Stoic.*1. 191. -στάλτως, Adv. = ἀνυποστόλως, ἐλευθεριάζοντες interpol. in Ammon.*in Cat.*2.8. -στασία, ἡ, gloss on ἀτλησία, Hsch. *-στασις, εως, ἡ, *unsubstantiality*, Sch.E.*Hec.*702 (leg. -στασίαν). -στᾰτος, ον, *not to be withstood, irresistible*, δύναμις Pl.*Lg.*686b; ἀνάγκη X.*Lac.*10.7; φρόνημα, πόλις, Id.*Cyr.*5.2.33, *Mem.*4.4.15; τολμήματα D.54.38; ἀ. τισὶν ἀνταγωνισταί D.Chr.8.17. Adv. -τως Aristobul.ap. Eus.*PE*8.10. II. *without sure foundation*, ἡ τῆς ὑποθέσεως ἀρχὴ ἀ. Plb.1.5.3, cf. 12.25ᶠ.4; ἀ. εἶναι τὰς τῶν ὅλων ἀρχάς D.L.9.99, cf. Ath. 3.98c. 2. *without sediment*, οὖρα Aret.*SD*1.13, cf. *CD*1.13, Hp. *Epid.*2.2.23. 3. *unsubstantial*, *Stoic.*2.117, Syrian.*in Metaph.*25. 3; of accidental or secondary qualities, Syn.Alch.p.62B.; *non-existent*, Ps.-Archyt.ap.Simp.*in Ph.*785.17; μαντικαί D.L.7.149; τὸ ἀ... τῆς μαντικῆς Diogenian.Epicur.4.79; κειμήλιον Secund.*Sent.* 11. 4. *without significance*, φωνή Them.*in Ph.*124.27. *-στολος, ον, *using no concealment, frank, fearless*, ῥήτωρ Poll.4.21; τὸ ἀ. τῆς ὀργῆς J.*AJ*16.3.1. Adv. -λως D.Chr.13.16, Phld.*Rh.*1.109S., Alciphr.3.39, etc. -στρεπτος, ον, *unreturning*, Suid. s.v. ἄνοστος. Adv. -τί *without turning back*, Pythag.ap.Phlp.*in de An.*116. 32. *-στροφος, ον, *from which none return*, Orph.*H.*56; ὁδός Lyd.*Mag.*3.14. 2. of diseases, *without relapse*, Hp.*Epid.*6.3. 4. -τακτέω, *to be unruly, insubordinate*, Sch.Od.19.179. -τακτος, ον, of persons or things, *not made subject*, τινί *Ep.Hebr.*2.8, cf. J.*AJ*11.6.6, Arr.*Epict.*4.1.161; ἀ. ὁ βασιλεύς Artem.2.30; *unrestrained, free*, Ph.1.473, cf. Arr.*Epict.*2.10.1. 2. *not to be classified under heads, confused*, Plb.3.36.4; *irregular*, ποιήματα, of dithyrambs, Demetr.Lac.*Herc.*1014.12, Zen.2.15. II. of persons, *independent*, Ptol.*Tetr.*61; in bad sense, *unruly*, 1*Ep.Ti.*1.9, *Ep.Tit.*1.6 and 10, *PMag.Par.*1.1367. Adv. -τως *impatiently*, Hsch. s.v. ἀστέκτως. III. of Verbs, *having no first aorist*, *AB*1087. -ταξία, ἡ, *indiscipline*, Phld.*Lib.*p.63O. *-τίμητος [ῐ], ον, *that cannot be adequately punished*, ἀσέβεια J.*AJ*16.11.8, cf. 15.7.10. Adv. -τως *without fear of punishment*, 16.9.1. -τλητος, ον, *not to be borne*, Sch.E.*Ph.*93.

**ἀνύπουλος**, ον, *without disguise*, Ph.2.435; γνώμη *without arrière-pensée*, Chor.*Milt.*50.

**ἀνύπους**, ὁ, ἡ, only in Hsch. ἀνύποδας· ταχύποδας, ἀπὸ τοῦ τοῖς ποσὶν ἀνύειν, prob. due to a misreading of S.*Aj.*837 Ἐρινῦς τανύποδας.

**ἀνυπο-φόρητος**, ον, *insufferable*, *EM*115.18. -χώρητος, gloss on ἀνύπεικτος, Hsch.

**ἀνύπτιος**, ον, *not passive*, of reciprocal Verbs, D.L.7.64.

**ἄνυρις**· ἄδικος, ἀσεβής, and **ἄνυρος**· ἄδικος, Hsch.

**ἀνῠ-σιεργός**, όν, *finishing work, industrious*, Theoc.28.14 [ᾰ metri gr.], cf. Phld.*Hom.*p.30O. -σιμος, ον, (ἀνύω) = ἀνυστικός, *efficacious, effectual*, πρός τι Pl.*Lg.*716d: Comp., εἰς τι οὐδὲν -ώτερον X. *Cyr.*1.6.22, cf. Aret.*CA*1.10, Jul.*Or.*5.178a: Sup. -ώτατος Pl. l.c., Luc.*Cal.*16; λόγος D.Chr.39.8. Adv. -μως Pl.*Tht.*144b, Ps.-Ale Aphr.*in SE*164.33: Sup. -ώτατα Pl.*R.*518d. 2. Pass., *capable accomplishment*, J.*BJ*5.5.1, cf. Porph.*VP*27, Serapion in *Cat.Co Astr.*1.100. -σις, εως, ἡ, (ἀνύω) *accomplishment*, ἄ. δ' οὐκ ἔσσετ αὐτῶν Il.2.347; οὐκ ἄνυσίν τινα δήομεν we find no *end, accompli* nothing, Od.4.544; χρήμασιν ὧν ἄ. γίνεται οὐδεμία Thgn.462; οὐ ἄνυσις there is no *respite*, Theoc.25.93.—Poet. and late Pros as Plu.2.77b. -σμα, ατος, τό, *accomplishment, end*, Sch.Od. 299. -στέον or -στέα, *one must accomplish*, Suid. -στικό ή, όν, *effective, practical*, Arist.*Phgn.*813ᵃ4; τὸ ἀ. D.H.*Vett.Cens.*5.2 Comp. -ώτερος Plb.8.5.3, cf. Archig.ap.Gal.8.154: Sup., [Longin. *Rh.*p.182H. -στός, όν, *to be accomplished, practicable*, οὐκ ἐστ ἀνυστὸν τόνδε σοι κατακτανεῖν E.*Heracl.*961, cf. D.Chr.12.34; τ γὰρ μερόπεσσιν ἀ.; Opp.*H.*2.4: neut., ὡς ἀνυστόν [ἐστι], like ὡ δυνατόν, ὡς ἀ. κάλλιστα Diog.Apoll.3; ὡς ἀ. ἀνθρωπίνῃ γνώμῃ Hp *Nat.Puer.*29; σιγῇ ὡς ἀ. as silently *as possible*, X.*An.*1.8.11; ἀ. μετριωτάτῳ Id.*Lac.*1.3; τὰ ἀνθρώπῳ ἀ. Arist.*Fr.*44. 2. o persons, *able, ready*, πρὸς λόγους Hp.*Decent.*3. -τής, οῦ, ὁ, = Lat. *exactor*, Just.*Nov.*163(2)(pl.). *-τικός, ή, όν, = ἀνυστικός, *effective*, X.*Eq.Mag.*2.6 (Comp.), *Oec.*20.22 (Sup.), Plb.8.3.3 (Comp.); λόγοι S.E.*M.*9.182 (Sup.); of persons, J.*BJ*5.9.1 (Comp.), 1.17.8 (Sup.). 2. *rapid*, ἀνυτικωτέραν ποιεῖν τὴν κίνησιν Arist.*PA*682ᵇ1. Adv. -κῶς [Longin.]*Rh.*p.190H. -τω or **ἀνύτω**, Att. form of ἀνύω.

**ἀνῠφ-αίνω**, *weave anew*, ἀ. τὸ ἀνατριβόμενον *renew* that which wears out, Pl.*Phd.*87d, cf. Olymp.*Vit.Pl.*p.3W., *in Alc.*p.198C. -άντης, ου, ὁ, *one who weaves anew*, Suid.:—fem. -άντρια, Eust.1764.60.

**ἀνυφαίρετος**, ον, f.l. for ἀναφ-, D.H.*Dem.*34.

**ἀνύφαντος**, ον, *not woven*, Ael.Dion.*Fr.*80.

***ἀνυψόω**, *raise up, exalt*, Lxx *Ps.*112(113).7, al., *PGen.*51.27 (iii A.D.):—Med., *AP*7.748 (Antip. Sid.):—Pass., ὁ λόγος -οῦται πρὸς θεῖον δικαστήν Lyd.*Mag.*2.16.

***ἀνύω** (ἀνῦ), Il.4.56, Ar.*Ra.*606, Att. **ἀνύτω** or **ἁνύτω** Th.2.75, Pl.*R.*486c, al.: impf. ἤνυον Hdt.9.66, E.*Hec.*1167: fut. ἀνύσω [ῠ], S.*Aj.*607, Ar.*Ra.*649, Ep. ἐξ-ανύω Il.11.365: aor. ἤνῠσα Od.24. 71, A.*Pers.*726, etc.; poet. ἤνυσσα (Dor. ἀν-) Pi.*P.*12.11, A.R.4. 413, Ep. ἄνυσσα [ᾰ] Hes.*Th.*954, Maiist.57 (ὑπ-): pf. ἤνῠκα Pl.*Plt.* 264b:—Pass., pf. ἤνυσμαι Plb.8.29.1, etc., δι-ήνυσμαι X.*Cyr.*1.4.28: aor. ἠνύσθην Plb.32.3.17, D.Chr.3.127: fut. ἀνυσθήσομαι J.*AJ*1.19.1, Ael.*VH*1.21:—Med., ἀνύομαι Pi.*P.*2.49, Bion *Fr.*4.6: impf. ἠνυτόμην A.*Ag.*1159: fut. ἀνύσομαι (v. infr.): aor. ἠνυσάμην A.*Pr.*700, S.*Tr.* 995 (lyr.), inf. ἀνύσασθαι X.*An.*7.7.24 (Valck.).—Non-thematic forms are found in poets: impf. Act. ἄνῠμες, Dor. for ἤνυμεν, Theoc.7.10: pres. Pass. ἄνυται Opp.*H.*3.427, Nic.*Al.*599: impf. Pass. ἤνῠτο Od.5. 243 (nisi leg. ἤνετο); Dor. ἄνῠτο Theoc.2.92. [ῠ in all parts: hence ἀνῦσαι in Tryph.126, ἀνῦσάμενοι in *AP*10.12 should be written with σσ: ἀνῦων is corrupt in Nonn.*D.*21.16]:—*effect, accomplish*, ἤνυτο δ' ἔργον Od.5.243 (v. supr.), cf. A.*Pers.*726, etc.; πρὸς θανάτῳ θάνατον ἀνύσασα S.*Tr.*886; ἀρωγάν Id.*Ph.*1145 (lyr.); τοὔπος ὡς ἄρ' ὀρθὸν ἤνυσας Id. *Ant.*1178, cf. *OC*454: abs., οὐδὲν ἤνυε he *did no good*, Hdt.9.66; εἴ τι ἔμελλεν ἀνύτειν whatever was likely *to forward the work*, Th.2.75; σμικρὸν ἀνύτειν Pl.*Sph.*230a, al.; ἧσσον ἀνύτειν Th.2.76; οὐδὲν ἤνυε τούτοις D.21.104; ἀ. εἴς τι *to conduce* towards.., Pl.*Ax.*369d: c. acc. et inf., Ἀπόλλων.. ἐκεῖνον ἤνυσε φονέα γενέσθαι *brought it to pass* that .., S.*OT*720:—Med., *accomplish for one's own advantage*, ἀνύσσεσθαι τάδε ἔργα (if not in pass. sense, *will be accomplished*) Od.16.373, cf. Hp.*Ep.*27; θεός.. τέκμαρ ἀνύεται Pi.*P.*2.49, cf. Ar.*Pl.*196, dub. in Pl.*Phd.*69d. 2. *make an end of, destroy*, φλόξ σε ἤνυσεν Od.24.71; *kill*, Pi.*P.*12.11. 3. c. dupl. acc., *make, cause to be*, ἠνύσατ' ἐκτοπίαν φλόγα S.*OT*166 (lyr.), Nic.*Al.*400. 4. *make*, εἰκόνα *AP* 12.56 (Mel.). 5. *finish a journey*, ὅσσον τε πανημερίη γλαφυρὴ νηῦς ἤνυσεν (sc. ὁδοῦ) as much as a ship *gets over* in a day, Od.4.357; so πολλὴν κέλευθον ἤνυσεν A.*Pers.*748; πορείαν Onos.6.1: c. acc. loci, ὄφρα τάχιστα νηῦς ἀνύσειε θαλάσσης.. ὕδωρ Od.15.294, cf. Thgn.511, S.*Ant.*231. 6. in Trag. freq. abs. (sc. ὁδόν or κέλευθον), *make one's way, win*, πρὸς πόλιν Id.*Tr.*657 (lyr.); ἐπὶ ἀκτάν E.*Hipp.*743; also θάλαμον ἀνύτειν (i.e. εἰς θάλαμον) *reach* the bridal chamber, S.*Ant.* 805 (lyr.); ἐς Ἀΐδαν Id.*Aj.*607 (lyr.), E.*Supp.*1142 (lyr.): metaph., ζυγὰ ἤνυσε δούλια Τροία (s.v.l.) Id.*Tr.*599 (Τροίᾳ Sch.): rarely with inf. instead of acc., στρατὸς ἤνυσε περᾶν *succeeded in* crossing, A.*Pers.* 721: with Adj., *come to be*, εὐδαίμων ἀνύσει καὶ μέγας S.*Ph.*720 (lyr.). 7. in Pass. of Time, *come to an end*, χρόνος ἄνυτο Theoc. 2.92, cf. Eus.Mynd.63. 8. in Pass. of persons, *grow up*, ἠνυτόμαν τροφαῖς (lyr.) A.*Ag.*1159. 9. *get, obtain*, γαστρὶ φορβὰν S.*Ph.*711 (lyr.), cf. Theoc.5.144; τίνος χρείας ἀνύσαι; i.e. τίνος χρείας προσπίπτετε, ὥστε ἀνύσαι αὐτήν; S.*OC*1755:—Med., χρεῖαν ἠνύσασθε ye obtained it, A.*Pr.*700, cf. *Ch.*858, S.*Tr.*995 (lyr.); τοῦτο ἐκ Μοιρέων ἠνύσατο *AP*7.506 (Leon.). II. c. part., οὐκ ἀνύω φθονέουσα *I gain* nothing by grudging, Il.4.56. 2. in Com., *do quickly, make haste*, οὐ μέλλειν.., ἀλλ' ἀνύειν Ar.*Pl.*607, cf. *Ra.*606; οὐκ ἀνύσεις τι; *make haste!* ib.649; ἀλλ' ἄνυσον, οὐ μέλλειν ἐχρῆν *Fr.*102: c. part., ἄνυε πράττων *make haste* about it, *Pl.*413; ἄνυσον ὑποδησάμενος *make haste* and get your shoes on, *V.*1168, cf. *Av.*241; ἄνυσόν ποτ' ἐξελθών Pherecr.40: more freq. in part. ἀνύσας, or ἀνύσας τι with a Verb, ἄνοιγ', ἄνοιγ' ἀνύσας *make haste* and open the door, Ar.*Nu.*181; ἀνάβαιν' ἀνύσας *V.*398; σὺ δ' ἔγχεον πιεῖν ἀνύσας τι *Eq.*119, cf. *V.*202,847, 1158, *Pl.*648,974; βοηθησάτω τις ἀνύσας *Ach.*571; νῦν οὖν ἀνύσαντε φροντίσωμεν *Eq.*71; ἀκολουθήσεις ἐμοὶ ἀνύσας τι *Nu.*506, cf. 1253; ἀπόδωμεν ἀνύσαντε *Pax*872. (The distinction of meaning ἀνύτω *accomplish, make way*, ἀνύω *hasten*, is doubtful, cf. *AB*411.—Att.

ύω acc. to Hdn.Gr.1.541, Phryn.*PS*p.23B., cf. καθανύσαι X.*HG* 1.15 (Hsch.); but κατανύειν (q.v.) occurs in Trag., cf. ταῦτ' ἀνύεται Ar.*Pl.*196.) (I.-E. *sen*-, pres. stem *s̥neu*-, cf. Skt. *sanoti* wins'.)

ἄνω (A), imper. ἀνέτω S.*Ichn.*70, inf. ἄνειν Pl.*Cra.*415a, part. ἄνων, ipf. ἦνον, etc. (v. infr.): aor. ἤνεσα *IG*7.3226 (Orchom. Boeot.), *Hymn.Is.*35, prob. in *AP*7.701.1 (Diod.) (ἤνεσ' codd.):—= ἀνύω, ἀνύτω, *accomplish, finish*, ἦνον ὁδόν Od.3.496; οὔτ' ἄν τι θύων οὔτ' ἐπισπένδων ἄνοις A.*Fr.*161 (Dobree, cf. *AB*406); ἀλλ' οὐδὲν ἦνεν E.*Andr.* 132; ἢ τὸ δέον..ἤνομεν; S.*Ichn.*98; ταῦτα πρὸς ἀνδρός ἐστ' ἄνοντος ἐς σωτηρίαν (cf. ἀνύω 1.6) Ar.*V.*369; ἀρυσσάμενοι ποτὸν ἤνομεν *AP* 1.64 (Agath.). II. Pass., *come to an end, be finished*, mostly of period of time, μάλα γὰρ νὺξ ἄνεται night *is quickly drawing to a close*, Il.10.251; ἔτος ἀνόμενον the *waning* year, Hdt.7.20; ἦμαρ ἀνόμενον A.R.2.494; ἀνομένου τοῦ μηνός *SIG*577.30 (Milet., iii/ii B.C.); also ὅππως..ἔργον ἄνοιτο Il.18.473; ἤνετο τὸ ἔργον Hdt.1.189, 8.71; ἀνομένων βημάτων A.*Ch.*799; ὁππόταν θήρης..ἔργον ἄνηται Opp.*H.*5.442: impers., λιταῖς ἄνεται, = λιταὶ ἀνύονται, Pi.*O.*8.8. [ᾱ Hom., exc. Il.18.473: afterwds. common, cf. A. l.c., Opp.*H.* l.c. Orig. ἄνϝω, cf. ἀνύω.]

*ἄνω (B), Aeol. ὄνω, Adv., (ἀνά): I. with Verbs implying Motion, *upwards*, ἄ. ὤθεσκε ποτὶ λόφον Od.11.596; ἄ. ἀπὸ θαλάσσης ἀναπλεῖν *up* stream, Hdt.2.155; ἄ. ποταμῶν χωροῦσι παγαί E.*Med.*410 (lyr.), hence "ἄ. ποταμῶν", proverbial, D.19.287, etc.; κόνις δ' ἄ. φορεῖτο S. *El.*714; κονιορτὸς ἄ. ἐχώρει Th.4.34; ἡ ἄ. ὁδός the *upward* road, Pl. *R.*621c; ἄ. ἰόντι going *up the country* (i.e. *inland*, v. infr. II.1f), Hdt.2.8; ἄ. κάτω, v. infr. II. 2; πέμπειν ἄ., i.e. from the nether world, A.*Pers.*645 (lyr.), cf. *Ch.*147; σύριγγες ἄ. φυσῶσι μέλαν μένος S. *Aj.*1412 (lyr.). II. with Verbs implying Rest, *aloft, on high*, ib.240, etc.; τὸ ἄ. Pl.*Phdr.*248a, etc. b. *on earth*, opp. *the world below*, νέρθε κἀπὶ γῆς ἄ. S.*OT*416; ἡνίκ' ἦσθ' ἄ. Id.*El.*1167; ἄ. βλέπειν Id. *Ph.*1348; ἄ. ἐπὶ [τῆς] γῆς Pl.*Phd.*109c; οἱ ἄ. the *living*, opp. οἱ κάτω the *dead*, S.*Ant.*1068, cf. *Ph.*1348, etc.; τὰ ἄ. πράγματα the world *above*, Luc.*Cont.*1. c. *in heaven*, opp. *earth*, οἱ ἄ. θεοί the gods *above*, S.*Ant.*1072; κῆρυξ τῶν ἄ. τε καὶ κάτω A.*Ch.*124: esp. in *NT*, ἐκ τῶν ἄ. εἰμί *Ev.Jo.*8.23; ἡ ἄ. Ἱερουσαλήμ *Ep.Gal.*4.26; ἡ ἄ. κλῆσις *Ep.Phil.*3.14. d. generally, of relative position, ὁ δῆμος ἄ. καθῆτο *in the upper quarter* of the city, i.e. the Pnyx, D.18.169; ἡ ἄ. βουλή, i.e. the Areopagus, Plu.*Sol.*19; βαλλόμενοι ὑπὸ τῶν ἄ. by those *above on the roofs*, Th.4.48; τὰ ἄ. X.*An.*4.3.25; τὰ ἄ. τῆς οἰκίας, opp. θεμέλια, Id.*Eq.*1.2; οἱ ἄ. τόποι *OGI*111.17. e. geographically, *on the upper side*, i.e. *on the north*, ἄ. πρὸς βορέην Hdt.1.72; οὔτε τὰ ἄ. χωρία οὔτε τὰ κάτω [οὔτε τὰ πρὸς τὴν ἠῶ οὔτε τὰ πρὸς τὴν ἑσπέρην] Id.1.142; ὁ ἄ. τόπος Pl.*R.*435e. f. *inward from the coast*, ἡ ἄ. Ἀσίη Hdt.1.95; τὰ ἄ. τῆς Ἀσίης ib.177; ἡ ἄ. ὁδός the *upper* or *inland* road, Id.7.128, X.*An.*3.1.8; ἡ ἄ. πόλις, opp. *the Piraeus*, Th.2.48; in full, οἱ ἀπὸ θαλάσσης ἄ. ib.83; ἡ ἄ. Μακεδονία Plu.*Pyrrh.*11; ὁ ἄ. βασιλεύς the king *of the upper country*, i.e. of Persia, X.*An.*7.1.28. g. in the race-course, τὰ ἄ. *turning-post*, Pl.*R.*613b; cf. κάτω. h. in the body, τὰ ἄ. the *upper* parts, opp. τὰ κάτω, Arist.*GA*741b28, al.; ἡ ἄ. κοιλία Id.*Mete.*360b23. i. of Time, *formerly, of old*, εἰς τὸ ἄ. reckoning *upwards* or *backwards*, of generations, Pl.*Tht.*175b; οἱ ἄ. men *of olden time*, Id.*Criti.*110b; οἱ ἄ. τοῦ γένους Id.*Lg.*878a; αἱ ἄ. μητρός the mother's *lineal ancestors*, Id.*R.*461c, cf. infr. C; ἐν τοῖς ἄ. χρόνοις D.18.310. k. *above*, in referring to a passage, Pl.*Grg.* 508e; ἐν τοῖς ἄ. λόγοις *R.*503d, cf. Arist.*Rh.*1412b33, etc. l. of tones in the voice, οἱ ἄ. τόνοι Plu.*Cic.*3. m. metaph., ἄ. βαίνειν walk *proudly*, Philostr.*VA*1.13; ἄ. φρονεῖν Hld.7.23. n. *higher, more general*, of κατηγορίαι, Arist.*APo.*82a23. 2. ἄ. καὶ κάτω *up and down, to and fro*, εἶρπ' ἄ. τε καὶ κάτω E.*HF*953; ἄ. καὶ κ. φεύγειν Ar.*Ach.*21; ἄ. τε καὶ κ. κυκᾶν Id.*Eq.*866; περιπατεῖν ἄ. κ. Id.*Lys.* 709. b. *upside-down, topsy-turvy*, τὰ μὲν ἄ. κ. θήσω, τὰ δὲ κ. ἄ. Hdt.3.3; πάντ' ἄ. τε καὶ κ. στρέφων τίθησιν A.*Eu.*650; τρέπουσα τύρβ' ἄ. κ. Id.*Fr.*311, cf. Ar.*Av.*3; ἄ. κ. συγχεῖν E.*Ba.*349; ἄ. καὶ κ. ποιεῖν τὰ πράγματα D.9.36; τοὺς νόμους στρέφειν 21.19; πόλλ' ἄ., τὰ δ' αὖ κ. κυλίνδοντ' ἐλπίδες Pi.*O.*12.6; πολλάκις ἐμαυτὸν ἄ. κ. μετέβαλλον *backwards and forwards*, Pl.*Phd.*96a, cf. *Prt.*356d. 3. ἄ. ἔχειν τὸ πνεῦμα *pant* or *gasp*, Men.23, cf. Sosicr.1.

B. as Prep. with gen., *above*, ἡ ἄ. Ἅλυος Ἀσίη Hdt.1.130, cf. 103, Call.*Jov.*24; αἱ ἄ. μητρός (v. supr. II. 1 i); ἄ. τοῦ γόνατος *above* the knee, Thphr.*Char.*4.4; ἀπὸ ἄ. τῆς χθονὸς ταύτης Lxx 3*Ki.*14. 15. 2. with partitive gen., αἰθέρος ἄ. ἐλεῖν dub. in S.*Ph.*1092, cf. E.*Or.*1542; γῆς ἥκοντ' ἄ. Id.*HF*616; μικρὸν προαγαγὼν ἄ. τῶν πραγμάτων Aeschin.2.34.

C. Comp. ἀνωτέρω, abs., *higher*, ἀ. θακῶν..Ζεύς A.*Pr.*314; ἀ. οὐδὲν τῶν πρηγμάτων προκοπτομένων not getting on any *farther*, Hdt. 1.190; ἀδελφῷ ἢ πατρὶ ἢ ἔτι ἀ. Pl.*Lg.*880b; οὐ προήϊσαν ἀ. τὸ πρὸς ἑσπέρης Hdt.8.130. 2. c. gen., ἀ. Σάμου ib.132; ἀ. γίγνεσθαί τινων X.*An.*4.2.25; ἀ. τῶν μαστῶν *above* them, ib.1.4.17; later ἀνώτερον Plb.1.7.2, etc.; cf. ἀνώτερος. II. Sup. ἀνωτάτω, ἐς τοὺς ἀ. (sc. στάντας) Hdt.7.23; ἡ ἀ. κώμη X.*An.*7.4.11; ἀνῳκίσανθ' ὅπως ἀ. Ar.*Pax* 207; ἡ ἀ. ἄσκησις the *highest*, Arr.*Epict.*3.24.84, cf. Ph.1.33, al.; τὰ ἀ. τῶν γενῶν Arist.*Metaph.*998b18, cf. Zeno *Stoic.*1.51, S.E.*P.* 1.138; τὰ ἀ. τρία Ph.1.321; ἡ ἀ. διαίρεσις Ps.-Alex.Aphr.*in SE*20.27.

*ἄνωγα, old Ep. pf. with pres. sense: ἄνωγα, -ας, -ε, without augm., Il. and Trag., Hdt.3.81; 1 pl. ἄνωγμεν *h.Ap.*528: imper. ἄνωγε E.*Or.*119, more freq. ἄνωχθι Il.23.158, A.*Ch.*772, E.*Alc.*1044; 3 sg. ἀνωγέτω Od.2.195, ἀνώχθω Il.11.189; 2 pl. ἀνώγετε Od.23.132, ἄνωχθε 22.437, E.*Rh.*987; subj. ἀνώγῃ Il.7.74, Hdt.7.104, ἀνώγωμεν Herod.3.31; inf. ἀνωγέμεν Il.13.56; part. ἀνώγουσα Herod.7.101: plpf. with impf. sense, 3 sg. ἠνώγει Il.6.170, S.*OC*1598; without augm. ἀνώγει Od.2.385; Ion. ἠνώγεα ib.9.44, 17.55:—but ἀνώγει in Il.6. 439, 19.102, Od.5.139, 357, Hes.*Th.*549, Hdt.7.104 is pres. in sense, and must be referred to pres. ἀνώγω (unless corrected to ἄνωγεν); also 2 dual ἀνώγετον Il.4.287, and (later) 2 sg. ἀνώγεις Q.S.13.238:—from this pres. are formed impf. ἤνωγον Il.9.578, Od.14.237, or ἄνωγον Il.5.805, Od.3.35, etc.; ἤνωγες Maiist.17; ἤνωγε *h.Cer.*297, Hes.*Op.*68; 3 pl. ἄνωγον *Inscr.Cypr.*135 H.: fut. ἀνώξω Od.16.404: aor. ἤνωξα Hes.*Sc.*479; subj. ἀνώξομεν, Ep. for -ωμεν, Il.15.295; inf. ἀνῶξαι Od.10.531. Il.7.394, the impf. ἠνώγεον implies pres. ἀνωγέω:—Pass., ἄνωκται· κελεύεται, Hsch.:—poet. and Ion. Verb, also in Cypr., *Inscr.Cypr.* l.c., *command, order*, esp. of kings and masters, Il.5.899, etc.; also of equals and inferiors, *advise, urge*, 16.8, Od.2.195, etc.: constr. c. acc. pers. et inf., σιωπᾶν λαὸν ἀνώγει *bade* the people keep silence, Il.2.280, cf. 4.287, etc.; πατὴρ ἄνωγέ σ'.. αὐδᾶν A.*Pr.*947, cf. 1037, etc.; πράσσειν ἄνωγας οὖν με..τάδε; S.*Tr.* 1247; σιγᾶν ἄνωγα (sc. σε) Id.*El.*1458: in Hom. also c. dat. pers., Od.10.531, 20.139 sq., cf. A.R.1.693: c. acc. pers. only, θυμὸς ἄνωγέ με my spirit *bids, prompts* me, freq. in Hom.: abs., ἐποτρύνει καὶ ἀνώγει Il.15.43; κέλομαι καὶ ἄνωγα Od.3.317.

ἀνώγαιον or ἀνώγεον, τό, (ἄνω, γαῖα) *anything raised from the ground*: *the upper floor of a house*, used as a granary, X.*An.*5.4.29 (s.v.l.), Antiph.312; as a dining-room, *Ev.Marc.*14.15, *Ev.Luc.*22. 12. 2. *prison*, Suid. (ἀνώγεον in *GDI*1581 (Dodona); ἀνάγαιον and ἀνώκαιον are also found in codd., cf. *AB*405, Suid.)

*ἀνωγή, ἡ, (ἄνωγα) *command, exhortation*, A.R.1.1134; θείαν δι' ἀνωγάν *Philol.*71.6 (Argos).

ἄνωδα, Arc., = ἄνωθε, dub. in *IG*5(2).262.17 (Mantinea, v B.C.).

ἀνωδίνω [ῑ], *to be in labour, bring forth*, Nonn.*D.*41.167.

ἀνωδόρκας· βρίγκος ἢ ἰχθύς (Theb.), Hsch.

ἄνῳδος, ον, *songless*, Arist.*HA*488a34.

ἀνωδῠν-ία, ἡ, *freedom from pain*, Protag.9, Plot.1.4.6: in pl., *pain-free periods*, Philagr.ap.Aët.12.20. -ος, ον, (ὀδύνη) *free from pain*, οἰδήματα Hp.*Prog.*7, cf. D.Chr.32.57; τὸ ἐν ἀ. καὶ ἀνάλγητον Arist.*Xen.*974a19; of persons, S.*Ph.*883; -ώτερος γίγνεσθαι *suffer less pain*, Hp.*Prorrh.*2.7; τὸ ἀνώδυνον, = ἀνωδυνία, Plu.2.102d. Adv. ἀνωδύνως, τίκτεσθαι Hp.*Coac.*527, cf. Plu.*Cic.*2; ἰᾶσθαι D.Chr.41.9: Sup. -ώτατα Hp.*Acut.*4. 2. *causing no pain, harmless*, τὸ μὴ φρονεῖν γὰρ κάρτ' ἀ. κακόν S.*Aj.*554b; ἁμάρτημα ἢ αἶσχος ἀ., definition of τὸ γελοῖον, Arist.*Po.*1449a35. Adv. -ως, ἰάσασθαι τὴν πατρίδα Plu. *Cleom.*10. II. Act., *allaying pain*, Hp.*Aph.*5.22, Dsc.4.68 (Comp. and Sup.); φάρμακον ἀ. *anodyne*, Plu.2.614c:—the epitaph of a physician in *IG*14.1879 combines both signfs., πολλούς τε σώσας φαρμάκοις ἀνωδύνοις, ἀνώδυνον τὸ σῶμα νῦν ἔχει θανών.

*ἄνωθεν and ἄνωθε (Ar.*Ec.*698), Dor. ἄνωθα *Tab.Herad.*1.17: (ἄνω):—Adv. of Place, *from above, from on high*, θεοὺς ἄ. γῆς ἐποπτεύειν ἄχη A.*Ag.*1579; ὕδατος ἄ. γενομένου Th.4.75; βάλλειν ἄ. Id.7. 84; *from the interior* of a country, Id.1.59, X.*An.*7.7.2; esp. from inner Asia, Plu.*Dem.*14; from the north, Hdt.4.105. 2. like ἄνω, *above, on high*, opp. κάτωθεν or κάτω, A.*Ag.*871 (dub.): of the gods, Id.*Supp.*597 (lyr.), Pl.*Lg.*717b; of men on earth, οἱ ἄ. the *living*, A.*Ch.*834 (lyr.), E.*Hel.*1014; those *on deck* (in a ship), Th.7.63; of birds *of the air*, S.*El.*1058 (lyr.); ἡ ἄ. Φρυγία *upper* Phrygia, D.23. 155. b. rarely c. gen., ἄ. τοῦ στρατοπέδου Hdt.1.75; τοῦ καρποῦ Hp.*Art.*80; τῆς νεώς Plu.*Them.*12. II. in narrative or inquiry, *from the beginning, from farther back*, ἄ. ἄρχεσθαι, ἐπιχειρεῖν, Pl.*Phlb.* 44d, *Lg.*781d; ἄ. ἐξετάζειν τὸ γένος D.44.69, cf. Men.*Epit.*23; in quotations, *above, earlier*, Sch.E.*Ph.*249, etc.: οἱ ἔμπροσθεν καὶ ἄ. γονεῖς *ancestors*, Pl.*Ti.*18d; Κορίνθιαι εἰμὲς ἄ. *by descent*, Theoc.15.91, cf. 22. 164, Call.*Aet.*3.1.32; πονηρὸς ἄ. a *born* rogue, D.45.80; ἐκ προγόνων ἄ. τετιμημένος *IG*2².1072; ἄ. ἀναμάρτητον *from early life*, Phld. *Sto.Herc.*339.17.16; ἐν τοῖς ἄ. χρόνοις D.9.41. 2. τὰ ἄ. *higher, more universal principles*, Pl.*Phd.*101d, cf. Arist.*APo.*97a33. 3. *over again, anew, afresh*, φιλίαν ἄ. ποιεῖται J.*AJ*1.18.3, Artem.1.14, cf. *Ev.Jo.*3.3; πάλιν ἄ. *Ep.Gal.*4.9, cf. Harp. s.v. ἀνάδικοι κρίσεις; κτίστης ἄνωθε γενόμενος *IG*7.2712.58.

*ἀνωθέω, *push up* or *forth*, ἀνώσαντες πλέον (sc. ναῦν) they *pushed off from shore* and sailed, Od.15.553; ἀ. τὴν πόλιν εἰς τοὺς πολεμίους Th.8.93:—Pass., *to be thrust upwards*, Arist.*Pr.*931b35. 2. *push back*, Hp.*Art.*80; ὅστις σῖτον..ἐσαχθέντα ἀνωθοίη *SIG*37 A 10 (Teos):—Med., *repel, repulse*, οὗτοι ἦσαν οἱ βασιλέα..ἀνωσάμενοι Hdt.7.139, cf. 8.109. 3. *support*, of buoyant water, Olymp.*in Mete.*81.23, al. 4. metaph., *hand over*, τὰ πράγματα πρὸς τὸν δῆμον D.C.52. 17; *refer*, τὰς ἐλαττώσεις εἰς τοὺς στρατηγήσαντας Id.*Fr.*43.18. 5. intr., *push one's way up*, εἰς τὸ πρόσαντες J.*BJ*3.7.5.

ἄνωθον· ὀξύν, Hsch. (fort. ἄνωθρον).

ἀνωΐσ-τί [ῐ], Adv. of sq., *unlooked for*, Od.4.92. *-τος (A), ον, (οἴομαι) *unlooked for, unexpected*, ἀ. κακόν Il.21.39; ἀνωΐστων πολέων περ Hom.*Epigr.*5; βέλεα Mosch.2.75; κλάδοι Epic.Anon.*Oxy.* 214.1. Adv. -τως A.R.1.680. -τος (B), ον, prob. f.l. for ἀνοιστός, *referred*, ἀνωΐστου γενομένου ἐς τὴν Πυθίην the matter having been *referred to*.., Hdt.6.66. 2. *lifted up, raised*, Aret.*SA*2.11.

ἀνώλεθρος, ον, (ὄλεθρος) *indestructible*, Parm.8.3; ἀθάνατος καὶ ἀ. Anaximand.15, Pl.*Phd.*88b, 95b, Arist.*Mu.*396a31, Ocell.1.2; of roots, Thphr.*HP*3.12.2. II. Act., *not deadly, harmless*, ὄφεις Paus.10.17.12; of symptoms, *not fatal*, Aret.*SD*1.5.

ἀνωλέως· ἰσχυρός, Hsch.

ἀνωλόφυκτος, ον, (ὀλοφύζω) *unbewailed*, Hsch.

**ἀνωμᾰλ-έω**, *suffer ups and downs of fortune*, Nech.ap.Vett.Val. 279.28, cf. 65.6, Heph.Astr.2.28. **-ής**, ές, = ἀνώμαλος, Epicur. *Ep.*2 p.53 U., Arist.*Pr.*918$^a$11; ἡ φωνὴ μεταβάλλει ἐπὶ τὸ..ἀνωμαλέστερον Id.*HA*581$^a$18. Adv. -λῶς Id.*Ph.*265$^b$12. ⊛**-ία**, ἡ, *unevenness, irregularity*, Pl.*R.*547a, Arist.*HA*495$^b$2; of shape, Str.16.1.21; ἀ. τῶν στοιχείων, as cause of disease, Diocl.*Fr.*30: pl., Epicur.*Ep.*2 p.53 U. **2.** Astron., *irregular motion, anomaly*, ἀ. τῆς κινήσεως Gem.1.20, cf. Ptol. *Alm.*3.3, etc.; ἀ. ἐκλειπτικαί, of the moon's orbit, Plu.*Aem.*17. **II.** of conditions, *irregularity*, ἀ. καὶ ταραχή Isoc.2.6; ἀ. τῆς κτήσεως Arist.*Pol.*1270$^a$15; τύχης D.S.20.30, cf. 18.59: pl., Vett.Val.38.17. **III.** of persons, *inconsistency*, Aeschin.2.7 and 54, Plb.6.44.2, Plu.*Alc.*16; of style, *unevenness*, Id.2.45b. **IV.** Gramm., *deviation from rule, irregularity*, title of work by Chrysipp., *Stoic.*2.6, cf. Gell.2.25, etc.; *variety, diversity*, Arist.*GA*788$^a$24, A.D.*Adv.*205.18. **V.** *indisposition, 'malaise'*, Hld.7.19, Gal.7.435. **-ίζω**, *to be subject to vicissitude*, Vett.Val.57.4, 85.28. ⊛**-οκράς**, *unevenly mixed*, Hsch. **-ος**, ον, (ἀ- priv., ὁμαλός) *uneven, irregular*, χώρα Pl.*Lg.*625d; φύσις Id.*Ti.*58a; τὸ ἀ. τῆς ναυμαχίας Th.7.71 (cj.), cf. Arist.*Pr.*885$^a$15: and in Sup., Hp.*Aër.*13; of movements, Arist.*Ph.*228$^b$16, al.; of periods of time, Id.*GA*772$^b$7; of the voice, ib.788$^a$1. Adv. -λως, κινεῖσθαι Id.*Ph.*238$^a$22, cf. Pl.*Ti.*52e. **II.** of conditions, fortune, and the like, φεῦ τῶν βροτείων ὡς ἀ. τύχαι E.*Fr.*684; πόλις, πολιτεία, Pl.*Lg.*773b, *Mx.*238e; θέα Plot.6.7.34. Adv. -λως Hp.*Prog.*3, Isoc.7.29; ἀ. διατεθῆναι τὸ σῶμα fall into *precarious* health, Prisc.p.333 D. **III.** of persons, *inconsistent, capricious*, ὁμαλῶς ἀ. Arist.*Po.*1454$^a$26; ὄχλος, δαιμόνιον, App.*BC*3.42, *Pun.*59; πίθηκος Phryn.Com.20; τύχη *AP*10.96. Adv. -λως Isoc.9.44. **IV.** Gramm., of words *which deviate from a general rule, anomalous*, Diom.1.327 K.; but τὸ ἀ. τῆς συντάξεως *diversity* of construction, A.D.*Synt.*291.17. Adv. -λως Sch.Th.*Oxy.*853 v 18. **-ότης**, ητος, ἡ, = ἀνωμαλία, Pl.*Ti.*57e, 58c, *Placit.*2.30.2. **-ωσις**, v. ἀνομάλωσις.

**ἀνωμολογ-ημένως**, Adv. *admittedly*, Lib.*Decl.*50.39 (s.v.l.). ⊛**-ητος**, ον, *inconsistent*, Ptol.*Tetr.*47.

**ἄνωμος**, ον, *without shoulder*, Πελοπίδαι Suid.

**ἀνωμο-τί**, Adv. of sq., *without oath*, καὶ ὀμνύντας καὶ ἀ. Hdt.2.118. **-τος**, ον, (ὄμνυμι) *unsworn, not bound by oath*, ἡ γλῶσσ' ὀμώμοχ', ἡ δὲ φρὴν ἀ. E.*Hipp.*612; ἀ. μάρτυρες Antipho 5.12, cf. D.21.86; θεῶν ἀνώμοτος E.*Med.*737. Adv. -τως Aristid.*Or.*28(49).94. **II.** *not sworn to*, εἰρήνη D.19.204.

⊛**ἀνωνίς**, ίδος, ἡ, = ὄνωνις, Dsc.3.18, v.l. in Poet.ap.Plu.2.44e, cf. 485a.

**ἀνωνόμαστος**, ον, *nameless, ineffable*, E.*Hec.*714 (lyr.); ἀ. ὀσμή Ar.*Av.*1715.

**ἀνωνῠμ-εί** and **-ί**, Adv. *without name*, v.l. in Sch.D.T.p.18 H., *EM*764.22. ⊛**-ία**, ἡ, *namelessness*, Arat.146. ⊛**-ος**, ον, (from ὄνυμα, Aeol. for ὄνομα) *without name*, οὐ μὲν γάρ τις πάμπαν ἀ. ἔστ' ἀνθρώπων Od.8.552; ἡ Εὐρώπη..ἦν ἀ. Hdt.4.45; θεαί, i.e. the Furies, E.*IT*944; Ὅρκου παῖς ἐστὶν ἀ. Orac.ap.Hdt.6.86, cf. Pl.*Ti.*60a, Arist.*EN*1107$^b$2, prob. in *Po.*1447$^b$9, cf. Tz.*Diff.Poet.*11. **2.** *anonymous*, μήνυσις Lys.13.22, cf. D.C.66.11. **3.** *not to be named, unspeakable*, Aristid.*Or.*50(26).8. **4.** *difficult to name*, in Comp., Arist.*EE*1221$^a$40, Alex.Aphr.*in Mete.*197.23. **5.** Adv. -μως *without mentioning a name*, Men.Rh.p.391 S. **II.** *nameless, inglorious*, γῆρας Pi.*O.*1.82; γῆ πατρὶς οὐκ ἀ. E.*Hel.*16, cf. *Hipp.*1; ὄνομα ἀ. Ar.*Lys.*854; of persons, S.*Tr.*377, Pl.*Lg.*721c; ἀ. καὶ ἄδοξοι D.8.66, cf. Herod.6.14. Adv. -μως Poll.5.160.

⊛**ἄνωξις**, εως, ἡ, = ἀνωγή, Hsch.

**ἀνώξω**, v. ἄνωγα.

**ἀνώπιον**, τό, (ὀπή) *the part above the door*, Poll.2.53 (pl.).

**ἀνώπιστος**, ον, *unseen, unnoticed*, Hsch.

**ἀνωρέας**· οὐκ ἀπολλυμένους, Hsch.

**ἀνωρ-ία**, Ion. -ίη, ἡ, *untimeliness*, ἀ. τοῦ ἔτεος πολεμέειν *the bad season* of the year for war, opp. ὥρα ἔτους, Hdt.8.113. ⊛**-ος**, ον, v.l. for ἄωρος, ἄ. ἀποθανών Id.2.79, cf. *Leg.Gort.*7.29.

**ἀνώροφος**, ον, (ὄροφος) *unroofed, uncovered*, Lyc.350, D.C.37.17.

**ἀνωρύομαι** [ῡ], *howl aloud, utter with a howl*, πένθος *AP*7.468 (Mel.), Hld.10.16.

**ἀνῶσαι**, v. ἀναφέρω.

**ἀνωστικῶς**, Adv. *by pushing upwards*, S.E.*P.*3.69.

**ἀνωστόν**· ἔγκλητον, Hsch.

**ἀνώτατος**, η, ον, Sup. Adj. formed from ἄνω (B), *topmost*, τὰ ἀνώτατα Hdt.2.125; θεῶν τῶν ἀνωτάτων νοητικός Euryph.ap.Stob.4.39.27 (ἀνωτάτω Mein.); ἡ ἀ. χάρις D.Chr.31.32. Adv. **ἀνωτάτω**, v. ἄνω (B).

**ἀνωτερικός**, ή, όν, *upper* in point of place, *inland* (v. ἄνω (B) A. II. 1 f), *Act.Ap.*19.1. **2.** of a medicine, *given by the mouth*, τροχίσκος Archig.ap.Aët.9.42, cf. Cass.Fel.48. **II.** τὸ -κόν *medicine which takes effect upwards, emetic*, Hp.*Superf.*29, Gal.10.969.

⊛**ἀνώτερος**, α, ον, Comp. Adj. from ἄνω (B), *upper, higher*, Arist.*HA*496$^b$35, D.H.*Rh.*1.1, Luc.*Asin.*9; ἐπιβουλῆς ἀ. γέγονεν got *the better of*, Nic.Dam.p.25 D.; neut. as Adv., Arist.*HA*503$^b$18; *above*, Lxx *Le.*11.21; *earlier* in a book, *Ep.Hebr.*10.8, cf. Plb.3.1.1; *to a higher place*, *Ev.Luc.*14.10. Adv. **ἀνωτέρω**, v. ἄνω.

**ἀνωτέρωθεν**, Adv. *from above, from a higher place*, Hp.*Oss.*5.

**ἀνωτικός**, ή, όν, = ἀνωτερικός I, *CIG*6849 (Ilium), cf. *Eranos* 13.89.

⊛**ἀνωφάλακρος** [φᾰ], ον, *bald on top*, Ptol.*Tetr.*143.

**ἀνωφέλ-εια**, ἡ, *uselessness*, D.L.9.78, Aq.*Je.*4.14; *inconvenience*, *PHaw.*56.20 (i A.D.). ⊛**-ής**, ές, *unprofitable, useless*, ἁβροσύναι Xenoph.3.1; γόοι A.*Pr.*33; σκιά S.*El.*1159; πάντα ἀ. ἦν Th.2.47; ἀ. αὐτῷ τε καὶ τοῖς ἄλλοις Pl.*R.*496d, al. **2.** *hurtful, prejudici*[al], Th.6.33; τινί Pl.*Prt.*334a, X.*HG*1.7.27: Comp. -έστερος E.*Fr.*4[..], X.*Cyn.*13.11, Pl.*Hp.Ma.*284e. Adv. -λῶς Arist.*EN*1095$^a$5, *PLon*[d.] 3.908.28 (ii A.D.). ⊛**-ητος**, ον, *unprofitable, useless*, τινί *to* one, [A.] *Ch.*752: abs., S.*Ant.*645, *El.*1144; γῆ X.*Cyr.*1.6.11. **II.** *helpless*, ἄνθρωπος Eup.377; ἀ. καὶ θεοῖς ἐχθρός Stratt.9 D. **-ιμος**, ο[ν], = foreg., Phld.*Rh.*2.69 S.

**ἀνωφέρ-εια**, ἡ, *motion upwards*, opp. κατωφ., Alex.Aphr.*Pr.*1.92. **-ής**, ές, *borne upwards, ascending*, opp. κατωφερής, of air an[d] fire, Chrysipp.*Stoic.*2.143, cf. 290, Aristid.Quint.3.19; ὀσμαί Arist.*Pr.*908$^a$25, cf. Herm.*in Phdr.*p.178 A.; τὸ ἀ. Plu.2.649c. **2.** o[f] wine, *heady, intoxicating*, Ath.1.32c. **II.** Act., *bearing upwards*, Arist.*Ph.*217$^a$3.

**ἀνώφλῐον**, τό, (φλιά) *lintel* of a door, Suid.

**ἀνώ-φοιτος**, ον, *mounting upwards*, of air and fire, Zeno *Stoic.*1.27, cf. Ph.2.513, etc. **-φορέω**, *bear up, raise*, freq. in Eust., esp. in Pass. as 40.36, al.:—Act., 695.54. **-φορος**, ον, = ἀνωφερής, S.E.*M.*10.9, Alex.Aphr.*Pr.*1.96, Herm.*in Phdr.*p.132 A.

**ἄνωχθι, ἀνώχθω, ἄνωχθε**, v. ἄνωγα.

**ἄνωχμον**· κελευστικόν, Hsch.

⊛**ἀνώχῡρος**, ον, = ἀνόχυρος, *not fortified*, X.*Ages.*6.6, *SIG*569.7 (Halasarna, iii B.C.). **II.** *open, clear*, χώρα, f.l. for ἄνυδρος, Hp.*Aër.*24.

**ἄξαλλα**, ἡ, a herb found on the Euphrates and used as a remedy for fever, Chryserm.ap.Ps.-Plu.*Fluv.*20.3 (translated by θερμόν).

**ἄξεινος**, ον, Ion. for ἄξενος, q.v. **ἀξ-έμεν, -έμεναι**, v. sub ἄγω.

**ἀξενάγητος**, ον, *without a guide*, ψυχή Diog.*Ep.*39.2.

**ἀξενᾰγώγητος**, ον, *not received* or *guided as a guest*, Eust.*Prooem.*1.10.

**ἀξεν-ία**, ἡ, *inhospitality*, Eratosth.ap.Str.17.1.19, D.S.1.67. **-ος**, Ion. and poet. **ἄξεινος**, ον, *inhospitable*, of persons, opp. πολύξεινος, Hes.*Op.*715; ἀνὴρ ξένοισιν ἄ. E.*Fr.*736; ἄ. καὶ ἄγριον Pl.*Sph.*217e; of places, ὅρμος S.*Ph.*217 (lyr.); γῆ, στέγη, E.*IT*94, *Cyc.*91: Comp. and Sup. -ώτερος, -ώτατος, Id.*Alc.*556, *Med.*1264. **II.** Ἄξεινος (sc. πόντος) *the Axine*, afterwds. called *the Euxine*, Pi.*P.*4.203, E.*Andr.*793 (lyr.); in full, πόρος, πόντος Ἄ., Id.*IT*253, 341.

**ἄξεστος**, ον, *unwrought*, πέτρος S.*OC*19, cf. *Fr.*322, *AP*7.657 (Leon.): metaph. of a poet, *rough, uncouth*, Sch.Ar.*Ra.*86.

⊛**ἀξία**, Ion. -ίη, ἡ, (ἄξιος) *worth, value*, τῶν φορτίων Hdt.4.196; τοῦ τιμήματος τῆς ἀξίας E.*Hipp.*623; ἡ ἀ. τοῦ δούλου Pl.*Lg.*936d; then, simply, *money-value, price, amount*, κατ' ἀξίην ἑκάστου ἀδικήματος ἐδικαίευ Hdt.1.100; ὑποτελέειν ἀξίην βασιλέϊ Id.4.201; τῆς ἀ. τιμᾶσθαι estimate the penalty *at the real amount*, Pl.*Ap.*36b, cf. e; τὴν ἀξίαν τῆς βλάβης ἀπογράφεσθαι Id.*Lg.*845e; προσάπτειν ἑκάστῳ τῶν ἁμαρτημάτων τὴν ἀ. τοῦ πάθους ib.876d; μὴ κατ' ἀξίαν τῆς οὐσίας X.*Cyr.*8.4.32; σκοποῦμαι..εἰ ἄρα ὥσπερ τῶν οἰκετῶν, οὕτω καὶ τῶν φίλων εἰσὶν ἀξίαι Id.*Mem.*2.5.2; κατὰ τὴν τῆς ὀλιγωρίας ἀ. according to *the amount* of his neglect, Decr.ap.D.18.74; ἡ κατ' ἀ. ἰσότης *proportionate* equality, Arist.*Pol.*1302$^a$8; τὸ κατ' ἀ. ἴσον ib.1301$^b$30; παρὰ τὴν ἀ. Id.*EN*1122$^b$29, al. **2.** of persons, *reputation, dignity*, Th.6.68, D.13.18, cf. 18.63; ἡ τῆς ἀρχῆς ἀ. Pl.*Lg.*945b; ἡ τῆς ἀ. τιμή ib.744b; οἱ ἐπ' ἀξίας persons *of dignity, official* personages, Luc.*Nigr.*24; ἐξεπορεύετο μετὰ μεγάλης ἀ. with great *dignity, pomp*, Plb.38.8.6; κατὰ δουλικὴν ἀξίαν κοσμεῖσθαι D.S.5.40. **3.** generally, a man's *due, merit, deserts*, τὴν μὲν ἀ. οὐ λάμψεαι, ἐλάσσω δὲ τῆς ἀξίης Hdt.7.39; εἰ τῆς ἀ. ἐτύγχανες Ar.*Av.*1223; κατ' ἀξίαν according to *desert* or *merit, duly*, E.*Hec.*374, Pl.*R.*496a, cf. *Phd.*113e, al.; ὑπὲρ τὴν ἀ. beyond *desert, undeservedly*, E.*HF*146, D.2.3; παρὰ τὴν ἀ., οὐ κατ' ἀ., Th.7.77, cf. D.1.23. **b.** *penalty*, τὴν ἀ. ἀποτίνειν, ὑπέχειν, Luc.*DMort.*30.1, *Pisc.*8. **4.** *moral value*, *Stoic.*3.30: pl., Cleanth.ib.1.129. **II.** *estimate of* a thing's *worth, opinion*, κατὰ τὴν ἰδίαν ἀ. D.S.14.10, cf. 107; esp. *estimate* of the moral value of actions, αἱ τῶν ἐκτὸς ἀξίαι Arr.*Epict.*1.2.7, cf. 1.25.17.

⊛**ἀξι-άγαστος** [ᾰγ], ον, *worth admiring, admirable*, X.*Lac.*10.2, Ael.*Fr.*116, Jul.*Or.*6.190d. **-άκουστος** [ᾰκ], ον, *worth hearing*, X.*Smp.*4.44. **-ακρόᾱτος**, ον, *worth listening to*, Id.*Lac.*4.2 (in Sup. -ότατος). **-απόλαυστος**, ον, *delectable*, *Stoic.*3.180. **-αφήγητος**, Ion. **-απήγητος**, ον, *worth telling*, Hdt.1.16, 177 (Sup.), J.*AJ*15.11.5 (Sup.), Arr.*An.*1 *Praef.*1 (Comp.).

⊛**ἀξιάω**, = ἀξιόω, *Hoffmann Inscr.*2 No.160.33 (Lampsacus), No.130.5 (Tenedos).

**ἀξι-ελέητος**, ον, *pitiable*, Diog.*Ep.*27. **-επαίνετος**, ον, = v.l. for sq., in X.*HG*4.4.6. **-έπαινος**, ον, *praiseworthy*, Id.*Cyr.*3.3.6, D.61.15; χρῆμα, of a dead ox, Ael.*NA*2.57, etc.: Sup. -ότατος X.*HG*4.4.6. Adv. -νως Apollon.*Vit.Aeschin.*11. **-επιθύμητος** [ῡ], ον, *worthy of desire*, Hsch. s.v. ἀξιέραστον. **-έραστος**, ον, *worthy of love*, X.*Cyr.*5.2.9, Chrysipp.*Stoic.*3.181, Plu.*Comp.Thes.Rom.*1, Luc.*DMar.*1.2, Aristaenet.1.27; οἰκονομία *PMag.Par.*1.2010: Comp., X.*Smp.*8.14. **-ήκοος**, ον, (ἀκοή) = ἀξιάκουστος, Diog.*Ep.*35 and 36. **-θεος, -θέωρος**, v. ἀξιόθεος.

**ἀξῑν-άριον**, τό, Dim. of sq., J.*BJ*2.8.7. ⊛**-η**, ἡ, *axe-head*, ἀξίνην εὔχαλκον ἐλαΐνῳ ἀμφὶ πελέκκῳ Il.13.612. **2.** *battle-axe* (expl. as δίστομος πέλεκυς by Hsch.), ib.15.711, cf. Hdt.7.64. **3.** *axe for hewing wood*, X.*An.*1.5.12, *Ev.Matt.*3.10, *Ev.Luc.*3.9. (Cf. Goth. *aqizi*, OE. *æx*, Lat. *ascia* (fr. *acsia).) ⊛**-ίδιον**, τό, Dim. of foreg., J.*BJ*2.8.9.

**ἀξῑνο-κράτημα** [ρᾰ], ατος, τό, *helve of an axe*, Zonar. s.v. στελεός. **-πληκτος**, ον, *struck by an axe*, *An.Par.*3.114, Sch.Il.1.1.

**ἀξινῶρυξ**· *acisculus, ligo*, Gloss.

**ἀξιο-βίωτος**, ον, *worth living for*, οὐκ ἀξιοβίωτόν ἐστιν X.*HG*4.

.6. **-δάκρῡτος**, ον, *worthy of tears*, Sch.E.*Med.*1221. **-δοτος**, ον, *deserving, honourable*, *IGRom.*4.1398 (Smyrna). **-εργός**, όν, *fit for, capable of work*, X.*Oec.*7.34. ❋**-ζηλος**, ον, *enviable*, Ael. *VH*12.64, Them.*Or.*13.175b (Sup.). Adv. -λως Suid. ❋**-ζήλωτος**, ον, = foreg., Phld.*Piet.*66 (Sup.); νίκη Plu.*Flam.*20. 2. *worthy of emulation*, Dsc.*Praef.*4. **-ζήτητος**, ον, *worth inquiry*, Oenom.ap.Eus.*PE*6.7. **-θάνᾰτος** [θᾰ], ον, *worthy of death*, Sch.A. *Th.*582. **-θαύμαστος**, ον, *wonder-worthy*, X.*Mem.*1.4.4 (Comp.), Callix.1, Aristeas 282. **-θέᾱτος**, Ion. -ητος, ον, *well worth seeing*, Hdt.1.14,184, al., X.*Smp.*1.10, Corn.*ND*17: Comp. -ότερος Plu. *Demetr.*43: Sup. -ότατος Hdt.2.176, X.*Lac.*4.2. **-θεος** (A), ον, (θεός) *worthy of God*, Oenom.ap.Eus.*PE*5.34. **-θεος** (B), ον, (θέα) *worth seeing*, Alciphr.3.55:—in poet. forms **ἀξίθεος** *Epigr.Gr.*981; **ἀξιθέωρος**, ον, ibid. (Philae). **-θρηνος**, ον, *worthy of lamentation*, E.*Alc.*904 (lyr.). **-θρῐάμβευτος**, ον, *worth being led in triumph*, Suet.*Calig.*47. **-καταφρόνητος**, ον, *deserving contempt*, Iamb.*VP* 31.206. **-κοινώνητος**, ον, *worthy of our society*, Pl.*R.*371e; *worthy to share in*, τοῦ συλλόγου *Lg.*961a. **-κτητος**, ον, *worth getting*, X.*Cyr.*5.2.10, Paus.1.9.5, Philostr.*Ep.*9; ἐς φιλίαν Aristid.Quint. 3.18. **-ληπτος**, ον, *worth acceptance, precious*, Hsch. ❋**-λογος**, ον, *worthy of mention, remarkable*, ὁ ἐν Ἐφέσῳ νηός Hdt.2.148, etc.; πόλεμος -ώτατος Th.1.1; τοῦτο -ώτερον X.*Cyr.*8.2.13; ἀλίθοι Suid. Adv. -γως X.*Mem.*1.5.5, Aristeas 72, Phld.*Rh.*1.2 S., al., Plu.2. 128e. 2. of persons, *of note, important*, τοὺς μάλιστα ἐν τέλει καὶ ἀξιολογωτάτους Th.2.10, etc. 3. ἀ. μιμήματα imitations of *worthy* objects, Pl.*Lg.*669e. **-μᾰθής**, ές, = sq., X.*Ep.*7 (Comp.). **-μάθητος** [ᾰ], ον, *worth being learnt*, Iamb.*VP*3.14. **-μᾰκάριστος** [κᾰ], ον, *worthy to be deemed happy*, X.*Ap.*34 (Sup.). **-μανεῖς**· δυνατώτεροι, Hsch. **-μᾰχος**, ον, *a match for* another *in battle* or *war*, τινί Hdt.7.157, Th.8.38; πρός τινα Plu.*Cat.Ma.*12, etc.: abs., Hdt. 3.19, 8.63, Th.8.80, Aen.Tact.2.5. 2. c. inf., *sufficient in strength* or *number*, νέες ἀξιόμαχοι τῇσι Αἰγινητέων συμβαλεῖν Hdt.6.89; νεῶν ..ἀξιομάχων δέκεσθαι τὸν ἐπιόντα Id.7.138, cf. 101; ἀξιόμαχόν τι δρᾶν D.C.43.4. Adv. -χως, τινὶ συνεστάναι Plu.*Sull.*19. **-μίμητος** [ῑ], ον, *worthy of imitation*, Ecphant.ap.Stob.4.7.65. **-μισής**, ές, *worthy of hate, hateful*, D.C.78.21. **-μίσητος** [ῑ], ον, = foreg., Plu.2. 10a, 537d, D.C.38.44:—also **ἀξιόμῑσος**, ον, A.*Eu.*366 (lyr.). **-μνημόνευτος**, ον, *worthy of mention*, Pl.*Prt.*343a, *Smp.*178a, X.*HG*4.8. 1, etc. **-μνηστος**, ον, = foreg., *Gloss.* **-μορφος**, ον, *shapely, beautiful*, Man.4.513. ❋**-νῖκος**, ον, *worthy of victory*, *worthy of being preferred*, X.*Cyr.*1.5.10: c. inf., -ότερος ἔχειν τοῦτο τὸ κράτος *more worthy* to hold this supremacy, Hdt.7.187, cf. 9.26: Sup., Luc. *Anach.*36. **-πενθής**, ές, *lamentable*, E.*Hipp.*1465. **-πιστεύομαι**, *to be worthy of belief*, Phld.*Po.*1676.11. **-πιστία**, ἡ, *trustworthiness*, Hipparch.1.1.7, Phld.*Rh.*1.45 S., D.S.1.23, Longin. 16.2, etc. 2. *plausibility*, J.*BJ*1.32.2; *credibility*, Alex.*Fig.*1. 17. **-πιστος**, ον, *trustworthy*, Pl.*Alc.*1.123b; ἀ. ἂν εἰκότως φαίνοιτο D.1.3; Κτησίας οὐκ ὢν ἀ. Arist.*HA*606ᵃ8, al.; ἀ. εἴς τι X.*Mem.* 1.5.2; ναύλοχα ἀ. πρὸς τοσαύτην ναυτιλίαν *sufficient for..*, Plu.*Caes.* 58: Comp., Phld.*Mus.*p.77 K. 2. of evidence, *trustworthy*, Arist. *GA*741ᵃ37. Adv. -τως, ἀ. συνῶπται 741ᵃ34. 3. in bad sense, *plausible*, in Adv. -τως Timae.70, Gal.17(2).139. **-πιστοσύνη**, ἡ, = -πιστία, Man.4.505. **-ποινος**, ον, *exacting due punishment*, of Athena at Sparta, Paus.3.15.6. ❋**-πρεπής**, ές, *proper, becoming*, σῶμα X.*Smp.*8.40 (Sup.), cf. Phld.*Rh.*2.30 S. **-προστάτευτος** [ᾰ], ον, *worthy of command*, Poll.1.178.

**ἀξιόρᾱτος**, ον, *worth seeing*, Luc.*Hist.Conscr.*32, Ph.1.441.

❋**ἄξιος**, ία, ιον (ος, ον Nonn.*D.*8.314), for *ἄγ-τιος, *counterbalancing*, cf. ἄγω VI: hence prop. *weighing as much, of like value, worth as much as*, c. gen., βοὸς ἀ. Il.23.885; νῦν δ' οὐδ' ἑνὸς ἄξιοί εἰμεν Ἕκτορος we are not—all together—*worth* one Hector, 8.234, cf. Hdt. 1.32, 7.21; πάντων Ζεὺς ἄξιον ἦμαρ ἔδωκεν Il.15.719; so πολλοῦ ἀ. *worth* much, X.*An.*4.1.28, Pl.*Smp.*185b, etc.; πλείονος ἀ. Id.*Phdr.* 235b, etc.; πλείστου ἀ. Th.2.65, Pl.*Grg.*464d, etc.; παντός, τοῦ παντὸς ἀ., E.*Fr.*275, Pl.*Sph.*216c; παντὸς ἀ., c. inf., Ar.*Av.*797; λόγου ἀ., = ἀξιόλογος, Hdt.1.133, Th.1.73, etc.; σπουδῆς, μνήμης ἀ., Plu.2. 35a, 172e:—opp. to these are οὐδενὸς ἀ. Thgn.456; ἢ παντὸς ἢ τὸ παράπαν οὐδενός Pl.*Phlb.*64d; ὀλίγου Id.*Grg.*497b, etc.; σμικροῦ Id. *R.*504d, etc.; βραχέος Id.*Lg.*692c; μείονος, ἐλάττονος ἀ., X.*Vect.*4.50, *Cyr.*2.2.14; πολλαπλασίου τιμήματος ἀ. κτήσεις Arist.*Pol.*1306ᵇ12; also εἰς ὀγδοήκοντα μνᾶς ἀ. *worth* up to a sum of.., D.27.10. 2. c. dat. pers., σοὶ δ' ἄξιον ἔσται ἀμοιβῆς 'tis *worth* a return to thee, i.e. will bring thee a return, Od.1.318; πολέος δέ οἱ ἄξιος ἔσται Il.23.562; βασιλεῖ ἂν πολλοῦ ἄξιοι γένοιντο X.*An.*2.1.14. 3. abs., *worthy, goodly*, ἄξια δῶρα Il.9.261; ἀ. ὦνος a *goodly* price, Od.15.429; ὅθεν κέ τοι ἄξιον ἄλφοι it would bring thee *a good price*, 20.383; φέροντες ὅ τι ἕκαστος ἄξιον εἶχε X.*Cyr.*3.3.2. b. in Att. in an exactly opposite sense, 'good value for the money', i.e. *cheap*, Ar.*Eq.*672,895: Comp., ib.645; ὡς ἀξιώτατον πρίασθαι Lys.22.18; ὡς ἀ. γεγόνασιν οἱ πυροὶ ἐν τῇ ἀγορᾷ Thphr.*Char.*3.3, cf. X.*Vect.*4.6. 4. *deserved, meet, due*, δίκη S.*El.*298, X.*Oec.*12.19; χάρις Id.*HG*1.6.11; ἄξια δράσας ἄξια πάσχων *fit* suffering for *fit* deeds, A.*Ag.*1527, cf. E.*Ion*735. 5. of persons, οἱ ἑωυτοῦ ἄξιοι those of one's own *rank*, his *peers*, Hdt.1.107. 6. *sufficient for*, c. gen., τοῦ πολέμου τὰ χρήματα D.14.27. 7. αἰδοῦς ἀξίαν..τὴν προθυμίαν μᾶλλον ἢ θράσους more *like* modesty than rashness, Arist.*Cael.*291ᵇ 25. II. after Hom., in moral relation, *worthy, estimable*, of persons and things, Hdt.7.224, etc.; οὐδὲν ἀξία nothing *worth*, A.*Ch.* 445; ἀξίαν κἀπ' ἀξίων Id.*Eu.*435; ἀξίων γεννητόρων ἤθη φυλάσσεις E. *Ion*735. 2. *worthy of, deserving*, mostly c. gen. rei, ἄξιον φυγῆς, ἄξια στεναγμάτων, γέλωτος, Id.*Med.*1124, *Or.*1326, *Heracl.*507; ἐγκωμίων τί ἀξιώτερον ἤ..; X.*Ag.*10.3: c. gen. pers., ποιεῖν ἄξια οὔτε ὑμῶν οὔτε πατέρων Th.2.71; ἄξιον τοῦ πατρός Isoc.9.80; ἄξια τοῦ Μαραθῶνος διανοεῖσθαι Plu.*Cim.*5. b. c. gen. rei et dat. pers., ἡμῖν δ' Ἀχιλλεὺς ἄξιος τιμῆς *is worthy of* honour *at our hands*, E.*Hec.*309; πολλῶν ἀγαθῶν ἀ. ὑμῖν Ar.*Ach.*633; ἀ. πλείστου Λακεδαιμονίοις Th. 4.81; θανάτου τῇ πόλει X.*Mem.*1.1.1, cf. 1.2.62; εἰμὶ δ' οὐ τούτων ὑμῖν ἀ. D.21.217; χάριτος ἀ. τῇ πόλει Antipho 6.10; later τιμῆς ἀ. παρὰ πάντων Luc.*Tox.*3. 3. c. inf., Προθοήνορος ἀντὶ πεφάσθαι ἀ. *worthy* to be killed instead of him, Il.14.472, cf. Th.1.76; τίεσθαι δ' ἀξιώτατος A.*Ag.*531; ἀ. θρήνων τυχεῖν S.*Aj.*924; ἄξιοι δουλεύειν *only fit* to be slaves, Arist.*Pol.*1254ᵇ36; also ἀ. σέβειν E.*Heracl.*315 (Elmsl.). b. ἄξιός εἰμι, like δίκαιός εἰμι, I *deserve* to.., ἄξιός εἰμι πληγὰς λαβεῖν Ar.*Ec.*324; ἄξιός εἰμι ἀπολαῦσαι X.*Cyr.*5.4.19: abs., the inf. being supplied, *authorized* to act, And.1.132; ἀ. γάρ, emphatically, Pl.*Tht.*143e. c. later ἀ. ἵνα *Ev.Jo.*1.27. 4. ἄξιόν [ἐστι] 'tis *meet, fit, due*, ἄξιον εἶναι τρεῖς ἑνὸς ἀντὶ πεφάσθαι Il.13.446; ἀ. μνήμην ἔχειν Hdt.1.14: later c. fut. inf., ἀ. διαπορήσειν Did.*in D.*9. 15. b. c. dat. pers. et inf., τῇ πόλει γὰρ ἄξιον ξυλλαβεῖν τὸν ἄνδρα 'tis *meet* for the city, is *worth* her *while*.., Ar.*Ach.*205; τί σοι ζῆν ἄξιον; Id.*Nu.*1074, cf. *Av.*548; ἄξιόν γε πᾶσιν ἐπολολύξαι Id.*Eq.*616; freq. in X. as ὡς οὐκ ἄξιον εἴη βασιλεῖ ἀφεῖναι κτλ. that it was not *meet* for him.., *An.*2.3.25. c. the inf. is sts. omitted, ἄξιον γὰρ Ἑλλάδι 'tis *meet* in the eyes of Hellas [so to do], Ar.*Ach.*8; and sts. the dat., ἄξιόν ἐστι *operae pretium est*, it is *worth while*, ἐνθυμηθῆναι D.1.21; γαμεῖν οὐκ ἄξιον E.*Alc.*628. III. Adv. ἀξίως, c. gen., ἐμάχοντο ἀξίως λόγου Hdt.6.112; οὔτε ἑωυτοῦ ἀ. Id.3.125; οὐκ ἀ. ἀπηγήσιος ibid.; τῆς ἀδικίας Th.3.39; ἀ. τοῦ θεοῦ, τῆς θεᾶς, *OGI*331.9 (Pergam.), *Inscr.Magn.*33.30, cf. 1*Ep.Thess.*2.12: abs., S.*OT*133, etc.; κολάσετε ἀξίως as they *deserve*, Th.3.40.

**ἀξιο-σέβαστος**, ον, *worthy of reverence, worshipful*, Eust.ad D.P. p.72.22. **-σκεπτος**, ον, *worth considering*, X.*HG*6.1.13. **-σπούδαστος**, ον, *worthy of zealous endeavours*, X.*Lac.*10.3 (Comp.), Plu. 2.5d. **-στράτηγος** [ρᾰ], ον, *worthy of being general* or *worthy of a great commander*, X.*An.*3.1.24 (Comp.), D.C.56.24 codd. (Sup.):—**-στρᾰτηγικός** is found as v.l. in Arr.*An.*4.11.9 and D.C.41.55, and **-στρᾰτήγητος** Id.45.42. **-σῦλος**, ον, *liable to seizure*, *GDI*1151.6 (Elis). **-τέκμαρτος**, ον, *worthy of being brought in evidence, credible*, ἀξιοτεκμαρτότερον τοῦ λόγου τὸ ἔργον deeds are *stronger proof* than words, X.*Mem.*4.4.10. **-τίμησις** [τῐ], εως, ἡ, *valuing, appraisement*, Sch.Aristid.p.281 F. **-τίμητος** [ῑ], ον, *highly prized, valuable*, Ph.1.461:—also **-τῖμος**, ον, Nic.Dam.p.94 D., X.*Ep.*2.3 (Comp.), App.*BC*3.19 (Sup.). **-φᾰνής**, ές, (φανῆναι) *reputable*, *PLond.*2.483.72 (vii A.D.). **-φίλητος** [φῐ], ον, *worth loving*, X.*Oec.* 10.3, *Stoic.*3.180. ❋**-χρεία**, ἡ, *sufficiency, guarantee*, in pl., *CPH* 97.13 (iii A.D.). **-χρείων**, ονος, = sq., ἐνέχυρα *SIG*672.30 (Delph.).

❋**ἀξιόχρεως**, εων, gen. εω, Ion. **ἀξιόχρεος**, ον, Hdt. (though the other form occurs as v.l. 1.156, al.) and Hp.*Art.*11; both forms in *Foed. Delph.Pell.*1 A 15, cf. 1 B 9: Boeot. acc. pl. ἀξιοχρειέας, implying nom. ἀξιοχρη(Ϝ)ής, prob. rest. in *IG*7.1739.9: neut. pl. ἀξιόχρεα Hdt. 5.65: dat. sg. written ἀξιοχρέῳ *IG*2².1183.28: Comp. and Sup. ἀξιοχρεώτερος, -ώτατος, Plb.4.3.3 (s.v.l.), 10.27.1: (χρέος):—*worthy of a thing*: hence, I. abs., like ἀξιόλογος, *noteworthy, considerable*, πόλις Th.1.10; of a person, ὑπὸ ἀξιοχρέου καὶ ἀποθανεῖν ἡμίσεα συμφορή Hdt.5.111. 2. *serviceable, sufficient*, ἀξιόχρεον πρόφασιν προτείνειν Id.1.156; ἐπ' οὐδεμιῇ αἰτίῃ ἀξιόχρεῳ Id.3.35; also of persons, ἀ. ἐγγυηταί *trustworthy, substantial*, Ar.*Ec.*1065, Pl.*Ap.*38c, cf. *Foed. Delph.Pell.* ll.cc.; εἰς ἀ. τὸν λέγοντα ἀνοίσω Pl.*Ap.*20e; στρατόπεδα ἀ. πρὸς μάχην Plb.1.19.1; τόλμα ἀ. πρὸς ἡγεμονίαν Plu.*Caes.*56. II. c. inf., *able, sufficient to* do.., Hdt.4.126, Th.5.13; ἀξιόχρεω..ἡμῖν ἀντιτάξασθαι D.3.27; ἦ οὐκ ἀξιόχρεως ὁ θεὸς..τὸ μίασμα λῦσαι; E.*Or.* 598. Adv. -χρέως Hsch. III. c. gen. rei, *worthy, deserving of*, ἀξιόχρεα ἀπηγήσιος, = ἀξιαπήγητα, Hdt.5.65; ἀ. τηλικούτου πράγματος *worthy of credit* in.., D.48.49, cf. 19.131.—Rare in poets, as E. l.c.

❋**ἀξιόω**, pf. ἠξίωκα Isoc.18.24:—Med., v. infr. III. 2:—Pass., fut. ἀξιωθήσομαι Id.9.6, but also ἀξιώσεται S.*Ant.*637: aor. ἠξιώθην: pf. ἠξίωμαι: (ἄξιος):—*think, deem worthy*, I. c. acc. et gen., whether in good sense, *think worthy of a reward*, ἡμᾶς ἀξιοῖ λόγου E.*Med.*962; ἑαυτὸν τῶν καλλίστων X.*An.*3.2.7; or in bad, *of a punishment*, γοργύρης Hdt.3.145; ἀ. τινὰ ἀτιμίας Philipp.ap.D.18.166; κακοῦ Pl.*Ap.* 38a:—Pass., ἀξιεύμενος θυγατρὸς τῆς σῆς Hdt.9.111; λέχη..τυράννων ἠξιωμένα *deemed worthy of* kings, E.*Hec.*366; ἀξιοῦσθαι κακῶν Antipho 3.2.10; τοῦ αὐτοῦ ὀνόματος Pl.*Phd.*103e, al. 2. c. acc. only, *esteem, honour*, S.*Aj.*1114, E.*Heracl.*918; ἀ. τινὰ προσφθέγμασιν *honour* one with words, A.*Ag.*903; of things, *value*, οὐκ ἐξ ἴσου πάσας ἀξιοῦμεν ὑπολήψεις Phld.*Herc.*1251.12:—Pass., καλοῖς ὑμεναίοις ἀξιοῦσθαι E.*Or.*1210: abs., τύμβον ἀξιούμενον δρᾶσθαι Id.*Hec.*319, cf. Th. 5.16. 3. *value at a certain price*, ὁπόσης ἂν τιμῆς ἀξιώσῃ τὸ πωλούμενον Pl.*Lg.*917d. II. c. acc. pers. et inf., *think* one *worthy* to do or be, σέ τοι ἠξίωσε ναίειν E.*Alc.*572; οὐκ ἀξιῶ 'γὼ 'μαυτὸν ἰσχύειν μέγα Ar.*Eq.*182; τί σαυτὸν ἀποτίνειν ἀξιοῖς; Pherecr.93:—Pass., Pi. *N.*10.39, A.*Pr.*242; διδάσκαλος ἀξιοῦσθαι *to be esteemed as* a teacher, Pl.*Tht.*161d. 2. *think fit, expect, require that..*, ἀ. τινὰ ἰέναι Hdt. 2.162; ἀ. τινὰ ἀληθῆ λέγειν Antipho 2.3.4; οὐκ ἀ. [ὑμᾶς] τὰ μὴ δεινὰ ἐν ὀρρωδίᾳ ἔχειν *we expect* that you do not.., Th.2.89, cf. 3.44; ἀ. σωτηρίαν ἐμοὶ γενέσθαι And.1.143; ἀ. καὶ παρακαλεῖν τινα c. inf., Decr.ap.D.18.165; ἀ. ἵνα.. *Inscr.Prien.*53.58, al.; simply, *ask, request*, *PEleph.*19.18, Apollon.Perg.1 *Praef.* (Pass.); esp. *pray*, τὸν θεὸν ὅπως.. Aristeas 245, cf. Lxx *Je.*7.16, *SIG*1181.1; τὰ -ούμενα *prayers*, Aristeas 18; also, *ask, inquire* of an oracle, Ps.-Callisth. 1.3. III. c. inf. only, ἀ. κομίζεσθαι, τυγχάνειν *think one has a right to* receive, *expect* to receive, Th.1.43, 7.15; προῖκα θεωρεῖν ἀ. Thphr. *Char.*6.4; ἄλλο τι ἀξιοῖς ἢ ἀποθανεῖν; Lys.22.5: with a neg., οὐκ ἀξιῶ ὑποπτεύεσθαι I *think I do* not *deserve* to be suspected, *have a right* not to be.., Th.4.86:—Pass., ὥστε ἀξιοῦσθαι λητουργεῖν so as *to be required* to.., D.27.64; νίφ προθύμως τἀξιούμενον ποιῶν *one's duty*, Men. 663. 2. *think fit, expect, consent, resolve*, etc., and so in various senses, ἀξιῶ θανεῖν I *consent* to die, S.*OT*944, etc.; *dare*, ἀξιῶσαι μάχην συνάψαι A.*Pers.*335; *deign* to do, εἴ τις ἀξιοῖ μαθεῖν Id.*Ag.*1661, cf. S.*OT*1413; ἀξιῶ χρήματα λαμβάνειν I *do not hesitate* to receive, Pl.*Hp.Mi.*364d, etc.; οἶμαι πάντας.. φέρειν ἀξιοῦν ἔρανον I think that all *should be glad* to bring, D.21.101:—freq. with neg., οὐδ' ἀξιῶ μνησθῆναι I *do* not *think* them *worth* mentioning, Hdt.2.20; οὐκ ἠξίωσαν οὐδὲ προσβλέψαι A.*Pr.*217; οὐκ ἀξιώσαντες.. τοῦτο παθεῖν Th.1.102 (but ἀξιοῦντε μὴ ἀντιδοῦναι δίκην 3.66); πεἰθεσθαι οὐκ ἀξιοῦντες *refusing*, X.*Oec.*21.4:—also in Med. (not in Att. Prose), ἀξιοῦσθαι μέλειν *deign* to care for, A.*Ag.*370; φονεὺς γὰρ εἶναι ἠξιώσατο *thought fit* to be, Id. *Eu.*425; οὐκ ἀξιεύμεναι ἀναμίσγεσθαι τῇσι ἄλλῃσι not *condescending* to.., Hdt.1.199; οὐκ ἀξιεύμενος ἐς τὸν.. θρόνον ἵζεσθαι not *deeming oneself worthy* to.., Id.7.16. 3. *think, deem*, ἀξιοῦντες ἀδικέεσθαι Id.6.87, cf. S.*OC*579, E.*HF*1343; ἑκάτεροι νικᾶν ἠξίουν *claimed* the victory, Th.1.55. IV. *make a claim*, Id.4.58; πάντες καθ' ὑπεροχὴν -οῦσιν Arist.*Pol.*1288a23; ἀξίωσιν ἀ. Plb.38.7.7; ἀξιοῦν τινά τι *make a claim on* a person, X.*Mem.*3.11.12. 2. ἐγὼ μὲν οὑτωσὶ περὶ τῆς τύχης ἀξιῶ *hold* this *opinion*.., D.18.255; ἐγὼ μὲν οὐκ ἀξιῶ I *think* not, Id.20.12: in philosophic language, *lay down, maintain* (cf. ἀξίωμα II.2), Arist.*APr.*37b10, cf. 41b10, Polystr.p.24 W.; ἐν τῷ τοιῷδε ἀξιοῦντι in such a *state of opinion*, v.l. in Th.3.43.

**ἄξῐφος**, ον, *without sword*, Lyc.50, A.D.*Synt.*187.10. Adv. **ἀξιφεί** Hdn.*Epim.*257.

**ἀξιώλεθρος**, ον, *pernicious*, ἐνθύμημα Procop.*Aed.*6.5, cf. *Goth.*4.30.

*__ἀξί-ωμα__, ατος, τό, *that of which one is thought worthy, an honour*, γάμων.. ἀξίωμ' ἐδέξατο E.*Ion*62; οἱ τὰς πόλεις ἔχουσι κἀξιώματα ib.605; κοινῆς τραπέζης ἀ. ἔχειν Id.*Or.*9; τὸ τῆς πόλεως ἀ. the *dignity* of the city's representative, D.18.149. 2. *honour, reputation*, E.*Supp.* 424, Th.2.65, etc.; ὢν ἐν ἀξιώματι ὑπὸ τῶν ἀστῶν Id.6.15; τὸ τῶν ἐλευθέρων γυναικῶν ἀ. D.59.113: c. gen. objecti, ἀ. ἔχειν ἀρετῆς *claim* on ground of merit, Arist.*Pol.*1281b25. 3. *rank, position*, ἀξιώματος ἀφάνεια Th.2.37; γένει καὶ τοῖς ἄλλοις ἀξιώμασιν Isoc.19.7. 4. of things, *worth, quality*, οὐ τῷ πλήθει ἀλλὰ τῷ ἀ. Th.5.8. 5. concrete, *things of dignity*, Philostr.*VS*2.5.4. II. *that which is thought fit, decision, decree*, δαιμόνων S.*OC*1452, cf. 1459; τὰ τῶν προγόνων ἀ. D.18.210; ἀ. κενὰ καὶ νομοθεσίαι Epicur.*Ep.*2 p.36 U. 2. in Science, *that which is assumed as the basis of demonstration, self-evident principle*, Arist.*Metaph.*997a7, 1005b33, *APo.*72a17, Polystr. p.16 W.:—Math., *axiom*, Arist.*Metaph.*1005a20, etc.; philosophical *doctrine*, τὸ Ζήνωνος ἀ. ib.1001b7, cf. *Xen.*979b22; logical *proposition*, Chrysipp.*Stoic.*2.53, 63, etc. 3. *request, petition*, ἱκετικὸν ἀ. *BGU*1053 ii 7 (i B.C.), cf. Plu.2.633c. *—__ωμᾰτικός__, ή, όν, *dignified, honourable*, προστασία Plb.10.18.8, etc.; *high in rank*, Plu. 2.617d: Comp., Dam.*Pr.*54. 2. in Literary Criticism, *dignified*, D.H.*Dem.*18, al.; ῥυθμός *Comp.*13: Comp., *Isoc.*3. Adv. -κῶς, κατεσκευάσθη *Dem.*43; λέγειν Hermog.*Id.*2.6. 3. *concerned with dignities*, Ptol.*Tetr.*163. II. *supplicatory*, Plb.20.9.9. III. *employing logical propositions*, ἐκφορά *Stoic.*2.61: Sup., D.L.4. 33. Adv. -κῶς *self-evidently*, Steph.*in Hp.*1.59 D. **-ωμάτιον**, τό, Dim., *petty dignity*, Arr.*Epict.*2.2.10. **-ωσις**, gen. εως, Ion. ιος, ἡ, *thinking worthy*, τῆς ἀξιώσιος εἵνεκα τῆς ἐξ ἐμεῦ γῆμαι for your *deeming* it *fit* to marry from my family, Hdt.6.130. 2. *being thought worthy*, one's *reputation, character*, διὰ τὴν προϋπάρχουσαν ἀ. Th.1.138, cf. 6.54; τὴν ἀ. μὴ ἀφανίζειν Id.2.61; *excellence*, τῶν ποιημάτων D.H.*Comp.*4. 3. *dignity, rank*, Id.6.71, al., App.*BC*1.79; λοχαγοῦ τάξις καὶ ἀ. Arr.*Tact.*12.4. 4. *dignity* of style, D.H.*Comp.* 18. II. *demand, claim*, on grounds of merit (opp. χρεία, on grounds of necessity), Th.1.37; ἀ. χάριτος ib.41, cf. Plb.1.67.10, *PRyl.*120.17 (ii A.D.), etc.; generally, *request*, ἐχθροῦ δεηθέντος μὴ ἀποστραφῆς τὴν ἀ. Epicur.*Fr.*215. b. *petition*, ἀ. ἔγγραφος Plu. *Demetr.*42; = *libellus*, D.C.60.30. III. *opinion, principle, maxim*, τὴν ἀ. ταύτην εἰλήφεσαν.. Th.2.88, cf. Aeschin.3.220. IV. ἀ. τῶν ὀνομάτων ἐς τὰ ἔργα *the established meaning* of words, Th.3. 82. **-ωτέον**, *one must think worthy*, τινά Arist.*EN*1159b18, Jul. *Ep.*89b; *insist on*, c. inf., Phld.*D.*3.2.

**ἀ-ξόᾰνος**, ον, *without carved images*, Luc.*Syr.D.*3.

**ἀξονήλᾰτος**, ον, *whirling on the axle*, σύριγγες A.*Supp.*181.

**ἀξόν-ιον**, τό, Dim., *small bolt* or *pin*, Hero *Spir.*1.30, Poll.10.31; of *bolts* used in twisting the strands of torsion-engines, Hero *Bel.*82. 7:—also **-ίσκος**, ὁ, Id.*Spir.*2.32, Ph.*Bel.*76.24. **-ιος**, α, ον, (ἄξων) *belonging to the axle*, *AP*9.117 (Stat. Flacc.).

**ἄξοος**, ον, *unwrought, not carved*, σανίς Call.*Fr.*105.

**ἄξος**, ὁ, Cret., = ἀγμός, St.Byz. s.v. Ὄαξος. B. Maced. word for ὕλη, Hsch.

*__ἀξουγγία__, ἡ, *tallow, grease*, Crateuas *Fr.*3, al., Gal.12.419:—also **ἀξούγγιον**, τό, Aët.12.1, Gal.13.57, *Hippiatr.*105; cf. ὀξούγγιον.

**ἀξουγγιασμός**, ὁ, *treatment with* ἀξούγγιον, *Hippiatr.*129.

**ἀξυγκρότητος**, ον, for ἀσυγκ–, *not welded together by the hammer*: metaph. of rowers, *not trained to pull together*, Th.8.95; of style, *not compact, rambling*, D.H.*Dem.*19.

*__ἀξῠλ-ία__, Ion. -ίη, ἡ, *want of wood*, Hes.*Fr.*206, Str.15.2. 10. **-ιστος**, ον, = sq. 1, Hsch. *__-ος__, ον, *with no timber cut from it*, ἄξυλος ὕλη an *unthinned*, i.e. *thick*, wood, Il.11.155 (ἀφ' ἧς οὐδεὶς ἐξυλίσατο Sch.Ven. ad loc.), wrongly expl. (as if ἀ- intens.) *thick with trees*, Corn.*ND*13. II. *without wood*, Hdt.4.61, 185, *AP*9.89 (Phil.); also, *without a load of wood*, Luc.*Asin.*32. III. *free from woody matter*, of galbanum, Dsc.3.83, Damocr.ap.Gal.13.916.

**ἀξυμ–, ἀξυν–**, v. sub ἀσυμ–, ἀσυν–.

**ἄξῡνος**, ον, = ἀκοινώνητος, Hsch., Suid.

**ἀξῠρής**, ές, and **ἄξῠρος**, ον, *not cutting, blunt*, Hsch.

**ἀξύστατος**, ον, v. sub ἀσύστατος.

**ἄξυστος**, ον, *not scraped*, Antyll.ap.Orib.4.11.13.

*__ἄξων__, ονος, ὁ, *axle*, Il.16.378; σιδήρεος 5.723; φήγινος ib.838, cf. Hes.*Op.*424, A.*Th.*153 (lyr.), etc. 2. *axis*, of a cone, Arist.*Mete.* 375b22; of a conic section, Apollon.Perg.1 *Def.*7; of a cylinder, Archim.*Con.Sph.Def.*1.260. 3. *axis of the celestial sphere*, Arist.*Mu.* 391b26, Arat.22, D.H.2.5; ἄ. νοητός Eust.1389.59. 4. metaph., *course, path* of action, Lxx *Pr.*2.9, 2.18. II. οἱ ἄξονες *the wooden tablets of the laws* in Athens, *made to turn upon an axis*, Plu.*Sol.*25: sg. in *IG*1.61, D.23.31. 2. in pl., *door-jambs*, Parm.1.19. III. in pl., *part of a bridle bit*, X.*Eq.*10.9 and 10. IV. *the second cervical vertebra*, Poll.2.132. (Cf. Skt. *ákṣas*, Lat. *axis*, OHG. *ahsa*, Lith. *ašis* 'axle'.)

**ἀογκέω**, *diminish in bulk*: hence, *weaken* an arch or vault, *BCH* 23.178 (Pisidia).

**ἄογκος**, ον, *not bulky, attenuated*, σῶμα ὡς ἀογκότατον Hp.*Nat.Hom.* 9. 2. *immaterial*, Syrian.*in Metaph.*143.22; *without mass* or *bulk*, Plot.6.1.26, 6.4.5, Porph.*Sent.*27: Comp., Dam.*Pr.*372.

**ἄοδμος**, ον, v. ἄνοδμος.

**ἀοζ-έω**, *serve, wait on*, A.*Fr.*54. *__-ία__, Ion. -ίη, ἡ, *attendance* on a god, *service*, *Epigr.Gr.*425 (Phryg.). *__-ος__, ὁ, = θεράπων, *servant, attendant*, esp. belonging to a temple, A.*Ag.*231 (lyr.), cf. Call.*Del.*249, *IG*9(1).976 (Corc.). (*sm̥-sod-yos*, root *sed-* 'go', Slav. *chodŭ*, cf. ὁδός.)

**ἄοζος**, ον, = ἄνοζος, q.v.

**ἀοῖα**, τά, trees cut down and dedicated to Aphrodite, Nassandros (sic) ap.Hsch. **ἄοιγον**· ὀλέθριον, Hsch. (leg. λοιγόν).

**ἀοιδάω**, = ἀοιδιάω, dub. in Simon.174, cf. Hdn.Gr.1.439.

*__ἀοιδ-ή__ [ᾰ], Att. contr. ᾠδή (q.v.), ἡ, : (ἀείδω):—*song*, whether: 1. *art of song*, αὐτὰρ ἀοιδὴν θεσπεσίην ἀφέλοντο Il.2.599; ὡς ἄρα τοι.. θεὸς ὤπασε θέσπιν ἀ. Od.8.498. 2. *act of singing, song*, οἱ δ' εἰς ἱμερόεσσαν ἀ. τρεψάμενοι 18.304; ὑπ' ὀρχηθμῷ καὶ ἀοιδῇ Hes.*Sc.*282. 3. *thing sung, song*, στονόεσσαν ἀ. οἱ μὲν ἄρ' ἐθρήνεον Il.24.721, cf. Od. 1.351, Hdt.2.79, Alc.*Supp.*4.24, Pi.*N.*11.18 (pl.), etc.; whether of joy or sorrow, cf. A.*Eu.*954 (lyr.) with S.*Ant.*883; λύρας ἀ. E.*Med.* 425 (lyr.). 4. *theme of song, person sung of*, ἵνα ἦσι καὶ ἐσσομένοισιν ἀ. Od.8.580, cf. Thgn.252, Theoc.12.11; στυγερὴ δέ τ' ἀ. ἔσσετ' ἐπ' ἀνθρώπους [Κλυταιμήστρα] Od.24.200. 5. = ἐπῳδή, *spell, incantation*, ὀχῆες ὠκείαις.. ἀναθρῴσκοντες ἀοιδαῖς A.R.4.42, cf. 59. Cf. ᾠδή. [Dissyll. in Hes.*Th.*48 (unless λήγουσί τ' ἀοιδῆς be read) and in Pi. l.c. (unless μελίζεν be read).] **-ιάω**, poet. for ἀείδω, Od.5.61, 10.227, Hermesian.7.13. **-ικός**, ή, όν, *musical*, prob. coined by Sch.Heph.p.130 C. *__-ιμος__, ον, *sung of, famous in song* or *story*, Hdt.2.79, 135, Pi.*P.*8.59, etc.; προφάταν Id.*Pae.*6.6; from Pi. (*Fr.*76) downwds. a favourite epith. of Athens; ἀ. πόμα a *glorious* draught, Id.*N.*3.79, etc.; ἀ. εὐνομίῃσιν *famous* for his justice, *IG*7.94 (Nisaea), cf. Luc.*Tim.*38, App.*BC*2.82, etc.: Sup., Plu.*Ant.*34:—only once in Hom., and in bad sense, *notorious, infamous*, ὡς.. ἀνθρώποισι πελώμεθ' ἀοίδιμοι Il.6.358. II. *won by song*, ἄγρα, of the Sphinx's victims, E.*El.*471 (lyr.).

**ἀοιδο-θέτης** [ᾰ], ου, ὁ, *lyric poet*, *AP*7.50 (Archim.). **-κῆρυξ**, Dor. -κᾶρυξ, ὁ, *herald who announces singers*, *IG*5(1).1314.15 (Thalamae, ii A.D.). **-μάχος** [ᾰ], ον, *fighting with verses*, λογολέσχαι *AP*11.140 (Lucill.). *__-πόλος__, ὁ, *one busied with song, poet*, like μουσοπόλος, *AP*7.594, 595 (Jul. Aegypt.), cf. *APl.*4.75 (Antip.). 2. *ode-devoted*, of lyric poetry, Aus.*Ep.*14.

*__ἀοιδός__ [ᾰ], ὁ, (ἀείδω) *singer, minstrel, bard*, Il.24.720, Od.3.270, al., Hes.*Th.*95, *Op.*26, Sapph.92, etc.; ἀ. ἀνήρ Od.3.267; θεῖος ἀ. 4.17, 8.87, al.; τοῦ ἀρίστου ἀνθρώπων ἀ. Hdt.1.24; πολλὰ ψεύδονται ἀ. Arist.*Metaph.*983a4: c. gen., γόων, χρησμῶν ἀοιδός, E.*HF*110, *Heracl.* 403; πρᾶτος ἀ., of the cock, Theoc.18.56. 2. fem., *songstress*, πολυΐδρις ἀ. Id.15.97; of the nightingale, Hes.*Op.*208; of the Sphinx, S.*OT*36, E.*Ph.*1507 (lyr.); ἀοιδὸς Μοῦσα Id.*Rh.*386 (lyr.). 3. *enchanter*, S.*Tr.*1000. II. as Adj., *tuneful, musical*, ἀοιδοτάταν ὄρνιθα E.*Hel.*1109 (lyr.), cf. Theoc.12.7, Call.*Del.*252, *IG*12(2). 443. 2. Pass., = ἀοίδιμος, *famous*, πολλὸν ἀοιδοτέρη Arcesil.ap. D.L.4.30. III. = εὐνοῦχος, Hsch.; cf. δοῖδος.

**ἀοιδοτόκος** [ᾰ], ον, *inspiring song*, *AP*9.364 (Nestor).

*__ἀοίκ-ητος__, ον, *uninhabited*, ἀ. καὶ ἔρημος ἡ Λιβύη Hdt.2.34, cf. 5.10, Pl.*Lg.*778b; *uninhabitable*, Arist.*Mete.*362b9. II. *houseless*, ποιεῖν τινα ἀοίκητον *banish* one *from home*, D.45.70, cf. Luc.*Gall.*17. **-ος**, ον, *houseless, homeless*, Hes.*Op.*602, E.*Hipp.*1029, Pl.*Smp.*203d, etc.; ἐπὶ ξένης χώρας ἄοικος S.*Tr.*300; of animals, Arist.*HA*488a 21: Comp., D.Chr.6.62. II. ἄ. εἰσοίκησις a *homeless*, i.e. *miserable*, home, S.*Ph.*534, cf. Nonn.*D.*17.42.

**ἄοιμος**, ον, = ἄρρητος, acc. to Hsch.; but also ἄοιμος· ἄπορος ἢ ἀληθὴς ἢ ἀπρόστυχος, Id.

**ἀοιν-έω**, *abstain from wine*, Hp.*Morb.*3.7. **-ία**, ἡ, *abstinence from wine*, Str.15.1.45. **-ος**, ον, *without wine*, ἄοινοι χοαί, offered to e Erinyes, A.Eu.107 (whence they are themselves called ἄοινοι, S. OC100); ἀοίνοις ἐμμανεῖς θυμώμασιν frenzied with the wine of wrath, A.Eu.860; ἄ. συμπόσιον Thphr.ap.Plu.2.679a; νηφαντικὴ καὶ ἄ. ψυχή Pl.Phlb.61c. 2. of men, having no wine, sober, X.Cyr.6.2.27; also of a place, having none, ib.26. 3. without use of wine, ἀοινοτέρα τροφή Arist.Pol.1336$^{a}$8; ἄοινος μέθη Plu.2.716a.

**ἀοκν-ία**, ἡ, not shrinking from, c. gen., πόνων Hp.Epid.6.4.18; censured by Poll.3.120. -ος, ον, without hesitation, resolute, ἀνήρ Hes.Op.495; φύλακα τροφῆς ἄοκνον S.Aj.563; ἄ. πρὸς μελλητάς Th.1.70; ἔψομαί γ' ἄ. Cleanth.Stoic.1.118; πρὸς τὰς ἀναγκαίας χρήσεις Epicur.Ep.3 p.64 U.; πρὸς τοὺς πόνους Plu.Pel.3; ἄ. βλάβη pressing, present mischief, S.Tr.841. Adv. -νως without hesitation, Hp. Art.38, Pl.Lg.649b, Orib.Syn.Praef.: Sup. -ότατα X.Cyr.1.4.2.

**ἀολλεῖ**· συνάγει, Hsch.

**ἀολλήδην**, Adv. of sq., in a body, together, Epic. in Arch.Pap.7.7, Opp.H.1.788; of two only, Mosch.2.49, cf. sq.

**ἀολλής**, ές, (v. εἴλω) all together, in throngs or crowds, freq. in Hom., esp. of warlike hordes, always in pl., Ἀργεῖοι δ' ὑπέμειναν ἀολλέες Il.5.498; βάλλον δ' εἰν ἐλεοῖσιν ἀολλέα they put [the joints] all together on the dressers, Od.14.432; τύραννον μέγ' ἐπαίνεντες ἀόλλεες Alc.37A, cf. Sapph.Supp.20b.2; χωρῶμεν δὴ πάντες ἀολλεῖς S.Ph.1469 (lyr.); of two only, together, Id.Tr.514 (lyr.); cf. foreg.

**ἀόλλησις**, εως, ἡ, etym. of ἀλλᾶς, EM68.31.

⊛**ἀολλίζω**, gather together, ἀόλλισσαν κατὰ ἄστυ γεραιάς Il.6.287; ἀολλίσσασα γεραιάς ib.270; ἀ. τὸν ὄχλον Pherecyd.11 J.:—Pass., come together, assemble, πάντες ἀολλίσθησαν Ἀχαιοί Il.19.54; πρίν περ ὅμιλον ἀολλισθήμεναι 15.588; νῆσοι ἀολλίζονται Call.Del.18. 2. later of things, gather together, heap up, ὄλβον AP9.649 (Maced.); Βάκχον ib.772 (Phoc.).

**ἀολλόπους, ἀόξοος**, ff.ll. for ἀελλόπους, ἄξοος, Hsch.

**ἀόμμᾰτος**, ον, = ἀνόμματος, Tz.H.1.538.

**ἄοπλος**, ον, without heavy armour on (cf. ὁπλίτης), Th.4.9, etc.: generally, unarmed, Pl.Prt.321c; τὰ τυφλὰ τοῦ σώματος καὶ ἄοπλα καὶ ἄχειρα, i.e. the back, X.Cyr.3.3.45; ἅρμα ἄ. a chariot without scythes, ib.6.4.16. Cf. ἄνοπλος.

**ἄοπος**, ον, (ὄψ) speechless, Hsch. II. = sq., Id.

**ἄοπτος**, ον, unseen, Antipho Soph.4.

**ἄορ** or **ἀορ**, ἄορος, τό (on the accent see Hdn.Gr.1.391): (ἀείρω):—properly, hanger or sword hung in a belt (cf. ἀορτήρ), Od.11.24; synon. with ξίφος, 10.294, cf. 321.—The masc. acc. pl., οὐκ ἄορας οὐδὲ λέβητας 17.222 (cf. Hsch.), is prob. f.l. for ἀορά γ'; Eust.1818.5 and the Scholl. ad loc. expl. ἄορας as = ὄαρας, women given as prizes (cf. ἀόρων· γυναικῶν, Hsch.), or = τρίποδας. 2. later, any weapon, ἄορ τριγλώχιν the trident, Call.Del.31; of the horn of the rhinoceros, Opp. C.2.553. [Hom. has ᾰ in dissyll. forms, as also Hes.Sc.457, Call. Hec.1.1.1; in the trisyll. forms, ᾰ Od.17.222, al., ᾱ Il.10.484, al. In Hes.Sc.221, and later Poets, ᾱ even in ἄορ, which must then be written ἆορ. Hes.Th.283 has ἄορ as monosyll., unless we read with Tricl. γένθ', ὃ δ' ἄορ χρύσειον ...]

**ἀορᾰ-σία**, ἡ, inability to see, blindness, Plb.12.25$^{g}$.4, Lxx Ge.19.11, al., IG12(9).955.8, 1179.26 (Euboea); failure to observe, στάσεων Inscr.Magn.114.4. ⊛-τος, ον, unseen, invisible, Pl.Phd.85e, etc.; ἀόρατος ὄψιν Alex.240.5; τραῦμ' ἀ., ἔρως APl.4.198 (Maec.); ἀ. τὸ μέλλον Isoc.1.29; τὸ ἀόρατον the unseen world, the unseen, ἐξ οὐρανοῦ καὶ τοῦ ἀ. Pl.Sph.246a, cf. Tht.155e, al.: τὰν ἀ. ἀτραπιτὸν βιότου obscure, Epigr.Gr.223 (Milet.); ἀ. κατὰ δόξαν Ath.12.511d; τὸν ἀ. ὡς ὁρῶν Ep.Hebr.11.27. Adv. -τως Ph.1.157, Placit.2.24.5. II. Act., not having seen, without experience of, παντὸς κακοῦ, δεινοῦ, Plb. 2.21.2, 3.108.6: abs., Luc.Halc.3.

**ἀόρβιτος**, ον, (orbis) without tyres, τροχοί Edict.Diocl.15.31a.

⊛**ἀοργ-ησία**, ἡ, a defect in the passion of anger, 'lack of gall', Arist. EN1108$^{a}$8, cf. 1126$^{a}$3:—in good sense, Plu., who wrote a treatise περὶ ἀοργησίας, cf. Nic.Dam.p.150 D., Andronic.Rhod.p.575 M., Gal. 5.30. -ητος, ον, not irascible, Arist.EN1108$^{a}$8:—in good sense, Phld.Ir.p.71 W., Plu.2.10c, Luc.Herm.12, Aret.CD1.4, etc. Adv. -τως Phld.Lib.p.7 O., Arr.Epict.3.18.6, Hierocl. in CA12 p.447 M. -ιστος, ον, = foreg., Sor.1.88.

⊛**ἀοριστ-αίνω**, = sq., Procl.Inst.124, Phlp. in GA191.34, Sch. Hermog.Stat. in Rh.4.82 W., Dam.Pr.436; to be undecided, uncertain (of a fact), Ps.-Alex.Aphr. in SE57.24. 2. make ἀόριστος, Iamb. in Nic.p.78 P. -εύω, = sq., Arc.142.4. -έω, to be indeterminate, Arist.Pr.941$^{b}$26. 2. to be without definite ideas, uncertain, Phld.Mus.p.48 K., cf. S.E.P.1.28, Porph.Sent.33, Asp. in EN74.27. 3. to be immoderate, opp. ἔχεσθαι ὅρου καὶ μέτρου, Epicur. Fr.465. ⊛-ία, ἡ, indefiniteness, indeterminateness, τῆς ὥρας Arist. Pr.941$^{b}$32, cf. Mete.361$^{b}$34, Thphr.Vent.52, Gal.4.406. 2. illimitability, Epicur.Sent.Vat.63. 3. indecision, τῆς ψυχῆς Plot.2.4.10. 4. lack of limit, κατὰ τὰς ἐπιθυμίας Carneisc.Herc.1027.14, cf. Phld.Herc.1251.3. 5. pl., irregularities, τὰς κατὰ τῶν φασμάτων τῶν τοῦ ἡλίου ἀοριστίας Epicur.Nat.11.6. -ος, ον, without boundaries, debatable, γῆ Th.1.139. 2. limitless, ὀρέξεις, φόβοι, ἐπιθυμίαι, Epicur.Fr.202, 203. II. indeterminate, Pl.Lg.643d, Arist.Metaph. 1087$^{a}$17, al.; οὐδὲν ἀνεξέταστον οὐδ' ἀ. D.4.36; ἄτακτα, ἀδιόρθωτα, ἀόρισθ' ἅπαντα ibid.; ἀ. ἀξιώματα indefinite propositions, Chrysipp. Stoic.2.5, al.; ἀ. καὶ κρίσεως προσδεόμενον, opp. ὡρισμένον, Epicur. Nat.p.31 G.; ἀ. [ἄρχων] one who holds office without limit of time, Arist.Pol.1275$^{a}$26; uncertain, ζωῆς τελευτή AP9.499: Comp. πρόληψις Phld.Rh.2.189 S., cf. Plot.3.9.2. Adv. -τως Pl.Lg.916e, Arist. Cat.8$^{b}$9, al. 2. ἀ. ὄνομα or ῥῆμα an indefinite term, as οὐκ-ἄνθρωπος Id.Int.16$^{a}$32, 16$^{b}$14; of pronouns, A.D.Pron.7.1, al. 3. ὁ ἀ. (sc. χρόνος) the aorist tense, D.T.638.24, A.D.Synt.276.5, al. -όω, in Pass., to be indefinite, ib.70.4, al. -ύς· ὁμιλία, Zonar.; cf. ἀόρκους (leg. ὀαριστύς). -ώδης, indefinite, φαντασία Hierocl. p.39 A., cf. A.D.Pron.5.14, Synt.27.4, al.; ἀ. χρόνος Eust.1755.58. Adv., A.D.Synt.70.1.

**ἀόρκτους**· ὁμιλίας, Hsch.; cf. ἀοριστύς.

**ἀόρμητος**, ον, without impulse, Ph.1.278.

**ἄορνος**, ον, (ὄρνις) without birds, λίμνη S.Fr.748; ἄ. ὕψη heights no birds can reach, Plu.2.327c; ἄ. λίμνη lake Avernus, Arist.Mir.839$^{a}$13; called ὁ Ἄορνος by Str.5.4.5; ἡ ἄ. πέτρα, a hill-fort on the Indus, D.S. 17.85, Plu.2.181c.

**ἄορον**· μοχλόν, πυλῶνα, θυρωρόν (Cypr.), Hsch. **ἄορος**· ἄυπνος (Methymn.), Id.

**ἀορτ-εύς** [ᾰ]· ἀορτήρ, Hsch. -έω, lengthd. form of ἀείρω, found only in aor. 1 part. Pass. ἀορτηθεὶς hung up, suspended, AP7.696 (Arch.). -ή, ἡ, (ἀείρω) in pl., = βρόγχια, Hp.Loc.Hom.14 (where Littré reads ἀορτρέων, -τρῃσι), Coac.394, cf. Ruf.Onom.159. 2. the arteries springing from the heart, i.e. aorta and pulmonary artery, Hp.Cord.10; esp. in sg., the aorta, Arist.HA496$^{a}$7, 513$^{b}$4, etc.: in pl., arteries, Poll.2.205. II. knapsack that hung from the shoulders, Men.331, Diph.40, Posidipp.10, cf. Poll.7.79, 10.139. III. point of suspension of a balance, Theol.Ar.29. ⊛-ήρ, ῆρος, ὁ, (ἀείρω) strap to hang anything to, sword-belt, Od.11.609: in pl., κουλεὸν.. χρυσέοισιν ἀορτήρεσσιν ἀρηρός Il.11.31 (also expl. as οἱ κρίκοι τῆς θήκης, Hsch.). 2. in Od.13.438 knapsack-strap, στρόφος ἀορτήρ, v. στρόφος. ⊛-ης, ὁ, = ἀορτή II (Maced.), Hsch. 2. = ἀορτήρ I, Id. -ρα, τά, lobes of the lungs, Hp.Morb.2.54.

**ἀόρχης**, ες, without ὄρχεις, gelded, D.C.75.14.

**ἄος**· πνεῦμα ἢ ἄημα (cod. ἴαμα), Hsch.

⊛**ἀοσμ-ία**, ἡ, want of perfume, opp. εὐοσμία, Thphr.CP6.16.3. -ος, ον, having no smell, v.l. in Hp.Acut.63, Arist.Sens.443$^{a}$10: Comp., ib.19; opp. εὔοσμος, Thphr.CP6.16.5; cf. ἄνοδμος, ἄνοσμος.

**ἀοσσ-έω**, aor. inf. ἀοσσῆσαι, help, τινί Mosch.4.110; cf. ἀοζέω. (sm-soq$^{u}$-io-, cf. Lat. socius, ἕπομαι.) ⊛-ητήρ, ῆρος, ὁ, assistant, helper, aider, Il.15.254, 22.333, Od.4.165, A.R.1.471, etc.

**ἄοστον**· ἄριστον, Hsch. (i.e. ἄωστον). **ἀούματα**, τά, chaff (Cypr.), Id. (fort. λούματα, = λύματα).

**ἄουτος**, ον, (οὐτάω) unwounded, unhurt, Il.18.536, Hes.Sc. 157. II. = ἀνήκοος, Hsch.

**ἀοχλ-ησία**, ἡ, freedom from disturbance, τοῦ σώματος Epicur.Ep.3 p.62 U.; ψυχῆς S.E.P.1.10, cf. Posidon.Stoic.3.5. -ητος, ον, undisturbed, calm, διαγωγή D.H.1.8: an Epicurean term, Epicur. Sent.Vat.79, cf. Luc.Par.11; τὸ τῆς σαρκὸς ἀ. Alciphr.3.55. Adv., Comp. -ότερον Gal.13.597: Sup. -ότατα Id.15.707. -ος, ον, not troublesome, Hp.Art.78 (Sup.). Adv. -ως Id.Fract.31.

**ἄοψ**, οπος, ὁ, ἡ, without eyes, Hsch.

**ἀπαβοιδῶρ** (Lacon., = ἀπαοιδῶς), out of tune, Hsch.

**ἀπαγγ-ελεύς**, έως, ὁ, = ἀπαγγελτήρ, Man.2.263. ⊛-ελία, ἡ, report, e.g. of an ambassador, D.19.5, al., Arist.Rh.Al.1438$^{b}$10; ἀ. ποιεῖσθαι Lycurg.14; in Psychology, reports of the senses, Plot.4.6.3. 2. narrative, recital, description, ὧν.. βραχεῖα ἡ ἀ. ἀρκεῖ Th. 3.67; lyric poetry is said to be δι' ἀπαγγελίας αὐτοῦ τοῦ ποιητοῦ Pl. R.394c, cf. Phld.Po.5.1425.2; dramatic poetry is expressed by action καὶ οὐ δι' ἀπαγγελίας Arist.Po.1449$^{b}$26, cf. ib.11, D.H.Comp. 20. II. diction, Id.Dem.25, Plu.Dem.2.

⊛**ἀπαγγ-έλλω**, fut. -αγγελῶ, Ion. -έω Simon.5.18: aor. 1 -ήγγειλα: pf. -ήγγελκα Plu.Fab.16:—Pass., pf. -ήγγελμαι Pl.Chrm.153c: aor. -ηγγέλθην Hdt.2.121.ε', E.Hec.672, later -ηγγέλην Plu.Galb.25: 1. of a messenger, bring tidings, report, τινί τι Il.9.626, etc., Pi.P.6.18, Hdt.3.25, etc.; τι πρός τινα A.Ch.266, X.An.6.3.22, etc.; ἀ. εἰς τὴν Ἑλλάδα, εἰς τὸ στρατόπεδον, ib.2.4.4, 6.4.25; τὰ παρά τινος ib.2.3.4; ταῦτα περί σου οἴκαδε Pl.Men.71c, cf. Hp.de Arte 11, Th.4.122; ἀ. ἡδονάς, φόνον, E.IT642, Andr.1241: folld. by relat. clause, ἐκέλευε τὸν ἄγγελον ἀπαγγέλλειν ὅτι.. Hdt.1.127, cf. X.An.2.3.5; ἀ. ὡς.. Lys.9.6: abs., πάλιν ἀ. bring back tidings, report in answer, Od.9.95:—Pass., ἐξ ὧν.. ἀπηγγέλλετό μοι as he was reported to me, D.21.25: c. part., ἀπηγγέλθη.. ὁ νέκυς ἐκκεκλεμμένος was reported to have been stolen away, Hdt.2.121.ε'. 2. of a speaker or writer, report, relate, ὄψις ἀπαγγέλλει Id.1.210, cf. Arist.Rh.1417$^{b}$9, Po.1448$^{a}$21, D.H. Comp.20; ὧν ὁ παθὼν ἔνια.. οὐδ' ἂν ἀπαγγεῖλαι δύναιθ' ἑτέρῳ D.21.72; describe, Hp.Prorrh.2.3 (Pass.), cf. Plu.Fab.16; [Ῥωμαίους] ἡττημένους ὑπὸ τοῦ συγγραφέως ἀπηγγέλθαι Plb.1.15.11. 3. recite, declaim, Chor. in Rev.Phil.1.220. II. explain, interpret, a dream or riddle, Lxx Ge.41.8, Jd.14.12. ⊛-ελσις, εως, ἡ, = ἀπαγγελία, AB438. -ελτήρ, ῆρος, ὁ, one who reports, messenger, Phryn. Trag.(?) ap.Phot.p.154 R.: metaph. of a cork, ἀ. κύρτου AP6.5 (Phil.). ⊛-ελτικός, ή, όν, reporting, αἴσθησις Plot.4.4.17; narrative, Sch.Ar.Ach.9. II. Rhet., of or for expression: τὸ ἀ. power of expressing, Arr.Epict.2.23.2. Adv. -κῶς S.E.P.1.197.

**ἀπαγγή**· φανερὸν ποιῶ, Hsch.

**ἄπᾰγε**, (imper. of ἀπάγω) away! begone! Lat. apage! ἄ. ἐς μακαρίαν Ar.Eq.1151; κἄπαγ' ἀπὸ τῆς ὀσφύος hands off! Id.Pax 1053: abs., Luc.Prom.Es 7, Am.38, etc.: rarely c. part., ἄπαγε τὰ πάρος εὐτυχήματ' αὐδῶν E.Ph.1733: pl., D.C.38.46.

**ἀπαγελάζω**· abgrego, Gloss.

**ἀπάγελος** [ᾰγ], ον, not yet received into the ἀγέλη, of boys under 17, Cret. word, Palch. in Cat.Cod.Astr.5(1).188.31 (prob. l.), Hsch.

**ἀπαγής**, ές, (πήγνυμι) not firm or stiff, πῖλοι ἀπαγέες Hdt.7.61;

of water, ἀ. καὶ ἀσύστατον Plu.2.949b, cf. Gal.8.677; ὀστοῦν ἔτι ἄ. Antyll.ap.Orib.46.27.5; of flesh, *flabby*, D.L.7.1, Poll.1.191.

**ἀπᾰγῑνέω**, Ion. for ἀπάγω, esp. *pay* tribute, ἀ. φόρον Hdt.3.89,94.

**ἀπαγκῠλόω**, *make crooked*, χεῖρα v.l. in Ath.15.667c; σπάρτον *make a loop in* a rope, Hero *Aut.*27.4.

***ἀπαγκωνίζομαι**, *bare the elbows*, aor. -ισάμενος Archipp.1 D.; ἀπηγκωνισμένη πάντα *elbowing* all *aside*, utterly *unabashed*, Philostr. *VA*6.11; γλῶττα ἀπηγκωνισμένη καὶ γυμνή Id.*VS*2.1.11. II. Act. in Eust.1221.58, *bind* one's *hands behind* him.

***ἀπαγλαΐζω**, *deprive of ornament*, τινά τινος *AP*5.219 (Agath.), cf. Poll.1.217:—Pass., Tim.*Pers.*20. II. *honour to the full*, *IG*.12(5).292 (Paros).

**ἀπάγλαυται**· διόλου κατάνυται, Hsch.

**ἄπαγμα**, ατος, τό, *fracture at a joint*, Gal.ap.Orib.46.6.1, Gal.10.424.

**ἀπαγνίζω**, Ion. for ἀφαγνίζω, q.v.

***ἀπάγνῡμαι**, *to be fractured at a joint*, Gal.ap.Orib.46.6.3.

**ἀπαγοράζω**· *redimo*, *Gloss.*

**ἀπαγόρευ-μα**, ατος, τό, *prohibition, interdict*, Plu.2.1037d; προστάγματα καὶ ἀ. Arr.*Epict.*3.24.98. **-σις**, εως, ἡ, *prohibition*, ἐπίρρημα -εύσεως D.T.642.5, cf. A.D.*Synt.*246.4, al. II. *failure of strength, exhaustion*, Luc.*Anach.*37, Plu.*Ant.*45. **-τέον**, *one must give up*, Luc.*Herm.*47; *one must issue a prohibition*, περί τινος D.Chr.7.133 (dub.). **-τικός**, ή, όν, *prohibitory*, Plu.2.1037f; τινός Corn.*ND* 16; of particles, A.D.*Conj.*229.16. Adv. -κῶς Aristeas 131; gloss on ἀπηλεγέως, Sch.Il.1.309. ***-ω**, mostly in pres. and impf. only (ἀπερῶ being used as fut. by correct writers, ἀπεῖπον as aor., ἀπείρηκα as pf., and ἀπορρηθήσομαι, ἀπερρήθην, ἀπείρημαι as Pass. fut., aor., and pf.): aor. ἀπηγόρευσα Pl.*Tht.*200d (v.l.), D.40.44, 55.4, freq. in later writers: pf. ἀπηγόρευκα Arist.*Phgn.*808$^a$11, Plu.2.1096f, etc.; Arist. (v. infr.) has pf. Pass. ἀπηγορευμένος:—*forbid*, μὴ ποιεῖν τι Hdt.1.183, 3.51, Ar.*Ach.*169, etc.; ἀ. τινὶ μὴ ποιεῖν Hdt.4.125, Pl.*Prt.*334c, al.; ἀ. μηδένα βάλλειν X.*Cyr.*1.4.14; τινὶ ποιεῖν τι D.S.20.18; ἔμοιγε ἀπηγόρευες ὅπως μὴ.. ἀποκρινοίμην Pl.*R.*339a; τοῦ νόμου ἀπαγορεύοντος ἐάν τις.. Lys.9.6; ἀ. τι Id.10.6; περὶ ὧν ὁ νόμος ἀ. μὴ κινῶσιν Arist.*Pol.*1298$^a$38; τὰ ἀπηγορευμένα things *forbidden*, ib.1336$^b$9, cf. S.E.*P.*1.152. 2. *dissuade*, πολλὰ ἀπαγορεύων οὐδὲν ἤνυε Hdt.9.66, cf. 3.124; ἀ. τινί τι Plu.*Arat.*35. II. intr., *bid farewell to*, c. dat., ἀ. τῷ πολέμῳ *give up*, *renounce* war, Pl.*Mx.*245b: c. acc., τὴν ἀγκιστρείαν Aristaenet.1.17; *lose*, στρώματα εἰς τὴν βαφὴν Eun.*VS*p.487 B.: c. part., *give up doing*, οὔτε λέγων οὔτε ἀκούων ἀ. X.*Cyn.*1.16: also, *grow weary of*, ἀ. θεώμενος Id.*Eq.*11.9: abs., *give up, flag, fail*, Pl.*R.*368c, 568d, *Tht.*200d (answering to ἀπεροῦμεν above); ἀ. γήρᾳ *by* old age, X.*Eq.Mag.*1.2; ἀ. ὑπὸ πόνων *to be exhausted* by.., Id.*An.*5.8.3; ταχὺ ἀ. οἱ ἵπποι Arist.*IA*712$^a$32; ἀ. πρὸς στρατείαν Plu.*Cor.*13; πρὸς κρύος Luc.*Anach.*24, cf. Eun.*Hist.* p.272 D.: also of things, τὰ ἀπαγορεύοντα *worn out and useless*, X.*Cyr.*6.2.33. III. *make an announcement, proclamation from*, ἀπὸ τῶ λάω ὧ ἀπαγορεύοντι *Leg.Gort.*10.36, 11.13.

**ἀπαγορία**, Dor. for ἀπηγορία, dub. in Pi.*Fr.*122.6.

**ἀπαγρεύω**, *carry off, take away*, Hsch.

**ἀπαγρι-όομαι**, *become wild* or *savage*, μή μ' ἐκπλαγῆτ'.. ἀπηγριωμένον S.*Ph.*226, cf. Pl.*Plt.*274b; ὑπὸ τῶν στατήρων ἦν ἀπηγριωμένη had been *made saucy* by riches, Epicr.3.16. II. of plants, *revert to wild state*, Thphr.*HP*2.2.9, 3.2.2. **-ωσις**, εως, ἡ, *reversion to wild state*, Id.*CP*4.5.6.

**ἄπαγρος**, ον, (ἄγρα) *unlucky in the chase*, Hsch.

**ἀπαγχον-άω**, = sq. in Pass., D.C.72.7:—also -έω, in Pass., Steph. in *Hp.*2.334 D. **-ίζω**, *hang by a noose, strangle*, Ant.Lib.13.7; αὑτόν *AP*11.111 (Nicarch.):—Pass., Hp.*Virg.*1; γυναῖκας ἀπ' ἐλαίας ἀπηγχονισμένας D.L.6.52. II. *release from a noose*, Luc.*Lex.*11.

**ἀπάγχω**, *strangle, throttle*, ὁ μὲν λάε νεβρὸν ἀπάγχων Od.19.230; γαλῆν ἀ. Ar.*Pax*795, cf. Plu.*Mar.*27, Luc.*Lex.*11; ὃ μάλιστά μ' ἀπάγχει *chokes* me *with anger*, Ar.*V.*686:—Med., aor. ἀπηγξάμην, and Pass., *hang oneself, to be hanged*, Archil.67, Hdt.2.131, Hp.*Aph.*2.43, A.*Supp.*465, And.1.125, Philem.130, etc.; ἐκ δένδρων Th.3.81; ὥστε μ' ἀπάγχεσθ' *am ready to choke*, Ar.*Nu.*988; ἀπάγξασθαι ῥηγνύμενος Arr.*Epict.*2.20.31.

***ἀπάγω** [ᾰγ], *lead away, carry off*, ἀπάγουσι βόας καὶ ἴφια μῆλα Od.18.278; ἀ. τινὰ ἐκτόπιον S.*OT*1340 (lyr.), cf.121, etc.; προσάγειν.., ἀπάγειν, bring near.., *hold far off*, Arist.*GC*336$^a$18; ἀ. ἀχλὺν ἀπ' ὀφθαλμῶν *remove* it, Thphr.*HP*7.6.2; τὸ ἱμάτιον ἀπὸ τοῦ τραχήλου Plu.*Ant.*12; οὐκ ἀπάξετε ταῦτα; *stop* this *fooling!* Jul.*Or.*7.225a:—Med., *take away for* or *with oneself*, παρθένον Hdt.1.196, cf. 4.80, Ar.*Nu.*1105, etc.; or *that which is one's own*, X.*Cyr.*3.1.37, etc.:—Pass., ἐς ὀξὺ ἀπηγμένας *brought to a point, tapering off*, Hdt.7.64, cf. 2.28, Arist.*PA*658$^b$30. 2. *lead away, draw off* troops, τῆς στρατιῆς τὸ πολλὸν Hdt.1.164, cf. Th.1.28, al.; ἄπαγε τὸν ἵππον Ar.*Nu.*32. b. elliptically, *retire, withdraw*, Hdt.5.126, X.*HG*1.1.34, al.; 'go off', Apollod.*Epit.*3.3. 3. *abduct*, Aeschin.1.80, Luc.*Tim.*16:—Pass., πρὸς ὕβριν -εσθαι Id.*Anach.*13. II. *bring back, bring home*, Il.18.326; ἀπήγαγεν οἴκαδε Od.16.370, cf. S.*Ph.*941, X.*An.*1.3.14; ἀ. ὀπίσω Hdt.9.117. III. *return, render what one owes, pay*, τὸν φόρον Ar.*V.*707, cf. X.*Cyr.*2.4.12, Th.5.53; *render* service, honour, etc., κώμους πρὸς τάφον E.*Tr.*1184; θεωρίαν εἰς Δῆλον Pl.*Phd.*58b. IV. *arrest and carry off*, ἀπάγετε αὐτὸν παρ' ἐμέ Hdt.2.114, cf. 6.81; δεῖν κἀπάγειν ἐφίετο E.*Ba.*439:—Pass., ἀπαχθέντας παρ' ἑωυτὸν Hdt.6.119. 2. law-term, *bring before a magistrate and accuse* (cf. ἀπαγωγή III), Antipho 5.85; ἀσεβείας *for* impiety, D.22.27; ἀ. ὡς θεσμοθέτας Id.23.31; ἀ. τοῖς ἕνδεκα Id.24.113; τὴν ἐπὶ θανάτῳ -εσθαι Sch.Arist.*Rh.*1397$^a$30 ap.D.H.*Amm.*1.12. 3. *carry off to prison*, Pl.*Grg.*486a, Ar.*Ach.*57; εἰς τὸ δεσμωτήριον And.4.181, D.23.80, 35.47 (Pass.): abs., ὡς γόης ἀπαχθῆναι Pl.*Men.*80b; ἀπαχθεὶς Lys.25.15. V. *lead away, divert* from the subject, esp. by sophistry, ἀπὸ τοῦ ὄντος ἐπὶ τοὐναντίον Pl.*Phdr.*262b; ἀ. τινὰ ἀπὸ τῆς ὑποθέσεως D.19.242; ἀ. τὸ ὀργιζόμενον τῆς γνώμης *divert*.., Th.2.59; ἀπὸ δεινῶν ἀ. τὴν γνώμην ib.65. b. in Logic, *reduce*, εἰς ἀδύνατον Arist.*APr.*29$^b$9:—impers. in Pass., ἀπῆκται ἄρα εἰς.. Papp.798.11. c. in later Greek, *reduce, drive* an opposing disputant, ἐπὶ ψεῦδος S.E.*P.*2.233; εἰς ἀντίφασιν, εἰς ἄτοπον, Phlp.*in APr.*21.31, 58.14:—Pass., εἰς ἀδύνατον ἀπαχθῆναι Arr.*Epict.*1.7.25, cf. Phlp.*in APr.*129.2. 2. *receive*, ἀπ' ὄψεως.. τὰ δοξάζοντα ἀ. Pl.*Phlb.*39b. 3. *separate*, ἀπάγεται καὶ χωρίζεται Id.*Phd.*97b. VI. simply, *carry*, ἐν ἀριστερᾷ τόξον Id.*Lg.*795a.

**ἀπᾰγωγή**, ἡ, *leading away*, of troops, X.*An.*7.6.5; *dragging away, rape*, γυναικῶν Luc.*Phal.*1.3 (pl.). b. *leading into captivity*, Lxx *Is.*10.4, al. c. *separation, withdrawal*, σώματος (from the soul), Plot.4.4.19. II. *payment*, κατεστρέψατο ἐς φόρου ἀ. subjected them to *payment* of tribute, Hdt.1.6.27, 2.182. III. as Att. law-term, 1. *a summary process by which a person* caught in the act (ἐπ' αὐτοφώρῳ) *might be arrested* by any citizen and brought before the magistrates, Antipho 5.9, And.1.88, Lys.13.85f, D.24.113; ἀπαγωγῆς ἄξια Hyp.*Eux.*16. 2. *written complaint* handed in to the magistrates, ἀπάγειν τὴν ἀ. lay such *accusation*, Lys.13.86; παραδέχεσθαι ἀ., of the Eleven, *admit it*, ibid. IV. in Logic, *shifting of* the basis of argument: hence of argument based on a probable or agreed assumption, Arist.*APr.*69$^a$20, cf. Anon.*in SE*65.35; *reduction*, ἡ εἰς τὸ ἀδύνατον ἀ. *reductio per impossibile*, *APr.*29$^b$6; ἡ ἀ. μετάβασίς ἐστιν ἀπ' ἄλλου προβλήματος ἢ θεωρήματος ἐπ' ἄλλο, οὗ γνωσθέντος ἢ πορισθέντος καὶ τὸ προκείμενον ἔσται καταφανές Procl.*in Euc.*p.212 F.; τῶν ἀπορουμένων διαγραμμάτων τὴν ἀ. ποιήσασθαι ib.p.213 F. b. *reduction* of a disputant (cf. ἀπάγω v.1c), ἡ ἐπὶ τὸ ἄδηλον ἀ. S.E.*P.*2.234.

**ἀπᾰγωγός**, όν, *leading away, diverting*, λύπης Gorg.*Hel.*10, cf. Iamb.*Myst.*2.5.

**ἀπᾰγώνιος**, v. ἐπαγώνιος.

**ἀπᾰδεῖν**, Ion. -έειν, v. sub ἁφανδάνω.

**ἀπᾰδῐκέω**, *withhold wrongfully*, μισθὸν ἀ. τινός Lxx *De.*24.14. II. *wrong*, *PLond.*2.354.7 (i B.C., Pass.).

**ἀπᾳδόντως**, Adv. *unbefittingly*, Plot.3.5.5.

**ἀπᾴδω**, fut. -ᾴσομαι Pl.*Ti.*26d:—*sing out of tune*, ὅλῃ ἁρμονίᾳ Id.*Lg.*802e; ἐπὶ τὸ ὀξὺ Arist.*Pr.*919$^b$23: abs., Pl.*Hp.Mi.*374c, D.Chr.13.20, etc. II. metaph., *dissent*, ἀπ' ἀλλήλων Pl.*Lg.*662b; πρὸς τὴν καθεστῶσαν πολιτείαν Plu.*Lyc.*27: c. gen., ἐθῶν Luc.*Anach.*6; *to be at variance with*, τῆς ἀληθείας Ph.1.235; *fall short of*, τῆς διὰ τῶν νεύρων ἰσχύος Hero *Bel.*112.16. 2. *wander away*, πολὺ ἀπῇσας ἀπὸ τοῦ ἐρωτήματος Pl.*Hp.Ma.*292c. 3. in part., *unbefitting*, ἀπᾴδοντα τῷ θεῷ ἐγκώμια Jul.*Or.*4.132b; τῷ πράγματι Lib.*Or.*10.34; ξένον καὶ ἀπᾷδον τὸ ῥῆμα Porph.*Chr.*69.

**ἀπᾰείρω**, aor. -ήειρα, poet. form of ἀπαίρω, *depart*, E.*Fr.*773.68:—in Med., ἀπαειρόμενον πόλιος Il.21.563. II. trans., *remove*, ὀθόνην ἀπὸ γυίων Orac.ap.Porph.ap.Eus.*PE*5.9.

**ἀπᾰέξομαι**, poet. for ἀπαυξάνομαι, *grow out of*, Semon.7.85; plpf. ἀπηέξηντο Q.S.14.198 (dub.).

**ἀπᾰθᾰνᾰτ-ίζω**, *aim at immortality*, Pl.*Chrm.*156d, v.l. in Arist.*EN*1177$^b$33. II. trans., *deify*, D.S.2.20, Vett.Val.150.17; ἑαυτὸν Inscr.ap.Str.15.1.73; ἀ. τὴν ψυχήν *represent* it *as immortal*, Ascl.*in Metaph.*90.26; *make perpetual*, θεὸς ἀ. τὰ γένη Ph.1.9; διὰ τοῦ πυρὸς ἀ. τοῖς θεοῖς τὰς τιμάς Porph.*Abst.*2.5:—Pass., *become immortal, earn immortality*, ψυχαὶ ἀπαθανατιζόμεναι, opp. φθαρτὰ σώματα, Ph.1.427; *become a god*, D.C.45.7. **-ισις**, εως, ἡ, *immortalization, deification*, dub. l. in Id.60.35. **-ισμός**, ὁ, = foreg., Corn.*ND*31, *PMag.Par.*1.741, al.

**ἀπάθ-εια** [πᾰ], ἡ, *impassibility*, of things, opp. πάθος, Arist.*Ph.*217$^b$26, *Metaph.*1046$^a$13: pl., opp. πάθη, Epicur.*Ep.*1 p.25 U., S.E.*M.*10.224. II. of persons, *insensibility, apathy*, Arist.*EN*1104$^b$24, *de An.*429$^a$29; ἀ. τῶν κακῶν *insensibility to*.., Thphr.*HP*9.15.1; ἀ. περί τι Arist.*APo.*97$^b$23, *Rh.*1383$^b$16. 2. as Stoic term, *freedom from emotion*, Dionys.*Stoic.*3.35, cf. Arr.*Epict.*4.6.34, al., Plu.2.82f; spelt ἀπαθία in Antip.*Stoic.*3.109, Phld.*Sto.Herc.*339.7. III. *absence of injury*, σῴζεσθαι δι' ἀπάθειαν ἀνακαμπτόμενα for the sake of *immunity*, Arist.*PA*682$^b$21. **-έω**, *to be free from* πάθος, Phld.*Lib.* p.40 O.

**Ἀπᾰθηναῖοι**, ων, οἱ, *degenerate Athenians*, Theopomp.Hist.308; censured by Poll.3.58.

**ἀπᾰθής**, ές, *not suffering* or *having suffered*, c. gen., ἀ. ἔργων αἰσχρῶν Thgn.1177; κακῶν Hdt.1.32, 2.119, X.*An.*7.7.33, etc.; ἀεικείης Hdt.3.160; τῶν σεισμῶν τῶν τοῦ σώματος Pl.*Phlb.*33e; νόσων D.60.33, etc.; but also, *without experience of*, πόνων Hdt.6.12; καλῶν μεγάλων Id.1.207: abs., A.*Pers.*862 (lyr.), Th.1.26; πρός τινος Pi.*P.*4.297; χάριν ἴσθι ἐὼν ἀ. be grateful for going *unpunished*, Hdt.9.79: generally, *unaffected*, τὸ οἰκεῖον ὑπὸ τοῦ οἰκείου ἐστὶν ἀ. Arist.*Pr.*872$^a$11, cf. Thphr.*Ign.*42; πρός τι Plu.*Alc.*13, etc.: c. dat. modi, Luc.*Nav.*44. b. Medic., of organs, *unaffected, sound*, μόρια Aret.*SD*1.7, cf. Gal.5.122; τὰ ἀπαθῆ τῶν ᾠῶν *good* eggs, Alex.Aphr.*Pr.*2.76. II. *without passion* or *feeling, insensible, free from emotion*, Arist.*Top.*125$^b$23, cf. *Rh.*1378$^a$5, 1383$^a$28, *Stoic.*3.109, al., Pers.*Stoic.*1.99; of the Cynics, Polystr.p.20 W.; *unmoved by*.., τινός Phld.*Acad.Ind.*p.51 M. Adv. -θῶς, ἔχειν Plu.*Sol.*20: Comp. -έστερον Plot.

3.6.9: Sup. -έστατα Longin.41.1. 2. of things, *not liable to change, impassive*, Arist.*Metaph.*1019ᵃ31, al.; ἀ. αἱ ἰδέαι Id.*Top.*148ᵃ20, cf. *Metaph.*991ᵇ26; 'Αναξαγόρας τὸν νοῦν ἀ. φάσκων Id.*Ph.*256ᵇ25; ὁ δὲ νοῦς ἴσως θειότερόν τι καὶ ἀπαθές ἐστιν Id.*de An.*408ᵇ29, cf. 430ᵃ18; οὐσία ἀσώματος καὶ ἀ. Plu.2.765a; ἀ. ὑπὸ τῶν πολλῶν *unaffected* by the many, Dam.*Pr.*60. 3. Medic., *unaffected by disease, healthy*, περιταμὼν ἄχρι τῶν ἀπαθῶν Gal.5.122, cf. Antyll.ap.Orib.44.23.13. III. *exciting no feeling*, Arist.*Po.*1453ᵇ39; τὰ ἀπαθῆ *unemotional topics*, Id.*Fr.*134. IV. Gramm., *not modified*, of uncontracted verbs, Theodos.*Can.*p.36 H.; of patronymics, Eust.13.17; in Metric, *free from metrical licences*, Ps.-Plu.*Metr.*p.472 B. V. ἀπαθῆ, τὰ μὴ ὡς ἀληθῶς γεγονότα πάθη Antipho Soph.5.

**ἀπαθία**, v. ἀπάθεια.

**ἀπαί**, = ἀπό, Emp.134, D.P.51. **ἀπαιάζει**, corrupt in Hsch.

**ἀπαιγειρόομαι**, *to be changed into a poplar*, Str.5.1.9.

**ἀπαιδᾰγώγητος**, ον, *without teacher* or *guide*, Arist.*EN*1121ᵇ11; *uneducated, untaught*, τινός *in* a thing, Id.*Pol.*1338ᵇ33 (v.l. ἀπαιδάγωγος): -ητον, τό, *lack of education*, Sor.1.33.

**ἀπαιδ-ευσία**, Ion. -ιή, ἡ, *want of education*, Democr.212, Pl.*R.*514a, al.; μετὰ ἀπαιδευσίας Th.3.42; δι' ἀπαιδευσίαν Arist.*Rh.*1356ᵃ29; δι' ἀ. τῶν ἀναλυτικῶν Id.*Metaph.*1005ᵇ3, cf. 1006ᵃ6; ἀ. πλούτου ἐστὶ τὸ νεόπλουτον εἶναι Id.*Rh.*1391ᵃ17. 2. *stupidity*, Pl.*Grg.*527e, al., Aeschin.1.144; ἀπαιδευσίᾳ ὀργῆς *from bigotry* of passion, Th.3.84. -ευτέω, *to be* ἀπαίδευτος, A.D.*Conj.*235.19, Iamb.*in Nic.*p.9P.; *to be foolishly said*, Id.*Comm.Math.*7. *-ευτος, ον, *uneducated*, παιδεύσωμεν τὸν ἀ. E.*Cyc.*493, cf. Pl.*Tht.*175d; πιθανώτεροι οἱ ἀ. τῶν πεπαιδευμένων ἐν τοῖς ὄχλοις Arist.*Rh.*1395ᵇ27, cf. E.*Hipp.*989: c. gen. rei, *uninstructed in..*, X.*Cyr.*3.3.55. 2. *boorish, rude*, Pl.*Grg.*510b, etc.; ῥῆμα ἀ. Id.*Phdr.*269b; ἀ. βίος Alex.284; πνεῦμα Philem.213.11; ἀ. μαρτυρία *clumsy* evidence, Aeschin.1.70; ζητήσεις 2*Ep.Ti.*2.23: Comp., Nicoch.3. II. Adv. -τως Pl.*R.*559d; ἀ. ἔχειν E.*Ion*247, Alex.267.4, cf. Philostr.*VA*6.36; φληναφᾶσθαι Phld.*Rh.*1.227 S.

**ἀπαιδία**, ἡ, (ἄπαις) *childlessness*, Hdt.6.139, S.*OT*1024, Antipho 3.1.2, etc. II. = ἀπαιδευσία, *POxy.*33 ii 13 (ii A.D.) (s.v.l.).

**ἀπαιδοιόω**, = ἀποσκολύπτω (Aeol.), Poll.2.176 (Pass.); ἀπαιδοίωται· ἀπηναισχύντηκε, τέτμηται, Hsch.

**ἀπαιδοτρίβητος** [ῐ], ον, *not taught by a* παιδοτρίβης, *AB*419.

**ἀπαιθᾰλόω**, *burn to cinders* or *ashes*, f.l. in Thphr.*CP*4.12.8.

**ἀπαίθομαι**, *take fire*, Q.S.1.693.

**ἀπαιθριάζω**, *expose to the air, air*, Hp.*Morb.*3.17:—Pass., Herod.Med.ap.Orib.5.30.33. 2. ἀ. τὰς νεφέλας *clear away* the clouds, Ar.*Av.*1502. 3. intr., *clear up, grow fine*, of weather, Lib.*Or.*11.215: metaph., M.Ant.2.4.

**ἀπαιθύσσομαι**, *flare, stream*, of a torch, D.S.2.53.—Act. in *EM* 233.34, intr., of the eyes.

**ἀπαίνομαι**, v.l. for ἀναίνομαι, Il.7.185.

***ἀπαινύμαι**, = ἀποαίνυμαι (q.v.), Mosch.2.66.

**ἀπαιοθήκη**, ἡ, dub. sens., *PGrenf.*2.111.39 (inventory of church property).

**ἀπαιολάω**, *perplex, confound*, E.*Ion*549; ἀ. τινὰ τῆς ἀληθείας Babr.95.99:—also **ἀπαιολέω**, Sch.Ar.*Nu.*1150.

**ἀπαιόλ-η**, ἡ, (αἰόλος) *loss by fraud*, τέθνηκεν.. χρημάτων ἀπαιόλη A.*Fr.*186. II. *fraud*, cj. Herm. in E.*Hel.*1056; personified in Ar.*Nu.*1150. -ημα, ατος, τό, = foreg., A.*Ch.*1002, S.*Fr.*1018, Ar.*Nu.*729:—also -ησις, εως, ἡ, Hsch.

**ἀπαιρεθέω**, Ion. aor. 1 subj. Pass., and **ἀπαραιρημένος**, Ion. pf. part. Pass., from ἀφαιρέω.

***ἀπαίρω** (cf. ἀπαείρω), fut. ἀπᾰρῶ: aor. 1 ἀπῆρα E.*IT*967: pf. ἀπῆρκα Th.8.100, Aeschin.2.82: Ion. impf. ἀπαιρέεσκον, v.l. ἀπαίρεσκον, Hdt.1.186:—*lift off*, and so, *carry off, take away*, τὰ ξύλα ibid.; *remove*, τί τινος E.*Or.*1608; τινὰ Σπάρτης Id.*Hel.*1671; in *IT*967, perh. *get rid of*, νικῶν ἀπῆρα φόνια πειρατήρια:—Pass., ἀπαίρεται τράπεζα Achae.17.5; ἀπό τινος *Ev.Matt.*9.15. II. *lead* or *carry away*, τὰς νέας ἀπὸ Σαλαμῖνος Hdt.8.57; μελάθρων ἀ. πόδα E.*El.*774; ἀ. τινὰ ἐκ χθονός Id.*Hel.*1520. 2. elliptically (sc. ναῦς, στρατόν, etc.), *sail away, march away, depart*, ἀπαίρειν ἀπὸ Σαλαμῖνος Hdt.8.60, freq. in Th., X., etc.: c. gen., ἀπαίρειν χθονὸς *depart from* the land, E.*Cyc.*131; Σπάρτης ἀπῆρας νηὶ Κρησίαν χθόνα Id.*Tr.*944: c. acc. cogn., ἀ. πρεσβείαν *to set out on* an embassy, D.19.163.

**ἄπαις**, αιδος, ὁ, ἡ, *childless*, Hdt.6.38, S.*Fr.*4; τὰς ἄπαιδας οὐσίας, perh. *childless* estate, dub.l. in Id.*Tr.*911:—often c. gen., ἄ. ἔρσενος γόνου *without* male heirs, Hdt.1.109 (so ἄ. alone, 5.48,67); ἀ. ἔρσενος καὶ θήλεος γόνου Id.3.66; τέκνων ἄπαιδα E.*Supp.*810; ἄ. ἀρρένων παίδων And.1.117, X.*Cyr.*4.6.2; ἀρρένων τε καὶ θηλειῶν Pl.*Lg.*925c. II. Νυκτὸς παῖδες ἄπαιδες children of Night, *yet children none*, dub. l. in A.*Eu.*1034.

**ἀπαίσιος**, ον, *ill-omened*, ἡμέρα App.*BC*1.78; φωνή Plu.2.266d; ἄχθος ὀαίνης Opp.*H.*1.372; ἡμέρα Luc.*Pseudol.*12; ὄνομα Procl. *in Cra.*p.39 P. Adv. ἀπαισίως, αἰσίως καὶ ἀ. ἐπιγενησόμενα Gal.1.292.

**ἀπαΐσσω**, Att. -ᾴσσω, *spring from* a height, κρημνοῦ ἀπαΐξας Il.21.234. II. *dart away*, ὁπόταν μὲν ἀπαΐξῃ τέρεν αἷμα Emp.100.6, cf. ib.23; τοῦ δ' ἐγὼ κλύων ἀπῇξα S.*Tr.*190, cf. Ar.*Ra.*468; ἀπῇξε πέμφιξ S.*Fr.*337; φρένες.. γνώμης ἀπῇξαν Id.*Aj.*448. [ἀπᾱ- Hom., cf. ἀΐσσω.]

**ἀπαισχύνομαι** [ῡ], *shrink back* or *refuse through shame*, Pl.*Grg.*494c, Phld.*Lib.*p.34 O.

**ἀπαισχυντέω**, = foreg., Hld.8.5 (but better ἀπαναισχ-).

***ἀπαιτ-έω**, *demand back, demand to have returned*, esp. of things forcibly taken or rightfully belonging to one, Hdt.1.2; εἰ μὲν βούλεσθε, αἰτῶ, εἰ δὲ μὴ βούλεσθε, ἀπαιτῶ And.2.22; τὸ μισθάριον γὰρ ἂν ἀπαιτῇς Diph.43.34; τὸ τέλος ὁ χρόνος ἀπαιτεῖ *BCH*7.278 (Tralles); τὴν ψυχήν *Ev.Luc.*12.20; ἀ. τινά τι *demand* something *of* one, Hdt.8.122, E.*Hel.*963, Ar.*Av.*554, D.1.22; εὐθύνας ἀ. τινά Id.18.245; also ἀ. ὅπλα τοῦ πατρός S.*Ph.*362; χάριν ἀ. τινά Pl.*Phdr.*241a, etc.; τι παρά τινος Arist.*de An.*408ᵃ18; also ἀ. δίκην ἐξ ἀδίκων A.*Ch.*398; λόγον ἀ. τινὰ περί τινος Pl.*R.*599b; ἀ. ὑπέρ τινος ib.612d; ἀ. ὑποσχέσεις Arist.*EN*1164ᵃ17: c. inf., ἀ. τινὰ ποιεῖν τι E.*Supp.*385. b. *call down on oneself*, ποινάς Jul.*Or.*2.59a (and so Med., ib.58a). c. of things, *require*, νοῦσοι -έουσι σικύην Aret.*CA*1.10; περίοδος ἀ. μῆνα τρισκαιδέκατον Plu.*Agis*16: abs., ὅταν αἱ χρεῖαι -ῶσιν Ael.*Tact.*15.1. 2. *inquire*, ἀπαιτήσομεν αὐτὸν τίνες εἰσίν Str.12.3.24. II. Pass., of things, *to be demanded in payment*, Hdt.5.35. 2. of persons, *have demanded of one*, ἀπαιτεῖσθαι εὐεργεσίαν X.*Ap.*17; τὸ τῆς ψυχῆς χρέος Lxx *Wi.*15.8; ἀποδώσειν ὅταν ἀπαιτῆται *BGU*1058.33 (i B.C.); *yield to a request*, οὐκ ἀπαιτούμεσθα, answering to ἀπαιτῶ σκῆπτρα, E.*Ph.*602. -ημα, ατος, τό, *demand*, *BGU*1113.15 (i B.C.); *requirement*, Arr.*Epict.*4.6.35, M.Ant.5.15. II. *that which is demanded*, [ἄνθρωπος] γῆς ἀ. Secund.*Sent.*7. -ήσιμον, τό, *list of lands subject to dues*, *PTeb.*72.218 (ii B.C.), *BGU*457.4 (ii A.D.), *PFay.*40.3 (ii A.D.). 2. *demand* for services, *POxy.*136.17 (vi A.D.). -ησις, εως, ἡ, *demanding back*, Hdt.5.85; Ἑλένης ἀ., name of a play by S.; ἀ. ποιεῖσθαι make a *formal demand*, D.33.26, cf. *POxy.*272.13 (i A.D.); *claim, right to demand* a thing, τινὸς ἔχειν ἀ. ἀπὸ τῆς πόλεως *IG*9(1).61 (Daulis). -ητέον, *one must demand* or *require*, Arist.*EN*1098ᵃ33, Jul.*Or.*2.86a. 2. -τέος, α, ον, *to be demanded, required*, Arist.*EN*1104ᵃ3. *-ητής, οῦ, ὁ, *tax-gatherer*, *PAmh.*2.72, *POxy.*514.1 (ii A.D.), etc. -ητικός, ή, όν, *requiring*: -κόν, τό, *state of need*, Gal.1.205. -ίζω, = ἀπαιτέω, *demand back*, of things forcibly taken away, χρήματα Od.2.78, cf. Call.*Fr.*178; simply, *demand*, τινά τι Nonn.*D.*42.382, cf. Opp.*H.*5.443.

**ἀπαίων**, ωνος, ὁ, ἡ, *without the paean, cheerless*, ἀκτὰς ἀπαίωνας.. Ἀχέροντος S.*Fr.*523.

**ἀπαιώνιστος**, ον, = foreg., E.*Fr.*77.

***ἀπαιωρ-έομαι**, *hang down from, hover about*, Hes.*Sc.*234; ἀ. ἔνθεν καὶ ἔνθεν *hang without support* at either end, as a fractured limb supported only by the bandage at the fracture, Hp.*Fract.*7, cf. *Art.*63, J.*AJ*15.11.3, Antyll.ap.Orib.44.23.6, Meges ap.eund.44.24.13; τῆς ὕλης ἡ κόμη μετέωρος ἀπῃώρηται Procop.Gaz.*Ecphr.*p.158 B. 2. *to be uplifted*, Luc.*Astr.*19. II. later in Act. ἀπαιωρέω, *let hang down*, πλοκάμους Alciphr.3.55; *lift up* a garment, J.*AJ*11.6.9. -ημα, ατος, τό, *holder* for splints in surgical apparatus, Hp.*Fract.*30.

**ἀπακμάζω**, *go out of bloom, fade away*, v.l. in Pl.*Ax.*367b (ap. Stob.).

**ἀπακμή**, ἡ, *decline*, of genius, Longin.9.14.

**ἀπᾰκονάω**, *sharpen*, τὴν γλῶτταν καθάπερ μάχαιραν Porph.*Chr.*31:—Pass., *to be sharpened to a point*, ἄκραι εἰς λεπτὸν ἀπηκονημέναι J.*AJ*6.6.2.

**ἀπᾰκοντίζω**, *shoot away like a javelin, shoot off*, τὰς ἀποφυάδας Arist.*HA*501ᵃ32 (= Ctes.*Fr.*64); *spirt out* blood, Antyll.ap.Orib.7.10.2; *dart forth*, μαρμαρυγήν Nonn.*D.*40.414.

**ἀπάκρας μάχη** *single* combat (Lacon.), Hsch.

***ἀπακρῑβόομαι**, *to be highly wrought* or *finished*, πρὸς κάλλος Pl.*Lg.*810b; λόγος ἀπηκριβωμένος Id.*Ti.*29c, Isoc.4.11, cf. Pl.*Phlb.*59d; παιδεία Isoc.15.190; τὰ μάλιστ' ἀπηκρ. the most *perfect creatures*, Arist.*PA*666ᵃ28; of persons, ἀπηκριβωμένος ἐπί τινι *accurately versed* in a thing, Isoc.12.28; cf. ἀπηκριβωμένως. II. Med., *finish off, make perfect*, of sculpture, *APl.*4.172 (Alex.Aet.), cf. 5.342; ἀ. ταῖς γραμμαῖς Luc.*Im.*16 (Pass.).

**ἀπακταίνω**, *to be unequal to violent exercise*, Hsch.

**ἀπακ-τέον**, *one must lead away*, τινά τινος Plu.2.9f. -τός, όν, *that may be dragged to prison*, Arr.*Epict.*3.24.105 (Schweigh. for ἀπότακτος, q.v.).

**ἀπάλαιστος** [πᾰ], ον, *not to be thrown in wrestling, unconquerable*, Pi.*N.*4.94.

***ἀπάλαιστρος** [πᾰ], ον, *not trained in the palaestra, unskilled in wrestling*, *AP*12.222 (Strat.); opp. οἱ μετέχοντες τοῦ γυμνασίου, *CIG*3086 (Teos). 2. generally, *awkward, clumsy*, Cic.*Or.*68.229, Quint.*Inst.*9.4.56, Phld.*Rh.*1.88 S. (Sup.). II. *not customary in the palaestra, contrary to its rules*, *AP*5.213 (Mel.).

**ἀπᾰλαίωτος**, ον, *not growing old* or *decaying*, Hsch. s.v. ἀγήραος.

**ἀπάλαλκε** [πᾰ], 3 sg. aor. 2, opt. ἀπαλάλκοι: (with no pres., v. ἀλαλκεῖν and cf. ἀπαλέξω):—*ward off, keep off* something *from* one, τί τινος Il.22.348, cf. Od.4.766; νόσους Pi.*O.*8.85: later inf. ἀπαλαλκέμεν Theoc.28.20: 2 sg. ἀπάλαλκες Q.S.5.215.

**ἀπάλαμνος** [πᾰ], ον, poet. for ἀπάλαμος (cf. παλαμναῖος from παλάμη, νώνυμνος from νώνυμος), properly, *without hands*, i.e. *helpless*, ἀνὴρ ἀ. Il.5.597, cf. Simon.53; also οὐκ ἀ. λόγος Alc.49. Adv. -νως *AB*418. II. in Lyr. and Eleg., *reckless, lawless*, ἀ. φρένες Pi.*O.*2.57; of acts, ἔρδειν ἔργ' ἀ. Sol.28.12; ἀπάλαμνα μυθεῖσθαι Thgn.481; ἀνελέσθαι Id.281; ἀ. τι παθεῖν E.*Cyc.*598.

**ἀπᾰλᾰμος** [πᾰ], ον, = foreg., *helpless*, Hes.*Op.*20; βίος ἀ., of Tantalus, Pi.*O.*1.59. [ἀπ metri gr., Hes. l. c.]

**ἀπᾰλάομαι**, *go astray, wander*, ἀ. ἄλλῃ Hes.*Sc.*409.

**ἀπαλασίξαι** (i.e. ἀπαληθίσαι)· ὀμόσαι (Lacon.), Hsch.

**ἀπᾰλαστέω**, (ἄλαστος) *complain of grievous usage*, Hsch. (ἀτταλ- cod.).

**ἀπαλαύξινα**· εἰς αὐτὸν καταστρέφοντα, Hsch.

*ἀπαλγ-έω, *put away sorrow for*, τὰ ἴδια Th.2.61; ἀ. τὸ πένθος Plu. *Cleom.*22; τὸ πάθος Procop.*Arc.*16. II. generally, *to be despondent*, ἀ. ταῖς ἐλπίσιν Plb.9.40.4; πρὸς ἐλπίδα D.C.48.37: abs., Plb.1.35.5, *Ep.Eph.*4.19. **-ησις**, εως, ἡ, *ceasing to feel pain*, Hld.6.5.

**ἀπαλεῖν**· ἀμελεῖν, and **ἀπαλέντες**· ἀμελοῦντες, Hsch.

**ἀπ-ᾰλειπτέον**, *one must expunge*, M.Ant.11.19. **-ᾰλείφω**, pf. ἀπαλήλιφα D.52.29:—*wipe off, expunge*, esp. from a record or register, Id.45.44; ἀ. ἀπὸ ὀφλήματος καθ' ὅτι ἂν ἐκτίνῃ Id.58.50; ἀ. τι τῶν δεδογμένων *cancel* it, Aeschin.2.160; ἀ. ἀπὸ τῶν παρακαταθηκῶν *embezzle* part of the deposits, D.52.27:—Med., *erase*, Themist.*Ep.* 8:—Pass., *to be erased*, *POxy.*3414 (i A.D.). 2. metaph., μυρίας ἐπιστολὰς ἓν δάκρυον ἀπαλείφει μητρός Plu.*Alex.*39.

**ἀπᾰλέξ-αι, -ασθαι**, v. ἀπαλέξω. **-ησις**, εως, ἡ, *defence*, τινός *against* a thing, Phot., Suid. **-ητικός**, ή, όν, *helping, defending*, *EM*56.10. ***-ίκᾰκος**, ον, = ἀλεξίκακος, f.l. in Orph.*H.*67.5, dub. in *IG*12(7).253 (Amorgos); ἥλιος Porph.ap.Eus.*PE*3.11. ***-ω**, *ward off from*, c. acc. rei et gen. pers., καὶ δέ κεν ἄλλον σεῦ ἀπαλεξήσαιμι Il. 24.371: c. dat. pers., Ζεὺς.. μοι ἀπαλέξαι γάμον *may* he *avert* it *from* me, A.*Supp.*1053. 2. c. acc. pers. et gen. rei, οὐδ' ὥς τιν' ἔμελλεν ἀπαλεξήσειν κακότητος Od.17.364. II. Med., *defend oneself*, πρὸς ταῦτ' ἀπαλέξασθαι S.*Aj.*166 (lyr.), cf. *Fr.*303, Nic.*Th.*829.

**ἀπᾰλεύομαι**, *keep aloof from*, v.l. Nic.*Th.*395 (Sch.).

**ἀπᾰληθεύω**, *speak the whole truth*, πρός τινα X.*Oec.*3.12: c. acc., χρόνος ὁ πάντα ἐκκαλύπτων καὶ ἀπαληθεύων Ael.*Fr.*62.

**ἀπαλθαίνομαι**, fut. -ήσομαι, *heal thoroughly*, ἕλκε' ἀπαλθήσεσθον (-ονται Aristarch.) Il.8.419: impf., Q.S.4.404.

**ἁπᾰλία**, ἡ, (ἁπαλός) *softness*, τοῦ ἀέρος *Gp.*1.8.2.

***ἀπᾰλίας**, ου, ὁ, *a sucking pig*, D.L.8.20 (prob.); cf. ἀπάλιον· θῦμα δελφάκιον, Hsch.

**ἀπαλλ-ᾰγή**, ἡ, (ἀπαλλάσσω) *deliverance, release, relief from* a thing, πόνων, πημάτων, ξυμφορᾶς, A.*Ag.*1,20, *Pr.*754, S.*Ant.*1338, etc.: in pl., A.*Pr.*318, E.*Heracl.*811; ἀ. πραγμάτων Antipho6.35; ἀ. τοῦ πολέμου *putting an end to* the war, Th.7.2; οὐκ ἦν τοῦ πολέμου πέρας οὐδ' ἀ. D.18.145; of contracts, *release, discharge*, ἀ. συμβολαίων Id. 33.3; generally, *relief from*, τινός Arist.*HA*582b12. 2. abs., *divorce*, in pl., E.*Med.*236,1375: sg., *PRyl.*154.29 (i A.D.), etc. II. *removal*, Pl.*Lg.*736a. III. (from Pass.) *going away, means of getting away* or *escape*, Hdt.1.12, 7.207, al.; τέλος τῆς ἀ. the final *departure*, Id.2.139; ἡ ἀ. ἐγένετο ἀλλήλων *separation* of combatants, Th.1.51; ἐκ τῆς Αἰγύπτου τὴν ἀ. ποιήσασθαι D.S.15.43. 2. τοῦ βίου *departure* from life, Hp.*Epid.*7.89, X.*Cyr.*5.1.13; ψυχῆς ἀπὸ σώματος Pl.*Phd.*64c: hence ἀ. alone, *death*, Thphr.*HP*9.8.3, etc. 3. *avoidance*, τῆς μίξεως Sor.1.31. **-ακτέον**, *one must release from*, τινά τινος Plu.*Cor.*32. 2. *one must remove, make away with*, τι ἐκποδών D.H.6.51. II. (from Pass.) *one must withdraw from, get rid of*, τινός Lys.6.8, Pl.*Phd.*66e. **-ακτής**, οῦ, ὁ, *liberator from*, κακοῦ Max.Tyr.13.5. **-ακτιάω**, = ἀπαλλαξείω, M.Ant.10. 36. **-ακτικός**, ή, όν, *fit for ridding, removing*, στρόφων Dsc.3.72; νοσήματος Phld.*Rh.*1.345 S. 2. *fit for curing illness*, Arist.*Pr.* 959b26. 3. Adv. -κῶς, ἔχειν, = ἀπαλλαξείειν, *wish to depart*, D.H. *Rh.*11.8. **-αξείω**, Desiderat. of ἀπαλλάσσομαι, *wish to be delivered from* or *get rid of*, τινός Th.1.95, 3.84, Procop.*Arc.*4. **-αξίκακος**, = Ἀλεξίκακος, epith. of Heracles, Roussel *Cultes Égyptiens* 200 (Delos). ***-αξις**, εως, ἡ, = ἀπαλλαγή III, Hdt.9.13, Porph.*Marc.*9; ἀ. χροιῆς *loss of* colour, Hp.*Hum.*5, cf. Epicur.*Nat.*139 G.

**ἀπαλλᾶσθαι**· ἀπαντλεῖν, Hsch. (fort. ἐπαμᾶσθαι· ἐπαντλεῖν).

***ἀπαλλάσσω**, Att. -ττω, fut. -ξω Isoc.5.52: pf. ἀπήλλᾰχα X.*Mem.* 3.13.6: aor. ἀπήλλαξα Hdt.1.16, Ar.*V.*1537, etc.:—**Pass.**, pf. ἀπήλλαγμαι Id.*Pax*1128, Isoc.5.49, Ion. ἀπάλλαγμαι Hdt.2.144,167: aor. ἀπηλλάχθην, Ion. ἀπαλλ- Id.2.152, etc.; in Att. ἀπηλλάγην [ᾰ] as always in Prose; also in Trag. (for the most part metri gr., cf. however S.*Ant.*422, *El.*783 (v.l.), E.*Ph.*592 (v.l.), *Andr.*592): fut. ἀπαλλαχθήσομαι Id.*Hipp.*356, Ar.*Av.*940; in Prose, ἀπαλλαγήσομαι Th. 4.28, etc.:—Med., fut. (in pass. sense) ἀπαλλάξομαι Hdt.7.122, E. *Hel.*437, Th.8.83, etc.: aor. ἀπηλλάξαντο E.*Heracl.*317, cf. Plu.*Cat. Mi.*64.

A. Act., *set free, deliver from* a thing, παιδίον δυσμορφίης Hdt. 6.61; τινὰ πόνων, κακῶν, A.*Eu.*83, *Pr.*773; τινὰ ἐκ γόων S.*El.*292; ἐκ φόβου καὶ κακῶν And.1.59: c. acc. only, *release*, S.*Ant.*596, etc.; κόπος μ' ἀ. Id.*Ph.*880. 2. *put away from, remove from*, τί τινος, as ἀ. γῆς πρόσωπον, φρενῶν ἔρωτα, E.*Med.*27, *Hipp.*774 (lyr.); σφαγῆς χεῖρα *IT*994; χρυσὸν χερὸς *Hec.*1222; ἀ. τινά τινος *take away* or *remove from* one, Ar.*Ec.*1046; τινὰ ἀπὸ τῆς πολιορκίας D.C.43.32. 3. c. acc. only, *put away, remove*, τι E.*Hec.*1068, Pl.*Prt.*354d, etc.; μύθοις ἔργ' ἀ. κακά *do away* ill by words, E.*Fr.*282.26; *get rid of* creditors, And. 1.122; τοὺς χρήστας Is.5.28; *get rid of* an opponent, by fair means or foul, D.24.37; ἀ. τοὺς κατηγόρους Lys.29.1; τοὺς Πελοποννησίους ἐκ τῆς χώρας Th.8.48; *dismiss, send away*, τινά Id.1.90; *remove* or *displace* from an office, ib.129; ἀ. τοὺς ὑπηρέτας καὶ θεραπευτῆρας Plu. *Lyc.*11; also, *make away with, destroy*, Thphr.*HP*9.15.2; ἑαυτόν Plu.*Cat.Mi.*70; *bring to an end*, λόγον E.*Med.*790. 4. in Law, *give a release, discharge*, D.36.25, cf. 37.1; τοὺς δανείσαντας ἀ. 34.22, cf. *PTeb.*315.16 (ii A.D.); *discharge* a debt, D.C.59.1, etc.:—so in Pass., Id.51.17. II. intr., *get off free, escape*, esp. with an Adv. added, ῥηιδίως, χαλεπῶς ἀ., Hp.*VM*10,20, cf. X.*Cyr.*4.1.5; ὁ στόλος οὕτως ἀ. *came off, ended*, Hdt.5.63, cf. A.*Ag.*1288, E.*Med.*786; οὐκ ὡς ἤθελε ἀπήλλαξεν Hdt.1.16; κάκιον ἀ. Pl.*R.*491d, cf. Men.*Epit.*199; καταγελάστως ἀ. Aeschin.2.38; ἀλυσιτελῶς ἀ. Thphr.*Char.*8.11; ἀλύπως ἀ. *get along* well, *PPetr.*3 p.58: with part. or Adj., χαίρων ἀ. Hdt.3.69; ἀθῷοι ἀ. Pl.*Sph.*254d, etc.: c. gen., *depart from*, βίου E.*Hel.*302 (dub. l.); τοῦ ζῆν Pl.*Ax.*367c; so πῶς ἀπήλλαχεν ἐκ τῆς ὁδοῦ; X.*Mem.*3.13.6; ἄριστ' ἀπαλλάττεις ἐπὶ τούτου τοῦ κύβου *in respect of*.., Diph.73.

B. Pass. and Med., *to be set free* or *released from* a thing, *get rid of* it, ἀπαλλαχθέντας δουλοσύνης Hdt.1.170; τυράννων Id.5.78; τῶν παρεόντων κακῶν Id.2.120; πημονῆς A.*Pr.*471; φόβου S.*El.*783; πραγμάτων τε καὶ μαχῶν Ar.*Pax*293; στρατιᾶς Id.*Ach.*251; Κλέωνος Th.4.28; τῆς κακουχίας ἐπὶ τὴν αὐτοῦ σκηνήν Plb.5.15.6. 2. *get off, escape*, mostly with some Adj. or Adv. added (as in Act. II), ῥηιδίως ἀ. Hp.*VM*3; ἀγῶνος ἀ. καλῶς E.*Heracl.*346; ἀζήμιος ἀπαλλαγῆναι, ἀπαλλάττεσθαι, Ar.*Pl.*271, Pl.*Lg.*721d. 3. abs., *to be acquitted*, D.22.39. 4. of a point under discussion, *to be dismissed as settled*, τοῦτο ἀπήλλακται μὴ .. τὸ φίλον φίλον εἶναι Pl.*Ly.*220b, cf. *Phlb.* 67a. II. *remove, depart from*, ἐκ τῆς χώρης, ἐξ Αἰγύπτου, Hdt.1. 61, 2.139, al.; μαντικῶν μυχῶν A.*Eu.*180; γῆς ἀπαλλάσσεσθαι πόδα E.*Med.*729; δόξης, δέους Th.2.42; ἀ. παρά τινος Aeschin.1.78; *depart, go away*, ἐς τὴν ἑωυτοῦ Hdt.1.82, al.; ἐπὶ τῆς ἑωυτοῦ Id.9.11, cf. 5.64; πρὸς χώραν Pl.*Lg.*938a: abs., Hdt.2.93, al., Aen.Tact.10.19, 15.9. 2. ἀπαλλάσσεσθαι τοῦ βίου *depart from* life, E.*Hel.*102, *Hipp.*356; βίου ἀπαλλαγὴν ἀ. Pl.*R.*496e; freq. without τοῦ βίου, *depart, die*, E.*Heracl.*1000, Pl.*Phd.*81c, etc. 3. ἀ. λέχους *to be divorced*, E.*Andr.*592; ἀ. γυναῖκά τε ἀπ' ἀνδρὸς καὶ τὸν ἄνδρα ἀπὸ γυναικός Pl.*Lg.*868d. 4. ἀ. τῶν διδασκάλων *leave* school, Id.*Grg.*514c, cf. X.*Mem.*1.2.24. 5. ἀ. ἐκ παίδων *become a man*, Aeschin.1. 40. 6. *to be removed from, free from* the imputation of, ἀπηλλαγμένος εὐηθίης *many removes from* folly, Hdt.1.60; ξυμφορῶν Th.1. 122; αἰσχύνης Id.3.63: c. inf., κρῖναι ἱκανῶς οὐκ ἀπήλλακτο *was* not *far from* judging adequately, Id.1.138. b. πολλὸν ἀπηλλαγμένος τινός far *inferior to* him, Hdt.2.144. 7. *depart from, leave off from*, τῶν μακρῶν λόγων S.*El.*1335; σκωμμάτων Ar.*Pl.*316; ἀ. λημμάτων *give up the pursuit of*.., D.3.33; οὐκ ἀπήλλακται γραφικῆς *is* not *averse from*.., Luc.*Salt.*35. b. abs., *have done, cease*, of things, S.*Ant.*422; ὅταν ἡ μέθη ἀπαλλαγῇ Arist.*MM*1202a3. c. *throw up one's case, give up a prosecution*, D.21.151,198. d. c. part., εἰπὼν ἀπαλλάγηθι speak and *be done with it*, Pl.*Grg.*491c, cf. *Tht.*183c; ταῦτα μαντευσάμενος ἀπαλλάττομαι Id.*Ap.*39d; ἀπαλλάχθητι πυρώσας E. *Cyc.*600: also in part., with a Verb, οὐκοῦν ἀπαλλαχθεὶς ἄπει; *make haste* and begone, S.*Ant.*244. 8. *to depart from enmity*, i.e. *to be reconciled, settle a dispute*, πρὸς ἀλλήλους Pl.*Lg.*915c: abs., ib. 768c. 9. *recover from an ailment*, Aret.*SD*1.14.

**ἀπαλλητός**, όν, *marvellous*, Hsch.

**ἀπαλλοιόω**, *differentiate*, Phld.*Sto.Herc.*339.9.

**ἀπαλλότρι-ος**, α, ον, *given over to strangers*, πολιτεῖαι D.S.11. 76. ***-όω**, pf. ἀπηλλοτρίωκα Aeschin.2.194:—*estrange, alienate*, ἀφ' ὑμῶν τὸν ἐπὶ Θρᾴκης τόπον l.c.; λόγον -οῦντα κακίας Aristo *Stoic.*1.80; τινά τινος J.*AJ*4.1.1:—Pass., *to be alienated*, τινός *from* one, Plb.1.79.6, cf. Alex.Aphr.*in Top.*389.12; πρός τινα towards one, Isoc.*Ep.*7.13, D.S.18.48; ἀπηλλοτριωμένην πρὸς φυτείαν ἀμπέλου χώραν *ill-suited for*.., Id.3.73. 2. of property, *alienate*, Arist. *Rh.*1361a22, *IPE*1².32 *B*68 (Olbia, iii B.C.):—Pass., *PLond.*3.1157v iii3 (iii A.D.). 3. of things, *separate, distinguish*, Hp.*Art.*58 (Pass.). b. *alter*, Pl.*Ti.*65d (Pass.). c. *remove*, in Surgery, Archig.ap.Orib.46.26.13 (Pass.):—Act., Gal.14.789. **-ωσις**, εως, ἡ, *alienation*, λέγω ἀπαλλοτρίωσιν δόσιν καὶ πρᾶσιν Arist.*Rh.*1361a 22, cf. *CIG*3281 (Smyrna). 2. *estrangement*, γονέων Vett.Val.2. 37 (pl.); φιλτάτων Gal.19.181.

**ἁπαλοανθής**, v. ἁπαλοβραχέα.

**ἀπᾰλοάω**, poet. -οιάω, *thresh out*, σῖτος ἀπηλοημένος D.42.6. 2. metaph., *bruise, crush*, Il.4.522; generally, *destroy*, Nonn.*D.*9.320.

**ἁπᾰλο-βραχέα**· ἁπαλοανθῆ, Hsch. **-θριξ**, τρῐχος, ὁ, ἡ, *soft-haired*, E.*Ba.*1186 (lyr.).

**ἀπαλοῖξαι**· ὀμόσαι (Lacon.), Hsch. (cf. ἀπαλασίξαι).

***ἀπᾰλοιφή**, ἡ, (ἀπαλείφω) *effacing, expunging*, *Gloss.* II. prob. l. for ἀπαλειφή (sic), *paste, amalgam*, Zos.Alch.p.222 B. [Perh. ἀπαλιφή; cf. καταλιφή.]

**ἁπᾰλο-κουρίς**, ίδος, ἡ, = ἁπαλὴ κουρίς, or καρίς, cj. in Epich.44. 3. ***-κροκῶδες**, τό, name of an *eye-salve*, Sichel *Pierres sigillaires* p.59.

**ἄπαλον**· ἀνοχὴ ἀπὸ τοῦ παλαίειν, Hsch.

**ἀπαλ-όνυχος**, ον, dub. l. in Ph.2.397.

**ἁπᾰλό-παις**, αιδος, ὁ, *delicate child*, Hsch. s. v. δρυψόπαιδα. **-πάρῃος** [ᾰρ], ον, *with soft cheeks*, Eust.691.52. **-πλόκᾰμος**, ον, *with soft tentacles*, of cuttlefish, Philox.2.14. **-πους**, οδος, ὁ, ἡ, *tender-footed*, Hippiatr.116.

***ἁπᾰλός**, ή, όν, *soft to the touch, tender*: in Hom. mostly of the human body, ἁπαλὴν ὑπὸ δειρήν Il.3.371; παρειάων ἁπαλάων 18.123; ἁπαλοῖο δι' αὐχένος ἤλυθεν ἀκωκή 17.49; ἁ. πόδες 19.92; ἁ. τέ σφ' ἦτορ ἀπηύρα, i.e. the life of *young* animals, 11.115; ἵεσαν αὐδὴν ἐξ ἁπαλῶν στομάτων Hes.*Sc.*279; δέρα Sapph.*Supp.*23.16; of persons, *delicate*, παῖδες Alc.*Supp.*14.5; εὐμορφοτέρα.. τᾶς ἁπάλας Γυρίννως Sapph.76; of flowers, ἀνθρυσκα Ead.*Supp.*25.13; rare in Trag., and only in lyr., παρειά A.*Supp.*70; βρέφος ἁ. E.*IA*1285; βλέφαρον τέγγουσ' ἁ. *El.* 1339; more freq. in Com., σισύμβριον Cratin.239; κρέα Ar.*Lys.* 1063; δάκτυλοι Alex.48; θερμολουσίαις ἁπαλοί *Com.Adesp.*56; so in Prose, ἁ. ψυχή Pl.*Phdr.*245a; of *raw* fruit, Hdt.2.92, cf. X.*Oec.*19. 18; of *tender* meat, Id.*An.*1.5.2; *soft-boiled*, of eggs, Cael.Aur. *AP*2.18; of a *gentle* fire, Philem.79.8, D.S.3.25. II. metaph., *soft, gentle*, ἁπαλὸν γελάσαι laugh *gently*, Od.14.465; ἁ. δίαιτα *soft*, elicate, Pl.*Phdr.*239c; τῷ αὐτῷ..χρησώμεθα τεκμηρίῳ περὶ Ἔρωτα τι ἁπαλός Id.*Smp.*195e (also in Sup.); ἁ. εἴσπλους λιμένος, opp. ραχύς, Cratin.357. Adv. ἁπαλῶς, ὀπτᾶν to roast *moderately*, Sotad. om.1.16: Comp. ἁπαλωτέρως, ἅπτεσθαι Hp.*Art.*37. 2. in bad ense, *soft, weak*, ὡς ἁ. καὶ λευκὸς [οἶνος] Cratin.183; λευκός, ἐξυρη- ένος, γυναικόφωνος, ἁ. Ar.*Th.*192. [ἄπᾰλος; for καλάμῳ..ὑπᾱπάλῳ, n Theoc.28.4, is corrupt.]

**ἀπᾰλό-σαρκος**, *with soft* or *tender flesh*, Hp.*Liqu.*6, *Mul.*1.1; Diph.Siph.ap.Ath.8.355e. **-στομος**, ον, *delicate to the mouth*, Hsch. s.v. γλύξις. **-σύγκρῐτος**, ον, *of delicate texture*, σώματα Orib.44.14.4. **-σώματος**, ον, *of tender body*, Ar.*Fr.*54 D. **-της**, ητος, ἡ, *softness, tenderness*, Hp.*VM*22, Pl.*Smp.*195d, X.*Mem.*2.1. 22; δι' ἁπαλότητα Arist.*Pol.*1336ᵃ10. **-τρεφής**, ές, *well-fed, plump*, σίαλος Il.21.363; λειμῶνες *rich* pastures, *IG*14.1389 ii 11. **-φόρος**, ον, *wearing soft raiment*, *EM*4.16. **-φρων**, ον, gen. ονος, *soft-hearted*, *AP*7.403 (Marc. Arg.). **-χροος**, ον, contr. **-χρους**, χρουν; with heterocl. gen. ἁπαλόχροος, dat. -χροΐ, acc. -χροα:—*soft-skinned*, *h.Ven.*14, Hes.*Op.*519, Thgn.1341, E.*Hel.*373 (lyr.):—also* **-χρως**, χρωτος, ὁ, ἡ, Phryn.*PS*p.30 B.

**ἀπᾰλ-υντής**, οῦ, ὁ, *worker of hides, currier*, Zonar. ***-ύνω** [ῡ], *soften*, ἵππου τὸ στόμα, τὰς τρίχας, X.*Eq.*4.5, 5.5; *make plump*, opp. ἰσχναίνω, Hp.*Art.*50. 2. *make tender* or *delicate*, τοὺς πόδας ὑποδήμασι X.*Lac.*2.1:—Pass., *to be softened*, metaph., Lxx 4*Ki.*22.19, *Ps.* 54(55).21.

**ἀπᾰλύσκομαι**, = ἀπαλεύομαι: ἀπαλύξασθαι v.l. for ἀπαλέξασθαι, Nic.*Th.*829.

**ἀπᾰλυσμός**, ὁ, *making plump*, Hp.*Art.*50.

**ἀπαλφῐτίζω**, *mix* wine *with barley-meal* or *groats*, in the Persian fashion, f.l. in Ath.10.432d.

**ἀπᾰμαλδύνω** [ῡ], *bring to naught, plunge into obscurity*, *AP*9.24 (Leon.); *quench*, μαρμαρυγήν Nonn.*D.*33.24; *turn pale*, ἔρευθος Q.S. 8.209.

**ἀπᾰμαυρόω**, *remove darkness*, ὄσσων..ἀπημαύρωσας ὁμίχλην Orph. *H.*6.6. II. *make obscure*, *Hymn.Is.*21. 2. Pass., *fall into obscurity, become antiquated*, μάθημα ἀπημαυρωμένον Ael.*Tact.Praef.* 2. b. Pass., *lose its power*, of a drug, Agatharch.97. III. Pass., *to be deprived of sight*, ἀ. τοῦ βλέπειν Lxx *Is.*44.18.

***ἀπᾰμάω** (A), fut. -ήσω, *cut off*, ἀπ' οὔατα νηλέϊ χαλκῷ ῥῖνάς τ' ἀμήσαντες Od.21.300, cf. Hes.*Th.*181; ἀπάμησον [τὸν πόδα] S.*Ph.*749:— in Med., Thphr.*Lap.*21; ἀπὸ στάχυν ἀμήσασθαι Q.S.13.242:—Pass., Nonn.*D.*4.413. [ἄπᾰ- in Ep.; but in S. ἀπᾱ-.]

**ἀπᾰμάω** (B), *sweep away*, γῆν *Gp.*2.6.44.

**ἀπαμβλίσκω**, *make abortive*, καρποὺς *produce abortive* fruit, Plu. *Arat.*32. II. intr., *miscarry*, aor. ἀπήμβλωσε, Id.*Pomp.*53.

**ἀπαμβλύνω** [ῡ], fut. -ῠνῶ (v. infr.), *blunt* or *dull the edge of*, τὰ ξίφη D.C.40.24 (Pass.). 2. mostly metaph., ἐλπίδα Pi.*P.*1.82 (tm.); of a person, τεθηγμένον τοί μ' οὐκ ἀπαμβλυνεῖς λόγῳ A.*Th.*715; τὰ λευκὰ τῶν τριχῶν ἀπαμβλύνει τὸν νοῦν Herod.1.67; φάος ὄσσων Opp.*H.*4. 525; *tone down, take the edge off* a phrase, Plot.3.6.12:—more freq. in Pass., *to be blunted, lose its edge* or *force*, ὥρη μὲν ἀπήμβλυνται, θυμὸς δὲ μενοινᾷ Hom.*Epigr.*12, cf. S.*Eleg.*6; γηράσκοντι συγγηράσκουσι αἱ φρένες καὶ ἐς τὰ πρήγματα πάντα ἀπαμβλύνονται Hdt.3.134; ἀπαμβλυνθήσεται γνώμην A.*Pr.*866; ἡμῖν -ύνεται ἡ δικαιοσύνη *is indistinctly seen*, Pl.*R.*442d. II. = foreg., J.*BJ*4.8.3 (s.v.l.).

***ἀπαμβρᾰκόομαι**, *to be patient, endure* (cf. ἀμβρακόομαι), Pl.Com.5 D.

**ἀπαμβροτεῖν**, v. ἀφαμαρτάνω.

**ἀπαμείβομαι**, fut. -ψομαι: aor. ἀπημείφθην X.*An.*2.5.15: plpf. ἀπάμειπτο *AP*14.2, Nonn.*D.*8.165:—*reply, answer*, freq. in Hom., but always with a second more definite Verb, as ἀπαμειβόμενος προσέφη Il.1.84, al.; ἀπαμείβετο φώνησέν τε 20.199, al.; ὧδε ἀ. X. l.c.; τινά Theoc.8.8.

**ἀπᾰμείρω**, *deprive one of share in* a thing, τινά τι A.R.3.186:— Med., τί τινος Nonn.*D.*29.158:—Pass., *to be bereft*, τίνος *of* a thing, prob. l. in Hes.*Th.*801, cf. *Op.*578; v.l. for ἀποαίνυνται, Od.17.322.

**ἀπᾰμέλγω**, *suck out* milk from the breast, Sor.1.105.

**ἀπᾰμελέομαι**, Pass., *to be neglected utterly*, ἀπημελημένος Hdt.3. 129, 132, S.*Ph.*652.

**ἀπᾰμέργομαι**, Med., only pres. and impf., *take* or *carry off for oneself*, Nic.*Th.*861, *Al.*306.

***ἀπᾰμέρδω**, = ἀπαμείρω, Q.S.4.422, Man.3.26, Agamestor ap.Sch. Lyc.179.

**ἀπᾰμεύς**, έως, ὁ, *harvester*, *PStrassb.*35.14 (iv/v A.D.).

**ἀπᾰμήτωρ**, ορος, *shearing off*, μηδέων ἀ. ἄνδρες Man.4.220.

**ἀπαμμένος**, Ion. pf. part. Pass. of ἀφάπτω.

**ἀπᾰμοιβή**, ἡ, *alternation*: ἐξ -ῶν masonry laid in courses *of headers and stretchers*, *IG*2.1054c60.

**ἀπαμπαίομαι**, Cret. for ἀπαναπ., *beat off*, of dogs, *GDI*4998 ii 17 (Gortyn).

**ἀπαμπίσχω**, *take off*, ἐσθῆτα Ph.2.43:—Med., *doff*, 1.653: and metaph., ψυχῇ ἀ. τὸ ἀδικεῖν ib.569. II. metaph., *lay bare, reveal*, 2.74, al.

**ἀπαμπλᾰκεῖν**, inf. of aor. ἀπήμπλακον (no pres. in use), = ἀφαμαρτεῖν, *fail utterly*, S.*Tr.*1139.

**ἀπαμυνταί**· βοηθοί, Hsch. (-τοί cod.).

**ἀπᾰμύνω** [ῡ], *keep off, ward off*, with collat. notion of defence, τί τινι something *for* (i.e. *from*) another, Αἰτωλοῖσιν ἀπήμυνεν κακὸν ἦμαρ Il. 9.597; ἡμῖν ἀπὸ λοιγὸν ἀμύνειν 1.67; later τί τινος Luc.*Cyn.*13: c. acc. only, ἀ. τῶν ἐπιόντων κακῶν τὰ ἡμίσεα Hdt.7.120; ἀ. τὸν βάρβαρον *repulse* him, 9.90; τὰς μυίας Ar.*V.*597; τοὺς ἔξωθεν Pl.*R.*415e. 2. *requite, take vengeance on*, τινά *AP*5.6 (Asclep.). II. Med., *keep off from oneself, drive back, repel*, ἄνδρ' ἀπαμύνασθαι Od.16.72; so ἀ. μίαν [ναῦν] καὶ ὀλίγῳ πλεῦνας Hdt.5.86; τὴν πενίην καὶ τὴν δεσποσύνην Id.7.102, cf. 3.110. 2. abs., *defend, protect oneself*, ὁ δ' οὐκ ἀπαμύνετο χερσίν Od.11.579; πόλις ᾗ ἀπαμυναίμεσθα by which we *may protect ourselves*, Il.15.738; μεγέθει Arist.*Long.*467ᵃ3.

**ἀπαμφι-άζω**, *take off* a garment, *doff* it, Plu.2.406d, Ph.2.393: metaph., γαῖαν *AP*7.49 (Bianor); ἀπαμφιάσαντες τὴν ψυχήν Them. *Or.*21.249d:—Med., ἀπαμφιάσασθαι τὰ περίαπτα Ph.1.288: metaph., *lay bare, reveal*, τὰ κεκρυμμένα Id.2.310:—Pass., γυμνὴ καὶ ἀπημφιασμένη ἀλήθεια Id.1.362. 2. *strip off*, βῶλον *AP*7.76 (Diosc.):— hence Subst. **-ασις**, εως, ἡ, *putting off*, dub. in J.*AJ*19.2.5. **-ασμός**, ὁ, = foreg., metaph., τοῦ τρόπου Corn.*ND*30.

**ἀπαμφιέννυμι** [ῠ], *strip off garments*, στέρν' ἀπημφιεσμένοι *having* them *stripped bare*, Xenarch.4.5. 2. *strip off*, τοίχους Plu.2.516f, cf. Ph.1.117.

**ἀπαμφίζω**, Att. fut. -ιῶ, = ἀπαμφιάζω, *strip from* one, τί τινος Men. 339:—also **ἀπαμφίσκω**, Ph.2.319.

**ἀπαναγιγνώσκω**, *read amiss*, A.D.*Synt.*126.15.

**ἀπᾰναγκάζω**, *force away*, τι ἀπό τινος Hp.*Art.*2; opp. προσαναγκάζω, ib.14; simply, = ἀναγκάζω, ib.58, cf. Str.2.1.31, *PFay.*122.18 (100 A.D.):—freq. as f.l. for ἐπαν-, as Plb.4.46.6, 5.24.1, Them.*Or.* 33.367a.

**ἀπανάγνωσμα**, ατος, τό, *fault in reading, faulty reading*, A.D. *Synt.*146.24, al.

**ἀπαναιδεύομαι**, Dep., = ἀναισχυντέω, mentioned by Thom.Mag. p.21 R. as an Att. word.

***ἀπᾰναίνομαι**, *disown, reject*, οἱ δ' οὐ γιγνώσκοντες ἀπηνήναντο Il.7. 185; ἀπανήνασθαι θεοῦ εὐνήν Od.10.297; εὐθὺς δ' ἀπανάνατο νύμφαν Pi.*N.*5.60; part. ἀπανηνάμενος A.*Eu.*972 (lyr.); of a woman, τὸν ἄνδρα ἀπαναίνεται Hp.*Mul.*2.179; pres. also in Plu.2.132c.

**ἀπαναισιμόω**, *use up, consume*, [ὑγρασίη] -οῦται Hp.*Gland.*9.

**ἀπαναισχυντέω**, *behave with effrontery*, c. acc. cogn., ἀ. τοῦτο Pl. *Ap.*31b; c. inf., Alex.Aphr.*in Top.*524.5: abs., D.29.20, cf. 54.33; *put away shame*, Hld.8.5.

**ἀπᾰνᾱλ-ίσκω**, fut. -ανᾱλώσω, Alciphr.3.47: pf. ἀπανάλωκα Th.7. 11: aor. 1 Pass. -ηλώθην ib.30: plpf. ἀπανηλώμην D.S.12.40: pf. -ηλωμένος J.*AJ*12.9.5:—*use quite up, utterly consume*, ll. cc.:—part. Pass. ἀπαναλούμενος in Ti.Locr.101d. II. *spend from* a given sum, *IG*1.32.26. **-ωσις**, εως, ἡ, *consumption*, D.S.1.41, Sor.1.42, Antyll.ap.Orib.6.10.18.

**ἀπανᾶν**· καλεῖν, Hsch.; cf. ἀπανεῖ.

**ἀπαναπαύομαι**, *take one's rest*, Sch.Opp.*H.*3.236.

**ἀπανάστᾰσις**, εως, ἡ, *migration*, Str.4.1.13, J.*BJ*1.15.3; *departure*, D.H.9.6, Philostr.*Ep.*11.

**ἀπαναστομόω**, = ἀναστομόω, for which it is v.l. in D.H.3.40.

**ἀπανατέλλω**, poet. ἀπαντ-, *make to rise, raise up from*, v.l. in Opp.*C.*2.97, 563.

**ἀπαναχωρ-έω**, *pass away*, Olymp.*in Grg.*p.367 J.; v.l. for ἐπ-, J. *BJ*2.21.5:—Subst. **-ησις**, εως, ἡ, v.l. for ἐπ-, D.S.25.6.

**ἀπανδόκευτος**, ον, *without an inn to rest at*, ὁδός Democr.230.

**ἀπανδρίζομαι**, *stand manfully*, πρός τι Callistr.*Stat.*4.

**ἀπανδρόομαι**, *become a man, come to maturity*, E.*Ion*53, Luc. *Am.*26; ἀπηνδρώθησαν αἱ μῆτραι *viro maturae factae sunt*, Aret.*SD* 1.6.

**ἀπανεῖ**· καλεῖ, and aor. imper. ἀπάνεσον· κάλεσον (Lacon.), Hsch.; cf. ἀπανᾶν.

**ἀπᾰνεμία**, ἡ, *shelter from wind*, Sch.Opp.*H.*1.602.

**ἀπᾰνεμόομαι**, *to be blown down*, Hsch. (leg. ἀπηνεμώθη for -ήθη).

**ἀπάνευθε** [ᾰν], and before vowels **-θεν**, strengthd. for ἄνευθε, Adv. *afar off, far away*, ἀ. κιὼν Il.1.35; φεῦγον ἔπειτ' ἀ. 9.478, etc. II. as Prep. with gen., *far from, aloof from*, τῶν ἄλλων ἀ. θεῶν ib.14.189, cf. 20.41; ἀ. τοκήων Od.9.36; ἀ. θεῶν *without* their *knowledge*, Il.1. 549. 2. *out from, issuing from*, τοῦ δ' ἀ. σέλας γένετ' 19.374.

**ἀπανθ-έω**, *finish blooming*, Thphr.*HP*1.13.3, al.; *fade*, Hp.*Genit.* 9: mostly metaph., Ar.*Ec.*1121; ἀνανθεῖ..καὶ ἀπηνθηκότι καὶ σώματι καὶ ψυχῇ Pl.*Smp.*196a; so in Arist.*Rh.*1410ᵇ15, old age is compared to straw, ἄμφω γὰρ ἀπηνθηκότα, cf. Luc.*DMort.*18.2, al.; of athletes, ἀ. ὑπὸ τῶν πόνων Philostr.*Gym.*48. II. of wine, *lose its sweetness*, i.e. *ripen*, Alex.45. III. *break out*, of skin-eruptions, Sor.1.121, Orib.*Inc.*24.2. **-ησις**, εως, ἡ, *time of blossoming*, ταχεῖαν εἶναι τὴν ἀ. Thphr.*HP*7.7.4.

***ἀπανθ-ίζω**, *pluck off flowers*: metaph., ματαίαν γλῶσσαν ἀπανθίσαι *cull the flowers of* idle talk, A.*Ag.*1662; Ἄρης φιλεῖ..τὰ λῷστα πάντ' ἀπανθίζειν (Kidd for πάντα τἀνθρώπων) *cut off* all the best, Id.*Fr.* 100; ἀπανθίζειν ἐπεχείρει τοὺς Φρύγας Ἀχιλλεύς Polion ap.Phryn.*PS* p.162 B.:—Med., *gather honey from flowers*, Luc.*Pisc.*6; *pick out flowers*, *Asin.*54: metaph., *cull the best of* a thing, Plu.2.30d, Luc. *Merc.Cond.*39, Philostr.*VS*2.1.14. 2. Pass., *to be withered*, Phryn. *PS*p.9 B. **-ισμα**, ατος, τό, *inflorescence*, τὸ ἀκρότατον τῆς ψυχῆς καὶ τὸ ἀ. Olymp.*in Alc.*p.226 C.; *flower plucked* or *culled*, Eust.782.21; τὸ τερπνὸν τῆς πορφύρας ἀ., rhetorical description of the emperor Constant. Porphyrog., *Gp.Prooem.*11. **-ισμός**, ὁ, *plucking of flowers*, Sch.Il.5.629.

**ἀπανθρᾰκ-ίζω**, *broil on the coals, roast*, βοῦν ἀπηνθράκιζ' ὅλον Ar. *Ra.*506, cf. *Av.*1546, Ph.1.665, Philostr.*VA*5.25. **-ίς**, ίδος, ἡ, *cake baked on coals*, Diocl.*Fr.*116 (v.l. ἐπ-), cf. Hsch. **-ισμα**, ατος, τό, *broil*, Hsch. s.v. χναύματα. **-όω**, *burn to a cinder*, ἀπηνθράκωσεν Luc.*DMort.*20.4:—Pass., Id.*DMar.*11.1, *Peregr.*1.

**ἀπανθρωπ-έομαι**, *shun like a misanthrope*, rejected by Poll.2.5, but used by Hp.*Ep.*12 ἀπανθρωπέονται ξύμφυλον ὄψιν, cf. Tz.*H.*7.880, 885 (ubi -οῦνται). **-ία** (-εία Poll.8.14), ἡ, *dislike of men*, Luc. *Tim.*44. 2. *unfitness for social intercourse*, J.*BJ*1.17.3. II. *unsociability, moroseness*, Hp.*Coac.*472 (pl.); *inhumanity*, *POxy.*298.52 (i A.D.), J.*AJ*17.11.2. **-ίζομαι**, *become a man*, opp. a *beast*, Herm.ap.Stob.1.49.69. ※**-ος**, ον, *far from man*: hence, I. *desert, desolate*, τῷδ' ἀπανθρώπῳ πάγῳ, of Caucasus, A.*Pr.*20; ἀ. ἡ γῆ Luc.*Prom.*11. 2. ἀπάνθρωπον, τό, *violence, drastic nature*, of remedies, Philum.*Ven.*2.5. II. of men and their deeds, *inhuman, savage*, S.*Fr.*1020; ἀπάνθρωπα διαπεπραγμένοι D.H.6.81; ἀ. ἐπιστολαί *PFlor.*367.4 (iii A.D.); *unsocial, misanthropic*, τρόπος Pl.*Ep.*309b (Comp.), cf. J.*AJ*8.4.3, Gal.5.54 (Comp.). Adv. -πως J.*AJ*6.13.6, Luc.*Tim.*35, Philostr.*VA*1.21. 2. χρόα οὐκ ἀ. not *unpleasing*, Plu.2.54e, *Cat.Mi.*5. III. ἀπάνθρωπον, τό, = σταφὶς ἀγρία, Ps.-Dsc.4.152.

**ἀπανιζόμενοι**· ξηραινόμενοι, Hsch.

**ἀπανίστημι**, *make rise up and depart, send away*, τὴν στρατιήν Hdt. 3.156, 6.133; *cause to depart*, τοὺς Ἀθηναίους Th.2.70. II. Pass., with aor. 2 and pf. Act., and fut. Med., *arise and go away, depart again*, Hdt.9.87; ἀπὸ τῆς πόλιος ib.86; ἐκ τῆς Μακεδονίας Th.1.61; Ποτειδαίας ib.139; esp. *leave one's country, emigrate*, ib.2.

※**ἀπάνουρ-γευτος**, ον, *guileless*, *EM*163.6. Adv. -τως Sch.D.22.20. **-γος**, ον, = foreg., Plu.2.966b. Adv. -γως S.E.*M.*2.77.

**ἀπαντᾰχ-ῆ**, Adv., (ἅπας) *everywhere*, E.*Fr.*218, Jul.*Or.*4.134b. **-όθεν**, *from all sides*, D.S.20.57, Jul.*Or.*1.35b, al.: c. gen., γῆς Luc. *DMort.*9.2. **-όθι**, = ἀπανταχοῦ, Luc.*Prom.*12, Them.*Or.*25.310b. **-οῖ**, *to every quarter*, Is.9.14 (Reiske for -χῇ). **-οῦ**, *everywhere*, E.*IT*517, Alex.152, Men.*Epit.*16; ἀ. γῆς D.C.69.13.

※**ἀπαντάω**, impf. ἀπήντων Th.4.127, Dor. 3 sg. ἀπάντη Bion *Fr.*9.7: fut. ἀπαντήσω Arist.*Rh.Al.*1432ᵇ35, Plb.4.26.5, etc.; but better -ήσομαι Th.4.77, 7.2 and 80, X.*HG*1.6.3, Lys.2.32, etc.: aor. ἀπήντησα E.*Ph.*1392, Th.2.20: pf. ἀπήντηκα Ar.*Lys.*420, D.18.15:—the Med., used in act. sense by Polyaen.1.21.1 (impf.), al., is censured by Luc.*Lex.*25; so also pf. ἀπήντημαι Plb.2.37.6, D.H.6.88, etc. I. mostly of persons, *move from* a place *to meet* a person, and generally, *meet, encounter*, τινί Hdt.8.9, E.*Supp.*772, etc.; ἐξ ἐναντίας ἀ. Pl.*Lg.*893e; ἀ. ταῖς ὁμοίαις φύσεσι *encounter, fall in with* them, D.60.20: abs., ὁ ἀεὶ ἀπαντῶν *any one that meets you, any chance person*, Pl.*R.*563c; οἱ ἀπαντῶντες D.36.45, Alex.78, cf. 87. b. freq. with a Prep., ἀ. τινὶ εἰς τόπον *come* or *go* to a place *to meet* him, *meet* him at a place, Hdt.2.75; ἐς τὠυτό 6.84; ἐπὶ Τριποδίσκον Th.4.70; τὸν μὲν ἐς τὰς Σίφας ἀ., τὸν δ' ἐπὶ τὸ Δήλιον ib.89: without dat. pers., *present oneself* at a place, Id.7.1; εἰς Κύζικον X.*HG*1.3.13; ἀ. ἐνθάδε Ar.*Lys.*13; δεῦρο πάλιν ἀ. Pl.*Tht.*210d, etc. c. c. dat. loci, *light upon, come to*, τόπῳ Lxx *Ge.*28.11. 2. freq. in hostile sense, *meet* in battle, ἀ. δορί (dat. pers. being omitted) E.*Ph.*1392; ὅπλοις *HF*542; τοῖς βαρβάροις Μαραθῶνάδε And.1.107; ἀ. Ἀθηναίοις ἐς Τάραντα Th.6.34, cf. 2.20, 3.95; ἀ. πρός τινα Isoc.4.86,90; generally, *resist, oppose* in any way, νομοθέτῃ ἀ. λέγων.. Pl.*Lg.*684d; διὰ λόγων νουθετικῶν ἀ. prob. ib.740e; ἀ. τραχέως πρὸς τὰς τῶν πλησιαζόντων ὀργάς Isoc.1.31; ἀ. τοῖς εἰρημένοις *rejoin, reply*, Id.11.30; τοῖς θορύβοις Arist.*Rh.Al.*l.c.; πρὸς ἕκαστον D.21.24. b. abs., *present oneself* in arms, *attend the muster*, E.*Ba.*782. c. *face, meet*, αἰκίαις καὶ θανάτοις Hecat.Abd.ap.J.*Ap.*1.22. 3. freq. as a law-term, *meet in open court*, τῷ καλεσαμένῳ Pl.*Lg.*937a, cf. D.39.3, etc.: without dat. pers., ἀ. πρὸς τὴν δίκην *present oneself* at the trial, Pl.*Lg.*936e; πρὸς ἣν [δίκην] οὐκ ἀπήντα *did not appear to defend* his cause, D.21.90; ἀ. πρὸς τὸν διαιτητήν, etc., *come before* him, Id.40.11, etc.; εἰς ἡμέραν τὴν συγκειμένην ἀ. εἰς τὸ Ἡφαιστεῖον 33.18; ἐπὶ τὰ ἱερά 42.7; ἐπὶ τὴν δίαιταν Test.ap.eund.21.93; ἀ. ἐπὶ τοῖς ἀλλοτρίοις ἀγῶσι *to be present at* other people's suits, *meddle with* them, D.21.205: abs., *appear in court*, 40.16, etc. 4. ἀ. εἰς.. *enter into* a thing, *attempt* it, εἰς τὸν ἀγῶνα Pl.*Lg.*830a; ἀ. εἰς τὴν τίμησιν *come to* the question of rating, Aeschin.3.198; ἀ. εἰς τὰς χρείας Arist.*EN*1158ᵃ8; ἀ. πρὸς τὰς μαθήσεις Pl.*Tht.*144b; πρὸς τὴν ἐρώτησιν, τὸ πρόβλημα, Arist. *Metaph.*1036ᵃ14, *Ph.*213ᵇ3; ἀ. πρὸς τὴν τροφήν *go to seek* it, Id.*deAn.*421ᵇ12; ἀ. ἐπί.. *have recourse to*.., D.21.151, 24.193, etc.; ἐπὶ ταύτας τὰς οἰκίας ἀ. οἱ τραγῳδοποιοί Arist.*Po.*1454ᵃ12. II. of things, *come upon* one, *meet* or *happen to* one, ἀ. δάκρυά μοι E.*Ion*940, cf. Bion l.c.; τοῖς πρὸς ὑμᾶς ζῶσι τοσαύτην κωφότητα.. παρ' ὑμῶν ἀπαντᾶν D.19.226; ἐπὶ τῷ κεφαλαίῳ τῶν πραγμάτων ἀ. [ἡ ῥᾳθυμία] 'comes home to roost', 10.7; ἀ. αὐτῷ κραυγὴ παρὰ τῶν δικαστῶν Aeschin.1.163; μή τίς σοι ἐναντίος λόγος ἀ. Pl.*Phd.*101a, cf. D.H.4.33, etc. 2. abs., *happen, occur, turn out*, Ar.*Lys.*420, Pl.*Ep.*358e, Arist.*Pol.*1302ᵃ6, *Top.*160ᵃ23, al.; τούτων ἀπαντώντων Hdt.8.142:—Pass., Plb. 2.7.4, Phld.*Herc.*1251.9.

※**ἀπαντή**, ἡ, = ἀπάντησις, Lxx *Jd.*4.22, al.

**ἀπάντη**, Adv., (ἅπας) *everywhere*, κύκλῳ ἀ. *all* round about, Od. 8.278; κῆρυξ δὲ φέρων ἀν' ὅμιλον ἀ. δεῖξε (sc. τὸν κλῆρον) Il.7.183, cf. 186; ἀ. πλανώμενος Pl.*Lg.*752a.

**ἀπάντ-ημα**, ατος, τό, (ἀπαντάω) *meeting*, E.*Or.*514. II. *chance*, Lxx *Ec.*9.11. ※**-ησις**, εως, ἡ, = foreg., S.*Fr.*828, Epicur.*Ep.*1 p.10 U., Plb.5.26.8, D.S.18.59; εἰς -σίν τινι ἐξελθεῖν Lxx *Jd.*11.31, *Ev.Matt.*25.6; *escort*, Plb.5.43.3, etc. II. *meeting in argument, reply*, πρός τι Arist.*SE*176ᵃ23, *Metaph.*1009ᵃ20, cf. Phld.*Sign.*19,28; ἀ. ποιεῖσθαι *to reply*, Plb.5.63.7; προσφιλὴς κατ' ἀ. *in conversation*, Id.10.5.6, cf. Phld.*Vit.*p.13 J., Id.*Herc.*1457.4, Plu.2.803f (pl.). III. *steadfastness in face of opposition*, Hp.*Decent.*5. **-ητέον**, *one must present oneself, appear*, ἀ. μοι εἰς τὴν στοάν Pl.*Tht.*210d; *one must rejoin, reply*, πρὸς τοὺς λόγους Arist.*SE*182ᵇ5; τοῖς θορύβοις *Rh.Al.*1432ᵇ33; *one must counteract*, Antyll.(?)ap.Orib.8.6 tit. ※**-ητήριον**, τό, *hostelry, inn*, *PSI*3.175.5 (v A.D.), *PLand.*17 (vi/vii A.D.), *Gloss.* **-ητής**· *deversorianus*, ib. **-ητικός**, ή, όν, *combative*, Asp. in *EN*82.27. Adv. -κῶς *obviam*, *Gloss.* **-ιάζω**, *meet*, ἀλλάλοις Archyt.1; v.l. for ὑπ- in Procop.*Goth.*3.6. **-ίζορα**· ἐναντία, Hsch.

**ἀπαντικρύ**, Adv. (in Att. Inscr. ἀπαντροκύ *IG*2.834*b*i 25, cf. 2(5) p.204), strengthd. for ἀντικρύ, *right opposite*, τῆς Ἀττικῆς D.8.36, cf. Hp.*Cord.*2, Thphr.*Char.*21.7, Luc.*Am.*5; ὁ ἀ. λόφος X.*HG*6.4.4. 2. *in the first instance*, opp. ἀνὰ χρόνον, Hp.*Art.*41.

**ἀπαντινά**· ἀνέντροπα, ἐκτετημένα (sic), Hsch.

**ἀπαντίον**, Adv., strengthd. for ἀντίον, like ἀπεναντίον, *right opposite*, ἐς τὴν ἀ. ἀκτήν Hdt.7.34, cf. Scyl.111.

**ἀπαντλ-έω**, *draw off from*, ἀ. χθονὸς ὕβρισμα θνητῶν E.*Or.*1641; *lighten*, τί σοι οἷοί τε θνητοὶ τῶνδ' ἀπαντλῆσαι πόνων; A.*Pr.*84; ἀ. τὸ ὑγρόν Arist.*Pr.*870ᵇ16; opp. ἐπιχέω, Pl.*R.*407d. II. c. acc. only, *lighten, lessen*, βάρος ψυχῆς E.*Alc.*354; τῶν ἐγκαλουμένων ἀπηντληκώς τι *having shed* some of his faults, Phld.*Lib.*p.35 O.:—in Pass., Ph. 1.266, Plu.*Alex.*57. **-ησις**, εως, ἡ, *drawing off*, of moisture, Arist. *Pr.*869ᵇ38; of blood, with menses, Sor.1.29. **-ητέον**, *one must draw off*, as water, *Gp.*6.18.

**ἀπάντομαι**, *entreat one not to do a thing*, E.*Rh.*901 (lyr., tm.). II. poet., = ἀπαντάω, Phryn.254.

**ἀπάντοτε**, Adv. *always*, A.D.*Synt.*263.2, al.

**ἀπαντροκύ**, v. ἀπαντικρύ.

**ἀπᾰνύω** [ῡ], *finish entirely*, νῆες ἀπήνυσαν οἴκαδε (sc. ὁδόν) the ships *performed the voyage* home, Od.7.326:—Pass., Q.S.5.1.

**ἀπάνωθεν**, *from above, from the top*, τοῦ τείχους Lxx *2Ki.*11.20, al.

※**ἅπαξ** [ᾰπ], Adv. *once, once only, once for all*, first in Od., ὅτε τ' ἄλλοι ἅ. θνήσκουσ' ἄνθρωποι 12.22; ἅ... ἀπὸ θυμὸν ὀλέσσαι ib.350; ἀπαλλάχθηθ' ἅ. E.*Cyc.*600; οὐχ ἅ. μόνον more than once, A.*Pr.*211; ἅ.. κοὐχὶ δίς S.*OC*1208; πολλάκις καὶ οὐχὶ ἅ. Hdt.7.46; πολλάκις τε κοὐχ ἅ. S.*OT*1275; μὴ ἅ. ἀλλὰ πολλάκις Antipho 1.3, cf. Pl.*Lg.*711a; μὴ δίς, ἀλλ' ἅ. μόνον Arist.*Pol.*1299ᵃ10; of the self-creation of Νοῦς, τὴν ποίησιν αὐτοῦ.. ἅ. εἶναι Plot.6.8.21; ἅ. ἔτι *yet* this *once*, A.*Ag.*1322; τὸ ἅ. τοῦτο *at* this *moment*, Lxx *2Ki.*17.7; ἅ. δυοῖν ποδοῖν, i.e. *two* square feet (1 × 2), opp. δυοῖν δίς (2 × 2), *four*, Pl.*Men.*82c. 2. c. gen., ἅ. τοῦ ἐνιαυτοῦ, ἔτεος ἑκάστου ἅ., Hdt.2.59, 4.105; also ἐν τῷ ἐνιαυτῷ ἅ. Id.2.132. 3. *once on a time, formerly*, ἅ. καὶ ἅ. Lxx *Jd.*20.30. II. without any notion of number, after conditional and temporal Particles, if *once*, when *once*, εἴπερ ἐσπείσω γ' ἅ. if *once* you have made a treaty, Ar.*Ach.*307, cf. 923; ἢν ἅ. ἁλῷ Id.*V.*898, cf. *Av.*342; ἂν ἅ. τις ἀποθάνῃ Amphis 8; ἐπειδήπερ γ' ἅ. ἐμοὶ σεαυτὸν παραδέδωκας Ar.*V.*1129; ἐπεὶ ἅ. ἐταράχθησαν Th.7.44; ὡς ἅ. ἤρξατο X.*HG*5.4.58; ἐπεὶ ἅ. αὐτοῖς φίλος ἐγένετο Id.*An.*1.9.10, cf. 3.2.25, Isoc.12.242; ὡς ἅ. ἐγκλήματα ἐταράχθη D.18.151: so with part., ἐπὶ γᾶν ἅ. πεσὸν.. αἷμα A.*Ag.*1019 (lyr.); ἅ. θανόντος οὔτις ἔστ' ἀνάστασις Id.*Eu.*648; ἅ. ἐλθόντες Pl.*Prm.*165e, cf. *Ep.Hebr.*6.4, etc. (ἁ- = *sm̥* (cf. εἷς); -παξ akin to πήγνυμι.)

**ἁπαξ-άπᾱς** [ξᾰ], ᾱσα, ᾰν, *all together, the whole*, περιτρέχων τὴν γῆν ἁπαξάπασαν Hermipp.4.3; ἡμέρα ἁ. Stratt.36.2; ἁπαξάπαν Xenarch. 7.16; ἁπαξαπάσης τιμῆς Phld.*Mort.*23: mostly in pl., *all at once, all together*, Ar.*Pl.*111,206, etc. ※**-απλῶς**, Adv., strengthd. for ἁπλῶς, *in general*, Hierocl.p.51 A., *PLips.*27.29 (ii A.D.), S.E.*M.*7.428, Luc. *Peregr.*3, etc.

※**ἀπαξί-α**, ἡ, (ἄξιος) opp. ἀξία, *disvalue*, Zeno *Stoic.*1.48, cf. Antip. ib.3.251, Arr.*Epict.*1.2.10, S.E.*M.*11.62. **-ος**, ον, = ἀνάξιος, *unworthy of*, τινός Pl.*Lg.*645c. II. οὐκ ἀ. [ἐστι], c. inf., Id.*Ep.*324b. Adv. -ίως Iamb.*Myst.*5.6. **-όω**, *disclaim as unworthy, disown*, τι or τινά, Th.1.5, Plb.1.67.13, Plot.5.8.3; ἀ. τινὸς μή, c. inf., Paus. 10.14.6. 2. ἀ. ἑαυτὸν τῶν καλλίστων Arist.*Mu.*391ᵃ6; but τί τινος *deem* a thing *unworthy* of one, Luc.*Dom.*2:—Med., ἀνέχας ἀπηξιώσατο *deemed* them *unworthy of*.., *banished* them *from*.., A.*Eu.*367.

※**ἄπαξις**, εως, ἡ, = ἀπαγωγή, *arrest*, *POxy.*33 iii 15 (ii A.D.).

**ἀπαξίωσις**, εως, ἡ, *rejection, contempt*, Plb.*Fr.*10, D.H.1.9; τῆς ἀρχῆς 5.71.

**ἀπαξοί**· μοναχοί, Hsch.; perh. to be read in Hdt.2.79, 7.96.

**ἀπάορος**, ον, Dor. for ἀπήορος, q.v.

**ἀπαπαῖ**, = ἀππαπαῖ, Ar.*V.*309.

**ἀπάπη**, ἡ, *dandelion, Taraxacum officinale*, Thphr.*HP*7.7.1, 7.8.3 and 11.3 (ex cod. Urb. pro vulg. ἀπάτη vel ἀφάκη), cf. Plin.*HN*21.99.

**ἀπαππᾰπαῖ**, = ἀππαπαῖ, S.*Ph.*746.

**ἄπαππος**, ον, *with no grandfather*: metaph., φάος οὐκ ἄπαππον Ἰδαίου πυρός light not *unfathered by* the Idaean flame, A.*Ag.*311.

**ἀπάπτω**, Ion. for ἀφάπτω.

※**ἀπαρά-βᾰτος**, ον, *unalterable*, εἱρμὸς αἰτιῶν *Stoic.*2.266; ἐπιπλοκή, of causation, Chrysipp.ib.293; τάξις Plu.2.410f; ἡ τῆς κινήσεως ἰδέα Ocell.1.15; *infallible*, προρρήσεις Iamb.*VP*28.135, cf. Philum.*Ven.*4.14; also of persons, *Cat.Cod.Astr.*8(4).215. Adv. -τως Chrysipp.*Stoic.*2.279. 2. *inviolable*, κύρια καὶ ἀ. *PRyl.*65.18 (i B.C.), cf. *PGrenf.*1.60.7 (vi A.D.). 3. *permanent, perpetual*, ἱερωσύνη *Ep.Hebr.*7.24. 3. Act., *not transgressing*, J.*AJ*18.8.2; ἀ. τῶν καθηκόντων Hierocl. in *CA*10p.435M. Adv. -τως Arr.*Epict.*2.15.1. **-βλαστος**, ον, *not branching laterally*, Thphr.*HP*1.2.5, *CP*1.1.3; *not budding laterally*, Id.*HP*3.17.2. ※**-βλητος**, ον, *incomparable*, *PLond.*2.232.5 (iv A.D.), f.l. for -βατος in Ph.2.509. **-βολος**, ον, *without deposit made*, κρίσιν ἀπάρβολον *IG*9(1).694.115; δίκα *GDI*5017 (Gortyn, prob.). II. Adv. -λως *without danger*, Sch.Il.13.141.

**ἀπαράγγελτος**, ον, *without formal declaration*, πόλεμος Ἀρχ.Ἐφ. 920.84 (Itanos, ii B.C.). Adv. -τως *without signal of battle*, Plb.16. .1, *Fr.*11.

**ἀπαρα-γνώστως**, Adv. *without reading*, Suid. s. v. Πουλχε-ρία. **-γρᾰφος**, ον, *incapable of definition*, ποσότης Plb.16.12.10.

**ἀπαράγωγος** [ἄγ], ον, *not to be turned aside*, Hierocl.*in CA*13 p.450 M. Adv. -γως ib.8 p.431 M.

***ἀπαρα-δειγμάτιστος**, ον, *not liable to censure*, Ptol.*Tetr.*170. **-δεικτος**, ον, *not returned, unregistered*, ἐδάφη *BGU*915.6 (ii A.D.). **-δεκτος**, ον, *inadmissible*, Phld.*Sign.*17 (-δεικτον Pap.), A.D.*Synt.*59.18, al.; *unacceptable*, Olymp.Hist.p.465 D. II. Act., *not receiving* or *admitting*, c. gen., μαθημάτων Memn.2.2; [τῶν ἀγαθῶν] Phld.*D.*3 *Fr.*42 (dub. rest.); τέχνης Ph.1.311; διαβολῆς *Stoic.*3. 153; esp. in Gramm., τῶν ἄρθρων A.D.*Synt.*16.18, al. **-δίσκευτος**, ον, *not defeated in discus-throwing*, *Ephes.*2 No.72 (iii A.D.). **-θετος**, ον, *not padded out with quotations*, D.L.7.181: hence in Gramm., ἀπαράθετα *words* or *phrases without quoted authority*, prob. for ἀπαρένθ-, *Et.Gud.* s. v. ἀεί. **-θραυστος**, ον, *unshaken, not to be shaken*, Olymp.*in Phlb.*p.274 S., Eustr.*in EN*297.26.

**ἀπαραιρημένος**, Ion. pf. part. Pass. of ἀφαιρέω.

***ἀπαραίτητος**, ον, I. of gods or persons, *not to be moved by prayer, inexorable*, δαίμων Lys.2.78; θεοί, θεαί, Pl.*Lg.*907b, *IG*12(2). 484 (Lesb.); Δίκη D.25.11; ἀνάγκη Epicur.*Ep.*3 p.65 U.; δικασταί Lycurg.2; ἀ. εἶναι περί τι Plu.*Pyrrh.*16:—τὸ ἀ. τινος πρὸς τοὺς πονηρούς Id.*Publ.*3. Adv. -τως *implacably, inexorably*, Th.3.84; ἀ. ἔχειν πρός τινα Plb.21.31.15. II. of punishments, etc., *not to be averted by prayers, inevitable, unmerciful*, τιμωρίαι Din.1.23; κολάσεις Ti. Locr.104d; νόμος J.*Ap.*2.30; ὀργή, κατηγορία, Plb.1.82.9, 12.12.6; = ἀνήκεστος, βουλεύεσθαί τι ἀ. Id.4.24.6; ἁμαρτία *unpardonable*, Id. 33.10.5. Adv. -τως *obstinately*, Sor.1.107. 2. *not to be evaded*, ἱκέτευμα Plu.2.950f; χρεία *POxy.*900.12 (iv A.D.), cf. *PFlor.*6.11 (iii A.D.); *indispensable*, ἀριθμός Philostr.*VA*3.30; *irresistible*, προθυμία Orib.*Fr.*57. Adv. -τήτως *without evasion*, *PMag.Leid.W.*17.2.

***ἀπαρα-κάλυπτος** [κᾰ], ον, *undisguised*, γυμνὴ καὶ ἀ. κατηγορία Hld. 10.29. Adv. -τως Pl.*R.*538c, *Euthd.*294d: Comp. -ότερον D.C.67. 3. 2. *open-hearted*, ἀ. τὰς ψυχάς Ptol.*Tetr.*155. ***-κλητος**, ον, *unsummoned, volunteering*, Th.2.98; εὔνοια *Inscr.Prien.*108.43 (ii B.C.); καὶ παρακαλούμενος καὶ ἀ. Plu.2.403b, cf. *CIG*2271.27 (Delos). II. *not to be consoled*, Sch.A.*Pr.*185.

**ἀπαρᾰκολούθητος**, ον, *not to be reached* or *attained*, Tz. ad Lyc. 5. II. Adv. -τως *inconsequently*, M.Ant.2.16, Plot.4.3.28.

**ἀπαρᾰκόντιστος**, ον, *not defeated in javelin-throwing*, *Ephes.*2 No. 72 (iii A.D.).

**ἀπάρακτος**, ον, (παράγω) gloss on ἀνώπιστος, Hsch.

**ἀπαρά-λειπτος**, ον, *unintermittent*, Simp.*in Ph.*213.34. Adv. -τως Syrian.*in Metaph.*132.23, Procl.*in Prm.*p.833 S. 2. *complete*, Alex.Trall.5.1. **-λεκτος**, ον, *with disordered hair*, Pherecr. 195. ***-λήκτως**, Adv. *unceasingly*, *CIG*2271.7 (Delos).

**ἀπαράλλακτος**, ον, *precisely similar, indistinguishable*, *Stoic.*2.26, al., cf. Phld.*Sign.*15, al., D.H.2.71, D.S.1.91, Plu.*Alex.*57, Plot.5. 7.3; ἀ. ἁρμονία πρὸς τὸ ἀρχέτυπον Jul.*Or.*2.93a: c. gen., *indistinguishable from*, Phld.*Po.*994.26: c. dat., *exactly like*, D.S.2.50. Adv. -τως *unchangeably*, Lxx *Es.*3.13, *BMus.Inscr.*481*.402 (Ephesus), Theo Sm.p.172 H.; *in precisely similar terms*, Ath.1.26a, etc.; *indistinguishably*, *Stoic.*2.190, al., Plot.2.1.2.

**ἀπαραλλαξία**, ἡ, *indistinguishability*, *Stoic.*2.34 (pl.), cf. Phld. *Sign.*6, 37; ὁμοιότης κατ' -ίαν S.E.*M.*7.108. II. *unshakable determination*, *Stoic.*3.73.

**ἀπαρα-λόγιστος**, ον, *not to be deceived*, τῶν καθηκόντων τήρησις Hierocl.*in CA*10 p.437 M.; *not liable to error*, Nicom.*Harm.*6. Adv. -τως *undoubtedly*, Ruf.ap.Orib.45.30.55. II. Act., *not deceiving*, Hsch. s. v. ἀπαράσημον. **-λογος**, ον, *not without reason* or *method*, Iamb.*VP*30.182. **-λῠτος**, *irrevocable*, λόγος *PGrenf.*1.60.31 (vi A.D.). **-μῑγής**, ές, *unmixed*, Sch.Od.2.341.

**ἀπαρᾰμίλλητος**, ον, *unrivalled*, J.*AJ*8.7.3.

**ἀπαρά-μονος**, ον, *not abiding, transient*, Secund.*Sent.*14, Vett.Val. 39.30, al. **-μύθητος** [ῡ], ον, *not to be persuaded* or *entreated, inexorable*, Pl.*Epin.*980d, Plu.2.629a. 2. *incorrigible*, in Adv. -τως Pl.*Lg.*731d. II. of conditions, *comfortless*, Plu.2.332d; *not admitting consolation*, πάθος Jul.*Or.*8.245c; κακόν Hld.1.14. 2. of persons, *inconsolable*, Id.2.33. Adv. -τως Jul.*Or.*8.252a. **-μῡθος**, ον, = foreg., *inexorable*, κέαρ A.*Pr.*185 (lyr.); *restive*, ὄμμα πωλικόν E.*IA*620. [In A. ἀπ- metri gr.]

**ἀπαράντινα**· ἀπαράλλακτα, Hsch.

**ἀπᾰράομαι**, *propitiate*, τοῖς θεοῖς Mim. in *POxy.*413[v] ii 133.

**ἀπαρά-πειστος**, ον, *not to be seduced*, D.H.8.61. **-πόδιστος**, ον, *free from embarrassment* or *interference*, Arr.*Epict.*1.1.10, al., *BGU* 1124.44 (i B.C.); ὁρμή Hld.3.13; *clear*, διάνοια Hices.ap.Ath.15. 689c. Adv. -τως Arr.*Epict.*2.13.21, S.E.*M.*1.178, *PLond.*3.1168.12 (i A.D.), Gal.4.725.

**ἀπαραποιήτως**· ἀπλάστως, Hsch.

**ἀπαρα-σήμαντος**, ον, *unnoticed*, ἀ. τι ἀφιέναι, ἐᾶσαι, Lxx 2 *Ma.*15.36, *Mon.Ant.*23.61 (Seleucia), cf. *Michel* 546.21 (Anisa, i B.C.). **-σημείωτος**, ον, = foreg., Dsc.*Prooem.*1. ***-σημος**, ον, *not counterfeit*, Hsch. II. κατηγορία φόνου ἀ. with *no* defendant *named*, Antipho 2.1 tit. **-σκευᾰσία**, ἡ, *want of preparation*, Hp.*Acut.*65. **-σκεύαστος**, ον, = sq., X.*An.*1.5.9 (Comp.), 2 *Ep.Cor.*9.4, J.*AJ*4.8.41. Adv. -τως Arist.*Rh.Al.*1430[a]3. **-σκευος**, ον, *without preparation, unprepared*, Antipho 5.18 (Sup.), Th.2.87; ἀπαράσκευόν τινα λαβεῖν X. *Cyr.*7.5.25; ἀ. ληφθῆναι D.40.30; ἀ. πρὸς τὸ μέλλον Plb.1.49.4: c. gen., *unprovided with*, τῶν ἐπιτηδείων J.*BJ*3.7.32; also of things, ἀπόστασις Th.3.13: Sup., X.*An.*1.1.6. Adv. ἀπαρασκεύως, ἔχειν, διακεῖσθαι, Plb.1.45.7, 14.10.7. **-στᾰτος**, ον, *not having appeared in person*, *PLond.*2.260.128 (i A.D.).

**ἀπᾰράσσω**, Att. -ττω, *strike off*, ἀντικρὺ δ' ἀπάραξε [τὴν αἰχμήν] Il.16.116; ἀπήραξεν δὲ χαμᾶζε.. κάρη 14.497; ἀ. τοῦ ἵππου τοὺς πόδας Hdt.5.112; κρᾶτα S.*Tr.*1015 (lyr.). 2. *knock* or *sweep off*, τοὺς ἐπιβάτας ἀπὸ τῆς νεός Hdt.8.90; τοὺς ἀπὸ τοῦ πολεμίου καταστρώματος ὁπλίτας ἀ. Th.7.63:—Pass., aor. part. ἀπαραχθείς D.H.8. 85. 3. *crush*, ἀπὸ δ' ὀστέον ἄχρις ἄραξε Il.16.324:—Pass., -άσσεται τὴν κεφαλήν J.*BJ*3.7.23.

**ἀπαρα-σχημάτιστος**, ον, *not parallel in formation*, *EM*13.33: c. dat., ἀ. οὐδετέρῳ *having no corresponding* neuter, Eust.94. 30. **-τᾰτος**, ον, *unextended*, Simp.*in Ph.*640.21. Adv. -τως *without extension*: of Time, *in a moment*, τὴν ἀφὴν ἀθρόως καὶ ἀ. γίνεσθαι Id.*in Cael.*313.22. ***-τήρητος**, ον, *not observed*, *IG*2[2].1035.11 (i B.C.). Adv. -τως *without precautions*, Plb.3.52.7, 14.1.12, J.*BJ*4.3. 3, Ph.*Fr.*105 H. **-τιλτος**, ον, *with hairs not pulled out*, Ar.*Lys.* 279, Luc.*Salt.*5. **-τρεπτος**, *not turned*, of clothes, Phryn.*PS* p.52 B. II. of laws, *not to be perverted*, Plu.2.745d; of persons, Poll.8.10. Adv. -τως M.Ant.1.16.1.

**ἀπάραυξος**, ον, *not subject to increase*, dub. in Gal.8.913.

**ἀπαρά-φθορος**, ον, *free from damage*, ἔργον *IG*12(3).326 (Thera). **-φύλακτος** [ῠ], ον, *not to be guarded against*, Sch.Il.11.297. II. (from Med.) *careless, heedless*, Sch.E.*Hipp.*657. **-χάρακτος** [χᾰ], ον, *not counterfeit*, Damocr.ap.Gal.14.135, Hsch. s. v. ἀπαράσημον. **-χῠτος**, ον, *without anything poured in, unmixed*, οἶνος Gal.13.721, cf. 10.832; ὕδωρ Hld.5.16: generally, *pure*, Plu.2. 968c. **-χώρητος**, ον, *not giving ground, staunch*, Plb.1.61.3. Adv. -τως, διακεῖσθαι περί τινος Id.5.106.5. 2. *refusing to retire, unyielding*, τὸ ἀ. τῆς ἐξουσίας D.H.10.19; φιλαρχία ἀ. 10.54, cf. Plu. 2.1ca. II. Pass., *not permitted*, Sch.Opp.*H.*5.416.

**ἀπάρβολος**, v. ἀπαράβολος.

**ἀπαργία**, ἡ, *hawk's-beard, Crepis Columnae*, Thphr.*HP*7.8.3.

***ἄπαργμα**, ατος, τό, = ἀπαρχή (q. v.), in pl., Ar.*Pax* 1056, Lyc. 106. II. = μασχαλίσματα, *EM*118.22.

**ἀπαργῠρ-ίζω**, *appraise at cash value*, ὄψα Them.*Or.*23.292d:—Med., *buy off*, πολέμους Lyd.*Mag.*3.45. **-ισμός**, ὁ, *selling for ready money*, *Gloss.* II. = Lat. *adaeratio*, *PFlor.*377.4 (vi A.D.), Just.*Nov.*43.1 *Intr.*, 130.4. **-όω**, = ἀπαργυρίζω, Artem.1.50.

**ἀπαρ-εγκλῐτος**, ον, *direct*, Gal.*UP*15.8; *inflexible*, νόμοι φυσικοὶ ἀ. Nicom.*Ar.*1.23; πρόνοια Hero *Deff.*136.57. 2. *straight*, εὐθεῖα (sc. γραμμή) Phlp.*in Mete.*21.10, cf. Ammon.*in Porph.*9.1. Adv. -τως Gal.18(2).726; *not diverging from the perpendicular*, Eustr.*in EN*74. 9. II. *unimpaired*, ὑγίεια Iamb.*VP*3.13. **-εγχείρητος**, ον, *not to be tampered with, inviolable*, Ti.Locr.95a, Arr.*Epict.*4.1.161, J.*AJ*15.8.1. Adv. -τως *inimitably, perfectly*, D.S.4.78. **-έγχῠτος**, ον, = ἀπαράχυτος, Ath.1.27a. **-εμπόδιστος**, ον, = ἀπαραπόδιστος (for which it occurs as a v. l.), Sor.1.3; ἡ τοῦ κόσμου διοίκησις Chrysipp.*Stoic.*297, cf. S.E.*M.*1.147. Adv. -τως Aët.16.61, Hdn.*Fig.* p.96 S., Alex.Aphr.*in Top.*46.3. **-έμφᾰτος**, ον, (παρεμφαίνω) *not determinative* or *indicative*, c. gen., A.D.*Synt.*239.8, cf. Herm.*in Phdr.* p.124 A., Ps.-Alex.Aphr.*in SE*36.17. Adv. -τως Hsch. II. ἡ ἀπαρέμφατος (sc. ἔγκλισις) the *infinitive mood* (cf. παρεμφατικός), D.H.*Comp.*5, A.D.*Synt.*226.20, Ps.-Alex.Aphr.*in SE*34.28; τὸ ἀ. S.E.*P.*1.204. Adv. -τως *in the infinitive mood*, ἀναγνῶναι take *as an infinitive*, A.D.*Synt.*76.16. ***-ενθύμητος** [ῡ], ον, *not considering, carelessly*, M.Ant.10.8. Adv. -τως Id.6.53. **-ενόχλητος**, ον, *undisturbed*, συμβίωσις Phld.*Ir.*p.78 W.; ὑπό τινων *BGU*1140.24 (i B.C.), cf. *IGRom.*4.2927 (Pergam.), *PTeb.*41.24, Plu.2.118b.

**ἀπαρές**· ὑγιές, Hsch.; cf. ἀπηρής.

**ἀπᾰρέσκω**, *to be disagreeable to*, τινί Th.1.38, Plu.2.6b. 2. c. acc. pers., *displease*, Pl.*Tht.*202d, Jul.*Mis.*365d. 3. abs., τὰ ἀπαρέσαντα J.*AJ*8.14.1. II. Med., οὐ.. γάρ τι νεμεσσητὸν βασιλῆα ἄνδρ' ἀπαρέσσασθαι it is no disgrace for a king *to approve* a man (or, *to appease* a man of royal birth), Il.19.183, cf. Sch. and Eust. ad loc. III. ἀπαρέσκεσθαί τινι *to be displeased with*, Hdn.5.2.5, cf. 5.6.1, 6.1.10, Lyd.*Mag.*2.7.

**ἀπᾰρεστός**, όν, *unpleasing*, Stob.2.7.11[k].

**ἀπαρηγόρητος**, ον, *unconsoled*, Plu.*Dem.*22; *admitting of no consolation*, συμφορά J.*AJ*7.6.1. II. *not to be controlled*, Men.798, Plu.*Mar.*2, *Ant.*6; *inexorable*, Hp.*Decent.*4. Adv. -τως *inflexibly*, Ph.2.196.

***ἀπαρήγορος**, ον, *unconsoling*, θρῆνος *Epigr.Gr.*344.2 (Mysia).

**ἀπαρθένευτος**, ον, *unmaidenly, unfitting a maiden*, E.*Ph.*1739 (lyr.), neut. pl. as Adv., cf. Id.*IA*993. II. *deflowered*, Sch.Theoc. 2.41. III. *virginal* (as if from παρθενεύω, = κορεύω), S.*Fr.*304, *Carm.Pop.*8.

***ἀπάρθενος**, ον, *no more a maid*, Theoc.2.41; νύμφην ἄνυμφον παρθένον τ' ἀπάρθενον 'virgin wife and widowed maid', E.*Hec.*612.

**ἀπαρθρ-όομαι**, Pass., *to be jointed*, ἀπό τινος Hp.*Art.*30. **-ωσις**, εως, ἡ, *articulation*, Gal.18(1).433.

***ἀπᾰριθμ-έω**, *count over, take an inventory of*, X.*Oec.*9.10; *reckon up*, Id.*Cyr.*5.2.35; μύθους ἀ. *recount*, Arist.*Po.*1453[a]18:—Pass., Ps.-Alex. Aphr.*in SE*64.11, al. II. *reckon* or *pay back, repay*, X.*Cyr.*3.1.42, D.H.4.10, etc. III. Med., *secure payment of* a sum owing, *IG*1. 32, cf. ib.2[2].1122; but, 2. = Act. in Men.*Epit.*164, cf. Alex.Aphr. *in Top.*422.3; ἀ. προγόνους δυνάστας Jul.*Or.*2.83b; *enumerate*, σοφῶν ὀνόματα Id.*Gal.*176b. **-ησις**, εως, ἡ, *counting over*, ὀνομάτων Th. 5.20, cf. Alex.Aphr. *in Top.*425.8, Procl. *in Prm.*p.908 S., *in Ti.*1.15 D., al. :—Adj. **-ητικός**, ή, όν, Sch.Hermog.*Id.* in Rh.7.1027 W.

**ἀπαρίνη** [ῐ], ἡ, *cleavers, Galium Aparine*, Thphr.*HP*7.14.2, Plu.2.709e, Dsc.3.90, Gal.11.834. **2.** = ἄρκιον, Ps.-Dsc.4.106. **3.** = ξάνθιον, Dsc.4.136.

**ἀπαρῑνής**, ές, *of the* ἀπαρίνη, χυλός Nic.*Th.*953.

**ἀπ-άριστα**, neut. as Adv., (ἄριστον) *after luncheon*, *Tab.Defix.Aud.*187.63. **-αριστάω**, *finish luncheon*, *Gloss.*

***ἀπαρκέω**, *suffice, be sufficient*, Sol.5 (ap.Arist.*Ath.*12.1), A.*Pers.*474, S.*OC*1769 (lyr.), E.*Fr.*892; πρός τι S.E.*P.*1.185: abs., οὐκ ἀπήρκει *it was* not *enough*, Ar.*Fr.*457, cf. D.H.11.1. **II.** *to be contented, acquiesce*, ὥστ' ἀπαρκεῖν A.*Ag.*379 (lyr.) :—Pass., Cerc.18 ii 13, Lyc.1302.

**ἀπαρκής**, ές, *sufficient*, Hsch.

**ἀπαρκίας**, v. ἀπαρκτίας.

**ἀπαρκούντως**, Adv., (ἀπαρκέω) *sufficiently*, Poll.9.154 (perh. f.l. for ἐπ-).

**ἀπαρκτεῖν**· ἀποτυχεῖν, Hsch.

**ἀπαρκτέον**, (ἀπάρχομαι) *one must offer as first-fruits, sacrifice*, Ph.1.533, Them.*Or.*11.142a, Porph.*Abst.*2.61.

***ἀπαρκτίας**, ου, ὁ, (ἄρκτος) *north wind*, Arist.*Mete.*363$^b$14, al., Thphr.*Sign.*2.35. The form **ἀπαρκίας**, mentioned by Eust.1156.17, 1535.16, but censured by Phryn.*PS*p.31 B., occurs (= *Septentrio*) in *IG*14.1308, *Gloss.*

**ἀπάρκτιος**, α, ον, *northerly*, πνοαί Lyc.27.

***ἀπαρν-έομαι**, fut. -ήσομαι Pl.*Grg.*461c: aor. ἀπηρνησάμην Call.*Cer.*75,107, A.R.3.1133 (v.l.), *Ev.Matt.*16.24, al., but in Trag. and Att., -ηρνήθην S.*Tr.*480, E.*Hipp.*1266, Th.6.56, etc. :—*deny utterly*, Hdt.6.69; κλέψαντες ἀπαρνεῖσθαι Antipho 2.3.4; μὴ.. ἀπαρνηθεὶς γένη Pl.*Sph.*217c; ἀπαρνηθῆναί τι *to refuse, reject* it, Th. l.c., etc.; ἀ. μή c. inf., τὸν.. ἀπαρνηθέντα μὴ χρᾶναι E. l.c.; οὐκ ἀπαρνοῦμαι τὸ μή (sc. δρᾶσαι) S.*Ant.*443, *Aj.*96; τίνα οἴει ἀπαρνήσεσθαι μὴ οὐ..; Pl.*Grg.*461c; οἷός ἐστι μὴ ἂν ἀ. χαρίσασθαι Id.*Phdr.*256a. **2.** in Logic, opp. κατηγορεῖν, *deny*, Arist.*APr.*41$^a$9 :—Pass., ib.63$^b$37. **3.** ἀ. ἑαυτόν *deny* oneself, *Ev.Matt.*16.24, al. **II.** Pass., fut. ἀπαρνηθήσεται *it shall be denied* or *refused*, S.*Ph.*527, cf. *Ev.Luc.*12.9, dub. in Lxx *Is.*31.7: aor. ὤνθρωπος ἐν μὲν οἶδεν, ἐν δ' ἀπηρνήθη *was refused*, Herod.4.74. **-ησις**, εως, ἡ, *denial, renunciation*, Ph.2.438. **-ητής**, οῦ, ὁ, *one who denies*, *Gloss.* **-ητικός**, ή, όν, *denying*, Eust.29.44.

**ἄπαρνος**, ον, (ἀρνέομαι) *denying utterly*, ἄ. ἐστι μὴ νοσέειν Hdt.3.99, cf. Antipho 1.9 and 10: c. gen., ἄ. οὐδενὸς καθίστατο she *denied* nothing, S.*Ant.*435. **II.** Pass., *denied*, ᾧ.. οὐδὲν ἄπαρνον τελέθει to whom nothing is *denied*, A.*Supp.*1039 (lyr.).

**ἀπαρ-όδευτος**, ον, *inaccessible*, κρημνοί D.S.17.67. **-όξυντος**, ον, *without paroxysms*, Alex.Trall.8.2. **-όρμητος**, ον, *not excitable*, Theag.ap.Stob.3.1.116. **-ουσιάστως**, Adv., (παρουσία) *without bodily presence*, Olymp. *in Alc.*p.13 C. **-οχος**, ον, *niggardly*, Vett.Val.85.24; *impraestans*, *Gloss.*

**ἀπαρόω**, aor. ἀπήροσα, *plough up*, Suid. (expl. by ἀπηροτρίασα).

**ἀπαρρενόω**, *produce male plants*, opp. ἀποθηλύνομαι, Thphr.*HP*7.4.3 (Pass.).

**ἀπαρρησίαστος**, ον, *deprived of freedom of speech*, Thphr.*Fr.*103; πολιτεία Plb.22.12.2; *having no right of speech*, Cic.*Att.*9.2.2; *not frank*, Phld.*Herc.*1457.12, Id.*Rh.*2.158 S. **II.** *not speaking freely*, J.*BJ*4.5.4, Plu.2.51c, al., Luc.*Cal.*9. Adv. **-τως**, εὐλαβεῖσθαι Ph.1.477. **b.** *not acting freely*, of reptiles, Herm.ap.Stob.1.49.69. **III.** Pass., *not freely spoken of*, Ph.2.428.

***ἄπαρσις**, εως, ἡ, (ἀπαίρω) *setting out, departure*, D.H.3.58, Lxx *Nu.*33.2, J.*AJ*17.9.3.

**ἀπαρτάω**, *hang up*: ἀ. δέρην *strangle*, E.*Andr.*412; *swing freely*, of a stone in a sling, Arist.*Mech.*852$^b$1 :—Pass., *hang loose*, X.*Eq.*10.9, Arist.*Aud.*802$^a$38; ἀπό τινος πρός τι Id.*GA*740$^a$29; ἔκ τινος Luc.*Pisc.*48; τινός Babr.17.2. **2.** metaph., *make dependent upon*, ἀ. ἐλπίδας ἐξ ἑαυτοῦ Luc.*Tim.*36 :—Med., *make dependent on oneself*, νόμοις τὸ πλῆθος Plu.*CG*8. **II.** *detach, separate*, τὸν λόγον τῆς γραφῆς D.18.59, cf. Arist.*Rh.*1407$^a$24 :—Pass., ὥστε τὴν χώραν πολὺ τῆς πόλεως ἀπηρτῆσθαι Id.*Pol.*1319$^a$34; ὁ πλεύμων.. πολὺ ἀπηρτημένος τῆς καρδίας Id.*HA*508$^a$33; οἱ πόροι.. ἀπήρτηνται ἀλλήλων, opp. συμπίπτουσι, ib.495$^a$18 :—but that from which one is separated is often omitted, and the Pass. used absolutely, ἀπηρτημένοι καὶ ταῖς παρασκευαῖς καὶ ταῖς γνώμαις *detached*, D.4.12; συνεχεῖς καὶ οὐκ ἀπηρτημένοι not *detached*, Arist.*HA*509$^b$13, cf. 506$^b$19, al.; of Time, τοῖς καιροῖς οὐ μακρὰν ἀπηρτῆσθαι Plb.12.17.1, cf. Plu.*TG*3; λόγος ἀπηρτημένος *discrepant*, Str.7.3.2; λίαν ἀπηρτ. far *different*, Ph.1.300, cf. Phld.*Rh.*1.288 S. **III.** intr. in Act., *remove oneself, go away*, ἐς ἀλλοτρίαν ἀπαρτᾶν Th.6.21, cf. D.C.40.15; *to be away, distant*, ἀπό τινος Id.51.4; πρὶν ἀπαρτηθῆναι 44.38 is perh. f.l. for ἀπαντ-.

**ἀπαρτής**, ές, *raised up*, βίς Hp.*Art.*38 (v.l. ἀπαρτητήν).

***ἀπάρτησις**, εως, ἡ, *hanging from, appendage*, τῶν πτερυγίων Arist.*GA*720$^b$12. **2.** *attachment*, Hp.*Art.*8 (with v.l. ἀπάρτισις): metaph., *dependence*, Plot.5.1.2. **II.** *detachment, separation*, Ph.1.209.

***ἀπαρτί** [ῐ], Adv. *completely*, and, of numbers, *exactly, just*, ἡμέραι ἀ. ἐνενήκοντα Hdt.5.53, cf. 2.158; φρόνιμος ὢν ἀ. ταύτης τῆς τέχνης Telecl.37; ἀ. ἐναρμόζειν πρός τι Hp.*Art.*73: of Time, ἀ. ἐν καιροῖσι.. Id.*Acut.*41. **II.** *just the contrary*, τί.. ἀποτίνειν τῷδ' ἀξιοῖς; — ἀ. δή που προσλαβεῖν παρὰ τοῦδ' ἐγὼ μᾶλλον *on the contrary*, I expect to receive.., Pherecr.93, cf. 71, Ar.*Pl.*388. **III.** ἀπάρτι, properly ἀπ' ἄρτι, of Time, *from now, henceforth*, *Ev.Matt.*23.39, etc. **2.** *just now, even now*, *Ev.Jo.*13.19, etc. (This is not an Att. use, hence Pl.Com.143 must be incorrectly interpr. by *AB*79.)

**ἀπαρτία**, Ion. -ίη, ἡ, = ἀποσκευή, *household utensils, movables, chattels*, Hippon.26, Thphr.ap.Poll.10.19, Lxx *Ex.*40.36. **2.** *spoil*, including captives, ib.*Nu.*31.17,18. **II.** *public auction*, *PStrassb.*59.3 (i B.C.), *PGnom.*241 (-εία, ii A.D.), Poll. l.c. **III.** ἀπαρτίαν· μετάβασιν, ἀποσκευήν, τέλος, ἀπαρτισμόν, Hsch.

**ἀπαρτιζόντως**, Adv. *adequately, precisely*, λόγος κατ' ἀνάλυσιν ἀ. ἐκφερόμενος Antip.*Stoic.*3.247, cf. Apollod.ib.3.260; Alex.Aphr. *in Top.*42.27; of division, *without remainder*, Theo Sm.p.76 H.

***ἀπαρτίζω**, fut. ἀπαρτιῶ Mitteis *Chr.*88 iii 13 (ii A.D.) :—*make even*, σπουδὴ.. οὐκ ἀπαρτίζει πόδα does not *allow* his feet *to move evenly, regularly*, A.*Th.*374 (Herm. οὐ καταργίζει); *produce an even result*, Arist.*GA*780$^b$10; ἀ. ὥστε σφαιροειδῆ εἶναι *make* it *perfectly* spherical, Id.*Mete.*340$^b$35; *fasten off* the ends of a phylactery, *PMag.Par.*1.2703. **II.** generally, *get ready, complete*, Plb.31.12.10; *finish*, λόγον Iamb. *in Nic.*p.35 P.; *dispose of*, δίκας Mitteis *Chr.* l.c., cf. Charito 6.1; *educate* an apprentice *thoroughly*, *POxy.*724.11 (ii A.D.) :—Pass., *to be brought to perfection*, Arist.*Fr.*282; *to be completed, be exactly made up*, ἀπηρτισμένης ⟨τῆς⟩ πρώτης περιόδου Hp.*Morb.*4.48; ἀπαρτίζεται εἰς ἑπτὰ κεφαλάς, of the golden candlestick, J.*AJ*3.6.7: metaph., *end, result in*, εἴς τι ib.16.8.2; of multiplication, *make*, Paul.Al.*E.*1; ἀπηρτισμένος *complete, perfect*, D.H.*Dem.*50; στίχος verse *coinciding with a sentence*, Hdn.*Vers.*86; πρὸς τὸ τέλος Phld.*Mus.*p.31 K., cf. *Piet.*66. **2.** intr., *to be complete*, τῆς ὀκταμήνου ἀπαρτιζούσης Hp.*Epid.*2.3.17; ἀ. ὁ τόπος καὶ τὸ σῶμα *fit exactly*, Arist.*Ph.*205$^a$32; ἀ. πρός τι *square with, suit exactly*, Id.*Pol.*1313$^a$7; ἡ ἀπαρτίζουσα ὥρα the *fitting* season, Id.*HA*542$^a$31; τῶν ὀργάνων οὐθὲν ἀπαρτιζόντων Epicur.*Nat.*11.6; οἱ -οντες *corresponding precisely to definition*, *Stoic.*2.128. Adv. ἀπαρτισμένως (sic) Simp. *in Ph.*949.17; cf. ἀπηρτισμένως.

**ἀπαρτικός**· πρὸς ἄπαρσιν καὶ ἀποδημίαν ἕτοιμος, Hsch.

**ἀπαρτι-λογέω**· ἄρτια βάζω, Eust.1594.1. **-λογία**, Ion. -ίη, ἡ, *an even number* or *sum*, Hdt.7.29, Lys.*Fr.*28 S., Antipho Soph.99.

**ἀπάρτιον προγράφειν**, (ἀπαρτία) put up *goods to public sale*, Plu.*Cic.*27, 2.205c.

**ἀπάρτ-ισις**, εως, ἡ, *arrangement*, νεύρων Hp.*Art.*8 (with v.l. ἀπάρτησις, q.v.). **-ισμα**, ατος, τό, = sq., Sm.3*Ki.*7.9(46). **-ισμός**, ὁ, *completion*, *Ev.Luc.*14.28; ἔργων *PGiss.*67.9 (ii A.D.); λογοθεσίας Mitteis *Chr.*88 iv 25 (ii A.D.); κατ' ἀπαρτισμόν *precisely*, Chrysipp.*Stoic.*2.164; οὐ κατ' ἀπαρτισμὸν ἀλλ' ἐν πλάτει *not narrowly but broadly*, D.H.*Comp.*24. **2.** *rounding off*, βαλάνου Antyll.ap.Orib.50.3.1.

**ἀπαρτίως**, Adv., (ἄρτιος) = ἀπαρτί, Gal.17(2).437; f.l. in Hp.*Hum.*6 (to which Gal. refers).

**ἀπαρτύειν**· ἀποκηρύσσειν (Tarent.), Hsch.; **ἀπαρτῦναι**· τάξαι, Id.

**ἀπαρυστέον**, (ἀπαρύω) *one must draw off*: metaph., ἀ. τῶν ἀπειλῶν Ar.*Eq.*921.

**ἀπάρυστρον**, τό, = ἀρυστήρ, *IG*11(2).110.27 (Delos, iii B.C.).

***ἀπαρύω** or -ύτω [ῠ], fut. -ύσω, *draw off*, τὸ ἐπιστάμενον ἀπαρύσαντες *having skimmed off* the cream, Hdt.4.2, cf. D.S.5.37. **2.** metaph., *draw off, take off the force of* a thing, χαλκῷ ἀπὸ ψυχὴν ἀρύσας Epic.ap.Arist.*Po.*1457$^b$14; *exhaust, come to the end of*, Plu.2.463c, etc. :—Med., c. gen., ὁ τῆς μνήμης τῶν ἀγαθῶν ἀπαρυτόμενος *skimming the cream of* memory, ib.610e :—Pass., aor. part., ἀπαρυθεὶς τὴν ἄνω.. ἄνοιαν ἐπιπολάζουσαν *having it skimmed off* the surface, Alex.45.

**ἀπαρχαΐζω**, *compare to something ancient*, τινί τι Ath.1.20c. **II** *assign antiquity to*, αἵρεσιν Gal.14.683; τὸ παγκράτιον Sch.Pi.*N.*3.27.

**ἀπαρχαιόομαι**, Pass., *to be* or *become ancient*, ἀπηρχαιωμένα *old-fashioned songs*, Antiph.85; ἀ. λέξις, φράσις, D.H.*Th.*24, Aristid.*Rh.*2 p.508 J.

***ἀπαρχή**, ἡ, mostly in pl. ἀπαρχαί (cf. ἄπαργμα): **1.** *beginning of a sacrifice, primal offering* (of hairs cut from the forehead), ἀπαρχαὶ κόμης E.*Or.*96, cf. *Ph.*1525 (lyr.); later, a *banquet* held on this occasion, Plu.2.40b. **2.** *firstlings* for sacrifice or offering, *first-fruits*, ἁπάντων ἀπαρχαί Hdt.4.71; ἀπαρχὰς ἄγειν θεοῖσι S.*Tr.*183; ἀπαρχὰς θύειν E.*Fr.*516; ἀ. σκυλευμάτων *Ph.*857; ἐπιφέρειν ἀ. τῶν ὡραίων Th.3.58; τῶν ὄντων Is.5.42, cf. Epicur.*Fr.*130, etc. :—so also in sg., λείας ἀ. S.*Tr.*761; ἀ. τῶν πατρῴων χρημάτων Hdt.1.92, etc.; ἀνθρώπων ἀ. εἰς Δελφοὺς ἀποστέλλειν Arist.*Fr.*485; ἀ. ἀπό τινος ἀνατιθέναι Hdt.4.88; inscribed on votive offerings, [ἀνέθηκεν].. τόδ' ἀ. *IG*1.382, etc.; freq. in Lxx, as *Ex.*25.2, al., cf. *Ep.Rom.*11.16, and metaph., ἀ. τῶν κεκοιμημένων 1*Ep.Cor.*15.20; τῶν κτισμάτων *Ep.Jac.*1.18. **3.** metaph., ἀπαρχαὶ τῶν ἐμῶν προσφθεγμάτων E.*Ion* 402; ἀπαρχὴν τῆς σοφίας ἀνέθεσαν Pl.*Prt.*343b, etc.; ἀ. ἀπὸ φιλοσοφίας Plu.2.172c. **4.** *tax on inheritances*, *PTaur.*1.7.10; *tax* paid by Jews, *Stud.Pal.*4.72 (i A.D.). **5.** *entrance fee*, *PTeb.*316.10 (i A.D.), al. **6.** *board of officials* (cf. sq.), *IG*12(8).273 (Thasos). **7.** *birth-certificate* of a free person, *PTeb.*316.10 (i A.D.), *PGnom.*131 (ii A.D.): perh. metaph. in *Ep.Rom.*8.23.

**ἀπάρχης**, ου, ὁ, title of *official* (or perh. *ex-magistrate*) in Lesbos, *IG*12(2).68.5, 69 b 6 (Mytil.).

**ἀπάρχομαι**, *make a beginning*, esp. in sacrifice; τρίχας ἀπάρχεσθαι *begin the sacrifice with* the hair, i.e. by cutting off the hair from the forehead and throwing it into the fire, κάπρου ἀπὸ τρίχας ἀρξάμενος Il.19.254; ἀλλ' ὅ γ' ἀπαρχόμενος τρίχας ἐν πυρὶ βάλλεν Od.14.422: abs., 3.446. **II.** later c. gen., *cut off part* of a thing, *offer*

, τοῦ ὠτὸς τοῦ κτήνεος Hdt.4.188; ἀ. κόμης E.*El.*91; τῶν κρεῶν καὶ πλάγχνων *offer part of* them, Hdt.4.61: hence, 2. *offer the first-ngs* or *first-fruits*, πάντων of all sacrifices, Id.3.24: abs., *begin a acrifice*, Ar.*Ach.*244, *Pax* 1056, etc.; ἀ. τοῖς θεοῖς X.*Hier.*4.2; ἀπηργ-ένοι, of eunuchs, *having had their first-fruits offered*, Anaxandr.39. 1. 3. metaph., *take as the first-fruits, take as the choice* or *best*, ικαστήν Pl.*Lg.*767c: abs., *offer first-fruits*, Theoc.17.109. III. generally, *offer, dedicate*, χρυσᾶς (sc. δραχμάς) *IG*2.652*B*19, cf. Plu. *Sull.*27, *AP*7.406 (Theodorid.). IV. later, = ἄρχομαι, *begin*, . gen., πημάτων Lyc.1409: c. inf., v.l. in Luc.*Nigr.*3; *practise, prelude on*, ὀργάνων Him.*Or.*17.2.

***ἄπαρχος**, ὁ, f.l. for ἔπαρχος, A.*Pers.*327.

**ἀπάρχω**, fut. -ξω (v. infr.), *lead the way*, εἰς νᾶσον B.11.6 (s.v.l.): esp. in dancing, ὁ ἀπάρχων τῶν ὀρχηστῶν dub. l. in D.H.7.73; ὔμμι δ' ἀπάρξει *shall lead* you *in the dance*, *AP*9.189. II. prob. *reign far away* from home, of Teucer, Pi.*N.*4.46.

**ἀπᾰρφδήτως**, Adv. *without alteration*, Eust.1090.12.

**ἅπᾱς**, ἅπᾱσα (also ἅπανσα *SIG*56.25 (Argos, v B.C.)), ἅπαν (ἀ- = *sm-*, cf. εἷς), strengthd. for πᾶς, *quite all, the whole*, and in pl. *all together*, freq. from Hom. downwds.; ἅπασι *in all things*, Hdt.1.1; τοῖσι ἅπασι 91; ἐν ἅπασι Hp.*Coac.*156; ἐφ' ἅπασι Ph.2.365. 2. with Adj., ἀργύρεος δὲ ἔστιν ἅ. *all* silver, i.e. of *massive* silver, Od.4.616, 15.116; ἅ. δὲ τραχὺς ὅστις ἂν νέον κρατῇ A.*Pr.*35; μικκός γα μᾶκος.. ἀλλ' ἅπαν κακόν Ar.*Ach.*909, cf. Theoc.15.19,148; ἡ ἐναντία ἅπασα ὁδός the *exactly* contrary way, Pl.*Prt.*317b. 3. with abstract Subst., *all possible, absolute*, ἅπασ' ἀνάγκη Ar.*Th.*171; σπουδῇ D.H.6.23; ἀτοπία Plb.39.1.7; εἰς ἅπαν ἀφικέσθαι ἀνοίας Paus. 7.15.8. 4. sts. c. Art., Hdt.3.64, al., A.*Pr.*483, Th.2.13. II. after Hom. in sg., *every one*, neut. *everything*, Pl.*Phd.*108b; οὐ πρὸς [τοῦ] ἅπαντος ἀνδρός not in the power of *every* man, Hdt.7.153; οὐκ ἐξ ἅπαντος δεῖ τὸ κερδαίνειν φιλεῖν S.*Ant.*312; ἐξ ἅπαντος εὖ λέγει *in any cause whatever*, Id.*OC*807; σῖγα νῦν ἅπας ἔχε σίγαν Cratin.144; ἅπαν γένοιτ' ἂν ἤδη *nihil non*.., Ar.*Th.*528: with Subst., ἅπαντι λόγῳ in *every* matter, Cratin.231; τὸ ἅπαν, as Adv., *altogether*, Pl.*Phdr.*241b; καθ' ἅπαν as *a whole*, Ti.Locr.96d; ἐς ἅπαν Th.5.103; εἰς ἅπαν *at all*, Lib.*Or.*18.266; πρὸς ἅπαν Ph.2.493; ἐξ ἅπαντος Luc.*Merc.Cond.*41. [ἅπᾰν Od.24.185, etc., Pi.*P.*2.49; but ἅπᾱν Men.129, Metrod.57, Theoc.2.56, and Att. acc. to Hdn.Gr.2.12; ἅπᾰν in anap., Ar.*Pl.*493: the use of ἅπας for πᾶς is chiefly for the sake of euphony after consonants.]

**ἀπασβολόομαι**, *turn to soot, become sooty*, Dsc.5.76.

**ἀπασιτόν**· τὸ δεσμωτήριον, Hsch. (fort. ἀπλίκιτον).

**ἀπασκᾰρίζω**, fut. -ιῶ Men.839:—*struggle, be convulsed*, like a dying fish, ἀ. ὡσπερεὶ πέρκην χαμαί Ar.*Fr.*495; ἀπασκαριῶ γέλωτι Men. l.c.; ἀπησκάρισεν *gave up the ghost*, prob. for ἀπεσκ-, *AP*11.114 (Nicarch.).

**ἀπασπάζομαι**, *take leave of*, ἀλλήλους *Act.Ap.*21.6, v.l. in Lxx *To.* 10.13; ᾠδῇ καὶ μέλει χορόν Him.*Ecl.*11.1.

**ἀπασπαίρω**, *gasp away*, θνῄσκει δ' ἀπασπαίρουσα E.*Ion* 1207.

**ἀπασσεῖον** (sic)· παμποίκιλον, οἱ δὲ λινοῦν χιτῶνα, οἱ δὲ μαλλωτόν, Hsch.

**ἀπαστακώς**· ἁμαρτών, Hsch.

**ἀπαστ-ί**, Adv. of ἄπαστος, *fasting*, Hsch. **-ία**, ἡ, *abstaining from food, fast*, ἀ. ἄγειν Ar.*Nu.*621. **-ος**, ον, (πατέομαι) *not having eaten, abstaining from food, fasting*, Il.19.346, Arist.*HA* 563ᵃ 23, Call.*Cer.*6, Euph.57, v.l. in *h.Merc.*168. 2. c. gen., ἄπαστος ἐδητύος ἠδὲ ποτῆτος *without having tasted* meat or drink, Od.4.788, cf. 6.250, *h.Cer.*200: ἐδητύος ἔργον ἄπαστον a meal *which feeds not*, Opp.*H.*2.250. II. Pass., *not eaten*, Ael.*NA*11.16.

**ἀπαστρά-πτω**, *flash forth*, Arat.430, Opp.*C.*1.220; αὐγὴ ἀ. λίθων J.*AJ*3.8.9: c. acc. cogn., φέγγος Ph.1.150, al.; αἴγλην Opp.*C.*3.479; φάος Procl.*Hymn.*7.31, cf. Luc.*Gall.*7, Iamb.*Myst.*2.3. **-ψις**, εως, ἡ, *lightning*, Tz.*H.*9.106.

**ἀπαστύς**, ύος, ἡ, = ἀπαστία, *EM*118.50.

**ἀπασφᾰλίζω**, *make secure, fasten* or *shut up*, Ps.-Porph. in Bentley *Epistola ad Millium* p.303 (where ἀποσφαλίσει for ἀπασφαλίσῃ), Sch.E.*Or.*1108.

**ἀπασχολ-έω**, *leave* one *no leisure, keep* him *employed*, Luc.*Philops.* 14, Hld.2.21:—Pass., *to be wholly occupied* or *engrossed*, so as to attend to nothing else, περί τινα Luc.*Charid.*19, cf. Olymp. *in Mete.* 108.22; τινί ib.107.13; ἀ. ἐπὶ τῆς ἀλλοδαπῆς *to be absent* on foreign service, *POxy.*71 ii 8 (iv A.D.). II. τῆς συνεχείας τῶν φυτῶν ἀπασχολούσης ἐς ἑαυτὴν τὰ βέλη *rendering* them *of none effect*, Hdn.7.2.5. III. ἀ. τινὰ τῶν ἡδίστων *detain* him *from*.., Hld. 10.23. **-ητέον**, *one must be engrossed*, βιωτικαῖς πράξεσι Aët. 9.23. **-ία**, ἡ, *detention by business*, Str.6.4.2 (pl.).

**ἀπᾰτᾰγί**, Adv., (πάταγος) *noiselessly*, Suid.

***ἀπᾰτάω** [ἀπ], late Ion. -έω Luc.*Syr.D.*27 (Pass.): impf. ἠπάτων E.*El.*938, Ion. ἐξ-απατάσκον Orac. in Ar.*Pax* 1070: fut. -ήσω: aor. ἠπάτησα, Ion. ἀπ- Il.9.344, S.*Tr.*500 (lyr.): pf. ἠπάτηκα Id.*Ph.* 929:—Pass., fut. ἀπατηθήσομαι Arist.*APr.*67ᵃ38, cf. (ἐξ-) Pl.*Cra.* 436b, Aeschin.2.123; also in Med. form ἀπατήσομαι Pl.*Phdr.*262a, (ἐξ-) X.*An.*7.3.3: aor. ἠπατήθην Pl.*Cri.*52e: pf. ἠπάτημαι Th.5.46, etc.: (ἀπάτη):—*cheat, deceive*, Il.19.97, Od.17.139, etc.; *cheat* one's *hopes*, Hes.*Op.*462; οἵ' ἠπάτηκας S.*Ph.*929; κλέμματα.. ἃ τὸν πολέμιον ἀπατήσας Th.5.9: abs., *to be deceptive* or *fallacious*, Arist.*Rh.* 1376ᵇ28:—Pass., *to be self-deceived, mistaken*, Pi.*Fr.*182, S.*OT*594, Pl.*Phdr.*262a, etc.; ἔγνωκα.. φωτὸς ἠπατημένη S.*Aj.*807; τί γὰρ οὐκ.. ἔρχεται ἀγγελίας ἀπατώμενον; comes not *belied by* the result? Id.*El.*170; ἀ. περί τ. Arist.*Rh.*1368ᵇ22; περί τινος Id.*Sens.*442ᵇ8; ἀ. ταύτην τὴν ἀπάτην Id.*APo.*74ᵃ6; also ἀπατᾶσθαι ὡς.. *to be deceived into thinking* that.., Pl.*Prt.*323a.—The compd. ἐξαπατάω is more common, esp. in Hdt. and Att. Prose; the simple Verb is used in Lxx *Ge.*3.13, al., but not by Plb., and is rare in later Greek, Plu. 2.15d.

**ἀπάτειρα** [πᾰ], fem. of ἀπάτωρ, epith. of Isis, *POxy.*1380.19.

***ἀπάτερθε** [πᾰ], before a vowel -θεν, Adv. *apart, aloof*, ἀ. δὲ θωρήσσοντο Il.2.587, cf. Thgn.1059, Pi.*O.*7.74. II. as Prep. c. gen., *far away from*, ἀπάτερθεν ὁμίλου Il.5.445, cf. Thgn.1153; γόων ἀ. *IG*14. 2123.

**ἀπᾰτ-εύω**, = ἀπατάω, Xenoph.11. **-εών**, ῶνος, ὁ, *cheat, rogue*, Hp.*Art.*42, Democr.63, Pl.*R.*451a, X.*Cyr.*1.6.27, Epicur.*Fr.*236, etc.:—as Adj., ἀ. λόγος Max.Tyr.2.1. ***-η**, ἡ, *trick, fraud, deceit*, νῦν δὲ κακὴν ἀπάτην βουλεύσατο Il.2.114, cf. 4.168: in pl., *wiles*, οὐκ ἄρ' ἔμελλες.. λήξειν ἀπατάων, says Athena to Ulysses, Od.13. 294, cf. Il.15.31; σκολιαὶ ἀπάται Pi.*Fr.*213. 2. *guile, treachery*, ἄταν ἀπάτᾳ μεταγνούς A.*Supp.*111, cf. S.*OC*230; ἀπάτης δικαίας οὐκ ἀποστατεῖ θεός A.*Fr.*301, cf. *Pers.*93; ἀ. ἐρώτων S.*Ant.*617; διαβολὴ καὶ ἀ. Antipho6.7, etc.; ἀ. εὐπρεπής, opp. βία ἐμφανής, Th.4.86; ἡ βίᾳ ἢ ἀπάτῃ 2.39; ἀ. λεχέων *a being cheated out of* the marriage, S.*Ant.*630; ἄνευ δόλου καὶ ἀπάτης 'without fraud or *covin*', Hdt.1.69; μετὰ σκότους καὶ ἀ. Pl.*Lg.*864c. 3. Ἀπάτη, personified, Hes.*Th.*224, Luc.*Merc.Cond.*42. II. *beguiling* of time, *pastime* (not Att., Moer.65), Plb.4.20.5; ψυχῆς Dicaearch.1.1; ψυχαγωγίαι καὶ ἀπάται τῆς πόλεως D.Chr.32.5. III. as name of a plant, f.l. for ἀπάρη (q.v.). **-ήλιος**, ον, poet. Adj. *guileful, wily*, ἀπατήλια εἰδώς skilled in *wiles*, Od.14.288; ἀ. βάζειν ib.127; of a person, Nonn.*D.*46.10, al. **-ηλογεῖν**, gloss on γελγιθεύειν, Hsch. **-ηλός**, ή, όν (ος, ον Pl.*Criti.*107d), = ἀπατήλιος, Il.1.526; κόσμος Parm.8.52; λόγου στόλος Emp.17.26; δέσποινα X.*Oec.*1.20; κακοῦργος καὶ ἀπατηλή Pl.*Grg* 465b; ἀ. λόγος Id.*Lg.*892d; τὸ ἀ. ἐν λόγοις Id.*Cra.*407e; σκιαγραφία ἀ. *producing illusion*, Id.*Criti.*107d; στρατηγός App.*BC*1.112 (Sup.); also, *deceptive*, opp. γνήσιος, Eus. Mynd.63. Adv. -λῶς Iamb.*Myst.*3.26, Poll.9.135. **-ημα**, ατος, τό, *deceit, stratagem*, Aen.Tact.23.6; *beguilement*, δόξης Gorg.*Hel.* 10 (pl.); πόθων *AP*7.195 (Mel.). ***-ήμων**, ον, gen. ονος, = ἀπατήλιος, Orac.ap.Zos.1.52. ***-ήνωρ**, ορος, ὁ, ἡ, (ἀνήρ) *beguiling men*, τέχνη Tryph.137. II. epith. of Dionysus, Call.*Fr.*36 P. **-ησις**, εως, ἡ, *beguiling*, Lxx *Ju.*10.4, Phld.*Ir.*p.9 W. (pl.), Id.*D.*1.16. **-ητής**, οῦ, ὁ, *deceiver*, *Gloss.* **-ητικός**, ή, όν, *fallacious*, of sophistry, Pl. *Sph.*240cd, 264d, Arist.*APo.*80ᵇ15, al.: Comp. -κώτερος *more effective in deceiving*, X.*Eq.Mag.*5.5. Adv. -κῶς Poll.4.24.

**ἀπάτητος** [πᾰ], ον, *untrodden*, *AP*6.51. II. *not trodden down*: hence metaph., *unusual*, Democr.131.

**ἀπᾱτῐμ-άζω**, = sq., ἀπητιμασμένη A.*Eu.*95. **-άω**, *dishonour greatly*, ἀπητίμησε Il.13.113.

**ἀπατμ-ίζω**, *evaporate*, ἀπατμίζει τὸ ὑγρόν Arist.*Mete.*359ᵃ31, cf. *Somn.Vig.*457ᵇ31, *PA*653ᵃ36. **-ισις**, εως, ἡ, *evaporation*, Mich. *in EN*55.6.

***ἄπατος**, ον, (ἄτη) *immune from punishment*, *Leg.Gort.*2.1, al.

**ἀπατουργόν**· κωλυτικόν, Hsch.

***Ἀπᾰτουρεών**, ῶνος, ὁ, name of a *month*, answering to Att. Pyanepsion, *CIG*3661 (Cyzicus), *IPE*1².47 (Olbia):—written -ιών *IG* 11.203*A*32,53 (Delos, iii B.C.), ib.12(5).824.33 (Tenos), *SIG*169.1 (Iasus): Ἀπατοριών *IG*12(7).412 (Amorgos, iii B.C.).

***Ἀπᾰτούρια**, τά, *the Apaturia*, a festival celebrated by the members of φρατρίαι at Athens and most Ionic cities, Hdt.1.147, And. 1.126, X.*HG*1.7.8, D.39.4, Thphr.*Char.*35, etc.

**Ἀπᾰτουρία**, ἡ, title of Aphrodite at Troezen, Paus.2.33.1:—also **Ἀπατούρη** *IPE*2.28 (Panticapaeum); **Ἀπατουριάς** ib.352 (Phanagoria):—also **Ἀπάτουρον** (leg. -ούριον) τὸ τῆς Ἀφροδίτης ἱερόν, at Phanagoria, Str.11.2.10. (ἀ- copul., πατήρ, cf. ὁμοπάτορες.)

***ἀπατρία** (Ep. -ίη), ἡ, *exile*, *CIG* 632 (Ilium).

**ἄπᾰτρις**, ιδος, ὁ, ἡ, *without country*, Tz.*H.*7.436.

**ἀπάτυλλα** [πᾰ], ἡ, Dim. of ἀπάτη, dub. in Cerc.*Oxy.*1082 *Fr.*39.

**ἀπάτωρ** [πᾰ], ορος, ὁ, ἡ, (πατήρ) *without father*, of deities, αὐτοπάτωρ, ἀ. Orph.*H.*10.10; ἀ.. ἀμήτωρ Nonn.*D.*41.53, cf. *Ep.Hebr.* 7.3; *fatherless, orphan*, ἀοίκους ἀπάτοράς τε S.*Tr.*300; ἀμήτωρ ἀ. τε E.*Ion* 109 (lyr.); ἀ. πότμος Id.*IT*864 (lyr.), cf. Vett.Val.103.35: neut. pl., ἀπάτορα τέκεα E.*HF*114 (lyr.); *disowned by the father*, Pl.*Lg.* 929a: also c. gen., ἀ. ἐμοῦ *not having* me *for a father*, S.*OC*1383. 2. *of unknown father*, like σκότιος, Plu.2.288e, *PGrenf.*2.56.3 (ii A.D.).

**ἀπάτωρος**, ον, = foreg., [Hes.] ap.Sch.Il.*Oxy.*1087.50.

***ἀπαυαίνω**, aor. part. ἀπαυάνας Orph.*Fr.*31.20:—*make to wither away*, Thphr.*CP*3.10.7; *parch* with thirst, Orph. l.c.:—Pass., *to be withered*, Q.S.1.66, al.; cf. ἀφ-.

**ἀπαυγ-άζω**, *flash forth*, ἀπὸ τῶν ὀφθαλμῶν σέλας Hld.3.4; χροιάν, χρῶμα, Id.4.8, Philostr.*VA*3.8. II. Med., *see from far*, Call.*Del.* 125,181. **-ασμα**, ατος, τό, *radiance, effulgence*, of light *beaming from* a luminous body, φωτὸς ἀϊδίου Lxx *Wi.*7.26; δόξης *Ep.Hebr.*1.3, cf. Ph.1.337, al., Hld.5.27, Dam.ap.Simp. *in Ph.*775.15. **-ασμός**, ὁ, *efflux of light, radiance, effulgence*, Plu.2.83d, 934d.

**ἀπαυγής**, ές, *bright*, Hsch.

***ἀπαυδ-άω**, *forbid*, abs., ἐγὼ δ' ἀπαυδῶ γ' S.*Ph.*1293; freq. folld. by μή c. inf., τὸν ἄνδρ' ἀπηύδα.. στέγης μὴ ἔξω παρήκειν Id.*Aj.*741; τὸν ἄνδρ' ἀπαυδῶ τῆσδε γῆς.. μή εἰσδέχεσθαί τινα Id.*OT*236, cf. E.*Rh.*934, *Supp.*468, Ar.*Eq.*1072: with implied neg., ἀ. ἐξίστασθαι μύσταισι χοροῖς Id.*Ra.*369. II. *decline, refuse*, οὔκουν ἀπαυδᾶν δυνατόν ἐστι μοι πόνους E.*Supp.*342; *renounce*, νεῖκος ἀ. Theoc.22.129; *say no*, *APl.*4.299. III. *to be wanting towards*, *fail*, φίλοισι E.*Andr.*87: hence abs., *fail*, of wood, Thphr.*HP*5.6.1; ἀ. πρὸς τὸ περίπατον Antyll.ap.Orib.6.21.11; *become speechless*, of hysterical patients, Hp.*Mul.*1.74, cf. Ps.-Luc.*Philopatr.*18; ἀ. τὰ μαντεῖα the oracles *are dumb*, Plu.2.431b; *faint*, *fail*, Thphr.*Char.*8.14; ἀ. ὑπὸ λιμοῦ Luc. *Luct.*24; κόπῳ Babr.7.8; πόνοις *AP*5.167; *die* (of patients), Herod. Med. in *Rh.Mus.*58.80. —ησις, εως, ἡ, *exhaustion*, Agathin.ap. Orib.10.7.10.

**ἀπαυθᾰδιάζοντες**· μεγαλοφρονοῦντες, *AB*419, Hsch., Suid.:—Med., -ιάζομαι, = sq., Phlp.*in Mete.*7.35; *reject boldly*, Hld.7.19.

**ἀπαυθᾰδίζομαι**, *speak* or *act boldly*, Pl.*Ap.*37a; freq. in late Prose, in bad sense, Ph.2.441; μέχρι παντός J.*BJ*3.7.11, cf. Plu.2.766c, Them.*Or.*10.131d, 135a, 23.290c.

**ἀπαυθημερίζω**, *do on the same day*; esp. *go* or *return the same day*, εἰς τὸ στρατόπεδον X.*An.*5.2.1; ἐκ Πίσης εἰς Αἴγιναν Ael.*VH*9.2.

**ἀπαυλεῖσθαι**· τὸ μὴ προαυλεῖν κατὰ τρόπον, Hsch.

***ἀπαύλια**, ων, τά, (αὐλή) *sleeping alone*, esp. the night before the wedding, when the bridegroom slept alone in the father-in-law's house, Poll.3.39; cf. ἐπαύλια:—*EM*119.14 is confused.

**ἀπαυλ-ίζομαι**, aor. -ηυλίσθην, *sleep* or *live away from*, τῆς πόλεως D.H.8.87; ἀπὸ τῆς νύμφης Poll.3.39. -ισμός, ὁ, seems to be used of *a moon-stroke* or *fit caused by sleeping in the moonlight*, Poet. *de herb.*173. -ιστήριος, α, ον, *belonging to the* ἀπαύλια, ἀ. χλανίς a garment *presented on this day*, Poll.3.40.

**ἄπαυλος**, ον, *lying alone*, Hsch.

***ἀπαυλόσῦνος**, ον, *away from the* αὐλή, *AP*6.221 (Leon.).

**ἀπαυξάνομαι**, pf. part. ἀπηυξημένος *in 'irrational' proportion to the* χρόνοι πρῶτοι, Gal.8.913.

***ἀπαύξησις**, εως, ἡ, *decrease*: hence, *disesteem*, πίπτειν εἰς ἀ. Longin 7.3.

**ἀπαυράω**, v. ἀπούρας.

**ἀπαυρίσκομαι**, *derive nourishment*, ἀπὸ τῆς ἰκμάδος Hp.*Nat.Puer.*26.

***ἀπαυστί**, Adv. of sq., *unceasing*, *incessant*, D.C.37.46.

**ἀπαυστίας**· παραχύτας, Hsch.

**ἄπαυστος**, ον, *unceasing*, *never-ending*, Parm.8.27; αἰών A.*Supp.*574 (lyr.); βίος Pl.*Ti.*36e; ἄτα S.*Aj.*1187 (lyr.); ἀ. καὶ ἀθάνατος φορά Pl.*Cra.*417c, etc. Adv. -τως Arist.*Mu.*391ᵇ18, Corn.*ND*34. 2. *not to be stopped* or *assuaged*, *insatiable*, δίψα Th.2.49; γνάθοι Antiph. 237.4; ἐπιθυμίη χρημάτων Eus.Mynd.1. II. c. gen., *never ceasing from*, γόων E.*Supp.*82 (lyr.).—Cf. ἄπαυτος.

**ἀπαυτίκα**, Adv. strengthd. for αὐτίκα, *on the spot*, dub. l. in D.C. 40.15

**ἀπαυτομᾰτίζω**, *do a thing of oneself*, Plu.2.717b; *produce spontaneously*, Ph.1.36:—Pass., Id.2.182:—Act., intr., *occur spontaneously*, Id.1.571; -ίζουσα φορά ib.387; of the menses, Orib.7.20.1.

**ἀπαυτομολέω**, *go of one's own accord*, *desert*, Th.7.75; πρός τινα D.H.*Orat.Vett.*2; τινός D.C.36.17.

**ἄπαυτος**, ον, *unceasing*, Thphr.*Metaph.*5; cf. ἄπαυστος.

**ἀπαυχενίζω**, *cut off by the neck*, D.S.34.2.22. II. ταῦρον ἀ. *tame* a bull *by forcing back his neck*, Philostr.*Her.*12ᵇ, cf. Philostr. Jun.*Im.*2. III. *shake off* the yoke *from the neck*, *get free by struggling*, Phld.*Lib.*p.34 O., Ph.1.305.

**ἀπαφίνιον**, τό, *stone kneading-trough* (Lacon.), Hsch.

**ἀπᾰφίσκω**, *cheat*, *beguile*, mostly in compos. with παρά and ἐξ:—of the simple word Hom. has only ἀπαφίσκει Od.11.217: aor. opt. ἀπάφοιτο in act. sense, 23.216:—later, ἀπάφῃ *APl.*4.108 (Jul.); ἀπαφών Opp.*H.*3.444; ἤπαφες, ἤπαφε, Q.S.3.49, Nonn.*D.*5.512: aor. 1 ἀπάφησε ib.8.129, Q.S.13.280, 2 sg. ἀπάφησας 3.502.

**ἀπαφός**· ἔποψ, Hsch.

**ἀπαφούλιστορ**· σταφυλῖνος (Lacon.), Hsch.

***ἀπαφρίζω**, *skim*, esp. of honey, *Gp.*8.29 and 32, Orib.5.33.4:—Pass., Gal.6.283, *Gp.*8.27.2, Philagr.ap.Orib.5.21.1.

**ἀπάχεια** [πᾰ], ἡ, *thinness*, Eust.641.33.

**ἀπᾰχής**, ές, *without thickness* or *solidity*, Eust.641.35.

**ἀπαχλυόομαι**, *have blurred vision*, Aret.*SD*2.3.

**ἀπαχλύω**, *free from darkness*, Q.S.1.79.

**ἄπᾰχος**, ον, paraphrase of νεαρής, f. l. in Procl.*Par.Ptol.*43.

**ἀπᾰχῠρίζω**, (ἄχυρον) *winnow*, Sch.Nic.*Th.*114.

**ἀπεγγυᾰλίζω**, *give up*, *deliver again*, Hsch.

**ἀπεγνωσμένως**, Adv. pf. part. Pass. of ἀπογιγνώσκω, *desperately*, Plu.*Nic.*21.

**ἀπεδᾰνός**, όν, = ἠπεδανός, Hsch. s. h. v.

**ἀπέδεσθαι**, **ἀπεδήδοκα**, v. ἀπεσθίω.

**ἀπεδίζω**, (ἄπεδος) *level*, ἠπέδιζον τὴν ἀκρόπολιν Clitod.22.

***ἀπέδῑλος**, ον, *unshod*, A.*Pr.*135, Nonn.*D.*5.407, al.:—also -δίλωτος, ον, Call.*Cer.*124.

**ἀπεδοποιέω**, v. ἀπειδοποιέω.

**ἄπεδος**, ον, (ἀ- copul., πέδον) *level*, *flat*, χώρη Hdt.1.110, cf. 9.25, 102, Th.7.78, X.*Cyn.*6.9:—Subst. ἄπεδον, τό, *flat surface*, Hdt.4.62.

**ἄπεζος**, ον, (πέζα) *footless*, Lyc.629.

**ἀπεθίζω**, *disaccustom*, τιμωρίαις ἀ. τινά Aeschin.1.58: c. inf., ἀ. μὴ ποιεῖν *accustom* or *teach not* to do something, ib.152; τινὸς τινα Philostr.*VS*1.25; τινὸς τὸ σῶμα Epicur.*Fr.*458, cf. Gal.16.141: pf. part. ἀπειθικώς Plu.*Alex.*40:—Pass., ἀπειθισμένος J.*BJ*5.13.4.

**ἀπεθιστέον**, *one must disuse*, *unteach*, *Gp.*14.7.5.

**ἀπεῖδον**, inf. ἀπιδεῖν, aor. 2 with no pres. in use, ἀφοράω being used instead:—*look away from other things at*, and so simply, *look at*, πρός or ἔς τι Th.7.71, Luc.*DMar.*9.2, al.; πόρρωθεν ἀπιδεῖν Timocl. 21. II. *look away from*, and so, *despise*, Plu.2.1070f (dub. l.) (In later Greek ἀφ-, ἀφίδω *Ep.Phil.*2.23.)

***ἀπειδοποιέω**, *construct according to a pattern*, *Inscr.Milet.* (Haussoullier p.163), in form ἀπειδοποιήθη; but more prob. from ἀπεδοποιέω, *make flat*, *smooth*, κατεξέσθη τὸ ὑπέρθυρον καὶ ἀ.

**ἀπειθ-αρχία**, ἡ, *disobedience to command*, Antipho Soph.72, D.C. *Fr.*57.17. -εια, ἡ, *disobedience*, X.*Mem.*3.5.5, D.H.9.41, Arr. *Epict.*3.24.24; υἱοὶ τῆς ἀπειθείας *Ep.Eph.*5.7; later ἀπειθία, ἡ, *BGU* 747 ii 14 (ii A.D.), etc., *Gloss.* -έω, Att. form of ἀπῑθέω (though even Trag. preferred ἀπιστέω, q.v. II), *to be disobedient*, *refuse compliance*, A.*Ag.*1049; opp. πείθομαι, Pl.*Phdr.*271b: freq. c. dat., *disobey*, οὐκ ἀπειθήσας θεῷ E.*Or.*31; ἀ. ἅμα νόμῳ καὶ τῷ θεῷ Pl.*Lg.*741d, etc.; τὰ μεγάλα ἀ. τινί *in* great matters, Id.*R.*538b; ἀ. ταῖς ἐνεχυρασίαις *not to abide by* them, Id.*Lg.*949d: later c. gen., ψαφίσματος *GDI*3705.111 (Cos); ἐντολῶν Lxx *Jo.*5.6. 2. of animals, X.*Cyr.* 7.5.62; of ships, τοῖς οἴαξιν ἀ. D.S.13.46. 3. of a woman, *refuse compliance*, Aristaenet.2.20.

**ἀπείθη**, **ἀπείθησαν**, Ion. aor. 1 Pass. of ἀφίημι.

**ἀπειθήνιος**, ον, *disobedient*, *BGU*747 i 6 (ii A.D.).

***ἀπειθής**, ές, *disobedient*, S.*Fr.*45; ἀ. τοῖς νόμοις Pl.*Lg.*936b; of ships, τοῖς κυβερνήταις ἀπειθεστέρας τὰς ναῦς παρεῖχον *less obedient to* them, Th.2.84, cf. D.C.50.29 (Comp.), Orph.*A.*247; στράτευμα X.*Eq.* 3.6; of horses, Id.*Eq.Mag.*1.3; ἀπειθέα τεύχειν work *disobedience*, Call.*Dian.*66. Adv. ἀπειθῶς, ἔχειν πρός τινα Pl.*R.*391b. b. *unbelieving*, Nonn.*D.*8.306. 2. of things, *inflexible*, *rigid*, κέντρον Ael. *NA*1.55; σιδήρου καὶ ἀδάμαντος ἀπειθέστεροι Ph.2.87; ὀδόντες ἀ. *unyielding*, Opp.*C.*2.511; χῶρος ἀ. *impracticable*, of Hades, Hermesian. 7.3; δίκη ἀ. Νεμέσεως *IG*4.444. II. Act., *not persuasive*, *incredible*, μῦθος Thgn.1235; *uninviting*, πρὸς τὴν γεῦσιν Hices.ap.Ath.3.87b, c; τὴν γεῦσιν Id.323a; of places, *difficult of access*, Ael.*Fr.*120.

**ἀπεικ-άζω**, fut. -άσομαι X.*Mem.*3.11.1, -άσω Plu.2.1135a:—Pass., aor. ἀπεικάσθην E.*El.*979, Pl.*Cra.*419d: fut. -ασθήσομαι Them.*Or.*2.33a: pf. ἀπείκασμαι Pl.*Cra.*420d (on the augment v. εἰκάζω):—*form from a model*, *represent*, *express*, *copy*, of painters, ἀ. τὰ καλὰ τῶν ζῴων Isoc.1.11; τὸ σὸν χρῶμα καὶ σχῆμα Pl.*Cra.*432b, cf. *Criti.*107d, e; διὰ χρωμάτων ἀ. X.*Mem.*3.10.1; χρώμασι καὶ σχήμασιν Arist.*Po.*1447ᵃ 19: metaph., ἀ. ἑαυτόν τινι *conform* oneself *to*.., Pl.*R.*396d:—Pass., *become like*, *resemble*, τινί ib.563a, *Cra.*419c; ἀπεικασθεὶς θεῷ *in a* god's *likeness*, E.*El.*979. 2. *express by a comparison*, ἔχοιμ' ἂν αὐτὸ μὴ κακῶς ἀπεικάσαι S.*Fr.*149.2, cf. Pl.*Tht.*169b; οἷος γὰρ Ἀχιλλεὺς ἐγένετο ἀπεικάσειεν ἄν τις Βρασίδαν Id.*Smp.*221c; τὸ θάλλειν τὴν αὔξην μοι δοκεῖ ἀπεικάζειν τὴν τῶν νέων the word θάλλειν seems *to express* the growth.., Id.*Cra.*414a; ἀ. διὰ τοῦ ῥῶ *to express* by the sound of ρ, ib. 426e:—Pass., *to be copied* or *expressed by likeness* τοῖς ὑπὸ τῶν κάτω ἀπεικασθεῖσι Id.*R.*511a; τὰ ἄλλα ἀπείργαστο εἰς ὁμοιότητα ᾧπερ (sc. τούτου ᾧ) ἀπεικάζετο Id.*Ti.*39e; ἀ. πρός τι *to be copied* in reference to.., i.e. from.., ib.29c. 3. *liken*, *compare with*, τινί τι E.*Supp.* 146, Pl.*Phd.*76e, *Grg.*493b, *Smp.*221d, al.; οὐ τοιοῦτόν ἐστιν ᾧ σὺ ἀπεικάζεις it is not such [as that] to which you *compare* it, Id.*Phd.*92b:—Pass., *to be likened* or *compared*, ἄρχουσιν Id.*Lg.*905e, al.; [τὸ ἀναγκαῖον] ἀπείκασται τῇ πορείᾳ Id.*Cra.*420d; [τὸ ψεῦδος] ἀπείκασται τοῖς καθεύδουσι ib.421b. II. ὡς ἀπεικάσαι, = ὡς ἐπεικάσαι, *as one may guess*, *to conjecture*, S.*OC*16, *Tr.*141, E.*Or.*1298. III. *imagine*, ἀ. χειρώσεσθαι (-ασθαι codd.) τὴν Σπάρτην D.S.15.65. -ασία, ἡ, *representation*, μίμησις καὶ ἀ. Pl.*Lg.*668b, *Criti.*107b, Hierocl. *in CA*27 p.484 M. -ασμα, ατος, τό, *copy*, *representation*, Pl.*Cra.*402d, 420c. -ασμός, ὁ, *representation*, Porph.*Abst.*4.7. -αστέον, *one must represent as like*, τινά τινι Pl.*Phdr.*270e; ἀπεικαστικὰ τὰ ῥήματα ἀ. X.*Mem.*3.10.8; *one must compare*, τί τινι Plot.5.6.4, cf. Men. Rh.p.349 S.

**ἀπεικον-ίζω**, (εἰκών) *represent in a statue*, *AP*12.56 (Mel.); *express*, ψυχῇ κάλλος ib.127 (Mel.); generally, *represent*, Porph.*Sent.*44:—Pass., *to be modelled*, Ph.1.106, al.; *to be described*, 1.561. 2. Med., *reflect*, *symbolize*, τὴν [τῶν ἀπορρήτων] δύναμιν Procl. *in Alc.* p.25 C., cf. *Inst.*209, Aristaenet.2.5. -ισμα, ατος, τό, = ἀπείκασμα, Socr.*Ep.*20, Ph.1.4, al., *BMus.Inscr.*481*.24 (Ephesus, ii A.D.), Phlp. *in Ph.*316.24.

**ἀπεικότως**, **ἀπεικώς**, v. ἀπέοικα.

**ἀπειλέω** (A), Elean ἀποϝηλέω, *keep away*, ἀπὸ τῶ βωμῶ *GDI*1159, cf. 1150; ἀπὸ μαντείας 1154:—Pass., ἐς ἀπορίην ἀπειληθεὶς or ἀπειλημένος *brought* into great straits, Hdt.1.24, 2.141; ἐς ἀναγκαίην ἀπειλημένος Id.8.109; ἀπειληθέντες ἐς στεινόν *forced* into narrow compass, Id.9.34. II. *unroll*, *roll off*, Hero *Aut.*5.5.

***ἀπειλέω** (B), 3 dual impf. Act. ἀπειλήτην, Ep. for ἠπειλείτην, Od. 11.313: later Ep. pres. ἀπειλείω Musae.122, Nonn.*D.*20.204:—*hold out* either in the way of *promise* or *threat*, and therefore: I. sts. in good sense, *promise*, οὐδ' ἠπείλησεν ἄνακτι.. ῥέξειν κλειτὴν ἑκατόμβην Il.23.863, cf. 872; also, *boast* or *brag*, ὥς ποτ' ἀπειλήσει 8.150; ἦ μὲν ἀπείλησας βητάρμονας εἶναι ἀρίστους Od.8.383, cf. Jul.*Or.*2. 57a. II. commonly in bad sense, *threaten*, in Hom. either abs., as Il.2.665, Od.21.368: or (more freq.) c. dat. pers., ib.20.272, etc.: c. acc. cogn., αἶψα δ' ἀναστὰς ἠπείλησεν μῦθον *spake a threatening* speech, Il.1.388; ἀπειλὰς ἀ., v. ἀπειλή; δεῖν' ἀπειλήσων ἔπη E. *Supp.*542: freq. with neut. Pron. or Adj., ἀ. τόγε θυμῷ Il.15.212; ταῦτα, πολλὰ ἀ., Hdt.7.18, 1.111, Th.8.33, etc.; πύργοις ἀ. δεινὰ A. *Th.*426; τοῦτ' ἀπειλήσας ἔχεις S.*OC*817. 2. with acc. of the thing threatened, θάνατον ἀ. ὃς ἄν.. Hdt.4.81; ξίφος Plu.*Pomp.*47; ζημίας ἀ. κατά τινος Id.*Cam.*39; ἠπείλησαν τοὺς ἄρχοντας *threatened* them with the prefects, Lib.*Or.*47.7. **3.** dependent clauses were added in fut. inf., γέρας.. ἀφαιρήσεσθαι ἀπειλεῖς Il.1.161, cf. 15.179, Od.11.313; σφέας.. ἀπείλεε ἐκτρίψειν Hdt.6.37; ἀ. δράσειν τι E.*Med.* 287; ἀ. ἀποκτενεῖν Lys.3.28: rarely in pres. inf., ἠπ...ἐλκέμεν Il. 9.682: after Hom. in aor. inf., X.*Mem.*3.5.4, *HG*5.4.7, Theoc.24. 16. **4.** ἀ. ὅτι.., ὡς.., Ar.*Pl.*88, X.*An.*5.5.22, etc.; ἀ. τινί, εἰ μή .. Id.*Cyr.*4.5.12. **III.** Pass., ἀπειλοῦμαι, of persons, *to be terrified by threats*, Id.*Smp.*4.31. **2.** of things, τὰ ἀπειληθέντα, = ἀπειλαί, Pl.*Lg.*823c. **IV.** later in Med., with aor. 1 -ησάμην App.*BC*3.29, Polyaen.7.35.2: c. inf., *forbid with threats*, ἀπειλησώμεθα αὐτοῖς μηκέτι λαλεῖν *Act.Ap.*4.17.

**ἀπειλ-ή**, ἡ, mostly in pl., *boastful promises, boasts*, ποῦ τοι ἀπειλαὶ ἃς.. ὑπίσχεο οἰνοποτάζων; Il.20.83; μέχρι τῶν ἀπειλῶν γενναῖος Lib. *Or.*59.118, cf. Eust.704.28. **II.** commonly in pl., *threats*, ποῦ τοι ἀπειλαὶ οἴχονται τὰς Τρωσὶν ἀπείλεον υἷες Ἀχαιῶν; Il.13.219; οὐδὲ.. λήθετ' ἀπειλάων τὰς ἀντιθέῳ Ὀδυσῆι πρῶτον ἐπηπείλησεν Od.13.126, cf. Il.16.200, Hdt.6.32; εὐθύνειν ἀπειλαῖς καὶ πληγαῖς Pl.*Prt.*325d, cf. A.*Pr.*175(lyr.): in sg., S.*Ant.*753, Th.4.126; ἀπειλῆς ἕνεκα τοῖς ἐν τῷ Ταρτάρῳ Arist.*APo.*94b33. **2.** of threatening conditions, ἀ. πνιγμοῦ Alex.Aphr.*Pr.*2.60; τὰ ἐν ἀπειλῇ ἀποστήματα Heras ap.Gal.13. 815; of storms, J.*BJ*1.21.5, Ael.*NA*7.7. **-ημα**, ατος, τό, = ἀπειλή, S.*OC*660(pl.). **-ησις**, εως, ἡ, *threat*, Phld.*Herc.*1251.8. **-ητήρ**, ῆρος, ὁ, *threatener, boaster*, Il.7.96, Call.*Del.*69, *AP*6.95 (Antiph.): as Adj., Nonn.*D.*4.378, al.:—fem. **-ήτειρα**, ib.2.257. **-ητήριος**, α, ον, *of* or *for threatening*, λόγοι Hdt.8.112. **-ητής**, οῦ, ὁ, = ἀπειλητήρ, D.S.5.31, J.*BJ*1.10.4. **-ητικός**, ή, όν, = ἀπειλητήριος, ῥήσεις Pl.*Phdr.*268c; νόμιμα Id.*Lg.*823c; ὄμματα X.*Mem.*3.10.8. Adv. **-κῶς** Phryn.*PS*p.61 B.

**ἀπείλλω**, v. ἀπίλλω.

***ἄπειμι** (A), (εἰμί *sum*), impf. ἀπῆν (later ἀπήμην *POxy.*1204.23 (iii A.D.)), 2 sg. ἀπῆσθα S.*Ph.*379; Ep. ἀπέην Il.20.7, 3 pl. ἄπεσαν ib.10. 357: fut. ἀπέσομαι Ar.*Nu.*887; Ep. ἀπέσσομαι Od.8.150, 3 sg. ἀπεσσεῖται ib.19.302:—*to be away* or *far from*, c. gen., ὁππότε πάτρης ἧς ἀπέῃσιν ἀνήρ ib.169, cf. 20.155, al.; ἐὰν δ' ἀπῇ τούτων τὸ χαίρειν S. *Ant.*1169; ἀ. τῶν ἰδίων Th.1.141: c. dat., φίλοισιν E.*Med.*179 (lyr.), cf. *Tr.*393, Hdt.4.1, Th.2.61, etc.: but mostly, **2.** abs., *to be away* or *absent*, and of things, *to be wanting*, οἵ τ' ὄντες οἵ τ' ἀπόντες, i.e. all that are, every one, S.*Ant.*1109; τὰς οὔσας τέ μου καὶ τὰς ἀπούσας ἐλπίδας Id.*El.*306; of the dead, v.l. in E.*Hec.*312; τοῦ θεοῦ ἀπεόντος the god *not being counted*, Hdt.6.53:—in 3 pl. impf., ἀπῆσαν and ἀπῇσαν are freq. confused in codd., as in Th.4.42.

***ἄπειμι** (B), (εἶμι *ibo*), serving as fut. of ἀπέρχομαι: inf. ἀπιέναι, in *AP*11.404 (Lucill.) ἀπίναι:—*go away, depart*, Od.17.593, al.; οὐκ ἄπει; = ἄπιθι, *begone*, S.*OT*431: ἀπιὼν οἴχεσθαι D.18.65, Isoc.17.43; οἱ πρέσβεις περὶ τῶν σπονδῶν ἀπῇσαν Th.4.39; of soldiers, ἀπίασι οὐδενὶ κόσμῳ *will retreat*, Hdt.8.60.γ'; ἀ. πρὸς βασιλέα *desert* to him, X.*An.* 1.9.29; ἀ. πάλιν *return*, ib.1.4.7, cf. 15; ἄπιτε ἐπὶ τὰ ὑμέτερα αὐτῶν *return* to your homes, Hdt.6.97; ἄπιμεν οἴκαδε Ar.*V.*255; ἀπῇσαν ἐπ' οἴκου Th.5.36; εἰς τὴν πατρίδα Arr.*Epict.*2.23.36; of the Nile, *recede*, Hdt.2.108; ἀ. ἐπί τι *go* in quest of.., X.*Cyr.*7.5.80; μηνὸς ἀπιόντος, for the common φθίνοντος, Decr.ap.D.18.37, *CIG*3658 (Cyzicus); *die*, Luc.*Tim.*15, Philostr.*Im.*2.9. **2.** c. acc. cogn., πολλὴν καὶ τραχεῖαν ἀπιέναι (sc. ὁδόν) Pl.*Phdr.*272c. **3.** *to be discharged*, Hp.*Mul.*8, al.

***ἀπεῖπον**, inf. ἀπειπεῖν, Ep. ἀποειπεῖν, ἀποειπέμεν, and part. ἀποειπών, i.e. ἀποϝειπών, Il.19.35, etc.: less freq. aor. 1 ἀπεῖπα Hdt.3.153, S.*Ant.*405: fut. in use is ἀπερῶ, pf. ἀπείρηκα, mostly in signf. IV. 3:—**Med.**, aor. 1 ἀπειπάμην Hdt.1.59, 5.56, Arist.*EN*1163b19, but never in correct Att.:—**Pass.**, fut. ἀπορρηθήσομαι Lys.22.14: aor. ἀπερρήθην Pl.*Lg.*929a, D.33.21:—pres. and impf. are supplied by ἀπαυδάω, ἀπόφημι, and in Att. Prose by ἀπαγορεύω:—*speak out, tell out, declare*, μῦθον Il.9.309, cf. 431; ἀγγελίην 7.416; ἀληθείην 23.361; ἐφημοσύνην Od.16.340; μνηστήρεσσιν ἀπειπέμεν (prob. μνηστῆρσ' ἀποειπέμεν) *to give* them *full notice*, ib.1.91; ἀπηλεγέως ἀποειπεῖν Il. 9.309, cf. Od.1.373; ῥῆσιν ἀπερέοντα *to deliver* a *verbal* message, Hdt. 1.152: in aor. Med., ἀπείπασθαι θανάτῳ ζημιοῦν τοὺς πλευσομένους Arist.*Mir.*837a2. **II.** *deny, refuse*, ὑπόσχεο καὶ κατάνευσον, ἢ ἀπόειπ' Il.1.515, cf. 9.510, 675; σύμφαθι ἢ ἄπειπε Pl.*R.*523a: c. acc., βοήθειαν Plu.*Tim.*2. **III.** *forbid* (cf. ἀπαγορεύω I), freq. in Prose, ἀ. τινὶ μὴ ποιεῖν *forbid* one *to do, tell* him *not to* do, Hdt.1.155, S.*OC*1760, Ar. *Av.*556; also without μή, Plb.2.52.8: with inf. omitted, ἀπειπὼν εἴργει μελάθρων A.*Ag.*1333, cf. S.*Ant.*405; ἀ. τινί τι *forbid* him *the use of* it, Arist.*Pol.*1264a21:—Pass., ἀπειρῆσθαι γάρ οἱ.. μηδενὶ ἐπιδεικνύναι Hdt.6.61; τὸ ἀπειρημένον a *forbidden* thing, Id.3.52, Antipho 3.2.7; ἀπείρηται δὲ τοῦτο τῷ νόμῳ Xenarch.7.7; ἀπειρημένον, abs., *contrary to orders*, Arist.*Rh.*1373b10. **IV.** *renounce, disown, give up*, c. acc. rei, ἀ. μῆνιν Il.19.35; and not seldom in Prose, as εἴτε.. ἀπερέουσι.. τὴν συμμαχίην Hdt.7.205; ἀπειπεῖν.. κηρύκων ὕπο.. πατρῴαν ἑστίαν *renounce* it by public proclamation, E.*Alc.*737; τὸν υἱὸν ὑπὸ κήρυκος ἀ. Pl.*Lg.*928d; πόνους E.*HF*1354; προξενίαν Th.5.43, 6.89; ὁμιλίαν Lys.8.6; ταῦτα μὲν οὖν ἀπείποι τις ἂν D.21.113; ἀ. τὴν στρατηγίαν *to resign* it, X.*An.*7.1.41; τὴν ἀρχήν Arist.*Pol.*1272b5; ἐλπίδας Plb.14.9.6; ἀ. γυναῖκα *divorce* her, Plu.*Luc.*38:—in Pass., αἱ σπονδαὶ οὐκ ἀπείρηντο *had* not *been renounced*, remained in force, Th.5.48; τὰς σπονδὰς μέλλειν ἀπορρηθήσεσθαι Lys.22.14:—in Med., ἀπείπασθαι παῖδα Hdt.1.59; συμμαχίην 4.120, 125; φιλίαν Plb.33.10. 5; ἀ. ὄψιν *averruncare*, Hdt.5.56; ἀ. υἱόν, πατέρα, Arist.*EN*1163b 19; ἀποϝειπάθθω (Cret. for ἀπειπάσθω) *let him renounce* the inheritance, *Leg.Gort.*11.11; ἀ. γνώμας *withdraw, retract* them, Plu.*Caes.* 8. **2.** *refuse*, c. inf., Nonn.*D.*4.30. **3.** intr., *fail, tire, sink from exhaustion*, ἐπεὶ δ' ἀπεῖπε S.*Tr.*789, cf. Ar.*Pax* 306, Pl.*Phdr.*228b, etc.; ἀπειρηκὸς σῶμα Antipho 5.93; γῆ ἀπειρηκυῖα Thphr.*CP*3.20.3; οὐ γάρ που ἀπεροῦμέν γέ πω *shall* not *give in* yet, Pl.*Tht.*200d; ἕως ἂν ἀπείπωσιν D.54.25, cf. 27; οἱ διὰ τὸν χρόνον ἀπειρηκότες Arist.*Pol.* 1329a33; οὐδ' ἀπεῖπεν.. φάτις *was* not *unfulfilled*, A.*Th.*840. **b.** c. dat. pers., *fail* or *be wanting to* one, οὐκ ἀ. φίλοις E.*Med.*459. **c.** c. dat. rei, *fail* or *fall short in* a thing, ἀπειρηκότων δὲ χρήμασι *now that they are bankrupt*, D.3.8; ἀ. σώμασι Isoc.4.92, Lycurg.40; but, **d.** ἀ. κακοῖς, ἄλγει, *give way to, sink under* them, E.*Or.*91, *Hec.*942; ἀ. ὑπὸ πλήθους κακῶν X.*HG*6.3.15. **e.** ἀ. πρὸς τὸν φόνον *to be tired* of butchery, Plu.*Cam.*18; ἀ. ἐν τοῖς δράμασι Antiph.191. 14. **f.** c. pres. part., ἀ. ταλαιπωρούμεναι Ar.*Lys.*778; φέροντες ἀπεροῦσιν they *will be tired of* paying, Th.1.121; ἀ. λέγων *give over* speaking, Pl.*Lg.*769e; ἀπειρήκη τὰ ὄντα σκοπῶν I *had failed to*.., Id.*Phd.*99d, etc.

**ἀπειρ-ἄγἄθέω**, *act without right knowledge*, Paul.Aeg.6.50. **-ἄγἄθία**, ἡ, *ignorance of goodness, folly*, Hierocl.p.54A. **-άγἄθος**, ον, *unacquainted with goodness, foolish*, Lxx *Es.*8.13. Adv. **-θως** D.S.15.40.

**Ἀπειραῖος**, α, ον, *Apeiraean*, and **Ἀπείρηθεν**, Adv. *from Apeire*, both in Od.7.8,9 γρηῢς Ἀπειραίη.., τήν ποτ' Ἀπείρηθεν νέες ἤγαγον. *Apeire* seems to be *Limitless-land* (from ἄπειρος B), an imaginary place; Hsch. expl. by ἠπειρωτική.

***ἀπειράκις**, Adv., (ἄπειρος B) *times without number*, Arist.*Ph.*193a 28, *Xen.*975a26, Plu.2.426e; πολλάκις, μᾶλλον δ' ἀ. Arist.*Pol.*1329b 27; οὐχ ἅπαξ οὐδὲ δὶς ἀλλ' ἀ. Id.*Cael.*270b19, cf. Phld.*D.*3*Fr.*35; ἀπειράκις ἄπειρος Ph.1.499, Dam.*Pr.*21.

**ἀπείρανδρος**, ον, *that has not known man*, Hsch. s.v. μνηστή.

**ἀπείραστος**, ον, *incapable of being tempted*, κακῶν *Ep.Jac.*1. 13. **II.** *without experience*, τῶν ἀβουλήτων Alciphr.3.37. **III.** *not experienced*, Gal.13.459; *untried*, τέχνη Phld.*Rh.*1.45S.

**ἀπείρᾶτος**, ον, Dor. and Att. for ἀπείρητος.

***ἀπείρᾶτος**, ον, (-περ-τος, cf. πειραίνω) *impenetrable*, Pi.*O.*6.54. **II.** = ἄπειρος (B), v.l. in Hp.*Flat.*7, dub. in Dam.*Pr.*107.

**ἀπειράχῶς**, Adv. *in an infinite number of ways*, Plu.2.732f, Procl. *in Prm.*p.581S.

**ἀπείργἄθον**, Ep. ἀποέργαθον (also ἀπεργ– Hsch.), poet. aor. 2 of ἀπείργω:—*keep away*, Πηλείωνα δόλῳ ἀποέργαθε λαοῦ Il.21.599; ῥάκεα μεγάλης ἀποέργαθε οὐλῆς he *pushed back* the rags *from* the scar, Od. 21.221; ἤν μή μ' ὁ κραίνων τῆσδε γῆς ἀπειργάθῃ S.*OC*862.

**ἀπείργω**, Ion. and Ep. ἀπέργω, in Hom. also ἀποέργω i.e. ἀποϝέργω), also ἀπεέργει Hsch.: fut. ἀπείρξω: aor. ἀπείργαθον (q.v.); aor. also ἀπεῖρξα S.*Aj.*1280, Th.4.37, etc.:—**Pass.**, pf. inf. ἀπεῖρχθαι Phld.*Mus.*p.19 K.: *keep away from, debar from*, c. gen., ὁ δὲ Τρῶας.. αἰθούσης ἀπέεργεν Il.24.238; σφέας θυσιέων ἀπέρξαι Hdt.2. 124; ἀ. πόλεως ζυγόν A.*Th.*471; ἐγώ σφ' ἀπείργω.. χαρᾶς S.*Aj.*51 (dub. sens.); οὐκ ἔστιν ὅτε ἀπειργομέν τινα.. μαθήματος ἢ θεάματος Th.2.39, cf. 3.45; νόμων ἡμᾶς ἀπείργεις; do you *exclude* us *from* their benefit? Ar.*V.*467; δείπνου ἀ. τινά Cratin.57; ἀ. τινὰ ἀπό τινος Hdt.9.68:—Med. like Act., ἱκέτην ἀπείργεται A.*Ch.*569; but also, *keep one's hands off, keep away from*, ξένου Pl.*Lg.*879d. **2.** *keep from* doing, *prevent* (ἀπείργω τὸν βουλόμενον ἐνεργεῖν τι, ἀνείργω τὸν ἀρξάμενον *AB*331), c. acc. et inf., αὐγὰς ἀπείρξω σὴν πρόσοψιν εἰσιδεῖν S.*Aj.*70, cf. E.*Rh.*432, Antiph.126; μὴ ποιεῖν E.*Hel.*1559; ἀ. τι μὴ γίγνεσθαι Pl.*Lg.*837d:—Pass., *to be debarred from* doing, ἅπτεσθαί τινος Id.*Prm.*148e. **3.** c. acc., *keep back, keep off, ward off*, μικρὸς δὲ λίθος μέγα κῦμ' ἀποέργει Od.3.296; ἀπὸ πάμπαν εἴργοντες (sc. τοὺς πολεμίους) Pi.*O.*13.59; τίς ταῦτ' ἀπεῖρξεν; S.*Aj.*1280; νόσους ἀ. E.*Ion* 1013; abs., ἀλλ' ἀπείργοι θεός God *forfend!* S.*Aj.*949; ὅπου μὴ.. καῦμα ἀπείργει Pl.*Ti.*22e, etc. **b.** νόμος οὐδεὶς ἀπεῖργε *checked* them, Th.2.53, cf. Democr.259; τὴν βίαιον τροφὴν ἀ. *prohibit* it, Arist.*Pol.*1338b41:—Pass., φυγῇ ἀπειργόμενος X.*HG*1.4.15. **c.** τὸ ἀπεργμένον the old bed of the Nile laid dry by *barring* or *damming off* the river, Hdt.2.99; ὁ ἀγκών.. ὡς ἀπεργμένος ῥέῃ *dammed off*, ibid. **II.** *part, divide, separate*, ὅθι κληῒς ἀποέργει αὐχένα τε στῆθός τε Il.8.325:—and so, *bound, skirt*, of seas and rivers, etc., ὁ Ἅλυς ἔνθεν μὲν Καππαδόκας ἀπέργει, ἐξ εὐωνύμου δὲ Παφλαγόνας Hdt.1.72; πρὸς βορῆν ἄνεμον ὁ Κεραμεικὸς κόλπος ἀπέργει ib.174, cf. 204, 2.99, 4.55. **2.** of travellers, ἐπορεύετο ἐν ἀριστερῇ μὲν ἀπέργων Ῥοίτειον πόλιν κτλ. *keeping* Rhoeteium on the left.., Id.7.43; ἐκ δεξιῆς χειρὸς τὸ Πάγγαιον ὄρος ἀ. ib.112, cf. 109, 8.35. **III.** *shut up, confine*, αἱ ἐσχατιαὶ τὴν ἄλλην χώρην ἐντὸς ἀ. Id.3.116; ἀπεργμένον ἐν τῇ ἀκροπόλει Id.1.154, cf. 5.64; ἐν τῷ ἱρῷ Id.6.79.

***ἀπειρέσιος**, α, ον, *boundless, immense*, γαῖα, ὀϊζύς, Il.20.58, Od.11. 621; δῆρις Batr.4; *countless*, ἄνθρωποι πολλοί, ἀπειρέσιοι Od.19.174, cf. Hes.*Fr.*134.4, Theoc.25.100; ὄρνιθες Simon.40; ἀ. εἶδος *untold* beauty, Hes.*Fr.*33; once in Trag., ἀ. πόνοι S.*Aj.*928(lyr.): neut. as Adv., Q.S.2.179, 3.386. (Like ἀπερείσιος, by metrical lengthening for *ἀπερέσιος; root *per*– in πεῖραρ, ἄπειρος B.)

**Ἀπείρηθεν**, v. Ἀπειραῖος. **ἀπείρηκα**, v. ἀπεῖπον.

**ἀπείρητος**, Dor. and Att. **ἀπείρᾶτος**, ον, also η, ον *h.Ven.*133; *without trial*, and so: **I.** Act., *without making trial of, without making an attempt upon*, c. gen., ἀπείρητος.. σταθμοῖο, of a lion, Il. 12.304: abs., *making no attempt* or *venture*, Pi.*I.*4(3).30. **2.** *without trial* or *experience of, unknowing of*, φιλότητος *h.Ven.* l.c., cf. J.*BJ*3.4.1, Plu.2.681c, etc.; στρατὸν μηδ' ἀπείρατον καλῶν Pi.*O.*11 (10).18; ἀλλοδαπῶν οὐκ ἀ. δόμοι not *unvisited by*.., Id.*N.*1.23; ἀ. πολεμίας σάλπιγγος *that never heard* an enemy's bugle, Demad.12: abs., *inexperienced*, opp. εὖ εἰδώς, Od.2.170, cf. Pi.O.8.61. Adv. ἀπειράτως, ἔχειν τινός Paus.10.7.1. II. Pass., *untried, unattempted*, οὐ μὰν ἔτι δηρὸν ἀ. πόνος ἔσται.. ἤτ' ἀλκῆς ἤτε φόβοιο Il.17.41 (where however Nicanor took it in signf. 1.2); ἔστω μηδὲν ἀ. Hdt.7.9.γ'; οὐδὲν ἦν ἀπείρατον τούτοις κατ' ἐμοῦ D.18.249, cf. J.*BJ*7.8.1, Luc. *Tox.*3.

**ἀπειρία** (A), ἡ, (ἄπειρος A) opp. ἐμπειρία, *want of skill, inexperience, ignorance*, Hp.*Lex*4, Th.1.80; ἐμπειρία τε τῆς ἀπειρίας κρατεῖ E.*Fr.*619; ἡ μὲν ἐμπειρία τέχνην ἐποίησεν ἡ δ' ἀπειρία τύχην Polus ap. Arist.*Metaph.*981ᵃ5; ὑπὸ ἀπειρίας Pl.*Tht.*167b; δι' ἀπειρίαν Id.*Grg.*518d. 2. c. gen. rei, τοῦ θανεῖν E.*Fr.*816.10; ἀ. μέθης *want of skill* to carry it discreetly, Antipho 4.3.2; ἀ. ἔργου And.3.2; μουσικῆς ἀπειρίᾳ Philetaer.18; δι' ἀπειρίαν τοῦ ἐρωτᾶν καὶ ἀποκρίνεσθαι Pl.*R.*487b; ἀπειρείησι νόοιο (sic) *Epigr.Gr.*1078.5 (Adana).

**ἀπειρία** (B), ἡ, (ἄπειρος B) *infinity, infinitude*, τὴν τῶν ὁμοιομερῶν ἀ. Anaxag.ap.Arist.*Metaph.*988ᵃ28; opp. πέρας, Pl.*Phlb.*16c; ἡ ἀ. καὶ ὁ αἰών Metrod.37, cf. Phld.*D.*3.11; ἀ. χρόνου Pl.*Lg.*676a; ἀ. τῶν κόσμων Epicur.*Ep.*1 p.9 U.; τῶν ἀτόμων Dam.*Pr.*98; τῶν ἀριθμῶν Ph. 1.10. 2. *eternity*, Arist.*Cael.*279ᵃ26.

※**ἀπείρῐτος**, ον, = ἀπειρέσιος, Od.10.195, Hes.*Th.*109; *boundless, immense*, νῆσος D.P.4; γαῖα Orph.*Fr.*91, al.: neut. pl. as Adv., ἀπείριτα δηριόωντες Timo 12.

**ἀπειρκτικός**, ή, όν, *keeping out*, Alex.Aphr.*in Sens.*23.18.

**ἀπειρο-βίως**, Adv. *without experience of life*, Hierocl.p.55 A. **–γᾰμος**, ον, *unwedded*, νύμφα Eub.35; of Athene, Nonn.*D.*47.416, *Cat.Cod.Astr.*7.227. **–γονος**, ον, *infinitely generative*, δύναμις Dam.*Pr.*98,99. **–γρᾰφος**, ον, f.l. for ἀπερίγραφος, ib.272. **–γωνος**, ον, *with an infinite number of angles*, *Theol.Ar.*1. **–δακρυς**, υ, *ignorant of tears*, A.*Supp.*71. **–διοικήτης**, ου, ὁ, *director of the infinite*, *PMag.Par.*1.1354(pl.). **–δροσος**, ον, *unbedewed, parched*, E.*El.*735 (lyr.). **–δύναμος** [ῠ], ον, *of infinite potentiality*, ἡ τῆς ψυχῆς φύσις Porph.*Sent.*37, cf. Procl.*Inst.*84, Id.*in Prm.*p.642 S., Dam.*Pr.*117, al., Simp.*in Ph.*608.36:—Subst. **–δῠναμία**, ἡ, *infinite potentiality*, Procl. *in Prm.*p.873 S., Simp. *in Ph.*1329.10. **–ειδής**, ές, *resembling the infinite*, Procl.*Inst.*159, Dam.*Pr.*210, Simp. *in Ph.*528.13. **–θάλαττος** [θᾰ], ον, *unused to the sea*, Philostr.Jun.*Im.*12. **–κᾰκος**, ον, *without experience of evil*: τὸ ἀ. *unsuspiciousness*, Th.5.105. II. *unused to evil* or *misery*, E.*Alc.*927. **–κᾰλεύομαι**, *lack taste*, Aeschin.*Ep.*10.1. **–κᾰλία**, ἡ, *ignorance of the beautiful, want of taste*, ἀμουσία καὶ ἀ. Pl.*R.*403c; ὑπ' ἀπειροκαλίας ib.405b; ἀ. περὶ χρήματα *vulgar* extravagance, Arist.*EN*1107ᵇ19; of literary style, D.H.*Dem.*23: in pl., *vulgarities*, X.*Cyr.*1.2.3. **–κᾰλος**, ον, *ignorant of the beautiful, tasteless, vulgar*, ἀ. καὶ ἀπαίδευτος Pl.*Lg.*775b, cf. D.H.*Pomp.*2, etc.; περὶ λόγους ἀ. Plu.2.44d; ἀ. ἡγοῦμαι πάντων μεμνῆσθαι Ael.*Tact.*1.2; τὸ ἀ., = ἀπειροκαλία, X.*Mem.*3.10.5. Adv. –λως Pl.*Phdr.*244c, etc.; *foolishly, rashly*, Onos.11.4. **–λεχής**, ές, (λέχος) = ἀπειρόγαμος, Ar.*Th.*119; Φοίβη Orac. ap.Eus.*PE*4.23. **–λογία**, ἡ, (λόγος) *interminable argument*, S.E.*P.*2.151 (pl.), prob. l. in Phld.*Rh.*1.7 S. **–μάχας** [μᾰ], α, ὁ, (Dor.) *unused to battle, untried in war*, Pi.*N.*4.30. **–μεγέθης**, ες, *immensely large*, S.E.*P.*3.44; διαστήματα Ph.1.605, cf. Cleom.2.1: metaph., χωρίον ἐπιστήμης Ph.1.627. **–μείζων**, ον, *infinitely greater*, v.l. for ἀπείρῳ μείζων, Cleom.2.1.

**ἀπειρόμενος**· ἀποφεύγων, Cyr., cf. Hsch.

**ἀπειρό-μοθος**, ον, *unused to toil*, Κυθερείη Nonn.*D.*24.294. 2. = ἀπειρομάχης, κεμάδες ib.20.260. **–πλᾰσίων**, ον, gen. ονος, *infinitely more, many thousand-fold*, Phlp.*in Mete.*17.15, Eust.89.8. **–πληθής**, ές, *infinitely great* or *numerous*, Id.562.37, Sch.Nic.*Th.*310:—Subst. **–πλήθεια** or **–πληθία**, ἡ, Eust.202.43. **–πλους**, ουν, *ignorant of navigation*, Luc.*Dom.*12. **–ποιός**, όν, *producing infinitude*, δυνάμεις Procl.*in Prm.*p.567 S., cf. p.602 S., Dam.*Pr.*91 bis. **–πόλεμος**, ον, *inexperienced in war*, App.*Mith.*51; τὸ ἀ. D.H.8.37. Adv. –μως App.*BC*2.71. **–πονος**, ον, *unused to toil*, Κυθερείη Nonn.*D.*24.276.

**ἄπειρος** (A), ον, (πεῖρα) *without trial* or *experience of* a thing, *unused to, unacquainted with*, ἄθλων Thgn.1013; καλῶν Pi.*I.*8(7).70; κακότητος Emp.112.3; τυράννων Hdt.5.92.α'; τῆς ναυτικῆς Id.8.1; Περσέων Id.9.58, cf. 46; πόνων, νόσων, A.*Ch.*371, *Fr.*350.2; γνώμης S.*Ant.*1250; δικῶν Antipho 1.1; πολέμων Th.1.141; τοῦ μεγέθους τῆς νήσου Id.6.1; γραμμάτων Pl.*Ap.*26d; ἀνδρῶν ἀγαθῶν Lys.2.27; of a woman, ἄ. ἄλλων ἀνδρῶν *not having known* other men (beside her husband), Hdt.2.111; ἄ. λέχους E.*Med.*672: abs. in same sense, ib.1091 (lyr.). 2. abs., *inexperienced, ignorant*, Pi.*I.*8(7).48, etc.; γλυκὺ δ' ἀπείροισι πόλεμος Id.*Fr.*110; δίδασκ' ἄπειρον A.*Ch.*118. Adv. ἀπείρως, ἔχειν τῶν νόμων Hdt.2.45; πρός τι X.*Mem.*2.6.29; περί τινος Isoc.5.19: Comp. ἀπειρότερον, παρεσκευασμένοι Th.1.49; –οτέρως Isoc.12.37, Arist.*Resp.*470ᵇ9.

※**ἄπειρος** (B), ον, (πεῖραρ, πέρας) *boundless, infinite*, σκότος Pi.*Fr.*130.8; τὸν ὑψοῦ τόνδ' ἄ. αἰθέρα E.*Fr.*941; ἤπειρον εἰς ἄ. ib.998; of number, *countless*, πλῆθος Hdt.1.204; ἀριθμὸς ἄ. πλῆθει Pl.*Prm.*144a; ἄ. τὸ πλῆθος Id.*R.*525a, al.; εἰς ἄ. τὴν ἀδικίαν αὐξάνειν Id.*Lg.*910b; χρόνος ἄ. *OGI*383.113 (i B.C.): Comp. –ότερος Dam.*Pr.*50, Phlp.*in Mete.*17.15; τὸ ἄ. *the Infinite*, as a first principle, Arist.*Ph.*203ᵃ3, etc.; esp. in the system of Anaximander, D.L.2.1, etc.; but τὰ ἄπειρα *individuals*, opp. τὰ εἴδη, Arist.*Top.*109ᵇ14, cf. *Metaph.*999ᵃ27, al.; ἄπειρος, opp. πεπερασμένος, *Ph.*202ᵇ31; εἰς ἄ. ἰέναι, προϊέναι, ἥκειν, etc., *APo.*81ᵇ33, *Ph.*209ᵃ25, *EN*1113ᵃ2, etc.; [γῆ] ἐπ' ἄπειρον ἐρριζωμένη Str.1.1.20; also, *indefinite*, ὕλη *Stoic.*2.86. 2. in Trag., freq. of garments, etc., *in which one is entangled past escape*, i.e. *without outlet*, ἀμφίβληστρον A.*Ag.*1382; χιτών S.*Fr.*526; ὕφασμα E.*Or.*25. 3. *endless*, i.e. *circular*, ἀ. δακτύλιος a simple hoop-ring, = ἄλιθος (Poll.7.179), Arist.*Ph.*207ᵃ2; cf. ἀπείρων (B) 1.3. Adv. –ρως, θρυφθῆναι *into an infinite number of* fragments, Id.*Pr.*899ᵇ16.

**ἀπειροσύνη**, ἡ, = ἀπειρία (A), E.*Hipp.*196, *Med.*1094, Cleanth.1.33.

**ἀπειρο-τέρμων**, ονος, ὁ, *limitless*, of God, *Corp.Herm.*18.12. **–τεχνής**, f.l. for –λεχής in Orac.ap.Eus.*PE*4.23. ※**–τοκος**, ον, *not having brought forth*, παρθενίη *AP*6.10 (Antip. Sid.). **–χρόνιος**, ον, *of infinite duration*, διαμονή Phld.*D.*3 *Fr.*24.

**ἀπειρόω**, *multiply to infinity*, Dam.*Pr.*25 bis (Pass.).

**ἀπειρωδίν**, ῖνος, ἡ, *knowing not the pains of child-birth*, Nonn.*D.*16.152.

**ἀπείρων** (A), ον, gen. ονος, (πεῖρα) = ἄπειρος (A), *without experience, ignorant*, S.*OT*1088 (lyr.), *Fr.*266.

※**ἀπείρων** (B), ον, gen. ονος, (πεῖραρ, πέρας) Ep. form of ἄπειρος (B), *boundless, endless*, ἐπ' ἀπείρονα γαῖαν Od.1.98, Hes.*Th.*187; Ἑλλήσποντος ἀ. Il.24.545; δῆμος ἀ. a *countless* people, ib.776; ὕπνος ἀ. *seeming endless*, i.e. *profound* sleep, Od.7.286; ἀπείρονα γῆς βάθη Emp.39, cf. 28; τῶν ἀλιθίων ἀ. γενέθλα Simon.5.6; δόξα Pi.*P.*2.64; κύκλος a *vast* concourse, B.8.30. 2. = ἄπειρος (B) 2, *without end* or *escape*, δεσμοὶ ἀπείρονες Od.8.340. 3. In Att., = ἄπειρος (B) 3, *having no end, circular*, δακτύλιος ἀ. Ar.*Fr.*250, cf. *IG*2.709.5, 11(2).161*B*81 (Delos, iii B.C.); ἐν λόχῳ ἀπείρονι, of persons standing in *a circle*, A.*Fr.*379.

**ἀπείς**, v. sub ἀφίημι.

**ἀπεισουτῆρες**· σκόλοπες, Hsch.

**ἄπειστος**, ον, (πείθω) *not to be persuaded*, πρὸς δωροδοκίαν Hyp.*Dem.Fr.*4.

※**ἀπέκ**, Prep. with gen., *away out of*, v.l. in *h.Ap.*110.

**ἀπεκ-βαίνω**, *turn out, come to be*, ὥσπερ τι τέρας Eust.1062.61. **–βάλλω**, *turn out*, Sch.A.*Pr.*84. **–βιόω**, aor. ἀπεξεβίω, *cease living*, Hsch. **–βολή**, ἡ, (ἀπεκβάλλω) *expulsion*, Sch.Dosiad.*Ara.* ※**–γονος**, ὁ, ἡ, *great-great-grandchild*, Simon.112.3. ※**–δέχομαι**, *expect anxiously, await eagerly*, σωτῆρα *Ep.Phil.*3.20; θάνατον Alciphr.3.7; τὸ μέλλον Hld.2.35, cf. S.E.*M.*2.73. II. *misunderstand, misinterpret*, Hipparch.1.6.11, al. b. *understand* a word *from* the context, A.D.*Conj.*226.20. **–δίδωμι** *relet* (after cancelling a contract), *CIG*2266 (Delos); simply, *contract for*, στήλην *Michel*468.72 (Iasus); ὅπως στήλη κατασκευασθῇ ib.481.31 (Priene). **–δῐκέω**, = τιμωρέω, Sch.E.*Hec.*749. **–δοσις**, εως, ἡ, *contract*, –σιν ποιῆσαι *Milet*6.36 (–ἐγδ– lapis), cf. *PPetr.*2 p.34; *performance of* work *contracted for*, ἐν τῇ ἀ. τῶν ἔργων *PSI*4.352.5 (iii B.C.). **–δύομαι**, fut. –δύσομαι [ῡ]: aor. 1 –εδυσάμην:—*strip off oneself*: metaph., *put off*, τὸν παλαιὸν ἄνθρωπον *Ep.Col.*3.9. II. *strip off for oneself, despoil*, τινά ib.2.15. **–δῠσις**, εως, ἡ, *putting off* (like clothes), ib.11.

**ἀπεκεῖθεν**, Adv. *thence*, Olymp.*in Mete.*119.28 (better divisim).

**ἀπεκέλλερεν**· ἀπέκλεψεν, Hsch.

**ἀπέκιξα**, v. κίκω.

**ἀπεκ-λανθάνομαι**, *forget entirely*, τινος, found only in aor. 2 imper., ἀπεκλελάθεσθε δὲ θάμβευς Od.24.394. **–λέγομαι**, *pick out and reject*, Dsc.1.7, Antip.*Stoic.*3.252, Arr.*Epict.*4.7.40. **–λεκτικός**, ή, όν, *fit for rejection*, ἀπαξία *Stoic.*3.28, cf. Antip.ib.251. **–λογή**, ἡ, *rejection*, opp. ἐκλογή, Diog.Bab.*Stoic.*3.219, cf. S.E.*M.*11.133: pl., Ph.*Fr.*8 H. **–λούομαι**, v.l. for ἐκλ. in Dsc.1.99. **–λύω**, *relax, weaken*, Alex.Aphr.*Fr.*1.120 (dub.). **–ρίπτω**, *throw away*, *PMag.Par.*1.59. **–ρῦσις**, f.l. for ἀπέρασις, q.v. **–τᾰσις**, εως, ἡ, *spreading out*, Lxx *Jb.*36.29, Gal.19.447; f.l. for ἐπέκτασις in Ph.*Bel.*72.28:—also **–τανσις**, Anon.*in Rh.*146.1. **–τείνω**, *draw off*, τῆς θερμασίας ἐν τοῖς ἀγγείοις ἀπεκταθείσης Gal.17(1).114.

**ἀπέκτητος**, ον, = sq., *AP*5.269 (Paul. Sil.).

**ἄπεκτος**, ον, lit. *uncombed*: hence, *unshorn*, of sheep less than a year old, μὴ σφάττειν πρόβατον ἄ. ἢ ἄτοκον Androt.41, cf. Philoch.64.

**ἀπεκφορέω**, gloss on ἀπεξιηνσάμην, Hsch.

**ἀπελᾰσία**, ἡ, (ἀπελαύνω) *driving away*, *POxy.*1252ʳ6 (iii A.D.), *PLond.*2.403.12 (iv A.D.).

**ἀπέλᾰσις**, εως, ἡ, *retirement* of cavalry, Arr.*Tact.*16.10 (pl.).

**ἀπέλαστος**, ον, *unapproachable*, dub. in Simon.29.

**ἀπελᾰτέος**, α, ον, *to be driven away*, Philostr.*VA*6.16.

**ἀπελάτης** [λᾰ], ου, ὁ, *driver away, cattle-lifter*, Ptol.*Tetr.*180, Just.*Nov.*22.15.1.

※**ἀπελαύνω**, also ἀπέλα as imper. from pres. ἀπελάω, X.*Cyr.*8.3.32; Dor. impf. ἀπήλαον vulg. in Ar.*Lys.*1001 (but prob. ἀπήλααν, = ἀπήλασαν, should be read): fut. –ελάσω Lxx *Ez.*34.12; Att. –ελῶ (also in Hdt.8.102): pf. –ελήλακα X.*Cyr.*4.2.10:—Pass., aor. –ηλάθην [ᾰ]: pf. part. ἀπεληλαμένος Artem.4 *Prooem.*:—Med., aor. –ηλασάμην *AP*7.303 (Antip. Sid.):—*drive away, expel from* a place, τινὰ δόμων, πόλεως, etc., E.*Alc.*553, etc.; ἀπὸ τόπου X.*Cyr.*3.2.16; ἀ. τινά *drive away, banish* him, S.*OC*93,1356, etc.; *expel* (from a society), X.*An.*3.1.32; *exclude, keep at a distance*, Ar.*Eq.*58; *remove*, φόβον τινὶ X.*Cyr.*4.2.10; *exclude from* a thing, Id.*HG*3.2.31:—Med., ἀ. τί τινος *ward off, avert from* him, *AP*l.c. 2. ἀ. στρατιήν *lead away* an army, Hdt.4.92: freq. abs. like ἀπάγω, *march, depart*, ἐς τὰς Σάρδις Id.1.77, cf. 5.25, etc.; πυρώσας τὰς Ἀθήνας ἀπελᾶς Id.8.102; also (sc. ἵππον) *ride away*, X.*Smp.*9.7, etc. II. Pass., *to be driven away*, ἐνθεῦτεν Hdt.5.94; ἐντεῦθεν εἰς ἄλλον τόπον X.*Cyr.*1.2.3; γῆς ἐμῆς πρός τινος S.*OC*599; *to be excluded from* a thing, ἁπάσης [τῆς στρατιῆς] *from* the command, Hdt.7.161, cf. X.*Cyr.*1.2.15; τῆς πολιτείας Lys.18.5; τῶν ἀρχῶν Pl.*R.*564d; ἀ. τῆς φροντίδος *to be far* *from*, Hdt.7.205; ἐς πατέρ' ἀπηλάθην τύχης *was barred from* [good] fortune on my father's side, E.*HF*63; ἀ. φιλίας Them.*Or.*7.90c.

**ἀπελεγκτής**, οῦ, ὁ, *one who refutes*, Oenom.ap.Eus.*PE*6.7.

**ἀπελεγμός**, ὁ, *refutation, exposure*, *Act.Ap.*19.27.

**ἀπελέγχω**, strengthd. for ἐλέγχω, *convict, expose, refute*, Antipho 5.19; τινά τινος Ph.1.205; εὐχέρειαν ἑαυτοῦ ib.193; τὴν διάνοιαν, εἰ .. M.Ant.8.36: abs., *procure a conviction*, *CIG*4325*k* (Olympus); *vindicate*, ἀ. τὸν τόκον γνήσιον Jul.*Or.*2.81d:—Pass., *to be convicted*, πείσας *of* having persuaded, Antipho 5.21.

**ἀπέλεθρος**, ον, *immeasurable*, ἵν' ἀπέλεθρον ἔχοντας Il.5.245, cf. Od. 9.538; ἀπέλεθρον ἀνέδραμε sprang back *immeasurably*, Il.11.354; *countless*, Nonn.*D.*19.330.

**ἀπελέκητος**, ον, *unhewn, unwrought*, Lxx 3*Ki.*6.1, al.: metaph., φωνή Crantor ap.D.L.4.27.

**ἀπελευθερ-ία**, Ion. -ίη, ἡ, *enfranchisement of a slave*, Aeschin.3. 41, Man.4.600. II. *status of a freedman*, Poll.3.83. ⊛-**ιάζω**, *to be free, act freely*, -άζουσα κίνησις Ph.1.419, cf. 277; in bad sense, ὑπ' αὐθαδείας Id.2.31. -**ικός**, ή, όν, *in the condition of a freedman*, ἄνθρωπος Plu.*Sull.*1, *Cic.*7; γυνή *PGnom.*83 (ii A.D.); γένος Str.8. 6.23. II. *relating to freedmen*, νόμοι D.ap.Poll.3.83. -**ισμός**, ὁ, *manumission*, *IG*9(1).109 (Elatea). -**ίωσις**, εως, ἡ, = foreg., ib.190 (Phocis). -**ιωτής**, οῦ, ὁ, *freedman*, Str.5.3.7 (v.l. ἀπελευθέρων). -**ος**, ὁ, *restored to freedom*, S.*Ichn.*193; *emancipated slave, freedman*, Pl.*Lg.*930d; ἀ. τινος Lys.7.10; opp. δοῦλος and μέτοικος, X.*Ath.*1.10, Arist.*Pol.*1278a2; ἀ. ἀφιέναι τινά Aeschin.3. 41: metaph., ἀ. Κυρίου 1*Ep.Cor.*7.22:—fem. **ἀπελευθέρα**, Ion. -έρη, ἡ, Hp.*Epid.*5.75, Is.6.19, D.59.18, Men.436. -**όω**, *emancipate* a slave, Pl.*Lg.*915a sq., *POxy.*722.18 (i A.D.):—Pass., Pl.*Lg.*915b; αἱρεῖται ἐπίτροπον ὁ ἀπελευθερούμενος Arist.*Rh.*1408b25. -**ωσις**, εως, ἡ, *emancipation*, δούλων D.17.15, cf. Plu.*Publ.*7, *PGnom.*60 (ii A.D.), *BGU*96.10 (iii A.D.). -**ωτικός**, ή, όν, *concerning manumission*, νόμοι *SIG*1210 (Calymna); δίκαια *SIG*2868.9 (ibid.).

**ἀπέλευσις**, εως, ἡ, *dropping out*, of a letter, Eust.191.13.

**ἀπέληκα** (cf. λακίς)· ἀπέρρωγα (Cypr.), Hsch.

**ἀπελίσσω**, *unroll, unwind*, ἀγαθίδα Aen.Tact.18.15:—Pass. in Ion. form ἀπειλισσομένης Hero *Aut.*2.7. II. *roll up*, aor. 1 ἀπείλιξαν D.C.46.36.

**ἀπέλκω**, Ion. for ἀφέλκω.

⊛**ἀπελλάζω**, Lacon. for ἐκκλησιάζω, Plu.*Lyc.*6.—Hsch. writes ἀπελάζειν, but quotes ⊛**ἀπέλλαι**· σηκοί, ἐκκλησίαι; ἐν ταῖς μεγάλαις ἀπέλλαις *IG*5(1).1144.21, 1146.41 (Gythium, i B.C.).

⊛**ἀπελλαῖα**, τά, *sacrifice at meeting of a* φρατρία, *Michel*995*A* 4 (Delph.).

⊛**Ἀπελλαῖος**, ὁ, sc. μήν, name of a month in various Dorian states, as Delphi, *GDI*1721, al.; Epidaurus, *IG*4.925.1, etc.:—also **Ἀπελλαιών**, ῶνος, ὁ, at Tenos, ib.12(5).872.15.

**ἀπελλακάς**· ἱερῶν κοινωνούς, Hsch. **ἀπέλλειν**· ἀποκλείειν, Id.

**ἀπέλλητος**, ὁ, = ἀνταγωνιστής, A.*Fr.*415.

**ἀπελλόν**· αἴγειρος, Hsch.

⊛**Ἀπέλλων**, ὁ, Dor. form of Ἀπόλλων, *IG*5(1).145 (Amyclae), *GDI* 5075 (Cret.), etc.; cf. Ἀπείλων *Inscr.Cypr.*140 H.

**ἄπελος**, τό, *wound not skinned over*, Call.*Fr.*343.

**ἀπελπ-ίζω**, Att. fut. -ιῶ D.S.19.50: pf. -ήλπικα:—*despair of*, τῆς πόλεως τὴν σωτηρίαν Hyp.*Ath.*35; τὸ μέλλον Epicur.*Ep.*3 p.62 U.; πράξεις Plb.1.19.12, etc.:—Pass., *to be given up in despair*, τὰ πράγματα Id.10.6.10; of persons, *to be despaired of*, οἱ ἀπηλπισμένοι Lxx *Is.*29.19, cf. Plb.9.5.2; ὑπὸ τῶν ἰατρῶν D.S.1.25, D.L.8.69, cf. *IG* 14.966 (ἀφηλπ-). 2. ἀ. τινός *despair of*, Plb.1.55.2, al.; οὐκ ἀ. τινός *to be confident of*, Gal.8.365; περὶ τῆς νίκης D.S.2.25. 3. abs., *hope* that a thing will *not* happen, D.L.1.59. II. causal, *drive to despair*, τινά *AP*11.114 (Nicarch.). III. *hope to receive back*, μηδὲν (v.l. μηδένα) ἀπελπίζοντες *Ev.Luc.*6.35 (dub.). -**ισμός**, ὁ, *hopelessness, despair*, Plb.30.32.11. -**ιστέον**, *one must despair*, Posidon. ap.Aët.6.20, Ph.2.422, Orib.14.42.3. -**ιστία**, ἡ, *despair*, Tz.*H.* 11.18 (pl.). -**ιστος**· *desperatus*, *Gloss.*

**ἀπεμέσῳ**· ματαίῳ, Hsch.

**ἀπεμέω**, Ep. aor. -έσσα, *spit up, vomit forth*, Il.14.437, Hp.*Aff.*15, Opp.*H.*1.560, Arist.*Pr.*871a21, Ael.*NA*9.66, Luc.*Cont.*7, Gal.14. 163:—Pass., ἀπεμούμενα Arist.*Pr.*926b26.

⊛**ἀπεμπολ-άω**, *sell*, ἀπημπόλα με λάθρα E.*Ion*1371; ἀ. τι ἀντί τινος *to sell for* a thing, Id.*Cyc.*257; τί τινος X.*Smp.*8.21, cf. Herod.7.65; ἀ. τινὰ εἰς λατρείαν Luc.*Merc.Cond.*23; *sell*, i.e. *betray*, ἡ μὲν Ἄργος βαρβάροις ἀπημπόλα E.*Tr.*973; ἀ. ψυχάς *barter* your lives, Id.*Ph.* 1228; τίς ὢν σὺ τήνδ' ἀπεμπολᾷς χθονός; *dost* thou *smuggle* her *out of* the country? Id.*IT*1360; ἀ. νόμους τοῖς δεομένοις Procop.*Pers.*1. 24:—Pass., ἀπεμπολώμενοι 'bought and sold', Ar.*Ach.*374.—An Ion. form ἀπεμπολέω is found in D.H.7.63, Max.Tyr.33.8, Luc.*Tox.* 28. ⊛-**ή**, ἡ, *sale*, Hsch.; also, = sq., Id. -**ησις**, εως, ἡ, *riddance*, ἀκαθαρσίας Hp.*Decent.*5. -**ητής**, οῦ, ὁ, *seller, dealer*, Lyc.341.

**ἀπεμ-φαίνω**, *to be incongruous, inconsistent*, Plb.6.47.10, A.D. *Synt.*324.23; ἀπεμφαῖνον *incongruous*, *Stoic.*2.51, Str.8.3.17, Jul.*Or.* 7.217c, Dam.*Pr.*229; *to be absurd*, A.D.*Synt.*47.8, S.E.*P.*3.112; -οντες θρῆνοι *discordant*, Marin.*Procl.*33; of verses faulty in metre, Aristid.Quint.1.28; τοῦ ἀπεμφαίνοντος ὀνόματος of a word similar in meaning but *different in form* (?), Demetr.Lac.*Herc.*1012.74:—Pass., *to be distinguished*, A.D.*Pron.*46.1. II. *display*, ἀλαζονείαν .. διὰ τῶν προσώπων Malch.p.397 D. -**φασις**, εως, ἡ, *incongruity, absurdity*, Str.10.2.12; *contradiction*, εἰς -σιν περικλείεσθαι S.E.*M.* 11.162. -**φερής**, ές, *unlike*, Thphr.*HP*8.8.5.

**ἀπέναντι**, Adv., (ἔναντι) *opposite*, c. gen., Plb.1.86.3, Lxx *Ge.*21. 16, *PGrenf.*1.21.14 (ii B.C.), *IG*2.489*b*17, *Ev.Matt.*27.61; *before, in the presence of*, ἀ. ὑμῶν *Act.Ap.*3.16; *against*, c. gen., Lxx *Si.*37.4, *Act.Ap.*17.7. 2. abs., εἰς τὸν ἀ. βουνόν *Inscr.Prien.*37.168. 3. = κατὰ ἀνατολὰς νότου, Hsch.

**ἀπεναντίον**, Adv. = foreg., ἡ ἀ. (sc. χώρα) the *opposite* shore, ἐς τὴν ἀ. Hdt.7.55, cf. Str.7.6.2, D.S.19.38: c. dat., Gal.*UP*1.9: c. gen., *from before*, Lxx *Ca.*6.4: Geom., of angles, ἡ ἀ. γωνία the *opposite* angle, Euc.1.16, al.; of sides of a figure, Archim.*Aequil.*2.1, hence, II. Adj. **ἀπεναντίος**, ον, Procop.*Aed.*1.11. Adv. -ίως v.l. in Luc.*Nigr.*36.

⊛**ἀπεναρίζω**, (ἔναρα) *strip of arms*, c. dupl. acc., τοὺς ἐνάριζον ἀπ' ἔντεα Il.12.195, 15.343.

**ἀπενάσσατο**, 3 sg. aor. 1 Med. of ἀποναίω.

**ἀπενδονικώς**· φυγών, Hsch.

**ἀπένεικα, ἀπενείχθην**, v. ἀποφέρω.

**ἀπενεόομαι**, Pass., (ἐνεός) *become mute*, Thd.*Da.*4.16.

**ἀπενέπω**, v. ἀπεννέπω.

⊛**ἀπενθ-ής**, ές, *free from grief*, A.*Pr.*956; νεβρός B.12.87; θυμός *Fr.*7.2, cf. Plu.*Flam.*11, Tryph.599. -**ητος**, ον, = foreg., A.*Ag.* 895, *Eu.*912. 2. Pass., *unlamented*, Lxx 2*Ma.*5.10, *Epigr.Gr.* 436 (Berytus).

**ἀπενιαυτ-έω**, = -ίζω, Pl.*Lg.*866c, 868c. -**ησις**, εως, ἡ, *banishment for a term of years*, τριετεῖς ἀ. ib.868e (v.l. -ισις). -**ίζω**, *go into banishment for a term of years*, X.*Mem.*1.3.13, Nic.Dam. p.18 D., Philostr.*VA*1.13; ἐνιαυτοὺς τρεῖς ἀ. Pl.*Lg.*868d. II. *outlive the year* after a thing, D.C.46.49. -**ισμός**, ὁ, = ἀπενιαύτησις, *AB*421, Hsch.

**ἀπεννέπω**, Trag. word, also **ἀπενέπω** (only lyr. E.*IA*552), *forbid*: abs., A.*Th.*1058, E.*Ph.*1657; ἀ. τι *forbid* it, S.*OC*209; more freq. c. acc. et inf., ἀ. τινὰ ποιεῖν E.*Med.*813, *Heracl.*556; ἀ. τινὰ μὴ ποιεῖν Id.*Ion*1282, *HF*1295; ἀ. τινὰ θαλάμων *order* him *from* the chamber, Id.*IA*552 (lyr.). 2. c. acc. rei, *deprecate*, ἀνδροκμῆτας δ' .. ἀπεννέπω τύχας A.*Eu.*957 (lyr.).

**ἀπεντάσσω**, *put back in its place*, of the prolapsed uterus, Sor.2.88.

**ἀπεντεῦθεν**, Adv. *at this point*, Plb.39.1.1. II. *henceforth*, *POxy.*93.16 (iv A.D.), Eustr. *in EN*339.16.

**ἀπέξ**, v. ἀπέκ.

⊛**ἀπεξ-αιρέω**, *take out, remove*, τί τινος E.*IT*1278 (tm.). -**αρτάω**, *hang out*, τι ἐκ τόπου Anon.ap.Suid. s.v. κυνζόμενον. -**έβαι**· τὸ ἀποπατεῖν (Cret.), Hsch. ⊛-**ηγέομαι**, *narrate*, cj. in X.Eph.5. 9. -**ινόω**, *purge*, prob. in Timocl.39; also aor. Med. ἀπεξινησάμην (from -άω) Hsch. -**ισάζω**, *equalize*, Steph. *in Int.*16. 33. -**ωθέω**, *drive out, expel*, *AB*1454.

**ἀπέοικα**, *to be unlike, differ from*, c. gen., Plu.*Per.*8, Arr.*Ind.*6.8, Lib.*Or.*59.157:—in early writers found only in part. **ἀπεοικώς**, Att. **ἀπεικώς**, υῖα, ός, *unreasonable, unnatural*, οὐκ ἀπεικός (v.l. ἀπεοικός) Hp.*VM*4, Antipho 2.2.5; οὐκ ἀπεικός not *unlikely*, Plb.2.62.8, cf. Philostr.*VA*3.34; ἀπεοικὼς πρὸς τὰ καλά *unfitted, indisposed* for noble deeds, Plb.6.26.12: c. dat., *unlike*, Heph.15.4. Adv. ἀπεοικότως *unreasonably*, Th.6.55; but οὐκ ἀπεικότως Th.1.73, 2.8, 8.68, cf. Porph.*Abst*.1.46; D.Chr. has ἀπεοικότως 12.35, ἀπεικότως 31.116.

**ἀπέπαντος**, ον, (πεπαίνω) *not ripened, unripe*, Thphr.*CP*2.8.4, *AP* 9.561 (Phil.), Dsc.5.34; cf. ἀπεπαν[ό]τος· ὁ μὴ παλαιούμενος, Hsch.

**ἀπεπείγομαι**, *hasten away*, ἄλλοσε Man.5.239.

**ἀπέπειρος**, ον, *unripe*, ὀπώρα *AP*9.78 (Leon.).

⊛**ἄπεπλος**, ον, *unrobed*, i.e. *in her tunic only*, of a girl, ἄπεπλος ὀρούσαισ' ἀπὸ στρωμνᾶς Pi.*N.*1.50; λευκῶν φαρέων ἄπεπλος, i.e. clad in black, E.*Ph.*324 (lyr.).

**ἀπεποριάνεν**· ἀπεχλωρίασεν, Hsch.

**ἀπεπτέω**, *suffer from indigestion*, Luc.*Par.*57, Plu.2.136d, Arr. *Epict.*1.26.16, Cass.*Pr.*74. 2. Pass., of food, *to remain undigested*, Gal.6.628, Mich. *in EN*56.21.

**ἄπεπτος**, ον, (πέσσω) *uncooked*: *undigested*, of food, Hp.*Epid.*1. 26.β', Arist.*deAn.*416b5, al.; of humours, *crude, unconcocted*, Hp. *VM*19; οὖρον Id.*Acut.*42; φύματα Id.*Art.*41, cf. Arist.*Mete.*384a33: Comp., Id.*GA*750b25: Sup., ib.745b20. Adv. -τως Hp.*Epid.*1. 5. 2. metaph., Arist.*Mete.*371a3, Plu.2.495b. II. *suffering from indigestion*, Ruf.ap.Orib.7.26.99, Aret.*SD*2.3; τὸ στόμα τῆς γαστρὸς Alex.Aphr.*Pr.*1.45. III. χῶραι ἄ. countries *where fruits ripen ill*, Thphr.*CP*6.18.12 (Comp.).

**ἅπερ**, neut. pl. of ὅσπερ, q.v.

**ἀπεραντο-λογέω**, *talk without end*, Str.13.1.41. -**λογία**, ἡ, = ἀπειρολογία, Cic.*Att.*12.9, Luc.*DMort.*10.10, Gal.18(1).254. -**λόγος**, ον, *talking without end*, γλῶσσαι Thal.4 Bgk., cf. Ph.1.216: Comp. -ώτερος Gal.18(1).254.

⊛**ἀπέραντος**, ον, (περαίνω) *boundless, infinite*, of space, πεδίον Pi.*N.* 8.38 (who also has ἀπείραντος ἀλκά *P.*9.35); πόντου κλῇδ' ἀ. E.*Med.* 213 (lyr.); τὸν ἀέρα τόνδ' ὄντ' ἀ. Ar.*Nu.*393; ὁδός Pl.*Tht.*147c; of time, *endless*, τὸ χρῆμα τῶν νυκτῶν ὅσον· ἀπέραντον Ar.*Nu.*3; χρόνος Pl.*Plt.*302a; of number, *countless, infinite*, ἀ. ἀριθμὸς ἀνθρώπων Id. *Criti.*119a; ἀ. κακά Id.*R.*591d, al.; λῦπαι Plu.*Sol.*7; πένθη *Fab.*17; *unlimited*, τιμωρίαι D.23.39; generally, of events, business, etc., ἀπέραντον ἦν there was *no end to it*, Th.4.36; μακρὸν καὶ ἀ. φαίνεται Arist.*EN*1101a26; ἀπέραντα περαίνειν represent as concluded *what is not concluded*, Luc.*Philops.*9 (with allusion to signf. III); μηδὲν ἀβασάνιστον μηδ' ἀ. Plb.4.75.3. Adv., τὸ ἀπεράντως διεστηκός of *unlimited* dimensions, Arist.*Ph.*204b21, *Metaph.*1066b33. II. *allowing no escape, whence none can pass*, Τάρταρος, δίκτυον, A.*Pr.*153, 1087 (both lyr.). III. in Logic, *inconclusive*, λόγος Phld.*Ir*.p.97 W., cf. *Stoic*.2.77. IV. *incomplete, imperfect*, of persons, ἀτελὴς καὶ ἀ. Artem.1.12.

**ἀπέρᾱσις**, εως, ἡ, (ἀπεράω) *spitting out, vomiting*, Plu.2.134e, Philum.*Ven*.17.6: metaph., Str.8.8.4 (ἀπέκρυσις codd.). II. *carrying off of moisture*, Thphr.*CP*2.9.8: metaph., Iamb.*Myst*.3.9.

**ἀπέραστος**, ον, *unsurpassed*, Aristeas 156 (v.l. ἀπέραντον).

**ἀπερᾱτέον**, *one must vomit*, Orib.*Fr*.53.

**ἀπέρᾱτος**, ον, (περάω) *not to be crossed* or *passed*, ποταμός Plu.2.326e, Luc.*VH*2.30: metaph., Διὸς οὐ παρβατός ἐστιν μεγάλα φρὴν ἀ. A.*Supp*.1049.

**ἀπέρᾰτος**, ον, (πέρας) *boundless*, Ph.1.554, al.; v.l. for ἀπέραντος in Pl.*Tht*.147c (Anon.*in Tht*.23.48), Sch.Ar.*Nu*.3.

**ἀπεράτωτος** [ᾰτ], ον, *unbounded*, Plu.2.424d, Dam.*Pr*.178; of fate (with play on πεπρωμένη), Plu.2.1056d.

***ἀπεράω**, fut. -άσω [ᾱ], *vomit, disgorge*, Archig.ap.Gal.13.174, Philum.*Ven*.17.6, Alciphr.3.7. II. of moisture, generally, *carry off*, Str.1.3.6:—Pass., prob. in Thphr.*CP*1.17.10.

***ἀπεργ-άζομαι**, pf. -είργασμαι, sts. Act., Pl.*Lg*.704c, *Ti*.30b, al., sts. Pass., *R*.566a, *Phdr*.272a, al.: aor. -ειργάσθην always in pass. sense, Id.*R*.374c, al.:—*finish off, complete, bring to perfection*, τὰ ξύλινα τοῦ τείχους Ar.*Av*.1154; freq. in Pl., ἔργον ἀ. *Grg*.454a, *R*.353c, 603a, al.; εὐδαίμονα πόλιν ἀ. *Lg*.683b; τόν τε πολιτικὸν ἀ. καὶ τὸν φιλόσοφον *Plt*.257a; ἡ τέχνη ἐπιτελεῖ ἃ ἡ φύσις ἀδυνατεῖ ἀπεργάσασθαι Arist.*Ph*.199ᵃ16. 2. of a painter, *fill up with colour, represent in a finished picture*, opp. ὑπογράψαι (*sketch*), ἀ. ἀκριβῶς Pl.*R*.548d. 3. *finish a contract*, X.*Mem*.1.6.5. II. *cause, produce*, Pl.*Ti*.28e, al.; τὸ πλέον καὶ τὸ ἔλαττον Id.*Phlb*.24e; δόξαν ψευδῆ ib.40d; νίκην καὶ σωτηρίαν Id.*Lg*.647b; πανουργίαν ἀντὶ σοφίας ib.747c; ὀσμήν Arist.*Fr*.368, etc.; folld. by inf., *enable*, τὸ ἀπεργαζόμενον ὀρθῶς χρῆσθαι Pl.*Euthd*.281a. III. c. dupl. acc., *make* so and so, ἀγαθόν ἀ. τινα X.*Smp*.8.35; τοὺς παῖδας ἀ. δειλοτέρους Pl.*R*.381e, cf. *Plt*.287a, al.: pf. in pass. sense, ἀπειργασμένος τύραννος *finished* tyrant, *R*.566a; τέχνη ἀπειργασμένη *Phdr*.272a; ἀνὴρ ἀ. καλὸς κἀγαθός X.*Oec*.11.3. 2. ἀ. τινά τι *do* something *to* one, ὅ τι ἀγαθὸν ἡμᾶς ἀπεργάζεται Pl.*Chrm*.173a, cf. *Riv*.135e; ὅπερ ὕδωρ γῆν ἀ. as water *acts upon* earth, Id.*Ti*.61b. IV. *work off* a debt, Men.*Her*.36. -**ασία**, ἡ, *finishing off, completing*, of painters, πρὸς τὴν ἀ. τὴν τῶν εἰκόνων Pl.*Prt*.312d; *execution, workmanship*, Arist.*Po*.1448ᵇ18. II. *causing, producing*, ἀ. χάριτος καὶ ἡδονῆς Pl.*Grg*.462c; ἔργου, ὑγιείας, *Euthphr*.13d, e; ἐνύλων εἰδῶν Iamb.*Comm.Math*.9. III. *working off* of a debt, *IG*5(1).1390.77. IV. ἡ ἀ. τῶν νόσων *treatment*, Pl.*Alc*.2.140b; τοῦ χώματος *upkeep*, *POxy*.729.8 (ii A.D.). V. *efficacy*, ἡ ἐν ταῖς θυσίαις ἀ. Iamb.*Myst*.5.8, al. -**αστικός**, ή, όν, *fit for finishing, effecting, causing*, c. gen., Pl.*R*.527b, Epicur.*Sent*.26, Phld.*Rh*.1.345 S., S.E.*M*.4.4, etc.: ἡ -κή (sc. τέχνη) *the art of making*, τινός Pl.*Epin*.975c.

***ἄπεργος**, ον, *idle*, f.l. for ἀργός, Artem.1.42. II. *obsolete*, Phld.*Rh*.1.354 S.

**ἀπέργω**, v. ἀπείργω.

**ἀπέρδω**, *bring to an end, finish*, ἱρήϊα Hdt.4.62.

**ἀπερεί**, Adv. = ὡσπερεί, from ἅπερ, S.*El*.189 (lyr.).

***ἀπερείδω**, *fix, settle*, τὰς ὄψεις Plu.2.681f; τὴν ὄψιν πρός τι Luc.*Dem.Enc*.17; δι' ἄλλα τὴν γνῶσιν *support*, Iamb.*Protr*.5. 2. intr., = Pass., ἔνθα ἡ ὄψις ἀπερείδῃ Luc.*DDeor*.20.8; but, II. used by earlier writers in Med. with pf. Pass. in med. sense, *support oneself upon, rest upon*, ἀ. ἐν τῷ χαλινῷ, of a horse, *lean upon* the bit, X.*Eq*.10.7; ὀκτὼ τοῖς μέλεσι ἀ. *supporting himself on*.., Pl.*Smp*.190a, cf. *Ti*.44e, Arist.*PA*684ᵃ3; πείσμασιν, of a ship, Archimel.ap.Ath.5.209d, al.; ἀ. εἰς τοῦτο *to be fixed steadily on*.., Pl.*R*.508d; εἰς ἓν κεφάλαιον ἀ. *rest entirely on*.., ib.581a; ἀ. ἐπί τι *rely on*, Plb.28.20.8; πρὸς τὴν γῆν Hp.*Art*.52: abs., Arist.*IA*705ᵃ9. III. Med. in act. sense, ἀ. εἰς τοῦτο [τὸ οὖς] X.*Cyn*.5.32; τὴν χεῖρα πρός τινα Plu.*Sull*.35; τὰς ὄψεις εἴς τι Id.2.521d; ἀ. ἐλπίδας εἴς τινα, ἐπί τινα, *fix one's* hopes *upon* one, Plb.23.5.3, 28.2.3, cf. Plu.*Dio*42; ἀ. ὀργὴν εἴς τινα, χάριν ἐπί τινα, *direct one's* anger, *one's* gratitude, *towards* him, Plb.1.69.7, 23.3.6, cf. Plu.2.775e; ἀ. εἰς Περικλέα τὴν ὑπόνοιαν Id.*Per*.32; of Fortune, τὴν νέμεσιν εἰς τὸν οἶκον Id.2.198d; ἀ. ἄγνοιαν ἐπί τινας *throw the blame of* their ignorance *upon*.., Plb.38.9.5; ἐπὶ τὴν τύχην τοὺς ὀδυρμοὺς Plu.2.168a. 2. ἀ. λείαν εἰς τόπον *place, deposit in*.., Plb.3.92.9; τὰς δυνάμεις εἰς ἀσφαλὲς ἀπηρεῖσθαι Id.3.66.9; ὠδῖνας Call.*Del*.120.

**ἀπερείσιος**, ον, = ἀπειρέσιος (q.v.); ἀπερείσι' ἄποινα *countless* ransom, Il.1.13, al.; ἔδνα 16.178; δῶρα A.R.1.419; ἄλγος *AP*7.363.

**ἀπέρει-σις**, εως, ἡ, *leaning upon, pressure, resistance*, Pl.*Cra*.427a; ἀ. πρὸς τὰς χεῖρας Arist.*IA*705ᵃ18, cf. *Pr*.885ᵇ1. II. *infliction*, τιμωρίας Plu.2.1130d. ***-σμα**, ατος, τό, *prop, stay*, Hsch.

**ἀπερεύ-γομαι**, *belch forth, disgorge*, τι Hp.*Morb*.2.60, Nic.*Al*.380, etc.; ἀ. ἄχνην, of a river, *empty itself*, D.P.693, 981. -**ξις**, εως, ἡ, *belching forth*, Aret.*SA*1.9.

**ἀπερημόομαι**, *to be left destitute of*, τῆς τοῦ δαίμονος ἐπιμελείας Pl.*Plt*.274b; *to be isolated*, ἀπὸ τῶν ὄντων Id.*Sph*.237d; ἀπηρημωμένος *in isolation*, ἐν ψιλὸν ἀ. Plot.6.6.11.

**ἀπέρημος**, ον, strengthd. for ἔρημος, Sch.Pi.*N*.4.88.

**ἀπερητύω** [ῡ], *keep back, hinder*, A.R.1.772.

**ἀπερι-άγνιστος**, ον, *not purified*, prob.l. for ἀπεριόριστος, Hsch. -**βλεπτος**, ον, *not looked at from all sides*: hence, *limitless*, ἀ. καὶ παμπληθὴ θεωρίας ἔκτασιν Iamb.*VP*29.162, cf. *AB*421; *incomprehensible*, Hsch., Suid. II. Act., *regardless*, Phryn.*PS*p.10 B. -**βλητος**, ον, *without* περιβολή (q.v.), λόγος Hermog.*Id*.1.11. -**γένητος**, ον, *not to be overcome*, D.S.3.30; φύσις Corn.*ND*31. ***-γραπτος**, ον, *not cancelled, valid*, διαθήκη *PLond*.1.77.51. -**γράφος**, ον, *not rounded*, περιόδου βάσις D.H.*Comp*.22. 2. *not circumscribed*, Ph.1.5, al., Procl.*Inst*.93, Dam.*Pr*.71; *undetermined*, of time, Chrysipp.*Stoic*.2.67. 3. *unlimited*, ἀριθμῷ *Stoic*.3.79. Adv. -φως Ph.1.47, Corn.*Rh*.p.396 H. -**έργαστος**, ον, *not wrought carefully, simple*, in Adv. -τως Hierocl.*Prov*.p.464 B. -**εργία**, ἡ, *artlessness*, Perict.ap.Stob.4.28.19. -**εργος**, ον, *not over-busy, artless, simple*, Hp.*Decent*.3; ἀγωγή Gal.13.168; of things, Dsc.*Eup*.1.35, Sor.2.11; ἀφελὴς καὶ ἀ. χρῆσις Ath.6.274a: Sup., ib.b; τὸ ἀ. *simplicity*, Plu.2.1144f, Ach.Tat.5.27. Adv. -γως Ceb.21, D.H.*Dem*.9, Sor.1.46, S.E.*P*.1.240, Ael.*VH*12.1.

**ἀπερίζομαι**, *contend*, Suid.

**ἀπερι-ήγητος**, ον, *not traced out*, ἀ. καθάπερ τινὶ περιγραφῇ Pl.*Lg*.770b; ἀ. τῷ πλήθει *innumerable*, Simp.*in Ph*.178.29. -**ήχητος**, ον, *not encompassed by sound*, *AB*422. -**θλάστως**, Adv. *without crushing*, Sor.2.60. -**κάθαρτος** [κᾰ], ον, *unpurified, impure*, Lxx *Le*.19.23, Ph.1.346. ***-κάλυπτος** [κᾰ], ον, *uncovered, exposed*, in Adv. -τως *undisguisedly*, Hld.8.5. -**κοπος**, ον, *without hindrance* or *interruption*, in Adv. -πως Tz.ad Lyc.1432. -**κτητος**, ον, *not gaining wealth*, Ptol.*Tetr*.182. -**κτύπητος** [ῠ], ον, *not surrounded with noise*, Suid. -**λάλητος** [λᾰ], ον, *not to be out-talked* or *without skill in circumlocution*, Ar.*Ra*.839:—cf. Hsch. ἀπεριλάλητον (ἀπεριάλλητον cod.)· ἀνεξαπάτητον, ἀφελῆ. -**ληπτος**, ον, *uncircumscribed*, ἐξουσία ἀ. *absolute* power, Plu.*Pomp*.25; *indeterminate*, *Theol.Ar*.58; *not to be embraced* or *comprehended*, λόγῳ Ph.2.24; ἐπιστήμη Iamb.*VP*29.159: abs., τῷ ἀ. τῆς δυνάμεως Plot.6.9.6, cf. Procl.*Inst*.150; *incomprehensible*, Iamb.*Myst*.1.7, Dam.*Pr*.7; ἀ. κατὰ τὸν ἀριθμὸν κόσμοι Gal.8.159, cf. A.D.*Synt*.5.14; *indefinite* (opp. *infinite*) οὐχ ἁπλῶς ἄπειροι ἀλλὰ μόνον ἀ. Epicur.*Ep*.1 p.8 U., cf. *Placit*.1.3.8, Corn.*ND*9. -**λῠτος**, ον, *not annulled* or *cancelled, valid*, *BGU*1170.58 (i B.C.), *POxy*.713.39 (i A.D.). -**μάχητος** [μᾰ], ον, *not worth contending for*, δόγμα Ph.1.2. II. *free from need of contention*, βίος Max.Tyr.36.1. -**μέριμνος**, ον, in Adv. -νως *unthinkingly*, Ar.*Nu*.136. -**νόητος**, ον, *incomprehensible*, v.l. in S.E.*P*.2.70, Ph.1.581, Dam.*Pr*.4, *PMag.Par*.1.1138. 2. *inconceivable*, i.e. *indefinitely short*, χρόνος Epicur.*Ep*.1 p.10 U. II. *unintelligent*, Eust.644.43. III. Adv. -τως *inadvisedly*, Plb.4.57.10. 2. *imperceptibly*, S.E.*P*.3.145 codd. -**οδος**, ον, *not periodic*, D.H.*Comp*.23, cf. 26. -**οπτος**, ον, *unregarding, reckless of*, πάντων Th.1.41, J.*AJ*19.1.11: abs., Onos.1.22. Adv. -τως Poll.3.117. -**όριστος**, ον, *unlimited, infinite*, Longin.16.1, 44.6, Ph.1.187; ἐπιστήμαις ἀ. *undefinable*, Iamb.*Comm.Math*.7. Adv. -τως Gal.7.469. 2. of poems in uniform metre, *indefinite in length*, Heph.*Poëm*.6.2. -**ουσίαστος**, ον, *without wealth*, Eust.1768.54. -**πλάνητος** [λᾰ], ον, *without wandering* or *deviating*, Id.1308.46. -**πνευστος**, ον, *sheltered from wind*, Agathin.ap.Orib.10.7.16. -**πτυκτος**, ον, *not wrapped up*, J.*AJ*3.7.5. -**πτωτος**, ον, *not liable to*, τινός or τινί (dub. l.) Dsc.2.47; τινί D.L.7.122, cf. *Stoic*.3.152. II. *not stumbling*, of the Stoic sage, Arr.*Epict*.1.1.31, al. Adv., Comp. -ότερον 4.6.26. -**σάλπιγκτος**, ον, *not surrounded by the sound of trumpets*, Pyrrhus ap.Stob.4.13.60. -**σκεπτος**, ον, *inconsiderate, thoughtless*, Th.4.108, D.C *Fr*.57.25. Adv. -τως Th.4.10, 6.57, Ph.2.340, al., D.H.6.10: Comp. -ότερον Th.6.65, Chrysipp.*Stoic*.3.125. II. Pass., *uninvestigated*, πολλὰ ἀ. καταλιπεῖν Ph.1.387. -**σκοπος**, ον, = foreg., Suid. s.v. ἀπερίγραπτοι. ***-σπαστος**, ον, *not drawn hither and thither, not distracted* or *hindered*, Plb.2.67.7; ὕπνος Philum.ap.Orib.45.29.57; θεωρία Porph.*Abst*.1.36; τὸ ἀ. *freedom from distractions*, Plu.2.521c, Lxx *Si*.41.1; παρέχεσθαί τινα ἀ. *guarantee against annoyance*, *BGU*1057.22 (i B.C.); but ἀ. τῆς σῆς εὐεργεσίας *not able to be roused by* it, Lxx *Wi*.16.11. Adv. -τως Plb.2.20.10, 1 *Ep.Cor*.7.35; καθῆσθαι Arr.*Epict*.1.29.59. 2. *uninterrupted, free from digressions*, D.H.*Th*.9; τὸ ἀ. τῆς ἐξουσίας *the fact of* power *not passing from hand to hand*, Plu.*Arist*.5. Adv. -τως *continually*, ἐπαινεῖ τὸν οἶνον Ath.1.16c.

**ἀπερίσσευτος**, = ἀπέριττος, Phint.ap.Stob.4.23.61ᵃ.

**ἀπέρισσος**, ον, v. ἀπέριττος.

**ἀπερισσοτρύφητος** [ῠ], ον, *not luxuriously fed*, δίζυς Timo 3.

**ἀπερι-στᾰτος**, ον, *not stood around*: and so, I. *unguarded*, ῥαστῶναι Plb.6.44.8. 2. *solitary*, Ps.-Phoc.26, Arr.*Epict*.4.1.159; *not crowded*, D.L.7.5. 3. Medic., of wounds or ulcers, *free from complications*, Gal.13.498, al. II. *without explanatory circumstances*, Hermog.*Stat*.1. III. *not encompassed by dangers*, βίος Max.Tyr.36.3. -**στικτος**, ον, *not dotted round*, opp. περιεστιγμένος, ἀ. διπλῆ Sch.Il.p.xlii Dind., etc.; εὐθεῖα Gal.19.750. ***-τμητος**, ον, *uncircumcised*, Lxx *Ge*.17.14, al., J.*BJ*1.1.2: metaph., καρδίᾳ Lxx *Ez*.44.7, cf. *Act.Ap*.7.51, al. II. *not clipped* or *circumscribed*, φύσις Plu.2.495c. ***-τρεπτος**, ον, *not to be turned* or *moved, immutable*, Sm.*Ps*.95(96).10, Plu.2.983c. Adv. -τως S.E.*M*.1.53. -**τροπος**, ον, *unheeding*, S.*El*.182 (lyr.).

**ἀπέριττος**, ον, *without superfluity, plain, simple*, λιτοὶ καὶ ἀ. Zeno *Stoic*.1.57, cf. D.H.*Lys*.15, Plu.2.267f, Philostr.*VS*1.23.2; τὸ ἀ. τῆς τροφῆς Luc.*Nigr*.26; μηροί, γαστήρ, *perfectly modelled*, Philostr.Jun.*Im*.14,15. Adv. -ττως *plainly*, D.S.12.26; *frugally*, Simp.*in Epict*.p.33 D.

**ἀπεριττότης**, ητος, ἡ, *simplicity*, λόγου S.E.*M*.2.23.

***ἀπερίττωτος**, ον, *without* περιττώματα, φύσις, τροφή, Thphr.*CP*6.10.3, 17.9.

**ἀπερι-φερής**, ές, *not round* or *rounded*, Thphr.*CP*6.1.6. **-φραστος**, ον, *without circumlocution*, Eust.1941.59. Adv. -τως ib.1112.42. **-φρονήτως**, Adv. *without malice prepense*, ἀ. καὶ ἀκαταγνώστως *Sammelb.*4774.5. **-ψυκτος**, ον, *free from chill*, τηρεῖν Gal. 11.475, cf. Sor.2.14.

**ἀπερκτικός**, = ἀπειρκτικός, prob.l. for παρεκτικός, Alex.Aphr.*in Sens.*97.

**ἀπεροπεύς**, έως, ὁ, = ἠπεροπευτής, *EM*433.45.

**ἀπερριμμένως**, Adv. pf. part. Pass. of ἀπορρίπτω, *negligently*, Aristeas 28.

**ἀπέρρω**, *go away, be gone*, E.*HF*260; ἄπερρε *away! begone!* Ar. *Nu.*783, *Ec.*169; οὐκ ἀπερρήσεις σὺ θᾶττον; Cratin.123.

**ἀπερρωγώς**, υῖα, ός, (ἀπορρήγνυμι) *broken*, i.e. *unsound, unreliable*, σημεῖον S.E.*M.*8.165.

**ἀπερυγγάνω**, aor. ἀπήρῠγον, *belch forth, disgorge*, τὴν κραιπάλην Alciphr.3.32, cf. Nic.*Th.*253: metaph., *vent*, D.L.5.77, Ph.1. 639. II. abs., *eructate*, Arist.*Pr.*962ᵃ8.

**ἀπερυθριάω**, *to put away blushes, to be past blushing*, Ar.*Nu.*1216; ἀπερυθριᾷ πᾶς, ἐρυθριᾷ δ' οὐδεὶς ἔτι Men.782, cf. Plu.2.547b, Luc.*Jud. Voc.*8, Lib.*Decl.*15.43; πρὸς πάντας Jul.*Or.*6.196d. Adv. **ἀπηρυθριᾰκότως**, *shamelessly*, Apollod.Com.13.10. 2. *cease to be red* or *flushed*, Luc.*Lex.*4.

**ἀπερῠκάνω**, = sq., Epic.Anon.*Oxy.*422.6.

**※ἀπερύκω** [ῡ], impf. ἀπήρυκον Plb.16.1.3: aor. ἀπήρυξα X.*An.*5.8. 25, Isyll.74 (tm.), Maiist.45 (tm.):—*keep off* or *away*, εἰ γὰρ Ἀθήνη.. βελέων ἀπερύκοι ἐρωήν Il.17.562; σύας τε κύνας τ' ἀ. Od.18.105; ἀπερύκοι.. Φοῖβος κακὰν φάτιν S.*Aj.*186 (lyr.); πολέμιον X.l.c., cf. Plb.16.1.3: c. gen., στρατὸν.. Μήδων ἀπέρυκε τῆσδε πόλεος Thgn. 775: c. acc. et inf., *prevent* one *from*.., οὔτε σε κωμάζειν ἀπερύκομεν οὔτε καλεῦμεν Id.1207:—less freq. in Prose, ἀ. τινί τι *keep off from*, ταῦτα ἡ εὐτυχίη οἱ ἀπερύκει Hdt.1.32, cf. X.*Oec.*5.6; τοὺς λύκους ἀπὸ τῶν προβάτων *Mem.*2.9.2, cf. Arist.*HA*620ᵃ12:—Pass., πατρῴης γῆς ἀπερυκόμενος *debarred from*.., Thgn.1210:—Med., ἀλλήλων ἔριδος (v.l. ἔριδας) δὴν (δῆγμ' Bgk.) ἀπερυκόμενοι *desisting from*.., Id. 494; ἀπερύκου (sc. φωνῆς) *abstain from* speech, S.*OC*169 (lyr.):—later in act. sense, ἀπερύκεο νούσους, to be read in Maced.*Pae.*23. 2. *withhold*, σῖγα νόον βουλήν τ' ἀπερύκων A.R.3.174.

**ἀπερῠσῑβόω**, (ἐρυσίβη) *destroy by mildew*, Thphr.*CP*5.10.3 (Pass.). 2. *produce mildew*, ib.5.9.13.

**ἀπερύω** [ῠ], *tear off from*, ῥινὸν ἀπ' ὀστεόφιν ἐρύσαι Od.14.134; πόρτιν μητρὸς ἀπειρύσσαντες Q.S.14.259:—Med., *AP*7.730 (Pers.) (tm.).

**※ἀπέρχομαι**, fut. -ελεύσομαι (Att. fut. ἄπειμι): pf. -ελήλυθα: aor. -ῆλθον:—*go away, depart from*, c. gen., πάτρης Il.24.766; οἴκου Od. 2.136, cf. S.*OC*1165, etc.; λόγου E.*IT*546; ἀ. ἀπὸ τοῦ βουλευτηρίου Th.8.92; ἐκ τῆς χώρας Id.1.89, etc.: metaph., ἀ. ἐκ δακρύων *cease from* tears, E.*Or.*295. 2. with εἰς, implying *departure from* one place *and arrival at* another, ἀ. ἐς τὰς Σάρδις Hdt.1.22; ἀ. εἰς Θουρίους οἰκήσοντες And.4.12; παρά τινα Luc.*Tim.*11; ἀ. ἐπ' οἴκου *depart* homewards, Th.1.92; ἀθῷος οἴκαδε Archipp.40; ἀπῆλθεν ὅθεν.. *went back to* the place whence he came, Men.481.3: metaph., ἀ. εἰς τὴν ἀρχαίαν φύσιν Pl.*Smp.*193c. 3. abs., Hdt.1.190, etc.; ταχεῖ' ἀπέρχεται (sc. ἡ νόσος) S.*Ph.*808; κατ' ὀφλὼν ἀ. Ar.*Ach.*689; ἄπελθε τουτονὶ λαβών take him and *be off!* Id.*Av.*948; ἀπελθόντος ἐνιαυτοῦ Pl.*Lg.*954d; νυκτὸς -ομένης Arat.315. 4. c. part., ἀ. νικῶν *come off* conqueror, Aristid.2.2 J., cf. Plu.*Ages.*7, etc. 5. *spread abroad*, ἀπῆλθεν ἡ ἀκοὴ αὐτοῦ εἰς Συρίαν *Ev.Matt.*4.24. II. *depart from life*, ἀ. κάτω E.*Alc.*379, cf. S.*Ant.*818 (lyr.): abs., D.L.3.6, *AP*11.335, cf. Ph.1.513, Plot.4.7.15; εἰς τοὺς θεοὺς *PPetr.*2p.45 (iii B.C.).

**ἀπερῶ**, Ion. ἀπερέω, v. ἀπεῖπον.

**ἀπερωεύς**, έως, ὁ, *thwarter*, ἐμῶν μενέων ἀπερωεύς Il.8.361.

**ἀπερωέω**, *retire* or *withdraw from*, τῷ κε τάχα.. πολέμου ἀπερωήσειας Il.16.723.

**ἀπερωπός**, όν, *inconsiderate, cruel*, A.*Ch.*600; expl. by ἀναιδής, σκληρός, οἷον ἀπερίοπτος καὶ ἀπερίβλεπτος by Phryn.*PS*p.10 B., cf. *EM*120.41, Hsch. Adv. -πῶς· θαυμαστῶς, ἀδοκήτως, Id.

**ἀπέρωτος**, ον, (ἔρως) *loveless, unloving*, ἔρως ἀπέρωτος, like γάμος ἄγαμος, read by M² in A.*Ch.*600; but v. foreg.

**ἄπες**, Ion. for ἄφες, v. sub ἀφίημι.

**ἄπεσθαι** (= ἕπ-)· ἀκολουθῆσαι, Hsch.

**ἀπεσθέομαι**, Med., (ἐσθής) *undress oneself*, Luc.*Lex.*5 (in pf. part. ἀπησθημένοι).

**ἀπεσθίω**, fut. ἀπέδομαι Ar.*Av.*26: aor. part. ἀποφαγών Id.*Eq.*497: pf. ἀπεδήδοκα Id.*Ra.*984:—Pass., aor. 1 ἀπηδέσθην Pl.Com.138: pf. ἀπεδήδεμαι Arist.*HA*591ᵃ5:—*eat, gnaw off*, τοὺς δακτύλους Hermipp. 24, cf. Ar.*Av.*26; ἀπεσθίει μου τὴν ἀκοήν Hermipp.52; τίς τὴν κεφαλὴν ἀπεδήδοκεν τῆς μαινίδος; Ar.*Ra.*984; ἀπεσθίει τὴν ῥῖνα τἀνθρώπου D.25.61. II. *leave off eating*, τὰ πετραῖα τῶν ἰχθυδίων Theopomp. Com.62.

**ἀπεσκής**, ές, (πέσκος) *without a bow-case*, τόξα S.*Fr.*626.

**ἀπέσκληκα**, v. ἀποσκλῆναι.

**ἀπεσκληρυμμένως**, Adv., (ἀποσκληρύνω) ἀ. ἔχων, = ἀπεσκληκώς, *AB*422.

**ἀπεσσία**, = ἄφεσις, Hsch. (dub.).

**ἀπεσσούα**, *he is gone off*, Lacon. for ἀπεσσύη, ἀπεσσύθη, aor. Pass. of ἀποσεύω, X.*HG*1.1.23 (dub.).

**ἀπεσσύμεθα**, -συτο, Ep. sync. aor. Pass. of ἀποσεύω.

**ἀπεστώ**, οῦς, ἡ, Ion. Noun, (ἄπειμι, cf. εὐεστώ) *absence*, ἐπαισχυνομένους τῇ ἀπεστοῖ τῆς μάχης Hdt.9.85, cf. Call.*Fr.*340.

**ἀπεσχᾰρ-όω**, *remove a scab*, Zopyr.ap.Orib.14.61.2:—Pass., Eust. 1575.43. **-ωτικός**, ή, όν, *removing scabs*, Paul.Aeg.4.34, 6.66.

**※ἀπέτηλος**, ον, *leafless*, *AP*6.190 (Gaet.).

**ἄπετρος**, ον, *without stones*, Eust.1736.9.

**ἀπευδιασμός**, ὁ, (εὐδιάζω) *making calm*, Porph.*VP*29 (pl.).

**ἀπευδοκιμῶ**· *depudesco*, *Gloss.*

**ἀπευήκασιν**· ἐξηραμμέναι εἰσίν, Hsch.

**ἀπευθᾰνᾰτίζω**, *die well* or *happily*, Lxx 2 *Ma.*6.28.

**ἀπευθής**, ές, (πυνθάνομαι) *not inquired into, unknown*, κείνου δ'.. ὄλεθρον ἀπευθέα θῆκεν Od.3.88, cf. Arat.259, etc.; ἀ. ἀκοῇ Max.Tyr. 17.9. II. Act., *not inquiring, ignorant*, ἦλθον.. ἀπευθής Od.3.184, cf. Cerc.5.3: c. gen., D.P.194, *APl.*4.303.

**ἀπευθ-υνσις**, εως, ἡ, *adjustment, setting*, Paul.Aeg.6.92. **-υντέον**, *one must set straight, adjust*, Sor.2.60. **-ύνω**, fut. -υνῶ S. *Ichn.*161:—*make straight, restore*, πάντα ὀρθὰ ἀ. Pl.*Ti.*71d; χέρας δεσμοῖς ἀ. *bind* his arms *straight*, i.e. *behind* him, S.*Aj.*72: metaph., ἀπευθύνεται τὸ ὑποκλάζον τοῦ πυρετοῦ Paul.Aeg.2.47. b. in military drill, *dress*, λόχον Ascl.*Tact.*12.11, etc. 2. *guide aright, direct*, δεῦρ' ἀ. μολεῖν A.*Ag.*1667; ἀ. βροτῶν τοὺς ἀγνωμοσύνην τιμῶντας *corrects, chastises* them, E.*Ba.*884 (lyr.); ἐκ πρύμνης ἀ. *to steer*, Pl.*Criti.* 109c; πλήκτροις ἀ. τρόπιν S.*Fr.*142, cf. *Ichn.*l.c.; ἀ. πόλιν *govern, rule*, Id.*OT*104; ἀ. τὰ κοινὰ Aeschin.3.158; κλήρῳ ἀ. [τὴν ἰσότητα] *regulate*, Pl.*Lg.*757b, cf. *Alt.*282e; ἀ. τι πρός τι *to adjust*, Arr.*Epict.*4.12.16, cf. Luc.*Im.*12; ταῖς συλλαβαῖς ἀ. τοὺς χρόνους D.H.*Comp.*11. II. τὸ ἀπευθυσμένον (sc. ἔντερον) *intestinum rectum*, Dsc.1.99, Heliod.ap. Orib.44.23.55, Gal.2.573, etc.

**ἄπευκος**, ον, *without resin*, Thphr.*HP*3.9.3 (in Comp. -ότερος).

**ἀπευκτ-αῖος**, α, ον, = ἀπευκτός, Pl.*Ax.*369b (Sup.), Plu.2.289b; τάραχοι *CPHerm.*119ʳiv 16 (iii A.D.), cf. A.D.*Synt.*252.10. Adv. -αίως *to the loss of our hopes*, [τελευτῆσαι] *POxy.*1114.24 (iii A.D.). **-ικός**, ή, όν, *deprecatory*, ὕμνοι Men.Rh.p.342 S. **-ός**, ή, όν, Luc.*Pseudol.*12, Hld.7.25: (ἀπεύχομαι):—*to be deprecated, abominable*, πήματα A.*Ag.*638; ἀ. τὸ δεηθῆναι τούτων Pl.*Lg.*628c; τὰ ἀ. Id.*Ep.*353e.

**ἀπεύλογον**, τό, *of irregular shape*, dub. in Hero*Stereom.*2.32.

**※ἀπευλῠτέω**· *expedio, explico, exploro*, *Gloss.*

**ἀπευνάζω**, *lull to sleep*, ἀπευνασθέντος κακοῦ (ἀπ' εὐνασθέντος κ. cod. L) S.*Tr.*1242.

**ἄπευστος**, ον, = ἀπευθής, Hsch.

**※ἀπευτακτέω**, *deliver* or *pay regularly*, τοὺς φόρους Str.4.6.9:—Pass., Id.7.4.6, *UPZ*42.15 (ii B.C.).

**ἀπευτελεῖσθαι**· ἀπάρξασθαι, Hsch.

**ἄπευτος**, ον, = ἄπευστος, Hsch.

**ἀπευφημ-έω**, *deprecate*, v.l. for ἐπ-, Philostr.*VA*5.19, 7.10. **-ισμός**, ὁ, -οῦ χάριν out of *politeness*, Phld.*Lib.*p.56 O.

**※ἀπευχᾰριστέω**, *show gratitude*, τινί *IG*5(1).1145.35 (Gythium).

**ἀπεύχετος**, ον, = ἀπευκτός, A.*Ch.*155, 625 (lyr.).

**ἀπευχή**, ἡ, *deprecation*, Men.Rh.p.343 S. (pl.).

**ἀπεύχομαι**, *wish* a thing *away, wish* it *may not happen*, c. acc. rei, ἀπεύχου ταῦτα, πρὸς θεῶν E.*Hipp.*891; τί μάλιστ' ἂν ἀπευξαίμεθα; D.20.157; ἀ. τι τοῖς θεοῖς μηδαμῶς γίγνεσθαι *pray* the gods it *may not be*, Pl.*Lg.*687d, cf. D.8.51: without μή, ἀπεύχεσθε ἰδεῖν Id.6.23, cf. 20.106: also τοῦτο.. μὴ γένοιτο.. ἀπεύχομαι Ar.*Th.*714. II. *reject, despise*, μητρὸς αἷμα A.*Eu.*608. III. *avert by prayer*, Philostr.*VA* 6.41.

**ἀπεύω**, *scorch off*, v. ἀφεύω.

**ἀπευωνίζω**, *cheapen*, dub. in Luc.*Nigr.*23.

**ἀπεφεισμένως**, *abundantly*, dub. in Str.15.1.24.

**※ἀπέφθῐον**, v. ἀποφθίω.

**※ἄπεφθος**, ον, by dissimilation for ἄφεφθος, (ἀφέψω) *boiled down*, ἄ. χρυσὸς *refined* gold, Thgn.449, Hdt.1.50; χρυσίον Th.2.13; ὕδωρ ἄ. water *purified by boiling*, Alex.198; μέλι ἄ. *despumated*, Sor.1.118.

**ἀπέφρυσεν**· ἀπέζεσεν, ἀπέβαλεν, Hsch.

**ἀπεχθαίρω**, *hate utterly, detest*, τινά Il.3.415, Opp.*H.*5.420, Jul.*Or.* 2.86b, Vett.Val.349.14:—Med., aor. 1 ἀπηχθήραντο Q.S.13.255. II. *make utterly hateful*, ὅς τέ μοι ὕπνον ἀ. καὶ ἐδωδήν Od.4.105.

**ἀπεχθάνομαι**, Od.2.202, Ar.*Pl.*910, Pl.*Ap.*24a, etc.: impf. ἀπηχθανόμην Cratin.36, X.*An.*7.7.10: fut. ἀπεχθήσομαι Hdt.1.89, E.*Alc.*71, Pl.*Phlb.*28d, etc.; ἀπεχθᾰνοῦμαι Them.*Or.*26.322c: pf. ἀπήχθημαι Th.1.75, 2.63, X.*An.*7.6.34, etc.: aor. ἀπηχθόμην Il.24.27, etc.; subj. ἀπέχθωμαι ib.4.53; inf. ἀπεχθέσθαι (not ἀπέχθεσθαι), v. ἀπέχθομαι; part. ἀπεχθόμενος Pl.*Min.*321a: (ἔχθος):—Pass., *to be hated, incur hatred*, ἀπεχθάνεαι δ' ἔτι μᾶλλον Od.2.202; elswh. in Hom. always in aor., mostly c. dat. pers., *to be* or *become hateful to* one, *incur* his *hate*, ἀπήχθετο πᾶσι θεοῖσι Il.6.140; ἶσον γάρ σφιν πᾶσιν ἀπήχθετο κηρὶ μελαίνῃ 3.454; οὔτε τί μοι πᾶς δῆμος ἀπεχθόμενος χαλεπαίνει nor does the people *roused to hate against* me distress me, Od.16.114; σοὶ ἐμέθεν ἀπήχθετο φροντίσδην Sapph.41, Hdt.1.89, 3.1, Antipho6.11, Th.1.136, etc.; ἀ. πρός τινα *to be hateful* in his eyes, E.*Med.*290; *to be irritated* against, πρὸς τὴν ἡγεμονίαν Plu.*Galb.*18, cf. J.*AJ*13.9.3: c. dat. rei, *to be hated for* a thing, Pl.*Ap.*24a, cf. Th.2.63 (but also in act. sense, *dislike*, τῇ φιλοσοφίᾳ, τῷ οἴνῳ Philostr.*VA*3.22, *Im.*2.17): c. part., ἀ. ποιῶν And.4.10; θριάμβους ἀναρύτουσ' ἀπηχθάνου Cratin. 36. II. causal, λόγοι ἀπεχθανόμενοι language *that causes hatred*, opp. οἱ πρὸς φιλίαν ἄγουσι, X.*Smp.*4.58.

**ἀπέχθεια**, ἡ, *hatred*, 1. felt towards another, πρός τινα D.18. 36, Arist.*Pol.*1305ᵃ23; διὰ τὴν ἀ. τοῦ πάθους *for* it, ib.1274ᵃ40. 2. felt by others towards one, *enmity, odium*, ὁ πράξας τὴν ἀ. αὐτῶν δίκαιος φέρεσθαι Antipho3.4.2, cf. Pl.*Ap.*28a, D.3.13, etc.: in pl., *enmities*, Pl.*Ap.*23a, interpol. in D.9.64; θεοῖς δι' ἀπεχθείας ἐλθεῖν to be *hated* by them, A.*Pr.*121 (lyr.); δι' ἀ. γίγνεταί τι it becomes *hateful*, X.*Hier.*9.2; οὔτ' ἐκείνου πρὸς χάριν οὔτ' ἐμοῦ πρὸς ἀπέχθειαν D.5.7; ἀπέχθειαν φέρει τι it brings *odium*, Id.*Prooem.*44; πολλὴν ἔχει ἀ. Arist.*Pol.*1322$^a$2; δείσας τὴν πρὸς ὑμᾶς ἀ. *enmity* with you, Isoc.8.38; μετὰ πολλῆς ἀ. Plb.1.66.9.

**ἀπεχθές**, Adv. *yesterday*, A.D.*Synt.*235.26:—divisim ἀπ' ἐχθές *AP*11.35 (Phld.).

**ἀπεχθ-ήεις**, εσσα, εν, Adj. *odious, noxious*, Androm.ap.Gal.14.33. **-ημα**, ατος, τό, *object of hate*, E.*Tr.*425. **-ήμων**, ον, gen. ονος, worse form for sq., Poll.8.153. **-ής**, ές, *hateful*, S.*Ant.*50; *hostile*, Theoc.1.101; τὸ ἀ. Onos.37.3: Sup., Ph.1.604. II. *hated*, Isoc.1.12 (dub. l.); δάκρυα *IG*4.622 (Argos). Adv. -θῶς, ἔχειν τινί D.5.18; διακεῖσθαι D.Chr.32.70; πρός τινας D.H.7.31: Sup. -έστατα Poll.5.116. **-ητικός**, ή, όν, *full of hatred, envious*, opp. κόλαξ, Arist.*MM*1193$^a$22, *EE*1221$^a$26, 1233$^b$32. **-ομαι**, later form of ἀπεχθάνομαι, Theoc.7.45, Lyc.116, *AP*5.176 (Mel.), Plu.*Marc.*22, etc.; for in E.*Hipp.*1260 ἐπάχθομαι is the better reading; and the inf. ἀπέχθεσθαι freq. found in codd. should be written ἀπεχθέσθαι, cf. ἀπεχθάνομαι. **-ρεύω**, *to be hostile*, Phld.*Rh.*2.162 S. **-ρῶς**· ἐχθρωδῶς, Hsch.

⊛**ἀπέχω**, fut. ἀφέξω, and (Od.19.572) ἀποσχήσω: aor. ἀπέσχον:—*keep off* or *away from*, αἴ κεν Τυδέος υἱὸν ἀπόσχῃ Ἰλίου ἱρῆς Il.6.96,277; ἑκὰς νήσων ἀπέχων εὐεργέα νῆα Od.15.33; κληῖδες ἀπ' ὤμων αὐχέν' ἔχουσιν the collar-bone *parts* the neck *from* the shoulders, Il.22.324; Εὐβοίης ἀπέχειν.. αἶγας Orac.ap.Hdt.8.20, cf. 22; ἄπεχε τῆς βοὸς τὸν ταῦρον A.*Ag.*1125 (lyr.), cf. *Pr.*687 (lyr.). 2. c. dat. pers., τοι.. χεῖρας ἀφέξω Od.20.263. 3. with a Prep., ἀ. φρένα περισσῶν παρὰ φωτῶν E.*Ba.*427 (lyr.); ῥῖνα ἀπὸ κάκκης Ar.*Pax*162. 4. c. acc. only, *keep off* or *away*, σκοτεινὸν ἀ. ψόγον Pi.*N.*7.61; ἀ. φάσγανον E.*Or.*1519. 5. οὐδὲν ἀπέχει c. inf., nothing *hinders, debars* one *from* doing, Pl.*Cra.*407b, Plu.2.433a. II. Med., κακῶν ἄπο χεῖρας ἔχεσθαι *hold one's* hands *off* or *away from*.., Od.22.316; κυάμων ἄπο χεῖρας ἔχεσθε Emp.141; ἀθανάτων ἀ. χεῖρας A.*Eu.*350 (lyr.), cf. *Supp.*756, Pl.*Smp.*213d, 214d:—but mostly, 2. ἀπέχεσθαί τινος *hold oneself off* a thing, *abstain* or *desist from* it, πολέμου Il.8.35, al.; βοῶν Od.12.321; οὐδὲ.. σευ ἀφέξομαι *will* not *keep my hands off* thee, ib.19.489; Δεκελέης *abstain from ravaging* D., Hdt.9.73, cf. 1.66, 4.118, al., Th.1.20, etc.; *keep away from*, πόλεως X.*HG*7.3.10: in pf. Pass., μηδὲ τῶν μικρῶν ἀπεσχημένον D.27.47; ἀγορᾶς ἀπεσχ. Arist.*Pol.*1278$^a$25. 3. c. inf., ἀπέχεσθαι μὴ στρατεῦσαι *abstain from* marching, Th.5.25; λαμβάνειν ἀπέσχετο Philem.94.3; ἀπέχεσθαι τοῦ ποιεῖν X.*Mem.*4.2.3; οὐκ ἀ. τὸ μὴ οὐ ποιεῖν Id.*Cyr.*1.6.32, Pl.*R.*354b: also c. part., Jul.*Or.*1.43d. 4. abs., *refrain oneself*, D.21.61. III. intr. in Act., *to be away* or *far from*, c. gen. loci, τῶν Ἐπιπολῶν ἓξ ἢ ἑπτὰ σταδίους Th.6.97; ἀ. ἀπὸ Βαβυλῶνος, etc., Hdt.1.179, cf. 3.26, al.; ἀπὸ θαλάττης.. δώδεκα ὁδὸν ἡμερῶν ἀ. Euphro11.3; ἀ. παμπόλλων ἡμερῶν ὁδόν X.*Cyr.*1.1.3; τὸ μέσον ἴσον τῶν ἐσχάτων ἀ. Pl.*Prm.*145b; πλεῖστον ἀ. κατὰ τόπον Arist.*Mete.*363$^a$31; ἀ. τὴν ἡμίσειαν διάμετρον Id.*Cael.*293$^b$30, etc. b. *project, extend*, Id.*GA*781$^a$11; τὰ ἀπέχοντα *prominent parts*, *PA*655$^a$32. c. ἀποσχὼν τεσσαράκοντα μάλιστα σταδίους μὴ φθάσαι ἐλθὼν *failing to arrive in time by*.., Th.5.3. 2. of actions, *to be far from*, ἀπεῖχον τῆς ἐξευρέσιος οὐδὲν ἔλασσον *were* just *as far from* the discovery, Hdt.1.67; τοσοῦτον ἀπέχω τοῦ ποιεῖν τι ὥστε.. Isoc.6.70; τοσούτῳ πλέον ἡμῶν ἀπέχεις τοῦ πιστὰ λέγειν ὅσον.. ib.11.32; ἀπέχει τοῦ μὴ μετ' ὀργῆς [πράττειν] D.21.41; πλεῖστον ἀ. τινός *to be* as *far* as possible *from* doing, X.*Mem.*1.2.62; but τοσοῦτ' ἀπέχει τῶν χορηγῶν so far *is it from the thoughts of*.., D.21.59. 3. generally, *to be far removed from*, πολιτείας, μοναρχίας, Arist.*Pol.*1289$^b$2, 1293$^a$17; τοῦ μέσου Id.*EN*1109$^a$10. 4. *differ from*, οὐδέν τι ἀπεῖχε γαμετῆς γυναικός Hdn.1.16.4. 5. διαφύσιες.. ἧσιν οὐδὲν ἀπέχει ἀγγεῖα εἶναι nothing *is wanting*, Hp.*de Arte*10. IV. *have* or *receive in full*, τὴν ἀπόκρισιν Aeschin.2.50; τὸ χρέος ἀ. *receive* payment *in full*, Call.*Epigr.*55; χάριτας ib.51; ἀπέχω in receipts, *BGU*612.2 (i A.D.), etc.; ἀ. τὸν μισθόν Plu.*Sol.*22, *Ev.Matt.*6.2, al.; καρπὸν ἀ. τῶν πονηθέντων Plu.*Them.*17; ἀ. τὸ μέτριον Id.2.124e. 2. impers., ἀπέχει *it sufficeth, it is enough*, *Ev.Marc.*14.41, cf. *Anacreont.*15.33.

⊛**ἀπεψία**, ἡ, (ἄπεπτος) *indigestion*, etc.; δι' ἀπεψίαν Arist.*PA*668$^b$8: in pl., Id.*Mete.*381$^b$9, Plu.2.127d, Gal.8.34, S.E.*P.*1.131.

**ἀπέψω**, Ion. for ἀφέψω.

**ἀπέωσε**, v. ἀπωθέω. **ἀπεωστόν**· ἀπόθητον, Hsch. **ἀπηγενέες**· ἀποτεταγμένοι, Id.

**ἀπηγέομαι, ἀπήγημα, ἀπήγησις**, Ion. for ἀφηγ-.

**ἀπηγορ-έομαι**, Med., *defend oneself*, like ἀπολογέομαι, Arist.*Pr.*951$^a$23:—Act., *defend*, Simp.*in Cat.*17.2. **-ευμα**· ἀπολόγημα, Hsch. **-ημα**, ατος, τό, *defence*, opp. κατηγόρημα, Pl.*Lg.*765b. **-ία**, Dor. **ἀπαγ-**, ἡ, dub.l. in Pi.*Fr.*122.6 (pl.).

**ἀπήδᾰλος**, ον, *without rudder*, Arist.*IA*710$^a$8.

⊛**ἀπηθ-έω**, *strain off, filter*, Ar.*Ra.*943, Thphr.*HP*9.8.3. **-ημα**, ατος, τό, *that which is filtered off*, Asclep.ap.Gal.14.142, *Hippiatr.*6, 11. **-ητέον**, *one must strain off*, Dsc.5.88.

**ἀπήκει**· ἀπέχει, ἢ εἰς ὀξὺ συνάγει, Hsch. **ἀπηκολλύρισεν**· ἐν τῷ παραβεβλῆσθαι ἀπέστρυφε (Lacon.), Id.

**ἀπήκοος**, ον, (ἀκοή) *disobedient*, opp. ὑπήκοος, Hsch.

**ἀπηκρῑβωμένως**, Adv., (ἀπακριβόω) *exactly*, Plu.*Agis* 2 (v.l.); *sparingly*, Alex.213.4.

**ἄπηκτος**, ον, *not capable of being solidified*, Arist.*Mete.*385$^b$1, *GA*735$^b$30, *HA*520$^a$8. 2. *not solid*, θεμέλια Sor.1.47.

**ἀπηλγημένως**, Adv., (ἀπαλγέω) gloss on ἀπηλεγέως, Sch.Il.9.309.

**ἀπηλεγ-έω**, *neglect*, A.R.2.17. ⊛**-έως**, Adv. *without caring f*[or] *anything, outright, bluntly*, Hom. only in phrase μῦθον ἀπηλεγέω[ς] ἀποειπεῖν Il.9.309, Od.1.373; ἀ. πεπύθοιτο A.R.4.1469; νίσσετ[αι] ἀπηλεγέως *straightforwards, without looking about*, Id.1.785; *sternly* 4.687; prob. f.l. for ἀνηλ-, Q.S.1.226:—also **ἀπηλεγές**, Nic.*Th.*495, Opp.*C.*2.510. (From ἀλέγω, like νηλεγής, ἀνηλεγής.)

**ἀπηλιαστής**, οῦ, ὁ, opp. φιληλιαστής, *one who keeps away from the* Ἡλιαία, i.e. an enemy to law, with a play on ἥλιος (*not fond of basking in the sun*), Ar.*Av.*110.

**ἀπηλῐθιόομαι**, Pass., *become stupid, fatuous*, Dsc.5.17.

**ἀπῆλιξ**, Ion. for ἀφῆλιξ.

**ἀπηλῐ-ώτης** (with or without ἄνεμος), ου, ὁ, *east wind*, Hdt.4.22, 7.188, E.*Cyc.*19, Th.3.23; opp. ζέφυρος, Arist.*Mete.*363$^b$13, cf. *Mu.*394$^b$23, *Vent.*973$^a$13, al.—The Ion. form ἀπηλιώτης is retained in Att., and appears on the Tower of Andronicus Cyrrhestes, *CIG* 518; ἀφηλιώτης on a later table of the winds, *IG*14.1308, and in Latin authors, Catull.26.3, Seneca *QN*5.16.4, Gell.2.22.8. **-ωτικός**, ή, όν, *from the quarter of the* ἀπηλιώτης, Arist.*Mete.*364$^a$21, *POxy.*985 (i A.D.), Ptol.*Geog.*1.11.1.

⊛**ἀπηλλαγμένως**, Adv., (ἀπαλλάσσω) c. gen., *apart from*, ὀργῆς dub.l. in J.*AJ*17.5.6.

**ἀπηλλάζεις**· ἀπηλλαγμένος ἔσῃ, Hsch.

⊛**ἀπήμαντος**, ον, *unharmed, unhurt*, Od.19.282, cf. Hes.*Th.*955; ἀ. βίοτος a life *free from misery*, Pi.*O.*8.87; ἔστω δ' ἀπήμαντον be *misery far away*, A.*Ag.*378 (lyr.). II. Act., *unharming*, σθένος Id.*Supp.*576 (lyr.); of snakes, Nic.*Th.*492. Adv. -τως Tz. ad Lyc.886.

**ἀπήμβροτον**, v. ἀφαμαρτάνω.

**ἀπημελημένως**, Adv., (ἀπαμελέω) *carelessly*, Procop.*Vand.*1.4, al.

**ἀπήμιος**, ὁ, *averter of ill*, Ζεύς Paus.1.32.2.

**ἀπημονία**, ἡ, = sq., Call.*Jov.*92.

**ἀπημοσύνη**, ἡ, *freedom from harm, safety*, Thgn.758, *IG*12(5).215 (Paros). 2. *harmlessness*, Opp.*H.*2.647.

**ἀπήμων**, ον, gen. -ονος, (πῆμα) like ἀπήμαντος, *unharmed, unhurt*, ἀδάκρυτος καὶ ἀ. Il.1.415, al.; σὺν νηυσὶν ἀπήμονες ἦλθον Ἀχαιοί Od.4.487; νόστος ἀ. ib.519, cf. νῆες ἀπήμονες Opp.*H.*5.676; ὄλβος Pi.*Pae.*9.8; μοῖρα A.R.1.422; *without sorrow* or *care*, ἀ. κραδία κᾶδος ἀμφ' ἀλλότριον Pi.*N.*1.54, cf. *P.*10.22: c. gen., ἀ. πάσης οἰζύος A.*Eu.*893.—Rare in Prose, as Hdt.1.42, 4.179, Pl.*Phdr.*248c, Ph.1.393. II. Act., *doing no harm*: hence, *kindly, propitious*, οὖρον ἀπήμονά τε λιαρόν τε Od.7.266, cf. 12.167; πόντος Hes.*Op.*670; ὕπνον ἀπήμονά τε λιαρόν τε Il.14.164; μῦθος 13.748; πομποί Od.8.566; *without hostile intent*, A.*Supp.*186; πλοῦς νεῶν ἀ. *free from harm to* them, E.*IA*1575.

⊛**ἀπηναῖος**· ἀπήνης, Hsch.

**ἀπήνεια**, ἡ, (ἀπηνής) *rudeness, discourtesy*, Thphr.*Char.*15.1: in pl., A.R.2.1202. 2. *stiffness*, Heliod.ap.Orib.44.23.56, Sor.1.44.

**ἀπήνεμος**, ον, (ἄνεμος) *without wind*, D.Chr.6.33, *AB*424; ἀ. λιμήν Poll.1.100.

⊛**ἀπήνη** [ᾰ], ἡ, *four-wheeled wagon*, drawn by mules, ἡμίονοι ἕλκον τετράκυκλον ἀπήνην Il.24.324, cf. Od.6.57 with 69,72,73,82; much the same as ἅμαξα, cf. Il.24.266 with 324, Od.6.72 with 73: of a *racing-car*, drawn by mules, ἡμιόνοις ξεστᾷ τ' ἀπήνᾳ Pi.*P.*4.94, cf. *O.*5.3, Arist.*Fr.*568; ἦν γὰρ δὴ ἀπήνη.. ἡμιόνους ἀνθ' ἵππων ἔχουσα Paus.5.9.2. 2. later, any *car* or *chariot*, A.*Ag.*906, S.*OT*753; ἀ. πωλική ib.803; *war-chariot*, Str.4.5.2; cf. καπάνα. 3. metaph., *any conveyance*, ναΐα ἀ. *ship*, E.*Med.*1123; πλωταῖς ἀπήνησι *Lyr.Adesp.*117 (= *Trag.Adesp.*142); τετραβάμονος ὡς ὑπ' ἀπήνας, of the Trojan horse, E.*Tr.*517 (lyr.). 4. metaph., like ζεῦγος, *pair*, e.g. of brothers, ἀ. ὁμόπτερος Id.*Ph.*329 (lyr.). 5. in pl., the *alae nasi*, Poll.2.80.

**ἀπηνής**, ές, Ep. Adj. *ungentle, rough, hard*, of persons, Il.1.340; ὅτι τοι νόος ἐστὶν ἀ. 16.35, cf. Od.18.381; θυμὸς ὑπερφίαλος καὶ ἀ. Il.15.94; μῦθον ἀπηνέα τε κρατερόν τε ib.202, cf. Od.18.381, al.; ὃς μὲν ἀπηνὴς αὐτὸς ἔῃ καὶ ἀπηνέα εἰδῇ *cruel* himself and full of *cruel thoughts*, 19.329.—Rare in Att. (never in Trag.), ὅπως τοῖς ἔξωθεν μηδὲν δείξειαν ἀπηνές Ar.*Nu.*974 (anap.); ἀπηνές τι εἰπεῖν Pl.*Phdr.*257b (but ἀπηχές (q.v.) Hermias ad loc.), cf. *Lg.*950b, Call.*Iamb.*1.257; freq. in later Prose, as Onos.42.23, Phld.*D.*3 *Fr.*69, D.S.9.24, Plu.2.678b, 970c, Luc.*Nec.*18; τὸ ἐς ἀλλήλους ἀ. Procop.*Goth.*4.35: Comp. -έστερος J.*BJ*5.7.4, Adam.2.44: Sup. -έστατος Ael.*NA*3.26; τοῖς φίλοις J.*BJ*1.24.8. Adv. -νῶς D.Chr.32.53, Plu.2.19b; πρὸς φίλους ἀπηνῶς ζῆν ib.525d: Comp. -έστερον J.*AJ*11.6.9. II. in physical sense, σπλὴν ἀ. *hard*, Aret.*SD*1.14, cf. 2.12; *unpleasant to taste*, *CA*1.5. (Cf. προσ-ηνής, Goth. *ansts* 'favour'.)

**ἀπῆνθον**, Dor. aor. 2 of ἀπέρχομαι, Theoc.2.84, al.

**ἀπηνόφρων**, ον, gen. ονος, *harsh-minded*, Sch.A.*Pr.*159.

**ἀπηξία**, ἡ, (πήγνυμι) *want of solidity, liability to flux*, σώματος Ptol.*Tetr.*204; *incapacity for solidification*, Ar.Byz.*Epit.*15.9.

**ἀπηόριος**, α, ον, = sq., *hanging*, of branches, *AP*9.71.

**ἀπήορος**, Dor. **ἀπάορος**, ον, (ἀείρω) *hanging on high, far distant*, ἀστέρες οὔτε τι πολλὸν ἀ. οὔτε μάλ' ἐγγύς Arat.396: c. gen., ἀπάορος ἐχθρῶν *aloof from* them, Pi.*P.*8.86.

**ἀπηρεμέω**, *take a thorough rest*, Sor.1.80, Orib.*Fr.*74.

**ἀπηρής**, ές, = ἄπηρος, *unharmed*, A.R.1.888 (ap.*EM*122.4; ἀπήμοσιν codd.), v.l. A.R.1.556 (on the accent v. Hdn.Gr.1.7).

**ἀπήρῑνος**, ον, (πηρίν) *without scrotum*, restored (for ἀπύρηνος) by Coraës in Archestr.8.9.

⊛**ἄπηρος**, ον, *unmaimed*, Hdt.1.32, *AP*7.110 (D.L.), Hsch.

®**ἀπηρτημένως**, Adv., (ἀπαρτάω) *consistently with*, τινί Plu.2.105e. II. ἀ. ἔχειν to be *discontinuous*, M.Ant.4.45.

**ἀπηρτισμένως**, Adv., (ἀπαρτίζω) *adequately, completely*, D.H.1.90; *precisely*, Procl.*Hyp.*4.80.

**ἀπηρυθριᾱκότως**, v. ἀπερυθριάω.

**ἀπήρωτος**, ον, *intact, unimpaired*, Thphr.*CP*3.5.1, Gal.5.234. Adv. -τί Theognost.*Can.*159.

**ἀπήτρια**, Dor. for ἠπ-, Hsch.

**ἀπηύρων**, ας, α, v. sub ἀπούρας.

**ἀπήχ-εια**, ἡ, *discord, enmity*, Lys.*Fr.*88: **ἀπηχία**, Phryn.*PS* p.25 B. ®-**έω**, *sound back, re-echo*, Arist.*Pr.*899$^a$24, 918$^a$35. 2. *utter*, φωνάς Arr.*Epict.*2.17.8. II. *to be out of tune*, Phryn.*PS* p.25 B., Suid.; *to be discordant*, Ph.1.693, 2.44. ® -**ημα**, ατος, τό, *echo*: metaph. of *sayings repeated by rote*, Pl.*Ax.*366c; *faint echo*, τῆς ἐκεῖ ζωῆς Procl.*in Alc.*p.99 C., cf. p.135 C. 2. *echo*, 'ring', μεγαλοφροσύνης Longin.9.2. 3. Medic., *fracture from contre-coup*, Sor.*Fract.*8. ®-**ής**, ές, (ἦχος) *discordant*, v.l. in Pl.*Phdr.*257b (Hermias), cf. Aristid.*Or.*40(5).8, Luc.*Vit.Auct.*10; *out of tune with* one's surroundings, Alciphr.3.70. -**ησις**, εως, ἡ, *echo*: metaph. of *posthumous fame*, M.Ant.4.3. 2. *sounding, resonance*, φωνῆς, πνεύματος, D.T.629.26, Gal.19.380, cf. Phlp.*in Ph.*47.1 (pl.).

**ἀπηχθημένως**, Adv., (ἀπεχθάνομαι) *hostilely*, Philostr.*VA*7.36.

**ἀπήωρος**, ον, *high in air*, ἀ. δ' ἔσαν ὄζοι Od.12.435; cf. ἀπήορος.

**Ἀπία γῆ**, v. sub ἄπιος (B).

**Ἀπιακός**, ἡ, όν, *of Apis*, ἄρτοι *PSI*4.425.40 (iii B.C.); cf. Ἀ. ἄρτος· Μεμφιτικός, Hsch.

**ἀπιάλλω**, fut. -ιαλῶ Hsch., Dor. for ἀποπέμπω, Th.5.77; μεγάλου δ' ἀπὸ χεῖρας ἴαλλε *keep* them *off*, Archestr.*Fr.*29.

**ἀπίαλος**, Dor. for ἠπ-, Hsch.

**ἀπιάπτω**, *tear away*, only in tmesi, ὁππόσων ἀπὸ θυμὸν ἴαπτε Q.S.1.9.

**ἀπίαστος**, ον, *not to be caught*, Hsch. s. v. ἄναπτος.

**ἀπιᾶτον**, τό, *wine flavoured with celery*, *Gp.*8.30, Alex.Trall.10.

**ἀπιδέα**, ἡ, *pear-tree*, *Gp.*10.3.6 (ἀπιδ- codd.).

**ἀπίδιον**, τό, Dim. of ἄπιον, *pear*, Sch.Od.7.115 codd., Alex.Trall.*Febr.*3.

**Ἀπιεῖον**, τό, *the temple of Apis*, *OGI*90.33 (Rosetta).

**ἀπίεστος** [ῐ], ον, (πιέζω) *incompressible*, Arist.*Mete.*385$^a$15, 386$^b$8, Thphr.*Lap.*8.

®**ἀπῐθᾰνος** [ῐ], ον, *incredible, unlikely*, Pl.*Lg.*663e, Arist.*Po.*1461$^b$12; φαντασίαι *Stoic.*2.25: Comp. ἔτι -ώτερον εἰ.. Str.1.2.22. 2. of persons, *not to be trusted* or *relied on*, πρός τι in a matter, Aeschin.2.3. b. *unpersuaded, unconvinced*, ἀ. ἂν εἴη Pl.*Prm.*133c. II. *not having confidence* to do a thing, c. inf., Plu.*Nic.*3. III. *not persuasive, unconvincing*, λόγος Pl.*Phdr.*265b, cf. Arist.*Rh.*1406$^b$14, 1408$^b$22; ὁρίζειν τὸν ἀριθμὸν ἀπίθανον Ael.*Tact.*8.1; ἀ. λέγειν, of persons, Plu.2.812e, cf. 819c; ἀ. ζωγράφος Luc.*Ind.*22; ἀ. ἐν τῇ ὑποκρίσει Id.*Pseudol.*16. Adv. -νως *not persuasively, coarsely, rudely*, Isoc.5.26, D.H.*Lys.*17, Epicur.*Ep.*2 p.35 U., etc.

**ἀπῐθᾰνότης**, ητος, ἡ, *improbability*, αἰτίας Aeschin.2.64, J.*Ap.*1.34.

**ἀπῑθέω**, (πείθω) Ep. form of ἀπειθέω, c. dat., freq. in Hom. usu. with neg., οὐκ ἀπίθησε μύθῳ he *disobeyed* not the words, Il.1.220, cf. 6.102, al.: abs., ib.16.458: once c. gen., οὐδ' ἀπίθησε θεὰ.. ἀγγελιάων *h.Cer.*448: used in S.*Ph.*1447 (anap.). II. *fail to persuade*, οὐδ' ἀπίθησέ νιν (ϝιν Herm.) Pi.*P.*4.36.

**ἀπῑθής**, ές, poet. for ἀπειθής I, *AP*5.86 (Rufin.); for ἀπειθής II, *lacking in persuasion*, Timo 26.

**ἀπῑθύνω**, = ἀπευθύνω, of setting bones, in pf. Pass., Hp.*Fract.*7; of drawing lines, *AP*6.67 (Jul. Aegypt.); ἀ. τῆς ὄψιος τὰ διάστροφα Aret.*CA*1.5.

**ἀπικμάω**, *winnow*, σῖτον Thphr.*CP*4.16.2.

®**ἄπικρος**, ον, *not bitter*, τῷ ἤθει Arist.*VV*1250$^a$42, cf. Ptol.*Tetr.*158.

**ἀπικρόχολος**, ον, *free from bitter bile*, Hsch.

**ἀπίλητος**, ον, (πιλέω) *not to be pressed close*, i.e. either *incompressible* or *elastic*, Arist.*Mete.*385$^a$17, 387$^a$16.

**ἀπίλλω**, *exclude*, Lys.10.18 (nisi leg. ἀπείλλ-).

**ἀπίμελος**, ον, (πιμελή) *without fat, not fat*, Diocl.*Fr.*136, Arist.*HA* 519$^b$8, *PA*675$^b$11, al.: Comp. -ώτερος ib.672$^a$23: Sup. -ώτατος *HA* 520$^a$19.

**ἀπῑνής**, ές, (πίνος) *without dirt, clean*, Ath.14.661d.

**ἀπῑνόω**, (ἀπινής) *clean*, Hsch. (Pass.).

**ἀπῑνύσσω**, (πινυτός) *lack understanding*, δοκέεις δέ μοι οὐκ ἀπινύσσειν Od.5.342, 6.258; κῆρ ἀπινύσσων, of one *lying senseless*, Il.15.10; cf. Apollon.*Lex.* s.v. **ἀπινυτέω**.

**ἀπινύτως**, Adv. *unwisely*, Hsch. s. v. ἀπινύσσων.

**ἄπιξις**, εως, ἡ, Ion. for ἄφιξις.

**ἀπιοειδής**, ές, φύλλα *like those of the pear-tree*, Thphr.*HP*3.10.3, cf. Gal.19.137.

®**ἄπιον**, τό, (ἄπιος A) *pear*, Pl.*Lg.*845b, Theoc.7.120, Thphr.*CP*6.14.4. 2. = ἄπιος (A), *pear-tree*, ib.1.15.2.

®**ἄπιος** (A), [ᾰ], ἡ, *pear-tree*, *Pyrus communis*, Arist.*HA*552$^b$2, Thphr.*HP*1.3.3, *CP*1.15.2, Dsc.1.116, Gal.11.834. 2. = ἄπιον, *pear*, Ar.*Fr.*569.3; ἀπ' Εὐβοίας ἀπίους Hermipp.63.17, Alex.33, Gal.6.603. II. *Euphorbia Apios, tuberous spurge*, Thphr.*HP*9.9.5, Dsc.4.175. III. = ἀστράγαλος, Ps.-Dsc.4.61.

**ἄπιος** (B), η, ον, *far away, far off, distant*, τηλόθεν ἐξ ἀπίης γαίης Il.1.270, 3.49, Od.16.18, cf. S.*OC*1685. II. Ἄπιος, α, ον, *Apian*, i.e. *Peloponnesian*, said (in this sense) to be derived from Ἆπις, Apis, a mythical king of Argos, A.*Supp.*260, cf. Paus.2.5.7; Ἀπία γῆ, Ἀπία χθών, or Ἀπία alone, *the Peloponnese*, esp. *Argolis*, A.*Ag.*256, S.*OC*1303, Ath.14.650b, etc.; cf. Ἀπίς prob. in A.R.4.1564. [The former word has ᾰ, the latter ā; yet S.*OC*1685 uses signf. I with ā, and later Ep. Poets have signf. II with ᾰ, cf. Rhian.13.] (Commonly derived from ἀπό, as ἀντίος from ἀντί; and Hsch. expl. ἐξ ἀπίης γαίης by ἀλλοτρίας ἢ ξένης ἢ μακρὰν οὔσης, cf. Str.8.6.9.)

**ἀπῑπόω**, *press* the juice *from* anything, Hdt.2.94.

®**Ἆπις**, ιδος, εως, and Ion. ιος, ὁ, *Apis*, a bull worshipped in Egypt, Hdt.2.153, etc. 2. a mythical king of Argos, v. ἄπιος (B) II. II. **Ἀπίς**, = Ἀπία γῆ, Theoc.25.183, prob. in A.R.4.1564.

**ἀπισόω**, *make equal*, αὐτὸν ἀ. τοῖς κλιντῆρσιν, in reference to Procrustes, Plu.*Thes.*11, cf. Luc.*Pr.Im.*13:—Pass., *to be made equal*, τῇ ἀξίῃ τῶν φορτίων *to* their value, Hdt.4.196, cf. Sch.Il.*Oxy.*1086i 22 (in form ἀφ-).

®**ἀπίσσωτος**, ον, (πισσόω) *unpitched*, ἄγγη Str.11.10.2, cf. Dsc.1.71 (interpol.).

**ἀπιστ-εύω**, incorrect form for sq., ἀ. εἰ.. *POxy.*237$^v$5 (ii A.D.). ® -**έω**, fut. Pass. ἀπιστηθήσομαι D.S.32.10, but ἀπιστήσομαι in pass. sense, Pl.*R.*450c:—*to be* ἄπιστος, and so: I. *disbelieve, distrust*, ἐγὼ τὸ μὲν οὔ ποτ' ἀπίστεον Od.13.339; τύχην ἀ. E.*Alc.*1130; πάντα Ar.*Ec.*775, cf. Th.7.28 (s. v.l.), X.*Ages.*5.6, 8.7:—Pass., τὴν γνῶσιν τοῦ οἰκείου ἀπιστεῖσθαι *was distrusted*, i.e. no one could be sure of knowing, Th.7.44; ἀ. ἐν μαρτυρίαις Antipho 2.2.7; ἐπειδὰν γνῶσιν ἀπιστούμενοι, οὐ φιλοῦσι τοὺς ἀπιστοῦντας X.*Cyr.*7.2.17, cf. *Hier.*4.1; ὑπὸ τῆς πατρίδος Id.*Smp.*4.29, cf. Pl.*Plt.*271b, Isoc.5.49:—but mostly, 2. c. dat. pers., κρατέουσιν Emp.5.1, cf. Th.8.83, Pl.*Prt.*319b, etc.: so c. dat. rei, τῷ χρησμῷ Hdt.1.158; πῶς ἀπιστήσω λόγοις; S.*Ph.*1350, cf. Th.6.86; ἀ. τῇ ἐξ αὐτῶν ξυνέσει Id.3.37; τοῖς ἰάμασιν *IG*4.951.24 (Epid.); ἡμῖν αὐτοῖς Arist.*EN*1112$^b$10; ἀ. τινί τι *disbelieve* one in a thing, Hdt.3.122; περί τινος Id.4.96; οἷς ἠπίστησαν ἔχειν.. whom they *suspected of* having, Plb.4.18.8. 3. c. inf., οὐδέν σ' ἀπιστῶ καὶ δὶς οἰμῶξαι I nothing *doubt* that.., S.*Aj.*940; ἀ. μὴ γενέσθαι τι *to doubt* that it could be, Th.1.10; ἀπιστοῦντες αὐτὸν μὴ ἥξειν Id.2.101, cf. 4.40, Pl.*Plt.*301c, *R.*555a; also ἀ. μὴ οὐκ ἐπιστήμη ᾖ ἡ ἀρετή Id.*Men.*89d; ἀ. πῶς.. *Phd.*73b; ἀ. εἰ.. *APl.*4.52 (Phil.), Ph.2.555; ὅτι.. Pl.*Men.*89d; ὡς *R.*450c:—Pass., τὸ ἐπιτήδευμα ἀπιστεῖται μὴ δυνατὸν εἶναι it *is not believed* to be possible, Id.*Lg.*839c, cf. *Chrm.*168e. 4. abs., *to be incredulous*, Hdt.8.94, cf. *Ev.Marc.*16.16, etc.; νᾶφε καὶ μέμνασ' ἀπιστεῖν Epich.250; ἐπὶ τοῖς λεγομένοις Ph.2.92. II. = ἀπειθέω, *disobey*, τινί Hdt.6.108, freq. in Trag. and Pl., A.*Pr.*640, S.*Ant.*381 (lyr.), *Tr.*1183, 1224, Pl.*Ap.*29c, al.: abs., *to be disobedient*, τοῖς ἀπιστοῦσιν τάδε *in* these things, S.*Ant.*219, cf. 656; ἢν δ' ἀπιστῶσι but if they *refuse to comply*, E.*Supp.*389, cf. Pl.*Lg.*941c. 2. *to be faithless*, εἰ ἡμεῖς ἀπιστοῦμεν, ἐκεῖνος πιστὸς μένει *2Ep.Tim.*2.13. 3. νεκρὸς τὸν θάνατον ἀπιστούμενος *belying* death, Polem.*Call.*55. III. τὸ σῶμ' οὐκ ἀπιστήσω χθονί, i.e. I *will* not *hesitate to commit* it.., E.*Heracl.*1024; τούτῳ ἠπίστησεν ἀποθανοῦσαν ἑαυτὴν ἐπιτρέψαι Lys.31.21. -**ητέον**, *one must mistrust, disbelieve*, c. dat., Plb.4.41.8; of persons, Str.8.4.10, etc.; ἀ. ἡμῖν περί.. Hp.*Cord.*2. -**ητικός**, ή, όν, *incredulous*, M.Ant.1.6.

®**ἀπιστία**, Ion. -ίη, ἡ, *unbelief, distrust*, πίστεις.. ὁμῶς καὶ ἀπιστίαι ὤλεσαν ἄνδρας beliefs and *disbeliefs*, Hes.*Op.*372; πίστει χρήματ' ὄλεσσα, ἀπιστίῃ δ' ἐσάωσα Thgn.831 [ῑ]; τῶν θείων τὰ πολλὰ ἀπιστίῃ διαφυγγάνει μὴ γινώσκεσθαι Heraclit.86, cf. Pl.*Grg.*493c; τοῖσι παρεοῦσι ἀ. πολλὴ ὑπεκέχυτο Hdt.3.66, cf. 2.152; ὑπὸ ἀπιστίης Id.3.153, al.; ὑπὸ ἀ. μὴ γενέσθαι τι from *disbelief* that.., Id.1.68; ἀ. πρὸς ἑαυτόν *lack of* self-*confidence*, Th.8.66; ἀπιστίᾳ λόγους ἐνδέχεσθαι E.*Ion* 1606; πέφευγε τοὔπος ἐξ ἀπιστίας A.*Ag.*268; ἀπιστίαν ἔχειν περί τινος to be *in doubt*, Pl.*Phd.*107b; σώφρων ἀ. E.*Hel.*1617; πρὸς -ίαν τοῦ κατηγόρου *to discredit* him, Arist.*Rh.*1398$^a$10; ἡ ἀ. ἡ πρὸς ἀλλήλους Id.*Pol.*1297$^a$4; ἀ. ἡ καθ' αὑτοῦ Longin.38.2; πρός τι Pl.*Sph.*258c. 2. of things, τὰ εἰρημένα ἐς ἀ. πολλὴν ἀπῖκται Hdt.1.193; πολλὰς ἀπιστίας ἔχει it admits of many *doubts*, Pl.*R.*450c; ὁ λόγος εἰς ἀ. καταπίπτει Id.*Phd.*88d; καταβαλεῖν τινὰ εἰς ἀ. ib.c; ἀ. παρέχειν ib.86e (interpol.); ἀτοπία καὶ ἀπιστία *incredibility*, Isoc.17.48; ταῦτ' ἀπιστίαν ἔχει D.10.44. II. *want of faith, faithlessness*, θνῄσκει δὲ πίστις βλαστάνει δ' ἀ. S.*OC*611; *treachery*, And.3.2, X.*An.*2.5.21; βλέπειν ἀπιστίαν Eup.309.

®**ἄπιστος**, ον, I. Pass., *not to be trusted*, and so: 1. of persons and their acts, *not trusty, faithless*, ὑπερφίαλοι καὶ ἄ. Il.3.106; θεοῖσίν τ' ἐχθρὲ καὶ ἀνθρώποισιν ἄπιστε Thgn.601; ἄ. ὡς γυναικεῖον γένος E.*IT*1298; ἄ. λῃστορες *Sammelb.*4309.14 (iii B.C.); δολοπλοκίαι Thgn.226; ἄ. ποιεῖν τινά *mistrusted*, Hdt.8.22, cf. 9.98; τὰ ἑαυτοῦ πιστὰ ἀ. ποιεῖν X.*An.*2.4.7; ἄπιστος ἑταιρείας λιμήν S.*Aj.*683; θράσει ἀ. ἐπαιρόμενος by *untrustworthy, groundless* confidence, Th.1.120; *shifty, unreliable*, Pl.*Lg.*775d. 2. of reports and the like, *incredible*, dub. in Archil.74.5, cf. Pi.*O.*1.31, Hdt.3.80; τέρας A.*Pr.*832; ἄ. καὶ πέρα κλύειν Ar.*Av.*418; ἄ. ἐνόμιζον εἰ.. Ph.2.556; τὸ ἐλπίδων ἄ. *undreamed of* even in hope, S.*Ph.*868: Comp. -ότερος, λόγος Aeschin.3.59: Sup., πίστις ἀπιστοτάτη And.1.67, cf. Pl.*Ep.*314b. II. Act., *mistrustful, incredulous, suspicious*, θυμὸς δέ τοι αἰὲν ἄ. Od.14.150; ὦτα.. ἀπιστότερα ὀφθαλμῶν *less credulous*, Hdt.1.8; ἄ. πρὸς Φίλιππον *distrustful* towards him, D.19.27; ἄ. εἶ.. σαυτῷ you do *not believe* what you say yourself, Pl.*Ap.*26e; ἤθη ἄ. Id.*Lg.*705a; τὸ ἄ., = ἀπιστία, Th.8.66; δούλοις πῶς οὐκ ἄπιστον; Gorg.*Pal.*11. b. in *NT*, *unbelieving*, 1*Ep.Cor.*6.6, al. 2. *disobedient, disloyal*, S.*Fr.*627: c. gen., A.*Th.*876; ἔχειν ἄπιστον.. ἀναρχίαν πόλει, i.e. ἀναρχίαν ἔχειν ἀπειθοῦσαν τῇ πόλει, ib.1035, cf. E.*IT*1476. III. Adv. ἀπίστως: 1. Pass., *beyond belief*, ἀ. ἐπὶ τὸ μυθῶδες ἐκνενικηκότα Th.1.21; οὐκ ἀ. not *incredibly*, Arist.*Rh.Al.*1438$^a$22, 1438$^b$2. 2. Act., *distrustfully, suspiciously*, Th.3.83; ἀ. τινὰ διαθεῖναι D.20.22. b. *treacherously*, Ph.1.516.

**ἀπιστοσύνη**, ἡ, = ἀπιστία, E.*Med.*422 (lyr.).

**ἀπιστούντως**, Adv. = ἀπίστως 2, Numen.ap.Eus.*PE*14.7.

**ἀπιστόφῐλος**, ον, *loving unbelief*, Orac.ap.Phleg.*Mir.*10.

**ἀπισχν-αίνω**, *make lean* or *thin*, Philem.98.7, Arist.*HA*574$^b$6. **-αντέον**, *one must make thin*, Id.*Pr.*865$^a$37. **-όω**, in Pass., *shrink*, Hp.*Int.*3, *Morb.Sacr.*8, cf. Sor.1.53.

**ἀπισχῡρ-ίζομαι**, *oppose firmly, give a flat denial*, πρός τινα Th.1.140, cf. Plu.*Per.*31; πρὸς τὰς ἡδονάς Id.*Agis*4, al.; *hold out against*, πρὸς δίψος Them.*Or.*11.149c. II. *set oneself to affirm, maintain* a thing, ib.28.342c, Eust.1278.53, etc. III. *cling firmly*, of the λεπάς, Sch.Ar.*Pl.*1096. **-ιστικῶς**, Adv. *positively*, Eust.1861.41.

**ἀπίσχω**, = ἀπέχω, *keep off, hold off*, Od.11.95; χεῖρας ἔργου J.*BJ* 1.7.3.

⊛**ἀπίσωσις** [πῐ], εως, ἡ, *equalization*, Nicom.*Ar.*1.23; as a rhetorical figure, coupled with παρίσωσις, Poll.4.27 (pl.).

**ἀπῐτέον**, (ἄπειμι B) *one must go away*, Hp.*Ep.*13, X.*An.*5.3.1, Amphis 1, Luc.*Herm.*82.

**ἀπίτευτος**, ον, *unwatered*, *BCH*21.554 (Thesp.); cf. πιτεύω.

**ἀπίτης** [ῑ], (sc. οἶνος), ου, ὁ, (ἄπιον) *perry*, Dsc.5.24, *Gp.*8.5 (ἀππ-).

**ἀπῐτητέον**, pl. έα, = ἀπιτέον, Luc.*Lex.*2.

**ἀπιχθυόομαι**, Pass., *to become a fish*, Herm.ap.Stob.1.49.69.

**ἄπιχθυς**, υ, *eating no fish*, Ar.*Fr.*564 (= E.*Fr.*366). 2. Subst., *paltry little fish*, Eust.1720.24.

**ἀπίων** [ῑ], ον, gen. ονος, *not fat*, Diph.Siph.ap.Ath.4.120e, Aret.*CD*1.5.

**ἀπλᾰγιάστως**, Adv., (πλαγιάζω) *not obliquely*, Eust.1229.41.

**ἄπλαγκτος** [λᾰ], ον, = ἀπλανής, Nonn.*D.*4.313.

**ἁπλαῖ**, v. sub ἁπλοῦς.

**ἀπλακέω, ἀπλακία**, etc., v. sub ἀμπλακέω, etc.

**ἀπλάκουντος** [λᾰ], ον, *without cakes*, Pl.Com 113.

**ἀπλάν-εια** [λᾰ], ἡ, *constancy, unchangeableness*, Suid. **-ῆ**· πολλά (Cypr.), Hsch. **-ής**, ές, *not wandering, steady, fixed*, Pl.*Plt.*288a, al.: c. gen., ἀπλανὲς ἀπηργάσατο ἐκείνων [κινήσεων] made it *free from* their *influence*, Id.*Ti.*34a. 2. Astron. of stars, *fixed*, opp. *planets*, ib 40b, cf. Arist.*Mete.*343$^b$9, *Metaph.*1073$^b$10, Arat.461, *AP*9.25 (Leon.); ἡ ἀ. σφαῖρα *Corp.Herm.*2.6. II. of a line, *straight*, *AP*6.65 (Paul. Sil.). III. *unwavering*, θεωρία Epicur.*Ep.*3p.62 U. 2. *not erring*, S.E.*M*7.195, Longin.2.2 (Sup.), etc. Adv. **-νῶς** *without going astray*, Max.Tyr.5.2; *accurately*, Alciphr.3.59. **-ησία**, ἡ, *freedom from error*, S.E.*M.*7.394. **-ητος**, ον, *that cannot go astray* or *err*, Lxx *Jb.*12.20, Babr.50.20, *POxy.*237 vi 30 (ii A. D.).

**ἄπλαντα**· ῥυπαρά, Hsch. (leg. ἄπλυντα).

**ἀπλαστία**, ἡ, *sincerity*, Pl.*Def.*412e.

⊛**ἄπλαστος**, ον, *not capable of being moulded*, Arist.*Mete.*385$^a$15. 2. *not moulded*: hence, *natural, unaffected*, φρόνημα, εὔνοια, προθυμία, ἦθος, etc., Plu.*Aem.*37, *Vit.Philonid.*p.10 C., Them.*Or.*4.56d, etc.; of persons, Lxx *Ge.*25.27, Ceb.20. Adv. **-τως** *naturally, without disguise*, γελᾶν Pl.*Ep.*319b codd.; αὐλεῖν Thphr.*HP*4.11.4; λέγειν D.H.*Rh.*10.11; ἀποκρίνεσθαι Ael.*VH*9.27. 3 *not feigned*: hence, *true*, opp. *mythical*, Plu.2.16c, 62c. 4. *not fully shapen, unformed*, Ph.2.317. II. v.l. for ἄπλᾱτος (q.v.).

⊛**ἀπλᾰτής**, ές, *without breadth*, γραμμή Arist.*APr.*49$^b$36; μῆκος ἀ., opp. πλάτος ἔχον, Id.*Top.*143$^b$14: metaph., Gal.7.410; ἀ. ὑγίεια *without latitude*, i.e. variation, Id.6.28. Adv. **-τῶς** Iamb.*in Nic.*p.56 P.

⊛**ἄπλᾱτος**, Dor. and Trag. for Ep. ἄπλητος (q.v.), ον, (πελάζω) *unapproachable*, always with a notion of *terrible, monstrous*, Hes.*Op.*148, *Th.*151; ἄ. πῦρ Pi.*P.*1.21 (whence it must be restored for ἀπλήστου in A.*Pr.*373); ὀφίων κεφαλαί, Τυφών, Pi.*P.*12.9, *Fr.*93; Ἔχιδνα B.5.62, cf. 12.51; θρέμμα S.*Tr.*1093; αἶσα Id.*Aj.*256 (lyr.); ἄπλατον ἀξύμβλητον ἐξεθρεψάμην Id.*Fr.*387.—In many places ἄπλαστος is a v.l., Id.*Aj.*256, E.*Med.*151 (lyr.); cf. ἄπληστος. 2. = ἄπλετος, κυψέλη *Com.Adesp.*620; ἄπλατοι ὅσοι Phld.*Rh.*1.3 S., al.; γάλα Diog.Oen.39, cf. Epicur.*Nat.*11.154.14, Phld.*Oec.*p.41 J., Porph.*Abst.*1.55; cf. ἄπλητος.

**ἀπλέητον**· ἀπροσπέλαστον, Hsch.

**ἀπλεκής**, ές, = sq., Nonn.*D.*42.87.

**ἄπλεκτος**, ον, *unplaited*, χαίτη *AP*7.412 (Alc. Mess.), *Epigr.Gr.*790.8 (Dyme).

**ἀπλεόναστος**, ον, *without an extra letter*, Eust.947.16.

**ἀπλεονέκτητος**, ον, *free from avarice*, Chaerem.ap.Porph.*Abst.*4.6. 2. *without excess*, *Theol.Ar.*34.

⊛**ἀπλετομεγέθης**, ες, *unapproachably great*, λίθος Sch.A.R.3.41.

⊛**ἄπλετος**, ον, *boundless, immense*, ἠέρος ὕψος Emp.17.18; αὐγή Id.135; δόξα Pi.*I.*4(3).11; βάρος S.*Tr.*982; also found in Prose, χρυσὸς ἄ. Hdt.1.14, 50, al.; ἅλες, ὕδωρ, 4.53, 8.12; οἰμωγή 6.58; μάχη Pl.*Sph.*246c; ἄ. καὶ ἀμήχανον [χρόνου πλῆθος] Id.*Lg.*676b; ἐν χρόνου μήκεσιν ἀπλέτοις ib.683a; χιών X.*An.*4.4.11; πλῆθος Arist.*GA*755$^b$26; ποταμοὶ ἄπλετοι τὸ μέγεθος Id.*Mete.*355$^b$23; ῥαφανίδες ἄ. τὸ πάχος Id.*Pr.*924$^a$27; θόρυβος Plb.1.50.3, al.; φύσις Plot.5.5.6; δύναμις 4.8.6.

**ἄπλευρος**, ον, *without sides* or *ribs*, ἄ. στῆθος *narrow* chest, Arist.*Phgn.*810$^a$3, cf. 809$^b$7 (Comp.); of persons, *narrow-chested*, opp. εὔπλευροι, ib.810$^b$13, Teles p.55.3 H., Mnesith.ap.Orib.21.7.6 (Sup.).

**ἄπλευστος**, ον, *not navigated*: τὸ ἄ. part of the sea *not yet navigated*, X.*Cyr.*6.1.16.

**ἀπληγής**, ές, of verses, *free from metrical defect*, Diom.p.498 K.

**ἀπλήγιος**, ον, *clad in a single garment*: generally, = ἁπλοῦς, Eup.222.

**ἀπληγίς**, ίδος, ἡ, = ἁπλοΐς (as Subst.), *a single upper garment* or *cloak*, opp. διπληγίς, S.*Fr.*777, Ar.*Fr.*54, Herod.5.18.

⊛**ἄπληγος**, ον, (πληγή) *not smitten* with disease, etc., *PMag.Par.*1.1063.

**ἀπλήθυντος**, ον, *not multiplied, without plurality*, Porph.*Sent.*33, Procl.*in Prm.*p.535 S. Adv. **-τως** Porph.*Sent.* l.c., Procl.*Inst.*62.

**ἄπληκτος**, ον, *unstricken*, of a horse *needing no whip* or *spur*, Eup.232, Pl.*Phdr.*253d: metaph., Plu.2.721e; *unwounded, without receiving a blow*, φρουροὶ δ' ἄ. E.*Rh.*814; *immune from stings*, Dsc.2.118; of a plant, *uninjured*, Thphr.*HP*9.14.1. 2. Act., *not striking*, in Adv. **-τως** *without pulsation*, Procl.*in Cra.*p.37 P. II. Act., *not irritating* or *pungent*, Sor.2.59: Comp., *not too stimulating*, Herod.Med.ap.Aët.5.116. Adv. **-τως** Ruf.ap.Orib.8.24.53.

**ἀπλημμελῶς**, Adv. *without discord*, Dam.*Pr.*424.

**ἀπλήμων**, ον, = ἄπληστος, Hsch.

**ἀπλήξ**, ῆγος, ὁ, ἡ, = ἄπληκτος I, Arr.*Epict.*4.1.124; sens. obsc., Luc.*Am.*54.

**ἀπλήρωτος**, ον, *insatiable*, Phld.*Mus.*p.78 K., Ph.2.266, al., Luc.*Merc.Cond.*39; Ἅιδης *IG*14.1754; πάντων Plu.2.524b; *unsatisfied*, Gal.17(1).597. 2. *unfilled*, Poll.1.121; τὸ ἀ. *absence of satiety*, Plot.5.8.4.

**ἀπλησίαστος**, ον, = ἄπλατος, Sch.Pi.*P.*12.15, Sch.S.*Aj.*247.

**ἀπληστ-εί**, Adv. of ἄπληστος, Hdn.*Epim.*257. **-εύομαι**, *to be insatiable*, τινός *in* a thing, Hipparch.ap.Stob.4.44.81; ἔν τινι Lxx *Si.*34(31).17. **-ία**, ἡ, *insatiate desire, greediness*, whether of food or money, ὑπὸ τῆς ἀπληστίας Pherecr.156; εἰς τοσαύτην ἀ. ἀφίκοντο Lys.12.19, cf. D.36.44; διὰ τὴν ἀ. Pl.*Grg.*493b; ἀ. τρόπων D.22.67 (interpol.); γαστρός Ph.1.360. 2. c. gen. rei, *insatiate desire of*, πλούτου, χρυσοῦ, Pl.*R.*562b, *Lg.*831d; λέχους E.*Andr.*218; τῆς εὐχῆς, referring to Midas, Arist.*Pol.*1257$^b$16; τοῦ θεωρεῖν Ph.1.12. **-οινος**, ον, *insatiate in wine*, ἀρύταιναι Timo 4. **-ος**, ον, *insatiate, greedy*, Thgn.109, S.*El.*1336, Arist.*HA*591$^b$2, etc.; sts. confounded with ἄπλαστος (i.e. ἄπλατος), q.v. 2. c. gen., ἄ. χρημάτων, αἵματος, Hdt.1.187, 212, Pl.*Lg.*773e, etc.; κακῶν A.*Eu.*976 (lyr.). II. Adv. **-τως**, ἔχειν Pl.*Grg.*493c, al.; ἀ. διακεῖσθαι or ἔχειν πρός τι X.*Cyr.*4.1.14, Isoc.5.135, 8.7: also neut. pl. as Adv., αἰάξας ἄπληστα *CIG*2240 (Chios).

⊛**ἄπλητος**, Ep. and Ion. form of ἄπλᾱτος (q.v.), ον, dub. in *h.Cer.*83; μαίνεται ἄπλητον Semon.7.34; = ἄπλετος, *great*, χεύματα Orph.*A.*1051; αἰθήρ Q.S.8.222; δῶρα Id.9.510.

**ἄπλια**, name of a *throw at dice*, Poll.7.204.

**ἀπλίκιτ-ον**, τό, *camp-prison*, *PLond.ined.*2487 (iv A. D.):—hence **-άριοι**, οἱ, *warders*, Lyd.*Mag.*3.8.

**ἀπλοδίσημος**, ον, (also written ἁπλοτίσ-) dub. sens., ἔργον, apptly. of embroidery or weaving, *PLond.ined.*2132.

**ἁπλο-ειδής**, ές, *simple* or *single*, *Theol.Ar.*52 (Comp.). **-θριξ**, ὁ, ἡ, gen. τριχος, *with plain hair*, Ptol.*Tetr.*143, Alex.Aphr.*Pr.*1.2.

⊛**ἄπλοια**, ἡ, Ion. and poet. **ἀπλοΐη**, Call.*Dian.*230, prob. in *AP*7.640 (Antip.). (ἄπλους):—*impossibility of sailing, detention in port*, esp. from stress of weather, A.*Ag.*188; ἀπλοίᾳ χρῆσθαι E.*IA*88, cf. *IT*15; ἡσύχαζεν ὑπὸ ἀπλοίας Th.4.4, cf. 6.22: pl., ἀποπλέειν .. ὁρμημένον αὐτὸν ἴσχον ἄπλοιαι Hdt.2.119.

**ἁπλοΐδιον**, τό, Dim. of ἁπλοΐς, *PPetr.*3p.18 (iii B. C.).

**ἁπλοΐζομαι**, (ἁπλοῦς) *behave simply, deal frankly*, πρὸς τοὺς φίλους X.*Mem.*4.2.18; *to be simple in habits*, D.C.65.7; *to be reduced to simplicity*, Dam.*Pr.*32.—Act. in same sense, Sch.Od.6.187.

⊛**ἁπλοϊκός**, ή, όν, *simple, natural, plain*, Phint.ap.Stob.4.23.61$^a$, Luc.*Tim.*56, A.D.*Synt.*200.18, Hermog.*Id.*2.9, Demetr.*Eloc.*244, etc.: Comp. **-ώτερος** Simp.*in Ph.*337.11: Sup. **-ώτατος** Philostr.*VS*2.9.2, Luc.*Alex.*4. Adv. **-κῶς** D.H.*Dem.*45.

**ἄπλοιοι**· οἱ μὴ δυνάμενοι πλεῖν, Hsch.

**ἁπλοΐς**, ίδος, ἡ, *simple, single*, ἁπλοΐδες χλαῖναι Il.24.230, Od.24.276: as Subst., *single garment*, = ἀπληγίς, *AP*5.293 (Agath.).

**ἁπλόκᾰμος**, ον, *having shorn her hair*, *AP*7.146 (Antip. Sid.).

**ἄπλοκος**, ον, (πλέκω) = ἄπλεκτος, Opp.*H.*3.469: metaph., *unconnected*, cj. in Longin.19.1.

**Ἁπλοκύων**, ὁ, nickname of *a Cynic who wore his coat single* instead of double, Plu.*Brut.*34, D.L.6.13.

⊛**ἁπλόος**, η, ον, contr. **ἁπλοῦς**, ῆ, οῦν, opp. διπλόος *twofold*, and so, I. *single*, ἁπλῆ γὰρ οἶμος εἰς Ἅιδου φέρει A.*Fr.*239, cf. X.*Cyr.*1.3.4 (Comp.); ἁπλῷ τείχει περιτειχίζειν Th.3.18; δὶς τόσ' ἐξ ἁπλῶν κακά S.*Aj.*277; ὅπως ἂν ἡ χάρις ἐξ ἁπλῆς διπλῆ φανῇ Id.*Tr.*619; ἁπλᾶς δὲ λύπας ἐξὸν οὐκ οἴσω διπλᾶς E.*IT*688. b. ἁπλαῖ (sc. κρηπῖδες), αἱ, *single-soled shoes*, Stratt.24, D.54.34. II. *simple, plain, straightforward*, κελεύθοις ἁπλόαις ζωᾶς Pi.*N.*8.36; ἁ. ὁ μῦθος A.*Ch.*554; ἁ. λόγῳ Id.*Pr.*610, al.; ὡς ἁ. λόγῳ ib.46, Ar.*Ach.*1151; ἁ. λόγος the matter is *simple*, E.*Hel.*979; ἁ. διήγησις *simple* narrative (without dialogue), Pl.*R.*392d; οὐκ ἐς ἁπλοῦν φέρει leads to no *simple issue*, S.*OT*519; ἁπλᾶ γε καὶ σαφῆ λέγω μαθεῖν Alex.240.7; οὐδὲν ἔχω ἁπλούστερον λέγειν X.*Cyr.*3.1.32; of *single-membered* periods, Demetr.*Eloc.*17, etc.; of habits, ἁπλούστατος βίος Plb.9.10.5; νόμοι λίαν ἁ. καὶ βαρβαρικοί Arist.*Pol.*1268$^b$39; ἁπλοῦν ἦν .. ἀποθανεῖν *a plain course*, Men.14. b. of persons, or their words, thoughts, and acts, *simple, open, frank*, ἁπλᾶ γάρ ἐστι τῆς ἀληθείας ἔπη A.*Fr.*176; ἁ. καὶ γενναῖος Pl.*R.*361b, etc.; ἁ. τρόποι E.*IA*927; opp. δόλος, Ar.*Pl.*1158; πρὸς τοὺς φίλους ὡς ἁπλούστατον εἶναι X.*Mem.*4.2.16. c. *simple-minded*, ὁ κριτὴς ὑπόκειται εἶναι ἁ. Arist.*Rh.*1357$^a$12, cf. *HA*608$^b$4 (Comp.), *Rh.*1367$^a$37; in bad sense, *simple, silly*, Isoc.2.46; λίαν γὰρ ἁπλοῦν τὸ νομίζειν.. Arist.*Mete.*339ᵇ34. III. *simple*, opp. *compound* or *mixed*, Pl.*R.*547e, etc.; opp. μεμιγμένος, κεκραμένος, Arist.*Metaph.*989ᵇ17, *Sens.*447ᵃ18; ἁ. χρώματα Id.*Col.*791ᵃ1; ἁ. ὀνόματα, opp. διπλᾶ, Id.*Po.*1457ᵃ31; also of nouns, *without the article*, A.D.*Synt.*98.17, al.; of the *positive* adjective, Plu.2.412e, etc. b. ἁ. βιβλία rolls *containing a single author*, Id.*Ant.*58. c. of precious metals, *unalloyed, pure*, *SIG*901.9 (Delph., iv A.D.), *PCair.*67041. d. ἁ. ἐπίδεσμος, a kind of *bandage*, Hp.*Off.*7, etc. 2. *absolute, sheer*, ἀκρασία Arist.*EN*1149ᵃ2; συμφορά Lys.24.8, etc. 3. *simple, unqualified* (cf. ἁπλῶς II. 3), οὐ πάνυ μοι δοκεῖ..οὕτως ἁπλοῦν εἶναι ὥστε.. Pl.*Prt.*331b, cf. *Smp.*206a, *Tht.*188d, al. 4. *general*, opp. ἀκριβής, Arist.*Metaph.*1025ᵇ7 (Comp.), cf. 1030ᵃ16. IV. Adv. ἁπλῶς, v. sub voc. V. Comp. and Sup. ἁπλούστερος, ἁπλούστατος, v. supr.; irreg. Sup. ἁπλότατος *AP*6.185 (Zos.). (Cf. δι-πλόος; ἁ- = *sm*; -πλόος perh. identical with πλοῦς 'voyage', cf. Serb. *jedan put* '(*one journey*, hence) *once*'; transition from 'once' to 'simple' as in Lett. *vienkaršs* 'simple' (cf. Lith. *vienkart* 'once').)

**ἄπλοος**, ον, contr. **ἄπλους**, ουν: I. Act., of ships, *unseaworthy*, τριήρεις And.3.5; ναῦς ἄπλους ποιεῖν Th.7.34; νῆες ἄπλοι ἐγένοντο ibid.: of persons, ναύκληρον..ποιήσας ἄπλουν Crito Com.3: Comp., ἀπλοώτεραι νῆες *less fit for sea*, Th.7.60 (codd.; ἀπλούστεραι Suid.). II. Pass., of the sea, *not navigable, closed to navigation* (cf. ἄπλοια), ἄπλους ἡ θάλαττα ὑπὸ τῶν..λῃστῶν γέγονεν D.18.241; ἅλμη A.R.4.1271; Πόντος Plb.4.38.7: metaph., αἰθήρ Nonn.*D.*6.358. III. *no seafarer*, Ἠχώ ib.319.

**ἁπλοπαθής**, ές, (πάθος) *simply passive*, S.E.*P.*3.108 (-πάθεια, ἡ, is f.l. ib.47).

**ἁπλός**, ή, όν, late form for ἁπλόος, *An.Ox.*2.331.

**ἁπλοσύνη**, ἡ, = ἁπλότης, Lxx *Jb.*21.23.

**ἁπλοσχήμων**, ον, *of simple form*, Str.*Chr.*2.28.

***ἁπλότης**, ητος, ἡ, *singleness*, τῆς φωνῆς Arist.*Aud.*801ᵃ19. II. *simplicity*, πόλεως X.*HG*5.1.18; κατὰ τὴν μουσικήν Pl.*R.*404e; τῆς τροφῆς D.S.3.17: of literary style, D.H.*Rh.*9.14: pl., ἁπλότητες λόγων ibid. 2. of persons, *simplicity, frankness, sincerity*, X.*Cyr.*1.4.3, Lxx *Wi.*1.1, Plb.1.78.8, D.S.5.66, etc.; ἡ εἰς τὸν Χριστὸν ἁ. 2*Ep.Cor.*11.3. 3. *open-heartedness*: hence, *liberality*, ib.8.2, 9.11, cf. *IG*14.1517.

**ἁπλο-τομέω**, *cut by a simple incision*, τι Antyll.ap.Orib.44.8.1:—Pass., Aët.8.26:—hence -**τομητέον**, Id.16.123. -**τομία**, ἡ, *simple incision*, Antyll.ap.Orib.44.8.6, Gal.14.781.

***Ἄπλουν**, ὁ, Thess., = Ἀπόλλων, Pl.*Cra.*405c, *IG*9(2).512.19 (Larissa), etc. **ἁπλοῦς**, v. ἁπλόος.

**ἄπλουτος**, ον, *without riches*, S.*Fr.*835; ἁβρὸς καὶ οὐκ ἄ. Philostr.*VA*6.36; ἄ. ἀπεργάσασθαι τὸν πλοῦτον Thphr.*Fr.*78.

**ἀπλόφυλλον**, τό, = ἄλυσσον, Ps.-Dsc.3.91 (prob.l.).

**ἁπλόω**, (ἁπλοῦς) *make single, unfold, spread out*, οὐρήν Batr.74 (v.l.), cf. 80; σῶμα *AP*11.107 (Lucill.); ἱστία Orph.*A.*360, etc.; σαγήνην Alciphr.3.3; φάλαγγα Paus.4.11.2; δακτύλους Sor.1.73; ἁ. τὸν ἄργυρον *beat* it *thin*, *Anacreont.*4.5; *expose* a wound, Just. *Nov.*111 *Pr.*:—Pass., ἀγρευθεὶς εἰς τὸ πλοῖον ἡπλώθη [the fish] *lay stretched out*.., Babr.4.5; ἀσπάραγος χαίρει γῇ ἡπλωμένῃ *open* ground, *Gp.*12.18.1; ἁπλωθέντων ἱστίων Lib.*Or.*11.264:—Med., *AP*10.9, Orph.*A.*278, D.P.235. 2. metaph., ἅπλωσον σεαυτόν *be simple*, M.Ant.4.26:—Pass., *to be simplified*, Plot.6.7.35; but, *to be expanded*, Id.3.5.9 (fort. ἐξαπλ-). 3. *make plain*, ὁδόν Lxx *Jb.*22.3.

**ἀπλυσία** (A), ἡ, (ἄπλυτος) *filthiness, filth*, *AP*7.377 (Eryc.).

**ἀπλυσία** (B), ἡ, a kind of *sponge*, so called because *it cannot be cleaned*, Arist.*HA*549ᵃ4, Plin.*HN*9.150, prob.l. in Thphr.*HP*4.6.10.

***ἄπλυτος**, ον, (πλύνω) *unwashen, unwashed*, of clothes, ἄλουτος ἀπλύτοις ἐν εἵμασιν Semon.7.5; ῥαφανίδες Eup.312, cf. Pherecr.175; of sponges, Arist.*HA*548ᵇ29; of parts of the body, Ar.*V.*1035; ἀ. ποσὶ διεξιέναι τὰ φανερώτατα D.Chr.12.43; ἄ. ἄρτος Gal.6.500. Adv. -τως, λοιδορεῖν with *foul* language, Phld.*Ir.*p.45 W.

***ἅπλ-ωμα**, ατος, τό, (ἁπλόω) *that which is unfolded, expanse*, Sch.Ar. *Av.*1218. *-**ῶς**, Adv. of ἁπλοῦς, *singly, in one way*, μένειν ἁ. ἐν τῇ αὑτοῦ μορφῇ Pl.*R.*381c, etc.; ἁ. λέγεσθαι *in one sense*, opp. πολλαχῶς, Arist.*Top.*158ᵇ10; ἁ. λεγόμενα, opp. συμπλεκόμενα, Id.*Metaph.*1014ᵃ19, cf. *Ph.*195ᵇ15; opp. κατ' ἀλλήλων λέγεσθαι, *without distinction of subject and predicate*, *Metaph.*1041ᵇ1; ἐσθλοὶ μὲν γὰρ ἁ. παντοδαπῶς δὲ κακοί Poët.ap.*EN*1106ᵇ35, etc. II. *simply, plainly*, ἀλλ' ἁ. φράσον A.*Supp.*464; ἁ. τι φράζουσ' Id.*Ch.*121; ἁ. εἰπεῖν Isoc.4.154; λαλεῖν Anaxil.22.23. b. *openly, frankly*, Isoc.3.52, X.*HG*4.1.37; *in good faith*, D.18.308, etc.: in bad sense, ἁ. ἔχειν to be *a simpleton*, Isoc.4.16. c. *in its natural state, uncooked*, of food, Jul.*Or.*6.192b. 2. *simply, absolutely*, ἁ. ἀδύνατον Th.3.45; τῶν νεῶν κατέδυ οὐδεμία ἁ. no ship was *absolutely* sunk (though some were disabled), Id.7.34; ἁ. οὐδὲ ἕν..συνίημι Philem.123; ὅσ' ἐστὶν ἀγαθὰ..ἁ. *simply* all the good things there are, Ar.*Ach.*873; ἔδωκ' ἐμαυτὸν ὑμῖν ἁ. D.18.179; ἁ. *absolutely*, opp. κατά τι (*relatively*), Arist.*Top.*115ᵇ12; opp. πρός τι, *APr.*41ᵃ5; opp. πρὸς ἡμᾶς, *APo.*72ᵃ3; opp. τινί, *Top.*116ᵃ21; ἁ. βαρύ, κοῦφον, μαλακόν, etc., *Cael.*311ᵃ17,27, *Mete.*386ᵇ32, al.; τὸ ἁ. καλόν, τὸ ἁ. ἀγαθόν, etc., *EN*1136ᵇ22, 1134ᵇ4, al.; opp. ὁτιοῦν (*in some particular*), *Pol.*1301ᵃ29; strengthd. ἁ. οὑτωσὶ Pl.*Grg.*468c, D.21.99; τὴν ἁ. δίκην *absolute, strict* justice, opp. τοὐπιεικές and χάρις, S.*Fr.*770; ἡ τελεία καὶ ἁ. κακία Arist.*EN*1138ᵃ33; τὸ ἁ. the *absolute*, Dam.*Pr.*5: Comp. ἁπλούστερον Is.4.2; -τέρως Str.6.2.4: Sup. ἁπλούστατα Pl.*Lg.*921b. 3. *in a word*, E.*Rh.*851, X.*Cyr.*1.6.33, *Mem.*1.3.2, etc. 4. *generally*, opp. σαφέστερον, Arist.*Pol.*1341ᵇ39, al.; ὡς ἁ. εἰπεῖν ib.1285ᵃ31, *EN*1115ᵃ8, al.; ἁ. δηλῶσαι *Hell.Oxy.*11.4; τὸν ἀκριβῶς ἐπιστάμενον λέγειν ἁ. οὐκ ἂν δυνάμενον εἰπεῖν Isoc.4.11, cf. Demetr.*Eloc.*100,243: in bad sense, *loosely, superficially*, λίαν ἁ. Arist.*Metaph.*987ᵃ21, *GA*756ᵇ17, al.; οὐχ ἁ. φέρειν not *lightly*, E.*IA*899. 5. *foolishly*, Plu.2.72b. -**ωσις**, εως, ἡ, *simplification*, Plot.6.9.11. -**ωτέον**, *one must simplify* Dam.*Pr.*256. -**ωτικός**, ή, όν, *simplifying*, c.gen., ib.39.

***ἄπλωτος**, ον, (πλώω) *not navigated, not navigable*, Arist.*Mir.*839ᵇ13; πελάγη Ph.2.108; ἄπλωτα πάντα ἦν *navigation was stopped*, App.*Mith.*93.

**ἀπνεής**, ές, corrupt in *AP*9.420 as epith. of πῦρ (metaph. of love).

**ἀπνεύ-μάτος**, ον, (πνεῦμα) *without wind* or *current of air*, μεσημβρία Arist.*Pr.*911ᵇ2, cf. Thphr.*CP*1.8.3. -**μων**, ον, gen. ονος, *without breath* or *life*, νεκρὰ καὶ ἀ. Simp. *in Epict.*p.6 D., Orac.ap.Dam.*Pr.*453, *Tab.Defix.Aud.*22.8 (Curium, iii A.D.). -**στί**, Adv. of ἄπνευστος, *without breathing*, ζῆν Arist.*Pr.*898ᵇ24, *Resp.*475ᵃ23; ἀ. ἔχειν *hold* one's *breath*, Pl.*Smp.*185d; *without drawing breath*, Hp.*Int.*12; λόγους συνείρειν σαφῶς καὶ ἀ. D.18.308 (-τεί), cf. Thphr.*Char.*2.9; ἀ. ἕλκειν, ἐκπίνειν, Antiph.74.14, Alex.244.3; *without breathing*, i.e. *lifeless*, ἀ. κεῖσθαι Plu.2.642d; φεύγειν ἀ. *breathlessly*, Porph.*Chr.*49. -**στία**, ἡ, *holding of the breath, not breathing*, Arist.*Pr.*881ᵇ13, 961ᵇ21. -**στιάζω**, *hold the breath*, ib.962ᵇ31. -**στος**, ον, *breathless*, ἄ. καὶ ἄναυδος Od.5.456, cf. Theoc.25.271. 2. *lifeless, dead*, Nonn.*D.*26.115; *without life*, φαρέτρη ib.15.269. II. = ἀπνεύματος, τόποι Thphr.*CP*5.12.7 (Sup.). Adv. -τως, = ἀπνευστί (q.v.), Plu.2.844f.

**ἄπνιγμος**, ον, = οὐ πεπνιγμένος, κνώδων Anon.ap.Hsch.

**ἀπνοέω**, *suffer from breathlessness*, Orib.*Syn.*9.44.1.

**ἄπνοια**, ἡ, *freedom from wind*, Hp.*Epid.*3.2. 2. *windlessness, calm*, Arist.*Pr.*944ᵇ12, Plb.34.11.19 (v.l.); *want of wind*, Thphr.*CP*2.7.5: *shelter from wind*, Arist.*GA*785ᵃ29. 3. *absence of respiration*, Gal.7.959.

***ἄπνοος**, ον, contr. **ἄπνους**, ουν:—*without wind, with but little air*, ἔαρ Hp.*Epid.*3.2, cf. Arist.*Mete.*361ᵇ6, Thphr.*CP*2.9.1. 2. *unventilated*, οἰκία Plu.2.515b; *air-tight*, κώρυκος Herod.8.74. II. *breathless*, Theopomp.Com.71. 2. *lifeless*, *AP*7.229 (Diosc.), *IG*14.1787. 3. *without breathing* or *respiration*, Heraclid.Pont.*Fr.*72,75 Voss, Arist.*HA*492ᵃ13.

***ἀπό**, Aeol., Thess., Arc., Cypr. **ἀπύ** Sapph.44, cf. 78, Alc.33, Theoc.28.16, *IG*12(2).6.45 (Mytil.), ἀπυδόμεναι ib.9(2).594 (Larissa), 5(2).6 (Tegea), etc.:—Prep. usually with Gen. but v. infr. B. (Cf. Skt. *ápa*, Lat. *ab*, Umbr. *ap-ehtre* 'ab extra', Goth. *af*, OE. *af, æf, of*, etc.) Orig. sense, *from*. [ᾰπό: where ᾱπό is found in Ep. before ϝ or liquids (as ἀπὸ ἔθεν Il.6.62, ἀπὸ νευρῆς 11.664, Hes. *Sc.*409) ἀπαί was sometimes written in later texts, cf. Eust.625.11:—ᾱ metri gr. in Ep. compds., such as ἀπονέεσθαι.]

I. OF PLACE, the earliest, and in Hom. the prevailing sense: 1. of Motion, *from, away from*, ἐσσεύοντο νεῶν ἄπο καὶ κλισιάων Il.2.208; pleonastic, ἀ. Τροίηθεν ib.24.492; ἀπ' οὐρανόθεν 8.365 (later with Advbs., ἀπὸ ἔμπροσθεν Lxx *Ec.*1.10, etc.); strengthd., ἐκτὸς ἀ. κλισίης Il.10.151; also ἀπ' αἰῶνος νέος ὤλεο, implying *departure from* life, ib.24.725; opp. ἐξ, of relatively superficial motion, λαμβάνομεν οὔτε ἐκ τῆς γῆς οὐδέν, οὔτ' ἀπὸ τῶν οἰκιῶν X.*Mem.*2.7.2; similarly of the cause or ground, ἐξ ὧν προηγώνισθε καὶ ἀφ' ὧν εἰκάζω Th.4.126:—freq. of warriors fighting *from* chariots, etc., οἱ μὲν ἀφ' ἵππων, οἱ δ' ἀ. νηῶν..μάχοντο Il.15.386; ἀφ' ἵππων μάρνασθαι Od.9.49; so ἡ μάχη ἦν ἀφ' ἵππων Hdt.1.79; λαμπὰς ἔσται ἀφ' ἵππων *on horseback*, Pl.*R.*328a; ἀφ' ἵππου θηρεύειν X.*An.*1.2.7; ἀ. νεῶν πεζομαχεῖν Th.7.62; ἐν ταῖς ναυσὶν αἱρόμενος τοὺς ἱστοὺς ἀ. τούτων ἐσκοπεῖτο X.*HG*6.2.29; ὀμμάτων ἄπο..κατέσταζον γένυν, of tears, E.*Hec.*240: joined with ἐκ, ἐκ Κορίνθου ἀ. τοῦ στρατοπέδου Pl.*Tht.*142a. 2. of Position, *away from, far from*, μένων ἀ. ἧς ἀλόχοιο Il.2.292 (cf. ἀπ' ἀνδρὸς εἶναι *to live apart from* a man or husband, Plu.*CG*4); κεκρυμμένος ἀπ' ἄλλων Od.23.110; μοῦνος ἀπ' ἄλλων *h.Merc.*193; ἀπ' ὀφθαλμῶν, ἀπ' οὔατος, *far from* sight or hearing, Il.23.53, 18.272, cf. 22.454; ἀ. θαλάσσης ᾠκίσθησαν Th.1.7, cf. 46; αὐλίζεσθαι ἀ. τῶν οἴκων Id.6.64; ἀπ' οἴκου εἶναι Id.1.99; σπεύδειν ἀ. ῥυτῆρος *far from*, i.e. *without using* the rein, S.*OC*900; in Hom. freq. strengthd., τῆλε ἀ..., νόσφιν ἀ..., Il.23.880, 5.322; in measurement of distances, ὅσον ιε' στάδια ἀ. Φυλῆς X.*HG*2.4.4, etc.; but later the numeral follows ἀ., πηγὰς ἔχων ἀ. μ' σταδίων τῆς θαλάσσης D.S.4.56; ἀ. σταδίων κ' τῆς πόλεως Plu.*Phil.*4; κατεστρατοπέδευσεν ἀ. ν' σταδίων fifty stades *away*, Id.*Oth.*11, cf. D.Chr.17.17. 3. of the mind, ἀ. θυμοῦ *away from*, i.e. *alien from*, my heart, Il.1.562; ἀ. δόξης 10.324; οὐ..ἀ. σκοποῦ οὐδ' ἀ. δόξης Od.11.344; ἀ. τοῦ ἀνθρωπείου τρόπου Th.1.76; οὐδὲν ἀ. τρόπου not *without* reason, Pl.*R.*470b; οὐκ ἀ. σκοποῦ, καιροῦ, Id.*Tht.*179c, 187e; οὐκ ἀ. γνώμης S.*Tr.*389; οὐκ ἀ. τοῦ πράγματος D.24.6; μάλα πολλὸν ἀπ' ἐλπίδος ἔπλετο A.R.2.863. 4. in pregnant sense, with Verbs of rest, previous motion being implied (cf. ἐκ), ἀνὰ δ' ἐβόασεν..ἀ. πέτρας σταθεὶς E.*Tr.*523; ἀ. τῆς ἐμῆς κεφαλῆς τὴν [ἐκείνου] κεφαλὴν ἀναδήσω, i.e. taking the chaplet *off* my head, and placing it on his, Pl.*Smp.*212e: with Verbs of hanging, where ἐκ is more common, ἀψαμένη βρόχον ἀ. μελάθρου Od.11.278. 5. with the Article, where the sense of motion often disappears, οἱ ἀ. τῶν οἰκιῶν φεύγουσιν, i.e. οἱ ἐν ταῖς οἰκίαις φεύγουσιν ἀπ' αὐτῶν, X.*Cyr.*7.5.23; οἱ ἀ. τῶν πύργων..ἐπαρήξουσι ib.6.4.18; αἴρειν τὰ ἀ. τῆς γῆς Pl.*Cra.*410b; αἱ ἵπποι αἱ ἀ. τοῦ ἅρματος v.l. in Hdt.4.8; ὁ Ἀθηναῖος ὁ ἀ. τοῦ στρατεύματος X.*An.*7.2.19; τὸν ἀ. γραμμᾶς κινεῖ λίθον Theoc.6.18. 6. partitive, λαχὼν ἀ. ληΐδος αἶσαν part *taken* *from* the booty, a share *of* it, Od.5.40; αἱρεσθαι ἀ. τῶν καλπίδων Ar. *Lys.*539; ἀ. ἑκατὸν καὶ εἴκοσι παίδων εἷς μοῦνος Hdt.6.27; ὀλίγοι ἀ. πολλῶν Th.7.87, cf. A.*Pers.*1023. 7. Math., of figures described *upon* a base, κῶνον ἀναγράφειν ἀ. κύκλου Archim.*Sph.Cyl.*1.19, etc.; τὸ ἀ. τῆς AB τετράγωνον the square *on* AB, Euc.1.47, cf. 48; εἴδεα ἀ. .. Archim.*Spir.*10,11. 8. ἀ. ἀνθρώπου ἕως γυναικός man *and* woman, Lxx 1*Es.*9.40; ἀ. ἀρσενικοῦ ἕως θηλυκοῦ ib.*Nu.*5.3. 9. *from being, instead of*, ἀθανάταν ἀ. θνατᾶς.. ἐποίησας Βερενίκαν Theoc.15.106. 10. privative, *free from, without*, ἀ. πάσης ἀκαθαρσίας *PLips.*16.19 (ii A.D.); ἀ. ζημίας *PTeb.*420.4 (iii A.D.). II. of Time, *from, after*, Hom. only in Il.8.54 ἀ. δείπνου θωρήσσοντο rising up *from*, i.e. *after*, cf. Hdt.1.133; ἀ. δείπνου εἶναι or γενέσθαι, Id.1.126, 2.78, 5.18, al.; ἀ. τοῦ σιτίου πίνειν Hp.*Salubr.*5; ἀ. τῶν σίτων διαπονεῖσθαι X.*Lac.* 5.8; in narrative, τὸ ἀ. τούτου or τοῦδε, *from* this point *onwards*, Hdt.1.4, 2.99; ἀ. τούτου τοῦ χρόνου Id.1.82, X.*An.*7.5.8; τὸ ἀπ' ἐκείνου Luc.*Tox.*25; ἡμέρη δεκάτη ἀφ' ἧς.. Hdt.3.14, etc.; δευτέρῃ ἡμέρῃ ἀ. τῆς ἐμπρήσιος Id.8.55, cf. X.*An.*1.7.18, etc.; ἀφ' οὗ χρόνου Id.*Cyr.* 1.2.13; more often ἀπ' or ἀφ' οὗ, Hdt.2.44, Th.1.18, etc.; ἀφ' οὗπερ A.*Pers.*177; ἀφ' ἧς Plu.*Pel.*15; εὐθὺς ἀ. παλαιοῦ, ἀ. τοῦ πάνυ ἀρχαίου, *of* olden time, Th.1.2, 2.15; ἀπ' ἀρχᾶς Pi.*P.*8.25, etc.; ἀ. γενεᾶς X. *Cyr.*1.2.8; ἀφ' ἑσπέρας *from the beginning of* evening, i.e. *at* eventide, Th.7.29; ἀ. πρώτου ὕπνου ib.43; ἀ. μέσων νυκτῶν Ar.*V.*218; ἀπ' ἀγροῦ *fresh from* field-work, *Ev.Marc.*15.21, cf. 7.4; ἀ. νουμηνίας X.*An.*5.6.23; χρονίζειν ἀ. τοῦ καιροῦ tarry *beyond* the time, Lxx 2*Ki.* 20.5; ἀ. τέλους ἐννέα μηνῶν *at* the end of.., ib.24.8; γενόμενος ἀ. τῆς ἀρχῆς Plu.*Caes.*5: hence ἀ. ἀγωνοθετῶν an *ex*-ἀγωνοθέτης, *IG*3. 398; ἀ. λογιστῶν *POxy.*1103.3 (iv A.D.); οἱ ἀ. ὑπατείας, = *consulares*, Hdn.7.1.9, etc.; but ἀ. τινος the *freedman of*.., *IG*5(2).50.59 (Tegea, ii A.D.), cf. ib.5(1).1391 (Andania), 1473. III. of Origin, Cause, etc.: 1. of that *from* which one is born, οὐ γὰρ ἀ. δρυός ἐσσι οὐδ' ἀ. πέτρης not *sprung from* oak or rock, Od.19.163; γίγνονται δ' ἄρα ταί γ' ἔκ τε κρηνέων ἀ. τ' ἀλσέων 10.350, cf. S.*OT*415, *OC*571, etc.: sts. ἀπό denotes remote, and ἐκ immediate, descent, τοὺς μὲν ἀ. θεῶν, τοὺς δ' ἐξ αὐτῶν τῶν θεῶν γεγονότας Isoc.12.81, cf. Hdt.7.150; πέμπτη ἀπ' αὐτοῦ γέννα A.*Pr.*853; τρίτος ἀ. Διός third *in descent from* Zeus, Pl.*R.* 391c; οἱ ἀ. γένους τινός his descendants, Plu.*Them.*32; Περσέως ἀφ' αἵματος E.*Alc.*509: of the place one *springs from*, ἵπποι.. ποταμοῦ ἄπο Σελλήεντος Il.2.839, cf. 849; Ἡρακλεῖδαι οἱ ἀ. Σπάρτης Hdt.8.114, cf. Th.1.89, etc.; τοὺς ἀ. Φρυγίας X.*Cyr.*2.1.5, etc.: hence, b. metaph. of things, Χαρίτων ἄπο κάλλος ἔχουσαι Od.6.18; θεῶν ἄπο μήδεα εἰδώς ib.12; γάλα ἀ. βοός A.*Pers.*611; μῆνις ἀφ' ἡμῶν Id.*Eu.*314; ἡ ἀφ' ὑμῶν τιμωρία Th.1.69; ὁ ἀ. τῶν πολεμίων φόβος fear *inspired by* the enemy, X.*Cyr.*3.3.53. c. of persons, οἱ ἀ. τῆς χώρας, τῆς πόλεως, country *folk*, towns*folk*, Plb.2.6.8, 5.70.8; and so of connexion with the founder or leader of a sect, οἱ ἀ. Πυθαγόρου Luc.*Herm.*14; οἱ ἀ. Πλάτωνος Plu.*Brut.*2; οἱ ἀ. τοῦ περιπάτου, ἀ. τῆς Στοᾶς, etc., Luc.*Conv.* 6; generally οἱ ἀ. φιλοσοφίας καὶ λόγων philosophers and learned men, ibid.; οἱ ἀ. σκηνῆς καὶ θεάτρου stage players, Plu.*Sull.*2; οἱ ἀ. τῆς βουλῆς Id.*Caes.*10, etc.; ὁ ἀφ' ἑστίας παῖς, v. ἑστία; ἀπ' ἐξωμίδος *with only* an ἐξωμίς, S.E.*P.*1.153. 2. of the material *from* or *of* which a thing is made, εἵματα ἀ. ξύλου πεποιημένα Hdt.7.65; ἀπ' ὄμφακος τεύχειν οἶνον A.*Ag.*970, cf. S.*Tr.*704; ὅσσα ἀ. γλυκερῶ μέλιτος Theoc.15.117; ἔνδυμα ἀ. τριχῶν καμήλου *Ev.Matt.*3.4: hence στέφανος ἀ. ταλάντων ἑξήκοντα *of* or *weighing* 60 talents, Decr.ap.D. 18.92, cf. Plb.24.1.7, *IG*2.555.10, al.: hence of value, θύειν αἶγα ἀ. δραχμᾶν εἴκοσι *GDI*3707 (Cos); κρᾶσις ἀ. τε τῆς ἡδονῆς συγκεκραμένη καὶ ἀ. τῆς λύπης Pl.*Phd.*59a; so, by an extension of this use, εἰδεχθής τις ἀ. τοῦ προσώπου ugly *of* countenance, Thphr.*Char.*28.4; θῆλυν ἀ. χροιῆς Theoc.16.49; σεμνὸς ἀ. τοῦ σχήματος Luc.*DMort.*10. 8. 3. of the instrument *from* or *by* which a thing is done, τοὺς.. πέφνεν ἀπ' ἀργυρέοιο βιοῖο by arrow *shot from* silver bow, Il.24.605; τόξου ἄπο κρατεροῦ ὀλέκοντα φάλαγγας 8.279; ἐμῆς ἀπὸ χειρός 10.371, 11.675; so ἀ. χειρὸς ἐργάζεσθαι μεγάλα Luc.*Hist.Conscr.*29; γυμνάζεσθαι ἀ. σκελῶν, χειρῶν, τραχήλου, X.*Lac.*5.9; μάχεσθαι ἀ. κόντος Str.17.3.7; ἡ ἀ. τοῦ ξίφους μάχη D.S.5.29; βάπτειν τὸν δάκτυλον ἀ. τοῦ αἵματος Lxx *Le.*4.7. 4. of the person *from* whom an act comes, i.e. *by* whom it is done, οὐδὲν μέγα ἔργον ἀπ' αὐτοῦ ἐγένετο Hdt.1.14; ζήτησιν ἀ. σφέων γενέσθαι Id.2.54; ἐπράχθη οὐδὲν ἀπ' αὐτῶν ἔργον ἀξιόλογον Th.1.17, cf. 6.61; ἀ. τινος ὀνασθαι Pl.*R.*528a, etc.; so τἀπ' ἐμοῦ, τἀπὸ σοῦ, E.*Tr.*74, S.*OC*1628; τὰ ἀ. τῶν Ἀθηναίων Th.1.127: in later Greek freq. of the direct agent, Plb.1.34.8, Str.5.4.12, D.H.9.12, *Ev.Luc.*9.22, J.*AJ*20.8.10, etc.; in codd. this may sts. be due to confusion with ὑπό, but cf. *PMag.Par.*1.256, *BGU* 1185.26 (Aug.), *SIG*820.8 (Ephesus, i A.D.), etc. 5. of the source *from* which life, power, etc., are sustained, ζῆν ἀπ' ὕλης ἀγρίης Hdt.1. 203; ἀ. κτήνεων καὶ ἰχθύων ib.216; ἀ. πολέμου Id.5.6; ἀπ' ἐλαχίστων χρημάτων X.*Mem.*1.2.14; ἀ. τῆς ἀγορᾶς Id.*An.*6.1.1; τρέφειν τὸ ναυτικὸν ἀ. τῶν νήσων Id.*HG*4.8.9, cf. Th.1.99; ἀ. τῶν κοινῶν πλουτεῖν Ar.*Pl.*569, cf. D.24.124; ἀ. μικρῶν εὔνους.. γεγένησαι Ar.*Eq.* 788, cf. D.18.102; ἀφ' ὥρας ἐργάζεσθαι *quaestum corpore facere*, Plu. *Tim.*14. 6. of the cause, means, or occasion *from, by*, or *because of* which a thing is done, ἀ. τούτου κριοπρόσωπον τὤγαλμα τοῦ Διὸς ποιεῦσι Hdt.2.42; ἀ. τινος ἐπαινεῖσθαι, θαυμάζεσθαι, ὠφελεῖσθαι, Th.2.25, 6.12, X.*Cyr.*1.1.2; ἀ. τῶν ξυμφορῶν διαβάλλεσθαι Th.5.17; τὴν ἐπωνυμίαν ἔχειν ἀ. τινος Id.1.46; ἀ. λῃστείας τὸν βίον ἔχειν X.*An.* 7.7.9; ἀπ' αὐτῶν τῶν ἔργων κρίνειν D.2.27; ἀ. τοῦ πάθους *in consequence of*.., Th.4.30; βλάπτειν τινὰ ἀ. τινος Id.7.29; κατασκευάσαντα τὸ πλοῖον ἀφ' ὧν ὑπελάμβανε σωθήσεσθαι D.18.194; τρόπαιον ἀ. τινος εἱστήκει *on occasion of* his defeat, Id.19.320; τλήμων οὐδ' ἀπ' εὐτόλμου φρενός A.*Ag.*1302, cf. 1643; ἀ. δικαιοσύνης *by reason of* it (v.l. [ὑπό]), Hdt.7.164; ἀ. τῶν αὐτῶν λημμάτων *on* the same *scale* [of] profits, D.3.34, etc.; for ὅσον ἀ. βοῆς ἕνεκα, v. ἕνεκα: hence in [ha]adverbial usages, ἀ. σπουδῆς in earnest, eagerly, Il.7.359; ἀ. τοῦ ἴσο[υ], ἀ. τῆς ἴσης, or ἀπ' ἴσης, equally, Th.1.99, 15, D.14.6, etc.; ἀπ' ὀρθ[ῆς] καὶ δικαίας τῆς ψυχῆς Id.18.298; ἀ. ἀντιπάλου παρασκευῆς Th.1.91; ἀ. τοῦ προφανοῦς openly, ib.35; ἀ. τοῦ εὐθέος straightforwardly, Id. 3.43; ἀ. τοῦ αὐτομάτου *of* free-will, Pl.*Prt.*323c; ἀ. γλώσσης *by wor[d]* of mouth, Hdt.1.123 (but also, *from* hearsay, A.*Ag.*813); ἀ. στό[μα]τος Pl.*Tht.*142d; ἀπ' ὄψεως *at* sight, Lys.16.19; ἀ. χειρὸς λογίζεσθαι *on* your fingers, Ar.*V.*656; πεύθομαι δ' ἀπ' ὀμμάτων νόστον A.*Ag* 988; ὀμμάτων ἄπο *in* the public gaze, E.*Med.*216; ἀ. τοῦ κυάμου ἄρχοντας καθίστασθαι X.*Mem.*1.2.9; ἡ βουλὴ ἡ ἀ. τοῦ κυάμου Th.8.66, cf. *IG*1.9; τοὺς ἀ. τοῦ κυάμου δισχιλίους ἄνδρας Arist.*Ath.*24.3; τριηράρχους αἱρεῖσθαι ἀ. τῆς οὐσίας Decr.ap.D.18.106; ἀφ' ἑαυτοῦ *from* oneself, *on* one's own *account*, Th.8.6, etc.; ἀφ' ἑαυτοῦ γνώμης Id.4.68; ἀ. συνθήματος, ἀ. παραγγέλματος, *by* agreement, *by* word of command, Hdt.5.74, Th.8.99; ἀ. σάλπιγγος *by sound of* trumpet, X.*Eq.Mag.*3. 12 (s.v.l.); ἐπίτροπος ἀ. τῶν λόγων, = Lat. *procurator a rationibus*, *Ann.Épigr.*1913.143a (Ephesus, ii A.D.). 7. of the object spoken of, τὰ ἀ. τῆς νήσου οἰκότα ἐστί the things *told from* or *of* the island.., Hdt.4.195, cf. 54, 7.195; νόμος κείμενος ἀ. τῶν τεχνῶν Ar.*Ra.*762.

B. in Arc., Cypr., ἀπύ takes dat., ἀπὺ τᾶ [ἀμέρᾳ] *IG*5(2).6 (Tegea); ἀπὺ τᾶ ζᾶ *Inscr.Cypr.*135.8 H. (Idalion). 2. in later Greek ἀπό is found c. acc., *PLond.*1.124.30 (iv/v A.D.).

C. in Hom. frequent with Verbs in tmesi, as Il.5.214, etc., and sts. in Prose, as Hdt.8.89.

D. in Compos.: 1. *asunder*, as ἀποκόπτω, ἀπολύω, ἀποτέμνω: and hence, *away, off*, as ἀποβάλλω, ἀποβαίνω; denoting, *removal* of an accusation, as ἀπολογέομαι, ἀποψηφίζομαι. 2. *finishing off, completing*, ἀπεργάζομαι, ἀπανδρόω, ἀπανθρωπίζω, ἀπογλαυκόω. 3. *ceasing from, leaving off*, as ἀπαλγέω, ἀποκηδεύω, ἀπολοφύρομαι, ἀποζέω, ἀπανθίζω, ἀφυβρίζω. 4. *back again*, as ἀποδίδωμι, ἀπολαμβάνω, ἀπόπλους: also, *in full*, or *what is one's own*, as ἀπέχω, ἀπολαμβάνω: freq. it only strengthens the sense of the simple. 5. *by way of abuse*, as in ἀποκαλέω. 6. almost = ἀ- priv.; sts. with Verbs, as ἀπαυδάω, ἀπαγορεύω; more freq. with Adjectives, as ἀποχρήματος, ἀπότιμος, ἀπόσιτος, ἀπόφονος.

E. ἄπο, by anastrophe for ἀπό, when it follows its Noun, as ὀμμάτων ἄπο S.*El.*1231, etc.; never in Prose. 2. ἄπο for ἄπεστι, Semon.1.20, Timocr.9.

**ἀποαγνέω·** ἀποκαθαίρω, Hsch.

**ἀποαίνυμαι,** v. ἀπαίνυμαι.

**ἀποαιρέομαι,** poet. for ἀφαιρέομαι, Il.1.275.

**ἀποᾰφύσσω,** aor. 1 ἀποήφυσα, *draw off*, Euph.131.

**ἀπόβα,** v. ἀποβαίνω.

**ἀποβᾰδίζω,** Att. fut. -ιῶ, *go away*, οἴκαδε Ar.*Fr.*475.

***ἀποβάθρα,** Ion. -βάθρη, ἡ, *ladder for disembarking, gangway*, Hdt.9.98, Th.4.12, Luc.*DMort.*10.1. II. = λάσανον 1, Suid.

**ἀπόβαθρα,** τά, *sacrifices on disembarkation*, D.C.40.18; perh. to be read in S.*Fr.*415.

***ἀποβαίνω,** fut. -βήσομαι, with Ep. aor. 1 -εβήσετο Il.2.35: aor. 2 ἀπέβην: pf. ἀποβέβηκα—in these tenses intr. (pres. not in Hom.):— *step off from* a place, νηὸς ἀ. *alight, disembark from* a ship, Od.13.281; ἀπὸ τῶν νεῶν, ἀπὸ τῶν πλοίων, Hdt.5.86, 4.110; ἐκ τῶν νεῶν X.*HG*5.1. 12: abs., *disembark*, Hdt.2.29, Th.1.111, etc.; ἀ. ἐς χώρην Hdt.7.8.β', cf. E.*Fr.*705, Th.4.9, Lys.2.24; ἐς τὴν γῆν Th.1.100; ἐξ ἵππων ἀ. ἐπὶ χθόνα *dismount* from a chariot, Il.3.265, cf. 11.619; ἵππων 17.480; but in D.61.23 τὸ ἀποβαίνειν seems to be the art of *leaping from* horse to horse (cf. ἀποβάτης); τῇ συνωρίδι τοῦ ἀποβάντος *IG*9(2).527.10 (Larissa): generally, ἀβάτων ἀποβάς *having stepped off* ground on which none should step, S.*OC*167. 2. *go away, depart*, Il.1.428, 5.133, etc.; ἀπέβη πρὸς μακρὸν Ὄλυμπον 24.468; πρὸς δώματα, κατὰ δῶμα, Od.4.657,715; μετ' ἀθανάτους Il.21.298: c. gen., ἀ. πεδίων E. *Hec.*142; ἀπὸ τῆς φάτνης X.*Eq.Mag.*1.16; of death, ἀπὸ δὲ φθίμενοι βεβᾶσι E.*Andr.*1022; of hopes, *vanish, come to nought*, Id.*Ba.*909 (lyr.). II. of events, *issue, result from*, τὰ ἔμελλε ἀποβήσεσθαι ἀπὸ τῆς μάχης Hdt.9.66; τἀναντία ἀπέβη *resulted*, Pl.*Phlb.*39a, cf. *Lg.* 782e; ὅ τι ἀποβήσεται Id.*Prt.*318a, etc.; τὸ ἀποβαῖνον, contr. τὠποβαῖνον, *the issue, event*, Hdt.2.82, etc.; τὰ ἀποβαίνοντα, τὸ ἀποβάν, *the results*, Th.1.83, 2.87; τὰ ἀποβησόμενα *the probable results*, Id.3. 38, cf. S.E.*M.*5.103. 2. freq. with an Adv. or other qualifying phrase, σκοπέειν.. τὴν τελευτὴν κῇ ἀποβήσεται how it will *turn out, issue*, Hdt.1.32; ἀ. τῇ περ εἶπε ib.86; ἀ. κατὰ τὸ ἐόν ib.97; ἀ. παρὰ δόξαν, ἀ. τοιοῦτον, Id.8.4, 7.23; τοιόνδ' ἀπέβη τόδε πρᾶγμα E. *Med.*1419, cf. X.*Cyr.*1.5.13; πολέμου τοιοῦτον ἀπέβη τὸ τέλος Plb.26. 6.15; οὐδὲν αὐτῷ.. ὡς προσεδέχετο ἀπέβαινεν Th.4.104, cf. 3.26; παρὰ γνώμαν ἀ. 5.4; opp. κατὰ γνώμαν ἀ. Theoc.15.38; πῶς ἡ φήμη δοκεῖ ὑμῖν ἀποβῆναι; And.1.131. 3. abs., *turn out well, succeed*, ἡ ὑπόσχεσις ἀπέβη Th.4.39, cf. 5.14; of dreams, *turn out true*, Arist.*Div. Somn.*463b10. 4. of persons, with an Adj., *turn out, prove to be* so and so, ἀ. οὐ κοινοί *prove* partial, Th.3.53; ἀ. χείρους Pl.*Lg.*952b; φρενιτικοὶ ἀ. Hp.*Coac.*405; τύραννος ἐκ βασιλέως ἀ. Plb.7.13.7; also of a wound, ἰάσιμον ἀ. Pl.*Lg.*878c. b. with εἰς.., ἀ. εἰς τὰ πολιτικὰ οἱ τοιοῦτοι *prove fit* for public affairs, Id.*Smp.*192a; ἐς ἀλαθινὸν ἄνδρ' ἀ. Theoc.13.15. c. of conditions, etc., ἀπέβη ἐς μουναρχίην *things ended in* a monarchy, Hdt.3.82; εἰς ἓν τέλεον καὶ νεανικόν Pl.*R.*425c; ἀποβήσεται εἰς μαρτυρίαν *Ev.Luc.*21.13. 5. of space, μέγεθος μὲν ἦν πρὸς τὸν Ἠριδανὸν ἀποβεβηκυῖα *reaching, extending to*

.., Pl.Criti.112a. 6. τῷ ἀποβεβηκότι ποδί with the hind foot, opp. τῷ προβεβηκότι, Arist.IA706a9.

B. causal, in aor. 1 ἀπέβησα, cause to dismount, disembark, land (in which sense ἀποβιβάζω serves as pres.), ἀ. στρατιήν Hdt.5.63, 6.107; ἐς τὴν Ψυττάλειαν Id.8.95. II. hence, in Pass., τὸ ἀποβαινόμενον σκέλος a leg put out so as not to bear the weight of the body, Hp.Art.52:—Act., Id.Mochl.20.

**ἀποβάλλω**, fut. -βαλῶ, throw off, ἀπὸ δὲ χλαῖναν βάλε Il.2.183, cf. 21.51; ἀπὸ φροντίδος ἄχθος.. βαλεῖν A.Ag.166: c. gen., throw off from, ἀ. ὀμμάτων ὕπνον E.Ba.692:—Med., throw off from oneself, cast off, δύναμιν βασιλέως And.3.29. 2. throw away, h.Merc.388, Hdt.3.40, etc.; ἀ. τὴν ἀσπίδα Ar.V.22, And.1.74, Lys.10.9, etc.; τὸν ἄνδρα τὸν πάρος ἀ. reject him, E.Tr.663, cf. Pl.Tht.151c, etc.; ἀ. τὰ κέρατα, τὰς ὁπλάς, cast, shed, Arist.HA500a10, 604a15, al.:—Med., Pl.Lg.802b; οὐδεὶς ἀ. ἑκὼν jettisons cargo, Arist.EN1110a9; ἀ. τὸν φιλέοντα Theoc.11.19; expose a child, Leg.Gort.4.9; despise, reject, Hp.Ep.10:—Pass., ἀποβληθεὶς τῆς τυραννίδος Plu.Comp.Dion.Brut.3. b. throw away, sell too cheap, X.Oec.20.28. 3. lose, τὴν τυραννίδα Hdt.1.60; τὰ πατρῷα, τὸν στρατόν, τὴν κεφαλήν, Id.3.53, 8.65, al.; βιοτάν S.Fr.593; τὴν οὐσίαν Ar.Ec.811, Pl.Cri.44e, etc.; ἱκανὸν μέρος τῶν ὄντων Antipho 2.1.6, etc.; opp. κτᾶσθαι, Isoc.6.57, Arist.Pol.1291b41; ἀ. δόξαν, τέχνην, Id.deAn.428b5, Metaph.1047a1, al.; ἀ. τι ὑπό τινος X.Smp.4.32; ἀ. πολλοὺς τῶν στρατιωτῶν Th.4.7; τὸν εὐεργέταν E.HF878:—in Med., ἀγαθὸν πολίτην SIG730.20 (Olbia). b. Gramm., drop a letter, etc., A.D.Pron.36.21, al. 4. degrade, Pl.Lg.630d.

**ἀπόβαμμα**, ατος, τό, water drawn from a sacred spring, IG4.1607 (Cleonae). II. tincture, infusion, Sch.Nic.Al.51.

**ἀποβάπτω**, dip, plunge, ἑωυτόν Hdt.2.47; ἐς τὴν κύλικα ἀκινάκεα Id.4.70; εἰς ποταμὸν τὰ γιγνόμενα Arist.Pol.1336a16; λίθον ἐν οἴνῳ Id.HA607a25; φαρμάκῳ τοὺς ὀϊστούς Id.Mir.845a1: metaph., ἀ. τὴν λέξιν εἰς νοῦν Plu.Phoc.5:—Pass., ὅστις ἐν ἅλμῃ..ἀπεβάφθη Ar.Fr.416; περιστερὰς ἀποβεβαμμένας εἰς μύρον Alex.62.3. 2. ἀ. ὕδωρ draw water, Lxx 2Ma.1.21.

**ἀποβᾰσῐλεύς**, έως, ὁ, ex-king, AB1089.

*__ἀπόβᾰσις__, εως, ἡ, (ἀποβαίνω) stepping off, disembarking, ἀπὸ τῶν νεῶν ἐς τὴν Λοκρίδα ἀποβάσεις ποιησάμενοι Th.3.103, cf. 115; ἡ ναυτικὴ ἐπ' ἄλλους ἀ. landing from ships in the face of an enemy, Id.4.10: abs., ποιεῖσθαι ἀ. disembark, land, Id.2.26; ἀ. ἔστι a landing is possible, Id.4.13, cf. 6.75; οὐκ ἔχει ἀπόβασιν does not admit of landing, or has no landing-place, Id.4.8; ἐν ἀποβάσει τῆς γῆς, = ἀποβάντες ἐς τὴν γῆν, Id.1.108. 2. in Plb.8.4.4 ἐξ ἀποβάσεως ἰσοϋψὴς τῷ τείχει, of a ladder, equal in height to the wall, when planted at the proper distance from its foot, cf. Id.9.19.7. II. way of escape, Plu.Sol.14. III. result, issue, τῶν εἰρημένων Aret.SA2.4, Luc.Hes.6(pl.), Artem.4.83; of prophecies, Phld.D.1.25; success in a race (prob.), Tab.Defix.Aud.234.59 (Carthage, i A.D.), al. IV. = ἀγὼν ἀποβατικός, IG7.4254 (Oropus, iv B.C.). V. numerical sequence, Theol.Ar.60.

**ἀπόβασκε**· ἀπελθέ, Theodos.Gramm.p.64 G.

*__ἀποβᾰ-τήριος__, α, ον, of Zeus, as protector of persons landing, Arr.An.1.11.7; of Artemis, IGRom.4.1539 (Erythrae). II. τὰ ἀ. (sc. ἱερά) offerings made on landing, St.Byz. s. v. Βουθρωτός, Poll.2.200. III. ἀ. τόπος place of landing, of Mt. Ararat, J.AJ1.3.5. **-της**, ου, ὁ, one that dismounts; but in usage, one who rode several horses leaping from one to the other, ἀποβάτην ἀγωνίσασθαι Plu.Phoc.20, cf. IG2.966, al., D.H.7.73, AB198,426, EM124.31, Suid. **-τικός**, ή, όν, of or for an ἀποβάτης, ἀγών IG9(2).527,531 (Larissa). Adv. -κῶς EM124.31.

**ἀποβδελύττομαι**, reject with abhorrence, Eustr. in EN19.4.

**ἀποβελίζω**, take off the spit, f.l. in Sotad.Com.1.10.

**ἀποβημᾰτίζω**, degrade from one's rank or station, Plu.Nob.21.

**ἀποβήσσω**, cough up, Hp.Aph.5.11, Prog.23: fut. -βήξομαι Id.Mul.1.41.

**ἀπο-βῐάζομαι**, force away, force back, τὸ ὑγρὸν Arist.IA714a19; τὸ κωλῦον Id.Pr.903b5, cf. GA737b29, Mete.368b10, PPetr.3p.39 (iii B.C.):—Pass., to be forced away or back, X.Cyr.4.2.24, Arist.Mete.364a29; ἀ. εἰς ἐλάττω τόπον to be forced into.., ib.366b11. 2. treat with violence, τινά Plb.16.24.5: abs., 33.9.5, cf. SIG629.20 (Delph., ii B.C.), Wilcken Chr.11 A 30 (ii B.C.): metaph., κατὰ τὰς λέξεων ὁμιλίας Phld.Oec.p.59 J. II. abs., use force, X.Cyr.3.1.19, Arist.Mete.364b8, al.; force its way, ib.351a6:—Act. -βιάζω, Sch.Theoc.6.18. **-βιάομαι**, = foreg., Hp.Morb.1.24.

**ἀποβῐβ-άζω**, causal of ἀποβαίνω B, make to get off, esp. from a ship, disembark, put on shore, τινά Th.6.97, etc.; τινὰ εἰς τόπον Hdt.8.76, Pl.Grg.511e; ἐς τὴν πολεμίαν ἀποβιβάζων τὸν πόδα Ar.V.1163; ἀ. τινὰ ὅποι αὐτὸς κελεύοι X.HG7.4.3:—Med., ἀποβιβάσασθαί τινας ἀπὸ τῶν νεῶν cause them to be put on shore, Hdt.9.32. **-ασμός**, ὁ, disembarkation, Iamb.VP3.17.

*__ἀποβιβρώσκω__, eat off, in aor. Pass. χεῖρας ἀποβρωθέντα AP7.294 (Tull. Laur.).

*__ἀποβι-όω__, cease to live, λάθε ἀποβιώσας Philostr.VA8.28; ἀπεβίω Hld.4.7, cf. Ant.Diog.10. **-ωσις**, εως, ἡ, ceasing to live, death, Plu.2.389a, CIG4253 (Lycia), al. **-ώσκομαι**, = ἀποβιόω, Herm. in Phdr.p.202 A.

**ἀποβλάπτω**, ruin utterly, Pi.N.7.60, Pl.Lg.795d:—Pass., ἀποβλαφθῆναι φίλου to be robbed of a friend, S.Aj.941.

**ἀποβλαστ-άνω**, shoot forth from, spring from, ἀπέβλαστον ματρὸς ὠδῖνος S.OC533, cf. Plu.2.954c, Hierocl. in CA17p.459 M., Iamb.Myst.3.20. **-ημα**, ατος, τό, shoot, Thphr.CP1.20.1: metaph., τὸ ἑαυτοῦ ἀ. πᾶς φιλεῖ Pl.Smp.208b. **-ησις**, εως, ἡ, shooting forth, growth, νεύρων Hp.Art.45, cf. Gal.UP8.6; of roots, Dsc.2.183.

**ἀπό-βλεμμα**, ατος, τό, steadfast gaze, Phryn.Com.75. **-βλεπτέον**, one must consider, Gal.11.407. **-βλεπτος**, ον, gazed on by all, admired, E.Hec.355, Procop.Arc.9, al. ***-βλέπω**, fut. -βλέψομαι Luc.Somn.12, etc., but -βλέψω Hero Spir.2.34: pf. -βέβλεφα Antip.Stoic.3.254 codd. Stob.:—**Med.**, pres., Luc VH2.47 (v.l.): aor., Sch.Od.12.247:—Pass., Ar.Ec.726:—look away from all other objects at one, gaze steadfastly, ἐς ἐμέ Hdt.7.135; εἴς σε E.Andr.246, cf. Pl.Chrm.162b, al.; ἐς ἀκτάς E.Hipp.1206; ἐς μίαν τύχην Id.Hel.267; πρὸς τὸ Ἡραιον Hdt.9.61, cf. Pl.R.431b; πρός τινα Id.Phd.115c, Phdr.234d, al. 2. pay attention to, regard, ἐς τὸ κακόν Ar.Ra.1171; πρὸς τὰ κοινὰ E.Supp.422; εἰς τὰ πράγματα ἀ. φαύλως ἔχοντα D.2.29; εἰς τὸ κέρδος μόνον Demetr.Com.Vet.4; εἰς τὴν μισθαποδοσίαν Ep.Hebr.11.26; ἐπί τι Pl.Phlb.61d; κατά τι Luc.DMort.18.1; πρός τι Pl.R.477c, al.; εἰς τὰ πράγματα καὶ πρὸς τοὺς λόγους ἀ. D.3.1: c. acc., Thphr.Vert.8, Plu.Luc.26, etc. 3. of places, etc., look, face in a particular direction, πρὸς ὁδόν D.C.76.11 (of a statue); Ῥήνου προχοάς AP9.283 (Crin.); ἐπὶ τὴν ἀνατολήν J.AJ11.5.5. 4. look upon with love, wonder or admiration, look at as a model, c. acc., οὐ χρὴ..μέγαν ὄλβον ἀ. S.Fr.593; ἀ. τινά Luc.Vit.Auct.10, cf. D.19.265; προϊόντα ἴσα θεῷ ἀπέβλεπον Philostr.VA5.24; more freq. with a Prep., εἰς ἔμ' Ἑλλὰς..ἀ. E.IA1378; ἡ σὴ πατρὶς εἰς σὲ ἀ. X.HG6.1.8, cf. Th.3.58; εἰς τὴν εὐσέβειαν τῆς θεοῦ SIG867.11 (Ephesus); so ἀ. πρός τινα E.IT928, X.Mem.4.2.30, Thphr.Char.2.2; of a vain person, ἀ. εἰς τὴν ἑαυτῆς σκιάν X.Mem.2.1.22; of entire dependence, πάντα ἀ. εἰς τὸν ἐραστήν Pl.Phdr.239b; εἰς ἀλλοτρίαν τράπεζαν X.An.7.2.33; look longingly, ἐς τὸν ἀγρόν Ar.Ach.32:—Pass., to be looked up to, Id.Ec.726, Aeschin.Socr.Fr.56 D.; ὡς εὐδαίμων ἀ. Luc.Nigr.13, cf. Somn.11. 5. ἐς τοιόνδ' ἀποβλέψας μόνον τροπαῖον αὐτοῦ στήσομαι with a single look, E.Andr.762. II. look away, D.Chr.21.13: c. gen., Philostr.Im.1.1; ἀ. ἀπ' ἀμφοτέρων face both ways, dub. in X.HG2.3.31; ἀπὸ τοῦ συμφέροντος Antip. l. c. III. Med., look at each other, ταυρωπὸν ἀποβλεψάμενοι Ph.1.602. **-βλεψις**, εως, ἡ, of a place, ἀ. ἔχειν πρὸς βορρᾶν look towards.., Gp.2.3.7.

**ἀπό-βλημα**, ατος, τό, anything cast away, Lxx Wi.13.13, Sch.Ar.Eq.412. **-βλήσιμος**, ον, fit to be cast away, CPHerm.119r vi 5 (iii A.D.). **-βλησις**, εως, ἡ, outpouring; μέθης ἀ., of exclamations uttered in liquor, Eust.1767.59. **-βλητέος**, α, ον, to be thrown away, rejected, Pl.R.387b, Luc.Herm.18. II. ἀποβλητέον one must reject, A.D.Conj.226.10. **-βλητικός**, ή, όν, apt to throw off, καρπῶν Thphr.CP2.9.3. **-βλητος**, ον (η, ον D.L.7.127, Iamb.Myst.1.19), to be thrown away or aside, as worthless, οὔ τοι ἀπόβλητ' ἐστὶ θεῶν ἐρικυδέα δῶρα Il.3.65; οὔ τοι ἀπόβλητον ἔπος ἔσσεται 2.361; γίγαρτον Simon.88, etc., cf. Hp.Ep.10 and late Prose, as Ph.2.294, Luc.Tox.37, Plu.2.821a, Plot.6.7.31, Procop.Arc.11. 2. capable of being thrown off, Iamb. l. c.; capable of being lost, D.L. l. c.

**ἀποβλίττω**, cut out the comb from the hive: hence, steal away, carry off, ὁ δ' ἀπέβλισε θοἰμάτιόν μου Ar.Av.498: aor. Med. ἀπεβλίσατο cj. Reisk. in AP7.34 (Antip. Sid.).

**ἀπο-βλύζω**, spirt out, ἀ. οἴνου spirt out some wine, Il.9.491, cf. Archil.32; ὑδαρὲς ἀ. Aret.SD2.6. II. intr., flow forth, πηγαὶ ἀ. τῶν ὀρῶν Philostr.Im.1.9, cf. Procop.Aed.2.2, al. **-βλυστάνω**, = foreg., πηγαὶ ἀ. ὕδωρ ib.1.11. **-βλύω**, = foreg., Orph.A.1066.

*__ἀποβλώσκω__, go away, A.R.3.1143.

**ἀποβολ-εύς**, έως, ὁ, one who has lost, ὅπλων Pl.Lg.944b. **-ή**, ῆς, ἡ, throwing away, e.g. ὅπλων ib.943e sq.; jettison, Ph.2.413; in Gramm., dropping of a letter, etc., A.D.Pron.55.7, al.; τόνου Synt.130.1. 2. loss, opp. κτῆσις, χρημάτων Pl.La.195e, Arist.EN1115a21, etc.; ἐπιστήμης Pl.Phd.75d, cf. Euphro 1.27: pl., τὰς τῶν κακῶν ἀ. Arist.Rh.1362a36, cf. Isoc.3.32. **-ιμαῖος**, ον, apt to throw away, c. gen., τῶν ὅπλων Ar.Pax678. 2. Pass., usually thrown away, worthless, Gloss. **-ον**· ἀποβεβλημένον, Hsch.

**ἀποβόομαι**, Pass., of Io, become a cow, Eust.278.32.

**ἀποβορρότατος**, ον, most northerly, POxy.506.26 (ii A.D.).

**ἀπο-βοσκέω**, = sq., EM120.5. **-βόσκομαι**, feed upon, καρπόν Ar.Av.749,1066.

**ἀποβουκολ-έω**, lead astray, as cattle, βοῦς ἐς τὴν ἰδίαν ἀγέλην Longus 1.27. 2. lead away shepherds from the sheep, τῶν θρεμμάτων Chor.p.92 B. 3. let stray, lose (as a bad shepherd does his sheep), χαρίεν γὰρ εἰ..τῇ θυγατρὶ τὸν παῖδα ἀποβουκολήσαιμι.. if I were to lose my daughter her son, X.Cyr.1.4.13:—Pass., stray, lose one's way, Luc.Nav.4. 4. beguile, soothe, Id.Am.16; lead astray, seduce, Id.Bis Acc.13. **-ίζω**, = ἀποβουκολέω 3, Chor. in Rh.Mus.49.522.

*__ἀπό-βρασμα__, ατος, τό, that which is thrown off, Alex.Trall.Febr.6; scum, Hsch.; chaff, Id., Suid. ***-βρασμός**, ὁ, throwing off of scum, S.E.M.9.103. **-βράσσω**, Att. -ττω, Poll.6.91: mostly in aor. -έβρασα:—throw out froth, like boiling water, and metaph., shake, sift out the bran from the meal, Call.Fr.232:—Pass., spirt out, Hp.Nat.Puer.31; to be cast ashore, Thphr.Fr.30.3; νεκροὶ ἀπεβράσθησαν εἰς τοὺς αἰγιαλοὺς Ph.2.174. 2. metaph., εἰς τὰ τῆς ἐσχατιᾶς ib.354. II. intr., cease to boil, Alciphr.1.23.

**ἀπό-βρεγμα**, ατος, τό, infusion, Agatharch.61, Str.16.4.17, Dsc.4.81, Aret.CA1.1, Plu.2.614b. **-βρεξις**, εως, ἡ, moistening, Aq., Sm.Nu.6.3, Gal.6.652. **-βρέχω**, steep well, soak, Thphr.CP2.5.5, IG4.955.9 (Epid.): metaph., τὴν γλῶσσαν εἰς νοῦν ἀ. Zeno Stoic.1.67, cf. Suid. s. v. Ἀριστοτέλης:—Pass., aor. part. -βρεχθεὶς Thphr.HP

5.9.5; –*βραχείς* Dsc.1.110: metaph., ὡς τὰ ἄχη τῆς ψυχῆς ἀποβρέχοιτο Philostr.*VA*7.22.

**ἀποβρίζω,** *go off to sleep, go sound asleep*, Od.9.151: aor. imper. ἀπόβριξον Theoc.*Ep*.19; ὕπνον ἀ. Call.*Epigr*.18; βαιὸν ἀποβρίξαντες Q.S.5.661.

**ἀποβρόξαι,** aor. of *ἀποβρόχω, *swallow, gulp down part of a thing* (cf. ἀναβρόξειε), prob. l. *AP*7.506 (Leon.); cf. ἀποβρύκω.

**ἀποβροχή,** ἡ, v.l. for βροχή (q.v.), Dsc.1.43.

**ἀποβροχθίζω,** *gulp down*, Ar.*Fr*.236.

**ἀποβροχ-ίζω,** *ligature*, Sor.1.80, Gal.14.784. II. *bind tightly*, λαιμόν *AP*9.410 (Tull. Sab.). III. *strangle*, ἑαυτόν Polyaen. 8.63. **–ισμός,** ὁ, *making a ligature*, Antyll.ap.Orib.45.24. 3. **–ιστέον,** *one must make a ligature*, Archig.ap.Orib.47.13.5.

**ἀποβρύκω** [ῡ], *bite off, eat greedily of*, τῶν κρεῶν (partit. gen.) Eub. 42: abs., *bite in pieces*, Archipp.35; ἀπέβρυξεν is v.l. (Planud.) for –έβροξεν in *AP*7.506 (Leon.).

**ἀπόβρωμα,** ατος, τό, *something devoured*, Ps.-Callisth.3.15.

**ἀποβύω** [ῡ], *stop up*, *AB*426.

⊛**ἀποβώμιος,** ον, *far from an altar, godless*, Κύκλωψ E.*Cyc*.365. II. in Eust.1720.28, literally, *not offered on an altar*, but on the ground. 2. *not suitable for an offering*, *IG*5(2).403 (Lusi, dub.).

**ἀπόγαιος,** v. ἀπόγειος.

**ἀπογαιόω,** *make into land*, Heraclit.*All*.22 (Pass.): Medic., *form a stone*, Gal.19.648,672; cf. ἀπογεόομαι.

**ἀπογᾰλακτ-ίζω,** *wean from the mother's milk*, Diph.74, Lxx *Ge*.21. 8, Sor.1.116, *POxy*.37 i 22 (i A.D.), *PLips*.31.20 (ii A.D.). **–ισις,** εως, ἡ, *weaning*, Ar.Byz.*Epit*.42.14. ⊛**–ισμός,** ὁ, = foreg., Hp. *Dent*.16. **–ιστέον,** *one must wean*, Sor.1.78. **–όομαι,** Pass., *to become milky*, Antyll.ap.Orib.4.11.6. ⊛**–ος,** ον, *weaned*, Aët. 4.29.

**ἀπογᾰληνίζω,** *calm down*, ἑαυτόν prob. in Plu.2.655b.

**ἀπογᾰληνιόομαι,** Pass., *become calm*, Ps.-Democr.*Symp.Ant.* p.4 G.

**ἀπογᾰληνόομαι,** *calm down*, of physical disturbances, Sor.1.46.

**ἀπόγαλον,** τό, = ἀβρότονον, Ps.-Dsc.3.24.

⊛**ἀπόγειος,** α, ον, (γῆ) *from land, coming off land*, ἄνεμοι, πνεῦμα, Arist.*Mu*.394$^{b}$14, *Mete*.363$^{a}$1, cf. Thphr.*CP*2.3.1; ἡ ἀ. (sc. αὔρα) *land-breeze*, Arist.*Pr*.940$^{b}$24; αἱ ἀπόγεαι ib.945$^{a}$4; τὰ ἀ. ib.940$^{b}$18. 2. ἀπόγαιον or ἀπόγειον, τό, *mooring cable*, Plb.33.9.6, Luc.*VH*1.42, Polem.*Call*.26, Lib.*Or*.59.139, 61.21, etc.; in full, ἀπόγεια (–γυια cod.) σχοινία Hsch. s.v. γύαια; cf. ἀπόγυον. II. *far from the earth*, Plu.2.933b, cf. Olymp.*in Mete*.10.14, al.: Comp., Cleom.2.6, Ptol.*Alm*.9.1: Sup., Theo Sm.p.157 H.; τὸ ἀ. (sc. σημεῖον), in Astronomy, a planet's *greatest distance from the earth, apogee*, Ptol. *Alm*.3.3. 2. *from the shore*, Luc.*Lex*.15.

⊛**ἀπογεισ-όω,** *crown with a cornice*, γείσοις Κορινθίοις *IG*2$^{2}$.463.71, cf. *BCH*35.12 (Delos): metaph., *make to jut out like a cornice*, ὀφρύσι ἀ. τὰ ὑπὲρ τῶν ὀμμάτων X.*Mem*.1.4.6:—Pass., *jut out like a cornice*, Arist.*GA*781$^{b}$13. **–ωμα,** ατος, τό, *projecting cornice*: metaph. of eyebrows, Arist.*PA*658$^{b}$16.

**ἀπόγεμε·** ἄφελκε (Cypr.), Hsch.

**ἀπογεμίζομαι,** Pass., of a ship, *discharge her cargo*, D.H.3.44; *to be emptied of contents*, Ps.-Luc.*Philopatr*.24.

**ἀπογενεσία,** ἡ, = sq., *PMag.Par*.1.721.

**ἀπογένεσις,** εως, ἡ, *decease*, τὰς τῶν ψυχῶν γενέσεις καὶ ἀ. Porph. *Antr*.31, cf. 24, Plot.3.4.6.

**ἀπογενν-άω,** *produce*, Hp.*Morb*.1.25 (Pass.); τὸ ὅμοιον Thphr.*CP* 1.16.12; γάλα Sor.1.27; συμπτώματα Gal.7.200; of atoms *generating* bodies, Epicur.*Nat*.22 G., cf. Diog.Oen.20, Aen.Gaz.*Thphr.* p.42 B.; ἀ. δυσμένειαν Demad.15:—Pass., Epicur.*Ep*.2 p.40 U.; τὰ ὑπὸ μεγαλοφροσύνης –ώμενα Longin.15.12, cf. Ph.1.144, Plot.6.1.6, etc. II. *destroy*, ἐγώ εἰμι ὁ γεννῶν καὶ ὁ ἀπογεννῶν *PMag. Lond*.46.155. **–ημα,** ατος, τό, *offspring*, Ti.Locr.97e, Ael.*NA* 15.8. **–ησις,** εως, ἡ, *generation*, Sch.Epicur.*Ep*.3 p.47 U., Jul. *Or*.4.153c, Procl.*Inst*.152.

**ἀπογεόομαι,** Pass., *to be changed into earth*, Ph.2.508 (cj.).

**ἀπογεύ-ω,** *give* one *a taste of*, *AP*4.3.39 (Agath.); opp. ἀποπληρόω, Herod.Med.ap.Orib.5.30.21. II. Med., *take a taste of*, σιτίων, Hp.*Epid*.7.2, cf. Pl.*R*.354b, *Tht*.157d, X.*Cyr*.1.3.4, Plb.3.57.8; ἑκάστου μικρὸν ἀ. Eub.42, cf. Antiph.326: metaph., ἐλπίδος Ph.2. 338. **–σις,** εως, ἡ, *tasting*, τῶν παθῶν Olymp.*in Alc*.p.6 C., cf. *PMag.Leid.W*.9.34.

**ἀπογεφῡρόω,** *bank off, fence with dykes*, τὴν Μέμφιν Hdt.2.99.

**ἀπογηράσκω,** *grow old*, Thgn.821, Hp.*Aph*.2.20; part. ἀπογηράς dub. l. Alex.278; inf. ἀπογηρᾶν, of senile dementia, Gal.16.696; ἀπεγήρασα Thphr.*HP*7.13.6; of vines, ὅσσαι δέ κα..ἀπογηράσκωντι *fail from old age*, *Tab.Heracl*.1.170.

**ἀπογίγνομαι,** Ion. and later Att. **–γίνομαι,** fut. –γενήσομαι:—*to be away from, have no part in*, τῆς μάχης Hdt.9.69: τῶν ἁμαρτημάτων Th.1.39; *to be freed from*, κακῶν ἀπογεγονότες J.*AJ*19.2.2. II. abs., *to be taken away*, opp. προσγίγνομαι, Zeno Eleat.2, Pl.*Ti*.82b, *Lg*.850a; ἀπεγίγνετο οὐδέν..προσεγίγνετο δέ Th.2.98: generally, *to be away, absent*, Antipho 2.3.5, Pl.*Phd*.69b, D.8.35: ἀπό τινος Aeschin.2.126; of diseases, opp. προσπίπτω, Hp.*Morb.Sacr*.1 (dub. l.). 2. esp. of death, ἀ. ἐκ τῶν οἰκίων *depart* from the house, *die* out of it, Hdt.2.85; ἀπογενέσθαι alone, *to be dead*, ib.136, cf. *IG*9(1).334. 37 (Locr.), Ocell.1.14; οἱ ἀπογενόμενοι *the dead*, Th.2.34; ὁ ὕστατον αἰεὶ ἀ. he who *died* last, Hdt.6.58, cf. 5.4; οἱ ἀπογιγνόμενοι *the dying*, Th.2.51, Hdt.3.111. 3. *fall away, be lost*, Th.5.74; opp. ἐκβλαστάνω, Paus.5.12.1. III. *arrive at*, ἀ. δωδεκαταῖος Hp.*Epid.* 4.11. IV. *turn out, become*, τράχηλος σκληρὸς ἀ. ib.12 (dub. l.); νωθροὶ ἀ. Id.*Prorrh*.1.117 (dub. l.). V. ἀ. τὸ ἕκτον μέρος εἰς τρίχας καὶ αἷμα *goes into, is consumed in forming*.., Arist.*HA*595$^{b}$1.

⊛**ἀπογιγνώσκω,** Ion. and later Att. **–γῑνώσκω,** fut. –γνώσομαι:—*depart from a judgement, give up a design* or *intention* of doing, τοῦ μάχεσθαι X.*An*.1.7.19, cf. Plb.1.29.5, etc.; ἀ. τὸ κατὰ γῆν πορεύεσθαι X.*HG*7.5.7; ἀ. διώκειν Plu.*Ant*.34, cf. *Thes*.6; ἀ. μὴ βοηθεῖν *resolve not* to help, D.15.9, cf. *IG*2$^{2}$.457.30: c. gen., *give up* a notion, Simp. *in Ph*.610.9. II. c. gen. rei, *despair of*, τῆς ἐλευθερίας Lys.2. 46; οὐδενὸς χρὴ πράγματος ὅλως ἀπογνῶναι Men.131; ὡς ἀνιάτων D.Chr.32.97; ὑπὲρ σφῶν Jul.*Or*.2.61c: abs., *despair*, D.4.42 (where some codd. supply ἑαυτῶν), Babr.43.18: c. fut. inf., αἱρήσειν ἀ. Arr. *An*.3.20.3; ἀκούσεσθαι Luc.*Icar*.10: c. aor. inf., τὴν πόλιν ἀπέγνω ἑλεῖν Arr.*An*.1.5.8, cf. D.Chr.32.9. 2. c. acc., *give up as hopeless* or *desperate*, τὴν σωτηρίαν Arist.*EN*1115$^{b}$2; τὰς πρεσβείας Plb.5.1.5, al.; τὰς ἐλπίδας Id.2.35.1; ἀ. τι ἀπὸ τῶν παρόντων App.*Hisp*.37; ἀρετῆς ἀκρίβειαν Porph.*Antr*.36; ἀ. αὐτόν Plb.21.26.14:—Pass., *to be given up*, τὰ παρ' ὑμῶν D.19.54; ἐλπίς D.H.5.15; ἐλευθερία Luc. *Tyr*.6; ἀπεγνωσμέναι ἐλπίδες *forlorn* hopes, Plb.30.8.3; ἐπιβουλὴ –μένη Hdn.4.4.3; ἀπεγνωσμένοι ἄνθρωποι *desperate* men, Id.1.16.4 (but ἄνθρωποι ἀπεγνωκότες Plu.*Alex*.16); ὑπὸ τῶν ἰατρῶν ἀ. *to be despaired of*.., Id.*Per*.13. Adv. ἀπεγνωσμένως *in despair*, Id.*Nic*.21. b. *renounce, reject*, τι Hp.*Medic*.4, cf. D.3.33; τινάς Id.6.16, cf. D.C.73. 15; φιλίαν Iamb.*VP*22.102. III. as law-term, *refuse to receive* an accusation, *reject*, γραφήν, ἔνδειξιν, D.22.39, 58.17: hence, 2. ἀ. τινός (sc. δίκην vel γραφήν) *reject* the charge *brought against* a man, i.e. *acquit* him, opp. καταγιγνώσκειν τινός, Id.40.39, cf. Aeschin.2.6, etc.; ἀ. τί τινος Is.5.34: c. inf., ἀ. τινὸς μὴ ἀδικεῖν *acquit* him of wrong, Lys.1.34; also οὐκ ἀπέγνω τῆς δίκης D.34.21.

**ἀπογκ-έω,** (ὄγκος) *swell up*, Hp.*Aff*.5. **–όω,** *stuff*, χόρτῳ dub. l. in Porph.*Abst*.2.30 (ἐπ– Nauck).

**ἀπογλαυκ-όομαι,** Pass., *suffer from* γλαύκωμα of the eyes, Aristeas 316, D.S.3.24, Plu.*Tim*.37; τοὺς ὀφθαλμούς Vett.Val.69.10; Ἀπεγλαυκωμένος, title of a play of Alexis. 2. *become grey-blue*, of the pupil, Dem.Ophth.ap.Aët.7.53; *to be dyed blue*, *PHolm*.26. 32. **–ωσις,** εως, ἡ, *formation of a* γλαύκωμα, Dsc.1.54, Ptol.*Tetr.* 149 (pl.), Orib.*Syn*.3.151.

**ἀπογλάφομαι** [λᾰ], *scrape off from oneself, obliterate*, τὸν ἄνδρα.. ἀπεγλαψάμην *Com.Adesp*.574, cf. Paus.Gr.*Fr*.109.

**ἀπόγλουτος,** ον, *with small rump*, Suid. s.v. λίσποι.

**ἀπογλῠκαίνω,** *sweeten*, D.S.1.40, cf. Ruf.ap.Orib.8.47*b*7; ἀπεγλυκασμένος Diph.Siph.ap.Ath.2.55f.

**ἀπογλῠφ-ή,** ἡ, *place scraped bare*, Asclep.Jun.ap.Gal.12.694. **–ω,** *scrape* or *peel off*, Aret.*CD*1.2, Alciphr.3.60; *scrape thin*, Heliod. ap.Orib.48.33.3; *carve*, of sculpture, *Rev.Phil*.44.251 (Didyma, ii B.C.).

**ἀπογλωττίζομαι,** Pass., *to be deprived of tongue*, Luc.*Lex*.15.

**ἀπόγνοια,** ἡ, (ἀπογιγνώσκω) *despair*, τοῦ κρατεῖν Th.3.85.

**ἀπογνώμων,** ον, = ἀγνώμων III, Hsch., Suid.

**ἀπο-γνώσιμος,** ον, *desperate*, of errors of conduct, Phld.*Lib.* p.22 O. **–γνωσις,** εως, ἡ, = ἀπόγνοια, τοῦ βίου D.H.1.81, Aret.*SA* 2.2; πραγμάτων Luc.*Somn*.17; ἐλπίδος Ph.2.300: abs., Aristaenet. 1.13. II. *rejection*, φίλου Iamb.*VP*22.102. **–γνωστέον,** *one must give up in despair*, ἐλπίδας Ph.1.455, cf. Aristaenet.1.17. 2. *one must reject the view*, Plot.4.9.2: c. gen., Simp.*in Ph*.610.9. **–γνωστής,** οῦ, ὁ, *desperate man*, Hsch. **–γνωστικῶς,** Adv. *in a desperate way, as in a hopeless case*, Arr.*Epict*.3.1.24.

**ἀπο-γομή,** ἡ, *discharge* of cargo, *PBaden* 26.73,75. **–γομόω,** *unload* cargo, *Stud.Pal*.8 No.1094.

**ἀπογονή,** ἡ, *issue, posterity*, *Gloss.*

⊛**Ἀπογονικός,** ὁ (sc. μήν), name of a month in Cyprus, *Hemerolog. Flor.*

⊛**ἀπόγονος,** ον, *born* or *descended from*, Γλαύκου οὔτε τι ἀ. ἐστι has no *descendant*, Hdt.6.86.δ': in pl., *descendants*, Id.1.7, 4.148, al., Th.1. 101; σαὶ..ἀπόγονοι thy *offspring*, S.*OC*534 (lyr.): metaph., ἀ. τοῦ ἐφθαρμένου πνεύματος Hp.*Ep*.19 (*Hermes* 53.65); ἀ. τέταρτος, ἕβδομος Paus.4.15.32: fem. ἀπογόνη *Milet*.3 No.176. II. *viable*, Hp.*Epid.* 2.3.17.

**ἀπογραΐζω,** *skim off*, ἀφρὸν γάλακτος Sch.Nic.*Al*.91.

**ἀπογρᾰφ-εύς,** έως, ὁ, *registrar*, Sch.Pl.*Lg*.850c. **–ή,** ἡ, *register, list*, of lands or property, Pl.*Lg*.745d, 850d, etc.; of the πεντηκοστολόγοι, D.34.7; ἀ. τῆς οὐσίας *IG*2.476.14; ἐφήβων *CIG* (add.) 1997c (Maced.); *list* of moneys claimed by the state from private persons, Lys.17.4, D.20.32. 2. *register of persons liable to taxation*, *Ev.Luc.* 2.2, J.*AJ*18.1.1; ἡ κατ' οἰκίαν ἀ. *PLond*.2.260.79 (i A.D.), etc.; of the Roman *census-lists*, Plu.*Cat.Ma*.16 (pl.); *muster-roll* of soldiers, Plb.2.23.9. 3. generally, ἐξ ἀπογραφῆς λέγειν from *a written list*, Sotad.Com.1.35. II. as Att. law-term, *copy of a declaration* made before a magistrate, *deposition* or *information* laid, Lys.9.3, 29.1, Lex ap.D.35.51; ποιεῖσθαι ἀ., = ἀπογράφειν, D.53.1; τινὸς κατά τινος And.1.23, cf. Harp. s.v. 2. any *written declaration* before a magistrate, ἀ. ποιείσθωσαν δηλοῦντες κτλ. *POxy*.237 vii 33 (i A.D.), etc.; esp. *declaration* of property or persons liable to taxation, *BGU*1147. 26 (i B.C.), etc. **–ος,** ον, *copied*:—as Subst., ἀ., ὁ, *a copy*, D.H.*Is.* 11, D.L.6.84; ἀπόγραφον, τό, Cic.*Att*.12.52.3. ⊛**–ω,** *write off, copy*, and in Med., *have* a thing *copied, have a copy made of*, τι Pl.*Chrm.* 156a, Plu.2.221b; *commit to writing*, ὀνόματα Pl.*Criti*.113b. II. *enter in a list, register*, ἔθνος ἐν ἕκαστον ἀπέγραφον οἱ γραμματισταί Hdt.

7.100:—Pass., *to be registered*, παρὰ τοῖς ἄρχουσι Pl.*Lg*.914c, cf. Men. 272; πρὸς τὸν ἄρχοντα Is.6.44:—freq. Med., *register as one's own property*, ἄρνας δέκα δύο *POxy*.246.10 (i A.D.); *declare* as liable to taxation, *PTaur*.1 vii 11 (ii B.C.), etc. 2. Med. also, *register, note for one's own use*, τὰ ἔτεα Hdt.2.145, 3.136, cf. Heraclid.Pont.ap. Ath.11.554e, etc. 3. Med., *register oneself*, οἱ Ἐλευσῖνάδε ἀπογραψάμενοι Lys.25.9; πρὸς τὸν ταξίαρχον εἰς τὴν τάξιν X.*Cyr*.2.1.18; ἔξεστι πᾶσιν ἀπογραψαμένοις ἐκκλησιάζειν Arist.*Pol*.1297$^a$24; φυλῆς ἧστινος ἂν ἀπογράψηται *IG*2.54*b*11 (iv B.C.); ἀπεγράψανθο ἐμ πελτοφόρας ib.7.2823 (Boeot.); ἀ. εἰς ἀγῶνας πυγμὴν ἢ παγκράτιον *enter oneself for*.., Plb.39.1.8; but ἀπογραψάμενος πύκτης *AP*11.75 (Lucill.); γέρδιος -όμενος *POxy*.252.4 (i A.D.); ἐπὶ στρατηγίαν ἀ. *enter as candidate for*.., Plu.*Sull*.5; also ἀπογράφομαι ἐμαυτόν *PGrenf*.1.45.6 (ii B.C.); αὐτοὺς ἀ. Plu.*Nic*.14. b. metaph., *subscribe to*, τῇ ἐμῇ αἱρέσει Vett.Val.271.18. III. as Att. law-term, 1. ἀ. τινά *enter* a person's name for the purpose of accusing him, *give in a copy of the charge* against him, And.1.12, etc.; generally, *inform against, denounce*, X.*HG*2.3.11: c. acc. et inf., ἀ. τινὰ μορίαν ἀφανίζειν Lys.7.29: Med., *enter one's name as an accuser, indict*, τινά Antipho6.37: abs., ibid.; of the magistrate who receives the charge, ἀπογράφεσθαι τὴν δίκην Antipho6.41:—in Pass., of the person accused, ἀ. φόνου δίκην ib.36, Lys.7.2, etc. 2. *hand in a list* or *inventory* of property alleged to belong to the state, but held by a private person, Id. 17.4, al., D.53.1,2; ἀ. οὐσίαν τινὸς ὡς δημοσίαν οὖσαν Hyp.*Eux*.34; generally, *give in a list* or *statement* of property, τοῖς ἄρχουσι τὸ πλῆθος τῆς αὑτῶν οὐσίας Pl.*Lg*.754d; τὰ χωρία καὶ τὰς οἰκίας D.22.54:—Pass., 40.22:—Med., *have such list given in, see it done*, Lys.12.8, al.; ἀπογραφὴν ἀπογράψασθαι D.42.16; τίμημα μικρὸν Is.7.39, cf. 11.34; ἀ. ἀπόλειψιν *have it registered*, D.30.17. b. c. acc. pers., ἀπέγραψεν ταῦτα..ἔχοντα αὑτόν *gave a written acknowledgement* that he was in possession of.., Id.27.14; but ἔχειν ib.47:—in Pass., *to be entered in the list* [of debts], Id.25.71.

ἀπόγυιοι· εὐχαί· σιωπώμεναι, Hsch.

ἀπογυιόω, *enfeeble, unnerve*, μή μ' ἀπογυιώσῃς μένεος Il.6.265, cf. Ath.1.10b; *tire out*, cj. for ἀπογυμνώσῃ, Thphr.*Char*.7.4.

ἀπογυμνάζω, *bring into hard exercise*, ἀ. στόμα *ply* one's tongue *hard*, A.*Th*.441; αὐτούς Arist.*HA*624$^a$25.

*ἀπογυμν-όω, *strip bare*, esp. of arms: hence, in Pass., μή σ' ἀπογυμνωθέντα κακὸν καὶ ἀνήνορα θήῃ Od.10.301; ἀπογυμνωθεὶς *with the person exposed*, Hes.*Op*.730; ἀ. τινά *vanquish*, Thphr.*Char*.7.4:—Med., *strip oneself*, X.*Mem*.3.4.1; ἀπογυμνοῦσθαι τὰ ἱμάτια *strip off one's* clothes, Arist.*Pr*.866$^a$21:—Pass., τῆς σχέσεως Them.*in Ph*. 26.8. 2. metaph., *lay open, reveal, explain*, Paus.4.22.4, App.*BC* 1.57; σόφισμα Jul.*Mis*.357c. 3. Pass., *become visible*, of land from the sea, Str.1.1.20. -ωσις, εως, ἡ, *stripping bare*, Plu.2.751f; ξιφιδίων App.*BC*1.64.

ἀπογυναίκωσις, εως, ἡ, *making womanish*, Plu.2.987f.

ἀπόγυον, τό, *mooring cable*, Poll.1.93 (v.l.); cf. ἐπίγυον, ἀπόγειος 2.

ἀπογώνιον, τό, = ὡροσκοπικὴ μοῖρα, Vett.Val.349.22: in pl., *tables* of such degrees for calculating expectation of life, Critodem.ibid., cf. 304.21.

ἀπογωνιόομαι, Pass., *become angular*, Thphr.*CP*2.16.4.

ἀποδαιμονίζει· ἀποκαρτερεῖ ἐν τῷ ἐνθουσιᾶν, Hsch.

ἀποδάκνω, *bite off a piece of*, ἄρτου Aristomen.14:—Pass., μῆλα ἀποδεδηγμένα *with pieces bitten out*, Luc.*Tox*.13: also c. acc., *bite off*, τὴν αὑτῆς γλῶσσαν Polyaen.8.45. 2. abs., *bite, gnaw*, ὀδάξ Cratin.164, cf. X.*Smp*.5.7, *Tab.Defix.Aud*.237.18 (Carthage, i A.D.):—Pass., *have one's tongue bitten*, as by a pungent substance, Arist.*Pr*.958$^b$7.

ἀποδάκρ-υσις, εως, ἡ, *flow of tears*, Cass.*Pr*.18. -υτικός, ή, όν, *calling forth tears*, κολλύρια ibid., cf. Antyll.ap.Orib.8.14.1. *-ύω [ῡ], *weep much for, lament loudly*, τινά Pl.*Phd*.116d; τι Plu.*Sull*. 12. 2. ἀ. γνώμην *weep away* one's judgement, *be melted to tears contrary to* it, Ar.*V*.983. 3. *to be made to weep* by the use of collyrium, and so *have* the eyes *purged*, Arist.*Pr*.958$^b$6, Luc.*Peregr*.45, Gal.12.751. 4. of trees, *weep, drip* gum, etc., ἀ. ῥητίνην Plu.2.640d. II. *cease to weep*, ἀπολοφυράμενοι καὶ ἀποδακρύσαντες Aristox. *Fr.Hist*.90, cf. *AB*427.

ἀποδαπανάω, *waste*, τὸν καιρόν Herod.Med.ap.Orib.7.8.2.

ἀποδάπτω, = ἀποκόπτω, Hsch.

ἀποδαρθάνω, aor. -έδαρθον, inf. -δραθεῖν Them.*Or*.7.91a (but v. infr.):—*sleep*, μικρόν Plu.*Dio*26; ἀποδαρθεῖν τὸν ἀηδόνιον ὕπνον Nicoch.4 D. (cf. ἀηδόνιος). II. *wake up*, Ael.*NA*3.13.

ἀπόδαρ-μα, ατος, τό, *hide*, Hdt.4.64 (v.l. -δερμα). -μός· *ingluvies*. *Gloss*.

ἀποδάσ-μιος, ον, *parted off*, Φωκέες ἀ. *parted from* the rest, Hdt. 1.146; ἀ. αἶσα a share *apportioned*, Opp.*H*.5.444. -μός, ὁ, (ἀποδατέομαι) *division, part of a whole*, Th.1.12; *separation*, χώρας ἀποδασμῷ ζημιωθῆναι by *loss* of territory, D.H.3.6. -τος, ον, *divided off*, Hsch. (-δατοι cod.). -τύς, ύος, ἡ, = ἀποδασμός, Id.

ἀποδατέομαι, fut. -δάσομαι [ᾰ], Ep. -δάσσομαι: Ep. aor. -δασσάμην Theoc.17.59, inf. -δάτταθθαι *Leg.Gort*.4.29:—*portion out* to others, *apportion*, ἥμισυ τῷ ἑνάρων ἀποδάσσομαι Il.17.231; Ἀχαιοῖς ἄλλ' ἀποδάσσεσθαι 22.118; σοὶ δ' αὖ..τῶνδ' ἀποδάσσομαι ὅσσ' ἐπέοικεν 24.595; πάντων ἶσον Pi.*N*.10.86, cf. Call.*Del*.9, etc. II. *part off, separate*, ἀποδασάμενος μόριον ὅσον δὴ τῆς στρατιῆς Hdt.2.103.

ἀποδαυλίζω, f.l. for ἀποκαυλίζω, E.*Supp*.717.

ἀποδαψιλεύομαι, *to be liberal of* a thing, *Gloss*.

ἀποδέδεγμαι, pf. of ἀποδέχομαι: also Ion. for ἀποδέδειγμαι, pf. Pass. of ἀποδείκνυμι.

ἀποδεδειγμένως, Adv., (ἀποδείκνυμι) *demonstrably*, Cyr.

ἀποδεδειλιακότως, Adv., (ἀποδειλιάω) *in a cowardly way*, censured by Poll.5.123.

*ἀποδεής, ές, (δέω B) *empty*, ἀγγεῖον Arist.*Fr*.224, Plu.2.967a; ναῦς ἀ. *not fully manned*, Id.*Ant*.62: metaph. of persons, Id.2.473e.

ἀποδεῖ, Ion. ἀποδέει, v. ἀποδέω.

ἀποδειδίσσομαι, *frighten away*, Il.12.52 (tm.).

*ἀποδείκ-νῡμι (and -ύω X.*Smp*.8.20, Plb.7.14.3), Ion. -δέκνῡμι *GDI*5653*b*14 (Chios, v B.C.), fut. -δείξω, Ion. -δέξω:—*point away from* other objects *at* one, and so: I. *point out, display, make known*, whether by deed or word, σφι γνώμας Hdt.1.171, al.; τάφους καὶ συγγένειαν Th.1.26; ἦθος τὸ πρόσθε τοκήων A.*Ag*.727; ἀρετήν Hyp.*Epit*.29; τὰ τῆς τέχνης ἐξευρήματα Hp.*Praec*.9; *proclaim*, τὴν ἡμέρην *GDI* l.c.:—Pass., τῶν οὔρων ἀποδεχθέντων *SIG*124.2 (Milet., iv B.C.). 2. *bring forward, produce*, μαρτύρια τούτων Hdt.5.45; πολλοὺς παῖδας Id.1.136, cf. S.*OT*1405, Isoc.19.6, X.*Cyr*. 1.2.5; ἐπόχους 8.1.35; ἀ. τρόπαια And.1.147; χρήματα πλεῖστ' ἀ. ἐν τῷ κοινῷ Ar.*Eq*.774; μορφὴν ἑτέραν E.*Fr*.839.14 (v.l. ἐπέδειξεν): c. part., ὑγιέα τινὰ ἐόντα ἀ. *produce* him safe and sound, Hdt.3.130, cf. 134. 3. *produce, deliver* accounts, τὸν λόγον Id.7.119; ἀ. τετρακόσια τάλαντα τετελεσμένα ib.118. 4. *publish* a law, Lys. 30.11, X.*HG*2.3.11. 5. *appoint, assign*, τέμενος ἀ. τινί Hdt.5.67, 89; βωμόν τινι Id.7.178; ἐν βουλευτήριον Th.2.15; γῆς ὅρους ib.72; τὴν τρίτην ἀ. ἐκκλησίαν *to fix, prescribe* it, D.24.25:—Pass., τοῖσί ἐστι χῶρος ἀποδεδεγμένος Hdt.1.153; τροφὴ αὐτοῖσι τοιαύτη ἀποδέδεκται Id.2.65. b. c. inf., κώμας ὅθεν ἀπέδειξαν οἱ ἡγεμόνες λαμβάνειν τὰ ἐπιτήδεια whence *they appointed* that they should receive .., X.*An*.2.3.14:—Pass., τοῖσι ἀποδεδέχθαι.. ἕλκειν (impers.) *it had been appointed* them to draw, Hdt.2.124. 6. *show by argument, prove, demonstrate*, Ar.*Nu*.1334, Arist.*APo*.75$^b$37, etc.; ἀ. σαφεῖς τὰς ἀποδείξεις And.2.3; ἀ. ὡς.. Ar.*V*.548, Pl.*R*.472d; ὅτι .. Id.*Prt*.323c, etc.; πότερον..ἢ.. Id.*Alc*.1.114b: c. dupl. acc., *prove* one so and so, οὓς ἀποδείξω λέκτρων προδότας E.*Ion*879, etc.; τοιούτους τινάς Hp.*Decent*.4: folld. by part., ἀ. λόγῳ..οὐδὲν μετεὸν Hdt.5.94; ἀ. τινὰ λέγοντα οὐδέν *make it evident* that.., 7.17, cf. 2. 133. II. *show forth* a person or thing *as* so and so, hence: 1. *appoint, proclaim, create*, ἀ. τινὰ στρατηγόν X.*An*.1.1.2, al.: c. inf., στρατηγὸν εἶναι Hdt.5.25; ἀ. τούτους τὴν πόλιν νέμειν ib.29; ἑαυτὸν ὅτι ἐστὶ θεός 2*Ep.Thess*.2.4:—Pass., *to be so created*, Hdt.1.124,162; μελεδωνοὶ ἀποδεδέχαται τῆς τροφῆς 2.65; ἀπεδέχθη εἶναι ἵππαρχος 7.154; αὐτοκράτωρ ἀποδέδεικται *POxy*.1021.7 (i A.D.); ὕπατος ἀποδεδειγμένος, = Lat. *consul designatus*, *OGI*379.5 (Tiflis), etc. 2. *make, render*, mostly with an Adj., ἀ. τινὰς μοχθηροτάτους *make* them finished rascals, Ar.*Ra*.1011; ἀ. κρατίστους τοὺς λόχους X.*Cyr*.2. 1.23; γοργότερον ἀ. τὸν ἵππον Id.*Eq*.1.10; ζῷον ἀγριώτερον Pl.*Grg*. 516b: with a Subst., γέλωτα ἀ. τινά Id.*Tht*.166a, cf. *Phd*.72c: c. part., βλέποντ' ἀποδείξω σ' ὀξύτερον τοῦ Λυγκέως Ar.*Pl*.210; ἀ. τινὰς ἀλλοτρίους ὄντας Pl.*Smp*.179c:—Pass., πολέμιοι ἀποδεδειγμένοι *declared* enemies, X.*An*.7.1.26, cf. D.23.200. 3. *represent as*, ἀ. παῖδα πατρὸς ἑωυτῶν ἕκαστον ἐόντα Hdt.2.143, cf. Lys.32.17:—Pass., ἀνδραγαθίη δ' αὕτη ἀποδέδεκται *is represented, considered as*.., Hdt.1.136; οὐδὲ..οὗτοι ἐν τοῖσι ἄλλοισι θεοῖσι ἀποδεδέχαται *have not been considered, admitted* among.., 2.43:—these two last examples may be pass. usages of ἀποδέχομαι. 4. c. inf., *ordain* a thing or person to be, X.*Oec*.7.30, *Lac*.10.7. 5. *dedicate, consecrate*, θέατρον Plu.*Luc*.29:—Pass., νεὼς ἀποδέδεικται Luc.*Tox*.5.

B. Med., *show forth, exhibit* something of one's own, ἀποδέξασθαι τὴν γνώμην *deliver one's* opinion, Hdt.1.170,207, cf. Th.1.87; also ἀ. μεγάλα ἔργα Hdt.1.59, al.; ἀξιαπηγητότατα ib.16; οὐδὲν λαμπρὸν ἔργον ib.174; ἀ. ἀρετάς *display* high qualities, Pi.*N*.6.49 (cf. supr. A.I.2); πνεύματα εἰς ἄλληλα στάσιν.. ἀποδεικνύμενα A.*Pr*. 1088; of buildings and the like, μνημόσυνα ἀ. Hdt.2.101; χώματα ἀξιοθέητα 1.184; οὐδεμίαν στρατηίην ἀ. not *to have* any military service *to show*, 2.111:—Pass., ἔργα μεγάλα καὶ θαυμαστὰ..ἀποδεχθέντα Id. *Prooem*., cf. 9.27. 2. Med. in act. sense, ἀποδεδειγμένοι ἦσαν ὅτι *had declared* that.., X.*An*.5.2.9.

C. Pass., v. supr. I. 5, II. 1,2,3: aor. ἀπεδείχθην is always Pass., as Hdt.7.154; and so mostly pf. ἀποδέδειγμαι, 1.136, Antipho2.4.10, X.*An*.7.1.26; but the part. of the latter is sts. Act., v. supr. B.2. -τέον, *one must show, prove*, Pl.*Phdr*.245b. 2. c. dupl. acc., *one must make* one so and so, σκαπανέα αὐτὸν ἀ. Luc.*Vit.Auct*. 7. -τικός, ή, όν, *affording proof, demonstrative*, ὁ ἀ. συλλογισμός Arist.*APo*.74$^b$10; ἕξις ἀ. Id.*EN*1139$^b$31; πίστεις ἀ. Id.*Rh*.1358$^a$1, etc.: Comp. -ώτερος Phlp.*in Ph*.9.20: Sup. -ώτατος, λόγος Ph.2.499. Adv. ἀποδεικτικῶς, ἐπίστασθαι Arist.*APo*.75$^a$12; εἰρηκέναι Phld.*Mus*. p.12 K. 2. ἀ. ἱστορία, διήγησις, in which the facts are *regularly set forth and explained*, Plb.2.37.3, 4.40.1, cf. Plu.2.243a. Adv. -κῶς Sch.Iamb.*in Nic*.p.129 P. 3. of persons, *scientific, exact*, Gal.4. 649. 4. ἀ., τά, *sights, attractions*, *SIG*685.70 (Crete, ii B.C.). -τός, ή, όν, *demonstrable* or *to be demonstrated*, Arist.*APo*.76$^b$33, al. 2. *demonstrated*, Id.*EN*1140$^b$32.

ἀποδειλί-ασις, εως, ἡ, *cowardice*, Plb.3.103.2; ἀ. πρός τινα Plu.*Alex*. 13. -ατέον, *one must flinch*, Pl.*R*.374e, Marin.*Procl*.31. *-άω, fut. -άσω [ᾱ], *to be very fearful, play the coward, flinch from danger* or *toil*, X.*Mem*.3.12.2, Pl.*Grg*.48cc, al.; ἀ. ἐν ἰσχυροῖς μαθήμασιν Id.*R*. 535b, cf. 504a; ταῖς ψυχαῖς Plb.1.15.7; πρός τινα or τι Id.11.16.2, cf. Onos.33.6, Luc.*DMort*.10.9, etc. 2. ἀ. τοῦ διαπονεῖσθαι *shrink from*.., X.*Lac*.10.7. 3. ἀ. τὴν μάχην *to be afraid of*, Plb.5.84.5.

*ἀπόδειξις, Ion. -δεξις, εως, ἡ, (ἀποδείκνυμι) *showing forth, making* *known, exhibiting,* δι' ἀπειροσύνην..κοὐκ ἀπόδειξιν τῶν ὑπὸ γαίας E.*Hipp.*196. 2. *setting forth, publication,* 'Ηροδότου..ἱστορίης ἀπόδεξις Hdt.*Prooem.*; ἀρχῆς ἀ. *an exposition, sketch* of it, Th.1.97; ἀ. περὶ τὸν πολιτικόν Pl.*Plt.*277a; περί τινος *R.*358b. 3. *proof,* βουλομένοισί σφι γένοιτ' ἂν ἀ. Hdt.8.101; ἀ. ποιεῖσθαι Lys.12.19, etc.; esp. by words, ἀποδείξεις εὑρίσκειν τινός Isoc.10.3; ἀ. λέγειν Pl.*Tht.* 162e; -ξεις φέρειν Plb.12.5.5; χρῆσθαί τινι ἀποδείξει τινός use it *as a proof* of a thing, Plu.2.160a: in pl., *proofs,* or *arguments in proof* of, τινός D.18.300, cf. Pl.*Phd.*73a; λέγειν τι ἐς ἀπόδειξιν τοῦ περιέσεσθαι τῷ πολέμῳ Th.2.13; ἄνευ ἀποδείξεως Pl.*Phd.*92d; μετ' ἀ. Plb.3.1.3, al.; ἀ. λαμβάνειν..τῶν μανθανόντων *test* them by examination, etc., Plu.2.736d; ἀ. ποιεῖσθαι τῶν ἐφήβων *IG*2.470.40; ἀ. τέχνης *specimen,* Dionys.Com.3.4; ἀ. αὐτοῖς δοῦναί τινος Plu.2.79f, etc.; *citation,* ποιητῶν καὶ ἱστοριαγράφων ἀποδείξεις *SIG*685.93 (Crete, ii B.C.). b. in the Logic of Arist., *demonstration,* i.e. *deductive proof by syllogism,* *APo.*71b17, al., cf. Epicur.*Ep.*1 p.25 U., *Stoic.*2.89; opp. inductive proof (ἐπαγωγή), Arist.*APo.*81a40:—sts. in a loose sense, ἀ. ῥητορικὴ ἐνθύμημα Id.*Rh.*1355a6. 4. *appointment,* θεωρῶν *SIG*402.29 (Delph., iii B.C.). II. (from Med.) ἀ. ἔργων μεγάλων *display, achievement* of mighty works, Hdt.1.207, cf. 2.101,148.

**ἀποδειπν-έω,** *finish supper,* Ath.15.622e, Iamb.*VP*21.98. **-ίδιος,** ον, *of* or *from supper, AP*6.302 (Leon.). **-ος,** ον, = ἄδειπνος, Hsch.

**ἀποδειρο-τομέω,** *slaughter by cutting off the head,* or *cutting the throat,* of men, Il.18.336, 23.22, Luc.*DMeretr.*13.3; μῆλα ἐς βόθρον Od.11.35; κεφαλὴν ἀ. Hes.*Th.*280. **-τόμησις,** εως, ἡ, *slaughtering,* Eust.1145.63.

**ἀποδείρω,** Ion. for ἀποδέρω.

**ἀποδεισιδαιμονέω,** *brood over with superstitious fear,* Sch.Th.7.50.

**ἀποδεκάτ-ευσις,** έως, ἡ, *tithing, Gloss.* **⊛-εύω,** v.l. for sq., *Ev.Luc.*18.12.

**ἀποδεκᾰτίζω,** = sq., δεκάτην Lxx *To.*1.7.

**ἀποδεκᾰτόω,** *tithe, take a tenth of,* τι Lxx 1*Ki.*8.16; πάντα *Ev.Luc.* 18.12; ἀ. τὸν λαόν *take tithe of* them, *Ep.Hebr.*7.5; δεκάτην ἀ. τινός Lxx *De.*14.22. II. *pay tithe of,* τι Lxx *Ge.*28.22, *Ev.Matt.*23.23, etc.

**ἀποδέκομαι,** Ion., etc., for ἀποδέχομαι.

**ἀποδεκ-τέον,** (ἀποδέχομαι) *one must receive from others,* τὰ εἰσφερόμενα X.*Oec.*7.36. 2. *one must accept, allow, admit,* c. acc. rei, λόγον Pl.*Lg.*668a: c. gen. et part., ἀ. τινὸς λέγοντος Id.*Tht.*160c, *R.*379c; μὴ ἄλλως ἀ. λεγομένης τέχνης; Id.*Phdr.*272b. 3. Adj. **-τέος,** α, ον, Vett.Val.329.16, Zos.Alch.p.229 B. **-τήρ,** ῆρος, ὁ, = sq., X.*Cyr.* 8.1.9, Arist.*Mu.*398a25. **⊛-της,** ου, ὁ, *receiver*: in pl., *financial officials,* established by Cleisthenes, *IG*2.38, D.24.162, Arist.*Ath.*48, *Pol.*1321b33, Harp.: also at Thasos, *IG*12(8).608; in Egypt, σίτου *Ostr.*1217; ἀχύρου *POxy.*43r iii 8 (iii A.D.), cf. Poll.8.114; ἀ. τῶν πολιτικῶν χρημάτων *Jahresh.*21/2 *Beibl.*255 (ii A.D.):—hence **-τεύω,** *hold office of* ἀποδέκτης, *IG*12(8).391,610 (Thasos). **-τός,** όν (ή, όν prob. l. in Phld.*Ir.*p.63 W.), *acceptable, welcome, OGI*441.100, 1*Ep.Ti.*2.3, S.E.*M.*11.83, Plu.2.1061a: Comp. -ότερος Dsc.*Eup.*1 *Praef.* Adv. -τως *An.Ox.*3.139, Sch.E.*Or.*1680.

**ἀποδενδρόομαι,** Pass., *grow into a tree,* Thphr.*HP*3.17.2, cf. 1.3. 2; *to be turned into a tree,* Luc.*VH*1.8, Heraclit.*All.*36.

**ἀποδέξασθαι,** aor. I of ἀποδέχομαι, but also, II. Ion. for ἀποδείξασθαι, cf. ἀποδείκνυμι.

**⊛ἀπόδεξις,** εως, ἡ, (ἀποδέχομαι) *acceptance,* τῶν ἀπονεμομένων M.Ant. 10.8; πρὸς τοὺς φίλους *OGI*227.13 (Milet., iii B.C.). II. Ion. for ἀπόδειξις.

**ἀποδέρκομαι,** = ἀποβλέπω, Trag. (Satyric) in *POxy.*1083.21.

**ἀπόδερμα,** v. ἀπόδαρμα.

**ἀποδερμᾰτ-ίζω,** *flay, strip,* Androm.ap.Gal.12.991, Sch.Nic.*Al.* 301, Hsch. **-ισμός,** ὁ, *flaying, Gloss.* **-όομαι,** Pass., of shields, *to have their leather covering destroyed,* ὑπ' ὄμβρου Plb.6.25.7: —late in Act., *flay,* κεφαλὴν ξίφει Zos.Alch.p.108 B.

**ἀποδερτρόω,** (δέρτρον) *disembowel, eviscerate,* Sch.Od.11.579.

**⊛ἀποδέρω,** Ion. **-δείρω** (also in Ar.*V.*1286):—*flay, skin completely,* τὸν βοῦν Hdt.2.40, cf. 42, 4.60; ἀ. τὴν κεφαλήν *scalp,* 4.64:—Pass., πρόβατα ἀποδαρέντα X.*An.*3.5.9; *become excoriated,* Philum.ap.Orib. 45.29.61. 2. *flay by flogging, fetch the skin off one's back,* Ar.*Lys.* 739. 3. sens. obsc., ib.953. 4. Medic., *separate by avulsion,* Gal.2.896. II. *strip off,* ἀ. πᾶσαν ἀνθρωπηΐην (sc. δορήν) Hdt.5.25.

**ἀπόδεσις,** εως, ἡ, *tying up,* ἡ τοῦ ὀμφαλοῦ ἀ. τοῖς παιδίοις Arist.*HA* 587a12; ἀ. ἐκ τοῦ πασσάλου Nicom.*Harm.*6, cf. Iamb.*VP*26.118.

**ἀποδεσμ-εύω,** *bind fast,* Lxx *Pr.*26.8, *Hippiatr.*77. **-έω,** = foreg., Pherecyd.119 J., Tim.Gaz.ap.Ar.Byz.*Epit.*143.14, Olymp.*in Mete.*96.7. **-ίς,** ίδος, ἡ, prob. f.l. for ὑπο-, Gal.14.794. **-ος,** ὁ, *band, breastband, girdle,* Ar.*Fr.*320.13, Luc.*DMeretr.*12.1. II. *bag, case, receptacle,* Plu.*Dem.*30, Paul.Aeg.3.41; στακτῆς *sachet,* Lxx *Ca.*1.13. 2. *bundle,* ἐπιστολῶν *PRyl.*78.36 (ii A.D.), etc.

**ἀποδεχθείς,** Ion. for ἀποδειχθείς, Hdt.

**⊛ἀποδέχομαι,** Ion. **-δέκομαι,** fut. -δέξομαι: aor. -εδεξάμην: pf. -δέδεγμαι (for possible pass. usages of this tense v. ἀποδείκνυμι A.II.3): —*accept,* καὶ οὐκ ἀπεδέξατ' ἄποινα Il.1.95, cf. Ar.*Ec.*712, X.*An.*6.1.24, etc.; ἀ. γνώμην παρά τινος *accept* advice from him, Hdt.4.97; ἀπόδεξαί μου ὃ λέγω Pl.*Cra.*430d. 2. *accept as a teacher, follow,* X.*Mem.*4.1. 1, etc.; ἀ. τινὰ σύμβουλον Pl.*Prt.*323c. 3. *admit* to one's presence, τοὺς πρεσβευτάς Plb.21.35.5; ἀ. αὐτὸν καὶ τὰ ῥηθέντα φιλοφρόνως 21. 22.1, cf. 3.66.8. 4. mostly of *admitting into the mind,* a. *receive favourably, approve,* ἀπολογίαν Antipho 3.2.2; κατηγορίας, διαβολάς, Th.3.3, 6.29; τοῖσι μὴ ἀποδεκομένοισι, c. acc. inf., those who do not *accept the story* that.., Hdt.6.43; freq. in Pl., δοῦναί τε καὶ ἀ. λόγον *R.*531e; τὴν ἀπόκρισιν *Prt.*329b; λόγον παρά τινος *Smp.*194d, etc.; τι παρά τινος *Ti.*29e; τί τινος Th.1.44, 7.48, Pl.*Phlb.*54a, etc.: c. gen. pers. mostly with part. added, ἀ. τινὸς λέγοντος *receive* or *accept* a statement *from* him, i.e. *believe* or *agree with* his statements, Id.*Phd.*92a,e; μὴ ἀποδέχεσθε τούτου φενακίζοντος ὑμᾶς D.56.31; ἀ. μαθηματικοῦ πιθανολογοῦντος Arist.*EN*1094b26, cf. *Rh.*1395b8: without part., οὐκ ἀποδέχομαι ἐμαυτοῦ ὡς τὸ ἓν δύο γέγονεν I cannot *satisfy* myself *in thinking* that.., Pl.*Phd.*96e, cf. *Euthphr.*9e, *R.*329e: abs., *to accept a statement, to be satisfied,* D.18.277, Arist.*Pol.*1263b 16; ἀ. ἐάν.. Pl.*R.*336d, 525d: c. gen. rei, *to be content with,* τῆς προαιρέσεως Lib.*Or.*24.2; τῶν εἰρημένων ib.59.9. b. generally, *approve, acknowledge,* τὴν τῶν ἐφήβων ἀρετὴν *IG*2.481.60, al. c. *take* or *understand* a thing, ὀρθῶς ἀ. τι X.*Mem.*3.10.15, cf. *Cyr.*8.7.10; ἱκανώτατα Pl.*R.*511d; τὰ τοιαῦτα δυσχερῶς πως ἀποδέχομαι Id.*Euthphr.* 6a; ὑπόπτως Th.6.53: c. gen. pers. (the acc. rei being understood), οὕτως αὐτοῦ ἀποδεχώμεθα let us *understand* him thus (referring to what goes before), Pl.*R.*340c; μὴ χαλεπῶς ἀλλὰ πρᾴως ἀποδεχώμεθα ἀλλήλων Id.*Lg.*634c. II. *receive back, recover,* Hdt.4.33; opp. ἀποδιδόναι, Th.5.26. III. *sustain, hold out against,* Plb.3.43.3, 5.51.1.

**ἀποδέω** (A), *bind fast, tie up* the navel, Pl.*Smp.*190e; generally, *bind,* Lxx *Jo.*9.4, J.*AJ*4.8.21:—Pass., ἐν δερματίῳ ἀποδέδεταί τι Pl. *Erx.*400a, cf. Arist.*HA*587a14, Erasistr.ap.Gal.11.148.

**ἀποδέω** (B), *to be in want of, lack,* often in accounts of numbers, τριακοσίων ἀποδέοντα μύρια 10,000 *lacking* or *save* 300, Th.2.13, cf. 4.38, etc.; δυεῖν χιλιάδων ἀποδέοντες εἶναι δισμύριοι D.H.7.3; generally, τοσοῦτον ἀποδέω τινός so *far am I from..,* Pl.*Ax.*366b, 372a: c. inf., ὀλίγου ἀποδεῖν εἶναι *want* little *of* being, Plu.2.978f; *fall short of, be inferior to,* τινός Luc.*Merc.Cond.*36, cf. Plu.2.1088c; πλήθει οὐ πολὺ ἀποδέοντες ἀλλήλων not *differing* much in number, D.H.3.52, cf. Plu.*Luc.*28; *come short of, miss,* τῆς ἀληθείας Pl.*Ax.*369d.

**ἀποδηλ-όω,** *make manifest,* A.*Fr.*304.2, Hp.*Int.*23; *indicate,* πλήθος Corn.*ND*13; *explain, expound,* ὅτι.. Plb.21.37.8, cf. Plu.*Phil.* 13:—Pass., Str.2.5.16. II. intr., *become manifest,* Arist.*Mir.* 834b33. **-ωσις,** εως, ἡ, *communication by speech,* Diog.Oen.10.

**⊛ἀποδημ-έω,** Dor. **-δᾱμέω,** pf. ἀπεδήμηκα dub. in Hermipp.66:— *to be away from home, be abroad* or *on one's travels,* Hdt.1.29, 4.1,152, Ar.*Nu.*371, etc.; of foreign service, Id.*Lys.*101; opp. ἐπιδημεῖν, X.*Cyr.*7.5.69: metaph., *to be absent,* Pi.*P.*10.37; ὁ νοῦς παρὼν ἀποδημεῖ Ar.*Eq.*1120: sts. c. gen., ἀποδημεῖν οἰκίας Pl.*Lg.*954b; ἀπὸ τῆς ἑωυτῶν Hdt.9.117; ἐκ τῆς πόλεως Pl.*Cri.*53a; οὐκ ἔξεστι ἀποδημεῖν τοῖς Λακεδαιμονίοις Arist.*Fr.*543. 2. *go abroad,* παρά τινα to visit him, Hdt.3.124; ἀ. ἐς Αἴγιναν κατὰ τοὺς Αἰακίδας *go abroad* to Aegina to fetch the Aeacidae, Id.8.84; ἀ. ἐπὶ δεῖπνον εἰς Θετταλίαν Pl.*Cri.*53e; ἐνθένδε εἰς ἄλλον τόπον Id.*Ap.*40e; κατ' ἐμπορίαν Lycurg.21,57 (v.l. ἐπί); πρὸς τὰ ἱερά X.*HG*4.7.3; ποῖ γῆς ἀπεδήμεις; Ar.*Ra.*48; ἄλλοσε ἀ. Pl.*Lg.*579b; ἐκεῖσε Id.*Phd.*61e. **-ησις,** εως, ἡ, = ἀποδημία, Alciphr.1.29, *CIG*1813b8 (Nicopolis, dub.). **-ητής,** οῦ, ὁ, *one who goes abroad, is not tied to his home,* opp. ἐνδημότατος, Th.1.70. **-ητικός,** ή, όν, *fond of wandering* or *travelling,* Dicaearch.1.9, Vett.Val. 98.7; παράστασις ἀ. banishment *to foreign parts,* of ostracism, Arist. *Pol.*1308b19: metaph., *migratory,* i.e. *mortal,* Arr.*Epict.*3.24.4, cf. ib.60,105. **⊛-ία,** Ion. **-ίη,** ἡ, *going* or *being abroad,* ἀ. ἐξ οἴκου Hdt. 6.130, cf. Lys.3.10; ἀ. ποιεῖσθαι Pl.*Cri.*52b; ἔξω τῆς χώρας Id.*Lg.* 949e, cf. 950a; ἀ. ἡ εἰς Ὀλυμπίαν And.4.30; περὶ τῆς ἀ. τῆς ἐκεῖ as to my *life in* that *foreign land,* i.e. beyond the grave, Pl.*Phd.*61e, cf. 67c, *Ap.*41a (but in pl. of earthly life, as *exile from* heaven, Porph. *Marc.*5); ἐξ ἀποδημίας τινὸς προσήει from *a long journey,* X.*Cyr.*3. 1.7. **⊛-ος,** Dor. **-δᾱμος,** ον, *away from one's country, abroad,* οὐκ ἀ. Ἀπόλλωνος τυχόντος Pi.*P.*4.5, cf. Plu.2.799f, etc.; ἀ. ἐπέρχεσθαι *from abroad, CIG*3344 A (Smyrna); ἀ. στρατεία Luc.*Am.*6: metaph., τῆς ἐμῆς γνώμης Hp.*Ep.*17:—less Att. than ἔκδημος, Moer.143, cf. Poll.1.177.

**ἀπόδησις,** f.l. for ἐπίδησις, Sor.ap.Gal.13.43.

**ἀποδία,** ἡ, (πούς) *absence of feet,* Arist.*PA*642b23, 690b15.

**ἀποδιαγράφω** [ρᾰ], *order payment to be made, SIG*976.30 (Samos, ii B.C.), *PTheb.Bank* 12.7 (ii B.C.).

**ἀποδιαιρέω,** *distribute,* v.l. in Lxx *Jo.*1.6; *divide off, distinguish from,* δημιουργοῦ τὸν Ἄττιν Jul.*Or.*5.165b; ἐγχέλυας ἰχθύων Eust. 1221.36:—Pass., *PStrassb.*92.6 (iii B.C.).

**ἀποδιαιτάω,** *pronounce in* one's *favour in an arbitration,* opp. καταδιαιτάω (q.v.), ὅπως τὴν δίαιταν αὐτῷ ἀποδιαιτήσομεν Test.ap.D.21. 93:—Pass., ib.96: hence ἀ. τινός (sc. τὴν δίκην) *decide for* one, Id. 40.17; τὰ ἀποδιαιτηθέντα μου λύσας ib.43.

**ἀποδιά-κειμαι,** Pass., *have a distaste,* πρός τι Aët.8.76. **-κλασμός,** ὁ, *mental perturbation,* Gal.19.514. **-κρίνω** [ρῐ], *separate completely,* Dam.*Pr.*36. **-λαμβάνω,** *set apart,* Syrian.*in Metaph.* 64.40; *discuss separately,* Dex.*in Cat.*59.16, Herm.*in Phdr.*p.115 A., etc. **-ληπτός,** ή, όν, *separable,* ἀ. καθ' ἑαυτήν *Stoic.*2.126. **-ληψις,** εως, ἡ, *division into parts,* Iamb.*Myst.*1.9, Procl.*in Prm.*p.674 S.; *abstraction,* Dex.*in Cat.*40.9 (pl.). **-λύω,** *dissipate,* νωθρότητας Antyll.ap.Orib.6.21.36. II. *confute utterly,* λόγον Phld.*Herc.* 19.16. **-νομή,** ἡ, *distribution, assignment,* Ecphant.ap.Stob. 4.7.66. **-πέμπομαι,** *divert,* ἡμᾶς τῆς ματαίας πλάνης Syn.Alch. p.59 B. **-σείω,** gloss on ἀπεστυφέλιξεν, Hsch. **-στᾰσις,** εως, ἡ, *distance,* τῶν ἀστέρων Vett.Val.227.14. **⊛-στέλλω,** *divide, PTaur.* 8.22.48 (ii B.C.), Lxx *Jo.*1.6 (v.l.):—Pass., *to be set apart, forbidden,* ib.2*Ma.*6.5. **-στολή,** ἡ, *division, PRyl.*65.4 (ii B.C.). **-στρέ-**

**φω**, *divert*, Phld.*Lib*.p.29 O. **-τίθεμαι**, *to be weaned*, Theol.*Ar*. 49. **-τρίβω** [ῐ], *waste time*, Aeschin.2.49; *spend time*, περὶ ὀρχηστάς D.C.54.17 (Pass.); ἐν πόλει Agath.1.19, cf. 3.16, 4.13. **II.** c. acc. pers., *detain*, D.C.44.19; *defer*, τὰς χειροτονίας App.*BC*2.20: abs., *delay*, ib.13. **III.** *divert*, τὰς χεῖρας ἀπὸ τῶν σφαγῶν D.C. 77.14.

⊛**ἀποδῐδάσκω**, *teach not* to do, Hp.*Fract*.1.

**ἀποδιδρασκίνδα** (sc. παιδιά), Adv. a *game in which all but one ran away*, described by Poll.9.117.

⊛**ἀποδῐδράσκω**, Ion. -ήσκω, fut. -δράσομαι, Ion. -δρήσομαι: pf. -δέδρᾱκα Men.*Sam*.143, Phld.*Rh*.1.199 S.: aor. ἀπέδραν, Ion. -έδρην, opt. ἀποδραίην Thgn.927, imper. ἀπόδρᾱθι Ph.1.90, inf. ἀποδρᾶναι, Ion. -δρῆναι, part. ἀποδράς—the only form found in Hom.; the other tenses in Hdt., etc., pf. part. ἀποδεδρακότες X.*An*.6.4.8:—*run away, escape* or *flee from*, esp. *by stealth*, Hom. (never in Il.), ἐκ νηὸς ἀποδράς Od.16.65; νηὸς ἀ. 17.516; ἀ. ἐκ τῆς Σάμου Hdt.3.148; ἐς Σάμον 4.43; ἐπὶ θάλασσαν 6.2; ἀποδρᾶσα ᾤχετο And.1.125, cf. 4.17, Ar.*Ec*.196, Pl.*Tht*.203d; of runaway slaves, X.*An*.1.4.8 (ἀποδρᾶναι τὸ ἀναχωρήσαντά τινα εὔδηλον εἶναι ὅπου ἐστίν, ἀποφεύγειν δὲ τὸ μὴ δύνασθαι ἐπιληφθῆναι Ammon.p.19V.); σώματα ἀποδράντα *IG*2². 584; of soldiers, *desert*, X.*An*.5.6.34; ἀποδιδράσκοντα μὴ δύνασθαι ἀποδρᾶναι *attempting to escape* not to be able *to escape*, Pl.*Prt*.317a, cf. 310c. **2.** c. acc., *flee, shun*, Hdt.2.182, Ar.*Pax*234, etc.; ἀπέδρασαν αὐτόν Th.1.128; *evade*, τὸν νόμον Arist.*Pol*.1270b35; οὐκ ἀπέδρα τὴν στρατείαν D.21.165; ὅτε..τὸ σὸν ὄμμ' ἀπέδραν (poet. for ἀπέδρασαν) S.*Aj*.167.—Rare in Trag. (Cf. Skt. *drāti* 'run'.)

**ἀποδῐδύσκω**, = ἀποδύω, τινάς Artem.2.69:—Med., Parth.15.3; *cast off, slough off*, γῆρας Artem.2.13, 14.

⊛**ἀποδίδωμι**, fut. -δώσω: aor. 1 ἀπέδωκα: aor. 2 ἀπέδων A.D.*Synt*. 276.9, shortened inf. ἀποδοῦν prob. in Hsch.:—*give up* or *back, restore, return*, τινί τι Hom., etc.: esp. *render what is due, pay*, as debts, penalties, submission, honour, etc., τοκεῦσι θρέπτρα Il.4.478; ἀ. τινὶ λώβην *give* him *back* his insult, i.e. *make atonement for* it, ib.9. 387 (tm.); τὴν πλημμέλειαν Lxx*Nu*.5.7; εὖ ἔρδοντι κακὴν ἀ. ἀμοιβήν Thgn.1263; ἀ. τὴν ὁμοίην τινί Hdt.4.119; ἀμοιβὰς Democr.92; κακὸν ἀντ' ἀγαθοῦ Id.93; ἀ. τὸ μόρσιμον *pay the debt of* fate, Pi.*N*.7.44; τὸ χρέος Hdt.2.136; τὸν ναῦλον Ar.*Ra*.270; τὴν ζημίαν, τὴν καταδίκην, Th.3.70, 5.50; τὴν φερνήν *PEleph*.1.11 (iv B.C.); εὐχάς X.*Mem*.2.2. 10; ἀ. ὀπίσω ἐς Ἡρακλείδας τὴν ἀρχήν Hdt.1.13, etc.; πόλεις ἀ. τοῖς παρακαταθεμένοις Aeschin.3.85; ἀ. χάριτας Lys.31.24; οὐκ ἐς χάριν ἀλλ' ἐς ὀφείλημα τὴν ἀρετὴν ἀ. Th.2.40; ἀ. χάριν τινός Isoc.6.73; [τὴν πόλιν] ἀ. τοῖς ἐπιγιγνομένοις οἵανπερ παρὰ τῶν πατέρων παρελάβομεν X.*HG*7.1.30:—Pass., ἕως κ' ἀπὸ πάντα δοθείη Od.2.78; ἀ. μισθός, χάριτες, Ar.*Eq*.1066, Th.3.63. **2.** *assign*, ταῖς γυναιξὶ μουσικὴν καὶ γυμναστικήν Pl.*R*.456b; τὸ δίκαιον καὶ τὸ συμφέρον Arist.*Rh*.1354b3, cf. 1356a15; τὸ πρὸς ἀλκὴν ὅπλον ἀ. ἡ φύσις Id. *GA*759b3, etc. **b.** *refer* to one, as belonging to his department, εἰς τοὺς κριτὰς τὴν κρίσιν Pl.*Lg*.765b; ἀ. εἰς τὴν βουλὴν περὶ αὐτῶν *refer* their case to the Council, Isoc.18.6, cf. Lys.22.2, etc. **3.** *render, yield*, of land, ἐπὶ διηκόσια ἀποδοῦναι (sc. καρπόν) *yield fruit* two hundred-fold, Hdt.1.193; τἄλλα δ' ἄν τις καταβάλῃ ἀπέδωκεν ὀρθῶς Men.*Georg*.38; ἣν ἡ χώρη κατὰ λόγον ἐπιδιδοῖ ἐς ὕψος καὶ τὸ ὅμοιον ἀποδιδοῖ ἐς αὔξησιν *renders, makes* a like increase in extent, Hdt.2.13:—hence perh. metaph., τὸ ἔργον ἀ. Arist.*EN*1106a16; ἀ. δάκρυ E.*HF*489. **4.** *concede, allow*, c. inf., *suffer* or *allow* a person to do, ἀ. τισὶ αὐτονομεῖσθαι Th.1.144, cf. 3.36; εἰ δὲ τοῖς μὲν..ἐπιτάττειν ἀποδώσετε D.2.30; ἀ. κολάζειν Id.23.56; τῷ δικαστηρίῳ ἀποδέδοται τοῦ φόνου τὰς δίκας δικάζειν Lys.1.30; ἀ. τινὶ ζητεῖν Arist.*Pol*.1341b30, cf. *Po*.1454b5; also οὔτε ἀπολογίας ἀποδοθείσης And.4.3; ἐπειδὰν αὐτοῖς ὁ λόγος ἀποδοθῇ when right of speech is *allowed* them, Aeschin.3.54. **5.** ἀ. τινά with an Adj., *render* or *make* so and so, like ἀποδείκνυμι, ἀ. τὴν τέρψιν βεβαιοτέραν Isoc.1.46; τέλειον ἀ. τὸ τέκνον Arist.*GA*733b1; δεῖ τὰς ἐνεργείας ποιὰς ἀ. Id.*EN* 1103b22; μετριωτέραν τὴν ὑπερηφανίαν D.H.7.16. **b.** *exhibit, display*, τὴν ὑπάρχουσαν ἀρετήν And.1.109; ἀ. τὴν ἰδίαν μορφὴν *render, express* it, Arist.*Po*.1454b10; ἀ. φαντασίαν τινός *present* appearance of, Phld.*Ir*.p.71 W., al. **6.** *deliver over, give up*, e.g. as a slave, E. *Cyc*.239; ἀ. τὸν μιαρὸν τῷ χρόνῳ φῆναι Antipho4.4.11. **7.** ἀ. ἐπιστολήν *deliver* a letter, Th.7.10, cf. E.*IT*745. **8.** ἀ. τὸν ἀγῶνα ὀρθῶς καὶ καλῶς *bring* it *to a conclusion*, Lycurg.149. **9.** λόγον ἀ. *render* an account, D.27.48:—Pass., μαρτυρίαι ἀ. Test.ap.D.18. 137. **10.** ἀ. ὅρκον, v. ὅρκος. **11.** *give an account* or *definition* of a thing, *explain* it, E.*Or*.150; ἀ. τί ἐστί τι Arist.*Cat*.2b8, cf. 1a10, *Metaph*.1040b30, al.; ἑπομένως τούτοις ἀ. τὴν ψυχήν Id.*deAn*.405a4, cf. *Ph*.194b34, al.; also, *use by way of definition*, ὁ μὲν τὴν ὕλην ἀποδίδωσιν, ὁ δὲ τὸ εἶδος Id.*deAn*.403b1; simply, *define*, τὸν ἄνθρωπον S.E.*M*.7.272; *expound*, Phld.*D*.3.14, cf. Epicur.*Nat*.14.3, 119 G., 143 G.; *render, interpret* one word *by* another, ἀ. τὴν κοτύλην ἥλεισον Ath.11.479c; *explain, interpret*, τὸ "φωνὴν αἵματος βοᾶν" Ph.1.209:—Pass., βέλτιον ἀποδοθήσεται Epicur.*Ep*.1p.15 U.; ἀκριβεστέρως ἀποδοθήσεται A.D.*Synt*.45.21; ἀ. τι πρός τι *use with reference to*, Olymp.*inMete*.281.10, cf. Sch.Ar.*Pl*.538. **12.** *attach* or *append, make dependent upon*, τί τινι or εἴς τι Hero *Aut*.24.5, 6. 2. **13.** ἀ. τί τινος *assign* a property *to* a thing, Arist.*Top*.128b 28. **II.** intr., *return, recur*, Id.*GA*722a8, *HA*585b32. **2.** Rhet. and Gramm., *introduce a clause answering to the πρότασις*, Id. *Rh*.1407a20; διὰ μακροῦ ἀ. D.H.*Dem*.9, etc.; cf. ἀπόδοσις II. 2; οὐκ ἀποδίδωσι τὸ ἐπεί *has* no *apodosis*, Sch.Od.3.103; esp. in similes, *complete the comparison*, Arist.*Rh*.1413a11. **3.** in Tactics, *turn back to face the enemy*, εἰς ὀρθόν Ascl.*Tact*.10.12, etc. **4.** Medic. in Pass., *to be evacuated*, σὺν τοῖς περιττώμασιν Dsc.4.82. **III.** Med., *give away of one's own will, sell*, Ar.*Av*.585, Hdt.1.70, etc.; ἀ. τι ἐς τὴν Ἑλλάδα *take* to Greece *and sell* it there, Id.2.56: c. gen. pretii, Ar.*Ach*.830, *Pax*1237; οὐκ ἂν ἀπεδόμην πολλοῦ τὰς ἐλπίδας Pl.*Phd*.98b; ἀ. τῆς ἀξίας, τοῦ εὑρίσκοντος, *sell for* its worth, *for* what it will fetch, Aeschin.1.96; ὅταν τις οἰκέτην πονηρὸν πωλῇ (= offer for sale) καὶ ἀποδῶται τοῦ εὑρόντος X.*Mem*.2.5.5, cf. Thphr. *Char*.15.4; διδοῦσι [τὰς νέας] πενταδράχμους ἀποδόμενοι Hdt.6.89; ἀ. εἰσαγγελίαν *sell*, i.e. *take a bribe to forgo*, the information, D.25. 47; οἱ δραχμῆς ἂν ἀποδόμενοι τὴν πόλιν X.*HG*2.3.48; at Athens, esp. *farm out* the public taxes, D.20.60, opp. ὠνέομαι: metaph., οἷον πρὸς ἄργυρον τὴν δόξαν τὰς ψυχάς Jul.*Or*.1.42b:—Act. and Med. are distinguished in Lex ap.And.1.97 πάντα ἀποδόμενος τὰ ἡμίσεα ἀποδώσω τῷ ἀποκτείναντι: but Act. is used in med. sense in Th.6. 62 (s. v. l.), cf. *Foed.Delph.Pell*.2 *A* 22, and possibly in E.*Cyc*.239, Ar.*Ra*.1235: Med. for Act. in Antipho *Fr*.54:—Pass., *to be sold*, Hsch.

**ἀποδιηθέω**, *strain off, filter*, *Gp*.9.20.

**ἀποδιΐστημι**, *separate*, ἀποδιαστῆσαι καὶ διαχωρίσαι Plu.2.968d, cf. Vett.Val.214.17:—Pass., Hsch. **II.** intr., *to be distant*, [πόλεις] θαλάσσης ἀποδιέστησαν Lib.*Descr*.8.1, cf. Paul.Al.*F*.1.

⊛**ἀποδῐκάζω**, *acquit*, opp. καταδικάζω, Antipho6.47, Arist.*Pol*.1268b 18; ἀ. δίκην Critias71 D., *PPetr*.3p.44 (iii B.C.).

**ἀποδῐκεῖν**, inf. of ἀπέδικον, poet. aor. with no pres., *throw off*, E. *HF*1205; *throw down*, A.*Ag*.1410.

⊛**ἀποδῐκέω**, (δίκη) *defend oneself on trial*, X.*HG*1.7.21, Antiph.313.

**ἀπόδῐκος**, ον, = ἀπολελυμένος τοῦ ἐγκλήματος, πόλις *GDI*1432 (Hypata). **2.** *rejected*, δίκα *IG*9(1).692.3 (Corcyra, ii B.C.).

**ἀποδινέω**, (δῖνος III) *thresh* corn, Hdt.2.14; 3 pl. subj. -δίνωντι *Tab.Heracl*.1.102.

**ἀποδίομαι**, poet. for ἀποδιώκω, αἴ κεν Ἄρηα..μάχης ἐξ ἀποδίωμαι (with ᾱ metri gr.) Il.5.763.

**ἀποδιοπομπ-έομαι**, fut. -ήσομαι (in pass. sense, Themist.*Ep*.4.5; act. form in Eust.1935.12):—*escort out of* the city the δῖον κῴδιον (v. κῴδιον): hence generally, *conjure away*, Pl.*Cra*.396e, Onos.5, Ph.1. 239, Lib.*Decl*.15.34; μετ' εὐπρεπείας τοὺς φιλοσόφους ἐκ τῆς πόλεως Plu.*Cat.Ma*.22; τινὰς τοῦδε τοῦ γράμματος Gal.*Thras*.37. **2.** generally, *set aside, waive*, τὸ προβληθέν Ath.9.401b, cf. Theo Sm. p.200 H. **II.** καθήρασθαι καὶ ἀ. τὸν οἶκον *free* it *from pollution*, Pl. *Lg*.877e; πόλιν καθαίρειν καὶ ἀ. Lys.6.53. ⊛**-ησις**, εως, ἡ, *offering of an expiatory sacrifice*, Pl.*Lg*.854b. **-ητέον**, *one must reject with abhorrence*, Plu.2.73d.

**ἀποδιορ-ίζω**, *mark off by dividing* or *defining*, Arist.*Pol*.1290b26; (sc. ἑαυτούς) *Ep.Jud*.19. **-ισμός**, ὁ, *division, separation*, v.l. for ἀπομερισμός, Herm.*inPhdr*.p.166 A. **-ιστέον**, *one must mark off, separate*, τινά τινος Sever.*Clyst*.p.35 D.

**ἀποδιπλόομαι**, Pass., *to be unfolded*, Eust.1661.60.

**ἀποδίς**, Adv. *twice*, A.D.*Synt*.339.14, al.

**ἀποδισκεύω**, *throw like a discus*, in Pass., Eust.1591.31.

**ἀποδιφθερόομαι**, Pass., *to be covered with hides*, δέρμασι Lyd.*Ost*. 45.

**ἀποδιψάω**, *cease from thirst, be relieved of it*, Eust.871.5.

**ἀποδιωθέω**, *thrust away*, Hices.ap.Ath.3.87d, cf. Hp.*Mul*.2.201, Aspasia ap.Aët.16.72:—Med., Ar.Byz.*Epit*.10.9.

**ἀπο-δίωγμα** [ῐ], ατος, τό, *pursuit*, a ceremony performed at the Thesmophoria, Hsch. s. v. δίωγμα. **-δῐωκτέον**, *one must drive away*, κύνας Lib.*Fab*.1.1. **2.** -διωκτέος, α, ον, *to be driven away*, Hdn.*Epim*.165. **-δίωκτος** [ῐ], ον, *thrust out*, ib.103. **-δῐώκω**, fut. -διώξομαι, *chase away*, Th.3.108, 6.102; ἀπὸ τῆς θηλείας Arist. *HA*614a16; οὐκ ἀποδιώξει σαυτὸν ἐκ τῆς οἰκίας; *take* yourself *off*, Ar. *Nu*.1296; τὸ λυποῦν ἀποδίωκε τοῦ βίου Men.410; intr., *move*, Olymp. in *Mete*.43.2:—Pass., *to be ridden at full speed*, of a horse, Aët.3. 7. **-δίωξις** [ῐ], εως, ἡ, *expulsion*, πνεύματος Antyll.ap.Orib.6.36.4, cf. *Gp*.13.1.1.

**ἀποδοκεῖ**, impers., (δοκέω) mostly c. μή et inf., ἀπέδοξέ σφι μὴ τιμωρέειν it *seemed good* to them not to do, they *resolved not*.., Hdt. 1.152; ἐπεί σφι ἀ. μὴ ἐπιδιώκειν Id.8.111; without μή, X.*An*.2.3.9: sts. with inf. omitted, ὥς σφι ἀπέδοξε when they *resolved not* (to go on), when they *changed their mind*, Hdt.1.172.

⊛**ἀποδοκῐμ-άζω**, *reject on scrutiny* or *trial, reject* a candidate *from want of qualification*, Hdt.6.130, Lys.13.10, Archipp.14:—Pass., λαχὼν ἀπεδοκιμάσθη ἄρχειν Din.2.10, cf. D.25.30. **2.** generally, *reject as unworthy* or *unfit*, πασσόφους ἄνδρας Pl.*Tht*.181b; ἵππον X. *Eq.Mag*.1.13; νόμους Id.*Mem*.4.4.14; ἀργύριον Thphr.*Char*.4.11; τὴν [τοῦ αὐλοῦ] χρῆσιν ἐκ τῶν νέων Arist.*Pol*.1341a26, cf. 37 (Pass.); [ἡ ὄρνις] ἀ. τὰ αὑτῆς Id.*HA*618a17; τὴν τοιαύτην διατριβήν Timocl. 8.12; τὸ ποιεῖν τι X.*Cyr*.8.1.47: c. inf., Phlp.*inPh*.584.26. **II.** *conclude, judge*, Dam.*Pr*.117. **-ᾰσία**, ἡ, *rejection after trial*, etc., *Gloss*. **-αστέον**, *one must reject*, Xen.*Eq*.3.8, Onos.1. 19. **2.** -αστέος, α, ον, *to be rejected*, Arist.*Po*.1462a8, Luc.*Herm*. 18. **-αστής**, οῦ, ὁ, *one who rejects*, *Gloss*. **-αστικός**, ή, όν, *rejecting, disapproving*, δύναμις δοκιμαστικὴ ἢ ἀ. Arr.*Epict*.1.1.1. **-άω**, = ἀποδοκιμάζω, *reject*, Hdt.1.199. **-ος**, ον, *worthless*, Dsc.1.64; *rejected*, λίθος *BCH*20.324 (Lebad.); πῶροι ib.6.20 (Delos, ii B.C.).

**ἀπόδομα**, ατος, τό, *gift, offering*, Lxx*Nu*.8.13 sq.

**ἄποδον**· βραδύ, ἡ ἀπαγόρευσις, Hsch.

**ἀποδόντωσις**, εως, ἡ, *cleansing of the teeth*, Poll.2.48.

**ἀποδορά**, ᾶς, ἡ, *peeling of the skin*, Agathin.ap.Orib.10.7.18 (pl.).

**ἄποδος**, ἡ, Ion. for ἄφοδος. II. = ἄπους, *not having the use of one's feet*, *Tab.Defix.Aud.*159A44 (Rome, ca. 400 A.D.).

®**ἀπο-δόσιμος**, ον, *restored*, ἀ. γίγνεσθαι Sch.Th.3.52. 2. -μον, τό, *receipt*, *PSI*3.237.6 (v/vi A.D.). ®-**δοσις**, εως, ἡ, (ἀποδίδωμι) *giving back*, *restitution*, *return*, τῶν ἵππων Hdt.4.9; τῶν χωρίων Th.5.35, Pl.*R.*332b; dist. from δόσις, Arist.*Pr.*950ᵃ37. 2. *payment*, *IG*1². 32*A*5, etc.; ἡ ἀ. τοῦ μισθοῦ Th.8.85; φόρου Luc.*VH*1.36: generally, *giving*, Pl.*Lg.*807d; *rendering*, i.e. *performance*, ἔργου Dam.*Pr.* 64. 3. *assignment*, *attribution*, Plot.5.1.6. II. *rendering by way of definition*, Arist.*Cat.*7ᵃ8, *Top.*108ᵇ9, al.; *definition*, S.E.*P.*3. 242, etc. 2. in a sentence, *clause answering to* the πρότασις, διὰ μακροῦ τὰς ἀ. λαμβάνειν D.H.*Th.*52, al.; cf. ἀποδίδωμι II. 2. 3. Gramm., *interpretation*, *explanation*, A.D.*Synt.*155.25, cf. Heliod.ap. Orib.48.70.5: generally, *account*, *explanation*, Epicur.*Ep.*2p.41 U. (pl.), Simp.*in Ph.*614.13; but ψιλὴ ἀ. bare *statement*, Theodor.ap. Corn.*Rh.*p.363 H. III. (from Med.) *sale*, Poll.3.124. -**δόσιμος**, Arc. **ἀπυδόσιμος**, *saleable*, κόπρος *IG*5(2).3 (Tegea, iv B.C.). -**δοσμός**, Arc. **ἀπυ-**, (ἀποδίδωμι) *sale*, ib.343.28 (Orchom. Arc., iv B.C.). -**δοτέον**, *one must give* to another as his *due*, Arist.*EN* 1163ᵃ8, ᵇ20; *one must refer*, *assign*, τί τινι Pl.*R.*452a, etc. 2. *one must describe*, *represent*, οἷος τυγχάνει ὁ θεὸς ὤν.. ἀ. ib.379a. 3. *one must explain*, *interpret*, Sch.Pi.*N.*5.25. 4. *one must allow*, *permit*, Jul.*Or.*2.73c. II. -**δοτέος**, α, ον, *to be referred*, *ascribed*, *assigned*, Pl.*R.*456b; ἕτερος ἂν εἴη ὁρισμὸς -τέος Arist.*Top.*142ᵃ1. -**δοτήρ**, ῆρος, ὁ, *a giver back*, *repayer*, Epich.116. -**δοτικός**, ή, όν, *productive of*, τινός Sor.1.28, S.E.*M.*11.253; *assigning*, Iamb.*in Nic.* p.18 P. 2. *concerning* ἀπόδοσις II.1, S.E.*P.*1.67. 3. *of* or *for* ἀπόδοσις III, *EM*763.8. Adv. -κῶς Eust.920.55. -**δοτος**, ον, *liable to be repaid*, φερναί *SIG*364.60 (Ephesus).

**ἀποδοῦ**· ἀπόδυσον, Hsch.

**ἀπόδουλος**, ὁ, *freedman*, Suid. s. v. Ἀριστοφάνης.

**ἀποδοχ-εῖον**, τό, *storehouse*, Lxx*Si.*1.17. 2. *cistern*, ib.50.3; also ἀποδόχιον *PHib.*1.85 (iii B.C.), *BCH*1.55 (Tralles). -**εύς**, έως, ὁ, = ἀποδέκτης, *IG*5(2).434 (Megalopolis), Epist.ap.J.*AJ*16.6.2, Them.*Or.*15.192c. 2. *keeper of archives*, ἀ. δημοσίων γραμμάτων *IGRom.*4.1248 (Thyatira), *Jahresh.*21/2 *Beibl.*255 (ii A.D.). ®-**ή**, Aeol. **ἀπυδοχά**, ἡ, *receiving back*, *having restored to one*, opp. ἀπόδοσις, Th.4.81. 2. *entertainment*, *reception*, ξένων J.*AJ*12.2.12 (s.v.l.). 3. *place of reception*, γῆ ἀ. πάντων Secund.*Sent.*15. II. *acceptance*, *approbation*, *favour*, ἀποδοχῆς τυγχάνειν παρά τινι Plb.1. 5.5, cf. J.*AJ*6.14.4; ἀ. ἀξιοῦσθαι Plb.2.56.1, cf. D.S.12.53; μετ' εὐχαριστίας καὶ ἀποδοχῆς Phld.*D.*3.2; εἶναι ἐν ἀ. τῷ δήμῳ *SIG*807.21 (Magn. Mae., i A.D.); εἶναι ἐν τῇ καλλίστῃ ἀ. *AJA*18.324 (Sardes); ἐν ἀ. ἔχειν τινά *GDI*311 (Cyme); πάσης ἀ. ἄξιος 1*Ep.Ti.*1.15, cf. *SIG* 867.21 (Ephesus, ii A.D.), Hp.*Ep.*20. III. *acceptation*, *meaning* of terms, S.E.*M.*1.232.

**ἀποδοχμόω**, *bend sideways*, Od.9.372, Orph.*Fr.*149.

**ἀπόδραγμα**, ατος, τό, *part taken off*, Hsch.

**ἀποδρᾶθεῖν**, v. ἀποδαρθάνω.

**ἀποδρᾶπετεύω**, *run away from*, τι Tz. in *An.Ox.*4.80.

**ἀποδράς**, v. ἀποδιδράσκω.

**ἀπόδρᾶσις**, Ion. -**δρησις**, εως, ἡ, (ἀποδιδράσκω) *running away*, *escape*, τὴν ἀ. ποιεῖσθαι Hdt.4.140; βουλεύειν Luc.*DMort.*27.9; οὐκ ἔστιν ἀ. Plu.*CG*1. 2. c. gen., *escape from*, *avoidance of*, στρατείας D.21.166; *evasion*, τῆς ἐρωτήσεως Plu.2.641c.

**ἀποδρασκάζω**, = ἀποδιδράσκω, Tz.*H.*1.502.

**ἀποδρεπᾰνίζω**, *prune*, *lop with a* δρέπανον, Suid. s. v. δρεφθῆναι.

**ἀπο-δρέπτομαι**, = sq., σοφίην *AP*10.18 (Marc. Arg.). -**δρέπω**, *pluck off*, ἀπόδρεπε οἴκαδε βότρυς *pluck and take* them home, Hes.*Op.* 611; *pluck off* hair, Hp.*Mul.*2.106: metaph., ἀ. καρπὸν ἥβας Pi.*P.*9. 110, cf. *O.*1.13; τὸν ἀφροδισίων κῆπον Archipp.2 D.:—Med., μαλθακᾶς ὥρας ἀπὸ καρπὸν δρέπεσθαι Pi.*Fr.*122.8, cf. *AP*6.303 (Aristo), Plu. 2.79d. -**δρεψις**, εως, ἡ, *plucking off*, *Corp.Herm.*18.11.

**ἀπο-δρῆναι**, Ion. for -δρᾶναι, v. ἀποδιδράσκω. -**δρησις**, v. ἀπόδρᾶσις.

®**ἀποδρομή**, ἡ, *harbour of refuge*, σκάφαις dub. in *Peripl.M.Rubr.* 3.

**ἀπόδρομος**, ον, (δραμεῖν) *apart from the race*, whether as *too old* or *too young* (as in Crete, *Leg.Gort.*7.35) *to share it*, Eust.727.18, 1592. 55 sqq.; or *left behind by others*, Hsch., cf. S.*Fr.*73.

**ἀποδρύπτω**, aor. 1 ἀπέδρυψα: aor. 2 ἀπέδρῠφον:—*tear off the skin*, *lacerate*, μή μιν ἀποδρύφοι ἑλκυστάζων Il.23.187; μή σε νέοι διὰ δώματ' ἐρύσσωσ'.. ἀποδρύψωσί τε πάντα Od.17.480; σάρκας ὀνύχεσσι Theoc. 25.267:—Pass., ἀπὸ χειρῶν ῥινοὶ ἀπέδρυφθεν Od.5.435, cf. 426; ἀποδρυφθῆναι χαλάζῃ *AP*11.365 (Agath.):—Med., *scrape oneself*, *grow thin*, dub. in Alciphr.3.51.

**ἀποδυνᾰμία**, ἡ, *lack of power*, Olymp.*in Grg.*p.251 J.

**ἀποδύνω** [ῡ], = ἀποδύω, *strip off*, ἀπέδυνε βοείην Od.22.364.

**ἀπ-οδυρμός**, ὁ, *bewailing*, *lamentation*, *Gloss.* ®-**οδύρομαι** [ῡ], *lament bitterly*, τι πρὸς τὤγαλμα Hdt.2.141; τύχας A.*Pr.*637; ἐμαυτὴν καὶ γένος τὸ πᾶν S.*El.*1122; τινί *to* a person, Apollod.1.9.8 (dub.): abs., Pl.*R.*606a. 2. *take one's fill of lamentation* (cf. ἀπολοφύρομαι), *IG*14.63.

**ἀπόδῠσις**, εως, ἡ, (ἀποδύομαι) *stripping*, *undressing*, J.*AJ* 2.5.1, Plu.2.751f, Porph.*Abst.*1.31. II. gloss on Lat. *obitus*, *POxy.* 1099ᵛ42.

**ἀποδυσ-πετέω**, *desist through impatience*, Arist.*Top.*163ᵇ19; περὶ αὐτὴν τὴν ἐπιθυμίαν Plu.2.502e; πρός τι Luc.*Rh.Pr.*3; σχέτλια ἀ. Alciphr.3.74. (πετ-, root of πίπτω.) -**πέτημα**, ατος, τό, = sq., Sch.Luc.*Tim.*3 (pl.). -**πέτησις**, εως, ἡ, *discouragement*, *despair*, Corn.*ND*35.

**ἀπο-δῠτέον**, *one must strip*, τινά Luc.*Herm.*38; *one must put off*, χιτῶνας Porph.*Abst.*1.31. II. (from Pass.) ἀ. ταῖς γυναιξίν they *must strip off their clothes*, Pl.*R.*457a. ®-**δῠτήριον**, τό, *undressing room* in the bath, X.*Ath.*2.10, Pl.*Ly.*206e, etc.; in the palaestra, Id.*Euthd.*272e. ®-**δύω**, I. in fut. -δύσω, aor. 1 -έδῡσα (for pf. -δέδῠκα v. infr. II. 1), trans. used by Hom. (esp. in Il.) of *stripping* armour *from* the slain, 1. c. acc. rei, *strip off*, τεύχεα δ' Ἕκτωρ δῃώσας ἀπέδυσε Il.18.83, cf. 4.532, etc.; ἀπὸ μὲν φίλα εἵματα δύσω 2. 261; ἀ. τί τινος Pl.*Chrm.*154e. 2. c. acc. pers., *strip*, ἀπέδυσε τὰς.. γυναῖκας Hdt.5.92.η', cf. Pl.*Epigr.*12.3; ἵνα μὴ ῥιγῶν ἀποδύῃ (sc. τοὺς ὁδοιπόρους) Ar.*Av.*712, cf. *Th.*636, *Ec.*668: c. dupl. acc., τὴν ἐσθῆτά τινα ἀ. Luc.*Nigr.*13:—Pass., *to be stripped of* one's clothes, οὔ τοι τοῦτον ἀποδυθήσομαι (sc. τὸν τρίβωνα) Ar.*V.*1122; ἵνα μή ποτε κἀποδυθῇ μεθύων Id.*Ra.*715, cf. *Pl.*930; θοἰμάτιον ἀποδεδύσθαι Lys. 10.10; ἀποδυόμενος *stripped of its shell*, of the nautilus, Arist.*HA* 622ᵇ18. II. Med., fut. -δύσομαι: aor. 1 -εδυσάμην Od.5.349 (v.l.), Pl.*R.*612a (v.l.), Lys.*Fr.*232 S., etc.; mostly with intr. aor. 2 Act. ἀπέδυν, pf. ἀποδέδῡκα (used trans. by X.*An.*5.8.23 πολλοὺς ἤδη ἀποδέδυκεν):—*strip off oneself*, *take off*, εἵματα ταῦτ' ἀποδὺς Od.5.343; ἀπόδυθι.. θοἰμάτιον Ar.*Th.*214; τῶν ἱματίων ἀποδυσας (aor. 2 part. pl. fem.) *having stripped off* some of them, ib.656; σῶμ' ἀποδυσάμενος *Epigr.Gr.*403 (Galatia): metaph., ἀ. τὴν ὑπόκρισιν J.*AJ*13.7.1. 2. abs., ἀποδυσάμενος *having stripped*, v.l. for ἀπολυσ-, Od.5.349; ἀποδύντες *stripped naked*, Th.1.6, cf. Pl.*Mx.*236d: metaph., ἀποδύεσθαι πρὸς τὸ λέγειν, εἰς ἀγορανομίαν, Plu.*Dem.*6, *Brut.*15; οἱ ἀποδυόμενοι εἰς τὴν παλαίστραν those who *strip for* the palaestra, who *practise* there, Lys.*Fr.*45.1; εἰς τὸ γυμνάσιον *IG*14.256 (Phintias); πρὸς τὸ ἀχανὲς πέλαγος Jul.*Or.*4.142c; ἀποδύντες τοῖς ἀναπαίστοις ἐπίωμεν *let us strip* and attack the anapaests, Ar.*Ach.*627, cf. *Ra.*641.

**ἀποδωρέω**, *give away*, Ἀρχ.Ἐφ.1918.170.106 (Epid., iv B.C.), Critias6.3 D.

**ἀποδωσείω**, Desiderat., *wish to give back*, Procop.*Goth.*3.34.

**ἀποείκω**, *withdraw from*, θεῶν ἀπόεικε κελεύθου Il.3.406 (Aristarch.).

**ἀπο-ειπεῖν**, -**ειπών**, v. ἀπεῖπον. -**εργάθω**, v. ἀπείργαθον. -**έργω**, v. ἀπείργω.

**ἀπόερσε**, Ep. aor. almost always in 3 pers. (imper. ἀπόερσον Nic. *Th.*110):—*swept away*, ἔνθα με κῦμ' ἀπόερσε Il.6.348; ὅν ῥά τ' ἔναυλος ἀποέρσῃ 21.283; μή μιν ἀποέρσειε μέγας ποταμὸς ib.329; cf. ἀπούρας.

®**ἀποζάω**, *live off*, ὅσον ἀποζῆν enough *to live off*, Th.1.2: c. dat., ἀ. ἐλύμοις Procop.*Pers.*1.12, al. 2. *live poorly*, Luc.*Tox.*59, Ael.*NA* 16.12, Lib.*Or.*11.253. 3. *live out*, ἰδιώτην βίον J.*AJ*9.10.4.

**ἀπό-ζεμα**, ατος, τό, (ἀποζέω) *decoction*, *Gp.*13.12.2, Apollon.ap. Philum.*Ven.*33.5. -**ζέννῡμι**, = ἀποζέω, Dsc.1.94 (Pass.), etc. -**ζεσμα**, ατος, τό, = ἀπόζεμα, *PHolm.*15.40, al.

**ἀπο-ζευγέω**, aor. inf. -ῆσαι, lit. *unyoke*: metaph., *discontinue treatment*, Hp.*Loc.Hom.*12. ®-**ζεύγνῡμι**, *separate*, *part*, ἀ. συνεύνων Man. 3.85; ἀ. τὸ τείχισμα Malch.p.412 D. II. mostly in Pass., -ζεύγνυμαι, aor. -εζύγην [ῠ] (v.infr.), also -εζεύχθην E.*El.*284, *AP*12.226 (Strat.):—*to be loosed from the yoke*, [βοῦς] εἰς νομὰς ἀπεζεύχθη Babr. 37.6; but usually metaph., *to be parted from*, τέκνων γυναικός τ' E.*HF* 1375, cf. *Med.*1017; εἰ γάμων ἀπεζύγην if I *were free from*.., Id.*Supp.* 791; ὀρφανὸς ἀποζυγεὶς Id.*Ph.*988; ὥσπερ δεῦρ' ἀπεζύγην πόδας as I *unharnessed* my feet, i.e. took rest, A.*Ch.*676. -**ζευκτέον**, *one must part*, *separate*, τινά τινος Them.*Or.*13.179c. ®-**ζευξις**, εως, ἡ, *unyoking*, Sch.Od.6.88.

®**ἀποζέω**, *boil till the scum is thrown off*, Hp.*Acut.*(*Sp.*)63, Diph.17. 9; simply, *boil*, κρέα *IG*12(7).515.78 (Amorgos). 2. intr., *cease boiling* or *fermenting*: metaph., Alex.45.3.

®**ἀποζημιόω**, v. ἀπίθετο.

**ἀποζίννυνται**· ἀποσβέννυνται, Hsch. (-ξινν- cod.).

**ἀπο-ζῠγή**, ἡ, *deed of divorce*, *PGrenf.*2.76.19 (iv A.D.). -**ζῠγος**, ον, of numbers, *odd*, Vett.Val.361.13.

**ἀπόζῡμος**, ον, *in a state of fermentation*, Hp.*Prorrh.*2.23.

**ἀπόζω**, *smell of* something, τινός Luc.*DMar.*1.5, Plu.2.13f: abs., Longus4.1. II. impers., ἀπόζει τῆς Ἀραβίης *there comes an odour from* Arabia, Hdt.3.113, cf. Luc.*Cyn.*17.

**ἀποζωγρᾰφέω**, *portray*, τἀναντία φαντάσματα Pl.*Ti.*71c.

**ἀπο-ζώννῡμι** and -ύω, aor. -έζωσα, *take the girdle off* one, Chor. p.28 B.; esp. when *discharging* him *from service*, Hdn.2.13.8. -**ζωσις**, εως, ἡ, *ungirding*, *Gloss.*

**ἀποϝειπάθθω**, v. ἀπεῖπον.

**ἀποϝηλέω**, v. ἀπειλέω.

**ἀποθᾰλασσόω**, *make into sea*, Eust.ad D.P.511.

**ἀποθᾰνετέον**, (ἀποθνῄσκω) *one must die*, Arist.*EN*1110ᵃ27.

**ἀποθαρρέω** and -**θαρσέω**, *take courage*, *have full confidence*, X.*Oec.* 16.6: c. inf., *to have the boldness to*.., Longin.32.8, J.*AJ*15.7.3: c. acc., ἀ. τὸ πρόσω τῆς πορείας Paus.10.19.5: c. dat., *use rashly*, Aët.12.23.

**ἀποθαρρύνω**, *encourage*, τοὺς φίλους App.*Hann.*12.

**ἀποθαυμάζω**, Ion. -**θωυμάζω** or -**θωμάζω**, *marvel much at* a thing, ἄφαρ δ' ἀπεθαύμασ' ὄνειρον Od.6.49; ἀ. τὰ λεγόμενα, τὸ λεχθέν, Hdt. 1.11, 30; πολλὰ ἄλλα Id.2.79: abs., *wonder much*, Id.1.68, X.*Oec.* 2.17, Luc.*Am.*13, *POxy.*1242 iii 53 (iii A.D.): c. part., ἀ. ὁ ἐών Hdt. 1.88; folld. by εἰ, *wonder* that.., Aeschin.1.94, 119.—Rare in Trag., A.*Ag.*318, S.*OC*1586.

**ἀποθεάομαι**, *look attentively at*, τι J.*BJ*2.15.1.

**ἀποθειάζω**, = ἀποθεόω, Them.*Or.*20.239d.

**ἀποθει-όω,** *clothe in mystical language,* λόγον Philostr.*Im.*16.2; = ἀποθεόω, in Pass., *AP*12.177. **-ωσις,** εως, ἡ, *fumigation,* Onos. 10.28 (pl.)

**ἀποθεμελιόω,** *destroy utterly,* Suid. s.v. ἀπογαιῶσαι.

**ἄποθεν,** freq. as f.l. for ἄπωθεν (q.v.) in codd., as Th.2.81, Arist. *Pol.*1280$^b$18, etc., cf. Hsch.

**ἀπόθε-ος,** ον, *far from the gods, godless,* S.*Fr.*267. ⊛**-όω,** *deify,* *PTeb.*5.78 (ii B.C.), Plb.12.23.4, Plu.*Num.*6, etc.:—Pass., Γανυμήδης.. ἀποθεούμενος Nicol.Com.1.35; μετὰ τὸ ἀποθεωθῆναι *CIG*2831.7 (Aphrodisias); cf. -θειόω. **2.** in magic, *drown* a sacred animal and thus liberate its divine element, *PMag.Berol.*1.5, *PMag.Lond.* 121.629 (Pass.); ἀ. ἱέρακα ἐν ὕδατι Afric.ap.Sch.Tz.*H.*9.161.

**ἀποθεράπ-εία,** ἡ, *regular worship,* θεῶν Arist.*Pol.*1335$^b$15. **II.** *restorative treatment* after fatigue, Antyll.ap.Orib.6.21.1, Gal.*Thras.* 47. **-ευσις,** εως, ἡ, = θεράπευσις, Hsch. s.v. ἀκέσεων (pl.). **-ευτέον,** *one must treat by* ἀποθεραπεία, τὸ σῶμα Sor.2.11: abs., *one must conclude the treatment,* σὺν ἀλείμματι Id.1.49. **-ευτικός,** ή, όν, *of, connected with* ἀποθεραπεία, Antyll.ap.Orib.6.21.4, Gal.6.197. Adv. -κῶς ib.262. ⊛**-εύω,** *treat with attention and honour,* D.H.3.71, Phld.*Herc.*1457.11, etc. **2.** *cure,* τινά Hp.*Praec.*5; τὸ ἀλγοῦν τινι Plu.2.118c; *apply* ἀποθεραπεία *to,* τὰ μέρη Antyll.ap.Orib.7.16.10, Gal.6.201 (Pass.).

**ἀποθερίζω,** poet. aor. ἀπέθρῐσα (also in late Prose, Porph.*Abst.*2. 10):—*cut off,* ἶνας μεδέων ἀπέθρισεν Archil.138; ἄκρας ὡς ἀπέθρισεν κόμας E.*Or.*128, cf. *Hel.*1188, *AP*6.107 (Phil.), etc.; καυλόν Dsc.3. 70; of persons, μνηστῆρας Nonn.*D.*48.96; regul. form -θέρισα in Ael.*NA*1.5, Apollod.1.9.23; ἀπεθέρισα τοὺς προφήτας σου Lxx*Ho.*6. 6(5):—Med., aor. ἀπεθρισάμην *AP*5.236 (Agath.); ἀποθρίξασθαι, of the *tonsure* of monks, Procop.*Arc.*1, al., perhaps from a mistaken etymology, cf. ἀποθρίξαντες τὴν χαίτην Ael.ap.Ar.Byz.*Epit.*149.13.

**ἀποθέρισμα,** ατος, τό, v. sub ἀπόθρισμα.

**ἀπόθερμος,** ον, = ἄθερμος, Aret.*SD*2.1. **II.** as Subst., = μελιτοῦττα, Sch.Ar.*Pl.*1122; = ἄμυλος, Sch.Theoc.9.21. **2.** a kind of *drink,* Hp.*Mul.*1.44, 2.207. **3.** a *condiment,* Gal.6.519.

**ἀποθέσιμος,** ον, *stored away,* χρήματα J.*AJ*16.7.1.

**ἀπόθεσις,** εως, ἡ, (ἀποτίθημι) *laying up in store,* σκευῶν *SIG*1106. 107 (Cos); εἰς ἀ. γενέσθαι to be *stored up,* Pl.*Lg.*844d; γάλα χρήσιμον εἰς ἀ. Arist.*HA*522$^a$26; ἡ ἀ. τῆς τροφῆς, of bees, 622$^b$26; τὴν ἀ. τῆς θήρας ποιεῖσθαι 623$^a$12; *preserving,* of fish, Philum.ap.Aët.9. 23. **2.** *the final movement in setting* a dislocated or fractured limb, Gal.18(2).332, al., Pall.*in Hp.Fract.*12.273C.; f.l. in Hp.*Off.* 19. **3.** κατ' ἀπόθεσιν, of *internal* abscesses, Gal.17(1).103. **II.** *putting aside, making away with, getting rid of,* ῥύπου 1*Ep.Pet.*3. 21, cf. 2.1.14. **2.** *exposure* of children, Arist.*Pol.*1335$^b$19; cf. ἀποτίθημι II.7. **3.** *resignation* of an office, App.*BC*1.3, cf. *SIG* 900.16 (iv A.D.). **4.** ἀ. κώλου, περιόδου, *close* or *cadence* of a phrase, Demetr.*Eloc.*19, cf. Sch.Ar.*Nu.*176; so in metres, = κατάληξις, Heph.4 tit. **III.** = ἀποδυτήριον, Luc.*Hipp.*5.

**ἀπο-θεσπίζω,** *utter as an oracle,* ἀ. ἔμμετρα Str.9.3.5, cf. Plu.*Luc.* 2; *prophesy,* D.H.6.43. **-θέσπισις,** εως, ἡ, *oracle given,* Str.17. 1.43.

**ἀπόθεστος,** ον, *despised,* δὴ τότε κεῖτ' ἀ. Od.17.296, cf. Lyc.540, Call.*Fr.*302, Plu.2.159f. (From θέσσασθαι, cf. πολύθεστος.)

**ἀπό-θεται,** ων, αἱ, a place in Lacedaemon, into which misshapen children were thrown as soon as born, Plu.*Lyc.*16. **-θετέον,** *one must set aside, lay by,* Dsc.2.76. **-θετικός,** ή, όν, *completing,* τῆς διανοίας Sch.Ar.*Pl.*8. **II.** of verbs, *deponent,* *An.Bachm.* 2.303,304. ⊛**-θετος,** ον, (ἀποτίθημι) *laid by, stored up,* Dsc.5.9, Plu.*Caes.*35, Luc.*Merc.Cond.*5: ἀπόθετα, τά, *stores,* *PRyl.*153.16 (ii A.D.). **2.** *hidden, secret, mysterious,* ἔπη Pl.*Phdr.*252b; βίβλοι D.H.11.62, cf. Philostr.*Im.*1.10, 2.16, Plu.*Crass.*16. **3.** *reserved for special occasions, special,* φίλος Lys.8.17; δωρεά D.59.93. **4.** ἀπόθετος, ὁ (sc. νόμος), name of an aulodic nome, Plu.2.1132d, Poll. 4.79. **II.** f.l. for ἀπόθεστος, Plu.2.159f. **III.** ἀπόθετον· *deponens,* *Gloss.*; cf. foreg. II.

**ἀποθέω,** *run away,* Hdt.8.56, X.*Cyr.*7.5.40.

**ἀποθεωρ-έω,** = ἀποθεάομαι, Arist.*Mir.*839$^b$3, Plb.27.4.4, D.S.4.38, Polycharm.1; *observe,* Plu.*Lyc.*25; *examine, consider,* πίστεις Phld. *Rh.*2.116 S., cf. *Oec.*p.74 J. **-ησις,** εως, ἡ, *serious contemplation,* Plu.*Pel.*25; *wide view,* τόπος τὴν ἀ. πανταχόθεν εὐφυής D.S.19. 38. **-ητέον,** *one must consider, contemplate,* Plu.2.30a. **2.** ἀ. μή.. *one must take care* not.., Herod.Med.ap.Orib.7.8.10.

⊛**ἀποθέωσις,** εως, ἡ, *deification,* Str.6.3.9, *CIG*2832 (Aphrodisias), Cic.*Att.*1.16.13, Senec.*Apoc.* tit., *PGen.*36.18 (ii A.D.), Hierocl.*in CA*27 p.483 M.

⊛**ἀπο-θήκη,** ἡ, *any place wherein to lay up* a thing, *magazine, storehouse,* Th.6.97; ἀ. βιβλίων Luc.*Ind.*5; ἀ. σωμάτων *burial-place,* Id.*Cont.*22. **2.** *refuge,* Philist.59. **II.** *anything laid by, store,* ἀποθήκην ποιεῖσθαι ἐς τὸν Πέρσην lay up *store* of favour with him, Hdt. 8.109. **-θήκιον,** τό, *larder,* Cael.Aur.*CP*1.11.93.

**ἀποθηλ-άζω,** *suck,* Sor.1.118, Paul.Aeg.3.28. **-ασμός,** ὁ, (θηλάζω) *sucking, sucking out,* Erasistr.ap.Dsc.*Ther.Praef.*, Sor.1. 77, Paul.Aeg.3.35.

**ἀποθηλύνω,** *make effeminate, enervate,* Plu.*Ant.*53; *weaken,* τὰς ὀσμάς Thphr.*Od.*66; ἄκρατον Plu.2.692d:—Pass., Clearch.6. **II.** *produce female* plants, Thphr.*HP*7.4.3.

**ἀποθηρευτής,** οῦ, ὁ, *drinking-cup used after hunting,* *IG*11(2).113. 17 (Delos, iii B.C.), al.

**ἀποθηρι-όω,** *change into a beast,* τινά Eratosth.*Cat.*1:—Pass., Str. 3.2.7; prob. in Herm.ap.Stob.1.49.69. **2.** *make quite savage,* τὸν βίον Plu.2.995d; *exasperate,* τινὰ πρός τινα Plb.1.79.8:—Pass., *to become* or *be so,* ib.67.6; τὴν ψυχήν D.S.17.9; of wounds, Plb.1.81. 5. **II.** Pass., *to be full of savage creatures,* ἀποτεθηρίωται ὁ Νεῖλος Alciphr.2.3. **-ωσις,** εως, ἡ, *changing into a wild beast,* Hsch. s.v. Αἰαίη. **II.** (from Pass.) *fury* or *rage* against any one, πρός τινα D.S.34/5.20.

**ἀποθησαυρ-ίζω,** *store, hoard up,* Lxx *Si.*3.4, D.S.5.40, Luc. *Alex.*23; ἑαυτοῖς τι 1*Ep.Ti.*6.19:—Pass., J.*BJ*7.8.4, Vett.Val.16. 21. ⊛**-ισμός,** ὁ, *laying by, storing up,* D.S.2.29.

**ἀπόθητος,** ον, *not desired,* Hsch., dub. in Call.*Fr.*302 (leg. ἀπόθεστος).

**ἀποθῑνόομαι,** Pass., *to be silted up,* Plb.1.75.8.

⊛**ἀπο-θλίβω** [ῑ], *squeeze out,* τοὺς ὄρχεις Arist.*HA*632$^a$17; ὑπόστασιν Thphr.*Od.*29; τὸν ἐκ τοῦ βότρυος ἀποθλιβόμενον οἶνον D.S.3.62; τῆς χώρας *from* the place, Luc.*Jud.Voc.*2. **2.** *press* or *force back,* τὸ αἷμα Arist.*HA*587$^a$22:—in E.*Cyc.*237 Ruhnken restored ἀπολέψειν. **3.** *press tightly,* τὰ κράσπεδα Diph.43.30; ἀ. τινά *press upon, crowd,* *Ev.Luc.*8.45. **4.** *crush,* Lxx *Nu.*22.25. **II.** Gramm., *drop* a letter in the middle of a word, A.D.*Adv.*185.3 (Pass.). **III.** *oppress much,* Aq.*Ex.*3.9, Sm.*Jd.*10.12:—Pass., πρὸς τὸ τὴν πόλιν ἀποθλιβῆναι Wilcken *Chr.*11 *A* 9 (ii B.C.). **-θλιμμα,** ατος, τό, *expressed juice,* Dsc.1.110. **II.** *solid residue after expression of juice,* Gal.11.845. **-θλιμμός,** ὁ, *oppression,* Aq.*Ex.* 3.9. **-θλιψις,** εως, ἡ, *pressing,* βοτρύων D.S.3.63. **II.** *squeezing out of one's place,* Luc.*Jud.Voc.*2.

**ἀποθνῄσκω,** fut. -θᾰνοῦμαι, Ion. -θανέομαι or -εῦμαι Hdt.3.143, 7.134:—strengthd. for θνῄσκω, *die,* Hom. (v. infr.), Pi.*O.*1.27, and once in Trag. (E.*Fr.*578.6); in Com. and Prose the usual form of the pres.; σεῦ ἀποτεθνηῶτος Il.22.432; ἀποθνῄσκων περὶ φασγάνῳ Od.11. 424; βόες δ' ἀποτέθνασαν ἤδη 12.393; ἐκ τῶν τρωμάτων Hdt.2.63; ὑπὸ λιμοῦ Th.1.126: c. dat., βρόμῳ κεραυνοῦ Pi. l.c.; νόσῳ Th.8.84: c. acc. cogn., θάνατον ἀ. X.*Mem.*4.8.3, etc.; εἰς ἕτερον ζῆν ἀ. Pl.*Ax.* 365d; *to be ready to die,* of laughter, etc., Ar.*Ach.*15; ἀ. τῷ δέει Arist.*MM*1191$^a$35. **II.** serving as Pass. of ἀποκτείνω, *to be put to death, slain,* ὑπό τινος Hdt.1.137, 7.154; esp. by judicial sentence, ἀποθανεῖν ὑπὸ τῆς πόλεως Lycurg.93, cf. Pl.*Ap.*29d, 32d, al., Arist. *Rh.*1397$^a$30 (v.l.). **III.** *renounce,* νόμῳ *Ep.Gal.*2.19; ἀπό τινος *Ep.Col.*2.20.

**ἀποθορεῖν,** aor. 2 inf. Act. of ἀποθρῴσκω.

**ἀποθρᾰσύνομαι,** *to be very courageous, dare all things,* D.61.20:—later **-θαρρύνομαι,** Diog.*Ep.*32.3.

**ἀπό-θραυσις,** εως, ἡ, *breaking, fracture,* Paul.Aeg.6.89,117; κατὰ ἀπόθραυσιν Sor.*Fract.*10. **II.** *breaking up,* νεφῶν Arist.*Mu.*394$^a$ 33. **-θραυσμα,** ατος, τό, *piece broken off,* Str.10.5.16. **-θραύω,** *break off,* νεὼς κόρυμβα A.*Pers.*410; τοὺς ὑπερέχοντας τῶν σταχύων D.H.4.56: metaph., τῆς ἐλευθερίας τὸ κεφάλαιον Jul.*Mis.*356b; τοῦ ἑνὸς τὸ μερικόν Dam.*Pr.*51:—Pass., *to be broken off,* Arist.*Pr.*967$^b$5, Arr.*Tact.*2.4: metaph., ἀποθραυσθῆναι τῆς εὐκλείας *to be broken off from* one's fair fame, *make shipwreck of* it, Ar.*Nu.*997.

**ἀπόθρεκτα·** φευκτά, Hsch.

**ἀποθρηνέω,** *lament much,* Plu.*Fab.*18, *Crass.*27, Babr.12.3.

**ἀποθρῑάζω,** properly, *strip of fig-leaves*: metaph., *circumcise,* Ar. *Ach.*158; cf. θρῖον.

⊛**ἀποθριγκόω,** *furnish with coping,* τοῖχον *IG*11(2).144 *A* 84, al. (Delos, iv B.C.). **2.** *wall off,* Procop.*Aed.*5.7, al.

**ἀποθρίζω,** v. ἀποθερίζω.

**ἀπόθριξ,** τρῐχος, ὁ, ἡ, = ἄθριξ, Call.*Fr.*341; = ἄνηβος, Poll.2.22.

**ἀπόθρισμα,** ατος, τό, *that which is cut off,* Orph.*A.*1000.

**ἀποθρύπτω,** *crush, crumble to pieces,* J.*BJ*3.7.23: metaph., *break in spirit, enervate,* τὰς ψυχὰς συγκεκλασμένοι τε καὶ ἀποτεθρυμμένοι Pl. *R.*495e.

**ἀποθρῴσκω,** aor. ἀπέθορον, *leap off from,* νηός Il.2.702; ἀπὸ τῶν ἵππων, ἀπὸ νεός, Hdt.1.80, 7.182; ἰοὶ ἀπὸ νευρῆφι θορόντες Il.16.773: abs., *spring away,* Opp.*H.*1.206. **2.** *leap up from, rise from,* καπνὸν ἀποθρῴσκοντα νοῆσαι ἧς γαίης Od.1.58. **3.** *rebound from,* ἔρως ἀντιτύπου κραδίης ἀ. *AP*9.443 (Paul. Sil.). **4.** *break off,* of rocks, ἀφ' ὑψηλῆς κορυφῆς Hes.*Sc.*375.

**ἀποθυμαίνω,** dub. in S.*Ichn.*122.

**ἀποθῡμίᾱσις,** εως, ἡ, *rising of smoke* or *vapour,* Plu.2.647f (nisi leg. ὑπο-).

**ἀποθῡμιάω,** *smoke out,* [μῦς] Arist.*HA*580$^b$23.

⊛**ἀποθύμιος** [ῡ], ον (fem. -ίη in Semon.7.35): (θῡμός):—*not according to the mind, unpleasant, hateful,* ἔπος Hes.*Op.*710; ἀποθύμια ἔρδειν τινί to do one *a disfavour,* Il.14.261; οὔ τι ἀποθύμιον ποιῆσαι Hdt.7.168; μή μοί τι τέκνοις ἀ. ἕρπῃ Mosch.4.93.

**ἀπόθῡμος,** ον, f.l. for ἀπρόθυμος, Plu.2.87f.

**ἀποθυννίζω,** *dismiss as worthy of a tunny,* in Pass., Luc.*JTr.*25, cf. Eust.1720.63.

**ἀποθῠρίζω,** *put out of doors,* *Gloss.*:—also **-θυρόω,** Hsch. (Pass.).

**ἀπο-θύσκειν·** ἀποτυγχάνειν, Hsch. **-θύσσει·** ἀποπνεύσει, Id.

**ἀποθυστάνιον,** τό, *drinking-vessel,* Polem.Hist.20.

**ἀπο-θῠτέον,** *one must perform a sacrifice,* Them.*Or.*11.142a. **-θύω,** fut. -θύσω *IG*4.951.45 (Epid.):—*offer up* as a votive sacrifice, χιμαίρας X.*An.*3.2.12; ἡγεμόσυνα 4.8.25; εὐχήν Diph.43.10; ἴατρα *IG* l.c.

**ἀποθωρᾱκίζομαι,** *put off one's coat of mail,* Procop.*Goth.*4.32.

**ἀποθωυμάζω** or **-θωμάζω,** Ion. for ἀποθαυμάζω.

**ἀποιδ-έω,** *swell up,* Hp.*Mul.*1.52. **-ησις,** εως, ἡ, *swelling,* ὑφάλου γῆς Str.1.3.10 (pl.). **-ίσκομαι,** = ἀποιδέω, Hp.*Int.*41.

**ἀποϊερόω,** = ἀφιερόω, *CIG*2827.9 (Aphrodisias).

**ἀποίζειν·** ἀπομωκᾶσθαι, Hsch.

**ἀποιητικός,** ή, όν, *unpoetical*, Sch.D.P.289.

®**ἀποίητος,** ον, *not done, undone*, πεπραγμένων ἀποίητον θέμεν ἔργων τέλος Pi.*O*.2.18; ἀ. πάμπολλ' ἐστίν Men.113. 2. *not to be done, impossible*, Plu.*Cor*.38. II. *not artificial, unpolished*, D.H. *Lys*.8; esp. *unpoetical*, ἀ. λόγος, opp. ποιητική, Id.*Comp*.1; τὰ ἀποίητα, opp. τὰ πεποημένα, Phld.*Po*.1081; ἀ. ὑπόθεσις *not used as material for poetry*, ibid.; τὸ ἀ. *simplicity, naïveté*, Aristid.*Or*.31(11). 4. Adv. -τως D.H.*Dem*.39. III. of land, *unsuitable*, εἴς τι *Gp*. 10.75.12.

**ἀποικει-όω,** *absorb completely, assimilate*, Anon.Lond.24.26:—hence **-ωσις,** εως, ἡ, ib.24.35. II. *keep apart*, Hero *Spir.Praef*. p.146 S. (Pass.), s. v. l.

**ἀποικ-εσία,** ἡ, = ἀποίκησις, esp. of *the Captivity*, Lxx 4*Ki*.24.15, al. ®**-έω,** *go away from home*, esp. as a colonist, *settle in a foreign country, emigrate*, ἐκ πόλεως Isoc.4.122; ἐς Θουρίους Pl.*Euthd*.271c: so c. acc. loci, Καλλίσταν ἀπῴκησαν νᾶσον Pi.*P*.4.258, cf. Porph.*VP* 2. II. *dwell afar off*, μακρὰν ἀ. Th.3.55; πρόσω ἀ. X.*Oec*.4.6; ἀ. τινὸς πρόσω E.*HF*557, cf. *IA*680; ἐν νήσῳ Arist.*Pol*.$1272^{b}$1; ἀ. τῶν πεδίων Philostr.*Im*.1.9: c. acc., *live a long way off* a person, Theoc. 15.7 (s. v. l.):—Pass., ἡ Κόρινθος ἐξ ἐμοῦ..μακρὰν ἀπῳκεῖτο Corinth *was inhabited* by me *at a distance*, i.e. I *settled far from* Corinth, S. *OT*998. **-ησις,** εως, ἡ, = sq., *emigration*, Hsch., Suid.; dub. in D.H.2.36. ®**-ία,** Ion. **-ίη,** ἡ, (ἄποικος) *settlement far from home, colony*, Pi.*O*.1.24, S.*Fr*.373.6, Hdt.1.146, *IG*1.31, etc.; correlative to μητρόπολις, Th.1.34; εἰς ἀ. στέλλειν, ἄγειν, send, lead to form *a settlement*, Hdt.4.147, 5.124; ἀ. κτίσαι A.*Pr*.814; ἀ. ἐκπέμπειν Th.1.12; ἀ. κηρύσσειν ἐς τόπον ib.27; ἀ. ποιεῖσθαι Pl.*Lg*.702c; στέλλειν (of the οἰκιστής) Str.8.6.22; ἀποστέλλειν (of the μητρόπολις) Aeschin.2.176; ἡ κώμη ἀ. οἰκίας is *an offshoot from*.., Arist.*Pol*.$1252^{b}$17. 2. *migration*, Ph.2.410. II. *charter* granted to a colony, Hyp.*Fr*. 73. **-ίζω,** Att. fut. ἀποικιῶ A.*Fr*.304.10:—*send away from home*, ἐς νῆσον Od.12.135; ἐκ τόπων S.*Tr*.955 (lyr.), cf. *OC*1390; ἀ. δόμων τινά E.*El*.1008, cf. *Hipp*.629; of the queen-bee, X.*Oec*.7.34:—Pass., *to be settled in a far land*, ἐν μακάρων νήσοις ἀπῳκίσθαι Pl.*R*. 519c; *emigrate*, ἐκ τῆσδε τῆς πόλεως Id.*Euthd*.302c; ἀπὸ πατρὸς ἀποικισθῆναι *dwell apart from*.., Arist.*GA*$740^{a}$7. 2. metaph., *banish*, τὰς ψευδεῖς δόξας Ph.2.221:—Pass., εἰς τὸ μέσον ἀπῳκίσθη τῶν ἐσχάτων Pl.*Plt*.284e; ἀνάγκης οὐκ ἀ. πολύ is not far *removed from*.., Chaerem.18. II. *colonize* a place, *send a colony to* it, c. acc., Hdt. 1.94, Th.1.24; δρυμοὺς ἐρήμους καὶ πάγους ἀποικιεῖ A. l. c.

**ἀποίκῐλος,** ον, *unadorned, simple*, ἀληθείας στολή Ph.1.369, al.; *homogeneous*, σῶμα ὁμοιομερὲς καὶ ἀ. Plot.6.7.13, cf. Iamb.*VP*23.103. Adv. -λως Vett.Val.343.36.

**ἀποίκιλτος,** ον, *not elaborated, without convolutions*, ἐγκέφαλος Gal.*UP*8.13. 2. = foreg. in Adv. -τως Sch. A.*Pr*.317.

**ἀποίκ-ις,** ίδος, ἡ, pecul. fem. of ἄποικος, ἀ. πόλις *a colony*, Hdt.7. 167, Plu.*Cor*.28; and without πόλις, Str.10.4.17. **-ισις,** εως, ἡ, *leading out a colony*, D.H.3.31 (s. v. l.). **-ισμός,** ὁ, *settlement of a colony*, ἀ. εἰς Ἐλέαν, title of work by Xenoph., D.L.9.20; μετὰ τὸν ἀ. Arist.*Pol*.$1304^{b}$32. II. = ἀποικεσία, Lxx *Je*.26(46).19, al. **-ιστέον,** *one must send away*, Paul.Aeg.4.1. ®**-ιστής,** οῦ, ὁ, *leader of a colony*, *IG*1.31.4, Men.Rh.p.356S.

**ἀποικοδομέω,** *cut off by building, wall up, barricade*, τὰς θύρας, τὰς ὁδούς, Th.1.134, 7.73; χαράδραν D.55.5:—Pass., Plu.*Caes*.49. 2. *rebuild* (nisi leg. ἀν-), Jul.*Or*.2.66a.

**ἀποικονομ-έω,** *manage so as to get rid of* a thing, Antyll.ap.Orib. 6.6.1:—Med., πᾶν πάθος καὶ νόσημα τῆς ἑαυτοῦ ψυχῆς *get rid of* them *by one's manner of life*, Hierocl.p.51 A., cf. Plot.1.4.6, 5.9.1, Procl. *in Prm*.p.497 S.:—Pass., *to be removed*, Herod.Med.ap.Orib.10.37. 17. **-ησις,** εως, ἡ, *getting rid of* a thing, Cass.*Pr*.70. **-ητέον,** *one must get rid of*, φλεγμονήν Orib.*Fr*.42, cf. Herod.Med.in *Rh.Mus*. 58.76. **-ητος,** ον, *to be got rid of*, Arr.*Epict*.4.1.44. **-ία,** ἡ, *rejection*, opp. ἐκλογή, Alex.Aphr.*de An*.160.25.

®**ἄποικος,** ον, *away from home, abroad*, ἄ. πέμπειν τινὰ γῆς to send *away from* one's native land, S.*OT*1518. II. mostly as Subst., 1. of persons, *settler, colonist*, Hdt.5.97, Th.1.25, 38, 7. 57, etc. 2. of cities, πόλιν Σινωπέων ἄποικον ἐν τῇ Κολχίδι χώρᾳ X.*An*.5.3.2, cf. 6.2.1, Ar.*Lys*.582: hence A. calls iron Χάλυβος Σκυθῶν ἄ. *Th*.729 (lyr.).

**ἀποικτίζομαι,** *complain loudly of* a thing, πρὸς πατέρα ἀποικτίζετο τῶν..ἤντησε (sc. ταῦτα ὧν ἤντησε) Hdt.1.114.

**ἀποίμαντος,** ον, *untended*, ἀγέλη, of bees, *AP*6.239 (Apollonid.).

**ἀποιμώζω,** *bewail loudly*, τι A.*Ag*.329, S.*Ph*.278; τινά A.*Fr*.138, Antipho 5.41; ἀ. τι πρός τινα E.*Med*.31; ἀ. ἑαυτόν τινος D.H.5.8.

**ἄποινα,** τά, (by haplology for ἀπό-ποινα (ποινή), cf. ἀπετίνυτο ποινήν Il.16.398; τὰ χρήματα ἄποινα ὠνόμαζον οἱ παλαιοί D.23.33): I. Hom. (only in Il.), *ransom* or *price paid*, whether *to recover one's freedom* when taken prisoner, φέρων ἀπερείσι' ἄ. Il.1.13; οὐκ ἀπεδέξατ' ἄ. ib.95, al., cf. Hdt.6.79; or *to save one's life*, Il.6.46, 10.380, al., Thgn.727; or *for the corpse of a slain friend*, ὃς ἄ. φέροι καὶ νεκρὸν ἄγοιτο Il.24.139: freq. with gen. of the person ransomed, ἄ. κούρης, υἷος, *ransom for* them, 1.111, 2.230; νεκροῖο δὲ δέξαι ἄ. 24.137. II. generally, *atonement, compensation, penalty*, ἂψ ἐθέλω ἀρέσαι δόμεναί τ' ἀπερείσι' ἄ. 9.120, cf. Hdt.9.120; ὕβρεως, μιασμάτων ἄ., *for* violence, etc., A.*Pers*.808, *Ag*.1420, cf. 1670, E.*Ba*.516, *Alc*.7; in *IT* 1459 τῆς σῆς σφαγῆς ἄ. prob. *redemption, rescue* from death.—Rare in Prose, ἀποίνοις ἐξιλασθῆναι Pl.*Lg*.862c, cf. Hdt. l. c., Parth.8. 5. 2. in good sense, *recompense, reward*, freq. c. gen., ἄποιν' ἀρετᾶς Pi.*P*.2.14, cf. *O*.7.16, al.: in sg., τοῦτο γὰρ ἀντ' ἀγαθοῖο νόου εἴληχεν ἄποινον *IG*14.1389 i 10.

**ἀποινάω,** *demand the fine* due from the murderer (cf. ἄποινα II), Lex ap.D.23.28, cf. 33:—Med., *hold to ransom*, E.*Rh*.177, cf. 66 (lyr., dub.).

**ἀποινέω,** *cease to ferment*, v. l. in Alex.45.4.

**ἀποινί,** Adv. *unpunished*, Agath.4.19.

**ἀποινό-δῐκος,** ον, *exacting penalty, atoning*, δίκαι E.*HF*888. **-δορπος,** ον, *ransom-devouring*, Lyc.902.

**ἄποινον,** τό, v. ἄποινα II. 2.

**ἄποινος,** ον, = ἄοινος, Eust.727.19.

**ἄποιος,** ον, (ποιός) *without quality* or *attribute*, στοιχεῖα *Placit*.1.15. 8; ὕλη Zeno *Stoic*.1.24, Chrysipp.*Stoic*.2.111; ποιότης Plot.1.8.10; γεῦσις Aret.*SA*2.7; τὸ ἄ. Porph.*Abst*.1.30; ἀ. ὕδωρ *pure* water, Ath.1.33c (Sup.); ἄ. βοτάνη Orib.*Fr*.52. II. (ποιεῖν) *inert*, ἄ. δὲ καὶ ἀδύναμον (v. l. ἀδύνατον) τὸ σῶμα καθ' αὑτό Procl.*Inst*.80, cf. eund. *in Ti*.3.337 D.

**ἀποιστέον·** *perferendum*, *Gloss*.

**ἀποϊστεύω,** *kill with arrows*, *AP*7.743 (Antip.).

**ἀποίσω,** v. ἀποφέρω.

**ἀποίχομαι,** fut. -οιχήσομαι: impf. -ῳχόμην:—*to be gone away, to be far from, keep aloof from* a thing, c. gen., ἀποίχονται πολέμοιο Il.11.408; ἀποίχεαι ἀνδρός *hast forsaken* him, 19.342. 2. abs., *to be gone, to have departed*, ὅππως δὴ δηρὸν ἀποίχεται how long *he has been gone*, Od.4.109; ἀνδρὸς ἀποιχομένοιο πολὺν χρόνον 21.70, cf. 1.253; περὶ πατρὸς ἀποιχομένοιο ἐρέσθαι his *absent* father, 1.135, cf. E.*Hel*.1306 (lyr.); ἀ. εἰς τάξιν πάλιν Id.*Heracl*.818: imper. ἀποίχεσθε *begone!* Hecat.30 J. 3. *to have perished*, ἀποίχεται χάρις E. *HF*134 (lyr.); of persons, *to be dead and gone*, ἀπολιπών μ' ἀποίχεται Ar.*Ra*.83; in full, ἀ. βιότοιο v. l. in *AP*10.59 (Pall.); οἱ ἀποιχόμενοι, = οἱ τελευτήσαντες, Pi.*P*.1.93, cf. 3.3, *SIG*1219.10 (iii B. C.). 4. μηνὸς ἀποιχομένου, = φθίνοντος, Arat.810. 5. ἀποιχομένου μίτου, of a *broken* lyre-string, *AP*6.54 (Paul. Sil.).

®**ἀποιων-ίζομαι,** *shun as an ill-omen*, Lat. *abominari*, *Gloss*. **-ισμός,** ὁ, = *deprecatio*, Charis.p.553 K.

**ἀποκαθαίρω,** aor. inf. -ῆραι Gal.11.129, but subj. -άρῃ Thphr.*CP* 1.17.10:—*clear, cleanse* or *clean quite*, ἀ. τὴν χεῖρα εἰς τὰ χειρόμακτρα upon the towels, X.*Cyr*.1.3.5; τοῖς προσθίοις ἀ. σκέλεσιν, of flies, Arist.*PA*$683^{a}$29:—Pass., Id.*Pr*.$958^{b}$5:—Med., *rid oneself of*, ib. $880^{a}$32. 2. *refine* metal *by smelting*, Str.9.1.23; ῥητίνη ἀποκεκαθαρμένη *purified*, Dsc.1.25: metaph., ἀποκεκαθάρθαι τὴν φωνήν *to be pure in* dialect, Luc.*Hist.Conscr*.21. II. *cleanse off, clear away*, τὰς τραπέζας Ar.*Pax*1193; ἀ. τὰς βαναύσους τέχνας εἰς οἰκετῶν καὶ μετοίκων χέρας Plu.*Comp.Lyc.Num*.2; *remove by purging* or *clearing*, ἴκτερον Dsc.4.71; ἀ. ἄνω *purge* by emetics, Hp.*Morb*.3.9:—Pass., *to be removed by purging*, Id.*VM*19: generally, *to be got rid of*, Pl.*Ti*. 72d, Arist.*HA*$568^{b}$9; *to be thrown off*, Id.*Mete*.$383^{a}$24:—Med., ἀποκαθήρασθαί τι *get rid of* a thing, Ti.Locr.104b, Demoph.*Sim*.25; τινός *rid oneself of*.., X.*Cyr*.2.2.27.

**ἀποκαθαριεύω,** = sq., Sch.Il.1.1.

®**ἀποκᾰθᾰρ-ίζω,** fut. -ιῶ, *cleanse, purify*, Lxx *Jb*.25.4. **-ισμα,** ατος, τό, = κάθαρμα, *EM*483.12. ®**-μα,** ατος, τό, *that which is cleared off, excretion*, ἀ. ἡ χολή Arist.*PA*$677^{a}$29, cf. *HA*$546^{b}$24; *by-product, dross*, $624^{a}$15; *dregs*, τῶν ὄντων Jul.*Or*.5.170d; *offscourings, slops*, St.Byz. s. v. Ἀζανία (pl.). **-σις,** εως, ἡ, *purging*: hence, of *dross*, Arist.*Mete*.$383^{b}$4, cf. Str.4.2.1; of animal *secretions*, Arist.*GA*$726^{a}$ 13, cf. *HA*$587^{b}$1; ἀποκαθάρσεις χολῆς Th.2.49. 2. *cleansing*, πνεύματος *Gp*.12.22.11; *sifting* of grain, *PRev.Laws*39.10 (iii B. C.), *PLond.ined*.$2361^{r}$ (iii B. C.). II. *lustration, expiation*, Plu.*Rom*.21, Iamb.*Comm.Math*.15; νείκους Hierocl.*in CA* 24 p.473 M. **-τέον,** *one must purify*, Aristid.*Or*.46(3).3. ®**-τικός,** ή, όν, *clearing off, cleansing*, c. gen., Dsc.3.23; ψυχῶν Iamb.*Myst*.2.5.

**ἀποκαθέζομαι,** *sit down*, *Gloss*.

®**ἀποκαθεύδω,** *sleep away from home*, ἐς τὸ ἱερόν Philostr.*VS*2.4.1; of a woman separated from her husband, *sleep apart*, Eup.399. II. *fall asleep over* a thing, Them.*Or*.1.13d.

**ἀποκάθ-ημαι,** *sit apart*, ἀτιμώμενοι ἀποκατέαται (Ion. for -κάθηνται) Hdt.4.66; ἐν τῷ τεύχει Arist.*HA*$625^{a}$26; ἐν τῷ γυμνασίῳ *SIG* 739.7 (Delph., i B. C.); ἀποκαθημένη, = αἱμορροοῦσα, Lxx *Le*.20.18, al., cf. Ph.1.578; θεαταὶ ἀ. τῶν κινδύνων J.*BJ*4.6.2. II. *sit idle*, Ael. *VH*6.12. **-ίζω,** *sit apart*, of a judge, ἐν τῷ γυμνασίῳ Plb.31. 6.3. II. *sit down*, Plu.2.649c; of the uterus, *slip down*, Sor. 2.85. **-ισμα,** ατος, τό, *residuatio*, *Gloss*.

**ἀποκαθιστάνω,** = sq., *SIG*²588.56 (ii B. C.), Plb.3.98.9, D.S.18.57:—also ®**-ιστάω,** v. l. in Arist.*Metaph*.$1074^{a}$3.

®**ἀποκαθίστημι,** fut. -καταστήσω: aor. ἀποκατέστησα, later ἀπεκατέστησα *PTeb*.413.4 (ii/iii A. D.): pf. -καθέστᾰκα Plb.21.11.9, *SIG* 798.7 (i A. D.):—*re-establish, restore, reinstate*, X.*Lac*.6.3; τὰν πολιτείαν Decr.Byz.ap.D.18.90; πολίτας Plu.*Alex*.7; συνθήκας εἰς τὸ ἐξ ἀρχῆς D.H.3.23; ἀ. τινί τι *restore, return* it *to* one, Plb.3.98.7, D.S. 18.65, etc.; ἀ. εἰς αὐτάν (sc. φύσιν) Ti.Locr.100c, cf. Arist.*MM*$1204^{b}$ 37; εἰς τὸ αὐτό Id.*Metaph*.$1074^{a}$3; εἰς ἀκέραιον, = *restituere in integrum*, *CIL*1.203; τινὰ ἐς οἶκον Plb.8.27.6, cf. Thphr.*Char*.7.6; ἀ. σαυτὸν εἰς ἐκεῖνον τὸν χρόνον *carry* yourself *back*.., Plu.2.610d; ἐπί .. D.S.5.23; *cure*, δασυσμοὺς φωνῆς Dsc.1.64, etc. 2. *pay* what is due, ἀργύριον Lxx *Ge*.23.16. 3. *hand over, deliver*, τοῖς φυλακίταις τὸ σῶμα *PSI*4.359.9 (iii B. C.). 4. in drill, *restore* a formation, etc., εἰς ὀρθὸν ἀ., = εἰς ὀρθὸν ἀποδοῦναι, Ael.*Tact*.26.3 (cf. ἀποδίδωμι

II. 3); ἀποκατάστησον *as you were!* Ascl.*Tact.*12.11, etc. II. Pass., with pf. ἀποκαθέστᾰμαι, aor. -εστάθην [ᾰ]: also aor. 2 Act. -κατέστην :—*to be restored*, Arist.*Cat.*9ᵇ25, al.; τῷ θεῷ *SIG*459.7 (Beroea, iii B.C.); *return* from captivity, Vett.Val.68.24; μέχρι τοῦ τὰ πράγματ' ἀποκαταστῆναι till affairs *are settled*, Wilcken *Chr.*10 (ii B.C.); ἀ. εἰς τὴν ἐξ ἀρχῆς κατάστασιν *return, settle down* into.., Plb.25.1.1, cf. 2.41.14, Porph.*Antr.*34; of planets, *complete a revolution*, Cleom. 2.7, al.; of the periodic *return* of the cosmic cycle, *Stoic.*2.190; of stars, *return* to their place in the heavens, Phlp.*in Mete.*112.21; of a revolving figure, *return* to the original situation, Archim.*Con. Praef.*; of sicknesses, *subside*, Hp.*Aph.*6.49; ἀ. εἴς τι *turn out* so and so, Thphr.*HP*4.14.5; of sediment, *settle*, Dsc.5.89; of a spring, *recoil*, Ph.*Bel.*70.46, cf. 71.2. 2. *to be detached from* the mainland, of an island, Anon.Vat.40.

**ἀποκαίνῠμαι**, *surpass, vanquish*, τῇ δ' αὖτ'.. ἀπεκαίνυτο πάντας in wrestling again he *vanquished* all, Od.8.127; οἷος δή με.. ἀπεκαίνυτο τόξῳ ib.219, cf. A.R.2.783.

**ἀποκαίριος**, ον, = ἄκαιρος, *unseasonable*, S.*Ph.*155 (lyr.).

**ἀποκαισᾰρόομαι**, Pass., *assume the monarch*, M.Ant.6.30.

***ἀποκαίω**, Att. -κάω, aor. ἀπέκηα Il. (v. infr.), -έκαυσα D.25.95, Philippid.25.4:—*burn off*, of cautery, X.*Mem.*1.2.54, D. l. c.; of intense cold, θύελλαν ἥ κεν ἀπὸ Τρώων κεφαλὰς .. κήαι Il.21.336; ἄνεμος βορρᾶς.. ἀποκαίων πάντα X.*An.*4.5.3; ἀπέκαυσεν ἡ πάχνη τοὺς ἀμπέλους Philippid. l. c., cf. Thphr.*CP*2.3.1, al.:—Pass., ἀπεκαίοντο αἱ ῥῖνες their noses *were frozen off*, X.*An.*7.4.3. 2. *calcine*, Dsc. 5.125.

**ἀποκᾰκ-έω**, (κάκη) *sink under a weight of misery*, Lxx *Je.*15. 9. **-ησις**, εως, ἡ, *cowardice*, Hsch. s. v. ἀπόκνησις.

**ἀποκᾰλᾰμουργέω**, *free from reeds*, in Pass., *PLond.*3.1003.7 (vi A.D.).

**ἀποκᾰλέω**, *recall*, esp. from exile, Hdt.3.53, X.*Cyr.*1.4.25. 2. *call away* or *aside*, Id.*An.*7.3.35. II. *call by a name*, esp. by way of disparagement, *stigmatize as..*, τὸν τοῦ μανέντος.. ξύναιμον ἀποκαλοῦντες S.*Aj.*727; ὀλιγαρχικοὺς καὶ μισοδήμους ἀ. And.4.16; ὡς ἐν ὀνείδει ἀ. μηχανοποιόν Pl.*Grg.*512c; ἀργόν, σοφιστὴν ἀ. τινά, X. *Mem.*1.2.57, 1.6.13; οὓς νῦν ὑβρίζει καὶ πτωχοὺς ἀ. D.21.211; ὡς ἐν αἰσχρῷ φιλαύτους ἀ. Arist.*EN*1168ᵃ30; παράσιτον ἀ. Timocl.19; χαριεντισμὸν ἀ. *call* it *a sorry* jest, Pl.*Tht.*168d; sts. without any bad sense, τοὺς χαλεπαίνοντας ἀνδρώδεις ἀ. Arist.*EN*1109ᵇ18, cf. X.*Eq.* 10.17, Plu.2.776e.

**ἀποκαλλωπίζω**, *strip of ornament*, esp. of foliage, Poll.1.236.

***ἀπο-κάλυμμα** [κᾰ], ατος, τό, *a revelation*, Lxx *Jd.*5.2. **-κᾰλυπτέος**, α, ον, *to be revealed*, Them.*Or.*23.294c. ***-κᾰλύπτω**, aor. 2 Pass. -καλύφην *CPR*1.239.5 (iii A.D.), etc.:—*uncover*, τὴν κεφαλήν Hdt.1. 119; τὰ στήθη Pl.*Prt.*352a:—in Pass., of land *left* cultivable by the Nile (cf. ἀποκάλυφος), ἀρούρας β' ἀποκαλυφείσης.. αἰγιαλοῦ *PLand.*27. 12, cf. 27.60 (i/ii A.D.):—Med., ἀποκαλύπτεσθαι τὴν κεφαλήν Plu. *Crass.*6. 2. *disclose, reveal*, τόδε τῆς διανοίας Pl.*Prt.*352a; τὴν τῆς ῥητορικῆς δύναμιν Id.*Grg.*455d, cf. 460a:—Med., *reveal one's whole mind*, Plu.*Alex.*55, 2.880e:—in Pass., Lxx 1 *Ki.*2.27, al.; ἀποκαλύπτεσθαι πρός τι *let one's designs* upon a thing *become known*, D.S.17.62, 18.23:—Pass., *to be made known*, *Ev.Matt.*10.26, etc.; of persons, 2 *Ep.Thess.*2.3,6,8, etc.; λόγοι ἀποκεκαλυμμένοι *naked*, i.e. *shameless*, words, Ps.-Plu.*Vit.Hom.*214. 3. *unmask*, τινά Luc.*Cat.*26, *Vit.Auct.*23. II. of the epiglottis, *raise*, Arist. *de An.*422ᵃ2 (Pass.). **-κάλῠφος** [κᾰ], ον, *uncovered*, κεφαλή Ph.1.141 (s. v. l.); ἀ. αἰγιαλός land cultivable only *when* the water *receded*, *BGU*640, *CPR* 32.7 (s. v. l.); ὀψ[ί]μως ἀποκάλυφο(ι) (ἄρουραι) ε̄ *CPHerm.*45.6. **-κάλυψις** [κᾰ], εως, ἡ, *uncovering*, of the head, Phld.*Vit.*p.38 J.; *disclosing*, of hidden springs, Plu.*Aem.*14: metaph., ἁμαρτίας Id.2.70f; *revelation*, esp. of divine mysteries, *Ep.Rom.*16.25, etc.; of persons, *manifestation*, 2 *Ep.Thess.*1.7, etc.; title of *the Apocalypse*.

**ἀποκάμνω**, *grow quite weary, fail, flag utterly*, mostly abs., S.*OC* 1776 (lyr.), Pl.*R.*445b, *AP*5.46 (Rufin.); τῷ μήκει τοῦ χρόνου Jul. *Or.*2.91d: c. part., ἀ. ζητῶν, μηχανώμενος, *to be quite weary of* seeking, etc., Pl.*Men.*81d, X.*Mem.*2.6.35. 2. c. inf., *cease* to do, μοχθεῖν οὐκ ἀ. E.*Ion* 135 (lyr.); μὴ ἀποκάμῃς σαυτὸν σῶσαι *do not hesitate..*, Pl.*Cri.*45b. 3. c. acc., ἀ. πόνον *flinch from* toil, X.*HG* 7.5.19; ἀ. πρὸς τὰς διαμαρτίας *to be disheartened by..*, Plu.*Arat.*33.

**ἀπο-καμπτός**, όν, *bent*, Sch.Opp.*H.*1.205. ***-κάμπτω**, intr., *turn aside, wheel*, opp. ὀρθοδρομεῖν, X.*Eq.*7.14; ἀ. ἐκ τῆς ὁδοῦ Thphr. *Char.*22.9; ἀ. ἔξω τοῦ τέρματος, of chariots, Arist.*Rh.*1409ᵇ23. 2. ἀποκεκαμμένον ῥάμφος *curved* beak, Horap.2.96.

**ἀποκαπν-ίζω**, *fumigate*, *PMag.Par.*2.23. **-ισμός**, ὁ, *fumigation* (v. l. for ὑπο-), Dsc.3.112.

**ἀποκᾱπύω**, (v. καπνός) *breathe away*, aor. 1 in tmesi, ἀπὸ δὲ ψυχὴν ἐκάπυσσεν she *gasped forth* her life, Il.22.467, cf. Q.S.6.523.

**ἀποκᾰρᾰδοκ-έω**, *expect earnestly*, c. acc., Plb.16.2.8, al., Aq.*Ps.* 36(37).7, J.*BJ*3.7.26. **-ία**, ἡ, *earnest expectation*, *Ep.Rom.*8.19, *Ep.Phil.*1.20.

**ἀποκᾰρᾱτομέω**, *behead*, Sch.Pi.*O.*10(11).19.

**ἀποκαρδιουργέω**, *extract the heart of a victim*, Hsch. s. v. δσιουργῆσαι.

**ἀπόκαρμα**, ατος, τό, in pl., *hair-clippings*, Iamb.*Protr.*21.λβ'.

**ἀποκαρόω**, *stupefy*, prob. in Dsc.4.75.

***ἀποκαρπ-ίζω**, *gather fruit*:—Pass., *to be stript of fruit*, Poll.1. 236. II. metaph. in Med., *reap the fruits of, enjoy*, c. acc. rei, *IG* 14.1934 *f* 12. **-όω**, *throw off, send out*, φλέβας Hp.*Oss.*17:—Med., *enjoy the fruits of*, τι *PAmh.*2.142.15 (iv A.D.).

**ἀποκαρτέον**, (ἀποκείρω) *one must clip off*, Eup.400.

**ἀποκαρτερ-έω**, *kill oneself by abstinence, starve oneself to death*, Hp. *Acut.*56; Ἀποκαρτερῶν, title of work by Hegesias, Cic.*Tusc.*1.34. 84, cf. Plu.*Num.*21, Luc.*Macr.*19; -οῦντα ἀποθνήσκειν Phld.*Mort.*6; ὥστε μᾶλλον ἂν θέλειν ἀποκαρτερεῖν ἢ τοῦτ' ἀκούων καρτερεῖν *Com. Adesp.*336.8; οὐκ ἀπεκαρτέρησε.., ἀλλ' ἐκαρτέρησ' Timocl.18. ***-ησις**, εως, ἡ, *suicide by hunger*, Quint.*Inst.*8.5.23. **-ητέον**, *one must abstain from food*, Philum.ap.Aët.9.23.

**ἀποκαρφολογέω**, = καρφολογέω, v. l. in Hp.*Prog.*4.

**ἀποκαρφόομαι**, Pass., *to be parched, dried up*, Sever.*Clyst.*p.12 D.

**ἀποκαταβαίνω**, *dismount*, D H.9.16.

**ἀποκάτ-αγμα**, ατος, τό, *fragment broken off*, φιάλης *IG*7.3498.60 (Oropus). ***-άγνῡμι**, *break, rend off*, Hsch. s. v. ἀπαράσσεται. **-άγω** [ᾰγ], *bring back*, Vett.Val.319.19.

**ἀποκαταλαμβάνω**, *intercept*, Autol.2.13 (Pass.).

**ἀποκαταλλάσσω**, Att. -ττω, *reconcile again*, *Ep.Eph.*2.16; τὰ πάντα εἰς αὐτόν *Ep.Col.*1.20.

**ἀποκαταπτῦσαι**· τελειῶσαι, Hsch.

**ἀποκατα-ρρέω**, *flow down from*, ἀπό τινος Hp.*Aph.*7.30. **-ρρίπτω**, *plunge*, σιδηρᾶ εἰς ὕδωρ Gal.14.208.

**ἀποκατα-στᾰσία**, ἡ, *restitution*, *PTeb.*424.7 (iii A.D.). ***-στᾰσις**, εως, ἡ, *restoration, re-establishment*, τοῦ ἐνδεοῦς Arist.*MM*1205ᵃ4; εἰς φύσιν ib.1204ᵇ36, 1205ᵇ11; *return to* a position, Epicur.*Ep.*1 p.8 U.; esp. of military formations, *reversal* of a movement, Ascl.*Tact.*10.6, etc.; generally, πάντων *Act.Ap.*3.21; of the soul, Procl.*Inst.*199 (pl.); τῆς φύσιος ἐς τὸ ἀρχαῖον Aret.*CD*1.5; *recovery from sickness*, Id. *SA*1.10; τῶν ὁμήρων εἰς τὰς πατρίδας Plb.3.99.6; εἰς ἀ. ἐλθεῖν, of the affairs of a city, Id.4.23.1; *return* to original position, Ascl.*Tact.* 10.1; ἀ. ἄστρων *return* of the stars to the same place in the heavens as in the former year, Plu.2.937f, D.S.12.36, etc.; *periodic return* of the cosmic cycle, *Stoic.*2.184,190; of a planet, *return* to a place in the heavens occupied at a former epoch, Antioch.Astr.ap.*Cat.Cod.Astr.* 7.120,121; but, *zodiacal revolution*, Paul.Al.*T.*1; opp. ἀνταπ. (q. v.), Doroth.ap.*Cat.Cod.Astr.*2.196.9; *restoration* of sun and moon after eclipse, Pl.*Ax.*370b. **-στᾰτικός**, ή, όν, *bringing back* to a point, σελήνης Ph.1.24; χρόνος Gem.18.17; μοῖρα Vett.Val.213.27; ἀ. ἀριθμοί *recurrent*, in which the last digit is identical in all powers, Nicom.*Ar.*2.17; πᾶσα περίοδος τῶν ἀϊδίων -κή Procl.*Inst.*199; ἀ. βίος Herm. *in Phdr.*p.152 A.; ἀ. διάλαμψις, of star positions at the nativity of the terrestrial universe, Paul.Al.*T.*1. II. *for restitution*, *POxy.*144.9 (vi A.D.). **-σχεσις**, εως, ἡ, *abstentatio*, *Gloss.* **-τίθημι**, *lay aside*, ἀποκάτθετο (sync. aor. Med.) κυνέην A.R.3.1287: c. gen., ib.817. **-φαίνομαι**, Pass., *to be clearly visible*, Aristaenet. 1.3. **-ψύχω** [ῡ], *cool*, Gal.11.555.

**ἀποκατεῖδον**, inf. -ιδεῖν cited from Hp.*Prog.*7 (where ἐπι- codd.) by Metrod.*Herc.*831.2.

**ἀποκατ-έχω**, *hold bound*, ἐσχάταις τιμωρίαις *IG*14.872 (Cumae, dub. l.). **-ημαι**, Ion. for ἀποκάθημαι. **-ορθόω**, *recover one's prosperity*, Arist.*EE*1247ᵇ10.

**ἀπο-κάτω** [κᾰ], *from below*, Sch.D.T.p.23 H. **-κάτωθεν** [κᾰ], *from the bottom upwards*, Olymp.*in Mete.*179.17, al., *PMag.Leid.W.* 5.49:—better written divisim.

**ἀποκαυλ-ίζω**, (καυλός) *break off by the stalk*: hence, *break short off*, E.*Supp.*717, Th.2.76:—Pass., *to be so broken, to be fractured across*, Hp.*Fract.*45, *Art.*33. **-ισις**, εως, ἡ, *breaking off by the stalk*: *snapping*, πηδαλίων Luc.*Merc.Cond.*1. **-ιστέον**, *one must break off*, Antyll.ap.Orib.44.23.20.

**ἀπόκαυλος**, ον, f. l. in Thphr.*HP*7.2.4.

**ἀπό-καυμα**, ατος, τό, *firebrand*, Sm.*Ps.*101(102).4. 2. *blister* caused by a burn, Hierocl.*Facet.*135, Eust.1123.24; *chilblain*, Id. ad D.P.916, Sch.Nic.*Th.*677. ***-καυσις**, εως, ἡ, (ἀποκαίω) *burning, scorching*, Str.16.4.20. ***-καυσμός**, ὁ, *burning*, πάγων Judeich *Altertümer von Hierapolis* p.142. **-κάω**, v. ἀποκαίω.

**ἀπόκειμαι**, fut. -κείσομαι, used as Pass. of ἀποτίθημι, *to be laid away from*, προμαθείας ἀπόκεινται ῥοαί the tides of events *lie beyond* our foresight, Pi.*N.*11.46, cf. Arat.110. II. abs., *to be laid up in store*, of money, ἀ. ἔνδον ἀργύριον Philetaer.7.6; σῖτος D.42.6; παρά τινι Lys.19.22; τινί for one's use, X.*An.*2.3.15; χάρις.. ξύν' ἀπόκειται (as Reisig for ξυναπόκειται) *is laid up* as a common possession, S.*OC*1752: hence, *to be kept in reserve*, X.*Cyr.*3.1.19, etc.; πολύς σοι [γέλως] ἐστὶν ἀποκείμενος you have great *store* of laughter *in reserve*, ib.2.2.15; ἀ. εἰς.., *to be reserved for* an occasion, Pl.*Lg.*952d; τὸ τῆς συγγνώμης ὠφέλιμον, ἔλεος ἀ. τινί, D.23.42, D.S.13.31; σοφία ἐς ἐκείνας [τὰς τέχνας] ἀποκείσθω *let* the name of wisdom *be reserved for..*, Philostr.*Gym.*1; ἐφ' ὑμῖν ἀπόκειται τὸ πεισθῆναι you *reserve* your acquiescence, D.Chr.38.5: c. inf., ἀτυχήματα ἀπόκειταί τινι ἐνευδοκιμεῖν D.18.198; ὅσα τοῖς κακουργοῖς ἀ. παθεῖν D.H.5.8, cf. Luc. *Syr.D.*51; ἀ. τοῖς ἀνθρώποις ἅπαξ ἀποθανεῖν *Ep.Hebr.*9.27; πᾶσι.. τὸ θανεῖν ἀπόκειται *Epigr.Gr.*416.6 (Alexandria). 2. *to be buried*, *Not. Scav.*1923.49. III. *to be laid aside, neglected*, ἀ. πόρρω Cratin.367, cf. Plu.2.159f, Philostr.*VA*8.21. 2. ἀποκειμένη καὶ παλαιὰ φύσις *stale*, of perfume, D.S.3.46. IV. *to be exposed, lie open, to*, χώρα ἀ. βαρβάροις Procop.*Aed.*4.2, cf. 2.9.

***ἀποκείρω**, aor. -έκειρα, Ep. -έκερσα (v. infr.):—Pass., pf. -κέκαρμαι E.*Hec.*910:—*clip, cut off*, properly of hair, mostly in Med., ξανθὴν ἀπεκείρατο χαίτην Il.23.141; ἀποκείρασθαι τὰς κεφαλάς *to have their* hair *shorn close*, Hdt.6.21: abs., ἀποκείρασθαι *cut off one's hair*, Ar. *Nu.*836; esp. in token of mourning, Is.4.7:—in Act., X.*Eq.*5.8, Thphr.*Char.*21.3, Luc.*Pisc.*46; *tear out*, ἧπαρ Id.*Prom.*2:—Pass., δὶς ἀποκαρέντα πρόβατα twice *shorn* or *clipped*, D.S.1.36; ἀποκεκαρμένος ἐν χρῷ, ἀ. σκάφιον, of peculiar fashions of *hair-cutting*, Ar.*Th.* 838, Luc.*DMeretr.*5.3: c. acc., ἀπὸ στεφάναν κέκαρσαι πύργων thou *hast been shorn of* thy crown of towers, E.*Hec.*910; but ἀ. τινὰ τῶν γενείων Philostr.*VA*7.34. 2. metaph., *cheat*, τοὺς παχεῖς Luc. *Alex.*6. II. generally, *cut through, sever*, ἀπὸ δ' ἄμφω κέρσε τένοντε Il.10.456; ἀπὸ δὲ φλέβα πᾶσαν ἔκερσεν 13.546. III. metaph., *cut off, slay*, ἀποκείρεται σὸν ἄνθος πόλεως E.*HF*875 (lyr.); ἀπέκειρε τὴν ἀκμὴν τῆς Σπάρτης Demad.12.

**ἀποκεκᾰλυμμένως**, Adv. *openly*, Isoc.8.62, D.H.*Rh.*8.3, Lib.*Or* 1.37, al.

**ἀποκεκινδῡνευμένως**, Adv. *venturously*, Them.*Or.*8.107c.

**ἀποκεκρυμμένως**, Adv. *by stealth*, Theon *Prog.*8, Procop.*Goth.*4.27.

**ἀποκέλλω**, *get out of the course* or *track*, *AB*428.

⊛**ἀπόκενος**, ον, *not quite full*, ἀγγεῖα Dsc.5.36, cf. Gal.17(2).163; *empty*, Hero *Spir.*2.24.

**ἀποκενόω**, *drain, exhaust*, Hp.*Nat.Puer.*15; ἀ. τοὺς πόδας (where τοὺς π., more Hebraico, = τὴν γαστέρα) Lxx *Jd.*3.24; *evacuate*, τὸ περιττὸν γυμνασίοις Sor.1.27:—Pass., Arist.*Fr.*224.

**ἀποκεντ-έω**, *pierce through*, Hp.*Ulc.*25, Lxx *Nu.*25.8, al., D.L. 9.26. **-ησις**, εως, ἡ, *piercing*, Lxx *Ho.*9.13.

**ἀπόκεντρος**, ον, *away from a cardinal point*, Man.3.269.

**ἀποκένωσις**, εως, ἡ, *evacuation*, αἵματος Orib.7.20.11, cf. Sor.1.36, Gal.1.392.

**ἀποκερᾰμόω**, *cover with tiles*, τὴν πάροδον τοῦ τείχους *SIG*[2]587.110.

**ἀποκερδαίνω**, pf. -κεκέρδαγκα D.C.43.18:—*have benefit, enjoyment from* or *of* a thing, c. gen., ποτοῦ E.*Cyc.*432; ἀ. βραχέα *make* some small *gain* of a thing, And.1.134: abs., ἔνεσται ἀποκερδᾶναι Luc. *DMort.*4.1.

**ἀποκερμᾰτίζω**, *break into small pieces*, Porph.*Sent.*37. 2. metaph., ἀ. τὸν βίον *dissipate* one's whole substance, *AP*7.607 (Pall.).

**ἀποκεστίλλαι**· ἐκδεῖραι, Hsch. **ἀπόκετον**· ἀποκομίζων, Id.

**ἀποκεφᾰλαιόομαι**, Pass., *to be summed up*, Eust.1769.4.

**ἀποκεφᾰλ-ίζω**, *behead*, Arr.*Epict.*1.1.24, Lxx *Ps.*151.7, v.l. in Artem.1.35; of a fish, Dorio ap.Ath.7.287e:—Pass., Phld.*Sign.*13, 29, Arr.*Epict.*1.1.19. **-ισμα**, ατος, τό, *dirt that comes off the head*, Poll.2.48. **-ισμός**, ὁ, *beheading*, Plu.2.358e, Procl.*Par.Ptol.* 280. **-ιστής**, οῦ, ὁ, *headsman*, Str.11.14.14.

**ἀποκεχωρισμένως**, Adv. *separately*, Apollon.*Lex.* s.v. τμήδην.

⊛**ἀποκηδεύω**, *cease to mourn for*, τινά Hdt.9.31.

**ἀποκηδέω**, Dor. **-κᾱδέω**, = ἀκηδέω, *to be remiss*, Il.23.413; *to be faint*, Sophr.78.

**ἀποκηδής**, ές, = ἀκηδής, *negligent*: Adv., Comp. -έστερον Hp.ap. Gal.19.84.

**ἀποκήλειν**· ἀποδιώκειν, Hsch.

**ἀπόκηρος**, (κήρ) *free from fate* or *death*, prob. l. in Emp.147.

**ἀποκήρ-υκτος**, ον, *publicly renounced*: 1. of a son, *disinherited, disowned*, Theopomp.Hist.309, Poll.4.93, Luc.*Icar.*14, Hermog.*Stat.* 2. ⊛**-ύξιμος**, ον, *to be sold by public auction*, *IG*2.476. **-υξις**, εως, ἡ, *public announcement*, esp. *public renunciation* of a son, *disinheriting*, Plu.*Them.*2, Luc.*Abd.*5, Hermog.*Inv.*4.13. ⊛**-ύσσω**, Att. **-ττω**, *offer* a thing *for public sale, sell by auction*, Hdt.1.194, Pl.Com. 121; ἀ. ὅ τι ἂν ἀλφάνῃ Eup.258:—Pass., *to be sold by auction*, Lys. 17.7, Luc.*Pisc.*23, D.Chr.66.4. II. *renounce publicly*, ἐξέστω τῷ πατρὶ τὸν υἱὸν ἀ. Pl.*Lg.*928e sq., cf. D.39.39, Luc.*Abd.*1:—Pass., *to be disinherited*, ὑπὸ τοῦ πατρός Aeschin.Socr.*Oxy.*1608.39. 2. *declare outlawed, banish*: metaph., φιλοσοφίας Max.Tyr.32.2; τῆς σοφίας Philostr.*VA*4.30. III. *forbid by proclamation*, ἀποκεκήρυκται μὴ στρατεύειν X.*HG*5.2.27, cf. Thphr.*HP*4.4.5. IV. *manumit* by public renunciation of ownership, οἱ ἀποκαρυχθέντες ἐλεύθεροι, ἀπελεύθεροι, *IG*5(2).274, 342*a* (Mantinea, i/ii A.D.).

**ἀποκῐδᾰρόω**, *take the* κίδαρις *off*, τὴν κεφαλήν Lxx *Le.*10.6, 21.10.

**ἀποκίδνᾰμαι**, *spread abroad from* a place, A.R.4.133, Arat.735, D.P.48.

**ἀποκίκω**, 3 pl. aor. ἀπέκιξαν, *dash to the ground*, Ar.*Ach.*869 (Boeot.).

**ἀποκινδύν-ευσις** [ῡ], εως, ἡ, *venturous attempt*, τύχης Th.7.67 codd. **-ευτέον**, *one must make a desperate venture*, τῇ βίᾳ τῶν σωμάτων Polyaen.1 *Praef.*4. **-εύω**, *make a desperate venture, try a forlorn hope*, πρός τινα *against* another, Th.7.81; οὐ τῶν εὐτυχούντων ἦν τὸ ἀ. Arist.*Fr.*159; ἀ. ἔν τινι *to make trial in* his *case, upon* him, X.*Mem.* 4.2.5, Aeschin.2.104; ἀ. πάσαις ταῖς δυνάμεσι D.H.3.52; ἀ. περὶ τῶν ὅλων Plu.*Alex.*17: c. acc. cogn., ἀ. τοῦτο *to make* this *venture*, Lys. 4.17: c. inf., ἀποκινδυνεύετον..σοφόν τι λέγειν Ar *Ra.*1108:—Pass., ἡμῖν..ἀποκεκινδυνεύσεται τὰ χρήματα *will be put to the uttermost hazard*, Th.3.39. II. *shrink from the dangers of* another, *abandon* him *in danger*, τινός Philostr.*VA*7.15.

**ἀποκῑνέω**, *remove* or *put away from*, ἀποκινήσασκε τραπέζης Il.11. 636; μή μ' ἀποκινήσωσι θυράων Od.22.107; τῆς ὀδύνης Hp.*Morb.*2. 69. II. intr., *move off, abscond*, Aen.Tact.10.5, Polyaen.1.43.2.

**ἀπόκῑνος**, ὁ, (κινέω) *comic dance*, of an indecent nature, Cratin.120, Ar.*Fr.*275, Poll.4.101, Ath.14.629c: metaph., ἀπόκινον εὑρέ find *some way of dancing off* or *escaping*, Ar.*Eq.*20.

**ἀποκιρνάομαι**, *become unmixed*, κιρνᾶται πάντα καὶ ἀποκιρνᾶται Zos. Alch.p.110B.

**ἀποκιρσ-όομαι**, Pass., *become varicose*, φλέβες ἀ. Archig.ap.Gal. 8.90. **-ωσις**, εως, ἡ, *formation of a varex*, Paul.Aeg.6.64.

**ἀποκισσόομαι**, Pass., *develop into* κισσός, of ἕλιξ, Thphr.*HP*3.18. 7. II. *to be deprived of the ivy-wreath*, *IG*3.80.

**ἀπόκιστος**, ον, gloss on ἀπέκτητος and ἄποκος, Hsch.

**ἀποκλᾰδεύω**, *lop off the branches*, Ph.Bybl.ap.Eus.*PE*1.10.

**ἀπο-κλάζω** (A), aor. -έκλαγξα, *ring* or *shout forth*, A.*Ag.*156 (lyr.), *AP*7.191 (Arch.).

**ἀπ-οκλάζω** (B), *bend one's knees*: hence, *rest*, Ar.*Fr.*109 (but cf. ἀποκλάω 2).

⊛**ἀποκλαίω**, Att. **-κλάω** [ᾱ], fut. -κλαύσομαι: aor. -έκλαυσα:—*weep aloud*, Hdt.2.121.γ', etc.; ἀ. στόνον S.*Ph.*695 (lyr.). 2. ἀ. τινά or τι *bewail much, mourn deeply for*, Thgn.931, A.*Pr.*637; ἐμαυτόν Pl.*Phd.*117c:—Med., ἀποκλαύσασθαι κακά *bewail one's* woes, S.*OT* 1467; τὴν πενίαν Ar.*V.*564; τερπνὸν τὸ λέξαι κἀποκλαύσασθαι E.*Fr.* 563. II. Med., also, *cease to wail*, Luc.*Syr.D.*6.

**ἀποκλᾳξον**, v. ἀποκλείω.

**ἀπόκλᾱρος**, ον, Dor. for ἀπόκληρος.

**ἀπό-κλᾰσις**, εως, ἡ, *breaking*, of a wave, *EM*8.41. **-κλασμα**, ατος, τό, *fracture near a joint*, Hp.*Off.*23. 2. *morsel* of bread, Alex.Trall.7.9.

**ἀπόκλαυμα**, ατος, τό, *loud wailing*, γραῶν Arr.*Epict.*2.16.39 (pl.).

**ἀποκλάω**, *break off*, τὸ κέρας Str.10.2.19: aor. 2 part. ἀποκλάς Anacr.17:—Med., *AP*7.506 (Leon.):—Pass., σὺν ἱστίῳ.. ἄρμεν' ἀποκλασθέντα Theoc.22.14. 2. *dress vines*, Ar.*Fr.*109 (unless from ἀπ-οκλάζω (B), q.v.). 3. dub. sens. in Hp.*Off.*14 (s.v.l.).

**ἀποκλάω** [ᾱ], v. sub ἀποκλαίω.

**ἀπό-κλεισις** or **-κλησις**, εως, ἡ, (ἀποκλείω) *a shutting up*, ἀ. μου τῶν πυλῶν *a shutting* the gates *against* me, Th.4.85. II. *a shutting out*, ἀποκλήσεις γίγνεσθαι (sc. ἔμελλον) there would be *a complete stoppage to their works*, Id.6.99. **-κλεισμα**, ατος, τό, *guard-house*, Lxx *Je.*36(29).26. **-κλεισμός**, ὁ, *exclusion*, Arr.*Epict.*4.7.20, Artem.3.54; but, *prison*, Aq.*Ps.*141(142).8. **-κλειστος**, ον, *shut off, enclosed*, Lxx 3*Ki.*6.21.

⊛**ἀποκλείω**, fut. -κλείσω X.*An.*4.3.20: Ion. **-ηίω**: Att. **-ῄω**, fut. -κλῄσω Ar.*V.*775: Dor. aor. imper. -κλᾳξον Theoc.15.43:—*shut off from* or *out of*, τινὰ τῶν πυλέων Hdt.5.104; δωμάτων A.*Pr.*670; ἀ. τινά *shut* her *out*, Theoc.15.43, 77; τινὰ τῇ κιγκλίδι Ar.*V.*775; τῇ θύρᾳ Id.*Ec.*420:—Med., ἀ. τινὰ τῆς διαβάσεως Th.6.101:—Pass., ἀ. τῆς διεξόδου [ὕδωρ] Hdt.3.117; τῆς ὀπίσω ὁδοῦ ib.55; τοῦ ἄστεος ib. 58; ἀ. τῶν πυλῶν Ar.*Lys.*423 codd.; τῆς θύρας Timocl.23; ὑπὸ τῆς ἵππου Hdt.9.50. 2. *shut out* or *exclude from*, τούτων Id.1.37, etc.; ἀ. τινὰ τῶν ὑπαρχόντων D.28.17; ἀπὸ τῶν ἀγαθῶν Ar.*V.*601; also ἀποκεκλῄκαμεν..θεοὺς μηκέτι..διαπερᾶν πόλιν Id.*Av.*1263:—Pass., ἀ. τοῦ σίτου, τῶν προσηκόντων, *turn away from* food, *have no appetite*, Hp.*Int.*1; τῶν σιτίων Id.*Vict.*3.81, cf. D.54.11; ἀ. τοῦ λόγου τυχεῖν Id.45.19; πρὸς τὰς ὁτουδήποτε ἀποκλείονται μεταδόσεις *refuse*, Phld.*Herc.*1251.17. II. c. acc. only, *shut up, close*, τὰς πύλας, τὰ ἱρά, Hdt.1.150, 2.133; τὰ..πρὸς τὴν ἠῶ ἔχοντα τό τε Πήλιον ὄρος καὶ ἡ Ὄσσα ἀποκληΐει, of Thessaly, 7.129; ἀ. τὰς ἐφόδους τῶν ἐπιτηδείων X.*HG*2.4.3:—Pass., *to be closed*, ἀ. αἱ πύλαι Hdt.3.117; ἀ. ἡ Σκυθικὴ ὑπὸ Ἀγαθύρσων, i.e. *is bounded* by them, Id.4.100; of a road, Babr. 8.4. 2. *shut up*, as if in prison, δέμας S.*OT*1388, Ar.*V.*719; τὴν πόλιν ἀ. μοχλοῖς Id.*Lys.*487; ἀ. τινὰ ἔνδον D.59.41:—Pass., ἀποκλῄεσθαι ἐν δωματίῳ Lys.1.17. 3. *shut out*, ἀ. τὴν ὄψιν *intercept*, Hdt.4.7; ἀ. τὴν βλάστην τοῦ πτεροῦ *bar* its growth, Pl.*Phdr.*251d:—Pass., τὸ φῶς ἀποκέκλεισται Arist.*Pr.*904$^{b}$18.

⊛**ἀποκλέπτω**, fut. -ψω, *to steal away, run away with*, τι *h.Merc.*522:—Pass., aor. 2 ἀπεκλάπην, *to be robbed of*, τι interpol. in Artem.2.59.

⊛**ἀποκληΐω**, v. -κλείω: later **-κλῄζω**, *IG*3.900.

**ἀπο-κληρόνομος**, ον, = sq., *disinherited*, Arr.*Epict.*3.8.2, *BGU*326. 7 (ii A.D.), Just.*Nov.*2.3 *Intr.* ⊛**-κληρος**, Dor. **-κλᾱρος**, ον, *without lot* or *share of*, πόνων Pi.*P.*5.54; ἀχέων Emp.147. II. abs., *disinherited*, Arist.*Top.*112$^{b}$19.

⊛**ἀποκληρ-όω**, *choose by lot from* a number, Hdt.2.32; ἀ. ἕνα ἐκ δεκάδος Id.3.25; ἀπὸ πάντων τῶν λόχων Th.4.8: at Athens, *choose* or *elect by lot*, πρυτάνεις Id.8.70, cf. And.1.82; σιτοφύλακας ἀ. Lys.22. 16:—Pass., *to be so chosen*, D.25.27, *Marm.Par.*16: hence, *choose at random*, prob. in Phld.*Rh.*1.114S.:—Med., much like Act., Ph.2. 508, Plu.2.826f. 2. *allot, assign by lot*, χώραν τινί Plu.*Caes.*51, cf. Hld.4.2:—Pass., *to be allotted, fall to* one's *share*, τινί Luc.*Merc. Cond.*32, Ph.2.577; *have allotted to one*, τι Ph.1.214. II. *eliminate by lot*, Arist.*Pol.*1298$^{b}$26. **-ωσις**, εως, ἡ, *selection by lot*, δικαστῶν D.C.39.7; *choice by lot* or *chance, unreasoning choice*, Plu.2.1045f: hence, *absurdity, absence of reason*, in the phrase τίς ἡ ἀ. τοῦ..; what is there *unreasonable* in.., A.D.*Synt.*267.17, cf. Alex.Aphr. *de An.*22.25, S.E.*M.*8.351, Dam.*Pr.*34, al.; κατ' ἀποκλήρωσιν *without reason, at random, fortuitously*, Gal.1.135, al. **-ωτέον**, *one must decide by lot*, Arist.*Pol.*1318$^{b}$1. **-ωτικός**, ή, όν, *choosing* or *acting by lot* or *chance, at random*, τὸ -κόν S.E.*P.*3.79; *absurd*, λόγος Phlp.*in Mete.*82.35, cf. Simp.*in Cael.*158.3, 161.21. II. *assigning, allotting*, δυνάμεις τοῦ κατ' ἀξίαν ἀ. Simp.*in Epict.*p.104 D.

**ἀπόκλησις**, **ἀποκλῄω**, v. ἀπόκλεισις, ἀποκλείω.

**ἀπόκλητος**, ον, (ἀποκαλέω) *called* or *chosen out, select*; οἱ Ἀπόκλητοι, in the Aetolian League, *members of the select council*, Plb.20.1.1, etc.

**ἀπόκλῐμα**, ατος, τό, *a slope*, *EM*374.35, Aristeas 59. II. Astrol., *cadent place*, preceding one of the four κέντρα, *Cat.Cod.Astr.* 1.100; opp. ἐπαναφορά (q.v.), S.E.*M.*5.14, Paul.Al.*P.*2, etc.

⊛**ἀποκλῑμάκωσις**, εως, ἡ, *ladder*, *JHS*12.232 (Cilicia).

**ἀπο-κλῑνής**, ές, *on the decline*, Man.6.62. ⊛**-κλίνω** [ῑ], fut. -ῐνῶ:—Pass., aor. -εκλίθην, poet. -εκλίνθην Theoc.3.37:—*turn off* or *aside*, ὄνειρον Od.19.556; αὐγήν Sor.1.100; *turn back*, *h.Ven.*168: metaph., τὴν διάνοιαν Simp.*in Ph.*1164.39:—Pass. (cf. III. 1), *slope away*, of countries, τὰ πρὸς τὴν Γελῴαν ἀποκεκλιμένα D.S.13.89; of the day, *decline towards evening*, ἀποκλινομένης τῆς μεσαμβρίης, τῆς ἡμέρης, Hdt.3.104,114, 4.181. II. Pass., *to be upset*, D.55.24, Plu.*Galb.* 27. III. more freq. intr. in Act., 1. of countries, *slope*, ὡς πρὸς τὰς ἄρκτους Plb.3.47.2. 2. *turn aside* or *off the road*, X.*An.* 2.2.16, Theoc.7.130: hence, τὸ πρὸς τὴν ἠῶ ἀποκλίνοντι *as one turns to go eastward*, Hdt.4.22. 3. *slip off*, στέφανον -κλίνοντα τῆς κεφαλῆς Philostr.*Im.*1.14. 4. with a bad sense, *fall away, decline*, S.*OT*1192 (lyr.); ἐπὶ τὸ ῥαθυμεῖν D.1.13; πρὸς θηριώδη φύσιν Pl.*Plt.* 309e: generally, *tend, incline*, πρὸς τὰς ἡδονάς Arist.*EN*1121$^b$10, cf. Pl.*R.*547e; ἀ. ὡς πρὸς τὴν δημοκρατίαν, πρὸς τὴν ὀλιγαρχίαν, Arist. *Pol.*1293$^b$35, 1307$^a$15; ἀ. εἴς τινα τέχνην Pl.*Lg.*847a; πρὸς τὸ κόσμιον ib.802e; *to be favourably disposed*, πρός τινα D.23.105. 5. Astrol., of planets, *enter the* ἀπόκλιμα (q.v.), opp. ἐπίκεντρος εἶναι, Plot.2.3.1, cf. 3, Ptol.*Tetr.*115. -κλἴσις, εως, ἡ, *slope*, Cleom.1.1, Ph.1. 459. II. *turning off, decline*, of fortune, Plu.2.611a; of disease, Gal.7.424, Herod.Med. in *Rh.Mus.*58.98. III. *stooping, descent*, Plu.2.970d; of the sun, Id.*Aem.*17; of a ship, *rolling*, Id.*Pomp.*47 (pl.); of a crowd, *swaying to and fro*, Id.*Pyrrh.*33. IV. Astrol., *passing away from* a κέντρον, Vett.Val.57.14. V. *turning aside*, Corn.*Rh.*p.384 H. -κλἴτέον, *one must incline*, πρός τι Arist.*EN* 1165$^a$4. -κλἴτος, ον, *declining, waning*, Plu.2.273e.

*ἀπο-κλύζω, *wash off*, [πίσσαν] εἰς οἶνον Erasistr.ap.Philum.*Ven.*17. 12: metaph., τὸν λόγον ἀ. τῆς ψυχῆς Plu.*Cic.*32; *wash clean*, σέρεις Diog.*Ep.*32.1; ἔρια *PHolm.*27.2; *rinse* the mouth, *Gp.*14.17.5:— Pass., Thphr.*HP*8.6.5, Arist.*Mu.*397$^a$34. II. in Med., D.S.4.51: metaph., ποτίμῳ λόγῳ ἁλμυρὰν ἀκοὴν ἀ. Pl.*Phdr.*243d: hence, *avert by purifications*, ὄνειρον Ar.*Ra.*1340. -κλῦσις, εως, ἡ, *washing off*, ἐπικλύσεις καὶ ἀ. flow and ebb, Them.*Or.*13.167b.

ἀπό-κλωμα· ἀπολογία ἐπὶ τὸ χεῖρον, Hsch. -κλωνεῖ· ἀποστροφεῖ (Tarent.), Id.

ἀποκμητέον, (ἀποκάμνω) *one must grow weary*, Pl.*R.*445b (Bekk. for ἀποκνητέον).

ἀπό-κναισις, εως, ἡ, *affliction, vexation*, Hsch. -κναίω, Att. -κνάω, inf. -κνᾶν dub. l. Pl.*Phlb.*26b: aor. -έκναισα Id.*R.*406b:— *scrape, rub off*, τι Antiph.245:—Med., Hsch. II. ἀ. τινά *wear* one *out, worry to death*, Ar.*Ec.*1087, Pl. ll. cc., f. l. in Thphr.*Char.*7.4; σύ μ' ἀποκναίεις περιπατῶν Men.341; ἀποκναίει γὰρ ἀηδίᾳ δήπου καὶ ἀναισθησίᾳ D.21.153, cf. D.H.*Dem.*20:—Pass., *to be worn out*, Pl.*R.* 406b; εἰσφοραῖς X.*HG*6.2.1.

ἀποκν-έω, *shrink from*, c. acc., τὸν κίνδυνον Th.3.20; τὸν πλοῦν Id.8.12; πρός τι Zos.5.40:—c. inf., *shrink from* doing, Th.4.11, Pl. *Phd.*84c, *Tht.*166b. 2. abs., *shrink back, hesitate*, Th.3.55, 6.18, Pl.*Lg.*780d, etc. -ησις, εως, ἡ, *shrinking from*, στρατειῶν Th. 1.99; ἀ. πρὸς τοὺς πολιτικοὺς ἀγῶνας Plu.2.783b. -ητέον, Pl. *R.*349a, 372a, Isoc.8.62; οὐκ ἀ. τὸ φάναι μὴ συνιέναι Arist.*Top.* 160$^a$21.

ἀπο-κνίζω, fut. -ίσω, *nip* or *snip off*, τι Hp.*Steril.*214, Ar.*Ach.*869, Sotad.Com.1.23, Thphr.*HP*6.8.2; κηφῆνος πτερόν Arist.*HA*554$^b$5; ἀπό τινος D.S.2.4; τινός Plu.2.977b; *wring off*, κεφαλήν Lxx *Le.*1.15; ἀ. τὰ ὄμματα, perh. f.l. for ἀπόκναισον, *Tab.Defix.Aud.*242.59 (Carthage, iii A.D.). -κνῖσις, εως, ἡ, *nipping off*, Thphr.*CP*5.9.11 (pl.). -κνισμα, ατος, τό, *that which is nipped off, a little bit*, Ar. *Pax*790.

ἀποκογχίζω, *draw out with a* κόγχη I.2, Dsc.1.30.

ἀποκοιμάομαι, Pass. with fut. Med. -ήσομαι:—*sleep away from home*, νύκτα -ηθείς Pl.*Lg.*762c; ἐν Λακεδαίμονι Eup.208. II. *get a little sleep*, esp. of troops on duty, Hdt.8.76, Ar.*V.*213, X.*Cyr.*2.4. 22 and 26, Plb.3.79.10; simply, *fall asleep*, Polyaen.8.23.1. III. *die an easy death*, Vett.Val.126.28.

ἀποκοιμίζω, *put to sleep*, Alciphr.1.39:—Pass., *go to sleep*: metaph., Socr.*Ep.*1.6.

ἀπο-κοιτέω, *sleep away from* one's post, Decr.ap.D.18.37, cf. *PPetr.*3p.204 (iii B.C.). -κοιτος, ον, *sleeping away from*, τῶν συσσίτων Aeschin.2.127; οὐκ ἀ. παρὰ Ῥέας Luc.*DDeor.*10.2; μήτε ἀ. μηδ' ἀφήμερος ἀπὸ τῆς οἰκίας *BGU*1058.34 (i B.C.): abs., Men.*Inc.* 2.10. 2. *separate from*, c. gen., ἀρουρῶν *BGU*915.14 (i/ii A.D.).

ἀποκολᾰκεύω· *eblandior*, Gloss.

ἀποκόλαστος, ον, *unpunished*, Zos.Alch.p.241 B.

ἀποκολλάω, *unglue, dissolve*, Gal.18(1).481 (Pass.): metaph., σῶμα διαλυόμενον ἤδη καὶ ἀποκολλώμενον, Eun.*Hist.*p.264 D.; *strip off*, τί τινος Eust.854.33.

ἀποκολοκύντωσις, εως, ἡ, (κολοκύνθη) *transformation into a pumpkin*, a travesty of the ἀποθέωσις of the Emperor Claudius, attributed to Seneca, D.C.60.35.

ἀποκολούω, *cut short off*, πόδας dub. in Hp.*Nat.Mul.*8, cf. Call. *Jov.*90 (tm.), *AB*435, Hsch. s.v. ἀποσκόλυπτε.

ἀποκολπόομαι, Pass., *form a bay*, Arist.*Mu.*393$^a$26.

*ἀποκολυμβάω, *dive and swim away*, Th.4.25, D.C.49.1.

ἀποκομάω, *lose one's hair*, Luc.*Lex.*5.

ἀποκομ-ιδή, ἡ, *carrying away*, Plb.24.6.3. II. (from Pass.) *getting away* or *back, return*, Th.1.137. -ίζω, *carry away, escort*, X.*Cyr.*7.3.12; *carry away captive*, ἐς πόλιν Th.7.82:—Pass., *to be carried off*, οἴκαδε And.1.61, cf. D.54.9; *take oneself off, get away*, ἐς τὴν Ἠιόνα Th.5.10; ἐπ' οἴκου Id.4.96. II. *carry back*, A.R.4. 1106:—Pass., ὀπίσω ἀ. *return*, Hdt.5.27. -ιστής, οῦ, ὁ, *one who leads away*, Sch.E.*Andr.*1268: pl., ib.*Hec.*222. II. *messenger, bearer* of a letter, *Cat.Cod.Astr.*2.193. *-ιστικός· *ablativus*, Gloss.

ἀπόκομμα, ατος, τό, *splinter, chip*, πέτρας ἀπόκομμ' ἀτεράμνου (of a man) Theoc.10.7; ἀ. τῶν τοῦ χαλκοῦ πετάλων *PHolm.*1.40; ἀ. ἀραχνίου *shred*, Luc.*VH*1.18; *block* of wood, of an idol, Aq.*Ez.*20.7; of stone, πώρων ἀ. *IG*11.158*A*32 (Delos, iii B.C., pl.).

ἀποκομπάζω, of lyre strings, *break with a snap*, *AP*6.54 (Paul. Sil.); *declare blatantly*, Simp.*in Ph.*1143.8.

ἀποκονδῠλόομαι, *become condylomatous*, Paul.Aeg.3.75.

ἀποκονίω [ῑ], said to be an Aetol. word for *kick up the dust*, i.e. *run*, dub. in Hygin.*Astr.*3.11.

*ἀποκοντόω, (κοντός) *thrust away* or *out*, τὰ ὀπίσω Procop.*Arc.*9.

ἀπο-κοπέομαι, = ἀποκόπτομαι III, Hsch. *-κοπή, ἡ, (ἀποκόπτω) *cutting off*, κρατός A.*Supp.*841, cf. Hp.*Mochl.*34; *lopping off* a shoot *for grafting*, M.Ant.11.8: Medic., *amputation*, Archig.ap. Orib.47.13.3; *stoppage*, ἐμμήνων Sor.1.26. 2. πεδίων ἀ., prob. their *abrupt terminations*, Plu.*Phil.*4, cf. *Gp.*12.41.1. 3. φωνῆς ἀ. *loss* of voice, Dsc.2.120, cf. Gal.13.31. II. ἀποκοπαὶ χρεῶν *cancelling* of all debts, And.1.88, Pl.*R.*566a, Jusj.ap.D.24.149, etc. III. *abruptness*, esp. of literary style, Demetr.*Eloc.*238; ἀ. ῥυθμοῦ *broken* rhythm, ib.6; ἐξ ἀποκοπῆς *abruptly*, D.H.*Th.*52; also of disease, ἐξ ἀ. λυθῆναι to be *suddenly* cured, Gal.7.441. IV. *section, extract*, λόγου Tryph.*Trop.*7. V. in Gramm., *apocope, cutting off of* one or more letters, esp. at the end of a word, Arist.*Po.*1458$^b$2 (pl.), cf. A.D.*Synt.*6.11; κατ' ἀποκοπήν Str.8.5.3; also of elliptical expressions, such as νὴ τόν, Ph.2.271. *-κοπος, ον, *castrated*, Str.13.4. 14, Vett.Val.113.28; τὸ ἀ. *castration*, Ph.2.264. II. *abrupt, precipitous*, ὄρη *Peripl.M.Rubr.*32.

ἀποκοπρόομαι, *turn into excrement*, Anon.Lond.25.41.

ἀπο-κοπτέον, *one must hew off*, χεῖρα Ph.1.668, cf. Paul.Aeg.6. 74. -κοπτικός, ή, όν, *fit for cutting off*, Procl.*in R.*2.182, 296 K. -κοπτός, ή, όν, *severed from others, special*, νίκη Eust. 1468.3. *-κόπτω, *cut off, hew off*, freq. in Hom., of men's limbs, κάρη ἀπέκοψε Il.11.261; ἀπό τ' αὐχένα κόψας ib.146, al.; in Prose, χεῖρας ἀ. Hdt.6.91, etc.; ἀγκύρας X.*HG*1.6.21; γεφύρας Plu.*Nic.*26; *amputate*, Archig.ap.Orib.47.13.2; νηῶν ἀποκόψειν ἄκρα κόρυμβα Il.9.241; ἀπὸ πείσματ' ἔκοψα νεός Od.10.127; ἀΐξας ἀπέκοψε παρήορον he *cut loose* the trace-horse, Il.16.474:—Pass., ἀποκεκόψονται, of buds, *will be cut off*, Ar.*Nu.*1125, cf. M.Ant.11.8; ἀ. τὴν χεῖρα *have it cut off*, Hdt.6.114; ἀ. τὰ γεννητικά, of eunuchs, Ph.1.89: abs., ἀποκεκομμένος *eunuch*, Lxx *De.*23.1, cf. Luc.*Eun.*8:—Med., *make oneself a eunuch*, *Ep.Gal.*5.12, cf. Arr.*Epict.*2.20.19. 2. metaph., ἀπ' ἐλπίδα φημὶ κεκόφθαι ναυτιλίης νόστου τε A.R.4.1272, cf. Plb.3.63.8; ἔλεον D.S.13.23; ἀ. τὸ ἀμφίβολον τῆς γνώμης *decide summarily*, Alciphr.1.8; also ἀποκοπῆναι τῆς ἐλπίδος Plu.*Pyrrh.*2; διὰ τὸ μὴ ἀποκόπτειν τὴν πολυχρόνιον ζωὴν *exclude from the reckoning, despair of*, Phld.*Herc.*1251.22; *reject, exclude*, Id.*Sign.*7, *D.*3.13:—Med., dub. in Id.*Mort.*23. 3. esp. of voice or breath, *cut short*, τὸν τοῦ πνεύματος τόνον D.H.*Comp.*14, cf. 22:—Pass., ἀποκέκοπταί τινι ἡ φωνή Plu.*Dem.*25, cf. Dsc.*Eup.*1.85. 4. of literary periods or phrases, *bring to an abrupt close*, δεῖ τῇ μακρᾷ -κόπτεσθαι Arist.*Rh.* 1409$^a$19, cf. Demetr.*Eloc.*18,238. 5. Gramm., in Pass., *to be cut short by* ἀποκοπή (q.v.), Eust.487.10, *EM*609.54. 6. *abstract* an idea or word from its context, τὸ "ἀγαθὸς" ἀποκοπέν Anon.*in SE*57. 31. II. ἀ. τινὰ ἀπὸ τόπου *beat off from* a strong place, of soldiers, X.*An.*3.4.39, 4.2.10. III. Med., *smite the breast in mourning*: c. acc., *mourn for*, νεκρόν E.*Tr.*628.

ἀποκορέννῡμι, *make quite satisfied*, Gloss.

ἀποκορέω, *wipe off*, Hsch.

ἀποκορσόομαι, Med., (κόρση) = ἀποκείρομαι, A.*Fr.*248.

ἀποκορῠφ-όω, *bring to a point*, Plb.3.49.6:—Pass., *rise to a head*, εἰς ὀξύ Hp.*Prog.*7; *run to a point*, φλὸξ ἀ. Thphr.*Ign.*53: metaph., *culminate*, εἰς ἓν -κορυφοῦται ἡ νόησις Dam.*Pr.*213. 2. metaph., ἀπεκορύφου σφι τάδε *gave* them this *summary answer*, Hdt.5.73; *cause to culminate*, διδασκαλίαν εἰς θεολογίαν Simp.*in Ph.*1359.8, cf. *in Cael.*126.3. -ωσις, εως, ἡ, *concentration*, εἰς ἕν Prisc.Lyd.22.3.

ἄποκος, ον, *without nap*, *An.Ox.*2.238; *not shorn*, Suid.

ἀποκοσμέω, *restore order by clearing away, clear away*, ἀπεκόσμεον ἔντεα δαιτός Od.7.232; *dismantle*, ἡρῷον *IG*3.1423; *deform*, ἀμπέλους Corn.*ND*30; πόλιν Lib.*Or.*30.23; τὸ βασίλειον τῆς πρώτης εὐδαιμονίας J.*AJ*16.8.5, cf. Longus 4.7:—Pass., *to be disfigured*, D.C.*Fr.* 102.9:—Med., *put off one's ornaments*, Paus.7.26.9:—Pass., *to be stripped of them*, Aristid.*Or.*43(25).39. II. *remove from the world, kill*, Lxx 2*Ma.*4.38.

ἀποκοττᾰβ-ίζω, *dash out the last drops of wine*, as in playing at the cottabus, X.*HG*2.3.56, cf. Ath.15.665e. 2. metaph., *vomit*, Herod.Med.ap.Orib.10.8.12. -ισμός, ὁ, *dashing out the last drops*, Ath.15.666a, cf. 667c (pl.). 2. *vomit*, Herod.Med.ap.Orib.5.27.9.

ἀποκουφίζω, *lighten, set free from*, τινὰ κακῶν, παθέων, E.*Or.*1341, *Hec.*104 (lyr.), cf. *AP*9.372; *relieve*, Plu.*Cleom.*18; *lighten* a cargo, Str.5.3.5 (Pass.).

ἀποκόψιμος, *that can be cut off*, Gloss.

ἀπόκοψις, εως, ἡ, *cutting off*, ὀστέων Hp.*Art.*68.

ἀπο-κρᾰδίζω, (κράδη) *pluck from the fig-tree*, ἐρινούς Nic.*Al.* 319. -κράδιος [ρᾰ], ον, *plucked from the fig-tree*, *AP*6.300 (Leon.).

ἀποκράζω, *cry out under, complain of*, βίαν Simp.*in Epict.*p.132 D.

*ἀποκραιπᾰλ-άω, *sleep off a debauch*, Plu.*Ant.*30. II. *waste in debauch*, Theognet.2. -ίζομαι, = foreg., Suid. -ισμός, ὁ, *sleeping off a debauch*, Hsch.

ἀποκρᾰνίζω, *strike off from the head*, κέρας *AP*6.255 (Eryc.). II. *cut off the head*, Eust.1850.30.

ἀποκρᾰτέω, *exceed all others*, ὁ Νεῖλος πλήθεϊ [ὕδατος] ἀ. Hdt.4.50, cf. 75. II. trans., *control, remedy*, ἐντεροκήλας Dsc.4.9. 2. *withhold, retain*, τροφήν Plu.2.494d; *keep one's hands from*, ξιφῶν J.*BJ*4.5.4. 3. *retain* in memory, c. gen., μαθημάτων Sor.1.3.

**ἀπόκρᾰτος**, ον, *without strength, exhausted*, Ph.1.209.

**ἀπο-κρεμάζω**, = ἀποκρεμάννυμι, Suid. s. v. Ὑπέρβολον. ⊛**-κρέμᾰμαι**, Pass., *hang down from, hang on by*, Arist.*HA*553ᵇ3; τὰ ἀποκρεμάμενα *appendages*, ib.620ᵇ14; impf. ἀπεκρεμάμην Q.S.11.197; aor. ἀπεκρεμάσθην Luc.*DDeor*.21.1; ἀποκρεμάμενος τὴν ῥῖνα *hook-nosed*, Philostr.*Her*.3.3. **-κρεμάννῡμι**, fut. -κρεμάσω, Att. -κρεμῶ:—*let hang down*, αὐχέν' ἀπεκρέμασεν, of a dying bird, Il.23.879; χορδὰν πλῆκτρον ἀπεκρέμασε the plectrum *broke* the string *so that it hung down*, *AP*9.584; ἡ προβολὴ τῶν χειρῶν ἀ. τὸ σῶμα *renders unsteady*, Philostr.*Gym*.34; ἰσχὺν *relax*, ib.53:—Pass., *hang down*, Arist.*Pr*.948ᵇ4; *break forth from*, πηγὰς -υμένας τῶν ὀρῶν Philostr.*VA*6.26: metaph., *become detached*, γνώμη μὴ -υσθω οὗ ζητεῖ Id.*VS*2.9.2; οὐσίαι ἀποκεκρεμασμέναι τῶν οἰκείων ἑνάδων Dam.*Pr*.213. II. *hang up, suspend*, τὸν φαρετρεῶνα Hdt.1.216. **-κρέμᾰσις**, εως, ἡ, *hanging down*, Aët.3.7. **-κρέμασμα**, ατος, τό, = foreg., αὐχένος Eust.1334.2. **-κρεμαστός**, ή, όν, *hanging from* a thing, Epigr.ap. Philostr.*Her*.19.17 (tm.). **-κρεμάω**, = ἀποκρεμάννυμι, Arist.*HA* 540ᵇ26, Luc.*Asin*.30. **-κρεμής**, ές, *hanging down*, Ruf.*Onom*. 101, Eust.1587.20.

**ἀποκρήμνημι**, = ἀποκρεμάννυμι, Sor.1.71, Diog.*Ep*.30.3.

⊛**ἀπο-κρημνίζω**, *throw from a cliff's edge*, Hld.2.8. **-κρημνος**, ον, *sheer, precipitous*, ὄρος ἄβατον καὶ ἀ. Hdt.7.176, cf. 3.111; χῶρος ἀ. Id.8.53, cf. Th.4.31, etc.: Sup., Diog.*Ep*.37.4: metaph. of an advocate's case, *full of difficulties*, πάντα ἀ. ὁρῶ D.25.76. **-κρημνόω**, *walk over a precipice*, David *Proll*.148.26.

**ἀπο-κρῐδόν**, Adv., (ἀποκρίνω) *apart from*, c. gen., A.R.2.15: abs., Opp.*H*.1.548, cf. *IG*3.1416*a*:—also **-κριδά**, Hdn.Gr.1.496.

⊛**ἀπόκρῐμα**, ατος, τό, *judicial sentence, condemnation* (= κατάκριμα, Hsch.), τὸ ἀ. τοῦ θανάτου 2*Ep.Cor*.1.9. 2. (from Med.) *answer*, δοῦναί τισι Plb.12.26ᵇ.1; esp. of the *answers* given by Emperors to *legationes*, ὁ ἐπὶ τῶν Ἑλληνικῶν ἀ. *SIG*804.5 (Cos, i A.D.); ἐπὶ τῶν ἐπιστολῶν καὶ πρεσβειῶν καὶ ἀ. Suid. s.v. Διονύσιος, cf. *IG*12(1).2.4 (Rhodes, i A.D., pl.), J.*AJ*14.10.6; also of a proconsul of Asia, *OGI* 494.18 (Milet., ii A.D.). b. *rescript*, θεοῦ Ἀδριανοῦ *PTeb*.286.1 (ii A.D.).

⊛**ἀποκρίνω** [ῑ], fut. -κρῐνῶ, *separate, set apart*, prob. in Alc.*Supp*. 5.7, Pherecr.23, Ael.*VH*12.8; χωρὶς ἀ. Pl.*Plt*.302c, al.:—Pass., *to be parted* or *separated*, ἀποκρινθέντε *parted from the throng* (of two πρόμαχοι), Il.5.12 (nowhere else in Hom.); πίθηκος ᾔει θηρίων ἀποκριθεὶς Archil.89.3; of the elements in cosmogony, Emp.9.4, Anaxag.2, Democr.167; ἀπεκρίθη..τοῦ βαρβάρου ἔθνεος τὸ Ἑλληνικόν Hdt.1.60; χωρὶς θηρίων ἡ δίαιτα ἀποκέκριται Id.2.36; ἀποκεκρίσθαι εἰς ἓν ὄνομα *to be separated and brought* under one name, Th.1.3; οὐ βεβαίως ἀπεκρίθησαν, of combatants, *separated* without decisive result, Id.4.72. 2. Medic. in Pass., *to be distinctly formed*, Hp.*Prog*.23; of the embryo, Arist.*HA*561ᵃ17; τὰ ἐν τῷ σώματι -όμενα bodily *secretions*, Hp.*VM*14; τὰ ἐς τὴν κοιλίην ἀ. Id.*Vict*.4.89; but ἐς τοῦτο πάντα ἀπεκρίθη all illnesses *determined* or *ended* in this *alone*, Th.2.49; also ᾗ τὰ περιττώματα ἀποκρίνεται *are voided*, Arist.*PA*665ᵇ24, cf. *GA*773ᵇ35. 3. *mark by a distinctive form, distinguish*, πρύμνην Hdt.1.194; νόσημά τι ἀποκεκριμένον *specific*, Pl.*R*.407d, cf. Arist.*Mete*.369ᵇ29. II. *choose*, ἕνα ὑμῶν ἀ. ἐξαίρετον Hdt.6.130; ἀ. τοῦ πεζοῦ, τοῦ στρατοῦ, *choose from*.., Hdt.3.17,25; δυοῖν ἀποκρίνας κακοῖν *having set apart*, i.e. *decreed*, one of two, S.*OT*640. 2. *exclude*, πλήθει τῶν ψήφων Pl.*Lg*.946a. III. *reject on examination*, κρίνειν καὶ ἀ. ib.751d; ἐγκρίνειν καὶ ἀ. ib.936a; ἀ. τινὰ τῆς νίκης *decide* that one *has lost* the victory, *decide* it *against* one, Arist.*Pol*.1315ᵇ18:—Med., Pl.*Lg*.966d. IV. Med., ἀποκρίνομαι, fut. -κρῐνοῦμαι, etc.: Pl. uses pf. and plpf. Pass. in med. sense, *Prt*.358a, *Grg*.463c, etc., but also in pass. sense (v. infr.):—*give answer to, reply to* a question, dub. l. in Hdt.5.49, 8.101 (elsewh. ὑποκρ-), cf. E.*Ba*.1271, *IA*1354; ἀ. τινί Ar.*Nu*.1245, etc.: metaph., ἀ. τοῖς πράγμασιν ὡς ἐπὶ τῶν ἐρωτημάτων Arr.*Epict*.2.16.2; ἀ. πρός τινα, πρὸς τὸ ἐρωτώμενον, *to* a questioner or question, Th.5.42, Pl.*Prt*.338d; ἀ. εἰ.. Ar.*V*.964; ἀ. ὅτι.. Th.1.90: c. acc., ἀποκρίνεσθαι τὸ ἐρωτηθὲν *to answer* the question, Id.3.61, cf. Pl.*Cri*.49a, *Hp.Ma*.287b, Arist.*Metaph*.1007ᵃ9: c. acc. cogn., ἀ. οὐδὲ γρῦ Ar.*Pl*.17; οὐδὲν ξυμβατικόν Th.8.71; ἀ. ἀπόκρισιν Pl.*Lg*.658c:—Pass., τοῦτό μοι ἀποκεκρίσθω *let* this *be* my *answer*, Id.*Tht*.187b; καλῶς ἄν σοι ἀπεκέκριτο your *answer would have been* sufficient, Id.*Grg*.453d, cf. *Men*.75c, *Euthd*.299d. 2. *answer charges, defend oneself*, Ar.*Ach*.632; ὁ ἀποκρινόμενος *the defendant*, Antipho6.18, cf. 2.4.3; ἀπεκρινάμην freq. in legal documents, *PHib*.1.31.24 (iii B.C.), etc. 3. aor. Pass. ἀπεκρίθη, = ἀπεκρίνατο, he *answered*, condemned by Phryn.86, is unknown in earlier Att., exc. in Pherecr.51, Pl.*Alc*.2.149b; but occurs in Macho ap.Ath.8.349d, *UPZ*6.30 (ii B.C.), *SIG*674.61 (Narthacium, ii B.C.), *IG*4.679 (Hermione, ii B.C.), Plb.4.30.7, etc.; once in J., *AJ*9.3.1, twice in Luc., *Sol*.5, *Demon*.26; regular in Lxx (but sts. ἀπεκρινάμην in solemn language, as 3*Ki*.2.1) and prevails in *NT* esp. in the phrase ἀποκριθεὶς εἶπεν *Ev.Matt*.3.15; ἀ. λέγει *Ev.Marc*.8.29, al., cf. X.*An*.2.1.22 codd.: fut. ἀποκριθήσομαι in same sense, Lxx*Is*.14.32, al., *Ev.Matt*.25.45, Hermog.*Inv*.4.6.

⊛**ἀπο-κρῐσιάριος**, ὁ, *secretary*, *POxy*.144.15 (vi A.D.). ⊛**-κρῐσις**, εως, ἡ, *separation*, Anaxag.4; κάθαρσις ἀ. χειρόνων ἀπὸ βελτιόνων Pl.*Def*.415d. 2. Medic., *excretion* or *secretion*, γονῆς Hp.*Genit*.2, σιτίων *Vict*.4.93, cf. Arist.*HA*582ᵃ4, *Pr*.878ᵃ23, etc.; ἀ. σπερματική, περιττωματική, *PA*681ᵇ35; σπέρματος Epicur.*Nat.Herc*.908.3. 3. ἀ. νοσηρή *exhalation, miasma*, Hp.*Nat.Hom*.9. II. (from Med.) *decision, answer*, first in Thgn.1167, cf. Hdt.1.49, 5.50 codd. (ὑπόκρισις edd.), Hp.*Decent*.3, *Steril*.213, E.*Fr*.977; ἀ. πρὸς τὸ ἐρώτημα Th.3.60, cf. X.*Hier*.1.35. 2. *defence*, Antipho5.65. 3. *rescript*, Procop.*Pers*.2.23; = *responsum*, *Gloss*. 4. *embassy, commission*, Chor. in *Rev.Phil*.1.79. III. a kind of *dance*, Hsch. **-κρῐτέον**, *one must reject*, opp. ἐγκριτέον, Pl.*R*.377c, 413d, cf. Lib.*Or*.25.53. II. *one must answer*, Pl.*Prt*.351d, *Alc*.1.114e, etc. **-κρῐτικός**, ή, όν, *secretory*, δύναμις τῶν περιττωμάτων ἀ. Gal.8.9; ἀ. δύναμις faculty *of ejection*, Olymp. *in Mete*.201.7; *separative*, Simp. *in Ph*.1190.22. II. *proper to answers*, Theon *Prog*.5. ⊛**-κρῐτος**, ον, *separated, chosen*, Inscr. in Sauciuc *Andros* 130, Opp.*H*.3.266.

**ἀποκροτ-έω**, *snap the fingers*, Str.14.5.9. II. *dash against the ground*, χαμαί Babr.119.4. **-ημα**, ατος, τό, *snap of the finger*, Aristobul.6.

**ἀπόκροτος**, ον, *beaten* or *trodden hard*, γῆ, χωρίον, Th.7.27, X.*Eq*.7.15, cf. Hero *Aut*.2.1: generally, *hard*, χηλαὶ καὶ ὁπλαί Plu.2.98d: Medic., ἀρτηρία Gal.19.405; πῶρος ib.442: metaph., ψυχὴ λιθίνη καὶ ἀ. Ph.2.165, cf. Ptol.*Tetr*.155. Adv. -τως *without fail*, *PGrenf*.2.89.3 (vi A.D.), etc.; cf. Hsch. s. v. διακρότως. II. of style, *sonorous*, Anon. *in Rh*.191.20, 225.11.

**ἀποκρουνίζω**, *spout, gush out*, Plu.2.699d.

**ἀπό-κρουσις**, εως, ἡ, (ἀποκρούομαι Pass.) *retiring, waning*, τῆς σελήνης Colum.2.10.10, Alex.Trall.8.2, *PMag.Leid.V*.11.28, Horap.1.4, etc. **-κρουστέον**, *one must repel*, Them.*Or*.22.278a. **-κρουστικός**, ή, όν, *able to drive off, dispel*, Dsc.1.116; δυνάμεις Gal.1.396; *repulsive*, D.L.2.87. 2. *waning*, ἀ. σελήνη Ptol.*Tetr*.149, cf. Paul.Al.*G*.4; δέλτος ἀ. πρὸς σελήνην *PMag.Par*.1.2241.

**ἀπόκρουστος**, ον, *beaten back*, Nic.*Th*.270.

⊛**ἀποκρούω**, *beat off, drive away, from* a place or person, X.*HG*5.3.22, *AP*11.351 (Pall.); ὕπνον, νόσον, Porph.*Abst*.1.27,53:—more freq. in Med., *beat off from oneself*, τὰς προσβολάς Hdt.4.200, Th.2.4; αὐτοὺς ἐπιόντας Hdt.8.61, etc.; generally, *repel*, opp. ἐπισπᾶσθαι, S.E.*M*.7.400; *shake off*, Plot.4.7.10, Hierocl. *in CA*19p.461 M.; τινάς Jul.*Or*.2.67b; ἀλληλοφαγίας τοὺς ἀνθρώπους Porph.*Abst*.1.23; *refute* an opponent, D.H.*Comp*.25; κατηγορίαν Chor. in *Rev.Phil*.1.245:—Pass., *to be beaten off*, of an assault, Th.4.107, etc.; ἀποκρουσθέντες τῆς πείρας Id.8.100, cf. X.*HG*6.4.5; ἀ. τῆς μηχανῆς dub. in Plb.21.28; τῆς Ἰβηρίας Plu.*Sert*.7, etc. II. *knock off*, *IG*3.1417.12:—Pass., κοτυλίσκιον τὸ χεῖλος ἀποκεκρουμένον a cup *with* the lip *knocked off*, Ar.*Ach*.459. III. Pass., also, *to be thrown from horseback*, X.*Eq.Mag*.3.14; *to be stranded*, πρὸς χωρίον λιμνῶδες ἀπεκρούσθη Gal.2.221.

**ἀποκρῠβή**, ἡ, *concealment*, Lxx*Jb*.24.15, Aq.*Is*.16.4, *Cat.Cod.Astr*.2.161, Eust.974.45.

**ἀποκρύβω**, = ἀποκρύπτω, v.l. in D.S.3.25.

⊛**ἀποκρύπτω**, used by Hom. only in aor. 1, Ep. impf. ἀποκρύπτασκε Hes.*Th*.157:—Pass., aor. -εκρύβην [ῠ] Lxx*Jb*.3.23: fut. -κρῠβήσομαι ib.*Ps*.18(19).6, Gal.*UP*10.12:—Med., aor. 2 -εκρυβόμην Apollod.3.2.1:—*hide from, keep hidden from*, c. acc. et gen., αἲ γάρ μιν θανάτοιο..δυναίμην νόσφιν ἀποκρύψαι Il.18.465: c. dat. pers., ἀπέκρυψεν δέ μοι ἵππους 11.718: c. dupl. acc., *hide* or *keep back from* one, οὔτε σε ἀποκρύψω τὴν ἐμὴν οὐσίαν Hdt.7.28; τι ἀπό τινος Lxx4*Ki*.4.27:—Med., ἀποκρύπτεσθαί τινά τι Pl.*Lg*.702c, X.*Mem*.2.6.29, etc.; ἀ. τι *keep* it *back*, Pl.*Prt*.348e, cf. 327a: c. acc. pers., X.*Cyr*.8.7.23, *Smp*.1.6. 2. *hide from sight, keep hidden, conceal*, Od.17.286, etc.; ἔθηκε νύκτ' ἀποκρύψας φάος Archil.74.3; τὸν ἥλιον ὑπὸ τοῦ πλήθεος τῶν ὀϊστῶν ἀ. Hdt.7.226; ἀποκρύψει φάος νύξ A.*Pr*.24; χιὼν ἀ. τι X.*An*.4.4.11; ἀ. τὴν σοφίαν Pl.*Ap*.22e; ἀ. τὴν οὐσίαν ἐν ταῖς οἰκίαις Isoc.1.42; εἰς τὸ ἄδηλον -κρύπτων X.*Eq.Mag*.5.7:—Med., Ar.*Eq*.424,483; ἀ. ἑαυτὸν *efface* oneself, Pl.*R*.393c: c. inf., ἀποκρύπτεσθαί τι μὴ καθ' ἡδονὴν ποιεῖν *to conceal one's* doing, Th.2.53; περὶ ὧν ἀποκρυπτόμεθα μηδένα εἰδέναι Lys.7.18; pf. Pass. in med. sense, οὐκ ἀποκέκρυπται τὴν οὐσίαν D.28.3: abs., ἀποκρύψασθαι πρός τινα Isoc.11.2:—Pass., τὸν Ἑλλήσποντον ὑπὸ τῶν νεῶν ἀποκεκρυμμένον Hdt.7.45; τοὺς ἀποκρυπτομένους those who *withdraw from public*, Alex.265. 3. *obscure*, E.*Fr*.153, Arist.*Po*.1460ᵇ4, Alcid.*Soph*.30, Lib.*Or*.63.26, Jul.*Or*.1.44c. II. ἀ. γῆν *lose from sight*, of ships running out to sea, opp. ἀνοίγνυμι 1.3, φεύγειν εἰς τὸ πέλαγος..ἀποκρύψαντα γῆν Pl.*Prt*.338a, cf. Lib.*Or*.59.147; ἐπειδὴ ἀπεκρύψαμεν αὐτοὺς when we *got out of sight of* them, Luc.*VH*2.38, cf. Th.5.65 (sc. αὐτούς); τὴν θάλατταν (i.e. by marching inland) Aristid.1.473J.; ἀποκρύπτουσι Πελειάδες (sc. ἑαυτούς) *disappear*, Hes.*Fr*.179; ἄστερες ἄμφι σελάνναν ἀ. εἶδος Sapph.3; but also Pass. of ships, Hero *Aut*.22.5.

**ἀποκρυσταλλόομαι**, Pass., *become all ice*, Sch.Il.23.281.

**ἀποκρῠφή**, ἡ, *hiding-place*, Lxx*Jb*.22.14, al.

**ἀπόκρῠφος**, ον, *hidden, concealed*, E.*HF*1070 (lyr.); ἐν ἀποκρύφῳ in *secret*, Hdt.2.35; ἀ. θησαυροὶ *hidden, stored up*, *Ep.Col*.2.3; *underhand*, μηδὲν ἀ. πεποιῆσθαι *Vit.Philonid*.p.2 C. 2. c. gen., ἀπόκρυφον πατρὸς *unknown to* him, X.*Smp*.8.11. II. *obscure, recondite, hard to understand*, Id.*Mem*.3.5.14; γράμματα Call.*Fr*.242; ἀ. σύμβολα δέλτων, of hieroglyphics, *Hymn.Is*.10; στήλη *PMag.Par*.1.1115; [βίβλος] *PMag.Leid.W*.25.14; -κρύφων μύσται Vett.Val.7.30; ἀ. αἰτία Procl. *in Ti*.1.53D., cf. eund. *in Prm*.p.549S. III. Adv. -φως *secretly*, Aq.*Hb*.3.14, Vett.Val.301.5.

**ἀπόκρῠψις**, εως, ἡ, *disappearance*, ἀ. ποιεῖσθαι Arist.*Cael*.294ᵃ2.

**ἀποκτάμεν, -κτάμεναι, -κτάμενος**, v. ἀποκτείνω.

**ἀποκτάομαι**, *lose possession of, alienate*, Hsch. II. metaph., *clear out of the way, refute*, Gal.1.132.

**ἀποκτείνυμι** or **-κτίννυμι** (the former is the more correct spelling, cf. best codd. in Pl.*Grg*.469a, Plb.2.56.15, etc., Hdn.Gr.2.539), = sq., CratesCom.17, Lys.12.7, Pl. l. c., X.*An*.6.3.5, D.20.158, etc.: —also **-κτιννύω**, X.*HG*4.4.2, 5.2.43, etc.

**ἀποκτείνω** (later -κτέννω (q. v.): -κταίνω 2*Ep.Cor*.3.6, etc.), fut. -κτενῶ, Ion. -κτενέω Hdt.3.30: aor. 1 ἀπέκτεινα Il.: pf. ἀπέκτονα Isoc.12.66, Pl.*Ap*.38c, X.*Ap*.29, D.22.2; plpf. 3 pl. -εκτόνεσαν Id.19.148, Ion. 3 sg. -εκτόνεε Hdt.5.67; later ἀπεκτόνηκα Arist.*SE* 182$^b$19, Parth.24.2, Plu.*Tim*.16; also ἀπέκταγκα Men.344, Arist.*Pol*.1324$^b$16,18, Lxx 1*Ki*.24.12, etc.; ἀπέκτᾰκα Plb.11.18.10: aor. 2 -έκτᾰνον Il., poet. 1 pl. ἀπέκταμεν Od.23.121, inf. -κτάμεναι, -κτάμεν, Il.20.165, 5.675:—Pass., late (ἀποθνήσκω being used as the Pass. by correct writers), pres. in Palaeph.7: aor. ἀπεκτάνθην D.C.65.4, Lxx 1*Ma*.2.9: aor. 2 inf. ἀποκτανῆναι Gal.14.284: pf. inf. ἀπεκτάνθαι Plb.7.7.4, Lxx 2*Ma*.4.36:—but aor. Med. in pass. sense ἀπέκτατο Il. 15.437, 17.472; part. ἀποκτάμενος 4.494, etc.; cf. ἀποκτείνυμι:—stronger form of κτείνω, *kill, slay*, Ep., Ion., and the prevailing form in Att. (cf. ἀποθνήσκω): once in A.*Ag*.1250, never in S., freq. in E., *Hec*.1244, al. 2. of judges, *condemn to death*, Antipho 5.92, Pl.*Ap*.30d sq., etc.; also of the accuser, And.4.37, X.*HG*2.3.21, Th.6.61; *put to death*, Hdt.6.4: generally of the law, Pl.*Prt*. 325b. 3. metaph., τὸ σεμνὸν ὥς μ' ἀ. τὸ σόν E.*Hipp*.1064; σὺ μή μ' ἀπόκτειν' Id.*Or*.1027.

**ἀποκτενείω**, Desiderat. of ἀποκτείνω, dub. in Lib.*Narr*.18.

**ἀποκτέννω**, later form for ἀποκτείνω, Plb.1.69.11, *AP*.11.395 (Nicarch.), Lxx *To*.6.13.

**ἀπόκτησις**, εως, ἡ, *deed of gift*, *PGrenf*.2.70.26 (iii A. D.). 2. *loss*, θάνατος ἀ. βίου Secund.*Sent*.19, cf. Paul.Al.*N*.4.

**ἀπόκτισις**, εως, ἡ, *planting of a colony*, Call.*Ap*.74, D.H.1.49.

**ἀποκτῠπέω**, *sound loudly from*, τῆς γλώττης Philostr.*VS*1.25.7; *make a noise by striking*, μάστιξι Suid. s. v. τύμπανα, cf. *AB*208.

**ἀποκῠᾰμεύω**, *select by lot*, ταμίας *IG*1.32.13.

**ἀποκῠβεύω**, *run hazard* or *risk*, περὶ βασιλείας D.S.17.30, Polyaen. 8.14.1.

✻**ἀποκῠβιστάω**, *plunge headlong off* a place, εἰς ὕδωρ Clearch.73 (dub.).

✻**ἀποκῠδαίνω**, *glorify greatly*, Hierocl.p.59 A., *IG*3.1367.

**ἀποκῠ-έω**, *bear young, bring forth*, c. acc., Arist.*Fr*.76, interpol. in D.H.1.70, Plu.*Sull*.37: abs., Luc.*DMar*.10.1: metaph., ἡ ἁμαρτία ἀ. θάνατον *Ep.Jac*.1.15, cf. Ph.1.214:—Pass., of the child, Plu. *Lyc*.3, Hdn.1.5.5 (Pass. part. ἀποκυόμενα Ph.2.202,397). **-ησις**, εως, ἡ, *bringing forth, birth*, Plu.2.907c, Dsc.2.120, Ph.2.396, Sor. 1.46, etc. **-ητικός**, ή, όν, *favourable for bringing forth*, ἡμέρα Paul.Al.*R*.1; ὥρα Palch. in *Cat.Cod.Astr*.1.114. **-ΐσκω**, = ἀποκυέω, Ael.*NA*9.3, D.L.8.29: metaph. in Pass., ἀριθμὸς ἀ. Herm. *in Phdr*.p.134 A.

**ἀπο-κῠλινδέω**, = ἀποκυλίω, J.*BJ*3.7.28 (Pass.). **-κύλισμα** [ῠ], ατος, τό, *rolling-machine*, Longin.40.4. ✻**-κῠλίω**, *roll away*, Lxx *Ge*.29.3, al., D.S.14.116, *Ev.Matt*.28.2, Apollod.3.15.7:—Pass., Luc. *Rh.Pr*.3.

**ἀποκῡμᾰτίζω**, *make to swell with waves, boil up*, Plu.2.734e: metaph., ἀ. τὰς ψυχάς ib.943d; ἦχον D.H.*Comp*.23.

**ἀπόκῠνον**, τό, (κύων) *dog's-bane, Marsdenia erecta*, Dsc.4.80, Gal. 11.835. II. name of a *poisoned cake for dogs*, Hsch.

**ἀποκῠνόω**, *turn into a dog*, Eust.1714.42.

**ἀποκυπαρῶσαι**· ἀποκτεῖναι, Hsch.

**ἀποκύπτω**, *stoop away from* the wind, Ar.*Lys*.1003, in pf. ἀποκέκῡφα, but Reiske ἐπικεκύφαμες (prob. l.).

**ἀποκῡριάζειν**· ἀποκακεῖν, ἀποφεύγειν, ἀποσκιρτᾶν, Hsch.; cf. ἀνακυρτᾶσαι.

**ἀποκῡρόω**, *annul*, Lat. *abrogare*, *Gloss*.

**ἀποκυρτόομαι**, *rise to a convex shape*, v.l. for ἀποκορυφόομαι, Hp. *Prog*.7.

**ἀποκύρωσις** [ῡ], εως, ἡ, *ratification by vote*, Sch.E.*Hec*.259.

**ἀποκωκύω**, *mourn loudly over*, τινά A.*Ag*.1544.

**ἀποκώλ-ῡσις**, εως, ἡ, *hindering*, X.*Eq*.3.11, J.*AJ*14.11.5. **-ῡτέον**, *one must forbid*, Sor.2.42. ✻**-ύω**, fut. -ύσω [ῡ], *hinder* or *prevent from* a thing, or its use, τινὰ τῆς ὁδοῦ X.*An*.3.3.3; ἀπό τινος Lxx *Ec*.2.10: c. inf., *prevent from* doing, E.*Med*.1411, Pl.*Tht*.150c, al.; ἀ. τοῦ ποιεῖν X.*Hier*.8.1; ἀ. μὴ ἐλθεῖν Id.*An*.6.4.24. II. c. acc. only, *keep off, hinder*, Orac.ap.Hdt.1.66, cf. Th.3.28. III. abs., *stop the way*, Id.1.72: impers., οὐδὲν ἀποκωλύει *there is* nothing *to prevent* it, Pl.*R*.372e, al. IV. *shut up*, τέκνα εἰς οἶκον Lxx 1*Ki*.6.10.

**ἀποκωφόομαι**, *become deaf*, Lxx *Mi*.7.16, Arr.*Epict*.2.20.37, etc.

**ἀπολάβειον** [λᾰ], τό, *clamp, holdfast*, Ph.*Bel*.61.15.

**ἀπο-λᾰγαίω**, *set at liberty*, ἐλεύθερον *GDI*5008, al. (Gortyn). **-λάγαξις**, εως, ἡ, *setting at liberty*, ib.5010.

**ἀπολαγνεύω**, *spend in debauchery*, in pf. Pass., Hsch. (-λαχν- cod.).

**ἀπολαγχάνω**, *obtain a portion of* a thing *by lot*, λαγχάνειν ἄπο μοῖραν ἐσθλῶν B.4.20; τῶν κτημάτων τὸ μέρος ἀ. Hdt.4.114, cf. 115; τὴν Ταναγρικὴν μοῖραν Id.5.57; τῆς γῆς Id.4.145; μόριον ὅσον αὐτοῖσι ἐπέβαλλε Id.7.23; ὡς ἀλλὰ ταὐτά γ' ἀπολάχωσ' οἴκων πατρός that they *may obtain*.., E.*HF*331; cf. Antipho *Fr*.63, *Leg.Gort*.5.4, al. II. *fail in drawing lots*, ἀ. κριτῆς Lys.4.3, cf. Plu.*Cat.Mi*.6, 2.102e: generally, *lose one's all, be left destitute*, E.*Ion* 609.

**ἀπολάζυμαι**, poet. for ἀπολαμβάνω, E.*Hel*.911.

**ἀπολαΐζομαι**, *become stone*, prob. l. in Hsch. s. v. ἀπολελασμένον.

**ἀπολάκημα**, ατος, τό, *box on the ear*, Hsch.

**ἀπολακτ-ίζω**, *kick off* or *away, shake off*, ἀνίας Thgn.1337; ὕπνον A.*Eu*.141; βαρεῖαν κωφείαν Phld.*D*.1.24 (dub.); *inimicos* Plaut.*Epid*. 678. 2. *spurn*, λέχος τὸ Ζηνός A.*Pr*.651; τὰ καλὰ καὶ σωτήρια Plu. *Ant*.36. II. abs., *kick out, kick up*, ἀμφοτέροις with both legs, Luc. *Asin*.18. **-ισμα**, ατος, τό, *kick*, Theodos.Gramm.p.6 G. **-ισμός**, ὁ, *a kicking off* or *away*, ἀ. βίου, of a violent death, A.*Supp*.937: Medic., of a form of haemorrhage, *diapedesis*, Steph. *in Hp*.1.124 D.

**ἀπολᾰλέω**, *blurt out*, πρός τινα ὅτι J.*AJ*6.9.2, cf. Luc.*Nigr*.22, Poll.2.127.

**ἀπολαμβάνω**, fut. -λήψομαι, in Hdt. -λάμψομαι 3.146, 9.38: Att. pf. ἀπείληφα, Pass. ἀπείλημμαι, Ion. ἀπολέλαμμαι: in Act. aor. 2 ἀπέλαβον, but in Pass. aor. 1 ἀπελήφθην, Ion. ἀπελάμφθην Hdt.:—*take* or *receive from* another, correlat. to ἀποδιδόναι, Pl.*R*.332b; οὐδὲν ἀ. τοῦ βίου χρηστόν (v.l. ἀπολαύ-) Plu.2.258b. 2. *receive what is one's due*, μισθόν Hdt.8.137; ἀ. τὸν ὀφειλόμενον μισθόν X.*An*.7.7.14; τὴν σὴν ξυνάορον E.*Or*.654; τὰ χρήματα Ar.*Nu*.1274; τὰ παρὰ τοῦ πατρός Antiph.196; ἀ. χρέα *have* them *paid*, And.3.15; ὑπόσχεσιν παρά τινος ἀ. X.*Smp*.3.3; τὰ δίκαια Aeschin.1.196: opp. λαμβάνω, Epist.Phil.ap.D.12.14, cf. D.7.5; ἀ. ὅρκους *accept* them *when tendered*, Id.5.9, 18.27. 3. *take of, take a part of* a thing, Th.6.87, Pl.*Hp.Mi*.369b; ἀ. μέρος τι Id.*R*.392e, cf. Arist.*Po*.1459$^a$35: abs. in aor. part., ἀπολαβὼν σκόπει consider it *separately*, Pl.*Grg*.495e, cf. *R*.420c. 4. *take away*, Plb.21.43.8,17; *take off*, τὸ βάρος Arist. *IA*711$^a$24. 5. *hear, learn*, Pl.*R*.614a. II. *regain, recover*, τὴν τυραννίδα, τὴν πόλιν, Hdt.1.61, 2.119, 3.146, al.; τι παρά τινος Th.5. 30; τὴν ἡγεμονίαν Isoc.4.21; τὴν αὐτὴν εὐεργεσίαν 14.57: metaph., ἀ. ἑαυτόν *recover* oneself, Porph.*Sent*.40, al. 2. *have rendered to one*, λόγον ἀ. *demand* an account, Aeschin.3.27,168. III. *take apart* or *aside*, of persons, ἀ. τινὰ μοῦνον Hdt.1.209; αὐτὸν μόνον Ar. *Ra*.78, cf. Lxx 2*Ma*.6.21; of things, μὴ μόνος τὸ χρηστὸν ἀπολαβὼν ἔχε E.*Or*.451:—Med., ἀπολαβόμενος *taking* him *aside*, *Ev.Marc*.7. 33:—Pass., οἱ ἀπειλημμένοι those *set apart, recluses*, *UPZ*60.10 (ii B. C.). IV. *cut off, intercept*, λέγων ὡς ἀπολάμψοιτο συχνούς Hdt.9. 38; ἀ. τείχει wall *off*, Th.4.102; ἰσθμοὺς Id.1.7, cf. 4.113; ἀ. εἴσω *shut up* inside, Id.1.134; of contrary winds, ὅταν τύχωσιν οἱ ἄνεμοι ἀπολαβόντες αὐτούς Pl.*Phd*.58c; κἂν ἄνεμοι τὴν ναῦν ἀπολάβωσιν Philostr.*Her*.14; τὴν ἀναπνοὴν ἀ. τινός *stop* his breath, *choke* him, Plu.*Rom*.27; τὸν ἀντίπαλον ἐς πνῖγμα Philostr.*Im*.1.6; ἀ. τῶν σιτίων *spoil the appetite*, Hp.*Prorrh*.2.22:—freq. in Pass., ὑπ' ἀνέμων ἀπολαμφθέντες *arrested* or *stopped* by contrary winds, Hdt.2.115, 9.114; ὑπὸ ἀπλοίας Th.6.22; νόσῳ καὶ χειμῶνι καὶ πολέμοις ἀποληφθεὶς D.8.35; ἐν ὀλίγῳ ἀπολαμφθέντες Hdt.8.11; ἀπολαμφθέντες πάντοθεν Id.5.101; ἐν τῇ νήσῳ Id.8.70,76; ἐν τῇ Εὐρώπῃ ib.97,108; ἐν τοῖς ἰδίοις λόγοις ἀ. *to be entangled* in.., Pl.*Euthd*.305d; ἐν τούτῳ τῷ κακῷ Id.*Grg*. 522a; ἐς στενόν Philostr.*VS*1.19.1; of an afflux of blood, *to be checked*, Hp.*Fract*.4; κοιλίη, κύστις ἀπολελαμμένη, Id.*Prorrh*.1.88,115, etc. V. Math., *cut off*, ἡμικύκλιον ἀποληφθήσεται Arist.*Mete*.375$^b$ 27, cf. Archim.*Quadr*.15, etc.; *intercept*, Id.*Sph.Cyl*.1.10; -ομένη, ἡ, *abscissa*, Apollon.Perg.*Con*.1.11, al.—A prose word, used by E. ll. cc.

**ἀπολαμπρύνω**, *make bright* or *famous*, Lib.*Or*.64.87:—Pass., *become so*, ἔργοισι by one's deeds, Hdt.1.41; ἔργοισί τε καὶ γνώμῃσι Id.6.70.

**ἀπολάμπω**, *shine* or *beam from*, αἰχμῆς ἀπέλαμπ' εὐήκεος (sc. φῶς) Il.22.319, cf. Ar.*Av*.1009; ἀστὴρ ὣς ἀπέλαμπεν Il.6.295, Od.15.108:—Med., χάρις ἀπελάμπετο grace *beamed from* her, Il.14.183, cf. Od. 18.298; χρυσοῦ ἀπολάμπεται *gleams with* gold, Luc.*Syr.D*.30. 2. *reflect light*, Epicur.*Ep*.2 p.51 U. II. c. acc. cogn., αὐγὴν ἀ. Luc. *Dom*.8; ἀστραπῆς κάλλος Callistr.*Stat*.5; θεῖόν τι Philostr.*Im*.1.16.

**ἀπόλαμψις**, εως, ἡ, Aeol., = ἀπόληψις, *IG*12(2).28 (Mytil.).

**ἀπολανθάνομαι**, dub. for ἐκλ-, Longus 3.7.

**ἀπολάντιον**, τό, perh. name of a grass, σπάρτα ἀπολαντίου *PMag. Lond*.1.121.209.

**ἀπολάπτω**, *lap up* like a dog, *swallow greedily*, Ar.*Nu*.811.

✻**ἀπό-λαυσις**, εως, ἡ, *act of enjoying, fruition*, Th.2.38, *OGI*669. 8 (Egypt, i A. D.); ἀ. ἀνεύφραντος Secund.*Sent*.9. II. *result of enjoying, pleasure*, αἱ ἀ. αἱ σωματικαί Arist.*Pol*.1314$^b$28, cf. *EN* 1148$^a$5, etc.; ὁ κατ' ἀπόλαυσιν βίος a life of *pleasure*, Id.*Top*.102$^b$ 17. 2. c. gen., *advantage got from* a thing, σίτων καὶ ποτῶν X.*Mem*.2.1.33, cf. Hp.*VM*1; ἀγαθῶν Isoc.1.27; ἀπόλαυσιν εἰκοῦς (acc. abs.) *as a reward for* your resemblance, E.*Hel*.77, cf. *HF*1370; ἀ. ἑαυτῶν ἔχειν Pl.*Ti*.83a; ἀ. ἀδικημάτων *advantage, fruit* of them, Luc.*Tyr*.5. **-λαυσμα**, ατος, τό, *enjoyment*, Aeschin.*Ep*.5.4 (pl.), J.*AJ*18.6.10, Plu.2.125d, *Aem*.28. **-λαυστέον**, *one must enjoy*, τῶν θεωρημάτων Iamb.*Protr*.2. **-λαυστικός**, ή, όν, *devoted to enjoyment*, βίος Arist.*EN*1095$^b$17; οἱ -κοί Plu.2.1094f; *producing enjoyment*, ἀρεταί Arist.*Rh*.1367$^a$18. Adv. -κῶς, ζῆν Id.*Pol*.1312$^b$ 23. II. *choice*, οἶνος Plb.12.2.7; μήκωνες Hices.ap.Ath.3.87e (Comp.); *luxurious*, δίαιτα Gal.18(2).463. **-λαυστός**, όν, *enjoyed, enjoyable*, Epicur.*Ep*.3 p.60 U., Phld.*Ir*.p.84 W., Ph.1.572, Diotog. ap.Stob.4.7.62, Plu.*Comp.Arist.Cat*.4. **-λαύω**, fut. -λαύσομαι Ar. *Av*.177, Pl.*Chrm*.172b, etc.; later -λαύσω D.H.6.4, Plu.*Pyrrh*.13, etc. (in earlier writers corrupt, as Hyp.*Epit*.30): aor. ἀπέλαυσα E.*IT*526, Ar.*Av*.1358, etc.: pf. -λέλαυκα Pl.Com.169, Isoc.19.23:—Pass., pf. -λέλαυται Philostr.*VA*6.19, but ἀπολελαυσμένος Plu.2. 1089c, 1099e (ἐν-): aor. ἀπελαύσθην Ph.1.37.—The double augm.

ἀπήλαυον, ἀπήλαυσα, is found in codd. of Id.1.435, etc., prob. in *LW* 1046.5 (Blaudos). (The simple λαύω is not found, but was = λάϝω, expl. by Aristarch. as ἀπολαυστικῶς ἔχω, cf. Apollon.*Lex.*, Sch.Od. 19.229) :—*have enjoyment of* a thing, *have the benefit of* it, c. gen. rei, τῆς σῆς δικαιοσύνης Hdt.6.86.α′ ; τῶν σιτίων Hp.*VM*11, cf. Pl.*R.* 354b ; ἰχθύων, λαχάνων, ἐδεσμάτων, etc., *enjoy* them, Amphis26, Aristopho10.3, Antiph.8 ; ποτῶν, ὀσμῶν, X.*Cyr.*7.5.81, *Hier.*1.24, etc. ; τῶν ἀγαθῶν Isoc.1.9, Pl.*Grg.*492b ; σχολῆς Id.*Lg.*781e ; τῆς σιωπῆς ἀ. *take advantage of* it, D.21.203 ; τῆς ἐξουσίας Aeschin.3. 130. **2.** with acc. cogn. added, ἀ. τί τινος *enjoy* an advantage *from* some source, τί γὰρ..ἂν ἀπολαύσαιμι τοῦ μαθήματος; Ar.*Nu.* 1231, cf. *Th.*1008, *Pl.*236 ; ἐλάχιστα ἀ. τῶν ὑπαρχόντων Th.1.70 ; τοῦ βίου τι ἀ. Id.2.53 ; ζῴων τοσαῦτα ἀγαθὰ ἀ. ὁ ἄνθρωπος X.*Mem.*4.3. 10, cf. Pl.*Euthd.*299a, etc. ; τοσοῦτον εὐερίας ἀπολέλαυκε Pl.Com. 169. **3.** c. acc. (instead of gen.), ἀ. τὸν βίον Diph.32.6 (ἀποβάλλειν cj. Kock) ; ἀ. καὶ πάσχειν τι Arist.*Sens.*443$^{b}$3. **4.** abs., οἱ ἀπολαύοντες, opp. οἱ πονοῦντες, Id.*Pol.*1263$^{a}$13 ; ἧττον ἀ. *to have* less *enjoyment*, Id.*HA*584$^{a}$21 ; ἡδόμενοι καὶ -οντες Plu.2.69e. **II.** in bad sense (freq. ironically), *have the benefit of*, τῶν Οἰδίπου κακῶν ἀ. E.*Ph.*1205 ; ἀ. τι τῶν γάμων Id.*IT*526 ; ἧς ἀπολαύων Ἅιδην..καταβήσει Id.*Andr.*543 (lyr.) ; τῶν ἁμαρτημάτων, τῶν ἀσεβῶν ἀ., Hp.*VM* 12, Pl.*Lg.*910b ; φλαῦρόν τι ἀ. Isoc.8.81, cf. Pl.*Cri.*54a : with Preps., ἀπὸ τῶν ἀλλοτρίων [παθῶν] ἀ. Id.*R.*606b ; ἐκ τῆς μιμήσεως τοῦ εἶναι ἀ. ib.395c ; ἀπ' ἄλλου ὀφθαλμίας ἀ. Id.*Phdr.*255d. **2.** abs., *have a benefit, come off well*, Ar.*Av.*1358. **III.** *make sport of*, συνοδοιπόρου Thphr.*Char.*23.3, cf. Lys.6.38.—Chiefly Att. ; Trag. only in E. (Cf. Lat. *lu-crum*, Goth. *laun* 'payment', Slav. *loviti* 'capture' ; cf. Dor. λᾱΐα, Att. λεία 'booty'.)

**ἀπολεαίνω** or **-λειαίνω**, *smooth*, παρειάς D.S.5.28 : metaph., *polish*, περιόδους Plu.2.350e, cf. 384a. **II.** *erase, cancel* an entry, *IG*7.1737.17 (Thesp.).

***ἀπολέγω**, *pick out from* a number, and so : **1.** *pick out, choose*, τὸ ἄριστον Hdt.5.110, cf. 3.14, Ar.*V.*580, Aen.Tact.1.5, 3.2 :—freq. in Med., *pick out for oneself*, τριήκοντα μυριάδας τοῦ στρατοῦ *from* the army, Hdt.8.101 ; ἐκ πάντων Th.4.9 :—Pass., ἀπολελεγμένοι *picked men*, Hdt.7.40 ; ἀπειλεγμένοι X.*Eq.Mag.*8.12. **2.** *pick out* for the purpose of rejecting, τριβόλους Ar.*Lys.*576 ; ἀ. τινὰ ἐκ τῶν δικαστῶν Plu.*Cat.Mi.*48. **II.** later, *decline, refuse*, ἀ. τὸ χορηγεῖν Plb.2.63.1 ; ἀ. περί τινος Id.4.9.3 :—Med., *decline* something *offered to one*, ἀρχήν Id.*Fr.*16 ; ἱκεσίαν, δέησιν, Plu.*Sol.*12, *Cat.Mi.*2 ; *renounce, give up*, τὰ πρωτεῖα, τὴν νίκην, τὸν βίον, Id.*Luc.*42, *Nic.*6, 2. 1060d ; τὴν ψυχήν Lxx *Jn.*4.8 : abs. (sc. τὸ ζῆν), Ph.1.274 ; also, *give in, make no resistance*, Plu.*Lyc.*22, *Pomp.*23 :—so in Act., *lose heart*, as pres. of ἀπεῖπον, τῇ ταλαιπωρίᾳ Procop.*Vand.*2.19 ; ταῖς δυνάμεσι Herod.Med.ap.Orib.10.5.9. **III.** *speak of fully*, Ael.*NA* 8.17 (Pass.), cf. ἀπολέγει· παραγγέλλει, and ἀπολέξω· ἐρῶ, δηλώσω, Hsch.

**ἀπολειαίνω**, v. ἀπολεαίνω.

**ἀπολείβραξαι**· ἀπολεῖψαι, ἐκνοτίσαι· ἄλλοι, πορρωτέρω ἀπελθεῖν, Hsch.

***ἀπολείβω**, *let drip* : hence, *pour a libation*, ἀπολλείψας Hes.*Th.* 793 ; δένδρον ἀπολεῖβον μέλι *dropping* honey, D.S.17.75 ; δάκρυα τῶν ὀφθαλμῶν Alciphr.3.21 : metaph., ἴχνη ὥραν ἀπολείβει *Com.Adesp.* 39 :—Pass., *drop* or *run down from*, τινός Od.7.107 ; ἔραζε Hes.*Sc.* 174.

**ἀπόλειμμα**, ατος, τό, *a remnant*, Ar.Byz.*Epit.*22.18, D.S.1.46.

**ἀπολεῖνα**· ἀποστρέφειν (Lacon.), Hsch.

**ἀπολειόω**, *erase*, ἐπιγραφήν *CIG*3966 (Apamea Cibotus) ; Arc. ἀπυλιῶναι (pres. inf.) dub. in *IG*5(2) p.xxxvi *D* 1.20 (Tegea, iv B.C.).

**ἀπολειπής**, f.l. for ἐπιλειπής, Hp.*Nat.Puer.*20.

**ἀπο-λειπτέον**, (ἀπολείπομαι) *one must stay behind*, X.*Oec.*7. 38. **2.** (from Act.) *one must leave behind*, Hld.2.17 ; *one must desert, abandon*, οὐκ ἀ. Plu.2.263f ; *one must omit, pass over*, Jul.*Or.* 3.106c. ***-λείπω**, aor. ἀπέλῐπον (ἀπέλειψα late, Them.*Or.*25.310d, Ps.-Phoc.77) :—*leave over* or *behind*, οὐδ' ἀπέλειπεν ἔγκατα Od.9.292, cf. Heraclit.56, etc. ; κλέος καὶ φήμην Critias44D. ; *bequeath, Test. Epict.*2.3, cf. Mosch.3.97 ; ἀ. κληρονόμον *leave as* one's heir, *POxy.* 105.3 (ii A.D.) ; *bequeath to posterity*, of writings, D.L.8.58, cf. 7. 54. **2.** *leave hold of, lose*, ψυχάν Pi.*P.*3.101 (tm.) ; βίον S.*Ph.* (lyr., tm.) ; νέαν ἁμέραν ἀπολιπὼν θάνοι E.*Ion*720 (lyr.) : conversely, ἐμὲ μὲν ἀπολέλοιπεν ἤδη βίοτος S.*El.*185 (lyr.). **3.** *leave behind* in the race, *distance* : generally, *surpass*, X.*Cyr.*8.3.25, Lys.2.4 ; τινὰ περί τι Isoc.4.50 :—more freq. in Med. and Pass., v. infr. **4.** *leave undisputed* : hence, *admit*, Chrysipp.*Stoic.*3.173, Phld.*Piet.*17, S.E.*M.*7.55, D.L.7.54 ; αἰτίαν νόσων ἀ. τὸ αἷμα Meno*Iatr.*11.43 ; [ὁ Διοκλῆς] τὴν φρόνησιν περὶ τὴν καρδίαν ἀ. Herod.Med. in *Rh.Mus.*49. 540. **5.** *leave, allow*, ὑπερβολὴν οὐδὲ ταῖς ἑταίραις Jul.*Or.*7. 210d. **II.** *desert, abandon*, one's post, etc., οὐδ' ἀπολείπουσιν κοῖλον δόμον, of bees, Il.12.169, cf. Hdt.8.41, al. ; ἀ. (sc. τὴν πολιορκίην) Id.7.170 ; τὴν ξυμμαχίαν, τὴν ξυνωμοσίαν, Th.3.9,64 ; of persons, καί σ' ἀπολείψω σου λειπόμενος E.*El.*1310 ; ξεῖνον πατρώϊον ἀ. *leave* him *in the lurch*, Thgn.521 ; ἀπολιπὼν οἴχεται Hdt.3.48, cf. 5.103, Ar.*Ra.* 83 ; of a wife, *desert* her husband, And.4.14, D.30.4 (not of the husband, Luc.*Sol.*9) ; of sailors, *desert*, τὴν ναῦν D.50.14. **2.** c. inf., ἀ. τούτους κακῶς γηράσκειν *leave* them to grow old, X.*Oec.* 1.22. **3.** *leave undone* or *unsaid*, ὅσα ἀπέλιπε κτείνων τε καὶ διώκων..σφέα ἀπετέλεσε Hdt.5.92.η′ ; ὕβρεως οὐδ' ὁτιοῦν ἀ. D.54. 4, cf. Pl.*R.*420a ; *omit*, συχνὰ ἀπολείπω ib.509c. **III.** *leave open, leave a space*, ἀ. μεταίχμιον οὐ μέγα Hdt.6.77 ; ἀ. ὡς πλέθρον X.*An.* 6.5.11 ; μικρὸν ἀ. *leaving* a small *interval*, Hero*Aut.*27.1. **IV.** intr., *cease, fail*, τάων οὔποτε καρπὸς ἀπόλλυται οὐδ' ἀπολείπει Od.7. 117 ; opp. γίνεται, Diog.Apoll.7 ; of rivers, *fall, sink*, Hdt.2.14,93 ; ἀ. τὸ ῥέεθρον Id.2.19 ; τῆς θαλάττης τὰ μὲν ἀπολειπούσης, τὰ δ' ἐπιούσης Arist.*Mete.*353$^{a}$22 ; of swallows, δι' ἔτεος ἐόντες οὐκ ἀπολείπουσι Hdt.2.22 ; of youth, *begin to decay*, X.*Smp.*8.14 ; *fail, flag, lose heart*, Id.*Cyr.*4.2.3 ; of the moon, *wane*, Arist.*APo.*98$^{a}$33. **2.** c. gen., *to be wanting of* or *in* a thing, προθυμίας οὐδὲν ἀ. Th.8.22, cf. Pl.*R.* 533a : freq. of numbers, μηδὲν ἀ. τῶν πέντε κτλ. Id.*Lg.*828b ; τῶν εἴκοσιν ὀλίγον ἀ. Arist.*HA*573$^{b}$16, etc. ; ἀπὸ τεσσέρων πηχέων ἀ. τρεῖς δακτύλους *wanting* three fingers *of* four cubits, Hdt.1.60, cf. 7.117 ; μήτ' ἄρ' ὑπερβάλλων βοὸς ὁπλὴν μήτ' ἀπολείπων Hes.*Op.*489 : c. inf., ὀλίγον ἀπέλιπον ἐς Ἀθήνας ἀπικέσθαι *wanted* but little of coming, Hdt.7.9.α′ ; βραχὺ ἀ. διακόσιαι γενέσθαι Th.7.70 ; οὐδὲν δ' ἀπολείπετε οὕτω πολεμεῖν D.4.40 ; ἡ πόλις μικρὸν ἀπέλιπεν ἔρημος εἶναι Plu.*Tim.* 1. **3.** c. part., *leave off* doing, ἀ. λέγων X.*Oec.*6.1 : abs., ὅθεν ἀπέλιπες from the point at which.., Pl.*Grg.*497c, cf. *Phd.*78b, Is.5. 12. **4.** *depart from*, ἐκ τῶν Συρακουσῶν Th.5.4 ; ἐκ τοῦ Μηδικοῦ πολέμου Id.3.10, cf. Pl.*Phd.*112c.

**B.** Med. (aor. ἀπελιπόμην in A.R.1.399 (tm.)), like Act.1.1, *bequeath to posterity*, Hdt.2.134 codd. ; cf. ἀπολείψεται· ἐάσεται, Hsch.

**C.** Pass., *to be left behind, stay behind*, Th.7.75 (v.l. for ὑπο-), X. *Cyr.*1.4.20 ; μόνος ἀπολελειμμένος Antipho1.3 ; *to be unable to follow* an argument, *be at a loss*, Pl.*Tht.*192d. **2.** *to be distanced by, inferior to*, ἀ. [ἀπὸ] τῶν ἄλλων θηρίων Diocl.*Fr.*145 ; *to be inferior*, ἔν τισι Isoc.12.61. **II.** *to be absent* or *distant from*, c. gen., πολὺ τῆς ἀληθηΐης ἀπολελειμμένοι Hdt.2.106, cf. Pl.*R.*475d ; ἥβας E.*HF* 440 (lyr.) : c. gen. pers., X.*Mem.*4.2.40, Pl.*Smp.*192d : abs., E.*Or.* 80, Pl.*Phdr.*240c ; *to be deprived of*, τοῦ σοῦ..μὴ ἀπολείπεσθαι τάφου S.*El.*1169 ; πατρῴας μὴ ἀ. χθονός E.*Med.*35 ; τῶν πρὶν ἀπολειφθεὶς φρενῶν Id.*Or.*216. **2.** *to be wanting in, fall short of*, ὅτι τοῦ σκώπτειν ἀπελείφθη Ar.*Eq.*525 ; τοῖς ἀπολειφθεῖσι (sc. τῆς παιδείας) D.18. 128, cf. Isoc.12.209 ; ἀπολειφθεὶς ἡμῶν *without* our *cognizance*, D.19. 36 ; ἀπολειφθῆναι τῶν πραγμάτων *to be left in ignorance of..*, Id.27.2 ; καιροῦ ἀ. *miss* the opportunity, Id.34.38, cf. Isoc.3.19 ; θεάματος, ἑορτῆς ἀ., Luc.*DMar.*15.1, *Sacr.*1 ; εἰσβολῆς Isoc.14.31. **3.** *remain to be done*, Plb.3.39.12 : impers., ἀπολείπεται λέγειν, διδάσκειν, D.L.7.85, S.E.*M.*7.1.

***ἀπολειτουργέω**, *complete required service*, D.L.3.99, M.Ant.10.22.

***ἀπολείχω**, *lick off*, ἕλκη, v.l. for ἐπι-, A.R.4.478, cf. Epic. in *Arch. Pap.*7.6, Ath.6.250a, Sch.Il.*Oxy.*221 ii 33 ; *lick clean*, c. gen. partit., φόνου *Ev.Luc.*16.21.

***ἀπόλειψις**, εως, ἡ, (ἀπολείπω) *abandonment*, ἡ ἀ. τοῦ στρατοπέδου Th.7.75 ; *defection*, Id.4.126 ; *desertion* of a husband by his wife (cf. ἀπολείπω II. 1), D.30.15 ; ἀπόλειψιν ἀπογράφεσθαι (v. ἀπογράφω III. 2) ib.17 (but also, = ἀπόπεμψις, ἀ. γράψασθαι Plu.2.100e) ; *desertion* by soldiers, seamen, etc., X.*HG*4.1.28, D.50.11. **II.** intr., *deficiency*, of rivers, *failing*, Arist.*Mete.*351$^{a}$21 (pl.) ; of the moon, *waning*, Id. *GA*767$^{a}$5 ; of the sun, *departure to southern hemisphere*, Jul.*Or.*4. 137d. **2.** *death*, δοιὴ δὲ θνητῶν γένεσις, δοιὴ δ' ἀ. Emp.17.3 ; ἀ. τοῦ ζῆν Hyp.*Epit.*24 ; ἐκ τοῦ ὄντος Porph.*Sent.*20. **III.** in Law, *default*, *Cod.Just.*1.4.18.

**ἀπόλεκτος**, ον, (ἀπολέγω) *chosen, picked*, Th.6.68, X.*An.*2.3.15, Aen.Tact.26.10. **II.** ἀπόλεκτον, τό, *choice cut off* the πηλαμύς (q.v.), Xenocr.70.

**ἀπολέλασται**· ἀπολέλεκται, Hsch.

**ἀπολελεγμένως**, gloss on ἀπηλεγέως, Hsch.

**ἀπολελῠμένως**, Adv. *absolutely*, opp. κατὰ σχέσιν, S.E.*M.*8.162, cf. Ptol.*Tetr.*127. **II.** Gramm., *in the positive degree*, opp. κατὰ σύγκρισιν ('in the comparative'), Phryn.*PS*p.1B. **III.** Rhet., *without regular pauses*, ἀ. λέγειν, opp. διακόψαι, Hermog.*Id.*1.9.

**ἀπολέμητος**, ον, *not warred on*, Plb.3.90.7, Luc.*DDeor.*20.12.

**ἀπόλεμμα**, ατος, τό, (ἀπολέπω) *skin*, D.C.68.32.

***ἀπόλεμος**, Ep. **ἀπτόλεμος**, ον, *unwarlike*, ἀ. καὶ ἄναλκις Il.2.201, al., cf. X.*Cyr.*7.4.1, Jul.*Or.*2.87a ; ἀ. χειρὶ λείψεις βίον, i.e. by *a woman's* hand, E.*Hec.*1034 (lyr.). **2.** *unwarlike, peaceful*, εὐνομία Pi.*P.*5.66 ; εὐναί E.*Med.*640 ; ἡσυχία D.H.2.76, etc. Adv. -μως, ἴσχειν Pl.*Plt.*307e. **II.** *invincible*, A.*Ag.*768, *Ch.*55 (lyr.). **III.** πόλεμος ἀ. a war *that is no war*, a hopeless struggle, Id.*Fr.*904 (lyr.) (Dind. metri gr. proposes ἀπολέμιστος), E.*HF*1133.

**ἀπολεοντόομαι**, Pass., (λέων) *become a lion*, Heraclit.*Incred.*12.

**ἀπολεπιδόομαι**, Pass., *exfoliate*, of bones, Hp.*Fract.*33.

***ἀπολεπ-ίζω**, = ἀπολέπω, *peel*, *Gp.*10.58. **-ισμα**, ατος, τό, *husk*, Sch.Ar.*Ach.*469.

**ἀπολεπτ-ύνω**, *fine down*, esp. *of reducing temperature* or *fever*, Plu.2.695e, Alex.Trall.*Febr.*5 :—more freq. in Pass., *become quite fine* or *thin*, ἀπολεπτυνθέντος τοῦ πικροῦ *being fined away*, Pl.*Ti.*83b ; πλάτος ἀπολελεπτυσμένον Arist.*HA*489$^{b}$33 ; of fever, v.l. in Hp. *Epid.*1.25. **-υσμός**, ὁ, *attenuation*, Antyll.ap.Orib.6.10.17.

**ἀπολέπω**, aor. 2 Pass. ἀπελέπην Hsch. :—*peel, skin*, ἀ. μάστιγι τὸ νῶτον cj. Ruhnk. in E.*Cyc.*237 ; ὥσπερ ᾠὸν τὸ λέμμα Ar.*Av.*673 ; θρίδακος ἀπολελεμμένας τὸν καυλόν *with* the stalk *peeled*, Epich. 158. **2.** *lop off*, στεῦτο ἀπολεψέμεν οὔατα χαλκῷ Il.21.455 (dub. l.).

**ἀπολέσκετο**, Ep. iterative of ἀπόλλυμι.

**ἀπολευκ-αίνω**, *make all white*, Hp.*Prorrh.*2.20 ; τὸν ἀέρα Plu.*Eum.* 16 :—Pass., *to be* or *become so*, Arist.*Fr.*350, Archig.ap.Orib.44.26. 1. **-όω**, = foreg., *Hippiatr.*69.

**ἀπό-ληγμα**, ατος, τό, *skirt, hem* of a robe, Aq.*Ex.*28.33. ***-λήγω**, *leave off, desist from*, c. gen., ἀλλ' οὐδ' ὣς ἀπέληγε μάχης Il.7.263; οὐκ ἀπολήγει ἀλκῆς ib.21.577; νέον δ' ἀπέληγεν ἐδωδῆς ib.24.475; ἀ. ἔρωτος Pl.*R.*490b. 2. c. part., *leave off* doing, Il.17.565, Od.19.166; [γενεὴ] ἡ μὲν φύει, ἡ δ' ἀπολήγει Il.6.149: abs., *cease, desist*, ib.13.230, 20.99; κλέος..οὐδ' ἀπολήξει Xenoph.6.3; opp. γίνεται, Emp.17.30; of the wind, *fall*, Theoc.22.19. 3. ἀ. εἰς ἕν *end* in.., Arist.*Mu.*399ᵃ13, cf. Str.13.4.1, Plu.2.496a, Luc.*Im.*6; ἐς ὀξὺ *taper* to a point, Arr.*Tact.*16.7: Rhet., of the close of a sentence, ἀ. εἰς συνδέσμους Demetr.*Eloc.*257. b. τὸ ἀπολῆγον [τοῦ βουνοῦ] the *extremity* of the hill, *Inscr.Prien.*37.168 (ii B.C.): so Medic., τὰ ἀ. μέρη the *extremities*, Ruf.ap.Orib.49.33.11, al. II. trans., = ἀποπαύω, A.R.4.767. [ἀπολλ. Il.15.31, Od.13.151, 19.166, Theoc. l.c., al.] **-ληκέω**, *snap the fingers*, Hellanic.63(b) J., Hsch. (-λεκ- cod.), Suid. s. v. Σαρδαναπάλλους. **-ληξις**, εως, ἡ, *cessation*, ἐνεργείας M.Ant.9.21; καταμηνίων Sor.1.62; esp. *decline* of life, Hp. *Praec.*14. II. *close* of a sentence or period, Demetr.*Eloc.*182, al. III. *termination* of a fistula, Antyll.ap.Orib.44.22.7.

**ἀποληπτ-έον**, *one must admit, accept*, κριτήριον τὴν φαντασίαν (nisi leg. -λειπτέον, cf. ἀπολείπω I.4) S.E.*M.*7.388. **-ικός**, ή, όν, *pertaining to the receipt of a debt*, ὁμολογία *Cod.Just.*4.21.16.

**ἀποληρέω**, *chatter at random*, D.19.182, Longus 1.17; ἔς τινα D.C.53.23; τι Id.72.4. 2. *outdo in foolish talk*, τινά Plb.34.6.15.

**ἀπόληρος**· ἡ τοῦ θανάτου γραφή (Tarent.), Hsch.

**ἀπόληψις**, εως, ἡ, (ἀπολαμβάνω IV) *intercepting, cutting off*, ὁπλιτῶν Th.7.54; *stoppage*, ἐπιμηνίων, οὔρων, Hp.*Prorrh.*1.51, 2.7, etc.; ὑδάτων Thphr.*CP*3.21.1; *imprisonment*, πνεύματος ἐν τῇ γῇ Epicur.*Ep.*2 p.48 U.; ἀ. ποδὸς *constrained position*, Hp.*Art.*62. b. *refutation*, Gal.5.261. 2. *reception*, τῆς φιλίας Phld.*D.*3*Fr.*84, cf. Str.10.2.25. 3. *clamp, holdfast*, Ph.*Bel.*57.44. 4. *repayment*, Phalar. *Ep.*27.

**ἀπολῐβάζω**, *cause to drop off, throw away*, Pherecr.42. II. intr., *drop off, vanish*, οὐκ ἀπολιβάξεις εἰς ἀποικίαν τινά; Eup.206, cf. Ar.*Av.*1467.

**ἀπολῐγαίνω**, *speak with a shrill voice, bluster*, ἦν δ' ἀπολιγαίνῃ Ar. *Ach.*968. II. *make shrill music*, Plu.2.713a.

**ἀπολῐγωρέω**, *esteem little*, πόλεμον Sch.Th.1.140, cf. Steph. *in Gal.* 1.285 D.

**ἀπολῐθ-όω**, *turn into stone, petrify*, Arist.*Pr.*937ᵃ17, cf. Hellanic. 191 J., Pherecyd.77 J.:—Pass., ἀ. ὑπὸ τοῦ ἡλίου Thphr.*HP*4.7.2; *become stone*, Arist.*Pr.*937ᵃ14, *Mir.*838ᵃ14, Str.5.4.13, Palaeph.31; *become hard*, *PHolm.*4.38. **-ωσις**, εως, ἡ, *petrifaction*, Pherecyd. 12 J., Thphr.*Lap.*50, Sch.Il.2.319: metaph., Arr.*Epict.*1.5.3.

**ἀπολιμνόομαι**, Pass., *become a lake* or *pool*, Eust.267.47.

***ἀπολιμπάνω**, Aeol. ἀπυ-, collat. form of ἀπολείπω, ἀέκων σ' ἀ. Sapph.*Supp.*23.5, cf. Luc.*Cat.*7, Gal.*UP*4.11, *POxy.*1426.12 (iv A.D.):—Pass., Plu.*Them.*10.

**ἀπόλινον**, τό, = θυμελαία, Dsc.4.172 (v.l.).

**ἀπολῐν-όω**, *tie up with a thread*, of surgeons, Paul.Aeg.6.5. **-ωσις**, εως, ἡ, *operation by ligature*, ibid.

**ἀπόλιον**· θαῦμα, Hsch. (fort. θῦμα, cf. ἀπάλιον).

**ἀπολῐόρκητος**, ον, *impregnable*, Str.12.3.31, Plu.2.1057e.

**ἀπολιόω**, v. ἀπολειόω.

**ἀπολῐπαίνω**, *oil*, Antig.*Mir.*135.

***ἄπολις**, ι: gen. ιδος or εως, Ion. ιος: dat. ἀπόλι Hdt.8.61:—*without city, state* or *country*, Id.7.104, 8.61, etc.; *outlaw, banished man*, ἄ. τινα τιθέναι, ποιεῖν, S.*OC*1357, Antipho 2.2.9, Pl.*Lg.*928e, etc.; προβαλέσθαι S.*Ph.*1018; ἀ. ἀντὶ πολιτῶν Lys.20.35; ἄ. τῆς ἀρχαίας (sc. πόλεως) Aristid.*Or.*26(14).75. 2. *no true citizen*, opp. ὑψίπολις, S.*Ant.*370. II. of a country, *without cities*, Plu.*Tim.*1, Philostr.*VA*1.24. III. πόλις ἄπολις a city *that is no city*, a ruined city, ἄ. Ἰλίου πόλιν ἔθηκας A.*Eu.*457, cf. E.*Tr.*1292; also, one *that has no constitution, no true* city, Pl.*Lg.*766d.

***ἀπολισθ-άνω**, later -αίνω Poll.1.116, v.l. in Hp.*Acut.*17, Plu.*Alc.* 6, etc.: aor. ἀπώλισθον Ar.*Lys.*678, etc.; later ἀπωλίσθησα *AP*9.158:—*slip off* or *away*, Th.7.65, Arist.*Pr.*961ᵃ27, Plot.3.6.14: c. acc. cogn., ἐκ τέγεος πέσημα *AP* l.c. 2. c. gen., *slip away from*, τινός Ar.*Lys.*678; τῆς μνήμης prob. in Alciphr.3.11; ἀ. τινός, also, *cease to be intimate with* one, τοῦ Σωκράτους Plu. l. c.; ἀ. εἴς τι Luc.*Dem. Enc.*12; ἐπὶ τὴν δόξαν Iamb.*Myst.*9.8. b. ἀ. τοῦ ρ *make a slip* in pronouncing ρ, Plu.2.277d. **-ησις**, εως, ἡ, *slipping off*, Plot.6.6.3.

**ἀπόλιστος**, ον, = ἄπολις, Man.4.282.

**ἀπολῐταργίζω**, Att. fut. -ιῶ, *hop off, pack off*, οὔκουν ἀνύσας τι.. ἀπολιταργιεῖς; Ar.*Nu.*1253.

***ἀπολ-ίτευτος** [ῐ], ον, *without political constitution* (πολιτεία), of nations, Arist.*Pol.*1327ᵇ26. II. *not fitted for public affairs, unstatesmanlike*, Plu.*Mar.*31; ὑπατεία, λόγοι, Id.*Crass.*12, 2.1034b. 2. *withdrawn from public life, private*, βίος ib.1098d; θάνατος Id.*Lyc.*29. 3. *not in current use*, λέξις Id.2.7a. **-ίτης** [ῑ], ου, ὁ, v.l. for ἀποπολίτης, q.v. **-ῐτικός**, ή, όν, *unstatesmanlike*, Cic.*Att.* 8.16.1 (Sup.).

**ἀπολίτρωσις**, εως, ἡ, = ἀπονίτρωσις, Orib.*Fr.*74.

**ἀπολιχμάζω**, = sq., Opp.*C.*2.175 (tm.).

**ἀπολιχμάομαι**, *lick off*, αἷμα Il.21.123:—later in Act., D.H.1.79. II. *lick*, τὸ πρόσωπον Longus 1.5.

**ἀπολλαπλάσιος**, ον, *without multiplicity*, Dam.*Pr.*47.

**Ἀπολλόδωρος**, ὁ, pr. n., *Apollodorus*, Th.7.20, etc.:—hence Adj. **-δώρειος**, ον, αἵρεσις Str.13.4.3.

***ἀπόλλῡμι** or -ύω (Th.4.25, Pl.*R.*608e, Arist.*Pol.*1297ᵃ12, but f.l. in Men.580; the form is rejected by Phryn.*PS* p.10 B., Moer.12), impf. ἀπώλλυν A.*Pers.*652 (lyr.), S.*El.*1360, ἀπώλλυον And.1.58: fut. ἀπολέσω, Ep. ἀπολέσσω, Att. ἀπολῶ, Ion. ἀπολέω Hdt.1.34, al.: aor. ἀπώλεσα, Ep. ἀπόλεσσα: pf. ἀπολώλεκα:—freq. in tmesi in Ep.; Prep. postponed in Od.9.534:—stronger form of ὄλλυμι, *destroy utterly, kill*, in Hom. mostly of death in battle, ἀπώλεσε λαὸν Ἀχαιῶν Il.5.758, al.; ἐκπάγλως ἀπόλεσσαν ib.1.268; also of things, *demolish, lay waste*, ἀπώλεσεν Ἴλιον ἱρήν ib.5.648, etc.; generally, βίοτον δ' ἀπὸ πάμπαν ὀλέσσει *will waste* my substance, Od.2.49; οἵ μ' ἀπωλλύτην *sought to destroy* me (impf. sense), S.*OT*1454; in pregnant sense, ἐπεί με γᾶς ἐκ πατρίας ἀπώλεσε *drove* me *ruined* from.., E.*Hec.*946; τῆς παρ' ἡμέραν χάριτος τὰ μέγιστα τῆς πόλεως ἀ. for the sake of.., D.8.70. 2. λόγοις or λέγων ἀ. τινά *talk* or *bore* one *to death*, S.*El.*1360, Ar.*Nu.*892 (lyr.): hence, alone, in fut. ἀπολεῖς με Id.*Ach.*470; οἴμ' ὡς ἀπολεῖς με Pherecr.108.20; ἀπολεῖ μ' οὑτοσί by his questions, Antiph.222.8, etc. 3. *ruin* a woman, Lys.1.8. II. *lose*, πατέρ' ἐσθλὸν ἀπώλεσα Od.2.46, cf. Il.18.82, Democr.272; ἀπώλεσε νόστιμον ἦμαρ Od.1.354; ἀπὸ θυμὸν ὀλέσσαι *lose* one's life, Il.16.861, Od.12.350; θυμὸν οὐκ ἀπώλεσεν *loses* not his spirit, S.*El.*26; ἔλεον ἀπώλεσεν Il.24.44; freq. of things, ἡ τοῦ πλέονος ἐπιθυμίη τὸ παρεὸν ἀπόλλυσι Democr.224; ἵππους ἑβδομήκοντα ἀπολλύασι Th.7.51; ἀπώλεσαν τὴν ἀρχὴν ὑπὸ Περσῶν X.*An.*3.4.11, cf. 7.2.22; μηδὲν ἀπολλὺς τοῦ ὄγκου Pl.*Tht.*155c; ἀ. οὐσίαν, = ἀπόλλυσθαι, Id.*Prm.*163d.

B. Med., ἀπόλλυμαι: fut. -ολοῦμαι, Ion. -ολέομαι Hdt.7.218: aor. 2 -ωλόμην: pf. -όλωλα, whence the barbarous impf. ἀπόλωλο Ar.*Th.*1212: plpf. in Att. Prose sts. written ἀπωλώλειν in codd., as Th.4.133, 7.27:—*perish, die*, Il.1.117, etc.; *cease to exist*, opp. γίγνεσθαι, Meliss.8, Pl.*Prm.*156b, etc.: sts. c. acc. cogn., ἀπόλωλε κακὸν μόρον Od.1.166; ἀπωλόμεθ' αἰπὺν ὄλεθρον ib.9.303: c. dat. modi, ἀπώλετο λυγρῷ ὀλέθρῳ (v.l. λυγρὸν ὄλεθρον) ib.3.87; ἀ. ὑπό τινος Hdt.5.126; simply, *to be undone*, αὐτῶν..ἀπωλόμεθ' ἀφραδίῃσιν Od.10.27; ἀπωλώλει τῷ φόβῳ μή.. X.*Cyr.*6.1.2: freq. in Att., esp. in pf., ἀπόλωλας you *are lost*, Ar.*Nu.*1077; ἀπωλόμεθ' ἂν εἰ μὴ ἀπολώλειμεν Plu.2.185f; ἱκανὸν χρόνον ἀπολλύμεθα καὶ κατατετρίμμεθα Ar.*Pax*355; βλέπειν ἀπολωλός Philostr.Jun.*Im.*2:—as an imprecation, κάκιστ' ἀπολοίμην εἰ.. Ar.*Ach.*151, al.; κακὸς κακῶς ἀπόλοιτ' ὅστις.. Eub.116; ἐξώλης ἀπόλοιθ' ὅστις.. Men.154; ἀπολλύμενος, opp. σῳζόμενος, Isoc.6.36, cf. Plu.2.469d: freq. in part. fut., ὦ κάκιστ' ἀπολούμενε o *destined to* a miserable *end!* i.e. o *thou villain, scoundrel, knave!* Ar.*Pl.*713, cf. 456, *Ach.*865, *Pax*2; ὁ κάκιστ' ἀνέμων ἀ. Luc.*DDeor.*14.2. 2. in *NT*, *perish*, in theol. sense, *Ev.Jo.*3.16, al.; οἱ ἀπολλύμενοι, opp. οἱ σῳζόμενοι, 1*Ep.Cor.*1.18. II. *to be lost*, ὕδωρ ἀπολέσκετ' (of the water eluding Tantalus) Od.11.586; οὔποτε καρπὸς ἀπόλλυται never *falls untimely*, ib.7.117; ἀπό τέ σφισιν ὕπνος ὄλωλεν Il.10.186; γέλως ἐξ ἀνθρώπων ἀπόλωλεν X.*Smp.*1.15; ἀπολόμενον ἀργύριον Antipho Soph.54; ἀπώλοντο οἱ ὄνοι Lxx 1*Ki.*9.3.

**ἀπόλλω**, late form of ἀπόλλυμι, Lxx 4*Ma.*6.14, v.l. in Eust.712.55, etc.

***Ἀπόλλων**, ὁ, *Apollo*: gen. ωνος (also ω *An.Ox.*3.222): acc. Ἀπόλλω *IG*1.9, al., A.*Supp.*214, S.*OC*1091, *Tr.*209 (lyr.) (mostly in adjurations, νὴ τὸν Ἀπόλλω, etc.), Ἀπόλλωνα Pl.*Lg.*624a, freq. later, Agatharch.7, etc.: voc. Ἄπολλον Alc.1, A.*Th.*159 (lyr.), Cratin.186, etc.; Ἀπόλλων A.*Ch.*559; cf. Ἀπέλλων, Ἄπλουν. II. Pythag. name of a number, Porph.*Abst.*2.36.

***Ἀπολλ-ώνεια**, τά, = Lat. *ludi Apollinares*, D.C.47.18. **-ωνιακός**, ή, όν, = Ἀπολλώνιος I, Ph.2.560, Dam.*Pr.*95, Olymp.*Vit.Pl.* p.1 W. ***-ωνιασταί**, οἱ, *worshippers of Apollo*, *IG*12(1).163 (Rhodes). **-ώνιος**, α, ον, *of* or *belonging to Apollo*, Pi.*P.*6.9, etc.:—fem. **-ωνιάς** (sc. πόλις or νᾶσος), άδος, ἡ, i.e. Delos, Id.*I.*1.6: also, = δάφνη, Hsch. II. ***-ώνιος**, ὁ, (sc. μήν) name of month at Elis, Methymna, etc., Sch.Pi.*O.*3.35, *IG*12(2).505, etc. III. **-ώνιον**, τό, *temple of Apollo*, Th.2.91, Arist.*Mir.*840ᵃ21, *GDI*5726.45 (Halic.):—also **-ώνειον**, D.S.14.16, etc., cf. Eust.1562.54. IV. **-ώνια**, τά, *festival of Apollo*, *IG*11(2).105 (Delos), etc. **-ωνίσκος**, ὁ, Dim. of Ἀπόλλων, Ath.14.636f. 2. *statuette of Apollo*, Roussel *Cultes Égyptiens* 221 (Delos, ii B.C.). **-ωνιών**, ῶνος, ὁ, (sc. μήν) name of month at Halicarnassus, *BCH*14.106.

**Ἀπολλωνό-βλητος**, ον, *stricken by Apollo*, = ἡλιόβλητος, Macrob. 1.17.11. **-νησοι**, formed in illustration of ἑκατόννησοι, Str.13.2.5. **-τρᾰφής**, ές, *nourished by Apollo*, Sch.Il.23.291.

***ἀπολογ-έομαι**, aor. ἀπελογησάμην E.*Ba.*41, Antipho 5.13, but f.l. in Pl.*Sph.*261c, X.*An.*5.6.3; also aor. Pass. ἀπελογήθην Antipho 2.3.1, al., Alex.12 (prob. spurious in X.*HG*1.4.13): pf. ἀπολελόγημαι And.1.33, Isoc.12.218 (in pass. sense, Pl.*R.*607b):—*speak in defence, defend oneself*, opp. κατηγορεῖν, περί τινος *about* a thing, Antipho 5.7, Th.1.72; πρὸς τὴν μαρτυρίαν *in reference* or *answer to* the evidence, Antipho 2.4.3, cf. Th.6.29; πρός τινας *before*.., Eup.357, cf. Plb.22.6.4: later, c. dat., κατηγορίαις Plu.*Them.*23; ἀ. ὑπέρ τινος *speak* in another's *behalf*, Hdt.7.161, E.*Ba.*41, Pl.*R.*488a, etc.; ἀ. ὑπέρ τινος *speak in support of* a fact, Antipho 3.2.1; ὑπὲρ τῆς ἀδικίας Pl. *Grg.*480b; πρὸς Μέλητον *in answer to* him, Id.*Ap.*24b: abs., παρὼν ἀ. Hdt.6.136, Ar.*Th.*188; ὁ ἀπολογούμενος *the defendant*, Id.*V.*778, And.1.6. 2. c. acc. rei, *defend oneself against*, ἀ. τὰς διαβολὰς Th.8.109; τὰς πράξεις *defend* what one has done, Aeschin.1.92. 3. ἀ. τι ἔς τι *allege in one's defence* against a charge, Th.3.63; ἀ. πρὸς τὰ κατηγορημένα μηδὲν Lys.12.38; τί ποτε ἀπολογήσεσθαι μέλλει μοι; Antipho 1.7 codd.; ταῦτα ἀ. ὡς.. Pl.*Phd.*69d; ἔργοις καλλίστοις ἀ. ὡς.. Lys.2.65; ἀ. ὅτι οὐδένα ἀδικῶ X.*Oec.*11.22; ἀ. ἀπολογίαν Luc.

Hes.6. 4. ἀ. δίκην θανάτου *speak against* sentence of death *passing on one*, Th.8.68.—Prose word, used once in Trag., v. supr.—The Prep. ἀπό implies the *removal* of a charge. **-ή**, ἡ, (ἀπολέγω) *selection*, or possibly *challenging of jurors*, ἐξ ἀπολογῆς *OGI*484.54 (Pergam.). **-ημα**, ατος, τό, *plea alleged in defence*, Pl.*Cra.*436c; ὑπὲρ τῆς πόλεως πρὸς Ῥωμαίους Plu.*Cim.*1. **-ητέον**, *one must make one's defence*, Antipho 4.4.1; *one must defend*, Pl.*Ap.*19a: also in pl., -ητέα Philostr.*VA*8.7; ἐκεῖνα -ητέα ἦν ὅτι.. D.H.6.44. **-ητικός**, ή, όν, *suitable for defence, apologetic*, Arist.*Rh.Al.*1421ᵇ10. **-ία**, ἡ, *speech in defence*, opp. κατηγορία, Antipho 6.7, Th.3.61, Pl.*Ap.*28a, etc.; ἀ. ποιεῖσθαι to make *a defence*, Is.6.62; ἀ. ποιεῖσθαι τὸν ἑαυτοῦ βίον τῶν τοῦ πατρὸς ἀδικημάτων Lys.14.29; τῶν κατηγορηθέντων τὸ μὴ λαβὸν ἀπολογίαν Hyp.*Eux.*31; ἀ. τοῦ εὐαγγελίου *Ep.Phil.*1.16; expl. by πληροφορία, Hsch. **-ίζομαι**, fut. -ιοῦμαι Phld.*Lib.* p.50 O., D.C.*Fr.*109: aor. ἀπελογισάμην Pl.*Sph.*261c (prob.); Dor. -ιξάμην *IG*9(1).694.97 (Corcyra): pf. ἀπολελόγισμαι ib.2.594.19, 329.16, D.H.*Pomp.*1.17 codd.: in pass. sense, X.*Oec.*9.8:—*render an account*, ἀ. κατ' ἐνιαυτόν Id.*HG*6.1.3; ἀ. τὰς προσόδους *render an account of* the receipts, Aeschin.3.25, cf. *IG*7.303.21 (Orop.); τῇ βουλῇ καὶ τῷ δήμῳ ib.2.594.19:—Pass., τὰ ἀπολελογισμένα *the estimates*, X.*Oec.*9.8. 2. ἀ. εἴς τι *refer to* a head or class, Pl.*Phlb.*25b. II. *reckon on* a thing, *calculate that* it will be.., c. acc. et inf., D.19.20; ἀπολογιεῖται πεῖσαι.. *will count on* persuading, Phld. l.c.; *calculate fully*, ἀ. πότερον.. Pl.*Sph.* l.c. III. *give a brief account of*, τι Arist.*Rh.Al.*1433ᵇ38; περί τινος ib.1444ᵇ31; but, *recount at length*, τι Plb.21.3.2; περί τινος Id.8.24.7; ὡς.. Id.4.25.4.—Prose word: Act., *reject*, Suid. **-ισμός**, ὁ, *giving account, statement of reasons*, etc., v.l. in Aeschin.3.247, Plb.10.11.5. 2. *account kept, record*, ἀναλωμάτων Luc.*Dem.Enc.*33; ἀπολογισμὸν ποιήσασθαι *Klio* 18.276 (Delph., ii B.C.), cf. Plu.*Per.*23, *POxy.*297.5 (i A.D.): in pl., Plu.2.822e. 3. *narration*, Plb.10.21.8. 4. = ἀπολογία, Zeno *Stoic.*1.55; τοῦ βίου, τῶν πράξεων, Plu.2.726b, *Sull.*34. **-ιστής**, οῦ, ὁ, *accountant, bookkeeper*, *POxy.*34 vi 8 (ii A.D.). **-ος**, ὁ, *story, tale*, Ἀλκίνου ἀπόλογος, of long and tedious stories (from that told by Odysseus to Alcinous in Od.9–12), Pl.*R.*614b, Arist.*Rh.*1417ᵃ13, *Po.*1455ᵃ2. II. *fable, apologue, allegory*, Cic.*Orat.*2.66.264, Quint.*Inst.*6.3.44, Gell.2.29.20. III. *account rendered*, *Test.Epict.*8.36, *IG*14.952 (Agrigent.), Hsch. IV. = λογιστής, *IG*12(8).267 (Thasos), *BCH*45.154 (ibid., iii B.C.), *AJA*19.446 (Halae, iii B.C.).

**ἀπολοιδορέω**, *abuse violently*, Plb.15.33.4.

**ἀπολοίμιον φανόν**· τὸν ἐπὶ δόλῳ, Hsch.

**ἀπολοιπασία**, ἡ, *remainder*, in subtraction, Hero *Geom.*12.32. II. *list of arrears*, *POxy.*1147.1 (vi A.D.), cf. ib.1855.4 (vi A.D.).

**ἀπόλοιπος**, ον, *remaining over, left behind*, Lxx *Ez.*41.15, al.; ἀπόλοιπα, τά, *unpaid arrears*, = Lat. *residua*, *IG*5(1).1434 (Messene).

**ἀπολοίφειν**· ἀποτελεῖν, Hsch.

**ἀπολοπίζω**, = ἀπολέπω, *skin, peel*, prob. l. for -λογίζειν, -λογίζων, Ar.*Fr.*135, Antiph.128, cf. Phryn.*PS* p.44 B.

**ἄπολος**, ον, = ἀκίνητος, ἀστρεφής, *immovable*, Hsch.

**ἀπό-λουμα**, ατος, τό, = ἀποκάθαρμα, Sch.Ar.*Eq.*1401, Eust.1560.32. **-λουσις**, εως, ἡ, *ablution*, Pl.*Cra.*405b, Sor.1.83. **-λούτριος**, ον, *washed off*: τὰ ἀπολούτρια (sc. ὕδατα) water *which has been used for washing*, Ael.*NA*17.11:—also **-λουτρον**, τό, Sch.Ar.*Eq.*1401. ⊛**-λούω**, I. c. acc. rei, *wash off*, λούειν ἄπο βρότον Il.14.7:—Med., ὄφρ'.. ἅλμην ὤμοιϊν ἀπολούσομαι that I *may wash* the brine *from off my* shoulders, Od.6.219; of baptism, ἀ. τὰς ἁμαρτίας *Act.Ap.*22.16. 2. c. acc. pers., *wash clean*, Ar.*V.*118 (ἀπέλου for ἀπέλοε, v. λούω), Pl.*Cra.*405b, 406a:—Med., *wash away from oneself*, λούσασθαι ἄπο βρότον αἱματόεντα Il.23.41; τὸ σῶμα ἀπελούετο Longus 1.13: in archaic style, ἀπολούμενος Luc.*Lex.*2, cf. Ath.3.97e, 98a. 3. c. acc. pers. et rei, ὄφρα τάχιστα Πάτροκλον λούσειαν ἄπο βρότον *might wash* the gore *off* him, Il.18.345: c. gen. rei, καί μ' ἀπέλουσε λύθρου *Epigr.Gr.*314.6 (Smyrna). 4. ἀπολουσέμεναι· κολ[λ]οβώσειν (Cypr.), Hsch.; cf. ἀπολέπω.

⊛**ἀπολοφ-ύρομαι** [ῠ], *bewail loudly*, ἐμαυτόν And.3.16, cf. X.*HG* 1.1.27; συμφοράν Antipho Soph.54: abs., *indulge one's sorrows to the full*, Th.2.46, Pl.*Mx.*249c. **-υρσις**, εως, ἡ, *lamentation*, Sch.S.*Aj.*596.

**ἀπολοχμόομαι**, *make too much wood*, Thphr.*HP*6.6.6.

**ἀπόλυγμα[τος]**· ἀπογύμνωσις (Cypr.), Hsch.

**ἀπόλῡμα**, ατος, τό, *filth*, Harp. s.v. ὀξυθυμία: in pl., *fragments of tissue*, Heliod.ap.Orib.44.10.13, Gal.19.422.

**ἀπολῡμ-αίνομαι**, Med., (λῦμα) *cleanse oneself by bathing*, esp. *from an* ἄγος, Il.1.313, 314, A.R.4.702, cf. Paus.8.41.2; ἀπολυμήνασθαι καὶ ἀφαγνίσαι τὸ μίασμα Agath.2.7. **-αντήρ**, ῆρος, ὁ, (λύμη) *destroyer*: δαιτῶν ἀ. *one who destroys* one's pleasure at dinner, *kill-joy* (or *a devourer of remnants, lick-plate*), Od.17.220, 377.

**ἀπολύουσα**, = κώνειον, Ps.-Dsc.4.78.

**ἀπολυπραγμ-όνητος**, ον, *not meddled with*, prob. in *SIG*399.24 (Delph.). Adv. -τως Hsch. s.v. ἀπεριέργως. **-ων**, ον, gen. ονος, *not meddlesome*, M.Ant.1.5, Ptol.*Tetr.*159.

**ἄπολυς**, υ, *without plurality*, expl. of ἁπλοῦς, Dam.*Pr.*21, 26.

**ἀπο-λῠσίδιον**, τό, *order for delivery*, *PFlor.*131.7 (iii A.D.), al.; οἴνου *PFay.*133.14. ⊛**-λύσιμος** [ῠ], ον, (ἀπολύω) *deserving acquittal*, Antipho 4.4.9. II. *released from* public service, *PLond.*2.445.7 (i A.D.); ἀπὸ στρατείας *CPR*1.3 (i A.D.). ⊛**-λυσις**, εως, ἡ, *loosing*, e.g. of a bandage or cord, Hp.*Fract.*10, Hero *Aut.*2.9. 2. *release, deliverance*, Pl.*Cra.*405b, Plb.33.1.5: c. gen., κατὰ τὴν ἀ. τοῦ θανάτου as far as *acquittal from* a capital charge went, Hdt.6.136; ἀ. κακῶν θάνατος Plu.*Arat.*54; ἀ. πένθους *end* of mourning, *OGI*56.53 (Canopus). 3. *getting rid of a disease*, Hp.*Coac.*378, etc. 4. *spell for releasing* a divine being, *PMag.Par.*1.1056, al. II. (from Pass.) *separation, parting*, Arist.*GA*718ᵃ14; τῆς ψυχῆς Id.*R.*479ᵃ22: abs., *decease, death*, Thphr.*HP*9.16.8, Lycon ap.D.L.5.71; ἀ. ποιεῖσθαι to take one's *departure*, of an army, Plb.3.69.10. **-λῠτέον**, *one must acquit*, τινά τινος Gorg.*Hel.*6; *one must disengage*, ὀστέον Heliod.ap.Orib.46.12.2. **-λῡτήριον**, τό, = ἐκλ., Sch.E.*Ph.*969. ⊛**-λῠτικός**, ή, όν, *disposed to acquit*. Adv. -κῶς, ἔχειν τινός *to be minded to acquit* one, X.*HG*5.4.25. ⊛**-λῠτος**, ον, *loosed, free*, Plu.2.426b; ἀ. ψυχαί souls *at large* before being embodied, Porph.ap.Stob.1.49.40; ἀ. θεοί Dam.*Pr.*351, cf. Procl.*in Cra.*p.74 P. 2. *absolute, unconditional*, Arr.*Epict.*2.5.24, S.E.*M.*8.273, Plot.6.1.18 and 22. Adv. -τως S.E.*M.*8.161, Men.Rh.p.434 S., Lyd.*Mens.*4.7; opp. κατὰ σχέσιν, Procl.*in Prm.*p.733 S. 3. τὸ ἀ. the *positive* degree of comparison, Hdn.*Fig.*p.85 S., Sch.Ar.*Av.*63. 4. ἀ. χάραγμα *independent* coinage of Alexandria, Just.*Edict.*11, *POxy.*1448 (vi A.D.). 5. Rhet., *unfinished*, μερισμός, e.g. μέν not folld. by δέ, Hermog.*Id.*2.7. b. ἀ. χαρακτήρ *loose, unconstrained* style, Aphth.*Prog.*11. 6. Medic., = ἀπολελυμένος (ἀπολύω C. II. 1), Heliod.ap.Orib.46.14.2, Ruf.*Syn.Puls.*3.4. Adv. -τως ib.5.

**ἀπολυτρ-όω**, *release on payment of ransom*, Men.*Mis.*21: c. gen. pretii, ὡς ἐχθροὺς ἀ. τῶν μακροτάτων λύτρων Pl.*Lg.*919a, cf. Philipp. ap.D.12.3; *restore for a ransom*, τὰ ἐλεύθερα σώματα καὶ τὴν πόλιν αὐτοῖς Plb.2.6.6, cf. J.*BJ*2.14.1:—Med., Polyaen.5.40. **-ωσις**, εως, ἡ, *ransoming*, αἰχμαλώτων Plu.*Pomp.*24 (pl.), cf. J.*AJ*12.2.3, Ph.2.463. II. *redemption by payment of ransom, deliverance*, Ev. *Luc.*21.28, *Ep.Rom.*3.24, al.; of Nebuchadnezzar's *recovery*, Lxx *Da.*4.30c; in *NT*, *redemption*, *Ep.Rom.*3.24, al. **-ωτικός**, ή, όν, *for ransom*, Suid. s.v. θυσία.

⊛**ἀπολύω** [v. λύω], fut. -λύσω, etc.: fut. Pass. ἀπολελύσομαι X.*Cyr.*6.2.37:—*loose from*, ἱμάντα θοῶς ἀπέλυσε κορώνης Od.21.46; ὄφρ' ἀπὸ τοίχους λῦσε κλύδων τρόπιος the sides of the ship *from* the keel, ib.12.420; *undo*, ἀπὸ κρήδεμνον ἔλυσεν ib.3.392; ἐπιδέσματα Hp.*Fract.*25. 2. *set free, release, relieve from*, ἀ. τινὰ τῆς φρουρῆς Hdt.2.30; τῆς ἐπιμελείας X.*Cyr.*8.3.47; τῶν ἐκεῖ κακῶν Pl.*R.*365a; τὴν ψυχὴν ἀπὸ τῆς τοῦ σώματος κοινωνίας Id.*Phd.*65a, cf. 67a; ἀ. τῆς μετρήσεως *save* them *from the trouble* of measuring, Arist.*Pol.*1257ᵃ40:—Pass., *to be set free*, τῶν δεινῶν, φόβου, Th.1.70, 7.56, etc. b. freq. in legal sense, ἀ. τῆς αἰτίης *acquit of* the charge, Hdt.9.88, X.*An.*6.6.15; opp. καταψηφίζω, Democr.262; τῆς εὐθύνης Ar.*V.*571: c. inf., ἀ. τινὰ μὴ φῶρα εἶναι *acquit of* being a thief, Hdt.2.174; so ἀπολύεται μὴ ἀδικεῖν Th.1.95, cf. 128: abs., *acquit*, Ar.*V.*988, 1000, Lys.20.20, etc. II. in Il. always, = ἀπολυτρόω, *release on receipt of ransom*, οὐδ' ἀπέλυσε θύγατρα καὶ οὐκ ἀπεδέξατ' ἄποινα 1.95; Ἕκτορ' ἔχει.. οὐδ' ἀπέλυσεν 24.115, al.:—Med., *set free by payment of ransom, ransom, redeem*, χαλκοῦ τε χρυσοῦ τ' ἀπολυσόμεθ' *at a price of*.., Il.22.50 (but Act. in Prose, ἀπολύειν πολλῶν χρημάτων X.*HG*4.8.21). 2. *let go, let alone, leave* one, of an illness, Hp.*Coac.*564. III. *discharge, disband* an army, ἀ. οἴκαδε X.*HG*6.5.21; generally, *dismiss, discharge*, ἐμὲ.. ἀπέλυσ' ἄδειπνον Ar.*Ach.*1155, cf. Bion 1.96. 2. *divorce* a wife, *Ev.Matt.*1.19, etc.; τὸν ἄνδρα D.S.12.18. 3. *do away with, remove*, αἰσχύνην D.20.47:—Pass., Antipho 2.1.5. 4. *discharge* or *pay* a debt, Pl.*Cra.*417b; *pay*, ἀ. τὸν χαλκόν *PTeb.*490 (i B.C.); *pay off* a mortgage, *POxy.*509.15. 5. *dismiss* a charge, εἰσαγγελία ὑπὸ τοῦ κατηγόρου ἀπολελυμένη Hyp.*Eux.*38. IV. ἀ. ἀνδράποδα Θρᾳξίν *sell*, Antipho 5.20; ἀ. οἰκίαν τινί *sell* a mortgaged house *outright*, Is.6.33. V. *deliver*, τί τινι *PFlor.*123.2 (iii A.D.):—Pass., ib.228.6 (iii A.D.). VI. *begin to count*, [μοίρας] ἀπό.. Vett.Val.135: abs., Id.19.19, Paul.Al.*Q.*2. VII. intr., *depart* (cf. B. IV, C. 2), Plb.3.69.14, al.

B. Med. with aor. 2 ἀπελύμην (in pass. sense), Opp.*C.*3.128:—*redeem*, v. supr. A. II. II. ἀπολύεσθαι διαβολάς *do away with, refute* calumnies *against one*, Th.8.87, Pl.*Ap.*37b, al.: abs., Arist.*Rh.*1416ᵇ9. 2. τὴν αἰτίαν, τὰς βλασφημίας, τὰ κατηγορημένα, Th.5.75, D.15.2, 18.4: c. gen., τῶν εἰς Ἀριστόβουλον -σασθαι J.*AJ*15.3.5. b. *refute*, τοὺς ἐναντίους λόγους Dam.*Pr.*126 ter: abs., ὁ δὲ ἀπολυόμενος ἔφη *in defence*, Hdt.8.59. III. like Act., *acquit*, τοῦ μὴ κακῶς ἔχειν ἀλλ' ὀρθῶς Pl.*Lg.*637c. 2. *release from*, τοὺς Ἕλληνας ἀ. δουλείας Id.*Mx.*245a. IV. like Pass. (C. II), *depart*, S.*Ant.*1314; also, *put off*, πνεῦμα ἀ. *AP*9.276 (Crin.); but πνεῦμα μελῶν ἀπέλυε *IG*14.607e (Carales).

C. Pass., *to be released*, ἐλπίζων τοὺς υἱέας τῆς στρατηίης ἀπολελύσθαι *from* military service, Hdt.4.84, cf. X.*Cyr.*6.2.37; τῆς ἀρχῆς ἀπολυθῆναι βουλόμενοι *to be freed from* their rule, Th.2.8; τῶν δεινῶν μηδέποτε οἴεσθαι ἀπολυθήσεσθαι Id.1.70; τῆς ὑποψίας Antipho 2.4.3; τῆς μιαρίας ib.3.11: abs., *to be acquitted*, Th.6.29; *to be absolved from*, τῶν ἀδικημάτων Pl.*Phd.*113d. II. of combatants, *to be separated, part*, οὐ ῥᾳδίως ἀπελύοντο Th.1.49; generally, *to be separated* or *detached*, ἀλλήλων or ἀπ' ἀλλήλων, Arist.*Metaph.*1031ᵇ3, *Ph.*185ᵃ28; ἀ. τὰ ᾠὰ τῆς ὑστέρας Id.*GA*754ᵇ18, al.; ἀπολελυμένος, abs., *detached*, αἰδοῖον, γλῶττα, ὄρχεις, Id.*HA*500ᵇ2, 533ᵃ27, 535ᵇ2; τὴν γλῶτταν ἀ. *having* its tongue *detached*, Id.*Fr.*319, al.; also, *distinct, differentiated*, Id.*HA*497ᵇ22. 2. *depart*, ἔθανες, ἀπελύθης, S.*Ant.*1268 (lyr.), cf. Plb.6.58.4, al., Lxx *Nu.*20.29, al.; cf. supr. B. IV. III. of a child, *to be brought forth*, Hp.*Superf.*11, cf. 24, Arist.*GA*745ᵇ11; of the mother, *to be delivered*, Hp.*Epid.*2.2.17. IV. *to be annulled*, Arist.*EN*1156ᵃ22. V. ἀπολελυμένος, η, ον, *absolute*, esp. in Gramm., D.T.636.15, A.D.*Synt.*97.20, al.: also, *general*, of meaning, Olymp.Alch.

p.72 B. VI. of metres, *irregular, without strophic responsion*, Heph.*Poëm*.5.

**ἀπολῠώρητος,** ον, *not highly esteemed*, Phld.*Oec*.p.67 J.

**ἀπολωβάω,** *dishonour*, aor. Pass. ἀπελωβήθην S.*Aj*.217 (lyr.).

**ἀπολωπίζω,** (λῶπος) = λωποδυτέω, S.*Fr*.1021.

⊛**ἀπολωτίζω,** = ἀπανθίζω, *pluck off flowers*: generally, *pluck off*, κόμας E.*IA*792; ἀ. νέους *cut off* the young, Id.*Supp*.449.

**ἀπολωφ-άω,** Ion. -έω, *appease*, Hp.*Ep*.17 (Pass.); δίψαν A.R.4.1418 (tm.). II. intr., *abate*, Procop.*Aed*.1.1, 5.5:—Subst. **-ησις,** εως, ἡ, *lightening, relief*, *An.Ox*.3.188.

**ἀπόλωψεν·** ἀπώλετο, Hsch.

**ἀπομαγ-δᾰλία** or **-ιά,** ἡ, (ἀπομάσσω) *the crumb* or *inside of the loaf*, on which the Greeks wiped their hands at dinner, and then threw it to the dogs: hence, *dog's meat*, Ar.*Eq*.415, Alciphr.3.44, Plu.*Lyc*.12. **-δᾰλίς,** ίδος, ἡ, = foreg., Eust.1857.17. ⊛**-μα,** ατος, τό, *anything used for wiping* or *cleaning*, Hp.*Medic*.2. 2. *dirt washed off*, S.*Fr*.34. II. *impression of a seal*, Thphr.*CP*6.19.5, *Lap*.67.

**ἀπομᾰδ-άω,** of the hair, *fall off*, Arist.*Mir*.$836^{a}$1. **-ίζω,** *make quite bald*, Crito ap.Gal.12.454, Sch.Ar.*Eq*.373.

**ἀπομάζιος,** (μαζός) *taken from the breast*, Opp.*C*.4.93.

**ἀπομάθημα** [ᾰθ], ατος, τό, *unlearning*, Hp.*Fract*.25.

⊛**ἀπομαίνομαι,** aor. 2 ἀπεμάνην [ᾰ], *go mad*, Luc.*DDeor*.12.1.

**ἀπομᾰκᾰρίζω·** *ebeo*, *Gloss*.

**ἀπομακ-τέον,** *one must wipe*, τὰ μέλη Aët.9.1. **-της,** ου, ὁ, *one who wipes, rubs*, or *cleans*, *Com.Adesp*.589, *AB*431; esp. in magical rites, Poll.7.188. **-τρια,** ἡ, fem. of ἀπομάκτης, Poll.7.188. **-τρον,** τό, *strickle*, Ar.*Fr*.712.

**ἀπομᾰλᾰκίζομαι,** *to be weak* or *cowardly, show weakness*, πρός τι in a thing, Arist.*HA*$613^{a}$1, cf. Plu.*Lyc*.10.

**ἀπομαλθᾰκίζομαι,** = foreg., Plu.2.1097a, prob. l. (for -όομαι) Id.*Pel*.21.

**ἀπομανθάνω,** *unlearn*, ταῦτα ἃ πρὸ τοῦ ᾤμην εἰδέναι Pl.*Phd*.96c, cf. *Prt*.342d, X.*Cyr*.4.3.14, Antisth.ap.D.L.6.7: c. inf., Plu.*Lyc*.11.

**ἀπομαντ-εία,** ἡ, *negative divination*, opp. κατα-, Jul.Laod. in *Cat.Cod.Astr*.5(1).190. **-ευμα,** ατος, τό, *divination*, v.l. in Hp.*Ep*.27. **-εύομαι,** *divine by instinct, presage*, τὸ μέλλον ἥξειν Pl.*R*.516d; τι εἶναι ib.505e; τρίτον ἀ. τι τὸ ὄν Id.*Sph*.250c, cf. Plot.5.5.12, Jul.*Or*.4.149c. **-ευτικός,** ή, όν, *of negative divination*, *PAmh*.2.14.15.

**ἀπόμαξις,** εως, ἡ, (ἀπομάσσω) *wiping off*, Plu.*Rom*.21. II. *taking an impression*: metaph., *copying, imitation*, Iamb.*Protr*.21.

**ἀπομᾰρ-αίνω,** *cause to waste away*, αἱ συλλήψεις ἀ. τὰ σώματα Sor.1.30, cf. Chor.p.22 B.; τὴν ἀκμὴν τῶν αἰσθήσεων Callistr.*Stat*.2; ἡδονὰς τὰς τὸ θυμοειδὲς -ούσας Philostr.*VA*7.4; *obliterate* from memory, Chor.*Milt*.19:—Pass., *waste, wither away, die away*, ἡ ῥητορικὴ ἐκείνη ἀ. Pl.*Tht*.177b; αἱ κατὰ τὸ σῶμα ἡδοναὶ ἀ. Id.*R*.328d; of a tranquil death, X.*Ap*.7, cf. Plu.*Num*.21; of comets, ἀπομαρανθέντες κατὰ μικρὸν ἠφανίσθησαν Arist.*Mete*.$343^{b}$16; of wind, *die down*, ib.$367^{b}$11; ἡ φύσις ἀ. Ocell.1.12, etc. **-ανσις,** εως, ἡ, *wasting* or *dying away, disappearance*, opp. φάσις, παρηλίων Thphr.*Vent*.36.

**ἀπομαρξάμενοι·** ἀπομαξάμενοι, Hsch.; cf. ὄμαρξον.

**ἀπομαρτῠρ-έω,** *testify, bear witness*, ἀ. τισὶν ὅτι εἰσὶν πολῖται *Milet*.3 No.313 (iii B.C.): c. acc. et inf., Plb.30.31.20; τι Plu.2.860c:—Pass., περὶ τούτων ἀπομεμαρτύρηται αὐτῷ ὅτι *IG*2.377.9. **-ομαι** [ῡ], *maintain stoutly*, τι Pl.*Sph*.237a.

⊛**ἀπομάσσω,** Att. **-ττω,** *wipe off*, δάκρυα χλαμύδι Plb.15.26.3, cf. Plu.*Rom*.21:—Med., *wipe off oneself*, ὕδατος ἄχνην Call.*Del*.14; τὸν κονιορτόν τισι *Ev.Luc*.10.11; *wipe*, τι *POxy*.1381.133: abs., *dry oneself*, Jul.*Or*.6.203b. 2. *wipe clean*, esp. in magical ceremonies, ἀπομάττων [αὐτοὺς] τῷ πηλῷ καὶ τοῖς πιτύροις D.18.259, cf. Luc.*Nec*.7, Hsch. s. vv. μαγίδες, μαγμόν:—Med., *wipe for oneself*, Ἀχιλλείων ἀπομάττει you *wipe your hands on* the finest bread, Ar.*Eq*.819; χεῖρας χειρομάκτρῳ ἀ. Ath.9.410b: abs., *wipe one's mouth*, Eratosth.30; of a serpent, ἀ. τὸν ἰὸν *get rid of* its poison, Arist.*Fr*.372. II. *wipe off* or *level* corn in a measure *with a strickle*: hence χοίνικα ἀ. *give scant* measure, Luc.*Nav*.25; κενεὰν ἀπομάξαι (sc. χοίνικα) *level* an empty measure, i.e. labour in vain, Theoc.15.95. III. *take an impression of*, ἔν τισι τῶν μαλακῶν σχήματα ἀ. Pl.*Ti*.50e:—Med., *model*, as a sculptor, Philostr.*VA*6.19, *APl*.4.120 (Arch. or Asclep.): metaph., *take impressions*, ὅθεν ἡμὴ φρὴν ἀπομαξαμένη Ar.*Ra*.1040; τὰς ἰδέας Gal.18(2).655; ἀ. παρ' ἀλλήλων one from another, Arist.*EN*$1172^{a}$12: generally, *copy, imitate*, D.H.*Vett.Cens*.3.2; ἤθεα ἀ. τεκούσης Nonn.*D*.46.18, cf. 48.229: c. gen., *model oneself upon*, Call.*Epigr*.27.

**ἀπομαστῑγόω,** *scourge severely*, Hdt.3.29, 8.109.

⊛**ἀπομαστίδιον,** τό, *suckling*, E.*Hyps.Fr*.64.94.

**ἀπομᾰτᾰΐζω,** *behave idly* or *unseemly*, euphem. for ἀποπέρδω, Hdt.2.162, Favor.ap.Stob.4.50.25; cf. ἀποματαιάσαι· ἐξευτελίσαι, Hsch.

**ἀπομαύρωσις,** εως, ἡ, *dullness*, διανοίας Archig.ap.Aët.6.27.

**ἀπο-μάχομαι** [μᾰ], fut. -μαχοῦμαι, *fight from* the walls of a fort or town, τεῖχος ἱκανὸν ὥστε ἀπομάχεσθαι ἐκ τοῦ ἀναγκαιοτάτου ὕψους Th.1.90; βασίλεια ἱκανὰ ἀ. high or strong enough *to fight from*, X.*Cyr*.3.1.1: abs., *fight desperately*, Id.*An*.6.2.6; πρός τι Plu.*Brut*.5, Hld.5.1; τινί *against* a thing, Plu.*Caes*.17. II. ἀ. τι *fight off* a thing, *decline* it, ἀπεμαχέσαντο τοῦτο Hdt.7.136: abs., ὁ μὲν δὴ ταῦτα λέγων ἀπεμάχετο Id.1.9; ἀ. μὴ λαβεῖν τὴν ἀρχήν D.H.2.60. III. ἀ. τινά *drive off in battle*, X.*HG*6.5.34. IV. *finish a battle, fight it out*, Lys.3.25; *resist*, Arist.*Pr*.$870^{b}$23. V. metaph., *counteract*, ταῖς ἀποφοραῖς Aët.16.24. **-μᾰχος,** ον, (μάχη) *unfit for service, disabled*, X.*An*.3.4.32, 4.1.13, Arr.*Tact*.12.4, Agath.3.22. II. *absent from the fight*, of Achilles, *AP*9.467 tit., cf. Agath.2.7.

**ἀπομεθίημι** ψυχὴν *give up* the ghost, A.R.1.280 (tm.).

**ἀπομειλίσσομαι,** Att. **-ττομαι,** *appease, allay*, θεοῦ μῆνιν D.H.1.38; πεῖναν Ph.2.477; τινά J.*AJ*19.9.2; θεούς Porph.*Marc*.2. II. *expiate*, τὰς τῶν πολλῶν ἁμαρτίας Id.*Abst*.4.5.

**ἀπομειουρ-ίζω** or **-μυουρίζω,** (μείουρος) *make to taper off to a point*, Nicom.*Ar*.2.13; of a root, Herod.Med.ap.Orib.8.4.3. ⊛**-ισμός,** ὁ, *curtailment*, Dam.*Pr*.59 (pl.).

⊛**ἀπομειόω,** *diminish*, Aët.3.162.

⊛**ἀπομείρομαι,** *distribute*, αἶσαν Hes.*Op*.578. 2. Pass., *to be parted from*, Id.*Th*.801, Arat.522:—in each place with v.l. ἀπαμείρομαι (q.v.).

**ἀπομελ-αίνομαι,** *turn black*, of grapes, Thphr.*HP*2.7.5; of cinders, Ruf.*Fr*.70.14. 2. *to be blackened by mortification*, Hp.*Art*.69. ⊛**-ανσις,** εως, ἡ, = λεύκωσις, Olymp.Alch.p.91 B.

**ἀπόμελι,** ιτος, τό, *honey-water*, an inferior kind of *mead*, Dsc.5.9. 2. = ὀξύγλυκυ, τό, Antyll.ap.Orib.5.29.8, Philagr.ib.5.17, Gal.6.274.

**ἀπομελίζω,** *enervate*, = ἀπογυιόω, Eust.641.23.

⊛**ἀπομέμφομαι,** *rebuke*, E.*Rh*.900 (lyr.); φανερῶς J.*BJ*1.24.2, Plu.2.229b (s.v.l.); τῇ ἀποτυχίᾳ Oenom.ap.Eus.*PE*5.20 (v.l.).

⊛**ἀπομένω,** dub. sens. in *PFlor*.378.6 (v A.D.); *remain behind*, Alciphr.3.60, dub. l. in Polyaen.4.6.13.

**ἀπομερίζω,** *divide off, separate*, Pl.*Plt*.304a; ἑαυτοὺς τῆς ὁμιλίας Hierocl. *in CA* 24 p.472 M.:—Pass., *to be distinguished*, ἑτέρων συγγενῶν Pl.*Plt*.280b. 2. *detail* for special service, Plb.8.30.1; πρός or ἐπί τι, Id.3.101.9, 16.21.8:—Pass., πρός τι, Id.10.16.2; ἀπομερισθῆναι ἀριστίνδην *to be selected* by merit, Pl.*Lg*.855d:—also in Act., *take as one's special province*, Bito 56.3. b. *assign a detachment to* a commander, τῆς δυνάμεώς τινι Plb.3.35.5. 3. *impart*, δεκάτην τινί J.*AJ*4.4.4. 4. *send out branches*, [ἡ ἀορτὴ] ἀ. ἑαυτῆς ἁπάσας τὰς ἀρτηρίας Gal.5.199.

⊛**ἀπομεριμνάω,** *rest from labour*: hence, *die*, Eust.821.36.

**ἀπομερισμός,** ὁ, = ἀπονομή, of water from an aqueduct, *Ephes*.2 No.18 (i A.D.), cf. Hsch. s.v. ἀπόδραγμα, al. 2. *fragmentation*, οὐ γὰρ ἀ. τοῦ παράγοντος τὸ παραγόμενον Procl.*Inst*.27. 3. *division*, τῆς ψυχῆς Herm. *in Phdr*.p.166 A. 4. *banishment*, ἐλλογίμων ἀνδρῶν *Cat.Cod.Astr*.8(3).185.25, al. 5. v.l. for ἐπιμερίζω (q.v.), Vett.Val.164.19, al.

**ἀπομερμηρίζω,** aor. -ιξα *AB*431:—*sleep off care, forget one's cares in sleep*, Ar.*V*.5, D.C.55.14.

**ἀπομεστόομαι,** Pass., *become filled to the brim*, Pl.*Phdr*.255c, Plot.2.3.18.

**ἀπομετρ-έω,** fut. Med. -ήσομαι *IG*7.3073.77 (Lebad.):—*measure off* or *out*, θριγκούς l.c.; δακτυλίους μεδίμνοις Luc.*DMort*.12.2:—Med., μεδίμνῳ ἀπομετρήσασθαι τὸ ἀργύριον X.*HG*3.2.27:—Pass., *to be measured off*, Plb.6.27.2, Str.2.1.27. II. *measure out, distribute*, X.*Oec*.10.10; σῖτόν τινι J.*AJ*2.5.7, cf. Ath.Med.ap.Orib.*Inc*.5.6. **-ημα,** ατος, τό, *servant's allowance*, *Gloss*. ⊛**-ησις,** εως, ἡ, *measuring out, distribution*, Vett.Val.346.13. **-ον,** τό, in pl., *emoluments* of a priest, *IG*$2^{2}$.1357, 1363 (Eleusis), *Leg.Sacr*.2.10 *B* 10.

**ἀπομήκης,** ες, prob. f.l. for ἐπι-, Sophon. *in de An*.75.13.

**ἀπομηκύνω,** *prolong, draw out*, λόγον Pl.*Sph*.217e, cf. *Prt*.336d, Luc.*Herm*.67, etc.: abs., *to be prolix*, Them.*Or*.2.39d, etc.:—Pass., *to be prolonged, extended*, Sor.1.57, Luc.*DMar*.1.2.

**ἀπομηνίω,** *to be very wroth, persevere in wrath*, κεῖτ' ἀπομηνίσας Ἀγαμέμνονι (where Eust. expl., *having departed from wrath* against him) Il.2.772; ἐμεῦ ἀπομηνίσαντος ib.9.426, 19.62; opp. μεθησέμεναι, Od.16.378; ἀ. εἴς τινα *PBodl.ined*.32478. II. *cease from wrath*, *AB*431, Suid.

**ἀπομηρῡκάομαι,** aor. -ήσατο, *ruminate*, Porph.*Chr*.32.

**ἀπομηρύομαι** [ῡ], *draw up from, out of*, βυθῶν Opp.*C*.1.50.

**ἀπομῑμ-έομαι,** *express by imitation, copy* or *represent faithfully*, ἦθος X.*Mem*.3.10.3; πρᾶξιν Pl.*Lg*.865b; τὴν Κλεοφῶντος πολιτείαν Aeschin.3.150; τὸ ἵεσθαι διὰ τοῦ ῑ ἀ. *endeavour to express* motion by the sound of *i*, Pl.*Cra*.427a sq.: pf. in pass. sense, Moschio ap.Ath.5.207f. **-ημα,** ατος, τό, *imitation, copy*, Hp.*Vict*.1.22, Bato Sinop.4, D.S.16.26. **-ησις,** εως, ἡ, *imitation*, Hp.*Vict*.1.10, Arist.*Rh.Al*.$1420^{b}$16, Phld.*Lib*.p.45 O., J.*AJ*3.7.7, Plu.*Num*.14.

**ἀπομιμνήσκομαι,** fut. -μνήσομαι, aor. -εμνησάμην:—*remember, recognize*: hence, *repay*, τῷ οἱ ἀπεμνήσαντο [χάριν] Il.24.428; ἀπεμνήσαντο χάριν εὐεργεσιάων *for* benefits, Hes.*Th*.503; αὐτῷ δὲ.. χάριν ἀπομνήσεσθαι ἀξίαν Th.1.137, cf. E.*Alc*.299.

**ἀπομίμνω,** *remain away from*, c. gen., παρθενικῆς Nonn.*D*.42.439.

**ἀπομῐνύθω,** = μινύθω, Orph.*L*.624.

**ἀπομίσγομαι,** *draw off and mix*, οἶνον Max.Tyr.1.5.

**ἀπομῑσέω,** = μισέω, Eratosth.*Cat*.9, Them.*Or*.15.189c.

**ἀπόμισθ-ος,** ον, *away from* (i.e. *without*) *pay, unpaid* or *underpaid*, X.*HG*6.2.16; ἄθλιοι ἀ. ξένοι D.4.46; *defrauded of pay*, Lys.*Fr*.138 S. II. *paid off, discharged*, ἀ. γίγνεται παρὰ Τιμοθέου D.23.154, cf. Aen.Tact.5.2 and 11.4; λευκή με θρὶξ ἀ. ποιεῖ *Com.Adesp*.226. **-όω,** *let out for hire*, γῆν ἐπὶ δέκα ἔτη Th.3.68; χωρίον τινί Lys.7.9; ὥσπερ.. ἀπομεμισθωκότες τὰ ὦτα Pl.*R*.475d; *farm out* by contract, *IG*1.26*a*10, al.; ἀναγραφήν *Milet*.7.69 (Didyma), etc.: c. inf., ἀ. ποιεῖν τι ὡς ἂν δύνωνται ὀλιγίστου *contract for*.., Lex ap.D.43.58.

**ἀπομιτρόω,** *take away the mitre*, Lxx *Le*.21.10, Ph.1.562.

**ἀπομνημόν-ευμα,** ατος, τό, *memorial, record*, τινός D.S.1.14, Plu.

*Pomp.*2; ἀ. σύντομον *memorandum, PSI*1.85 (iii A.D.): in pl., *memoirs*, as those of Socrates by X., D.H.*Rh.*9.12, Plu.*Cat.Ma.* 9. **-ευτις**, εως, ἡ, *recounting, summarizing*, τῶν λόγων Arist.*Top.* 164a3, cf. Plu.2.44e. II. *commemoration, BSA*17.233 (Pamphyl.). **-εύω**, *relate from memory*, Pl.*Phdr.*228a, etc.:—Pass., *to be recorded*, ἀπομνημονεύεται ὁκόστος ἐγένετο X.*Ages.*1.2. 2. *remember, call to mind*, Pl.*Plt.*268e, *Phd.*103b, *Ly.*211a, D.19.13, Aeschin.3.16, etc.; *keep in mind*, διδαχήν Pl.*Plt.*273b, al. 3. ἐπὶ τούτου τὠυτὸ οὔνομα ἀπεμνημόνευσε τῷ παιδὶ θέσθαι *gave* his son the same name *in memory of* a thing, Hdt.5.65. 4. ἀ. τινί τι *bear* something *in mind against* another, X.*Mem.*1.2.31, Aeschin.1.129, 3.208; οὐδὲ μνησίκακος· οὐ γὰρ μεγαλοψύχου τὸ ἀ. Arist.*EN*1125a 4. 5. τινί τι *bear in mind favourably*, πατρικὰς εὐεργεσίας D.*Ep.* 3.19; χάριν Luc.*Sacr.*2, *JTr.*40.

**ἀπομνησῐκᾰκέω**, *bear a grudge against*, τινί Hdt.3.49; πρός τινα Eus.Mynd.45.

**ἀπόμνῡμι** or **-ύω** (Pi.*N.*7.70), fut. -ομοῦμαι: 3 impf. ἀπώμνυ Od. 2.377:—*take an oath away from*, i.e. *swear that one will not do* a thing, ἡ δ' αὐτίκ' ἀπώμνυεν ib.10.345, cf. 12.303, 18.58; μέγαν ὅρκον ἀπόμνυ ib.2.377; ἀπώμοσα καρτερὸν ὅρκον ib.10.381. 2. *deny on oath*, Hdt.2.179, 6.63; ἀ. Ζηνὸς σέβας S.*Ph.*1289; ταῦτ' ἀ. μοι τοὺς θεούς Ar.*Nu.*1232, cf. *Eq.*424; also ἀ. τἀναντία κατὰ τῆς θυγατρὸς *swear to* the contrary *by*.., D.29.52: freq. c. μή et inf., ἀ. μὴ ὅρσαι Pi. l.c., cf. E.*Cyc.*266; τοὺς θεοὺς ἀ. ἦ μὴν μὴ εἰδέναι.. Pl.*Lg.*936e, cf. X.*Cyr.*6. 1.3; ἀ. μηδὲ ὀβολόν (sc. ἔχειν) Id.*Smp.*3.8; ἀ. ὡς οὐκ εἴρηκε D.21. 120. 3. c. acc., ἀ. υἱόν *deny, disown* a son *on oath*, And.1.127:—Med., ἀπωμόσατο τὴν ἀρχήν, = Lat. *eieravit, solemnly laid it down*, Plu.*Cic.*19. II. strengthd. for ὄμνυμι, *take a solemn oath*, ἦ μὴν .. Th.5.50 codd.

⊕**ἀπό-μοιρα**, ἡ, *portion*, σιτηρᾶς *OGI*55.15 (iii B.C.); esp. of a *revenue assigned* to the gods, τὰς καθηκούσας ἀ. τοῖς θεοῖς.. μένειν ib. 90.15 (Rosetta), cf. *PEleph.*14.3 (iii B.C.), *PRev.Laws*25.15, al., *PLond.*2.195.9 (i A.D.), etc.: generally, λαφύρων J.*AJ*6.14.6; ὀρνίθων Paus.8.22.6. b. θεία ἀ. *particle* of divinity, M.Ant.2.1. 2. *distribution* of parts of a victim, *BCH*29.524 (Delos). **-μοιράζω**, = sq., Sch.A.*Th.*727. **-μοιράομαι**, *give as a share*, J.*AJ*18.8. 7. **-μοίρια**, τά, *portion dedicated to a god*, *AP*6.187 (Alph.). **-μοιρος**, ον, *forming a branch* or *portion* of a nation, etc., Zos.3.6.

**ἀπομολῠβδόω**, *turn into lead*, Lyd.*Mens.*4.107:—also written **-μολυβδόω**, *detach by melting off the lead, Gloss.*

**ἀπομονόομαι**, Pass., *to be excluded*, τῆς ξυμβάσεως *from* the agreement, Th.3.28; ἐκ συμμείξεως Pl.*Ti.*60d. 2. *to be left alone*, ἐν πολεμίοις Plu.*Phil.*18.

**ἀπόμοργ-μα**, ατος, τό, *that which is wiped off*, Eust.218.12. **-νῦμι**, fut. -μόρξω, *wipe off* or *away from*, ἀπ' ἰχῶ χειρὸς ὀμόργνυ Il.5.416; αἷμ' ἀπομόργνυ ib.798; πεύκης ἀπὸ δάκρυ' ὀμ. v.l. in Nic.*Al.*547:—Med., *wipe off from oneself*, ἀπομορξαμένω κονίην Il.23.739; ἀπομόρξατο δάκρυ *wiped away his* tears, Od.17.304; ἀφρὸν ἀπὸ στομάτων Mosch. 2.96; abs. in same sense, ἀπομόρξασθαι Ar.*Ach.*706; ἀ. ἱδρῶτα ib. 696:—Pass., τὴν ὀργὴν ἀπομορχθεὶς *having* my anger *wiped off*, Id.*V.* 560; ἀπωμοργμένος *rubbed bare*, Arist.*Phgn.*810b3. 2. *wipe clean*, σπόγγῳ δ' ἀμφὶ πρόσωπα.. ἀπομόργνυ Il.18.414:—Med., ἀπομόρξατο χερσὶ παρειάς *wiped her* cheeks, Od.18.200.

**ἀπο-μορφόομαι**, Pass., *receive their form*, Thphr.*Fr.*171.9. II. late in Act., ἀ. τινὰ εἰς πτηνόν *change* one *into the form of*.., Eust. 1598.64. **-μορφος**, ον, *of strange form, strange*, S.*Fr.*1022. **-μόρφωσις**, εως, ἡ, *form*, Sch.Ptol.76.

**ἀπομοσία** στήλη record *of an oath, OGI*573.22 (Cilicia).

**ἀπομοτικός**, ή, όν, *of abjuration*, λόγος Simp.*in Cat.*406.9.

**ἀπόμουσος**, ον, *away from the Muses, untutored, rude*, E.*Med.* 1089. Adv., κάρτ' ἀπομούσως ἦσθα γεγραμμένος wast *unfavourably* painted, A.*Ag.*801.

**ἀπομοχλεύω**, *move as with a lever*, Hp.*Art.*70, cf. Ph.*Bel.*70.47.

**ἀπομυζ-άω**, *suck away*, Artem.5.49:—Pass., Them.*Or.*22.282c.

⊕**-ουρις**, ιδος, ἡ, obscene name of a courtesan, *Com.Adesp.*1352.

**ἀπομῡθέομαι**, *dissuade*, μάλα γάρ τοι ἔγωγε πόλλ' ἀπεμυθεόμην Il. 9.109. II. = ἀπολογέομαι, Stratt.72.

**Ἀπόμυιος**, ὁ, *Averter of flies*, epith. of Zeus and Heracles, Paus. 5.14.1, *EM*131.23.

**ἀπομῡκάομαι**, *bellow loud*, *AP*9.742 (Phil.).

**ἀπο-μυκτέον**, (ἀπομύσσομαι) *one must wipe one's nose*, E.*Cyc.* 561. **-μυκτηρίζω**, *turn up the nose at*, Hsch. s.v. ἀποσκαμυνθίζειν:—also **-μυκτίζω**, Luc.*DMeretr.*7.3 (s.v.l.).

**ἀπομυλλαίνω**, *make mouths at*, *EM*125.25; μὴ ἀπομυλλαίνῃ ἡ γνάθος, of a broken jaw, in which the fractured parts *override* each other, Hp.*Art.*33 (-σμιλ- in Gal. ad loc.).

**ἀπομυξία**, ἡ, *dirt from the nose*, *AB*432, Hsch.

**ἀπόμυξις**, εως, ἡ, *blowing one's nose*, Plu.2.1084c.

⊕**ἀπομύσσω**, Att. **-ττω**, *wipe* the nose, ῥῖνα *AP*11.268; σεαυτόν Arr.*Epict.*1.6.30:—Med., *blow one's nose*, Ar.*Eq.*910, X.*Cyr.*1.2.16, Thphr.*Char.*19.4, *AP*7.134, etc.; ὑδατώδη ἀ. Arist.*Pr.*897a31; βραχίονι, ἀγκῶνι ἀ., Plu.2.631d, D.L.4.46. II. metaph., *stop* his *drivel*, Pl.*R.*343a. 2. Pass., *to be wiped clean*, i.e. *cheated*, γέρων ἀπεμέμυκτ' ἄθλιος Men.493 (Act. in Hsch.). III. *snuff* a wick, *Com. Adesp.*847. (Cf. μυκτήρ, μύξα, Lat. *mūcus, emungo*.)

⊕**ἀπομύω**, fut. -ύσω [ῡ], *shut* the eyes *close*: hence, *die*, Call.*Epigr.* 41.

**ἀπομφολύγωτος** [ῠ], ον, *making no bubbles*, Dsc.5.99.

**ἀπομωκάομαι**, v. ἀποίζειν.

**ἀπομωλέω**, *contend*, of litigants, *Leg.Gort.*6.26.

**ἀπομωλύνομαι**, *to be absorbed, disappear*, Hp.*Epid.*7.105.

**ἀπομωρόω**, *stupefy*, Dsc.4.75:—Pass., Asclep.ap.Aët.6.16.

**ἀπόναϝε**, perh. for ἐπόνησε, *wrought*, *IG*5(1).920 (Sellasia).

**ἀπόναιο, ἀποναίατο**, v. ἀπονίναμαι.

⊕**ἀποναίω**, *remove, send away*, used by Hom. only in aor. 1, ὡς ἂν.. περικαλλέα κούρην ἂψ ἀπονάσσωσιν Il.16.86, cf. A.R.4.1492:—Med., *wend one's way back*, Δουλίχιόνδ' ἀπενάσσατο Il.2.629, cf. Od.15. 254. II. aor. Med. in trans. sense, ἀπενάσσατο παῖδα *sent away her* child, E.*IT*1260 (lyr.):—Pass., aor. ἀποնασθῆναι, *to be taken away, depart from* a place, σᾶς πατρίδος ib.175 (lyr.); πατρὸς καὶ πόλεως Id. *Med.*166.

**ἀποναρκ-άω**, *to be quite torpid*, πρὸς πόνους Plu.2.8f. **-ησις**, εως, ἡ, = ἀπονάρκωσις, Plu.2.652e. **-όομαι**, *become torpid, stupefied*, Hp.*Coac.*478, cf. *Acut.*(*Sp.*)55; ἀπονεναρκωμένος Pl.*R.*503d, Hp.*Ep.* 21. **-ωσις**, εως, ἡ, *insensibility*, Id.*Art.*46, Arist.*Pr.*875b7.

**ἀπονείφω**, *snow* or *rain down*, δρόσον Ph.2.112 (dub. l.).

**ἀπονεκρ-όω**, *destroy*, Dsc.*Eup.*1.204; esp. of cold, *benumb*, Tz.*H.*1.332:—Pass., *to be quite killed, be benumbed*, τοὺς πόδας D.S. 2.12, cf. Luc.*VH*2.1: metaph., τὸ αἰδῆμον ἀπονενέκρωται Arr.*Epict.* 4.5.21; τῆς ψυχῆς -ουμένης ib.1.5.4. **-ωσις**, εως, ἡ, *benumbing*, ibid.

**ἀπονέμ-ησις**, εως, ἡ, (ἀπονέμω) *distribution*, M.Ant.8.6, Porph. *Sent.*40, Hierocl.*in CA*7 p.430 M. II. *branch*, Gal.4.565, Orib. 22.2.6, cf. 8.62. **-ητέον**, *one must assign*, Arist.*EN*1165a18. 2. **-ητέος**, α, ον, *to be assigned*, φρόνησις ἐν -τέοις Zeno *Stoic.*1.49, Chrysipp.ib.3.72. **-ητής**, οῦ, ὁ, *distributor, Gloss.* **-ητικός**, ή, όν, *disposed to distribute*: τὸ ἀ. [ἦθος] disposition *to give every one his due*, M.Ant.1.16; ἑκάστῳ τῶν πρὸς ἀξίαν Gal.19.384; *distributive*, Asp.*in EN*158.22. Adv. -κῶς D.L.7.126. (ἀπονεμετ- is a f.l.) ⊕ **-ω**, fut. -νεμῶ Pl.*Phlb.*65b:—*portion out, impart, assign*, ἡμῖν.. ταῦτ' ἀπένειμε τύχη Simon.100; βωμοὺς καὶ ἀγάλματα θεοῖσι Hdt.2.4; τὸ πρέπον ἑκατέροις Pl.*Lg.*757c; τῷ θεῷ τοῦτο γέρας Id.*Prt.*341e; τοῖς θεοῖς χάριτας *SIG*708.33, cf. 1*Ep.Pet.*3.7; τὸ καλῶς ἀποθανεῖν ἴδιον τοῖς σπουδαίοις ἡ φύσις ἀπένειμεν Isoc.1.43; aor. imper. ἀπόνειμον *render, impart*, Pi.*I.*2.47; τῇ συγγνώμῃ πλέον ἢ τῷ δικαίῳ ἀπονέμει Din.1. 55:—Med., *assign* or *take to oneself*, τι Pl.*Sph.*267a, *Lg.*739b; ἀπονέμεσθαί τι *feed on*, Ar.*Av.*1289; ἀπονέμεσθαι τῶν πατρῴων *help oneself to a share* of.., Pl.*R.*574a:—Pass., *to be assigned*, τοῖς ἀγαθοῖς Arist. *EN*1123b35; *to be rendered*, θεῷ Porph.*Marc.*11. II. *part off, divide*, of logical division, ἐπὶ τἀναντία ἀ. τοῖς ὀνόμασι Pl.*Plt.*307b:— in Pass., ib.276d, 280d. III. Pass., *to be taken away, subtracted*, Id.*Lg.*771c, 848a.

**ἀπονένεται**· ἀποστρέφεται, Hsch.

**ἀπονενοημένως**, Adv., (ἀπονοέομαι) *desperately*, X.*HG*7.2.8, Luc. *DMort.*19.2, etc.; ἀ. ἔχειν πρὸς τὰ γεύματα to be *obstinately averse* to food, Hp.*Epid.*3.17.ιβ'; ἀ. διακεῖσθαι πρὸς τὸ ζῆν to be *recklessly indifferent* to life, Isoc.6.75.

**ἀπονέομαι**, *go away, depart*, freq. in Hom., only in pres. (sts. with fut. sense, as Il.2.113) and impf., always at the end of the line, with the first syll. long, metri gr., ἀπονέεσθαι Il. l.c., etc.; ἀπονέωνται Od. 5.27; ἀπονέοντο Il.3.313, al.

**ἀπονεοττεύω**, *hatch the young*, Arist.*HA*563a3.

**ἀπόνευμα**, ατος, τό, *slope*, Suid. s.v. ἀπόκλιμα.

**ἀπονευρ-όομαι**, Pass., *become tendinous*, Gal.2.252, etc. 2. *become a nerve*, Id.5.191. 3. ἀπονευρούμενος· ὁ τὰ νεῦρα κοπτόμενος, Hsch.; *to be unnerved*, Suid. **-ωσις**, εως, ἡ, *end of the muscle*, where it becomes *tendinous*, Gal.4.368, 13.603.

**ἀπόνευσις**, εως, ἡ, *bending* or *turning off*, *Stoic.*2.289, Them.*Or.*20. 236b. II. *dissent*, opp. κατάνευσις, Anon.*Fig.*p.179 S.

**ἀπονεύω**, *bend away from* other objects towards one, *turn off* or *incline towards*, εἰς τοὐπίσω Plb.3.79.7; σκηναὶ ἀπονενευκυῖαι πρὸς ἓν μέρος τῆς πόλεως Id.15.29.2: metaph., πρὸς τὴν γεωμετρίαν Pl.*Tht.* 165a; πρὸς τὸ δικολογεῖν Arist.*Rh.*1355a20; πρός τινα Plb.21.6.4; ἐπὶ τὴν ἁρπαγήν Id.16.6.7; ἀπὸ τοῦ ἀληθοῦς Arr.*Epict.*4.10.2. II. abs., *hang the head*, of barley, Thphr.*CP*3.22.2. III. Astron., *pass away from* a cardinal point, Vett.Val.95.1.

**ἀπονέω** (A), *unload*:—Med., *throw off a load from*, στέρνων ἀπονησαμένη (expl. by ἀποσωρεύσασα in *AB*432, Hsch.) E.*Ion*875; ἀπενήσω· ἀπέβαλες *AB*421; ἀπὸ δ' εἵματα.. νήσαντο A.R.1.364.

**ἀπονέω** (B), (ἄπονος) *to be without pain*, Hsch. s.v. ἀωδυνεῖν.

**ἀπονήμενος**, v. ἀπονίναμαι.

**ἀπονήνισι**· τιμὴν ἀποδοῦναι, Hsch.

**ἀπονηρευσία**, ἡ, (πονηρεύομαι) *innocence*, gloss on εὐήθεια, Sch.D. 2.6.

**ἀπόνηρος**, ον, (πονηρός) *not vicious, harmless*, Ptol.*Tetr.*163. 2. Medic., *not malignant*, πυρετοί Antyll.ap.Orib.5.29.8. II. (πόνηρος) *not taking pains*, c. inf., D.H.*Lys.*15.

**ἀπονηστίζομαι**, *break one's fast*, Herod.9 tit.

**ἀπονητί**, Adv. of ἀπόνητος, *without fatigue*, Hdt.3.146, E.*Fr.lyr.*3, Luc.*Rh.Pr.*8, al.

**ἀπόνητο**, v. ἀπονίναμαι.

**ἀπόνητος**, ον, *without toil* or *trouble*. Adv., Sup. ἀπονητότατα *with least toil* or *trouble*, Hdt.2.14, 7.234. 2. *without suffering*, S.*El.* 1065 (lyr.).

**ἀπονήχομαι**, *escape by swimming, swim away*, Plb.16.3.14, Luc. *Pisc.*50: metaph., τοῦ σώματος *escape from*.., Plu.2.476a; πόλεως J.*BJ*2.20.1.

**ἀπονία**, ἡ, (ἄπονος) *non-exertion, laziness*, X.*Cyr.*2.2.25, Arist.*Rh.*

1370ᵃ14 (pl.); *exemption from toil*, of women, Id.*GA*775ᵃ37, cf. Plu. *Rom*.6. II. *freedom from pain*, Epicur.*Fr*.2, Chrysipp.*Stoic*.3.33, Dsc.*Eup*.1.67, Aret.*SA*2.1, etc.

**ἀπονίζω**, later -νιπτω D.S 4.59, Plu.*Phoc*.18, and once as v.l. in Hom., v. infr.:—*wash off*, ἀπονίψαντες..βρότον ἐξ ὠτειλῶν Od.24.18), cf. Il.7.425 (tm.):—Med., *wash off from oneself*, ἱδρῶ πολλὸν ἀπονίζοντο θαλάσσῃ ib.10.572. II. *wash clean*, esp. of the hands and feet, τὴν ἀπονίζουσα φρασάμην I perceived it (the scar) *as I was washing his feet*, Od.23.75; ὅταν ἡ θυγάτηρ μ' ἀπονίζῃ καὶ τὼ πόδ' ἀλείφῃ Ar.*V*.608, cf. Men.*Georg*.60; ἓ μὲν ἔφη ἀ. τὸν παῖδα Pl.*Smp*. 175a:—Med., χρῶτ' ἀπονίπτεσθαι *wash one's* body, v.l. in Od.18.179, cf. 172; χεῖράς τε πόδας τε ib.22.478: abs., οἷον εἴ τις εἰς πηλὸν ἐμβὰς πηλῷ -νίζοιτο Heraclit.5; *wash one's hands* (esp. after meals, cf. Ar.Byz.ap.Ath.9.408f), Hp.*Mul*.1.89; ἐγὼ μὲν ἀποτρέχων ἀπονίψομαι Ar.*Av*.1163; ἀπονίψασθαι δοτέον *water to wash with*, Alex.250, cf. Antiph.136; so in pf. Pass., ἀπονενίμμεθ' Ar.*V*.1217; ἀπονενιμμένος Id.*Ec*.419; also in late Prose, v. supr.; τῆς κρήνης -νιψάμενος Alciphr.3.1; but ἀπονίψασθαι τὸ πρόσωπον ἀπὸ τᾶς κράνας *IG*4.951.63 (Epid.). 2. rarely of things, ἀ. τὴν κύλικα Pherecr.41.

**ἀπονῑκάω**, *overpower*, J.*AJ*15.3.4:—Pass., Arist.*MA*703ᵃ27.

**ἀπόνιμμα**, ατος, τό, (ἀπονίπτω) = ἀπόνιπτρον, Plu.*Sull*.36: esp. *water for purifying the dead* or *the unclean*, Clidem.(or Anticlid.)ap. Ath.9.409f, cf. 410a.

**ἀπονίνᾰμαι**, Med., fut. ἀπονήσομαι Hom.: Ep. aor. 2 without augm. ἀπονήμην, ἀπόνητο Hom.; 2 sg. opt. ἀπόναιο Il.24.556, 3 pl. ἀπο-ναίατο *h.Cer*.132, S.*El*.211 (lyr.); inf. ἀπόνασθαι A.R.2.196; part. ἀπονήμενος Od.24.30: later aor. 1 ἀπωνάμην Luc.*Am*.52, Procl.*in Alc*.p.89C.:—*have the use* or *enjoyment of* a thing, ἧς ἥβης ἀπόνητο Il. 17.25; τῶνδ' ἀπόναιο *mayest* thou *have joy of* them, ib.24.556; τιμῆς ἀπονήμενος Od. l. c.; μηδέ ποτ' ἀγλαΐας ἀποναίατο S.*El*.211: without gen., ἦγε μὲν οὐδ' ἀπόνητο married her but *had no joy* [of it], Od.11. 324; θρέψε μὲν οὐδ' ἀπόνητο ib.17.293, cf. 16.120; πόλιν κτίσας οὐκ ἀπόνητο Hdt.1.168.

**ἀπό-νιπτρον**, τό, *water used for washing, dirty water*, ἀ. ἐκχεῖν Ar. *Ach*.616. **-νίπτω**, v. ἀπονίζω.

**ἀπονίσσομαι**, *go away*, Thgn.528, A.R.3.899: aor. -νισσαμένη *AP*9.118.

**ἀπονιτρόω**, *rub off with* νίτρον (q. v.), Hp.*Ulc*.18.

**ἀπόνιψις**, εως, ἡ, *washing off* or *away*, Herod.Med.ap.Orib.*Fr*.106, prob. l. for ἄποψις in Callix.2.

**ἀπονοέομαι**, *have lost all sense*, 1. of fear, *to be desperate*, ἀπονοηθέντας διαμάχεσθαι X.*HG*6.4.23; ταῖς γνώμαις Plb.16.31.1; ἄνθρωποι ἀπονενοημένοι *desperate* men, Th.7.81, cf. X.*HG*7.5.12. 2. of shame or duty, ἀπονενοημένος *abandoned fellow*, Thphr.*Char*. 6.1, cf. Isoc.8.93, D.19.69:—later in Act., *make desperate*, J.*AJ*18. 1.6.

***ἀπόνοια**, ἡ, (νοῦς) *loss of all sense*, 1. of fear and hope, *desperation*, εἰς ἀ. καταστῆσαί τινα to make one *desperate*, Th.1.82, 7.67, cf. Nicol.Com.1.43, Plb.2.35.2, D.H.6.23. 2. of right perception, *madness*, D.18.249, 25.32, Phld.*Lib*.p.11O., *PGiss*.8.7.8 (ii A.D.), Alciphr.1.3: in pl., Plb.1.70.5. 3. *rebellion*, ἀ. καὶ στάσις Antig. ap.Heph.Astr.2.18.

**ἀπόνοιμον**· ἀπογύμνωσιν, Hsch.

**ἀπονομή**, ἡ, = ἀπονέμησις, *distribution, assignment*, τινός τινι Ph. 2.345. 2. *a portion*, Harp.

**ἀπονομίζω**, *forbid by law*, Mnaseas32.

***ἄπονος**, ον, *without toil* or *trouble*, βίος Simon.36; χάρμα Pi.*O*.10 (11).22; οἶκος A.*Pers*.862 (lyr.); τύχη S.*OC*1585; ἄ. ὕπνον εὕδεις *Eranos*13.87; ἀπονώτατος τῶν θανάτων *easiest*, Pl.*Ti*.81e; ἄ. τινι χάρις *costing* one *no trouble*, And.2.22; ἄ. τὸ εὖ πάσχειν Arist.*EN*1168ᵃ24; -ώτερον τὸ ὀξύ, in playing the flute, Thphr.*Fr*.89.6; opp. μετὰ βίας, Arist.*PA*668ᵇ19. b. *painless*, τοξικόν Str.3.4.18. 2. of persons, *work-shy, lazy*, μαλακὸς καὶ ἄ. X.*HG*3.4.19; ἄ. πρός τι Pl.*R*.556b; of the heaven, *free from the necessity of labour*, Arist.*Cael*.284ᵃ15. b. *free from pain*, Dsc.3.96, Aret.*SA*2.1; in Sup., *least painful*, Id.*CA*1. 6. 3. *relieving pain*, Id.*CD*2.12. II. Adv. -νως Hdt.9.2; ἀπόνως ἔχειν feel *easy*, of a sick person, Hp.*Prog*.23 (but with v. l. ἀποβήσσειν ἀ.); ἀπόνως λιπαροί, opp. ἐπιπόνως αὐχμηροί, X.*Mem*.2.1.31. III. irreg. Comp. ἀπονέστερος Pi.*O*.2.68; regul. Comp. -ώτερος Hp.*Art*. 79, cf. supr. Adv., Comp. -ώτερον Th.1.11.

**ἀπονοσέω**, *fall into a morbid state*, Hp *Septim*.6.

***ἀπονοστ-έω**, *return, come home*, Hom. in phrase ἂψ ἀπονοστήσειν Il.1.60, al.; ἀ. ἀπὸ τάφου Hes.*Op*.735; ἀ. ὀπίσω Hdt.4.33; ἀ. σῶς Id. 3.124, 4.76; ἀπ' ἡμων Id.1.42, al.; ἐς Σπάρτην Id.1.82; rare in Trag. and Prose, ἀπονοστήσας χθονὸς *when he returns from*.., E.*IT*731; ἀ. ἐπ' οἴκου Th.7.87; ἐκ πυρός Iamb.*Protr*.21.ι': abs., X.*An*.3.5. 16. **-ησις**, εως, ἡ, *return*, Arr.*An*.7.4.3, 7.12.1.

**ἀπονόσφι**, before a vowel -νόσφιν, Ep. Adv. *far apart, aloof*, ἀ. κατίσχεαι Il.2.233; ἀ. τραπέσθαι Od.5.350. II. c. gen., following its case, *far away from*, ἐμεῦ ἀ. ἐόντα Il.1.541; φίλων ἀ. ὀλέσθαι Od. 5.113; φίλων ἀ. ἑταίρων ib.12.33.

***ἀπονοσφίζω**, *put asunder, exclude from*, τινὰ δόμων *h.Cer*.158. 2. *bereave* or *rob of*, ὅπλων τινά S.*Ph*.979:—Pass., *to be robbed of*, ἐδωδήν *h.Merc*.562. 3. Med., *embezzle*, τὰ κοινά *OGI*515.49 (Mylasa), prob. in *SIG*37 (Teos, v B.C.). II. c. acc. loci, *flee from, shun*, S.*OT*480 (lyr.), cf. *Ichn*.131.

**ἀπονυκτερεύω**, *pass a night away from*, τοῦ στρατοπέδου Plu.*Fab*. 20: abs., Id.2.195e.

**ἀπονύμφης**, ου, ὁ, or -νυμφος, ον, = μισογύνης, Poll.3.46.

**ἀπονυστάζω**, *to be sleepy and sluggish*: metaph., Plu.*Cic*.24, cf. Arr.*Epict*.4.9.16.

**ἀπονῠχ-ίζω**, *pare the nails*, Men.996:—Med., ἀπονυχίσασθαι τὰς χεῖρας Hp.*Mul*.1.70:—Pass., *have them pared*, ἀκριβῶς ἀπωνυχισμένος *with* carefully *pared nails*, Thphr.*Char*.26.4; ὑπὸ σμίλης ἀπωνυχίσθη Babr.98.14, cf. Sor.1.69. 2. metaph., *scratch out*, τὰ σιτία Ar. *Eq*.709. II. = ὀνυχίζω III, *polish by the nail*, τὰ ῥήματα Jul.*Or*.2. 77a. III. = ἐξονυχίζω, Paul.Aeg.3.59. **-ισμα**, ατος, τό, *nail-paring*, D.L.8.17, Iamb.*Protr*.21.λβ'. ***-ιστικός**, ή, όν, *polishing to the nail*: -κή (sc. -τέχνη), ἡ, Sch.D.T.p.110H.

***ἀπονωτίζω**, *turn one's back and flee*, S.*Fr*.713; trans. in causal sense, ἀ. τινὰς φυγῇ E.*Ba*.763.

**ἀποξαίνω**, *scarify, tear*, in Pass., Lxx4*Ma*.6.6, Asclep.Jun.ap.Gal. 13.1022.

**ἀποξανᾶν**· κακοπαθεῖν, Hsch.

**ἀποξενῑτεύομαι**, *dwell away from home*, Sch.E.*Hec*.1208.

**ἀπο-ξενολογέω**, *hire for mercenary service*, J.*AJ*13.16.2; *finish recruiting*, prob. in *Vit.Philonid*.p.12C. **-ξενος**, ον, *alien to guests, inhospitable*, stronger than ἄξενος, ὅρμος S.*OT*196 (lyr.). 2. c. gen. loci, *far from* a country, τῆσδε γῆς ἀπόξενος A.*Ag*.1282, *Ch*.1042; τοῦδ' ἀ. πέδου *banished from*.., Id.*Eu*.884. ***-ξενόω**, *drive from house and home*: generally, *estrange, banish from*, εἰς βαρβάρους τινὰ τῆς Ἑλλάδος Plu.2.857e, cf. Id.*Alex*.69; *drive into exile*, τινά Id.*Phil*.13:—Pass., *live away from home*, φυγὰς ἀπεξενοῦτο S.*El*.777; γῆς ἀπεξενωμένοι E.*Hec*.1221; of troops on service, ἀ. ἔξω τῆς οἰκείας Arist.*Pol*. 1270ᵃ2; ἑτέρωσε ἀ. *migrate* to some other place, Pl.*Lg*.708b: generally, *alienate oneself from, be averse from*, τινός D.S.3.47, cf. Luc. *Dom*.2. 2. *wean*, Sor.1.117:—Pass., *become disused to*, λουτρῶν Agathin.ap.Orib.10.7.1. 3. *to be convicted of* ξενία, Is.*Fr*.46. 4. Med., *disguise oneself*, Lxx3*Ki*.14.5. II. metaph., τοῦ ποιητοῦ ἀ. τὰ ἔπη *estrange* the verses *from* him, i. e. *deny that* they *are* his, Ath. 2.49b; but in Pass., ἀπεξενωμένος *outlandish*, of words, Hdn.Gr.2. 910; μαθήματα Iamb.*VP*1.2. **-ξένωσις**, εως, ἡ, *living abroad*, Plu. *Pomp*.80. 2. *exile*, Paul.Al.*E*.2 (pl.), al. **-ξενωτέος**, α, ον, *to be rejected*, Aret.*CD*1.2.

**ἀπό-ξεσις**, εως, ἡ, *smoothing, polishing*, *SIG*244ii39 (Delph., iv B.C.). **-ξεσμα**, ατος, τό, *scraping, shred*, ἐντέρων Orib.8.26.1, cf. Eust.230.4. **-ξέω** (contr. ἀποξοῦσιν *SIG*²587, subj. ἀποξῶμεν Herod.Med.ap.Orib.10.37.17), *cut off*, ἀπὸ δ' ἔξεσε χεῖρα Il.5.81. II. *wipe, scrape*, τινὰ σπόγγοις Herod.Med. l. c. 2. *scrape off*, ἀποξέων τὸν κηρόν Luc.*Somn*.2; *scrape*, τὸ ὀστοῦν Aët.15.11. 3. metaph., ἀπέξεσας τὴν αἰδῶ τοῦ προσώπου *strip* it *off* like a mask, Alciphr.3.2, cf. Luc.*Vit.Auct*.10 (v.l. -ξυσον). III. *scrape to a point*, in pf. part. Pass. -εσμένος Hp.*Nat.Mul*.109. 2. metaph., *polish, finish off*, Eust.1.16, al.; ἀπεξεσμένος *polished, precise*, Suid.

**ἀποξηραίνω**, *dry up*, τὸ ἀρχαῖον ῥέεθρον -ξηρῆναι Hdt.2.99:—Pass., *to be dried up*, of rivers, ἀποξηρανθῆναι Id.1.75; ἀπεξηρασμένου τοῦ.. ῥεέθρου ib.186, cf. 7.109. 2. generally, *dry completely*, τὰς ναῦς *lay* them *up*, Th.7.12:—Pass., ἀπεξηραμμένα κρεάδια Alex.124.11, cf. Thphr.*HP*8.11.3.

**ἀποξίννυται**, v. ἀποζίννυται.

**ἀποξῐφίζομαι**, = ἀπορχέομαι, *AB*432: but ἀπεξίφισται· ἀποδεδοκίμασται, Hsch.

**ἀποξῠλίζω**, *deprive of its woody fibre*, κράμβην Arist.*Pr*.873ᵇ4 (v.l. ἀποχυλίζοντες).

***ἀποξῠλόομαι**, *become hard like wood*, *Gp*.17.2.1, 19.2.5.

**ἀποξύνω**, *bring to a point, make taper*, ἀποξύνουσιν ἐρετμά Od.6. 269, cf. 9.326, Luc.*DMar*.2.2:—Pass., Thphr.*Ign*.52: pf. part. ἀπωξυμμένος or -υσμένος, Plb.18.18.13, 1.22.7; ὦτα -ξυσμένα Gal.7. 30. II. *make sharp and piercing*, τὴν φωνήν Plu.*TG*2. b. *intensify*, θερμότητα Id.2.695d. III. *make sour*, [τὴν τροφήν] Hp. *Vict*.3.76, cf. Asclep.Jun.ap.Gal.13.164:—Pass., Sor.1.107.

**ἀποξῠρ-άω** or -έω, *shave clean*, c. dupl. acc., τὸν δοῦλον ἀποξυρήσας τὴν κεφαλὴν Hdt.5.35; ἀποξυρεῖν ταδί Ar.*Th*.215; ἀπεξύρησε ib.1043; τὴν κόμην ἀπεξύρησε Luc.*Sacr*.15:—Pass., τὰς κεφαλὰς ἀπεξυρημένοι Polyaen.7.35.1. **-ησις**, εως, ἡ, *shaving off*, τριχῶν Orib.46.8.1. **-ίζω**, *scalp*, Sch.E.*Tr*.1026. **-ος**, ον, (ξυρόν) *cut sharp off, abrupt, sheer*, πέτραι Luc.*Rh.Pr*.7, *Prom*.1, cf. *Peripl.M.Rubr*.40. **-ω**, = ἀποξυράω, aor. part. -ξύρας Polyaen.1.24:—Med., -ξυράμενος *get shaved*, ibid., cf. Plu.*Oth*.2:—Pass., opp. κείρεσθαι, D.C.57.10.

**ἄποξυς**, υ, *tapering*, Hp.*Art*.33, *Off*.9 (with vv. ll. ἀπόξυρα, ἀπόξηρα), Dsc.2.114, Gal.15.330.

**ἀπόξῠσις**, εως, ἡ, *sharp point*, *Gp*.10.75.11. II. *making smooth*, of stone, *IG*4.481 (Nemea).

**ἀπόξυσμα**, ατος, τό, (ἀποξύω) *that which is shaved* or *scraped off*: *shavings, filings*, Dsc.*Eup*.1.175, Sch.Ar.*Pax*48.

**ἀποξυσμός**, ὁ, *becoming acid*, Aët.9.10.

**ἀποξυστρόομαι**, Pass., *become bent* or *blunted*, Plb.2.33.3.

***ἀποξύω** [ῡ], fut. -ξύσω, = ἀποξέω, *scrape off*, τι Thphr.*HP*9.4.4; τὸν καττίτερον *IG*7.303.15 (Oropus), cf. Dsc.5.79:—Med., φάρμακον D.Chr.32.44: abs., *scrape oneself*, Plin.*HN*34.62. 2. metaph., *strip off* as it were a skin, γῆρας ἀποξύσας θήσει νέον Il.9.446, cf. Nosti *Fr*.6; κόρυζαν ἀποξύσας (prob. f.l. for ἀπομύξας) Luc.*Nav*.45; τὸ ἐρυθριᾶν ἀ. τοῦ προσώπου v.l. in Id.*Vit.Auct*.10: so in Pass., ἀπέξυσται τὴν αἰδῶ τοῦ προσώπου Alciphr.3.40:—Med., *scrape off*, φάρμακον D.Chr.32.44.

**ἀποπᾰγιόομαι**, gloss on ἀποκλεΐζομαι, Gal.15.129 (ad Hp.*Nat. Hom*.10).

**ἀποπαιδᾰγωγέω**, *lead away*, ἀπό τινος Iamb.*Protr*.21.

⊛**ἀποπαιδαριόω**, dub. sens. in *PSI*4.418.17 (iii B.C.).

**ἀπόπᾰλαι**, Adv. *from of old*; condemned by Phryn.32.

**ἀποπᾰλαιόω**, *abrogate*, dub. in Hsch.

**ἀποπάλησις**, εως, ἡ, gloss on ἐκπάλησις, read by Erot. in Hp. *Fract.*42, cf. Gal.19.84.

**ἀπο-πάλλω**, *hurl* or *cast*, βέλη Luc.*Am.*45; *radiate*, αὐγήν J. *BJ*5.5.6:—Pass., *rebound*, Epicur.*Fr.*293; ἀ. πάλιν Arist.*Pr.*$891^{a}$3, cf. Plu.*Alex.*35, S.E.*M.*10.73, etc. **–παλμός**, ὁ, *rebounding*, Epicur.*Ep.*1 p.8 U. **–παλσις**, εως, ἡ, = foreg., ib.2 p.50 U.; gloss on ἐκπάλησις, Gal.19.84; *shock*, Archig.ap.Orib.8.2.10. **–παλτικός**, ή, όν, *rebounding*. Adv. –κῶς S.E.*M.*10.223.

**ἀποπαλώσει**· ἀποπαλαιώσει, Hsch.

⊛**ἀπόπαξ**· ξύμπαν, Hsch.

**ἀποπαππόομαι**, Pass., *become pappose*, of dandelions, Thphr.*HP* 7.11.4.

**ἀποπαπταίνω**, *look about one, look round*, as if to flee, Ion. fut. ἀποπαπτανέουσιν Il.14.101.

**ἀποπάρδαξ**, ακος, ὁ, *qui crepitum ventris emittit*, Hsch. (ἀποπαρδακᾶ cod.).

**ἀποπαρθεν-εύομαι**, *lay aside virginity*, Hp.*Aër.*17:—also **–όω**, *deflower*, νεανίδα Lxx *Si.*20.4.

**ἀπόπαστος**, ον, *fasting*, Opp.*H.*1.299.

**ἀποπάσχω**, opp. πάσχω, a Stoic term, *reject an impression*, ἀπόπαθε ὅτι ἡμέρα ἐστί Arr.*Epict.*1.28.3.

**ἀποπᾰτ-έω**, fut. –ήσομαι Ar.*Pl.*1184, but –ήσω Hp.*Morb.*2.66: aor. subj. –πατήσω Ar.*Ec.*354:—*retire to ease oneself*, Cratin.49, Ar. ll. cc., M.Ant.10.19, D.C.78.5, etc. II. *pass with the excrement, void*, τι Ar.*Ec.*351. **–ημα**, ατος, τό, *dung*, ἀλώπεκος Eup.284, cf. Ael. *NA*3.26. **–ησις**, εως, ἡ, *going to stool*, Gal.15.607. **–ητέον**, *one must ease oneself*, Ar.*Ec.*326. **–ος**, ὁ (ἡ only in Greg.Cor. p.521 S.) *ordure*, Hp.*Prorrh.*2.4, Plu.2.727e, Luc.*Trag.*168. 2. = ἄφοδος, *privy*, Ar.*Ach.*81, Poll.10.44.

**ἀπό-παυσις**, εως, ἡ, (from Med.) *cessation* of an attack, Aret.*SA* 1.5. **–παύστωρ**, ορος, ὁ, = ἀποπαύων, Orph.*H.*39.3. **–παύω**, *stop* or *hinder from, make to cease from*, τοὺς μὲν.. εἴασαν ἐπεὶ πολέμου ἀπέπαυσαν Il.11.323; πένθεος ἀ. τινά Hdt.1.46; ἐρώτων S.*Aj.*1205 (lyr.); λόγου δέ σε μακροῦ 'ποπαύσω E.*Supp.*639: c. inf., *hinder* from doing, ἀ. τινὰ ἀλητεύειν, ὁρμηθῆναι, Od.18.114, 12.126:—Med. and Pass., *leave off, cease from*, c. gen., πολέμου δ' ἀποπαύεο πάμπαν Il.1.422, cf. 8.473; ἀοιδῆς Od.1.340; τοῦ δάκνειν X.*Cyr.*7.5.62; ἐκ καμάτων S.*El.*231 (lyr.): abs., *leave off*, opp. ἄρχεσθαι, Thgn.2; *terminate*, Arat.51. 2. c. acc., *stop, check*, νὺξ ἀπέπαυσε.. Πηλεΐωνα Il. 18.267; Ἀλκμήνης δ' ἀ. τόκον 19.119, al.; so ἀ. κῶμον Thgn.829; μερίμνας E.*Ba.*381 (lyr.); ὠδῖνα Pl.*Tht.*151a, etc. II. intr. in Act., ἀπόπαυσον *stop! cease!* E.*Fr.*118; οὐκ ἀπὸ πυγμαχίης ἀποπαύσετε; *AP*9.217 (Scaev.).

**ἀποπεῖν**· ἀπελθεῖν, Hsch.

**ἀπό-πειρα**, ἡ, *trial, venture*, ἀ. ποιεῖσθαι τῆς μάχης make *trial* of their way of fighting, Hdt.8.9; ναυμαχίας ἀ. λαμβάνειν Th.7.21; δοῦναι ἀ. εὐσεβείας give *proof* of it, Ph.1.650. **–πειράζω**, *make trial of, prove*, ἀ. εἰ.. Arist.*Mir.*$831^{a}$29. 2. *make an attempt upon*, Μεγάρων App.*Pun.*117. ⊛**–πειράομαι**, fut. –άσομαι [ᾱ]: aor. Pass. ἀπεπειράθην, Ion. –ήθην, v. infr.:—*make trial* or *proof of*.., τῶν μαντηΐων, τῶν δορυφόρων, Hdt.1.46, 3.128; ἀ. ἑκάστου εἰ ναυμαχίην ποιέοιτο Id.8.67, cf. 9.21; ἀ. γνώμης [ἑκάστου] Id.3.119; τῆς γνώμης ἀποπειρῶ Ar.*Nu.*477, cf. And.1.105; ἀ. τινὸς εἰ δύναιτο ἀληθεύειν X. *Cyr.*7.2.17, cf. 2.3.5; ναυμαχίας ἀποπειρᾶσθαι *to venture* it, Th.4.24: abs., ἐπεὰν ἀποπειρηθῇ Hdt.2.73; freq. in Pl., to express the dialectical *trial* of an opponent, *Prt.*311b, 349c, al. II. Act., esp. in Th., τῆς Καρχηδονίων ἀρχῆς καὶ αὐτῶν ἀποπειράσοντες 6.90; ὅπως ναυμαχίας ἀποπειράσωσι 7.17; ἀποπειρᾶσαι τοῦ Πειραιῶς *make an attempt on* the Piraeus, etc., 2.93, cf. 4.121: abs., κατὰ γῆν ἀ. 4.107, cf. 7.36; τῶν τειχῶν App.*BC*5.36, etc. **–πειρᾱτέον**, *one must make trial of*, τῶν λόγων Isoc.9.11, cf. Gal.10.376.

⊛**ἀποπέκω**, *shear off* wool:—Pass., ἀποπέπεκται Hsch.:—Med., ἀπὸ χαίταν πέξηται *comb* her hair, Call.*Lav.Pall.*32, cf. *AP*6.155 (Theodorid.).

**ἀποπελεκ-άω**, *hew* or *trim with an axe*, Ar.*Av.*1156, Thphr.*HP* 5.5.6:—also **–ίζω**, *AB*438. **–ημα**, ατος, τό, *chip*, Hsch. s.v. λατύπη.

**ἀποπελιόομαι**, (πελιός) *become livid*, Hp.*Acut.*(*Sp.*)9.

⊛**ἀποπεμπτικός**, ή, όν, *valedictory*, ὕμνοι Men.Rh.p.336 S.

⊛**ἀπόπεμπτος**, ον, *dismissed*, dub. in *PPetr.*2 p.52 (iii B.C.); cf. Hsch.

**ἀποπεμπτόω**, *give a fifth part of*, τι Lxx *Ge.*47.26. II. *take a fifth part of*, ib.41.34.

**ἀποπέμπω**, *send off* or *away, dispatch, dismiss*, Il.21.452, Od.24. 312, al.; τῷ κε τάχα στυγερῶς μιν ἐγὼν ἀπέπεμψα νέεσθαι 23.23; ἐπί τι, ἔς τι, for a purpose, Hdt.1.38, 47; ἀ. τοὺς πρέσβεις *dismiss* them, Th.5.42, cf. Ar.*Nu.*1244; ἀ. ἀσινέας Hdt.7.146:—Med., *send away from oneself*, τὸν παῖδα ἐξ ὀφθαλμῶν ἀ. Id.1.120; ἀ. τὴν γυναῖκα *put away, divorce* her, Id.6.63 (so in Act., D.59.52, Men.994); ἀ. τὰς ναῦς ὁμολογίᾳ *get rid of*.., Th.3.4; ἀ. ἡδονὴν *get rid of* it, Arist.*EN*$1109^{b}$11; *send from home*, A.*Pers.*137. II. of things, *send back*, Od. 17.76; ἀ. ἐξοπίσω Hes.*Op.*87. 2. *send off, dispatch*, ἀναθήματα ἐς Δελφούς Hdt.1.51; *export*, τἀπόρρητα Ar.*Ra.*362:—so in Med., X. *Vect.*1.7. 3. Med., *get rid of*, τὸ ὕδωρ Hdt.2.25. 4. *emit, discharge*, Pl.*Ti.*33c. 5. Med., *avert* by sacrifice, etc., ἔννυχον ὄψιν E.*Hec.*72 (lyr.), cf. Orph.*H.*39.9; *banish, exorcise* disease, αἶγας ἐς ἀγριάδας τὴν ἀποπεμπόμεθα Call.*Aet.*3.1.13.

**ἀπόπεμψις**, εως, ἡ, *sending away, dispatching*, τῶν κατασκόπων Hdt 7.148. 2. *dismissal, divorcing*, D.59.59; δίκη ἀποπέμψεως Lys. *Fr.*307 S.

**ἀποπενθέω**, *mourn for*, τινά Plu.*Cor.*39.

**ἀποπεραίνω**, *complete, finish*, in fut. ἀποπερᾰνῶ, Hsch.

**ἀπο-περαιόω**, *terminate*, Ammon.*in Int.*54.29. **–περᾰτίζω**, = foreg., Sch.Ar.*Nu.*1454. **–περᾰτόω**, = foreg., Porph.*in Cat.* 132.33, Sch.Ar.*Th.*1033:—freq. in Pass., –οῦσθαι εἴς τι Hierocl. *in CA*26 p.478 M., Paul.Aeg.6.77, Steph.*in Hp.*1.188 D., al.; ἔν τινι Phlp.*in Mete.*31.1. **–περάτωσις**, εως, ἡ, *termination* of a fistula, Antyll.ap.Orib.44.22.9, Paul.Aeg.6.77: generally, *completion, end*, Syrian.*in Metaph.*49.29; *final term*, Procl.*Inst.*147 (pl.), Dam.*Pr.* 114, al.

**ἀποπεράω**, *carry over*, Plu.*Pomp.*62, *Mar.*37, al.

**ἀποπέρδομαι**, fut. –παρδήσομαι Ar.*Ra.*10: aor. Act. –έπαρδον Id. *Eq.*639, *Pl.*699, etc.:—*break wind*, Ar. ll. cc., etc.: metaph., ἀνὴρ ἀποπέρδεται ἵππον, i. e. *desinit in equum*, of a Centaur, *APl.*4.115.

**ἀποπερισπάω**, *draw off, divert*, τὴν διάνοιαν Sor.1.117, cf. Sch.Ar. *Nu.*721.

**ἀποπερκόομαι**, (πέρκος) *colour*, of ripening grapes, S.*Fr.*255.6.

**ἀποπέρνημι**, *sell*, Aeol. aor. subjunct. ἀποπεράσσει Schwyzer 646. 13 (Cyme, ii B.C.): Ion. aor. inf. ἀποπεράσαι *GDI*5533*f* 2 (Zelea); 3 pl. ἀπεπέρασαν *SIG*45.32 (Halic., v B.C.).

**ἀποπερονάω**, *fix with a buckle* or *pin*, Hp.*Mochl.*5:—Pass., πρὸς τοὺς παραστάτας Ph.*Bel.*66.43.

**ἀποπετάννῡμι**, *spread out*, τρίβωνα D.L.6.77:—also **ἀποπετάζω**, Aq.*Ex.*5.4, al.

**ἀποπέτομαι**, fut. –πετήσομαι Ar.*Pax*1126: aor. ἀπεπτάμην, part. –πτάμενος, inf. –πτάσθαι Hdt.7.13: also ἀπεπτόμην Ar.*Av.*90; aor. 2 ἀπέπτην, 3 pl. ἀπέπταν Emp.2.4; inf. ἀποπτῆναι *AP*5.211 (Mel.):—*fly off* or *away*, esp. of dreams, ᾤχετ' ἀποπτάμενος Il.2.71; ψυχὴ δ' ἠΰτ' ὄνειρος ἀποπταμένη πεπότηται Od.11.222; ἀπέπτετο Ar.*Av.*90; ἐς τἀπὶ Θρᾴκης ἀποπέτου ib.1369; οἴχεται ἀποπτάμενος Pl.*Smp.*183e; συχνὸν ἀποπτάς Arist.*HA*$619^{a}$32; ψυχῆς ἐκ μελέων ἀποπταθείσης *IG* 9(1).883.6 (Corcyra).

**ἀποπεφασμένως**, Adv., (ἀποφαίνω) *openly, clearly, plainly*, D.59.67.

**ἀποπήγνῡμι**, *make to freeze, freeze*, τἀντικνήμια Ar.*Ra.*126:—Pass., of men, *to be frozen*, in fut. –πᾰγήσομαι X.*Mem.*4.3.8. 2. of blood, *congeal*, Hp.*Morb.Sacr.*9:—Pass., X.*An.*5.8.15.

**ἀποπηδ-άω**, *leap off*, esp. of riders, *dismount*, Plu.*Fab.*16, Jul.*Or.* 2.60a, etc. II. *start off from, turn away from*, ἀπό τινος Hp.*Art.* 47; ἀ. ἀπὸ τῆς φύσιος *from* its natural position, of a joint, ib.61; metaph., ἀπὸ τοῦ λόγου Pl.*Tht.*164c; Σωκράτους X.*Mem.*1.2.16: abs., *leap off*, Pl.*R.*613b; *stalk off*, οἴχεται ἀποπηδήσας πρὸς ἄλλον Id.*Lg.* 720c; ἐς τὰ Περσῶν ἤθη Procop.*Goth.*1.24. 2. *rebound*, Arist. *Aud.*$803^{b}$1, Ph.1.610. **–ησις**, εως, ἡ, *leaping off*, Plu.2.769f.

**ἀποπηλώσειν**· ἀποπηδώσειν, Hsch.

**ἀποπηνίζομαι**, *become unwound, unrolled*, Thphr.*HP*8.10.4.

**ἀποπήσσω**, late form for ἀποπήγνυμι, *benumb*, τὸν νοῦν Herm.ap. Stob.1.49.45.

**ἀποπῑδύω**, *ooze out, spread*, Hp.*Nat.Puer.*21.

**ἀπο-πῐέζω**, *squeeze out*, τὸ αἷμα ἐκ.. Arist.*Pr.*$889^{b}$28. II. *squeeze tight*, Hp.*Aph.*5.46, al.; *press outwards* or *away from* a spot, Id. *Fract.*30:—Pass., ὅταν [οἱ πόδες] ἀποπιεσθῶσιν ἀπὸ καθέδρας Thphr.*Fr.* 11:—also **–πῐάζω**, Lxx *Jd.*6.38, Archig.ap.Orib.8.1.21. **–πίεσις** [πῐ], εως, ἡ, *squeezing* or *wringing out*, Thphr.*Ign.*11, cf. Archig.ap. Gal.8.110. ⊛**–πίεσμα** [ῐ], ατος, τό, *pressure outwards* or *off*, used of rods slightly bent, Hp.*Fract.*30.

**ἀποπιμπλάνω**, rare form of sq., Agath.5.21.

⊛**ἀποπίμπλημι**, later **–πιμπλάω**: poet. also **ἀποπίπλημι, –άω**:—*fill up* a number, τὰς τετρακοσίας μυριάδας Hdt.7.29. II. *satisfy, fulfil*, in Pass., ἀποπλησθῆναι τὸν χρησμόν Id.8.96. 2. *satisfy, appease*, ἀ. αὐτοῦ τὸν θυμόν Id.2.129, cf. Th.7.68; ἀ. τὰς ἐπιθυμίας Pl. *Grg.*492a, al. 3. *satisfy* an inquirer, τινά Id.*Cra.*413b.

**ἀποπίμπρημι**, only in aor. ἀπέπρησεν· ἀπεδάκρυσεν, ἀπεφύσησεν, ἀπέμαρεν, Hsch.

**ἀποπῑνόω**, *dirty, soil*, prob. l. for ἀπινοῦται, Hsch.

**ἀποπίνω** [ῑ], *drink up, drink off*, Hdt.4.70; ὅσον ἂν ἀποπίῃ Critias 33: abs., Philostr.*Ep.*60.

**ἀποπιπράσκω**, *sell off*, ξύλων τῶν ἀποπραθέντων *BCH*6.20 (Delos, ii B.C.).

**ἀποπίπτω**, *fall off from*, ἐκ πέτρης Od.24.7; ἀπὸ τῶν φιαλέων Hdt. 3.130; τοῦ κολεοῦ ἀ. ὁ μύκης ib.64, cf. Hecat.22 J.; ἀ. τῶν ἵππων *slip off*, Plb.11.21.3. 2. abs., *fall off*, στιλπναὶ δ' ἀπέπιπτον ἔερσαι Il. 14.351, cf. Th.4.4, Arist.*HA*$557^{b}$29. II. *miss* or *fail in obtaining*, τῆς ἐλπίδος ἀ. Plb.9.7.1; τἀγαθοῦ Procl.*Inst.*13; *fail to record, let slip*, τῶν ἀναγκαιοτέρων D.S.13.84: abs., *to be disappointed, fail*, Plb.4.36. 5, *UPZ*70.27 (ii B.C.).

**ἀπόπισθεν**, *from behind*, better divisim, Sch.E.*Hec.*900.

**ἀποπιστεύω**, *trust mistakenly*, τοῖς ἐπιπέδοις Plb.3.71.2, cf. $12.26^{d}$.4, J.*AJ*15.7.6; τοῖς ἰδίοις λογισμοῖς (opp. τῷ θεῷ πεπιστευκέναι) Ph. 1.132, cf. Gal.8.90. 2. *confide strongly in*, τῇ τῶν ἰδεῶν ὑποθέσει Procl.*in Prm.*p.480 S.

**ἀποπλάζω**, *lead away from*, ἀοιδῆς A.R.1.1220, cf. Hsch.:—Pass., only aor., *stray away from*, πολλὸν ἀπεπλάγχθης σῆς πατρίδος Od. 15.382; Τροίηθεν 9.259; ἀπὸ θώρηκος.. πολλὸν ἀποπλαγχθεὶς [ὀϊστός] *glancing off* the hauberk, Il.13.592; –πλαγχθέντες ἑταίρων Theoc.22. 35; τῆλε δ' ἀπεπλάγχθη σάκεος δόρυ Il.22.291: abs., *wander*, Od.8.573; *to be separated*, Emp.22.3; τρυφάλεια ἀποπλαγχθεῖσα a helm *struck off*, *falling from the head*, Il.13.578:—also ἀποπλασθεῖσα· ἀποκρουσθεῖσα, Hsch.

**ἀποπλᾰν-άω**, fut. -ήσω, *lead astray, make to digress*, λόγον Hp. *Art.*34, Luc.*Anach.*21; ἀ. τινὰ ἀπὸ τῆς ὑποθέσεως Aeschin.3.176:—Pass., *wander away from*, τῆς ὑποθέσεως Isoc.7.77: abs., of leaderless wasps, Arist.*HA* 554$^{b}$23; *wander from the truth*, Alex.Aphr. *in Metaph.*139.12, Chrysipp.*Stoic.*3.33. II. *distribute*, in Pass., ἀποπλανᾶται ἐς πάντα αἷμα καὶ πνεῦμα Hp.*Alim.*33. III. metaph., *seduce, beguile*, τοὺς ἐκλεκτούς *Ev.Marc.*13.22. **-ημα**, ατος, τό, *deception*, Hsch., Suid. s.vv. ἀπαιόλημα, αἰόλημα. **-ησις**, εως, ἡ, *digression*, Pl.*Plt.*263c, Licymn.ap.Arist.*Rh.*1414$^{b}$17. II. *wandering*, Lxx *Si.*31(34).11. **-ίας**, ου, ὁ, *a wanderer, fugitive*, *AP*9.240 (Phil.), 548 (Bianor). ※**-ος**, ὁ, *fallacy*, Cratin.Jun.7. 2. *impostor*, Hsch.

**ἀποπλάσσομαι**, Med., fut. -πλάσομαι, aor. -πλασάμην: —*model* or *mould from* a thing: hence, *represent, model, portray*, Plu.*Aem.*28, *AP*5.14 (Rufin.), 7.34 (Antip. Sid.), etc.; ἀ. πρᾶξιν Call.*Fr.*194.

**ἀποπλάστωρ**, ορος, ὁ, *copier*, Man.4.343.

**ἀποπλέκω**, *separate*, Pass., συμπλέκονται τὰ πάντα καὶ -ονται Zos. Alch.p.110 B.: esp. in pf. part. -πεπλεγμένος, η, ον, *divorced, separated*, γυνή *PGen.*19.3 (ii A.D.); ἀνήρ *BGU*1118 ii 11 (ii A.D.).

**ἀποπλευστέον**, *one must sail away*, Ar.*Fr.*142.

**ἀποπλέω**, Ep. -πλείω, Ion. -πλώω v.l. in Hdt.4.156,157, cf. Arr. *Ind.*26.9: fut. -πλεύσομαι Hdt.4.147; -πλευσοῦμαι Pl.*Hp.Mi.*371b:—*sail away, sail off*, οἴκαδ' ἀποπλείειν Il.9.418, etc.; ἐπ' Αἰγύπτου Hdt. 1.1, cf. Ar.*Ra.*1480; ὀπίσω ἀ. Hdt.4.156; ἐκ τῆς Σικελίας ὡς ἐς τὰς Ἀθήνας Th.6.61; ἐπ' οἴκου Id.1.55.

**ἀπο-πληγία**, ἡ, = ἀποπληξία, Gal.16.672. **-πληκτεύομαι**, *to be senseless*, Phld.*Po.*2.40. **-πληκτικός**, ή, όν, *paralysed*, ἀ. τὰ δεξιά, τὰ ἀριστερά, Hp.*Coac.*467, cf. Arist.*Rh.*1411$^{a}$21; τὰ ἐξαίφνης ἀ. *apoplectic seizures*, Hp.*Coac.*470; τὰ ἀ. νοσήματα Arist.*Pr.*954$^{b}$30. **-πληκτος**, ον, (ἀποπλήσσω) *disabled by a stroke*, 1. in mind, *struck dumb, astounded*, Hdt.2.173, cf. S.*Ph.*731; ἀ. ποδί Id. *Fr.*248; *senseless*, οὐχ οὕτως ἄφρων οὐδ' ἀ. D.21.143, cf. Men.*Epit.* 344, Phld.*Ir.*p.82 W., D.Chr.11.100; ἀ. καὶ παντελῶς μαινόμενος D. 34.16; ὁ νυνὶ ποεῖς ἀ. ἐστι Men.*Pk.*246; -ότερος μῦθος D.Chr.11. 54. 2. in body, *paralysed, crippled*, Hdt.1.167, Pl.Com.130; ἀ. τὰς γνάθους *struck dumb*, Ar.*V.*948. 3. Medic., *stricken with paralysis*, Hp.*Aph.*6.57; μέρος *paralysed*, Id.*Flat.*13; so σκέλος Id.ap. Aret.*SD*1.7; ἀπόπληκτοι *cases of apoplexy*, Id.*Aph.*3.16. **-πληκτώδης**, ες, = ἀπόπληκτος, Gal.19.110. **-πληξία**, Ion. -ίη, ἡ, *madness*, Phld.*Rh.*1.145 S., *Vit.*p.7 J.; μάντεων Phleg.*Mir.*2. 2. of body, *apoplexy*, Hp.*Aph.*2.42, Aret.*SD*1.7; ἀ. μέρους *paralysis*, Arist.*Pr.*905$^{a}$17: in pl., ib.860$^{a}$33, al. **-πλήξιος**, ον, *apoplectic*, πυρετός Alex.Aphr.*Pr.*2.42 (s.v.l.). **-πληξις**, εως, ἡ, = ἀποπληξία, σώματος Hp.*Aph.*6.56.

※**ἀποπληρ-όω**, = ἀποπίμπλημι, *fill up*, Hp.*Art.*45 (in irreg. form -πληρέουσιν), *VM*22. 2. *satisfy*, τὰς βουλήσεις, τὰς ἐπιθυμίας, Pl. *R.*426c, *Lg.*782e; *satisfy* an inquirer, κἀμὲ τάχ' ἂν ἀποπληρώσαις ὡς .. Id.*Chrm.*169c, cf. *Plt.*286a; τοῦτό μοι ἐν τῇ ψυχῇ ἀποπλήρωσον *make* this *complete* for me, *satisfy* me in this, Id.*Prt.*329c:—Pass., Arist.*Rh.*1369$^{b}$14. II. *complete*, ἑβδομήκοντα ἔτη *PFlor.*382.10 (iii A.D.). III. *discharge* a function, ib.2.23 (iii A.D.). 2. *pay* a debt, Hsch. s.v. ἐκτετικότας. 3. *fulfil* a promise, Hdn.2.7.1.—Prose word, also in E.*Oen.*4.6 A. (Pass.). **-ωματικός**, ή, όν, = -ωτικός, δύναμις Iamb.*Myst.*3.10. ※**-ωσις**, εως, ἡ, *filling, satisfying*, Plu.2.48c, Porph.*Abst.*3.18, Jul.*Or.*4.144d. 2. *accomplishment, fulfilment*, ἐνέργεια ἡ τοῦ οἰκείου ἔργου ἀ. Dam.*Pr.*64, cf. Iamb.*Myst.* 5.26, al. **-ωτής**, οῦ, ὁ, *one who completes* or *fulfils*, τῶν αἱρεθέντων Pl.*R.*620e, cf. Jul.*Or.*2.90c, Iamb.*Myst.*5.10, al. **-ωτικός**, ή, όν, *completing, fulfilling*, Jul.*Or.*4.137b; τῶν εὐχῶν Iamb.*Myst.*5.26; *supplying with content*, τὸ νοητὸν -κὸν τοῦ νοῦ Dam.*Pr.*70.

**ἀποπλήσσω**, Att. -ττω, *cripple by a stroke, disable in body* or *mind*: —Pass., *lose one's senses, become dizzy* or *astounded*, S.*Ant.*1189. 2. Med., *push off from oneself*, Arist.*Pr.*899$^{b}$24.

**ἀποπλίσσομαι**, *trot off*, Ar.*Ach.*218.

**ἀπόπλοια**, ἡ, = ἀπόπλους (A), Lib.*Eth.*4.1.

※**ἀποπλοκή**, ἡ, *chemical separation*, opp. συμπλοκή, Zos.Alch.p.110 B.

**ἀποπλοκίαι**· ἐμπλοκαί (Lacon.), Hsch.

※**ἀπόπλοος** (A), contr. **-πλους**, ὁ, *sailing away*, ἐνθεῦτεν Hdt.8.79, Arist.*Po.*1454$^{b}$2. 2. *voyage home* or *back*, X.*An.*5.6.20; of the Greeks at Troy, Arist.*Po.*1457$^{b}$7.

**ἀπόπλοος** (B), ον, contr. **-πλους**, ουν, *starting on a voyage*, *AP*5. 177 (Mel.). II. *unseaworthy*, Hsch.

**ἀπό-πλῠμα**, ατος, τό, *water in which anything has been diluted* or *dissolved*, ἀ. κηρίων *mead*, ἀ. τιτάνου *lime-water*, D.S.5.26,28; κρεῶν Sor.1.59. **-πλυνσις**, εως, ἡ, *cleansing*, Sophon.*in de An.*96. 2. **-πλύνω** [ῡ], fut. -ῠνῶ, *wash well, wash away*, λαΐγγας.. ἀποπλύνεσκε θάλασσα Od.6.95; τὸ περὶ τὴν γλῶτταν Pl.*Ti.*65d; τὰς χεῖρας Ath.9.409c; τινὰ βαφῆς ἀτόπου Philostr.*VA*8.22. 2. *wash away*, Arist.*Sens.*443$^{b}$7 (Pass.). ※**-πλῠσις**, εως, ἡ, *washing away*, Alex. Aphr. *in Sens.*94.13. **-πλῠτέον**, *one must wash, cleanse*, *Gp.*16. 18.2.

**ἀποπλώω**, Ion. for -πλέω: **ἀποπνείω**, Ion. for -πνέω.

**ἀποπνευματ-ίζω**, *breathe out, expire*, in Pass., Hsch. s.v. ἀπεψύχη: also, = ἀποπέρδω, Sch.Ar.*Pax*891. **-ισμός**, ὁ, Hsch. s.v. πετραδεῖλαι. **-ωσις**, εως, ἡ, = foreg., Eust.866.18. **-ος**, ον, *away from the wind, sheltered*, Thphr.*Vent.*30.

※**ἀποπνέω**, Ep. -πνείω (as always in Hom.), fut. -πνεύσομαι, later -πνεύσω *Gp.*2.21.3:—*breathe forth*, of the Chimaera, δεινὸν ἀποπνείουσα πυρὸς μένος Il.6.182; [φῶκαι] πικρὸν ἀποπνείουσαι ἁλὸς.. ὀδμήν Od.4.406; ἀ. ἔπος στόματος Pi.*P.*4.11; θυμὸν ἀποπνείων *giving up* the ghost, Il.4.524; so without θυμόν, Batr.99, Nic.Dam.p.61 D., Phleg.*Mir.*3; ἀ. ψυχήν Simon.52; ἡλικίαν Id.115, Pi.*I.*7(6).34; ἀ. τὴν δυσμένειαν *to blow* it *off, get rid of* it, Plu.*Them.*22:—Pass., ἀποπνεῖται ἡ ἀτμίς Arist.*Pr.*937$^{a}$7. b. causal in Pi.*N.*1.47 χρόνος ἀπέπνευσεν ψυχάς *made* them *give up* the ghost. 2. *breathe hard, take breath*, Arist.*HA*587$^{a}$5; *exhale, evaporate*, ψυχὰς ὥσπερ ὁμίχλας ἀποπνεούσας τῶν σωμάτων Plu.2.560c. 3. in Com., = ἀποπέρδω, *AB*439. II. *smell of a thing*, c. gen., Luc.*Hist.Conscr.*15; χθιζῆς μέθης Plu.2.13f; but also τοῖον ἀπέπνεε λείψανα so they *smelt*, A.R. 2.193; τοῦ χρωτὸς ἥδιστον ἀ. Plu.*Alex.*4; ἀ. τι τοιοῦτον Id.2. 695e. 2. *exhale* (*and so lose*) *the scent*, Thphr.*HP*9.16.2, cf. Plu. 2.692c; τὸ βρομῶδες ib.791b. III. *blow from* a particular quarter, αὔρη οὐκ ἀ. ἀπὸ θερμῶν χωρέων Hdt.2.27, cf. 19; ἀπὸ τῆς γῆς Arist. *Mete.*366$^{a}$33, al.; τὸ ἀποπνέον Id.*Pr.*933$^{a}$39: impers., ἀποπνεῖ ἀπὸ τῆς θαλάττης *there is a breeze from* the sea, ib.933$^{a}$27, 943$^{b}$4. IV. Pass., *to be blown out*, of a light, Plu.2.281b.

※**ἀποπνίγω** [ῑ], fut. -πνίξω Pl.Com.198, Antiph.171: aor. inf. ἀποπνεῖξαι *GDI*2171.18 (Delph., i B.C.):—*choke, throttle*, Hdt.2.169, al.; τὰς ἀναπνοάς Hp.*Morb.Sacr.*9; τοὺς πατέρας τ' ἦγχον.. καὶ τοὺς πάππους ἀπέπνιγον Ar.*V.*1039; *suffocate*, Id.*Eq.*893; of plants, *choke*, *Ev.Matt.*13.7, *Ev.Luc.*8.7:—Pass., fut. -πνῐγήσομαι Ar.*Nu.*1504; also -πεπνίξομαι Eun.*VS* p.463 B.: aor. 1 ἀπεπνίχθην Aret.*SA*1.7: aor. 2 ἀπεπνίγην [ῐ] (v. infr.): pf. part. -πεπνιγμένος Hdt.4.72:—*to be choked, suffocated*, τρώγων ἐρεβίνθους ἀπεπνίγη Pherecr.159, cf. Alex. 266; *to be drowned*, Democr.172, D.32.6, Aesop.352. b. generally, *cut off, kill*, λιμῷ τινα Aret.*CA*1.9:—Pass., πόλις ἀ. τῇ τῶν ἀναγκαίων σπάνει Procop.*Arc.*26. 2. metaph., *choke one with vexation*, ἀποπνίξεις με λαλῶν Antiph. l.c.; ἡ γάρ [με] γειτονεῦσ' ἀποπνίγεις Call.*Iamb.*1.300:—Pass., *to be choked with rage*, ἐπί τινι *at* a thing, D.19.199, cf. Alex.16.7; πρός τι Lib.*Or.*63.15.

**ἀπο-πνοή**, ἡ, *exhalation, evaporation*, Arist.*Pr.*863$^{a}$7, Thphr.*HP* 9.7.2, al. II. *breeze blowing from* a place, Arist.*Pr.*943$^{b}$12. III. *death*, D.L.4.21 (prob. for ἀναπνοῆς). **-πνοια**, ἡ, = foreg. 1, Hp. *de Arte* 12. 2. = foreg. II, Thphr.*CP*5.12.2.

**ἀποποι-έω**, *unmake*, *Corp.Herm.*9.6. 2. *deduct*, τὸ ἀποποιηθέν *BGU*475$^{r}$5 (ii A.D.). II. Med., *put away from oneself, reject*, Lxx *Jb.*14.15, Plu.2.152a; *refuse*, δῶρον Plot.4.3.14; *deny, disclaim*, εἰδέναι τι Max.Tyr.24.4; *do away with, kill*, *Cat.Cod.Astr.*7.135. 29. **-ησις**, εως, ἡ, *disclaimer, disavowal*, Phoeb.*Fig.*2.3.

**ἀποπολεμέω**, *fight off* or *from*, (sc. τοῦ ὄνου) *from* ass-*back*, Pl. *Phdr.*260b.

**ἀπόπολις**, poet. **-πτολις**, ι, gen. ιδος and εως, *far from the city*, *banished*, ἀ. ἔσει A.*Ag.*1410 (lyr.), cf. S.*OT*1000, *OC*208, E.*Hyps.* *Fr.*44; ἀπόπτολιν ἔχειν τινά S.*Tr.*647 (lyr.).

**ἀποπολῑτεύω**, *dissolve political community*, *IG*9(2).205.16 (Melitaea):—in Med., ib.9(1).32 (Stiris).

**ἀποπομπ-αῖος**, α, ον, *carrying away evil*, of the scapegoat, Lxx *Le.*16.8 sq., Ph.1.338, al.; ἀ. θεοί Hsch. II. *to be cast out, abominable*, Ph.1.238. **-έω**· ἀποπέμπομαι, Hsch. **-ή**, ἡ, (ἀποπέμπω) *sending away*, Lxx *Le.*16.10. b. *valediction*, Men.Rh.p.333 S. 2. *divorce*, *PSI*1.36$^{a}$16 (i A.D.), etc., Poll.8.31. 3. *averting* an ill omen, etc., ἀ. ποιεῖσθαι Isoc.5.117; *getting rid*, πυρετῶν Luc.*Philops.* 9. **-ιμος**, ον, = ἀποπομπαῖος, πάθος Ph.1.75; ἡμέραι, = ἀποφράδες, Hsch.

**ἀποπονέω**, *finish a work*, τὰ πλεῖστα γὰρ ἀποπεπόνηκας Ar.*Th.*245.

**ἀποποντόω**, (πόντος) *cast into the sea*, Sch.S.*Aj.*1297.

**ἀποπορδή**, ἡ, *crepitus ventris*, prob. in Alex.Aphr.*Pr.*1.144.

**ἀποπορ-εία**, ἡ, *return*, πορεία καὶ ἀ., of machinery at work, Hero *Aut.*12.1. 2. *departure*, D.C.*Fr.*104.4, Agath.2.31, 3.23; *retreat*, Procop.*Pers.*1.23, al. **-εύομαι**, Pass., *depart*, X.*An.*7.6.33, *IG* 9(2).205.18 (Melitaea), etc. II. *go back, return*, ἐκ βαλανείου Plb. 24.7.6; of machinery (cf. foreg.), Hero *Aut.*6.3. **-ευτέα**, *one must go away*, Agath.2.22.

**ἀποπορπάω** or -ίζω, *fix in the safety-pin and excise*, *Hippiatr.*12.

**ἀπόπρᾱμα**, ατος, τό, *sub-letting*, *PRev.Laws*18.16 (iii B.C.), *UPZ* 112.3 (ii B.C.).

**ἀποπράσσω**, *demand the return of*, χρήματα *IG*12(7).42 (Amorgos):—Pass., ib.4.752.9 (Troezen):—Med., *exact to the uttermost*, τὸν μισθόν Them.*Or.*21.260b.

**ἀποπρᾱτίζομαι**, (πιπράσκω) *sell*, Lxx *To.*1.7.

**ἀποπρᾱΰνω**, *soften matters down*, Plu.*Sert.*25.

**ἀποπρεσβ-εία**, ἡ, *an ambassador's report*, Plb.23.9.5, al., cf. *AJA* 18.324f (Sardes, 5 B.C.). **-εύω**, *report as ambassador*, τὰ παρ' ἐκείνων Pl.*Lg.*941a: abs., *make such a report*, Plb.7.2.5.

※**ἀποπρηνίζω**, (πρηνής) *throw headlong*, Nonn.*D.*18.271 (aor. -ιξεν).

**ἀποπρίασθαι** [ῐ], aor. with no pres., ἀποπρίω (for -πρίασο) τὴν λήκυθον *buy* it *off* or *up*, Ar.*Ra.*1227.

※**ἀπό-πρῐσις**, εως, ἡ, *sawing off*, Paul.Aeg.6.77. ※**-πρισμα**, ατος, τό, *shavings*, prob. l. Arist.*Mir.*841$^{a}$16. **-πριστέον**, *one must saw off*, Paul.Aeg.6.77. **-πρίω** [ῑ], *saw off*, Hdt.4.65, *AP*11.14 (Ammian.); ὀστέον Hp.*Fract.*33:—Pass., Isid.Char.20, Plu.2.924b, prob. in Archil.122.

**ἀποπρό**, Adv. *afar off*, πολλὸν ἀ. φέρων Il.16.669. 2. as Prep. c. gen., *away from*, τυτθὸν ἀ. νεῶν ib.7.334, cf. E.*HF*1081, *Or.*142, etc.

※**ἀποπρο-άγω** [ᾰγ], only in pf. Pass., mostly part., ἀποπροηγμένα *in* *the second rank*, of things neither good nor bad, opp. προηγμένα, Zeno *Stoic*.1.48; the distn. was rejected by Aristo ib.1.83, but cf. *Stoic*.3.29, al.: inf. -ῆχθαι Aristo l. c. **-αιρέω**, *take away from*, σίτου ἀποπροελὼν δόμεναι *having taken some of* the bread to give it away, Od.17.457. **-βάλλω**, *throw far away*, A.R.3.1311.

**ἀπόπροθε**, before vowels -θεν, Adv., prop. *from afar*, λύζουσιν ἀ. οὐδ' ἐθέλουσιν ἀντίον ἐλθέμεναι Il.17.66; ἀ. εἰς ἓν ἰόντες A.R.1.39, cf. 1244, etc.; but in Hom., = ἀπόπροθι, *afar off, far away*, αὖθι μένειν παρὰ νηυσὶν ἀ. Il.10.209, cf. 17.501; στῆθ' οὕτω ἀ. Od.6.218; ἀ. εἰν ἁλὶ κεῖται 7.244, cf. 9.188, 17.408, Thgn.595, S.*Ichn*.3. 2. c. gen., *far away from*, ὀφθαλμῶν Archil.25; αἰζηῶν Q.S.1.414.

**ἀποπροθέω**, *run away from*, *AP*9.679 (better divisim).

**ἀπόπροθι**, Adv. *far away*, ἀ. δώματα ναίεις Od.4.811, al., cf. Theoc. 13.61, etc.; μάλα πολλοὶ ἀ. πίονες ἀγροί fields *extending far and wide*, Il.23.832, cf. Od.4.757.

**ἀποπρο-θορεῖν**, aor. 2 inf. of ἀποπροθρῴσκω, *spring far from*, νηός A.R.3.1280, Orph.*A*.545. **-ἵημι**, *send away forward, send on*, [κύνα] ἀποπροέηκε πόλινδε Od.14.26; ἑταίρους Orph.*A*.1216. 2. *send forth, shoot forth*, ἰὸν ἀποπροΐει Od.22.82; *let fall*, [ξίφος] ἀποπροέηκε χαμᾶζε ib.327.

**ἀποπροικίζω**, (προίξ) *give a dowry*, Sch.Od.2.53.

**ἀποπρο-λείπω**, *leave far behind*, Ἄργος ἀποπρολιπών Hes.*Fr*.144, cf. A.R.1.1285, Hermesian.7.21,44. **-νοσφίζω**, Att. fut. -ιῶ, *remove afar off, carry far away*, E.*IA*1286 (lyr., better divisim ἀποπρὸ νοσφ-).

**ἀπόπροσθεν**, Adv. = ἀπόπροθε, Hp.*VC*10. 2. c. gen., νεφῶν καὶ ὑδάτων ἀ. Pl.*Epin*.987a.

**ἀποπροσποιέομαι**, Med., *reject*, τὸ προβληθέν Ath.9.402a, Eust. 769.14; *dissemble*, ἑκοντὶ ἀποπροσποιησάμενος τὰ λεχθέντα πρὸς αὐτοῦ εἰδέναι Men.Prot.p.44 D., cf. p.125 D.

**ἀποπροσωπίζομαι**, Med., *clean one's face*, Pherecr.9: also, = ἐσοπτρίζεσθαι, Hsch.

**ἀποπρο-τέμνω**, *cut off from*, νώτου ἀποπροταμών *after he had cut a slice from* the chine, Od.8.475, cf. Nic.*Th*.572. **-φεύγω**, *flee away from, escape*, δίψαν *AP*12.133 (Mel.).

**ἀποπρωΐ**, *early*, Gloss.

**ἀποπτάω**, *roast sufficiently*, Sor.1.51, Lyd.[*Mens*.]p.182 W.; of ores, *smelt*, in Pass., Ph.*Bel*.70.4 and 6.

**ἀποπτερνίζω**, *thrust off with the heel*, Philostr.*Her*.6.

**ἀπο-πτερῠγίζομαι**, *clap the wings vehemently*, Thphr.*Sign*.18; *spread the wings and fly away*, metaph. of ἔρως, Eust.397.5. **-πτερῠγόομαι**, *lose the* πτέρυγες, of a rudder, Vett.Val.287.36. **-πτερύσσομαι**· ἀποπτερυγίζομαι, Hsch.

**ἀποπτεύω**, *have a view*, εἰς θάλασσαν J.*AJ*15.9.6.

**ἀποπτήσσω**, strengthd. for πτήσσω, f.l. for ὑπο-, Hsch. s. v. καταμεμυκέναι, dub. in Opp.*H*.4.370.

**ἀπό-πτισμα**, ατος, τό, (πτίσσω) *chaff, husks*, dub. l. for ἀπόπρισμα, Arist.*Mir*.841ᵃ16. **-πτίσσω**, *strip the husk off*, Dieuch.ap.Orib. 4.6.4 (Pass.).

**ἀποπτοέω**, poet. -πτοιέω, *scare* or *drive away*, Call.*Fr.anon*.93:— Pass., *to be startled, to shy*, of horses, Plb.3.53.10.

**ἀπόπτολις**, v. ἀπόπολις.

**ἄποπτος**, ον, (ἀπόψομαι) *seen* or *to be seen from* a place, ὅπως μὴ ἄ. ἔσται ἡ Κορινθία ἀπὸ τοῦ χώματος Arist.*Pol*.1274ᵃ40, cf. Arr.*Ind*.4.7; ἐν ἀπόπτῳ ἔχειν *in a conspicuous place*, Id.*An*.2.10.3; ἐν ἀ. ἑστιᾶσθαι J.*AJ*13.14.2, etc. II. *out of sight of, far away from*, τοῦδ' ἄποπτος ἄστεως S.*OT*762; ἄποπτος ἡμῶν Id.*El*.1489: abs., *far away*, ἐξ ἀπόπτου μᾶλλον ἢ 'γγύθεν σκοπεῖν Id.*Ph*.467; ὡς ἐξ ἀ. θεώμενος Pl.*Ax*. 369a; τόπος ἐξ ἀπόπτου καταφανής Plu.*Eum*.15; οὐδ' ἐξ ἀ. Phld.*Rh*.1. 149 S., *Piet*.27, cf. Gal.4.628. 2. *dimly seen*, S.*Aj*.15. 3. *out of sight*, ἐν ἀπόπτῳ τίθενται τὸν χάρακα D.H.2.54; ἐξ ἀπόπτου τῶν Ῥωμαίων παρεμβαλόντες Id.6.14.

**ἀπόπτυγμα**, ατος, τό, (πτύσσω) *portion of the* χιτών *folded back*, *IG* 2.652*A* 20.

**ἀποπτύρω**, *scare*, Gloss.

**ἀπό-πτυσμα**, ατος, τό, *that which is spat out*, *AB*223; v. l. in Arist. *Mir*.841ᵃ16. **-πτύσσω**, *fold back*, -πτύξαντες τοῦ χιτωνίσκου Aen. Tact.31.23. **-πτυστήρ**, ῆρος, ὁ, *one that spits out*: ἀ. χαλινῶν a horse *that will not bear* the bit, Opp.*H*.2.11. **-πτυστος**, ον, *spat out*: hence, *abominated, detested*, θεοῖς A.*Eu*.191: abs., S.*OC*1383, E. *Med*.1373, Ar.*Eq*.1285, etc. **-πτύω**, *spit out*, ὄνθον ἀποπτύων Il. 23.781; of the sea, ἀποπτύει ἁλὸς ἄχνην 4.426, cf. Emp.115.10; ἀ. σίαλον ἐκ τοῦ στόματος X.*Mem*.1.2.54: abs., *spit*, A.*Fr*.354, X.*Cyr*. 1.2.16 codd., Thphr.*Char*.19.11:—Pass., Ph.1.20, Gal.15.472; *to be washed ashore*, Alciphr.1.10. 2. *abominate, spurn*, ἀποπτύουσι δέ τ' ἀράς Hes.*Op*.726; ἀποπτύεις λόγους A.*Eu*.303; ἀπέπτυσαν εὐνὰς ἀδελφοῦ Id.*Ag*.1192, cf. *Pr*.1070 (lyr.), Ar.*Pax*528, E.*Andr*.607; *disown*, A.*Ch*.197:—aor. ἀπέπτυσα freq. used in pres. sense, ἀπέπτυσα μὲν λόγον E.*Hel*.664, cf. *IA*874: freq. abs., ἀπέπτυσα *omen absit*, Id. *Hipp*.614, *Hec*.1276, *IT*1161; ἀ. χαλινόν, of a horse, Philostr.*Im*.1. 12. 3. *ward off*, Epic. in *BKT*5(1).122. [ῡ of pres. long in Ep.; ῠ of fut. and aor. short in Trag.]

**ἀπό-πτωμα**, ατος, τό, *unlucky chance, misfortune*, Plb.11.2. 6. II. *error*, Vett.Val.238.26. **-πτωσις**, εως, ἡ, *falling off* or *away*, ὀστέων Hp.*Mochl*.35; ἀνθέων Dsc.*Praef*.8. 2. ἀ. τῆς ἀρχῆς *deposition*, Ath.12.530a. 3. *direction in which a force is exerted*, Ph. *Bel*.73.7. 4. *vanishing, disappearance, negation*, τὸ μηδαμῶς ὂν ἀ. ἐστι τοῦ ὄντος Dam.*Pr*.8; *eclipse*, τοῦ εἰδώλου ib.433. II. *declension from*, καθήκοντος Chrysipp.*Stoic*.2.51, M.Ant.10.12, Procl.*Inst*.209 (pl.); τῆς εὐσεβείας Hierocl.*in CA*11 p.442 M.; κατὰ ἀπόπτωσιν, opp. κατὰ κατόρθωσιν, Herm.*in Phdr*.p.166 A.

**ἀποπῡδαρίζω**, v. πυδαρίζω, Ar.*Eq*.697.

**ἀποπῡ-έω**, *suppurate*, Hp.*Epid*.2.2.6. **-ημα**, ατος, τό, *suppuration*, ib.4.25. **-ητικός**, ή, όν, *suppurative*, Id.*Coac*.282, *Epid*.2.3. 6. **-ΐσκω**, (πνέω) *to promote suppuration*:—Pass., *suppurate*, Id. *Morb*.2.28.

**ἀποπυκνόομαι**, Pass., *to be condensed, consolidated*, f.l. in Epicur. *Ep*.2 p.49 U.

**ἀποπυνθάνομαι**, *inquire* or *ask of*, ἀ. [αὐτοῦ] εἰ.. *asked of* him whether.., Hdt.3.154; παρά τινος J.*AJ*12.4.9.

**ἀποπυργίζοντες** λόγοι, title of work by Diagoras, Suid. s. v. Διαγόρας.

**ἀπο-πῡρίας** (sc. ἄρτος), ου, ὁ, a kind of *toasted bread*, Cratin.99, Ath.3.111e. **-πῡριατέον**, *one must foment*, Gal.12.840, Aët. 8.16. **-πῡριάω**, *foment*, Antyll.ap.Orib.7.22.21, Gal.13.245, al. **-πῡρίζω**, *roast on the fire*, Epich.124, cf. Hsch. **-πυρίς**, ίδος, ἡ, small fish like ἐπανθρακίς, Clearch.16. II. *fry*, τῶν μαινίδων ἀπόπυριν ποιήσας Teles p.41 H. III. *sacrifice of fish*, *SIG*1106.42 (Cos).

**ἀποπῡτίζω**, stronger form of πυτίζω, Hp.*Epid*.7.25, Ar.*Lys*.205, Arist.*HA*527ᵇ22.

**ἀπο-πωμάζω**, *remove lid*, Zos.Alch.p.221 B., *PHolm*.9.40, al. **-πωμᾰτίζω**, = foreg., Gal.14.268.

**ἀπόρανθρον**, τό, v. ἀπόρρανθρον.

**ἀποράξ**· ἀπόρροια, ἀπόσπασμα, ἀπότμημα, Hsch.

**ἀπορᾰφᾰνίδωσις**, εως, ἡ, v. ῥαφανιδόω, Sch.Ar.*Pl*.168.

**ἀποργάζω**, *work up* mortar, *IG*2².463.84.

**ἀποργ-ής**, ές, *wrathful*, Antiph.73 (dub.):—Comp. -έστερον Erot. is a variant for ἀστεργέστερον Hp.*Fract*.16. **-ίζομαι**, Pass., *to be angry*, Men.*Sam*.338, Lxx 2*Ma*.5.17.

**ἀπορέγχω**, *snore to the end*, *AP*11.4 (Parmen.).

**ἀπορέγω**, *stretch out*, Hp.*Fract*.1.

**ἀπορέπω**, *slink away*, *AP*9.746 (Polem. Rex).

**ἀπόρευτος**, ον, *that cannot or may not be travelled*, ὁδός Plu.*Cam*. 26, *Mar*.39. 2. *not to be traversed*, πέλαγος Ph.2.112, al. 3. *pathless*, Λιβύη Agatharch.7.

**ἀπορέω** (A), Ion. for ἀφοράω.

**ἀπορ-έω** (B), Lacon. 1 pl. ἀπορίομες X.*HG*1.1.23: aor. ἠπόρησα Th.1.63, etc.: pf. ἠπόρηκα Pl.*Sph*.244a, etc.:—Pass., fut. ἀπορηθήσομαι (συν-) S.E.*M*.10.5, but Med. in pass. sense ἀπορήσομαι Arist. *MM*1200ᵃ11: aor. ἠπορήθην, pf. ἠπόρημαι, both in act. and pass. sense (v. infr.):—*to be* ἄπορος, i. e. *without means* or *resource*: hence, 1. *to be at a loss, be in doubt, be puzzled*, mostly folld. by relat. clause, ἀ. ὅκως διαβήσεται Hdt.1.75; ὅτῳ τρόπῳ διασωθήσεται Th.3.109; ὅ τι λέξω δ' ἀπορῶ S.*OT*486 (lyr.); ἀ. ὅπῃ, ὁπόθεν, ὅποι, Th.1.107, 8.80, X. *HG*5.4.44: ὅ τι χρὴ ποιεῖν Id.*Cyr*.4.5.38; τίνα χρὴ τρόπον.. D.3.3; ἀ. εἰ.. Pl.*Prt*.326e; πότερα.. X.*Mem*.1.4.6; ἀ. ὁποτέραν τῶν ὁδῶν τράπηται ib.2.1.21; ἀ. μή.. *fear lest*.., Pl.*Alc*.2.142d: with acc. added, ἀ. τὴν ἔλασιν ὅκως διεκπερᾷ *to be at a loss about* his march, how to cross, Hdt.3.4: c. acc. only, ἀ. τὴν ἐξαγωγήν *to be at a loss about* it, Id.4. 179, cf. Ar.*Ec*.664, Pl.*Prt*.348c, al.: also c. inf., *to be at a loss how to* do, Ar.*V*.590, Pl.*Plt*.262e, Lys.9.7:—also ἀ. περί τινος Pl.*Phd*.84c, *Grg*.462b, al.; ἀ. διὰ τὸ πλῆθος τῶν ἁμαρτημάτων ὅθεν ἄρξομαι And. 4.10; ἐς πολλὰ S.*Tr*.1243: abs., Hdt.6.134; οὐκ ἀπορήσας without *hesitation*, Id.1.159; τὸ δ' ἀπορεῖν ἀνδρὸς κακοῦ E.*HF*106, etc.:— Med. used like Act., Hdt.2.121.γ'; ὡς ἠπόρημαι.. τάδε E.*IA*537; ἠπορούμην ὅτι χρησαίμην Lys.3.10, cf. Pl.*Prt*.321c: so in aor. Pass., πολλὰ.. ἀπορηθείς D.27.53. 2. in Dialectic, *start a question, raise a difficulty*, ἀπορία ἣν ἀπορεῖς Pl.*Prt*.324d; ἀ. περί τινος Arist.*Ph*. 194ᵃ15, al.; τὰ αὐτὰ περί τινος *Metaph*.1085ᵃ35; ἀ. πότερον.. *Pol*. 1283ᵇ36; ἀπορήσειε δ' ἄν τις τί.. *EN*1096ᵃ34, cf. 1145ᵇ21, Plb.1.64. 1, al.:—Pass., τὸ ἀπορούμενον, τὸ ἀπορηθέν, *the difficulty just started, the puzzle before us*, Pl.*Sph*.243b, *Lg*.799c, cf. Hp.*VM*1; τὰ ἠπορημένα Arist.*Pol*.1281ᵃ38; ἀπορεῖται *there is a question* or *difficulty*, πότερον.. Id.*EN*1099ᵇ9; μή.. ib.1159ᵃ6. 3. Pass., of things, *to be left wanting, left unprovided for*, τῶν δεομένων γίγνεσθαι οὐδὲν ἀπορεῖται X.*Lac*.13.7, cf. *Oec*.8.10; *to fail, turn out a failure*, opp. εὐπορεῖσθαι, Hp.*Art*.47. II. c. gen. rei, *to be at a loss for, in want of*, ἀπορεῖς δὲ τοῦ σύ; S.*Ph*.898; ἀλφίτων Ar.*Pax*636; πάντων Id.*Pl*.531; τροφῆς Thuc.8.81; ξυμμάχων X.*Cyr*.4.2.39; τοσαύτης δαπάνης Id. *Mem*.1.3.5; λόγων Pl.*Smp*.193e:—Med., Id.*Lg*.925b. III. ἀ. τινί *to be at a loss* by reason of, by means of something, X.*An*.1.3.8, Isoc.4. 147. IV. *to be in want, be poor*, opp. εὐπορέω, in Med., ὅταν ἀπορῆταί τις Antiph.123, but Act., Timocl.11, E.*Fr*.953.19; opp. πλουτέω, Pl. *Smp*.203e:—Pass., ἄνθρωπος ἠπορημένος *Com.Adesp*.249.—Chiefly Prose and Com.; never in A., thrice in S., twice in E. **-ημα**, ατος, τό, *matter of doubt, question, puzzle*, Pl.*Phlb*.36e, Arist.*Metaph*. 1011ᵃ6, etc. 2. esp. in the Dialectic of Arist., *objection raised to an* ἐπιχείρημα (q. v.), Id.*Top*.162ᵃ17. 3. *practical difficulty*, Plb. 31.13.8. **-ηματικός**, ή, όν, = ἀπορητικός, S.E.*P*.1.221, v. l. in Gal. *Nat.Fac*.2.9. 2. *expressive of doubt*, of particles, D.T.642.26, A.D. *Conj*.258.15. Adv. -κῶς S.E.*M*.8.1. **-ησία**, ἡ, = ἀπορία, Eub. 141:—also **-ησις**, εως, ἡ, Thphr.*Od*.12. **-ητέον**, *one must raise the question*, τί δήποτε.. Ph.1.336; περί τινος Plu.*Fr*.2.6. **-ητικός**, ή, όν, *inclined to doubt*, Id.*Aem*.14, S.E.*P*.1.221, al.; ἀ. καὶ σκεπτικοί D.L.9.69, cf. Gell.11.5.6. Adv. -κῶς S.E.*M*.7.30, Procl.*in Prm*. p.562 S. 2. *dubitative*, ἐπίρρημα Gal.7.661; ὕμνοι Men.Rh.p.343 S.

**ἀπόρθητος**, ον, *not sacked, unravaged*, Πριάμοιο.. ἀ. πόλις ἔπλεν

Il.12.11; ἀρχαγοὺς ἀπορθήτων ἀγυιῶν B.8.52, cf. 99; Θάσον ἀ. λείπειν Hdt.6.28; ἀ. χώρα *Hell.Oxy.*16.3; of Attica, E.*Med.*826, cf. A.*Pers.* 348; of Laconia, Din.1.73, cf. Lys.33.7; οὐκ ἐφύσων οἱ Λάκωνες ὡς ἀπόρθητοί ποτε; Antiph.117.

**ἀπορθ-όω,** *make straight,* τὸ στόμα τῶν μητρέων Hp.*Nat.Mul.* 40. II. *guide aright,* γνώμας S.*Ant.*636; πρός τι according to a standard, Pl.*Lg.*757e. III. *restore to health,* dub. in Men. *Georg.*59. ※**-ωμα,** ατος, τό, *erection, IG*9(1).691.2 (Corcyra, iii B.C.). **-ωσις,** εως, ἡ, *guiding aright,* τῆς γνώσεως Eust.1531. 66.

※**ἀπορία,** Ion. -ίη, ἡ, (ἄπορος) *being* ἄπορος: hence, I. of places, *difficulty of passing,* X.*An.*5.6.10. II. of things, *difficulty, straits,* in sg. and pl., ἐς ἀπορίην πολλὴν ἀπιγμένος, ἀπειλημένος, Hdt.1.79, 2. 141; ἐν ἀπορίῃ or ἐν ἀπορίῃσι ἔχεσθαι, Id.9.98, 4.131, cf. Antipho 5.66; ἀπορίῃσιν ἐνείχετο Hdt.1.190; ἀπορίην ἐρωτηθέντι παρασχεῖν Hp.*VM*13, cf. Lys.19.1; ἀπορίᾳ τελέθει, c. inf., Pi.*N.*7.105, cf. Pl. *Lg.*788c; εἰς φρέατα καὶ πᾶσαν ἀ. ἐμπίπτων Id.*Tht.*174c: c. gen. rei, ἀ. τοῦ μὴ γινώσκειν Hp.*Morb.Sacr.*1; ἀ. τοῦ μὴ ἡσυχάζειν *impossibility* of keeping quiet, Th.2.49; ἀ. τῆς προσορμίσεως Id.4.10; ἀ. τοῦ ἀνακαθαίρεσθαι Pl.*Lg.*678d. 2. *not providing* a thing, Id.*Men.* 78e. III. of persons, *difficulty of dealing with* or *getting at,* τῶν Σκυθέων Hdt.4.83; τοῦ ἀποκτείναντος Antipho 2.4.2. 2. *being at a loss, embarrassment, perplexity,* ἀ. τοῦ δυστυχεῖν E.*Ion*971, cf. Th. 7.44,75, etc.; ἀ. ἐν τῷ λόγῳ συμβᾶσα Aeschin.2.41; *distress, discomfort,* in illness, Hp.*Epid.*5.42, Aret.*SA*2.5: hence metaph., ὠδίνουσι καὶ ἀπορίας ἐμπίμπλανται Pl.*Tht.*151a. 3. ἀ. τινός *lack of* a person or thing, σοφῶν ἀνδρῶν Ar.*Ra.*806; τροφῆς, χρημάτων, etc., Th.1.11, 7.48; ἀπώλλυντο.. ἀπορίᾳ τοῦ θεραπεύοντος *for want of one* to attend to them, Id.2.51; ἀ. λόγων Pl.*Ap.*38d; ἀ. πλοίων *shortage* of ships, *CPHerm.*6.10: abs., *need, poverty,* Th.1.123; ἀ. καὶ πενία And.1.144; opp. εὐπορία, Arist.*Pol.*1279$^{b}$27: in pl., D. 19.146. IV. in Dialectic, *question for discussion, difficulty, puzzle,* ἀπορίᾳ σχόμενος Pl.*Prt.*321c; ἀ. ἣν ἀπορεῖς ib.324d; ἡ ἀ. ἰσότης ἐναντίων λογισμῶν Arist. *Top.*145$^{b}$1, al.; ἔχει ἀπορίαν περί τινος Id. *Pol.*1285$^{b}$28; αἱ μὲν οὖν ἀ. τοιαῦταί τινες συμβαίνουσιν Id.*EN*1146$^{b}$6; οὐδεμίαν ποιήσει ἀ. Id.*Metaph.*1085$^{a}$27; ἀ. λύειν, διαλύειν, Id.*MM* 1201$^{b}$1, *Metaph.*1062$^{b}$31; ἀπορίᾳ ἀπορίαν λύειν D.S.1.37.

**ἀπορικός,** ή, όν, *of* or *for persons without means,* ὀνόματα *BGU*390. 8 (iii A.D.), cf. *PTeb.*267 *Intr.* (ii A.D.).

**ἀπορνε-όω,** *turn into a bird,* Apollod.1.7.4, Sch.Ar.*Av.*251:—Pass., Herm.ap.Stob.1.49.69, Apollod.1.8.3. **-ωσις,** εως, ἡ, *being changed into a bird,* Sch.Ar.*Av.*212.

**ἀπορνῑθόομαι,** *become a bird,* Str.6.3.9, Heraclit.*Incred.*35, Sch. Ar.*Av.*100.

※**ἀπόρνῡμαι,** *start from* a place, ἀπορνύμενον Λυκίηθεν Il.5.105, cf. Hes.*Th.*9, A.R.1.800.

**ἀποροποίητος,** ον, *impermeable,* S.E.*M.*8.309.

※**ἄπορος,** ον, first in Hdt. and Pi. (v. infr.), *without passage, having no way in, out,* or *through*: hence, I. of places, *impassable,* πέλαγος, πηλός, Pl.*Ti.*25d, *Criti.*108e; ὁδός, ὄρη, X.*An.*2.4.4, 2.5. 18. II. of states or circumstances, *impracticable, difficult,* Hdt. 5.3, etc.; ἄ. ἀλγηδών, πάθη, S.*OC*513 (lyr.), *Ph.*854; τἄπορον ἔτος ib.897; ἄ. χρῆμα E.*Or.*70; ἀγών, κίνδυνος, Lys.7.2 and 39 (Sup.); αἰσχύνη Pl.*Lg.*873c; σωτηρία λεπτὴ καὶ ἄ. ib.699b, cf. *R.*453d; φόβος *Lg.*698b; βίος Men.*Kith.Fr.*1.10; νύξ Longin.9.10:—ἄπορον, τό, and ἄπορα, τά, as Subst., ἐκ τῶν ἀπόρων in the midst of their *difficulties,* Hdt.8.53, cf. Pl.*Lg.*699b; εὔπορος ἐν τοῖς ἀ. Alex.234.6; ἄπορα πόριμος A.*Pr.*904; ἐν ἀπόροις εἶναι to be in *great straits,* X.*An.* 7.6.11; εἰς ἄπορον ἥκειν, πεσεῖν, E.*Hel.*813, Ar.*Nu.*703; ἐν ἀπόρῳ εἴχοντο, ἦσαν, they were *at a loss* how to.., Th.1.25, 3.22; ἐτεῇ οἶον ἕκαστον γιγνώσκειν ἐν ἀπόρῳ ἐστί Democr.8: ἄπορόν [ἐστι] c. inf., Pi.*O.*10(11).40, Th.2.77, Aeschin.Socr.53, etc.; ἄπορά [ἐστι] Pi.*O.*1.52: Comp. -ώτερος, ἡ λῆψις Th.5.110. 2. *hard to discover* or *solve,* ἀνεξερεύνητον καὶ ἄπορον Heraclit.18; ἄ. ἐρωτήσεις, = ἀπορίαι IV, Plu.*Alex.*64, Luc.*DMort.*10.8; ζήτησις Pl.*Plt.*284b; λόγοι D.L. 7.44. 3. *hard to get, scarce,* ἐν δυστυχίῃ [φίλον εὑρεῖν] πάντων -ώτατον Democr.106; θῦμα Pl.*R.*378a; ἄπορα [ὀφλήματα] *bad* debts, D.50.9. III. of persons, *hard to deal with, unmanageable,* E.*Ba.* 800, Pl.*Ap.*18d (Sup.), cf. Th.4.32 (Sup.): c. inf., ἄ. προσμίσγειν, προσφέρεσθαι, *impossible* to have any dealings with, Hdt.4.46, 9.49; βορῆς ἄνεμος ἄ. *against which nothing will avail, which there is no opposing,* Id.6.44; ἄ. τὸ κακὸν καὶ ἀνίκητον Id.3.52. 2. *without means* or *resources, helpless,* ἔρημος, ἄ. S.*OC*1735 (lyr.), cf. Ar.*Nu.*629, etc.; ἄ. ἐπὶ φρόνιμα S.*OT*691 (lyr.); ἐπ' οὐδέν Id.*Ant.*360 (lyr.); ἄ. γνώμῃ Th.2.59. 3. *poor, needy,* Id.1.9, Pl.*R.*552a; opp. εὔπορος, Arist.*Pol.* 1279$^{b}$9, 1289$^{b}$30; ἄ. λειτουργεῖν *too poor* to undertake liturgies, Lys. 31.12, cf. *PRyl.*75.5 (ii A.D.), etc.; ἄ. καὶ τῶν ἐλαχίστων κατέστησαν D.Chr.17.18; also of states of life, δίαιτα ταπεινὴ καὶ ἄ. Pl.*Lg.* 762e. IV. Adv. -ρως Simon.46, etc.; τὸ πρᾶγμα ἀ. εἶχε πατρί E. *IA*55; ἀ. ἔχει μοι περί τινος Antipho 1.1; ἀ. ἔχειν, c. inf., D.H.6.14; ἀ. διατεθῆναι Lys.18.23: Comp. -ώτερον Th.1.82; but -ωτέρως διακεῖσθαι Antipho 3.2.1: Sup. -ώτατα Pl.*Ti.*51b. etc.

**ἀπορούω,** *dart away,* Ἰδαῖος δ' ἀπόρουσε Il.5.20, etc.; esp. *start back,* Od.22.95; ἀλλήλων Orph.*A.*705. 2. *spring up from,* πρέμνων Pi.*Fr.*88.

**ἀπορρ-,** ρ is regularly doubled in all compds. after ἀπό; but in Poets it sts. remains single.

**ἀπορραγεῖς·** οἱ καθαρμοί, Hsch.

**ἀπορρᾰθῡμ-έω,** *leave off in faintheartedness* or *laziness,* τινός X. *Mem.*3.7.9: abs., Pl.*R.*449c, D.8.75. Adv. **-ήτως,** v. l. for ἀπαραμυθήτως, Jul.*Or.*8.252a.

**ἀπορραίνω,** *spirt out, shed about,* τοῦ θοροῦ, τῶν ᾠῶν (partit. gen.), Hdt.2.93: c. acc., Arist.*HA*567$^{a}$31:—Pass., Dsc.*Eup.*1.235, al. II. *sprinkle, douche,* Epict.*Ench.*4:—esp. in Med., *sprinkle* by way of lustration, *IG*1.121, al. III. Pass., *to be dissolved,* Olymp.*in Mete.*228.6 (dub.).

**ἀπορραΐς,** v.l. for αἱμορροΐς in Arist.*HA*530$^{a}$19: in *Gloss.* expld. by *murex.*

**ἀπορραίω,** *bereave* one *of* a thing, c. dupl. acc., ὅστις σ' ἀέκοντα βίηφι κτήματ' ἀπορραίσει' Od.1.404; ἀπορραῖσαι [αὐτὸν] φίλον ἦτορ *bereave* him *of* life, 16.428; θυμὸν ἀπορραῖσαι (sc. ἄνδρας) Emp.128: c. gen. rei, μή τιν' ἀπορραίσειν γεράων Hes.*Th.*393.

**ἀπόρραυθρον,** τό, = sq., *IG*12(3).248.18 (Anaphe; ἀπόρανθρον lapis), *Inscr.Prien.*158.

**ἀπορραντήριον,** τό, (ἀπορραίνω) *a vessel for sprinkling with holy water,* E.*Ion*435, *IG*1.143, al.

**ἀπορραντίζω,** = ἀπορραίνω, Alex.Trall.1.13.

**ἀπόρραξις,** εως, ἡ, a *game of ball,* Poll.9.103,105, Eust.1601.33.

**ἀπορρᾰπίζω,** *beat back, drive away,* Apollod.*Poliorc.*141.1; *reject,* Mich.*in EN*56.22, Eust.561.41:—Pass., Arist.*Div.Somn.*464$^{a}$ 26. II. τῆς γλώσσης ἄκρας ἀπορραπιζούσης τὸ πνεῦμα *causing* the breath *to vibrate,* in the pronunciation of *r,* D.H.*Comp.*14 (but v. ἀπορριπ-).

**ἀπορρᾰπιστέον,** *one must reject,* Eust.310.23.

**ἀπορράπτω,** *sew up again,* τοῦ λαγοῦ τὴν γαστέρα Hdt.1.123: metaph., τὸ στόμα τινός Aeschin.2.21, cf. Ph.1.476; γεράνων ὄμματα Plu.2.997a:—Pass., τὰ ἀπερραμμένα Gal.18(2).671.

**ἀπορράσσω,** *beat off,* τοὺς Ῥωμαίους ἀπὸ τοῦ λόφου D.H.6.5, cf. D.C.56.14.

**ἀπορραψῳδέω,** *speak in fragments of epic poetry,* X.*Cyr.*3.3.54.

**ἀπορρέζω,** fut. -ρέξω, *sacrifice,* χίμαρον v.l. in Theoc.*Ep.*4.15; *offer part of* ., Is.*Fr.*105.

**ἀπορρέμβομαι,** *wander from,* c. gen., τῆς παρατηρήσεως M.Ant.3. 4: abs., *hesitate,* Id.4.22.

**ἀπό-ρρευμα,** ατος, τό, *that which distils,* as from a tree, Theognost. *Can.*79. **-ρρευματίζω,** v.l. for -φλεγματίζω, Ps.-Diocl.*Epist. ad Antig.*ap.Paul.Aeg.1 fin. **-ρρευσις,** εως, ἡ, *flowing from,* ἔχειν τὰς ἀ. to be *the source of streams,* Plb.10.28.4; ἀέρος οὐ δεχομένου τὰς ἀ. Plu. 2.933c. II. Astrol., = ἀπόρροια 3, Vett.Val.146.32; μανίας καὶ λύττης ἀ. Junc.ap.Stob.4.50.27. (ἀπόρρυσις (q. v.) shd. perh. be read in these passages.) III. *folly,* = ἀφροσύνη, Aq.*De.*22.21, 1*Ki.*25.25.

※**ἀπορρέω,** Ep. -ρείω Nic.*Th.*404, fut. ἀπορρεύσω Serapio in *Cat. Cod.Astr.*1.101,102, but ἀπορρυήσομαι Dsc.5.75: aor. ἀπερρύην, part. ἀπορρυείς A.*Ag.*1294; ἀπέρρευσα Plb.5.15.7, Ath.9.381b:—Pass., ἀπορρέοιτο Gal.6.709:—*flow* or *run off,* ἀπό τινος Hdt.4.23; ἐκ κρήνης Pl.*Criti.*113e, etc.: abs., *stream forth,* of blood, A.*Ag.*1294; τὸ ἀπορρέον *the juice that runs off,* Hdt.2.94, 4.23; φλόγα τῶν σωμάτων -ουσαν Pl.*Ti.*67c; λιγνὺς ἀπὸ τῆς φλογὸς ἀ. *emanating from,* Arist.*Mete.*374$^{a}$ 25, cf. *Mu.*394$^{a}$13: metaph., ὥσπερ ἐκ πηγῆς ἀ. τῆς ἡμερότητος Plu. *Cat.Ma.*5; τὸ ἀπορρέον ἐκ νοῦ λόγος Plot.3.2.2. II. *fall off,* of fruit, Hdt.1.193; feathers, Pl.*Phdr.*246d; leaves, D.22.70; hair, Arist. *HA*518$^{a}$14; flesh, σάρκες ἀπ' ὀστέων ἀπέρρεον E.*Med.*1201: generally, *run to waste,* Plot.2.1.3; of riders, ἀπορρυέντες εἰς γῆν Plu.*Eum.* 7, cf. *Pyrrh.*30, al. 2. *fall away, decay, perish,* ἀ. δαίμων, ἀ. μνῆστις, S.*El.*999, *Aj.*523; τῶν καλῶν ἡ μνήμη ταχέως ἀπορρεῖ Longin.33. 3. 3. of persons, *fall away, drop off from,* ἀλλήλων Pl.*Lg.*776a; ἀπό τινος Plb.5.26.11; τῆς αὐλῆς Plu.*Arat.*51: abs., *slip away, decamp,* Plb.5.15.7. 4. *fall away, decline from,* τῆς δόξης Plu.2. 199a. 5. Astrol., *to be 'separated',* ἀπό.. Serapio ll. cc.

**ἀπόρρηγμα,** ατος, τό, *fragment,* Plu.*Dio*46, Sch.Il.2.755.

※**ἀπορρήγνῡμι** or -ύω, *break off,* δεσμὸν ἀπορρήξας Il.6.507, cf. Hdt. 3.32; ἧκε δ' ἀπορρήξας κορυφὴν ὄρεος Od.9.481; πνεῦμ' ἀπέρρηξεν βίου *snap the thread* of life, *die,* A.*Pers.*507; ἀ. πνεῦμα, βίον, E.*Or.*864, *IT*974, cf. *Tr.*756; ἀ. ψυχὴν *AP*7.313; τὰ μακρὰ τείχη ἀ. ἀπὸ τῆς τῶν Μεγαρέων πόλεως Th.4.69; ἀ. τῆς εἰρήνης τὴν ξυμμαχίαν, a phrase of D. censured by Aeschin.3.72; ἀ. πάνυ τείνουσαι τὸ καλῴδιον Luc. *DMeretr.*3.3. 2. causal, ἀ. τὸν θυμόν *let* one's rage *burst forth,* D.H.*Rh.*9.5, cf. Luc.*Am.*43; *burst out with* a remark, App.*BC*2.81:—Pass., πόλεμος.. ἀπερρήγνυτο ἐς ἔργον Id.*Syr.*15. 3. ἀ. ἑαυτόν τινος *tear* oneself *away, break away* from, Plu.*Marc.*27; τῶν τοῦ πατρὸς ἐπιτηδευμάτων J.*AJ*10.3.1; *deprive,* τοὺς ἀδελφοὺς τῆς βασιλικῆς ἐλπίδος Id.*BJ*1.23.2. II. Pass., freq. in aor. ἀπερράγην [ᾰ] Hdt.8. 19, etc.: pf. ἀπέρρηγμαι Ph.2.510; but 3 sg. ἀπορέρηκται Gal.ap.Orib. 46.21.22:—*to be broken off* or *severed from,* ἀπό τινος Hdt.l.c., ib.37: abs., *to be broken off, severed,* Id.2.29, Th.5.10, etc.; *break away from* one's allegiance, *rebel,* J.*BJ*2.14.3. 2. Act., pf. ἀπέρρωγα in pass. sense, Archil.47, etc.; φωνὴ ἀπερρωγυῖα a *broken* voice, Hp. *Acut.*(*Sp.*)10, Arist.*Aud.*804$^{b}$20; ἀπερρωγώς *broken in character, dissolute,* Luc.*Pseudol.*17; οἵ γε μὴ τελέως -ότες Muson.*Fr.*12 p.64 H.; *absurd,* S.E.*M.*8.165. III. intr. in aor. 1 Act., ἀπορρήξας ἀπὸ δεσμῶν *AP*9.240 (Phil.); κακὸν ἀπέρρηξε Luc.*Abd.*6.

**ἀπορρηθῆναι,** aor. 1 inf. Pass. of ἀπερῶ.

**ἀπόρρημα,** ατος, τό, (ἀπερῶ) *prohibition,* Pl.*Plt.*296a.

**ἀπόρρηξις,** εως, ἡ, *bursting,* e.g. of an abscess, Aret.*SA*2.1. 2. *breaking away from,* ὁδῶν J.*AJ*19.3.1.

**ἀπόρρησις,** εως, ἡ, (ἀπερῶ) *forbidding, prohibition,* Pl.*Sph.*258c; *interdiction* of judgement, παρὰ τὴν ἀ. D.33.31; δίκη τῆς ἀ. Is.2. 29. II. (ἀπείρηκα) *giving up,* Pl.*R.*357a; ἀ. μαρτυρίας *refusal to give* testimony, Plu.*Mar.*5; *renunciation of a truce*, Plb.14.2.14. III. *disowning* of a son, = ἀποκήρυξις, Suid. IV. *giving in, flagging*, -σιν ποιήσασθαι Aristid.1.374 J.

***ἀπορρήσσω**, late form of ἀπορρήγνυμι, Paus.10.15.5, Iamb.*Myst.* 3.16.

**ἀπο-ρρητέον**, (ἀπερῶ) *one must prohibit*, D.Chr.7.133. ***-ρρητος**, ον, *forbidden*, ἀπόρρητον πόλει *though it was forbidden to* the citizens, S.*Ant.*44, cf. E.*Ph.*1668; τἀπόρρητα δρᾶν Ar.*Fr.*622; τὰ ἀ. *forbidden exports*, τὰ. ἐξάγειν, ἀποπέμπειν, Id.*Eq.*282, *Ra.*362; ἀπόρρητον μηδὲν ποιούμενοι Pl.*Lg.*932c; πράξεις ἀ. Phld.*Ir.*p.54 W. II. *not to be spoken, secret*, ἀ. ποιεῖσθαι make *a secret of*. Hdt.9.94; esp. of state *secrets*, Ar.*Eq.*648; ἐν -τῳ ποιεῖσθαι X.*An.*7.6.43; τἀπόρρητα ποιοῦνται Lys.12.69; ὁ ἐπὶ τῶν ἀπορρήτων τοῦ βασιλέως Plu.*Luc.*17, cf. *OGI* 371; ὁ τῶν ἀ. γραμματεύς, = *a secretis*, Procop.*Pers.*2.7; ἀπόρρητα ποιεύμενος πρὸς μηδένα λέγειν ὑμέας keep them *secret* so that you tell them not to any one, Hdt.9.45; ἐν ἀπορρήτῳ τὴν ἀλήθειαν λέγειν tell *as a secret*, Pl.*Tht.*152c; ἐν ἀ. εἰδέναι And.2.19; φυλάττειν ἐν ἀπορρήτοις keep *as a secret*, Arist.*Fr.*662; ἐν ἀπορρήτῳ ξυλλαμβάνειν arrest *secretly*, And.1.45; δι' ἀπορρήτων ἐξαγγέλλειν, ἀκούειν, Lycurg.85, Pl.*R.*378a; κύριον καὶ ῥητῶν καὶ ἀπορρήτων D.1.4; τἀπόρρητ' οἶδεν Id. 21.200; ὁ ἐν ἀπορρήτοις λεγόμενος λόγος of *the esoteric doctrines* of the Pythagoreans, Pl.*Phd.*62b; τὰ ἀ. τῆς κατὰ τὰ μυστήρια τελετῆς *SIG* 873.9 (Eleusis, ii A.D.); ἐν ἀπορρήτοις in *cipher*, D.S.15.20: Comp. -ότερος Paus.2.17.4, Philostr.*VA*6.19. 2. of sacred things, *ineffable, secret*, φλόξ E.*IT*1331; μυστήρια Id.*Rh.*943; τἀπόρρητ'.. ἐκφέρειν Ar.*Ec.*442, cf. Pherecr.133; ἐνεργείας Jul.*Or.*4.151b. b. γόης καὶ ἀ. a 'man of mystery', Philostr.*VA*8.7.9. 3. *unfit to be spoken, abominable*, Lys.10.2; ἀ. ἀδικίαι Pl.*Lg.*854e; τίς οὐκ οἶδεν.. τὰς ἀπορρήτους, ὥσπερ ἐν τραγῳδίᾳ, τὰς τούτου γονάς; D.21.149; of *foul abuse*, κακῶς τὰ ἀπόρρητα λέγειν ἀλλήλους Id.18.123, etc.; in Att. Law of words (e.g. ῥίψασπις) whose use was punishable, Isoc.20.3. 4. of words, *not in common use*, ἀ. καὶ ἔξω πάτου Luc.*Hist.Conscr.* 44. 5. τὰ ἀπόρρητα, = τὰ αἰδοῖα, Plu.2.284a, cf. Ar.*Ec.*12, Longin. 43.5. III. Adv. ἀπορρήτως *ineffably, inexpressibly*, Philostr.*VS* 2.18; *covertly*, ἀπορρήτως τὰ γραφόμενα κατεχλεύαζε διὰ τῆς εἰκόνος Eun.*Hist.*p.263 D.

**ἀπορρῑγ-έω**, 2 pf. ἀπέρριγα, *shrink shivering from* a thing: generally, *shrink from doing* it, c. inf., νέεσθαι Od.2.52. **-όω**, *shiver with cold*, Arist.*Pr.*862$^b$37.

**ἀπορριζόω**, *pull out by the roots*, τρίχας Alciphr.3.66.

**ἀπορρῑν-άω**, *file off*, κέρατα Str.7.3.18. **-ήματα**, τά, *filings, scraps*, Daphitas ap. eund.14.1.39.

**ἀπορριπίζω**, *blow away*, τὴν ἀναθυμίασιν Arist.*Pr.*947$^a$20; *blow out* or *back*, v.l. in D.H.*Comp.*14; cf. ἀπορραπίζω.

**ἀπο-ρριπτέον**, *one must reject, cast aside*, Hld.7.17; ὄκνον Them.*Or.* 22.274c. **-ρριπτος**, ον, *cast aside*, Procop.Gaz.*Ep.*116. **-ρρίπτω**, poet. **ἀπορίπτω** Pi.*P.*6.37, later **ἀπορριπτέω** X.*HG*5.4.42, Plu.*Caes.* 39, *Cat.Ma.*5, Luc.*Tim.*12, Hdn.4.9.2, D.C.74.1, fut. -ρρίψω Hes.*Sc.* 215: pf. ἀπέρριφα Plb.1.40.15:—*throw away, put away*, μῆνιν, μηνιθμόν, Il.9.517, 16.282; ἀπὸ κρόκεον ῥίψαις.. εἷμα Pi.*P.*4.232; ἀπορρίψοντι ἐοικώς like one *about to cast* [a net], Hes.*Sc.*215; ἀ. ἀπὸ τοῦ στόματος *spit*, Thphr.*Char.*19.4; *vomit*, τὴν τροφήν Asclep.Jun.ap. Gal.13.162; *cast up*, of a river, τοὺς νεκροὺς τῶν ῥευμάτων Jul.*Or.*2. 60c. II. *cast forth from* one's country, A.*Ch.*914; ἀπωστὸς γῆς ἀπορριφθήσομαι S.*Aj.*1019; ἀπερριμμένοι *outcasts*, D.18.48, cf. D.H. 9.10; of things, *reject*, *PBaden*19.12 (ii A.D.); τὰ φαῦλα καὶ ἀπερρ. τῶν ἐδεσμάτων Hdn.4.12.2. 2. *disown, reject*, Pi.*O.*9.38, S.*El.* 1018. 3. *throw aside, set at naught*, ἡ ἡμετέρη εὐδαιμονίη οὕτω τοι ἀπέρριπται ἐς τὸ μηδέν Hdt.1.32; Κύπρις δ' ἄτιμος τῷδ' ἀ. λόγῳ A.*Eu.* 215; ὅταν.. τὰ χρηστὰ ἀπορρίπτηται D.25.75. III. of words, *utter*, esp. in disparagement, ἔς τινα Hdt.1.153, 4.142 (Pass.), 8.92: generally, ἀ. ἔπος *let fall* a word, Id.6.69; χαμαιπετὲς ἔπος ἀ. Pi.*P.* 6.37; λόγον ἀχρεῖον Ant.Lib.11.3; μηδ' ἀπορριφθῇ λόγος A.*Supp.* 484. IV. intr., *throw oneself down, leap off*, *Act.Ap.*27.43, Charito 3.5. **-ρριφή**, ἡ, *being cast out*, Sch.E.*Hec.*675. **-ρρίψιμος**, ον, *that should be thrown away*, Artem.5.85. **-ρριψις**, εως, ἡ, *throwing off*, ἱματίων Hp.*Acut.*42 (pl.), cf. Luc.*Symp.*15.

**ἀπο-ρροή**, ἡ, (ἀπορρέω) *flowing off, stream*, αἵματος ἀπορροαί E.*Hel.* 1587; *outflow*, Sabin.ap.Orib.9.15.6; *surface from which water flows off*, D.S.2.8. 2. *falling* of a river, Aristid.*Or.*36(48).36. 3. *exhalation*, Plu.*Sol.*23. 4. *effluence, emanation*, ἀπορροὴ τοῦ κάλλους Pl.*Phdr.*251b; πάντων ἀπορροαὶ ὅσσ' ἐγένοντο Emp.89, cf. Arist. *Pr.*908$^a$21, Plot.2.3.2; ἔστι χρόα ἀπορροὴ σχημάτων ὄψει ξύμμετρος Pl. *Men.*76d. II. *falling away, loss*, τὰ ἐκεῖ ταχθέντα κατὰ φύσιν μένοντα οὐδεμίαν πάσχει ἀ. Plot.2.1.4. ***-ρροια**, ἡ, = foreg. I. 1, X.*HG* 5.2.5. 2. = foreg. I. 4, Arist.*Sens.*438$^a$4, al., Epicur.*Ep.*1 p.9 U., Porph.*Abst.*2.46, etc.; αἴγλης Orph.*L.*173; Medic., *effluvia*, Gal.15. 625 (pl.), etc. 3. Astrol., *separation*, opp. συναφή, Serapio in *Cat. Cod.Astr.*1.100: but, *influence* of planets, Gem.2.14. II. = foreg. II, Plot.2.3.11. (Less correct than ἀπορροή, Phryn.*PS* p.50 B.)

**ἀπορροιβδέω**, *shriek forth*, οὐκ εὐσήμους ἀ. βοάς, of birds of prey, S.*Ant.*1021; ἰωήν Nonn.*D.*2.257.

**ἄπορρον**· πάλιν, Hsch. (fort. ἄψορρον).

**ἀπόρροος**, ον, contr. -ρους, ουν, (ἀπορρέω) *streaming out of*. αἰγῶν ἀ. θρόμβος Antiph.52.8. II. Subst., *outflow*, κρήνης E.*Antiop.* iv B 57 Arn.; *branch* of a river or sea, Νείλου Aristid.*Or.*36(48).74; θαλάσσης ib.87, cf. 44(17).17 (pl.).

**ἀπορροφέω**, *swallow some of*, τοῦ οἴνου X.*Cyr.*1.3.10 codd.

**ἀπο-ρρῡ́σκω**, *run off*, of whey in making cheese, Eust.1625. 65. **-ρρῠπαίνω**, *tarnish*, prob. in S.*Ichn.*153 (Pass.). **-ρρῠπόω**, = sq., Hsch. s.v. ἀπινοῦται. **-ρρύπτω**, *cleanse thoroughly*, Asp.*in EN*25.1, Luc.*Gall.*9; τοὺς πόρους Gal.11.745:—Med., *cleanse oneself*, Plu.*Sull.*36, Ael.*NA*9.62: c. acc., ἀ. τὰς ἐκ παθῶν καὶ νοσημάτων κηλῖδας Ph.2.487, cf. Iamb.*Protr.*21.ιά. 2. *wash away*, μελεδωνάς prob. cj. in *AP*9.815. **-ρρῠσις**, εως, ἡ, *sinking down*, τῶν προσκεφαλαίων Herod.Med. in *Rh.Mus.*58.74; cf. ἀπόρρευσις.

**ἀπορρυταλίξαι**· ἀποσπάσαι, Hsch.

**ἀπόρρῠτος**, ον, = ἀπόρροος, *running*, κρήνη Hes.*Op.*595; ἀ. ὕδωρ, opp. στάσιμον, Hp.*Aër.*7. II. *subject to efflux*, opp. ἐπίρρυτος, Pl.*Ti.*43a; οὐκ ἀ., of the sea, Arist.*Mete.*353$^b$32; *having an outflow*, πηγή Porph.*Sent.*44. III. ἀ. σταθμά stables *with drains* or *a sloping floor*, X.*Eq.*4.3.

**ἀπόρρυψις**, εως, ἡ, *cleansing*, Ath.9.409c; in medic. sense, Philagr.ap.Orib.5.21.4, Ruf.ib.8.24.5: metaph., *purification*, τῆς ψυχῆς Iamb.*VP*17.74 (pl.).

**ἀπο-ρρωγάς**, άδος, v.l. for sq., Lxx 2*Ma.*14.45. ***-ρρώξ**, ῶγος, ὁ, ἡ, (ἀπορρήγνυμι) *broken off, abrupt, sheer, precipitous*, ἀκταί Od.13. 98; πέτρα X.*An.*6.4.3, cf. Arist.*HA*611$^a$21, Call.*Lav.Pall.*41. 2. Subst., *cliff, precipice*, Plb.7.6.3, etc.; ἀκμή *AP*7.693 (Apollonid.); *abyss*, J.*BJ*1.21.3. II. fem. Subst., *piece broken off*, Κώκυτός θ' ὃς δὴ Στυγὸς ὕδατός ἐστιν ἀ. *branch* of the Styx, Od.10.514, cf. Il. 2.755; ἀλλὰ τόδ' ἀμβροσίης καὶ νέκταρός ἐστιν ἀ. is *an efflux, a distillation* of nectar (ἀπόσταγμα Hsch.), Od.9.359; ἀ. Ἐρινύων *limb* of the Furies, Ar.*Lys.*811 (lyr.); ἡ δὲ προφητείη δίης φρενός ἐστιν ἀ. Orac.ap.Luc.*Alex.*40; μελέων ὀλίγη τις ἀ. some small *portion* of melody, *AP*7.571 (Leont.); ἀ. δραχμαίη *portion* of a drachm's weight, Nic.*Th.*518; ἀπορρῶγες σπλάγχνου Aret.*SD*1.10; ἀπορρὼξ τῆς πόλεως, of Samos, Demad.ap.Ath.3.99d; μουνογενής τις ἀ. φύλου ἄνωθεν Χαλδαίων Orph.*Fr.*247.23.

**ἀπορύσσω**· *refodio*, Gloss.

**ἀπορφᾰνίζω**, *bereave*, τινὰ παιδός *BCH*46.345:—Pass., *to be orphaned*, A.*Ch.*249; ἀπό τινος ἀ. *to be torn away from*.., 1*Ep.Th.*2.17.

**ἀπόρφῡρος**, ον, *without purple attire*, Plu.2.528b; esp. of a garment, *without purple border*, Id.*Ant.*71, *POxy.*1741.21 (iv A.D.).

**ἀπορχέομαι**, *dance away, lose by dancing*, γάμον Hdt.6.129.

**ἆπος**, v.l. for αἶπος (q.v.).

**ἀποσᾰλεύω**, *lie in the roadstead, ride at anchor*, Th.1.137; ἐπ' ἀγκύρας D.50.22, cf. Arist.*HA*523$^b$33, *PA*685$^a$34: metaph., ἀ. ἐν φόβοις J. *BJ*7.3.4; *keep aloof from*, τινός Plu.2.493d. b. ἀποσαλεύσας· ἐπιτηρήσας, Hsch., *EM*125.48. 2. trans., *shake, cause to move*, Gal. 6.141:—Pass. (with fut. -σαλεύσομαι), *to be loosened, shaken away*, Ruf.*Ren.Ves.*12.3; *be shaken from one's opinion*, Arr.*Epict.*3.26.16.

**ἀποσαρκόομαι**, dub. sens., σὰρξ ἀποσαρκοῦται Arist.*Pr.*865$^b$30 (fort. ἀποστρακοῦται), cf. 966$^a$26.

**ἀποσάττω**, *unsaddle, unpack*, opp. ἐπισάττω, Lxx *Ge.*24.32. II. *stop up, caulk*, Din.*Fr.*89.10; *stuff with food*, σαυτὸν ἀποσάξεις (Casaub. for -τάξεις) Diph.43.41:—Med., *stuff oneself*, Philem.68.

**ἀποσᾰφέω**, (σαφής) *make clear, indicate*, οὐδὲν ἀπεσάφει.. ὁπότερα ποιήσοι Pl.*Prt.*348b, cf. *Cra.*384a, Gal.8.678, Luc.*Hist.Conscr.*52; ὑπέρ τινος Jul.*Gal.*138a.

***ἀποσᾰφηνίζω**, = foreg., Luc.*JTr.*27.

**ἀποσβαίῳ**· νεκρῷ, Hsch.

**ἀπο-σβέννῡμι** (-ύω A.D.*Pron.*36.4, Plu.2.681e), *extinguish, quench*, τὸ φῶς *Trag.Adesp.*9; τοὺς λύχνους Ar.*V.*255; τὸ πῦρ Pl.*Hp. Ma.*290e, etc.; also ἀ. τὸ κακόν Id.*R.*556a; τὸ γένος καὶ ὄνομα X.*Cyr.* 5.4.30; ψυχήν *AP*7.303 (tm.); ἰόν ib.11.321 (Phil.); τὰς ὁράσεις Plu. l.c.; Gramm., *extinguish*, i.e. *lose*, τὸν τόνον, cf enclitics, A.D.*Pron.* l.c. II. Pass., pres. in Heraclit.30, Hp.*Aër.*4, X.*Lac.*13.3, etc.:—Med., fut. ἀποσβήσομαι Pl.*Lg.*805c: aor. 2 and pf. Act. intr., ἀπέσβην E.*Med.*1218, X.*Cyr.*l.c., Call.*Fr.*1.10 P., Theoc.4.39, etc.; ἀπέσβηκα X.*Cyr.*8.8.13, Pl.*Plt.*269b, etc.: aor. 1 Pass. ἀπεσβέσθην Ar.*Lys.* 293, Lys.1.14, v.l. in Luc.*Cat.*27: pf. ἀπέσβεσμαι Parm.8.21, Porph. *Abst.*3.7:—*to be extinguished, go out, vanish, die, cease*, ll.cc.; of a woman's milk, Hp.*Aër.* l.c., Arist *GA*777$^a$14; ὁ μαστός Id.*HA* 618$^b$7: metaph., ἔρωτος ἀπέσβη πυρσὸς *AP*12.182 (Strat.). **-σβεσις**, εως, ἡ, *extinction*, πυρός Arist.*APo.*93$^b$10; ζωῆς Procl.*in R.*2.113 K.

**ἀποσειρόω**, *strain, filter off*, Philum.*Ven.*23.3, Aët.1.113, *PMag. Leid.V.*6.19, *PHolm.*23.21, etc.

**ἀπό-σεισις**, εως, ἡ, *shaking off*: *licentious dance*, Poll.4.101. **-σεισμα**, ατος, τό, f.l. for ὑπο-, Gal.13.784. ***-σείω**, *shake off*, Men.61, Thphr.*CP*1.20.3:—Pass., ξίφος ἀποσεσεῖσθαι τοῖς αὐχέσιν ἐπαιωρούμενον Hdn.5.2.1:—Med., *shake off from oneself*, πάντ' ἀποσεισάμενος Thgn.348; of a horse, *throw* his rider, Hdt.9.22, X.*Cyr.* 7.1.37; τειχέων θριγκοὺς ἀ. *throw* them *off*, S.*Fr.*506: metaph., ἀποσείεσθαι λύπας, γῆρας, Ar.*Ra.*346, *Lys.*670; νέφος Id.*Nu.*288; ἑταίρους Luc.*DMeretr.*13.2; ὕπνον Id.*Tim.*6:—Pass., ὑπὸ τῶν ἐρωμένων Them.*Or.*24.302c. 2. Med., *shake oneself*, Arist.*HA*560$^b$8.

***ἀποσεμνύνω**, *extol, glorify*, Pl.*Tht.*168d, D.S.2.47, etc. II. Pass., with fut. Med., *give oneself solemn airs*, Ar.*Ra.*703; ἀποσεμνύνεῖται πρῶτον ib.833, cf. Procop.*Arc.*17; ὀψὲ ἀπεσεμνύνθη, of Tragedy, *assumed a dignified form*, Arist.*Po.*1449$^a$20; ἀποσεμνυνάμενοι Aristid.26(14).63. 2. c. dat., *pride oneself on*, πατρίδι, κάλλει, etc., Procop.*Aed.*4.1, 1.1, al.

***ἀποσεύω**, *chase away*, Nic.*Th.*77, *AP*9.642 (Agath.):—Pass., *run away, flee*, Hom. only in syncop. aor. 2 ἀπέσσυτο Il.6.390, etc.; ἀπεσσύμεναι θύγατρες B.10.82: also aor. ἀπεσσύθην [ῡ] Hes.*Th.*183; ἀποσυθὲν αἷμα, *haemorrhage*, v.l. for ἀποχυθέν in Hp.*Acut.*(*Sp.*)29:—Med., = Act., ἀπεσσεύοντο γυναῖκας A.R.1.805.

**ἀποσήθω,** *sift off, separate by sifting,* Dsc.5.88. 2. metaph., *riddle completely, rob,* Herodic.ap.Ath.13.591c.

**ἀποσηκόω,** (σηκός) *shut up in a pen,* Hsch.

**ἀποσημ-αίνω,** *announce by signs* or *signals, give notice,* περί τινος Hdt.5.20: abs., *give a sign* or *signal,* Pl.*Euthd.*276b; νοσήματα ἀ. *show themselves,* Arist.*Pr.*954ᵇ30. 2. c. acc., *indicate by signs* or *symptoms.* οὐδὲν ἀ. Hp.*Epid.*1.9; = δηλῶσαι, S.*Fr.*676; *denote, represent,* J.*AJ*3.7.7, Plu.*Sull.*7, etc.; *indicate,* J.*AJ*1.3.8, al.; *declare,* ib.1.8.1, al.:—Med., *show by signs* or *proofs,* Hdt.9.71; *guess by signs,* Ael.*NA*6.58. II. ἀ. εἴς τινα *allude to* him, Th.4.27, cf. Plu.2.177b; πρός τινα Philostr.*VA*6.10. III. *give adverse signs, be unpropitious,* τινί ib.2.33. IV. in Med., *seal up as confiscated, sequestrate,* Ar.*Fr.*432, X.*HG*2.3.21; of persons, *proscribe,* ib.2.4.13 (also Act., ἀποσημανῶ· ἀποδιώξω, Hsch.). 2. generally, *seal up,* γράμματα Hdn.4.12.6. -άντωρ, ορος, ὁ, *a sealer, recorder,* Eust.1590.6. -ασία, ἡ, *enunciation,* Phld.*Po.*2.16.

**ἀποσημει-όομαι,** *note down, make notes,* Phlp.*in Cat.*3.29. ⊛-ωσις, εως, ἡ, *record, note, abstract,* second title of Hippocrates' προγνωστικόν, Steph.*in Hp.*1.54D., cf. Herm.*in Phdr.*p.96A.

**ἀποσήπομαι,** Pass., aor. ἀπεσάπην [ᾰ] Hp.*Aph.*6.58: fut. -σαπήσομαι Id.*Prorrh.*2.1: with pf. Act. ἀποσέσηπα (v. infr.):—*lose by rotting* or *mortification,* ὑπὸ τοῦ ψύχους τοὺς δακτύλους τῶν ποδῶν ἀποσεσηπότες *having lost* the toes by frost-bite, X.*An.*4.5.12, cf. 5.8.15, Luc.*Ind.*6. 2. of water, *throw off impurities* by boiling, joined with ἀφέψεσθαι, Hp.*Aër.*8. II. causal in Act., *cause to putrefy, remove by putrefaction,* Id.*Haem.*2; γάλα Id.*Gland.*17; τινὰ ἐκ τοῦ σώματος Gal.11.820, cf. Aët.1.18.

**ἀποσήχειν·** ἀποδιώκειν, Hsch.

**ἀπόσηψις,** εως, ἡ, *rotting away,* Plu.9.1087e (pl.).

**ἀποσῑγ-άω,** *keep silent about, make no mention of,* c. acc., Demetr.*Eloc.*149, Ps.-Plu.*Vit.Hom.*213. -ησις, εως, ἡ, *keeping silence,* Hp.*Decent.*3 (pl.).

**ἀποσῑμ-όω,** *make flat-nosed*:—Pass., ἀποσεσιμώμεθα τὴν ῥῖνα *we have snub noses,* Luc.*DMort.*24.2. 2. = τὸ ἐπικύψαι καὶ τὴν πυγὴν προτεῖναι γυμνήν Philippid.1. II. ἀ. τὰς ναῦς *cause to swerve,* Th.4.25, cf. Gal.18(2).347. -ωσις, εως, ἡ, *turning* a ship *aside,* App.*BC*4.71 (pl.).

**ἀποσιόομαι,** Ion. for ἀφοσιόομαι.

**ἀποσῑτ-έω,** *cease to eat, starve,* Luc.*Asin.*33; *lose appetite,* Orib.*Inc.*6.25. -ία, ἡ, *aversion to food, want of appetite,* Hp.*Aph.*6.3, Aret.*SD*1.12. 2. *fasting,* Porph.*Abst.*1.27. -ίζομαι, *get to eat,* f.l. for ἐπι-, τι Aristaenet.1.3. -ικός, ή, όν, *exciting distaste for food,* Hp.*Prorrh.*1.100. -ος, ον, = ἄσιτος, *having eaten nothing,* ἡμερῶν τοσούτων ἀ. Hld.8.7, cf. Ael.ap.Ar.Byz.*Epit.*82.14, Luc.*Hist.Conscr.*21. 2. *hungry,* Philonid.1. II. *having an aversion for food, without appetite,* Hp.*Epid.*1.26.ς', Plu.2.635c, Gal.16.654, Jul.*Or.*6.190d.

**ἀποσῑωπ-άω,** *maintain silence,* Isoc.12.215, Plb.30.19.9, etc.; *cease speaking and be silent,* μεταξὺ λέγων ἀ. Plu.*Alc.*10; as a rhetorical figure (cf. sq.), Demetr.*Eloc.*44,253. II. trans., *keep secret,* ὄνομα Luc.*Pseudol.*21; *leave unsaid,* Id.*Pisc.*29; *leave unnoticed,* *POxy.*237 vii 24 (ii A.D.). ⊛-ησις, εως, ἡ, *becoming silent,* Plu.*Alex.*52, Herod.Med.in *Rh.Mus.*58.71. 2. a rhetorical figure, when for emphasis, modesty, etc., the sentence is *abruptly broken off,* Quint.*Inst.*9.2.54, Demetr.*Eloc.*103,264, Plu.2.1009e, Hermog.*Id.*2.7. 3. *breaking off* of friendship, Ptol.*Tetr.*192 (pl.).

**ἀποσκάλλω,** *scratch, scrape off,* *AB*428.

**ἀποσκαμυνθίζειν·** ἀπομυκτηρίζειν, Hsch.

**ἀποσκάπτω,** fut. Pass. -σκᾰφήσομαι Polyaen.5.10.3:—*cut off* or *intercept by trenches,* X.*An.*2.4.4. II. strengthd. for σκάπτω, Pl.*Lg.*760e.

**ἀποσκᾰρίζω,** = ἀπασκαρίζω (q. v.), Lxx *Jd.*4.21.

**ἀποσκεδάννῡμι** or -ύω, fut. -σκεδάσω, contr. -σκεδῶ S.*OT*138 (poet. also ἀποκεδ- A.R.3.1360, tm.):—*scatter abroad, disperse,* ἄλλους μὲν ἀπεσκέδασεν βασιλῆας Il.19.309; ψυχὰς μὲν ἀπεσκέδασ' ἄλλυδις ἄλλῃ Od.11.385; σκέδασον δ' ἀπὸ κήδεα θυμοῦ 8.149; ἀ. μύσος S. l. c.; ἀντιπάλων ὕβριν ἀπεσκέδασαν Epigr.ap.D.18.289:—Pass., *to be scattered,* τῶν ἐκ Τροίης ἀποσκεδασθέντων Hdt.7.91; *straggle away from,* ἀπὸ τοῦ στρατοπέδου X.*An.*4.4.9; τῆς φάλαγγος Id.*HG*5.4.42:—Med., *repel and scatter,* τὸν τοιόνδε φλύαρον Pl.*Ax.*365e.

**ἀποσκελίσαι·** παιδικὴν ὄρχησιν ὀρχήσασθαι, Hsch. (-ῆσαι cod.).

***ἀποσκέλλω,** v. ἀποσκλῆναι.

**ἀποσκεπάζω,** *uncover,* Sch.A.*Pr.*83, *Gp.*7.15.4 (Pass.).

**ἀποσκεπαρνισμός,** ὁ, (σκέπαρνον) *chipping off with an adze*: name for a particular kind of *wound in the head,* Gal.ap.Orib.46.21.3, Sor.*Fract.*1,7.

**ἀπο-σκεπτέον,** *one must look,* πρός τι Arist.*Pol.*1327ᵇ4. -σκέπτομαι, not found in pres. (v. ἀποσκοπέω), fut. ἀποσκέψομαι: aor. ἀπεσκεψάμην:—*examine,* Plu.2.582d, ἔς τι Hp.*Mul.*1.11.

**ἀποσκέπω,** *give shelter from,* τὸν βορέαν Arr.*Epict.*3.22.65. II. *strip,* τὸ δέρμα Hsch. s. v. ἀπεσκόλυπτεν.

**ἀποσκευάζω,** *pull off,* τὴν ὀροφὴν Lycurg.128; *clear away* tables, Suid.; *strip of furniture,* οἰκίαν Lxx *Le.*14.36. 2. = ζημιόω, Hsch. II. mostly in Med., *pack up and carry off,* ἀ. τι τῶν ἰδίων *SIG*633.68 (Milet., ii B.C.), cf. 588.50 (ib., ii B.C., Pass.), Plb.2.26.6, D.H.9.23: abs., *pack up and depart,* *Act.Ap.*21.15. 2. *get rid of,* τὰ ἐνοχλοῦντα (= ἀποπατέω, cf. Poll.5.91), Hdn.4.13.4; *remove,* τῆς φιλίας τινά Luc.*Cal.*12; *make away with, kill,* Id.*Tyr.*1, Hdn.2.5.1; *get rid of, confute,* τοὺς σοφιστάς Gal.8.19:—Pass., *to be expelled,* τῶν σωμάτων Dsc.*Ther.Praef.* 3. *repel,* αἰτίαν, διαβολάς, J.*BJ*2.16.5, 1.24.4. 4. *reject,* Simp.*in Ph.*888.15. 5. *defer,* διήγησιν Hld.5.1. 6. *transfer,* ἔς τινας τὰς αἰτίας Jul.*Or.*2.66d.

⊛**ἀποσκευή,** ἡ, *removal, riddance,* i.e. *assassination,* J.*AJ*18.2.4. II. *baggage,* in sg. and pl., Plb.2.3.7, 1.66.7, Plu.2.174a, etc.; *household stuff,* Lxx *Ge.*34.29, *UPZ*110iii90 (ii B.C.), etc.; δόμων ἀ. Ezek.*Exag.*209. III. *ordure, filth,* v.l. Str.14.1.37. [Scanned ⏑ – ⏑ – by Ezek. l. c.]

**ἀπόσκημμα,** ατος, τό, *support, prop,* A.*Fr.*18. II. = ἀπόσκηψις, Ruf.ap.Orib.45.30, Gal.18(2).133, Simp.*in Epict.*p.37D.

**ἀποσκην-έω,** *encamp apart,* πόρρω ἀπεσκήνουν τῶν Ἑλλήνων X.*An.*3.4.35. -ος, ον, (σκηνή) *encamping apart, living and messing alone,* opp. σύσσιτος, Id.*Cyr.*8.7.14. -όω, *keep apart from,* τὰ ὦτα τῶν Μουσῶν Plu.2.334b: also intr. in Act., μακρὰν ἀ. τῶν ἰδίων Id.2.627a, cf. *Eum.*15, *Demetr.*9. 2. *remove one's habitation,* Lxx *Ge.*13.18.

**ἀποσκήπτω,** *hurl from above,* ἐς οἰκήματα τὰ μέγιστα.. ἀποσκήπτει βέλεα (sc. ὁ θεός) Hdt.7.10.ε': metaph., ἀ. τὴν ὀργὴν εἴς τινα *discharge* one's rage upon one, D.H.6.55, cf. J.*AJ*13.1.5; φθορὰν εἰς τὴν πόλιν ib.6.1.1; ἀ. τιμωρίαν D.S.1.70. II. intr., *fall suddenly,* ὀργαὶ δ' ἔς σ' ἀπέσκηψαν θεᾶς her wrath *fell* upon thee, E.*Hipp.*438; μὴ οὖν εἰς ἀθρόους ἀλλ' εἰς ἕνα ἀποσκήψατε Aeschin.1.182; ἀ. τὸ ὕδωρ εἰς τοὺς ὀφθαλμούς Arist.*Mir.*846ᵃ2; αἱ πληγαὶ τῶν ξιφῶν εἰς τὰς χεῖρας Plu.*Pomp.*19; ἡ δίκη ἀ. ἐς ὀφθαλμοὺς καὶ ἐς χεῖρας Philostr.*VA*1.6; ἀποσκήψαντος τοῦ ἐνυπνίου ἐς φλαῦρον *come to* a sorry *ending,* Hdt.1.120; ποῖ ταῦτα ἀποσκήψει; Cic.*Att.*12.5.1; εἰς μέγα τι κακόν, ἐς ὄλεθρον ἀ., D.H.7.15, Alciphr.1.37. 2. Medic., of humours, *determine,* εἴς τινα τῶν ἀκυροτέρων μορίων Gal.15.783, cf. 17(1).54; ἐς τὸ πᾶν Aret.*SD*1.12.

**ἀπόσκηψις,** εως, ἡ, *determination* of humours to one part of the body, Hp.*Aph.*6.56, *Prorrh.*2.7; ἀ. νούσου ἐς ἕν τι Aret.*SD*1.9; wrongly expl. as = ἀπόσχασις by Gal.19.84.

**ἀποσκῐ-άζω,** *cast a shade* or *shadow,* σκιαὶ δι' ἑτέρου.. φωτὸς ἀποσκιαζόμεναι shadows *cast*.., Pl.*R.*532c, cf. D.C.36.49. II. *cloud over, dull the brightness* of metallic surfaces, Zos.Alch.p.223B. -ασμα, ατος, τό, *shadow,* ἀ. τροπῆς *a shadow cast by* turning, *Ep.Jac.*1.16, cf. Porph.*in Ptol.*193, Suid. s. v. ἀνθήλιος. II. *illusion, deceit,* Men.Prot.p.118D. -ασμός, ὁ, *the casting a shadow,* ἀ. γνωμόνων *measures of time by the shadow* on the sun-dial, Plu.*Per.*6 (pl.).

**ἀπο-σκίδνημι,** *scatter,* Ph.2.100:—elsewh. in Pass., -σκίδνᾰμαι, Μυρμιδόνας δ' οὐκ εἴα ἀποσκίδνασθαι Il.23.4; of soldiers, ἀ. ἔς τι *to disperse* for a purpose, Hdt.4.113: abs., Th.6.98; cf. ἀποκίδναμαι.

**ἀποσκίμπτω,** = ἀποσκήπτω:—Pass., δύο ἄγκυραι ἀγαθαὶ ἐκ ναὸς ἀπεσκίμφθαι it is good *to have* two anchors *fastened to* the ship, Pi.*O.*6.101.

**ἀποσκίρρωμα,** ατος, τό, *a callous, hard lump,* Sch.Ar.*Ach.*553.

**ἀποσκιρτάω,** *skip away,* τῆς ἀγελῆς Hellanic.111J.; in Str.17.1.31 *to have a bout of skipping* or *capering*: metaph., *to be restive* or *rebellious,* Luc.*Merc.Cond.*23, Them.*Or.*7.87b.

⊛**ἀποσκλῆναι,** aor. 2 inf. of *ἀποσκέλλω (cf. σκέλλω), *to be dried up, wither,* Ar.*V.*160: pf., λιμῷ ἀπεσκληκέναι Luc.*DMort.*27.7: and abs., ἀπέσκλη *died of starvation,* Men.*Her.*30: fut. ἀποσκλήσῃ *AP*11.37 (Antip.).

**ἀπόσκληρ-ος,** ον, strengthd. for σκληρός, *very hard,* Philum.*Ven.*15.4, 22.1, Simp.*in Ph.*304.27. 2. *harsh* to the taste, of water, Myia *Ep.*4. ⊛-ύνω, *harden,* Hp.*Coac.*515:—Pass., Arist.*Mir.*836ᵇ5, Thphr.*CP*3.16.2; ἀπεσκληρυμμένοι, gloss on ναρκώδεις, Erot.

**ἀπόσκλησις,** εως, ἡ, *drying up, withering,* Corn.*ND*33.

**ἀποσκνίπτω,** aor. subj. ἀποσκνίψῃς, *scatter,* Hsch.

**ἀποσκνῐφόω,** *obscure, darken,* Emp.42.2.

**ἀποσκολοπίζω,** *remove stumbling-blocks,* Aq.*Is.*57.14, al.

⊛**ἀποσκολύπτω,** *skin, strip off,* Archil.124 (sens. obsc.), S.*Fr.*423; also ἀπεσκολυμμένος, = περιτετμημένος, Hsch., Ael.Dion.*Fr.*432.

**ἀπο-σκοπεύω,** = sq., Lxx *La.*4.17, Ph.1.677 codd., etc.; cf. ἀποσκωπεύω. -σκοπέω, (with fut. -σκέψομαι) *look away from* other objects *at* one, and so *look steadily,* πρός τινα or τι, S.*OT*746, Pl.*Plt.*291e, Arist.*Pol.*1284ᵇ5, etc.; ἔς τι S.*OC*1195; πόρρω ποι ἀ. Pl.*R.*432e; *keep watch,* Luc.*DMar.*6.2. 2. c. acc., *look to, regard,* E.*Hec.*939 (lyr.), D.H.6.72, Procop.*Goth.*4.15:—Med., ἀποσκοπεῖσθαι τὸ μέλλον Plu.*Pomp.*79; πρός τι Procl.*in Prm.*p.549S. 3. ἀποσκοπεῖν εἰ.. E.*Supp.*236. 4. Pass., ἡ πόλις ἐκ περιωπῆς -εῖται *is visible from a distance,* Procop.*Aed.*1.1. -σκοπιάζω, = foreg., Q.S.6.114. -σκόπιος, ον, *far from the mark,* ἀ. ἀφάμαρτον *App.Anth.*3.59 (Ptol.). -σκοπος, ον, *erring from the mark,* οὐκ.. ἀ. οὐδ' ἀδαήμων Emp.62.3. II. *beholding from afar,* Hsch.

**ἀποσκορᾰκ-ίζω,** (ἐς κόρακας) *wish* one *far enough, curse, damn,* Lxx *Is.*17.13, Plu.2.740a, Alciphr.1.38, Iamb.*VP*25.112. ⊛-ισμός, ὁ, *casting off utterly,* Lxx *Is.*66.15, Hsch.

**ἀποσκορπίζω,** = σκορπίζω, Lxx 1*Ma.*11.55, *Gp.*20.12.1, Aët.15.15.

**ἀποσκοτ-ίζω,** *darken,* c. gen., τῆς ἐκείνου [θεοῦ] ἐνοράσεως ἑαυτὸν ἀπεσκότισε Porph.*Marc.*13. II. *remove darkness,* σμικρὸν ἀποσκοτίσαι κελεύοντος *stand out of his light,* Plu.2.605e; ἀποσκότησόν μου is f.l. in D.L.6.38. -όομαι, *to be darkened, blinded,* ὑπὸ λιγνύος Plb.1.48.6; of the mind, Ath.10.446b; σελήνη ἀποσκοτοῦται Eust.1769.19; ἀποσκοτοῦσθαι τὰς ὄψεις Plu.*Sert.*17, Sch.Pi.*P.*4.89.—The Act. only in Poll.1.118, ἀ. τὰ ὄμματα. II. *to be shaded off,* in painting, Ar.*Fr.*712. -ωσις, εως, ἡ, *darkening, loss of sight,* Nech.ap.Vett.Val.279.33.

**ἀποσκουτλόω,** *deprive of its paving,* ἡρῷον *IG*3.1423 sq.

**ἀποσκῠβᾰλ-ίζω**, *treat as vile refuse*, Sch.Pi.*P*.3.22; *pollute* a tomb, prob. in *CIG*3927 (Hierapolis):—Pass., *to be cast forth as excrement*, Epict.*Gnom*.19:—hence Subst. **-ισις**, εως, ἡ, Sch.Ar.*Pl*.1184.

**ἀποσκυδμαίνω**, *to be enraged with*, μὴ..ἀποσκύδμαινε θεοῖσι Il.24.65.

**ἀποσκύζω**, = foreg., Procop.*Arc*.10, Hsch.

**ἀποσκῠθίζω**, *scalp* (*as the Scythians did*), Lxx 4*Ma*.10.7. 2. metaph. in Pass., *to be shaved bare*, κρᾶτ' ἀπεσκυθισμένη E.*Tr*.1026; τὴν ἐφ' ὕβρει κουρὰν ἀπεσκυθίσθαι Ath.12.524f.

**ἀποσκῠλεύω**, *carry off as spoil from*, τί τινος Theoc.24.5.

**ἀποσκύλλω**, *pull, tear off*, aor. Med. ἀποσκύλαιο λάχνην Nic.*Th*.690.

**ἀπόσκωμμα**, ατος, τό, *banter, raillery*, Hsch.

**ἀποσκωπεύω**, *dance the figure* σκώπευμα (q. v.); ὁ -εύων, painting by Antiphilus, Plin.*HN*35.138; confused with ἀποσκοπεύω by Ath. 14.629f.

**ἀποσκωπτικῶς**, Adv. *in a jeering way*, Sch.Luc.*Lex*.15.

**ἀποσκώπτω**, *banter, rally*, Θαλῆν ἀστρονομοῦντα..θεραπαινίς ἀποσκῶψαι λέγεται Pl.*Tht*.174a; ἀ. πρός or εἴς τινα, *jeer at* one, D.C.48.38, Luc.*Herm*.51, etc.; ἐπί τινι D.C.60.33; εἴς τινα ἐπίγραμμα D.L. 5.11.

**ἀποσμ-άω**, *wipe off*, οὐλάς Dsc.5.91, Diocl.*Fr*.141, Apollon.ap. Gal.12.477; ῥύπον Luc.*Anach*.29. II. *wipe clean*, Id.*Pisc*. 14 (Pass.). **-ηκτέον**, *one must wipe clean*, Sor.1.78, Aët.12. 1. **-ηξις**, εως, ἡ, *wiping, cleaning*, Archig.ap.Aët.9.35, Hsch. s. v. ἔκνιψις. **-ήχω**, = ἀποσμάω, Pherecyd.33 J., Sor.1.81, Paus. 5.5.11, Luc.*Tim*.54, Them.*Or*.32.359c:—Pass., c. dat., *to be smeared with*, *Gp*.16.18.2.

**ἀποσμῑκρύνω**, *diminish*, Luc.*Merc.Cond*.21, etc.:—also **ἀποσμῑκρόω**, Tim.*Lex*. s. v. ὑποκορίζεσθαι.

**ἀποσμιλαίνω**, f. l. for ἀπομυλλαίνω.

**ἀποσμίλ-ευμα** [ι], ατος, τό, *a chip, shaving*, Suid. **-εύω**, *plane off, polish off*, ῥήματα, λέξιν, Jul.*Or*.2.77a, Them.*Or*.21.251b.

***ἀποσμύχομαι** [ῡ], Pass., *to be consumed as by a slow fire, waste, pine away*, Luc.*D Mort*.6.3.

***ἀποσοβ-έω**, *scare away*, as one does birds, τοὺς ῥήτορας Ar.*Eq*.60, cf. *V*.460: metaph., ἀποσοβῆσαι τὸν γέλων Id.*Ra*.45; ἀ. ἀπὸ τῶν ὀφθαλμῶν τὰ λυποῦντα *to keep off*, X.*Eq*.5.6; ἀ. τινὰ ὁμιλίας Plu.2. 11d:—Med., *keep off from oneself*, X.*Eq*.5.7:—Pass., *to be scared*, ἀποσοβηθῆναι ταῖς διανοίαις Plb.30.5.16. II. intr., *to be off in a hurry*, οὐκ ἀποσοβήσεις; i.e. *be off!* Ar.*Av*.1032,1258, cf. Luc.*Nav*. 4; ἀποσοβῶμεν *let's be off*, Men.997. **-ημα**, ατος, τό, *that which averts evil*, Sch.Opp.*H*.1.46, Sch.E.*Med*.1322; = sq., Sch.rec.A.*Th*. 69. ***-ησις**, εως, ἡ, *scaring away*, Sch.A.*Pers*.215. **-ητέον**, *one must shun*, v.l. Phryn.295. **-ητήρ**, ῆρος, ὁ, *one that scares away*, Sch.Od.14.531. **-ητήριος**, α, ον, gloss on ἀλεξητήριος, Hsch. **-ητής**, οῦ, ὁ, = -ητήρ, Sch.Ar.*Pl*.359. **-ητικός**, ή, όν, *driving away, averting*, μιασμῶν Iamb.*Protr*.21.ιϛ', cf. Sch.Pi.*O*.9.143.

**ἄποσος**, ον, *non-quantitative*, Plot.4.7.5, Phlp.*in Ph*.401.4.

**ἀποσοφίζομαι**, *become wise*, Arr.*Epict*.1.18.10.

**ἀποσπάδιος** [ᾰδ], α, ον, (ἀποσπάω) *torn off* or *away from*, τινός Orph.*H*.18.13; τὸ ἀ. = ἀπόσπασμα, *AP*6.102 (Phil.).

**ἀποσπάδων**, οντος, ὁ, = σπάδων, Suid.

**ἀποσπαίρω**, *beat convulsively*, σφυγμῶν -όντων Aët.16.67.

***ἀποσπᾰλᾰκόω**, (σπάλαξ) *blind*: metaph. in Pass., ὁ τᾶς Δίκας ὀφθαλμὸς ἀπεσπαλάκωται Cerc.4.17.

**ἀποσπάρ-αγμα** [πᾰ], ατος, τό, = ἀπόσπασμα, *AP*13.21 (Theodorid.). **-άσσω**, *tear off*, E.*Ba*.1127.

**ἀποσπαργᾰνόω**, *take off the swaddling-clothes*, Sor.1.100:—Pass., Lyd.*Mens*.4.26.

**ἀποσπαρθάζω**, *quiver*, Hp.*Morb*.2.10.

***ἀπο-σπάς**, άδος, ἡ, *torn off from*, τινός Nonn.*D*.1.289, al.: metaph., βασσαρίδες ἀποσπάδες ἠθάδος ὕλης ib.34.347, etc. II. as Subst., *slip for propagating*, *Gp*.11.9, etc.; *vine-branch* or *bunch of grapes*, *AP*6.300 (Leon.): metaph., *branch* of a river, Eust.1712.6. **-σπᾰσις**, εως, ἡ, *avulsion, separation*, αὐτόματος ἀ. Aret.*CD*1.4. **-σπασμα**, ατος, τό, *that which is torn off, a piece, rag, shred*, Pl.*Phd*. 113b; *branch, division of a tribe*, Str.9.5.12, cf. Agatharch.57: generally, *a detached portion* or *particle*, ψυχῆς καὶ σώματος ἀ. τὸ σπέρμα Epicur.*Fr*.329, Zeno*Stoic*.1.36, Chrysipp.ib.2.191, Ph.1.119; μύθου Corn.*ND* 7. 2. *avulsion, tearing apart* of bones, Hp.*Off*.23, cf. Gal.18(2).887. **-σπασμάτιον**, τό, Dim. of foreg., *fragment*, Cic.*Att*.2.1.3. **-σπασμός**, ὁ, *tearing away, severing*, Plu.2. 77c; νεύρου Gal.18(1).736. II. *being torn away, separation, severance*, ὁ τῆς συνουσίας ἀ. Str.8.3.17; τῶν ἀναγκαιοτάτων D.H.5. 55, cf. Phld.*Lib*.p.4O.; -μοὶ τῆς ψυχῆς ἀπὸ τοῦ σώματος Id.*Mort*. 9. **-σπαστέον**, *one must sever*, Ph.*Bel*.92.30. ***-σπαστος**, ον, *separated*, ἀπ' ἀλλήλων prob. l. in Theag.ap.Stob.3.1.117. **-σπάω**, fut. -σπάσω [ᾰ], *tear* or *drag away from*, τινός S.*Aj*.1024, Pl.*R*. 491b, etc.; ἀ. τινὰ ἀπὸ γυναικὸς καὶ τέκνων Hdt.3.1, cf. 102; ἀποσπάσας..περόνας ἀπ' αὐτῆς S.*OT*1268; μή μου τὸ τέκνον ἐκ χερῶν ἀποσπάσῃς E.*Hec*.277: rarely ἀ. τινά τι *tear* a thing *from* one, S.*OC* 866; ἀ. τινὰ *tear* him *away*, Hdt.6.91; ἀ. τι τῆς λείας *detach, abstract* some of it, Plb.2.26.8: metaph., ἀ. τινὰ ἐλπίδος S.*OT*1432; and reversely also ἀ. τῆς φρενὸς αἵ μοι μόναι παρῆσαν ἐλπίδων Id.*El*.809; *detach, withdraw*, πλήρωμα a gang of labourers, *PPetr*.3 p.129 (iii B.C.); τινὰ ἀπό τινος *BGU*1125.9 (i B.C.), cf. infr. 5; μαθητὰς *Act.Ap*.20.30; ἀ. πολίτας τῆς θαλάσσης Plu.*Them*.19; ἀπὸ τοῦ φρονεῖν τινά Ar.*Ra*.962:—Med., τὴν μάχην οὕτω μακρὰν τῆς ναυτικῆς βοηθείας Plu.*Pomp*.76:—Pass., *to be dragged away, detached, separated from*, τινός Pi.*P*.9.33, E.*Alc*.287, etc.; ἐξ ἱροῦ Hdt.1.160; ἀπὸ τῶν ἱερῶν Th.3.81; of a bone, *to be torn off*, Hp.*Art*.13; ἀκρώμιον -σπασθέν Id.*Mochl*.6. 2. ἀ. τινὰ κόμης *drag away* by the hair, A. *Supp*.909. 3. ἀ. πύλας, θύρας, *tear off* the gates, doors, Hdt.1.17, 3.159, etc.: metaph., πινακηδὸν ἀποσπῶν [ῥήματα] Ar.*Ra*.824. 4. ἀ. τὸ στρατόπεδον *draw off, divert* the army, X.*HG*1.3.17: abs., ἀποσπάσας *having drawn off*, Id.*An*.7.2.11:—Pass., of troops, *to become separated* or *broken*, Th.7.80, Plb.1.27.9. 5. *withdraw, reclaim*, *POxy*.496.9. 6. ἀπεσπασμένος, ὁ, *eunuch*, Lxx*Le*.22. 24. II. intr. (sc. ἑαυτόν), *separate* (i.e. *be separated*) *from*, Ael. *NA*10.48, Luc.*Icar*.11, D.C.56.22; and in X.*An*.1.5.3 the best Mss. give πολὺ γὰρ ἀπέσπα (for ἀπέπτα) φεύγουσα [στρουθός].

**ἀποσπείρω**, *scatter like seed*, τι ἐς γῆν Luc.*Somn*.15, cf. *Theol.Ar*.6.

**ἀποσπένδω**, *pour out wine*, as a drink-offering, at sacrifices, εὔχετ' ἀποσπένδων Od.3.394; ὤμοσ' ἀποσπένδων 14.331; ἀ. μέθυ E.*Ion* 1198, cf. Antipho 1.20; τινί Pl.*Phd*.117b:—Pass., *AP*5.54 (Diosc.).

**ἀποσπερμ-αίνω**, aor. -ηνα, *shed semen*, εἴς τι Apollod.3.14.6, Palaeph.51. **-ατίζω**, = foreg., Arist.*GA*728ᵃ11; δυνάμεις Porph. *Antr*.16. **-άτισις** [ᾰτ], εως, ἡ, *emission of semen*, Sch.Aristid. p.329 F. **-ᾰτισμός**, ὁ, = foreg., Tz.ad Lyc.598.

**ἀποσπερμᾰτόομαι**, *to be converted into semen*, Steph.*in Hp*.1. 124 D.

**ἀποσπεύδω**, fut. -σπεύσω, *to be zealous in preventing, dissuade earnestly*, τὴν συμβολήν the engagement, Hdt.6.109: c. acc. et inf., ἀ. Ξέρξεα στρατεύεσθαι Id.7.17: abs., opp. ἐπισπεύδω, ib.18, Th.6.29.

**ἀποσπινθηρ-ίζω**, *emit sparks*, Arist.*Mete*.341ᵇ30. **-ισμός**, ὁ, *the emission of sparks*, Hsch.

***ἀπόσπληνος**, ἡ, *rosemary*, Apul.*Herb*.79.

***ἀποσπογγ-ίζω**, *wipe off as with a sponge*, Antipho 5.45, Antyll.ap. Orib.6.9.1:—Med., Sch.Od.8.88. **-ισμα**, ατος, τό, *dirt wiped off with a sponge*, Rh.3.530 W. **-ισμός**, ὁ, *sponging off*, Antyll.ap. Orib.9.23.2, Sor.1.67. **-ιστέον**, *one must wipe off*, Orib.*Fr*.38.

**ἀποσποδέω**, *wear quite off*, τοὺς ὄνυχας *walk* one's toes *off*, Ar. *Av*.8:—Pass., = ἀπερρίφθαι, ἀποθανεῖν, Hsch. II. ἀπεσποδηκότων· φλεγομένων ἐν τῇ τέφρᾳ, Id. (-ικώτων cod.).

**ἀπόσπονδος**, ον, (σπονδή) stronger form for ἄσπονδος (q.v.), Poll. 6.30.

**ἀπόσπορος**, ον, *born from*, θαλάσσης Musae.249, cf. Nonn.*D*.11. 145.

**ἀποσπουδάζω**, *dissuade eagerly*, τινά τινος Philostr.*VA*4.2. II. *slight, despise*, τοὺς Ἐπικούρου λόγους ib.1.7; *show lack of interest in*, τινός Id.*VS*1.17.2.

**ἀποσσεύω**, poet. for ἀποσεύω.

**ἀπόσσῠτος**, ον, *rushing away*, Opp.*H*.2.560, Nonn.*D*.2.686, al.; *thrown out of* a chariot, ib.28.165; *starting from* a mark, of racers, Opp.*H*.4.102; *departing from*, ὠκεανοῖο Tryph.668.

**ἀπόστα**, for ἀπόστηθι, aor. 2 imper. of ἀφίστημι.

**ἀπόσταγμα**, ατος, τό, *that which trickles down*, κυκεῶνος Tz. ad Lyc. 607, *EM*538.16.

**ἀποστᾰδά** [δᾰ], *standing apart*, Od.6.143.

**ἀποστᾰδόν**, Adv., (ἀφίσταμαι) *from afar*, Il.15.556. II. ἀπόσταδον· δίκτυον μεμολυβδωμένον καὶ καλάμῳ περιεννημένον, Hsch.

**ἀποστάζω**, *let fall drop by drop, distil away*, δακρύων ἀποστάζει αἰδῶ A.*Supp*.579 (lyr.); ἀμβροσίαν ἀ. Theoc.15.108: of grains, κρῖμνον κυκεῶνος ἀποστάζοντος ἔραζε Call.*Fr*.205: metaph., φάος Id. *Dian*.118; φωνήν *AP*15.9 (Cyrus). II. intr., *trickle*, Hp.*Coac*.328; μανίας ἀποστάζει μένος fury *distils from* madness, or *trickles away*, i.e. *passes off*, S.*Ant*.959 (lyr.); λόγων ἀ. χρυσός Luc.*Electr*.6; of grain, Herod.6.6: metaph., ῥίνημ' αὐτῆς ἂν οὐκ ἀποστάξαι not a brass farthing would *come off* the price, Id.7.82.

**ἀποστάλ-αγμα** [τᾰ], ατος, τό, = ἀπόσταγμα, αἰγείρων Scymn.397. **-άζω**, = ἀποστάζω II, Luc.*Am*.45: c. acc., ἀποσταλάξει τὰ ὄρη γλυκασμόν Lxx *Jl*.3(4).18 ( = *Am*.9.13). **-άω**, = ἀποστάζω I, Opp.*C*. 3.370, 4.198.

**ἀπόσταλ-μα**, ατος, τό, gloss on ἄφεμα, *EM*176.4. **-τέον**, *one must send away*, Alex.*Fig*.1.1.

**ἀποστάνομαι**, = ἀφίσταμαι, *PGen*.53.21 (iv A.D.).

***ἀπόσταξις**, εως, ἡ, *nose-bleeding*, Hp.*Acut*.(*Sp*.)29.

**ἀπο-στᾰσία**, ἡ, late form for ἀπόστασις, *defection, revolt*, v.l. in D.H.7.1, J.*Vit*.10, Plu.*Galb*.1; esp. in religious sense, *rebellion against God, apostasy*, Lxx*Jo*.22.22, 2*Ep.Th*.2.3. 2. *departure, disappearance*, Olymp.*in Mete*.320.2. 3. *distinguishing*, c. gen., Elias *in Cat*.119.7. 4. *distance*, Archim.*Aren*.1.5. ***-στᾰσίου** δίκη action against a freedman *for having forsaken his* προστάτης and chosen another, ἀ. ὀφλεῖν D.25.65, cf. 35.48, Arist.*Ath*.58.3, prob. in *IG*2.776. II. ἀποστασίου βιβλίον writing or bill *of divorce*, Lxx *De*.24.1, *Ev.Matt*.19.7, *Ev.Marc*.10.4: so ἀποστάσιον *Ev.Matt*.5.32. III. ἀποστασίου συγγραφή deed *of cession, conveyance*, *PHib*.1.96.3 (iii B.C.), cf. *PGiss*.36.21 (ii B.C.), etc.; ἀντίγραφον -ίου *BGU*919.23 (ii A.D.); with συγγραφή omitted, esp. in phrase πρᾶσις καὶ ἀποστασίου *PTeb*.561ʳ (i A.D), etc. **-στᾰσις**, εως, ἡ, (ἀφίστημι) *causing to revolt*, συμμάχων Th.1.122; Ἰώνων ἀπὸ τῆς Λακεδαιμονίων συμμαχίας Arist.*Ath*.23.4. B. (ἀφίσταμαι) *emanation*, εἰδώλων -σεις Epicur.*Fr*.320. 2. *slackness*, of bandages, Gal.18(2).806. 3. *defection, revolt*, ἀπό τινος Hdt.3.128; τὴν Κυπρίων ἀ. πρῆξαι Id.5.113; τὴν Αἰγύπτου ἀ. παρασκευάζεσθαι Id.7.4; ἀ. ἐκ τῆς ξυμμαχίας Th.5.81; ἀ. πρός τινα Id.1.75; διπλῆν ἀ. ἀποστήσεσθαι Id.3.13; ἀ. τῶν Ἀθηναίων, for ἀπὸ τ. Ἀ., Id.8.5; but τὰς

Μεσσηνίων ἀ. Pl.*Lg.*777c. 4. *departure from*, βίου E.*Hipp.*277; *separation* of effect *from* cause, Procl.*Inst.*35; *giving up, cession*, ἀ. τῶν κτημάτων D.19.146; *desisting from, disuse of*, φάσεως S.E.*P.*1.192; τῶν ἀπροαιρέτων Arr.*Epict.*4.4.39. 5. *distance*, ἁ ἀφ' ἁμῶν ἀ. Archyt.1; ἀφεστάναι τῇ αὐτῇ ἀ. ᾗπερ.. Pl.*Phd.*111b; ἀπόστασιν ὅσην ἀφεστηκὼς γίγνεται Id.*R.*587d, cf. 546b; ἐκ μικρᾶς ἀ. Arist.*Aud.*800b7; τῇ ἀπὸ τῆς γῆς ἀ. Id.*HA*503a21; ἐκ τῶν ἀ. according to their *distances*, Id.*Cael.*290b22; of time, κατὰ τὴν πρὸς τὸ νῦν ἀ. Id.*Ph.*223b5; ἐξ ἀποστάσεως at *a certain distance*, Plb.3.114.3; ἐν ἀποστάσει Id.3.113.4, Phld.*Herc.*19.25; κατ' ἀποστάσεις Hanno *Peripl.*13. 6. Rhet., *employment of detached phrases*, Hermog.*Id.*1.10, Aristid.*Rh.*1 p.462S., Philostr.*VS*1.9.1 (pl.), *Ep.*73. 7. *lapse, declension*, Plot.1.8.7, 5.1.1. II. *place where something is put away, repository, storehouse*, Str.17.1.9, Philippid.14, Heraclid.*Pol.*72. III. Medic., *suppurative inflammation, throwing off the peccant humours left by fever*, etc., Hp.*Epid.*3.4 (pl.), Aret.*SD*1.0, Aristid.*Or.*47(23).68. 2. of diseases, *transition from one to another*, Hp.*Epid.*1.6; στραγγουριώδης ἀ. ib.3.ια'. 3. *lesion* of continuity, Gal.18(2).820. 4. *degree* of heat, cold, etc., Id.11.561. al. **-στᾰτέον**, (ἀφίσταμαι) *one must stand off from*, i.e. *give up, abandon*, πολέμου Th.8.2, etc.; οὐκ..ἀ. τῇ πόλει τούτων D.18.199: abs., οὐκ ἀ. πρίν.. Pl.*Plt.*257c. II. later, (ἀφίστημι) *one must keep apart, detain*, ἵππον ἀπὸ τῶν ἔργων *Gp.*16.1.4. ⊛**-στᾰτέω**, *stand aloof from*, τινός A.*Ch.*826 (lyr.), *Fr.*161, 301; οὔκουν πάρος γε σῆς ἀπεστάτουν φρενός S.*Ant.*993; μορφῆς δὲ τῆς σῆς οὐκ ἀπεστάτει was not *far from*.., Id.*OT*743; *fall off from, fail* one, κοὐκ ἀποστατῶ φίλων Ar.*Av.*312; βουλευτέον ὅπως μηδεὶς τῶν νῦν παρόντων ἀποστατήσει ἡμῶν συμμάχων X.*Cyr.*4.5.24; ἀ. τῶν ὄντων *to be absent from*, Pl.*Prm.*144b, cf. *Tht.*205a. 2. of the soul, etc, *fall away* from the divine, Plot.5.1.5, 5.3.16. II. abs., *stand aloof, be absent*, A.*Ch.*444 (lyr.); ἑκάς, πρόσω ἀ., Id.*Ag.*1104 (lyr.), *Eu.*65; σμικρὸν ἀ. Pl.*Cra.*428d. **-στᾰτήρ**, ῆρος, ὁ, *one who has power to dissolve an assembly* or *to decide a question*, Lex Lyc. ap. Plu.*Lyc.*6; cf. ἀφίστημι. **-στάτης** [τᾰ], ου, ὁ, *deserter, rebel*, ἀ. τοῦ βασιλέως Plb.5.57.4, cf. Wilcken *Chr.*10 (ii B.C.), Plu.*Cim.*10; *seceder*, *SIG*705.41,50 (Delph., ii B.C.). II. *runaway slave*, Plu.*Rom.*9; ἀ. κύων *runaway* dog, Id.2.821d. III. Lat. *apostata, apostate*, *Cod.Theod.*16.7.7. **-στᾰτικός**, ή, όν, *of* or *for rebels, rebellious*, θράσος Plu.*Rom.*7. Adv. -κῶς, ἔχειν to be *ready for revolt*, Id.*Pel.*15: Comp. -ότερον, φρονούντων *PLond.*2.354.6 (i B.C.); -κῶς πράττειν τοῦ λόγου Chrysipp. ap. Gal.5.406. II. *disposed to exfoliate*, of bones, Hp.*Fract.*25, Antyll. ap. Orib.6.1.6. III. Rhet., *belonging to* ἀπόστασις B.I.6; -κόν, τό, Hermog.*Id.*1.10; σχήματα ibid., Aps.p.259H.; λόγος Eust.1389.28. Adv. -κῶς Id.635.58. **-στάτις** [τᾰ], ιδος, ἡ, pecul. fem. of ἀποστάτης, ἀ. πόλις Lxx 1*Es.*2.18, J.*AJ*11.2.1.

**ἀποσταυρόω**, *fence off with a palisade*, Th.4.69, 6.101, X.*HG*7.4.32, Plb.4.56.8, Plu.*Arat.*40:—Pass., Pherecr.17.

**ἀποστᾰφῐδόομαι**, Pass., = σταφιδόομαι, Thphr.*CP*2.8.3.

**ἀποστᾰχύω**, *to be in the ear*, of corn, *Gp.*2.24.3.

**ἀποστεγ-άζω**, *uncover*, πυκινὸν ῥόον Emp.100.14 (prob. in 42.1); ἀ. τὸν νεών *unroof* it, Str.8.3.30, cf. 4.4.6 (Pass.), *IG*12(3).325.30 (Thera, ii A.D., Pass.); ἀ. τὸ τρῆμα *open* it, Sotad.2. 2. *take off* a covering, τὴν στέγην *Ev.Marc.*2.4. II. = ἀποστέγω I, *cover closely*, Thphr.*CP*5.6.5, Arist.*Pr.*924a37. **-ασμα**, ατος, τό, *protection against*, ψύχους Thphr.*CP*5.13.3. **-ασσις** (Dor. for -στέγασις), εως, ἡ, *plastering*, πλίνθων, τοίχων, *IG*4.823.24,25 (Troezen). **-νόω**, *cover close*, Moschio ap. Ath.5.207b:—Pass., *to be blocked*, of the intestines, Hp.*Acut.*(*Sp.*)51; *to be luted* or *sealed up close*, Hero *Spir.*1.23, 2.10. **-ω**, *shelter* or *protect*, αἱ ὀφρύες ἀ., οἷον ἀπογείσωμα, τῶν ὑγρῶν Arist.*PA*658b16: c. acc. only, *protect*, Id.*Pr.*924b1; ἀ. καὶ τηρεῖ τὴν ζωὴν [ὁ φλοιός] Thphr.*CP*1.4.5. II. *keep out* or *off*, τὸ ὕδωρ Arist.*Pr.*924a26, cf. Emp.84.10, Pl.*Lg.*844b; τὸ ψῦχος Arist.*Pr.*939b17; τὴν ἁλμυρίδα Thphr.*CP*3.6.3, al.; θερμότητα καὶ ὑγρότητα ib.4.12.2, cf. 5.12.9, Plu.2.665f: metaph., ὄχλον πύργος ἀποστέγει A.*Th.*234 (lyr.); ἀ. πληγὰς λίθων Plb.6.23.5.

**ἀποστείνομαι**, gloss on ὀρέχθεον, Sch.Il.23.30.

**ἀποστεινόω**, poet. for ἀποστενόω.

**ἀποστείχω**, aor. ἀπέστῐχον, *go away, go home*, οἴκαδ' ἀ. Od.11.132, etc.; imper. ἀπόστιχε Il.1.522: aor. part. ἀποστιχόντων Hdt.9.56; ἐς νύκτ' ἀποστείχοντος ἡλίου A.*Supp.*769, cf. S.*El.*799, etc.

⊛**ἀποστέλλω**, fut. -στελῶ: aor. ἀπέστειλα (v. infr.):—*send off* or *away from*, μή μ'..τῆσδ' ἀποστείλητε γῆς S.*El.*71, cf. E.*Med.*281; τῆσδ' ἀ. χθονός Id.*Cyc.*468; ἔξω χθονὸς Id.*Ph.*485; ἐκ τῆς πόλεως Pl.*R.*607b; *send away, banish*, τὰ δίκαια S.*Ph.*450; τινά E.*Hec.*731:—Pass., *go away, depart*, S.*OT*115; ἀποστέλλου χθονὸς E.*Supp.*582; δόμων..τῶν ἐμῶν ἀπεστάλης Id.*Hel.*660; φυγὰς ἀποσταλεὶς Id.*Ph.*319 (lyr.); πρὸς σὲ δεῦρ' ἀπεστάλην Id.*IT*1409. II. *dispatch*, on some mission or service, S.*Ph.*125, 1297, etc.; freq. of messengers or forces, Hdt.1.46,123; νέας ἐπὶ χώρην Id.7.235, cf. 8.64; στρατὸν παρά τινα Id.5.32; ναῦς αὐτοῖς ἀ. βοηθοὺς Th.1.45; also ἀ. ἀποικίην Hdt.4.150; οἰκιστάς (as a form of banishment), Arist.*Pol.*1306b31; πρεσβείαν Th.3.28; ἀγγέλους X.*An.*2.1.5, etc.; ἀπαρχὴν εἰς Δελφοὺς Arist.*Fr.*485:—Pass., c. inf., οἱ ἀποσταλέντες στρατεύεσθαι Id.3.26, cf. 5.33; ἀποσταλθέντες *GDI*5186.4 (Cret.). III. *put off, doff*, θαἰμάτια Ar.*Lys.*1084. IV. intr., *retire, withdraw*, of the sea, Th.3.89; of persons, οἴκαδε D.32.5.

**ἀποστενοχωρέω**, *straiten, cramp*, Ath.Mech.40.1, Gal.19.408.

**ἀποστενόω**, poet. -στεινόω, *straiten*, Thphr.*Ign.*54 (Pass.), Alex.Aphr.*Pr.*1.75; ὄμματα ἀπεστείνωτο Theoc.22.101; τόπος ἀπεστενωμένος D.S.3.37: metaph. in Pass., *to be contracted*, γνῶσις ἀπεστενωμένη Simp.*in Ph.*18.4; ἐπιχείρησις -μένη *hampered*, Alex.Aphr.*in Top.*56.3; τὸν τοῦ ἑνὸς ἀπεστενωμένον ἰδιασμόν Dam.*Pr.*28bis.

**ἀποστένω**, *bewail*, πόθον Aristaenet.2.18.

**ἀποστέν-ωσις**, εως, ἡ, *straitening, straits*, Sch.Il.23.330. 2. *contraction*, Dam.*Pr.*59 (pl.). **-ωτικός**, ή, όν, *straitening*, i.e. *condensing*, opp. πλατυντικός, Eust.315.11.

**ἀποστεπτικός**, ή, όν, *of* or *for discrowning*, ᾆσμα, a bridal chant, *EM*131.38.

**ἀποστέργω**, *get rid of love, love no more*, Theoc.14.50; μητέρα ἀ. Philostr.*VS*2.25.2; *loath, reject*, τι A.*Ag.*499; ἀοιδάν Terpand.5; πόθους τινός Theoc.*Ep.*4.14; πίστιν Doroth. in *Cat.Cod.Astr.*2.175. II. *empty of love, harden*, καρδίαν Lxx *De.*15.7.

**ἀποστερεόω**, *harden*, Ph.*Bel.*79.4, 81.4:—Pass., *become solid*, Arist.*Mir.*837b13, 844a14: metaph., -όομαι πρός τι *persist stubbornly in*, Phld.*Rh.*2.31S.

**ἀποστέρ-εσις**, εως, ἡ, = ἀποστέρησις II, *POxy.*71.10 (iv A.D.). **-έω**: —Pass., fut. -στερηθήσομαι Lys.12.70, v.l. in D.1.22; also -στερήσομαι E.*HF*137 (lyr.), Th.6.91, D.24.210; ἀποστεροῦμαι And.1.149: pf. ἀπεστέρημαι, etc.:—*rob, despoil, defraud* one *of* a thing, c. acc. pers. et gen. rei, χρημάτων ἀ. τινά Hdt.5.92.έ; τὸν πατέρα τῆς τυραννίδος Ar.*Av.*1605; τῆς ψυχῆς Antipho 4.1.6: c. acc. pers. et rei, μή μ' ἀποστερήσῃς ἡδονάν S.*El.*1276 (lyr.), cf. Antipho 3.3.2, X.*An.*7.6.9, Is.8.43, etc.: abs., *commit fraud*, Ar.*Nu.*487; ἀπεστερηκὼς ὑπ' ἀνάγκης being constrained to *become a defaulter*, Pl.*Phdr.*241b; συνέστιον ὢν ἔκγονον ἢ ἀδελφὸν ἀπεστέρηκε γίγνεσθαι Id.*Lg.*868d:—Pass., *to be robbed* or *deprived of*, c. gen., Ἑλλάδος ἀπεστερημένος Hdt.3.130; σοῦ τ' ἀπεστερημένη καὶ πατρός S.*El.*813; ἡδονῶν Ar.*Nu.*1072; ἁπάντων ἂν ἀπεστερήμην D.21.106: c. acc., ἵππους ἀπεστέρηνται X.*Cyr.*6.1.12, etc.: abs., εἰ δ' ἀπεστερήμεθα if we *have been frustrated*, S.*Aj.*782. 2. ἀ. ἑαυτόν τινος *detach, withdraw* oneself *from* a person or thing, τῶν [ἀγαλμάτων]..ἀπεστέρησ' ἐμαυτόν Id.*OT*1381; οὐκ ἀποστερῶν γε τῶν ἐς τὴν πόλιν ἑαυτὸν οὐδενὸς Antipho 5.78; ἄλλου ἑαυτὸν ἀ. Th.1.40; ἀ. ἑαυτὸν τοῦ φρονεῖν Crobyl.3; ἐκείνους..ἀ. μὴ ἂν.. ἀποτειχίσαι *deprive* them *of* the power of walling off, Th.7.6:—reversely, ἀ. τὸν ἔλεον ἑαυτοῦ Plu.*Aem.*26, cf. *Dem.*4. 3. c. acc. pers., *defraud, rob*, Hdt.7.155, Ar.*Pl.*373, 1*Ep.Cor.*6.7, etc.; θεούς Pl.*Lg.*917d. 4. c. acc. rei only, *filch away*, S.*Ph.*931; *withhold*, A.*Pr.*777, S.*OT*323, Ar.*Nu.*1305; *refuse payment* of a debt, D.21.44, etc.; *refuse to give up*, παρακαταθήκην Arist.*Rh.*1383b21; Ζεὺς ἀποστεροίη γάμον *may he avert* it, A.*Supp.*1063 (lyr.). 5. τὸ σαφές μ' ἀποστερεῖ certainty *fails* me, E.*Hel.*577. II. in Logic, *draw a negative conclusion*, Arist.*APr.*44b23. (ἀποστέρω is f.l. in Isoc.12.243.) **-ησις**, εως, ἡ, *deprivation*, τῆς ἀκοῆς Th.7.70; ἐπ' ἀποστερήσει τοῦ δούλου for the purpose of *depriving* him *of* the slave, Pl.*Lg.*936d. II. *withholding what is due*, Antipho Soph.107, D.24.111; ἐπ' ἀποστερήσει τῶν ἐμῶν in order to *avoid payment* of my claims, Id.30.5. **-ητέον**, *one must defraud*, τινά τινος Plu.2.931d. **-ητής**, οῦ, ὁ, *one who withholds*, Arist.*EE*1232a15; esp. *one who withholds what is due, a defrauder, cheat*, Pl.*R.*344b, *POxy.*745.7 (i A.D.); ἀποστερητὴν ἀγοράσας ἀγρόν a farm *that costs money* instead of bringing it in, *Com.Adesp.*109. **-ητικός**, ή, όν, *of* or *for withholding* by fraud, γνώμη ἀ. τόκου a device *for cheating* one of his interest, Ar.*Nu.*747, cf. 728. **-ητρίς**, ίδος, ἡ, fem., *for cheating*, γνώμη ib.730. **-ίζω**, = sq., *carry off*, ἀ. τὴν πλεονεξίην τοῦ σώματος Hp.*Gland.*17 (s.v.l.). **-ίσκω**, = ἀποστερέω, S.*OC*376.

**ἀποστερνίζω**, *expectorate*, *Gloss.*

⊛**ἀποστεφᾰνόω**, *rob of the crown, discrown*, Charito 1.5, etc.:—Med., aor. inf. -ώσασθαι *lay aside one's crown*, D.L.2.54, Max.Tyr.5.9:—Pass., Luc.*JTr.*10, Jul.*Caes.*310c.

⊛**ἀποστηθίζω**, (στῆθος) *repeat by heart*, *EM*277.56, David *Proll.*5.22.

⊛**ἀπό-στημα**, ατος, τό, *distance, interval*, ἀ. τοῦ ἡλίου πρὸς τὴν γῆν Arist.*Cael.*294a4; τῶν σφαιρῶν Id.*Metaph.*1073b33, cf. Phld.*Sign.*9, etc.; ἐξ ἀ. θεωρεῖσθαι Epicur.*Ep.*2 p.39U.; ὅπλα τὰ ἐξ ἀ. λεγόμενα Ascl.*Tact.*1.2. 2. *degree* of descent from an ancestor, τοῖς ἀ. πρὸς τοὺς γονεῖς παντοδαπῶς ἔχειν Arist.*EN*1100a26. 3. *abscess*, Hp.*Aph.*7.36, Arist.*Pr.*885b31, Thphr.*Od.*59. **-στημᾰτίας**, ου, ὁ, *one who has an abscess*, Aret.*SD*1.9. **-στημᾰτικός**, ή, όν, *due to an abscess*, Heliod. ap. Orib.44.23.74. II. *at a distance*, οὐδὲν ἀ. παρεμφαίνουσα Chrysipp.*Stoic.*2.245. **-στημάτιον** [ᾰτ], τό, Dim. of ἀπόστημα, Gal.17(1).326, Heliod. ap. Orib.44.14.10. ⊛**-στημᾰτώδης**, ες, *of the nature of an abscess*, Hp.*Coac.*141.

**ἀποστήρ-ιγμα**, ατος, τό, *stay, support*, Hp.*Off.*25, cf. *EM*125.17. 2. *determination* of humours, Hp.*Flat.*9. **-ίζομαι**, Med., *fix firmly*, βάκτρον ἐς γᾶν *APl.*4.265.9. 2. *support oneself firmly, throw one's weight upon*, τοῖς μηροῖς Arist.*Pr.*882b30: πρὸς τὸ ὑποκείμενον Id.*IA*705a8, cf. *MA*699a5. II. Medic., of diseases, *to be confirmed*, Hp.*Prorrh.*2.2. 2. ἀ. ἐς.., of humours, *determine* towards a particular part of the body, Hp.*Hum.*7; of labour pains, Arist.*HA*586b28: also in Act., Hp. l.c., cf. *Prorrh.*2.14. ⊛**-ιξις**, εως, ἡ, *fulcrum* or *rest for a lever*, Hp.*Mochl.*42.

**ἀποστῐβής**, ές, (στίβος) *off the road, solitary*, S.*Fr.*558.

**ἀποστίζω**, *mark with points* or *lines*, f.l. for ὑπ- in Gal.17(1).560, al.

**ἀποστιλβόω**, *make to shine*, κύπελλον *AP*7.329.

**ἀπο-στίλβω**, Ep. impf. ἀπεστίλβεσκε Epic. in *Arch.Pap.*7.7:—*to be bright from* or *with*, ἀποστίλβοντες ἀλείφατος Od.3.408: c. dat., Lyc.253; ἐθείραις *AP*5.25, cf. Luc.*Asin.*47: c. gen., χρυσοῦ Id.*JTr.*8, cf. *Hipp.*6; φῶς ἀπό τινος Plot.2.1.7. 2. abs., φαίνεται τὸ ὕδωρ ἀποστίλβον τῆς νυκτὸς *phosphorescent*, Arist.*Mete.*370a14; *shine brightly*, Thphr.*Sign.*26, Agatharch.95, Luc.*DMar.*14.2, etc.; ἀκτὶς ἀ. εἰς πέλαγος Alciphr.1.1. 3. Act., *shed* light, etc., Μήνη σέλας -ουσα κεραίης Nonn.*D*.5.165; καθαρότητα Iamb.*Myst*.2.8. **-στιλψις**, εως, ἡ, *emission of light*, Sch.A.R.3.1377 (pl.), Hsch. s. v. αἰγίς.

**ἀποστλεγγ-ίζω**, *scrape with a* στλεγγίς (q. v.), Philostr.*Gym*.18,51:—Med., *scrape oneself clean*, X.*Oec*.11.18; pf. part. Pass. ἀπεστλεγγισμένοι *scraped clean, fresh from the bath*, Ar.*Eq*.580; -ισάμενοι Arist.*Pr*.867ᵇ4; censured as archaic by Luc.*Rh.Pr*.17. **-ισμα**, ατος, τό, *scrapings with the* στλεγγίς, Str.5.2.6.

***ἀποστολ-εύς**, έως, ὁ, *one who dispatches*, ἀ. τῶν ἐνσωματωμένων ψυχῶν Herm.ap.Stob.1.49.69: but mostly, 2. at Athens, *magistrate who had to fit out* a squadron for service, D.18.107, 47.26, Aeschin.2.177, Philoch.142, *IG*2.809ᵇ20. ***-ή**, ἡ, (ἀποστέλλω) *sending off* or *away*, E.*IA*688, *Ph*.1043 (lyr., pl.); *dispatching*, νεῶν Th.8.9; *sending forth on their journey*, ξένων ὑποδοχὰς καὶ ἀ. Arist.*EN*1123ᵃ3, cf. *IG*2.238.15; δοῦναί τι ἀποστολάς τινι *as a parting gift*, Lxx 3*Ki*.9.16, cf. 1*Ma*.2.18. 2. *shooting, discharge*, βέλους Ph.*Bel*.68.33. 3. *discharge from service*, οὐκ ἔστιν ἀ. ἐν ἡμέρᾳ πολέμου Lxx *Ec*.8.8. 4. *payment* of tribute, Jul.*Ep*.204. II. (from Pass.) *expedition*, Th.8.8. 2. *apostleship*, 1*Ep.Cor*.9.2, *Ep.Gal*.2.8. ***-ικός**, ή, όν, *sung on departure*, μέλη Procl.ap.Phot.p.322 B. **-ιμαῖος**, α, ον, *sent off, missive*, φίλημα Ach.Tat.2.9. II. *connected with dismissal*, φράσις Eust.790.44. **-ιον**, τό, *tax for escort* of caravans, *OGI*674.4 (Coptos, i A.D.). ***-ος**, ὁ, *messenger, ambassador, envoy*, ὁ μὲν δὴ ἀ. ἐς τὴν Μίλητον ἦν Hdt.1.21; ἐς Λακεδαίμονα τριήρεϊ ἀ. ἐγίνετο he went off *on a mission* to Laced., Id.5.38. b. *commander of a naval force*, Hsch. 2. *messenger from God*, Lxx 3*Ki*.14.6; esp. of the *Apostles*, *Ev.Matt*.10.2, al. II. = στόλος, *naval squadron* or *expedition*, Lys.19.21; ἀπόστολον ἀφιέναι, ἀποστέλλειν, ποιεῖσθαι, D.3.5, 18.80,107, *IG*2.809ᵇ190. 2. *colony*, D.H.9.59. 3. = ἀποστολή, of envoys, J.*AJ*17.11.1. 4. ἀπόστολον, τό, with or without πλοῖον, *packet*, Pl.*Ep*.346a, Ps.-Hdt.*Vit.Hom*.19. 5. ἀπόστολος, ὁ, *order for dispatch*, of a vessel, *CPHerm*.6.11 (iii A.D., pl.), *PAmh*.2.138.10 (iv A.D.), cf. *Dig*.49.6.1. 6. *export-licence*, *PGnom*.162 (ii A.D.). 7. gen. dub., *cargo dispatched by order*, *POxy*.522.1, al. (ii A.D.), *PTeb*486 (ii/iii A.D.).

**ἀποστομ-ατίζω**, (στόμα) *teach by word of mouth, teach by dictation*, γράμματα ἀ. Pl.*Euthd*.277a: abs., ὅταν ἀ. ὑμῖν ὁ γραμματεύς ib.276c:—Pass., τὸ ἀποστοματιζόμενον *dictated lesson*, ibid., Arist.*SE*165ᵇ32. 2. *interrogate, catechize*, as a master his pupil, *Ev.Luc*.11.53, cf. Pl.ap.Poll.1.102 (Pass.). II. *repeat by heart*, Ath.8.359d, Antyll. ap.Orib.6.9.4: generally, *recite, repeat*, Plu.*Thes*.24. **-ίζω**, *deprive of an edge*, πέλεκυς ἀπεστομισμένος Philostr.*Im*.2.17. II. = foreg. II, Hsch. III. = φιμόω, Id. **-όω**, *stop the mouth of*, Cerc.11.7: hence, *block, stop up*, τὰς διώρυχας Plb.*Fr*.117. II. = ἀποστομίζω I, ὅπλα ἀπεστομωμένα τὰς ἀκμάς D.H.6.14, cf. Luc.*Tim*.10. ***-ωσις**, εως, ἡ, *laying open, opening*, τῶν πόρων Arist.*Pr*.888ᵃ28.

**ἀπόστοργος**, ον, *devoid of affection*, ἀ. γίγνεσθαι Plu.2.491c. Adv. -γως, ἔχειν τινός Lib.*Decl*.51.13. II. = ἀπεχθής, *unlovable*, Hsch.

**ἀποστράβοομαι** [ρᾰ], Pass., *become squinting*, Sor.1.106.

**ἀποστραγγᾰλίζω**, *kill by strangling*, D.S.14.12, Str.17.1.11.

**ἀποστραγγίζω**, *check*, *Theol.Ar*.49 (Pass.).

**ἀποστρᾰκ-ίζω**, *bake to a hard crust*, of a quick fire, Gal.6.484. II. *banish by ostracism*, Hsch., Suid. **-όομαι**, *become dry like a potsherd*, Hp.*VC*16, Dsc.2.4, Hippiatr.25; *to be ossified*, Phlp.*in GA*113.1.

**ἀποστράπτω**, *flash forth*, φλόγα A.R.3.1018 (tm.).

***ἀποστρᾰτεύομαι**, *to be discharged from military service*, App.*BC*5.26.

**ἀποστράτηγος** [ρᾰ], ὁ, *retired general*, ἀ. ποιεῖν τινά *to remove* him *from the command, supersede* him, D.23.149; also, *general who has completed his term of office*, Plu.*Marc*.22.

**ἀποστρᾰτοπεδεύομαι**, *remove one's camp from, encamp away from*, τινός X.*An*.3.4.34; ἀ. προσωτέρω *encamp at a* greater *distance*, ib.7.7.1.

**ἀποστρεβλόομαι**, Pass., *to be horribly tortured*, Lxx 2*Ma*.9.7.

**ἀπο-στρεπτικός**, ή, όν, *repellent*, Gal.4.819. **-στρεπτος**, ον, *turned back*, = ἀποστραφείς, Phryn.*PS*p.15 B. 2. *hostile, unacceptable*, Diogenian.Epicur.4.62. ***-στρέφω**, Dor. aor. ἀποστράψαι *SIG*244 ii 16 (Delph.); Ion. aor. ἀποστρέψασκε Il.22.197, etc.: pf. ἀπέστροφα Lxx 1*Ki*.6.21:—Pass. and Med., fut. -στρέψομαι X.*Cyr*.5.5.36, Plu.2.387c: aor. -εστράφην [ᾰ], S.*OC*1272, etc.; later -εστρεψάμην Lxx *Ho*.8.3, prob. in Ar.*Nu*.776: fut. -στρᾰφήσομαι Lxx *Nu*.25.4, al.: pf. -έστραμμαι Hdt.1.166, etc.: Ion. 3 pl. plpf. -εστράφατο ibid.; -έστρεμμαι *PSI*4.392.11 (iii B.C.):—*turn back*: hence, either *turn to flight*, ὄφρ'..Ἀχαιοὺς αὖτις ἀποστρέψῃσιν Il.15.62, etc., cf. Hdt.8.94; or *turn back from flight*, X.*Cyr*.4.3.1; *send home again*, Th.4.97, 5.75; ῥῆμα *bring back* word, Lxx 4*Ki*.22.9; ἀποστρέψαντε πόδας καὶ χεῖρας *having twisted back* the hands and feet so as to bind them, Od.22.173,190, cf. S.*OT*1154; τὸν ὦμον Ar.*Eq*.263; ἀποστρέφετε τὰς χεῖρας αὐτῶν, ὦ Σκύθαι Ar.*Lys*.455; ἀ. τὸν αὐχένα Hdt.4.188; *guide back again*, ἀποστρέψαντες ἔβαν νέας Od.3.162; ἴχνι' ἀποστρέψας *having turned* the steps of the oxen *backwards* so as to make it appear that they had gone the other way, *h.Merc*.76; *turn away, avert*, αὐχέν' ἀποστρέψας Thgn.858; ἀπέστρεψ' ἔμπαλιν παρηΐδα E.*Med*.1148; but τὸ πρόσωπον πρός τινα Plu.*Publ*.6; *bring back, recall*, ἐξ Ἰσθμοῦ X.*An*.2.6.3; φῶτας ἀπέστρεψεν Περσεφόνης θαλάμων [Emp.]156.4. 2. *turn away* or *aside, divert*, v.l. in Th.4.80, etc.; ὕδατα *cut off* water from a besieged town, Ph.*Bel*.97.4; τὸν Κάϋστρον *SIG*839.14 (Ephesus); τὸν πόλεμον ἐς Μακεδονίαν Arr.*An*.2.1.1; *avert* a danger, an evil, etc., πῆμ' ἀ. νόσου A.*Ag*.850 (Porson); *prevent*, Dsc.2.136; *rebut*, δίκην Ar.*Nu*.776 (v. supr.); ἀ. τύχην μὴ οὐ γενέσθαι Antipho6.15 codd.; ἀ. εἰς τοὐναντίον τοὺς λόγους Pl.*Sph*.239d; τὰς πράξεις εἰς τοὺς ἀντιδίκους Arist.*Rh.Al*.1442ᵇ6. 3. ἀ. τινά τινος *dissuade from*, X.*Eq.Mag*.1.12; τινὰ ἀπὸ τοῦ λήμματος Din.2.23; πότων ἀ. τοὺς στομάχους D.H.*Dem*.15. II. as if intr. (sc. ἑαυτόν, ἵππον, ναῦν, etc.), *turn back*, Th.6.65; ἀ. ὀπίσω Hdt.4.43; ἀ. πάλιν S.*OC*1403. 2. *turn away* or *aside*, Hdt.8.87; of a river, Id.4.52; τἀναντία ἀ. X.*HG*3.4.12.

B. Pass., *to be turned back*, ἀπεστράφθαι τοὺς ἐμβόλους, of ships, *to have* their beaks *bent back*, Hdt.1.166; ἀποστραφῆναι..τὼ πόδε *to have* one's feet *twisted*, Ar.*Pax*279; τρίχες ἀπεστραμμέναι *close-curled*, Arist.*Phgn*.809ᵇ26. II. Med and Pass., *turn oneself from* or *away*, ἀπεστραμμέναι ἀπ' ἀλλήλων Id.*HA*611ᵃ6; ἀπεστραμμένοι *back to back*, Apollod.*Poliorc*.145.2: esp., 1. *turn one's face away from, abandon*, c. acc., Phoc.2, Sallust.3; ἐχθροῦ ἀξίωσιν Epicur.*Fr*.215; μή μ' ἀποστραφῇς S.*OC*1272; μή μ' ἀποστρέφου E.*IT*801, cf. Ar.*Pax*683, X.*Cyr*.5.5.36, *PSI* l.c.; τὸ θεῖον ῥᾳδίως ἀπεστράφης E.*Supp*.159: also c. gen., ἄψορρος οἴκων τῶνδ' ἀποστραφείς S.*OT*431: c. dat., ἀστεφανώτοισι ἀπυστρέφονται Sapph.78: abs., μὴ πρὸς θεῶν ..ἀποστραφῇς S.*OT*326; ἀπεστραμμένοι λόγοι *hostile* words, Hdt.7.160; τὴν διάνοιαν ἀποστρέφεσθαι *to be alienated*, Phld.*Lib*.p.8 O. 2. *turn oneself about*, X.*Cyr*.1.4.25; ἅρματα ἀπεστραμμένα ὥσπερ εἰς φυγήν ib.6.2.17; ἀποστραφῆναι λυγιζόμενος *escape* by wriggling, Pl.*R*.405c. 3. ἀποστραφῆναί τινος *fall off from* one, *desert* him, X.*HG*4.8.4. ***-στροφή**, ἡ, *turning back*, X.*Eq*.9.6; ἀ. νώτων Max.Tyr.9.8; ἀ. λαμβάνειν make *a bend*, of a stream, Plu.*Luc*.27, cf. Luc.*Hipp*.2. 2. *twisting*, ὀρχέων ἀποστροφαί Trag.(Satyr.)*Oxy*.1083.10. II. *turning away from, escape, refuge*, c. gen., τύχης, κακῶν, A.*Pr*.769, E.*Fr*.444; ζημίας Id.*Med*.1223. 2. *resort, recourse*, Hdt.8.109, Th.4.76; ἥκει βίου τελευτή κοὐκέτ' ἔστ' ἀ. S.*OC*1473, cf. E.*Med*.603; οὐκ ἔχων ἀ. D.4.8, cf. Hyp.*Dem.Fr*.5; in pl., Antip.*Stoic*.3.255: c. gen. objecti, οὔ σφί ἐστι ὕδατος οὐδεμία ἄλλη ἀ. no other *means for getting* water, Hdt.2.13; so σωτηρίας ἀ. Th.8.75; βίου Luc.*DMeretr*.6.1; ἀ. τοῦ δήμου ποιεῖσθαι secure a *refuge with*.., Philostr.*VS*2.1.4. III. Rhet., *apostrophe*, when *one turns away from all others to one*, and addresses him specially, Phld.*Lib*.p.11 O., Quint.*Inst*.9.2.38, Longin.16.2, Hermog.*Inv*.4.4, *Id*.1.10 (pl.), Phoeb.*Fig*.1.1, Alex.*Fig*.1.20. IV. *aversion*, Plot.1.1.1; opp. ἐπιθυμία, Simp.*in de An*.15.36; γευμάτων Aret.*SD*2.6; σιτίων Gal.11.261; ὀσμῆς *Gp*.12.39.8. V. *diversion, amusement*, Plu.2.133b (pl.). VI. *elision*, A.D.*Pron*.46.1 (ubi leg. ἑ). VII. = προδοσία, Hsch. **-στροφία**, ἡ, *she that turns away*, epith. of Aphrodite, Paus.9.16.3. **-στροφος**, ον, *turned away, averted*, ἀποστρόφους αὐγὰς ἀπείρξω S.*Aj*.69: *turned away from*, c. gen., σελήνης Man.1.57: also c. dat., δισσοῖς σελάεσσιν ἀ. οἶμον ἰοῦσα Id.6.127. Adv. -φως Lyd.*Ost*.15. b. Astrol., *not conjoined*, Vett.Val.53.24, etc. 2. *to be turned from, dreadful*, epith. of the Erinyes, Orph.*H*.70.8. II. as Subst., **-στροφος**, ἡ, *apostrophe*, Sch.D.T.p.135 H., etc.; *mark of elision*, *EM*638.19, etc. 2. *turning away* of chorus from stage in Comic parabasis, Platon.*Diff.Com*.8.

**ἀποστρυθάομαι**, perh. = *disturb, move*, dub. in *IG*5(1).1155.2 (Gythium).

**ἀποστρώννῡμι**, *pave*, τὸ καταπεσὸν ἀνοικοδομήσαντι καὶ -ώσαντι *IG*11(2).203*A*41 (Delos, iii B.C.). II. *take off the trappings*, Hsch. s. v. ἀπέσαξεν.

***ἀποστῠγ-έω**, aor. 1 -εστύγησα S.*OC*692 (lyr.), -έστυξα Opp.*H*.4.370: aor. 2 ἀπέστῠγον Call.*Aet*.1.1.11, *Del*.223, Nic.*Al*.406, Parth.36.2: pf. with pres. sense, -εστύγηκα Hdt.2.47:—*hate violently, abhor*, Hdt. l. c., S.*OC*186,692, E.*Ion*488 (lyr. in S. and E.); ἀ. ὕδωρ (in comparison with wine) Melanipp.4; ἄμυστιν Call.*Aet*.l.c.: c. inf., ἀ. γαμβρὸν ἄν οἱ γενέσθαι Ἱπποκλείδεα Hdt.6.129. **-ησις**, εως, ἡ, *abhorrence*, Sch.A.*Ch*.79.

**ἀποστῠπάζω**, *drive off with blows*, Archil.127. (Cf. στύπος.)

**ἀποστῠφελίζω**, *drive away by force from*, τινά τινος Il.18.158, *AP*7.603 (Jul. Aegypt.).

**ἀποστύφω** [ῡ], *draw up, contract*, of the effect of astringents, δριμέα..ὥστε ἀποστύφειν Arist.*Pr*.863ᵃ18, cf. Thphr.*CP*2.8.1; χείλεα ἀ. *screw* them *up*, *AP*7.536 (Alc.):—Pass., pf., οὖρα δ' ἀπέστυπται *are stopped*, Nic.*Th*.433. 2. of preparing tissues for dyes, *mordant*, *PHolm*.9.14. 3. ἀποστύφων· τῇ φωνῇ σκληρός, Hsch.

**ἀποσυγχωρέω**, *give up, withdraw*, Sch.Ar.*Nu*.107.

***ἀποσῡκ-άζω**, *gather figs*, Amips.33 (Pass.). 2. *squeeze figs*, to try whether they are ripe: metaph. of informers, with a play on συκοφαντία, Ar.*Eq*.259. **-ίζω**, = foreg. 1, Sch.Nic.*Al*.319.

**ἀποσῡλάω**, *strip off spoils from* a person: hence, *strip off* or *take away from*, τί τινος Pi.*P*.4.110. II. *rob, defraud* one *of* a thing, ὅς μ'..ἀπεσύλησεν πάτρας S.*OC*1330; ὅτε ἐκράτησεν ἡμῶν ἀπεσύλησεν ἃ ἐδύνατο Is.5.30; ἀ. τινά τι E.*Alc*.870 (lyr.), X.*An*.1.4.8:—Pass., ἀποσυλᾶσθαί τι A.*Pr*.172 (lyr.); ἱερὰ -συληθέντα τῶν ἀνεθημάτων Jul.*Or*.7.228b. III. *carry off*, τὴν Ἄρτεμιν Luc.*Tox*.2.

**ἀποσυμβαίνω**, *to be absent*, of an accidental quality, S.E.*M*.7.282; ἀποσυμβεβηκότα *negative symptoms*, e.g. absence of pain, Gal.18(2).86.

***ἀποσυμβιβ-άζω**, *make good a deficiency*, *POxy*.136.25 (vi A.D.):—hence **-ασμός**, ὁ, ib.2035 (vi A.D.).

**ἀποσυμβολ...**· συναντᾶν, Hsch.

**ἀποσυμβουλεύω**, *dissuade*, τινὶ ποιεῖν τι Arr.*Epict*.1.23.3, cf. Phalar.*Ep*.58. II. metaph., *divert*, of a stream of blood meeting another, ἀ. τῷ ἐπιρρέοντι Hp.*Loc.Hom*.3.

**ἀποσυμμίγνῡμι**, *mingle*, Thd.*Da*.11.6.

**ἀποσυν-άγω** [ᾰγ], *recover* a man *from*, ἀπὸ λέπρας Lxx 4*Ki*.5.3. **-άγωγος** [ᾰγ], ον, *expelled from the synagogue*, *Ev.Jo*.9.22, etc. **-εθίζω**, *wean* one *from*, τὸ βρέφος τοῦ μαστοῦ Sor.1.116:—Pass., ibid. **-εργέω**, *thwart, oppose*, ib.27, al., S.E.*P*.1.212; of planetary influence, Ptol.*Tetr*.3. **-έργησις**, εως, ἡ, *adverse influence*, Id.*Phas.Praef*.8. ***-ίστημι**, *appoint a representative*, τινὰ κατελθεῖν εἰς Ἀλεξάνδρειαν *POxy*.1274.9 (iii A.D.):—Pass., *PGen*.44.28 (iii A.D.). 2. *recommend, introduce* one person to another, c. acc. et dat., *PHamb*.27.1, *AB*436. ***-τάσσω**, *order to be supplied*, *PSI*4.418 (iii B.C.).

**ἀποσῡριγγόω**, *make a channel for*, Hp.*Oss*.18:—Pass., Id.*Loc. Hom*.12.

***ἀποσῡρίζω**, *whistle aloud* for want of thought, or to show indifference, μάκρ' ἀποσυρίζων *h.Merc*.280:—Pass., *sound like whistling*, Luc. *VH*2.5.

***ἀπόσυρμα**, ατος, τό, *that which is peeled off, abrasion*, Hp.*Liqu*.2, Dsc.1.30. 2. *mark left by a rope dragged along*, *POxy*.69.8 (ii A.D.). II. *rubbish* left in working mines, Arist.*Mir*.833ᵃ29.

***ἀποσύρω** [ῡ], *tear away*, S.*Fr*.416, *EM*127.19; φλυκταίνας Philum. *Ven*.33.3; τὸ -σεσυρμένον *torn flesh*, Gal.13.457, cf. Orib.44.18.2 (Pass.); τὰς ἐπάλξεις Th.7.43; but τοὺς πολεμίους (sc. ἀπὸ τοῦ τείχους) Plb.10.15.1; *lay bare, strip*, μέτωπον ἐς ὀστέον Theoc.22.105; τὴν ἐπιπολῆς γῆν Plb.34.10.10; *skim off*, τὸ πιμελῶδες Sor.2.13.

**ἀποσυσσῑτέω**, *absent oneself from the public table* (συσσίτια), Pl. *Lg*.762c.

**ἀποσυστᾰτικὰ** γράμματα letter *of recommendation, power of attorney*, *PSI*3.236.20 (iii/iv A.D.), *PLond.ined*.2222 (iv A.D.); τὸ ἀ. *POxy*.1642.8 (iii A.D.), *PLond*.ibid.

**ἀπόσφαγμα**, ατος, τό, = ὑπόσφαγμα, Ael.*NA*1.34.

***ἀποσφάζω**, in Att. Prose **-σφάττω** Lys.13.78, Pl.*Euthphr*.4c, etc.: plpf. -εσφάκειν D.C.78.7:—Pass., aor. -εσφάγην [ᾰ] Hdt.4.84: fut. -σφᾰγήσομαι Ar.*Th*.750:—*cut the throat of* a person, ἀ. τινὰ ἐς ἄγγος so that the blood runs into a pail, Hdt.4.62: generally, *slay*, Ar.*Ach*.327, Th.7.86, Pl. l. c., etc.:—Med., *cut one's throat*, X.*Cyr*.3.1.25:—Pass., ἀποσφαγείην πρότερον ἂν ἢ καθυφείμην Men.*Epit*.184.

**ἀποσφαιρ-ίζομαι**, Pass., *to be thrown off like a ball*, Arist.*Pr*.936ᵇ36. II. later in Act., *jerk away like a ball*, Tz. ad Lyc.17. **-ισις**, εως, ἡ, *throwing off, flinging as a ball*, ibid.

**ἀποσφαιρόω**, *round off, make into balls*, Ath.2.42f.

**ἀποσφᾰκελ-ίζω**, *to have one's limbs frost-bitten and mortified*, ἵπποι ἐν κρυμῷ ἑστεῶτες ἀ. Hdt.4.28, cf. Ar.*Fr*.424. II. *fall into convulsions*, Plu.*Lyc*.16. **-ισις**, εως, ἡ, *gangrene*, σαρκῶν Hp.*Art*.69 (pl.).

**ἀποσφάλλω**, aor. 1 -έσφηλα (v. infr.):—*lead astray, drive in baffled course*, ὅντινα πρῶτον ἀποσφήλωσιν ἄελλαι ἐς πέλαγος Od.3.320; μή ..σφας ἀποσφήλειε πόνοιο lest he *balk* them *of* the fruits of toil, Il.5.567. 2. *cause to err*, Lib.*Or*.59.147. II. mostly in Pass., esp. in aor. 2 ἀπεσφάλην [ᾰ], *to be balked* or *disappointed of*, τῆς ἐλπίδος Hdt.6.5; *to be deprived of*, φρενῶν Sol.33.4, A.*Pr*.472; γνώμης Id.*Pers*.392; οὐσίας ἀρετῆς ἀπεσφαλμένοι *mistaken as to* the nature of.., Pl.*Lg*.950b; *fail in reaching*, Ἰταλίας Plu.*Pyrrh*.15: abs., *make a mistake*, D.26.3; ἀποσφάλλεσθαι εἴς τι *go astray*, Plu.2.392b: rare in literal sense, *miss one's footing*, ἀποσφαλεὶς ἐξ ὕψους ἔπεσε Id. *Per*.13.

**ἀποσφαλμάω**, *fall headlong*, of a horse, Plb.*Fr*.18.

**ἀποσφάξ**, ᾶγος, ὁ, ἡ, *broken off, abrupt*, βῆσσα Nic.*Th*.521.

**ἀποσφάττω**, v. ἀποσφάζω.

**ἀποσφενδον-άω**, *hurl from* or *as from a sling*, D.S.2.50, Luc.*JTr*.33:—Pass., Lxx 4*Ma*.16.21, Plu.2.1062a. **-ητος**, ον, *driven away by the sling*, ib.293b.

**ἀποσφηκόω**, *untie, loosen*, Nonn.*D*.21.152, al.

***ἀποσφήλωσις**, εως, ἡ, *failure*, Suid.

**ἀποσφην-όω**, *wedge tight in*, ἀποσφηνωθεὶς δένδρῳ τὰς χεῖρας Eust. ad D.P.369; λίθος εἰς φυτὸν -ωθεὶς Aët.16.21; *compress as by a wedge*, Ph.*Bel*.76.25, Hero *Bel*.77.3. 2. sens. obsc., Mim.*Oxy*.413.17. II. *plug* a tooth, Paul.Aeg.6.28. **-ωμα**, ατος, τό, *wedge-shaped block*, *PFay*.331 (ii A.D.). **-ωσις**, εως, ἡ, *impaction* of an infant in childbirth, Paul.Aeg.3.76.

***ἀπο-σφίγγω**, *squeeze tight, compress, bind up*, τραῦμα cj. Littré in Hp.*Art*.69; σιαγόνας Luc.*Luct*.19; λόγος ἀπεσφιγμένος *a close-packed style*, Id.*Rh.Pr*.9. **-σφιγξις**, εως, ἡ, *squeezing tight*, Hp.*Fract*.11 (pl.), *Art*.69 (pl.):—in form **-σφιξις**, *ligature* above a poisonous bite, Philum.*Ven*.22.4, cf. Leonid.ap.Orib.45.23.78, Antyll.ib.7.9.2.

**ἀποσφρᾱγ-ίζω**, *seal up*, Plu.*Alex*.2 (Pass.):—Med., E.*Or*.1108, Theopomp.Hist.265. II. *unseal*, D.L.4.59. **-ισμα**, ατος, τό, *impression of a seal*, Plin.*Ep.Traj*.74, Ath.13.585d; also, *the seal itself, signet*, Lxx *Je*.22.24. II. *sealed copy*, *IG*12(7).237.69 (Amorgos, i B.C.). III. *stamped receipt* for goods taken, *PRev.Laws* 31.19 (iii B.C.). **-ιστής**· *resignator*, *Gloss*.

**ἀποσφρ-αίνω**, *make to smell*, γλήχωνι αὐτὸν ἀποσφραίνει he *gives* himself *a whiff of* pennyroyal, *AP*11.165 (Lucill.), cf. Sor.2.85, Orib.8.6.1:—Pass., ἥρμοσεν ἀποσφρανθὲν *when smelt at*, Dsc.1.54. **-αντέον**, *one must cause to smell*, αὐτὰς τοῖς δυσώδεσι Aspasia ap.Aët.16.72.

**ἀποσφύδου**· καρτερεῖν *AB*436, Suid.

**ἀποσφῡρηλατέω**, *shape on the anvil*, Lib.*Decl*.51.16.

**ἀποσχάζω**, stronger form of σχάζω, ἀ. φλέβα *open* a vein, Crates Com.41, Arist.*HA*514ᵇ2:—Pass., *to be lanced*, of a γαργαρεών, Hp. *Prog*.23. 2. *scarify*, Antyll.ap.Orib.7.18.2. II. *let go*, σχαστηρίαν Hero *Bel*.79.3:—Med., *let go* a stage machine, Id.*Aut*.20.4.

**ἀποσχᾰλίδωμα**, ατος, τό, (σχαλίς) *forked piece of wood for propping hunting-nets*, X.*Cyn*.10.7.

***ἀπό-σχᾰσις**, εως, ἡ, *opening of a vein*, Hp.*Epid*.7.66 (but possibly *scarification*). II. *letting go*, in an engine, Ph.*Bel*.74.51. **-σχαστέον**, *one must scarify*, Paul.Aeg.4.21. **-σχάω**, = ἀποσχάζω 1, Hp.*Morb*.2.38, Arist.*HA*512ᵃ30.

**ἀποσχεδιάζω**, = αὐτοσχεδιάζω, *make offhand*, νόμος ἀπεσχεδιασμένος Arist.*EN*1129ᵇ25, cf. Ael.*Tact*.21.2. 2. *act offhand* or *at random*, τὰ πολλά Jul.*Ep*.89a, cf. Sch.Ar.*Pax*990, etc. 3. *write offhand*, περί τινος Plb.12.3.7; *extemporize*, Ath.3.125c, Philostr. *VA*5.37:—Pass., τὰ μυθικῶς -εσχεδιασμένα Phld.*Sign*.38.

**ἀπό-σχεσις**, εως, ἡ, *abstinence*, τινός Plu.2.123c (pl.): abs., ib. 125d (pl.); τῶν βρωμάτων Str.16.2.37 (pl.). II. *division*, χρόνου Artem.4.2 (pl.). **-σχετέον**, (ἀπέχομαι) = ἀφεκτέον, *one must abstain*, οἴνου Hp.*Acut*.63. **-σχετική**· *dimissoria*, *Gloss*.

**ἀποσχετλιάζω**, strengthd. for σχετλιάζω, Phryn.*PS* p.63 B.

***ἀπόσχημα**, ατος, τό, *figure, copy*, τινός Sch.Stob.p.463 Heeren.

**ἀποσχημᾰτίζω**, *shape, fashion*, in Pass., ἐργασίαι εἰς ζῷα -εσχηματισμέναι Socr.*Ep*.28, cf. Philostr.*VS*1 *Praef*.

**ἀπο-σχίζω**, *split, cleave off*, ἀπὸ δ' ἔσχισεν αὐτήν [τὴν πέτρην] Od.4.507; *tear off*, E.*Alc*.172, Opp.*H*.2.623. 2. *sever, detach from*, τινὰ ἀπὸ τοῦ συμμαχικοῦ Hdt.6.9; ἀ. Λυδοὺς *part* them *off, separate* them, Pl.*Plt*.262e; τὴν ἰδίαν ψυχὴν τῆς τῶν λογικῶν M.Ant.4.29:—Pass., ἀποσχισθῆναι ἀπό.., of a river *being parted from* the main stream, Hdt.2.17, 4.56; of a tribe *detached from* its parent stock, Id.1.58, 143; ἀπὸ τῆς μεγάλης φλεβὸς -σχίζεται Arist.*HA*514ᵇ10: c. gen., ἀποσχισθέντες τῆς ἄλλης στρατιῆς Hdt.8.35, cf. 7.233, Pl. *Plt*.267b, etc.:—Med., *separate oneself*, Id.*Lg*.728b; τοῦ σοφιστοῦ Lib.*Or*.3.24. 3. metaph., ἀ. τινὰ τοῦ λόγου *cut* him *off from* his speech, *interrupt* him *in* it, Ar.*Nu*.1408. **-σχίς**, ίδος, ἡ, mostly in pl., ἀποσχίδες *branches* of veins, Hp.*Oss*.6, Aret.*CA*2.2; ὀστῶν Gal.18(2).781; of a mountain, *spurs*, Str.11.12.4. II. sg., *branch* of the bile-duct, Gal.2.578. **-σχίσις**, εως, ἡ, *division, branching*, of a vein, Arist.*HA*514ᵃ13, Aret.*CA*2.2. **-σχισμα**, ατος, τό, *that which is severed*, M.Ant.4.29.

**ἀποσχοινίζω**, *separate by a cord*: hence generally, *bar, exclude*, ἀπεσχοινισμένος πᾶσι τοῖς ἐν τῇ πόλει δικαίοις D.25.28: abs., Plu.2.443c; ἀρετῆς Ph.1.205; ἀ. τινά τινος ib.219, cf. Lib.*Decl*.23.45.

***ἀποσχολάζω**, *rest, recreate* oneself, ἔν τινι Arist.*EN*1176ᵇ17. 2. *have leisure for, devote oneself to*, τῷ οἴνῳ Ael.*VH*12.1. 3. *spend one's leisure with* one, *go to* him *for teaching*, Ps.-Hdt.*Vit.Hom*.5, 34.

**ἀπόσχολος**, ον, *shunning the schools*, f.l. in Timo 50.

***ἀποσῴζω**, *save* or *preserve from*, νόσου S.*Ph*.1379; ἐκ τῶν ναυαγίων -σωθέντες Luc.*Herm*.86; ἀ. οἴκαδε *bring safe* home, X.*HG*7.2.19, cf. *An*.2.3.18. 2. *keep safe*, Pl.*Phlb*.26c, *Lg*.692c, *IG*2.268; ἀ. πατρὸς γνώμας *keep* them *in mind, remember*, E.*Fr*.362.2. 3. *preserve*, τὴν τάξιν, of the pulse, Gal.14.635. II. Pass., ἀποσωθῆναι ἐς.. *to get safe* to a place, Hdt.5.87, 7.229, X.*HG*1.3.22; ἐπὶ θάλατταν ib.3.1.2: abs., *get off safe*, Hdt.2.107, al. III. intr. in Act., ἀ. γενομένη *come safely* into being, Pl.*Ep*.336b.

**ἀποσωμάτωσις** [ᾰτ], εως, ἡ, *conversion from corporeal substance*, ὑδάτων Zos.Alch.p.107 B.

**ἀποσωρεύω**, *heap up, accumulate*, *AB*432, Hsch. s. v. ἀποθησαμένη.

**ἀποτᾰγή**, ἡ, (ἀποτάσσω) *renunciation* of a claim, *PLond*.3.1007.18 (vi A.D.). II. *disinheriting*, *PMasp*.97 ii 53 (vi A.D.).

**ἀποτᾰγηνίζω**, v. ἀποτηγανίζω.

**ἀπόταγμα**, ατος, τό, *prohibition*, Iamb.*VP*28.138 (pl., dub.).

**ἀποτάδην** [ᾰδ], Adv., (τείνω) *stretched at length*, Luc.*Zeux*.4, Ael. *NA*4.21; ἀ. τρέχειν Poll.6.175. 2. *diffusely, prolixly*, Philostr. *VS*1 *Praef*., cf. 1.15.4; ξυνέστειλε τοὺς χοροὺς ἀ. ὄντας Id.*VA*6.11; ἀ. φθεγγόμενον [φθέγμα κηρύκων] Poll.4.94; also with κατά, τῶν κατὰ ἀ. λόγων ἀκήκοας Herm.*in Phdr*.p.184 A.

**ἀποτάδων**· ἐκτεταμένων, Hsch.

**ἀπο-τακτέον**, *one must exclude*, Ἡρακλέα τῶν χθονίων θεῶν Philostr. *VA*8.7.9. **-τακτήρ**, ῆρος, ὁ, *anchorite, hermit*, *POxy*.1311 (v A.D.). **-τακτικός**, ὁ, = foreg., *PFlor*.71.722 (iv A.D.). **-τακτῖται**, οἱ, name of a heretical sect, *Anatolian Studies* p.86 (iv/v A.D.):—**-τισταί** (= -τῆρες) is f.l. in Jul.*Or*.7.224b. **-τακτος**, ον, *set apart for a special use*, σιτία Hdt.2.69; ἀπότακτον, τό, 'speciality', Philem.76; ἀ. χρεία Heliod.ap.Orib.49.4.7. 2. *settled, appointed*, ἡμέρα Critias 6.27 D.; *fixed*, ἐκφόριον *PTeb*.42.12 (ii B.C.); φόρος *POxy*.280.17 (i A.D.), etc.:—Subst. **-τακτον**, τό, *fixed rent*, ib.1124.9 (i A.D.); *prescribed sum*, *PFay*.39 (ii A.D.), Porph.*Abst*.4.17; ἱερὸν ἀ. imperial *assessment*, *POxy*.1662.14 (iii A.D.). 3. *set apart* for punishment, Herod.3.69; cf. ἄπακτος. II. Adv. **-τως** *in isolation*, Phld.*D*.3 *Fr*.1.

**ἀπο-τάμία**, ἡ, *larder*, Cael.Aur.*CP*3.21 (fort. -ιεία):—Adj. **-τᾰμιακός**, ή, όν, *Cat.Cod.Astr*.8(4).338.

***ἀποτᾰμιεύομαι**, *lock up, keep*, Ael.*VH*1.12, cf. *PSI*4.428.28 (iii B.C.).

**ἀποτάμνω**, Dor. and Ion. for ἀποτέμνω.

**ἀποτᾰνύω**, = ἀποτείνω, τὴν χεῖρα Hp.*Fract*.8.

**ἀποτάξιον**· ἀπόπομπον, Hsch.

**ἀπόταξις**, εως, ἡ, (ἀποτάσσω) *separate assessment* for tribute, Antipho *Fr*.55.

**ἀποταρτᾰρόομαι**, metaph., *suffer hell*, ἐν ταῖς ἀποβολαῖς ταῖς χρημάτων Phld.*Herc*.1251.20.

⊕ἀπότᾰσις, εως, ἡ, *lengthening, prolongation*, ὅσων ἔστιν ἀ. τῆς φωνῆς, i.e. ὅσων ἀποτείνεται ἡ φωνή, Arist.*HA*545ᵃ17. cf. *de An.*420ᵇ 8. 2. *stretching out*, τῆς χειρός Sor.1.101; τῶν ποδῶν Plu.2.670d; τετάνου ἴδιον ἡ ἐς εὐθὺ ἀ. Aret.*SA*1.6. 3. *distension*, of the breast, Sor.1.87. 4. *reference*, ἡ ἀ. πρὸς Κλυταιμήστραν Sch.S.*El.*1070, cf. A.D.*Synt.*35.28, al.

⊕ἀποτάσσω, Att. -ττω, *set apart, assign specially*, χώραν τινί Pl.*Tht.* 153e; *detach* soldiers, Plb.6.35.3, etc., cf. *POxy.*475.27 (ii A.D.):—Pass., ἀποτεταγμένη ἀρχή *distinct* office, Arist.*Pol.*1322ᵃ26; ἀποτεταγμένοι τῇ κατοικίᾳ χρηματισταί *PFay.*12 (ii B.C.): generally, *to be fixed, appointed*, χῶρος Plu.2.120b; *ear-mark*, ἀργύριον εἰς δημοθοινίαν -τεταγμένον *IG*12(7).515.91 (Amorgos), cf. *BCH*46.397 (Mylasa). II. *appoint, settle definitely*, Arist.*HA*585ᵇ36. III. *remove, exclude*, τόπον τοῦ κόσμου Philostr.*VA*3.35; ἑαυτόν τινων Id. *Im.*2.19. IV. Med., ἀποτάσσομαί τινι *bid adieu to* a person, *part from* them, *Ev.Luc.*9.61, *Act.Ap.*18.21, *Ev.Marc.*6.46, J.*AJ*11.8.6, *BGU*884 ii 14 (ii/iii A.D.), Aesop.64, Lib.*Decl.*45.28; *have done with, get rid of* a person, *POxy.*298.31 (i A.D.); ἀ. τῷ βίῳ *commit suicide*, *Cat.Cod.Astr.*8(3).136.17: also c. dat. rei, *renounce, give up*, τοῖς ἑαυτοῦ ὑπάρχουσιν *Ev.Luc.*14.33; τροφῇ J.*AJ*11.6.8; ταῖς μίξεσι, of the Vestals, Sor.1.32; πάθεσι Ph.1.116, cf. Iamb.*VP*3.13, Phryn.15.

⊕ἀποταυρόομαι, Pass., *to be like a bull*, δέργμα λεαίνης ἀποταυροῦται δμωσίν *casts* the *savage* glance of a lioness on them, E.*Med.*188 (lyr.). 2. of Io, *to be changed into a heifer*, Erot. s. v. κερχνώδεα.

ἀπόταυρος, ον, *apart from the bull*, Arist.*HA*595ᵇ19.

ἀπότᾰφος, ον, *not buried in one's ancestral tomb*, Din.*Fr.*16.5. II. *buried separately*, *IG*12(1).656 (Rhodes), Hsch., *EM*131.43.

ἀποταφρ-ευσις, εως, ἡ, *circumvallation*, D.H.9.9 (pl.). -εύω, *fence off with a ditch*, X.*An.*6.5.1, *HG*5.4.38; for defence or offence, D.H.2.37, 3.41.

ἀποτέγγω, *dip*, Hp.*Morb.*2.56.

ἀπότεγμα, ατος, τό, (τίκτω) *product*, νοῦ καὶ λόγου Sophon.*in de An.* 52.30.

ἀποτείνω, 3 pl. pf. Pass. ἀποτέτανται Luc.*Zeux.*4: —*stretch out, extend*, μέρος τι αὑτοῦ Arist.*GA*723ᵇ22; ἀ. ἐκεῖ τὴν διάνοιαν Id.*Mem.* 452ᵇ10; τὼ πόδε Luc.*Merc.Cond.*13:—Pass., δρέπανα ἐκ τῶν ἀξόνων εἰς πλάγιον ἀποτεταμένα X.*An.*1.8.10; ἡ ὄψις ἀπὸ μικροῦ ἐνόπτρου πόρρω ἀποτεινομένη Arist.*Mete.*377ᵇ33, etc. 2. *extend, prolong*, of the line of an army, X.*HG*5.2.40 (Pass.); μακροτέρους ἀ. μισθοὺς *extend* rewards much further, Pl.*R.*363d; esp. of speeches, λόγον Id. *Grg.*466a; ἀ. μακροὺς λόγους *to make long* speeches, Id.*Prt.*335c, al.; συχνὸν λόγον Id.*Grg.*465e; μακρὰν ῥῆσιν ἀ. Id.*R.*605d; of brazen vessels, μακρὸν ἠχεῖ καὶ ἀ. [τὴν ἠχήν] Id.*Prt.*329a; φωνὴ σάλπιγγος ὀξὺν ἀ. φθόγγον Plu.*Sull.*7; ἱστορίας μέχρι μέσων νυκτῶν ἀ. Id.2.60a: —Pass., προοίμια ἀποτεταμένα ὡς ἐν διηγήσεως τρόπῳ D.H.*Rh.*10.13; ἀποτεινομένου τοῦ ποτοῦ Luc.*Merc.Cond.*18. 3. *strain, tighten*:—Pass., παραδείγματα ἀκριβῶς ἀποτεταμένα ταῖς γραμμαῖς severely *drawn*, Luc.*Rh.Pr.*9:—Med., *exert oneself*, ὑπέρ τινος about a thing, Id.*Am.*17; ἀποτείνεσθαι πρός τινα *inveigh* against.., D.L.5.17, Gal. 18(1).255. 4. *refer, allude*, πρός τινα Luc.*Nigr.*13:—Med., Simp. *in Ph.*242.23:—Pass., impers., ἀποτείνεται ἐπί.. *the reference is* to.., Sch.Il.*Oxy.*221 xi 25. II. intr., *extend*, ἀπὸ.., εἰς.., Arist.*HA* 503ᵇ16, 514ᵃ34; μέχρι.. Id.*Mete.*343ᵇ22; ἀ. πόρρω *to go* too *far*, Pl. *Grg.*458b: c. part., *continue doing*, ἀ. μαχόμενοι Plu.2.60a.

ἀπο-τεισις, v. ἀπότισις. -τεισμα, ατος, τό, *payment*, *IG* 2.1058.26, 12(7).62.15 (Amorgos).

ἀποτειχ-ίζω, *wall off*, 1. by way of *fortifying*, ἀ. τὸν Ἰσθμόν Hdt.6.36:—Pass., Id.9.8. 2. by way of *blockade*, ὁ τοὺς θεοὺς ἀποτειχίσας Ar.*Av.*1576; τοὺς ἐν τῇ ἀκροπόλει Th.4.130, cf. 1.64, X. *HG*1.3.4, 2.4.3:—Pass., Th.6.96: metaph., *shut out*, ἑαυτῷ τὴν φυγήν Hld.9.20. 3. *keep off by fortification*, τὰς καταδρομάς Plu. *Per.*19. 4. *wall off, separate*, ὄρη ἀποτειχίζοντα τὴν Ἰταλίαν ἀπό τε Ἰλλυριῶν καὶ Γαλατῶν Jul.*Or.*2.72b. 5. Med., *build a party-wall*, πρὸς ἀλλήλους Luc.*Am.*28. II. *unblock by razing a wall*, χάσμα Polyaen.1.3.5; *dismantle*, τὴν ἀκρόπολιν Arr.*Epict.*4.1. 88. -ισις, εως, ἡ, *walling off of a town, blockading*, τῆς Ποτειδαίας Th.1.65. II. *razing of fortifications*, Polyaen.2.22.3. -ισμα, ατος, τό, *lines of blockade*, Th.6.99, 7.79, X.*HG*1.3.7. -ισμός, ὁ, = ἀποτείχισις I, Plu.*Nic.*18, etc. -ιστέον, *one must wall off*: metaph., διαβολήν Them.*Or.*22.278a.

⊕ἀποτεκμαίρομαι, *draw signs* or *proofs from* a thing, *conclude*, c. acc. et inf., A.R.4.1538.

ἀποτεκνόομαι, Pass., *to be deprived of children*, Lxx *Ge.*27.45.

ἀπότεκνος, ον, *sterile*, Vett.Val.119.30.

ἀποτέλει-ος, ὁ, (τέλος) title of a *magistrate* of the Achaean League, Plb.16.36.4: in pl., Id.10.23.9; ἀ. τῶν πεζῶν *subordinate commander*, *IG*5(2).293 (Mantinea). -όω or -τελεόω, *bring to maturity*, Aristid. *Or.*43(1).13:—Pass., *come to maturity*, Arist.*HA*576ᵇ7. -ωσις, εως, ἡ, *bringing to perfection*, Plu.*Nob.*7.

ἀποτελ-έσιμος, η, ον, *effective*, Hsch. s. v. θεμινήσασα. -εσις, εως, ἡ, *production*, ὑγρασίας Epicur.*Ep.*2 p.50 U., cf. *Theol.Ar.*44. 2. Astrol., *influence*, Paul.Al.*F.*1. ⊕-εσμα, ατος, τό, *full completion*, μηνός Arist.*Mu.*397ᵃ14; τέχνης Plb.4.78.5, Plu.*Lyc.*30. 2. *event, result*, Plb.2.39.11, D.S.1.89, Phld.*Rh.*1.129 S. (pl.), Antyll.ap.Orib. 45.26.4, M.Ant.6.42, etc.; *effect*, opp. αἰτία, *Stoic.*2.118, al., Herm. ap.Stob.1.41.6, Procl.*Inst.*18. 3. *finished product*, Olymp.*in Mete.* 143.15; *created objects*, in pl., Ph.2.472. II. Astrol., *result of certain positions of the stars on human destiny*, τἀπὸ ἀποτελεσμάτων προρρηθέντα Phld.*D.*1.25, cf. Plu.*Rom.*12, Artem.1.9, *PTeb.*276 (ii/iii A.D.); title of works by Helicon and others, Suid. s. v. -εσμᾰτικός, ή, όν, *productive of material objects*, τέχνη ἀ., opp. θεωρητική and πρακτική, S.E.*M.*11.197: generally, *productive*, τινός Sor.1.48, Gal.19.475. II. *astrologically influential*, Ptol.*Tetr.*90; *of* or *for astrology*, λόγος Vett. Val.332.1; -κή (sc. τέχνη), ἡ, Eust.900.34, Simp.*in Ph.*293.11; ἀποτελεσματικά, name of a *work on astrology* by Paul.Al.; οἱ -κοί *astrologers*, Eust.193.7. -εσμᾰτογρᾰφία, ἡ, *nativity plan*, Vett.Val.29. 10, Paul.Al.*L.*1, Porph.*in Ptol.*201. -εσμᾰτολόγος, ὁ, *writer on astrology*, *Theol.Ar.*53. -εστέον, *one must complete*, τὴν ἐκτομήν Dsc.*Ther.*2. -εστικός, ή, όν, *causative, productive*, τινός Epicur. *Ep.*1 p.14 U., *Stoic.*2.149, Polystr.p.32 W., Pl.*Def.*412c, Plu.2.652a, etc.; *final, conclusive*, ἀποχή *PTeb.*397.25 (ii A.D.). 2. prob. f.l. for -ματικός II, Porph.*Plot.*15. II. Gramm., *final*, σύνδεσμος A.D. *Synt.*265.27, al. Adv. -κῶς ib.268.28.

ἀποτελευτ-άω, intr., *end*, ἐς τεταρταίους Hp.*Aër.*10, cf. Alex.Aphr. *Pr.*2.57; εἰς ἀνίας, εἰς ἡδονάς, Pl.*Prt.*353e, 354b; ἀποτελευτῶν *at last*, Id.*Plt.*310e; εἰς τοὐναντίον καὶ τὸ ἄμεινον Arist.*Metaph.*983ᵃ18; ἡ ὀλιγαρχία εἰς δῆμον ἀπετελεύτησεν Id.*Pol.*1305ᵇ11. -ή, ἡ, = sq., ἀ. εἴς τι ποιεῖσθαι Antyll.ap.Orib.44.22.1. -ησις, εως, ἡ, *ending*, εἴς τι Hp.*Loc.Hom.*3, Thphr.*Ign.*54. II. *result*, δόξα διανοίας ἀ. Pl.*Sph.*264a; *completion, accomplishment*, Dam.*Pr.*67, 113.

⊕ἀποτελέω, fut. -τελέσω, Att. -τελῶ, *bring to an end, complete* a work, Hdt.5.92.η', X.*HG*3.2.10, Pl.*Plt.*308e, etc.:—Pass., Th.4.69: pf. part. ἀποτετελεσμένος *perfect*, ἐπίτροπος X.*Oec.*13.3. 2. *produce*, νοσήματα Pl.*Ti.*84c, cf. Epicur.*Ep.*1 p.20 U., M.Ant.10.26, etc.: —Pass., Arist.*Cael.*268ᵇ26. 3. *pay* or *perform what is due*, τὰς εὐχὰς σφι ἀ. Hdt.2.65; τῷ θεῷ τὰ πάτρια Id.4.180; of rent or tribute, τὰ νομιζόμενα X.*Cyr.*3.2.19; ἀπαρχὴν τῶν ἐκ τῆς γῆς Pl.*Lg.*806e; *pay* or *suffer*, παραπλήσια τοῖς Καμβύσου παθήμασιν ib.695e. 4. *accomplish, perform*, τὰ καθήκοντα X.*Cyr.*1.2.5; προσταχθέντα Pl.*Lg.*823d; τὰ προσήκοντα Id.*Criti.*108d; ἀ. ἄρτον *accomplish the making of* bread, Hp.*VM*3; ἐν ὑφ' ἑνὸς ἔργον ἄριστ' ἀποτελεῖται Arist.*Pol.*1273ᵇ10. b. esp. of astral influences, Ptol.*Tetr.*1, D.C.45.1, etc.; cf. ἀποτέλεσμα. c. Astrol., *make a forecast*, περὶ ζωῆς Ps.-Ptol.*Centil.*215. 5. *render* of a certain kind, τὴν πόλιν ἀ. εὐδαίμονα *make* the state *quite* happy, Pl.*Lg.*718b; ἀμείνους ἐκ χειρόνων ἀ. Id.*Plt.*297b, cf. *Lg.*823d; τοιούτους ἄνδρας ὥστε.. Plb.6.52.11:—in Med., ἄμεμπτον φίλον ἀποτελέσασθαι *make* him without blame *towards himself*, X.*Lac.*2.13:—Pass., τύραννος ἀντὶ προστάτου ἀποτετελεσμένος Pl.*R.*566d; ἐνύπνιον τέλεον ἀ. *turns out* .., ib.443b. 6. *fill up, satiate*, τὰς ἐπιθυμίας Id. *Grg.*503d:—Pass., Id.*R.*558e, al. II. Pass., *to be worshipped*, Id. *Smp.*188d.

⊕ἀποτελωνέομαι, *get discharge from the customs*, *PLond.ined.*2092 (iii B.C.).

ἀποτεμᾰχίζω, (τέμαχος) *cut a portion off, sever*, Herm.*in Phdr.* p.92 A.:—Pass., τῆς ἀποτετεμαχισμένης ψυχῆς ib.p.166 A., cf. Syrian. *in Metaph.*40.35.

⊕ἀποτέμνω, Ep., Ion., and Dor. -τάμνω, fut. -τεμῶ: aor. 2 Ion. and Dor. -έταμον, Att. -έτεμον:—Pass., fut. ἀποτμηθήσομαι Lys.6.26: —*cut off, sever*, παρηορίας ἀπέταμνε Il.8.87; ἀπὸ στομάχους ἀρνῶν τάμε 3.292, etc.; κρῶτ' ἀπὸ πάντα καὶ ἄρθρα τεμῶ χερί S.*Ph.*1207; τὴν κεφαλήν Hdt.2.39, cf. *IG*4.952.2 (Epid.); τὰ σκέλεα Hdt.2.40; τὴν ῥῖνα καὶ τὰ ὦτα Id.3.154, etc.; *amputate*, X.*Mem.*1.2.54, Hp.*Art.*69; *excise*, Id.*Haem.*2, cf. Dsc.*Eup.*1.12 (Pass.); *decapitate*, ἀλεκτρυόνα *PMag.Par.*1.38:—Pass., *to be cut off*, τὰ ἀκρωτήρια ἀποτμηθήσεσθαι Lys.6.26; τὴν γλῶτταν ἀποτμηθείς Aeschin.1.168 (s. v. l.; ἐκτμ. Suid.); τὴν κεφαλὴν Luc.*Nav.*33; τὸν τράχηλον Arr.*Epict.*1.2.27. 2. *cut off, divide, sever*, in a geographical sense, ὁ Ἅλυς.. ἀποτάμνει σχεδὸν πάντα τῆς Ἀσίης Hdt.1.72; ὄρεα ὑψηλὰ ἀ. [τὴν χώρην] Id.4. 25: mathematically, ἥμισυ.. ἡ γραμμὴ ἀ. Pl.*Men.*85a, cf. Arist.*Mech.* 849ᵃ17:—Med., Pl.*Phlb.*42b:—Pass., of troops, *to be cut off from* the main body, X.*An.*3.4.29. 3. *cut off, check, put an end to*, τὰς μηχανάς Cratin.289 (s. v. l.). 4. *cut off, separate* in argument, Pl. *Lg.*653c:—Med., Arist.*Metaph.*1003ᵃ24:—Pass., *to be so cut off* or *abstracted*, Id.*Ph.*202ᵇ8. 5. ἀ. τὰ βαλλάντια *to be a cut-purse*, Pl. *R.*348d. 6. *cut open*, ἱερεῖον Plu.*Cim.*18. b. ἀποτεμεῖν· ἁγνίσαι, Hsch. II. Med., *cut off for oneself*, ἀποταμνόμενον κρέα ἔδμεναι Il. 22.347; ἀ. πλόκαμον Hdt.4.34; τὴν χώρην ἀ. τάφρον ὀρυξάμενοι ib.3; ἀ. τοῦ ὠτὸς *cut off a bit of*.., ib.71. 2. *cut off*, with a view of appropriating, πεντήκοντ' ἀγέλης ἀπετάμνετο.. βοῦς *h.Merc.*74; τὰς Θυρέας ἐούσας τῆς Ἀργολίδος μοίρης ἀποταμόμενοι ἔσχον Hdt.1.82; χώραν, ὀργάδα, Isoc.5.122, D.13.32, etc. (in Pass., of the country *cut off*, Hdt.1.82, etc.); ἀ. ὡς μέγιστα τῶν Ἀθηναίων *cut off* as much power as possible *from* them, Th.8.46: also c. gen., χώρας ἀποτάμνεσθαι *cut off a part of*.., *SIG*56.24 (Argos, v B.C.), cf. Isoc.1.88; Φοινίκης ἀ. Ἀραβίας τε *to have a slice* or *portion of*.., Theoc.17.86. 3. *cut off from common use, consecrate*, ὕλας Luc.*Sacr.*10. 4. *subtend*, of the chord of an arc, S.E.*M.*1.304.

ἀπότεξις, εως, ἡ, *bringing to the birth*, Ph.2.466, Hierocl.p.7 A., Sor.1.6, S.E.*M.*5.53, Olymp.*Vit.Pl.*p.1 W.

ἀποτερᾰτεύομαι, Pass., (τέρας) *to be astonished as by a prodigy*, Ps.-Callisth.3.17.

ἀποτερμᾰτ-ίζω, *bound, limit, define*, Anon.*Geog.Comp.*19, cf. 10 (Pass.); *bring to an end*, λόγον dub. in Phld.*D.*3.14. II. Med., *look towards*, εἴς τι prob. for ἀποτελμ- in Hp.*Decent.*3. -ισμός, ὁ, *limitation*, τῆς ὁράσεως Gem.16.5. -ωσις, εως, ἡ, = foreg., *EM*583.17.

ἀποτετερμᾰτισμένως, Adv. *definitely*, Hsch. s. v. ἀμφιτέρμως.

ἀποτετρᾰγωνίζω, *square*, Hero *Stereom.*2.60.3.

ἀποτετραίνω, aor. 1 part. -τρήσας, *perforate*, Hp.*Steril.*222.

**ἀπό-τευγμα,** ατος, τό, *failure*, Arist.*VV*1251$^{b}$20, Phld *Rh.*1.67S., *Vit.*p.35J., D.S.1.1, Cic.*Att.*13.27.1, etc. **-τευκτέω,** = ἀποτυγχάνω, Phot. s.v. οὐκ ἀποτευκτήσεις. **-τευκτικός,** ή, όν, *causing failure* or *miscarriage*. τινός Hippod.ap.Stob.4.39.26; *liable to failure*, Phld.*Rh.*1.72S., Arr.*Epict.*3.6.6, 3.26.14, Ptol.*Tetr.*161. Adv. -κῶς *without success*, Arr.*Epict.*4.10.6. **-τευξις,** εως, ἡ, *miscarriage, failure*, Pl.*Ax.*368d, Phld.*Mus.*p.14K.(pl.); ἐλπίδος Plu.*Galb.*23; of an electoral *defeat*, Id.*Mar.*5.

**ἀποτεφρόω,** *reduce to ashes*, Dsc.5.81, Poll.1.167:—Pass., τῶν -τεφρουμένων ὑλῶν Lyd.*Mag.*3.70.

***ἀποτηγᾰνίζω,** (τήγανον) *eat off the gridiron, eat broiled*, Pherecr. 123, Phryn.Com.57, Machoap.Ath.13.582e; written ἀπεταγήνισα in Sotad.Com.1.1.

***ἀποτήκω,** *melt away from*, αὐτῆς τῆς φύσεως ἀ. *melt away a part of*.., Pl.*Ti.*65d; τετυλωμένα βλέφαρα ἀ. *reduce* them, Dsc.5.99: metaph., Plu.2.451f:—Pass., ἀπετάκη αὐτοῦ τρία τάλαντα Hdt.1.50, cf. Epicur. *Ep.*2p.49U.; ἀπετάκησαν οἱ μασθοί (prob. for ἀπετάθησαν), Luc. *DMort.*28.2.

**ἀπο-τῆλε,** *afar off*, ἠϊόνων *AP*7.637 (Antip.), cf. *APl.*4.86. **-τηλόθεν·** μακρόθεν, Hsch. **-τηλόθι,** = foreg., A.R.4.728. **-τηλοῦ,** = foreg., Od.9.117, A.R.4.1092, etc.

**ἀπότηξις,** εως, ἡ, *melting away, discharging*, Hp.*Morb.Sacr.*5; of snow, Str.4.1.12.

**ἀποτηρέω,** *wait for, watch for*, D.S.14.21 (Dind. ἐπιτ-).

**ἀποτίβᾰτος,** ον, Dor. and poet. for ἀπρόσβατος, S.*Tr.*1030 (lyr.).

***ἀποτίθημι,** *put away, stow away*, δέπας δ' ἀπέθηκ' ἐνὶ χηλῷ Il.16. 254, cf. X.*An.*2.3.15: ἀ. εἰς δεσμωτήριον Lycurg.112: metaph., 'pigeon-hole', *class*, Phlp.*in Ph.*361.22. **2.** *expose* a child, Pl.*Tht.* 161a. **II.** Med. (aor. 1 part. ἀποθησαμένη Hsch.), *put away from oneself, lay aside*, τεύχεα κάλ' ἀποθέσθαι ἐπὶ χθονί Il.3.89; τὴν Σκυθικὴν στολὴν ἀ. *put* it *off*, Hdt.4.78; ἀ. κόμας *cut* it *off*, in mourning, E.*Hel.* 367 (lyr., tm.); ἀ. τὸν νόμον *set aside*, i.e. *disregard*, the law, Th.1.77; ἀ. τὰν Ἀφροδίταν *quell* desire, E.*IA*558 (lyr.); ἀ. ῥαθυμίαν D.4.8, 8.46; ὀργήν Plu.*Cor.*19; ἀρχήν Id.*Pomp.*23. **2.** *put away from oneself, avoid*, ἀποθέσθαι ἐνιπήν *wipe away* the reproach, Il.5.492, cf. Hes.*Op.* 762; νόστον ἔχθιστον ἀπεθήκατο Pi.*O.*8.68, cf. 10(11).40. **3.** *put by for oneself, stow away*, Ar.*Eq.*1219, X.*Cyr.*6.1.15; ἀ. τροφὴν τοῖς νεοττοῖς Arist.*HA*619$^{a}$20; ἀ. τινὰ εἰς φυλακήν Plb.23.10.8; freq. of drugs, Dsc.4.136, al., cf. *PEleph.*12 (iii B.C.); ἐν φυλακῇ *Ev.Matt.* 14.3. **b.** *bury*, *IG*14.1974. **4.** ἀποτίθεσθαι εἰς αὖθις *put off, defer*, E.*IT*376, Pl.*Grg.*449b, X.*Smp.*2.7, etc.; εἰς τοὺς παῖδας ἀ. τὰς τιμωρίας Lys.*Fr.*53.3. **5.** *reserve, keep back*, Pl.*Lg.*887c, Din.1. 30. **6.** ἀπεθήκατο κόλπων, of a woman, *laid down the burden of* her womb, i.e. bore a child, Call.*Dian.*25; ἀ. ὠδῖνας Str.10.5.2: but, **7.** μηδὲν ἀποτίθεσθαι τῶν γιγνομένων *expose* none of *one's* children, Arist.*Pol.*1335$^{b}$22. **8.** ἀ. χρόνον εἴς τι *employ, bestow* time upon it, Plb.18.9.10. **9.** *set* a fracture, Pall.*in Hp.Fract.*12. 276C.; cf. ἀπόθεσις.

**ἀποτίθησιν·** ἀποθνήσκει, Hsch.

**ἀποτίκτω,** *bring to the birth*, Pl.*Tht.*150c, 182b, Arist.*HA*544$^{a}$3, al.:—Pass., ib.10, Philostr.*VA*1.5, Iamb.*Comm.Math.*4; χθονὸς ἧς ἀπετέχθην *IG*9(1).882.5 (Corcyra).

**ἀποτῑλάω,** *pass*, of excrement, τι αἱμοειδές *Hippiatr.*75; *defile*, Suid.

**ἀπο-τίλλω,** fut. -τῐλῶ Cratin.123: aor. ἀπέτῑλα Ar.*Fr.*686:—*pluck, pull out*, τὰς τρίχας Hdt.3.16; οὐδὲν ἀποτίλας without *pulling off* any of the fur, Id.1.123. **II.** *pull the hair off, pluck bare*, τὰς κεφαλάς Ar.*Lys.*578, cf. Luc.*Gall.*28; ἀποτιλῶ σε τήμερον Cratin. l.c.:—Pass., ἀποτετιλμένος σκάφιον Ar.*Av.*806, cf. *Ec.*724. **2.** of a fish, σαπέρδην ἀποτῖλαι Id.*Fr.*686. **-τιλμα,** ατος, τό, *piece plucked off*, γραιᾶν ἀποτίλματα πηρᾶν *pluckings*, Theoc.15.19. **-τιλμός,** ὁ, *tearing away*, Sor.1.71.

**ἀποτίμαστος** [ῐ], ον, *dishonoured*, Hsch.

***ἀποτῑμ-άω,** *fail to honour, slight*, *h.Merc.*35, Call.*Fr.*103, *IG*14. 1389 ii 33. **2.** Pass., *to be disfranchised*, Phleg.*Olymp.Fr.*14. **II.** *value*, τὰ χρήματα, of the owner, J.*AJ*18.1.1:—Med., of the valuer, ibid., cf. 17.13.5; *fix a price by valuation*, δίμνεως ἀποτιμησάμενοι *having fixed their price* at two minae a head, Hdt.5.77; ἀ. πολλοῦ αἰσχροὶ εἶναι *value it* at a high price (i.e. to offer a great deal) *that they may not* be ugly, Hp.*Art.*37:—Pass., *to be valued*, πλειόνων χρημάτων Catalog.ap.D.18.106. **2.** *measure*, μέτρον γῆς J.*AJ*5.1. 21. **III.** as law-term, **1.** in Act., *mortgage* a property, D.30. 28, 41.7. **2.** Pass., of the property, *to be pledged* or *mortgaged*, Id.30.4; τινὶ εἰς προῖκα *IG*12(7).57 (Amorgos), cf. ib.2.1138. **-ημα,** ατος, τό, *mortgaged property, security*, Lys.*Fr.*84S., Is.6.36, D.30.7, *IG*2.1059.4. ***-ησις,** εως, ἡ, *pledging of a property, mortgaging*, D. 31.11. **II.** = Lat. *census*, Plu.*Crass.*13, J.*AJ*.18.2.1. **2.** *valuation*, Just.*Nov.*2.4. **III.** *tax*, *AB*437, cf. *OGI*476.2 (Dorylaeum, i A.D.). **-ητής,** οῦ, ὁ, *one who receives in pledge*, *AB*437. **II.** official *valuer* of property, Lys.*Fr.*84S., Harp.

**ἀπότῑμος,** ον, *put away from honour*, stronger than ἄτιμος, Hdt.2. 167 (Comp.), S.*OT*215 (lyr.).

**ἀποτίν-αγμα** [ῐ], ατος, τό, *tow*, Lxx *Jd.*16.9, Sm.*Is.*1.31. **-άσσω** [ῐ], *shake off*, E.*Ba.*253:—Med., ἀποτινάξασθαι Gal.6.821; ἀποτετίνακται τὸ ῥῆμα τῶν ὄνων *has got rid of* it, Lxx 1*Ki.*10.2.

***ἀπο-τίνῡμι** [ῐ, cf. sq.], Dor. inf. -τινύμεν *Supp.Epigr.*1.410.9 (Crete, iv B.C.); 3 sg. imper. ἀποτεινύτω *GDI*5100.11 (ib.), *SIG*$^{2}$680. 8 (Syros):—later -τίννῡμι, inf. -τιννύναι, part. -τιννύντες, Them.*Or.* 23.289c, 3.40d, imper. -τιννύτω J.*AJ*4.8.36, *SIG*1109.79 (Athens, ii A.D.):—also -τιννύω Lxx *Ge.*31.39, al., Ph.2.596; ἀποτεινυέτω *PAvrom.*1 *A* 26:—for Med. v. sq. II.1.

***ἀποτίνω,** Arc. ἀπυτείω *IG*5(2).6.43 (Tegea, iv B.C.), fut. -τείσω: aor. -έτεισα; Thess. 3 sg. aor. imper. ἀππεισάτου ib.9(2).1229 (ii B.C.):—*repay*, τιμὴν δ' Ἀργείοις ἀποτινέμεν Il.3.286; εὐεργεσίας ἀποτίνειν Od.22.235. **2.** *pay for* a thing, πρὶν..μνηστῆρας ὑπερβασίην ἀποτεῖσαι ib.13.193; Πατρόκλοιο δ' ἕλωρα..ἀποτείσῃ *may atone for* making a prey of Patroclus, Il.18.93; σύν τε μεγάλῳ ἀπέτεισαν *made atonement* with a great price, ib.4.161; ἀ. αἷμα A.*Ag.*1338 (lyr.); πληγὰς τῶν ὑπεραύχων S.*Ant.*1352. **3.** more freq., *pay in full*, τίσιν οὐκ ἀποτείσει Orac.ap.Hdt.5.56, cf. 3.109; ζημίην Id.2.65; ἀργύριον Ar.*V.*1255; ἐγγύας Antipho 2.2.12, cf. 5.63; χρήματα Lys. 1.29; ἀξίαν Luc.*DMort.*30.1; ἀπότεισον *pay* the wager! Ar.*Pl.*1059; in Law παθεῖν ἢ ἀποτεῖσαι are opposed to denote personal or pecuniary penalties, e.g. Lexap.D.21.47, cf. ib.25; τί ἄξιός εἰμι παθεῖν ἢ ἀ.; Pl.*Ap.*36b, cf.*Plt.*299a, *Lg.*843b, al. **4.** c. acc. pers., ἀλάστωρ.. τόνδ' ἀπέτεισεν *made* him *the price*, A.*Ag.*1503 (lyr.). **5.** τὸ πεπρωμένον ἀ. *pay the debt of* fate, i.e. *die*, *Epigr.Gr.*509 (Thess.). **II.** Med., ἀποτίνομαι, poet. ἀποτίνῡμαι (freq. written -τίννυμαι) Il.16. 398, Hes.*Op.*247 (s.v.l.), Thgn.362, Hdt.6.65: fut. -τείσομαι:—*to get paid one, exact* or *require* a penalty *from*, πόλεων δ' ἀπετίνυτο ποινήν Il.16.398, etc.: c. dupl. acc., ἀποτείσασθαι δίκην ἐχθρούς E. *Heracl.*852; δέκα τάλαντ' ἀ. Eup.317 (dub.), etc. **2.** c. acc. pers., ἀποτείσασθαί τινα *avenge oneself on* another, *punish* him, Od.5.24, X. *Cyr.*5.4.35, etc. **3.** c. acc. rei, *take vengeance for* a thing, *punish* it, εἴ κέ ποτέ σφι βίας ἀποτείσεται Od.3.216, cf. 16.255; τὰ παράνομα ..θεὸς ἀ. Ar.*Th.*684: c. gen. rei, ἀ. τῶν..ἱρῶν κατακαυθέντων Hdt.6. 101, v.supr. I.2: abs., *take vengeance*, Thgn. l.c., Sol.4.16. [ἀποτίνω has ῑ by position before νϝ in Ep., ῐ in Att. For ἀποτίνυμαι, which has ῑ by nature, ἀποτείνυμαι should perh. be read in early texts; cf. foreg.]

**ἀποτίπλαστος,** ον, Dor. for ἀπροσπέλαστος, Hsch.

**ἀπότῐσις** (better ἀπότεισις), εως, ἡ, *repayment*, Ath.11.503b.

**ἀποτιστέον** (better ἀποτειστέον), *one must pay*, ζημίαν X.*Lac.*9.5, cf. *PTeb.*71, Aristid.*Or.*46(3).2.

**ἀπότιστος,** ον, *unwatered*, *PTeb.*1.71.8–9 n. (ii B.C.).

**ἀπότιτθος,** ον, *put from the breast, weaned*, Ph.2.83, 332.

***ἀπο-τμήγω,** Ep. for ἀποτέμνω, *cut off from*, μοῦνον ἀποτμήξας πόλιος Il.22.456; τὸν..λαοῦ ἀποτμήξαντε 10.364, etc. **2.** *cut off, sever*, χεῖρας ἀπὸ ξίφεϊ τμήξας 11.146; μήδεα Hes.*Th.*188; κλιτῦς τότ' ἀποτμήγουσι χαράδραι *plough* the hill-sides, Il.16.390:—Pass., μοῦνοι ἀποτμηγέντες A.R.4.1052: c. gen., τοῦ ἑνός Dam.*Pr.* 34. **-τμημα,** ατος, τό, *anything cut off, piece*, Hp.*Art.*38, *Gp.*1.14. 12. **-τμήξ,** ῆγος, ὁ, ἡ, *cut off, sheer*, like ἀπορρώξ, σκοπιή A.R.2. 581. **-τμηξις,** εως, ἡ, *cutting off*, Anon.Lond.32.51. **-τμησις,** εως, ἡ, *cutting off*, ἀγκυρίων Ph.*Bel.*100.33 (pl.). **-τμητέον,** *one must cut off*, τῆς τῶν πλησίον χώρας *a portion of* it, Pl.*R.*373d; *one must excise*, τὴν μήτραν Sor.2.89.

**ἄποτμος,** ον, *unhappy, ill-starred*, Il.24.388, Od.20.140; βοά A. *Pers.*280 (lyr.); πότμος ἄ. E.*Hipp.*1144 (lyr.): Comp. -ότερος Mosch. 4.11: Sup. -ότατος Od.1.219.

**ἀπότοκος** (A), ὁ, *propagation*, νοσήματος Hp.*Art.*49 (pl.).

**ἀπότοκος** (B), ον, *resulting from*, τινός Aret.*SD*1.16, 2.3.

**ἀποτολμ-άω,** *make a bold venture upon*, τινί Th.7.67: c. inf., ἀ. ἐπιχειρῆσαι Lys.7.28; λέγειν Aeschin.3.131, cf. Plb.2.45.2, Ph.1. 233, etc.:—pf. part. Pass. in act. sense, δι' ἐλευθερίας λίαν ἀποτετολμημένης too *presumptuous* liberty, Pl.*Lg.*701b, cf. Plu.*Galb.*25: in pass. sense, εἰπεῖν τὰ νῦν ἀποτετ. Pl.*R.*503b: abs., ἀποτολμᾷ καὶ λέγει *Ep.Rom.*10.20: c. acc., ἀναίρεσιν J.*AJ*7.8.3. **-ητέον,** *one must venture*, c. inf., λέγειν Plu.2.11d.

**ἀπότολμος,** ον, *bold, daring*, Heph.Astr.3.34, Sch.Opp.*H.*1.112.

***ἀποτομ-άς,** άδος, ἡ, pecul. fem. of ἀπότομος, *abrupt, sheer*, πέτρα D.S.4.78, cf. 2.13. **2.** as Subst., *split* or *hewn piece of wood*, J. *AJ*3.1.2; *javelin used in athletic games*, Poll.10.64, Hsch. **3.** fiery *dart*, prob. l. in Tim.*Pers.*28. **-εύς,** έως, ὁ, = foreg. 2, Poll. 3.151. **-ή,** ἡ, *cutting off*, τῶν χειρῶν X.*HG*2.1.32: in pl., Ti. Locr.97d. **2.** *piece, segment*, ἀπὸ τοῦ ἀπείρου Epicur.*Ep.*2p.37U.; γῆς Ph.2.77, cf. ib.124 (pl.), Diog.Oen.24; κόσμου Ocell.3.3; τοιαύτας ἔχειν τὰς ἀ., of the moon in eclipse, Arist.*Cael.*297$^{b}$25, cf. 294$^{a}$4, Plot.6.4.7; *end cut off*, Dsc.5.120. **b.** in Music, *difference between* λεῖμμα *and* τόνος, Gaud.*Harm.*14; τοῖς ἡμιτονίοις τῷ τε ἐλάσσονι καὶ τῷ μείζονι, τουτέστι τοῦ τε λείμματος καὶ τῇ ἀ. ib.16. **c.** Math., *compound irrational straight line equivalent to binomial surd with negative sign*, Euc.10.83, al. **3.** *branching off*, τῶν φλεβίων Arist.*HA*497$^{a}$17; *place where roads intersect*, Plb.6.29.9. **4.** *division* of an argument *into sections*, D.H.*Is.*15. **5.** in Tactics, = φαλαγγαρχία (q.v.), Ascl.*Tact.*2.10, etc. **-ία,** ἡ, *severity*, νόμων D.S.12.16, *POxy.*237 vii 40 (i A.D.); ἐπιτιμημάτων Plu.2.13d; ἀναβάσεως *BGU*1208.16 (Aug.); Φαλάριδος Demetr.*Eloc.*292; περὶ τὰ δίκαια D.H.8.61; of tortures, Ph.2.287; καῦσις διὰ τὴν ἀ. Archig.(?) ap.Aët.9.35. **II.** *cutting off*, Dem.Ophth.ap.Aët.7.81. **III.** *sheer madness*, Ps.-Callisth.2.12. ***-ος,** ον, *cut off*, στροφέων ἀ. μῆκος πήχεων πέντε *IG*11(2).287*A*49 (Delos, iii B.C.); esp. *sheer, precipitous*, ἀ. ἐστι ταύτῃ ἡ ἀκρόπολις Hdt.1.84, cf. 4.62; ἀ. ἐκ θαλάττης Pl.*Criti.*118a; τὰ ἀ. *precipices*, Philostr.*VA*3.4; ἀπότομον ὤρουσεν εἰς ἀνάγκαν, metaph. from one who comes suddenly *to the edge of a cliff*, S.*OT*877 (lyr.). Adv. -μως, ἔχειν Philostr.*VA*2.5. **2.** metaph., *severe, relentless*, λῆμα E.*Alc.*981 (lyr.); κρίσις Lxx *Wi.*6.6. Adv. -ως ib.5.22, Plb.18.11.2, Plu.*Crass.*3, etc.; *brusquely*, prob. l.

in Cic.*Att.*10.11.5. b. of persons, *severe*, Ph.2.268. c. of gladiatorial combats, a fight *to a finish*, ἐνόζυγον ἀπότομον *IGRom.* 4.1632; ἀπότομα alone, Μουσεῖον καὶ Βιβλ.1876/8 No.153; μονομαχιῶν τρεῖς ἡμέρας ἀποτόμους *Inscr.Magn.*163.10, cf. *IGRom.*3.360.9 (Sagalassus), *CIG*2880 (Branchidae). 3. *concise*, συγκεφαλαίωσις Plb.9.32.6. 4. c. gen., οἱ καθηγητῶν οὕτως ἀπότομοι γενηθέντες *offshoots* of our founders, Phld.*Lib.*p.22 O. 5. ἀπότομοι· οὐκ ἐνεργοί, Hsch.: ἀπότομον· τὸν μὴ ἄξιον προσόψεως, Id. II. *absolute*: Adv. -μως *absolutely*, οὐδὲν τῶν τοιούτων ἐστὶν ἀ. οὔτε κακὸν οὔτ' ἀγαθόν Isoc.6.50, cf. D.61.4; ἀ. ἀληθής Phld.*Mus.*p.98 K.; *precisely, in the strictest sense*, τοῖς ὀνόμασι χρῆσθαι Isoc.9.10.

**ἀποτοξεύω**, *shoot off arrows*, ἀπὸ δένδρων D.C.37.2: metaph., *shoot off like an arrow*, ῥηματίσκια Pl.*Tht.*180a, cf. Luc.*Rh.Pr.*17:—Pass., Id.*Prom.Es*2. 2. *shoot* a person, τινά τινι Id.*Vit.Auct.*24 (codd., κατατοξ- Cobet). II. *keep off by shooting*, λοιμόν Id.*Alex.*36.

**ἀποτορεύω**, dub. l. for sq., Ph.1.505 (Pass.), Jul.*Or.*3.112a.

**ἀποτορν-εύω**, *round off* as by the lathe, εἰς σφαῖραν -τετορνευμένος Ph.1.505: metaph. of *polished* language, σαφῆ καὶ στρογγύλα.. τὰ ὀνόματα ἀποτετόρνευται Pl.*Phdr.*234e (imitated by Plu.2.45a); κέγχρους Jul.*Or.*3.112a; περιόδους ib.2.77a. **-ωσις**, εως, ἡ, *rounding off* as by the lathe, Heliod.ap.Orib.49.7.4.

**ἄποτος**, ον, *not drinkable*, ὕδωρ Hdt.4.81, Pherecr.70, etc. 2. *not drunk from*, ποτήριον Philostr.*VA*4.20. II. Act., *never drinking*, ὄνοι Hdt.4.192; of grasshoppers, Pl.*Phdr.*259c; of birds of prey, Arist.*HA*594ᵃ1. 2. *not drinking, without drink*, ἄσιτος ἀνήρ, ἄ. S.*Aj.*324, cf. X.*Cyr.*7.5.53; ἄ. ἀνέχεσθαι Arist.*HA*596ᵃ1; *not given to drinking*, ἐδωδοὶ καὶ ἄ. Hp.*Aër.*1; but, *unable to drink*, Id.*Epid.*2.3.7. 3. in Architecture, ἁρμοὶ ἄ. *not admitting water*, of close-fitting joints, *IG*2².244.90.

**ἀποτρᾰγεῖν**, v. ἀποτρώγω.

**ἀποτράγημα** [ᾰγ], ατος, τό, *remains of a dessert*, v.l. for ἀποπάτημα, Eup.284.

**ἀποτρᾰγοπώγων**, = λάδανον, Gal.12.423.

**ἀποτρᾰχηλίζω**, *strangle*, σχοινίοις Eun.*Hist.*p.272 D.

**ἀποτρᾰχύνω**, pf. ἀποτετράχυκα D.H.*Comp.*22:—*make rough* or *hard*: metaph., τὴν ἁρμογήν l.c.; but ἀ. τὴν ἀκοήν *grate on* the ear, Id.*Dem.*43:—Pass., *to be* or *become rough* or *hard*, Thphr.*HP*6.4.2.

**ἀποτρέκω**, = ἀποτρέχω, barbarism in Ar.*Th.*1214.

**ἀποτρεπ-τέον**, *one must turn away, divert*, Arist.*Rh.Al.*1425ᵃ35; τὴν ὄρεξιν ἐπὶ τὰ λιτά Plu.2.125d. 2. -τέος, α, ον, *to be diverted*, ῥεύματα Gal.16.152. ❋-**τικός**, ή, όν, *fit for dissuading from* a thing, τινός Ps.-Luc.*Philopatr.*8; ἀ. εἶδος τῶν λόγων Arist.*Rh.Al.*1421ᵇ9. 2. *preventive*, τῶν νομῶν Dsc.1.70. **-τος**, ον, *abominable*, Them.*Or.*13.170c. ❋-**ω**, *turn away from*, εἰ δὲ σύ.. -τιν' ἄλλον.. ἀποτρέψεις πολέμοιο Il.12.249, cf. 20.256; ὅθεν.. ἀπέτραπε λαὸν Ἀθήνη 11.758; *deter* or *dissuade from*, τινός τινα Th.3.39; τινὰ τῆς κακουργίας Id.6.38; τῆς γνώμης And.3.21, etc.: c. inf., ἀ. προσωτέρω τὸ μὴ πορεύεσθαι Hdt.1.105; ἀ. βοὰν A.*Supp.*900 (lyr.); δηλοῦν D.60.26, cf. X.*Mem.*4.7.5,6: c. part., ἀ. τινὰ ὑβρίζοντα A.*Supp.*880:—Pass., ὁ παραβαίνειν τι βουλόμενος τῷ μὴ προὔχων ἂν ἐπελθεῖν -τρέπεται Th.3.11, cf. Plu.*Fab.*19. 2. c. acc. pers. only, *turn away* or *back*, πάντας ἀπέτραπε καὶ μεμαῶτας Il.15.276: c. dat. modi, οὔ μ' ἐπέεσσιν ἀποτρέψεις μεμαῶτα 20.256, cf. 109; τοὺς ἀλαζόνας ἀ. *deter* them, Pl.*Chrm.*173c; opp. παροξῦναι, D.21.37; opp. συμβουλεύω, Arist.*Rh.*1391ᵇ33, etc. 3. c. acc. rei, *turn back again*, ποτὶ χέρσον ἔντεα ναὸς Pi.*N.*4.69. 4. *turn aside, avert*, ἀπὸ δὲ.. ἔγχεος ὁρμὴν ἔτραπε Hes.*Sc.*455; *pervert*, δίκας κέλευθον ὀρθᾶς B.10.27; τὸ σφάλμα ἀ. *prevent, avert* it, Hdt.1.207; τὸ μέλλον γενέσθαι Id.3.65, cf. 8.29, al.; ἀ. βλάβην, συμφοράν, Pl.*Grg.*509b, *Phdr.*231d; ἀ. τὴν εἰρήνην *prevent* its being made, X.*HG*6.3.12. 5. *turn from* others *against* one, ἐπὶ τῷδε.. οὐκ ἔγχος τις.. ἀποτρέψει; v.l. in S.*Tr.*1013 (lyr.):—Pass., ἀποτετράφθαι πρὸς τὴν ἄλλην Ἰταλίαν Plu.*Fab.*19:—Med., ἀποτραπόμενος πρὸς θυσίαν, i.e. *turning away from other objects to* this one, Id.*Rom.*7; εἰς τὴν μεσογείαν -τραπόμενος Luc.*Tox.*52. II. Med. and (later) Pass., *turn from, desist from*, c. part., ἀπετράπετ' ὄβριμος Ἕκτωρ ὀλλὺς Ἀργείους Il.10.200: c. inf., λέγειν E.*Or.*410, cf. Antipho 5.32, D.*Prooem.*23 (b); ἀ. ἐκ κινδύνων Th.2.40; ἀ. τοῦ ἐρωτήματος X.*Oec.*15.13. 2. *turn away, turn a deaf ear*, οὐδέ.. ἀπετράπετ' οὐδ' ἀπίθησεν Il.12.329: abs., Pl.*Smp.*206d. 3. c. acc. rei, *turn away from, shrink from*, δεῖμα πολιτῶν A.*Th.*1065 (anap.); τἀληθές E.*IA*336 (lyr.), cf. Th.3.68, and late Prose, Plu.*Cleom.*9, etc. 4. *turn back, return*, ἐπ' οἴκου Th.5.13; ἐς τὴν πόλιν Id.3.24; ἀποτρεπόμενοι ἵεντο X.*HG*7.2.13. 5. *dissuade, deter*, τινά Plb.7.13.1. 6. *beat off, repulse*, Plu.*Brut.*42.

**ἀποτρέφω**, *feed, support*, τὴν στρατιὰν ἡ χώρα ἀ. Str.16.2.10; τινά Lyd.*Mag.*1.34, al.; γαμετάς Just.*Nov.*43.1.2:—Pass., *live off* a thing, Poll.6.32, Just.*Nov.*80.5 *Intr.*; συσσιτίων ἀ. Eust.1.14.

❋**ἀποτρέχω**, fut. -θρέξομαι Ar.*Nu.*1005, but -θρέξω Pl.Com.232; also -δρᾰμοῦμαι X.*An.*7.6.5: aor. 2 ἀπέδρᾰμον Hdt.4.203:—*run off* or *away*, ll.cc., X.*An.*5.2.6; οἴχεσθαι ἀποτρέχων Pl.*Tht.*171d. II. *run hard*, of one training for a race, Ar. l.c. III. *run home*, οἴκαδε X.*Oec.*11.18; *run off the track*, Pl.*R.*613c. IV. *depart*, Foed.ap.Plb.3.24.11; of manumitted slaves, ἀποτρεχέτω ἐλευθέρα *GDI*2038 (Delph.), etc. V. of workers, *abscond, strike*, *PSI*4.421.8 (iii B.C.).

**ἀπότρεψις**, εως, ἡ, (from Med.) *aversion*, Hp.*Liqu.*2 (pl.).

**ἀποτριάζω**, *to be victorious in wrestling* (cf. τριακτήρ), Sch.A.*Ch.* 339 (Pass.); *to be victorious in the* πένταθλον, Poll.3.151: = τρεῖς πληγὰς δοῦναι, *AB*438, Hsch.

**ἀπο-τρῐβή**, ἡ, *rubbing away, wearing out, depreciation*, τῶν σκευῶν D.50.28; *damage*, ὥστε μηδεμίαν ἀ. τῷ δημοσίῳ συμβῆναι, = *ne quid detrimenti res publica caperet*, D.C.37.31. ❋-**τρίβω** [ῑ], fut. -ψω, strengthd. for τρίβω, *wear out*, πολλά οἱ.. σφέλα.. πλευραὶ ἀποτρίψουσι his ribs will *wear out* many a footstool (thrown at him), Od.17.232. II. *rub clean*, ἀ. ἵππον *rub down* a horse, X.*Eq.*6.2:—Med., ἀ. τὸ αἰδοῖον Plu.2.1044b. III. *rub off*, ἰόν Theoc.16.17: metaph., πρὶν γῆρας ἀποτρῖψαι νεότητα Id.24.133:—Pass., *to be rubbed off*, Arist.*Col.*793ᵃ25:—Med., *get rid of*, ἀδοξίαν D.1.11; ἐγκλήματα Aeschin.1.179; τὸ πάθος Arist.*EN*1105ᵃ2; διαβολάς D.S.17.5; τὸν πόλεμον, τὸν κίνδυνον, Plb.3.8.10, 10.14.1; τοὺς πελάζοντας ἀ. *brush* them *away*, Id.3.102.5; τὸν ἄνθρωπον Plu.*Mar.*40; quartanam Cic.*Att.*7.5.5; λιμὸν τῆς γαστρός Plu.2.1044b; *decline, reject*, ἡμέραν *Inscr.Prien.*27.17; τὴν πεῖραν Plu.*Thes.*26; δεήσεις Id.*Brut.*17; τὰ διδόμενα *OGI*315.82 (Pessinus, ii B.C.). 2. in Pass., ὥστε μηδὲν ἀπ' αὐτῆς ἀποτρῖβῆναι, = *ne quid detrimenti resp. caperet*, D.C.40.49, etc. -**τριμμα**, ατος, τό, *that which is rubbed off*, ἀκόνης Ναξίας *emery powder*, Dsc.5.149, Critoap.Gal.12.447. ❋-**τριπτος**, ον, *worn out*, *PLond.*2.191.12 (ii A.D.).

**ἀποτρίς**, Adv. *thrice*, A.D.*Synt.*339.14.

**ἀποτρῐτ-όω**, *boil down to a third part*, v.l. in Ps.-Dsc.4.137 (Pass.), cf. *Gp.*7.13.5, Alex.Trall.1.15. -**ωσις**, εως, ἡ, *boiling down to a third part*, ἑψέσθω εἰς -σιν Orib.*Fr.*51, cf. Aët.3.77.

**ἀπό-τρῐχος**, ον, *hairless*, Eust.581.13. -**τριψις**, εως, ἡ, *mashing*, *PSI*4.332.24 (iii B.C.).

**ἀποτροπ-άδην** [ᾰδ], Adv. *turned away*, Opp.*H.*3.612. ❋-**αιος**, ον, *averting evil*, freq. of Apollo, Ar.*Eq.*1307, *Av.*61, *Pl.*359, Orac.ap.D.21.53, *CIG*464: generally, θεοὶ ἀ. Hp.*Vict.*4.89, Pl.*Lg.*854b, X.*HG*3.3.4, Paus.2.11.1. 2. of sacrifices, D.H.5.54, Plu.2.290d, 292a. II. Pass., *that ought to be averted, ill-omened*, φαντασίαι Ph.2.433; δυσφημίαι Plu.2.587f; θέαμα Luc.*Tim.*5; ἄκουσμα Id.*Gall.*2, etc. ❋-**άομαι**, poet. for ἀποτρέπω, Ps.-Phoc.133 codd., Numen.ap.Ath.7.304f. -**ή**, ἡ, *turning away, averting*, A.*Pers.*217; ἄλλοσ' ἀποτροπὰ κακῶν γένοιτο, i.e. ἄλλοσε ἀποτρέποιτο κακά, E.*Hel.*360; λυπῶν ἀπαλλαγὰς τε καὶ ἀποτροπάς Pl.*Prt.*354b; τεράτων ἀ., Lat. *procuratio*, Plu.*Fab.*18. 2. *diverting*, of water, Pl.*Lg.*845d. 3. *prevention*, Th.3.45; ἀποτροπῆς ἕνεκα κολάζειν Pl.*Prt.*324b, cf. *R.*382c. 4. *dissuasion*, Id.*Thg.*128d; opp. προτροπή, Arist.*Rh.*1358ᵇ9, Chrysipp.*Stoic.*3.3. II. (from Med.) *desertion of one's party*, 'ratting', Th.3.82. ❋-**ία**, Ep. -ίη, ἡ, poet. for foreg. I, οὐ γάρ τις ἀ. θανάτοιο A.R.4.1504. -**ιάζω**, *utter a deprecatory prayer for*, τινά Aristaenet.1.1:—Med., *avert* evil *by sacrifice*, Lxx *Ez.*16.21; σημεῖον *POxy.*885.53, cf. Phleg.*Mir.*1, Sch.A.*Pers.*203. -**ιασμα**, ατος, τό, *sacrifice to avert evil*, Hsch. -**ιασμός**, ὁ, *averting by expiatory sacrifice*, *PTeb.*140: in pl., Beros.ap.J.*AJ* 1.3.6, Aesop.112b, D.L.8.32. -**ιαστής**, οῦ, ὁ, *averter*, Sch.A.l.c. -**ιαστικός**, ή, όν, *fit for averting*, Eust. ad D.P.723. -**ιμος**, ον, = ἀποτρόπαιος, Hsch. s.v. ὀξυθυμία. -**ιος**, ον, = foreg., Orph.*A.*481. ❋-**ος**, ον, (ἀποτρέπω) *turned away, far from men*, ἐγὼ παρ' ὕεσσιν ἀπότροπος Od.14.372; *turned away in flight*, Opp.*H.*4.254. 2. *from which one turns away, horrible*, ἀ. ἄγος A.*Ch.*155 (lyr.); τὸν ἀ. Ἅιδαν S.*Aj.*608 (lyr.); σκότου νέφος Id.*OT*1314; πῦρ Ar.*Ec.*792; γνώμη ἀ. a *stern, hostile* decree, Pi.*P.*8.94; κασιγνήτης ἀπότροπον.. εὐνήν Ps.-Phoc.182. II. Act., *turning away, averting*, κακῶν A.*Ch.*42, E.*Ph.*586; ἀ. δαίμονες A.*Pers.*203. 2. *preventing, saving from*, ἀ. αὐτοῖς ἐγένετο μή.., c. inf., Pl.*Lg.*877a.

❋**ἀποτροφ-ή**, ἡ, *nourishment, support*, *PSI*1.76.6 (vi A.D., pl.); f.l. for ἀποστρ- in D.H.7.28, dub. in Ph.1.617 (leg. ἀπ' οὐρανοῦ τροφήν). ❋-**ιμος**, ον, (prob. for -τρόφινος) *furnishing sustenance*, ἐπιτήδευμα τοῦ ζῆν ἀ. *means of* subsistence, *PFlor.*295.2 (vi A.D.). -**ος**, ον, *reared away from home*, Hdt.2.63; of birds, Arist.*HA*536ᵇ16: c. gen., ἀ. ἀλλήλων *reared apart from*, Plu.2.917c.

**ἀποτροχίζω**· *deporto*, *Gloss.*

**ἀπότροχος**, ὁ, (ἀποτρέχω) *race-course*, Ar.*Fr.*637 (pl.).

**ἀποτρῡγ-άω**, *pluck grapes or fruit*, Philostr.*VA*3.5; ἀ. πέπερι ib.3.4: metaph., ἀρχὰς ἐθνῶν ἀ. Lxx *Am.*6.1. -**ίζω**, (τρύξ) *rack off, decant*, εἰς ἀγγεῖα *Gp.*8.23.2.

**ἀποτρύζω**, *emit a sound*, σύριγμα Nonn.*D.*25.47.

❋**ἀποτρυπῶν**· λάθρα ἐξιών, Hsch.

**ἀποτρύχω** [ῡ], = sq., τινὰ πόνοις Ph.2.231:—Pass., ib.288, Plu.*Ant.*24; of land, Ph.2.371. (The form -**χόομαι** is dub. in Plu.*Ant.*38.)

**ἀποτρύω** [ῡ], *rub away, wear out*, ἐλπίδα S.*Tr.*125 (lyr.); ζῷον πόνοις Ph.2.341; χρόνῳ καὶ δαπάνῃ τινὰ ἀ. Plu.*Aem.*13:—Med., γῆν ἀποτρύεσθαι S.*Ant.*339 (lyr.):—Pass., ἀποτετρυμένος *harassed*, Hierocl.p.53 A., cf. Plu.*CG*6.

❋**ἀπο-τρώγω**, aor. 2 ἀπέτρᾰγον Ph.1.224, Gal.6.864, D.L.9.27:—*bite* or *nibble off*, πτόρθους Eup.14; τὸ ἱππομανὲς ἀ. Arist.*HA*605ᵃ4; γλῶτταν Ph. l.c., cf. Gal. l.c.: metaph., μισθοὺς ἀ. Ar.*Ra.*367, cf. Men.303; ἀ. τὸ ἀπορηθὲν 'gulp down', 'bolt' the difficulty, i.e. pass it by without trying to get at the heart of the matter, Arist.*Metaph.*1001ᵃ2. 2. c. gen., *nibble at*, πόης Babr.46.6: metaph., τᾶς αὔλακος οὐκ ἀποτρώγεις, i.e. you don't *gobble* your swathe, Theoc.10.6. -**τρωκτος**, ον, *bitten off*: metaph., *with the end cut off by apocope*, e.g. ἄλφι for ἄλφιτον, Hsch. and Suid. s.v. ἄλφι. -**τρωμάξαι**· ἀποφράξαι, Hsch. -**τρωξις**, εως, ἡ, *biting off*, μυκτήρων Phld.*Ir.*p.34 W.

**ἀποτρωπάω**, Frequentat. of ἀποτρέπω, τινὰ ὀπίσσω Il.20.119: abs., δέ κ' ἀποτρωπῶσι θεοί, παύσασθαι ἄνωγα Od.16.405. **B.** Med., . inf., Il.18.585: c. gen., τανυστύος Od.21.112, etc.: c. acc., πεῖραν A.R.3.16.

**ἀποτυγχάνω,** fut. -τεύξομαι Pl.*Lg.*898e:—Med., aor. ἀποτεύξασθαι· ἀποτυχεῖν, Hsch.: pf. Pass. in med. sense, Phld.*Rh.*1.220S.:—*fail in hitting* or *gaining*, τινός Hp.*VM*2, Pl.*Lg.*744a, X.*Mem.*4.2.27, etc.; τοῦ ὠφελιμωτάτου Pl.*Tht.*179a; τούτων τριῶν ἑνός γ' ἀ. Alex.211; μήτ' ἀξίως τυχεῖν τῆς ἀληθείας μήτε πάντως ἀ. Arist.*Metaph.*993b 1; *lose*, ὧν εἶχον ἀπέτυχον X.*Cyr.*1.6.45; κακοῦ ἀποτυχεῖν *escape from*, Philem.93.9. **2.** Pass., ἀποτυγχάνεται *a failure ensues*, Arist.*Ph.*199b3; of things, *to be missed*, τὸ μὴ ἐπιτευχθὲν ἀ. D.H.*Pomp.*2.14; τὰ προτεθεσπισμένα καὶ ἀποτετευγμένα prophesied and *not come to pass*, Luc.*Alex.*28; ἀποτετευγμένος *rejected, not finding a purchaser*, Dsc.5.79. **II.** abs., *miss one's object, fail*, X.*HG*7.5.14; ὅλως ἀ. D.11.12; λέγοντες οὐκ ἀποτευξόμεθα *shall* not *miss the truth* in saying, Pl.*Lg.*898e; ἀ. περί τινος X.*Eq.*1.16; τυγχάνειν καὶ ἀ. κατά τι Arist.*Po.*1450a3; τῷ γάμῳ D.S.12.12; ἐν ταῖς ἐπιβολαῖς Plb.5.98.6:—Med., ἀποτυγχανομένῳ πρὸς τὸν γάμον Ant.Lib.39.3.

**ἀποτῡλόω,** = ἀναφλάω, Pherecr.204, *AB*423.

⊛**ἀποτύμβιος,** ον, *away from the tomb*, λώβην ῥεθέων ἀ. ἴσχειν *BCH* 23.281 (Termessus).

⊛**ἀποτυμπᾰν-ίζω** (later **-τυπ-** *UPZ*119 (ii B.C.), *POxy.*1798.1.7), *crucify on a plank*, D.8.61, 9.61:—Pass., Lys.13.56, D.19.137, Arist.*Rh.*1383a5, Beros.ap.J.*Ap.*1.20. **2.** generally, *destroy*, Plu.2.1049d. ⊛**-ισμός,** ὁ, *crucifixion*, *Cat.Cod.Astr.*7.140.11.

⊛**ἀπό-τῠπος,** ον, *moulded*, εἰκόνες J.*AJ*20.9.4. **2.** Subst. ἀπότυπος, ὁ, *image*, Ἀπόλλωνος ἀ. ἀργυροῦς *IG*11(2).223*B*17 (Delos, iii B.C.); also as neut., Ἀπόλλωνος ἀπότυπον ἀργυροῦν ἐπίχρυσον ib.203*B*83 (ib.). **-τῠπόω,** *impress*, σφραγῖδα Luc.*Alex.*21; of stars, εἴδωλον *form* a constellation, Phlp.*in Mete.*112.36. **2.** *represent*, τὴν ἀσώματον θεόν Lib.*Eth.*11.3, cf. Porph.ap.Eus.*PE*3.7. **II.** Med., *stamp an impression* as on wax, *form as in an impression*, εἴς τι Pl.*Tht.*191d, cf. *Lg.*681b; πρὸς τὴν τοῦ παραδείγματος φύσιν Id.*Ti.*39e, cf. Hierocl.*in CA*23p.468M., Iamb.*Myst.*1.11. **2.** *model one's style on, imitate*, Ἰσοκράτην D.H.*Din.*8.

⊛**ἀποτύπτω,** *incise, open*, τὰς φλέβας Hp.*Morb.*2.55; *scarify*, τὴν ὀσχην ib.71. **2.** Med., *cease to beat oneself, cease mourning*, Hdt.2.40.

**ἀποτύπ-ωμα** [ῠ], ατος, τό, *impression*, Pl.*Tht.*194b, Iamb.*Myst.*2.10 (pl.). **-ωσις,** εως, ἡ, *impression*, ἀ. ποιεῖν ἀπό τινος Longin.13.4, cf. Thphr.*Sens.*51; v.l. for διατύπωσις, J.*AJ*12.2.8.

**ἀποτῡρόω,** *make into cheese*, Erot. s.v. ὀρὸν πίσσης (Pass.).

**ἀποτυφλ-όω,** *make quite blind*, τινά Arist.*Mir.*845a23; τὴν ὅρασιν D.S.3.37: metaph. of anger, Phld.*Ir.*p.68 W.:—Pass., *to be blinded*, Arist.*HA*602a2, 618b7; τῶν ὄψεων Porph.*Abst.*1.17: metaph., χρήμασι πολλοῖς ὑπό τινων J.*AJ*20.6.1. **2.** metaph., *cut out the bud* of a tree, Plu.2.529b. **3.** *make* a spring *fail*, ib.703b:—Pass., *to be obstructed*, ἀποτυφλωθῆναι τοὺς πόρους Arist.*Pr.*879b7; τὰς πηγάς Str.1.3.16; τὸν μαστόν Antig.*Mir.*45; τὰ ἀγγεῖα Aët.16.26. **-ωσις,** εως, ἡ, *making blind*, Lxx *Za.*12.4: metaph. of the veins, *blocking*, Herod.Med. in *Rh.Mus.*49.555.

**ἀποτύφω** [ῡ], *burn*, in pf. part. Pass. ἀποτεθυμμένος, Hsch.

**ἀποτῠχ-ής,** ές, *missing*, Pl.*Sis.*391c (Comp.). **-ία,** Ion. **-ίη,** ἡ, *failure*, Democr.243, Din.1.29 (as v.l.), Plb.5.98.5, Phld.*Rh.*1.73S., J.*AJ*16.9.1, etc.: c. gen., *failure to obtain*, στεφάνου, ὕδατος, Artem.5.78. **-ίζω,** (τύχος, = τύκος) = ἀποπελεκάω, Paus.Gr.*Fr.*62:—Pass., Hsch.

⊛**ἀπουλ-όω,** *cicatrize*, ἕλκη Dsc.5.79: metaph., τὴν ἀβελτερίαν Plu.2.46f:—Pass., of sores, ἀπουλωθῆναι Arr.*Epict.*2.21.22, cf. Alex. Aphr.*Pr.*1.114; ἀπουλωθήσεται Gal.13.719. ⊛**-ωσις,** εως, ἡ, *cicatrization*, v.l. in Dsc.2.4, cf. Crito ap.Gal.12.448, Aret.*CD*2.3, Alex. Aphr.*Pr.*1.111. ⊛**-ωτικός,** ή, όν, *causing to scar over, healing*, Dsc.2.4: c. gen., ἑλκῶν Id.5.84, cf. Gal.4.770. ⊛**-ωτος,** ον, *free from scar*, prob. in Plu.2.1091e (for ἀπουλώτιστος: ἀμωλώπιστος Bern.).

**ἀπουρᾱγέω,** *cover the rear*, τινί Plb.3.49.13, al.

**ἀπουραι,** = ἀφόρισαι, Eust.1774.36.

⊛**ἀπούρας,** Homeric aor. part. Act., cf. ἀπούραις Pi.*P.*4.149: aor. ind. ἀπηύρων, ας, α, Hom.; pl. ἀπηύρων Il.1.430: aor. part. Med. ἀπουράμενος Hes.*Sc.*173: fut. ἀπουρήσω Il.22.489 (Sch.Ven.B):—*take away* or *wrest from, rob of*, c. dupl. acc. pers. et rei, ἅμφω θυμὸν ἀπηύρα 6.17; ἁπαλόν τέ σφ' ἦτορ ἀπηύρα 11.115; τοὺς μὲν Τυδεΐδης.. τεύχε' ἀπηύρα ib.334; λάθον δέ ἑ θυμὸν ἀπούρας Od.13.270, etc. **2.** c. gen. pers., a doubtful construction in Ἀχιλλῆος γέρας αὐτὸς ἀπηύρων Il.19.89; κούρην..Ἀχιλῆος ἔβης κλισίηθεν ἀπούρας 9.107, cf. Od.18.273; τήν ῥα βίῃ ἀέκοντος ἀπηύρων Il.1.430 (where β. ἀ. may be taken together, 'in spite of him unwilling', cf. ἥ σε βίῃ ἀέκοντος ἀπηύρα νῆα Od.4.646). **3.** c. dat. pers., πολέεσσιν..θυμὸν ἀπηύρα Il.17.236; οἱ οὔ τιν' ἀπηύρα Od.3.192. **4.** c. acc. only, ἔχει γέρας αὐτὸς ἀπούρας Il.1.356; ἐλεύθερον ἦμαρ ἀ. 6.455, etc.:—Med., ἀπουράμενοι ψυχάς *having taken away each other's* lives, Hes.*Sc.*173. **II.** after Hom., *receive* good or ill, *enjoy* or *suffer*, first in Hes.*Op.*240 ξύμπασα πόλις κακοῦ ἀνδρὸς ἀπηύρα (v.l. ἐπαυρεῖ); φόνον πρὸς τέκνων ἀπηύρα E.*Andr.*1030 (lyr.). (ἀπο-Ϝρᾱ-, augmented ἀπ-η-Ϝρᾱ- (cf. ηὔδη, ἑώρων for ἠϜόρων); perh. cogn. with ἀπό-(Ϝ)ερσε.)

**ἀπουργοι** γωνίαι corners *used to shoot rubbish*, Suid., *AB*434.

**ἀπουρ-έω,** *pass urine*, Aret.*SD*2.2, Luc.*VH*1.23, etc.: c. acc., *pass in urine*, αἷμα Ruf.*Ren.Ves.*3.10; πηλόν Gal.13.330. **-ημα,** ατος, τό, *urine passed*, Anon.Lond.30.32. **-ησις,** εως, ἡ, *making water*, ib.30.6, Sor.1.66, Ruf.ap.Aët.11.29, Aret.*SD*2.3.

**ἀπουρία,** ἡ, *issue of free and slave*, Suid., Zonar.

**ἀπουρ-ίζω,** (οὖρος = ὅρος) only in Il.22.489 ἄλλοι γάρ οἱ ἀπουρίσσουσιν (Ion. for ἀφοριοῦνται, Sch.Ven.A) ἀρούρας others *will mark off the boundaries* of his fields, i.e. *take* them *away from* him; better ἀπουρήσουσι *will take away*; cf. ἀπούρας. **II.** v.l. for ἐπουρίζω, Ph.1.668. **-ικτικῶς·** ἀφελομένως, Hsch.

**ἄπουρος,** ον, (οὖρος = ὅρος) *far from the boundaries*, ἀ. πάτρας v.l. in S.*OT*194 (lyr.).

**ἀπουρόω,** (οὖρος A) *to be driven by foul winds*, Plb.16.15.4.

**ἄπους,** ὁ, ἡ, πουν, τό, gen. οδος, *without foot* or *feet*, Pl.*Phdr.*264c, Arist.*HA*487a23, Corn.*ND*16, etc. **2.** *without the use of one's feet, lame*, S.*Ph.*632; *bad of foot*, κύνες X.*Cyn.*3.3; κακόποδες οἱ διὰ τοῦτο καλοῦνται ἄποδες Arist.*HA*487b24, cf. *Metaph.*1022b35, *de An.*422a29. **II.** as Subst., = κύψελος, *sand-martin, Hirundo riparia*; possibly also, *the swift, Cypselus apus*, Id.*HA*618a31.

⊛**ἀπουσία,** ἡ, (ἀπεῖναι) *absence*, A.*Ag.*1259, E.*Hec.*962, Th.1.70, *Ep. Phil.*2.12, etc. **II.** *waste*, as in smelting ore, Arist.*Mete.*383b3, Agatharch.28; τρῖψις καὶ ἀ. *POxy.*1273.32 (iii A.D.). **III.** = ἀποσπερματισμός, Plu.2.364d.

⊛**ἀπουσιάζω,** *waste one's goods*, Suid.; εἴς τινα Artem.1.78: c. gen., *lose substance*, σωμάτων Zos.Alch.p.235 B.:—Pass., *to be expended*, εἰς τροφήν Sor.1.87.

**ἀποφᾰγεῖν,** aor. 2 inf. of ἀπεσθίω, *eat off, eat up*, Ar.*Eq.*497: later fut. ἀποφάγονται *POxy.*465.74.

**ἀποφαιδρύνω,** *cleanse off*, Q.S.5.616, 8.487:—Med., *bathe*, λουτροῖς *AP*9.419 (Crin.).

⊛**ἀποφαίνω,** *show forth, display*, Sol.15.33, etc.; ἀ. τινὶ ἐς ὄψιν Hdt.4.81; ἀ. τὴν φύσιν αὐτοῦ Ar.*Nu.*352; τινά S.*Fr.*1023, cf. 74 (Pass.); ἀ. παῖδας ἐκ γυναικός, i.e. *have* children by her, Is.6.22; of the woman, *produce*, ἔφεδρον βασιλέα..ἀ. Hdt.5.41; also of the descendants, ἑπτὰ πάππους πλουσίους ἀ. *produce* seven generations of wealthy ancestors, Pl.*Tht.*174e. **II.** *make known, declare*, ὡς εἰπὼν ἀπέφηνε Batr.144; γνώμην ἀ. περί τινος Hdt.1.40; δικαίην ζόην ἀ. *give evidence of* a legitimate mode of living, Id.2.177; cf. B.II. **2.** *show by reasoning, prove*, c. part., τοὺς μὲν ἀ. πεφευγότας Id.1.82; ἀπέφαινε τῷ λόγῳ μιν σκαιότατον ὄντα ib.129; πόλλ' ἂν ἀποφήναιμ' ἐκείνους.. ἀδικουμένους Ar.*Ach.*314; ἀποφαίνω ὑμᾶς κυριωτάτους ὄντας Th.2.62; ἀ. ἀγαθῶν..οὖσαν αἰτίαν ἐμέ Ar.*Pl.*547, cf. Isoc.4.139, Plb.1.15.7; with part. omitted, ἀ. τινὰ ἔνοχον Antipho4.2.3, cf. And.1.41; ἀ. τινὰ ἐχθρόν Philipp.ap.D.12.8. **b.** *represent, proclaim*, ἀ. σεαυτὸν ἀρετῆς διδάσκαλον Pl.*Prt.*349a; σοφὸν ἀ. τὸν Ἡσίοδον Id.*Lg.*718e; ἀντὶ φιλοσόφων μισοῦντάς τι ἀ. τινάς Id.*Tht.*168b; ἀ. ἡδονὴν τῶν φαύλων (sc. οὖσαν) Arist.*EN*1172a30, cf. *Rh.Al.*1438b19, etc. **3.** c. acc. et inf., *make plain that..*, Pl.*R.*338e, al.; *show*, ἀ. λόγῳ ὡς.. Hdt.5.84; ἀ. ὡς.., ὅτι.., Th.3.63, Pl.*Phd.*95c, etc. **4.** *denounce, inform against*, Antipho6.9, Lys.31.2; πρίν γ' ἂν τοῦτον ἀποφήνω..οἷος ὢν θρασύνεται Ar.*Ra.*845; ὃν ἡ ἐξ Ἀρείου πάγου βουλὴ ἀποπέφαγκεν χρήματ' ἔχειν Din.1.15:—Pass., ἀποπέφανται μισθαρνῶν ibid. **III.** *give an account of*, τὴν πρόσοδον, τὴν οὐσίαν, D.27.47, 42.11: esp. *pay in money* (to the treasury) *according to accounts delivered*, of public officers, Id.20.77, 80: generally, of private persons, ἕνδεκα μνᾶς τοῦ ἐνιαυτοῦ ἀπέφηνεν Id.27.19; ἅπαντα ἐς τὸ κοινὸν ἀ. X.*Oec.*7.13. **IV.** *render, make* so and so, Ἀθηναίους μικροπολίτας ἀ. Ar.*Eq.*817, cf. X.*Eq.*1.11, 10.5, Luc.*Somn.*8. **2.** *declare elected*, τινὰς ἄρχοντας Pl.*Lg.*753d; τοὺς πεντακισχιλίους Th.8.93:—in Med., ἀποφήνασθαί τινα ταμίαν v.l. in Pi.*N.*6.25 (cf. B.III):—Pass., ἀποφαίνεσθαι εὐδοκίμου στρατιᾶς *to be named* (chief) of a glorious army, A.*Pers.*858 codd.

**B.** Med., *display something of one's own*, Μοῦσαν στυγεράν A.*Eu.*309; καλὰ ἔργα Pl.*Smp.*209e: abs., *make a display of oneself, show off*, X.*Cyr.*8.8.13. **2.** ἀ. μαρτύρια *produce* evidence, Hdt.5.45; ἀ. νόμους *set forth, propound*, Pl.*Lg.*780a. **II.** ἀποφαίνεσθαι γνώμην *declare one's* opinion, Hdt.1.207, 2.120, al., E.*Supp.*335, Pl.*Grg.*466c, D.4.1; ἀ. δόξαν Pl.*R.*576e; δόξαν περί τινος Id.*Tht.*170d. **2.** abs., *give an opinion*, ταύτῃ ἀ. Hdt.7.143; ἀ. περί τινος Pl.*Ly.*214a: c. inf., ἀ. κινεῖσθαι τὰ πάντα Id.*Tht.*168b:—Pass., καθόλου ἀ. ἐπί τινος Arist.*Int.*17b3. **3.** *give a decision* or *award*, ὁ κριτὴς ἀ. Pl.*R.*580b; ἀ. περί τινος Id.*Phdr.*274e; ἀ. δίαιταν, of an arbitrator, D.33.19, 20:—Pass., τῆς διαίτης -φαινομένης Id.54.27. **III.** Med. used like the Act., Pi.*N.*l.c. supr.; ἀ. λογισμόν X.*Mem.*4.2.21: c. inf., *advise*, τὸν ..ὑπακούειν ἀποφηνάμενον D.18.204. **IV.** *define*, ἀ. τἀγαθὸν οὗ πάντες ἐφίενται Arist.*EN*1094a2.

**C.** Pass., *disappear, shade off*, θάλασσα κατὰ μικρὸν εἰς πέλαγος ἀποφαινομένη *Peripl.M.Rubr.*26.

**ἀποφᾰλακρόομαι,** Pass., *become bald*, Phryn.*PS*p.26B.

**ἀπόφαν-σις,** εως, ἡ, (ἀποφαίνω) *declaration, statement*, Arist.*APo.*72a11, *Rh.*1395b6 (as v.l.); δι' ἀποφάνσεων περαίνειν τὸ πᾶν Hermog.*Id.*2.11. **II.** in Logic, *predication*, κατά τινος or ἀπό τινος, *affirmative* or *negative*, Arist.*Int.*17a25, cf. Chrysipp.*Stoic.*2.59. **-τέον,** *one must pronounce*, Ph.2.461, Aristid.Quint.1.28, Plot.2.1.8. **-τικός,** ή, όν, *categorical*, λόγος ἀ. Arist.*Int.*17a8, cf. *Stoic.*2.61, al.; *declaratory*, ἐπιστήμη πάντων ἀληθῶν -κή ib.2.42. Adv. -κῶς dub. in Aristid.*Rh.*1 p.462S., cf. Sch.E.*Ph.*624, al.; λέγειν Hermog.*Id.*2.11. **-τος,** ον, *declared, asserted*, λεκτὸν αὐτοτελὲς ἀ. Chrysipp.*Stoic.*2.62; σχῆμα διηγήματος Hermog.*Prog.*2; χρεῖαι ib.3.

**ἀποφάργῡμι,** v. ἀποφράγνυμι. **ἀπόφαρσις·** ἡ ἑταίρα, Hsch.

⊛**ἀπόφᾰσις** (A), εως, ἡ, (ἀπόφημι) *denial, negation*, opp. κατάφασις, Pl.*Sph.*263e; ἀ. ἐστιν ἀπόφανσίς τινος ἀπό τινος *a predication* of one thing *away from* another, i.e. *negation* of it, Arist.*Int.*17a25, cf. *APo.*72a14; ἀ. τινός *negation, exclusion* of a thing, Pl.*Cra.*426d; δύο ἀ.

μίαν κατάφασιν ἀποτελοῦσι Luc.*Gall.*11. II. *negative particle*, e.g. οὐ, A.D.*Adv.*124.8, al.; *sign of negation*, *Stoic.*2.52 (pl.).

**ἀπόφᾰσις** (B), εως, ἡ, (ἀποφαίνω) = ἀπόφανσις, *sentence, decision*, of an arbitrator's *award*, διαιτητῆς D.47.45, cf. 33.21; κατά τινος, of an Amphictyonic decree, D.S.16.24; ἀ. ἔγγραφος *OGI*335.72 (Pergam.); of an emperor, *PTeb.*286.11 (ii A.D., pl.). 2. *catalogue, inventory*, ἀ. δοῦναι D.42.1, 14. 3. = ἀπόφανσις, *assertion, judgement*, Arist.*Rh.*1365$^{b}$27, Epicur.*Ep.*3p.60U., Phld.*Ir.*p.75W., Plb.1.14.8 (pl.), al.; περί τινος Plu.*Comp.Sol.Publ.*1, cf. Str.2.1.19; καταληπτικὴ ἀ. S.E.*P.*2.123. b. *answer*, Plb.22.13.7; πρὸς τὰ κατηγορούμενα Id.24.2.5. 4. *oracle*, Jul.*Ep.*89. 5. = φάσμα, *appearance, image*, sc. τοῦ ἡλίου, Diog.Oen.8.

**ἀποφάσκω**, = ἀπόφημι, only in pres. inf. and part., and impf.:—*deny*, Plu.2.393c; τί τινος Simp.*in Ph.*218.11:—Pass., Dam.*Pr.*445; in S.*OT*485 οὔτε δοκοῦντ' οὔτ' ἀποφάσκονθ' is interpreted by Sch. οὔτε πιστὰ οὔτε ἄπιστα 'neither commanding assent nor *suffering denial*' (but better referred to ἐμέ understood, 'neither assenting nor *denying*'):—ὁ ἀποφάσκων [λόγος], name of a sophism, Arr.*Epict.*3.9.21; title of work by Chrysippus, *Stoic.*2.8.

**ἀποφᾰτικός**, ή, όν, (ἀπόφημι) *negative*, opp. καταφατικός, λόγος Arist.*Cat.*12$^{b}$8, cf. Chrysipp.*Stoic.*2.55,69; ἐπίρρημα A.D.*Synt.*245.24. Adv. -κῶς Arist.*APr.*64$^{a}$14; also written for ἀποφαντικῶς, A.D.*Pron.*27.16. II. *conclusive*, *PLond.*5.1902$^{v}$ (vi A.D.).

**ἀποφαυλίζω**, = ἀποφλαυρίζω, Lib.*Decl.*48.68, *EM*789.51.

**ἀποφεῖν**· ἀπατῆσαι, Hsch. (fort. ἀπαφεῖν, sed cf. ἀποφώλιος).

**ἀποφενᾱκίζω**, *delude, mock*, Men.Prot.p.90D.

**ἀποφέρβομαι**, *feed on*, σοφίαν dub. l. in E.*Med.*826 (lyr.).

**ἀποφέρω**, Hom. only in fut. -οίσω (Dor. -οισῶ Ar.*Ach.*779, Med. -οίσομαι Theoc.1.3, Luc.*Bis Acc.*33) and Ion. aor. ἀπένεικα: Att. aor. -ήνεγκα Th.5.10: aor. 2 -ήνεγκον Ar.*Ach.*582, etc.: pf. -ενήνοχα D.27.20:—*carry off* or *away*, τεύχεα δέ σφ' ἀπένεικαν Od.16.360, etc.; of a wind, Il.14.255, Hdt.4.179: metaph., Plu.2.374e; of a disease, Hdt.3.66, 6.27; generally, ἀ. σῆμα S.*Tr.*614; βρέφος ἐς ἄντρον E.*Ion*16, cf. *Ev.Marc.*15.1, etc.:—Pass., *to be carried from one's course*, ὑπ' ἀνέμων Hdt.2.114, cf. 116; ἀπενεχθέντες ἐς Λιβύην Th.7.50, cf. 6.104. 2. *exhale, evaporate*, Anon.Lond.22.25:—Pass., *to be wafted*, Plu.2.681a. II. *carry* or *bring back*, αὖτις ἀποίσετον ὠκέες ἵπποι Il.5.257; ἂψ Ἕκτορι μῦθον ἀποίσειν 10.337; ἀ. οἴκαδις Ar.*Ach.*779:—so in Pass., of oracles, ταῦτα ἀπενειχθέντα Hdt.1.66,158,160: but in Pass., also of persons, *return*, Id.4.164, Th., etc.; ἀπηνέχθη εἰς.. ἔτι ζῶν *was carried home*, of a sick man, X.*HG*3.3.1; τεθνεὼς ἐκ δεσμωτηρίου ἀ. Lys.12.18. 2. *pay back, return*, Hdt.1.196, etc.: hence, *pay what is due* as tribute, etc., Id.4.35, 5.84, Th.5.31. 3. *bring in, return*, of slaves let out to labour for their master's profit, v.l. Aeschin.1.97, cf. Philostr.*Her.*2. 4. generally, *bring, hand over as required*, τί τινι Hdt.4.64; ὅπλα X.*Cyr.*7.5.34; εἰς τὰ δημόσια ἀ. ἱερὰ τὰ ἴδια Pl.*Lg.*910c. III. *hand in* an accusation, *render* accounts, returns, etc., ἀ. παρανόμων (sc. γραφήν) πρὸς τὸν ἄρχοντα Docum.ap.D.18.54, cf. 52.30; ἀπήνεγκε παρανόμων (sc. γραφήν) Δημοσθένει Decr.ap.D.18.105; λόγον..ἀπενήνοχεν ἀναλωμάτων D.27.20; λόγον πρὸς τοὺς λογιστάς, λόγον τῇ πόλει, Aeschin.3.22; ἀ. τοὺς ἱππεύσαντας *hand in a list of*.., Lys.16.6; ναύτας D.50.6; ἀ. ἐν τῷ λόγῳ δεδωκὼς *having entered* in the account, Id.49.16:—Pass., *to be returned as* so and so, ἀπηνέχθη ἀνώμοτος Id.21.86; διαιτητὴς ἀπενηνεγμένος Id.52.30. 2. *deliver* a letter, Id.34.8. IV. *bring home, receive as wages*, Luc.*Tim.*12 (which others refer to signf. II. 2).

B. Med., *take away with one*, Hdt.1.132, Isoc.6.74, etc.; *carry off* a prize, μετὰ Πᾶνα τὸ δεύτερον ἆθλον ἀποισῇ Theoc.l.c.; κάλλευς πρῶτ' ἀπενεγκαμέναν *APl.*4.166 (Even.); ἀ. δόξαν Hdn.1.5.7; *carry home* delicacies from a banquet, Luc.*Symp.*38 (less freq. in Act., Id.*Nigr.*25). 2. *take for oneself, gain, obtain*, λέχη ἀλλότρια E.*El.*1089 codd.; *receive to oneself*, μόρον Id.*Ph.*595. 3. *obtain* a decision, *win* a lawsuit, δίκην κενὴν θελόντων ἀ. *Inscr.Prien.*111.150 (i B.C.). II. *bring back for oneself*, ὀπίσω Hdt.7.152; ἀ. σημεῖα τοῦ θυμῷ μάχεσθαι X.*Ages.*6.2; ἀ. βίον μητρί, i.e. *return to* her alive, E.*Ph.*1161; νόστον Id.*IA*298 (lyr.).

C. Intr. in Act., *be off*, ἀπόφερ' ἐς κόρακας Ar.*Pax*1221.

**ἀπο-φεύγω**, fut. -φεύξομαι Pl.*Ap.*39a; -οῦμαι Ar.*Av.*932: pf. -πέφευγα X.*An.*3.4.9, etc.:—*flee from, escape*, c. acc., Batr.42,47; σοφίην ὁ σοφώτατος οὐκ ἀποφεύγει Thgn.1159; τὴν πεπρωμένην μοῖραν Hdt.1.91; τὴν μάχην Id.5.102; κῆρα S.*Ph.*1166 (lyr.), cf. Pl.*Ap.*39a; νόσον D.28.15; ἀ. ἐκ τῶν πλησίον κωμῶν X.*An.*3.4.9; ἐς Νίσαιαν Th.1.114: rarely c. gen., ἀ. τῆς φθορᾶς 2*Ep.Pet.*1.4: c. inf., *avoid*, λέγειν Phlp.*in Ph.*617.14: abs., *get safe away, escape*, Hdt.1.1, 9.102, etc.; *go free*, of manumitted slaves, *IG*2.786, al. II. as law-term, ἀ. πολλὸν τοὺς διώκοντας Hdt.6.82; τινά And.1.123; φεύγων ἂν ἀποφύγοι δίκην Ar.*Nu.*167, cf. 1151; γραφάς Antipho 2.1.16; εὐθύνας Pl.*Lg.*946d: c. dupl. acc. pers. et rei, ἀπέφυγον αὐτοὺς τὰς δίκας ἅς μοι ἐνεκάλουν D.40.19. 2. abs., *get clear off, be acquitted*, opp. ἁλίσκομαι, Hdt.2.174, Pl.*Ap.*35c, D.18.103; κἂν.. εἰσέλθῃ φεύγων οὐκ ἀποφεύγει Ar.*V.*579. 3. of a woman in child-birth, *bring to birth*, ἀ. τὸ παιδίον ἐν τῷ τόκῳ Hp.*Mul.*1.25; also ἀ. τοῦ παιδίου ib.33: intr., ἢν τὰ ὕστερα μὴ δύνηται ἀποφυγεῖν Id.*Nat.Mul.*56. **-φευκτικός**, ή, όν, *useful in escaping*, τὰ ἀ. *means of acquittal*, X.*Ap.*8. **-φευξις** or **-φυξις** (cod. Rav. in Ar.*V.*558,562,645 and *Nu.*874, cf. D.Chr.1.41), εως, ἡ, *escaping, means of getting off*, ἀ. δίκης *acquittal*, Ar.*Nu.*l.c., al., cf. Antipho 5.66.

**ἀποφηληκίζω**· ἀποπλανάω, *AB*439, Suid.

**ἀπόφημι**, fut. -φήσω: aor. 1 ἀπέφησα Pl.*Tht.*166a, al.:—*speak ou[t], declare flatly* or *plainly*, ἀντικρὺ δ' ἀπόφημι γυναῖκα μὲν οὐκ ἀποδώσ[ειν] κτλ. Il.7.362:—Med., ἀγγελίην ἀπόφασθε 9.422.—In this sense onl[y] Ep. II. *say no*, S.*OC*317, etc. 2. c. acc., *deny*, οὔτε σὺ φῄ[ς] ἃ ἐρωτῶ οὔτε ἀπόφῃς Pl.*Prt.*360d, cf. X.*Cyr.*6.1.32, Arist.*APo.*71$^{a}$14, al.; opp. κατάφημι, Id.*Int.*17$^{a}$31, al.: ἀ. τι κατά τινος, opp. καταφάναι Id.*Metaph.*1007$^{b}$22; *negative*, τι Id.*Rh.*1412$^{b}$10, *Po.*1457$^{b}$31; μὴ γεγονέναι Plu.*Alc.*23.

**ἀπόφημος**, ον, = δύσφημος, Ael.*NA*6.44.

**ἀποφθαλμόομαι**, *look askance at*: hence, *covet, envy*, *PLond.*1674.17 (vi A.D.).

**ἀποφθαναῖνον**· ἀποθνῄσκοντα, Hsch.

**ἀποφθαράξασθαι**, *snort*, Hsch.

**ἀπόφθαρμα**, ατος, τό, *abortion*, Hp.*Epid.*2.2.13, 5.53.

**ἀπο-φθέγγομαι**, *speak one's opinion plainly*, Luc.*Zeux.*1; *utter an apophthegm*, Plu.2.405e, Iamb.*VP*11.55; χρησμόν Luc.*Alex.*25, cf. D.S.16.27, Vett.Val.73.24: metaph. of vessels when struck, *ring*, σαπρὸν ἀ. Luc.*Par.*4. II. *chant hymns*, Lxx 1*Chr.*25.1. **-φθεγκτήριον**, τό, *an utterance*, Man.4.550. **-φθεγκτος**, ον, = ἄφθεγκτος, E.*IT*951. **-φθεγμα**, ατος, τό, *terse pointed saying, apophthegm*, of Theramenes, X.*HG*2.3.56; of Anaxagoras, Arist.*Metaph.*1009$^{b}$26; of Pittacus, Id.*Rh.*1389$^{a}$16; of the Spartans, ib.1394$^{b}$34: in pl., title of work by Plu. **-φθεγματίας**, ου, ὁ, *dealer in saws and proverbs*, Metrod.45. **-φθεγματικός**, ή, όν, *dealing in apophthegms, sententious*, Plu.*Lyc.*19, *Brut.*2, Demetr.*Eloc.*9; θορύβους ἐνθυμηματικοὺς καὶ -κούς, i.e. bare assertions, Epicur.*Nat.*14.9. Adv. -κῶς Eust.1870.46.

**ἀποφθείρω**, fut. -φθερῶ, *destroy utterly, ruin*, A.*Ch.*256; δέμας ἀσιτίαις E.*Supp.*1106. 2. *have an abortion, miscarry*, Hp.*Epid.*1.16. II. Pass., with fut. Med., *to be lost, perish*, E.*Tr.*508, v.l. in Th.2.49. 2. *to be gone, make off*, ἀποφθαρεὶς ἐκ τῆς πόλεως Men.*Sam.*282, cf. Alciphr.*Fr.*6.3: freq. in imprecations, οὐ γῆς τῆσδ' ἀποφθαρήσεται; i.e. *let him begone with a plague* to him, E.*HF*1290; οὐκ εἰς κόρακας ἀποφθερεῖ; Ar.*Eq.*892, *Nu.*789; ἀποφθείρου ταχὺ Men.*Sam.*158; ἀποφθάρηθι Lib.*Decl.*33.28.

**ἀπο-φθῐνύθω** [ῠ], poet. Verb, *perish*, ἀποφθινύθουσι δὲ λαοί Il.5.643, Hes.*Op.*243, cf. A.R.1.683. II. causal, *make to perish*, θυμὸν ἀποφθινύθουσι *lose* their life, Il.16.540. 2. *diminish*, τὰ μὲν αὔξεις τὰ δ' ἀ. E.*Fr.*916. **-φθίνω** [ῐ], I. intr. in pres., *perish utterly, die away*, A.*Ag.*857; ἀποφθίνει τὰ χρηστὰ S.*Ph.*457: also in pf. ἀπέφθῐκα Them.*Or.*28.341d: but mostly, II. causal, in fut. -φθίσω, aor. ἀπέφθισα [ῑ Ep., ῐ Trag.]:—*make to perish, waste away, destroy*, ἄνδρας ἀποφθίσειε θάλασσα Hes.*Op.*666; πρὸς γυναικὸς δ' ἀπέφθισεν βίον *had* his life *taken* by a woman's hand, A.*Ag.*1454 (lyr.); ἔμελλέ σ' Ἕκτωρ καὶ θανὼν ἀποφθίσαι S.*Aj.*1027; τὸν βαλόντ' ἀποφθίσαι χρῄζων Id.*Tr.*709; of disease, *cause death, be fatal*, Hp.*Aër.*11. 2. most freq. in Pass., = Act. intr., *perish, die*, esp. in aor. with plpf. form ἀπέφθιτο [ῐ] Od.15.268; imper. ἀποφθίσθω Il.8.429; opt. ἀποφθίμην [ῐ] Od.10.51; Ep. and Lyr. part. ἀποφθίμενος [ῐ] *dead*, Il.3.322, al., Ibyc.27, B.8.79 (not in Trag.): also in Ep. aor. 3 pl. ἀπέφθιθεν Od.5.110,133, 7.251 (v.l. ἀπέφθιθον). 3. Med., aor. 1 -φθίσασθαι [ῑ] Q.S.14.545. **-φθῐσις**, εως, ἡ, *waning* of the moon, Sch.Arat.799.

**ἀποφθορά**, ἡ, (ἀποφθείρω) = φθορά, σπέρματος A.*Eu.*187; esp. *abortion, miscarriage*, Hp.*Epid.*3.1.ι',ια'.

**ἀποφῑμόω**, *muzzle completely*, *AB*421.

**ἀποφλάσαι**· ῥογχάσαι (Cret., Sam.), Hsch.

**ἀποφλαυρίζω**, *treat slightingly, make no account of, disparage*, τι Pi.*P.*3.12, Hdt.1.86.

**ἀποφλεγμαίνω**, *cease to burn*, of inflammation, Hp.*Aph.*6.49: metaph. of anger, Plu.2.13d.

**ἀποφλεγμᾰτ-ίζω**, *purge away phlegm* or *cleanse from it*, Dsc.2.159, Antyll.ap.Orib.8.10.2; *promote the discharge of phlegm* or *mucus*, Gal.11.769, etc. **-ικός**, ή, όν, *promoting such discharge*, ibid. **-ισμός**, ὁ, *purging of phlegm*, Dsc.5.3, Antyll.ap.Orib.8.10 tit., Archig.ap.Gal.12.582. **-ιστέον**, *one must promote the discharge of phlegm*, Id.12.650.

**ἀπόφλησις**, εως, ἡ, *discharge of a debt*, Anon.*in Rh.*206.3.

**ἀποφλογίζω**, *burn up*, Hsch. s.v. εὔστρα (Pass.).

**ἀποφλογόομαι**, Pass., *grow fiery*, ἀ. τὰ ὄμματα Max.Tyr.24.8.

**ἀποφλοιόω**, (φλοιός) *peel, strip off*, καλύπτρην Nonn.*D.*14.380:—Med., λέοντος δέρμα *AP*6.263 (Leon.):—also **-φλοιάω**, *peel*, κύπερον Aët.1.129.

**ἀποφλύζω**, *give vent to, sputter out*, ὄφρ' ἀλεγεινὴν ὕβριν ἀποφλύξωσιν A.R.3.583: aor. ἀπέφλυσαν Archil.35 (-φλοσαν codd. Phot.):—Hsch. has **ἀποφλύειν**· ἀπερεύγεσθαι.

**ἀπόφλω**, *owe*, Tz.*H.*13.613.

**ἀποφοβέομαι**, *to be scared away*, Sch.Opp.*H.*3.510.

**ἀποφοιβάζω**, *utter by inspiration*, ποιήματα ὥσπερ ἀ. Str.14.5.15; *foretell*, τὰ μέλλοντα D.S.34.2; τὸν λόγον Id.31.10; ταῦτα περὶ τοῦ μέλλοντος ἀποπεφοίβακεν Plb.29.21.7.

**ἀποφοιβάομαι**, = foreg., *PMag.Par.*1.738.

**ἀποφοιτ-άω**, fut. -ήσομαι Thom.Mag.p.7R.:—*cease to attend a* master, ἀ. παρά τινος, of scholars, Pl.*Grg.*489d; ἀ. πρός τινα *go away to a new* master, Din.*Fr.*6.13: abs., *cease to go to school*, Lys.*Fr.*116; also ἀ. τῶν ἐκκλησιῶν Philostr.*VS*1.17.2, cf. *VA*7.25, Hld.3.13. 2. *desert, abscond*, πρός τινα Plu.*Lys.*4, cf. Aristid.*Or.*21(22).15; of ships in battle, Procop.*Goth.*4.23; simply, *depart*, Dionys.*Av.*1.11. **-ησις**· χωρισμός, ἀναχώρησις, Hsch.

**ἀπόφονος**, ον, φόνος, αἷμα ἀ., *unnatural* murder, E.*Or.*163,192 (both lyr.).

*__ἀποφορ-ά__, ἡ, (ἀποφέρω) *payment of what is due, tax, tribute*, Hdt. 1.109, Plu.*Thes.*23, etc.: esp. *money* which slaves let out to hire *paid* to their master, ἀποφορὰς πράττειν X.*Ath.*1.11; ἀ. κομίσασθαι And.1.38; φέρειν Aeschin.1.97, Men.431; ἀποδόντες Id.*Epit.*163: generally, *return, profit, rent*, ἀποφορὰν φέρειν Arist.*Pol.*1264a33; ἀποφέρειν Plu.2.239e; ἀ. βαλανείου *BGU*362 ix 2 (iii A.D.); *contribution, war-tax*, ἀ. τελεῖν Plu.*Arist.*24. II. *effluvia*, D.H.10.53, D.S.24.12, Plu.2.647f, Aret.*SA*1.10; ἡ ἀ. τοῦ πυρός Sch.Il.*Oxy.*221 xvii8. 2. *absorption* of περίττωμα, Anon.Lond.*Fr.*1.6. III. in Logic, = στέρησις, *privation*, Arist.*Metaph.*1046b15, cf. Alex.Aphr. ad loc. IV. *right to carry away* portions of sacrifice, *SIG*1025.46, al., 1026.4 (Cos, iv/iii B.C.). -έω, *carry away*, χοῦν *SIG*²587.45 (dub.). *-ησις, εως, ἡ, = ἀποφορά II, S.E.*P.*1.12. *-ητος, ον, *carried away*; τὰ ἀ. *presents which guests received* at table *to take home*, Ath.6.229c, cf. Petron.56, Suet.*Calig.*55, *Vesp.*19. *-ος, ον, *not to be borne* or *suffered*, μίασμα Phalar.*Ep.*141 (ἀπότροπον Ruhnk.). 2. *past bearing*, δένδρα Hsch.; cf. ἀποφόρος· ἀσθενέστερος, Id.

**ἀποφορτ-ίζομαι**, Med., *discharge one's cargo*, τὸν γόμον *Act.Ap.*21.3; *jettison*, abs., Ph.2.413; τῇ θαλάσσῃ τὰ περιττὰ τῶν φορτίων Timae. 61; *unload one's stomach*, Artem.2.26:—Pass., of περιττώματα, Sor. 1.40: generally, *jettison, get rid of*, τι Ph.2.434, etc. -ισμός, ὁ, *unloading*: hence of *vomiting*, Archig.ap.Orib.8.23.1.

**ἀποφράγνυμι** (better -φάργ-), *fence off, block*, τὰς ὁδοὺς ἀπεφάργνυσαν Th.7.74: metaph., ἀποφάργνυσαι κύκλῳ τὸ πρᾶγμα S.*Ant* 241.

**ἀποφράζω**, *explain*, Dam.*Pr.*111 (Pass.).

**ἀπόφραξις**, εως, ἡ, *blocking up*, τῆς ὁδοῦ X.*An.*4.2.25: pl., πόρων Ph.2.432.

*__ἀποφράς__, ἄδος, ἡ, (φράζω) *not to be mentioned, unlucky*; ἀ. ἡμέραι, opp. καθαραὶ ἡμ., Pl.*Lg.*800d, cf. Lys.*Fr.*53.2, Plu.*Alc.*34, Luc.*Pseudol.* 12; ἀ. πύλαι at Rome, = *portae nefastae*, Plu.2.518b. II. rarely as masc. Adj., *impious, wicked*, ἄνθρωπος Eup.309; βίος Luc.*Pseudol.*32.

**ἀποφράση**, ἡ, Cretan word for δούλη, Seleuc.ap.Ath.6.267c:—Eust.1090.57 writes -φράτη.

*__ἀποφράσσω__, Att. -ττω, fut. -ξω, = ἀποφράγνυμι, *block up, stop up*, Hp.*Carn.*18, *Mul.*1.1; τὰς διεξόδους Pl.*Ti.*91c; ἀ. καὶ παροικοδομεῖν D.55.17; τὰς φυγάς Onos.32:—Med., ἀποφάρξασθαι αὐτοὺς *bar* their *passage*, Th.8.104.

**ἀποφρέω**, aor. -έφρησα, = ἐκφρέω, Cratin.78.

**ἀπόφρικτος**, ον, (φρίσσω) *shivering*, Aret.*SD*1.12.

**ἀποφρύγω** [ῡ], *dry up*, ὑφ' ἡδονῆς ἀπεφρύγοντο Eun.ap.Suid. s.v. ἀπεφρύγοντο. II. aor. 2 Pass. -φρῠγῆναι *cool down*, Maria ap. Zos.Alch.p.238 B.

**ἀποφυάς**, άδος, ἡ, = ἀπόφυσις, *appendage*, τῶν ἐντέρων, of the *caeca* of birds and fishes, Arist.*HA*507b33, 509a17. 2. *outgrowth*, Thphr. *HP*7.2.5. 3. *branch* of a blood-vessel, Hp.*Oss.*11, Arist.*PA*667b 17. 4. *one of the spines* on the tail of the martichoras, Id.*HA*501a31.

**ἀποφυγγάνω**, = ἀποφεύγω, D.23.74, Them.*Or.*18.220b, al.

**ἀποφυγή**, ἡ, like ἀπόφευξις, *escape* or *place of refuge*, βραχείας τὰς ἀποφυγὰς παρέχειν Th.8.106; ἀ. κακῶν, λυπῶν, *escape from* ills, griefs, Pl.*Phd.*107d, *Phlb.*44c (pl.). 2. *excuse, plea*, Aristid.2.85 J.; *shift, subterfuge*, *PStrassb.*40.44 (vi A.D.).

**ἀποφυλάττω**, *store up*, Hsch. s.v. ἀποταμιεύεται:—Med., *ward off*, Id. s.v. ἀπαλέξασθαι.

**ἀποφύλιος** [ῠ], ον, *having no tribe*, i.e. *foreign*, A.*Fr.*287, Poll.3.56.

**ἀποφυλλίζω**, *strip* a plant *of its leaves*, Thphr.*HP*7.12.2, Dsc.1.49, Sch.Ar.*Pax*1147.

**ἀπόφυλλον τραχύ**, = ἄλυσσον, Ps.-Dsc.3.91.

**ἀπόφυξις**, εως, ἡ, v. ἀπόφευξις.

**ἀποφῡσ-άω**, *blow away*, Ar.*V.*330 (anap.); τὰ νέφη Arist.*Mete.*364b 8. II. *breathe out*, ἀ. ψυχίδιον Luc.*Nav.*26. 2. *throw off*, κονιορτόν Archig.ap.Orib.8.2.6. III. ἀποφυσήσασα· ἐγκρύψασα, Hsch. -ησις, εως, ἡ, *blowing away*, τῆς φλογός Sch.Pi.*P.*4. 412. -ητέον, *one must blow off, away*, Dsc.5.99.

**ἀπόφῠσις**, εως, ἡ, *side-shoot*, Thphr.*HP*6.4.4, Plb.18.18.10 (pl.): metaph., μιᾶς φύσεως ἀποφύσεις Dam.*Pr.*100. II. in Anatomy, *process* of a bone, i.e. the *prominence* to which a tendon is attached, Hp.*Art.*45; ἀ. ὀδοντοειδὴς *processus dentatus*, Gal.*UP*12.7, etc.; ἀ. στυλοειδεῖς Ruf.*Onom.*142; of the βρογχίαι, ib.159. 2. *branch* of an artery, Gal.8.319; of a nerve, Id.*UP*9.9; of the urethra, ib.15.3 (but ἀ. σκωληκοειδής is f.l. for ἐπίφυσις, ib.8.14; the two words distd. by Id.2.733). III. Archit., member connecting shaft and base of column, Vitr.4.7.3.

**ἀποφῠτ-εία**, ἡ, *propagation by slips*, Arist.*Long.*467a28, *Juv.*468b 18, Thphr.*CP*1.4.3. -εύω, *strike slips* or *cuttings*, Arist.*GA*761b 28, al., Thphr.*HP*7.2.1.

**ἀποφύω**, *produce*, ῥίζας Thphr.*HP*1.6.4; of veins, *send out* branches, ἀ. τὰς φλέβας Gal.15.532; τένοντας Id.18(2).979:—Pass., with aor. 2 and pf. Act., *grow afresh*, ἀπὸ τῶν ῥιζῶν Thphr.*CP*4.8.5; of branching veins, Gal.15.389; τρίχες ἀ. Archig.ap.Aët.6.55: metaph., Dam.*Pr.*89. II. *part asunder, separate*, Hsch.

**ἀποφώζω**, *dry*, λίνου σπέρμα ἀποπεφωσμένον Hp.*Mul.*1.63.

*__ἀποφώλιος__, ον, acc. to the Ancients, = ἀνεμώλιος, μάταιος, *empty, vain, idle*, Hom. only in Od., νόον ἀποφώλιός ἐσσι 8.177; οὐκ ἀποφώλια εἰδώς 5.182; οὐκ ἀ. ἦα οὐδὲ φυγοπτόλεμος 14.212; ἐπεὶ οὐκ ἀ. εὐναὶ ἀθανάτων are not *barren*, 11.249; νέκυς ἀ. Opp.*C.*3.447; ἀποφώλια μητιόων Man.6.565; ῥέξουσ' ἀποφώλια Orac.ap.Jul.*Ep.*89; of the Minotaur, ξύμμικτον εἶδος κἀποφώλιον τρέφος a *monstrous*, hybrid birth, E.*Fr.*996; in Nic.*Al.*524 στομίων ἀ. ἆσθμα is expld. by Sch. χαλεπόν, but perh. there is a play on φωλεύοντα (φωλεός, cf. Eust.) which occurs just before. (Perh. from ἀποφεῖν (q.v.), cf. ἁμαρτωλός: ἁμαρτεῖν; Hsch. has ἀποφώλια· ἀποφίλια (i.e. -φύλια).) -φωλος, ον, = foreg., Man.4.316.

*__ἀποφωνέω__, Cret. ἀποπωνίω, *depose in evidence*, *Leg.Gort.*1.13, al.

**ἀποφώρ**, ῶρος, ὁ, *thief*, Hsch.

**ἀποχάζομαι**, *withdraw from*, βόθρου Od.11.95; γραφίδων *APl.*4.181 (Jul. Aegypt.): abs., ἀποχασθῇ· ἀποθάνῃ, Hsch.:—Act., only in aor. imper. ἀπόχασον· ἀποχώρησον, Id.

**ἀποχαιρετίζω**, (χαῖρε) *say farewell, take leave*, Sch.rec.S.*Tr.*532.

**ἀποχᾰλάω**, *slack away*, ἀποχάλα τὴν φροντίδ' ἐς τὸν ἀέρα λινόδετον ὥσπερ μηλολόνθην τοῦ ποδός Ar.*Nu.*762; ἑαυτὸν ἀ. Plu.2.655b (s.v.l.).

**ἀποχᾰλῑνόω**, *unbridle*, X.*Eq.*11.7: metaph., ἀ. τὴν αἰδῶ Plu.2.794c.

**ἀποχαλκ-εύω**, *forge of copper*, X.*Cyn.*10.3. -ίζω, *strip of brass*, i.e. *of money*, pun on Χαλκίς in *AP*11.283 (Pall.).

**ἀποχᾰρακόω**, = ἀποσταυρόω, D.H.5.58, Plu.*Pomp.*35 (Pass.).

*__ἀποχάρ-αξις__ [χᾰ], εως, ἡ, *incision*, πολλὰς -ξεις λαμβάνειν Democr. 155; *scarification*, Gal.11.305, al. II. *enclosure*, Haussoullier *Milet* p.187, cf. *Rev.Phil.*44.251, 264. -άσσω, Att. -ττω, *erase, obliterate*, στήλην D.Chr.31.86. II. *incise*, *Hippiatr.*52. III. *characterize, mark*, ἀποχαράττει ταῦτα τὸν ἀγαθὸν ποιητήν prob. in Phld.*Po.*5.1425. 10.

**ἀποχᾰρ-ίζομαι**, *confer upon, present*, τί τινι *IGRom.*4.182 (Lampsacus), Alex.Aphr. *in Metaph.*483.25:—Pass., τάλαντον -ισθέν σοι *POxy.*1208.16 (iii A.D.). -ισμα, ατος, τό, *deed of gift*, *PMonac.* 8.29 (vi A.D.).

**ἀποχᾰριστέω**, *return thanks*, *Delph.*3(1).152 (ii B.C.).

**ἀποχειμάζω**, *blow over*, ὅταν ἀποχειμάσῃ when the wind *drops*, Arist.*Pr.*943b31.

**ἀπο-χειρίζω**, *cut off the hand*, only in Pass., ἀπεχειρίσθη τὴν δεξιάν Anon.ap.Suid., cf. Eust.1960.10. -χειρόβῐος, ον, = sq., Poll.1.50, Hsch. -χειροβίοτος or -ωτος [ῐ], ον, *living by the work of one's hands*, Hdt.3.42, X.*Cyr.*8.3.37. -χειρος, ον, *unprepared*, Plb.22.14.8. *-χειροτονέω, *vote by show of hands away from*; and so, I. *vote a charge away from* one, *acquit* him, τινός D.21.214. II. *reject as unfit*, ἀ. τινὰ ἀπὸ τῆς τῶν ἐφήβων ἐπιμελείας Din.3.15, cf. Arist. *Ath.*49.1; αὐτὸν ἀ. τῆς ἀρχῆς Plu.*Nic.*8: metaph., ἀ. τῆς ἡδονῆς τὸν ἄνδρα you *vote* his poetry *devoid of* sweetness, Max.Tyr.23.5. 2. *supersede, depose*, τὸν στρατηγόν D.23.168, cf. Arist.*Ath.*61.2:—Pass., D.49.9, Hp.*Ep.*10. 3. *abrogate, annul*, τὰς συνθήκας D.23.172:—Pass., of laws, Id.24.21; of a peace, *to be rejected*, ἐν τῇ ἐκκλησίᾳ Ar.*Pax*668. III. ἀ. μὴ φίλι' εἶναι.. *vote* that a thing is *not*.., D.24.12; μὴ μισθοῦν τοὺς οἴκους Is.6.37; ἀ. τῶν δικαστῶν ὡς οὐδὲν αὐτοῖς προσῆκεν ib.45. -χειροτονητέον, *one must reject a claim to*, τοῦ ἀρίστου Max.Tyr.22.5. -χειροτονία, ἡ, *deposition* of an official, D.58.28.

**ἀποχέτ-ευμα**, ατος, τό, *branch*, τῆς θαλάσσης Eust.ad D.P.38. -ευσις, εως, ἡ, *drawing off*, περιττωμάτων Ph.1.29. -εύω, *draw off* water *by a canal*, Pl.*Lg.*736b:—Pass., ὥσπερ ῥεῦμα ἀπωχετευμένον Id.*R.*485d, cf. Arist.*Pr.*867b13, M.Ant.12.2:—Med., metaph., Πλάτων ἀπὸ τοῦ Ὁμηρικοῦ νάματος εἰς αὐτὸν μυρίας παρατροπὰς -σάμενος Longin.13.3:—so in Act., 'canalize', τὴν Ὁμήρου ποίησιν Jul.*Or.*2. 51a. 2. metaph., ἀ. τὸ βάσκανον Plu.2.485e.

**ἀποχέω**, imper. ἀπόχει Dsc.1.53: aor. ἀπέχεα, Ep. -έχευα:—*pour out* or *off, spill, shed*, ἀπὸ δ' εἴδατα χεῦεν ἔραζε Od.22.20,85: poet. pres. Med., παγὰν ἂν ἀποχεύονται Κασταλίας δῖναι E.*Ion*148 (lyr.). 2. *pour off*, Hp.*Ulc.*12; τι εἴς τι Dsc.1.53. II. Pass., *to be poured off*, Plb.34.9.10; τοῦ μὲν ἀποχεομένου ὕδατος, τοῦ δὲ ἐπιχεομένου Dsc.2.76; *to be shed, fall off*, ἀποχυθέντα φύλλα Plu.2. 332b. 2. of plants, *come into ear*, Thphr.*HP*8.8.1, etc.; οὐκ εἰς στάχυν ἀλλ' οἷον φόβην ib.4.4.10:—Med., *make to shoot*, ἀ. ποίην Nic. *Th.*569 (s.v.l.); χαίτην ib.658.

*__ἀποχή__, ἡ, (ἀπέχω) *distance*, Phld.*Rh.*1.168 S., Ptol.*Geog.*1.11.2, al. II. *abstinence*, Phld.*Ind.Sto.*67, cf. *Piet.*36, Arr.*Epict.*2.15.5; ἀ. τροφῆς Plu.*Demetr.*38; ἐμψύχων Porph.*Abst.*tit. III. *receipt, quittance*, *PTeb.*11.14 (ii B.C.), *BGU*1116.41 (i B.C.), *AP*11.233 (Lucill.), Ulp.ap *Dig.*46.4.19, etc.: metaph., ἡ τελευταία ἀ., title of work by Zos.Alch.p.239 B.

**ἀποχηρόομαι**, Pass., *to be bereft of*, τινός Ar.*Pax*1013 (parod.).

**ἀπόχιμος**, ον, *of* or *for a receipt*, γράμματα *PCair.Preis.*14.13 (iv A.D.).

**ἀποχλωρίας**, ου, ὁ, *one whose complexion has become pale*, Hsch.

**ἀποχοιρ-ιάζειν**· ἀποσοβεῖν, ὡς χοῖρον ἐλαύνειν, Hsch., cf. *AB*439; ἀπεχοιρίασεν· ἀπεσκίρτησεν, Hsch. -ωσις, εως, ἡ, *transmutation into swine*, Eust.1656.32.

**ἀπόχοον**, τό, prob. = ἀπόχυμα, *PFay.*123.12 (i/ii A.D.).

**ἀποχορτάζω**, *fed to the full*, Sosith.2.13.

**ἄποχος**, ον, = ἀπόχιμος, γράμματα *PThead.*28.13 (iv A.D.), al. II. ἄποχον· ἀπότεχνον, ἄγροικον, μάταιον, Hsch.

**ἀποχραίνω**, *colour, tint evenly*, Pl.*Lg.*769a, cf. Tim.*Lex.* s.v. χραίνειν:—Pass., *take a tone*, Pl.*R.*586b; of fruit, *colour*, Arist.*Col.*796a 24.

**ἀπόχρανος**· ἀκάλυπτος, ἀπροφάσιστος, Hsch.

*__ἀποχράω__, Dor. -χρέω Archim.*Aren.*3.3, [Epich.]253: inf. -χρῆν D.4.22, Antiph.161, Luc.*Herm.*24 (-χρῆναι v.l. in D.H.3.22, condemned by *AB*81), Ion. -χρᾶν Hdt.3.138, but -χρῆναι Hp.*VC*14; part. -χρῶν, -χρῶσα, v. infr.: impf. ἀπέχρη, Ion. -έχρα Hdt.1.66: fut. -χρήσω: aor. -έχρησα:—*suffice, be sufficient, be enough*: 1. abs., in persons other than 3 sg., 1 sg. only in εἷς ἐγὼν ἀποχρέω [Epich.] l.c.; [θανάτῳ] δύ' ἀποχρήσουσιν μόνω Ar.*Pl.*484; ἀποχρήσει (sc. ἡ ὑφαντική) Pl.*Plt.*279b; τηλικαύτην ἀποχρῆν οἶμαι τὴν δύναμιν D.4.22; ἀποχρῶν ἀνὴρ ἔμοιγε πρὸς τὰ νῦν κακά Pherecr.145.6; ἡλικία ἀποχρῶσα Ar.*Fr.*489; σύμβουλος ἀποχρῶν τῇ πόλει Pl.*Alc.*2.145c; of ἀρετή, *Stoic.*3.50: c. inf., ἀποχρῶσι.. ἑκατὸν νέες χειρώσασθαι Hdt.5.31; Κνιδίους μούνους ἀποχρᾶν οἱ τοὺς κατάγοντας γίνεσθαι Id.3.138, cf. 9.48; πεδίον ἀποχρῶν τὴν Ἀσίαν πρὸς τὴν Εὐρώπην ἀντιτάξαι Philostr. *Im.*1.1. 2. mostly in 3 sg., c. dat., a. with a nom., [ποταμὸς] οὐκ ἀπέχρησε τῇ στρατιῇ πινόμενος *was* not *enough to supply* the army with drink, Hdt.7.43,196; often in the phrase ταῦτ' ἀπόχρη μοι Ar. *Av.*1603, cf. Pl.*Phdr.*279a; ἀπόχρη μοι τοσοῦτον ἐάν.. Isoc.5.28; οὐκ ἀπέχρησε δὲ αὐτῷ τοῦτο D.21.17; οὐδὲ ταῦτ' ἀπέχρησεν αὐτοῖς Isoc. 4.97. b. impers., c. inf., ἀποχρᾷ (-χρῇ) μοι ἡσυχίην ἄγειν, ποιέειν τι, etc., *'tis sufficient* for me to.., Hdt.1.66, 6.137, 9.79, Hp.*Mochl.*38; [ἔφασαν] ἀποχρήσειν σφι τὴν ἑωυτῶν φυλάσσειν Hdt.8.130: c. dat. part., ἀποχρᾶν σφι κατὰ τὸ ἥμισυ ἡγεομένοισι *it was enough* for them if they shared the command, Id.7.148; μέρος βαιὸν ἐχούσῃ πᾶν ἀπόχρη μοι *'tis* all *sufficient* for me to have a little, A.*Ag.*1574 (nowhere else in Trag.); τοσαῦτ' ἀπόχρη προσθήσειν Str.9.1.20. c. impers., ἀπόχρη τινός *there is enough of* a thing, Hp.*Mul.*1.12, *Vid.Ac.*4; ἀποχρῆν ἐνίοις ὑμῶν ἄν μοι δοκεῖ εἰ.. methinks *it would have satisfied* some of you, D.4.42: abs. in part., οὐκ ἀποχρῆσαν αὐτῷ *since it did* not *suffice* him, Arist.*Xen.*976$^b$21. 3. Pass., *to be contented with* a thing, c. dat., ἀποχρεωμένων τούτοισι τῶν Μυσῶν the Mysians *being satisfied* therewith, Hdt.1.37; τοῖς ὀνόμασι μόνον D.17.31. b. impers., οὐκ ἀπεχρᾶτο μούνων Μήδων ἄρχειν Hdt.1.102; ἀπεχρᾶτό σφι ἡσυχίην ἄγειν Id.8.14. II. *deliver an oracle*, Ael.*Fr.*59.

B. ἀποχράομαι *use to the full, avail oneself of*, ἐπικαιρότατον χωρίον.. ἀποχρῆσθαι Th.1.68; ἀποχρήσασθε τῇ.. ὠφελίᾳ Id.6.17, cf. 7.42; ὅταν.. ἀποχρήσωνται χρῶνται λοιπὸν ὡς προδόταις when they *have made all the use they can of* them, then they deal with them.., Plb.18.15.9. 2. *abuse, misuse*, c. dat., εἰς ταῦτα ἀποχρῆσθαι τῷ πλουτεῖν D.21.124; πλεονεκτικῶς ταῖς ἐξουσίαις ἀ. *OGI*665.16 (Egypt, i A.D.); ἀποχρωμένων μᾶλλον ἢ χρωμένων αὐτῷ Plu.*Comp.Alc.Cor.*2; οἷς μὲν χρῆσθαι, οἷς δ' ἀ. Id.2.178c: c. gen., θυγατρὸς Id.*Nob.*13. 3. c. acc., *destroy, kill*, Ar.*Fr.*358, Th.3.81, Poll.8.74, etc. 4. ἀ. τὰ χρήματα *make use of*, Arist.*Oec.*1349$^b$17. 5. ἀποχρησαμένοις· ἀποσεισαμένοις, Hsch.

**ἀπό-χρεμμα**, ατος, τό, *expectoration*, Hp.*Loc.Hom.*16. **-χρέμπτομαι**, *cough up, expectorate*, Id.*Acut.*58, *Loc.Hom.*14. **-χρεμψις**, εως, ἡ, *expectoration*, Id.*Aph.*4.47.

**ἀποχρεόντως**, v. ἀποχρώντως.

**ἀποχρέω, -χρη**, v. ἀποχράω.

**ἀποχρηματ-ίζω**, *carry to an end, close* a discussion, λόγον dub. in Phld.*D.*3.14; cf. ἀποτερματίζω. II. Pass., *to be deposited, registered*, of an official copy, ἐν τοῖς ἀρχείοις *Inscr.Magn.*293.5. **-ος**, ζημία ἀ. forfeiture *of my inheritance*, A.*Ch.*275.

**ἀπό-χρησις**, εως, ἡ, *getting rid of*, τῶν περιττῶν dub. in Plu.2. 267f. II. *consumption, using up*, *Ep.Col.*2.22. **-χρηστικῶς**, f.l. for -χρώντως, D.L.7.160.

**ἀποχριμφθέντα**· ἀποχωρισθέντα, Hsch.

**ἀποχρίω**· *relevio, relino*, *Gloss.*

**ἀποχρυσόω**, *turn into gold* or *money*, Pass., Artem.1.50, cf. Poll. 7.102.

**ἀποχρωμένως**, = ἀποχρώντως, dub. in Phld.*Rh.*2.87 S.

**ἀποχρώννυμι**, = ἀποχραίνειν, Poll.7.129.

**ἀποχρώντως**, Dor. **-χρεόντως** Archim.*Aren.*3.2, Adv. pres. part. of ἀποχράω:—*enough, sufficiently*, Th.1.21, 7.77, Pl.*R.*429a; ἀ. ἔχει τινί Antiph.191.16; ἀ. ἔχειν τιμῆς J.*AJ*15.2.7; μέρος ἀ. ἐξειργασμένον Phld.*Piet.*22.

**ἀπόχρωσις**, εως, ἡ, (ἀποχρώννυμι) *laying on colour*, ἀ. σκιᾶς Plu.2. 346a.

**ἀποχυλ-ίζω**, *extract the juice*, prob. in Arist.*Pr.*873$^b$4, cf. Dsc.1.86: —Pass., Antyll.ap.Orib.4.11.3. **-ισμα**, ατος, τό, *juice*, μαλάχης ἀγρίας *Gp.*15.6.1. **-όω**, = ἀποχυλίζω, Hp.*Mul.*1.93.

⊛**ἀπόχυμα**, ατος, τό, (χέω) *that which is poured out*, Ti.Locr.100a, *PFay.*95.25 (ii A.D.). 2. = ζώπισσα, Dsc.1.72. 3. Ὀρειβασίου ἀ., name of a kind of *plaster*, Aët.15.24.

**ἀποχύνω**, later form of ἀποχέω, Lxx 3*Ki.*22.35.

**ἀποχυρόω**, *fortify*:—Pass., ἀποχυρωθέντος τοῦ περιπολίου *SIG*569. 9 (Cos, iii B.C.); ἀπωχυρῶσθαι *form a fence*, of trees, Thphr.*HP* 4.7.7: metaph., ἀπωχυρωμένος πρὸς τὸ λαμβάνειν *incorruptible*, Plu. *Dem.*14.

⊛**ἀπό-χυσις**, εως, ἡ, (ἀποχέω) *pouring out* or *forth*, ἀκτίνων ἢ χρωμάτων S.E.*P.*3.51, cf. Gal.*UP*6.2, al.; of corn, *coming into ear*, ἐκβιάζεσθαι τὴν ἀ. Thphr.*HP*8.10.4: generally, *inflorescence*, ἡ καλαμώδης ἀ. φόβη ib.8.3.4. **-χυτήριον**, τό, *sewer*, Charis.p.553 K. **-χυτος**, ον, *poured out*, Hsch. s.v. ἀράμενοι.

**ἀποχωλεύω**, *make quite lame*, X.*HG*7.2.9, *Oec.*11.17.

**ἀποχωλόομαι**, Pass., *to be made quite lame*, Hp.*Aër.*22, Th.7.27, Paus.10.1.3.

**ἀποχώννυμι**, *bank up* a river, etc., X.*HG*2.2.4, 5.2.4; λιμένας ἀπεχώννυσαν Plu.*Phoc.*11.

⊛**ἀποχωρ-έω**, fut. -ήσομαι Th.3.13, D.25.78:—*go from* or *away from*, δόμων Ar.*Ach.*456; ἐκ τοῦ στρατοπέδου Pl.*R.*394a. 2. abs., *depart*, πάλιν ἀ. E.*IT*265; *withdraw*, ἐπὶ τὰ ἀναγκαῖα v.l. in X.*Cyr.* 1.6.36; esp. after a defeat, *retire, retreat*, Th.2.89, etc.; πρὸς τὴν πόλιν X.*HG*4.4.11; ἐπὶ τῆς Κορίνθου Th.2.94. 3. ἀ. ἐκ τῶν πόλεων *..withdraw from.., give up possession of*, X.*HG*5.2.13. b. metaph. *withdraw* or *dissent from* opinions, δοξῶν Gal.15.356, cf. Arr.*Epict.*4. 1.53. 4. *turn out, succeed*, Phld.*Rh.*1.105 S.; of persons, κατὰ τρόπον ἀ. *to be successful*, ib.2.259 S. 5. *have recourse*, εἰς, ἐπί τι D.25.78, 37.21. II. *pass off*, esp. of the excretions of the body, Hp.*Judic.*10, X.*Cyr.*1.2.16; τὰ ἀποχωροῦντα *excrements*, Id.*Mem.*1. 4.6; τὸ ἀποχωροῦν *excretion*, Arist.*GA*725$^b$15. III. of places, *to be distant*, μέρη ἀποκεχωρηκότα Plb.15.27.8; ἀ. ὡς πόδα *to be a foot apart*, Apollod.*Poliorc.*165.1. **-ήματα**, τά, *excretions*, Meno *Iatr.* 12.41. ⊛**-ησις**, εως, ἡ, *retreat*, Th.5.73; ποιεῖσθαι ἀ. Hdt.8.21; *place* or *means of safety*, Th.8.76 (pl.); *line of retreat*, Aen.Tact.16.4. 2. *death*, Eun.*VS*p.469 B. II. *voidance*, opp. πλήρωσις, Pl.*Ti.*65a, 81a; esp. of excretions, Arist.*GA*726$^a$21, al.; = ἀπόπατος 2, Plu.*Lyc.* 20. **-ητέον**, *one must depart*, Hld.7.11. **-ίζω**, *separate from*, τὸ χεῖρον ἀπὸ βελτίονος Pl.*Sph.*226d:—Pass., *to be separated from*, πυρός Id.*Ti.*59d; ἐξ ἰνῶν αἷμα ἀ. ib.84a. 2. *separate, set apart, detach*, Lys.16.16; ἀ. ὡς ἓν εἶδος *separate and put* into one class, Pl. *Plt.*262e; ἀπὸ βασιλικῆς τε καὶ πολιτικῆς πράξεως ib.289d. 3. Pass., *to be vomited*, Herod.Med. in *Rh.Mus.*58.99. **-ισις**, εως, ἡ, *separation*, Antyll.(?)ap.Orib.45.17.3. **-ιστέον**, *one must separate, remove*, *Gp.*16.1.5. **-ιστής**, οῦ, ὁ, *separator*, *Gloss.*

**ἀπόχωσις**, εως, ἡ, *damming up*, ἀ. ποταμοῦ *bar*, Plu.*Ant.*41.

**ἀποψάλακτος**, = ἀκρότητος II, Phot. s.v. οὐκ ἀ.

**ἀποψαλίζω**, = ψαλίζω, *cut off with shears*, Dsc.1.99, Heliod.ap. Orib.48.50.1.

**ἀπο-ψάλλω**, *pluck off*, τρίχας Hsch.; ἀ. πάγην *spring* a trap that is set, Lyc.407; *twang* a string, Id.915; ἡ γλῶττα ἀ. τὴν ἄκραν Ἀτθίδα *rings out* the purest Attic, metaph. from the lyre, Philostr.*VS* 2.1.7. **-ψαλμα**, ατος, τό, *the part of the string which the musician plucks*, Ptol.*Harm.*1.8 (pl.), al., Porph. *in Harm.*295.

**ἀποψαύω**, prob. f.l. for ἐπι-, Suid. s.v. μουσομανία.

**ἀποψάω**, fut. -ήσω: impf. 3 sg. ἀπέψη E.*IT*311 (Elmsl.: ἀπέψα codd., cf. Hsch.): aor. ἀπέψησα Dsc.1.68.8, Luc.*Gall.*6. I. c. acc. rei, *wipe off*, ἀφρόν τ' ἀπέψη E. l.c.; δάκρυ *AP*5.65 (Rufin.), cf. Nonn. *D.*8.205:—Med., *wipe* or *rub off from oneself*, τι Ar.*Eq.*572. 2. ἀ. νούσους *cure* diseases, of Apollo, Herod.4.17. II. c. acc. pers., *wipe clean*, Ar.*Lys.*1035:—Med. (v. ψάω) *wipe oneself, wipe one's nose*, μου πρὸς τὴν κεφαλὴν ἀποψῶ *wipe your nose* on my head, Id.*Eq.*910; *podicem detergere*, ἀποψώμεσθα Id.*Pl.*817; ἀπεψησάμην Id.*Ra.*490; ἀ. τὴν χεῖρα εἴς τι X.*Cyr.*1.3.5; prov. τὴν κόνιν ἀποψησάμενος ἀγωνίζεσθαι *renew the struggle*, Eust.1327.29. III. τὰ ἐπιτήδεια σφόδρα ἀποψῶν giving short measure, of a skinflint, Thphr.*Char.*30.11.

⊛**ἀποψέ**, Adv. *late*, A.D.*Synt.*304.16.

**ἀποψεύδομαι**, *cheat grossly*: c. acc., *forge*, πρόφασιν J.*BJ*4.3.5:— Pass., *to be quite cheated of*, τῆς ἐλπίδος Plu.*Marc.*29.

**ἀπό-ψηκτέον**, *one must wipe clean*, ὦτα καὶ ῥῖνας *Gp.*17.20.3. **-ψηκτος**, ον, *wiped clean*: hence metaph., *keen-witted, sharp*, S.*Ichn.*363 (lyr.). **-ψηκτρον**, τό, *cleanser*, name of a remedy for ὑπώπια, Gal. 12.818. ⊛**-ψημα**, ατος, τό, *wipings, refuse*, Dsc.5.75, Hsch. s.v. μαριλοκαυτῶν. **-ψηξις**, εως, ἡ, *scraping, scratching*, Orib.*Fr.*79, Paul.Aeg.4.15. **-ψηστρον**, τό, *strickle*, Hsch.

⊛**ἀποψηφ-ίζομαι**, Att. fut. -ιοῦμαι D.22.45: Dep., c. pf. Pass., D.C. 39.55:—*vote away from*, opp. καταψηφίζομαι, θάνατον ἀ. τινός *vote* death *away from* him, *refuse to condemn* him to death, Lycurg. 149. 2. *refuse to elect*, τινά Plu.*Cor.*15. II. ἀ. τινός (gen. pers.), 1. *vote a charge away from* one, i.e. *acquit*, Antipho 5.96, Lys.12.90, D.18.250; τινός Id.19.212: abs., *vote an acquittal*, Pl.*Ap.* 34d, 39e; ἀ. τινὸς ὡς οὐκ ἀδικεῖ Arist.*Pr.*951$^b$1. 2. *vote the franchise away from* one, *disfranchise*, D.57.11; τοῦ παιδός Id.59.59, cf. Aeschin.1.114; ἀ. μὴ εἶναι ἐλεύθερον Arist.*Ath.*42.1:—Pass., τὸν ἀποψηφισθέντ' Ἀντιφῶντα D.18.132; δικαίως ἔστ' ἀπεψηφισμένος Aristopho 11.1; ἀ. τοῦ πολιτεύματος Plu.*Phoc.*28. III. c. acc. rei, *reject*: of judges, ἀ. γραφήν *vote against receiving* the indictment, Aeschin.3.230; ἀ. τὸν νόμον (with play on νόμος 'tune') Pl.*Lg.*800d; ἃ Διοπείθης κατεψηφίσατο Is.5.34, cf. D.20.164; ἀποψηφιζόμενον μὲν κύριον δεῖ ποιεῖν τὸ πλῆθος to give them an absolute power *of rejection*, Arist.*Pol.*1298$^b$35. IV. folld. by μή c. inf., *vote against* doing, X.*HG*3.5.8, D.19.174; so ἢν δ' ἀποψηφίσωνται (sc. μὴ ἕπεσθαι) X.*An.*1.4.15; ἀποψηφίσασθαι ἔφη Id.*HG*7.3.2.—Act. only -ψηφίζοντες· *refragantes*, *Gloss.* **-ισις**, εως, ἡ, *acquittal*, Antipho 5.9. 2. *disfranchisement*, D.57.2 and 4 (pl.), cf. *IG*2.841*b*102. 3. *final vote*, *SIG*344.120 (Teos). **-ιστέον**, *one must acquit*, D.22.44. **-ος**, ον, *voting in the negative*, ἀ. ἐγένοντο τοῦ ἀποκτεῖναι Phryn.*PS* p.13 B.

**ἀποψήχω**, *wipe away*, δάκρυα Eun.*VS*p.481 B. II. *scrape* or *rub off*, Dsc.2.76, 5.78 (-ψώχω Wellm.):—Pass., Arist.*HA*630$^b$11.

**ἀποψιλ-όω**, *strip off hair, make bald*, Ar.*Th.*538; of a barber, ἀ. τὸ πύκνωμα τῶν τριχῶν Alciphr.3.66:—Pass., Ar.*Lys.*827. 2. *strip bare*, τὸ ὀστέον Hp.*Foet.Exsect.*1; τὸν Κύρου οἶκον ἀ. Hdt.3. 32. II. c. gen., *strip bare of*, φίλων τινά A.*Ch.*695. **-ωσις**, εως, ἡ, *stripping*, ἀμπέλων Thphr.*CP*5.9.11.

**ἀπόψιος**, α, ον, *far seen, conspicuous*, prob. l. in Dicaearch.1.1.

⊛**ἄποψις**, εως, ἡ, *outlook, view*, πεδίον πλῆθος ἄπειρον ἐς ἄποψιν boundless *in view*, Hdt.1.204; παραπλησίους πάντας ἐκ τῆς ἀ. all alike *to look at*, Plb.11.31.8; ἐν ἀπόψει εἶναι, γίγνεσθαι, to be *within view*, Str. 6.1.5, *AP*9.412 (Phld.). 2. *lofty spot* or *tower which commands a view, belvedere*, Str.17.1.16, Plu.*Comp.Cim.Luc.*1. II. *that on which one looks, view, prospect*, Arist.*Mir.*843$^a$17, Plu.2.133b.

**ἀποψίω**, pf. Pass. ἀπέψισται, *strip bare*, *EM*818.36.

⊛**ἀποψοφ-έω**, *break wind*, Hp.*Epid.*6.3.14, Arist.*HA*633$^b$7, *Pr.*895$^b$

, Macho ap.Ath.8.349e. II. *sound loudly*, φωνὴ ἐν λιμένι-ψοφοῦσα hphr.*Sign*.40. -ησις, εως, ἡ, *crepitus ventris*, Plu.2.866c.
ἀπό-ψυγμα, ατος, τό, *ordure*, Hsch. ⊛-ψυξις, εως, ἡ, *cooling*, *vaporation*, Thphr.*Fr*.171.10. II. *shivering fit, rigor*, Simp. *in Epict.* .50 D. (pl.). ⊛-ψῦχος, ον, *frigid*, of literary style, Longin. 2. ⊛-ψύχω [ῡ]:—Pass., aor. ἀπεψύχθην and ἀπεψύχην [ῠ], v. infr., lso ἀπεψύγην [ῠ] Hld.2.3:—*leave off breathing, faint, swoon*, τὸν δὲ.. λεν ἀποψύχοντα Od.24.348; ἀ. ἀπὸ φόβου *Ev.Luc*.21.26. 2. c. acc., πέψυξεν βίον *breathed out* life, S.*Aj*.1031; πνεῦμα *AP*12.72 (Mel.): bs., *expire, die*, Th.1.134. cf. Lxx 4*Ma*.15.17, D.C.43.11, al.; λεπτὸν . faintly *breathing out his life*, Bion 1.9:—also Pass., ἀποψύχεται Hp. *Morb*.1.19: aor. 2 ἀπεψύχη A.*Fr*.104. II. *cool, chill*, ὄψα Sosip. 54:—Pass. or Med., *to be cooled*, Hom. only in phrase ἱδρῶ ἀπεψύχοντο χιτώνων στάντε ποτὶ πνοιήν they *got* the sweat *dried off* their tunics, Il.11.621; ἱδρῶ ἀποψυχθείς (by bathing) 21.561 (also in Act., ἱδρῶ ἀποψύχοντε Orph.*A*.1091): generally, *grow cold*, Thphr.*HP*4. 7.3, etc.: metaph., ἀπεψυγμένοι πρὸς τὸ μέλλον *cold and indifferent* as to.., Arist.*Rh*.1383ᵃ4; ἀποψυχόμενοι *shivering with terror*, Arr.*Epict*. 4.1.145, cf. Alciphr.2.2; but, *to be refreshed*, Phryn.*PS* p.27 B. 2. impers., ἀποψύχει *it grows cool*, ἐπειδὰν ἀποψύχῃ Pl.*Phdr*.242a, ap. Phryn.*PS* p.45 B., sed leg. ἀποψυχῇ (aor. 2 Pass.). III. ἀποψύχειν· ἀποπατεῖν, ἀφοδεύειν, Hsch.; cf. ἀπόψυγμα. ⊛-ψωλέω, (ψωλός) sens. obsc., *praeputium retrahere alicui*, Ar.*Ach*.592; ἀπεψωλημένος *a lewd fellow*, ib.161. -ψώχω, v. ἀποψήχω.

ἄππα, = πάππα, ἄττα (Maced., acc. to *EM*167.32), Call.*Dian*.6, *BGU*714.15, al.

**ἀππαλλάζειν**· ἐκκλησιάζειν (Ion.), Hsch.; cf. ἀπελλάζω.

**ἀππαπαῖ**, an exclamation of grief or pain, Ar.*V*.235,309.

⊛**ἄππας**, ὁ, religious official, τοῦ Διονύσου *Inscr.Magn*.117.8 (ii A.D.), cf. *Ath.Mitt*.17.200, Buresch *Aus Lydien* 131. II. = τροφεύς, Hsch.

**ἀππασάμενος**, = ἀνακτησάμενος (cf. πάομαι), Corinn.*Supp*.2.78. (From ἀμ-πα-.)

**ἀππέμψει**, rare poet. contr. for ἀποπέμψει, Od.15.83.

**ἄππιλος**· ἀσπάργαντος, Hsch. **ἄππιρ**· ὕσπληξ (Lacon.), Id.

**ἀπρᾱγ-έω**, *do nothing, remain quiet*, θεοὺς ἀπρηγεῦντας (-ται Pap.) Call.*Iamb*.1.198, Plb.3.70.4, 4.64.7; *hold no office* or *employment*, Heph.Astr.2.28. II. *fare ill*, Pittac.ap.Stob.3.1.172. ⊛-ία, ἡ, *inaction*, Plb.3.103.2; *want of energy*, Plu.*Fab*.1 (so in physical sense, Aret.*SD*2.7); *unemployment*, Vett.Val.189.8.

**ἀπραγμ-άτευτος** [μᾰ], ον, *impracticable*, πόλις ἀ., i.e. an *impregnable* city, D.S.17.40; χωρίον Plb.4.75.2. II. *deprived of commerce*, Anon.ap.Suid. s.v. διακλεισθέντες. III. *costing no trouble*, Muson. *Fr*.18 B p.105 H., Eun.*VS* p.504 B. IV. *free from trouble*, Phld. *Piet*.66. V. *inexperienced*, *UPZ*39.21 (ii B.C.). VI. *not elaborate, simple*, *Vit.Aesch*. Adv. -τως D.H.*Is*.16; *without taking pains*, Jul.*Or*.6.191c. ⊛-οσύνη, ἡ, *freedom from politics, love of a quiet life*, Ar.*Nu*.1007, X.*Mem*.3.11.16; of states, Th.1.32; ἡ Νικίου τῶν λόγων ἀ. Id.6.18. 2. = ἀτέλεια λειτουργιῶν, *SIG*876.8 (Smyrna), Poll. 8.156. II. *love of ease, easiness of temper*, Th.2.63, D.21.141. III. *inexperience*, *POxy*.71 ii 16 (iv A.D.). IV. name of a *weed* which grew ἐν Ἀκαδημίᾳ, Ar.Byz.ap.Sch.Ar.*Nu*.1007. -ων, ον, gen. ονος, *free from business* (πράγματα), *easy-going, fond of quiet*, esp. of those who *refrain from meddling in politics*, opp. πολυπράγμων, ὅστις δὲ πράσσει πολλά..μωρὸς παρὸν ζῆν ἡδέως ἀπράγμονα E.*Fr*.193; τῶν ἀ. γε πόρνων κοὐχὶ τῶν σεμνῶν [τις ὤν] Eup.8.4D.; esp. with political connotation, *not meddling in public affairs*, 'mugwump', ἄν τιν' αὐτῶν γνῷς ἀπράγμον' ὄντα καὶ κεχηνότα Ar.*Eq*.261, cf. Antipho 3.2.1; αὐτουργοί τε καὶ ἀ. Pl.*R*.565a; ἀ. καὶ οὐ φιλόδικος D.40.32; ἀκάκους καὶ ἀ. Id.47.82; οἱ ἀ. οὐκ ἄδικοι Arist.*Rh*.1381ᵃ25; τὸν μηδὲν τῶνδε [τῶν πολιτικῶν] μετέχοντα οὐκ ἀπράγμονα ἀλλ' ἀχρεῖον νομίζομεν Th.2.40; πόλις ἀ. *keeping clear of foreign politics*, Id.6.18; ἡσυχία ἀ. Id.1.70; βίος ἀνδρὸς ἰδιώτου ἀπράγμονος Pl.*R*.620c; τὸ ἄ. Th.2.63; τόπος ἀ. a place *free from law and strife*, Ar.*Av*.44; ἀπόλαυσις ἀ. X. *Mem*.2.1.33. Adv. -μόνως *without trouble* or *care*, E.*Fr*.787; ἀ. ζῆν ἡδύ Apollod.Com.1.1. II. of things, *not troublesome* or *painful*, τελευτὴν..ἀπραγμονεστάτην τοῖς φίλοις X.*Ap*.7. Adv. -μόνως *without trouble*, Th.4.61, X.*HG*6.4.27; σῴζεσθαι Th.6.87; ὁ λόγος ἀ. εἴρηται *carelessly*, Arist.*Mete*.369ᵇ27: Comp. -έστερον X.*Ages*.4.1. 2. *simple*, ἐσθής Muson.*Ep*.4.

**Ἀπρᾱγόπολις**, εως, ἡ, *Castle of Indolence, Sans-souci*, as Augustus called his retreat on an island near Capri, Suet.*Aug*.98.

⊛**ἄπρᾱγος**, ον, = ἀπράγμων, Sm.*Jd*.9.4.

**ἀπρακτέω**, *do nothing, to be idle*, Arist.*EN*1095ᵇ33; opp. πράττειν, Id.*Pol*.1325ᵃ31. 2. *gain nothing*, παρά τινος X.*Cyr*.1.6.6. 3. *waste one's time*, Lyd.*Mag*.1.22. 4. *lose power*, of a drug, Paul. Aeg.3.4.

⊛**ἄπρακτος**, Ion. ἄπρηκτος, ον, Pi.*I*.8(7).7 codd.: I. Act., *unavailing, unprofitable*, ἄπρηκτον πόλεμον Il.2.121; ἀπρήκτους ἔριδας ib.376; ἄ. ἐλπίς Simon.5.16, cf. Pi. l. c.; ἄ. γίγνεταί τι D.9.40; ἄ. ἡμέραι days *when no business is done, holidays*, Plu.2.270a, cf. *BGU* 255.8 (vi A.D.); *restful*, παῦλα B.9.8; ἄ. ἑορτή *Proll.Hermog*. in Rh. 4.15 W. (s. v. l.); ἀ. χρόνος period *of inaction*, Plb.2.31.10. b. of a farm, *untilled*, Lys.7.6. 2. of persons, *unsuccessful*, ἄπρηκτος νέεσθαι Il.14.221; ἄ. ἀπιέναι, ἀπελθεῖν, ἀποχωρεῖν, Th.4.61,99,1.111; ἄ. γίγνεσθαι *gain nothing*, Id.2.59; ἄ. ἀποπέμπειν τινά Id.1.24: Comp., Socr.*Ep*.6.7. Adv. -τως *unsuccessfully*, Th.6.48; ἄπρακτ' ὀδυρόμενον *in vain*, B.*Fr*.8. 3. *not taking part in the action*, ἄ. κηδευτὴς ὁ χορός Arist.*Pr*.922ᵇ26; *doing nothing, idle*, Ti.Locr.104e, Arr.*Epict*.1.10.7. Adv. ἀεργῶς καὶ ἀ. *PFlor*.295.5 (vi A.D.). 4. *impotent*, μόρια Orib. *Fr*.67, cf. Dsc.3.101. Adv. -τως, βοηθεῖ οὐκ ἀ. Orib.*Fr*.129. II. Pass., *against which nothing can be done, unmanageable, incurable*, ὀδύναι, ἀνίη, Od.2.79, 12.223; μεληδόνες Simon.39; φόβων -ότατος καὶ ἀπορώτατος ὁ τῆς δεισιδαιμονίας Plu.2.165d. 2. *not to be done, impossible*, πρᾶγμα, ἔργμα, Thgn.1075,1031; ἄπρηκτα *impossibilities*, Id.461. 3. *not done, left undone*, X.*Mem*.2.1.2, D.19.278; ἄ. ποιῆσαί τι *undo* it, Id.*Prooem*.41. 4. c. gen., κοὐδὲ μαντικῆς ἄ. ὑμῖν εἰμί not *unassailed* even by your divining arts, S.*Ant*.1035.

**ἀπραξία**, ἡ, *non-action*, τὸ μέλλον ἴσον ἀπραξίᾳ λέγω intending to act is the same as *not-acting*, E.*Or*.426; οὐδεμίαν..πρᾶξιν οὐδ' ἀπραξίαν Pl.*Sph*.262c. 2. *rest from business, leisure*, Men.633: in pl., = Lat. *justitium*, Plu.*Sull*.8. II. *want of success*, κοινὴ ἀ. Aeschin. 1.188. 2. in pl., *futilities*, Phld.*Rh*.1.38 S.

**ἀπρᾱσία**, ἡ, *want of purchasers, no sale*, Eup.62, D.27.21, 34.8.

⊛**ἄπρᾱτος**, ον, *unsold, unsaleable*, dub. in Lys.7.6, cf. D.34.9, *BGU* 18.4 (ii A.D.), al.; *unprostituted*, Aeschin.2.23. Adv. ἀπρατί Sch. Il.1.99.

**ἀπρέπ-εια**, Ep. ἀπρεπίη, ἡ, *unseemliness*, Pl.*R*.465b, etc. 2. *impropriety* in writing, Id.*Phdr*.274b. II. *ugliness*, εἴδεος ἀπρεπίη *APl*.4.319, cf. Dsc.*Alex*.27. ⊛-ής, ές, *unseemly, unbecoming*, ἀ. τι ἐπιγνῶναι, πάσχειν, Th.3.57,67; ἀ. καὶ ἄσχημον Pl.*Lg*.788b; μέθη ..φύλαξιν -έστατον Id.*R*.398e; τό..τοιαυτὶ ποιεῖν ἀπρεπές Epicr.11. 33; τὸ ἀ., = ἀπρέπεια, Th.5.46, 6.11. Adv. -πῶς, poet. -πέως, *h.Merc*. 272, Pl.*Phdr*.274b, etc.: Comp. -έστερον Hdn.3.13.1. II. of persons, *disreputable, indecent*, ἀνδρίον Theoc.5.40.

**ἄπρηκτος**, Ion. for ἄπρακτος. **ἄπρητον**· ἀφλόγιστον, Hsch.

**ἀπρήϋντος**, ον, *implacable*, *AP*7.287 (Antip.), Nonn.*D*.28.1, al.

**ἀπρῐάτην** [ᾰ] (ἀπριάδην read by Rhian. in Hom.), Adv. of πρίασθαι, *without purchase-money*, ἔνθα με..ἐκομίσσατο Φείδων ἥρως ἀ. (speaking of a man) Od.14.317; so in late Prose ἥδετο ἀ. εὐωχούμενος Agath.4.22:—also as fem. of Adj. **ἀπρίατος**, μή με ἀπριάτην περάσαντες (sc. Δημήτερα) *h.Cer*.132; δόμεναι..κούρην ἀπριάτην ἀνάποινον Il.1.99: acc. pl., ἀπριάτας Pi.*Fr*.169.7.

**ἄπριγδα**, = ἀπρίξ, A.*Pers*.1057,1063 (lyr.).

**ἀπριγδόπληκτος**, ον, *struck unceasingly*, prob. l. for ἄπριγκτοι πληκτά in A.*Ch*.425 (lyr., Blomfield).

**ἀπρίξ**, Adv. *fast, tight*, ἀ. ὄνυξι συλλαβών S.*Aj*.310; ἀ. ἔχεσθαι τοῦ κερδαίνειν Id.*Fr*.328, cf. Theoc.15.68, Luc.*Nec*.5, Eun.*VS* p.475 B.; τοῖν χεροῖν λαβέσθαι τινός Pl.*Tht*.155e, cf. Plb.12.11.6; ἔχειν χείρεσσι Theoc.24.55; δράξασθαι *AP*5.247 (Paul. Sil.). II. Subst., a kind of ἄκανθα (Cypr.), *EM*132.53.

**ἄπριστος**, ον, *not to be sawed*, μοχλός Aen.Tact.20.2. 2. *unsawed*, Q.S.12.137, prob. in *CPHerm*.28.11 (iii A.D.).

**ἀπρίωτος** [ῑ], ον, in Surgery, *without the use of the trepan*, Hp.*VC*14; *not trephined*, ib.20.

**ἀπροαιρ-εσία**, ἡ, *inconsistency*, Hp.*Ep*.17; prob. in *Sammelb*. 4317.5 (ii/iii A.D.), for τῆς σῆς σαπροεραισει. -ετος, ον, *without set purpose, not deliberate*, of actions, Arist.*EN*1135ᵇ10, Arr.*Epict*.2. 16.1, Plot.1.2.5, etc. Adv. -τως Hp.*Prog*.2, Arist.*EN*1106ᵃ3, Phld. *Ir*.p.93 W., etc. 2. of things, *incapable of choice or purpose*, Hermog.*Id*.2.4; *not under the control of will*, Phld.*D*.3 *Fr*.75, M.Ant.6. 41, al.

**ἀπρόβᾰτος**, ον, *making no progress*, of persons, Phld.*Ir*.p.43 W. II. *not advancing matters, inconclusive*, λόγος Id.*Sign*.6 and 35.

**ἀπρόβολος**, ον, *unprotected*, Pall. *in Hp.Fract*.12.285 C.

**ἀπροβουλ-ευσία**, ἡ, *failure to look forward*, Phld.*Herc*.1251. 7. -ευτος, ον, *unpremeditated*, Arist.*EN*1135ᵇ11; λόγοι Thphr. *Char*.3.1; *not deliberated upon*, D.H.4.72, J.*BJ*3.5.6. 2. *not submitted to the* βουλή, D.22.5, Hyp.*Fr*.231, Plu.*Sol*.19; of the Roman Senate, App.*BC*1.59. II. Act., *without forethought* or *premeditation*, Arist.*EN*1151ᵃ3, Ceb.8. Adv. -τως Pl.*Lg*.867a,b; ἀ. τοῦ ἀποκτεῖναι *without purpose of*.., ib.866e. -ία, ἡ, *want of premeditation*, ib.867b. ⊛-ος, ον, = ἀπροβούλευτος, only in Adv. -λως *rashly*, A.*Ch*.620 (lyr.).

**ἀπρό-γρᾰφος**, ον, *not promulgated*, Hyp.*Fr*.231. -διηγήτως, Adv., (διηγέομαι) *without preface*, Tz.*Proll.Hes*.10. -δῐκος, ον, *without preliminary trial*, [δίκα] *GDI*5017 (Gortyn). -εδρος, ον, *without president*, ἐκκλησία Eun.*Hist*.p.209 D. -θεσμος, ον, *not fixed to any definite time*, opp. ἐμπρόθεσμος, Sor.1.33. -θέτως, Adv., (προτίθημι) *undesignedly*, Plb.9.12.6. -θῡμία, ἡ, *want of readiness*, Suid. s.v. ἀρρωστία. -θῡμος, ον, *unready, backward*, Hdt.7.220, Th.4.86, X.*An*.6.2.7, etc. Adv. -μως Pl.*Lg*.665e. ⊛-ϊδής [ῐ], ές, (προϊδεῖν) *unforeseen*, Nic.*Th*.2,18, *AP*7.213 (Arch.), 9.111 (Id.). Adv. -ῶς Archig.ap.Orib.8.2.19. 2. Act., *unforeseeing*, prob. in Nonn.*D*.9.102, 48.757.

⊛**ἄπροικος**, ον, (προίξ) *without portion or dowry*, ἄ. τὴν ἀδελφὴν διδόναι Is.3.29, cf. D.40.20; λαβεῖν Lys.19.15, Diod.Com.3.4, cf. Men.*Mon*. 371.

**ἀπρό-ϊτος** [ῐ], ον, *not proceeding* or *emanating* (cf. ἀπρόοδος), Dam. *Pr*.34; θερμή Gal.14.729. Adv. -τως Hsch. -κάλυπτος [κᾰ], ον, *undisguised*. Adv. -πτως Chio *Ep*.7.3, 13.3. -κατασκεύαστος, ον, *not elaborately prepared*, D.H.*Is*.14. ⊛-κοπία, ἡ, *lack of progress*, Sch.Luc.*Bis Acc*.21. -κοπος, ον, *making no progress*, Man.3. 375, Ptol.*Tetr*.156. -κρίτως [ῐ], *without discussion, admittedly*, *POxy*.1467.22 (iii A.D.). 2. = Lat. *sine praejudicio*, Just.*Nov*.17. 8. -ληπτος, ον, *unanticipated*, *Stoic*.3.149, Onos.8.1. 2. *not prejudged*, τὸ ἀ. τῶν πράξεων Hierocl. *in CA*24 p.459 M. 3. *unprejudiced*, Syrian. *in Metaph*.1.15.

**ἀπρομήθ-εια** or **-ία**, ἡ, *want of forethought*, Pl.*La*.197b, J.*BJ*3.5.6. **-ευτος**, ον, later form for ἀπρομήθητος. Adv. -τως Suid. s.v. ἀφειδῶς. **-ης**, ες, *not known beforehand*, τὸ ἀ. τῶν γεγονότων J.*AJ* 19.3.1; τὸ ἀ. *failure to take previous account in time*, ib.18.6.5. **-ητος**, ον, *unforeseen*, A.*Supp*.357.

**ἀπρονο-ησία**, ἡ, *improvidence*, Epicur.*Fr*.368, Alex.Aphr.*de An*. 178.22, Procl.*in Prm*.p.746S. **-ητέω**, *to be imprudent*, Sch.Il. 4.2. **-ητος**, ον, *unpremeditated*, ἀκρασία Arist.*MM*1203ᵃ30; χώρα ἀ. an *unguarded* country, Plb.4.5.5; τόποι ἀ. *unreconnoitred*, Id.3.48.4; *not the work of providence*, κόσμος Ph.2.411, cf. Hierocl.*in CA*11 p.442M. II. Act., *not considering beforehand*, ἡ ὀργὴ -τον X.*HG* 5.3.7; ἀ. καὶ ἀπαράσκευοι Plb.5.7.2, cf. Orph.*Fr*.233; ἀ. τῶν ἐσομένων J.*Vit*.13; τῶν ἐπὶ γῆς πραγμάτων Luc.*Bis Acc*.2, etc.; of the gods, *not exercising providence*, Epicur.*Fr*.368. Adv. -τως X.*Cyr*.1.4.21, etc.; ἀ. τινὸς ἔχειν Str.2.5.1; opp. προνοίᾳ, S.E.*P*.1.151; οἱ ἀ. θεώμενοι *without previous acquaintance*, Plb.10.14.8.

**ἀπρονόμευτος**· οὐ πρυτανευθείς· ἀπρονομή (sic) γὰρ ἡ ἐπὶ τῆς χώρας ἁρπαγή, Hsch.

**ἀπρόξενος**, ον, *without* πρόξενος, A.*Supp*.239.

**ἀπροξίς**, ίδος, ἡ, *burning bush, Dictamnus albus*, Pythag.ap.Plin. *HN*24.158.

**ἀπρό-οδος**, ον, *not proceeding* or *emanating*, ἡ [τοῦ ἑνὸς] φύσις Dam. *Pr*.34. **-οιμίαστος**, ον, *without preface*, Luc.*Hist.Conscr*.23, Corn. *Rh*.p.358H. Adv. -τως D.H.*Lys*.17. **-οπτος**, ον, *unforeseen*, A.*Pr*.1074 (lyr.); ἐξ -όπτου Aesop.330. Adv. -τως *PAmh*.2.154.7 (vi A.D.). II. Act., *not foreseeing, unwary*, Poll.1.179; ἀ. τοῦ μέλλοντος Id.3.117. Adv. -τως Sor.1.71, Ael.*NA*1.8. ❋**-όρᾱτος**, ον, = foreg. I, D.S.20.96, Corn.*ND*10, Iamb.*Protr*.21. 2. *not previously seen*, Gal.14.279. II. = foreg. II, Ph.2.268, Max.Tyr. 11.6; τοῦ μέλλοντος Ph.2.159. Adv. -τως Onos.22.1, D.L.9.62, Ach. Tat.2.6, Max.Tyr.31.1. **-πετία**, ἡ, *freedom from precipitancy*, Ti. Locr.102e.

**ἄπροπον**· ἀπρεπές, Hsch.

**ἀπρο-πτωσία**, ἡ, *freedom from precipitancy, deliberateness*, *Stoic*. 2.39, Chrysipp.ib.40, M.Ant.3.9. **-πτωτος**, ον, *not precipitate*, Chrysipp.*Stoic*.2.40; συγκατάθεσις Arr.*Epict*.2.8.29, cf. M.Ant.4.49. Adv. -τως Chrysipp.*Stoic*.3.50. **-ρρητος**, ον, *not foretold*, Pl.*Lg*. 968e, as Ast for ἀπόρρητος.

**ἀπροσ-ᾱγόρευτος**, ον, *without appellation*, *Proll.Hermog*. in Rh.4. 21W. **-άρμοστος**, ον, *not befitting*, τινί Eust.1271.58. **-άρτητος**, ον, *detached*, ζῷον ἤδη ἀ. *Theol.Ar*.46. **-αύδητος**, ον, *not accosted*, Plu.2.29b, 921f; *unapproachable*, Aristocl.ap.Eus.*PE*11.3. ❋**-βᾰτος**, Dor. **ἀποτίβατος**, ον, *inaccessible*, πέτραι Arist.*HA*563ᵃ5, cf. Plu.*Alex*. 58, Luc.*Prom*.1; ἀποτίβ. νοῦσος *unapproachable*, S.*Tr*.1030 (lyr.), cf. Max.Tyr.18.1. **-βλεπτος**, ον, *not to be looked at*, *EM*433. 49. **-βλητον**· γενναῖον, Hsch. **-δεής**, ές, *without want of* anything, Lxx 1*Ma*.12.9, al., Phld.*D*.3.13; φιλοσοφίας Plu.2.122f, cf. 381b, Luc.*Hist.Conscr*.36: abs., *self-sufficient*, Plu.*Comp.Arist.Cat*. 4, Plot.5.9.4. **-δέητος**, ον, = foreg., Plb.21.23.4; διδασκαλίας Phld.*Rh*.1.194S. **-δεικτος**, *not to be pointed out*, A.*Supp*.794 cod. (lyr., -μεικτος Headlam). ❋**-δεκτος**, ον, *inadmissible*, *BGU* 1113.21 (i B.C.), S.E.*P*.2.229. II. Act., *not giving heed to*, συμβουλίας Phld.*Vit*.p.34J., dub. in Id.*D*.3 *Fr*.42; *unacceptable*, Plb.36.12.4; θυσία *IG*3.73.14, 74.8; εὐχὴ ἀ. ὑπὸ θεοῦ Porph.*Marc*.24. ❋**-διόνῡσος**, ον, *unconnected with the worship of Dionysus*, Plu.2.671f. II. *not to the point, mal à propos*, proverbial like οὐδὲν πρὸς Διόνυσον, Cic.*Att*. 16.13ᵃ.1, Plu.2.612e, Luc.*Bacch*.6. **-διόριστος**, ον, *undefined*, Ulp.ad D.24.68; *unqualified*, Heliod.*in EN*109.19; of propositions, *indefinite in quantification*, Ammon.*in APr*.14.37. Adv. -τως *without distinction*, Gal.16.558; *par excellence*, Olymp.*in Mete*.123.3. **-δόκητος**, ον, *unexpected, unlooked for*, A.*Pr*.680, S.*El*.1017, etc.; εὐπραγία Th.3.39; πρᾶγμ' ἡμῖν ἰδεῖν ἀ. Ar.*Lys*.352; κακοπάθεια Antipho 3.2. 11; τύχη Pl.*Lg*.920d; ἀ. [ὁδὸν] πορευθεὶς X.*HG*6.4.3; ἐξ ἀπροσδοκήτου Hdt.1.191, 7.204. Adv. -τως Th.4.29, Lys.1.11, etc. II. Act., *not expecting, unaware*, ἐπιθέσθαι τισὶ ἀπροσδοκήτοις Th.2.33, cf. 7.39; ἀ. ἦσαν ὡς ἤδη μαχούμενοι Id.6.69; ἀ. μὴ ἄν ποτέ τινα σφίσιν ἐπιθέσθαι Id.7.29. **-δοκία**, ἡ, *non-expectation*, Pl.*Def*.412c. **-έγγιστος**, ον, gloss on ἀπρόσιτος, Hsch. **-ειλος**, *unsunned*, E.*Fr*. 845. **-εκτέω**, *to be heedless, inattentive*, Eustr.*in APo*.258.6. **-εκτος**, ον, *heedless, careless*, Tz. ad Lyc.314. Adv. -τως *unconcernedly*, Porph.*Sent*.32. **-έλευστος**, ον, *not taken up*, of an inheritance, Just.*Nov*.1.1.3, cf. Suid. **-εξία**, ἡ, *want of attention*, Arr.*Epict*. 4.12.5, Sext.*Sent*.280a, etc. **-ηγορία**, ἡ, *want of intercourse*, Poet.ap.Arist.*EN*1157ᵇ13. **-ήγορος**, ον, *not to be accosted, unapproachable*, of a man, S.*OC*1277; of a lion, Id.*Tr*.1093; *without intercourse* or *conversation*, Plu.2.679a. **-ηνής**, ές, *ungentle, harsh*, Sch.Pi.*P*.2.10. **-θετέω**, *suspend judgement*, Timo 80. ❋**-θετος**, ον, *not added to*, *Theol.Ar*.30. **-θικτος**, ον, *untouched, not to be touched*, Hsch. s.v. ἀπροτίμαστος. **-ικτος**, ον, *unattainable*, ἔρωτες Pi.*N*.11. 48. **-ῐτος**, ον, *unapproachable, inaccessible*, ὄρη Plb.3.49.7, cf. Str. 1.3.18; φῶς 1*Ep.Ti*.6.16; of persons, Cic.*Att*.5.20.6, cf. Plu.2.68e; καταφυγή D.S.19.96: metaph., λόγοις ἀ. παρρησία Plu.*Alc*.4; δύναμις τοῦ λόγου Luc.*Dem.Enc*.32. Adv. -τως Plu.2.45f. **-καίρως**, *unseasonably*, Sch.Ptol.*Tetr*.158.

**ἀπρό-σκεπτος**, ον, *unforeseen, not thought of*, X.*Lac*.13.7. II. Act., *improvident*, D.51.15. Adv. -τως Antiph.195.

**ἀπρόσ-κλητος**, ον, *without summons to attend a trial*, *IG*1.27a10, Hyp.*Fr*.2; ἀ. δίκη a prosecution *in support of which no* πρόσκλησις *has been issued*, D.53.15; ἐπιβολή ib.14; γνῶσις Id.21.92; *without notice*, ὑμέναιος Hld.6.8; *unsummoned*, Id.8.1. **-κόλλητος**, ον, *not adhering*, τινί Eust.1940.20.

**ἀπροσκοπεῖν**· μὴ προορᾶν, Hsch.

**ἀπρόσ-κοπος** (A), ον, *not stumbling, void of offence*, *Ep.Phil*.1.10; συνείδησις *Act.Ap*.24.16. 2. *free from harm*, ἄτρυτος καὶ ἀ. *IG*5(2). 20.19 (Tegea, i B.C.); [θεοί] σε διαφυλάσσουσιν ἀ. *PGiss*.17.7 (ii A.D.), cf. *PBaden*39iii14 (ii A.D.). Adv. -πως ib.79iv8 (ii A.D.). II. *giving no offence*, τινί S.E.*M*.1.195, 1*Ep.Cor*.10.32.

❋**ἀπρό-σκοπος** (B), ον, *unseeing*, A.*Eu*.105. II. *unexplored*, ὁδός Lxx *Si*.35(32).21.

**ἀπρόσ-κοπτος**, ον, *without offence*, *IG*14.404. Adv. -τως *without stumbling*, τρέχειν Eust.925.28. **-κορής**, ές, *not satiating* or *disgusting*, Men.Rh.p.340S., Hld.6.1. II. *insatiate*, πρὸς τὰς ἡδονάς *Cat.Cod.Astr*.8(4).178.19. **-κρουστος**, ον, *free from blows*, ἕλκη φυλάττειν ἀ. Hierocl.p.25A. II. *not taking offence*, πρός τινα Plu. *in Hes*.65. **-ληπτος**, ον, *not taking* or *admitting* a construction, A.D.*Pron*.14.15, *Synt*.63.21. ❋**-λογος**, ον, *not to the point*, Sch.Ar. *V*.1311, al. Adv. -γως Plb.9.36.6. **-μᾰχος**, ον, *irresistible*, S. *Tr*.1098; τινί Luc.*Tox*.48. **-μηχάνητος** [χᾰ], ον, *against whom no device avails*, Sch.Il.16.29. **-μήχᾰνος**, ον, = foreg., Sch.A.R.1. 1053. **-μῑγής**, ές, = sq., Steph.Byz. s.v. Σῆρες, Eust. ad D.P. 752. **-μικτος** (-μεικτος), ον, *holding no communion with*, ξένοισι Hdt.1.65: abs., *solitary, isolated*, Poll.3.64. Adv. -τως Id.5. 139. ❋**-όδευτος**, ον, *not turned to profit*, *JHS*38.188 (Iconium, dub.). ❋**-οδος**, ον, *without approach, inaccessible*, βίος Phryn.Com. 18; ὄρη Procop.*Goth*.4.16. II. *not yielding a return, unproductive*, Phld.*Oec*.p.35J. **-οιστος**, ον, *hard to associate with* or *deal with*, A.*Pers*.91 (lyr.). Adv. -τως *unsociably*, Isoc.9.49. **-όμῑλος**, ον, *unsociable*, γῆρας S.*OC*1236. **-οπτος**, ον, *not to be looked at, faced*, ἀστραπή Poll.1.117. **-όρᾱτος**, ον, *not to be looked on, frightful*, πόνος Pi.*O*.2.67; epith. of Κύρβας, Orph.*H*.39.2. **-όρμιστος**, ον, *where one cannot land*, D.S.20.74, Sch.S.*Ph*.214. **-πᾰθής**, ές, *without affection* or *passion*, Hierocl.*in CA*11 p.438M. **-πέλαστος**, ον, *unapproachable*, Str.1.2.9, Plu.*Ant*.70. **-πληστος**, = foreg., Hsch. **-πλοκος**, ον, *not to be interwoven*, Sch.Ar.*Ra*.1340. ❋**-ποίητος**, ον, *unfeigned*, in Adv. -τως D.S.32.24. **-πταιστος**, ον, = ἀπρόσκοπος (A), Hp.*Ep*.17. **-πτωσία**, ἡ, *freedom from error*, Alex. Aphr.*de An*.150.35. **-ρητος**, ον, *unaddressed*, ἀ. τινὰ καταλιπεῖν Jul.*Ep*.182, cf. Poll.5.137, 138.

**ἀπρο-στᾰσίαστος**, ον, *without* προστάτης or *guardian*, Ph.1.170; of the universe, ib.696. **-στᾰσίου γραφή** indictment of a μέτοικος *for not having chosen a* προστάτης or *patron*, D.35.48; ἀ. δίκη Arist.*Ath*. 58.3, Hyp.*Fr*.15. **-στάτευτος** [τᾰ], ον, *without a leader* or *guide*, J.*AJ*20.8.8, Ael.*NA*15.8, f.l. for sq. in Hierocl.p.54A. **-στάτητος** [τᾰ], ον, = foreg., M.Ant.12.14; οἶκος Hierocl.p.54A. **-στᾰτος**, ον, = foreg., dub. in D.C.78.20.

**ἀπροστίμητος** [ῑ], ον, *without penalty*, Ἀρχ.Δελτ.2.269 (Coronea, i B.C.). II. ἀπροστίματον· ἀπροσδόκητον, ἀπρόσβατον, Hsch.

**ἀπρόστομος**, ον, *without sharp edge*, ξίφος Magn.7.

**ἀπρόστυχος**, gloss on ἄσιμος, Hsch.

**ἀπρόσ-φῐλος**, ον, *unfriendly, hostile*, Hld.5.7. ❋**-φορος**, ον, *dangerous*, νήσους ναύταις ἀπροσφόρους E.*IA*287 (lyr.); *unsuitable*, Herod. Med.ap.Orib.10.18.6; *incongruous*, Tz. ad Hes.*Op*.735. Adv. -ρως Steph.*in Hp*.1.223D. **-φυής**, ές, *incongruous*, Eust.178.37; *unrelated*, Tz.*H*.8.158. Adv. -ῶς Eust.529.31. **-φῦλος**, ον, (φῦλον) *not belonging to the tribe*, Hld.4.8 (dub. l.). **-φωνητί**, Adv. of sq., *without accosting*, Aesop.35. **-φώνητος**, ον, *not accosted*, Cic.*Att*. 8.8.1. 2. *unnoticed, unremarked*, Plu.2.575b, Sch.A.R.1.645.

**ἀπρόσχημος**, = *aequiformis*, of verses, Diom.p.498K.

**ἀπρόσ-χωρος**, ον, *arrogant*, *Gloss*. **-ψαυστος**, ον, *not to be touched*, Hdn.*Epim*.57.

❋**ἀπροσωπόληπτος**, ον, *not respecting persons*, Suid. s.v. ἀδυσώπητος. Adv. -τως *without respect of persons*, 1*Ep.Pet*.1.17.

**ἀπρόσωπος**, ον, *without a face*, i.e. *without beauty of face*, opp. εὐπρόσωπος, Pl.*Chrm*.154d, cf. Ael.*NA*14.18; of a country, Chor. p.223B. II. *without a mask, undisguised*, ἀγνωμοσύνη Aristid. 1.409J. III. *impersonal*, Phld.*Lib*.p.29O., *AB*420. Adv. -πως Aphth.*Prog*.4.

❋**ἀπροτί-ελπτος**, ον, Ep. for ἀπρόσ-, *unhoped for*, Opp.*C*.3.422 (v.l. ἀπροτίοπτον). **-μαστος**, ον, Ep. for ἀπρόσμαστος, (μαίομαι) *untouched, undefiled*, of Briseis, Il.19.263. II. *unapproachable*, of Homer, Euph.118. **-όπιστος**· ἀπρονόητος, Hsch. **-οπτος**, ον, = ἀπρόσοπτος, *invisible, obscure*, Man.2.19, Opp.*H*.3.159, Q.S.7. 73, *Ath.Mitt*.27.339 (Acarn.).

**ἀπρο-φᾰνής**, ές, = ἀπρόφατος, *unexpected*, f.l. in Orph.*A*.787. ❋**-φάσιστος** [φᾰ], ον, *offering no excuse, unhesitating, ready*, προθυμία Th.6.83; εὔνοια Lys.*Fr*.114; σύμμαχοι X.*Cyr*.2.4.10; συνεραστής Timocl.8. Adv. -τως *without disguise*, Th.1.49, etc.; *without evasion, honestly*, Id.6.72, *IG*2.243, etc.; *unhesitatingly*, D.C.38.39. II. *admitting no excuse, implacable*, θάνατος E.*Ba*.1002. III. *inexcusable*, κακία Plu.*Cat.Mi*.44, cf. 2.742c. **-φᾰτος**, ον, *unforetold, unexpected*, Arat.424, 768, A.R.2.268, Nic.*Al*.598. Adv. -τως A.R. 1.1201, 2.580, Orph.*A*.787. II. *unutterable, terrific*, A.R.1. 645. III. *without parley*, in Adv. -τως Id.2.62, 4.1005. **-φύλακτος** [ῠ], ον, *not guarded against, unforeseen*, Th.4.55. Adv. -τως D.C.38. 41, Ach.Tat.8.1. 2. *unguarded*, Opp.*H*.5.106. II. Act., *using no precautions*, Hld.6.13. **-φώνητος**, ον, *not announced beforehand*, Sch.Od.4.727. **-χωστος**, ον, *not silted up*, λιμένες Men.Rh.p.351S.

**ἀπρῠτάνευτος** [τᾰ], ον, *without payment of* πρυτανεῖα (q. v.), δίκαι *Milet.*3 No.147.31.

**ἀπταισία**, ἡ, *smoothness* of rhythm in music, Pl.*Lg.*669e.

❋**ἄπταιστος**, ον, *not stumbling*, ἀπταιστότερον παρέχειν τὸν ἵππον *make a horse less apt to stumble*, X.*Eq.*1.6: metaph., ἀ. ἐν τῷ βίῳ Epict.*Gnom.*52; δώμασιν ἀ. Limen.43, cf. M.Ant.5.9; βίος Luc.*Am.*46; *infallible*, Plot.5.3.17, Alex.Aphr.*in Metaph.*713.12; ἀλήθεια Iamb.*Myst.*3.31; θεοὶ διδασκάλων -ότατοι Max.Tyr.38.1. Adv. -τως Pl.*Tht.*144b; *inevitably*, Gal.14.230. Comp. -ότερον *with greater precision*, Ptol.*Tetr.*177:—also -τί, Hdn.*Epim.*256. 2. *intact*, Plu.2.691d. II. *not causing to stumble, giving a good footing*, λεία καὶ ἀ. ὁδός Max.Tyr.5.2.

**ἀπτάν**· ἀναχωρήσιον, Hsch. II. cf. sq., Id.

**ἀπταντίτας**, derived from ἀπτάν, = πένης, τιτάν, = παιδεραστής, Hsch. **ἀπταρύσσεται**· πέτεται, Id.; cf. ἀπτερύσσομαι.

**ἀπτέον**, (ἅπτομαι) *one must cling to* a thing, *bestow pains upon* it, μουσικῆς Pl.*R.*377a, cf. Epicur.*Fr.*461; *one must partake of*, πλακοῦντος Alex.250, cf. Gal.11.371, Porph.*Abst.*2.44.

**ἀπτερέως**, Adv., (ἀ-, = *sm*-, πτερόν) *quickly, swiftly*, Hes.*Fr.*96.46, Parm.1.17, A.R.4.1765. (Expld. as = αἰφνιδίως by Hdn.Gr.2.230; cf. ἄπτερος III, ἀπτέρωτος II.)

**ἄπτερος**, ον, *without wings, unwinged*, Hom. only in Od., and always in phrase τῇ δ' ἄπτερος ἔπλετο μῦθος the speech was to her *without wings, remained unuttered*, opp. ἔπεα πτερόεντα, 17.57; ἀ. φάτις *unspoken* rumour, A.*Ag.*278; ἄπτερα πωτήματα *wingless* flight, Id.*Eu.*250; ἀ. δρόμος, of the Trojan horse, v.l. in Tryph.85. 2. ἄπτερα, opp. πτερωτά, *without wings*, of insects, Arist.*HA*523$^b$17; ἄπτερον, τό, Id.*PA*642$^b$33. II. *unfeathered*, of Harpies, A.*Eu.*51; ἄνθρωπος ζῷον ἀ. Pl.*Def.*415a; ὄρνις (i.e. the Chorus) E.*IT*1095 (lyr.); of arrows, Hdt.7.92. 2. of young birds, *unfledged, callow*, ἀ. ὠδὶν τέκνων E.*HF*1039, cf. Pl.*Phdr.*256d. III. (ἀ-, = *sm*-) ἀ. τάχος of great speed, *Trag.Adesp.*429; cf. ἄπτερα· ἰσόπτερα, ταχέα, ἡδέα, Hsch. Adv. -ρως Lyc.627 (ὁμοπτέρως, ταχέως, Sch.).

**ἀπτέρῠγος**, ον, *without wings*, Hedyle ap.Ath.7.297b.

**ἀπτερύομαι**, = πτερύσσομαι, *flap the wings*, Arat.1009.

**ἀπτερύσσομαι**, = foreg., Archil.49 Diehl (ap.Sch.Arat.1009); cf. ἀπταρύσσεται.

**ἀπτέρωτος**, ον, *unfeathered*, of arrows or bolts, *IG*2.809e19. II. ἀπτέρωτα· ταχέα, αἰφνίδια, Hsch.; cf. ἀπτερέως, ἄπτερος III.

❋**ἀπτήν**, ῆνος, ὁ, ἡ, (πτηνός) *unfledged, callow*, ἀπτῆσι νεοσσοῖσι Il.9.323: metaph. of men, ἀπτῆνα τυτθόν *Com.Adesp.*1291. II. *unwinged*, βροτοί Ar.*Av.*687; πεζοῖς τε καὶ ἀπτῆσι (sc. ζῴοις) Pl.*Plt.*276a.

**ἀπτικός**, ή, όν, (ἅπτομαι) *able to come into contact with*, ἀλλήλων Arist.*GC*322$^b$27. 2. abs., τὴν ἀ. αἴσθησιν the sense *of touch*, Id.*de An.*413$^b$9, cf. Alex.Aphr.*Pr.Praef.*; τὸ ἀ. Arist.*de An.*415$^a$3; γλῶττα ἀπτικωτάτη *most sensitive to touch*, Id.*PA*660$^a$21. Adv. -κῶς Olymp.*in Alc.*p.40C. 3. of medicines, *acting on*, c. gen., τοῦ νευρώδους Dsc.2.179.

**ἄπτῐλος**, ον, *unfledged*, Jul.*Ep.*191.

❋**ἄπτιστος**, ον, *not winnowed* or *ground*, Hp.*VM*14.

**ἀπτοεπής**, ές, *reckless in speech*, Il.8.209 (v.l. ἀπτοεπής: fort. ἀεπτο-επής *uttering unspeakable words* (for ἀϝεπτο-, cf. ϝέπος)).

**ἀπτόητος**, poet. **ἀπτοίητος**, ον, *undaunted*, Lxx *Je.*26(46).28, Nonn.*D.*22.355, Sch.Il.1.56, etc. Adv. -τως, θνήσκειν Phalar.*Ep.*103.2.

**ἀπτολέμ-ιστος**, ον, *unwarlike*, Orac.ap.Ath.12.524b. **-ος**, ον, poet. for ἀπόλεμος, Il.2.201, E.*Med.*640(lyr.), etc.

**ἄπτορος**· ἰσόπτερος, Hsch. (leg. ἄπτερος).

**ἀπτός**, ή, όν, (ἅπτω) *tangible*, ὁρατὰ ἢ ἀ. σώματα Pl.*R.*525d, cf. *Ti.*32b, al., Arist.*de An.*424$^a$12, Thphr.*Od.*64, etc. II. ἀπτά· φάρμακα, Hsch.

❋**ἄπτρα**, ἡ, Dim. **ἄπτριον**, τό, (ἅπτω B) *wick of a lamp*, Sch.D.T. p.195 H.

**ἄπτυστος**, ον, *without expectoration*, πλευρῖτις Hp.*Coac.*375, cf. Gal.17(1).491.

❋**ἅπτω**, fut. ἅψω: aor. ἧψα:—Pass., pf. ἧμμαι, Ion. ἅμμαι Hdt.1.86: fut. ἅψομαι Od.9.379, ἀφθήσομαι (συν-) Gal.3.311:—Med., v. infr. (cf. ἑάφθη):—*fasten* or *bind to*, used by Hom., once in Act., ἅψας ἀμφοτέρωθεν.. ἔντερον οἰός (of a lyre-string) Od.21.408; once in Med., ἁψαμένη βρόχον.. ἀφ' ὑψηλοῖο μελάθρου *having fastened* the noose to the beam (to hang herself), 11.278; so later ἅψεται ἀμφὶ βρόχον.. δείρᾳ E.*Hipp.*770; ἁψαμένη βρόχον αὐχένι A.R.1.1065:—Act., βρόχους ἅ. κρεμαστούς E.*Or.*1036; but βρόχῳ ἅ. δέρην Id.*Hel.*136, cf. *AP*7.493 (Antip. Thess.). 2. *join*, ἅ. χορόν A.*Eu.*307; πάλην τινὶ ἅ. *fasten* a contest in wrestling *on* one, *engage with* one, Id.*Ch.*868:—Pass., ἅπτεσθαι τὴν Μεγαρέων πόλιν καὶ Κορινθίων τοῖς τείχεσιν Arist.*Pol.*1280$^b$14. II. more freq. in Med., ἅπτομαι, fut. ἅψομαι, aor. ἡψάμην E.*Supp.*317, with pf. Pass. ἧμμαι S.*Tr.*1010(lyr.), Pl.*Phdr.*260e:—*fasten oneself to, grasp*, c. gen., ἅψασθαι γούνων Il.1.512; χειρῶν 10.377; ἁψαμένη δὲ γενείου Ὀδυσσῆα προσέειπεν Od.19.473; ἅπτεσθαι νηῶν Il.2.152; βρώμης δ' οὐχ ἅπτεαι οὐδὲ ποτῆτος; Od.10.379, cf. 4.60; ὡς δ' ὅτε τίς τε κύων συὸς.. ἅπτηται κατόπισθε.. ἰσχία τε γλουτούς τε Il.8.339; ἅπτεσθαι τοῦ ἐπεόντος ἐπὶ τῶν δενδρέων καρποῦ Hdt.2.32; τῶν τύμβων ἀπτόμενοι Id.4.172; ἅπτεσθαί τινος, Lat. *manus inicere alicui*, Id.3.137; οὔτ' ἔθιγεν οὔθ' ἥψαθ' ἡμῶν E.*Ba.*617; τῶν σφυγμῶν *feel* the pulse, Arr.*Epict.*3.22.73: metaph., *take hold of, cleave to*, Pl.*Lg.*967c. b. abs., τῶν μὲν γὰρ πάντων βέλε' ἅπτεται for the spears of all the Trojans *reach their mark*, Il.17.631; ἀμφοτέρων βέλε' ἥπτετο 8.67. c. ἅ. τῆς γῆς *land*, D.S.4.48. III. metaph., *engage in, undertake*, βουλευμάτων S.*Ant.*179; ἀγῶνος E.*Supp.*317; πολέμου *prosecute* it *vigorously*, Th.5.61; ἧπται τοῦ πράγματος D.21.155; ψυχὴ ἡμμένη φόνων Pl.*Phd.*108b, cf. E.*IT*381; τῶν μεγίστων ἀσεβημάτων Plb.7.13.6; so ἅ. τῆς μουσικῆς καὶ φιλοσοφίας Pl.*R.*411c; ἐπιτηδευμάτος ib.497e; γεωμετρίας Id.*Plt.*266a; τῆς θαλάττης Plb.1.24.7; ἅπτεσθαι λόγου E.*Andr.*662, Pl.*Euthd.*283a (but ἅπτεσθαι τοῦ λόγου *attack, impugn* the argument of another, Id.*Phd.*86d); τούτων ἥψατο *touched on* these points, *handled* them, Th.1.97; ἅ. τῆς ζητήσεως Arist.*GC*320$^b$34; but also, *touch on, treat superficially*, Pl.*Lg.*694c, Arist.*EE*1227$^a$1. b. abs., *begin, set to work*, ταῖς διανοίαις Ar.*Ec.*581. 2. *fasten upon, attack*, Pi.*N.*8.22, A.*Ag.*1608, etc.; μόνον τῷ δακτύλῳ Ar.*Lys.*365; τῆς οὐραγίας Plb.2.34.12; esp. with words, Hdt.5.92.γ'; of diseases, ἧπταί μου S.*Tr.*1010, cf. Gal.15.702; ἥψατο τῶν ἀνθρώπων Th.2.48; ὅσα ἅπτεται ἀνθρώπων all that *feed on* human flesh, ib.50. b. *lay hands on*, χρημάτων Pl.*Lg.*913a; τῶν ἀλλοτρίων Id.*R.*360b, etc. 3. *touch, affect*, ἄλγος οὐδὲν ἅπτεται νεκροῦ A.*Fr.*255, cf. S.*OC*955; ἅπτει μου τοῖς λόγοις τῆς ψυχῆς Pl.*Ion* 535a; τῆς ἐμῆς ἥψω φρενός E.*Rh.*916; ὥς μου χρησμὸς ἅ. φρενῶν Ar.*Eq.*1237; *make an impression upon*, ἡμῶν *OGI*315.56 (Pessinus, ii B.C.). 4. *grasp with the senses, perceive*, S.*OC*1550, Pl.*Phd.*99e; *apprehend*, τῆς αἰτίας Arist.*Resp.*472$^a$3. 5. *have intercourse with* a woman, Pl.*Lg.*840a, Arist.*Pol.*1335$^b$40, 1*Ep.Cor.*7.1; εὐνῆς E.*Ph.*946. 6. *come up to, reach, overtake*, X.*HG*5.4.43; *attain*, τῆς ἀληθείας Pl.*Phd.*65b; τοῦ τέλους Id.*Smp.*211b: in Pi., c. dat., ἀγλαΐαις *P.*10.28; στάλαισιν Ἡρακλείαις Id.*I.*4(3).12; but also c. gen., Ἡρακλέος σταλᾶν Id.*O.*3.44. 7. *make use of, avail oneself of*, τῆς τύχης E.*IA*56. 8. Geom., of bodies and surfaces, *to be in contact*, Arist.*Ph.*231$^a$22, cf. *Metaph.*1002$^a$34, al., S.E.*M.*3.35; of lines or curves, *meet*, Euc.3*Def.*2; *touch*, Id.4*Def.*5, Archim.*Sph.Cyl.*1.28; *pass through* a point, Euc.4*Defs.*2,6; of points, *lie on* a line or curve, ib.*Defs.*1,3; ἅπτεται τὸ σημεῖον θέσει δεδομένης εὐθείας *the locus* of the point *is* a given straight line, Id.ap.Papp.656.6, al.

B. Act., *kindle, set on fire* (i.e. by *contact* of fire), Hdt.8.52, etc. (so in Med., Call.*Dian.*116); ἐρείκης θωμὸν ἅψαντες πυρί A.*Ag.*295: metaph., πυρσὸν ὕμνων Pi.*I.*4(3).43:—Pass., *to be set on fire*, ὁ μοχλὸς ἐλάϊνος ἐν πυρὶ μέλλεν ἅψεσθαι Od.9.379; ὡς ἄφθη τάχιστα τὸ λήιον.. ἅψατο νηοῦ as soon as the corn *caught fire*, it *set fire to* the temple, Hdt.1.19; πυρῆς ἤδη ἁμμένης ib.86; ἧπται πυρί E.*Hel.*107. II. ἅ. πῦρ *kindle* a fire, ib.503:—Pass., ἄνθρακες ἡμμένοι *red-hot* embers, Th.4.100; δᾷδ' ἐνεγκάτω τις ἡμμένην Ar.*Nu.*1490, cf. *Pl.*301. III. *cook*, Alex.124.1.

**ἀπτώδιον**, τό, *brooch*, *POxy.*1273.8 (iii A.D.).

**ἀπτώξ**, ῶκος, ὁ, ἡ, *without hares*, Hdn.Gr.1.46.

❋**ἀπτώς**, ῶτος, ὁ, ἡ, (πίπτω) *not falling* or *liable to fall*, ἀ. δόλος, of a wrestler's art, Pi.*O.*9.92; λόγος Pl.*R.*534c; ἀ. ἑστάναι M.Ant.7.61; ἀ. ἑαυτὸν διατηρεῖν Plu.*Comp.Arist.Cat.*2.

**ἄπτωτος**, ον, = ἀπτώς, *never thrown*, of a wrestler, *IG*14.1106, *TAM*2.301. 2. metaph., *faultless*, Longin.33.4, cf. Ph.1.678. II. *without cases*, ῥῆμα στοιχεῖον λόγου ἄ. Apollod.*Stoic.*3.213, cf. D.T.638.3, A.D.*Synt.*176.5, al. 2. *not involving different cases*, of a geometrical problem, Procl.*in Euc.*p.222F. III. Adv. -τως, ἔχειν to be *secure*, Corn.*ND*9; *infallibly, with certainty*, S.E.*M.*8.187.

❋**ἀπύ**, Aeol., Arc., Thess. for ἀπό:—**ἀπυδόσμιος, -δοσμός**, v. ἀπο-.

❋**ἄπῡγος**, ον, *without buttocks*, Semon.7.76, Pl.Com.184.3.

❋**ἄπυθεν**, Aeol. for ἄποθεν, Hsch.

**ἀπύθμενος**, ον, *without bottom* or *base*, κύλιξ Thphr.*Fr.*94; φιάλη Parth.ap.Ath.11.501a, cf. Dsc.*Eup.*1.235; γῆ ἀπύθμενον θεώρημα Secund.*Sent.*14:—also **ἀπυθμένιστος**, ον, Eust.870.28: **ἀπύθμην**, ενος, ὁ, ἡ, Theognost.*Can.*86.

**ἀπύκαστον**· ἀσκέπαστον, Phot.

**ἄπυκν-ος**, ον, *not dense, not compressed*, Ptol.*Geog.*8.1.4. 2. in Music, of notes, *not included in the* πυκνόν (q. v.), Cleonid.*Harm.*4, etc. **-ωτος**, ον, = foreg. I, Eust.972.39.

**ἄπῠλος**, ον, = sq., metaph., Vett.Val.334.13.

**ἀπύλωτος** [ῠ], ον, *not secured by gates*, X.*HG*5.4.20; στόμα Ar.*Ra.*838 (v.l. ἀθύρωτον).

**ἀπυνδάκωτος** [δᾰ], ον, = ἀπύθμενος, S.*Fr.*611.

**ἄπῡος**, ον, *not suppurating*, Suid.

**ἄπυργ-ος**, ον, *untowered, unfortified*, E.*Fr.*749. **-ωτος**, ον, = foreg., *not girt with towers*, Od.11.264.

**ἀπύρεκτος** [ῠ], ον, = ἀπύρετος, Arr.*Epict.*4.6.21 (ex corr.), *Gp.*13.8.9, Gal.10.378, Aët.9.31.

**ἀπῠρεξία**, ἡ, *absence of fever, time* or *state free from fever*, Gal.17(1).69, cf. 19.399.

❋**ἀπύρετος** [ῠ], ον, *free from fever*, Hp.*Aph.*4.20, Luc.*Philops.*25, *POxy.*1582.9 (ii A.D.); *not inducing fever*, δίαιτα Hp.*Art.*69; βίος Antiph.226.6; *relieving fever*, ἀντίδοτος Archig.ap.Gal.13.173:—perh. to be read for **ἀπύρευτος** f.l. in Thphr.*Char.*3.6.

**ἀπῡρηνομήλη**, ἡ, *probe without a knob* (πυρήν), Hp.ap.Gal.19.85.

❋**ἀπύρηνος** [ῠ], ον, *without stone* or *kernel, pipless*, ῥοά Ar.*Fr.*118, Thphr.*HP*4.13.2; φοῖνιξ Arist.*de An.*422$^a$29, *Fr.*267. II. *with no spine*, ἰχθύς (i.e. ἔγχελυς) Archestr.*Fr.*8 codd.

**ἀπυρίτης** (sc. ἄρτος), ὁ, a kind of *loaf*, Poll.6.33.

❋**ἄπῡρος**, ον, *without fire*, in Hom. only of pots and tripods, *that have not yet been on the fire, brand-new*, ἕπτ' ἀπύρους τρίποδας Il.9.122, cf. 23.267. b. *not capable of standing on the fire*, σκευῶν ἐμπύρων καὶ ἀ. Pl.*Lg.*679a, cf. Ar.*Fr.*532. c. *not wasted by fire*, Max.Tyr.41.4. 2. ἄ. οἶκος *fireless*, i.e. *cold, cheerless*, Hes.*Op.*525. 3. *unfermented*, οἶνος Alcm.117; *uncooked*, σιτία Plu.2.349a; ἄκολος *AP*9.563 (Leon.), etc. 4. ἄ. χρυσίον *unsmelted*, opp. ἄπεφθον, Hdt.

3.97, *IG*2.652*B*28(but ἄ. χρυσός, of nuggets, or gold-dust, Arist.*Mir.* 833$^{b}$8, D.S.2.50, al.); ἄ. κύανος Thphr.*Lap.*55; ἄ. τέχναι Aristid.*Or.* 37(2).13; θεῖον ἄ. *native* sulphur, Gal.12.903. **5.** ἱερὰ ἄ. sacrifices *in which no fire was used*, i.e. offerings of fruit, grain, and wine, Pi.*O.* 7.48, cf. A.*Ag.*70 (lyr.), S.*Fr.*417; θυσίαν ἄπυρον παγκαρπείας E.*Fr.* 912.4; ἄ. βωμοί Ph.1.345; ἱερουργία Plu.2.578b. **6.** in A.*Pr.*880 (lyr.) ἄ. ἄρδις an arrow-point *but one not forged in fire*, i.e. the sting of the gad-fly; **ἄ.** δᾴς, of love, Luc.*DDeor.*19.1. II. Medic., *without fever*, Hp.*Epid.*1.1, cf. Aret.*SD*1.9. Adv. ἀπύρως Hp.*Prorrh.* 1.119. III. = νεκρός, Hsch.

**ἀπύρωτος** [ῠ], *ον*, *not exposed to fire, brand-new*, φιάλη Il.23.270; *uncooked*, Thphr.*Od.*10; of the moon in eclipse, *not fiery*, *Placit.*2. 29.2; *incombustible*, Thphr.*Lap.*19, 22.

⊛**ἄπυστος,** *ον*, *not heard of*, ᾤχετ' ἄϊστος ἄ. Od.1.242, cf. Sapph. *Supp.*25.19, Opp.*C.*1.236. **2.** of words, *inaudible*, ἄπυστα φωνῶν S.*OC*489. II. Act., *without hearing* or *learning* a thing, οὐδὲ δὴν ἦεν ἄ. Ζεύς Od.5.127: c. gen., μύθων 4.675; κακῶν ἔτι πάμπαν ἀπύστω *IG*14.1389ii16.

**ἀπύω,** Dor. for ἠπύω.

⊛**ἀπφά** or **ἄπφα,** a term of endearment used by brothers and sisters, also by lovers, Eust.565.23.

**ἀπφάριον** [φᾰ], Dim. of ἀπφά, Xenarch.4.15, *CIG*3277 (Smyrna).

**ἀπφίδιον** [φῑ], *τό*, Sch.Luc.*Cat.*12, and **ἀπφίον,** *τό*, Eust.565.23, Dim. of ἀπφά; also **ἀπφία** Poll.3.74, cf. Hsch.

**ἀπφῦς** (for the accent cf. Hdn.Gr.2.936), gen. ύος, ὁ, a term of endearment used by children to their father, *papa*, Theoc.15.14:— Eust. (v. foreg.) expld. as ὁ ἀφ' οὗ ἔφυ.

**ἀπώγων,** *ωνος, ὁ, ἡ, beardless*, Suid.

**ἀπῳδ-έω,** v.l. for ἀπᾴδω in Plu.2.1043b: metaph., *go wrong*, τοσοῦτον μόνον.. ἀπῴδησεν ὁ ἄνθρωπος prob. in Phld.*Po.*994.4. **-ός,** *όν*, *out of tune*, E.*Cyc.*490 (lyr.), Ph.1.375, Luc.*Icar.*17: metaph., *out of harmony with*, c. gen., Id.*Salt.*65: abs., Ph.2.170, Luc.*Pisc.*34, A.D. *Synt.*307.14. II. *having ceased to crow* or *sing*, ἀλεκτρυών Luc. *Lex.*6; of a person, Him.*Or.*22.5.

⊛**ἄπωθεν** (in late Poets also **ἄπωθε,** Q.S.6.647, *AP*7.172 (Antip. Sid.)), Adv. *from afar* or *afar*, S.*Ant.*1206, *Tr.*816, E.*Heracl.*674, Ar.*Av.*1184, etc.; οἱ ἄπωθεν *strangers, outsiders*, Arist.*Rh.*1371$^{a}$12, al. **2.** c. gen., *far from*, νεώς E.*IT*108, cf. Ar.*Pl.*674, Th.3.111, Babr.1.12; cf. ἄποθεν.

⊛**ἀπωθέω,** fut. inf. ἀπωσέμεν Il.13.367: aor. ἀπέωσα Od.9.81, ἀπῶσα prob. corrupt in S.*Fr.*479:—**Med.,** fut. ἀπεώσομαι Lxx 4*Ki.*21.14: aor. ἀπωσάμην Hom. (v. infr.), ἀπεωσάμην Th.1.32, etc., ἀπωθησάμην D.C.38.28 codd.: pf. ἀπῶσμαι· ἀπώθησα, Hsch., inf. ἀπεῶσθαι Th.2. 39:—**Pass.,** pf. part. ἀπωσμένος Phld.*Ir.*p.33 W.:—*thrust away, push back*, ᾤϊξε πύλας καὶ ἀπῶσεν ὀχῆας Il.24.446, cf. 21.537; ἀ. ἐπάλξεις *pushed* them *off* the wall, Th.3.23:—Med., *thrust away from oneself*, χερσὶν ἀπώσασθαι λίθον Od.9.305; ἀπώσατο ἦκα γέροντα *pushed* him gently *away*, Il.24.508; αἱ χεῖρες τὸ τόξον -οῦνταί τε καὶ προσέλκονται Pl.*R.*439b. **2.** *drive away*, ἠέρα μὲν σκέδασεν καὶ ἀπῶσεν ὀμίχλην [Ζεύς] Il.17.649; of the wind, *beat from* one's course, Βορέης ἀπέωσε Od.9.81 (so in Med., σφέας κεῖθεν ἀπώσατο ἶς ἀνέμοιο 13.276). **3.** c. gen., εἴ κέ μιν οὐδοῦ ἀπώσομεν 22.76, cf. 2.130; γῆς ἀπῶσαί [με] πατρίδος S.*OT*641:—Med., *thrust from oneself, drive away*, μνηστῆρας ἀπώσεαι ἐκ μεγάροιο Od.1.270:—Pass., *to be expelled*, Hdt.1.173; ἀπωθοῦμαι δόμων Ar.*Ach.*450; γῆς S.*OT*670. **4.** *thrust aside, spurn*, Id. *Aj.*446, al.:—Pass., τὸν δῆμον πρότερον ἀπωσμένον *pushed aside*, Hdt. 5.69. **5.** *repel, drive back*, in Med., Τρῶας ἀπώσασθαι Il.8.206; νεῖκος ἀπωσαμένους 12.276; ἀπώσασθαι κακὰ νηῶν 15.503; νηῶν μὲν ἀπωσάμενοι δήϊον πῦρ 16.301; πένθος Archil.9.10; νοῦσον *AP*6.190 (Gaet.):— also in Prose, Antipho 4.4.6, etc.: c. dupl. acc., τὴν ναυμαχίαν ἀπεωσάμεθα Κορινθίους Th.1.32. **6.** in Med., *reject*, τὸ ἀργύριον Hdt.1.199; τὸν αὐλόν S.*Tr.*216 (lyr.); φιλότητα Id.*Ph.*1122 (lyr.); τὰς σπονδάς Th.5.22; τὰ ἐξ ἀδικίας κέρδη Pl.*R.*366a; ἀ. πόνους *decline* them, E.*Fr.* 789; τὴν δουλοσύνην *shake off* slavery, Hdt.1.95; ὕπνον *shake off* sleep, Pl.*R.*571c: abs., *refuse*, ποιήσω κοὐκ ἀπώσομαι S.*Tr.*1249.

**ἀπώθ-ησις,** *εως, ἡ, rejection, repulsion*, χυμῶν Steph.*in Hp.*1.72 D. **-ητής,** *οῦ, ὁ, one who repels*, *Gloss.* **-ητος,** *ον*, *thrust* or *driven away, rejected*, Suid. **-ία,** *ἡ*, *refusal*, *PFay.*21.24 (ii A.D.) (fort. ἀπειθίας).

**ἀπώλεια,** *ἡ*, *destruction*, Arist.*EN*1120$^{a}$2, etc.: pl., Id.*Mete.*351$^{b}$ 11. II. *loss*, Id.*Pr.*952$^{b}$26; opp. τήρησις, Plb.6.59.5 Schweigh., cf. *BGU*1058.35, al. (i B.C.); τῶν χρόνων ἀ. Diog.Oen.1. **2.** *perdition*, *Ep.Rom.*9.22, 2*Ep.Thess.*2.3. **3.** *thing lost*, Lxx *Le.*6.3 (5.22).

**ἀπωλεσίοικος,** *ον*, *ruining one's house*, μειράκιον *Com.Adesp.*848.

**ἀπώλευτος,** *ον*, of horses, *unbroken*, Anon.ap.Suid.

**ἀπωλία,** *ἡ*, = ἀπώλεια, Pl.Com.199.

**ἀπώμ-αστος,** *ον*, (πῶμα) *without a lid*, Babr.60.1, Gal.17(2). 161. **-ος,** *ον*, = foreg., *Gp.*6.1.4, Zos.Alch.p.113 B.

**ἀπωμ-οσία,** *ἡ*, (ἀπόμνυμι) *denial upon oath*, as law-term, opp. ἐξωμοσία, Poll.8.54, cf. Hsch. **-οτικός,** *ή, όν, of* or *for denial on oath*, ἐπίρρημα (i.e. μά) D.T.642.15, Eust.54.23. Adv. -κῶς Id.92. 22, Sch.Il.1.85. ⊛**-οτος,** *ον*, *abjured, declared impossible on oath*, χρημάτων ἄελπτον οὐδέν ἐστιν οὐδ' ἀ. Archil.74; βροτοῖσιν οὐδέν ἐστ' ἀ. S.*Ant.*388; πρᾶγμ' ἀ. Eup.217; οὐδὲν ἀ. οὐδὲ ἄπρακτον ποιεῖσθαι D.Chr.4.102. II. of persons, *under oath not to do a thing*, καίπερ ὢν ἀ. S.*Ant.*394; κἂν ἀ. τις ᾖ *Trag.Adesp.*566.

⊛**ἀπωνέομαι,** *buy, purchase*, ἀπωνηθήσεται Theopomp.Com.84.

**ἀπωρῠγ-ίζω,** *dig up*, *PFlor.*369.5 (ii A.D.). **-ισμός,** *ὁ*, *layering of* ἀπώρυγες II, *POxy.*1692.14 (ii A.D.), cf. 1631.10 (iii A.D.).

**ἀπῶρυξ,** *υγος, ἡ*, (ἀπορύσσω) *canal from* a place, ἀπώρυγες συχνα[ί] Procop.*Vand.*2.19 (Scalig., for ἀπορρῶγες): metaph. of Samos, ἀ[πῶρυξ] τῆς πόλεως Demad.*Fr.*4 S., cf. Phld.*Rh.*1.181 S. II. *layer of a vine*, Lxx *Ez.*17.6, *Gp.*5.18.1, *POxy.*1631.10 (iii A.D.).

**ἀπωρ-ωσία,** *ἡ*, *absence of callus*, Paul.Aeg.6.110. ⊛**-ωτος,** *ον*, *not forming a callus*, of fractured bones, Dsc.1.70.

**ἀπωσί-κᾰκος** [ῐ], *ον*, *repelling evil*, θεοί *IG*14.957; ἄνεμοι ἀ. *BMus. Inscr.*370 (Delos). **-κύμᾰτος** [ῡ], *ον*, *repelling waves*, *AP*6.90 (Phil.).

**ἄπ-ωσις,** *εως, ἡ, thrusting* or *driving away*, διὰ τὴν τοῦ ἀνέμου ἄπωσιν αὐτῶν Th.7.34, cf. Aret.*SD*1.14. **2.** *repulsion*, opp. ἕλξις, Arist.*Ph.*243$^{a}$19. **-ωσμός,** *ὁ*, = foreg., Lxx *La.*1.7. **-ωστέον,** *one must reject*, E.*HF*294. **-ώστης,** *ου, ὁ, one that drives away*, ἄνεμος Eust.1741.22; cf. ἐξώστης. **-ωστικός,** *ή, όν, rejecting*, δύναμις Gal.*Nat.Fac.*3.8. **-ωστός,** *ή, όν, thrust* or *driven away from*, τῆς ἑωυτοῦ (sc. γῆς) Hdt.6.5, cf. S.*Aj.*1019. II. *that can be driven away*, οὐδὲ ἀπωστοὶ ἔσονται Hdt.1.71.

**ἀπωτάτω,** Sup. Adv. of ἄπωθεν, *farthest from*, τῆς Θρᾴκης D.23. 166, cf. *Trag.Adesp.*130 (lyr.).

**ἀπώτερος,** *α, ον*, Comp., (ἀπό) *farther off*, = μακρότερος, Suid.: neut. as Adv., ἡ ἀπώτερον (sc. γραμμή) Euc.3.15, al.; opp. ἔγγιον, Id. *Phaen.*p.4 M.

**ἀπωτέρω,** Comp. Adv. of ἄπωθεν, *farther off*, S.*OT*137, Ar.*Nu.* 771, Pl.*Phdr.*254c, etc.; γένει ἀ. ὄντες D.43.50: prov., ἀ. ἢ γόνυ κνάμα Theoc.16.18. **2.** c. gen., *farther from*, Cratin.229.

**ἀπωτέρως,** = foreg., *Gloss.*

⊛**ἄπωτος,** *ον*, *deaf*, dub. in *GDI*104 (Cypr.) (= *Inscr.Cypr.*171 H.); λιταῖς ἄπωτε cj. in Moschio Trag.2.

**ἀπωχραίνω,** *make pale*, v.l. for ἀποχραίνω, Arist.*Col.*796$^{a}$24.

**ἄρ,** v. sq.

⊛**ἄρᾰ,** Ep. **ῥά** (which is enclitic and used after monosyllables, ἤ, ὅς, γάρ, etc., or words ending in a vowel or diphthong, e.g. ἐπεί), before a consonant **ἄρ** (perh. cf. Lith. *ir̃* 'and'): expressing consequence, *then*, or mere succession, *there and then*, and in many derived uses.

A. Earlier usage: to denote, I. immediate transition, *there and then, straightway*, ὣς φάτο βῆ δ' ἄρ' Ὄνειρος Il.2.16: after a part., ὣς εἰπὼν κατ' ἄρ' ἕζετο 1.68, al.; πυθόμενος.. εἶπε ἄ. Hdt.4.134, cf. 9.9; ἐρωτώσης τῆς μητρὸς ἀπεκρίνατο ἄρα X.*Cyr.*1.3.2; with other Particles, δέ, ἤ, ὡς, etc., cf. ὁ δὲ Ἀστυάγης ἄ. εἶπεν ib.4.10: also after Advbs. of Time, τότε δή ῥα, τῆμος ἄρα, etc.; οὕτως ἄρα Pl.*Phdr.*259b; often in apodosi, as αὐτὰρ ἐπεὶ δὴ θηήσατο.. αὐτίκ' ἄρ' ἤλυθεν Od.5. 77; repeated τὼ μὲν ἄρ'.. κεῖντο ἡ δ' ἄρ'.. ἀγόρευε Il.21.426: in enumerations, e.g. in Homer's catalogue, *then, next*, οἱ δ' ἄρ' Ἀθήνας εἶχον 2.546; so in genealogies, Σίσυφος.. ὁ δ' ἄ. Γλαῦκον τέκεθ' υἱόν 6.154. **2.** to draw attention, *mark you!* τὸν τρεῖς μὲν ἐπιρρήσσεσκον.. τῶν ἄλλων Ἀχιλεὺς δ' ἄρ' ἐπιρρήσσεσκε καὶ οἶος 24.456; with imper., ἀλλ' ἄγε δὴ κατ' ἄρ' ἕζευ 24.522: to point a moral or general statement, φευγόντων δ' οὔτ' ἂρ κλέος ὄρνυται οὔτε τις ἀλκή 5. 532. II. connexion, such as, **1.** that of *antecedent* and *consequent*, οἰνοχόει.. ἄσβεστος δ' ἄρ' ἐνῶρτο γέλως 1.599, cf. 24.507; τοὔνεκ' ἄρ' ἄλγε' ἔδωκε 1.96; freq. with οὕνεκα in protasi, 7.140, al.: also in questions, τίς τ' ἂρ τῶν ὄχ' ἄριστος ἔην; who *then* (say you) was..? 2.761: with demonstr. Pronoun in recapitulation, ἀλλ' υἱὸν Πριάμοιο.. τόν ῥ' Ὀδυσεὺς βάλε *he it was, whom*.., 4.501: freq. in such phrases as ὣς ἄρα φωνήσας 2.35, al.; ὣς ἄρ' ἔφη 1.584, al.; ἦ ῥα 3. 355, al., thus, *then* he spoke.—This usage is universal in Greek. **2.** explanation of that which precedes, χωόμενον κατὰ θυμὸν ἐϋζώνοιο γυναικὸς τήν ῥα.. ἀπηύρων whom (*and for this cause* he was angry) they had taken away, 1.429; εἰ μὴ ὑπερφίαλον ἔπος ἔκβαλε.. φῆ ῥ' ἀέκητι θεῶν φυγέειν *for* he said, Od.4.504: freq. with οὕνεκα; so with relatives, ἐκ δ' ἔθορε κλῆρος ὃν ἄρ' ἤθελον αὐτοί the *very* one which.., Il.7.182.

B. Later usage, always with inferential force: **1.** in drawing conclusions (more subjective than οὖν), ἄριστον ἄ. ἡ εὐδαιμονία Arist.*EN*1099$^{a}$24; δῆλον ἄ. Id.*Pol.*1295$^{b}$33; in pseudo-syllogistic conclusions, Id.*SE*174$^{b}$11, *Rh.*1401$^{a}$3, al.: esp. by way of informal inference, *as it seems*, οὐκ ἄ. σοί γε πατὴρ ἦν Πηλεύς Il.16.33; οὐδ' ἄ. πως ἦν ἐν πάντεσσ' ἔργοισι δαήμονα φῶτα γενέσθαι 23.670; μάτην ἄρ', ὡς ἔοικεν, ἥκομεν S.*El.*772; οὕτω κοινόν τι ἄ. χαρᾷ καὶ λύπῃ δάκρυά ἐστιν *so true is it that*.., X.*HG*7.1.32; πολὺ γὰρ ἀμείνων ἄ. ὁ τοῦ ἀδίκου ἢ ὁ τοῦ δικαίου βίος Pl.*R.*358c; ἦν ἄ. πυρός γ' ἕτερα.. θερμότερα Ar.*Eq.* 382; ὦ τλῆμον ἀρετή, λόγος ἄρ' ἦσθα *Trag.Adesp.*374; so in announcing the discovery or correction of an error, as οὐκ ἐννενοήκαμεν ὅτι εἰσὶν ἄ... Pl.*R.*375d; φαίνεται πρὸ ποδῶν ἡμῖν κυλινδεῖσθαι καὶ οὐχ ἑωρῶμεν ἄρ' αὐτό ib.432d; εἰκότως ἄ. οὐκ ἐγίγνετο· ὡς γὰρ ἐγὼ νῦν πυνθάνομαι.. X.*An.*2.2.3. **2.** in questions, expressing the anxiety of the questioner, τίς ἄ. ῥύσεται; *who is there* to save? A.*Th.*92; so in exclamations to heighten the expression of emotion, οἵαν ἄρ' ἥβην ..ἀπώλεσεν *what* a band of youth was that..! Id.*Pers.*733; so ὡς ἄρα ib.472, S.*Fr.*577; τί μ' ἄ. τί μ' ὀλέκεις; Id.*Ant.*1285; τί οὖν.. ἄ. X.*Oec.*6.2; πῶς ἄ.; οὕτως ἄ., etc.; ἄ. alone, ἔζης ἄ. S.*Fr.*685: esp. in ironical comments, Ar.*Av.*476, 1371, etc. **3.** epexegetic, *namely*, ἐρῶ, ὡς ἄ... Pl.*Tht.*152d, cf. 156e. **4.** for τοι ἄρα, τἄρα, v. sub τοι II.2. **5.** εἰ (or ἐάν) μὴ ἄ. unless *perhaps*, Pl.*Ap.*38b, D.58.4; separated from εἰ μή, Id.9.20; with irony, εἰ μὴ ἄ. ἡ τῆς ἀρετῆς ἐπιμέλεια διαφθορά ἐστιν X.*Mem.*1.2.8. **6.** in hypothetical clauses, to indicate the improbability of the supposition, ἢν ἄ. ποτὲ κατὰ γῆν βιασθῶσιν Th.1.93, etc.; or simply, *perhaps* (sts. separated from εἰ), εἴ τις οὖν ὑμῶν ἄ... ὑπελάμβανεν D.21.8; εἴ τις ἰδίᾳ τινὰ δεδιὼς ἄ. ἀπρόθυμός ἐστιν Th.4.86.

C. In crasis, freq. τἄρα, μεντἄρα, οὐτἄρα: also δῆξομἄρα for ἥξομαι ἄ., Ar.Ach.325; οἰμώξετἄρα, κλαύσἄρα, Id.Th.248, Pax 32: also in Trag., E.Hyps.Fr.34.86.

D. ἄρα never stands first in the sentence in Classical Greek (Arist.Mech.851$^a$22 is corrupt), but is found at the beginning of an apodosis in Ev.Matt.12.28, Ep.Rom.10.17, and first in a sentence, Ev.Luc.11.48, Vett.Val.305.20; in conclusion of syllogism, Herm. ap.Stob.3.11.31.

*__ἆρα__, interrog. Particle implying *anxiety* or *impatience*, = Ep. and Lyr. ἦ ῥα: 1. alone, it simply marks the question, the nature of which is determined by the context: e.g. in D.35.44 a *negative* answer is implied in the question ἆρ' ἂν οἴεσθε..; but an *affirmative* in X.Cyr.6.4.4 ἆ. βέβληκα δὶς ἐφεξῆς; cf. ἆρ' εὐτυχεῖς..ἢ δυστυχεῖς; E.Ph.424.—To make it plainly neg., we have ἆ. μή..; A.Th.208, Pl.Phd.64c; and to make it plainly affirmative, ἆρ' οὐ; ἆρ' οὐχί; S. OC791, OT540; ἆρ' οὐχ οὕτως; Pl.Phlb.11d. 2. ἆ. οὖν; is used to draw an affirmative inference, Id.Grg.477a, La.190b; also when a neg. answer is expected, Id.Chrm.159b; with a neg., ἆρ' οὖν οὐ..; Id.Phdr.263a, etc. 3. in ἆρά γε, each Particle retains its force, γε serving to make the question more definite, Ar.Pl.546, X.Mem.1.5.4, etc. 4. less freq. with τίς interrog., τίνος ποτ' ἆρ' ἔπραξε χειρί S.Aj.905; τί δ' ἆρ' ἐγὼ σέ; E.IA1228; τίς ἆρ' ὁ φεύγων; Ar.V.893; with ἦν, E.Rh.118. 5. in indirect questions, σκεψώμεθα τοῦτο ἆ... Pl.Phd.70e, cf. R.526c, al., Arist.Ph.204$^b$3, etc. II. in Poets sts. like ἄρα, Archil.86,89, Pi.P.4.78, Ar.V.3; τοιοῖσδε χρησμοῖς ἆ. χρὴ πεποιθέναι; A.Ch.297, cf. 435; τῷ δὲ ξιφήρης ἆρ' ὑφειστήκει λόχος E. Andr.1114: in exclamations, βραδεῖαν ἡμᾶς ἆρ' ὁ τήνδε τὴν ὁδὸν πέμπων ἔπεμψεν S.Aj.738; ὀδυνηρὸς ἆρ' ὁ πλοῦτος E.Ph.566, cf. El.1229, Hipp.1086; ἦ δεινὸν ἆρ' ἦν Id.Fr.931; ἔμελλόν σ' ἆ. κινήσειν Ar.Nu. 1301, cf. Ach.347.

B. In Prose, ἆ. almost always stands first in the sentence, but cf. Pl.Grg.467e; καὶ ὑπὲρ τούτων ἆ.. Jul.Or.2.61c: in Poetry greater licence is taken, v. supr. 1.4, II.

*__ἀρά__, Ion. ἀρή, ἡ, *prayer*, Il.15.378,598, 23.199, Hes.Op.726, Pi.I. 6(5).43; ἀρὴν ἐποιήσαντο παῖδα γενέσθαι Ἀρίστωνι offered *prayers* that a child should be born, Hdt.6.63. 2. *vow*, Inscr.Cypr.83, 147 H. 3. *curse, imprecation*, ἐξ ἀρέων μητρὸς..ἥ ῥα θεοῖσι πόλλ' ἀχέουσ' ἠρᾶτο Il.9.566; freq. in Trag., mostly in pl., A.Pr.910, S.OT 295; ἀρὰς ἀρᾶσθαι, προστιθέναι, ἐξανιέναι, E.Ph.67, S.OC952,154(lyr.), 1375; ἐπεύχεσθαι Pl.Criti.119e; θέσθαι ἐπί τινας Plu.Cam.13: also in sg., πατρὸς δ' ἀ. κρανθήσεται A.Pr.910, cf. Ag.457 (lyr.), etc.; ἡ τοῦ νόμου ἀ. Pl.Lg.871b; ἀρᾷ..ἔνοχος ἔστω ib.742b, etc.: in pl., *imprecations*, freq. in Inscrr. on those who shall mutilate or remove them, Inscr.Magn.105.53 (ii B.C.), IG3.1417 sqq. II. Ἀρά personified as the goddess of destruction and revenge, ὦ πότνι' Ἀρὰ σεμναί τε θεῶν παῖδες Ἐρινύες S.El.111; δεινόπους Ἀρά Id.OT418; but in A.Eu.417 the Erinyes say that Ἀραί is their own name γῆς ὕπαι; Ἀρά τ' Ἐρινὺς πατρὸς ἡ μεγασθενής Id.Th.70; Ἀρᾶς ἱερόν Ar.Fr.575. (Hence the Verb ἀράομαι.) [Ep. always ἀρ, Att. always ᾱρ.] (From ἀρϝᾱ, cf. κατάρϝος.)

__Ἀρᾰβ-άρχης__, v. Addenda. *__-αρχία__, ἡ, *office of* Ἀραβάρχης, BGU665 ii 5 (i A.D.).

*__ἄραβδος__, v. ἄρραβδος. __ἀράβδωτος__, v. ἀρράβδωτος.

__ἀρᾰβέω__ [ἄρ], (ἄραβος) *rattle, ring*, Hom. (mostly in Il.), always of armour, δούπησεν δὲ πεσών ἀράβησε δὲ τεύχε' ἐπ' αὐτῷ Il.5.42, al.; of the teeth, *gnash*, Theoc.22.126; ἀραβεῖ δ' ἁ γνάθος Epich.21.2. 2. trans., *gnash, grind*, ὀδόντας Hes.Sc.249, A.R.2.281.

__Ἀρᾰβ-ία__, ἡ, *Arabia*, Hdt.2.8, etc. (also, = κόσμος γυναικός, Hsch.): poet. Ἀρραβία Theoc.17.86:—Adj. __Ἀράβιος__, α, ον, *Arabian*, οἱ Ἀ. Hdt.1.198, al.:—also *__Ἀραβικός__, ή, όν, χάραγμα PGen.29.8 (ii A.D.), Plu.Ant.69, Hsch.:—later Ἄραβες (v. Ἄραψ):—pecul. fem. __Ἀραβίς__, ίδος, Them.Or.34.56 *__Ἀράβισσα__, St.Byz. __-ίζω__, *take part with the Arabs*, Suid. __-ιστί__, Adv. *in Arabic*, Eust. ad D.P.954.

__ἀραβίδες__· αἱ μετὰ κονιορτοῦ πνοαί, Hsch.

__ἀραβίς__, ίδος, ἡ, = δράβη, Dsc. (post 2.185).

__ἄρᾰβος__ [ἄρ], ὁ, *gnashing* or *chattering* of teeth, ἄ. δὲ διὰ στόμα γίγνετ' ὀδόντων Il.10.375, cf. Hes.Sc.404, Hld.5.3; prob. f.l. for ἄραδος in Plu.2.654b. 2. generally, *rattling, ringing*, σάκεος Call.Del. 147. (Prob. onomatop.)

__ἀρᾰβοτοξότης__, ου, ὁ, *Arab archer*, employed for police duty in Egypt, PAmh.2.77.4 (ii A.D.), etc.

__ἀραβύλη__· ἀρβύλη, Hsch.

__ἀραβών__, v. ἀρραβών.

__ἀράγ-δην__ [ἄρ], Adv., (ἀράσσω) *with a rattle*, Luc.Lex.5. __-ειν__· σπαράσσειν, Hsch. __-μα__, ατος, τό, = sq., τυμπάνων ἀ. E.Cyc.205. II. = κάταγμα, Sor.Fract.10. *__-μός__, ὁ, *clashing, clattering, rattling*, A. Th.249; ἀ. πετρῶν *crashing shower* of stones, E.Ph.1143; στέρνων ἀ. *beating* of the breast in grief, S.OC1609; ἀ. χεροῖν Lyc.940.—Rare in Prose, Hellanic.167(c) J.

__ἀραδ(ήσ)ει__· θορυβήσει, ταράξει, and __ἀράδηται__· κεκόνηται (prob. -κίν-), συγκέχυται, Hsch.; cf. ἄραδος.

__ἀρᾰδιούργητος__, ον, *not dishonestly done*, AB357, Suid. s.v. ἀκαπήλευτον. Adv. -τως, = *sine fraude*, Just.Edict.7.7.

*__ἄρᾰδος__ [ἄρ], ὁ, *disturbance*, τοῦ χρωτὸς ἄ. ποιεῖν Hp.Morb.4.56; ἄ. ἐμποιεῖν Id.Acut.(Sp.)47; also of foods, ἄ. ἔχειν Id.VM15; ἔχον ἄ. κακόν Id.Acut.10; *palpitation* of the heart, ἄ. κακός Nic.Th.775; generally, ὁ ἐκ τῆς συνουσίας ἄ. καὶ παλμός prob. in Plu.2.654b. (Prob. onomatop., like ἄραβος.)

__ἀράδους__· βλαβεράς, λεπτάς, Hsch.

__ἀράζω__ or __ἀρράζω__, *snarl, growl*, of dogs, Ael.NA5.51, Poll.5.86, Ph.1.694 codd. (Onomatop., = *make the sound* ἀρ, ἀρρ.)

__ἀράη__· φιάλην, καὶ ἀράκτην, Hsch.; cf. ἀράκη, ἀρακτήρ.

__ἀραιά__, ᾶς, ἡ, *belly*, v. ἀραιός.

__ἀραιάκις__, = ὀλιγάκις, prob. in Hsch. s.vv. ἀδράκις, ἀρβάκις.

__ἀραιόδους__, οντος, ὁ, ἡ, *with thin-set teeth*, Arist.HA501$^b$23, cf. Pr. 963$^b$20 (dub. l.).

__ἀραιό-θριξ__, τρῐχος, ὁ, ἡ, *with thin hair*, Hsch. s.v. ψεδνή, cf. Moer. 421. __-πορος__, ον, *thinly porous, flaccid*, Alex.Aphr.Pr.1.2.

__ἀραῖος__ [ᾰ], α, ον, also ος, ον S.Ant.867 (lyr.): (ἀρά): I. Pass., *prayed to* or *entreated*, Ζεὺς ἀ., = ἱκέσιος, S.Ph.1182 (lyr.). 2. *prayed against, accursed*, γονά A.Ag.1565 (lyr.); πότμος ἀ. ἐκ πατρός Id.Th.898 (lyr.); μ' ἀραῖον ἔλαβες you adjured me *under a curse*, S. OT276. II. Act., *cursing, bringing mischief upon*, c. dat., φθόγγος ἀ. οἴκοις A.Ag.237 (lyr.); δόμοις ἀ. S.OT1291, cf. E.Med.608, IT 778; ἀ. γονεὺς ἐκγόνοις ὡς οὐδεὶς ἕτερος ἄλλος Pl.Lg.931c: abs., A. Ag.1398, S.Tr.1202.—Almost confined to Trag., exc. Pl. l. c.

__ἀραιός__ [ᾰ], ά, όν, (ἀρ- Hdn.Gr.2.108, v.l. in Il.18.411, al.) *thin, slender*, κνῆμαι, χείρ, γλῶσσαι, Il. l. c., 5.425, 16.161; γαστήρ Nic.Th. 133; *narrow*, εἴσοδος Od.10.90; of ships, Hes.Op.809; φάλαγγες ἀ., opp. βαθύτεραι, X.Lac.11.6, cf. Plu.Crass.23; ἀραιᾷ τροφῇ χρῆσθαι *meagre*, of diet, Arist.Pol.1335$^b$13. II. later, of the substance of bodies, *of loose texture*, opp. πυκνός, Anaximen.1, Meliss.7, Anaxag. 12,15, cf. Emp.104 (Sup.), Thphr.CP2.4.7, etc.; opp. πίων, Arist. Pr.880$^a$38; freq. in Hp., as VM22; δέρμα Aph.5.71; ὀστέον Art.33; εἴρια Mul.1.1; ὁμίχλη..νέφους ἀραιοτέρα Arist.Mu.394$^a$21, cf. Mete. 364$^b$25 (Comp.); σπόγγοι D.S.3.14. b. φλύκταιναι ἀ. *empty* blisters, Nic.Th.240 (v. Sch. ad loc.), cf. Theoc.12.24. 2. in Tactics, *in open order*, opp. πυκνός, τὸ ἀραιότατον [διάστημα] Ascl.Tact.4.1, etc. III. *intermittent*, πνεῦμα Hp.Epid.1.26.α', β'; ἆσθμα, βήξ, Aret.SD1.11, etc. Adv. -ῶς Hp.Nat.Puer.24; of the pulse, Gal.9.444, al. IV. *scanty, few and far between*, τρίχες Arist.Col.797$^b$27; ἀκτῖνες ib.791$^a$ 27; φωναί Id.Aud.803$^b$28; ὀδόντες Poll.2.94, etc. V. ἀραιά (sc. γαστήρ), ἡ, *flank, belly*, Ruf.Onom.171. VI. of the voice, *thin*, Theoc.13.59. (Homeric metre proves ϝαραιός.)

__ἀραιό-σαρκος__ [ἄρ], ον, *with porous, spongy flesh*, Hp.Nat.Puer.21, Mul.1.1, Hices.ap.Ath.7.288c (Comp.). __-στημος__, ον, *of thin warp, fine*, Hsch. s.v. μανοστήμοις. *__-στῦλος__, ον, *with columns widely spaced*, Vitr.3.31. __-σύγκρῐτος__, ον, *with loose tissues*, Gal.6.407. __-της__, ητος, ἡ, *looseness of substance, porousness, rarity*, opp. πυκνότης, Hp.Aph. 5.63, al., Arist.Pr.869$^b$30: pl., Id.Ph.260$^b$10, Epicur.Ep.2 p.49 U., Placit.3.12.1; τῶν πόρων Arist.Aud.802$^a$24; opp. πύκνωσις, Plu.Fr.inc. 149. __-τρητος__, ον, *with few pores*, opp. πολύτρητος, Gal.UP8.6 codd.

__ἀραι-όφθαλμος__ [ἄρ], ον, *with few eyes* or *buds*, κλῆμα Gp.5.8.2.

__ἀραιό-φυλλος__ [ἄρ], ον, *with scanty leaves*, Zonar. s.v. μανόφυλλον.

__ἀραιόω__ [ἄρ], *make porous, rarefy*, τὴν ἐπιδερμίδα Hp.Nat.Puer.20; τὴν σάρκα Id.Vict.3.78; opp. πυκνόω, Arist.Pr.884$^a$27, Aret.CA2.1, cf. SA2.2, etc. II. Pass., *to be rarefied*, Hp.Vict.1.13, Arist.Mu. 394$^a$36; ἀραιουμένων τῶν σωμάτων Ph.Bel.71.43.

__ἀραίρ-ηκα__, __-ημένος__, __-ητο__, v. αἱρέω.

__ἀραιώδης__ [ἄρ], ες, *loose of substance, porous*, Gal.14.680.

*__ἀραί-ωμα__ [ἄρ], ατος, τό, (ἀραιόω) *interstice, crevice, chink*, Str.4.4.1, D.S.1.39, Luc.VH1.30, Placit.3.3.11, Plu.2.98cc, etc.; of the body, Hp.Morb.4.45; *pore*, σώματος Hero Spir.1 Praef., al., cf. Sor.1.115; *a little bit*, Longin.10.17. __-ωσις__, εως, ἡ, *becoming* or *making porous, rarefaction*, opp. πύκνωσις, dub. in Epicur.Nat.14 Fr.11 (cf. Fr.6), cf. Plu.Strom.3, D.L.9.8 (Heraclit.), Corn.ND17, etc. 2. Medic., *porosity*, of the lungs, Hp.Oss.13, etc. 3. *mordanting*, PHolm. 8.3. __-ωτικός__, ή, όν, *of* or *for rarefying*, ὑγρῶν, v.l. in Dsc.1.62.

__ἀράκη__, ἡ, = φιάλη, Hsch. s. v. ἀράη (leg. ἀράκην), and s.v. ἐξ ἀρκιδῶν (leg. ἀρακιδῶν): so in Ath.11.502b Αἰολεῖς τὴν φιάλην ἀράκην (ἀρακίν cod.) καλοῦσιν.

__ἀρᾰκικός__, ή, όν, *of* or *from aracus*, φόρος PFlor.27.6 (iv/v A.D.).

__ἀράκιον__ [ᾰκ], τό, = sq., POxy.119.12 (ii/iii A.D.), Gal.13.68.

__ἀρᾰκίς__, ίδος, ἡ, and __ἀρᾰκίσκος__, ὁ, Dims. of ἄρακος, Gal.19.85.

__ἄρᾰκος__ [ἄρ], ὁ, a leguminous plant, *wild chickling, Lathyrus annuus*, Ar.Fr.412c, BGU636.12 (i A.D.), Gal.6.524. II. neut., ἄ. τὸ τραχὺ καὶ σκληρόν, a variety which grew as a weed among lentils, Thphr.HP8.8.3. III. Tyrrhen. word for ἱέραξ, Hsch.

__ἀρᾰκό-σπερμον__ [ἄρ], τό, *aracus-seed*, PRyl.143.16 (i A.D.). __-σπορος__, ον, *sown with aracus*, BGU1292.54 (i B.C.). __-χερσος__, ον, *dry and fit for sowing aracus* (sc. γῆ), CPHerm.120$^r$ iii 5.

__ἀρακτῆρα__· ἀμελκτῆρα, Hsch.: __ἀράκτης__, Id. s.v. ἀράη.

__ἀρᾰκώδης__ [ἄρ], ες, *like* ἄρακος: -ῶδες, τό, *tine-tare, Lathyrus tuberosus*, Thphr.HP1.6.12.

__ἄραμα__· βόρβορος, Hsch. __ἄραμεν__· μένειν, and __ἀράμεναι__· ἡσυχάζειν, Id. (perh. for ἠρεμεῖν). __ἀράμενοι__· τὰ ἀπόχυτα ὕδατα, Id. __ἄραμος__· ἐρῳδιός, Id. __ἀράνη__· μεσάγκυλον, Id. (order requires ἀραύη). __(ἄ)ρανις__· ἔλαφος, Id. __ἀράντισιν__· ἐρινύσι (Maced.), Id.

__ἄραξ__, ακος, ὁ, = ἄρακος, PMeyer12.23 (ii A.D.), PTeb.423.4 (iii A.D.), etc.

__ἀράξα__, ἡ, fabulous plant which grows by the Araxes, Ps.-Plu. Fluv.23.2.

__ἄραξις__, εως, ἡ, *dashing, beating*, Cass.Pr.25. II. kind of *bread* used in Athamania, Ath.3.114b.

__ἀραξίχειρος__ [ᾰ] [ῐ], ον, (ἀράσσω) *beaten with the hand*, τύμπανα AP 6.94 (Phil.).

*__ἀράομαι__, Aeol. inf. ἄρασθαι Sapph.Supp.5.22: fut. ἀράσομαι [ᾱ],

Ion. ἀρήσομαι: aor. ἠρησάμην, Aeol. 3 pl. ἀράσαντο Sapph.51: pf. ἤρᾱμαι (only in compds. ἐπήραμαι, κατήραμαι): (ἀρά): [ἄρ Hom., ἄρ Lyr., Trag.]:—poet. Verb (v. infr.), *pray to* a god, Ἀπόλλωνι Il.1.35; δαίμοσιν 6.115: once c. acc., *invoke*, στυγερὰς ἀρήσετ' Ἐρινῦς Od.2.135. 2. c. acc. et inf., *pray* that.., ἀρᾶται δὲ τάχιστα φανήμεναι Ἠῶ Il.9.240; τὰ ἐναντία.. ἀρέομαι ὑμῖν γενέσθαι Hdt.3.65 codd.; ἠρῶντο (sc. σφέας) ἐπικρατῆσαι *prayed* that they might prevail, 8.94; ἥ σε θεοῖς ἀρᾶται.. μολεῖν S.*Aj.*509, cf. Ar.*Th.*350. b. c. inf. only, πάντες κ' ἀρησαίατ' ἐλαφρότεροι πόδας εἶναι *would pray* to be, Od.1.164. c. folld. by optat., ἀρώμενος εἷος ἵκοιο *praying* till thou should'st come, ib.19.367. 3. *pray for*, ἔσλα τῷ γάμβρῳ Sapph.51; ἀ. τινὶ ἀγαθὰ Hdt.1.132: c. inf., σφῷν.. θεοῖς ἀρῶμαι μή ποτ' ἀντῆσαι κακῶν S.*OC* 1445; more freq. in bad sense, *imprecate*, τί τινι Id.*OT*251; ἀρὰς ἀ. τινί Id.*OC*952, And.1.31, cf. A.*Th.*633, *Pr.*912; and without an acc., ἀρᾶσθαι τινι *to curse* one, E.*Alc.*714, cf. S.*OT*1291. 4. c. fut. inf., *vow* that.., πατὴρ ἠρήσατο Πηλεὺς.. με.. σοί τε κόμην κερέειν ῥέξειν τε Il.23.144. II. Act. only in Ep. aor. inf., ἀρήμεναι μέλλεις you are like *to have prayed*, Od.22.322. III. the part. ἀρημένος (q.v.) does not belong to this Verb.

**ἀραρίζω**, = ἀράζω, Ammon. s.v. φωνεῖν. **ἄραριν**· ἀράχνην, Hsch. **ἀραρινοί** (sc. λίθοι), stones used *to fill chinks* in walls, Id. **ἄραρις**· ἔνορκος, Id.

***ἀρᾰρίσκω** (redupl. form of √ἀρ, *join, fit together*), only impf. ἀράρισκε Od.14.23, Theoc.25.103: the tenses in use (from *ἄρω) are mostly poet., v. infr.

A. trans.:—Ion. aor. 1 ἦρσα Il.14.167 (ἐπ-), Ep. ἄρσα Od.21.45, imper. ἄρσον 2.289, pl. ἄρσετε A.R.2.1062, part. ἄρσας Il.1.136 (also inf. ἀρᾶραι· ἁρμόσαι, πλέξαι, Hsch.): aor. 2 ἤρᾰρον, Ion. ἄρᾰρον, inf. ἀραρεῖν, part. ἀραρών (but ἄραρεν is used intr. in Il.16.214, Od.4.777, Simon.41; while for ἄρηρεν, in trans. sense (Od.5.248), ἄρασσεν is the true reading; ἐς οὐρανὸν ἤραρεν ὄσσε Orph.*A.*984 is by confusion with αἴρω:—Med., fut. ἄρσομαι Lyc.995 acc. to Sch. (possibly fr. αἴρω): aor. 1 ἠρσάμην, part. ἀρσάμενος Hes.*Sc.*320: 3 pl. aor. 2 opt. (in pass. sense) ἀραροίατο A.R.1.369: pf. subj. ἀρήρεται Hes.*Op.*431 (προσ-):—Pass., pf. part. ἀρηρεμένος or -έμενος A.R.3.833, al.; later incorrectly written ἀρηράμενος Q.S.2.265, Opp.*C.*2.384, etc.: aor. 1 ἤρθην, only 3 pl. ἄρθεν, for ἤρθησαν, Il.16.211:—*join together, fasten*, οἱ δ' ἐπεὶ ἀλλήλους ἄραρον βόεσσι when they had *knitted* themselves one to another with their shields, Il.12.105 (in Pass., μᾶλλον δὲ στίχες ἄρθεν 16.211); ἄγγεσιν ἄρσον ἅπαντα *pack up*, Od.2.289. II. *fit together, construct*, ὅτε τοῖχον ἀνὴρ ἀράρῃ πυκινοῖσι λίθοισιν Il.16.212:—Med., ἀρσάμενος παλάμῃσι Hes.*Sc.*320. 2. μνηστῆρσιν θάνατον καὶ Κῆρ' ἀραρόντες *having prepared, contrived*, Od.16.169. III. *fit, equip, furnish* with a thing, νῆ' ἄρσας ἐρέτῃσιν 1.280; καὶ πώμασιν ἄρσον ἅπαντας *fit* all [the jars] with covers, 2.353, cf. A.R.2.1062; καὶ ἤραρε θυμὸν ἐδωδῇ *furnished*, i.e. *satisfied*, his heart with food, Od.5.95:—in Pass., esp. pf. part., *fitted, furnished with*, πύλας ἀρηρεμένας σανίδεσσι A.R.1.787. 2. *please, gratify*, ἐμέ γ' ἁ στονόεσσ' ἄραρεν φρένας S.*El.*147 (lyr.); ἁ Νεμέα ἄραρε Nemea *smiled on* [him], Pi.*N.*5.44. IV. *make fitting* or *pleasing*, ἄρσαντες κατὰ θυμόν (sc. τὸ γέρας), Il.1.136.

B. intr.:—pf. ἄρᾱρα with pres. sense, Ion. and Ep. ἄρηρα, part. ἀρᾱρώς, ἀρηρώς, Hom., Trag., and late Prose (except that X. has προσαραρέναι *HG*4.7.6), Ep. fem. part. ἀρηρυῖα Hes.*Th.*608, and metri gr. ἀρᾰρυῖα Hom., εὖ ἀρᾰρός Opp.*H.*3.367: Ion. and Ep. plpf. ἀρήρειν or ἠρήρειν, with impf. sense, Il.10.265, 12.56, etc.:—Med. only aor. 2 part. sync. ἄρμενος, η, ον, also ος, ον Hes.*Op.*786 (cf. however ἀρημένος): on aor. 2 used intr. v. supr. A.1:—*to be joined closely together*, ἀρηρότες *in close order*, Il.13.800; ἄραρον κόρυθές τε καὶ ἀσπίδες 16.214; ἑξείης ποτὶ τοῖχον ἀρηρότες [πίθοι] *piled close* against the wall, Od.2.342: c. dat. instr., κόλλῃσιν ἀρηρότα Emp.96.4; in Tactics, ἀραρός, τό, = ὀμφαλός (q.v.), Ascl.*Tact.*2.6, etc. 2. abs., *to be fixed*, φρεσὶν ᾖσιν ἀρηρώς Il.10.553; θυμὸς ἀρηρὼς Theoc.25.113; ἄραρε φέγγος *shines for ever*, Pi.*N.*3.64; ἄραρεν ἤδε γ' ὠλένη *is fixed*, A.*Pr.*60: or metaph., θεῶν.. οὐκέτι πίστις ἄραρε E.*Med.*414 (lyr.); ὡς ταῦτ' ἄραρε ib.322; τὸ σόν τ' ἄραρε *is fixed*, ib.745: abs., ἄραρε *it is fixed, my mind is made up*, Id.*Or.*1330, Men.*Epit.*185; τὸ ἀραρὸς ἦθος *steadfastness*, J.*AJ*14.12.3; δόγματα ἀραρότα D.Chr.12.56; also of persons, ἀραρὼς τὴν γνώμην *steadfast*, Plu.*Dio*32; [θεοὶ] ἀραρότες τοῖς κρίμασιν Hierocl.p.48 A.; τοῖς λογισμοῖς ἀ. Id.p.51 A. II. *fit well* or *closely*, ζωστὴρ ἀρηρὼς a *close-fitting* belt, Il.4.134; πύλαι εὖ, στιβαρῶς ἀραρυῖαι, 7.339, 12.454; σανίδες πυκινῶς ἀ. 21.535; *fit* or *be fitted to* a thing, ἔγχος παλάμηφιν ἀρήρει *fitted* the hands, Od.17.4; κόρυθα κροτάφοις ἀραρυῖαν, κνημῖδες ἐπισφυρίοις ἀραρυῖαι, Il.13.188, 19.370; κυνέη ἑκατὸν πολίων πρυλέεσσ' ἀραρυῖα *fitting* a hundred champions, i.e. *large enough for* them, 5.744; also with Preps., κυνέη ἐπὶ κροτάφοις ἀραρυῖα Od.18.378, Hes.*Sc.*137; ὄφρ' ἄν.. δούρατ' ἐν ἁρμονίῃσιν ἀρήρῃ Od.5.361; κεραυνὸς ἐν κράτει ἀ. *fit* emblem in victory, Pi.*O.*10(11).83; ἀνθρώποισιν ἀρηρότα μυθίζεσθαι *befitting* men, Orph.*A.*191. III. *to be fitted, furnished with* a thing, [τάφρος] σκολόπεσσιν ὀξέσιν ἠρήρει Il.12.56; πόλις πύργοις ἀραρυῖα 15.737; ζώνη θυσάνοις ἀραρυῖα 14.181: hence, *furnished, endowed with*, χαρίτεσσιν ἀραρώς Pi.*I.*2.19; ἔθνεα θνητῶν παντοίαις ἰδέῃσιν ἀρηρότα Emp.35.17; κάλλει ἀραρώς E.*El.*948; πολλῇσιν ἐπωνυμίῃσιν ἀρηρώς D.P.28. IV. *to be fitting, agreeable, pleasing*, (cf. ἀρέσκω) once in Hom., ἐνὶ φρεσὶν ἤραρεν ἡμῖν it *fitted* our temper *well*, Od.4.777; ἄκοιτιν ἀρηρυῖαν πραπίδεσσι Hes.*Th.*608. V. syncop. aor. 2 part. Med. ἄρμενος, η, ον (ος, ον Id.*Op.*786), *fitting, fitted* or *suited to* (cf. ἀρμένως), c. dat., ἱστὸν.. καὶ ἐπίκριον ἄρμενον αὐτῷ *fitted* or *fastened to* the mast, Od.5.254 (cf. ἄρμενα, τά); τροχὸν ἄρμενον ἐν παλάμῃσιν Il.18.600; πέλεκυν.. ἐν π. Od.5.234. 2. *fit, meet*, μάλα γάρ νύ οἱ ἄρμενα εἶπεν Hes.*Sc.*116: rarely c. inf., ἡμέρα κούρῃσι γενέσθαι ἄρμενος a day *meet* for girls to be born, Id.*Op.*786. 3. *prepared, ready*, χρήματα δ' εἰν οἴκῳ πάντ' ἄ. ποιήσασθαι ib.407; ἄ. πάντα παρεῖχον Id.*Sc.*84, cf. Thgn.275; ἄ. ἐς τόδε ἔργον A.R.4.1461; ἄ. ἐς πόλεμόν τε καὶ ἐν νήεσσι μάχεσθαι Hermonax 1.3, cf. 8. 4. *agreeable, welcome*, ἄρμενα πράξαις, = εὖ πράξας, Pi.*O.*8.73; ἐν ἀρμένοις θυμὸν αὔξων Id.*N.*3.58; so of men, ἄ. ξείνοισιν Pl.*Epigr.*6. (Cf. Lat. *arma, armus, artus*, Goth. *arms*, etc.)

**ἀρᾱρότως** [ἄρ], (ἀραρίσκω) *compactly, closely, strongly*, A.*Supp.*945, E.*Med.*1192, Pl.*Phdr.*240d, D.Chr.3.79, Iamb.*Protr.*12: Comp. ἀραρότερον (-ώτερον Dind.) Them.*Or.*22.270c.

**ἀράσιμος** [ρᾰ], ον, (ἀράομαι) *accursed*, Suid.

***ἀράσσω**, Att. -ττω [ἄρ], Ion. and poet. impf. ἀράσσεσκον Pi.*P.*4.226: fut. ἀράξω (συν-) Hom., Dor. ἀραξῶ Theoc.2.160: aor. ἤραξα (ἀπ-) Hom., Ep. ἄραξα Hes.*Sc.*461:—Pass., aor. ἠράχθην, Ep. ἀράχθην (συν-) Hom.: fut. Med. in pass. sense, κατ-αράξεσθαι Plu.*Caes.*44:—*smite, dash in pieces*, (Hom. only in compds. ἀπαράσσω, συναράσσω); of any violent impact, with collat. notion of *rattling, clanging*, as of horses, ὁπλαῖς ἀ. χθόνα Pi. l.c.; ἄρασσε (sc. πύλας) *knock at* the door, E.*Hec.*1044; τὴν θύραν Ar.*Ec.*978, cf. Theoc.2.6 (Pass., of the door, *open with a crash*, Luc.*DMeretr.*15.2); *pound* in a mortar, ὅλμῳ ἀ. Nic.*Th.*508; ἀράσσειν στέρνα, κρᾶτα, *beat* the breasts, the head, *in mourning*, A.*Pers.*1054 (lyr.), E.*Tr.*279 (lyr.); ἄρασσε μᾶλλον *strike* harder, A.*Pr.*58; ὄψεις ἀράξας S.*Ant.*52; ἤρασσε βλέφαρα Id.*OT*1276:—in Pass., ὀμμάτων ἀραχθέντων Id.*Ant.*975 (lyr.); also ἀ. πέτροις τινά *strike with* a shower of stones, E.*IT*327:—Pass., πέτροισιν ἠράσσοντο A.*Pers.*460:—ἀ. κιθάρην *strike* the lyre, Orph.*A.*382; ὕμνον, μέλος, etc., Nonn.*D.*1.15,440, etc. 2. c. dat. modi, ἀράσσειν τινὰ ὀνείδεσι, κακοῖς, *assail with* reproaches or threats, S.*Aj.*725, *Ph.*374, cf. ἐξαράσσω. II. Pass., *to be dashed against*, πρὸς τὰς πέτρας Hdt.6.44; πρὸς τὴν γῆν Luc.*Anach.*11; of things, *dash one against the other*, A.R.2.553, Ael.*NA*16.39.—The simple Verb is poetic, used once by Hdt. and in late Prose, v. supr. (Akin to ῥάσσω, Ion. ῥήσσω (q.v.), cf. προσαρασσόμενον· προσρησσόμενον, Hsch.).

**ἀρασύνη**· πύελος, Hsch. **ἀρασχάδες**· τὰ περισινὰ κλήματα, Id.

**Ἀράτειον** [ᾱτ], τό, *shrine dedicated to Aratus*, Paus.2.9.4, Plu.*Arat.*53. ***-ειος**, ὁ, kind of *fig*, Thphr.ap.Ath.3.77a.

**ἀρατειχεύειν**· καταρᾶσθαι, οἱ δὲ στρατεύεσθαι, Hsch.

**ἀρᾱτ-ήριον**, τό, v. ἀρητήριον. **-ικός**, ή, όν, *of, for prayer* or *cursing*: ἀρατικόν, τό, *deprecation*, as a form of proposition, *Stoic.*2.60. ***-ός**, Ion. ἀρητός, ή, όν, (ἀράομαι) *prayed against, accursed*, ἀρητὸν γόος Il.17.37, 24.741; ἀρατὸν ἕλκος S.*Ant.*972 (lyr.). II. *prayed for, desirable*, Sapph.*Supp.*6.3; ἀ. καὶ σωτήριος γνώμη *SIG*656.17 (Abdera): hence Ἄρητος, Ἀρήτη, as pr. nn., *the Prayed-for*, Hom.: later Ἄρατος. [ᾱρ Ep., ᾰρ Att.]

**ἄρατρον**, τό, Cret., = ἄροτρον, *GDI*4992 a ii 5 (Gortyn).

**Ἀράτυος**, ὁ (sc. μήν), name of month in Locris, *SIG*[2]855.

**ἀράχιδνα**, ἡ, *ground-pease, Lathyrus amphicarpos*, Thphr.*HP*1.1.7, 1.6.12.

**ἀραχν-αῖος** [ἄρ], α, ον, *of* or *belonging to a spider*, νήματα *AP*6.206 (Antip. Sid.); *like a spider's web*, μίτος ib.39 (Arch.); ἀραχναίη, = ἀράχνη, ib.9.233 (Eryc.). **-άομαι**, *weave the spider's web*, Eust.285.41. ***-η**, ἡ, = ἀράχνης, ἀράχνης ἐν ὑφάσματι A.*Ag.*1492 (lyr.), cf. *AP*11.110 (Nicarch.); αἱ λειμώνιαι ἀ. Arist.*HA*555[b]7 (elsewh. ἀράχνης, q.v.). II. *spider's web*, Hp.*Cord.*10, S.*Fr.*286, *AP*11.106 (Lucill.). III. ἀ. λεπταί thin *lines*, Gal.*UP*10.12. IV. = σφονδύλιον, Ps.-Dsc.3.76. V. kind of *sundial*, Vitr.9.8.1. **-ήεις**, εσσα, εν, = ἀραχναῖος, Nic.*Th.*733, *Al.*492. **-ηκες**· ἀράχναι, Hsch. **-ης**, ου, ὁ, *spider*, Hes.*Op.*777, Pi.*Fr.*296, A.*Fr.*121, Call.*Com.*2, Arist.*HA*623[a]30, al.; ἀραχνᾶν ἱστοί B.*Fr.*3.7. II. a kind of *pulse*, Hsch. **-ικός**, ή, όν, = ἀραχναῖος, dub. ibid. **-ιον**, τό, *spider's web*, Od.8.280, 16.35, Cratin.190, Pherecr.142, Pl.Com.22, X.*Mem.*3.11.6, Arist.*HA*623[a]30. 2. a *disease* in olive-trees, prob. due to the tent-caterpillar, *Clisiocampa neustria*, Thphr.*HP*4.14.10, *CP*5.10.2. II. Dim. of ἀράχνη, *small spider*, Arist.*HA*555[a]27, 622[b]27. [ᾰρᾰχν Hom., ᾱρᾰχν Com. ll. cc.] ***-ιόω**, *spin a cobweb*, Arist.*HA*605[b]10:—Pass., *to be covered with cobwebs*, ib.625[a]8:—Act. in same sense, Nonn.*D.*38.14. II. *form a venous network over*, ἡ φλὲψ ἠραχνίωκε τοῦ σπληνὸς ἐναίμοισι φλεβίοισι Hp.*Oss.*18. **-ιώδης**, ες, *like a cobweb*, Id.*Dent.*24, Arist.*HA*622[b]12. 2. of liquids, *filled with filaments*, οὖρον Hp.*Coac.*571; γάλα Arist.*HA*583[a]34; ἀραχνιῶδες οὐρεῖν Dsc.4.65.

**ἀραχνοειδής** [ἄρ], ές, *like a cobweb*, of the scum of urine, λιπαρότητες Hp.*Prog.*12; also used of a *feeble* pulse, Gal.19.411; of *capillary* veins, Id.2.808; of nerves, ib.400; ἀπέφυσις -εστάτη ib.366; ἀ. χιτών in Medic., older name for the ἀμφιβληστροειδὴς χ. (q.v.), i.e. the *retina*, Herophil.ap.Cels.7.7.13, Ruf.*Onom.*153; but distinguished from it by Gal.10.47.

**ἄραχνος**, ὁ, = ἀράχνης, A.*Supp.*887.

***ἀραχνοϋφής** [ῠ], ές, *spun as by spiders*, i.e. *fine-spun*, ἀμπεχόναι Ph.1.666, cf. 2.479,637.

**ἀραχνώδης**, ες, = ἀραχνοειδής, Arist.*HA*554[b]28, Ael.*NA*8.16.

***ἄραχος**, ὁ, *wild vetch, Vicia Sibthorpii*, Gal.6.541.

***Ἄραψ**, ὁ, pl. Ἄραβες, οἱ, *Arab*, Str.1.2.34, J.*BJ*1.19.4:—as Adj., Ἄραψ ἀτμός, of incense, *Pae.Delph.*11; θώρηξ Nonn.*D.*36.326: dat. pl. Ἀράβεσσι ib.26.23.

**ἀράω**, *plough*, οὐδὲ τὰς ὁδὼς.. ἀρασόντι *Tab.Heracl.*1.133. (Cf. Lat. *arare.*)

**ἀρβάκις·** ὀλιγάκις, Hsch.

**ἀρβάλη·** τήγανον ὀστράκινον (Tarent.), Hsch.

**ἄρβηλος,** ὁ (Sch.Nic. l. c.), *semicircular knife*, used by cobblers, e. leather-workers (ἄρβηλοι γὰρ τὰ δέρματα Hsch. s. v. ἀνάρβηλα), Nic.*Th.*423. **II.** Geom., *figure resembling it in shape*, contained by three semicircles with coincident diameters, Papp.208.12.

**ἀρβίννη·** κρέας (Sicel), Hsch.; cf. Lat. *arvina*. **ἀρβόν·** διεστός, ἀραιόν, ἐλαφρόν, Id. **ἀρβύκη·** τοῦ ὑποδήματος, Id.

**ἀρβύλη** [ῠ], ἡ, *strong shoe* coming up to the ankle, *half-boot*, used by country people, hunters, travellers, A.*Ag.*944, *Fr.*259, E.*Or.*1470 (lyr.); πηλοπατίδες ἀ. Hp.*Art.*62; αὐταῖσιν ἀρβύλαισιν ἁρμόσας πόδα *with shoes* and all, E.*Hipp.*1189 (wrongly expld. by Eust. as = δίφρος, *the stand of the charioteer*), cf. *Ba.*1134; cf. ἄρμυλα.

**ἀρβῠλικός,** ή, όν, in form of an ἀρβύλη, ὀβελοί *IG*11(2).158*A*6, al. (Delos, iii B. C.).

**ἀρβῠλίς,** ίδος, ἡ, = ἀρβύλη, Theoc.7.26, *APl.*4.306 (Leon.).

**ἀρβῠλόπτερος,** ον, *with winged shoes*, Lyc.839.

**ἀρβύνδα·** λήκυθον (Lacon.), Hsch. (leg. ἀρυβαλλίδα).

**ἀργάδες·** εἶδος φυτοῦ, καὶ ἀργαὶ γυναῖκες, Hsch.

**Ἀργᾰδῆς,** οἱ, name of *one of the four Ionic tribes*, in Attica and elsewh., E.*Ion* 1580, cf. Hdt.5.66, *CIG*3664 (Cyzicus), etc.; also of a χιλιαστύς at Ephesus, *SIG*353.10 (sg.).

**ἀργάεις,** v. ἀργήεις.

**ἀργαίνω,** *to be white*, E.*Fr.*73, Philod.Scarph.126 (prob.), Opp.*C.*3.299:—in Pass., Nonn.*D.*34.145 (s. v. l.).

**ἀργαλεῖον,** τό, later form for ἐργαλεῖον (q. v.).

**ἀργᾰλέος,** α, ον, *painful, troublous*, ἄνεμοι Il.13.795; Ἔρις 11.3; νοῦσος 13.667; Ἄσκρη, χεῖμα κακή, θέρει ἀργαλέη (trisyll.), οὐδέποτ' ἐσθλή Hes.*Op.*640; νύξ Alc.*Supp.*12.11; *difficult* of attainment, ἀληθείη Emp.114.2; κάθοδος Anacr.43.5:—never in Trag., sts. in Com., ἀ. πρᾶγμα Ar.*Pl.*1; στάσις Id.*Th.*788; ἀργαλέας νύκτας ἄγειν Id.*Lys.*764: rare in Prose, πρᾶγμα X.*Hier.*6.4: Comp., Ph.1.224: Sup., Id.2.300. **2.** of persons, *troublesome, vexatious*, Thgn.1208 codd. (ἀρπ- Bgk.); βιότοιο κέλευθοι Emp.115.8, cf. Ar.*Nu.*450, Men.403.5: Sup., Ar.*Eq.*978: rare in Prose, ἀ. τὴν ὄψιν Aeschin.1.61. **II.** ἀργαλέον ἐστί, c. dat. et inf., ἀ. δέ μοί ἐστι διασκοπιᾶσθαι ἕκαστον Il.17.252, cf. 12.410, Od.13.312, etc.: rarely c. acc. et inf., ἀργαλέον δέ με πάντ' ἀγορεῦσαι Il.12.176; or without case, ἀ. δὲ πληκτίζεσθ' ἀλόχοισι Διός 21.498, cf. Od.7.241, etc.; also, **2.** agreeing with the object, ἀ... θεὸς βροτῷ ἀνδρὶ δαμῆναι God is *hard* to be subdued by mortal man, 4.397; ἀ. γὰρ Ὀλύμπιος ἀντιφέρεσθαι Il.1.589. **III.** Adv. -ως *AP*9.499. (By dissimilation from *ἀλγαλέος, cf. ἄλγος.)

**ἀργᾰλεότης,** ητος, ἡ, *grievousness*, Ph.1.346, Eust.892.32.

**ἀργαπέτης,** ου, ὁ, *commandant of a fort*, *IGRom.*3.1043, 1044 (Palmyra, iii A. D.) (Persian word).

**ἀργᾶς,** Dor. contr. for ἀργάεις, v. ἀργήεις.

**Ἀργεῖος,** α, ον, *of* or *from Argos, Argive*: Ἀργεῖοι in Hom., like Ἀχαιοί, for *the Greeks* in general:—ἡ Ἀργεία (sc. γῆ) *Argolis*, Th.2.27, al.; ἀργεῖαι, αἱ, *women's shoes*, Hsch.; ἀργεῖος (sc. βόλος), ὁ, name of a *throw at dice*, Id.

**ἄργειτε,** = ἄγρειτε, Antim.82.

**Ἀργειφόντ-ης,** ου, ὁ, voc. -φόντα *h.Hom.*29.7, Orph.*H.*28.3, Luc.*Tim.*32: (Ἄργος, *φόνος):—*slayer of Argus*, epith. of Hermes, Od.1.38, al., Hes.*Op.*77, etc.: variously expld. by Gramm., cf. Corn.*ND*16. **II.** acc. to Paus.Gr.*Fr.*65, from ἀργής, *serpent-slayer*, i. e. Apollo, S.*Fr.*1024, cf. Sch.A.*Pr.*569; of Telephus, Parth.*Fr.*33. **-ιάδας,** gen. αο, *son of Hermes*, Pancrat.*Oxy.*1085.9.

**Ἀργείωνας·** τοὺς Ἀργείους, Hsch.

**ἄργελλα,** ἡ, *vapour bath* (Maced.), Suid.

**ἀργέλοφοι,** οἱ, *the legs and feet of a sheep-skin*, and so generally, *offal*, Ar.*V.*672.

**ἄργεμον,** τό, *albugo*, a white speck on the eye, S.*Fr.*233, Hp.*Loc.Hom.*13, Thphr.*HP*7.6.2, 9.9.5, Dsc.2.78.2. **II.** = *Lappa canaria, Geum urbanum Avens*, Plin.*HN*24.176:—also **ἄργεμος,** ὁ, = λεύκωμα, Poll.2.65. **2.** *upper part of the finger-nail*, ib.146.

**ἀργεμώνη,** ἡ, *Papaver Argemone, wind-rose*, Crateuas *Fr.*9, Dsc.2.177, Orib.14.60.2, Gal.11.835. **2.** ἀ. ἑτέρα, = ἄργεμον II, Ps.-Dsc.2.178; written *argemonia* by Plin.*HN*25.102.

**ἀργεμώνιον,** τό, = ἀστὴρ Ἀττικός, Plin.*HN*26.92. **II.** = ἀνεμώνη, Dsc.2.176.

**ἀργένναος,** ον, = ἀργεννός, *AP*15.35 (Theoph.).

**ἀργεννός,** ή, όν, Aeol. for ἀργός, *white*, in Hom. almost always of sheep, ἀργεννῇς ὀΐεσσι Il.6.424, etc.; of woollen cloths, ἀργεννῇσι καλυψαμένη ὀθόνῃσι 3.141; later, ἀ. μόσχοι E.*IA*574 (lyr.); κρίνη Chaerem.8, cf. *AP*9.384.11; ὀθόναι ib.5.259 (Paul. Sil.); σέλα ib.9.46 (Antip. Thess.); γαῖα Opp.*H.*1.795.

**ἀργέντινος,** *silvery*, δελματικομαφόρτης *POxy.*1273.12 (iii A. D.):—also **ἀργέντιος,** ib.1310.

**ἀργεστής,** οῦ, ὁ, *clearing, brightening*, epith. of the south wind, Il.11.306, 21.334. **II.** *the north-west wind*, ἀ. Ζέφυρος Hes.*Th.*379, 870, cf. Acus.15 J.; Ἀργέστης, pr. n., Arist.*Mete.*363$^b$24, Thphr.*Sign.*35, D.S.1.39, Plu.*Sert.*8, *AP*9.42 (Jul.). **III.** = ἀργής, *white*, ἀργέσταο λίπευς ἰσόμοιρον ἐλαίου Nic.*Th.*592.

**ἀργέτι, ἀργέτα,** v. ἀργής:—nom. **ἀργέτις,** ἡ, = ἀργήεσσα, Ἠώς Nonn.*D.*16.124; voc. ἀργέτι *AP*5.253 (Paul. Sil.):—also nom. **ἀργέτᾰ** Μήνη Max.587; ἀργέται ἵπποι Orac.ap.Phleg.*Mir.*3.

**ἄργετος,** ὁ, = ἄρκευθος (Cret.), Hsch.

**ἀργεύομαι,** = ἀργέω: metaph. of a woman, Gal.17(1).498.

**ἀργεφάντης,** coined as etym. of ἀργειφόντης, Corn.*ND*16.

**ἀργέω,** fut. -ήσω: aor. ἤργησα *BGU*698.4 (ii A. D.): pf. ἤργηκα *POxy.*1160.14 (iii/iv A. D.): (ἀργός, ἀεργός):—*to be unemployed, do nothing*, Hp.*Mochl.*23, E.*Ph.*625, X.*Cyr.*1.2.15, Pl.*R.*426a, etc.; *keep Sabbath*, Lxx 2*Ma.*5.25; ἀ. τὴν ἑβδόμην J.*BJ*7.3.3; οἱ ἀργοῦντες *the idle*, *Trag.Adesp.*527; γῆ ἀργοῦσα *lying fallow*, X.*Cyr.*1.6.11, *PFlor.*262.9 (iii A. D.); ἀργῆσαν ἤμυσε στέγος S.*Fr.*864; φησὶν ἀργῆσαι τὸ ἐργαστήριον *is out of work*, D.27.19; of the senses, *to be at rest*, νυκτὸς τῆς ὄψεως ἀργούσης Arist.*Pr.*903$^a$21, cf. *Somn.Vig.*455$^a$30: c. gen. rei, ἀργήσει.. τῆς αὐτοῦ δημιουργίας *will be unoccupied in* his own work, Pl.*R.*371c. **II.** Pass., *to be left undone*, X.*Cyr.*2.3.3; *to be fruitless*, ἡ σκέψις ἂν ἀργοῖτο Id.*Hier.*9.9.

**ἀργεώτας,** ὁ, title of Apollo in Messenia, Paus.4.34.7.

**ἀργήεις,** εσσα, εν: Dor. **ἀργάεις,** contr. **ἀργᾶς,** gen. ᾶντος: (v. ἀργός):—*white, shining*, ταῦρον ἀργᾶντα Pi.*O.*13.69; ἐν ἀργάεντι (v. l. ἀργινόεντι) μαστῷ Id.*P.*4.8; οἰωνός.. ἔξοπιν ἀργᾶς, = πύγαργος, prob. in A.*Ag.*115 (lyr.). **2.** = ἀργεστής, ἀργήεσσιν ἀέλλαις Orph.*A.*128, cf. 685.

**ἀργής,** ῆτος, ὁ, ἡ, Ep. dat. and acc. ἀργέτι, ἀργέτα (v. infr.), gen. ἀργέος Nic.*Al.*305, and v. l. *Th.*856:—*bright, glancing*, mostly of *vivid* lightning, κεραυνός Il.8.133, Od.5.128, al., Ar.*Av.*1747; opp. ψολόεις κεραυνός, Arist.*Mete.*371$^a$20; Ζεὺς ἀργής, i. e. *fire*, Emp.6.2; ἀργέτι αὐγῇ Id.21.4; φύσις Orph.*H.*10.10. **2.** *shining, white*, of fat, ἀργέτι δημῷ Il.11.818; ἀργέτα δημόν 21.127; of a robe, ἑανῷ ἀργῆτι φαεινῷ 3.419; ἀργῆτι μαλλῷ A.*Eu.*45, cf. S.*Tr.*675; ἀργὴς Κολωνός because of its *chalky* soil, Id.*OC*670 (lyr.): neut., ἀργῆτος ἐλαίου Nic.*Th.*105; ἀργῆτα κέλευθα Opp.*C.*2.140.—Poet. word, cf. Arist. l. c.

**ἀργής,** Dor. **ἀργᾶς** (ἄργας *AB*442), ὁ, a kind of *serpent*, Achae.1, *Trag.Adesp.*199; ὄφις ἀργής Hp.*Epid.*5.86: also an obscure nickname of Demosthenes, Aeschin.2.99, Plu.*Dem.*4.

**ἀργηστής,** οῦ, ὁ, = ἀργής, *glancing, flashing*, πτηνὸς ἀ. ὄφις, of an arrow, A.*Eu.*181. **2.** *white*, ἀφρός Id.*Th.*60; κύκνοι Theoc.25.131.

**ἀργία,** ἡ, = ἀεργία, *want of employment*, πεσσοὺς κύβους τε, τερπνὸν ἀργίας ἄκος S.*Fr.*479.4; νεύρων καὶ ἄρθρων Hp.*Mochl.*23; τοῦ καλοῦ Hierocl. *in CA* 19 p.461 M.; ψυχῆς ἀργίη Democr.212; *idleness, laziness*, E.*HF*592; νόμος περὶ τῆς ἀργίας against those who *would not work*, D.57.32; γραφὴ ἀργίας *AB*310, cf. Plu.*Sol.*17, 31: in pl., Isoc.7.44. **b.** *quietism*, E.*Med.*296. **2.** in good sense, *rest, leisure*, τῶν οἰκείων ἔργων *from*.., Pl.*Lg.*761a (pl.), Lxx *Wi.*13.13, etc. **3.** in pl., *holidays*, Arr.*Epict.*4.8.33, = *feriae* or *justitium*, App.*BC*1.56, *PPetr.*3: sg., of the Sabbath, Lxx *Is.*1.14. **4.** *lapse of cultivation*, Thphr.*CP*4.5.6.

**ἀργῐ-βόειος,** ον, *with white kine*, of Euboea, Poet.ap.Ael.*NA*12.36 (ἀργίβοιος Lobeck). **-βρέντας,** ὁ, (βρέμω, βροντή) = sq., Pi.(?)*Oxy.*1792; cf. ἀναξιβρέντας. **-κέραυνος,** ον, *with bright, vivid lightning*, epith. of Zeus, Il.19.121, al., Orph.*Fr.*21a, 168, Pi.*O.*8.3, Cleanth.*Stoic.*1.122. **-κερως,** ὁ, ἡ, *white-horned*, αἶγες Orac.ap.D.S.7 *Fr.*16.

**ἀργικός,** ή, όν, = ἀργός (B), θάκοις ἀ. καθήμενοι E.*IT*795 codd. Stob.

**ἀργῐλίπης,** ές, Archil.160:—and **ἀργίλιψ,** ιπος, Nic.*Th.*213 (of serpents), *white*.

**ἄργιλλα** or **ἄργιλα,** ἡ, *underground dwelling*, so called in Magna Graecia, Ephor.45, Eust. ad D.P.1166; cf. ἄργελλα. **II.** = ἄργιλλος, Gal.12.438, 19.90.

**ἀργίλληψιν·** γῆ μὴ βλαστάνουσά τι, Hsch.

**ἄργιλλος** or **ἄργῑλος** (so Ἐφ.Ἀρχ.1893.31 (Acarn.)), ἡ, (ἀργός A) *white clay, potter's earth*, Arist.*Pr.*890$^a$26, Thphr.*CP*3.20.3, Opp.*H.*4.658.

**ἀργιλλοφόρητος** γῆ, dub. sens. in *PTeb.*702.

**ἀργιλλώδης** or **ἀργῑλώδης,** ες, *clayey*, ἀργιλωδεστέρην γῆν Hdt.2.12, cf. Arist.*Mete.*352$^b$10, Thphr.*HP*3.18.5, Antyll.ap.Orib.9.11.4; ὄχθαι Euph.11 (= Archyt.Amph.2).

**ἀργιλόεις,** = ἀργινόεις, Eust. ad D.P.1166.

**ἀργί-λοφος** [ῐ], *white-crested*, κολώνα Pi.*Fr.*200. **-μήτας,** ὁ, (*quick-witted*, acc. to Hsch.) epith. of bull which carried Europa, Phryn.Trag.16. **-νεφής,** ές, *clouded with white*, ὀπός S.*Fr.*534.2 (anap.).

**ἀργῐνόεις,** εσσα, εν, = ἀργός, *bright-shining, white*, epith. of Lycastus and Camirus, from their lying on *chalky* hills, Il.2.647, 656; νῆσοι Ἀργινοῦσαι X.*HG*1.6.27; of milk, *AP*7.23 (Antip. Sid.); χαλινά A.R.4.1607; μαστός, v. l. for ἀργάεις (q. v.), Pi.*P.*4.8.

**ἀργῐ-όδους,** όδοντος, ὁ, ἡ, *white-toothed, white-tusked*, λευκοὶ ὀδόντες ἀργιόδοντος ὑός Il.10.264, cf. Od.8.60, etc.; κύνες Il.11.292:—also **-όδων,** A.R.2.820.

**ἄργιον,** = ἀδίαντον, Ps.-Dsc.4.134. **ἀργιόπους·** ἀετός (Maced.), Hsch. **ἄργιος·** λευκός, ταχύς, Id.

**ἀργῐ-πόδης,** ου, Dor. **-ας,** ὁ, = sq., χίμαρος *AP*6.299 (Phan.). **-πους,** ὁ, ἡ, -πουν, τό, gen. ποδος, *swift-footed*, ἀργίποδας κύνας Il.24.211; of rams, S.*Aj.*237 (lyr.) (= λευκόποδας, Sch.); = ἀετός (Maced.), Hsch.

**ἀργίς,** ίδος, ἡ, = νύξ (διὰ τὴν ἀνάπαυσιν), Orph.*Fr.*33.

**ἀργῖτις** (sc. ἄμπελος), ιδος, ἡ, vine with *white* grapes, Virg.*G.*2.99, Plin.*HN*14.35, Isid.*Etym.*17.5.23.

**ἄργμα,** ατος, τό, (ἄρχω) only in pl. ἄργματα, = ἀπάργματα, *firstlings* at a sacrifice or feast, Od.14.446.

**ἀργό-βῐος,** ον, *sedentary*, Archig.ap.Aët.13.120. **-θάνᾰτος** [θᾰ], ον, *slow of dying*, Sch.Opp.*H.*1.142.

**Ἀργόθεν,** Adv. *from Argos*, S.*Ant.*106 (lyr.), E.*IT*70, *Heracl.*775 (lyr.).

**ἀργόθριξ,** τρῐχος, ὁ, ἡ, τό, *white-haired*, Archim.*Bov.*9.

**ἀργόλας,** α, ὁ, a kind of *serpent*, Suid.; cf. ἀργής. **II.** v. Ἄργος.

**'Αργολ-ίζω,** *take the part of the Argives,* X.*HG*4.8.34, Ephor. 137. **-ίς** (sc. γῆ), ἴδος, ἡ, *Argolis,* Hdt., etc. 2. as Adj., ὁ, ἡ, *of Argolis, Argolic,* ἐσθής A.*Supp.*236:—later ⊛**Ἀργολικός,** ή, όν, Plu. *Rom.*21. Adv. -κῶς Eust.722.63.

**'Αργολιστί,** Adv. *in Argive fashion,* S.*Fr.*462.

⊛**ἀργομέτωπος,** ον, *with rough-hewn faces,* λίθοι Ph.*Bel.*82.5.

**'Αργοναύτης,** ου, ὁ, *a sailor in the ship Argo, an Argonaut,* Arist. *Pol.*1284$^a$23, etc.; Ἀπολλώνιος ὁ τοὺς Ἀργοναύτας ποιήσας Str.14.2.13.

**ἀργο-ποιός,** όν, *making idle,* Plu.*Num.*22. **-πρακτος,** ον, *slothful,* Paul.Al.*N.*4.

⊛**Ἄργος,** εος, τό, name of several Greek cities, Ἄ. Ἀχαιϊκόν Il.9.141; Ἄ. Πελασγικόν 2.681, etc.; ἄργος = πεδίον acc. to Str.8.6.9, cf. Dionys. Epic.ap.St.Byz. s.v. Δώτιον, Call.*Fr.*45:—hence Adjs. Ἀργεῖος, Ἀργολίς, Ἀργολικός, qq. v.: **Ἀργόλας,** ὁ, E.*Rh.*41 (lyr.), Ar.*Fr.*298.

**ἀργός** (A), ή, όν, *shining, glistening,* of a goose, Od.15.161; of a sleek, well-fed ox, Il.23.30; in Hom. mostly in the phrase πόδας ἀργοί, of hounds, *swift-footed,* because all swift motion causes a kind of glancing or flickering light, 18.578, Od.2.11, etc.; κύνες ἀργοί Il. 1.50, 18.283, cf. D.S.4.41, Corn.*ND*16. 2. *white,* Arist.*Top.*149$^a$ 7. II. parox. as pr. n., Ἄργος, ὁ, name of a dog, *Swift-foot,* Od. 17.292: also of the herdsman *Argus* (i. e. *bright-eyed,* A.*Pr.*567 (lyr.), *Supp.*305) who was so called from his eyes being ever open and *bright.* (By dissimilation from *ἀργρός, cf. Skt. *ṛjrá-,* = (1) *shining,* (2) *swift,* Vedic pr. n. *Ṛji-śvan-,* lit. = *possessing* κύνες ἀργοί.)

⊛**ἀργός** (B), όν, later ή, όν Arist.*EN*1167$^a$11, *Mete.*352$^a$13, Thphr. *Lap.*27, Ath.Mech.12.11, etc.: (contr. from ἀεργός):—prop. *not working the ground,* Hdt.5.6; *idle, lazy,* opp. ἐργάτις, S.*Ph.*97, cf. Ar. *Nu.*53, etc.; γαστέρες ἀ. Epimenid.1; ἀ. ἐπιθυμίαι Pl.*R.*572e; ἀ. τὴν διάνοιαν ib.458a; τὸ πρὸς ἅπαν ξυνετὸν ἐπὶ πᾶν ἀ. Th.3.82; ἂν ἀ. ᾖ if he have *no trade,* Antiph.123.3; πότερον ἀνθρώπου οὐδὲν ἐστιν [ἔργον] ἀλλ' ἀργὸν πέφυκεν; Arist.*EN*1097$^b$30: c. gen. rei, *idle at* a thing, *free from* it, τῶν οἴκοθεν *from* domestic toils, E.*IA*1000; πόνων σφοδρῶν Pl.*Lg.*835d; γυναῖκας ἀργοὺς ταλασίας ib.806a; ἀ. αἰσχρῶν *slow to* evil, A.*Th.*411; ἀργότεραι ἐς τὸ δρᾶν τι Th.7.67; ἀ. περί τι Pl.*Lg.* 966d. 2. of things, δόρυ E.*Ph.*1387; of money, *lying idle, yielding no return,* opp. ἐνεργός, D.27.7 and 20; of land, *lying fallow,* Isoc.4. 132, X.*Cyr.*3.2.19, Thphr.*HP*9.12.2; opp. πεφυτευμένος, *IG*7.2226*B* (Thisbe, iii A.D.); διατριβὴ ἀ. *in which nothing is done, fruitless,* Ar. *Ra.*1498 (lyr.), Isoc.4.44; χρόνον ἀργὸν διάγειν Plu.*Cor.*31. Adv. ἀργῶς, ἐπιμέλεσθαι X.*Mem.*2.4.7; ἔχειν D.6.3: Comp. and Sup. ἀργότερον, -ότατα, X.*Oec.*15.6 and 1. b. ἀ. λόγος, name of a *sophism,* Chrysipp.*Stoic.*2.277, cf. Plu.2.574e. II. Pass., *unwrought,* ἁρμός, κυμάτιον, *IG*1.322*b*23,59; πυροὶ ἀ. *unprepared for eating,* Hp.*VM*13; ἄργυρος Paus.3.12.3; βύρσαι *undressed* hides, Ath.Mech. l. c.; *unpolished,* Thphr.*Lap.*27. 2. *not done, left undone,* κοὐκ ἦν ἔτ' οὐδὲν ἀ. S.*OC*1605; ἓν δ' ἐστὶν ἡμῖν ἀ. E.*Ph.*766; οὐκ ἐν ἀργοῖς not among *things neglected,* S.*OT*287; τὰ μὲν προβέβηκεν ἀμήχανόν ἐστι γενέσθαι ἀργά Thgn.584. 3. *unattempted,* μάχη Pl.*Euthd.*272a. 4. Astrol., τόπος ἀ., name of the 8th of the 12 'houses', Ptol.*Tetr.*128, Paul.Al.*M.*4; πλανήτης Plot.2.3.3; ζῴδιον S.E.*M.*5.15.

**ἀργῠρ-άγχη,** ἡ, (formed after κυνάγχη) *silver-quinsy,* which Demosthenes was said to have, when he abstained from speaking on the plea of quinsy, but really because he was bribed, Demad.*Fr.*5S., Plu.*Dem.*25. ⊛**-ᾰμοιβικός,** ή, όν, *of or for a money-changer*: ἡ -κή (sc. τέχνη), Poll.7.170; personified, Luc.*Bis Acc.*13,24. Adv. -κῶς Id.*Hist.Conscr.*10. ⊛**-ᾰμοιβός,** ὁ, *money-changer, banker,* Pl.*Plt.* 289e, Theoc.12.37, etc.: as Adj., ἀ. τιμή Maiist.32. **-άνθρωπος,** ὁ, *'silver-man',* symbol in alchemy, Zos.Alch.p.112B. **-ἄσπῐδες,** οἱ, *the silver-shielded,* a corps in the army of Alexander, D.S.17.57, Arr.*An.*7.11.3, Ath.12.539e, etc.; also in the armies of the Diadochi, Plb.5.79.4, etc. ⊛**-άφιον** [ᾰ], τό, Dim. of ἄργυρος, Theognost. *Can.*126.34, *AB*1339. **-ειος,** ον, = ἀργύρεος, ἀργύρεια μέταλλα *silver-mines,* Th.2.55, 6.91; τὰ ἀ. ἔργα X.*Vect.*4.5; τὰ ἔργα τὰ ἀ. D.21.167; τὰ ἀ. alone, X.*Mem.*2.5.2, Aeschin.1.101, Pl.*Lg.*742d. **-ένδετος,** ον, *overlaid with silver,* κύλικες *IG*11(2).161*B*79 (Delos, iii B.C.).

⊛**ἀργύρεος** [ῠ], α, ον, contr. **ἀργῠροῦς,** ᾶ, οῦν: *of silver,* of the bow of Apollo, Il.1.49, cf. Pi.*O.*9.32; κρητήρ Il.23.741, Od.4.615, cf. A.*Fr.* 184; τάλαρον Od.4.125; λάρναξ Il.18.412; ἀσάμινθοι Od.4.128, etc.; γένος Hes.*Op.*144, etc.; ἀ. πλοῦτος Pl.*Lg.*801d. 2. *silver-plated,* κλῖναι Hdt.9.82. II. as Subst., ἀργυροῦς, ὁ, *silver coin,* Lxx*Za.* 11.12, al., *SIG*731.20 (Tomi, i B.C.), Hero *Mens.*60.1, al.

**ἀργῠρ-ευτική,** ἡ, *silversmith's art,* Eustr. in *EN*296.10. **-εύω,** *dig for silver,* D.S.5.36, Str.3.2.9. **-ηλάτης** [ᾰτ], ου, ὁ, *silversmith,* Hsch. **-ήλᾰτος,** ον, *of wrought silver,* A.*Fr.*185; φιάλαι E.*Ion* 1181; *bearing silver,* πρὼν [Παγγαίου] A.*Fr.*25A. **-ηρός,** ά, όν, = ἀργυρικός, ἔρανος *IG*2.621.14. **-ίδιον** [ρῐ], τό, = ἀργύριον, generally (but not always, cf. Alciphr.3.38) in a contemptuous sense, Ar. *Pl.*147, *Fr.*547, Eup.113; ἀ. καὶ χρυσίδιον τὸν πλοῦτον ἀποκαλοῦντες Isoc.13.4, cf. Socr.*Ep.*36, Olymp. in *Grg.* p.275 J. ⊛**-ίζομαι,** Med., *get or extort money,* πάντοθεν Din.1.40, cf. *OGI*669.52 (Egypt, i A.D.); ἀργυρισάμενοι *for a bribe, Sammelb.*4416.19 (ii A.D.): τινά *from* one, J.*AJ*14.14.6. **-ικός,** ή, όν, *of, for,* or *in money*: φόρος *cash* rental, *AJA*16.13 (Sardes, iv B.C.); ἀργυρικά, τά, *taxes paid in money,* ἀργυρικῶν πράκτωρ, πρακτορεία, *BGU*15 i 13 (ii A.D.), *PLond.*2.306 (ii A.D.); ζημίαι ἀ. *IG*2$^2$.1028.81 (i B.C.), cf. D.S.12.21, Plu.*Sol.*23; τέλος Str.11.13.8, cf. *PRyl.*133.16 (i A.D.), etc. Adv. ἀργυρικῶς ἢ σωματικῶς κολασθήσονται *OGI*664.17 (Egypt, i A.D.).

⊛**ἀργύριον** [ῠ], τό, *small coin, piece of money,* Ar.*Fr.*262, X.*Oec.*19. 16, etc.: pl. (v. Poll.9.89), Ar.*Av.*600, Eup.155, X. l. c.: then, 2. collectively, *money,* Ar.*Pl.*156, 158, al.; ἀ. ῥητόν a fixed *sum,* Th. 70; εἰς ἀ. λογισθέντα calculated in *our money,* X.*Cyr.*3.1.33; καθαρόν 'hard *cash*', Theoc.15.36: in Com. with Art., τἀργύριον *money, the cash,* δανείζεσθαι Ar.*Nu.*756; ἀπαιτεῖν ib.1247; καταθεν... Antiph.124.14, etc.; so τὰ. καταβάλλειν Th.1.27, etc. II. = ἄργυρος, *silver,* πεντηκοσίας μνέας ἀργυρίου Hdt.3.13; ἀ. ἐπίσημον an... ἄσημον Th.2.13; χρυσίον καὶ ἀ. Pl.*Alc.*1.122e; ἀργυρίου ἄνθος *lead oxide,* Hp.*Nat.Mul.*33.

⊛**ἀργύριος** [ῠ], name of a *plant,* Hsch.; cf. ἄργυρος III. II. Aeol. = ἀργύρεος, πρόσωπον Alcm.23.55.

**ἀργῠρ-ίς,** ίδος, ἡ, *silver cup* or *vessel,* Pi.*O.*9.90, Pherecr.129, *IG* 1.127.16, *SIG*$^2$588.142 (Delos, ii B.C.), Ath.11.502a. 2. *plate* in general, πίνειν ἐξ ἀργυρίδων χρυσῶν Anaxil.40. II. = δραχμή, Heraclid.Lemb.5. **-ισμός,** ὁ, *getting money,* Str.7.3.7, Ph.1.145, al., D.C.59.15; ἀργυρισμοῦ πρόφασιν *OGI*669.37 (Egypt, i A.D.); ἐπ' ἀργυρισμῷ *Sammelb.*4416.11 (ii A.D.). **-ίτης,** ου, ὁ, fem. **-ῖτις,** ιδος, ἡ, *of* or *belonging to silver,* γῆ *containing silver-ore,* Posidon. 48, cf. Gal.12.184; ψάμμος Dsc.5.94; βῶλος Plb.34.9.10; more freq. ἀργυρῖτις, ἡ, as Subst., *silver-ore,* φλὲψ ἀργυρίτιδος X.*Vect.*1.5, cf. 4.4; κατεργασάμενος τὴν ἀ. Docum.ap.D.37.28; also a form of λιθάργυρος, Dsc.5.87. II. *of* or *for money,* ἀγὼν ἀργυρίτης a contest *in which the prize was money* (cf. στεφανίτης, Plu.2.820d, Lync. ap.Ath.13.584c. 2. *a moneyed man, AB*442. 3. fem. -ῖτις, = λινόζωστις ἄρρην, Ps.-Dsc.4.189.

**ἀργῠρό-βῐος,** ον, (βιός) *with the silver bow,* Eust.41.11. **-γνωμονικός,** ή, όν, *skilled in assaying silver,* Arr.*Epict.*2.3.2. **-γνώμων,** ονος, ὁ, ἡ, *assayer of silver,* Pl.*Virt.*378e, Arist.*Rh.*1375$^b$5, Plu.*Crass.* 2, Max.Tyr.2.2, etc. **-γρᾰφία,** ἡ, *writing in silver letters, PLeid.X.* 78. **-δάμας** [δᾰ], αντος, ὁ, name of a *precious stone,* Plin.37. 144. **-δίνης** [ῑ], ου, Dor. **-δίνας,** α, ὁ, (δίνη) *silver eddying,* epith. of rivers, Il.2.753, 21.8, 130, Hes.*Th.*340, B.7.48, Call.*Cer.*13, *Epic.Alex. Adesp.*5, Nonn.*D.*19.304; late Prose, Philostr.*VS*2.1.14. **-ειδής,** ές, *like silver, silvery,* δῖναι E.*IA*752 (lyr.), *Ion*95 (anap.); ὕδωρ Orph.*A.* 599; ἀργυροειδεῖ (prob. for ἀργυροδινεῖ) χαλκῷ Tryph.98; of the pupils in disease, Hp.*Prorrh.*2.20. **-εις,** εσσα, εν, = ἀργύρεος, Epigr.ap. Zonar.13.13, v.l. in Nic.*Al.*54. **-ηλος,** ον, *silver-studded,* ξίφος Il.2.45; θρόνος Od.7.162, etc. **-θήκη,** ἡ, *money-chest,* Diocl.Com. 1 D., Antiph.157, Thphr.*Char.*10.14, Poll.4.19. **-θρονος,** ον, *silver-throned,* Ἥρα Him.*Or.*1.20 (Sapph.133). **-θώραξ,** ᾶκος, ὁ, *with a silver breastplate,* Iamb. post Polem. p.49 Hinck. ⊛**-κοπεῖον,** τό, *silversmith's shop, mint,* Antipho *Fr.*36, And.*Fr.*5, Aeschin.Socr.39, Arist.*Pr.*936$^b$26, Plb.26.1.2:—also **-κόπιον,** *IG*2$^2$.1013.30, 12(5). 480. **-κοπέω,** *coin money,* Lxx *Je.*6.29. **-κοπία,** ἡ, *minting, coinage, SIG*253*U* (Delph., iv B.C.). **-κοπιστήρ,** ῆρος, ὁ, *coiner,* metaph., λόγων Cratin.226; *money-changer,* Hsch. ⊛**-κόπος,** ὁ, (κόπτω) *coiner,* Phryn.Com.5. II. *silversmith,* Plu.2.830e, *SIG* 1263 (Smyrna), Poll.7.102,103, Lxx *Jd.*17.4, *Act.Ap.*19.24, *PHaw.* 68.3 (i A.D.). **-κορίνθιος,** *of Corinthian silver, cratera CIL*6.302 (ii A.D.). **-κυκλος,** ον, *silver-wheeled,* Nonn.*D.*18.10. ⊛**-λογέω,** *levy money,* X.*HG*1.1.12: c. acc., *levy money upon, lay under contribution,* τὰ τῶν ξυμμάχων Th.8.3, cf. 2.69; τοὺς Ἕλληνας Aeschin. 3.159, etc.; ἀ. ἐκ πόλεων X.*HG*4.8.30; παρά τινος Them.*Or.*23. 289d. **-λόγητος,** ον, *subject to a levy in money,* Lxx 2*Ma.*11. 3. **-λογία,** ἡ, *levying of money,* X.*HG*1.1.8, etc. ⊛**-λόγος,** ον, (λέγω) *levying money,* ναῦς Ar.*Eq.*1071, Th.3.19, etc. **-μῑγής,** ές, *mixed with silver,* γῆ Str.3.2.9 codd. ⊛**-παστος,** ον, *silver-broidered,* ὅπλα Polyaen.4.16. **-πεζα,** ἡ, *silver-footed* (or *-sandalled*), epith. of Thetis, Il.1.538, al.; of Aphrodite, Pi.*P.*9.9, cf. Orph.*Fr.* 275; of Artemis, Nonn.*D.*34.47:—hence Adj. **-πεζος,** ον, *AP*5.59 (Rufin.). **-πηχυς,** υ, *silver-armed,* Nonn.*D.*42.419. **-ποιΐα,** ἡ, *production of silver,* in Alchemy, Ps.-Democr.Alch.p.49B. **-ποιός,** ὁ, *worker in silver, AP*14.50. **-πους,** ὁ, ἡ, πουν, τό, gen. ποδος, *with silver feet* or *legs,* κλίνη X.*An.*4.4.21; δίφρος *IG*2.646, D.24.129; φορεῖα Plb.30.25.18. ⊛**-πράτης** [ᾰ], ου, ὁ, *money-dealer, PSI*1.76. 2 (vi A.D.):—hence ⊛**-ᾱτικός,** ή, όν, Just.*Nov.*136. **-πρυμνον** (sc. πλοῖον), τό, *vessel with silver-plated stern-post, PSI*6.551.1 (iii B.C.). **-ριζος,** ον, (ῥίζα) *with silver root,* παγαὶ Ταρτησσοῦ ἀ., i. e. *having silver in the soil,* Stesich.5. ⊛**-ρρῠτος,** ον, (ῥέω) *beside a silver stream,* ὄχθαι Ἕβρου E.*HF*386 (lyr.).

⊛**ἀργῠρορύχη,** ἡ, (prob. for -υχή) in pl., *silver-mines, Mon.Ant.*23. 8 (Adalia).

⊛**ἄργῠρος,** ὁ, (ἀργός A) *white metal,* i. e. *silver,* ἐξ Ἀλύβης ὅθεν ἀργύρου ἐστὶ γενέθλη Il.2.857; so πηγὴ ἀργύρου A.*Pers.*238, etc.; ἀ. κοῖλος *silver plate,* Theopomp.Hist.283a, Arist.*Oec.*1350$^b$23, etc. 2. ἀ. χυτός *quicksilver,* Id. *de An.*406$^b$19, *Mete.*385$^b$4, Thphr.*Lap.*60. II. = ἀργύριον, *silver-money,* generally, *money,* A.*Supp.*935; ἐπ' ἀργύρῳ γε τὴν ψυχὴν προδοὺς S.*Ant.*322; εἴ τι μὴ ξὺν ἀργύρῳ ἐπράσσετ' by *bribery,* Id.*OT*124; in later Prose, coupled with χρυσός, *Ev.Matt.* 10.9, Alciphr.2.3. III. = λινόζωστις ἄρρην, Ps.-Dsc.4.189.

**ἀργῠρο-σκόπος,** ὁ, ἡ, = ἀργυρογνώμων, *IG*5(1).1390.48 (Andania, i B.C.), Phryn.*PS*p.30B. **-στερής,** ές, (στερέω) *robbing of silver,* βίος ἀ. *a robber's life,* A.*Ch.*1002. **-τᾰμεία** (for -ταμιεία), ἡ, *office of* ἀργυροταμίας, *CIG*2787, 2817 (Aphrodisias). ⊛**-τᾰμίας,** ου, ὁ, *treasurer of a city, IG*2$^2$.1100, *IGRom.*4.774, 775 (Apamea), etc.: of a club, *PLond.* 3.1178.74 (ii A.D.). **-τᾰμιευτικός,** ή, όν, *controlled by the treasurer,* χρήματα *IG*9(1).144 (Elatea, ii A.D.). **-τᾰμιεύω,** *hold office of* ἀργυροταμίας, *IGRom.*4.785 (Apamea), *IG*12(9).20.7 (Carystus). **-τέχνης,** ου, ὁ, *silversmith, Jahresh.*1 *Beibl.*107. **-τοιχος,** ον, *with silver sides,* δροίτη A.*Ag.*1539 (lyr.). ⊛**-τοξος,** ον, *with silver bow,* Homeric epith. of Apollo, Il.2.766, al.; also simply Ἀργυρότοξος *bearer of the silver bow*, ib.1.37. **-τράπεζα** [ρᾰ], ἡ, *bank*, Just.*Edict*.9.2.1. **-τρύφημα** [ῠ], ατος, τό, a sort of *blanc-mange*, Chrysipp.Tyan.ap.Ath. 14.647d, prob. in Gal.6.811. **-φάλᾰρος** [φᾰ], ον, *with silver trappings*, ἱππεῖς Plb.30.25.6. **-φεγγής**, ές, *silver-shining*, δίφρος Nonn. *D*.4.24; λιμός, of a poor dinner served on *silver* plate, *AP*11.313 (Lucill.). **-φλεψ**, φλεβος, ὁ, ἡ, *with veins of silver ore*, Sch.Pl.*Ti*. 25b. **-χάλῑνος** [ᾰ], ον, *with silver-mounted bridle*, ζεῦγος Philostr. *VS*1.25.2. **-χαλκος**, ὁ, *silver-copper alloy*, Maria ap.Zos.Alch. p.169B. ⊛**-χόος**, ὁ, (χέω) *melter of, worker in, silver*, Lxx *Wi*.15. 9. **-χροος**, ον, *silver-coloured*, Tz.*H*.11.483.

⊛**ἀργῠρόω**, *to cover with silver*, ὀστέον *Dialex*.2.13; βωμόν *IG*3.899.4: —Pass., *to be silvered, silver-plated*, ῥύπος ἠργυρωμένος Men.*Mon*.469; ἀργυρούμενα ἢ ἐνηργυρωμένα σκεύη Timae.Astr. in *Cat.Cod.Astr*.1.97. 4. II. metaph. of persons, ἀργυρωθέντες σὺν οἰνηραῖς φιάλαις *rewarded with silver* wine-cups, Pi.*N*.10.43; also ἀοιδαὶ ἀργυρωθεῖσαι πρόσωπα songs *with silvered* brow, i.e. *mercenary*, Id.*I*.2.8.

**ἀργῠρ-ώδης**, ες, *rich in silver*, τόπος X.*Vect*.4.3. **-ωμα**, ατος, τό, *silver plate*, mostly in pl., Lys.*Fr*.56, Antiph.243.3, Men.475, Plb.5. 2.10, etc.: dat. pl. -ωμάτοις *IG*14.427ii 15 (Tauromenium). II. *imitation silver*, an alloy of tin, copper, and silver, *PHolm*.1. 35. ⊛**-ωματικὴ γῆ** earth *for making moulds for silver reliefs*, *BMus. Inscr*.481*,542,549 (Ephesus, ii A.D.). ⊛**-ωμάτιον**, τό, Dim. of ἀργύρωμα, Arr.*Epict*.3.26.36. **-ώνητος**, ον, *bought with silver*, θεράποντες Hdt.4.72; ὑφαὶ A.*Ag*.949; ὁ ἀ., i.e. *slave*, Isoc.14.18; ἀ. σέθεν E.*Alc*.676; ἀ. ἄμπελος *PAvrom*.1*A* 16 (i B.C.), cf. *PLond*.2.198 (ii A.D.). **-ωρῠχεῖον**, τό, *silver-mine*, Sch.Aeschin.1.100. **-ωταί**, οἱ, name of a *board of officials*, *GDI*1267.16 (Sillyon).

**ἀργ-ύφεος** [ῠ], η, ον, Ep. Adj. *silver-shining, silver-white*, σπέος Il.18. 50; φᾶρος Od.5.230; ἐσθής Hes.*Th*.574; νάματα *AP*9.633 (Damoch.); ᾠεόν Orph.*Fr*.70, cf. *Mus.Belg*.16.71 (Athens, ii A.D.), Epic. in *POxy*. 421.6. **-ῠφος**, ον, = foreg., epith. of sheep, Il.24.621, Od.10.85.

**Ἀργώ**, όος, contr. οῦς, ἡ, (ἀργός, ή, όν) *Argo*, the ship in which Jason sailed to Colchis, *the Swift*, first in Od.12.70:—Adj. **Ἀργῷος**, α, ον, *of the Argo*, δόρυ, σκάφος, E.*Andr*.793 (lyr.), *Med*.477. 2. the constellation *Argo*, Eudox.ap.Hipparch.1.2.20, Arat.342, etc. 3. tree of whose timber the *Argo* was built, Hsch.

**ἀργώδης**, ες, *lazy*, Aesop.413.

**ἀργωπός**, όν, *white*, Nic.*Fr*.74.19.

**ἄρδᾰ**, ης, ἡ, *dirt*, τὴν ἄρδαν ἀπ' ἐμοῦ σπόγγισον Pherecr.53.

**ἀρδάλιον**, τό, *water-pot* or *trough*, Hsch.

⊛**ἄρδαλος**· ὁ μὴ καθαρῶς ζῶν, Erot.; cf. ἀρδάλους· εἰκαίους, Hsch.:— also **ἄρδαλος**· μόλυσμα, Id.

**ἀρδᾰλόω**, *smear*, Hp.*Nat.Mul*.67, Philem.59; *spread* a plaster, Hp.*Mul*.1.20:—Pass., ἠρδαλωμένος *filthy*, Lxx *Si*.22.1; also ἀρδαλωμένους· ταρασσομένους, Hsch.

⊛**ἀρδάνιον**, τό, = ἀρδάλιον, Ael.Dion.*Fr*.66, Poll.8.66, *AB*441.

**ἀρδ-εία**, ἡ, *irrigation*, Str.4.6.7, Plu.2.688a (pl.), *BGU*283.6 (ii A.D.); εἰς ἀρδείαν τῆς γῆς Wilcken *Chr*.461.24 (iii A.D.); of a horse, εἰς ἀρδείαν ἄγειν Ael.*NA*7.12. **-εύσιμος**, η, ον, *irrigated*, Hsch. s.v. κατάρρυτα. **-ευσις**, εως, ἡ, (ἀρδεύω) = foreg., Hp.*Hebd*.1.87, Plb.9.43.5 (pl.), Moschio ap.Ath.5.207d, J.*AJ*3.1.3. **-ευτέον**, *one must water, irrigate*, *Gp*.9.11.3. **-ευτής**, οῦ, ὁ, *waterer*, Man. 4.258. **-ευτός**, ή, όν, *watered*, Sosith.7. **-εύω**, = ἄρδω, *water, irrigate*, A.*Pr*.852, Arist.*HA*601$^b$13, *Pr*.924$^b$15, Thphr.*HP*7.5.2, etc.:—Pass., *Com.Adesp*.29 D., Plb.10.28.3, *PThead*.16.10 (iv A.D.); βόσκομαι καὶ ἀρδεύομαι M.Ant.5.4: metaph., [Θουκυδίδης] ὁ τὸν Δημοσθένην πολλάκις ἀρδεύσας Chor. in *Philol*.54.120:—Pass., Plot.2.9. 3. **-ηθμός**, ὁ, = ἀρδμός, Lyc.622, Nic.*Th*.401.

⊛**ἄρδην**, Adv. contr. for ἀέρδην, (ἀείρω) *lifted up on high*, of a vase carried on the head, S.*Ant*.430; φέρειν ἄ. E.*Alc*.608; πηδῶντος ἄ. Ἕκτορος τάφρων ὕπερ S.*Aj*.1279. II. *utterly, wholly*, εἰς Τάρταρον ἄ. ῥίψειε δέμας A.*Pr*.1051, cf. E.*Hec*.887; πᾶσαν ἄ. πόλιν ἀπολλύναι Pl.*R*.421a; ἄ. διαφθείρεσθαι Id.*Lg*.677c; Φωκέων ἄ. ὄλεθρος D.19.141; πεπτωκὸς ἄ. πολίτευμα Plb.1.35.5; ὕμνυμι πάντας ἄ. τοὺς θεοὺς all *together*, all *at once*, Ar.*Th*.274, cf. X.*An*.7.1.12; later εἰς ἄ., πόλιν ἐξελεῖν Hld.9.2.

**ἀρδικός**· φαρέτρα, Hsch.

**ἀρδιοθήρα**, ας, ἡ, (ἄρδις) *forceps to extract arrow-heads*, etc., Serv. ad Virg.*Aen*.8.453, 12.404.

⊛**ἄρδις**, ιος, ἡ, *point of an arrow*, acc. ἄρδιν Hdt.4.81; acc. pl. ἄρδις (Ion.) 1.215; gen. ἀρδίων 4.81:—on A.*Pr*.880 v. ἄπυρος. II. *arrow*, Lyc.63.

**ἀρδμός**, ὁ, *means of watering*, Il.18.521, Od.13.247, Nonn.*D*.26. 185; *watering-place*, A.R.4.1247. II. *draught*, νέκταρος prob. in Orph.*Fr*.189.

**ἀρδρομηκιαῖος**, α, ον, dub. in *POxy*.896.12 (iv A.D.); cf. ἀνδρο-.

**ἄρδω**, impf. ἦρδον Pl.*Ti*.76a, Ion. 3 sg. ἄρδεσκε Hdt.2.13: aor. ἦρσα Id.5.12, subj. ἄρσῃ Id.2.14, part. ἄρσας Id.2.14, 5.12: used by Att. only in pres. and impf.:—*water*: hence, 1. *give drink to* cattle, ἵππους ἄρσασα βαθυσχοίνοιο Μέλητος *from* or *at* the Meles, *h.Hom*. 9.3; ἄ. Σιμόεντος Euph.66; ἦρσε τὸν ἵππον Hdt.l.c.; of rivers, *furnish drink for* men, Pi.*O*.5.12:—Pass., *drink*, ἀρδόμενοι οὐρῆες ἀπὸ πηγέων *h.Ap*.263: metaph., ἄ. φωτί *to be drunk with* light, Plot. 2.9.3. 2. *water* land, of rivers, Hdt.2.14, A.*Pers*.487,806, etc.; of men, *irrigate*, μισθωτὸς ἄρδει πεδία Timocl.15.5, cf. Arist.*GC*335$^a$ 14; θεὸς ἄ. γῆν Ph.1.50:—Pass., *to be watered*, of countries, Hdt.2. 13; σῖτος χερσὶ ἀρδόμενος *watered* by hand, Id.1.193; ἐκ τοῦ ποταμοῦ ibid., cf. Ibyc.1, Ath.2.43c; καρποὺς ἀρδομέναν.. χθόνα *having its* corn *watered*, Ar.*Nu*.282; Νυμφάων ὅθεν ἄρδεται ἄστυ Ἀθήνης *IG*3.1354. 5. II. metaph., *foster, cherish*, ὄλβον ἄ. Pi.*O*.5.23; πάτραν Χαρίτων ἄρδειν δρόσῳ, i.e. cover with glory, Id.*I*.6(5).64; τὸ λογιστικὸν ἄ. καὶ αὔξειν Pl.*R*.550b, cf. 606d, etc.; ἄ. νοῦν οἴνῳ Ar.*Eq*.96; συμποσίοις ἄρδοντες αὐτοὺς Pl.*Phdr*.276d, cf. X.*Smp*.2.24. III. *guzzle*, πολὺν ἄκρατον Ph.1.639. IV. *pour forth*, θεὸς ἄ. χάριτας Id.2. 294:—Pass., ib.244. (ἀ acc. to Hdn.Gr.2.109.)

**Ἀρέθουσα** [ᾰρ], ἡ, name of several fountains, e.g. in Ithaca, Od. 13.408; at Syracuse, Str.6.2.4: pl., κρῆναι ἀρέθουσαι Choeril.2:— Adj. **Ἀρεθούσιος**, α, ον, ὕδωρ *AP*9.362.18. (A participial form; ἀρέθω is cited by Hdn.Gr.1.440 without expl.)

**ἀρειά** [ᾰρ], Ion. and poet. ἀρειή, ἡ, collective noun, *menaces, threats*, λευγαλέοις ἐπέεσσιν.. καὶ ἀρειῇ Il.20.109, but μειλιχίοις ἐπέεσσιν.. καὶ ἀρειῇ 21.339; πολλὰ δὲ μειλιχίοισι.. πολλὰ δ' ἀρειῇ 17.431.

**ἀρειάω** [ᾰρ], (ἀρειά) = ἀπειλέω, Hippon.65. (Cf. ἄρος· βλάβος ἀκούσιον, Hsch., Skt. *irasyā* 'malevolence'.)

**Ἀρειθῠ́σᾰνος** [ῠ], ὁ, *tassel of Ares*, word for a brave warrior, A. *Fr*.203. (Cf. Paus.Gr.*Fr*.67.)

**Ἀρεϊκός**, ή, όν, *belonging to Ares*, Dam.*Pr*.97 bis; κάλλος Them. *Or*.13.165b; δόξα Paul.Al.*M*.1.

**Ἀρει-μᾰνής** [ᾰρ], ές, (μαίνομαι) *full of warlike frenzy*, Simyl.ap.Plu. *Rom*.17; Ἀριμασποί D.P.31; Οὖννοι *AP*9.210. II. Ἀρειμανής· ὁ Ἀΐδης, παρὰ Πέρσαις, Hsch.; cf. sq. II. **-μάνιος** [μᾰ], ον, = foreg., θρασύτης Ph.1.375; δυνάστης Plu.2.321f, cf. 758f; κριός D.L.6.61; φῦλα J.*BJ*2.16.4. II. Ἀρειμάνιος, ὁ, as pr. n., = Avest. *angrō mainyuš*, a name given by the Magi to *the Spirit of Evil*, opp. Oromasdes (= Ahuramazda), Arist.*Fr*.6, Plu.2.369e, Dam.*Pr*.125 bis. **-μᾰνιότης**, ητος, ἡ, opp. ἀψυχία, Stob.2.7.25.

**ἀρεΐνος**, η, ον, (ἀρία) *made of oak*, ξύλον *IG*11(2).161*A* 70 (Delos, iii B.C.).

**Ἀρειο-πᾰγίτης**, **-πᾰγος**, v. Ἄρειος πάγος.

⊛**Ἄρειος** [ᾰ], ον, also α, ον E.*HF*413 (lyr.); Ion. **Ἀρήϊος**, η, ον; Aeol. **Ἀρεύϊος** Alc.*Supp*.1a.10: (Ἄρης):—*devoted to Ares, warlike, martial*; in Hom., mostly of warriors, Μενέλαος Ἀρήϊος Il.3.339, al.; Ἀρήϊοι υἷες Ἀχαιῶν 11.800, al.; of arms, Ἀρήϊα τεύχεα δύω 6.340, cf. 10.407; the Att. form only in the phrase τεῖχος Ἄρειον 4.407, al.; also in Hdt., ἀρήιοι ἀγῶνες conflicts *in real war*, opp. γυμνικοί, 9.33; ὅπλον ἀ. 4.23; of a man, as Subst., *warrior*, 6.98; Ἀθηνᾶ Ἀρεία *OGI* 229.70 (Smyrna), cf. *IG*12(5).913 (Tenos): Comp. ἀρειότερος (q.v.) Thgn.548 is prob. formed from ἀρείων, as χερειότερος from χερείων. 2. Ἄρειος (also Ἄρεος, Ἄρηος), ὁ (sc. μήν), name of month in Thessaly, *GDI*1449, etc. 3. Ἄρειον πεδίον, = *Campus Martius*, D.H.7.59, Plu.*Pomp*.53 (also name of a plain in Thrace, Plb.13.10. 7); τῶν τελῶν τὸ καλούμενον Ἄρειον, = *legio Martia*, App.*BC*3.45; Ἄρεια, τά, = *ludi Martiales*, D.C.56.46. 4. Ἄρειον, τό, = ξιφίον, Ps.-Dsc.4.20; = ἰσάτις, Id.2.184. II. = Ἄριος, Μάγοι καὶ πᾶν τὸ Ἄρειον γένος Dam.*Pr*.125.

**Ἄρειος πάγος** [πᾰ], ὁ, *the hill of Ares*, at Athens, Ἀρήϊος π. Hdt.8. 52, cf. A.*Eu*.685,690, etc.; ἡ βουλὴ ἡ ἐξ Ἀρείου πάγου *IG*1.38a (prob.), 2.476.59, al., D.18.133, cf. Lys.26.12, Arist.*Ath*.4.4; ἡ ἐν Ἀ. πάγῳ βουλή D.20.157, Aeschin.1.81, Arist.*Pol*.1273$^b$39; βουλὴ Ἀρεία *IG*3. 824; εἰς τὸν Ἄ. πάγον ἀναβῆναι become a member of the court, Isoc. 7.37, 12.154; ἐν Ἀ. πάγῳ δοῦναι δίκην Arist.*Rh*.1398$^b$26; ψευδομαρτύρια τὰ ἐξ Ἀ. πάγου Id.*Ath*.59.6.—The compd. **Ἀρειόπᾰγος** only in a late Att. Inscr., *IG*3.1005; but we find the noun **Ἀρεοπᾰγίτης** (Ἀρευ- ib.2.839.7) [ῑ], ου, ὁ, *Areopagite*, Aeschin.1.81, *IG*3.746, cf. 635, Arist.*Ath*.3.6, etc.: prov., Ἀρεοπαγίτου σιωπηλότερος 'as silent as the grave', Them.*Or*.21.263a; στεγανώτερος Alciphr.1.13:—Adj. **Ἀρεοπᾰγῖτις**, βουλή Arist.*Ath*.41.2, Alciphr.2.3; **Ἀρεοπᾰγῑτικός**, ή, όν, Isoc.7 tit., Str.6.1.8.

**ἀρειότερος** [ᾰ], α, ον, prob. = ἀρείων, Thgn.548, etc.; cf. Ἄρειος.

**Ἀρεί-τολμος**, ον, *warlike, bold*, *AP*9.40 (Zos.). **-φᾰτος**, Ep. **Ἀρηΐφατος**, ον, (cf. φόνος, πέφαται) *slain by Ares*, i.e. *slain in war*, Il.19.31, etc.; ψυχαί [Heraclit.]136, cf. 24; φόνοι Ἀ. E.*Supp*.603 (lyr.). 2. later, = Ἄρειος, *martial*, Ἀ. ἀγών, λῆμα, A.*Eu*.913, *Fr*. 147; κόποι E.*Rh*.124. 3. *slaying in war*, ἀνέρες Orph.*A*.514.

⊛**ἀρείων** [ᾰ], ον, gen. ονος, used as Comp. of ἀγαθός, cf. ἄριστος: —*better, stouter, braver*, in Hom. of all advantages of body, birth, and fortune, Il.1.260, al., cf. Hes.*Op*.207, Pi.*N*.7.101, A.*Th*.305 (lyr.), *Ag*.81 (lyr.):—rare in Prose, ἃ ὑμῖν ἄρειον μὴ γνῶναι Arist.*Fr*. 44. II. ἀρείονες, οἱ, a kind of *snail* or *slug*, Ael.*NA*10.5.

**ἄρεκτος**, ον, poet. for ἄρρεκτος, *unaccomplished*, Il.19.150, Simon. 69.

**ἀρέομαι**, Ion. for ἀράομαι (q.v.), v.l. in Hdt. II. fut. of ἄρνυμαι (q.v.), prob. l. in Pi.*P*.1.75.[ᾰ].

**Ἀρεοπαγίτης**, ου, ὁ, v. Ἄρειος πάγος.

**Ἄρεος**, α, ον, collat. form of Ἄρειος, Ἀρέα (sc. κρήνη) *the spring of Ares*, Pi.*N*.9.41.

**ἀρέσαι, ἀρέσασθαι**, v. ἀρέσκω. **ἀρεσίπονον**· σύμμετρον, ἀρέσκον, Hsch.

**ἄρεσις** [ᾰ], εως, ἡ, *good pleasure, favour*, ἀπόδειγμα τῆς πρὸς τὴν πόλιν ἀρέσεως *Inscr.Prien*.108.30 (ii B.C.).

**ἀρέσκ-εια** [ᾰρ], ἡ, (ἀρεσκεύομαι) *obsequiousness*, Arist.*EE*1221$^a$8, *MM*1192$^b$30, Thphr.*Char*.5, Plb.31.26.5, Phld.*Herc*.1457.5, Polystr. p.16 W.; ἀ. βασιλέως Plb.6.11$^a$.7, cf. J.*AJ*18.8.7. 2. in pl., = δόξαι, ἀρέσκοντα, αἱ ἀ. τῶν πολλῶν, of false *superstitions*, Ph.2.191; τὰ ταῖς κεναῖς σοφιστῶν ἀρεσκῄαις (sic) ὑπεναντία Demetr.Lac.*Herc*.1012. 73. 3. in good sense, πρὸς θεὸν καὶ ἀρετήν Ph.1.168; ἡ εἰς τὸ πλῆθος ἀ. *Inscr.Prien*.113.73 (i B.C.), cf. *IPE*2.5, *Ep.Col*.1.10; πρὸς τὴν ἑτέρων ἀ. βιοῦν Hld.10.14. **-ευμα,** ατος, τό, *act of obsequiousness*, Plu.*Demetr.*11, Epicur.*Fr.*177. ®**-εύομαι,** *to be complaisant to*, τινί Clearch.25, Hsch.: abs., *to be obsequious*, Plu.2.4d, M.Ant.5.5. **-ευτικός,** ή, όν, *obsequious*, Id.1.16, prob. in Phld.*Herc.*1457.11. **-όντως,** (ἀρέσκω) *agreeably*, ἀ. ἔχειν E.*IT*463 (lyr.), 581; ῥηθῆναι Pl.*R.*504b, X.*Oec.*11.19.

**ἄρεσκος** [ᾰ], η, ον, *pleasing*, mostly in bad sense, *obsequious, cringing*, Arist.*EN*1108$^{a}$28, 1126$^{b}$12, Thphr.*Char.*5.1. II. ἄρεσκος, ὁ, the staff borne by πορνοβοσκοί on the stage, Poll.4.120.

®**ἀρέσκω** [ᾰ], impf. ἤρεσκον Th.5.37, etc.: fut. ἀρέσω D.39.33, Ep. ἀρέσσω (συν-) A.R.3.901: aor. ἤρεσα Hdt.8.19, *Com.Adesp.*19.4D., etc., Ep. ἄρεσσα A.R.3.301, inf. ἀρέσαι Il., X.: pf. ἀρήρεκα Corn.*ND*24, S.E.*M.*1.238:—Med., fut. ἀρέσομαι A.*Supp.*655 (lyr.), Ep. ἀρέσσομαι Il.4.362: aor. ἠρεσάμην, Ep. ἀρ- Hes.*Sc.*255, Ep. part. ἀρεσσάμενος Il.9.112, Thgn.762: aor. Pass. in med. sense, S.*Ant.*500:—Pass., aor. ἠρέσθην Paus.2.13.8, J.*AJ*12.9.6. I. of pers. only, *make good, make amends*, ἂψ ἐθέλω ἀρέσαι Il.9.120:—Med., ταῦτα δ' ὄπισθεν ἀρεσσόμεθ' εἴ τι κακὸν νῦν εἴρηται 4.362, cf. Od.22.55, Q.S.4.377, 9.510; σπονδὰς θεοῖς ἀρέσασθαι *make full* drink-offerings to the gods, Thgn. l.c. 2. in Hom. also freq. in Med., c. acc. pers. et dat. modi, *appease, conciliate*, αὐτὸν ἀρεσσάσθω ἐπέεσσι καὶ δώρῳ Od.8.396; τὸν ξεῖνον ἀρέσσομαι ὡς σὺ κελεύεις ib.402; ὥς κέν μιν ἀρεσσάμενοι πεπίθωμεν δώροισι Il.9.112, cf. 19.179; καθαροῖσι βωμοῖς θεοὺς ἀρέσονται A.*Supp.*655; καί σε φίλως θυέεσσιν ἀρέσσατο Maiist.11: c. gen. rei, ἀρέσαντο φρένας αἵματος they *sated their* heart with blood, Hes.*Sc.*255. 3. after Hom., c. dat. pers., *please, satisfy*, οὔτε γάρ μοι Πολυκράτης ἤρεσκε δεσπόζων.. Hdt.3.142; δεῖ μ' ἀρέσκειν τοῖς κάτω S.*Ant.*75, cf. 89; ἀεὶ δ' ἀρέσκειν τοῖς κρατοῦσιν *to be obsequious to* them, E.*Fr.*93, cf. X.*Mem.*2.2.11; ἀ. τρόποις τινός *conform to* his ways, D.61.19; τὸ κολακεύειν νῦν ἀρέσκειν ὄνομ' ἔχει Anaxandr.42; πᾶσιν ἀρέσκω 1*Ep.Cor.*10.33; ἑαυτοῖς *Ep.Rom.*15.1:—Med., μάλιστα ἠρέσκοντό ⟨οἱ⟩ οἱ ἀπ' Ἀθηνέων *pleased* him most, Hdt.6.128. II. of things, c. dat. pers., *please*, εἴ τοι ἀρέσκει τὰ ἐγὼ λέγω Hdt.1.89; κάρτα οἱ ἤρεσε ἡ ὑποθήκη Id.8.58, cf. 3.40, 6.22; τῷ τοῦτ' ἤρεσεν; S.*El.*409; σοὶ ταῦτ' ἀρέσκει Id.*Ant.*211, etc.; τοῖς..πρέσβεσιν ἤρεσκεν [the proposal] *pleased* them, Th.5.37, cf. Pl.*Tht.*157d, al.: also in aor. Pass., μηδ' ἀρεσθείη ποτέ (sc. μηδὲν τῶν σῶν λόγων) S.*Ant.*500. III. c. acc. pers., οὐ γάρ μ' ἀρέσκει γλῶσσά σου τεθηγμένη Id.*Aj.*584; οὐδέ σ' ἀρέσκει τὸ παρὸν E.*Hipp.*185 (lyr.), cf. *Or.*210; τουτὶ.. μ' οὐκ ἀ. Ar.*Pl.*353, cf. *Ach.*189, *Ra.*103, Th.1.128; πότερός σε ὁ τρόπος ἀ.; Pl.*Cra.*433e, cf. 391c, *R.*557b, *Tht.*172d: hence in Pass., *to be pleased, satisfied*, οὐκ ἠρέσκετο λειπομένου Μαρδονίου ὑπὸ βασιλέος Hdt.9.66; τῇ κρίσι *with* the decision, Id.3.34; διαίτῃ Σκυθικῇ Id.4.78; τοῖς λόγοις Th.1.129, cf. 2.68; τῇ σῇ συνουσίᾳ Pl.*Thg.*127b; later in aor., ἠρέσθη τῇ γνώμῃ J. l.c., al.; ἀρεσθεὶς τῷ πώματι Paus. l.c. IV. ἀρέσκει is used impers. to express *the opinion* or *resolution* of a public body, ταῦτα ἤρεσέ σφι ποιέειν Hdt.8.19; ἦν δ' ἀρέσκῃ ταῦτ' Ἀθηναίοις Ar.*Eq.*1311; ἀρέσκει..εἶναι Δελφῶν *it is resolved* that.., *SIG*827*D*10; also of *prevailing opinions*, ἀρέσκει περὶ τρίψεως παραγγέλλοντας.. writers on massage *lay down the rule* that.., Gal.6.96; τὰ ἀρέσκοντα the *dogmas* of philosophers, Plu.2.448a, 1006d, etc.:—Med., ἐξεῖναι παρ' ὁποτέρους ἂν ἀρέσκηται ἐλθεῖν Th.1.35. V. part. ἀρέσκων, ουσα, ον, *grateful, acceptable*, ὅσοις τάδ' ἔστ' ἀρέσκονθ' S.*OT*274; μηδὲν ἀρέσκον λέγειν Th.3.34; ἀρέσκοντας ὑμῖν λόγους Isoc.8.5. 2. of persons, *acceptable*, τὸν ἀρέσκοντα αὑτῷ προσλαμβάνειν Pl.*Lg.*951e; τῇ πόλει ἀ. Lys.19.13. (Cognate with ἀραρίσκω.)

**ἀρέσμιον,** τό, *honorarium, perquisite*, *IG*9(1).32.25 (Stiris).

**ἀρεστέον** [ᾰ], *one must be pleased*, c. inf., Tz.*H.*8.212.

**ἀρεστ-ήρ** [ᾰ], ῆρος, ὁ, *a cake*, as a *propitiatory* offering, *IG*2.1651*B*6, cf. 1662, Ael.Dion.*Fr.*68, Poll.6.76. **-ήριος,** α, ον, *propitiatory*, θυσίαι D.H.1.67:—hence **ἀρεστηρία** (sc. θυσία), ἡ, *SIG*$^{2}$587.223, and ®**-ήριον,** τό, *IG*2.198*c*18 (iv B.C.). **-ής,** οῦ, ὁ, *EM*138.57.

**ἀρεστός** [ᾰ], ή, όν, *acceptable, pleasing*, Semon.7.46, Hdt.1.119, Men.*Epit.*71, Phld.*Po.*1676.1, etc.; ἔμοιγε οὐκ ἀρεστά Hdt.2.64; τῶν σῶν λόγων ἀ. οὐδέν S.*Ant.*500, cf. *OT*1096 (lyr.); τἀρεστὰ ὑμῖν αὐτοῖς αἱρεῖσθαι Lys.14.15; τὸ αἱρετὸν ἀρεστόν Chrysipp.*Stoic.*3.9; οἴνου παρέχειν ἀρεστόν a *sufficient* quantity, *IG*12(5).647.17 (Ceos); *satisfactory*, *PSI*3.171.16 (ii B.C.); of persons, *acceptable, approved*, τινί X.*Cyr.*2.3.7, *SIG*577.58 (Milet., iii/ii B.C.), etc. Adv., ἑωυτῷ ἀρεστῶς *quite to* his own *satisfaction*, Hdt.6.129; ἀ. τοῖς ναοποιοῖς *IG*7.3073.52 (Lebad.); ὄχλοις ἀρεστῶς λέγειν Plu.2.6b; ἐσθίειν ἀ. θεοῖς Arr.*Epict.*1.13.1.

**ἀρέσχαι·** κλήματα, βότρυες, Hsch.

**ἀρεταίνω,** = ἀρετάω, Hsch., Eust.1599.32.

**ἀρέταιχμος,** ον, *valiant with the spear*, ἥρως B.16.48.

**ἀρετᾱ-λογία** [ᾰρ], ἡ, *celebration of divine* ἀρεταί, Lxx*Si.*36.19(16), cf. Sm.*Ps.*29(30).6; as a profession, *recitation of* ἱεροὶ λόγοι, Str.17.1.17 (prob. l.), Man.4.447. ®**-λόγος,** ὁ, (ἀρετή, λέγω) *professional expounder of* ἀρεταί (v. ἀρετή), *writer of* ἱεροὶ λόγοι, μιμογράφου καὶ ἀρεταλόγου ἢ ἄλλου συγγραφέως prob. in Phld.*Po.*5.1425.9; ὀνειροκρίτης καὶ ἀ. *SIG*1133, cf. Suet.*Aug.*74, Juv.15.16, Aus.*Ep.*13.

**ἀρετάω** [ᾰρ], *thrive, prosper*, οὐκ ἀρετᾷ κακὰ ἔργα Od.8.329; λαοὶ ἀρετῶσι 19.114: in late Prose, ἀρετῶσα γῆ Ph.2.372, al.; διάνοια ib.280:—Med., ἐὰν ἀρετήσηται αὐτοῦ τὰ.. *PGiss.*67.15 (ii A.D.). II. *choose the path of valour*, Procop.*Goth.*4.35, cf. *Aed.*1 *Prooem.*

**ἀρετή** [ᾰ], ἡ, *goodness, excellence*, of any kind, in Hom. esp. of *manly* qualities, ποδῶν ἀρετὴν ἀναφαίνων Il.20.411; ἀμείνων παντοίας ἀρετὰς ἠμὲν πόδας ἠδὲ μάχεσθαι καὶ νόον 15.642; so of the gods, τῶν περ καὶ μείζων ἀ. τιμή τε βίη τε 9.498; also of women, Od.2.206; ἀ. εἵνεκα for *valour*, Hdt.8.92: pl., ἀ. ἀπεδείκνυντο displayed *brave deeds*, Id.1.176, 9.40. b. later, of the gods, chiefly in pl., *glorious deeds, wonders, miracles*, *SIG*1172, Str.17.1.17; ζῶσαι ἀ. *IG*14.966, cf. 1*Ep.Pet.*2.9: also in sg., ὄψιν ἰδοῦσα ἀρετὴν τῆς θεοῦ *IG*2.1426*b*, cf. Isyll.62, *BSA*21.169, 180. 2. generally, *excellence*, ἡ ἀ. τελείωσίς τις Arist.*Metaph.*1021$^{b}$20, cf. *EN*1106$^{a}$15, etc.; of persons, ἄνδρα πὺξ ἀρετὰν εὑρόντα Pi.*O.*7.89, cf. *P.*4.187, B.9.13, etc.; τὸ φρονεῖν ἀ. μεγίστη Heraclit.112: in pl., *forms of excellence*, μυρίαι ἀνδρῶν ἀ. B.13.8, cf. Gorg.*Fr.*8, etc.; δικαστοῦ αὕτη ἀ. Pl.*Ap.*18a; esp. *moral virtue*, Democr.179, 263, al., Gorg.*Fr.*6; opp. κακία, X.*Mem.*2.1.21, cf. Pl.*R.*500cd, *Lg.*963a, c sq., D.60.17, Arist.*EN*1102$^{a}$6, *Pol.*1295$^{a}$37, etc.; *good nature, kindness*, etc., E.*Fr.*163. b. of animals, things, as land, Hdt.4.198, 7.5, Th.1.2; ἡ ἐν ἀρετῇ κειμένη γῆ *productive* land, *PTeb.*5.165 (ii B.C.); ἵππου Hdt.3.88; κυνῶν, ἵππων, Pl.*R.*335b; σκεύους ib.601d; [ἀστακοῦ] Archestr.*Fr.*24; ἀ. βίου Pl.*R.*618c; πολιτείας *Lg.*886b, etc. 3. *prosperity*, Od.13.45. II. ἀ. εἴς τινα *active merit, good service* done him, ἐς τοὺς Ἕλληνας Th.3.58, cf. 2.40; ἀ. περί τινα X.*An.*1.4.8; ἀνταποδοῦναι ἀ. Th.4.19; ἀρετὰς παρασχέσθαι ὑπέρ τινος D.19.312; ἀρετῆς ἕνεκα, freq. in honorary Inscrr., *IG*2$^{2}$.107.14, etc. III. *reward* of excellence, *distinction, fame*, πλούτῳ δ' ἀρετὴ καὶ κῦδος ὀπηδεῖ Hes.*Op.*313, cf. Sapph.80, Pi.*N.*5.53, al.; ἀθάνατος ἀ. S.*Ph.*1420, Pl.*Smp.*208d; ἃ ἆθλα τοῦ πολέμου τοῖς ἀνδράσιν ἐστίν, ἐλευθερία καὶ ἀ. Lycurg.49; of God, δόξα καὶ ἀ. 2*Ep.Pet.*1.3: in pl., *glories*, Thgn.30, Pi.*N.*10.2, al.; πλοῦτος ἀρεταῖς δεδαιδαλμένος Id.*O.*2.53; γενναίων ἀ. πόνων E.*HF*357 (lyr.), cf. Lys.2.26; προγόνων ἀ. Pl.*R.*618b; in Lxx freq. of the *praises* of God, Is.42.8, al. IV. Ἀρετή personified, Prodic.1, Arist.*Fr.*675, Callix.2, *CIG*2786, *SIG*985.10, etc. V. ἡ ἀ. σου as a title, Your *worship*, *PLips.*13 ii 20, etc. VI. an *engine of war*, Ath.Mech.38.11. VII. a *plaster*, Androm.ap.Gal.13.531.

®**ἀρετηφόρος** [ᾰ], ον, *virtuous*, Phld.*Rh.*1.217S., *Mort.*35.

**ἀρετίδιον** [ᾰ], τό, Dim. of ἀρετή, Anon.*in Rh.*174.6.

**ἀρετόομαι** [ᾰ], Pass., *become excellent, grow in goodness*, Simp.*in Epict.*p.10D., Id.*in Ph.*1066.5.

**ἀρή** [ᾰ], ἡ, *bane, ruin*, ἀρὴν ἑτάροισιν ἀμύνειν Il.12.334; ἀρῆς ἀλκτῆρα γενέσθαι 18.100; ἀρὴν καὶ λοιγὸν ἀμῦναι 24.489, cf. Od.2.59; so in A.*Supp.*84 (lyr.), where the gloss of the Sch., βλάβης, confirms the reading ἀρῆς for ἄρης. (Cf. pf. part. ἀρημένος = βεβλαμμένος, and pr. n. Ἄρης (cf. Corn.*ND*20), perh. also ἄρος, ἀρειά, ἐπήρεια; perh. an old *ē* stem.)

**ἄρηαι,** Ep. 2 sg. subj. aor. 2 Med. from ἄρνυμαι, Il., Hes.

®**ἀρηβώ,** a kind of *cassia*, *Peripl.M.Rubr.*12, Gal.14.72.

**ἀρηγοσύνη** [ᾰ], ἡ, *help, aid*, *AP*9.788.8, *Epigr.Gr.*1050 (Ephesus).

®**ἀρήγω** [ᾰ], fut. -ξω *Com.Adesp.*12.5D., etc.:—*aid, succour*, τινί Il.2.363, al. (never in Od.); in Hom. always, *succour in war*, freq. c. dat. pers. et modi, μάχῃ Τρώεσσιν ἀ. 1.521, 5.507; ὄμοσσον ἦ μέν μοι..ἔπεσιν καὶ χερσὶν ἀ. 1.77: generally, *help, succour*, λέχει Ἀλκμήνας Pi.*N.*1.49; νεότατι ἀ. θράσος Id.*P.*2.63; θνητοῖς A.*Pr.*260, etc.; in mock Trag. passages of Com., γυναῖκες, οὐκ ἀρήξετ'; Ar.*Th.*696, cf. *Pl.*476: rare in Prose, Hecat.30J., etc.; ὁ ναυτικὸς τῷ πεζῷ ἀρήξει Hdt.7.236; τοῖς φίλοις ἀ. X.*Cyr.*1.5.13; ἀ. σὺν ὅπλοις τῇ χώρᾳ Id.*Oec.*5.7; *to be good for* a patient or his case, Hp.*Prorrh.*2.30, cf. *Acut.*65. 2. impers., c. inf., *it is good* or *fit*, φέρειν ἀρήγει Pi.*P.*2.94; σιγᾶν ἀρήγει A.*Eu.*571. II. c. acc. rei, *ward off, prevent*, ὄλεθρον v.l. in Batr.279; ἄρηξον..ἅλωσιν A.*Th.*119 (lyr.); ἀ. τινί τι *ward off from* one, φόνον τέκνοις E.*Med.*1275 (lyr.), cf. *Tr.*777. (Perh. cognate with Lat. *rēx*, Skt. *rājati* 'rule'.)

®**ἀρηγών** [ᾰ], όνος, ὁ, ἡ, *helper*, Il.4.7, 5.511, in fem.; masc. in Batr.280, etc.; ἀρηγόνος ἡνιόχοιο Opp.*H.*5.108.

**Ἀρηΐ-θοος** [ᾰ], ον, *swift in war*, αἰζηοί Il.8.298, 15.315, A.R.1.1042; ἄνδρες Simon.104. **-κτάμενος** [ᾱρ], η, ον, (κτείνω) *slain by Ares*, Il.22.72.

**Ἀρήϊος** [ᾰ], η, ον, also ος, ον, Ion. for Ἄρειος, Hom., etc.; δαίμων Ἀ. Jul.*Or.*4.154c:—pecul. fem. **Ἀρηιάς,** άδος, Q.S.1.187.

**Ἀρηΐ-φᾰτος** [ᾰ], ον, Ep. and Ion. for Ἀρείφατος (q.v.). **-φθορος,** ον, *slain in war*, πτώματα Corn.*ND*21. **-φῐλος,** η, ον, *dear to Ares*, epith. of warriors in Hom., Il.2.778, al., cf. Hes.*Th.*317, Pi.*I.*8(7).25, etc.; of the river Thermodon, Tryph.33.

**ἀρήμεναι,** v. ἀράομαι. **ἀρημένος** [ᾱ], η, ον, pf. part. Pass., expld. by Gramm. by βεβλαμμένος, *distressed, worn out*, once in Il., γήραϊ λυγρῷ κεῖται ἐνὶ μεγάροις ἀ. 18.435; more freq. in Od., ὕπνῳ καὶ καμάτῳ ἀ. 6.2; τίπτε τόσον, Πολύφημ', ἀρημένος ὧδ' ἐβόησας; 9.403; γήρᾳ ὑπὸ λιπαρῷ ἀ. 11.136; δύῃ ἀ. 18.53. [Prob. akin to ἀρή, Ἄρης.]

®**ἀρήν** (nom. only in Inscrr., *IG*1.4, 11.154*A*11 (Delos, iii B.C.), *SIG*1027.9 (Cos), ϝαρήν *GDI*4964.2 (Gortyn)); also **ἄρης** *PGurob.*22.40, 42 (iii B.C.), and **ἄρνον** ib.3, al.; acc. ἄρνα, gen. ἀρνός, dat. ἀρνί, dual. ἄρνε: pl. ἄρνες, ἄρνας, ἀρνῶν, dat. ἀρνάσι J.*AJ*3.8.10, Ep. ἄρνεσσι:—*lamb* (under a year old, Max.515, Istros ap.Eust.1672.12); ἀ. πρωτογόνων Il.4.102, etc.; γαλαθηνῶν Crates Com.1. II. *sheep* of either sex, ἄρν' ἕτερον λευκόν, ἑτέρην δὲ μέλαιναν Il.3.103; ἄρνες κεραοί Od.4.85. III. in pl., *stunted ears* of wheat, Thphr.*HP*8.7.5. (Skt. *úrā* 'sheep', *úraṇas* 'ram', 'lamb', *urabhras* 'ram', Arm. *garn* 'lamb'; cf. -ϝρην in πολύρρην.)

**ἀρηνοβοσκός,** ὁ, *shepherd*, Paus.Gr.*Fr.*69, dub. in S.*Fr.*655.

**ἄρηξις** [ᾰ], εως, ἡ, (ἀρήγω) *help, succour*, τινός *from* a person, A.*Pr.*547 (lyr.), S.*OC*829. II. c. gen. rei, *help against* a thing, *means of averting* it, πημάτων S.*El.*876.

**ἄρηρα, ἀρήρειν, ἀρηρεμένος,** v. ἀραρίσκω.

**ἀρηρομένος,** η, ον, v. ἀρόω.

®**Ἄρης,** ὁ, Ep. gen. Ἄρεος, Att. Ἄρεως A.*Th.*64, E.*El.*1258; but Ἄρεος never contr.) is required by the metre in A.*Th.*115 (lyr.), S *OC*947, *Ant.*125 (lyr.), *El.*1423 (lyr.), E.*Heracl.*275, *El.*950, *Fr.*16; dat. Ἄρεϊ, contr. Ἄρει; acc. Ἄρεα S.*OT*190 (lyr.), Att. Ἄρη (never Ἄρην, which is not found in Attic Inscrr. and is never required by the metre; Ἄρη' is the true reading in Il.5.909, Hes.*Sc.*59, cf. *AP*7.237 (Alph.), D.S. 5.72); voc. Ἄρες, Ep. (metri gr.) Ἆρες:—Ion. and Ep. declens. **Ἄρης,** ηος, ηι, ηα: Aeol. **Ἄρευς,** ευος, ευα, ευι, ευ, Sapph.66, Alc. 28 ff.:—*Ares*: in Trag., *the god of destruction* generally, S.*OT*190, etc.; ἐς Οἰδίπου παῖδε.. Ἄρης κατέσκηψ' Ar.*Fr.*558; in Com., Ἄρεως νεοττός chicken *of Ares*, Id.*Av.*835. **2.** the planet *Mars*, Arist. *Cael.*292$^{a}$5, Cleom.1.11.59, etc.; Ἄρεος ἡμέρα D.C.37.19. **II.** in Poets, Appellat. for *war, slaughter*, ξυνάγωμεν Ἄρηα Il.2.381; Ἄρη μείξουσιν S.*OC*1046 (lyr.); χρονίῳ σὺν Ἄρει Pi.*P.*11.36; Ἄρης ἐμφύλιος, Ἄ. τιθασός, A.*Eu.*862, 355; θηλυκτόνῳ Ἄρει δαμέντων Id.*Pr.*861; ναύφαρκτος Ἄ. Id.*Pers.*951 (lyr.); λιθόλευστον Ἄρη *death* by stoning, S.*Aj.*254 (lyr.); ἔνθα μάλιστα γίγνετ' Ἄ. ἀλεγεινὸς ὀϊζυροῖσι βροτοῖσι, of a *mortal wound*, Il.13.569. **2.** *warlike spirit*, A.*Ag.*78, E.*Ph.* 134; κἀν γυναιξὶν.. Ἄ. ἔνεστιν S *El.*1242; οὔτ' ὄλβος οὔτ' Ἄ. Id.*Ant.* 952; μέγαν ἐκ θυμοῦ κλάζοντας Ἄ. A *Ag.*48; Ἄρη βλέπειν Ar.*Pl.*328, Timocl.12.7: in Prose, ἔμφυτος Ἄ. Gorg.*Fr.*6. **3.** *the sword*, ὀξὺς Ἄ. Il.7.330, cf. *AP*.7.531 (Antip. Thess.), Plu.2.23c. **III.** epith. of Zeus, as the *avenger* of perjury, in oaths, *IG*5(2).343*c* (Arc.); of Ἐνυάλιος, ibid., Poll.8.106. (Akin to ἀρή, q. v.) [ᾰ in Hom., but α of voc. may be long, e.g. Ἆρες, Ἄρες βροτολοιγέ Il.5.31, and gen. Ἄρηος 2.767, Call.*Jov.*77 (s.v.l.), Ἄρεος A.R.3.1187, dat. Ἄρηϊ Id.2. 991: in Trag., regularly ᾰ, but A. uses ᾱ even in dialogue, as *Th.*244, 469; and S. in lyr., *Aj.*252, 614, *Ant.*139.]

**Ἀρησιών,** ῶνος, ὁ (sc. μήν), name of a month at Delos, *IG*11.158*A* 48 (iii B.C.).

**ἀρήτ-ειρα** [ᾱρ], ἡ, fem of ἀρητήρ, Call.*Cer.*43, Musae.68, A.R.1. 312, etc. **-εύω,** *to be president*, βωλᾶς *IG*12(3).1259 (Cimolus); Dor. ἀϝρ- ib.4.497.4 (Mycenae), *SIG*56.43 (Argos). (Always in 3 sg. impf. ἀϝρήτευε, ἀρήτευε, hence perh. for ἐ-ϝρήτευε, from ϝρητεύω, cf. ϝρήτρα.) **-ήρ** [ᾱ], ῆρος, ὁ, (ἀράομαι) *one that prays*: poet. for ἱερεύς (Arist.*Po.*1457$^{b}$35), *priest*, Il.1.11, 5.78, al.; also in metr. Inscrr., *IG*4.1007 (Epid.), 1538 (Apollo Maleatas), etc., cf. Orac.ap. Jul.*Ep.*89. **-ήριον** [ᾱ], τό, *a place for curses*, Plu.*Thes.*35. **-ός,** ή, όν, Ion. for ἀρᾱτός: **Ἀρήτη,** ἡ, as pr. n., Od.7.54, etc.

**ἀρητυμένος,** f.l. for ἀρυτήμενος, Alc.47.

**ἄρθεν,** v. ἀραρίσκω.

**ἄρθεος·** τράγος, Hsch.

**ἀρθμέω,** intr., *to be united*, ἐν φιλότητι ἀρθμήσαντε Il.7.302:—Pass., ἀρθμηθέντες A.R.1.1344.

**ἄρθμιος,** α, ον, *united*, οἵ δ' ἡμῖν ἄρθμιοι ἦσαν *in league with* us, Od. 16.427, cf. Hdt.7.101, al.; ἄ. ἠδὲ φίλος Thgn.1312; ἄρθμια, τά, *peaceful relations, friendship*, τέως μὲν δή σφι ἦν ἄ. ἐς ἀλλήλους, ἐκ τούτου δὲ πόλεμος Hdt.6.83; ἄ. ἔργα Emp.17.23, cf. 22.1. **2.** *calm*, βολαὶ ὀφθαλμῶν Hdn.1.7.5.

⊛**ἀρθμός,** ὁ, (ἀραρίσκω) *a bond, league, friendship*, ἀρθμῷ καὶ φιλότητι *h.Merc.*524, cf. A.*Pr.*193 (lyr.), Call.*Fr.*199.

**ἀρθρέμ-βολέω,** *insert* part of a machine, in Pass., Ath.Mech.34. 6. **-βόλησις,** εως, ἡ, *setting of a limb*, Apollon.Cit.1.1:—also **-βολία,** ἡ, Orib.49.9.5. **-βολον,** τό, (ἐμβάλλω) *instrument for setting limbs*, Gal.14.781: in pl., *instruments of torture*, Lxx 4*Ma.*8.13.

**ἀρθρίδιον,** τό, Dim. of ἄρθρον, v.l. for ἀγρίδιον, M.Ant.4.3.

**ἀρθρικός,** ή, όν, (ἄρθρον I) *of* or *for the joints*, Gal.19.85. **II.** (ἄρθρον II) *of, belonging to the article*, in Gramm., A.D.*Synt.*6.5, al. Adv. -ῶς ib.33.6.

**ἀρθρῑτικός,** ή, όν, (ἄρθρον) *of* or *for the joints*, νόμος Hp.*Art.* 18. **II.** *diseased in the joints, gouty*, Id.*Epid.*6.4.3, Damox.2.32, Cic.*Fam.*9.23: τὰ -κά Hp.*Epid.*7.100; ἀ. ἀλήματα Gal.17(2).125.

**ἀρθρῖτις,** ιδος, ἡ (acc. -ῖτιν Porph.*Abst.*1.53), as if fem. of ἀρθρίτης, which does not occur:—*of* or *in the joints*, νόσος Hp.*Aff.*30; ἡ ἀ. *gout*, Id.*Aph.*3.16 (pl.), Aret.*SD*2.12, etc.

**ἀρθροκηδής,** ές, *limb-distressing*, πόνοι Luc.*Trag.*15.

⊛**ἄρθρον,** τό, (ἀραρίσκω) *joint*, Emp.17.22, etc.; ἄρθρων πόνοι Hp. *Aph.*3.31, al.; ἅπαν κατ' ἄρθρον S.*Tr.*769; κρᾶτα καὶ ἄρθρα the head and *joints of the neck*, Id.*Ph.*1208 (lyr., codd.); esp. *the socket of the ankle-joint*, ὁ ἀστράγαλος ἐξεχώρησε ἐκ τῶν ἄ. Hdt.3.129; in Hp.*Art.* 1, al., *ball* of a joint, opp. *socket* (κοτύλη), cf. Gal.18(2).487 (but *socket* in Hp.*Loc.Hom.*6); μάρψας ποδός νιν ἄρθρον ᾗ λυγίζεται S.*Tr.*779, cf. *Ph.*1202 (lyr.). **2.** generally, of *limbs*, etc., esp. in pl., ἄ. ποδοῖν the ankles, Id.*OT*718, cf. 1032; of the legs, βραδύπουν ἤλυσιν ἄρθρων προτιθεῖσα E.*Hec.*67 (lyr.); ἄ. τῶν κύκλων eyes, S.*OT*1270; ἄ. στόματος the mouth, E.*Cyc.*625; θέναρ διηρημένον ἄρθροις *lines*, Arist.*HA*493$^{b}$33; τὰ ἄ. alone, *genitals*, Hdt.3.87, 4.2, Arist.*HA*504$^{b}$23, al.; τὰ ἐντὸς ἄ. the internal *organs*, Mnesith.ap.Orib.8.38.7: metaph., ἄ. τᾶν φρενῶν Epich.250: in sg., ἄρθρον τῆς φωνῆς vocal *articulation*, Arist.*HA*536$^{a}$ 3. **II.** Gramm., *connecting word*, Id.*Po.*1457$^{a}$6; esp. of the *article*, Id.*Rh.Al.*1435$^{a}$35, Chrysipp.*Stoic.*2.45, D.H.*Th.*37, al.

⊛**ἀρθροπέδη,** ἡ, *band for the limbs, fetter*, *AP*6.297 (Phan.).

**ἀρθρόω,** (ἄρθρον) *fasten by a joint*:—Pass., *to be jointed*, κνημὶς περὶ σφυρὸν -οῦται Hermipp.47.3; σώματα ἠρθρωμένα *well-jointed, well-knit*, Hp.*Aër.*20; κνῆμαι ἠρθρωμέναι Arist.*Phgn.*810$^{a}$28. **II.** mostly of words, *utter distinctly*, γλῶσσα ἀρθροῖ τὴν φωνὴν *produces articulate* sounds, X.*Mem.*1.4.12 (but ἀρθρῶσαι γλῶσσαν καὶ νόον *nerve* the tongue and mind, v.l. in Thgn.760); of persons, *render articulate*, καί μ' εἰς τοῦτο.. ἤρθρωσαν οἱ θεοὶ ὅπως.. Nic.Dam.p.65 D.

**ἀρθρ-ώδης,** ες, *well-jointed, well-knit*, X.*Cyn.*4.1, Arist.*Phgn.*810$^{b}$ 26. **2.** *articulated*, opp. ἄναρθρος, Id.*PA*667$^{a}$9 (Comp.); esp. in sense of sq., Gal.2.735. Adv. -δῶς ibid. **-ωδία,** ἡ, a particular kind of *articulation*, where the surfaces are only slightly concave and convex, ib.736. **-ωσις,** εως, ἡ, *jointing, compact connexion*, prob. in Str.2.1.30, cf. Ph.2.408. **2.** *articulation*, of speech, Phld.*D.* 3.14, cf. *Po.*994.6.

**ἀρθύσανοι·** ἀποσχίσματα καὶ ἀποκλαστήματα, Hsch.

**ἀρῐ-** [ᾰ], insep. prefix, like ἐρι-, strengthening the notion conveyed by its compd.: cogn. with ἀρείων, ἄριστος, chiefly denoting *goodness, excellence*: mostly in older Ep. and Lyr.

⊛**ἀρία,** ἡ, Dor. for φελλόδρυς, Thphr.*HP*3.16.3, al. (Prob. for ἀρέα, cf. ἀρέϊνος.)

**ἀριβάσκανος,** ον, *very envious*, Hsch.

⊛**ἀρί-γνως** [ᾰ], ωτος, ὁ, ἡ, = sq., in nom. pl. ἀριγνῶτες, Pi.*N.*5. 12. **-γνωτος,** η, ον, Od.6.108, Aeol. α, ον Sapph.*Supp.*25.4, also ος, ον Il.15.490:—*easy to be known*, ἀρίγνωτοι δὲ θεοί περ 13.72, cf. 15.490, Sapph. l.c.; δώματα Od.6.300; ῥεῖά τ' ἀριγνώτη πέλεται ib.108. **2.** in bad sense, *infamous*, ὦ ἀρίγνωτε συβῶτα 17.375.

**ἄρῑγος** or **ἄρρ-,** ον, *insensible to cold*, Arist.*Pr.*959$^{b}$17, Aret.*SD*1.14.

**ἀρίγων,** ωνος, ὁ, a kind of *spear*, Hdn.Gr.1.24, 2.279.

⊛**ἀρῐ-δάκρυος** [ᾰρ], ον, = sq., Arist.*Pr.*874$^{b}$8. **-δακρῦς,** υ, gen. υος, *very tearful*, γόος A.*Pers.*947 (lyr.); of persons, Arist.*HA*608$^{b}$9, *Pr.* 953$^{b}$11: prov., ἀριδάκρυες ἀνέρες ἐσθλοί Sch.Ven.Il.1.349; but in bad sense, Ph.2.269. **-δάκρῡτος,** ον, *much wept*, Hsch. **-δείκετος,** ον, *famous, glorious*: in Hom. mostly c. gen., ἀριδείκετος ἀνδρῶν Il. 11.248, al.; also υἱὸν.. ἀριδείκετον εἶναι Od.11.540; ἀ. τέκνα Hes.*Th.* 385; ἀριδείκετε δαῖμον Orph.*Fr.*155; of things, σκῆπτρον ib.101. **II.** *clear, distinct*, Emp.20.1. (Metr. lengthd. for ἀρι-δέκ-ετος, cf. Lat. *decus.*)

**ἀρίδες·** αἱ μετὰ κονιορτοῦ πνοαί, Hsch.

**ἀρί-δηλος** [ᾰρῐ], Dor. **-δηλος** (v. infr.), also **-δᾱλος,** ον, in pr. n., *IG*12(1).741 (Rhodes):—*clear, distinct, far seen*, Ὄσσα Simon.130, cf. Arat.94; *bright*, Ἀνταύγης Orph.*Fr.*237; ἀρίδηλον μνᾶμα *IG*7.52 (Megara), cf. Charito 4.1. **II.** *manifest*, τάδε γὰρ ἀ. Hdt.8.65, Ph. 1.276, al., Porph.*Chr.*35: Comp., Ph.1.331: Sup., ib.690; also f.l. for ἀΐδηλα in Tyrt.11.7. **III.** *conspicuous, magnificent*, ἀγῶνα τῶν πρόσθεν -ότερον Arr.*An.*7.14.10; *famous*, Eun.*VS* p.456 B. (Comp.). Adv. -λως Them.*Or.*2.26c, Sch.Ar.*Pl.*948: Comp., Ph.1.451: Sup. -ώτατα (sic) Hsch.—Ep., Ion., and later Prose.

**ἀρίδιον,** τό, Dim. of ἀρίς, *Hermes* 38.281.

⊛**ἀρί-ζηλος** [ᾰ], ον (Dor. -ζηλος *IG*9(1).270), also η, ον, v. infr.:—Ep. for ἀρίδηλος (-ζηλος from δγηλος, cf. δῆλος from δεγαλος and δέατο), *conspicuous*, of lightning, ἀρίζηλοι δέ οἱ αὐγαί Il.13.244, cf. Pi.*O.*2.61, S.*Ichn.*72; of sound, ὡς δ' ὅτ' ἀριζήλη φωνή Il.18.219; of persons whom all admire, ὥς τε θεῷ περ ἀμφὶς ἀριζήλω ib.510, *AP*4.1.3 (Mel.), etc.; ῥεῖα δ' ἀρίζηλον μινύθει καὶ ἄδηλον ἀέξει Hes.*Op.*6. Adv. ἀριζήλως, εἰρημένα a *plain* tale, Od.12.453. **II.** Dor. ἀρίζαλος (ζῆλος), = sq., Call.*Epigr.*52, Hsch. s. v. ἀρι-. **-ζήλωτος,** ον, *much to be envied*, Ar.*Eq.*1329 (anap.): **-ζήλητος** in Orac.ap.Eus.*PE*9.10.

**ἄριζος·** τάφος (Cypr.), Hsch.

**ἀρῐήκοος** [ᾰ], ον, *much heard of*, Call.*Del.*308. **II.** Act., *far-hearing, hearing readily*, A.R.4.1707, Dam.*Isid.*279; οὖας Procl.*H.* 2.14.

**ἀριῆνας·** ἀριστπώλους, Hsch.

⊛**ἀριθμ-έω** [ᾰ], impf. ἠρίθμεον as trisyll., Od.10.204, 3 sg. ἠρίθμει 13. 218:—Med., aor. ἠριθμησάμην Pl.*Phdr.*270d:—**Pass.,** fut. Med. in pass. sense ἀριθμήσομαι E.*Ba.*1318; fut. ἀριθμηθήσομαι Lxx 3*Ki.*3.8, Gal.10.68: Ep. aor. inf. ἀριθμηθήμεναι (for -ῆναι) Il.2.124:—*number, count, reckon up*, Od.4.411, Pi.*N.*10.46, etc.; αὐτὰρ ἐγὼ δίχα πάντας .. ἑταίρους ἠρίθμεον *counted* them so as to halve them, Od.10.204; ἀριθμήσαντες *after numbering* the army, Hdt.7.60; οὐδεὶς πώποτ'.. ἠρίθμησε *stopped to count* the enemy, Ar.*Eq.*570: poet., ἀριθμήσεις γαῖαν ἀπειρεσίην, = μετρήσεις, *AP*11.349 (Pall.):—Pass., Hdt.6.111, 9.32:—Med., ἠριθμοῦντο *counted each for himself*, πλίνθους Th.3. 20. **2.** *count out, pay*, χρυσίον, ἀργύριον, X.*Smp.*4.44, D.49.30, *IG* 5(1).1390.51 (Andania), *Mon.Anc.Gr.*7.22. **3.** *reckon, account*, ἐν εὐεργεσίας μέρει D.21.166; ἀ. τινὰ κλυτόπαιδα *AP*9.262 (Phil.); κέρδος τι ἀ. D.Chr.31.158:—Pass., *to be reckoned*, ἐν τοῖσι γενναίοισιν E.*Hel.* 729; ἐν γράμμασι Luc.*Jud.Voc.*2; εἴς τινας Hdn.1.1.1; ἀριθμεῖσθαι τῶν φιλτάτων *as one of*.., E.*Ba.*1318; μακάρων Theoc.13.72. [-ῐθμ- Ar.*V.*333, *Com.Adesp.*21.28 D.] **-ημα,** ατος, τό, *reckoning, number*, τῶν πάλων A.*Eu.*753; ἡμέρα ἀ. αἰώνιον Secund.*Sent.*4. ⊛**-ησις,** εως, ἡ, *counting, reckoning up*, Hdt.2.143, Str.9.5.3, *POxy.*1258.7 (i A.D.), Plot.4.4.11; *counting out, payment* of money, *IPE*1$^{2}$.32*B*35 (Olbia). **2.** *account*, *BGU*328 i 24 (ii A.D.), etc. **II.** = ἀριθμητική, ἡ, Hp.*Ep.*22. **-ητέος,** α, ον, *to be reckoned, counted*, Id.*Epid.* 2.3.17. **2.** ἀριθμητέον, *one must reckon, count*, Thphr.*Ign.*3, Porph. *Abst.*2.38. ⊛**-ητής,** οῦ, ὁ, *calculator*, Pl.*Just.*373b. ⊛**-ητικός,** ή, όν, *of* or *for reckoning, skilled therein*, ἄνθρωπος Id.*Grg.*453e. **II.** *arithmetical*, μέσα Archyt.2; ἀναλογία Arist.*EN*1106$^{a}$35; τὸ ἓν ἁπλῶς οὐκ ἦν ἀ. Dam.*Pr.*117; ἡ ἀριθμητική (sc. τέχνη) *arithmetic*, Pl.*R.*525a, al.; as a subject of competition, *Inscr.Magn.*107; ἡ ἀ. ἐπιστήμη Plu. 2.979e. Adv. -κῶς ib.643c, Theo Sm.p.116 H. **III.** -κόν, τό, *land-tax* in Egypt, τὸ τέλειον ἀ. *Sammelb.*4415.14 (ii A.D.), etc.; ἡμιτέλειον ἀ. *BGU*330.6 (ii A.D.). **-ητός,** ή, όν, *that can be counted*, οὐκ ἀ. Cratin.153, cf. *AP*12.145; ἠριθμημένον ἢ ἀ. Arist.*Ph.*223$^{a}$24; opp. μετρητόν, Id.*Metaph.*1020$^{a}$9. **2.** *easily numbered, few in number*, ἀριθμητοὺς ἀπὸ πολλῶν Theoc.16.87. **3.** οὐκ ἀ. *of* no *account*, Id.14.48. ⊛**-ιος,** α, ον, = *numerical*, Iamb.*Comm.Math.*9;

*by number*, ἀρίθμια σῦκα ρ′ *POxy.*529.6 (ii A.D.). 2. Astrol., *determining number*, κλῆρος Vett.Val.145.23; τόπος Id.278.30. II. *reckoned, counted*, μέτ' ἀθανάτοισιν ἀ. Rhian.1.16; ἐν καὶ ὄνος κείνοισιν ἀ. prob. in Opp.*H.*1.151; ἀνέρες ἐν Λιβύεσσιν ἀ. D.P.263; cf. μεταρίθμιος, ἐναρίθμιος. III. Subst. ἀρίθμιον, τό, *set, series*, *BGU*544.23 (iii A.D.).

**ἀριθμοποιός** [ᾰ], όν, *creating number*, Dam.*Pr.*245.

⊛**ἀριθμός** [ᾰ], (ἀρ- *IG*1.164), ὁ, *number*, first in Od., λέκτο δ' ἀριθμόν 4.451; ἀριθμῷ παῦρα Semon.3; ἐν ἀριθμῷ Hdt.3.6; ἀριθμὸν ἕξ Id.1.14, cf. 50; ἐς τὸν ἀ. τρισχίλια Id.7.97; πλῆθος ἐς ἀ. the amount in point of *number*, ib.60; τὸν ἀ. δώδεκα Euphro 11.11; δύο τινὲς ἢ τρεῖς . . εἰς τὸν ἀ. Men.165; ἔλαττον μήτε ὄγκῳ μήτε ἀριθμῷ Pl.*Tht.*155a; οὔτ' ἀριθμοῖς οὔτε μεγέθεσιν ἐλάττους Id.*Lg.*861e; σταθμῷ καὶ ἀ. X.*Smp.*4.45; δι' ἀ. καὶ μέτρου Plu.*Per.*16, cf. E.*Tr.*620: prov., λέγειν ποντιᾶν ψάφων ἀριθμόν 'count the pebbles on the shore', Pi.*O.*13.46, cf. 2.98; οὐ γιγνώσκων ψήφων ἀριθμούς, of a blockhead, Ephipp.19; οὔτ' ἀριθμὸν οὔτ' ἔλεγχον . . ἔχων Dionys.Com.3.13. 2. *amount, sum*, πολὺς ἀ. χρόνου Aeschin.1.78; ἀ. τῆς ὁδοῦ X.*An.*2.2.6; ἀ. [χρυσίου] a *sum* of money, Id.*Cyr.*8.2.16. 3. ἀριθμῷ, abs., *in certain numbers*, Hdt.6.58; but δένδρα ἀριθμῷ ὑμέτερα *by tale*, Th.2.72; ἀ. διδόναι Dionys.Com.3.6. 4. *item* or *term* in a series, ὁ δεύτερος ἀ. E.*Ion* 1014; τρίτον ὠδίνων ἀ. *Epigr.Gr.*574; ναῦς πολλοὺς ἀ. ἄγνυται ναυαγίων E.*Hel.*410, cf. Arist.*Po.*1461$^b$24; τοὺς ἀ. τοῦ σώματος *points* of the body, Pl.*Lg.*668d; τοὺς ἀ. ἑκάστου τῶν νοσημάτων Hp.*Acut.* 3; τὸ καλὸν ἐκ πολλῶν ἀ. ἐπιτελεῖσθαι Plu.2.45c: hence as a mark of *completeness*, πάντας τοὺς ἀ. περιλαβών Isoc.11.16; τοῦ καθήκοντος τοὺς ἀριθμούς the *sum total* of duty, M.Ant.3.1. 5. *number, account*, as a mark of station, worth, rank, μετ' ἀνδρῶν ἵζει ἀριθμῷ takes his place *among* men, Od.11.449; εἰς ἀνδρῶν μὲν οὐ τελοῦσιν ἀ. E.*Fr.*492; εἰς ἀ. τῶν κακῶν πεφύκαμεν Id.*Hec.*1186; ξενίας ἀριθμῷ πρῶτ' ἔχειν ἐμῶν φίλων *in regard of* friendship, ib.794; δειλοὶ γὰρ ἄνδρες οὐκ ἔχουσιν ἐν μάχῃ ἀριθμόν have no *account* made of them, Id.*Fr.*519; οὐδ' εἰς ἀ. ἥκει λόγων she comes not into my *account*, Id.*El.*1054; ἀ. οὐδεὶς οὐδὲ λόγος ἐστί τινος Plu.2.682f, cf. Call.*Epigr.*27.6, Orac.ap. Sch.Theoc.14.48. 6. *mere number, quantity*, opp. *quality*, ταῦτ' οὐκ ἀ. ἐστιν, ὦ πάτερ, λόγων *a mere set* of words, S.*OC*382; of men, οὐκ ἀ. ἄλλως not *a mere lot*, E.*Tr.*476; ἀριθμός, πρόβατ' ἄλλως Ar.*Nu.*1203; sometimes even of a single man, οὐκ ἀριθμὸν ἀλλ' ἐτητύμως ἄνδρ' ὄντα not *a mere unit*, E.*Heracl.*997; also ἀριθμὸν πληροῦν to be *a mere cipher*, Chor.*Milt.*66. II. *numbering, counting*, μάσσων ἀριθμοῦ past *counting*, Pi.*N.*2.23; esp. in phrases, ἀ. ποιεῖσθαι τῶν νεῶν to hold *a muster* of . ., Hdt.8.7; ποιεῖν X.*An.*7.1.7, etc.; παρεῖναι εἰς τὸν ἀ. ib.11; εἴ τι δυνατὸν ἐς ἀ. ἐλθεῖν can be stated *in numbers*, Th.2.72. III. *the science of numbers, arithmetic*, ἀριθμόν, ἔξοχον σοφισμάτων A.*Pr.*459; ἀριθμῶν καὶ μέτρων εὑρήματα S.*Fr.* 432; ἀ. καὶ λογισμὸν εὑρεῖν Pl.*Phdr.*274c, cf. *R.*522c: prov., εἴπερ γὰρ ἀριθμὸν οἶδα E.*Fr.*360.19. IV. in Philos., *abstract number*, Arist.*Cat.*4$^b$23, *Metaph.*990$^a$19, al.; ἀ. μαθηματικός ib.1090$^b$35; ἀ. οὐσιώδης, opp. τοῦ ποσοῦ, Plot.5.5.4; ἀ. ἐνιαῖος, οὐσιώδης, ἑτεροῖος, Dam.*Pr.*228. V. Gramm., *number*, *Stoic.*3.214, D.T.634.16, A.D.*Synt.*32.2, al.; cf. ἑνικός, δυικός, πληθυντικός. VI. *numeral*, ib.36.6, etc.; ὁ τέσσαρα ἀ. S.E.*M.*7.96; παιδὸς ἀ., = δεκάτη, E.*El.* 1132. VII. *unknown quantity* (*x*), defined as πλῆθος μονάδων ἀορίστων, Dioph.*Def.*2. VIII. Rhet., *rhythm* in Prose, in pl., D.H.*Comp.*23, *Dem.*52, cf. Arist.*Rh.*1408$^b$29; but also ἀριθμοὶ τῶν ἀρχαίων ποιητῶν *SIG*703.7 (Delph.). IX. *line* of a book, Apollon. Cit.2. X. *sum of numerical values* of letters in a name, *Apoc.*13.17, al.; φιλῶ ἧς ἀριθμὸς φμε' Pompeian Inscr. in *Rend.Linc.*10(1901). 257. XI. *unit* of troops, = Lat. *numerus*, *CIG*5187 (vi A.D.), *BGU*673 (vi A.D.), etc.; = *legio*, Jul. *ad Ath.*280d, Zos.5.26, *PLond.* 5.1711.69 (vi A.D.). XII. Astrol., mostly in pl., *degrees traversed in a given time*, Ptol.*Tetr.*112, Doroth. in *Cat.Cod.Astr.*6.107.30; τοῖς ἰδίοις ἀ. at her normal *speed*, of the moon, Gal.19.531; also of *degrees* of latitude, Heph.Astr.2.8,3.1. XIII. Medic., in pl., *precise conditions*, παρόντων τῶν πρὸς τὴν φλεβοτομίαν ἀριθμῶν Herod.Med. in *Rh.Mus.*58.71, cf. Aret.*CA*2.3, prob. in Herod.Med.ap.Aët.9.2; cf. supr. I.4. [ῐ E.*El.*1132, Ar.*Nu.*1203.] (ἀρῐ-θμός from root ἀρι-, cf. ἐπάριτος (q.v.), νήριτος.)

**ἀριθμοστόν** [ᾰ], τό, *fraction whose denominator is unknown* ($\frac{1}{x}$), Dioph.*Def.*2.

**ἀρίκεσι·** χαλεπαῖς, Hsch.

⊛**ἀρῐκύμων** [ᾰ] [ῡ], ον, gen. ονος, (κύω) *prolific*, Hp.*Superf.*23, prob. in *Aër.*5.

**ἄριλλα**, ἡ, dub. sens. in *IGRom.*4.1349.

**ἀριμάζω**, = ἁρμόζω, Hsch.

**Ἀριμασποί**, οἱ, Scythian word, meaning *one-eyed*, derived by Hdt. 4.27 from ἄριμα = ἕν, σποῦ = ὀφθαλμός; by Eust. ad D.P.31 from ἀρί = ἕν, μασπός = ὀφθαλμός: Ἀ. ἱπποβάμων A.*Pr.*805.

**ἀρίμηλον**, τό, a kind of *apple*, Antig.Car.ap.Ath.3.82b (sed leg. εἰαριμήλων).

**ἄριμος**, Tyrrhen., = πίθηκος, Str.13.4.6.

⊛**ἀρῖν**, v. ἄρριν.

**ἀρίξαι·** ὑποστηρίξαι, Hsch.

**Ἄριοι**, οἱ, ancient name of the *Medes*, Hdt.7.62; Μάγοι καὶ πᾶν τὸ Ἄριον (Ἄρειον codd.) γένος Eudem.ap.Dam.*Pr.*125bis; ἔκοψα κομμὸν Ἄριον (Ἄρειον codd.) a *Median* lament, A.*Ch.*423 (lyr.):—hence **Ἀριανή**, ἡ, name of the eastern *Iranian* highlands, Str.15.2.1: **Ἀριανοί**, οἱ, its inhabitants, D.S.2.37, cf. 1.94, Ael.*NA*16.16 (cf. Avest. *Airyana*). II. inhabitants of the Persian satrapy of Ἀρεία (Arr.*An.*3.25.1), Pers. *Haraiva*, Hdt.7.66; written Ἄρειοι, Id.3.93, Arr.l.c.

**Ἀριοντία**, ἡ, divinity worshipped at Sparta, *IG*5(1).213.40.

**ἀρί-πικρος** [ᾰρῐ], ον, *very bitter*, Hsch. **-πρέπεια**, ἡ, *glory*, of God, *Corp.Herm.*18.14. **-πρεπής**, ές, (πρέπω) *very distinguished*, ὡς καὶ σοὶ εἶδος μὲν ἀριπρεπές Od.8.176; δότε δὴ καὶ τόνδε γενέσθαι . . ἀριπρεπέα Τρώεσσιν Il.6.477; ἵππον ἀ. προὔχοντα 23.453; ἀ. βασιλῆες Od.8.390. 2. of things, *very bright*, ἔχε δ' αἰγίδα . . ἀριπρεπέα Il. 15.309; ἄστρα . . φαίνετ' ἀ. 8.556; ὅρμοι *Lyr.Alex.Adesp.*9.3; of a mountain, *conspicuous*, Νήριτον ἀ. Od.9.22; ἀ. εἶδος ἔχουσα Orph.*Fr.* 114: Comp., Them.*Or.*18.223b. 3. *famous*, σκῆπτρον Orph.*Fr.* 102. Adv. -πῶς, Ion. -πέως *IG*7.1684 (Plataea), etc. **-πρεπτος**, ον, = foreg., Ὑγίεια Maced.*Pae.*21.

⊛**ἆρις**, v. ἄρριν.

⊛**ἀρίς** [ᾰ], ίδος, ἡ, *bow drill*, Hp.*Art.*12, Call.Com.16, Apollod.*Poliorc.* 148.7, *AP*6.103 (Phil.), 205 (Leon.), Heliod.(?)ap.Orib.46.11.7. II. = φράκτης, *shrine*, Procop.*Aed.*2.3. III. = δρακοντία μικρά, Ps.-Dsc.2.167, Gal.19.85, *PMag.Par.*1.2308. 2. = sq., Plin.*HN*24. 151.

**ἀρίσαρον**, τό, *hooded arum*, *Arisarum vulgare*, Dsc.2.168.

**ἀρίσημος** [ᾰρῐ], ον, (σῆμα) *notable*, ἀρίσημα δὲ ἔργα τέτυκτο *h.Merc.* 12; καὶ τύμβος καὶ παῖδες ἐν ἀνθρώποις ἀρίσημοι Tyrt.12.29; ἀνήρ Hp. *Ep.*10; εἰκών *Epigr.Gr.*260 (Cyrene). II. *plain, visible*, τρίβος Theoc.25.158. Adv. -μως Hld.6.14.

**ἀρισθάρμᾰτος** [ᾰρ], ον, (ἄριστος, ἅρμα) *best in the chariot-race*, ἀ. γέρας the prize *of the best chariot*, Pi.*P.*5.30.

**ἀρίσκος·** κόφινος, Hsch.; cf. ῥίσκος.

**ἀρισκῠδής** [ᾰ], ές, (σκύζω) *very wrathful*, Call.*Fr.*108.

**ἀρίσπης**, f.l. for ἀρτιεπής, Hsch. **ἀρισπώλους**, v. ἀρῆναι.

**ἀρίσταθλος** [ᾰ], ον, *victorious in the contest*, *APl.*4.94 (Arch.).

**ἀρισταίνω·** ἀριστεύω, *AB*1340.

**Ἀρισταῖος**, ὁ, pr. n., Hes.*Th.*977: also epith. of Apollo, Pi.*P.*9. 65; of Zeus, Call.*Aet.*3.1.33.

**ἀρισταλκής** [ᾰρ], ές, *eminent in power*, σθένος B.7.7.

**ἀρισταρχαμία·** ἀριστία, Hsch.

**Ἀριστάρχειος**, α, ον, *of Aristarchus* (the critic), Str.2.3.8; αἱ Ἀ. (sc. ἐκδόσεις) Sch.Il.*Oxy.*221 iv 22, xi 15.

**ἀριστ-αρχέω** [ᾰρ], *rule in the best way*, Arist.*Pol.*1273$^b$5 codd. **-αρχος**, ὁ, *best-ruling*, epith. of Zeus, Simon.231, B.12.58.

**ἀριστάφῠλος** [ᾰρ], ον, (σταφυλή) *rich in grapes*, *AP*9.580.

**ἀριστάω**, inf. ἀριστᾶν, Ion. -ῆν Hp.*Vict.*3.68: pf. ἠρίστηκα X.*Cyr.* 4.2.39, Antiph.212.25; of this tense the Com. also used 1 pl. ἠρίσταμεν Ar.*Fr.*496, Theopomp.Com.22, inf. ἠριστάναι Hermipp.60:—Pass., pf. ἠρίστημαι, v. infr. [ᾱρ Ar.*Eq.*815, etc.; ᾰρ only late, *AP*11.387 (Pall.)]:—*take the* ἄριστον or *midday meal*, Ar.*Nu.*416, *Eq.*815; ἠρίστων, opp. ἐδείπνουν, X.*Mem.*2.7.12, cf. *An.*4.6.21: c. acc. rei, *breakfast on*, ἴα καὶ ῥόδα Diod.Com.2.37, cf. Pherecr.122. 5: pf. Pass. impers., ἠρίστηται δ' ἐξαρκούντως Ar.*Ra.*377. 2. *eat a second meal*, opp. μονοσιτέω, Hp.*VM*10, *Acut.*30.

⊛**ἀριστεία** [ᾰρ], Ion. -είη, ἡ, *excellence, prowess*, S.*Aj.*443, *AP*7.312 (Quadr.); γέρας ἀριστείας Alciphr.3.36: in pl., *Gorg.Fr.*11a, Pl.*Lg.* 942d: Il.5,11,17 are called respectively Διομήδους, Ἀγαμέμνονος, Μενελάου ἀριστεία; cf. Cic.*Att.*16.9.

⊛**ἀριστεῖα** [ᾰρ], Ion. -ήϊα, τά, *the meed of valour*, ἀ. διδόναι τῷ ἀξιωτάτῳ Hdt.8.123, cf. 124; ἀπαίτεε τοὺς Αἰγινήτας τὰ ἀ. demanded of them *the reward* (they had received) *for prowess*, ib.122; τὰ ἀ. τῆς νίκης φέρεσθαι Hp.*Aër.*23, cf. S.*Aj.*464, Pl.*Lg.*919e, Isoc.9.16, etc.; ἀ. τῆς θεοῦ offered to her, *IG*2.652*A*30, al.; ἀριστεῖον τῷ θεῷ ib.814$^a$*A*32, cf. *SIG*276*A*9 (Delph.), D.22.72: less freq. in sg. in same sense, Hdt.8.11, Luc.*DDeor.*22.3. 2. in sg., *monument of valour, memorial*, τοῦ πρὸς τοὺς βαρβάρους πολέμου D.19.272, cf. 59.97.

⊛**ἀριστεῖος** [ᾰ], ον, Adj. *belonging to the bravest, bestowed as the prize of valour*, στέφανοι, τιμαί, D.H.6.94, 9.13; γέρας Plu.*Thes.*26; Ἡρακλεῖ ποιήσειν θυσίαν ἀριστεῖον Id.*Pyrrh.*22.

**ἀριστερᾰχόθεν** [ᾰρ], *on the left*, *IG*7.3073.129,151 (Lebad.).

**ἀριστερεών**, ῶνος, ἡ, a plant, = περιστερεών, Plin.*HN*27.21, Orph. *A.*916, Ael.*NA*1.35.

**ἀριστερο-μάχος** [ᾰρ] [μᾰ], ον, *fighting left handed*, Herm.ap.Stob. 1.49.45. **-πηρος**, ον, *paralysed on the left side*, *BGU*367.8 (vi A.D.).

⊛**ἀριστερός** [ᾰ], ά, όν, *left, on the left*, ἐπ' ἀριστερά towards, i.e. on *the left*, Il.2.526, al.; ἐπ' ἀριστερὰ χειρός Od.5.277; ἐπ' ἀ. χειρῶν A.R. 2.1266; ἐξ ἀριστερῶν Hp.*Epid.*2.4.1; ἐν τοῖσι ἀριστεροῖσι ibid. 2. ἀριστερά (with or without χείρ), ἡ, *left hand*, ἐξ ἀριστερῆς χειρός on *the left hand*, Hdt.2.30; simply ἀριστερῆς χ. Id.4.34; ἐξ ἀριστερᾶς S.*Ph.*20, Pl.*Ti.*72c, etc.; οὐξ ἀριστερᾶς . . ναὸς S.*El.*7; ἐς ἀριστερὴν χεῖρα ἤιε, ἐν ἀριστερῇ ἔχειν, Hdt.7.42. 3. metaph., *boding ill, ominous*, because to a Greek, looking northward, unlucky signs came from the left, ἀ. ἤλυθεν ὄρνις Od.20.242. 4. *awkward, erring*, φρενόθεν ἐπ' ἀριστερὰ ἔβας turnedst to *the leftward* of thy mind, S.*Aj.* 182 (lyr.); ἐπ' ἀριστερὰ εἴληφας τὸ πρᾶγμα in a *sinister* sense, *Com. Adesp.*22.67 D.; τῷ ἀριστερῷ δέχεσθαι [λόγους] Plu.2.378b. (Prop. 'better', cf. ἄριστος; euphemism (cf. εὐώνυμος) to avoid ill-luck.)

**ἀριστεροστάτης** [ᾰρ] [τᾰ], ου, ὁ, *standing on the left*, esp. in the Trag. chorus, Cratin.215, Aristid.2.161 J.

**ἀριστερόφιν**, Ep. gen. of ἀριστερός, ἐπ' ἀ. Il.13.309.

**ἀριστερόχειρ** [ᾰ], χειρος, ὁ, ἡ, *left-handed*, Sor.1.111.

**ἀρίστ-ευμα** [ᾰ], ατος, τό, = ἀριστεία, *deed of prowess*, Eust.115.14 (pl.), *Gp.Praef.*2 (pl.). ⊛**-εύς**, έως, ὁ, dual ἀριστέοιν S.*Aj.*1304: (ἄριστος):—used by Hom. mostly in pl. ἀριστῆες *those who excel in valour,* *chiefs*, Il.2.404, al.; ἄνδρας ἀριστῆας Od.14.218, cf. Hdt.6.81, Alc. *Supp.*1a.8, Pi.*P.*9.107, Ant.Lib.2.2, etc.: sg., A.*Pers.*306; ἀνδρὸς ἀριστέως E.*IA*28 (lyr.); as an honorary title, *CIG*2881 (Milet.), *IG Rom.*4.914 (Cibyra). **-ευτής**, οῦ, ὁ, *improver*, πεδίων ἀ., of a husbandman, Secund.*Sent.*16. **-ευτικός**, ή, όν, *of, belonging to valiant deeds*, Max.Tyr.29.1, Plu.2.319b. **-εύω**, *to be best* or *bravest*, αἰὲν ἀριστεύειν καὶ ὑπείροχον ἔμμεναι ἄλλων Il.6.208; ὅς δέ κ' ἀριστεύῃσι μάχῃ ἔνι 11.409; ἐν ἀέθλοισιν ἀ. Pi.*N.*11.14; *gain the prize for valour* (v. ἀριστεῖα, τά), *gain the highest distinction*, Hdt.3.55, 9.105, Pl.*R.*468b, Isoc.9.16. 2. c. gen., ἀριστεύεσκε μάχεσθαι Τρώων he *was the best* of the Trojans.., Il.6.460, cf. Hdt.5.112, 7.106, al.; οὕνεκα βουλῇ ἀριστεύεσκεν ἁπάντων Il.11.627, cf. Pi.*N.*10.10. 3. c. inf., ἀριστεύεσκε μάχεσθαι *he was best at* fighting, Il 16.292,551, etc.; ἀριστεύεσκε μάχεσθαι Τρώων, v. supr. 4. c. acc. rei, ἀ. τι *to be best in* a thing, στάδιον Pi.*O.*10(11).64, cf. 13.43; ἰάλεμον Theoc.15.98. 5. c. acc. cogn., *win* as ἀριστεῖα, τὰ πρῶτα καλλιστεῖ' ἀριστεύσας S.*Aj.*435, cf. 1300; πάντα ἀ. Id.*Tr.*488, Pl.*R.*540a; μεμιγμένην ἀριστείαν ἀ. Plu.*Pel.*34. II. of things, *to be best*, ἀριστευοίσαν εὐκάρπου χθονὸς *best of all lands* on fruitful earth, Pi.*N.*1.14; τὸ κηδεῦσαι καθ' ἑαυτὸν ἀριστεύει μακρῷ A.*Pr.*890 (lyr.); of an opinion, *prevail*, Hdt.7.144.

**ἀριστέφᾰνος** [ἄρ], ον, *highly honoured with crowns*, *IGRom.*4.1273 (Thyatira).

**ἀριστήρ**, ῆρος, ὁ, title of magistrate at Elatea, *IG*9(1).101.9. (Perh. a mistake for ἀρτιστήρ.)

***ἀριστ-ητήριον** [ᾰ], τό, (ἀριστάω) *refectory*, τὸ ἱερὸν ἀ. τοῦ θεοῦ *BCH* 15.184. **-ητής**, οῦ, ὁ, *one who breakfasts*, i.e. *takes more than one full meal in the day*, Hp.*Aër.*1. ***-ητικός**, ή, όν, *fond of one's breakfast*, Eup.130: Comp., Id.7.13D. ***-ίζω**, *give one breakfast*, ἀπὸ σμικρᾶς δαπάνης ὑμᾶς ἀριστίζων ἀπέπεμψεν Ar.*Eq.*538; τούτους ἀρίστισον εὖ Id.*Av.*659; τὴν πόλιν ἀ. ἐπὶ πενταετίαν *IG*7.2712.62 (Acraephia):—Med., *breakfast*, Hp.*VM.*10.

***ἀριστίνδας**, ὁ, title at Sparta, *IG*5(1).680.6.

***ἀριστίνδην** [ᾰ], Adv., (ἄριστος) *according to birth* or *merit*, αἱρεῖσθαι *IG*1.61, cf. 9(1).333.12 (Locr. -δαν), Lex ap. D.43.57, Theopomp. Hist.217a; Ἀθηναίων πολλοὺς ἀπολέσαντες ἀ. καὶ τῶν συμμάχων And. 3.30, cf. Isoc.4.146, Pl.*Lg.*855c; κατ' ἐκλογὴν ἀ. κεκριμένοι Plb.6.10.9; opp. πλουτίνδην, Arist.*Pol.*1273$^a$23, cf. *Ath.*3.1, Plu.*Lys.*13.

**ἀριστό-βῐος** [ᾰ], ον, *living best*, Orac.ap.Hld.2.35. **βουλος**, η, ον, *best in counsel*, epith. of Artemis at Melite, Plu.*Them.*22, cf. Artem.2.37; at Rhodes, Porph.*Abst.*2.54:—hence **Ἀριστοβουλῐασταί**, οἱ, a confraternity of her worshippers, *IG*12(1).163 (Rhodes). ***-γᾰλᾰτίας**, ου, ὁ, title of *chief citizen of the province of Galatia*, *Class.Rev.*22.214. **-γένεθλος**, ον, *producing the best*, χῶρος *AP*9.686. **-γόνος**, ον, *bearing the best children*, μάτηρ Pi.*P.*11.3.

**ἀριστόδειπνον** [ᾰ], τό, *breakfast-dinner*, Alex.294, Men.998.

**ἀριστό-καρπος** [ᾰ], ον, *bearing fairest fruit*, Σικελία B.3.1. **-κρᾰτέομαι**, Pass., *to be governed by the best-born, live under an aristocracy*, Ar.*Av.*125, Pl.*R.*338d, Arist.*Pol.*1288$^a$41, etc. **-κράτης** [ρᾰ], ου, ὁ, *aristocrat*, Asp. *in EN*182.8. **-κρᾰτία**, ἡ, *rule of the best-born, aristocracy*, ἀ. σώφρων Th.3.82, cf. Henioch.5.17, Isyll.1, etc.; *rule of the rich*, Pl.*Plt.*301a. II. *ideal constitution, rule of the best*, Arist. *Pol.*1293$^b$1 sqq., *EN*1160$^a$33, Pl.*Mx.*238c,d, Plb.6.4.3. **-κρᾰτικός**, ή, όν, *aristocratical*, Pl.*R.*587d; ἀ. πολιτεία Arist.*Pol.*1288$^a$21, 1265$^b$33 (Comp.); κοινωνία, of man and wife, Id.*EN*1160$^b$32; παῖς Cic.*Att.*2.15.4 (Sup.). Adv. **-κῶς** Arist.*Pol.*1300$^a$41, 1317$^a$6, Cic.*Att.*2.3.4, Str.10.1.8. **-λόχεια** (-λοχία Thphr.*HP*9.20.4), ἡ, herb *promoting child-birth, birthwort, Aristolochia*, Nic.*Th.*509,937; ἀ. στρογγύλη, = *A. rotunda*, ἀ. μακρά, = *A. longa*, ἀ. κληματῖτις, = *A. Clematitis*, Dsc.3.4; ἀ. Κρητική, = *A. cretica*, Plin.*HN*25.95:—also **-λόχιον**, τό, Hp.*Nat.Mul.*32 (s.v.l.): **-λόχιος**, ἡ, Crateuas *Fr.*1, 2. **-λοχος**, ον, *well-born*, *App.Anth.*3.162. ***-μαντις**, εως, ὁ, *best of prophets*, S.*Ph.*1338. **-μάχος** [μᾰ], ον, (μάχη) *best in fight*, Pi.*P.*10.3. 2. as pr. n., Hdt., etc.:—hence Adj. **-μάχειος**, ον, *AP*13.8 (Theodorid.).

***ἄριστον**, τό, *morning meal, breakfast*, twice in Hom., ἐντύνοντ' ἄ. ἅμ' ἠοῖ Od.16.2, cf. Il.24.124; ἄριστα, δεῖπνα, δόρπα θ' αἱρεῖσθαι τρίτα A.*Fr.*182, cf. *Ag.*331: later, *breakfast* was called ἀκράτισμα, and ἄριστον was the midday meal, our *luncheon*, cf. Th.4.90, 7.81; ἄ. αἱρεῖσθαι, ποιεῖσθαι, Hdt.3.26, 6.78; ἀπ' ἀρίστου μέχρι δείλης Arist. *HA*619$^a$15. [ᾰ; contr. from ἀ(γ)ερι-στον, cf. Goth. *air*, OHG. *ēr* 'early', Avest. *ayarə* 'day'; also ἀ(γ)ερ- in ἦρι, ἠέριος; -στο- from -*d-to-*, root *ed-* 'eat'.]

**ἀριστό-νῑκος** [ᾰ], ον, *gaining glorious victory*, κράτος *Trag.Adesp.*97. **-νομία**, ἡ, (νέμω) = ἀριστοκρατία, Suid., Hsch. **-νοος**, ον, *excellent in wisdom*, *AP*9.213, *IG*5(2).156 (Tegea, iii/iv A.D.). **-πάλας** [πᾰ], ὁ, *best of wrestlers*, Epigr. in *BKT*5(1).77. **-πάτρα**, ἡ, *daughter of a peerless line*, of Artemis, B.10.106.

**ἀριστο-ποιέω** [ᾰ], *prepare breakfast*, τὰ ἀριστοποιούμενα things *prepared for breakfast*, X.*HG*4.5.1:—mostly in Med., *get one's breakfast*, Th.4.30, 8.95, X.*An.*3.3.1, 4.3.9, Onos.42.10, etc.; ἠριστοποίηντο X. *HG*4.5.8. **-ποιΐα**, ἡ, *preparation of breakfast*, Onos.12.1.

**ἀριστο-πολῑτευτής** [ᾰ], οῦ, ὁ, (πολιτεύω) *best of citizens*, honorary title, esp. at Sparta, *IG*5(1).335, al.:—also **-πολίτης** [λῑ], ου, ὁ, *best citizen*, αἰώνιος ἀ. ib.468, *IPE*2.29 (Panticapaeum; -πυλίτης lapis):—hence ***-πολῑτεία**, ἡ, *privileges of an* ἀ., *IG*5(1).65 (Sparta), *SIG*893*A* 9 (Messene). ***-πόνος**, ον, *working excellently*, χεῖρες Pi.*O.*7.51; μέλισσα Ps.-Phoc.171; ὑμέναιοι *AP*9.466: pl., ἀριστοπονῆες, as if from -πονεύς, Man.4.512. Adv. **-νως** *App.Anth.*3.182. II. *excellently wrought*, μέλαθρον Nonn.*D.*44.79. **-πόσεια**, ἡ, (πόσις) νύμφη wife *of a noble husband*, Opp.*C.*1.6. **-πρᾱγέω**, (πρᾶγος) = ἀριστεύω, Eust.621.39.

***ἄριστος** [ᾰ], η, ον, (with Art. Ep. ὤριστος Il.11.288, Att. ἄριστος) *best* in its kind, and so in all sorts of relations, serving as Sup. of ἀγαθός: I. of persons, 1. *best* in birth and rank, *noblest*: hence, like ἀριστεύς, *a chief*, Ἀργείων οἱ ἄριστοι Il.4.260, cf. 6.209; ἄ. ἔην πολὺ δὲ πλείστους ἄγε λαούς 2.580; θεῶν ὕπατος καὶ ἄ. 19.258; πατρὸς πάντων ἀ. παῖδα S.*El.*366; ἀνδρῶν τῶν ἀ. ὁμιλίη, opp. δῆμος, Hdt.3.81, cf. Cic.*Att.*9.4.2. 2. *best* in any way, *bravest*, ἀνδρῶν αὖ μέγ' ἄ. ἔην Τελαμώνιος Αἴας Il.2.768, cf. 7.50, etc.; οἰωνοπόλων, σκυτοτόμων ὄχ' ἄ., 6.76, 7.221. b. c. dat. modi, βουλῇ μετὰ πάντας.. ἔπλευ ἄ. 9.54, al.; ἔγχεσιν εἶναι ἀρίστους Od.4.211. c. c. acc. rei, εἶδος ἄριστε Il.3.39; ψυχὴν ἄ. Ar.*Nu.*1048. d. c. inf., ἄριστοι μάχεσθαι X.*Cyr.*5.4.44; ἄ. διαβολὰς ἐνδέκεσθαι *readiest* to give ear to calumnies, Hdt.3.80; ἀ. ἀπατᾶσθαι *best*, i.e. *easiest*, to cheat, Th.3.38. 3. *morally best*, εἴς τινα E.*Alc.*83 (lyr.); οἱ ἄ. ἁπλῶς κατ' ἀρετήν Arist.*Pol.*1293$^b$3. 4. *best, most useful*, πόλει E.*Fr.*194 codd. (leg. ἀρεστός); αὐτῷ Id.*Heracl.*5. II. of animals, things, etc., *best, finest*, ἵπποι Il.2.763; μήλων, ὑῶν, Od.9.432, 14.414; τεύχε' ἄριστα Il.15.616; χῶρος Od.5.442; ποταμῶν ἄ. τά τε ἄλλα καὶ ἀκέσασθαι Hdt.4.90; ἄριστα φέρεσθαι win an *excellent* reward, S.*El.*1097 (lyr.). III. neut. pl. as Adv., ἄριστα *best, most excellently*, ὄχ' ἄ. Il.3.110, Od.13.365, cf. Hdt.1.193, al., etc.; ἄριστά γε, in answers, *well said!* Pl.*Tht.*163c: later also ἀρίστως Iamb.*Myst.*3.14.

**ἀριστοσαλπιγκτής** [ᾰρ], ου, ὁ, *best of trumpeters*, Poll.4.87.

**ἀριστότατος**, η, ον, late superlative formation from ἄριστος, *Rev. Phil.*46.127 (Miscamus).

**Ἀριστοτελίζω**, *follow* or *imitate Aristotle*, Str.13.1.54:—Adj. **Ἀριστοτέλειος**, α, ον, *Aristotelian*, Cic.*Att.*13.19.4:—also **Ἀριστοτελικός**, ή, όν, Luc.*Demon.*56. Adv. **-κῶς** Iamb.*Comm.Math.*27.

**ἀριστο-τέχνης** [ᾰ], Dor. **-τέχνας**, ου, ὁ, *best of artificers*, of Zeus, Pi.*Fr.*57, cf. Hsch. **-τόκος**, ον, *bearing the best children*, γαστήρ Opp.*C.*3.62:—poet. fem. **ἀριστοτόκεια** [ᾰρ], Theoc.24.73, Tryph. 401, *IG*12(5).292 (Paros). II. Pass., ἀριστότοκος, ον, *born of the best parents*, γέννα E.*Rh.*909, cf. *Epigr.Gr.*896 (Syria).

**Ἀριστοφάνειος** [φᾱ], α, ον, *of Aristophanes*, μέτρον, the anapaestic tetrameter, D.H.*Rh.*11.10, Heph.8, Theon *Prog.*3.

**ἀριστοφόρον** [ᾰ], τό, *breakfast-tray*, *PGrenf.*1.14.7, *PEdgar*9.39 (iii B.C.), *PSI*4.428.47.

**ἀριστο-φυής** [ᾰ], ές, *of best nature*, Ecphant.ap.Stob.4.7.64 (in Sup. -έστατος). **-χαλκος**, ον, *with, producing finest brass*, Sch. Lyc.854. **-χειρ**, χειρος, ὁ, ἡ, *won by the stoutest hand*, ἀγών S.*Aj.*935 (lyr.). **-χειρουργός**, ὁ, *best of surgeons*, *POxy.*437.

**ἀριστώδῑν** [ᾰ], ῖνος, ὁ, ἡ, *bearing the best children*, Ἀθῆναι *APl.*4.221 (Theaet.).

**ἀρι-σφᾰλής** [ᾰρ], ές, *very slippery* or *treacherous*, οὐδός Od.17.196. **-τῑμος**, ον, *highly honoured*, *IG*5(1).add.722.

**ἀριτριλλίς**, = λινόζωστις, dub. l. in Ps.-Dsc.4.190 (ἀργυρῖτις Wellm.).

**ἀρι-φρᾰδής** [ᾰρ], ές, (φράζομαι) *clear, manifest*, σῆμα Il.23.326; ὀστέα.. ἀριφραδέα τέτυκται ib.240: so poet. Adv. **-δέως** *plainly*, ἀ. ἀγορεύει Theoc.25.176. 2. *clear to the sight, bright*, Id.24.39. II. *very thoughtful, wise*, S.*Ant.*347 (as cited by Eust.135.25). ***-φρων**, ον, gen. ονος, (φρήν) *very wise* or *prudent*, Suid.

**ἄριχα**· ἄρρεν πρόβατον, Hsch. **ἀρῑχάομαι** or **ἀρρῑχ-**, v. ἀναρριχάομαι. **ἀρίχεται**· γλίχεται, ἐπιθυμεῖ, Hsch. **ἀριχῶταν**· ἐκδύειν ζητῶν, Id.

**Ἀρκᾰδάρχης**, ου, ὁ, *president of Arcadian council*, *IG*5(2).132 (Tegea, iii A.D.).

**Ἀρκᾰδίζω**, *take the side of the Arcadians*, Polyaen.6.36.

**ἄρκαλα**, τά, *ear-rings* or *dry wood*, Hsch. **ἀρκαλέον**· ξηρόν, ῥυσσόν, Id. **ἀρκάνη**, ἡ, *bar to which the threads of the warp are fastened*, Id.

***ἀρκαρικός**, ή, όν, *of an arcarius*, *POxy.*126.14 (vi A.D.).

***ἀρκάριος**, ὁ, = *arcarius*, *POxy.*126.15 (vi A.D.).

***Ἀρκᾰδία**, ἡ, *Arcadia*, Il.2.603, etc.:—hence **-ίηνδε** A.R.2.1052: **-ίηθεν** Id.1.161. ***Ἀρκᾰδικός**, ή, όν, *Arcadian*, Men.462.8. **Ἀρκάς**, άδος, ὁ, *Arcadian*, pl. Ἀρκάδες ἄνδρες Il.2.611: also as Adj., ὁ, ἡ, Ἀ. κυνῇ prob. in S.*Fr.*262.

***ἀρκεθέωρος**, = ἀρχιθέωρος, *IG*2.181*a*, 11(2).219*B* (Delos, iii B.C.); cf. ἀρχεθέωρος, ἀρκιθέωρος.

**ἄρκειος**, α, ον, = ἄρκτειος, *of a bear*, στέαρ Dsc.1.125.3, 2.19; δέρματα D.Chr.7.43, cf. *Edict.Diocl.*8.33. 2. πνοὴ ἄρκειος a *northern* blast, A.*Fr.*127 (Lob. for ἄρκιος).

**ἀρκεόντως**, Att. contr. **ἀρκούντως**, (ἀρκέω) *enough, abundantly*, ἀ. ἔχει A.*Ch.*892, Th.1.22, Hp.*Mul.*2.162; ἀ. λέγεται Arist.*EN*1102$^a$27; τοῦ βίου ἀ. ἔχειν Ps.-Hdt.*Vit.Hom.*7; ἀ. ποδώκης swift *enough*, X.*Eq.*3.12.

**ἀρκεσίβουλος**, ον, *availing in council*, Cerc.*Oxy.*1082*Fr.*24 (prob.).

**ἀρκεσίγυιος**, ον, *limb-strengthening*, οἶνος dub. in Antiph.207.7 (= Philox.17).

**ἀρκ-έσιμος**, η, ον, *assisting*, θεός *CIG*9899 (Syria, Jewish). **-εσις**, εως, ἡ, (ἀρκέω) *help, aid*, S.*OC*73; οὐδὲ γὰρ -σιν ἔσχεν *IG*12(3).868 (Thera). **-εσμα**, ατος, τό, = foreg., Hsch. **-ετός**, ή, όν, *sufficient*, Chrysipp.Tyan.ap.Ath.3.113b, *Ev.Matt.*6.34, Herm.ap. Stob.1.49.44: c. inf., J.*BJ*3.6.3; of persons, *satisfactory*, ἀ. γενοῦ *BGU*33.5 (ii/iii A.D.); ἀρκετὸν [ἐστι] *it is enough*, c. inf., *AP*9.749 (Oenom.). Adv. **-τῶς** *Theol.Ar.*38.

**ἀρκευθιδίτης** οἶνος wine *made from* ἀρκευθίδες, Dsc.5.46 Sprengel (om. Wellm.).

**ἀρκεύθινος,** η, ον, *of juniper,* οἶνος Dsc.5.36. II. in Lxx, *of oleaster,* 3*Ki.*6.31; *of fir,* 2*Ch.*2.8.

***ἀρκευθίς,** ίδος, ἡ, *juniper-berry,* Hp.*Nat.Mul.*32, Thphr.*Od.*5 (prob. for -θος), Nic.*Th.*585, Plu.2.383e, Dsc.1.75. II. = sq., Ps.-Dsc. 1.75.

***ἄρκευθος,** ἡ, *juniper, Juniperus macrocarpa,* Hp.*Nat.Mul.*63, Theoc. 5.97, Nic.*Th.*584; ἀ. μεγάλη Dsc.1.75. II. *Phoenician cedar, Juniperus phoenicea,* Thphr.*HP*3.3.1, 3.12.3, *AP*6.253 (Crin.). III. *prickly cedar, Juniperus oxycedrus,* Musae.*Fr.*2 D. IV. ἀ. μικρά *dwarf juniper, Juniperus communis,* Dsc. l.c.

***ἀρκέω,** impf. 3 sg. ἤρκει Il.13.440, A.*Pers.*278: fut. ἀρκέσω: aor. ἤρκεσα, Dor. ἄρκεσα Pi.*O.*9.3:—**Med.,** aor. ἠρκεσάμην, 2 sg. ἠρκέσω dub. in A.*Eu.*213 (s.v.l.):—**Pass.,** inf. ἀρκέεσθαι Hdt.9.33, ἀρκεῖσθαι Poet.ap.Greg.Cor.p.425 S.: pf. ἤρκεσμαι Sthenid.ap.Stob.4.7.63: aor. ἠρκέσθην Plu.*Pel.*35, Luc.*Salt.*83: fut. ἀρκεσθήσομαι D.H.6.94, D.S.1.8, etc.:—*ward off, keep off,* c. dat. pers. et acc. rei, σάκος τό οἱ ἤρκεσε λυγρὸν ὄλεθρον Il.20.289, cf. 6.16; πατρίδι δουλοσύνην Simon. 101; κῆρας μελάθροις E.*El.*1300 (lyr.); ὅς οἱ ἀπὸ χροὸς ἤρκει ὄλεθρον Il.13.440, cf. 15.534; τοῦτό γ' ἀρκέσαι S.*Aj.*535; ὡς οὐκ ἀρκέσοι τὸ μὴ οὐ.. θανεῖν *would* not *keep off* death, ib.727. 2. c. dat. only, *defend,* πυκινὸς δέ οἱ ἤρκεσε θώρηξ Il.15.529; οὐδ' ἤρκεσε θώρηξ, without dat., 13.371. 3. *assist, succour,* 21.131, Od.16.261, S.*Aj.*824, *El.* 322, E.*Hec.*1164. II. c. acc. cogn., *make good, achieve,* οὐδ' ἔργα μείω χειρὸς ἀρκέσας ἐμῆς S.*Aj.*439. III. mostly in Trag., and always in Prose, *to be strong enough, suffice,* c. inf., first in Pi.*O.*9.3; ἀρκῶ σοι σαφηνίσαι (-σας Linwood) A.*Pr.*621 codd., cf. S.*OT*1209 (lyr.): c. part., ἀρκέσω θνῄσκουσ' ἐγώ my death *will suffice,* Id.*Ant.*547; cf. ἀρκοῦμεν ἡμεῖς οἱ προθνῄσκοντές σεθεν E.*Alc.*383; ἔνδον ἀρκείτω μένων *let him be content* to stay within, S.*Aj.*76; ἀρκεῖν γὰρ οἶμαι μίαν ψυχὴν τάδ' ἐκτίνουσαν Id.*OC*498; οὔτε ἰατροὶ ἤρκουν θεραπεύοντες Th.2.47; ellipt., σοφοὺς ὥσπερ σύ, μηδὲν μᾶλλον· ἀρκέσουσι γὰρ [σοφοὶ ὄντες] E.*Heracl.*576; ἀ. εἴς τι X.*Cyr.*8.2.5; πῶς ἡ πόλις ἀρκέσει ἐπὶ τοιαύτην παρασκευήν; Pl.*R.*369d; ταὐτὸν ἀρκεῖ σκῶμμα ἐπὶ πάντας *holds* equally for all, Id.*Tht.*174a; ὅτ' οὐκέτ' ἀρκεῖ [ἡ μάθησις] when it *avails* no more, S.*Tr.*711. 2. c. dat., *suffice for, satisfy,* οὐδὲ ταῦτά τοι μοῦνα ἤρκεσε Hdt.2.115, cf. S.*Ant.*308, etc. 3. *to be a match for,* c. dat., ψιλὸς ἀρκέσαιμι σοί γ' ὡπλισμένῳ Id.*Aj.*1123; πρὸς τοὺς πολεμίους Th. 6.84. 4. abs., *to be enough, avail, endure,* ἀρκείτω βίος A.*Ag.*1314; οὐδὲν γὰρ ἤρκει τόξα Id.*Pers.*278; *hold out, last,* ἐπὶ πλεῖστον ἀρκεῖν Th. 1.71, X.*Cyr.*6.2.31; οὐδ' ἔτ' ἀρκῶ I *can hold out* no longer, S.*El.*186 (lyr.); ὥστε ἀρκεῖν πλοῖα *to be sufficient* in number, X.*An.*5.1.13: freq. in part., ἀρκῶν, οῦσα, οῦν, *sufficient, enough,* βίος ἀρκέων ὑπῆν Hdt.1. 31, cf. 7.28; τἀρκοῦντα *a sufficiency,* E.*Supp.*865; ἀρκοῦσα ἀπολογία Antipho 2.4.10; ἀρκοῦντα or τἀρκοῦντα ἔχειν, X.*Mem.*1.2.1, *Smp.*4. 35; τῶν ἀρκούντων περιττὰ κτᾶσθαι Id.*Cyr.*8.2.21. 5. impers., ἀρκεῖ μοι *'tis enough* for me, I *am well content,* c. inf., οὐκ ἀρκέσει ποθ' ὑμὶν.. εἴκειν S.*Aj.*1242, cf. X.*An.*5.8.13: c. acc. et inf., ἐμοὶ μὲν ἀρκεῖ τοῦτον ἐν δόμοις μένειν S.*Aj.*80; ἀρκεῖ ἦν.., ὅτι.., X.*Cyr.*8.1.14, *Mem.* 4.4.9; ἔμ' ἀρκεῖ βουλεύειν *'tis enough* that I.., A.*Th.*248; οὐκ ἀρκοῦν μοί ἐστι, c. acc. et inf., Antipho 2.2.2; ἀρκεῖν δοκεῖ μοι it seems *enough,* seems *good,* S.*El.*1364. IV. in Pass., *to be satisfied with,* c. dat. rei, Poet.ap.Greg.Cor. l.c.; ἔφη οὐκέτι ἀρκέεσθαι τούτοισι Hdt.9.33, cf. Pl.*Ax.*369e, Arist.*EN*1107$^{b}$15, *AP*6.329 (Leon.), Plot.5.5.3: abs., ib.3.6, etc. 2. later, c. inf., *to be contented to* do, Plb.1.20.1, Ps.-Luc.*Philopatr.*29, etc.

**ἄρκη,** ἡ, Lat. *arca, CIG*3484 (Thyatira).

***ἄρκηλα,** *egg,* Hsch.; *hedgehog* (Cret.), Id.

***ἄρκηλος,** ὁ, *young panther,* Callix.2, Ael.*NA*7.47 (or a species of panther, ibid.); cf. ἄρκιλος.

**ἀρκής·** ταχύς, Hsch.

**ἀρκίθεωρος,** = ἀρχιθέωρος, *IG*11.287*B*33, al. (Delos, iii B.C.); cf. ἀρκεθέωρος.

**ἄρκιλος,** ὁ, *bear's cub,* Eust.1535.15; cf. ἄρκηλος, ἀρκτύλος.

**ἄρκιον,** τό, *burdock, Arctium Lappa,* Dsc.4.106.

***ἄρκιος** (A), α, ον Arat.741, ος, ον *AP*11.59 (Maced.): (ἀρκέω):—Ep. Adj. *to be relied on, sure, certain,* οὔ οἱ ἔπειτα ἄρκιον ἐσσεῖται φυγέειν he shall have no *hope* to escape, Il.2.393; νῦν ἄρκιον ἢ ἀπολέσθαι ἠὲ σαωθῆναι one of these is *certain,* to perish or be saved, 15.502; μισθὸς δέ οἱ ἄ. ἔσται a *sure* reward, 10.304, cf. Od.18.358, but, a *sufficient* reward in Hes.*Op.*370; βίος ἄ. ib.501, 577. II. *enough, sufficient,* ἄρκιον εὑρεῖν to be sure of having enough, ib.351, A.R.2.799, Theoc. 8.13; ὄφρα.. σφίσιν ἄρκιος εἴη that he might be *sufficient* for them, Id. 25.190; δέμας ἄρκιος Opp.*C.*3.185, cf. *H.*3.601; *helpful, useful,* παντὶ γὰρ ἄ. ἐστι Nic.*Th.*508, cf. Opp.*C.*3.173; ἄρκια νούσων *remedies against..,* Nic.*Th.*837: c. inf., *able to..,* Call.*Fr.*51a, cf. *Cer.*35. Adv. -ίως Hsch. III. in comp. sense, ἄρκιον ἦν θνᾴσκειν *it were better..,* *AP*9.154 (Agath.).

**ἄρκιος** (B), v. ἄρκειος.

**ἀρκόν·** σχολήν (Maced.), Hsch.

***ἄρκος** (A), ὁ and ἡ, = ἄρκτος, *bear,* Lxx 4*Ki.*2.24, *Apoc.*13.2, *AP*11. 231 (Ammian.), *IG*14.1302 (ii A.D.), *Tab.Defix.Aud.*249 (Carthage, i A.D.), Ael.*NA*1.31, Eust.1156.16, Suid. II. = ἄρκτος III, Hp. *Vict.*2.48. III. ἄρκου σταφυλή a plant, *bear-berry, Arctostaphylos Uva-ursi,* Gal.13.83.

***ἄρκος** (B), εος, τό, (ἀρκέω) *defence,* Alc.67: c. gen., βέλευς Id. 15.4.

**ἀρκούντως,** contr. for ἀρκεόντως (q.v.).

**ἀρκόφθαλμον,** = χρυσόγονον, Ps.-Dsc.4.56.

**ἄρκτειος,** α, ον, *of a bear,* στέαρ Heras ap.Gal.12.399.

**ἀρκτέον,** I. (ἄρχομαι) *one must begin,* τι πρᾶγμα S.*Aj.*853; πάλιν ἀ. ἀπ' ἀρχῆς *one must make a* fresh *start,* Pl.*Ti.*48b; ἀπὸ τοῦ πρώτου, τῶν πρώτων, τῶν γνωρίμων ἀ., Arist.*Metaph.*1013$^{a}$3, *GA*737$^{b}$25, *EN* 1095$^{b}$2, cf. Str.15.1.1. II. (ἄρχω) *one must govern,* τινί τινος Isoc. 14.10: abs., S.*OT*628, al. (*you must be ruled,* i.e. *obey*).

**ἀρκτεύω,** *serve as an* ἄρκτος II, Lys.*Fr.*82:—in Med., Sch.Ar. *Lys.*645.

**ἀρκτῆ** (sc. δορά), ἡ, *bearskin,* Anaxandr.65.

**ἀρκτικός** (A), ή, όν, (ἄρκτος I.2) *near the Bear, arctic, northern,* πόλος Arist.*Mu.*392$^{a}$3; κύκλος Hipparch.1.7.6, etc.: pl., Gem.5.10; -κά, τά, *the northern constellations,* Str.1.1.21: Comp. -ώτερος ib. 12, Gem.14.10: Sup., Str.1.1.6. II. *connected with the Great Bear,* δύναμις *PMag.Par.*1.1275.

**ἀρκτικός** (B), ή, όν, (ἄρχομαι) *initial, placed at the beginning,* of a sentence, A.D.*Synt.*28.19; ἀ. τεθεὶς σύνδεσμος Demetr.*Eloc.*56; of a word, συλλαβή Heph.1. 2. *originative,* c. gen., πυρετοῦ Gal. 17(2).299.

**ἀρκτικός** (C), ή, όν, (ἄρχω) *imperious,* Vett.Val.9.16.

**ἄρκτιον,** τό, *bearwort, Inula candida,* Dsc.4.105, Nic.*Th.*840, Plin. *HN*27.33.

**ἄρκτιος,** ον, *arctic, northern,* Nonn.*D.*38.329.

**ἀρκτόμορφος,** ον, *bear-like,* Tz. ad Lyc.481.

***ἄρκτος,** ἡ, *bear,* esp. *Ursus arctos, brown bear,* Od.11.611, *h.Merc.* 223, *h.Ven.*159, Hdt.4.191, etc.: the instances of the masc. are dub. (Arist.*Col.*798$^{a}$26 is inconclusive), the fem. being used even when both sexes are included, Id.*HA*539$^{b}$33. 2. Ἄρκτος, ἡ, the constellation *Ursa Major,* Ἄρκτον θ', ἣν καὶ Ἄμαξαν ἐπίκλησιν καλέουσιν Il.18.487, Od.5.273, cf. Heraclit.120, E.*Ion* 1154, etc.; τὰ ὑπὸ τὴν Ἄ. ἀοίκητα Hdt.5.10; Ἄρκτου στροφάδες κέλευθοι S.*Tr.*131 (lyr.); Ἄρκτου στροφάς τε καὶ Κυνὸς ψυχρὰν δύσιν Id.*Fr.*432.11: in pl., *the Greater and Lesser Bears,* Arat.27; Ἄ. μικρά, μεγάλη, Str.2.5.35, 36, cf. Cic.*ND*2.41.105. 3. *the north,* πρὸς ἄρκτον τετραμμένος Hdt. 1.148, cf. E.*El.*733 (lyr.), Aeschin.3.165, etc.; ἀπὸ ἄ. *IG*5(2).444.11 (Megalopolis), al.: pl., Hp.*Aër.*5 and 19, Pl.*Criti.*118b, etc. b. ἡ ἑτέρα ἄ. *the south pole,* Arist.*Mete.*362$^{a}$32. II. ἄρκτος, ἡ, at Athens *a girl appointed to the service of Artemis Brauronia* or Ἀρχηγέτις, E. *Hyps.Fr.*57, Ar.*Lys.*645. III. a kind of *crab,* prob. *Scyllarus arctus,* Arist.*HA*549$^{b}$23, cf. Speus.ap.Ath.3.105b, Mnesim.4.45, Archestr.*Fr.*56. IV. ἄρκτου δένδρον, = ἀκτῆ, Ps.-Dsc.4.173. (Cf. Skt. *ṛkṣas,* Lat. *ursus,* etc.)

**ἀρκτοτρόφος,** ον, *keeping bears,* Procop.*Arc.*9.

***Ἀρκτοῦρος,** ὁ, (οὖρος *guard*) the star *Arcturus, Bearward* (v. ἄρκτος I.2), Hes.*Op.*566, 610, Anaxag.20, etc. II. *the time of his heliacal rising,* i.e. *the middle of September,* Hp.*Aër.*10, S.*OT*1137; τὴν ὥραν τὴν τοῦ τρυγᾶν Ἀρκτούρῳ σύνδρομον Pl.*Lg.*844e (cf. Τρυγητής); Ἀρκτούρου ἐπιτολαί Th.2.78, etc.

**Ἀρκτο-φύλαξ** [ῠ], ακος, ὁ, *the constellation* Βοώτης, Eudox.ap. Hipparch.1.2.5, Arat.92. **-χειρ,** χειρος, ὁ, ἡ, *with bear's paws for hands,* Artem.5.49.

**ἀρκτύλος,** ὁ, *bear's cub,* Poll.5.15; cf. ἄρκιλος, ἄρκυλλος.

**ἀρκτῷος,** α, ον, (ἄρκτος) *of a bear,* γενύεσσιν Nonn.*D.*2.44. 2. *arctic, northern,* βορέας D.P.519, etc.; κρυμός Lib.*Or.*59.128; τὰ ἀ. *the arctic regions,* Luc.*Cont.*5.

**ἄρκυια,** dub. sens., epith. of Hecate, *Tab.Defix.Aud.*38.14 (Alexandria, iii A.D.).

**ἄρκυλλος,** ὁ, *young of the bear,* Sch.Opp.*H.*2.248; cf. ἄρκιλος.

**ἄρκυλον·** δίκτυον, Hsch. **ἄρκυμα·** ἀκρίς (Perga), Id. **ἄρκυον,** τό, = ἄρκυς, Id., *EM*144.11.

**ἀρκυοστασία,** v. ἀρκυστασία.

***ἄρκῠς** (ἄρκ- *Et.Gen.*, cf. Paus.Gr.*Fr.*73), υος, ἡ: pl., nom. and acc., ἄρκυες, -υας, Att. acc. ἄρκυς (v. infr.):—*net, hunter's net,* A.*Ag.*1116, *Ch.*1000: more freq. in pl., ἐξ ἀρκύων πέπτωκεν Id.*Eu.*147 (lyr.); ἀρκύων μολεῖν ἔσω E.*Cyc.*196; ἄρκυς ἱστάναι to set *nets,* X.*Cyn.*6.5; διωκόμενον τὸν λαγὼ εἰς τὰς ἄρκυς ib.10; πλεξάμενος ἄρκυς Ar.*Lys.* 790: metaph., ἄρκυες ξίφους *the toils,* i.e. *perils,* of the sword, E.*Med.* 1278. 2. *woman's hair-net,* Hsch.

**ἀρκυ-στᾰσία,** ἡ, *line of nets,* in pl., X.*Cyn.*6.6. (Also ἀρκυο- Artem. 2.11, 3.59.) **-στᾰτος,** η, ον, E.*Or.*1421 (lyr.): (ἄρκυς, ἵστημι):—*beset with nets,* ἐς ἀρκυστάταν μηχανὰν ἐμπλέκειν παῖδα into *the hunter's toils,* E. l.c. II. ἀρκύστατα, τά, *surrounding toils, a place beset with nets,* A.*Eu.*112, S.*El.*1476, cf. A.*Ag.*1375 Elmsl. **-ωρέω** [ῠ], *watch the nets,* of a spider, Ael.*VH*1.2. II. metaph., *keep carefully,* καλῴδια Eup.313 (ἁρκ- Eust.1535.18). **-ωρός** [ῠ], ὁ, *watcher of nets,* Cratin.79, X.*Cyn.*6.5, Lycurg.*Fr.*79, Poll.5.17, etc.

***ἅρμα,** ατος, τό, *chariot,* esp. *war-chariot,* Il.5.231, etc.; freq. in pl. for sg., ἑσταότ' ἐν θ' ἵπποισι καὶ ἅρμασι 4.366, etc.; τὰ Λυδῶν ἅρματα Sapph.*Supp.*5.19; ἵππους ὑφ' ἅρμασι ζευγνύναι A.*Pers.*190, E.*Hipp.*111; ἵππους ὑφ' ἅρματα ἄγειν A.*Pr.*465; πῶλον.. ζυγέντ' ἐν ἅρμασιν Id.*Ch.*795 (lyr.); opp. ἁρμάμαξα (q.v.); also, *racing-chariot* drawn by horses, opp. ὄχημα (a mule-car), Pi.*Fr.*106.5; ἅ. τέλειον *IG*2.967.45; ἁρμάτων ὀχήματα E.*Supp.*662, cf. *Ph.*1190; *travelling-chariot, Act.Ap.*8.28. 2. *chariot and horses, yoked chariot,* Il.2. 384, etc.; ἅ. τέθριππον Pi.*I.*1.14; ἅ. τετράορον, τέτρωρον, Id.*P.*10.65, E.*Alc.*483: metaph., τρίπωλον ἅ. δαιμόνων of three goddesses, E. *Andr.*277 (lyr.). 3. *team, chariot-horses,* ἅρμασιν ἐνδίδωσι κέντρον Id.*HF*881 (lyr.); ἅρματα.. φυσῶντα καὶ πνέοντα Ar.*Pax* 902; ἅρματα τρέφειν keep *chariot-horses for racing,* X.*Hier.*11.5; ἅρματος τροφεύς

Pl.*Lg.*834b. 4. metaph., ἅ. θαλάσσης *a ship*, Nonn.*D.*4.230,al., Opp.*H.*1.190. II. *a mountain district in Attica*, where omens from lightning were watched for: hence prov., ὁπόταν δι' Ἅρματος ἀστράψῃ, i.e. *seldom* or *never*, Str.9.2.11; δι' Ἅρματος alone, Plu.2.679c. III. Pythag. name for *unity*, *Theol.Ar.*6.

**ἅρμα** (A), ατος, τό, (αἴρω) *that which one takes*: *food*, used by Hp., acc. to Hellad.ap.Phot.p.533 B., cj. in Hes.*Th.*639 (pl.). II. *burden, load*, Aq.*De.*1.12, al.

**ἅρμα** (B), ἡ, (ἀραρίσκω) *union, love*, Delphic word, Plu.2.769a, Hsch.

***ἁρμακιάς·** στοάς, Hsch.

**ἁρμαλά**, = πήγανον ἄγριον, Dsc.3.46; Syrian for π. κηπαῖον, Ps.-Dsc.3.45:—also **ἁρμαρά**, *PMag.Par.*1.1294,1990. (Cf. Arabic *harmal* 'rue'.)

**ἁρμαλιά**, ἡ, *sustenance allotted, food*, Hes.*Op.*560,767; ἁ. ἔμμηνος Theoc.16.35; *stores* in a ship, A.R.1.393:—also **ἁρμολία**, ἡ, *PTeb.*112 (ii B.C.), 121.78 (i B.C.).

**ἁρμαλόομαι**, in aor. ἡρμαλώσατο, = συνέλαβεν, Hsch.

**ἁρμάμαξα** [μᾰμ], ης, ἡ, *covered carriage*, esp. used by Persians; [Ξέρξης] μεταβαίνεσκε ἐκ τοῦ ἅρματος ἐς ἁρμάμαξαν Hdt.7.41, cf. 83; of ambassadors to Susa, ἐφ' ἁρμαμαξῶν μαλθακῶς κατακείμενοι Ar.*Ach.*70; used by women, X.*Cyr.*3.1.40, 6.4.11.

**ἁρμάν·** πόλεμος (Phryg.), *EM*145.42.

***ἁρμαρίτης**, ου, ὁ, *bank-manager*, Just.*Edict.*9.2.1.

**ἁρμᾰσίδουπος** [ῐ], ον, *sounding in the chariot*, Pi.*Fr.*17.

***ἁρμᾰτάρακτα**, τά, (for ἁρματο-ταρ-) *spells for upsetting chariots in races*, *PMag.Par.*1.2210.

**ἁρμᾰτ-αρχία**, ἡ, *squadron of sixteen war-chariots*, Ascl.*Tact.*8, Ael.*Tact.*22.2. ***-ειος**, ον, *of* or *belonging to a chariot*, σύριγγες E.*IA*230; δίφρος X.*Cyr.*6.4.9, Ant.Lib.11.3 (ἁρμάτιον codd.); ἁρμάτινον, Apoll.*Lex.* s.v. δίφρον, is prob. corrupt; τροχός *Placit.*2.20.1; νόμος ἁ. name of a *melody for the flute*, Plu.2.335a, 1133e; ἁ. μέλος, stage-direction in E.*Or.*[1384]. **-εύω**, *drive a chariot*, ib.994. **-ηγός**, όν, (ἄγω) *driving a chariot*, τροχοί Parth.6.14. **-ηλᾰσία**, ἡ, *chariot-driving*, X.*Cyr.*6.1.27, Luc.*Dem.Enc.*23. **-ηλᾰτέω**, *go in a chariot, drive it*, Hdt.5.9, X.*Smp.*4.6. **-ηλάτης** [λᾰ], Dor. **-τας**, ου, ὁ, *charioteer*, Pi.*P.*5.115, S.*El.*700, X.*Smp.*2.27, etc. **-ηλᾰτικός**, ή, όν: μονομερής, διμερής, τετραμερὴς ἁ., names of *bandages*, Sor.*Fasc.*12.513C.(tit.). **-ήλᾰτος**, ον, *driven round by a chariot* or *wheel*, of Ixion, E.*HF*1297 Musgr. (-την codd.). 2. ὁδὸς ἁ. road *for chariots*, Archyt.ap.Iamb.*Protr.*4. **-ίζομαι**, *place in a chariot*: metaph., εἰς λάληθρον κίσσαν, i.e. the Argo, Lyc.1319. ***-ιον**, τό, Dim. of ἅρμα, *Gloss.* II. name of an *eyesalve*, Gal.12.779, Aët.7.41. ***-ίτης** [ῑ], ου, ὁ, *using chariots*, Λυδοί Philostr.*Im.*1.17.

**ἁρμᾰτο-δρομέω**, *race in a chariot*, Apollod.3.5.5. **-δρομία**, ἡ, *chariot-race*, Str.5.3.8. **-δρόμος**, ον, *running a chariot-race*, Sch.A.R.1.1333. **-εις**, εσσα, εν, = ἁρμάτειος, δίφρος Critias 2.11 D. **-εργος**, ον, (ἔργον) *building chariots*, Sch.Il.24.277. **-θεσία**, ἡ, (τίθημι) *chariot-race*, Eust.226.6. **-κτύπος** ὄτοβος *rattling* din *of chariots*, A.*Th.*204(lyr.). **-μᾰχέω**, *fight in* or *from a chariot*, Eust.1088.27. **-πηγέω**, *build chariots*, Poll.7.115. ***-πηγός**, όν, (πήγνυμι) *building chariots*: ἁ. ἀνήρ *wheelwright, chariot-maker*, Il.4.485, Theoc.25.247. **-πήξ**, ῆγος, ὁ, ἡ, = foreg., Theognost. in *AB*1340. **-ποιέω**, = ἁρματοπηγέω, Poll.7.113. **-ποιός**, όν, = ἁρματοπηγός, J.*AJ*6.3.5. **-τροφέω**, *keep chariot horses*, esp. for racing, X.*Ag.*9.6, D.L.4.17, Phld.*Acad.Ind.*p.47 M. **-τροφία**, ἡ, *keeping of chariot-horses*, X.*Hier.*11.5. ***-τροχιά**, Ep. **-ιή**, ἡ, *wheel-track of a chariot*, Il.23.505, Ph.1.312, Luc.*Dem.Enc.*23, Ael.*VH*2.27, Q.S.4.516.

**ἁρματωλία**, ἡ, acc. to the Sch. for ἁρματηλασία, with a play on ἁμαρτωλία, Ar.*Pax*415.

**ἁρμ-ελᾰτέω**, = ἁρματηλατέω, Ps.-Callisth.1.18. **-ελᾰτήρ**, ῆρος, ὁ, *charioteer*, κόσμοιο, of the Sun, *IG*14.2012.1 (Sulp. Max.). **-ελάτης** [λᾰ], ου, ὁ, = foreg., Orac.ap.Eun.*Hist.*p.229 D. 2. name of a *bandage*, Gal.12.497 Chart.

**ἄρμενα**, τά, *tackle* of a ship, *sails*, etc., Hes.*Op.*808, Aen.Tact.11.3, Theoc.22.13, *IPE*1².32 *B*52 (Olbia). 2. *accoutrements*, Alc.94. 3. *implements*, ὁπόσα ἀνθρώποις ἄ. μεμηχάνηται Hp.*Fract.*31, cf. Aen.Tact.18.11, *AP*6.205 (Leon.), etc.: in sg., πρὸς τὸ ἄ. Hp.*Fract.*2; ἄ. ἐργασίης *AP*6.47 (Antip. Sid.), 11.203. b. esp. of *surgical apparatus*, Hp.*Off.*2, cf. Bacch.ap.Erot.*Fr.*37. 4. *food*, Numen.ap.Ath.7.306c. Neut. of ἄρμενος, part. of ἀραρίσκω (q.v.).

***Ἀρμεν-ία**, ἡ, *Armenia*, ἡ μεγάλη and ἡ μικρά Str.11.12.3 and 4 sq., cf. App.*Mith.*105:—Adj.***Ἀρμένιος**, α, ον, *Armenian*: also ***Ἀρμενιακός**, ή, όν, Str.11.14.12: **-κόν**, τό, *apricot*, *Prunus Armeniaca*, Dsc.1.115, Gal.6.593 (also **Ἀρμενική** (sc. μηλέα) Id.12.76): **-κὸς λίθος** *limestone coloured blue by copper carbonate*, Id.5.105; χρυσόκολλα Ἀ. Dsc.5.89. **-ιάρχης**, ου, ὁ, *president of the* κοινὸν τῆς Ἀρμενίας, *Anatolian Studies* p.116. **-ιστί**, Adv. *in Armenian fashion*, ἐσκευάσθαι Str.11.3.3.

***ἁρμενίζω**, *sail*, *Gloss.*

**Ἀρμένιον**, τό, *copper carbonate, azurite*, Dsc.5.90. II. **ἀρμένια**, τά, Dim. of ἄρμενα, *small tools*, Hero *Aut.*24.2, Sch.Opp.*H.*1.222.

**ἀρμενοθήκη**, ἡ, *store for ship's tackle*, Hsch. s.v. καραδάλη.

**ἄρμενον**, v. ἄρμενα.

**ἀρμενοποιέω**, *sail*, Dosith.432.21.

**ἀρμένος**, v. ἀείρω III.1.

***ἀρμενοφόρος**, gloss on ἱστιοφόρος, Hsch.

**ἁρμή**, ἡ, (ἀραρίσκω) *junction*, Chrysipp.*Stoic.*2.154 (prob. for ὁρμήν); *fitting together*, of shields, Q.S.11.361; *suture* of a wound, Hp. ap.Erot.; of the skull-bones, Id.ap.Gal.19.86.

**ἁρμογή**, ἡ, (ἁρμόζω) *joining, junction*, Luc.*Zeux.*6; *fitting, arrangement*, Plb.6.18.1. 2. *joint* in masonry, J.*AJ*15.11.3, Hdn.3.3.7. 3. Lit. Crit., κώλων ἁ. *getting together, junction, arrangement* of clauses, D.H.*Comp.*8, cf. 23; ὀνομάτων ib.26; of letters, ib.22; *adjustment* of parts in an organized whole, ἁ. τοῖς ὅλοις Phld.*Po.*2.17; ἑλληνισμὸς ἀποτελεῖται καὶ ἁ. τις ib.18. 4. Medic., *joining of two bones without motion*, = σύμφυσις, opp. ἄρθρον, Gal.19.460. 5. in Music, = ἁρμονία, *method of tuning* a stringed instrument, Ptol.*Harm.*2.6; *modulation*, Eup.11; opp. ἀναρμοστία, Plot.3.6.2. 6. in Painting, *gradation* of tints in transition, Plin.*HN*35.29.

***ἁρμόδιος**, α, ον, (ἁρμόζω) *fitting together*, θύραι, metaph. of the lips, Thgn.422. II. *fitting*, ἥβη Id.724; δεῖπνον Pi.*N.*1.21; ἀνθρώποις ἁρμόδιόν [ἐστι] c. inf., Democr.187, cf. Aeschin.Socr.52; μέρη τῆς πολιτείας ἁ. τοῖς τηλικούτοις Plu.2.793a; πᾶν σῶμα ἁ. εἶναι ψυχῇ Aen.Gaz.*Thphr.*p.60 B.: Comp. **-ώτερος**, γάμος Hld.1.21: Sup. **-ώτατος**, ἔς τι Arr.*Tact.*16.4; also, *agreeable*, Parth.16.2. Adv. **-ως** Plu.*Arist.*24, *PGiss.*57.6 (vi/vii A.D.).

**ἁρμοδιοτῠπής**, ές, *of accordant mould* or *cast*, Hsch.

**ἁρμοζόντως**, *suitably*, χρείᾳ τινῶν D.S.3.15, cf. *SIG*559.10 (iii B.C.), *BGU*1060.31 (i B.C.); τοῖς παροῦσι J.*AJ*6.1.2; τῷ πάθει Gal.18(1).773; Att. **ἁρμοττόντως** Ph.*Bel.*82.4, Iamb.*Comm Math.*17, Sch.Ar.*Nu.*253.

***ἁρμόζω**, Att. **ἁρμόττω**, Dor. **ἁρμόσδω** Theoc.1.53 (ἐφ-); part. ἁρμόσσον Hp.*Art.*37: impf. ἥρμοζον, Dor. ἅρμ- Pi.*N.*8.11: fut. ἁρμόσω S.*Ant.*1318 (lyr.), Hp.*Fract.*31, Ar.*Th.*263: aor. ἥρμοσα Il.3.333, etc., Dor. ἅρμοξα Pi.*N.*10.12 (συν-): pf. ἥρμοκα Arist.*Po.*1459ᵇ32:—Med., Ep. imper. ἁρμόζεο Od.5.162, -όζου Philem.187: fut. -όσομαι Gal.10.971: aor. ἡρμοσάμην Hdt.5.32, etc., Dor. ἁρμοξάμην Alcm.71:—**Pass.**, pf. ἥρμοσμαι E.*Ph.*116 (lyr.), Pl.*La.*193d, Ion. ἅρμοσμαι Hdt.2.124; Dor. inf. ἁρμόχθαι Ocell.ap.Stob.1.13.2; Dor. 3 sg. ἅρμοκται Ecphant.ap.Stob.4.7.64: aor. ἡρμόσθην Pl.*Phd.*93a, Dor. ἁρμόχθην D.L.8.85: fut. ἁρμοσθήσομαι S.*OC*908:—*fit together, join*, esp. of *joiner's* work, ἥρμοσεν ἀλλήλοισιν (sc. τὰ δοῦρα) Od.5.247 (also in Med., *put together*, ἁρμόζεο χαλκῷ εὐρεῖαν σχεδίην ib.162; ναυπηγίαν ἁρμόζων E.*Cyc.*460; ἁρμόζειν χαίταν στεφάνοισι Pi.*I.*7(6).39; ἀρβύλαισιν ἁ. πόδα E.*Hipp.*1189; ἁ. πόδα ἐπὶ γαίας *plant* foot on ground, Id.*Or.*233; ἁ. ποδὸς ἴχνια Simon.182; ἐν ἀσυχαίᾳ βάσει βάσιν ἅρμοσαι (aor. imper. Med.) S.*OC*198; στόμ' ἅρμοσον *kiss*, E.*Tr.*763; ἁ. ψαλίοις ἵππους *furnish* them *with*.., Id.*Rh.*27 (lyr.). b. generally, *adapt, accommodate*, ἁ. δίκην εἰς ἕκαστον *award* each his just due, Sol.36.17; σφισὶν βίοτον ἁ. *accord* them life, Pi.*N.*7.98; *apply* a remedy, S.*Tr.*687; *make ready*, τοὐπτάνιον Hegesipp.Com.1.19:—Med., *accommodate, suit oneself*, πρὸς τὴν παροῦσαν πάντοθ' ἁρμόζου τύχην Philem. l.c.; πρός τινα Luc.*Merc.Cond.*30; ἁ. σύνεσιν *acquire* it, Hp.*Lex*2. 2. of marriage, *betroth*, Hdt.6.108; ἁ. κόρᾳ ἄνδρα Pi.*P.*9.117; ἁ. γάμον, γάμους, ib.13, E.*Ph.*411:—Med., *betroth to oneself, take to wife*, τὴν θυγατέρα τινός Hdt.5.32,47 (but Med. = Act., 2*Ep.Cor.*11.2); ἁ. ὡς ἐὰν αἱρῆται γάμῳ *POxy.*906.7 (ii/iii A.D.):—Pass., ἁρμόσασθαι θυγατέρα τινὸς γυναῖκα *have* her *betrothed* or *married to* one, Hdt.3.137; ὡς ἐκείνῳ τῇδέ τ' ἦν ἡρμοσμένα as *troth was plighted* between him and her, S.*Ant.*570. 3. *bind fast*, ἁ. τινὰ ἐν ἄρκυσι E.*Ba.*231. 4. *set in order, regulate, govern*, στρατόν Pi.*N.*8.11:—Pass., [νόμοις] οὐκ ἄλλοισιν ἁρμοσθήσεται S.*OC*908; κονδύλοις ἡρμοττόμην I *was ruled* or *drilled* with cuffs, Ar.*Eq.*1236. b. in the Spartan Constitution, *act as harmost*, ἐν ταῖς πόλεσιν X.*Lac.*14.2, etc.: c. acc., ἁρμοστὴν ὃς ἥρμοζε τὴν Ἀσίαν Luc.*Tox.*17. 5. in Music, *tune* instruments, τὸ σύμφωνον Pl.*Phlb.*56a, etc.:—Med., ἁρμόττεσθαι ἁρμονίαν Id.*R.*591d; ἁ. λύραν *tune one's* lyre, ib.349e; Δωριστὶ ἁ. λύραν Ar.*Eq.*989; αὐλόν Luc.*Harm.*1 (but μέλη ἔς τι ἁ. *adapt* them *to* a subject, Simon.184):—Pass., of the lyre, ἡρμόσθαι *to be tuned*, Pl.*Tht.*144e, cf. *Phd.*85e; ἁρμονίαν καλλίστην ἡρμ. Id.*La.*188d; ὁμονοητικὴ καὶ ἡρμοσμένη ψυχή *at harmony with itself*, Id.*R.*554e. 6. *compose*, ᾆσμα Philostr.*Her.*19.17. II. intr., *fit well*, of clothes or armour, ἥρμοσε δ' αὐτῷ [θώρηξ] Il.3.333; Ἕκτορι δ' ἥρμοσε τεύχε' ἐπὶ χροΐ 17.210; ἐσθὰς ἁρμόζοισα γυίοις Pi.*P.*4.80; ἆρ' ἁρμόσει μοι (sc. τὰ ὑποδήματα); Ar.*Th.*263; τοῖς τρόποις ἁ. ὥσπερ περὶ πόδα *fit* like a shoe, Pl.Com.129; θώραξ περὶ τὰ στέρνα ἁρμόζων X.*Cyr.*2.1.16. b. Math., *coincide with*, c. dat., Papp.612.14; *correspond*, Hero *Aut.*1.4. 2. *suit, be adapted for*, τινί S.*OT*902 (lyr.), *El.*1293, And.4.6; τόδ' οὐκ ἐπ' ἄλλον ἁρμόσει *shall* not *be adapted* to another, S.*Ant.*1318; κἂν ἐπὶ τῶν θηρίων ἁρμόσειε λόγος Arist.*Pol.*1281ᵇ19; εἴς τι, πρός τι, Pl.*Plt.*289b, 286d; πρὸς τὰς συνουσίας Isoc.2.34, cf. D.61.24; of medicines, Dsc.1.2, al.; of an argument, *apply*, Arist.*Ph.*209ᵃ9, al.; τὸ τοῦ Ξενοφάνους ἁρμόττει *is applicable*, Id.*Rh.*1377ᵃ19. 3. impers., ἁρμόζει *it is fitting*, c. acc. et inf., σιγᾶν ἂν ἁρμόζοι σε S.*Tr.*731: c. inf. only, λόγους οὓς ἁρμόσει λέγειν D.18.42; πάντα τὰ τοιαῦτα ἁρμόττει καλεῖν Id.21.166; οὔτε ἁ. μοι οἰκεῖν μετὰ τοιούτων Id.40.57; τὰ τοιαῦτα ῥηθῆναι μάλιστ' ἂν ἁρμόσειεν Isoc.9.72. 4. part. ἁρμόζων, ουσα, ον, *fitting, suitable*, Pi.*P.*4.129; ἡ ἁρμόζουσα ἀπόφασις the *appropriate* verdict, Archim.*Sph.Cyl.*1 *Praef.*; ἀλλήλοις Pl.*La.*188d, al.: c. gen., Plb.1.44.1; πρός τι X.*Mem.*4.3.5, etc. 5. *to be in tune*, λύραν ἐπίτειν' ἕως ἂν ἁρμόσῃ Macho 2.9.

**ἁρμοῖ**, Adv. *just, lately*, A.*Pr.*615, Theoc.4.51, Lyc.106, Call.*Fr.*44; *at once*, Hp.*Mul.*1.36. 2. *just, a little*, ib.4, *Steril.*213. 3. *tightly*, Id.*Cord.*12.—Written ἁρμῷ Pi.*Fr.*10, Pherecr.111, Hp.*Cord.* l.c., cf. *EM*144.49. (Old locative of ἁρμός.)

**ἁρμοίματα**· ἀρτύματα, Hsch.

**ἁρμο-κ[όπος]**, ὁ, *locksmith*, prob. in *BGU*344.14 (ii/iii A.D.). **-λογέω**, *join, pile together*, τάφον *AP*7.554 (Phil.):—Pass., τὰ μέλαθρα τῶν θυρίδων ἡρμολόγηται *PRyl.*233.6 (ii A.D.): metaph., ἡρμολογημένον τῷ πρὸ ἑαυτοῦ *closely connected with*.., S.E.*M.*5.78. **-λόγησις**, εως, ἡ, *joining, Gloss.* **-λόγος**, ον, *joining together*, Id.

***ἁρμονία**, ἡ, (ἁρμόζω) *means of joining, fastening*, γόμφοισιν.. καὶ ἁρμονίῃσιν ἄρηρεν Od.5.248; of a ship, ὄφρ' ἂν.. ἐν ἁρμονίῃσιν ἀρήρῃ ib.361. 2. *joint*, as between a ship's planks, τὰς ἁ. ἐν ὧν ἐπάκτωσαν τῇ βύβλῳ caulked the *joints* with papyrus, Hdt.2.96; τῶν ἁρμονιῶν διαχασκουσῶν Ar.*Eq.*533; also in masonry, αἱ τῶν λίθων ἁ. D.S.2.8, cf. Paus.8.8.8, 9.33.7. 3. in Anatomy, *suture*, Hp.*Off.*25, *Oss.*12; *union* of two bones by mere apposition, Gal.2.737; also in pl., *adjustments*, πόρων Epicur.*Fr.*250. 4. *framework*, ῥηγνὺς ἁρμονίαν ..λύρας S.*Fr.*244; βοὸς Philostr.*Im.*1.16; esp. of the *human frame*, ἁρμονίην ἀναλυέμεν ἀνθρώποιο Ps.-Phoc.102; νεύρων καὶ κώλων ἔκλυτος ἁ. *AP*7.383 (Phil.); τὰς ἁ. διαχαλᾷ τοῦ σώματος Epicr.2.19. b. of the mind, δύστροπος γυναικῶν ἁ. women's perverse *temperament*, E.*Hipp.*162 (lyr.). c. *framework* of the universe, *Corp.Herm.* 1.14. II. *covenant, agreement*, in pl., μάρτυροι.. καὶ ἐπίσκοποι ἁρμονιάων Il.22.255. III. *settled government, order*, τὰν Διὸς ἁ. A.*Pr.*551 (lyr.). IV. in Music, *stringing*, ἁ. τόξου καὶ λύρας Heraclit.51, cf. Pl.*Smp.*187a: hence, *method of stringing, musical scale*, Philol.6, etc., Nicom.*Harm.*9; esp. *octave*, ἐκ πασῶν ὀκτὼ οὐσῶν [φωνῶν] μίαν ἁ. συμφωνεῖν Pl.*R.*617b; ἑπτὰ χορδαὶ ἡ ἁ. Arist. *Metaph.*1093ᵃ14, cf. *Pr.*919ᵇ21; of the planetary spheres, in Pythag. theory, *Cael.*290ᵇ13, *Mu.*399ᵃ12, etc. 2. generally, *music*, αὐτῷ δὲ τῷ ῥυθμῷ μιμοῦνται χωρὶς ἁ. Id.*Po.*1447ᵃ26. 3. *special type of scale, mode*, ἁ. Λυδία Pi.*N.*4.46; Αἰολὶς or -ηῒς Pratin.Lyr.5, Lasus 1, cf. Pl.*R.*398e, al., Arist.*Pol.*1276ᵇ8, 1341ᵇ35, etc. b. esp. *the enharmonic scale*, Aristox.*Harm.*p.1 M., Plu.2.1135a, al. 4. ἁρμονίαν λόγων λαβών *a due arrangement* of words, fit to be set to music, Pl.*Tht.*175e. 5. *intonation* or *pitch* of the voice, Arist.*Rh.* 1403ᵇ31. 6. metaph. of persons and things, *harmony, concord*, Pl.*R.*431e, etc. V. personified, as a mythical figure, h.*Ap.*195, Hes.*Th.*937, etc.; Philos., like φιλότης, *principle of Union*, opp. Νεῖκος, Emp.122.2, cf. 27.3. VI. Pythag. name for *three, Theol. Ar.*16. VII. name of a *remedy*, Gal.13.61; of a *plaster*, Paul. Aeg.3.62.

**Ἁρμον-ίδης**, ου, ὁ, Patron., *son of a carpenter*, Il.5.60. **-ίζω**, *frame*, in Pass., μεμνημένος.. ἐξ οἵης ἡρμόνισαι (prob. for -ισας) καλάμης *AP*7.472.16 (Leon.). **-ικός**, ή, όν, *skilled in music*, Pl.*Phdr.* 268d; ἁ. οὐ μάγειρος *musician*, Damox.2.49 codd. II. *musical*: τὰ -κά *theory of music*, Pl.*Phdr.*268e, Arist.*Metaph.*1077ᵃ5; ἡ ἐν τοῖς μαθήμασιν -κή (sc. ἐπιστήμη) mathematical *theory of music*, ib.997ᵇ21; ἁ. πραγματεία a treatise *thereon*, Plu.2.1142f; ἁρμονικὰ στοιχεῖα, title of work by Aristoxenus; ἁρμονικοί, οἱ, *students of* -κή, οἱ κατὰ τοὺς ἀριθμοὺς ἁ. Arist.*Top.*107ᵃ16; with play on (b), Aristox. *Harm.*p.1 M. b. *of* or *in the enharmonic scale*, νόμος Plu.2. 1133e. c. ἁ. κίνησις, of the pulse, *in harmony with* physical state, Gal.19.376. III. Arith., *harmonic*, μέσα Archyt.2; ἁ. ἀναλογία Ph.1.27, Nicom.*Ar.*2.22, Theo Sm.p.114 H.; μεσότης Arist.*Fr.*47; λόγοι Ph.1.22 (Sup.); λόγοι κατ' ἀριθμὼς ἁ. συγκεκραμένοι Ti.Locr. 96a, cf. Arist.*de An.*406ᵇ29. IV. ἁ. γυμνάσιον training *by rule of thumb*, Philostr.*Gym.*53. V. metaph., *capable of harmonizing*, τακτικοὶ καὶ ἁ. Plu.2.618c; of God, ib.946f. VI. Adv. -κῶς ib.1138e, Iamb.*Comm.Math.*32. **-ιος**, ον, *fitting, harmonious*, Lxx *Wi.*16.20, dub.l. in D.H.*Dem.*22. Adv. -ίως J.*AJ*3.3.2, Ph.1. 179, Iamb.*VP*5.20. (Mostly with v.l. ἁρμοδ-.) **-ιώδης**, ες, = ἁρμόνιος, of friends, Socr.*Ep.*15 (Sup. -ωδέστατος).

**ἁρμοποιός**, όν, *uniting, joining*, Sch.Lyc.832.

***ἁρμός**, ὁ, (ἀραρίσκω) *joint*, in masonry, *IG*1.322; in metal-work, Ph.*Bel.*77.39; ὁ προσιών, ἀπιὼν ἁ., front and back *faces* of blocks, *IG* 7.3073.106, 112 (Lebad.), cf. 2².463.40: pl., *fastenings* of a door, E. *Med.*1315, *Hipp.*809; ἁ. χώματος λιθοσπαδής a fissure in the tomb made by tearing away the stones *at their joining*, S.*Ant.*1216; *chink in the fitting* of a door, ἁρμῷ τὴν ὄψιν προσβαλεῖν D.H.5.7, cf. Plu. *Alex.*3. 2. *bolt, peg*, ἁ. ἐν ξύλῳ παγείς E.*Fr.*360.12. 3. *shoulder-joint, Hippiatr.*34.

**ἅρμ-οσις**, εως, ἡ, *tuning*, Phryn.*PS*p.24 B. (pl.): metaph. of numbers, *Theol.Ar.*54 (pl.). **-οσμα**, ατος, τό, *joined work*, τρόπις δ' ἐλείφθη ποικίλων ἁρμοσμάτων E.*Hel.*411. **-οστέον**, *one must adapt*, A.D.*Pron.*79.9 codd.; *one must apply*, Ps.-Democr.Alch. p.47 B. **-οστήρ**, ῆρος, ὁ, = sq., X.*HG*4.8.39, *IG*5(1).937.2 (Cythera). II. = κοσμητής 1.2, Pl.Com.126. III. of stones, *laid with the grain*, Hsch. ***-οστής**, οῦ, ὁ, *one who arranges* or *governs*, esp. *harmost, governor* sent out by the Lacedaemonians to the περίοικοι and subject cities, Th.8.5, X.*HG*2.4.28, etc.; *governor of a dependent colony*, Id.*An.*5.5.19. 2. title of officials at Thessalonica, *IG*11(4).1053 (iii B.C.). 3. = *triumvir*, App.*BC*4.7; = *praefectus*, Luc.*Tox.*17, 32. 4. *betrothed husband*, Poll.3.35. ***-οστικός**, ή, όν, *fitted for joining*, v.l. for ἁρμονικός, *Theol.Ar.*34. **-οστός**, ή, όν, *joined, adapted, well-fitted*, Hero*Spir.*1.16, al.; τινὶ κατὰ τὸ πλάτος Plb.21.28.12; *suitable, fit*, ἁρμοστόν μοι λέγειν τοῦτο Philem. 4.4. Adv. -τῶς Plu.2.438a. **-οστρα**, τά, *sponsalia, Gloss.* **-όστωρ**, ορος, ὁ, *commander*, ναυβατῶν A.*Eu.*456.

**ἁρμόσυνοι**· ἀρχή τις ἐν Λακεδαίμονι ἐπὶ τῆς εὐκοσμίας τῶν γυναικῶν, Hsch.

**ἁρμόττω, ἁρμοττόντως**, Att. for ἁρμόζω, -ζόντως, qq.v.

***ἄρμυλα**, τά, *shoes* (Cypr.), Hsch. **ἀρμώατος**· σπασμός (Cypr.), Id. **ἄρμωλα**· ἀρτύματα (Arc.), Id.:— also **ἀρμώμαλα**, Id.

**ἄρνα**, acc. sg., dual ἄρνε, pl. ἄρνες; v. ἀρήν.

**ἀρναβώ**, ἡ, *zedoary*, Posidon.Jun.ap.Paul.Aeg.7.3:—also ***ἀρναβόν**, τό, Aët.7.135.

***ἀρνᾰκίς**, ίδος, ἡ, *sheepskin coat*, Ar.*Nu.*730, Pl.*Smp.*220b, Aristonym.6, Theoc.5.50. (Formed as if from *ἄρναξ, Dim. of ἀρνός.)

**ἄρναν**· τὸν ὅρκον (Clazom.), Hsch. **ἄρναπον**· τὸν ἄρνα, Id.

**ἀρνέα**, ἡ, = ἀρνακίς, Hdn.*Philet.*p.445 P. II. *lambing, POxy.* 297.8 (i A.D.).

***ἄρνειος**, α, ον, (ἀρήν) *of a lamb* or *sheep*, κρέα Orac.ap.Hdt.1.47, Pherecr.45.3, X.*An.*4.5.31; σπλάγχνα Eub.75.5; ἁ. φόνος slaughtered *sheep*, S.*Aj.*309. 2. Ἀρνεῖος, ὁ (sc. μήν), name of month at Argos, *Schwyzer*90.3 (-ῆος lapis), Conon 19. 3. ἄρνειον, τό, = ἀρνόγλωσσον, Ps.-Dsc.2.126. II. **ἀρνεῖον**, τό, *a shop where lamb is sold, butcher's shop*, Didym.ap.*EM*146.39.

**ἀρνειός**, ὁ, *ram, wether* ( = τριετὴς κριός, Hsch.), Il.2.550, al., Ister 53; ἀ. ὄϊς, opp. θῆλυς, Od.10.572, al.; but later, θῆλυς ἀ. A.R. 3.1033. 2. the constellation *Aries*, Max.72. (Orig. ἀρνηός, cf. ἀρνηάς and Att. ἀρνεώς. Deriv. of ἄρσην, as ἀρσ-ηϝ-ό-ς, cf. ἀρνευ-τήρ. No initial ϝ-.)

**ἀρνεοθοίνης**, ου, ὁ, *feasting on rams*, *APl.*4.235 (Apollonid.).

***ἀρνέομαι**, fut. -ήσομαι A.*Pr.*268, Ar.*Ec.*365; also ἀρνηθήσομαι S.*Ph.*527 (ἀπ-), *Ev.Luc.*12.9: aor. Pass. ἠρνήθην freq. in Att., Th. 6.60, etc.: also aor. Med. ἠρνησάμην Hom. (v. infr.), Hdt.3.1; rare in Trag. and Att., E.*Ion*1026, Aeschin.2.69, 3.324: pf. ἤρνημαι D. 28.24:—*deny, disown*, τεὸν ἔπος ἀρνήσασθαι Il.14.212, Od.8.358, etc.; ἀ. ἀμφὶ βόεσσιν h.*Merc.*390; ἀ. ἃ εἶπον E.*Hec.*303: abs., Hdt.2.174; ἀρνούμενοι ἔπαινοι *negative* praises, Plu.2.58a. 2. *refuse*, τόξον.. δόμεναι τε καὶ ἀρνήσασθαι Od.21.345, cf. Hes.*Op.*408, Hdt.3.1; ἀ. γάμον Od.1.249; ἀ. χρείαν *decline, renounce* a duty or office, D.18.282; διαθήκην Id.36.34; κληρονομίαν *PFlor.*61.49 (i A.D.); ζωὰν ἀ., of a suicide, *AP*7.473 (Aristodic.); δυνάμει τὸν βίον ἀ. S.E.*M.*11.163; ἀ. ἀνθρώπους *cast aside* humanity, Him.*Or.*2.10. 3. abs., *say No, decline*, ὁ δ' ἠρνεῖτο στεναχίζων Il.19.304; αὐτὰρ ὅ γ' ἠρνεῖτο στερεῶς 23.42, etc. 4. in expressing *denial*, c. inf., either without μή, *deny that*.., A.*Eu.*611, E.*IA*966; or with μή, *say that..not*.., Ar.*Eq.*572, Antipho 3.3.7, etc.; οὐδ' αὐτὸς ἀρνεῖται μὴ οὐ.. D.C.50.22; also οὐκ ἂν ἀρνοίμην τὸ δρᾶν S.*Ph.*118; ἀ. ὅτι οὐ.., ὡς οὐ.., X.*Ath.*2.17, Lys. 4.1, D.9.54. 5. in expressing *refusal*, c. inf., ἀ. εἶναι χρηστοὺς Hdt.6.13: poet. also c. part., οὐ γὰρ εὐτυχῶν ἀρνήσομαι E.*Alc.*1158, cf. *Or.*1582.

**ἀρνεός**, ὁ, = ἀρνειός, *PStrassb.*24.44 (ii A.D.).

**ἀρνευ-τήρ**, ῆρος, ὁ, *tumbler, acrobat*, Herod.8.42: metaph. of one falling headlong, ὁ δ' ἀρνευτῆρι ἐοικὼς κάππεσε Il.12.385, 16.742, Od. 12.413. 2. *diver*, Arat.656, Hsch. **-τήρια**, τά, *tumbling* or *diving tricks*, Id. (s.v.l.). (Acc. to D.H.ap.*Et.Gen.*, from ἀρήν, *one that plunges and butts like a lamb*; but rather from ἀρνεύω *butt* or *dive headlong like a ram* (*ἀρνεύς, cf. ἀρνειός).) **-τής**, οῦ, ὁ, = ἀρνευτήρ, epith. of the fish ἵππουρος, Numen.ap.Ath.7.322f, Eust. 1083.59. **-ω**, *frisk, tumble*, Lyc.465; *plunge, dive*, Id.1103.

**ἀρ(ν)εώνιον**· ὅρκον βασίλειον, Hsch.

**ἀρνεώς**, ὁ, *ram*, *IG*2.844.5: gen. pl. ἀρνέων read by Zenod. in Il. 3.273. (From ἀρνηϝός, cf. ἀρνειός.)

**ἀρνηάς**, άδος, ἡ, prob. some sort of *sheep*, ἔπεροι καὶ ἀρνηάδες ἐρίων ἀτελέες, ἀρνηάδων ἔταλα ἀτελέα *Schwyzer*644.15 (Aeol.). (Fem. of ἀρνεώς, q.v.)

***ἀρνηΐς**, ΐδος, ἡ, = ἀρνίς, Ael.*NA*12.34.

**Ἀρνῆος**, v. ἄρνειος 1.2.

**ἀρν-ήσιμος**, ον, *to be denied*, τούτων δ' οὐδέν ἐστ' ἀ. S.*Ph.*74. **-ησις**, εως, ἡ, *denial*, τούτου δ' οὔτις ἁ. πέλει A.*Eu.*588; τῶνδ' ἁ. οὐκ ἔνεστί μοι S.*El.*527, cf. *OT*578: foll. by τὸ μή c. inf., D.19.163. II. Gramm., *negation*, D.T.642.3, Lesb.Gramm.26; δύο ἁ. μίαν συγκατάθεσιν ποιοῦσι two *negatives* make an affirmative, Sch.S.*OT*1053. **-ητέον**, *one must deny*, Arist.*Top.*160ᵃ25, Hld.1.26. **-ητικός**, ή, όν, *denying, negative*, μόριον ἀξιώματος Chrysipp.*Stoic.*2.66, cf. Alex.Aphr.*in Metaph.*333.26; φαντασίαι Numen.ap.Eus.*PE*14.8; ἐπίρρημα Eust. 211.37. Adv. -κῶς Porph.*inCat.*136.27, Simp.*inPh.*812.17, Sch. Ar.*Ra.*1455.

**ἀρνίον**, τό, Dim. of ἀρήν, *a little lamb*, Lys.32.21, Eub.150.4, *PStrassb.*24.7 (ii A.D.). II. *sheepskin, fleece*, Luc.*Salt.*43.

***ἀρνίς**, ίδος, ἡ, festival at Argos, in which dogs were slain, Conon 19; cf. ἀρνηΐς.

**ἀρνό-γλωσσον**, τό, (γλῶσσα) *plantain, Plantago major*, Thphr. *HP*7.8.3, 7.10.3, Crateuas*Fr.*6, Luc.*Trag.*150; ἀ. τὸ μεῖζον Dsc.2. 126. 2. *haresfoot plantain, P. Lagopus*, ἀ. τὸ μικρὸν ibid. **-κόμης**, ου, ὁ, *with lamb's hair*, i.e. *curly hair*, epith. of Apollo, Macr.*Sat.*1. 17.45. **-πολέμιον**, τό, = σταφὶς ἀγρία, Ps.-Dsc.4.152.

**ἀρνορ(κ)ίη**· ὁ μετὰ τοῦ ἀρνὸς αἰρομένου γινόμενος ὅρκος, Hsch.

**ἀρνός**, ὁ, late nom., = ἀρήν, Aesop.274.

**ἀρνο-τροφία**, ἡ, *rearing of lambs*, *Gp.*18.1.2. **-φάγος** [ᾰ], ον, *lamb-devouring*, Man.4.255.

**ἄρνυθεν**· ἠγωνίζοντο, ἐνήργουν, Hsch.

***ἄρνῠμαι**, imper. ἄρνυσο Sapph.75, *Trag.Adesp.*4: fut. ἀρέομαι [ᾰ] Pi.*P.*1.75, Att. ἀροῦμαι S.*OC*460, *Aj.*75, Pl.*Lg.*969a: aor. 2 ἀρόμην [ᾰ] Il.11.625, 23.592 (augm. 3 sg. ἤρετο only as v.l. for ἤρατο, cf. ἀείρω); subj. ἄρηαι Hes.*Op.*632, ἄρηται Il.12.435; opt. ἀροίμην 18. 121, S.*El.*34, etc.; inf. ἀρέσθαι Il.16.88, S.*Aj.*246 (lyr.); part. ἀρόμενος A.*Eu.*168 (lyr.):—*win, gain,* esp. of honour or reward, in pres. and impf. often with additional idea of *striving,* ἀρνύμενος πατρός τε μέγα κλέος *maintaining..,* Il.6.446; κλέος ἐσθλὸν ἄροιτο 5.3; κῦδος ἀρέσθαι 9.303, Od.22.253, Pi.*N.*9.46; ἵν' οἴκαδε κέρδος ἄρηαι Hes.*Op.* 632; οὐχ ἱερήϊον οὐδὲ βοείην ἀρνύσθην Il.22.160; ἀέθλια ποσσὶν ἄροντο 9.124; ἀρνύμενος ἥν τε ψυχὴν καὶ νόστον ἑταίρων *trying to win, striving to secure..,* Od.1.5; *exact,* of atonement, τιμὴν ἀρνύμενοι Μενελάῳ Il. 1.159; ὅτῳ τρόπῳ πατρὸς δίκας ἀροίμην τῶν φονευσάντων πάρα S.*El.*34; simply, *receive,* καί κεν τοῦτ' ἐθέλοιμι Διός γε διδόντος ἀρέσθαι Od.1.390; ὧν..τὴν μάθησιν ἄρνυμαι S.*Tr.*711, etc.; κράτος ἄρνυται Id.*Ph.*838 (lyr.); τὴν δόκησιν ἄ. E.*Andr.*696; ἕλκος ἀρέσθαι Il.14.130; = λαβεῖν in ποδοῖν κλοπὰν ἀ. S.*Aj.*247 (lyr.); ἄγος ἀ. A.*Eu.*168 (lyr.); *win reputation for..,* δειλίαν ἀρῇ S.*Aj.*75 (cf. Hsch.); τόλμαν..ἀρομένῳ Pi.*N.*7.59: rare in Prose, exc. in the phrase μισθὸν ἄρνυσθαι Pl.*Prt.*349a, *R.*346c, *Lg.*813e, Arist.*Pol.*1287ᵃ36, cf. ἀρ[έσ]θαι μισθόν *IG*12(9).1273–4iii 1 (Eretria); also ἣ δ' ἂν ἄνδρα ἑωυτῇ ἄρηται Hp.*Aër.*17; δίκαν ἁρέσται καὶ δόμεν (= λαβεῖν καὶ δοῦναι) *IG*9(1).334.32 (Locr.); ζωὴν αἰσχρὰν ἄ. *strive to save,* Pl.*Lg.*944c: rarely in bad sense, ἀρνύμενος λώβαν λύμας ἀντίποιν' ἐμᾶς *reaping* destruction as the penalty of.., E.*Hec.*1073 (lyr.). II. *take up, bear, carry* (perh. by confusion with ἄρασθαι), οὐδ' ἂν νηῦς..ἄχθος ἄροιτο Il.20.247. (Root ϝ: *er: or,* cf. τιμά-ορος 'one who *exacts* atonement'.)

ἀρνυτός· εὔπνους, εὔνους, Hsch.

ἀρνῳδός, ὁ, *one who sings for the prize of a lamb,* Eust.6.26, cf. Hsch., *EM*146.55.

ἀρνών· *agnile, Gloss.*

ἄρξ, ὁ, *bear,* ἐγὼ εἰς κάτω μέρη λέων εἰμὶ καὶ εἰς ἄνω μέρη ἄ. εἰμί *OGI* 201.15 (Nubia), cf. *PMag.Lond.*121.782.

ἄρξιφος, Persian word, = *eagle,* Hsch. ἀροάτους· ἀβάτους, καὶ ἀνιαρούς, Id.

ἄροκλον, τό, = φιάλη, Nic.*Fr.*129 (dub.l.).

ἄρομα, ατος, τό, f.l. for ἄρωμα (q.v.), Luc.*Lex.*2, Ael.*NA*7.8, cf. *AB*450.

ἄρον, τό, *cuckoo-pint, Arum italicum,* Arist.*HA*600ᵇ11, Thphr.*HP* 1.6.10, Ph.*Bel.*89.44 (pl.), Ps.-Dsc.2.167. II. *Egyptian arum, Colocasia antiquorum,* Plin.*HN*19.96, Gal.6.650. III. = δρακόντιον, Thphr.*HP*7.12.2, Phan.ap.Ath.9.371d. IV. *Arum Dioscoridis,* ἄ. τὸ καλούμενον παρὰ Σύροις λοῦφα Dsc.2.167, cf. Gal.11.839.

ἀροπῆσαι· πατῆσαι (Cret.), Hsch. (fort. τροπῆσαι).

ἄρος [ᾰ], εος, τό, *use, profit, help,* f.l. in A.*Supp.*885, cf. Hsch., Eust.1422.19; cf. ἄρ-νυμαι. 2. = κοιλὰς ἐν αἷς ὕδωρ ἀθροίζεται ὀμβριον, Hsch. 3. = ἀκούσιον βλάβος, Id.; cf. ἀπαρές, ἀπηρής.

ἀρ-όσιμος [ᾰ], ον, (ἀρόω) *arable, fruitful,* γῆ *corn*-land, *POxy.*137.14 (vi A.D.), cf. Max.Tyr.5.4; ὀροπέδια Str.6.2.6; ἡ ἀ. Id.9.5.19, Hld. 9.5, Ph.Byz.*Mir.*1.3. II. metaph., *fit for engendering* children, S.*Ant.*569 (in form ἀρώσιμος). -οσις, εως, ἡ, *arable land, cornland,* Il.9.580, Od.9.134, Thphr.*CP*3.2.2, A.R.1.826. II. *ploughing,* Arat.1055, Arist.*Mu.*399ᵇ17, Ael.*NA*13.1.

ἀροσμός, ὁ, = ἄροσις, *PTeb.*49.10.

ἀρ(ο)σπάκες· δρύες ἐπικεκομμέναι, Hsch.

⊛ἀρ-οτήρ [ᾰ], ῆρος, ὁ, *plougher, husbandman,* Il.18.542, 23.835, Hecat.335 J., E.*El.*104, etc.: in Prose, Σκύθαι ἀροτῆρες, opp. νομάδες, Hdt.4.17, cf. 191, 1.125, 7.50. 2. as Adj., βοῦς ἀροτήρ steer *for ploughing,* Hes.*Op.*405, Arat.132, Plu.*Pyrrh.*5, *OGI*519.21 (Asia Minor, iii A.D.), etc.; ὁλκός Nonn.*D.*3.192; τέκνων Orph.*H.*40.8. II. metaph., *begetter, father,* τέκνων E.*Tr.*135 (lyr.); εὐτεκνίης *IG*14. 16 5. -ότης, ου, ὁ, = foreg., Pi.*I.*1.48, Hdt.4.2, Pherecr.130; βόες ἀ. Hp.*Art.*8, cf. Ael.*VH*5.14; Πιερίδων ἀρόται *workmen* of the Muses, i.e. *poets,* Pi.*N.*6.32; ἀ. κύματος *seaman,* Call.*Fr.*436. ⊛-οτήσιος, ον, *of* or *for ploughing,* ὧραι Arat.1053. -οτικός, ή, όν, *capable of ploughing,* βόες Gal.19.245.

ἄρ-οτος [ᾰ], ὁ, *corn-field,* οὔτ' ἄρα ποίμνῃσιν καταΐσχεται οὔτ' ἀρότοισιν Od.9.122: metaph., Ἄρη τὸν ἀρότοις θερίζοντα βροτοὺς ἐν ἄλλοις A.*Supp.*638 (lyr.). 2. *crop,* S.*OT*270: metaph., *seed,* τέκνων ὅν ἔτεκες ἄροτον E.*Med.*1281 (lyr.); ὅσον εὐσεβίᾳ κρατοῦμεν ἄδικον ἄροτον (cj. Barnes for ἄροτρον) ἀνδρῶν Id.*Ion* 1095. 3. *tillage, ploughing,* Hes.*Op.*384, 458; ζῆν ἀπ' ἀρότου live by *husbandry,* Hdt.4.46; ἄ. ἱερὸς ritual *ploughing,* ceremonial at Athens, Plu.2.144a: pl., Ar.*Ra.* 1034. 4. metaph., *procreation of children,* ὁ ἄ. ὁ ἐν γυναικί Pl.*Cra.*406b; παίδων ἐπ' ἀρότῳ γνησίων, in Athen. marriage-contracts, Men.720, cf. *Pk.*436, Luc.*Tim.*17; τέκνων ἀρότοισιν E.*Hyps.Fr.*1iii 25. II. *season of tillage, seed-time,* Hes.*Op.*450, Thphr.*HP*8.1.2, Arat.267, etc.: hence, *season, year,* τὸν παρελθόντ' ἄ. S.*Tr.*69; δωδέκατος ἄ. ib.825 (lyr.). -οτός, ή, όν, *arable,* Theognost.*Can.*95. II. ἀροτόν· τὸν ὁλκὸν τοῦ Ἕκτορος ἢ τὸ ἀντίσταθμον A.*Fr.*270 (ap.Hsch.).

ἀροτρ-αῖος [ᾰρ], α, ον, *of corn-land, rustic,* θαλάμη *AP*7.209 (Antip.). -ευμα, ατος, τό, *ploughing*: metaph., *generation,* φύσεως ἀ. καινοῖς Poet.ap.Stob.1.49.46. ⊛-εύς, έως, ὁ, = sq., Theoc.25.1, 51, Bion *Fr.*9.8, etc. -ευτήρ, ῆρος, ὁ, = ἀροτήρ, ἀρούρης *AP*9.299 (Phil.); πόντου ib.242 (Antiphil.). -εύω, *plough,* Pherecyd.105 J., Lyc. 1072, Nic.*Th.*6, Babr.21.5. -ήτης (or -ίτης), ου, ὁ, *belonging to the plough,* βίοτος, χαλκός, *AP*9.23 (Antip.), 6.41 (Agath.). ⊛-ιάζω, *plough,* in Pass., *PFlor.*383.89 (iii A.D.). ⊛-ίαμα, ατος, τό, *ploughed land,* Sch.Ar.*Pax* 1158. -ίασις, εως, ἡ, = sq., Lxx*Ge.*45.6, Ps.-Ptol.*Centil.*214. -ιασμός, ὁ, *ploughing, tillage,* Sch.Opp.*H.*2. 19. -ιαστής, οῦ, ὁ, *husbandman, EM*207.31. ⊛-ιάω, = ἀρόω, Call. *Dian.*161, Thphr.*HP*8.6.3, Babr.55.2, Corn.*ND*28 (Pass.). -ιος, ον, *of husbandry,* epith. of Apollo, Orph.*H.*34.3. -ιόω, = -ιάω, in Pass., v.l. in Lxx*Is.*7.25, cf. Ps.-Plu.*Fluv.*21.2. -ίτης, v. -ήτης.

ἀροτρο-δίαυλος [ᾰρ] [ῐ], ὁ, *plougher,* who goes backwards and forwards *as in the* δίαυλος, *AP*10.101 (Bianor). -ειδής, ές, *like a plough,* D.S.3.3.

⊛ἄροτρον [ᾰ], τό, (ἀρόω) *plough,* Od.18.374; πηκτὸν ἄ. Il.10.353, cf. Thgn.1201, Pi.*P.*4.224, etc.; ἰλλομένων ἀρότρων S.*Ant.*340; ἀρότρῳ ἀναρρηγνύντες αὔλακας Hdt.2.14: pl., Ar.*Pl.*515, Mosch.*Fr.*4.6. b. ἡ ἀπ' ἀρότρου πληγή, in boxing, *right-handed* blow, Paus.6.10.2, Philostr.*Gym.*20. 2. in pl., metaph. of the *organs of generation,* Nonn.*D.*12.46, al. II. ἄροτρα· γῆ, χώρα, πλέθρα, Hsch.

ἀροτρο-πόνος [ᾰ], ον, *working with the plough, AP*9.274 (Phil.). ⊛-πους, ποδος, ὁ, *ploughshare,* Lxx*Ju.*3.31. -φορέω, *draw the plough, AP*9.347 (Leon.).

ἀρόται, οἱ, *serfs* at Syracuse, Eust.295.33.

⊛ἄρουρα [ᾰρ] (ἀρωραῖος in Ar.*Ach.*762 is hyperdor., as shown by Aeol. ἄρουρα Sapph.*Supp.*25.11, Cypr. *a ro u ra i* (dat. sg.) *Inscr. Cypr.*135.20 H.), ἡ, (ἀρόω) *tilled* or *arable land,* Il.11.68, etc.; φυταλιῆς καὶ ἀρούρης 6.195; οὖθαρ ἀρούρης 9.141, al.; τέλσον ἀρούρης 18.544: in pl., *corn-lands, fields,* 14.122, 23.599: rare in Prose, Pl.*Ti.*22e, Arist.*Pol.*1284ᵃ30, *Inscr.Cypr.* l.c. 2. generally, *earth, ground,* ὀλίγη δ' ἦν ἀμφὶς ἄ. Il.3.115; σέο δ' ὀστέα πύσει ἄ. 4.174. 3. *land,* generally, = γῆ; πατρὶς ἄ. father-*land,* Od.1.407; ἄ. πατρία, πατρῴα, Pi.*O.*2.14, *I.*1.35. 4. *the earth,* ἐπὶ ζείδωρον ἄ. Il.8.486, Od.7.332; ἄχθος ἀρούρης Il.18.104, al. 5. metaph. of a woman as receiving seed and bearing fruit, Thgn.582, A.*Th.*754 (lyr.), S.*OT*1257, cf. *Tr.* 32; ἄ. θήλεια Pl.*Lg.*839a, cf. *Ti.*91d. II. *measure of land* in Egypt, 100 *cubits square,* Hdt.2.168, cf. 141, *OGI*90.30, *POxy.*45.12, Hecat. Abd.ap.J.*Ap.*1.22, *PRyl.*143.17 (i A.D.), etc. III. = σωρὸς σίτου σὺν ἀχύροις (Cypr.), Hsch.

ἀρουρᾰβάτης [ᾰρ] [βᾰ], ου, ὁ, *traversing the tilled land,* epith. of the Nile, Epic. in *BKT*5(1).119.

ἀρουρ-αῖος [ᾰρ], α, ον, *of* or *from the country, rural, rustic,* μῦς ἀ. *field*-vole, Hdt.2.141; σμίνθος A.*Fr.*227; ὦ παῖ τῆς ἀ. θεοῦ, of Euripides as the reputed son of a *herb*-seller, Ar.*Ra.*840; ἀ. Οἰνόμαος, of Aeschines, who played the part of Oenomaüs 'in the provinces', D. 18.242, cf. *AB*211 sq.; ἀ. λίθοι *rough* stones, *SIG*²587.21; φυτὰ ἀ. *field*-weeds, Thphr.*HP*7.6.1. -είτης (or -ίτης), ὁ, = foreg., μῦς ἀ. Babr.108.27. -ηδόν, τό, *surface measured in* ἄρουραι, *PRyl.* 157.5 (ii A.D.), *PStrassb.*112.10 (ii A.D.), etc. ⊛-ιον, τό, Dim. of ἄρουρα, *AP*11.365 (Agath.). -ισμός, ὁ, *measuring in* ἄρουραι, *PLond.*3.1171ᵛ(a)3 (i A.D.). -ίτης, v. -είτης.

ἀρουροπόνος [ᾰ], ον, *working in the field, AP*6.36, 104 (both Phil.).

ἄρους· τὰ λιβάδια, Hsch. ἀρόχεται· γλίχεται, ἐπιθυμεῖ, Id.

⊛ἀρόω [ᾰ], pres. inf. ἀρώμεναι Hes.*Op.*22: fut. ἀρόσω *AP*9.740 (Gem.), -ώσω or -όσσω ib.7.175 (Antiphil.): aor. ἤροσα Hes.*Op.*485, Pi.*N.*10.26, S.*OT*1497, etc. (ἄροσε Call.*Cer.*137), Ep. inf. ἀρόσσαι A.R.3.497:—Pass., pres. ἀροῦται Din.1.24: aor. ἠρόθην A.*Supp.*1007, S.*OT*1485: Ion. pf. part. ἀρηρομένος Il.18.548, Hdt.4.97:—*plough, till,* οὔτε φυτεύουσιν..οὔτ' ἀρόωσιν Od.9.108: metaph. of poets, Μοίσαισιν ἔδωκ' ἀρόσαι gave them *work to do* (cf. ἀρότης), Pi.*N.*10.26; πόντος..ἠρόθη δορί A. l.c. II. *sow,* ἀροῦν εἰς Ἀδώνιδος κήπους Pl.*Phdr.*276b:—metaph. in Pass., ἐν Διὸς κήποις ἀροῦσθαι..ὄλβους S.*Fr.* 320. 2. metaph. of the man, ἀλλοτρίην ἄρουραν ἀροῦν Thgn.582; τὴν τεκοῦσαν ἤροσεν S.*OT*1497; of the mother, *IG*7.581.1 (Tanagra):—Pass., of the child, ἔνθεν αὐτὸς ἠρόθην *was begotten,* S.*OT*1485. (Root ἀρο-, cf. Lat. *arāre,* Goth. *arjan,* Lith. *árti,* etc., 'plough'.)

ἁρπάγ-δην, Adv. *hurriedly, violently,* A.R.1.1017; *greedily,* Opp. *H.*3.219, Aret.*SA*2.12. -εύς [πᾰ], έως, ὁ, = ἅρπαξ, Them.*Or.*21. 247a. ⊛-ή, ἡ, *seizure, robbery, rape,* first in Sol.4.13; ὀφλὼν ἁρπαγῆς δίκην found guilty *of rape,* A.*Ag.*534; αἰτέειν δίκας τῆς ἁ. Hdt.1.2; ἁρπαγῇ χρησαμένους ib.5; ἁρπαγὴν ποιεῖσθαι, ποιεῖν, Th.6.52, X.*Cyr.* 7.2.12; ἐφ' ἁ. τραπέσθαι Th.4.104, X.*Cyr.*4.2.25; τοῦ κρητῆρος ἡ ἁ. Hdt.3.48: pl., of a single act, συνεπρήξαντο τὰς Ἑλένης ἁ. Id.5.94, cf. A.*Th.*351 (lyr.), *Supp.*510; Καδμείων ἁ., of the Sphinx, E.*Ph.*1021 (lyr.). II. *thing seized, booty, prey,* τοῦ φθάσαντος ἁ. A.*Pers.*752; ἁ. κυσί, θηρσί, Id.*Th.*1019, E.*El.*896; ἁρπαγὴν ποιεῖσθαί τι to make *booty* of a thing, Th.8.62. III. *greediness,* X.*Cyr.*5.2.17. IV. ἐν ἁρπαγῇ σελήνης when the moon is *invisible, PMag.Par.*1.750. ⊛-η, ἡ, *hook* for drawing up buckets, etc., Men.829, Poll.6.88; *grappling-iron,* D.C.66.4, 74.11. 2. *rake,* E.*Cyc.*33. -ιμαῖος, α, ον, = sq., Orph.*H.*29.14, Phryn.*PS*p.6 B.; σελήνη *scarcely visible,* at close of month, Sch.Arat.735. -ιμος, η, ον, *ravished, stolen,* Call.*Cer.*9, *Fr.*1.46 P., *AP*11.290 (Pall.), Doroth.20. ⊛-ιον, τό, = κλεψύδρα I, Alex.Aphr.*Pr.*1.95. -μα, ατος, τό, *booty, prey,* Lyc. 87, Lxx*Jb.*29.17, al.: in pl., ib.*Ez.*22.25. 2. ἁ. εὐτυχίας *windfall,* Plu.2.330d; οὐχ ἁ. οὐδ' ἕρμαιον ποιεῖσθαί τι Hld.7.20. -μός, ὁ, *robbery, rape,* Plu.2.12a; ἁ. ὁ γάμος ἔσται Vett.Val.122.1. 2. concrete, *prize to be grasped, Ep.Phil.*2.6; cf. ἅρπαγμα 2. -ος, ὁ, *hook,* ἅρπαγοι χεροῖν A.*Fr.*258 B:—as Adj., χερσὶν ἁρπάγοις S.*Fr.* 706.

⊛ἁρπάζω, fut. -άξω Il.22.310, Babr.89.2, -άσω X.*Eq.Mag.*4.17, (ἀν-) E.*Ion* 1303; in Att. more commonly ἁρπάσομαι Ar.*Pax* 1118, *Ec.*866, *Av.*1460, X.*Cyr.*7.2.5, (ἀν-) Hdt.9.59; contr. ἁρπῶμαι, ἁρπᾷ Lxx*Le.*19.13, al.: aor. ἥρπαξα Il.3.444, Pi.*N.*10.67, *IG*4.951.11 (Epid.); Trag. and Att. ἥρπασα E.*Or.*1634, Th.6.101 (also Il.13.528, 17.62, Hdt.2.156): pf. ἥρπακα Ar.*Pl.*372, Pl.*Grg.*481a:—Med., aor. ἡρπασάμην Luc.*Tim.*22, etc. (ὑφ-αρπάσαιο Ar.*Ec.*921):—Pass., pf. ἥρπασμαι X.*An.*1.2.27, E.*Ph.*1079 (ἀν-): 3 plpf. ἥρπαστο Id.*El.*1041; later ἥρπαγμαι Paus.3.18.7, inf. -άχθαι Str.13.1.11: aor. 1 ἡρπάσθην

Hdt.1.1 and 4, etc., -χθην Id.2.90 (v.l.), 8.115, D.S.17.74; later, aor. 2 ἡρπάγην [ᾰ] Lyc.505, etc.: fut. ἁρπᾰγήσομαι 1*Ep.Thess.*4.17, *J.BJ*5.10.3; part. ἁρπάμενος (as if from ἅρπημι) *AP*11.59 (Maced.), Nonn.*D.*1.340,al., (ὑφ-) *AP*9.619 (Agath.):—*snatch away, carry off*, ὅτε σε πρῶτον Λακεδαίμονος ἐξ ἐρατεινῆς ἔπλεον ἁρπάξας Il.3.444; ὡς δ' ὅτε τίς τε λέων.. ἀγέλης βοῦν ἁρπάσῃ ib.17.62; τοὺς δ' αἶψ' ἁρπάξασα φέρεν πόντονδε θύελλα Od.10.48, cf. 5.416; κλέψαι τε χἀρπάσαι βίᾳ S.*Ph.*644; ἁ. τοῦ βασιλέος τὴν θυγατέρα Hdt.1.2; ἁ. [χρυσὸν] ὑπὲκ τῶν γρυπῶν Id.3.116; ἁ. καὶ φέρειν Lys.20.17: abs., *to be a robber*, ὅτιὴ 'πιώρκεις ἡρπακώς Ar.*Eq.*428, cf. *Pl.*372; ἁρπάζειν βλέπει looks *thievish*, Men.*Epit.*181:—Pass. (or Med.), ἐκ χερῶν ἁρπάζομαι I *have her torn* from my arms, E.*Andr.*661. 2. *seize hastily, snatch up*, λᾶαν Il.12.445; δόρυ A.*Th.*624; τὰ ὅπλα X.*An.*6.1.8; ἁ. τινὰ μέσον *seize* him by the waist, Hdt.9.107; λίθος ἥτις τὸν σίδηρον ἁρπάζει, of the magnet, Hp.*Steril.*243: c. gen. of the part seized, ἁ. τινὰ τένοντος ποδός E.*Cyc.*400: c. gen. partit., ἁ. τούτων ἐνέτραγον Timocl.16.7: abs., ἀπογεύονται ἁρπάζοντες *greedily*, Pl.*R.*354b:—Med. in Luc. *Sacr.*3. 3. *seize, overpower, overmaster*, γλῶσσαν ἁ. φόβος A.*Th.*259; *seize, occupy* a post, X.*An.*4.6.11; ἁρπάσαι πεῖραν *seize* an opportunity of attacking, S.*Aj.*2; ἁ. τὸν καιρόν Plu.*Phil.*15; *snap up*, ὥσπερ εὕρημα Herod.6.30. 4. *seize, adopt* a legend, of an author, Hdt.2.156. 5. *grasp with the senses*, ὀσμαὶ -όμεναι ταῖς ὀσφρήσεσιν Plu.2.647e. 6. *captivate, ravish*, Lxx *Ju.*16.9, Plu. *Ant.*28. 7. *draw up* by means of a vacuum, Simp.*in Ph.*647.28. II. *plunder*, πόλεις, τὰ ἐκ τῶν οἰκιῶν, τὴν Ἑλλάδα, etc., Th.1.5, X.*Cyr.*7.2.5, D.8.55, etc.

**ἁρπάκ-τειρα**, ἡ, fem. of sq., *AP*7.172 (Antip. Sid.). **-τήρ**, ῆρος, ὁ, *robber*, Il.24.262, Opp.*H.*1.373; Περσεφονείης Nonn.*D.*6.92, Jul. *Or.*2.87a. **-τήριος**, ον, = ἁρπακτικός, Lyc.157. **-τής**, οῦ, ὁ, *robber*, Call.*Epigr.*2.6, *Gloss.* **-τί**, Adv. = ἁρπάγδην, *greedily*, ἁρπακτὶ πίε *CIG*8470b (vase). **-τικός**, ή, όν, *rapacious, thievish*, Luc.*Pisc.*34, Eun.*Hist.*p.243 D.: c. gen., ἁ. πυρός *readily catching* fire, Dsc.1.73. Adv. -κῶς, gloss on ἁρπαλέως, *EM*148.6, Hsch. ⊛**-τός**, ή, όν, *gotten by rapine, stolen*, Hes.*Op.*320. 2. *to be caught*, i.e. *to be got by chance, hazardous*, ib.684. **-τύς**, ύος, ἡ, Ion. for ἁρπαγή, Call.*Ap.*95.

**ἅρπαλα**· ἁρπακτικά, Hsch.

**ἁρπάλᾰγος** [πᾰ], ὁ, *hunting implement*, Opp.*C.*1.153.

**ἁρπᾰλ-έος**, α, ον, Ep. Adj., (ἁρπάζω): *devouring, consuming*, νοῦσος *IPE*2.167.3 (Panticapaeum); *greedy*, παλάμη *AP*9.576 (Nicarch.); ἁ. καὶ οἷον δὴ οὖν ἀεὶ τῶν ἀθνείων ἐφίεσθαι Agath.4.13: elsewh. only in Adv., *greedily, eagerly*, ἦ τοι ὁ πῖνε καὶ ἦσθε.. ἁρπαλέως Od.6.250, cf. 14.110; δέξεται ἁρπαλέως Thgn.1046; ἁ. εὕδειν *gladly, pleasantly*, Mimn.12.8; ἁ. ἐπεχήρατο *vehemently*, A.R.4.56; once in Ar., ἁ. ἀραμένη *Lys.*331 (lyr.). II. *attractive, alluring, charming*, κέρδεα Od.8.164; ἁ. ἔρως, opp. ἀπηνής, Thgn.1353; ἄνθεα ἥβης ἁρπαλέα Mimn.1.4; δόσιν gift *to be eagerly seized*, Pi.*P.*8.65, cf. 10.62. ⊛**-ίζω**, *catch up, be eager to receive*, τινὰ κωκυτοῖς A.*Th.*243:—also in Med., Hsch. 2. *exact greedily*, A.*Eu.*983 (lyr.). 3. ἁ. τὰ μετέωρά σου *settle* your outstanding transactions, *PLond.ined.*1561. **-ιμος**, η, ον, = ἁρπακτός, προσφιλής, Hsch.

**ἁρπάμενος**, η, ον, v. ἁρπάζω.

**ἁρπάναι**· μάνδραι βοσκημάτων, Hsch.

⊛**ἅρπαξ**, ᾰγος, ὁ, ἡ, (ἁρπάζω) *robbing, rapacious*, Ar.*Eq.*137, v.l. in *Fr.*628, X.*Mem.*3.1.6; λύκοι Lyc.1309 (v.l. Ἄτρακας): also c. Subst. neut., ἅρπαγι χείλει *AP*9.272 (Bianor): Sup. ἁρπαγίστατος Pl.Com. 57. II. mostly as Subst., 1. ἅρπαξ, ἡ, *rapine*, Hes.*Op.*356. 2. ἅρπαξ, ὁ, *robber, peculator*, τῶν δημοσίων Ar.*Nu.*351; ὁ μὲν κλέπτης ὁ δ' ἅ. Myrtil.4; πάντες εἰσὶν ἅρπαγες (sc. οἱ Ὠρώπιοι) Xeno 1. 3. species of *wolf*, Opp.*C.*3.304. 4. *grappling-iron*, used in sea-fights, App.*BC*5.118, Moschio ap.Ath.5.208d; *flesh-hook*, *J.AJ*3.3.7.

**ἁρπάξανδρος**, α, ον, *snatching away men*, A.*Th.*776, restored by Herm. (in fem. form ἁρπαξάνδραν) for ἀναρπ-.

**ἁρπαξίβῐος** [ξῐ], ον, *living by rapine*, στρατιῶται Archestr.*Fr.*61.

**ἁρπαξομίλης** [ῑ], ὁ, = ὁ ἁρπάζων τὰς ἀφροδισίους ὁμιλίας, *Com. Adesp.*949.

**ἅρπᾰσ-ις**, εως, ἡ, = ἁρπαγμός, Phryn.*PS*p.65 B. **-μα**, ατος, τό, Att. form of ἅρπαγμα, Pl.*Lg.*906d, Men.*Epit.*542; prob. in Aeschin. 3.222, cf. Plu.*Cat.Ma.*13, *IG*12(7).123 (Amorgos). **-μός**, = ἁρπαγμός, Plu.2.644a. ⊛**-ος**, ὁ, a *bird of prey*, Ant.Lib.20.6. **-τικός**, ή, όν, *rapacious*, like birds of prey, Arist.*Phgn.*813ᵃ19; κέρδους Phld. *Oec.*p.69 J.

**ἁρπάστιον**, Dim. of sq. 2, Arr.*Epict.*2.5.19.

⊛**ἁρπαστός**, ή, όν, *carried away* (as by a storm), *AP*12.167 (Mel.) (but ἁρπασταί, nom. pl. of **ἁρπαστής**, ὁ, *ravisher*, is prob. l.). 2. neut. as Subst., ἁρπαστόν, τό, *handball*, Ath.1.14f, Artem.1.55.

**ἀρπεδ-ής**, ές, *flat, level*, Nic.*Th.*420. **-ίζω**· ὁμαλίζω, ἐδαφίζω, Hsch. ⊛**-όεις**, εσσα, εν, = ἀρπεδής, Antim.Col.2 P. (From ἀρι-πέδον acc. to Did.ap.*EM*148.9, Hdn.Gr.2.247, but the best codd. of Nic. l.c. have ἀρπ-; cf. ἐρπεδίζω.)

**ἁρπεδον-άπται**, ῶν, οἱ, *rope-fasteners*, applied to Egyptian geometers, [Democr.]299. **-η**, ἡ, *cord*, for binding or snaring game, X.*Cyr.*1.6.28, *AP*9.244 (Apollonid.). 2. *yarn* of which cloth is made, Hdt.3.47, Aristias 2 (ap.Poll.7.31), *AP*6.160 (Antip. Sid.); *silk-worm's thread*, Paus.6.26.8; *bow-string*, *AP*5.193 (Posidipp. or Asclep.). II. ἁρπεδόναι· τῶν ἀμαυρῶν ἄστρων σύγχυσις (i.e. band of stars connecting Pisces), Hsch., cf. Vitr.9.5.3. **-ίζω**, *snare with a ἁρπεδόνη*, Hsch.: also, = λωποδυτέω, Id.

**ἁρπεδών**, όνος, ἡ, = ἁρπεδόνη, *AP*6.207 (Arch.), *J.AJ*3.7.2, Jul. *Gal.*135c.

⊛**ἄρπεζα**, ἡ, *hedge*, Nic.*Th.*393, 647 (pl.) (expl. by Sch. as *foot-hill*):—also ⊛**ἄρπεζος**, ἡ, *BCH*46.405 (Mylasa).

**ἀρπετόν**· ἀκόμιστον, Hsch.

⊛**ἅρπη**, ἡ, unknown *bird of prey*, prob. *shearwater*, [Ἀθήνη] ἅρπῃ εἰκυῖα τανυπτέρυγι λιγυφώνῳ Il.19.350; a *sea-bird* acc. to Arist.*HA* 609ᵃ24, cf. Ael.*NA*2.47, Dionys.*Av.*1.4 (describing the *Lämmergeier*). II. *sickle*, = δρέπανον, Hes.*Op.*573, S.*Fr.*424; καλαμητόμος A.R.4.987: hence, the *scimitar* of Perseus, Pherecyd.11 J., cf. E.*Ion* 192 (lyr., pl.). 2. *elephant-goad*, Ael.*NA*13.22. 3. metaph. of a hippopotamus' *tooth*, Nic.*Th.*567. 4. *bill-hook*, *J.AJ*14.15.5. 5. kind of *fish*, Marc.Sid.22. (Cf. Lat. *sarpio, sarpo*, etc.)

**ἄρπιξ**· εἶδος ἀκάνθης (Cypr.), Hsch.; cf. ἄπριξ.

**ἁρπίς**, ῖδος (but nom. pl. ἀρπίδες *EM*148.36, nom. sg. ἄρπις Suid.), ἡ, = κρηπίς, Call.*Fr.*66.

**ἄρπισαι**· αἱμασιαί, ἢ τάφρους, Hsch. **ἀρπίσθος**· φοῖνιξ· καὶ **ἀρπίαθος**, Id.

**Ἅρπυιαι**, (Ἀρεπ- on a vase from Aegina, *Arch.Zeit.*40.197, cf. *EM* 138.21, and prob. ἀρέπυιαι ἀνηρέψαντο shd. be read in Od. ll. cc.; v. ἀνερείπομαι) αἱ, *the Snatchers*, a name used in Od. to personify *whirlwinds* or *hurricanes* (so τυφῶσι καὶ ἁρπυίαις Ph.1.333); ἅρπυιαι ἀνηρείψαντο Od.1.241, 20.77: acc. pl., Hes.*Th.*267; πτηνά τ' Ἁρπυιῶν γένη Anaxil.22.5, cf. A.R.2.188: rarely in sg., Euph.113: as pr. n., Ἅρπυια Ποδάργη, mother of the horses of Achilles, Il.16.150; also name of one of Actaeon's hounds, A.*Fr.*245; cf. ἁρπυίας· ἁρπακτικοὺς κύνας, Hsch. 2. as Adj., ἁ. σκύλακες *Inscr.Perg.*203. (A quasi-participial form.)

**Ἁρπυιόγουνος**, ον, *Harpy-legged*, ἀηδόνες, of the Sirens, Lyc.653.

**Ἄρπυς**, ὁ, = Ἔρως, Parth.*Fr.*9 (Aeol. acc. to Hsch.).

**ἀρρ-**, in words beginning with ρ, ρ is doubled after a Prefix.

**ἀρρᾰβάσσω**, = ῥαβάσσω, and **ἀρράβαξ**, ὁ, = ὀρχηστής, Paus.Gr.*Fr.*74, Hsch.

**ἀρράβδωτος**, ον, *not ribbed*, Arist.*HA*528ᵃ26, *Fr.*304; of columns, *not fluted*, *IG*1.322.55 (ἀρά-), 65.

**ἀρράβη**· θύρα, οἷον γέρρον, Hsch.

⊛**ἀρρᾰβών**, ῶνος, ὁ, *earnest-money, caution-money*, deposited by the purchaser and forfeited if the purchase is not completed, ἀ. δοῦναί τινος Is.8.20, cf. Arist.*Pol.*1259ᵃ12, Stilpo ap.D.L.2.118, *BGU*446.18 (ii A.D.): pl., *deposits* required from public contractors, *IPE*1².32*B* 34 (Olbia). 2. generally, *pledge, earnest*, τὴν τέχνην ἔχοντες ἀ. τοῦ ζῆν Antiph.123.6; τοῦ δυστυχεῖν.. ἀ. ἔχειν Men.697, cf. Lxx *Ge.* 38.17, 18, *Ep.Eph.*1.14. 3. *present, bribe*, Plu.*Galb.*17. (Semitic, prob. Phoenician, word, Hebr. *'ērābōn*: freq. written ἀραβών, *UPZ* 67.14 (ii B.C.), *Ep.Eph.* l.c., etc.) II. ἀρραβών· πρόδομα, καὶ ἀγκιστρον, Hsch.

**ἀρρᾰβωνίζεται**· ἀρραβῶνι δίδοται, Hsch.

**ἀρρᾰγάδωτος**, ον, (ῥαγάς) *without chink*, Apollod.*Poliorc.*157.1.

**ἀρρᾰγής**, ές, (ῥήγνυμι) *unbroken*, ὀστέον Hp.*VC*12; βάσεις, ἁρμοί, *IG*7.3073.103, 117 (Lebad.); τάξις Ael.*Tact.*13.3; φάλαγξ Arr.*Tact.*12.4; σίδηρος Plu.*Demetr.*21; τὸ ἀ. *unbroken surface*, Arist.*Pr.*899ᵇ20. 2. *that cannot be rent* or *broken*, ξύλα Thphr.*HP*5.5.6; τείχεα D.P.1006: metaph., πόνος παιδείας Ph.1.471 (Sup.); νοῦς Max.Tyr. 41.2; ὁμολογία *Anatolian Studies* p.39 (Sardes, v A.D.), cf. *PLond.*1731.34. II. ἀ. ὄμμα an eye *not bursting into tears*, S.*Fr.*736.

**ἀρραγίδες**· στήμονες, κρόκαι, Hsch.

**ἀρράζω**, = ἀράζω, Ael.*NA*5.51, D.H.16.2.

**ἀρραθάγησεν**· ἐψόφησεν, Hsch.

**ἄρραιστος**, ον, *unhurt*, Sch.Od.13.259.

**ἄρραντος**, ον, (ῥαίνω) *unwatered, unwet*, Arat.868, Str.11.7.5.

**ἄρρᾱτος**, ον, = σκληρός, ἀμετάστροφος, Pl.*Cra.*407d; ἅ. καὶ μνήμων Id.*R.*535c; θάρσος prob. l. in Id.*Ax.*365a; ἀνέρος ἀρράτοιο Euph. 24.

**ἀρρᾰφής**, ές, = sq. 2, κεφαλαί Arat.*Iatr.*ap.Poll.2.38.

**ἄρρᾰφος**, ον, (ῥάπτω) *without seam*, *Ev.Jo.*19.23, *J.AJ*3.7.4. 2. *without sutures*, Gal.*UP*11.19.

**ἀρραχθές**· ἀσύνετον, Hsch.

**ἄρρεκτος**, ον, v. ἄρεκτος.

**ἀρρεν-**, see also ἀρσεν-.

**ἀρρενική**, ἡ, and **ἀρρενικόν**, τό, v. ἀρσενικόν.

⊛**ἀρρενικός**, ή, όν, (ἄρρην) *male*, σωμάτιον *POxy.*3717 (i A.D.); ᾠόν *PMag.Lond.*121.522, cf. Luc.*DDeor.*16.1; opp. θηλυκός, *IG*14.872.5 (Cumae): less Att. form ἀρσενικός Call.*Epigr.*27, *POxy.*38.7 (i A.D.), *AP*5.115 (Marc. Arg.); λίβανον ἀ. *PMag.Par.*1.906; cf. λίβανος. 2. *virile*, M.Ant.11.18 (Comp.); *of masculine gender*, Plu.2.1011c; πτῶσις Ph.1.294; (ἀρσ-) D.T.634.17, etc. Adv. -κῶς, opp. θηλυκῶς, Phld. *Piet.*12, cf. Ath.13.590b, (ἀρσ-) Str.8.3.11.

**ἀρρενο-γᾰμέω**, = τοὺς ἄρρενας γαμεῖν, Anon.*in EN*428.16. **-γονέω**, *beget* or *bear male children*, Thphr.*HP*9.18.5, Ph.1.262. ⊛**-γονία**, ἡ, *begetting* or *bearing of male children*, Arist.*HA*585ᵇ11. **-γόνος**, ον, *begetting* or *bearing male children*, ib.573ᵇ32, 585ᵇ13; αἱ σμικραὶ κοτυληδόνες ἀρσ. Hp.*Steril.*230; of drugs, *promoting the conception of males*, Dsc.3.140. 2. ἀρρενογόνον, τό, = φύλλον III, *dog's mercury*, *Mercurialis perennis*, Thphr.*HP*9.18.5, Dsc.3.125, Plin.*NH*26.162. ⊛**-κοίτης**, ου, ὁ, *sodomite*, *AP*9.686; (ἀρσ-) 1*Ep.Cor.*6.9. **-κυέω**, *bear male children*, Str.4.6.8. **-μᾰνής**, ές, *mad after males*, of men, *Cat.Cod.Astr.*8(2).43, v.l. in Heph.*Astr.*1.1. **-μίκτης**, ου, ὁ, = ἀρρενοκοίτης, (ἀρσ-) Man.4.590. **-μιξία**, ἡ, *sodomy*, S.E.*P.*1.152, 3.199.

⊛**ἀρρενόομαι**, *become a man, do the duties of one*, Luc.*Am.*19; of a woman, πλέον τῆς φύσεως ἀ. Ph.2.328; φρόνημα ἠρρενωμένον ib.53;

Astrol., of stars (cf. ἄρρην), *become masculine*, Heph.*Astr.*1.2, Ptol. *Tetr.*20.

**ἀρρενόπαις**, παιδος, ὁ, ἡ, *of male children*, γόνος (ἀρσ-) *APl.*4.134 (Mel.); γονή (ἀρσ-) *Epigr.Gr.*218. II. ἀ. Κύπρις, = *paedicatio*, *AP* 5.55 (Diosc.).

**ἀρρεν-οπίπης** [ῐ], ου, ὁ, *one who looks lewdly on males*, Eust.827.30.

**ἀρρενο-ποιέω**, *make masculine*, Ptol.*Tetr.*69. **-ποιός**, όν, *favouring the generation of males*, Ael.*NA*7.27. **-πρεπής**, ές, *befitting men, manly*, Aristid.Quint.2.13.

**ἀρρενότης**, ητος, ἡ, *manhood, manliness*, *Stoic.*3.66, Andronic. Rhod.p.575 M., Hierocl.p.63 A.; *masculinity*, opp. θηλύτης, Dam. *Pr.*198.

**ἀρρενο-τοκέω**, *bear male children*, Arist.*HA*574$^{a}$1, *GA*765$^{a}$24, Dsc. *Eup.*2.96. **-τοκία**, ἡ, *bearing of male children*, Aët.16.36. **-τόκιον**, τό, *drug promoting conception of males*, Dsc.*Eup.*2.96. **-τόκος**, ον, *bearing male children*, Arist.*GA*723$^{a}$27.

**ἀρρενουργός**, όν, = ἀρρενοποιός, Nicom.ap.Phot.*Bibl.*p.144 B.

**ἀρρενο-φανής**, ές, *masculine-looking*, Lyd.*Mag.*3.62. **-φθορία**, ἡ, = ἀρρενομιξία, Arg.A.*Th.*, Sch.Luc.*Am.*36. **-φρων**, ον, gen. ονος, (φρήν) *of manly mind*, Suid. s. v. Δεββώρα.

**ἀρρέντερος**, v. ἄρσην.

***ἀρρεν-ώδης**, ες, *brave*. Adv. -δῶς Lxx 2*Ma.*10.35. **-ωνυμέω**, (ὄνομα) *use in masculine gender, change into it*, of a feminine noun, Eust.560.15. **-ωπία**, ἡ, *manly look, manliness*, Pl.*Smp.*192a, Zeno *Stoic.*1.58. ***-ωπός**, όν, also ἡ, όν Luc.*Fug.*27: (ὤψ):—*masculine-looking, manly*, Pl.*Lg.*802e; γυναῖκες Arist.*GA*747$^{a}$1, cf. Sor. 1.35, Ruf.ap.Orib.*Inc.*2.15; εὐμορφία Luc.*Scyth.*11; τὸ ἀ., = ἀρρενωπία, D.S.4.6. 2. of things, *befitting a man, manly*, στολή Ael.*NA* 2.11; τὸ ἀ. τῆς ψυχῆς *manliness*, Chor.*Lyd.*8. Adv. -πῶς *Gloss.*:—irreg. fem. ***-ωπάς**, άδος, ἡ, = ἀνδρόγυνος, Cratin.389, cf. Hsch.

***ἀρρεπής**, ές, of a balance, *inclining to neither side*: hence, *without weight* or *influence*, ἀρρεπὲς πρὸς εὐδαιμονίαν Plu.2.1070a, cf. 1015a; *insignificant*, *Stoic.*3.35; *firm, unwavering*, of ἰσότης, ib.159, Dam. *Pr.*283. Adv. -πῶς Ph.1.409, Hierocl.p.31 A.:—also **-πί**, Hdn.*Epim.* 256.

***ἀρρευμάτιστος** [μᾰ], ον, *arresting discharge, astringent, styptic*, Gal.13.77. II. *not accompanied by discharge, free from discharge*, Ruf.ap.Orib.8.24.54, Aët.7.38, 12.68.

**ἄρρευστος**, ον, *without flux* or *change*, Dam.ap.Simp.*in Ph.*644.32, Eustr.*in EN*50.25. II. *not flowing*, Sch.A.*Ch.*185 (v.l. ἄγευστος); *not fusible*, Ps.-Democr.Alch.p.45 B.

***ἀρρεψία**, ἡ, *equilibrium* of the soul, *absence of bias*, D.L.9.74, S.E. *P.*1.190, etc.

**ἀρρήδην**, Adv. *negatively*, οὐ κατατιθέμενος τῇ ῥήσει, Hsch., cf. Poll.2.129.

***ἄρρηκτος**, ον, (ῥήγνυμι) *unbroken, not to be broken*, δεσμὸν.. χρύσεον ἄ. Il.15.20, cf. 13.37; τεῖχος χάλκεον ἄ. Od.10.4, cf. Il.14.56; ἵν' ἄ. πόλις εἴη 21.447; ἄ. νεφέλην 20.150; πτολέμοιο πεῖραρ.. ἄρρηκτόν τ' ἄλυτόν τ' 13.360; φωνή τ' ἄ. 2.490; ἄ. πέδαι A.*Pr.*6; σάκος Id.*Supp.* 190, S.*Aj.*576; ἄρρηκτος φυάν, i.e. *invulnerable*, Pi.*I.*6(5).47; δέρμα ἄ. ἐπὶ τοῦ νώτου, of the crocodile, Hdt.2.68, cf. Arist.*HA*503$^{a}$10; ἄ. χάλαζαι Theoc.22.16: metaph., θυμός Id.25.112; of land, *unploughed*, *Tab.Heracl.*1.19. Adv. -τως, ἔχειν Ar.*Lys.*182; *with unbroken courage*, Phld.*Mort.*39.

**ἀρρήμων**, ον, gen. ονος, *without speech, silent*, Poll.2.128.

**ἄρρην**, v. ἄρσην.

**ἀρρηνεῖν**· λοιδορεῖν, Hsch.; cf. sq.

**ἀρρηνής**, ές, *fierce, savage*, of dogs, Theoc.25.83, Hsch.

**ἄρρης**, late form for ἄρρην, *PMag.Par.*1.361; cf. ἄρσης.

**ἀρρῆσαι**· ἀβουλῆσαι, ἀπαγορεῦσαι, Hsch.

**ἀρρησία**, ἡ, (ἄρρητος) *silence*, Nicopho 23.

***ἀρρητο-ποιέω**, *practise unmentionable vice*, Artem.1.79. ***-ποιός**, όν, *practising such vice*, Anon.*in EN*172.29. II. pedantically, *celebrating mysteries*, Luc.*Lex.*10.

**ἀρρητόρευτος**, ον, *not taught rhetoric*, Tz.*H.*11.217; *unworthy of an orator*, Sopat.Rh.in Rh.8.58 W.

***ἄρρητος**, ον, also η, ον E.*Hec.*201:—*unspoken*, ἔπος προέηκεν ὅ πέρ τ' ἄρρητον ἄμεινον Od.14.466; ἄνδρες.. ῥητοί τ' ἄ. τε Hes.*Op.*4; ἔστω ἄ. τὰ εἰρημένα Pl.*Smp.*189b, etc., cf. Aeschin.3.217; οὐκ ἐπ' ἀρρήτοις γε τοῖς ἐμοῖς λόγοις not *without* warning *spoken* by me, S.*Ant.*556; ἄ. κατελῆ φυλάξομαι Id.*El.*1012. Adv. -τως, σιγᾶν Arist.*Fr.*44 codd. (ἀρρήκτως Reiske, ἀρράτως Bernays). II. *that cannot be spoken* or *expressed*, ἀδιανόητον καὶ ἄ. καὶ ἄφθεγκτον καὶ ἄλογον Pl.*Sph.*238c: hence, *unspeakable, immense*, App.*BC*3.4; ἐπιθυμία Phld.*Ir.*p.50 W.; εὐχαριστία Id.*Lib.*p.51 O. III. *not to be spoken*: hence, 1. *not to be divulged*, ἱοργίαι, ἱρά, Hdt.5.83, 6.135; σέβας ἀρρήτων ἱερῶν Ar. *Nu.*302; ἄ. σφάγια E.*IT*41; ἄ. ἀβακχεύτοισιν εἰδέναι Id.*Ba.*472; διδακτά τε ἄρρητά τ', i.e. things profane and *sacred*, S.*OT*301; ἄ. κόρη the maid *whom none may name* (i.e. Persephone), E.*Fr.*63, cf. *Hel.* 1307; ἀρρήτων θέσμια, sc. of Demeter and Persephone, *IG*3.713. 6. 2. *unutterable, horrible*, δεῖπνα S.*El.*203 (lyr.); λώβη E.*Hec.*200 (lyr.); ἄρρητ' ἀρρήτων 'deeds without a name', S.*OT*465 (lyr.). 3. *shameful to be spoken*, ῥητόν τ' ἄ. τ' ἔπος Id.*OC*1001, cf. *Aj.*214 (lyr.), 773; ῥητὰ καὶ ἄ. ὀνομάζων 'dicenda tacenda locutus', D.18.122; πάντας ἡμᾶς ῥητὰ καὶ ἄ. κακὰ ἐξεῖπον Id.21.79. Adv. -τως D.L.7. 187. IV. of numbers, ἄρρητα, τά, *irrationals, surds*, opp. ῥητά, Pl.*Hp.Ma.*303b, cf. *R.*546c.

**ἀρρητ-ουργέω**, = ἀρρητοποιέω, *An.Ox.*3.188. **-ουργία**, ἡ, *filthy lewdness*, Jul.*Or.*7.210d.

**ἀρρητο-φόρια**, τά, = ἀρρηφόρια, Sch.Luc.*DMeretr.*2.1. **-φόρος**, v. ἀρρηφόρος.

**ἀρρη-φορέω**, *serve as* ἀρρηφόρος, Ar.*Lys.*642, Din.*Fr.*6.4, *IG*2. 453$^{b}$14. II. applied to the service of the Jewish High Priest, Ph.1.377. **-φορία**, ἡ, *procession of* ἀρρηφόροι, Lys.21.5. **-φόρια**, τά, *festival at which this took place*, prob. for foreg. in Sch.Ar.*Lys.* 642, *EM*149.13. **-φόρος**, ἡ, at Athens, *maiden who carried the symbols* of Athena Polias in procession, Paus.1.27.3, Plu.2.839c, etc. (wrongly expl. by Gramm. as shortd. for ἀρρητο-: ἀρρη-, = ἔρση, q.v.; cf. Ἐρσηφόροι).

**ἀρρῑγ-ής**, ές, = sq. Adv. -γέως Hp.*Acut.*29. ***-ητος**, ον, *not shivering, daring*, *AP*6.219 (Antip.). **-ος**, ον, *insensible to cold*, Arist.*Sens.*438$^{a}$22 (Sup.). II. *without shivering*, Aret.*SD*1.14.

**ἄρριζος**, ον, *without roots*, Arist.*Resp.*478$^{b}$31, Thphr.*CP*3.5. 4. II. metaph., ῥῆμα ἄ. ἐκ τῆς ὀργῆς *not rooted* in.., Them.*Or.* 8.111b; ἄ. καὶ ἀνέστια ἐᾶν Str.1.2.18.

**ἀρρίζω**· ἀράζω, *AB*1452.

**ἀρρίζωτος** [ῐ], ον, *not rooted*, Arist.*HA*548$^{a}$5, Thphr.*CP*3.7.3.

**ἄρρινον**, τό, = νᾶπυ, Nic.*Fr.*84 (s.v.l.); cf. ἀνάρρινον.

**ἀρρίπιστος** [ῐ], ον, *not cooled* or *ventilated*, Gal.10.745.

**ἄρρῑς**, ῖνος, ὁ, ἡ, *without power of scenting*, X.*Cyn.*3.2 (with v.l. ἄρινες). II. *noseless*, Str.2.1.9.

***ἀρριχάομαι**, v. ἀναρριχάομαι.

**ἀρρῑχίς**, ίδος, ἡ, = sq., Ath.4.139c.

***ἄρρῑχος**, ἡ, *wicker basket*, Ar.*Av.*1309, Thphr.*CP*1.7.2: masc. in *AP*7.410 (Diosc.):—also **ἄρσῑχος**, D.S.20.41, *Marm.Par.*55, *IG*12 (7).162.22.42 (Amorgos).

**ἄρροια**, ἡ, *amenorrhoea*, Hp.*Loc.Hom.*47.

**ἄρροιζος**, ον, *without whistling*, Eust.1538.31.

**ἄρρυ**, a cry of boatmen, Theognost.*Can.*161: **ἀρῦ**, Eust.855.23.

**ἀρρυθμ-έω**, *to be out of rhythm*, ῥυθμῷ ἀ. Pl.*Lg.*802e. **-ία**, ἡ, *want of rhythm* or *proportion*, Pl.*R.*401a. **-ιστος**, ον, *not reduced to form, unorganized*, Arist.*Metaph.*1014$^{b}$27, *Ph.*193$^{a}$11. II. of stone, *undressed, rough-hewn*, Plot.5.8.1.

**ἀρρυθμοπότης**, ου, ὁ, *immoderate drinker*, Timo 4.2.

**ἄρρυθμος**, ον, of sounds, *unrhythmical*, opp. εὔρυθμος, Pl.*R.*400d; λέξις.. μήτ' ἔμμετρος μήτ' ἄ. Arist.*Rh.*1408$^{b}$22. Adv. -μως, βαδίζειν step *out of time*, Alex.263.2; *ungracefully*, Plu.*Ant.*29. II. metaph., *in undue measure*, E.*Hipp.*529 (lyr.); *ill-proportioned*, σώματα X. *Mem.*3.10.11; of persons, ἄ. ἐν τοῖς συγγράμμασιν Phld.*Rh.*2.135 S.

**ἀρρύπαντος** [ῠ], ον, *unsoiled*, Eust.598.43. Adv. -τως, gloss on καθαρῶς, Tz. ad Hes.*Op.*337.

***ἄρρῡπος**, ον, *clean*, δίαιτα Hierocl.*in CA*17 p.459 M.

**ἄρρυπτος**, ον, *unwashen*, Nic.*Al.*469.

**ἀρρύπωτος** [ῠ], ον, = ἀρρύπαντος, dub. l. in Sch.A.*Pers.*614.

**ἀρρῡσίαστος**, ον, *not carried off as a hostage*, A.*Supp.*610; *not liable to distraint*, D.H.6.41.

***ἀρ(ρ)ύσιος**, ον, = ἀρρυσίαστος, *Schwyzer*366 *A*3 (Tolophon, iii B.C.).

**ἀρρύσωτος**, ον, = sq., Sor.1.88.

**ἀρρῡτίδωτος** [ῐ], ον, *unwrinkled*, *AP*5.12 (Phld.), 6.252 (Antiphil.), Dsc.3.102, 4.122, Sor.1.56.

**ἀρρωδέω, ἀρρωδίη**, Ion. for ὀρρωδέω, ὀρρωδία.

**ἀρρώξ**, ῶγος, ὁ, ἡ, *without cleft* or *breach, unbroken*, γῆ S.*Ant.*251: also c. Subst. neut., ὅπλοις ἀρρώξιν, like ἀρρήκτοις, Id.*Fr.*156.

**ἀρρωστ-έω**, *to be unwell*, Heraclit.58, X.*Mem.*3.11.10, D.19.124: c. acc. cogn., ἀρρωστίην, ἀρρώστημα, Hp.*Coac.*579, Arist.*Rh.*1372$^{a}$ 28. **-ημα**, ατος, τό, *illness, sickness*, Hp.*Flat.*9, D.2.21, 26.26, Arist.*PA*671$^{b}$9: pl., of *epidemics*, *SIG*943.6 (Cos, iii B.C.). 2. moral *infirmity*, Plu.*Nic.*28. 3. Stoic, = νόσημα (of σῶμα or ψυχή) μετ' ἀσθενείας συμβαῖνον, *Stoic.*3.103, cf. Chrysipp.ib.121. **-ηματικός**, ή, όν, *sickly*, Vett.Val.68.17. **-ήμων**, ον, gen. ονος, = ἄρρωστος, Eup.63. ***-ία**, ἡ, *weakness, sickness*, Hp.*VM*6, etc.: pl., Arist.*EN* 1115$^{a}$2, *SIG*731.7 (Tomi, i B.C.): esp. *lingering ailment, bad state of health*, Phryn.*PS*p.10 B.; ἀ. τοῦ ἀδικεῖν Pl.*R.*359b. 2. *moral weakness*, D.*Prooem.*53; *loss of morale*, Th.7.47; ἀ. τις διανοίας Arist. *Ph.*253$^{a}$33: c. gen., ἀ. τοῦ στρατεύειν *lack of eagerness* to serve, Th. 3.15, cf. Phryn.*PS*p.10 B. ***-ος**, ον, (ῥώννυμι) *weak, sickly*, Arist. *HA*634$^{b}$14, Plu.2.465c. Adv. -τως, ἔχειν Aeschin.2.14, cf. D.H.7. 12; διακεῖσθαι Isoc.19.20. 2. in moral sense, *weak, feeble*, τὴν ψυχήν X.*Ap.*30, cf. *Oec.*4.2 (Comp.). 3. ἀρρωστότερος ἐς τὴν μισθοδοσίαν *remiss* in payment, Th.8.83. [ἄρωστος *AP*11.206 (Lucill.).]

**ἆρσαι, ἆρσον, ἄρσαντες, ἀρσάμενος**, v. ἀραρίσκω.

**ἄρσακες**· οἱ βασιλεῖς Περσῶν, Hsch.

**ἀρσενάκανθον**, = γλήχων, Ps.-Dsc.3.31.

***ἀρσενίκιον**, τό, Dim. of sq., Eust.913.59.

**ἀρσενικόν**, τό, *yellow orpiment*, Arist.*Pr.*966$^{b}$28, Thphr.*Lap.*40 (ἀρρεν-), Dsc.5.104, Str.15.2.14, Lyc.ap.Orib.8.25.15:—also **ἀρρενική**, ἡ, Gall.12.212. (Cf. Hebr. *zarnīq*.)

**ἀρσενικός**, v. ἀρρενικός.

**ἀρσένιον**, τό, Dim. of ἄρσην, *male child*, *PGiss.*77.9 (ii A.D.).

**ἀρσένιος**, = ἀρσενικός, *IG*5(2).498 (Teuthis, iii A.D.).

**ἀρσενο-γενής**, ές, *male*, γένος A.*Supp.*818 (lyr.). ***-θηλυς**, υ, gen. εος, *hermaphrodite, of both sexes*, Plu.2.368c; Pythag. epith. of unity, *Theol.Ar.*5:—also **ἀρρενόθηλυς**, Orph.*Fr.*56, Porph.ap.Eus. *PE*3.11, Man.5.140; of a vine twining about a wild fig, D.S.8 *Fr.*23. **-θυμος**, ον, *man-minded*, Procl.*H.*7.3, Nonn.*D.*34. 352. **-κοίτης**, v. ἀρρενοκοίτης. **-μίκτης**, v. ἀρρενομίκτης. **-μορφος**, ον, *of masculine form* or *look*, Orph.*H.*36. 7. **-πληθής** ἑσμός *crowding* swarm *of men*, A.*Supp.*29 (anap.).

**ἀρσέν-ωμα**, ατος, τό, *seed of the male*, Sch.Opp.*H.*1.494. **-ωπή**, = σταφὶς ἀγρία, Ps.-Dsc.4.152.

*****ἄρσην**, ὁ, ἡ, ἄρσεν, τό, gen. ἄρσενος, Ep., Ion., and Trag.: Att. ἄρρην *IG*2.678*B*55, Pl.*Smp.*191c, etc.: Aeol., Cret., Epid., and Hdt. ἔρσην, q.v.; ἀρσ- prevails in Lxx and *NT*, ἀρρ- is more common in Pap. (exc. Pap. Mag.): nom. ἄρσης *IG*5(1).364.10(Lacon.), *POxy.*465.147 (ii A.D.):—*male*, μήτε τις οὖν θήλεια θεὸς.. μήτε τις ἄρσην Il.8.7; βοῦν.. ἄρσενα 7.315; ἄρσενες ἵπποι 23.377, etc.; ἄρσην σπορά E.*Tr.*503; νηδύς Id.*Ba.*527 (lyr.) (of the birth of Bacchus); γονή Hp.*Genit.*7: ἄρσην, ὁ, or ἄρσεν, τό, *the male*, A.*Ag.*861, *Supp.* 393 (lyr.), Pl.*Lg.*665c, *Smp.*191c, etc.; Ἀπόλλωνι.. θῆλυ καὶ ἄρσεν.. προσέρδειν *IG*12(8).358(Thasos, v B.C.); οἱ ἄρσενες *the male sex*, Th.2.45; τὸ ἄρσεν A.*Eu.*737. 2. *masculine*, Id.*Supp.*951; φρένες E.*Or.*1204: metaph., *mighty*, κτύπος ἄρσην πόντου S.*Ph.* 1455 (lyr.); Ἀχέροντος ἄρσενας χοάς Id.*Fr.*480.3; ἄρσην βοή Ar.*Th.* 125 (lyr.); ἄ. φθόγγοι Aristid.Quint.2.12; of plants, *robust, coarse*, opp. θῆλυς (*tender, delicate*), Thphr.*HP*3.9.3, cf. 2.2.6, Dsc.3.1, al., S.*Tr.*1196. 3. of gender of nouns, *masculine*, ὀνόματα Ar.*Nu.* 682. 4. of sex in plants, ἀπὸ τοῦ ἄρρενος τοῖς θήλεσι βοήθεια Thphr. *HP*2.8.4:—but also, *coarse, tough*, γογγυλίς ib.7.4.3, cf. 3.9.3: Comp. form **ἀρρέντερος** (cf. θηλύτερος), κὰ τὠρρέντερον γένος in the *male* line, *IG*5(2).262.21(Mantinea, v B.C.). 5. Adv. ἀρρένως Diog.ap.Stob. 4.44.71. (Occurs without ϝ- on Cret. Inscrr. which preserve ϝ-; cf. Skt. *ṛṣabhás* 'bull', Avest. *aršan-* 'man'.)

**ἄρσηνος**, = ἄρσην, *PLond.*3.909ᵃ5. **ἄρσης**, v. ἄρσην.

*****Ἀρσῐνόεια**, τά, *festival in honour of Arsinoe*, *PSI*4.364.5 (iii B.C.).

**ἄρσιος**, ον, (ἀραρίσκω) *fitting, meet, right*, Hsch.

**ἀρσίπους** [ῐ], ὁ, ἡ, πουν, τό, gen. ποδος, contr. for ἀερσίπους, *raising the foot, active*, *h.Ven.*211, *AP*7.717.

*****ἄρσις**, εως, ἡ, (αἴρω) *raising* or *lifting*, τῶν σκελῶν Arist.*IA*711ᵇ25; πᾶσα πορεία ἐξ ἄρσεως καὶ θέσεως συντελεῖται Id.*Pr.*885ᵇ6; βοῶν, as an athletic feat, *IG*2.471.78 (pl.); μηχανήματος Plb.8.4.6; *taking up, examination*, δειγμάτων *POxy.*708.5,18(ii A.D.); *plucking, pulling up* of a herb, *PMag.Par.*1.2977. b. *distillation*, ὕδατος Ps.-Democr. ap.Zos.Alch.p.152B.; *sublimation*, νεφέλης ibid. 2. (from Pass.) *rising*, κυμάτων Arist.*Mu.*396ᵃ26. 3. *that which is lifted, burden*, Lxx 4*Ki.*8.9, al.; *that which is taken*, ἄ. βασιλέως *portion* from the king's table, ib.2*Ki.*19.42, cf. 11.8. 4. *dignity*, Aq.*Ge.*49.3. II. *removal*, τὴν ⟨ἐκ⟩ θαλάττης ἄ. [τῶν κητῶν] D.S.3.41; ἀκανθῶν *POxy.* 909.25 (iii A.D.); τριχῶν Dsc.5.146. 2. *taking away, removal, abolition*, dub. in Arist.*Metaph.*1019ᵇ16; τοῦ ὄντος Plu.2.1130a; τοῦ φόβου Metrod.*Herc.*831.16. b. Gramm., *omission*, e.g. of the reduplication, Rh.3.566 W. 3. *negation*, Phld.*Sign.*14, Procl.*in Prm.*p.850 S.; opp. θέσις, S.E.*P.*1.192, cf. Plot.5.5.6; = στέρησις, Id. 2.4.13. 4. *destruction, ruin*, *OGI*315.59(Pessinus, ii B.C.). III. *raising of the foot* in beating time, opp. θέσις, *downward beat*, Aristox.*Rhyth.*12.17, D.H.*Dem.*48, Aristid.Quint.1.13, Luc.*Harm.*1, etc. IV. ἄρσις· ζύμη, Hsch.

**ἄρσῐχος**, v. ἄρριχος.

*****ἄρσος**, εος, τό, only pl. ἄρσεα· λειμῶνες, Hsch.; cf. ἄλσος.

**ἄρσω**, Aeol. fut. of αἴρω.

**ἀρσωμίδες**· ὑπόδημα γυναικεῖον, Hsch.

*****ἀρτάβη**, ἡ, Persian measure, *artaba*, = 1 medimnus + 3 choenices, Hdt 1.192; or exactly 1 medimnus, Suid., Hsch. II. Egyptian measure of capacity, varying from 24 to 42 χοίνικες, *OGI*90.30 (Rosetta), *PLond.*2.265 (i A.D.), *POxy.*9ᵛ8 (iii/iv A.D.), etc.

**ἀρταβι-ειος**, α, ον, *of an* ἀρτάβη, σφυρὶς *PFlor.*369.14(ii A.D.). 2. **-ία**, ἡ (later **ἀρταβία**, ἡ, *CPR*1.16 (i A.D.)), *tax of one artaba per* ἄρουρα, *PTeb.*119.11 (ii B.C.), *PLond.*3.1171ᵛii 15 (i A.D.), *PFay.*99: —also neut. pl. -εια, τά, *PTeb.*5.59 (ii B.C.).

**ἀρτάδες**· οἱ δίκαιοι, ὑπὸ Μάγων, Hsch. **ἀρταῖοι**· οἱ ἥρωες, παρὰ Πέρσαις, Id.

*****ἀρτᾰμ-έω**, *cut in pieces*, ταῦρον E.*El.*816; ἄνδρας γναθοῖς Id.*Alc.* 494. **-ησις**, εως, ἡ, *slaughtering*, βοὸς *IG*7.2426.15 (Thebes).

*****Ἄρταμις**, **Ἀρταμίτιος**, **-μίτιον**, v. Ἀρτεμ-.

*****ἄρτᾰμος**, ὁ, *butcher, cook*, X.*Cyr.*2.2.4, Epicr.6, *IG*14.643; βοὸς Orac.ap.Phleg.10.39. 2. metaph., *murderer*, S.*Fr.*1025, Lyc.236, 797. (For ἀρτι-ταμος, = ὁ εἰς ἄρτια τέμνων, acc. to Eust.577.45.)

**ἀρτάνη** [ᾰ], ἡ, (ἀρτάω) *that by which something is hung up, rope, noose, halter*, A.*Ag.*875,1091 (lyr.), etc.; ἀ. κρεμαστή S.*OT*1266; πλεκταῖσιν ἀ. Id.*Ant.*54.

**ἀρτάρια**, τά, *felt shoes*, Suid.; cf. ἀρτήρ.

**ἀρταχήλας**· τὰ χέμνια (leg. χελύνια), τὰ χείλη, Hsch.

*****ἀρτάω**, fut. -ήσω *AP*6.245 (Diod.): aor. 1 ἤρτησα E.*Andr.*811, etc.: pf. ἤρτηκα (προσ-) Arr.*Epict.*1.1.14:—Pass., pf. ἤρτημαι E. *Hipp.*857, Ion. 3 pl. ἀρτέαται Hdt.1.125: aor. ἠρτήθην (προσ-) Man. 4.199:—*fasten to* or *hang* one thing *upon* another, τι ἀπό τινος Th.2. 76; ἀ. δέρην *hang*, E.*Andr.* l.c.; ἱμᾶσιν.. ἀρτήσας δέμας *having bound*, Id.*Hipp.*1222:—Med., βρόχους ἀρτωμένη *fastening* halters *to one's neck*, Id.*Tr.*1012; ἀρτήσαντο Orph.*A.*1096: but, II. more freq. Pass., *to be hung upon, hang upon*, ἠρτῆσθαι ἔκ τινος E.*Hipp.* 857, Pl.*Ion*533e, etc.; ἐν βρόχοις E.*Hipp.*779. 2. ἀρτᾶσθαι ἔκ τινος *depend upon*, Hdt.3.19, 6.109, al.; ἐξ ὧν ὦλλοι ἀρτέαται Πέρσαι on whom the rest of the Persians *depend*, i.e. whom they acknowledge as their chiefs, Id.1.125; so παρρησία ἐξ ἀληθείας ἠρτημένη D. 60.26; ἀπὸ ταὐτοῦ ἠ. Arist.*MM*1209ᵃ22; ἐντεῦθεν Id.*Juv.*469ᵇ15; τοῦ στόματος Ael.*NA*4.51; τῶν χειρῶν Philostr.*Im.*2.23, etc.; αἰτίου, ἀπ' αἰτίας, Porph.*Sent.*14. (Contr. from ἀερτάω (cf. ἀν-αερτάω), cf. ἀείρω 'attach'.)

**ἀρτεμ-έω**, *to be safe and sound*, Nonn.*D.*35.387. ***-ής**, ές, *safe and sound*, ζωόν τε καὶ ἀρτεμέα Il.5.515; σὺν ἀρτεμέεσσι φίλοισι Od. 13.43, cf. A.R.1.415, Call.*Iamb.*1.227.—Ep. word; etym. of Ἄρτεμις, Pl.*Cra.*406b. ***-ία**, ἡ, *soundness, health*, *AP*9.644(Agath.), Procl. *H.*1.42: pl., *recovery*, Max.184.

**ἀρτεμίδιον** or **-ιδῖον**, = δίκταμνος, Ps.-Dsc.3.32.

**Ἀρτεμῐδόβλητος**, ον, *stricken by Artemis*, Macr.*Sat.*1.17.11.

*****Ἄρτεμις**, ἡ, gen. ιδος, also ιτος, dat. ιτι *SIG*671 *A* 6 (Delph., ii B.C.), *GDI*1679 (Zacynthus), etc.: acc. ιν, also ιδα *h.Ven.*16: Dor. Ἄρταμις, ιτος (or ιδος as in Boeot. Inscrr. *IG*7.546, al.), *SIG*765 (Rhodes, i B.C.), *IG*2.545.12 (Delph.), etc.; dat. Ἀρτάμι ib.4.577 (Argos): pl., Ἀρτέμιδες πραεῖαι, = Εἰλειθυῖαι, ib.7.3101 (Lebad.):—*Artemis*, Od.11.172, etc. (Deriv. uncertain, but more prob. connected with ἄρταμος than with ἀρτεμής.)

**ἀρτεμισία**, ἡ, *wormwood*, ἀ. πλατυτέρα, = *Artemisia arborescens*, ἀ. λεπτοτέρα, = *A. campestris*, Dsc.3.113. 2. ἀ. μονόκλωνος, = *A. scoparia*, Ps.-Dsc.3.113. II. = ἀμβροσία, ib.114.

**Ἀρτεμισιασταί**, οἱ, guild of *worshippers of Artemis* at Athens, *Berl.Sitzb.*1888.324.

**Ἀρτεμίσιον**, τό, *temple of Artemis, place sacred to her*, Hdt.8.8 sq., Plu.2.264c, etc.: Dor. **Ἀρταμίτιον** Ar.*Lys.*1251, *SIG*56.26 (Argos, v B.C.); **Ἀρτεμίτιον** *IG*14.217.14 (Acrae). 2. **Ἀρταμίτια**, τά, *festival of Artemis*, *Michel*995 *D* 8 (Delph., v B.C.). II. Dim. of Ἄρτεμις, *small figure of Artemis*, as device on a signet, *SIG*²588.191 (Delos, ii B.C.); *image of A.*, Hyp.*Fr.*74.

*****Ἀρτεμίσιος**, Dor. **Ἀρταμίτιος**, ὁ (sc. μήν), a Spartan and Macedonian month, Th.5.19, Plu.*Alex.*16:—also ***Ἀρτεμισιών**, ῶνος, ὁ, at Erythrae, *SIG*410.1 (iii B.C.), etc. [The first ι in Ἀρτεμίσιον, -ίσιος, -ισιών, etc., is long (cf. Ar.*Th.*1200, Diph.124) and written ει in Inscrr. of late ii B.C., *IG*12(9).234.23, *SIG*708.1, etc.]

**ἀρτέμ-ων**, ονος, ὁ, (ἀρτάω) *foresail* of a ship, *Act.Ap.*27.40, dub. sens. in Lyd.*Mens.*2.12. II. *principal pulley* in a system, Vitr. 10.2.9 (in Latin form, = Gk. ἐπάγων). **-ώνιον**, τό, Dim. of foreg. I, Tz. ad Lyc.359. II. name of an *eye-salve*, Gal.12.780.

**ἀρτέομαι**, Ion. Verb, Pass., *to be prepared, make ready*, c. inf., οἱ δὲ αὖτις πολεμέειν.. ἀρτέοντο Hdt.5.120; ἀρτέετο ἐς πόλεμον Id.8. 97. II. Med., c. acc., οἳ οὐκ ἔων ναυμαχίην ἀρτέεσθαι Id.7.143. (Cf. ἀν-, πορ-αρτέομαι. Akin to ἀρτίζομαι, not to ἀρτάομαι.)

**ἀρτέον**, (αἴρω) *one must take away*, Socr.ap.Stob.3.13.63; τράπεζαν *one must clear*, Alex.250.1. 2. *one must deny*, Polystr. p.24W.

**Ἀρτεπίβουλος** [ῐ], ὁ, *Bread-thief*, name of a mouse in Batr.261.

*****ἄρτημα**, ατος, τό, (ἀρτάω) *hanging ornament, ear-ring*, Hdt.2.69; cf. λίθινος. II. *cord for suspension*, e.g. of the steelyard, Arist. *Mech.*853ᵃ34, ᵇ25, *IG*2.834 *c* 13, al.; ἐπὶ τὸ αὐτοῦ ἀ. νεύειν Str.1.1. 20. 2. *buoy*, Plu.*Cat.Mi.*38. 3. in pl., *ligaments*, Gal.8.125.

**ἀρτήρ**, ῆρος, ὁ, a kind of *felt shoe*, Pherecr.38. II. *that by which anything is carried*, Lxx *Ne.*4.17(11).

**ἀρτηρία**, Ion. -ίη, ἡ, *wind-pipe*, ἡ ἀ. μόλις ἀναπνεούσῃ ὑπεσύριζε Hp.*Epid.*7.25, cf.39, Pl.*Ti.*70d, Arist.*HA*493ᵃ8, *deAn.*420ᵇ29; ἡ τραχεῖα ἀ. (cf. II) Timoth.ap.Menon.*Iatr.*8.29, v.l. in Dsc.2.50, Luc.*Hist. Conscr.*7, S.E.*M.*9.178, etc.: in pl., *bronchial tubes*, ἆσθμα.. περὶ στῆθεα καὶ ἀρτηρίας Hp.*Epid.*7.12 (vulg. but prob. l. -ίην, = *trachea*), cf. Pl.*Ti.*78c; πλεύμονος ἀρτηρίαι S.*Tr.*1054. II. *artery*, as distinct from a vein, αἱ φλεβῶν καὶ ἀρτηριῶν κοινωνίαι Hp *Art.*45, cf. 69; τὰς δὲ φλέβας καὶ τὰς ἀ. συνάπτειν εἰς ἀλλήλας.. τῇ αἰσθήσει φανερὸν εἶναι Arist.*Spir.*484ᵃ1; ἀ. λεῖαι (cf. 1) Gal.*UP*8.1, al.; ἀ. φλεβώδης *pulmonary vein*, ib.6.10; believed to contain πνεῦμα by Erasistr., ib. 17, and derived fr. ἀήρ, τηρέω by Bacch.ap.Erot. s.v. ἀορτέων. III. = ἀορτή, *aorta*, δύο εἰσὶ κοῖλαι φλέβες ἀπὸ τῆς καρδίης, τῇ μὲν οὔνομα ἀρτηρίη τῇ δὲ κοίλη φλέψ Hp.*Carn.*5. IV. in pl. of the *ureters*, Id.*Oss.*10. (Contr. from ἀερτηρία, from ἀείρω 'attach' (q.v.), cf. ἀορτήρ, etc.)

**ἀρτηριακός**, ή, όν, *of* or *for the trachea* or *bronchi*, esp. -κή (sc. ἀντίδοτος), ἡ, *medicament for their treatment*, Plin.*HN*20.207, 23.136, Gal.13.1; δυνάμεις Androm.ib.14; φάρμακα Aët.8.54; -κὸν ἴσχαιμον styptic for *arterial* haemorrhage, Id.7.19; ἀ. πάθος, τὰ ἀ., affections *of these organs*, Paul.Aeg.3.28; ἡ -κή a medicine, Aët.8.54 sq.; ἡ ἀ. κοιλία τῆς καρδίας *left ventricle*, *Placit.*4.5.7; ἀ. φωνή, of the human voice, opp. ἡ τῶν ὀργάνων, Nicom.*Harm.*2.

**ἀρτηριᾶσις**, εως, ἡ, *bronchitis*, Isid.*Etym.*4.7.14.

**ἀρτηριο-τομέω**, *cut an artery*, in Pass., *have it cut*, Antyll.ap.Orib. 7.14.2, Gal.8.202. **-τομία**, ἡ, *severing of an artery*, Antyll.ap. Orib.7.14 tit., Gal.11.312.

**ἀρτηριώδης**, ες, *like an* ἀρτηρία, μέρη Gal.8.737; κοιλία τῆς καρδίας *left ventricle*, ibid.; ἀ. φλέψ *pulmonary artery*, Herophil.ap.Ruf.*Onom.* 203, cf. Gal.*UP*6.10.

**ἄρτ-ησις**, εως, ἡ, (ἀρτέομαι) *equipment*, Hdt.1.195 (v.l. ἄρτισις, q.v.). II. (ἀρτάομαι) *suspension*, Papp.1044.14. **-ησμός**, ὁ, (ἀρτάω) *hanging, suspension*, *AB*447. **-ητός**, όν, = κρεμαστός, Hsch.

*****ἄρτι** [ῐ], Adv. *just, exactly*, of coincidence of Time, *just now* (not in Hom.): 1. mostly of the present, with pres. tense, Thgn.998, Pi.*P.*4.158, A.*Th.*534; opp. πάλαι, with pf., τέθνηκεν ἄ. S.*Ant.*1283; βεβᾶσιν ἄ. Id.*El.*1386; ἄ. ἥκεις ἢ πάλαι; Pl.*Cri.*43a; more fully ἄ. νυνί Ar.*Lys.*1008; ἄ... νῦν or νῦν.. ἄ., Pl.*Plt.*291a, b; later, = νῦν, Theoc.23.26, *Ep.Gal.*1.9, J.*AJ*1.6.1; ἄ. καὶ πρώην *to-day* and *yesterday*, i.e. *very lately*, Plu.*Brut.*1, etc.; ἕως ἄ. till *now*, *Ev.Matt.*11.12; *POxy.*936.23 (iii A.D.): with Subst., ὁ ἄ. λόγος Pl.*Tht.*153e; ἡλικίαν..τὴν ἄ. ἐκ παίδων X.*HG*5.4.25; ἡ ἄ. ὥρα 1*Ep.Cor.*4.11, *PMag. Lond.*1.121.373; ἄ. μὲν..ἄ. δὲ.. *now..now..*, *at one time..at another..*, Luc.*Nigr.*4. 2. of the past, *just now*, with impf., ἄ. βλάστεσκε dub. in S.*Fr.*546, cf. E.*Ba.*677, Pl.*Grg.*454b: with aor., λέξας ἄ. S.*Aj.*1272; καθημάτωσεν ἄ. E.*Ph.*1160; opp. νῦν, ὃ ἄ. ἐρρήθη..νῦν δὲ.. Pl.*Alc.*1.130d, cf. 127c; ἐν τῷ ἄ., opp. ἐν τῷ νῦν καὶ ἐν τῷ ἔπειτα, Id.*Men.*89c. 3. in Antiph.26.7 (s.v.l.) and later also of the future, *just now, presently*, Luc.*Sol.*1, App.*Mith.*69, Astramps.*Orac.* 94.2; condemned by Phryn.12; also, *just at present*, πλεύσεις, ἄ. δὲ οὔ Astramps.*Orac.*92.7: with imper., Nonn.*D.*20.277, etc. (Perh. cogn. with Skt. *ṛtám* 'ordinance', *ṛtás* 'correct'.)

**ἀρτῐ-άζω**, (ἄρτιος) *play at odd and even*, Ar.*Pl.*816; ἀστραγάλοις ἄ. Pl.*Ly.*206e, prob. in Arist.*Div.Somn.*463b20. II. *count*, *AP* 12.145. **-άκις** [ᾰ], Adv. *an even number of times*, opp. περιττάκις, Pl.*Prm.*144a, Plu.2.429d; ἄρτια ἀ. *even times even*, of powers of two, Pl.*Prm.*143e, cf. Ascl.*Tact.*2.7. **-ακός**, ή, όν, *of even numbers*, only in Adv. **-κῶς**, τὸ ἥμισυ ἀ. ὠνομασμένον the half called *after the even number*, Nicom.*Ar.*1.9.

**ἀρτίαλα**, τά, Aeol., *ear-rings*, Poll.5.97.

**ἀρτιάλωτος**, ον, *newly caught*, Xenocr.34.

**ἀρτιασμός**, ὁ, *game of odd and even*, Arist.*Rh.*1407b3.

**ἀρτι-βλαστής**, ές, *newly budding*, Thphr.*CP*2.3.1. **-βλαστος**, ον, *recently sprouted*, Callix.1, Dsc.1*Praef.*9. **-βρεφής**, ές, *of young children*, v. ἀρτιτρεφής. **-βρεχής**, ές, *just steeped*, *AP*5.174 (Mel.). **-γάλακτος** [γᾰ], ον, *just weaned*, τέκνον *Epigr.Gr.*205 (Halic., ii B.C.), cf. *Ath.Mitt.*24.448 (Phryg.). **-γάλαξ** [γᾰ], ὁ, ἡ, gen. ακτος, = foreg., Hdn.Gr.1.352. ✻**-γάμος**, ον, *just married*, κούρη *IG*14.1835, cf. Opp. *H.*4.179, Nonn.*D.*48.298, al. **-γενέθλος**, ον, *just born*, Orph.*A.* 386. ✻**-γένειος**, ον, *with the beard just sprouting*, *AP*9.219 (Diod.), Nonn.*D.*18.135; as Subst., ἀ. ἐπίλεκτοι App.*Pun.*8; incorrectly used, = ἀρτιγέννητος, σολοικισμοί Luc.*Sol.*2. **-γενής**, ές, *just born* or *made*, Nic.*Al.*357, Ael.*NA*4.34, Sor.1.87. **-γέννητος**, ον, = foreg., βρέφη 1*Ep.Pet.*2.2, cf. Luc.*Alex.*13, Longus 1.9, al. **-γλῠφής**, ές, *newly carved*, Theoc.*Ep.*4. **-γνωστος**, ον, *newly known*, App.*BC*3.12. **-γονος**, ον, = ἀρτιγενής, μῆλα *AP*6.252 (Antiphil.); κάλυκες Nic.*Fr.*74.34, cf. Nonn.*D.*7.143, Opp.*C.*3.9. **-γρᾰφής**, ές, *just written*, Luc.*Lex.*1. ✻**-δᾰής**, ές, *just taught*, *AP*6.227 (Crin.). **-δαϊκτος** [δᾰ], ον, *just slain*, Nonn.*D.*15.393, al. **-δακρυς**, υ, *ready to weep*, E.*Med.*903, Luc.*Lex.*4. **-δίδακτος** [δῐ], ον, *just taught*, τῶν Ἑλληνικῶν App.*BC*3.20.

**ἀρτί-διον**, τό, Dim. of ἄρτος, *small loaf*, D.L.7.13; *piece of bread*, Sor.1.115; *food*, *POxy.*738.8 (i A.D.). **-δορος**, ον, *just stript off* or *peeled*, cj. Toup in *AP*6.22 (Zon.) for ἀντίδορος (q.v.). **-δρεπής**, ές, *just plucked*, Hld.2.23. **-δροπος**, ον, = foreg., v. ἀρτίτροπος. **-έπεια**, ἡ, Ep. fem. of sq., Hes.*Th.*29. **-επής**, ές, (ἄρτιος, ἔπος) *ready of speech, glib of tongue*, ἀ. καὶ ἐπίκλοπος ἔπλεο μύθων Il.22.281: in good sense, ἀπεφθέγξατο δ' ἀρτιεπὴς answered *clearly*, Pi.*O.* 6.61; ἀ. γλῶσσα Id.*I.*5(4).46. **-ζῠγία**, ἡ, *recent union*, ἀνδρῶν ἀ., i.e. *newly married* husbands, A.*Pers.*542.

**ἀρτί-ζω**, pf. ἤρτικα *PMag.Leid.W.*10.42:—*get ready, prepare*, *AP*10.25 (Antip.), *PMag.* l.c.:—Med., χορὸν ἀρτίζοντο Theoc.13.43; πρός τι D.S.14.20:—Pass., πρός τι *CIG*3601.9 (Ilium), S.E.*M.*11.208. **-ζωος**, ον, *not likely to live*, Hp.*Superf.*15. **-θᾰλής**, ές, *just budding* or *blooming*, *AP*5.197 (Mel.); ἐλπίδες *Epigr.Gr.*348 (Cius); of persons, Nonn.*D.*3.312, al. **-θᾰνής**, ές, *just dead*, E.*Alc.*600 (lyr.), Men. Prot.p.89 D. **-θέριστος**, ον, *newly reaped*, κριθή *Hippiatr.*1. **-θηρος**, ον, *newly caught*, Damocr.ap.Gal.14.93. **-καυστος**, ον, *freshly roasted*, Thphr.*Ign.*65. **-κολλος**, ον, *close-glued, clinging close*, ἀρτίκολλος ὥστε τέκτονος χιτών, = ἀρτίως κολληθεὶς ὡς ὑπὸ τέκτονος, S.*Tr.*768. II. metaph., *fitting well together*, ἀ. συμβαίνει τάδε turn out *exactly right*, A.*Ch.*580; εἰς ἀ. ἀγγέλου λόγον μαθεῖν *in the nick of time*, Id.*Th.*373. **-κόμιστος**, ον, *newly nursed*, Nonn.*D.*9.53, al. **-κροτέω**, = συγκροτέω, *equip*, στόλον Str.15.1.32; λόγους prob. in Pl.*Ax.*369d, cf. Phld.*Rh.*2.75 S.: —Pass., *to be brought to an agreement*, γάμοι Men.904. 2. *keep time*, of rowers, Hsch. **-ληπτος**, ον, *just taken*, App.*Mith.*108. ✻**-λῐθία**, ἡ, *exact superposition of joints*, in masonry, *IG*7.4255.27 (Oropus). **-λογία**, ἡ, *ready speech*, Poll.6.150. **-λόγως**, Adv. *speaking readily*, ibid. **-λόχευτος**, ον, *just born*, *APl.*4.122, Nonn.*D.*14.27, al. **-μαζές**· νέον, Hsch. **-μᾰθής**, ές, *having just learnt*, κακῶν E.*Hec.*687; λογικῆς θεωρίας Gal.11.466: abs., *beginner*, Sor.1.4, cf. Longus 3.20. **-μελής**, ές, *sound of limb*, Pl.*R.*536b, Sor.1.3, D.C.69.20; *perfect in all members*, τέχναι Them.*Or.*26.316c. **-μήτας**· νέους, Hsch.

**Ἄρτιμις**, barbarism for Ἄρτεμις, Tim.*Pers.*172.

**Ἀρτίμπασα**, ἡ, Scythian name for Aphrodite Urania, Hdt.4.59 (vv.ll. Ἀργίμπ-, Ἀρίππ-).

**ἀρτινεστέραν**· ὑγιεστέραν, Hsch.

**ἀρτίνοος** [ῐ], ον, contr. **-νους**, ουν, *sound of mind*, D.C.69.20.

**ἀρτῐο-γενής**, ές, *of the even class* (of powers of 2), Nicom.*Ar.*1.8 (v.l. ἀρτιοπληθής). **-γώνιος** (or **-γωνος**), ον, *having an even number of angles*, Archim.*Sph.Cyl.*1.44, al. **-δύνᾰμος** [ῠ], ον, *of even power*, of numbers the halves of which are *even*, Nicom.*Ar.*1.8. **-λογέω**, *speak distinctly*, Eust.1151.59. **-παγής**, ές, v. **-ταγής**. **-πέρισσος**, Att. **-ττος**, ον, *even-odd*, of *even* numbers, the halves of which are *odd*, as 6, 10, etc., Philol.5, Ph.1.3, Plu.2.1139f; of unity, Arist.*Fr.*199. **-πλευρος**, ον, *having an even number of sides*, of polygons, Archim.*Sph.Cyl.*1.21, al. **-πληθής**, v. ἀρτιογενής.

**ἄρτιος**, α, ον (ος, ον Aristid.Quint.1.25): (ἄρτι):—*complete, perfect of its kind, suitable, exactly fitted*, ἄ. ἀλλήλοισι σπόνδυλοι Hp.*Art.*45; ἄρτια βάζειν speak *to the purpose*, Il.14.92, Od.8.240; ὅτι οἱ φρεσὶν ἄρτια ᾔδη thought things *in accordance with* him, was of *the same* mind *with* him, Il.5.326, Od.19.248; ἄρτια μήδεσθαι Pi.*O.*6.94; *meet, right, proper*, Sol.4.40, Thgn.946; ἄ. εἴς τι *well-suited* for.., *IG*14.889.7 (Sinuessa); ἀρτιωτάτην ἔχειν τάξιν *most perfect*, Philostr.*VS*1.21.3. 2. *full-grown*, Thphr.*HP*2.5.5; *sound*, of body and mind, νόος, σώμασιν, Thgn.154, D.S.3.33, cf. 2*Ep.Ti.*3.17. 3. *prepared, ready*, c. inf., ἄρτιοι πείθεσθαι, ποιέειν, Hdt.9.27,48; καταβιῶναι Philostr.*VS*1.9. II. of numbers, *perfect*, i.e. *even*, opp. περιττός (*odd*), Epich.170.7, cf. Pl.*Prt.*356e, al.; ἄ. πόδες *even number of* feet, Arist.*HA*489b22; ἐν ἀρτίῃσι (sc. ἡμέρῃσι) happening on *the even* days, Hp.*Epid.*1.18; ἄ. χώρα, of the *even* feet in iambic and trochaic verse, Heph.5.1, Aristid.Quint. l.c. 2. *exact, precise*, ἐτῶν ἀριθμὸν ὀγδοήκοντ' ἀρτίων *Epigr.Gr.*222*b* (Milet.). III. Adv. ἀρτίως *just, newly*, = ἄρτι, [Epich.]251, freq. in S. 1. of present time, with pres., *Aj.*678, *OT*78, al.: with pf., *OC*892, al. 2. of the past, with impf., *Tr.*664,674, etc.: with aor., ib.346, *OT*243, etc. 3. with an Adj., ἀ. νεοσφαγής *Aj.*898. 4. *closely fitting*, καθηλῶσαί τί τινι Polyaen.3.11.13. IV. neut. pl. ἄρτια, = ἀρτίως 2, *AP*6.234 (Eryc.).

**ἀρτῐοτᾰγής**, ές, *occupying the even places* in a series, Iamb.*in Nic.* p.59 P., al.; prob. for **-παγής** in Nicom.*Harm.*11.3. II. *even in number*, Id.*Ar.*2.24.

**ἀρτῐότης**, ητος, ἡ, *soundness, entireness*, Arr.*Epict.*1.22.12, Gal. *Thras.*12, Stob.2.7.7a. 2. of numbers, *evenness*, opp. περιττότης, Arist.*Metaph.*1004b11.

✻**ἀρτῐ-πᾰγής**, ές, *just put together* or *made*, στάλικες Theoc.*Ep.*3; ναῦς *AP*9.32; σκῆνος Them.*Or.*4.60a. II. *freshly coagulated*, ἀλλ' τυρός *AP*9.412 (Phld.). **-παις**, παιδος, ὁ, *lately a boy*, prob. f. l. for ἀντίπαις, Thom.Mag. s. v. παῖς. **-πλακέες**· οἱ πεινῶντες, Hsch. **-πλουτος**, ον, *newly gotten*, χρήματα E.*Supp.*742. **-πνουν**· ὀρθόπνουν, Hsch. **-πόλεμος**, ον, *new to war*, App.*Syr.*37. ✻**-πους**, ὁ, ἡ, πουν, τό, gen. ποδος: Ep. nom. **ἀρτίπος**: I. (ἄρτιος, πούς) *sound of foot*, ὁ μὲν καλός τε καὶ ἀρτίπος, opp. χωλός, Od.8.310, cf. Hdt.3.130, Them.*Or.*21.255c. 2. generally, *strong* or *swift of foot*, ἡ δ' Ἄτη σθεναρή τε καὶ ἀρτίπος Il.9.505; ἀρτίποδες καὶ ἀρτίχειρες Pl.*Lg.*795d. II. (ἄρτι, πούς) *coming just in time*, S.*Tr.*58.

✻**ἄρτῐσις**, εως, ἡ, (ἀρτίζω) *equipment*, v.l. for ἄρτησις, ἡ περὶ τὸ σῶμα ἄ. Hdt.1.195.

**ἀρτίσκαπτος**, ον, *just dug*, *AP*7.465 (Heraclit.).

**ἀρτίσκιον**, τό, Dim. of sq. 2, Damocr.ap.Gal.14.96.

**ἀρτίσκος**, ὁ, Dim. of ἄρτος, *little loaf*, Hp.*Steril.*216, Sch.Ar.*Pax* 1196. 2. *pastille*, Dsc.2.172, Gal.12.317.

**ἀρτιστῆρες**, οἱ, magistrates at Elatea, *IG*9(1).97.22.

**ἀρτι-στομέω**, *to speak in good idiom, accurately*, Str.14.2.28. **-στομία**, ἡ, *distinctness* or *precision in speech*, Poll.6.150. **-στομος**, ον, *speaking in good idiom*, or *with precision*, Plu.*Cor.*38, Suid. Adv. **-μως** Poll.6.150. II. *with a good mouth* or *opening*, κόλπος Str.5.4.5; λιμήν Id.17.1.6. III. ἀ. βέλεα *evenly tipped*, i.e. *not sharp* or *jagged* (πανταχόθεν ὁμαλά Gal.19), Hp.*VC*11; so ἀ. ξοΐς *plain* chisel (not toothed), *IG*7.3073.148 (Lebad.). **-στράτευτος** [ρᾰ], ον, *young in military service*, App.*BC*3.49. **-σύλληπτος**, ον, *newly conceived* in the womb, Dsc.*Eup.*2.81. **-τέλεστος**, ον, *just completed*, Nonn. *D.*5.579, al. **-τελής**, ές, *newly initiated*, Pl.*Phdr.*251a. II. *fully formed*, Thphr.*HP*2.5.5; *just finished*, Nonn.*D.*26.46. **-τοκέω**, *produce normal issue*: metaph. of vines, *Gp.*5.41.1. **-τοκος**, ον, *new-born*, *AP*6.154 (Leon. or Gaet.), Luc.*DDeor.*7.1, Them. *Or.*25.311a; *new laid*, ᾠά Aret.*CA*1.10: metaph., σελήνη Opp.*C.* 4.123. II. parox. ἀρτιτόκος, ον, *having just given birth*, ib.3.119, *AP*7.729 (Tymn.), 9.2 (Tib. Ill.). **-τομος**, ον, *just cut* or *severed*, A.R.4.1515. II. parox. ἀρτιτόμος, ον, *having just cut* or *hewn*, Suid. **-τόνον**· εὔτονον, εὐάρμοστον, Hsch. **-τρεφής**, ές, *just nursed*, ἀρτιτρεφεῖς βλαχαί wailings *of young children*, A.*Th.* 350 cod. Med. (v.l. ἀρτιβρεφεῖς). **-τροπος**, ον, (ἄρτιος, τρόπος) *of modest manners* (but, *just of age*, acc. to Sch.), A.*Th.*333 cod. Med. (v.l. ἀρτιδρόποις *just plucked, of tender age*). **-φᾰής**, ές, *newly shining*, μήνη Nonn.*D.*5.165. ✻**-φᾰνής**, ές, *just seen*, *having newly appeared*, ib.12.5, al. **-φᾰτος**, ον, *just killed*, Opp.*H.*4. 256. **-φονος**, ον, *just slain*, Nonn.*D.*44.275 (prob.), Sch.Opp.*H.* 2.617.

**ἄρτιφος**· ὀρίγανον, Hsch.

✻**ἀρτί-φρων** [ῐ], ον, gen. ονος, (ἄρτιος, φρήν) *sound of mind, sensible*, οὔτε μάλ' ἀ. Od.24.261, cf. E.*Med.*294; ἀρτιμελεῖς καὶ ἀρτίφρονας Pl. *R.*536b; ἀ...πλὴν.. *quite in one's senses* except.., E.*IA*877: c. gen., ἐπεὶ δ' ἀ. ἐγένετο..γάμων when he came *to full consciousness of..*, A.*Th.*778 (lyr.). ✻**-φυής**, ές, *just born*, ἀ. ἔθανον *Epigr.Gr.* 334.11 (Ilium), cf. *Inscr.Cos* 343; *fresh*, κράμβη *AP*6.21, cf. Dsc.3.15; κύκλος ἰούλων Nonn.*D.*3.416. II. of number, *even*, Hp.*Septim.* 9. **-φῠτος**, ον, *just born, fresh*, ἄνθεα *AP*4.2.14 (Phil.); ἔρνεα Nonn.*D.*41.5. **-φωνία**, ἡ, = ἀρτιλογία, Poll.6.150. **-φωνος**, ον, only in Adv. **-νως**, = ἀρτιλόγως, ibid. **-χᾰνής**, ές, *just opening*, *AP* 6.22 (Zon.). **-χάρακτος** [χᾰ], ον, *newly graven*, γράμμα Epigr. ap.Ath.5.209d. 2. *newly ploughed*, Nonn.*D.*2.65. 3. *freshly wounded*, ib.25.498. 4. metaph. of darkness, *newly cleft* by light, ib. 27.5; of colour on ripening grapes, ib.12.311. **-χείλης**· ὑπερέχων τοῖς χείλεσιν, ὑπόμακρος, Hsch. **-χειρ**, ὁ, ἡ, gen. χειρος, *strong of hand* (cf. ἀρτίπους), Pl.*Lg.*795d. **-χνους**, ουν, gen. ου, = ἀρτιγένειος, *with the first bloom on*, μῆλον *AP*6.22 (Zon.); ἀ. ἴουλος a *young* beard, Philostr.Jun.*Im.*6; ἔρνος ἀρτίχνουν γονέων ἐλπίδα *Epigr.Gr.*

201.6 (Cos). -χόρευτος, ον, *recently celebrated in the dance*, Nonn.*D.* 7.46, al. -χριστος, ον, *fresh-spread*, φάρμακον S.*Tr.*687. -χῠτος, ον, *just poured* or *shed*, φόνος Opp.*H.*2.617; αἷμα Nonn.*D.*39.226. II. Act., μαζός ib.13.431. -ώνῠμος, ον, *of even denomination*, epith. of all *even* numbers, Nicom.*Ar.*1.8:—hence -ωνῠμέω, *to be even*, Iamb.*in Nic.*p.22 P.

ἀρτίως, v. sub ἄρτιος III.

ἀρτιωτά· βραχυτάτῳ χρόνῳ συντετελεσμένα, Hsch.

ἀρτο-δότης, ου, ὁ, *giver of bread*, Tz.ad Lyc.435. -ζήτης, ου, ὁ, *one who begs for bread*, Sch.Lyc.775. -θήκη, ἡ, *pantry*, *PFlor.*15.17 (vi A.D.); *bread-basket*, Sch.Ar.*Pl.*763. -κάπηλος [ᾰ], ὁ, *bread-seller*, *Stud.Pal.*10.233*c* 6 (v A.D.). -κλασμα, ατος, τό, *morsel of bread*, Tz.*H.*8.49. -κοπεῖον, τό, *bake-house*, Dsc.2.36, *BGU*1202.5 (i B.C.), *Gp.*1.6.2; -κόπιον Charis.p.553 K.; -κόπιν (sic) *OGI*177.19. -κοπία, ἡ, *baking*, *PThead.*31.35, 36.21 (iv A.D.). -κοπικός, ή, όν, *belonging to a baker* or *baking*, Lxx 1 *Ch.*16.3; τὸ ἀ., name of work by Chrysipp.Tyan.in Ath.14.647c. -κόπισσα, ἡ, fem. of sq., *POxy.*1146.8,9 (iv A.D.). ⊛-κόπος, ὁ, ἡ, *baker*, whether fem., Hdt.1.51; or masc., Id.9.82, Pl.*Grg.*518b (v.l. -ποιός), X.*An.*4.4.21 (v.l. -ποιός), *HG*7.1.38, *IG*3.1452, *IGRom.*4.1244. (Dissim. from ἀρτοπόπος, cf. Phryn.198, Hsch., Poll.7.21; cf. πέσσω.) ⊛-κρεας, τό, *bread and meat*, prob. = Lat. *visceratio*, *IGRom.*4.1348 (Lydia), Pers.6.50, *Gloss.*; *artocrea CIL*9.5309. -λάγᾰνον [λᾰ], τό, *savoury cake* made with spices, wine, oil, and milk, Cic.*Fam.*9.20.2, Ath.5.113d. ⊛-λάγῡνος [λᾰ] πήρα *bag with bread and bottle*, *AP*11.38 (Polem. Rex). -μελι, μέλιτος, τό, *plaster* or *poultice of bread and honey*, Gal.10.692, Aët.3.177. -πίναξ [ῐ], ακος, ὁ, *platter*, *PTeb.*140 (i B.C.). ⊛-ποιέω, *make into bread, bake*, c. acc., πόαν App.*BC*2.61, cf. *POxy.*1459.9 (ii A.D.): abs., *bake bread*, Longus 3.10:—Med., Str.3.3.7; σῖτον J.*AJ*4.4.4:—Pass., Dsc.2.189. -ποιΐα, ἡ, *baking*, Ar.*Fr.*313, X.*Mem.*2.7.6; -ποιεία *PFlor.*168.3 (iii A.D.), al. -ποιϊκός, ή, όν, *of* or *for baking*: -κόν, τό, title of work by Chrysipp.Tyan., Ath.3.113a, cf. Poll.10.112:—later -ποιητικός, ή, όν, Sch.E.*Hec.*359. -ποιός, ὁ, *bread-maker, baker*, X.*Cyr.*5.5.39, J.*AJ*15.9.2. -πόνος, ὁ, *one who bakes loaves* for Apollo Maleatas, *IG*4.1549 (Epid.). -ποπέω, *to be a baker*, Phryn.Com.27. -πόπος, v. ἀρτοκ-. -πράτης [ᾰ], ου, ὁ, *dealer in bread*, Hierocl.*Facet.*225, *BGU*317.15 (vi A.D.).

ἀρτ-οπτεῖον, τό, *place* or *vessel for baking*, Poll.10.112. ⊛-όπτης, ου, ὁ, (ὀπτάω) *baker*, Hsch. s. v. πάσανος. 2. *pan for baking bread*, Plin.*HN*18.107. -οπτίκιος ἄρτος bread *baked in a pan*, Chrysipp. Tyan.ap.Ath.3.113a, Plin.*HN*18.105.

ἀρτο-πωλέω, *deal in bread*, Poll.7.21. ⊛-πώλης, ου, ὁ, *baker*, *AJA*18.33 (Sardes, iii A.D.), Poll.7.21. -πωλία, ἡ, *dealing in bread*, ib.24, Phryn.*PS*p.33 B. ⊛-πωλικόν, τό, *tax on bakeries*, *IG*2.860. -πώλιον, τό, *baker's shop*, Ar.*Ra.*112, *Fr.*155: -εῖον, Suid. -πωλις, ιδος, ἡ, fem. of -πώλης, Ar.*V.*238, *Ra.*858, *PTeb.*119.50 (ii B.C.). 2. as Adj., τηλία ἀ. *baker's* tray, Poll.9.108.

ἄρτος, ὁ, *cake* or *loaf of wheat-bread*, mostly in pl., Od.18.120, al.; ἄρτος οὖλος a whole *loaf*, 17.343; collectively, *bread*, δούλιον ἄρτον ἔδων Archil.*Supp.*2.6; ἄ. τρισκοπάνιστος Batr.35; opp. μᾶζα (*porridge*), Hp.*Acut.*37.—Freq. in all writers. II. ἄρτος· βόλος τις, καὶ ὁ Ἀθηναίων ξένος, Hsch.

ἀρτο-σιτέω, *eat wheaten bread*, opp. ἀλφιτοσιτέω, X.*Cyr.*6.2.28. 2. *eat bread*, opp. ὀψοφαγέω, Pl.Com.172, Hp.*Vict.*3.68, v.l. in *Nat.Hom.*9. -σιτία, ἡ, *feeding on bread*, Id.*Mul.*1.66 (pl.), *Epid.*5.52. -στάσιον [ᾰ], τό, *fee for weighing bread*, *PTeb.*612 (ii/iii A.D.). -στροφέω, *turn bread*, as in baking, Ar.*Fr.*748. -τῡρος, ὁ, *bread and cheese*, *PMag.Lond.*46.181; perh. an Adj. (sc. καθαρμός).

ἀρτουργός, όν, = ἀρτοποιός, Tz.*H.*5.535.

ἀρτο-φᾰγέω, *eat bread*, Hdt.2.77, Hp.*Aff.*61; esp. *eat wheaten bread*, Id.*Acut.*37. -φάγος [φᾰ], ον, *bread-eater*, Hecat.*Fr.*323(b) J.: name of a mouse in Batr.210. -φοῖνιξ, ῖκος, ὁ, *cake of bread and dates*, *PLond.*2.90.37 (iii A.D.). -φόριον, τό, *bread-basket*, S.E.*M.*1.234: the form -φορίς, ibid., is prob. corrupt. II. ἀρτοφόρια, τά, a festival, *An.Ox.*3.277. -φόρος, ον, *holding bread*, κανοῦν Poll.6.32; τὸ ἀρτοφόρον, = foreg. 1, Ath.4.129e. -χᾰρις, kind of *cake*, Hsch. s. v. χάρις.

ἀρτυλία· διαθήκη, Hsch. (leg. ἄρτυμα). ἀρτύλλεν· λόγχην, ἀγκύλην, Id.

⊛ἄρτ-ῡμα, ατος, τό, *condiment, seasoning*, ἀρτύμασι παντοδαποῖσι Batr.41, cf. Hp.*Aff.*43, Dsc.3.36, etc.; βορᾶς ἀρτύματα S.*Fr.*675, cf. 709; τὰ παλαιὰ καὶ θρυλούμενα ἀρτύματα Anaxipp.1.5: metaph., ἡ ἀνάπαυσις τῶν πόνων ἄ. Plu.2.9c. II. = διαθήκη, δίκη, Hsch. (cf. ἄρτημα). -ῡμᾶς, ὁ, = sq., *BGU*9 iv 5 (iii A.D.). -ῡματᾶς, τᾶτος, ὁ, *dealer in condiments*, *POxy.*1517.14 (iii A.D.), al. -ῡματικός, ή, όν, *spicy, savoury*, Suid. s. v. ἄνηθον. -ῡμάτιον, τό, Dim. of ἄρτυμα, prob. in *PFay.*117.8 (ii A.D., pl.). -ῡματοποιΐα, ἡ, *making of condiments*, *POxy.*1731.16 (iii A.D.). ⊛-ῡματοπώλης, ου, ὁ, *dealer in condiments*, *Sammelb.*699 (i A.D.). -ῡματώδης, ες, *spicy*, Sor.1.115, Dsc.3.34.

ἀρτύνας [ῡ], α, ὁ, *a magistrate* at Argos and Epidaurus, Th.5.47:—also ἄρτῡνος, ὁ, Plu.2.291d, Hsch., cf. Hdn.Gr.1.56.

ἀρτύνω [ῡ], fut. -ῠνῶ, Ion. -ῠνέω Od.1.277: aor. Act. ἤρτῡνα, Med. -υνάμην, Pass. -ύνθην:— = ἀρτύω, chiefly used in Ep. (in later Prose, γηράσκουσα ἡ ἐπιστήμη σοφίαν ἀρτύνει Philostr.*VS*1.25.11), ψεύδεά τ' ἀρτύνοντες Od.11.366; λόχον ἀρτύναντες 14.469; μνηστῆρσιν θάνατον κακὸν ἀρτύναντε 24.153; ὑσμίνην ἤρτυνον Il.15.303; ἀρτύνθη δὲ μάχη 11.216; ἀρτυνέουσιν ἔεδνα Od.1.277; πυργηδὸν σφέας αὐτοὺς ἀρτύναντες *putting* themselves *in order, dressing* their ranks, Il.12.43, cf. 86, 13.152:—Med., πυκινὴν ἠρτύνετο βουλὴν *prepared his* counsel, 2.55; ἠρτύναντο ἐρετμὰ τροποῖς ἐν δερματίνοισι *fitted* them with.., Od.4.782, 8.53.

⊛ἀρτύς· σύνταξις, Hsch.; cf. ἀρτύν· φιλίαν καὶ σύμβασιν ἢ κρίσιν, Id. (cf. ἀραρίσκω, ἀρθμός).

ἀρτῡσία, ἡ, *art of seasoning*, cj. Mein.in Alex.36.9.

ἀρτῡσί-λᾱος or -λεως, ὁ, *a public servant* at Delos, Ath.4.173a (pl.):—also ἀρτῡσίτρᾰγοι (s. v.l.), ibid.

ἄρτ-ῡσις, εως, ἡ, (ἀρτύω) *dressing, seasoning*, Ph.*Bel.*86.32, D.S.2.59, Plu.2.99c, Gal.6.478; *mixing of metals in smelting*, Plu.2.395c. -ῡτήρ, ῆρος, ὁ, *director*, official of a college at Thera, *Test. Epict.*4.37, al. -ῡτικός, ή, όν, *fit for dressing, seasoning*, Sch.Ar.*Eq.*894: -κόν, τό, *spice*, *Sammelb.*5224.50.

ἀρτῡτοπώλης, ου, ὁ, dub. l. for ἀτυρτοπώλης in *Sammelb.*1805.

ἀρτῡτός, ή, όν, *seasoned, flavoured*, Str.15.1.59; ἅλες Dsc.2.147.

⊛ἀρτύω Od.4.771, impf. ἤρτυον Hom. (v. infr.), the only tenses in Hom.: fut. ἀρτύσω [ῡ] S.*Fr.*1122: aor. ἤρτῡσα Hdt.1.12, Cratin.303: pf. ἤρτῡκα (κατ-) A.*Eu.*473:—Pass., pf. ἤρτῡμαι Pherecr., Eup., Hp., v. infr.: aor. ἠρτύθην [ῠ] Ruf.ap.Orib.4.2.4: in Att. this Verb is chiefly used in compds. with κατά and ἐξ: (cf. ἀραρίσκω):—like ἀρτύνω, *arrange, prepare, make ready*, of things requiring skill or cunning, e.g. of a smith, τὰ δ' ἤρτυε Il.18.379; σοὶ δὲ.. δόλον ἤρτυε Od.11.439; τῷδ' ἤρτυεν.. ὄλεθρον 16.448, cf. 20.242; γάμον.. ἀρτύει 4.771; ἤρτυσαν τὴν ἐπιβουλήν Hdt.1.12; φόνον τινί Plb.15.25.2. II. in culinary sense, *dress savoury* meat, *season*, S.*Fr.*1122, Cratin.303; ἀ. τὰ ὄψα Arist.*EN*1118ᵃ29:—Pass., κίχλαι.. εἰς ἀνάβραστ' ἠρτυμέναι Pherecr.108.23; ὄψῳ πονηρῷ πολυτελῶς ἠρτυμένῳ Eup.335; τὰ πρὸς ἡδονὴν ἠρτυμένα Hp.*VM*14; ἠρτυμένος οἶνος Thphr.*Od.*51. III. *administer* property, *Leg.Gort.*12.32, *IG*5(2).3.27 (Tegea, iv B.C.), Epich.192. IV. *bequeath*, *Tab.Heracl.*1.106.

ἀρῦ, v. ἄρρυ. ⊛ἄρυα, τά, *walnuts*, Hsch.

ἀρῠβαλλίς, ίδος, ἡ, = sq., Hsch., *EM*150.54 (prob. l.).

ἀρύβαλλος [ῠ], ὁ, *bag* or *purse*, made so as to draw close, Stesich.11, Antiph.50. II. *globular oil-flask*, Ar.*Eq.*1094, Ath.11.783f.

⊛ἀρυβάσσαλον· κοτύλη, Hsch.

ἀρύπᾰρος [ῠ], ον, *not sordid*, γάμος *Cat.Cod.Astr.*1.149.8.

ἀρῠσαῖα, τά, *remains of ladles*, *SIG*²588.97 (Delos, ii B.C.).

ἀρῠσάνη [ᾰρ] [σᾱ], ἡ, v.l. for ἀρύταινα, Timo 4.

ἀρῠσᾶς, ᾶ, ὁ, = ἀρυστήρ, *IG*11(2).110, al. (Delos, iii B.C.).

ἀρύσιμος [ᾰρῠ], ον, *that may be drawn*, gloss on ἀφυσγετός, Sch. Nic.*Al.*584.

ἀρύσιος, v. ἀρρ-.

ἀρυσμεῖ (Ion. for ἀρρυθμεῖ)· ἀσχημονεῖ, ἀκοσμεῖ, Hsch.

ἀρυσμίη, ἡ, Ion. = ἀρρυθμία, Hsch.: ἄρυσμος (= ἄρρυθμος)· εὐσχήμων (leg. ἀσχήμων), *EM*151.1.

ἄρυσος, ὁ, *wicker-basket*, Hdn.Gr.1.213. II. = ἄρρυσος, *not wrinkled, smooth*, Aët.3.126.

ἀρύσσομαι [ᾰρ], Med., *draw for oneself*, Hdt.6.119; cf. ἀρύω.

⊛ἀρυστήρ [ᾰ], ῆρος, ὁ, = ἀρυτήρ, Alc.*Supp.*4.9, Semon.25, Hp.*Genit.*9, *Inscr.Cos*42ᵇ, *IG*11.154 *A*66, 161 *C*63 (Delos, iii B.C.): dat. pl. ἀρυστήρεσσι Call.*Aet.*1.1.17: name of a *liquid measure*, Hdt.2.168.

ἀρυστικός [ᾰ], ή, όν, *for drawing liquids*, ἀγγεῖον Ael.*NA*17.37.

⊛ἄρυστις [ᾰ], ἡ, = ἀρυτήρ, acc. pl. ἀρύστεις S.*Fr.*764:—also = ἄμυστις, *bumper*, Hsch.

⊛ἀρύστῐχος [ᾰ], ὁ, Dim. of ἀρυτήρ, Ar.*V.*855, Phryn.Com.40, *IG*4.39 (Aegina).

⊛ἀρυστρίς [ᾰ], ίδος, ἡ, = ἀρύταινα, *AP*6.306 (Aristo).

⊛ἀρύταινα [ᾰρῠ], ης, ἡ, fem. of ἀρυτήρ, Ar.*Eq.*1092, Antiph.25.3, Thphr.*Char.*9.8, *PMagd.*33.3 (iii B.C.).

ἀρυταινοειδής [ᾰ], ές, *shaped like an ἀρύταινα*, χόνδρος ἀ. *arytenoid* cartilage of the larynx, Gal.*UP*7.11, cf. 18(2).951.

⊛ἀρῠτήρ [ᾰ], ῆρος, ὁ, (ἀρύω) *ladle* or *cup*, Dsc.2.74. 2. perh. *irrigation*, ἐμίσθωσεν.. εἰς τὸν ἀρυτῆρα τοῦ ἐνεστῶτος ἔτους τὰς ἀρού[ρας.. *PLond.ined.*2210 (i B.C.).

ἀρῠτήσιμος [ᾰ], ον, *that can be drawn*: *drinkable*, *AP*9.575 (Phil.).

ἀρῠτός, ὁ, *dragging*, cj. in A.*Fr.*270.

ἀρυφῆνα· ῥυτίδα, Hsch.

⊛ἀρύω (A) [ᾰ], Simon.45, Att. ἀρύτω [ῡ] Pl.*Phdr.*253a; Aeol. part. ἀρυτήμενοι Alc.47: impf. ἤρυον Hes.*Sc.*301; ἄρυον Hsch.: aor. ἤρῠσα Pherecr.138, X.*Cyr.*1.3.9:—Med., ἀρύτομαι Ar.*Nu.*272; ἀρύομαι Aeschin.Socr.11, *AP*9.37 (Tull. Flacc.), etc.: fut. ἀρύσομαι [ῠ] *AP*9.230 (Honest.), Luc.*DMar.*6.1: aor. ἠρῠσάμην Plu.2.516c; opt. ἀρῠσαίμην E.*Hipp.*209 (lyr.); inf. ἀρύσασθαι X.*Cyr.*1.2.8; part. ἀρῠσάμενος Hdt.8.137, Ep. ἀρυσσάμενος Hes.*Op.*550:—Pass., aor. ἠρύθην, ἀπ-αρῠθεὶς Alex.45.6; also ἀρυσθεὶς Hp.*Nat.Puer.*25, Plu.2.690b:—*draw* water, wine, etc., τοὶ δ' ἤρυον others *drew off* the must, Hes.*Sc.*301; ἀρυόντεσσιν.. ὕδωρ Simon.45; ἐκ πιθῶν ἤρυσαν ἄκρατον Pherecr.l.c.; ἀρύσαντες ἀπ' αὐτῆς [τῆς φιάλης] τῷ κυάθῳ X.*Cyr.*1.3.9; μέλισσαι νέκταρ ἀρύουσιν *Lyr.Alex.Adesp.*7.18: metaph., κἂν ἐκ Διὸς ἀρύτωσιν if they *draw inspiration* from Zeus, Pl.*Phdr.*253a. II. Med., *draw water for oneself*, ἀρυσσάμενος ποταμῶν ἄπο *having drawn water* from.., Hes.*Op.*550; σφῷν ἀρύσασθαι Pherecr.130.5; ἀρύσασθαι ἀπὸ τοῦ ποταμοῦ X.*Cyr.*1.2.8; ἐκ τοῦ κρατῆρος Pl.*Criti.*120a: c. acc., ἀρύσασθαι ὑδάτων πῶμα E.*Hipp.*209; ἀ. ἐκ τῶν ποταμῶν μέλι καὶ γάλα Pl.*Ion*534a: c. gen. partit., ὑδάτων ἀ. πρόχοισι Ar.*Nu.*272; ἐς τὸν κόλπον τρὶς ἀρυσάμενος τοῦ ἡλίου *having* (as it were) *drawn* the rays of the sun into *his* bosom, Hdt.8.137: generally, *draw in*, τροφῆς καὶ πνεύματος Diog.Bab.ap.Gal.5.281; μαντικῆς Plu.2.411f; πλοῦτον Id.*Caes.*

29; καιροῦ καὶ τύχης Eun.*Hist.*p.256D. 2. of stars *rising from* the sea, οἵ τ' ὠκεανοῦ ἀρύονται ἀστέρες Arat.746.

**ἀρύω** (B), only in Lexx., ἀρύει· ἀντὶ τοῦ λέγει, βοᾷ, Hsch.; ἀρύουσαι· λέγουσαι, κελεύουσαι, Id. (Syrac., acc. to *EM*134.12):—Med., ἀρύσασθαι· ἐπικαλέσασθαι, Hsch.

**ἄρφα**· ἀρραβών (i.e. *arrha*), Hsch. **ἀρφύς**· ἱμάς (Maced.), Id. **ἀρφύταινον**· δίσκος (Lyd.), Id. **ἄρχα**· ἀρραβών, Id.; cf. ἄρφα.

***ἀρχάγγελος**, ον, *archangel*, Lxx *Da.*10.13, al., *Ep.Jud.*9, *PMag. Lond.*121.257 (iii A.D.), Nicom.ap.*Theol.Ar.*43, Dam.*Pr.*96, Procop. *Pers.*2.11, al.:—Adj. **-γελικός**, ή, όν, θεοί Dam.*Pr.*130, cf. Procl.*in Cra.*p.37P.

**ἀρχᾱγέτας, ἀρχᾱγός**, Dor., etc., = Att. ἀρχηγέτης, ἀρχηγός.

**ἀρχᾱΐζω**, *to be old-fashioned, copy the ancients* in manners, language, etc., D.H.*Rh.*10.7, Plu.2.558a.

***ἀρχᾱϊκός** (ἀρχαϊκός interpol. in Phryn.28), ή, όν, *old-fashioned*, in manners, etc., ἀρχαϊκὰ φρονεῖν Ar.*Nu.*821; ἐν τοῖς δ' ἐκείνων ἤθεσιν ἴσθ' ἀρχαϊκός Antiph.44; of literary style, D.H.*Comp.*22: Sup., Plu. 2.238c; τὰ Ἀρχαϊκά, title of work by Epicurus, *Juvenilia*, Phld.*Sto. Herc.*339.17. Adv. -κῶς Arist.*Metaph.*1089ᵃ2; ἀ. ἔχειν τοῖς σχήμασι *Chron.Lind.*B.90; *stupidly*, Aristid.1.482J.

**ἀρχαιο-γονία**, ἡ, *origin* of a race, Eust.1156.54, etc. **-γονος**, ον, *of ancient race, of old descent*, S.*Ant.*981. II. (perh. parox. ἀρχαιογόνος) *original, primal*, αἰτία Arist.*Mu.*399ᵃ26 (nisi leg. ἀρχέγονον). **-γράφος** [ρᾰ], ον, *writing of antiquities*, *Gloss.* **-ειδής**, ές, *old-fashioned, archaic*, Demetr.*Eloc.*245. ***-λογέω**, *discuss antiquities* or *things out of date*, Th.7.69; ἀ. τὰ Ἰουδαίων J.*BJProoem.* 6:—Pass., ἱστορία ἀρχαιολογουμένη a history *treated in an antiquarian manner*, D.H.1.74. II. *use an old-fashioned style*, Luc.*Lex.* 15. ***-λογία**, ἡ, *antiquarian lore, ancient legends* or *history*, Pl. *Hp.Ma.*285d, D.S.2.46, D.H.1.4, Str.11.14.12; title of works by Cleanthes, Josephus, and Hieronymus Aegyptius, cf. J.*AJ*1.3. 6. **-λογικός**, ή, όν, *skilled in antiquarian lore*, Str.10.2.9 (Comp.).

***ἀρχαιο-μελῐ-σῑδωνο-φρυνῑχ-ήρᾰτος**, ον, prob. in Ar.*V.*220 μέλη ἀ. *dear honey-sweet old* songs *from Phrynichus' Phoenissae* (ἀρχαῖα μελι- codd.).

**ἀρχαῖον**, τό, v. sub ἀρχαῖος.

**ἀρχαιό-νομος**, ον, *old-fashioned*, ἤθη Anon.ap.Suid. s.v. αἵρεσις. **-πῑνής**, ές, *with the patina of antiquity*, D.H.*Dem.*38. ***-πλουτος**, ον, *rich from olden time, of hereditary wealth*, A.*Ag.*1043, S.*El.*1393 (lyr.), Lys.19.49, Arist.*Rh.*1387ᵃ24. **-πρεπής**, ές, *time-honoured, venerable*, A.*Pr.*409, Pl.*Sph.*229e; παράκλησις Iamb.*Protr.*17: Comp., Dam.*Pr.*131. Adv. -πῶς ib.337. 2. of literary style, *old-fashioned*, σχήματα D.H.*Comp.*23; ὀνόματα Id.*Pomp.*2; ἑρμηνεία Simp.*in Ph.* 233.10 (Comp.). Adv. -πῶς ib.111.15.

***ἀρχαῖος**, α, ον, (ἀρχή I) *from the beginning* or *origin*: I. mostly of things, *ancient*, σκότος S.*OC*106; ἐσθής Hdt.5.88; δόμοις ἐπασσάλευσαν ἀρχαῖον γάνος A.*Ag.*579 codd.; Ζηνὸς ἀρχαίοις νόμοις S.*OC*1382; χερὸς σῆς πίστιν ἀρχαίαν faith *firm for ever*, ib.1632 codd. 2. *old-fashioned, antiquated*, A.*Pr.*317 (lyr.), Ar.*Nu.*984, D.22.14; of literary style, Demetr.*Eloc.*244. b. *simple, silly*, Ar.*Nu.*915, al., Pherecr. 205; -ότερος εἶ τοῦ δέοντος Pl.*Euthd.*295c, etc. 3. *ancient, former*, τὸ ἀ. ῥέεθρον Hdt.1.75; τοῦ ἀ. λόγου Id.7.160; οὐ γὰρ δὴ τό γ' ἀ. δέμας S.*OC*110; οἱ ἀ., opp. οἱ ὕστερον, Th.2.16; ἀ. φύσις A.*Ch.*281, Hp. *Art.*53, Pl.*Smp.*193c, etc.; φύσις καὶ κατάστασις ἀ. Democr.278; coupled with παλαιός, παλαιὸν δῶρον ἀρχαίου θηρός S.*Tr.*555, cf. Lys. 6.51, D. l.c. 4. *old, worn out*, ὑποδήματα X.*An.*4.5.14; πινάκια *BGU*781 i 1 (i A.D.). II. of persons, Θέμιν.. ἀρχαίαν ἄλοχον Διός Pi.*Fr.*6.5; ἀ. θεαί, of the Erinyes, A.*Eu.*728; Πέλοψ S.*Aj.*1292; οἱ ἀ. *the Ancients*, name given by Arist. to the pre-Socratics, *Metaph.* 1069ᵃ25, *GC*314ᵃ6; in Lit. Crit., *ancient, classical* writers, Demetr. *Eloc.*15, 67; in Plot., the philosophers down to Aristotle, 5.1.9; in *NT, the Fathers*, *Ev.Matt.*5.21, al. 2. *ancient, old*, βαλὴν ἀ., of Darius, A.*Pers.*657 (lyr.); λάτρις E.*Hec.*609; ἑταῖρος X.*Mem.*2.8.1; οἱ ἀ. κύριοι the *original* owners, *BGU*992 ii 6 (ii B.C.); τὰς ἀ. πόλεις (banished from) their *original* cities, Polystr.p.22W.; ἀ. μαθητής an *original* disciple, *Act.Ap.*21.16; ἀ. μύστης *Inscr.Magn.*215b; παιδαγωγὸς ἀ., i.e. *of old, formerly*, E.*El.*287, cf. 853. III. neut. as Adv., τὸ ἀρχαῖον, Ion. contr. τὠρχαῖον, *anciently*, Hdt.1.56, 173, al., Att. τἀρχαῖον A.*Supp.*326; ἀπὸ τοῦ ἀ. Hdt.4.117; ἐξ ἀρχαίων D.S.1.14. 2. regul. Adv. ἀρχαίως *in olden style*, καινὰ ἀ. λέγειν Pl.*Phdr.*267b, cf. Isoc.4.8, D.9.48; ἀ. καὶ σεμνῶς Aeschin.1.183. IV. irreg. Comp. ἀρχαιέστερος Pi.*Fr.*45 (on ἀρχέστατος v. h. v.); usual Comp. -ότερος Ar.*Av.*469: Sup. -ότατος Hdt.1.105, etc. V. as Subst., τὸ ἀρχαῖον, of money, *prime cost*, πλέον τοῦ ἀ. X.*Vect.*3.2; *principal*, mostly in pl., Ar.*Nu.*1156, etc.; τἀρχαῖα ἀποδιδόναι D.34.26, etc.; τῶν ἀρχαίων ἀπέστησαν lost their *capital*, Id.1.15: opp. ἔργον, Id.27. 10; opp. πρόσοδοι, Is.6.38. 2. ἀρχαίη, ἡ, = ἀρχή, Eust.475.1, etc.

**ἀρχαιότης**, ητος, ἡ, *antiquity, old-fashionedness*, Pl.*Lg.*657b, D.H. *Pomp.*2; *simplicity*, Alciphr.3.64; *pristine state*, ἀποκαταστῆσαι εἰς τὴν ἀ. τῆς αὐτονομίας *SIG*814.42 (Nero); *ancient history*, J.*Ap.*1.1, al.; *antiquity, ancient times*, D.Chr.31.94.

**ἀρχαιο-τροπία**, ἡ, *old fashioned ways*, Plu.*Phoc.*3. **-τροπος**, ον, *old-fashioned*, ἐπιτηδεύματα Th.1.71, cf. Ph.2.458, Iamb.*Protr.*21; of a person, D.C.59.29. Adv. -πως Dam.*Pr.*5. **-φᾰνής**, ές, *seeming ancient*, Lyd.*Mag.*1.18.

**ἀρχαιόομαι**, *become ancient*, ἐξ ἀρχαιωθέντος καὶ ἀμνημονεύτου χρόνου *POxy.*1915.5, al. (vi A.D.).

***ἀρχαιρ-εσία**, Ion. -ίη, ἡ, (αἵρεσις) *election of magistrates*, ἀ. συνίζει *an election* is held, Hdt.6.58: mostly in pl., Pl.*Lg.*752c, X.*Mem.* 3.4.1, Is.7.28, Arist.*Pol.*1281ᵇ33, etc. II. later neut. **-έσια**, τά, Plb.4.67.1, D.H.10.17, *OGI*458.82; = Lat. *comitia*, Plb.3.106.1, etc. **-εσιάζω**, *hold an assembly for the election of magistrates*, Is. *Fr.*47, Plu.*Cam.*9, etc.; *elect* a magistrate *in the assembly*, ib.42, D.H.2.14; simply, *vote*, Plu.*Crass.*14: c. acc. inf., ib.11. 2. *canvass for a magistracy*, Plb.26.1.5. ***-εσιακός**, ή, όν, *for* ἀρχαιρεσίαι, ἐκκλησία *IGRom.*3.474 (Lycia), al. **-εσιάρχης**, ου, ὁ, *leader of a political party*, Hdn.*Epim.*167. **-ετικός**, ή, όν, = ἀρχαιρεσιακός, ἐκκλησία *SIG*730.29 (Olbia), *IGRom.*4.293a ii 69 (Pergam., ii B.C.), *AJA*18.326 (Sardes, 4 B.C.).

**ἀρχαϊσμός**, ὁ, *old-world charm* of style, D.H.*Comp.*22. 2. *use of obsolete expressions*, ἀ. οὗτος ῥημάτων Men.11D., cf. Sch.E.*Hipp.* 23. 3. *ancient custom*, περὶ ἀρχαϊσμοῦ, title of work by Manetho, Porph.*Abst.*2.55.

**ἀρχε-**, insep. Prefix (from ἄρχω), = ἀρχι-, with which it is sometimes interchanged, cf. ἀρχιθέωρος, etc.

***ἀρχέβακχος**, ὁ, *leader of* Βάκχοι, title of Dionysus, *Wiener Denkschr.*44(16).104 (Seleucia ad Calycadnum).

**Ἀρχεβούλειον** μέτρον metre used by Archebulus, ⏑⏑–⏑⏑–⏑⏑–⏑⏑–⏑⏑–⏑–⏑––, Heph.8.9.

**ἀρχέγονος**, ον, *original, primal*, τὸ ἀ. ὑγρόν Corn.*ND*17, cf. Nonn. *D.*24.48, al.; οὐσία Gal.5.418: Comp. -ώτερος Ph.2.472: Sup., Id. 1.237. II. (perh. parox. ἀρχεγόνος) *first author* or *origin*, ἡ φύσις πάσης τέχνης ἀρχέγονόν ἐστ' Damox.2.8, cf. D.S.1.88; τῶν ὅλων Procl.*Inst.*152; Ὠκεανὸς ἀ. πάντων Corn.*ND*8.

***ἀρχ-εδέατρος**, ὁ, *chief seneschal* at the Ptolemaic court, *OGI*169.4 (Alexandria), 181.4 (Paphos).

**ἀρχε-δίκας** [ῐ], α, ὁ, *first, legitimate possessor*, Pi.*P.*4.110. ***-ζωστις**, ἡ, = ἄμπελος λευκή, Ps.-Dsc.4.182, Plin.*HN*23.21. ***-θέωρος**, = ἀρχι-, *IG*11(2).205A ᵃ9, al. (Delos, iii B.C.); cf. ἀρκεθέωρος.

**ἀρχείνη**, ἡ, title of *priestess*, *SIG*890.20 (Syros, iii A.D.).

***ἀρχεῖον**, Ion. ἀρχήϊον, τό, neut. of an Adj. ἀρχεῖος, α, ον: (ἀρχή II):—*town-hall, residence*, or *office of chief magistrates*, Hdt.4.62 (dub.), Lys.9.9, X.*Cyr.*1.2.3, Isoc.5.48, Arist.*Mu.*400ᵇ16; τὰ ἀ. καὶ βουλευτήρια D.10.53, cf. *IG*2.475.21, al., *OGI*268.18 (Nacrasa, iii B.C.), *PGrenf.*2.30, al. (ii B.C.). 2. τὰ ἀ. *public records, archives*, prob. in *SIG*684.7 (Dyme, ii B.C.), cf. D.H.2.26, *PTeb.*397.19 (ii A.D.). II. *college* or *board of magistrates, magistracy*, Arist.*Pol.*1298ᵇ28, 1304ᵃ 19: but in pl., *special boards*, ib.1299ᵃ36, 1331ᵃ25, Plu.*Ages.*33; ὀμόσαι τὰ ἀ. *IG*2.332.45, cf. *OGI*218.149 (Ilium), etc.; ὅσοι ἀρχείων μετέχουσιν καὶ δικαστηρίων *SIG*286.20 (Milet., iv B.C.). III. in the Roman camp, = *principia, head-quarters*, Plu.*Galb.*12.

**ἀρχειοφύλαξ** [ῠ], ακος, ὁ, *keeper of archives*, = Lat. *censualis*, Lyd. *Mag.*2.30 (ἀρχαιο- codd.).

***ἀρχεῖτις**, ἡ, acc. -τιν, title of *priestess* at Thasos, *IG*12(8).526.

**ἀρχειώτης**, ου, ὁ, Lat. *archeota, a municipal recorder*, *Dig.*50.4.18. 10:—hence **ἀρχειωτικὰ** δικαστήρια courts *of record*, Lyd.*Mag.*2.15 (ἀρχαιωτ- codd.).

**ἀρχέ-κᾰκος**, ον, *beginning mischief*, Il.5.63, Plu.2.861a, Hld.1.9, Ph.1.359, al., Porph.*Chr.*49.22. **-λᾱος**, ον, *leading the people, chief*, A.*Pers.*297 (in Ion. form ἀρχελείων for -λῃῶν); contr. **ἀρχέλᾱς** Ar.*Eq.*164.

**ἀρχελληνοδίκης** [ῑ], ου, ὁ, *chief* Ἑλληνοδίκης, *CPHerm.*121.4 (iii A.D.).

***ἀρχέμπορος**, ὁ, *president of a guild of merchants*, *OGI*646.8 (Palmyra, iii A.D.).

**ἀρχενόμενα**· ξύλα, Hsch. (perh. ἀρχενομέας *principal ribs*, cf. νομεύς).

**ἀρχενταφιαστής**, οῦ, ὁ, *president of guild of embalmers*, *UPZ*108. 10, 22 (i B.C.).

***ἀρχέ-πλουτος**, ον, = ἀρχαιόπλουτος, S.*El.*72. **-πολις**, ι, *ruling a city*, Pi.*P.*9.54. **-πρόβουλος**, ὁ, *chairman of* πρόβουλοι, *IG*12 (9).11 (Carystus), *IG*3.1306.

**ἀρχερᾰν-ίζω**, *to be president of an* ἔρανος (q.v.), *IG*12(5).672.3 (Syros). **-ιστέω**, = foreg., ib.83, 12(1).155 (Rhodes). ***-ιστής**, οῦ, ὁ, *president of an* ἔρανος, ib.2.630.4 (**ἀρχιερᾰνιστής** ib.2².1369, Hdn.Gr.1.82). **-ος**, = foreg., *IG*12(7).58.9 (Amorgos).

**ἀρχεσίμολπος** [ῐ], ον, *beginning the strain*, Μοῦσα Stesich.77.

**ἀρχέσπερος**, ον, v. ἀκρέσπερος.

**ἀρχέστατος**, irreg. Sup. of ἀρχαῖος, *most ancient*, A.*Fr.*187.

***ἀρχέτας**, ὁ, Dor. for ἀρχέτης, *leader, prince*, E.*El.*1149: as Adj., ἀ. θρόνος *princely* throne, Id.*Heracl.*753.

**ἀρχέ-τῡπικῶς**, Adv. *as a model*, Eust.931.22. ***-τῡπος**, ον, *first-moulded as a pattern* or *model, archetypal*, σφραγίς, παράδειγμα, Ph.1. 5, al.: Comp. -ώτερος Plot.6.8.14; *exemplary, ideal*, μαῖα Sor.1. 4. 2. Astrol., ἀ. κλῆρος, = κλῆρος τύχης, Serapio in *Cat.Cod.Astr.* 8(4).226, Vett.Val.67.3. II. ἀρχέτυπον, τό, *archetype, pattern, model*, opp. ἀπόγραφον, D.H.*Is.*11, cf. *APl.*4.204 ([Simon.]), Cic. *Att.*16.3.1; Philos., Plot.5.1.4, Procl.*in R.*2.296K.; *figure on a seal*, Luc.*Alex.*21; ἀ. Διδοῦς *a portrait* of Dido *as she really was*, *APl.*4.151; δαίδαλον ἀ. *IG*14.1188; of the nominative case, *Stoic.* 2.48.

***ἀρχεύω**, (ἄρχω) *command*, c. dat., ἀρχεύειν Τρώεσσι Il.5.200, cf. 2. 345: c. gen., ὁμάδοιο A.R.1.347; μετὰ παισίν Poet. in *POxy.*1015. 13. 2. *to be chief magistrate* or *official*, ἠρχευκὼς τῆς πόλεως *OGI* 166.3 (Paphos), cf. *SIG*1023.87 (Cos).

**ἀρχ-εφηβεύω**, *to be head of the* ἔφηβοι, *IG*4.589 (Argos). ***-έφηβος**, ὁ, *head of the* ἔφηβοι, ib.5(2).52 (Tegea, ii A.D.). **-εφοδεία**, ἡ, *function of an* ἀρχέφοδος, *POxy.*1063.5 (ii/iii A.D.). ®-έφοδος, ὁ, *chief of police*, *PTeb.*90 *Intr.* (i B.C.), *PRyl.*127.20 (i A.D.), *PTeb.* 331.15 (ii A.D.).

**ἀρχέχορος**, ον, *leading the chorus* or *dance*, πούς E.*Tr.*151; of a person, *IG*14.1618.

®**ἀρχή**, ἡ, (v. ἄρχω) *beginning, origin*, νείκεος ἀ. Il.22.116; πήματος Od.8.81; φόνου 21.4, etc.; opp. τέλος, Hdt.7.51, etc.; opp. τελευτή, Thgn.607, cf. Pl.*Lg.*715e, Hp.*Morb.*1.1; ἀ. γενέσθαι κακῶν Hdt.5.97; ἀ. ποιήσασθαί τινος Th.1.128, And.2.37, Isoc.12.120, etc.; ἀ. λαβεῖν τινός Aeschin.1.11; τὰς ἀρχὰς εἰληφέναι Plb.4.28.3; ἀρχὴν ὑποθέσθαι lay *a foundation*, D.3.2, etc.; βαλέσθαι Pl.*Ep.*326e (and Pass., ἀρχαὶ βέβληνται Pi.*N.*1.8); ἀρχὴν ἄρχεσθαί τινος Pl.*Ti.*36e; *source* of action, [ὁ ἄνθρωπος] ἔχει ἀρχὴν ἐλευθέραν Plot.3.3.4. b. with Preps. in adverbial usages, ἐξ ἀρχῆς from *the beginning*, from *the first*, from *of old*, Od.1.188, Xenoph.10, etc.; οὐξ ἀ. φίλος S.*OT*385; ἡ ἐξ ἀ. ἔχθρα D.54.3; τὸ ἐξ ἀ. X.*Cyn.*12.6; but πλουτεῖν ἐξ ἀ. πάλιν *anew, afresh*, Ar.*Pl.*221; λόγον πάλιν ὥσπερ ἐξ ἀ. κινεῖν Pl.*R.*450a; ὁ ἐξ ἀ. λόγος the *original* argument, Id.*Tht.*177c, etc.; τὰ ἐξ ἀ. the *principal sum*, Arist.*Pol.*1280ᵃ30:—also ἀπ' ἀ. Hes.*Th.*425, Hdt.2.104, Pi.*P.*8.25, A.*Supp.*344, Pl.*Tht.*206d; κατ' ἀρχάς in *the beginning*, at *first*, Hdt.3.153, 7.5; αὐτίκα κατ' ἀ. Id.8.94; τὸ κατ' ἀ. Pl.*Lg.*798a, al. c. acc. ἀρχήν, abs., *to begin with, at first*, Hdt.1.9, 2.28, 8.132; τὴν ἀρχήν And.3.20: pl., τὰς ἀρχάς Plb.16.22.8: freq. followed by a neg., not *at all*, ἀρχὴν μηδὲ λαβών Hdt.3.39, cf. 1.193, al.; ἀ. δὲ θηρᾶν οὐ πρέπει τἀμήχανα S.*Ant.*92; ἀ. κλύειν ἂν οὐκ.. ἐβουλόμην Id.*Ph.*1239, cf. *El.*439, Philol.3, Antipho 5.73, Pl.*Grg.*478c; sts. c. Art., τοῦτο οὐκ ἐνδέκομαι τὴν ἀ. Hdt.4.25; τὴν ἀ. γὰρ ἐξῆν αὐτῷ μὴ γράφειν D.23.93. 2. *first principle, element*, first so used by Anaximander, acc. to Simp. *in Ph.*150.23, cf. Arist.*Metaph.*983ᵇ11, etc.; Ἡράκλειτος τὴν ἀ. εἶναί φησι ψυχήν Id.*de An.*405ᵃ25; of ὕλη and θεός, opp. στοιχεῖα, *Placit.*1.3.25; *practical principle* of conduct, τῶν πράξεων τὰς ἀρχὰς καὶ τὰς ὑποθέσεις D.2.10; *principles* of knowledge, Arist.*Metaph.*995ᵇ8, al. 3. *end, corner*, of a bandage, rope, sheet, etc., Hdt.4.60, Hp.*Off.*9, E.*Hipp.*762, Aen.Tact.18.14, *Act.Ap.*10.11; of a compound pulley, Hero *Bel.*84.14. 4. Math., *origin* of a curve, τῆς ἕλικος Archim.*Spir.* 11 *Def.*2, etc.; ξυνὸν ἀ. καὶ πέρας ἐπὶ κύκλου περιφερείας Heraclit. 103. 5. *branch* of a river, Lxx *Ge.*2.10 (pl.). 6. *sum. total*, ib.*Nu.*1.2. 7. *vital organs* of the body, Gal.1.318, al. II. *first place* or *power, sovereignty* (not in Hom.), Διὸς ἀρχά Pi.*O.*2.64, cf. Hdt.1.6, etc.; γενέσθαι ἐπ' ἀρχῆς Arist.*Pol.*1284ᵇ2: metaph., μεγάλην μενταν ἀ. εἴης εὑρηκώς, of a stroke of fortune, D.21.196: pl., ἀρχαὶ πολισσονόμοι A.*Ch.*864 (lyr.); τὰς ἐμὰς ἀρχὰς σέβων S.*Ant.*744, etc.: c. gen. rei, τῆσδ' ἔχων ἀρχὴν χθονός S.*OT*737; ἀ. τῶν νεῶν, τῆς θαλάσσης, *power over* them, Th.3.90, X.*Ath.*2.7, etc.: prov., ἀ. ἄνδρα δείξει Bias ap.Arist.*EN*1130ᵃ1, cf. D.*Prooem.*48; *method of government*, οὐδὲ τὴν ἄλλην ἀ. ἐπαχθής Th.6.54. 2. *empire, realm*, Κύρου, Περδίκκου ἀ., Hdt.1.91, Th.4.128, etc. 3. *magistracy, office*, ἀρχὴν ἄρχειν, παραλαμβάνειν, Hdt.3.80, 4.147; καταστήσας τὰς ἀ. καὶ ἄρχοντας ἐπιστήσας Id.3.89; εἰς ἀ. καθίστασθαι Th.8.70; εἰς τὴν ἀ. εἰσιέναι D.59.72, etc.; ἀ. λαχεῖν to obtain *an office*, Id.57.25; Ἑλληνοταμίαι τότε πρῶτον κατέστη ἀ. Th.1.96; ἐνιαύσιος ἀ. Id.6.54; ἀ. χειροτονητή, κληρωτή, Lex ap.Aeschin.1.21; with sg. Noun, Κυθηροδίκης ἀ. ἐκ τῆς Σπάρτης διέβαινεν αὐτόσε Th.4.53; *term of office*, ἀρχῆς λοιποὶ αὐτῷ δύο μῆνες Antipho 6.42; ἀρχαὶ καὶ λειτουργίαι *POxy.*119.16 (iii A.D.). 4. in pl., αἱ ἀρχαί *the authorities, the magistrates*, Th.5.47, cf. Decr.ap.And.1.83; ἐν ταῖς ἀ. εἶναι Th.6.54; ἡ ἀρχή collectively, 'the board', D.47.22, cf. *IG*1.229, etc.; παραδιδόναι τινὰ τῇ ἀ. Antipho 5.48; but ἡ ἀ., of a single *magistrate*, *PHal.*1.226 (iii B.C.); κατ' ἀρχῆς γὰρ φιλαίτιος λεὼς against *authority*, A.*Supp.*485; πομποὺς ἀρχάς Id.*Ag.*124 (anap.). 5. *command*, i.e. *body of troops*, Lxx 1*Ki.*13.17, al. 6. pl., *heavenly powers*, *Ep.Rom.*8.38, al., cf. Dam.*Pr.*96; *powers of evil*, *Ep.Eph.*6.12, al. III. = εἶδος μελίσσης ἀκέντρου, Hsch.

**ἀρχηγενής**, ές, *originating, causing*, κλαυμάτων A.*Ag.*1628.

**ἀρχηγ-έσια**, τά, *festival of Apollo Archegetes*, *Inscr.Cos*105.16. -ετεύω, *to be chief leader*, τῶν κάτω Hdt.2.123. -ετέω, *make a beginning*, ἀπὸ τῶνδε S.*El.*83. ®-έτης, ου, ὁ, fem. **ἀρχηγέτις**, ιδος (dat. ἀρχηγέτι Ar.*Lys.*644); Dor. **ἀρχᾱγέτας**: (ἡγέομαι):—*first leader, author*, esp. *founder* of a city or family, Hdt.9.86, Pi.*O.*7.78, *IG*9(1).61.49 (Daulis); title of Apollo at Cyrene, Pi.*P.*5.60; at Naxos in Sicily, Th.6.3; of Heracles at Sparta, X.*HG*6.3.6; Asclepius in Phocis, Paus.10.32.12; Helios at Rhodes, Aristid.*Or.*24(44).50; freq. of ἥρωες, *IG*2.1191, *SIG*1024.40 (Myconos), etc.; so at Athens of ἥρωες ἐπώνυμοι, Ar.*Fr.*126, Orac.ap.D.43.66; ὁ δήμου ἀ. the *tutelary hero* of the deme, Pl.*Ly.*205d; at Sparta of the kings, ῥήτρα ap.Plu.*Lyc.*6; so at Thera, *IG*12(3).762; fem. ἀρχηγέτις, of Athena, *IG*3.65, al., cf. *BMus.Inscr.*481*.20 (Ephesus, ii A.D.); τἀρχηγέτι, = τῇ ἀρχηγέτιδι, Ar.*Lys.*644. 2. generally, *leader, chief*, A.*Supp.*184, 251, S.*OT*751, etc.; later, *governor*, Chor. in *Rev.Phil.*1.67: metaph., ἀ. φιλοσοφίας Jul.*Or.*6.188b; of a philosophical school, τῆς ἀγωγῆς Phld.*Sto.Herc.*339.12. 3. *first cause, author*, τύχης E.*El.*891; γένους Id.*Or.*555.

**ἀρχηγικός**, ή, όν, *original, primary, principal*, αἴτιον Ph.2.168 (Sup.), cf. Max.Tyr.17.8 (Sup.), Syrian. *in Metaph.*65.17, Procl. *in Alc.*p.250 C., Jul.*Or.*5.175b (Comp.); -κά, τά, Procl.*Inst.*70.

®**ἀρχηγός**, Dor. **ἀρχᾱγός**, όν, *beginning, originating*, λόγος ἀρχηγὸς κακῶν E.*Hipp.*881; *primary, leading, chief*, Τροίας ἀ. τιμάς Id.*Tr.*196 (lyr.); δύο φλέβες ἀ. Arist.*PA*666ᵇ25. II. as Subst., *founder*, of a tutelary hero, S.*OC*60; as fem., *ancestral heroine*, B.8.51; τοῦ γένους Isoc.3.28, cf. D.S.5.56; τῆς πόλεως θεὸς ἀ. τίς ἐστιν Pl.*Ti.*21e; *founder of a family*, Arist.*EN*1162ᵃ4. 2. *prince, chief*, Δία ἀ. θεῶν B.5.179, cf. A.*Ag.*259; *chief captain, leader*, Ἑλλάνων Simon.138; Βεβρύκων Theoc.22.110; ἀ. ἱερέων *CIG*6798 (Dijon), cf. 2882 (Milet.). 3. *first cause, originator*, κοπίδων Heraclit.81; πράγματος X.*HG*3.3.4, cf. Din.3.7, Isoc.12.101; συγχύσεως *SIG*684.8 (Dyme, ii B.C.); φόνου *POxy.*1241 iii 35; σωτηρίας *Ep.Hebr.*2.10; Θαλῆς ὁ τῆς τοιαύτης ἀ. φιλοσοφίας Arist.*Metaph.*983ᵇ20; τῆς τέχνης Sosip.1.14; τὸ ἀ. *the originating power*, Pl.*Cra.*401d, cf. *Sph.*243d; *primary, fundamental*, ἀρχηγὸν ἡ φωνή Phld.*Po.*2.19.

**ἀρχῆθεν**, Dor. -ᾱθεν, Adv. *from the beginning, from of old*, Pi.*O.*9.55, *I.*4(3).7, Hdt.1.131, 2.138, Hp.*Epid.*6.7.5; rare in Trag., A.*Fr.*416, S.*Fr.*126; condemned by Phryn.75; freq. in later Prose, as Plb.1.50.5, al., Plu.2.238e, etc.; *immediately*, Id.*Cat.Mi.*28. 2. with neg., κρέσσον.. ἀρχῆθεν μὴ ἐλθεῖν not *at all*, Hdt.5.18; cf. ἀρχή I. 1 c.

®**ἀρχηΐα**, ᾱ, Cret., = ἀρχεία, *term of office*, *GDI*5007 (Gortyn), al. (unless name of a tribe). **ἀρχήϊον**, τό, v. sub ἀρχεῖον. ®**ἀρχηΐς**, ίδος, ἡ, title of *priestess*, *IG*5(1).586 (Amyclae).

**ἀρχήν**, Adv., v. ἀρχή I. 1 c.

**ἀρχῐ-**, insep. Prefix, like ἀρχε-, from the same Root as ἄρχω, ἀρχός.

®**ἀρχ-ῐᾰριστάς**, ὁ, = ἀρχιερεύς, *IG*12(1).705 (Camirus), cf. *Michel* 1187 (Peraea). -ιατρεία, ἡ, *office of* ἀρχιατρός, *archiatriae dignitas* *Cod.Theod.*13.3. ®-ιᾱτρός (on the accent v. Hdn.Gr.1.229), Ion. -ιητρός, ὁ, *court* or *official physician*, *OGI*256.5 (Delos, ii/i B.C.), etc.; of the Roman Emperors, Gal.14.2, al.; of communities, *arch. populares* *Cod.Theod.*13.3, *Cod.Just.*10.52.10, al.: generally, *responsible practitioner*, Aret.*CA*2.5; cf. ἀρχιίατρος.

**ἀρχί-βακχος**, ὁ, *chief of college of* Ἰόβακχοι, *IG*2².1368.12, al. ®-βασσάρα [σᾰ], ἡ, *leader of Bacchanals*, *CIG*2052 (Apollonia in Thrace). -βδέλλιον, τό, = ἄγχουσα, Ps.-Dsc.4.23 Wellm.; spelt *archebion* in Plin.*HN*22.51. ®-βούκολος, ὁ, *chief herdsman*, Sch.Il.1.39. II. *president of college of* βουκόλοι, *SIG*1115.3 (Pergam., i A.D.): hence -βουκολέω, *Inscr.Perg.*487.5. ®-βουλευτής, οῦ, ὁ, *president of council*, *Sammelb.*1106. -βουλος, ον, *chief in council*, Suid. -γαλλος, ὁ, *head of college of* γάλλοι *in mystery-cult*, *Jahresh.*14 *Beibl.*136 (Cyme, i A.D.), *JHS*19.280 (Lycaonia), etc. -γένεθλος, ον, = ἀρχέγονος, Orph.*H.*14.8; Ζεύς Id.*Fr.*168.5. ®-γέρων, οντος, ὁ, *chief of a* γερουσία, *Sammelb.*2100 (i B.C.), *Cod.Just.*1.4.5. ®-γεωργός, ὁ, *chief cultivator*, *POxy.*477.4 (ii A.D.), *Ostr.Strassb.*727.6 (ii A.D.). ®-γραμμᾰτεύς, έως, ὁ, *chief clerk* or *secretary*, Plb.5.54.12, Plu.*Eum.*1, etc. -δαίμων, ονος, ὁ, *arch-demon*, *PMag.Par.*1.1349 (pl.). -δαφνηφορέω, Thess. -δαυχναφορέω, *to be chief* δαφνηφόρος, *IG*9(2).1234 (Phalanna). -δενδροφόρος, ὁ, *chief of* δενδροφόροι, *IGRom.*1.614 (Tomi). -δεσμοφύλαξ [ῠ], ακος, ὁ, *chief gaoler*, Lxx *Ge.*39.21, Ph.1.290 (pl.):—also -δεσμώτης, ου, ὁ, Lxx *Ge.*40.4. ®-διάκονος [ᾱ], ὁ, *chief deacon*, Just.*Nov.*123.3. -δῐκαστεία, ἡ, *function of* ἀρχιδικαστής, *PLond.*3.1222.4 (ii A.D.). -δῐκαστής, οῦ, ὁ, *chief judge*, D.S.1.48, Plu.2.355a; at Alexandria, *BGU*1155.6 (i B.C.), *OGI*136, 682, etc. -διοικητής, οῦ, ὁ, *chief administrator*, *Michel*546.13 (Anisa, i B.C.).

**ἀρχίδιον**, τό, Dim. of ἀρχή II. 3, *petty office*, Ar.*Av.*1111; ὑπηρετεῖν τοῖς ἀ. serve *the petty magistrates*, D.18.261. II. Dim. of ἀρχή I, ἐξ ἀρχιδίου dub. in Philol.21 (ἐξ ἀρχᾶς ἀιδίω Rose).

®**ἀρχιεπίσκοπος**, ὁ, *archbishop*, Just.*Nov.*3.2.1.

**ἀρχιεράνιστής**, v. ἀρχερανιστής.

®**ἀρχῐερ-άομαι**, Med., *to be high-priest* or *priestess*, Lxx 4*Ma.*4.18, J.*AJ*17.19.1, *OGI*544.14 (Ancyra), *IG*14.1878, *BSA*16.120 (Pisidia, iii A.D.), etc.: pf. part. ἠρχιερα μένους *IGRom.*3.1475 (Iconium). -ᾱτεία, ἡ, = Lat. *pontificatus maximus*, *Mon.Anc.Gr.*5.22. ®-ᾱτεύω (Ion. -ητεύω *Inscr.Magn.*221.2 (i B.C.)), *to be high-priest*, Lxx 1*Ma.*14.47, *PTeb.*407 (ii A.D.), *OGI*485.4 (Magn. Mae.), *IG*14.1045, etc. -ᾱτικός, ή, όν, *of the* ἀρχιερεύς, ἐκ γένους ἀ. *Act.Ap.*4.6, cf. J.*AJ*15.3.1, *OGI*470.21, *Jahresh.*15.51, etc.; θρόνοι Just.*Nov.*42.1.1. ®-εια, ἡ, *chief-priestess*, *SIG*846 (Delph.), 882 (Olympia), etc.: misspelt ἀρχειέρια *IG*5(2).313 (Mantinea, ii A.D.): = Lat. *virgo Vestalis maxima*, D.C.79.9. ®-εύς, έως, ὁ: Ion. ἀρχιέρεως, εω, Hdt.2.37, also in Pl.*Lg.*947a: acc. pl. ἀρχιρέας v.l. in Hdt.2.142:—*arch-priest, chief-priest*, ll. cc., freq. in Inscrr., νήσου *OGI*93.3 (Cyprus), etc.: esp. in Roman provinces, of the Imperial cult, ἀ. Ἀσίας ib.458.31, etc., cf. *PRyl.*149.2 (i A.D.), etc.:—at Rome, = *pontifex*, Plu.*Num.*9, etc.; ἀ. μέγιστος, = *pontifex maximus*, *SIG*832, etc. (but ἀρχιερεύς alone, *IG*7.2711, etc.):—at Jerusalem, *high-priest*, Lxx *Le.*4.3, *Ev.Matt.*26.3, etc. (Spelt ἀρχι-ιερεύς *IGRom.*4.882 (Themisonium)). -εύω, = ἀρχιερατεύω, Gal.13.600.

**ἀρχιερμηνεύς**, έως, ὁ, *chief dragoman*, *Izv.Arch.Comm.*40.113 (Panticapaeum, ii/iii A.D.).

**ἀρχῐερο-θῠτέω**, *to be president of* ἱεροθύται (q.v.), *IG*12(1).836 (Lindus):—Subst. ®-θύτης [ῠ], ου, ὁ, *president of* ἱεροθύται, ib.788, al.

®**ἀρχῐερωσύνη**, ἡ, *high-priesthood*, Ἀπόλλωνος *OGI*244.21 (Daphne, ii B.C.), cf. *BGU*362ᵛ11 (iii A.D.), etc.; = *pontificatus maximus*, Plu.*Pomp.*67; of the Jewish *high-priesthood*, Lxx 1*Ma.*7.21, J.*AJ*15.3.1, al.

**ἀρχι-εταῖρος**, ὁ, *chief friend* or *companion*, Lxx 2*Ki.*16.16 (due to mistranslation of pr. n. 'Arkī'). -ευνοῦχος, ὁ, *chief of the eunuchs*, ib.*Da.*1.3, Hld.8.3. ®-ζάκορος, ὁ, ἡ, *chief keeper of a temple*, *CIG* 4470 (Laodicea). ®-ζάπφης or -ος, ὁ, title of *religious official* at

Delos, Roussel *Délos Colonie Athénienne* 416. **-θάλασσος** [θᾰ], ον, *ruling the sea*, Ποσειδῶν *AP*6.38 (Phil.). **-θεωρέω**, *to be* ἀρχιθέωρος, D.21.115, *IG*12(5).946 (Tenos). **-θεώρησις**, εως, ἡ, = sq., Is.*Fr.* 148. ⊛**-θεωρία**, ἡ, *the office of* ἀρχιθέωρος, Lys.21.5, *Inscr.Prien.* 174.27 (ii B.C.). ⊛**-θέωρος**, ὁ, *chief of a* θεωρία or *sacred embassy*, And.1.132, Arist.*EN*1122ᵃ25, *SIG*²588.15, al. (Delos, ii B.C.):—also **ἀρχεθέωρος, ἀρκιθέωρος, ἀρκεθέωρος** (q.v.); Dor. **ἀρχιθέᾱρος** *SIG* 558.24 (Ithaca). ⊛**-θῐάσῑτης** [ῑ], ὁ, *leader of a* θίασος, *IG*11(4).1228. 4 (Delos, ii B.C.):—hence ⊛**-θῐασῑτεύω**, *OGI*591.5 (Delos), etc.; and ⊛**-θῐασεύω**, *BCH*31.446. **-θρονος**, ὁ, *occupying the chief seat, presiding*, Choerob. in *An.Ox.*2.182. **-θύρα** [ῠ], ἡ, *principal door* of a temple, *BCH*27.271 (Argos). ⊛**-θυρωρός**, ὁ, *chief door-keeper*, *Sammelb.*327. **-ἰατρος**, ὁ, = ἀρχίατρος, *IG*5(2).385 (Cleitor, i/ii A.D.), *POxy.*126.23 (vi A.D.). **-κᾰμῑνευτής**, οῦ, ὁ, *chief smelter*, *Ath.Mitt.*19.243 (Laureion). **-κέραυνος**, ον, *ruling the thunder*, Cleanth.1.31, v.l. for ἀργι- in Orph.*Fr.*21a. **-κερδέμπορος**, ὁ, *president of guild of merchants*, *IG*12(8).581 (Thasos). **-κήπουρος**, ὁ, *head-gardener*, *PHamb.*117 (iii B.C.), *BGU*1479 (ii B.C. (?)). **-κλοπος**, ὁ, *master-thief*, Suid. **-κλωψ**, ωπος, ὁ, *robber-chief*, Plu.*Arat.* 6. **-κοιτωνίτης**, ου, ὁ, *chief chamberlain*, *IPE*2.428 (Tanais).

⊛**ἀρχικός**, ή, όν, (ἀρχή) *of* or *for rule, royal*, πυθμήν A.*Ch.*260; γένος Th.2.80; *official*, δικαστήριον Chor. in *Rev.Phil.*1.219: neut. pl. ἀρχικά as Subst., perh. *presents demanded by officials on entering office*, *PTeb.* 3.57 *A* 22. 2. of persons, *fit for rule, command*, or *office*, Pl.*Prt.* 352b, al., Isoc.2.24; *having served as magistrates*, *CIG*2774 (Aphrodisias): c. gen., ἀνθρώπων X.*Mem.*1.1.16; νεώς Pl.*R.*488d; φύσει ἀρχικὸν πατὴρ υἱῶν Arist.*EN*1161ᵃ18; ἔστιν -κώτατα τῶν γενῶν Σκύθαι καὶ Θρᾷκες καὶ Πέρσαι Isoc.4.67. Adv. -κῶς, ἔχοντες Lib.*Or.*11. 148; ἱερατικῶς καὶ ἀ. φυλαττόμενα Just.*Nov.*58. 3. *dominant, sovereign*, ἡ ἀρχικωτάτη ἐπιστήμη the *sovereign* science, i.e. σοφία, Arist.*Metaph.*982ᵇ4; τὴν ἀ. χώραν ἔχειν Id.*PA*665ᵇ18; ἀ. ἀρετή, opp. ὑπηρετική, Id.*Pol.*1260ᵃ23:—Math., *principal*, ἀ. συμπτώματα, of the properties of a curve, Apollon.Perg.*Con.*1 *Praef.*; ἀ. διάμετροι *principal* diameters, ib.1.51. II. *belonging to* ἀρχαί 11. 6, Dam.*Pr.* 130,341. III. *primal, original*, γένεσις Phld.*D.*3.14; -κώτατον αἴτιον S.E.*M.*9.5. Adv. -κῶς ib.1.46. 2. ἀ. σχῆμα ποιήσεως in which the poet *commences with* an invocation of the Muses, Zeus, etc., Anon.*Fig.*p.149S.

⊛**ἀρχι-κῠβερνήτης**, ου, ὁ, *chief pilot*, Str.15.1.28, Plu.*Alex.*66, *PGrenf.* 2.80.8 (v A.D.). ⊛**-κυνηγός**, ὁ, *chief-huntsman*, a Ptolemaic court official, *OGI*99.2 (Ptol. V), 143.3 (Cyprus, Ptol. VIII), *Ostr.*1530, J.*AJ*16.10.3. **-λῃστής**, οῦ, ὁ, *robber-chief*, Id.*BJ*1.10.5, Ps.-Callisth.1.36, *PMasp.*2 iii 22 (vi A.D.).

**ἀρχιλλάν**· ἀρχιποίμενα (Cret.), Hsch.

**Ἀρχιλόχειος**, α, ον, *of* or *used by Archilochus*, μέτρον Heph. 15.2.

**ἀρχι-μάγειρος** [ᾰ], ον, *chief cook*, Lxx *Ge.*39.1, al., cf. Ph.2.63; title of a great officer in Oriental courts, Lxx *Da.*2.14, cf. J.*AJ*10.10.3, Plu.2.11b:—also ⊛**-μαγειρεύς**, έως, ὁ, *dignitary* in Mithraic cult, *BCH* 37.97 (Thessalonica). **-μάγος**, ὁ, *chief of the magi*, *Epigr.Gr.* 903 *b* 7 (Hypaepa), Rhetor. in *Cat.Cod.Astr.*8(4).147. ⊛**-μανδρίτης**, ου, ὁ, *chief of a* μάνδρα, *abbot*, Just.*Nov.*5.7. **-μάχιμος** [ᾰ], ὁ, *officer of native Egyptian troops*, *PTeb.*112.86 (ii B.C.), 121.128 (i B.C.). **-μηχᾰνικός**, ὁ, *chief engineer*, *Sammelb.*1113 (ii A.D.). ⊛**-μῖμος**, ὁ, *chief comedian*, Plu.*Sull.*36. **-μύστης**, ου, ὁ, *chief of the mystae*, *CIG* 2052 (Apollonia in Thrace), *Arch.Anz.*30.175 (Kara-Ornan), *BCH* 11.483 (Lydia), Jul.Laod. in *Cat.Cod.Astr.*4.105.33:—hence **-μυστέω**, *Eph.Epigr.*3.236 (Perinthus). **-νᾱκορέω**, *to be chief of* νακόροι (= νεωκόροι), *BCH*37.94 (Thessalonica). **-ναυφύλαξ** [ῠ], ακος, ὁ, *chief of naval guard*, *Annuario* 2.136 (Rhodes, i B.C.). ⊛**-νεᾱνίσκος**, ὁ, *chief of* νεανίσκοι, *CIL*6.2180. ⊛**-νεώκορος**, ὁ, *chief of* νεωκόροι, *Milet.*7.65 (i A.D.), *BCH*37.97 (ii/iii A.D.). **-νεωποιός**, ὁ, *chief of* νεωποιοί, *CIG*2811 (νεοπ- ib.2781, 2795). **-νυκτοφύλαξ** [ῠ], ὁ, *chief of night-guard*, *Sammelb.*4636.33 (iii A.D.). **-οινοχοεία**, ἡ, *office of chief cup-bearer*, Lxx *Ge.*40.13. **-οινοχόος**, ὁ, *chief cup-bearer*, ib.1 sq., Plu.*Alex.*74. **-ονηλάτης** [ᾰ], ου, ὁ, *chief donkey-driver*, *CPHerm.*127ʳ *Fr.*2 vii 19:—also **ἀρχονηλάτης**, *PLond.*1.131ʳ321 (i A.D.). **-παραφύλαξ** [ῠ], ακος, ὁ, *chief of* παραφύλακες (q.v.), *OGI*476.8. **-παρθενος**, ον, *chief among virgins*, *EM*702.6. **-παστοφόρος**, ὁ, *head of college of* παστοφόροι (q.v.), *Ostr.*1174, *POxy.*241.10 (i A.D.). **-πατριώτης**, ου, ὁ, *head of a family*, Lxx *Jo.*21.1. **-πεδῑοφύλαξ** [ῠ], ακος, ὁ, *chief of field-guards*, *Sammelb.*4525. **-πειράτης**, ου, ὁ, Lat. *archipirata* Cic.*Off.*2.11.40, al.:—*pirate-chief*, D.S.20.97, Plu.*Pomp.* 45, Petron.101. **-πλᾰνος**, ὁ, *nomad chieftain*, Luc.*Tox.*39. ⊛**-ποίμην**, ενος, ὁ, *chief shepherd*, 1 *Ep.Pet.*5.4, Sm.4*Ki.*3.4, *PLips.*97 xi 4 (iv A.D.). **-πολῐαρχέω**, Thess. ἀρχι-ττολιάρχεω, *to be president of board of magistrates*, *IG*9(2).1233 (Phalanna). **-πρεσβευτής**, οῦ, ὁ, *chief ambassador*, D.S.14.25, Str.17.1.11, *SIG*810.20 (Rhodes, i A.D.). **-πρόβουλος**, ὁ, *president of* πρόβουλοι, *CIG*4364 (Termessus). ⊛**-προστᾰτέω**, *hold office of chief* προστάτης συναγωγῆς, *Sammelb.*626 (Ptolem.). ⊛**-προστάτης** [ᾰ], ου, ὁ, *chief official of a synagogue*, *Arch.Pap.*2.430. **-προυρέω**, v. -φρουρέω. **-προφήτης**, ου, ὁ, *chief prophet*, Ph.1.594; *chief of* προφῆται (q.v.), *PGen.*7. 5 (i A.D.), Ps.-Callisth.3.34:—hence **-προφητεία**, ἡ, *PGen.*36.5 (ii A.D.). ⊛**-πρύτᾰνις** [ῠ], εως, ὁ, *chief president*, *OGI*494.3 (Milet.), *PTeb.*397.8 (ii A.D.), *Inscr.Prien.*246.20 (ii A.D.), etc.:—hence **-πρῠτᾰνεύω**, *BCH*11.70 (Isaura). ⊛**-ραβδοῦχος**, ὁ, *chief lictor*, *Gloss.*:—fem. **-ραβδούχισσα**, *leader of wand-bearers*, in cult of Cybele, *IG Rom.*1.614 (Tomi).

**ἀρχιρεύς**, v. ἀρχιερεύς.

**ἀρχίς**, ίδος, ἡ, fem. of ἄρχων, *IG*12(5).909, al. (Tenos).

**ἀρχι-σῑτοποιός**, ὁ, *chief baker*, Lxx *Ge.*40.1 sq., Ph.1.661. **-σκηπτοῦχος**, ὁ, *chief staff-bearer*, *CIG*2987.21 (Ephesus). **-στάτωρ** [ᾰ], ορος, ὁ, *chief usher*, *POxy.*294.17 (i A.D.). ⊛**-στολιστής**, οῦ, ὁ, *keeper of the sacred vestments*, *OGI*111.18 (ii B.C.), *Sammelb.* 4011. **-στράτηγος** [ᾰ], ὁ, *commander-in-chief*, Lxx *Jo.*5.15, al., J.*AJ*6.11.9, etc. ⊛**-συνάγωγος** [ᾰ], ὁ, *ruler of a synagogue*, *Ev.Marc.* 5.22, al., *IG*14.2304, Ramsay *Cities and Bishoprics* No.559:—hence ⊛**-συνᾰγωγέω**, *BCH*8.463 (Thessalonica, ii A.D.). II. *master of a guild* or *company*, *IGRom.*1.782 (Thrace), etc. **-σωμᾰτοφύλαξ** [ῠ], ακος, ὁ, *chief of the body-guard*, Lxx *Es.*2.21, *OGI*99.1 (ii B.C.), *PTeb.*79.52 (ii B.C.), J.*AJ*12.2.5. **-ταβλάριος**, ὁ, (*tabularium*) *keeper of records*, ἀ. Αἰγύπτου *OGI*707.6 (Tyre, ii A.D.).

**ἀρχιτεκτον-εύμα**, ατος, τό, *construction*, Bito 61.2. **-εύω**, = sq., Id.45 (Pass.). **-έω**, *to be architect, chief constructor*, or *commissioner of works*, Plu.*Per.*13, Sosip.1.16, *OGI*656, etc.: c. acc., *design, construct*, τριακοντήρη ib.39 (iii B.C.); βιβλιοθήκην Afric.*Cest. Oxy.*412.67:—Pass., τὴν οἰκίαν.. εὖ ἠρχιτεκτονῆσθαι Thphr.*Char.*2. 12. 2. generally, *contrive*, Ar.*Pax* 305, *Fr.*195; *supervise, direct*, -τεκτονοῦντος τοῦ Πλάτωνος Phld.*Acad.Ind.*p.15 M. **-ημα**, ατος, τό, *stroke of art, artifice*, Luc.*Asin.*25. **-ία**, ἡ, *architecture, construction*, Lxx *Ex.*35.32, Bito 49.2, Gal.5.68. **-ικός**, ή, όν, *of* or *for an* ἀρχιτέκτων or *his business and art*, Pl.*Plt.*261c; of persons, *fit to be a master-builder, skilled in his art*, Arist.*Pol.*1282ᵃ3. II. ἡ -κή (sc. τέχνη or ἐπιστήμη) *architecture*, Sosip.1.36. 2. *master-art* or *science*, which prescribes to all beneath it, as an ἀρχιτέκτων to his workmen, Arist.*EN*1094ᵃ14, *Metaph.*1013ᵃ14, al.; *professional knowledge*, Id.*Po.*1456ᵇ11.

⊛**ἀρχι-τεκτοσύνη**, ἡ, *conduct of office of* ἀρχιτέκτων, *BCH*10.500 (Pisidia). ⊛**-τέκτων**, ονος, ὁ, *chief-artificer, master-builder, director of works*, τοῦ ὀρύγματος, τῆς γεφύρας, Hdt.3.60, 4.87; opp. χειροτέχνης, Arist.*Metaph.*981ᵃ30; opp. ἐργατικός, Pl.*Plt.*259e; *commissioner of works*, *IG*2.403, al., ib.9(1).694.145 (Corcyra), *SIG*284.12 (Chios, from Erythrae), etc.; ἀ. τοῦ ναοῦ ib.494.3 (Delph.); ἀ. ἐπὶ τὰ ἱερά *IG*2.404. b. pl., *board of naval constructors*, Arist.*Ath.*46.1. 2. generally, *author, contriver*, E.*Cyc.*477; ἀ. κύριος τῆς ἡδονῆς Alex. 149.2; ἀ. τῆς ἐπιβουλῆς D.56.11; τοῦ τέλους Arist.*EN*1152ᵇ2; τοὺς ταῖς διανοίαις ἀ. τινός *those that direct activities* by thought, Id.*Pol.*1325ᵇ 23. II. at Athens, *manager of the state theatre and of the Dionysia*, D.18.28, *IG*2.335. **-τελώνης**, ου, ὁ, *chief toll-collector, chief-publican*, *Ev.Luc.*19.2. **-τρίκλῑνος**, ὁ, *president of a banquet* (*triclinium*), *Ev. Jo.*2.9. 2. *head-waiter*, Hld.7.27. **-υπασπιστής**, οῦ, ὁ, *chief of the men-at-arms*, Plu.*Eum.*1. ⊛**-υπηρέτης**, ου, ὁ, *chief minister*, *IG* 14.914 (iii A.D.), *BGU*21 iii 9 (iv A.D.):—also **ἀρχυπηρέτης**, *Sammelb.*599.61, *Ostr.*1538. **-φερεκίτης** [κῑ], ου, ὁ, *head of Jewish school*, Just.*Nov.*146.1.2. (Aram. *pirkā* 'lesson'.) **-φίλος**, ὁ, *principal friend*, dub.l. in J.*AJ*7.9.6 (prob. ἀρχαῖον φίλον). ⊛**-φρουρέω**, *command a* φρουρά, *IG*9(2).1059 (Thess.): also in form **-προυρέω**, ib.1058. ⊛**-φρουρος**, ὁ, *commandant of a* φρουρά, Ἀρχ.Ἐφ. 1911.124 (Gonnos). **-φῠλᾰκέω**, *hold office of* ἀρχιφύλαξ (q.v.), *OGI*565.12 (Oenoanda); ἠρχιφυλακηκότα Λυκίων τοῦ κοινοῦ *TAM*2. 143 (Lydae). **-φῠλᾰκία**, ἡ, *office of* ἀρχιφύλαξ, *OGI*566.17 (Oenoanda):—written **-φῠλᾰκεία**, *IGRom.*3.593 (Sidyma). ⊛**-φῠλᾰκίτης**, ὁ, *commandant of* φυλακῖται (q.v.), *PRev.Laws* 37.5 (iii B.C.), *PHib.*1.73, *PTeb.*5.142 (ii B.C.):—hence **-φῠλᾰκῑτεία**, ἡ, *office of* ἀ., ib.27.22 (ii B.C.), and **-φῠλᾰκῑτεύω**, *hold such office*, *PAlex.*9.4 (iii B.C. (?)). **-φύλαξ** [ῠ], ακος, ὁ, *commandant of guards*, in Egypt, *PGiss.*9.13 (ii A.D.). II. title of an *official of the Lycian league*, *TAM*2.199 (Sidyma). **-φύλαρχος** [ῠ], ὁ, *chief of the* φύλαρχοι, Zos. 3.22. **-φῦλος**, ὁ, *chief of a tribe*, Lxx *De.*29.10(9). **-φωρ**, ωρος, ὁ, = ἀρχίκλωψ, D.S.1.80. **-χορος**, ὁ, *leader of chorus*, *IG*12(2). 484.20 (Mytil.).

**ἄρχματα**· ἀπάρχματα θεοῖς, Hsch.

⊛**ἀρχο-γλυπτάδης**, ου, ὁ, *son of a place-hunter*, *Com.Adesp.* 84. **-ειδής**, ές, *of the nature of a principle*, Arist.*Metaph.*999ᵃ2, *APo.*86ᵇ38, Plu.2.1085c, *Theol.Ar.*8, al.: Comp., Alex.Aphr.*Febr.* 21, Simp. *in Ph.*7.21: Sup., Alex.Aphr.*Febr.*7, Dam.*Pr.*52 ter. Adv. -δῶς Procl.*Inst.*65, Syrian. in *Metaph.*3.23.

**ἀρχοινόχοος**, contr. -χους, ὁ, *chief butler*, *IG*9(1).486 (Thyrrheum), *PTeb.*72.447 (ii B.C.).

**ἀρχολαβῶν**· ἡ ἐργολαβῶν, Hsch.

**ἀρχονηλάτης**, v. ἀρχιονηλ-.

**ἀρχολῐπᾰρος** [ῑ], ον, *grasping at office*, *Com.Adesp.*84.

⊛**ἀρχοντ-εύω**, *hold office of* ἄρχων, *IPE*1².130.17 (Olbia, ii/iii A.D.). **-ιάω**, *wish to be ruler*, Sch.Ar.*V.*342, Lyd.*Mag.*1.28. ⊛**-ικός**, ή, όν, *of an archon*, πέλεκυς *AP*9.763 tit. (Jul. Aegypt.); ὑπηρεσία *PGrenf.*2.82.15 (400 A.D.): generally, *of a ruler*, *Corp.Herm.*1. 25. 2. *ex-archon*, *IG*14.756ᵃ (Naples), cf. 1789. **-ίς**, ίδος, ἡ, fem. of ἄρχων, *Cat.Cod.Astr.*2.177.8.

**ἀρχός**, ὁ, *leader, chief*, εἷς δέ τις ἀρχὸς ἀνήρ Il.1.144: c. gen., νηῶν 2.493; οἰωνῶν Pi.*P.*1.7; *ruler*, Τειχιούσσης *SIG*3 *d* (Milet., vi B.C.); πόλεως (opp. ἔτης), prob. in E.*Fr.*1014. 2. = ἄρχων, *IG*7.3301, al. 3. ἀ. ἑῴας, = *dux Orientis*, ib.14.1073 (iv A.D.). 4. of a god, *SIG*56.26 (Argos, v B.C.). II. *the rectum*, Hp.*Aph.*5.58, Arist. *HA*507ᵃ33, *Theol.Ar.*51. 2. *the anus*, Hp.*Haem.*2, *Epid.*5.20.

**ἀρχο-στάσια** [ᾰ], τά, = ἀρχαιρέσια, *IG*5(2).437 (Megalop., ii B.C.), Ἀρχ.Ἐφ.1917.2,10 (Perrhaebia). **-στάσιος** [ᾰ], ὁ (sc. μήν), month *in which elections were held* at Erineos, *GDI*2030. **-στάται** [ᾰ], οἱ, *electoral college for the appointment of magistrates* in Lycia, *IGRom.* 3.473.44.

**ἀρχυπηρέτης**, v. ἀρχιυπηρέτης.

**Ἀρχύτειος** [ῠ], α, ον, *belonging to Archytas*, Iamb.*Comm.Math.* 7 (-ιος cod.).

***ἄρχω**, Ep. inf. ἀρχέμεναι Il.20.154: impf. ἦρχον ib.2.378, etc.; Dor. ἆρχον Pi.*O.*10(11).51: fut. ἄρξω Od.4.667, A.*Pr.*940, Th.1. 144: aor. ἦρξα, Ep. ἄρξα Od.14.230, etc.: pf. ἦρχα *CIG*3487.14 (Thyatira), Decr.ap.Plu.2.851f:—**Med.**, Od.8.90, etc.; non-thematic part. ἄρχμενος Call.*Aet.*3.1.56, al.: impf., Il.9.93, Hdt.5.28: fut. ἄρξομαι (in med. sense, v. infr.) Il.9.97, E.*IA*442, X.*Cyr.*8.8.2; Dor. ἀρξεῦμαι Theoc.7.95: aor. ἠρξάμην Od.23.310, etc.:—**Pass.**, pf. ἦργμαι only in med. sense, v. infr. I. 2: aor. ἤρχθην, ἀρχθῆναι Th.6. 18, Arist.*Pol.*1277$^b$13, v. infr. II. 4:—*to be first*, I. in Time, *begin, make a beginning*, Act. and Med. (in Hom. the Act. is more freq., in Att. Prose the Med., esp. where personal action is emphasized), πολέμου ἄρχειν *to be the aggressor*, Th.1.53; π. ἄρχεσθαι *to begin one's* operations, X.*HG*6.3.6; ἄρχειν τοῦ λόγου *to open* a conversation, Id.*An.*1.6.6; ἄρχεσθαι τοῦ λόγου *to begin one's* speech, ib.3.2.7. Constr.: 1. mostly c. gen., *make a beginning of*, ἄρχειν πολέμοιο Il.4.335; μύθων Od.3.68; τῶν ἀδικημάτων πρῶτον τοῦτο ἄρξαι Hdt. 1.2; ἦρξεν ἐμβολῆς A.*Pers.*409; τοῦ κακοῦ ib.353; ἄρχειν χειρῶν ἀδίκων, ἄρχειν τῆς πληγῆς, *strike the first* blow, Antipho 4.2.1 and 2:—in Med. in religious sense, = ἀπάρχεσθαι, ἀρχόμενος μελέων *beginning with* the limbs, Od.14.428, cf. E.*Ion*651; but Act., σπονδαῖσιν ἄρξαι Pi.*I.*6(5).37. 2. c. gen., *begin from* or *with*.., ἐν σοὶ μὲν λήξω σέο δ' ἄρξομαι Il.9.97; ἄρχεσθαι Διός Pi.*N.*5.25; πόθεν ἄρξωμαι; A.*Ch.* 855; πόθεν ποτὲ ἦρκται Hp.*VM*5; ἄρχεσθαι, ἦρχθαι ἔκ τινος, Od.23. 199, Hp.*Off.*11; ἀπό τινος freq. in Prose, ἀρξάμενοι αὐτίκα ἀπὸ παιδίων *even* from boyhood, Hdt.3.12; but more commonly ἐκ παίδων, ἐκ παιδός, etc., Pl.*R.*408d, *Thg.*128d:—ἀπό in non-temporal relations, ἀρξάμενος ἀπὸ σοῦ, i.e. *including* yourself, Pl.*Grg.*471c, cf. D.18.297; ἀπὸ τῶν πατέρων X.*Mem.*3.5.15; μέχρι τῶν δώδεκα ἀπὸ μιᾶς ἀρξάμενος Pl.*Lg.*771c; ἀφ' ἱερῶν ἠργμένη ἀρχή ib.771a; ἀφ' Ἑστίας ἀρχόμενος Ar.*V.*846. 3. c. gen. rei et dat. pers., ἄρχε θεοῖς δαιτός *begin* a banquet to the gods, Il.15.95; τοῖς ἄρα μύθων ἦρχε 2.433, etc.; τῇσι δὲ.. ἄρχετο μολπῆς Od.6.101; ἦρξε τῇ πόλει ἀνομίας τὸ νόσημα Th.2. 53, cf. 12; τὴν ἡμέραν ἄρχειν ἐλευθερίας τῇ Ἑλλάδι X.*HG*2.2.23; ἡμῖν οὐ σμικρῶν κακῶν ἦρξεν τὸ δῶρον S.*Tr.*871. 4. c. acc., ἄρχειν ὁδόν τινι, *show* him the way, Od.8.107 (but also ἄρχειν ὁδοῖο *lead* the way, 5.237): abs. (sc. ὁδόν), ἄρχε δ' Ἀθήνη 3.12; σὺ μὲν ἄρχε Il.9.69; ἦ ῥα καὶ ἄρχε λέχοσδε κιών 3.447; ἦρχε δ' ἄρα σφιν Ἄρης 5.592, cf. infr. II. 2: with other accusatives, ἄρχειν ὕμνον Pi.*N.*3.10; ἅπερ ἦρξεν A.*Ag.*1529 (lyr.); λυπηρόν τι S.*El.*552; ὕβριν Id.*Fr.*368. 5. of actions, σέο δ' ἕξεται ὅττι κεν ἄρχῃ Il.9.102: freq. c. inf., τοῖσιν δ' ἦρχ' ἀγορεύειν among them, Il.1.571, etc.; ἦρχε νέεσθαι, ἦρχ' ἴμεν, 2.84, 13.329; ἄρχετε νῦν νέκυας φορέειν Od.22.437, etc.; ὑφαίνειν ἤρχετο μῆτιν Il.7.324; ἤρξαντο οἰκοδομεῖν Th.1.107; ἡ νόσος ἤρξατο γενέσθαι Id.2.47: c. part., of continued action or condition, ἦρχον χαλεπαίνων Il.2.378; ἦν ἄρξῃ ἀδικέων Hdt.4.119; ἡ ψυχὴ ἄρχεται ἀπολείπουσα X.*Cyr.*8.7.26; πόθεν ἂν ὀρθῶς ἀρξαίμεθα ἐπαινοῦντες; Pl.*Mx.*237a, cf. *Tht.*187a (but ἄ. ἐπαινεῖν Id.*Phdr.*241e); ἄρξομαι διδάσκων X.*Cyr.*8.8.2 (but ἦρξω μανθάνειν Id.*Mem.*3.5.22). 6. abs., ἄρχε *take the lead!* Il.9.69: generally, *begin*, ἄρχειν [τὴν ἐκεχειρίαν] τήνδε τὴν ἡμέραν Indut.ap.Th.4.118, cf. Lex ap.D.24.42; τὸ ἄρχον, opp. τὸ ἑπόμενον, Dam.*Pr.*234: part. ἀρχόμενος *at first*, X.*Eq.*9.3, *Cyn.*3.8, Isoc.2.54; *at the beginning*, ἀρχομένου δὲ πίθου καὶ λήγοντος Hes.*Op.*368, cf. *Fr.*192.4; ἀρχομένοισιν ἢ καταπαυομένοισι Ar.*Eq.* 1246; ἄρχεται ὁ πόλεμος ἐνθένδε Th.2.1; ἅμα ἦρι ἀρχομένῳ ibid.; θέρους εὐθὺς ἀρχομένου ib.47. 7. Gramm., of a word, ἄ. ἀπὸ φωνήεντος D.T.633.27; ἡ ἄρχουσα (sc. συλλαβή) A.D.*Synt.*130. 13. II. in point of Place or Station, *rule, govern, command*, 1. mostly c. gen., *rule, be leader of*.., Βοιωτῶν Il.2.494, cf. Hdt.5.1, etc. 2. less freq. c. dat., ἀνδράσιν ἦρξα Od.14.230, cf. 471, Il.2. 805, Pi.*P.*3.4, A.*Pr.*940, E.*Andr.*666, *IA*337, *IG*7.2830 (Hyettus, etc.; also ἐν δ' ἄρα τοῖσιν ἦρχ' *held command* among them, Il.13. 690, cf. Pl.*Phdr.*238a: c. inf. added, ἄρχε Μυρμιδόνεσσι μάχεσθαι *led* them *on* to fight, Il.16.65. 3. abs., *rule*, ὅσον τό τ' ἄρχειν καὶ τὸ δουλεύειν δίχα A.*Pr.*927, cf. *Pers.*774; esp. *hold a magistracy*, ὁκοῖόν τε εἴη ἄρχειν μετὰ τὸ βασιλεύειν Hdt.6.67; at Athens, etc., *to be archon*, D.21.178; ἀρχάς, ἀρχὴν ἄρχειν, Hdt.3.80, Th.6.54; ἄρχειν τὴν ἐπώνυμον (with or without ἀρχήν) *IG*3.659,693, *SIG*872.7. 4. Pass., with fut. ἄρξομαι Hdt.7.159, Pi.*O.*8.45, A.*Pers.*589, Lys.28.7; but ἀρχθήσομαι Arist.*Pol.*1259$^b$40, D C.65.10:—*to be ruled, governed*, etc., ὑπό τινος Hdt.1.127; ἔκ τινος S.*El.*264, *Ant.*63; ὑπό τινι Hdt.1.91, 103; σφόδρα ὑπό τινος Lys.12.92; ἀρχὲ πρῶτον μαθὼν ἄρχεσθαι Sol. ap.D.L.1.60, cf. Pl.*Prt.*326d; δύνασθαι καὶ ἄρχεσθαι καὶ ἄρχειν Arist. *Pol.*1277$^b$14; οἱ ἀρχόμενοι *subjects*, X.*An.*2.6.19, etc.

***ἄρχων**, οντος, ὁ, (part. of ἄρχω) *ruler, commander*, νεὸς Hdt.5.33: abs., A.*Th.*674, S.*Aj.*668, etc.; *chief, king*, Ἀσίας A.*Pers.*73; ἄ. τοῦ κόσμου τούτου, of Satan, *Ev.Jo.*16.11, al. II. as official title, *chief magistrate*, esp. at Athens, Th.1.126, etc.; οἱ ἐννέα ἄρχοντες *IG*2. 163; οἱ ἄ., at Sparta, *the authorities*, Hdt.6.106: sg., ὁ ἄρχων the *eponymous magistrate of the year*, *IG*1.52, al., Arist.*Ath.*3.3, etc.; so in Boeotia, at Delphi, Delos, and elsewhere, *IG*7.2407, *SIG*295. 18, *IG*2.814, etc.; = Lat. *consul*, Plb.1.39.1. 2. *governor* of a dependency or province, e.g. in the Athenian Empire, *IG*1.62$^b$19, etc.; of a Roman *governor*, *OGI*441.59; = *praefectus*, Plb.6.26.5. 3. generally, *magistrate, official*, Aeschin.3.29, etc.; opp. ἰδιώτης, *SIG* 672.16 (Delph.); *ruler* of a synagogue, *Ev.Matt.*9.18; *president* of a club, *PLond.*3.1178.6 (ii A.D.).

***ἀρχ-ωνέω**, *to be an* ἀρχώνης, *PRev.Laws* 14.3, al., *BCH*1.410 (Callipolis). **-ώνης**, ου, ὁ, *chief contractor* or *farmer of revenue*, And.1.133 (ἄρχων εἷς codd.), *PRev.Laws*10.10, al., *CIG* (add.)3912; ἀ. λιμένων, = *promagister portorii*, *Ephes.*2 No.29; ἀ. τεσσαρακοστῆς λιμένων Ἀσίας *promagister quadragesimae*.., *OGI*525.5 (Halic.).

**ἀρχωνίδας**, = δρῦς, Pl.Com.233.

**ἀρωγή** [ᾰ], ἡ, (ἀρήγω) *aid, succour*, Ζηνὸς ἀρωγῇ Il.4.408; ἐς μέσον.. δικάσσατε μηδ' ἐπ' ἀρωγῇ judge impartially and not in any one's *favour*, ib.23.574; πέμπειν ἀ. A.*Ch.*477 (lyr.); οὐδ' ἔχων ἀ. S.*Ph.*856 (lyr.); in parody of A., Ar.*Ra.*1267 sq.; ἀ. νόσου, πόνων, *help against*.., Pl. *Lg.*919c, *Mx.*238a. II. of persons, *an aid, succour*, διπλᾶς ἀρωγὰς μολεῖν, of Apollo and Artemis, S.*OC*1094 (lyr.); στρατιῶτιν ἀ., of the Greek host, A.*Ag.*47, cf. 73 (lyr.).—Poet. word, rare in Prose.

**ἀρωγονaύτης** [ᾰ], ου, ὁ, *helper of sailors*, *AP*9.290 (Phil.).

***ἀρωγός** [ᾰ], όν, (ἀρήγω) *aiding, succouring, propitious*, τινί Pi.*O.*2. 49, A.*Eu.*289: abs., Id.*Pr.*997, S.*OT*206 (lyr.):—rare in Prose, *beneficial*, medically, Hp.*Aër.*10; ἔλαιον.. ταῖς θριξὶ ἀ. Pl.*Prt.*334b. 2. c. gen., *serviceable, useful towards* a thing, ἀρωγὰ τῆς δίκης ὁρκώματα A.*Eu.*486; γένος ναΐας ἀρωγὸν τέχνας *serviceable* in sea-craft, S.*Aj.* 357; δίψους ἀ. *against* thirst, Antiph.150; πόνων Luc.*Trag.*54: with Preps., ἐπὶ ψευδέσσι Il.4.235; πρός τι Th.7.62: and c. dat., ῥίζας ἐχίεσσιν ἀ. *serviceable against*, Nic.*Th.*636. II. as Subst., *helper*, esp. in battle, ὅσοι Δαναοῖσιν ἀρωγοί Il.8.205, etc.; also, *defender* before a tribunal, *advocate*, ib.18.502; ἀρωγοὺς ξυνδίκους θ' ἥξω λαβών A.*Supp.*726.

**ἀρῳδιός**, v.l. for ἐρῳδιός, Lxx*Le.*11.19, al.

***ἄρωμα** (A) [ᾰρ], ατος, τό, *aromatic herb* or *spice*, Hp.*Aph.*5.28, X. *An.*1.5.1, prob. in *Supp.Epigr.*1.414 (Crete, v/iv B. C., pl.), Arist.*Pr.* 907$^a$13, *IG*5(2).514.17 (Lycosura, ii B. C., pl.), Plu.*Phoc.*20.

**ἄρωμα** (B) [ᾰρ], ατος, τό, (ἀρόω) *arable land, corn-land*, S.*Fr.*75 (pl.), Ar.*Pax*1158, Eup.304.

**ἀρωμάτ-ίζω** [ᾰρ], *spice*, στέαρ Dsc.1.66:—Pass., Id.2.76.10; ἠρωματισμένον ἔλαιον *Inscr.Prien.*112.62 (i B.C.). 2. intr., *have a spicy flavour* or *scent*, D.S.2.49, Str.16.2.41, Plu.2.623e. **-ικός**, ή, όν, *aromatic*, δυνάμεις Dsc.2.171, Plu.2.382f; **-κόν**, τό, ib.791b; **-κή** (sc. ὠνή), ἡ, *contract for supply of spices*, *Röm.Mitt.*13.121. **-ιστέον**, *one must spice, perfume*, Dsc.2.76.8. ***-ίτης**, ου, ὁ, fem.***-ῖτις**, ιδος, ἡ, = ἀρωματικός, οἶνος Id.5.54; σχοῖνος Str.16.2.16.

**ἀρωμᾰτο-πώλης** [ᾰρ], ου, ὁ, *dealer in spices*, Ptol.*Tetr.*179, Artem. 2.22. ***-φόρος**, ον, *spice-bearing*, [γῆ] Str.1.2.32; Ἀραβία Dsc.1. 13, cf. Plu.*Alex.*25, Luc.*Macr.*17. 2. Subst. -φόρος, ὁ, *servant in charge of spices*, J.*AJ*17.8.3.

**ἀρωμᾰτώδης** [ᾰρ], ες, *likespice, spicy*, Dsc.1.13, Gal.1.399, Ath.1.33e.

**ἀρώμεναι**, v. ἀρόω.

**ἀρωνία**, ἡ, = ἄρον, corrupt in Phan.ap.Ath.9.371d. 2. = μέσπιλον, Dsc.1.118.

**ἀρωραῖος**, hyperdor. for ἀρουραῖος, Ar.*Ach.*762.

**ἀρώσιμος** [ᾰ], ον, poet. for ἀρόσιμος (q. v.), S.*Ant.*569.

**ἄρωσις**, εως, ἡ, = ἄροσις, *POxy.*280.16 (i A. D.).

**ἄρωστος** [ᾰ], ον, poet. for ἄρρωστος, *AP*11.206 (Lucill.).

**ἆς**, Aeol., and **ἇς**, Dor., = ἕως, Sapph.25, Pi.*O.*10(11).51, Ar.*Lys.* 173, Theoc.14.70; esp. in sense *as long as*, *Leg.Gort.*4.27, al., *Tab. Heracl.*1.100.

**ἀσαγεύω**, dub. in B.8.13.

**ἀσάζειν**· λυπεῖσθαι, Hsch.

**ἆσαι**, contr. for ἀίσαι, v. ἀάω. **ἆσαι, ἄσαιμι**, v. ἄω. **ᾆσαι, ᾄσας**, v. ᾄδω. **ἀσαίνων**· ὑβρίζων, λυπῶν, Hsch.

**ἄσακτος**, ον, (σάττω) *not trodden down*, γῆ X.*Oec.*19.11.

**ἀσᾰλᾰμίνιος** [μῑ], ον, *not having been at Salamis*, Ar.*Ra.*204.

**ἀσάλγαν**· ὕβριν, ἀμέλειαν, Hsch. **ἀσαλγάνας**· φοβερός, Id.; cf. ἀσελγής.

**ἀσάλεια** [σᾰ], ἡ, (ἀσαλής) *carelessness*, Sophr.113.

**ἀσάλειν** [σᾰ]· ἀφροντιστῆναι, σάλα γὰρ ἡ φροντίς, Hsch.

**ἀσάλευτος** [σᾰ], ον, *unmoved, unshaken*, ἀ. ἡ γῆ Arist.*Mu.*392$^b$34; of Delos, *AP*9.100 (Alph.); ἔσται ἀσάλευτον πρὸ ὀφθαλμῶν Lxx*Ex.* 13.16, al.; πρῷρα *Act.Ap.*27.41; of the sea, prob. in Plu.2.982f: metaph. of the mind, E.*Ba.*391 (lyr.); ἀ. ἡσυχία Pl.*Ax.*370d; πίστις Polystr.p.10 W.; βασιλεία *Ep.Hebr.*12.28; στάλα ἀ. *Hymn.Is.*4; νίκη *IG*9(1).270 (Atalante); ἀ. μένειν, of ordinances, *PLips.*34.35 (iv A. D.), cf. *Sammelb.*4324.12. Adv. -τως Plb.9.9.8: neut. pl. as Adv., χείλεσι ἀσάλευτα μεμυκόσι *AP*12.183 (Strat.).

**ἀσαλής**, ές, *unthinking, careless*, μανία A.*Fr.*319; cf. ἀσάλεια.

**ἄσᾰλος**, ον, = ἀσάλευτος, Plu.2.981c.

**ἀσάλπικτος**, ον, *without sound of trumpet*, ὥρα ἀ. the hour *when no trumpet sounds*, i. e. midnight, S.*Fr.*389.

**ἀσάμβᾰλος**, = ἀσάνδαλος, Nonn.*D.*32.256, 44.14.

***ἀσάμινθος** [ᾰσᾰ], ἡ, *bathing-tub*, ἐς ῥ' ἀσάμινθον ἕσασα having made sit in it, Od.10.361; ἐκ ῥ' ἀ. βῆ 3.468; ἐς ῥ' ἀσαμίνθους βάντες ἐϋξέστας Il.10.576, al.; ἀργυρέας ἀ. Od.4.128: rare in Att., ἐξ ἀ. κύλικος λείβων from a cup *as large as a bath*, Cratin.234; later, Artem.1.56, *PStrassb.*29.37 (iii A. D.).

**ἄσᾱμος**, Dor. for ἄσημος.

**Ἀσάνα, Ἀσᾶναι, Ἀσᾱναῖος**, Lacon. for Ἀθην-, Ar.*Lys.*1300, 980, al.

**ἀσάνδᾰλος**, ον, *unsandalled, unshod*, Pherecyd.105 J., Bion 1.21.

**ἄσαντος**, ον, (σαίνω) *not to be soothed, ungentle*, θυμός A.*Ch.*422 (lyr.). II. = οὐ σαίνων, Hsch.

**ἀσᾰπής**, ές, (σήπομαι) *not decayed*, Hp.*Epid.*5.27, Arist.*Pr.*909$^{b}$4, Thphr.*HP*3.12.3. Adv. -έως, = ἀπέπτως (acc. to Gal. ad loc.), Hp. *Acut.*16.

**ἄσαρ**, = ἄσαρον (q. v.), Act.1.131, Suid.

**ἀσᾰρίτης** [ᾰσ] οἶνος wine *made from hazelwort* (ἄσαρον), Dsc.5.58, *Gp.*8.6 tit.

*****ἀσαρκ-έω**, causal, *make lean*, Hp.*Vict.*1.35. **-ία**, ἡ, *want of flesh, leanness*, Arist.*HA*493$^{b}$23, Aret.*SD*1.8,16, Luc.*Anach.*25. **-ος**, ον, *without flesh, lean*, opp. σαρκώδης, Hp.*VM*8, X.*Cyn.*4.1, Arist. *Pr.*867$^{b}$34 (Sup.), Opp.*C.*1.474 (Sup.); φύλλον Thphr.*HP*3.11.1 (Comp.); *bare of flesh*, Hp.*Fract.*18; ὀστᾶ *Com.Adesp.*1205; τέττιξ *AP*9.264 (Apollon. or Phil.): Comp., ib.5.101 (Marc. Arg.). 2. *not consisting in flesh*, δίαιτα Epicur.*Fr.*464; τροφή Porph.*Abst.*1.1. II. (ἀ- copul.) *fleshy*, Lyc.154. **-ώδης**, ες, *lean, meagre-looking*, Aret.*SD*1.8.

**ἄσᾰρον** [ᾰσ], τό, a plant, *hazelwort, Asarum europaeum*, Crateuas *Fr.*7, Dsc.1.10, Gal.11.840, Androm.ap.Gal.14.52. 2. = βάκχαρις, Ps.-Dsc.3.44.

*****ἄσᾰρος**, Aeol. for ἀσηρός, Sapph.77 (Comp.). **ἄσᾰρος**, ον, = sq., Hsch.

**ἀσάρωτος** [σᾰ], ον, *unswept*, οἶκος a room *paved in mosaic to look as if strewn with crumbs*, Plin.*HN*36.184.

**ἄσασθαι, ἄσεσθε**, v. ἄω. **ἄσατο**, contr. for ἀάσατο, v. ἀάω, *hurt*. **ἀσαυτόν**, v. αὑσαυτόν.

**ἀσάφ-εια** [σᾰ], ἡ, *want of clearness, uncertainty, obscurity*, opp. σαφήνεια, Pl.*R.*478c, cf. Plu.*Sol.*19, Arr.*Tact.*1.3; personified, Emp.122.4:—later **ἀσᾰφία**, ἡ, Plb.1.67.11; Ion. **ἀσᾰφίη** Hp.*Praec.*14. **-ήνιστος**, ον, *not explained, declared*, Sch.E.*Med.*722 (dub.). **-ής**, ές, *indistinct* (to the senses), *dim, faint*, σημεῖα Th.3.22; σκιαγραφία Pl.*Criti.*107d; *indistinct* (to the mind), *uncertain, obscure*, πάντ'.. αἰνικτὰ κἀσαφῆ λέγεις S.*OT*439; νὺξ διὰ τὸ σκοτεινὴ εἶναι ἀσαφεστέρα ἐστίν by night one sees *less distinctly*, X.*Mem.*4.3.4; ἀ. πέλαγος *AP* 12.156; *inarticulate*, γλῶσσα Hp.*Epid.*1.26.ιγ'; of sounds, Arist. *Aud.*801$^{b}$21; φθέγματα *Epigr.Gr.*1003.6. 2. of persons, *obscure*, διδάσκαλος Pl.*R.*392d. II. Adv. -φῶς *obscurely*, Id.*Cra.*427d; πολεμοῦνται ἀσαφῶς ποτέρων ἀρξάντων *without knowing* which began, Th.4.20.

*****ἀσάω** [ᾰσ], Thgn.593; elsewh. Pass. ἀσάομαι, imper. ἀσῶ, part. ἀσώμενος: aor. ἠσήθην: (ἄση):—orig. *glut oneself, take a surfeit*, and so perh. in Sapph.*Supp.*2.7; but usu., *feel loathing* or *nausea*, caused by surfeit, ἀσᾶται Hp.*Morb.Sacr.*25, *Int.*35; of pregnant women, Arist.*HA*584$^{a}$22: metaph., *to be disgusted* or *vexed at* a thing, c. dat., μηδὲν ἄγαν χαλεποῖσιν ἀσῶ φρένα Thgn.657, cf. 593; ὅταν δέ τι θυμὸν ἀσηθῇς Id.989; ἄσαιο Sapph. l. c.; ἐδίζητο ἐπ' ᾧ ἂν μάλιστα τὴν ψυχὴν ἀσηθείη Hdt.3.41; ἀσώμενος ἐν φρεσί Theoc.25.240; Aeol. ἀσάμενοι [σᾱ] *disgusted*, Alc.35.—Never in good Att.; in later Prose, πολλὰ ἀσώμενοι καὶ ἀδημονοῦντες Ph.*Fr.*74 H.

**ἄσβεσθε**· διέφθειρε (Cret.), Hsch.

**ἀσβεστήριοι**, οἱ, (ἄσβεστος II) *plasterers*, Hsch. s. v. κονιαταί.

**ἀσβέστινον** (sc. λίνον), τό, a *non-combustible* material, dub. l. in Plin.*HN*19.20.

*****ἄσβεστος**, ον, also η, ον Il.16.123:—*unquenchable, inextinguishable*, φλὸξ Il. l. c.; *not quenched*, πῦρ ἄ. D.H.3.67, Plu.*Num.*9; κλέος Od.4.584; γέλως Il.1.599; βοή 11.50; ἐργμάτων ἀκτὶς καλῶν ἄ. αἰεί Pi.*I.*4(3).42; ἄ. πόρος ὠκεανοῦ ocean's *ceaseless* flow, A.*Pr.*532 (lyr.); πῦρ, of hell, *Ev.Marc.*9.43. II. as Subst., ἄσβεστος (sc. τίτανος), ἡ, *unslaked lime*, Dsc.5.115, Plu.*Sert.*17, *Eum.*16; ἄ. κονία Lyc.ap. Orib.8.25.16. 2. a mineral or gem, Plin.*HN*37.146. **ἀσβεστώδης**· *tofus*, Gloss.

**ἀσβέστωσις**, εως, ἡ, *plastering*, Hsch. s. v. κονίασις.

**ἀσβηνοί**· ὄρνιθες, Hsch.

**ἀσβολαίνεται**· *fuscatur*, Gloss.

*****ἀσβολάω**, = foreg., Aesop.59.

**ἀσβόλη**, ἡ, = ἄσβολος, Semon.7.61, Dsc.5.161, Gal.8.378.

**ἀσβολθέν**· μέγα, ὑψηλόν, μέλαν, Hsch.

**ἀσβολοποιός**, όν, *turning into soot*, Eust.1949.36.

**ἄσβολος**, ἡ (ὁ, Hippon.105), more Att. form for ἀσβόλη, *soot*, Ar. *Th.*245, Alex.98.16, Thphr.*Ign.*39, Luc.*Tim.*2.

*****ἀσβολόω**, *cover with soot*, in pf. part. Pass. ἠσβολωμένος Macho ap. Ath.13.581e, cf. Plu.*Cim.*1, Arr.*Epict.*3.16.3.

**ἀσβολώδης**, ες, *sooty*, Dsc.1.68.6.

**Ἀσγελάτας**, epith. of Apollo, *IG*12(3).248.8,27 (Anaphe); cf. Αἰγλάτας:—hence **Ἀσγελαῖα**, τά, festival of Apollo, ib.249.22.

**ἄσδος**, = στήλη λιθίνη, Arc.45.5.

**ἄσε**, contr. for ἄασε, v. ἀάω.

**ἀσέβ-εια**, ἡ, *ungodliness, impiety*, opp. ἀδικία, διὰ τὴν ἐκείνων περὶ μὲν θεοὺς ἀ. περὶ δὲ ἀνθρώπους ἀδικίαν X.*Cyr.*8.8.7; ἀ. εἰς τοὺς θεοὺς Antipho 5.88, cf. Pl.*R.*615c, etc.; also ἀ. ἀπὸ τοῦ θεοῦ Lxx 2*Ki.*22.22; ἀ. ἀσκεῖν E.*Ba.*476; δίκη ἀσεβείας πρὸς τὸν βασιλέα Lys.6.11; ἀσεβείας γράφεσθαί τινα Pl.*Euthphr.*5c: at Rome, *disloyalty to the Emperor* (as θεός), D.C.57.9; of Christianity, Id.68.1: in pl., ἀσέβειαι ἀνθρώποις ἐμπίπτουσι νέοις Pl.*Lg.*890a. *****-έω**, *to be impious, act profanely, commit sacrilege*, Hdt.1.159; opp. ἀδικέω, Ar.*Th.*367; ἀ. ἐς τὸν νηὸν Hdt.8.129, cf. E.*Ba.*490, Antipho 5.93; περὶ τὰ ἱρά, τοὺς θεούς, Hdt.2.139, Antipho 4.1.2, cf. X.*Ap.*22, etc.; πρὸς τὰ θεῖα Id. *Cyn.*13.16: c. acc. cogn., ἀ. ἀσέβημα Pl.*Lg.*910e; ἀγγελίας καὶ ἐπιτάξεις παρὰ νόμον ἀ. ib.941a; περὶ οὗ τὴν ἑορτὴν ἀσεβῶν ἑάλωκε D.21.227. 2. c. acc. pers., *sin against*, ἢ θεὸν ἢ ξένον τιν' ἀσεβῶν A.*Eu.*271 (lyr.); ἀ. θεούς D.S.1.77, Plu.2.291c; τὸ ἱαρὸν *IG*7.2418 (Thebes, iv B. C.); τὸν Καίσαρα *POxy.*1612.23 (iii A. D.):—Pass., ἀσεβοῦνται οἱ θεοί Lys.2.7; ἠσεβῆσθαι πρός τινος D.C.57.9; of households, *to be affected with the consequences of sin*, ὅταν τις ἀσεβηθῇ τῶν οἴκων Pl. *Lg.*877e. 3. Pass. also of the act, ἐμοὶ ἠσέβηται οὐδὲν περί τινος And.1.10; τὰ ἠσεβημένα Lys.6.6. **-ημα**, ατος, τό, *impious* or *profane act, sacrilege*, opp. ἀδίκημα, Antipho 2.1.3, Th.6.27, D.21.104; τὰ περὶ τοὺς θεοὺς ἀσεβήματα Id.16.130. *****-ής**, ές, (σέβω) *ungodly, unholy, profane, sacrilegious*, opp. εὐσεβής, Pi.*Fr.*132.1, A. *Supp.*9 (anap.); τὸν ἀσεβῆ, of Oedipus, S.*OT*1382,1441; σκοπῶν τί ἀ. X.*Mem.*1.1.16: c. gen., θεῶν ἀσεβής *against* them, Paus.4.8.1; ἀσεβέστεροι περὶ θεούς X.*Cyr.*8.8.27; πρὸς ἀλλοτρίους J.*BJ*5.10.5. Adv. -βῶς, Sup. -έστατα D.C.79.9.

*****ἄσειρος**, ον, *without trace*, ἵππος Eust.1734.2.

*****ἀσείρωτος**, ον, *not drawn by a trace* (but by the yoke, cf. σειραφόρος), ὄχημα E.*Ion*1150.

*****ἀσειστος**, ον, *unshaken*, γῆ Max.Tyr.41.4: metaph., εὐδαιμονία Id. 4.5, cf. D.L.8.26. Adv. -τως *unshakably*, Epicur.*Ep.*2 p.36 U., Arr. *Epict.*2.17.33.

**ἄσεκτος**, ον, Dor. for ἄψεκτος, Rhinth.15.

**ἀσελγ-αίνω**, impf. ἠσέλγαινον D.21.31: fut. ἀσελγανῶ Id.24.143: aor. inf. ἀσελγᾶναι D.C.52.31:—Pass., pf. ἠσέλγημαι (v. infr.): plpf. ἠσέλγητο J.*AJ*17.5.6:—*to be* ἀσελγής, *behave licentiously*, And.4.7, Pl.*Smp.*190c; εἴς τινα D.54.5:—Pass., of acts, τὰ εἰς ἐμὲ ἠσελγημένα *outrageous acts*, Id.21.19. **-εια**, ἡ, *licentiousness, wanton violence*, Pl.*R.*424e, Is.3.13, etc., οἱ προεληλυθ' ἀσελγείας ἄνθρωποι D.4.9: joined with ὕβρις, Id.21.1; *insolence*, opp. κολακεία, Phld.*Lib.*p.42 O.; τῶν δημαγωγῶν Arist.*Pol.*1304$^{b}$22: Astrol., epith. of certain ζῴδια, Vett.Val.335.34. II. *licentiousness*, περὶ τὰς σωματικὰς ἐπιθυμίας Plb.36.15.4, etc. **-έω**, late form of ἀσελγαίνω, Sch.Ar.*Pl.*1093. **-ημα**, ατος, τό, *licentious act*, prob. in Plb.38.2.2, cf. Plu. *in Hes.*64, Suid. s. v. ἀστυνάσσα; *vulgar abuse*, in pl., *POxy.*903.21 (iv A. D.). *****-ής**, ές, *licentious, wanton, brutal*, And.4.40 (Sup.), D.2.19 (Comp.); εἰς ἔμ' ἀ. καὶ βίαιος Id.21.128, cf. Is.8.43; σκῶμμα Eup.244: generally, *outrageous*, ἄνεμος Id.320. Adv. -γῶς, πίονες *extravagantly* fat, Ar.*Pl.*560; ἀ. ζῆν D.36.45; ἀ. διακείμενος Lys.24.15; ἀ. τινὶ χρῆσθαι D.9.35. II. *lascivious, lewd*, Jul.*Caes.*315c.

**ἀσελγό-κερως**, ὁ, ἡ, *with outrageous horn*, κριός Pl.Com.210. **-μανέω**, *to be madly dissolute*, Ps.-Luc.*Philopatr.*7. **-ποιός**, όν, *producing licentious persons*, δεκανοί Antioch.Astr.in *Cat.Cod.Astr.*8(3).109.13.

**ἀσέληνος**, ον, *moonless*, νύξ Th.3.22, cf. Plb.7.16.3, App.*BC*5.114.

**ἀσέλῑνος**, ον, *without crown of celery*, νίκη D.C.68.19.

**ἀσεμνολόγητος**, ον, *not solemnly extolled*, Eust.342.39.

**ἄσεμνος**, ον, *undignified, ignoble*, Arist.*Mu.*398$^{b}$4, Ph.2.406, Hdn. 2.7.1; esp. in Lit. Crit., D.H.*Comp.*7, al., Demetr.*Eloc.*189, Longin. 43.1; *indecent*, Eust.1950.63. Adv. -νως A.D.*Conj.*232.9, al.; βίον ἀ. διῆγεν *BGU*1024 vii 22 (iv/v A. D.).

**ἀσεπτέω**, = ἀσεβέω, εἰς θεοὺς μηδὲν ἀσεπτεῖν S.*Ant.*1350 (lyr.).

*****ἄσεπτος**, ον, *unholy*, τὰ ἄσεπτα S.*OT*890 (lyr.); Πρωτέως ἀσέπτου παιδός E.*Hel.*542, cf. *Pae.Delph.*22.

*****ἄση** [ᾱ], Aeol. ἄσα, ἡ, *surfeit, loathing, nausea*, Hp.*Aph.*5.61 (pl.), *Acut.*(*Sp.*)14; ἄση περὶ τὴν καρδίαν *Epid.*7.10; ἄ. πλησμονή Sch.Il. *Oxy.*221 xi 18. 2. *distress, vexation*, Hdt.1.136, Andronic.Rhod. p.570 M.; ἔπαυσε καρδίαν ἄσης E.*Med.*245: pl., μή μ' ἄσαισι μήτ' ὀνίαισι δάμνα θῦμον Sapph.1.3, cf. Alc.*Supp.*14.11; λύπας καὶ ἄσας παρέχειν Pl.*Ti.*71c, cf. *Stoic.*3.100. 3. *longing, desire*, κῆρ ἄσᾳ βόρηται Sapph.*Supp.*25.17. II. = ἄσις, Luc.*Cyn.*1, Poll.1.49, Opp. *H.*3.433. (Cf. ἄω *satiate*.)

**ἀσηκορίς**· ἀδικία, Hsch. **ἀσήκορος**· ἀκηδιαστής, Id.

**ἀσημ-άνθρωπος**, ὁ, 'electron-man', Zos.Alch.p.207 B.; cf. ἀργυράνθρωπος. **-αντος**, ον, *without leader* or *shepherd*, μήλοισιν ἀσημάντοισιν ἐπελθών Il.10.485, cf. Tryph.616; δόμος Opp.*H.*3.361. II. *unsealed, unmarked*, Hdt.2.38, Pl.*Lg.*954a, Hyp.*Fr.*4; = ἀφύλακτος, Hsch. 2. *giving no sign*: hence, *unseen, unknown*, Nonn.*D.*3.95, 5.232; *unintelligible*, ἔπεα ib.10.31. III. ἀσήμαντοι τούτου ὃ .. σῶμα ὀνομάζομεν *not entombed* in this, which we call body, Pl.*Phdr.*250c, with play on signf. II. 1, cf. Dam.*Pr.*161. IV. *uncoined*, χρυσὸς καὶ ἄργυρος App.*Hisp.*23, *Pun.*66. V. Act., opp. σημαντικός, *without significance*, λέξις Diog.Bab.*Stoic.*3.213; φωνή Plu.2.1026a. Adv. -τως Paul.Aeg.3.15. **-αντρος**, ον, *without seal*, *PMasp.*151.10 (vi A. D.).

*****ἀσημείωτος**, ον, *unnoticed*, πηγὴν παρελθεῖν Ph.1.121; ἀσαμήωτον αὐτοῦ τὰν παρουσίαν ἀφέμεν *GDI*3059.22 (Byzantium, i A. D.). II. *without signposts*, of a road, Demetr.*Eloc.*202. III. *not capable of being inferred by signs*, ἀσημείωτα πάντα ποιοῦσι τἀφανῆ Phld.*Sign.*30.

**ἀσημοκλέπτης**, ου, ὁ, *thief of plate*, *AP*11.360.

*****ἄσημος**, Dor. ἄσᾱμος, ον, *without mark* or *token*, ἄ. χρυσός *uncoined* gold, bullion, or plate, Hdt.9.41; ἄ. χρυσίον, ἀργύριον, Th.2.13, 6.8, Alex.69; freq. in Inscrr., opp. ἐπίσημον, *IG*1.170.6, 2.652 *B* 22, etc., cf. Luc.*Cont.*10; also of cattle, *not branded*, *IG*7.3171; of persons, *without distinguishing marks* (e. g. οὐλαί), *PGrenf.*1.27.7, al.; ἄ. ὅπλα arms *without device*, E.*Ph.*1112: generally, *shapeless, formless*, Opp.*C.*3.160. 2. later τὸ ἄσημον (sc. ἀργύριον) *plate, silver*, Lxx *Jb.*42.11, *AP*11.371 (Pall.); μέταλλα ἀσήμου *silver*-mines, Ptol.*Geog.*7.2.17: also, = *electron*, alloy of gold and silver, or an imitation thereof, Ps.-Democr.Alch.p.49 B., etc.:—masc. **ἄσημος**, ὁ, *PLeid.X.*6, al. II. of sacrifices, oracles, and the like, *unintelligible*, χρηστήρια Hdt.5.92.β'; χρησμοί A.*Pr.*662; ἄ. ὀργίων μαντεύματα S.*Ant.*1013. III. *leaving no mark, indistinct,* a. to the hearing, πτερῶν γὰρ ῥοῖβδος οὐκ ἄ. ἦν ib.1004; of sounds and voices, *inarticulate, unintelligible,* ἄσημα φράζειν Hdt.1.86; ἄ. κνυζήματα Id.2.2; ἄσημα βοῆς, = ἄσημος βοή, S.*Ant.*1209. b. *without significance, meaningless,* [τοῦ διπλοῦ ὀνόματος] τὸ μὲν ἐκ σημαίνοντος καὶ ἀσήμου Arist.*Po.*1457ᵃ33, *Rh.*1405ᵃ35; ἄσημα τρίζειν, of a mouse, Babr.108.23; μόριον *Stoic.*2.46; λέξις Simp.*in Ph.*1164.4. c. to the eye, ἄσημον ἔχειν μυελόν Arist.*PA*652ᵃ1: generally, πρὸς τὴν αἴσθησιν -ότερα Id.*Aud.*802ᵃ14. d. generally, *unperceived, unnoticed,* A.*Ag.*1596, S.*Ant.*252; ἀσήμων ὑπὲρ ἑρμάτων *hidden, sunken* rocks, Anacr.38. IV. of persons, cities, etc., *of no mark, obscure, insignificant,* οὐκ ἄ. E.*HF*849, cf. *Ion*8; νὺξ οὐκ ἄ. a night *to be remembered* (being a feast), Antipho 2.4.8; τὸ τῆς πατρίδος ἢ τοῦ γένους ἄσημον Phld.*Sto.Herc.*339.16. V. Adv. -μως *without leaving traces,* Hp.*Epid.*1.1, *Morb.Sacr.*11; ἀ. πορεύεσθαι X.*Cyn.*3.4; ἀ. καὶ κενῶς φθέγγεσθαι *inarticulately,* Theopomp.Hist.250. 2. *ignobly,* οὐκ ἀ. D.S.5.52, Hdn.1.10.4.

**ἀσημότης·** *ignobilitas, Gloss.*

***ἀσήμων,** ον, gen. ονος, = ἄσημος III, S.*OC*1668.

**ἀσημωνία,** ἡ, *farming of trade in silver bullion, BGU*1242 (iii/ii B.C.).

***ἄσηπτος,** ον, *not liable to decay* or *corruption,* Hp.*Fist.*4, X.*Cyn.*9.13 (Sup.), Arist.*HA*521ᵃ1, etc.; ξύλα ἄ., of *Acacia tortilis,* Lxx *Ex.*25.5, cf. Thphr.*HP*4.2.8: Sup., κέδρος Ph.2.147. 2. *undigested,* σιτία Hp.*Aff.*24.

**ἀσηρής,** ές, = sq., *causing discomfort,* Gal.18(2).850.

**ἀσηρός** [ᾰ], όν, (ἄση) *causing discomfort,* Hp.*Fract.*22,33, Plu.2.713a. Adv. -ρῶς Poll.3.99. 2. *feeling disgust, disdainful,* Sapph.77 (Comp.): Medic., *feeling discomfort,* Ruf.ap.Orib.45.30.22.

**ἄσηρος,** ον, (σῆρες) *without worms,* Suid.

**ἄσηστος,** ον, (σήθω) *unsifted,* Diph.Siph.ap.Ath.3.115d, Sor.1.50.

**ἀσθέν-εια,** ἡ, *want of strength, weakness,* Th.1.3, etc.: in pl., ἰσχύες καὶ ἀ. Pl.*R.*618d; esp. *feebleness, sickliness,* Hdt.4.135; ἀ. τοῦ γήρως Antipho 4.3.2, Pl.*R.*330e; σωμάτων Th.4.36, etc. 2. *disease, sickness,* Id.2.49 (pl.), *OGI*244.11 (Daphne, ii B.C.), etc.; δι' ἀσθένειαν *Ep.Gal.*4.13. 3. ἀ. βίου *poverty,* Hdt.2.47, 8.51. 4. in moral sense, *feebleness, weakness,* τῆς ἀνθρωπίνης φύσεως Pl.*Lg.*854a, cf. Arist.*EN*1150ᵇ19; τοῦ ἀκροατοῦ Arist.*Rh.*1419ᵃ18.—Rare in poetry, as E.*HF*269. ***-έω,** *to be weak, feeble, sickly,* ἀ. μέλη *to be weak* in limb, E.*Or.*228; τοὺς ὀφθαλμοὺς ἀ. Pl.*Ly.*209e; ἀ. ἀσθένειαν Id.*Chrm.*155b: abs., E.*Hipp.*274, Th.7.47, *Ev.Matt.*10.8, etc.; ἠσθένησε he *fell sick,* D.1.13; ἀσθενέων *sick man,* Hp.*VM*12 (Phot. says that μαλακίζεσθαι is used of women); ἠσθενηκότα Plb.31.13.7. 2. *to be needy,* Ar.*Pax*636; ἠσθενηκότες, of those *unable to pay* taxes, *PTeb.*188 (i B.C.). 3. c. inf., *to be too weak* to do a thing, *not to be able..,* J.*BJ*2.15.5; εἰς τὸ θεωρεῖν Plot.3.8.4. 4. *decline,* ἠσθένησεν ἡ ἡμέρα εἰς τὴν ἑσπέραν Lxx *Jd.*19.9. **-ημα,** ατος, τό, *weakness, ailment,* Arist.*GA*726ᵃ15, *Gp.*12.27 (pl.); *weakness* of conscience, *Ep.Rom.*15.1 (pl.). **-ής,** ές, *without strength, weak,* 1. in body, *feeble, sickly,* τοὺς ἀσθενέας τῆς στρατιῆς Hdt.4.135, cf. Hp.*VM*12; ἀσθενεῖ χρωτὶ βαίνων Pi.*P.*1.55, etc.; ὁ παντάπασιν ἀ. τῷ σώματι D.21.165; ἀ. περὶ τὸν ὀφθαλμόν Luc.*Nigr.*4; τοὺς ἀσθενεστάτους ἐς τὰς ταλαιπωρίας *least able to bear* hardship, Hdt.4.134; ἀσθενέστερος πόνον ἐνεγκεῖν *too weak* to.., D.23.54. Adv. ἀσθενῶς, ἴσχειν Pl.*Lg.*659e, cf. *OGI*751.8 (Amblada, ii B.C.). 2. in mind, and the like, τὸ ἀ. τῆς γνώμης *the weakness,* Th.2.61. 3. in power, *weak, feeble,* ἀ. δύναμις Hdt.7.9.α', cf. 1.58; τέχνη δ' ἀνάγκης -εστέρα μακρῷ A.*Pr.*514; πόλιν ἑνὸς -εστέραν S.*OC*1033; εἰς ὠφέλειαν ἀ. D.*Ep.*2.15. 4. in property, *weak, poor,* οἱ χρήμασιν ἀσθενέστεροι Hdt.2.88: abs., ὅ τ' ἀ. ὁ πλούσιός τε E.*Supp.*433; οἱ ἀσθενέστεροι *the weaker sort,* i.e. *the poor,* X.*Cyr.*8.1.30, cf. Lys.1.2. 5. *insignificant,* οὐκ ἀσθενέστατος σοφιστὴς Ἑλλήνων Hdt.4.95; *paltry,* ἀ. σόφισμα A.*Pr.*1011; of streams, *petty, small,* Hdt.2.25; of fluids, *of small specific gravity,* Id.3.23; ἐς ἀσθενὲς ἔρχεται comes to *nothing,* Id.1.120. Adv. -νῶς *feebly, without energy,* Pl.*R.*528b; *on slight evidence,* ἀπαγγέλλεσθαι Onos.*Praef.*: Comp. ἀσθενεστέρως, ἐπιθυμεῖν Pl.*Phdr.*255e; -έστερον Id.*Chrm.*172b; -έστερα Th.1.141. **-ικός,** ή, όν, *weakly,* παιδίον Arist.*HA*587ᵃ20, Timo 26.1, Luc.*Tox.*19. Adv. -κῶς, αἰσθάνεσθαι Arist.*Insomn.*462ᵃ20.

**ἀσθενο-ποιέω,** *make weak,* App.*Mac.*9.6. **-ποιός,** όν, *causing weakness,* Archig.ap.Aët.12.1, Sch.A.R.2.205, Sch.Nic.*Th.*158. **-ρρῖζος,** ον, *with weak roots,* Thphr.*CP*4.14.4.

**ἀσθεν-όφθαλμον** ζῴδιον, of the Ram, Rhetor.in *Cat.Cod.Astr.*7.194.2, cf. 1.166.19.

**ἀσθενό-ψῡχος,** ον, *weak-minded,* Lxx 4*Ma.*15.5.

**ἀσθεν-όω,** *weaken,* X.*Cyr.*1.5.3. **-ωσις,** εως, ἡ, *weakness, faintness,* Hp.*Judic.*20.

***ἆσθμα,** ατος, τό, *short-drawn breath, panting,* ἆσθμα καὶ ἱδρώς Il.15.241; ἀργαλέῳ ἄσθματι ib.10; ὑπ' ἄσθματος κενοί A.*Pers.*484; ἄσθματι στρευγόμενος Tim.*Pers.*93; ὑπὸ ἄσθματος ἀδυνατεῖν Pl.*R.*568d, cf. 556d; as symptom of anger, Phld.*Ir.*p.27 W.; *death-rattle,* Pi.*N.*10.74. II. Medic., *asthma,* Hp.*Aph.*3.22 (pl.), etc. III. *breath, breathing,* Mosch.3.53, Luc.*DDeor.*11.2, Philum.*Ven.*36.3; *blast,* ἀρκτῴοις ἄσθμασι *AP*9.677 (Agath.): ἄ. φλογός Coluth.179; κεραυνοῦ Nonn.*D.*1.2. (On the accent v. Hdn.Gr.1.522.)

***ἀσθμ-άζω·** ἀσθμαίνω, *AB*451. **-αίνω,** *breathe hard*: used by Hom. in pres. part., *panting,* as after running, τὼ δ' ἀσθμαίνοντε κιχήτην Il.10.376; *gasping for breath,* of one dying, ὃ γ' ἀσθμαίνων.. ἔκπεσε δίφρου 5.585, cf. 10.496, Pi.*N.*3.48: pres. ind., Hp.*Morb.*3.7, Arist.*Pr.*905ᵇ33: impf., Luc.*DMeretr.*5.4; οὐδὲν ἀσθμαίνων without *an effort,* A.*Eu.*651; ἀ. τι *pant for* a thing, Hld.4.3: c. acc. cogn., ἀ. πυρὸς δριμεῖαν ὁμοκλήν Opp.*H.*4.14. **-άομαι,** = foreg., prob. in *PMag.Leid.W.*12.28. **-ατίας,** ου, ὁ, = sq., Adam.2.41. **-ατικός,** ή, όν, *suffering from dyspnoea* or *asthma,* Herod.Med.ap.Orib.10.8.9, Antyll.ib.6.8.4, Dsc.1.25, Gal.13.106; *panting,* Man.4.274. ***-ατώδης,** ες, = foreg., Hp.*Epid.*2.2.19, 4.21. **-ησις,** εως, ἡ, = ἆσθμα, *Gloss.*

***Ἀσία** [ᾱ], Ion. -ίη, ἡ, *Asia,* Pi.*O.*7.18, Hdt.1.4, 4.45, A.*Pr.*412; γῆ Ἀσία S.*OC*694, etc.:—Adj. ***Ἀσιᾱνός,** ή, όν, *Asian, Asiatic,* Th.1.6, etc.; Ἀ. ῥήτορες Theon *Prog.*2; Ἀ. ζῆλος Str.14.1.41, Plu.*Ant.*2. Adv. -νῶς, ἑστιᾶν τινά D.C.46.30:—fem. ***Ἀσιάς,** άδος, and **Ἀσίς,** ίδος [the latter with ᾰ], freq. in A. and E., never in S., Ἀσιάς being required by the metre in E.*Or.*1397 (lyr.), *Ba.*1168 (lyr.), *Cyc.*443, Ἀσίς in A.*Pers.*270 (lyr.), *Supp.*547 (lyr.), cf. Euph.34: Ἀσιάς (sc. γῆ), = Ἀσία, E.*Tr.*748, *Ion* 1356; also (sc. κιθάρα), *the Asian harp,* Ar.*Th.*120, cf. E.*Cyc.*443, Plu.2.1133c:—also **Ἀσιάτης,** -ᾱτις, Ion. -ήτης, -ῆτις, A.*Pers.*61 (lyr.), E.*Andr.*1, etc.: **Ἀσιᾱτικός,** ή, όν, Th.1.2.8: **Ἀσίηθεν,** Adv. *from Asia, CIG*6336. (Fem. of ἄσιος (q. v.).)

***Ἀσιᾱγενής,** ές, *of Asiatic descent,* D.S.17.77; = *Asiaticus,* cognomen of Scipio, Id.35.33: Ion. **Ἀσιηγενής,** Opp.*C.*1.235.

**ἀσίαρος·** ἐπισκάζων, ἢ ἀσίδαρος, Hsch.

**Ἀσι-άρχης,** ου, ὁ, *an Asiarch,* priest of the Imperial cult in the province of Asia, Str.14.1.42, *Act.Ap.*19.31, *IG*12(3).531, 14.2405, etc.; Ἀ. ναῶν τῶν ἐν Ἐφέσῳ *OGI*525.8 (Halic.):—hence **-αρχέω,** *BMus.Inscr.*481*.240 (Ephesus, ii A.D.), etc. ***-αρχία,** ἡ, *office of* Ἀσιάρχης, *Dig.*27.1.6.14. **-αρχος,** ὁ, = Ἀσιάρχης, *CIG*2990ᵃ (Ephesus).

**Ἀσιᾱτογενής,** ές, *of Asian birth,* A.*Pers.*12, Critias 6.6 D.

**ἀσῑγ-ησία,** ἡ, *inability to keep silence,* Plu.2.502c. **-ητος,** ον, *never silent,* Call.*Del.*286, Nonn.*D.*42.405, al.

**ἄσιγμος,** ον, *without sigma,* ᾠδαί D.H.*Comp.*14; ἄ. ᾠδή, name of a poem of Lasus *without a sigma in it,* Ath.10.455c:—hence **ἀσιγμοποιέω,** *compose such a poem,* ibid.

**ἀσίδα,** ἡ, = Hebr. *hᵃsidhah, stork,* Lxx *Jb.*39.13, *Je.*8.7: cf. **ἄσιδον·** ἐρωδιόν, Hsch.

***ἀσίδηρος** [ῐ], ον, *not of iron,* μοχλοί E.*Ba.*1104; *not made by iron,* αὖλαξ *AP*9.299 (Phil.). II. *without sword,* χείρ E.*Ba.*736; μάχη *sham* fight, Onos.10.4; βίος Max.Tyr.36.1.

**Ἀσιῆτις,** Ion. for Ἀσιᾶτις.

**ἄσικχος,** ον, *not nice as to food,* Plu.*Lyc.*16. II. *not easily causing satiety* or *disgust,* of food, Id.2.132b (Sup.).

**ἄσιλλα,** ἡ, *yoke,* like that of a milk-man, to carry baskets, pails, etc., Simon.163; ἄ. ἐπωμίους ἀνελόμενοι Alciphr.1.1 (prob.).

**ἀσιλλο-φορέω,** *carry a yoke,* Democr.132, prob. in *EM*160.34. **-φόρος,** ον, *carrying a yoke, PLond.*1.44.33 (ii B.C.).

***ἄσιλος,** ον, v. ἀνάσιλος.

***ἀσινής,** ές, *unhurt, unharmed,* τὰς εἰ μέν κ' ἀσινέας ἐάᾳς Od.11.110; ἀσινέα τινὰ ἀποπέμπειν Hdt.2.181; ἀ. ἀπικέσθαι, ἀναχωρέειν, Id.8.19, 116; ἀ. δαίμων *secure, happy* fortune, A.*Ag.*1341; βίοτος Id.*Ch.*1018; ἀσινὴς αἰῶνα διοιχνεῖ Id.*Eu.*315. 2. less freq. of things, *undamaged,* οἴκημα Hdt.2.121.γ'; ἐὰν τὰ ἐπιθέματα.. ἀσινῆ *IG*3.1418, 1419; ὑγιὴς καὶ ἀ. *POxy.*278.18 (i A.D.); of ships, App.*BC*5.98: metaph., κανόνες ἀληθείας Ph.1.215. II. Act., *doing no harm,* Sapph.80, Hdt.1.105, Hp.*Fract.*28, *Schwyzer*197.46 (Crete, iii B.C.); ἀσινέστεραι πηρώσιες Hp.*Art.*61; *harmless,* of wild asses, X.*Cyr.*1.4.7; *innocent,* ἡδοναί Pl.*Lg.*670d; ἀσινέσταται τῶν ἡδονῶν Id.*Hp.Ma.*303e. 2. *protecting from harm,* πόλεως ἀσινεῖ σωτῆρι A.*Th.*826. 3. Adv. -νῶς, Ion. -νέως Hp.*Epid.*1.1, Arist.*HA*617ᵃ3: Sup. -έστατα X.*An.*3.3.3.

**ἀσινότης,** ητος, ἡ, *innocence,* Eun.*VSp.*480 B.

**ἀσιογεῖαι,** αἱ, *mud-walls,* Sch.Il.21.231.

***ἄσιος,** α, ον, epith. of λειμών, Il.2.461, prob. *Asian,* but also expld. as ἰλυώδης, Eust. adloc., or *meadow of Asias* (reading Ἀσίῳ), Str.14.1.45, St.Byz.131.7.

***ἀσίρακος,** ὁ, *locust* without wings, = τρωξαλλίς, Dsc.2.52 codd.: **ἀσείρακος,** Gal.12.366.

**ἄσις** [ᾰ], εως, ἡ, *slime, mud,* Il.21.321, Nic.*Th.*176; ἐκ θαλάσσης Charito 2.2; cf. ἄσις· κόνις, ἢ εἶδος ὀρνέου, Hsch.

**ᾆσις,** εως, ἡ, *singing, song,* Ptol.ap.Eust.1312.41.

**Ἀσίς** [ᾰ], ίδος, ἡ, v. Ἀσία.

**ἀσῑτ-έω,** *abstain from food, fast,* E.*Hipp.*277, Pl.*Smp.*220a; ἀ. ἡμέρας δύο Arist.*HA*594ᵇ20. 2. *have no appetite,* Hp.*Aph.*2.32. **-ία,** Ion. -ίη, ἡ, *want of food,* Hdt.3.52, E.*Supp.*1105 (both pl.). II. *abstinence from food,* Hp.*Acut.*34, Arist.*EN*1180ᵇ9. 2. *want of appetite,* Hp.*Aph.*7.6. **-ος,** ον, *without food, fasting,* Od.4.788, S.*Aj.*324, E.*Med.*24, Th.7.40, Phryn.Com.3 D., etc.; ἰχθύς Pl.Com.29. Adv. -ως *Mantiss.Prov.*1.47: ἀσιτί Lxx *Jb.*24.6. II. *of forbidden food,* εὐωχία ἄ. Ph.2.398 (dub. l.).

**ἀσιχήρ·** δοτικός, Hsch.; cf. ἤσιχερ.

**ἀσιώπητος,** ον, *not to be left unspoken,* τὸ ἀληθὲς ἀ. Eun.*Hist.* p.261 D.

**ἀσκαίρω,** = σκαίρω (with ἀ- euph.), Q.S.5.495 (dub.).

**ἀσκάλᾰβος** [κᾰ], ὁ, = sq., *GDI*3123 (Corinthian vase), Nic.*Th.*484, Ant.Lib.24.3.

**ἀσκᾰλᾰβώτης,** ου, ὁ, *spotted lizard, gecko, Platydactylus mauretanicus,* Ar.*Nu.*170, Arist.*HA*538ᵃ27, 607ᵃ27; cf. σκαλαβώτης, καλαβώτης.

***ἀσκάλαφος,** ὁ, an unknown bird, perh. a kind of *owl,* Arist.*HA*509ᵃ21.

**ἀσκάλευτος** [ᾰ], ον, *unhoed*, Sch.Theoc.10.14. **ἀσκαλεῶς**· ἄγαν σκληρῶς, ἐπιμόνως, Hsch. (i.e. ἀσκελέως).

**ἀσκᾰληρής**, ές, *equilateral*, Democr.132 (prob. ἀσκαληνές, cf. σκαληνός).

**ἀσκάληρον**, τό, v.l. (ap.Ath.) for σκαλίας (q.v.), Thphr.*HP*6.4.11:—also ⊛**ἀσκαλία**, Plin.*HN*21.97.

**ἀσκᾰλίζω**, *hoe*, Phryn.*PS*p.42 B.

**ἀσκάλιστος** [ᾰ], ον, = ἀσκάλευτος, Sch.Theoc.10.14.

⊛**ἄσκᾰλος**, ον, = ἀσκάλευτος, Theoc.10.14:—also **ἄσκαλτος**, ον, Hsch.

⊛**ἀσκᾰλώνιον** κρόμυον *Syrian* onion, *Allium Cepa*, Diocl.*Fr.*120, Thphr.*HP*7.4.7, Pl.*HN*19.101. (Hence Eng. *shallot*, which however is applied to κρόμυον σχιστόν; v. κρόμυον.)

**ἀσκαλώπας**, ὁ, prob. *woodcock*, *Scolopax ruricola*, Arist.*HA*617ᵇ23.

**ἀσκᾰμωνία**, ἡ, = σκαμωνία, *Gp.*12.19.18, *Hippiatr.*31, Suid.

**ἀσκανδάλιστος** [δᾰ], gloss on ἀπρόσκοπος and ἀπρόσπταιστος, Hsch.

⊛**ἀσκανδής**· ἄγγελος, Hsch.; cf. Mandaic *ashganda* 'messenger'.

**ἀσκάνη**· ἀγανάκτησις, Id.

⊛**ἀσκάντης**, ου, ὁ, *pallet*, Ar.*Nu.*633, Luc.*Lex.*6. II. *bier*, *AP* 7.634 (Antiphil.).

**ἀσκαρδᾰμυκτ-έω**, *look without winking*, Sch.Ar.*Eq.*292. **-ης**, ου, ὁ, *one who does not blink*, Hp.*Epid.*2.6.1 (pl.). **-ί**, Adv. of sq., *without winking, with unchanged look*, X.*Cyr.*1.4.28, Luc.*Tim.*14, Gal.7.91, Poll.2.67, v.l. in Ar.*Eq.*292. **-ος**, ον, *not blinking* or *winking*, Ar.*Eq.*292, Adam.1.21. Adv. -τως Eust.756.59, v.l. in Ar. l. c.

**ἀσκᾰρής**, ές, *not hopping* or *skipping*, Hsch.:—also **ἄσκαρθμος**, ον, Id.

**ἀσκᾰρῐδώδης**, ες, *full of ascarides*, Hp.*Coac.*160.

⊛**ἀσκᾰρίζω**, fut. -ιῶ, Att. form of σκαρίζω (with ἀ- euph.), Hp.*Nat. Puer.*30, Cratin.26.

**ἀσκαρίς**, ίδος, ἡ, *worm in the intestines*, Hp.*Aph.*3.26, Arist.*HA* 551ᵃ10. II. *larva of the* ἐμπίς, ib.551ᵇ27.

**ἀσκάριστος**, ον, *without struggling*, Sch.S.*Aj.*833.

**ἄσκαρος**, ὁ, a kind of *castanet*, Poll.4.60, Hsch.; also a kind of *shoe*, Id.

**ἀσκαροφόρον**· φορτηγόν, Hsch.

**ἄσκαστος**, v. ἄσχαστος.

⊛**ἀσκαύλης**, ου, ὁ, (ἀσκός) *bagpiper*, Mart.10.3, *Gloss.*

⊛**ἄσκᾰφος**, ον, *not dug about*, ἄμπελοι Str.11.4.3.

⊛**ἀσκέδαστος**, ον, *not scattered*, τὸ ἓν ἀ. Eustr. *in EN*51.13; *that cannot be dissipated*, Procl.*Inst.*48.

**ἀσκεθής**, ές, v.l. for ἀσκηθής (q.v.), Od.14.255.

**ἀσκεία**, ἡ, (ἀσκέω) = ἄσκησις, Hsch.

**ἀσκελής**, ές, (ἀ- euph., σκέλλω) *dried up, withered, worn out*, ἀσκελέες καὶ ἄθυμοι Od.10.463. 2. neut. ἀσκελές as Adv., *toughly, stubbornly*, ἀ. αἰεί ib.1.68, 4.543; ἀ. αὔτως Nic.*Th.*278:—also ἀσκελέως αἰεί Il.19.68. II. (ἀ- priv., σκέλος) *without legs*, Pl.*Ti.*34a, Arist.*GA*717ᵇ17. 2. (ἀ- copul., σκέλος) = ἰσοσκελής, *even*, of a balance, Nic.*Th.*42.

**ἀσκελόν**· ἄγαν τὰ αὐτά, Hsch.

**ἀσκελοποιός**, όν, (ἀ- priv., σκέλλω, ποιέω) *not allowing to pine*, etym. of Ἀσκληπιός, Tz. ad Lyc.1054.

**ἀσκέπαρνος**, ον, *without the axe, unhewn*, βάθρον S.*OC*101.

**ἀσκέπαστος**, ον, *uncovered*, Dsc.5.114, Antyll.ap.Orib.6.23.10, *Gp.* 7.19.3, *PLond.*5.1722 (vi A.D.).

**ἀσκεπής**, ές, = foreg., *Lyr.Alex.Adesp.*7.17, *AP*5.259 (Paul. Sil.), Nonn.*D.*46.279, al.; γυμνὸς καὶ ἀ. Max.Tyr.2.4. 2. *not covering*, ἀ. νεφέων γυμνούμενος ἀήρ Nonn.*D.*22.214:—also ⊛**ἄσκεπος**, ον, *defenceless*, Amynt.*Epigr.* in *POxy.*662.37; *bare-headed*, Ps.-Luc.*Philopatr.* 21.

⊛**ἄσκεπτος**, ον, *inconsiderate, unreflecting*, οὐκ ἄσκεπτα λέγειν Ephipp. 14.5, cf. Pl.*R.*438a, Plu.2.45d: mostly in Adv. -τως *inadvisedly*, Th.6.21, Pl.*Chrm.*158e, etc.; ἀ. ἔχειν Id.*Cra.*440d; ἀ. ἔχειν τινός Id. *Grg.*501c: Comp. -ότερον Arist.*Pol.*1274ᵃ30, Plu.*Demetr.*1. II. *unconsidered, unobserved*, Ar.*Ec.*258, X.*Mem.*4.2.19; μὴ τὸ μέγιστον ἐπιστήμης πέρι τί ποτ' ἐστὶν ἄσκεπτον γένηται Pl.*Tht.*184a. 2. *unseen, hidden*, γάμοι Opp.*H.*1.773. 3. *too small to be observed, negligible*, ἐν ἀσκέπτῳ χρόνῳ Arist.*APo.*89ᵇ10.

⊛**ἀσκέρα**, ας, ἡ, *winter shoe with fur lining*, Hippon.19, Lyc.855, 1322, Herod.2.32:—Dim. **ἀσκερίσκος**, ὁ, metapl. pl. ἀσκερίσκα Hippon.18.

**ἀσκεύαστος**, ον, *not made by art, natural*, κάλλος Philostr.*Im.*2.9.

**ἀσκευής**, ές, *without the implements of his art*, Hdt.3.131. II. *without furniture*, Muson.*Fr.*14p.71 H.

**ἄσκευος**, ον, *unfurnished, unprepared*, οὐ ψιλὸν οὐδ' ἄ. S.*OC*1029; [τριήρης] *IG*2.804.268, al.: c. gen., ἄ. ἀσπίδων τε καὶ στρατοῦ *unfurnished with..*, S.*El.*36. II. ἄσκευοι, οἱ, *light-armed troops*, Paus.8.50.2.

**ἀσκευώρητος**, ον, *not searched thoroughly*, Str.8.6.23.

**ἀσκεψία**, ἡ, *want of consideration, heedlessness*, Plb.2.63.5.

⊛**ἀσκέω**, *work* raw materials, εἴρια, κέρα, Il.3.388, 4.110; *work curiously, form by art*, [κρητῆρα] Σιδόνες πολυδαίδαλοι εὖ ἤσκησαν ib. 23.743; ἑρμῖν' ἀσκήσας Od.23.198; πτύξασα καὶ ἀσκήσασα χιτῶνα having folded and *smoothed* it, ib.1.439; ἅρμα.. χρυσῷ καὶ ἀργύρῳ εὖ ἤσκηται Il.10.438; χορὸν ἤσκησεν ib.18.592; γόμφοις ἀ. Emp.87: added in aor. part. to Verbs, [θρόνον] τεύξει ἀσκήσας *elaborately*, Il.14. 240; [χρυσὸν] βοὸς κέρασιν περίχευεν ἀσκήσας Od.3.437; [ἑανὸν] ἔξυσ' ἀσκήσασα Il.14.179. 2. of personal adornment, *dress out, trick out*, ἀ. τινὰ κόσμῳ Hdt.3.1; ἐς κάλλος ἀσκεῖ *decks herself*, E.*El.*1073; δέμας Id.*Tr.*1023:—freq. in Pass., σκιεροῖς ἠσκημένα γυίοις *furnished with..*, Emp.61.4; πέπλοισι Περσικοῖς ἠσκημένη A.*Pers.*182; οὐ χλιδαῖς ἠσκημένον S.*El.*452; of buildings, παστὰς ἠσκημένη στύλοισι Hdt.2.169; Παρίῳ λίθῳ ἠσκημένα Id.3.57: abs., οἴκημα ἠσκημένον Id. 2.130; σῶμα λόγοις ἠσκ. *tricked out* with words only, not real, S.*El.* 1217:—Med., σῶμ' ὅπλοις ἠσκήσατο *adorned his own* person, E.*Hel.* 1379, cf. *Alc.*161. 3. in Pi., *honour* a divinity, *do him reverence*, δαίμον' ἀσκήσω θεραπεύων *P.*3.109; ἀσκεῖται Θέμις *O.*8.22. II. *practise, exercise, train*, esp. in Prose and Com., properly of athletic exercise, 1. c. acc. of person or thing, ἀ. τὸν υἱὸν τὸν ἐπιχώριον τρόπον Ar.*Pl.*47; ἀ. τὰ σώματα εἰς ἰσχύν X.*Cyr.*2.1.20, cf. *Mem.*1.2.19; ἐχθρὸν ἐφ' ἡμᾶς αὐτοὺς τηλικοῦτον ἠσκήκαμεν D.3.28:—Pass., σώματα εὖ ἠσκημένα X.*Cyr.*1.6.41; εἰς ἀγῶνα ἄμεινον ἡμῶν ἤσκηνται D.9.52; ἀσκεῖσθαι λέγειν Luc.*Dem.*4; τὴν Κυνικὴν ἄσκησιν Id.*Tox.*27; λόγοις D.C.45.2; ἐν παιδείᾳ Id.60.2; πρός τι D.S.2.54. 2. c. acc. of the thing practised, ἀ. τέχνην, πεντάεθλον, Hdt.3.125, 9.33; λόγους Democr.53ᵃ, 110; μανθάνειν καὶ ἀ. τι Pl.*Grg.*509e; ἀ. παγκράτιον, στάδιον, etc., Id.*Lg.*795b, *Thg.*128e; ἠσκηκέναι μηδεμίαν ἄσκησιν κυριωτέραν τῆς πολεμικῆς Arist.*Pol.*1271ᵇ5: metaph., ἀ. τὴν ἀληθείην, δικαιοσύνην, Hdt.7.209, 1.96; δίκαια S.*OC*913; ἀρετήν E.*Fr.*853, Pl. *R.*407a; κακότητα A.*Pr.*1066 (lyr.), cf. S.*Tr.*384; ἀσέβειαν E.*Ba.*476; τὰ δίκαια Crates Theb.12; λαλιάν Ar.*Nu.*931 (anap.): c. dupl. acc., ἀ. αὐτόν τε καὶ τοὺς σὺν αὐτῷ τὰ πολεμικά X.*Cyr.*8.6.10. 3. c. inf., ἄσκει τοιαύτη μένειν *practise, endeavour* to remain such, S.*El.*1024; λέγειν ἠσκηκότες Id.*Fr.*963; εὐσεβεῖν ἠσκηκότα E.*Fr.*1067; ἀ. γαστρὸς κρείττους εἶναι, τοὺς φίλους ἀγαθὰ ποιεῖν, X.*Cyr.*4.2.45, 5.5.12, cf. *Mem.*2.1.6; ἤσκει ἐξομιλεῖν παντοδαποῖς he *made a practice of* associating.., Id.*Ag.*11.4. 4. abs., *practise, go into training*, Pl.*R.*389c, X.*Cyr.*2.1.29; οἱ ἀσκέοντες *those who practise gymnastics*, Hp.*Acut.* 9; περὶ τὰς βαναύσους τέχνας Plb.9.20.9.

**ἄσκη**, ἡ, = ἄσκησις, Pl.Com.234.

**ἀσκηθής**, ές, *unhurt, unscathed*, in Hom. of persons, ἄψ εἰς ἡμέας ἔλθοι ἀ. Il.10.212; ἀ. ἱκόμην ἐς πατρίδα γαῖαν Od.9.79, cf. Epich.99. 10, Call.*Aet.*3.1.69; ἀσκηθέες (trisyll.) καὶ ἄνουσοι Od.14.255 (v.l. ἀσκεθέες); *sound, healthy*, *IG*4.952.109 (Epid.); ἀ. τινὰ πέμπειν Sol. 19.4; *unblemished*, *IG*5(2).3.5 (Tegea, iv B.C.); = ἀπαθής, θεός Timo 60, etc.; later of things, ἀ. νόστος *safe* return, A.R.2.690; ἀ. μέλι *pure, virgin* honey, Antim.16.2. (Perh. from ἀ- priv., and the root of *scathe*, Germ. *schaden* 'hurt'.)

⊛**ἄσκημα**, ατος, τό, *exercise, practice*, Hp.*Off.*7, X.*Cyr.*7.5.79; τὰ εἰς τὸν πόλεμον ἀ. Id.*Oec.*11.19, cf. *PLond.*3.1164 i 21 (iii A.D.); in warfare, *branch of the service, arm* (e.g. elephants or chariots), Arr. *Tact.*19.6.

**ἄσκηνος**, ον, *without tents, not under canvas*, Plu.*Sert.*12, App.*BC* 5.117.

**ἀσκηπτος**, ον, *that cannot be feigned*, μανία Ph.2.522.

**ἀσκηρά**· εἶδός τι τῶν καστανίων, Hsch.

**ἄσκ-ησις**, εως, ἡ, (ἀσκέω) *exercise, practice, training*, ἐξ ἀσκήσιος ἀγαθοὶ γίνονται Democr.242, cf. Protag.3, Pl.*Prt.*323d, al.; γυμνασίων καὶ ἀσκησίων ἐπιμελόμενοι Hp.*VM*4, cf. Th.2.39; πολεμικὴ X. *Cyr.*8.1.34; ἱππικὴ *IG*2.478ᵇ18: in pl., *exercises*, ἔθεσι καὶ ἀσκήσεσι Pl. *R.*518e, cf. *Plt.*294d. II. c. gen., ἄ. τινος *practice of* or *in* a thing, Th.5.67; ἀρετῆς X.*Mem.*1.2.20; δειλίας ἀλλ' οὐκ ἀνδρείας Pl.*Lg.* 791b. III. generally, *mode of life, profession*, Luc.*Vit.Auct.*7; of a philosophical sect, ἡ Κυνικὴ ἄ. Id.*Tox.*27. 2. of religious sects, *asceticism*, Str.15.1.61, 17.1.29, Ph.1.643, J.*BJ*2.8.10. IV. *adornment*, τῶν τριχῶν Aeschin.Socr.18. ⊛**-ητέος**, α, ον, *to be practised*, X.*Cyr.*5.3.43, Jul.*Ep.*89. II. ἀσκητέον *one must practise*, σοφίαν, σωφροσύνην, Pl.*Grg.*487c, 507d; ποῖα πρὸς ποίους ἀ. Arist.*Pol.*1325ᵃ 13. ⊛**-ητήρ**, ῆρος, ὁ, = sq., Poet.ap.Gal.*Protr.*13 (leg. ἀσκήτορες). ⊛**-ητής**, οῦ, ὁ, *one who practises any art or trade*, ἀ. τῶν καλῶν κἀγαθῶν ἔργων, opp. ἰδιώτης, X.*Cyr.*1.5.11; λόγων D.H.*Is.*2; σοφίης *IG*3.1322; esp. = ἀθλητής, Ar.*Pl.*585, Pl.*R.*403e sq., Isoc.2. 11; Διόνυσος ἀ., title of comedy by Aristomenes. II. *hermit* or *monk*, Ph.1.643. ⊛**-ητικός**, ή, όν, *laborious*, βίος Pl.*Lg.*806a; ἀ. νόσημα *such as is incident to an athlete*, Ar.*Lys.*1085; of persons, Ph.1. 552. Adv. -κῶς Poll.3.145. II. *ascetic*, μελέται Ph.1.646. **-ητός**, ή, όν, *curiously wrought*, νῆμα Od.4.134; λέχος 23.189; χρίματα Xenoph.3.6; εἵματα Theoc.24.140; *adorned, decked*, πέπλῳ *with..*, Id. 1.33, cf. *AP*6.219.3 (Antip.). Adv. -τῶς prob.l. in Simon.157. 2. *to be got* or *reached by practice*, οὐ διδακτὸν ἀλλ' ἀ., of virtue, Pl.*Men.* 70a, cf. X.*Mem.*1.2.23; μαθητὸν ἢ ἐθιστὸν ἢ καὶ ἄλλως πως ἀ. Arist.*EN* 1099ᵇ10. II. of persons, *exercised, practised in* a thing, Ἀθηναίης παλάμῃσιν Simon. l. c. (codd. D.L.); ἀνὴρ ἀ. καὶ σοφός Plu.*Lyc.* 30. ⊛**-ήτρια**, ἡ, fem. of ἀσκητής II, ἀ. γυναῖκες *Cat.Cod.Astr.*7.225. 29, cf. *Anatolian Studies* p.81. **-ήτωρ**, v. ἀσκητήρ.

**ἀσκίαστος** [ῐ], ον, *unshaded*, Onos.10.5, Eust.1550.63. II. *not clouded by rust*, etc., Maria ap.Zos.Alch.p.152 B., cf. ib.182 B.

**ἀσκῐαστ-όω**, *clear from rust*, Zos.Alch.p.183 B.:—hence **-ωσις**, εως, ἡ, ib.217 B.

**ἀσκίδιον**, τό, = sq., Ar.*Ec.*307, Posidon.30.

**ἀσκίον**, τό, Dim. of ἀσκός, Hp.*Liqu.*6, *Aff.*21, Plu.*Art.*12: prov. of *empty threats*, οὐκ ἀσκίῳ μορμολύττεσθαι Crates Com.8.

⊛**ἄσκῐος**, α, ον, *unshaded*, ὄρεα Pi.*N.*6.45 (v.l. δασκίοις); αὐγή, ἀκτῖνες, Ph.1.485, 579. II. *shadowless*, Theopomp.Hist.313, Cleom.1.10, Str.17.1.48, Hld.9.22. III. = ἀσκίαστος II, Zos.Alch.p.183 B. IV. (ἀ- intens.) *dull*, of colour, Thphr.*Sens.*78. 2. ἄσκιος ὕλη· ἡ δασεῖα ὕλη, Hsch.

⊛**ἀσκίπων** [ῐ], ον, gen. ονος, *not leaning on a staff*, *AP*9.298 (Antiphil.), 7.732 (Theodorid.); but ἀσκείπωνι γονῇ γῆρας ἐρειδόμενοι a child *too young to serve as a staff*, *BMus.Inscr.* 2.390.

**ἀσκίτης** [ῐ], ου, ὁ, (ἀσκός) kind of *dropsy, ascites*, Epicur.*Fr.*190, Aret.*SD*1.16, Gal.17(2).670. II. *patient suffering from the disease*, Herod.Med.ap.Orib.10.8.9.

*__ἀσκληπιάς__, άδος, ἡ, *swallow-wort, Vincetoxicum officinale*, Dsc.3.92, Gal.11.840. 2. = ἐλλέβορος λευκός, Ps.-Dsc.4.148 Wellm. 3. = δάφνη, Hsch.

**ἀσκληπιασμός**, ὁ, *bleeding from haemorrhoids*, Sever.*Clyst.*p.35 D.

*__Ἀσκληπιός__, Dor. **-ᾱπιός**, ὁ, *Asclepios*, Il.2.731, *h.Hom.*16, etc.:—hence **Ἀσκληπιάδης**, ου, ὁ, *son of Asclepios*, Il.4.204, al.: in pl., as a name for *physicians*, Thgn.432, Pl.*R.*405d: also **Ἀσκληπίδης**, ου, ὁ, in pl., S.*Ph.*1333:—*__Ἀσκληπιασταί__, Dor. **Ἀσκλᾱπ-**, οἱ, *guild of worshippers of A.*, *IG*2.617*b*, 12(1).162 (Rhodes), etc.:—*__Ἀσκληπιεῖον__, τό, *temple of Asclepios*, Plb.1.18.2, Str.17.3.14; **-ίεια**, τά, *festival of A.*, Pl.*Ion* 530a, *IG*2.741 *A*ᵃ14, etc. (also **Ἀσκληπίδεια** ib.5(1).659 (Sparta)):—*__Ἀσκληπιακός__, ή, όν, Aristid.*Or.*47(23).58, Dam.*Pr.*95:—**Ἀσκληπιάδειος** [στίχος], ὁ, metre *employed by* Ἀσκληπιάδης, *POxy.*220 xiv 9, Heph.10.3: also **Ἀ.**, ὁ, *physician of the school of Asclepiades*, Gal.11.794. (Ἀσκληπιοῦ is for -ιόο in Il.2.731. D. is said to have made it proparox. Ἀσκλήπιος, deriving it from ἤπιος, Plu.2.845b.)

**ἀσκο-δέτης**, ου, ὁ, *string for wineskins*, Nic.*Th.*928. **-δορέω**, *flay a person and make a bag of his skin*, Ps.-Callisth.3.8. **-θύλακος** [ῠ], ὁ, *leathern bag*, Ar.*Fr.*174, Archipp.4, Diocl.Com.3.

**ἀσκόλαχα**· ἀσκαλαβώτης, Hsch. **ἀσκόομαι**, only aor. 1 ἀσκώσατο (sic)· ἠχθέσθη, Id.

**ἀσκόπευτος**, ον, *free from intrusions*, πενία ἀ. οὐσία Secund.*Sent.*10.

**ἀσκοπήρα**, ἡ, *scrip, wallet*, Ar.*Fr.*577, Diph.55.2, prob. in Suet.*Ner.*45.

**ἄσκοπος** (A), ον, (σκοπέω) *inconsiderate, heedless*, Il.24.157, Timo 5, etc.; ὄμμα Parm.1.35; ἄσκοποί τινος *unregardful of..*, A.*Ag.*462 (lyr.). Adv. **-πως** *heedlessly*, Babr.95.39. II. Pass., *not to be seen, invisible*, πλάκες ἄ., of the nether world, S.*OC*1682 (lyr.), cf. E.*Hyps.Fr.*57.21 (lyr.). 2. *not to be understood, unintelligible*, ἔπος A.*Ch.*816 (lyr.), cf. S.*Ph.*1111 (lyr.); πρᾶγος Id.*Aj.*21; ἄ. χρόνος *unknown* time, Id.*Tr.*246; *unimaginable*, ἄ. ἁ λώβα Id.*El.*864 (lyr.); *bewildering, strange*, ἤργασαι δέ μ' ἄσκοπα ib.1315. 3. = ἄσκεπτος, *unconsidered*, Gal.7.432.

**ἄσκοπος** (B), ον, (σκοπός) *aimless*, βέλος D.H.8.86; κίνησις Phlp. *in Ph.*846.25; ἄσκοπα τοξεύειν Luc.*Tox.*62. Adv. **-πως**, εἰκῇ καὶ ἀ. χρήσασθαι τοῖς πράγμασιν Plb.4.14.6; πλανώμενος ἀ. Plu.*Dio* 49; ἀ. λόγους ῥίπτειν Longus 4.31, cf. Ath.Mech.3.9, Cleom.2.4, Phlp. *in Ph.*902.19; οὐκ ἀ. εἰκάζειν J.*AJ*2.2.3, cf. Gal.18(1).768, Alex.Aphr.*Pr.Anecd.*1.

**ἀσκοπῡτίνη** [ῐ], ἡ, *leathern canteen*, Antiph.150, Men.266, Lxx *Ju.*10.5.

**ἀσκορδίνητος** [ῐ], ον, *not stretching one's limbs*, *Com.Adesp.*952.

*__ἀσκός__, ὁ, *skin, hide*, *PFay.*121.9 (i/ii A.D.); but usually, *skin made into a bag*, esp. *wineskin*, οἶνον .. ἀσκῷ ἐν αἰγείῳ Il.3.247, Od.6.78; ἀσκὸν .. μέλανος οἴνοιο 5.265, 9.196; ἀσκὸς βοός, of the *bag* in which Aeolus bottled up the winds, Od.10.19, cf. 45, 47; ἀσκοὺς καμήλων *skins of* camel's *hide*, Hdt.3.9; ἀ. Μαρσύεω *bag made from the skin* of Marsyas, Id.7.26; ἀ. ἀφύσητος Hp.*Art.*47; εἴ μοι ἡ δορὰ μὴ εἰς ἀσκὸν τελευτήσει ὥσπερ ἡ Μαρσύου Pl.*Euthd.*285c; ἀσκοῖς καὶ θυλάκοις X.*An.*6.4.23, cf. Th.4.26; ἀσκοὶ πεφυσαμένοι, of mankind, Epich.246; ἄνθρωποι κενεῆς οἰήσιος ἔμπλεοι ἀ. Timo 11; ἀσκός, of the human *skin*, Ph.2.462. 2. *paunch, belly*, Archil.72; in oracular language, E.*Med.*679, Plu.*Thes.*3. 3. *bellows*, Plb.21.28.15, Ath.10.456d. 4. *bagpipes*, Gal.4.459. 5. prov., *wineskin*, of a toper, Antiph.19: prov., ἀεί ποτ' εὖ μὲν ἀ. εὖ δὲ θύλακος ἄνθρωπός ἐστι Alex.85; "ἀσκός, πέλεκυς" in a child's game, Thphr.*Char.*5.5; ἀσκὸν δείρειν *flay alive*, hence, *abuse, maltreat*, Ar.*Nu.*442:—Pass., ἀσκὸς δεδάρθαι Sol.33.7.

**ἀσκότονοι**· κυνορραῖσται, κρότωνες, Hsch. **ἀσκουρῶτις**· ἄ(ρ)κτος ἡ (cod. ἢ) μικρά Id.

**ἀσκο-φορέω**, *bear wineskins* at the feast of Bacchus, *AB*214:—Adj. **-φόρος**, ον, ibid.

**ἄσκρα**· δρῦς ἄκαρπος, Hsch.

*__ἀσκύλευτος__ [ῠ], ον, *not pillaged* or *stripped*, D.H.11.27, Hld.1.1.

**ἄσκυλτος**, ον, *not pulled about*, Heliod.ap.Orib.50.47.5, Philum. ap.Aët.9.23; *undisturbed*, S.E.*P.*1.71, *POxy.*532.14 (ii A.D.); ἱερὸν ἄ. *IG*12(9).15 (Carystus). Adv. **-τως** *without being mangled* or *hurt*, Eust.1252.55. II. Act., *without causing laceration*, Herod.Med. ap.Orib.10.7.1: Comp. **-ότερον** Sor.1.3.

**ἀσκυροειδές**, τό, = sq., Ps.-Dsc.3.155.

**ἄσκυρον**, τό (also **ἄσκυρος**, ὁ, Hsch.), *St. John's wort, Hypericum perforatum*, Dsc.3.155, Gal.11.829. II. = ἄλισμα, Ps.-Dsc.3.152.

**ἄσκῠφος**, ον, *without cup*, Hippoloch.ap.Ath.4.129f.

**ἀσκωληκόβρωτος**, ον, *not worm-eaten*, *PGrad.*7.11 (iii B.C.).

**Ἀσκώλια**, τά, second day of the rural Dionysia, Sch.Ar.*Pl.*1129.

**ἀσκωλι-άζω**, *hop on greased wineskins at the* Ἀσκώλια, Ar.*Pl.*1129 (cf. Sch.). II. *hop on one leg*, ἀσκωλιάζειν ῥᾷον ἐπὶ τοῖς ἀριστεροῖς Arist.*IA*705ᵇ33, cf. Ael.*NA*3.13, Plu.2.621f, Gal.11.106; also, *jump up and down with legs held together*, Sch.Orib.3 p.689 D. (Signf. II may be original and the connexion with ἀσκός due to popular etymology.) **-ασμός**, ὁ, *leaping on greased wineskins*, Poll.9.21.

**ἀσκωλίζω**, = -ιάζω II, Pl.*Smp.*190d, Phryn.*PS* p.42 B.

*__ἄσκωμα__, ατος, τό, (ἀσκός) *leather padding* or *lining* of the hole which served for the rowlock, Ar.*Ach.*97, *Ra.*364. 2. any *swelling*, such as on the female *breast*, Ruf.*Onom.*92, cf. Poll.2.163. 3. *leathern bellows*, Apollod.*Poliorc.*153.3:—Dim. **-άτιον**, τό, Hero *Spir.*1.39.

*__ἄσμα__, ατος, τό, = δίασμα, *AB*452; cf. ἄττω.

**ᾆσμα**, ατος, τό, (ᾄδω) *song*, esp. *lyric ode, hymn*, Pl.*Pht.*343c sq., Alex.19, Luc.*Salt.*16; ᾆ. μετὰ χοροῦ *SIG*648*B*7 (Delph., ii B.C.).

**ἀσμάρᾰγος** [μᾰ], ον, *noiseless*, Opp.*H.*3.428.

**ᾀσμάτιον**, τό, Dim. of ᾆσμα, Pl.Com.235.

**ᾀσμᾰτο-κάμπτης**, ου, ὁ, *twister of song*, of Trag. and Dithyrambic poets, Ar.*Nu.*333:—hence **-καμπέω**, Tz. in *An.Ox.*3.339.

**ᾀσμᾰτο-λογέω**, *repeat songs*, Artem.1.76. **-ποιός**, ὁ, *composer of songs*, Ath.5.181e.

**ἀσμεναίτατα**, **-έστατα**, v. sub ἄσμενος.

**ἀσμεν-έω**, (ἄσμενος) = ἀσμενίζω, only in Din.1.34 ἀσμενεῖν μεταβολὴν *wish for* a change. **-ής**, ές, dub. l. in Arist.*Phgn.*807ᵇ35. **-ίζω**, *take* or *receive gladly*, τι Plb.6.8.3; ἀγλαΐαν Plot.5.8.12; ἐπιστήμην, λόγους, Them.*Or.*33.364d, 8.107b; τὸν Ἰουδαϊσμόν Porph.*Chr.*27: intr., *to be satisfied with* a thing, τινί Plb.3.97.5; τῇ ἡδονῇ Muson.*Fr.*6 p.27 H., cf. Agathin.ap.Orib.10.7.10, Ph.2.37, etc.; ἀ. εἰ.. Plb.4.11.5: c. part., ἀ. ἐσθίοντες Plu.2.101d; ὡς χρησόμενοι App.*BC*3.40:—Med. as Dep., Aesop.45. **-ισμός**, ὁ, *gratification*, Ph.1.450; a form of ἡδονή, *Stoic.*3.97. **-ιστέον**, *one must take* a thing *gladly*, Hp.*Dent.*25, Gal.8.816, 10.648. *__-ιστός__, ή, όν, *acceptable, welcome*, S.E.*M.*11.85, Plot.6.7.30, Them.*Or.*16.205c; τινί J.*AJ*19.6.4.

**ἄσμενος**, η, ον, *well pleased, glad*, always with a Verb, φύγεν ἄ. ἐκ θανάτοιο he *was glad* to have escaped death, Il.20.350, cf. Od.9.63, Pi.*O.*13.74: freq. in Trag. and Att., ἄσμενος δὲ τἂν .. κάμψειεν γόνυ A.*Pr.*398; ἐκ θαλάσσης ἀσμένους πεφευγότας E.*Hel.*398; ἄ. αἱρεθείς Th.6.12; ἐκάθευδον ἄ. ἥκων ἐξ ἀγροῦ Lys.1.13; ἀσμένας εἰς τὸν λειμῶνα ἀπιούσας Pl.*R.*614e: freq. in dat., ἐμοὶ δέ κεν ἀσμένῳ εἴη *glad* would it make me! Il.14.108; ἀσμένῳ δέ σοι.. νὺξ ἀποκρύψει φάος *glad* wilt thou be when night shuts out the light, A.*Pr.*23; ὥς σφι ἀσμένοισι ἡμέρα ἐπέλαμψε Hdt.8.14; ἀσμένῃ δέ μοι.. ἦλθε S.*Tr.*18; ὡς ἀσμένοισιν ἦλθες Ar.*Pax* 582, cf. Pl.*Cra.*418c, etc. Adv. ἀσμένως *gladly, readily*, A.*Pr.*728, D.18.36, Alex.142, Timocl.14 (this Adv., which is common in later Greek, *Act.Ap.*21.17, etc., has sts. been substituted for the Adj., as in Th.4.21 (v.l.)): Sup. ἀσμεναίτατα (v.l. -έστατα) Pl.*R.*329c; -έστατα ib.616a (though the Adj. makes -ώτερος, -ώτατος, Hp.*Art.*8, cf. Phryn.*PS* p.18 B.). (Not to be connected with ἁνδάνω, since there is no ancient authority for rough breathing ἅσμ-.)

**ἄσμηκτος**, ον, *not cleansed with soap*, Pherecr.195.

**ᾀσμός**, ὁ, = ᾆσμα, Pl.Com.235.

**ἀσμόσσει**· ἀγνοεῖ, ἀναπνεῖ, Hsch.: **ἀσμωλεῖν**· ἀγνοεῖν, *EM*155.33: **ἀσμωλή**· ἀναπνοὴ ὀλίγη, ibid.

**ἀσολοίκ-ιστος**, ον, = sq., Eust.591.9. Adv. **-τως** Id.316.32. **-ος**, ον, *not barbarous*, S.*Fr.*629. 2. *correct, without solecism*, Zeno *Stoic.*1.23. Adv. **-κως** *AB*452. II. metaph., *uncorrupted, unspoiled*, κρέας Eub.7.8; ἀ. παιδιά *not coarse, refined*, Plu.*Cleom.*13; of persons, *unexceptionable*, Phld.*Acad.Ind.*p.52 M. Adv. **-κως** Id.*Vit.*p.7 J.

**ἀσοῦρ** or **ἀσούρ**, = κρατήρ (Phoenician word), Hsch., *EM*155.34.

*__ἀσοφία__, ἡ, *folly, stupidity*, Plu.*Pyrrh.*29, Luc.*Astr.*2; rejected by Poll.4.13.

**ἀσόφιστος**, ον, *not deluded by fallacies*, Arr.*Epict.*1.7.26; ἀ. λόγων παρασκευαῖς J.*Ap.*2.41.

*__ἄσοφος__, ον, *unwise, foolish*, Thgn.370, Pi.*O.*3.45, *Ep.Eph.*5.15, Plu.2.330a: Comp., Them.*Or.*15.185a. Adv. **-φως** D.S.2.29, Lib.*Decl.*2.27.

**ἄσπα**· ἵππος, ἡ ἐγγία, Hsch. (Perh. Persian *asp* = ἵππος.) **ἀσπάζει**· συμπεριπατεῖ, Id.

**ἀσπάζομαι**, Ep. aor. ἀσπάσσατο *Epigr.Gr.*990.9:—*welcome kindly, greet*, τινά Hom., etc.: freq. c. dat. modi, δεξιῇ ἠσπάζοντο ἔπεσσί τε μειλιχίοισι Il.10.542; χερσίν Od.3.35, al.; ἀδυπνόῳ φωνᾷ Pi.*I.*2.25; μεγάλως ἠσπάζοντο αὐτόν *received* him *with* great *joy*, Hdt.1.122, cf. 3.1; παρὰ τὴν πόσιν φιλοφρόνως ἀ. Id.2.121.δ'; εὖ νιν ἀσπάσασθε A.*Ag.*524: freq. with no modal word, S.*OT*596, etc.; esp. as the common form on meeting, Στρεψιάδην ἀσπάζομαι Ar.*Nu.*1145, cf. *Pl.*1042 (v. Sch.), Pl.*Euthd.*273c; αὐτὸν ἠσπάζοντο καὶ ἐδεξιοῦνθ' Ar.*Pl.*752; πόρρωθεν ἀ. *salute* from a distance, Pl.*Chrm.*153b; πρόσωθεν αὐτὴν ἁγνὸς ὢν ἀ. I *salute* her at a respectful distance, i.e. keep away from her, E.*Hipp.*102, cf. Pl.*R.*499a; ἀ. ταῖς κώπαις, of the *saluting* of ships, Plu.*Ant.*76; ἀ. τινὰ βασιλέα *to hail* or *salute as* king, D.H.4.39: metaph., ἀ. συμφοράν *to bid* the event *welcome*, E.*Ion* 587. b. *take leave of*, Id.*Tr.*1276; τὰ ὕστατα ἀ. *take a* last *farewell*, Lys.13.39. c. as a formula in closing letters, *Ep.Rom.*16.22, 23, *BGU* 1079.33 (i A.D.), etc. 2. from the modes of salutation in use, *kiss, embrace*, Ar.*V.*607; ἀ. τοῖς στόμασι Plu.*Rom.*1; of dogs, *fawn*, X.*Mem.*2.3.9, Pl.*R.*376a; *cling fondly to*, ἴσον σ' ὡς τεκοῦσ' ἀσπάζομαι E.*Ion* 1363, cf. X.*Cyr.*1.3.2; ἐγὼ ὑμᾶς ἀ. καὶ φιλῶ Pl.*Ap.*29d: metaph., φιλεῖν καὶ ἀ. τὸ ἄδικον Id.*Lg.*689a. 3. of things, *follow eagerly, cleave to*, ἀ. τὸ ὅμοιον, οἶνον, Id.*Smp.*192a, *R.*475a, cf. S.E.*M.*11.44; of dogs, ἀ. τὰ ἴχνη X.*Cyn.*3.7. 4. ἀ. ὅτι.. *to be glad* that.., Ar.*Pl.*324. 5. c. inf., *to be ready to..*, εὐωχεῖσθαι Philostr.*VA*2.7, cf. 31, *VS*2.25.4. (Act. ἀσπάζω in letters (cf. I. c), *POxy.*1158.18 (iii A.D.), al., cf. ἀσπάζομαι· ἀσπάζω, Hsch.

**ἀσπάθητος** [ᾰ], ον, (σπᾰθάω) *not struck close with the* σπάθη: hence, either *loosely woven* or *not woven* (i.e. of skin), χλαῖνα S.*Fr.*877: generally, *not in close order*, φάλαγξ D.H.16.3.

*ἀσπαίρω, impf. ἤσπαιρον, Ion. and Ep. ἀσπαίρεσκον Q.S.11.104: (ἀ- euph., σπαίρω):—*pant, gasp, struggle*, in Hom. always of the dying (so κραδίη ἀσπαίρουσα must be taken, Il.13.443), περὶ δουρὶ ἤσπαιρ' ὡς ὅτε βοῦς κτλ. ib.571; ζωὸν ἔτ' ἀσπαίροντα 12.203, cf. Od. 19.229, A.*Pers*.977 (lyr.), E.*IA* 1587; νεκροὶ -οντες Antipho 2.4.5; ἀ. ἄνω κάτω E.*El*.843; of an infant, Hdt.1.111; of fish taken out of the water, Id.9.120, Babr.6.5:—but in Hdt.8.5 Ἀδείμαντος ἤσπαιρε μοῦνος was the only one who still *made a struggle, resisted*; ἐβ᾽ ὧν τε καὶ ἤσπαιρον D.H.7.25.—Poet. and Ion. word.

ἀσπᾰκάζομαι, = ἀσπάζομαι, *Com.Adesp*.953:—ἀσπᾰκῶς· φιλοφρόνως, Hsch.

*ἀσπάλᾰθος [πᾰ], ὁ, Ar.*Fr*.749, but more commonly ἡ, as Pherecr. 109 (s.v.l.), Thphr.*Od*.33:—name of a *spinous shrub*, yielding a fragrant oil, = ἐρυσίσκηπτρον, *camel's thorn, Alhagi maurorum*, Thphr.9.7.3, *Od*.33, Dsc.1.20. 2. *thorny trefoil, Calycotome villosa* Thgn.1193(pl.), Arist.*Pr*.906ᵇ11, Theoc.4.57(pl.), 24.89. 3. *Genista acanthoclada*, used as an instrument of torture, ἐπ' ἀσπαλάθων τινὰ κνάμπτειν Pl.*R*.616a.

ἀσπάλαξ [πᾰ], ακος, ὁ, elsewh. σπάλαξ (q.v.), *blind-rat, Spalax typhlus*, Arist.*HA*533ᵃ3, Antig.*Mir*.10, *Stoic*.2.51, Ael.*NA*17.10; ἀσπαλάκων αὐτόχθονα φῦλα Opp.*C*.2.612: prov., τυφλότερος ἀσπάλακος Diogenian.8.25.

ἀσπᾰλία, ἡ, *angling*, Hsch., Suid.; perh. f.l. for -ιεία.

ἀσπᾰλι-εύομαι, *angle*, Suid.:—Act., fut. -εύσω, metaph. of a lover, Aristaen.1.17; ἀσπαλίσαι· ἀλιεῦσαι, σαγηνεῦσαι, *AB*183, may be f.l. for ἀσπαλιεῦσαι. -εύς, έως, ὁ, = sq., Nic.*Th*.704, Opp.*H*.3. 29, al. -ευτής, οῦ, ὁ, *angler*, Pl.*Sph*.218e, Aen.Gaz.*Thphr.* p.16 B. -ευτικός, ή, όν, *of* or *for an angler*: -κή (sc. τέχνη), ἡ, *angling*, Pl.*Sph*.219d, 221a, Gal.*Thras*.30.

ἄσπαλον· σκῦτος, Hsch. ἄσπαλος, ὁ, = ἰχθύς (Athaman.), Id. ἀσπάνιον· πάσσαλον, Id.

ἀσπᾰνιστία, ἡ, *superfluity*, Telesp.44 H.

ἀσπᾰραγία, ἀσπάραγος, ἀσπαραγωνία, v. sub ἀσφ-.

ἀσπάρακτος [πᾰ], ον, *not causing laceration*, τάσις Heliod.(?)ap. Orib.49.4.46.

ἀσπαρίζω, for σπαρίζω, = ἀσπαίρω, Arist.*PA*696ᵃ20, *Resp*.471ᵇ13.

ἄσπαρτος, ον, of land, *unsown, untilled*, Od.9.123; but ἡ ἄ. the sea, Lib.*Eth*.24.4. 2. of plants, *not sown, growing wild*, Od.9. 109, Numen.ap.Ath.9.371b.

ἀσπ-άσιος [πᾰ], α, ον, also ος, ον Od.23.233, Luc.*Nec*.1:—*welcome, gladly welcomed*, ἀσπασίη τρίλλιστος ἐπήλυθε νύξ Il.8.488, cf. 10.35; ὡς δ' ὅτ' ἂν ἀσπάσιος βίοτος παίδεσσι φανήῃ πατρός Od.5.394, etc. Adv. -ίως, ἀ. δ' ἄρα τῷ κατέδυ φάος ἠελίοιο 13.33. II. *well-pleased, glad*, ἀσπάσιοι δ' ἐπέβαν γαίης 23.238; ἀσπάσιον δ' ἄρα τόν γε θεοὶ κακότητος ἔλυσαν they released him *to his joy*, 5.397. Adv. -ίως *gladly*, Hom. with a Verb, to be *glad to*.., as φημί μιν ἀσπασίως γόνυ κάμψειν Il.7. 118, cf. 18.232, Od.4.523, etc.—Ep., exc. in Adv. -ίως *with glad welcome*, A.*Ag*.1555 (lyr.); *gladly*, Hdt.7.152, Jul.*Or*.2.71a. -ασμα, ατος, τό, = sq., esp. in pl., *embraces*, E.*Hec*.829, Ph.2.77, Artem.1.10, etc. II. *thing embraced, dear one*, Plu.2.608e. -ασμός, ὁ, *greeting, embrace*, Thgn.860 (pl.); οἱ ἔσχατοι, οἱ τελευταῖοι ἀ., D.11.4.4, Ph.2.45: generally, *salutation*, *Ev.Matt*.23.7, *Ev.Marc*.12.38, *POxy*. 471.67 (ii A.D.), Gal.10.76, Prisc.p.316 D. 2. *affection*, opp. μῖσος, Pl.*Lg*.919e. -αστέον, *one must welcome*, Id.*Phlb*.32d, Iamb.*Protr.* 5. -αστικός, ή, όν, *friendly*, ἔντευξις Plb.28.3.10; *used in salutation*, δάκτυλος Gal.14.451. Adv. -κῶς, ἐδέξατο τὴν ἀπόκρισιν Phld.*Acad. Ind*.p.41 M. -αστός, ή, όν, = ἀσπάσιος, *welcome*, Hom. (only in Od.), Ὀδυσῆ' ἀσπαστὸν ἔδυ φάος ἠελίοιο 13.35, cf. 5.398, 23.239; κάρτα ἀ. [τὸ πρᾶγμα] ἐποιήσαντο Hdt.5.98; τοῖσι ἡ τυραννὶς πρὸ ἐλευθερίης ἦν ἀσπαστότερον 1.62, cf. E.*Rh*.348 (lyr.), Them.*Or*.15.184d (Comp.). Adv. -τῶς Hdt.4.201, Lyc.1090; τὸ τῆς ζωῆς ἀ. Epicur.*Ep*.3 p.61 U.; neut. ἀσπαστόν as Adv., Hes.*Sc*.42. 2. *to be welcomed*, Pl.*Phlb*. 32d. II. ἄσπαστον, τό, an instrument of uncertain use, *BGU*544. 25 (ii/iii A.D.). -αστύς, ύος, ἡ, Ion. for ἀσπασμός, Call.*Fr*.427.

ἄσπεδος, ὁ, dub. in Epich.42; perh. ἀσπέτους as Adj. shd. be read.

ἄσπειστος, ον, (σπένδω) *to be appeased by no libations, implacable*, D.25.52; κότος Nic.*Th*.367; πόλεμοι ἄσπειστοι, = ἄσπονδοι, Plu.2. 537b, cf. S.E.*P*.3.175.

ἀσπερμί or -εί, *without the right to a loan of seed*, *PTeb*.61.307, 67.97, *PAmh*.2.90.6, etc.

ἄσπερμος, ον, *without seed*, i.e. *posterity*, Il.20.303, Luc.*Am*.35: metaph., καρπὸς λόγου Max.Tyr.31.5:—in literal sense, opp. πολύσπερμος, Arist.*GA*725ᵇ29; of plants, Thphr.*HP*7.4.4.

ἀσπερχές, *hotly, unceasingly*, Hom., who uses only the neut. form as Adv., esp. in phrase ἀσπερχὲς μενεαίνεις Il.4.32; ἀ. κεχολῶσθαι 16.61, al. (ἀ- intens., σπέρχομαι.)

ἄσπετος, ον, Ep. Adj. *unspeakable, unutterable*; mostly in sense of *unspeakably great*, ἄ. αἰθήρ, ῥόος Ὠκεανοῖο, ὕλη, ὕδωρ, Il.8.558, 18.403, 23.127, Od.5.101; ἀλκή Il.16.157; less freq. of number, *countless*, ἄσπετα πολλά Od.4.75; κρέα ἄσπετα 9.162; τρεῖτ' ἄσπετον ye tremble *unspeakably*, Il.17.332, cf. Q.S.11.127; φωνὴ ῥεῖ ἄσπετος flows on *unceasingly*, *h.Ven*.237; ἄσπετος αἰὼν *endless* time, Emp.16.—Chiefly Epic, but found in Lyric, ἄσπετοι μέριμναι B.18.34, and rarely in Trag., θαῦμα S.*Tr*.961 (lyr.); χάλαζα E.*Tr*.78; δρυὸς ἄ. ἔρνος *Cyc*. 615 (lyr.); later Prose, λείας ἄ. πλῆθος f.l. for ἄπλετον, Plb.3.92.8. (ἀ- priv. + root seqᵘ, cf. ἔννεπε, ἔσπετε (*ἐν-σπετε), Lat. *insece*.) A lengthd. form ἀάσπετος is used by Q.S.3.673, 7.193, al.

ἀσπῐδαποβλής, ῆτος, ὁ, *one that throws away his shield, runaway*, Ar.*V*.592.

*ἀσπῐδεῖον, τό, part of *shield*, *IG*2.720*B* i 16 (iv B.C.), cf. *Rev.Épigr.* 1.239 (Naples, ii A.D.): pl., defined as αἱ πτυχαὶ τῶν ἀσπίδων, Hsch. II. part of the *prow of a ship*, Id. III. = ἀσπίδιον (?), *POxy*.473.8 (ii A.D.), *BGU*362 x 6 (iii A.D.).

ἀσπῐδής, v. σπιδής.

ἀσπῐδη-στρόφος, ον, *shield-wielding*, λεώς A.*Ag*.825. -φόρος, ον, *shield-bearing*, of warriors, Id.*Th*.19; κῶμος ἀ. E.*Supp*.390: Subst., Id.*Ba*.781.

ἀσπίδιον [πῐ], τό, Dim. of ἀσπίς, *small shield*, Hermipp.16, *IG*2. 61.34, Men.765, etc. 2. = ἀτρακτυλίς, Ps.-Dsc.3.93. 3. = ἄλυσσον, ib.91.

*ἀσπῐδ-ίσκος, ὁ, Dim. of ἀσπίς, *boss*, Sch.Il.5.743; *wide end of a clyster-pipe*, Cael.Aur.*TP*4.3:—also*-ίσκη, ἡ, *boss, disk*, *Jahresh.* 16 *Beibl*.51 (Athens, iii B.C.), *SIG*²588.31 (Delos, ii B.C.), *Ausonia* 10. 171 (Perga), Lxx *Ex*.36.26(39.18); *small shield*, Ascl.*Tact*.1.2, Hero *Dioptr*.5, etc.; name of a *constellation*, Ptol.*Alm*.8.1: -ίσκιον, τό, *IG*2.733 *A* ii 7, Dsc.3.91, Gal.14.724; and -ισκάριον, τό, Lyd.*Mag.* 1.11.

ἀσπῐδιώτης, ου, ὁ, *shield-bearing, a warrior*, ἀνέρες ἀσπιδιῶται Il.2. 554, 16.167, Theoc.14.67, Plb 10.29.6, *AP*9.116: in pl., = Lat. *scutati*, Lyd.*Mag*.1.9:—so ἀσπῐδίτης [δῑ], ου, ὁ, S.*Fr*.426.

ἀσπῐδό-δηκτος, ον, *bitten by an adder* or *asp*, Dsc.2.34, Vett.Val. 127.20, Gal.14.300. -δουπος, ον, *clattering with shields*, Pi.*I*.1. 23. -ειδής, ές, *shaped like a shield*, Agatharch.105. II. *adorned with serpents*, βασίλειαι *OGI*90.44 (Rosetta). -εις, εσσα, εν, = foreg., Poet.ap.S.E.*M*.1.316. cf. Opp.*H*.1.397; but perh. *shield-covered*, and so of the *testudo, formed by shields*, Id.*C*.1.214. -θήρας, ου, ὁ, *snake-hunter*, *Gloss*. -θρέμμων, ον, gen. ονος, = ἀσπιδοφέρμων, Sch.E.*Ph*.796.

ἀσπῐδο-πήγιον, τό, *shield-manufactory*, D.36.4, Poll.7.155, Lib. *Or*.33.17. -πηγός, ὁ, *shield-maker*, Poll.1.149, Them.*Or*.15. 197c. -ποιΐα, ἡ, *the making of the shield*, Gramm. name for Il.18, Hermog.*Prog*.2, Eust.1154.41. -ποιός, ὁ, *shield-maker*, Poll.7. 155. -τροφος, ον, *feeding on adders* or *asps*, Gal.11.143.

ἀσπῐδοῦχος, ὁ, (ἔχω) *shield-bearer*, S.*Fr*.427, E.*Supp*.1144.

ἀσπῐδο-φέρμων, ον, gen. ονος, (φέρβω) *living by the shield*, i.e. *by war*, ἀ. θίασος E.*Ph*.796 (lyr.). -φορέω, *bear a shield*, Sch.Ar.*Nu*. 984. -φορικός, ή, όν, = sq.: -κή (sc. τέχνη), ἡ, Eustr.*in EN*11. 27. -φόρος, ον, *bearing a shield*, Thd.2*Ki*.11.4.

ἀσπίζω, *shield, protect*, τόπον *IGRom*.4.1349 (Lydia): pf. part. ἠσπικότες Hsch., Suid.

ἄσπῐλ-ος, ον, lit. *stainless*: hence, *faultless, without blemish*, λίθοι *IG*2.1054*c*4, cf. *AP*6.252 (Antiphil.), 1*Ep.Ti*.6.14, 1*Ep.Pet*.1.19, etc.; ἄ. ἀπὸ παντὸς κινδύνου *PMag.Leid.V*.8.11: Comp. and Sup. vv.ll. for sq. in Dsc.2.167. II. ἄσπιλος· χειμάρρους (Maced.), Hsch. -ωτος, ον, = foreg. I, Sext.*Sent*.449, Suid.; *without spots*, Dsc.2.167.

ἀσπί(ν)θιον, τό, prob. a vulgar form of ἀψίνθιον, Hsch.:—also ἀπίνθιον, *EM*183.25.

*ἀσπίς, ίδος, ἡ, *shield*, εὔκυκλος Il.14.428, al.; κυκλοτερής Hdt.1.194; ἀσπίδος κύκλος A.*Th*.489; ὀμφαλόεσσα Il.4.448, al.; opp. Thracian πέλτη and Persian γέρρον, X.*An*.2.1.6, *Mem*.3.9.2; ἀσπίδα ῥῖψαι, ἀποβαλεῖν, Anacr.28, Ar.*V*.19, cf. Hdt.5.95: to estimate a victory, ἀσπίδας ἔλαβον ὡς διακοσίας X.*HG*1.2.3: metaph., οὗτος γὰρ ἡμῖν ἀ. οὐ μικρὰ θράσους A.*Ag*.1437; τὴν ἀ. ἀποβέβληκεν τοῦ βίου Nicostr. Com.29, cf. Lib.*Or*.62.47. 2. collective, *body of men-at-arms*, ὀκτακισχιλίη ἀ. Hdt.5.30, cf. E.*Ph*.78, X.*An*.1.7.10. 3. military phrases, ἐπ' ἀσπίδας πέντε καὶ εἴκοσι τάξασθαι to be drawn up twenty-five *deep* or *in file*, Th.4.93; στρατιὰν τεταγμένην οὐκ ἐπ' ὀλίγων ἀσπίδων Id.7.79; ἵστασθαι ἐπὶ τρεῖς ἀσπίδας Ar.*Fr*.66; ἐπὶ μιᾶς ἀσπίδος in single line, Isoc.6.99; ἐπ' ἀσπίδα, παρ' ἀσπίδα (opp. ἐπὶ δόρυ), *on the left, towards* or *to the left*, because the *shield* was on the left arm, X.*Cyr*.7.5.6, *An*.4.3.26; παρ' ἀσπίδος A.*Th*.624; ἐξ ἀσπίδος Plb.11.23.5; but παρ' ἀσπίδα, literally, beside *the shield*, Il. 16.400; παρ' ἀ. στῆναι stand in *battle*, E.*Med*.250, *Ph*.1001; παρ' ἀ. βεβηκέναι ib.1073; ἐκπονεῖν Id.*Or*.653, cf. *Hel*.734; ἐς ἀσπίδ' ἥξειν Id.*Ph*.1326; ἀσπίδας συγκλείειν (cf. συγκλείω); ἀσπίδα τίθεσθαι *serve in the ranks*, Pl.*Lg*.756a; but θέσθαι τὰς ἀ. pile *shields*, X.*HG*2.4. 12; ἐπειδὰν ἀ. ψοφῇ when the *shields* ring, i.e. when two bodies of men meet in a charge, Id.*An*.4.3.29; ἀσπίδα ἀναδέξαι, ἆραι, as a signal, Hdt.6.115, X.*HG*2.1.27. 4. of a round, flat bowl, Aristopho 14. 5. *boss* on a door, *IG*4.1484.79 (Epid.). II. *asp, Egyptian cobra, Coluber haie*, Hdt.4.191, Men.702, Nic.*Th*.158, Ph.2.570, Ael.*NA*10.31; a play on signff. I and II, Ar.*V*.23. 2. *ornament* in this form, *OGI*90.43 (Rosetta).

ἀσπ-ιστήρ, ῆρος, ὁ, = sq., S.*Aj*.565, E.*Heracl*.277. -ιστής, οῦ, ὁ, *one armed with a shield, warrior*, Hom. (in Il.) always in gen. pl. ἀσπιστάων, Il.4.90, al.:—as Adj., ἀσπισταὶ μόχθοι τευχέων, i.e. the *shield* of Achilles, E.*El*.444 (dub.l.). -ιστικός, ή, όν, *composed of warriors*, φάλαγξ D.H.20.3. -ίστωρ, ορος, ὁ, = ἀσπιστής, κλόνοι ἀσπίστορες turmoil *of shielded warriors*, A.*Ag*.404 (lyr.).

ἀσπλαγχν-έω, *to be unmerciful*, Aq., Th.*Jb*.41.2. -ος, ον, *without bowels*, or rather, *without heart*: metaph., *dastard*, S.*Aj*.472; *unsympathetic, merciless*, Chrysipp.*Stoic*.2.249. Adv. -νως Hsch. s.v. ἀνηλεῶς. II. *not eating* σπλάγχνα, Pl.Com.113.

ἀσπλήνις· βοτάνης εἶδος, Hsch.

ἄσπληνον, τό (and -ος, ὁ, Dsc.3.134), (ἀ- euph., σπλήν) *miltwaste, Asplenium Ceterach*, supposed to be a cure for the *spleen*, Dsc. l.c., Zopyr.ap.Orib.14.50.1. 2. = ἄκορον, Dsc.1.2.

**ἄσπληνος,** ον, *spleenless*, Aët.15.14. 2. ἄσπληνος, ὁ, = κισσός, Ps.-Dsc.2.179.

**ἀσπόλην·** ἀρίστην, Hsch.

**ἀσπονδ-εί** (also **-ί,** *SIG*110 (Rhodes, v B.C.), 187 (Cnidus, iv B.C.), Adv. of ἄσπονδος :—*without truce, implacably*, πολεμεῖν Ph.2.195; φονᾶν ib.423. II. of peace, *without formal treaty*, ἀσυλεὶ καὶ ἀ. *SIG*168.9 (Erythrae, iv B.C.), *IPE*2.1 (Panticapaeum, iv B.C.), etc. **-ία,** ἡ, *being without truce* or *treaty*, *IG*2$^{2}$.28, Poll.8.139. II. *implacability*, Lib.*Vit.*1.22 (–εία codd.). ®**-ος,** ον, *without* σπονδή or *drink-offering* : hence, I. of a god, *to whom no drink-offering is poured*, ἄ. θεός, i.e. death, E.*Alc.*424. II. *without a regular truce* (ratified by σπονδαί), ἀνοκωχή Th.5.32; of persons, *without making a truce*, ἄ. ἀπιέναι Id.3.111, cf. 113; ἀσπόνδους τοὺς νεκροὺς ἀνελέσθαι take up their dead *without leave asked*, Id.2.22; τὸ εὐπρεπὲς ἄσπονδον the specious plea *of neutrality*, Id.1.37. 2. *admitting of no truce, implacable*, ἄσπονδόν τ' Ἄρη (ἀράν codd.) A.*Ag.*1235 (Pors.); πόλεμος D.18.262, Plb.1.65.6, etc.; ἔχθρα Plu.*Per.*30; ἀσπόνδοισι νόμοισιν ἔχθραν συμβάλλειν E.*El.*905 (lyr.); of persons, *implacable*, 2*Ep.Ti.*3.3. Adv. -δως, ἔχειν Ph.*Fr.*24H.

**ἀσπορ-έω,** *to be unsown*, of land, *PTeb.*61$^{b}$34 (ii B.C.), etc.; ἀσπορίσαι, written for -ῆσαι, Wilcken *Chr.*11*A*8. **-ία,** ἡ, *barrenness*, Man.4.585. ®**-ος,** ον, = ἄσπαρτος, χώρα D.19.123, *IG*2.379.9, Plu.*Alex.*66, *PRyl.*133.22 (i A.D.), etc. II. of plants, *unsown, growing without cultivation*, Luc.*Rh.Pr.*8, Nic.*Fr.*74.58. III. *begotten without impregnation*, of Hephaestus, Nonn.*D.*9.229; but, *producing without impregnation*, ἰλύς ib.40.433. IV. *barren*, Luc.*Am.*28, Nonn.*D.*2.221, al.; *not having issue*, ib.40.119. 2. Act., *preventing production*, αὐχμός ib.39.139.

**ἀσπούδ-αστος,** ον, *not zealously pursued* or *courted*, γυνή E.*Fr.*501; ἀσπούδαστα, τά, *matters of no interest*, Hp.*Ep.*17. 2. *not to be sought for, mischievous*, σπεύδειν ἀσπούδαστα E.*Ba.*913, *IT* 202. II. Act., *not in earnest*, τὸ ἀ. *want of earnestness*, περί τι D.H.5.72. Adv. -τως *carelessly*, Ael.*NA*10.30, *PFlor.*187.3 (iii A.D.). **-ί** [ῑ] or **-εί,** Adv. *without effort* or *trouble*, Il.8.512, 15.476; *without a struggle, ignobly*, μὴ μὰν ἀσπουδί γε..ἀπολοίμην 22.304, cf. Arr.*An.*6.9.5; *carelessly*, D.C.54.18. **-ος,** ον, *without ambition*, Eup.234. 2. = ἀσπούδαστος 2, *Stoic.*3.38.

**ἀσπράτουρα,** ἡ, (*asper*) *rough*, i.e. *unworn, coin*, *OGI*484.25 (Pergam.); cf. κόλλυβος· *aspratura*, *Gloss.*

**ἄσπρις,** ἡ, *Turkey oak, Quercus Cerris*, Thphr.*HP*3.8.7.

®**ἄσπρος,** α, ον, = Lat. *asper*, Ael.*NA*1.26. II. ἄ. γράμματα *invisible* writing, *Cat.Cod.Astr.*1.108 (the signf. *white* is very late); ἄσπρον, τό, *white of an egg*, [Gal.]14.560. III. name of an *ingredient of incense*, Aët.16.146, 148.

®**ἄσσα,** Ion. for ἅτινα, neut. pl. of ὅστις, Il.10.208, al., Hdt.1.47, al.; Att. **ἅττα** Pl.Com.49, etc. II. **ἄσσα,** Ion. for τινά, Att. **ἄττα,** *something, some*, Hom. only once, ὁπποῖ' ἄσσα *what sort*, Od.19.218; πόσ' ἄττα; Ar.*Ra.*173; δείν' ἄ. ib.925; οἶ' ἄττα βαΰζει Cratin.6, etc.: with numerals, δύ' ἄττα ὀνόματα, τρία ἄττα γένη, Pl.*Sph.*255c, *Ly.*216d: added to a temporal Conj., πηνίκ' ἄττα..; Ar.*Av.*1514, etc. (ἄσσα (ἄττα) arises from false division of groups like ὁποῖά σσα where σσα = τι̯-α, neut. pl. of τις, cf. Megarian σά.)

**ἀσσαριαῖος,** α, ον, *at the rate of* 12 *asses per denarius per month*, τόκος *BMus.Inscr.*481*.66 (Ephesus, ii A.D.).

**ἀσσάριον,** τό, (Lat. *assarius* (sc. *nummus*)), D.H.9.27, *SIG*$^{2}$869.5 (Calymna), *OGI*484.9, al. (Pergam., ii A.D.), Plu.*Cam.*13, *Ev.Matt.*10.29. II. a sort of *valve*, Hero *Spir.*1.10.

**ἀσσέως·** ἐπὶ σοῦ, Hsch. (Fort. ἆος· ἕως, ⟨μ⟩έ⟨χρ⟩ις οὗ.)

**ἀσσιδάριος,** ὁ, = *essedarius*, Artem.2.32.

**ἄσσιος·** προκόλπιος, Hsch.

®**ἆσσον** (Dor. **ἄσσιον** acc. to Eust.1643.32), Adv. Comp. of ἄγχι :—*nearer*, esp. of hostile approach, ἆσσον ἴτ' Il.1.567, al., cf. Hes.*Th.*748; τείχεος ἆ. ἴσαν Il.22.4, cf. Hdt.4.3, Ar.*Eq.*1306; simply of approach, γυναῖχ' ὁρῶ στείχουσαν ἡμῶν ἆ. S.*OC*312, cf. *El.*900; of a woman, ἥτις ἀνδρῶν ἆ. οὐκ ἐλήλυθεν Ar.*Eq.*1306; δίφρον ἆ. ἕλκεται πυρός Semon.7.26: c. dat., S.*OC*722: with double Comp., ἕρποντι μᾶλλον ἆσσον Id.*Ant.*1210: Sup. ἄσσιστα A.*Fr.*6; ἄσιστα *IG*5(2).159.17 (Tegea), *Michel* 1334 (Elis, iv B.C.). II. hence new Comp. **ἀσσοτέρω,** with or without gen., Od.19.506, 17.572; later Comp. Adj. **ἀσσότερος,** = ἐγγύτερος, Arat.878: Sup. Adv. ἀσσοτάτω *AP*9.430 (Crin.): Sup. Adj. ἀσσότατος ib.6.345 (Id.).

**Ἀσσύριοι** [ῠ], οἱ, *the Assyrians*, Hdt.1.193, al.:—**Ἀσσυρία,** Ion. **-ίη** (sc. γῆ), ἡ, *their country*, Id.2.17, etc.:—®**Ἀσσύριος,** α, ον, as an Adj., Theoc.2.162, al.; later **Ἀσσυρικός,** ή, όν, St.Byz., al.

**ἀσσύτεροι,** = ἐπασσύτεροι, Opp.*C.*4.121, 202; cf. **ἀσσυτία·** ἄλλα ἐπ' ἄλλοις, Hsch.

**ᾄσσω,** Att. contr. for ἀΐσσω.

**ἀσταγανά·** ἱμάς, Hsch.

®**ἀστᾰγής,** ές, *not trickling*, ἀ. κρύσταλλος *hard-frozen* ice, dub. l. in S.*Fr.*149.4 (prob. εὐπαγῆ). II. *not merely trickling*, i.e. *gushing, in a stream*, A.R.3.805, Nic.*Th.*307.

**ἀστᾰθής,** ές, (ἵσταμαι) *unsteady, unstable*, κινήσεις Phld.*Ir.*p.26W.; αὖραι *AP*10.74 (Paul. Sil.), cf. Nonn.*D.*8.140, al.; διάνοια Lxx 3*Ma.*5.39.

**ἀστάθμ-ευτος,** ον, *not encamped*, App.*BC*2.74. **-ητος,** ον, *unsteady, unstable*, ἀστέρες, = πλανῆται, X.*Mem.*4.7.5; of persons, ὁ δῆμος -ότατον πρᾶγμα D.19.136, cf. Ar.*Av.*169, Pl.*Ly.*214d; of life, ἀ. αἰών E.*Or.*981 (lyr.); τὸ ἀ. τοῦ μέλλοντος *the uncertainty* of.., Th.4.62; τῆς συμφορᾶς Id.3.59; τύχης -ότερον οὐδέν Ph.2.85. Adv. -τως D.Chr.4.122. **-ος,** ον, *unweighed, without record of weight*, *IG*1.121.4, al., *Epigr.Gr.*805.

**ἀσταίνει·** δυσπαθεῖ, ἁμαρτάνει, μοχθεῖ, Hsch.

®**ἀστακός,** ὁ, *the smooth lobster*, Philyll.13, Arist.*HA*526$^{a}$11, 549$^{b}$14, Matro *Conv.*66, Archestr.*Fr.*24.1; ὁ ἐν τοῖς ποταμοῖς ἀ. *the* river *cray-fish*, Arist.*HA*530$^{a}$28. II. *hollow of the ear*, Poll.2.85. (By assimilation from ὀστακός, the Att. form acc. to Ath.3.105b.)

**ἀστακτ-ί,** Adv. of sq., *not in drops*, i.e. *in floods*, S. (who has -ῑ in *OC*1646, -ῐ 1251), Pl.*Phd.*117c. **-ος,** ον, = ἀσταγής II, E.*IT*1242 (lyr.), Orph.*Fr.*47.

**ἀστάλακτος** [τᾰ], ον, *not damp*, ἀήρ Plu.*Crass.*4.

**ἀστάλη,** ἡ, *polypus in the nose*, Hsch. 2. = σκώληξ οὐρὰν ἔχων, Id.

**ἀστᾰλής,** ές, (στέλλομαι) *unarmed, unclad*, Call.*Fr.*266.

**ἀσταλύζω,** *weep and sob*, Hsch. (-ύχειν cod.).

®**ἀστάνδης,** ου, ὁ, *courier*, Plu.*Alex.*18, 2.326f; cf. Armen. *astandel* 'wander'.

®**ἀστᾰσία,** ἡ, *unsteadiness, inconstancy*, Man.1.19: pl., Vett.Val.38.3.

**ἀστᾰσίαστος** [ῐ], ον, *not torn by faction*, Ἀττική Th.1.2; στρατός App.*Hisp.*72; βίος Eus.Mynd.26. 2. *not liable to disturbance*, νομή *Sammelb.*5174 (iv A.D.), etc. II. of persons, *free from faction* or *party-spirit*, Lys.2.55, Pl.*R.*459e, etc.; of forms of government, Arist.*Pol.*1302$^{a}$9. Adv. -τως D.S.17.54, Herm. *in Phdr.*p.186A.: Comp., D.C.52.30: Sup. -ότατα Pl.*R.*520d.

**ἀστᾰταίνω,** = sq., Gal.19.493.

**ἀστᾰτέω,** *to be never at rest*, πόλοιο φορὰν..-έουσαν *App.Anth.*3.146.4 (Theon); of the sea, Plu.*Crass.*17; βλέμμα ἀστατοῦν *Hippiatr.*3. 2. *to be unsettled, to be a wanderer*, 1*Ep.Cor.*4.11; *to be inconstant*, περὶ τοὺς γάμους Vett.Val.116.30.

®**ἄστᾱτοι,** οἱ, = Lat. *hastati*, Plb.6.23.1.

®**ἄστᾰτος,** ον, (ἵσταμαι) *never standing still, unresting*, τὸ κύκλῳ σῶμα Arist.*Metaph.*1073$^{a}$31; ἄ. τροχός Mesom.*Nem.*7. Adv. -τως, φορεῖσθαι Ph.1.181, cf. Vett.Val.27.1. 2. *unsteady, unstable*, τύχη Epicur.*Ep.*3p.65U., cf. Phld.*Rh.*1.166S. (Sup.), Ph.1.230, al., Diog.Oen.18, Diogenian.Epicur.2.60, Plu.2.103f; of persons, ἄ. τὴν διάνοιαν Onos.3.3; ἄ. αἰών *IG*7.2543; θνητῶν βίος *Epigr.Gr.*699, cf. Ph.1.651; of a house, *ruinous*, *PLond.ined.*2194. 3. *uncertain*, θεωρία Plb.6.57.2. 4. Act., *making it impossible to stand*, πόνος, πάθος, Luc.*Ocyp.*36, 71. II. *unweighed*, *IG*1.32*B*25, al., Nic.*Th.*602.

**ἀστᾰφῐδίτης,** ου, ὁ, fem. **-ῖτις,** ιδος, *of raisins*, ἀσταφιδῖτις ῥώξ bunch *of raisins*, *AP*9.226 (Zon.).

®**ἀστᾰφίς,** ίδος, ἡ, sg. as collect. noun, *dried grapes, raisins*, *IG*5(1).1.13 (Tegea, v B.C.), Hdt.2.40, Alex.127.4, etc.: pl., ἡ Ῥόδος ἀσταφίδας [παρέχει] Hermipp.63.16, cf. X.*An.*4.4.9, Arist.*HA*595$^{b}$10; ἀσταφίδος οἶνος *raisin*-wine, Pl.*Lg.*845b: **ὀστᾰφίς,** v.l. ap.Phot. as in Cratin.121 (pl.), Nicopho 21; **στᾰφίς,** Hp.*Acut.*64, Theoc.27.9, etc. II. = σταφὶς ἀγρία, Ps.-Dsc.4.152, Gal.11.842, Plin.*HN*23.17. (ἀσταφίς is prob. by assimilation from ὀσταφίς; cf. ἀστακός.)

**ἀστᾰφῠλῖνος,** = σταφυλῖνος, Diocl.*Fr.*123.

®**ἀστάφῠλος** [ᾰ], ον, *without grapes*, χῶρος Aus.*Ep.*12.24.

**ἄστᾰχυς,** υος, ὁ, (στάχυς with prothetic α) :—*ear of corn*, Il.2.148, Hdt.5.92.ζ', Call.*Cer.*20, etc.: metaph., βοστρύχων ἀστάχυες Philostr.*Im.*1.7, cf. Luc.*Charid.*3. II. *bandage*, Gal.18(1).813.

®**ἀστέγαστος,** ον, *uncovered*, ἀγγεῖον Gal.17(2).153: of a ship, *undecked*, Antipho 5.22, cf. Apollod.*Poliorc.*185.10; *roofless*, *PGen.*11.7 (iv A.D.); διὰ τὸ ἀ. from their *having no shelter*, Th.7.87.

**ἀστεγής,** f.l. for ἀσταγής, δάκρυ *App.Anth.*3.198.

**ἄστεγος,** ον, (στέγη) *without roof, houseless*, Ps.-Phoc.24, Lxx *Is.*58.7, App.*Hisp.*78; *unprotected, exposed*, Ph.1.574. II. (στέγω) Act., *not holding*: metaph., ἄ. χείλεσι *unable to keep* one's mouth *shut, given to prating*, Lxx *Pr.*10.8; στόμα ἄ. ib.26.28.

**ἀστειεύομαι,** = sq., Sch.Ar.*Ach.*1058, *Pax*370, Sch.Arat.956.

**ἀστεΐζομαι,** *write* or *talk wittily* or *eloquently*, Str.13.4.11, J.*Ap.*2.9, Demetr.*Eloc.*149, Plu.*Marc.*21; *talk speciously*, Ph.2.123 :—Act. in St.Byz. s.v. ἄστυ.

**ἀστειο-λογία,** ἡ, *clever talking, wit*, Arist.*Rh.Al.*1436$^{a}$20 (pl.), M.Ant.1.7. **-μελής,** ές, *with graceful limbs*, Heph.Astr.1.1. **-ρρημονέω·** ἀστεΐζομαι, Zonar.

®**ἀστεῖος,** α, ον, also ος, ον Diph.73: (ἄστυ) :—*of the town* (but in the literal sense ἀστικός is used). II. *town-bred, polite*, Pl.*Phd.*116d; opp. ἄγροικος, Plu.*Mar.*3; γένοιτ' ἀστεῖος οἰκῶν ἐν πόλει Alc.Com.26; *charming*, Isoc.2.34. 2. of thoughts and words, *refined, elegant, witty*, διάλεκτον ἀστείαν ὑποθηλυτέραν, opp. ἀνελεύθερον ὑπαγροικοτέραν, Ar.*Fr.*685; ἀστεῖόν τι λέξαι Id.*Ra.*901; ἀστεῖον λέγεις (where there is a play on the double sense, *witty* and *popular*) Id.*Nu.*204; ἀ. καὶ δημωφελεῖς οἱ λόγοι Pl.*Phdr.*227d; ἀστεῖον εἰπεῖν *Com.Anon.*248 Mein., cf. Axiop.1.14; ἀστειοτάτας ἐπινοίας Ar.*Eq.*539; of persons, οἱ ἀ. *the wits*, Pl.*R.*452d; τὰ ἀ. *witty sayings, witticisms*, Arist.*Rh.*1411$^{b}$21, al. Adv. -ως J.*AJ*12.4.4, Plu.2.123f, Luc.*Nigr.*13. 3. as a general word of praise, of things and persons, *pretty, charming*, βοσκήματε Ar.*Ach.*811; ἑορτή Pl.*Grg.*447a; ἀ. καὶ εὐήθης Id.*R.*349b, cf. *Phdr.*242e, Hp.*Ep.*13; ἐστὶ γοῦν ἁπλῆ τις;—ἀστεία μὲν οὖν Anaxil.21; ἀστεῖόν [ἐστι] ὅτι ἐρυθριᾷς it is *charming* to see you blush, Pl.*Ly.*204c; ἀστεῖον πάνυ εἰ.. Men.*Sam.*149. b. ironically, ἀ. κέρδος a *pretty* piece of luck, Ar.*Nu.*1064; ἀστεῖος εἶ Diph.73. 4. of outward appearance, *pretty, graceful*, Lxx *Ex.*2.2, al.; οἱ μικροὶ ἀ. καὶ σύμμετροι, καλοὶ δ' οὔ Arist.*EN*1123$^{b}$7; *handsome*, Lxx *Jd.*3.17 (of Eglon): in Comedy, of *dainty* dishes, κραμβίδιον, κρεΐσκον, Antiph.6, Alex.189. 5. *good* of its kind, αἷμα Hp.*Alim.*44; ἐλλέβορος Str.9.3.3; οἶνος Plu.2.620d; of persons, *good*, Ph.1.97, Plu.*Them.*5; ἀστεῖα *good qualities*, opp. φαῦλα, Demetr.*Eloc.*114. Adv. -είως *honourably*, πράττων Lxx 2*Ma.* 12.43, cf. Ph.1.244.

**ἀστειοσύνη**, ἡ, = sq., Lib.*Or.*11.154, Chor. in *Rev.Phil.*1.81.

***ἀστειότης**, ητος, ἡ, *prettiness, daintiness* of person, Vett.Val.161.17; *politeness, wit*, μακαρισμὸς καὶ ἀ. Andronic.Rhod.p.570M., cf. Lib.*Or.*11.270, Sch.Ar.*Pax* 370.

**ἄστειπτος**, ον, v. ἄστιπτος.

**ἀστέ-ϊσμα**, ατος, τό, *witticism*, Tz.*H.*4.780. ***-ϊσμός**, ὁ, *wit*, D.H.*Dem.*54, Demetr.*Eloc.*128 (pl.), 130, Phld.*Rh.*1.181 S.: pl., *forms of wit*, Longin.34.2, Philostr.*VS*1.25.9; esp. of ironical self-depreciation, *mock-modesty*, Phld.*Acad.Ind.*p.52M., Alex.*Fig.*1.18, Trypho *Trop.*24; = παράλειψις, Hdn.*Fig.*p.98S.

**ἄστεκτος**, ον, (στέγω) *insufferable*, Hsch., A.*Fr.*224 ap.*AB*456 (Hsch. ἄστερκτα), Paul.Aeg.5.16, Dsc.*Ther.*13. Adv. -τως Hsch.

**ἀστέλεφος**, ὁ, *leathern case for a lyre*, Hsch.:—also **ἀστελοφοῦν**· δέρμα τὸ εἰς τὰ ἄκρα, Id.

**ἀστελέχης**, ες, *without main stem*, Thphr.*HP*1.3.1.

**ἀστέλεχος**· ὁ δακτύλιος, ἕδρα, Hsch.

**ἀστέμβακτος**, ον, = sq., Euph.123, Lyc.1117.

***ἀστεμφής**, ές, *unmoved, unshaken*, βουλή Il.2.344; βίη A.R.4.1375; ἀστεμφὲς ἔχεσκε [τὸ σκῆπτρον] he held it *stiff*, Il.3.219; οὐδός Hes.*Th.*812; ἀ. οἵη νέκυς Opp.*H.*2.70. Adv., ὑμεῖς ἀστεμφέως ἐχέμεν you hold *fast!* Od.4.419, cf. 459; ἀστεμφῶς τὸν βίον διενήξατο Marin.*Procl.*15: neut. ἀστεμφές as Adv., *stiffly, starkly*, Mosch.4.113; νεφέλαι.. ἀ. μελανεῦσαι dark *without relief*, Arat.878. 2. of persons, *stiff*, ποιηταὶ σκληροὶ καὶ ἀ. Ar.*Fr.*579; ἀ. Τελαμών *unflinching*, Theoc.13.37; as pr. n. of a Titan, Emp.123. 3. metaph., of a trap, *relentless*, *AP*6.296 (Leon.); ζυγός, δεσμός, Opp.*H.*1.417, 2.84; νύξ *AP*9.424 Duris).—Poet. word, also in late Prose, Agath.1.21. (Cf. στέμβω, στέμφυλον, Skt. *stabhnā́ti* 'supports', 'holds fast'.)

**ἀστένακτος**, ον, *without sigh* or *groan*, ἀ. κἀδάκρυτος S.*Tr.*1200, cf. 1074; ἄκλαυτος ἀ. E.*Alc.*173; ἀ. ἡμέρα a day *free from groans*, Id.*Hec.*691 (lyr.), cf. Pl.*Ax.*370d, *Mél.Nicole* 308 (Panticapaeum). Adv. -τως Plu.2.107a:—also **ἀστενακτί**, A.*Fr.*307, Ar.*Ec.*464.

**ἀστέον**, *one must sing*, Ar.*Nu.*1205, Pl.*R.*390e.

**ἄστεπτος**, ον, (στέφω) *uncrowned*, τίς ἄ. θεῶν; E.*Heracl.*440.

***ἀστεργ-άνωρ** [ᾰν], ορος, ὁ, ἡ, *without love of man, unwedded*, παρθενία, of Io, A.*Pr.*898 (lyr.). **-ής**, ές, *without love, implacable*, ὀργή S.*Aj.*776; ἀ. τι παθεῖν something *intolerable*, Id.*OT*229. II. *repellent*, Hp.*Gland.*16; *unyielding*, -έστερον ξύλον Id.*Fract.*16 (s.v.l.), cf. Ruf.ap.Orib.49.28.3.

**ἀστερ-ιαῖος**, α, ον, *like a star*, Cleom.1.11; *decorated with stars*, prob. in *PHamb.*10.44 (ii A.D.). **-ίας**, ου, ὁ, *starred*: hence, I. a fish, *Squalus stellaris*, Philyll.1.2, Arist.*HA*543ᵃ17. II. a bird, 1. perh. *bittern, Ardea stellaris*, ib.609ᵇ22. 2. a kind of *hawk*, ib.620ᵃ18; = χρυσάετος, Ael.*NA*2.39. ***-ίζω**, *arrange in constellations*, Hipparch.1.4.5 (Pass.), al.; *mark with stars*, Ptol.*Geog.*1.23.3 (Pass.); *cast a nativity*, Vett.Val.187.15. **-ικός**, ή, όν, *planetary*, κινήματα *Theol.Ar.*37. ***-ιος**, α, ον, also ος, ον, *starred, starry*, Arat.695; ἀ. ἅμαξα, = Ἄρκτος, Call.*Fr.*146; κύτος, of the sphere *of the fixed stars*, Vett.Val.172.32. 2. *of a star*, [σῶμα] Porph.*Chr.*35; ὕλη Orph.*Fr.*353. II. ἀστέριον, τό, a kind of *spider*, Nic.*Th.*725. III. ἀστέριον, τό, name of a *plant*, Crateuas *Fr.*10; = κορωνόπους, Ps.-Dsc.2.130 (prob. for ἄστριον); = σφονδύλιον, Id.3.76; = κάνναβις ἥμερος, ib.148; = ἀστὴρ Ἀττικός, Id.4.119. IV. ἀστέριον, τό, = ἀστήρ VI, Dsc.*Eup.*2.30. V. ἀστέριος λίθος *meteoric* stone, D.P.328. **-ίσκιον**, τό, Dim. of sq., *little star, boss, knob* on a helmet, Apollon.*Lex.* **-ίσκος**, ὁ, Dim. of ἀστήρ, *little star*, Call.*Iamb.*1.120, Hipparch.3.5.22 (pl.). 2. = ἀστερίσκιον, Eust.424.5. II. *asterisk*, the mark ⁜ by which Gramm. distinguished fine passages in Mss., Id.599.34, etc.; also used as a metrical sign, Heph.*Poëm.*p.74C. III. = ἀστὴρ Ἀττικός, *blue daisy*, Thphr.*HP* 4.12.2, Ps.-Dsc.4.119. IV. *capsule of the poppy*, Dsc.4.64. V. *small wheel with projections*, Hero *Aut.*24.5. VI. a *geometrical figure*, Id.*Stereom.*1.77. **-ισμός**, ὁ, *marking with stars*, Ptol.*Geog.*1.22.4, Sch.Arat.205; *arrangement of constellations*, τῆς Ἀργοῦς Hipparch.1.8.1, cf. 2.1.12; *a starry ornament*, f.l. for foreg. in D.S.19.34. II. = καταστερισμός, Herm.ap.Stob.1.49.44. **-ίτης** (sc. λίθος), ὁ, name of a *mythical precious stone*, Ptol.Heph.ap.Phot.p.153B., Ps.-Democr.Alch.p.50B.

**ἄστερκτος**, ον, = ἀστεργής, v. ἄστεκτος.

**ἀστερο-βλής**, βλῆτος, ὁ, ἡ, *star-flung*, κεραυνός *IG*14.641i. **-δίνητος**, ον, (δινέω) *brought by the revolution of the stars*, Procl.*H.*1.49. **-ειδής**, ές, *star-like*, Ph.1.20,633 (Sup.), Plu.2.933e. Adv. -δῶς Dsc.1.19. II. *starred, starry*, E.*Fr.*114 ap.Ar.*Th.*1067. **-εις**, εσσα, εν, = foreg. II, οὐρανός Il.4.44, *IG*9(1).882.15 (Corc.), etc. II. *like a star, sparkling*, θώρηξ Il.16.134; Ἡφαίστου δόμος 18.370. III. ἀ. πέδιλα, of the Senators' buskins which had a *half-moon* in front, *IG*14.1389 i 23. **-θεν**, Adv. *from the stars*, Arat.1013 (v.l. οὐρανόθεν). **-μαρμᾰρῡγή**, ἡ, *the brightness of the stars*, v.l. in Sch. Arat.328. **-νωτος**, ον, *with starry back*, οὐρανός Nonn.*D.*2.335.

**ἀστεροόμμᾰτος**, ον, *star-eyed*, epith. of night, Orph.*H.*34.13.

**ἀστεροπ-ᾱγερέτας**, α, ὁ, *lightning-compeller*, Cerc.4.25. **-αῖος**, ον, = ἀστεροπητής, Corn.*ND*9. **-ή**, ἡ, = στεροπή, ἀστραπή, *lightning*, Il.10.154 (v.l. for στεροπή), Pi.*N.*9.19, Ar.*Av.*1746, 1748 (anap.). **-ής**, ῆτος, ὁ, ἡ, *lightening*, κεραυνός *IG*14.641. **-ητής**, οῦ, ὁ, *lightener*, of Zeus, Il.1.580, Hes.*Th.*390, S.*Ph.*1198 (dact.).

**ἀστερο-πληθής**, ές, *full of stars*, Orac.ap.Eus.*PE*5.8. **-πληκτος**, ον, *struck* '*sine fulmine*' (by a meteoric bolt), Seneca *QN*1.15.

***ἀστεροπός**, όν, = ἀστερωπός, Ζεύς Achae.2.3 (anap.).

**ἀστερο-σκοπέω**, *watch the stars*, S.E.*M.*5.68:—hence Subst. **-σκοπία**, ἡ, ib.80 (pl.). **-σκόπος**, ον, *astronomer* or *astrologer*, Artem.2.69. **-φεγγής**, ές, *shining with stars*, αἰθήρ Orph.*H.*5.5; νύξ ib.3.3. ***-φοιτος**, ον, *traversing the stars*, esp. of constellations, Ἠριδανός Nonn.*D.*23.298, al. II. *traversed by stars*, κύκλος Ὀλύμπου ib.32.10, al.

**ἀστερόω**, *turn into stars*, πέτρους ἠστερωκέναι *Placit.*2.13.3:—Pass., *to be marked by stars*, opp. εἶναι ἀνάστερα, Sch.Arat.273.

**ἀστερόωνται**, f.l. for ἀστερόεντες in Arat.548.

**ἀστερ-ώδης**, ες, = ἀστεροειδής, Ποταμός Sch.Arat.355. **-ωπός**, όν, *star-faced, star-like, bright-shining*, ὄμμα Δητῴας κόρης A.*Fr.*170; νυκτὸς ἀ. σέλας E.*Hipp.*851 (lyr.), cf. *Ph.*129 (lyr.). II. *star-eyed, starry*, αἰθήρ E.*Ion* 1078 (lyr.); ἀ. οὐρανοῦ δέμας Critias 25.33D. **-ωτός**, ή, όν, *starred*, φιάλη *IG*11(2).199*B*8,42 (iii B.C.); πῖλος Sallust.4.

**ἀστέφᾰν-ος**, ον, *without crown, ungarlanded*, mostly in token of defeat, E.*Hipp.*1137 (lyr.); ἁμίλλας ἔθετ' ἀστεφάνους Id.*Andr.*1021. **-ωτος**, ον, *uncrowned, forbidden to be crowned*, Sapph.78, Pl.*R.*613c, D.18.319; ἀ. ἐκ τῶν νόμων Aeschin.3.176. 2. *without the nuptial crown, unwedded*, *Epigr.Gr.*314.27.

**ἀστεφής**, ές, = ἀστέφανος, Man.6.517:—also **ἄστεφος**, ον, A.D.*Pron.*31.15.

***ἀστή**, ἡ, fem. of ἀστός, Hdt.1.173, al., Ar.*Th.*541, *BGU*1104.4 (i B.C.), etc.

**ἄστηθι**, = ἀν-στ-, Herod.8.1, cf. ἀνίστημι.

**ἄστηλος**, ον, *without tombstone*, *AP*7.479 (Theodorid.).

**ἀστηνεῖ**· ἀδυνατεῖ, Hsch., cf. sq.

***ἄστηνος**, ον, *miserable*, *BCH*29.410 (Rhenea, ii B.C.): heterocl. pl. ἀστῆνες Hsch.; expld. παρὰ τὸ μὴ στάσιν μηδ' οἴκησιν ἔχειν in *EM* 159.11, cf. Suid.

***ἀστήρ**, ὁ, gen. έρος: dat. pl. ἀστράσι Il.22.28,317 (Aristarch.; ἄστρασι Sch.Ven., Choerob.):—*star* (v. ἄστρον), ἀστέρ' ὀπωρινῷ Il.5.5; οὔλιος ἀ. 11.62; Σείριος ἀ. Hes.*Op.*417; ἀ. Ἀρκτοῦρος *the chief star* in the constellation, ib.565, etc.; *shooting star* or *meteor*, Il.4.75; οἱ διατρέχοντες ἀ. Ar.*Pax* 838; ᾄττοντας ὥσπερ ἀστέρας Pl.*R.*621b, cf. Arist.*Mete.*341ᵃ33, Plu.*Agis* 11. 2. *flame, light, fire*, E.*Hel.*1131 (lyr.). 3. ἀστὴρ πέτρινος *meteoric* stone, *Placit.*2.13.9. II. metaph. of *illustrious* persons, etc., φανερώτατον ἀστέρ' Ἀθήνας E.*Hipp.*1122 (lyr.); Μουσάων ἀστέρα καὶ Χαρίτων *AP*7.1.8 (Alc. Mess.) III. *star fish*, Hp.*Nat.Mul.*32, Arist.*HA*548ᵃ7, *PA*681ᵇ9, etc. IV. name of a *bird*, perh. *goldfinch*, Dionys.*Av.*3.2. V. *blue daisy, Aster Amellus*, Nic.*Fr.*74.66, Dsc.4.119. VI. *Samian clay* used as sealing-wax, and in Medicine, Thphr.*Lap.*63, Dsc.5.153, Gal.12.178, al. VII. architectural *ornament*, *IG*4.1484.83 (Epid.), *SIG*241*B*111 (Delph., iv B.C.). VIII. *bandage*, Gal.18(1).823. 2. name of various *remedies*, Id.12.761, al. IX. *birth-mark in form of star*, Carcin.ap.Arist.*Po.*1454ᵇ22: in Palmistry, a *mark* on the hand, τῷ ὑποστοιχείῳ παραπλήσιον *Cat.Cod. Astr.*7.238.28. (Cf. Skt. *stár-* 'star', Lat. *stella* (from *stēr-la*), Goth. *stairnō*.)

**ἀστήρει**· σῖτος, Hsch.

**ἀστηρίδιον**, τό, Dim. of ἀστήρ, *ornament in shape of star*, *PHamb.*10.44 (ii A.D.).

**ἀστήρικτος**, ον, *not supported by a staff*, *AP*6.203 (Lacon or Phil.); *unstable*, Longin.2.2, 2*Ep.Pet.*3.16, Gal.*UP*2.15, al.; ἀ. λογισμοῦ Vett.Val.242.3; *not remaining still*, of persons, Nonn.*D.*10.14, al.; of water, ib.32.8, al.

**ᾄστης**, ου, ὁ, (ᾄδω) *singer*, Gloss.

**ἀστιάγγας**· τὰς ὑποφυλλίδας τῶν βοτρύων, οἱ δὲ ἀκτῖνος αὐγάς, ἔνιοι **ἄστριγγας**, καὶ **ἀστρίγας** ἄλλοι, *EM*159.38; cf. **ἄστιγγας**· αἶγας, ἢ ἄστριγγας, Hsch. (Cf. ἄστλιγξ, ὄστλιγξ.)

**ἀστίαρχος**, = ἀστύαρχος, *BGU*1024.

***ἀστῐβής**, ές, (στείβω) *untrodden*, τινί A.*Th.*859 (lyr.): hence, 2. *desert, pathless*, χῶρος S.*Aj.*657; ἀ. πόρος, of the sea, Arion 1.16; ὁδός *Hymn.Is.*149. 3. *not to be trodden, holy*, ἄλσος S.*OC*126; rare in Prose, as X.*Mem.*3.8.10. II. Act., *leaving no track*, τροχός Mesom.*Nem.*7.

**ἀστίβητος** [ῐ], ον, = foreg., Lyc.121, Procop.*Arc.*14; ἀ. οἶκοι· ἄδυτα, Hsch.:—also **ἄστῐβος**, ον, *AP*7.745 (Antip. Sid.).

**ἀστῐγής**, ές, *unpunctuated*, βιβλίον St.Byz. s. vv. Ἀνακτόριον, Βάβρας.

***ἀστικός**, ή, όν, (ἄστυ) *of a city* or *town*, opp. *country*, λεὼς ἀ. A.*Eu.*997; βωμοί Id.*Supp.*501; epith. of Hecate, *IG*9(2).575 (Larissa, v B.C.); τὰ ἀ. Διονύσια (= τὰ κατ' ἄστυ) Th.5.20; *home*, opp. ξενικός (*foreign*), A.*Supp.*618; ἀ. δίκαι suits *between citizens*, Lys.17.3; ἀ. δικαστήριον *IG*12(7).3.32 (Amorgos); ἀ. νόμοι *POxy.*706.9 (ii A.D.). 2. as Subst., = ἀστός, *TAM*2.377,886 (Xanthus). b. ἀστικοί, οἱ, = Lat. *cohortes urbanae*, D.C.56.32, 59.2; ἀστικόν, τό, Id.55.24. II. *fond of the town* or *town life*, D.55.11. 2. = ἀστεῖος, *polite*, ἀστικά, as Adv., opp. ἀγροίκως, Theoc.20.4.—In codd. often written ἀστυκός.

**ἄστικτος**, ον, *not marked with* στίγματα, *not tattooed*, τὸ ἄστικτον Hdt.5.6. II. χωρίον ἄ. an estate *not pledged* or *mortgaged* (those that were so being *marked by* στῆλαι or ὅροι), Lys.*Fr.*3S, Men.1D., Poll.3.85.

**ἀστιλάζει**· συμπεριπατεῖ, Hsch.

**ἀστιξία**, ἡ, *want of punctuation*, *An.Ox.*4.51.

**ἄστιος,** α, ον, = ἀστικός, δίκα *GDI*4976 (Crete), *IG*5(2).357.26 (Stymphalus, iii B.C.); πεντηκοστὴ ἡ ἀ. ib.11.287*A*9 (Delos, iii B.C.).

**ἀστίοχος,** ὁ, *stink-pot*, Hsch. **ἄστιππος·** ἱππέων ἑβδομήκοντα, Id.

**ἄστιπτος,** ον, = ἀστιβής, *untrodden*, ἀκτὴ..βροτοῖς ἄ. S.*Ph.*2, v.l. ἄστειπτος, which is prob. in *OGI*606 (Syria).

**ἀστίτης** [ῑ], ου, ὁ, (ἄστυ) *townsman, citizen*, S.*Fr.*92; spelt **ἀστείτης** in *CIG*2134*b*23.

**ἀστλέγγιστος,** ον, *not scraped clean*, *AP*6.298 (Leon.).

**ἄστλιγξ,** ιγγος, ἡ, = ὄστλιγξ, Philet.ap.Sch.A.R.1.1297, Hdn.Gr. 1.44.

**ἄστοβος,** ον, = ἀλοιδόρητος, Hsch.

**ἀστοιχείωτος,** ον, *ignorant of the first elements*, Ph.1.337.

**ἄστοιχος,** ον, *not in a row*, of the grains in an ear of wheat, Thphr. *HP*8.4.2.

**ἀστολόγος,** ὁ, title in Egypt, *Sammelb.*969.

***ἄστολος,** ον, (στέλλω) *ungirded*, χιτών S.*Fr.*872. **2.** of Charon's boat, A.*Th.*857 (lyr.) (ἄστονος cod. M).

**ἀστομάχητος** [ᾰ], ον, *without anger* (i.e. *not angered*), *PBaden* 35.17 (i A.D.), Alciphr.2.2. Adv. -τως *IG*14.2095.

**ἀστόμιος,** α, ον, = ἄστομος II, Nonn.*D.*7.244.

**ἄστομ-ος,** ον, *speechless*, S.*Fr.*76, Arr.*Epict.*2.24.26; ἄ. πεποιηκέναι reduce to *silence*, Luc.*Lex.*15. **2.** *with no mouth*, ἄ. καὶ ἄρρινες Str.2.1.9, cf. Plu.2.938c, 940b. **3.** *with no outlet*, λίμνη Str.7. 3.15. **II.** of horses, *hard-mouthed*, S.*El.*724, Plu.*Art.*9. **III.** of dogs, *soft-mouthed, unable to hold with the teeth*, X.*Cyn.*3.3. **IV.** of meat and drink, *unpalatable*, Hices.ap.Ath.7.323a, Dsc.1.110, al.: Comp., Sor.1.95. **V.** of metal, *soft, incapable of a fine edge*, Plu. *Lys.*17. **-ωτος,** ον, *with no orifice*, Sor.1.57, Orib.45.3.8, prob. in Gal.18(2).795. **II.** *unsharpened, untempered*, of metal, Hsch. s.v. ἄβαπτος.

**ἀστονάχητος** [ᾰ], ον, = sq., *IG*14.2111.

**ἄστονος,** ον, *without sighs*, πότος ἄ. a potion *to chase away sighs*, dub. in *Anacreont.*50.6, cf. Max.Tyr.3.9. **II.** (ἀ- intens.) = μεγαλόστονος, Hsch.

**ἀστόξενος,** ὁ, ἡ, *public guest of a city*, A.*Supp.*356.—Expld. by Ael. Dion.*Fr.*282, Hsch., as *a blood-relation, though a foreigner by birth*.

**ἀστοργ-ία,** ἡ, *want of natural affection*, Antipho *Fr.*73, Men.522, D.H.3.18. ***-ος,** ον, *without natural affection*, ἄστοργος ψυχήν Aeschin.2.146; ὤστοργος *the heartless one*, Theoc.2.112, cf. *Lyr.Alex. Adesp.*6.9; ἄ. γυνή Theoc.17.43; ἄ. πρὸς τὰ ἔκγονα Clytus 1, cf. *IG* 12(5).14 (Ios); ἄ. θάνατος *cruel*, *AP*7.662 (Leon.), *IG*3.1374. **2.** *without attraction*, Plu.2.926f:—also **ἀστόργης** (sic) *An.Ox.*1.50.

**ἀστορής,** ές, *without bedding*, χαμεῦναι Nonn.*D.*16.93.

**ἀστόριον·** μέγα καὶ διακεχυμένον, Hsch.

***ἀστός,** ὁ, (ἄστυ) *townsman, citizen*, Il.11.242, Od.13.192, etc.; dist. from πολίτης, ἀστός being *one who has civil rights* only, πολίτης *one who has political rights* also, Arist.*Pol.*1278$^{a}$34; ἀ. πικρὸς πολίταις E. *Med.*223; οἱ ἀ. *the commons*, opp. οἱ ἀγαθοί, Pi.*P.*3.71, cf. Isoc.3.21; opp. ξένος, Pi.*O.*7.90, Hdt.2.160, 3.8; esp. at Athens, Lys.6.17, Pl. *Ap.*30a, Isoc. l.c., cf. S.*OT*817, *OC*13, etc.; opp. μέτοικος, ξένος, Pl. *R.*563a; in Egypt, *citizen of Alexandria* (cf. ἄστυ II.3), *PGnom.*38, al. —Fem. ἀστή, q.v., but Ἀστός fem. as epith. of Κόρη, *IG*12(5).225 (Paros, v B.C.). (ϝασστός and ϝαστός, *IG*9(1).333.14 (Locr., v B.C.), 9(2).1226 (Phalanna, v B.C.).)

**ἀστόχ-αστος,** ον, *not aimed*, D.H.14.10; *not aimed at, not considered*, πλήθους καὶ ποιότητος ἀστοχάστων Phld.*D.*3*Fr.*89. **2.** *hard to guess at*, Thphr.ap.Stob.4.11.16. **3.** Act., *missing the mark*, Phld.*Rh.*1.191S. ***-έω,** *miss the mark, miss*, τοῦ συμφέροντος *IG* 9(2).517.28 (letter of Philip V to Larissa); τινός Plb.5.107.2, al., Phld.*Rh.*1.219S.; τοῦ μετρίου Plu.2.414f; ἀμφοῖν Luc.*Am.*22; *fail*, περί τινος Plb.3.21.10; περὶ τὴν πίστιν, τὴν ἀλήθειαν, 1*Ep.Ti.*6.21, 2. 2.18; ἔν τινι J.*BJ*2.8.12: abs., Alciphr.3.53.—Rare in poetry, ἠστόχηκέ μου *Lyr.Alex Adesp* 4.21. **-ημα,** ατος, τό, *failure, fault*, Plu. 2.520b. **-ία,** ἡ, *missing the mark, failing*, Phld.*Vit.*p.41 J. (pl.), Plu.2.800a (pl.); ἀστοχίαι τῶν ἔργων *Cat.Cod.Astr.*2.162.6. **2.** *imprudence, thoughtlessness, error*, Plb.2.33.8, etc. **-ίζομαι,** = ἀστοχέω, S.*Fr.*442.4. **-ος,** ον, *missing the mark, aiming badly at*, τινός Pl.*Ti.*19e, *AP*9.370 (Tib. Ill.). **2.** abs., *aiming amiss, random*, οὐκ ἀστόχου διανοίας Arist.*HA*587$^{a}$9; κατηγορία *aimless, absurd*, Plb.5.49.4; of a person, Phld.*Ind.Sto.*32. Adv. -χως *amiss*, Alex.116.14, Plb.1.74.2, Phld.*Mort.*33.

**ἀστρᾰβᾰλίζω,** *make level*, *EM*159.59, Hsch. (-οβίζειν cod.).

**ἄστραβδα** (or **-αβδά**), παίζειν dub. sens. in Herod.3.64: perh. fr. ἀστράπτω, or *without turning* (ἀ- priv., στρέφω).

**ἀστρᾰβ-εύω,** *ride a mule*, Pl.Com.39. **-η,** ἡ, *mule's saddle, an easy padded saddle*, used by effeminate persons (Sch.D. l.c. infr.), ἐπ' ἀστράβης ἂν ὠχούμην Lys.24.11; ἐπ' ἀστράβης ὀχούμενος ἀργυρᾶς (v.l. ἐξ Ἀργούρας) D.21.133; τῶν ὑποζυγίων τὰ τριχώματα γίνεται λευκὰ ἐκ προστρίψεων τῆς ἀστράβης Arist.*Col.*interpol.post 798$^{a}$19; εὐτελῶς ἐπ' ἀστράβης Macho ap.Ath.13.582c; μαλακίζομαι ἐπ' ἀστράβης ὀχηθείς Luc.*Lex.*2: prov., σοφόν γ' ὁ βοῦς ἔφασκεν ἀστράβην ἰδών, *Com.Adesp.*563.—Expld. as εἶδος ἁμάξης in Hdn Gr.1.308; as the *pommel* of a saddle, *EM*159.50, Hsch.; of the *mule* itself, Id., Harp., Eust 1625.40. **2.** Δημοσθένους ἀ., a kind of *surgical appliance*, Heliod ap.Orib.49.4.34. **-ηλάτης** [λᾰ], ου, ὁ, *muleteer*, Luc.*Lex.*2, Poll.7.185. **-ηλος,** ὁ, = στράβηλος (with ἀ- euph.), a kind of *shell*, Agias 1, Dercyl.1. **-ής,** ές, = ἀστραφής, *not twisted, straight, steadfast*, Τροίας κίων (i.e. Hector) Pi.*O.*2.90; γέννες Hp.*Art.*31; τρίγωνον Pl.*Ti.*73b; τὸ σῶμα ποιεῖν ἀ. Arist.*Pol.*1336$^{a}$12; βάσεις *IG*7. 3073.104 (Lebad.); of timber, Thphr.*HP*3.9.2: Comp., ib.5.1.11: Sup., ib.5.3.5; *rigid, stiff*, ἀ. ἐντέταται Aret.*SA*1.6. Adv. -βῶς Ael.*NA*2.11. **-ίζω,** (ἀστράβη) *ride pillion*, καμήλους ἀστραβιζούσας A.*Supp.*285 (dub.). ***-ιστήρ,** ῆρος, ὁ, *instrument used in levelling*, Hsch.

**ἀστρᾰγάλ-ειος** [γᾰ], α, ον, *covering the ankles*, = Lat. *talaris*, χιτών Aq.*Ge.*37.3. ***-η,** ἡ, Ion. for ἀστράγᾰλος, Anacr.46, Herod.3.7, Ael.Dion.*Fr.*359. **II.** = ἡ τῆς ἴρεως ῥίζα, Hsch. **III.** = κακοήθης κύων, Id. ***-ίζω,** *play with* ἀστράγαλοι, Pl.*Ly.*206e, *Alc.*1. 110b; ἀ. ἄρτοις Cratin.165, cf. Telecl.1.14. **-ῖνος,** ὁ, *goldfinch*, elsewh. ποικιλίς, Dionys.*Av.*3.2. **-ισις,** εως, ἡ, *playing with* ἀστράγαλοι, Arist.*Rh.*1371$^{a}$2 (pl.). **-ίσκος,** ὁ, Dim. of ἀστράγαλος, Roussel *Cultes Égyptiens* 218 (Delos, ii B.C.), Poll.6.99; name of a *surgical appliance*, *PMed.Lond.*2.14. **-ιστής,** οῦ, ὁ, *dice-player*; in pl., name of a comedy by Alex. Aet., Sch.Il.23.86 (Mein. for ἀστρολογισταί). **-ιστικός,** ή, όν, *of the dice*, βόλος Eust.1397.47. **-ῖτις,** ιδος, ἡ, = ἶρις Ἰλλυρική, Gal.12.422.

**ἀστρᾰγᾰλόμαντις,** εως, ὁ, *divining from* ἀστράγαλοι, Artem.2.69.

***ἀστράγᾰλος** [ρᾰ], ὁ, (v. ὀστέον) *one of the vertebrae*, esp. of the neck, Il.14.466, Od.11.65, *AP*7.632 (Diod.); votive object, *IG*5 (2).125 (Tegea, ii A.D.). **II.** *ball of the ankle joint* (not to be confused with σφυρόν, Ruf.*Onom.*124), Hdt.3.129; in horses, X.*Eq.*1. 15; of various animals, Hp.*Int.*20, 30. **2.** οἱ μὲν πόδες ἀστράγαλοί τευ, as a compliment, i.e. *well-turned*, Theoc.10.36. **III.** *wrist*, Lxx *Da.*5.5, 24. **IV.** pl., ἀστράγαλοι *knucklebones* used as *dice* or *a game played with dice*, ἀμφ' ἀστραγάλοισι χολωθείς Il.23.88, cf. Hdt.1.94, Menecr.Com.1D.; ἀ. διάσειστοι Aeschin.1.59, cf. Men. 423; ἀ. μεμολιβδωμένοι loaded *dice*, Arist.*Fr.*913$^{a}$36, cf. Eust.1397. 34; later, *dice proper*, ἀντ' ἀστραγάλων κονδύλοισι παίζετε Pherecr. 43. **V.** ἡ ἐκ τῶν ἀστραγάλων μάστιξ scourge of *strung bones*, Luc. *Asin.*38; cf. ἀστραγαλωτός. **VI.** *moulding* in the capital of the Ionic column, *IG*1.322, Vitr.3.5.7. **VII.** *milk vetch, Orobus niger*, Dsc.4.61, Gal.11.841. **VIII.** *prism of wood*, Aen.Tact.31.17, al. **IX.** *ear-ring*, ξύλινοι ἀ. Anacr.21.4.

**ἀστρᾰγᾰλ-ώδης,** ες, *shaped like an* ἀστράγαλος, Tz.*H.*10.231. ***-ωτός,** ή, όν, *made of* ἀστράγαλοι, μάστιξ Crates Com.35, Plu.2. 1127c; ἱμάς Posidon.9. **II.** -ωτή, ἡ, name of a *plant*, Philum. *Ven.*7.11; dub. in Harp.Astr. in *Cat.Cod.Astr.*8(3).150.26. **2.** (sc. στυπτηρία) a kind of *alum*, Gal.12.237.

**ἀστραῖος,** α, ον, (ἄστρον) *starry*, Orac ap.Porph.ap.Eus.*PE*3.14, Nonn.*D.*1.191, al.

**ἀστρακλεῖν·** ἀδυνατεῖν, Hsch.

**ἀστραλός,** ὁ, = ψαρός (Thess.), Hsch. (Cf. Lat. *sturnus*, OHG. *stara*, OE. *stær.*)

***ἀστρᾰπ-αῖος,** α, ον, *of lightning*, ἄνεμος ἀ. a wind *with thunderstorms*, Arist.*Mete.*364$^{b}$30, cf. Thphr.*Sign.*37; τὰ ἀ. τῶν ὑδάτων *thunder*-showers, Plu.2.664c; Ζεὺς ἀ. Arist.*Mu.*401$^{a}$16, Corn.*ND*9, *IGRom.*3.17 (Bithyn.). ***-ή,** ἡ, = ἀστεροπή, στεροπή, *flash of lightning, lightning*, βροντὴ καὶ ἀ. Hdt.3.86, cf. X.*HG*7.1.31, etc.; βροντὴ δ' ἐρράγη δι' ἀστραπῆς S.*Fr.*578, cf. Pl.*Ti.*68a, *Cra.*409c, Arist.*Mete.*369$^{b}$6; personified, as subject of painting, Plin.*HN*35.96, Philostr.*Im.* 1.14: freq. in pl., *lightnings*, τὰς ἀ. τε καὶ κεραυνίους βολάς A.*Th.* 430; τᾶν πυρφόρων ἀστραπᾶν κράτη νέμων S.*OT*201 (lyr.). **2.** *light* of a lamp, A.*Fr.*386, *Ev.Luc.*11.36. **3.** metaph., ἀστραπήν τιν' ὀμμάτων *flashing* of the eyes, S.*Fr.*474; βλέπων ἀστραπάς Ar.*Ach.* 566; ἐκτυφλοῦν τιν' ἀστραπὴ [εἰμί] Antiph.195.4, cf. Ach.Tat.6.6.

**ἀστρᾰπη-βολέω,** *hurl lightnings*, Eust.1060.43. **-βόλος,** ον, (βάλλω) *hurling lightnings*, Id.1682.5. **-δόν,** Adv. *like lightning*, Aristobul.ap.Eus.*PE*8.10. ***-φορέω,** *carry lightnings*, Ar.*Pax* 722. **-φόρος,** ον, *flashing*, πῦρ E.*Ba.*3.

***ἀστράπιος** [ᾰ], ον, = ἀστρᾰπαῖος, Orph.*H.*15.9, 20.5.

**ἀστρᾰπο-ειδής,** ές, *like lightning, forked*, *Gloss.* **-κτῡποδίωκτα,** prob. in *PMag.Lond.*1.46.20 for ἀστραποκυποδωκε. **-πληκτος,** ον, *lightning-stricken*, v.l. for ἀστερόπληκτος in Seneca *QN*1.15.

**ἀστραπτικός,** ή, όν, *lightening*, Sch.Il.1.580.

***ἀστράπτω** (cf. στράπτω), Ep. impf. ἀστράπτεσκον Mosch.2.86: fut. ἀστράψω Cratin.53, Nonn.*D.*33.376: aor. ἤστραψα Il.17.595, etc.:—*lighten, hurl lightnings*, freq. of omens sent by Zeus, ἀστράπτων ἐπιδέξι' Il.2.353; Κρονίδης ἐνδέξια σήματα φαίνων ἀστράπτει 9.237; ὡς δ' ὅτ' ἂν ἀστράπτῃ πόσις Ἥρης 10.5; ἀστράψας δὲ μάλα μεγάλ' ἔκτυπε 17.595; οὑλύμπιος ἤστραπτεν, ἐβρόντα Ar.*Ach.*531, cf. *V.* 626. **2.** impers., ἀστράπτει *it lightens*, ἤστραψε *it lightened*, οὐρανοῦ δ' ἄπο ἤστραψε S.*Fr.*578, cf. Arist.*Rh.*1392$^{b}$27. **II.** *flash* or *glance like lightning*, πᾶς γὰρ ἀστράπτει χαλινός S.*OC*1067 (lyr.); κατάχαλκον ἀ. πεδίον *gleams* with brass, E.*Ph.*111; so ἀ. χαλκῷ X. *Cyr.*6.4.1; of the face, εἶδον τὴν ὄψιν..ἀστράπτουσαν Pl.*Phdr.*254b; ἀ. τοῖς ὄμμασι X.*Cyn.*6.15; of flowers, ἀνεμωνίδες ἀστράπτουσαι *bright*, Nic *Fr.*74.64: c. acc. cogn., ἐξ ὀμμάτων δ' ἤστραπτε..σέλας (sc. Τυφών) *flashed* flame from his eyes, A.*Pr.*358; ἵμερον ἀστράπτουσα κατ' ὄμματος *AP*12.161 (Asclep.), cf. Mosch. l.c.; ἤστραψε γλυκὺ κάλλος *AP*12.110 (Mel.). **2.** of persons, *to be brilliant, conspicuous*, ἔν τινι Opp.*C.*1.361, 2.23. **III.** trans., *consume with lightning*, dub. in Cratin.53. **2.** *illuminate*, τι Musae.276.

**ἀστράρχη,** ἡ, *queen of stars*, of the moon, Orph.*H.*9.10:—also **ἀστροάρχη,** Hdn.5.6.4.

**ἀστρᾰτ-εία,** ἡ, *exemption from service*, Ar.*Pax* 526, Ph.2.373. **2.** *avoidance of service*, φεύγειν γραφὴν ἀστρατείας Ar.*Eq.*443; ἀστρατείας ἀλῶναι, ὀφλεῖν, Lys.14.7, And.1.74; γραφαὶ περὶ τῆς ἀ. Pl.*Lg.*943d; δίκη ἀστρατείας D.39.16. II. *she that stops an invasion*, of Artemis, Paus.3.25.3. -ευσία, ἡ, = foreg.1, *Sammelb.*4224.14. ☼-ευτος, ον, *without service*: hence, 1. *exempt therefrom*, Lys.9.15. 2. *never having seen service* Ar.*V.*1117, Aeschin.3.176; ἀ. καὶ λιποτάκτης Ph.1.144. Adv. -τως Poll.1.159.

ἀστρᾰτηγ-ησία, ἡ, *in apacity for command*, D.H.9.31. ☼-ητος, ον, *never having been general*, Pl.*Alc.*2.142a. 2. *incapable of command, no general*, Cic.*Att.*7.13.1, cf. 8.16.1 (Sup.), Onos.33.5. Adv. ἀκόσμως καὶ -τως App.*BC*1.47, cf. Hierocl.p.17 A. II. *without a general*, J.*BJ*2.12.4. -ία, ἡ, *lack of a general*, Phryn.*PS*p.42 B.

ἀστρᾰφής, ές, = ἄστρεπτος I. 2, S.*Fr.*418; *fixed, immovable*, *IG*2.1054*f*20. II. = ἄστρεπτος II, πύλαι Epic.ap.Aristid.*Or.*49(25).4.

☼ἀστραφιστήρ, ῆρος, ὁ, dub. sens. in *IG*2.808$^d$65; cf. ἀστραβιστήρ.

ἀστραψις, εως, ἡ, = ἀστραπή, Suid. s.v. μαρμαρυγή.

ἀστρεκίας· ἀστροφανίας, Hsch.

☼ἄστρεπτος, ον, *without turning the back*, Theoc.24.96. Adv. -τεί *AP*7.436 (Hegem.). 2. *unbending, rigid*, δόγμα ib.103 (Antag.), cf. 6.71 (Paul. Sil.); τὸ θεῖον Max.Tyr.11.3. II. *whence none return*, Ἅιδης Lyc.813.

ἀστρεφής, ές, = ἀστραφής, Hsch. s. v. ἄπολον. ἀστρηνές, = στρηνές, Id. ἄστρητα, τά, = τὰ ἐγγώνια τὰ ἐντὸς τοῦ δίφρου, Poll.1.143.

ἀστρίζω, (ἄστρις) = ἀστραγαλίζω, Poll.9.99.

ἀστρικός, ή, όν, *of or concerning the stars*, μαντεία Philostr.*VA*3.41; ἡ -κή *astronomy* or *astrology*, Tz.*H.*5.270; ἡ ἰδία τινὸς ἀ. (sc. μοῖρα or εἱμαρμένη) *destiny*, *PMag.Leid.W.*14.37; ἀ., ὁ, = ἀστρολόγος, *Cat. Cod.Astr.*8(4).174.

ἄστριον, τό, Dim. of ἀστήρ, *an architectural ornament*, *IG*4.1495.61. II. = ἀστερίτης λίθος, Plin.*HN*37.132, Isid.*Etym.*16.13.7. III. = κορωνόπους, Ps.-Dsc.2.130 (nisi leg. ἀστέριον).

ἄστρις, ιος, ἡ, = ἀστράγαλος, Call.*Fr.*238, 239:—also ἄστρῖχος, ὁ, Antiph.92.

ἀστρο-άρχη, v. ἀστράρχη. -βλέφᾰρος, ον, *with starry eyes*, Orph.*L.*672 (s.v.l.). -βλής, ῆτος, ὁ, ἡ, *sun-scorched*, Arist.*HA* 602$^b$22. -βλησία, ἡ, prob. l. for -βολησία (q.v.). -βλητος, ον, = ἀστροβλής, *sun-scorched*, Id.*Juv.*470$^a$32, Thphr.*HP*4.14.7. -βοᾶν, f.l. for ἀστρ(β)ολον, Hsch. -βολέομαι, Pass., *to be sun-scorched*, Thphr.*HP*4.14.2, etc.:—Act. in Porph.*Plot.* 10. -βολησία, ἡ, *sun-scorch*, in plants, Thphr.*CP*5.9.4 (nisi leg. ἀστροβλησία). -βόλητος, ον, = ἀστροβλής, Hsch., v.l. in Thphr. for -βλητος (q.v.). -βολία, ἡ, = ἀστροβολησία, Id.*CP*5.9.2. -βολίζομαι, Pass., = ἀστροβολέομαι, *Gloss.* -βολος, ον, *lightning-like, swift*, Hsch. Adv. -λως Id. -βρόντης, ου, ὁ, *thundering from the stars*, epith. of Mithras, *IG*14.998. -γείτων, ον, gen. ονος, *near the stars*, κορυφαί A.*Pr.*721. -δάμας [δᾰ], αντος, ὁ, *subduing the stars*, *PMag.Par.*1.603. -δίαιτος [ῐ], ον, *living under the stars*, i. e. *in the open air*, Orph.*H.*11.5 codd. -δίφης [ῑ], ου, ὁ, = ἀστρονόμος, Herod.3.54. -δώρητος, ον, *endowed by the stars*, φύσις Vett.Val. 221.22. -ειδής, ές, *starlike, starry*, Ph.1.485 (Sup.), Hierocl. *in CA*27 p.483 M.; ἀ. περίοδος *like that of the stars*, Str.3.5.8. -θεάμων [ᾰ], ονος, ὁ, (θεάομαι) *observing the stars*, ἱστορία Dam.*Pr.*23; ἐπιστήμη Id.*Isid.*145. -θεσία, ἡ, *group of stars, constellation*, Ath.11.490f; *arrangement of planets*, Vett.Val.157.24. -θετέω, *class* or *group the stars* (in constellations), Str.1.1.6 (Pass.). -θέτημα, ατος, τό, *a group of stars, constellation*, Suid. s.v. ἀστήρ. ☼-θέτης, ου, ὁ, *one who classes the stars*, Orph.*H.*64.2. -θετος, ον, *astronomical*, κανών *AP*7.683 (Pall.). -θύτης [ῠ], ου, ὁ, *star-worshipper*, D.L.*Prooem.*8, Sch.Pl.*Alc.*1.122a.

☼ἀστροΐτης, ου, ὁ, prob. for *astriotes*, a magical gem, Plin.*HN*37.133.

ἀστρο-κύων [ῠ], κύνος, ὁ, *the dog-star*, Horap.1.3. -λάβος, ὁ, *armillary sphere*, Ptol.*Alm.*5.2, al., Procl.*Hyp.*6; ἀ. στερεός Simp. *in Cael.*462.30:—also as Adj., ἀ. ὄργανον Ptol.*Alm.*5.9, al., *Geog.* 1.2.2 (pl.); κύκλοι Id.*Alm.*5.1, 7.2. II. *planisphere*, Phlp. in *Rh.Mus.*6(1839).127. -λογέω, *study* or *practise astronomy*, Thphr.*Sign.*4, Sosip.1.15, Plb.9.20.5; τὰ -λογούμενα Cleom.2.1. -λόγημα, ατος, τό, *astronomy*, Tz.ad Lyc.363. -λογία, ἡ, *astronomy*, X.*Mem.*4.7.4, Isoc.11.23; a branch of mathematics, Arist. *Ph.*193$^b$26, *Metaph* 989$^b$33, cf.997$^b$35; γεωμετρίατε καὶ ἀ. *Vit.Philonid.* p.4 C.; ἀ. ναυτική Arist.*APo.*78$^b$40. 2. later, *astrology*, S.E.*M.* 5.1. -λογικός, ή, όν, *of* or *for astronomy*, ἐμπειρία, ἐπιστήμη, Arist. *APr.*46$^a$19, *APo.*78$^b$39; τὰ -κά Id.*Cael.*291$^b$21. -λόγος, ὁ, *astronomer*, X.*Mem.*4.2.10, Epigr.ap.D.L.1.34. 2. later, *astrologer*, Epicur.*Ep.*2 p.40 U., Lxx *Is.*47.13, *SIG*771.2 (Delph., i B.C.), S.E.*M.* 5.2, etc. -μαντεία, ἡ, = sq., D.S.36.5. -μαντική (sc. τέχνη), ἡ, *astrology*, ibid., S.E.*M.*9.132. -μαντις, εως, ὁ, *astrologer*, Poll. 7.188, Jul.*Or.*4.131a.

☼ἄστρον, τό, mostly in pl., *the stars*, Il.8.555, Od.12.312, A.*Pr.*458, *Ag.*4, etc.; τοῦ κατ' ἄστρα Ζηνός, = τοῦ ἐν οὐρανῷ, S.*Tr.*1106; ἄστρων εὐφρόνη, = εὐφρ. ἀστερόεσσα, Id.*El.*19: sg., like ἀστήρ, freq. of Sirius (in full, σήριον ἄστρον prob. l. in Alcm.23.63), Alc.39,40, X.*Cyn.*4.6, Thphr.*CP*6.10.9, al.; περὶ τὸ ἄ. in the *dog-days*, Hp.*Epid.*7.7; poet. of the sun, Pi.*O.*1.6, Pl.*Def.*411b: seldom of *any common star*, Gal.17(1).16, Sch.Arat.11; of the fixed stars, Arist.*Cael.*290$^a$20; ἄστρα πλανητά, opp. ἀπλανῆ, Pl.*Ti.*38c; opp. ἐνδεδεμένα, Arist.*Mete.* 346$^a$2; opp. ἀστέρες, Herm.ap.Stob.1.21.9; ἐπὶ τοῖς ἄστροις at the times of *the stars'* rising or setting, Hp.*Aër.*10, Arist.*HA*568$^a$18; ἄστροις σημαίνεσθαι, τεκμαίρεσθαι, guide oneself by *the stars*, Ael. *NA*2.7, 7.48; ἄστροις τὸ λοιπὸν ἐκμετρούμενος χθόνα knowing its place only by *the stars*, S.*OT*795: metaph., ἐχθροῦς ἀ. ὡς λάμψειν Id. *El.*66. II. of something *brilliant, admirable*, Ἀκροκόρινθον Ἑλλάδος ἄ. *AP*7.297 (Polystr.), cf. 9.400 (Pall.), *APl.*4.295; Σωκρατικῆς σοφίης ἄ. *IG*3.770a.

ἀστρονομ-έω, *study astronomy*, Ar.*Nu.*194, Pl.*Tht.*174a:—Med., D.L.1.34, Iamb.*VP*25.112:—Pass., ὡς νῦν ἀστρονομεῖται as *astronomy is now practised*, Pl.*R.*530c. ☼-ημα, ατος, τό, *observation of the stars*, Timo 23. -ία, ἡ, *astronomy*, Hp.*Aër.*2, Ar.*Nu.*201, Pl.*Smp.*188b, etc.; title of a work ascribed to Hesiod, and Ptolemy's σύνταξις, Olymp. *in Mete.*68.20, al. -ικός, ή, όν, *skilled in astronomy*, Pl.*R.*530a, etc.; ἀστρονομικώτατον ἡμῶν Id.*Ti.*27a; τὰ -κά Thphr. *Sign.*1: Comp. -ώτερος Str.1.2.24. Adv. -κῶς Poll.4.16. II. of questions, *pertaining to astronomy*, Pl.*Prt.*315c. III. name of *ninth sign of* ἀποτελεσματογραφία, Paul.Al.*M.*4.

ἀστρο-νόμος, ὁ, (νέμω) *astronomer*, Pl.*R.*531a, etc.; ὁ ἀ. the *astronomer par excellence*, i. e. Ptolemy, Olymp. *in Mete.*188.33:—as Adj., Nic.Dam.p.3 D. -πληγος, ον, = ἀστροβλής, *Gp.*5.36.1. -ποιέω τι *make a constellation of* it, *An.Ox.*3.164. -σκοπέω, *observe the stars*, E.ap.Satyr.*Vit.Eur.Fr.*38 iii 12. -σκοπία, ἡ, *the study of the stars*, Herm. *in Phdr.*p.109 A. -τέχνημα, ατος, τό, *celestial globe*, Tz.*H.*5.282.

ἀστρούθιστος, ον, *not washed with* στρουθίον, Dsc.2.74.

ἀστρο-φᾰής or -φάνής, ές, *shining like a star*, Eumolp.ap.D.S. 1.11. -φεγγής, ές, *shining with the light of heavenly bodies*, *PMag. Par.*1.2071. -φόρος, ον, (φέρω) *bearing stars*, *Hymn.Is.*23.

ἄστροφος, ον, (στρέφω) *without turning round* or *away*, *fixed*, ὄμματα A.*Ch.*99; ἀφέρπειν ἄ. go away *without turning back*, S.*OC* 490. 2. *without turning* or *twisting*, Pl.*Plt.*282d. II. *without strophe*, Heph.*Poëm.*5.

☼ἀστροχίτων [ῑ], ον, gen. ωνος, *star-clad*, of night, Orph.*A.*513, 1028, Nonn.*D.*40.408.

ἀστρώδης, ες, = ἀστροειδής, Lyd.*Mens.*4.73.

ἀστρῷος, α, ον (also ος, ον Sch.A.R.1.936), *starry*, οἶκος *AP*9.400 (Pall.); ἀ. ἀνάγκη the law *of the stars*, ib.505.14; ἀ. οὐρανοῦ διάθεσις Phlp. *in Mete.*117.20; ἀ. θεοί Procl. *in Cra.*p.49 P.; ψυχαί ib.p.87 P., Herm. *in Phdr.*p.130 A.; σώματα Alex.Aphr.*Pr.*1.116.

ἀστρωπός, όν, = ἀστερωπός, E.*HF*406 (lyr.).

ἀστρ-ωσία, ἡ, *practice of sleeping without bedding*, Pl.*Lg.*633c (pl.). -ωτος, ον, *without bed* or *bedding*, εὕδω Epich.35.14, cf. Pl. *Smp.*203d, *Plt.*272a. 2. *uncovered*, Id.*Prt.*321c: metaph., *bare*, πέδον E.*HF*52. 3. of a horse, *without trappings*, Arr.*Tact.*2.3, Suid.

☼ἄστυ, τό, Ep. and Ion. gen. εος (disyll. in Semon.7.74), Att. and Trag. εως (ἄστεος is never required by the metre, ἄστεως (trisyll.) is necessary in E.*Or.*761, *Ph.*842, *El.*246, and is the only form found in Att. Inscrr., as *IG*2.584.7, 2$^2$.463.76; it is a disyll. in E.*El.*298, *Ba.* 840): pl., ἄστη Id.*Supp.*952; ἄστεα Hdt.1.5:—*town*, ἀ. μέγα Πριάμοιο Il.2.332, al.: with name in gen., Σουσίδος, Σούσων ἄ., A.*Pers.*119, 535; ἄ. Θήβης S.*OC*1372, *Tr.*1154, etc. 2. *lower town*, opp. *acropolis*, Hdt.1.176, al. II. in Attica, *town* (i.e. *Athens*), opp. ἀγρός (*country*), mostly without Art., στυγῶν μὲν ἄ. Ar.*Ach.*33; ἐξ ἄστεως νῦν εἰς ἀγρὸν χωρῶμεν Id.*Fr.*107; ἔγημα.. ἄγροικος ὢν ἐξ ἄστεως I married a *town* girl, Id.*Nu.*47; τῶν κατ' ἄστυ πραγμάτων Men.*Georg.* *Fr.*4: also with Art., πρὸς τὸ ἄ. Pl.*R.*327b, 328c, al. 2. *Athens*, opp. *Phalerum* or *Piraeus*, Id.*Smp.*172a, D.20.12, Arist.*Pol.*1303$^b$12, al.; τὸ ἄστυ τῆς πόλεως, opp. *Piraeus*, Lycurg.18; ἄρχοντος ἐν ἄστει, opp. ἐν Σαλαμῖνι, *IG*2.594. 3. in Egypt, *Alexandria*, *PHal.*1.89 (iii B.C.), St.Byz. s. v. ἄστυ, etc. III. *town* in the material sense, opp. πόλις (*the civic body*), Il.17.144. IV. Adv. ἄστυδε (q.v.). (ϝάστυ, cf. ϝαστυόχος *IG*5(2).77 (Tegea): gen. ϝάστιος ib.7.3170 (Orchom. Boeot.): but prob. not cogn. with Skt. *vásati* 'dwell', which has *e* in the root.)

ἀστῠ-άναξ [ᾰν], ακτος, ὁ, *lord of the city*, epith. of certain gods, A. *Supp.*1018 (lyr.): in Hom. only as pr. n., *Astyanax*, the son of Hector:—hence Adj. Ἀστυανάκτειος, α, ον, *AP*9.351 (Leon.). II. by an obscene pun, = ἄστυτος, Eust.849.54. III. name of a *fish*, Hsch. ☼-αρχος, ὁ, title of *magistrate* in Alexandria, *BGU*1024$^v$8 (iv A.D.; ἀστί- Pap.). -βοώτης, ου, ὁ, (βοάω) *crying* or *calling through the city*, epith. of a herald, Il.24.701. (Prop. -βοήτης, Ion. contr. -βώτης, by 'distraction' -βοώτης.) -γειτνιάω, *to be neighbouring, adjacent*, τὰς -γειτνιώσας πόλεις *CIG*2820 *A* 20 (Aphrodisias). -γειτονέομαι χθόνα *dwell in a neighbouring* land, A.*Supp.* 286. -γειτονικός, ή, όν, *of* or *with neighbours*, πόλεμος Plu.2. 87e. -γείτων, ον, gen. ονος, *near or bordering on a city*, σκοπαί A.*Ag.*309; πόλιες Hdt.6.99, cf. 9.122, E.*Hipp.*1161, Plu.*Rom.*23; πόλεμοι Arist.*Pol.*1330$^a$18. 2. as Subst., *neighbour to the city*, *borderer*, Hdt.2.104, 5.66, Th.1.15, X.*HG*1.3.2., *SIG*633.10 (Milet., ii B.C.), etc.

ἄστῠδε, Adv. *into, to*, or *towards the city*, Il.18.255, Od.17.5, and in late Prose, as Alciphr.1.1.

ἀστῠ-δίκης [ῑ], ου, ὁ, = Lat. *praetor urbanus*, Lyd.*Mens.*1.19. -δρομέομαι, Pass., ἀστυδρομουμένα πόλις *filled with the turmoil of pursuers and pursued*, A.*Th.*221 (lyr.). -θεμις, ὁ, *just ruler of cities*, B.4.3.

ἀστυκός, v. ἀστικός.

ἀστυλάζει· λυπεῖ μετὰ κλαυθμοῦ, Hsch. ἀστυλίς· φυτόν, ὅθεν ὁ ἰξός, Id. ἀστυλόν· τὸ τραχὺ ἱμάτιον, Id.

ἄστῡλ-ος, ον, *without pillar* or *prop*, οἶκος *AP*7.648 (Leon.). -ωτος, ον, gloss on ἀνερμάτιστος, Sch.Ael.*NA*1.11.

ἀστύ-νῑκος [ῠ] πόλις Athens *the victorious city*, A.*Eu.*915. -νομέω, *to be an* ἀστυνόμος, D.*Prooem.*55, *OGI*483.1 (Pergam.), *IG*11(4).

1145 (Delos). 2. at Rome, *to be praetor urbanus*, D.C.42.22. **-νομία**, ἡ, *the office of ἀστυνόμος*, Arist.*Pol.*1321ᵇ23. 2. at Rome, *the city praetorship*, D.C.42.22. ***-νομικός**, ή, όν, *of or for an ἀστυνόμος* or *his office*, Pl.*R.*425d, Arist.*Pol.*1264ᵃ31; νόμος *PHal.*1.237 (iii B.C.). **-νόμιον**, τό, *the court of the ἀστυνόμοι*, Pl.*Lg.*918a. **-νόμος**, ὁ, (νέμω) *protecting the city*, θεοί A.*Ag.*88; ἀγλαΐαι ἀ. *public* festivals, Pi.*N.*9.31; ὀργαὶ ἀ. the feelings *of law-abiding* or *social life*, S.*Ant.* 355 (lyr.). II. as Subst., *a magistrate who had the care of the police, streets, and public buildings* at Athens, Is.1.15, D.24.112, Arist.*Ath.* 50.1, *SIG*313.17, *Com.Adesp.*25aD.: in other cities, as Tenos, *IG* 12(5).883.14; Iasos, *SIG*169.10; Rhodes, *IG*12(1).1; Pergamum, *OGI*483.7, etc., cf. Pl.*Lg.*759a, al. 2. = Lat. *praetor urbanus*, D.C. 53.2. **-ξενοι**, οἱ, *those who have no house in the city* (Tarent.), Hsch. ***-όχος**, ον, (ἔχω) *protecting the city*, τεῖχος *AP*9.764 (Paul. Sil.); μέριμνα *APl.*4.36 (Agath.). (ϝάστ-, cf. ἄστυ fin.) **-πολέω**, *go up and down in a city, live in it, frequent the streets*, Theopomp. Hist.114a, Max.Tyr.8.1 and 9. **-πολία**, ἡ, *residence in a city*, Hierocl.p.62A.

***ἄστῠρον**, τό, Dim. of ἄστυ, Call.*Fr.*19, *Aet.*3.1.74, *Hec.*1.1.6, Nic. *Al.*15.

**ἀστῠσία**, ἡ, *impotence*, D.C.79.16.

**ἀστῠτίς**, ίδος, ἡ, *lettuce*, used as an anti-aphrodisiac, Lycus ap.Ath. 2.69e, *Gp.*12.13.2.

**ἄστῠτος**, ον, (στύω) *impotent*, paratrag. for ἄστυλος in Xenarch.1.

**ἀστύτριψ**, ῖβος, ὁ, ἡ, (τρίβω) *always living in the city*, Critias 72 D., Philostr.*Im.*2.26.

**ἀστῠφέλικτος**, ον, *unshaken, undisturbed*, βασιλεία X.*Lac.*15.7; θεός Call.*Del.*26; Ἅιδης *Epigr.Gr.*540.3; ὕπνου χάριν *AP*9.764 (Paul. Sil.); σῶμα Orph.*Fr.*168.22; ἀσκηθὴς ἐν νευσὶ καὶ ἀ. ἐπ' αἴη *Sammelb.* 5829.3.

**ἀστύφελος** [ῠ], η, ον (ος, ον *AP*9.413 (Antiphil.)), *not rugged*, πατρίς Thgn.1044.

**ἀστυφία**, ἡ, = ἀστυσία, Anon.ap.*EM*197.53, *AB*456.

**ἄστῠφος**, ον, (στύφω) *not astringent*, Alex.Trall.2. II. *not over-dry*, Aët.7.102. III. *not mordanted*, *PHolm.*17.42.

**ἀσυγγενής**, ές, *not akin*, Hsch. (ἀξ-).

**ἀσυγ-γνωμόνητος**, ον, = sq., Phint.ap.Stob.4.23.61ᵃ, Sch.A.*Pr.* 34. **-γνώμων**, ον, gen. ονος, *not pardoning, merciless*, D.21.100, Plu.2.59e: irreg. Sup. -έστατος Phint.ap.Stob.4.23.61. ***-γνωστος**, ον, = foreg., Jul.*Ep.*184. II. *unpardonable*, Gal.1.13, Phalar. *Ep.*6, Him.*Ecl.*5.10, Lib.*Or.*59.144. Adv. -τως Phld.*Mort.*20.

**ἀσύγγρᾰφος**, ον, *without bond*, ἀσύγγραφα δανείζεσθαι D.S.1.79.

**ἀσυγγύμναστος**, ον, *unexercised*, Luc.*Par.*6.

**ἀσυγκατα-θετέω**, *withhold one's assent*, S.E.*M.*7.157. **-θετος**, ον, *withholding assent*, διάθεσις Chrysipp.*Stoic.*2.40; γνώμη Ph.1.287, cf. Aristocl.ap.Eus.*PE*14.18. Adv. -τως Chrysipp.*Stoic.*3.42, Ph. 1.78.

**ἀσυγκέραστος**, ον, *untempered*, φύσις *AP*9.180 (Pall.).

**ἀσυγκίνητος** [ῑ], ον, *without agitation*, Antyll.ap.Orib.6.21.16.

**ἀσύγκλαστος**, ον, *hard, pitiless*, πρὸς τοὺς ὁμοφύλους Phld.*Herc.* 1251.20.

**ἀσύγκλειστος**, ον, *not enclosed*, πλευραῖς Arist.*PA*688ᵇ35.

**ἀσύγκλωστος**, ον, *not interwoven, disconnected, disjointed*, πράγματα Cic.*Att.*6.1.17, cf. Porph.*Abst.*3.18; λόγος Herm.*in Phdr.*p.187A.; ἐξηγήσεις Porph.*Chr.*39; *incompatible*, συγκλώθειν τὰ ἀ. Phlp.*in Ph.* 34.14; πρὸς τὸ ἓν ἀ. καὶ ἀσύμβατος Dam.*Pr.*5.

***ἀσυγκόλλητος**, ον, *made in one piece*, Sch.Il.14.200.

**ἀσυγκόμιστος**, ον, *not gathered in*, καρπός X.*Cyr.*1.5.10.

**ἀσύγκρᾶτος**, ον, *incapable of blending, discordant*, δόξαι Plu.2.418d; δυνάμεις, of herbs, cj. ib.134d; φωνή Nicom.*Harm.*12.

***ἀσύγκρῐτος**, ον, *not comparable*, Thphr.*Fr.*89.7, Phld.*D.*1.15, *AP* 5.64; τοῖς ἄλλοις Plu.*Marc.*17; ἀσύγκριτος ἄνθρωπος ἀλόγῳ ζῴῳ Phld. *D.*1.11. Adv. -τως *without the use of the comparative form*, D.T.635. 15. 2. *incomparable, surpassing*, θεός Ph.1.578, cf. Plu.*Dio* 47, *BGU*613.20 (ii A.D.), etc., *Ath.Mitt.*12.174 (Prusias); of remedies, Gal.14.112. Adv. -τως *incomparably*, Hierocl.*in CA*3p.424M., *CIG* 3493.14 (Thyatira). II. *antagonistic, of alien kind*, Plu.2.134d (but v. foreg.).

**ἀσυγκρότητος**, ον, v. ἀξυγκρότητος.

**ἀσύγκτητος**, ον, *not capable of being acquired with other things*, κάλλος ἀ. πρᾶγμα Secund.*Sent.*14.

**ἀσύγχριστος**, ον, *unanointed*, Antyll.ap.Orib.10.13.20.

**ἀσύγχῡμος**, ον, *not turned into syrup*, Orion s. v. χυλός.

**ἀσύγχῠτος**, ον, *not confused*, ἐπίνοιαι, δυνάμεις, Ph.1.6,434, cf. Plu. 2.735b, Procl.*Inst.*176; *not mingled together*, Arr.*Epict.*4.11.8. Adv. -τως *without confusion*, ib.8.20.

**ἀσυγχώρητος**, ον, *forbidden*, D.S.1.78; *not to be conceded* or *admitted*, Agatharch.8, S E.*M.*7.380; *not duly authorized*, ἐπιγραφαί *SIG*793.8 (Cos, i A.D.).

**ἀσύζευκτος**, ον, *not paired*, Suid. s. v. ἀσυνδύαστος. Adv. -τως *AB*456.

**ἀσύζῠγος**, ον, *without exact correspondence*, Habron ap.A.D.*Synt.* 100.27. Adv. -γως Archig.ap.Gal.8.592,625. 2. *unique*, αἰτία Anon.*in Prm.* in *Rh.Mus.*47.617.

**ἀσῡκοφάντητος**, ον, *not plagued by informers*, Aeschin.3.216, Plu. 2.756d; ἑορτή *OGI*383.157 (Commagene, i B.C.); πενία ἀ. κτῆμα Secund.*Sent.*10; *free from misrepresentation*, Onos.*Praef.*10. II. *unexceptionable*, *BGU*1059.8 (Aug.), Luc.*Hist.Conscr.*59, *Salt.*81. III. Adv. -τως *without quibbling*, Phld.*Rh.*1.8 S., Plu.2.529d.

**ἀσῡλ-αῖος**, α, ον, *of an asylum*, θεός Plu.*Rom.*9. ***-εί** or **-ί**, Adv. of ἄσυλος, *inviolably*, *IG*1.41, *Supp.Epigr.*1.362.23 (Samos), *SIG*110.10 (Rhodes), Theognost.*Can.*165.10. **-ητος**, ον, = ἄσυλος 1, E.*Hel.*449, J.*AJ*19.1.1, D.C.75.14. ***-ία** ἡ, *inviolability*, i.e., 1. *safety to the person*, of suppliants, ἀ. βροτῶν A.*Supp.*610; of competitors at games, Plu.*Arat.*28; in Inscrr., as a privilege bestowed on one who has deserved well of the state, εἶμεν δὲ αὐτῷ ἀτέλειαν καὶ ἀ. καὶ κατὰ γᾶν καὶ κατὰ θάλασσαν *IG*7.11 (Megara), cf. 2.551.80, 5(1).1226 (Lacon.), etc. 2. *sanctity, inviolability* of character, ἀ. ἱερέως D.H.11.25. 3. of a place of refuge, *right of sanctuary*, Plb.4.74.2; ἀσυλίαν παρέχειν Plu.2.828d; freq. in Inscrr., ἀ. πόλεως καὶ χώρας *IG*12(5).1341 (Paros), etc. 4. *exemption from contributions*, Ph.2.250.

**ἀσυλ-λήπτος**, ον, *not conceiving*, Dsc.4.19; *preventing conception*, φάρμακον Aët.16.17. **-ληψία**, ἡ, *inability to conceive, barrenness*, Dsc.3.34, Aët.16.26.

**ἀσυλλογ-ιστία**, ἡ, *inconclusiveness, faultiness of logic*, Ps.-Alex. Aphr.*in SE*135.31. ***-ιστος**, ον, *non-syllogistic, formally* or *materially invalid*, χρῆσις Arist.*APo.*91ᵇ23, cf. *Rh.*1357ᵇ24, Phld. *Rh.*2.24S.; *irrelevant*, ἀ. πρὸς τὸ προκείμενον Anon.*in SE*16.33. 2. *unattainable by reasoning, incalculable*, Men.355.1, J.*AJ*4.7.1, al., Plu.2.24b, 580d. II. Act., *not reasoning justly, unreasoning*, Arist. *SE*167ᵇ35, cf. Plb.12.3.2; ἀσυλλόγιστόν ἐστιν ἡ πονηρία Men.768: c. gen., *not rationalizing*, διάθεσις ἀ. τινῶν Chrysipp.*Stoic.*3.117; ἀ. τοῦ συμφέροντος *not calculating* it, J.*AJ*9.12.3; τοῦ χρησίμου Porph.*Abst.* 1.7. Adv. -τως, λέγειν Arist.*APo.*77ᵇ40; ἀ. ἔχειν τινός Plu.*Caes.*59.

***ἄσῠλος**, ον, *safe from violence, inviolate*, ἐπεὶ πᾶν ἐστιν ἄ. Parm.8. 48; μενεῖς ἄ. E.*Med.*728; ἐκπεμπέτω ἄσυλον Pl.*Lg.*866d; of the persons of magistrates, D.H.7.45, 10.39; τὸ ἄ. *right of sanctuary*, *GDI*4940.13 (Allaria). 2. *not liable to reprisals* (cf. σῦλαι), *IG*9(1). 333 (Locr.). 3. c. gen., γάμων ἄ. *safe from* marriage, E.*Hel.* 61. II. of places, γῆν ἄ. παρασχεῖν make the land *a refuge*, Id. *Med.*387; ἱερὸν ὃ ἄσυλον νενόμισται Plb.4.18.10, cf. *SIG*635.5, *BGU* 1053 ii 9 (i B.C.), etc.; ἄσυλον, τό, *sanctuary*, ib.304.28: metaph., νόμον τηρεῖν ἄ. *OGI*383.115 (Commagene, i B.C.); ἄ. γράμματα, στῆλαι, ib.8.110; so κόμην ἄ. φυλάξαι *uncut*, Philostr.*VA*4.16.

***ἀσύλωτος** [ῠ], ον, = foreg., πύργος *BSA*17.231 (Pamphyl.).

**ἀσύμ-βᾰμα**, ατος, τό, *not a σύμβαμα* or *full predicate*, Priscian.*Inst.* 18.1.4. **-βᾰτος**, Att. ἀξ-, ον, *not coming to terms*, τὸ ἀξ. Th.3.46; ἀ. ἐχθρός Ph.1.223; ἀντίθεσις ἀ. *irreconcilable*, Plu.2.946e, cf. Procl. *Inst.*28, Dam.*Pr.*5. Adv. -τως, ἔχειν to be *irreconcilable*, Ph.*Fr.*24 H., Plu.*Cic.*46: neut. pl. as Adv., ἀσύμβατα μνησικακοῦντες Ph.2. 520. 2. *not comparable, disparate*: εἰς ἕτερα ἀ. *incongruous* in other respects, Gal.5.540. 3. τραῦμα ἀ. wound *that will not close up, heal*, Aret.*CA*2.2. II. Act., *bringing no agreement*, κοινολογία Plb.15.9.1. **-βίβαστος** [ῐ], ον, *not to be brought into union, not to be reconciled* or *harmonized*, Eust.1658.40. **-βλητος**, Att. ἀξ-, ον, *not addible*, Arist.*Metaph.*1080ᵇ9; *not comparable*, ib.1055ᵃ7; ἀ. πρός τι or τινί, *incomparable with, far superior to*, Epicur.*Ep.*1p.31 U., *Fr.*556, cf. Plu.2.1125c. 2. *incommensurable*, Theo Sm.p.73H.; *indeterminate*, μῆκος Gal.18(1).773. 3. of weights or measures, *not true according to the standard*, *IG*2.476.17. II. *not to be guessed, unintelligible*, ἀξύμβλητον ἀνθρώπῳ μαθεῖν S.*Tr.*694, cf. Ael.*NA*6. 60. III. *unsocial*, ἄπλατον ἀξ. S.*Fr.*387. **-βολέω**, *pay no contribution towards*, τινός Ach.Tat.8.17 (dub.). **-βολος**, ον, *without contribution* (cf. συμβολή), freq. in later Com.: I. of the dinner, δεῖπνον ἀ. *to which no one brings anything*, Alex.257.2, Amphis 39; δείπνων ἡδοναῖς ἀ. Timocl.8.10: metaph., ἀ. βίος *unsocial, solitary*, Plu.2.957a. II. of persons, *not contributing* to a feast, *not paying one's scot* or *share*, δεῖπνα δειπνεῖν ἀσύμβολον Aeschin.1.75, cf. Dromo 1.2; ἀ. κινεῖν ὀδόντας Timocl.10.4; τὸν ἀ. εὗρε γελοῖα λέγειν Ῥαδάμανθυς Anaxandr.10; τρέφειν τινὰ ἀ. Men.*Sam.*258, cf. Diph.73. 8; ἔστω ἀ. ἐν συνόδοις πάσαις *Michel* 998.44 (Delos); ἡδονὴ ἀ. Plu.2. 646b. Adv. -λως, δειπνεῖν Ath.4.162f (ἀσυμβόλῳ Kaib.). **-μᾰχος**, ον, *without allies*, E.*Antiop.*iv B 32 A. **-μετρία**, *incommensurability*, Arist.*Metaph.*1061ᵇ1. II. *disproportion, want of proportion* or *harmony*, Pl.*Grg.*525a; πρός τι Arist.*Mete.*380ᵃ32: in pl., αἱ τῶν πράτων δυναμίων ἀ. Ti.Locr.102b. **-μετρος**, Att. ἀξ-, ον, *incommensurable*, ταῖς μεγίσταις συμμετρίαις Pl.*Ti.*87d: abs., Arist.*Sens.* 439ᵇ30, al., Pl.*Lg.*918b; ἁ. ἡ διάμετρος καὶ ἡ πλευρά Arist.*EN*1112ᵃ 23. Adv. -ρως Dam.*Pr.*427. II. *disproportionate*, X.*Cyn.*2.7; ἀ. πρός τι *disproportionate* to it, Arist.*IA*708ᵃ15; *ill-proportioned*, Id.*Po.*1461ᵃ13; ὑπόμνημα *of excessive length*, Demetr.Lac.*Herc.* 1014.67 F.; κινήματα Phld.*Mort.*9. Adv. -ρως ib.8, Attic.ap.Eus. *PE*15.7. III. *unsuited*, πρὸς δημοκρατίαν Plu.*Per.*16, cf. *Them.* 22; τινί *Phoc.*3: c. inf., *not of fit size to*.., Arist.*GA*719ᵇ12. **-μικτος**, ον, *incapable of blending*, στοιχεῖα D.H.*Comp.*22. **-μνημόνευτος**, ον, *not remembered in connexion*, Dsc.1*Praef.*3. **-πᾰγής**, ές, *not compact*, Luc.*Anach.*24. **-πάθεια** [πᾰ], ἡ, *want of fellow-feeling*, S.E.*M.*5.44. **-πᾰθής**, ές, *without fellow-feeling* or *sympathy*, ἑαυτῷ Plu.*Cor.*21; πρός τινα Id.2.976c, cf. Phld.*Herc.*1251. 20, Plot.2.9.16, Procl.*Inst.*28; πρὸς τὸν λόγον Arr.*Epict.*2.9.21. Adv. -θῶς D.S.13.111, Porph.*Sent.*32. II. Medic., *unaffected* by an operation, Sor.2.60. III. Astrol., epith. of certain ζῴδια, *Cat. Cod.Astr.*1.135.13. Adv. -θῶς Vett.Val.146.24. **-πάθητος** [πᾰ], ον, = foreg. 1, *An.Ox.*2.340. **-πέραντος**, ον, *inconclusive*, Arist.*Ph.*186ᵃ 25. **-πέραστος**, ον, *unfinished*, Sch.Pi.*I.*1 (Arg.). **-περίφορος**, ον, *unaccommodating*, Phld.*Ir.*p.54 W., Ptol.*Tetr.*159. **-πλεκτος**, ον, *unconnected*, Thphr.*CP*6.10.3. **-πλήρωτος**, ον, *not filled up*,

Dsc.1.70. **-πλοκος**, ον, *unconnected, absolute*, Ph.2.19. Adv. -κως *AB*456. **-ποτος**, ον, *made of non-absorbent material*. κυθρίδιον Afric.ap.Olymp.Alch.p.75 B. **-πτωτος**, ον, *not falling in, full*, of face or body, Hp.*Hum*.4, Gal.11.25, al.; *not closing*, of the edges of a wound, ἀ. χείλη Antyll.ap.Orib.7.11.10; *not liable to collapse*, Anon.Lond.26.50. II. *not touching*, τῇ ψυχῇ Plu.*Lib*. 7. 2. esp. in Math., of lines or planes *which never meet*, e.g. parallel straight lines, Hero *Deff*.70; of lines *which do not cut* a curve, *non-secant*, ἀ. τῇ τομῇ αἱ ΓΔ, ΓΕ Apollon.Perg.*Con*.2.1, cf. 14; ἀσύμπτωτος (sc. γραμμή), ἡ, *asymptote*, of the hyperbola, ib.2. 3, etc.; of the conchoid, Procl. *in Euc*.p.366 F. **-πώρωτος**, ον, (πωρόομαι) *not become callous*; of fractured bones *that have not united*, Dsc.1.112. **※-φάνής**, ές, *dark*, ὑπόνομος Arist.*Mir*.836ᵇ19; *obscure*, Porph.*in Ptol*.181: Sup., Dam.*Pr*.38. Adv. -νῶς *obscurely*, Arg.4 Ar.*Ra*., Suid. **-φθαρτος**, ον, *without blending*, κρᾶσις Porph.*Gaur*. 10.6. **-φιλος**· ἀνόητος, ἄτιμος, Hsch., and **ἀσύμφηλος**, Cyr., Zonar., i.e. ἀσύφηλος (q.v.). **-φορος**, Att. ἀξ-, ον, *inconvenient, prejudicial*, φυτοῖσιν Hes.*Op*.782, cf. Hp.*Acut*.56, Antipho 2.1.10, Th.3.40; ἔς τι Id.1.32; πρός τι Id.2.91: Sup., E.*Tr*.491; ἀσυμφορώτατον ὑμῖν ἔθος εἰσάγειν D.19.2. Adv. -ρως, ἔχειν X.*HG*6.3.1; ζῆν πρὸς τὴν πολιτείαν Arist.*Pol*.1308ᵇ21. **-φυής**, ές, *not growing together*, μόρια *Placit*.5.19.5; τῇ κτίσει Hsch. **-φῦλος**, ον, *not akin, unlike*, Dsc.1 *Praef*.3, J.*AJ*11.6.5, Luc.*Hist.Conscr*.11; *incompatible, unsuitable*, Plu.2.709b, etc. Adv. -λως Sch.Il.9.643. **-φῦτος**, ον, *not growing together* or *uniting*, Hp.*de Arte* 10; *not able to unite*, Aret. *CA*1.7, Gal.10.336: generally, *detached*, *PLond*.1207.6 (i B.C.).

**ἀσυμφων-έω**, *to be out of harmony with*, παντὶ λόγῳ Plot.1.1. 12. **-ία**, ἡ, *want of harmony, discord*, Pl.*Lg*.861a, Ph.1.5; *incoherence*, πολλῆς ἀσυμφωνίας ἔγεμεν ὁ λόγος Carneisc.*Herc*.1027. 10. **-ος**, Att. ἀξ-, ον, *not harmonious*, Pl.*R*.402d; χορδή D.H. *Comp*.11. 2. metaph., *discordant, at variance*, ἐμαυτῷ Pl.*Grg*. 482c; ἕξεις Ocell.4.13; πρὸς ἀλλήλους *Act.Ap*.28.25, Arr.*An.Prooem*. (Comp.). Adv. -νως Pl.*Lg*.860c; τοῖς αὐτοῖς Arg.Str.1. II. *not speaking the same language*, πρὸς ἄλληλα Pl.*Plt*.262d, cf. *Lg*.777d; ἀ. ταῖς διαλέκτοις D.S.17.53.

**ἀσυν-αίρετος**, ον, Medic., *not contracted* or *shortened*, Paul.Aeg.6. 107. II. Gramm., *uncontracted*, Eust.50.36. Adv. -τως Id.16. 32. **-αίσθητος**, ον, *not perceptible*, Simp.*in Ph*.707.4. **-ἀκόλουθος**, Att. ἀξ-, ον, *without attendants*, Antiph.16. **-ακτος**, ον, *incompatible, incoherent, illogical*, Phld.*Sign*.14, Epict.*Ench*.44, S.E.*P*.2. 137. **-άλειπτος** [ᾰλ], ον, (συναλείφω) *without synaloephe*, Hdn. Gr.2.912. Adv. -τως Eust.19.39, Sch.Ven.Il.3.150.

**ἀσυνάλλ-ακτος**, ον, *without intercourse*, Plu.2.416f; *unsociable*, D.H.1.41, 5.66. **-αξία**, ἡ, *lack of intercourse*, πρὸς ἀλλήλους *SIG* 684.14 (Dyme, ii B.C.), cf. Stob.2.7.25.

**ἀσυν-άντητος**, ον, *not to be met, unsocial*, Hsch. s.v. ἀξύμβλητον. **-απτος**, ον, *not joined*, Arist.*HA*516ᵃ30; *not connected*, συλλογισμοὶ ἀ. πρὸς ἀλλήλους Id.*APr*.42ᵃ21. **-αρθρος**, ον, Gramm., *without the article*, D.T.641.9, A.D.*Synt*.101.5, al. Adv. -ρως Sch.Il. 2.1. II. *inarticulate*, βοή prob. in *Corp.Herm*.1.4 (-ρως codd.). **-άρμοστος**, ον, *unfitting, unsuitable*, Plu.2.709b; τὸ ἀ. *incongruity*, S.E. *P*.1.43. **-άρτητος**, ον, *disconnected, incoherent*, D.H.*Th*.6, Gal.15. 468, Sch.S.*OC*1560. II. in Metric, ἀσυνάρτητοι στίχοι verses *compounded of independent* κῶλα, Heph.15, Sch.Ar.*Ra*.1316, etc. **※-δεξίαστος**, ον, *not entering into engagements*, Ptol.*Tetr*.166. **-δετος**, ον, *unconnected, loose*, X.*Cyn*.5.30, Apollod.*Poliorc*.160.8; *independent*, κίνησις Plu.2.386a: Astrol., of signs, Κριὸς πρὸς Σκορπίον ἀ. Gal. 19.333. II. of language, *without conjunctions*, Arist.*Int*.17ᵃ17; of style, Id.*Rh*.1413ᵇ29 (but ib.1407ᵇ38 ἄνευ μὲν συνδέσμου, μὴ ἀσύνδετα δέ without conjunction, but not *without connexion*); τὸ ἀ., in Rhet., *style without conjunctions*, Demetr.*Eloc*.268, cf. 192; σχῆμα Hermog.*Id*.2.1, al. Adv. -τως Philostr.*VS*1.16.4, Hermog.*Id*.1.9, Tib.*Fig*.40. **-δηλος**, ον, strengthd. for ἄδηλος, Plu.*Lyc*.28. **-δύαστος** [ῠ], ον, = ἀσύμπλοκος, Hsch.; = ἀσύζευκτος, Suid. **-εγκλῖτος**, ον, Gramm., *not undergoing enclisis at the same time*, Trypho *Fr*.5 V. **-είδητος**, ον, (σύνοιδα) *not privy to* a thing, ψυχαὶ ἀ. κακῶν Onos.4.2. Adv. -τως, τοῖς ἄλλοις Plu.2.214e, cf. *POxy*.123.16 (iii/iv A.D.). **-είκαστος**, ον, *not to be guessed, unintelligible*, Sch.S. *Tr*.694. **-έλευστος**, ον, *non-coagulating*, ἄτομοι Diog.Oen.20: Gramm., *not forming a compound*, A.D.*Pron*.45.24; *not entering into composition*, τὰ τοῦ τόνου Id.*Synt*.304.9. **-έμπτωτος**, ον, *not coinciding in form*, Eust.879.30, al. II. *not denoting coincidence in time*, A.D.*Synt*.210.14. **※-έξωστος**, ον, *not to be dislodged*, of an athlete, *IG*14.1102, *CPHerm*.7 ii 3. **-έργητος**, ον, *not affording help*, Phld.*Oec*.p.67 J., *Vit*.p.24 J., Carneisc.*Herc*.1027.14. II. *unassisted*, Antyll.ap.Orib.10.30.8.

**ἀσυν-εσία**, Att. ἀξ-, ἡ, (ἀσύνετος) *want of understanding, stupidity*, E.*Ph*.1727 (lyr.), Th.1.122; opp. σύνεσις, Arist.*EN*1142ᵇ34 codd. **-ετέω**, *to be without understanding*, τὰ μέγιστα Hp.*Fract*.25, cf. Lxx *Ps*.118(119).158, Hsch. s.v. φελγύνει:—Aeol. **-έτημι**, *fail to understand*, τὰν ἀνέμων στάσιν Alc.18. **-ετίζομαι**, = foreg., Aq.*Je*.10.8. **ἀσυνετοποιός**, όν, *nonsensical*, Sch.Ar.*Ra*.1286.

**※ἀσύνετος**, Att. ἀξ-, ον, *void of understanding, witless*, Hp.*Fract*.31: Comp., Hdt.3.81, E.*Or*.493, Th.1.142; φρὴν ἀ. Ar.*Av*.456; τί τάδ' ἀσύνετα; what *folly* is this? E.*Hel*.352 (lyr.). Adv. -τως Plu.2. 141b. 2. c. gen., *not able to understand*, λόγου Heraclit.1, cf. Plu.2.713b, Jul.*Or*.7.218b. II. *not to be understood, unintelligible*, E.*Ion* 1205, *Ph*.1731. Adv. -τως Hipparch.1.8.11.

**ἀσυν-εχής**, ές, *not continuous*; of winds, *variable*, Thphr.*Vent*. 11. **-ήθεια**, ἡ, *unfamiliarity*, Arist.*Metaph*.995ᵃ2, Thphr.*HP*9. 17.2; ἀ. τοῦ δικολογεῖν *inexperience in*.., Arist.*Rh*.1368ᵃ21, cf. Plb. 15.32.7. **-ήθης**, ες, gen. εος, *unaccustomed*, χῶρος, τόπος, Emp. 118, Aen.Tact.16.19; τὰ ἀ. Hp.*Aph*.2.50; ἀσύνηθες τοῖς ζῴοις τὸ πίνειν Arist.*HA*606ᵇ26; φαντασία ἀ. πράγματος *Stoic*.3.98, al.; *not customary*, ὅπερ οὐκ ἀσύνηθες ὀνομάζειν Phld.*D*.3.2. II. of persons, *unaccustomed, inexperienced*, Hp.*Aph*.2.49, Plb.10.47.7. Adv. -θως Plu.2.678a. 2. *unfamiliar*, of persons, Arist.*EN*1126ᵇ 26; ἐν ἀνδράσιν ἀ. amongst men *unknown to them*, D.H.8.44. **※-ήμων**, ον, gen. ονος, *not comprehending*, A.*Ag*.1060. **-θεσία**, ἡ, *breach of covenant, transgression*, Lxx 2*Es*.9.2,4. II. *being uncompounded* or *uncombined*, A.D.*Pron*.32.10; opp. σύνθεσις, Phlp.*in Ph*.113. 11. **-θετέω**, *break covenant, be faithless*, Lxx *Ps*.72(73).15, al.; opp. εὐσυνθετέω, Chrysipp.*Stoic*.2.63. **※-θετος**, ον, (συντίθημι) *uncompounded*, Pl.*Phd*.78c, *Tht*.205c, Arist.*Pol*.1252ᵃ19; freq. in Gramm., as A.D.*Synt*.172.27, al.; ἀ. φωνή a word *standing alone*, Chrysipp.*Stoic*.2.50. Adv. -τως Eust.17.6. II. (συντίθεμαι) *bound by no covenant, faithless*, ὁ δῆμός ἐστιν πρᾶγμα τῶν πάντων ἀσυνθετώτατον D.19.136 (v.l. ἀσυνετ-), cf. *Ep.Rom*.1.31; *making no covenants*, ἀ. διατελοῦσι Phld.*Herc*.1251.19. **-θηκέω**, = ἀσυνθετέω, Sm.*Is*.63.8. **-θηκος**, ον, = ἀσύνθετος II, Onos.37.2. Adv. **-θηκεί**, *through breach of contract*, *POxy*.904.2 (V A.D.). **-νευστος**, ον, *non-convergent*; ἀ. σύννευσις, of curve and asymptote, Procl. *in Euc*. p.177 F. **-νεφής**, ές, *unclouded*, Sch.Pi.*O*.1.16; *not bringing clouds*, ἄνεμοι Thphr.*Vent*.11. **-νόμως**, Adv. *irregularly*, ἐπιπλέκεσθαι Vett.Val.119.4. **-νοος**, ον, contr. **-νους**, ουν, *thoughtless*, ἀργία Pl.*Sph*.267d. **-οπτος**, ον, *not easily perceived*, opp. εὐσύνοπτος, Aeschin.2.146, J.*BJ*7.6.1, Secund.*Sent*.1, 15.

**ἀσύνορον**· ἀσύμφωνον, Hsch.

**ἀσυν-τακτικός**, ή, όν, *against the rules of syntax*, Sch.E.*Hec*. 970. **-τακτος**, Att. ἀξ-, ον, *disorganized*, X.*Cyr*.8.1.45; of soldiers, *not in battle-order*, opp. συντεταγμένοι, X.*HG*7.1.16, J. *BJ*1.13.3, al.: c. dat., *not ranked on an equality with*.., Syrian. *in Metaph*.11.29. 2. *undisciplined, disorderly*, X.*Cyr*.7.5.21, D.13. 15; στρατός Ph.2.120; πόλις Aen.Tact.3.1; ἀξ. ἀναρχία Th.6.72; ἡ πρόνοια τυφλόν τι κἀσύντακτον Nicostr.Com.19.5. Adv. -τως Plu. *Nic*.3. 3. *loosely put together, ill-proportioned*, σῶμα X.*Cyn*.3.3. 4. *ungrammatical, irregular*, Choerob. *in Theod*.2 p.18 H.; τὸ ἀ., a figure of speech, Ps.-Plu.*Vit.Hom*.41:—but of books, *not comprehended in a list*, D.L.9.47. 5. *not in the same order* or *class*, Dam.*Pr*.2. 6. Adv. -τως *without previous intimation* or *arrangement*, *UPZ* 61 (ii B.C.). II. Act., *not having composed a speech, without premeditation, unprepared*, Plu.2.6d. **-ταξία**, ἡ, *incapacity of entering into construction*, A.D.*Pron*.14.3, *Synt*.304.24; *irregularity*, Choerob. *in Theod*.2 p.18 H. II. *disorder, indiscipline*, App.*BC*2.20, *Gall*. 15. **-τᾰτος**, ον, (τείνω) v.l. for ἄτυτος in Xenarch.1. II. *without exertion*, περίπατος Antyll.ap.Orib.6.21.8. **-τέλεστος**, ον, *incomplete*, *IPE*1².32 *B* 57 (Olbia, iii B.C.), D.S.4.12, Plu.2.1056d, *POxy*.707.30 (iii A.D.); *not executed*, *Annuario* 4/5.225 (Rhodes, ii B.C.). **-τελής**, ές, *not contributing, useless*, τοῖς κοινοῖς Them.*Or*.31.352c; πρός τι *Hippiatr.Praef*.2. Adv. ἀσυντελῶς, ἔχειν πρός τινας Sch.Pi.*O*.3. 81. II. = ἀσυντέλεστος, βίος M.Ant.3.8. **-τήρητος**, ον, *inaccurate*, παράδοσις Eust.300.43. **-τονος**, ον, *slack, lazy*. Adv., Sup. -ώτατα X.*Cyr*.4.2.31. **-τρητος**, ον, *imperforate*, Heliod.ap.Orib.44.23. 59, Gal.19.438. **-τριπτος**, ον, *not easily rubbed* or *crushed*, Ph.*Bel*. 65.47. **※-τροφον**, = βάκτος, Ps.-Dsc.4.37. **-τρόχαστος**, ον, *incompatible*, Simp.*in Cat*.380.25. **-ύπαρκτος**, ον, *incapable of coexisting*, A.D.*Conj*.221.8, Alex.Aphr.*Quaest*.97.28, S.E.*P*.2.202, Simp.*in Cat*.381.13.

**※ἀσυρής**, ές, *lewd, filthy*, ἄνθρωπος Plb.4.4.5; βίος Id.18.55.7; λοιδορία Id.38.20.6; ἀπαιδευσία Lxx *Si*.23.13. Adv. -ρῶς Phld.*Rh*.1.348 S.

**ἀσύρρηκτος**, ον, *not burst* or *rent*, Gal.10.817.

**ἀσυσκεύαστος**, ον, *not arranged, not ready*, X.*Oec*.8.13.

**ἀσυ-στᾰσία**, ἡ, *want of union, confusion*, Archig.ap.Gal.8.626. **-στᾰτέω**, *to be incapable of*, c. gen., A.D.*Conj*.228.14. **※-στᾰτος**, Att. ἀξ-, ον, (συνίσταμαι) *not solidified*, γῆ ἀ. ὑπὸ βίας Pl.*Ti*.61a; *not cohesive*, ὕδωρ Plu.2.949b, etc.; τὸ ἀ. *want of cohesion*, ib.697a; γάλα ἀ. εἰς τυρόν *that will not curdle*, Aret.*CD*1.13. 2. *unformed*, ἔμβρυα Antyll.ap.Orib.6.31.5: metaph., *incoherent*, of Aeschylus, Ar.*Nu*.1367. 3. *that cannot be composed, incurable*, ἄλγος A.*Ag*. 1467 (lyr.). 4. *incapable of subsistence*, ἀ. καὶ ἀνύπαρκτος *Stoic*. 3.91; τὰ ἀ. Hermog.*Stat*.1. 5. Gramm., *irregular, inadmissible*, A.D.*Pron*.55.11, al. 6. *chaotic, confused*, Plu.2.1025a. 7. of self-evident propositions, *incapable of proof* (cf. σύστασις), Alex. Aphr.*in Top*.84.8. 8. of legal status, *not determined*, *POxy*.1680. 11 (iii/iv A.D.). **-στᾰτόω**, *regard as* ἀσύστατος, τοὺς τὴν ἀστρονομίαν μὴ οἰομένους εἶναι τέχνην ἀλλ' ἐθέλοντας αὐτὴν ἀσυστατοῦν Sch. Ptol.*Tetr*.1.

**ἀσύστροφος**, ον, *not forming a solid mass*, Hp.*Gland*.13. II. of style, *not condensed*, D.H.*Din*.8. III. *slack, careless*, ἕξις, opp. εὐσύστροφος, Olymp.*in Grg*.p.258 J. IV. dub. sens., of the pulse, Archig.ap.Gal.8.650.

**ἀσύφη**, ἡ, a kind of κασία, *Peripl.M.Rubr*.12, Dsc.1.13 (v.l. ἀσυφήμων).

**※ἀσύφηλος** [ῠ], ον, *headstrong*, or perh. *foolish*, ὥς μ' ἀσύφηλον ἐν Ἀργείοισιν ἔρεξεν ὡς εἴ τιν' ἀτίμητον μετανάστην Il.9.647; οὔ πω σεῦ ἄκουσα κακὸν ἔπος οὐδ' ἀσύφηλον 24.767, cf. Q.S.9.521: also in late Prose, as Eun.*VS*p.481 B. Adv. -λως *foolishly*, Diusap.Stob.4.21.16.

**ἀσφᾰγής**, ές, *not to be sacrificed*, Ph.2.323.

**ἀσφάδαστος** [φᾰ], ον, *without convulsion* or *struggle*, esp. in dying, A.*Ag.*1293, S.*Aj.*833 (fort. -ᾳστος).

**ἀσφάζει·** ἀντέχεται, Hsch.

**ἀσφακέλιστος,** ον, *not gangrened* or *mortified*, Hsch.

**ἄσφακτος,** ον, *unslaughtered*, E.*Ion* 228.

**ἀσφάλαθος,** v. ἀσπ-.

***ἀσφάλαξ** [φᾰ], ἄκος, ὁ, = ἀσπάλαξ, Babr.108.13, Str.15.1.44, Hdn. Gr.2.630.

***ἀσφάλ-εια** [φᾰ], gen. ας, Ion. ης, ἡ, (ἀσφᾰλής) *security against stumbling* or *falling*. ἀ. πρὸς τὸν πηλόν Th.3.22; *steadfastness, stability*, ἀσφαλείᾳ..ἀνόρθωσον πόλιν raise up the city *so that it stand fast*, S. *OT*51; κατασκευάζειν τὴν [τῆς πολιτείας] ἀ. Arist.*Pol.*1319$^b$39. 2. *assurance from danger, personal safety*, A.*Supp.*495, etc.; τηρεῖν ἀ. ἐπιβουλῆς Antipho 2.2.8; ἀ. τῆς ἐπαναφορᾶς *precaution regarding* it, And.3.33, cf. Th.4.68, 8.4; ἡ ἰδία ἀ., opp. ὁ τῆς πόλεως κίνδυνος, Lys. 31.7; δεηθεὶς τῆς ἀ. ἔτυχε *safe-conduct*, Hdt.3.7; ἀ. διδόναι, παρέχειν, X.*HG*2.2.2, *Cyr.*4.5.28: freq. with Preps., ἀσφαλείης εἵνεκεν Hdt.4. 33; ἀσφαλείας οὕνεκα Ar.*Av.*293; δι' ἀσφαλείας τὰς πόλεις οἰκεῖν Th. 1.17; τὸ σῶμ' ἐν ἀσφαλείᾳ καθιστάναι, καθεστάναι, Isoc.9.30, X.*Hier.* 2.10; κατ' ἀσφάλειαν in *safety*, Th.4.128; μετ' ἀσφαλείας Id.1.120, Pl. *Ti.*59b: pl., ἀσφάλειαι *seasons of safety*, Isoc.8.21. 3. *caution*, σῴζονται ὑπ' ἀσφαλείας Alciphr.1.10, cf. Heliod.(?)ap.Orib.46.11.27 and 14.4: in Lit. Crit., *circumspection*, Demetr.*Eloc.*287. 4. *assurance, certainty*, ἀ. πολλὴ μὴ ἂν ἐλθεῖν αὐτούς Th.2.11; ἀ. ἐργάζεσθαι τὴν γῆν *security* for agriculture, X.*Cyr.*7.4.5. 5. ἀ. λόγου *convincing nature, certainty* of an argument, Id.*Mem.*4.6.15, cf. *Ev.Luc.* 1.4. 6. as law-term, *security, bond*, Arr.*Epict.*2.13.7; *pledge*, *BGU*1149.24 (i B.C.): in pl., = Lat. *cautiones*, Just.*Nov.*72.6. 7. Pythag. name for *eight*, *Theol.Ar.*56. ***-ειος** (with collat. form -ιος, q.v.), ον, epith. of Poseidon, the *Securer*, Ar.*Ach.*682, Paus.3. 11.9, 7.21.7, Plu.*Thes.*36. ***-ής,** ές, (σφάλλομαι, σφαλῆναι) *not liable to fall, immovable, steadfast*, in Hom. only once as Adj. (cf. infr. III), θεῶν ἕδος ἀ. αἰεί Od.6.42, cf. Hes.*Th.*128, Pi.*N.*6.3, Theoc.2.34, etc.; ἀσφαλῆ θεῶν νόμιμα S.*Ant.*454; *unshaken*, of purpose, ἀ. ὁ νοῦς Id. *Fr.*351. 2. of friends and the like, *unfailing, trusty*, οὐ γὰρ οἱ..εὐρύνωτοι φῶτες ἀσφαλέστατοι Id.*Aj.*1251; ἀ. στρατηλάτης E.*Ph.*599, cf. Th.1.69: c. inf., φρονεῖν γὰρ οἱ ταχεῖς οὐκ ἀσφαλεῖς the hasty in counsel are not *safe*, S.*OT*617, cf. Pl.*Sph.*231a; σῴζειν τὰ κοινὰ πράγματ' ἀσφαλέστατα E.*IT*1062; of things, *sure, certain*, Th.4.108, etc. 3. *assured from danger, safe*, ἀ. αἰών Pi.*P.*3.86; ἀσφαλεῖ σὺν ἐξόδῳ S.*OC*1288; ἀ. ὅρος X.*Lac.*12.1; ὁδὸς -εστέρα Id.*HG*5.4.51; ἐν τῷ ἀσφαλεῖ in *safety*, Th.1.137, 8.39, cf. Pl.*Lg.*892e; ἐν ἀσφαλεῖ τοῦ μὴ παθεῖν X.*Cyr.*3.3.31; τοῦ λαλεῖν Men.*Sam.*25; ἐν -εστέρῳ, -εστάτῳ, X.*Cyr.*7.1.21, *An.*1.8.22; ἐν ἀ. βίου E.*Hipp.*785; μένειν ἐν τῷ ἀ. X. *An.*4.7.8; ἐξ ἀσφαλοῦς from *a place of safety*, Id.*Eq.Mag.*4.16; τοῦ ἀσφαλέος εἵνεκα Hdt.1.109; τὸ ἀ., = ἀσφάλεια, Th.6.55, etc.; μετὰ τοῦ αὐτῆς ἀ. with *no risk to* herself, Plot.4.8.7; ἀσφαλές [ἐστι], c. inf., *it is safe* to.., Hdt.3.75, E.*Ph.*891, Ar.*Av.*1489: abs., ἀλλ' οὐκ ἀσφαλές Pl.*Phlb.*61d, etc.; φεύγειν αὐτοῖς ἀσφαλέστερόν ἐστιν ἢ ἡμῖν X.*An.*3.2.19. 4. ἀ. ῥήτωρ a *convincing* speaker, Id.*Mem.*4. 6.15. 5. in Lit. Crit., *sound, not risky*, of language or rhythm, Demetr.*Eloc.*19, 41. Adv. -ῶς, ἐρεῖ ib.78. II. Subst. ἀσφαλές, τό, = ἀσφάλεια 6, *BGU*984.14 (iv A.D.), etc. III. Ep. Adv. ἀσφαλέως, ἔχειν, μένειν, to be, remain *firm, steady*, Il.23.325, Od.17. 235: neut. ἀσφαλές as Adv., Il. (v. infr.); δρακεῖσ' ἀσφαλές Pi.*P.*2. 20; ἀ. ἀγορεύει *without faltering*, Od.8.171, Hes.*Th.*86; ἔμπεδον ἀσφαλέως Il.13.141, Od.13.86; ἔμπεδον ἀσφαλὲς αἰεί Il.15.683. Adv. ἀσφαλῶς (-έως) is used in all senses of the Adj., -έως βεβηκὼς ποσσί Archil.58.4; *in safety, with certainty*, S.*OT*613; ἀ. βουλεύειν And.3. 34; ἀ. ἔχει Hdt.1.86: c. inf., Lys.27.6; ἀ. προσθεῖναι *as a precaution*, Alex.Aphr.*in Mete.*14.10: Comp. -έστερον Hdt.2.161, Pl.*Phd.*85d; but -εστέρως Hp.*Prorrh.*2.15, Th.4.71: Sup. -έστατα Hp.*Prorrh.* 2.23, Pl.*R.*467e.

***ἀσφᾰλίζω** Plb.18.30.3:—mostly in Med., fut. -ιοῦμαι J.*BJ*2.21.4, but -ίσομαι Id.*AJ*13.5.11, and so D.S.20.24: pf. ἠσφάλισμαι Plb.5. 43.6: plpf. ἠσφάλιστο ib.7.12: aor. ἠσφαλισάμην Id.2.22.11; ἠσφαλίσθην J.*Vit.*62: some of these tenses are used in pass. sense (v. infr.):—*fortify*, τὸν τόπον Plb.18.30.3, etc.:—Pass., Id.1.42.7, 4.70.9, *Ev.Matt.*27.64. b. *secure*, *BGU*829.9 (i A.D.). 2. more freq. in Med., *secure*, ἑαυτόν Epicur.*Fr.*215; τὰς εἰσβολάς, τὴν χώραν, etc., Plb.2.65.6, 4.60.5, etc.; τόπους Hero *Bel.*101.7; τὸν ὕσπληγγα *CIG* 2824 (Aphrodisias); *shut up, close*, πύλην Lxx *Ne.*3.15; ὀφθαλμοὶ ἠσφαλισμένοι, opp. ἀνεῳγμένοι, Polem.*Phgn.*55; τοὺς πόδας ἠσφαλίσατο εἰς τὸ ξύλον *made* them *fast*, *Act.Ap.*16.24. 3. *secure the person of, arrest*, τινά *PTeb.*283.19 (i B.C.), cf. *PRyl.*68.19 (i B.C., Pass.); *seize*, τὰ γενήματα ib.53.29 (ii B.C.). 4. Med., *certify*, ib. 2.77.40 (ii A.D.). II. Med., *secure oneself against, ward off*, τὰς καταφορὰς τῶν μαχαιρῶν Plb.6.23.4, cf. 9.3.3: abs., *safeguard oneself*, J.*AJ*13.5.10, *POxy.*1033.13 (iv A.D.). 2. metaph. in Rhet., *safeguard* a risky metaphor, ἀ. τὰς μεταφοράς Demetr.*Eloc.*85:—Pass., λέξις ἠσφαλισμένη τοῖς συνδέσμοις ib.193. (The word is βάρβαρον acc. to *AB*456.)

***Ἀσφάλιος,** = Ἀσφάλειος (q.v.), Opp.*H.*5.680, *IG*5(1).559.14 (Amyclae), Aristid.*Or.*46(3).1, *BGU*96.6 (iii A.D.).

***ἀσφάλ-ισμα** [φᾰ], ατος, τό, *pledge, security*, *BGU*248.8 (i A.D.), 601.7 (ii A.D.). **-ιστός,** όν, *made secure*, Hdn.*Epim.*178.

**ἀσφαλός,** ὁ, name of a *bird*, Hsch. s.v. ἐνθύσκος.

**ἀσφαλτίας,** ου, ὁ, (ἀ- priv., σφάλλω) *not failing*, σφόνδυλος ἀ. *lowest vertebra*, Poll.2.179 (v.l. -τίτης).

**ἀσφαλτίζω,** *smell like asphalt*, Dsc.5.128.

**ἀσφάλτιον,** τό, = τρίφυλλον, *treacle clover*, *Psoralea bituminosa*, Dsc.3.109. 2. = πολύγονον ἄρρεν, Ps.-Dsc.4.4. 3. = πεντάφυλλον, ib.42.

**ἀσφαλτίτης** [ῑ], ου, ὁ, fem. **-ῖτις,** ιδος, *bituminous*, βῶλος Str.7.5.8; λίμνη Ἀ. the Dead Sea, D.S.19.98, cf. J.*BJ*1.33.5; πόα, = ἀσφάλτιον, Philum.ap.Orib.45.29.27, Archig.ap.Aët.5.84. II. v. ἀσφαλτίας.

**ἀσφαλτόπισσα,** ἡ, = πισσάσφαλτος, Lxx *Ex.*2.3.

***ἄσφαλτος,** ἡ (also ὁ, Gal.13.784), *asphalt, bitumen*, Hdt.1.179, 6.119, Theoc.16.100, Dsc.1.73; ἄ. ὀρυκτή Arist.*Mir.*842$^b$15:—also **ἄσφαλτον,** τό, Hp.*Aër.*7, Ti.Locr.99c. II. a kind of *petroleum*, Dsc.1.99. III. *pitch*, Lxx *Ge.*6.14. (Ph.1.420 derives it from σφάλλω.)

**ἀσφαλτοφόρος,** ον, *producing bitumen*, λίμνη J.*AJ*17.6.5.

**ἀσφαλτ-όω,** *smear with pitch*, Lxx *Ge.*6.14. **-ωδεύομαι,** *to be soaked in pitch*, Aët.2.73. **-ώδης,** ες, *full of* or *like asphalt*, Arist. *Sens.*444$^b$33, Str.7.5.8, etc. **-ωσις,** εως, ἡ, gloss on πίσσωσις, Suid.

**ἀσφαλών,** ῶνος, ὁ, perh. *safe, cash-box*, *PGrenf.*1.14.8.

**ἀσφᾰραγέω,** (ἀ- euph., σφαραγέω) *resound, clang*, of armed men, Theoc.17.94 (dub. l.).

**ἀσφᾰρᾰγία,** ἡ, *root-stock of asparagus*, Thphr.*HP*6.4.2.

***ἀσφάρᾰγος** (A) [φᾰ], ὁ, = φάρυγξ, *throat, gullet*, Il.22.328, Plu.2. 698e, Q.S.11.82.

**ἀσφάρᾰγος** (B) [φᾰ], ὁ, *stone sperage*, *Asparagus acutifolius*, Cratin. 325, Amips.25, Antiph.301, Theopomp.Com.68, etc.; *the edible shoots thereof*, Thphr.6.4.2, Dsc.2.125, *AP*11.325 (Autom.), Gal.6.641. II. *the shoots* of other plants, Nic.*Th.*883, etc.; κράμβης Diph.Siph ap. Ath.2.62f; of ἄμπελος λευκή, Dsc.4.182. (ἀσφ- Attic, Phryn.89, *PS*p.41 B.: ἀσπ- in Antiph.301, Aristopho 16, and later writers, as Nic. l. c., Plb.34.8.5, etc.)

**ἀσφᾰρᾰγωνία,** ἡ, *wreath of asparagus*, Plu.2.138d.

**ἄσφε, ἄσφι,** Aeol. for σφέ, σφί, v. σφεῖς.

**ἄσφηλοι·** ἀσθενεῖς, σφηλὸν γὰρ τὸ ἰσχυρόν, Hsch.

**ἀσφίγγωτος,** ον, = sq., *Corp.Herm.*13.6 codd.

**ἄσφιγκτος,** ον, *not tightly bound, loose*, Gal.12.373, 18(2).627.

**ἀσφοδέλινος,** η, ον, *of asphodel*, ναῦς ἀ. a ship *built of asphodel stalks*, Luc.*VH*2.26.

**ἀσφόδελος,** ὁ, *asphodel*, *Asphodelus ramosus*, Hes.*Op.*41, Arist. *HA*627$^a$8, Thphr.*HP*1.10.7, 7.13.2, Crateuas *Fr.*5, Theoc.7.68, Dsc. 2.169, etc.; cf. σφοδελός. II. oxyt., as Adj., ἀσφοδελὸς λειμών the *asphodel* mead which the shades of heroes haunted, Od.11.539, 24. 13: generally, *flowery* mead, *h.Merc.*221, 344. (On the accent v. Hdn.Gr.1.160.)

**ἀσφοδελώδης,** ες, *like asphodel*, Thphr.*HP*6.6.9.

**ἀσφράγιστος** [ᾱ], ον, *not sealed*, *Klio* 18.264 (Delph., iii B.C.), *SIG*953.35 (Cnidus, ii B.C.), Harp. s.v. ἀσήμαντα, Horap.1.49; μόσχοι *PGnom.*183 (ii A.D.). II. *not assigned to a* σφραγίς, γῆ *BGU*659 ii 9 (iii A.D.).

**ἀσφυ-γμία,** ἡ, = *pulsus defectio*, opp. ἀσφυξία, Cael.Aur.*CP*1.2. **-κτέω,** *to be without pulsation*, Dsc.*Alex.Praef.*, Gal.7.194, al., Herod. Med. in *Rh.Mus.*58.71. **-κτος,** ον, (σφύζω) *without pulsation, lifeless*, Gal.2.647, *AP*11.211 (Lucill.): metaph. of the mind, *without impulse, calm*, Plu.2.446d; *moderate*, ἂν ἰάσιμον ᾖ τὸ χεῖρον καὶ ἄ. ib. 500c. II. Act., *causing no violent pulsation*, ib.132e. **-ξία,** ἡ, *stopping of the pulse*, Aret.*SA*2.11; *pulsus amputatio*, opp. ἀσφυγμία, Cael.Aur.*TP*4.3.

**ἀσχᾰδής,** ές, (σχάζω) *not to be restrained*, A.*Fr.*418.

**ἀσχᾰλάω,** only pres. (exc. fut. -ήσω Thal.ap.D.L.1.44), 3 sg. ἀσχαλάᾳ Il.2.293; 3 pl. ἀσχαλόωσι 24.403; inf. ἀσχαλάαν 2.297; part. ἀσχαλόων 22.412; imper. ἀσχάλα Archil.66.6; inf. ἀσχαλᾶν E.*IA* 920:—more freq. **ἀσχάλλω,** once in Hom. ἀσχάλλῃς Od.2.193, cf. S.*OT*937, E.*Or.*785, and so always in Prose, X.*Eq.*10.6, D.21.125, Onos.1.17, Eus.Mynd.6: impf. ἤσχαλλον Hes.*Fr.*76.3, Hdt.3.152, 9.117; imper. ἄσχαλλε Thgn.219: 3 sg. fut. ἀσχαλεῖ (prob. for -αλᾷ) A.*Pr.*764:—*to be distressed, grieved*, abs., ἀσχαλάαν παρὰ νηυσί Il.2. 297, cf. 22.412, etc.: the cause of distress is added by Hom. either in part., μένων ἀσχαλάᾳ Il.2.293, cf. Od.1.304; ἥν κε (sc. θωὴν) τίνων ἀσχάλλῃς 2.193: or in gen., ἀσχαλάᾳ δὲ πάϊς βίοτον κατεδόντων *is vexed because of*.., 19.159; κτήσιος ἀσχαλόων τήν οἱ κατέδουσιν Ἀχαιοί ib.534: later in dat., ἀ. τινί *at* a thing, Archil. l. c., A.*Pr.*764, E.*IA*920; ἐπὶ τῷ διδόναι δίκην ἀσχάλλειν D. l. c., cf. Ph.2.521; πρός τι Longus 3.8: c. acc., θάνατον ἀ. πατρῷον E.*Or.*785.

**ἀσχαλιάζω,** = ἀσκωλιάζω II, Hsch.

**ἄσχαστος,** ον, *unshakable, firm*, λίθοι *IG*7.3073.163 (Lebad.), cf. *BCH*29.468 (Delos):—written **ἄσκαστος** *IG*7.4255 (Oropus). II. *without a gap*, Eutoc. *in Archim.*3 p.94 H.

**ἀσχέδωρος,** ὁ, *wild boar*, in Magna Graecia, A.*Fr.*261, Sciras 1.

**ἀσχέλιον·** τραχύ (Cret.), Hsch.

**ἄσχετος,** Ep. also **ἀάσχετος,** ον, (σχεῖν) *not to be checked, ungovernable*, πένθος ἄσχετον οὐκ ἐπιεικτόν Il.16.549; ἀάσχετον ἵκετο πένθος 24.708; μένος ἄσχετοι υἷες Ἀχαιῶν *resistless* in might, Od.3. 104; μητρός τοι μένος ἐστὶν ἀάσχετον οὐδ' ἐπιεικτόν Il.5.892; κάκον ἄ. Alc.92; ὕβρις Epic. in *Arch.Pap.*7.6: in later Prose, ἄ. δίψος Luc. *Dips.*9; ἄ. ὁρμή Aret.*SA*2.12; of a person, *ungovernable, unmanageable*, γυνή *PMag.Par.*1.2071, cf. *PMag.Lond.*121.593. Adv. -τως Pl.*Cra.*415d: neut. ἄσχετον, -τα, as Adv., A.R.4.1738, 1087. 2. *not held together*, Phlp. *in Ph.*533.4. 3. *unrelated*, πρός τι Anon. *in*

Prm. (Rh.Mus.47.605), cf. Jul.Or.5.163b, Dam.Pr.3, al., Procl.in Cra.p.57 P., al.; ἀ. σχέσις Ps.-Alex.Aphr.inSE152.24; unqualified, ὕλη Dex.inCat.51.21. Adv. -τως Procl.Inst.122, inCra.p.70P.

***ἀσχημάτιστος** [μᾰ], ον, without form or figure, Pl.Phdr.247c, Arist.Ph.191$^a$2. 2. that cannot be represented by a figure, Theol. Ar.11. 3. Astrol., not in aspect with other planets, Vett.Val.102. 8, Anon.in Ptol.Tetr.104. II. not employing figures of speech, of orators, Plu.2.835b; φράσις D.H.Pomp.5, cf. Demetr.Eloc.67. Adv. -τως D.H.Rh.10.11.

**ἀσχημ-ονέω**, behave unseemly, disgrace oneself, E.Hec.407, Cratin. 151, Pl.R.506d, etc.: c. acc. cogn., ἀ. ἄλλα ἄ.. D.22.53; ἀ. τὰ δεινότατα Id.60.25; μηδὲν ἀ. Arist.Pol.1273$^a$34, cf. EN1119$^a$30: c. part., Plu.2.178d:—Pass., πολλὰ ἀσχημονεῖται many unseemly things are done, D.H.2.26. **-όνησις**, εως, ἡ, = ἀσχημοσύνη, Sm.Ps.43(44). 16. ***-ος**, ον, late form for ἀσχήμων, Phld.Herc.1457.9 (Comp.), PRyl.144.18 (i A.D.), Polem.Phgn.13, Hippiatr.55: Sup. -όνατος D.L.2.88. Adv. -μως Sch.S.Aj.916. **-οσύνη**, ἡ, want of form, ἀ. καὶ ἀμορφία Arist.Ph.190$^b$15, cf. 188$^b$20, Simp.in Cael.129.26. 2. ungracefulness, Pl.Smp.196a, R.401a; awkwardness, Id.Tht.174c; disfigurement, τοῦ προσώπου, in playing on the flute, Arist.Pol.1341$^b$ 5. 3. ἀ. φέρει brings discredit, disgrace, Id.EN1126$^b$33. II. in moral sense, indecorum, obscene or disgraceful conduct, Ep.Rom.1. 27: in pl., Ph.1.78, Vett.Val.61.31. III. euphem. for αἰδοῖον, Lxx Le.18.7, al.; for ἀπόπατος, ib.De.23.13(14). **-ων**, ον, gen. ονος, (σχῆμα) misshapen, ugly, Hp.Art.27, Procl.inPrm.p.624S. II. unseemly, shameful, E.Hel.299, Pl.Phlb.46a, Arist.Pol.1336$^b$14, etc. 2. of persons, ἀ. γενέσθαι to be indecorous, Hdt.7.160; ἀσχημονέστερος Arist.EN1127$^b$13. III. Adv. -νως J.BJ2.12.1, Phld. Sign.29: Sup. -έστατα very meanly, Pl.Lg.959d.

**ἀσχῐδής**, ές, (σχίζω) uncloven, undivided, ἰσχάδες Arist.Pr.930$^b$33; of animals, ἀσχιδῆ οἷον τὰ μώνυχα Id.HA499$^b$11, cf. PA642$^b$29; φύλλα Thphr.HP3.10.1.

**ἀσχίον**, τό, puff-ball, Lycoperdon giganteum, Thphr.HP1.6.9.

**ἀσχιστόπους**, ουν, gen. ποδος, not having cloven hoofs, Alex.Aphr. in Metaph.521.24.

**ἄσχιστος**, ον, uncloven, of solid-hoofed animals, opp. σχιζόπους, Arist.Metaph.1038$^a$14. 2. not curdled, γάλα Philum.ap.Orib.45. 29.12. II. undivided, Pl.Ti.36d; πτερὸν ἄ. Arist.HA519$^a$28; δάκτυλοι ib.517$^a$32; φλέψ ib.513$^b$13; of logical division, Pl.Sph. 221e. 2. indivisible by fission, Arist.Mete.385$^a$16, 386$^b$26, cf. Opp. C.2.528; not liable to split, Thphr.Ign.72.

**ἀσχολ-έω**, engage, occupy, τινά Luc.Zeux.7:—Med., impf. ἠσχολεῖτο (v. infr.): fut. -ήσομαι M.Ant.12.2, Aristid.1.423J.; -ηθήσομαι Lxx Si.39.1: pf. ἠσχόλημαι D.C.71.10: aor. ἠσχολησάμην Gal.7. 657, and -ήθην D.S.4.32, Luc.Macr.8:—to be occupied, busy, Alex. 205, Men.999, Epicur.Fr.204, etc.; ἀσχολούμεθα ἵνα σχολάζωμεν Arist.EN1177$^b$4; περί or ἐπί τι, D.S.2.40, 17.94; πρός τινας Aristid. l.c., cf. 2.178J.: c. part., λαλῶν ἠσχολεῖτο Alex.261.12, etc.: c. acc. cogn., ἀ. ἀσχολίας ἀνωφελεῖς D.Chr.47.23; exercise a function, POxy.44.7,23 (i A.D.). II. Act. intr., in same sense as Med., Arist.Pol.1333$^a$41, 1338$^a$4, Philem.220; to be engaged in one's own business, Arist.Pol.1299$^b$33.—Not used in the best Att. **-ημα**, ατος, τό, business, engagement, Str.10.3.9 (pl.), Iamb.Protr.21.κβ' (pl.); performance of a public function, BGU8ii23 (iii A.D., pl.). **-ημᾰτικός**, ή, όν, hard working, Vett.Val.233.18. **-ία**, ἡ, occupation, business, engagement, πρᾶγμα ἀσχολίας ὑπέρτερον Pi.I.1.2, cf. Th.1.90, 8.72, Pl.Phd.58d; πρᾳότης καὶ ἀ. Lys.6.34; ἀ. καὶ ἀπραγμοσύνη D.21.141; opp. ἡσυχία, Th.1.70; ἐμοί τις ἀ. ἐστίν I have an engagement, Pl.Prt. 335c; δι' ἀσχολίαν because of business, Eub.119.12; later, office, function, BGU1202.3 (i B.C.). II. want of time or leisure, ἀ. ἄγειν φιλοσοφίας πέρι to have no leisure for pursuing it, Pl.Phd.66d; ἀ. ἄγειν to be engaged or occupied, Id.Ap.39e; ἀ. ἔχειν πρός τι Plu.Comp. Sol.Publ.2; opp. σχολή, Arist.Pol.1333$^a$35; ἐν ἀσχολίᾳ λέγειν Pl. Tht.172d; ἀ. παρέχειν τινί cause one trouble, X.Cyr.4.3.12; μυρίας.. ἡμῖν παρέχει ἀσχολίας τὸ σῶμα Pl.Phd.66b: c. inf., hinder one from doing, X.Cyr.8.1.13; ἀ. μοι ἦν παρεῖναι I had no time, Antipho6.12; πολλήν ἀ. ἔχειν τοῦ ἐπιμεληθῆναι X.Mem.1.3.11; τοῦ (prob. for τὸ) εὐφραίνεσθαι πολλὰς ἀ. παρέχει Id.Cyr.8.7.12; ἀ. ἔχει τὸ μὴ [εἰς τὸ] πράττειν τὸ δεόμενον Id.HG6.1.16. **-ος**, ον, (σχολή) of persons, without leisure, engaged, busy, Pl.Lg.832b, D.3.27; ἄ. συγγόνου προσεδρίᾳ E.Or.93; ἄ. ἐς σοφίην busily engaged upon (or, with no leisure for).., Hdt.4.77; ἄ. περί τι busy about.., Plu.Tim.12; πρὸς τοῖς ἔργοις Arist.Pol.1305$^a$20: c. inf., having no time to.., Pi.P.8.29; ἄσχολοί εἰσιν ἐπιβουλεύειν Arist.Pol.1313$^b$20; ἄ. ὥστε μὴ ἐκκλησιάζειν ib.1318$^b$12. Adv. -λως, ἔχειν D.33.25; πρός τι Aristid.Or.23 (42).61. II. of actions, etc., πάντα χρόνον ἄ. ποιεῖν fully occupied, Pl.Lg.831c; ἄ. πράξεις not leisured, Arist.EN1177$^b$8; κίνησις ἄ. unresting, Id.Cael.284$^a$31.

**ἄσχυ**, τό, inspissated juice of the fruit of the bird-cherry, Prunus Padus, Hdt.4.23.

**ἀσῶ**, = βλάπτω, coined by EM39.42.

***ἀσώδης** [ᾰ], ες, (ἄση) attended with nausea, ὀδύνη prob. in Hp.Art. 19; suffering from nausea, Id.Acut.67; ἀ. στόμαχοι Dsc.1.17; surfeited, Plu.2.974b. Adv. -δως Gal.10.437. II. (ἄσις) slimy, muddy, A.Supp.31 (lyr.).

**ἀσωμᾰτ-ία**, ἡ, incorporeality, Porph.Abst.1.31, Iamb.Comm.Math. 15,33, Procl.in Prm.p.686S. ***-ος**, ον, disembodied, incorporeal, Pl.Phd.85e, al., Arist.Ph.209$^a$16, de An.404$^b$31, al., Epicur.Ep.1 p.22U., Stoic.2.117, etc.; σῶμα ἀσωματώτατον Arist.de An.409$^b$21: Comp. -ώτερος Id.Ph.215$^b$5. Adv. -τως Iamb.Myst.5.16, Procl. Inst.122, Dam.Pr.376. II. non-metallic, Maria ap.Zos.Alch. p.196B. III. in Law, not specified in the body of a document, PSI 6.709.19. **-ότης**, ητος, ἡ, incorporeality, Ph.1.44,76. **-όω**, demetallize, Maria ap.Zos.Alch.p.196B. (Pass.).

**ἄσωμος**, ον, = ἀσώματος, EM161.40.

**ἄσωστος**, ον, (σῴζω) not to be saved, past recovery, ἄσωστά οἵ ἐστιν Ael.NA13.7, PFay.12.24 (ii B.C.). Adv. -τως, διατίθεσθαι, ἔχειν, Dsc.2.141, Gal.15.753.

***ἀσωτ-εῖον**, τό, abode of a prodigal, Stratt.51, Longus 4.17. **-εύω**, lead a profligate, spendthrift life, PSI1.41.12 (iv A.D.):—usu. Dep. -εύομαι, Arist.Pol.1316$^b$15, Babr.108.12, PFlor.99.7 (i/ii A.D.): pf. ἠσώτευμαι S.E.M.8.201. 2. c. acc., squander in riotous living, χρήματα Ael.VH5.9.

**ἀσωτία**, ἡ, prodigality, wastefulness, Pl.R.560e, Arist.EN1107$^b$10; τὴν ἀ. ὑγρότητα προσαγορεύουσιν Crobyl.4. 2. profligacy, Ep.Eph. 5.18, al.: pl., ἐν ἀσωτίαις καὶ κραιπάλαις Hdn.2.5.1.

**ἀσωτοδῐδάσκᾰλος**, = ἀσωτίας διδάσκαλος, name of a play of Alexis, Ath.8.336d.

**ἄσωτος**, ον, (σῴζω) having no hope of safety, in desperate case, Arist. Pr.962$^b$5. Adv. -τως, ἔχειν to be past recovery, Plu.2.918d. II. in moral sense, abandoned, τᾶς ἀσώτου Σισυφιδᾶν γενεᾶς S.Aj.189 (lyr.); spendthrift, Pl.Lg.743b, Arist.EN1107$^b$12, 1120$^a$1, al.: Sup., D.C.67.6; profligate, Vett.Val.18.2. Adv. -τως Theopomp.Hist. 217a, D.40.58, Ev.Luc.15.13: Comp. -ότερον D.C.62.27. III. Act., ἄσωτος γένει bringing destruction on the race, A.Ag.1597.

**ἀσωφρόνως**, Adv. = ἀσελγῶς, Sch.Ar.Pl.560.

**ἄτα**· ὦτα (Tarent.), Hsch.

**ἀτᾱβῡρίτης** [ῑ] ἄρτος, a kind of loaf, Sopat.9.

**ἀτᾱγία**, ἡ, absence of a ταγός (q.v.) in Thessaly, IG9(2).257.

**ἀταής**· ἀγύμναστος, Hsch. (fort. ἀτλής, cf. ἄτλας). **ἀταθήνιον**· χαλκός, ἔλυτρον, Id. **ἆται**· πληροῦται, Id. **ἄταιθα**· λαμυρά, Id.

**ἀταῖος**, = ὑοσκύαμος, Ps.-Dsc.4.68: cf. ἄτη.

**ἀταισόν**· ἀναδενδράς (Tyrrhen.), Hsch.

***ἀτακτ-έω**, of a soldier, to be undisciplined, opp. εὐτακτέω, X.Cyr. 7.2.6, D.3.11; τοὺς ἀτακτοῦντας τῶν τριηράρχων IG2².809$^b$13.—Pass., πολλὰ γὰρ ἠτάκτητο αὐτοῖς J.AJ17.10.10: generally, neglect one's duty, fail to discharge obligation, PEleph.2.13 (iii B.C.), 2Ep.Thess.3. 7, POxy.275.24 (i A.D.). 2. generally, lead a disorderly life, Lys. 14.18, X.Oec.7.31: c. gen., τῆς πατρίου ἀγωγῆς to desert it, Plu.2. 235b. 3. raise a riot or rebellion, OGI200.6 (iv A.D.). **-ημα**, ατος, τό, disorderly or contumacious act, irregularity, Stoic.3.136, OGI 483.58 (Pergam., ii B.C.), Vett.Val.116.13. ***-ος**, ον, not in battle-order, of troops, Hdt.6.93, Th.8.105 (Comp.). 2. not at one's post, Lycurg.39. II. undisciplined, disorderly, θόρυβος Th.8.10; ποιεῖν τὴν πολιτείαν ἀτακτοτέραν Arist.Pol.1319$^b$15; irregular, πυρετὸς Hp. Coac.26; οὐδὲν ἄ. τῶν φύσει Arist.Ph.252$^a$11; φθορὰ ἄ. casual, Id.HA 556$^a$12; of sensual excess, irregular, inordinate, ἡδοναί, Ἀφροδίτη, Pl.Lg.660b, 840e; in Music, without rhythm, μελῳδίαι Aristid.Quint. 1.13; Medic., irregular, σφυγμός Gal.8.458. 2. uncivilized, lawless, βίος Critias25.1D. 3. Math., ἄτακτα προβλήματα indeterminate, not admitting of a definite solution, Procl.inEuc.p.220F.

B. Adv. -τως in an irregular, disorderly manner, of troops, ἀ. καὶ οὐδενὶ κόσμῳ προσπίπτοντες Th.3.108; ἀ. διώκειν Id.2.91; ἀτακτότερον προσπεσόντες Id.6.97, cf. X.Cyr.1.4.22, Hell.Oxy.6.4; ἀ. φέρεσθαι Isoc.1.32; οὐθὲν ἀ. θεῷ πράττεται Epicur.Ep.3p.65U. 2. irregularly, of fevers, Hp.Epid.1.7; ζῆν Isoc.2.31. 3. Comp. ἀτακτοτέρως somewhat negligently, Demetr.Eloc.53.

**ἀτᾰλαίπωρος**, ον, not painstaking, οὕτως ἀ. τοῖς πολλοῖς ἡ ζήτησις τῆς ἀληθείας Th.1.20. Adv. -ρως, οὕτως αὐτοῖς ἀ. ἡ ποίησις διέκειτο Ar.Fr.254; οὐκ ἀ. τινὰς χειροῦσθαι D.C.49.35; ἀ. διάγειν Ph.1.18; ἀ. ἀκούειν Simp.in Cael.143.16. II. of persons, not given to hard work, Hp.Art.1; lazy, ἀνθρωπάρια Arr.Epict.1.29.55. 2. incapable of bearing fatigue, prob. in Hp.Aër.21. Adv. -ρως without incurring fatigue, Id.Acut.33. III. of stagnant water, sluggish, Ruf.ap.Orib.5.3.1:—also **-πώρητος**, ον, Poll.4.28; easy, Sor.2.11. Adv. -τως Hsch. s.v. ἀνοίκτως, Sch.E.Hec.204.

***ἀτάλαντος** [ᾰτᾰ], ον, (ἀ- copul., τάλαντον) equal in weight, equivalent to, like, ἀ. Ἄρηϊ Il.5.576; Διὶ μῆτιν ἀ. equal to Zeus in wisdom, 2.169, etc.: generally, like, ἀστέρι A.R.2.40. 2. in equipoise, Arat.22.

**ἀτᾰλάφρων** [ᾰτ], ον, gen. ονος, (φρονέω) tender-minded, of a child in arms, Il.6.400, Q.S.13.122:—also in form **ἀταλόφρων**, IG12(8). 600.14 (Thasos).

**ἀτάλλω** [ᾰ], (ἀταλός) only in pres. and impf., skip in childish glee, gambol, ἄταλλε δὲ κήτε' ὑπ' αὐτοῦ Il.13.27, cf. Mosch.2.116, Philostr. Im.2.3. II. Act., bring up a child, rear, foster, Hom.Epigr. 4.2; νέαν ψυχὴν ἀτάλλων S.Aj.559: metaph., ἐλπὶς ἀτάλλοισα καρδίαν Pi.Fr.214:—Pass., grow up, wax, h.Merc.400:—Act., intr. in this sense, ἐτρέφετ' ἀτάλλων [ᾰτ] Hes.Op.131.—Poet. and later Prose.

**ἄταλμα** [ᾰ], ατος, τό, frolic, Hsch. (pl.).

***ἀτᾰλός** [ᾰτ], ή, όν, tender, delicate, of youthful persons, as of maidens, Od.11.39; of fillies, Il.20.222; ἀταλὰ φρονέοντες of young, gay spirit, 18.567, cf. Hes.Th.989, h.Cer.24; μάτηρ E.El.699 (lyr.) (unless it = suckling her lamb); ἀ. χερσί, of the aged, tremulous, A.Pers.537 (anap.): c. dat., ἀταλὸς πατρί, i.e. subject, amenable to him, Pi.N.7.91. Adv. -λῶς Sch.Il.5.271: Sup. -ώτατα, παίζει IG1. 492a.

**ἀτᾰλό-φρων** [ᾰτ], ονος, v. ἀταλάφρων. **-ψῡχος**, ον, *soft-hearted*, θηλύτεραι *AP*5.296 (Agath.).

**ἀτάλυμνος** [ᾰτᾰ], ὁ, = κοκκυμηλέα, Nic.*Al.*108.

**ἀτᾰμίευτος**, ον, *that cannot be stored*, Ph.2.113; *that cannot be regulated*, Arist.*GA*788$^{a}$34; *uncontrolled, inordinate*, J.*BJ*4.1.6. Adv. -τως, ὑπὸ θυμοῦ ἐπισπασθείς Plu.*Arat.*37. **2.** *not needing to be husbanded*, Max.Tyr.3.9, al. **II.** Act., *not husbanding, prodigal, lavish*, χάριτες Ph.1.5: c. gen., ἡδονῶν Plu.2.12c. Adv. -τως, ταῖς ὀργαῖς χρώμενος Pl.*Lg.*867a; ἀ. πάντα χαρίζεσθαι Ph.2.274.

**ἀταξία**, Ion. -ίη, ἡ, *indiscipline*, prop. among soldiers, opp. εὐταξία, Hdt.6.11, Th.2.92, X.*HG*3.1.9, etc. **2.** generally, *disorder, confusion*, ἀ. καὶ ἀκολασία Pl.*Cri.*53d; ἀμαθία καὶ ἀ. X.*Ath.*1.5; ἀ. καὶ ἀναρχία Arist.*Pol.*1302$^{b}$28; εἰς τάξιν ἤγαγεν ἐκ τῆς ἀ. Pl.*Ti.*30a; ἀπὸ τύχης καὶ ἀ. Arist.*PA*641$^{b}$23: in pl., ἀταξιῶν, opp. τῶν ἐν ταῖς κινήσεσι τάξεων, Pl.*Lg.*653e. **3.** c. gen., διαίτης ἀ. *irregularity*, Hp.*Coac.*211; νόμων Aeschin.3.38.

***ἀτάομαι** [ᾱτ], Pass., (ἄτη) *suffer, be in distress*, in Trag. always in pres. part. ἀτώμενος S.*Aj.*384, *Ant.*17,314, E.*Supp.*182, exc. ἀτώμεσθα S.*Aj.*269; ἀτασθῶσιν is dub. in Hes.*Cat.Oxy.*1358*Fr.*2.13. **II.** as law-term, αἴ τις ἀταθείη the *injured party*, *Leg.Gort.*4.29; but ὁ ἀταμένος the *loser* in a suit, ib.10.21; ἀϝατᾶται *suffers a penalty*, *IG*5(1).1155 (Gythium):—Act., ἀτάω, aor. subj. 3 sg. ἀτάσῃ dub. in *Leg.Gort.*6.23,43.

**ἀτᾰπείνωτος**, ον, *not humbled*, Zeno *Stoic.*1.53, Arr.*Epict.*4.6.8, Plu.*Cor.*21.

**ἀταποῦ**· χαλεπῆς, Hsch.

***ἀτάρ** [ᾰτᾰ], Ep. also **αὐτάρ** (q.v.); ἀϝυτάρ *IG*1.477:—Conj., *but, nevertheless*, marking a strong contrast; freq. in Hom. to introduce an objection or correction, Il.1.506, etc.; in form of a question, E.*Hec.*258, X. ll. cc. infr., etc. it begins a sentence or clause, and, in apostrophe, is placed after the voc., Ἕκτορ, ἀ. που ἔφης *truly* thou didst say, Il.22.331; Ἕκτορ, ἀ. σύ μοί ἐσσι πατὴρ..ἀλλ' ἄγε νῦν ἐλέαιρε 6.429; γε is freq. added, with a word between, 16.573, E.*Med.*84: ἀ. sts. answers to μέν, more emphatic than δέ, Il.21.41, Od.3.298, Hdt.6.133, al.; ἀεὶ μὲν δή..ἀτὰρ οὖν καὶ τότε Pl.*R.*367e, cf. *Prt.*335d, *Tht.*172c; πῶς παισὶ μὲν πληθύεις ἀτὰρ..οὐ πέμπεις τινά; S.*Tr.*54, cf. Pl.*Sph.*225c: sts. after ἐπειδή, when it may be translated *then*, Il.12.144; ἀτὰρ ἠδέ is peculiar to Aret., *SD*1.9, al. **2.** freq. in Pl. and Trag. to mark a rapid transition to another thought, A.*Pr.*343, S.*OT*1052, Pl.*Phdr.*227b, etc.; ἀτὰρ δή E.*Tr.*63 (also later, Eus.Mynd.63). **3.** without real contrast, μὰψ ἀτὰρ οὐ κατὰ κόσμον Il.2.214, cf. 3.268,270, etc.—More freq. in Poetry (esp. Ep.) than in Prose, though found in Pl. ll.cc., *Tht.*142d, X.*Cyr.*1.6.9, *An.*4.6.14, etc.: also in Com., Cratin.188.

**ἀτᾰρ-ακτέω**, *keep calm*, Epicur.*Ep.*1 p.30U., J.*AJ*15.10.3, S.E.*P.*1.12. **-ακτοποιησία**, Ion. **-ποιησίη**, ἡ, *acting with perfect composure*, dub. in Hp.*Decent.*12. **-ακτος**, ον, *not disturbed, uniform*, περίοδοι Pl.*Ti.*47c. **II.** *not disturbed, without confusion, steady*, of soldiers, X.*Cyr.*2.1.31: generally, *quiet*, Id.*Eq.*7.10 (Sup.). Adv. Sup. -ότατα Id.*Eq.Mag.*2.1. **III.** *not excited, calm*, Arist.*HA*630$^{b}$12: Comp., M.Ant.4.24; of the sea, prob. in Arist.*Pr.*944$^{b}$23. Adv. -τως, ζῆν Phld.*Herc.*1003. **-αξία**, Ion. -ίη, ἡ, *impassiveness, calmness*, Democr.ap.Stob.2.7.3$^{i}$, Hp.*Ep.*12, Epicur.*Ep.*1 p.30U., Phld.*Oec.*p.63J., Cic.*Fam.*15.19.2, Hero *Bel.*71.2, Plu.2.101b, Plot.1.4.1, etc.; prob. f.l. for ἀταξία in Hp.*Praec.*14. **-ᾰχος**, ον, = ἀτάρακτος, ἐν τοῖς φοβεροῖς Arist.*EN*1117$^{a}$31, cf. 1125$^{b}$34, Epicur.*Sent.Vat.*79, Str.1.3.21, Onos.2.2, etc.; ἀτάραχον, τό, an *eyesalve*, Gal.12.786; of a will, *unchallengeable* *PMasp.*151.142 (vi A.D.). Adv. -χως *unconfusedly*, Epicur.*Ep.*1 p.14U.; *calmly*, Hero *Bel.*72.4, Phld.*Herc.*1003, D.S.17.54, J.*AJ*14.9.1, Archig.ap.Orib.46.26.1, Plu.*Fr.inc.*140: Comp. -ώτερον Arr.*Epict.*4.1.47. **-ᾰχώδης**, ες, *not liable to be disturbed*, Arist.*Div.Somn.*464$^{a}$14 (Comp.).

**ἀτάρβακτος**, ον, *unaffrighted*, γνώμα Pi.*P.*4.84; γυνά B.5.139; cf. ἀτάρμυκτος.

**ἀταρβ-ής**, ές, *fearless*, Il.13.299, Pi.*P.*5.51; ἀ. τῆς θέας *having no fear about* the sight, S.*Tr.*23; later of things, δοῦρας ἀ. *AP*6.97 (Antiphil.). **2.** *causing no fear*, A.*Pr.*849. **-ητος**, ον, = foreg., ἐνὶ στήθεσσιν ἀ. νόος ἐστίν Il.3.63, cf. Hes.*Sc.*110, A.*Fr.*199: neut. pl. as Adv., ὕβρις ἀτάρβητα ὁρμᾶται stalks abroad *without fear*, S.*Aj.*196. Adv. -τως Suid. **II.** *not dreaded*, κάματοι *IG*14.1003.2, cf. ib.7.96. **-ίζεται**· ἀτηρὸς φαίνεται, Hsch.

**ἀταρβομάχας** [μᾰ], α, ὁ, *fearing not the fray*, B.15.28.

**Ἀταργατῖς**, gen. ῖδος, acc. ῖν (cf. Hdn.Gr.1.107, 2.761): dat. Ἀταργατεῖτι *IG*12(3).188 (Astypalaea): also gen. Ἀταργάτιος *BCH*6.499 (Delos); dat. Ἀταργάτει *SIG*1135 (Delos), Ἀταργάτι *IG*12(3).178 (Astypalaea):—*Atargatis*, a Syrian divinity, Mnaseas 32, Str.16.1.27, Corn.*ND*6, etc.:—also **Ἀταργάτη**, *LW*1890, v.l. in Str.16.4.27: **Ἀτταγάθη**, Hsch.

**ἀτᾰρίχευτος** [ῑ], ον, *not desiccated*, Arist.*Pr.*926$^{a}$35; *not salted*, Gal.12.321.

**ἀτάρμυκτος**, ον, *unblenching, unflinching*, ὄμμα Euph.124; φρενὸς οἶστρος Nic.*Al.*161.

**ἀτάρνη**· βρόχος, Hsch. (leg. ἀρτάνη).

***ἀταρπῑτός, ἀταρπός**, Ion. for ἀτρ- (qq.v.).

**ἀταρτ-άομαι** [ᾰτ], *hurt*, Hsch. **-ηρός**, όν, *mischievous, baneful*, ἀταρτηροῖς ἐπέεσσιν Il.1.223; of a person, Μέντορ ἀταρτηρέ Od.2.243; γενέθλη Hes.*Th.*610; στόμα Πόντου Theoc.22.28; of wild beasts, Q.S.4.223, 12.40.

**ἄταρχον** (ἀτάραχον cod., post ἀταρτηροῖς)· ἀχείμαστον, Hsch.; cf. τάρχη.

**ἀτάρχῡτος**, *unburied*, Ps.-Phoc.99, Lyc.1326; cf. ἀταρίχευτος.

**ἀτασθᾰλία** [ᾰτ], Ion. **-ίη**, ἡ, *presumptuous sin, recklessness, wickedness*, Hom., always in pl.; σφετέρῃσιν or σφῇσιν ἀτασθαλίῃσιν, Il.4.409, Od.1.34, al.; ἀτασθαλίαι δέ οἱ οἴῳ ἐχθραὶ ἔσαν 21.146; δι' ἀτασθαλίας ἔπαθον κακόν 23.67; ἀτασθαλίῃσι κακῇσιν 12.300:—after Hom. in sg., ἀτασθαλίῃ μέγα ῥέξαι, of the Titans, Hes.*Th.*209; εἵνεκ' ἀτασθαλίης τε καὶ ἠνορέης ὑπερόπλου ib.516; βασιλῆος ἀ. Pi.*Parth.*2*Fr.*1.31; οὐκ ἤρθη νοῦν ἐς ἀτασθαλίην Simon.111.4; ἀτασθαλίῃ χρησάμενον Hdt.2.111: in later Prose, Alcid.ap.Arist.*Rh.*1406$^{a}$9, Luc.*Astr.*15; ἀ. ἡ εἰς τὸ θεῖον Arr.*An.*7.14.5; of an elephant, Id.*Ind.*13.13.

**ἀτασθάλλω** [ᾰτ], *to be insolent*, only in pres. part., μή τις..πλήξῃ ἀτασθάλλων Od.18.57; οὔ τις..γυναικῶν λήθει ἀτασθάλλουσα 19.88.

**ἀτάσθᾰλος** [ᾰτ], ον, *reckless, presumptuous, wicked*, of men, ἀνέρα..ἀ. ὀβριμοεργόν Il.22.418; ἀ. ἀνδρὶ ἔοικας Od.8.166, etc.; so in Hdt., ἄνδρα ἀνόσιόν τε καὶ ἀ. 8.109; ἀνὴρ δεινὸς καὶ ἀ. 9.116, cf. Him.*Ecl.*13.28, al. **2.** of men's acts, words, etc., Τρωσὶν τῶν μένος αἰὲν ἀ. Il.13.634; λίην γὰρ ἀ. ὕβριν ἔχουσιν Od.16.86; ἄνδρες δραῖσιν ἀτάσθαλα Alc.*Supp.*27.11; λέγειν βάρβαρά τε καὶ ἀ. Hdt.7.35; ἔρδειν πολλὰ καὶ ἀ. Id.3.80; πρῆγμα ἀ. ποιήσαντες ib.49; ἀ. οὐδὲν ἔρεξας Theoc.22.131.—Ep., Aeol., and Ion. word, used for comic effect by Strato Com.1.38; also in later Prose, Luc.*Cont.*3, Arr.*An.*6.27.4, etc.—In *EM*261.56 also **ἀτασθάλεος**, ον.

**ἀταύρωτος**, ον, A.*Ag.*245, also η, ον Ar.*Lys.*217:—*unwedded, maiden*, A. l.c.; *chaste*, Ar. l.c., v. Scholl. ad locc., Poll.2.173.

**ἀτᾰφία**, ἡ, *want of burial*, J.*AJ*13.15.5, Luc.*Salt.*43, Plu.*Marc.*30.

**ἄτᾰφος**, ον, *unburied*, Hdt.9.27, S.*Ant.*29, *OC*1732 (lyr.), Th.2.50, etc. **II.** ἄ. πράξεις modes of *refusal of burial*, Pl.*Lg.*960b.

**ἀτάω**, v. ἀτάομαι.

***ἅτε**, properly acc. pl. neut. of ὅστε (as in Il.11.779, 22.127). **I.** *just as, as if, so as*, ἅ. σήριον ἄστρον prob. in Alcm.23.62, cf. Pi.*O.*1.2, *P.*4.30, Hdt.5.85, S.*Aj.*168 (lyr., s.v.l.); τιμᾶν τινα ἅ. ἱεροφάντιν Jul.*Or.*7.221c. **II.** causal, *inasmuch as, seeing that*, with part., ἅτε τὸν χρυσὸν ἔχων Hdt.1.154, cf. 102; Cratin.295, Ar.*Pax*623, Th.4.130, etc.: with gen. abs., ἅτε τῶν ὁδῶν φυλασσομένων Hdt.1.123, cf. Pl.*Smp.*223b, etc.:—with part. omitted, δίκτυα δοὺς [αὐτῷ] ἅτε θηρευτῇ [ὄντι] Hdt.1.123, etc.; ἅ. γένους προμάτωρ dub. in A.*Th.*140 (lyr.); ἅ. δή Hdt.1.171; ἅ. δὴ οὖν Pl.*Prt.*321b; ὡς ἅ. freq. in Olymp. *in Mete.*39.12, al.—Rare in Trag., and only in lyr.

**ἆτε**, Lacon. = ὥς, *IG*5(1).213.

***ἄτεγκτος**, ον, *not to be softened by water*, χαλκός Arist.*Mete.*385$^{b}$13; κηρός Plu.2.15d (s.v.l.). **II.** metaph., *not to be softened*, παρηγορήμασιν A.*Fr.*348: abs., *hard-hearted, relentless*, S.*OT*336, E.*HF*833, Ar.*Th.*1047, and in late Prose, D.H.5.8, J.*BJ*5.9.4, Plu.*TG*12, Luc.*DMeretr.*12.3, etc. Adv. -τως, πρὸς ἔρωτας ἔχειν Philostr.*Ep.*5.

***ἀτειρής**, ές, *not to be rubbed* or *worn away, indestructible*, in Hom. mostly of brass or iron, Il.5.292, al. **II.** metaph., *stubborn, unyielding*, αἰεί τοι κραδίη πέλεκυς ὥς ἐστιν ἀ. ib.3.60, cf. 15.697; [Hercules] μένος αἰὲν ἀ. Od.11.270; φωνή Il.13.45, 17.555; ὄμματα Emp.86; ἀτειρέσιν ἀκτίνεσσιν Id.84.6; ἀγαθόν Pi.*O.*2.36; of persons, κἀν μύθοισι καὶ ἐν προσόδοισιν ἀ. *stubborn*, Theoc.23.6; ἀτειρὴς οἴνῳ *AP*12.175 (Strat.); τὸ ἀτειρές *stubbornness*, Pl.*Cra.*395b; Pythag. etym. of τριάς, *Theol.Ar.*15.—In Archig.ap.Gal.8.87 **ἀτειρός**. Adv., Comp. -ότερον Gal.8.110, prob. in D.L.6.99.

***ἀτείχιστος**, ον, *unwalled, unfortified*, Th.1.2, 8.62, Lys.33.7: metaph., χάριν θανάτου πάντες ἄνθρωποι πόλιν ἀ. οἰκοῦμεν Epicur.*Sent.Vat.*31. Adv. -τως Sm.*Za.*2.4(8); ἀ. τετειχισμένοι, of Brahmans living in the open air, Philostr.*VA*3.15, 6.11. **2.** *not walled off*, Th.1.64.

***ἀτέκμαρτος**, ον, *without distinctive mark, obscure, baffling*, χρηστήριον Hdt.5.92.γ'; μοῖρα A.*Pers.*910 (Sup.); ἐρημία *trackless*, Plu.*Luc.*14; ἀτέκμαρτον προνοῆσαι *without mark* whereby to judge it, Pi.*P.*10.63; ἀ. δέος Th.4.63, cf. Pl.*Lg.*638a. Adv. -τως, ἔχειν ὅτου ἕνεκά ἐστι X.*Mem.*1.4.4: neut. pl. as Adv., *bafflingly*, Pi.*O.*7.45. **2.** of persons, *uncertain, inconsistent*, Ar.*Av.*170. **II.** *boundless, unlimited*, ὕδωρ Orph.*A.*1150: metaph., γαστήρ dub. in Opp.*H.*2.206.

**ἀτέκμων**, ονος, ἡ, (τεκεῖν) *childless, barren*, Man.4.584.

**ἀτεκν-έω**, *have no children*, v.l. in Hp.*Steril.*217, cf. Lxx *Ca.*4.2, *Ho.*9.12. **-ία**, ἡ, *childlessness, barrenness*, Arist.*Pol.*1265$^{b}$10, Ph.1.201, etc.: pl., Arist.*Pol.*1265$^{a}$41. **-ος**, ον, *without children, childless, barren*, Hes.*Op.*602, A.*Th.*828 (lyr.), S.*El.*164 (lyr.), Arist.*EN*1099$^{b}$4, *Tab.Heracl.*1.151, etc.; of animals and fishes, Arist.*HA*577$^{a}$3, *GA*755$^{b}$19: also c. gen., ἄ. ἀρσένων παίδων E.*Ba.*1305. Adv. -νως Sch.E.*Or.*206. **II.** in causal sense, λειχὴν ἄφυλλος ἄ. A.*Eu.*785. [ᾰτε͞κνος S. l.c., ᾰτε̆κνος A. and E. ll.cc.] ***-όω**, *make childless*:—Pass., of the earth, *to be barren*, Lxx 4*Ki.*2.19. **-ωσις**, εως, ἡ, *barrenness*, Aq.*Ps.*34(35).12.

***ἀτέλ-εια**, Cret. **ἀτέλεα** *GDI*5040.22, ἡ:—*incompleteness, imperfection*, Arist.*Ph.*261$^{a}$36, *GA*758$^{b}$20, *Mete.*380$^{a}$31, Thphr.*CP*4.13.1. **II.** *exemption from public burdens* (τέλη), ἀ. στρατηΐης καὶ φόρου Hdt.3.67; ἔδοσαν Κροίσῳ..ἀτελείην καὶ προεδρίην Id.1.54, cf. 9.73, D.20.47; ἁπάντων ib.60; τοῦ ἄλλου (sc. φόρου) *IG*1.40; μετοικίου ib.2.121; στρατείας ib.551; ὧν ἂν εἰσάγῃ ἢ ἐξάγῃ *OGI*10.13; ἐς τὴν ἀ. to purchase *immunity*, *IG*2.570; ἀ. τινὸς ποιεῖν Alex.276.6; εὑρέσθαι, ἔχειν, enjoy *it*, D.20.1,19: generally, τοιούτων πραγματειῶν ἀ. Isoc.12.147; ἀ. ἐπικραίνειν confirm *immunity*, A.*Eu.*362; ἐξ ἀτελείας *without payment, gratis*, D.59.39, Philonid.1 D., Poll.4.46. ***-ειος**, α, ον, =

ἀτελής, Phld.*Rh.*1.5 S. **-ειότης**, ητος, ἡ, *insufficiency*, Zos.Alch. p.245 B. **-είωτος**, ον, *unfinished, incomplete*, Arist.*Fr.*70, Sor.1.33: neut. pl. as Adv., Sch.Nic.*Th.*456 (v.l. -τως). **-εσιούργητος**, ον, *not brought to an issue*, ὠδῖνες *Theol.Ar.*55. ***-εστος**, ον, *without end, issue*, or *effect, unaccomplished*, ἅλιον θεῖναι πόνον ἠδ' ἀ. Il.4.26, cf. 57,168, Od.2.273; σῖτον ἔδοντες μὰψ αὔτως ἀ. 16.111; τὰ δέ κεν θεὸς ἢ τελέσειεν ἤ κ' ἀτέλεστ' εἴη 8.571, cf. *Tab.Defix.Aud.*68$^{b}$: rare in Prose, of prayers, *not deserving of accomplishment*, Antipho 1.22; ἀ. κῶνος *truncated* cone, Hero *Stereom.*1.16: neut. pl. as Adv., *inconclusively*, ἀ. λαλεῖν *AP*12.21 (Strat.). II. *uninitiated in*.., c. gen., βακχευμάτων E.*Ba.*40: metaph., ἀ. ἱερῶν καὶ μυστηρίων τῆς πολιτείας Plu.*Flam.*2: abs., ἀ. καὶ ἀμύητος Pl.*Phd.*69c, cf. Arist.*Rh.*1419$^{a}$4, Phld.*Acad.Ind.*p.4 M.; ἀ. τῷ θεῷ Ael.*VH*3.9; prob. *unmarried*, *Tab. Defix.Aud.*68$^{a}$. III. = ἀτελής III, χώρα D.*Prooem.*55. IV. *endless, eternal*, Parm.8.4.

**ἀτελεσφόρητος**, ον, *not brought to accomplishment*, Sm.*Jb.*31.40.

**ἀτελεύτ-ητος**, ον, *not brought to an end* or *issue, unaccomplished*, ἀτελευτήτῳ ἐπὶ ἔργῳ Il.4.175, cf. 1.527. 2. *without an end, interminable*, Parm.8.32, Arist.*Ph.*204$^{a}$5, *Cael.*273$^{a}$5; *everlasting*, τὸ πᾶν Ocell.1.2, cf. Plu.2.114f, etc. II. of a person, *impracticable*, ἄτεγκτος κἀτελεύτητος S.*OT*336. **-ος**, ον, *endless, eternal*, ὕπνος A.*Ag.*1451 (lyr.).

***ἀτελής**, ές, *without end*, i.e., 1. *not brought to an end* or *issue, unaccomplished*, τῷ κε καὶ οὐκ ἀ. θάνατος μνηστῆρσι γένοιτο Od.17.546; εἰρήνη ἐγένετο ἀ. the peace was *not brought about*, X.*HG*4.8.15; τὰ μὲν λελεγμένα ἄρρητ' ἐγώ σοι κἀτελῆ φυλάξομαι *unaccomplished*, i.e. *harmless*, S.*El.*1012. 2. *incomplete, unfinished*, ἀτελῆ σοφίας καρπὸν δρέπειν Pi.*Fr.*209; ἀτελεῖ τῇ νίκῃ .. ἀνέστησαν Th.8.27; of a building, ib.40; *without end* or *purpose*, ἡ φύσις οὐθὲν .. ἀτελὲς ποιεῖ Arist.*Pol.*1256$^{b}$21. 3. *inchoate, imperfect*, of growth, Hp.*Art.*41 (Comp.); ᾠὰ ἀ. Arist.*GA*733$^{a}$2; ζῷα ib.774$^{b}$5; πολῖται ἀ., of minors, Id.*Pol.*1275$^{a}$17; ἀ. συλλογισμός Id.*APr.*24$^{a}$13; ἀ. ποιεῖν τινά *castrate*, Luc.*DSyr.*20: Comp. -έστερος *less highly developed*, Phlp.*in Ph.*898.29. Adv. -λῶς *incompletely*, Arist.*Pol.*1275$^{a}$13, dub. in Plu.2.472f. 4. *never-ending*, Δαναΐδων ὑδρεῖαι ἀ. Pl.*Ax.*371e. 5. *indeterminate*, Id.*Phlb.*24b; τὸ μὲν ἄπειρον ἀ. ἡ δὲ φύσις ἀεὶ ζητεῖ τέλος Arist.*GA*715$^{b}$14, cf. *Pol.*1256$^{b}$21. II. Act., *not bringing to an end, not accomplishing one's purpose, ineffectual*, ἀτελεῖ νόῳ Pi.*N.*3.42; of persons, ἀποπέμπειν τινά Pl.*Smp.*179d; ἀ. περὶ τὸ κρίνειν *imperfectly fitted for*.., Arist.*Pol.*1281$^{b}$38; ἀ. εἴς τι Ph.2.417: c. inf., *unable* to do *effectually*, ἄκυρος καὶ ἀ. σῶσαι And.4.9; *invalid*, δίκα *Michel* 196 (Elis). 2. *not giving accomplishment to* a thing, μαντεύμασι Pi.*P.*5.62. III. (τέλος IV) *free from tax* or *tribute*, Hdt.2.168, 3.91, Lys.32.24: c. gen., ἀ. τῶν ἄλλων *free from* all other *taxes*, Hdt.1.192; καρπῶν ἀ. *free from tithe on* produce, Id.6.46; *exempt*, λητουργιῶν D.21.155; στρατείας ib.166, cf. *IG*2$^{2}$.1132.12, Arist.*Pol.*1270$^{b}$4; τοῦ ἄλλου (sc. φόρου) *IG*1.40; μετοικίου ib.2.121. b. of things, *untaxed*, ἀ. τὸν σῖτον ἐξάγειν D.34.36; ὅσα οἱ νόμοι ἀ. πεποιήκασιν Id.42.18. 2. of sums, *without deduction, nett*, ὀβολὸς ἀ. an obol *clear gain*, X.*Vect.*4.14 sq.; τριάκοντα μνᾶς ἀτελεῖς ἐλάμβανε τοῦ ἐνιαυτοῦ D.27.9. 3. *not costly*, S.*Fr.*268, Amphis 29, Paus.Gr.*Fr.*305. IV. (τέλος V) *uninitiated*, c. gen., ἱερῶν *h.Cer.*481; ἀ. τῆς θέας Pl.*Phdr.*248b; prob. *unmarried*, *Tab.Defix.Aud.*68$^{a}$: metaph., ἔρημον καὶ ἀ. φιλοσοφίαν λείπειν Pl.*R.*495c.

**ἀτελώνητος**, ον, *untaxed*, Zen.1.74, Hierocl.*Facet.*246, Just.*Nov.*106 *Pr.*

**ἀτέμβιος**· μεμψίμοιρος, *EM*163.32.

**ἀτέμβω** [ᾰ], only pres., *maltreat*, οὐ καλὸν ἀτέμβειν .. ξείνους Τηλεμάχου Od.20.294, 21.312; *afflict, perplex*, ἀτέμβει θυμὸν ἐνὶ στήθεσσιν Ἀχαιῶν 2.90:—Pass., c. gen., *to be bereft* or *cheated of* a thing, ἀτέμβονται νεότητος they *have lost their* youth, Il.23.445; ἀτεμβόμενός γε σιδήρου ib.834; μή τίς οἱ ἀτεμβόμενος κίοι ἴσης 11.705, cf. Od.9.42. II. Med. like Act., Q.S.5.147,173: c. dat., *blame, be dissatisfied with*, A.R.2.56, 3.99: c. inf., ἀτεμβόμενος τοῖον στόλον ἀμφιπένεσθαι Id.2.1199.

***ἀτεν-ής**, ές, *stretched, strained*, κισσός S.*Ant.*826 (lyr.); freq. of the eyes, *staring*, Arist.*HA*492$^{a}$11; τὸ ἀ. τῆς ὄψεως καὶ ἄτεγκτον D.H.5.8; τὴν ὄψιν εἰς τὸ ἀ. ἀπερείδεσθαι *intently*, Luc.*Icar.*12. 2. *intense, excessive*, ὀργαί A.*Ag.*71 (lyr.); ὀδυρμοί Call.*Fr.*1.7 P. 3. *straight, direct*, ἥκω δ' ἀτενὴς ἀπ' οἴκων *straight* from home, E.*Fr.*65. 4. of diseases, *obstinate*, ἰσχιάς prob. for ἀγεννής in Archig.ap.Aët.12.1. II. of men's minds and speech, *intent, earnest*, ἀτενεῖ .. νόῳ Hes.*Th.*661, Pi.*N.*7.88; ἁπλοῖ καὶ ἀ., of men, Pl.*R.*547e; ἀ. παρρησία E.*Fr.*737; ἀ. ψυχή Luc.*Nigr.*4. 2. *unbending, stubborn*, ἀ. ἀτεράμων τε Ar.*V.*730 (lyr.); ἀστένακτος καὶ ἀ. D.H.5.8: Comp., Phld.*Lib.*p.44 O. III. Adv. ἀτενῶς, Ion. -έως Hp.*Prorrh.*1.24; ἀ. ἐμβλέπειν Agatharch.41; δυσπειθῶς καὶ ἀ. ἔχειν πρός τι to be *obstinately averse to*, Plu.*Galb.*25:—more freq. in neut., ἀτενὲς ἴκελοι *exceeding* like, Pi.*P.*2.77; ἀ. ἀπ' ἀοῦς from dawn *onwards*, Epich.124.1; καταμαθεῖν ἀ. Id.172.4; ἀ. τηρεῖν Diph.61; ἀ. βλέπειν Plb.18.53.9. **-ίζω**, *look intently, gaze earnestly*, τοῖς ὄμμασιν *stare*, Hp.*Epid.*7.10; εἴς τι Arist.*Mete.*343$^{b}$12; πρός τι Id.*Pr.*959$^{a}$24; of the eyes, ἀτενίζοντες αὐτῷ *Ev.Luc.*4.20, cf. *Act.Ap.*23.1, *Placit.*1.7; εἴς τι Plb.6.11.12, J.*BJ*5.12.3, S.E.*P.*1.75, etc.; εἴς τινα *Act.Ap.*6.15; εἰς τὸν θεόν Them.*Or.*4.51b; πρὸς τὸ ἐκείνου πρόσωπον Luc.*Merc.Cond.*11: abs., also of the eyes, Arist.*Pr.*957$^{b}$18:—Pass., *to be gazed upon*, *APl.*4.204 (Praxit.). II. metaph. of the mind, ἀ. τὴν διάνοιαν πρός τι Arist.*Ph.*192$^{a}$15; εἰς τὴν προαίρεσιν ἀτενίζοντα πράττειν Phld.*Ir.*p.96 W.; *to be obstinate*, Lync.ap.Ath.7.313f. **-ισις**, εως, ἡ, *straining of the eyesight*, Paul.Aeg.6.21. **-ισμός**, ὁ, *intent observation*, Thphr.*Vert.*9. 2. *fixed stare*, τῶν ὀμμάτων, in apoplexy, Herod.Med.in *Rh.Mus.*58.80. **-ιστός**, ή, όν, *that may be gazed at*, Sch.Il.1.98.

***ἄτερ** [ᾰ], Ep., Ion., Trag. Prep. with gen., *without, apart from*, Hom.; κράτιστον Ἀχιλέος ἄ. Pi.*N.*7.27; ἄ. Ζηνός *without* his will, Il.15.292, cf. *POxy.*936.18 (iii A.D.); οὐ θεῶν ἄ. 'non *sine* dis', Pi.*P.*5.76; ἄ. μόχθου Democr.223; ἄ. πυρετοῦ καὶ ὀδύνης Hp.*Prorrh.*2.4. II. *aloof, apart from*, ἄ. ἥμενον ἄλλων Il.1.498; νόσφιν ἄ. τε κακῶν Hes.*Op.*91:—freq. in Trag., mostly after its case, A.*Supp.*377, etc.; but before it in Id.*Pr.*456, *Supp.*703 (lyr.), *Ch.*338 (lyr.), S.*Ph.*703 (lyr.), *El.*866:—also in late Prose, as Lxx 2*Ma.*12.15, D.H.3.10, *Ev. Luc.*22.6, Plu.*Cat.Mi.*5, Vett.Val.136.9, al. III. c. dat., ἄτερ ἄστρασιν Anub.87.

**ἀτεραμν-ία** [ᾰτ], Ion. -ίη, ἡ, *harshness, hardness*, ὑδάτων Hp.*Aër.*4. **-ος**, ον, *unsoftened, hard*, ὕδατα ib.1, Arist.*GA*767$^{a}$34; πέτρα Theoc.10.7; ἀ. κοιλία *costive*, Hp.*Aër.*4; of food *that will not cook*, Plu.2.701c, Gal.17(2).157. II. metaph., *stubborn, unfeeling, merciless*, κῆρ Od.23.167; ὀργή A.*Pr.*192; βροντῆς μύκημ' ἀ. ib.1062. **-ότης**, ητος, ἡ, *stubbornness*; ἀ. πρὸς τὴν βλάστησιν *slowness* to germinate, Thphr.*CP*4.3.2. **-ώδης**, ες, *not to be softened*, ὕδατα Gal.17(2).187.

***ἀτεράμων** [ᾰτ] [ρᾰ], ον, gen. ονος, Att. for ἀτέραμνος, *hard, tough*, Μαραθωνομάχαι Ar.*Ach.*181, cf. Pl.*Lg.*853d, 880e, Eub.1 D.; *hard to cook*, Thphr.*HP*2.4.2, cf. 8.8.6, *CP*4.12.8.

**ἀτεράτευτος** [ρᾰ], ον, *nowise prodigious* or *wonderful*, Eust.918.5.

**ἀτερέα**· ὄρος, γοργόν (Cret.), Hsch. **ἀτέρεμνος**, ον, = ἀτέραμνος, Id. **ἀτερέψατο**· ἠθέτησεν, Id. **ἀτερήσιον**· ἀπρόμηθες, Id. (ἀρετή- cod.).

**ἀτερηδόνιστος**, ον, *not worm-eaten*, Dsc.1.16.

***ἄτερθε** [ᾰ], before a vowel **-θεν**, Aeol. **ἄτερθα** Hdn.Gr.2.192, = ἄτερ, Pi.*O.*9.78, etc.: c. gen., ἄ. πτερύγων A.*Supp.*783 (lyr.); λατρῶν ἄ. ib.1011; ἄ. τοῦδε S.*Aj.*645 (lyr.). II. as Adv., *aloof, apart*, Pi.*P.*5.96.

**ἀτέριγε**· χωρίς, Hsch.

**ἀτερμ-άτιστος** [μᾰ], ον, *unbounded*, ἐπιθυμία D.S.19.1, cf. Gal.19.472. II. = ἀβέβαιος, ἀθεμελίωτος, Hsch. **-ων**, ον, gen. ονος, *without bound* or *end*, αἰών Arist.*Mu.*401$^{a}$16; ὕπνος Mosch.3.104; ἐνόπτρων ἀ. αὐγαί the mirror's *countless* rays, E.*Hec.*926; ἀ. πέπλος *having no end* or *issue, inextricable*, A.*Eu.*634.

**ἀτεροῖον**· τὸ ἑτέρωθεν καὶ χωρίς, Hsch.

**ἀτερόπλευρος**, ον, = ἑτερο-, *SIG*247 K$^{1}$.13 (Delph.).

**ἀτερόπτιλλος**, ον, Dor. = ἑτερόφθαλμος, *IG*4.951.34 and 72 (Epid.).

***ἄτερος** [ᾰ], Dor. etc. for ἕτερος, *IG*9(1).694.17 (Corc.); Aeol. **ἄτερος** Alc.41, al., etc.; τὸ ἄτερον, Megarian in Ar.*Ach.*813. 2. ἅτερος [ᾱ], Att. contr. for ὁ ἅτερος, *Com.Adesp.*14.23 D., Pl.*Lg.*695b, etc.; also neut. θἄτερον, gen. θᾰτέρου, dat. θᾰτέρῳ, θᾰτέρᾳ, or with mark of crasis, θἀτέρου, etc.; but contr. forms when the Art. ends with a conson., are incorrect, as θάτερον τὸν τόπον Str.2.1.20, cf. Luc.*DMort.*26.1, *Hist.Conscr.*22: also nom. θάτερος Polem.*Cyn.*4; ὁ θάτερος Men.846; τὰ θάτερα Arist.*Mu.*397$^{a}$2; ἅτερον for τὸν ἕτερον Luc.*Pseudol.*29. (sm̥-τερος; v. ἕτερος.)

**ἀτέρπ-εια**, Ion. -είη, -ίη, ἡ, = ἀτερψία, Democr.4,174, D.L.7.97. ***-ής**, ές, *unpleasing, joyless*, λιμός Il.19.354; of the nether world, νέκυας καὶ ἀτερπέα χῶρον Od.11.94, etc.; πέτρης .. καὶ ἀτερπέϊ χώρῳ, of a rocky shore, 7.279; νούσων ἑσμός A.*Supp.*685 (lyr.), cf. *Pr.*31, Simon.37.6; λόγοι E.*El.*293; γῆρας Mosch.4.114; ἀτερπέστερον ἐς ἀκρόασιν *less attractive* to the ear, Th.1.22; ἦχοι ἀ., opp. ἐπιτερπεῖς, Phld.*Po.*994.23, cf. *Mus.*p.82 K.; εἴ τις ὑπερβάλλοι τὸ μέτριον τὰ ἐπιτερπέστατα ἀτερπέστατα ἂν γίγνοιτο Democr.233, cf. Ph.1.396 (Sup.); of persons, ἀ. καὶ κακὸς ὀρχηστής Plu.*Cor.*25. Adv. -πῶς, οὐκ ἀ. ἱστορείσθω Gal.14.237; but ἀ. ζῆν *without enjoyment*, Plu.2.1100d. **-νος**, ον, = ἄγρυπνος, Stesich.78, Ibyc.52. **-ος**, ον, = ἀτερπής, Il.6.285 (dub. l.).

**ἀτερψία**, Ion. -ίη, ἡ, *unpleasantness*, Luc.*Vit.Auct.*14.

**ἀτετόν**· λευκόν, Hsch. **ἀτετῶς**· ἀφροντίστως, Id.

**ἀτευκτ-έω**, *fail in gaining*, τῆς πατρίου ἀγωγῆς Plu.2.235b; τῶν οἰκείων χρειῶν Phld.*Ir.*p.47 W., cf. ib.p.9 W., Herm.ap.Stob.1.49.44. II. Pass., *to be unsuccessful*, of an operation, Antyll.ap.Orib.45.25.6. **-ος**, ον, *not gaining* or *obtaining*, Max.Tyr.11.8, Hsch.

**ἀτευξία**, ἡ, *not obtaining, privation*, A.D.*Synt.*56.26, Dam. in *AB*1345.

**ἀτευχ-ής**, ές, (τεῦχος) *unequipped, unarmed*, E.*Andr.*1119, *AP*9.320 (Leon.). **-ητος**, ον, = foreg., ib.543 (Phil.), *Epic.Alex.Adesp.*8.2.

**ἄτεφρος**, ον, epith. of δάφνη, *PMag.Par.*1.2582.

**ἀτέχν-αστος**, ον, *artless*, Them.*Or.*2.39d. **-έω**, *to be* ἄτεχνος, *to be unskilful*, Sch.Ar.*Nu.*296. ***-ής**, ές, = ἄτεχνος, S.E.*M.*7.395, interpol. in Babr.75.4: Comp. -έστερος v.l. in Hp.*Fract.*16. ***-ία**, ἡ, *want of art* or *skill*, Hp.*Lex*4, Pl.*Phd.*90d, al., Arist.*EN*1140$^{a}$21, Chrysipp.*Stoic.*2.269: pl., Simp. in *Stoic.*3.49. **-ίτευτος** [ῐ], ον, *artless, simple*, D.H.*Lys.*8:—hence Verb **-ῑτεύομαι**, Hsch. s.v. ἐρρωπίζομεν. **-ος**, ον, *without art, unskilful*, Pl.*Plt.*274c; esp. *ignorant of the rules* or *principles of art*, opp. ἔντεχνος or τεχνίτης, *unskilled, unprofessional*, of persons, Id.*Sph.*219a, Gal.6.134, S.E.*P.*3.262; *having no trade* or *profession*, *PFlor.*4.14 (iv A.D.); *unsystematic*, διδασκαλία Anon.*in SE*67.31; of pursuits, ἄ. τριβή Pl.*Phdr.*260e, cf. 262c, *Lg.*938a; πίστεις ἄ. proofs *not invented by the orator*, Arist.*Rh.*1355$^{b}$35, 1375$^{a}$22; ἀποδείξεις Ph.1.355; αἰσχρὸν καὶ ἄ. *not workmanlike*, Hp.*Fract.*30; πῦρ *uncreative*, opp. τεχνικόν, Zeno *Stoic.*1.34; φαντασία ib.2.24.

**ἀτέχνως**, Adv. of ἄτεχνος, *without art, without rules of art, empirically*, X.*Mem*.3.11.7, Pl.*Grg*.501a. **II.** **ἀτεχνῶς** (with penult. short), Adv. of ἀτεχνής, *simply*, i.e. *really, absolutely*, freq. in Com., Pl., etc.; ἀ. ἥκω παρεσκευασμένος Ar.*Ach*.37, cf. *Nu*.408,1174, al.; καλὸν ἀ. *simply* beautiful, Id.*Av*.820; ἀ. γε παμπόνηρα Id.*Ra*.106; ῥύγχος ἀ. ἔσθ' ὑός *simply* a swine's snout, Pherecr.102; ἀ. μὲν οὖν σκύτη βλέπει Eup.282; ἀ. τὸ τοῦ Ὁμήρου ἐπεπόνθη Pl.*Smp*.198c; *bona fide, sincerely*, opp. κόμπου ἕνεκα, Philostr.*VA*6.20: freq. in comparisons, ἀ. ὥσπερ *just* like, Pl.*Phd*.90c, etc.; ἀ. οἷον Id.*Lg*.952e: with neg., οὐδ' ἂν διαλεχθείην γ' ἀ. would *just* not have spoken a word to him, Ar.*Nu*.425; ἀ. οὐδείς *simply* no one, Id.*Av*.605, cf. *Pl*.362, Pl.*Plt*.288a.—On ἀτέχνως and -νῶς v. Sch.Ar.*Pl*.109.

⊛**ἀτέω** [ᾰ], part. ἀτέων *demented, reckless*, c. gen., θεῶν *defying* the gods, Il.20.332 (Aristarch.); Μουσέων Call.*Fr*.537: abs., Hdt.7.223.

**ἀτεώροχοι**· ἄγαν αὐθάδεις, Hsch. (leg. ἀγέρωχοι).

⊛**ἄτη**, ἡ, Dor. **ἄτα**, Aeol. **αὐάτα** (ἀϜ–), v. infr.:—*bewilderment, infatuation*, caused by *blindness* or *delusion* sent by the gods, mostly as the punishment of guilty rashness, τὸν δ' ἄτη φρένας εἷλε Il.16.805; Ζεῦ πάτερ, ἦ ῥά τιν' ἤδη.. βασιλήων τῇδ' ἄτῃ ἄασας 8.237; Ζεὺς καὶ Μοῖρα καὶ.. Ἐρινὺς.. φρεσὶν ἔμβαλον ἄγριον ἄτην 19.88 (so ἀλλ' ἐπεὶ ἀασάμην καί μευ φρένας ἐξέλετο Ζεύς ib.137); ἄτην δὲ μετέστενον ἣν Ἀφροδίτη δῶχ' ὅτε μ' ἤγαγε κεῖσε, says Helen, Od.4.261. **2.** Ἄτη personified, *the goddess of mischief*, author of *rash actions*, πρέσβα Διὸς θυγάτηρ, Ἄτη, ἣ πάντας ἀᾶται Il.19.91, cf. 9.504, Hes.*Th*.230, Pl.*Smp*.195d; Ἄτης ἂν λειμῶνα Emp.121.4; coupled with Ἐρινύς, A.*Ag*.1433. **II.** of the consequences of such visitations, either, **1.** Act., *reckless guilt* or *sin*, Ἀλεξάνδρου ἕνεκ' ἄτης Il.6.356: in pl., *deceptions*, 10.391: or, **2.** Pass., *bane, ruin*, 24.480, Hdt.1.32; ἐγγύα, πάρα δ' ἄτα prov. in Thales ap.Stob.3.1.172: τὸ πῆμα τῆς ἄτης the anguish of the *doom*, S.*Aj*.363 (lyr.); ὕβρις γὰρ ἐξανθοῦσ' ἐκάρπωσε σταχὺν ἄτης A.*Pers*.822; Πειθὼ προβουλόπαις.. ἄτης Id.*Ag*.386 (lyr.): pl., Id *Pers*.653 (lyr.), 1037 (lyr.), S.*Aj*.848, etc.; *strokes of fate*, ἀνδρείη τὰς ἄτας μικρὰς ἔρδει Democr.213. **3.** Trag., of persons, *bane, pest*, δίκην ἄτης λαθραίου A.*Ag*.1230; δύ' ἄτα S.*Ant*.533. **b.** *ill-fated person*, A.*Ag*.1268 codd.—Not in Comedy (unless read for αὐτῆς, Ar.*Pax*605) nor in Att. Prose (exc. as pr. n. and in quotations of ἐγγύα, πάρα δ' ἄτα Cratin.Jun.12, Pl.*Chrm*.165a), but found in Arist.*VV*$1251^{b}$20; κῆρας καὶ ἄτας D.H.8.61; τοιαύτας κακὰς ἄτας such *abominations*, of certain Epicurean expressions, Cleom.2.1. **III.** *fine, penalty*, or *sum lost* in a lawsuit, *Leg.Gort*.11.34, al. (From ἀάω, q.v.: orig. ἀϜάτη, Aeol. αὐάτα Alc.*Supp*.23.12, Pi.*P*.2.28, 3.24, *Lyr.Adesp*.123.) [ᾱάτη, ἄτη; ἄτη is dub. in Archil.73.]

⊛**ἄτηκτος**, ον, *not melted* or *to be melted* by fire, χιών Pl.*Phd*.106a; ἄ. πυρί Arist.*GA*$762^{a}$31, cf. *Mete*.$388^{b}$24. **2.** *insoluble* in oil, Dsc.5.160. **II.** metaph., *not to be softened* or *subdued*, νόμοις ἄτηκτοι Pl.*Lg*.853d.

**ἀτημέλ-εια** [ᾰτ], ἡ, *carelessness*, Plu.2.608f, Agath.5.13. **–έω**, *take no heed of, neglect*, pf. part. Pass. ἀτημελημένος f.l. in Procop.*Vand*.1.21 (for ἀπ–), cf. Sch.A.R.1.609. **–ής**, ές, *neglected*, κόμη Plu.*Ant*.18. **II.** of persons, *careless, neglectful*, χρημάτων E.*Fr*.184. Adv. –λῶς, ἔχειν τινός Plu.*Agis* 17; ἀτημελέως ἀλάλητο A.R.1.812 (v.l. –λέες). **–ητος**, ον, *unheeded, unnoticed*, X.*Cyr*.5.4.18, 8.1.14, and so prob. in A.*Ag*.891. Adv. –τως, ἔχειν to be *uncared for*, X.*Cyr*.8.1.15. **2.** *slovenly*, οὐκ ἀ. τοὺς κικίννους Alciphr.3.55; τὸ ἀ. τῶν τριχῶν Jul.*Mis*.365d. **–ία**, poet. –ίη, ἡ, = ἀτημέλεια, A.R.3.830.

**ἀτηνεῖν**· μοχθεῖν, Hsch. (leg. ἀστηνεῖν).

⊛**ἀτηρής** [ᾱ], ές, = ἀτηρός, f.l. in Hp.*Aër*.24.

**ἀτήρητος**, ον, *unobserved, unnoticed*, Them.*Or*.23.294c.

**ἀτηρία** [ᾱ], ἡ, *mischief, evil*, Pl.Com.182, X.*Mem*.3.5.17 (v.l. ἀπειρία).

**ἀτηρόγνωμος**· *durus*, *Gloss*.

**ἀτηρός** [ᾱ], ά, όν, *blinded by* ἄτη, *hurried to ruin*, Thgn.433,634; φρήν S.*Fr*.264. **II.** *baneful, mischievous*, δύη A.*Pr*.746; τύχη Id.*Ag*.1483 (lyr.); κακόν E.*Andr*.353; ναυτιλίη *AP*9.23 (Antip.); τὸ ἀ. *bane, mischief*, A.*Eu*.1007 (anap.); μή τι ἀ. ποιέωσι [οἱ παῖδες] Democr.279.—Once in Com., ἀτηρότατον κακόν an 'outrageous' nuisance, Ar.*V*.1299; and so Adv. –ῶς 'awfully' as a slang word, Phld.*Mus*.p.105 K.: in Pl.*Cra*.395b and c introduced only for an etym. purpose: also in later Prose, D.L.6.99.

⊛**Ἀτθίς**, ίδος, ἡ, *Attic*, esp. (with or without γῆ) *Attica*, E.*IA*247 (lyr.) (unless –ίδας ναῦς be read); γῆς ἀπ' Ἀτθίδος Epin.1.6. **2.** (sc. γλῶττα) *the Attic dialect*, Str.8.1.2. **3.** (sc. ἱστορία) *history of Athens*, οἱ τὴν Ἀ. συγγράψαντες Id.9.1.6, cf. D.H.1.8, J.*Ap*.1.3. **4.** *Athens*, written Ἀθθίς in *Pae.Delph*.8,14.

**ἀτίετος** [ῐ], ον, (τίω) *unhonoured*, A.*Eu*.385, 839 (both lyr.). **II.** Act., *not honouring* or *regarding*, φίλων E.*Ion* 701 (lyr.).

⊛**ἀτίζω** [ᾰ], mostly in pres. part.; 2 and 3 sg., E.*Rh*.327, 253 (lyr.); inf., S.*OC*1153: fut. ἀτίσεις [ῑ] A.*Fr*.105: aor. subj. ἀτίσῃς [ῑ] Id.*Eu*.542 (lyr.); Ep. aor. ἄτισσα A.R.1.615:—Pass., Gal.18(2).642:—*not to honour, not to heed*, ὁ δὲ πρῶτον μὲν ἀτίζων ἔρχεται *unheeding*, Il.20.166: c. acc., *slight, treat lightly*, θεοὺς ἀτίζων A.*Th*.441, cf. E.*Supp*.19, Rhian.1.5: c. gen. rei, *deprive of honour* due, γεράων μιν ἄτισσαν A.R. l.c.—Never in early Prose; for Nic.*Al*.193 v. ἀτύζω.

**ἀτῐθάσ-ευτος** [θᾰ], ον, *untamable, wild*, Agatharch.74, Aesop.342, Plu.*Art*.25, 2.728a; κακία App.*BC*4.8; τοῦ νόμου τὸ λίαν ἀκριβὲς καὶ ἀ. Agath.4.21. **–ος**, ον, = foreg., dub. in Hdn.5.6.9; λύτται Ph.1.20, al.

**ἀτίθηνος** [ῐ], ον, *without a nurse*, Man.4.368.

**ἀτῑμᾰγελ-έω**, (ἀγέλη) *forsake the herd, stray*, Arist.*HA*$572^{b}$19, $611^{a}$2, Theoc.9.5: metaph., *try to escape*, Luc.*Lex*.10. **–ης**, ου, Dor. **–ας**, α, ὁ, *despising the herd*, i.e. *straying, feeding alone*, S.*Fr*.1026, Theoc.25.132, *AP*6.255 (Eryc.).

⊛**ἀτῑμ-άζω**, fut. –άσω A.*Eu*.917 (lyr.), Pl.*R*.465a, etc.: aor. ἠτίμασα S.*OC*49, Pl.*Euthd*.292e, etc.: pf. ἠτίμακα And.4.31, Pl.*Plt*.266d:—Pass., pf. ἠτίμασμαι E.*Med*.20, Pl.*Smp*.219d, Ephor.*Fr*.3.21 B.: aor. ἠτιμάσθην Pi.*Fr*.123.5, Pl.*Lg*.931b: fut. ἀτιμασθήσομαι A.*Ag*.1068, S.*OT*1081: (ἄτιμος):—*hold in no honour, esteem lightly*, c. acc., once in Il.9.450 ἀτιμάζεσκε δ' ἄκοιτιν; freq. in Od., τούσδε γ' ἀτιμάζει κατὰ δῆμον 6.283; οἶκον ἀτιμάζοντες ἔδουσιν 21.332, cf. 427; ἀ. τοκῆας Thgn.821: freq. in Trag., A.*Th*.1023, *Eu*.712, 917, al.; μή μ' ἀτιμάσας γένῃ Phryn.Trag.20 (= Id.Com.80), cf. D.40.26, etc.; ἀ. καὶ κολάζειν, opp. ἐπαινεῖν καὶ τιμᾶν, X.*Cyr*.1.6.20; τὴν ἀνθρωπίνην ἀσθένειαν ἀ. Pl.*Phd*.107b, al.; *bring dishonour upon*, τὴν πόλιν And.4.31: c. acc. cogn., ἔπη ἃ ἀτιμάζεις πόλιν the words thou *speakest in dishonour of* the city, S.*OT*340:—Pass., *suffer dishonour, insult*, etc., πρός τινος Pi.*Fr*.123.5, Hdt.1.61; τινί S.*Aj*.1342; οὐκ ἀτιμασθήσομαι Id.*OT*1081, cf. D.21.74; τῷ γεγενημένῳ *put to shame by*.., Lys.2.27: c. neut. pl., ἀνάξι' ἠτιμασμένη E.*IA*943. **2.** c. gen. rei, *treat as unworthy of*, μηδ' ἀτιμάσῃς λόγου (sc. ἐμέ) A.*Pr*.783; μή μ' ἀτιμάσῃς ὧν σε προστρέπω φράσαι, = τούτων ἃ σε πρ. φρ., S.*OC*49, cf. *Ant*.22. **3.** c. inf., ὦ θάνατε Παιάν, μή μ' ἀτιμάσῃς μολεῖν *do* not *deem* me *unworthy* of thy visit, A.*Fr*.255.1; μήτοι μ' ἀτιμάσῃς τὸ μὴ οὐ θανεῖν σὺν σοί *deem* me not *unworthy* to die, S.*Ant*.544; but also οὐκ ἀτιμάσω θεοὺς προσειπεῖν *will* not *disdain* to.., E.*HF*608, cf. Pl.*La*.182c. **II.** in legal sense, *disfranchise*, ὑπὸ τῆς πόλεως ἠτιμασμένος Ephor. l.c.; at Rome, of the Censors, *punish with ignominia*, D.C.38.13. **–αλφέω**, *fail to fetch a price*, Hsch. **–ασμός**, ὁ, *dishonour*, Lxx 1*Ma*.1.40 (v.l.), Aristeas 269. **–αστέος**, α, ον, *to be despised*, Hp.*Fract*.31, Pl.*Phdr*.266d, Jul.*Or*.6.198d. **2.** ἀτιμαστέον *one must dishonour*, X.*Smp*.4.17, *Hippiatr.Praef*. **–αστήρ**, ῆρος, ὁ, *dishonourer*, A.*Th*.637. **–αστής**, οῦ, ὁ, = foreg., *Gloss*. **–αστός**, όν, *dishonoured*, γυναιξίν Mimn.1.9. ⊛**–άω**, Ep. impf. ἀτίμων: fut. ἀτιμήσω: aor. ἠτίμησα: pf. ἠτίμηκα Gal.1.10:—Pass., aor. –ήθην Id.5.44:—used by Hom. for ἀτιμάζω, *dishonour, disdain*, σὲ δ' ἀτιμᾷ Od.16.307; ὃν τότ' ἀτίμα 21.99; τὸν πάντες ἀτίμων 23.28; τὸν Χρύσην ἠτίμασεν Il.1.11, cf. 94, al.; νῦν δέ σ' ἀτιμήσουσι 8.163, cf. Hes.*Op*.185; used once by Pi. in Dor. aor. ἠτίμᾱσα, *P*.9.80; once by S. in imper. ἀτίμα, *Aj*.1129; ἀτιμῶσι v.l. for –οῦσι in X.*Ath*.1.14; also in later Ep., Call.*Dian*.260, Mosch.4.6, Nonn.*D*.17.313, al.; and in later Prose, Gal. l.c. **–ητεί**, Adv. *without a valuation*, *OGI*218.69 (Ilium, iii B.C.). **–ητέον**, *one must hold in disesteem*, συκοφάντας Isoc.15.175. **–ητος**, ον, *unhonoured, despised*, ὡς εἴ τιν' ἀτίμητον μετανάστην Il.9.648; οὐκ ἀ. not *unrewarded*, X.*Hier*.9.10. **II.** (τιμή II) *not valued* or *estimated*, Is.3.35: esp. δίκη ἀ. a cause *in which the penalty is not assessed in court*, but fixed by law beforehand, D.21.90, Aeschin.3.210; opp. τιμητός (where the penalty is settled in court), D.27.67, cf. Poll.8.54,63, Harp. s.v.; Suid. erroneously reverses this explanation. **2.** *invaluable, priceless*, Lxx *Wi*.7.9, Eust.781.19. **3.** *not assessed*, *IG*5(1).1433.45 (Messene); *not capable of being valued*, ἄγαλμα *Epigr.Gr*.805. ⊛**–ία**, Ion. –ίη, ἡ, *dishonour, disgrace*, ἀτιμίῃσιν ἰάλλειν Od.13.142, Pi.*O*.4.21, S.*El*.1035, etc.; ἐν ἀτιμίῃ τινὰ ἔχειν Hdt.3.3; ἀτιμίην προστιθέναι τινί Id.7.11; ὄνειδος καὶ ἀ. ἔχειν ib.231; ἀτιμίης κυρεῖν πρός τινος ib.158; θεῶν ἀ. *dishonour done to* the gods, E.*Heracl*.72, Pl.*Hipparch*.229c; οὐκ ἀτιμίᾳ σέθεν A.*Eu*.796: pl., ταῖς μεγίσταις κολάζειν ἀ. Pl.*Plt*.309a, cf. 310e, *R*.492d, al.; ὕβρεις καὶ ἀτιμίας D.18.205, 21.23; *indignities*, Arist.*Pol*.$1336^{b}$11. **2.** *deprivation of privileges*, A.*Eu*.394 (lyr.); esp. *of civic rights*, And.1.74, X.*Lac*.9.6, D.9.44; coupled with θάνατος and φυγή, *IG*1.27*a*74. **II.** of things, ἐσθημάτων ἀ., i.e. *sorry* garb, A.*Pers*.847; κόμη.. ἀτιμίας πλέως Cratin.9. [Ep. ἀτιμῑη Hom. l.c., Tyrt.10.10.]

**ἀτῑμοπενθής**, ές, *sorrowing for dishonour*, A.*Eu*.792 (lyr.).

**ἄτῑμ-ος**, ον, (τιμή I) *unhonoured, dishonoured*, Il.1.171; μετὰ πᾶσιν ἀτιμοτάτη θεός εἰμι ib.516; ἀτιμότερον δέ με θήσεις 16.90; ἀτιμότεροι, opp. λαχόντες τιμῆς, Thgn.1111; ἄ. μόρος *dishonourable*, A.*Th*.589; ἄτιμα δ' οὐκ ἐπραξάτην, i.e. they have met their deserts, Id.*Ag*.1443; ἄτιμος Ἀργείοισι *by* them, S.*Aj*.440; ἔκ γ' ἐμοῦ *by* me, Id.*OC*51. **b.** c. gen., ἄ. δωμάτων *without the honour of*.., *not deemed worthy of*.., A.*Ch*.409 (lyr.); πάντων ib.295; ἐκφορᾶς Id.*Th*.1029; χάρις οὐκ ἄ. πόνων no *unworthy* return for.., Id.*Ag*.354; ὧν μὲν ἱκόμην ἄτιμον ἐξέπεμψεν S.*OT*789. **2.** *deprived of civic rights* (cf. ἀτιμία), ἄτιμα τὰ τέκνα γίνεται Hdt.1.173, cf. *IG*1.37, 9(1).334 (Locr.), etc.; opp. ἐπίτιμος, Ar.*Av*.766, *Ra*.692, And.1.80; ἄ. τὰ σώματα ib.74: c. gen., ib.75; ἄ. γερῶν *deprived of* privileges, Th.3.58; ἄ. τοῦ τεθνηκότος *debarred from all rights in* him, S.*El*.1214; ἄ. τοῦ συμβουλεύειν *deprived of the right of* advising, D.15.33; ἄ. τῆς πόλεως καθιστάναι τινά Lys.12.21; ἄ. εἶναι καθάπαξ D.21.32, Arist.*Ath*.22.8. **3.** of things, *not honourable*, Hdt.5.6 (Sup.); ἄτιμον ποιεῖσθαί τι hold *in dishonour*, S.*Ant*.78; ἄτιμα ποιεῖν ἔς τινα Hdt.2.141; ἄ. τοὔργον Ar.*Av*.166; ἕδρα ἀτιμοτέρα *less honourable*, X.*Cyr*.8.4.5; of parts of the body, τὸ τιμιώτερον καὶ τὸ ἀτιμότερον Arist.*PA*$672^{b}$21; ἀ. σκεῦος D.S.17.66. **II.** (τιμή II) *without price* or *value*, τοῦ νῦν οἶκον ἄτιμον ἔδεις thou devourest his substance *without payment*, Od.16.431; *of little price, cheap*, opp. τίμιος, X.*Vect*.4.10. **2.** *unavenged*, ἐκ θεῶν A.*Ag*.1279, cf. E.*Hipp*.1417. **3.** *unpunished*, Pl.*Lg*.855c. **III.** Adv. –μως *dishonourably, ignominiously*, A.*Pr*.197,919, *Th*.1026, S.*OC*428, v.l. in Lys.32.17, etc.: Comp. –ότερον Pl.*Ep*.309b, D.S.1.67: Sup.

ἀτιμότατα Pl.*Lg.*728b. -όω, fut. -ώσω: aor. ἠτίμωσα A.*Supp.* 644 (lyr.), etc.: pf. ἠτίμωκα D.21.103:—Pass., pf. ἠτίμωμαι E.*Hel.* 455, D.21.91: plpf. ἠτίμωτο Hdt.7.231, *IG*1.61*a* 10: aor. -ώθην A.*Ch.*636 (lyr.), And.1.33, etc.: fut. ἀτιμωθήσομαι Isoc.5.64; ἠτιμώσομαι D.19.284:—*dishonour*, A.*Supp.*644:—Pass., *suffer dishonour* or *indignity*, Hdt.4.66, 7.231, A.*Ch.*636, E.*Hel.*455. II. *punish with* ἀτιμία 2, Ar.*Pax* 742, And.1.33, D.18.82, Arist.*Ath.*53.6 (Pass.); ἀτιμωθῆναι ἐπὶ αἰτίᾳ Lys.6.25; ἐκπεσόντα ἢ ἀτιμωθέντα Pl.*R.*553b.

**ἀτῑμώρ-ητεί** or -τί, Adv. of sq., *EM*664.37. -ητος, ον, *unavenged*, i.e., I. *unpunished*, ἀ. γίγνεσθαι *to escape punishment*, Hdt.2.100, Th.6.6, etc.; ἀ. ἁμαρτημάτων *unpunished for..*, Pl.*Lg.* 959c. Adv. -τως *with impunity*, ib.762d. II. *for whom no revenge has been taken*, Antipho 3.3.7; ἀτιμώρητον ἐᾶν θάνατον Aeschin. 1.145. III. *undefended, unprotected*, Th.3.57.

**ἀτίμωσις** [τῐ], εως, ἡ, *dishonouring*, c. gen., τραπέζας A.*Ag.*702 (lyr.); πατρὸς Id.*Ch.*435 (lyr.). II. = *capitis deminutio*, J*AJ*19.1.1.

**ἀτίνακτος** [ῐ], ον, *unshaken, immovable*, Opp.*H.*2.8, Nonn.*D.*10.166, al.

**ἀτῑσανδρέω**· ἀτιμάζω ἄνδρα, Hsch.

**ἀτῐτάλλω**, aor. 1 ἀτίτηλα Il.24.60, *IG*14.2005:—Med., aor. 1 ἀτιτήλατο Opp.*C.*1.271: (ἀταλός):—redupl. form of ἀτάλλω, *rear, tend*, θρέψα τε καὶ ἀτίτηλα Il. l. c.; παῖδα δὲ ὣς ἀτίταλλε Od.18.323; οἵ μ' ἐν σφοῖσι δόμοισιν ἐῢ τρέφον ἠδ' ἀτίταλλον Il.14.202, cf. 16.191, Hes.*Th.* 480, Pi.*N.*3.58; also of animals, τοὺς μὲν [ἵππους]..ἀτίταλλ' ἐπὶ φάτνῃ Il.5.271:—Pass., χῆν' ἥρπαξ' ἀτιταλλομένην ἐνὶ οἴκῳ Od.15.174. 2. metaph., *cherish*, καί σε Κόως ἀτίταλλε Theoc.17.58: c. dat., καλοῖς Id.15.111; in bad sense, *beguile, cajole*, σκιράφοις ἀ. Hippon.86.—Poet. and late Prose, as Them.*Or.*20.234b.

✱**ἀτῐτάλτας**, α, ὁ, *foster-father*, *GDI*4978 (Gortyn).

**ἀτίταν**· ὁ μὴ ἔχων ἀποτῖσαι, Hsch. s. v. Τιτᾶνες.

**ἀτῑτέω**, = ἀτίω, D.P.1158: but **ἀτιτεῖν**· ἀδικεῖν, and **ἀτίται**· ἄδικοι, Hsch.

**ἀτίτης** [ῐ], ου, ὁ, (τίνω) *unpunished*, A.*Eu.*257 (lyr.). II. *unable to pay*, Hsch. III. (τίω) *unhonoured*, ἀτῖται σαρκὶ παλαιᾷ A.*Ag.*72 (anap.). IV. v. foreg.

**ἀτίτηστον**· ἀπρόμηθες, Hsch.

**ἄτῑτος**, ον, (τίνω) *unavenged*, Il.13.414. 2. *unpaid*, ποινή ib.14.484 [where ῐ]. 3. *not liable to penalty*, *IG*4.498 (Mycenae). II. (τίω) *unhonoured*, Menecr.Xanth.4.

**ἀτίω** [ῐ], = ἀτίζω, ἀτίει Thgn.621; ἀτίουσι Orph.*L.*62.

**Ἀτλᾱγενής**, ές, (γένος) *sprung from Atlas*, of the Pleiads, Hes.*Op.* 383.

**Ἀτλαντικός**, ή, όν, *of Atlas*, τέρμονες Ἀ. the pillars of Hercules, E.*Hipp.*3, 1053; τὸ Ἀ. πέλαγος Pl.*Ti.*24e, Arist.*Pr.*946a29; ἡ Ἀ. θάλασσα Id.*Mu.*392b22:—also **Ἀτλάντειος**, α, ον, Critias 18.5 D.:—fem. **Ἀτλαντίς**, ίδος, as Patron., Hes.*Th.*938; title of work by Hellanicus (also **Ἀτλαντιάς**, Harp. s. v. Ὁμηρίδαι); θάλασσα ἡ Ἀ. καλουμένη Hdt.1.202; ἡ Ἀ. νῆσος, a fabulous island in the far West, Pl.*Ti.*25a, Str.2.3.6.

**Ἄτλας**, αντος, ὁ, acc. also Ἄτλαν A.*Pr.*428 (lyr.), cf. Sch.: (ἀ- euph., and τλάς, v. *τλάω):—*Atlas*, Od.1.52: later, one of the Titans, Hes.*Th.*517, A.*Pr.*350, 428 (lyr.); αἱ δ' ἑπτ' Ἄτλαντος παῖδες Id.*Fr.*312. II. in hist. writers, *Mount Atlas* in West Africa, regarded as *the pillar of heaven*, Hdt.4.184, Str.17.3.2, etc.: pl., D.P.66. 2. *the Atlantic Ocean*, Id.30. 3. *axis* of the earth, Hsch. III. Ἄτλαντες, in Architecture, *colossal statues* as supports for the entablature (cf. τελαμῶνες), Moschio ap.Ath.5.208b, Vitr.6.7.6; κείονας Ἄτλαντάς τε *Epigr.Gr.*1072.7. IV. *seventh of the neck-vertebrae*, which supports the head, Poll.2.132. V. Pythag. name for *ten*, *Theol.Ar.*59. [ᾰτλ A.*Fr.* l.c.]

✱**ἄτλας**, αντος, ὁ, *not enduring* or *daring*, Hsch.; cf. ἀταής.

**ἀτλησία**· ἀμηχανία, ἀνυποστασία, Hsch.

**ἀτλησίφρων** [ῐ]· οὐδεμιᾶς τόλμης ἔννοιαν ἔχων, Hsch. (ἀτμ- cod.).

**ἀτλητέω** (Dor. ἀτλᾱτέω, Hsch.), *to be impatient, not to endure* or *submit to* a thing, S.*OT*515.

✱**ἄτλητος**, Dor. ἄτλᾱτος, ον, *not to be borne, insufferable*, πένθος, ἄχος, Il.9.3, 19.367, cf. Orac.ap.Hdt.5.56, Pi.*O.*6.38; ἀγγελία S.*Aj.* 223 (lyr.). 2. *not to be dared*, ἄτλητα τλᾶσα A.*Ag.*408 (lyr.). II. Act., *incapable of bearing, impatient of*, c. gen., μόθων ἄ. *AP*9.321 (Antim.?). Adv. -τως, φέρειν Ael.*NA*16.28.

**ἄτματα**· καθάρματα, Hsch.

**ἀτμενία**, ἡ, (ἀτμήν) *slavery*, Man.6.59, *AP*9.764 (Paul. Sil.).

✱**ἀτμένιος**, ον, *toilsome, prepared with trouble*, Nic.*Al.*178, 426.

**ἄτμενος**, ὁ, = ἀτμήν, Archil.ap.Sch.Il.*Oxy.*1087, Call.*Fr.*538, Hsch., Eust.1750.62:—as Adj., ἄτμενον οἶτον Hsch.

**ἀτμεύω**, for ἀτμενεύω, *to be a slave*, Nic.*Al.*172.

✱**ἀτμή**, ἡ, = ἀτμός, ἀτμίς, Hes.*Th.*862.

✱**ἀτμήν**, ένος, ὁ, *slave, servant*, Call.*Aet.*1.1.19, Epic.in *Arch.Pap.* 7.4, *Et.Gen.*, Sch.Nic.*Al.*172, 426.

**ἀτμησίφρων**, v. ἀτλησίφρων.

**ἄτμητος**, ον, *not carved*, *IG*1.322; λίθοι Ph.2.253; *uncut*, ἔθειραι A.R.2.708; *unwounded*, S.*Fr.*124; *not laid waste, unravaged*, γῆ Th.1.82: and so metaph., ὑγίεια Gal.6.18; ἄμπελοι *unpruned*, Plu. *Num.*14; *unreaped*, Ph.2.390; λίβανος ἄ. *in lumps*, *PMag.Par.*1. 1991; ἀργυρεῖα ἄ. silver-mines *as yet unopened*, X.*Vect.*4.27; of animals, *entire*, Arist.*HA*632a9. II. *indivisible*, Pl.*Phdr.*277b, Arist.*EE* 1230a29, Ph.1.505, al., Iamb.*Comm.Math.*4. Adv. -τως Hero*Geom.* p.85 H. III. *that cannot be cut*, Arist.*Mete.*387a6, *Metaph.*1023a2.

**ἀτμιάω**, (ἀτμή) *steam, emit vapour*, Hp.*Morb.*4.49.

**ἀτμῐδ-όομαι**, Pass., *to be turned into vapour*, Arist.*Mete.*346b25. -οῦχος, ον, (ἔχω) *containing vapour, damp*, Hsch. -ώδης, ες, *vaporous*, ἀναθυμίασις Arist.*Mete.*341b8 (Comp.), 360a9; ὁ βορέας ib.358a35; ἀήρ Id.*GA*786a12. II. *full of vapour*, γῆ Clidem.ap. Thphr.*CP*3.23.2.

**ἀτμ-ίζω**, pf. ἥτμικα Arist.*Pr.*930b36:—*smoke*, βωμὸς ἀτμίζων πυρί S.*Fr.*370; of water, *steam*, X.*An.*4.5.15: generally, *emit vapour*, of hot meat, ἥδιστον ἀ. Pherecr.108.15 codd. Ath. (ἀπατμ- edd.); of perspiration, interpol. post Hp.*Prog.*6; of fresh-burnt tiles, Arist.*Mete.* 383a24, cf. 388b32. II. *to be vaporized*, ib.349b23, 358b16, al. -ίς, ίδος (-ῖτος *PMag.Lond.*1.121.639), ἡ, = ἀτμός, Hdt.4.75, Pl.*Ti.*87a, Nicostr.15.5: properly, *moist vapour, steam*, opp. καπνός (but ἀτμὶς καπνοῦ LXX *Jl.*2.30(3.3)), Arist.*Mete.*359b30, cf. 346b32, Ph.2.223, etc.; ἡ ἀ. συνίσταται εἰς ὕδωρ Arist.*Mete.*384a6. II. *sublimate* or *deposit* of colouring matter, *PHolm.*4.21. III. *poultice*, Crito ap. Gal.13.879. IV. = σπινθήρ, ἀπαύγασμα, Hsch. -ιστός, ή, όν, *capable of being turned into vapour*, Arist.*Mete.*387b8, dub. in Alex. Trall.*Febr.*5.

**ἀτμοειδής**, ές, = ἀτμιδώδης, S.E.*M.*7.119, Alex.Aphr.*Pr.*2.67. Adv. -δῶς Anon.Lond.22.19, Gal.*Nat.Fac.*1.16.

**ἀτμός**, ὁ, *steam, vapour*, A.*Eu.*138; ὅταν ἐκ γῆς ἀ. ἀνίῃ..ὑπὸ τοῦ ἡλίου Arist.*Pr.*862a4; Ἄραψ ἀ., of incense, *Pae.Delph.*11: in pl., *vapours*, A.*Fr.*205; *clouds* of steam, Jul.*Mis.*341d; esp. of *odours*, A.*Ag.*1311, Arist.*Pr.*908a21, Ph.1.96, al., Lib.*Or.*12.79 (pl.), etc.; distd. from ἀτμίς, as dry from moist, by Olymp. *in Mete.*165.25. [ᾰτμ A.*Fr.*205.]

**ἀτμώδης**, ες, = ἀτμιδώδης, Arist.*Mu.*394a14, Thphr.*CP*3.16.4. Adv. -δως Gal.*Nat.Fac.*3.7.

**ἄτοιχος**, ον, *unwalled*, E.*Ion*1133, D.C.74.4.

**ἀτοκ-εῖον**, τό, = *contraceptive*, *SIG*985.20 (Philadelphia, i B.C.). -έω, *not to bring forth, to be barren*, Ph.1.478. -ί, Adv. of ἄτοκος, D.C.58.21, *PTeb.*342.30 (ii A.D.), *BGU*725.23 (vii A.D.). ✱-ία, ἡ, *unfruitfulness, barrenness*, Muson.*Fr.*15 Ap.77 H. ✱-ιος, ον, *causing barrenness*, Dsc.1.81; ἀτόκιον (sc. φάρμακον), τό, *a medicine for causing it*, Hp.*Mul.*1.76, Dsc.1.77. II. = λυχνὶς ἀγρία, Ps.-Dsc. 3.101. -ος, ον, *having never yet brought forth*, Hdt.5.41, E.*El.* 1127; ἄ. ὑπὸ νούσου *barren..*, Hp.*Aër.*3; δι' ἡλικίαν Pl.*Tht.*149c; of mules, Arist.*APr.*67a35. II. *not bearing interest*, χρήματα Pl.*Lg.* 921c, cf. D.53.12, *SIG*330.7 (Ilium), etc.: neut. pl. as Adv., *PAmh.* 2.50.10 (ii B.C.), al. 2. *not paying interest*, Arist.*Oec.*1350a11.

**ἀτολμ-έω**, *to be* ἄτολμος, *be disheartened*, Hp.*Epid.*6.7.3: c. inf., *lack courage to..*, περαιτέρω προχωρῆσαι D.C.78.34:—also -όω, *AB* 407 (ἀτολμάω, Suid., is incorrect). -ηρος, ον, = ἄτολμος, Gal. 14.603 (Comp.). -ητος, Dor. -ᾱτος, ον, = ἄτλητος, *not to be endured, insufferable*, μόχθος Pi.*I.*8(7).11; of men, dub. in A.*Ag.* 375. 2. *not to be dared*, οὐδὲν [τοῖς ποιηταῖς] ἀ. Aristid.*Or.*45(8). 2, cf. Gal.8.260; τῷ πλουσίῳ οὐδὲν ἀ. Him.*Ecl.*4.24. -ία, ἡ, *want of daring, cowardice*, E.*Fr.*364 (v.l. ἀνανδρία), Th.2.89, X.*HG*5.3.22, etc. 2. *bashfulness*, D.61.20. -ος, ον, *daring nothing, cowardly*, Pi.*N.*11.32, Th.2.39 (Comp.), etc.; λῆμα..οὐκ ἄ. ἀλλ' ἕτοιμον Ar.*Nu.* 458; ἄ. καὶ μαλακός D.8.68, etc.; of women, ἄ. αἰχμά A.*Ch.*630 (lyr.); of things, ἄ. ἐπινόημα Jul.*Or.*2.75d: c. inf., ἄ. εἰμι..δῆσαι I have *not the heart* to bind, A.*Pr.*14. Adv. -μως Plb.3.103.3, Plu.2.47c: Comp. -ότερον *less boldly*, Gal.6.37.

**ἄτομος**, ον, *uncut, unmown*, λειμών S.*Tr.*200; ἄ. πώγωνος βάθη Ephipp.14.7; ἄ. λίβανος *in lumps*, Dsc.1.68.1; ἄτομον, τό, = ὑοσκύαμος, dub. in Ps.-Dsc.4.68 (cf. ἀταῖος). 2. Gramm., of words, *not compound*, D.H.*Th.*22. II. *that cannot be cut, indivisible*, γραμμαί Arist.*Ph.*206a17, cf. *LI*968a1; μεγέθη Id.*Ph.*187a3; esp. of particles of matter, ἐτεῇ ἄτομα (sc. σώματα) καὶ κενόν Democr.9, 125, cf. Arist.*de An.*404a2, *Metaph.*1039a10; in full, ἄ. σώματα Id. *Cael.*303a21, Epicur.*Nat.*14 *Fr.*5: sg., ἄτομόν ἐστι σῶμα στερεόν.. Id.p.129.24 U.; also ἄ. φύσεις Democr.ap.Diog.Oen.5, Epicur.*Ep.*1 p.7 U.; ἄτομοι, αἱ, ib.p.14 U., al., Phld.*Sign.*5, al., Alciphr.1.34. 2. of Time, οὐχ οἷόν τε εἰς ἀ. χρόνους διαιρεῖσθαι τὸν χρόνον Arist.*Ph.*263b 27; κατ' ἄ. χρόνον Id.*Sens.*447b18; ἐν ἀτόμῳ in a *moment*, Id.*Ph.* 236a6, 1*Ep.Cor.*15.52; ἐν ἀ. ὀργῆς Sm.*Is.*54.8. b. metaph., *infinitely small*, διαφοραί Plu.*Phoc.*3. III. in Logic, *individual*, of terms, Pl.*Sph.*229d; of the εἶδος, Arist.*Metaph.*1034a8, *de An.*414b 27. 2. *individual*, Id.*APo.*96b11, al.: Subst. ἄτομον, τό, Id.*Cat.* 1b6, 3a38, *Metaph.*1058a18 (pl.), Plot.6.2.2, al. 3. of the *summum genus*, πρὶν εἰς τὰ ἄ. ἐλθεῖν Arist.*Metaph.*994b21. Adv. ἀτόμως, ὑπάρχειν *immediately, without the intervention of a middle term*, Id. *APo.*79a33.

**ἀτομόω**, *leave undivided*, τὸν λόγον Olymp.*in Alc.*p.181 C.:—Pass., *to be individualized*, Simp.*in Ph.*255.28; *to be unified*, Id.*in de An.* 217.36.

✱**ἀτον-έω**, *to be relaxed, exhausted*, Arist.*Pr.*945a17, Plu.*Cor.*25; ὁδοιπορίαις *Epigr.Gr.*613.4; στόμαχος ἀτονῶν Dsc.1.109: c. inf., *to be too weak to..*, D.L.4.14. -ία, ἡ, *slackness, enervation, debility*, Hp.*Aër.*20; *laziness*, Epicur.*Nat.*54 G.; ψυχῆς Plu.2.535d; ἀσθένεια καὶ ἀ. Luc.*Nigr.*36; ἰνῶν ἀ. καὶ τρόμος Phld.*Acad.Ind.*p.76 M.; as Stoic term, *lack of* τόνος (q.v.), Chrysipp.*Stoic.*3.120, 123, Arr.*Epict.* 2.15.4, etc.; in oratory, *lack of vigour* in delivery, Hermog.*Inv.*4. 3. ✱-ος, ον, *not stretched, slack, relaxed*, of the limbs, Hp.*Aër.*3 (Comp.), 19; *lacking in elasticity*, of strands in torsion-engine, Ph. *Bel.*58.18; πνοαί D.S.1.41; σφυγμοί Aret.*SD*2.9; of fruit, *insipid*, Dsc. 1.112 (Comp.), al.; τὸ ἄ. τῆς γεύσεως v.l. ib.127; φωνεῖν ἄτονον Arist.*Phgn.*813b3: Medic., of the stomach, Ath.3.79f (Comp.), etc.:

c. inf., *too weak to..*, D.L.7.35; of oratorical style, D.H.*Dem.*20, cf. Hermog.*Id.*2.11 (Comp.), Eun.*VS*p.493 B. (Comp.). Adv. -νως Plu. *Lyc.*18: Comp. -ώτερον J.*BJ*4.1.5; -ωτέρως Archig.ap.Orib.8.2. 26. **2.** as Stoic term, *lacking* τόνος (q. v.), σπέρμα Sphaer.*Stoic.*1. 141; opp. εὔτονος, Chrysipp. ib.2.155, 3.121. **-όω,** *weaken*, Aq. *Ps.*68(69).24. **-ώδης,** ες, ἠτρία dub. in *AP*9.350 (Leon.).

**ἀτόξ-ευτος,** ον, *out of bow-shot*, πέτρα Plu.2.326e. **-ος,** ον, *without bow or arrow*, Luc.*DDeor.*19.1.

**ἀτόπ-αστος,** ον, *not to be guessed*, A.*Fr.*119. **°-ημα,** ατος, τό, *absurdity*, S.E.*M.*1.80. **2.** *strange sight* or *occurrence*, *POxy.*1557. 6 (iii A.D.), al. **3.** *offence*, *PTeb.*303.11 (ii A.D.), Procop.*Pers.*1. 24. **-ηματοποιός,** ὁ, *one who commits absurdities* or *offences*, Gloss. **-ία,** ἡ, *being out of the way*, hence, **1.** *absurdity*, Ar.*Ra.* 1372; of persons, Id.*Ach.*349; *singularity*, Pl.*Smp.*215a; of sounds or words, *uncouthness*, D.H.*Comp.*12. **2.** *extraordinary nature*, νοσήματος Th.2.51; τῶν τιμωριῶν Id.3.82; τοῦ πάθους Pl.*Phdr.*251d. **3.** *logical absurdity*, S.E.*P.*3.240. **4.** *wickedness, misdeed*, Lxx *Ju.* 11.11: pl., Phld.*Vit.*p.34 J. **-ος,** ον, *out of place, out of the way*: hence, **1.** *unwonted, extraordinary*, of symptoms, Hp.*Aph.*4.52: Comp., ibid.; ἄ. ἀδονά E.*IT*842 (lyr.), cf. Arist.*EN*1149$^a$15; ὄρνις Ar.*Av.*276; πόθος Id.*Ec.*956. **2.** *strange, paradoxical*, δοῦλοι τῶν αἰεὶ ἀτόπων slaves to every new *paradox*, Th.3.38; ἄτοπόν τι πάσχειν And.4.34; τῶν -ωτάτων μέντἂν εἴη D.1.26; ἄτοπα τῆς σμικρολογίας *absurd* pettinesses, Pl.*Tht.*175a; ἄ. ἡδονῆς καὶ λύπης μεῖξις Id.*Phlb.*49a; ἄτοπόν ἐστι, c. inf., Pherecr.91, Eub.125; οὐδὲν ἄ. εἰ ἀποθάνοιμι Pl.*Grg.*521d, cf. Arist.*Cat.*11$^a$37, al., etc. **b.** of persons, Isoc.12.149; ἄ. παιδευτής Pl.*R.*493c; ἄ. καὶ δυσχερεῖς D. 19.308; τὸν ἄτοπον φεύγειν ἀεί Men.203c; ἄ. φαγεῖν *given to strange* food, Philostr.*VA*3.55. **3.** *unnatural, disgusting, foul*, πνεῦμα Th. 2.49; *monstrous*, ἀτοπώτατον πρᾶγμα ἐξευρών Lys.3.7; later, *wicked, wrong*, Lxx *Jb.*27.6, *Ev.Luc.*23.41; of persons, opp. χρηστός, Phld. *Sign.*1; of things, *bad, harmful*, *Act.Ap.*28.6. Adv. -πως *in an unfavourable position*, κεῖσθαι, of planets, Vett.Val.63.12. **4.** Adv. -πως *marvellously* or *absurdly*, Th.7.30, Pl.*Phd.*95b, al., Arist.*EN* 1136$^a$12, etc.; ἀ. καθίζων, = ἀνυπόπτως, Eup.180. **II.** *non-spatial*, τῆς ἰδέας μενούσης ἐν ἀτόπῳ αὐτὸ τόπους γεννῆσαν Plot.6.5.8. Adv. -πως *non-spatially*, opp. τοπικῶς, Porph.*Sent.*33.

**ἀτόρητος,** ον, *not to be pierced, invulnerable*, Nonn.*D.*14.380.

**ἀτόρνευτος,** ον, *not turned in the lathe, not rounded*, Gloss.

**ἀτόρῡ(νη)τος,** ον, *not stirred with a ladle*, Orib.4.9.1.

**ἆτος,** ον, contr. for ἄατος.

**ἀτρᾰγῳδ-ητος,** ον, *not treated tragically*, Luc.*Merc.Cond.*19; τὸ ἀ. *absence of display* or *pomp*, Ph.2.76. **-ος,** ον, *untragical, unsuitable to tragedy*, ἀτραγῳδότατον τοῦτο.. Arist.*Po.*1452$^b$37, cf. Plu.2. 519a. Adv. -δως *without noise* or *fuss*, M.Ant.1.16.3.

**ἀτρακίς,** ίδος, ἡ, name of a *spinous plant*, Gal.6.623.

**°ἀτράκτιον,** τό, Dim. of ἄτρακτος, Epic. in *Arch.Pap.*7.9: pl. (written ἀτράκτεια), *POxy.*1740.2 (iii/iv A.D.).

**ἀτρακτοειδής,** ές, *spindle-shaped*, ῥαβδία Dsc.4.36.

**°ἄτρακτος,** ὁ, and in Plu.2.271f, ἡ:—*spindle*, ἄτρακτον στρέφειν Hdt.5.12, cf. 4.34,162, Pl.*Plt.*281e, etc.; λίνου μεστὸν ἄ. Ar.*Ra.*1348 (lyr.); Ἀνάγκης ἄ. Pl.*R.*616c; τῶν Μοιρῶν Arist.*Mu.*401$^b$15, cf. *IG* 12(7).447 (Amorgos). **II.** *arrow*, ἄ. τοξικός A.*Fr.*139; ἄ. alone, S.*Ph.*290, *Tr.*714. In this sense specially Lacon., Th.4.40. **III.** *upper part of a ship's mast*, Poll.1.91. **IV.** *spindle-shaped cautery*, Hp.*Int.*28, *Vid.Ac.*4. (Cf. ἀτρεκής, Lat. *torqueo*.)

**°ἀτρακτῠλίς** or **ἀτρακτυλλίς,** ίδος, ἡ, *spindle-thistle*, used for making spindles, *Carthamus lanatus*, Arist.*HA*627$^a$8, Thphr.*HP* 6.4.6, Theoc.4.52 (pl.), Dsc.3.93:—also **ἀτρακτύαλος** (leg. -τυλλος), Hsch.

**ἀτρακτώδης,** ες, *like a spindle*, Eust.1328.46.

**ἀτρᾱνής,** ές, Adv. -νῶς *not plainly*, Hsch. s.v. ἀσήμως.

**ἀτράνωτος** [ρᾱ], ον, *unexplained, not understood*, φόβος Diog.Oen. 30.

**ἀτράπεζος** [ρᾰ], ον, (τράπεζα) *unsocial*, Man.4.563.

**ἀτράπελος** [ρᾰ], ον, = δυστράπελος, Sch.S.*Aj.*913, v.l. in Lxx *Jb.* 39.9.

**ἀτρᾰπ-ίζω,** (ἀτραπός) *go through, traverse*, τὰς ἁρμονίας Pherecr. 26. **-ῑτός,** ἡ, = sq., Od.13.195, A.R.4.123, etc.: metaph. of studies, Πλατώνειοι ἀ. *BCH*36.230 (Rhodes), cf. *AP*9.540:—also **ἀταρπῑτός** [ᾰτ], Od.17.234: **ἀτρᾱπητός,** *AB*460. **°-ός,** Ep. **ἀταρπός,** as always in Hom., e. g. Il.17.743, ἡ:—*short cut*, or generally, *path*, Hom., Hdt.7.215, Ar.*Nu.*76, Th.4.36, etc.; ἀεὶ μίαν ἀ. πάντες βαδίζουσι [μύρμηκες] Arist.*HA*622$^b$25. **2.** metaph., *walk of life*, ἡ πολιτικὴ ἀ. Pl.*Plt.*258c; μύθων Emp.24; ἱστορίης *IG*3.716; ἀ. μυρμηκος, v. μυρμηκιά.

**°ἀτραυμάτιστος,** ον, *not caused by a wound*, πόνοι Luc.*Ocyp.*36, cf. Aët.7.9.

**ἀτράφαξυς** [ᾰτρᾰ], υος, ἡ, *orach*, *Atriplex rosea*, Hp.*Vict.*2.54, Thphr.*HP*7.1.2, al., Dsc.2.119, Gal.6.633. (The correct form is implied by the compound ψευδ-ατράφαξυς Ar.*Eq.*630, cf. *EM*565.17; other spellings are **ἀδράφαξυς** (ἀδρ- Eust.539.5) Thphr. l. c., **ἀνδράφαξυς** Dsc. l. c., Hp. l. c., **ἀτράφαξις** v.l. Dsc. l. c., Gal.11.843, cf. Hdn.Gr.1.539, 2.49,467.)

**ἀτρᾰφής,** ές, (τρέφω) *wasting, atrophic*, Thphr.*CP*2.6.4.

**°ἀτράχηλος** [ρᾰ], ον, *without neck*, of the crab, *AP*6.196 (Stat. Flacc.). **II.** *short-necked, bull-necked*, Teles p.55 H., Gal.5.383.

**ἀτράχυντος** [ρᾰ], Ion. ἀτρήχ-, ον, *without asperity*, Aret.*SD*2.12; ἔλαιον Id.*CA*1.10:—also **ἄτρᾱχυς,** υ, Eust.340.21.

**ἀτρεής,** ές, = ἄτρεστος: acc. ἀτρέα for ἀτρεέα, Euph.125; also, *not to be feared*, pl., ἀτρεῖες (for ἀτρεέες) ἀνάγκαι *IG*14.1389ii18.

**Ἀτρείδης,** ου, Ep. **Ἀτρεΐδης,** εω, Dor. **Ἀτρείδας,** α, *son of Atreus*, Hom., etc.

**ἀτρέκ-εια,** ἡ, Ion. -είη, also -ιη Man.3.229: (ἀτρεκής):—*precise truth, certainty*, Pi.*Fr.*213.4; τῶν ἡμεῖς ἀτρεκείην ἴδμεν Hdt.4.152, cf. 6.1; μαθεῖν.. τὴν ἀ. ὅτι οὐκ αἱρέει learnt *for certain* that he is unable to take it, ib.82, cf. *IG*9(1).880 (Corc.): in pl., τὰς -ας τὰς λεγομένας Hp.*Prorrh.*2.3. **II.** Ἀτρέκεια personified, *Strict Justice*, Pi. *O.*10(11).13, E.*Fr.*91. **-έω,** *to be sure*, ἀτρεκήσασα ib.315. **°-ής,** ές, *strict, precise, exact*, ἀλάθεια, καιρός, Pi.*N.*5.17, *P.*8.7; ἀριθμός Hdt. 7.187; δίαιτα Hp.*Mochl.*42; βιότου ἀ. ἐπιτηδεύσεις *over-nice, precise*, E.*Hipp.*261; τὸ ἀ., = ἀτρέκεια, φράσαι, εἰπεῖν τὸ ἀ., Hdt.5.9, 7.60; τὸ -έστερον τούτων *more precise details*, Id.5.54; τὸ -έστατον Id.7.214; ἐγγὺς τοῦ -εστάτου ἥκειν Hp.*VM*12; rarely of persons, *exact, strict*, Ἑλλανοδίκας Pi.*O.*3.12. **2.** *sure, certain*, ποδὶ ἀτρεκεῖ Id.*N.*3.41; ἀ. δόξα E.*Hipp.*1115 (lyr.). **II.** Hom. has only Adv. ἀτρεκέως (neut. as Adv., ἀτρεκὲς.. βαλών *accurately*, Il.5.208 (expld. as Adj. by Eust. ad loc.); δεκὰς ἀ. *precisely*, Od.16.245): mostly with the Verbs ἀγορεύειν, καταλέξαι, tell *truly, exactly*, Il.2.10, Od.1.169, etc.; ἀ. μαντεύσομαι 17.154; ἀ. ἔφρασεν *IG*3.716; ἀ. ὀλίγοι Thgn. 636; freq. in Hdt., ἀ. εἰπεῖν 1.57, al.; εἰδέναι 1.209, al.; ἐπίστασθαι 3.130; ἐκμαθεῖν 7.10.η′; διακρῖναι 1.172; διασημῆναι 5.86; φαίνειν 2.49; ἀ. ἀριθμεῖσθαι Hp.*Prog.*20; ἀ. ὅμοιον *precisely* similar, Diog. Apoll.5. **2.** ἀ. ἀποκυλισθεῖσα broken *straight across*, opp. παραμηκέως, Hp.*Art.*14. **3.** neut. as Adv. (cf. supr. II. 1), τὸ δ' ἀτρεκὲς ὄλβιος οὐδείς Thgn.167; ἐπ' ἀτρεκές *IG*9(1).880 (Corc.).—The word and its derivs. are rare in Trag. and not found in Att. Prose, ἀκριβής and its derivs. being used instead: freq. in Ion. Prose, esp. in Hp. and Aret., *SD*2.12, al., and in later Prose, cf. ἐπιστήμη καὶ γνώμη ἀ. Plb.1.4.9, ἀ. τριακάς Plu.*Rom.*12; ὁ σενᾶτος ἀτρεκῶς γερουσίαν σημαίνει *strictly*, ib.13; οὐκ ἔφυγον δ' ἀτρεκῶς not *really*, *Epigr. Gr.*339.5; of persons, *truthful, accurate*, J.*BJ*3.8.9. (Cf. ἄτρακτος.)

**ἀτρεκότης,** ητος, ἡ, = ἀτρέκεια, Sch.E.*Hipp.*1114.

**°ἀτρέμ-ᾰ,** (τρέμω) = ἀτρέμας, usually before a conson., once in Hom., αἰγίδα.. ἔχ' ἀ. Φοῖβος Il.15.318; proleptic, ἀτρέμ' ἀμπαύσας μεριμνᾶν B.5.7; μέν'.. ἀ. σοῖς ἐν δεμνίοις E.*Or.*258, cf. *Ba.*1072; ἔχ' ἀ. keep *still!* Ar.*Nu.*743, *Av.*1244, cf. Alciphr.3.2; elided before a vowel, Ar.*Ra.*339; ἀτρέμα ἑστάναι Antipho 3.4.7 s. v. l. (but ἀτρέμας ἑστάναι 3.3.10); ἀ. διαπορεύεσθαι X.*Cyn.*5.31, cf. 9.5; freq. in Plu., μειδιάσας ἀ. *Per.*28, cf. *Alex.*46. **b.** *at leisure, at ease*, ἀ. σκοπούμενοι Pl.*Grg.*503d. **2.** *fixedly*, i. e. *precisely, accurately*, χρονικοῖς ἀ. συντεταγμένοις Plu.*Them.*27. **3.** *slightly*, Diocl.*Fr.* 141. **-αῖος,** α, ον (ος, ον E.*Or.*147 (lyr.)), = ἀτρεμής, βοά a whisper, l. c.: neut. pl. as Adv., Id.*HF*1053 (lyr.); regul. Adv. -αίως Call.*Iamb.* 1.241; οὐκ ἀτρεμαῖοι Hp.*Morb.Sacr.*15, cf. J.*AJ*15.7.5. **-αιότης,** ητος, ἡ, *calmness*, Hp.*Praec.*13. **-ᾱς,** Adv. *without trembling, without motion*, ἀ. ἑσταότα Il.13.438; ὀφθαλμοὶ δ' ὡς εἰ κέρα ἕστασαν ἠὲ σίδηρος ἀ. ἐν βλεφάροισι Od.19.212; ἀ. εὕδειν Il.14.352, Od.13. 92; ἀ. ἧσο sit *still!* Il.2.200; ἀ. ἔχειν to keep *quiet*, Hdt.5.19, 8.16; ἀ. εἶχον τὸ στρατόπεδον Id.9.53; σφέας αὐτοὺς ib.54; ἀ. ἴθι E.*Or.* 149 (lyr.); ἔχ' ἀ. Ar.*Av.*1200, Luc.*Herm.*41; ἀ. ἅπτεσθαί τινος *gently, softly*, E.*Hipp.*1358; ἀ. βαδίζειν, opp. ταχύ, D.37.55. **-εί,** Adv. of ἀτρεμής, ἀτρεμί Ar.*Nu.*261; ἀτρεμεί dub. in Alex.124.12. **-έω,** fut. -ήσω Plu.*Pomp.*58, App.*Syr.*2, etc.: aor. ἠτρέμησα v. l. in Hdt. (v. infr.), Hp.*Morb.Sacr.*14:—*not to tremble, to keep still* or *quiet*, ἵνα τοι τρίχες ἀτρεμέωσι Hes.*Op.*539; οὐδαμά κω ἠτρεμήσαμεν, of a restless people, Hdt.7.8.α′ (as v. l., cf. ἀτρεμίζω), etc.; of a state of health, *remain stationary*, Hp.*Aph.*1.3; ἀτρεμέει ἡ χολή Aret.*SD*1.15; of the patient, *endure*, ib.1.1; σχεδὸν οὐκ ἀναπνέων ἠτρέμει Luc.*Am.* 16, al.; of water, *to be calm*, Antyll.ap.Orib.10.3.9:—ἀτρέμ' ἔσεσθαι shd. be read for inf. Med. ἀτρεμέεσθαι in Thgn.47.—Found in Arist.*Xen.*977$^b$17, but ἠρεμέω is the Att. equivalent. **-ής,** ές, *unmoved, calm*, ἦτορ Parm.1.29; θάλασσα Semon.7.37; φάσματα Pl.*Phdr.*250c; ὄμμα X.*Smp.*8.3; ἀτρεμές, τό, *calmness*, Id.*Ages.*6.7. Adv. -έως Thgn.978; ἀ. ἔχειν Hp.*Epid.*3.17.ε′. **II.** *stable, firm*, δόρυ Plb.6.25.9; ὁδοί Plu.*CG*7. **-ητον·** ἀσάλευτον, Hsch. **-ί,** v. ἀτρεμεί. **-ία,** ἡ, *keeping still*, ἀτρεμίαν ἔχειν X.*Cyr.*6.3.13, cf. Max.295; ἀ. λιμένων *AP*9.555.6 (Crin.); ἐν ἀτρεμίᾳ Cerc.5.7: pl., Arist.*HA*537$^a$4. **2.** *intrepidity*, Pi.*N.*11.12. **-ίζω,** fut. -ιῶ Hdt.8.68.β′: aor. ἠτρέμισα Hp.*Morb.Sacr.*7:—*keep quiet*, Thgn. 303: in Ion. Prose, mostly with neg., ἀσπίδος.. οὐδαμὰ ἀτρεμιζούσης never *being kept still*, Hdt.9.74; of restless, aggressive kings or nations, οὐκ ἀτρεμίζειν Id.1.185,190; of people attacked, οὔτε αὐτοὺς οἶκος.. ἀτρεμιεῖν Id.8.68.β′; without a neg., γνώμην εἶχον ἀτρεμίζοντά σε μακαριστὸν εἶναι Id.7.18, cf. Hp.*Morb.Sacr.*14, *Vict.* 1.10.—Not in good Att., exc. Antipho 2.4.9 (opp. νεωτερίζειν), cf. 3.4.4 and 5: also in later Prose, Ti.Locr.104b, D.C.43.35, Them.*Or.* 26.317a, etc.

**ἀτρεπί,** = ἀτρεπτί, Hdn.*Epim.*256.

**ἄτρεπτος,** ον, *unchangeable*, opp. παθητός, οὐσία Chrysipp.*Stoic.* 2.158; *unmoved, inflexible*, Arist.*Mu.*401$^b$19; *irreparable*, φόνος A.R. 4.704; Μοῖρα *IG*9(2).317, cf. 14.1839; ἀτρέπτους κἀπαραιτήτους Phld. *D.*1.18; ἀ. τὸ πρόσωπον Luc.*VH*2.23; ἀ. πρὸς κινδύνους J.*BJ*7.8.7; πρὸς τὸ κακῶς ἀκούειν *indifferent* to ill-repute, *not caring*, Plu.*Alc.*13. Adv. -τως Ph.2.87, J.*BJ*7.9.1; *without hesitation*, D.S.34.2, Ael. *NA*17.17:—also -πτί, Hdn.*Epim.*256. **II.** Medic., of food, *undigested*, Aret.*SD*1.16, Gal.16.800.

**ἄτρεστος,** ον, (τρέω) *not trembling, fearless*, Trag., and Pl.*Cra.*395c:

c. gen., ἀ. μάχας *fearless of* fight, A.*Pr.*416 (lyr.); ἀ. ἐν μάχαις S.*Aj.* 365 (lyr.); ἀ. εὕδειν *securely*, Id.*OT*586. Adv. -τως A.*Supp.*240: neut. pl. ἄτρεστα as Adv., E.*Ion* 1198.

**ἀτρεφής**, v. ἀτραφής.

**ἀτρεχής**, ές, Dor. for ἀτρεκής, *Et.Gud.*91.56,611.20.

**ἄτρητος**, ον, *not perforated, without aperture*, Pl.*Plt.*279e, Arist. *HA*516$^a$26; with *imperforate* anus, Ptol.*Tetr.*150; of a virgin, Procop.*Arc.*17. II. Act., *not making holes*, ζῷα interpol. in Arist. *HA*488$^a$25.

**ἀτρήχυντος**, Ion. for ἀτρᾱχ- (q. v.).

**ἀτριάκαστος**, ον, *not belonging to a* τριακάς, Hsch.

**ἀτρίακτος** [ῐ], ον, *unconquered*, A.*Ch.*339.

**ἀτρίαστος** [ῐ], ον, *not admitting triplicity*, Dam.*Pr.*117.

**ἀτρίβ-αστος** [ῐ], ον, = sq., *not worn*, ἵππος ἀ. πρὸς τραχέα a horse *whose hoofs have not been worn off* on rough ground, X.*Eq.Mag.*8.3 (dub. l.). -ής, ές, *not rubbed*: hence, 1. of places, *not traversed, pathless*, Th.4.8,29, Ph.2.257, al.; of roads, *not worn* or *used*, X.*An.*4.2.8, App.*Hisp.*62: generally, *fresh, new*, X.*Mem.*4.3.13, cf. *Cyr.*8.7.22 (v. l. ἀκρ-). 2. of the neck, *not galled*, Pl.*Amat.* 134b; ἀ. ζεύγλης Babr.37.1. II. *not practised in*, πολεμικῶν ἀγώνων D.H.3.52. Adv. -βῶς Poll.5.145. -ος, ον, = ἀτριβής II, ἀρετῆς dub.l. in Ph.1.325. -ων, ον, gen. ονος, poet. for ἀτριβής, *unskilled in*, λέσχης E.*Fr.*473.

**ἀτρίζεται**· πένεται (fort. πηνίζεται, cf. sq.), Hsch.

⊛ **ἄτριον**, τό, Dor. for ἤτριον, Theoc.18.33, *AP*15.27 (Simm.).

**ἄτριπτος**, ον, = ἀτριβής, χεῖρας ἀτρίπτους ἁπαλάς *not worn hard by work*, Od.21.151; of corn, *not threshed*, X.*Oec.*18.5; of bread, *not kneaded*, Arist.*Pr.*929$^a$17; μᾶζα *not pounded*, Hp.*Vict.*2.40; ἀ. ἄκανθαι *trackless* thorns, Theoc.13.64; κέλευθοι ἀ. *untrodden* ways, Opp.*H.*4.68: metaph., ἀ. φρονήσεως ὁδοί Ph.1.316. 2. metaph., *unknown, strange*, Artem.4.63; of a problem, Simp.*in Ph.*520.23.

**ἀτριστ-ος**, ον, (τρίζω) *not crackling*, i.e. *stiff*, of tin, Zos.Alch. p.161 B.:—hence -όω, *make stiff*, Id.p.162 B.

**ἀτριχέω**, *not to be hairy*, Orib.10.15.2.

**ἄτριχος**, ον, = ἄθριξ, *without hair*, Call.*Dian.*77, Gal.4.572. 2. Subst., *serpent*, Hes.*Fr.*96.91. 3. *preventing the growth of hair*, Aët.1.19.

**ἀτριχόσαρκος**, ον, *smooth-skinned, not hairy*, Procl.*Par.Ptol.*202.

**ἄτριψ**, ῐβος, ὁ, = ἀτριβής II, Phryn.*PS*p.17 B.: c. gen., Suid.

**ἀτριψία**, ἡ, *inexperience, amateurishness*, Cic.*Att.*13.16.1.

**ἀτρομ-έω**, = ἀτρεμέω, Opp.*H.*3.355. -ητος, ον, = sq., B.12.123, *AP*6.256 (Antip.). ⊛-ος, ον, *fearless*, ἐν δέ τε θυμὸς στήθεσιν ἀ. ἐστι Il.16.163; μένος..ἀ. 5.126, 17.157; σῶμα Orph.*Fr.*168.23; νεῦρα Aret.*CA*1.2; ἀ. ὕπνος *calm, undisturbed*, *AP*6.69 (Maced.). Adv. -μως Plu.2.474d, 475f.

⊛ **ἀτροπάμπαις**, παιδος, dub. sens. in *IG*5(1).278,279 (Sparta); cf. πρατοπάμπαις. (ἀτρο- perh. = ἀδρο- 'mature', cf. Βατρόμιος: Βαδρόμιος.)

**ἀτροπ-ία**, ἡ, *inflexibility*, κρέσσων τοι σοφίη..ἀτροπίης Thgn.218; *rigour, cruelty*, ἀτροπίῃ A.R.4.387; ἀτροπίῃσι ib.1006. II. ἀτροπίη· ἀωρία, μεσονύκτιον, Hsch. ⊛-ος, ον, *not to be turned, unchangeable, eternal*, ὕπνος Theoc.3.49. 2. *inflexible, rigid*, Ἀίδης *AP*7.483; ἀρετή ib.10.74 (Paul. Sil.): pr. n., Ἄτροπος, ἡ, name of one of the Μοῖραι, Hes.*Th.*905, al., Pl.*Lg.*960c, Chrysipp.*Stoic.*2.264; ἀ. Κλωθώ *IG*3.1337: hence of the decrees of fate, ἄτροπα γραψάμεναι *Epigr. Gr.*153.4; ἀ. νόμος ib.288 (Cypr.). 3. *uncourteous, unseemly*, ἔπεα Pi.*N.*7.103. II. *not turned by the plough, untilled*, Call.*Del.*11.

**ἀτροφ-έω**, *have* or *get no food*, Ael.*NA*10.21, etc.; *waste away*, Arist.*Mu.*395$^b$28, Plu.*Arat.*24; of trees, Thphr.*CP*5.9.9, cf. Plu. *Rom.*20; of fire, *have no fuel*, Ph.2.620. -ής, ές, = ἄτροφος I, Man.6.25. -ία, ἡ, *want of food* or *nourishment*, of trees, Thphr. *CP*5.9.9; φθινούσης ἀ. φλογός Plu.2.949a. 2. *atrophy*, Arist. *Pr.*888$^a$10, Antyll.ap.Orib.6.21.7. 3. *starvation-diet*, καύσεις καὶ τομαὶ καὶ ἀ. Alex.Aphr.*in Top.*202.17. -ος, ον, *ill-fed*, X.*Mem.* 3.3.4; -ώτερος εἶναι Ael.*NA*12.20; *ill of atrophy, pining away*, Plu.2.912e. b. *non-viable*, of infants, Ptol.*Tetr.*127. 2. Act., *not nutritious*, Thphr.*CP*2.5.1, 2.6.4, Diph.Siph.ap.Ath.2.54a (Comp.); so prob. in Arist.*Mete.*384$^a$25 (but possibly, *that will not curdle* (τρέφω I)). 3. ἄτροφος τυρός· ὁ πησσόμενος (Lacon.), Hsch.

⊛ **ἀτρύγετος** [ῠ], ον, later η, ον *IG*3.900:—*unharvested, barren*, freq. in Hom. as epith. of the sea, παρὰ θῖν' ἁλὸς ἀτρυγέτοιο Il.1.316, al.; πόντον ἐπ' ἀ. Od.2.370, al.; also δι' αἰθέρος ἀτρυγέτοιο Il.17.425, Hes. *Cat.Oxy.*1358.2.34, *h.Cer.*67,457: Ep. Adj., borrowed by S.*Fr.*476, Ar.*V.*1521, *Av.*1338 (all lyr.). 2. metaph., ἀ. νύξ, of death, *AP* 7.735 (Damag.). (Expld. as if from ἀ-priv., τρυγάω by Sch.Od.l.c., etc.: but = ἄτρυτος, *never worn out, unresting*, acc. to Hdn.Gr.2.284.)

**ἀτρυγ-ής**, ές, (τρυγάω) *not gathered*, μέλι *AP*7.622 (Antiph.). -ητος, ον, = foreg., Arist.*Pr.*925$^b$15; ἀ. γενήματα *PGnom.*233 (ii A.D.).

**ἀτρυγηφάγον**· πολυφάγον, Hsch.; cf. ὀτρυγηφάγος.

**ἄτρυγος**, ον, (τρύξ) *without lees, clarified, pure*, οἶνος, opp. τρυγίας, Orac.ap.Arist.*Fr.*597; ἔλαιον Lxx *Ex.*27.20.

**ἀτρύμων** [ῠ], ον, gen. ονος, = ἄτρυτος, c. gen., ἀ. κακῶν *not worn out by* ills, A.*Th.*876 (lyr.).

**ἀτρύνων**· ἐγείρων, Hsch. (leg. ὀτρύνων).

⊛ **ἀτρύπητος** [ῠ], ον, = ἄτρητος, τὸ οὖς ἔχειν ἀ. Plu.*Cic.*26, 2.205b.

⊛ **ἄτρῡτος**, ον, *not worn, untiring, unwearied*, πούς A.*Eu.*403; *indefatigable*, φεῦ τῶν ἀ. οἷα κωτιλίζουσι Call.*Iamb.*1.277, cf. Plu.*Pomp.* 26; ironical in Herod.8.4. Adv. -τως, κάματον ἐκδέχεσθαι Ph.1. 19; ὑπομένειν τι J.*AJ*11.5.8, cf. Jul.*Or.*7.226c, Orph.*Fr.*71. 2. of things, *unabating*: hence, *limitless*, πόνος Pi.*P.*4.178, Hdt.9.52; χρόνος B.8.80; χάος Id.5.27; κακά S.*Aj.*788; ἄλγεα Mosch.4.69; Ἰξίονος μοῖρα ἀΐδιος καὶ ἀ. Arist.*Cael.*284$^a$35; τὸ ἀ. Id.*EN*1177$^b$22; ἀνάγκαι Ph.2.434; Πόνος Chaerem.ap.Porph.*Abst.*4.8; of a road, *wearisome, never-ending*, Theoc.15.7; ὁδοιπορίαι Plu.*Caes.*17: Sup., Ph.1.418. 3. = ἀτρύγετος, αἰθήρ Corn.*ND*20.

**Ἀτρυτώνη**, ἡ, *the Unwearied*, title of Pallas Athene, Il.2.157, Od. 4.762, etc. (Lengthd. form of ἀτρύτη, as Ἀϊδωνεύς of Ἅιδης.)

**ἀτρύφερος** [ῠ], ον, *not delicate* or *luxurious*, Eup.69; *plain, simple*, στολή Ceb.20; ὄψον Teles p.7 H.

**ἀτρύφητος**, ον, (τρυφάω) = foreg., Plu.2.10b (s. v. l.); cf. ἀτύφωτος.

**ἄτρυφος**, ον, = ἄθρυπτος, τυρός Alcm.34, cf. Hierocl.*in CA*17 p.458 M.

**ἀτρώς**, ῶτος, ὁ, ἡ, = ἄτρωτος, Choerob.*in Theod.*p.159 H.

**ἀτρωσία**, ἡ, *invulnerability*, Sch.A.R.1.57.

⊛ **ἄτρωτος**, ον, *unwounded*, κραδία Pi.*N.*11.10; ἀ. οὖθαρ ὑπὸ στύγους A.*Ch.*532; ἄτρωτον οὐ μεθῆκ' ἄν S.*OC*906, cf. Eub.107.4 (hex.), etc. II. *invulnerable*, παῖδες θεῶν Pi.*I.*3.18, cf. Acus.22 J., E.*Ph.* 594, Arist.*Rh.*1396$^b$18; σιδήρῳ D.S.4.11, Nonn.*D.*2.452: metaph., ἀ. χρήμασιν Pl.*Smp.*219e; κακίας Philostr.*VA*1.11; πρὸς σώματος ὥραν Lib.*Or.*59.122. Adv. -τως, ἔχειν Ph.1.384 (s.v.l.). III. of capital, *intact*, *PLond.*2.483.81 (vii A.D.).

**ἄττα** (A), Att. for ἅσσα, (q.v.). II. ἄττα for ἄσσα, = ἅτινα, Pl.Com.49, etc.

**ἄττα** (B), a salutation used to elders, *father*, ἄττα γεραιέ Il.9.607, cf. Od.16.31, etc.; said to be Thess. by Eust.777.54. (From child-language.)

**ἀτταβυγάς**, a *bird* (perh. = ἀτταγᾶς), Hsch.

**ἀττᾰγᾶς**, ᾶ, ὁ, *francolin, Tetrao orientalis*, Alex.Mynd.ap.Ath.9. 387f; πτερυγοποίκιλος, ποικίλος, Ar.*Av.*247, 761; a delicacy, Hippon.36.1, Ar.*Ach.*875, *Fr.*433: prov., τὸν πηλὸν ὥσπερ ἀ. τυρβάσεις βαδίζων Id.*V.*257.

⊛ **ἀττᾰγεινός**, ὁ, a *fish*, = σκεπινός, Dorio ap.Ath.7.322c.

**ἀττᾰγήν**, ῆνος, ὁ, = ἀτταγᾶς, Phoenicid.2.5, Arist.*HA*617$^b$25, 633$^b$1, Thphr.*Fr.*180. -ηνάριον, τό, Dim. of foreg., Gramm. in Gaisford *Choeroboscus* 1 p.43. -ῆς, έος, ὁ, = ἀτταγήν, Opp.*C.*2. 405, 427.

**ἀττάκης**, ου, ὁ, a kind of *locust*, Lxx *Le.*11.22 (ἀττακύς Al. ibid.):—also **ἄττακος**, ὁ, Aristeas 145, Ph.1.85.

**ἀτταλαγώσεται**· μολυνθήσεται, Hsch.

**ἀτταλασίξαι**· ὀμόσαι, Hsch.; cf. ἀπαλασίξαι, ἀπαλοῖξαι.

**Ἀττᾰλεῖον**, τό, *meeting-place of* Ἀτταλισταί (q.v.), *CIG*3069. II. Ἀττάλεια, τά, festival at Delphi, *SIG*672.53.

**ἀττάλη**· φάρυξις (Phryg.), Hsch.

**Ἀτταλιανόν**, τό, kind of *garment*, *PGiss.*21.6 (ii A.D.).

**ἀτταλίζομαι**· πλανῶμαι (Sicel), Hsch.

**Ἀτταλίς**, ίδος, ἡ, φυλή tribe at Athens, *IG*2.444.

**Ἀττᾰλισταί**, οἱ, *guild of worshippers of Attalus*, *Michel* 1307 (ii B.C.).

⊛ **ἀττάμιος**, ον, Elean, = ἀζήμιος, *Michel* 1334 (iv B.C.).

**ἄττανα**· τήγανα, Hsch.:—hence ⊛**ἀττᾰνίτης**, ου, ὁ, a kind of *cake*, coupled with τηγανίτης, Hippon.36.3:—also **ἀττανίδες**, αἱ, Hsch.

⊛ **ἀττάρᾰγος** [τᾰ], ὁ, *crumb, morsel of bread*, Ath.14.646c: metaph., *the least crumb, bit*, οὐδ' ὅσον ἀττάραγόν τυ δεδοίκαμες Call.*Epigr.*47.9.

**ἀττάρυμα**· πόμα, σόφισμα Κρητικόν, Hsch. **ἄττασι**· ἀνάστηθι (Lacon.), Id.

**ἀτταταῖ**, a cry of pain or grief, S.*Ph.*790, etc.; doubled, Ar.*Ach.* 1190.

**ἀττέλᾰβος**, Ion. -εβος (both forms in Lxx *Na.*3.17 codd.), ὁ, *locust*, Hdt.4.172, Arist.*HA*550$^b$32, 556$^a$8, Thphr.*Fr.*174.3, Plu.2.636e:—also **ἀττελάβη**· ἀκρίδας, Hsch.

**ἀττελεβόφθαλμος**, ον, *with locust-eyes*, i.e. *with prominent, staring eyes*, Eub.107.10.

**ἀττηγός**, ὁ, *he-goat*, Ion. word, *SIG*589.51 (Magn. Mae., ii B.C.), Eust.1625.35. (*Attagus* Phryg. for *hircus* acc. to Arn.5.6.)

**Ἄττης** Ὕης, mystic formula recited by the priests of Cybele, D. 18.260, cf. *AB*207.

**Ἀττίδεια** [τῐ], τά, *festival of Attis*, *IG*2.622.10.

**Ἀττῐκ-ηρῶς**, Adv. *in Attic fashion*, Alex.213.4. -ιανός, ή, όν, *of Atticus*: ἀντίγραφα manuscripts *collected by A., copied for A.*, or *written by A.*, Gal.*in Pl.Ti.*3, Harp. s.v. Ἀργᾶς. ⊛-ίζω, *side with the Athenians*, Th.3.62, X.*HG*1.6.13, *Hell.Oxy.*12.1. II. *speak Attic*, Eup.8.3 D., Pl.Com.168.1; opp. Ἑλληνίζω, Posidipp. 28. -ισις, εως, ἡ, *Attic style, Atticism*, Luc.*Lex.*14, Philostr. *VS*2.3. -ισμός, ὁ, *siding with Athens, loyalty to her*, Th.3.64, 4.133. II. = foreg., Alciphr.2.4: pl., ibid., cf. Cic.*Att.*4.19. 1. -ιστής, οῦ, ὁ, *one who affects* or *collects Attic expressions*, Iamb. *VP*18.80, *EM*527.54, etc.; title of work by Moeris. -ιστί, Adv. *in the Attic dialect*, D.*Prooem.*8 (= Id.16.2, v. Ἀττικός III); Ἀ. λέγειν Antiph.97; λαλεῖν Alex.195. -ίων, a comic Dim., *little Athenian*, Ar.*Pax*214.

**ἀττῐκοπέρδιξ**, ῑκος, ὁ, *Attic partridge*, nickname of an actor, Ath. 3.115b.

⊛ **Ἀττικός**, ή, όν, *Attic, Athenian*, Sol.2, Alc.32, A.*Eu.*681, etc.; σφόδρ'..Ἀττικάς *of* true *Attic breed*, Ar.*Lys.*56; Ἀ. πάροικος, prov. of a *troublesome neighbour*, Arist.*Rh.*1395$^a$18. II. ἡ Ἀττική (sc. γῆ) *Attica*, Hdt.5.76, etc.; cf. Ἀτθίς. III. Gramm., Ἀττικοί, οἱ, *Attic writers*, Longin.34.2, Phryn.302, etc.; Ἀ. γράμματα the *Attic* alphabet, D.59.76, Paus.6.19.6; 'Α. σχῆμα, use of nom. for voc., A.D.*Synt.*214.2; χρῆσις ib.59.20; -κόν, τό, *the Attic style*, Plu.2.79d: Comp. -ώτερος Cic.*Att.*1.13.5 (with play on the name *Atticus*): Sup., ib.15.1b.2. Adv. -κῶς D.16.2 codd., Luc.*Sol.*6: Comp. -ώτερον A.D.*Adv.*132.20. IV. 'Αττικόν, τό, *a remedy*, Hp.*Epid.*4.47.

**'Αττἰκ-ουργής**, ές, *wrought in Attic fashion*, ῥήματα Men.1000. **-ωνικός**, ή, όν, comic alteration of 'Αττικός, after the form of Λακωνικός, Ar.*Pax*215.

**ἄττομαι**, = διάζομαι, Hermipp.2.

**ᾄττω**, Att. for ἄσσω, ἀΐσσω.

**ἀτυζηλός**, ή, όν, *frightful*, δεῖμα A.R.2.1057.

**ἀτύζομαι**, in Hom., Lyr., Trag. only pres. and aor. part. Pass.:—*to be distraught from fear, bewildered*, ἀτυζομένους ὑπὸ καπνοῦ Il.8.183; ἀτυζομένω πεδίοιο *fleeing bewildered* o'er the plain, Il.6.38, cf. 18.7, Od.11.606: abs., ἀτύζονται, ἀτυζόμενος, Pi.*P.*1.13, *O.*8.39, B.12.116; *to be distraught with grief*, ἀτυζόμενος S.*El.*148 (lyr.), E.*Andr.*131, A.R.4.39: c. acc., *to be amazed at* a thing, ὄψιν ἀτυχθεὶς Il.6.468, cf. Tryph.685: c. inf., ἀτυζομένην ἀπολέσθαι *terrified* even to death, Il.22.474; ἀ. περὶ νύμφην *to be distressed* for... *AP*7.528 (Theodorid.). II. in later Ep. Act. **ἀτύζω**, *strike with terror* or *amazement*, A.R.1.465: aor. opt. ἀτύξαι Theoc.1.56; ἠέρα παῦρον ἀτύζει *draws* short breaths, Nic.*Al.*193 (vv.ll. ἀτίζει, ἀλύξει).—Ep. Verb, used by Trag. only in lyr.

**ἄτυκτος**, ον, *undone*, οὐκέτι γὰρ δύναται τὸ τετυγμένον εἶναι ἄτυκτον Ps.-Phoc.56.

**ἄτυλλα**· ἀγκύλη, Hsch. (ἄττ- cod.). **ἀτυλόν**· μικρόν, ἀγενές, Id.

⊛ **ἀτύλωτος** [ῡ], ον, (ἀ- euph.) *made callous by labour, hardened*, ὦμοι Call.*Dian.*213 (Toup for ἀσύλωτοι). II. (ἀ- priv.) *that will not cicatrize*, Archig.ap.Gal.13.730.

⊛ **ἀτύμβ-ευτος**, ον, *without tomb*, θάνατος *AP*9.439 (Crin.); ὕβρις contemptuous *neglect of burial*, Onos.36.2; τάφος ἀ. burial *but not in a tomb*, Opp.*H.*5.346. **-ος**, ον, *without burial, without a tomb*, Luc.*Cont.*22. Adv. -βως prob. in *Anatolian Studies* p.118.

**ἀτυπῆδες**· κριθαὶ ἀπίτυροι, Hsch.

⊛ **ἄτῡπ-ος**, ον, *speaking inarticulately, stammering*, Gell 4.2.5. II. *conforming to no distinct type* (of illness), Gal.7.471 (Sup.). **-ωτος**, ον, *unformed, shapeless*, Ael.*NA*2.19, Plu.2.636c; ἀ. ψυχή *uninfluenced* by good or evil, *Stoic.*3.52. 2. = ἄσκαλτος, Hsch.

**ἀτῡράννευτος**, ον, *not ruled by tyrants, free from tyrants*, Th.1.18, D.C.37.22, Chor.p.208 B.:—also **ἀτύραννος**, ον, Phryn.*PS*p.30 B.

**ἀτύρωτος** [ῡ], ον, *not curdled* or *coagulated*, Dsc.3.34, Orib.*Fr.*137.

⊛ **ἀτῡφ-ία**, ἡ, *freedom from arrogance*, Men.304, Plu.2.82b, Jul.*Or.*7.214b. **-ος**, ον, *not puffed up*, Pl.*Phdr.*230a, Timo 9.1; esp. of the Stoic sage, Cleanth.*Stoic.*1.127: Comp., Plu.*Alex.*45: Sup., D.L.4.37. Adv. -φως Plu.2.32d, M.Ant.1.16.4: Comp. -ότερον Hierocl.*in CA* 19 p.461 M.: Sup. -ότατα Ael.*Fr.*137:—also **ἀτῡφί**, dub. in *IG*14.2094. **-ωτος**, ον, = foreg., Plu.2.10b.

⊛ **ἀτῠχ-έω**, fut. -ήσω Ar.*Nu.*427, Eup.114: aor. ἠτύχησα Hdt.9.111, Antipho 4.2.6: pf. ἠτύχηκα D.20.53, Men.149, Philem.107: rarely in Pass. (v. infr.):—*to be unfortunate, fail, miscarry*, Ar.*Nu.*427, Th.1.32, etc.; opp. κατορθόω, Isoc.3.24, etc.; ἀ. ἔν τινι Id.12.105; πεζῇ Arist.*Pol.*1303ᵃ8; οἱ ἀτυχοῦντες, = οἱ ἀτυχεῖς, Antipho 2.4.9: euphem. for ἀτιμοῦσθαι, D.21.60. 2. c. gen., *fail of* a thing, *fail in getting* it, τῆς ἀληθείας Pl.*Tht.*186c; τῶν δικαίων οὐδενός X.*HG*3.1.22: c. part., ἀ. κτώμενοι Th.2.62, cf. Men.*Epit.*470: c. inf., Vett.Val.358.30: c. acc., τὸ ἀγαθόν Eun.*VS* p.469 B. 3. *fail in one's request, meet with a refusal*, Hdt.9.111; πρός τινα X.*Cyr.*1.3.14; παρὰ θεῶν ib.1.6.6; τι παρά τινος *IG*2.86; ἀ. τινός Eup.114:—Pass., τὰ ἀτυχηθέντα *mischances, failures*, D.18.212; τὰ ἠτυχημένα J.*AJ*16.8.6; ἠτύχητο ἡ μάχη D.H.*Isoc.*9.—Chiefly in Com. and Att. Prose, never in Trag. **-ημα**, ατος, τό, *misfortune, miscarriage*, Antipho 3.4.5 (v.l.), Timocl.6.18. 2. *fault of ignorance, mistake*, D.23.70; opp. ἀδίκημα, ἁμάρτημα, Gorg.11, Arist.*Rh.*1374ᵇ6, *EN*1135ᵇ12: euphem., *crime*, ἀ. πρὸς τὸ δημόσιον Is.10.20, cf. Plb.12.14.2. **-ής**, ές, *unfortunate*, Antipho 2.2.1 (Sup.); οὐ γὰρ οὕτως ἄφρων οὐδ' ἀ. εἰμι D.3.21; euphem., ἀ. γενέσθαι 'get into trouble', Pl.*Lg.*905a: fem. acc. fem. ἀτυχήν *Annales du Service* 22.10 (i B.C./i A.D.). Adv. -χῶς Isoc.12.15: Sup. -έστατα Longin.33.5. II. *missing, without share in*, τινός Ael.*NA*11.31, Max.Tyr.20.5. **-ία**, ἡ, *ill-luck*, Amphis 3. II. = ἀτύχημα, *miscarriage, mishap*, Hp.*Fract.*25, Antipho 2.2.13, X.*Mem.*3.9.8 (pl.), Men.674; *defeat* in war, Aeschin.3.55. 2. euphem. for ἀτιμία, D.21.59; for *crime*, Din.1.77, Plb.12.13.5, etc. 3. of a person, ἀ. κοσμουμένα Axiop.4.5. 4. *failure to obtain*, τινός Aret.*SD*1.5.

⊛ **ἀτῶμαι**, v. ἀτάω.

**ἄτωρ**· μελία (Egypt.), Hsch.

⊛ **αὖ**, Adv. of repeated action, *again, anew, afresh, once more*, Il.1.540, etc.: freq. after numerals, δεύτερον αὖ, τρίτον αὖ, etc., Hom.; τὸν δὲ πέμπτον αὖ λέγω A.*Th.*526, cf. *Ch.*1066 (lyr.); in a question, expressing impatience, τίς δὴ αὖ τοι..; Il.1.540. II. generally, *again*, i.e. *further, moreover*, ib.2.493, etc.; καὶ ἔτι γε αὖ Pl.*Tht.*192b. 2. *on the other hand*, following δέ, τούτῳ μὲν.. τούτῳ δ' αὖ.. Il.4.417; also, *in turn*, οἱ δ' ἄρα..'Ηλίδα δῖαν ἔναιον..τῶν αὖ τέσσαρες ἀρχοὶ ἔσαν ib.2.618; ἥξει γὰρ ἄλλος αὖ τιμάορος A.*Ag.*1280: hence = δέ, even when μέν precedes, Il.11.109, Od.4.211; freq. joined with δέ, ὃν δ' αὖ δήμου τ' ἄνδρα ἴδοι Il.2.198; ὦ πολλὰ μὲν τάλαινα πολλὰ δ' αὖ σοφή A.*Ag.*1295, cf. *Eu.*954 (lyr.); ὁ μὲν ἥμαρτε ὁ δ' αὖ..κατειργάσατο X.*Cyr.*4.6.4; οὐκ..οὐδ' αὖ S.*OT*1373, *El.*911, cf. Pl.*Tht.*160b: with τε, X.*Cyr.*1.1.1, Pl.*Prt.*326a, etc. III. in pleon. phrases, esp. in Trag. (v. αὖθις, ἔμπαλιν, πάλιν), μάλ' αὖ A.*Eu.*254, S.*El.*1410. IV. *on the contrary*, ἆρ' ὀρθῶς.. ἢ αὖ; Pl.*R.*468a. V. of Place, *backward*, only in the incorrect orthography αὖ ἔρυσαν, cf. αὐερύω.—Not placed first in a sentence. [αὖ before a vowel, Pl.Com.153.3, Archestr.ap.Ath.6.300e (both hex.).] (Cf. αὐτάρ, αὖτε, αὖτις, Lat. *aut.*)

**αὖ αὖ**, *bow wow*, of a dog, Ar.*V.*903.

**Αὐαίνου λίθος** *the Withering stone*, Ar.*Ra.*194.

**αὐαίνω**, Att. **αὑ-** (cf. ἀφ-, ἐπαφ-αυαίνω), impf. (καθ-)αύαινον Luc.*Am.*12: fut. αὐανῶ S.*El.*819: aor. ηὔηνα or αὔ- Hdt.4.172, inf. αὐῆναι Hp.*Mul.*1.84, part. αὐήνας Id.*Morb.*3.17:—**Pass.**, impf. Ar.*Fr.*613: aor. ηὐάνθην or αὐ- (v. infr.), ἐξ- Hdt.4.151: fut. αὐανθήσομαι (cf. ἀφ-):—but also **Med.** αὐανοῦμαι in pass. sense, S.*Ph.*954: Mss. and editors differ with regard to the augm.: (v. αὔω):—*dry*, αὐανθέν (of a log of wood) Od.9.321; αὐ. ἰχθῦς πρὸς ἥλιον Hdt.1.200, 2.77, cf. 92, 4.172; αὐαίνεσθαι ὑπὸ τοῦ καύματος, διὰ ξηρότητα, X.*Oec.*16.14, 19.11, cf. *An.*2.3.16, etc. 2. *wither*, Thphr.*HP*3.7.1 (Pass.): metaph., εὐνομίη αὐαίνει ἄτης ἄνθεα Sol.4.36; αὐανθεὶς πυθμήν A.*Ch.*260; αὐανῶ βίον I *shall waste* life *away, pine away*, S.*El.*819; αὐανοῦμαι I *shall wither away*, Id.*Ph.*954; ηὑαινόμην θεώμενος Ar.*Fr.*613. II. intr., *to be dry*, μήτε ὑγραὶ μήτε λίαν αὐαίνουσαι Hp.*Mul.*1.17.—The Act. is comparatively rare, esp. in Attic.

**αὐᾰλέος**, α, ον, (αὖος) *dry, parched, withered*, αὐ. χρὼς ὑπὸ καύματος Hes.*Op.*588; of hair, *rough*, dub. in Simon.37.9, cf. *AP*7.141 (Antiphil.); of plants, Orph.*A.*246; of the mouth, Call.*Cer.*6; of eyes, *sleepless*, *AP*5.279 (Agath.); αὐαλέη ἐνὶ κόγχῳ prob. in Timo 3.—Late in Prose, Aret.*SD*2.2, al. (αὐ- Call. l. c.)

**αὔανσις**, εως, ἡ, *drying up*, Arist.*Mete.*379ᵃ5, *GA*785ᵃ26; equivalent to γῆρας in plant-life, Id.*Resp.*478ᵇ28.

**αὐαντή** (sc. νόσος), ἡ, *wasting, atrophy*, Hp.*Morb.*2.66.

⊛ **αὐαρά**· τὰ Ποντικὰ κάρυα, Hsch.

**Αὔασις**, ἡ, = Ὄασις (q.v.), Str.2.5.33, al.

**αὐασμός**, ὁ, *drying, dryness*, Hp.*Hum.*4, *AB*462.

**ἀϝάτα**, i.e. ἀϝάτα, Aeol. for ἄτη (q.v.).

⊛ **αὐγάζω**, fut. -άσω: aor. ηὔγασα *AP*7.726 (Leon.):—**Pass.**, v. infr.: (αὐγή):—*view in the clearest light, see distinctly, discern*, S.*Ph.*217 (lyr.), *AP*9.221 (Marc. Arg.); τὸν ἴδιον νοῦν οἷα πρὸς κάτοπτρον Ph.2.156:—also in Med., Il.23.458, Hes.*Op.*478, A.R.1.155, Call.*Dian.*129, *AP*9.349 (Leon.); αἱ δὲ λῇς αὐγάσδεο *Carm.Pop.*18:—Pass., αὐγασθεῖσα *being mirrored* in the smooth water, dub. in S.*Fr.*598.6; simply, *appear*, Max.11, al., dub. in Orph.*Fr.*284. II. of the sun, *illumine*, τινά E.*Hec.*637 (lyr.):—Pass., Id.*Ba.*596 (lyr.). 2. metaph., *enlighten*, 2*Ep.Cor.*4.4; *set in a clear light*, Ph.1.659, al. III. intr., *appear bright* or *white*, Lxx *Le.*13.25, al.; *shine*, *PMag.Par.*1.2558, 2.143.

**αὔγαρος**· ἄσωτος (Cypr.), Hsch.

**αὐγ-ασμα**, ατος, τό, *brightness, whiteness*, Lxx *Le.*13.38. **-ασμός**, ὁ, *radiance, flashing*, ἡλίου *Lacit.*3.5.10. **-άστειρα**, ἡ, *light-giving*, of the moon, Orph.*H.*9.5.

**αὐγεῖν**· ἀλγεῖν, Hsch.

**αὔγειον**, τό, = ὠκιμοειδές, Ps.-Dsc.4.28.

**αὐγέω**, *to shine, glitter*, Lxx *Jb.*29.3.

⊛ **αὐγή**, ἡ, *light of the sun*, and in pl., *rays, beams*, πέπτατο δ' αὐ. ἠελίου Il.17.371, cf. Od.6.98, 12.176; ἠελίου ἴδεν αὐγάς, i.e. was born, Il.16.188; ὑπ' αὐγὰς ἠελίοιο, i.e. still alive, Od.11.498, 619; Διὸς αὐγάς Il.13.837; αὐγὰς ἐσιδεῖν see *the light*, i.e. to be alive, Thgn.426, cf. E.*Alc.*667; λεύσσειν A.*Pers.*710; βλέπειν E.*Andr.*935; ὑπ' αὐγὰς λεύσσειν or ἰδεῖν τι hold up to *the light* and look at, Id.*Hec.*1154, Pl.*Phdr.*268a, cf. Plb.10.3.1; ὑπ' αὐγὰς δεικνύναι τι Ar.*Th.*500 (πρὸς and ὑπ' αὐγήν, *in a full* and *in a side light*, Hp.*Off.*3); δυθμαὶ αὐγῶν *sun*-set, Pi.*I.*4(3).65; ξυνορθρον αὐγαῖς dawning with *the sun*, A.*Ag.*254 (lyr.); κλύζειν πρὸς αὐγάς rise surging towards *the sun*, ib.1182; λαμπροτάτη τῶν παρεουσέων αὐγέων brightest *light* available, Hp.*Fract.*3, cf. Arist.*PA*658ᵃ3, *Pr.*912ᵇ14, al.: metaph., βίου δύντος αὐγαί 'life's setting *sun*', A.*Ag.*1123 (lyr.); ἤδη γὰρ αὐγὴ τῆς ζόης ἀπήμβλυνται Herod.10.4. 2. αὐγαὶ ἠελίοιο or αὐγαί alone, *the East*, D.P.84, 231. 3. *dawn, day break*, *Act.Ap.*20.11, *PLeid.W.*11.35. 4. generally, *any bright light*, πυρὸς αὐγή Od.6.305, cf. Il.2.456; ἀρίζηλοι δέ οἱ αὐγαί, of lightning, 13.244; βροντῆς αὐ. S.*Ph.*1199 (lyr.); of a beacon, Il.18.211, A.*Ag.*9; λαμπάδος Cratin. post 150; distd. from φλόξ, Chrysipp.*Stoic.*2.186. 5. of the eyes, ὀμμάτων αὐγαί S.*Aj.*70; αὐγαί alone, *the eyes*, E.*Andr.*1180 (lyr.), *Rh.*737: metaph., ἀνακλίναντας τὴν τῆς ψυχῆς αὐ. Pl.*R.*540a. 6. *gleam, sheen*, of bright objects, αὐ. χαλκείη Il.13.341; χρυσὸς αὐγὰς ἔδειξεν Pi.*N.*4.83; ἀμβρόσιος αὐ. πέπλου E.*Med.*983 (lyr.); ἠλεκτροφαεῖς αὐ. Id.*Hipp.*741 (lyr.); αὐ. τῆς κρόκης Men.561; of gems, Philostr.*Im.*2.8.—Mostly poet., but freq. in Arist., chiefly in the sense of *sunlight*.

**αὐγήεις**, εσσα, εν, *bright-eyed, clear-sighted*, Nic.*Th.*34.

**αὐγής**, ές, f.l. for διαυγής, ὕδατα Alex.Aphr.*Pr.*1.116.

**αὔγιον**, τό, = ἰσάτις, dub. in Ps.-Dsc.2.184.

**αὐγ-ίτης** (sc. λίθος), ὁ, *a precious stone*, Plin.*HN*37.147:—fem. **-ῖτις**, ιδος, ἡ, = ἀναγαλλὶς ἡ Φοινική, Ps.-Dsc.2.178.

**αὐγοειδής**, ές, *of the nature of light*, πνεῦμα, as the source of sight, *Stoic.*2.231; αἰσθητήριον, of the eye, Gal.*UP*8.6; *brilliant*, χρόα Plu.2.922d: metaph., ψυχή ib.565d; σῶμα, πνεῦμα, Iamb.*Myst.*5.10, 3.11; ὄχημα *luminous* vehicle, Procl.*in Ti.*2.81 D.: Comp., Ph.1.6: Sup., ib.504, al., Eus.Mynd.63. Adv. -δῶς dub. in Ph.2.487.

**αὖγος**, εος, τό, *the morning light, dawn*, Hsch. s. v. ἠώς.

⊛ **Αὔγουστος**, ὁ, *Augustus*, used as an Adj., = Gr. σεβαστός, Paus.

3.11.4, etc. :—hence **Αὐγούστειος**, ον, D.C.61.20: **Αὐγουστεῖον**, τό, *temple of Augustus*, Id.57.10: **Αὐγούστεια**, τά, *festival of A.*, *IG*3.129, 14.739 :—⊛**Αὐγουστάλιος**, ον, *Augustalis*, τὰ Αὐγουστάλια *ludi Augustales*, D.C.54.34; -άλιος, ὁ, *praefectus Augusti*, Lyd.*Mag.*2.3. II. the month *August*, Plu.*Num.*19.

**Αὐγώ**, *Daybeam*, name of a dog, X.*Cyn.*7.3.

⊛**αὐδάζομαι**, Dep., (αὐδή) *cry out*, *speak*, αὐδάξασθαι φωνῇ ἀνθρωπηΐῃ Hdt.2.55, cf. 5.51, Euph.48; τοῦτ' ἔπος ηὐδάσατο Call.*Aet.*3.1.21. 2. *name*, Opp.*H.*1.127 :—Act., fut. αὐδάξω Lyc.892: aor. ηὔδαξα Id.360, dub. l. in *AP*6.218 (Alc.):—Pass., aor. αὐδαχθεῖσα Orph.*H.*27.9.

⊛**αὐδάω**, impf. ηὔδων Il.3.203, Hdt.2.57, S.*OT*568, etc.: fut. αὐδήσω, Dor. -άσω [ᾱ] Pi.*O.*1.7, S.*OT*846; Dor. αὐδασοῦντι *APl.*4.120 (Archel. or Asclep.): aor. ηὔδησα, Dor. αὔδασα Pi.*I.*6(5).42, etc.; part. αὐδήσας Il.10.47, Dor. αὐδάσαις Pi.*P.*4.61; Ion. 3 sg. αὐδήσασκε Il.5.786: pf. ηὔδηκα (ἀπ-) Hp.*Gland.*14:—Pass., impf. ηὐδώμην (v. infr.): aor. part. αὐδηθείς S.*Tr.*1106, Dor. αὐδαθείς E.*Med.*174 (lyr.): pf. ηὔδημαι Maiist.3: fut. αὐδηθήσομαι Lyc.630: Ep. pres. 3 pl. αὐδώωνται Opp.*H.*1.776 :—also Med., **αὐδάομαι**, A.*Pr.*766, *Eu.*379, S.*Ph.*130: impf. ηὐδᾶτο Id.*Aj.*772: fut. αὐδήσομαι, Dor. αὐδάσομαι Pi.*O.*2.101: (αὐδή). I. c. acc. rei, 1. *utter sounds*, *speak*, Il.1.92, etc.; τόσον αὐδήσασχ' ὅσον ἄλλοι πεντήκοντα 5.786; ὥς δέ τις.. αὐδήσασκεν 17.420; αὐδᾶν κραυγήν *utter* a cry, E.*Ion*893 (lyr.). 2. *speak*, *say*, ὁμοκλήσας ἔπος ηὔδα Il.6.54; αὔδα δ' τι φρονέεις 18.426; so οὐκ αὐδᾶν ἔσθ' ἃ μηδὲ δρᾶν καλόν S.*OT*1409; τί τινι Id.*OC*25 :—Med., Id.*Ph.*130, 852 (lyr.):—Pass., ηὐδᾶτο γὰρ ταῦτα so *'twas said*, Id.*OT*731, cf. 527; ὡς ηὐδᾶτ' ἐκεῖ ib.940. 3. of oracles, *utter*, *proclaim*, ib.392, etc.; οὕστινας κομπεῖς γάμους αὐδᾶν *speak out concerning them*, A.*Pr.*948. 4. αὐ. ἀγῶνα *sing of* a contest, Pi.*O.*1.7. 5. abs., *speak*, *utter*, of the statue of Memnon, *Epigr.Gr.*988 (Balbilla), al. II. c. acc. pers., 1. *speak to*, *address*, *accost*, ἀντίον αὐδᾶν τινά Il.3.203, al.; ἔπος τέ μιν ἀντίον ηὔδα 5.170; αὐδῶν δεινὰ πρόσπολον κακά E.*Hipp.*584; *call on* or *invoke* a god, Id.*HF*499, 1215. 2. c. acc. et inf., *bid*, *order* to do, αὐ. σε χαίρειν Pi.*P.*4.61, cf. S.*OC*1630; αὐ. σε μὴ.. *forbid*, A.*Th.*1048, etc.; αὐδῶ τινὶ ποιεῖν E.*IT*1226; αὐδῶ σιωπᾶν S.*OC*864; αὐδήσας χαίρειν *Epigr.Gr.*205.7 (Halic.); αὐδῶ καὖθις ἀπαυδῶ Ar.*Ra.*369 :—Med., S.*Aj.*772. 3. *call by name*, λεώς νιν Θετίδειον αὐδᾷ E.*Andr.*20 :—Med., ὅν τε λέοντα αὐδάξαντο Nic.*Th.*464 :—more freq. in Pass., αὐδῶμαι παῖς Ἀχιλλέως S.*Ph.*240; Ζηνὸς αὐδηθεὶς γόνος Id.*Tr.*1106; αὐδᾶσθαι νεκρόν Id.*Ph.*430; κάκιστ' αὐδώμενος most ill *reported of*, A.*Th.*678; ὁ παραμασήτης ἐν βροτοῖς αὐδώμενος Alex.236 (paratrag.). 4. *mean* such an one, E.*Hipp.*352.—Never in good Att. Prose.

**αὐδή**, Dor. **αὐδά**, ἡ, *human voice*, *speech* (but distd. fr. φωνή, *Stoic.*2.44), μέλιτος γλυκίων ῥέεν αὐ. Il.1.249. 2. generally, *sound* or *twang* of the bow-string, καλὸν ἄεισε χελιδόνι εἰκέλη αὐδήν Od.21.411; of a trumpet, E.*Rh.*989; of the τέττιξ, Hes.*Sc.*396; of the *sound* emitted by the statue of Memnon, *Epigr.Gr.*990.7 (Balbilla). II. *report*, *account*, ἔργων ἀΐοντες αὐδήν S.*OC*240 (lyr.), cf. E.*Supp.*600 (lyr.), *Hipp.*567. 2. *oracle*, Id.*IT*976. 3. *song*, *ode*, Pi.*N.*9.4. (Cf. Skt. *vadati* 'speaks', v. ἀείδω.)

⊛**αὐδήεις**, εσσα, εν, *speaking with human voice*, ἀνθρώπων.. σχεδὸν αὐδηέντων Od.6.125; [Ἰνὼ] ἣ πρὶν μὲν ἔην βροτὸς αὐδήεσσα 5.334; of Achilles' horse, αὐδήεντα δ' ἔθηκε θεά Il.19.407; θνητοὶ αὐδήεντες, opp. ἀθάνατοι, Hes.*Th.*142b; of divinities, *using human speech*, of Calypso and Circe, Od.10.136, 11.8, 12.150, 449 (οὐδήεσσα or αὐλήεσσα Arist.*Fr.*171, Chamael.ap.Sch.Od.5.334); χθόνιαι θεαὶ αὐδήεσσαι A.R.4.1322; Ἀργοῦς.. αὐδῆεν (Hartung for αὔδασον) ξύλον A.*Fr.*20. 2. *vocal*, κόσμον αὐδάεντα λόγων Pi.*Fr.*194; αὐδάεις λόγος *rumour*, B.14.44; of the statue of Memnon, *Epigr.Gr.*1000, al.; opp. ἄναυδος, Epigr.ap.Paus.10.12.6. 3. *famous*, Hsch.

**αὔδρ-ία**, ἡ, = ἀνυδρία, Pl.*Lg.*844a, Thphr.*HP*8.6.6. **-ος**, ον, = ἄνυδρος, Id.*CP*2.4.10.

⊛**Αὐδυναῖος**, ὁ (sc. μήν), name of month in Macedonia, Crete, etc., *Hemerolog.Flor.*; **Αὐδουν-**, *IG*12(3).254 :—also **Αὐδν-**, **Αὐτναῖος**, *PPetr.*3 p.4, *PPar.*3, etc.

**αὐειρόμεναι**, v. ἀείρω. **αὐεκίζει**· σφακελίζει (Cypr.), Hsch.

⊛**αὐεοῦλλαι**, = ἄελλαι, dub. in Alc.125.

**αὔερος**, v. αὐήρ.

⊛**αὐερύω**, i. e. ἀϝ-ϝερύω, Ep. for ἀν-ϝερύω, = Att. ἀναρρύω: aor. αὐέρυσα :—*draw back* or *backwards*, τὰς [στήλας] οἵ γ' αὐέρυον *pulled* them *backwards*, Il.12.261; τόξον αὐερύοντα παρ' ὦμον 8.325: mostly abs., in sacrifice, *draw* the victim's head *back*, so as to cut its throat, αὐέρυσαν μὲν πρῶτα καὶ ἔσφαξαν 1.459, cf. Pi.*O.*13.81, Theoc.25.241, *AP*6.96 (Eryc.). II. of leeches, *suck*, Opp.*H.*2.603.

**αὐετής**, i. e. ἀ-ϝετής, ές, (ἀ- copul., ἔτος) = αὐτοετής, Hsch.

**αὖηλαι**· αἶσαι, Hsch.

**αὐήρ**, i. e. ἀϝήρ, Aeol. for ἀήρ, Greg.Cor.p.612 S.; cf. **αὐερός**· σκιά, Hsch.

**αὐηρός**, ά, όν, = αὐαλέος, *AP*12.121 (Rhian.). **αὐήτω**· ἔπνεον, Hsch.

**αὐθάγιος** [ᾰ], α, ον, *absolutely holy*, θεός *PMag.Leid.W.*7.18.

⊛**αὐθάδ-εια** [θᾰ], poet. and later Prose (*SIG*1243.27) **-ία**, ἡ, *wilfulness*, *stubbornness*, A.*Pr.*79, S.*OT*549, Ar.*Th.*704, Pl.*R.*590a, *BGU*1187.21 (i B.C.), *IG*7.2725.27 (Acraephia, ii A.D.), etc.; opp. εὐβουλία, A.*Pr.*1034; *surliness*, Thphr.*Char.*15.1; mean betw. ἀρέσκεια and σεμνότης, Arist.*EE*1221$^a$8; αὐθαδίαν αὐθαδίᾳ [ἐξελαύνειν] Antiph.300.4; ἡ αὐ. τῶν συνθηκῶν ὅτι οὐ μετὰ κοινῆς γνώμης αὐτὰς ἔπραξεν D.H.9.17. ⊛**-ης**, ες, *self-willed*, *stubborn*, ἦσάν τε αὐθαδέστεροι Hdt.6.92; τὰς ὀργὰς αὐ. Hp.*Aër.*24, cf. Arist.*Rh.*1367$^a$37; *surly*, Thphr.*Char.*15.1; αὐθάδη φρονῶν A.*Pr.*907; of a dog, X.*Cyn.*6.25. 2. metaph. of things, *remorseless*, σφηνὸς γνάθος αὐ. A.*Pr.*64. 3. Adv. **-δως** Ar.*Ra.*1020, *POxy.*1242.41: Comp. -έστερον Pl.*Ap.*34c; cf. αὐτάδης. (From αὐτο-άδης, cf. Arist.*MM*1192$^b$33.) ⊛**-ιάζομαι** or **-ειάζομαι**, late form for sq., J.*BJ*5.3.4, Polem.*Call.*24, S.E.*P.*1.237, Procop.*Arc.*14.15, Lib.*Decl.*15.47. **-ίζομαι**, aor. -ισάμενος Them.*Or.*34 p.467 D.:—*to be self-willed*, οὐκ αὐθαδιζόμενος Pl.*Ap.*34d; *to be puffed up*, *arrogant*, Them.*Or.*29.346b. **-ικός**, ή, όν, *like an* αὐθάδης, *self-willed*, Ar.*Lys.*1116. **-ισμα**, ατος, τό, *act of self-will*, *wilfulness*, A.*Pr.*964 (pl.). **-όστομος**, ον, *presumptuous of speech*, Ar.*Ra.*837.

⊛**αὐθ-αίμων**, ον, gen. ονος, (αἷμα) *of the same blood*, *brother*, *sister*, *kinsman*, S.*Tr.*1041 (lyr.):— also **-αιμος**, ον, Id.*OC*1078, *AP*7.707 (Diosc.). ⊛**-αίρετος**, ον, *self-chosen*, *self-elected*, στρατηγοί X.*An.*5.7.29; στεφανηφόρος *voluntary*, i. e. undertaking the duty at one's own expense, *Ath.Mitt.*36.159 (Syros, ii A.D.), cf. *IG*12(5).660, 668; γυμνασίαρχος *OGI*583.8; συνήγορος *POxy.*1242.10. Adv. **-τως** *Inscr. Magn.*163.15, *PLond.*2.280.7 (i A.D.). II. *by free choice*, *of oneself*, E.*Supp.*931; αὐ. ἐξῆλθε 2*Ep.Cor.*8.17; *independent*, *free*, εὐβουλία Th.1.78; ἡ τοῦ τέλους ἔφεσις οὐκ αὐ. Arist.*EN*1114$^b$6. III. of things, *due to one's own choice*, ὄλβος B.*Fr.*20; usu. of evils, *self-incurred*, πημοναί S.*OT*1231; οὐκ αὐθαίρετοι βροτοῖς ἔρωτες E.*Fr.*339; νόσοι.. αἱ μέν εἰσ' αὐ. ib.292.4; κίνδυνοι, δουλεία, Th.1.144, 6.40; θάνατος X.*HG*6.2.36; λῦπαι Men.634; δυστύχημα Id.618. Adv. **-τως** *of free choice*, Lxx 2*Ma.*6.19, al., Mitteis *Chr.*361 (iv A.D.); πείθεσθαί τινι Plu.*Pel.*24, *independently*, Luc.*Anach.*34.

⊛**αὖθε**, Thess., = αὖθι, αὖθέ περ *IG*9(2).271 (Cierium).

**αὐθ-έδραστος**, ον, *self-established*, *self-supported*, Eustr. *in EN*347.13. ⊛**-έκαστος**, ον, *one who calls things by their right names*, *downright*, *blunt*, Arist.*EN*1127$^a$23, cf. Cleanth.*Stoic.*1.127; οὐκ ἔστ' ἀλώπηξ ἡ μὲν εἴρων.. ἡ δ' αὐ. Philem.89.7, cf. Posidipp.40; in later Prose, λόγος Phld.*Piet.*102 (Comp.), cf. Ph.2.51, Plu.*Cat.Ma.*6. Adv. **-τως** *bluntly*, Phld.*Sign.*32. 2. of style, *inartificial*, *plain*, D.H.*Comp.*22. 3. in bad sense, *self-willed* (αὐτάρεσκος, Hsch.; = ἀπαρέγκλητος, Suid.), αὐ. τὸν τρόπον, τῷ τρόπῳ, Men.843, *Sam.*205, cf. Luc.*Phal.*1.2, Plu.2.11e; οὐ γὰρ αὐθάδης οὐδὲ αὐ. ὁ σώφρων ἀνήρ ib.823a, cf. Phld.*Vit.*p.30 J. 4. *self-controlled*, ζῷον οὐ μονῆρες καὶ αὐ. ἀλλὰ κοινωνικὸν καὶ πολιτικόν Them.*Or.*34 p.446 D. Adv. **-τως** Plu.*Lys.*21. **-εκαστότης**, ητος, ἡ, *bluntness*, condemned by Phryn.330.

**αὐθεντ-έω**, *to have full power* or *authority over*, τινός 1*Ep.Ti.*2.12; πρός τινα *BGU*1208.37 (i B.C.): c. inf., Lyd.*Mag.*3.42. 2. *commit a murder*, Sch.A.*Eu.*42. **-ημα**· *auctoramentum*, *Gloss.* ⊛**-ης**, ου, ὁ, (cf. αὐτοέντης) *murderer*, Hdt.1.117, E.*Rh.*873, Th.3.58; τινός E.*HF*1359, A.R.2.754; *suicide*, Antipho 3.3.4, D.C.37.13: more loosely, *one of a murderer's family*, E.*Andr.*172. 2. *perpetrator*, *author*, πράξεως Plb.22.14.2; ἱεροσυλίας D.S.16.61: generally, *doer*, Alex.*Rh.*p.2 S.; *master*, δῆμος αὐθέντης χθονός E.*Supp.*442; voc. αὐθέντα ἥλιε *PMag.Leid.W.*6.46; condemned by Phryn.96. 3. as Adj., ὅμαιμος αὐ. φόνος, αὐ. θάνατοι, murder *by one of the same family*, A.*Eu.*212, *Ag.*1572 (lyr.). (For αὐτο-έντης, cf. συν-έντης, ἀνύω; root *sen-*, *sn-*.) ⊛**-ία**, ἡ, *absolute sway*, *authority*, *CIG*2701.9 (Mylasa), *PLips.*37.7 (iv A.D.), *Corp.Herm.*1.2, Zos.2.33. 2. *restriction*, Lxx 3*Ma.*2.29. 3. αὐθεντίᾳ ἀποκτείνας *with his own hand*, D.C.*Fr.*102.12. **-ίζω**, *take in hand*, *BGU*103.3. ⊛**-ικός**, ή, όν, *principal*, ἄνεμοι *Gp.*1.11.1. 2. *warranted*, *authentic*, χειρογραφία, ἀποχή, διαθήκη, *POxy.*260.20 (i A.D.), *Ostr.*1010, *BGU*326 ii 23 (ii A.D.); *original*, ἐπιστολαί *PHamb.*18 ii 6 (iii A.D.); ἐπιθύματα *PMag.Leid.W.*9.15; ὄνομα ib.14.25; *authoritative*, Ptol.*Tetr.*182. Adv. **-κῶς**, *loqui* make an *authoritative* statement, Cic.*Att.*9.14.2; αὐ. *nuntiabatur* ib.10.9.1: Comp. -ώτερον *with higher authority*, Ptol.*Tetr.*177. **-ρια**, ἡ, fem. of αὐθέντης, = κυρία, Keil-Premerstein *Zweiter Bericht* 142.

**αὐθεύρετος**, ον, *self-discovered*, Simp. *in Ph.*1250.14.

**αὐθέψης**, ου, ὁ, (ἕψω) Lat. *authepsa*, *self-boiler*, *urn*, Cic.*Rosc. Amer.*46.133, *Hist.Aug.Elag.*19.

**αὐθημερ-εί** or **-ί**, Adv. = αὐθημερόν, *Inscr.Prien.*28.17 (ii B.C.), *IG*2.471.71, 3.73, v.l. in Sch.Aeschin.1.128. **-ίζω**, *return on the same day*, Poll.1.64. ⊛**-ινός**, ή, όν, = sq., *ephemeral*, ποιηταί Cratin.306. 2. μίσθιος αὐ. *day*-labourer, Lxx *Jb.*7.1. 3. σοφὸς αὐ., = αὐτοσχέδιος, Eust.44.14. 4. = sq., Thphr.*Sign.*10. ⊛**-ος**, ον, *made* or *done on the very day*, αὐ. ἀναπλάσσεσθαι Hp.*Art.*37; λόγοι *extemporaneous* speeches, prob. f.l. for -ημερόν in Aeschin.3.208. 2. φάρμακον αὐ. curing *in one day*, Gal.12.755. II. Adv. **αὐθημερόν** (on the accent v. Hdn.Gr.1.491) *on the very day*, *on the same day*, *immediately*, A.*Pers.*456, Ar.*Ach.*522, al., Th.2.12, D.21.89 :—also **αὐθήμερα** Hp.*Fract.*24, *Mochl.*42; Ion. **αὐτημερόν** Hdt.2.122, 6.139 (but αὐθ- in Hp.*Prog.*17, *Aph.*4.10); Locr. **αὐταμαρόν** *IG*9(1).334.33; Dor. **αὐθαμέραν** *SIG*559.57 (Megalop.); Cret. **αὐταμερίν** *GDI* 4999 (Gortyn).

⊛**αὖθι**, Adv. shortd. for αὐτόθι, of Place, *on the spot*, *here*, *there*, Il.1.492, etc.; αὖθ' ἐπὶ τάφρῳ 11.48; ἐνθάδε κ' αὖθι μένων Od.5.208; ἐν Λακεδαίμονι αὖθι Il.3.244; αὖθι ἔχειν to keep him *there*, *as he is*, Od.4.416. 2. of Time, *forthwith*, *straightway*, Il.5.296, 6.281, etc.—Ep. word, borrowed by S.*Fr.*522; cf. αὐτόθι. 3. later, = αὖθις, Lyc.732, Call.*Dian.*241, *AP*9.343 (Arch.):—also **αὖθιν** (said to be Rhegian) acc. to Theognost.*Can.*161, 163.

**αὐθιγενής**, ές, *born on the spot*, *born in the country*, *native*, Μοῦσα B.2.11; θεός Hdt.4.180; ἔθνος D.H.1.9, cf. Luc.*Herm.*24; αὐ. ποταμοὶ Σκυθικοί the Scythian rivers *that rise in the country*, Hdt.4.48; τὸ ὕδωρ.. αὐ. μὲν οὐκ ἔστι not *from a natural spring*, Id.2.149; δόκος E.*Fr.*472.5 (lyr.); οἶνος Anaxandr.41.71; αὐ. καὶ ἄκρατος ἀλλοτρίοις ἤθεσι βίος τῶν ἐνύδρων Plu.2.976a; αὐ. καὶ αὐτόχθων ἐλευθερία *IG*7.2713.38 (speech of Nero). **2.** *genuine, sincere*, ἰάλεμος E.*Rh.*895 (lyr.).

**αὐθίξας**· κινήσας, Hsch.

⊛**αὖθις**, Ep. and Ion. **αὖτις** (also in S.*Ichn.*227,229, *Fr.*599, cod. Laur. in Id.*OC*234 (lyr.), 1438, and Men.*Epit.*362, *Sam.*281,292), Adv., a lengthd. form of αὖ: **I.** of Place, *back, back again*, αὖτις ἰών Il.8.271, al.; ἂψ αὖτις ib.335; τὴν αὐτὴν ὁδὸν αὖτις 6.391; rare later, δευρὶ καὖθις ἐκεῖσε Ar.*Ra.*1077. **II.** of Time, *again, anew*, Il.4.222, etc.; freq. strengthd., ὕστερον αὖ. 1.27, cf. S.*Aj.*858; ἔτ' αὖ. Il.9.375; πάλιν αὖ. 5.257, S.*Fr.*487; αὖ. πάλιν Id.*OC*364, etc.; αὖ. αὖ πάλιν ib.1418 codd.; αὖ πάλιν αὖθις Ar.*Nu.*975; μάλ' αὖ. A.*Ch.*654,876, *Ag.*1345; βοᾶν αὖθις cry *encore!* X.*Smp.*9.4. **2.** *in turn*, αὖθις ἐγὼ αὐτοὺς ἀνηρώτων Pl.*Chrm.*153d. **3.** of future Time, *hereafter*, ταῦτα μεταφρασόμεσθα καὶ αὖ. Il.1.140, cf. A.*Ag.*317, S.*Aj.*1283, Antipho 5.94, Isoc.4.110; ὁ αὖ. χρόνος Pl.*Lg.*934a; οἱ αὖ. *posterity*, S.E.*M.*1.53. **III.** of sequence, *in turn*, A.*Th.*576, S.*OT*1403, Pl.*Ap.*24b; *on the other hand*, οὔτ' ἀβέλτερος οὔτ' αὖ. ἔμφρων Alex.245.8; sts. in apodosi for δέ, τοῦτο μέν.. τοῦτ' αὖθις.. S.*Ant.*167; πρῶτα μέν.. αὖτις δέ.. Hdt.7.102.

**αὐθίτελής**, ές, *decided on the spot*, δίκαι prob. in *OGI*7.4 (Cyme).

**αὐθ-όμαιμος**, strengthd. for ὅμαιμος, S.*OC*335, Lyc.222. **-ομολογέομαι**, *confess of oneself*, πρᾶγμα αὐθομολογούμενον a thing *that speaks for itself*, Luc.*Herm.*59 (dub. for αὖθις ὁμ.).

**αὐθόρης**· αὐτὸς βλέπων, Hsch. **αὐθορόν**· σύντομον, and **αὐθορίτους**· συντόμους, Id.; cf. αὐθωρός.

**αὐθ-όρμητος**, ον, *self-impelled*, Eustr.*inEN*33.29, Eust.1148.13. Adv. -τως Id.1370.23:—also **-ορμητικῶς** Sch.E.*Hec.*1227. **-ύπαρκτος**, ον, *self-subsistent*, Hsch. Adv. -τως Zonar.s.v. ἕνωσις. ⊛**-υπόστᾰτος**, ον, *self-substantial*, Jul.*Or.*4.139d, Iamb.ap.Stob.2.8.45, Procl.*in Prm.*p.610S. Adv. -τως Phlp.*in de An.*52.19. **-υπότακτος** (sc. χρόνος), ὁ, *the subjunctive aor.* 2, sts. also, *aor.* 1, Hdn.*Epim.*278, *AB*1086. Adv. -τως *in the subjunctive of this tense*, ibid. **-ωρός**, όν, *in that very hour*, ἀγώγιμον αὐθωρόν, of a spell, *taking immediate effect*, *PMag.Lond.*121.300. Adv. -ρόν *immediately*, Hp.*Mochl.*2, Str.3.5.7, *PFlor.*186.10 (iii A.D.), Eun.*VS*p.471B., Agath.3.9:—also **αὐθωρεί** or -ρί, Lxx *Da.*3.15, 3*Ma.*3.25, Cic.*Att.*2.13.1, Plu.2.512e.

**αὐΐᾰχος** [ῐ], ον, (i.e. ἀ-ϝίαχος) either, **1.** (from ἀ- copul., ἰαχή) *joining in a shout*, or, **2.** (from ἀν- or ἀ- priv.) *noiseless*, ἄβρομοι αὐΐαχοι Il.13.41, cf. Q.S.13.70:—ἀνίαχοι is v.l. in Il. l.c. and read by codd. in Q.S. l.c., cf. Hsch.

**αὐίδετος**, i.e. ἀ-ϝίδετος, ον, *unseen*, Hsch. **αὐκάν**· ἀλκάν (Cret.), Id. **αὐκήλως**· ἕως (Tyrrhen.), Id. **αὐκηρεσίη**· ἀφθάρτη, Id. **αὐκυών**· ἀλκ- (Cret.), Id.

**αὐλά**· πανδέκτης, Hsch.

**αὐλαϝυδός**, ὁ, later Boeot. for αὐλῳδός, *IG*7.3195 (Orchom. Boeot.).

**αὐλαία**, ἡ, (αὐλή) *curtain*, Hyp.*Fr.*139, Thphr.*Char.*5.9, Men.834, *Michel*832.26 (Samos, iv B.C.), Plu.*Alex.*49; esp. in the theatre, Men. l.c.; *hunting-net*, Plu.*Alex.*40: in pl., *screens* to protect a wall against missiles, Ph.*Bel.*95.34.

**αὐλαῖος**, α, ον, = αὔλειος, θύρα Lxx 2*Ma.*14.41:—as Subst., perh. *doorkeeper*, Baillet *Inscriptions des tombeaux des rois à Thèbes* 199.

**αὐλᾰκ-εργάτης** [γᾰ], ου, ὁ, (αὖλαξ) *tracing furrows*, *AP*9.742 (Phil. (?)). **-ίζω**:—Med., fut. -ίσομαι *PFlor.*326.10 (ii A.D.):—*trace furrows on, plough*, ἐδάφη *PFlor.* l.c.:—Pass., ib.331.7 (ii A.D.); αὐλακισμέναν ἀρούν, prov. of doing work over again, Pratin.Lyr.3: metaph. of a shooting star *leaving a trail*, *Cat.Cod.Astr.*8(3).182.4. **-ιον**, τό, Dim. of αὖλαξ, Sch.D.T.p.196 H. **-ισμός**, ὁ, *ploughing*, *PFlor.*354.3 (ii A.D.).

**αὐλᾰκο-ειδής**, ές, *furrow-like*, γραμμή Eust.598.34. **-εις**, εσσα, εν, *furrowed*, Max.506. **-τομέω**, *cut into furrows*, οὐσίαν S.E.*M.*9.40 (Pass.).

**αὐλᾰκώδης**, ες, *like a furrow*, φυτεία Eust.831.59.

⊛**αὖλαξ**, ᾰκος, ἡ (also ὁ, *AP*9.274 (Phil.), Aret.*SD*2.13), also **ἄλοξ**, οκος (q.v.); **ὦλξ**, found only in acc. ὦλκα, ὦλκας; Dor. **ὦλαξ** *EM* 625.38:—*furrow* made in ploughing, [βόε] ἱεμένω κατὰ ὦλκα hastening along *the furrow*, Il.13.707; κατὰ ὦλκας A.R.3.1054; εἰ ὦλκα διηνεκέα προταμοίμην Od.18.375; [βόε] ἐρίσαντε ἐν αὔλακι Hes.*Op.*439; ἰθεῖαν κ' αὔλακ' ἐλαύνοι ib.443; ὀρθὰς αὔλακας.. ἤλαυνε Pi.*P.*4.227; ἀρότρῳ ἀναρρηγνύντες αὔλακας Hdt.2.14; αἰθέρος αὔλακα τέμνων Ar.*Av.*1400 (lyr.); ἐξ ἀλόκων ἐπετειᾶν A.*Ag.*1015; βαθεῖαν ἄλοκα διὰ φρενὸς καρπούμενος Id.*Th.*593; ἐν ἄλοκι Ar.*Av.*234 (lyr.). **b.** *furrow's breadth*, Thphr.*HP*8.8.7, *CP*4.12.1. **2.** metaph., *wife*, σπείρειν τέκνων ἄλοκα E.*Ph.*18; αἱ πατρῷαι ἄλοκες thy father's *wife*, S.*OT*1211. **3.** metaph., *furrow in the skin, gash, wound*, ὄνυχος ἄλοκι νεοτόμῳ A.*Ch.*25 (lyr.); δορὸς ἄλοκα E.*HF*164; of the line drawn by the stile in writing, ποίαν αὔλακα; Ar.*Th.*782 (anap.), cf. *AP* 6.68 (Jul. Aegypt.). **4.** *swathe*, Theoc.10.6. **5.** αὐ. ὑδροφόρος aque-*duct*, *IG*14.453 (Catana). **b.** αὔλακας· κοίλους τόπους, Hsch.—Chiefly poet., never in good Att. Prose; Hom. only in acc. ὦλκα; αὖλαξ only is used by Pi. and Hdt., ἄλοξ only by Trag.; both αὖλαξ and ἄλοξ by Ar. (Cf. Lac. εὐλάκα 'plough', Lith. *velkù*, Slav. *vlěką* 'pull'.)

**αὐλαρός**· αὐλωρός, Hsch.

**αὐλ-άρχης**, ου, ὁ, *chief of the court, mayor of the palace*, Lxx 2*Ki.*8.18:—hence Subst. **-αρχία**, ἡ, ib.3*Ki.*3.1.

**αὐλάχα**· ἡ ὕννις, Hsch.

**αὐλεία**, ἡ, = αὐλαία, *IG*5(1).1390.35 (Andania, i B.C.).

**αὔλειος**, α, ον, sts. also ος, ον (cf. infr.):—*of* or *belonging to the court*, ἐπ' αὐλείῃσι θύρῃσι at the door *of the court*, i.e. the *outer* door, *house*-door, Od.11.239, cf. Pi.*N.*1.19, Hdt.6.69; αὔλειοι θύραι Sol.4.28; ἐπὶ προθύροις.. οὐδοῦ ἔπ' αὐλείου Od.1.104; ἐκτὸς αὐ. πυλῶν S.*Ant.*18; πρὸς αὐλείοισιν ἑστηκὼς πύλαις E.*Hel.*438: sg., ἡ αὔλειος θύρα Lys.1.17, Pl.*Smp.*212c, Thphr.*Char.*28.3, Men.546; ἡ αὐλεία θύρα *IG*11(2).287*A*146 (Delos, iii B.C.), Thphr.*Char.*18.4; ἡ αὐλεία alone, Ar.*Pax*982, *Fr.*255, *SIG*²587.122; ἡ αὔλειος Plu.*Pomp.*46, 2.516f, Luc.*Tox.*17; αἱ αὔλειοι Plb.5.76.4.

**αὐλείτης**, ου, ὁ, = αὐλίτης, A.R.4.1487 codd.; for Boeot. αὐλειτάς v. αὐλητής.

⊛**αὐλέω**, Boeot. part. αὐλίων *IG*7.3211,3212 (Orchom. Boeot.): (αὐλός):—*play on the flute*, Φρύγιον αὔλησεν μέλος Alcm.82, cf. Hdt.1.141, 2.60, Pl.*Prt.*327a: c. dat. pers., X.*Smp.*2.8, etc.; αὐ. ἔξοδον *play* a finale, Ar.*V.*582; αὐ. εἰρεσίαν, of the boatswain, Plu.*Alc.*32:—Pass., of tunes, *to be played on the flute*, ὁ Βακχεῖος ῥυθμὸς ηὐλεῖτο X.*Smp.*9.3; αὐλεῖται πᾶν μέλαθρον *is filled with music*, E.*IT*367. **2.** of persons, *play to*, Philostr.*VA*2.34, cf. A.D.*Synt.*302.1:—mostly in Pass., *to be played to, hear music*, X.*An.*6.1.11, *Cyr.*4.5.7, Arist.*Pr.*917ᵇ19 (but possibly Med. as in Pl.*Lg.*791a), Thphr.*Char.*19.10, 20.10. **II.** generally, *play*, κέρατι Luc.*DDeor.*12.1, cf. Poll.4.74.

⊛**αὐλή**, ἡ, *open court* before the house, *courtyard*, Il.4.433, 11.774, *SIG*1044.17 (Halic., iv/iii B.C.), etc. **2.** *steading* for cattle, αὐλῆς ὑπεράλμενον Il.5.138, cf. Od.14.5. **II.** later, *court* or *quadrangle*, round which the house was built, Hdt.3.77, Ar.*V.*131, Pl.*Prt.*311a, etc. **III.** generally, *court, hall*, Ζηνὸς αὐ. Od.4.74, cf. Il.6.247; τὴν Διὸς αὐλὴν A.*Pr.*122 (lyr.); αὐ. νεκύων E.*Alc.*260 (lyr.); *court* of a temple, ἱεροῦ *IG*2².1299.28 (Eleusis, iii B.C.), cf. ib.1126.35, Lxx *Ps.*83(84).3; *any dwelling, abode, chamber*, S.*Ant.*946 (lyr.), etc.; of a cave, Id.*Ph.*153 (lyr.); ἀγρόνομοι αὐλαί *homes* of dwellers in the wild, Id.*Ant.*786 (lyr.); later, *country-house*, D.H.6.50. **IV.** ἡ αὐλή *the Court*, αὐλὰς θεραπεύειν Men.897, Diph.97, *Com.Adesp.*145, cf. Plb.5.26.9; οἱ περὶ τὴν αὐλήν the *courtiers*, ib.36.1, cf. *OGI*735.4 (ii B.C.), *Inscr.Mus.Alex.*31; at Rome, Arr.*Epict.*1.10.3; ἡ βασίλειος αὐ. Hdn.3.11.7. (Wrongly expld. as τόπος διαπνεόμενος (cf. αὐλός) by Ath.5.189b.)

⊛**αὔλημα**, ατος, τό, *piece of music for the flute*, Ar.*Ra.*1302, Pl.*Smp.*216c, al.

**αὔληρα** (i.e. ἄϝληρα, cf. ἄβληρα), τά, Dor. for εὔληρα (q.v.), Epich.178: sg. in Hsch.

⊛**αὔλ-ησις**, εως, ἡ, *flute-playing*, Pl.*Prt.*327b,c, al., Arist.*Pol.*1341ᵃ25, etc. **-ητήρ**, ῆρος, ὁ, = αὐλητής, Hes.*Sc.*283, 298, Archil.123, Thgn.825, Ar.*Fr.*566. **-ητηρία**· αὐλῶν θήκη, Hsch. ⊛**-ητήριον**, τό, a place at Tarentum, Id. ⊛**-ητής**, οῦ, ὁ, *flute-player*, Thgn.941, Hdt.1.141, 6.60, 129, Ar.*V.*581, And.1.12, Pl.*Prt.*327b, *OGI*51.62 (iii B.C.); Boeot. **αὐλειτάς** *IG*7.3195 (Orchom. Boeot.). **II.** kind of *wasp*, Hsch. **III.** αὐ. ὑπονόμων sanitary *engineer*, Procl.*Par.Ptol.*250. **-ήτης**, ου, ὁ, (αὐλή III), = αὐλίτης, Hsch. ⊛**-ητικός**, ή, όν, *of* or *for the flute*, Pl.*Ap.*27b; δάκτυλοι Pl.Com.211; κάλαμος *used for making flutes*, Thphr.*HP*4.10.1, Sch.Il.*Oxy.*221 ix 12; τέλος Plot.1.4.15: -κή (sc. τέχνη), ἡ, *flute-playing*, Pl.*Grg.*501e, Arist.*Po.*1447ᵃ15. Adv. -κῶς, δεῖ καρκινοῦν τοὺς δακτύλους Antiph.55.15, cf. Plu.2.404f. **2.** *fitted for flute playing*, ψυχή Pl.*Hp.Mi.*375b (Comp.). ⊛**-ητρία**, ἡ, = αὐλητρίς, D.L.7.62. **-ητρίδιον**, τό, Dim. of sq., Theopomp.Hist.205, *Com.Adesp.*25.34 D., D.L.7.13. ⊛**-ητρίς**, ίδος, ἡ, *flute-girl*, Simon.178, Ar.*Ach.*551, X.*HG*2.2.23, Pl.*Prt.*347d, *BCH*6.24 (Delos, ii B.C.), etc.

**αὐλία**· ἔπαυλις, ἢ ἡ μικρὰ αὐλή, *AB*463.

**αὐλία** [ῠ], ἡ, (ὕλη) *immateriality*, Hierocl.*in CA*26 p.479 M., Syrian.*in Metaph.*27.30, Nicom.*Ar.*1.3.

⊛**αὐλιάδες** νύμφαι, (αὖλις) nymphs *protecting cattle-folds*, *APl.*4.291 (Anyte).

**αὐλίδιον**, τό, Dim. of αὐλή, *place of athletic exercises, ring*, Thphr.*Char.*5.9. **II.** (αὐλός) *small tube*, Alex.Trall.3.3.

**αὐλιεῖον**, τό, = αὔλιον II (nisi leg. αὔλειον), *Epigr.Gr.*1075.6 (Erythrae).

⊛**αὐλίζομαι**, aor. 1 ηὐλισάμην always in Th., as 4.13, 6.7, cf. (κατ-) Plu.*Tim.*12; ηὐλίσθην always in X., as *An.*4.1.11, al.; both in Hdt., as 8.9 (ἐν-), 9.15: late fut. αὐλισθήσομαι Lxx *To.*6.10: pf. ηὔλισμαι Arr.*An.*3.29.7, J.*BJ*1.17.5:—*lie in the* αὐλή or *courtyard*, μυκηθμοῦ.. βοῶν αὐλιζομενάων Od.12.265; κλαγγὴ.. συῶν αὐλιζομενάων 14.412; *take up one's abode, lodge, live* in a place, ἐν ἄντρῳ, of sheep, Hdt.9.93; περὶ τὴν λίμνην, of birds, 3.110, cf. Arist.*HA*619ᵃ30; οἷοις ἐν πέπλοις αὐ. E.*El.*304; ἄδειπνος.. ηὐλιζόμην *passed the night*, Eup.322; esp. as military term, *encamp, bivouac*, Hdt.8.9: Medic., of blood, *lodge* or *settle* in a place, Aret.*SA*2.2 (nisi leg. ἀλισθέν): metaph., τὸ ἑσπέρας αὐλισθήσεται κλαυθμός Lxx *Ps.*29(30).6. **II.** Act., *cause to dwell*, ib.*Je.*38(31).9, D.Chr.35.16.

**αὐλικός**, ή, όν, (αὐλή) *of the court, courtier-like*, κατὰ τὴν φύσιν Plb.23.5.4; αὐ. ἀγχίνοια 15.34.4; αὐ. βίος, opp. ὁ φιλόσοφος βίος, Phld.*Ind.Sto.*13: Comp., ἐξ αὐλικωτέρων γονέων Id.*Lib.*p.45 O.: as Subst., *courtier*, Plb.16.20.8, Plu.2.778b, *Demetr.*17. **II.** αὐλικούς· κιθαρῳδούς, Suid.

**αὐλίκουροι**· φύλακες, Hsch. **αὐλίξ**· φλέψ, Id. **αὐλίξαι**· στασιάσαι (leg. σταδ-), δραμεῖν, Id.

⊛**αὔλιον**, τό, *country-house, cottage*, *h.Merc.*103; *fold, stable*, etc.,

E.*Cyc.*345,593, X.*HG*3.2.4, etc.: prov., βοῦς ἐν αὐλίῳ 'round peg in a square hole', Cratin.32. **II.** *chamber, cave, grotto,* ἀμφιτρὴς αὐ. S.*Ph.*19, cf. 954, al., *AP*6.334 (Leon.).

⊛ **αὔλιος**, α, ον, (αὐλή I) *belonging to folds,* ἀστὴρ αὔλιος 'star *that bids the shepherd fold*', A.R.4.1630, cf. Call.*Fr.*539; ὅταν αὐλίοις συρίζῃς, ὦ Πάν, τοῖς σοῖσιν ἐν ἄντροις dub. l. in E.*Ion* 500 (lyr.). **II.** αὔλιος θύρα dub. l. in Men.546; cf. αὐλία θύρα· πυλών, Hsch.

⊛ **αὖλις**, ιδος, ἡ, *tent* or *place for passing the night in,* αὖλιν ἔθεντο Il. 9.232; αὖλιν ἐσιέμεναι to go to *roost,* of birds, Od.22.470, cf. *h.Merc.* 71, E.*Cyc.*363, Call.*Dian.*87, Theoc.25.18, Arat.1027; αἰγινόμων *AP*6.221 (Leon.).

**αὔλισις**, εως, ἡ, = αὐλισμός, Ael.*NA*4.59.

**αὐλίσκος**, ὁ, (αὐλός I. 2) *small reed, pipe,* λιγύφθογγος Thgn.241; αὐλίσκων ὑπὸ λωτίνων cj. in Pi.*Parth.*2.14: prov., φυσᾷ οὐ σμικροῖσιν αὐλίσκοις makes a great bluster, S.*Fr.*768. **II.** generally, *small pipe* or *tube,* Arist.*Ath.*68.2, Plb.27.11.2, Mnesith.ap.Orib.8.38.3; *catheter,* Hp.*Morb.*1.6. **III.** = αἰδοῖον, Ptol.*Tetr.*187, Sch.Opp. *H.*1.582, Anon.*in Ptol.Tetr.*157. **IV.** *ear-ring* (Persian), Hsch.

**αὔλ-ισμα**, ατος, τό, = sq., Sch.Opp.*H.*3.5 (pl.). **-ισμός**, ὁ, *lodging,* Sm.*Is.*10.29: = διανυκτέρευσις, Hsch. **-ιστέον**, *one must fold* or *house* cattle, *Gp.*18.3.8. **-ιστήριον**, τό, *stall, steading,* Herm.ap.Stob.1.49.68, Aq.*Is.*10.29, Hsch. s.v. συοβαύβαλοι.

**αὐλίτης** [ῑ], ου, ὁ, (αὐλή III) *farm-servant,* S.*Fr.*502, A.R.4.1487; cf. αὐλείτης, αὐλήτης.

⊛ **αὐλο-βόας**, ὁ, ἡ, *sounding the flute, flute-playing, IG*3.82. **-δόκη**, ἡ, *flute-case, AP*5.205 (Leon.). **-θετέω**, *make flutes* or *pipes,* ib.6.120 (Leon.). **-θήκη**, ἡ, *flute-case,* Hsch.s.v. συρβηνεύς, Sch.Ar.*Th.* 1197. **-μᾰνέω**, *play the flute in mystic orgies,* D.S.36.4. **-μᾰνής**, ές, *flute-inspired,* Nonn.*D.*8.29. **-μελῳδία**, ἡ, *flute-* or *pipe-music,* Ps.-Callisth.1.46. **-ποιΐα**, ἡ, *flute-making,* Poll.7.153. **-ποιϊκή** (sc. τέχνη), ἡ, = foreg., Pl.*Euthd.*289c:—also **-ποιητική**, Asp.*in EN* 15.24: hence Adv. -ητικῶς Poll.7.153. ⊛ **-ποιός**, ὁ, *flute-maker,* Pl.*R.*399d, 601d, Arist.*Pol.*1277$^b$29, Dsc.2.75.

⊛ **αὐλός**, ὁ, *pipe, flute, clarionet,* Il.10.13, 18.495, *h.Merc.*452; Λύδιος Pi.*O.*5.19; Ἔλυμος, i.e. Φρύγιος (q.v.), S.*Fr.*398; Λίβυς E.*Alc.*347; αὐ. γυναικήιος, ἀνδρήιος, Hdt.1.17; αὐ. ἀνδρεῖοι, παιδικοί, παρθένιοι, Ath.4.176f, Poll.4.81; ὁ παρθένιος αὐ. τοῦ παιδικοῦ ὀξύτερος Arist. *HA*581$^b$11; διδύμοις αὐλοῖσιν ἀείσαι Theoc.*Ep.*5.1; ἐμφυσᾶν εἰς αὐλούς D.S.3.59; αὐ. Ἐνυαλίου, i.e. *a trumpet, AP*6.151 (Tymn.); ὑπ' αὐλοῦ to the sound of *the flute,* Hdt.l.c.; πρὸς τὸν αὐ., ὑπὸ τὸν αὐ., X.*Smp.*6.3, etc.: pl., αὐλοὶ πηκτίδος *pipes* of the πηκτίς, *IG*4.53 (Aegina). **2.** *hollow tube, pipe, groove,* περόνη τέτυκτο αὐλοῖσιν διδύμοισι the buckle was furnished with two *pipes* or *grooves* (into which the tongue fitted), Od.19.227; ἐγκέφαλος παρ' αὐλὸν ἀνέδραμε spirted up beside *the vizard* (cf. αὐλῶπις), or beside *the socket of the spear-head* into which the shaft fitted, Il.17.297; but in Od. 22.18 αὐλὸς παχύς means the *jet* of blood *through the tube* of the nostril; αὐλὸς ἐκ χαλκείου the smith's *bellows,* Hp.*Art.*47,77, cf. Th.4.100; *tube* of the clepsydra, Arist.*Pr.*914$^b$14; βλέπειν δι' αὐλοῦ Id.*GA*780$^b$19. **3.** in animals, *blow-hole* of cetacea, Id.*HA*589$^b$19, *PA*697$^a$17; *funnel* of a cuttle-fish, Id.*HA*524$^a$10; *conus arteriosus* in fishes, ib.507$^a$10, *Resp.*478$^b$8; *duct,* prob. in Id.*GC*322$^a$ 28. **4.** *stadium* (cf. δίαυλος), Lyc.40. **5.** *haulm* of grain, Sch. Theoc.10.46. **6.** *cow-bane, Cicuta virosa,* Ps.-Plu.*Fluv.*10.3. **7.** εἶδος ἀκολάστου σχήματος, *EM*170.28. **II.** *razor-shell,* = σωλήν (q.v.), Diph.Siph.ap.Ath.3.90d, Plin.*HN*32.103.

**ἄϋλος** [ῡ], ον, *immaterial,* dub. in Arist.*GC*322$^a$28 (v. foreg. I. 3); ἀρετή Plu.2.440e; θεός ib.1085c; οὐσία Jul.*Or.*4.140c; τὸ ἄ. Hierocl. *in CA*26 p.481 M.: Comp. -ότερος, νοῦς Ph.1.61. Adv. -λως Plot.1. 3.6, Iamb.*Myst.*5.15, Simp.*in Cael.*441.4, etc. **2.** v. ἄνυλος.

**αὐλοστατέω**, *set up a farmstead, Schwyzer* 197.54,62 (Crete, iii B.C.).

⊛ **ἀϋλότης**, ητος, ἡ, *immateriality,* Plot.1.2.7.

**αὐλο-τρύπης** [ῠ], ου, ὁ, *flute-borer,* Stratt.3, Arist.*Pr.*919$^b$7. **-τρῡπητικῶς**, Adv. *belonging to flute-boring,* Poll.7.153.

**αὐλουρός**, ὁ, *keeper of the court* or *fold,* Hsch.

**αὐλῳδ-έω**, *sing to the flute,* Sch.Ar.*Nu.*971. **-ία**, ἡ, *song to the flute,* Pl.*Lg.*700d, Plu.2.1132f. **-ικός**, ή, όν, *belonging to* αὐλῳδία, νόμοι ib.1132c, etc. **-ός**, ὁ, *one who sings to the flute, SIG*457.19 (Thespiae, iii B.C.), Plu.2.150a, Ath.14.621b; cf. αὐλαῳδός.

**αὐλωλάζειν**· τὸ συρ(ίττ)ειν διὰ τῶν δακτύλων, Hsch.

⊛ **αὐλών**, ῶνος, ὁ, also ἡ S.*Fr.*549, Ar.*Av.*244, Carc.1, Philostr.*Im.* 2.6:—*hollow* between hills or banks, *defile, glen, h.Merc.*95, Hdt.7. 128,129, Ar.l.c. (lyr.); expld. as οἱ στενοὶ καὶ ἐπιμήκεις ποταμοί Sch. Il.*Oxy.*221 xiv 19. **2.** *channel, trench,* A.*Fr.*167 A, Hdt.2.100,127, X.*An.*2.3.10. **3.** *strait,* Μαιωτικός A.*Pr.*731; πόντιαι αὐ. *sea-straits, channels,* S.*Tr.*100 (lyr.). **4.** *pipe, conduit,* Pl.*Ti.*79a; metaph. of *windpipe* or *duct,* Arist.*PA*664$^a$27, Gal.*UP*4.14. **5.** *furrow* in an elephant's hide, Aret.*SD*2.13.

**Αὐλωνεύς**, έως, ὁ, title of Dionysus, *IG*3.193.

**αὐλωνιάς**, άδος, ἡ, *glen-nymph,* Orph.*H.*51.7.

⊛ **αὐλωνίζω**, *live in an* αὐλών, Hsch.

**αὐλωνίσκος**, ὁ, Dim. of αὐλών, Thphr.*HP*9.7.1.

**αὐλωνοειδής**, ές, *full of valleys,* D.S.19.17; *in the shape of an* αὐλών, εἰσβολὴ νήσου Id.3.68.

**αὐλωπίας**, ου, ὁ (Dor. gen. ια Archestr.*Fr.*33), a large fish, similar to ἀνθίας, perh. *Serranus gigas,* Arist.*HA*570$^b$19, Henioch.3.4, Ael. *NA*13.17; cf. αὐλωπός.

**αὐλῶπις**, ιδος, ἡ, (ὤψ) in Il. always epith. of τρυφάλεια, helmet *with a tube-like opening* between the cheek-pieces (acc. to Sch. *with a tube* (αὐλός) *to hold the* λόφος), Il.5.182, al.; λόγχη *with a socket* to hold the shaft, S.*Fr.*1027; περικεφαλαία *conical,* Ath.5.189c, cf. Hsch.

**αὐλωπός**, ὁ, = αὐλωπίας, Opp.*H.*1.256.

**αὐλωτός**, ή, όν, *furnished with pipes,* φιμοί A.*Fr.*326. **II.** *pipe-shaped,* Ath.Mech.24.3.

**αὖμα**· ἅλμα (Cret.), Hsch.

**αὐνή**, ἡ, prob. f.l. for Ἄχνη in Hecat.365 J.; cf. St.Byz. s.v. Ἴχναι.

**αὐξάνιος** [ᾰ], ον, (αὔξω, ἀνία) *increasing grief,* δάπεδον *JHS*34.18 (Xanthus).

⊛ **αὐξάνω** Pi.*Fr.*153, Hdt.7.16.α', A.*Pers.*756, E.*Supp.*233, *Fr.*362. 28, Pl.*Ti.*41d:—also **αὔξω** (poet. ἀέξω, q.v.) Thgn.823, Pi.*O.*5.4, Emp.37, S.*Tr.*117 (lyr.), Ar.*Ach.*227, X.*Smp.*7.4, Pl.*R.*573a, D. 3.26, etc. (so Att. Inscrr. and Ptolemaic Pap.; both forms in *NT*): impf. ηὔξανον only Ps.-E.*Fr.*1132.25; ηὖξον Hdt.9.31, etc.: fut. αὐξήσω Th.6.40, etc. (αὐξανῶ only in Lxx *Ge.*17.6, al.): aor. 1 ηὔξησα Sol. 11, X.*HG*7.1.24: pf. ηὔξηκα Pl.*Ti.*90b, X.*Hier.*2.15:—Pass., αὐξάνομαι Hdt.2.14, E.*Med.*918, Ar.*Av.*1065, Isoc.4.104, Pl.*Phd.*96c, D. 18.161; αὔξομαι Emp.26.2, Ar.*Ach.*227, Pl.*R.*328d, etc., impf. ηὔξετο Hes.*Th.*493, Hdt.3.39 (v. l. αὔξετο): pf. ηὔξημαι E.*IA*1248, Pl.*R.* 371e, Ion. αὔξ- Hdt.1.58: plpf. ηὔξητο Id.5.78: aor. ηὐξήθην Th.1.89, Pl.*Prt.*327c: fut. αὐξηθήσομαι D.56.48; αὐξήσομαι X.*Cyr.*6.1.12, Pl.*R.* 497a:—*increase,* not in Hom. (only ἀέξω), Pi.*Fr.*153, etc.; ὕβριν αὐ. Hdt.7.16.α'; ὄλβον A.*Pers.*756; opp. ἰσχναίνειν, Pl.*Plt.*293b; εἰς ἄπειρον αὐ. τι Id.*Lg.*910b; ἐπὶ τὸ ἔσχατον Id.*R.*573a; ἐπὶ πλεῖον ηὖξον τὴν μαγειρικὴν τέχνην Athenio1.16, etc. **2.** *increase in power, strengthen,* αὐ. τὰ Ἑλλήνων *increase* their power, Hdt.8.30; νόμοισιν αὐ. πόλιν S.*Ant.*191, cf. X.*Mem.*3.7.2; *exalt by one's deeds, glorify,* πόλιν, πάτραν, Pi.*O.*5.4, *P.*8.38, cf. *IG*2$^2$.834, etc.; *exalt by praise, extol,* ἐπαινεῖν καὶ αὔξειν τινά Pl.*Ly.*206a; σέ γε.. καὶ τροφὸν καὶ ματέρ' αὔξειν *honour* thee *as*.., S.*OT*1092 (lyr.); of an orator, *amplify, exaggerate,* αὔξειν καὶ μειοῦν Arist.*Rh.*1403$^a$17. **3.** with an Adj., τρέφειν καὶ αὐ. τινὰ μέγαν *bring up* to manhood, Pl.*R.*565c; μείζω πόλιν αὐ. E.*IA*572 (lyr.); τὸν ὄγκον.. ἄπειρον αὐξήσει Pl.*R.*591d. **4.** αὔξειν ἔμπυρα *to sacrifice,* Pi.*I.*4(3).62; cf. ἀέξω. **5.** in Logic, = καταπυκνόω (q.v.), Arist.*APo.*79$^a$30, al.; but ὁ αὐξόμενος λόγος, name of a *fallacy,* Plu.*Thes.*23, 2.559b. **II.** Pass., *grow, increase,* in size, number, strength, power, etc., Hes.*Th.*493, Pi.*P.*8.93, D.61.5, etc.; αὐ. ἐς πλῆθος, ἐς ὕψος, Hdt.1.58, 2.14; of a child, *grow up,* Id.5.92.ε'; ἐν γὰρ τοῖς πόνοισιν αὔξεται, of Theseus, E.*Supp.*323; ηὐξανόμην ἀκούων I *grew taller* as I heard, Ar.*V.*638; of the wind, *rise,* Hdt.7.188; ηὔξηται ἡ πόλις ὥστ' εἶναι τελέα Pl.*R.*371e. **2.** with an Adj., αὔξεσθαι μέγας *wax* great, *grow* up, E.*Ba.*183; αὐ. μείζων A.*Supp.* 338, Pl.*Lg.*681a; αὐ. ἐλλόγιμος Id.*Prt.*327c; μέγας ἐκ μικροῦ.. ηὔξηται D.9.21. **III.** later, Act. intr., like Pass., ἡ σελήνη αὐξάνει Arist. *APo.*78$^b$6, cf. *HA*620$^a$21, Aristeas 208, D.S.4.64, *Ep.Col.*2.19, D. Chr.4.128, D.C.48.52, etc. **IV.** of Verbs, *take the augment,* both Act. and Pass., Hdn.*Epim.*280; αὔξουσα (sc. συλλαβή), ἡ, *augment,* ibid. (Cf. ἀέξω.)

**αὔξ-η**, ἡ, = αὔξησις, dub. l. in Hp.*Nat.Puer.*16, the form preferred by Pl.; σώματος αὐ. καὶ φθίσις *R.*521e; τὴν γένεσιν καὶ αὔξην καὶ τροφήν ib.509b, cf. Chrysipp.*Stoic.*2.157: also in pl., Pl.*Phlb.*42d. **II.** *dimension,* ἡ τῶν κύβων αὐ. Id.*R.*528b. **-ημα**, ατος, τό, = foreg., Hp.*Oct.*11, E.*Hyps.Fr.*3 ii 5 (lyr.). **-ηρός**, όν, dub. l. in Nic.*Al.* 588. ⊛ **-ησία**, Ion. -ίη, ἡ, *the goddess of growth,* Hdt.5.82, *IG*5(1). 363 (i A.D.). ⊛ **-ησις**, εως, ἡ, *growth, increase,* Hp.*VM*6; τῶν ἐχθρῶν Th.1.69, cf. Plu.*TG*13; κατὰ τὸ ποσὸν Arist.*Metaph.*1069$^b$ 11; of the Delta, Hdt.2.13: in pl., *increments,* Pl.*R.*546b; *multiplications,* Ascl.*Tact.*2.7. **2.** *amplification,* in Rhet., Arist.*Rh.*1368$^a$ 27, 1413$^b$34; μετ' αὐξήσεως ἐξαγγέλλειν Plb.10.27.8, cf. D.H.*Th.*19 (pl.). **3.** Gramm., *the augment, EM*338.47. **-ησίφως**, *increasing light,* epith. of a solar divinity, *PMag.Par.*1.601. ⊛ **-ητέον**, *one must amplify, exaggerate,* Men.Rh.p.359 S. **-ητής**, οῦ, ὁ, *increaser,* Orph.*H.*11.11, 15.8. **-ητικός**, ή, όν, *growing, of growth,* ἡ αὐ. ζωή Arist.*EN*1098$^a$1; ψυχή Id.*Juv.*469$^a$26; αὐ. εἰς μῆκος Thphr. *HP*1.9.1. Adv. -κῶς, κινεῖσθαι Ph.1.492. **II.** Act., *promoting growth,* c. gen., σπληνός Hp.*Acut.*62; μεγέθους S.E.*M.*3.24: abs., τροφή Arist.*GA*745$^a$3; -κόν, τό, Id.*Cael.*310$^a$29. **2.** metaph., *amplificatory,* in Rhet., Id.*Rh.*1368$^a$10, Longin.11.2, etc. Adv. -κῶς Id.38. 2, Sch.Il.*Oxy.*221 ix 31. **III.** *productive,* Aq.*Is.*32.12. **-ητός**, όν, *that may be increased,* Arist.*Cael.*310$^a$28. **II.** *increased,* ἀριθμός Antioch.Astr. in *Cat.Cod.Astr.*1.112.34.

⊛ **αὖξι**, *prosper!* in epitaphs, *Princeton Exp.Inscr.*568, al.; cf. αὐξίτω ib.159 (V A.D.).

**αὐξί-δημος** [ῐ], *increasing the people,* epith. of Hermes, Hsch. **-θᾰλής**, ές, (θάλλω) *promoting growth,* Orph.*H.*26.3. **-κερως**, ω, *with rising horns,* Archipp.11 (Dind.).

**αὔξῐμος**, ον, *promoting growth,* Hp.*Vict.*2.65 (Comp.), v.l. in Emp. 100.15, X.*Cyn.*7.3. **II.** intr., *growing,* Hp.*Art.*58, *Vict.*1.25, A. *Fr.*51, E.ap.*Lex.Sabb.*1.4, *Com.Adesp.*37 D.

⊛ **αὖξις**, εως, ἡ, = αὔξησις, Hsch.

⊛ **αὐξίς**, ίδος, ἡ, Byz. for κορδύλη or σκορδύλη, *young of the tunny,* Phryn.Com.56, Arist.*HA*571$^a$17, Nic.*Al.*469.

**αὐξί-τροφος** [ῐ], ον, *promoting growth,* Orph.*H.*10.17, 51.13. ⊛ **-φαής**, ές, *increasing light,* Man.5.174, *Cat.Cod.Astr.*8(4).217. ⊛ **-φωνος**, ον, *strengthening the voice,* Philem.Lex.s.v. ἀλεξίκακος. **-φωτέω**, *increase in light, wax,* of the moon, Vett.Val.196.16, Paul Al.*M.*4. **-φωτία**, ἡ, *increase of light,* Lyd.*Mens.*4.71. ⊛ **-φωτος**, ον, *waxing in light, EM*59.40.

**αὐξο-βίος** [ῐ], ον, *increasing in wealth*, Cat.Cod.Astr.8(4).119. **-μειόω**, *cause to wax and wane*, Ptol.*Alm*.6.7:—Pass., αὐξομειουμένη Σελήνη Vett.Val.331.28. ❀ **-μείωσις**, εως, ἡ, *rise and fall of the tide*, Str.*Chr*.3.26 (pl.). II. *waxing and waning of the moon*, Ant. Diog.4 (pl.; also περὶ τοὺς οἰκείους ὀφθαλμούς ibid.), Ptol.*Alm*.2.1 (pl.); *variation in period*, ζῳδίων Cat.Cod.Astr.1.163.13. **-σέληνον**, τό, *increase of the moon, the waxing moon*, *AP*5.270 (Maced.).

**αὐξύνω**, aor. Pass. ηὐξύνθην, late form of αὐξάνω, Aesop.51.

**Αὐξώ**, οῦς, ἡ, (αὐξάνω) *goddess of growth*, called to witness in an Athenian citizen's oath, Paus.9.35.2, Poll.8.106.

**αὔξω**, v. αὐξάνω.

**αὐόκωλος**, ον, *withered of limb*, Semon.7.76 (prob. αὐτόκ-).

**αὐονή** (A), ἡ, (αὖος) *dryness, withering, drought*, Archil.125, A.*Eu*. 333 (lyr.), Herod.8.2.

**αὐονή** (B), ἡ, (αὔω B) *cry*, Semon.7.20.

❀ **αὖος**, η, ον, Att. **αὗος**, α, ον, also ος, ον Arist.*Pr*.860a28, Philostr. *VS*1.21.1:—*dry*, ξύλον *a pole*, Il.23.327; αὖα παλαί, περίκηλα, of timber, Od.5.240, cf. Pl.*Lg*.761c; αὔην καὶ διερὴν ἀρόων (sc. γῆν) Hes.*Op*.460; βόας αὔας shields of ox-hide, Il.12.137, cf.17.493; so, of hippopotamus' hide, Hdt.2.71; τρύφος ἄρτου *stale*, *AP*6.105 (Apollonid.); *withered*, στέφανος Ar.*Eq*.534. 2. of sound, αὖον ἀϋτεῖν or αὔειν give *a dry, rasping* sound, κόρυθες δ' ἀμφ' αὖον ἀΰτευν Il.12.160; αὖον ἄϋσεν [θώρηξ] 13.441; αὖον δέ μοι οἶκος ἀϋτεῖ prob. in Epic. *Oxy*. 1794.8. 3. αὖον ἀπὸ χλωροῦ τάμνειν, i.e. to cut the nail from the quick, Hes.*Op*.743. 4. *drained dry, exhausted*, Alex.158, Theoc.8. 48 (Comp.), prob. in Ant.Lib.24.1. 5. *thirsty*, δίψῃ αὔη *IG*14.638 (Petelia), cf. *GDI*4959a (Eleutherna), Luc.*Luct*.8. 6. *trembling, shivering* (like a dry leaf), of the aged, Ar.*Lys*.385; esp. of fear, αὖός εἰμι τῷ δέει Men.*Epit*.480, cf.*Pk*.163, J.*BJ*1.19.5: abs., ib.6.4.2, Hld.1.12. 7. metaph., 'stony broke', *without money*, Luc.*Tox*. 16, *DMeretr*.14.1, Alciphr.3.70. 8. of lit. style, *dry*, ἰδέα λόγων Philostr.*VS*1.20.2. 9. αὔη ψυχὴ σοφωτάτη dub. in Heraclit.118. (Cf. Lith. *saũsas* 'dry', OE. *séar*.)

**αὐότης**, Att. **αὑότης**, ητος, ἡ, *dryness*, Arist.*HA*518a11.

**ἀϋπν-έω**, *to be sleepless*, Philostr.*Gym*.53:—Med., ἀϋπνέομαι Phryn. *PS*p.9 B. ❀ **-ία**, ἡ, *sleeplessness*, Pl.*Lg*.807e, Max.Tyr.5.1; ἐν ὕπνῳ ἀ. Aret.*SD*2.6. ❀ **-ος**, ον, *sleepless, wakeful*, of persons, Od.9.404, 10.84, 19.591, A.*Pr*.32, E.*Or*.83, X.*Cyr*.2.4.26: Sup. **-ότατος**, τῶν στρατηγῶν D.C.72.8; ἔχειν ἀΰπνους ἄγρας, of fishermen, S.*Aj*.880; of the eye, ἄϋπνά τ' ὀμμάτων τέλη E.*Supp*.1137: metaph., *sleepless, never-resting*, ἄ. πηδάλια dub. in A.*Th*.206 (lyr.); κρῆναι S.*OC*685 (lyr.); ἀκταί E.*IT*423 (lyr.). Adv. **-νως** Sannyr.2 D. 2. of nights, *sleepless*, πολλὰς μὲν ἀΰπνους νύκτας ἴαυον Il.9.325, Od.19.340; also ὕπνος ἄ. a sleep *that is no sleep, from which one easily awakes*, S.*Ph*.848 (lyr.). **-οσύνη**, ἡ, = ἀϋπνία, Q.S.2.155.

❀ **αὔρα**, Ion. **αὔρη**, ἡ, *breeze*, esp. *a cool breeze* from water (cf. Arist. *Mu*.394b13), or *the fresh air* of morning, once in Hom., αὔρη δ' ἐκ ποταμοῦ ψυχρὴ πνέει Od.5.469, cf. *h.Merc*.147, Hes.*Op*.670, etc.: rare in early Prose, αὔρας ἀποπνεούσας [ὁ Νεῖλος] μοῦνος οὐ παρέχεται Hdt. 2.19; αὔρα φέρουσα ἀπὸ χρηστῶν τόπων ὑγίειαν Pl.*R*.401c, cf. X.*HG* 6.2.29, *Smp*.2.25. 2. metaph., θυμιαμάτων αὖραι *the steam* of incense, Ar.*Av*.1717; ἐνθαῖσιν αὔραις σῶμα πᾶν ἀγάλλεται, of a well-fried fish, Antiph.217.22; δεῖπνον ὄζον αὔρας Ἀττικῆς Dionys.Com. 2.40; αὔρη φιλοτησίη of the attractive influence of the female, Opp. *H*.4.114. 3. metaph., of *the changeful course of events*, μετάτροποι πνέουσιν αὖ. δόμων E.*El*.1148 (lyr.); πολέμου μετάτροπος αὖ. Ar.*Pax* 945; of a bodily *thrill*, E.*Hipp*.166; ψυχᾶς ἀδόλοις αὔραις guileless *movements* of soul, Id.*Supp*.1029 (lyr.), cf. 1048. 4. Αὖραι personified, Q.S.1.684, Orph.*A*.340. 5. *epileptic aura*, Gal.8.94, Alex. Trall.1.15. (Cf. ἀήρ (ἀ*ϝ*έρ-), ἄελλα, ἄημι.)

❀ **αὔρηκτος**, Aeol. for ἄ-ϝρηκτος, *unbroken*, Hdn.Gr.2.171, Eust.548. 31.

**αὖρι**, = ταχέως, *AB*464.

**αὐρῐβάτης** [βᾰ], ου, ὁ, (v. foreg.) *swift-striding*, A.*Fr*.280.

**αὐρίγαμμος**, ον, (*aurum*, γάμμα) *adorned with a golden* Γ, παραγαῦδαι Lyd.*Mag*.2.4.

**αὐρίζω**, *procrastinate*, Hsch., *EM*171.57; also, = ῥιγοῦν, ibid. (Cypr. acc. to Hsch.).

**αὐρινός**, ή, όν, *of the morrow*, Gloss.

❀ **αὔριον**, Adv. *to-morrow*, Il.9.357, Od.1.272, etc.; αὔ. τηνικάδε *to-morrow* at this time, Pl.*Phd*.76b; ἐς or εἰς αὔ. *on the morrow*, Il.8. 538 (or *till morning*, Od.11.351), Nicoch.15, Anaxandr.4.4; *for the morrow*, καλέσαι ἐπὶ δεῖπνον εἰς αὔ. *IG*2².17, etc. 2. *presently, shortly*, φάγωμεν καὶ πίωμεν, αὔ. γὰρ ἀποθνήσκομεν 1*Ep.Cor*.15.32; opp. σήμερον, *Ev.Matt*.6.30. II. Subst., αὔ. ἣν ἀρετὴν διαείσεται *the morrow* will distinguish.., Il.8.535. III. ἡ αὔ. (sc. ἡμέρα) *the morrow*, S.*Tr*.945 (*OT*1090 is corrupt); τὴν αὔ. μέλλουσαν E.*Alc*. 784; ἡ αὔ. ἡμέρα X.*Oec*.11.6, Lys.26.6; also ἡ ἐς αὔ. ἡμέρα S.*OC*567; τὸ ἐς αὔριον Id.*Fr*.593.5; εἰς τὴν αὔ. Alex.241.3, *Act.Ap*.4.3; ἐπὶ τὴν αὔ. ib.5; ὁ αὔ. χρόνος E.*Hipp*.1117; ἡ Αὔ. personified by Simon.210 B.; δαίμονα τὸν Αὔριον Call.*Epigr*.16. (Cf. Lith. *aušrà* 'dawn', Skt. *usrás* 'of the dawn'; v. ἄγχαυρος, ἕως.)

**αὖροι**· λαγοί, ἢ σαῦροι, Hsch. (λόγοι ἴσαυροι cod.).

**αὐροστχάς**, άδος, ἡ, name of a *vine*, Ἰκαριωνείης Parth.*Fr*.17; also, = τὸ [illegible] βότρυν κλῆμα, Eratosth.37.

**αὐροφόρητος**, ον, *wind-borne*, Sch.Ar.*Ra*.1485.

**αὔσαις**· πνοαῖς, κραυγαῖς, Hsch.

❀ **αὐσαυτοῦ**, τᾶς, τοῦ, Dor. for ἑαυτοῦ, τῆς, τοῦ, *IG*5(2).265.18 (Mantinea), *GDI*1696, al. (Delph.), 4959 (Eleutherna), *IG*4.840.3 (Calauria); cf. αὖς· αὐτός (Cret., Lacon.), Hsch.: Delph. αὐσωτόν, αὐσωτῶν, *GDI*1696, *SIG*703.11: Boeot. ἀσαυτῦ, = ἑαυτῷ, *IG*7.3303 (Chaeronea); cf. αὐταυτοῦ.

**αὔσιος**, = τηΰσιος, Ibyc.12; cf. αὔτως.

**αὖσις**, εως, ἡ, *drying*, *EM*170.44.

❀ **αὐσόν**· ξηρόν, Hsch.

❀ **Αὐσονία**, poet. **-ίη**, ἡ, *Italy*, *AP*14.121 (Metrod.): **Αὐσονίηθεν** *App.Anth*.2.712b.14:—Adj. **Αὐσόνιος**, α, ον, *AP*7.342, al.: **Αὐσόνιοι**, οἱ, *Italians*, ib.363, al.:—also **Αὔσονες**, οἱ, Arist.*Pol*.1329b20, *IG*14.1374, Ael.*VH*9.16 (of the aborigines): fem. **Αὐσονίς**, ίδος, *IG* 14.2067, 2137.

**αὖσος**· ἄλσος (Cret.), Hsch.

**αὐσταλέος**, α, ον, Ep. **ἀϋσταλέος**, (αὔω A) *dried up, sunburnt*, Od. 19.327, Hes.*Sc*.265, Theoc.14.4, Call.*Cer*.16, A.R.2.200, etc.

**αὐστήρ**· μέτρου ὄνομα, Hsch.

**αὐστηρία**, ἡ, = αὐστηρότης, στρυφνότης καὶ αὐ. Thphr.*CP*6.12. 6. 2. metaph. of men, *austerity*, ἠθῶν Plb.4.21.1, Cat.Cod.Astr. 2.160.6, etc.; as a virtue, *Stoic*.3.66.

**αὐστηρόπρακτος**, ον, *austere in conduct*, Ptol.*Tetr*.159.

**αὐστηρός**, ά, όν, (αὔω) *harsh, rough, bitter*, ὕδωρ Pl.*Phlb*.61c, cf. *Ti*.65d; οἶνος αὐ., opp. γλυκύς, Hp.*Acut*.52, *Fract*.29, Arist.*Pr*.872b 35, 934a34; ὀσμή Id.*de An*.421a30; of country, *rugged*, τόποι *OGI* 168.57 (i B.C.): metaph., *harsh, crabbed*, ποιητής Pl.*R*.398a (Comp.); *severe, unadorned*, ἡ πραγματεία ἔχει αὐ. τι Plb.9.1.2, cf. D.H.*Dem*. 47; γυμνάδος αὐστηρὸν .. πόνον *severe*, *Epigr.Gr*.201. Adv. **-ρῶς**, κατεσκευάσθαι D.H.*Dem*.43. b. in moral sense, *rigorous, austere*, Arist.*EE*1240a2; τοῖς βίοις Plb.4.20.7 (Sup.), cf. Phld.*Hom*.p.23 O. (Comp.); αὐ. καὶ αὐθάδης D.H.6.27, cf. *Stoic*.3.162, Vett.Val.75.11; *strict, exacting*, *Ev.Luc*.19.21, *PTeb*.315.19 (ii A.D.); αὐστηρότερον, τό, *excessive rigour*, *BGU*140.18 (ii A.D.). Adv. **-ρῶς** Satyr.*Vit.Eur*. *Fr*.39 iv 19: Comp. **-ότερον** Lxx 2*Ma*.14.30.

**αὐστηρότης**, ητος, ἡ, *harshness, roughness*, X.*An*.5.4.29; οἴνου, opp. γλυκύτης, Pl.*Tht*.178c, Thphr.*HP*7.9.5. 2. metaph., *harshness, crabbedness*, τοῦ γήρως Pl.*Lg*.666b, cf. D.C.56.3.

**αὐτ-άγγελος**, ὁ, *carrying one's own message*, S.*Ph*.568; *bringing news of what oneself has seen*, Th.3.33: c. gen. rei, λόγων S.*OC*333; πάθους Plu.2.489e, cf. Arr.*An*.4.2.6, Max.Tyr.14.2, Nonn.*D*.8. 222. **-άγητος** [ᾰ], ον, (ἄγαμαι) = αὐθάδης, Anacr.142; *conceited*, Ion Trag.8. **-αγρεσία**, ἡ, *free choice*, ἐξ αὐταγρεσίης Call.*Fr*.120. 2. **-άγρετος**, ον, (ἀγρέω) poet. for αὐθαίρετος, *self-chosen, left to one's choice*, εἰ γάρ πως εἴη αὐτάγρετα πάντα βροτοῖσι Od.16.148; σοὶ δ' αὐτάγρετόν ἐστι δαήμεναι *h.Merc*.474. 2. *taken by one's own hands* or *exertions*, A.R.4.231. II. Act., *choosing freely*, Semon.1.19, Opp.*H*.5.588.

**αὐτ-άγρευτος**, ον, = αὐτόπλεκτος, Sch.Opp.*H*.4.440. **-άδελφος**, ον (η, ον Sch.E.*Hec*.944) *brother's* or *sister's*, αἷμα A.*Th*.718, *Eu*.89; αὐ. Ἰσμήνης κάρα S.*Ant*.1. II. Subst., *one's own brother* or *sister*, ib.503,696:—later **-αδέλφη**, ἡ, Sch.E.*Ph*.135.

**αὐταιώρητος**, ον, *self-suspended*, Hsch.

**αὐτάλεν**· ἐσκίρτα, Hsch. **αὐτάλκης**· ζωμός, also = αὐτάρκης, Id.

**αὐταμαρόν, αὐταμέριν**, v. αὐθήμερος II.

**αὐτ-ανδρί**, Adv. of sq., Plb.3.81.11. ❀ **-ανδρος**, ον, (ἀνήρ) *together with the men, men and all*, ναῦς αὐτάνδρους ἀπέβαλον Plb.1.23.7, cf. Sosyl.p.31 B., A.R.3.582, Luc.*Bacch*.2, etc.; πόλεις αὐ. ἀπρῆσθαι D.H.7.60: hence αὐ. λαός the people, *every man of them*, J.*BJ*3.7. 31. **-ανέψιος**, ὁ, *own cousin*, A.*Supp*.984, E.*Heracl*.987, Pl.*Euthd*. 275b: Adj. αὐ. στόλος A.*Supp*.933:—fem. **-ανεψία**, Lyc.811.

**αὐτανίδας**· αὖθις, πάλιν, Hsch. **αὐτάντας**· ὁ προεστώς τινος πράγματος καὶ αὐθεντῶν, Id.

❀ **αὐτάρ** (ἀ*ϝ*υτάρ *IG*1².1012), Conj. = ἀτάρ (Ep. and Cypr., *Inscr. Cypr*.57 H.):—*but, besides, moreover*, prop. to introduce a contrast, Od.13.286, al.; used also to mark a rapid succession of details, Il.2.406, al.; opp. μέν, Ἥφαιστος μέν .. αὐ. ἄρα Ζεύς .. ib.102 sq., cf. Od.19.512 sq.; αὐτάρ τοι *but nevertheless*, Il.15.45.—In an Epic reminiscence, Hermipp.63.17 (hex.). II. αὐτάρ· αὐτομάτη, ἑκουσία, Hsch.

**αὐτάρεσκ-εια**, ἡ, *self-satisfaction, self-indulgence*, Sm.*Ec*.6.9. **-έω**, *to be self-satisfied*, Tz.*H*.9.279. **-ος**, ον, *self-satisfied, self-willed*, Hsch. s.v. αὐθέκαστος:—also **αὐτάρεστος**, Id.

**αὐτάρκ-εια**, ἡ, *self-sufficiency, independence*, Democr.246, Hp.*Ep*. 17, Pl.*Phlb*.67a, Arist.*EN*1097b7, Epicur.*Ep*.3 p.63 U., etc.; αὐ. ζωῆς Arist.*Rh*.1360b15; κτήσεως Id.*Pol*.1256b32; ἡ τῆς τροφῆς αὐ. Id.*GA*776b8. II. concrete, *a sufficiency*, *PFlor*.242.8 (iii A.D.); *a competence*, Vett.Val.289.32. **-εσία**, ἡ, *sufficiency*, *Psalm.Solom*. 5.18. **-έω**, *supply with necessaries*, αὐτάρκησεν ἑαυτὸν ἐν ἐρήμῳ Lxx *De*.32.10. II. *to be sufficient*, Arist.*EE*1242a8, *PLips*.29.11 (iii A.D.). **-ης**, ες, (ἀρκέω) *sufficient in oneself, self-supporting, independent* of others, ἀνθρώπου σῶμα ἓν οὐδὲν αὐ. ἐστιν Hdt.1.32; αὐ. εἰς πάντα Pl.*Plt*.271d; εἰς εὐδαιμονίαν, of ἀρετή, Zeno *Stoic*.1.46; οὐκ αὐ. ἀλλὰ πολλῶν ἐνδεής Pl.*R*.369b; ὁ σοφὸς -έστατος Arist.*EN*1177b1, cf. Epicur.*Sent.Vat*.45; αὐτάρκη φρονεῖν E.*Fr*.29; νηδὺς αὐ. τέκνων *helping itself, acting instinctively*, A.*Ch*.757; αὐ. βοή a *self-reliant* shout, S.*OC*1057 (s.v.l.); πόλις αὐ. θέσιν κειμένη Th.1.37, cf. 2.36 (Sup.); οἰκία -έστερον ἑνός, πόλις δ' οἰκίας Arist.*Pol*.1261b11; τὸ τέλειον ἀγαθὸν αὐ. εἶναι δοκεῖ Id.*EN*1097b8; σῶμα αὐ. πρός τι *strong enough* for a thing, Th.2.51, cf. X.*Mem*.4.8.11: c. inf., *able of oneself* to do a thing, εἰ γὰρ αὐτάρκη τὰ ψηφίσματα ἦν ἢ ὑμᾶς ἀναγκάζειν κτλ. D.3.14, cf. X.*Cyr*.4.3.4. Adv. **-κως**, ἔχειν Arist.*Rh*.1362a27: Sup. **-έστατα**, ζῆν X.*Mem*.1.2.14. II. *sufficient* in quantity, ἀργύριον αὐ. εἰς σιτωνίαν Ph.2.69; ὕδωρ αὐ. τοῖς ποιμνίοις J.*AJ*2.11.2, cf. *PLond*.3.

1166.6 (i A.D.), *POxy.*729.19 (ii A.D.); ὄξους τὸ -έστατον Gal.13.1046. Adv. -κως *sufficiently*, *BGU*665.18 (i A.D.), Plot.3.3.3, *Theol. Ar.*45.

**αὐταρχ-έω**, *to be an absolute ruler*, Pi.*Pae.*4.37, D.C.44.2. **-ος**, ον, *autocratic*, ἰσχύς Id.61.7: as Subst., *IGRom.*4.1612 (Hypaepa).

**αὐταύλης**, ου, ὁ, *soloist on the flute*, condemned by Phryn.145.

**αὐταυτόθεν**, *of oneself*, Euryph.ap.Stob.1.6.19. ⊛ **αὐταυτοῦ** or **-τῶ, αὐταυτῆς** (-τᾶς), Dor. for ἑαυτοῦ, ἑαυτῆς, πεπαίδευται γὰρ αὐταυτᾶς ὕπο Epich.172.7, cf. *IG*14.646 (Heraclea), Archyt.2, Philol.5, Axiop.1.15, Diotog.ap.Stob.4.7.62: acc., αὐταυτόν Ecphant.ap.Stob. 4.7.64; αὐταυτόν *IG*4.156 (Aegina): as Adj., ταῖς αὐταυταῖς χερσίν Sophr.19 (-τᾶς Pors.):—also **αὐτοῦτα**, for ἑαυτοῦ, *IG*14.287, 288 (Segesta): pl., αὐτῶντα ib.316 (Thermae Himeraeae).

⊛ **αὖτε**, Adv., (αὖ, τε):—used by Hom. like αὖ, I. of Time, *again*, Il.1.202, 2.105,370, al.; freq. δὴ αὖτε 1.340, 2.225, and with crasis, δαὖτε Alcm.36, δηὖτε Archil.60, Sapph.40, Alc.19.1, Hippon. 78. II. to mark Sequence or Transition, *again, furthermore*, ἕκτον δ' αὖτ' Ὀδυσῆα Il.2.407; Δαρδανίων αὖτ' ἦρχεν.. Αἰνείας ib.819, cf. 826, etc.; esp. in speeches, τὸν δ' αὖτε προσέειπε.. him *in turn* addressed.., 3.58, al.; ἀμφί μοι αὖτε ἄναχθ' ἑκαταβόλον ἀειδέτω φρήν Terp.2, cf. Ar.*Nu.*595; ἧδ' αὖθ' ἕρπει S.*Tr.*1009 (lyr.). 2. *on the other hand, on the contrary*, sts. opp. μέν (instead of δέ), Il.1.237, Od. 22.6; coupled with δέ, *h.Cer.*137, A.*Pers.*183, *Th.*5, *Ag.*553.—Freq. in A., once in S., never in E.; not in Prose; Com. only in Dact. and Anap. in Epic reminiscences, Cratin.169, Ar.*Pax*1270, Metag. 4.2 (prob.); νῦν αὖτε λεῴ προσέχετε τὸν νοῦν Ar.*V.*1015.

**αὐτέγγυος**, ον, *one's own security*, *PEdgar*30.21 (iii B.C.).

⊛ **αὐτεῖ**, Adv., Dor. for αὐτοῦ, Isyll.73, *IG*12(3).248.19 (Anaphe), A.D.*Synt.*238.9; Boeot. αὐτῖ, *Schwyzer*462*A* 5 (Tanagra, iii B.C.).

**αὐτ-έκμαγμα**, ατος, τό, *one's very image*, Ar.*Th.*514. **-ενέργεια**, ἡ, *self-moving energy*, Eustr.*in EN*330.27: **αὐτοενέργεια**, Phlp.*in de An.*35.1. **-ενέργητος**, or **αὐτοεν-**, ον, *spontaneous*, ζωή Procl. *in Prm.*p.611 S. (αὐτ-), *in Alc.*p.18 C. (αὐτο-), *Theol.Plat.*6.22, Iamb. *Myst.*4.3. ⊛ **-ενιαυτός**, όν, *of the year, this year's*, γένη *BGU*1120. 34 (i B.C.), al.; κόπρος *Gp.*2.21.10; οἶνος Orib.*Fr.*142: neut. as Adv., Epigr. in *Supp.Epigr.*2.431. **-εξούσιος**, ον, *in one's own power, free*, ποιῶν τὸ αὐ. Chrysipp.*Stoic.*2.284, cf. Diogenian.Epicur. 3.61, Plot.1.4.8, Iamb.*Myst.*3.14; of persons, Muson.*Fr.*12 p.66 H., Arr.*Epict.*4.1.62, *PLips.*29.6 (iii A.D.); of captives, *freed unconditionally*, D.S.14.105; *absolute*, βασιλεία J.*AJ*15.7.10; δύναμις Plot.6.8. 20; αὐ., τό, *freedom of choice*, Procl. *in Alc.*p.143 C., etc.; αὐ. ἀρχή Plot.3.2.10. Adv. -ως J.*BJ*5.13.5, Plot.6.8.20, Procl.*Theol.Plat.* 6.16; cf. αὐτοεξούσιος. ⊛ **-εξουσιότης**, ητος, ἡ, *free will*, v.l. in Lxx 4*Ma.*2.21: αὐτο- Eustr.*in EN*390.11. **-επάγγελτος**, ον, *offering of oneself, of one's free will*, αὐ. ἠθέλησε συμβαλέσθαι χρήματα Hdt.7.29; αὐ. ὑποστῆναι E.*HF*706; παρεῖναι, χωρεῖν, Th. 1.33, 4.120; βοηθεῖν Isoc.1.25; ἐθελονταί D.18.68. Adv. -τως Ph. 2.173. II. *self invited*, dub. in Luc.*JTr.*37. **-έπαινος**, ον, *self-laudatory*, Sch.Il.*Oxy.*1087 i 17. **-επιβούλευτος**, ον, *self-destructive*, Ath.Mech.32.9, [Hero] *Poliorc.*p.269 W. **-επίβουλος**, ον, *plotting against oneself*, interpol. in Aesop.18; = αὐτοφονεύς, Hsch. **-επίσπαστος**, ον, *drawn on oneself, self-incurred*, Id. s. v. αὐθαιρέτῳ. **-επιστατέω**, *to be present oneself*, and Subst. **-επιστᾰσία**, ἡ, Sch.Theoc.7.6. **-επιστήμη**, ἡ, *absolute science*, Procl.*Theol.Plat.*4.14, Plot.5.8.4 (αὐτο-). **-επίστροφος**, ον, *returning upon oneself*, Olymp.*in Alc.*p.209 C. **-επιτάκτης**, ου, ὁ, *one who rules absolutely*, Pl.*Plt.*260e. **-επιτακτικός**, ή, όν, *belonging to absolute power*: -κή (sc. τέχνη), ἡ, ibid., etc. II. *ordaining by authority*, τῆς τριαδικῆς διαιρέσεως Dam.*Pr.*98. **-επίτακτος**, ον, *self-bidden, spontaneous*, Poll.1.156. **-επώνῠμος**, ον, *of the same surname with*, σοῦ πατρός E.*Ph.*769. **-ερέτης**, ου, ὁ, *one who rows himself*, i. e. *rower and soldier at once*, αὐ. καὶ μάχιμοι Th.1.10, cf. 3.18, 6.91. 2. *rowing one's own boat*, *AP*7.305 (Adaeus).

**ἀϋτέω** [ῡ], used by Hom. only in 3 pers. impf., and in Trag. (never in S.) only in pres. and impf.: ἠΰτησα Nonn.*D.*11.185, *Epigr.Gr.* 995.7: (αὔω B):—*cry, shout*, μακρὸν ἀΰτει Il.20.50; καί μέγ' ἀΰτει 21.582; κληδὼν ἀΰτεῖ A.*Ag.*927: c. acc. cogn., τοιαῦτ' ἀϋτῶν Id.*Th.* 384; ἀϋτεῖ δ' ὀξύ Id.*Pers.*1058 (lyr.); τί τινι E.*El.*757, etc. 2. c. acc. pers., *call to*, ἀΰτει πάντας ἀρίστους Il.11.258; ἀΰτευν Ἄρτεμιν E.*Hipp.*167 (lyr.); τί Ζῆν' ἀϋτεῖς; why *call on* Zeus? Ar.*Lys.*717: c. acc. pers. et inf., E.*Rh.*668. 3. c. acc. rei, *call for*, βοὰν ἀ. *call for* help, Id.*Hec.*1092 (lyr.). 4. *proclaim*, c. inf., Man.4.39,428.

⊛ **ἀϋτή** [ῡ], ἡ, (αὔω B) *cry, shout*, esp. *battle-shout, war-cry*, ἀϋτὴ δ' οὐρανὸν ἷκεν Il.2.153; ἀϋτή τε πτόλεμός τε 6.328; κίνδυνος ὀξείας ἀϋτᾶς Pi.*N.*9.35: generally, γλώσσης ἀϋτὴν Φωκίδος A.*Ch.*564; of the *blast* of the trumpet, Id.*Pers.*395; of the *creaking* of the axle, Parm.1.6. (ἀϝῡτά *IG*9(1).868 (Corc.).)

**αὐτ-ήκοος**, ον, (ἀκούω) *one who has himself heard, ear-witness*, αὐ. τινος γενέσθαι Th.1.133, Pl.*Lg.*658c. II. *hearing oneself*, i. e. *a law unto oneself*, Ph.2.2, al., Suid.; so, *self-acquired*, ἀρετή, ἐπιστήμη, Ph.1.371,354. ⊛ **-ῆμαρ**, Adv. = αὐθημερόν, *on the self-same day*, Il.18.454, Od.3.311; *for that day*, Il.1.81. ⊛ **-ημερόν**, Ion. for αὐθημερόν, Hdt.2.122.

⊛ **αὐτίκα** [ῐ], Adv. *forthwith, at once, in a moment*, which notion is strengthd. by Hom. in αὐ. νῦν, μάλ' αὐ. *on the spot*, Od.10.111, al.: c. part., αὐτίκ' ἰόντι *immediately* on his going, 2.367; beginning a sentence, Sapph.*Supp.*20a.13: in Prose, αὐ. γενόμενος *as soon as* born, Hdt.2.140; αὐ. μάλα Id.7.103, *IG*1².39.47, Pl.*Prt.*318b; αὐ. δὴ μάλα *presently* (at the end of a sentence), D.21.19,23; αὐ. νυκτός Theoc.2.119. 2. *now, for the moment*, αὐ. καὶ μετέπειτα Od.14. 403; ὁ μὲν αὐτίχ' ὁ δ' ἥξει A.*Ch.*1020; ἡδὺ μὲν γὰρ αὐ.. ἐν δὲ χρόνῳ.. E.*Andr.*781 (lyr.); Th. opposes τὸ αὐ. and ὁ μέλλων πόλεμος 1.36, cf. 2.41: with a Subst., τὴν μὲν αὐτίχ' ἡμέραν S.*OC*433; ὁ αὐ. φόβος *momentary* fear, Th.3.112, cf. 1.41,124. 3. in a slightly future sense, *immediately, presently*, αὐτίκ' ἀκούσεσθε D.19.17, cf. S.*Ph.*14, 1001, Ar.*Pl.*347, etc.; opp. νῦν, Pl.*Grg.*459c, *R.*420c; ἐμπέπτωκεν εἰς λόγους οὓς αὐ. μᾶλλον.. ἁρμόσει λέγειν D.18.42. II. *for example, to begin with*, Hp.*Epid.*1.25, *Acut.*16; αὐ. γὰρ ἄρχει διὰ τίν' ὁ Ζεύς; Ar.*Pl.*130, cf. *Av.*166,574, Pl.*Prt.*395e, *R.*340d, *Dialex.*2. 2, al.; αὐ. δὴ μάλα *for example now*, D.25.29; *at any rate*, Plu.2. 1137d. III. = αὖθις, Arat.880,1076 (but = εὐθέως, Sch.).

⊛ **αὖτις**, v. αὖθις: Cret. αὖτιν *Leg.Gort.*4.3.

⊛ **αὐτίτης** [ῑ], ου, ὁ, (αὐτός) *by oneself, alone*, Arist.*Fr.*668. II. as Subst., αὐτίτης (sc. οἶνος), ὁ, *home-made wine*, Telecl.9, Polyzel.1, Hp.*Morb.*3.14.

**ἀϋτμενόπης** (-πις cod.)· πεφυσημένος, πεπνευσμένος, Hsch.

⊛ **ἀϋτμή**, ἡ, (ἄημι) *breath*, εἰς ὅ κ' ἀ. ἐν στήθεσσι μένῃ Il.9.609; τεῖρε δ' ἀ. Ἡφαίστοιο *the fiery breath* of Hephaistos, 21.366; ὅσσον πυρὸς ἵκετ' ἀ. Od.16.290 (hence abs. for *heat*, 9.389): in pl., περισχίζοντο δ' ἀϋτμαὶ Ἡφαίστου Q.S.13.329; of bellows, εὔπρηστον ἀ. ἐξανιεῖσαι Il.18.471; ἀνέμων ἀμέγαρτον ἀϋτμήν Od.11.400. 2. *scent, fragrance*, με κνίσης ἀμφήλυθεν ἡδὺς ἀ. 12.369, cf. Il.14.174; θήρειος ἀ. *scent* of game, Opp.*C.*1.467.

**ἀϋτμήν**, ένος, ὁ, = ἀϋτμή, χέ' ἀϋτμένα Il.23.765; ἀνέμων ἐπ' ἀϋτμένα χεῦεν Od.3.289.

**αὐτο-ᾰγᾰθός**, ή, όν, *good in itself*, Plot.1.8.13: esp. in neut. -ᾰγᾰθόν, τό, *the ideal good, the Form of good*, Arist.*Metaph.*996ᵃ28, Plot. 6.6.10. **-ᾰγᾰθότης**, ητος, ἡ, *absolute goodness*, Procl.*Inst.* 127. **-ᾴδης** [ᾱ], etym. of αὐθάδης, Arist.*MM*1192ᵇ33. **-ᾱήρ**, έρος, ὁ, *air by itself*, Herm.ap.Stob.3.11.31. **-ᾰληθές**, τό, *the true-in-itself*, Alex.Aphr. *in Metaph.*301.6. **-ᾰληθῶς**, *in very truth*, Suid. s. v. αὐτό. **-άλφα**, **-βῆτα**, τό, *the very* ἄλφα, βῆτα, Arist.*Metaph.* 1087ᵃ9 (al. divisim). **-άνθρωπος**, ὁ, *the ideal man, the Form of man*, Id.*EN*1096ᵃ35, *Metaph.*991ᵃ29, etc. II. *a very man*, of a statue, Luc.*Philops.*18. **-άνισον**, τό, *inequality in the abstract*, Alex.Aphr. *in Metaph.*809.14. **-ανόσιον**, τό, *abstract impiety*, Procl. *in Prm.* p.773 S. **-απειρία**, ἡ, *infinity itself*, Id.*Inst.*92. **ἄπειρος**, ον, *infinite in itself*, Plot.2.4.7. **-απλότης**, ητος, ἡ, *simplicity itself*, of a person, ὁ βασιλεὺς τὸν τρόπον ἦν αὐ. Anon.ap.Suid. s. v. **-ἀριθμός**, ὁ, *abstract number*, Alex.Aphr. *in Metaph.*109.17, al. **-αρχή**, ἡ, *ideal rule*, Epist.Gall. in Jul.*Ep.*455b. **-βᾰφής**, ές, *self-dipped*, Nonn. *D.*30.123. **-βῆτα**, τό, v. αὐτοάλφα. **-βλάβη** [ᾰ], ἡ, *very mischief*, Sch.rec.S.*El.*301. **-βλᾰβής**, ές, *self-harming*, Sch.A.*Th.* 917. **-βοάω**, *bear testimony of oneself*, *AB*465, Suid. **-βοεί**, Adv. *by a mere shout, at the first shout*, αὐ. ἑλεῖν take *without a blow*, Th.2.81, 3.113, 8.62, etc.; αὐ. λαβεῖν κλέπτοντα, = ἐπ' αὐτοφώρῳ, *AB* 465. **-βοήθητος**, ον, *self-supporting*, of an argument, Simp. *in Ph.*354.29. **-βόητος**, ον, *self-sounding*, ὄργανον Nonn.*D.*1. 432. **-βορέας**, ου, ὁ, *a very Boreas*, Luc.*Tim.*54. **-βούλησις**, εως, ἡ, *the abstract will*, v.l. in Arist.*Top.*147ᵃ8. **-βουλήτως**, *of one's own purpose*, Hsch. s. v. ἐθελοντής. **-βουλος**, ον, *self-willing, self-purposing*, A.*Th.*1058. **-βοῦς**, βοός, ὁ, *ideal ox*, Alex.Aphr. *in Metaph.*758.31. **-βρᾰδύτης**, ητος, ἡ, *ideal slowness*, Procl. *Hyp.*1.1. **-γᾰμος**, ον, = αὐτογόνος II, Nonn.*D.*40.405. ⊛ **-γένεθλος**, ον, = sq., *Orac.Chald.*32; ἥλιος Hymn.*Mag.*4.24; κάνθαρος, of Kheper, *PMag.Par.*1.943. 2. *self-producing*, φύσις Nonn.*D.*41. 52. **-γενέτωρ**, τορος, = foreg. 2, *PMag.Par.*2.1561, *PMag.Leid. W.*7.6. **-γενής**, ές, *self-produced*, δαίμων v.l. in Herm.ap.Stob.1. 49.44, cf. Ph.1.618, Max.Tyr.16.6, Procl.*in Prm.*p.893 S., Orph.*Fr.* 245.8. 2. αὐτογενές, τό, = νάρκισσος, Ps.-Dsc.4.158; ὀστοῦν αὐ., = κολοκυνθίς, ib.176. II. *sprung from the same stock, kindred*, A. *Supp.*8 (cj. Bamberger for αὐτογένητον). **-γένητος**, ον, *self-generated*, Simp. *in Ph.*824.16 (s. v. l.). **-γεννητικός**, ή, όν, *of itself productive of..*, Procl. *in Prm.*p.821 S. **-γέννητος**, ον, = αὐτογενής: αὐ. κοιμήματα μητρός a mother's intercourse *with her own child*, S. *Ant.*864. **-γεωργός**, f.l. for αὐτουργός, Ph.1.685. **-γῆ**, ἡ, *ideal earth, archetype of earth*, Plot.6.7.11, Herm.ap.Stob.3.11.31. **-γλῠφος**, ον, *self-engraved*, λίθος Ps.-Plu.*Fluv.*12.2. **-γλώχῑν**, ῑνος, ὁ, ἡ, *in one piece with the point*, οἰστός Hld.9.19. **-γνωμονέω**, *act of one's own judgement*, X.*HG*7.3.6. **-γνώμων**, ον, gen. ονος, *on one's own judgement, at one's own discretion*, κρίνειν αὐ., opp. κατὰ γράμματα, Arist.*Pol.*1270ᵇ29, cf. 1272ᵃ39. Adv. -όνως Plu.*Demetr.*6: —hence Subst. **-οσύνη**, ἡ, Zonar. **-γνῶσις**, εως, ἡ, *absolute knowledge*, Olymp. *in Phd.*p.100 N., Procl. *in Alc.*p.88 C. **-γνωτος**, ον, *self-determined, self-willed*, ὀργή S.*Ant.*875.—also **γνωστος**, ον, *knowable in itself*, Simp. *in Ph.*1250.14, Dam.*Pr.*80. **-γονος**, ον, *self-produced*, Nonn.*D.*8.103, Syrian. *in Metaph.*187.9, Procl. *in Cra.*p.17 P. Adv. -νως Syrian. *in Metaph.*142.17, Procl. *in Prm.*p.897 S. II. Act., (-γόνος) *self-producing, breeding alone*, Nonn.*D.*9.229, Iamb. *Myst.*10.6. **-γραμμή**, ἡ, *line in itself*, Arist.*Metaph.*1036ᵇ14, Plot. 6.6.17. ⊛ **-γρᾰφος**, ον, *written with one's own hand*, ἐπιστολαί D.H. 5.7, Plu.*Sert.*27; τὸ αὐ. *one's own writing*, Id.2.1115c. **-γύος**, ον, ἄροτρον αὐ. a plough *whose* γύης *is of one piece with the* ἔλυμα *and* ἱστοβοεύς, not fitted together (πηκτόν), Hes.*Op.*433, A.R.3.232, 1285. **-δᾰής**, ές, *self-taught*, ἀρετά Diagor.1; ὀρχήματα S.*Aj.* 700 (lyr.). **-δάϊκτος** [ᾰ], ον, *self-slain*, *AP*9.293 (Phil.), Opp.*H.* 2.349; *mutually slain*, A.*Th.*735 (lyr.). **-δαίμων**, ονος, ὁ, *arche-*

*typal* δαίμων, Plot.3.5.6. **-δαιτος**, ον, of a guest, *bringing his own share to a feast*, Lyc.480. ⊛ **-δακὴς** μῆνις· μικρά, Hsch., cf. sq.

**αὐτ-οδάξ**, Adv. *with the very teeth*, γυναῖκες αὐτοδὰξ ὠργισμέναι women angered *even to biting*, Ar.*Lys*.687; τὸν αὐτοδὰξ τρόπον your *ferocious* temper, Id.*Pax* 607.

**αὐτο-δεής**, ές, *insufficient in itself*, dub. in *Corp.Herm*.10.10. **-δειπνος**, ον, = αὐτόδαιτος, Hsch. **-δεκα**, *just ten*, Th.5.20. **-δεκάς**, άδος, ἡ, *the series 1, 2, . . 10*, Plot.6.6.14. **-δερμος**, ον, *skin, bark and all*, Hsch. s.v. αὐτόφλοιον. **-δέσμητος**, ον, = αὐτάγρευτος, Sch.Opp.*H*.4.449. **-δεσποτεία**, ἡ, *absolute rule*, Procl. *in Prm*. p.736 S. **-δεσπότης**, ου, ὁ, *absolute master*, Eustr. *in EN*387.8. **-δέσποτος**, ον, *at one's own will, free*, Hierocl.*Prov*.ap.Phot. *Bibl*.p.172 B.; *absolute master*, παθῶν Lxx 4 *Ma*.1.1. **-δετος**, ον, *self-bound*, Opp.*C*.2.376. **-δηλος**, ον, *self-evident*, A.*Th*.848 (lyr.). **-δημιούργητος**, ον, *self-made*, i.e. *in the natural state*, Hsch. s.v. αὐτόξυλον. **-διᾱκονία**, ἡ, *self-service*, Chrysipp.*Stoic*.3.177, Teles p.54 H. **-διᾱκονέω**, *serve oneself*, Eust.732.65. **-διάκονος** [ᾱ], ον, *serving oneself*, Str.16.4.26. ⊛ **-δίδακτος** [ῐ], ον, *self-taught*, Od.22.347; αὐ. ἔσωθεν θυμὸς A.*Ag*.991 (lyr.); φιλοσοφία D.H. 5.12; of instinct, τὸ τῶν ὀργάνων αὐ. Gal.8.445. Adv. -τως *instinctively*, Id.19.175, cf. Alex.Aphr.*Pr*.1.14; *without instruction*, Phld. *Rh*.1.129 S. (dub.). **-διήγητος**, ον, *narrated in the first person*, opp. dialogue, D.L.9.111. **-διηγούμενος**, η, ον, *narrating in the first person*, ibid. **-δίκαιον** [ῐ], τό, *abstract right*, Aristid.2.182 J., Procl. *in Prm*.p.773 S., Dam.*Pr*.60. **-δῐκαιοσύνη**, ἡ, *very righteousness*, Plot.1.2.6, Herm. *in Phdr*.p.144 A. **-δῐκέω**, *to be* αὐτόδικος, Din. *Fr*.60.4, Poll.8.24. **-δῐκος**, ον, *with independent jurisdiction, with one's own courts*, Th.5.18, J.*AJ*19.2.2, *GDI*4985 (Gortyn).

**αὐτόδῐον**, Adv. *straightway*, Od.8.449.

**αὐτο-διπλάσιον**, τό, *the ideal double, its Form*, Arist.*Metaph*.990ᵇ32. **-δίπουν** [ῐ], ποδος, τό, *ideal biped*, Alex.Aphr. *in Metaph*.105.5. **-δοξα**, ἡ, *opinion in the abstract*, Arist. *Top*.162ᵃ30. ⊛ **-δόξαστον**, τό, *the object of opinion in the abstract*, Suid. s.v. αὐτό. **-δορος**, ον, *hide and all*, Plu.2.694b. **-δουλεία**, ἡ, *absolute servitude*, Procl. *in Prm*.p.736 S. **-δρομέω**, *run of itself*, Dion.Byz.53. **-δρομος**, ον, *running* or *moving of itself*, Hp.*Hebd*.2. **-δυάς**, άδος, ἡ, *the ideal number two*, Alex.Aphr. *in Metaph*.87.9, Phlp. *in de An*.77.8. **-δύνᾰμις** [ῠ], εως, ἡ, *abstract potentiality*, Procl.*Inst*.92. **-ε(θεί)ρας**· κόμας ἢ καὶ κόσμους, Hsch. **-ειδής**, ές, *true to its own* εἶδος, M. Ant.11.12 (s.v.l.), Olymp. *in Alc*.p.16 C. 2. *of ideal, abstract nature*, Dam.*Pr*.340. **-εἶδος**, τό, *abstract form*, read by Alex.Aphr. in Arist.*Metaph*.1087ᵃ6. **-ἕκαστος**, ον, = αὐθέκαστος, Arist. *Top*.162ᵃ27; τὸ αὐ. *the idea of each object*, Id.*EN*1096ᵃ35, cf. Dam.*Pr*.427. **-εκτᾰτος**, ον, (ἐκτείνω) *long by nature*, of syllables, Eust.943.59. **-ελαιουργός**, ὁ, dub. sens. in *PPetr*.3 p.169. **-ελέφας**, αντος, ὁ, *ideal elephant*, Alex.Aphr. *in Metaph*.761.30. **-έλικτος**, ον, *returning into itself*, κύκλος Nonn.*D*.33.272, al. ⊛ **-έν**, τό, *abstract unity*, Alex.Aphr. *in Metaph*.87.9, al., Plot.5.3.12, 6.2.5, Procl. *in Prm*.p.547 S., *Inst*.2, al. **-ενάς**, άδος, ἡ, *ideal* ἑνάς, ib. 128. **-ενέργεια**, -ητος, v. αὐτεν-. **-εννεάς**, άδος, ἡ, *the ideal number nine*, Alex.Aphr. *in Metaph*.836.25. **-εντεί**, Adv. *with one's own hand*, D.C.58.24 (v.l. αὐτοεντίᾳ, as in *Fr*.13.2). **-έντης**, ου, ὁ, in S., = αὐθέντης, *a murderer*, *OT*107, *El*.272: also in late Prose, D.C. 58.15 (s.v.l.). **-εντία**, ἡ, = αὐθεντία, Id.*Fr*.13.2. **-εξάς**, άδος, ἡ, *ideal* ἑξάς, Sch.Arist.833ᵃ2. ⊛ **-εξούσιος**, ον, *autonomous*, Anon. *in EN*139.17. Adv. -ίως ib.139.18. **-έπαινος**, ον, *praising oneself*, τὸ αὐ. Sch.Il.16.70. **-επιθυμία**, ἡ, *the Form of desire*, v.l. in Arist. *Top*.147ᵃ8. **-επίπεδον**, τό, *ideal surface, plane in itself*, Alex. Aphr. *in Metaph*.128.3. **-επιστήμη**, ἡ, *abstract science*, Procl. *in Prm*.p.738 S. **-ετεί**, Adv. of -ετής, Theoc.28.13, Thphr.*CP*3.12.1. **-ετερότης**, ητος, ἡ, *abstract difference*, Plot.2.4.13, Dam.*Pr*.322. ⊛ **-ετής**, ές, (ἔτος) *in* or *of the same year*, of trees, αὐτοετεῖς αὐαίνονται Thphr.*HP*3.7.1; ἔριφος J.*AJ*3.9.3. Adv. αὐτοετές *within the year*, Od.3.322, D.C.36.37; γεννᾶν Arist.*HA*562ᵇ12; *at one year old*, ὀχεύεσθαι ib.545ᵃ24. **-ετίτης**, ου, ὁ, f.l. for αὐτο-ετής, Gal.19.87. **-ζήμιος**, ον, *self-punished*, Hsch. s.v. αὐτόκαρνος. **-ζήτητος**, ον, *self-sought*, i.e. *unsought*, *EM*173.13. **-ζῷον**, τό, *animal in the abstract*, Arist. *Top*.137ᵇ11, Simp. *in Ph*.824.17, Dam.*Pr*.88. II. ⊛ **-ζῳος**, ον, *self-existent*, ψυχή Herm. *in Phdr*.p.118 A., but usu. **-ζως**, ζων, *having life in itself*, Plot.3.8.8; πᾶσα ψυχὴ αὐ. ἐστι Procl.*Inst*.189, cf. Dam.*Pr*.80. **-ηδύ**, τό, *pleasure in the abstract*, v.l. in Arist. *Top*.147ᵃ8. **-ήλιος**, ὁ, *ideal sun*, Alex.Aphr. *in Metaph*.198.15. **-θαΐς**, ίδος, ἡ, *Thais herself*, Luc.*Rh.Pr*.12. **-θάνᾰτος** [θᾰ], ον, *dying by one's own hand*, Plu.2.293e.

**αὐτόθε**, v. αὐτόθεν.

**αὐτο-θελεί**, Adv. of sq., *voluntarily*, *AP*7.470 (Mel.). **-θελής**, ές, *of one's own will*, ib.9.79 (Leon.), 5.21 (Rufin.). Adv. -λῶς Eust. 771.20.

**αὐτόθεν**, before a conson. sts. **αὐτόθε**, Theoc.5.60, *Supp.Epigr*.2.293 (Delph., iii/ii B.C.): Adv. I. of Place, = ἐξ αὐτοῦ τοῦ τόπου, *from the very spot*: freq. with a Prep., αὐ. ἐξ ἕδρης *straight* from his seat, without rising, Il.19.77; αὐ. ἐξ ἑδρέων Od.13.56, cf. 21.420; ἐκ τοῦ Ἄργους αὐ. Th.5.83; Ἄργεος ἐξ ἱεροῖο αὐ. Theoc.25.171: rare in Trag., σὺ δ' αὐ. μοι χαῖρε *from where you stand, not coming nearer*, S. *OC*1137; τῶν μὲν αὐ. τῶν δὲ ἀπὸ Στρυμόνος some *from the country* itself, others . ., Hdt.1.64; αὐ. παρασκευῇ ἐπιέναι with a force *raised on the spot*, Th.6.21; αὐ. πολεμοῦντα βιοτεύειν live *on the country*, Id.1.11; ὅπως αὐ. αὐτῷ τὰ σώματα καὶ τὴν γνώμην παρασκευάζοιντο X.*Ages*.1.28; οἱ αὐ. *the natives*, Th.2.25, 6.21, cf. 4.129; χρυσὸς αὐ. καθαρὸς *in its native state*, Plb.34.10.12; ἐνθένδ' αὐ. Ar.*Ach*.116; ὕδωρ αὐ. ποθὲν συλλειβόμενον Luc.*Alex*.13. 2. *from oneself, of one's own accord, spontaneously*, Demetr.*Eloc*.32; αὐ. εἰδέναι τι Dam. *Pr*.351. II. of Time, as we say *on the spot*, i.e. *at once, immediately*, Il.20.120, A.*Supp*.102, Hdt.8.64, Th.1.141; δῆλός ἐστιν αὐ. Ar.*Eq*.330, cf. *Ec*.246, Pl.*Grg*.470e; λέγετε αὐ. Id.*Smp*.213a. 2. *obviously*, αὐ. ἐκφανής *self-*evident, Cleom.1.8; αὐ. γνώριμος Muson. *Fr*.1 p.2 H.; αὐ. πρόδηλον S.E.*P*.2.164; αὐ. φαίνεσθαι Plu.2.930a; αὐ. ἐναργής Plot.5.5.1. 3. *hastily*, Plb.5.35.13, al., D.S.1.37. III. *merely, only*, dub. in Pl.*Sph*.220b, cf. Plu.2.631d, Luc.*Merc.Cond*.4.

**αὐτό-θεος**, ὁ, *very God*, Procl. *in Prm*.p.856 S., Eustr. *in EN*287.34. **-θεότης**, ητος, ἡ, *very Godhead*, Procl. *in Prm*.p.866 S. **-θερμος**, ον, *warm in itself*, Olymp. *in Pl.d*.p.226 N. **-θετος**, ον, *self-placed*, Sch.D.T.p.220 H. **-θηκτος**, ον, *self-sharpened*, epith. of cold-forged iron, A.*Fr*.356. **-θήρευτος**, ον, *self-caught* or *taken*, Sch.Opp.*H*.5.588.

**αὐτόθῐ**, Adv. = αὐτοῦ, *on the spot*, αὐτόθ' ἔασε κεῖσθαι Il.5.847, etc.; παρ' αὐ. (vv.ll. αὐτόφι, αὐτίκα) 23.147, cf. Hdt.1.93, 2.44,56, al.: also in Com. and Att. Prose, Ar.*Eq*.119, Pherecr.84, Lys.23.11, Pl. *Prt*.314b, al. II. later of Time, *on the spot*, Luc.*Cal*.24.

**αὔτοικος** λεώς, prob. *a slave with his house*, *GDI*5533 e 6.

**αὐτό-ϊππος**, ὁ, *ideal horse*, Arist.*Metaph*.1040ᵇ33. **-ἴσον**, τό, *ideal equality*, Alex.Aphr. *in Metaph*.79.14, Procl. *in Prm*.p.676 S., Herm. *in Phdr*.p.121 A. **-ἰσότης**, ητος, ἡ, *abstract equality*, Procl. *in Prm*.p.676 S. ⊛ **-κάβδᾰλος**, ον, *done carelessly, slovenly*, Arist. *Rh*.1415ᵇ38; αὐ. σκάφος a bark *built offhand*, Lyc.745. Adv. -λως *extempore*, περὶ εὐόγκων λέγειν Arist.*Rh*.1408ᵃ12. II. αὐτοκάβδαλοι, οἱ, *buffoons, improvisers*, Eup.200, Semus 20, Luc.*Lex*.10. **-κᾰκον**, τό, *evil in itself, radical evil*, Plot.1.8.8, Herm. *in Phdr*.p.156 A. 2. masc. -κακος, ὁ, *self-tormentor*, Theopomp.Com.20. **-καλές**· τὸ ἐπιτυχόν, συμβεβηκός, Hsch. **-καλλονή**, ἡ, *ideal, absolute beauty*, Procl.*Theol.Plat*.1.24; also **-καλλος**, τό, ib.5.14, Herm. *in Phdr*. p.157 A., Procl. *in Prm*.p.667 S. **-κᾰλον**, τό, *ideal beauty*, Aristid.2.182 J., Plot.1.8.13. **-καρνος**, ον, = αὐτοζήμιος, Hsch. **-καρπος**, ον, *self-fructifying*, *AB*464. ⊛ **-κᾰσιγνήτη**, ἡ, *own sister*, Od.10.137, E.*Ph*.136 (lyr.), etc. ⊛ **-κᾰσίγνητος**, ὁ, *own brother*, Il.2.706, al. **-κατάκρῐτος**, ον, *self-condemned*, *Ep.Tit*.3.11, Ph.2.652. **-κατασκεύαστος**, ον, *self-made, natural*, Sch.A.*Pr*.298, 301. ⊛ **-κέλευθος**, ον, *going one's own road*, Tryph.314, *AP*9.362.5, Nonn.*D*.6.369: neut. pl. as Adv., ib.21.167. **-κέλευστος**, ον, *self-bidden*, i.e. *unbidden*, X.*An*.3.4.5, D.H.8.66, *AP*5.21 (Rufin.); προθυμία Ph.2.90, al. Adv. -τως Aristeas 9. **-κελής**, ές, = foreg., Hdt.9.5. **-κεραs**, (κεράννυμι) *self-mixed*, Poll.6.24; used as Adv. acc. to Phryn.*PS* p.1 B. **-κέραστος**, *self-mixed*, i.e. *unmixed*, properly of light wines that need no water, dub., ibid. **-κερκίς**, ίδος, ἡ, *ideal shuttle*, Procl. *in Prm*.p.773 S. **-κῆρυξ**, ῡκος, ὁ, *self-heralded*, prob. in Phryn.*PS* p.5 B. **-κῑνέω**, *have the principle of motion in oneself*, f.l. in Procl.*Inst*.20, Serv. ad Virg.*Aen*.10.304. ⊛ **-κίνησία**, ἡ, = sq., Procl.*Inst*.20, Iamb.*Myst*.1.4, Dam.*Pr*.16, etc. **-κίνησις** [ῐ], εως, ἡ, *self-motion*, Syrian. *in Metaph*.45.26, etc.; ἔστιν ἡ ἐπιστήμη αὐ. Plot.6.2.18, cf. 6.6.6. **-κῑνητίζομαι**, *to be self-moved*, Dam.*Pr*.18. ⊛ **-κίνητος** [ῐ], ον, *self-moved*, Arist.*Ph*.258ᵃ2, Plu. 2.952e, etc.; λογικὴ φύσις Ph.1.36, cf. Procl.*Inst*.14, Dam.*Pr*.78; of *live-*stock, πράγματα κινητά τε καὶ ἀκίνητα καὶ αὐ. *PMasp*.122.3 (vi A.D.), etc. Adv. -τως Procl.*Inst*.195, Olymp. *in Alc*.p.61 C. **-κλᾰδος**, ον, *branches and all*, Luc.*VH*1.40. **-κλητος**, ον, *self-called*, i.e. *uncalled, unbidden*, A.*Eu*.170 (lyr.), S.*Tr*.392, Pl. *Ep*.331b; συμβουλεῦσαι αὐ. Phld.*Ir*.p.46 W.; αὐ. ἐπίκουροι *natural* allies (of parents and children), Hierocl.p.57 A.; δῆμος εἰς τοὺς πολέμους αὐ. Him.*Ecl*.5.14; *personally invited*, Plu.2.707f. **-κμής**, ῆτος, ὁ, ἡ, (κάμνω) = αὐτοπόνητος, Opp.*H*.1.718. **-κομος**, ον, *with natural hair, shaggy*, λοφιά Ar.*Ra*.822. II. *leaves and all*, Luc.*VH*1.40. **-κρᾱνος**, ον, *self-accomplishing*, λόγος prob. in A.*Fr*.295. II. Pass., *self-accomplished, self-evident*, Hsch., *EM* 173.34. III. *monolith*, Hsch. **-κρας**, = αὐτοκέραστος, Poll. 6.24. **-κρᾰσία**, ἡ, = sq., *PTaur*.8.67. **-κράτεια** [ρᾰ], ἡ, *power over oneself*, Pl.*Def*.412d. **-κράτειρα** [ρᾰ], ἡ, fem. of αὐτοκράτωρ, Orph.*H*.70.8. **-κρᾰτής**, ές, *ruling by oneself, absolute, independent*, νοῦς Anaxag.12; τύχη Hp.*Loc.Hom*.46; φρὴν E.*Andr*.482 (lyr.); ἀπειθὴς τε καὶ αὐ. Pl.*Ti*.91b; γένεσις οὐδεμία αὐ. ἐστιν Dam.*Pr*.394; τὸ αὐ. Plu.2.1026d. Adv. -κρατῶς Lyd. *Mag*.1.33. **-κράτητος** [ᾰ], ον, = αὐτάγρευτος, Sch.Opp.*H*.4.449. **-κρᾰτορεύω**, *to be* or *become Emperor*, D.C.69.4, *POxy*.33 ii 9 (ii A.D.). **-κρᾰτορία**, ἡ, *sovereignty*, of the Emperors, D.C. 67.12; also **-εία**, ἡ, *reign of an Emperor*, *PFlor*.56.13 (iii A.D.), etc. **-κρᾰτόρια**, τά, *festival in honour of the Emperor*, *IGRom*.3.682. **-κρᾰτορικός**, ή, όν, *of* or *for the Imperator*, ἐσθής D.H.8.59, cf. Gal.8.355, *BGU*970.23 (ii A.D.), etc. Adv. -κῶς *despotically*, Plu. *Ant*.15. **-κρᾰτορίς**, ίδος, ἡ, *the residence of a sovereign*, J.*AJ* 18.2.1. **-κρᾰτος**, ον, = αὐτοκέραστος, Ath.1.32f, Phryn.*PS* p.29 B. ⊛ **-κράτωρ** [ᾰ], ορος, ὁ, ἡ, (κρᾰτέω) *one's own master*: hence, 1. of persons or states, *free, independent*, Th.4.63, *IG*12(9).189.44, etc.: of a youth *that has come of age*, X.*Mem*.2.1.21. 2. of ambassadors and commissioners, *possessing full powers, plenipotentiary*, αὐτοκράτορά τινα ἑλέσθαι Ar.*Pax* 359; αὐ. ἥκομεν Id.*Av*.1595; πρεσβευτής Lys.13.9; ξυγγραφεῖς Th.8.67; αὐ. βουλή And.1.15; ἀποδεῖξαι ἄνδρας ἀρχὴν αὐτοκράτορας, opp. a reference to the assembly, Th.5.27. 3. of rulers, *absolute*, στρατηγοί Id.6.72; ἄρχων X. *An*.6.1.21; ἀνυπεύθυνος καὶ αὐ. ἄρχειν Pl.*Lg*.875b, cf. *Plt*.299c; τὸ πᾶν αὐ. διαθεῖναι manage all *at their pleasure*, Th.1.126; ἦρχε τῶν ἀκολουθούντων αὐτὸς αὐτοκράτωρ, of Philip, D.18.235; μόναρχοι Arist.*Pol.* 1295$^{a}$12; στρατηγία ib.1285$^{a}$8 (dub.); νοῦς αὐ. (cf. αὐτοκρατής) Anaxag. ap.Pl.*Cra.*413c: hence, = Lat. *Dictator*, Plb.3.86.7, etc.; = *Imperator*, Plu.*Pomp.*8; of *the Emperor*, Id.*Galb.*1, etc. **4.** αὐ. λογισμός *peremptory* reasoning, Th.4.108. **II.** c. gen., *complete master of..*, πόλις οὐκ αὐ. οὖσα ἑαυτῆς Id.3.62; τῆς τύχης Id.4.64; τῆς αὐτοῦ πορείας Pl.*Plt.*274a; τῆς ἐπιορκίας αὐ. *having full liberty to* swear falsely, D.17.12: c. inf., αὐ. κολάσαι *having full power* to punish, Id. 59.80. **-κρηής**, ές, = αὐτοκέραστος, Nic.*Al.*163. **-κρῐτος**, ον, (κρίνω) *self-interpreted*, κρίσεις ὀνείρων Artem.4.72. **-κτητος**, ον, *acquired* or *possessed by oneself*, χωρία *Test.Epict.*1.32. **-κτίστης**, ου, ὁ, *itself the creator*, Plu.*Nob.*12. **-κτῐτος**, ον, (κτίζω) *self-produced*, i.e. *made by nature, natural*, αὐτόκτιτ' ἄντρα A.*Pr.*303; αὐ. δόμους S.*Fr.*332. **-κτονέω**, *slay one another*, restored in S.*Ant.* 56 for the f.l. αὐτοκτενοῦντε. **-κτόνος**, ον, *self-slaying*, χεὶρ αὐ., of Medea, *who slew her own children*, E.*Med.*1254 (lyr.). Adv. -νως *with one's own hand*, A.*Ag.*1635. **2.** *slaying one another*, χέρες Id.*Th.*810; θάνατος αὐ. *mutual* death *by each other's hand*, ib.681; δῶρα αὐ. *AP*7.152 (Leont.). Adv. -νως A.*Th.*734 (lyr.). **-κῠβερνήτης**, ου, ὁ, *one who steers himself*, *AP*9.438 (Phil.). ⊛ **-κυκλος**, ὁ, *the ideal circle, the Form of circle*, Them.*Or.*13.165a, Procl. *in Prm.* p.773 S. **-κύλιστος** [ῠ], ον, *self-rolled* or *moved*, Opp.*H.*2.604, Nonn.*D.*2.434. **-κωλος**, 'skin and bone', *a mere skeleton*, prob. in Semon.7.76. **-κωπος**, ον, *with haft* and blade *in one*, βέλη αὐ., i.e. *swords*, A.*Ch.*163 (lyr.). **-λᾰβος**, ον, = foreg., Hsch. **-λάλητής**, οῦ, ὁ, *one who talks to himself*, Timo 50.

**αὐτόλειον**· λειτόν, Hsch.

**αὐτο-λεξεί**, Adv. *with the very words, in express words*, Ph.2. 597. ⊛ **-λήκῠθος**, ὁ, *one who carries his own oil-flask, one who has no slave to do so*: hence, *wretchedly poor*, Antiph.16, Men.105; αὐ., οἱ, 'the Beggars', name of a club, D.54.14. **II.** *flatterer, parasite*, Luc.*Lex.*10, Plu.2.50c. **-ληπτον**, gloss on αὐτάγρετον, Apollon. *Lex.Hom.* ⊛ **-λόχευτος**, ον, *self-engendered*, Nonn.*D.*4.427. **-λύκιον**, τό, *white hellebore*, *Hippiatr.*26. **-λῠρίζων** ὄνος an ass *that plays the lyre to himself*, prov. in Luc.*DMeretr.*14.4. **-λῠσις**, εως, ἡ, *couple* or *leash for hounds*, Hsch. ⊛ **-μάθεια** [μᾰ], ἡ, *self-teaching* or *learning*, Plu.2.973e:—also **-μᾰθία**, Aristid.Quint.2.9. **-μᾰθής**, ές, *having learnt of oneself*, Ph.1.35, al., Plu.2.992a; τινός *self-taught*, of persons, *in* a thing, *AP*6.218 (Alc.); of that which is learnt, ἐπιστήμη Ph.1.164; *spontaneous*, συγγένειαν εἶναι μούσαις αὐτομαθῆ Phld.*Po.*2.47. Adv. -θῶς Philostr.*VS*1.15.2, Ph.1.62. **-μαρτῠς**, ῠρος, ὁ, ἡ, *oneself the witness*, i.e. *eyewitness*, A.*Ag.*989 (lyr.).

**αὐτομᾰτ-εί** or **-τί**, Adv. of -ματος, Nonn.*D.*4.153 (dub.). **-έω**, = αὐτοματίζω, Hsch. s.v. αὐτοφαρίζειν. **-ία**, ἡ, *the goddess of chance*, Plu.*Tim.*36, 2.542e, 816e. ⊛ **-ίζω**, *act of oneself, act offhand* or *unadvisedly*, X.*Cyr.*4.5.21:—Pass., *to be done spontaneously* or *at random*, Plu.*Ages.*23, Procl. *in Ti.*1.297 D.; but ηὐτοματισμένη παράδοσις *haphazard*, Id.*Hyp.*7.35. Adv. ηὐτοματισμένως Id. *in Prm.* p.650 S. **2.** *introduce the agency of chance*, of Anaxagoras, Simp. *in Ph.*327.27. **3.** of things, *happen of themselves, casually*, Hp. *Acut.*(*Sp.*)33; φήμη D.S.16.92:—Pass., *to be self-produced*, Ph.1. 441. **4.** of natural agencies, *act spontaneously*, ὥσπερ αὐτοματιζούσης τῆς φύσεως Arist.*GA*715$^{b}$27, cf. D.H.*Comp.*20. ⊛ **-ισμός**, ὁ, *that which happens of itself, chance*, Hp.*Acut.*(*Sp.*)57, Alcid.*Soph.* 25 (pl.), D.H.1.4, J.*AJ*10.11.7; κατ' αὐτοματισμόν Phleg.*Mir.*1.

**αὐτομᾰτοποιητική** (sc. τέχνη), ἡ, *art of making marionettes*, and τὰ αὐ. *treatise thereupon*, Hero *Aut.*1.1.

⊛ **αὐτό-μᾰτος**, η, ον, Hom. and Att.; ος, ον Hes.*Op.*103, Arist.*GA* 762$^{a}$9, Philetaer.1 D., Hp.*Ep.*19 in *Hermes* 53.65. **1.** of persons, *acting of one's own will, of oneself*, αὐ. δέ οἱ ἦλθε Il.2.408; αὐ. φοιτῶσι Νοῦσοι Hes.*Op.*103; αὐ. ἥκω Ar.*Pl.*1190, cf. Th.6.91, D.S.2.25, etc. **2.** of inanimate things, *self-acting, spontaneous*, of the gates of Olympus, αὐτόμαται δὲ πύλαι μύκον οὐρανοῦ Il.5.749; of the tripods of Hephaistos, which ran of themselves, ὄφρα οἱ αὐτόματοι..δυσαίατ' ἀγῶνα 18.376, cf. Pl.Com.188; ὅπλα.. αὐ. φανῆναι ἔξω προκείμενα τοῦ νηοῦ Hdt.8.37; τὰ αὐ. *marionettes*, Arist.*GA*734$^{b}$10, Hero *Aut.* passim: generally, *spontaneous*, βίος Pl.*Plt.*271e; ἔπαινος Epicur. *Sent.Vat.*64. **3.** of natural agencies, ὁ ποταμὸς αὐ. ἐπελθών *of itself*, Hdt.2.14; of plants, *growing of themselves*, αὐ. ἐκ τῆς γῆς γίνεται Id.3.100; αὐ. φύεσθαι Id.2.94, Thphr.*Fr.*171.11; κύτισος αὐ. ἔρχεται Cratin.98.8: metaph., αὐτόματα πάντ' ἀγαθὰ..πορίζεται Ar. *Ach.*976, cf. Cratin.160; of philosophers, αὐ. ἀναφύονται Pl.*Tht.* 180c. **4.** of events, *happening of themselves, without external agency*, αὐ. δεσμὰ διελύθη E.*Ba.*447; αὐ. θάνατος *natural* death, D. 18.205; κόποι αὐ. *not to be accounted for externally*, Hp.*Aph.*2.5; ἀπό τινος αἰτίας αὐτομάτης Pl.*Sph.*265c; *without visible cause, accidental*, opp. ἀπὸ πείρης, Hdt.7.9.γ'. **II.** αὐτόματον, τό, *accident*, τὸ αὐ. αἰτιᾶσθαι Lys.6.25; σε ταὐ. ἀποσέσωκε Men.*Epit.*568; διὰ τὸ αὐ. Arist.*Ph.*195$^{b}$33; τὸ αὐ. ἀγαπῶντες Id.*Ath.*8.5; τῷ αὐ., opp. τέχνῃ, Id.*Metaph.*1070$^{a}$7: most freq. in the form ἀπὸ τοῦ αὐτομάτου or ἀπὸ ταὐτομάτου, ἀποθανέειν ἀπὸ τοῦ αὐ. Hdt.2.66, cf. Th.2.77, Pl. *Ap.*38c, al., Arist.*Po.*1452$^{a}$5, al., Men.*Pk.*31; ἐκ τοῦ αὐ. X.*An.*1. 3.13; τὸ Αὐ. personified, *Ath.Mitt.*35.458 (Pergam.); ταὐτόματόν ἐστιν ὡς ἔοικέ που θεός Men.291. **III.** Adv. -τως, = ἀπὸ ταὐτομάτου, v.l. in Hdt.2.180, Hp.*Fract.*43, Arist.*PA*640$^{a}$27, al., Theoc.21. 27; *of itself*, κοχλίας αὐ. βαδίζων Plb.12.13.11:—also αὐτοματεί or -τί (q.v.). **-μάττιτα**· σπέρμα ἀνδρός, Hsch. **-μᾰχέω**, (μάχομαι) *fight for oneself, plead one's own cause*, in a law-court, Lys.*Fr.*102 S., Hsch., Suid. **-μέγεθος**, ους, τό, *abstract magnitude*, Procl. *in Prm.* pp.663, 676 S. **-μέλαθρος**, ον, *united with her abode*, of a Hamadryad, Nonn.*D.*48.519. **-μέλιννα**, ἡ, *a very Melinna*, *AP*6.353 (Noss.). **-μενίς**, ἡ, dub. sens. in *BGU*387 ii 4 (ii A.D.). **-μετάβλητος**, ον, *self-changed*, Dam.*Pr.*405. **-μετρος**, ον, *self-measured*, Simp. *in Ph.*767.2. **-μήκης**, ες, *self-lengthened*, i.e. *square*, of a number, opp. ἑτερομήκης, Iamb. *in Nic.*p.74 P. **-μῆκος**, ους, τό, *abstract length*, prob. in Arist.*Top.*143$^{b}$24. **-μηνί**, Adv. *in the very month*, Attic.ap.Eus.*PE*15.4. **-μήνῡτος**, ον, *self-revealed* or *betrayed*, Phryn.*PS* p.51 B. **-μήτωρ**, ορος, ἡ, *very mother herself*, or *her mother's very child*, dub. in Semon.7.12. **-μοιρος**, ον, *with a single share*, S.*Fr.*250 (= μονόμοιρος, Hsch.).

**αὐτομολ-έω**, *desert*, Hdt.8.82, Ar.*Eq.*26, Th.3.77, etc.; αὐ. πρὸς τοὺς Πέρσας Hdt.1.127, etc.; ἐς αὐτούς Id.3.154, al.; ἐς Ἀθήνας ἐκ Περσέων ib.160; παρά τινος X.*An.*1.7.13; εἰς τοὺς πολεμίους αὐτομολήσας οἴχεσθαι And.1.44. **II.** metaph., αὐ. ἐν τῇ πολιτείᾳ *keep changing sides, rat*, Aeschin.3.75; αὐ. πρὸς τὴν ἐλευθερίαν D.S.2. 26. **III.** *come of one's own accord*, τὰ θηρία πρὸς τὰς παγίδας -μολήσει Lyd.*Ost.*39. ⊛ **-ησις**, εως, ἡ, = sq., Ph.1.272; rejected by Thom.Mag.p.128 R. ⊛ **-ία**, ἡ, *desertion*, Th.7.13, etc. ⊛ **-ος**, ον, *going of oneself, without bidding*, Opp.*H.*3.360; *coming of oneself*, *AP* 5.21 (Rufin.):—but mostly, **2.** as Subst., *deserter*, Hdt.3.156, al., Th.4.118, al.; παρά τινος X.*An.*1.7.2; γυνὴ αὐ. Hdt.9.76. Adv. -λως *treacherously*, S.*Fr.*691.

**αὐτομόλπως** and **-πα**· ὁμοίως ἐκείνοις, Hsch.

**αὐτό-μορφος**, ον, *self-formed, natural*, E.*Fr.*125. **-νεκρος**, ον, *verily dead, a mere corpse*, Alciphr.3.7.

**αὐτονομ-έομαι**, Dep. c. aor. Pass. -ήθην Str.12.3.11:—*to be independent*, Th.1.144, D.4.4, etc. **-ία**, ἡ, of a state, *freedom to use its own laws, independence*, Th.3.46, X.*HG*5.1.36, Isoc.9.68, *IG*2$^{2}$. 34, etc. **2.** αὐ. ποιητική, poetic *licence*, Him.*Or.*1.1. **3.** *dogmatism*, Olymp. *in Mete.*151.21. **-ος**, ον, *living under one's own laws, independent*, of persons and states, Hdt.1.96, 8.140.α', Cratin. 15 D., etc.; freq. in Th., αὐ. ἐπὶ σφῶν αὐτῶν οἰκεῖν Id.2.63; ἀφιέναι αὐ. τινα Id.1.139; αὐ. ποιεῖν τινα Id.5.33; αὐ. ἀπό τινος X.*HG* 5.1.36, cf. *Lac.*3.1; πόλις.. ἐλευθέρα καὶ αὐ. *IG*3.481, al.; αὐ. πολιτεία Plu.*Rom.*27. **2.** generally, *of one's own free will*, ἀλλ' αὐ... Ἀΐδην καταβήσει S.*Ant.*821 (lyr.). **3.** of animals, *feeding and ranging at will*, *AP*7.8 (Antip. Sid.).

⊛ **αὐτο-νοέω**, *think for oneself*, prob. in Meno *Iatr.*20.24. **-νοος**, ον, contr. **-νους**, ουν, of the Phaeacian ships, *instinct with sense*, Eust. 1153.32, with allusion to the nymph Autonoe. **-νους**, ὁ, *pure intellect*, Plot.3.2.16; νοῦ [ἕτερος] αὐτόνους Id.5.9.13. **-νυκτί**, Adv. = sq., J.*AJ*17.9.5. **-νῠχί** [ῑ] or **-χεί**, Adv., (νύξ) *that very night*, Il.8.197, Aristid.*Or.*48(24).16; *in the same night*, Arat.618, A.R.4. 1130. **II.** **αὐτ-ανῠχί**, (ὄνυξ) *with the nail*, *EM*173.57. **-νύχιος** [ῠ], ον, *nightly*, Hsch. s.v. ἔννυχος. **-νῠχίς** and **αὐτονῠχηδίς**, = αὐτονυχί 1, Theognost.*Can.*163.17. **-ξενεῖν** (-ξένειν cod.)· ἐν ἴσῳ τῷ προξενεῖν, Hsch. **-ξεστος**, ον, = αὐτοσχέδιος, Anon. *in Rh.*186. 2. ⊛ **-ξῠλος**, ον, *of one piece of wood*, ἔκπωμα S.*Ph.*35, cf. *APl.*4.235 (Apollonid.), Str.11.4.3. **-ολον**, τό, *abstract totality*, Dam.*Pr.* 427. **-ολότης**, ητος, ἡ, = foreg., Procl.*Inst.*69. **-όμοιον**, τό, *abstract similarity*, Id. *in Prm.*p.588 S. **-ομοιότης**, ητος, ἡ, = foreg., Herm. *in Phdr.*p.151 A. **-όν**, όντος, τό, *self-existence*, Dam.*Pr.*28, Them. *in Ph.*9.29: pl., **αὐτοόντα** Procl.*Inst.*128. **-ουσία**, ἡ, *full* or *perfect being*, Plot.6.8.12. **-πᾰγής**, ές, (πήγνυμι) *compact of itself*, γῆ Ephor.108; *rough*, πέτροι Agatharch.32; ϑαλάμαι, of a swarm of bees in the air, *AP*9.404 (Antiphil.). **-πάθεια** [πᾰ], ἡ, *one's own experience*, ἐξ αὐ. διατίθεσθαι τοὺς λόγους Plb.3.108.2, cf. D.H.*Dem.* 22, Plu.*Lib.*1; = ἰδιοπάθεια, *primary affection*, Gal.8.78. **2.** Gramm., of words that are *reflexive*, opp. transitive, A.D.*Synt.*147. 21. **-πᾰθής**, ές, *speaking from one's own feeling* or *experience*. Adv. -θῶς Plb.3.12.1, Plu.*Cat.Mi.*54; *instinctively*, αὐ. φεύγομεν τὴν ἀλγηδόνα Epicur.*Fr.*66, etc. **II.** Gramm., of pronouns, *reflexive*, opp. ἀλλοπαθεῖς, A.D.*Pron.*44.11; of verbs, opp. μεταβατικά, *Synt.* 281.15. **-παίδευτος**, ον, *self-educated*, Anatolius in *Cat.Cod.Astr.* 8(3).188. **-παις**, παιδος, ὁ, ἡ, *the own child*, τῷ Διὸς αὐτόπαιδι S.*Tr.*826 (lyr.); prob. *a mere child*, Id.*Fr.*1029; dub. l. in *PPetr.* 3 p.110. **-πάμων** [ᾱ], ον, gen. ονος, (πέπᾱμαι) *sole heir*, Hsch. (αὐτόπομα cod.). **-παστοι πύλαι**· παστάδας ἔχουσαι, ποικίλαι, Id. **-πάτωρ** [ᾰ], ορος, ὁ, ἡ, *self-engendered*, φύσις Orph.*H.*10. 10, Iamb.*Myst.*8.2; of Zeus, Aristid.*Or.*43(1).9. **-πέδη**, *fetter*, dub. in Nonn.*D.*21.50. **-πεδον**, = αὐτοποδητί, Hsch. **-πειρος**, ον, *learnt by one's own experience*, Dam.*Isid.*121.

**αὐτοπέλις**· κλῖμαξ, Hsch.

**αὐτο-περίγρᾰφος**, ον, *self-circumscribed*, Dam.*Pr.*261,2,6. **-πήμων**, ον, gen. ονος, *for one's own woes*, γόος A.*Th.*917 (lyr.). **-πηρίτης** [ῑ], ου, ὁ, *with only a wallet*, Menipp.*Ep.*tit. **-πιστος**, ον, *credible in itself*, ἀξιώματα Hero *Deff.*136.6, cf. Olymp. *in Phd.*p.225 N., Heliod. *in EN*117.36, Simp. *in Ph.*649.12; f.l. in Oenom.ap.Eus.*PE* 5.33. **-πλεκτος**, ον, *self-twined*, Opp.*H.*4.449. **-πληθος**, ους, τό, *abstract plurality*, Procl.*Theol.Plat.*3.21, Dam.*Pr.*202. **-ποδητί**, Adv. = sq., Luc.*Lex.*2. **-ποδί**, Adv. *on one's own feet, on foot*, D.C.50.5. **-ποδία**, ἡ, *use of one's own feet, walking*, αὐτοποδίᾳ κομισθῆναι D.C.44.8, cf. Stratt.5 D. **-ποιητικός**, ή, όν, opp. εἰδωλοποιϊκός, *making not a copy, but the thing itself*, Pl.*Sph.* 266a. **-ποίητος**, ον, = αὐτοπαγής, Sophr.13. ⊛ **-ποιός**, όν, *self-produced*, i.e. *not planted by man, naturally grown*, of the Athenian olive, S.*OC*698 (lyr.); *made by one's own hand*, of votive offerings,

*IG*4.222 (Corinth). **-πόκιστος**, ον, = sq., Hsch. **-ποκος**, ον, *made of wool only, all wool*, ἱμάτιον *Com.Adesp.*854. **-πολις** πόλις *free, independent* state, Th.5.79. **-πολίτης** [ῐ], ου, ὁ, *citizen of a free state*, prob. in X.*HG*5.2.14. **-πόνητος**, ον, *self-wrought, natural*, ῥεῦμα μελισσῶν *AP*9.404 (Antiphil.). **-πονος**, ον, = foreg., Nic.*Th.*23. **-πορος**, ον, *self-moving*, Nonn.*D.*1.308, 6.370. **-ποσόν**, τό, *abstract quantity*, Plot.4.3.2. **-πους**, ὁ, ἡ, -πουν, τό, gen. ποδος, *on foot, on one's own feet*, Luc.*Tim.*24. **-πρᾱγέω**, *act independently*, Str.8.3.30; *do one's own work*, Procl.*in R.*1.23K. ⊕**-πρᾱγία**, ἡ, *free, independent action*, Pl.*Def.*411e, Chrysipp.*Stoic.*3.176, Ph.2.51, Procl.*in Prm.*p.664S.; ἐξουσία αὐτοπραγίας *Stoic.*3.86. **-πραγμᾰτεύτως**, dub. l. (for ἀπραγμ-) in D.H.*Is.*16. **-πρακτος**, ον, *enjoying the privilege of collecting one's own taxes*, *PMasp.*19.3 (vi A.D.); αὐ. σχῆμα ib.2 iii 8, cf. *Cod.Theod.*11.22.4. ⊕**-πρεμνος**, ον, *together with the root, root and branch*, τὰ δ' ἀντιτείνοντ' αὐτόπρεμν' ἀπόλλυται (sc. δένδρα) S.*Ant.*714, cf. Antiph.231.7; ἀνασπᾶν αὐτοπρέμνοις τοῖς λόγοισιν Ar.*Ra.*903 (paratrag.); αὐ. τι νέμειν give *in absolute possession*, A.*Eu.*401. **-πρεπής**, v. αὐτοτροπήσας. ⊕**-προαίρετος**, ον, *self-chosen*, κακία Hierocl.*in CA*24 p.473 M., cf. Ps.-Plu.*Vit.Hom.*105. Adv. -τως, κολάζεσθαι Simp.*in Epict.*p.108 D. II. Act., *self-acting, acting of free will*, *Proll.Hermog.* in Rh.4.27 W.; τὸ αὐ. τε καὶ αὐτεξούσιον *free will*, Olymp.*in Grg.*p.264 J. **-προθύμως** [ῡ], Adv. *voluntarily*, *EM*173.8. **-πρόσωπος**, ον, *in one's own person, without a mask*, of an actor, Ath.10.452f, cf. Jul.*Mis.*367b; αὐ. φανῆναι Luc.*Pr.Im.*3; αὐ. ὁρᾶν τὸ κάλλος Id.*Tim.*27; λέγειν Id.*JTr.*29; *speaking in one's own person*, Sch.Il.*Oxy.*1086.64, al.; συγγράμματα αὐ. *in which the author speaks in his own person*, Ammon.*in Cat.*4.16; cf. αὐτοδιήγητος. Adv. -πως, θεσπίσαι Ph.2.208; εἰσάγειν τοὺς κωμῳδουμένους Hermog.*Stat.*11 (v.l. -πους); ὑποκρινόμενος Him.*Ecl.*2.21; ἀντεπιστεῖλαι *CPR*20 ii 5 (iii A.D.). **-πτερος**, ον, *with his own wings*, Aristid.*Or.*37(2).24.

**αὐτοπτ-έω**, *see with one's own eyes*, Paus.4.31.5, Hld.3.1; esp. *witness* a divine manifestation, Porph.ap.Eus.*PE*4.20:—Pass., φάσματα -ούμενα Marin.*Procl.*28. **-ης**, ου, ὁ, *seeing oneself, eyewitness*, Hdt.2.29, 3.115, al., Pl.*Lg.*900a, Euang.1.4, Din.3.15, D.22.22, etc.:—fem. **αὐτόπτις**, ἡ, Sch.Il.*Oxy.*1086.96. **-ικός**, ή, όν, *of an eyewitness*, πίστις Scymn.129; opp. λογικός, Gal.16.600. Adv. -κῶς Id.13.350. II. *concerned with a direct vision of divinity*, λεκανομαντ⟨ε⟩ία *PMag.Par.*1.221 (αὐθ-); αὐ. λεκάνης ἐνέργεια *a personal and active* power of dish-divination, Harp.Astr. in *Cat.Cod.Astr.*8(3).136.10; λόγος *PMag.Lond.*46.53, cf. 121.335; δεῖξις Iamb.*Myst.* 2.6. **-ος**, ον, *self-revealed*, Jul.*Or.*7.221b, Suid.; ἐπ' αὐτόπτῳ, gloss on ἐπ' αὐτοφώρῳ, Hsch. II. = αὐτοπτικός II, *PMag.Lond.* 121.319,727, *PMag.Par.*1.162.

**αὐτό-πτυκτος**, *folded on itself*, φύλλα *Gloss.* **-πῡρ**, πῡρος, τό, *very fire*, Herm.ap.Stob.3.11.31. **-πῡρος**, ὁ, *of whole wheaten meal*, ἄρτος Alex.121, Gal.15.577, *PPetr.*3p.179; opp. σητάνειος, Plu.2.466d.—also ⊕**-πῡρίτης** [ῑ], ου, ὁ, Phryn.Com.38, Hp.*Int.*20,22, Luc.*Pisc.*44. **-πώλης**, ου, ὁ, *selling one's own products*, Pl.*Plt.*260c; αὐ. περί τι Id.*Sph.*231d, cf. Sch.Ar.*Pl.*1155. **-πωλικός**, ή, όν, = foreg.: -κή (sc. τέχνη), ἡ, *trade of an* αὐτοπώλης, opp. ἐμπορική, καπηλική, Pl.*Sph.*223d, cf. 224e. **-ρέγμων**, ον, gen. ονος, (ῥέζω) *self-wrought*, πότμος A.*Fr.*117. **-ρήτωρ**, ορος, ὁ, *a self-made orator*, Eust.1301.32.

**αὐτ-όροφος**, ον, *self-covered, roofed* or *vaulted by nature*, πέτρα Opp.*H.*1.22; καλάμων σκηναί D.H.1.79; αὐ. στέγη *a natural roof*, Ael.*NA*16.17.

**αὐτό-ρρεκτος**, ον, *self-produced*, Opp.*C.*2.567, *H.*1.763. **-ρρῖζος**, ον, *together with the roots*, D.S.4.12: poet. **αὐτόρῐζος**, Babr.36.1. II. *self-rooted, self-founded*, ἑστία E.*Rh.*288. **-ρριφής**, ές, (ῥίπτω) *self-precipitated*, Sch.E.*Ph.*640. **-ρρῠτος**, ον, (ῥέω) *self-flowing, flowing unbidden*, *AP*9.669 (Marian.); of resin, Gal.13.626: poet. ⊕**αὐτόρῠτος**, χρυσός Pi.*P.*12.17.

⊕**αὐτός** (Cret. ἀϝτός *GDI*4976, al.), αὐτή, αὐτό (also αὐτόν *Leg.Gort.*3.4, al.), reflexive Pron., *self*:—in oblique cases used for the personal Pron., *him, her, it*:—with Art., ὁ αὐτός, ἡ αὐτή, τὸ αὐτό (also ταὐτόν), etc., *the very one, the same*.

I. *self, myself, thyself*, etc., acc. to the person of the Verb: freq. joined with ἐγώ, σύ, etc. (v. infr. 10), 1. *one's true self*, the *soul*, not the body, Od.11.602; reversely, *body*, not soul, Il.1.4; *oneself*, as opp. others who are less prominent, as king to subject, 6.18; Zeus to other gods, 8.4; bird to young, 2.317; man to wife and children, Od.14.265; warrior to horses, Il.2.466, or to weapons, 1.47; shepherd to herd, Od.9.167, cf. Il.1.51; Trojans to allies, 11.220; seamen to ships, 7.338: generally, whole to parts, ib.474; so later ἡ σίδη καὶ αὐτὴ καὶ τὰ φύλλα Thphr.*HP*4.10.7, cf. X.*Ath.*1.19, Pl.*Grg.*511e, etc.; αὐτή τε Μανδάνη καὶ τὸν υἱὸν ἔχουσα X.*Cyr.*1.3.1; αὐ. τε καὶ τὰ ποιήματα βουλόμενος ἐπιδεῖξαι Pl.*R.*398a: abs., *the Master*, as in the Pythag. phrase Αὐτὸς ἔφα, Lat. *Ipse dixit*; so τίς οὗτος..;—Αὐτός, i.e. Socrates, Ar.*Nu.*218; ἀνάβλεψον Αὐτόν ib.219; ἀνοιγέτω τις δώματ'· Αὐτὸς ἔρχεται *the Master*, Id.*Fr.*268, cf. Pl.*Prt.*314d, Thphr.*Char.*2.4, Men.*Sam.*41: αὐ. ἀϋτεῖ Theoc.24.50: neut., αὐτὸ σημανεῖ *the result* will show, E.*Ph.*623; αὐτὸ δηλώσει D.19.157; αὐτὰ δηλοῖ Pl.*Prt.*329b; αὐτὸ διδάξει ib.324a; esp. αὐτὸ δείξει Cratin.177, Pl.*Hp.Ma.*288b, cf. *Tht.*200e; in full, τάχ' αὐτὸ δείξει τοὔργον S.*Fr.*388; τοὔργον τάχ' αὐτὸ δείξει Ar.*Lys.*375; redupl., αὐτός θ' ὁ χρήσας αὐτὸς ἦν ὁ μαρτυρῶν A.*Eu.*798; of things, *the very*, ὑπὸ λόφον αὐτόν, i.e. *just, exactly* under.., Il.13.615; πρὸς αὐταῖς ταῖς θύραις *close* by the door, Lys.12.12; αὐτὸ τὸ δέον *the very* thing needed, X.*An.*4.7.7; αὐτὸ δ' μάλιστα ἔδει ῥηθῆναι Pl.*R.*362d; αὐτὸ τὸ περίορθρον *the point* of dawn, Th.2.3; αὐτὰ τὰ ἐναντία the *very* opposite, X.*Mem.*4.5.7; αὐτὰ τὰ χρήσιμα καὶ ἀναγκαῖα D.H.*Th.*23; *even*, οὔ μοι μέλει ἄλγος οὔτ' αὐτῆς Ἑκάβης Il.6.451; εἴ περ ἂν αὐταὶ Μοῦσαι ἀείδοιεν 2.597.—In these senses αὐτός in Prose either precedes both the Art. and Subst., or follows both, e.g. αὐτὸς ὁ υἱός or ὁ υἱὸς αὐτός. The Art. is sts. omitted with proper names, or Nouns denoting individuals, αὐτὸς Μένων X.*An.*2.1.5; αὐτὸς βασιλεύς ib.1.7.11. 2. *of oneself, of one's own accord*, ἀλλά τις αὐ. ἴτω Il.17.254; σπεύδοντα καὶ αὐτὸν ὀτρύνεις 8.293; καταπαύσομεν· οἱ δὲ καὶ αὐτοὶ παυέσθων Od.2.168; ἥξει γὰρ αὐτά S.*OT*341; also, *in person*, τῶν πραγμάτων ὑμῖν.. αὐτοῖς ἀντιληπτέον D.1.2. 3. *by oneself* or *itself, alone*, αὐτός περ ἐών although *alone*, Il.8.99; αὐτὸς ἐγείναο παῖδ', i.e. *without a mother*, 5.880, cf. Hes.*Th.*924; ἀνακομισθῆναι αὐτὸν ἐς Φάληρον *by himself*, Hdt.5.85; αὐτοί γάρ ἐσμεν we are *by ourselves*, i.e. *among friends*, Ar.*Ach.*504, cf. *Th.*472, Pl.*Prm.*137b, Herod.6.70, Plu.2.755c, Luc.*DDeor.*10.2; αὐτοῖς τοῖς ἀνδράσι.. ἢ καὶ τοῖς ἄλλοις X.*An.*2.3.7; ἄνευ τοῦ σίτου τὸ ὄψον αὐτὸ ἐσθίειν Id.*Mem.*3.14.3; τὸν τρίβωνα ὃν αὐτὸν φορεῖ Thphr.*Char.*22.13 (prob.); αὐτὰ γὰρ ἔστιν ταῦτα these *and no others*, Emp.21.13, al.: strengthd., αὐτὸς κτήσατο οἶος *himself* alone, Od.14.450; αὐτὸς μόνος, v. μόνος II; αὐτὸς καθ' αὑτόν, v. ἑαυτοῦ. 4. in Philosophy, *by* or *in itself*, of an abstract concept or idea, δίκαιον αὐτό Pl.*Phd.*65d; αὐτὸ τὸ ἕν Id.*Prm.*143a, al., cf. Arist.*Metaph.*997ᵇ8: neut., αὐτό is freq. in this sense, attached to Nouns of all genders, οὐκ αὐτὸ δικαιοσύνην ἐπαινοῦντες ἀλλὰ τὰς ἀπ' αὐτῆς εὐδοκιμήσεις Pl.*R.*363a; less freq. with Art., τί ποτ' ἐστὶν αὐτὸ ἡ ἀρετή Id.*Prt.*360e; more fully, εἰ αὐτὸ τοῦτο πατέρα ἠρώτων, ἆρα ὁ πατήρ ἐστι πατήρ τινος, ἢ οὔ; Id.*Smp.*199d; ἀδελφός, αὐτὸ τοῦτο ὅπερ ἔστιν *the ideal, abstract* brother, ibid.e: later, in compos., αὐτοαγαθόν, αὐτοάνθρωπος, etc. (q.v.), cf. Arist.*Metaph.*1040ᵇ33; less freq. agreeing with the Subst., ἵνα αὐτὴ δικαιοσύνη πρὸς ἀδικίαν αὐτὴν κριθείη Pl.*R.*612c, etc.; doubled, ἐκ τῆς εἰκόνος μανθάνειν αὐτήν τε αὑτήν, εἰ καλῶς εἴκασται *its very self*, Id.*Cra.*439a. 5. in dat. with Subst., *in one, together*, ἀνόρουσεν αὐτῇ σὺν φόρμιγγι he sprang up lyre *in hand*, Il.9.194; αὐτῇ σὺν πήληκι κάρη helmet *and all*, 14.498, cf. Od.13.118; αὐτῷ σὺν ἄγγει E.*Ion*32, cf. *Hipp.*1213; also without σύν, αὐτῇ κεν γαίῃ ἐρύσαι Il.8.24: so freq. in Prose and Poetry, αὐτοῖς ἀνδράσι men *and all*, Hdt.6.93; αὐτοῖσι συμμάχοισι allies *and all*, A.*Pr.*223 (lyr.); αὐτοῖς μελάθροις διακναιομένους E.*Med.*164: with Art., αὐτοῖσι τοῖσι ἱματίοισι ἀπ' ὧν ἔβαψε ἑωυτόν Hdt.2.47; αὐτοῖσι τοῖς πόρπαξι Ar.*Eq.*849, etc.; αὐτοῖς τοῖς ἵπποις κατακρημνισθῆναι X.*Cyr.*1.4.7. 6. added to ordinal Numbers, e.g. πέμπτος αὐτός *himself* the fifth, i.e. *himself* with four others, Th.1.46, cf. 8.35, X.*HG*2.2.17, *Apoc.*17.11, etc.:—αὐτός always being the chief person. 7. freq. coupled with οὗτος, τοῦτ' αὐτό ἐστι τὸ ζητηθέν Pl.*Plt.*267c, etc.; αὐτὸ τοῦτο μόνον Id.*Grg.*500b; also λεγόντων ἄλλο μὲν οὐδέν.. αὐτὰ δὲ τάδε Th.1.139; πόλεις ἄλλας τε καὶ αὐτὸ τοῦτο τὸ Βυζάντιον X.*An.*7.1.27; ταῦτα ἥκω αὐτὰ ἵνα.. Pl.*Prt.*310e. 8. καὶ αὐτός *himself* too, Od.7.73, 14.45, X.*An.*5.5.9, etc. 9. repeated in apodosi for emphasis, αὐτὸς ἐπαγγειλάμενος σώσειν..αὐτὸς ἀπώλεσεν Lys.12.68, cf. A.*Fr.*350, X.*An.*3.2.4. 10. in connexion with the person. Pron., ἐγὼν αὐτός Od.2.194; σέθεν αὐτοῦ Il.23.312; νωΐτερον αὐτῶν 15.39 (always divisim in Hom.); folld. by an enclit. Pron., αὐτόν μιν Od.4.244; so αὐτὸν γάρ σε δεῖ Προμηθέως A.*Pr.*86; also αὐτὸς ἔγωγε Pl.*Phd.*59b, etc.:—after Hom. in the oblique cases αὐτός coalesces with the Pron., ἐμαυτοῦ, σεαυτοῦ (these not in Alc. or Sapph., A.D.*Pron.*80.10 sqq.), ἑαυτοῦ, etc. (q.v.). b. with person. Pron. omitted, αὐτός.. ἧσθαι λιλαίομαι, for ἐγὼ αὐτός, Il.13.252; αὐτὸν ἐλέησον, for ἐμὲ αὐτόν, 24.503; αὐτῶν γὰρ ἀπωλόμεθ' ἀφραδίῃσιν Od.10.27; in 2.33 οἱ αὐτῷ is simply a strengthd. form of οἱ; and so in Att., when σὲ αὐτόν, ἐμοὶ αὐτῷ, etc., are read divisim, they are emphatic, not reflexive; in this case αὐτός generally precedes the person. Pron., cf. X.*Cyr.*6.2.25 with 6.1.14. c. with the reflexive ἑαυτοῦ, αὑτοῦ, etc., to add force and definiteness, αὐτὸς καθ' αὑτοῦ A.*Th.*406; αὐτοὶ ὑφ' αὑτῶν ib.194; αὐτοὶ καθ' αὑτούς X.*Mem.*3.5.4; αὐτὸ καθ' αὑτό Pl.*Tht.*201e; sts. between the Art. and reflex. Pron., τοῖς αὐτὸς αὑτοῦ πήμασιν βαρύνεται A.*Ag.*836, cf. *Pr.*762; τούς γ' αὐτὸς αὑτοῦ πολεμίους S.*Aj.*1132: also κατ' αὐτὺ (Boeot for αὐτοὶ) αὐτῶν *IG*7.3172.121 (Orchom. Boeot.). d. αὐτοῦ, αὐτῶν with possess. Pron., πατρὸς κλέος ἠδ' ἐμὸν αὐτοῦ Il.6.446; θρῆνον.. ἐμὸν τὸν αὐτῆς A.*Ag.*1323; ἐχθροὺς ὧν τοῖς σοῖσιν αὐτοῦ S.*OT*416; τοῖς οἴοιν αὐτοῦ ib.1248; αὐτῶν σφετέρῃσιν ἀτασθαλίῃσιν Od.1.7; τοῖς ἡμετέροις αὐτῶν φίλοις X.*An.*7.1.29. e. αὐτὸς ἑαυτοῦ with Comp. and Sup. Adj., αὐτὸς ἑωυτοῦ ῥέει πολλῷ ὑποδεέστερος Hdt.2.25; τῇ εὐρυτάτη ἐστὶ αὐτὴ ἑωυτῆς Id.1.203. 11. αὐτός for ὁ αὐτός, *the same*, Il.12.225, Od.8.107, 16.138, Pi.*N.*5.1 (never in Trag.), and in later Prose, αὐταῖς ταῖς ἡμέραις *IG* 14.966 (ii A.D.), cf. *Ev.Luc.*23.12. 12. Comp. αὐτότερος Epich.5: Sup. αὐτότατος *his very self*, Ar.*Pl.*83: neut. pl. αὐτότατα dub. in Phld.*Piet.*80. Adv., Comp. αὐτοτέρως Gal.18(2).431.

II. *he, she, it*, for the simple Pron. of 3 pers., only in oblique cases (exc. in later Gk., *Ev.Luc.*4.15, etc.), and rarely first in a sentence, Pl.*La.*194e, and later, *Ep.Eph.*2.10, etc.: rare in Ep., Il.12.204 (where Hdn. treated it as enclitic), and mostly emphatic, ib.14.457, Od.16.388; so in Trag., E.*Hel.*421: in Prose, to recall a Noun used earlier in the sentence, ἐγὼ μὲν οὖν βασιλέα.. οὐκ οἶδα ὅ τι δεῖ αὐτὸν ὀμόσαι X.*An.*2.4.7; πειράσομαι τῷ πάππῳ.. συμμαχεῖν αὐτῷ Id.*Cyr.*1.3.15; ἄνδρα δή.. εἰ ἀφίκοιτο εἰς τὴν πόλιν, προσκυνοῖμεν ἂν αὐτόν Pl.*R.*398a; after a Relative, ὅς κε θεοῖς ἐπιπείθηται.. ἔκλυον αὐτοῦ Il.1.218; οὓς μὴ ηὕρισκον, κενοτάφιον αὐτοῖς ἐποίησαν X.*An.*6.

4.9, cf. 1.9.29; esp. where a second Verb requires a change of case in the Pron., οἳ ἂν ἐξελεγχθῶσι..ὡς προδότας αὐτοὺς ὄντας τιμωρηθῆναι Id.*An.*2.5.27; ἐκεῖνοι οἷς οὐκ ἐχαρίζονθ' οἱ λέγοντες οὐδ' ἐφίλουν αὐτούς D.3.24; in subdivisions, ὅσοι..οἱ μὲν αὐτῶν.. X.*Cyr.*1.1.1, cf. Pl.*Chrm.*168e; later, pleonastically after a Relative, ὧν ὁ μὲν αὐτῶν Call.*Epigr.*43, cf. *Ev.Luc.*3.16, *Apoc.*7.2, etc.: in S.*Ph.*316 αὐτοῖς is emphatic 'in their own persons'.

**III.** with Art. ὁ αὐτός, ἡ αὐτή, τὸ αὐτό, and Att. contr. αὑτός, αὑτή, ταὐτό and ταὐτόν (as required by the metre, cf. S.*OT*734 with 325, and in Prose to avoid hiatus): gen. ταὐτοῦ, dat. ταὐτῷ, pl. neut. ταὐτά; Ion. ὡυτός, τὠυτό:—*the very one, the same*, rare in Hom., Il. 6.391, Od.7.55,326; ὁ αὐ. εἰμι τῇ γνώμῃ Th.3.38, cf. 5.75; ἐπὶ τὸ αὐ. αἱ γνῶμαι ἔφερον Id.1.79: c. dat., to denote sameness or agreement, esp. in Prose, τὠυτὸ ἂν ὑμῖν ἐπρήσσομεν Hdt.4.119; τὸν αὐτὸν χῶρον ἐκλιπὼν ἐμοί A.*Ch.*543; ὁ αὐτὸς τῷ λίθῳ *the same as* the stone, Pl. *Euthd.*298a; ἐν ταὐτῷ εἶναί τινι to be *in the place with..*, X.*An.*3.1. 27; προσίεσθαί τινα ἐς ταὐτὸ ἑαυτῷ to have a person *meet* one, ib.30, cf. A.*Ch.*210; κατὰ ταὐτὰ τῷ Νείλῳ Hdt.2.20; τῇ αὐτῇ..καί Id.4. 109; τὴν αὐτὴν διάνοιαν καὶ κατ' ἐκείνην ἡλικίαν Isoc.5.83; ὁ αὐτός.. ὥσπερ Pl.*Phd.*86a; ἐς ταὐτὸν ἀλλήλοις *face to face*, Jul.*Or.*2.52c. **2.** in later Greek, *the said, the above-named*, Ἡρώδης ὁ αὐ. *PLille* 23.8 (iii B.C.), etc.

**IV.** Adverbial phrases: **1.** αὐτὸ μόνον *simply, merely*, Ph. 2.252, etc.; αὐ. μόνον ἐργάτης Luc.*Somn.*9; αὐ. μόνον τὸ ὄνομα τῆς φωνῆς A.D.*Synt.*22.20. **2.** αὐτό as Adv., = ἄρτι, *Epigr.Gr.*540.1 (Thrace). **3.** αὐτὸ τοῦτο as Adv., *PGrenf.*1.114 (ii B.C.), 2*Ep.Pet.* 1.5; τῆς αὐτὸ τοῦτο κινουμένης σφαίρας Iamb.*Comm.Math.*17. **4.** with Preps., ἐπὶ τὸ αὐτό *added together, making a total*, *PLond.*2. 196.37 (ii A.D.); κατὰ τὸ αὐτό *together, at the same time*, *Act.Ap.*14. 1, etc.; but κατ' αὐτό *just then*, Hdn.1.12.3.

**V.** In Compos.: **1.** *of* or *by oneself, self-..*, as in αὐτοδίδακτος, αὐτογνώμων, αὐτόματος: and so, *independently*, as in αὐτοκράτωρ, αὐτόνομος. **2.** hence, *as a second self, very.., bodily*, as with proper names, Αὐτοθαΐς. **3.** *in the abstract, the ideal*, v. supr. 1.4. **4.** *precisely*, as in αὐτόδεκα. **5.** rarely with reflex. sense of ἀλλήλων, as in αὐτοκτονέω. **6.** *in one piece with, together with*, as in αὐτόκωπος, αὐτοχείλης, αὐτόπρεμνος, αὐτόρριζος. **7.** *by itself*: hence, *only*, as in αὐτόξυλος, αὐτόποκος.—For αὐτοῦ, αὐτῶς, etc., v. the respective Arts.

**αὑτός,** v. sub αὐτός III.

**αὐτοσανδᾰράκη** [ρᾰ], ἡ, *very* σανδαράκη, οἷον τὸ χρῶμα γυναικός, αὐ. Alciphr.*Fr.*4.

⊛ **αὐτοσαυτόν,** Dor. = ἑαυτόν, *GDI*1749, al. (Delph.), *UPZ*1: gen. αὐτοσαυτοῦ *IG*2.550.5 (Delph.), 5(1).1432.28 (Messene, i B.C.), *Tab. Defix.*p.xxxi: gen. pl. αὐτοσαυτῶν *Tab.Heracl.*1.124.

⊛ **αὐτόσε,** Adv. *thither, to the very place*, ἀπιέναι v.l. in Hdt.3.124; καταβαίνειν Ar.*Lys.*873; αὐτομολεῖν Th.7.26, etc.; σφενδόνῃ οὐκ ἂν ἐφικοίμην αὐτόσ' Antiph.55.20.

**αὐτοσί,** emphatic form of αὐτός, *GDI*1339 (Dodona).

**αὐτο-σίδηρος** [ῐ], Dor. -**ᾱρος**, ον, *of sheer iron*, ἅμιλλα αὐ. 'with cold steel', E.*Hel.*356 (lyr.). **-σῖτος,** ον, *bringing one's own provisions*, Com. of a παράσιτος, Crobyl.1. **-σκᾰπᾰνεύς,** έως, ὁ, *very digger*, Alciphr.3.70. **-σκεύαστος,** ον, *self-made*, i.e. *natural*, Sch.Opp. *H.*1.22, Hsch. s.v. αὐτόστυλον. **-σκευος,** ον, = αὐτουργός II, Poll. 10.14; *artless*, φύσεως ἔρευθος αὐ. Aristaenet.2.21. **-σκωμμα,** ατος, τό, *essence of wit*, in pl., Alciphr.3.43. **-σμῑκρόν,** τό, *abstract smallness*, Procl.*in Prm.*p.676 S. **-σμῑκρότης,** ητος, ἡ, = foreg., ib.p.677 S. **-σοφία,** ἡ, *very wisdom*, Them.*Or.*6.73a. ⊛ **-σοφος,** ον, *of, with native mother-wit*, Tz.*H.*8.437. **-σπορος,** ον, *self-sown*, A.*Fr.*196; *self-begotten*, Nonn.*D.*7.73, al.

**αὐτόσσῠτος,** ον, *self-sped*, A.*Eu.*170 (lyr.), S.*Fr.*559.

**αὐτο-στᾰδίη** (sc. μάχη), ἡ, *stand-up fight, close fight*, Ep. word, used only in dat., ἔν γ' αὐτοσταδίῃ Il.13.325. **-στᾰσις,** εως, ἡ, *pure rest*, Plot.3.7.2, Procl.*in Prm.*p.793 S. **-στᾰτέω,** (ἵσταμαι) *to be independent, self-sufficient*, Ph.1.688. **-στᾰτος,** ον, *standing on its own base*, κανοῦν *IG*2.698 ii 17. **-στεγος,** ον, = αὐτόροφος, σπῆλυγξ Dionys.Trag.1. **-στέρῐφος,** ον, *strong in itself*, Hsch. **-στοιχος,** ον, *going by oneself, independent*, Anon.ap. Suid. s.v. **-στολος,** ον, *self-sent, going* or *acting of oneself*, S.*Ph.* 496, cf. *AP*7.585 (Jul.): metaph. of Leander swimming, νηῦς Musae. 255; αὐτόστολον ναυλοῦν to let a ship *by private contract*, *OGI*572. 41 (Myra). **-στονος,** ον, *lamenting for oneself*, γόος A.*Th.*916 (lyr.). **-στράτηγος** [ᾰ], ὁ, *general in independent command*, D.C. 44.4. **-στροφος,** ον, perh. *revolving*, ἐσχάρα *IG*2.816.9. **-στῦλον·** αὐτοσκεύαστον, Hsch. **-σύμμετρος,** ον, *ideally symmetrical*, Alex. Aphr.*in Metaph.*79.15. **-συμφῠής,** ές, f.l. for συμφυής, Porph. *Antr.*5. ⊛ **-σύστᾰτος,** ον, *self-constituting*, Dam.*Pr.*89. **-σφᾰγής,** ές, *slain by oneself* or *by kinsmen*, both in S.*Aj.*841 (prob. spurious), cf. E.*Ph.*1316. **-σχεδά,** v. αὐτοσχεδόν. **-σχεδές,** τό, a kind of woman's *shoe*, Hsch.; cf. αὐτοσχιδής.

**αὐτοσχεδι-άζω,** aor. part. Pass. -ασθείς Stratt.4 D.: (αὐτοσχέδιος):—*act* or *speak offhand, extemporize*, Pl.*Cra.*413d, *Mx.*235c, X. *Mem.*3.5.21. **2.** c. acc., *extemporize*, τὰ δέοντα Th.1.138, cf. X.*HG* 5.2.32. **II.** mostly in bad sense, *act, speak*, or *think unadvisedly*, v.l. in Pl.*Euthd.*278e; αὐ. καὶ καινοτομεῖν περὶ τῶν θείων Id.*Euthphr.*5a, cf. *Ap.*20c, Isoc.9.41, D.61.43; περί τι Pl.*Euthphr.*16a, Arist.*Pol.*1326$^b$ 19; εἰς τὰ τῶν Ἑλλήνων σώματα Aeschin.3.158. **-ασμα,** ατος, τό, *work done offhand, impromptu, improvisation*, Arist.*Po.*1448$^b$23, Pl.Com.87. **-ασμός,** ὁ, *extemporaneous speaking*, Alcid.*Soph.* 18 (pl.). ⊛ **-αστής,** οῦ, ὁ, *one who acts* or *speaks offhand*: and so, *raw hand, bungler*, opp. τεχνίτης, X.*Lac.*13.5. **-αστικός,** ή, όν, *extemporary*, Arist.*Po.*1449$^a$9:—also **-αστός,** όν, Alcid.*Soph.*16,17. ⊛ **-ος,** α, ον, also ος, ον Plu.*Sull.*7:—*hand to hand*: used by Hom., in dat., αὐτοσχεδίῃ (sc. μάχῃ) *in close fight, in the mêlée*, αὐτοσχεδίῃ μεῖξαι χεῖράς τε μένος τε Il.15.510: acc. fem. as Adv., = αὐτοσχεδόν I, Ἀντιφάτην δ'..πλῆξ' αὐτοσχεδίην 12.192, 17.294; αὐτοσχεδίην οὐτασμένος Od.11.536: also ἔς τ' αὐ. καὶ προμάχους ἰέναι Tyrt.11.12. **II.** *offhand, improvised, rough and ready*, ἐξ αὐτοσχεδίης πειρώμενος *h. Merc.*55; ποιήματα αὐ. D.H.2.34; μαντικὴ αὐ. Plu.*Sull.*7; τετρήρη ναυπηγεῖν αὐ. Arist.*Fr.*600; βωμός, τείχη, D.H.1.40, 3.67; μνῆμα Hld.2. 4; ναῦς Max.Tyr.12.2; of persons, αὐτοσχέδιος ὢν περὶ τὰς ἰσηγορίας Plu.2.642a; σοφιστής Ach.Tat.5.27; ἐκ τοῦ αὐτοσχεδίου εἰπεῖν D.C. 73.1; τὸ αὐ., opp. τὸ περιπτωτικόν, in Empiric medicine, Gal.1.66. Adv. -ίως, γεννηθῆναι Lxx *Wi.*2.2; οἰκοδομεῖσθαι Paus.6.24.3. **2.** *ready to hand*, ὕλη Id.10.32.15; *wild, natural*, ἄνθη Lib.*Decl.*13.50.

⊛ **αὐτο-σχεδόν,** Adv. *near at hand, hand to hand*, in Hom. always of close fight, ξιφέεσσ' αὐ. οὐτάζοντο Il.7.273; δῄουν ἀλλήλους αὐ. 15.708; αὐ. ὁρμήθησαν 13.496, cf. Od.22.293:—once also αὐτοσχεδὰ δουρὶ..ἐπόρουσε Il.16.319; cf. αὐτοσχέδιος. **2.** c. gen., *near, close to*, ἀλλήλων Arat.901. **II.** of Time, *on the spot, at once*, A.R. 1.12, 3.148. **-σχῐδής,** ές, *simply slit*: *simple*, ὑπόδημα Hermipp.18, cf. αὐτοσχεδές. **-σχολος,** ον, = ἑαυτῷ σχολάζων, Timo 50. **-σωκράτης** [ᾰ], ὁ, *the 'form' of Socrates*, Plot.5.7.1. **-σωμα,** ατος, τό, *abstract, ideal body*, Herm.*in Phdr.*p.151 A. **-σωφροσύνη,** ἡ, *abstract moderation* or *temperance*, ib.p.144 A. **-τᾱγος,** ον, *without a master, independent*, dub. in Hsch., cf. *EM*173. 47. **-τᾰχος,** ους, τό, *abstract velocity*, Procl.*Hyp.*1.1. **-τέγον·** ἀπηρτισμένον, πλῆρες, Hsch. **-τέλεια,** ἡ, *perfection, completeness*, Ocell.1.9. **II.** *complete sentence, proposition*, A.D.*Synt.*12.4, al.; αὐ. τοῦ λόγου ib.5.20. **-τέλειος,** ον, *self-complete, perfect*, Procl. *Inst.*78 (Comp.). **-τελειότης,** ητος, ἡ, *perfection*, Iamb.*Myst.*1. 15. **-τέλεστος,** ον, *self-accomplished, spontaneous*, Opp.*H.*1.763, *AP*1.19.6 (Claudian.), Nonn.*D.*43.232, al. ⊛ **-τελής,** ές, *ending in itself, complete in itself*, ὁρισμός Arist.*Top.*102$^b$13, cf. Ocell.1.7; θεωρίαι αὐ. καὶ αὑτῶν ἕνεκα Arist.*Pol.*1325$^b$20; esp. in Gramm., λεκτόν *Stoic.*2.58; λόγος A.D.*Synt.*3.5, al.; ἀξίωμα S.E.*M.*8.79; διάνοια Hdn.*Fig.*p.93 S.; ῥῆμα an *intransitive* verb, A.D.*Synt.*116. 11; of unity, *Theol.Ar.*5, cf. Orph.*Fr.*247.10. Adv. -λῶς, opp. κατὰ συναφήν, *independently, separately*, Epicur.*Ep.*2 p.36 U. **b.** *perfect, complete, fully-grown*, Nonn.*D.*7.154, al. **2.** *self-sufficing*, αὐ. καὶ ἀπροσδεᾶ φιλοσοφίας Plu.2.122e; of personal character, *independent*, προχείρου ἀ. εὐβούλου Phld.*Herc.*1457.5. **3.** *absolute, with full powers*, στρατηγός Plu.2.754d, cf. D.C.52.22; αὐ. κρίνειν, opp. προανακρίνειν, Arist.*Ath.*3.5, cf. 53.2. **4.** *final*, ψήφισμα *without appeal*, Hyp.*Eux.*15; δίκη Hsch., Suid.; διαλήψεις Plb.3.4.4; αὐ. πρὸς γνῶσιν καὶ σαφήνειαν ib.36.2; αἰτίαν Chrysipp.*Stoic.*2.292. Adv. -λῶς *at one's own discretion, arbitrarily*, οὐκ αὐ. ἀλλ' ἀκριβῶς Lys.*Fr.* 38, cf. Plb.3.29.3; ἂν αἱ φαντασίαι ποιῶσιν αὐ. τὰς συγκαταθέσεις Chrysipp.*Stoic.*2.291; αὐ. διαιτᾶν control, govern *absolutely*, Phld.*D.* 1.22. **5.** *sufficing for oneself*: also, *supporting oneself*, ἱππεῖς Luc. *Tox.*54. **6.** *entirely due to*, c. gen., νίκη τῶν ἡγουμένων Plb.5.12. 4. **II.** (τέλος IV) *taxing oneself, self-taxed*, Th.5.18, Stob.2.7. 3$^a$. **-τετράς,** άδος, ἡ, *abstract number four*, Phlp.*in de An.*77. 9. **-τεχνος,** ον, *self-instructed*, πρὸς ἴασιν Plu.2.991e.

⊛ **αὐτότης,** ητος, ἡ, *identity*, S.E.*M.*10.261, v.l. in Porph.*Sent.*39.

**αὐτό-τμητος,** ον, *self-severed*, Sch.Opp.*H.*2.349. **-τοκος,** ον, *young and all*, A.*Ag.*137: but, **II.** parox. αὐτοτόκος, ον, Act., *self-producing*, Nonn.*D.*8.81, etc. **-τρᾰγικὸς** πίθηκος *a very* ape *of tragedy*, D.18.242. **-τράπεζος** [ᾰ], ον, *eating at the same table with*, ἀθανάτοις Emp.147.1. **-τρῐάς,** άδος, ἡ, *the abstract number three*, Alex.Aphr.*in Metaph.*836.24, Phlp.*in de An.*77.9. **-τρίγωνον** [ῐ], τό, *the ideal triangle, the Form of triangle*, Arist.*GC*316$^a$12, Them.*Or.* 13.165a. **-τροπήσας,** in *h.Merc.*86 ὁδὸν αὐ., as if from αὐτοτροπέω, *to be like oneself*, i.e. *unique*, v.l. αὐτοπρεπὴς ὥς, in same sense. **-τροφος,** ον, = αὐτόσιτος, condemned by Phryn.179. **-τῠπος,** ον, *self-inflicted*, ὠτειλαί Opp.*H.*2.358.

**αὐτοῦ,** Dor. **αὐτῶ** and **αὐτεῖ,** Adv., prop. gen. of αὐτός:—*just there* or *just here*, Hom., etc.; ἐπίσχες αὐτοῦ stop *there!* Cratin.66:—freq. with the place added, αὐτοῦ ἐνὶ Τροίῃ, μέν' αὐτοῦ τῷδ' ἐνὶ χώρῳ, *here in* Troy, etc., Il.2.237, Od.10.271; αὐτοῦ ἔνθα Il.8.207; που αὐτοῦ ἀγρῶν somewhere *there* on the farm, Od.4.639; αὐτοῦ ὑπὲρ κεφαλῆς 8.68; αὐτοῦ περὶ τεῖχος A.*Ag.*452 (lyr.); αὐτοῦ ταύτῃ in this *very* place, *exactly* here, Hdt.1.214, 3.77, 4.135; αὐτοῦ τῇ περ ἔπεσε Id.1.30:—so that αὐτοῦ usu. precedes; but κεῖθι αὐτοῦ *h.Ap.*374; κατ' οἴκους αὐτοῦ Ar.*Pax* 89; ἐνθάδ' αὐτοῦ Sol.36.11, Ar.*Pl.*1187; τοῖς ἐνθάδ' αὐτοῦ μὴ κατ' ἄστυ δημόταις S.*OC*78.

**αὑτοῦ,** Att. contr. for ἑαυτοῦ.

**αὐτοϋγίεια,** ἡ, *health in the abstract*, Alex.Aphr.*in Metaph.*79.12, Herm.*in Phdr.*p.151 A.

**αὐτουδέτερος,** ον, *absolutely neuter*, *An.Bachm.*2.302:—Subst. **-ότης,** -ητος, ἡ, ibid.

**αὐτοΰδωρ,** ατος, τό, *very water*, Herm.ap.Stob.3.11.31.

**αὐτοΰπαρκτος,** ον, = αὐθύπαρκτος, Hsch.

**αὐτουργ-έω,** *to be an* αὐτουργός, *work with one's own hand*, Hierocl. p.63 A., Luc.*DMar.*6.1; of the Creator, *to be his own workman*, Procl.*Theol.Plat.*5.17, cf. 18; *act directly*, Gal.18(1).780; esp. *farm one's own land*, *PTeb.*302.29 (i A.D.):—Pass., κτήματα -ούμενα *BGU* 475$^a$9 (ii A.D.). **II.** c. acc., *execute, fulfil of oneself*, τὰ ἐπὶ τῆς γῆς Arist.*Mu.*398$^a$5; τὴν μαντηΐην Luc.*Syr.D.*36; τὴν ἐπιβουλήν Philostr.

*VS*1.21.4. **-ημα**, ατος, τό, *a piece of one's own work*, D.Chr.12.57: pl., ἴδια αὐ. *PMasp*.244 (vi A.D.). **-ητος**, ον, *self-wrought, rudely wrought*, *AP*6.33.5 (Maec.). **-ία**, ἡ, *working on oneself*, i.e. *self-murder* or *murder of kin*, A.*Eu*.336 (lyr., pl.). II. *personal labour*, opp. slave-labour, Plb.4.21.1, Plu.*Cat.Ma*.1, Porph.*Marc*.34. 2. *farming oneself*, *PLips*.97 xxvii 10 (iv A.D.). III. *experience*, Plb.9.14.4. **-ικός**, ή, όν, *willing* or *able to work with one's own hand*, M.Ant.1.5; *industrious*, Muson.*Fr*.11 p.57 H. II. **-κή** (sc. τέχνη), ἡ, *art of making real things*, not semblances (εἴδωλα), Pl.*Sph*. 266d (dub.). ❀**-ός**, όν, *self-working*, αὐτὸς αὐτουργῷ χερί S.*Ant*.52, cf. Aen.Tact.18.2; αὐ. βίος D.H.10.19. 2. mostly Subst., *one who works his land himself* (not by slaves), *husbandman*, E.*Or*.920, Th.1.141, X.*Oec*.5.4, etc.: generally, *one who works for himself*, Pl.*R*.565a, Arist.*Rh*.1381ᵃ24. b. metaph., αὐ. τῆς φιλοσοφίας *one that has worked at* philosophy *by himself*, without a teacher, X.*Smp*.1.5; αὐ. τῆς ταλαιπωρίας *engaging in* hard service *oneself*, Plb.3.17.8: Sup., Jul.*ad Them*.264a. II. Pass., *self-wrought*, i.e. *rudely wrought*, D.H.*Dem*.39, *Comp*.19 (Comp.); *simple, native*, μέλος *AP* 9.264 (Apollonid. or Phil.). **-ότευκτος**, ον, = foreg. II, Lyc.747.

**αὐτοῦτα**, v. αὐταυτοῦ.

**αὐτο-φάγος** [ᾰ], ον, *self-devouring*, Hsch. s. v. αὐτόφορβος. **-φάής**, ές, = sq., Procl.*Phil.Chald*.p.1 J. (s. v. l.). **-φανής**, ές, (φανῆναι) *self-appearing, personally appearing*, Iamb.*Myst*.2.4; *self-revealing*, Syrian. *in Metaph*.187.9; αὐ. τῆς οὐσίας θεωρία Procl.*in Alc*.p.9 C.

**αὐτοφαρίζω**· αὐτοματέω, Hsch.

**αὐτόφι, -φιν**, Ep. case-forms of αὐτός, in Hom. always with Prep., ἀπ' αὐτόφιν from *the very spot*, Il.11.44; so παρ' αὐτόφιν or -φι, 12.302, 13.42, etc.; ἐπ' αὐτόφιν on *the spot*, 19.255.

**αὐτο-φίλαυτος** [ῐ], ον, *wholly given to self-love*, J.*AJ*5.6.3. **-φλοιος**, ον, *with the bark on*, βάκτρον Theoc.25.208, cf. *Ep*.4.3, *AP*6.99 (Phil.). **-φονεύς**, gloss on αὐτεπίβουλος, Hsch. **-φόνευτος**, ον, *self-slain*, Sch.A.*Th*.735. **-φονία**, ἡ, = αὐτουργία I, ib.*Eu*.336 (pl.). ❀**-φόνος**, ον, *murdering one's kin*, αὐτοφόνα κακά A.*Th*.850 (lyr.), *Ag*.1091 (lyr.); παλάμη *AP*7.149 (Leont.). Adv. -νως A.*Supp*.65 (lyr.). 2. *suicidal*, Opp.*C*.2.480. 3. *slaying with one's own hand*, ib.4.290. **-φόντης**, ου, ὁ, *murderer of kin*, E.*Med*.1269; prob. corrupt in S.*El*.272; στρῆνος Lyc.438. **-φορβος**, ον, (φέρβω) = αὐτοφάγος, A.*Fr*.114. **-φόρητος**, ον, *self borne*, Nonn.*D*.10.150. ❀**-φορτος**, ον, *travelling with one's own cargo*, S.*Fr*.251; dub. sense in *bearing one's own baggage*, A.*Ch*.675, Cratin.248. II. *cargo and all*, ὁλκάδες Plu.*Aem*.9, cf. 2.467d. **-φρόνησις**, εως, ἡ, *absolute prudence*, Him.*Ecl*.32.12. **-φρων**, ον, gen. φρονος, = ὁμόφρων, Ion Trag.ap.*Lex.Sabb*. ❀**-φυής**, ές, *self-grown*, στρωμνὴ οἰκεία τε καὶ αὐ., of the fur of beasts, Pl.*Prt*.321a; *self-existent*, Critias 19.1 D. 2. *self-grown, of home production*, ἀγαθά X.*Vect*.2.1; ὦ πόλι φίλη Κέκροπος, αὐτοφυὲς Ἀττική Ar.*Fr*.110. 3. *natural*, opp. artificial, οὐδός Hes.*Th*.813; λιμήν Th.1.93; χρυσὸς αὐ. *native* gold, D.S.3.45; κύανος αὐ. Thphr.*Lap*.39; αὐ. λόφοι hills *in their natural state*, not quarried or mined, X.*Vect*.4.2; κορύναν αὐτοφυῆ *a natural growth*, Theoc.9.24; opp. χειροποίητος, Plb.9.27.4; opp. τὰ διὰ τέχνης, *wild, not cultivable*, Thphr.*CP*3.1.1; of a horse, τὸν αὐτοφυῆ (sc. δρόμον) διατροχάζειν to have *natural* paces, X.*Eq*.7.11; αὐ. γηρύματα '*native wood-notes wild*', of birds, opp. language, Plu.2.973a; of style, *natural, simple*, D.H.*Din*.7; αὐ. αἴσθησις, opp. ἐπιστημονική, Phld.*Mus*.p.11 K., cf. p.63 K.: Comp. -έστερος *more natural*, of an explanation, Simp.*in Ph*.149.18. Adv. -φυῶς, ὅμοιον like *by nature*, opp. μιμητής, Pl.*Grg*.513b; αὐ. ἀγαθοί Id.*Lg*.642c. 4. τὸ αὐ. *one's own nature*, Id.*R*.486e; *natural state*, opp. τὸ ἐπίκτητον, Arist.*Rh*.1365ᵃ29. II. Act., *bearing, producing of itself*, γῆ αὐ. ὢν φέρει Philostr.*Im*.2.18. Adv. -φυῶς *spontaneously*, Syrian. *in Metaph*.123.22; αὐ. κινούμενοι Plot.6.5.1. **-φύσις**, εως, ἡ, *abstract nature*, Phlp.*in de An*.99.16. ❀**-φυτος**, ον, *self-engendered*: hence, *arising naturally*, ἕλκεα Pi.*P*.3.47, cf. Antipho Trag.ap.*Lex.Sabb*.; *native*, ἀρετή D.C.44.37. 2. *natural, primitive*, ἐργασία Arist.*Pol*.1256ᵃ40. **-φωνία**, ἡ, *direct utterance*, title of work on oracles by Oenomaus, Jul.*Or*.7.209b. **-φωνος**, ον, *self-sounding*, χρησμὸς αὐ. an oracle *delivered by the god himself*, Luc.*Alex*.26. **-φώρᾱτος**, ον, *self-betrayed, self-revealed*, S.E.*M*.8.173. **-φωρία** (-φορία cod.)· τὸ ἐπὶ αὐτῇ φωρᾷ (φορᾷ cod.), Hsch. ❀**-φωρος**, ον, (φώρ) *self-detected*, ἀμπλακήματα S.*Ant*.51. II. mostly in the phrase ἐπ' αὐτοφώρῳ λαμβάνειν to catch *in the act*, Lys.13.85, D.19.132; ἑλεῖν E.*Ion* 1214; ἐλέγχειν Lys.7.42: with pass. Verbs, ἐπ' αὐτοφώρῳ ἁλῶναι Hdt.6.72; εἰλῆφθαι Ar.*Pl*.455, Eup.181: hence, 2. in a more general sense, *notoriously, manifestly*, ἐπιβουλεύοντας φανῆναι ἐπ' αὐ. Hdt.6.137; ἐπ' αὐ. αὐτὸν ἐλέγξω Lys.13.30; τὸν θάνατόν τινος ἐπ. αὐ. μηχανωμένη Antipho 1.3; ἐπ' αὐ. καταλαμβάνειν τινὰ ἀμαθέστερον ὄντα Pl.*Ap*.22b, cf. *R*.359c; ἐπ' αὐ. εἴλημμαι πλουσιώτατος ὢν X.*Smp*.3.13; ἀξιῶ σε.. ἐπ' αὐ. ταὐτά μοι ἐπιδεῖξαι Lys.1.21; ἐπ' αὐ. κλέπται ὄντες ἐξελεγχόμενοι Aeschin.3.10. **-φως**, ωτος, τό, *very light*, ὁ ἥλιος αὐ. ἐστι καὶ πηγὴ φωτός Herm. *in Phdr*.p.118 A., cf. Dam.*Pr*.29, Aen.Gaz.*Thphr*.p.52 B. **-χάρακτος** [ᾰ], ον, *self-engraven* or *impressed*, of an image in a mirror, Nonn.*D*.5.599. **-χᾰρις**, ιτος, ἡ, *very grace*: αὐτοχάριτες Ἀττικαί *the essence of* Attic *graces*, Alciphr.3.43. ❀**-χειλής**, ές, *with the natural rim*, i.e. in one piece, λήκυθοι S.*Fr*.138. **-χειρ**, χειρος, ὁ, ἡ, *with one's own hand, creative*, A.*Supp* 592 (lyr.); αὐ. λούειν, παίειν, κτείνειν, S.*Ant*.900, 1315, *Aj*. 57; τίνες ᾠκοδόμησαν;—ὄρνιθες αὐτόχειρες Ar.*Av*.1132 sq., cf. *Lys*. 269, Theopomp.Com.86, *Act.Ap*.27.19, etc.: c. gen., *very doer, perpetrator of* a thing, αὐ. τοῦδε τοῦ τάφου S.*Ant*.306; τῆς ἀσελγείας ταύτης D.21.60; αὐ. οὔτε τῶν ἀγαθῶν οὔτε τῶν κακῶν *men who accomplish* neither.., Isoc.5.150. II. abs., *one who kills himself, suicide*, S.*Ant*.1175; αὐ. ἑαυτῶν Arist.*Fr*.502; simply, *murderer*, S.*OT*231, D.21.116; αὐτὸν..νομίζω αὐτόχειρά μου γεγενῆσθαι τούτοις τοῖς ἔργοις ib.106: c. gen., αὐ. καὶ φονεῖς τῶν πολιτῶν Isoc.4.111, cf. Men.*Sam*.216; in full, τὸν αὐ. τοῦ φόνου S.*OT*266, cf. *El*.955, D.18.287. III. as Adj., *murderous*, esp. of murder *committed by one's own hand* or *by kinsmen*, αὐ. θάνατος, σφαγή, μοῖρα, E.*Ph*.880, *Or*.947, *Med*.1281 (lyr.); πληγέντες αὐτόχειρι σὺν μιάσματι, of brothers smitten by *mutual slaughter*, S.*Ant*.172; φόνος Pl.*R*.615c. 2. αὐτόχειρα γράμματα *written with one's own hand, autograph*, D.C.59.4. **-χειρί**, Adv. of foreg., *with one's own hand*, Lycurg.122, Paus.7.16.6, Onos.33 tit.; dub. l. in E.*Or*.1040. ❀**-χειρία**, ἡ, *murder perpetrated by one's own hand*, Pl.*Lg*.872b; δι' αὐτοχειρίας Nic.Dam.p.46 D. II. mostly in dat. αὐτοχειρίᾳ, Ion. -ίῃ, used adverbially, = αὐτοχειρί, mostly of slaughter, αὐ. κτείνειν Hdt.1.140; ἀπολέσαι Id.3.74, cf. 66: generally, αὐ. διελεῖν Id.1.123; διασπείρειν Id.3.13, cf. Ar.*Fr*.33 D.; λαβεῖν D.25.57; καὶ αὐ. καὶ κελεύων καὶ ψήφῳ [κτείνειν] Democr. 260. **-χειρίζω**, *do a thing* or *commit a murder with one's own hand*, Philist.60 ap.Poll.2.154, where the word is called παμμίαρον. **-χείριος**, α, ον, = αὐτόχειρ, Sch.E.*Med*.1269, A.D.*Pron*. 70.2. **-χειρος**, ον, = foreg., Hsch. Adv. -ρως, = αὐτοχειρί, Sch. E.*Or*.1040, v.l. in Hierocl.*Facet*.152. **-χειροτόνητος**, ον, *self-elected*, D.19 Arg.ii 9. **-χερί**, Adv. of αὐτόχειρ, poet. for αὐτοχειρί, Call.*Epigr*.22: c. gen., αὐτοχερὶ ποσίων ἐδάμησαν Man.3.200.

**αὐτοχθηδόν**· αὐτοποίητον, Hsch.

**αὐτό-χθονος**, ον, *country and all*, A.*Ag*.536. ❀**-χθων**, ον, gen. ονος, *sprung from the land itself*; αὐτόχθονες, οἱ, *not settlers, of native stock*, Hdt.1.171, Th.6.2, etc.: c. gen., αὐ. Ἰταλίας D.H.1.10: esp. of the Athenians, E.*Ion* 29, al., *Fr*.360.8, Ar.*V*.1076, Isoc.4.24, 12.124. II. Adj., *indigenous, native*, τὰ μὲν δύο αὐτόχθονα τῶν ἐθνέων Hdt.4.197; αὐ. Αἰγύπτιοι *PGiss*.99.5 (ii A.D.); ἀρετή Lys.2.43; λάχανα τῶν αὐτοχθόνων Polioch.2.6; κόσμος Philod.Scarph. 127; *urbanitas*, *racy of the soil*, Cic.*Att*.7.2.3. **-χόλωτος**, ον, *their own enemy*, γένος ἀνθρώπων *AP*7.688 (Pall.). **-χορήγητος**, ον, *self-furnished*, Pl.*Ax*.371d. **-χόωνος**, ον, Ep. for αὐτοχόανος, -χωνος, *rudely cast, massive*, of a lump of iron used as a quoit, Il.23.826. **-χρημα**, Adv. *in very deed*, Ar.*Eq*.78, Luc.*Dem.Enc*.13, Procop.Gaz.*Ep*.58, Iamb.*Myst*.5.20; dub. in S.*Ichn*.38. 2. *just, exactly*, Ael.*NA*2.44, Aristid.2.228 J. II. *straightway*, Jul.*Or*.6.181b. **-χροΐνδον**· πρὸς τὸν χρῶτα, Hsch. **-χρονος**, ον, *being its own time*, οὔτε ἡ ψυχὴ ἔγχρονος ἀλλ' αὐ. Simp. *in Ph*.785.2. ❀**-χροος**, ον, contr. -χρους, ουν, *with its own, natural colour*, Plu.2.270f. 2. *of one and the same colour*, ib.330a. **-χρῡσος**, ον, *of very gold, precious*, Hsch. ❀**-χῠτος**, ον, *poured out of itself, self-flowing*, θάλαμος Hes.*Fr*.96.102; ὕδωρ Aristid.*Or*.39(18).7,16, cf. Sch.Pi.*O*.7.12; γάλα Nonn.*D*.24.131. **-χωνον**· αὐτοχώνευτον, Hsch. **-χωρέω**, *absorb into oneself, partake of*, τοῦ ἀγνώστου Anon. *in Prm*. in *Rh.Mus*. 47.603 (dub.).

**αὐτ-οψεί** or **-ψί**, Adv. of αὔτοπτος, *with one's own eyes*, Jul.*Ep*.204, *PSI*3.238.11 (vi A.D.). **-οψία**, ἡ, *seeing with one's own eyes*, Dsc.*Praef*.5, *PTeb*.286.20 (ii A.D.), Luc.*Syr.D*.1; in Medic., as t.t. of the Empiric school, Gal.1.67; ἐπὶ τῆς αὐ. *SIG*827 *D* 4 (Delph., ii A.D.), cf. *POxy*.1272.19 (ii A.D.); ἐπὶ τὴν αὐ. ἐλθεῖν *IG*9(1).61.17. II. *supernatural manifestation, vision*, Procl.*in Alc*.p.92 C. (pl.), Iamb.*Myst*.2.4 (pl.), 7.3 (pl.); [δαίμων] κληθεὶς εἰς αὐ. Porph.*Plot*.10, cf. Dam.*Isid*.13 (pl.); opp. ὄνειρος, Ps.-Callisth.1.6; *magical operation* for the production of such a manifestation (αὐθ.), *PMag.Par*.1.950, *PMag.Leid.W*.16.38.

**αὐτοψυχή**, ἡ, *absolute soul*, αὐ. καθαρά Herm. *in Phdr*.p.75 A., cf. Plot.5.9.13, Jul.*Ep*.89b (pl.).

**αὐτ-ώδης**, ες, Ion. for αὐθάδης, acc. to A.D.*Pron*.74.9, Hsch.: but Hdt.6.92 has αὐθαδέστεροι. **-ώλης**, ες, = αὐτόχειρ II, Hsch. **-ωνητής**, οῦ, ὁ, *one that buys for himself*, Din.*Fr*.89.11. **-ώρης**, ες, (ὄρνυμαι) *acting spontaneously*, of an oracle giving a response unquestioned, Call.*Fr*.264.

**αὔτως**, Adv.: I. *in this very manner, even so*, γυμνὸν ἐόντα αὔ. ὥς τε γυναῖκα unarmed *just as I am* like a woman, Il.22.125; *in the self-same way, likewise*, σὺν δ' αὔ. ἐγώ S.*Ant*.85, cf. Numen.ap.Ath. 7.328d; αὔ. ὅπωσπερ.. S.*Aj*.1179; αὔ., ὧδ' αὔ., ὥς μ' ὤλεσεν Id.*Tr*.1040 (lyr.); αὔ. ὡς.. Hes.*Th*.702, A.R.1.890: c. dat., γυναιξὶν αὔ. Anacr.21.14: hence ὡσαύτως (q.v.), in Hom. always ὡς δ' αὔτως, as in Pl.*Phd*.102e, X.*An*.5.6.9. 2. in a contemptuous sense, *just so*, τίη σὺ κήδεαι αὔ. ἀνδρῶν; why take you *no better* care? v.l. for οὕτως in Il.6.55; οἴχεται αὔ. has gone off *just as he pleased*, Od.4.665: joined with words implying contempt, νήπιος αὔ. a *mere* child, Il.24.726, cf. 6.400; μὰψ αὔ. 20.348; ἀνεμώλιον αὔ. 21.474; αὔ. ἄχθος ἀρούρης Od.20.379, etc.; so, *in vain*, οὐκ αὔ. μυθήσομαι 14.151, cf. Il. 2.342, etc. II. in reference to the past, *just as before, as it was*, ἧσθαι, κεῖσθαι, Il.1.133, 18.338, Od.20.130; λευκὸν ἔτ' αὔ. still white *as when new*, Il.23.268; ἔτι κεῖται αὔ. ἐν κλισίῃσι *just as he was*, 24.413; καὶ αὔ. *still, unceasingly*, 1.520. (From αὐτός, hence αὔτως in Homer, cf. Il.23.268, Od.14.151 (from αὐτῇ with Aeol. psilosis acc. to Eust.235.5, al.); but αὔτως is usu. written in codd. of Trag. Gramm. were divided as to etym. and accent, cf. A.D.*Adv*.174.1, *EM*172.34, and distd. αὔτως 'likewise' from αὔτως 'in vain'. Dam.*Pr*.178 uses αὔτως, = *of itself* (from αὐτοῦ).)

**αὔφην**, Aeol. for αὐχήν, Jo.Gramm.*Comp*.3.16.

**αὔφιτα**, = ἄλφιτα, *Supp.Epigr*.1.414 (Gortyn, v/iv B.C.).

**αὐχᾰλέος**, α, ον, (αὔχη) *boastful*, Xenoph.3.5, Hsch.

**αὐχάττειν**· ἀναχωρεῖν, Hsch.; cf. ἀναχάζω.

**αὐχεν-ίας**, ου, ὁ, *bull-necked*, Gloss. **-ίζω**, (αὐχήν) *cut the throat of*.., S.*Aj*.298. 2. *seize by the throat*: metaph., κῆρες αὐ. ψυχήν Ph.1.654; λόγους παλαίσμασι ib.676:—Pass., 2.372. 3. *bind the neck with a ligature*, *Hippiatr*.10. **-ιον**, τό, Dim. of αὐχήν, *An. Ox*.2.356. II. = αὐχήν II. 5, Eust.1533.46. ⊛ **-ιος**, α, ον, *belonging to the neck*, τένοντες αὐ. *neck*-sinews, Od.3.450, Pancrat.*Oxy*. 1085.29; χαίτη Opp.*C*.3.255; τρίχες Hld.10.28. 2. *stiff-necked, haughty*, γίγαντες *PMag.Par*.1.3058. II. a kind of *tunic*, Antiph. 315. **-ιστήρ**, ῆρος, ὁ, βρόχος αὐ. *halter*, Lyc.1100; *ligature for neck*, *Hippiatr*.10.

⊛ **αὐχέω**, chiefly pres. and impf. ηὔχουν, fut. αὐχήσω E.*Fr*.857, Luc. *DMort*.22.2, *AP*7.373 (Thall.): aor. ηὔχησα ib.6.283, 15.4, Apollod. 2.4.3: (αὔχη):—*boast, plume oneself*, ἐπί τινι on a thing, Batr.57, *AP*6.283; τινί E.*IA*412: with neut. Adj., τοσοῦτον αὐχεῖν Hdt.7.103; μέγ' αὐ. E.*Heracl*.353 (lyr.); μηδὲν τόδ' αὔχει Id.*Andr*.463; μεγάλα *Ep.Jac*.3.5: c. acc. objecti, *to boast of*, ἀστέρας *AP*7.373 (Thall.). II. c. acc. et inf., *boast* or *declare loudly* that.., αὐχέοντες κάλλιστα τιθέναι ἀγῶνα Hdt.2.160; ἀπεῶσθαι Th.2.39; σώσειν (σῶσαι codd.) E.*Andr*.311, cf. *Ba*.310: c. acc. only, αὐχῶ Σεβήραν *boast* (that I hold her), *IG*14.2001, cf. 3.172. 2. c. inf. fut., *say confidently, to be proudly confident* that, αὐχῶ γὰρ αὐχῶ τήνδε δωρεὰν ἐμοὶ δώσειν Δί' A.*Pr*.340, cf. 688 (lyr.), *Pers*.741, Cratin.1: with a neg., οὐ γάρ ποτ' ηὔχουν.. μεθέξειν I never *thought* that.., A.*Ag*.506, cf. *Eu*.561 (lyr.), E.*Heracl*.931. III. Med., αὐχήσασθαι· καυχήσασθαι, Hsch.—Never in S. (ἐπ-, ἐξ-αυχέω, *El*.65, *Ant*.390); rare in Com. and Prose.

⊛ **αὔχη**, ἡ, *boasting, pride*, κενεόφρονες αὖχαι Pi.*N*.11.29; αὐχάν· καύχησιν, Hsch.

⊛ **αὐχ-ήεις**, εσσα, εν, *braggart, proud*, Opp.*H*.2.677; [βοῦς] *AP*6. 114 (Simm.). ⊛ **-ημα**, ατος, τό, *thing boasted of, object of pride, the pride, boast*, ⟨χθονός⟩ S.*OC*710 (lyr.); *cause for boasting, glory*, σὺ γάρ νιν εἰς τόδ' εἶσας αὐ. ib.713, cf. Th.7.75. II. = αὔχη, *boasting, self-confidence*, Id.2.62, 7.66; ὀπιθόμβροτον αὔ. δόξας Pi.*P*.1.92: in pl., ποῦ τὰ πρόσθεν αὐ.; Pl.*Ax*.365a. **-ημᾰτίας**, ου, ὁ, *boaster*, Sch. Luc.*Pr.Im*.10, Eust.537.42:—Adj. **-μᾰτικός**, ή, όν, Id.1967.9.

⊛ **αὐχήν**, ένος, ὁ, *neck, throat*, of men and beasts, Il.7.12, Hes.*Op*. 815, Arist.*HA*493$^a$5, *PA*691$^b$29: rarely, *gullet*, Nic.*Th*.350: in pl., of *one neck*, S.*Fr*.659.4, Orph.*L*.137, *AP*5.27 (Rufin.). 2. metaph., τὸν αὐ. ἱστάναι to be *high-spirited*, Philostr.*VA*7.23; αὐχένα ὑψηλὸν ἀποθέσθαι Vett.Val.261.16. II. metaph., *any narrow band* or *connexion* (*like a neck*): 1. *neck of land, isthmus*, Hdt.1.72, 6.37, X.*An*.6.4.3. 2. *narrow sea, strait*, of the Bosporus, Hdt.4.85, 118; αὐ. πόντου, of the Hellespont, A.*Pers*.72 (lyr.); of the point at which the Danube spreads from a single stream into several branches, Hdt.4.89. 3. *mountain-pass, defile*, Id.7.223. 4. *neck* of the thigh-bone, Hp.*Art*.55; *cervix uteri*, Id.*Steril*.230, Poll. 2.222 (but, *pars vaginalis*, Gal.*UP*14.3); *root* of the tongue, Ruf. *Onom*.57. 5. *handle of the steering-paddle* in a ship, Poll.1.90: in pl., Polyaen.3.11.14, Hld.5.28. 6. an architectural member, αὐχένες δρύινοι *SIG*$^2$587.308. (Cf. αὔφην; ἄμφην Theoc.30.28.)

⊛ **αὔχ-ησις**, εως, ἡ, (αὐχέω) *boasting, exultation*, Th.6.16; cf. **αὐχῆτις** (sic)· σεμνότης, Hsch. **-ητής**, οῦ, ὁ, *boaster*, blamed by Poll. 9.146. **-ητικός**, ή, όν, = αὐχήεις, Sch.Pi.*O*.1.4. Adv. -κῶς Eust. 750.23.

**αὐχμ-ᾰλέος**, α, ον, = αὐχμηρός, Choeril.4.4, Epigr. in *POxy*.662 (Amynt.).

**αὐχμέω**, (αὐχμός) *to be squalid* or *unwashed*, αὐχμεῖς τε κακῶς καὶ ἀεικέα ἕσσαι Od.24.250, cf. Ar.*Nu*.442; *to be parched*, Pl.*R*.606d; αὐχμεῖ [φυτά] *dry up*, Thphr.*HP*4.10.7:—also **αὐχμάω**, part. αὐχμῶσαι interpol. in Hp.*Prog*.2; αὐχμώσης Arist.*Mete*.360$^b$11; αὐχμῶντες Thphr.*HP*8.10.4; αὐχμῶντα Plu.2.187d, Luc.*Vit.Auct*.7; αὐχμῶσαν Id.*Apol*.6, etc.; Ep. αὐχμώοντα Nonn.*D*.26.108, etc.—αὐχμέω is always used exc. in part. acc. to Phryn.*PS* p.10 B.; αὐχμᾷς is cited from Phryn.Com.76 by Poll.2.34; other forms are ambiguous, αὐχμῶν Ar.*Pl*.84, Anaxandr.34.6, Thphr.*Char*.26.5; αὐχμήσῃ Pl.*Phdr*. 251d. etc.

**αὐχμή**, ἡ, = αὐχμός, Q.S.9.372, Phryn.*PS* p.10 B.

**αὐχμήεις**, εσσα, εν, = αὐχμηρός, *h.Hom*.19.6.

**αὐχμηρία**, ἡ, = αὐχμός, *Cat.Cod.Astr*.2.161.1, 8(3).125.24.

**αὐχμηρό-βῐος**, ον, *squalid, sordid*, Pl.Com.16 D. **-κόμης**, ου, ὁ, *with squalid hair*, Anaxandr.41.9.

⊛ **αὐχμηρός**, ά, όν, *dry, without rain*, χειμών Hp.*Aph*.3.11, cf. *Aër*. 10; ἔτη Arist.*HA*605$^b$19; ἔαρ Id.*Pr*.860$^a$13; of places, *dry, parched*, τόποι Pl.*Lg*.761b (Sup.), cf. 2*Ep.Pet*.1.19; χωρία Thphr.*HP*9.11.10, etc.; καρποί D.S.2.53. b. *parching*, νόσοι Emp.121.3. 2. *dry, rough, squalid*, οὖδας E.*Alc*.947; σκληρὸς καὶ αὐ. Pl.*Smp*.203d; esp. of hair (cf. foreg.), S.*Fr*.475, E.*Or*.387, Theoc.25.225; βίος Luc.*Salt*. 1. Adv. -ρῶς, ἔχειν τοῦ προσώπου Philostr.*VA*4.10. 3. *miserable*, Man.2.169: c. gen., βιότοιο ib.454: irreg. Sup. αὐχμότατος dub. l. in Pl.Com.169.

**αὐχμηρ-ότης**, ητος, ἡ, *squalor*, metaph., Men.Rh.p.402 S. **-ώδης**, ες, = αὐχμηρός, Sch.Arist.25$^a$30.

⊛ **αὐχμός**, ὁ, *drought*, Emp.111.6, Hdt.2.13, 4.198, Hp.*Aph*.3.7: in pl., Th.1.23, Isoc.9.14, Plu.*Num*.13: metaph., ὥσπερ αὐχμός τις τῆς σοφίας *drought, dearth of*.., Pl.*Men*.70c; so perh. αὐχμὸς τῶν σκευαρίων Ar.*Pl*.839. 2. *effects of drought, squalor*, μεστὰς αὐχμοῦ τε καὶ κόνεως Pl.*R*.614d. 3. of style, *dryness, meagreness*, D.H.*Dem*. 44. 4. *thirst*, D.Chr.7.152. (Perh. akin to αὖος.)

**αὐχμώδης**, ες, *dry*, τὸ αὐ. *drought*, Hdt.1.142; ἔτη Arist.*HA* 602$^a$13; χώρα αὐχμωδεστέρα Thphr.*HP*8.1.6; *arid*, *CP*3.10.1; *squalid*, κόμη E.*Or*.223; σάρξ Plu.2.688d; of colour, *dull*, αἱματῖτις Thphr.*Lap*.37.

**αὔχμωσις**, εως, ἡ, *dirt, squalor*, of the hair, [Gal.]16.88.

⊛ **αὖχος**, ους, τό, = αὔχημα, Sch.A.*Pers*.871.

**αὔω** (A), *get a light, light a fire*, ἵνα μή ποθεν ἄλλοθεν αὔοι Od.5.490: —Med., *take fire*, Arat.1035.—Only poet. (Cf. ἐναύω, etc.; from αὔσγω, cf. ONorse *ausa* 'sprinkle', Lat. *haurio, haustum*.)

⊛ **αὔω** (B), fut. ἀΰσω E.*Ion* 1446: aor. ἤϋσα (v. infr.):—*cry out, shout, call aloud*, freq. in Hom., αὖε δ' Ἀθήνη Il.20.48, cf. Call.*Dian*.56 sq.; κέκλετ' ἀΰσας Il.4.508, cf. 6.66, etc.; μακρὸν ἄϋσε 5.101; ἤϋσε.. μέγα τε δεινόν τε ὄρθια 11.10; ἤϋσεν δὲ διαπρύσιον ib.275, etc.:—also in Trag., αὔειν λακάζειν A.*Th*.186; μηδὲν μέγ' ἀΰσῃς S.*El*.830 (lyr.); δεινὸν δ' ἀΰσας *OT*1260: c. acc. cogn., *utter*, στεναγμὸν.. ἀΰσατ' E. *Supp*.800 (lyr.); τίν' αὐδὰν ἀΰσω; Id.*Ion* 1446. 2. c. acc. pers., *call upon*, αὖε δ' ἑταίρους Il.11.461, 13.475, cf. Od.9.65, Theoc.13.58. 3. rarely of things, *ring*, καρφαλέον δέ οἱ ἀσπὶς.. ἄϋσεν Il.13.409 (v. sub αὖος 2); of the sea, *roar*, A.R.2.566. [In pres. and impf. αὐ- is a diphthong; in fut. and aor. a disyll. ἀΰσω, ἤϋσα.]

**αὔω** (C), = ἄω (A) II, ἰαύω, Nic.*Th*.263, 283.

**αὔω**, = ξηραίνω, Hdn.Gr.2.132.

**αὔως**, Aeol. for ἀώς, ἠώς, Sapph.*Oxy*.1787.1 + 2.18, al.

**ἀφάβρωμα**, ατος, τό, Megarian name of a *woman's garment*, Plu. 2.295b; cf. ἄβρωμα.

**ἀφαγν-εύω**, = sq., Plu.2.943c. **-ίζω**, fut. -ιῶ Lxx *Le*.14.52: aor. -ήγνισα Paus.2.31.8, Lxx *Le*.14.49:—**Med.**, fut. -ιοῦμαι Hp. *Morb.Sacr*.1: aor. -ηγνισάμην E.*Alc*.1146:—**Pass.**, fut. -αγνισθήσομαι Lxx *Nu*.19.19: aor. -ηγνίσθην ib.19.12:—*purify, consecrate*, χθόνα E. in *Gött.Nachr*.1922.6, Paus.2.31.8; πυρκαϊὴν χρὴ ἀφαγνίσαι .. οἴνῳ *Epigr.Gr*.1034.28 (Thrace):—Med., τοῖς νερτέροις θεοῖς E. *Alc*.1146, cf. Hsch., Suid. II. ἀφαγνίσας· ἀποδύσας, συλήσας, Hsch. **-ισμός**, ὁ, *purification*, Sch.E.*Alc*.98.

⊛ **ἀφᾰδία**, ἡ, (ἀφανδάνω) *enmity*, Eup.34:—also **ἀφάδιος** or **ἀφάδειος**, = ἐχθρός, Hdn.Gr.2.480.

**ἄφᾰδος**, ον, *displeasing, odious*, *EM*174.50.

**ἀφαδρύνομαι**, Pass., *mature, ripen*, Thphr.*CP*4.6.8.

**ἀφάζει**· ἀναδέχεται, Hsch.

⊛ **Ἀφαία**, ἡ, name of divinity in Aegina, *IG*4.1580; cf. Ἀφαία· ἡ Δίκτυννα, καὶ Ἄρτεμις, Hsch.

⊛ **ἀφαιάσαι**· ἀπαλγῆσαι, ἀπολειτουργῆσαι, καὶ ἀπολέσαι, Hsch.

**ἀφαιλέω**, Cret., = ἀφαιρέω (q.v.).

**ἀφαίμαξις**, εως, ἡ, *bleeding*, Archig.ap.Aët.8.76, *Hippiatr*.42.

**ἀφαιμάσσω**, Att. -ττω, *draw blood*, of leeches, Sor.2.11; *bleed*, *Hippiatr*.69.

**ἄφαιμοι**· ἀπόγονοι, εὐγενεῖς, Hsch.

**ἀφαίρ-εμα**, ατος, τό, *that which is taken away as the choice part*, Lxx *Ex*.35.21, *Nu*.18.27 sq., al., J.*AJ*14.10.12. 2. *tribute*, Lxx 1*Ma*.15.5. 3. *deduction*, *POxy*.1731.10 (ii A.D.). 4. *coarse grits made from* ζέα, Plin.*HN*18.112. ⊛ **-εσις**, εως, ἡ, *taking away, carrying off, removal*, Pl.*Cri*.46c (pl.); *putting off*, τοῦ θνητοῦ Hierocl. *in CA*27 p.483 M.; opp. πρόσθεσις, Plu.*Lyc*.13 (pl.). 2. as law-term, *assertion of freedom of a reputed slave*, Hyp.*Fr*.23. 3. *amputation*, Archig.ap.Orib.47.13.4. II. in Logic, *abstraction*, ἐξ, δι' ἀφαιρέσεως, Arist.*Cael*.299$^a$16, *EN*1142$^a$18; esp. τὰ ἐξ ἀ. *mathematics*, Id.*APo*.81$^b$3, *Metaph*.1061$^a$29, al.; opp. ἐκ προσθέσεως, ib. 1077$^b$9; also τὰ ἐν ἀ. ὄντα Id.*de An*.429$^b$18, al.:—Cicero jokes on this term, *Att*.6.1.2. 2. Gramm., *removal* of initial letters, as in σῦς ὗς, Choerob. *in Theod*.1 p.148 H., cf. A.D.*Pron*.55.13, al.; also of medial letters, ib.93.13; of feet in verse, opp. πρόσθεσις, *POxy*. 220 iii 3. **-ετέον**, *one must take away*, Hp.*Aph*.1.10, Pl.*R*.361a; *one must exclude*, Id.*Plt*.291c; *one must take away in thought*, Thphr. *Metaph*.6. II. ἀφαιρετέος, έα, έον, *to be taken away, removed*, Pl. *R*.398e, cf. Jul.*Or*.8.249d. **-ετέω**, *pick off*, Ion Hist.1. **-έτης**, ου, ὁ, *one who deprives*, χρόνων Vett.Val.55.18, cf. Ptol.*Tetr*.189, Sch. Od.13.224, Suid. s.v. ἐξαίτης. ⊛ **-ετικός**, ή, όν, *fit for taking away*, τινός A.D.*Adv*.165.12; χρόνος ἐλπίδος ἀ. Vett.Val.281.4; τὰ ἀ. τῶν βοηθημάτων *evacuant* remedies, prob. l. in Herod.Med. in *Rh.Mus*. 58.87. II. Astrol., *retrograde*, of planetary motion, Ptol.*Tetr*. 52, etc. **-έτις**, ιδος, ἡ, *one that takes away*, Μοῖραι ἀ. θνητοῖσιν ἀνάγκης Orph.*H*.59.18. ⊛ **-ετός**, όν, *to be taken away, separable*, Pl.*Plt*.303e, Arr.*Epict*.3.24.3. 2. *deducted*, *PRev.Laws* 55.1 (iii B.C.). ⊛ **-έω**, Ion. **ἀπαιρέω**, fut. -ήσω: pf. ἀφῄρηκα, Ion. ἀπαραίρηκα: aor. ἀφεῖλον, later inf. ἀφέλαι *GDI*4940.35 (Cret.); ἀφῄρησα Gal.11.121:—*take away from*:—Constr.: mostly ἀ. τί τινι, σῖτον μέν σφιν ἀφεῖλε *took it from* him, Od.14.455, cf. A.*Eu*.360 codd., etc. (but also, *relieve* one *of* a duty, X.*Cyr*.7.1.44): less freq. ἀ. τί τινος Ar.*Pax* 560, X.*Lac*.4.7; κῆρα χώρας A.*Th*.777 (lyr.); ἔκ τινος Id.*Eu*.444; also τινά τι prob. l. ib.360, S.*Ph*.933, v. infr. II. 1, III: c. gen., *take from*, τιμῆς οὔτ' ἀφελὼν οὔτ' ἐπορεξάμενος Sol.5.2; μηδὲν ἀφαιρῶμεν τοῦ ἀδίκου (*from* the unjust man) ἀπὸ τῆς ἀδικίας Pl.*R*.360e; τοῦ πλήθους *diminish* the number, X.*Vect*.4.4: c. acc. only, ἀπελὼν τὰ ἄχθεα *having taken* them *off*, Hdt.1.80; βασιλέων.. ὀργὰς ἀφῄρουν *took away*, E.*Med*.455, cf. Ar.*Pl*.22, *Ra*.518. 2. *set aside*, κρέα *SIG* 1044.41 (Halic., iv B.C.). b. *exclude, separate*, τὸ Ἑλληνικὸν ὡς ἓν ἀπὸ πάντων ἀφαιροῦντες χωρὶς Pl.*Plt*.262d; opp. προστιθέναι, Id. *Phd*.95e, etc. 3. Math., ἀ. ἀπό.. *subtract* from, Euc.*Ax*.3 (Pass.), etc.; of ratios, *divide out* from both sides of an equation, Apollon. Perg.1.41 (Pass.); *intercept*, in Pass., Procl.*Hyp*.2.27. 4. in

Logic, *abstract*, c. acc., Arist.*APo*.74ᵃ37, al.: abs., Id.*Metaph*.1030ᵃ 33. II. Med., fut. ἀφαιρήσομαι (in pass. sense, v.l. for ἀπαιρεθήσεσθαι, Hdt.5.35, cf. Antipho *Fr*.57), later ἀφελοῦμαι Timostr.5, Plb.3.29.7: aor. ἀφειλόμην, later ἀφειλάμην Ph.2.586, D.C.41.63, cf. Phryn.116: pf. ἀφῄρημαι (in med. sense) X.*Cyr*.7.5.79 (spelt ἀφείρ- *Sammelb*.4309 (iii B.C.)):—from Hom. downwds. more freq. than Act., *take away for oneself*; also in reciprocal sense, ἀφαιρεῖσθον τύχην ye *have received each* the fortune *of the other*, E. *El*.928:—Constr. like Act., ἀφαιρεῖσθαί τί τινι, as καὶ δή μοι γέρας.. ἀφαιρήσεσθαι ἀπειλεῖς Il.1.161; τί τινος 5.673,691, 9.335, Th.3.58, Lys.24.13, etc. (also τεύχεα.. ὤμοιϊν ἀφελέσθαι Il.13.510); τι πρός τινος E.*Tr*.1034; τι ἀπό τινος Ar.*V*.883; ἔκ τινος X.*Cyn*.12.9: c. dupl. acc. rei et pers., *bereave* or *deprive of*, μήτε σὺ τόνδ'.. ἀποαίρεο κούρην Il.1.275, cf. Hdt.1.71, 7.104; freq. in Att. and Trag., Lys. l. c., Th.8.74, D.20.46, etc.; τέκνα ἀ. τινά E.*Andr*.613, cf. Ar.*Ach*. 464: rarely c. acc. pers. et gen. rei, ἀ. τὰς κύνας τοῦ εὑρεῖν X.*Cyn*.6. 4; τῆς ἀρχῆς τινά Plu.*Ant*.60; τὴν Ἀμαζόνα τοῦ ζωστῆρος Paus.5.10. 9. 2. c. acc. rei, ἀ. ψήφισμα *cancel* or *rescind*, And.2.24; ἀφελομένης τῆς νυκτὸς τὸ ἔργον *having broken off* the action, Th.4.134; ἕως κελαινῆς νυκτὸς ὄμμ' ἀφείλετο A.*Pers*.428: abs., μέχρι σκότος ἀφείλετο (sc. τὴν δίωξιν) X.*HG*1.2.16; ἀ. τὴν μνήμην πολλῶν ἀγαθῶν D.22. 13. 3. folld. by μή c. inf., *prevent, hinder from* doing, τί μ' ἄνδρα.. ἀφείλου μὴ κτανεῖν; S.*Ph*.1303, cf. E.*Tr*.1146; κἄκτεινας, ἤ τις συμφορά σ' ἀφείλετο [μὴ κτεῖναι]; Id.*Andr*.913; c. inf. Pass., τὸν τὰ ὕστερον ἀφείλετο ἀδικήματα εὐεργέτην μὴ ὀνομασθῆναι Paus.8.52.2; c. inf. only, Pi.*I*.1.62: simply, *obstruct*, ἀρχήν Pl.*Lg*.958c. 4. ἀ. τινὰ εἰς ἐλευθερίαν, Lat. *vindicare in libertatem, claim* as free, Pl.*Lg*. 914e, Isoc.12.97, D.58.19, cf. Lys.23.10, Aeschin.1.62. III. Pass., fut. -αιρεθήσομαι E.*Hel*.938; -ήσομαι Antipho *Fr*.57: pf. ἀφῄρημαι, Ion. ἀπαραίρημαι Hdt.7.159, etc.:—*to be robbed* or *deprived of* a thing, τι A.*Ch*.962 (lyr.), Hdt.3.137, etc.; τι πρός or ὑπό τινος, Id.1.70, 3.65, 7.159; ἀφῃρέθην τὰ ἐνέχυρα ὑπό τινος D.47.41; ἐκ χερῶν ἀφῃρέθην *had* them *taken* out of my hands, E.*Tr*.486: c. inf., ἀφῃρέθη Σκίρωνος αὐτὰς ὄμμα τοὐμὸν εἰσορᾶν *was deprived of, hindered from* seeing them, Id.*Hipp*.1207: less freq. μηδὲν τοῦ ἐμοῦ ὄγκου ἀφαιρεθέντος ἀλλὰ σοῦ αὐξηθέντος Pl.*Tht*.155b. 2. ὁ ἀφαιρεθείς, in Law, *the person from whom* a slave *has been claimed*, Id.*Lg*.915a. **-ημα**· ἀνάθημα, δῶρον, Hsch. **-ηματικῶς**, *abstractly*, interpol. in Phlp. *in APo*.242.24.

**ἄφακες**· εὐήθεις, Hsch.

**ἀφάκη** [ἀφᾰ], ἡ, *tare, Vicia angustifolia*, Pherecr.188, Arist.*HA* 596ᵃ25, Thphr.*HP*8.8.3, Dsc.2.148, etc.

⊛ **ἀφάλλομαι**, aor. inf. ἀφάλασθαι Ael.*VH*6.14; Ep. aor. part. ἀπάλμενος Bion *Fr*.10.15:—*spring off* or *down from*, πήδημα κοῦφον ἐκ νεὼς ἀφήλατο A.*Pers*.305; ἐπὶ τὴν κεφαλὴν.. ἀφήλατο *jumped off* on to his head, Ar.*Nu*.147; ἀφαλόμενος τοῦ ἵππου Plu.*Caes*.27, cf. Ael. l.c.; of a river, τῆς πέτρας πλεῖον ἢ στάδιον ἀ. τὴν καταφοράν Plb.10.48. 5. 2. *jump, bound*, of a quick pulse, Ruf.*Syn.Puls*.7.5. II. *rebound, glance off*, ἀπὸ τῶν λείων Arist.*de An*.420ᵃ22; πέτρου Nic. *Th*.906: abs., *AP*9.159; *to be reflected*, πῦρ ἀπὸ πυρός Plu.2.931b.

**ἀφ-αλμός**, ὁ, *springing off*, Antyll.ap.Orib.6.31 tit. **-αλσις**, εως, ἡ, *jumping exercise*, Aret.*CD*1.3, Philum.ap.Orib.45.29.37, Antyll.ib.6.31.1. **-αλτος**, ον, *springing off* or *back*, Hsch.

**ἄφᾰλος**, ον, *without* φάλος, κυνέη Il.10.258, *BGU*1190.3 (i B.C.?).

⊛ **ἀφᾰμαρτάνω**, aor. part. ἀφαμαρτήσαντος Orph.*A*.643; Ep. aor. ἀπήμβροτεν Il.15.521, 16.466,477, Pancrat.*Oxy*.1085.7:—*miss* one's mark, c. gen., καὶ τοῦ μέν ῥ' ἀφάμαρτεν Il.8.119, etc.; θηρός Pancrat. l.c.: also in Prose, X.*HG*6.1.15, D.14.13. II. *lose, be deprived of* what one has, σεῦ ἀφαμαρτούσῃ Il.6.411; φίλου ἀπὸ πατρὸς ἁμαρτών 22.505.

**ἀφᾰμαρτοεπής**, ές, = ἁμαρτοεπής, *talking at random*, Il.3.215.

**Ἀφάμιος**, ὁ (sc. μήν), name of month at Thronium, *Klio* 16.170; at Ambryssus, *GDI*2256.5.

**Ἀφαμιῶται**, ῶν, οἱ, name of *serfs* in Crete, like the Helots in Laconia, Str.15.1.34, Ath.6.263f (written Ἀμφ-); cf. ἀφημοῦντας, ἀφημιάστους.

**ἀφαμμᾰτ-ίζω**, *fasten off*, Antyll.ap.Orib.45.24.4:—hence **-ιστέον**, Sor.1.56.

**ἀφάνα**, = σκινδαψός, Suid. s. h. v.

**ἀφανδάνω**, Ion. aor. inf. ἀπαδεῖν Hdt.2.129:—*displease, not to please*, εἰ δ' ὑμῖν ὅδε μῦθος ἀφανδάνει Od.16.387; σοὶ τἄμ' ἀφανδάνοντ' ἔφυ S.*Ant*.501.

**ἀφᾰν-εί**, Adv. of ἀφανής, *invisibly, obscurely*, Hdn.*Epim*.255. ⊛ **-εια**, ἡ, *obscurity, uncertainty*, τύχας Pi.*I*.4(3).49: metaph., ἀξιώματος ἀ. *want of illustrious* birth or rank, Th.2.37. 2. *invisibility*, Dam. *Pr*.6. II. *disappearance, destruction*, A.*Ag*.384 (lyr.), Procl. *in Prm*.p.840S.—The form **ἀφανία** is mentioned by A.D.*Synt*.341. 8. **-έω**, *fail to put in an appearance*, dub. in *PTeb*.43.22 (ii B.C.):— but **ἀφᾱνέω**, *thrash, beat*, Ar.*Eq*.394; cf. ἄφηνα· ἔκοψα, and ἀφῆναι· τὸ τὰς ἐπτισμένας κριθὰς ταῖς χερσὶ τρῖψαι, Hsch.; v. αἴνω. ⊛ **-ής**, ές, (φαίνομαι) *unseen*, esp. of the nether world, Ταρτάρου πυθμὴν Pi *Fr*.207, cf. A.*Th*.860 (lyr.); ἀ. κἂν Ἀΐδα δόμῳ φοιτάσῃς Sapph.68; χάσμα ἀ. a *blind* pit, Hdt.6.76; ἡ ἀ. θεός, of Persephone, S.*OC*1556 (lyr.); ὁ ἀ. πόλος, i. e. the south pole, Arist.*Cael*.285ᵇ21, *Mu*.394ᵇ31 (but ἀ. κόσμος *starless*, Vett.Val.6.22). 2. ἀ. γίγνεσθαι, = ἀφανίζεσθαι, *disappear*, ὑπὸ γῆν Hdt.3.104, cf. E.*IT*757, Pl.*R*.360a; so ἀ. ἦν *disappeared*, Hdt.7.37, cf. X.*An*.1.4.7; of soldiers *missing* after a battle, Th.2.34; *runaway, absconded*, *PGen*.5.4 (ii A.D.). b. στήλας ἀ. ποιῆσαι *obliterate*, *SIG*38.38 (Teos). 3. *unnoticed, secret*, ἀ. νόος ἀθανάτων Sol.17; ἀ. νεῦμα *a secret* sign, Th.1.134; ἀ. χωρίον *out of sight*, Id.4.29, cf. ib.67; ἀ. ξιφίδιον *concealed*, Id.8.69; δι' ἐπιστολῶν ἀφανῶν *secret* or *invisible* writings, Ph.*Bel*.102.29: c. part., ἀ. εἶναι ἀπιόντες depart *without being noticed*, X.*An*.4.2.4; ἀ. ὄντες ἠδίκουν Th.1.68; μαντικῇ χρώμενος οὐκ ἀ. ἦν he was *well known to* do.., X.*Mem*.1.1.2. b. *uncertain, doubtful*, ἀ. νοῦσοι Hdt.2.84; σὺν ἀφανεῖ λόγῳ on an *uncertain* charge, S.*OT*657 (lyr.); ἐν ἀφανεῖ λ. Antipho 5.59; μόρος S.*OC*1682 (lyr.); ὄνομα E.*Tr*.1322 (lyr.); ἐλπίς Th.5.103; πρόφασις ἀφανεστάτη λόγῳ Id.1.23; οὐκ ἀ. τεκμήρια X. *Ages*.6.1; μεθέντας τἀφανῆ, opp. τὸ πρὸς ποσί, S.*OT*131; ἀ. χάρις a favour *from an unknown hand*, D.19.240; ἐς ἀφανὲς τὸν μῦθον ἀνενείκας Hdt.2.23; μισῶ μὲν ὅστις τἀφανῆ περισκοπῶν S.*Fr*.737; τὰ ἀ. μεριμνᾶν Ar.*Fr*.672; ὑπὲρ τῶν ἀ. φανεροῖς μαρτυρίοις χρῆσθαι Arist. *EN*1104ᵃ13; of what is *beyond the evidence of sense*, opp. φανερόν, ἁρμονίη ἀ. φανερῆς κρείττων Heraclit.54, cf. Phld.*Sign*.1, al.; τἀφανῆ διὰ τοῦ φαινομένου συλλογίζεσθαι Epicur.*Nat*.14.4; τὸ τῆς τύχης ἀ. οἷ προβήσεται E.*Alc*.785; τὸ ἀ. τοῦ κατορθώσειν Th.2.42; ἐν ἀφανεῖ ἔτι κεῖσθαι, ἐν τῷ ἀ. εἶναι, Id.1.42, 3.23; ἐν ἀ. κεκτῆσθαί τι *secretly*, Pl.*Lg*. 954e; ἐκ τοῦ ἀφανοῦς Th.1.51, 4.96, etc.; ἐξ ἀ. A.*Fr*.57.9, Ar.*Ra*. 1332: neut. pl. as Adv., E.*Hipp*.1289 (lyr.). Regul. Adv. ἀφανῶς Th. 3.43, etc.: Sup. -έστατα X.*HG*5.1.27. 4. of persons and things, *unnoticed, obscure*, E.*Tr*.1244; also οὐ γὰρ ἀ. κρινεῖτε τὴν δίκην Th.3. 57; ἀ. καὶ ταπεινὴ φύσις D.61.35. 5. ἀ. οὐσία *personal* property, as money, *which can be secreted and made away with* (cf. ἀφανίζω 1.7), opp. φανερά (*real*, as land, Lys.32.4, cf. *BCH*27.219 (Crete); opp. ἐμφανής, *IG*12(2).15.8 (Mytil.), *SIG*554.17; but simply, *concealed*, ἀφανῆ καταστῆσαι τὴν οὐσίαν Lys.20.23: in lit. sense, ἀ. πλοῦτος Ar. *Ec*.602; πλοῦτος ἀ. δν σὺ κατορύξας ἔχεις Men.128.16. ⊛ **-ίζω**, Att. fut. -ιῶ X.*An*.3.2.11, Pl.*Tht*.184a: pf. ἠφάνικα D.36.18:—*make unseen, hide*, νεφέλη.. ἠφάνισεν ἥλιον X.*An*.3.4.8; *hush up*, ἔργον Pl.*Smp*. 217e: hence, *lose sight of*, Eub.107.18; ἀ. τὸ συμφορώτατον *do away with, reject*, Hp.*VM*21 (v.l. for ἀφαιρέοντας); *make away with* a person, Hdt.3.126, X.*Mem*.1.2.53, Th.4.80; μή μ' ἀφανίσῃ λαβών Men. *Epit*.210:—Pass., τὴν γνώμην μηδὲν.. ἀφανισθεῖσαν in no part *concealed* or *suppressed*, Th.7.8. 2. *do away with, remove*, ἄχος S. *OC*1712 (lyr.); τινὰ πόλεος *carry* one *off from* the city, E.*Ph*.1041 (lyr.); Μούσας ἀ. Ar.*Nu*.972; ἀ. αὑτὸν εἰς τὸν νεών *disappear* into the temple, Id.*Pl*.741. 3. *destroy*, Ἀθήνας X.*An*.3.2.11, cf. Plb.1.81.6, Lxx *De*.7.2; ὅλως ἀ. ἱερά D.21.147, cf. *Epigr.Gr*.376.8 (Aezani). 4. *obliterate* writing, Th.6.54; footsteps, X.*Cyn*.5.3, etc.; traces of bloodshed, Antipho 5.45; *spirit away* a witness, ib.52; *get rid of*, δίκην Ar.*Nu*.760. 5. *secrete, steal*, X.*Oec*.14.2. 6. *obscure, mar* one's good name, etc., πατρικὰς ἀρετάς, ἀξίωσιν, δόξαν, Th.7.69, 2.61: in good sense, ἀ. ἀγαθῷ κακόν *wipe out* ill deeds by good, ib.42; δύσκλειαν Id.3.58; τὰ χρώματα ἀ. ἐκ τοῦ σώματος, of the *wasting* effect of grief, Antiph.98; τρίχα βαφῇ ἀ. *disguise* it by dyeing, Ael.*VH*7.20; ἀ. τὰ πρόσωπα (cf. ἀπρόσωπος), *of artificial disfigurement*, *Ev.Matt*.6.16, cf. Lxx *Jl*.2.20, *Za*.7.14. b. *spoil*, οἶνον, ὕδωρ, Sor.1.90, Gal.9.645. 7. *make away with* property, etc., ἀργύριον, ναυτικόν, ἀνθρώπους, Aeschin. 1.101, 3.222, D.28.12; ἀ. τὴν οὐσίαν Aeschin.1.103; but, *conceal the existence of*, ἐργαστήριον, οὐσίαν, D.27.26,44. 8. *drain* a cup of wine, Eub.82. 9. ἀφανίσαι· σκεπάσαι, προνομεῦσαι, Hsch. II. Pass., *disappear, be missing*, Hdt.4.8,124, S.*Ant*.255; of persons *buried* by a sand-storm, Hdt.3.26; or *lost* at sea, Th.8.38, X.*HG*1.6.33; ἀ. κατὰ τῆς θαλάσσης, of islands, Hdt.7.6; ὑποβρύχιος ἠφ. Plu.*Crass*.19; ἀ. ἐκ τῶν Θρηίκων Hdt.4.95; ἐξ ἀνθρώπων Lys.2.11; ἀ. εἰς ὕλην *disappear* into it, X.*Cyn*.10.23; καταγελασθὲν ἠφανίσθη was laughed down and *disappeared*, Th.3.83. 2. *live retired*, X.*Ages*.9.1. **-ῐσις**, εως, ἡ, *getting rid of*, τῆς δίκης Ar.*Nu*.765; τῶν συνθηκῶν D.33.22; *destruction*, λόγων Pl.*Sph*.259e. II. (from Pass.) *disappearance*, Hdt.4. 15, Arist.*Pr*.953ᵃ17, Epicur.*Ep*.2 p.52 U. **-ισμός**, ὁ, *extermination, destruction*, Plb.5.11.5; πόλεων D.S.15.48; σώματος καὶ ψυχῆς Plu.2.107d; ἀφανισμῷ ἀφανίζειν Lxx *De*.7.2. II. = foreg. II, Arist. *HA*580ᵇ21, Luc.*Alex*.19; ἄστρων Thphr.*Sign*.2 (pl.), cf. Cleom.2.5; *occultation*, Theo Sm.p.137H.; Περὶ ἀ. ἡλιακῶν, title of work by Eudoxus, on *occultations* of stars by the sun, Phld.*D*.1.21; τῆς σελήνης Plu.2.67cc; ἐγγὺς ἀφανισμοῦ *Ep.Hebr*.8.13. **-ιστέος**, έα, έον, *to be suppressed*, [λόγος] Isoc.12.233. **-ιστής**, οῦ, ὁ, *destroyer*, dub. l. in Plu.2.828f, cf. Sch.A.*Th*.175, etc.; *scavenger*, *PLond*.2.387.9 (iii A.D.):—fem. **-ίστρια**, Sch.Opp.*H*.2.487:—hence **-ιστικός**, ή, όν, *causing to disappear*, τινός A.D.*Pron*.33.15; τριχῶν Archig.ap. Aët.6.63, cf. Crito ap.Gal.12.447; *destroying*, Sch.A.*Th*.145. Adv. -κῶς Sch.Il.21.220, al.

**ἄφανος**, ον, dub. sens., λίθος *PMag.Par*.2.195.

**ἀφαντ-ἀσίαστος**, ον, *not manifested*, *Corp.Herm*.5.1, Olymp. *in Phd*.p.35N. Adv. -τως Ascl. *in Metaph*.151.6, Olymp. *in Phd*.p.38 N. **-ασίωτος**, ον, *unable to imagine* a thing, Plu.2.960d, *Cat. Cod.Astr*.7.215.7. **-αστος**, ον, *without* φαντασία, φύσις *Stoic*.2. 304, al.: c. gen., ψυχὴ ἀ. τοῦ ὄντος Ph.1.230. Adv. -τως, κινεῖσθαι, opp. ὁρμῇ καὶ φαντασίᾳ χρῆσθαι, Id.1.641, cf. Porph.*Gaur*.7.3. 2. *without dreams*, Gal.16.221,525. II. *not sensibly presented*, εἶδος, of pure form, Syrian. *in Metaph*.92.5.

**ἀφαντικά**, τά, *derelict lands*, *Cod.Theod*.13.11.3, prob. in Lyd.*Mag*. 3.70; cf. *afanticius* *Cod.Theod*.5.11.9.

⊛ **ἄφαντ-ος**, ον, (φαίνομαι) *made invisible, blotted out*, ἀκήδεστοι καὶ ἄ. Il.6.60; ἄσπερμος γενεὴ καὶ ἄ. ὄληται 20.303, etc.; *hidden*, ἄ. ἕρμα A.*Ag*.1007 (lyr.); ἔφην ἄφαντον φῶς S.*Ph*.297; ἄ. ἔπελες Pi.*O*.1.46; ἐκ βροτῶν ἄ. βῆναι S.*OT*832; ἀνὴρ ἄ. ἐκ.. στρατοῦ he has *disappeared*, A.*Ag*.624; ἄ. οἴχεσθαι ib.657, Jul.*Or*.2.59a; ἔρρειν S.*OT*560; ἀρθεῖσ' ἄ. E.*Hel*.606; ἐκ χερῶν Id.*Hipp*.827 (lyr.); ἴχνος πλατᾶν ἄ. *disappear-*

*ing*, A.*Ag*.695 (lyr.); *invisible*, νύξ Parm.9.3. 2. *in secret*, ἄφαντα βρέμειν Pi.*P*.11.30. 3. *obscure*, Id.*N*.8.34; θεοῖς δῆλος θνητοῖσι δ' ἄ. Epimenid.11.—Poet. and late Prose, ἄ. γενέσθαι D.S.3.60, 4.65, *Ev.Luc*.24.31; τὰ ἄφαντα φήναντες Aristid.1.260 J., cf. Sch.Arat. 899. -όω, *make* ἄφαντος, *hide*, Eust.882.45:—Pass., *disappear*, Sch.Arat.899; *evaporate*, Syn.Alch.p.67 B.; *to be sublimated*, Zos. Alch.p.163 B.

**ἀφάπαξ** [φᾰ], *once for all*, *PFlor*.158.10 (iii A.D.).

**ἀφ-απτέον**, *one must fasten*, Antyll.ap.Orib.45.24.10. -άπτω, aor. ἀφῆψα, imper. ἄφαψον Ph.*Bel*.65.37:—*fasten from* or *upon*, ἄμματα ἀπάψας *having tied* knots *on a string*, Hdt.4.98, cf. Hp.*Fist*.4:—Med., Lxx *Pr*.3.3, al.:—Pass., *to be hung on, hang on*, pf. part. ἀπαμμένος (Ion. for ἀφημμ-) Hdt.2.121.δ'; ἀφημμένος ἐκ ποδεώνων Theoc. 22.52. 2. metaph. of argument, Gal.16.82.

**ἄφᾰρ** [ἄφ], poet. Adv. *straightway, forthwith*, in Hom. mostly at the beginning of a clause, with δέ following, ἄ. δ' ἤνυσε καρήατι Il.19.405, cf. Od.2.95: without δέ, *thereupon, after that*, Il.11.418. 2. *suddenly, quickly*, ἄ. κεραοὶ τελέθουσι Od.4.85: strengthd. ἄ. αὐτίκα Il. 23.593; πέμπε δράκοντας ἄ. Pi.*N*.1.40, cf. 10.63, *Pae*.6.81, Emp.35.6, 110.8.—Rare in Trag., A.*Pers*.469; ἄ. βέβακε S.*Tr*.133, 529, cf. E. *IT*1274 (lyr. exc. in A. l.c.): also in later Ep. as A.R.2.539, etc. 3. intens., *very*, Il.17.417, Od.2.169. II. in Thgn.716 as if Adj., *swift, fleet* (cf. ἀφάρτερος), παῖδες Βορέω τῶν ἄφαρ εἰσὶ πόδες.

**ἄφαρβαν**· ἐλεύθερον, Hsch.

**ἀφαρεί**, Adv. = ἄφαρ I.2, *EM*175.24, Hsch., Suid.

**ἀφαρεύς**, έως, ὁ, supposed *belly-fin of female tunny*, dub. in Arist. *HA*543a13.

⊛ **ἀφαρής**, ές, *without* φᾶρος, *unclad, naked*, of the Χάριτες, Euph. 87; cf. ἄφᾱρος.

**ἀφάρκη**, ἡ, an evergreen tree, *hybrid arbutus, Arbutus hybrida*, Thphr.*HP*1.9.3, 3.3.1.

⊛ **ἀφαρκίδευτον**· ἄγρευτον, ἀθυσίαστον, Hsch.

**ἄφαρκτος**, ον, v. ἄφρακτος.

**ἀφαρμάκ-ευτος** [μᾰ], ον, *without medicine, not physicked*, Hp.*Acut*. (*Sp*.)27; *without cosmetics*, ξανθίζειν ἀφαρμάκευτα Alciphr.*Fr*.5. 4. -ος, ον, *without medicinal properties*, Gal.6.650. II. *without bloom*, χρῶμα Eust.1416.2, Hsch. -τος, ον, *unanointed*, Nic. *Th*.115; *unpoisoned*, κύλιξ ἀ. Luc.*DMort*.7.2.

**ἀφαρμόζω**, Att. -ττω, *not to suit*, Oenom.ap.Eus.*PE*5.24.

**ἀφᾰρόζωμος** [ἄφ], ὁ, *improvised*, 'hasty' *broth*, Eust.1191.13.

**ἄφᾱρος**, ον, = ἀφάρωτος, Call.*Fr*.183. II. **ἄφᾱρος**, ον, = ἀφαρής, Hsch.

⊛ **ἀφαρπᾰγή**· *abreptio*, Gloss.

⊛ **ἀφαρπάζω**, fut. Ep. -άξω, Att. -άσομαι:—Pass., pf. -ήρπασμαι X. *Cyn*.9.18: aor. 1 -ηρπάσθην Id.*HG*5.4.17; -ηρπάγην *IPE*1.26 (Olbia):—*tear off* or *from*, Ἕκτωρ δ' ὡρμήθη κόρυθα.. κρατὸς ἀφαρπάξαι Il. 13.189; *snatch away, steal from*, τί τινος Ar.*Eq*.1062: c. acc. only, *snatch eagerly*, S.*Tr*.548, E.*Ion*1178; ἀ. τὸν στέφανον D.21.64; of death, *IG*12(7).52.9 (Amorgos):—Pass., Lys.19.31; φωτὸς ἀφαρπασθείς, of one *dead*, *IG*14.1386, cf. 12(7).400 (Amorgos).

**ἀφάρτερος** [ἄφ], α, ον, Comp. Adj. (from ἄφαρ) *more fleet*, τῶν δ' ἵπποι μὲν ἔασιν ἀφάρτεροι Il.23.311; cf. Dionys.Epic.ap.St.Byz. s.v. Κάσπειρος.

**ἀφάρυμος**· ἄτολμος, Hsch.

**ἀφᾰρωτος**, ον, (φᾰρόω) *unploughed, untilled*, Call.*Fr*.82c.

**ἀφᾱσία**, ἡ, (ἄφατος) *speechlessness*, caused by fear or perplexity, ἔκπληξιν ἡμῖν ἀφασίαν τε προστιθεῖς E.*Hel*.549; ἀ. μ' ἔχει Id.*IA*837, cf. Ar.*Th*.904; ἀ. ἡμᾶς λαμβάνει τί ποτε χρὴ λέγειν Pl.*Lg*.636e; εἰς ἀ. τινὰ ἐμβάλλειν Id.*Phlb*.21d; εἰς ἀ. ἐμβάλλειν πράγματος *inability to say anything* about it, S.E.*P*.2.211, cf. Dam.*Pr*.7.

**ἀφάσσω**, Ion., Ep., and late Prose, = ἀφάω, *feel*, Hp.*Nat.Mul*.11, etc.; ἄφασον αὐτοῦ τὰ ὦτα Hdt.3.69, cf. A.R.2.710, 4.428, v.l. in Call. *Fr*.317, cf. Musae.82, etc.; ὥσπερ ἐν σκότει ἀφάσσων *groping*, Dam. *Pr*.42, cf. Iamb.*Myst*.3.6, etc.:—Med., A.R.4.181:—Pass., Hp. *Morb*.2.30 and 41.

**ἀφατέω**, dub. sens. in *IG*5(1).209.34.

**ἀφατῆλες**· μαστοί, θηλαί, Hsch.

**ἄφᾰτος**, ον, *not uttered* or *named, nameless*, ἄνδρες ὁμῶς ἄ. τε φατοί τε Hes.*Op*.3. 2. *unutterable, ineffable*, λόγος E.*Ion*782 (lyr.); ἄ. μέλεα *monstrous*, Pi.*N*.1.47; κεφαλαί *AP*6.112 (Pers.); ἄ. χρήματα *untold* sums, Hdt.7.190; ἄ. νέφος, κτύπος, S.*OT*1314 (lyr.), *OC*1464 (lyr.); ὀρνιθαρίων ἄφατον (Schw. for -των) πλῆθος Anaxandr.41.63; πώλων ἄφατον τάχος *IG*14.2012.4 (Sulp. Max.); ἡδονή Phld.*D*.3.14; ὑπερβολὴ δυνάμεως Hermog.*Inv*.1.4; δύναμις Plot.4.8.6; ἄφατον ὡς.. *there's no saying* how.., i.e. *marvellously, immensely*, Ar.*Av*.428, *Lys*.198. Adv. -τως Dsc.1.13.

⊛ **ἀφαυαίνω**, aor. part. -ήνας Lyc.ap.Orib.8.25.8, *PHolm*.12.12, but inf. -ᾶναι Plot.4.4.32:—*starve, wither*, Thphr.*HP*3.18.9:—Pass., ib. 4.2.11; *to be parched*, δίψῃ ἀφαυανθήσομαι Ar.*Ec*.146, cf. Arist.*Pr*. 896a14, Lyc.ap.Orib.8.25.17; ἵνα μὴ ζητῶν τὸν σύαγρον ἀφαυανθῇς Ath.9.401e. 2. *grill, roast*, Hld.2.19 (prob.), Porph.*Abst*.4.20. (Cf. ἀπαυαίνω.)

**ἀφαυρ-ός**, ά, όν, *feeble, powerless*, ἠΰτε παιδὸς ἀφαυροῦ Il.7.235, cf. Nic.*Th*.198; *dim*, Arat.256; almost always Comp. and Sup., σέο πολλὸν ἀφαυρότερος Il.7.457; ἵνα μή οἱ ἀφαυρότερον βέλος εἴη 12.458; οὔ μιν ἀφαυρότατος βάλ' Ἀχαιῶν 15.11, cf. Od.20.110, Hes.*Op*.586, Pi.*P*.4.272 (Comp.), Theoc.21.49 (Comp.); ἀνδρὸς γηρέντος πολλὸν -ότερος Xenoph.9, etc.; ῥείθρων ἀφαυροτέρην, of a bridge, *too weak to resist* the stream, *Epigr.Gr*.1078.6 (Adana): so in Prose, σιτία -ότερα *less nutritious*, Hp.*Mul*.1.67; [κενεὼν] -ότατόν ἐστι X.*Eq*.12.8; Posit., Democr.285, Ti.Locr.102c, Arist.*EN*1101b2, *Hymn.Is*. 122. Adv. -ρῶς *AP*6.267 (Diotim.): Comp. -ότερον, τροχάει Arat. 227. -ότης, ητος, ἡ, *feebleness*, τῶν αἰσθήσεων Anaxag.21. -όω, *make weak*, Erot. s.v. ἀμαλδύνεται (v.l. ἀμαυροῦται).

⊛ **ἀφαύω**, (αὔω) *dry up, parch*, v.l. for ἀφᾱνέω in Ar.*Eq*.394.

**ἄφαψις**, ἡ, dub. sens. in Gal.19.368.

**ἀφάω**, (ἀφή) Ep. Verb, *to handle*, θώρηκα καὶ ἀγκύλα τόξ' ἀφόωντα *rubbing and polishing* them, Il.6.322; ὠτειλὰς ἀφόωσιν Opp.*H*.5.329; ἀφόων θησαυρόν *AP*11.366 (Maced.).

**ἀφέγγ-εια**, ἡ, *want of light*, Max.Tyr.40.4. -ής, ές, *without light*, φῶς ἀ. a light *that is no light* (i.e. to the blind), S.*OC*1549; νυκτὸς ἀφεγγὲς βλέφαρον, of the moon, E.*Ph*.543; simply, *dark*, σπῆλυγξ Opp.*C*.2.324; ὀμίχλη *AP*9.675; δηϊοτής a *night* battle, Nonn. *D*.24.165; Ἀΐδα.. τὸν ἀφεγγέα χῶρον *Epigr.Gr*.372.13 (Cotiaeum), cf. D.H.8.52. 2. *not visible to the eye*, ὀδμά A.*Pr*.115. 3. metaph., εἴ τι.. τυγχάνεις ἀφεγγὲς φέρων something *ill-starred, unlucky*, S.*OC*1481 (lyr.). 4. *obscure*, ἔκδοσις Olymp.Alch.p.70 B.

**ἀφέδιτος** (prob. ἀφείδ-, cf. φειδίτια) ἡμέρα day *when no sacrifice is offered*, at Sparta, Hsch. (leg. ⟨οὐ⟩ θύουσιν).

**ἀφεδνήν**· ἀναιδῆ, Hsch.

**ἀφεδρ-εία**, ἡ, *menstruation*, Dam.ap.Suid. s.v. διαγνώμων. -εύω, = ἐπὶ δίφρῳ καθίσαι, Hsch.

**ἀφεδρῆ**· ἀποπνίγη, Hsch.

⊛ **ἀφεδριατεύοντες**, οἱ, title of *Boeotian magistracy*, *IG*7.3207 (Orchom. Boeot.), al.

**ἄφεδρος**, ἡ, *menses muliebres*, Lxx *Le*.15.19, al., Dsc.2.75, Gal.14. 208. II. Εἰλειθυίας ἄ. *exudation from* silver fir, Thphr.*HP*5.9.8.

**ἀφεδρών**, ῶνος, ὁ, (ἕδρα) *privy*, *OGI*483.220 (Pergam.), *Ev.Matt*. 15.17.

⊛ **ἀφειδ-έω**, *to be unsparing, lavish of*, ψυχῆς S.*El*.980; τοῦ βίου Th. 2.43; σφῶν αὐτῶν ib.51; τῶν σωμάτων Lys.2.25: abs., ἀφειδήσαντες [πόνου, or the like] *ungrudgingly*, Hp.*Art*.37; *recklessly*, E.*IT* 1354. II. *take no care for, neglect*, εἴ τις τοῦδ' ἀφειδήσοι πόνου S.*Ant*. 414 (s.v.l.); *reck not of*, μαινομένης θαλάσσης Musae.303; βασιλῆος, ἀέθλων, τοκήων A.R.2.98 (ἀκήδησαν Choerob.), 869, 3.630; Ἀφροδίτης Nonn.*D*.8.217: also in Prose, Str.1.2.6. ⊛ -ής, ές, (φείδομαι) *not sparing of*, νεῶν καὶ πεισμάτων A.*Ag*.195 (lyr.); ἀ. δείματος *lightly regarding* it, A.R.4.1252; ἀ. πρὸς τὸν ἔρωτα Call.*Epigr*.47.7: Sup. -έστατοι, τῶν ἀγαθῶν D.Chr.1.24. 2. of things, ἀ. ὁ κατάπλους καθεστήκει the landing was made *without regard to cost* or *risk*, Th.4.26; *not spared, lavishly bestowed*, χρυσός Call.*Cer*.128; δῶρα *AP*11.59 (Maced.). II. Adv. -δῶς, Aeol. and Ion. -δέως Alc.34, Hdt.1. 163, al., Ep. -δείως A.R.3.897:—*freely, lavishly*, Alc.l.c.; διδόναι Hdt. l.c., D.18.88; ἀ. ἀπιέναι τὰ τοξεύματα Hdt.9.61: Comp. -έστερον, ταῖς λέξεσι χρῆσθαι Hermog.*Id*.2.11; *unsparingly*, ὁρμῆσαι πρὸς τὸν πόλεμον D.11.2. 2. *without mercy*, κατακόψαι Hdt.1.207; φονεύειν Id.9.39; χρώμενον Democr.159; κολαζόντων ἀφειδέστερον ἢ ὡς δεσπόται, -έστατα τιμωρεῖν, X.*Cyr*.4.2.47, *An*.1.9.13; ἀ. ἔχειν ἑαυτῶν Arist. *Pol*.1315a29, cf. Paus.4.4.8. -ία, ἡ, *generosity, liberality*, Pl.*Def*. 412c, Plu.2.762d. 2. *unsparing treatment*, σώματος *Ep.Col*.2.23.

**ἀφείδιτος**, v. ἀφέδιτος.

**ἀφείργω**, = ἀπείργω (q.v.), pf. part. Pass. ἀφειργμένη Ael.*NA*12.21.

**ἀφεκάς** [ᾰς], Adv. *far away*, Nic.*Th*.674.

**ἀφεκτ-έον**, (ἀπέχομαι) *one must abstain from*, τινός X.*Mem*.1.2. 34; τροφῆς Porph.*Abst*.1.38, etc.; *one must leave alone*, τινός Gal. 17(2).359: so in pl. -τέα, Ar.*Lys*.124; cf. ἀποσχετέον. -ικός, ή, όν, (ἀπέχομαι) *abstemious*, Arr.*Epict*.2.22.20; τὸ ἀ. Porph.*Abst*. 3.26: c. gen., ib.3.1.

**ἀφελγύνουσα**· κακοῦσα, Hsch.

⊛ **ἀφέλ-εια**, Ion. -είη, ἡ, *simplicity*, Hp.*Decent*.3, Antiph.163.8; περὶ τὴν δίαιταν Plb.6.48.3; of style, Ath.15.693f, Hermog.*Id*.1.1, al.; opp. σφοδρότης, ib.11; of terminology, Gal.10.269. -έον· συνηγμένον, κοινόν, Hsch. ⊛ -ής, ές, (φελλεύς) *without a stone, even, smooth*, διὰ τῶν ἀφελῶν πεδίων Ar.*Eq*.527. II. *artless, simple*, of persons, S.*Fr*.723, D.*Ep*.4.11, Luc.*DDeor*.4.3; εὔκολος καὶ ἀ. Plu.*Cat. Ma*.6; ἀφελέστατοι τῶν πρότερον Phylarch.43; *frater* ἀφελέστατος Cic.*Att*.1.18.1; ἀ. κατὰ τὴν ἐσθῆτα Plb.11.10.3; also ἀ. ἐντεύξεις Id. 18.49.4; ἀ. ψυχή *simple*, in good sense, *IG*14.1839. Adv. -λῶς, ἔχειν Plb.38.7.4; μετρίως καὶ ἀ. οἰκεῖν Plu.*Pomp*.40; *naively*, Cic.*QF* 1.2.3 (prob.); πολλὰ ἀ. πιστεύσας ἀπώλεσεν Vett.Val.168.23. b. in bad sense, *bold, brazen*, *AP*5.41 (Rufin.). Adv. -λῶς, παίζουσα dub. l. in Thgn.1211; κατηγορίαν ποιήσασθαι Aristid.2.116 J. 2. Rhet., *simple, not intricate* or *involved*, opp. ἐν κώλοις, περίοδος Arist. *Rh*.1409b16: generally, of style, *affecting simplicity* or *artlessness*, τὸ ἀ. D.H.*Comp*.22; λέξις λιτὴ καὶ ἀ. Id.*Dem*.2; φράσις ἰσχνὴ καὶ ἀ. Id.*Pomp*.2; λέξις ἀ. καὶ ἄθρυπτος Plu.*Lyc*.21; ἀφέλεια -εστέρα Hermog.*Id*.2.12. Adv. -λῶς, γράφειν ib.10.

**ἀφελκόω**, *make an incision, tap* a tree, Thphr.*HP*9.1.5, 9.2.1 (Pass.):—Pass., *to be ulcerated*, f.l. in Hp.*Epid*.4.41, Arist.*Pr*.889b13; *to be abraded*, Thphr.*CP*5.5.2.

**ἀφέλκ-ῠσις**, εως, ἡ, *dragging away*, Gloss. -υστέον, *one must draw off*, Antyll.ap.Orib.7.21.7. ⊛ -ω, Ion. ἀπέλκω, fut. ἀφέλξω E. *Hec*.142 (lyr.): aor. ἀφείλκῠσα (v. infr.): pf. ἀφείλκῠκα M.Ant.3.6:—*drag away*, ἱκέτας ἐκ τοῦ ἱροῦ Hdt.3.48, cf. S.*OC*844, E.*Heracl*.113; πῶλον ἀπὸ μαστῶν Id.*Hec*.142 (lyr.); τινὰς ἀπὸ τέκνων καὶ γονέων καὶ γυναικῶν Lys.12.96; *drag* a speaker *from* the βῆμα, Pl.*Prt*.319c; ἀ. τὰς τριήρεις *drag* or *tow* ships *away*, Th.2.93, cf. 7.53, 74; *draw aside, divert*, ἐπὶ τὰ ἡδέα X.*Mem*.4.5.6; τὸ δέρμα ἀ. *to draw* it *off*, Hp.*Art*.

11:—Pass., ibid. II. *draw off* liquor, κάδων πώματα Archil.4; θρόμβους οὓς ἀφείλκυσας φόνου A.*Eu*.184. 2. Med., τοῦ δόρατος ἀφελκύσωμαι τοὔλυτρον *let me draw off* the sheath *from*.., Ar.*Ach*.1120.

**ἀφέλκωσις**, εως, ἡ, *abrasion of plant-stem*, Thphr.*CP*5.5.3.

⊛ **ἀφελληνίζω**, *hellenize*, i.e. *civilize thoroughly*, τὴν βάρβαρον Ph.2.567:—Pass., aor. -ηλλήνισθη D.Chr.37.26.

**ἀφελλίαι**· μέλανος ἀλφός, Hsch. **ἄφελμα**· τὸ κάλλυντρον, Id.; cf. ὄφελμα.

**ἀφελόζωος**, ον, *living simply*, *PMag.Par*.1.1371.

**ἀφελότης**, ητος, ἡ, *simplicity*, *unworldliness*, *Act.Ap*.2.46, Vett.Val.240.15.

**ἀφελπίζω**, = ἀπελπ-, *IG*14.966 (Pass.).

**ἄφεμα**, ατος, τό, *that which is let go*: *remission of tribute* or *taxation*, Lxx 1*Ma*.10.28 (pl.), al., *PTeb*.226 (ii B.C.), *PFlor*.379.37 (ii A.D.).

**ἀφενάκιστος** [νᾱ], ον, *free from cajolery*, *straightforward*, Ph.1.564.

**ἄφενος**, εος, τό, *revenue*, *riches*, *wealth*, *abundance*, ἄφενος καὶ πλοῦτον ἀφύξειν Il.1.171, cf. 23.299, Thgn.30; μύρμηκος Crates Theb.10.7; of the *wealth* of the gods, Hes.*Th*.112: masc. acc. ἄφενον v.l. in Id.*Op*.24: gen. οιο Call.*Jov*.96, *AP*9.234 (Crin.); cf. ἄφνος.

**ἄφεος**· ἄφωνος, Hsch.

**ἄφεξις**, εως, ἡ, (ἀπέχομαι) *abstinence*, τινός *from* a thing, Aret.*CD*1.2.

**ἀφέργω**, = ἀπείργω, *keep off*, *withhold*, *Tab.Heracl*.1.131.

**ἀφεργοπον-ία**, ἡ, *incapacity for bearing labour*, Eust.222.28. **-ος**, ον, *incapable of labour*, Vett.Val.77.1, 150.27, Ptol.*Tetr*.156, Sch.A.R.1.269. Adv. -νως *carelessly*, Simp.*in Ph*.43.4.

**ἀφέριστα**· ἄχρηστα, Hsch.

**ἄφερκτος**, ον, (ἀφείργω) *shut out from*, A.*Ch*.446 (lyr.).

**ἀφερμηνεύω**, *interpret*, *expound*, τὸ λεχθὲν παρ' αὐτῶν ἀ. Pl.*Sph*.246e: abs., ὡς σὺ κατ' Αἴγυπτον ἀ. Id.*Lg*.660c; *translate*, Plu.*Rom*.21.

**ἄφερνος**, ον, *dowerless*, Hsch. s.v. ἄεδνον.

**ἀφερπετόομαι**, Pass., *become a reptile*, prob. in Herm.ap.Stob.1.49.69.

**ἀφερπυλλόομαι**, Pass., *change into* ἕρπυλλος, Thphr.*CP*5.7.2.

**ἀφέρπω**, *to creep off*, *steal away*, S.*Tr*.813, *OC*490: generally, *go away*, *retire*, Id.*Aj*.1161, Theoc.4.29, Herod.6.98; *die*, Pempel.ap.Stob.4.25.52.

**ἀφέρτεροι**· ἥσσονες, Hsch.; but ἀφερτέρους· πολὺ φερτέρους, ταχυτέρους, Id.; cf. ἀφάρτερος.

**ἄφερτος**, ον, *insufferable*, *intolerable*, A.*Ag*.386 (lyr.), al.; κακόν Id.*Eu*.146 (lyr.).

**ἀφέσιμος** ἡμέρα *holiday*, Arist.*Ath*.43.3, Aristid.*Or*.50(26).98:—also of persons, *released from payment*, *PTeb*.224 (ii B.C.).

**Ἀφέσιος**, ὁ, *Releaser*, epith. of Zeus, Arr.ap.*EM*176.32, Paus.1.44.9.

⊛ **ἄφεσις**, εως, ἡ, (ἀφίημι) *letting go*, *release*, περὶ τῆς τῶν πλοίων ἀφέσεως Philipp.ap.D.18.77, cf. Pl.*Plt*.273c; καρπῶν *PAmh*.2.43.9 (ii B.C.); γῆ ἐν ἀφέσει land *in private hands*, opp. βασιλική, *PTeb*.5.37 (ii B.C.), etc. b. of persons, *dismissal*: in ritual, λαοῖς ἄ. Apul.*Met*.11.17; *release*, Plb.1.79.12, *IG*2.314.21, *Ev.Luc*.4.18. 2. c. gen., ἀ. φόνου *quittance from* murder, Pl.*Lg*.869d: so abs., Hermog.*Stat*.8; *discharge from* a bond, D.33.3; ἄ. ἐναντίον μαρτύρων ποιήσασθαι Id.45.41; opp. ἀπόδοσις χρημάτων, Isoc.17.29; *exemption from attendance*, *leave of absence*, Arist.*Ath*.30.6; ἀ. τῆς στρατείας *exemption from* service, Plu.*Ages*.24; *remission* of a debt, ταλάντου *Michel*1340*B*7 (Cnidus, ii B.C.); χρημάτων *IPE*1².32*B*70 (Olbia, iii B.C.); sc. καταδίκης, *Inscr.Magn*.93*c*16. b. *forgiveness*, *Ev.Marc*.3.29; ἁμαρτιῶν *Ev.Matt*.26.28. 3. *relaxation*, *exhaustion*, Hp.*Epid*.3.6. 4. *divorce*, τινὶ πέμπειν Plu.*Pomp*.42. 5. *starting* of horses in a race, ἵππων ἄ. ποιεῖν D.S.4.73: hence, *starting-post* itself, ἰσώσας τἀφέσει (Musgr. for τῇ φύσει) τὰ τέρματα having made the winning-post one with the *starting-post*, i.e. having completed the δίαυλος and come back to the *starting-post*, dub. cj. in S.*El*.686, cf. Paus.5.15.5, 6.20.9: metaph., *the first start*, *beginning* of anything, Man.3.405, etc. 6. *discharge*, *emission*, ὕδατος Arist.*PA*697ᵃ24; βέλους D.S.17.41; τοῦ θοροῦ, τοῦ ᾠοῦ Arist.*GA*756ᵃ12; τοῦ κυήματος Id.*HA*608ᵃ1; *the dropping* of a foal, ib.576ᵃ25. b. *discharge*, *release* of an engine, Ph.*Bel*.58.24. 7. = ἀφεσμός, Arist.*HA*625ᵃ20 (pl.). 8. *release*, ὕδατος *PPetr*.2p.34 (iii B.C.): hence, in concrete sense, *conduit*, *sluice*, ib.3p.88, *PFlor*.388.44 (iii A.D.): pl., ἀφέσεις θαλάσσης *channels*, Lxx 2*Ki*.22.16. 9. Astrol., *reckoning of the vital quadrant*, Ptol.*Tetr*.127, cf. Vett.Val.136.2 (but ἀπὸ Λέοντος τὴν ἄφεσιν ποιούμενοι, simply, *starting from*.., Id.31.8).

**ἀφεσμός**, ὁ, *swarm of bees*, Arist.*HA*629ᵃ9.

⊛ **ἀφεσοφῠλᾰκία**, ἡ, *supervision of sluices* (cf. ἄφεσις 8), *PStrassb*.55.8 (ii A.D.).

**ἀφεσταίη**, 3 sg. opt. pf. of ἀφίστημι.

**ἀφεστήξω**, Att. intr. fut. from ἀφέστηκα, I *shall be absent*, *away from*, τινός Pl.*R*.587b; I *shall desert*, X.*An*.2.4.5.

**ἀφεστήρ**, ῆρος, ὁ, at Cnidus, *president of the* βουλή, *GDI*3505.19, Plu.2.292a.

**ἀφεστής**· ἀγαθός, Hsch.

**ἀφεστίᾱσις**, εως, ἡ, *feasting*, Sch.Pl.*Ti*.17b.

**ἀφέστιος**, ον, *far from hearth and home*, dub. l. in Lxx *Si*.37.11.

⊛ **ἀφέταιρος**, ον, *friendless*, Theopomp.Hist.308; cf. ἀπέταιρος.

**ἀφετ-έον**, *one must dismiss*, τὴν σκέψιν, τὸ νῦν λεχθέν, etc., Pl.*R*.376d, *Phdr*.260a, al. 2. ἀφετέος, έα, έον, *to be let go*, *dismissed*, Id.*Euthphr*.15d, Phld.*Mus*.p.89K. **-εύω**, Astrol., *to be* ἀφέτης I.2, *Cat.Cod.Astr*.8(4).236. **-ήρ**, ῆρος, ὁ, = ἀφετήριον, *starting-point*, Iamb.*Protr*.21.λη'. ⊛**-ήριος**, α, ον, (ἀφίημι) *for letting go*, ἀ. ὄργανα engines *for throwing stones*, etc., J.*BJ*3.5.2, cf. 5.6.3. 2. ἀφετηρία (sc. γραμμή), ἡ, *starting-point of a race*, *CIG*2758iii*D*7 (Aphrodisias), Sch.Ar.*Eq*.1156: hence ἀ. Διόσκουροι, whose statues adorned the race-course, Paus.3.14.7; ἀ. ἕρμα *AP*9.319 (Philox.): metaph., ἀφετήριον πρὸς μάθησιν S.E.*M*.1.41; ἀ. ἡ ῥητορική Phld.*Rh*.1.223S. 3. ἀφετηρία· ἀρχή, ἡγεμονία, Hsch. 4. ἀφετήριον (sc. πλοίων), τό, *outlet of a harbour*, Str.11.2.4. 5. *gate* of a sluice, *PLond*.3.1177.291 (ii A.D.). ⊛ **-ης**, ου, ὁ, (ἀφίημι) *one who lets off a military engine*, Plb.4.56.3. b. *teacher of ballistic*, *IG*2.465.22. c. *starter* in races, *POxy*.152.1 (vii A.D.). 2. Astrol., *prorogator*, heavenly body which determines the vital quadrant, Ptol.*Tetr*.131. II. Pass., *a freed-slave* among the Spartans, Myro2. **-ικός**, ή, όν, *determining the vital quadrant*, τόποι Ptol.*Tetr*.127. **-ις**, ιδος, ἡ, fem. of ἀφέτης I.2, ib.133. **-ος**, ον, (ἀφίημι) *let loose*, *ranging at large*, esp. of sacred flocks that *were free from work*, ἄ. ἀλᾶσθαι γῆς ἐπ' ἐσχάτοις ὅροις A.*Pr*.666; ἀφέτων ὄντων ταύρων ἐν τῷ.. ἱερῷ Pl.*Criti*.119d; νέμονται ὥσπερ ἄφετοι Id.*Prt*.320a, cf. *R*.498c, Isoc.5.127, Call.*Del*.36. II. of persons, *dedicated*, *free from worldly business*, E.*Ion*822, Plu.2.768b; [γένη] ἀπόλυτα καὶ ἄ. Iamb.*Myst*.1.8; ἄ. παντὸς τοῦ δεινοῦ Max.Tyr.3.9. 2. of things, ἄ. ἡμέραι *holidays*, Poll.1.36; νομὴ ἄ. *free* range, of horses, Plu.*Lys*.20; ὁρμαί Ph.2.380, cf. Plu.2.12a; δρόμοι Id.*Cleom*.34; ἐξουσία τοῦ λέγειν Phld.*Herc*.862.10; κακουργίαι Id.*Piet*.21; τὸ ἄ. τῆς κόμης Luc.*Dom*.7; τοῦ λόγου Hermog.*Id*.1.6. Adv. -τως, ὁρμᾶν *freely*, Ph.1.135, cf. Dam.*Pr*.307; ἀπολαύει Phld.*D*.3*Fr*.89. 3. of style, *rambling*, *prolix*, Luc.*Tox*.56. III. Ἀφέται, pr. n., the place *whence* the Argonauts *loosed* their ship, Hdt.7.193.

**ἄφευκτος**, ον, *fixed*, *fast*, of gilding or silvering, Zos.Alch.p.157B.:—hence **ἀφευκτότης**, ητος, ἡ, *incapacity for sublimation*, Olymp.Alch.p.77B., and **ἀφευξία**, ἡ, ibid.

**ἀφεύρεμα**, ατος, τό, *deficiency*, *UPZ*112, *PTeb*.8.23 (iii B.C.), *BGU*1118.14 (ii B.C.); *loss* on resale, *PPetr*.3p.232 (iii B.C.).

**ἀφευρίσκω**, pf. ἀφεύρηκα, *to be deficient*, *PTeb*.8.19 (iii B.C.).

**ἀφεύς**· ἀδύνατος, Hsch.

⊛ **ἀφεύω**, aor. 1 ἄφευσα Semon. (v. infr.), Ar.*Th*.590: pf. part. Pass. ἠφευμένος A.*Fr*.310: aor. part. ἀφευθείς Suid.:—*singe off*, ἀφεύων τὴν.. τρίχα Ar.*Ec*.13: abs., *singe clear of hair*, Id.*Th*.216, al.:—Pass., καλῶς ἠφευμένος ὁ χοῖρος well *singed*, A. l. c. 2. *toast*, *roast*, κρέα Semon.24; φασήλους Ar.*Pax*1144.

⊛ **ἀφέψᾰλος**, ον, *without a spark of fire*, Hsch.

**ἀφεψ-εῖν**· βάπτειν τρίχα, Hsch. **-ημα**, ατος, τό, *decoction*, Dsc.2.107, Lyc.ap.Orib.8.25.2, Ruf.ib.7.26.67, Gal.13.9. ⊛ **-ησις**, εως, ἡ, = ἄφεψις, *PPetr*.3p.315, Sch.Lyc.156.

**ἀφεψιάομαι**, *retire from intercourse*, ἀφεψιασάμην, = ἀφωμίλησα, S.*Fr*.138; v. ἑψία.

**ἄφεψις**, εως, ἡ, *boiled down pitch*, Thphr.*HP*9.2.5.

⊛ **ἀφέψω** (later -άω, part. -ῶντες Olymp.*in Mete*.164.35), Ion. ἀπέψω:—*purify* or *refine by boiling off* the refuse, *boil down*, καρπόν Hdt.2.94; τι εἰς τὸ τρίτον Dsc.5.6; esp. *free of dross*, *refine*, χρυσίον καθαρώτατον ἀπεψήσας Id.4.166; τὸν Δῆμον ἀφεψήσας.. καλὸν ἐξ αἰσχροῦ πεποίηκα Ar.*Eq*.1321, cf. 1336:—Pass., ὕδωρ ἀπεψημένον Hdt.1.188, cf. Hp.*Aër*.8, Dsc.2.107. 2. *boil off*, τοῦ ὕδατος μέρος τι Arist.*Mete*.359ᵃ30:—Pass., ἀφέψεται τὸ ἁλμυρόν Id.*Pr*.933ᵇ15; τοῦ ὀγδόου μόνον ἀφεψηθέντος Plb.34.10.12; cf. ἄπεφθος.

**ἀφέωνται**, v. ἀφίημι.

⊛ **ἀφή**, ἡ, (ἅπτω) *lighting*, *kindling*, περὶ λύχνων ἀφάς about *lamp-lighting* time, Hdt.7.215, cf. *PTeb*.88.12 (ii B.C.), D.H.11.33, D.S.19.31, Ath.12.526c. II. (ἅπτομαι) *touch*, ἐπώνυμον δὲ τῶν Διὸς γέννημ' ἀφῶν (Wieseler for γεννημάτων) τέξεις.. Ἔπαφον A.*Pr*.850. 2. *sense of touch*, Pl.*R*.523e, cf. Arist.*EN*1118ᵇ1, *de An*.424ᵃ12; ἀκριβεστάτην.. τῶν αἰσθήσεων τὴν ἁφήν Id.*HA*494ᵇ16; ἡ ἁφὴ ἐν ταῖς αἰσθήσεσι παρέσπαρται Luc.*Salt*.70. 3. *touch of the harp-strings*, metaph., ἐμμελοῦς ἁφῆς καὶ κρούσεως Plu.*Per*.15; οὐχὶ συμφώνους ἁφάς Damox.2.42. 4. *grip*, in wrestling, etc., ἁφὴν ἐνδιδόναι αὐτοῦ Plu.2.86f: metaph., τοῖς ἀθληταῖς τῆς λέξεως ἰσχυρὰς τὰς ἁ. προσεῖναι δεῖ καὶ ἀφύκτους τὰς λαβάς D.H.*Dem*.18; ἁφὰς ἔχει καὶ τόνους ἰσχυρούς Id.*Lys*.13; ἁ. εἶχεν ἡ συνδιαίτησις ἄφυκτον, of Cleopatra, Plu.*Ant*.27. 5. *sand sprinkled over wrestlers*, *to enable them to get a grip of one another*, Arr.*Epict*.3.15.4; ἀφῇ πηλώσασθαι *IG*4.955 (Epid., ii A.D.). 6. Math., *contact* of surfaces, etc., Arist.*Ph*.227ᵃ17, *Metaph*.1014ᵇ22, al.; *point of contact*, Euc.*Phaen*.p.16M., al.; *of intersection*, Papp.988.9, cf. Alex.Aphr.*in Top*.24.16. 7. in pl., *stripes*, *strokes*, Lxx 2*Ki*.7.14, al. 8. *infection*, esp. of *leprosy*, ib.*Le*.13.6, al.: generally, *plague*, Aq.*Ge*.12.17, Aq., Sm.*Ex*.11.1. III. *junction*, *point of contact* in the body, Arist.*GC*326ᵇ12, 327ᵃ12; *ligament*, *Ep.Eph*.4.16, *Ep.Col*.2.19.

**ἀφηβάω**, *to be past the prime of life*, ἀφηβηκώς Lib.*Decl*.23.59; τὴν ἀκμὴν τῶν παθῶν ἀφηβῶντες Ph.1.516; ἀφηβηκότες κλάδοι Poll.1.236: pf. part. Pass., Id.2.10,18.

**ἀφηγ-έομαι**, Ion. ἀπηγ-, *lead the way from* a point, and so generally, *lead the way*, *go first*, Pl.*Lg*.760d, etc.; οἱ ἀφηγούμενοι *the van*, X.*HG*4.8.37; ἀ. τῆς ἀποικίας, τῆς ἀγέλης, *to be leader of*.., Arist.*Fr*.514, *Mir*.831ᵃ22; πρεσβείας Str.1.3.1; τῆς σχολῆς D.L.4.14; τῆς Ἀκαδημείας Phld.*Acad.Ind*.p.57M.; ζῴων Porph.*Abst*.2.38; οὐκ ἀφηγησαμένῳ δὴ τὸ τέλος ἐγένετο died without ever *taking up his command*, Phld.*Acad.Ind*.p.61M. II. *tell*, *relate*, Hdt.1.24, al., E.*Supp*.186; *assert*, Aret.*CA*2.7:—pf. in pass. sense, ἀπήγηταί μοί τι Hdt.5.62; τὸ ἀπηγημένον *what has been told*, Id.1.207, cf. 9.26. **-ημα**, Ion. ἀπήγ-, ατος, τό, *tale*, *narrative*, Hdt.2.3. II. *guiding*, *leading*, Lxx 4*Ma*.14.6. **-ημᾰτικός**, ή, όν, *narrative*, λόγος Hermog.*Id*.1.

10; σχήματα Aristid.*Rh.*1 p.500 S., cf. D.H.*Rh.*1.8. Adv. -κῶς Hermog.*Id.*1.1, Procl.*in Prm.*p.477 S. -ήμων, ονος, ὁ, = ἀφηγητής, Hsch. (prob. should be ἀφηγεμών). -ησις, εως, Ion. ἀπήγ-, ιος, ἡ, *narration*, ἀξιωτάτη ἀπηγήσιος worth *telling*, Hdt.2.70; οὐκ ἀξίως ἀ. in a way not fit *to be told*, Id.3.125; ἱστορίας D.H.2.7; πραγμάτων J.*BJ*1.11.4, cf. Arr.*An.Prooem.*2, Luc.*Hist.Conscr.*30, Aristid.1.154 J., Hermog.*Id.*1.1, al.; *report*, *SIG*578.54 (Teos, ii B.C.). -ητέον, *one must explain*, Porph.*Chr.*94. -ητήρ, ῆρος, ὁ, *guide*, κελεύθου *AP*14.114 (-ήτορα cod.). -ητής, οῦ, ὁ, = foreg., Hsch. -ητικός, ή, όν, *tending to make*, Vett.Val.15.27. -οῦσα· μεταστρέφουσα, Hsch.

**ἀφηδύνω**, (ἡδύς) *sweeten*, Luc.*Am.*3; τὰς ἀκοάς Ph.1.353:—Pass., τὸ ἦθος Plu.*Dio* 17.

**ἀφηθέω**, *filter off*, Thphr.*Lap.*56.

**ἀφηκές**· εὔηθες, Hsch.

**ἀφήκω**, *arrive at* or *have arrived*, οἷ πάντα δεῖ ἀφήκειν Pl.*R.*530e; ἐς θεούς D.C.52.4; ἐς πρῖσιν ἀ. *is a case* for operation, Hp.*VC*9. II. *depart*, πολὺ ἀπό τινων D.C.41.8.

**ἀφηλῐκιότης**, ητος, ἡ, *childhood, nonage*, Eust.1282.24, *PLond.*1.113(1).18 (vi A.D.). ❋**ἀφήλῐκος**, ον, = sq., *PMasp.*6.2 (vi A.D.).

❋**ἀφῆλιξ**, Ion. ἀπῆλιξ, ῐκος, ὁ, ἡ, *beyond youth, elderly*, ἀνὴρ ἀπηλικέστερος Hdt.3.14, cf. Hp.*Mul.*2.120, Alciphr.1.6; ἀφηλικεστάτην Pherecr.206: acc. to Phryn.*PS* p.1 B., only in Comp. and Sup.; but Posit. in *h.Cer.*140, Cratin.369, Phryn.Com.67 (who used it of *young* persons, cf. ἀφηλικεστέραν· νεωτέραν, Hsch., and so later Aristobul.Jud.ap.Eus.*PE*8.10). II. *minor, infant*, in law, *POxy.*487.5.

**ἀφηλῐώτης**, ου, ὁ, = ἀπηλιώτης (q.v.), *IG*14.1308, Apion ap.J.*Ap.*2.2:—hence Adj. **ἀφηλῐωτικός**, ή, όν, Ptol.*Geog.*1.11, Gem.2.11.

**ἀφηλόω**, (ἧλος) *detach*, in Pass., *Stud.Pal.*22.54.16 (ii A.D.); τοῦ σώματος Porph.*Abst.*1.57:—hence Subst. **ἀφήλωσις**, εως, ἡ, *Gloss.*

**ἄφημαι**, *sit apart*: part. ἀφήμενος Il.15.106.

**ἀφημερεύω**, *to be absent for a day*, μήτ' ἀ. μήτ' ἀποκοιτεῖν Decr.ap.D.18.37, cf. *PHib.*148 (iii B.C.), etc.

**ἀφημερινός**, ή, όν, *daily*, Alex.Aphr.*Pr.*1.83; πυρετός *POxy.*1151.36 (v A.D.). **ἀφήμερος**, ον, *absent for a day*, *PGiss.*2.27 (ii B.C.), *PTeb.*104.28 (i B.C.), etc. **ἀφημιάστους**· ἀγροικίας, Hsch.

**ἀφημίζεσθαι**· ἀθερίζεσθαι, Hsch.

**ἀφήμιστος**, ον, = sq., Vett.Val.104.22.

**ἄφημος**, ον, and **ἀφήμων**, ον, (φήμη) *unknown*, Hsch.: also Adv. ἀφήμως· ἐν κόσμῳ, ἡσυχῇ, Id., cf. *h.Ap.*171 ap.Th.3.104.

**ἀφημοῦντας**· ἀγροίκους, Hsch.; cf. ἀφημιάστους.

**ἄφηνα, ἀφῆναι**, v. ἀφανέω.

**ἀφηνῐ-άζω**, (ἡνία) *refuse to obey the reins*, Ph.1.85, Luc.*DDeor.*25.1; of persons, *turn restive, rebel*, Ph.1.125, al., Str.17.3.25, Hdn.1.4.5: c. gen., *rebel against*, συντάγματος J.*BJ*4.7.1, cf. Luc.*Bis Acc.*20. II. Med. or Pass., ἀφηνιάζετο· ἐχωρίζετο, Hsch. -ᾰσις, εως, ἡ, = sq., Hierocl. *in CA*16 p.456 M. -ασμός, ὁ, *refusal to obey the reins*, Ph.1.311 (pl.): metaph., *rebellion*, ib.171, al. -αστής, οῦ, ὁ, *refusing the reins*, ἵππος ib.114; *rebellious*, ib.337, al.

**ἀφηράαν**· μακράν, Hsch.

**ἀφηρωΐζω**, aor. -ηρώϊξα, (ἥρως) *canonize as a hero*, *IG*12(3).864, al. (Thera).

**ἀφής**· ἀδύνατος, ἄλαλος (ἄλλος cod.), Hsch., cf. ἀφεύς; perh. to be read in Call.*Hec.*1.2.3.

**ἀφήσασθαι**· ἅψασθαι, Hsch.

**ἀφησῠχάζω**, *settle down, be quiet*, Hp.*Ep.*12, Plb.2.64.5, *CPR*232.4 (ii/iii A.D.). II. c. acc., *pass over in silence*, Ph.2.3.

**ἀφητορεία**· μαντεία, Hsch.

**ἀφήτωρ**, ορος, ὁ, (ἀφίημι) *archer*, epith. of Apollo, Il.9.404:—the Sch. gives an alternative expl., *prophet* (from ἀ- copul., and φημί), cf. Orac. in *App.Anth.*6.149.7; cf. ὁμοφήτωρ.

❋**ἄφθα** (A), ἡ, (ἅπτω) *an infantile disease, thrush*, mostly in pl., ἄφθαι Hp.*Aph.*3.24.

**ἄφθα** (B), or **ἄφθα**, ἡ, = νάφθα, Ph.*Bel.*94.9: **ἄφθας**, α, ὁ, Str.*Chr.*16.8.

**ἀφθαρ-σία**, ἡ, *incorruption, immortality*, Epicur.*Ep.*1 p.28 U., Phld.*D.*3.9, al., Lxx *Wi.*2.23, Ph.1.37, al., *Ep.Rom.*2.7, Simp.*in Cael.*298.16, etc. II. *integrity, sincerity*, *Ep.Eph.*6.24. ❋ -τος, ον, *uncorrupted, undecaying*, Ph.*Bel.*67.37. II. *incorruptible*, Epicur.*Ep.*1 p.29 U., al., Phld.*D.*3 *Fr.*88b, al., Diog.Oen.63, al. 2. *eternal*, Arist.*APo.*85$^b$18, *Cael.*270$^a$21; *immortal*, πνεῦμα Lxx *Wi.*12.1; τὸ πᾶν Ocell.1.10, D.S.1.6; ψυχαί D.H.8.62; θεός *Ep.Rom.*1.23; γένος Ph.1.689; οἱ νεκροὶ ἐγερθήσονται ἄ. 1*Ep.Cor.*15.52; of poems, Μοῦσαι *Epigr.Gr.*226.5 (Teos). Adv. -τως, τιμᾶν ib.919.10 (Lycia).

**ἄφθας**, v. ἄφθα (B).

**ἀφθάστως**, Adv., gloss on ἀκιχήτως, Sch.Il.17.75.

**ἀφθάω**, *suffer from* ἄφθαι, Hp.*Nat.Mul.*60, al.

**ἀφθεγγής**, ές, *speechless*, *AB*473.

**ἀφθεγκ-τέω**, *to be speechless*, Poll.5.146. -τί, Adv. of sq., *without speech*, ib.147. -τος, ον, = ἄφθογγος, *voiceless*, μηνυτήρ A.*Eu.*245; στόμα (of a pen) *AP*9.162; ἀστράγαλοι ib.7.427.14 (Antip. Sid.). 2. of places, etc., *where none may speak*, τῷδ' ἐν ἀφθέγκτῳ νάπει S.*OC*156 (lyr.). II. Pass., *unspeakable, unutterable*, B.*Fr.*2.2, Pl.*Sph.*238c. Adv. -τως Iamb.*Myst.*7.4.

**ἄφθησις**, εως, ἡ, = ἄφθα (A), *Hippiatr.*61.

**ἀφθιβόρος**, *one who eats greedily*, Hsch.

**ἀφθῐτό-μητις**, ιος, ὁ, *of immortal counsel*, Orph.*Fr.*66. -μῖσος, ον, *of undying hatred*, Man.4.234.

❋**ἄφθῐτος**, ον, (φθίνω) *not liable to perish, undecaying, imperishable*, freq. in Hom. (mostly in Il.) and Trag.: 1. of things, σκῆπτρον πατρώϊον ἄ. αἰεί Il.2.46; χρυσέη ἴτυς ἄ. 5.724; καλὸν θρόνον ἄ. αἰεί 14.238; Ἡφαίστου δόμος 18.370; ἄ. ἄμπελοι Od.9.133; ἄντρον Pi.*I.*8(7).41; πυρὸς φέγγος A.*Ch.*1037; Γᾶ S.*Ant.*339 (lyr.). 2. of persons, *immortal*, of the gods, *h.Merc.*326; Στύξ Hes.*Th.*389,397; of Tantalus, Pi.*O.*1.63; ἄ. ὑμνοπόλος, of Anacreon, Simon.184; ἀφθίτους θεῖναι βροτούς A.*Eu.*724; γέννας ἀφθίτου λαχόντες S.*Fr.*278. 3. of men's thoughts, etc., Ζεὺς ἄφθιτα μήδεα εἰδώς Il.24.88, Hes.*Th.*545; κλέος ἄ. Il.9.413; ἄ. ὄπις *unceasing* care, Pi.*P.*8.72 (v.l. ἄφθονος); ἄ. γνῶμαι *unchanging, unchangeable*, S.*Fr.*414; ἄφθιτα μηδομένοισι Ar.*Av.*689.—Poet. and later Prose, δόξα Plu.2.723e; prob. in Arist.*Cael.*270$^a$26.

**ἀφθογγία**, ἡ, *speechlessness*, λίθου Callistr.*Stat.*9.

**ἄφθογγος**, ον, *voiceless, speechless*, *h.Cer.*198, Hdt.1.116; φόβῳ ἄ. A.*Pers.*206; ἄ. εἶναι remain *silent*, Id.*Eu.*448; ἄ. ἄγγελος a beacon-fire, Thgn.549; ἀφθόγγῳ φθεγγομένα στόματι, of an epitaph, *Epigr.Gr.*234.4 (Smyrna). 2. ἄφθογγα (sc. γράμματα) *mutes*, Pl.*Phlb.*18c, *Cra.*424c. II. Pass., = ἄφατος, *not to be spoken of*, γάμοι S.*Fr.*618 (dub.).

**ἀφθόν-ητος**, ον, *unenvied*, A.*Ag.*939; *beyond the reach of envy*, αἶνος Pi.*O.*10(11).7. II. Act., *bearing no grudge against*, τινί ib.13.25. Adv. -τως Eust.823.8. 2. *bountiful*, *BGU*984.27 (iv A.D.). -ία, ἡ, *freedom from envy* or *grudging, liberality*, πᾶσαν προθυμίαν καὶ ἀφθονίαν εἴχομεν ἀλλήλους διδάσκειν Pl.*Prt.*327b. II. of things, *plenty, abundance*, Pi.*N.*3.9; τῶν ὠφελούντων Pl.*Ap.*24e, cf. 23c; κακῶν Men.589; ἀφθονίας οὔσης ὀργίζεσθαι *abundance of matter* for.., Lys.12.2; ἀ. ἦν καταπίνειν Telecl.1.10; τοσαύτην ἀ. κατηγοριῶν D.21.102; εἰς ἀ. in *abundance*, X.*An.*7.1.33; opp. ἀφορία, Id.*Smp.*4.55: pl., καρπῶν ἀφθονίῃσι Emp.78. III. = κακία, Hsch. -ος, ον, *without envy*: hence, I. Act., *free from envy*, Pi.*O.*6.7; ἄνδρα τύραννον ἄ. ἔδει εἶναι Hdt.3.80, cf. Pl.*R.*500a. Adv. -νως Id.*Lg.*731a. 2. *ungrudging, bounteous*, of earth, ἄφθονε δαῖμον *h.Hom.*30.16; ἀφθόνῳ μένει, ἀφθόνῳ χερί, A.*Ag.*305, E.*Med.*612; ἀ. λειμῶνες Pl.*Sph.*222a, cf. *Ax.*371c. II. more freq. (esp. in Prose) *not grudged, plentiful*, ἄ. πάντα παρέσται *h.Ap.*536; καρπὸν πολλόν τε καὶ ἄ. Hes.*Op.*118; πλοῦτος Sol.33.5; χρυσὸς ἄ. Hdt.6.132, cf. 7.83; χώρη..ἄ. λίην Id.2.6; ἄ. βίοτος A.*Fr.*196; πόλιν ἀφθονεστάτην χρήμασιν Eup.307; χώρα πολλὴ καὶ ἄ. X.*An.*5.6.25; ἄφθονα καὶ πολλὰ ἔχων εἰπεῖν Aeschin.3.203; λόγοι ἄ. D.21.136; ἐν ἀφθόνοις βιοτεύειν to live in *plenty*, X.*An.*3.2.25; ἐν ἀφθόνοις τραφείς D.18.256; τὸ χαίρειν ἄφθονον εἰπών *IG*12(7).445 (Amorgos). 2. *unenvied, provoking no envy*, ὄλβος A.*Ag.*471 (lyr.). III. irreg. Comp. -έστερος Pi.*O.*2.104, A.*Fr.*72, Pl.*R.*460b: Sup. -έστατος Eup. l. c.; regul. forms -ώτερος, -ώτατος, X.*An.*7.6.28, *Cyr.*5.4.40, etc. IV. Adv., πάντα δ' ἀφθόνως πάρα Sol.38; ἀ. ἔχειν τινός to have *enough* of it, Pl.*Grg.*494c; ἀ. διδόναι Arist.*Pol.*1314$^b$4; πολλά με διδάσκεις ἀ. Philem.154; ξένων καὶ ἐντοπίων ἀ. ζήσας *IG*5(2).491 (Megalop., ii/iii A.D.).

**ἀφθορία**, ἡ, *incorruption*, prob. l. for ἀδιαφθορία in *Ep.Tit.*2.7, cf. Them.*in Ph.*82.22.

**ἄφθορος**, ον, *uncorrupt*, of young persons, Artem.5.95; κούρη *AP*9.229 (Marc. Arg.), cf. Lxx *Es.*2.3, D.S.4.7; παῖς Sor.1.81; of a man, *IG*14.2088. II. *pure, unadulterated*, γάλα *BGU*1107.7 (i B.C.), al.

❋**ἀφθώδης**, ες, *suffering from* ἄφθαι, στόματα Hp.*Epid.*3.3.

**ἀφία**, ἡ, *lesser celandine, Ranunculus Ficaria*, Thphr.*HP*7.7.3.

**ἀφίας**· βωμός, Hsch.

**ἀφιδρόω**, *sweat off, get rid of* a thing *by sweating*, Hp.*Epid.*7.58, Arist.*Pr.*868$^a$37, *Com.Adesp.*3 D.:—Pass., *exude*, ἀπό τινος Dsc.5.1.

❋**ἀφίδρ-ῠμα**, ατος, τό, *thing set up*, esp. *image* of the gods (cf. Suid. s.v.), *IG*2$^2$.1046.13, *Inscr.Prien.*112.115, D.H.2.22, Str.12.5.3, Plu.*Num.*8, etc.; χρυσοῦς μόσχος, τὸ Αἰγυπτίων ἀ. Ph.1.256. 2. *shrine, temple*, Cic.*Att.*13.29.1(2), Str.6.2.5, 16.4.4. II. *copy taken from such image* or *shrine*, D.S.15.49; ἱερὸν Ἀσκληπιοῦ ἀ. τοῦ ἐν Τρίκκῃ Str.8.4.4. -ῠσις, εως, ἡ, *setting up* a statue, Id.8.7.2, Plu.2.1136a. -ῠσμα· ἱερόν, Hsch. ❋ -ύω, *remove to another settlement, transport*, in Med., πατρίδος θεοί μ' ἀφιδρύσαντο γῆς ἐς βάρβαρ' ἤθη E.*Hel.*273:—Pass., *to be transferred*, of a cult, ἀφιδρυθῆναι ἐκ Κρήτης D.S.4.79. II. *make statues* or *temples after a model*, Δήλιον τὸ ἱερὸν Ἀπόλλωνος ἐκ Δήλου -υμένον Str.9.2.7, cf. 12.3.32. III. simply, = ἱδρύω, *set up*, in Pass., Harp. s.v. Πάνδημος, Jul.*Or.*1.29d, *APl.*4.260 (in later form of aor. -ύνθην). [ῠ in pres., ῡ in fut., aor. 1, pf. Pass.]

**ἀφίδρ-ωσις** [φῐ], εως, ἡ, *sweating off*, Arist.*Pr.*867$^a$13 (pl.), Thphr.*Sud.*22 (pl.), Sor.2.46 (pl.). -ωτήριον, τό, *natural vapour-bath*, Herod.Med.ap.Orib.10.40.1 (pl.).

**ἀφιερ-ισμένα**· περικεκαθαρμένα, Hsch. -όω, *hallow, consecrate*, τῷ Κρόνῳ Ath.3.110b, cf. D.S.1.90 (Pass.), Plu.2.271a; πόλιν τῇ Λητῷ καὶ τῷ Ἀπόλλωνι *OGI*746.2 (Xanthus, ii B.C.). II. Pass., ταῦτ' ἀφιερώμεθα I *have had* these *expiatory rites performed*, A.*Eu.*451. -ωσις, εως, ἡ, *hallowing, dedication*, D.S.1.90, Plu.*Publ.*15; χρημάτων *BMus.Inscr.*481*.386 (Ephesus, ii A.D.).

**ἀφιζάνω**, *rise from one's seat*, Suid.:—also **ἀφίζω**, Hsch.

❋**ἀφίημι**, 2 sg. ἀφίης Pl.*Phlb.*50d, etc., 3 sg. ἀφίησι, also ἀφίει, Ion. ἀπίει Hdt.2.96, 1 pl. ἀφίεμεν Ar.*Nu.*1426; imper. ἀφίει Id.*V.*428: impf. ἀφίειν, with double augm. ἠφίειν Pl.*Euthd.*293a; 3 sg. ἀφίει Il.1.25, *IG*2$^2$.777.15, D.6.20, Ion. ἀπίει Hdt.4.157, ἠφίει Th.2.49, Pl.*Ly.*222b, ἤφιε *Ev.Marc.*11.16; 2 pl. ἀφίετε D.23.188; 3 pl. ἀφίεσαν

E.*Heracl.*821, Th.2.76, D.21.79, etc., ἠφίεσαν X.*HG*4.6.11, ἠφίουν Is. 6.40 (dub.): fut. ἀφήσω Il.2.263, etc., Ion. ἀπ– Hdt.7.193: pf. ἀφεῖκα X.*An.*2.3.13, D.56.26: aor. 1 ἀφῆκα, Ion. ἀπ–, Ep. ἀφέηκα, used in ind. only, Il.23.841, etc.: aor. 2 ind. only in dual and pl., ἀφέτην, ἀφεῖμεν, ἀφεῖτε or ἄφετε, ἀφεῖσαν or ἄφεσαν; imper. ἄφες, subj. ἀφῶ, opt. ἀφείην (2 pl. ἀφεῖτε Th.1.139), inf. ἀφεῖναι, part. ἀφείς:—**Med.**, ἀφίεμαι, Ion. ἀπίεμαι, Hdt.3.101, Th.2.60, etc.: impf. 3 sg. ἀφίετο Od.23.240, D.25.47: fut. ἀφήσομαι E.*Hel.*1629: aor. 2 ἀφείμην X.*Hier.*7.11; imper. ἀφοῦ, ἄφεσθε, S.*OT*1521, Ar.*Ec.*509; inf. –έσθαι Isoc.6.83, part. –έμενος Pl.*R.*354b; Arc. inf. ἀφεῶσθαι *SIG*306.19 (Tegea, iv B.C.):—Pass., pf. ἀφεῖμαι S.*Ant.*1165, Pl.*Lg.*635a; inf. ἀφεῖσθαι *SIG*577.77 (Milet., iii/ii B.C.): plpf. 2 sg. ἀφεῖσο Men.*Epit.*572: rarer pf. 3 pl. ἀφέωνται *Ev.Jo.*20.23, imper. ἀφεώσθω *IG*5(2).6.14: aor. ἀφείθην E.*Ph.*1377, ἀφέθην Batr.87, Ion. ἀπείθην Hdt.6.112; later Aeol. inf. ἀφέθην *Milet.*3 No.152.34 (ii B.C.): fut. ἀφεθήσομαι Pl.*R.*472a, etc. [ῐ mostly in Ep. (except in augm. tenses): ῑ always in Att. Hom. also has ἀφῑετε, metri gr., Od.7.126]:—*send forth, discharge*, of missiles, ἔγχος, δίσκον ἀφῆκεν, Il.10.372, 23.432; ἀφῆκ' ἀργῆτα κεραυνόν 8.133; ἀπῆκε βέλος Hdt.9.18, etc.: hence in various senses, ἀ. ἑαυτὸν ἐπί τι *throw oneself* upon, *give oneself up* to it, Pl.*R.*373d; ἀ. αὑτὸν εἰς τὴν πολιτείαν Plu.*Alc.*13; ἀ. γλῶσσαν *let loose* one's tongue, *make* utterance, Hdt.2.15, E.*Hipp.*991; ἀ. φθογγήν ib.418; ἔπος S.*OC*731; φωνάς D.18.218; γόους E.*El.*59 (v. infr. II. 2); ἀρὰς ἀφῆκας παιδί Id.*Hipp.*1324; ἀ. θυμὸν ἔς τινας *give vent to*.. (v. infr. II. 2), S.*Ant.*1088; ὀργὴν εἴς τινα *vent* upon.., D.22.58; ἀ. δάκρυα *shed* tears, Aeschin.3.153; ἀ. παντοδαπὰ χρώματα *change* colour in all ways, Pl.*Ly.*222b; freq. of liquids, etc., *emit*, ἀ. τὸ ὑγρόν, τὸν θολόν, τὸ σπέρμα, etc., Arist.*HA*487$^{a}$18, 524$^{a}$12, 489$^{a}$9; ἀ. τὸ ᾠόν, τὸ κύημα, ib.568$^{b}$30, $^{a}$22; of plants, ἄνθος ἀφιεῖσαι *putting forth*, Od.7.126, cf. Thphr.*HP*7.7.3; of a spider, ἀ. ἀράχνιον Arist.*HA*555$^{b}$5; ἱδρῶτα Plu.*Mar.*26; *put forth, produce*, καρπόν Thphr.*HP*3.4.5; φύλλον ib. 6.5.1 (but ἀ. σπέρμα *leave* issue, *Ev.Marc.*12.22):—Pass., *to be emitted*, Il.4.77 (tm.); of troops, *to be let go, launched* against the enemy, Hdt.6.112. **2.** *let fall* from one's grasp, Il.12.221; opp. κατέχω, Plu.2.508d; πόντιον ἀ. τινά E.*Hec.*797. **3.** *give up* or *hand over to*, τὴν Ἰωνίην τοῖσι βαρβάροισι Hdt.9.106; ἐχθροῖς αἶαν A.*Th.*306; ἀ. τινὰ δημόσια εἶναι Th.2.13:—Pass., ἡ Ἀττικὴ ἀπεῖτο ἤδη Hdt.8.49. **II.** *send away*, **1.** of persons, κακῶς ἀφίει Il.1.25; αὐτὸν δὲ κλαίοντα.. ἀφήσω 2.263. **b.** *let go, loose, set free*, ζωόν τινα ἀ. 20.464; *let loose*, βοῦς Hdt.4.69; περιστεράς Alex.62.3; ἀ. Αἴγιναν αὐτόνομον Th.1.139; ἀ. ἐλεύθερον, ἀζήμιον, Pl.*R.*591a, *Lg.*765c; τινὰς ἀφορολογήτους Plb.18.46.5; ἀφέντ' ἐᾶν τινα S.*Aj.*754, cf. E.*Fr.*463; ἐς οἴκους, ἐκ γῆς, S.*OT*320, E.*IT*739: c. acc. pers. et gen. rei, *release from* a thing, ἀποικίης Hdt.4.157: in legal sense, *acquit of* a charge or engagement, φόνου τινα D.37.59 (abs., ἐὰν αἰδέσηται καὶ ἀφῇ ibid.); συναλλαγμάτων Id.33.12: c. acc. only, *acquit*, Antipho 2.1.2, etc. (v. infr. 2 c):—Pass., κινδύνου ἀφιέμενοι Th.4.106; τοὺς γέροντας τοὺς ἀφειμένους *released* from duty, Arist.*Pol.*1275$^{a}$15; ἐγκλημάτων ἀφεῖσο Men.*Epit.*572. **c.** *let go, dissolve, disband*, of an army or fleet, Hdt.1.77, etc.; *dismiss*, δικαστήρια (opp. λύειν ἐκκλησίαν) Ar.*V.*595. **d.** *put away, divorce*, γυναῖκα Hdt.5.39; ἀ. γάμους *break off* a marriage, E.*Andr.*973; ἀ. τὸν υἱόν *disown* him, Arist.*EN*1163$^{b}$22 (but with metaph. from *releasing* a debtor). **e.** *dedicate*, τὰ νεογνὰ τῷ θεῷ X.*Cyn.*5.14; ἱερὸν .. ἄβατον ἀφεῖτο Pl.*Criti.*116c. **2.** of things, *get rid of*, ἀφέτην πολυκαγκέα δίψαν Il.11.642; ἀφίει μένος [ἔγχεος] *slackened* its force, 13.444; ἀ. ὀργήν *put away* wrath (v. supr. I. 1), A.*Pr.*317; ὀργήν τινι Arr.*An.*1.10.6; γόους (v. supr. I. 1) E.*Or.*1022; νόσημα Hp.*Prorrh.*2.39; ἀ. πνεῦμα, ψυχήν, *give up* the ghost, E.*Hec.*571, *Or.*1171: in Prose, *give up, leave off*, μόχθον Hdt.1.206; ξυμμαχίαν, σπονδάς, Th.5.78, 115, etc.:—Med., ἀ. τὸ προλέγειν D.S.19.1. **b.** ἀ. πλοῖον ἐς.. *loose* ship for a place, Hdt.5.42. **c.** in legal sense (v. supr. I b), c. dat. pers. et acc. rei, ἀ. τινὶ αἰτίην *remit* him a charge, Id.6.30; τὰς ἁμαρτάδας Id.8.140.β', cf. *Ev.Matt.*6.12, al.; τὰς δίκας.. ἀφίεσαν τοῖς ἐπιτρόποις D.21.79; ἀ. τινὶ εἰς ἐλευθερίαν χιλίας δραχμάς Id.59.30, cf. *IG*2$^{2}$.43 *A*27; ἀ. πληγάς τινι *excuse* him a flogging, Ar.*Nu.*1426; ἀ. ὅρκον Jusj. in Lexap.And.1.98; φόρον Plb.21.24.8 (Pass.); δάνειόν τινι *Ev.Matt.*18.27. **III.** *leave alone, pass by*, Hdt.3.95, etc.; *neglect*, τὰ θεῖα S.*OC*1537; τὸν καιρόν D.1.8; λέκτρων εὐνάς A.*Pers.*544: folld. by a predicate, ἀφύλακτον ἀ. τὴν ἑωυτῶν *leave* unguarded, Hdt.8.70; ἄτιμον, ἔρημον ἀ. τινά, S.*OC*1279, *Ant.*887; ἀ. τινὰς ὀρφανούς *Ev.Jo.*14.18; ἀ. τι ἀόριστον Arist.*Pol.*1265$^{a}$39; *leave*, περὶ κινήσεως, ὅθεν ὑπάρχει, τοῖς ἄλλοις ἀφεῖσαν Id.*Metaph.*985$^{b}$20, cf. 987$^{b}$14:—Pass., esp. in pf. imper., ἀφείσθω ἐπὶ τοῦ παρόντος *missum fiat*, Id.*EN*1166$^{a}$34, cf. *Pol.*1286$^{a}$5, 1289$^{b}$12. **2.** c. acc. et inf., ἀ. τὸ πλοῖον φέρεσθαι *let* the boat be carried away, Hdt.1.194; μὴ ἀφεῖναί με ἐπὶ ξένης ἀδιαφορηθῆναι *PLond.*2.144.14 (i A.D.). **IV.** c. acc. pers. et inf., *suffer, permit* one to do a thing, ἀ. τινὰ ἀποπλέειν Hdt.3.25, cf. 6.62, al., etc.: with inf. understood, ἡνίκα προῖκ' ἀφιᾶσιν (sc. θεᾶσθαι) οἱ θεατρῶναι Thphr.*Char.*30.6: c. subj., ἄφες ἐκβάλω *Ev.Matt.*7.4, cf. Arr.*Epict.*1.9.15; ἄφες ἐγὼ θρηνήσω *POxy.*413.184 (i A.D.); ἄφες ἵνα .. Arr.*Epict.*4.13.19; οὐκ ἤφιεν ἵνα.. *Ev.Marc.*11.16:—Pass., ἀφείθη σχολάζειν Arist.*Metaph.*981$^{b}$24. **V.** seemingly intr. (sc. στρατόν, ναῦς, etc.), *break up, march, sail*, etc., Hdt.7.193; ἀ. ἐς τὸ πέλαγος Th.7.19; cf. II. 2 b. **2.** c. inf., *give up* doing, ἀφεὶς σκοπεῖν τὰ δίκαια Diph.94.

**B.** Med., *send forth from oneself*, much like Act.; θορήν Hdt.3.101. **2.** *loose* something *of one's own from*, δειρῆς δ' οὔ πω.. ἀφίετο πήχεε λευκώ she *loosed* not *her* arms *from off* my neck, Od.23.240. **3.** freq. in Att. c. gen. only, τέκνων ἀφοῦ *let go of* the children! S.*OT*1521; τοῦ κοινοῦ τῆς σωτηρίας ἀ. Th.2.60; λόγων Pl.*Grg.*458c, Aeschin.1.178; μὴ ἀφίεσο τοῦ Θεαιτήτου, ἀλλ' ἐρώτα Pl.*Tht.*146b, etc.; ἀφεῖσθαι τοῦ δικαίου τούτου D.37.1; ἀφέμενος τῆς ἰαμβικῆς ἰδέας Arist.*Po.*1449$^{b}$8.

**ἀφῐκάνω** [ᾱ], Ep. = ἀφικνέομαι, only pres. and impf., *arrive at*, mostly c. acc., Od.14.159, al.; πρὸς τεῖχος .. ἀφικάνει Il.6.388: c. gen., A.R.1.177.

**ἀφικλῶντο** (fort. ἀφικμ–, cf. ἱκμάω)· ἀπεσείοντο ἢ ἀποελῶντο (fort. ἀπηλοῶντο), Hsch.

**ἀφικνέομαι**, Ion. ἀπ– Hdt.2.28, al.: impf. ἀφικνεῖτο Th.3.33: fut. ἀφίξομαι Il.18.270, etc., Ion. 2 sg. ἀπίξεαι Hdt.2.29, 3 sg. ἀπίξεται Theoc.29.13: pf. ἀφῖγμαι Od.6.297, Att. 2 sg. ἀφῖξαι A.*Pr.*305, 3 sg. ἀφῖκται S.*OC*794: plpf. ἀφῖκτο ib.1590, Ion. 3 pl. ἀπίκατο Hdt.8.6: aor. ἀφῑκόμην Il.18.395, etc.; inf. ἀφικέσθαι; Dor. imper. ἀφίκευσο Theoc.11.42: aor. 1 part. ἀφιξάμενος *Epigr.Gr.*981.9 (Philae):—*arrive at, come to, reach*: Constr., in Hom., Pi., and Trag. mostly c. acc. loci, Il.13.645, Pi.*P.*5.29, A.*Pers.*15, etc.; ὅνδε δόμονδε Hes.*Sc.*38: in Hom. also c. acc. pers., μνηστῆρας ἀ. *came up to* them, Od.1.332, cf. 11.122, etc.; ὅτε μ' ἄλγος ἀφίκετο *came to* me, Il.18.395; similarly, τοῦτον νῦν ἀφίκεσθε *come up to* this throw! Od.8.202; freq. also with Preps., ἀ. ἐς.. Il.24.431, Od.4.255, etc.; less freq. ἐπί.. Il.10.281, 22.208; still more rarely κατά.., ποτί.., 13.329, Od.6.297; ἀ. πρὸς τέλος γόων S.*OC*1622; ἐπὶ τῶν νήσων X.*HG*5.1.2; ἄχρι τοῦ μὴ πεινῆν ἀ. Id.*Smp.*4.37; θανάτου τοὖτ' ἐγγυτάτω τοὔπος ἀφῖκται S.*Ant.*934; παρά τινος ἀ. Id.*OT*935, etc.: abs., *arrive*, ὁπποίης ἐπὶ νηὸς ἀφίκεο Od.1.171; ὅταν ἀ. ὥρη Thgn.723; σῖτος ἀφικνούμενος D.20.31; ὁ ἀφικνούμενος *the stranger, newcomer*, *IG*1$^{2}$.118.11:—Phrases: **1.** ἀ. ἐπὶ or εἰς πάντα, *to try* every means, S.*OT*265, E.*Hipp.*284; ἀ. ἐς πᾶσαν βάσανον Hdt.8.110; ἐς διάπειράν τινος ἀ. Id.2.28, 77; ἐπὶ τὸ τέμνειν μῦς ἀ. Gal.2.230. **2.** *come into* a certain condition, ἀ. ἐς πᾶν κακοῦ Hdt.7.118; ἐς ἀπορίην πολλήν Id.1.79; ἐς τοσοῦτο τύχης, ἐς τοῦτο δυστυχίας, *come into* such a.., ib.124, Th.7.86; ἐς ὀλίγον ἀ. νικηθῆναι *come* within little of being conquered, Id.4.129; εἰς τὸ ἴσον ἀ. τινί *attain* equality with.., X.*Cyr.*1.4.5; εἰς ὀργήν Men.*Pk.*44; ellipt., ἐς ἄνδρ' ἀφίκου *reachedst* man's estate, E.*Ion*322. **3.** of intercourse with others, ἀ. τινὶ ἐς λόγους *hold* converse with one, Hdt.2.28; ἐς ἔχθεα, ἐς ἔριν ἀ. τινί, Id.3.82, E.*IA*319; διὰ μάχης, δι' ἔχθρας ἀ. τινί, Hdt.1.169, E.*Hipp.*1164; διὰ λόγων ἐμαυτῇ Id.*Med.*872. **b.** less freq. c. dat. pers., ἀ. τινί *come at* his *call*, Pi.*O.*9.67, Hdt.5.24, Th.4.85. **4.** εἰς τόξευμα ἀ. *come* within shot, X.*Cyr.*1.4.23, etc. **5.** of things, ἐς ὀξὺ ἀ. dub. l. for ἀπηγμένα, –μένας in Hdt.2.28, 7.64; ὁ λόγος εἰς ταὐτὸν ἀ. Arist.*EN*1097$^{a}$24, cf. 1167$^{a}$12, al. **II.** the sense of *return* is sts. implied in the context, but is not inherent in the word, as Od.10.420, Pi.*P.*8.54, E.*El.*6, Pl.*Chrm.*153a.

**ἀφικτός** and **ἀφικτρός**, *impure*, Hsch.

**ἀφίκτωρ**, ορος, ὁ, = ἱκέτης, A.*Supp.*241. **2.** Ζεὺς ἀφίκτωρ, = ἱκέσιος, ib.1.

**ἀφίκω**, = ἀφικνέομαι, *extend, reach*, Hp.*Epid.*5.26.

**ἀφῐλ-άγᾰθος** [ᾰγ], ον, *not loving the good*, 2*Ep.Ti.*3.3. **–ανθρωπία**, ἡ, *lack of human feeling*, Arist.*VV*1251$^{b}$3, Phld.*Oec.*p.68 J. **–άνθρωπος**, ον, *not loving men*, Plu.2.1098d, Lib.*Decl.*51.10. **–αργῠρία**, ἡ, *freedom from avarice*, Hp.*Decent.*5, Onos.1.8, D.S.9.12. **–άργῠρος**, ον, *not loving money*, *Inscr.Prien.*137.5 (ii B.C.), D.S.9.11, 1*Ep.Ti.*3.3, *Ep.Hebr.*13.5, Sor.1.4, *POxy.*33 ii 11 (ii A.D.). Adv. –ρως *IG*2$^{2}$.1343.25 (i B.C.), *SIG*708.17 (Istropolis, ii B.C.).

**ἀφῐλᾰρ-όω**, *brighten, cheer*, Phld.*Mus.*p.84 K. **–ύνω**, = foreg., in Pass., *have a cheerful expression*, *Stoic.*3.43.

**ἀφῑλάσκομαι**, *appease*, θυμόν Pl.*Lg.*873a; ἀφειλαξόμενον (sc. the gods) Polystr.p.9 W.

**ἀφίλ-αυτος** [ῐ], ον, *not showing self-love*, Plu.2.542b. **–έχθρως**, Adv. *with no disposition towards enmity*, Sch.Od.8.77. **–ήδονος**, ον, *not liking sensuality*, Ph.2.458, M.Ant.5.5.

**ἀφίλης**· καθαρός, ὑγιής, ὁλόκληρος, Hsch.

**ἀφίλ-ητος** [ῐ], ον, *unloved*, S.*OC*1702 (lyr.), Phld.*D.*1.1. **–ία**, ἡ, *want of friends*, Arist.*EN*1115$^{a}$11, *Rh.*1386$^{a}$9, Phld.*Oec.*p.67 J., Plu.*Sol.*7. **–ίωτος**, ον, *not to be made a friend of* or *reconciled*, Hsch. s.v. ἀσύμβατον.

**ἀφῐλο-δοξέω**, *to be free from ambition*, prob. in Phld.*Vit.*p.7 J. **–δοξος**, ον, *free from conceit* or *ambition*, Id.*Rh.*2.273 S., *Lib.*p.42 O.; τὸ ἀ. Cic.*Att.*2.17.2, Ph.2.458.

**ἀφῐλοικτίρμων**, ον, gen. ονος, *unmerciful*, Hsch.

**ἀφῐλο-κάλητος** [κᾰ], ον, *without adornment*, δόμος Procl. ad Hes.*Op.*746, cf. Eust.669.41. **–κᾰλία**, ἡ, *character of the* ἀφιλόκαλος, Ath.1.3a (cf. Eup.366). **–κᾰ⟨λοκᾱ⟩γᾰθία**, ἡ, *dishonesty*, *POxy.*33 ii 13 (ii A.D.). **–κᾰλος**, ον, *without love for beauty* or *honour*, Plu.2.672e, Gal.5.39. **–λογος**, ον, *without love for learning literature*, Plu.2.673a. **–νείκητος**, ον, = sq., Hdn.*Epim.*177. **–νεικος**, ον, *not fond of strife*, Arist.*VV*1250$^{a}$43, 1251$^{a}$15, Andronic.Rhod.p.575 M., Ph.2.5; ἡγεμονία ib.555. Adv. –κως, παραχωρεῖν τινός τινι Plb.21.20.1, cf. Ph.1.324, al., Luc.*Symp.*37. **–ξενος**, ον, *inhospitable*, Eust.1733.20. **–πλουτία**, ἡ, *contempt for wealth*, Plu.*Comp.Lys.Sull.*3. **–πονος**, ον, *disliking work*, Plb.12.27.4 (Comp.). **–πρωτία**, ἡ, *want of ambition*, Men.Prot.p.90 D.

**ἄφῐλος**, ον, of persons, *friendless*, A.*Ch.*295, S.*El.*819, Pl.*Lg.*730c, *R.*580a; ἄ. ἔρημον ἄπολιν S.*Ph.*1018; ἄκλαυτος ἄ. Id.*Ant.*876 (lyr.): c. gen., ἄ. φίλων E.*Hel.*524 (lyr.); τὸ ἄ. Ph.2.662. **II.** of persons and things, *unfriendly, hateful*, A.*Th.*522, S.*OC*186; ἄφιλα παρ' ἀφίλοις ἔπεσε..'Ατρείδαις Id.*Aj.*620; λίαν ἄφιλον φαίνεται Arist. *EN*1101ᵃ23; *unsociable*, γῆρας S.*OC*1237: perh., c. gen., *hostile to*, ἀσφαλείας Phld.*Lib.*p.36 O.; τὸ λαθραιοπραγεῖν -ώτατον ib.p.20 O., cf. Carneisc.*Herc.*1027.16. Adv. -λως *in unfriendly manner*, A.*Ag.* 805.

**ἀφῐλο-σόφητος**, ον, *not versed in philosophy*, ὄχλος D.H.2.20, Phld.*Herc.*1005.11. II. *without philosophical significance*, Arg. Sch.Od.1. **-σοφία**, ἡ, *contempt for philosophy*, Pl.*Def.*415e. **-σοφος**, ον, of persons, *without taste for philosophy*, Id.*Sph.*259e, Ph. *Fr.*35 H.; γένος Pl.*Ti.*73a; συγγραφεύς *unphilosophical*, Plb.12.25.6. 2. of conditions, *unphilosophic*, δίαιτα Pl.*Phdr.*256c; ἀ. τήρησις S.E.*M.*11.165. **-στάχυος** [τᾰ], ον, *without ears of corn, starving*, πενία *AP*6.40.8 (Maced.). **-στοργία**, ἡ, *absence of natural affection*, implied in punning phrase of Timagenes, ἡ πρὸς τὰ ἔκγονα φιλοστοργία (ἔκγον' ἀ.) Plu.2.634f. **-στοργος**, ον, *without natural affection*, ib.140d. **-τῑμία**, ἡ, *want of due ambition*, Arist.*EN* 1125ᵇ22. **-τῑμος**, ον, *lacking in ambition*, Is.7.35, Lycurg.69, Arist.*EN*1107ᵇ29: Sup., Plb.6.48.8; βίος ἀ. εἰς δόξαν *Inscr.Prien.* 112.11, cf. Eun.*VS*p.491 B. Adv. -μως Plb.12.23.8; πρὸς πολίτας ζῆν Plu.2.525d; but also, *without fear* or *favour, impartial*, *IG*(2). 517.34 (Epist. Philipp.). 2. simply, *indifferent*, πρὸς κάλλος J. *AJ*2.9.6. Adv. -μως *lukewarmly*, *PPetr.*2p.5. II. of things, *not honourable, paltry*, ἡ ἀπὸ μικρῶν δόξα ἀ. Plu.2.35a. **-χρημᾰτία**, ἡ, *contempt for riches*, Plu.*Comp.Ag.Gracch.*1, Socr.*Ep.*5.2:—hence Adj. **-ᾰτος**, ον, Ph.2.458, Eun.*Hist.*p.243 D. **-ψῡχος**, ον, *not cowardly*, prob. in Plu.2.761c.

**ἀφῑμᾰτόω**, (ἱμάτιον) *strip of clothing*, Suid.

**ἀφίμωσις**, εως, ἡ, an operation connected with the manufacture of vegetable oils, *PPetr.*3p.315.

**ἄφιξις**, εως, Ion. **ἄπιξις**, ιος, ἡ: (ἀφικνέομαι):—*arrival*, Hdt.1.69, al.; τὴν ἀπὸ Κορίνθου ἄ. *arrival* from C., Id.5.92.ζ'; ἐς Θήβας Id.9.17; ἄ. ἐπὶ Σαρπηδονίης ἄκρης ποιεῖσθαι Id.7.58; μέρος αὐτῆς ἀπίξιος παρὰ τὸν μάγον her turn *for going in* to him, Id.3.69, cf. Pl.*Ep.*337e, Aristeas 173, J.*Ap.*1.18, etc.; ἄ. εἰς τοὺς πολεμίους ποιησάμενος D.5.8; ἄ. εἰς Κύπρον Isoc.9.53; ἡ ἐνθάδε ἄ. Hdt.2.145, Lys.2.26; ἡ οἴκαδε ἄ. *home again*, D.*Ep.*1.2, 3.39. 2. *departure*, J.*AJ*2.2.4, *Act.Ap.*20.29. II. = ἱκεσία, A.*Supp.*483.

**ἀφιππ-άζομαι**, aor. -ασάμην Hld.7.29, etc.:—*ride off* or *away*, Plb. 29.6.18, Str.7.2.1, J.*AJ*14.13.5, Plu.*Aem.*19, Luc.*Tox.*50. ❀**-εύω**, *ride off, away*, or *back*, X.*An.*1.5.12, D.S.2.19, Plu.*Arat.*40:—also Med., Hld.4.18. **-ία**, ἡ, *awkwardness in riding*, X.*Eq.Mag.*8.13.

**ἀφιππο-δρομά**, ἡ, *contest of riders who dismounted while racing*, *IG* 9(2).527 (Larissa). **-λαμπάς**, άδος, ἡ, *torch-race on horseback*, ib. 531 (ibid.).

**ἄφιππος**, ον, *unsuited for cavalry*, Καρία X.*HG*3.4.12, cf. Plu.*Ant.* 47. II. of persons, *unused to riding*, opp. ἱππικός, Aeschin.Socr. *Oxy.*1608 *Fr.*1.15; *ignorant of horsemanship*, Pl.*Prt.*350a, *R.*335c, Luc.*Nav.*30. 2. *without cavalry*, Polyaen.4.6.6.

❀ **ἀφιπποτοξότης**, v. ἀμφιππ-.

**ἀφίπτᾰμαι**, = ἀποπέτομαι, *fly away*, E.*IA*1608, Luc.*Somn.*16, Lib. *Decl.*51.15, Aët.7.103.

**ἀφιστάνω**, later form of ἀφίστημι, *CPR*5.14 (ii A.D.), Dsc.3.87, Luc.*Sol.*7:—Pass., ἀφιστάνομαι *renounce*, τινί τινος *PRyl.*117.22 (iii A.D.):—also **ἀφιστάω**, Ath.1.9b, Lib.*Decl.*51.14; opt. ἀφιστῴην dub. in X.*Smp.*2.20 (v. sq. A. II), cf. Luc.*Sol.*7.

❀ **ἀφίστημι**: A. causal in pres. and impf., in fut. ἀποστήσω, and aor. 1 ἀπέστησα, as also in aor. 1 Med. (v. infr.):—*put away, remove, keep out of the way*, τὸ ἀσθενέστατον τοῦ στρατεύματος X.*HG*7.5.23; ἄχος A.*Ch.*416 (lyr.); of diseases, Dsc.2.96, Gal.13.846; τὰ συγκείμενα ἀ. ἀπ' ἀλλήλων Pl.*Plt.*282b; ἀ. τῆς ἐλάας τὸν φλοιόν Thphr.*CP*3.3.2; ἀ. τινὰ λόγου *hinder from..*, E.*IT*912; ἀ. τὰς τῶν πολεμίων ἐπιβουλάς *frustrate* them, Th.1.93; ἀ. τὸν ἄρχοντα *depose* him, X.*HG*7.1.45:—aor. Med., 'Αργείων δόρυ πυλῶν ἀπεστήσασθε *removed* it *from your own* gates, E.*Ph.*1087:—in Hdt.9.23 ἀποστήσαντες, = ἀποστάντες, *having retired*. 2. *cause to revolt*, of allies, Id.8.19, Ar.*Eq.*238, Th.1.81; τινὰ ἀπό τινος Hdt.1.76,154, etc.; τινά τινος And.3.22. 3. in geom. constructions, *cut off*, Procl.*Hyp.* 6.7. II. *weigh out*, X.*Smp.*2.20; ἀποστησάτωσαν τὰ χρυσία *IG*7. 303.19 (Oropus); *pay*, δραχμὰς ηʹ ἀργυρίου *UPZ*93.2 (ii B.C.): also in aor. 1 Med., μή..ἀποστήσωνται 'Αχαιοὶ χρεῖος lest they *weigh out* (i.e. *pay in full*) the debt, Il.13.745, cf. *IG*1².91.20, al.:—in strict sense of Med., ἀποστήσασθαι τὸν χαλκόν *to have* the brass *weighed out to one*, D.49.52.—Hom. has it trans. only in l.c. III. Med., *give a final decision* (or *break up, dismiss* the assembly), ῥήτρα ap.Plu. *Lyc.*6.

B. intr., in Pass., as also in aor. 2 ἀπέστην, imper. ἀπόστηθι Ar. *Th.*627, ἀπόστα Men.375: pf. ἀφέστηκα in pres. sense, sync. in pl. ἀφέστᾰμεν, -στᾰτε, -στᾶσι, as in inf. ἀφεστάναι, part. ἀφεστώς, -ῶσα, -ός or -ώς: plpf. ἀφεστήκειν, Att. -κη Pl.*Tht.*208e: fut. Med. ἀποστήσομαι E.*Hec.*1054, Th.5.64, etc. (while aor. 1 Med. is causal (v. supr.)): for fut. ἀφεστήξω v. h. v.:—*stand away* or *aloof from, keep far from*, ὅσσον δὲ τροχοῦ ἵππος ἀφίσταται Il.23.517; οὐ μέν κ' ἄλλη γ' ὧδε γυνὴ.. ἀνδρὸς ἀφεσταίη Od.23.101; ἀποστᾶσ' ἐκποδών E.*Hel.*1023; ἐς ἄλλο σχῆμ' ἀ. βίου Id.*Med.*1039; ἀποσταθῶμεν πράγματος τελουμένου A.*Ch.*872; ὡς γραφεὺς (or βραβεὺς) ἀποσταθείς E.*Hec.*807; μακρὰν τόποις καὶ χρόνοις ἀ. D.S.13.22: hence in various relations, ἀφεστάναι φρενῶν *lose* one's wits, S.*Ph.*865; φύσεος Ar.*V.*1457 (lyr.); οὐδενὸς ἀποστήσονται ὅσα ἂν δίκαια λέγητε *depart from, object to* right proposals, Th.4.118; ἀ. φόνου E.*Or.*1544; ἀ. ἀρχῆς *to be deposed from* office, Pl.*Lg.*928d; simply, *resign*, *SIG*527.105 (Crete, iii B.C.); ἀ. τῶν πραγμάτων, τῆς πολιτείας, etc., *withdraw from* business, politics, *have done with* it, D.10.1, 18.308, etc.; ἔργων ἢ πόνων ἢ κινδύνων *shun* them, Isoc.4.83, cf. X.*HG*7.5.19, etc.; ὧν εἷλεν ἀποστάς *giving up all claim to* what he had won (at law), D.21.181; τῶν αὐτῆς Id.19.147, cf. 35.4; ἀφίστασθαι τῶν τοῦ ἀδελφοῦ ib.44; οὐδενὸς τῶν ἀνηκόντων τῇ πόλει *Inscr.Magn.*53.65; τὴν πολιτείαν.. τὴν ἀφεστηκυῖαν τοῦ μέσου πλεῖον further *removed from..*, Arist.*Pol.* 1296ᵇ8; ἀποστὰς τῶν πατρῴων Luc.*DMort.*12.3; ἀ. ἐκ Σικελίας *withdraw* from the island, *give up* the expedition, Th.7.28; *retire*, ἐς 'Ιθώμην Id.1.101: rarely c. acc., *avoid, shrink from*, τὸν ἥλιον X.*Cyn.* 3.3; τὸν πόλεμον Id.*An.*2.5.7; τινάς E.*Fr.*1006; πυγμήν Philostr. *Gym.*20 (prob. cj.). 2. in Prose, ἀ. ἀπό τινος *revolt* from.., Hdt. 1.95,130, etc.; τινός Id.2.113; οὐκ ἀποστήσομαι ἀπὸ τοῦ δήμου 'Αθηναίων *IG*1².39.21; but 'Αθηναίων τοῦ πλήθους ib.10.22; also ἀ. εἰς or πρός τινας, Hdt.2.30,162, cf. X.*An.*1.6.7; ἐς δημοκρατίαν ἀ. Th.8.90: abs., *revolt*, Hdt.1.102, etc.; ὑπό τινος at his instigation, Th.8.35 (ἀπό codd.). 3. ἀ. τινί *make way for* another, *give way to* him, E. *Hec.*1054, D.8.37. 4. c. gen., *shrink from*, τῶν κινδύνων Isoc.9.29: also c. inf., *shrink from* doing, ἀπέστην τοῦτ' ἐρωτῆσαι σαφῶς E. *Hel.*536. 5. abs., *stand aloof, recoil* from fear, horror, etc., τίπτε καταπτώσσοντες ἀφέστατε; Il.4.340; πολλὸν ἀφεσταότες 17.375; παλίνορσος ἀπέστη 3.33, Pi.*O.*1.52, *P.*4.145; ἐγὼ οὐδέν τι μᾶλλον ἀ. Pl.*Tht.*169b, cf. D.19.45, etc.; *desist*, μὴ νῦν -ώμεθα Pl.*Lg.*960e; δοῦλος ἀφεστὼς *a runaway*, Lys.23.7. 6. Medic., ἀφίσταται, = ἀπόστασις γίγνεται, εἰς ἄρθρα Hp.*Aph.*4.74; ἀ. ὀστέον *exfoliates*, ib. 6.45; also ἀ. ἀπὸ τῶν ὀστῶν Pl.*Ti.*84a; τὸ δέρμα ἀ. X.*Eq.*1.5; also, *project, stand out*, ὦτα ἀφεστηκότα *PLond.*3.1209.12 (i B.C.). b. *to be separated* by the formation of an abscess, Gal.11.116, al. (also in Act., τὸ πύον ἀφίστησι 7.715).

**ἀφιστορέω**, *observe from* a place, τινὰ ἀπὸ τοῦ ὄρους Philostr.*Im.*2. 18; *explore, visit for information*, Id.*VA*1.27.

**ἀφλάσαι**· ἀπολέσαι, Hsch.

❀ **ἄφλαστον**, τό, *curved poop of a ship* with its ornaments, Il.15.717, Asclep.Tragil.31 J., Sch.A.R.1.1089: in pl., of a single ship, Hdt. 6.114.

**ἄφλεβος**, ον, (φλέψ) *without veins*, Thphr.*HP*1.5.3; *without visible veins*, Gal.18(1).598:—Eust.54.16 has **ἀφλεβής**, ές.

**ἀφλεγ-ής**, ές, *not burnt* or *burning*, Nonn.*D.*40.475, 45.100. ❀**-μαντος**, ον, *free from inflammation*, Hp.*Acut.*46, *Fract.*31; *not liable to it*, Arist.*Pr.*863ᵃ15; ἐπίδεσις -οτάτη *least inflammatory*, Gal. 10.451. Adv. -τως *without causing inflammation*, Aët.15.14. 2. *relieving* or *checking inflammation*, παντὸς τραύματος Thphr.*Od.*35, cf. Heliod.ap.Orib.46.8.1, Dsc.1.73. 3. of food, *not heating*, τράπεζαι Ion Lyr. in *PLG*2.257. II. *without phlegm*, πύον Hp.*Coac.* 396.

**ἄφλεκτος**, ον, (φλέγω) *unburnt, unconsumed by fire*, πέλανοι E. *Hel.*1334; πεῦκαι *Epigr.Gr.*241 a1 (Smyrna); *uncooked by fire*, ἄφλεκτα ἔδοντες A.R.1.1074.

**ἀφλετῆρες**· μαστοί, θηλαί, Hsch.; cf. ἀφατῆλες.

**ἀφλόγ-ιστος**, ον, *not inflammable*, Arist.*Mete.*387ᵇ18. **-ος**, ον, (φλόξ) *without flame* or *fire*, Lyc.36.

**ἄφλοιος**, ον, *without integument* or *bark*, Thphr.*HP*7.9.4, *Carm. Pop.*33, Epigr.ap.Plu.*Flam.*9, Ath.Med.ap.Orib.1.11.1.

**ἄφλοισβος**, ον, *without rushing noise*, Nonn.*D.*1.89, al.

**ἀφλοισμός**, ὁ, *foaming at the mouth*, ἀφλοισμὸς δὲ περὶ στόμα γίγνετο, of an angry man, Il.15.607, cf. Euph.51.4. (Cf. πεφλοιδέναι, ἔφλιδεν, Hsch.)

**ἀφλοῦς**· ἀφλοῖο, Hsch. (fort. ἄφλους· ἄφλοιος).

**ἀφλύᾱρος** [ῠ], ον, *not chattering idly*, M.Ant.5.5.

**ἀφλυκταίνωτος**, ον, *free from blisters*, Dsc.5.156.

❀ **ἀφνειός**, όν, also ἡ, όν Hes.*Fr.*134.2, Pi.*O.*7.1, A.R.1.57, etc.: (ἄφενος):—*rich, wealthy*, Il.2.825, etc.; *in* a thing, c. gen., ἀφνειὸς βιότοιο 5.544; χρυσοῖό τε ἐσθῆτός τε Od.1.165 (Comp.): c. acc., φρένας ἀφνειός Hes.*Op.*455: c. dat., ἀ. ἀρούραις, μήλοις, Theoc.24.108, 25. 119; *abundant*, ἄγρη Opp.*H.*3.648; δάκρυα Nonn.*D.*2.156; 'Α., title of Ares in Arcadia, Paus.8.44.7: irreg. Sup. -έστατος Antim. 73: regul. Comp. and Sup., Od. l.c., Il.20.220:—also **ἀφνεός**, ά, όν, Thgn.188,559, and generally in Lyr. and Trag., Pi.*O.*1.10, al., B.1.62, al., A.*Pers.*3 (anap.), *Fr.*96, S.*El.*457 (Comp.). [ᾰφν in Hom.; ᾰφν A.; ἀφνεώτερος in S. l.c.: Thgn. has ᾰ in ll. cc.]

**ἀφνήμων**, ον, gen. ονος, = ἀφνεός, Antim.67.

**ἀφνιδία**· ἀφνίδαν, ἄφνω, and **ἀφνός**· ἐξαίφνης, Hsch.

**ἄφνος**, εος, τό, = ἄφενος, Pi.*Fr.*219.

❀ **ἀφνύει**· ἀφνύνει, ὀλβίζει, Hsch.

**ἄφνω**, Adv. *unawares, of a sudden*, A.*Fr.*195, E.*Med.*1205, *Alc.* 420, Eup.268, etc.: in Prose, Th.4.104, 7.37, D.21.41, *Act.Ap.*2.2, etc.:—also **ἄφνως**, *Epigr.Gr.*468.

**ἀφοβ-έω**, *to be fearless*, Sch.Opp.*H.*3.355. **-ητος**, ον, *without fear of*, Δίκας S.*OT*885 (lyr.): abs., *fearless*, *AP*9.59 (Antip.). **-ία**, ἡ, *fearlessness*, Pl.*Lg.*649a sq., Arist.*EN*1107ᵇ1, Plu.*Cleom.*9, Onos. 13.3.

**ἀφοβοποιός**, όν, *removing fear, calming*, Sch.A.*Pr.*849.

❀ **ἄφοβος**, ον, *without fear*, and so: 1. *fearless, intrepid*, Pi.*I.*5(4). 40, S.*OC*1325, etc.; πρὸς ἐρημίαν, περὶ τοῦ μέλλοντος, Plu.*Lyc.*16, *Galb.*23: c. gen., *having no fear of*, τῶν ἀρχόντων D.Chr.2.52; τὸ ἄφοβον, = ἀφοβία, Pl.*La.*197b. Adv. -βως X.*Hier.*7.10, Pl.*Lg.* 682c, *PTeb.*24.74 (ii B.C.). 2. *causing no fear, free from fear*, A.

*Pr.*902; λόγος οὐκ ἄ. εἰπεῖν Pl.*Lg.*797a. **3.** ἄ. θῆρες, in S.*Aj.*366, is an oxymoron, beasts *which fear not men* or *which no one fears, tame* beasts, *cattle.*

**ἀφοβόσπλαγχνος,** ον, *fearless of heart,* Ar.*Ra.*496.

**ἀφόδ-ευμα,** ατος, τό, *excrement,* Dsc.*Eup.*1.89, *Gp.*12.11, Aesop. 400: in pl., Sch.Ar.*Pl.*1185 (also **-ήματα** ib.1184). **II.** ἀ. κροκοδείλου, = Αἰθιοπικόν, *ajowan, PMag.Leid.V.*12.30, *W.*6.27. **-ευσις,** εως, ἡ, *voiding of excrement,* Erot. s. v. ἀπόπατοι (pl.). **-ευτήριον,** τό, *night-stool,* Sch.Ar.*Pl.*1184. **-ευτικὸς** δίφρος *night-stool,* Gal. 19.104. **-εύω,** *go to stool, discharge excrement,* Hp.*Fist.*9, Pl.Com. 5, Arist.*HA*$627^{a}10$, al.

**ἀφόδιοι·** ἐχθροί, Hsch.; cf. ἀφάδιος.

**ἄφοδος,** Ion. **ἄποδος,** ἡ (ὁ, v. infr. II), *going away, departure,* Hdt. 5.19, 9.55, X.*An.*6.4.13, etc.; *departure out of life, death,* Hierocl. p.58 A., Plot.4.3.25. **2.** *going* or *coming back, return,* Hdt.4.97; *retreat,* X.*HG*6.5.20, *An.*5.2.21; ἄ. λείπειν τινί ib.4.2.11. **II.** *privy,* Hp.*Fract.*16, Ar.*Ec.*1059, Antiph.40.5. **2.** *excrement,* Hp. *Acut.*30, al., Arist.*Mir.*$830^{a}22$ (masc.), Dsc.2.80, Artem.2.26. **3.** in pl., *seminal ducts,* Aret.*CD*2.5.

**ἀφοίβαντος,** ον, *uncleansed, unclean,* A.*Eu.*237, *Fr.*148.

**ἀφοιδεῖν·** μὴ φροντίζειν, Hsch. (leg. ἀφειδεῖν).

**ἀφοίνικτος,** ον, *unreddened,* Ach.Tat.3.7.

**ἀφοίνους·** ἀφόνους, ὑγιεῖς, Hsch.

**ἀφοίτητος,** ον, *untrodden, inaccessible,* Opp.*H.*2.527.

⊛ **ἀφολίδωτος** [ῐ], ον, *not sheathed in scales,* Porph.*Abst.*4.14.

**ἀφ-ολκή,** ἡ, *evacuation, depletion,* Archig.ap.Orib.8.1.38. **-ολκος,** ον, (ὁλκή) *not having weight,* δραχμῇ ἀφολκότερον *too light* by a drachm, Str.15.3.22.

**ἀφομῑλέω,** *avoid, escape, a comitatu* Cic.*Fam.*16.17.2; cf. Hsch. s. v. ἀφεψιασάμην.

**ἀφόμοι-ος,** ον, *unlike,* Dsc.5.102:—but, **2.** *likened, made like,* in Subst. **ἀφόμοιον,** τό, *copy,* Lxx *Si.Prol.*21. **-όω,** *make like,* τινί τι X.*Eq.*9.9; τοῖς γράμμασι τὰ ἔργα Pl.*Cra.*427c; μαινομένοις .. ἀ. αὐτούς Id.*R.*396a; [τῶν θεῶν] τὰ εἴδη ἑαυτοῖς ἀ. οἱ ἄνθρωποι Arist. *Pol.*$1252^{b}27$:—also in Med. or Pass., *become* or *be made like,* τινί Pl. *R.*396b, al.; πρός τι Id.*Sph.*240a, etc. **II.** *compare,* τινί τι Id. *R.*517b, 564b. **III.** c. acc. rei, *portray,* of painters, X.*Mem.*3. 10.2: abs., *make a copy,* Pl.*Cra.*424d. **-ωμα,** ατος, τό, *resemblance, copy,* Id.*R.*395b. **-ωμᾰτικός,** ή, όν, *assimilative,* θεοί Procl.*Theol.Plat.*6.3, cf. Lyd.*Mens.*1.15. Adv. -κῶς Procl.*in Alc.* p.52 C. ⊛ **-ωσις,** εως, ἡ, *making like, comparison,* τὰς ἀ. ποιεῖσθαι Plu.2.988d, Iamb.*Myst.*1.11; *representation of..,* ἐπ' ἀφομοιώσει τῶν ἐμφάσεων Phld.*Po.*2.24. **-ωτέον,** *one must compare,* Thphr.*HP*1. 1.5. **-ωτικός,** ή, όν, *assimilative,* δύναμις Procl.*in Prm.*p.565 S.; διακόσμησις, θεοί, Dam.*Pr.*338, 340, Iamb.*Myst.*5.11.

**ἀφοπλ-ίζω,** *disarm,* τινά D.S.11.35, *APl.*4.171 (Leon.), Luc. *DDeor.*19.1:—Pass., D.S.14.64:—Med., ἀφοπλίζεσθαι ἔντεα *put off one's* armour, Il.23.26:—Pass. (in Lacon. form ἀφοπλίττονται), *to be discharged from service,* Hsch. ⊛ **-ισμός,** ὁ, *disarming, Cod.Just.* 12.40.12. **-ιστής,** οῦ, ὁ, *one who disarms,* Just.*Nov.*8.12.

⊛ **ἀφορ-άω,** Ion. **-έω,** fut. ἀπόψομαι: aor. ἀπεῖδον:—*look away from* all others at one, *have in view,* Hdt.8.37; *look at,* τι Lycurg.17; of a distant object, D.*Ep.*2.20; πρός τι Th.7.71; τι πρός τι *compare,* Pl. *R.*585a; ἀ. ὅθεν .. *look to the point* whence .., ib.584d; εἴς τι or τινα, Plu.*Lyc.*7, Luc.*Philops.*30; εἰς τὸν θεόν Arr.*Epict.*2.19.29; εἰς τὸν Ἰησοῦν *Ep.Hebr.*12.2: hence, *obey,* Nic.Dam.p.22 D.; ἐπί τινα Plu.*Cat. Mi.*52; πρός τινα Id.*Cat.Ma.*19, Arr.*Epict.*3.24.16:—in Med., Ar.*Nu.* 281. **b.** of Places, *look towards,* εἰς βόρειον ὠκεανόν App.*Praef.*3, cf. Philostr.*Im.Prooem.* **2.** *to view from a place,* ἀπὸ δενδρέου Hdt.4.22; πόρρωθεν ἀπιδών Timocl.21.6. **II.** rarely, *look away, have the back turned,* prob. in Thphr.*HP*4.16.6; ἀφορῶντας παίειν X.*Cyr.*7.1. 36. **-ᾱσις,** εως, ἡ, *looking away,* ἡ εἰς τὸ πλῆθος ἀ. Procl.*in Alc.* p.251 C.

**ἀφόρδιον,** τό, *excrement,* γαστρός Nic.*Th.*692, *Al.*140.

**ἀφορέω,** (ἄφορος) *to be barren,* Xenag.ap.Macrob.*Sat.*5.19.30, f.l. for ἀφοράω in Thphr.*HP*4.16.6, cf. Ph.2.249; *dry up,* of a river, Id. 1.690.

**ἀφόρητος,** ον, *unendurable,* κρυμός Hdt.4.28; χειμῶνος χρῆμα ἀφόρητον Id.7.188; μεγέθει βοῆς ἀφόρητοι Th.4.126; οὐκ ἔστιν .. οὐδὲν τῆς ὕβρεως -τότερον D.21.46; ἀ. κακόν Arist.*EN*$1126^{a}13$, cf. Epicur. *Fr.*447, Phld.*Lib.*p.17 O.; *irresistible,* Jul.*Or.*1.28d. Adv. -τως Poll. 3.130. **II.** *not worn, new,* censured by Luc.*Lex.*9, Ath.3.98a.

**ἀφορητότης·** *intolerabilitas, Gloss.*

**ἀφορία,** ἡ, (ἄφορος) *not bearing*:—hence, **1.** c. gen. objecti, *non-production, dearth,* καρπῶν -ίαι X.*Vect.*4.9; πίττης Thphr.*HP*9. 2.4; παίδων Pl.*Lg.*740c (pl.); ἀρετῆς Ph.1.430: abs., *dearth,* αἱ ἀ. γίγνονται Antipho 2.1.10, cf. Lycurg.84, Arist.*Mete.*$351^{b}14$ (pl.). **2.** in subj. sense, *barrenness, sterility,* ἀ. ψυχῆς τε καὶ σωμάτων Pl.*R.* 546a; ψυχῶν κρειττόνων εὐφορίαι ἢ ἀ. Chrysipp.*Stoic.*2.337; φρενῶν X.*Smp.*4.55.

⊛ **ἀφορ-ίζω,** *mark off by boundaries,* ἐξελόντας [τὸ ὄρος] τῷ θεῷ καὶ ἀφορίσαντας Hyp.*Eux.*16; οὐσία ἀφωρισμένη property *marked out by boundary-pillars,* D.49.61:—Med., *mark off for oneself, appropriate to oneself,* χώραν ὅτι πλείστην Isoc.5.120: metaph., ἀ. τιμάς E.*Alc.*31:—Pass., ἡ ὑπό τινος ἀφορισθεῖσα χώρα Isoc.4.36. **b.** *border on,* τοὺς ὅρους -ίζοντας τὸν Ἀσωπόν Pl.*Criti.*110e. **2.** *determine, define,* Id.*Sph.*240c:—also Med., περὶ φύσεως ἀφοριζόμενοι Epicr.11.13:—Pass., χρόνος ἀφωρισμένος a *determinate* time, Pl.*Lg.*785b; ὅροι -ισμένοι *well-defined,* Id.*Criti.*110d; ἀφωρισμένα *definite cases,* Arist. *Rh.*$1354^{b}8$: part. ἀφορίσας *definitely,* D.25.29. **3.** *separate, distinguish,* Antipho Soph.*Oxy.*1364.290 (Pass.); *exclude,* Pl.*R.*501d, al., ἀ. χωρίς Arist.*Pol.*$1331^{a}27$; ἀ. τί τινος Pl.*Hp.Ma.*298d; ἱππέων ἕδρας ἀπὸ τῶν ἄλλων D.C.36.42:—Med., Pl.*Lg.*644a, *Chrm.*173e; τι ἀπό τινος Id.*Sph.*227c:—Pass., ἀφορίζεσθαι ἀπό τινος Id.*Smp.*205c: abs., ἀγνοίας ἀφωρισμένον εἶδος *distinct* species, Id.*Sph.*229c; ἐπιστήμη ἀφωρισμένη Arist.*Rh.*$1354^{a}3$. **4.** *bring to an end, finish,* βίβλους Plb.2.71.10:—Med., λόγον Isoc.15.58. **5.** *grant as a special gift,* τᾷ κάλλος ἀφώρισε Κύπρις *Epigr.Gr.*244.3 (Cyzicus). **II.** c. acc. pers., **1.** *banish,* καί μ' ἀπὸ γᾶς ὥρισε E.*Hec.*940 (lyr.). **2.** *separate, Act.Ap.*19.9, etc.:—Pass., ἱερέων γένος ἀπὸ τῶν ἄλλων -ισμένον Pl.*Ti.*24a; ἐκ τινῶν ἀφωρισμένων from *a definite class* of persons, Arist.*Pol.*$1292^{b}4$; ἀφωρισμένος τέχνην *having a definite* art *assigned one,* Pl.*Sph.*231e. **b.** *set apart* for rejection, *cast out, excommunicate, Ev.Luc.*6.22. **c.** *set apart for* some office, *appoint, ordain, Act.Ap.*13.2, *Ep.Rom.*1.1 (Pass.), *Ep.Gal.*1.15. **d.** Pass., ἀρχὴ ἀφωρισμένη πρὸς τὰς θυσίας Arist.*Pol.*$1322^{b}26$; of a treatise, *to be devoted to,* c. dat., Olymp.*in Mete.*9.15. **-ιος·** θρασύς, ἄπιστος, Hsch. **-ῐσις,** εως, ἡ, = sq., *Gloss.* ⊛ **-ισμα,** ατος, τό, *that which is set apart: the wave-offering,* Lxx *Ex.*29.24, al. ⊛ **-ισμός,** ὁ, *delimitation, assignment of boundaries, SIG*827 *F*7; γῆς *PFreib.*11.7 (iv A. D.); θέσεως Simp. *in Ph.*626.20. **II.** *separation, distinction,* Thphr.*CP*3.14.2; ἀπὸ τοῦ λαοῦ Thd.*Is.*56.3: hence, *banishment,* = Lat. *relegatio,* Lyd.*Mag.* 3.17 (pl.), *Ost.*9c (pl.). **2.** *determination,* Arist.*Cat.*$3^{b}22$. **3.** *attainment of definiteness,* Thphr.*Metaph.*28; *distinctive character* or *feature,* Alex.Aphr.*in Top.*74.14. **4.** *pithy sentence, aphorism* (such as those of Hp.), Critias 39 D., Ph.1.636, Hermog.*Id.*1.6. **5.** *fixed rule,* Thphr.*HP*9.2.1. **-ιστέον,** *one must reject,* Arist.*EN* $1097^{b}34$. **II.** *one must define* or *assign,* Ph.*Bel.*92.49, Iamb.*Myst.* 2.1, Dam.*Pr.*448; *one must separate,* τί τινος Gal.9.379, cf. Plot.6.3. 1. **-ιστικός,** ή, όν, *delimiting,* Simp.*in Ph.*541.4, al.; *separative,* Sch.Luc.*Nav.*1; *aphoristic,* διδασκαλία Gal.11.802. Adv. -κῶς ibid.; *pithily, sententiously,* D.H.*Is.*7.

**ἀφορμ-άω,** Dor. part. dat. ἀφορμίοντι (-ιῶντι codd.) Archyt.ap. D.L.3.22:—*make to start from* a place:—Pass., *start, depart,* ναῦφιν Il.2.794, cf. Od.2.375, 4.748, Sapph.*Supp.*6.7, etc.: c. gen., *from* a place, οἷον ἄρ' ὁδοῦ τέλος Ἄργους ἀφωρμήθημεν S.*OC*1401; δόμων E. *Or.*844; ἐκ Κεγχρειῶν Th.8.10; *to* a place, δεῦρο Ar.*Nu.*607. **II.** intr. in Act. in same sense as Pass., ἀ. χθονός E.*Rh.*98; ἐκ δόμων Id. *Tr.*939, cf. Th.4.78; οἴκαδε Aeschin.2.40; εἰς Λιβύην Plb.1.39.1; of lightning, *to break forth,* S.*OC*1470 (lyr.): c. acc. cogn., τί τήνδ' .. ἀφορμᾷς πεῖραν; Id.*Aj.*290. **2.** *feel aversion,* opp. ὁρμάω, Arr.*Epict.* 1.4.14, Simp.*in Epict.*p.22 D. **-ή,** ἡ, *starting-point,* esp. in war, *base of operations,* ἀναχώρησίς τε καὶ ἀ. Th.1.90, cf. Plb.1.41.6, etc.; *place of safety,* E.*Med.*342. **2.** generally, *starting-point, origin, occasion* or *pretext,* ἀφορμαὶ λόγων Id.*Hec.*1239, *Ph.*199; ἀφορμὴν παρέχειν D.18.156; δεδωκέναι Id.21.98, cf. 2*Ep.Cor.*5.12; λαβεῖν ἀ. Isoc.4.61, *Ep.Rom.*7.8; εὑρεῖν *BGU*615.6 (ii A. D.), 923.22 (i/ii A. D.); ἵνα ἀ. γένοιτο τιμῆς *Inscr.Prien.*105.16 (i B. C.); ἀ. καὶ πρόφασις Plb. 2.52.3; *occasion, origin* of an illness, Hp.*Epid.*2.1.11, Sor.1.29; εἰ δέ τις οἴεται μικρὰν ἀ. εἶναι σιτηρέσιον τοῖς στρατευομένοις ὑπάρχειν a small *inducement,* D.4.29; τὸ γὰρ εὖ πράττειν παρὰ τὴν ἀξίαν ἀ. τοῦ κακῶς φρονεῖν Id.1.23; *instigation, incitement, POxy.*237 vii 21 (ii A. D.). **3.** *means with which one begins* a thing, *resources,* ἀ. τοῦ βίου Lys.24.24; εἰς τὸν βίον X.*Mem.*3.12.4; τίνας εἶχεν ἀφορμὰς ἡ πόλις; D.18.233; ἀφελεῖν τὴν ἀ. δι' ἣν ὑβρίζει Id.21.98; πίστις ἀ. μεγίστη πρὸς χρηματισμόν good faith is the best *asset* for business, Id.36.44, cf. 11.16; ἀ. ἐπί .. Id.3.33; esp. *means of war,* And.1.109; ἀ. εἰς ξένους χιλίους *means for levying* 1000 mercenaries, X.*HG*4.8.33; ἀ. ἔργων *means for undertaking* .., Id.*Mem.*2.7.11, cf. 3.5.11; πρὸς ἀφορμὴν ἐμπορίας ἢ γεωργίας Arist.*Pol.*$1320^{a}39$; πάντων ἀ. τῶν καλῶν Philem.110. **4.** *capital* of a banker, etc., Lys.*Fr.*1.2, X.*Mem.*2.7.12, Lycurg.26, D.14. 30, 36.11; ἀφορμῆς δίκη suit for *restitution of capital,* Arg.D.36. **5.** Rhet., *food for argument, material, subject,* ὑποθέσεις καὶ ἀφορμαὶ λόγων Luc.*Rh.Pr.*18, cf. Men.Rh.p.334 S., Aps.p.264 H. **6.** *aptitude, inclination,* εἰς φιλανθρωπίαν Phld.*Ir.*p.53 W. (pl.). **II.** Stoic term for *repulsion* (opp. ὁρμή), Chrysipp.*Stoic.*3.42, cf. 40, Simp. *in Epict.*p.22 D. **III.** *release* of water from sluice, *PAmh.*2.143. 17 (iv A. D.). **-ητικός,** ή, όν, (cf. foreg. II) *of repulsion,* δύναμις, opp. ὁρμητικός, Arr.*Epict.*1.1.12. ⊛ **-ίζομαι,** Med., *loose one's* ships *from harbour,* ναῦς E.*IT*18.

**ἀφόρμικτος,** ον, *without the lyre,* of melancholy music, A.*Eu.*332 (lyr.).

**ἄφορμος,** ον, = ἀφορμηθείς, *moving off from, departing from,* αὖθις ἄφορμος ἐμᾶς χθονός S.*OC*234.

**ἀφορολογ-ησία,** ἡ, *exemption from tribute, BCH*10.300 (Alabanda, ii B. C.). **-ητος,** ον, *not subjected to tribute, IG*$2^{2}$.1009.41, *GDI*5160. 10 (Cret.), *OGI*223 (Erythrae, iii B. C.), Plb.4.25.7, Lxx 1*Es.*4.50, Plu. *Flam.*10.

**ἄφορος,** ον, *not bearing, barren,* δένδρεα Hdt.2.156; γῆ X.*Oec.*20. 3; of females, *barren,* περὶ ἀφόρων Hp.*Steril.* tit. **2.** *causing barrenness,* σταλαγμός A.*Eu.*784 (lyr.); νοῦσος Hp.*Mul.*1.38; χρόνος ib.6. **II.** *exempt from tribute,* ἄ. καὶ ἀτελής Str.15.1.39, cf. *BGU* 889.24 (ii A. D.). **III.** Pass., *not to be borne,* νόσημα v. l. for ἄπορος in Hp.*VM*8.

**ἄφορτος,** ον, opp. φορτικός (q. v.), πολιτικὸς καὶ ἄ. καὶ εὐγνώμων Antip.*Stoic.*3.254. Adv. -τως, φέρειν bear *easily,* Teles p.15 H. **II.** at Sparta, *not having undergone the Lycurgean training,* Hsch.

**ἀφόρυκτος,** ον, *unspotted, unstained, AP*9.323 (Antip.).

**ἄφος·** τραγάκανθα, Hsch.

**ἀφόσι-ος,** α, ον, *unholy*, ἀσεβήματα *Annales du Service* 19.40 (i B.C.). ❀**–όω,** Ion. **ἀποσ–,** *purify from guilt* or *pollution*, τὴν πόλιν Pl.*Lg.*873b; σεαυτόν Id.*Euthphr.*4c; πόλιν τὰ πρὸς τοὺς θεούς Aeschin.3.120. 2. *dedicate, devote*, κόρας ἑταιρισμῷ Clearch.6. 3. *establish, consecrate*, θυσίας *OGI*383.202. II. Med., *satisfy one's conscience*, Pl.*Phd.*60e; *make atonement* or *expiation*, Id.*Phdr.*242c; ἀποσιοῦσθαι τῇ θεῷ Hdt.1.199; ἀ. ὑπὲρ αὐτοῦ Pl.*Lg.*874a. 2. c. acc. rei, *acquit oneself of* an obligation, ἀποσιεύμενος τὴν ἐξόρκωσιν *quit oneself conscientiously of* one's oath, Hdt.4.154; ἀ. λόγιον *quitting oneself of the orders of* an oracle, ib.203; τὰ πρὸς τοὺς θεούς Jul.*Mis.*361b. b. *avert* a curse or the consequence of crime, ἄγος Plu.*Cam.*18, cf. *Alc.*33, al.; διαβολάς D.H.4.79; τὴν ἀσθένειαν τῆς φύσεως Sallust.18 (prob.l.). c. *do* a thing *for form's sake*, i.e. *do it perfunctorily*, οὐδ' ἀφοσιούμενος ἀλλ' ὡς οἷόν τ' ἄριστα παρασκευαζόμενος Is.7.38; ἀ. περί τινος Pl.*Lg.*752d, cf. *Ep.*331b; προβολήν Plu.*Per.*10. d. *allege as an excuse*, τὴν ἀνάγκην Id.*Them.*24. e. *eschew on religious grounds, hold in abomination*, κρόμυον, κυάμους, Id.2.353f, 286d: abs., *Ant.*28. III. Pass., ἀφωσιωμέναι· ἀνόσιαι, ἄποθεν τοῦ ὁσίου γεγενημέναι, S.*Fr.*253. **–ωμα,** ατος, τό, *act of purification, expiation*, Hsch. ❀**–ωσις,** εως, ἡ, *purification, expiation*, D.H.2.52: pl., Plu.2.302b; defined as ὁσιότητος παραλελειμμένης ἀποπλήρωσις Herm.*in Phdr.*p.94A. 2. *doing as matter of form*, ἀφοσιώσεως ἕνεκεν for *form's* sake, Plu.*Eum.*12; τιμῆς ἀ. *outward, formal* respect, Id.*Tim.*39; κατὰ ἀφοσίωσιν Dam.*Pr.*171.

❀ **ἀφουλωτικός,** ή, όν, *causing to scar over*, Paul.Aeg.6.5.

**ἄφρα,** ἡ, a kind of *plaster*, Aët.15.14.

**ἀφρᾰδ-έω,** only in pres., *to be senseless, behave thoughtlessly*, σοὶ .. μαχήσομαι ἀφραδέοντι Il.9.32; αἰεὶ γάρ τε νεώτεροι ἀφραδέουσι Od.7.294. **–ής,** ές, (φράζομαι) *insensate, reckless*, μνηστῆρες ib.2.282, cf. Nonn.*D.*5.349; of the dead, *without sense, senseless*, Od.11.476. Adv. ἀφραδέως *senselessly, recklessly*, Il.3.436, etc. **–ία,** Ion. **–ίη,** ἡ, *folly, thoughtlessness*, in Hom. always in dat. pl., ἀνέρος ἀφραδίῃσι Il.5.649; ποιμένος ἀφραδίῃσι 16.354; exc. δι' ἀφραδίας Od.19.523, and ἀφραδίῃ πολέμοιο Il.2.368.—Ep. word, ἀφροσύνη being used for it in Prose; ἀφραδίῃσι in a mock heroic line, Ar.*Pax*1064 (hex.). **–μων,** in Trag. **ἀφράσμων,** ον, gen. ονος, = ἀφραδής, c. inf., ἀφράδμονες προγνώμεναι *without sense* to foresee, *h.Cer.*256; γυναικὸς ὡς ἀφράσμονος A.*Ag.*1401, cf. S.*Fr.*613. Adv. ἀφρασμόνως A.*Pers.*417.—Only poet.

**ἀφράζω,** = sq., cited from Hp. by Gal.19.87; cf. ἀφράσει· ἀσυνετεῖ, Hsch.

**ἀφραίνω,** (ἄφρων) *to be foolish*, Il.2.258, 7.109, Od.20.360, Phoc.5.—Poet. and Hp.*Gland.*12; later as a philosophic term, Chrysipp.*Stoic.*3.166, Plu.2.1037d, S.E.*M.*11.94, Plot.5.8.3.

**ἄφρακτος,** ον, old Att. **ἄφαρκτος** (though this form has generally been altered by the copyists), *unfenced, unfortified, unguarded*, οἴκησις, στρατόπεδον, Th.1.6, 117: c. gen., ἀ. φίλων *by* friends, S.*Aj.*910 (lyr.); of ships, *not decked*, *IG*12(1).44 (Rhodes); of horses, opp. πεφραγμένοι, Arr.*Tact.*2.5. 2. *not obstructed*, Gal.17(1).598. 3. *not to be kept in, irrepressible*, σταγόνες A.*Ch.*186 (with v.l. ἄφραστοι). II. *unguarded, off one's guard*, ἠρέθην E.*Hipp.*657; ληφθήσεσθε Th.6.33, cf. Ar.*Th.*581; πρός τινα Th.3.39.

**ἀφράσμων,** v. ἀφράδμων.

**ἄφραστ-ος,** ον, (φράζω) *unutterable, marvellous*, ἄ. ἠδ' ἀνόητα *h.Merc.*80; οὐδὲν –ότερον πέλεται νόου ἀνθρώποισιν Hom.*Epigr.*5.2; πέδη S.*Tr.*1057; *inexpressible*, μέριμνα A.*Pers.*165 codd.; *too wonderful for words*, φάτις S.*Tr.*694. II. (φράζομαι) *not perceived, unseen*, *h.Merc.*353; *not to be observed, known*, or *guessed*, A.*Supp.*95 (lyr.); *incomprehensible*, Orph.*L.*46; κατακρύπτει ἐς τὸ –ότατόν οἱ ἐφαίνετο εἶναι [χωρίον] the place *least likely to be thought of*, Hdt.5.92.δ'; *unforeseen*, A.R.2.824. Adv. **–τως** *beyond thought*, S.*El.*1262 (lyr.). III. Act., of persons, *beside themselves*, Nic.*Th.*776. 2. *giving no sign*, Nonn.*D.*9.134, 22.82. **–ύς,** ύος, ἡ, Ion. for ἀφραδία, Call.*Fr.anon.*9 (pl.).

❀ **ἀφρατίας·** ἰσχυρός (Cret.), Hsch.

**ἀφρᾶτον,** τό, Lat. *aphratum, soufflé, mousse*, Isid.*Etym.*20.2.29, Alex.Trall.*Febr.*3, Steph.*in Hp.*1.87 D.

**Ἄφραττος·** ἡ Ἑκάτη (Tarent.), Hsch.

**ἄφρενος,** ον, = ἄφρων, dub. l. in Beros.1.3.

**ἀφρέω,** (ἀφρός) *foam*, Hp.*Morb.Sacr.*7, etc. II. c. acc., *befoam, cover with foam*, ἵπποι ἄφρεον στήθεα (disyll.) Il.11.282.

**ἀφρηλόγος,** ον, poet. for ἀφρολόγος (which does not occur), *gathering froth, skimming*, λίπους *AP*6.101 (Phil.).

**ἀφρηστής,** οῦ, ὁ, *foamer*, of a dolphin, *AP*7.214 (Arch.).

**ἀφρήτωρ,** ὁ, Ion. for ἀφράτωρ, *without brotherhood* (φρήτρη), i.e. *bound by no social tie*, Il.9.63.

**ἀφρ-ιάω,** poet. for ἀφρέω, Opp.*H.*1.772, Porph.ap.Eus.*PE*3.11. **–ίζω,** = ἀφρέω, *foam*, S.*El.*719, Hp.*Mul.*2.123, Thphr.*CP*6.1.5; of a wine-cup, Antiph.174.6, Alex.119.3.

**ἀφρικτί,** Adv., (φρίσσω) *without shuddering*, Call.*Dian.*65.

**ἀφρῖνον·** τάλαρον τῶν ἑλκυσμάτων τῶν ἐρίων, Hsch.

**ἀφριόεις,** εσσα, εν, (ἀφρός) *foamy*, γένειον *AP*7.531 (Antip.Thess.); γάλακτος τεῦχος Nic.*Al.*206, cf. *Hymn.Is.*164.

❀ **Ἄφριος,** ὁ, epith. of Zeus in Thessaly, Ἀρχ.Ἐφ.1913.219: also, name of month, *IG*9(2).206 iii *c*, al.

**ἀφρίους·** ἀθέρας, Hsch. **ἀφρίς·** μύρτον, Id.

**ἀφρισμός,** ὁ, (ἀφρίζω) *foaming*, Archig.ap.Philum.*Ven.*14.3, Paul.Aeg.3.13, Sch.Il.9.539.

**ἄφρισσα,** ἡ, a plant, = ἀσκληπιάς, Apul.*Herb.*15.

**ἀφριστής,** οῦ, ὁ, *foamer*, Sch.Il.1.535.

**ἀφρῖτις,** ιδος, ἡ, = ἀφρός III, Arist.*Fr.*309, Ath.7.325b, Opp.*H.*1.776.

**ἀφρό-γᾰλα,** ακτος, τό, *frothed milk*, Gal.10.468. **–γένεια,** ἡ, *foam-born, Aphrodite*, Mosch.2.71, Coluth.167; the planet *Venus*, Max.402, Doroth.ap.*Cat.Cod.Astr.*2.82.2: ❀**ἀφρογενής,** ές, = foreg., Ἀφροδίτην ἀφρογενῆ Orph.*Fr.*183, cf. *APl.*4.211 (Stat. Flacc.); the planet *Venus*, Doroth.ap.Heph.Astr.1.6.

**Ἀφροδίσ-ια** [δῐ], τά, v. Ἀφροδίσιος. **–ιάζω,** *have sexual intercourse*:—Act., of the man, Hp.*Vict.*2.73, al., Pl.*R.*426a, X.*Mem.*1.3.14, etc.:—Pass., of the woman, Id.*Hier.*3.4, Arist.*HA*$581^{b}$17, etc. **–ιακός,** ή, όν, *sexual*, τέρψεις D.S.2.23; [λίθος] a precious stone *with aphrodisiac properties*, Plin.*HN*37.148; ἔλαιον *POxy.*1292.5 (ii A.D.). ❀**–ιάς,** άδος, ἡ, *sacred to Aphrodite*, name of an island, Hdt.4.169. II. = ἄκορος, Apul.*Herb.*6. **–ιασμός,** ὁ, *sexual intercourse, lustfulness*, Hp.*Aph.*6.30, Arist.*GA*$725^{b}$17 (pl.). ❀**–ιαστής,** οῦ, ὁ, *voluptuary*, Polem.*Phgn.*14. 2. *lessee of public brothel*, *POxy.*511.3. 3. in pl., *worshippers of Aphrodite*, at Rhodes, *IG*12(1).162. **–ιαστικός,** ή, όν, = ἀφροδισιακός, χάρις Arist.*Pol.*$1311^{b}$16; συνδυασμοί Gal.1.339. 2. of men and animals, *lecherous, salacious*, Arist.*HA*$488^{b}$4, Gal.1.624. II. *aphrodisiac*, ἐδέσματα Arist.*Pr.*$954^{a}$3, cf. Gal.14.241. ❀**–ιος,** α, ον, also ος, ον D.H.2.24, Luc.*Am.*12, Ael.*NA*1.2:—*belonging to the goddess of love*, ἔργον Semon.7.48; ἄγρα S.*Fr.*166; ὅρκος Pl.*Smp.*183b; ἀθύρματα Crates Com.2 D.; λόγος Pl.Com.2 D.; κῆπος Archipp.2 D.; ὑμέναιον Pherecr.12 D. II. Ἀφροδίσια, τά, *sexual pleasures*, Hp.*Mochl.*36, freq. in Pl., as *Phd.*81b, al.; τέρπν' ἄνθε' Ἀ. Pi.*N.*7.53; τὰ τῶν ὡραίων Ἀ. X.*Mem.*2.6.22; ἔργα Ἀ. Hp.*Jusj.*:—also as concrete, = *amasius*, X.*Mem.*1.3.8. 2. *festival of Aphrodite*, Ἀ. ἄγειν Id.*HG*5.4.4, Alex.253.1. 3. *pudenda*, Luc.*Nigr.*16. III. Ἀφροδίσιον, τό, *temple of Aphrodite*, X.*HG*5.4.58, *GDI*5075.70 (Crete); *her statue*, Plu.*Thes.*21, *PPetr.*3 p.113. 2. in pl., *brothels*, *PTeb.*6.29 (ii B.C.). IV. Ἀφροδίσιος, ὁ (sc. μήν), name of a month in Cyprus, Porph.*Abst.*2.54, etc. ❀**–ιών,** ῶνος, ὁ (sc. μήν), name of a month at Demetrias, *SIG*1157.52.

**Ἀφροδῑτ-ᾰρίδιον** [ῐδ], τό, 'darling', Pl.Com.3 D. **–άριον,** τό, name of an *eyesalve*, Gal.12.752. II. name of a *horse-medicine*, *Hippiatr.*129.

❀ **Ἀφροδίτη** [ῑ], ἡ, (ἀφρός) *Aphrodite*, *h.Hom.*5, Hes.*Th.*195; διὰ τὴν τοῦ ἀφροῦ γένεσιν Ἀφροδίτη ἐκλήθη Pl.*Cra.*406c. II. as Appellat., *sexual love, pleasure*, Od.22.444; ὑπ' Ἀπόλλωνι ψαύειν Ἀφροδίτας Pi.*O.*6.35; ἔργα Ἀφροδίτης *h.Ven.*1, 9, etc.; μὰ τὴν Ἀ., νὴ τὴν Ἀ., a woman's form of oath, Ar.*Lys.*208, *Ec.*189, etc. 2. generally, *vehement longing* or *desire*, E.*IA*1264; Ἀ. τιν' ἡδεῖαν κακῶν *enjoyment*, Id.*Ph.*399. 3. *beauty, grace, charm*, ἔρρει πᾶσ' Ἀ. A.*Ag.*419 (lyr.); τοιαύτην Ἀ. ἐπὶ τῇ γλώττῃ .. ἔχει Luc.*Scyth.*11; πολλὴν Ἀ. τῷ λόγῳ περιτιθέναι D.H.*Comp.*3. III. ὁ τᾶς Ἀφροδίτας [ἀστήρ] *the planet Venus*, Ti.Locr.97a, cf. Pl.*Epin.*987b, Arist.*Metaph.*$1073^{b}$31, etc. IV. Pythag. name for *five*, *Theol.Ar.*31. V. *seedtime*, Orph.*Fr.*33. VI. name of various *plasters*, Aët.12.48, 15.15.

**ἀφρό-κομος,** ον, lit. *foam-haired*, but always metaph., ῥαθάμιγξ Musae.262, Nonn.*D.*2.618; στόματα ib.46.161. **–λιτρον,** τό, Att. for ἀφρόνιτρον (q.v.).

**ἀφρον-εύομαι,** = ἀφρονέω, Lxx *Je.*10.21, Sm.*Jb.*1.22. **–ευσις,** εως, ἡ, *playing the fool*, opp. φρονίμευσις, *Stoic.*3.25. **–έω,** (ἄφρων) *to be silly, act foolishly*, Il.15.104, *AP*10.66 (Agath.); τὸ ἀφρονεῖν Ceb.41. 2. trans., *make foolish* or *vain*, f.l. in Aq.2 *Ki.*15.31. **–η,** ἡ, = ἀφροσύνη, *AB*472. **–ησις,** εως, ἡ, = foreg., J.*AJ*19.1.14 (dub.). **–ίζω,** *make foolish*, prob. in Aq.2 *Ki.*15.31. **–ικός,** ή, όν, = ἄφρων, Sch.Luc.*Bis Acc.*22.

❀ **ἀφρόνιτρον,** Att. **ἀφρόλιτρον** (the two distd. by Gal. l.c., cf. *Gp.*2.28), τό, a form of *native sodium carbonate* (cf. νίτρον), distd. by Gal.12.212 from the finer ἄνθος νίτρου, cf. Herod.Med.ap.Orib.6.20.5: in Hp. and correct Greek divisim ἀφρὸς νίτρου: hence ἀφρόνιτρον is condemned by Phryn.272.

**ἄφροντ-ις,** ιδος, ὁ, ἡ, *free from care, careless*, c. gen., ἄ. τοῦ θανεῖν E.*Fr.*958; τῶν καθηκόντων Plu.2.45d; περί τινος Luc.*Dem.Enc.*25: abs., δίαιτα Plu.2.792b (in acc. ἄφροντιν), cf. Max.Tyr.3.9: Comp. –έστερος Steph.*in Hp.*1.263 D. **–ιστέω,** *to be heedless*, Pl.*Lg.*917c. 2. *have no care of, pay no heed to*, ἀρχόντων ib.885a, v.l. in X.*An.*5.4.20, cf. Plb.9.13.1; περί τινος Hp.*Praec.*7 (dub.); ὑπὲρ τῆς βασιλείας Philostr.*VA*1.38. **–ιστητέον,** *one must disregard*, c. gen., Plb.9.16.5. **–ιστί,** Adv. of –ιστος, *thoughtlessly*, Ath.14.632d. **–ιστία,** ἡ, *heedlessness*, τοῦ συμμέτρου Them.*Or.*15.186c; τοῦ βίου Porph.*Plot.*7. II. in pass. sense, *being unheeded*, ὑπ' ἀνθρώπων Phld.*Mort.*36. **–ιστος,** ον, *thoughtless, heedless*, X.*Smp.*6.6; Ἔρως Theoc.10.20; ἐς τὸ ἀ. ἐπαίρεσθαι D.C.47.11. Adv. **–τως** *without taking thought, inconsiderately*, S.*Tr.*366, Timo 67.3; ἀ. ἔχειν to be *heedless*, X.*Cyr.*1.6.42; πρὸς τὸ μέλλον Plb.3.79.2; euphem. for ἄφρων εἶναι, S.*Aj.*355. 2. *without causing anxiety*, Ruf.ap.Orib.45.30.20. II. Pass., *unthought of, unexpected*, ἐμοὶ δ' ἀγὼν ὅδ' οὐκ ἀ. .. ἦλθε A.*Ag.*1377.

**ἀφρόομαι,** Pass., *become frothy*, *Theol.Ar.*40.

❀ **ἀφρός,** ὁ, *foam*, of the sea, ῥόος Ὠκεανοῖο ἀφρῷ μορμύρων Il.18.403, etc.; of a river, 5.599. 2. of persons and animals, *foam, slaver, froth*, περί τ' ἀ. ὀδόντας γίγνεται 20.168; ἀ. περὶ στόμα Hp.*Aph.*2.43, cf. *Ev.Luc.*9.39; μέλαν' ἀπ' ἀνθρώπων ἀφρόν *frothy blood*, A.*Eu.*183, cf. *Fr.*372; θρομβώδεις ἀφροί S.*Tr.*702; βακχίου παλαιγενοῦς ἀφρῷ, of wine, Antiph.237; κύλικα .. ἀφρῷ ζέουσαν Theophil.2. II.

ἀφρὸς νίτρου, = ἀφρόνιτρον, Hp.*Mul.*1.75; ἀ. alone, Arist.*Col.*794$^a$20. 2. ἀ. αἵματος, = σπέρμα, Diog.Apoll.A 24 D. III. a kind of ἀφύη, Arist.*HA*569$^a$29, $^b$28, Ath.7.325b; Ionic, acc. to Archestr. *Fr.*9.2, but cf. Hsch. s.v. ἀφύων τιμή. (*mbhrós*, cf. Skt. *abhrám* 'cloud', Lat. *imber.*)

⊕ **ἀφροσέληνος**, ὁ, = σεληνίτης, Ps.-Democr.ap.Zos.Alch.p.122B., Dsc.5.141.

**ἀφροσῐβόμβαξ**, ακος, ὁ, *puffing, bustling fellow*, Timo 29.

**ἀφρόσκορδον**, τό, *African* σκόροδον, i.e. *Cyprian garlic, Allium sativum*, Colum.11.3.20.

**ἀφροσύνη**, ἡ, (ἄφρων) *folly, thoughtlessness*, freq. in pl., παῖδας καταπαυέμεν ἀφροσυνάων Od.24.457, cf. 16.278: in sg., οὐδέ τί σε χρὴ ταύτης ἀφροσύνης Il.7.110, cf. Democr.254, Hdt.3.146, 9.82; κοῦφαι ἀ. S.*OC*1230 (lyr.); καταφρόνησιν ἢ.. ἀ. μετωνόμασται Th.1.122; opp. σωφροσύνη and σοφία, Pl.*Prt.*332e; συμβαίνει ἡ ἀ. μετὰ ἀκρατίας ἀρετῇ Arist.*EN*1146$^a$27.

⊕ **ἀφροτόκος**, ον, *producing foam, foaming*, Nonn.*D.*45.156.

**ἀφρουρ-έω**, *leave unguarded*, τὰ οἶκοι Str.15.1.53. ⊕ **-ητος**, ον, *unguarded*, Pl.*Lg.*760a, Plu.2.340f; *ungarrisoned*, Plb.4.25.7, al., Plu.*Flam.*10: metaph., Gal.18(1).321. **-ος**, ον, *off one's guard*, Pl.*Phdr.*256c; ἄ. καὶ ἄνοπλοι Plu.*Demetr.*32. 2. *free from military duty*, Arist.*Pol.*1270$^b$4.

**ἀφροφυής**, ές, *foamy*, of a lettuce, from its milky juice, *AP*9.412 (Phld.).

**ἄφρυκτος**, ον, *unroasted*, κριθαί Poll.6.77, Harp.s.v. προκώνια, Gal. 11.807, etc.

**Ἀφρώ**, οῦς, ἡ, = Ἀφροδίτη, Nic.*Al.*406.

**ἀφρώδης**, ες, *foamy*, αἷμα Diog.Apoll.6, Hp.*Aph.*5.13, cf. *Acut.*53; στόματος ἀ. πέλανος E.*Or.*220; ὄμβρος Tim.*Pers.*71 (dub.); γένος Pl. *Ti.*60b; σπέρματα Corn.*ND*24. II. μήκων ἀ. *frothy* poppy, *Silene inflata*, Dsc.4.66; = πέπλος, ib.167 (but, = πεπλίς, Plin.*HN*27.119); = χαμαισύκη, Ps.-Dsc.4.169.

**ἄφρων**, ον, gen. ονος, (φρήν) *senseless*, of statues, X.*Mem.*1.4.4:— and so, *crazed, frantic*, ἄφρονα κούρην Il.5.875, cf. 761, A.*Eu.*377 (lyr.); *silly, foolish*, Il.3.220, Hes.*Op.*[210], S.*El.*941, etc.; φρένας ἄ. Il.4.104; τὸ ἄ., = ἀφροσύνη, Th.5.105, X.*Mem.*1.2.55; τῷ φρονίμῳ τῆς γνώμης παύοντες τὸ ἄ. ⟨τῆς ῥώμης⟩ Gorg.*Fr.*6; ἐξ ἄφρονος σώφρων γεγένηται X.*Cyr.*3.1.17: Comp. -ἐστερος Pl.*Cra.*392c: Sup. -ἐστατος X.*Mem.*2.1.5. Adv. -νως *senselessly*, S.*Aj.*766, X.*HG*5.1.19; opp. νοῦν ἐχόντως, Isoc.5.7: Comp. -εστέρως Pl.*La.*193c; -έστερον Jul.*Or.*7.224d. 2. ἄφρων, = κώνειον, Ps.-Dsc.4.78.

**ἀφυβρίζω**, *work off youthful passion, sow one's wild oats*, Men. 377. 2. of wine, *to be done fermenting*, Alex.45.4. II. *give a loose rein* to passion, *indulge freely*, εἰς τρυφάς Plu.*Demetr.*19; ἀ. ἔς τινα *vent* upon.., Agath.1.20, 4.19.

**ἀφῠγής**, ές, (φυγεῖν) *without strength to flee*, Timo 72.1.

**ἀφῠγι-άζω**, *cure, heal*, Archig.ap.Gal.12.821, Philum.*Ven.*5.3, 17.5 (Pass.), Iamb.*VP*25.114, Paul.Aeg.5.4. **-ασμός**, ὁ, *healing*, Iamb.*VP*15.64 (pl.).

**ἀφυγραίνω**, *moisten*, Arist.*HA*637$^b$29 (Pass.).

**ἀφύδιον** [ῠ], τό, Dim. of ἀφύη, Ar.*Fr* 507.

**ἀφυδραίνω**, *wash clean*:—Med., *wash oneself, bathe*, καθαραῖς δρόσοις E.*Ion* 97 (lyr.).

**ἄφυδρος**, ον, *without water*, dub. in Hp.*Aër.*13.

**ἄφυζα**, *unfleeing*, of the lion, Hes.*Fr.*235.

**ἄφυζε**· ἀπόλαβε, Hsch.

⊕ **ἀφύη** [ῠ], ἡ (gen. pl. ἀφύων, not ἀφυῶν, Hdn.Gr.1.425.13), *small fry* of various fishes (cf. ἀφρός III), Epich.60,89,124, Ar.*Ach.*640, Hices.ap.Ath.7.285b; = μεμβράς, Hsch.; nickname of ἑταίρα, Ath. 13.586b: prov., ἀφύα πῦρ or εἶδε πῦρ ἀ. 'no sooner said than done', Zen.2.32, Eust.1150.40.—Not used in sg. by Att., acc. to Hsch. s.v. ἀφύων τιμή.

**ἀφυής**, ές, acc. ἀφυῆ S.*Ph.*1014 codd.: (φυή):—*without natural talent, not clever, dull*, opp. εὐφυής, πρός τι Pl.*R.*455b; οὐκ ἀ. *no fool*, Id.*Lg.*832a; ἀ. πρὸς ταύτην τὴν σκέψιν *wanting wit* for it, Id.*Phd.*96c; ἐς μάθησιν Democr.85, cf. *AP*14.62. 2. in good sense, *simple, unschooled*, S. l.c. II. *naturally unsuited*, οὐκ ἀ. πρὸς τὸ φιλοκερδεῖν X.*Cyr.*1.6.32; of places, ταῖς δυνάμεσι Plb.1.30.7; πρός τι Id.4.38.1 (Sup.). Adv. ἀφυῶς, διακεῖσθαι πρός τι Id.1.88.11; ἀ. ἔχειν πρός τι Arist.*IA*710$^a$5, Plu.*Aem.*2: Comp. -έστερον Anon.Rhythm.*Oxy.*9. iii 11. III. = δυσφυής (as etym. of ἀφύη), Ath.7.324d.

**ἀφυΐα**, ἡ, *want of natural power* or *faculty*, τῆς κάμψεως Arist.*PA* 659$^a$29; φωνητηρίων ὀργάνων Str.14.2.28; ψυχῆς Plu.2.104c; ἀ. πρὸς τὸ ἡδέως ζῆν *natural unfitness* for.., ib.1088b; in pl., ἀφυΐαι, opp. εὐφυΐαι, Porph.*Abst.*3.8, cf. Colot.*in Euthd.*2. (Written ἀφύεια in Colot. l.c., Epicur.*Nat.Herc.*1420.)

**ἄφῠκος**, ον, *without cosmetics*, Hsch.

**ἄφυκτος**, ον, (φεύγω) *not to be shunned*, δῶρα θεῶν Sol.13.64; *from which none escape*, θάνατος Simon.39.3; χείρ, γυιοπέδαι, Pi.*I.*8(7).65, *P.*2.41; θεῶν ὄμμα A.*Pr.*903; κακῶν τρικυμία ib.1016; ἄ. κύνες, of the Erinyes, S.*El.*1388; of an arrow, *unerring*, Id.*Ph.*105, *Tr.*265, E.*Med.*634 (lyr.); λαβή Nicoch.3 D.; of a question, *admitting no escape, inevitable*, Pl.*Tht.*165b; λόγος Aeschin.3.17; ἄφυκτα ἐρωτᾶν Pl.*Euthd.*276e; λόγοι ἄ. Ar.*Eq.*757: Comp. -ότερος Hp.*Acut.*(*Sp.*) 10. Adv. -τως Lyc.493, etc. II. Act., *unable to escape*, μέσον λαβὼν ἄ. Ar.*Nu.*1047; dub. l. in A.*Supp.*784 (lyr.). Adv. -τως Lxx 3*Ma.*7.9: Comp. ἀφυκτοτέρως ἂν διακέοιντο Aen.Tact.16.12.—In codd. freq. written ἄφευκτος, Philem.115.4, Plu.*Lys.*29; ἄφευκτος ἀνάγκη *IG*14.803 (Naples).

**ἀφ-ῠλακτέω** (A), *bark out*, λόγοι ἀφυλακτούμενοι Luc.*Am.*17.

**ἀ-φῠλακτέω** (B), *to be off one's guard*, X.*An.*7.8.20, *Eq.Mag.*5.15: c. gen., *to be careless about*, Id.*Cyr.*1.6.5:—Pass., *to be ill-guarded*, Plb.5.73.10, cf. Onos.42.15.

**ἀφύλ-ακτος** [ῠ], ον, (φυλάσσω) *unguarded, unwatched*, ἀφέντες τὴν ἑωυτῶν ἀφύλακτον Hdt.8.70, cf. Th.2.13,93; ἀ. ἡ τήρησις *no* watching is *sufficient*, E.*Fr.*162. II. (φυλάσσομαι) *unguarded, off one's guard*, ἀφυλάκτῳ τινὶ ἐπιπεσεῖν, ἐπιγενέσθαι, Hdt.9.116, Th.7.32; πρὸς τὸ ἀδικεῖσθαι Arist.*Rh.*1372$^a$19; ἀφύλακτον εὕδειν εὐφρόνην sleep *securely* through the night, A.*Ag.*337; ἀ. τινα λαμβάνειν catch one *off his guard*, X.*Cyr.*1.6.37; ἵνα.. ἀ. ληφθῇ D.4.18; τὸ ἀ. *want of precaution*, Th.3.30: Comp. -ότερος J.*AJ*5.7.4: Sup. -ότατος, νυκτὸς ὥρα D.H.2.38. Adv. -τως X.*HG*4.1.17; διακεῖσθαι Plb.4.36.4; ὁμιλεῖν Phld.*Ir.*p.30 W.; ῥαθύμως καὶ ἀ. D.H.9.19: Comp. -ότερον ἔχειν Paus.7.16.2. 2. of things, *against which no precautions are* or *can be used, not guarded against*, Arist.*Rh.*1372$^a$24; *inevitable*, τύχη D.H.9.25; τὸ πεπρωμένον Plu.*Caes.*63; Ἐρινὺς *Epigr.Gr.*218. 7; ἀκωκή *IG*12(7).115.7 (Amorgos); βέλος *APl.*4.211 (Stat. Flacc.); Ἔρως ib.198 (Maec.). **-ακτηρίαστος**, ον, *not protected by a phylactery*, *PMag.Par.*1.2507. **-αξία**, ἡ, *carelessness in watching*, X.*Oec.*4.10; *negligence*, Antipho 3.4.7; *absence of guards*, X.*Hier.*6.4, D.C.55.15.

**ἀφῡλ-ίζω**, *strain off*, *AP*6.191.5 (Corn. Long.), f.l. in Dsc.2.76.8. **-ισμα**, ατος, τό, *whey*, Hsch. s.v. ὀρὸς γάλακτος. ⊕ **-ισμός**, ὁ, *cleaning out*, or (ὕλη) *clearing of brushwood*, χωμάτων *PColumbia Inv.*56.

**ἀφυλλάκανθος** [λᾰ], ον, *without prickles on the leaves*, Thphr.*HP*6.4.8.

**ἀφυλλ-άνθης**, ες, *with no ray-florets*, ἄνθεμον *wild chamomile, Matricaria Chamomilla*, var. *eradiata*, Thphr.*HP*7.8.3. **-ος**, ον, *leafless*, Il.2.425, Thphr.*HP*1.14.3, Plu.2.648f; *stripped of leaves*, στέφανος Xenarch.13; ἀ. στόματος λιταί prayers *not seconded by the suppliant's olive-branch*, E.*Or.*383. II. Act., *stripping off the leaves, blighting*, λειχήν A.*Eu.*785 (lyr.). **-ωτος**, ον, *bare of foliage, treeless*, πέτρα S.*Fr.*299.

**ἄφῡλος**, ον, *without a tribe*, Max.Tyr.21.4, prob. in *EM*178.39.

**ἀφύξιμος**, ον, (ἀφύσσω) κυάθῳ τρὶς ἀ. οἴνην thrice *drawn* into the cyathus, i.e. 3 cyathi, Nic.*Th.*603.

**ἄφυξις**, εως, ἡ, (ἀφύσσω) *drawing out, ladling*, dub. in Hsch., Cyr.

**ἀφυπν-ίζω**, *awaken from sleep*, E.*Rh.*25, Plu.*Nic.*9, Longus 1.25, etc.:—Pass., *wake up, keep awake*, Cratin.306 (lyr.), Pherecr.191 (lyr.): intr. in Act., Philostr.*VA*2.36. **-ισμός**, ὁ, *keeping awake*, Eust.1297.31. ⊕ **-όω**, *awake from sleep*, *AP*9.517 (Antip. Thess.), Ant. Diog.9. II. *fall asleep*, *Ev.Luc.*8.23, Paul.Aeg.1.98:—Med., Hld.9.12 (v.l. ὑφυπν-). **-ώττω**, = ἀφυπνόω II, Sch.Pi.*I.*7(6).23.

**ἀφύρᾱτος** [ῠ], Ion. -ητος, ον, *not kneaded*, Hp.*VM*14.

**ἀφυρεῖν**· ἀκαθαρσία, Hsch.

**ἄφυρτος**, ον, *unmixed*. Adv. -τως Nic.Dam.p.144 D.

**ἀφυσγετός** (ἀφύσγετος Tyrannio ap.Sch.Il.11.495), ὁ, *mud and rubbish* which a stream carries with it, Il.11.495, Opp.*H.*1.779. II. as Adj., *filthy*, ὕδρωψ Nic.*Al.*342. 2. (ἀφύσσω) *abundant*, νέκταρ ib.584.

**ἀφύσητος** [ῠ], ον, *not inflated*, ἀσκός Hp.*Art.*47,77.

**ἀφύσικος** [ῠ], *unphilosophical, unscientific*, Arist.ap.S.E.*M.*10.46. 2. *contrary to the laws of nature*, ib.250.

**ἀφύσιμος**, = ἀρύσιμος, Sch.Nic.*Al.*584.

**ἀφῠσιολόγ-ητος**, ον, *not to be explained by science*, Epicur.*Fr.*141, 200. II. *without knowledge of natural laws*, in Adv. -τως, φαντάζεσθαι prob. in M.Ant.10.9. **-ος**, ον, *not versed in natural philosophy*, prob. l. in Id.9.41.

**ἀφυσμός**, ὁ, *drawing off*, of liquids, Suid.

**ἄφῡσος**, ον, (φῦσα) *without flatulence*, Hp.*Hum.*3. **2.** *causing no flatulence*, Diocl.*Fr.*128, Gal.6.540. **3.** *expelling flatus*, Ruf. *Fr.*1, Gal.12.101.

**ἄφυσσα**, ἡ, = κοτύλη, (Tarent.), Hsch.

⊕ **ἀφύσσω**, Ep. impf. ἄφυσσον Call.*Cer.*70: fut. ἀφύξω, Dor. -ξῶ Theoc.7.65: aor. ἤφῠσα Od.9.165, Ep. ἄφυσσα 2.379, E.*IA*1051 (lyr.), imper. ἄφυσσον Od.2.349:—Med., aor. ἠφυσάμην, Ep. ἀφύσσατο Il.16.230:—*draw* liquids, esp. from a larger vessel with a smaller, νέκταρ ἀπὸ κρητῆρος ἀφύσσων Il.1.598, cf. Od.9.9; οἶνον ἐν ἀμφιφορεῦσιν ἠφύσαμεν 9.165; εἰς ἄγγε' ἀφύσσαι δῶρα Διωνύσου Hes. *Op.*613:—Pass., πίθων ἠφύσσετο οἶνος *was drawn from* the wine-jars, Od.23.305: metaph., ἄφενος καὶ πλοῦτον ἀφύξειν *draw full draughts of* wealth, i.e. *heap it up*, τινί for another, Il.1.171; ἀ. νέκταρ ἐρώτων *AP*5.225 (Paul. Sil.). 2. *sound, probe*, ἰητὴρ ἕλκος ἀ. Opp.*H.*2.597. II. Med., *draw for oneself, help oneself to*, οἶνον ἀφυσσόμενος Il.23.220; ἀπὸ Κηφισοῦ ῥοὰς.. ἀφυσσαμέναν, of Aphrodite, E.*Med.*836 (lyr.); φύλλα ἠφυσάμην I *heaped me up* a bed of leaves, Od.7.286, cf. 5.482: metaph., αἰῶνος σπειρήματ' ἀφυσσάμενος *App.Anth.*3.186.—Trag. only in E. l.c. and *IA*1051.

**ἀφύστα**· κοτύλη, στάμνος, Hsch.

⊕ **ἀφυστερέω**, *come too late, be behindhand*, Plb.1.52.8, 21.22.2, D.H. 10.26; ἐὰν ἀφυστερῇ τὸ βαλανεῖον καύμασι *PLond.*3.1166.13 (i A.D.). II. *withhold*, Lxx *Ne.*9.20.

**ἀφύτευτος** [ῠ], ον, *not planted*, χῶρος X.*Oec.*20.22.

**ἀφύτρις**· ἀρύταινα (ἄρπαινα cod.), Hsch. (leg. ἀρυστρίς).

**ἀφύω**, *to become white* or *bleached*, Hp.*Int.*40.

**ἀφυώδης**, ες, *whitish, like an* ἀφύη, χρῶμα Hp.*Mul.*2.110,116.

**ἄφωκτος**, ον, *not roasted*, Dieuch.ap.Orib.4.7.21, Gal.12.619.

**ἀφώλιος**, = ἀποφώλιος, Theognost.*Can.*57.

**ἀφων-έω**, *to be speechless*, Hp.*Epid.*1.26.ιγ'. **-ητέω**, = foreg., Sch.A.*Ag.*241. **-ητος**, ον, *unspeakable, unutterable*, ἄχος Pi.*P.*4.237. II. *voiceless, speechless*, παρέσχε φωνὴν τοῖς ἀ. S.*OC* 1283. ※ **-ία**, Ion. **-ίη**, ἡ, *speechlessness*, Hp.*Epid.*3.17.γ', Pl.*Smp.* 198c. II. *mispronunciation*, Philostr.*VA*6.36. **-ος**, ον, (φωνή) *voiceless, dumb*, Thgn.669, Hdt.1.85, D.18.191; ῥήτωρ Antiph.196.14; κακὸν ἄ. *Com.Adesp.*8 D.; stronger than ἄναυδος (q.v.), Hp.*Epid.* 3.17.γ'; εἴδωλα 1*Ep.Cor.*12.2; *unable to speak*, of a child, Sapph.118: c.gen., ἄ. τῆσδε τῆς ἀρᾶς *unable to utter* it, S.*OC*865. Adv. -νως ib.131 (lyr.): neut. pl. as Adv., ἄφωνα σημανοῦσιν.. ὡς.. A.*Pers.*819. 2. *with a poor voice*, τραγῳδός D.T.631.21. 3. *intestate*, *Tab.Heracl.*1.151. 4. ἄφωνα (sc. γράμματα, στοιχεῖα) *consonants*, ἄ. καὶ φωνοῦντα (fort. ἄ. φωνήεντα) E.*Fr.*578.2; τοῖς ἄλλοις φωνήεσί τε καὶ ἄ. Pl.*Cra.*393e; τὸ σῖγμα τῶν ἀ. ἐστί Id.*Tht.*203b: but esp. of *mutes*, τὰ ἄφθογγα καὶ ἄ. Id.*Phlb.*18c, cf. *Cra.*424c; opp. ἡμίφωνα, Arist.*Po.*1456$^b$28, cf. Phld.*Po.*2.16, *Herc.*994.28, D.H.*Comp.*14, D.T.631.20, S.E.*M.*1.102.

**ἀφωντεύς**, fem. **ἀφώντισσα**, title of doubtful meaning, *BGU*1249 (ii B.C.).

**ἀφώρᾱτος**, ον, *not detected*, Oenom.ap.Eus.*PE*5.20. Adv. -τως Ph.2.521.

**ἀφωρισμένως**, (ἀφορίζω) *definitively*, Arist.*Cat.*12$^b$39; *separately, specially*, Plu.2.466a, Aristid.Quint.1.21, Artem.4.84, etc.

**ἄφως**, ωτος, *without light*, Eust.968.48.

**ἀφώτιστος**, ον, *dark, obscure*, J.*AJ*13.11.2, Arr.*Epict.*1.14.10, Plu. 2.931c, Onos.10.13, S.E.*M.*10.164, Orph.*Fr.*272, etc.; ἀ. τοῦ ἡλίου *unlit by* the sun, Gem.11.3: metaph., ψυχή Ph.1.638; φῶς Anon.*in Prm.* in *Rh.Mus.*47.608; σελήνη Nonn.*D.*6.91; *unenlightened*, Plot. 1.2.4.

**ἀχά**, ἡ, v. sub ἠχέω, ἰαχή.

※ **Ἀχαία**, Ion. **Ἀχαιΐη**, ἡ, epith. of Demeter in Attica, Hdt.5.61; also in Boeotia, Plu.2.378e; Ἀχέα at Thespiae, *IG*7.1867. II. **ἀχαιά**, ἡ, = ἔριθος, Philet.ap.Gramm. post Orionem p.185 S. (Acc. to Hsch. from ἄχος *grief* for the loss of her daughter: also **Ἀχηρώ** Id.) **Ἀχαΐα**, v. Ἀχαιός.

**ἀχαίας**· λύπας, Hsch. **ἀχαΐζειν**· ἑλληνίζειν, Id.

※ **Ἀχαικός**, ή, όν, (Ἀχαιός) *of* or *for the Achaians, Achaian*, A.*Ag.* 185,624, E.*Tr.*236, al.

※ **Ἀχαιΐς**, ΐδος, ἡ, *the Achaian land*, with or without γαῖα, Il.1.254, 3.75, etc. 2. (sc. γυνή) *Achaian woman*, Ἀχαιΐδες οὐκέτ' Ἀχαιοί 2.235, etc.:—also ※ **Ἀχαιϊάς**, άδος, 5.424, etc.

**ἀχαιμενίς**, ίδος, ἡ, = πόλιον, Ps.-Dsc.3.110. II. = *Euphorbia antiquorum*, Plin.*HN*24.161.

**ἀχαίνει**· σαίνει, παίζει, κολακεύει, Hsch.

**ἀχαΐνη**, ἡ, a kind of *large loaf*, baked by the women at the Thesmophoria, Semus 13.

**ἀχαΐνης** [ῐ] ἔλαφος *brocket, two-year stag*, Arist.*HA*611$^b$18: gen. ἀχαΐνεω *AP*6.165 (Phal.):—also fem. ἀχαΐνη Arist.*HA*506$^a$24; also ἀχαιΐνη *deer*, Babr.95.87; poet. ἀχαιΐνέη A.R.4.175, Opp.*C.*2.426.

**ἀχαιόμαντις**, εως, ὁ, title of diviner in Cyprus, Hsch.

※ **Ἀχαιός**, ά, όν, *Achaean*, Hom., etc.: hence as Subst., 1. Ἀχαιοί, οἱ, *the Achaeans*, in Hom. for the *Greeks* generally, Il.2.235, etc. 2. **Ἀχαΐα**, ἡ, *Achaia* in Peloponnese, Th., etc.; under the Romans, *the province of Greece*.

**ἄχαιος**, perh. = ἀχήν, *IG*3.1385.

**Ἀχαϊστί**, = *Graeco ritu*, Orac.ap.Phleg.*Mir.*10.

**ἀχάλέπως**, Adv. *without difficulty*, Ph.*Bel.*92.15.

**ἀχάλῑν-ος** [χᾰ], ον, *unbridled*, στόματα E.*Ba.*386 (lyr.), cf. *HF*382 (lyr.), Ar.*Ra.*838, Pl.*Lg.*701c; ἀχάλινα λέγειν *APl.*4.223; ἀ. ὑπ' ἀργύρου, i.e. *uncorrupted* by bribes, *IG*9(1).270 (Atalante): neut. pl. as Adv., E.*HF* l.c. **-ωτος** ον, *unbridled*, ἵππος X.*Eq.*5.3, D.H.9.65, Ph.1.313; στόματα *AP*11.177 (Lucill.); ἀνάγκαι Orph.*H.*55.13.

**ἀχάλιον**, τό, = σιδηρῖτις, = ἀλθαία, *Hippiatr.*11.

**ἀχάλκ-εος**, ον, *without a* χαλκοῦς, *penniless*, ἀ. οὐδός (with a pun on χάλκεος οὐδός) *AP*11.403 (Lucill.). **-ευτος**, ον, *not forged of metal*, πέδαι A.*Ch.*493, Critias 20 D.; τρύπανα S.*Fr.*708. **-έω**, (χαλκοῦς) *to be penniless*, *AP*11.154 (Lucill.). **-ής**, ές, *without brass*, ὁπλαί Tryph.87. **-ος**, ον, *without brass*, ἄχαλκος ἀσπίδων, i.e. ἄνευ ἀσπίδων χαλκείων S.*OT*191 (lyr.). **-ωτος**, ον, lit. *not brazened*: *without money*, κυνοῦχος *AP*6.298 (Leon.).

**ἀχανά**· κλήματα, Hsch.

**ἀχανδής**, ές, dub. in *Anacreont.*56.35.

**ἀχάνεια** [χᾰ], ἡ, (ἀχᾰνής II) *immensity, infinite expanse*, τοῦ ὀπίσω καὶ πρόσω αἰῶνος M.Ant.12.7; *infinite void*, Syrian. *in Metaph.*60.5; εἰς ἀ. λήγειν Olymp. *in Mete.*82.22; ἡ τοῦ ἀπείρου ἀστάθμητος ἀ. Dam. *Pr.*53. 2. Medic., *wide opening, cavity*, Heliod.(?)ap.Orib.46.19.12, Paul.Aeg.6.107.

**ἀχάνη**, ἡ, name of a *Persian* (also, *Boeotian*, Arist.*Fr.*566) *measure*, = 45 μέδιμνοι, Ar.*Ach.*108, 109. 2. *chest, box*, Phanod.25, Plu.*Arat.*6. [ἀχᾱ Ar.*Ach.* ll. cc.]

**ἀχᾰνής**, ές, (χάσκω, χανεῖν) *not opening the mouth*, of one mute with astonishment, Hegesipp.Com.1.25, Plb.7.17.5, Luc.*Icar.*23, Alciphr. 3.20; also δι' ἀχανοῦς through *a narrow opening*, Thphr.*Vent.*29. II. *yawning*, κρημνός Timae.28; χάσμα *AP*9.423 (Bianor), J.*AJ*7.10.2; *without a lid*, Hero *Aut.*28.4; *wide-mouthed*, τεῦχος Diocl.ap.Orib. 5.4.2, cf. Antyll.ib.44.8.12; *open*, ἀ. καὶ ἀνώροφος νεώς D.C.37.17; *open, unoccupied*, of building land, *POxy.*1702.3 (iii A.D.); χάσμα Parm.1.18; σκότος Lxx *Wi.*19.17, cf. Lyr.Anon. in *PFay.*2 ii 20; τὸ ἀχανές *the yawning gulf*, Arist.*Mete.*367$^a$19; ἡ ἀ. χώρα Ph.1.7; ἀχανές· τὸ μὴ ἔχον στέγην.. ἐπὶ τοῦ λαβυρίνθου, S.*Fr.*1030; ὄψει πάντα ἀχανῆ *PMag.Par.*1.1107. 2. generally, *vast, immense*, στράτευμα Plu. 2.866b; πέλαγος Id.*Cic.*6, Jul.*Or.*4.142c.

**ἀχανόωσαν**· ἐπιθυμοῦσαν, Hsch.; cf. ἰχανάω.

※ **ἀχάντιον**, τό, Ion. for ἀκάνθιον, Greg.Cor.pp.414, 649 S.

**ἀχάρακτος** [χᾰ], ον, *not marked* or *branded*, κάμηλος *BGU*13.8 (iii A.D.); *not stamped*, *Ath.Mitt.*33.384 (Pergam.); of ships, *without emblem* or *figurehead*, *PLille*22.6; *not graven* or *cut*, Nonn.*D.* 13.84; *that cannot be cut*, σιδήρῳ γυῖα ἀ. ib.16.158, cf. 26.242.

**ἀχᾰράκωτος** [ρᾰ], ον, *not palisaded*, Plb.10.11.2, Plu.*Mar.*20: metaph., *defenceless, friendless*, Philostr.*VA*5.35. Adv. -τως, αὐλίσασθαι App.*BC*3.70.

**ἀχαρές**· λυπηρόν, Hsch.

**ἀχᾰριότης**, ητος, ἡ, *awkwardness, stupidity*, with a play on the name Χαριμόρτης, dub. in Plb.18.55.2.

※ **ἄχᾰρις**, ὁ, ἡ, ἄχαρι, τό, gen. ιτος, dat. ἀχάρι Hdt.1.41 codd.:—*without grace* or *charm*, συμπόσιον γίνεται οὐκ ἄχαρι Thgn.496, cf. 1236; of an immature girl, Sapph.34. 2. *unpleasant, disagreeable*, οὐδὲν ἄ. πείσεται Hdt.2.141, cf. 6.9; πρός τινος 8.143; οὐδὲν ἄ. παριδεῖν τινι 1.38,108; ἐνδιδόναι οὐδὲν ἄ. 7.52; esp. as euphem. for a *grievous* calamity, ἄ. συμφορή 1.41, 7.190; τὸ τέλος σφι ἐγένετο ἄ. 8.13; [βίος] οὐκ ἄ. εἰς τὴν τριβήν Ar.*Av.*156. II. *ungracious, thankless*, ἄ. τιμή a *thankless* office, Hdt.7.36; χάρις ἄχαρις *graceless* grace, *thankless* favour, A.*Pr.*545 (lyr.), *Ag.*1545 (lyr.); κακῆς γυναικὸς χάριν ἄχαριν ἀπώλετο E.*IT*566.

**ἀχᾰριστ-έω**, *show ingratitude*, Antipho Soph.54, Phld.*Herc.*1251.17, *Hom.*p.59 O.; πρὸς τοὺς φίλους X.*Mem.*2.2.2; τινί *Vit.Philonid.* p.13 C., Plu.*Phoc.*36; τινί τινος D.H.7.60. 2. *disoblige*, τοῖς κακοῖς καὶ νοσώδεσιν ἀ. Pl.*Smp.*186c, cf. *SIG*495.159 (iii B.C.), Luc.*DMar.* 9.2, Nic.Dam.p.5 D. 3. Pass., *to be treated ungratefully*, Plb.22.11.8, Corn.*ND*16, J.*BJ*2.16.4, Plu.*Cam.*13, Just.*Nov.*98 *Pr.*; ὑπό τινος Plu.*Mar.*28. **-ία**, ἡ, *ingratitude*, X.*Cyr.*1.2.7; εἰς ἀ. ἄγειν D.18.316: in pl., ἀχαριστίαι πρὸς ἀνθρώπους Phld.*Herc.*1251.10; ὀλιγωρίας καὶ ἀ. ib.1457.9. 2. *ungraciousness*, ἀρρυθμία καὶ ἀ. Pl.*R.*411e. **-ος**, ον, (χᾰρίζομαι) *ungracious, unpleasant*, οὐκ ἀχάριστα μεθ' ἡμῖν ταῦτ' ἀγορεύεις Od.8.236: irreg. Comp., δόρπου ἀχαρίστερον (for -ιστότερον) 20.392; *without grace* or *charm*, οὐκ ἀχάριστα λέγειν X.*An.*2.1.13; φωνή Epicur.*Sent.Vat.*75; -ότερον ἐπιμέλημα a *more thankless* business, X.*Oec.*7.37; ἀ. ἐξέτασις D.H.*Pomp.*1. II. of persons, *ungracious, unfavourable*, Thgn.841 (-τως Bgk.), Phld.*Ir.*p.60 W. 2. *ungrateful, thankless*, Hdt.1.90, X.*Cyr.*1.2.7, Crates Theb. 19, etc.; δῆμος Hdt.5.91; προδότας E.*Ion*880 (lyr.), cf. *Med.*659 (lyr.); ἀ. πρὸς τοὺς γονέας X.*Mem.*2.2.14; τινί E.*Hec.*138 (lyr.); σπείρων εἰς ἀχάριστα sowing in *thankless soil*, *IG*14.2012 (Sulp. Max.). Adv. -τως, ἀποπέμψασθαι εὐεργέτας X.*An.*7.7.23, cf. Lys.30.6. 3. Pass., *unrequited*, ἀ. εἶναι τὰ ἀνηλωμένα Lys.21.12. Adv. οὐκ ἂν ἀχαρίστως μοι ἔχοι πρός τινος *thanks* would not be *refused* me by.., X. *An.*2.3.18. 4. Adv. -τως *with a bad grace, with an ill will*, ἀ. ἕπεσθαι follow *sulkily*, Id.*Cyr.*7.4.14; τὰς χάριτας ἀ. χαρίζεσθαι Isoc.1.31. 5. ἀχάριστον, τό, *antidote*, *PGrenf.*1.52.1,12 (iii A.D.), Marcell. Empir.20: also ἀχάριστος, ἡ, Alex.Trall.*Febr.*7. b. name of an *eyesalve*, Cels.6.6.7, Gal.12.749.

※ **ἀχάρῑτος** [χᾰ], ον, = foreg., *unseemly*, Plu.*Sol.*20; euphem., παθήματα ἀ. ἐόντα μαθήματα γέγονε Hdt.1.207. Adv. οὐκ -τως ἔφη Ath.7.281c, cf. Hermog.*Id.*2.11, D.C.66.9. 2. *ungrateful, thankless*, δῆμον εἶναι συνοίκημα ἀχαριτώτατον Hdt.7.156; χάρις ἀ. A.*Ch.*42 (lyr., Elmsl.), E.*Ph.*1757 (lyr.).

**Ἀχαρναί**, ῶν, αἱ, *Acharnae*, a famous deme of Attica, Th.2.19 sq.:—**Ἀχαρνεύς**, έως, ὁ, *inhabitant of Acharnae*, pl. Ἀχαρνῆς, title of play by Ar.: poet. **Ἀχαρνηΐδαι** Ar.*Ach.*322:—Adj. **Ἀχαρνικός**, ή, όν, ib. 180; Ἀ. κισσός, = κορυμβίας, Thphr.*HP*3.18.6:—also **Ἀχαρνίτης**, ου, ὁ, κισσός *AP*7.21 (Simm.):—Adv. **Ἀχαρνῆσι** *at Acharnae*, Luc.*Icar.* 18: **Ἀχαρνῆθεν** *from Acharnae*, Anaxandr.41.18.

**ἀχαρνώς**, ώ, ὁ, = ὀρφώς, a *sea-fish*, prob. *bass*, Callias Com.3: **ἄχαρνος** in Ath.3.286b: **ἀχάρνας** Arist.*HA*602$^a$12; gen. ἀχάρνου ib. 591$^b$1:—also **ἀχάρνα** and **ἄχερλα**, names of *fish* in Hsch.

**ἀχάσμητος**, ον, *without hiatus*, Eust.919.35.

**ἀχάτης** [ἄχᾱ], ου, ὁ, *agate*, Thphr.*Lap.*31, J.*AJ*3.7.5, D.P.1075, Nonn.*D.*5.170.

**ἀχεδών**, Dor. for ἠχεδών, f.l. in Mosch.3.54.

**ἄχει** or **ἄχι**, τό, *reed-grass*, Lxx *Ge.*41.2, al.; used for *lamp-wick*, *PMag.Par.*1.1091,1101. (Egyptian word.)

**ἀχείμ-αντος**, ον, *not stormy*, βληχρῶν ἀνέμων ἀ. πνόαι Alc.16; *not vexed by storms*, Μέμφις B.*Fr.*22:—also **-αστος**, ον, θάλασσα J.*AJ* 3.5.3: **-ᾰτος**, ον, A.*Supp.*136 (lyr.): **-ερος**, ον, Arat.1121: **-ων**, ον, gen. ονος, Nonn.*D.*1.142.

※ **ἄχειρ**, ρος, *without hands*, ἄποδα καὶ ἄ. [ζῷα] Arist.*HA*515$^b$24; ἄ. καὶ ἄποδας [Ἑρμᾶς] Plu.2.797f, cf. Corn.*ND*16; τὰ ἄ. *hinder parts*, X. *Cyr.*3.3.45.

**ἀχειρ-ἄγώγητος**, ον, *untamed*, Ph.1.680. **-άπτητος**, ον, *not touched by hand*, Iamb.*VP*29.157. ※ **-ής**, ές, = ἄχειρ, καρκίνοι Batr. 298: metaph., = ἀχρεῖος, Hsch. II. *not made with hands*, ἄγαλμα B.9.11. **-ία**, ἡ, *want of hands*: hence, *awkwardness*, Hp.*Morb.* 1.1, Apollon.Cit.1. **-ίδωτος** [ρῐ], ον, *without sleeves*, *Dialex.*2.9, Sch.Luc.*Vit.Auct.*7.

**ἀχειρο-ποίητος**, ον, *not made by hands*, of buildings and statues, *Ev.Marc.*14.58, 2*Ep.Cor.*5.1; ἀ. περιτομή, i.e. *spiritual*, *Ep.Col.*2.11. **-τόνητος**, ον, *not elected*, D.19 Arg. ii 13. II. *not granted by vote*, τιμή Max.Tyr.12.5.

**ἀχειρούργητος**, ον, = sq., Poll.2.154.

**ἀχείρωτος**, ον, *untamed, unconquered*, Th.6.10, D.S.5.15. II. ἀ. φύτευμα, of the olive, *not planted by man's hand*, S.*OC*698 (lyr.).

**ἀχέλιον**· τὸ λεπτομερές, Hsch. **ἀχέλουρις**· ποίμνη τις (Tarent.), Id.

⊛ **Ἀχελωΐδες** (sc. νῆσοι), αἱ, *islands at the mouth of the Achelous*, A. *Pers.*869 (lyr.).

⊛ **Ἀχελῷος**, poet. **Ἀχελώϊος**, ὁ, *Achelous*, name of several rivers, Il.21.194, 24.616, Hes.*Th.*340, Str.9.5.10, etc. II. in Poets, *any stream*: generally, *water*, S.*Fr.*5, E.*Ba.*625, Ar.*Fr.*351, Achae.9, Ephor.27.

**ἄχερδος** [ᾰ], ἡ (less freq. ὁ, Theoc.24.90), *wild pear, Pyrus amygdaliformis*, Od.14.10, S.*OC*1596, Pherecyd.33 J., Theoc. l.c.; ἀ. τῆς ἀκραχολωτάτης Pherecr.164: special kind at Ceos, Arist.*Mir.*845ᵃ15.

**Ἀχερδούσιος**, *inhabitant of the deme* Ἀχερδοῦς: hence with play on ἄχερδος, *Crabby*, μοχθηρὸς ὢν καὶ τὴν γνώμην Ἀχερδούσιος *Com. Adesp.*1277; cf. ἀχραδούσιος.

**ἄχερλα**, v. ἀχαρνώς.

**Ἀχερόντειος**, α, ον, *of Acheron*, ναῦς Call.*Hec.*31.3:—also **Ἀχερόντιος**, E.*Alc.*443 (lyr.), Ar.*Ra.*471:—fem. **Ἀχεροντιάς**, άδος, νύξ *AP*5.240 (Paul. Sil.): and **Ἀχερούσιος**, α, ον (also ος, ον A. *Ag.*1160), Th.1.46:—fem. **Ἀχερουσιάς**, άδος, X.*An.*6.2.2, Pl.*Phd.*113a.

**ἀχερωΐς**, ΐδος, ἡ, *white poplar, Populus alba*, elsewh. λευκή, Il.13.389, A.R.4.1476. (Expld. with ref. to Ἀχέρων, from the legend that it had been brought from the nether world by Hercules, Paus.5.14.2.) II. Ἀχερωΐδες ὄχθαι *of* the river *Acheron* in Asia Minor, Nic.*Al.*13.

**Ἀχέρων**, οντος, ὁ, *Acheron*, river in the nether world, Od.10.513, etc.; of other rivers, Th.1.46, Str.6.1.5, etc.

**ἀχέτας** or **ἀχέτᾱ**, Dor. and Att. for ἠχέτης (q.v.).

⊛ **ἀχεύω** and **ἀχέω** (A) [ᾰ], Ep. Verbs used in pres. part., *grieving, mourning*, ὀδυρόμενος καὶ ἀχεύων Il.9.612, Od.2.23; κεῖτ' ἀχέων Il.2.724; ἀχέουσά περ ἔμπης Od.15.361, cf. Sapph.*Supp.*1.11: c. acc., κῆρ ἀχέων *grieving in* heart, Il.5.399; θυμὸν ἀχεύων ib.869, 18.461, Hes. *Op.*399: c. neut. Adj., πυκινόν περ ἀχεύων Od.11.88; μέγ' ἀχεύων 16.139: c. gen. causae, τῆς ἀχέων *sorrowing for* her, Il.2.694, 18.446; Ὀδυσσῆος μέγ' ἀχεύων Od.16.139; so ἕνεκ' ἀλλοτρίων ἀχέων Il.20.298; τοῦγ' εἵνεκα θυμὸν ἀχεύων Od.21.318; later ἐπὶ σφετέροις ἀχέουσα παισί A.R.3.643. II. other forms (chiefly Ep.): 1. in causal sense, *vex, annoy*, redupl. aor. 2 ἤκαχε (but part. ἀκαχών intr., *grieving*, Hes.*Th.*868): hence redupl. pres. **ἀκᾰχίζω**, fut. **ἀκαχήσω**, aor. 1 **ἀκάχησα**: c. acc. pers., μέγα δ' ἤκαχε λαόν Il.16.822, cf. Od.16.427; ἐμὲ μεγάλως ἀκαχίζεις ib.432; θανὼν ἀκάχησε τοκῆας by his death, Il.23.223; ἐ μάλιστα ἤκαχ' ἀποφθιμένη Od.15.357; ἀκαχήσεις μηλοβοτῆρας *h.Merc.*286. 2. Pass., **ἄχομαι, ἄχνῠμαι, ἀκᾰχίζομαι**, imper. ἀκαχίζεο, -ίζευ, Il.6.486, Od.11.486: pf. ἀκάχημαι 8.314, Ep. 3 pl. ἀκηχέδαται (with v.l. ἀκηχέαται) Il.17.637; imper. ἀκάχησο A.R.4.1324; inf. ἀκάχησθαι Il.19.335; part. ἀκαχήμενος (accent. as a pres.) ib.312, Ep. also ἀκηχέμενος 5.364, 18.29: plpf. ἀκαχήατο 12.179: aor. 2, 3 pl. ἀκάχοντο Od.16.342; opt. ἀκαχοίμην, -οιτο, -οίμεθα, 1.236, Il.13.344, 16.16, etc.:—in later Ep. pres. ἀκάχονται, impf. ἀκάχοντο, Q.S.3.224, 5.652:—Constr.: abs., ἄχομαι Od.18.256, 19.129; ἄχνυται Il.18.62; ἀχνύμενος, like ἀχέων or ἀχεύων, 1.103, 241, etc.; ἀχνυμένη κραδίη 24.584; ἀχνύμενος κῆρ 7.428, 431, etc.; ἀκαχήμενος ἦτορ Od.9.62, etc.; θυμὸν ἀκηχέμεναι Il.18.29; ἀκαχήατο θυμόν 12.179: less freq. c. dat., ἀκαχίζεο θυμῷ 6.486; also κῆρ ἄχνυται ἐν θυμῷ, ἄχνυτο.. θυμὸς ἐνὶ στήθεσσιν 6.524, 14.38: c. gen. causae, *grieve for*, sts. with a part., ἀχνύμενός περ ἑταίρου, υἷος ἑοῖο, etc., 8.125, 24.550, etc.; σεῖο.. ἀχνύμεθα φθιμένοιο Od.11.558, cf. 14.376, Il.16.16; less freq. c. dat., οὔ κε θανόντι περ ὧδ' ἀκαχοίμην Od.1.236; ἀχνυμένη περὶ παιδί *h.Cer.*77: later c. acc., *lament*, τὸ δ' ἄχνυμαι Pi.*P.*7.16; ἀχνύμενος μόρον Ἀντιγόνης S.*Ant.*627: with part., δρόων ἀκάχημαι Od.8.314, cf. Il.17.637; μή τι θανὼν ἀκαχίζευ Od.11.486, cf. Il.6.486.—Once in Trag., S. l.c.; never in Prose.

**ἀχέω** (B) [ᾰ], poet. form for ἰᾰχέω, *utter*, *h.Cer.*479, prob. l. in *h.Hom.*19.18; ἣν ἄτην ἀχέων Hes.*Sc.*93 codd.; ὕμνον ἀχέων Ion Trag.39: fut. ἀχήσεται *Trag.Adesp.*237.

**ἀχέω** (C) [ᾱ], Dor. for ἠχέω (q.v.).

**ἄχηλος**, ον, *with undivided hoof*, Gal.2.431.

**ἀχήλωτος**, ον, *not barbed*, Ph.*Bel.*73.43, 75.35.

⊛ **ἀχήν** [ᾱ], ὁ, ἡ, Dor., = ἠχήν (q.v.), *poor, needy*, Theoc.16.33: dat. pl. ἀχήνεσσιν Epigr. in *BCH*11.161 (Lagina).

**ἀχηνεῖς**· κενοί, Hsch.

**ἀχηνία** [ᾰ], ἡ, *need, want*, χρημάτων A.*Ch.*301; φίλων ἀχηνίᾳ Ar. *Fr.*20, cf. 1 D.; ὀμμάτων ἐν ἀχηνίαις in the eyes' *blank gaze*, A.*Ag.*418 (lyr.).

**ἀχηρής**, v.l. for ἀχθηρής, Suid.

**ἄχηρον**· ἀκρίδα (Cret.), Hsch. **Ἀχηρώ**, v. Ἀχαία. **ἀχητεῖς**· ἀζήτητοι, ἀσύνετοι, ἄποροι, Id.

**Ἀχθεία**· ἡ Δημήτηρ, μυστικῶς, Hsch.

**ἀχθ-εινός**, ή, όν, (ἄχθος) *burdensome, oppressive*, of persons, E. *Hipp.*94; of things, Id.*Hec.*1240; τὸ -ότατον τοῦ βίου X.*Mem.*4.8.1; βοοκτασία, i.e. *that cost* the slayer *dear*, *AP*6.263 (Leon.). Adv. -νῶς *unwillingly*, οὐκ ἀ. δρᾶν τι X.*HG*4.8.27. II. *laborious*, βόες *IG*14.2012.16 (Sulp. Max.). ⊛ **-έω**, *load*, in aor. part. ἀχθήσας, Hsch. **-ηδών**, όνος, ἡ, *weight, burden*, ἀ. κακοῦ A.*Pr.*26. 2. metaph., *vexation, annoyance*, Th.2.37, Pl.*Lg.*734a; ἐρέσθαι τινὰ δι' ἀχθηδόνα for the sake of *teasing*, Th.4.40; μὴ πρὸς ἀχθηδόνα μου ἀκούσῃς Luc.*Tox.*9. **-ήεις**, εσσα, εν, *grievous*, κάματος Marc. Sid.96. **-ήμων**, ον, gen. ονος, *suffering*, Man.4.501. **-ηρής**, ές, = sq., Hsch. ⊛ **-ηρός**, όν, *grievous*, dub. l. in Antiph.94. **-ηφορέω**, v.l. for ἀχθοφορέω, D.H.4.81, Ph.2.604, D.C.72.12:—so **ἀχθηφόρος**, for -οφόρος, Id.62.6. **-ίζω**, *load*, Ἄραψ κάμηλον ἀχθίσας Babr.8.1.

**ἄχθομαι**, Pass.: fut. Med. ἀχθέσομαι Ar.*Nu.*865, 1441, *Av.*84, Pl.*R.*603e, *Hp.Ma.*292e; Pass., ἀχθεσθήσομαι And.3.21, Pl.*Grg.*506c, v.l. in X.*Cyr.*8.4.10, (συν-) Aeschin.3.242: pf. ἤχθημαι Lyc.827: aor. ἠχθέσθην Hdt.2.103, A.*Pr.*392, Th.6.15, Isoc.12.17:—*to be loaded*, ὅτε δὴ κοίλη νηῦς ἤχθετο Od.15.457: c. gen., τράπεζα τυροῦ καὶ μέλιτος πίονος ἀχθομένη Xenoph.1.10: c. dat., ἐλάτην.. ἀχθομένην ὄζοις A.R.1.1191. II. mostly of mental oppression, *to be vexed, grieved*:—Constr.: abs., ἤχθετο γὰρ κῆρ Il.11.274, cf. A.*Pr.*392; ὅτῳ μὴ ἀχθομένῳ εἴη (constr. like ἀσμένῳ, βουλομένῳ ἐστί) X.*Cyr.*4.5.21; ἀχθομένην ὀδύνῃσι Il.5.354; ἄ. τινί *at* a thing, or *with* a person, Hdt. 2.103, 3.1, al., Ar.*Ach.*62, *Pax*119, Th.6.28, etc.; μοι μὴ ἄχθεσθε λέγοντι τἀληθῆ Pl.*Ap.*31e, cf. *Men.*99e: with Preps., ἐπί τινι X.*HG* 7.1.32, etc.; ἐφ' ἑκάστου Pl.*Prm.*130a; περὶ τῶν νεῶν Hdt.8.99; ὑπέρ τινος Ar.*Lys.*10, Pl.*Ap.*23e; διά τινα Isoc.12.17: also c. acc., λίην ἄχθομαι ἕλκος Il.5.361: c. neut. Adj., τοῦτο X.*An.*3.2.20; μεῖζον Pl. *Smp.*216c: c. gen., τῆς οἰκίας Plu.*Publ.*10: c. part., either of subject, οὐκ ἄχθομαί σ' ἰδών τε καὶ λαβὼν φίλον S.*Ph.*671, cf. Ar.*Pl.*234, Th.1.92, X.*Cyr.*3.3.20, Pl.*Prt.*342c, etc.; or of object, ἤχθετο δαμναμένους *at* their being conquered, Il.13.352; Ἀρίσταρχον στρατηγοῦντ' ἄ. Eup.43: but the part. of the object is also put in gen., οὐδὲν ἤχθετο αὐτῶν πολεμούντων he *had no objection to*.., X.*An.*1.1.8, cf. Th.1.95: folld. by a relat. clause, ἄ. εἰ.., or ἤν.., E.*IA*1413, Th.8.109, Pl.*Hp.Ma.*292e; less freq. ἄ. ὅτι.. Ar.*Pl.*899, X.*Cyr.*3.3.13, Pl.*R.*549c.

⊛ **ἄχθος**, εος, τό, *burden, load*, Il.12.452, Hes.*Op.*692, Tyrt.6, etc.; ἄχθεα δυνατώτεραι φέρειν, of camels, Hdt.3.102, cf. 1.80, Ar.*Ra.*9, Th.4.115; ἄ. οὐκ εὐάγκαλον A.*Pr.*352; ἄ. ἀρούρης *cumberers of* the ground, Il.18.104, Od.20.379, etc.; περισσὸν ἄ. γυναικῶν *plague* of women, S.*El.*1241 (lyr.); γῆς ἄλλως ἄχθη Pl.*Tht.*176d; ἄ. μυρία γαίης *pests*, Nic.*Th.*9: but φίλτατον ἄχθος, of a corpse, E.*Rh.*379 (lyr.): metaph., δίδυμον ἄ. double *burden* of praise, Pi.*N.*6.57. II. *load of grief*, χάρμα καὶ ἄ. Hes.*Sc.*400; ἀπὸ φροντίδος ἄ... βαλεῖν A. *Ag.*166; λύπης ἄ. S.*El.*120 (lyr.), cf. *Ant.*1172; φέρειν ἄχθη κακῶν E.*IT*710; ἄ. φέρειν bring or cause *sorrow*, X.*Ep.*1.

**ἀχθο-φορέω**, *bear burdens*, Plb.4.32.7, Plu.*Mar.*13; *to be loaded*, ἡ κοιλία Hp.*Acut.*28. 2. *bear as a burden*, νέκυν *AP*7.468 (Mel.); κριόν *IG*14.1301; ὄστρακον *APl.*4.333 (Antiphil.). **-φορία**, ἡ, *bearing of burdens*, βαρῶν Plu.2.113cd (pl.), cf. Luc.*Asin.*19; μυρμήκων M.Ant.7.3; *any heavy pressure*, Hp.*Art.*63. **-φόρος**, ον, *bearing burdens*, κτήνεα Hdt.7.187; ὑποζύγια D.H.1.85; μύρμηκες Ael.*NA* 2.25. II. as Subst., *porter*, Gell.5.3.2, Luc.*Herod.*5.

**ἀχι**, v. ἄχει.

**ἀχίαστος** [ῐ], ον, *not arranged chiastically*, περίοδος Sch.Isoc.8.102. Adv. -τως Jo.Sic. in Rh.6.343 W.

**Ἀχίλλειος**, α, ον, *of Achilles*, E.*Tr.*39, etc.; poet. Ἀχιλλήϊος Theoc. 29.34: Ion. **Ἀχιλλήϊος** Hdt.4.55, 76; used in lyr. by S.*Fr.*152:—fem. **Ἀχιλλῆτις** (v. infr.), also **Ἀχιλλεΐτις**, ιδος, D.L.1.74. II. Ἀχίλλειαι κριθαί, *a fine* kind of barley, Ath.3.114f; also κριθαὶ Ἀχιλλήϊδες Hp.*Morb.*3.17; κριθὴ Ἀχιλλῆτις Thphr.*HP*8.10.2; Ἀ. μᾶζαι cakes *of fine barley*, Pherecr.130.4; Ἀχιλλείων ἀπομάττεσθαι (v. sub ἀπομάσσω) Ar.*Eq.*819; Ἀχίλλειον, τό, a *cake of this sort*, Eust.1414.33. 2. Ἀ. (sc. σπόγγος), ὁ, *fine* kind of *sponge*, used as padding for the inside of helmets, greaves, etc., Arist.*HA*548ᵇ1 and 20. 3. Ἀχίλλειος, ὁ, = μυριόφυλλον, Ps.-Dsc.4.114. b. *Achilles woundwort*, Crateuas *Fr.*3, Dsc.4.36, Plin.*HN*25.42.

⊛ **Ἀχιλλεύς**, Ep. also **Ἀχιλεύς**, gen. Ἀχιλλέως (either quadrisyll. or trisyll., as the metre requires, cf. S.*Ph.*4, 50 with 57, 364): acc. Ἀχιλλέα ib.331, 358, voc. Ἀχιλλεῦ: Ep. gen. Ἀχιλλῆος, etc.:—*Achilles*. II. the fallacy vulgarly called '*Achilles* and the Tortoise', invented by Zeno of Elea, Arist.*Ph.*239ᵇ14, D.L.9.29.

**ἄχῑλος**, ον, *without grass*, or (with ἀ- intens.) *rich in grass*, both senses in Hsch. s.v. ἄχειλον.

**ἀχιόνιστος**, ον, *not snowed upon*, Sch.Od.6.44.

**ἀχίτων** [ῐ], ον, gen. ωνος, *without tunic*, i.e. wearing the ἱμάτιον only, of Socrates, X.*Mem.*1.6.2; of Agesilaus, Ael.*VH*7.13, Plu.2.210b, cf. 276c; of Cleanthes the Stoic, D.L.7.169; of Gelon, ἀ. ἐν ἱματίῳ D.S.11.26.

**ἀχλαιν-ία**, ἡ, (χλαῖνα) *want of a cloak* or *mantle*, E.*Hel.*1282. **-ος**, ον, *without cloak* or *mantle*, Simon.167.3, Call.*Dian.*115, Lyc.763; βίος ib.635.

**ἄχλαξ**· κάχληξ, Suid.

**ἀχλάς**, άδος, ἡ, late form of ἀχράς (q.v.), Sch.Theoc.1.134.

**ἄχλοος**, ον, contr. **ἄχλους**, ουν, (χλόα) *without herbage*, E.*Hel.*1327 (lyr.). II. *sere, withered*, Opp.*H.*2.496. III. *discoloured*, Hp.*Coac.*596.

**ἀχλυδιᾶν**· θρύπτεσθαι, Hsch.

**ἀχλύμενος**· λυπούμενος, Hsch. (leg. ἀχν-).

**ἀχλύνω**, = ἀχλύω II, Q.S.2.550 (Pass.).

⊛ **ἀχλῠό-εις**, εσσα, εν, *dark, gloomy, dismal*, δεσμός Epigr.ap.Hdt.5.77; *darkened*, καπνῷ ἀ. αἰθὴρ πέλεν A.R.4.927, cf. Arat.908, Nonn. *D.*9.65, al.; of colour, ἰχώρ Opp.*H.*3.163; *cloudy*, of urine, Ruf.*Fr.*79.26. 2. *secret*, γάμος Musae.3. **-πεζα**, ἡ, *fringed* or *bordered with gloom*, ἠώς Tryph.210.

**ἀχλυόω**, *darken, make dim*, Aret.*CD*1.3:—Pass., *become gloomy, grow dark*, Thphr.*Vent.*35; *become dim*, Syn.Alch.p.58 B.

**ἀχλύς**, ύος, ἡ, (acc. ἀχλύα Orph.*A.*341) *mist*, Od.20.357; elsewh. in Hom. of *a mist over the eyes*, as of one dying, κατὰ δ' ὀφθαλμῶν κέχυτ' ἀ. Il.5.696; as result of ulceration, ἀχλύες Hp.*Prorrh.*2.20, cf. Thphr.*HP*7.6.2, Dsc.2.78 (pl.), Aët.7.27; or in emotion, Ἔρως πολλὴν κατ' ἀχλὺν ὀμμάτων ἔχευεν Archil.103; of drunkenness, πρὸς ὄμμ' ἀ. ἀμβλωπὸς ἐφίζει Critias 6.11 D.; of one whom a god deprives of the power of seeing and knowing others, κατ' ὀφθαλμῶν χέεν ἀχλύν Il.20.321; ἀπ' ὀφθαλμῶν σκέδασ' ἀχλύν ib.341, cf. 5.127, 15.668:—personified as *Sorrow*, πὰρ δ' Ἀχλὺς εἱστήκει ἐπισμυγερή τε καὶ αἰνή, χλωρή, ἀϋσταλέη Hes.*Sc.*264. 2. metaph., δνοφεράν τιν' ἀχλύν.. αὐδᾶται A.*Eu.*379 (lyr.), cf. *Pers.*668 (lyr.); ἀχλὺν ἀπὸ τῆς ψυχῆς ἀφελεῖν D.C.38.19; διάνοια ἀχλύος γέμουσα Plu.2.42c. 3. ἀ. ὑγρή liquid emitted by cuttlefish, Opp.*H.*3.158.—Mostly poet., but used by Hp. (v. supr.) and Arist.*Mete.*367ᵇ17, 373ᵇ12 (pl.): also in later Prose, Plb.34.11.15, Str.6.2.8, and v. supr. 2. [ῡ in nom. and acc. sg., Hom., Hes.: ῠ in later poets.]

**ἄχλυσις**, εως, ἡ, *dimming, clouding*, Syn.Alch.p.58 B.

**ἀχλύω**, aor. 1 ἤχλῡσα, *to be* or *grow dark*, ἤχλυσε δὲ πόντος ὑπ' αὐτῆς (sc. νεφέλης) Od.12.406; ὄμματα δ' αὔτως ἤχλυσαν A.R.3.963. II. trans., *darken*, Q.S.1.598, Nonn.*D.*4.368, Pancrat.*Oxy.*1085.12.

**ἀχλῠώδης**, ες, *hazy, misty*, νότοι Hp.*Aph.*3.5, Arist.*Mete.*367ᵃ20; ἀέρες Str.17.3.8; ἡμέρα App.*Syr.*33; κορυφή D.Chr.1.68; *dim*, of sight, ὄψις -εστέρα Gal.16.224; *dark*, of complexion or appearance, Aret.*CA*2.4, *SD*2.13.

**ἀχνάζω**, Aeol. **ἀχνάσδημι**, (ἄχος) *to be miserable*, Alc.81.

**ἄχνη**, Dor. **ἄχνα**, ἡ, *anything that comes off the surface*: I. of liquids, *foam, froth*, in Hom. of the sea, Od.12.238, al.; ἁλὸς ἀ. 5.403, cf. Tim.*Pers.*95, A.R.2.570; θοὴν ἀπερεύγεται ἄχνην, of a river, D.P.693: Medic., *exudation*, Hp.*Int.*1; οἰνωπὸς ἀ. *froth* of wine, E.*Or.*115; ἄχνα οὐρανία *dew* of heaven, S.*OC*681 (lyr.); δακρύων ἄχνα *dewy* tears, Id.*Tr.*848 (lyr.); also ἄχνη πυρός, i.e. smoke, A.*Fr.*336. II. of solids, *chaff*, in pl., ὡς δ' ἄνεμος ἄχνας φορέει Il.5.499; καρπόν τε καὶ ἄχνας ib.501; *down* on the quince, μῆλον λεπτῇ πεποκωμένον ἀ. *AP*6.102 (Phil.); ἄχνη ἡ ἀφ' ἡμιτυβίου *fluff, shreds*, used for *lint*, Hp.*Art.*37; ὀθονίου Id.*Mochl.*2; ἀ. Λυδῆς κερκίδος, of *fine-spun* fabrics, S.*Fr.*45; ἀ. χαλκίτιδος metallic *dust*, Plu.2.659c, cf. Orph.*L.*455; ἄχναι *wall-decorations*, dub. in Aret.*CA*1.1 (*stramina* Cael. Aur.). III. ἄχνην in acc., as Adv., *morsel, the least bit*, ἣν δ' οὖν καταμύσῃ κἂν ἄχνην Ar.*V.*92. IV. πυρὸς ἀ., = χαμελαία, Dsc.4.171; = θυμελαία, ib.172. V. ἄχναν· τὴν οἴκησιν, Hsch.

**ἀχνηκώς**, v. ἄγω. **ἄχνημος**· νῆστις, Hsch. **ἀχνητόν**· δαψιλές, κτλ., Id.

**ἄχνοος**, ον, contr. **ἄχνους**, ουν, *without down*, Ἑρμῆς *AP*6.259 (Phil.), cf. 242 (Crin.), Q.S.4.431, Nonn.*D.*10.180: metaplast. acc. pl. ἄχνοας Man.1.126.

**ἀχνοῦχος**, ὁ, dub. sens. in *PMag.Leid.W.*8.21 (perh. 'Lord of the Foam').

**ἄχνυλα**· κάρυα (Cret.), Hsch.

**ἄχνυμαι**, v. ἀχεύω, ἀχέω.

**ἀχνύς**, ύος, ἡ, = ἄχος, Call.*Fr.anon.*79.

**ἀχνώδης**, ες, *like, of the nature of* ἄχνη, Hsch.

**ἄχολος**, ον, *lacking gall*, Hp.*Prorrh.*1.98; *lacking a gall-bladder*, ἧπαρ ἀ. Arist.*HA*506ᵇ2; τὰ μώνυχα ἀ. Id.*PA*677ᵃ33; *deficient in bile* (with allusion to signf. 2), Plot.4.4.28. 2. metaph., πόλιος τᾶς ἀχόλω Alc.37 A, cf. Plu.*Daed.*2. II. Act., *allaying bile* or *anger*, φάρμακον.. νηπενθές τ' ἄχολόν τε Od.4.221.

**ἄχομαι**, v. ἀχεύω, ἀχέω.

**ἄχονδρος**, ον, *without cartilage*, Arist.*Spir.*484ᵃ29.

**ἄχορα**· τὰ πίτυρα, ἔνιοι δὲ κρανίον, Hsch.

**ἄχορδος**, ον, *without strings*, μέλος Poet.ap.Arist.*Rh.*1408ᵃ6: φόρμιγξ ἀ., metaph. of a bow, Thgn.Trag.1 (= *Lyr.Adesp.*127).

**ἀχόρευτος**, ον, *not trained in the dance* or *chorus*, Pl.*Lg.*654a; *not joining in the dance*, Nonn.*D.*44.125, al. II. *not attended with the dance*, γάμος Musae.274; esp. in bad sense, *ill suiting it, joyless*, ὀνείδη S.*El.*1069 (lyr.); ἆται E.*Tr.*121 (lyr.); φάρα Telest.1.8.

**ἀχορηγ-ησία**, ἡ, *want of supplies*, Plb.5.28.4, 28.8.6. **-ητος**, ον, *without supplies*, *IG*1².187, Arist.*EN*1099ᵃ33; ἀ. τῶν ἀναγκαίων Id.*Pol.*1288ᵇ32.

**ἄχορος**, ον, *without the dance*, epith. of Ares, to mark the horrors of war, A.*Supp.*681 (lyr.); of death, μοῖρ'.. ἄλυρος, ἀ. S.*OC*1222 (lyr.); ἀ. στοναχαί v.l. in E.*Andr.*1037 (lyr.).

**ἀχόρτ-αστος**, ον, *unfed, starving*, τύχη Men.690, Sm.*Ps.*58(59).16; = ἄπληστος, Hsch.:—hence Subst. **-ασία**, ἡ, *ravenous hunger*, Sm.*De.*28.20.

**ἄχος** [ᾰ], εος, τό, *pain, distress*, in Hom. always of mind, ἄχος αἰνόν, ἄλαστον, ἄτλητον, ὀξύ, Il.4.169, al.; ἄχεος νεφέλη μέλαινα 17.591; ἄχε' ἄκριτα 3.412; τὸν δ' εἷλεν ἄχος κραδίαν B.10.85; also of physical ills, Pi.*P.*3.50 (pl.); δειμάτων ἄχη A.*Ch.*586 (lyr.); ἀκοῦ δ' ἄχος, with a play on the words, S.*Tr.*1035; οὐράνι' ἄχη A.*Pers.*573 (lyr.); ἐμοὶ δ' ἄχε', ἄχεα κατέλιπε Ar.*Ra.*1353 (paratrag.), cf. 1531 (hex.).—Rare in Prose, ἡ παῖς ἀπήγξατο ὑπὸ ἄχεος Hdt.2.131; ἀ. αὐτὸν ἔλαβεν X.*Cyr.*5.5.6, cf. Plu.*Cor.*20.

**ἀχος**, Dor. for. ἦχος.

**ἀχράαντος** [ρᾱ], ον, poet. for ἄχραντος (q.v.), Call.*Ap.*111.

**ἀχραδῆναι**· ζῷά τινα ξυλοφάγα, Hsch.

**ἀχράδινος** [ρᾰ], η, ον, *of the* ἀχράς, ξύλον Dsc.*Alex.*23.

**Ἀχρᾰδούσιος**, formed from ἀχράς, as if the name of a δῆμος, *Crabby*, Ar.*Ec.*362; cf. Ἀχερδούσιος.

**ἀχρᾱής**, ές, gen. έος, = sq., Nic.*Th.*846; ψυχρὸν ἀ. *pure* cold water, *AP*9.314 (Anyte).

**ἀχρᾰνής**, ές, = sq., Hsch.

**ἄχραντος**, ον, *undefiled, immaculate*, E.*IA*1574, A.R.4.1025; μίτρη Mosch.2.73: c. gen., ἡδονῶν M.Ant.3.4; ἐμψύχου βρώσεως Philostr.*VA*6.11; αἵματος Opp.*H.*2.648: metaph., τεκμήριον καθαρὸν καὶ ἄ. Pl.*Alc.*1.113e; ἄ. ἰδέα Luc.*Dem.Enc.*13, cf. *Am.*22; οἰκειότητες Jul. *Or.*1.9c; τὸ ἄ. δικαστήριον, freq. in Pap., as *POxy.*59.10 (iii A.D.); ἄ. πυρί, of a cup, Ion Trag.1, cf. Theoc.1.60. Adv. -τως Iamb.*Myst.*5.9, Procl. *in Alc.*p.32 C.

**ἀχράς**, άδος, ἡ, a kind of *wild pear*, *Pyrus amygdaliformis*, Teleclid.32, Ar.*Ec.*355, Dsc.1.116; used for the tree as well as the fruit, cf. Arist.*HA*627ᵇ17 with 595ᵃ29, Thphr.*HP*1.4.1 with *CP*2.8.2; cf. ἄχερδος.

**ἄχρατοι**· οἱ πολέμιοι, Hsch. **ἀχρέα**· βλάσφημον, κτλ., Id.

**ἀχρεία**, ἡ, *rubbish*, Sch.E.*Hec.*159.

**ἀχρειόγελως**, ων, *untimely-laughing*, epith. of the Athenians, Cratin.323, cf. *AB*475.

**ἀχρειοποιός**, όν, *rendering useless*, Eust.217.38.

**ἀχρεῖος** (Att. ἄχρειος acc. to Hdn.Gr.1.136), ον, also α, ον *IG*7.303.10 (Oropus), Dsc.4.5, Polem.*Phgn.*69: Ion. **ἀχρήϊος**:—*useless, unprofitable*, ἀχρήϊος ἀνήρ Hes.*Op.*297; ἐπέων νομός ib.403; δέμας A.*Pr.*365, cf. Hp.*Int.*39; οἰκητήρ S.*OC*627; opp. εὐγενής, Id.*Fr.*667; ἐρινὸς ἀ. ὢν ἐς βρῶσιν ib.181; ἀ. κοὐ σοφός E.*Med.*299; δοῦλος *Ev.Matt.*25.30; οὐκ ἀπράγμονα ἀλλ' ἀχρεῖον νομίζομεν Th.2.40; λόγον ἀχρεῖον ἀπέρριψαν Ant.Lib.11.3: Comp. -ότερος, ὄρνιθες Chrysipp.*Stoic.*3.195: c. inf., *unfit* to do, ἀ. πράττειν τι Pl.*R.*371c: c. dat., ἀ. τοῖς σώμασι Agatharch.*Fr.Hist.*3, cf. Them.*Or.*26.326a. 2. esp. *unfit for war*, ἀ. ὅμιλος Hdt.3.81; τὸ ἀ. τοῦ στρατοῦ *the unserviceable part* of an army, Id.1.191; οἱ ἀχρειότατοι Th.1.93, 2.6, cf. X.*HG*7.2.18; τὸ ἀ. τῆς ἡλικίας Th.2.44. Adv. -είως, ἔχειν πρὸς ναυμαχίαν App.*BC*5.84. II. neut. ἀχρεῖον, as Adv., twice in Hom., ἀχρεῖον ἰδών giving a *helpless* look, looking *foolish*, of Thersites after being beaten, Il.2.269; ἀχρεῖον δ' ἐγέλασσε laughed *without cause*, made a *forced* laugh, of Penelope trying to disguise her feelings, Od.18.163; ἀχρεῖον κλάζειν bark *without need* or *cause*, Theoc.25.72. III. Adv. ἀχρείως γέλασόν με (cf. ἀχρειόγελως) *APl.*4.86, cf. Them.*Or.*33.367b: neut. pl. as Adv. ἀχρεῖ' ἀσπαίροντος *helplessly*, Euph.44.

**ἀχρει-οσύνη**, ἡ, = sq., *Gloss.* **-ότης**, ητος, ἡ, *unprofitableness, worthlessness*, Lxx *To.*4.13. **-όω** or **-χρεόω** (*OGI*573.16), pf. ἠχρείωκα:—*render useless, disable, damage*, Dicaearch.2.3, Plb.3.64.8, Lxx *Da.*4.11, *OGI* l.c.:—Pass., ἀχρεῶσθαι *SIG*569.31 (Crete, iii B.C.), cf. Plb.1.14.6, *BCH*35.286 (Delos, ii B.C.); *to be corrupted*, Lxx *Ps.*13(14).3; δι' ἀπειρίαν ἠχρειώθησαν Apollon.Cit.1.1.

**ἀχρεοκόπητος**, ον, *free from debt*, i.e. *undiminished*, δύναμις *PMag.Par.*1.527.

**ἄχρεος**, ον, = ἀχρεῖος, Epic. in *Arch.Pap.*7.10, Tryph.125.

**ἀχρήεις**, εσσα, εν, = ἀχρεῖος, v.l. in Man.4.76:—also **ἀχρήϊστος**, ον, Musae.328, Nonn.*D.*24.266. **ἀχρήϊος**, ον, Ion. for ἀχρεῖος.

**ἀχρημ-ατέω**, *to be without money*, Hsch. s.v. πένεται. **-ατία**, ἡ, *want of money*, Th.1.11, D.H.7.24, Eus.Mynd.7. **-άτιστος** [μᾰ], ον, ἡμέρα ἀ. a day *on which no public business was done*, Plu.2.273e, cf. Sch.Luc.*Tim.*43. II. *disused*, φρέαρ *PMag.Lond.*46.345. III. dub. sens. in *Sammelb.*2276. IV. Astrol., *unprofitable, bringing no advantage*, τόποι Antioch.Astr. in *Cat.Cod.Astr.*8(3).106; of planets, Vett.Val.5.8. **-ατος**, ον, *without money* or *means*, Hdt.1.89, Timocl.9.7; ἀ. τὴν πόλιν ποιεῖν Arist.*Pol.*1271ᵇ16; μήτ' ἀχρημάτοισι λάμπειν φῶς *on the poor*, A.*Pers.*167. **-ονέω**, *to be in want of money*, Poll.6.196. **-οσύνη**, ἡ, *want of money*, Od.17.502, Thgn.156. **-ων**, ον, gen. ονος, *poor, needy*, Sol.13.41, Pi.*Fr.*218; once in Trag., E.*Med.*461.

**ἀχρησ-ία**, ἡ, (χράομαι) *disuse, non-user*, Anon. *in Rh.*17.37. **-ιμος**, ον, *useless*, ἐν ἀ. διαθέσει *CPHerm.*119ʳiv9 (iii A.D.), cf. Sopat. in Rh. 8.10 W., *Hippiatr.*14. **-ιμότης**, ητος, ἡ, *uselessness*, *Gloss.* **-τεύω**, Gramm., *not to be in use*, Sch.D.T.p.195 H. **-τέω**, *to be useless*, S.E.*M.*1.259. **-τία**, Ion. -τίη, ἡ, *uselessness, unfitness*, Hp.*Praec.*9, Pl.*R.*489b, *AP*15.38 (Comet.), Them.*Or.*26.326a. II. *non-usance* of a thing, Pl.*R.*333d, Plu.2.135c. **-τολογέω**, *to speak unprofitably* or *amiss*, *EM*463.25. **-τος**, ον, *useless, unprofitable*, μετάνοια Batr.70; νέες Hdt.1.166; ὁ ὀφθαλμὸς γίνεται Hp.*Prorrh.*2.19; οὐκ ἀ. ἥδ' ἡ ἄνοια Th.6.16; χρεομένῳ ἄχρηστα *useless* if you try to use them, Hp.*Art.*14; πεσεῖν ἀ. θέσφατον *without effect*, E.*IT*121; ἀ. ἐς πόλεμον Hdt.8.142, Lycurg.53; πρός τι Arist.*HA*560ᵇ14: c. gen. rei, ἀ. τῶν ἔργων Id.*Oec.*1345ᵃ35; ἀ. τινι *useless* to a person, Hdt.1.80, cf. X.*Oec.*8.4 (Sup.); τῇ πόλει E.*Heracl.*4; τὸ διηπορηκέναι οὐκ ἀ. Arist.*Cat.*8ᵇ24. 2. = ἀχρεῖος (which it almost superseded in the Oratt. and later Greek), *useless, do-nothing*, D.19.135 (Comp.), etc.; ἀ. πολῖται Is.7.37; σοφισταί prob. l. in Lys.33.3; *non-effective, unwarlike*, Eun.Hist.p.239 D.; so (with a pun—*not having received an oracle*) Ath.3.98c. Adv. -τως, ἔχειν πρός τι D.61.43. II. *unkind, cruel*, θεοί Hdt.8.111; λόγος Id.9.111. III. Act., *making no use of*, c. dat., ξυνέσει τ' ἄχρηστον τῇ φύσει τε λείπεται E.*Tr.*672. IV. *not used*, i.e. *new*, ἱμάτια Luc.*Lex.*9, Ath.3.97e. 2. *obsolete*, Eust.118.25, Sch.rec.S.*El.*132. 3. *not to be used, unseemly*, *EM*463.26. **-τόω**, *make useless*, Horap.1.50; *corrupt*, τὴν Ἑλλάδα φωνήν Eust.367.40.

**ἄχρι** and **ἄχρις** (v. sub fin.): I. Adv. *to the uttermost*, τένοντε καὶ ὀστέα λᾶας ἀναιδὴς ἄχρις ἀπηλοίησεν Il.4.522; ἀπὸ δ' ὀστέον ἄχρις ἄραξε 16.324, cf. 17.599. 2. after Hom., before Preps., ἄχρι εἰς Κοτύωρα X.*An.*5.5.4; ἄ. ἐς ποταμόν *Tab.Heracl.*1.17; ἄχρι πρὸς τὸν σκοπόν, πρὸς τὴν πόλιν, Luc.*Nigr.*36, *Herm.*24; ἄχρις ἐπ' ἀκνηστιν A.R.4.1403; ἐπ' ὀστέον *IG*12(7).115.9 (Amorgos); ἄχρι ἐπὶ πολὺ τῶν πλευρῶν Thphr.*Char.*19.3; ἄχρις ἐς ἠῶ Q.S.6.177; ἄχρι ὑπὸ τὴν πυγήν Luc.*DMort.*27.4: less freq. after the Noun, ἐς τέλος ἄχρις Q.S.2.617, cf. Nonn.*D.*5.153, etc.: rarely c. acc., ἄχρι.. θρόνον ἦλθεν *IG*14.2012 (Sulp. Max.): with an Adv., ἄχρι πόρρω *still* farther, Luc.*Am.*12; ἄχρι δεῦρο S.E.*M.*8.401. II. Prep. with gen., *even to, as far as,* 1. of Time, *until,* ἄχρι μάλα κνέφαος *until* deep in the night, Od.18.370; ἄχρι τῆς τήμερον ἡμέρας D.9.28; ἀπὸ τῆς ἀρχῆς ἄχρι τῆς τελευτῆς Id.18.179; ἄχρι γήρως Apollod.Com.2; ἄχρι δὲ τούτου *until* then, Sol.13.35; ἄχρι τοῦ νῦν Timostr.1, *Ep.Rom.*8.22; ἄχρι νῦν Luc. *Tim.*39, LXX *Ge.*44.28; ἄχρι παντὸς *continually,* Plu.*Cic.*6. 2. of Space, *as far as, even to,* ἄχρι τῆς ἐσόδου τοῦ ἱροῦ Hdt.2.138 (who elsewh. has μέχρι); ἄ. τῆς ὁδοῦ *IG*1².893; ἄ. τῆς πυλίδος *SIG*²587.25; ἄ. τοῦ Πειραιῶς D.18.301; ἔδακνεν ἄχρι τῆς καρδίας *Com.Adesp.*475; ἄχρις ἥπατος Ti.Locr.101a, cf. 100e; ἄχρι τῆς πόλεως D.H.2.43; ἄ. τοῦ δεῦρο Gal.10.676: after its case, ἰνίου ἄχρις Euph.41. 3. of Measure or Degree, ἄχρι τούτου *up to* this point, D.23.122; ἄχρι τοῦ μὴ πεινῆν X.*Smp.*4.37; ἄχρι τοῦ θορυβῆσαι D.8.77; ἄ. θανάτου *Act.Ap.* 22.4; ἄχρι τῆς πρὸς τὸν πλησίον δοξοκοπίας Polystr.p.19W. III. as Conj., ἄχρι, ἄχρις with or without οὗ, 1. of Time, *until, so long as,* ἄχρι οὗ ὅδε ὁ λόγος ἐγράφετο X.*HG*6.4.37; ἄχρις ὅτου *Epigr. Gr.*314.24 (Smyrna); ἄχρι οὗ ἄν or ἄχρι ἄν with Subj., ἄχρι ἂν σχολάσῃ *till* he should be at leisure, X.*An.*2.3.2; ἄχρις οὗ ἂν δοκέῃ Hp.*Fist.*3; ἄχρις ἂν αἱ ἡμέραι παρέλθωσιν Id.*Int.*40; ἄχρι ἂν ἔχῃ τὸ ἴδιον ἐντελὲς [ἡ ἱστορία] Luc.*Hist.Conscr.*9: without ἄν, ἄχρις ῥεύσῃ Bion 1.47; ἄχρι οὗ τελευτήσῃ (v.l. -σει) Hdt.1.117; ἄχρι οὗ ἐπιλάμψῃ Plu.*Aem.*17; ἄχρι ἄν, c. inf., Epist.Mithr. in *SIG*741.37: c. inf. only, ἄχρις ἱκέσθαι ὀστέον Q.S.4.361. 2. of Space, *so far as,* διώξας, ἄχρι οὗ ἀσφαλὲς ᾤετο εἶναι X.*Cyr.*5.4.16: c. subj., αὐξάνεται εἰς μῆκος, ἄχρι οὗ δὴ ἐφίκηται τοῦ ἡλίου Thphr.*HP*5.1.8; cf. μέχρι throughout. —Ep. poets use ἄχρι or ἄχρις, as the metre requires: in Ion. μέχρι is preferred (v. supr.): but ἄχρι, -ις are more common in Hom. than μέχρι: the only Att. forms are ἄχρι, μέχρι, before both consonants and vowels, cf. Phryn.6, Moer.34; and so in Att. Inscrr. (where it is somewhat less freq. than μέχρι): ἄχρι ἄν with hiatus in *IG*2.2729, Hegesipp.Com.1.26; but ἄχρις Men.*Sam.*179.—Never in Trag. (ἄχρι, = ἠ-χρι, cf. μέχρι.)

**ἀχρισατέες**· ἀληθέες, Hsch.

**ἀχροέω** and **ἀχροιέω**, (ἄχροος) *to be colourless*: *to be discoloured, ill-coloured,* Hp.*Fract.*25, Sor.2.43.

**ἄχροια**, ἡ, *absence of colour,* Plot.2.4.10. 2. *loss of colour, paleness,* Hp.*Prorrh.*2.24, Arist.*Pr.*967$^a$8; opp. εὐχροια, Thphr.*Sud.* 39. II. (ἀ- copul.) *likeness in colour,* Hsch.

**ἄχρονος**, ον, *without time, instantaneous,* Gal.7.448; ἡ ἄ. φύσις Dam.*Pr.*404; *short-lived,* of infants, Ptol.*Tetr.*125, cf. *Placit.*5.18. 6. 2. *independent of time,* S.E.*M.*10.225; *non-temporal,* ἄ. πᾶσα ἡ νόησις Plot.4.4.1. Adv. -νως *timelessly,* Alex.Aphr. *in Mete.*129.5, *in Sens.*135.14, Procl.*Inst.*124, Herm. *in Phdr.*p.159 A.; *instantaneously,* Ph.1.571, al., Them.*Or.*15.196b.

**ἀχρονοτρίβής**, ές, *not wasting time,* Hsch.

**ἄχροος**, ον, contr. **ἄχρους**, ουν, *colourless,* Arist.*de An.*418$^b$27, Nic. *Th.*236, Ocell.2.3, Plot.2.4.12. II. *ill-complexioned, pallid,* opp. εὔχροος, Hp.*Aër.*6, *VC*19, Arist.*Pr.*966$^b$35, al.: Comp. ἀχρούστερος Hp.*Prorrh.*2.4, Arist.*HA*584$^a$14: also -ώτερος Hp.*Vict.*2.63. 2. ἄχροοι· πυρραὶ ἡμίονοι, Hsch.; also ἄχροον· πονηρόν· Λάκωνες νόθον, Id.

**ἄχρῦσος**, ον, *without gold,* ἄ. καὶ ἀνάργυροι Pl.*Lg.*679b, cf. Ath.6. 231e.

**ἀχρωμ-άτιστος** [μᾰ], ον, *uncoloured,* Arist.*Mete.*371$^b$9, 377$^b$1, Thphr.*Od.*31. Adv. -τως [Lib.]*Decl.*30.5. **-ᾰτος**, ον, *colourless,* Pl.*Phdr.*247c, Plu.2.97b, etc. 2. *unblushing, shameless,* Suid. s.v. ἄχρωμος. **-ος**, ον, = foreg. 2, Hp.*Epid.*7.122, Artem.4.44: Comp., οὐδὲν -ότερον Hierocl.*Facet.*203:—hence Subst. ⊛**ἀχρωμία**, ἡ, *Gloss.*

**ἄχρως**, ων, gen. ω, = ἄχροος, Hp.*Epid.*7.85, Pl.*Chrm.*168d, Arist. *Metaph.*989$^b$9.

**ἄχρωστος**, ον, (χρώζω) *untouched,* ἄ. γόνατα χερῶν ἐμῶν E.*Hel.* 831. II. *uncoloured, colourless,* Democr.ap.Plu.2.1111a.

**ἀχρώτιστος**, ον, = ἀχρωμάτιστος, σαμψοῦχον *PMag.Par.*1.3010, cf. *PMag.Berol.*1.7 (-τως Pap.).

**ἄχυ**, Hebr. *āhū, quill-cassia,* Dsc.1.13.

**ἀχῦλ-ία**, ἡ, *insipidity,* Diocl.*Fr.*138 (pl.). **-ος**, ον, *without juice, insipid,* Thphr.*CP*6.19.4, Xenocr.18, Diocl.*Fr.*138: Comp., Ath.Med. ap.Orib.1.2.14. **-ωτος**, ον, *not converted into chyle,* διαχωρήματα Gal.7.446, cf. 6.575.

**ἄχῡμ-ος**, ον, *without flavour,* Arist.*Metaph.*989$^b$10, *Sens.*443$^a$11, Xenocr.45; *tasteless,* of water, Thphr.*CP*6.3.1. **-ωτος**, ον, = foreg., Gal.1.584, Suid.

**ἀχύνετος** [ῠ], ον, (χέω, χύνω) *far-spread, copious,* ὕδωρ Nic.*Al.*174.

**ἀχύνωψ**, = κύνωψ (q.v.), *fleawort, Plantago Psyllium,* Thphr.*HP*7. 11.2, Plin.*HN*21.89, 101.

**ἀχῠρ-ᾰγωγός** [ᾰχ], όν, *for the conveyance of chaff,* prob. for ἀγυρατωγά, Hsch. s.v. σαργάναι. **-άριος**, ὁ, = ἀχυροπράκτωρ, *Theb. Ostr.*106. ⊛**-ηγέω**, *carry chaff,* *BGU*698.22 (ii A.D.), 14iii17 (iii A.D.). ⊛**-ικὸν** τέλος tax *on chaff,* *Sammelb.*1092. **-ινος**, η, ον, *fed by chaff,* φλόξ Plu.2.658d. ⊛ **-ιος**, ὁ, = ἀχυρός, *Tab.Heracl.*1. 139 sq. **-ῖτις**, ιδος, ἡ, *of chaff,* dub. in *AP*9.438.5 (Phil.). **-μιά**, ἡ, *heap of chaff,* Il.5.502, *AP*9.384.15. **-μιος**, α, ον, *consisting mainly of chaff,* ἀμητός Arat.1097. **-μός**, οῦ, ὁ, v. ἀχυρός.

**ἀχῠρο-βολών** [ᾰ], ῶνος, ὁ, *barn for chaff,* *PHamb.*23.18 (vi A.D.), Ael.Dion.*Fr.*88. **-δόκη**, ἡ, *chaff-holder,* X.*Oec.*18.7. **-θήκη**, ἡ, = foreg., *PLond.*5.1768 (vi A.D.), *PMasp.*279.18 (vi A.D.), Sch.Il. 5.202.

⊛ **ἄχῠρον** [ᾰ], τό, mostly in pl. ἄχυρα, *chaff, bran, husks* left after threshing or grinding, Hdt.4.72, Pherecr.161, Antiph.226.2, X. *Oec.*18.1; ἐν τοῖς ἀ. κυλινδομένην Hermipp.47: sg., Thphr.*HP*8.4.1, *Ev.Matt.*3.12, etc.: prov., ὗνος εἰς ἄχυρα 'pig in clover', of unexpected good fortune, Philem.188, cf. Ar.*Fr.*76: metaph., ἄχυρα τῶν ἀστῶν, of μέτοικοι, Id.*Ach.*508; ἄχυρα ἀπὸ τοῦ τοίχου ἀποσπᾶν, of dying persons, Hp.*Prog.*4. II. in pl., ἄ. χρυσοχοϊκά *slag* from gold-smelting, *PHolm.*5.7.

**ἀχῠρο-πᾰροχία** [ᾰχ], ἡ, *supply of chaff,* *Arch.Pap.*4.116 (iii A.D.). **-πράκτωρ**, ορος, ὁ, *collector of chaff* (or *of the tax thereon*), *Ostr.*1012 (ii A.D.).

⊛ **ἀχῠρός** or **ἄχῠρος** [ᾰ], ὁ, *chaff-heap,* Eup.299, Ar.*Fr.*10D., Pl. Com.6, and in the best Mss. of Ar.*V.*1310: but ἀχυρμός should be read.

**ἀχῠρότριψ** [ᾰ], ῖβος, ὁ, ἡ, *threshing out the husks,* τρίβολοι *AP*6.104 (Phil.).

⊛ **ἀχῠρόω** [ᾰ], *mix chaff* or *straw* with mud, Thphr.*HP*4.8.8:— Pass., μᾶζαν ἠχυρωμένην *mixed with chaff,* Polioch.2; πηλὸς ἠχ. *IG* 2².463.18; ἠχ. ἀμόργῳ Ph.*Bel.*86.44; *to be strewn with straw,* of the orchestra, Arist.*Pr.*901$^b$30. **-ώδης**, ες, *like chaff, chaffy,* ib. 928$^a$20 (Sup.); θρίσσαι Hices.ap.Ath.7.328c; of an eruption, f.l. in Hp.*Liqu.*6. II. ἀχυρῶδες, = ἄχυρον, Dsc.2.93. **-ών**, ῶνος, ὁ, *storehouse for chaff,* *IG*11(2).287 *A* 149, al. (Delos, iii B.C.), *Gp.*6.2. 8. **-ωσις**, εως, ἡ, *mixing of chaff with mud* or *straw,* compared with the swallow's nest-building, Arist.*HA*612$^b$22.

**ἀχύτλωτος**, ον, *unbathed, unanointed,* Nonn.*D.*9.25.

⊛ **ἄχῠτος**, ον, *insoluble,* τὰ ἀ. Gal.17(2).15.

*ἄχω, v. ἀχέω. **ἀχώ**, ἡ, Dor. for ἠχώ.

⊛ **ἀχώνευτος**, ον, = ἄκαυστος, Hsch.

**ἄχωρ** [ᾰ], ορος, ὁ, *scurf, dandriff,* Ar.*Fr.*410, etc. (ἀχώρ, ῶρος, in Alex.Trall.1.8, Paul.Aeg.3.3, Dsc.1.33, al., cf. Phryn.*PS*p.8 B., *AB* 475, after the analogy of ἰχώρ, ῶρος, but ἄχωρ acc. to Hdn.Gr.2.937.)

**ἀχωρέω** or **ἀχωριάω** [ᾰ], *suffer from* ἄχωρ, in part. ἀχωροῦντας or -ιῶντας, prob. cj. for ἰχωρροοῦντας in Paul.Aeg.3.3.

**ἀχώρητος**· ὁ μὴ χωρούμενος, Hsch.

**ἀχωριστ-έω**, *to be inseparable,* Phld.*D.*3.9. **-ία**, ἡ, *inseparability,* Id.*Mus.*p.94K. ⊛ **-ος**, ον, (χωρίζω) *not parted, undivided,* Pl.*R.*524c; *inseparable,* Arist.*EN*1102$^a$30, *de An.*427$^a$2; ἀρετὴ ἀ. ἡδονῆς Epicur.*Fr.*506, cf. *Ep.*3p.64U., Gal.16.521, al. Adv. -τως Phld.*Sign.*20. II. (χῶρος) *without a place assigned one,* X.*Lac.* 9.5.

**ἄχωρος**, ον, *without resting-place, homeless,* Ael.*Fr.*77; εἴ τι μέλλει ἐργάζεσθαι, ἀνόνητα γένοιτο καὶ ἄχωρα *Tab.Defix.*97.11, cf. 96. 17.

**ἀχωρώδης** [ᾰ], ες, *like* ἄχωρ, ἐξανθήματα Aët.8.15, v.l. in Hp.*Liqu.*6.

**ἄχωστος**, ον, *not heaped up,* Hld.9.3.

**ἄψ**, Adv. of Place, (ἀπό, Lat. *abs*) *backwards, back again,* freq. in Hom., mostly with Verbs of motion, freq. before ἐς, ἀπό, ἐκ, ἄ. ἐς Ὄλυμπον ἵκεσθον Il.8.456, cf. 10.211, etc.; with trans. Verbs, ἄ. ἐς κουλεὸν ὦσε 1.220, cf. 15.418; ἄ. ἐπὶ νῆας ἔεργε 16.395; ἄ. ἵππους στρέψαι 13.396, cf. 18.224. 2. of actions, *again, in return,* ἄ. διδόναι Il.22.277; ἄ. ἀφελέσθαι 16.54; ἄ. ἀπολύειν 6.427; ἄ. ἀρέσαι 9. 120; ἄ. τέτατο ὑσμίνη 17.543; ἄ. ἐπιμισγομένων 5.505; [ἂψ ἀπαγγ]εῖλαι prob. in Epich.99; ἄ. λαμβάνειν, = ἀναλαμβάνειν, Theoc.25.65: pleon., ἄ. αὖτις *yet* again, Il.8.335, 15.364; ἄ. πάλιν 18.280.

**ἀψάκειν** or **ἀψακεῖν**· ἀποτυχεῖν, Hsch.

**ἀψαλά**· ἀψοφητὶ πορεύεται, Hsch., Cyr., Zonar.

**ἀψάλακτος** [ψᾰ], ον, *untouched, unhandled,* S.*Fr.*550. 2. *scot-free,* Crates Com.46, Ar.*Lys.*275.

**ἀψάμαθος** and **ἄψαμμος**, ον, *without sand, not sandy,* Hsch.

**ἀψαυστ-έω**, *leave untouched,* σώμασι App.*Gall.*14:—Pass., Poll. 1.9. **-ί**, Adv. of ἄψαυστος, *without touching,* Plu.2.665f. **-ία**, ἡ, *want of contact,* Iamb. *in Nic.*p.57 P. **-ος**, ον, *untouched,* Hdt. 8.41, Thphr.*HP*5.5.6, Ph.2.14; *not to be touched, sacred,* Th.4.97; χρήματα App.*BC*2.41. II. Act., *not touching,* c. gen., ἄ. ἔγχους S.*OT*969; ἄ. τέκνων, of persons dying young, *Epigr.Gr.*241.2 (Smyrna).

**ἀψεγής**, ές, *blameless,* S.*El.*497 (lyr.). Adv. ἀψεγέως A.R.2.1022.

**ἄψεκτος**, ον, = foreg., Thgn.799; *not disapproved,* Gal.17(2).184.

**ἀψελές**· ὑγιές, Hsch. **ἄψερον**, = ὕστερον, πάλιν, Alc.*Supp.*26. 11, Hsch., Zonar.

**ἀψευδ-εια**, ἡ, *truthfulness,* Corinn.*Supp.*2.70, Pl.*R.*485c, Iamb. *Protr.*20; *reliability,* of times and seasons, Arist.*Mu.*397$^a$11: -ία, Ph. *Fr.*110 H., Them.*Or.*21.257c. ⊛ **-έω**, *not to lie, to speak truth,* πρός τινα S.*Tr.*469, Aeschin.2.95: abs., Ar.*Fr.*751; *not to err,* Pl.*Tht.*196b; περί τι Arist.*SE*165$^a$25. II. *observe faithfully,* *IG*5(2).343.38, 57 (Orchom. Arc., iv B.C.). **-ής**, ές, *without deceit, truthful,* esp. of oracles and the like, Hes.*Th.*233, Hdt.1.49, 2.152 (Sup.), al.; μάντις ἀ., of Apollo, A.*Ch.*559, cf. *Fr.*350.5, Cratin.29 D. (Sup.); θεὸς *Ep.Tit.*1.2; ἀψευδεῖ τέχνῃ, of augury, A.*Th.*26; ἦθος E.*Supp.*860; *unerring,* Pl. *Tht.*160d, etc.; μάρτυς -έστατος Plu.2.341. 2. of things, *uncorrupt,* *pure from all deceit*, ἀ. πρὸς ἄκμονι χάλκευε γλῶσσαν Pi.*P*.1.86. 3. ἀψευδής, = κώνειον, Ps.-Dsc.4.78. II. Adv. -δέως, Att. -δῶς, *really and truly*, οἱ ἀ. ἄριστοι Hdt.9.58, cf. Ph.1.19, al., Iamb.*Myst*.2.2: Sup. -έστατα, ἐρεῖν Ph.1.34.

**ἀψευδόμαντις**, *of no false diviner*, τέχνη Nicoch.ap.*Lex.Sabb*.

**ἀψευστ-έω**, later form of ἀψευδέω, Plb.3.111.8; πρός τινα Phalar. *Ep*.123. **-ος**, ον, later form of ἀψευδής, Ph.*Fr*.51 H.; νόμος Plu. *Art*.28; *unfeigned*, πένθος *AP*7.638.6 (Crin.). Adv. -τως *PMag. Lond*.121.248.

⊛ **ἀψεφ-έω**, *neglect*, Hsch. ⊛ **-ής**, ές, (ψέφω) = ἀφρόντιστος, *free from care*, S.*Fr*.692.

**ἄψηκτος**, ον, (ψήχω) *untanned*, κόθορνος Ar.*Lys*.658; *uncombed*, χαῖται A.R.3.50.

**ἀψηλάφητος** [λᾰ], ον, *not tried* or *tested*, Plb.8.19.5. II. *untouched*, Hsch.; gloss on ἄψαυστος, Id.

**ἄψητος**· ἀνυπότακτος, Hsch.

**ἀψήφιστος**, ον, *not having voted*, Ar.*V*.752. II. *not voted for, unwelcome*, πενία ἀ. οὐσία Secund.*Sent*.10.

**ἄψηφος**, ον, *without a stone*, δακτύλιος Artem.2.5. II. = πολύ, μέγα, ἰσχυρόν, Hsch.

**ἀψηφοφόρητος**, ον, *not having yet voted*, Plb.6.14.7.

**ἀψίαι**· ἑορταί (Lacon.), Hsch.

**ἀψῖδο-ειδής**, ές, *arched, vaulted*, D.C.68.25; *wheel-shaped*, Eudox. *Ars* 19.13. **-ομαι**, Pass., *to be tied in a circle* or *curve*, δικτύοις μόλυβδον ἡψιδωμένον *AP*6.90 (Phil.).

**ἀψῖδωτός**, όν, *vaulted*, Gloss. 2. *with tyres*, τροχός *Edict.Diocl*. 15.32.

**ἀψῐ-κάρδιος**, ον, (ἅπτομαι) *heart-touching*, M.Ant.9.3. **-κορία**, ἡ, *rapid satiety*, Plb.14.1.4, Plu.2.504d, Andronic.Rhod.p.572M.; *fickleness*, δίχα ὕβρεως καὶ ἀ. *PLond*.5.1711 (vi A.D.). ⊛ **-κορος**, ον, *quickly sated*: hence, *fickle*, Pl.*Ax*.369a; ἀ. πρὸς τὰς ἐπιθυμίας οἱ νέοι Arist.*Rh*.1389ᵃ6, cf. D.Chr.32.28, Ph.2.312, al.; ποικιλώτατος καὶ ἀ. βίος Posidon.41: τὸ ἀ., = ἀψικορία, Plu.*Cor*.4, Luc.*Cal*.21. Adv. -ρως Ph.1.214, Hsch. II. Act., *quickly sating*, χάρις Plu.2.20b; λόγος ib.7b.

**ἄψιλον**· ἄπτερον ἢ πολύπτερον, Hsch.

**ἀψι-μᾰχέω**, *skirmish with an enemy*, Hyp.*Fr*.131, Plb.18.8.4, D.S. 11.52; *entice* or *lead on to fight*, Plu.*Crass*.10, *Dio* 39. **-μᾰχία**, ἡ, *skirmishing*, D.S.20.29, Plu.*Brut*.39, al.: metaph., *altercation*, ῥητόρων Aeschin.2.176, cf. Hyp(?).*Oxy*.1607.11 26, Plb.5.49.5, Plu.*Lyc*.2, *PPetr*.3p.104: pl., ἀ. χειρῶν *personal encounters*, D.H.6.22; λόγων τε καὶ ἔργων ib.34. **-μᾰχικός**, ή, όν, = sq., *Gloss*. **-μᾰχος**, ον, = φιλοκίνδυνος, Alex.Aphr.*de An*.185.26. Adv. -χως *provocatively*, D.H.6.59. **-μῖσία**, ἡ, (μῖσος) *trivial and transient enmity*, Hsch., Suid.

⊛ **ἀψινθ-ᾶτον**, τό, *draught of wormwood*, Aët.3.69, Alex.Trall.1.15: —also **ἀψινθάτιον** (leg. -ιᾶτον) *PLond*.3.1259.32 (iv A.D.). **-ινος**, η, ον, *flavoured with wormwood*, ἔλαιον Alex.Trall.1.15. **-ιον**, τό, *wormwood, Artemisia Absinthium*, Hp.*Morb*.3.11, *Mul*.1.74, X.*An*. 1.5.1, Thphr.*HP*1.12.1, Dsc.3.23; ἀψινθίῳ κατέπασας Ἀττικὸν μέλι Men.708:—also ⊛ **ἄψινθος**, ἡ, Aret.*CD*1.13, but ὁ, *Apoc*.8.11; and **ἀψινθία**, ἡ, Alex.Trall.1.10. II. ἀψίνθιον, = ἀβρότονον, Ps.-Dsc.3. 24. 2. = *Artemisia monosperma*, Aq.*Pr*.5.4. 3. ἀ. θαλάσσιον, = σέριφον, Dsc.3.23. **-ίτης** [ῑ] οἶνος wine *prepared with wormwood*, ibid.

**ἀψίον**· τὸ πρόσωπον, Hsch. **ἀψίορ**· μέγα, πλατύ, πολύ, ἰσχυρόν, Id.

⊛ **ἀψίς**, Ep. and Ion. **ἀψίς**, ῖδος, ἡ, (ἅπτω) *loop, mesh*, such as form a net, ἀψῖσι λίνου Il.5.487; ἀψῖδες *nets*, A.R.3.138, Opp.*H*.4.146. 2. *felloe* of a wheel, Hes.*Op*.426, Lyr. in *PLG*3.740; the *wheel* itself, Hdt.4.72, E.*Hipp*.1233; κύκλος ἀψῖδος the potter's *wheel*, *APl*.4.191 (Nicaenet.). 3. in Archit., *dowel-pin*, *IG*11(2).161 *A* 70 (Delos, iii B.C.). 4. *disk*, τὴν ἡμερίαν ἀψῖδα, of the sun, E.*Ion* 88; *segment* cut off by rainbow, Arist.*Mete*.371ᵇ28, cf. Poet.ap.Plu.2.103f. 5. *arch* or *vault* (cf. ψαλίς II), ἐπὶ τὴν ὑπουράνιον ἀψῖδα Pl.*Phdr*.247b, cf. Suid. s.v. αἰθεροβατεῖν, *Epigr.Gr*.1078 (Adana), *IGRom*.3.975, *PMag. Lond*.46 41; κατὰ τὴν ἀψῖδα ποτώμενος Luc.*Bis Acc*.33; *triumphal arch*, D.C.53.22,26, etc.: metaph., κάμπτειν ἐπῶν ἀψῖδας Ar.*Th*. 53. b. σελάνας ἐς δεκάταν ἀψῖδα in the moon's tenth *orbit*, i.e. the tenth month, *Hymn.Is*.38. c. ἡ ἀνωτάτω ἀ. θεάτρου uppermost *tier*, D.C.61.17. (ἄψῖδα in late Poets, *Epigr.Gr*.440.9, 445.4.)

**ἅψις**, εως, Ion. ιος, ἡ, (ἅπτομαι) *touching*, Hp.*Epid*.7.5; *contact*, Pl. *Prm*.149a, Arist.*HA*621ᵃ11: pl., Pl.*Prm*.149c. 2. metaph., ἅ. φρενῶν *distraction of mind*, Hp.*Acut*.52.

⊛ **ἄψογος**, ον, *blameless*, *Sammelb*.625, Poll.3.139. Adv. -γως Eust. 19.17.

**ἄψοος**· θηρίον τι κατεσθίον ἀμπέλους, Hsch.

**ἀψόρροος**, ον, contr. **-ρρους**, ουν, (ἄψ, ῥέω) *back-flowing, refluent*, Homeric epith. of Ocean, regarded as a stream *encircling* the earth and *flowing back* into itself, Il.18.399, Od.20.65.

**ἄψορρος**, ον, *going back, backwards*, ἄψορροι κίομεν Il.21.456; ἄψορροι προτὶ Ἴλιον ἀπονέοντο 3.313; ἐκ δόμων ἄ... περᾷ S.*Ant*.386, cf. *OT*431: mostly in neut. ἄψορρον as Adv., *backward, back again*, ἄψορρον.. ἔβη Il.7.413; ἄ. οἱ θυμὸς ἀνέρθη 4.152; ἄ. προσέφην Od.9. 282; ἄψορρον ἥξεις A.*Pr*.1021, cf. S.*El*.53; ὦ παῖδες, οὐκ ἄψορρον (sc. ἄπιτε); ib.1430; οὐκ ἄ. ἐκνεμῇ πόδα; Id.*Aj*.369 (lyr.). (For ἄψ-ορσος, cf. παλίν-ορσος.)

**ἄψος**, εος, τό, (ἅπτω) *juncture, joint*, λῦθεν δέ οἱ ἄψεα πάντα all his *joints* were relaxed [by sleep], Od.4.794, cf. Nic.*Al*.541; ἄψεα δεσμοῦ Opp.*H*.3.538: in pl., *limbs*, *AP*5.217 (Agath.), al.

⊛ **ἀψοφ-ητί** or **-ητεί**, Adv. of sq., Pl.*Tht*.144b, D.25.90, Arist.*HA* 533ᵇ32, Men.298, Ph.1.643; λέξις ὥσπερ ἔλαιον ἀ. ῥέουσα D.H.*Dem*. 20. **-ητος**, ον, (ψοφέω) *noiseless*, c. gen., ἀ. κωκυμάτων *without sound of..*, S.*Aj*.321. **-ία**, ἡ, *noiselessness*, Arist.*Ph*.244ᵇ17, Plot.2.1.6. **-ος**, ον, = ἀψόφητος, S.*Tr*.967 (lyr.), E.*Tr*.887, *Com. Adesp*.1310, Arist.*de An*.420ᵃ7. Adv. -φως and -φέως *EM*183.22.

**ἀψυδρακίωτος**, ον, *without pustules* or *pimples*, σῶμα Dsc.2.72.

**ἀψῡθής**, ές, = ἀψευδής, Hsch.

⊛ **ἄψυκτος**, ον, *not capable of being cooled*, Pl.*Phd*.106a.

**ἀψῡχ-ᾰγώγητος**, ον, *not rejoicing the heart*, Plb.9.1.5. Adv. -τως *without being comforted*, Jul.*Or*.8.252a. **-εί**, Adv. of ἄψυχος, Hdn. *Epim*.257. ⊛ **-έω**, *swoon*, Hp.*Morb*.2.5, *Epid*.7.1. **-ία**, Ion. **-ίη**, ἡ, *swooning, syncope*, Id.*VM*10, *Coac*.222. II. *want of spirit, faint-heartedness*, A.*Th*.259,383, E.*Alc*.642, etc. **-οποιός**, όν, *making lifeless* or *faint*, Eust.611.5. ⊛ **-ος**, ον, *lifeless, inanimate*, πέθῳ Archil.84; μνημεῖ' ἄψυχ' ἐμψύχων Simon.106.4, cf. E.*Fr*.655, *Tr*. 623; λωτὸς ἄ. ἔμπνουν ἀνίει Μοῦσαν Sopat.10; ἄ -ότατα τῶν ὀστῶν *with least life* or *sensation*, Pl.*Ti*.74e, cf. Arist.*de An*.413ᵃ21, etc.; ἄ. θεοί, of statues, Timae.127. 2. ἄ. βορά *non-animal* food, E.*Hipp*. 952. II. *spiritless, faint-hearted*, κάκη A.*Th*.192; ἀνήρ *Trag. Adesp*.337: ἀψυχότεραι αἱ θήλειαι [ἐλέφαντες] Arist.*HA*610ᵃ21; of style, *lifeless*, D.H.*Dem*.20. Adv. -χως Poll.2.227. III. *materialistic*, λόγος Porph.*Gaur*.14.4 (Comp.).

⊛ **ἄω** (A), = ἵημι (q.v.), *blow*, only in impf. ἄεν, A.R.1.605, 2. 1228. II. = αὔω, ἰαύω, *sleep*, only in aor., ἐνὶ κοίτῃ ἄεσα Od.19. 342; νύκτα μὲν ἀέσαμεν 3.151; ἔνθα δὲ νύκτ' ἄεσαν ib.490; contr., νύκτ' ἄσαμεν 16.367.

**ἄω** (B), *hurt*, contr. from ἀάω (q.v.); cf. ἄτη.

⊛ **ἄω** (C), Ep. inf. ἄμεναι: fut. ἄσω Il.11.818: aor. 1 subj. ἄσω 18.281, inf. ἆσαι (v. infr.): aor. 2 subj. 1 pl. ἕωμεν 19.402:—Med., Ep. 3 sg. ἆαται Hes.*Sc*.101; cf. ἆται· πληροῦται, Hsch.: fut. ἄσομαι Il.24.717: aor. ἀσάμην 19.307:—*satiate*, αἵματος ἆσαι Ἄρηα *to give* him *his fill of* blood, 5.289: but, II. mostly intr., *take one's fill of* a thing, ἱεμένη χροὸς ἄμεναι 21.70; λιλαιομένη χροὸς ἆσαι ib.168, cf. 15.317; γόοιο μὲν ἔστι καὶ ἆσαι 23.157:—Med., ἄσεσθε κλαυθμοῖο 24.717; ποτῆτος ἄσασθαι φίλον ἦτορ 19.307. (Root *sā*: *sa*, cf. ἄ-ατος, ἄ-δην.)

**ἀῶ**· ὑγεία, ἡμέρα, Hsch.

**ἀώδης**, ες, (ὄζω) *without smell*, Thphr.*Od*.18, Plu.2.1014f.

**ἀωδῠνεῖν**, *to be free from pain*, Hsch.

**ἆωθεν**, Adv., Dor. for ἠῶθεν, Theoc.15.132.

⊛ **ἀωΐλιον**, τό, Egyptian measure of capacity, = 2 *cubic* πήχεις, *PPetr*. 2 p.14, al. (iii B.C.):—also **αὐωΐλιον**, ib.p.118.

**ἀῷος**, for ἠῷος, ἀστήρ Ion Lyr.10, prob. in B.*Fr*.3.11.

**ἀώλυπον**· τὸ οὐκ ἀπολλύμενον, Hsch.

**ᾀών**, ᾀόνος, ἡ, Dor. for ἠϊών, v.l. in Mosch.3.122.

**ἀών** [ᾱ], όνος, ὁ, a kind of *fish*, Epich.63. II. a kind of *garment*, *PAmh*.2.3aii 21 (iii A.D., pl.).

**ἄωρ**, ὁ, v. ἄορ.

**ἀωρέω**, *to be careless* (ἀ- priv., ὥρα), Hsch., Suid.:—also, = φυλάττειν (ἀ- intens.), Hsch.

⊛ **ἀωρί** (-εί *PFay*.19.2 (ii A.D.)), Adv. of ἄωρος, *at an untimely hour, too early*, Heraclid.Com.1.2, Luc.*Bis Acc*.1, *AP*12.116; ἀ. θανάτῳ ἀπέθανεν Ar.*Fr*.663 cod.; νυκτὸς ἀωρί *at dead of* night, Theoc.11.40, 24.38; ἀωρὶ τῶν νυκτῶν Antipho 2.1.4, 2.4.5; ἀωρὶ νύκτωρ (v.l. νυκτῶν) Ar.*Ec*.741, Phalar.*Ep*.141.2.

**ἀωρία**, ἡ, *wrong time*: hence, *untimely fate* or *death*, Hld.10.16; but ἀωρίη *old age*, Herod.3.29; *bad condition*, πραγμάτων Procop. *Arc*.14: pl., ἀωρίαι *bad seasons*, Plu.2.371b; ἀωρία *midnight, dead of night*, Pherecr.6D., Ael.*Fr*.81; in full, ἦν ἀ. τῆς νυκτὸς μεσούσης Alciphr.3.47: metaph., ἀωρίη τοῦ πρήγματος Aret.*CD*1.4; *darkness* (figure of *calamity*), prob. in Lxx *Is*.59.9: acc. as Adv., ἀωρίαν ἥκειν to have come *too late*, Ar.*Ach*.23; ποῦ βαδίζεις ἀωρίᾳ; whither *so late?* Luc.*Asin*.24.

**ἀωρῐλουστής**, οῦ, ὁ, *an early bather*, better written divisim in M.Ant.1.16.8.

⊛ **ἀώριος**, α, ον, = ἄωρος (A), Thphr.*CP*2.2.2, Arat.1076, *AP*7.600 (Jul. Aegypt.); ἀώριος *IG*1².980: nom. pl. fem. ἀώριαι Ἐφ.Ἀρχ.1911. 59 (Peraea, iv B.C.).

**ἀωρο-βόρος**, ον, *devouring those who die untimely*, *PMag.Par*.1. 2867. **-θάνᾰτος** [θᾰ], ον, *untimely dead*, Ar.*Fr*.663 (cj. Dind. for ἀωρὶ θαν., cf. Phryn.*PS* p.42 B.). ⊛ **-θανής**, ές, = foreg., *CIG*3846*q* (Aezani), Calder *Philadelphia and Montanism* 35. **-λειος**, ον, *unnaturally smooth*, esp. men who by pulling out their beards tried to make themselves look young, Cratin.10; of a youth, *beardless*, Ael.*NA*13.27. **-μορος**, ον, *dying untimely*, *IG*12(8).444 (Thasos). **-νυκτος**, ον, *at midnight*, ἀ. ἀμβόαμα ἔλακε A.*Ch*.34 (lyr.).

⊛ **ἄωρος** (A), ον, (ὥρα) *untimely, unseasonable*, χειμών, τύχαι, A.*Pers*. 496, *Eu*.956 (lyr.); θάνατος E.*Or*.1030; τελευτή Antipho 3.1.2; ξυνουσίη Aret.*CD*1.4 (but ἄ. γάμος *too late*, D.H.4.7); πένθος Lxx *Wi*. 14.15; μετὰ μάχην ἱκετεύειν ἄωρον ἐδόκει J.*BJ*5.11.1; ἄ. θανεῖν E.*Alc*. 168, cf. Hdt.2.79; οἱ ἄ. those *who die untimely*, Apollod.Com.4, cf. Philostr.*VA*6.4; esp. of those dying *unmarried*, *PMag.Par*.1.342, cf. 2725; in Epitaphs, ὤλετ' ἄ. *IG*1².977: Sup. ἀωρώτατε (sic) *Sammelb*. 1420; ἕνεκα χρόνου πάντες ἐσμὲν ἄ. *unripe* (for death), Metrod.52; ἀώροις περιπέσοιτο συμφοραῖς *Epigr.Gr*.376 (Aezani): Comp. γήρως ἀωρότερα πράττειν things *unbecoming* old age, Plu.*Sull*.2. 2. *unripe*, of fruit, Dsc.1.126, Lxx *Wi*.4.5; of fish, *out of season*, opp. ὥριμος, Nicom.Com.1.21: metaph., ἄωρος πρὸς γάμον Plu.*Lyc*.15; ἄ. ὥρα Id.

Comp.*Thes.Rom.*6. 3. *without youthful freshness, ugly*, Eup.69, X.*Mem.*1.3.14 (Sup.), Pl.*R.*574c. Adv. -ρως J.*AJ*4.8.19.

**ἄωρος** (B), ον, of the πλεκτάναι or polypus-like legs of Scylla, τῆς ἤ τοι πόδες εἰσὶ δυώδεκα πάντες ἄωροι Od.12.89; one of the Sch. expld. it as κρεμαστοί, ἀπὸ τοῦ αἰωρῶ, but more prob. = ἄκωλοι, as Sch.HQ, from Ion. ὤρη B. II. ἄωροι πόδες *fore*-feet, οὐ τοὺς ἀώρους εἶπά σοι..πόδας πρίασθαι; σὺ δὲ φέρεις ὀπισθίους Philem.145.

⊛ **ἄωρος** (C), contr. **ὦρος**, ὁ, *sleep*, Sapph.57; ἤλασ' ἄωρον prob. for ἤλασας ὦρον in Call.*Fr.*150.

⊛ **ἀωροσύνη**, ἡ, *untimeliness, immaturity*, dub. in *Epigr.Gr.*414.

**ἀωρότοκος**, ον, *laid prematurely*, of soft-shelled eggs, *Hippiatr.*22.

**ἄωρτο**, Ep. plpf. Pass. of ἀείρω.

⊛ **ἄως**, Boeot., = ἕως, *IG*7.2228.

**'Αώς**, ἡ, Dor. for 'Ηώς, Ἕως; ἐπ' ἀϝῶ c. gen., *to east of*, *Mnemos.* 42.332 (Argos, iv B.C.).

**'Αωσφόρος**, ὁ, = 'Εωσφόρος (q.v.).

**ἀωτ-έω** [ᾰ], *sleep*, Ep. Verb, only pres., τί πάννυχον ὕπνον ἀωτεῖς; Il.10.159; μηκέτι νῦν εὕδοντες ἀωτεῖτε γλυκὺν ὕπνον Od.10.548: abs., Simon.37.5:—in Hsch., **ἀωτεύειν**· ἀπανθίζεσθαι (also ἀωτεῖτε· ἀπανθίζετε τὸν ὕπνον), but expld. by ὑφαίνειν, *AB*476, cf. Suid. s.v. ἀωτεμεῖν (sic); perh. to be read (in signf. *sleep*) in B.8.13 for ἀσαγεύω. **-ίζομαι**, *cull the choicest* or *best*; v. λωτίζομαι.

⊛ **ἄωτον** [ᾰ], τό, and **ἄωτος**, ὁ, *the choicest, the flower of its kind*: in Hom. mostly of the *finest wool*, οἰὸς ἄωτον Il.13.599,716, Od.1.443; without οἰός (which must be supplied from the context), *flock, down*, 9.434; once of the *finest linen*, λινοῖό τε λεπτὸν ἄωτον Il.9.661; of the golden fleece, χρύσεον ἄωτον A.R.4.176, cf. Orph.*A.*1336; ἄκρον ἄωτον [ὕδατος], of *pure* water, Call.*Ap.*112; of the *foam* on a wave, κύματος ἄκρῳ ἀ. Id.*Hec.*1.4.3; μέλιτος ἀ. γλυκύς Pi.*Pae.*6.59: freq. in Pi., ἀ. ζωᾶς *the prime* or *flower* of life, Id.*I.*5(4).12; ἀ. στεφάνων *the fairest* of.., ib.6(5).4, cf. *O.*5.1; Χαρίτων ἀ. their *fairest gift*, Id.*I.* 8 (7).16; σοφίας ἄκρος ἀ. the *choicest gift* of minstrel's art, ib.7(6).18; ἀ. γλώσσας, i.e. a song, ib.1.51; ὕμνων Id.*P.*10.53; δίκας ἀ. Id.*N.*3. 29; 'Αφροδίτας..ἄωτον A.*Supp.*666 (lyr.): rarely in pl., στεφάνων ἄωτοι Pi.*O.*9.19; ἡρώων ἄωτοι Id.*N.*8.9; ῥόδων ἄωτοι Simon.148: in Epitaphs, θνήσκω..ἀκμᾶς ἐν ἀώτῳ *in the flower* of youth, *IG*3.1328; τὸν..ἄωτον τοῦ δήμου *CIG*2804, cf. *Epigr.Gr.*455. II. *that which gives honour and glory* to a thing, ἀ. ἵππων *a song in praise of* horses, Pi.*O.*3.4; χειρῶν ἀ. ἐπίνικον Id.*O.*8.75.—The gender is indeterminate in Hom. and A.; Pi. always has ἄωτος, and so Theoc.13.27; A.R. and later Ep. ἄωτον (Opp.*C.*4.154, οἰὸς ἄωτα in pl.).

⊛ **ἄωτος**, ον, (οὖς) *without ears*, Plu.2.963b; of vessels, *without lugs*, Philet.ap.Ath.11.783a, dub. in Call.*Fr.*115, cf. Aët.1.138.

# B

**B** β, **βῆτα**, indecl., second letter of the Gr. alphabet: hence as numeral, β' = δύο and δεύτερος, but ͵β = 2,000. II. to represent ϝ, freq. in Hsch., esp. in Lacon. words, cf. βείκατι, etc.

**βᾶ**, shortd. form of βασιλεῦ, *king!* A.*Supp.*892 (lyr.). II. an exclam. *baa!* (with ref. to the *baaing* of a lamb), Hermipp.19.

**βαβάζω**, *speak inarticulately*, or *shout*, Hsch.; but aor. inf. βαβάξαι *dance*, Id. (Cf. βαβάκτης.)

**βαβαί**, exclam. of surprise or amazement, *bless me!* E.*Cyc.*156, Ar.*Av.*272, etc.; doubled, *hurrah!* Achae.28, cf. Chrysipp.*Stoic.*3. 178; οὐχὶ τῶν μετρίων, ἀλλὰ τῶν βαβαὶ βαβαί, to denote persons *extravagant* in their expressions, Alex.206: c. gen., βαβαὶ τοῦ λόγου *bless me* what an argument! Pl.*Phlb.*23b, cf. Jul.*Caes.*309b, etc. (On the accent, cf. Hdn.Gr.1.502; βάβαι cod. B in Pl. l.c.)

**βαβαιάξ**, strengthd. for βαβαί, Ar.*Ach.*64, al.; βαβαὶ βαβαιάξ Id. *Pax*248.

**βάβακα**· τὸν γάλλον, Hsch.

⊛ **βαβάκινος**· χύτρας εἶδος, Hsch.

**βάβακοι**, in Elis, = τέττιγες; in Pontus, = βάτραχοι, Hsch.

**βαβάκτης**, *reveller*, of Pan, Cratin.321, cf. Eust.1431.46; of Dionysus, Corn.*ND*30; expld. by ὀρχηστής, *EM*183.45, Hsch.

**βάβαλον**· αἰδοῖον, Hsch.: also βάβαλον· κραύγασον (Lacon.), Id.

**βάβαξ**, ακος, ὁ, *chatterer*, Archil.33, Lyc.472.

**βαβέλιος**, Pamph., = ἀέλιος, ἥλιος, Eust.1654.20.

**βαβήρ**· ὁ Ἄρης, Hsch.

**βαβίζω** or **-ύζω**, = βαΰζω, Zenod.ap.Ammon.p.231 V.

**βάβιον**, τό, Syrian word for *child*, Dam.*Isid.*76.

**βαβράζω**, *chatter, chirp*, of the grasshopper, Anan.5.6.

⊛ **βάβρηκες**, οἱ, *gums*, or *food in the teeth*, Hsch. **βαβρήν**, *lees of olive-oil* (Maced.), Id. **βαβύας**, ὁ, *mud*, Id.:—also **βαβύλας**, Suid.

**βαβυκώς**, = πελεκάν, Philet.ap.Hsch.

**Βᾰβῠλών**, ῶνος, ἡ, *Babylon*, Alc.*Supp.*16.10, etc.:—**Βᾰβῠλώνιοι**, οἱ, *Babylonians*, Hdt.1.77, etc., and **Βᾰβῠλωνία**, ἡ, *Babylonia*, Arist. *Oec.*1352$^b$27:—also **Βᾰβῠλωνεύς**, έως, ὁ, St.Byz.; fem. **Βᾰβῠλωνίς**, ίδος, Nonn.*D.*40.303:—Adj. ⊛ **Βᾰβῠλώνιος**, α, ον, Hdt.1.106, etc.; ος, ον, Arr.*An.*6.29.6; or **Βᾰβῠλωνιακός**, ή, όν, Alex.308.

**βαβύρας**· πίων, Cyr.

⊛ **βαβύρτας**· ὁ παράμωρος, Hsch. (Cf. Lat. *baburrus*.)

**βαγαῖος**· μάταιος, Hsch. II. title of Zeus in Phrygia, Id. (Cf. Slav. *bogŭ* 'god'.)

**βαγαρόν**· χλιαρόν (Lacon.), Hsch. **βαγεῖ**· εἰσελθοῦσαι, Id. **βάγιον**· μέγα, Id., Suid.

**βάγμα**, ατος, τό, (βάζω) *speech*, A.*Pers.*637 (lyr., pl.).

⊛ **βάγος**· κλάσμα ἄρτου, Hsch.

⊛ **βαγός**· βασιλεύς, καὶ στρατηγός (i.e. Lacon., = ἀγός), Hsch.

**βαγώας**, ὁ, Lat. *Bagoas* and *Bagōus*, Persian word, said to be = εὐνοῦχος, as pr. n. in Str.15.3.24, etc.

**βαδάς**· κίναιδος, Amerias ap.Hsch. **βαδελεγεῖ**· ἀμέλγει, Id. (βαδέλγει Cyr., alii alia).

**βαδδίν**· βύσσινον ἔνδυμα ἐξαίρετον, Hsch.

**βάδην** [ᾰ], Adv., (βαίνω) *step by step*, β. ἀπιόντος Il.13.516; ἄραχνος ὡς β. A.*Supp.*887; *in marching step*, ἦγε β. Hdt.9.57; ἡγοῦ β. Ar.*Lys.*254; β. ταχὺ ἐφέπεσθαι *at quick march*, opp. δρόμῳ θεῖν, X.*An.*4.6.25; θᾶττον ἢ β. Id.*HG*5.4.53, Men.837, Aristaenet.2.14; β. ὑποχωρεῖν Arist.*HA*629$^b$14. 2. *gradually, more and more*, πεινῆν Ar.*Ach.*535. II. *on foot*, opp. ἐφ' ἵππων, ἐπὶ ναῶν, A.*Pers.* 19 (anap.); opp. ἐπ' ἀπήνης, App.*Gall.*1.

**βᾰδίζω**, Att. fut. βαδιοῦμαι Ar.*Th.*617, *Pl.*495, Pl.*Smp.*190d, etc.; later βαδίσομαι Gal.*UP*12.10, and βαδιῶ Nicol.*Prog.*p.69 F., Ael.*Tact.* 36.4, (δια-) Luc.*Dem.Enc.*1; βαδίσω D.Chr.10.8: aor. ἐβάδισα Hp.*Int.* 44, Pl.*Erx.*392b, Arr.*An.*7.3.2, etc.: pf. βεβάδικα Arist.*Metaph.*1048$^b$ 31, J.*Ap.*2.39:—Med., imper. βαδίζου Cratin.391:—*walk*, ἐπιστροφάδην δ' ἐβάδιζεν h.*Merc.*210; β. ἀρρύθμως Alex.263; opp. τρέχω, X.*Cyr.* 2.3.10, etc.; of horsemen, interpol. in Id.*An.*6.3.19; ἐπὶ κτήνους β. D.Chr.34.5; *go by land*, opp. πλέω, D.19.164,181; also of *sailing*, X. *Oec.*16.7; of a ship, Lxx *Jn.*1.3; *march*, of armies, Ael.*Tact.* l.c.; of certain animals, κατὰ σκέλη β., v. σκέλος I: c. acc. cogn., βάδον β. Ar.*Av.*42; ὁδὸν Hp. l.c., X.*Mem.*2.1.11; ἀεὶ μίαν ἀτραπὸν Arist.*HA* 622$^b$25; ὁδῷ β. Luc.*Tim.*5; βάδιζε *go!* Men.*Epit.*159, *Sam.*43. 2. *go about*, βῆ βῆ λέγων β. Cratin.43, al.; κατὰ ζυγά in pairs, Arist.*HA* 544$^a$5. 3. generally, *go, proceed*, Antipho 5.24; ἐπ' οἰκίας β. *enter* houses, D.18.132, cf. Test.ap.eund.21.121; β. ἐπί τινα ψευδοκλητείας *proceed* against him for.., D.53.15; εἰς τὸ πολίτευμα, εἰς τὰς ἀρχάς, εἰς τὰ ἀρχεῖα, Arist.*Pol.*1293$^a$24, 1298$^a$15, 1299$^a$36; β. εἰς τὰ πατρῷα *enter* on one's patrimony, Is.3.62; *proceed* (in argument), πρὸς τὰ κατηγορήματα D.18.263, cf. Arist.*APo.*97$^a$5; εἰς ἄπειρον β., of an infinite *process*, *Metaph.*1000$^b$28; ὁμόσε τῇ φήμῃ β. Plu.*Thes.*10. 4. of things, αἱ τιμαὶ ἐπ' ἔλαττον ἐβάδιζον prices *were getting* lower, D. 56.9; τὸ πρᾶγμα πορρωτέρω β. Id.23.203.—Very rare in Poets: [ἥλιος] β. τὸν ἐνιαύσιον κύκλον E.*Ph.*544.

**βάδιλλος**, ὁ, = Lat. *batillus, shovel*, β. σιδηροῦς *POxy.*521.13 (ii A.D.).

**βάδιον**, τό, Dim. of βάδος or βάτος, a measure, = 50 ξέσται, *PBaden* 43.10 (iii A.D.), *POxy.*1658.4 (iv A.D.).

**βάδ-ισις** [ᾰ], εως, ἡ, *walking, going*, Ar.*Pl.*334; βαδίσει χρῆσθαι Hp.*Aër.*15; of hares, τεχνάζειν τῇ β. X.*Cyn.*8.3; opp. πτῆσις, ἅλσις, Arist.*EN*1174$^a$31. **-ισμα**, ατος, τό, *walk, gait*, X.*Ap.*27, D.37. 55: pl., Luc.*Herm.*18; ἐλθὼν ἐν ἠρεμαίῳ β. Palaeph.31. **-ισμᾰτίας**, ου, ὁ, *a good walker*, Cratin.392. **-ισμός**, ὁ, = βάδισις, Pl. *Chrm.*160c. **-ιστέον**, *one must walk* or *go*, σοὶ β. πάρος S.*El.* 1502, Str.17.1.54; *one must proceed*, ἐπὶ τὸ καθόλου Arist.*EN*1180$^b$21: pl., βαδιστέα Ar.*Ach.*394. ⊛ **-ιστηλάτης** [λᾰ], ὁ, *driver of riding-donkeys*, *PTeb.*262 (ii B.C.), *POxy.*1514.2 (iii A.D.), etc. **-ιστής**, οῦ, ὁ, *goer*, ταχὺς β. a quick *runner*, E.*Med.*1182; ἵππος β. Hsch. s.v. κάλπις: ὄνος β. *riding*-donkey, *PGrenf.*2.14$^b$5 (iii B.C.); β. alone, = ὄνος, *PFlor.*376.23 (iii A.D.). ⊛ **-ιστικός**, ή, όν, *good at walking*, Ar.*Ra.*128, Thphr.*Fr.*180; *able to walk*, Simp.*in Ph.*887.17; τὸ β. *that which is capable of walking*, Arist.*Int.*21$^b$16; πούς.. ὄργανον β. Gal.*UP*2.9. Adv. -κῶς Porph.*Gaur.*1.3. II. *for riding animals*, στάβλον *POxy.*146.1 (vi A.D.). **-ιστός**, ή, όν, *that can be passed on foot*, Arr.*Ind.*43.10:—but ⊛ **βάδιστοι**· βαδύτατοι, Hsch. (i.e. ἡδ-).

**βάδομαι**· ἀγαπῶ, Hsch. (For ἥδομαι.)

**βάδος**, ὁ, *walk*, βάδον βαδίζειν, coined by Ar.*Av.*42. II. v. βάτος.

**Βαδρόμιος, Βαδρομιών**, v. Βοηδρόμιος, Βοηδρομιών.

**βᾱδύς** (i.e. ϝαδύς), Elean for ἡδύς, Pherecyd.*Fr.*79 J., Paus.5.3.2, cf. **βάδηδοι**· ἠχεῖοι (leg. βαδύ· ἡδύ· 'Ηλεῖοι), Hsch.

**βάζω**, poet. Verb, used chiefly in pres. and impf.: aor. ἔβαξα Hsch.: pf. Pass. (v. infr.):—*speak, say*, ἄρτια βάζειν Il.14.92, al.; ἀνεμώλια β. Od.4.837; πεπνυμένα βάζεις Il.9.58; οἵ τ' εὖ μὲν βάζουσι κακῶς δ' ὄπιθεν φρονέουσιν Od.18.168; νήπια β. Pi.*Fr.*157; ἐβληχημένα β. *AP*7.636 (Crin.): c. dupl. acc., ταῦτά μ' ἀγειρόμενοι θάμ' ἐβάζετε Il.16.207, cf. E.*Hipp.*119; πολλὰ κακῶς β. ἑστίαν 'Ατρειδᾶν Id. *Rh.*719 (lyr.); καθεύδουσιν μάτην ἄκραντα β. A.*Ch.*882: c. dat. modi, χαλεποῖς βάζοντες ἔπεσσι *address* with sharp words, Hes.*Op.*186; κακοῖσι β. πολλὰ Τυδέως βίαν A.*Th.*571; ὑπέραυχα β. ἐπὶ πτόλει ib. 483; εἴ τι μὴ ψεῦδος ἡ παροιμίη βάζει Herod.2.102; Διωνύσῳ ὄργια βάζων *IG*14.1642:—Pass., ἔπος.. βέβακται a word *has been spoken*, Od.8.408. (Cf. βάξις, βάσκειν (for βάκ-σκειν), ἀβακής.)

**βακίζων**· κακῶς ἕρπων, Hsch. **βαθάλη**· κρήνη, Amerias ap. eund. **βαθανίαν**· νεοσσιάν (Cret.), Hsch. ⊛ **βαθάρα**· πυκλιή (Maced.), πυρλός (Athaman.), Id.

**βαθίων, βάθιστος**, Comp. and Sup. of βαθύς.

**βαθμ-ηδόν**, Adv., (βαθμός) *by steps*, Gal.18(1).793, Ath.1.1c. ⊛ **-ίς**, ή, gen. ῖδος Pi.*N.*5.1, ἴδος *AP*7.428.4 (Mel.):—*step* or *threshold*, ἀκρᾶν βαθμίδων ἄπο Pi.*P.*5.7, cf. J.*AJ*15.11.5; cf. βασμίς. II. *base, pedestal*, Pi.*N.*5.1. 2. *socket*, Hp.*Fract.*2: generally, *hollow* in a joint, ib.37. **-οειδής**, ές, *like steps*, Democr.155, Zos.Alch. p.176 B. ⊛ **-ός** or **βασμός**, ὁ, (βαίνω) *step, threshold*, Lxx 1*Ki.*5.5,

[S.]*Fr.*1127; *degree* on the dial, Lxx 4*Ki.*20.9 sq.; *fifteen degrees* of the zodiac, Vett.Val.31.2; *interval* in a musical scale, Iamb.*VP*26. 120. 2. *rung* of a ladder, Luc.*Trag.*221. 3. *base* or *plinth* of a tower, *GDI*5524.10 (Cyzicus). II. metaph., *step, degree* in rank (οἱ β. κλίμακος προκοπὴν σημαίνουσι Artem.2.42), 1*Ep.Ti.*3.13, Procop.*Arc.*24, Lyd.*Mag.*2.8, al.; οἱ τᾶς ἀξίας βάσμοι *IG*12(2).243. 16 (Mytil.); simply, *degree*, τολμημάτων βαθμοί J.*BJ*4.3.10; ὥσπερ ἡδονῆς κλίμακα συμπηξάμενος ἔρως πρῶτον ἔχει β. ὕψεως Luc.*Am.*53; *step* in an argument, Simp.*in Cael.*718.35; of a genealogy, ἀπωτέρω δυοῖν β. two *steps* farther back, i.e. farther back than one's grandfather, D.Chr.41.6. III. *tax paid on stairs*, *POxy.*574 (ii A.D.): acc. to Phryn.296, Moer.97, βαθμός is Ion., βασμός Att., but βασμός occurs *GDI*5524.10 (Cyzic.), *Jahresh.*3.55 (Scepsis). **-ώδης**, expl. of βαλβιδώδης, Bacch.ap.Erot.*Fr.*42.

❀ **βαθόημι**, Aeol., = βοηθέω, impf. ἐβαθόη *IG*12(2).645.21 (Nesus); dat. part. βαθόεντι ib.526.27 (Eresus).

❀ **βάθος** [ᾰ], εος, τό, (βαθύς) *depth* or *height*, acc. as measured up or down, Ταρτάρου βάθη A.*Pr.*1029; αἰθέρος βάθος E.*Med.*1297, cf. Ar. *Av.*1715; βάθους μετέχειν to be a solid, possessing *depth* as well as length and breadth, Pl.*R.*528b; εἴτ' ἐν βάθεσιν εἴτ' ἐν τάχεσιν Id.*Plt.* 299e; βάθους αὔξη Id.*R.*528d; opp. μῆκος, πλάτος, Arist.*Ph.*209ᵃ5; μεγέθους τὸ ἐπὶ τρία [συνεχὲς] β. Id.*Metaph.*1020ᵃ12: with Preps., ἐκ βάθεος *in depth*, Hdt.1.186; ἐκ βάθους *through and through*, Plot. 5.8.10; εἰς βάθος Arist.*Mete.*386ᵃ23, al.; ἐν βάθει Id.*Sens.*440ᵃ14, etc.; κατὰ βάθους Id.*Mete.*339ᵇ12; κατὰ βάθος *in a descending scale*, metaph. of causation, Dam.*Pr.*95: freq. in military sense, *depth* of a line of battle, X.*HG*3.4.13, etc.; ἐπὶ βάθος τάσσεσθαι *in depth of line*, Th.5.68; ἐς β. ἐκτάξαι Arr.*An.*1.2.4; β. τριχῶν, of *long thick* hair, Hdt.5.9; ἄτομα πώγωνος βάθη Ephipp.14.7; *interior* of a country, Str.3.3.7, al.; *depth*, of perspective in a picture, Procop.Gaz.*Ecphr.* p.157 B.: pl., βάθη *depths*, Pl.*Ti.*44d, etc.; *deep water*, opp. shallows near shore, Lxx *Ps.*68(69).2, al., *Ev.Luc.*5.4; ἐν τοῖς βάθεσιν Arist. *HA*599ᵇ9. b. Astron., = ταπείνωμα, Vett.Val.241.26. 2. metaph., κακῶν δρῶν β. A.*Pers.*465; ἡ μακροῦ πλούτου βάθει S.*Aj.*130, cf. *Ep.Rom.*11.33; β. ἡγεμονίας Plu.*Pomp.*53; *depth of mind*, β. τι ἔχειν γενναῖον, of Parmenides, Pl.*Tht.*184a; ἐν βάθει πόσιος *deep* in drink, Theoc.14.29; β. καρδίας ἀνθρώπου Lxx *Ju.*8.14; τὰ β. τοῦ θεοῦ, τοῦ Σατανᾶ, 1*Ep.Cor.*2.10, *Apoc.*2.24. 3. of lit. style, *bathos*, ὕψους ἢ β. Longin.2.1. (Substituted for βένθος under the influence of βαθύς.)

**βάθρα**, ἡ, = βαθμός, Ar.*Fr.*513, cf. Poll.10.47, *Sammelb.*402 (iii A.D.), Lyd.*Mag.*1.3; = βάσις, *Et.Gud.*: = ἀποβάθρα, dub. in Plu.2. 347b.

**βαθράδιον**, τό, Dim. of βάθρον, Ar.*Fr.*514 codd. Poll.(10.47): leg. βαθρίδιον.

**βάθρακος**, v. βάτραχος.

**βαθρεία**, ἡ, = βάθρον, A.*Supp.*860 (dub. l.).

**βαθρίδιον**, v. βαθράδιον.

❀ **βαθρικόν**, τό, *base*, *IGRom.*4.835 (Hierapolis); *stairway*, *Rev.Ét. Gr.*19.265 (Aphrodisias).

**βαθρίον**, τό, Dim. of βάθρον, Suid. s.v. κλινίς:—also **βαθρεῖον**, τό, Cumont *Études Syriennes* 336 (Cyrrhus, pl.).

❀ **βάθρον**, τό, (βαίνω) *that on which anything steps* or *stands*, hence, 1. *base, pedestal*, τὸ β. καὶ ὁ θρόνος Hdt.1.183; of a statue, Id.5.85, X.*Eq.*1.1; δαιμόνων ἱδρύματα.. ἐξανέστρεπται βάθρων A. *Pers.*812; *throne*, ὑψηλὸν Δίκας β. S.*Ant.*854. 2. *stage, scaffold*, Hdt.7.23. 3. generally, *solid base*, ἀμφιρύτου Σαλαμῖνος β. S.*Aj.* 135 (anap.), cf. *Ph.*1000, *OC*1662; ὦ πατρῷον ἑστίας β., i.e. *house* of my father, Id.*Aj.*860: metaph., Εὐνομία βάθρον πολίων Pi.*O.*13. 6: pl., *foundations*, Ἰλίου.. ἐξαναστήσας βάθρα E.*Supp.*1198; ἐν βάθροις εἶναι stand *firm*, Id.*Tr.*47; ἐκ βάθρων ἀνῃρῆσθαι *utterly*, Id. *El.*608, cf. D.H.8.1, Lyc.770, *AP*9.97 (Alph.). 4. *step*, S.*OC* 1591; *rung of a ladder*, E.*Ph.*1179. 5. *bench, seat*, S.*OT*142, *OC* 101, Phryn.Com.3.5; τὰ β., of a lecture-room or school, Pl.*Prt.*315c, 325e, etc.; τὰ βάθρα σπογγίζων D.18.258; *seats* in the council-chamber, Lys.13.37. 6. β. Ἱπποκράτους *machine for reducing dislocation*, Ruf.ap.Orib.49.26. 7. metaph., πόνους ἀφῖγμαι κἀπὶ κινδύνου βάθρα *the verge* of danger, E.*Cyc.*352.

**βάθρωσις**, εως, ἡ, *stand* in the Delphic stadium, *BCH*23.567.

**βᾰθῠ-αγκής**, ές, *with deep dells*, Ἄλπεις *AP*9.283 (Crin.); τὰ β. Thphr.*HP*3.11.4. **-αίδοιος**, ον, *mentulatus*, of Priapus, *EM*2.24, Sch.Lyc.831. **-βουλος**, ον, *deep-counselling*, φροντὶς A.*Pers.*142 (lyr.). **-γειος**, ον, Call.*Ap.*65, Thphr.*HP*4.11.9, Str.6.3.5, D.S. 20.109: Sup., Ph.1.332, al.: Ion. **-γαιος** Hdt.4.23; Att. **-γεως**, ων, Thphr.*CP*2.4.10:—*with deep soil, productive*, ll. cc. **-γένειος**, ον, *with deep, full beard*, Poll.2.88, Jul.*Mis.*349c. **-γηρως**, ων, gen. ω, *in great old age*, S.E.*M.*6.13; *decrepit*, *AP*6.247.7 (Phil.). ❀ **-γλωσσος**, ον, *of unintelligible speech*, λαός Lxx *Es.*3.5: but expld. by ἐλλόγιμος, Hsch., Suid. **-γνώμων**, ον, gen. ονος, *of profound wisdom*, Ἀληθίη Babr.126.5, cf. Eun.*VS* p.481 B., *Hist.*p.254 D. **-δείελος**, ον, *steeped in sunshine*, πόλις B.1.29; cf. εὐδείελος. **-δενδρος**, ον, *deep-wooded*, *Lyr.Adesp.*96; Ἑλικών *Pae.Delph.*1. **-δίνης** [ῑ], ου, ὁ, *deep-eddying*, ποταμός Il.20.73, etc.; ὠκεανός Hes.*Op.*171:—also ❀**-δινήεις**, εσσα, εν, Il.21.15:❀**-δίνης**, ες, Dem.Bith.4.4: **-δινήτης**, Doroth.11. **-δοξος**, ον, *far-famed, illustrious*, Pi.*P.*1.66, *Pae.* 2.58. **-εργέω**, *plough deep*, *Gp.*2.23.14 (Pass.). **-ζωνος**, ον, *deep-girded* (cf. βαθύκολπος), βαθυζώνους τε γυναῖκας Il.9.594, Od.3.154; βαρβάρων γυναικῶν τὸ ἐπίθετον Sch.Od.l.c.; βαθυζώνων.. Περσίδων A.*Pers.*155 (lyr.); but epith. of Leto, B.10.16, Pi.*Fr.*89; Χάριτες Id.*P.*9.2, B.5.9; [Μοῦσαι] Pi.*I.*6(5).74; νύμφα βαθύζωνε S.*Ichn.*227 (lyr.).—Not in E. **-θριξ**, τρῐχος, ὁ, ἡ, *with thick, long mane*, Opp.*C.*1.314; of sheep, *with thick* or *long wool*, *h.Ap.*412. **-καμπής**, ές, *strongly curved*, *AP*6.306 (Ariston). **-κάρδιος**, ον, *of profound mind*, Procl.*Par.Ptol.*222. **-καρπος**, ον, *rich in fruits*, εἰρήνη *IG*3.170. **-κήτης** πόντος *deep yawning* sea, Thgn.175; cf. μεγακήτης. **-κλεής**, ές, = βαθύδοξος, *AP*9.575 (Phil.). **-κληρος**, ον, *with rich lands*, of persons, Hom.*Epigr.*16. II. *very rich*, of land, Coluth.218, Man.3.239. ❀ **-κνήμῖς**, ῖδος, *wearing high greaves*, Q.S.1.55. **-κνημος**, ον, *with high mountain-spurs*, Πλαταιαί Nonn.*D.*4.336. **-κολπος**, ον, *with dress falling in deep folds* (cf. βαθύζωνος), epith. of Trojan women, Il.18.122,339,24. 215; of Nymphs, *h.Cer.*5, *Ven.*257; Muses, Pi.*P.*1.12; παρθένος (of Aegina) Id.*Pae.*6.135: hence, *with deep, full breasts*, ἐκ β. στηθέων A.*Th.*864 (lyr.): metaph. of the earth, *deep-bosomed*, Pi.*P.*9. 101. 2. simply, *very deep*, χειή Nonn.*D.*12.327; *with deep foundations*, ib.40.534; *set deep*, ὀχῆα ib.21.94. 3. = ἀρχαία, παλαιά, κοίλη, Hsch. **-κόμης**, ου, *with thick hair*, Poll.2.24. **-κομος**, ον, *with thick leaves*, ὄρεα β. *covered with thick forests*, Ar.*Fr.*698 (lyr.). **-κρημνος**, ον, *with high cliffs*, ἅλς Pi.*I.*4(3).56; β. ἀκταί *deep and rugged* banks, Id.*N.*9.40; Συήνη D.P.244, cf. 618. **-κρήπῑς**, ῖδος, ὁ, ἡ, *with deep foundations*, Ἄβυδος Musae.229. **-κτέᾰνος**, ον, *with great possessions, wealthy*, Μῆδοι *Eleg.Alex.Adesp.*2.13; τύχη *AP*10.74 (Paul. Sil.); ῥέεθρον Nonn.*D.*12.126. ❀ **-κύμων** [ῡ], ον, gen. ονος, *deep in waves*, ὄχθαι Musae.189; φωνή, of Oceanus, Nonn. *D.*23.320, cf. Antioch.Astr. in *Cat.Cod.Astr.*1.110. **-λειμος**, ον, = sq., Il.9.151,293. **-λείμων**, ον, gen. ονος, *surrounded by rich meadows*, πέτρα β., i.e. Cirrha, where the land was forbidden to be ploughed, Pi.*P.*10.15. **-λήϊος**, ον, *with deep crop, very fruitful*, τέμενος, v.l. for βασιλήϊον in Il.18.550, cf. A.R.1.830, *AP*9.110 (Alph.). **-μαλλος**, ον, *thick-fleeced*, Pi.*P.*4.161, App.*Mith.* 103. **-μητᾱ**, ὁ, Aeol. for βαθυμήτης, *deep-counselling*, Pi.*N.* 3.53. **-νοος**, ον, contr. **-νους**, ουν, *of deep mind*, Νέστωρ [Arist.] *Pepl.*9.

❀ **βαθύνω**:—Pass., plpf. βεβάθυντο Nonn.*D.*39.305: (βαθύς):—*deepen, hollow out*, βάθυνε δὲ χῶρον ἅπαντα, of a torrent, Il.23.421; ἔσκαψε καὶ ἐβάθυνε dug and *dug deep*, *Ev.Luc.*6.48; ἐβάθυνε πέδον ταρσῷ, of a dog, Nonn.*D.*47.239: metaph., ὁ λιμὸς βαθύνει ἑαυτόν J. *BJ*5.12.3: esp. as military term, *deepen*, τὴν φάλαγγα X.*Cyr.*6.3.23, 8.5.15, cf. Arr.*Tact.*25.11:—Pass., *become deep, be deepened*, λίμνη β. Thphr.*HP*4.11.3; κρημνὸς βαθύνεται εἰς ἀπορρῶγα J.*BJ*1.21.3; νάσως βαθυνομένας ἀπὸ ῥιζᾶν, of Delos, *Hymn.Is.*160; τὸ βαθυνόμενον τῆς ῥηγμῖνος Agath.2.2; of a deep wound, Nonn.*D.*39.305; βαθυνομέναις χερσί in or *with the hollowed* hands, ib.11.180. 2. Math., *add a third dimension*, β. τὰ ἐπίπεδα Procl.*in R.*2.52 K., cf. *in Ti.*1. 146 D.:—Pass., κυκλικῶς βαθυνθέντες Simp.*in Ph.*59.17. II. intr., *sink deep*, Ph.1.248, 2.402; *sink, crumble*, Apollod.*Poliorc.*157. 8. 2. metaph., *go deeply into a subject*, βαθύνας θεωρῆσαι Procl.*in Prm.*p.622 S.

**βᾰθῠ-ξῠλος**, ον, *with deep wood*, ὕλης ἐν βαθυξύλῳ φόβῃ E.*Ba.*1138; β. δρυμοί Arist.*Mu.*392ᵇ18. 2. *built high with wood*, [πυρά] B.12. 169. b. *deeply carved*, γλυφαί, of coffered ceilings, J.*AJ*15.11. 5. **-ορυγή**, ἡ, *deep excavation*, *PHal.*1.81 (iii B.C.). **-πεδος**, ον, *with deep plain, lying low* (between hills), of Nemea, Pi.*N.*3.18 (prob. for -πεδίῳ). **-πελμος**, ον, (πέλμα) *thick-soled*, εὔμαρις *AP* 7.413 (Antip.). **-πεπλος**, ον, *with long robe*, Q.S.13.552. **-πικρος**, ον, *intensely bitter*, ἀψίνθιον Ps.-Dsc.3.23. **-πλεκής**, ές, *close-knit*, Opp.*H.*4.638. **-πλευρος**, ον, *deep-flanked*, *Gp.*17.2. 1. **-πλήξ**, ῆγος, ὁ, ἡ, *deep-striking*, σκορπίος Nic.*Fr.*31. **-πλόκᾰμος**, ον, *with thick hair*, B.10.8 (prob.), A.R.1.742, Mosch.2.101, Orph. *Fr.*114. **-πλοκος**, ον, (πλέκω) *deeply involved*, in Comp. -ώτερα πρὸς ἀπιστίαν Eun.*Hist.*p.259 D. **-πλοος**, ον, *going deep in the water*, ναῦς prob. in D.S.3.40. **-πλούσιος**, ον, = sq., Poll.3. 109. ❀**-πλουτος**, ον, *exceeding rich*, ζωά B.3.82; χθών A.*Supp.*554 (lyr.); Εἰρήνα E.*Fr.*453, copied by Ar.*Fr.*109; of persons, Ph.1.635, Alciphr.3.10; β. κατασκευαὶ οἰκιῶν D.H.20.4. **-πόλεμος**, ον, *plunged deep in war*, Pi.*P.*2.1. **-πόνηρος**, ον, *deeply depraved*, Ptol.*Tetr.*159, Vett.Val.104.4. ❀ **-πορος**, ον, *causing heavy going*, πεδίον, cj. for βαθύτερον in Plu.*Eum.*16. **-πτερος**, ον, *deep-winged*, Epic. in *Arch.Pap.*7 p.4. **-πύθμην**, ὁ, ἡ, gen. ενος, *with deep foundations*, *AB*1339, *EM*696.35. **-πώγων**, ον, gen. ωνος, *with thick beard*, D.S.34.1, Plu.2.710b, Luc.*JTrag.*26. **-ρρείτης**, ου, ὁ, (ῥέω), = βαθύρροος, Ep. gen. βαθυρρείταο Il.21.195, Hes.*Th.* 265. **-ρρείων**, ον, gen. οντος, = βαθύρροος, A.R.2.659,795. **-ρρηγαλῆ**, ἰκτῖνος (Lydian), Hsch. **-ρρηνος**, ον, (ῥήν) *with thick wool*, τάπης *AP*6.250 (Antiphil.). **-ρρῐζία**, ἡ, *depth of root*, Thphr.*HP*1. 7.1. **-ρρῐζος**, ον, *deep-rooted*, δρῦς S.*Tr.*1195, cf. A.R.1.1199, Q.S. 4.202; πέτρα, i.e. *lofty*, *Trag.Adesp.*203: Comp. -ριζότερος Thphr. *HP*1.7.2. ❀ **-ροος**, ον, contr. **-ρους**, ουν, *deep-flowing*, Ὠκεανός Il. 7.422, cf. Hes.*Cat.Oxy.*1358.2.23, etc.; β. ποταμὸν Εὔηνον S.*Tr.*559. [βᾰθῠρους Poet. *de herb.*118.] **-ρρωχμος**, ον, (ῥωχμή) *with deep clefts*, Q.S.1.687.

❀ **βᾰθύς**, βαθεῖα Ion. βαθέα, βαθύ; fem. βαθύς Call.*Del.*37, Eratosth. 8; gen. βαθέος, βαθείας Ion. βαθέης: dat. βαθεῖ, βαθείῃ Ion. βαθέῃ: Comp. βαθύτερος, poet. βαθίων [ῑ Att., ῐ Theoc.5.43], Dor. βάσσων (q.v.): Sup. βαθύτατος, poet. βάθιστος:—*deep* or *high*, acc. to one's position, Hom., etc.; βαθείης ἐξάλλεται αὐλῆς a court *within a high fence*, Il.5.142, cf. Od.9.239; ἠϊόνος προπάροιθε βαθείης *the deep*, i.e. *wide*, shore, Il.2.92; τάφρος 7.341, al.; κρατήρ S.*Fr.*563; κύλικες Id.

*Aj.*1200 (lyr.); βαθὺ πτῶμα a fall *from a high rock*, A.*Supp.*796; πλευρὰ βαθυτάτη (vulg. βαρυτάτη), of an athlete, Ar.*V.*1193; of a line of battle, βαθύτεραι φάλαγγες X.*Lac.*11.6, cf. *HG*2.4.34; β. τομή, πληγή, a *deep* cut, Plu.2.131a, Luc.*Nigr.*35. 2. *deep* or *thick* in substance, of a mist, ἠέρα βαθεῖαν Il.21.7, cf. Od.9.144; of sand, ἀμάθοιο βαθείης Il.5.587; ἐπὶ θῖνα βαθύν Theoc.22.32; of ploughed land, νειοῖο βαθείης Il.10.353; β. γῆ, opp. to stony ground, E.*Andr.*637, Thphr.*CP*1.18.1; of luxuriant growth, *deep*, *thick*, of woods, etc., βαθείης τάρφεσιν ὕλης Il.5.555; βαθείης ἐκ ξυλόχοιο 11.415; βαθὺ λήϊον 2.147, Thgn.107; τοῦ λητου τὸ..βαθύτατον Hdt.5.92.ζ; λειμών A.*Pr.*652; σῖτος X.*HG*3.2.17; χλόα E.*Hipp.*1139 (lyr.); χαίτη, τρίχες, πώγων, Semon.7.66, X.*Cyn.*4.8, Luc.*Pisc.*41. b. *deep*, of colour, *PHolm.*21.9: Comp., Ael.*VH*6.6, Lyd.*Mag.*2.13, πορφύριον -ύτερον *PLond.*3.899.4 (ii A.D.). 3. of quality, *strong*, *violent*, βαθείῃ λαίλαπι Il.11.306. b. generally, *copious*, *abundant*, β. κλᾶρος Pi.*O.*13.62; β. ἀνήρ *a rich* man, X.*Oec.*11.10; β. οἶκος Call. *Cer.*113; β. πλοῦτος Ael.*VH*3.18, Jul.*Or.*2.82b; β. χρέος *deep* debt, Pi.*O.*10(11).8; στεφάνων β. τέρψις S.*Aj.*1200 (lyr.); β. κλέος Pi.*O.*7.53; κίνδυνος Id.*P.*4.207; β. ὕπνος *deep* sleep, Theoc.8.65, *AP*7.170, cf. Luc.*DMar.*2.3; εἰρήνη Id.*Tox.*36; σιωπή App.*Mith.*99, *BC*4.109 (Sup.). 4. of the mind, ἄχος ὀξὺ κατὰ φρένα τύψε β. in the *depths* of his soul, Il.19.125; but also, *profound*, φρήν Pi.*N.*4.8; φροντίς A.*Supp.*407; μέριμνα Pi.*O.*2.60; βαθεῖαν ἄλοκα διὰ φρενὸς καρπούμενος A.*Th.*593; μουσικὴ πρᾶγμ' ἐστὶ β. Eup.336; βαθύτερα ἤθη *more sedate* natures, Pl.*Lg.*930a (but, *more recondite*, i.e. *civilized*, manners, Hdt.4.95): of persons, *deep*, *wise*, β. τῇ φύσει στρατηγός Posidipp.27.4; ταῖς ψυχαῖς Plb.6.24.9; also, *deep*, *crafty*, Men.1001; ἦθος Ph.2.468. 5. of time, β. ὄρθρος *dim* twilight, Ar.*V.*216, Pl.*Cri.*43a, etc.; β. νύξ *a late hour* in the night, Luc.*Asin.*34; περὶ ἑσπέραν β. Plu.2.179e, cf. Paus.4.18.3; βαθὺ τῆς ἡλικίας Ar.*Nu.*514; β. γῆρας cj. in *AP*7.163 (Leon.), cf. Eun.*VS*p.457 B., al.; β. ὥρα ἔτους Charito 1.7. II. Adv. -έως Theoc.8.66; *profoundly*, Procl.*in Prm.*p.475 S.: Sup. βαθύτατα, γηρῶν Ael.*VH*2.36. (βn̥θύς, cf. βένθος.)

**βᾰθύσαρκος** [ῠ], ον, *fleshy*: τὰ β. *Hippiatr.*71,72.

**βαθύσικος**, ὁ, kind of *cheese*, Gal.6.697 (Lat. *vatusicus*).

**βᾰθύ-σκαρθμος**, ον, (σκαίρω) *high-leaping*, Nonn.*D.*10.238. **-σκᾰφής**, ές, *deep-dug*, S.*El.*435. **-σκῐος**, ον, *deep-shaded*, *dark*, πέτρης κευθμῶνα *h.Merc.*229, cf. Theoc.4.19; ὗλαι Babr.92.2; οἰκίαι Ath.Med.ap.Orib.*inc.*23.18. II. Act., *throwing a deep shade*, ἀστήρ Musae.111. **-σκόπελος**, ον, *with high cliffs*, Orph.*A.*638, Q.S.1.316. **-σκοτος**, ον, *murky*, θύελλα Tz.*H.*10.294.

**βάθυσμα** [ᾰ], ατος, τό, *deep place*, λίμνης Thphr.*HP*4.11.8.

**βᾰθυ-σμῆριγξ**, ιγγος, ὁ, ἡ, *thick-haired*, Nonn.*D.*1.528. **-σοφός**, gloss on γλαφυρός, *EM*233.44. **-σπῆλυγξ**, υγγος, ὁ, ἡ, *with deep caves*, Nonn.*D.*40.260. **-σπορος**, ον, *deep-sown*, *fruitful*, E.*Ph.*648 (lyr.). 2. -σπόρος, = βαθεῖαν σπείρων γῆν, Hsch. **-στερνος**, ον, *deep-chested*, λέων Pi.*I.*3.12; β. αἶα *deep bosomed* earth, Cypr.*Fr.*1; χθών Pi.*N.*9.25; πόντος Orph.*H.*17.3. **-στολέω**, *wear long flowing robes*, Str.11.14.12. **-στολμος**, ον, *with deep, full robe*, prob. cj. in *AP*7.413 (Antip.). **-στομος**, ον, *deep-mouthed*, *deep*, σπήλαια Str.16.2.20. II. *cutting deep*, βουπλήξ Q.S.1.337. **-στρωτος**, ον, *deep strewn*, *well-covered*, λέκτρα Musae.266; κοίτη Babr.32.7. **-σχῖνος**, ον, *deep-grown with* σχῖνος, *AP*9.744 (Leon.). **-σχοινος**, ον, *deep-grown with rushes*, Ἀσωπός Il.4.383; χλόη Babr.46.2. **-τέρμων**, ον, gen. ονος, *deep*, *large*, ναῦς Opp.*C.*2.87.

⊛ **βᾰθύτης**, ητος, ἡ, = βάθος, *depth*, Luc.*Icar.*5: metaph. of character, Phld.*Ir.*p.60 W.; of mental *profundity*, Cic.*Att.*4.6.3, al.

**βᾰθύ-τῑμος** [ῠ], v. βαρύτιμος. **-τομέω**, *cut deeply*, τὸν μαστόν Leonid.ap.Aët.16.44. **-ϋδρος**, ον, *with deep water*, Sch.Il.16.3. **-ϋπνος**, ον, *in deep sleep*, Nic.*Th.*394. **-φροσύνη**, ἡ, *profundity of mind*, *Cat.Cod.Astr.*2.161.5. **-φρων**, ον, gen. ονος, = βαθύβουλος, Sol.33.1; Μοῖραι Pi.*N.*7.1. **-φυλλος**, ον, *thick-leafed*, *leafy*, Mosch.*Fr.*1.11. ⊛ **-φωνος**, ον, *of deep*, i.e. *hollow*, *voice*, Lxx *Is.*33.19. **-χάϊος** or **-χαῖος**, ον, *of old nobility*, A.*Supp.*858 (lyr.); cf. χάϊος. **-χαιτήεις**, εσσα, εν, = sq., A.*Eleg.*4. **-χαίτης**, ου, ὁ, *with thick long hair*, Hes.*Th.*977, Ph.2.479; Ἄδωνις Orph.*H.*56.7. **-χεύμων**, ον, gen. ονος, (χεῦμα) = βαθυκύμων, Procl.*H.*3.6. **-χθων**, ον, gen. ονος, = βαθύγειος, αἶα A.*Th.*306 (lyr.). **-χρήμων**, ον, gen. ονος, = βαθύπλουτος, Man.4.66. **-χροος**, ον, contr. **-χρους**, ουν, *deep-coloured*, Dsc.5.94.

⊛ **βαΐα**, ἡ, *nurse*, Str.*Chr.*5.39.

**βαῖβυξ**, υκος, ὁ, = πελεκάν, Hdn.Gr.2.741, Philet.ap.Hsch.

**βαίδειον**· ἕτοιμον (Elean), Hsch. **βαιδυμῆν**· ἀροτριᾶν (Boeot.), Id.:—also **βαιτρεύειν**, Id. **βαίεσσα**· βότρυς, Id. **βαῖκαν**· κρῆτες, Id. **βαίκυλος**· προβατώδης, Id. **βαιμάζειν**· βασιλεύειν, ἢ βαστάζειν, Id.

**βαϊνός**, όν, (βάϊς) *of palm-leaves*, Sm.*Ge.*40.16: **βαϊνή**, ἡ, *palm-rod*, Lxx 1*Ma.*13.37.

⊛ **βαίνω** (inf. βαίμεναι Hsch.), fut. βήσομαι Il.2.339, etc., Dor. βᾱσεῦμαι Theoc.2.8, etc.: pf. βέβηκα Il.15.90, etc., Dor. βέβᾱκα Pi.*I.*4(3).41, etc., with shortd. forms βεβάᾱσι Il.2.134, contr. βεβᾶσι A.*Pers.*1002 (lyr.), *Eu.*76, etc.; subj. βεβῶσι (ἐμ-) Pl.*Phdr.*252e; inf. βεβάμεν Il.17.359, βεβάναι E.*Heracl.*610 (lyr.); part. βεβαώς, -αυῖα Il.14.477, Hom.*Epigr.*15.10, contr. βεβώς: plpf. ἐβεβήκειν Il.11.296, etc., Ep. βεβήκειν 6.495; sync. 3 pl. βέβᾰσαν 17.286, etc.: aor. 2 ἔβην Il.17.112, etc., Dor. ἔβᾱν Pi.*O.*13.97, etc.; Ep. 3 sg. βῆ Il.13.297, Ep. 3 dual βάτην [ᾰ] 1.327, 3 pl. ἔβαν A.*Pers.*18 (lyr.), (κατ-) S.*Tr.*504 (lyr.), Ep. βάν Il.20.32; imper. βῆθι, Dor. βᾶθι S.*Ph.*1196 (lyr.); βᾶ in compds. ἔμβα, κατάβα, etc., 2 pl. βᾶτε A.*Supp.*191, *Eu.*1033 (lyr.); subj. βῶ, Ep. 3 sg. βήῃ (ὑπερ-) Il.9.501, βήω 6.113, ἐμ-βέῃ *GDI*5075.4 (Cret.), Dor. βᾶμες (for βῶμεν) Theoc.15.22; opt. βαίην; inf. βῆναι (Att. Prose only in compds.), Ep. βήμεναι Od.19.296, Dor. βᾶμεν Pi.*P.*4.39; part. βάς βᾶσα βάν, Dor. pl. ἐκ-βῶντας Th.5.77:—**Med.**, Ep. aor. 1 ἐβήσετο (ἀπ-) Il.1.428:—**Pass.**, pres. (v. infr. A. II. 1): in compds., aor. ἀν-, παρ-, ξυν-εβάθην, X.*Eq.*3.4, Th.3.67, 4.30; later παρ-εβάνθην D.C.48.2, al.; ἀνα-, παρα-, ξυμ-βέβᾰμαι, X.*Eq.Mag.*1.4, Th.1.123, 8.98; παρα-βέβασμαι D.17.12: fut. παρα-βαθήσομαι Sch.E.*Hec.*802.—For the Act. fut. and aor. 1, v. infr. B; for pres. part. βιβάς, v. βίβημι.—In correct Att. Prose the pres. βαίνω is almost the only tense in use; but in compds. Prose writers used all tenses freely.

A. in the above tenses, I. intr., *walk*, *step*, prop. of motion *on foot*, ποσὶ βήσετο Il.5.745, etc.; but also of all motion *on ground*, the direction being commonly determined by a Prep.:—the kind of motion is often marked by a part., βῆ φεύγων, βῆ ἀΐξασα, Il.2.665, 4.74: c. part. fut., denoting purpose, βῆ ῥ' Ἶσον..ἐξεναρίξων *he went to* slay, Il.11.101: with neut. Adj. as Adv., σαῦλα ποσὶν β. *h.Merc.*28; ἁβρὸν β. παλλεύκῳ ποδί E.*Med.*1164, cf. 830 (lyr.); ἴσα or ὁμοίως β. τινί, D.19.314, X.*Eq.*1.3; ἐν ποικίλοις β. A.*Ag.*936, cf. 924; *march* or *dance*, μετὰ ῥυθμοῦ, ἐν ῥυθμῷ, Th.5.70, Pl.*Lg.*670b: freq. c. inf. in Hom., βῆ δ' ἰέναι *set out* to go, *went* his way, Il.4.199, etc.; βῆ δ' ἴμεν 5.167, etc.; βῆ δὲ θέειν *started* to run, 2.183, etc.; βῆ δ' ἐλάαν 13.27: c. acc. loci, νέας Od.3.162, cf. S.*OT*153 (lyr.), *OC*378; ἐπὶ νηὸς ἔβαινεν *was going* on board ship, Od.11.534; but ἐν δὲ ἑκάστῃ [νηΐ]..ἑκατὸν καὶ εἴκοσι βαῖνον *were on board*, Il.2.510; ἐφ' ἵππων βάντες *having mounted* the chariot, 18.532; ἐπὶ πώλου βεβῶσα *mounted* on.., S.*OC*313; ἐς δίφρον Il.5.364; ἐς ἅρματα E.*El.*320; βαίνειν δι' αἵματος *wade* in blood, Id.*Ph.*20. 2. in pf., *stand* or *be* in a place, χῶρος ἐν ᾧ βεβήκαμεν S.*OC*52; βεβηκὼς σφόδρα firmly *poised* (opp. κρεμάμενος) Pl.*Ti.*62c; β. μάχη *steady* fight, Plu.*Phil.*9: freq. almost, = εἰμί (*sum*), εὖ βεβηκώς *on a good footing*, well *established*, *prosperous*, [θεοὶ] εὖ βεβηκότας ὑπτίους κλίνουσ' Archil.56.3; τυραννίδα εὖ βεβηκυῖαν Hdt.7.164, cf. S.*El.*979; εὖ βίου βεβηκότα prob. for ἐν βίῳ βεβιωκότα Nicom.Com.2; ἀσφαλέως βεβηκὼς ποσσί Archil.58.4; ἐπισφαλῶς βεβ. Lxx *Wi.*4.4; ἄγαλμα βεβηκὸς ἄνω τὰ κάτω δὲ κεχηνός Eub.107.23; οἱ ἐν τέλει ἐόντες, βεβῶτες, they who *are* in office, Hdt.9.106, S.*Ant.*67; τοῦτον οὐχ ὁρῇς ὅκως βέβη[κεν] ἀνδριάντα; Herod.4.36; [λίθους] ἐν ταῖς ἰδίαις χώραις βεβηκότας *IG*7.3073.163 (Lebad.); ἐν κακοῖς βεβ. S.*El.*1057; μοίρᾳ οὐκ ἐν ἐσθλᾷ β. ib.1095 (lyr.); βοῦς, κλεὶς ἐπὶ γλώσσῃ βέβηκεν, v. βοῦς IV, κλείς 4; φρόνει βεβὼς ἐπὶ ξυροῦ τύχης S.*Ant.*996. b. Geom. of figures, *stand* on a base, ἐπί τινος Arist.*IA*709[a]24, cf. Apollon.Perg.*Con.*3.3; πυραμὶς ἐπὶ τετραγώνου βεβηκυῖα Hero *Ster.*1.31; of an angle, *stand* on an arc, ἐπί τινος, πρός τινι, Euc.3*Def.*9, cf. 16.26. c. βεβηκὼς ῥυθμός *stately* rhythm, Syrian.*in Hermog.*1 p.69 R.; ἀνάπαυσις ib.p.18 R. 3. *go away*, *depart*, ἐν νηυσὶ φίλην ἐς πατρίδ' Il.12.16; ἔβαν ἄγοντες, ἔβαν φέρουσαι, *have gone* and taken away, 1.391, 2.302; ἄφαρ βέβακεν S.*Tr.*134; θανάσιμος βέβηκεν Id.*OT*959, cf. 832; βεβᾶσι φροῦδοι E.*IT*1289; βέβηκα euphem. for τέθνηκα, A.*Pers.*1002 (lyr.); of things, ἐννέα ἐνιαυτοὶ βεβάασι nine years *have come and gone*, Il.2.134; πῇ ὅρκια βήσεται; ib.339, cf. 8.229. 4. *come*, τίπτε βέβηκας; 15.90; *arrive*, S.*OT*81, *Aj.*921. 5. *go on*, *advance*, ἐς τόδε τόλμης, ἐς τοσοῦτον ἐλπίδων, Id.*OT*125, 772; ἐπ' ἔσχατα Id.*OC*217 (lyr.). 6. c. part. as periphr. for fut., βαίνω καταγγέλλων *PMag.Par.*1.2474. II. c. acc., *mount*, Hom. only in aor. Med. βήσασθαι δίφρον Il.3.262, Od.3.481: in Act. (fut. part. Med. βησόμενος Them.*Or.*21.248b), of the male, *mount*, *cover*, Pl.*Phdr.*250e, Achae.28, Arist.*HA*575[a]13, etc.:—in Pass., ἵπποι βαινόμεναι *brood* mares, Hdt.1.192. 2. c. acc. cogn., β. Δωρίαν κέλευθον ὕμνων Pi.*Fr.*191; Καλλαβίδας Eup.163; ἔβα ῥόον *went down* stream, i.e. *died*, Theoc.1.140. b. metaph. of metre, *scan*, D.H.*Comp.*21 (Pass.), Aristid.Quint.1.23, 24, etc.; βαίνεται τὸ ἔπος *is scanned*, Arist.*Metaph.*1093[a]30. 3. χρέος ἔβα με debts *came on* me, Ar.*Nu.*30; ὀδύνα μ' ὀδύνα βαίνει E.*Hipp.*1371 (lyr.). 4. Poet. with acc. of the instrument of motion, βαίνειν πόδα E.*El.*94, 1173 (lyr.). 5. βαίνειν· φιλεῖν, κολακεύειν, Hsch.

B. Causal, in fut. βήσω, (ἐπι-) Il.8.197, (εἰσ-) E.*IT*742: aor. 1 ἔβησα:—*make to go*, φῶτας βῆσεν ἀφ' ἵππων *he made* them *dismount*, Il.16.810; ἀμφοτέρους ἐξ ἵππων βῆσε κακῶς *he brought* them *down* from the chariot in sorry plight, 5.164; ὄφρα βάσομεν ὄκχον Pi.*O.*6.24.—Rare in Trag. (exc. in compds.), E.*Med.*209 (lyr.).—The simple Verb is uncommon in later Gr. (For βάμ-yω, cf. Lat. *venio*, Skt. *gamyáte*; βάσκω corresponds to Skt. *gácchati* ($g^{u}m̥$-*sk*-); root $g^{u}em$- in OHG. *quëman* 'come'; ἔβην, βήσομαι fr. root $g^{u}ā$-, Skt. *jigāti*, aor. *ágāt*.)

**βάϊον**, τό, = βάϊς, *Ev.Jo.*12.13; for gen. pl. βαΐων v. βάϊς. II. *measuring-rod*, β. δικαίῳ ἐξαπήχει *PFlor.*37.3 (v/vi A.D.), cf. *BGU* 1094.12 (vi A.D.).

⊛ **βαιός**, ά, όν, *little*, *small*, βαιὰ ποικίλλειν ἐν μακροῖσιν κτεάνων Pi.*P.*9.77; β. νῆσος A.*Pers.*448; μέρος β. ἔχειν Id.*Ag.*1574 (lyr.); ὄλβος prob. in E.*Fr.*825; γλῶττα Ar.*Nu.*1013; μαλλὸς εἰρίων Herod.8.12; *scanty*, and of number, *few*, σῦκα βαιά Anan.3, cf. Hp.*Lex* 1; βαιά γ' ὡς ἀπὸ πολλῶν A.*Pers.*1023 (lyr.); β. κύλιξ a *scanty* cup, i.e. one only, S.*Fr.*42, Lyc.*Fr.*3; ῥάκη β. *a few*, *paltry*, S.*Ph.*274; εἶπε πρός με βαιά *few words*, Id.*Aj.*292; but βαιὰν..λόγων φάμαν *low-spoken*, Id.*Ph.*845 (lyr.); ἥσθην δὲ βαιά, πάνυ δὲ βαιά, τέτταρα Ar.*Ach.*2; ἐχώρει βαιός he was going *with scanty escort*, i.e. *alone*, S.*OT*750; of condition, *mean*, *humble*, βαιοί, opp. οἱ μεγάλοι, Id.*Aj.*

160 (anap.); ἐκ κάρτα βαιῶν γνωτὸς ἂν γένοιτ' ἀνήρ from *a low condition*, Id.*Fr.*282; οὐχὶ βαιὰ τἀνθυμήματα Id.*OC*1199; βαιᾷ τῇδ' ὑπὸ στέγῃ Id.*Ph.*286; of time, *short*, Sol.10, S.*Tr.*44; βαιῆς ἄπο from *infancy* (of a girl), *IG*14.1892: neut. βαιόν as Adv., *a little*, S.*Aj.* 90, *Ph.*20: of time, Id.*OC*1653, *Tr.*335: pl., βαιά, φρονήσει τύχη μάχεται Democr.119; κατὰ βαιόν *by little and little*, D.P.622: Comp. βαιότερος, opp. μείζων, Parm.8.45, cf. Opp.*C.*3.86: Sup. –ότατος *AP*9.438 (Phil.).—Poet., Ion., and later Prose, as Phld.*Rh.*1.195, 244S., Id.*Ir.*p.95 W.

**βαϊο-φορέω,** *bear a palm-leaf*, of a priest, *PTeb.*294.10 (ii A.D.): **-φορία,** ἡ, ib.295.11 (ii A.D.).

**βαιόχρονος,** ον, *brief*, [βίος] *Inscr.Prien.*287 (i B.C.).

**βάϊς,** ἡ, acc. βάϊν Horap.1.3:—*palm-leaf* (Coptic *bai*), Chaerem. ap.Porph.*Abst.*4.7, *PMag.Leid.V.*7.16, *PLond.*1.131r384 (i A.D.), etc.; gen. pl. βαΐων *PMag.Leid.V.*7.17, Lxx 1 *Ma.*13.51.

**βαισήνης·** παρ' Ἰνδοῖς τὸ στρατόπεδον, Hsch. **βαίσηνος·** ὁ στρατός, Id. **βαισσόν·** βάθος, Id. **βαιτάς,** άδος, ἡ, = εὐτελὴς γυνή, Id.

⊛ **βαίτη,** ἡ, Dor. **βαίτα** Sophr.38:—*shepherd's* or *peasant's coat of skins*, Hdt.4.64, Theoc.3.25, *IG*5(2).268.48 (Mantinea, circ. i A.D.); τὴν β. θάλπουσαν εὖ δεῖ καὶ ῥάπτειν 'one good turn deserves another', Herod.7.128. **II.** *tent of skins*, S.*Fr.*1031. **III.** **βαίτης,** ου, ὁ, *warmed hall*, *Inscr.Magn.*179.12,15, *IG*5(2).268.48 (Mantinea, i B.C.). (Thracian word; Goth. *paida* 'garment'.)

**βαίτιον,** τό, = δίκταμνος, Ps.-Dsc.3.32, Hsch.

⊛ **βαιτοφόρος,** ον, (βαίτη) *wearing a coat of skin*, prob. for βαττ– in D.S.*Fr.*29.

**βαιτρεύειν,** v. βαιδυμῆν.

⊛ **βαίτῡλος,** ὁ, *meteoric stone*, held sacred, because it fell from heaven, Dam.*Isid.*94,203; of the stone swallowed by Kronos, Hsch.

**βαῖτυξ,** υγος, ἡ, *leech*, Hsch., *AB* 199. **βαιτῶνα·** τὸν εὐτελῆ ἄνδρα, Hsch.

**βαιῶμφαι·** αἱ αἶγες, ἐν ἱερατικοῖς, Hsch., Suid.

⊛ **βαιών,** όνος, ὁ, = βλέννος, Epich.64: prov., μή μοι β.· κακὸς ἰχθύς Ath.7.288a. **II.** at Alexandria, *a measure*, Hsch.

**Βαιῶτις,** ἡ, title of Aphrodite at Syracuse, Hsch.

**βακάϊον·** μέτρον τι, Hsch.

⊛ **βάκανον,** τό, *cabbage*, *PFay.*117.12 (pl.); also, *cabbage-seed*, Aët. 10.2, Alex.Trall.9.1, Paul.Aeg.7.11.42.

⊛ **βάκηλος** [ᾰ], ὁ, *eunuch in the service of Cybele, Gallus*, Luc.*Eun.*8, *Sat.*12. **II.** *womanish*, Antiph.113, Men.477, Telesp.24H., Zen.2.62.

**βακίας·** πηλός (Tarent.), *EM*186.1.

**Βᾰκίζω,** *prophesy like Bacis*, Ar.*Pax* 1072.

**Βακίνθιος,** v. Ὑακίνθιος.

**Βᾰκίς,** ἴδος, ὁ, Boeotian prophet, Hdt.8.20,77, al.; acc. Βάκιν Ar. *Pax* 1071; others are mentioned in Sch.Ar. l.c.: hence in pl., Βακίδες, οἱ, *soothsayers*, Arist.*Pr.*954a36.

**βάκκαρ,** τό, = ἄσαρον, Plin.*HN*21.29,30.

⊛ **βάκκᾰρις,** ἡ, gen. ιδος, dat. ιδι Ar.*Fr.*319, Magnes 3, but βακκάρῑ Semon.16, Hippon.41: acc. –ιν Hp.*Nat.Mul.*6: pl., βακκάρεις A.*Fr.* 14, Ion Trag.24:—*unguent* made from ἄσαρον, ll. cc. (Lydian word, Sch.A.*Pers.*42: one kind, = μύρον Λύδιον, Hsch.)

**βάκλον,** τό, = Lat. *baculum, stick, cudgel*, Aesop.188, Sch.Ar.*Pl.* 476 (pl.): pl., βάκυλα, = Lat. *fasces*, Plu.*Rom.*26:—hence **βακλίζω,** *cudgel*, *PMasp.*5.18 (vi A.D.).

**βακνίδες·** εἶδος ὑποδημάτων, Hsch. **βάκοα·** βάθρον, Id. **βακοίας·** πηλός, Id. **βακόν·** πεσόν (Cret.), Id. **βάκται·** ἰσχυροί, Id.

**βακταρικροῦσα,** barbarous word in Ar.*Av.*1629.

**βακτηρ-εύω,** = βακτρεύω, Suid. ⊛ **-ία,** ἡ, *staff, cane*, Ar.*Ach.*682, Th.8.84, Lys.24.12, X.*Eq.*11.4, etc.; συκίνη β., = σ. ἐπικουρία (q.v.), Alciphr.1.39, Macar.7.83. **II.** *wand*, as a badge of office, carried by δικασταί, D.18.210; ὁ λαβὼν τὴν β. βαδίζει εἰς τὸ δικαστήριον τὸ ὁμόχρων τῇ β. Arist.*Ath.*65.2. (Cf. Lat. *baculum, imbēcillus*, OIr. *bacc* 'crook, curved stick'.) **-ίδιον,** τό, Dim. of βακτηρία, Hsch. s.v. κάλιον. **-ιον,** τό, Dim. of βακτηρία, Ar.*Ach.*448, Men.*Sam.* 232. **-ίς,** ίδος, ἡ, = βακτηρία, prob. in Achae.21.

**Βάκτρα,** τά, *Balkh*, Hdt.9.113, Arist.*Mir.*833b14, Str.11.8.9: the people were **Βάκτριοι,** Hdt.3.102; or **Βακτριανοί,** Str. l.c.; cf. Βακτριανή, ἡ, Id.11.9.2:—the Bactrian camels were famous, Arist. *HA*498b8.

**βάκτρ-ευμα,** ατος, τό, *a staff*, βακτρεύμασι τυφλοῦ ποδός *by support lent to*.., E.*Ph.*1539 (lyr.). **-εύω,** *support as a staff*, ἀλαὸν πόδα, of Antigone, Arg.metr.S.*OC.* **-ιασμός,** ὁ, f.l. in Poll.4.101 for μακτρισμός.

⊛ **βάκτρον,** τό (cf. βακτηρία), *stick, cudgel*, A.*Ag.*202, *Ch.*362, E.*Ph.* 1719 (all lyr.), Theoc.25.207: metaph., τοκέων β. prob. in *Epigr.Gr.* 257.2 (Cyprus).

**βακτρο-προσαίτης,** ου, ὁ, *going about begging with a staff*, epith. of a Cynic, *AP*11.410 (Lucill.). **-φόρας,** ου, ὁ, *the staff-bearer*, epith. of Diogenes the Cynic, Cerc.1.2.

**βάκχαρ,** τό, = ἄσαρον, Ps.-Dsc.1.10; cf. βάκκαρ. **βάκχαρι,** τό, *unguent* prepared therefrom, Aret.*CA*2.10.

**βάκχᾰρις,** ἡ, *sowbread, Cyclamen hederaefolium*, Cephisod.3, Dsc. 3.44.

**Βακχᾶς,** ὁ, = Βακχευτής, S.*Fr.*674.

**Βακχάω,** *to be in Bacchic frenzy, to rave*, A.*Th.*498.

**Βακχέβακχον** ᾆσαι sing *the song* (to Bacchus) beginning with Βάκχε Βάκχε! Ar.*Eq.*408.

⊛ **Βακχ-εία,** ἡ, *Bacchic frenzy, revelry*, Βακχείας καλῆς A.*Ch.*698, cf. E.*Ba.*232, Arist.*Pol.*1342b4; ἡδονῇ δοὺς ἔς τε Β. πεσών (prob. for –εῖον) E.*Ph.*21; τῆς φιλοσόφου μανίας τε καὶ Βακχείας the madness and *frenzy* of philosophy, Pl.*Smp.*218b: in pl., *Bacchic orgies*, E.*Ba.* 218,1293. **-ειακός,** ή, ον, = Βακχεῖος II.3, μέτρον Heph.13.1, al. ⊛ **-εῖον,** τό, *Bacchic revelry*, Ar.*Lys.*1: pl., Id.*Ra.*357; Βάκχια, dub. l. in E.*Ba.*126. **2.** *congregation of Bacchic worshippers*, *IG*7.107 (Megara, ii A.D.), *Archives des Missions* 1876.150 (Perinthus). **b.** = τελεστήριον, νάρθηξ, Hsch. **-ειος** or **Βακχεῖος,** α, ον, also **Βάκχιος,** α, ον (to suit the metre), fem. ος Luc.*Ocyp.*171:—*of* or *belonging to Bacchus* and *his rites*, βότρυς S.*Fr.*255.2; νόμος E.*Hec.*686 (lyr.); ῥυθμός X.*Smp.*9.3, etc.: hence, *frenzied, rapt*, Β. Διόνυσος *h.Hom.*19.46, cf. Hdt.4.79; ὁ Β. θεός S.*OT*1105 (lyr.); Βάκχειε δέσποτ' Ar.*Th.*988 (lyr.), cf. *IG*4.558.20 (Argos), etc.; τὸν Β. ἄνακτα, of Aeschylus, Ar.*Ra.*1259. **II.** as Subst., Βάκχιος, ὁ, = Βάκχος, S.*Ant.*154 (lyr.), E.*Cyc.*9:—also, = οἶνος, Id.*IT*953, *Cyc.*519, Antiph. 237. **2.** **Βάκχια** or **-εῖα,** τά, v. Βακχεῖον. **3.** Βακχεῖος (sc. πούς), ὁ, *the bacchius, a metrical foot of three syllables*, – – ⏑, D.H.*Comp.*17 (opp. ὑποβ. ⏑ – –); but later ⏑ – –, Heph.3 (opp. παλιμβ. – – ⏑), etc.; also β. ἀπὸ τροχαίου (– ⏑ ⏑ –), ἀπ' ἰάμβου (⏑ – – ⏑), Aristid.Quint. 1.17, cf. Anon.Rhythm.*Oxy.*9 iii 12; = ⏑ ⏑ – –, Bacch.*Harm.* 101. **-ειοχόρειος** (sc. πούς), ὁ, the foot – – ⏑ – ⏑, Diom.p.482 K. **-ευμα,** ατος, τό, in pl., *Bacchic revelries*, E.*Ba.*40,317, Plu.*TG* 10. **-εύς,** έως, ὁ, = Βάκχος, A.*Fr.*341, S.*Ant.*1121, E.*Ba.*145, etc. (only in lyr.), Orph.*H.*45.2, *APl.*4.156, *SIG*1014.147 (Erythrae), 1024.27 (Myconos). **-εύσιμος,** ον, *Bacchanalian, frenzied*, E.*Ba.* 298. **-ευσις,** εως, ἡ, *Bacchic revelry*, ib.357. **-ευτής,** οῦ, ὁ, *a Bacchanal, any one full of Bacchic frenzy* or *of wine*, Orph.*H.*11.21, 47.6; β. θεός *APl.*4.290 (Antip.):—fem. **-εύτρια** *AB*225, Hsch. s.v. Βάκχου Διώνης. **II.** as Adj., Β. ῥυθμός *AP*11.64.2 (Agath.). **-ευτικός,** ή, όν, *disposed to Bacchic revels*, Arist.*Pol.*1342b26. **-εύτωρ,** ορος, ὁ, = Βακχευτής, *CIG*38, *AP*9.524. **-εύω,** *celebrate the mysteries of Bacchus*, Hdt.4.79. **2.** *speak* or *act like one frenzy-stricken*, S.*Ant.* 136 (lyr.), E.*Ion* 1204, etc.: also of places, β. στέγη A.*Fr.*58, cf. E. *IT*1243 (lyr.). **II.** causal, *inspire with frenzy*, αὗταί σε βακχεύουσι συγγενῆ φόνον; E.*Or.*411, cf. *HF*966:—Pass., Id.*Or.*835; φιλοσοφία εὖ μάλα βεβακχ. *full of mysticism*, Plu.2.580c. **2.** *initiate in the Bacchic mysteries*, in Pass., *Schwyzer*792 (Cyme, v B.C.).

**Βακχέχορος,** ον, *leading the Bacchic dance*, Διώνυσος Orph.*H.*57.3, 75.1.

**Βάκχη,** ἡ, *Bacchante*, A.*Eu.*25, S.*Ant.*1122 (lyr.), Ar.*Nu.*605, Pl. *Ion* 534a, etc.: generally, Βάκχη Ἅιδου *frantic handmaid* of Hades, E.*Hec.*1077; β. νεκύων Id.*Ph.*1489 (lyr.). **II.** a kind of *pear*, Nic. *Al.*354, *Th.*513.

**Βακχ-ιάζω,** = Βακχεύω I, E.*Cyc.*204; = βακχεύω II, Id.*Ba.*931, Philod.Scarph.14. **-ιακός,** ή, όν, = Βάκχιος, νύκτες Orph.*H.*79. 9. **-ιάς,** άδος, ἡ, poet. fem. of Βάκχειος, ὀπώρη *AP*6.72 (Agath.), Nonn.12.296, al. ⊛ **-[ια]στής,** οῦ, Dor. **-τάς,** ὁ, *Bacchic reveller*, Philod.Scarph.144. ⊛ **-ικός,** ή, όν, = Βάκχειος, Arist.*Pr.*922b22; ἔπη D.S.1.11; –κόν, τό, Str.10.3.10: Sup. –ώτατος Luc.*Bis Acc.*9. Adv. –κῶς Str.15.1.8: Comp. –ώτερον Duris 24. ⊛ **-ιος,** α, ον, = Βάκχειος (q.v.). **-ιόω,** *fill with the divine presence*, βεβακχιωμένην.. Νῦσαν S. *Fr.*959. **-ίς,** ίδος, ἡ, = Βάκχη, Νύμφαι Id.*Ant.*1129. **-ισταί,** οἱ, *worshippers of Bacchus*, *IG*12(3).1296 (Thera). ⊛ **-ιών,** ῶνος, ὁ, name of a month at Myconos, *SIG*1024.26. ⊛ **-ιώτης,** ου, ὁ, = Βακχευτής, S.*OC*678 (lyr.).

**βακχόαν·** βόθρον (Aeol.), Hsch.; cf. βάκοα, βακοίας.

⊛ **Βάκχος,** ὁ, *Bacchus*, name of Dionysus, first in S.*OT*211 (lyr.), cf. E.*Hipp.*560 (lyr.), al., Limen.19, Theoc.*Epigr.*18.3, etc. **2.** Ζεὺς Β. *Epigr.Gr.*1035.22. **II.** *wine*, E.*IA*1061 (lyr.), etc. **III.** *Bacchanal*, Heraclit.14, E.*Ba.*491: generally, *any one inspired, frantic*, Ἅιδου Βάκχος Id.*HF*1119; πολλοὶ μὲν ναρθηκοφόροι, Β. δέ τε παῦροι Orph.*Fr.*5. **2.** *branch* carried by initiates, Xenoph.17. **IV.** a kind of *grey mullet*, Hices.ap.Ath.7.306e; = ὀνίσκος II, Dorio ap. Ath.3.118c, cf. Xenocr.1. **V.** *garland*, βάκχοισιν κεφαλὰς περιάνθεσιν ἐστέψαντο Nic.*Fr.*130. **VI.** = κλαυθμός (Phoenician), Hsch.

**βακχούρια,** τά, Hebr. word in Lxx, = πρωτογεννήματα, *Ne.*13.31.

**βάκχῠλος,** ὁ, *bread baked in hot ashes*, Elean word, Nic.*Fr.*121.

**Βακχ-ώδης,** ες, (Βάκχος) *filled with the spirit of Bacchus*, Arr.*Ind.* 8.1 (Sup.). **-ων,** ωνος, ὁ, Dim. of Βακχυλίδης, Sch.D.T.p.227 H.

**βάλαγρος,** ὁ, a fresh-water fish, prob. a kind of *carp*, Arist.*HA* 538a15.

**βάλαικες·** δεσμωτήριον, καὶ **βαλαικάκες,** Hsch.:—also **βάλεκες,** Id., and **βάλακες, βαλάδες,** Cyr.

**βαλαιόν·** μέγα, πολύ, οἱ δὲ ταχύ, Hsch.

**βαλακρός,** Maced. = φαλ–, Plu.2.292e.

⊛ **βᾰλᾰν-άγρα,** ἡ, *key* or *hook for pulling out the* βάλανος II.4, Hdt. 3.155, X.*HG*5.2.29, Aen.Tact.18.9: in pl., = βάλανος II.4, Plb.7.16.5, Them.*Or.*26.315d. ⊛ **-άριον,** τό, *bath-towel* (or *-bag*), *PAmh.*2.126. 45 (ii A.D.), *POxy.*921.18 (iii A.D.). **-ειόμφᾰλος,** ον, *with a boss like the valve of a bath*, φιάλη β. a cup *with a round bottom*, Cratin. 50. ⊛ **-εῖον,** τό, *bath, bathing-room*, Ar.*Nu.*837,1054, etc.; β. δημόσιον *BGU*1130.9 (i B.C.): more freq. in pl., Ar.*Nu.*991, *Eq.*1401, etc. **2.** *bath* taken, Aristo *Stoic.*1.88, Gal.11.46.—Prose word for poet. λουτρά. **-είτης,** ου, ὁ, = sq., Plb.30.29.4. **-εύς,** έως, ὁ, *bath-man*, Ar.*Eq.*1403, *Ra.*710, Pl.*R.*344d, etc.: prov., βαλανεὺς ἐπὶ τῶν πολυπραγμόνων Diogenian.3.64. **-ευτής,** οῦ, ὁ, = βαλανεύς,

*PSI*5.584 (iii B.C.), *PTeb.*401.24 (i A.D.), etc. :—fem. **-εύτρια**, Poll 7.166, Lib.*Decl.*26.19. ⊛ **-ευτικός**, ή, όν, *of* or *for baths*, ἔλαιον *PTeb.*117.61 (i B.C.); κονία *Gp.*10.29.4; ἡ -κή (sc. τέχνη), Pl.*Sph.* 227a. **-εύω**, *heat the bath*, Ar.*Lys.*337 ; but β. ἑαυτῷ *to be* one's own *bath-man*, Id.*Pax* 1103 ; *drench like a bath-man*, οἴνῳ κατὰ τοῦ κεράμου β. Pherecr.130.6 :—Pass., Timocl.2 (dub.). **2.** *bawl, shout*, Hsch. **-ηρός**, ά, όν, (βάλανος) *of the acorn type*, Thphr.*HP*1.11.3.

**βᾰλᾰνη-φᾰγέω**, *live on acorns*, App.*BC*1.50. **-φᾰγία**, ἡ, *a living on acorns*, Ph.2.409. **-φάγος** [φᾰ], ον, *acorn-eating*, esp. of Arcadians, Alc.(?).91, Orac.ap.Hdt.1.66, Plu.*Cor.*3, Nonn.*D.*13.287, Them.*Or.*26.316c. **-φόρος**, ον, *bearing dates*, φοίνικες Hdt.1.193.

**βᾰλᾰν-ίδιον**, τό, *small bathing-establishment*, δημόσιον β. *POxy.* 1430.13 (iv A.D.). **-ίζω** δρῦν, *shake acorns from* the oak, hence as prov. answer to beggars, ἄλλην δρῦν βαλάνιζε *AP*11.417, Zen. 2.41, etc. **II.** (βάλανος II.6) β. τινά *administer a suppository to* him, Hp.ap.Poll.10.150. ⊛ **-ικός**, ή, όν, *of* or *for the bath* : τὸ β., = ἐπίλουτρον, Sch.Luc.*Lex.*2. **-ῐνος**, η, ον, *made of* βάλανος, β. ἔλαιον oil *of zukkum*, Thphr.*Od.*29, Dsc.1.34, cf. 19. **2.** *of the colour of* β., *POxy.*265.3 (i A.D.). **-ιον**, τό, *decoction of acorns*, used as a restorative after drunkenness, Nicoch.15. **2.** = βάλανος II.6, Hp. *Mul.*1.92, Ruf.ap.Orib.8.39, Dsc.4.176. **-ίς**, ίδος, ἡ, *pessary*, Hp.*Mul.*2.155, *Steril.*221. **2.** *peg, stopper*, *PLond.*3.1177.178 (ii A.D.). **II.** = βαλάνισσα, Suid. **-ῐσις**, εως, ἡ, = sq., *Gloss.* **-ισμός**, ὁ, *administration of a suppository*, Aët.8.49, Cael. Aur.*TP*4.7.105. ⊛ **-ισσα**, ἡ, fem. of βαλανεύς, *bathing-woman*, *AP*5.81. **-ιστέον**, *one must administer a suppository*, Archig.ap. Aët.9.27, Paul.Aeg.2.98. **-ιστής**, οῦ, ὁ, *one who collects acorns*, Zen.2.41. **-ίτης** [ῑ], ου, ὁ, *acorn-shaped*, β. λίθος a precious stone, Plin.*HN*37.149. **II.** β. βίος of *those who live on acorns*, Eust. 1859.47. **-ῖτις**, ιδος, ἡ, a sort of *sweet chestnut*, Plin.*HN*15.93.

**βᾰλᾰνο-δόκη**, ἡ, (δέχομαι) *socket in a door-post to receive the* βάλανος (II.4), Aen.Tact.18.3, al. **-ειδής**, ές, *like an acorn*, Dsc.5. 137. **-κάστᾰνον**, τό, *chestnut*, prob. for βολβο-, Alex.Trall.5.6.

⊛ **βάλᾰνος** [βᾰ], ἡ, *acorn*, Od.10.242, 13.409, Arist.*HA*603$^{b}$31, Thphr.*HP*3.8.3 : *any similar fruit, date*, Hdt.1.193, X.*An.*2.3.15, Arr.*Ind.*11.8 ; Διὸς β. v. Διοσβάλανος ; β. μυρεψική *bān*, *Balanites aegyptiaca*, Dsc.4.157, cf. Thphr.*HP*4.2.1. **2.** *tree which bears* βάλανοι, ib.6, Plb.34.8.1, Lxx *Ge.*35.8. **II.** from similarity of shape, **1.** a sea shell-fish, *barnacle*, Arist.*HA*535$^{a}$24, 547$^{b}$22, Xenocr.ap.Orib.2.58.50. **2.** *glans penis*, Arist.*HA*493$^{a}$27, Ar.*Lys.* 413, Gal.10.381. **3.** *air-vessel* of a seaweed, *bladder-wrack*, *Fucus vesiculosus*, Thphr.*HP*4.6.9. **4.** *iron peg, bolt-pin*, Ar.*V.*200, Th.2. 4, Aen.Tact.18.1, al. **5.** *fastening for necklaces*, Ar.*Lys.*410. **6.** Medic., *suppository*, Hp.*Epid.*1.26.α', Aret.*CA*1.1. **b.** *pledget, pessary*, Hp.*Mul.*1.84. **7.** *ballot-ball*, Arist.*Ath.*63.2. (Lat. *glans*, Slav. *želądĭ*, Lith. *gìlė*.)

**βᾰλᾰνο-φᾰγέω**, = βαλανηφαγέω, Sch.Od.19.163. **-φάγος** [φᾰ], = βαλανηφάγος, *EM*790.36.

**βᾰλᾰνόω**, *fasten with a* βάλανος (II.4), βεβαλάνωκε τὴν θύραν Ar.*Ec.* 361 :—Pass., *to be shut close, secured*, Id.*Av.*1159 : metaph. in pf. part. Pass., *constipated*, Id.*Ec.*370.

**βαλαντίδιον, βαλάντιον, βαλαντιοτομέω, -τόμος**, v. βαλλ-.

**βᾰλαντῐοκλέπτης**, ου, ὁ, *cutpurse*, Phryn.201 (who condemns the form βαλαντο-).

**βᾰλᾰν-ώδης**, ες, *acorn-like*, Thphr.*CP*4.3.4, *HP*3.16.1. **-ω[σις]**, εως, ἡ, *right of gathering acorns*, prob. in *IG*5(2).456 (Megalopolis). **-ωτός**, ή, όν, (βαλανόω) *fastened with a* βάλανος (II.4), ὀχεύς Parm.1.16 ; θύρα X.*Oec.*9.5. **II.** *adorned with acorns*, φιάλη Ath.11.502b.

**βάλαρες**· οἱ βλαισοί, **βαλάρα** γὰρ γυνὴ παρὰ Βοιωτοῖς, Hsch.

**βάλαρις**, = βρύον θαλάσσιον, Ps.-Dsc.4.98. **2.** = βοτάνη τρίφυλλος, Hsch. **3.** (βάλλ-), = λυχνὶς στεφανωματική, Ps.-Dsc.3.100.

**βαλαρός**, ὁ, Corsican word for φυγάς, Paus.10.17.9.

**βαλάσαι**· ἀγοράσαι, Hsch.

**βαλαύστιον**, τό, *flower of the wild pomegranate*, Dsc.1.111, Gal.11. 847 :—hence Adj. **βαλαύστινος**, *PSI*4.333.8 (iii B.C.). **βαλαυστιουργός**, ὁ, *dyer* (?), dub. in Alciphr.1.2.

**βαλαύστρινος**, η, ον, *of the colour of pomegranate flowers*, *Stud.Pal.* 20.41 (ii A.D.).

**βαλβῑδοῦχος**, ὁ, *judge* in races, Hsch.

**βαλβῑδώδης**, ες, *with cavities* or *grooves*, Hp.*Mochl.*1.

**βαλβίς**, ῖδος, ἡ, prop. *rope drawn across the race-course at the starting and finishing-point* : mostly in pl., *posts to which this rope was attached*, Ar.*Eq.*1159 : so in sg., *turning-post*, νῆσος β. ξεστῇ εἴκασται Philostr.*VA*5.5 : also, *platform from which the quoit was thrown*, Id.*Im.*1.24 : hence, *any starting-point*, Antipho Soph.69 ; βαλβίδων ἄπο E.*HF*867, cf. Ar.*V.*548 : metaph., ἕρπε πρὸς βαλβῖδα λυπηρὰν βίου E.*Med.*1245 ; ἐκ β. εἰς τέρμα Them.*Or.*13.177d ; β. λόγου βέβληται Philostr.*VS*2.20.3 ; βιβλίου *AP*4.3b.75 (Agath.) ; but, *edge*, ib.39. **II.** since *the starting-point* was also *the goal*, βαλβῖδες was used for *any point to be gained*, as *the battlements* (by one scaling a wall), S.*Ant.*131 (lyr.), cf. Lyc.287, Opp.*C.*1.513. **III.** = κοιλότης παραμήκης, Gal.19.87 ; v. foreg.

**βάλε**, *O that! would God!* c. opt., Alcm.26, Call.*Hec.*26.2 ; cf. ἄβαλε.

⊛ **βάλερος** or **βαλῖνος**, ὁ, kind of *carp*, Arist.*HA*568$^{b}$27 :—also **βαλλιρός**, ib.602$^{b}$26 ; cf. βάλαγρος.

**βαλήν**, ὁ, v. βαλλήν.

**Βάλησς**, epith. of Zeus in Bithynia, *Ath.Mitt.*19.373.

**βαλία**· ὀφθαλμία, καὶ τὸν **βάλιον** πηρόν (Cret.), Hsch.

⊛ **βαλιδικός**, ή, όν, epith. of a kind of *nut*, κάρυα βαλιδικά *PPetr.*3 p.332.

**βαλικιώτης** (ϝαλ-), Cret. for ἡλικιώτης, Hsch. **βαλῖνος**, v. βάλερος.

**βᾰλιός**, ά, όν, *spotted, dappled*, ἔλαφος, λύγκες, E.*Hec.*90, *Alc.*579 (both lyr.) ; πέρδιξ *AP*7.203 (Simm.). **2.** parox., Βαλίος, as name of one of Achilles' horses, *Piebald, Dapple*, Il.16.149, al., cf. E.*IA* 222. **II.** *swift*, Opp.*C.*2.314, Tryph.84, Nonn.*D.*9.156, al.

**βαλίς**, = σίκυς ἄγριος, Ps.-Dsc.4.150.

**βαλιῶται**· πρόγονοι, Hsch. **βάλλαι**· βαθμοί (Cypr.), Id. (Aeol. = βηλός).

**βαλλαντιατόμος**, v. βαλλαντιοτόμος.

**βαλλαντίδιον** [ῐ], τό, Dim. of sq., to be read for βαλ- in Eup.23, Hld.2.30.

⊛ **βαλλάντιον**, τό, *bag, pouch, purse*, [Simon.]178, Epich.10 (βαλ-), Ar.*Eq.*707, al., Thphr.*Char.*17.5 ; παῖς ἐκ βαλλαντίου a supposititious child, Teleclid.41. **II.** *javelin* (as if from βάλλω), a pun in Dionys. ap.Ath.3.98d. (The spelling βαλλ- is better attested than that with βαλ-, cf. Phld.*Rh.*1.354S., etc. ; cf. βαλλαντιοτομέω, -τόμος.)

**βαλλαντιο-τομέω**, *cut purses*, Pl.*R.*575b, X.*Mem.*1.2.62 (βαλ-). **-τόμος**, ὁ, *cutpurse, footpad*, Ecphantid.4, Teleclid.15, Aeschin.3. 207, v. l. in Pl.*R.*552d (leg. βαλλαντιᾱτόμοι (βαλ- codd. AF)) ; τοῖσι βαλλαντιοτόμοις, prob. for τοῖς βαλαντιοτόμοις, Ar.*Ra.*772.

**βαλλαχράδαι**, οἱ, *pear-throwers, nickname among boys at Argos*, Plu.2.303a.

**βάλλεκα**· ψῆφον, Hsch. **βαλλήιαι**· οἱ ἀκροβολισμοί, Id.

**βαλλήν**, ὁ (not βαλήν Hdn.Gr.2.923), *king*, A.*Pers.*657, S.*Fr.*515. —Prob. Phrygian word acc. to Hsch., but Thurian acc. to Hermesianax Hist.ap.Ps.-Plu.*Fluv.*12.4 : **βαλληναῖον** ὄρος, = βασιλικόν (in Phrygia) and **βαλλήν**, a fabulous precious stone, Ps.-Plu.*Fluv.*12. 3,4.

**Βαλλήνᾰδε** βλέπειν, a pun between βάλλω and the Attic deme Παλλήνη, Ar.*Ach.*234.

**βαλλητύς**, ύος, ἡ, *throwing*, Ath.9.406d, 407c ; festival of Demeter at Athens with a sham fight, Hsch.

⊛ **βαλλίζω**, *dance, jump about*, in Sicily and Magna Graecia, Epich. 79, Sophr.11,12, Ath.8.362bsq.

**βαλλίον**, τό, = φαλλός, Herod.6.69. **βαλλιρός**, ὁ, v. βάλερος.

**βάλλις**, εως, ἡ, *plant* with wonderful medicinal properties, Xanth. 16.

**βαλλισμός**, ὁ, *jumping about, dancing*, Alex.107, Ath.8.362b.

**Βαλλιστής**, οῦ, ὁ, a constellation, *Cat.Cod.Astr.*7.204.14.

**βαλλίστρα**, ἡ, *catapult, engine of war*, Procop.*Goth.*1.22, al., Steph. *in Hp.*2.384D.

⊛ **βάλλω**, fut. βᾰλῶ (in Att. Prose only in compds.), Ion. βαλέω Il. 8.403, βαλλήσω Ar.*V.*222,1491 : aor. 2 ἔβᾰλον, Ion. προ-βάλεσκε Od. 5.331 ; later aor. 1 ἔβαλα Lxx 3*Ki.*6.1 (5.18) ; Ep. and Ion. inf. βαλέειν Il.2.414, al., Hdt.2.111, al., but βαλεῖν Il.13.387, 14.424 ; opt. βλείης in Epich.219, part. βλείς Id.176, as if from ἔβλην (v. συμβάλλω) : pf. βέβληκα : plpf. ἐβεβλήκειν, Ep. βεβλήκειν Il.5.661 :—**Med.**, Ion. impf. βαλλέσκετο Hdt.9.74 : fut. βᾰλοῦμαι (προ-) Ar.*Ra.*201, (ἐπι-) Th.6.40, etc., Ep. βαλεῦμαι (ἀμφι-) Od.22.103 : aor. 2 ἐβᾰλόμην, Ion. imper. βαλεῦ Hdt.8.68.γ', used mostly in compds. :—**Pass.**, fut. βληθήσομαι X.*HG*7.5.11, (δια-) E.*Hec.*863 ; also βεβλήσομαι Id. *Or.*271, Hld.2.13, (δια-) D.16.2 ; part. δια-βεβλησόμενος Philostr. *VA*6.13 (Ep. fut. ξυμ-βλήσομαι, v. συμβάλλω) : aor. ἐβλήθην Hdt.1. 34, Th.8.84, etc. : Hom. also has an Ep. aor. Pass., ἔβλητο Il.11. 675, ξύμβλητο 14.39 ; subj. βλήεται Od.17.472 ; opt. βλῇο or βλεῖο Il.13.288 ; inf. βλῆσθαι 4.115 ; part. βλήμενος 15.495 : pf. βέβλημαι, Ion. 3 pl. βεβλήαται 11.657 (but 3 sg. *h.Ap.*20), opt. δια-βεβλῆσθε And.2.24 : plpf. ἐβεβλήμην (περι-) X.*HG*7.4.22, (ἐξ-) Isoc.18.17 ; Ion. 3 pl. περι-εβεβλέατο Hdt.6.25.—Ep. pf. βεβόλημαι in special sense, v. βολέω.

**A.** Act., *throw* : **I.** with acc. of person or thing aimed at, *throw so as to hit, hit* with a missile, freq. opp. *striking* with a weapon in the hand, βλήμενος ἠὲ τυπείς Il.15.495 ; τὸν βάλεν, οὐδ' ἀφάμαρτε 11.350, cf. 4.473, al. ; so even in ἐγγύθεν ἐλθὼν βεβλήκει .. δουρί 5.73 ; and δουρὶ ὤμων μεσσηγὺς σχεδόθεν βάλε 16.807 ; but later opp. τοξεύειν, D.9.17, X.*An.*4.2.12 ; ἐκ χειρὸς β. ib.3.3.15 : c. dat. instrumenti, β. τινὰ δουρί, πέτρῳ, κεραυνῷ, etc., Il.13.518, 20.288, Od.5. 128, etc. : βλήμενος ἢ ἰῷ ἢ ἔγχεϊ Il.8.514 : c. dupl. acc. pers. et partis, μιν βάλε μηρὸν ὀϊστῷ 11.583 : c. acc. partis only, 5.19,657 ; so τὸν δ' Ὀδυσεὺς κατὰ λαιμὸν .. βάλεν ἰῷ Od.22.15 ; δουρὶ βαλὼν πρὸς στῆθος Il. 11.144 : c. acc. cogn., ἕλκος .., τό μιν βάλε Πάνδαρος ἰῷ 5.795 ; also βάλε Τυδεΐδαο κατ' ἀσπίδα *smote upon* it, ib.281. **2.** less freq. of things, ἡνίοχον κονίης ῥαθάμιγγες ἔβαλλον 23.502 ; of drops of blood, 11.536, cf. A.*Ag.*1390 : metaph., κηλὶς ἔβαλέ νιν μητροκτόνος E.*IT* 1200, cf. *HF*1219 ; of the sun, ἀκτῖσιν ἔβαλλεν [θάμνους] Od.5.479 ; ἔβαλλε .. οὐρανὸν Ἠώς A.R.4.885 (so Pass., σελήνη .. δι' εὐτρήτων βαλλομένη θυρίδων *AP*5.122 (Phld.)) ; *strike* the senses, of sound, ἵππων ὠκυπόδων ἀμφὶ κτύπος οὔατα βάλλει Il.10.535, cf. S.*Ant.*1188, *Ph.*205 (lyr.) ; of smell, ὀσμὴ β. τινά Id.*Ant.*412 ; τάχ' ἂν πέμφιξ σε βροντῆς καὶ δυσοσμίας β. Id.*Fr.*538. **3.** metaph., β. τινὰ κακοῖς, φθόνῳ, ψόγῳ, *smite* with reproaches, etc., Id.*Aj.*1244, E.*El.*902, Ar. *Th.*895 ; στεφάνοις β. τινά Pi.*P.*8.57 (hence metaph., *praise*, Id.*O.*2. 98) ; φθόνος βάλλει A.*Ag.*947 ; φίλημα βάλλει τὴν καρδίαν Ach.Tat. 2.37. **II.** with acc. of the weapon thrown, *cast, hurl*, of missiles, rare in Hom., βαλὼν βέλος Od.9.495 ; χαλκὸν ἐνὶ στήθεσσι βαλών Il.5.

346, cf. Od.20.62; ἐν νηυσὶν.. πῦρ β. Il.13.629: c. dat., of the weapon, *throw* or *shoot with* a thing, οἱ δ' ἄρα χερμαδίοισι.. βάλλον 12.155; βέλεσι Od.16.277: in Prose abs., β. ἐπί τινα *throw* at one, Th.8.75; ἐπὶ σκοπόν X.*Cyr*.1.6.29; ἐπίσκοπα Luc.*Am*.16; alone, οἱ ψιλοὶ βάλλοντες εἶργον Th.4.33: c. gen., βάλλοντα τοῦ σκοποῦ *hitting* the mark, Pl.*Sis*.391a. 2. generally of anything thrown, εἰς ἅλα λύματ' ἔβαλλον Il.1.314; τὰ μὲν ἐν πυρὶ βάλλε Od.14.429; [νῆα] β. ποτὶ πέτρας 12.71; εὐνὰς β. *throw out* the anchor-stones, 9.137; 3. σπόρον *cast* the seed, Theoc.25.26; β. κόπρον *POxy*.934.9 (iii A.D.): hence β. ἀρούρας *manure*, *PFay*.118.21 (ii A.D.): metaph., ὕπνον.. ἐπὶ βλεφάροις β. Od.1.364; β. σκότον ὄμμασι E.*Ph*.1535 (lyr.); β. λύπην τινί S.*Ph*.67. b. of persons, β. τινὰ ἐν κονίῃσιν, ἐν δαπέδῳ, Il.8.156, Od. 22.188; γῆς ἔξω β. S.*OT*622; β. τινὰ ἄθαπτον Id.*Aj*.1333; ἄτιμον Id. *Ph*.1028:—Pass., ὑπὸ χλαίνῃ βεβλημένος *AP*5.164 (Mel.); βεβλημένος *on a sick-bed*, *Ev.Matt*.8.14: then metaph., ἐς κακὸν β. τινά Od. 12.221; ὅς με μετ'.. ἔριδας καὶ νείκεα β. Il.2.376; β. τινὰ ἐς ἔχθραν, ἐς φόβον, A.*Pr*.390, E.*Tr*.1058; also ἐν αἰτίᾳ or αἰτίᾳ β. τινά, S.*OT*657, *Tr*.940 (but in E.*Tr*.305 β. αἰτίαν ἔς τινα); κινδύνῳ β. τινά A.*Th*. 1053. 3. *let fall*, ἑτέρωσε κάρη βάλεν Il.8.306, cf. 23.697; β. ἀπὸ δάκρυ παρειῶν Od.4.198, cf. 114; κατὰ βλεφάρων β. δάκρυα Thgn. 1206; κατ' ὄσσων E.*Hipp*.1396; αἵματος πέμφιγα πρὸς πέδῳ β. A.*Fr*. 183; β. τοὺς ὀδόντας *cast*, *shed* them, Arist.*HA*501$^{b}$2, etc.; so βάλλειν alone, ib.576$^{a}$4; βοῦς βεβληκώς *SIG*958.7 (Ceos). 4. of the eyes, ἑτέρωσε βάλ' ὄμματα *cast* them, Od.16.179; ὄμματα πρὸς γῆν E.*Ion* 582; πρόσωπον εἰς γῆν Id.*Or*.958: intr., ὀφθαλμὸς πρὸς τὸ φῶς βαλὼν *aiming at*.., Plot.2.4.5; βαλὼν πρὸς αὐτὸ *directing one's gaze* at.., Id.3.8.10. 5. of animals, *push forward* or *in front*, τοὺς σοὺς [ἵππους] πρόσθε βαλών Il.23.572; πλήθει πρόσθε βαλόντες (sc. ἵππους) ib.639; βάλλε κάτωθε τὰ μοσχία Theoc.4.44: metaph., β. ψυχὰν ποτὶ κέρδεα Bion *Fr*.5.12. 6. in a looser sense, *put*, *place*, with or without a notion of haste, τὼ μὲν.. βαλέτην ἐν χερσὶν ἑταίρων Il.5. 574, cf. 17.40, 21.104; μῆλα.. ἐν νηῒ β. Od.9.470; ἐπὶ γᾶν ἴχνος ποδὸς β. E.*Rh*.721 (lyr.); φάσγανον ἐπ' αὐχένος β. Id.*Or*.51; τοὺς δακτύλους εἰς τὰ ὦτα *Ev.Marc*.7.33; β. πλίνθους *lay* bricks, *Edict.Diocl*.7.15; *pour*, οἶνον εἰς ἀσκούς *Ev.Matt*.9.17; εἰς πίθον Arr.*Epict*.4.13.12, cf. Dsc.1.71.5 (v.l. for ἐμβ.): metaph., ἐν στήθεσσι μένος βάλε ποιμένι λαῶν Il.5.513; ὅπως.. φιλότητα μετ' ἀμφοτέροισι βάλωμεν *may put* friendship between them, 4.16; μαντεύσομαι ὡς ἐνὶ θυμῷ ἀθάνατοι βάλλουσι Od.1.201; ἐν καρδίᾳ β. Pi.*O*.13.16; but also θυμῷ, ἐς θυμὸν β., *lay* to heart, A.*Pr*.706, S.*OT*975. b. esp. of *putting round*, ἀμφ' ὀχέεσσι θοῶς βάλε καμπύλα κύκλα Il.5.722; of clothes or arms, ἀμφὶ δ' Ἀθήνη ὤμοις.. βάλ' αἰγίδα 18.204; *put on*, φαιὰ ἱμάτια Plb. 30.4.5. c. *place* money *on deposit*, ἀργύριον τοῖς τραπεζίταις *Ev. Matt*.25.27. d. *pay*, *PLond*.3.1177 (ii A.D.), *POxy*.1448.5 (iv A.D.). 7. of dice, *throw*, τρὶς ἓξ βαλεῖν A.*Ag*.33, cf. Pl.*Lg*.968e; ἄλλα βλήματ' ἐν κύβοις βαλεῖν E.*Supp*.330: so prob. ψῆφος βαλοῦσα, abs., *by its throw*, A.*Eu*.751: metaph., εὖ or καλῶς βάλλειν *to be lucky*, *successful*, Phld.*Ir*.p.51 W., *Rh*.1.10 S. III. intr., *fall*, ποταμὸς Μινυήϊος εἰς ἅλα βάλλων Il.11.722, cf. A.R.2.744, etc.; ἄνεμος κατ' αὐτῆς (sc. νεώς) ἔβαλε *Act.Ap*.27.14; [ἵππους] περὶ τέρμα βαλούσας *having run* round the post, Il.23.462; ἐγὼ δὲ.. τάχ' ἐν πέδῳ βαλῶ (sc. ἐμαυτήν) A.*Ag*.1172 (lyr.); λίμνηθεν δ' εἰς ἁλὸς οἶδμα βάλητε *arrive* at.., A.R.4.1579; εἴσω β. *enter* a river's mouth, Orac. ap.D.S.8.23; βαλὼν κάθευδε *lie down and* sleep, Arr.*Epict*.2.20.10; τί οὖν, οὐ ῥέγκω βαλών; ib.4.10.29; βαλὼν ἐπὶ τῆς στιβάδος ἐπεχείρει καθεύδειν Anon.ap.*POxy*.1368.51; cf. A. II.4. 2. in familiar language, βάλλ' ἐς κόρακας *away with you! be hanged!* Ar.*V*.835, etc.; βάλλ' ἐς μακαρίαν Pl.*Hp.Ma*.293a, cf. Men.*Epit*.389.

B. Med., *put for oneself*, ὡς ἐνὶ θυμῷ βάλλεαι that thou *may'st lay it* to heart, Il.20.196, cf. Od.12.218; σὺ δ' ἐνὶ φρεσὶ βάλλεο σῇσιν Hes.*Op*.107; εἰ μὲν δὴ νόστον γε μετὰ φρεσὶ.. βάλλεαι Il.9.435; ἐς θυμὸν βαλέσθαι τι Hdt.1.84, etc.; εἰς or ἐπὶ νοῦν, εἰς μνήμην, Plu.*Thes*. 24, Jul.*Or*.2.58a, etc. (v. supr. A. II.6); ἐπ' ἑωυτῶν βαλόμενοι *on their* own *responsibility*, Hdt.4.160, cf. 3.71, al.; ἑτέρως ἐβάλοντο θεοί, v.l. for ἐβόλοντο in Od.1.234; θεοὶ δ' ἑτέρωσε βάλοντο Q.S.1.610. 2. τόξα or ξίφος ἀμφ' ὤμοισιν βάλλεσθαι *throw about one's* shoulder, Il.10. 333, 19.372, etc.; ἐπὶ κάρα στέφη β. E.*IA*1513 (lyr.). 3. ἐς γαστέρα βάλλεσθαι γόνον *conceive*, Hdt.3.28. 4. *lay as foundation*, κρηπῖδα βαλέσθαι Pi.*P*.7.3, cf. 4.138, Luc.*Hipp*.4; also, *lay the foundations of*, *begin to form*, οἰκοδομίας Pl.*Lg*.779b; χάρακα Plb.3.105.10, Poll. 8.161; simply, *build*, ἱερὸν περί τι Philostr.*VA*4.13; β. ἄγκυραν *cast* anchor, Hdt.9.74, etc.; καθάπερ ἐξ ἀγκυρῶν βαλλόμενος ψυχῆς δεσμούς Pl.*Ti*.73d. II. rarely, χρόα βάλλεσθαι λουτροῖς *dash oneself* with water, *bathe*, *h.Cer*.50 (but λουτρὰ ἐπὶ χροῒ βαλεῖν E.*Or*.303). (Arc. -δέλλω in ἐσ-δέλλοντες, = ἐκ-βάλλοντες, *IG*5(2).6.49; ζέλλειν· βάλλειν, Hsch. Root *g*ʷ*el*- 'throw', Skt. *galati* 'trickle', OHG. *quellan* 'spurt up', Lith. *gulėti* 'lie'.)

**βαλλωτή**, ἡ, *black horehound*, *Ballota nigra*, Dsc.3.103.

**βαλμός**, ὁ, = στῆθος, Hsch., Suid. **βαλοιτήσειρον**· παρὰ τὸ διεστραμμένον εἶναι τοὺς πόδας, Hsch.

**βαλός**, ὁ, Dor. for βηλός (q.v.).

**βαλσᾰμ-έλαιον**, τό, = σίλφιον, Sch.Ar.*Pl*.926. **-ίνη**, ἡ, = βούφθαλμον, Ps.-Dsc.3.139; *balsaminum*, = ὀποβάλσαμον, Plin.*HN*23. 92. **-ον**, τό, *balsam-tree*, *Balsamodendron Opobalsamum*, Thphr. *HP*9.6.1, Dsc.1.19; ξύλα βαλσάμου *BGU*953.6 (iii/iv A.D.). 2. the fragrant oil of this tree, *Mecca balsam*, Arist.*Fr*.110, Thphr.*HP*9. 4.1, *POxy*.1052 (βαρσ-, iv A.D.). II. *an aromatic herb*, *costmary*, *Chrysanthemum Balsamita*, *Gp*.11.27 tit.—Prob. Semitic. [βάλσᾰμον in Nic.*Th*.947, but ᾰ in Androm.ap.Gal.14.39, and Damocr.ap.Gal. 14.97, as in *balsămum* in Lat. Poets.] **-ῶδες**, τό, a *bark* like cassia, Plin.*HN*12.97.

**βαλώστιον**, τό, = βαλαύστιον, *PSI*5.489 (iii B.C.).

**βάμβα**, = βάμμα (Syrac.), Hsch.

⊛ **βαμβαίνω**, onomatop. word, *chatter with the teeth*, Il.10.375; *stammer*, Bion *Fr*.6.9, *AP*5.272 (Agath.), Procop.*Arc.Praef*.:—so also ⊛ **βαμβᾰκύζω**, *chatter with cold*, Hippon.17:—also **βαμβᾰλύζω**, Phryn.*PS*p.54 B., Hsch.; possibly to be restored (for βομβυλιάζω) in Arist.*Pr*.949$^{a}$13.

**βαμβᾰκ-εία**, **-κεύτρια**, ἡ, = φαρμακεία, -κεύτρια, Hsch.: **βάμβᾰκος**, ὁ, = φαρμακός (Cilic.), *AB*85.

**βαμβάκιον** [ᾰ], τό, *cotton*, Suid. s.v. πάμβαξ.

**βαμβᾰκοειδής**, ές, *like cotton*, v.l. for βομβυκ-, Dsc.3.16.

**βαμβάκτης**, ου, ὁ, *highway*, *causeway*, Cyr.Dresd.

**βάμβαλα**· χειμερινὰ ἱμάτια, Hsch.: in sg. also, = τὸ αἰδοῖον (Phryg.), Id. **βαμβᾰλεῖν**· τρέμειν, ψοφεῖν τοῖς χείλεσι, Id.

⊛ **βαμβᾰλύζω**, v. βαμβαίνω.

**βαμβρᾰδών**, όνος, ἡ, = βεμβράς, Epich.60, Sophr.65.

**βαμβράσσει**· ὀργίζεται, and **βαμβρασμός**· καχλασμός, Cyr.Dresd.

**βᾶμες**, Dor. for βῶμεν, 1 pl. subj. aor. 2 of βαίνω, Theoc.15.22.

⊛ **βάμμα**, ατος, τό, (βάπτω) *that in which a thing is dipped*, *dye*, Pl.*Lg*. 956a; βάμμα Σαρδιανικόν, Κυζικηνικόν, v. βάπτω I.2: in pl., διάφορα β. *POxy*.914.7 (v A.D.); β. λευκώματος a whitish *tinge*, Arist.*Phgn*. 813$^{a}$28. II. *sauce*, Nic.*Th*.622, cf. Hsch. s.v. βάμβα. III. = ὄα, *AB*362.

**βάν** [ᾰ], Ep. for ἔβαν, ἔβησαν, 3 pl. aor. 2 of βαίνω.

**βᾰνά**, Boeot. for γυνή, Corinn.21: pl., βανῆκες, Hsch.

**βᾰναυσ-ία**, ἡ, *handicraft*, Hdt.2.165, Pl.*R*.590c, etc. II. *the habits of a mere artisan*, *vulgarity*, *bad taste*, Arist.*EN*1107$^{b}$19, *Pol*. 1317$^{b}$41, *UPZ*62.3 (ii B.C.). 2. *quackery*, *charlatanism*, Hp.*Morb. Sacr*.18. **-ικός**, ή, όν, *of* or *for artisans*: τέχνη β. *handicraft*, X. *Smp*.3.4, *Oec*.4.2; τὸ β. Arist.*Pol*.1321$^{a}$6.

⊛ **βάναυσος** [ᾰ], ον, (for βαύναυσος, from βαῦνος, αὔω acc. to *EM*187. 40, cf. βαναυσία· πᾶσα τέχνη διὰ πυρός, Hsch.; βαναύσων seems to be f.l. for βαύνων in Heraclit.*All*.69):—epith. of the class of handicraftsmen or artisans, τὸ β., = τὸ περὶ τὰς τέχνας ὧν ἄνευ πόλιν ἀδύνατον οἰκεῖσθαι Arist.*Pol*.1291$^{a}$1, etc.; ὁ β. δῆμος, opp. ὁ γεωργικός, ὁ ἀγοραῖος, ib.1289$^{b}$33: as Subst., *artisan*, ib.1277$^{b}$35; ἡ βελτίστη πόλις οὐ ποιήσει β. πολίτην ib.1278$^{a}$8; τὸ β., = οἱ βάναυσοι, ib.1329$^{a}$20. II. τέχνη β. a *mechanical* art, *handicraft*, S.*Aj*.1121, Pl.*Tht*.176c (pl.); β. ἔργον Arist.*Pol*.1337$^{b}$8; βαναυσόταται τῶν ἐργασιῶν ib.1258$^{b}$37; β. βίον ζῆν a *mere mechanic's* life, ib.1278$^{a}$21, 1328$^{b}$39; β. πόνοι Plu.*Num*. 14: hence, 2. *vulgar*, *in bad taste*, Arist.*EN*1123$^{a}$19, Pl.*Ep*. 334b; of persons, Axiop.1.4. Adv. -σως, προσβλέπειν *unworthily*, *meanly*, Phld.*D*.1.11. 3. later, *fastidious*, *AP*11.326 (Autom.), 12.237 (Strat.).

**βᾰναυσοτεχνέω**, = sq., Str.16.4.25.

**βᾰναυσουργ-έω**, *follow a mere mechanical art*, Poll.7.6. **-ία**, ἡ, *handicraft*, Plu.*Marcell*.14. **-ός**, ὁ, *handicraftsman*, Poll.7.6.

**βανθῶσαι**· σκοτοδινιᾶσαι, Hsch. **βάνισος**· εἶδος θυμιάματος, Id. **βανκόν**· μωρόν, Id. **βάννας**· βασιλεύς (Ital.), Id. **βαννάται**· αἱ λοξοὶ ὁδοί (Tarent.); also **βάνναγροι**, Id. **βάννεια** and **βάννιμα**, τά, = ἄρνεια, Id. **βανοί**· τέχναι, Id. **βανόν**· λεπτόν, Id. **βάνος**· κλάσμα, μωρός, καὶ τυφλός, Id. **βανούς**· ὄρη στρογγύλα, Id. **βανύσει**· μωραίνει, ἐπιμαίνεται, Id.

⊛ **βανωτός**, ὁ, a kind of *vase* used as a measure, *PSI*4.428.12 (iii B.C.), 5.535.23 (iii B.C.), Callix.2:—Dim. **βανώτιον**, τό, *PSI*4.428. 22 (iii B.C.).

**βάξις**, εως, ἡ, (βάζω) poet. Noun, *saying*, esp. *an oracular saying*, *inspired utterance*, κλύειν εὐηκέα β. Emp.112.11; ἐναργὴς β. ἦλθεν Ἰνάχῳ A.*Pr*.663; θεσφάτων β. S.*Tr*.87. 2. *report*, *rumour*, μιν.. β. ἔχει χαλεπή Mimn.15; β. ἀργαλέη Id.16; θεῶν ἐποπίζεο μῆνιν βάξιν τ' ἀνθρώπων Thgn.1298; β. ἀλγεινήν, β. καλὴν λαβεῖν, S.*Aj*.494, *El*. 1006; σπείρειν ματαίαν β. ἐς πᾶσαν πόλιν ib.642, cf. 638; διὰ δὲ πόλεως ἔρχεται β. E.*Hel*.224 (lyr.); ὀξεῖα γάρ σου β.. διῆλθ' Ἀχαιούς *a report concerning* thee, S.*Aj*.998; ἁλώσιμος β. *tidings* of the capture, A.*Ag*.10; θανόντος β. ἀνδρός E.*Hel*.351 (lyr.); so τὴν τ' ἀμφὶ Θησέως β. Id.*Supp*.642. II. *voice*, *Epigr.Gr*.989.2.

**βάξον** (i.e. ϝάξον)· κατάξον (Lacon.), Hsch.

**βαπαίνει**· παρακαλεῖ, Hsch.

⊛ **βάπτης**, ου, ὁ, *dipper*, *bather*: in pl. of those who celebrated the mysteries of Cotytto; title of play by Eupolis, cf. Luc.*Ind*.27, Sch. Juv.2.91.

⊛ **βαπτ-ίζω**, *dip*, *plunge*, ξίφος εἰς σφαγήν J.*BJ*2.18.4; σπάθιον εἰς τὸ ἔμβρυον Sor.2.63:—Pass., of a trephine, Gal.10.447; βάπτισον σεαυτὸν εἰς θάλασσαν Plu.2.166a; β. Διόνυσον πρὸς τὴν θάλασσαν ib. 914d:—in Pass., *to be drowned*, Epict.*Gnom*.47; of ships, *sink* or *disable* them, Plb.1.51.6, 16.6.2 (Pass.); ἐβάπτισαν τὴν πόλιν *flooded* the city, metaph., of the crowds who flocked into Jerusalem at the time of the siege, J.*BJ*4.3.3; β. τινὰ εἰσφοραῖς D.S.1.73; β. τινὰ ὕπνῳ *AP*11.49 (Even.); ὕπνῳ βεβαπτισμένος Archig. and Posidon.ap.Aët. 6.3:—Pass., ὡς ἐκ τοῦ βεβαπτίσθαι ἀναπνέουσι Hp.*Epid*.5.63; *to be drenched*, Eub.68: metaph., βεβαπτισμένοι *soaked in wine*, Pl.*Smp*. 176b; ὀφλήμασι βεβ. *over head and ears* in debt, Plu.*Galb*.21; γνοὺς βαπτιζόμενον τὸ μειράκιον seeing that he was *getting into deep water*, Pl.*Euthd*.277d; β. εἰς ἀναισθησίαν καὶ ὕπνον J.*AJ*10.9.4; ὁ τῷ θυμῷ βεβαπτισμένος καταδύεται Ach.Tat.6.19; ψυχὴ βεβαπτισμένη λύπῃ Lib.*Or*.64.115. 2. *draw wine by dipping* the cup in the bowl, Aristopho 14.5; φιάλαις β. ἐκ.. κρατήρων Plu.*Alex*.67. 3. *baptize*, τινά *Ev.Marc.*1.4; ἐν ὕδατι εἰς μετάνοιαν *Ev.Matt.*3.11:—Pass., βαπτισθήτω ἕκαστος εἰς ἄφεσιν ἁμαρτιῶν *Act.Ap.*2.38; εἰς Χριστόν *Ep.Rom.*6.3, etc.:—Med., *dip oneself*, Lxx 4*Ki.*5.14; *get oneself baptized*, *Act.Ap.*22.16, 1*Ep.Cor.*10.2:—Pass., *perform ablutions*, *Ev.Luc.*11.38. **-ικός**, ή, όν, *for dyeing*, χρώματα Sch.Lyc.1138. **II.** *suited for gilding* or *silvering*, opp. σμηκτικός, Ps.-Democr.Alch. p.47 B.: Comp., *more suited for a wash*, Zos.Alch.p.129 B. **-ῐσις**, εως, ἡ, *dipping*: *baptism*, J.*AJ*18.5.2. **-ισμα**, ατος, τό, *baptism*, *Ev.Matt.*3.7, etc.; β. εἰς τὸν θάνατον *Ep.Rom.*6.4. **-ισμός**, ὁ, *dipping in water*, *immersion*, *Ev.Marc.*7.4, *Ep.Hebr.*9.10, Antyll.ap. Orib.10.3.9. **2.** metaph., εἰς κακίας β. οἰχήσεται *Theol.Ar.*30. **3.** *lethargic sleep*, Archig. and Posidon.ap.Aët.6.3. **4.** *baptism*, J.*AJ* 18.5.2. ⊛ **-ιστήριον**, τό, *swimming-bath*, Plin.*Ep.*2.17.11. **-ιστής**, οῦ, ὁ, *one that dips*: *baptizer*, ὁ β. *the Baptist*, *Ev.Matt.*3.1, cf. J.*AJ* 18.5.2, etc.: metaph. of the Passion, *Ev.Luc.*12.50. **-ός**, ή, όν, *dipped*, *dyed*, D.S.5.30; *bright-coloured*, ὄρνις Ar.*Av.*287; ἱμάτια Id. *Pl.*530; τὰ βάπτ' ἔχοντες *dyed*, i.e. *black*, garments, Hegesipp.1.13, cf. Plu.*Ages.*30. **2.** *for dyeing*, χρώματα Pl.*Lg.*847c. **II.** of water, *drawn by dipping vessels*, E.*Hipp.*123 (lyr.). **-ρια**, ἡ, fem. of βάπτης, Eup.401.

⊛ **βάπτω**, fut. βάψω (ἐμ-) Ar.*Pax*959: aor. ἔβαψα S.*Aj.*95, etc.:—**Med.**, fut. βάψομαι Ar.*Lys.*51: aor. ἐβαψάμην Arat.951, *AP*9.326 (Leon.):—**Pass.**, fut. βᾰφήσομαι Lxx *Le.*11.32, M.Ant.8.51: aor. ἐβάφθην *AP*6.254 (Myrin.), (ἀπ-) Ar.*Fr.*416; in Att. generally ἐβάφην [ᾰ] Pl.*R.*429e, etc.: pf. βέβαμμαι Hdt.7.67, Ar.*Pax*1176. **I.** trans., *dip*, ὡς δ' ὅτ' ἀνὴρ χαλκεὺς πέλεκυν.. εἰν ὕδατι ψυχρῷ βάπτῃ (so as to temper the red-hot steel) Od.9.392; β. εἰς ὕδωρ Pl.*Ti.*73e, cf. Emp.100.11; τἄρια θερμῷ Ar.*Ec.*216; εἰς μέλι, εἰς κηρόν, Arist.*HA* 605$^{a}$29, *de An.*435$^{a}$2:—Pass., βαπτόμενος σίδηρος iron *in process of being tempered*, Plu.2.136a; and of coral, *become hard*, Dsc.5.121 (s.v.l.). **b.** of slaughter in Trag., ἐν σφαγαῖσι βάψασα ξίφος A.*Pr.*863; ἔβαψας ἔγχος εὖ πρὸς Ἀργείων στρατῷ; S.*Aj.*95; φάσγανον εἴσω σαρκὸς ἔβαψεν E.*Ph.*1578 (lyr.); in later Prose, εἰς τὰ πλευρὰ β. τὴν αἰχμήν D.H.5.15; β. τὸν δάκτυλον ἀπὸ τοῦ αἵματος Lxx *Le.*4.17. **c.** also, *dip in poison*, ἔβαψεν ἰούς S.*Tr.*574; χιτῶνα τόνδ' ἔβαψα ib.580. **2.** *dye*, ἔβαψεν..ξίφος the sword *dyed* [the robe] *red*, A.*Ch.*1011; β. τὰ κάλλη *dye* the beautiful cloths, Eup.333; β. ἔρια ὥστ' εἶναι ἁλουργά Pl.*R.*429d; εἵματα βεβαμμένα Hdt.7.67; τρίχας βάπτειν *AP*11.68 (Lucill.): abs. in Med., *dye the hair*, Men.363.4, Nicol.Com.1.33; *glaze* earthen vessels, Ath.11.480e; of *gilding* and *silvering*, Ps.-Democr.Alch.p.46 B.: Com., βάπτειν τινὰ βάμμα Σαρδιανικόν *dye* one in the [red] dye of Sardes, i.e. give him a bloody coxcomb, Ar. *Ach.*112; but βέβαπται β. Κυζικηνικόν *he has been dyed in* the dye of Cyzicus, i.e. is an arrant coward, Id.*Pax*1176 (v. Sch.). **3.** *draw* water *by dipping* a vessel, ἀνθ' ὕδατος τᾷ κάλπιδι κηρία βάψαι Theoc. 5.127; ἀρύταιναν..ἐκ μέσου βάψασα τοῦ λέβητος ζέοντος ὕδατος *draw* water *by dipping* the bucket, Antiph.25, cf. Thphr.*Char.*9.8; βάψασα ποντίας ἁλός (sc. τὸ τεῦχος) *having dipped* it *so as to draw* water from the sea, E.*Hec.*610. **4.** *baptize*, Arr.*Epict.*2.9.20 (Pass.). **II.** intr., ναῦς ἔβαψεν the ship *dipped*, *sank*, E.*Or.*707; β. εἰς ψυχρὸν [αἱ ἐγχέλυς] Arist.*HA*592$^{a}$18; εἰ δ' ὁ μὲν (sc. ἠέλιος) ἀνέφελος βάπτοι ῥόου ἑσπερίοιο Arat.858 (ῥόον Sch.): c. acc., νῆα..βάπτουσαν ἤδη κῦμα κυρτόν *dipping into*.., Babr.71.2:—also Med., ποταμοῖο ἐβάψατο Arat. 951. **2.** βάψας (sc. τὴν κώπην) Ar.*Fr.*225. (Cf. ONorse *kuefia* 'dip'.)

**βάρα·** νόσημά τι καρηβαρικόν, ἢ θρέμματα (Lacon.), Hsch.

**βᾰραγχιάω, βᾰράγχια**, = βραγχ-, Hdn.Gr.2.481, Hsch.

⊛ **βάραγχος** [βᾰ], ὁ, = βράγχος, Hippon.106.

⊛ **βάραθρον** [βᾰ], Ep. and Ion. **βέρεθρον** (q.v., cf. ζέρεθρον), shortd. **βέθρον** (q.v.), τό, *gulf*, *pit*, Arist.*Pr.*947$^{a}$19; esp. at Athens, *a cleft* into which criminals were thrown, Hdt.7.133, Ar.*Nu.*1450, *Com.Adesp.* 24.10 D., Pl.*Grg.*516c, *AB*219, Sch.Ar.*Pl.*431. **2.** metaph., ἐν τῷ β. χειμάζειν D.8.45; *ruin*, *perdition*, Luc.*Am.*5, etc.; name of a courtesan, Theophil.Com.11. **II.** a woman's *ornament*, Ar.*Fr.* 320.8. **III.** = βράθυ, f.l. for βόρατον, Dsc.1.76. (Root *g$^{w}$er* 'devour', cf. βορά.)

**βάραθρος** [βᾰ], ὁ, *one that ought to be thrown into the pit*, Luc. *Pseudol.*17 (but perh. neut.).

**βᾰραθρώδης**, ες, *like a pit* or *gulf*, Str.13.1.67, Plu.*Lyc.*16; β. πέλαγος *abysmal*, of a dangerous sea, Ph.2.514; *precipitous*, of a road, Str.5.1.11: metaph., θολερὸς καὶ β. βίος Ph.1.322; of a person, τὴν ψυχὴν ἄδικος καὶ β. Agath.2.23.

**βαρακινῆσιν·** ἀκάνθαις, σκόλοψι, Hsch. **βαρακίς·** γλαύκινον ἱμάτιον, Id.

⊛ **βάρακος**, a kind of *fish*, Hsch.; also = βάτραχος, Id.

**βάραξ**, ακος, ὁ, a kind of *cake*, Epil.3; cf. βήρηξ.

⊛ **βάρβαξ** or **βάραξ**, a Libyan bird, Hsch.

**βαρβάρα**, ἡ, a kind of *plaster*, Alex.Trall.5.5.

**βαρβᾰρ-ίζω**, *behave* or *speak like a barbarian*, Hdt.2.57, Philostr. *VA*1.21, Arr.*An.*7.6.5; *speak broken Greek*, *speak gibberish*, Pl. *Tht.*175d codd. (sed leg. βατταρίζων); βαρβαριζόντων ἑτεροφώνων Phld.*Po.*994.6; *violate the laws of speech*, *commit barbarisms*, τῇ λέξει β. Arist.*SE*165$^{b}$21, cf. Plb.39.1.7, Str.14.2.28, Luc.*Rh.Pr.*17, 23, etc.; distd. from σολοικίζω, Phld.*Rh.*1.154 S. **2.** trans., '*murder*', *mangle*, τὴν Ῥωμαίων φωνήν Luc.*Merc.Cond.*24. **II.** *side with the barbarians*, i.e. *the Persians*, X.*HG*5.2.35, Max.Tyr.4. 2. **-ίκιον**, τό, name of a *foreign garment*, *POxy.*1684.5, 9 (iv A.D.). ⊛ **-ικός**, ή, όν, *barbaric*, *non-Greek*, χείρ Simon.136; ψυκτήρ *OGI*214.47 (Didyma, Seleucus I); τὸ β., = οἱ βάρβαροι, Th.1.6, 7. 29; τὰ β. ἔθνη Arist.*Pol.*1257$^{a}$25, etc.; νόμιμα β. *leges barbarorum*, name of a treatise by Arist.; νόμοι λίαν ἁπλοῖ καὶ β. *Pol.*1268$^{b}$40; esp. of the Persians, X.*An.*1.5.6; ἐς τὸ β. *in barbaric fashion*, Luc.*DMort.* 27.3; β. ἐπιδρομή inroad *of barbarians*, *PMasp.*321.5 (vi A.D.); ἐς τὸ βαρβαρικώτερον *more in the Persian fashion*, Arr.*An.*4.8.2: Sup. -ώτατος Sch.Th.7.29. Adv., ἐβόα καὶ -κῶς καὶ Ἑλληνικῶς, i.e. both *in Persian* and Greek, X.*An.*1.8.1, cf. Phld.*Lib.*p.13 O.; κεκλημένον β. *in the language of the country*, Arist.*Mir.*846$^{a}$32; *in foreign fashion*, App. *Hisp.*72. **II.** *barbarous*, *violent*, πένθη Plu.2.114e. Adv. -κῶς *barbarously*, ὠμῶς καὶ β. Id.*Dio*35: Comp. -ώτερον Id.*Alex.*2. ⊛ **-ισμός**, ὁ, *use of a foreign tongue* or *of one's own tongue amiss*, *barbarism*, Arist.*Po.*1458$^{a}$26, Diog.Bab.*Stoic.*3.214, Ph.1.124, Plu.2.731e; μιᾶς λέξεως κακία ὁ β., ἐπιπλοκῆς δὲ λέξεων ἀκαταλλήλων ὁ σολοικισμός A.D.*Synt.*198.7. **-ιστί**, Adv. *in barbarous fashion*, Plu.2.336c. **II.** *in barbarian* or *foreign language*, κεκράξονται β. Ar.*Fr.*79; ἀξύνετα βαρβαριστὶ παρακαλούντων App.*Mith.*50, cf. A.D.*Adv.*162.5.

**βαρβᾰρό-γλωσσος**, ον, = βαρβαρόφωνος, Sch.Lyc.276. **-κτόνος**, ον, *slaughtering barbarians*, Thom.Mag.p.141 R.

**βάρβᾰρος**, ον, *barbarous*, i.e. *non-Greek*, *foreign*, not in Hom. (but cf. βαρβαρόφωνος); β. ψυχαί Heraclit.107; esp. as Subst. βάρβαροι, οἱ, originally *all non-Greek-speaking peoples*, then specially of the Medes and Persians, A.*Pers.*255, Hdt.1.58, etc.: generally, opp. Ἕλληνες, Pl.*Plt.*262d, cf. Th.1.3, Arist.*Pol.*1252$^{b}$5, Str.14.2.28; βαρβάρων Ἕλληνας ἄρχειν εἰκός E.*IA*1400; β. καὶ δοῦλον ταὐτὸ φύσει Arist.*Pol.* 1252$^{b}$9; οἱ β. δουλικώτεροι τὰ ἤθη φύσει τῶν Ἑλλήνων ib.1285$^{a}$20; β. πόλεμον war *with the barbarians*, Th.2.36 codd.; ἡ βάρβαρος (sc. γῆ), opp. αἱ Ἑλληνίδες πόλεις, Th.2.97, cf. A.*Pers.*187, X.*An.*5.5.16. Adv. -ρως, opp. Ἑλληνικῶς, Porph.*Abst.*3.3. **2.** esp. of language, φωνὴ β. A.*Ag.*1051, Pl.*Prt.*341c; γλῶσσα β. S.*Aj.*1263, cf. Hdt.2.57, Str. l.c. supr., etc.; συγγραφαί Hippias 6 D.; of birds, Ar.*Av.*199. Adv., βαρβάρως, ὠνόμασται have *foreign* names, Str.10.3.17. **3.** Gramm., of *bad Greek*, Gell.5.20.5; τὸ β., of style, opp. Ἑλληνικόν, S.E.*M.*1. 64. **II.** after the Persian war, *brutal*, *rude*, ἀμαθὴς καὶ β. Ar.*Nu.* 492; τὸ τῆς φύσεως β. καὶ θεοῖς ἐχθρόν D.21.150; σκαιὸς καὶ β. τὸν τρόπον Id.26.17; β. ἀνηλεής τε Men.*Epit.*477: Comp. -ώτερος X. Eph.2.4: Sup., πάντων βαρβαρώτατος θεῶν Ar.*Av.*1573, cf. Th.8.98, X.*An.*5.4.34. **III.** used by Jews of *Greeks*, Lxx 2*Ma.*2.21. **IV.** name for various *plasters*, Androm. and Heras ap.Gal.13.555. (Onomatopœic acc. to Str.14.2.28.)

**βαρβᾰρο-στομία**, ἡ, (στόμα) *barbarous way of speaking*, Str.14.2. 28. **-της**, ητος, ἡ, *nature* or *conduct of a* βάρβαρος, Tz.*H.*9.972, Sch.E.*Hec.*1129. **-φωνέω**, *speak Greek barbarously*, Str.14.2. 28. **-φωνος**, ον, *speaking a foreign tongue*, Κᾶρες Il.2.867; of the Persians, Orac.ap.Hdt.8.20, 9.43. **II.** *speaking bad Greek*, Str. 14.2.28.

**βαρβᾰρ-όω**, *make barbarous*: only used in Pass., *to become barbarous*, E.*Or.*485, Antipho Soph.*Oxy.*1364.274; οἱ βαρβαρωθέντες τόποι *PLond.*5.1674.22 (vi A.D.); κακῷ κλάζοντας οἴστρῳ καὶ βεβαρβαρωμένῳ *unintelligible*, of birds, S.*Ant.*1002. **-ώδης**, ες, *barbaric*, Sch.Ar.*Pax*752: Comp., Tz.*H.*4.601.

**βάρβῐλος**, ἡ, *seedling peach-tree*, *Gp.*10.13.5 (v.l. βράβιλος).

**βαρβῐτ-ίζω**, *play on the barbiton*, Ar.*Fr.*752. **-ιστής**, οῦ, ὁ, *player on the barbiton*, name of play by Magnes, Sch.Ar.*Eq.* 519. ⊛ **-ος**, ἡ or ὁ, *musical instrument of many strings* (πολύχορδος Theoc.16.45), invented by Terpander, Pi.*Fr.*125; freq. used for *the lyre*, Anacr.143, B.*Scol.Oxy.*1361.1.1, E.*Cyc.*40, Ar.*Th.*137, etc.: fem. in *Anacreont.*23.3, but masc. in 14.34: in earlier Poets the gender is not determined:—later ⊛ **βάρβῐτον**, τό, as in Latin, Neanth. 5, D.H.7.72, Ath.4.175e, etc. (Prob. a foreign word, Str.10.3. 17.) **-ῳδός**, όν, *singing to the barbiton*, Luc.*Lex.*14.

**βαρβός**, ὁ, = μύστρον, Ar.*Fr.*341.

**βαρδῆν·** τὸ βιάζεσθαι γυναῖκας (Ambrac.), Hsch.; cf. **βαρδίσαγνος·** ὁ τὰς γυναῖκας βιαζόμενος, Suid., Zonar.

**βάρδιστος**, η, ον, poet. for βράδιστος, Sup. of βραδύς, Il.23.310, Theoc.15.104, Doroth.(?)ap.Heph.Astr.3.30: Comp. βαρδύτερος Theoc.29.30.

⊛ **βάρδοι**, οἱ, *poets of the Celts*, *bards*, Posidon.23, D.S.5.31, Str.4. 4.4. **II.** βάρδος, ὁ, *sumpter animal*, *BGU*276.11 (iii A.D.).

**βαρδύνω**, = βραδύνω, Babr.110.4.

⊛ **βαρέω**, Aeol. **βορ-**, v. infr., fut. -ήσω Luc.*DMort.*10.4: pf. βεβάρηκα D.C.78.17:—Pass., v. infr.:—*weigh down*, *depress*, βαρήσει ταῦτα τὸ πορθμεῖον Luc. l.c. (censured, Id.*Sol.*7); τὴν τῆς δίκης ῥοπὴν β. Procop.*Arc.*14; ὅταν τὰ πράγματα βαρῇ τοὺς ἀντιδίκους Hermog. *Inv.*2.7; ἵνα μὴ τὴν πόλιν βαρῶμεν *IG*14.830.15 (Puteoli), cf. *POxy.* 1159.2 (iii A.D.); τὸ ἔθνος ἐβάρει ταῖς εἰσφοραῖς J.*BJ*2.14.1, cf. D.C. l.c.:—Pass., κῆρ.. βόρηται Sapph.*Supp.*25.17; β. διά τινα Diog. Oen.64, cf. *POxy.*525.3 (ii A.D.); β. τῷ ἐκφορίῳ *PGiss.*6.7 (ii A.D.): c. acc., *to be indignant at*, αὐτῶν τὴν εὐγένειαν Hdn.8.8.1; οὓς βαροῦνται M.Ant.8.44. **2.** *charge* an account, *POxy.*126.8 (vi A.D.). **II.** intr. in Ep. pf. part. βεβαρηώς *weighed down*, *heavy*, οἴνῳ βεβαρηότες Od.3.139, cf. 19.122:—later, pf. part. Pass. βεβαρημένος, μεθυσθεὶς τοῦ νέκταρος β. ηὗδεν Pl.*Smp.*203b; οἴνῳ β. Ph.1.373; τοὺς ὀφθαλμοὺς β. ὑπ' οἴνου ib.377; ὠδίνεσσιν Theoc.17.61; ὕπνῳ *AP* 7.290 (Stat. Flacc.), *Gp.*13.1.8, *Ev.Luc.*9.32 (without ὕπνῳ *Ev.Matt.* 26.43); β. τὰ πρόσωπα πένθει Plu.*Aem.*34; τὰ σώματα πλησμονῇ β. Id.*Mar.*19; γυνὴ πολλοῖς ἔτεσι β. *PTeb.*327.25 (ii A.D.); οἷον βεβαρημένος as though *pregnant*, Plot.3.8.8:—Pass., pres. βαρέεται Hp. *Morb.*4.49: aor. ἐβαρήθην Parth.9.8: pf. βεβάρηται *Placit.*3.12.2.

**βάρηκες**, *gums*, *cheeks*, or *particles of food adhering to the teeth*; also, = τολύπη, *EM*188.37.

**βάρ-ημα** [βᾰ], ατος, το, *burden, load*, v. l. in D H.10.16. **–ησις**, εως, ἡ, *pressure, oppression*, Iamb.*Protr*.21.κε′: pl., *SIG*888.141 (Thrace, iii A. D.).

**βᾱρίβας** [ῐ], ὁ, *one that goes in a boat*, S.*Fr*.517.

**βαρίη**, ἡ, = βάρος, τοῦ ἠέρος Aret.*SD*1.11 (sed leg. ἀπορίη).

**βαρινακέδα**· τὸν δούριον ἵππον, Hsch.

**βαρῖνος**, ὁ, v.l. for βάλαγρος (q. v.).

**βάριον**· πρόβατον and **βάριχοι**· ἄρνες (Lacon.), Hsch. (β for ϝ, cf. ἀρήν, ἄριχα.)

⊛ **βᾶρις**, ιδος (also –εως J.*AJ*14.16.2, cf. *Et.Gud.*, *AB*84), Ion. ιος, ἡ: acc. βᾶριν J.*AJ*10.11.7, Iamb.*Myst*.6.5; dat. βάρει J.*AJ*11.4.6: pl. βάρεις Lxx 2*Ch*.36.19, al., Ion. βάριες Hdt.2.41; gen. βαρέων Lxx*Ps*.44(45).8; poet. dat. pl. βαρίδεσσι A.*Pers*.553 (lyr.):—*flat-bottomed boat*, used in Egypt, Id.*Supp*.874 (lyr.), Hdt.2.41,96,179, *PHib*.100.13 (iii B.C.), Procop.*Aed*.1.6; βάρβαροι βάριδες E.*IA*297 (lyr.); of Odysseus' *raft*, Lyc.747. 2. later, *large house, tower*, Lxx*Ps*.44(45).8, *Da*.8.2, al., J. ll. cc., Kalinka *Antike Denkmäler in Bulgarien* 142 (Apollonia, ii A.D.); λέγεται β. ἡ οἰκία, ὡς Ποσείδιππος, καὶ ἡ συνοικία ὡς Ἔφορος St.Byz. (Egyptian word.)

**βαρισίκται**· οἱ μὴ γεννῶντες, Hsch.

**βαρίτης** [ῑ], ου, ὁ, a *bird*, Dionys.*Av*.3.2.

**βάριχοι**, v. βάριον. **βαρκάζω**· βαρβαρίζω, *EM*188.43. **βάρκαλις**, v. βώκκαλις. **βαρκίων**, name of an *Egyptian plant*, Hsch. **βαρμίγκαλλος**· ὑπέρκαλλος, Id.

⊛ **βάρμος**, ὁ, = βάρβιτος, Alc.*Supp*.23.4, Phillis ap.Ath.14.636c:—also **βάρωμος**, Euph.*Fr.Hist*.8.

**βάρνακα**· ἄγρια λάχανα δύσπλυτα, *EM*291.46 (cf. βράκανα).

⊛ **βάρνᾰμαι**, = μάρναμαι, *IG*1$^{2}$.943, 9(1).868 (Corc.).

⊛ **βάρος** [ᾰ], ους, Ion. εος, τό, *weight*, Hdt.2.73, etc. II. *a weight, burden, load*, τέκνων A.*Ch*.1000, etc.; β. περισσὸν γῆς S.*Fr*.945: pl., βάρη *weights*, Arist.*Mech*.850$^{a}$30. III. *oppressiveness*, τὸ τῆς ὀσμῆς ἀφόρητον β. Lxx 2*Ma*.9.10; βάρος φέρειν to give *trouble*, τινί *POxy*.1062.14 (ii A.D.). IV. *heaviness, torpor*, β. ναρκῶδες Plu.2.345b; σπληνὸς βάρεα Hp.*Acut*.(*Sp*.)4; βάρη καὶ δυσαρεστήματα perh. *feeling of oppression*, Antyll.ap.Stob.4.37.15. V. metaph., *heavy weight*, σιγῆς β. S.*Ant*.1256; βάρος πημονῆς, συμφορᾶς, Id.*El*.939, *Tr*.325; χρὴ τοῦ βάρους μεταδιδόναι τοῖς φίλοις X.*Mem*.2.7.1; ὥσπερ βάρους μεταλαμβάνειν Arist.*EN*1171$^{a}$31; τὰ β. ὅσα ψυχὴν καθέλκοι Ph.2.674: hence alone, *grief, misery*, A.*Pers*.946 (lyr., pl.), S.*OC*409; κεφαλῆς πόνος καὶ β. Arist.*HA*603$^{b}$8; τὸ β. ἔχειν Id.*EN*1126$^{a}$23; ἐν συνοχαῖς καὶ βάρεσι Vett.Val.292.6; of *oppressive* demands, β. τῶν ἐπιταγμάτων, τῶν φόρων, Plb.1.31.5, 1.67.1; τῆς λειτουργίας *BGU*159.5 (iii A.D.); οὐκέτι δυνάμεθα φέρειν τὰ β. *SIG*888.67 (Thrace, iii A.D.); κουφίσαι τὰ β. *PGiss*.7.13 (ii A.D.). VI. in good sense, *abundance*, πλούτου, ὄλβου, E.*El*.1287, *IT*416; αἰώνιον β. δόξης 2*Ep.Cor*.4.17; *strength*, στρατοπέδων Plb.1.16.4; β. τῆς ὑλακῆς *violence* of.., Alciphr.3.18. VII. *weight, influence*, Plb.4.32.7, D.S.19.70, Plu.*Per*.37, etc.; *gravity, dignity* of character, Id.2.522e; opp. χάρις, Id.*Demetr*.2. VIII. Gramm., *stress* of accent, A.D.*Synt*.98.1. IX. in Music, = βαρύτης, *low pitch*, Aristid.Quint.1.11.

**βᾶρος**, ὁ, or **βᾶρον**, τό, a kind of *spice*, Mnesim.4.62.

⊛ **βᾰρουλκός** (sc. μηχανή), ἡ, *lifting-screw*, invented by Archimedes, Papp.1060, al., prob. in Vitr.10.1.1.

**βάρπυργος**· πορμεῖο περὶ ἀμφωδῶν, Hsch. **βαρραχεῖν**· ἠχεῖν, σκιρτᾶν, Id. **βαρρεῖ**· ἀπολεῖ, Id.

**βαρύ**, τό, *perfume* used in incense, *AB*225.

⊛ **βᾰρῠ-āής**, ές, *breathing hard*, ὕπνος Opp.*C*.3.421. II. *strong-smelling*, Nic.*Th*.43. **–αλγής**, ές, *grievously suffering*, Orph.*H*.69.7. II. = sq., νοῦσος *Epigr.Gr*.228 (Ephesus), 803 (Delos). **–άλγητος**, ον, *very grievous*, neut. pl., –άλγητα καγχάζειν S.*Aj*.199 (lyr.). **–αρον**· ἰσχυρόν, στερέμνιον, Hsch. **–ᾱχής**, ές, Dor. for βαρυηχής, ταῦροι *bellowing*, B.15.18; Ὠκεανός, βρονταί, Ar.*Nu*.278, *Av*.1750; μέλισσαι *Lyr.Alex.Adesp*.7.15. II. *awakening sore lament*, S.*OC*1561, Sch. (al. βαρυαχεῖ). **–αχθής**, ές, *very heavy*, τὸ κατὰ γαστρὸς β. Sor.1.55; *very burdensome*, Nonn.*D*.40.155. **–βάμων** [ᾱμ], ον, gen. ονος, *slowly moving*, φλόξ Man.4.318. **–βόας**, ου, ὁ, *heavy-sounding*, πορθμὸς Ἀχέροντος Pi.*Fr*.143.2. ⊛ **–βρεμέτης**, ου, ὁ, *loud-thundering*, Ζεύς S.*Ant*.1117:—also **–βρομήτης** πέτρος prob. in *AP*7.394 (Phil.):—fem. **–βρεμέτειρα** Orph.*H*.10.25. **–βρομος**, ον, *loud-roaring*, βαρύβρομα θωύσσοντες Hom.*Fr*.25; πέλαγος B.16.76; Trag. only in lyr., βρονταί, κῦμα, E.*Ph*.183, *Hel*.1305; ἀκταί Id.*Hyps.Fr*.41.80; *loud-sounding*, αὐλός, τύμπανα, Id.*Hel*.1351, *Ba*.156, cf. Ar.*Nu*.313; β. ἁρμονία Αἰολίς Lasus 1. **–βρώς**, ὁ, ἡ, gen. βρῶτος, *gnawing, corroding*, στόνος S.*Ph*.695 (lyr.). **–γδουπος**, ον, *loud-thundering, loud-roaring*, Ζεύς Pi.*O*.8.44; ἄνεμοι Id.*P*.4.210, cf. *AP*9.674; ἔρωτες Ion Lyr.9.3. **–γέτας**· ἀλαζών, *EM*206.23, cf. Hsch. ⊛ **–γλωσσος**, ον, *grievous of tongue*, v.l. for βαθυ–, Lxx*Ez*.3.5. **–γουνος**, ον, *heavy-kneed, lazy*, Call.*Del*.78, Coluth.121:—also **–γούνατος** Theoc.18.10. **–γυιος**, ον, *weighing down the limbs, wearisome*, κέλευθα Opp.*H*.5.63; νοῦσος *AP*6.190.9 (Gaet.). **–δαιμονέω**, *to be grievously unlucky*, Ar.*Eq*.558. **–δαιμονία**, ἡ, *grievous ill-luck*, Antipho 2.2.2. II. *surliness, churlishness*, Lys.4.9, Ph.1.487,558. **–δαίμων**, ον, gen. ονος, *pressed by a heavy fate, luckless*, πόλις Alc.37 A, cf. E.*Alc*.865, Ar.*Ec*.1102, *Cat.Cod.Astr*.2.162.30. **–δάκρυος**, ον, = sq., Nonn.*D*.40.194. **–δακρυς**, υ, *weeping grievously*, ἀηδών *AP*9.262 (Phil.).

**βαρυδάνιν, βαρύδαν** (leg. βαρίβαν ἢ βαριβάν)· τὸν ναυσιβάτην, Hsch.

**βαρύ-δεσμος** [ῠ], ον, *loaded with chains*. Nonn.*D*.25.140, al. **–δῐκος**, ον, *taking heavy vengeance*, ποινά A.*Ch*.936.

**βᾰρύδιον**, Dim. of βάρος, *small weight*, f.l. for βαρύλλιον, Hero *Spir*.2.4.

**βᾰρῠ-δότειρα**, ἡ, *giver of ill gifts*, Μοῖρα A.*Th*.977. ⊛ **–δουπος**, ον, = βαρύγδουπος (q. v.), Mosch.2.120; θρῆνος *Epigr.Gr*.344.13. **–δρόμου**· μεγαλοφώνου, Hsch. (fort. βαρυβρ–). **–εγκέφᾰλος**, ὁ, *heavy-headed*, Epicur.*Fr*.237. **–εργέω**, *plough deep*, *Gp*.2.23.14 (Pass.). **–εργής**, ές, *strongly influenced*, ἐς τὰ τοιαῦτα App.*BC*1.83.

**βαρύες**· δένδρα, Hsch.

**βᾰρύ-ζηλος**, ον, *exceeding jealous* or *envious*, Lyc.57; Ἔρως *AP*5.242 (Maced.). **–ηκοέω**, *to be hard of hearing*, Hp.*Morb*.2.4. ⊛ **–ηκοΐα**, ἡ, *hardness of hearing*, Id.*Aph*.3.17. **–ήκοος**, ον, (ἀκούω) *hard of hearing*, Aret.*SD*1.4, Poll.2.81. II. Act., *impairing the hearing*, νότοι Hp.*Aph*.3.5, cf. Ph.2.99, S.E.*M*.6.49. **–ηχής**, ές, *deep-voiced*, ταῖς φωναῖς D.S.5.31, cf. Opp.*H*.4.317; *deep-roaring*, θάλασσα Orph.*Fr*.168.28; θόρυβος Lxx 3*Ma*.5.48. **–ηχος**, ον, = foreg., *AB*225: Sup. –ηχότατος Agath.5.8. **–θροος**, ον, *deep-* or *loud-sounding*, Mosch.2.123. **–θῡμέω**, *to be weighed down*: *to be melancholy* or *indignant*, Lxx*Nu*.15.16, App.*BC*2.20; ἐπί τινι D.S.20.41:—Med., Plu.*Sull*.6. **–θῡμία**, ἡ, *sullenness*, Arist.*VV*1251$^{a}$4, Andronic.Rhod.p.570 M.; *heaviness of heart, depression*, J.*AJ*16.10.5, Plu.*Mar*.40: pl., Id.2.477e. **–θῡμος**, ον, *heavy in spirit*: *indignant, sullen*, ὀργή E.*Med*.176, cf. Call.*Cer*.81, etc.; opp. ὀξύθυμος, Plu.2.13e: Sup., Phld.*Ir*.p.64 W. Adv. –μως, ἔχειν Alciphr.2.3; rejected by Poll.3.99.

**βᾰρύθω** [ῠ], *to be weighed down*, βαρύθει δέ μοι ὦμος ὑπ' αὐτοῦ [τοῦ ἕλκεος] Il.16.519; βαρύθει δέ θ' ὑπ' αὐτῆς (sc. ὕβρεως) Hes.*Op*.215; καμάτῳ A.R.2.47; ὑπὸ κύματος Nic.*Th*.135. 2. abs., *to be heavy*, στάλα *AP*7.481 (Philet.); βαρύθεσκε..γυῖα A.R.1.43:—Pass., Max.212, Q.S.13.6.

**βάρυκα**· αἰδοῖον (Tarent.), Hsch. **βαρύκαν**· σφῦραν, Id.

⊛ **βᾰρῠ-κάρδιος**, ον, *heavy, slow of heart*, Lxx*Ps*.4.2. **–καρπέω**, *bear a heavy crop of fruit*, *Aegyptus* 5.129 (ii B.C.). **–κέφᾰλος**, ον, *large-* or *heavy-headed*, of dogs, Arr.*Cyn*.4.4. II. metaph., *top-heavy*, Vitr.3.3.5. **–κομπος**, ον, *loud-roaring*, λέοντες Pi.*P*.5.57. **–κοτος**, ον, *heavy in wrath*, A.*Eu*.780 (lyr.). **–κτῠπος**, ον, *heavy-sounding, loud-thundering*, epith. of Zeus, *h.Cer*.3, Hes.*Op*.79; of Poseidon, Id.*Th*.818, Pi.*O*.1.72, *Pae*.4.41; also of the sea, *AP*9.753 (Claudian). **–λαῖλαψ**, ᾰπος, ὁ, ἡ, *loud-storming*, αὖραι ib.247 (Phil.).

⊛ **βᾰρύλλιον**, τό, Dim. of βάρος: *instrument to find the weight of liquids*, Hero *Spir*.1.39, al.

**βᾰρύ-λογος** [ῠ], ον, *vented in bitter words*, ἔχθεα Pi.*P*.2.55; *offensive*, of certain Stoic tenets, Phld.*Sto.Herc*.339.12. **–λῡπος**, ον, *very sad*, Plu.2.114f (Sup.). **–μαστος**, ον, *with large, heavy breasts*, Str.17.3.4. **–μελής**, ές, (μέλος) *with heavy limbs*, Sch.Opp.*H*.1.360. **–μηνιάω**, *to be exceedingly wrathful*, Hld.1.15. **–μήνιος**, ον, Dor. **–μάνιος**, = sq., ἥρως Theoc.15.138. ⊛ **–μηνις**, ι, *heavy in wrath, exceeding wrathful*, δαίμων A.*Ag*.1482; ἡ β. Κλωθώ *IG*14.1466; of persons, Ph.2.94, al., Hld.7.20: βαρύμηνι, τό, Ph.2.108. **–μηνος**, ον, = foreg., πρόσωπα Doroth.(?) ap.Heph.Astr.3.4. **–μισθος**, ον, *largely paid, grasping*, *AP*5.1. ⊛ **–μοχθος**, ον, *toilsome*, γραμματική *AP*10.97 (Pall.); *painful*, οἶστρος Nonn.*D*.42.170. II. *hard-working*, κύων ib.5.469; epith. of Heracles, *APl*.4.102.

**βᾰρῠμωροκάρδιος**, ον, *stubborn and foolish*, Sm.*Pr*.14.14.

**βάρυν-σις** [ᾰ], εως, ἡ, *oppression, annoyance*, Artem.1.17. II. *weighing down*, Plot.4.3.15. **–τέον**, *one must mark with the grave accent*, Sch.Il.14.264. II. *one must bear hardly*, D.Chr.7.115. **–τικός**, ή, όν, *weighing down*, Arist.*Cael*.310$^{a}$32. II. *retracting the accent*, Αἰολεῖς *EM*548.19, *AB*663. ⊛ **–ω**, Pi.*P*.1.84, Pl.*Phdr*.247b: impf., Od.5.321: fut. –ῠνῶ X.*Ap*.9: aor. ἐβάρῡνα Plu.2.127c, etc.:—**Pass.**, pres., Il.19.165, etc.: fut. βαρυνθήσομαι S.*Fr*.697, Plb.5.94.9, Lxx*Si*.3.26: aor. ἐβαρύνθην Il.20.480, etc.: pf. βεβάρυμμαι Hp.*Ep*.17, Arist.*Phgn*. (v. infr.), Lxx*Na*.2.9(10): (βαρύς):—*weigh down, oppress, depress*, εἵματα γάρ ῥ' ἐβάρυνε Od.5.321; βάρυνε δέ μιν δόρυ μακρὸν ἑλκόμενον Il.5.664, etc.; ἥν σε βαρύνῃ δίψος Epigr.ap.Sotion.p.39 W.:—Pass., λάθρῃ γυῖα βαρύνεται *he is heavy*, i.e. *weary*, in limb, Il.19.165; χεῖρα βαρυνθεὶς *disabled* in hand, 20.480; βεβαρύνθαι *to be oppressed* by surfeit, etc., Arist.*Phgn*.810$^{b}$22, cf. *HA*582$^{b}$8, Ph.1.38; ὑπὸ κόπου D.H.1.39; βαρύνεσθαι τὴν γαστέρα *to be pregnant*, Luc.*Merc.Cond*.34, cf. X.*Mem*.2.2.5; τόκοις E.*IT*1228; β. alone, Nonn.*D*.26.270; βαρύνεταί τινι τὸ σκέλος Ar.*Ach*.220, cf. Pl.*Phd*.117e; ὄμμα β., of one dying, E.*Alc*.385; βαρυνόμεν' ἔνθα καὶ ἔνθα ἐκ παθέων Timo 9; also ὁ αὐταῖς ἐβαρύνθη *weighed upon* them, Plot.4.3.15. 2. metaph., *oppress, weary*, ἀστῶν ἀκοὰ κρύφιον θυμὸν β. Pi.*P*.1.84; τοὺς δικαστάς X.*Ap*.9; of cold, Arist.*Somn.Vig*.456$^{b}$26; *make more grievous*, ἀνίαν Ph.2.425:—Pass., *to be oppressed, distressed*, Simon.184.5, Pi.*N*.7.43, S.*El*.820, Th.8.1; πήμασιν *by* calamities, A.*Ag*.836, cf. 189 (lyr.); χόλῳ S.*Aj*.41; κακῇ ὀσμῇ Id.*Ph*.890; ὀσμῆς Id.*Fr*.697; ξυντυχίᾳ Cratin.166; διά τι Th.5.7; ὑπό τινων Nic.Dam.p.38 D.; ἐβαρύνθη ἡ καρδία *was made stubborn, was hardened*, Lxx*Ex*.8.15(11), al.; also c. acc., τὰ λυπηρὰ τῆς τύχης D.H.4.14; γῆρας J.*BJ*1.32.2, cf. Plu.*Cor*.31, D.Chr.43.6; τινά Id.40.1, Plu.*Thes*.32, *POxy*.298.26 (i A.D.); τὸν πλοῦτον *to be overloaded with*, Eun.*Hist*.p.248 D. II. *mark with the grave accent*, Hdn.Gr.1.18, A.D.*Synt*.120.4, Ath.2.52f.—βαρύνω I is replaced by βαρέω in later Greek.

**βᾰρύ-νωτος** [ῠ], ον, *with heavy back*, κόγχαι Emp.76. **–οδμία**, ἡ, *oppressiveness of smell*, Aret.*SA*1.5. **–οδμος**, ον, *of oppressive smell*, Nic.*Th*.51, cf. Aret.*CA*1.6. **–οζος**, ον, (ὄζω) = foreg., Dsc.5.

106. ⊛ **-ολκός**, = βαρουλκός, ἡ β. Tz.*H*.2.155. **-ὀπᾶς**, ὁ, (ὄψ) *loud-voiced*, of Zeus, in acc. -ᾶν, Pi.*P*.6.24. **-όργητος**, ον, *exceeding angry*, Πιερίδες *AP*5.106 (Phld.). **-οσμος**, ον, = βαρύοδμος, Arist.*Mir*. 831ᵇ24, Sor.2.29: Comp., Dsc.3.121. II. metaph., 'in bad odour', *PSI*2.158.25. **-πᾰθέω**, *to be much annoyed*, Plu.2.167f (v.l.). **-πά-λᾰμος** [πᾰ], ον, *heavy-handed*, χόλος Pi.*P*.11.23. **-πένθεια**, ἡ, *heavy, deep affliction*, Plu.2.118b. **-πενθής**, ές, = sq., Ph.2.269, *IG*12(5).675.6 (Syros), Orph.*Fr*.32c:—a fem. form **-πενθάς** *Epigr. Gr*.367 (Cotiaeum). II. *causing grievous woe*, μάχαι B.13.12; τόξα *APl*.4.134 (Mel.). ⊛ **-πένθητος**, ον, *mourning heavily*, *AP*7.743 (Antip.). **-πεσής**, ές, *heavy-falling*, πούς A.*Eu*.369 (lyr.). **-πήμων**, Dor. **-πάμων**, ον, gen. ονος, *miserable*, *Hymn.Is*.44, Suid. **-πλουτος**, ον, *very wealthy*, Nic.Dam.p.144 D. **-πνείων**, οντος, *blowing fiercely*, ἀῆται Musae.216,309. **-πνοια**, ἡ, *laboured breathing*, Sor.2.26. **-πνοος**, ον, = βαρυαής II, Nic.*Th*.76, *Al*.338. **-πο-τμος**, ον, = βαρυδαίμων, of persons, S.*Ph*.1096 (lyr.); of sufferings, *grievous*, Id.*OC*1449 (lyr.): Comp. -ότερος Plu.2.989e: Sup. -ότατος Id.*TG*5, Ph.1.637; but ξυμφορᾶς βαρυποτμωτάτας (metri gr.) E.*Ph*. 1345 (lyr.). **-πους**, ὁ, ἡ, πουν, τό, gen. ποδος, of a club, *heavy at the end*, *APl*.4.104 (Phil.). **-πρεπής**, ές, = μεγαλοπρεπής, εὐωχία Anon.ap.Suid. **-πυκνος**, ον, *in the lower part of the* πυκνόν (q.v.), φθόγγοι Aristid.Quint.3.10, Cleonid.*Harm*.4, etc. **-ρρήμων**, ον, gen. ονος, *using heavy words*, Sch.Ar.*Ra*.863.

⊛ **βᾰρύς**, εῖα, ύ, poet. gen. pl. fem. βαρεῶν dub. in A.*Eu*.932 (anap.): Comp. βαρύτερος, Sup. βαρύτατος:—*heavy in weight*, β. ἀείρεσθαι, opp. κοῦφος, Hdt.4.150, cf. Pl.*Tht*.152d, Arist.*Cael*.310ᵇ25, etc.: in Hom. mostly with collat. notion of *strength and force*, χεῖρα βαρεῖαν Il.1.219, cf. 89; ἀκμᾷ βαρύς Pi.*I*.4(3).51; β. τὸ σῶμα App.*Mac*.14; of athletes, Philostr.*Gym*.31; ὀφρύς *bushy*, ib.48; but also, *heavy with age*, *infirmity* or *suffering*, νόσῳ S.*Tr*.235; σὺν γήρᾳ Id.*OT*17; ἐν γήρᾳ Id. *Aj*.1017; ὑπὸ γήρως Ael.*VH*9.1; ὑπὸ τῆς μέθης Plu.2.596a; *pregnant*, *PGoodsp.Cair*.15.15 (iv A.D.); β. βάσις *heavy, slow*, S.*Tr*.966; τυπάδι βαρείᾳ Id.*Fr*.844. Adv. κοῦφον βαρέως Pl.*Tht*.189d. 2. *heavy to bear, grievous*, ἄτη, ἔρις, κακότης, Il.2.111, 20.55, 10.72; Κλῶθες Od.7.197; κῆρες Il.21.548; β. κὴρ τὸ μὴ πιθέσθαι A.*Ag*.206 (lyr.); βαρὺ or βαρέα στενάχειν *sob heavily*, Od.8.95,534, Il.8.334, etc.: in Trag. and Prose, *burdensome, grievous, oppressive*, β. ξυμφορά, τύχαι, καταλλαγαί, etc., A.*Pers*.1044 (lyr.), *Th*.332 (lyr.), 767 (lyr.), etc.; ἡδονή S.*OC*1204; ἀγγελία β. ἦν ἐν τοῖς βαρύτατ' ἂν ἐνέγκαιμι Pl.*Cri*.43c; πόλεμος D.18.241; βαρὺ κοὐχὶ δίκαιον Id.21.66; νόσος *causing disgust*, S.*Ph*.1330; αὐδά, ἠχώ, ib.208 (lyr.), E.*Hipp*.791; *unwholesome*, χωρίον X.*Mem*.3.6.12; πλησμονή Id.*Cyn*.7.4; *indigestible*, Ath.3.115e; β. νότος Paus.10.17.11. Adv. -έως, φέρειν τι *take a thing ill, suffer it impatiently*, Hdt.5.19; β. φέρειν ἐπί τινι Plb.15.1.1 (but β. φέρειν *bear with dignity*, D.S.26.3); β. ἔχειν, c. part., Arist.*Rh.Al*. 1424ᵇ5; πρός τι Id.*Pol*.1311ᵇ9; τοῖς λογίοις Arg.E.*Heracl*.: Comp. βαρυτέρως τινὶ ἐναντιωθῆναι Lxx 3*Ma*.3.1; βαρέως ἀκούειν *hear with disgust*, X.*An*.2.1.9. 3. *violent*, ὀργή S.*Ph*.368; μῆνις Id.*OC*1328; ἀπέχθειαι Pl.*Ap*.23a (Sup.); θυμός Theoc.1.96. 4. *weighty, grave*, ἐπιστολαί 2*Ep.Cor*.10.10; αἰτιώματα *Act.Ap*.25.7; τὰ βαρύτερα τοῦ νόμου *Ev.Matt*.23.23; *ample*, βαρυτάτην εὐδαιμονίαν τοῖς ἀρχομένοις παρέξειν Hdn.2.14.3. II. of persons, *severe, stern*, β. ἐπιτιμητής A. *Pr*.77; εὔθυνος Id.*Pers*.828, cf. S.*OT*546; Κύπρι βαρεῖα Theoc.1.100; *wearisome, troublesome*, E.*Supp*.894, Pl.*Tht*.210c, etc.; ξύνοικος A. *Supp*.415, S.*Fr*.753; γείτονες Plb.1.10.6. 2. *overbearing*, σεμνότεροι ἢ βαρύτεροι Arist.*Rh*.1391ᵃ27 (but σεμνὸς καὶ β. Str.14.1.42); ὑπερήφανοι καὶ β. Plu.2.279c; *important, powerful*, πόλις Plb.1.17.5, etc. 3. of soldiers, *heavy-armed*, X.*Cyr*.5.3.37 (s.v.l.); of the ὁπλίτης Pl.*Lg*.833b (Comp.); τὰ β. τῶν ὅπλων Plb.1.76.3. 4. *difficult*, ὅρκος γὰρ οὐδεὶς ἀνδρὶ φηλήτῃ β. S.*Fr*.933. III. of impressions on the senses, 1. of sound, *strong, deep, bass*, opp. to ὀξύς, Od.9.257, S.*Ph*.208, Pl.*Prt*.332c, Arist.*EN*1125ᵃ14, etc.; βαρὺ ἀυβόασον A.*Pers*. 572 (lyr.); φθέγγονται βαρύτατον ἀνθρώπων Hp.*Aër*.15; βαρύτατα ὑπακούειν, of diseases, Id.*Prorrh*.2.39; πενθεῖν Ael.*VH*12.1; esp. of musical pitch, *low*, opp. ὀξύς, βαρυτάτη χορδή Pl.*Phdr*.268e; ἆχος, φωνά, Archyt.1, cf. Arist.*EE*1235ᵃ28, Aristox.*Harm*.p.3 M.; of accent, *grave*, ἀντὶ ὀξείας τῆς μέσης συλλαβῆς βαρεῖαν ἐφθεγξάμεθα Pl. *Cra*.399b; ὀξείᾳ καὶ βαρείᾳ καὶ μέσῃ φωνῇ Arist.*Rh*.1403ᵇ30, etc.: hence ἡ βαρεῖα (sc. προσῳδία) *accentus gravis*, D.T.630.1, etc.; β. τάσις D.H.*Comp*.11, A.D.*Synt*.307.13; β. τόνος D.T.674.13, cf. A.D.*Pron*. 36.5; β. συλλαβή *unaccented*, Id.*Synt*.100.8, al. Adv. βαρέως *with the accent thrown back*, Id.*Pron*.51.1, Ath.2.53b: Comp. -ύτερον, opp. ὀξύτερον (οὐ opp. οὗ), Arist.*SE*178ᵃ3 (but, *on a lower note*, αὐλεῖν Id.*GA* 788ᵃ22). 2. of smell, *strong, offensive*, Hdt.6.119. 3. Adv. βαρέως *slowly*, ἐπισπᾶσθαι Hero *Aut*.26.6. ($g^u\underline{r}$-u- from $g^u\bar{r}$-u-, Skt. *gurús* 'heavy', Lat. *gravis* (from fem. $g^u$rəwī-), Goth. *kaurus* 'heavy'.)

**βᾰρύ-σαρκος**, ον, = βαθύσαρκος, *Hippiatr*.30 (s.v.l.). **-σίδηρος** [ῐ], ον, *heavy with iron*, Plu.*Aem*.18. **-σκελής**, ές, *heavy in the legs, slow*, *Trag.Adesp*.250. **-σκίπων** [ῐ], ον, gen. ωνος, *with a heavy club*, Call.*Fr*.120. **-σμάρᾰγος** [σμᾰ], ον, = βαρύκτυπος, Nonn.*D*.1.156. **-σπλαγχνος**, ον, *ill-tempered*, Ph.2. 269. **-σταθμέω**, *weigh heavy*, Ps.-Dsc.1.26. ⊛ **-σταθμος**, ον, *weighing heavy*, Ar.*Ra*.1397, Canthar.2, Arist.*EN*1142ᵃ22; νόμισμα Plu.*Lys*.17. **-στένακτος**, ον, = βαρύστονος, Sch.Opp.*H*.5. 152. **-στενάχων** [νᾰ], ουσα, *sobbing heavily*, better written βαρὺ στ- divisim, Il.1.364, etc. ⊛ **-στομος**, ον, *heavy in pronunciation*, of the first syllable of σκῆπτρον, Phld.*Po*.2.14 (dub.). 2. *of heavy*, i.e. *abusive, mouth*, Nonn.*D*.48.420. 3. of a weapon, *cutting deeply*, Opp.*H*.4.481. **-στονος**, ον, *groaning heavily*, τοῖς βαρυστόνοις ἐπικαλουμένοις.. ὑποκριταῖς nicknamed *the bellowers*, D.18.262, cf. Epicur.*Fr*.114,237; *resounding*, λίθος *AP*9.246 (Marc. Arg.). Adv. -νως A.*Eu*.794. II. of things, *heavily lamented, grievous*, S.*OT* 1233, Orac.ap.Paus.10.9.11. **-σύμφορος**, ον, *weighed down by ill-luck*, in Sup. -ώτατος Hdt.1.45, App.*Mac*.19. Adv. -ώτατα D.C.78. 41. 2. Act., *calamitous*, πόλεμος Them.*Or*.15.184c (Sup.). **-σφά-ρᾰγος** [φᾰ], ον, = βαρυσμάραγος, *loud-thundering*, of Ζεύς, Pi.*I*.8(7). 23. **-σωμος**, ον, *heavy in body*, Sch.Pi.*N*.8.41. **-τάλαντος** [τᾰ], ον, = *weighing heavily*, Zonar. s.v. ὁλκός. **-ταρβής**, ές, *terrifying*, εἰκών A.*Fr*.57.11. **-τελής**, ές, *heavily taxed*, *PLond*.5.1674. 33 (vi A.D.).

**βᾰρύτης** [ῠ], ητος, ἡ, (βαρύς) *weight, heaviness*, νεῶν Th.7.62, cf. Plb.1.51.9; opp. κουφότης, Thphr.*HP*5.3.1; *heaviness* of limb, β. ναρκώδης Plu.2.978c; of digestion, ἀπεψία καὶ β. ib.128b. II. of men, *troublesomeness, importunity*, ἀηδίαι καὶ βαρύτητες Isoc.12.31; *disagreeableness*, D.18.35, Plu.*Cor*.30, al.; β. φρονήματος Id.*Cat.Mi*. 57. 2. *arrogance*, Arist.*Rh*.1391ᵃ28; *gravity*, τοῦ ἤθους Plu. *Fab*.1 codd. III. of sound, *depth, low pitch*, opp. ὀξύτης, Pl.*Prt*. 316a, Arist.*GA*778ᵃ19, *de An*.422ᵇ30, Aristox.*Harm*.p.3 M., D.H. *Comp*.11, etc.; *the grave accent*, opp. ὀξύτης, Arist.*Po*.1456ᵇ33; *absence of accent*, A.D.*Pron*.38.15, al. IV. Rhet., *adoption of an injured tone*, Aps.p.331 H.

⊛ **βᾰρῠ-τῑμέω**, *raise the price of goods*, *EM*759.5, Suid. s.v. τιμουλκέω. **-τῑμος**, ον, *punishing severely*, of the gods below, A.*Supp*. 24. II. *very costly*, Str.17.1.13, *Ev.Matt*.26.7. III. *selling dearly*, Hld.2.30 (s.v.l.). **-τλητος**, Dor. **-τλᾱτος**, ον, *bearing heavy weight*, dub. in Naumach.ap.Stob.4.22.32; *unfortunate*, Ἀττικὴ β. *AP*7.343. II. Pass., *ill to bear*, συμφορά B.13.4; ὀδύναι *APl*.4.245 (Leont.). **-τονέω**, *pronounce with the grave accent*, D.H.2.58: abs., *use the grave accent*, Cleonid.*Harm*.12. **-τόνησις**, εως, ἡ, *grave accentuation*, Eust.70.45. **-τονητέος**, α, ον, *to be marked with the grave accent*, Sch.Ar.*Ra*.864, al. **-τονος**, ον, (τόνος) *deep-sounding*, β. φωνεῖν, of dogs, Arist.*Phgn*.813ᵇ2; so prob. β. στῆθος X.*Cyn*.5. 30; *deep*, of musical notes, Bacch.*Harm*.32. 2. Gramm., of enclitics, *unaccented*, A.D.*Pron*.35.25; of words, *not oxytone*, ib.38. 12, D.T.674.18, etc. Adv. -νως *POxy*.1012 *Fr*.16.16, Eust.41.3, Moer.109. **-ϋπνος**, ον, *sleeping heavily*, Nonn.*D*.48.765. **-φθέγκτης**, ου, ὁ, = sq., λέων Pi.*Fr*.239. **-φθογγος**, ον, *loud-roaring*, λέων *h.Ven*.159, B.8.9; *deep-lowing*, of cows, Arist.*GA*787ᵃ33; β. νευρά *loud-twanging* bowstring, Pi.*I*.6(5).34; *deep-toned*, αὐλοί *AP*6. 51. ⊛ **-φθονος**, ον, *heavy with envy*, χείρ *Epigr.Gr*.376a (Aezani), al. **-φλοισβος**, ον, *loud-roaring*, γενέθλη Procl.*H*.1.20. **-φορτος**, ον, *heavy-burdened*, i.e. *pregnant*, Nonn.*D*.48.769. **-φροσύνη**, ἡ, *melancholy*, Plu.2.710f (pl.), *Fr.inc*.146; *indignation*, Id.*Cor*.21, Porph.ap.Stob.1.49.60 (prob.). **-φρων**, ον, gen. ονος, (φρήν) *heavy of mind, melancholy, gloomy*, συντυχίαι *Lyr.Adesp*.140.8; Αἰήτης A.R.4.731; *savage*, ταῦρος Lyc.464; *cruel*, δαίμων Opp.*H*.4. 174. 2. *weighty of purpose, grave-minded*, Theoc.25.110. **-φωνέω**, *utter low-pitched sounds*, Arist.*Pr*.900ᵇ13. **-φωνία**, Ion. -ίη, ἡ, *deepness of voice, a bass voice*, Hp.*Aër*.8, Alex.311, Arist.*GA*786ᵇ 35. **-φωνος**, ον, *with a deep, bass voice*, opp. ὀξύφωνος, Hp.*Aër*. 6, Arist.*GA*786ᵇ7, etc. **-χειλος**, ον, *thick-lipped*, *APl*.2.20 (Ammian.). **-χείμων**, ον, gen. ωνος, *with heavy storms*, Theognost.*Can*. 460. **-χορδος**, ον, *deep-toned*, φθόγγος *AP*12.187 (Strat.). **-χρους**, ουν, *deep-coloured*, v.l. for βαθυ-, Dsc.5.94. **-ψῡχος**, ον, *heavy of soul, dejected*, S.*Aj*.319, *Cat.Cod.Astr*.7.198. **-ώδης**, ες, (ὄζω) = βαρύοδμος, Nic.*Th*.895. **-ώδῠνος**, ον, (ὀδύνη) *suffering grievous pangs*, Nonn.*D*.47.163. 2. *causing grievous pangs*, ib.48.808. **-ωπέω**, *to be dim-sighted*, Lxx *Ge*.48.10.

**βασά**· αἰσχύνη· ὅ ἐστι δρῦς, Hsch. **βασαγεῖ**· ἀλεσχοῖ, Id.

**βασαγίκορος**, = ὁ θᾶσσον συνουσιάζων, Hippon.107.

**βᾰσᾰν-αστρᾰγάλη** [γᾰ], Dor. -α, ἡ, *plague of the joints*, of the gout, in voc., Luc.*Trag*.199. **-εύω**, = -ίζω, Hsch. (Pass.). **-ηδόν**, Adv. *by means of torture*, Man.4.197. ⊛ **-ίζω**, Att. fut. -ιῶ Ar.*Ra*. 802,1121, *Ec*.748: aor. ἐβασάνισα, subj. βασανίσω v.l. in Id.*Ra*.618 cod. R:—Pass., aor. ἐβασανίσθην: pf. βεβασάνισμαι:—*rub upon the touch-stone* (βάσανος), χρυσὸν Pl.*Grg*.486d: hence, *put to the test, prove*, Arist.*GA*747ᵃ3 (Pass.), etc.; *investigate scientifically*, Hp.*Aër*.3; of the instances used in inductive inference, ἀπὸ τῶν πανταχόθεν βεβασανισμένων [μεταβαίνομεν] Phld.*Sign*.29. II. of persons, *examine closely, cross-question*, Hdt.1.116, 2.151, Ar.*Ach*.110, *Ra*.802, etc.; βεβασανισμένος εἰς δικαιοσύνην *having* his love of justice *put to the test*, Pl.*R*.361c, cf. 413e, *Smp*.184a; ὑπὸ δακρύων βασανίζεσθαι, i.e. *to be convicted* of being painted by tears (washing off the cosmetic), X.*Oec*.10.8. 2. *question by applying torture, torture, rack* (v. βάσανος III), Ar.*Ra*.616,618; [δούλους] πάντας παραδίδωμι βασανίσαι Antipho 2.4.8, cf. 5.36:—Pass., *to be put to the torture*, Th.7.86, Lys.4. 14, Arist.*Rh.Al*.1443ᵇ31; αἰωνίοις ἀμοιβαῖς βασανισθησόμενοι πρὸς τῶν θεῶν Phld.*D*.1.19; *to be tortured* by disease (censured by Luc.*Sol*.6), *Ev.Matt*.8.6; ὑπὸ τῶν κυμάτων ib.14.24; of animals, Philostr.*VA* 1.38: metaph. of the earth, ib.6.10. 3. metaph. of style, *strain*, Longin.10.6; βεβασανισμένος *forced, unnatural*, D.H.*Th*.55. **-ισμός**, ὁ, *torture*: ὁ γὰρ Κορίνθιος (sc. οἶνος) β. ἐστι Alex.290, cf. *Apoc*.9. 5. **-ιστέος**, α, ον, *to be proved* or *tested under suffering*, Ar.*Lys*. 478, Pl.*R*.540a. II. βασανιστέον *one must put to the test, prove*, τινά ib.503a, Max.Tyr.24.4, Gal.17(1).337, Jul.*Or*.7.226a, Them. *Or*.23.287c; *one must put to the torture*, D.29.35. ⊛ **-ιστήριον**, τό, *question-chamber*, Theopomp.Com.63, Polyaen.8.62, Phalar.*Ep*.82, 115; of the stocks, Sm.*Je*.20.2. II. in pl., *instruments of torture*,

Plu.2.315d, Charito 4.2, Them.*Or.*13.175c. **III.** *touchstone, test,* χρυσοῦ, πορφύρας ib.21.247b: metaph., ib.248a. **-ιστήριος,** ον, *of* or *for torture,* ὄργανα J.*BJ*2.8.10. **-ιστής,** οῦ, ὁ, *examiner, questioner, torturer,* Antipho 5.32, D.37.40, Plu.2.498d; *gaoler, Ev. Matt.*18.34. **II.** *one who tests,* Them.*Or.*21.247c:—fem. -ίστρια, *examiner,* ἐπῶν Ar.*Ra.*826. **-ιστικός,** ή, όν, *given to* or *for torturing,* Vett.Val.78.15, *AB*306, *EM*769.11. **2.** *for testing,* Them. *Or.*21.247c. **-ίτης** λίθος, = sq., Hsch. ⊛ **-ος,** ἡ, *touchstone,* on which pure gold leaves a yellow streak, ἐς βάσανον δ' ἐλθὼν παρατρίβομαι ὥστε μολύβδῳ χρυσός Thgn.417; χρυσὸν τριβόμενον βασάνῳ Id.450, cf. 1105; παρατρίβεσθαι πρὸς τὰς β. Arist.*Col.*793b1, cf. *HA* 597b2: metaph., β. τοῦ ἀρώματος (sc. τοῦ κινναμώμου) τὴν αἶγα εἶναι Philostr.*VA*3.4. **II.** *the use of this as a test,* χρυσὸς ἐν β. πρέπει Pi.*P.*10.67: generally, *test, trial of genuineness,* οὐκ ἔστιν μείζων β. χρόνου [Simon.]175.1; δόμεν τι βασάνῳ ἐς ἔλεγχον Pi.*N.*8.20; σοφὸς ὤφθη βασάνῳ θ' ἁδύπολις S.*OT*510 (lyr.), cf. 494; β. ἰσαυτον λαμβάνειν περί τινος Pl.*Lg.*648b; εἰς β. εἶ χερῶν wilt come to *a trial* of strength, S. *OC*835; πλοῦτος β. ἀνθρώπου τρόπων Antiph.232.5; [νόσου] ἔσχ' ἐπὶ σοὶ βάσανον had *experienced* it in you, i.e. you had had it first, *IG*14. 1320; βάσανον ὑποκείσονται will be subjected to *a test,* of candidates, *POxy.*58.25 (iii A.D.). **III.** *inquiry by torture,* ἐς πᾶσαν β. ἀπικνέεσθαι Hdt.8.110; εἰς β. αἰτεῖν Herod.2.88; ἐξετάσαι διὰ βασάνων *SIG*780.12 (Astypalaea, Aug.); esp. at Athens, used to extort evidence from slaves, εἰς β. δέχεσθαι Antipho 1.12; εἰς β. παραδοῦναι Is.8.17; ἐκ βασάνων εἰπεῖν ib.12: in pl., *confession upon torture,* D. 53.24, Hyp.*Fr.*5, Arist.*Rh.*1355b37. **2.** *agony* of battle, ἡ κατὰ τὸ ἔργον β. S.E.*M.*6.24; *tortures* of disease, *Ev.Matt.*4.24; cf. ἐπάγρυπνος β. Vett.Val.211.28; also ψυχικαί Id.182.19; *torments* of hell, *Ev.Luc.*16.23. **3.** *trespass-offering,* Lxx 1*Ki.*6.17.—Oriental word.

⊛ **βασείδιον,** τό, Dim. of βάσις, *BGU*781 iii 6 (i A.D.).

**βασίαρξ,** dub. in *BGU*630 i 22 (ii A.D.).

⊛ **βασίλ-εια** [ῐ], ἡ, βασιλέα Pi.*N.*1.39: fem. of βασιλεύς:—*queen, princess,* Od.4.770, A.*Ag.*84 (lyr.), Hdt.1.11, etc.; of goddesses, Κύπρις β. Emp.128.3, cf. *Hymn.Is.*1, etc.; β. θεά Ar.*Pax* 974; β. γύναι A.*Pers.*623 (lyr.), E.*El.*988 (lyr.). ⊛ **-εία,** Ion. **-ηΐη,** ἡ, *kingdom, dominion,* Hdt.1.11, etc.; παιδὸς ἡ β. Heraclit.52; *hereditary monarchy,* opp. τυραννίς, ἐπὶ ῥητοῖς γέρασι πατρικαὶ β. Th.1.13; βασιλείας εἴδη τέτταρα Arist.*Pol.*1285b20; ἡ πρώτη πολιτεία μετὰ τὰς β. after *the age of monarchies,* ib.1297b17: metaph., ἐποίησεν ἡμᾶς β. *Apoc.*1.6; β. τῶν οὐρανῶν *Ev.Matt.*3.2; τοῦ θεοῦ ib.6.33, etc. **2.** *kingly office,* β. καὶ στρατηγία Arist.*Pol.*1273a37. **3.** at Athens, *the office of the archon* βασιλεύς, Paus.1.3.1. **4.** Pass., *being ruled by a king,* τῆς ὑπ' ἐκείνου βασιλείας Isoc.9.43. **II.** *diadem,* D.S.1.47, *OGI*90.43 (Rosetta). **III.** *reign,* ib.331.40 (Pergam.), D.S.17.1, *POxy.*1257.7 (iii A.D.); so αἱ β. *the reigns of the Kings,* title of book of *VT*; *accession to the throne, BGU*646.12 (ii A.D.). **IV.** concrete, *His Majesty,* Lxx 4*Ki.*11.1, 1*Ma.*6.47. **-ειάω,** Desid., *aim at royalty, Com.Adesp.*958, J.*BJ Praef.*2, 1.4.1. ⊛ **-είδης,** ου, ὁ, *prince,* τῶν δέκα βασιλειδῶν Pl.*Criti.*116c. **-είδιον,** τό, Dim. of βασιλεύς, *tiny king,* Plu.*Ages.*2. ⊛ **-ειον,** Ion. **-ήϊον,** τό, *kingly dwelling, palace,* X.*Cyr.*2.4.3, etc.; more common in pl., Hdt.1.30, 178, Arist.*Oec.*1352a11, etc. **b.** *seat of empire, capital,* Plb.3.15.3, D.S.19.18, Str.1.2.25. **2.** *royal treasury,* Hdt.2.149: pl., Isoc. 3.31. **II.** *tiara, diadem,* Lxx 2*Ki.*1.10, Roussel *Cultes Égyptiens* 233 (Delos, ii B.C.), *OGI*90.45 (Rosetta), Plu.2.358d, Porph.ap.Eus. *PE*3.11, Horap.1.15: metaph., τὸ β. τῆς εὐπρεπείας *diadem* of beauty, Lxx *Wi.*5.16. **III.** = ἅλιμος, Ps.-Dsc.1.91; = λευκόϊον, Id.3. 123. **IV.** Βασίλεια, τά, *festival of Zeus Basileus,* in Boeotia, *IG*7. 552, Sch.Pi.*O.*7.153, *IG*12(1).78; at Olbia, *IPE*1.105. ⊛ **-ειος,** ον, also α, ον A.*Pers.*589, *IG*1².115; Ion. and Aeol. **-ήϊος,** η, ον, also **-ηος** Melinno ap.Stob.3.7.12, *Hymn.Is.*138:—*royal,* δεινὸν δὲ γένος βασιλήϊόν ἐστι κτείνειν Od.16.401; ὁ β. θρόνος Hdt.1.14, etc.; used by Trag. in lyr., β. οἶκοι, μέλαθρα, A.*Ag.*157, *Ch.*343; ἰσχύς, τιάρα, Id.*Pers.*589, 661; νόστος ὁ β. *the king's* return, ib.8; τοῖς β. νόμοις S.*Ant.*382; cf. πῆχυς. **2.** *of the archon* βασιλεύς, ἡ β. στοά *IG*1². 115, Arist.*Ath.*7.1, Paus.1.3.1 (also of the *basilica* of Herod at Jerusalem, J.*AJ*15.11.5). **3.** 'royal', i.e. *choice,* μύρον Sapph.*Supp.*23. 19, Crates Com.2; cf. βασίλεια· γένος ἰσχάδων, Hsch. **4.** Ἄρτεμις βασιληΐη, divinity in Thrace, Hdt.4.33.

⊛ **βᾰσῐλ-εύς,** ὁ, gen. έως, Ep. ῆος, Cypr. ῆϝος *Inscr.Cypr.*104, 135 H.: acc. βασιλέα, contr. -ῆ Orac.ap.Hdt.7.220, E.*Fr.*781.24 (lyr.): nom. pl. βασιλεῖς, Aeol. -ηες Sapph.*Supp.*6.4, *IG*12(2).6 (Mytil.), -εες ib. 646 a 45, al., Ep. -ῆες, old Att. -ῆς S.*Aj.*188, 960 (both lyr.), cf. Hdn. Gr.1.430: acc. pl. βασιλέας *IG*1².115, later βασιλεῖς ib.2.243, etc.:—*king, chief,* Hom., etc.: freq. with collat. sense of *captain* or *judge,* Hes. *Op.*202; διοτρεφέες β. Il.2.445, etc.; θεῖοι Od.4.691, etc.; later, *hereditary king,* opp. τύραννος, Arist.*EN*1160b3, etc.; but also of tyrants, as Hiero, Pi.*O.*1.23; of Gelo, Hdt.7.161; of Pisistratus, Eup.123, cf. Sch. Ar.*Ach.*61: joined with a Subst., βασιλεὺς ἀνήρ Il.3.170, etc.; ἀνὴρ β. Hdt.1.90; ἄναξ β. lord *king,* A.*Pers.*5, cf. B.17.1: c. gen., β. νεῶν A. *Ag.*114 (anap.); οἰωνῶν β., of the eagle, ibid., Pi.*O.*13.21: Comp. βασιλεύτερος *more kingly,* Il.9.160, 392, Od.15.533, Tyrt.12.7: Sup. βασιλεύτατος Il.9.69. **b.** of the gods, Ζεὺς θεῶν β. Hes.*Th.*886, cf. Pi.*O.*7.34, Emp.128.2, etc. (in this sense Hom. uses ἄναξ); as cult title of Zeus, *IG*7.3073.90 (Lebad.), *SIG*1014.110 (Erythrae), etc. (but Ζεὺς β., = Ahuramazda, X.*Cyr.*3.3.21, al., Arr.*An.*4.20.3); ὁ μέγας β., of *God,* Lxx *Ps.*47(48).2, Ph.2.107: Sup. βασιλεύτατοι τῶν θεῶν Max.Tyr.29.5. **2.** as a title of rank, *prince,* β. εἰσὶ καὶ ἄλλοι πολλοὶ ἐν.. Ἰθάκῃ Od.1.394, cf. 8.390, etc.; of Cyrus, X.*Oec.* 4.16. **b.** *descendant of a royal house,* esp. in Ionia, Arist.*Ath.* 41.3; βασιλέων οἶκοι 'estates *of the royal house*', name of a district in Chios, Ἀθηνᾶ 20.168. **3.** generally, *lord, master,* Il.18.556, Pi.*O.*6.47. **4.** metaph., πόλεμος πάντων β. Heraclit.53; νόμος ὁ πάντων β. Pi.*Fr.*169. **II.** at Athens, *the second of the nine Archons, IG*1².76, al., Antipho 6.38, Lys.6.4, Arist.*Pol.*1285b17, *Ath.* 57, etc.; ἡ τοῦ β. στοά Pl.*Euthphr.*2a. **2.** title of magistrates in other Greek states, as βασιλᾶες at Elis, *GDI*1152, cf. *IG*12(2).6 (Mytil.), etc., Arist.*Pol.*1322b29. **3.** at Rome, β. τῶν ἱερῶν, = *rex sacrorum,* D.H.5.1, cf. D.C.54.27. **III.** after the Persian war (without Art.), *the king of Persia,* Hdt.7.174, al.; ἄναξ Ξέρξης β. A.*Pers.*5, cf. 144, Ar.*Ach.*61, Th.8.48, *IG*2².141 (βασιλῆς βασιλέως ὕπoχοι μεγάλου, of the Satraps, A.*Pers.*24, cf. 44, S.E.*M.*2.22); less freq. ὁ βασιλεύς Hdt.1.132, 137, Arist.*Pol.*1304b13; β. ὁ μέγας Hdt. 1.188. **2.** of Alexander and his successors, usually with Art., *IG*2².641, 687, Men.293, 340 (pl.); Σέλευκος Antiph.187; Ἀντίγονος Alex.111; Πτολεμαῖος Id.244; Ὀσυμανδύας βασιλεὺς βασιλέων D.S. 1.47; title used by Parthian *kings,* Plu.*Pomp.*38, D.C.37.6, etc.; by Antony, Plu.*Ant.*54; of *God, Apoc.*17.14, 19.16. **3.** of the Roman *emperors, AP*10.25 (Antip. Thess.); β. Ῥωμαίων *BGU*588. 10 (i A.D.), etc., cf. 1*Ep.Ti.*2.2, J.*AJ*14.15.14; β. αὐτοκράτωρ *IG*3. 13 (Hadrian), Hdn.1.6.5; without Art., Paus.10.32.19. **IV.** of any *great man,* πένησί τε καὶ βασιλεῦσιν Ps.-Phoc.113. **2.** *first* or *most distinguished of any class,* Ἡρώδην τὸν β. τῶν λόγων Philostr. *VS*2.10.1, cf. Luc.*Rh.Pr.*11; *winner* at a game, Poll.9.106, Sch.Pl. *Tht.*146a; Stoic *sage,* μόνος β. Luc.*Herm.*16; βασιλέως ἐγκέφαλος 'morsel fit for a king', Clearch.5; β. σῦκα, name of a *choice* kind, Philem.Lex.ap.Ath.3.76f., cf. Poll.6.81. **V.** = συμποσίαρχος, Plu.2.622a, Luc.*Sat.*4. **VI.** *wren,* Arist.*HA*592b27. **VII.** *queen-bee,* ib.623b9, *GA*759a20, etc. (The form βασιλέα is scanned ⏑ ⏑ – in Pi.*N.*1.39; codd. βασίλεια.) **-ευτός,** ή, όν, *suited for monarchical rule,* Arist.*Pol.*1288a8. **-εύτωρ,** ορος, ὁ, = βασιλεύς, Antim.5. ⊛ **-εύω,** *to be king, rule, reign,* οὐ μέν πως πάντες βασιλεύσομεν ἐνθάδ' Ἀχαιοί Il.2.203; ἶσον ἐμοὶ βασίλευε 9.616; ἐν ὑμῖν.. βασίλευε *was king* among you, Od.2.47; ὄφρ' Ἰθάκης κατὰ δῆμον.. βασιλεύοι 22.52; also of a woman, ἡ βασίλευεν ὑπὸ Πλάκῳ *reigned as queen,* Il.6.425; ἡ δὲ Πύλου βασίλευε Od.11.285: in aor., *to have become king,* Hdt.2.2: c. gen., *to be king of, rule over,* ἐν.. Ἰθάκῃ βασιλεύσει Ἀχαιῶν Od.1.401, etc.; βασιλεύοντος βασιλέων Ἀρσάκου *PAvrom.*1 A 1: c. dat., *to be king among,* Γιγάντεσσιν βασίλευεν Od. 7.59; later β. ἐπὶ τὰς δύο βασιλείας Lxx 1*Ma.*1.16:—Pass., *to be governed by a king,* Pl.*R.*576d, e, al., Arist.*Pol.*1284b39, etc.: c. acc. cogn., βασιλείαν πασῶν δικαιοτάτην βασιλεύεσθαι Pl.*Lg.*680e: generally, *to be governed* or *administered,* Pi.*P.*4.106, etc.; ὑπὸ νόμου Lys. 2.19: hence, *submit to the king,* Plu.*Sull.*12. **b.** *to be* ἄρχων *β.* at Athens, Isoc.18.5, *IG*1².776, al.; of other magistrates, *SIG*709 (Chersonesus), 1054 (Samothrace). **c.** later ἡ βασιλεύουσα πόλις the *imperial* city, of Rome, Ath.3.98c, cf. *CPHerm.*125 ii 3. **2.** *enjoy as master,* τῷ χρυσῷ β. Theoc.21.60 codd. **3.** abs., *live royally,* β. ἐν πενίᾳ Plu.2.101d, cf. 1*Ep.Cor.*4.8. **II.** causal, *appoint as king,* τινά Lxx *Jd.*9.6; but β. τισὶ βασιλέα *make* them *a king,* ib.1*Ki.*8.22, 12.1. **-η,** ἡ, = βασίλειᾰ, *queen, princess,* S.*Fr.*310, cf. Hdn.Gr.1. 275. **2.** a divinity, worshipped with Neleus and Codrus at Athens, *IG*1².94, Pl.*Chrm.*153a. **-ηΐη, -ήϊος,** Ion. for βασιλείᾱ, -λειος. ⊛ **-ηΐς,** ΐδος, ἡ, pecul. fem. of βασίλειος, *royal,* τιμή Il.6.193, Hes.*Th.*462, E.*Hipp.*1280 (lyr.). **2.** = βασίλειᾰ, *a queen,* Man.1. 283, *Epigr.Gr.*989.3 (Memnon). **-ίζω,** *to be of the king's party,* Plu. *Flam.*16: also, c. acc., ἐγώ εἰμι ὁ βασιλίζων τὸν τόπον εἰς ὀνόματι (sic) Μωυσ[ῆ] *Stud.Pont.*3 No.109 (Amisus):—Med., *affect, assume the state of a king,* App.*BC*3.18; so in Act., J.*AJ*1.10.4. ⊛ **-ικός,** ή, όν, *royal, kingly,* ποιέεις οὐδαμῶς -κά Hdt.2.173; β. γένος A.*Pr.*869; β. [μοναρχία] Pl.*Plt.*291e; opp. τυραννικός, Arist.*Pol.*1285b3; βασιλικοὶ ἀπέβησαν proved themselves *truly kingly,* Plb.8.10.10; βασιλικὸν [ἐστι] πράττειν μὲν εὖ, κακῶς δ' ἀκούειν Arr.*Epict.*4.6.20; ἦθος β. X. *Oec.*21.10; τὸ β. Id.*Cyr.*1.3.18: βασιλική (sc. τέχνη), ἡ, *art of ruling,* Andronic.Rhod.p.574 M.: Comp. **-ώτερος** Herm.ap.Stob.1.49.45, Jul.*Or.*2.54d: Sup. βασιλικώτατος καὶ ἄρχειν ἀξιώτατος X.*An.*1.9.1, cf. Isoc.2.29; -ωτάτη χάρις Plu.*Alex.*21. Adv. **-κῶς,** παρών *as a king, with kingly authority,* X.*Cyr.*1.4.14; β. ἄρχειν Arist.*Pol.*1259b 1. **2.** *of* or *belonging to a king,* οἱ β. *the king's friends* or *officers,* Plb.8.12.10; ἐγκλήματα β. charges *of high-treason,* Id.25.3.1; ὀφειλήματα β. debts *to the king,* ib.3; β. πρόσοδοι *PPetr.*3 p.56; γραμματεύς (cf. II. 1) Wilcken *Chr.*233.2 (ii B.C.), etc.; γεωργοί *PTeb.*5. 200 (ii B.C.), etc.; ὁδὸς β. the *king's* highway, Lxx *Nu.*20.17, *PPetr.*3 p.65 (iii B.C.); μὴ εἶναι β. ἀτραπὸν ἐπὶ γεωμετρίαν no *royal* road, Euc. ap.Procl.*in Euc.*p.68 F.; β. νόμος *OGI*483.1, *Ep.Jac.*2.8; αἱ β. βίβλοι the books *of Kings,* Ph.1.427. **3.** *choice* (cf. βασίλειος 3), μίνδαξ Amphis 27. **4.** κάρυα β. *walnuts,* Dsc.1.125; καρύαι *PSI*4.428. 65 (iii B.C.). **b.** β. κύμινον, = ἄμι, Dsc.3.62. **II.** as Subst., **1.** βασιλικός (sc. γραμματεύς), ὁ, official in Egyptian νομοί, *POxy.*1219. 15 (iii A.D.). **b.** (sc. οἶκος) *basilica, CIG*2782.25 (Aphrodisias). **c.** (sc. ὄρνις) = ἀκαλανθίς, Sch.Ar.*Pax* 1078. **d.** (sc. ἀστήρ) = βασιλίσκος V, *Cat.Cod.Astr.*7.201.23. **2.** βασιλικὴ στοά *hall* divided into aisles by columns, *IG*12(3).326.18 (Thera), Str.5.3.8 (pl.); β. alone, *OGI*511.15 (Aezani), Lat. *basilica,* Vitr.5.1.4, 6.3.9, cf. Plu.*Publ.*15, *Cat.Mi.*5, App.*BC*2.26. **3.** βασιλικόν (sc. ταμιεῖον), τό, *treasury,* εἰς τὸ β. ἀπομετρῆσαι, τελεῖν, *PSI*4.344.17 (iii B.C.), D.S.2.40, etc.; ὀφείλειν *PRev.Laws* 5.1, al.; *royal bank, OGI*90.29 (Rosetta),

*PRein.*13.19,al., *BGU*830.18 (i A.D.). b. (sc. δῶμα) *palace*, D.C. 60.4. c. (sc. πρόσταγμα) *royal decree*, Lxx *Es.*1.19. d. (sc. φάρμακον) name for various remedies, = τετραφάρμακον, Gal.12.601; of other compounds, ibid.; *a plaster*, Id.13.184; *an eyesalve*, Id.12.782 (also -κός, ὁ, *a bandage*, Id.18(1).777). e. (sc. φυτόν) *basil, Ocimum basilicum*, Suid. f. βασιλικά, τά, *communications received from kings*, *SIG*333.23 (Samos), 426.26 (Teos); also, *interests* or *revenues of the crown*, *PRev.Laws* 15.4 (iii B.C.), *PTeb.*5.256 (ii B.C.), Lxx 1 *Ma.*10.43; *prerogatives*, ib.15.8.

**βασῖλῖναῦ**, barbarism for βασίλιννα (i.e. βασίλειά), Ar.*Av.*1678.

**βᾰσῐλ-ίνδα**, Adv., ἡ β. παιδιά 'king of the castle', a game, Poll.9.110, *AB*1353. ⊛ **-ιννα**, v. βασίλισσα. ⊛ **-ίς**, ίδος, ἡ, = βασίλειά, *queen, princess*, S.*Ant.*941 (dub. l.), E.*Hec.*552; β. νύμφη, γυνή, E.*Med.*1003, *Hipp.*778: in Prose, β. γυναικῶν Pl.*Lg.*694e, cf. Plu.*Alex.*21; of a Roman Imperial *princess*, Philostr.*VA*1.3. b. = βασίλισσα 2, Eust. 1425.42. 2. as Adj., *royal*, ἑστία, εὐναί, E.*Rh.*718, *IA*1307 (lyr.); of cities, β. Ῥώμη *IG*14.830 (Puteoli); β. πόλις, of Rome, Gal.14.796; of Constantinople, *OGI*521.22 (Abydos), Them.*Or.*11.144a, Agath.1.4, etc.; so β. alone, Lyd.*Mag.*2.14; also β. χώρα, = Rome, Vett.Val.226.14. b. metaph., καρδίη β. Hp.*Nat.Hom.*6. II. *kingdom*, D.S.29.22. **-ίσκος**, ὁ, Dim. of βασιλεύς, *princelet, chieftain*, Plb.3.44.5, *OGI*200.18 (Axum); also, = βασιλείδιον, Ath.13.566a. II. *kind of serpent, basilisk*, perh. *Egyptian cobra*, Hp.*Ep.*19 (*Hermes* 53.65), Lxx *Ps.*90(91).13,al., Hld.3.8, Artem.4.56, Horap. 1.1, Democr.[300], Plin.8.78. III. *wren*, Aesop.ap.Plu.2.806e, Ruf.*Fr.*117, Artem.4.56; *gold-crest*, Philagr.ap.Aët.11.11. IV. *sea-fish*, Opp.*H.*1.129, Marc.Sid.26. V. *the star α Leonis, Regulus*, Gem.3.5, Heph.Astr.2.18, etc. VI. kind of *shoe*, Poll.7.85. ⊛ **-ισσα**, ἡ, = βασίλειά, *queen*, Alc.Com.6, X.*Oec.*9.15, Philem. 16.1, Arist.*Fr.*179, *Supp.Epigr.*1.366.34 (Samos, iii B.C.), Theoc.15.24, *IG*2.614*b*; ἡ β. τῶν μελισσῶν Arr.*Epict.*3.22.99; condemned by Phryn.202, but cf. Ael.Dion.*Fr.*91. 2. *wife of the ἄρχων βασιλεύς at Athens*, Poll.8.90:—also **βασίλιννα**, D.59.74, Men.907. 3. the Roman *Empress*, Hdn.1.7.4, etc. 4. = βασιλεύς VI, *PMag.Leid. V.*1.31. **-ισταί**, οἱ, guild of worshippers of Ptolemy Euergetes II, *OGI*130.6, *IG*12(3).443 (Thera).

**βάσῐμος** [ᾰ], ον, (βαίνω) *passable, accessible*, D.S.5.44,al. (dub. sens. in Tim.*Pers.*65); τόποι S.E.*M.*1.78: metaph. of a rhetorical τόπος, D.25.76, cf. D.S.23.15,al.; χρόνος ἱστορίᾳ β. Plu.*Thes.*1. II. *fixed, stable*, Eustr. *in EN*98.3.

**βάσις** [ᾰ], εως, ἡ, (βαίνω) *stepping, step*, and collectively, *steps*, A.*Eu.*36, S.*Aj.*8, etc.: metaph., ἡσύχῳ φρενῶν βάσει A.*Ch.*452 (lyr.); οὐκ ἔχων β. *power to step*, S.*Ph.*691 (lyr.); τροχῶν βάσεις the *rolling* of the wheels, the *rolling* wheels, Id.*El.*718; ἀρβύλης β. the *print* of the sandal, E.*El.*532; ποίμναις τήνδ' ἐπεμπίπτει βάσιν S.*Aj.*42. 2. *measured step* or *movement*, β. χορείας Ar.*Th.*968, cf. Pi.*P.*1.2: hence, *rhythmical* or *metrical movement*, Pl.*R.*399e, *Lg.*670d: in Rhet., *rhythmical close* of a sentence, Hermog.*Id.*1.6,al.; *clause forming transition from* πρότασις *to* ἀπόδοσις, Id.*Inv.*1.5: and in Metric, *metrical unit, monometer*, Arist.*Pol.*1263$^b$35, *Metaph.*1087$^b$36, Heph.11, Longin.*Proll.Heph.*3, Mar.Vict.p.47.3K., etc. 3. *order, sequence*, θέσις καὶ β. Epicur.*Ep.*1p.10U. II. *that with which one steps, a foot*, Pl.*Ti.*92a, Arist.*GA*750$^a$4; ποδῶν β. E.*Hec.*837; θηλύπους β. their women's *feet*, Id.*IA*421; β. δίχηλος, of the ostrich, D.S.3.28. 3: abs., αἱ βάσεις Ph.1.226, *Act.Ap.*3.7; σφὶγξ εἶχε β. λέοντος Apollod.3.5.8; *leg*, Id.1.3.5; βάσεων ἀποκοπαί Diog.Oen.39. III. *that whereon one stands, base, pedestal*, [κρατῆρος] Alex.119; of statues, *OGI*705.6, etc.; τρία ἔργα.. ἐπὶ μιᾶς β. Str.14.1.14, cf. Luc.*Philops.*19; λεβήτων Plb.5.88.5; of an engine, Hero *Bel.*88.1, al.; of a column, *PLond.*3.755$^v$6 (iv A.D.): Medic., τοῦ ἐγκεφάλου Herophil.ap.*Placit.*4.5.4, cf. Plu.*Per.*6; τραχήλου Id.*Pyrrh.*34; κοῖλαι βλεφάρων ἰοτυπεῖς βάσιες *AP*5.86 (Rufin.); αἱ ἐν ὀφθαλμοῖς β. Sor. 1.27, cf. Archig.ap.Aët.16.101(91); of the heart, Gal.*UP*6.13; ἐπανόρθωσις τὴν τοῦ κενουμένου βάσιν ἀναπληροῦσα Id.1.474; *foundation, basement*, ῥίζα πάντων καὶ β. ἁ γᾶ ἐρήρεισται Ti.Locr.97e; so, of the soil, πεδίων σπορίμα β. *Hymn.Is.*162. 2. Geom., *base* of a solid or plane figure, Pl.*Ti.*55b, Arist.*APr.*41$^b$15,al.; [κώνου] Democr.155; πυραμίδος Speus.ap.*Theol.Ar.*63. IV. *position, fixedness*, opp. φορά, etym. of βέβαιος, Pl.*Cra.*437a. V. Astrol., = ὡροσκόπος, Vett.Val.88.6, Paul.Al.*T.*2, *Cat.Cod.Astr.*8(4).132.

**βάσκα**· μακέλη, Hsch.; cf. μάσκη.

⊛ **βασκ-αίνω**, fut. -ανῶ Lxx *De.*28.56: aor. ἐβάσκηνα Philostr. (v. infr.), -ᾱνα Arist.*Pr.*926$^b$24:—Pass., aor. ἐβασκάνθην (v. infr.):—*bewitch* by the evil eye, etc., Arist. l.c., Lxx *De.*28.56: metaph., *Ep.Gal.*3.1; ἐβάσκηνε πάντα.. τύχη Hdn.2.4.5:—Pass., ὡς μὴ βασκανθῶσι Arist.*Fr.*347; ὡς μὴ βασκανθῶ τρὶς ἔπτυσα Theoc.6.39. II. c. acc., *malign, disparage*, Pherecr.174, D.8.19; ἄν τι δύσκολον συμβαίνῃ τοῦτο βασκαίνει Id.18.189; εἰσίν τινες.. οὓς τὸ βασκαίνειν τρέφει Dionys.Com.11:—Pass., ὑπὸ τῶν ἀντιτέχνων βασκανθῆναι Str.14.2.7. 2. c. dat., *envy, grudge*, D.20.24, etc.; τινί τινος *grudge* one a thing, D.Chr.78.37, Philostr.*VA*6.12; τινὶ ἐπί τινι D.Chr. 78.25: abs., Luc.*Nav.*17: τινός *keep to oneself*, Id.*Philops.*35. 3. c. acc. et inf., μὴ βασκήνας γελᾶσαι καὶ ἄλλον Ael.*VH*14.20. **-ᾰνία**, ἡ, *malign influence, witchery*, Pl.*Phd.*95b; β. φαυλότητος ἀμαυροῖ τὸ καλόν Lxx *Wi.*4.12; βασκανίας φάρμακον τὸ πήγανον Arist.*Pr.*926$^b$20. 2. *malignity*, ἀγνωμοσύνη καὶ β. D.18.252; ὄχλος καὶ β. Id. 19.24: pl., Lxx 4 *Ma.*2.15. 3. *jealousy*, ἥεισεν κρέσσονα βασκανίης Call.*Epigr.*23, cf. Ph.2.81,al. **-άνιον** [ᾰ], τό, *charm, amulet*, Ar.*Fr.*592, Str.16.4.17, cf. Phryn.68. II. in pl., *malign influences*, 'Αϊδεω β. *Epigr.Gr.*381 (Aezani). ⊛ **-ᾰνος**, ὁ, *one who bewitches, sorcerer*, as a term of abuse, D.21.209, Men.*Pk.*279, Str. 14.2.7; β. καὶ φθοροποιός St.Byz. s.v. Θίβα. 2. *slanderer*, D.18.132, Vett.Val.358.5. II. Adj. βάσκανος, ον, *slanderous, malicious*, Ar.*Eq.*103, *Pl.*571; ὁ συκοφάντης πανταχόθεν βάσκανον D.18.242, cf. Str.14.1.22; δύσκολος καὶ β. Plu.*Fab.*26; β. πρᾶγμα.. ποιοῦντες D. 18.317; β. ἔσσ', 'Αΐδα Erinna 6.3; κώμων β. ἐστι λίθος *AP*9.756 (Aemil.); μ' ὁ β. ἥρπασε δαίμων *Epigr.Gr.*345; freq. in sepulchral inscriptions, *IG*14.1362, etc.: Sup. -ώτατος *Com.Adesp.*359. Adv. -νως J.*AJ*11.4.9, Porph.*VP*53. 2. β. ὀφθαλμός *evil* eye, Plu.2.680c, cf. Alciphr.1.15. **-αντικός**, ή, όν, *envious*, φθονητικὴ καὶ β. ἕξις Plu.2.682d, cf. Phld.*Vit.*p.42J.

**βασκᾰρίζειν** (i.e. ϝασκ-)· (ἀ)σκαρίζειν (Cret.), Hsch.

**βασκάς** (or -ᾶς), άδος, ἡ, a kind of *duck*, Ar.*Av.*885; cf. βοσκάς, φασκάς.

⊛ **βασκαύλης**, ου, ὁ, perh. = Lat. *vasculum*, *POxy.*109.22 (iii/iv A.D.).

**βάσκειν**· λέγειν, κακολογεῖν, καὶ ἀνίστασθαι, Hsch.; cf. βάζω.

**βασκευταί**· φασκίδες, ἀγκάλαι, Id.:—also **βάσκιοι**· δεσμαὶ φρυγάνων, Id. **βάσκιλλος**· κίσσα, Id. ⊛ **βάσκον**· χῶρον, Id.

**βασκοσύνη**, ἡ, poet. for βασκανία, Poet.*de herb.*51,131, *PMag. Lond.*122.34, *PMag.Par.*1.1400.

⊛ **βάσκω** (akin to βαίνω), only imper., βάσκ' ἴθι *speed thee! away!* Il.2.8, etc.; βάσκετ', ἐπείγετε Ar.*Th.*783; but βάσκε *come!* A.*Pers.* 663,671 (both lyr.); βάσκ', ἔλαστε *Mim.Oxy.*413.60. (βάσκου· πορεύου is prob. f. l. in Hsch.).

**βασμιαῖος** λίθος *flat* block *used as a base*, Haussoullier *Milet* p.172, *Rev.Phil.*43.188.

**βασμίς, βασμός**, v. βαθμ-. **βᾶσσα**, ἡ, Dor., = βῆσσα:—hence **βᾱσσαίας**· τὰς ἐν βήσσῃ γεγονυίας, Hsch.

⊛ **βασσάρ-α** [ᾰρ], ἡ, = ἀλώπηξ, *fox*, Sch.Lyc.771 (Cyren. acc. to Hsch.). II. *dress of Thracian bacchanals*, made of *fox*-skins, *AB* 222, Hsch. 2. *Thracian bacchanal*, in pl., title of play by A., Sch. Ar.*Th.*142, cf. Callix.2. 3. *impudent woman, courtesan*, Lyc.771, 1393. **-εύς**, έως, ὁ, name of Bacchus, Corn.*ND*30, Hor.*Od.*1.18. 11. **-έω**, = βακχεύω, v. ἀναβασσαρέω. **-ικός**, ή, όν, = βακχικός, θίασος *AP*6.165 (Phalaec.): βασσαρικά, τά, = Διονυσιακά, Soterich.ap. Suid. **-ιον**, τό, Dim. of βασσάρα I, *little fox*, Hdt.4.192. **-ίς**, ίδος, ἡ, = βασσάρα I, Hsch. s.v. ψυῖαι. II. = βασσάρα II. 2, Anacr. 55, *AP*6.74 (Agath.). **-ος**, ὁ, = Βασσαρεύς, Orph.*H.*45.2. II. = βασσάρα I, *EM*191.1.

**βάσσος**, εος, τό, = βασσάρα, *EM*191.1.

**βάσσων**, ον, gen. ονος, Dor. Comp. of βαθύς, Epich.188. 2. *baggage-train*, Petr.Patr.p.434D.

**βαστά**· ὑποδήματα (Ital.), Hsch.

**βαστᾰγ-άριος**, ὁ, *transport-worker*, *Stud.Pal.*20.82.5 (iv A.D.). ⊛ **-ή**, ἡ, *transport*, τῶν ἀναγκαίων Lyd.*Mag.*1.13.

**βαστάγιον**, τό, *baldric*, Eust.828.35.

**βάσταγμα**, ατος, τό, *that which is borne, burden*, E.*Supp.*767, Plb. 36.6.7, Plu.2.59b, etc.; εἶναι βαρὺ β. βασιλείαν J.*AJ*19.9.2.

⊛ **βαστάζω**, Od.11.594, etc.: fut. -άσω A.*Pr.*1019, S.*Aj.*920; late -άξω Ps.-Callisth.1.45, etc.: aor. ἐβάστασα Od.21.405, Ar.*Th.* 437 (lyr.), etc.; late ἐβάσταξα *PFay.*122, Lxx *Si.*6.25, J.*AJ*3.8.7, Epigr.ap.Stob.1.49.52:—Pass., fut. βασταχθήσομαι Ps.-Callisth.1.42: aor. ἐβαστάχθην Nic.Dam.p.114D., D.L.4.59, Ath.15.693e: aor. 2 βασταγῆναι Artem.2.68: pf. βεβάσταγμαι (ἐμ-) Luc.*Ocyp.*14:—*lift up, raise*, λᾶαν βαστάζοντα.. ἀμφοτέρῃσι Od.11.594; ἐπεὶ μέγα τόξον ἐβάστασε 21.405; πεπτῶτα β. τινά S.*Aj.*827, etc.; *lift* a veil, Id.*El.* 1470:—Pass., of sluice-gates, *PRyl.*81.6 (ii A.D.). 2. metaph., *lift up, exalt, ennoble*, Pi.*O.*12.19; β. τινὰ χαρίτεσσιν Id.*I.*3.8. II. *bear, carry*, A.*Pr.*1019, etc.; χεροῖν β. τινά S.*El.*1129, cf. 1216; δόρυ Hermipp.46.2 (anap.), Theoc.16.78; ὅπλα Men.*Epit.*107. 2. *hold in one's hands*, S.*El.*905; χεροῖν Id.*Ph.*657, cf. 1127 (lyr.); of books, συνεχῶς β. Epicur.*Ep.*2p.35U.:—in Pass., *to be popular*, Arist.*Rh.* 1413$^b$12. 3. β. ἐν γνώμῃ *bear* in mind, *consider, weigh*, A.*Pr.*888; φρενί Ar.*Th.*437 (lyr.); β. προβούλευμα *deliberate on*.., Eup.73; βαστάσας αἱρήσομαι *on consideration*, Id.303. 4. *bear, endure*, οὐκέτι βαστάζω τὴν σεῖο διαζυγίην *AP*5.8 (Rufin.). 5. *produce, yield*, of land, *PGiss.*6iii8 (ii A.D.). III. *carry off, take away*, *Ev.Jo.*20.15; *steal*, Plb.32.15.4, J.*AJ*1.19.9, D.L.4.59, Luc.*Asin.*16, *PTeb.*330.7 (ii A.D.), perh. also in *Ev.Jo.*12.6, Ath.2.46f (Pass.). 2. in Pass., *to be sublimated*, Zos.Alch.p.198B. IV. in Trag., *touch*, χέρα ἄνακτος.. τῇδε β. χερί A.*Ag.*35; *embrace*, σῶμα S.*OC*1105.—Not in Att. Prose: Pass. first in Plb.

**βάστακες**· πλούσιοι καὶ εὐγενεῖς (Boeot.), *EM*191.12.

**βαστακ-τέον**, *one must bear*, Sch.E.*Or.*769. II. Adj. **βαστακτέος**, α, ον, *to be borne* or *carried*, Sch.Ar.*Ach.*258. **-τής**, οῦ, ὁ, *bearer, porter*, *Gloss.* **-τικός**, ή, όν, *fit for bearing*: Adv. -κῶς, gloss on ἀέρδην, Sch.A.*Ag.*240. **-τός**, ή, όν, *borne*, *AP*12.52 (Mel.).

**βάσταχας**· τοὺς τραχήλους (Boeot.), and **βασταχάζει**· τραχηλίζει, Hsch. (βαστρ- cod.):—also **βάστραχες**, Boeot., = οἱ τράχηλοι, and ⊛ **βαστραχαλίσαι**, = τραχηλιάσαι, *EM*191.11.

⊛ **βαστέρνιον**, τό, Lat. *basterna, closed litter*, *Cod.Just.*8.10.12, *Cat.Cod.Astr.*1.103:—hence **βαστερνάριοι**, οἱ, *litter-bearers*, *IG*3. 1433.7.

**βασυνίας** (sc. πλακοῦς), ὁ, a kind of *cake*, Semus 3.

**βαταίνει**· καλεῖ, Hsch. **βαταΐς**· πορφυρίσιν, ἢ ὁδοί, Id.

**βᾰτᾰλίζομαι**, *live like a* βάταλος, Theano *Ep.*1.3:—later in Act., β. τὰ ὀπίσθια *wriggle*, of a horse, *Hippiatr.*30.

**βάτᾰλος** [βᾰ], ὁ, = πρωκτός, Eup.82; cf. βάτας, βατέω. **II.** *stammerer* (cf. βατταρίζω), a nickname given to Demosthenes, Aeschin. 2.99, cf. D.18.180. (Codd. vary between βάταλος and βάτταλος: Βάτταλος is pr. n. in Hedyl.ap.Ath.4.167d.)

⊛ **βᾰτάνη** [τᾰ], ἡ, = πατάνη, Matro *Conv.*85:—Dim. ⊛**βᾰτάνιον**, τό, Antiph.95, Eub.38, Alex.24,172.18, *POxy.*739.9 (i A.D.), Bilabel Ὀψαρτ.p.18, Zos.Alch.p.222 B. (Sicel word for λοπάδια, Hsch.)

**βάτας**· ὁ καταφερής (Tarent.), Hsch. (Fort. βατᾶς, = βάταλος.)

**βᾰτε**, Dor. imper. aor. 2 of βαίνω.

⊛ **βᾰτεία**, ἡ (scanned -εῐα), *bush, thicket*, Pi.*O.*6.54.

**βάτελλα**, ἡ, = Lat. *patella*, *POxy.*741.18 (ii A.D.):—Dim. **βατέλλιον**, τό, *Ostr.*1218, *POxy.*1657.5 (iii A.D.).

⊛ **βᾰτεύω**, perh. *trample, damage*, τὰ βεβατ[ευ]μένα *BGU*45.21 (iii A.D.).

**βᾰτ-έω**, (βαίνω) *cover*, τὰς χιμάρας ἐβάτευν *AP*9.317:—Pass., of she-goats, οἷα βατεῦνται Theoc.1.87. **II.** at Delphi, = πατέω, Plu. 2.292e. **-ήρ**, ῆρος, ὁ, *that on which one treads, threshold*, ἐπ' αὐτὸν ἥκεις τὸν β. τῆς θύρας, prov. of those who 'come to the point', 'hit the nail on the head', Amips.26; *base* of a statue, *IG*11(2).147.18 (Delos, iv B.C.), Ἀρχ.Ἐφ.1913.7 (Nisyros, iii B.C.). **2.** *place from which one jumps*, *AB*224, Hsch., Eust.1404.56. **3.** = βακτηρία, Nic.*Th.*377. **4.** *bridge* of a lyre, Nicom.*Harm.*6; also, *part of flute*, ib.10. **5.** *one who walks*, Hsch. **-ηρία**, Ion. -ίη, ἡ, = βακτηρία, Herod.8.60. ⊛ **-ήριον** λέχος (cf. βάτης), = ὀχεία, Ps.-Phoc.188. **-ηρίς**, ίδος, ἡ, κλίμαξ β. a *mounting* ladder, *AP*7.365 (Zon. or Diod.). **-ῆρος**· ἐξ ἐχίνου σφάκελος, Hsch. ⊛ **-ης**, ου, ὁ, *one that treads* or *covers*, expld. by πίθηκος, ἀναβάτης, Id.

**βᾰτῐάκη** [ᾰκ], ἡ, a kind of *cup*, Diph.80; β. χρυσαῖ, χαλκαῖ, Alexandr.Epist.ap.Ath.11.784a, Arist.*Mir.*834ᵃ4, *IG*11(2).137 (Delos, iv B.C.):—Dim.⊛**βᾰτῐάκιον**, τό, dub. in Philem.87, cf. *IG*11.199*B*8 (Delos, iii B.C.).

**βᾰτῐδοσκόπος**, ον, *looking after skates, greedy for them*, Ar.*Pax* 811.

**βάτινον**, τό, *fruit of* βάτος, *blackberry*, Gal.6.589, 12.920.

⊛ **βάτιον**, τό, Dim. of βάτος (A), Salaminian name for *mulberry*, Parth.ap.Ath.2.51f.

**βᾰτίς**, ίδος, ἡ, a flat fish, perh. *skate* or *ray*, Epich.59.1, 90.1, Ar.*V.*510, Hermipp.45.2, Arist.*HA*565ᵃ22, al. **II.** *bird that frequents bushes*, possibly *stone-chat*, ib.592ᵇ17. **III.** *samphire, Crithmum maritimum*, Plin.21.86, 174, Colum.12.7.

**βάτνος**· αὐλός (Messen.), Hsch.

**βᾰτοδρόπος**, ον, *pulling up brambles*, *h.Merc.*190.

**βᾰτόεις**, εσσα, εν, (βάτος A) *thorny*, Nic.*Al.*267.

⊛ **βάτον** [ᾰ], τό, *blackberry*, D.S.1.34.

**βάτος** (A) [ᾰ], ἡ, *bramble, Rubus ulmifolius*, Od.24.230, Aen.Tact.28.6, Theoc.1.132; ὁ, Hp.*Mul.*2.112, Ar.*Fr.*754 (Att. acc. to Moeris), Thphr.*HP*1.5.3, Lxx *Ex.*3.2: whence ἐπὶ τοῦ (v.l. τῆς) βάτου in *Ev.Marc.*12.26: fem., Dsc.4.37, *Ev.Luc.*20.37. **II.** β. Ἰδαία *raspberry, Rubus Idaeus*, Dsc.4.38; = β. ὀρθοφυής Thphr.*HP*3.18.4. **III.** β. Μοσυλῖτις, a kind of *cassia*, Dsc.1.13. **IV.** = ἑλένιον, *elecampane*, Ps.-Dsc.1.28.

**βάτος** (B), ὁ, a *fish*, a kind of *skate*, Epich.59.2, 90.2, Arist.*HA* 489ᵇ6, al.

⊛ **βάτος** (C), ὁ, the Hebrew liquid measure *bath*, = Egypt. ἀρτάβη or Att. μετρητής, Lxx 2*Es.*7.22, *Ev.Luc.*16.6, J.*AJ*8.2.9:—also **βάδος**, v.l. in Lxx l.c., Hsch.

⊛ **βᾰτός**, ή, όν, (βαίνω) *passable, accessible*, τοῖς ὑποζυγίοις X.*An.* 4.6.17, cf. Men.924, Arr.*An.*4.21.3, Nonn.*D.*1.54, al.; = βέβηλος, opp. ἄβατος, Porph.*Abst.*4.11: metaph., *permissible*, Just.*Nov.*30.8 *Intr.* **II.** Act., *speeding*, πούς Nonn.*D.*2.96, 18.55.

⊛ **βᾰτρᾰχ-ειος** [ρᾰ], ον, (βάτραχος) *of* or *belonging to a frog*: βατράχεια (sc. χρώματα) *frog-colour, pale-green*, Ar.*Eq.*523:—also **βατράχεος**, α, ον, Nic.*Fr.*85.5. **-ίδιον**, τό, Dim. of βάτραχος, Plu.*Nob.* 21. **-ίζω**, *to be* or *move like a frog*, Hippiatr.26. **-ιον**, τό, *Ranunculus*, Hp.*Nat.Mul.*32, Dsc.2.175 (which incl. *R. asiaticus, garden r.*, β. χρυσάνθεμον *Gp.*2.6.30, and *R. sardous, hairy crowfoot*, cf. Dsc.*Alex.*14). **II.** = βάτραχος 1, Paus.9.21.1. **III.** = βάτραχος III, Ptol.*Phas.*p.27 H., al. **IV.** *malachite*, Syn.Alch. p.64 B. **-ιοῦν**, τό, *a court of law* at Athens, so called from its colour (cf. Φοινικιοῦν), Paus.1.28.8:—Adj. **βατρᾰχε(ι)οῦς** *IG*2. 758 *B* ii 23. **-ίς**, ίδος, ἡ, *frog-green garment*, Ar.*Eq.*1406, *IG*2. 754.16, D.C.59.14. **2.** = βατράχιον 1, Alex.Trall.3.6: but, **II.** **βᾰτρᾰχίς**, ῖδος, Dim. of βάτραχος, Nic.*Th.*416. **-ίσκοι**, οἱ, *part of the* κιθάρα, Hsch. ⊛ **-ίτης** λίθος, ὁ, *a frog-green* stone, Plin.37. 149.

**βᾰτρᾰχομῡομᾰχία**, ἡ, *battle of the frogs and mice*, title of mock-epic poem ascribed to Homer, cf. Plu.2.873f.

**βάτρᾰχος** [βᾰ], ὁ, *frog*, Batr.6, 18, 59, al., Hdt.4.131, etc.: prov., ὕδωρ πίνειν βάτραχος *a very frog* to drink, Aristopho 10.3; βατράχοις οἰνοχοεῖν, of those who give what is not wanted, Pherecr.70.5; μέλει μοι τῶν τοιούτων ἧττον τῶν ἐν τοῖς τέλμασι β. Jul.*Mis.*358a; χλωρὸς β., of the tree-*frog*, Thphr.*Sign.*15. **II.** = ἁλιεύς, a kind of *fish, fishing-frog* or *sea-angler, Lophius piscatorius*, Arist.*GA*749ᵃ23, Ael.*NA*13.5. **III.** *frog of a horse's hoof*, *Gp.*16.1.9, *Hippiatr.*8: hence Astron., of the star β Centauri, Ptol.*Alm.*8.1. **IV.** ἐσχάρας εἶδος, Hsch. **V.** *swelling under the tongue*, Aët.8.39.—Dial. forms are cited by Gramm., **1.** Ion. βάθρακος, cited from Hdt. (prob. 4.131) by Sch.Il.4.243, Eust.1570.11, and found in *PLond.*1.124.31 (iv/v A.D.); Ion. also βότραχος Hp.ap.Gal.19, βρόταχος Xenoph.40 (as pr. n., *GDI*5577, 5592). **2.** βράταχος Hsch. (as pr. n., *GDI*5727 *d* 29). **3.** Cypr. βρούχετος Hsch. **4.** Phoc. βριαγχόνη Id. **5.** Pontic βάβακος Id. Cf. βύρθακος, βρύτιχος.

**βάτταλος**, ὁ, v. βάταλος.

**βαττᾰρ-ίζω**, onomatop. word, *stammer*, Hippon.108, Pl.*Tht.*175d (prob. l.), Cic.*Att.*6.5.1, Luc.*JTr.*27. **-ισμός**, ὁ, *stuttering*, Phld.*Rh.*2.136 S., Porph.*Hist.Phil.Fr.*11; also, *twittering* of swallows, Eust.1914.32. **-ιστής**, οῦ, ὁ, *stutterer*, Hsch.

**βάττικες**· γυναῖκες (Boeot.), Hsch.

⊛ **βαττο-λογέω**, = βατταρίζω, *speak stammeringly, say the same thing over and over again*, *Ev.Matt.*6.7, Simp.*in Epict.*p.91 D. **-λογία**· ἀργολογία, ἀκαιρολογία, Hsch. (βατο- cod.).

**βάττος**, ὁ, *stammerer, lisper*, Hsch.

**βατύλη**, ἡ, *she-dwarf*, dub. name of a play by Theopompus, Sch. Ar.*Pl.*1012.

**βᾰτώδης**, ες, *thorny*, Str.4.3.5. **2.** *like a blackberry*, τὸ μόρον τὸ β. Phan.Hist.33. **II.** *overgrown with thorns*, Plb.2.28.8.

**βαύ, βαύ**, *bow, wow*, imit. of a dog's bark, *Com.Adesp.*1304.

**βαῦ**, a kind of *flower*, Hsch.

**βαυβᾰλίζω**, = βαυκαλάω, Alex.229 (βαβ- cod. Hsch.).

**βαυβάω**, *sleep*, E.*Fr.*694, *Trag.Adesp.*165, Canthar.3. **II.** Act., *lull to sleep*, Hsch.

**βαύβυκες**· πελεκᾶνες, Hsch.

⊛ **βαυβώ**, ἡ, = κοιλία, Emp.153.

**βαυβών**, ῶνος, ὁ, = ὄλισβος, Herod.6.19.

**βαΰζω** (βαύζω disyll. Lyc.1453 is f.l. for βάζω), Dor. **βαΰσδω**, onomatop. word, *cry* βαὺ βαύ, *bark*, Theoc.6.10; of angry persons, *snarl, yelp*, παῦσαι βαΰζων Ar.*Th.*173, cf. 895; τάδε σῖγά τις βαΰζει thus they *snarl* in secret, A.*Ag.*449 (lyr.); οἷ' ἄττα β. Cratin.6. **II.** trans., *shriek aloud for*, τινά A.*Pers.*13; of dogs, *bark at*, τινά Heraclit.97 codd.

**βαΰθει**· μασᾶται, Hsch.

**βαυκᾰλ-άω**, *lull to sleep*, Crates *Ep.*33, Luc.*Lex.*11 (wrongly said to be Att. by Moer.102): metaph., *nurse, look after*, Aret.*SD*2. 11. **-η**, ἡ, *cradle*, Sor.1.106, 109. **-ημα**, ατος, τό, *lullaby*, Socr.*Ep.*27. **-ησις**, εως, ἡ, *lulling* a child to sleep, Ruf.ap.Orib.*inc.*20. 26, Crat.*Ep.*33. **-ίζω**, = βαυκαλάω, *AB*85, Hsch. ⊛ **-ιον**, τό, *narrow-necked vessel, that gurgles when water is poured in* or *out*, *POxy.*936.6 (iii A.D.), Olymp.*in Mete.*93.6: pl., Alex.Aphr.*Pr.*1.94 (καυκ- codd.). **-ις**, ιδος, ἡ, *vessel for cooling wine* or *water in*, elsewh. ψυκτήρ, *AP*11.244; β. ἡ τετράκυκλος Sopat.24.—Alexandr. word acc. to Ath.11.784b; on the accent cf. Hdn.Gr.1.90.

**βαύκαλον**· μαλακιζόμενον, τρυφερόν, καὶ ὡραϊστόν, *EM*192.20.

**βαυκανήσεται**· βοήσεται, Hsch. (For βυκ-.)

**βαυκίδες**, αἱ, a kind of *woman's shoes*, Ar.*Fr.*342, Alex.98.7, Herod. 7.58.

**βαυκ-ίζω**, (βαυκός) *to play the prude*, *AB*225:—Med., Alex.222.9, Hsch. **-ισμα**, ατος, τό, *coyness, affectation*, *AB*225 (pl.), Hsch. (pl.). **-ισμός**, ὁ, kind of *dance*, Poll.4.100, Hsch.

**βαυκοπᾰνοῦργος**, ὁ, *humbug*, Arist.*EN*1127ᵇ27.

⊛ **βαυκός**, ή, όν, *prudish, affected*, Arar.9.

⊛ **βαῦνος** or **βαυνός**, ὁ, *furnace, forge*, Eratosth.24, Max.Tyr.22.3, Asp.*in EN*104.23; also, = χυτρόπους, Poll.10.100:—in Hsch. also **βαύνη**, ἡ.

**βαυρία**, ἡ, = οἰκία, Messapian word, *EM*389.25.

**βαυριόθεν** (cf. foreg.), = οἴκοθεν, Cleon Sic.2.

**βαΰστικός**, ή, όν, *inclined to bark*, Sch.Opp.*H.*1.721.

**βαφά**· ζωμός (Lacon.), Hsch.

**βαφ-εῖον**, τό, *dyer's house* or *workshop*, Str.16.2.23, *PLond.*2.371.3 (i A.D.). **-εύς**, έως, ὁ, (βάπτω) *a dyer*, Pl.*R.*429d, Diph.72, Plu.*Per.*12, etc.; the βαφεῖς formed a guild at Thyatira, *IGRom.*4.1265; also in the νομὸς Ἀρσινοΐτης, *PTeb.*287.3 (ii A.D.). **II.** *gilder*, Zos.Alch.p.154 B. ⊛ **-ή**, ἡ, *dipping* of red-hot iron in water, S.*Aj.* 651: hence, *temper* or *edge* of a blade or tool *produced thereby*, τὴν β. ἀφιᾶσιν ὥσπερ ὁ σίδηρος εἰρήνην ἄγοντες Arist.*Pol.*1334ᵃ8, cf. Plu.*Alex.* 32, *Pyrrh.*24; τὰ σιδήρια τὴν β. ἀνίησι lose *their edge*, Thphr.*HP*5.3.3, cf. *CP*1.22.6; χαλκοῦ βαφαί prob. poet. for σιδήρου β. in A.*Ag.*612 (v. Sch. ad loc., but cf. βάψις): metaph., *temper*, τῆς ἀνδρείας οἷον β. τις ὁ θυμός ἐστι καὶ στόμωμα Plu.2.988d; of wine, ib.650b. **II.** *dye*, Thphr.*HP*4.6.5; πορφυρᾶ β. A.*Pers.*317 (metaph. of blood), cf. Pl.*R.* 430a; κρόκου βαφάς the saffron-*dyed robe*, A.*Ag.*239 (lyr.); βαφαὶ ὕδρας *the arrows dipped* in the hydra's blood, E.*HF*1188 (lyr.); χειλέων β. Philostr.*Ep.*22: metaph., β. τυραννίδος Plu.2.779c. **III.** *enamelling*, χαλκοῦ . . βαφῇ κυάνου στίλβοντος ib.395b. **2.** *gilding, silvering*, αἱ δύο β. Zos Alch.p.168 B., cf. p.208 B. **IV.** *infection*, Aret.*CD*2.13. **-ικός**, ή, όν, *fit for dyeing*, κόκκος Dsc.*Eup.*1.37; βοτάνη Luc.*Alex.*12: **-κή** (sc. τέχνη), ἡ, *art of dyeing*, Ph.1.353, Plu.2.228b, *PRyl.*98.2 (ii A.D.). **II.** βίβλοι βαφικαί, in Alchemy, books *on gilding and silvering*, Ps.-Democr.ap.Syn.Alch.p.57 B.; καῦσις β. Zos.Alch.p.208 B. **III.** βαφικόν, τό, form of ἰνδικόν, Dsc.5.92. **-ιον**· ὀξύβαφον (Tarent.), Hsch. **-ισ(σ)α**, ἡ, *female dyer*(?), *Sammelb.*1957.

**βάχθει**· τέλμα ὕδατος, ἢ βάθος, Hsch.

⊛ **βάψιμος**, ον, *to be dyed*, Lysis ap.Iamb.*VP*17.76.

**βάψις**, εως, ἡ, *dipping, tempering*, χαλκοῦ καὶ σιδήρου Antipho Soph. 40. **II.** *a dye*, Perict.ap.Stob.4.28.19.

**βάω**, = βαίνω, only in compds.

**βδᾰλεύς**, έως, ὁ, *milk-pail*, Sch.Luc.*Hes.*4.

**βδάλλω**, aor. part. βδάλας Alciphr.3.16: aor. opt. Med., βδήλαιο

Nic.*Al.*262:—*milk* cows, πολὺ βδάλλων *milking* many kine, rich in kine, Pl.*Tht.*174d; β. τινά ibid.; ὁ βδάλλων *the milker*, Arist.*HA* 522$^{b}$17; β. γάλα Procop.*Aed.*3.6:—Med., *yield*, of the cow, βοΐδια.. ὧν ἕκαστον βδάλλεται γάλα πολύ Arist.*HA*522$^{b}$15; βόες βδάλλονται ἑκάστη ἀμφορέα ib.16: also in sense of Act., νέον γλάγος Nic.l.c. II. *suck*, Arist.*GA*746$^{a}$20, cf. Gal.7.130:—Pass., Arist.*HA*522$^{a}$5,20.

**βδαλοί**· ῥαφίδες θαλάσσιαι, καὶ φλέβες κρισσώδεις, Hsch.

**βδάλσις**, εως, ἡ, *suction*, Gal.7.131, Aët.9.19.

**βδαροί**· δρύες, δένδρα, Hsch.

**βδέλλ-ᾰ**, ἡ, (βδάλλω) *leech*, Hdt.2.68, Arist.*IA*709$^{a}$29, Theoc.2.56, Nic.*Al.*500, Lxx*Pr.*24.50(30.15): metaph., β. σπιλάδων, of a fisherman, *AP*6.193 (Flacc.). 2. *lamprey*, Str.17.3.4. II. = βδέλλιον, J.*AJ*3.1.6, *Peripl.M.Rubr.*37, al., *Edict.Diocl.*32.54, Democr.ap. Gal.14.129, *PMag.Berol.*1.286, *PMag.Leid.V.*12.24. **-άζεται**· ἀμέλγεται, Erot. (perh. v.l. for ἐκθηλάζεται Hp.*Mul.*1.73). **-ίζω**, *bleed with leeches*, in Pass., Antyll.ap.Orib.7.21.3, Gal.11.317.

**βδέλλιον**, τό, the aromatic gum obtained from *Balsamodendrum africanum* and *B. Mukul*, Dsc.1.67, Democr.ap.Gal.14.118, Plin. *HN*12.35, Aq., Sm., Thd.*Ge.*2.12. (Semitic word.)

**βδελλιστέον**, *one must apply leeches*, Herod.Med.in *Rh.Mus.*58.113.

**βδελλολάρυγξ** [ᾰ], υγγος, ὁ, *leech-throat*, name for *a greedy parasite*, Cratin.44.

**βδέλλων**· τρέμων ἢ βδέων, Hsch.; cf. **βδέλεσθαι**· κοιλιολυτεῖν, Id.

**βδέλυγ-μα**, ατος, τό, *abomination*, τοῖς Αἰγ. πᾶς ποιμὴν β. Lxx*Ge.*43.32, etc.; β. τῶν ἐρημώσεων, ἐρημώσεως, of an idol, ib.*Da.*9.27, 1*Ma.*1.54, cf. *Ev.Matt.*24.15. **-μία**, ἡ, *nausea, sickness*, Cratin.251, X.*Mem.*3.11.13. 2. *filth, nastiness*, Hp.*Fist.*1. **-μός**, ὁ, *abomination*, Lxx1*Ki.*25.31, *Na.*3.6.

**βδελυκ-τός**, ή, όν, *disgusting, abominable*, Lxx*Pr.*17.15, *Ep.Tit.*1.16, Ph.2.261. **-τροπος**, ον, = foreg., A.*Eu.*52.

**βδελῠρ-εύομαι**, *behave in a beastly manner*, D.17.11. **-ία**, ἡ, *beastly, coarse*, or *objectionable behaviour*, And.1.122, Is.8.42 (pl.), D.22.52, Aeschin.1.105, Thphr.*Char.*11, Plu.*Caes.*9. 2. *disgust, nausea*, Hp.*Int.*26, Jul.*Or.*6.190d. **-ός**, ά, όν, *disgusting, loathsome, blackguardly*, Ar.*Ra.*465, Pl.*R.*338d, Thphr.*Char.*11; θεοῖς ἐχθρὸς καὶ β. D.21.197; θρασὺς καὶ β. Plu.2.10c: Comp. -ωτέρα, πολιτεία Jul.*Or.*7.210c: Sup. -ώτατος D.19.206,208. Adv. -ρῶς Ph.1.209. II. of things, *disgusting*, Gal.12.291; τὸ β. Alex.Trall.4.1. III. βδελυρά, = χαμελαία, Ps.-Dsc.4.171.

⊛ **βδελύσσομαι**, Att. **-ττομαι**, fut. -ύξομαι Hp.*Mul.*1.39,41 (Act. βδελύξειν wrongly cited by Erot.): aor. ἐβδελύχθην Ar.*V.*792, Plu.*Alex.*57, etc.; later ἐβδελυξάμην Lxx*Ge.*26.29, al., J.*BJ*6.2.10, Jul.*Or.*7.210d:—*feel a loathing for food*, Hp. ll.cc.; *to be sick*, Ar.*V.*792. 2. c. acc., *feel a loathing at*, Id.*Ach.*586, Lxx l.c., al., Plu.*Alex.*57; β. [τραγῳδίας] Jul.l.c.; ὠμοφαγίαν ib.6.193c: β. ἀπό τινων Lxx*Ex.*1.12. II. later causal, in Act., *cause to stink, make loathsome* or *abominable*, fut. -ύξω Lxx*Le.*20.25: aor. ἐβδέλυξα ib.*Ex.*5.21:—Med. and Pass., *to be loathsome*, fut. -υχθήσομαι ib.*Si.*20.8: aor. -ύχθην ib.*Ps.*13(14).1: pf. ἐβδέλυγμαι ib.*Pr.*8.7; οἱ ἐβδελυγμένοι *the abominable* (in ref. to the use of βδέλυγμα as *an idol*), *Apoc.*21.8:—this pf. in causal sense, Lxx*Pr.*28.9. (Cf. βδέω.)

**βδελυχρός**, ά, όν, Dor. for βδελυρός, Epich.63.

**βδέννυμαι**· ἐκκενοῦμαι τὴν κοιλίαν, Suid.; **βδένεσθαι** (sic), Hsch.

**βδέσμα**, ατος, τό, (βδέω) *stench*, Gloss.

**Βδεῦ**, (βδέω) comic parody on Ζεῦ, ὦ Βδεῦ δέσποτα *Com.Adesp.*28.

**βδέω**, poet. aor. βδέσα *AP*11.242 (Nicarch.); later ἔβδευσα Hierocl. *Facet.*233, al.:—*break wind*, Ar.*Pl.*693, *Pax*151, etc.: c. acc. cogn., οὐ λιβανωτὸν βδέω Id.*Pl.*703:—Med. or Pass., Id.*Eq.*900. 2. of the cockroach, σίλφης κατοικιδίου τῆς βδεούσης τὸ στέαρ Archig.ap. Aët.8.35, cf. Gal.12.861. (Onomatopoeic word: root *bzd*, cf. Czech *bzditi*, Slov. *pezděti*, Lat. *pēdo*.)

**βδόλος**, ὁ, *stench, stink*, *Com.Adesp.*781.

**βδύλλω**, *to be in deadly fear of*, τινάς Ar.*Lys.*354, cf. *Eq.*224, Luc.*Lex.*10.

⊛ **βέβαιος**, ον (so always in Th., Pl.), also α, ον (v. infr.): (βαίνω):—*firm, steady*, κρύσταλλος Th.3.23; ὄχημα Pl.*Phd.*85d (Comp.); γῆ β. *terra firma*, Arr.*An.*2.21.5; *steadfast, durable*, ὁμιλία.. πιστὴ καὶ βέβαιος S.*Ph.*71; ἀρετῆς βέβαιαι.. αἱ κτήσεις μόνης Id.*Fr.*194; ψῆφος βεβαία E.*El.*1263; τὴν χάριν βέβαιον ἔχειν Th.1.32; οὐδέπω βέβαιος ἦν ἡ σωτηρία And.1.53; εἰρήνην βεβαίαν ἀγαγεῖν Isoc.4.173; φιλία βέβαιος Pl.*Smp.*182c; βεβαίου τε καὶ καθαρᾶς ἡδονῆς γεύεσθαι Id.*R.*586a; δόξαι καὶ πίστεις βέβαιοι καὶ ἀληθεῖς Id.*Ti.*37b, etc. b. *sure, certain*, τέκμαρ A.*Pr.*456; ἄκεα Id.*Eu.*506 (lyr.); τοξεύματα S.*Ant.*1086; πύλας β. παρέχειν make *safe, secure*, Th.4.67; βεβαιότερος κίνδυνος a *surer* game, Id.3.39: Sup. -ότατος Id.1.124; βέβαιόν ἐστί τινι ὅτι.. D.H.3.35; τὰ παρ' ἀνθρώπων αὐτῷ β. ἦν ibid.; but β. παρέχειν τὰν ὠνάν *confirm, guarantee*, *GDI*1867, al. (Delph.); μένειν κυρίαν καὶ β.. συγχώρησιν *BGU*1058.47 (i B.C.). 2. of persons, etc., *steadfast, constant*, φίλος A.*Pr.*299 (Comp.), cf. Th.5.43, etc.: c. inf., βεβαιότεροι μηδὲν νεωτεριεῖν *more certain* to make no change, Th.3.11. 3. τὸ β. *certainty*, Hdt.7.50, cf. Pl.*Phlb.*59c, etc.; but τὸ β. τῆς διανοίας *firmness, resolution*, Th.2.89. b. *security, guarantee*, τὸ δημόσιον β. *IG*1$^{2}$.189. II. Adv. -ως A.*Ag.*15; β. κλητόν Th.2.17; β. οἰκεῖσθαι Id.1.2; ἔχειν, γνῶναι, δημοκρατεῖσθαι, D.8.41,39, 10.4: Comp. -ότερον, οἰκεῖν Th.1.8; -οτέρως Isoc.8.60, Porph.*Abst.*1.11: Sup. -ότατα Th.6.91.

**βεβαιότης**, ητος, ἡ, *steadfastness, stability*, τῆς οὐσίας Pl.*Cra.*386a; μετὰ ἡσυχίας καὶ βεβαιότητος ζῆν Id.*R.*503c, cf. *Lg.*735a, 790b, Arist. *EN*1100$^{b}$12. 2. *assurance, certainty*, Pl.*Phdr.*277d; *security, safety*, βεβαιότητος ἕνεκα Th.4.66; β. καὶ ἀσφάλεια Plu.*Fab.*19.

**βεβαιότροπος**, ον, *firm, resolute*, Dam.*Isid.*16.

⊛ **βεβαι-όω**, *confirm, establish, make good*, τοῖς δικασταῖς τὴν δόξαν Pl.*Cri.*53b; δωρεὰν Is.1.18; εἴτε δεξιὰς δοῖεν ἐβεβαίουν X.*Cyr.*8.8.2, etc.; ἔργῳ βεβαιούμενα, opp. ἀκοῇ λεγόμενα, Th.1.23; β. λόγον *make good* one's word, Lys.20.32; β. τὴν πρᾶξιν X.*An.*7.6.17; *treat as valid*, τὰς αὐτῶν αἰσθήσεις Metrod.1, cf. Epicur.*Sent.*24; β. τινί τι *secure* one *the possession of* a thing, οὐδ' ἡμῖν αὐτοῖς βεβαιοῦμεν [τὴν ἐλευθερίαν] Th.1.122; τοῖς θεοῖς βεβαιοῦντες τοὺς νόμους οὓς ἐψηφίσασθε Lys.6.29, cf. D.21.30; τὴν ἀρχήν τινι Plu.*Sull.*22; τὸν λόγον *Ev.Marc.*16.20:—Med., *establish for oneself, secure*, σφᾶς αὐτοὺς Th.1.33; τὴν ἀρχήν, τὴν φιλίαν τινός, Id.6.10,78; β. τινάς *confirm* them *in one's interest*, ib.34; βασιλείαν Paus.3.11.4; τὰ περὶ τῆς βοηθείας Plb.2.51.5. 2. Med., *secure one's ground* in argument, Pl.*Tht.*169e; *confirm* oneself in an opinion, Id.*Grg.*489a, *Prt.*348d. 3. *guarantee the validity of* a purchase, *warrant* the purchaser's title, β. τινὶ τὸ βαλανεῖον Is.5.23, cf. Din.1.42, D.37.12, *SIG*46.4 (Halic., v B.C.); τὴν μίσθωσιν *BGU*1119.47 (i B.C.): generally, β. τοὺς κανόνας Arr.*Epict.*2.11.24. II. intr., *determine, show itself positively*, τοῖσιν ἐνδοιαστῶς ἔχουσι.. ἐβεβαίωσε [ἡ νοῦσος] Hp.*Epid.*1.2. **-ωμα**, ατος, τό, *confirmation, proof*, J.*AJ*2.12.4, 17.1.1. **-ωσις**, εως, ἡ, *confirmation*, β. γνώμης Th.1.140, cf. 4.87, Demetr. Lac.*Herc.*1012.38F., Ph.1.486, al., D.H.*Rh.*10.18, Hermog.*Prog.*5; εἰς β. *in perpetuity*, ἡ γῆ οὐ πραθήσεται εἰς β. Lxx*Le.*25.23. 2. legal *warranty*, Aeschin.3.249 (pl.), *PTeb.*311.27 (ii A.D.), etc.; βεβαιώσεως δίκη Poll.8.34. **-ωτέον**, *one must confirm*, ὅρκους Ph.2.272; ὑπόσχεσιν Id.1.23. ⊛ **-ωτήρ**, ῆρος, ὁ, = sq. 2, *GDI*1684 (Delph.), al. ⊛ **-ωτής**, οῦ, ὁ, *one who gives assurance of* a thing, *authority*, ἀμφισβητουμένων Plb.4.40.3 (pl.); ἱστορίας D.H.1.28, cf. 3.67, al.; *confirmatory*, λόγοι Phld.*Sign.*29. 2. legal *surety*, τοῦ μόνιμον τὴν ὁμόνοιαν γενέσθαι Plb.2.40.2; β. τῆς πίστεως παρέχεσθαι Plu.*Flam.*4; *warrantor* in sales, *SIG*$^{2}$832 (Amphipolis), etc. **-ωτικός**, ή, όν, *confirmatory*, Epict.*Ench.*52, S.E.*P.*1.169, etc. II. **-κόν**, τό, *tax paid to the Government as warrantor of sales*, *BGU*156.9 (iii A.D.). **-ώτρια**, ἡ, fem. of βεβαιωτής, ib.994iii7 (ii B.C.), *PStrassb.*88.29 (ii B.C.), etc.

**βεβάμεν**, v. βαίνω. **βεβαρηώς**, v. βαρέω. **βέβᾰσαν**, v. βαίνω.

**βεβᾰσᾰνισμένως**, Adv. *with severe scrutiny*, Poll.6.150.

**βέβασις**· τὸ εὐζόμενον, Hsch.

⊛ **βέβηλ-ος**, ον, Dor. **βέβᾱλος** *IG*3.3845, Ps.-Lysis ap.Iamb.*VP*17.75: (βαίνω, βηλός):—*allowable to be trodden*, prob. of ground (opp. ἱερός, D.H.7.8); καὶ πῶς β. ἄλσος ἂν ῥύοιτό με; A.*Supp.*509; ἢ πρὸς βεβήλοις ἢ πρὸς ἄλσεσιν θεῶν either on *profane ground* or.., S.*OC*10; ἔς τε τἄβατα καὶ πρὸς βέβηλα Id.*Fr.*88: hence generally, *permitted*, καὶ βέβηλα καὶ κεκρυμμένα λόγια *public, current*, E.*Heracl.*404; ἐν βεβήλῳ Th.4.97; βέβηλα *permitted meats*, Ath.2.65f. II. of persons, *unhallowed*, = ἀμύητος, S.*Fr.*154, Orph.*Fr.*245; *impure*, E.*Fr.*648; β. τε καὶ ἄγροικος Pl.*Smp.*218b; β. καὶ ἀνόσια ἐνθυμήματα Ph.2.165: c. gen., *uninitiated*, τελετῆς *AP*9.298 (Antiphil.); ἀποδεικτικῆς μεθόδου Gal.*UP*12.6. Adv. -λως Ph.1.523. **-όω**, *profane*, τὸ σάββατον Lxx*Ex.*31.14, *Ev.Matt.*12.5; τὰ ἀνθρώπινα Jul.*Or.*7.228d. 2. *pollute, defile*, τινά Lxx*Le.*21.9, Hld.2.25. **-ωσις**, εως, ἡ, *profanation*, Lxx*Le.*21.4, Ph.1.523.

**βεβῐασμένως**, Adv. *of necessity*, D.S.3.25; *with effort*, Marcellin.*Puls.*311.

**βέβλειν** and **βέβλεσθαι**, = μέλλειν, Hsch.

**βεβολήατο, βεβολημένος**, v. βάλλω.

**βεβουλευμένως**, Adv. *advisedly, designedly*, D.21.41.

**βεβράδα**· ἀθερίνην, Hsch. **βεβράξαντα**· συντόνως κεκραγότα, Id. **βέβρηκες**· τὸ ἔνδον τῶν σιαγόνων μέρος, Id. **βέβροξ**· ἀγαθός, χρηστός, καλός, Id.

**βεβρός**, ά, όν, *stupid*, δεσπότεω βεβροῦ Hippon.64; also **βεμβρός**, Hsch.

⊛ **βέβρῡχε**, v. βρύχω. **βεβρώθοις**, v. βιβρώσκω.

**βεβυκῶσθαι** (βεβηκ- codd.)· πεπρῆσθαι (Thess.), Hsch.; cf. βύκτης. **βεβυλλῶσθαι**· βεβύσθαι, Id.

**βεβώς, βεβῶσα**, v. βαίνω.

⊛ **βέδυ**, τό, Phryg., = ἀήρ, Philyll.20; also, = ὕδωρ, Orph.*Fr.*219.

**βέη**, v. βέομαι.

**βέθρον**, τό, contr. from βέρεθρον, Euph.148, Crates ap.*EM*194.22.

**βειέλοπες**· ἱμάντες, used as crowns for victors at Sparta, Hsch. **βεικάδες**, *the skins of animals which die naturally* (Lacon.), Id. **βεικάσθων**· κατ' ὀλίγον προβάς, Id. (leg. βιβάσθων). **βείκατι** (β = ϝ), = εἴκοσι (Lacon.), Id. **βείκηλα**· νωχελῆ, ἀχρεία (Lacon.), Id. **βειλαρμόστας, βειλάρχας**, = Ϝιλ- (Tarent.), Id. **βείλομαι**, Boeot., = βούλομαι (q.v.). **βείομαι, βείω**, v. sub βέομαι. **βείρακες**· ἱέρακες, Hsch. **βειρακή**· ἡ ἁρπακτική, Id. **βείριξ**· ἔλαφος, Id. **βειρόν**· δασύ, Id.

**βεκκεσέληνος**, ον, (βέκος, cf. προσέληνος, and v. Hdt.2.2) = ἀρχαῖος, *superannuated, doting*, coined by Ar.*Nu.*398, cf. Plu.2.881a.

⊛ **βέκος** or **βεκός**, τό, gen. βέκους Aristid.2.3J.:—*bread*, Phryg. acc. to Hdt.2.2, cf. *Jahresh.*8*Beibl.*95; but Κυπρίων β. Hippon.82.

**βεκῶς**· μακρόθεν, Hsch. (ϝεκάς).

**βέλα**· ἥλιος καὶ αὐγή (Lacon.), Hsch.:—also **βελλάσεται**· ἡλιωθήσεται, Id. **βελάς**· εἴρων καὶ καταγελαστής, Id.

**βελεηφόρος**, ον, *bearing darts*, *AP*14.111.

**βέλεκκοι**, οἱ, = ὄσπρια, Ar.*Fr*.755.

⊛ **βέλεμνον**, τό, poet. for βέλος, *dart*, *javelin*, Il. only in pl., πικρὰ β. 22.206: later in sg., ἀμφιτόμῳ β. A.*Ag*.1496 (lyr.), cf. 1520, Theoc. 11.16; poet., of *hail-stones*, Orph.*L*.597.

**βελενκώθιον**, τό, *basket* (?), *PFay*.118.20 (ii A.D.).

**βελεσσιχᾰρής**, ές, *joying in darts*, of Apollo, *AP*9.525.3.

**βελικός**, ή, όν, *of* or *belonging to projectiles*: βελικά, τά, work by Agesistratus, Ath.Mech.8.6.

**βελίτης** [ῑ] κάλαμος reed used *for making darts*, *Gp*.2.6.23.

**βέλλαι**· ῥαφίδες θαλάσσιαι, Hsch. **βέλλιον**· ἀτυχές (Cret.), Id. **βέλλιρ**· τρυφάλεια (Lacon.), Id. **βέλλομαι**, v. βούλομαι. ⊛**βελλούνης**· τριόρχης, Id.

⊛ **βελοθήκη**, ἡ, *quiver*, Lib.*Decl*.30.9.

**βελόνη**, ἡ, (βέλος) *needle*, Batr.130, Eup.259, Arist.*Cael*.313$^a$19; βελόνας διείρειν Aeschin.3.166. **II.** *pipe-fish*, *Syngnathus*, Arist. *HA*567$^b$23; *garfish*, *Belone acus*, ib.506$^b$10, Dorio ap.Ath.7.319d; but prob. f.l. for βάλανος, Archipp.24.

**βελονίς**, ίδος, ἡ, Dim. of foreg., *little needle*, Hermipp.49. **II.** a little *fish*, Sch.Opp.*H*.3.577.

**βελονο-ειδής**, ές, *needle-shaped*, σχήματα Thphr.*Sens*.77; β. ἔκφυσις *styloid* process of the temporal bone, Gal.*UP*7.19, al. **-θήκη**, ἡ, *needle-case*, Sch.Ar.*Pl*.175. **-ποικίλτης**, ου, ὁ, *embroiderer*, Hsch. **-πώλης**, ου, ὁ, *needle-seller*, Critias 70 D., Ar.*Pl*.175:—fem. **-πωλις**, ιδος, Poll.7.197.

**βελο-ποιΐα**, ἡ, *manufacture of missiles*, Hero *Bel*.72.6, Poll.7.156:—also **-ποιϊκή** (sc. τέχνη), ἡ, Hero *Bel*.74.11. **-ποιός**, όν, *making missiles*, Ph.*Bel*.58.50, Poll.7.156.

**βέλος**, εος, τό, *missile*, esp. *arrow*, *dart*, freq. in Hom.; of the piece of rock *hurled* by the Cyclops, πόντονδε βαλὼν β. Od.9.495; of an ox's leg *thrown* by one of the suitors at Ulysses, 20.305; of a stool, 17.464; ὑπὲκ βελέων out *of the reach of darts*, out *of shot*, Il.4.465; ἐκ βελέων 11.163; ἔξω βελῶν X.*Cyr*.3.3.69, etc.; ἔξω βέλους Arr.*An*.2.27.1, Luc.*Hist.Conscr*.4; opp. ἐντὸς βέλους, D.S.20.6, Arr.*An*.1.2.5; εἴσω β. παρελθεῖν ib.1.6.8. **2.** used of *any weapon*, as *a sword*, Ar.*Ach*.345, cf. S.*Aj*.658; an *axe*, E.*El*.1159; *the sting* of a scorpion, A.*Fr*.169; of the gad-fly, Id.*Supp*.556. **3.** ἀγανὰ βέλεα of Apollo, Il.24.759, Od.3.280, and of Artemis, ib.5.124, denote *sudden*, *easy death* of men and women respectively; βέλος ὀξύ, of Ilithyia, *pangs* of childbirth, Il.11.269, cf. Theoc.27.29. **4.** after Hom. of *anything swift-darting*, Διὸς βέλη *the bolts* of Zeus, lightnings, Pi.*N*.10.8, cf. Hdt.4.79, etc.; Ζηνὸς ἄγρυπνον β. A.*Pr*.360; πύρπνουν β. ib.917; βέλεσι πυρπνόου ζάλης, of a storm, ib.373; πάγων δύσομβρα β. S.*Ant*.358: metaph., ὀμμάτων β. *glance* of the eye, A.*Ag*.742; φίλοικτον β. a piteous *glance*, ib.241 (lyr.); ἱμέρου β. the *shaft* of love, Id.*Pr*.649; θυμοῦ βέλη S.*OT*893 (s.v.l.); of arguments, πᾶν τετόξευται β. A.*Eu*.679, cf. Pl.*Phlb*.23b; β. τὰ ἀπὸ τοῦ στόματος, of invective, Lib.*Or*.51.8; of *mental anguish* or *fear*, ἄτλατον β. Pi.*N*.1.48 (v.l. δέος); ὁ φθόνος αὐτὸς ἑαυτὸν ἑοῖς βελέεσσι δαμάζει *AP*10.111. **5.** *engine of war*, Ph.*Bel*.82.8: pl., *artillery*, ib.97.10. (Cf. βάλλω, Lith. *gélti* 'sting', *gēlà* 'sharp pain', OHG. *quelan* 'feel sharp pain'. Root *g$^w$el-* 'pierce', cf. δέλλιθες.)

⊛**βελο-στᾰσία**, ἡ, *range* or *battery of warlike engines*, Ath.Mech.22.11. ⊛ **-στᾰσις**, εως, ἡ, = foreg., Plb.9.41.8, Ph.*Bel*.81.17, D.S.20.85. **-σφενδόνη**, ἡ, *dart wrapped with pitch and tow, and thrown while on fire from an engine*, Plu.*Sull*.18.

⊛ **βελουλκ-έω**, *draw out darts*, αὐτὸς ἑαυτὸν βελουλκεῖ *extracts the weapon* (i.e. *hook*) *from* itself, Plu.2.977b. **-ητέον**, *one must draw out darts*, Paul.Aeg.6.88. **-ία**, ἡ, *drawing out of darts*, Eust.464.41 (pl.). **-ικός**, ή, όν, *of* or *for* βελουλκία, Paul.Aeg.6.88. **-ός**, ὁ, *instrument for drawing out darts*, ibid. **II.** = δίκταμνος, Ps.-Dsc.3.32.

**βελοφόροι**, οἱ, = Lat. *sagittarii*, Lyd.*Mag*.1.46.

**βέλτ-ερος**, α, ον, = βελτίων, poet. Comp. of ἀγαθός, *better*, *more excellent*, Hom. only in neut., βέλτερόν [ἐστι] *it is better*, c. inf., Il.15.511, 21.485: c. dat. pers. et inf., Od.17.18; βέλτερον εἰ.. 6.282, cf. Thgn.92, A.*Th*.337, etc.: Sup. **βέλτατος**, η, ον, Id.*Eu*.487, *Supp*.1054. **-ιότης**, ητος, ἡ, *superiority*, Sch.Pi.*O*.1.5. **-ιόω**, *improve*, Ph.1.202, al., *Stud.Pal*.1.7 ii 20 (v A.D.), etc.:—Pass., Ph.1.169, al., Plu.2.85c, *SIG*888.5 (Thrace, iii A.D.), Antyll.ap.Orib.10.23.18, etc.; οὔτε βελτιοῦσι τὴν αἰτίαν τῶν παθῶν *give* no *better reason for*, Posidon.ap.Gal.5.469. **-ιστος**, η, ον, Dor. **βέντ-**, Sup. of ἀγαθός, *best*, *most excellent*, β. ἀνὴρ γενενῆσθαι περὶ τὸν δῆμον Ar.*Eq*.765; ὦ βέλτιστε or β., a common mode of address, *my dear friend*, Id.*Pl*.1172, Antiph.289, Pl.*R*.337e, etc.; ὦ βέλτιστε σύ Eub.106; ὦ β. ἀνδρῶν Pl.*Grg*.515a; ὦ ἄριστε καὶ β. Id.*Lg*.902a; βέντισθ' οὗτος Theoc.5.76; ὑπὲρ τὸ β. A.*Ag*.378; οἱ β. or τὸ β. *the aristocracy*, X.*HG*5.2.6, *Cyr*.8.1.16, *Ath*.1.5, etc.; τὸ β., in Philos., *the highest good*, Pl.*Phd*.99a,b, Epict.*Ench*.51, etc.; τὰ β. βουλεύειν Th.4.68; οὐκ ἀπὸ τοῦ β. ἀναστρέφεσθαι *SIG*593.7 (ii B.C.), *PTeb*.282.8 (ii A.D.). Adv. βέλτιστα X.*Oec*.7.29, etc.; βελτίστως Simp.*in Cael*.419.25. ⊛ **-ίων**, ον, gen. ονος, Comp. of ἀγαθός, *better* (not in Hom.), βέλτιόν [ἐστι] *it is fitting*, *convenient*, Arist.*Pol*.1264$^b$28; μανθάνειν βελτίονα [S.]*Fr*.1120.5; ἐπὶ τὸ β. χωρεῖν *improve*, *advance*, Th.7.50; ἐπὶ τὸ β. ἐλθεῖν Din.1.65; ἄγειν ib.29; τὰ βελτίω προσδοκᾶν ἀεί Apollod.Com.9. Adv. βελτιόνως, ἔχειν Hp.*Mul*.1.2, cf. Pl.*R*.484a. [ῑ Att., but βέλτῐον Mimn.2.10.] ⊛ **-ίωσις**, εως, ἡ, *improvement*, Ph.1.30, al., Plu.2.702c, S.E.*M*.7.23; *putting in repair*, *PMasp*.97.69 (vi A.D.). **-ιώτερος**, α, ον, = βελτίων, prob. in Telesill.6.

**βελτός**· βλητός, Hsch. **βέλφιν**, Aeol., = δελφίς, *EM*200.24.

**Βελφός**, **-οί**, Boeot. and Aeol. for Δελφ-.

**βεμβεύει**· δινεύει, Hsch. **βεμβίδιον**, a small *fish*, Id. (leg. βεμβρ-, cf. βεμβράς).

**βεμβῑκ-ιάω**, (βέμβιξ) *spin like a top*, Ar.*Av*.1465. **-ίζω**, *set a-spinning*, ἑαυτούς Id.*V*.1517. **-ώδης**, ες, *like a top*, Ath.11.496a.

⊛ **βέμβιξ**, ῑκος, ἡ, *whipping-top*, Ar.*Av*.1461, Call.*Epigr*.1.9. **II.** *whirlpool*, Opp.*H*.5.222. **III.** *cyclone*, Hsch. **IV.** *buzzing insect*, Nic.*Al*.183, *Th*.806, Parmeno 4.

**βέμβλετο**, v.l. for μέμβλετο in Il.21.516, Sch.Il.*Oxy*.221 xi 35: **βεμόλετο** (sic) Hsch., who also gives **βέμβλωκα** for μεμβλ-.

**βεμβράς**, άδος, ἡ, = μεμβράς, Aristomen.7, Numen.ap.Ath.7.287c:—Dim. **βεμβ⟨ρ⟩ίδιον**, Hsch.

**βεμβρᾰφύη** [ῠ], ἡ, *a dish of* μεμβράδες *and* ἀφύαι, Aristonym.2.

**βεμβρεῖ**· δινεύει, Hsch. **βεμβρός**, v. βεβρός. **βεμεῖ**· δονεῖ, Id. **βεμόλετο**, v. βέμβλετο. **βεμόριξ** (prob. for βέμβριξ), = βέμβιξ, Id.

**Βενδῖς**, ῖδος, ἡ, acc. Βενδῖν (not Βένδις, ιδος, Hdn.Gr.1.107):—*Bendis*, *the Thracian Artemis*, worshipped under this name at the Piraeus, Hippon.120, *IG*1$^2$.310, Luc.*JTr*.8, Orph.*Fr*.200:—hence **Βενδίδ-ειον**, τό, *temple of Bendis*, X.*HG*2.4.11: **-εια**, τά, *her festival*, Pl.*R*.354a, *IG*2.741 (written -εα): **-ειος**, ὁ (sc. μήν), name of month in Bithynia, *Hemerolog.Flor.*

**Βενετιανός**, ὁ, *a favourer of the blues*, M.Ant.1.5, *IG*14.1503.

**βένετος**, ον, = καλλάϊνος, *blue*, Lyd.*Mens*.4.30: esp. of *the blue faction* in the Circus, *Tab.Defix.Aud*.166.38 (Rome, iv/v A.D.), Lyd. l.c., Procop.*Pers*.1.24: Adj. **Βενέτειος**, ον, *of the* Βένετοι, στοά ibid.

**βένθος**, εος, τό, poet., = βάθος, *depth* of the sea, κατὰ βένθος ἁλός Il.18.38,49; ἁλὸς βένθοσδε Od.4.780, 8.51: in pl., ὅστε θαλάσσης πάσης βένθεα οἶδεν 1.53; ἐν βένθεσσιν ἁλός Il.1.358; βένθεσι λίμνης 13.21, 32; also βαθείης βένθεσιν ὕλης Od.17.316: metaph., βένθεϊ σῆς κραδίης *AP*5.273 (Paul. Sil.).—Used also by Emp.35.3, al., Pi.*O*.7.57, and in lyr., E.*Fr*.304, Ar.*Ra*.666. (Cf. βαθύς.)

**βέντιστος**, α, ον, v. βέλτιστος.

**βέομαι** and **βείομαι**, Homeric subj. used as fut., I *shall live*, οὔ τι Διὸς βέομαι φρεσίν Il.15.194; οὐδ' αὐτὸς δηρὸν βέῃ 16.852, cf. 24.131; τί νυ βείομαι αἰνὰ παθοῦσα; 22.431. (Cf. βιόμεσθα, βίονται (v. βιόω), whence βίομαι, βίε' should perh. be restored in Hom.)

**Βερβεία**, title of Aphrodite in Cyprus, Eriph.2.13.

**βέρβερι**, εος, τό, *pearl-mussel*, foreign word, Androsth.ap.Ath.3.93b.

**βερβερίζω**, = βατταρίζω, in later Greek, *EM*191.35.

⊛ **βερβέριον**, τό, *shabby garment*, Anacr.21.3.

**βερβίνια**, τά, *pegs for hanging up vases*, Hermipp. in Gloss.*Oxy*.1801.57, Hsch.

**βεργαΐζω**, *romance*, St.Byz. s.v. Βέργη: **βεργαῖος** ὕθλος Alex. in Gloss.*Oxy*.1801.50; β. διήγημα Str.2.3.5 (Antiphanes of Berga in Thrace was proverbial for his 'tall' stories).

**βέρεδος**, ὁ, = Lat. *veredus*, *post-horse*, Procop.*Pers*.2.20:—hence **βερεδάριος**, ὁ, Id.*Aed*.5.3:—also written **βερηδάριος**, τί ἐστὶ ναύτης; θαλάσσης β. Secund.*Sent*.18.

**βέρεθρον**, Ep. and Ion. for βάραθρον, Il.8.14, Pherecyd.51(b) J., Epic. in *Arch.Pap*.7 p.7; of the *underground course* of a river, Thphr. *HP*3.1.2, 5.4.6, Posidon.55.

**βερεκύνδαι**· δαίμονές τινες, Hsch.

**Βερέκυντες**, οἱ, a Phrygian people, Str.10.3.12, 12.8.21: acc. sg. Βερέκυντα A.*Fr*.158; Βερέκυντα βρόμον, of the *Phrygian* flute, S.*Fr*.513:—also **Βερέκυνται**, Hsch.:—Adj. **Βερεκύνθιος**, α, ον, *Phrygian*, *devoted to Cybele*, Call.*Dian*.246; **Βερεκύντιος**, Hsch.

**Βερεκυντίας**, ὁ, = ἀπηλιώτης (Pontic word), Thphr.*Vent*.62.

**Βερενίκη** [ῑ], ἡ, Macedon. form for Φερενίκη, freq. pr. n. in the time of the Ptolemies:—also **Βερνίκη** *Act.Ap*.25.13: **Βερενίκης** πλόκαμος, a *constellation*, Gem 3.8, etc.; also, a *throw of the dice*, Hsch.:—hence **βερενίκιον**, τό, a *plant*, Hsch.; also, *nitre* of the best quality, Gal.13.568:—Dim. **βερενικάριον** or **βερνικάριον** νίτρον, Orib.*Fr*.107, Aët.6.54:—**βερενικίδες**, αἱ, women's *shoes*, Hsch.

**Βερέσχεθοι**, οἱ, *the Powers of Folly*, Ar.*Eq*.635; βερέσχετοι *Gloss.Oxy*.1801.

⊛ **βερίκοκκον**, τό, *apricot*, *Gp*.10.73.2:—Dim. **βερικόκκιον** ib.3.1.4, Artem.1.73; β. μῆλον Herod.Med. in *Rh.Mus*.58.100. (Lat. *praecoqua*.)

**βέρκιος**· ἔλαφος (Lacon.), Hsch. **βερκνίς**· ἀκρίς, Id. (cf. βρεῦκος). **βερνώμεθα**· κληρωσώμεθα (Lacon.), and **βερρέαι**· κληρῶσαι (prob. = μείρεαι), Id. **βέρρης**, ου, ὁ, = δραπέτης, *a fugitive*; and **βερρεύω**, = δραπετεύω, Id. **βερρόν**, = βειρόν, Id. **βερωνετῶν**· ἀλλὰ ἀνετῶν, Id. **βέσκεροι**· ἄρτοι (Lacon.), Id. **βεσόν**· ἔθος, Id. (prob. Lacon. = ϝεθόν). **βεστικός**· ὁ τῶν ἐσθήτων ἔμπειρος cj. in Id. s.v. βεσόν. (Cf. *vestis*.)

⊛ **βεστίον**, τό, *clothing*, *PLond*.5.1654 (iv A.D.).

**βέστον** and **βέττον**, = ἱμάτιον, Diogenian.ap.*EM*195.45.

⊛ **βεττονική**, ἡ, = βρεττανική, interpol. post Dsc.4.2 (p.170 Wellm.). **2.** *Paul's betony*, *Sideritis purpurea*, Paul.Aeg.7.3. **3.** = κέστρος (q.v.), ibid.

⊛ **βεῦδος**, εος, τό, *woman's dress*, Sapph.155, Call.*Fr*.155, Nicaenet.(?) ap.Parth.11.4 (pl.). **II.** = ἄγαλμα, at Hermione, *EM*195.52.

**βέφῡρα**, Boeot. for γέφυρα, Stratt.47.5.

**βῆ βῆ**, *baa*, the cry of sheep, βῆ βῆ λέγων βαδίζει Cratin.43, cf. Ar.*Fr*.642, Varro *RR*2.1:—hence **βηβήν**· πρόβατον, and **βήζει**· φωνεῖ, Hsch.

**βῆγμα**, ατος, τό, (βήσσω) *expectoration*, *phlegm*, Hp.*Morb*.2.47.

**βήθυλος**· εἶδος ὀρνέου, *EM*196.54. **βῆκα**· ἀναδενδράς, Hsch.

**βήκη**· χίμαιρα, Id.

**βηκία**, τά, = προβάτια, Hp.ap.Gal.19.88: but **βηκία** and **βηκίον** (which = ἐλελίσφακος, Ps.-Dsc.3.33, and = ψευδοδίκταμνος, ib.32), = βήχιον, Erot., Ps.-Dsc.3.112. **βηκώνιον**· εἶδος βοτάνης, Hsch. (leg. μηκ-).

**βηλά**, ῶν, τά, = πέδιλα, Panyas.23.

**βῆλημα** (i.e. ϝηλ-), ατος, τό, = κώλυμα, φράγμα ἐν ποταμῷ (Lacon.), Hsch., cf. *IG*5(1).1390.104 (Andania).

**βηλήσσει**· βληχᾶται, Hsch.

**βηλόθῠρον**, τό, *door-curtain, portière*, Sch.Ar.*Ra*.969.

**βήλομαι**, v. βούλομαι.

**βηλός**, Dor. **βᾱλός** (also used in Trag., *AB*224), ὁ: (βαίνω):—*threshold*, Il.1.591, A.*Ch*.571, Porph.*Antr*.14; β. ἀστερόεις Q.S.13.483.

**βῆμα**, Aeol. and Dor. **βᾶμα**, ατος, τό, (βαίνω) *step, pace*, *h.Merc*.222, 345, Pi.*P*.3.43, A.*Ch*.799 (lyr.); σπουδῇ.. βημάτων πορεύεται E.*Andr*. 880; τοσόνδε β. διαβεβηκώς Ar.*Eq*.73; *footfall*, ἔρατον βᾶμα Sapph. *Supp*.5.17; Διὸς εὔφρονι βήματι μολεῖν to journey under the kindly *guidance* of Zeus, S.*El*.163 (lyr.); *gait*, β. οὐκ ὀρθὸν *Hippiatr*.27. 2. *step*, as a measure of length, = 10 παλαισταί, about 2½ feet, Hero *Deff*. 131. 3. metaph., *step*, '*moment*', πρόοδος ἐν τρισὶ β. διισταμένη Dam.*Pr*.258. II. = βάθρον, *step, seat*, S.*OC*193 (lyr.). 2. *raised place* or *tribune* to speak from in a public assembly, etc., Th.2.34, Lxx *Ne*.8.4, etc.; in the Pnyx at Athens, ἐπὶ τὸ β. ἀναβῆναι enter *public life*, D.18.66; αἱ ἀπὸ τοῦ β. ἐλπίδες Id.4.45; also in the law-courts, Id.48.31, Aeschin.3.207; of a suppliant, ἐπὶ τοῦ β. καθεζόμενον Ar.*Pl*.382; in the βουλευτήριον, Antipho 6.40. b. *tribunal* of a magistrate, τοῦ ἡγεμόνος β. *PTeb*.434 (ii A.D.). 3. = θυμέλη, Poll.4.123; β. θεήτρου *IG*3.239. 4. *base, pedestal*, *OGI*219.36 (Ilium, iii B.C.), 290.15 (Pergam., ii B.C.).

**βῆμα**· πρόβατα, Hsch.

**βημᾰτ-ίζω**, (Act. only in Hsch.) *measure by paces*, Plb.3.39.8 (Pass.); ὁδὸς βεβηματισμένη κατὰ μίλιον Str.7.7.4:—Med., ὄμματι βηματίσαισθε τὸν ἀέρα Dionys.Eleg.3.5. II. *step, walk*, Aesop. 322b. **-ιστής**, οῦ, ὁ, *one who measures by paces*, Ath.10.442c. II. *quartermaster*, *SIG*303 (Olympia, iv B.C.).

**βήμεναι**, v. βαίνω. **βηνῶσα**· ἡ φωνὴ τῶν προβάτων, Hsch.

**βήξ**, βηχός, *cough*, ὁ, Th.2.49; ἡ, Hp.*Prog*.14, Phryn.Com.60, Arist.*de An*.420b33, Thphr.*HP*3.18.3.

**βηράνθεμον** (i.e. ϝηρ-)· νάρκισσος, Hsch.

**βήρβη**· κωδύα (-δία cod.) μήκωνος, Hsch.

**βήρηξ**, ηκος, ὁ, a kind of *loaf*, Ar. in Gloss.*Oxy*.1801.59 (pl.), Ath.3.114f, *AB*226, Hsch. (who also has **βῆραξ**); cf. βάραξ, πάραξ.

**βηρίδες**, = ἐμβάδες, Hsch. **βηρίχαλκον**· μάρα[ν]θον (Lacon.), Id.

**βηρύλλιος**, = ἀείζωον τὸ μέγα, Ps.-Dsc.4.88. 2. = ἀνεμώνη ἡ Φοινική, Osthanes ap.eund.2.176; cf. Hsch. s.v. βήρυλλος.

**βήρυλλος**, ἡ, *gem of sea-green colour, beryl*, Lxx *To*.13.17, D.P. 1012, Tryph.70, *PHolm*.8.10, al.; Ἰνδὴ β. *AP*9.544 (Adaeus); β. λίθος Luc.*VH*2.11:—Dim. **βηρύλλιον**, τό, Lxx *Ex*.28.20, D.S.2.52.

**βηρυσσεύειν**· σπείρειν (perh. σπειρᾶν), Hsch.; cf. μηρύειν.

**βῆρυς**· ἰχθύς, Hsch.; cf. μῆρυξ.

**βήσαλον** (or **βισ-**), τό, *brick*, Alex.Trall.9.2:—hence **βησαλικόν**, τό, *brick-work*, Hero *Stereom*.1.76.

**βησασά**, usu. indecl., but acc. βησασᾶν v.l. in Dsc.3.46:—*Syrian rue*, Antyll.ap.Orib.10.23.26, etc.: **βησάς**, ἡ, *PMag.Par*.1.800.

**βήσετο**, v. βαίνω. **βησίον**, v. βησσίον.

**βῆσσα**, Dor. **βᾶσσα**, ἡ, poet. Noun, *wooded combe, glen*, in Hom. mostly οὔρεος ἐν βήσσῃς in the mountain *glens*, Il.3.34, al.; ἐν καλῇ βήσσῃ 18.588, cf. Od.19.435; κοίλη δ' ὑποδέδρομε βῆσσα τρηχεῖα *h.Ap*.284: pl. for sg., ἐν βήσσῃσι Od.10.210: used also by Pi., twice by S. (lyr.), *OC*673, *Aj*.197, and Arist.*HA*618b24. II. *drinking-cup* at Alexandria, broader below and narrower above, Ath.11.784b.

**βησσήεις**, εσσα, εν, *of* or *like a glen, woody*, ἄγκεα, δρία, Hes.*Op*. 389,530; οὔρεα D.P.1183; νομός Coluth.41.

**βησσίον**, τό, *cup*, *PHolm*.16.3, Hsch., prob. in *PMag.Par*.1.750: **βησίον** *Stud.Pal*.20.67 (ii/iii A.D.).

**βήσσω**, Att. -ττω, fut. βήξω Hp.*Mul*.1.41: aor. ἔβηξα Hdt.6.107, Hp.*Prog*.8: (βήξ):—*cough*, ll.cc., Ar.*Ec*.56, etc.:—Med. in act. sense, Hp.*Morb*.2.52:—Pass., τὰ βησσόμενα Id.*Epid*.1.3.

**βῆτα**, τό, indecl., *the letter* β, Pl.*Cra*.393e, Arist.*Metaph*.1087a8, *AP*11.437 (Arat.), Luc.*Herm*.40, etc. (Aram. *bēthā'*.)

**βηταρμός**, ὁ, *dance*, β. ἐνόπλιον ὠρχήσαντο A.R.1.1135.

**βητάρμων**, ονος, ὁ, *dancer*, in pl., Od.8.250,383, Man.2.335:—later, as Adj., καπνός Nonn.*D*.36.297; κάπρος ib.22.44. (βαίνω, ἀραρίσκω.)

**βηχία**, ἡ (or **βηχίας**, ὁ), (βήξ) *hoarseness*, Nicom.*Harm*.11, *Exc*. 4 (pl.), Menipp.*Ep*.

**βηχικός**, ή, όν, *suffering from cough*, γραίῃ f.l. in Hp.*Epid*.7. 105. 2. *good for a cough*, φάρμακα Gal.11.769, al., cf. Alex.Trall.5.

**βήχιον**, τό, *colt's-foot, Tussilago Farfara*, used to allay cough, Hp. *Art*.63, Dsc.3.112. II. *slight cough*, Id.*Eup*.2.31.

**βηχώδης**, ες, *coughing*, Hp.*Epid*.1.3. 2. *accompanied by, productive of coughing*, κατάρροοι Id.*Aph*.2.31, cf. Id.*Art*.49 (Comp.).

**βία**, Ion. **βίη** [ῐ], ἡ: Ep. dat. βίηφι Od.6.6:—*bodily strength, force*, Hom., etc.; χειρῶν βία B.10.91:—in Hom., periphr. of strong men, βίη Ἡρακληείη Il.2.658, where the part. masc. πέρσας follows, cf. 11.690; βίη Ἐτεοκληείη, Ἰφικλείη, 4.386, Od.11.290, etc.; βίη Διομήδεος Il.5.781; also ἴς.. βίης Ἡρακλῆεις Hes.*Th*.332: so in Lyr. and Trag., Πέλοπος βία B.5.181; Τυδέως βία, Πολυνείκους β., A.*Th*. 571, 577; φίλτατ' Αἰγίσθου β. Id.*Ch*.893; θήρειος β., = Κένταυροι, S. *Tr*.1059. 2. personified, Κράτος Βία τε A.*Pr*.12. 3. of the mind, οὐκ ἔστι βίη φρεσίν Il.3.45. b. of an argument, βίαν οὐκ ἔχειν πρὸς (τὸ) ἀποδεῖξαι Phld.*Sign*.9. II. *act of violence*, ὕβρις τε βίη τε Od.15.329: mostly in pl., κείνων γε βίας ἀποτείσεαι 11.117; βίας ὑποδέγμενος ἀνδρῶν 16.189; βίαι ἀνέμων Il.16.213. 2. βίᾳ τινός *against* one's *will, in spite of* him, A.*Th*.746 (lyr.), S.*Ant*.79, Th.1. 43, etc.; β. φρενῶν A.*Th*.612; β. καρδίας Id.*Supp*.798; β. alone as Adv., *perforce*, Od.15.231, B.17.10, A.*Pr*.74, al.; βίῃ ἐπειρᾶτο Hdt. 6.5; opp. κατὰ φύσιν, Arist.*Ph*.215a1; also πρὸς βίαν τινὸς A.*Eu*.5; πρὸς βίαν ἄγειν τινά Id.*Pr*.210, cf. S.*OT*805, Eup.8.10D., Ar.*V*.443, etc.; opp. ἑκών, Pl.*Phdr*.236d; ἐκ βίας S.*Ph*.563, al., Herod.5.58; ὑπὸ βίης Hdt.6.107; ἀπὸ βίας D.S.20.51; of Zeus, εὐμενεῖ βίᾳ κτίσας A.*Supp*.1068 (lyr.). 3. in Att. law, *rape*, βίας δίκη Sch.Pl.*R*.464e; βίᾳ αἰσχύνεσθαί τινα Lys.1.32. 4. = Lat. *vis*, βίας γραφή D.C.37. 31, cf. 33; μαρτύρομαι τὴν βίαν *POxy*.1120.11 (iii A.D.). (Cf. Skt. *jyā jiyā* 'preponderating power', *jināti* 'oppress'.)

**βιάζω**, *constrain*, Act. once in Hom., ἦ μάλα δή με βιάζετε Od.12. 297; ἐβίασε τὴν γυναῖκά μου Alc.Com.29: abs., εἰ πάνυ ἐβίαζον if *they used force*, Hp.*Epid*.2.24; cf. infr.1.2:—Pass., fut. βιασθήσομαι Paus. 6.5.9: aor. ἐβιάσθην, pf. βεβίασμαι (v. infr.):—*to be hard pressed* or *overpowered*, βελέεσσι βιάζεται Il.11.589; βιάζετο γὰρ βελ. 15.727; βιασθέντες λύᾳ Pi.*N*.9.14; νόσῳ Ar.*Fr*.20 (= *Trag.Adesp*.70); *to be forced* or *constrained* to do, c. inf., Id.*Th*.890: c. acc. cogn., βιάζομαι τάδε S.*Ant*.66, cf. 1073; βιασθεὶς Id.*El*.575; ἐπεὶ ἐβιάσθη Th.4. 44; ὑπό τινος Id.1.2; opp. ἀδικεῖσθαι, ib.77; βιασθεὶς ἄκων ἔπραξεν D.6.16; ἵνα ἢ συγχωρήσωσιν.. ἢ βιασθῶσιν Id.18.175; βιαζόμενος ὑπό τινος ἐξήμαρτεν Antipho 4.4.5; βεβιασμένοι *forcibly made slaves*, X.*Hier*.2.12; πόλεις βεβ. Id.*HG*5.2.23; βιαζόμενος ὑπὸ τῆς παρούσης ἀπορίας Th.7.67; τὸ βιασθέν *those who are forced*, Arist.*Pol*.1255a 11; of things, τοὐνειδος ὀργῇ βιασθὲν *forced from one* by anger, S.*OT* 524; τὸ βεβιασμένον *forced* to fit a hypothesis, Arist.*Metaph*.1082b2; βεβ. σχήματα *forced* figures of speech, D.H.*Th*.33, cf. Porph.*Antr*. 36. 2. Act., *make good, suffice to discharge* a debt, *PFlor*.56. 13. II. more freq. βιάζομαι, aor. Med. ἐβιασάμην, pf. βεβίασμαι D.19.206, Men.*Sam*.63, D.C.46.45:—*overpower by force, press hard*, ἦ μάλα δή σε βιάζεται ὠκὺς Ἀχιλλεύς Il.22.229, etc.; β. τοὺς πολεμίους *dislodge* them, X.*An*.1.4.5; β. νόμους *to do* them *violence*, Th. 8.53; βιασάμενος ταῦτα πάντα *having broken through* all these restraints, Lys.6.52; β. γυναῖκα *force* her, Ar.*Pl*.1092; opp. πείθειν, Lys.1.32; β. αὑτόν *lay violent hands on* oneself, Pl.*Phd*.61c,d; β. τινά, c. inf., *force* one to do, X.*An*.1.3.1; τί με βιάζεσθε λέγειν; Arist. *Fr*.44: with inf. omitted, β. τὰ σφάγια *force* the victims [*to be favourable*], Hdt.9.41; β. ἄστρα Theoc.22.9: c. dupl. acc., αὐδῶ πόλιν σε μὴ β. τόδε A.*Th*.1047. 2. c. acc. rei, *carry by force*, βιάσασθαι τὸν ἔκπλουν *force* an exit, Th.7.72; τὴν ἀπόβασιν Id.4.11: c. acc. neut., And.4.17, X.*HG*5.3.12. 3. abs., *act with violence, use force*, A.*Pr*. 1010, *Ag*.1509 (lyr.), S.*Aj*.1160, etc.; πρὸς τὸ λαμπρὸν ὁ φθόνος βιάζεται *Trag.Adesp*.547.12; opp. δικάζομαι, Th.1.77; β. διὰ φυλάκων *force one's way*, Id.7.83; β. ἐς τὸ ἔξω, ib.69, X.*Cyr*.3.3.69; δρόμῳ β. Th.1.63: c. inf., β. πρὸς τὸν λόφον ἐλθεῖν Id.7.79; βιαζόμενοι βλάπτειν *using every effort* to hurt me, Lys.9.16; but βιαζόμενοι μὴ ἀποδιδόναι refusing *with violence* to repay, X.*HG*5.3.12: esp. in part., ἵνα βιασάμενοι ἐκπλεύσωσι may sail out *by forcing their way*, Th.7.67; συνεξέρχονται βιασάμενοι X.*An*.7.8.11; ἐπὶ μᾶλλον ἔτι β. (of a famine) *grow worse and worse*, Hdt.1.94. 4. *contend* or *argue vehemently*, c. inf., Pl.*Sph*.246b; β. τὸ μὴ ὂν ὡς ἔστι κατά τι ib. 241d: abs., *persist in assertion*, D.21.205.

**βιαιοελυπίου**, dub. in *PPetr*.3p.317.

**βῐαιο-θᾰνᾰσία**, ἡ, *violent death*, Vett.Val.94.1, Paul.Al.*N*.2. **-θᾰνᾰτέω**, *die a violent death*, Vett.Val.67.8, Ps.-Plu.*Fluv*.7.3. **-θάνᾰτος** [θᾰ], ον, *dying a violent death*, most freq. of *suicides*, Vett.Val.74. 29, Paul.Al.*M*.2, Olymp. in *Phd*.p.243 N., *PMag.Par*.1.1950, Suid. s.v. κυνήγιον.—Freq. written βιοθάνατος. **-κλώψ**, ῶπος, ὁ, (κλέπτω) *stealing forcibly*, Lyc.548. **-μάχος** (cod. Pal. -μάχας) [ᾰ], ὁ, *fighting violently*, *AP*6.129 (Leon.). **-μᾰχέω**, *fight at close quarters*, of ships, opp. ταχυναυτεῖν, Plb.1.27.12: generally, Id.5. 84.2, Phld.*Rh*.1.195 S.

**βίαιος** [ῐ], α, ον, also ος, ον Pl.*R*.399a, Philostr.*VA*1.33: (βία):—*forcible, violent*: Adj. once in Hom., ἔρδειν ἔργα βίαια Od.2.236, Adv. twice, *by force, perforce*, κατέδουσι βιαίως οἶκον Ὀδυσσῆος 2.237; γυναιξὶ παρευνάζεσθε βιαίως 22.37: freq. in all writers, ἔργα β. Thgn. 1343; νόμος ἄγει δικαιῶν τὸ βιαιότατον Pi.*Fr*.169; of persons, βιαιότατος τῶν πολιτῶν Th.3.36; χρόνος καταψήχει καὶ τὰ βιαιότατα Simon. 176; β. θάνατος a *violent* death, Hdt.7.170, Pl.*R*.566b, etc.; β. νόσος S.*Ant*.1140 (lyr.); β. ἄνεμος Arist.*Mete*.370b9; ἐπάρδευσις Epicur.*Ep*. 2p.44 U. (Comp.); ὁ πόλεμος β. διδάσκαλος teaches *by violence*, Th. 3.82; δίκη βιαίων an action *for forcible rescue*, Harp.; τοῖς β. or τῶν βιαίων ἔνοχος, Lys.23.12, Pl.*Lg*.914e; βιαίων [ἐγκαλεῖ] D.37.33; τὰ [περὶ] τῶν βιαίων ibid.; συναλλάγματα β., λαθραῖα, *obligationes ex delicto*, Arist.*EN*1131a8; κλοπαῖα καὶ β. Pl.*Lg*.934c. Adv. βιαίως, ἀποθανεῖν Antipho 1.26; β. σέλμα σεμνὸν ἡμένων *in their irresistible might*, A.*Ag*.182 (lyr.); χαλεπῶς καὶ β. by struggling and *forcing their way*, Th.3.23; *firmly*, σχεδίας β. ζεύξαντες Plb.3.46.1: neut. pl. as Adv., A.*Supp*.821 (lyr.); πρὸς τὸ β. Id.*Ag*.130; ἐκ τοῦ βιαιοτάτου D.H.10. 36. 2. esp. of magic, β. τέχνη Philostr.*VA*1.33. Adv. βιαίως, σοφὸς a *wizard*, ib.1.2. II. Pass., *forced, constrained*, opp. ἑκούσιος, πράξεις Pl.*R*.603c; β. κίνησις, = παρὰ φύσιν κ., Arist.*Ph*.254a9, cf. Pl.*Ti*.64d; τὸ β., = οὗ ἔξωθεν ἡ ἀρχὴ μηδὲν συμβαλλομένου τοῦ βιασθέντος Arist.*EN*1110b15; ἡ β. τροφή, of the diet of athletes, Id.

*Pol.*1338$^{b}$41 ; πόνοι μὴ β. ib.1335$^{b}$9 ; ὁ χρηματιστὴς (sc. βίος) β. τίς ἐστιν, Id.*EN*1096$^{a}$6 ; βιαιότερος λόγος Jul.*Or.*6.191d. Adv. -ως, = παρὰ φύσιν, κινεῖσθαι Arist.*Ph.*253$^{b}$34 : Comp. -οτέρως Gal.17(1). 19. **2.** = βιαιοθάνατος, *PMag.Par.*1.332.

**βῐαιότης**, ητος, ἡ, *violence*, β. καὶ παρανομία Antipho5.8, And.4. 10, cf. Lys.23.11.

**βῐ-αρκής**, ές, (βίος II, ἀρκέω) *supplying the necessaries of life*, *AP*6. 179(Arch.). **2.** *life-giving*, Nonn.*D.*17.370. ❋**-αρχος**, ὁ, (βίος II, ἄρχω) *commissary-general*, Lyd.*Mag.*1.48, al., *BGU*316.4 (iv A.D.).

**βῐασ-μός**, ὁ, *violence*, Aen.Tact.24.15, Eup.64 ; *rape*, παρθένου Men.*Epit.*236, cf. Satyr.*Vit.Eur.Fr.*39vii8 (pl.) ; ἁρπαγὴ καὶ β. Plu. 2.755d, cf. D.H.1.77. **II.** Medic., = τεινεσμός, interp. in Dsc. 3.94. **-τέον**, *one must do violence to*, τύχην E.*Rh.*584 ; ἀλόγως β. Phld.*Oec.*p.56 J. **-τήρ**, ῆρος, ὁ, = sq., prob. in Gorg.*Hel.* 12. **-τής**, οῦ, ὁ, = βιατάς, *Ev.Matt.*11.12. **-τικός**, ή, όν, *forcible, violent*, νόμος Pl.*Lg.*921e, Arist.*MA*703$^{a}$22 : Comp., ἀνάγκη Ph.2.295 : Sup., φίλτρον ib.28 ; *cogent*, τὸ β. [τοῦ λογικοῦ] Jul.*Or.*7.216a. Adv. -κῶς *violently*, *EM*197.11 : of a *forced* construction, Sch.Philostr. *Her.*p.484 B. : Comp. -ώτερον, ἐπιτάττειν S.E.*M.*6.7 : also, *cogently*, ἀποδείκνυται Gal.5.48c. **-τός**, ή, όν, *violent*, πράγματα Chor. in Lib.4.793 Reiske.

❋ **βῐᾱτάς**, α, ὁ, *forceful, mighty*, Pi.*Pae.*6.84, al. ; σοφοὶ καὶ χερσὶ βιαταί Id.*P.*1.42 ; β. νόος Id.*O.*9.75 ; of wine, *potent*, Id.*N.*9.51 ; Ἄρης *AP*7.492 (Anyte).

**βιάτωρ**· κυάθιον μικρόν, κοχλιάριον, Hsch.

**βῐάω**, Ep. form of βιάζω, *constrain*, Act. only in the pf., ἄχος, χρειὼ βεβίηκεν Ἀχαιούς, Il.10.145,172, 16.22 :—Pass., *to be forcibly driven*, of fire, ἀνέμῳ βιώμενον Hdt.1.19 ; πῦρ βεβιημένον *AP*9.546 (Antiphil.) ; θανάτῳ βιηθεὶς Hdt.7.83, cf. Hp.*Mul.*1.40 : fut., οὐ βιήσεται (in pass. sense) *will not yield to force*, ib.2.132 ; βιωομένη (v.l. βιαζ-) Mosch.2.13. **II.** freq. as Dep. (pres. imper. βιάσθω Parm.1.34, fut. βιήσεται Emp.4.6) in act. sense, οἳ κεῖνον βιόωνται Od.11.503, cf. 23.9, Pl.*Ti.*63c ; ὥς εἴ ἑ βιῷατο (opt.) . . Τρῶες *should press* him *hard*, Il.11.467 ; βιήσατο κῦμ' ἐπὶ χέρσον it *forced* me upon . ., Od.7.278 ; ψεύδεσσι βιησάμενος over-reaching, Il.23. 576 ; τότε νῶϊ βιήσατο μισθὸν ἅπαντα *wronged us, deprived us of* our wages, 21.451 ; τὸ δοκεῖν καὶ τὰν ἀλάθειαν βιᾶται Simon.76, cf. Pi.*N.* 8.34, B.12.200 ; *force, ravish*, παρθένον Hdt.4.43 ; *drive* or *urge on*, βιᾶται δ' ἁ τάλαινα πειθὼ A.*Ag.*385 (lyr.).

**βιβ-άζω**, fut. βιβάσω, Att. βιβῶ, with part. βιβῶν S.*OC*381, (δια-) Pl.*Lg.*900c, D.23.157, (ἐμ-) X.*An.*5.7.8, (προσ-) Ar.*Av.*426, Pl. *Phdr.*229e (but διαβιβάσοντες codd. in X.*An.*4.8.8, 5.2.10) : aor. ἐβίβασα (ἀν-) Id *HG*4.5.3, (ἀπ-) Pl.*Grg.*511e :—**Med.**, pres. (ἀνα-) Th.7. 33 : fut. βιβάσομαι, Att. βιβῶμαι (ἀνα-) Amips.30, Aeschin.2.146, D.19. 310, but ἀναβιβάσομαι codd. in And.1.148, Lys.18.24 : aor. ἐβιβασάμην (ἀν-) Th.7.35, Lys.20.34, etc. :—**Pass.**, fut. βιβασθήσομαι (δια-) D.S. 13.81 : aor. βιβασθεὶς Arist.*HA*577$^{a}$30 : pf. βεβίβασται (συμ-) S.E. *M.*7.283 :—causal of βαίνω, mostly used in compds., *cause to mount, exalt*, πρὸς οὐρανὸν βιβῶν S.*OC*381 : simply, *cause to go*, μή με τᾶσδ' ἐξ ὁδοῦ βίβαζε Id.*Ichn.*368. **II.** of animals, *put the female to the male*, Alc.Com.18, Arist.*HA*573$^{b}$7 ; also of the male, Horap.1.48 :—Pass., of the female, Arist.*HA*577$^{a}$29, Lxx *Le.*18.23. **-άσθω**, = βιβάω, only in part., μακρὰ βιβάσθων *long-striding*, Il.13.809, 16.534. **-ᾰσις**, εως, ἡ, *a Spartan dance*, Poll.4.102. **II.** = ὀχεία, *Gloss.* **III.** = κοίτη, στιβάς, Hsch. **-αστής**, οῦ, ὁ, *stallion*, *Gloss.* **-άω**, poet. collat. form of βαίνω, *stride*, πέλωρα βιβᾷ he *takes* huge *strides*, *h.Merc.*225 ; ἐβίβασκε, Ion. impf., *h.Ap.*133 : elsewh. only part., μακρὰ βιβῶντα (βιβάντα Aristarch.), μακρὰ βιβῶσα, Il.3.22, Od.11.539 ; κοῦφα βιβῶν lightly *stepping*, Pi.*O.*14.17. **-ημι**, poet. collat. form of βαίνω, *to stride*, used by Hom. only in part., μακρὰ βιβάς Il.7.213, al. ; ὕψι βιβάντα 13.371, al. (v. foreg.) : Dor. 3 sg. βίβαντι Epigr.Lacon.ap. Poll.4.102.

**βιβλ-, βυβλ-**, v. βίβλος.

**βιβλ-αρίδιον**, τό, Dim. of βίβλος, *small roll*, *Apoc.*10.2. **-άριον**, τό, = foreg., *PLille* 1.7.7 (iii B.C.), *AP*11.78 (Lucill.).

**βιβλιαγράφος**, v. βιβλιογράφος.

**βιβλ-αίγισθος**, Ἀνδρέας ὁ ἰατρὸς ἐπεκλήθη ὑπὸ Ἐρατοσθένους ὅτι λάθρα αὐτοῦ τὰ βιβλία μετέγραψε *EM*198.20. **-ακός**, ή, όν, *versed in books*, Phld.*Ir.*p.90 W. (βυβλ-) ; ἐν ἱστορίᾳ βιβλιακώτατος Plu. *Rom.*12 ; *pedantic*, χαρακῖται Timo 12 ; ἕξις Plb.12.25$^{h}$.3. **2.** *of a book*, σελίδες *AP*7.594 (Jul.) ; *in* or *of books*, συντάξεις Chaerem. ap.Porph.*Abst.*4.7. **-αρίδιον**, τό, = βιβλαρίδιον, Gal.16.5. **-άριον**, τό, = βιβλάριον, Antisth.ap.D.L.6.3.

❋ **βιβλιᾱφόρος**, ον, *letter-carrier*, Plb.4.22.2, D.S.2.26 : **βυβλιοφόρος** *PHal.*7.6 (iii B.C.).

**βιβλιδάριον**, τό, = βιβλάριον, Ar.*Fr.*756, Agatharch.111.

**βιβλίδιον** [ῐδ], τό, Dim. of βιβλίον, D.56.1, Plb.23.2.5 (βυβλ-), *SIG*663.20 (Delos, iii/ii B.C.), *AP*12.208 (Strat.), Antiph.162 : **βιβλείδιον**, τό, *petition*, Lat. *libellus*, *POxy.*1032.4 (ii A.D.), etc. ; ἐπὶ βιβλειδίων, = Lat. *a libellis*, *IG*14.1072 :—written **βυβλείδιον** Demetr. Lac.*Herc.*1012.35 F., 1013.12 F.

❋ **βίβλινος**, η, ον, *made of* βίβλος (βύβλος), *BGU*544.4 (ii A.D.).

**βιβλιο-γρᾰφία**, ἡ, *writing of books*, Dsc.1.85, D.L.7.36. ❋**-γράφος** [ᾰ], ὁ, *writer of books, scribe*, Antiph.197, Lib.*Ep.*263 :—also **βιβλιᾰγράφος** (correct form acc. to Phryn.67), Cratin.249, Luc.*Ind.* 24. **-θήκη**, ἡ, *book-case*, Cratin.Jun.11 (βυβλ-). **2.** *library, collection of books*, Plb.12.27.4, Lxx *Es.*2.23, Posidon.41, Phld.*Sto. Herc.*339.13 (βυβλ-), Str.13.1.54, al., J.*AJ*12.2.1 ; β. ἔμψυχος, of Longinus, Eun.*VS*p.456 B. **3.** *record-office, registry*, *PTeb.*389. 18 (ii A.D.) ; β. ἐγκτήσεων *BGU*76.1 (ii/iii A.D.) ; β. δημοσίων [λόγων] *PRyl.*291.1 (iii A.D.). **4.** *compilation* from various sources, title of works by Apollod. and D.S. **-κάπηλος** [ᾰ], ὁ, *dealer in books*, Luc.*Ind.*4, 24. **-λάθας** [λᾱ], α, ὁ, (λήθη) *book-forgetting*, nickname of Didymus the Gramm., who had written so many books (3,500) that he could not remember them, Demetr.Troez.ap.Ath.4. 139c. **-μᾰχέω**, *present a counter-petition*, *POxy.*68.33 (ii A.D.).

**βιβλίον** or **βυβλίον**, τό, *strip of* βύβλος, Thphr.*HP*4.8.4 : hence, *paper, document*, Hdt.1.123, 3.128, Ar.*Av.*974, etc. ; τὸ β. τοῦ ψηφίσματος *IG*2$^{2}$.1.61 ; β. ἀποστασίου *notice* of divorce, *Ev.Matt.*19.7. **2.** = βιβλίδιον, *petition* to the Government, = Lat. *libellus*, *BGU*422 (ii A.D.), *POxy.*86.16 (iv A.D.), etc. **3.** = δέλτος, *tablet*, Lxx *To.*7. 14. **II.** *book*, Eup.304, Theognet.1.8, Pl.*Ap.*26d, etc. ; μέγα β. ἴσον τῷ μεγάλῳ κακῷ Call.*Fr.*359. **2.** *book* as the division of a work, ἐν τῷ πρώτῳ β. Dsc.2 *Praef.*, Ph.1.329, etc. **3.** τὰ β. *place in which books are kept, library*, ἀνεθήκατε εἰς τὰ β. D.Chr.37.8. **4.** τὰ β. τὰ ἅγια the sacred *books* or *Scriptures*, Lxx 1*Ma.*12.9 ; τὰ β. τοῦ νόμου ib.1.56.

**βιβλιο-πωλεῖον**, τό, *bookseller's shop*, Ath.1.1e, Gal.*Lib.Propr.*1. ❋**-πώλης**, ου, ὁ, *bookseller*, Theopomp.Com.77, Nicoph.19.4, Aristomen.9, Arist.*Fr.*140. **-φόριον**, τό, *book-* or *letter-case*, *AB* 314. ❋**-φῠλᾰκέω**, *to be a librarian*, *PBodl.ined.* (MS. Gr. Class. d 86 P 19). **-φῠλᾰκία**, ἡ, *office of* βιβλιοφύλαξ, *PRyl.*374.8 (i/ii A.D.). ❋**-φῠλάκιον** [ᾰ], τό, *place to keep books in*, τὰ βασιλικὰ β. the royal *archives*, Lxx 1*Es.*6.21, 23, *PTeb.*318.23 (ii A.D.). ❋ **-φύλαξ** [ῠ], ακος, ὁ, *keeper of archives*, ib.112 *Intr.*10 (ii B.C.), *PFay.*31.3 (ii A.D.) : βυβλ- *Milet.*6.36 (Didyma), *POxy.*483.32, *CPR*1.18.41 (ii A.D.).

❋ **βιβλίς**, ίδος, ἡ, = βιβλίον, *EM*197.30. **II.** pl., *cords of* βίβλος, ibid.

**βιβλοπώλης**, = βιβλιο-, Phryn.*PS*p.52 B. **βίβλος**, ἡ, v. βύβλος.

**βιβρώσκω**, Babr.108.9, (cf. βράζω, βορά) : βρώσομαι Philostr.*VA*3. 40 : aor. ἔβρωσα (ἀν-) Nic.*Th.*134 ; inf. βρῶξαι (κατα-) Epic. in *Arch. Pap.*7.5 : Ep. aor. 2 ἔβρων Call.*Jov.*49, (κατ-) *h.Ap.*127 : pf. βέβρωκα Il.22.94, Eup.68 ; sync. part. βεβρώς, ῶτος, S.*Ant.*1022 ; opt. βεβρώθοις, as if from pf. βέβρωθα, Il.4.35 :—Pass., pres., Hp.*Aff.*4 : fut. βρωθήσομαι Lyc.1421, S.E.*P.*3.227 ; βεβρώσομαι Od.2.203 : aor ἐβρώθην Hp.*Acut.*37, etc., (κατ-) Hdt.3.16 : pf. βέβρωμαι A.*Ag.*1097 (lyr.), (δια-) Pl.*Ti.*83a, (κατα-) *SIG*$^{2}$587.310 : plpf. ἐβέβρωτο Hp.*Epid.*4.19. —In Ion. Prose and Lxx βέβρωκα ἐβρώθην βέβρωμαι take the place of Att. ἐδήδοκα ἠδέσθην ἐδήδεσμαι :—*eat, eat up*, βεβρωκὼς κακὰ φάρμακ' Il.22.94, etc. ; οὐδὲν βεβρ. Eup.68 : c. gen., *eat of* a thing, [λέων] βεβρωκὼς βοὸς Od.22.403 ; τῶν μελῶν βεβρωκότες Ar.*V.*463 ; κρειῶν τε καὶ αἵματος Theoc.25.224 : abs., βεβρωκώς, opp. πεινῶν, Arist.*HA* 629$^{b}$9 ; β. καὶ πεπωκὼς Id.*Fr.*232, cf. Plb.3.72.6, *Ev.Jo.*6.13 :—Pass., *to be eaten*, Hp.*Acut.*37 ; of teeth, *decay*, Id.*Epid.*4.19 ; χρήματα δ' αὖτε κακῶς βεβρώσεται *will be devoured*, Od.2.203 ; βεβρωμένοι ἄρτοι *mouldy* bread, Lxx *Jo.*9.12 ; ῥίζα βεβρ. *worm-eaten*, Dsc.3.9 ; *to be bitten*, ὑπὸ τῶν κροκοδείλων Gal.14.246.

**βίδην**, εἶδος, κροῦμα· ἄλλοι **βίθυν**, S.*Fr.*60 (ap.Hsch.) ; cf. βυδοί.

**βιδιαῖοι**, οἱ, *officers* at Sparta, whose duties were connected with the charge of the ephebi, five in number, acc. to Paus.3.11.2 ; but six in Inscrr. :—written **βίδεοι** *IG*5(1).32 *B*, al., **βίδυοι** ib.41 : sg. **βίδυιος** ib.1498.13 (Messenia, ii B.C.). (For ϝίδυιοι, i. e. *overseers.*)

❋ **βιζάριον**, τό, *she-camel* or *suckling camel*, *PLond.ined.*1821.

**βιζῆαι**· κοῖται, στιβάδες, Hsch.

**βῑημάχος** [ᾰ], ον, = βιαιομάχας, Ἔρως *AP*5.292.1 (Paul. Sil.) ; βασιλεύς ib.4.3b.2 (Agath.).

**βίθυν**, v. βίδην.

❋ **Βῑθῡνῐ-άρχης**, ου, ὁ, *President of the Provincial Council of Bithynia*, *OGI*528.10 (Prusias), al. : **-αρχία**, ἡ, *his office*, *Dig.*27.1.6.14, *IGRom.* 3.1427 (Βειθ-).

**βῖκας**· σφίγγας, Hsch.

❋ **βῑκίον**, τό, Dim. of βῖκος, v.l. in Dsc.2.78 ; β. ὑέλινον *Gp.*10.69.1 :—also **βῑκίδιον**, Suid.

❋ **βῑκίον**, τό, *vetch*, *Vicia sativa*, Gal.6.550 :—also ❋**βῖκία**, ἡ, *Edict. Diocl.*17.6, *Gp.*3.6.7 :—hence Adj. ϝίκειος, χόρτος *Hippiatr.*104.

❋ **βῖκος**, ὁ, *jar* or *cask*, Hdt.1.194, X.*An.*1.9.25, *PHal.*7.5 (iii B.C.), *PHib.*1.49 (iii B.C.), Lxx *Je.*19.1, etc. **2.** *drinking-bowl*, Pollux Par.ap.Ath.11.784d. **3.** *a measure*, *BGU*112.15 (i A.D.), *PTeb.* 472 (ii A.D.). [ῑ, v. Ephipp.8.2, Archestr.*Fr.*38.2.]

**βῑκόστομον**, τό, *opening of a receiving vessel*, of a still, Zos.Alch. p.224 B.

**βιλίσκος**, vulg., = ὀβελίσκος, *PLond.*2.329.

❋ **βιλλαρικός**, ή, όν, perh. = Lat. *villaticus*, *POxy.*1026.12 (v A.D.).

❋ **βιλλᾶς**, dub. sens. in Hdn.Gr.1.55. **βιλλίν**· τὸ αἰδοῖον, ib. 158. **βίλλος**, = foreg., ibid. **βιμβικίζεται**· περικρούεται, Hsch. **βίμβλινος**, = βίβλινος, Id.

❋ **βῑνέω**, *inire, coïre*, of illicit intercourse, opp. ὀπυίω, Sol.ap. Hsch., Ar.*Ra.*740 : c. acc. pers., Id.*Av.*560, etc. :—Med., Ion. impf. βινεσκόμην Id.*Eq.*1242 :—Pass., of the woman, Eup.351.2, Philetaer. 9.4.

**βῑνητιάω**, Desiderat. of βινέω, *coïre cupio*, of the woman, Ar.*Lys.* 715, Machoap.Ath.13.583c ; of the man, Luc.*Pseudol.*27.

**βῐο-γρᾰφία**, ἡ, *biography*, Dam.*Isid.*8. **-δότης**, ου, ὁ, *giver of livelihood*, θεὸς Pl.*Lg.*921a. **-δωρος**, ον, *life-giving*, ἀμαχανίας ἄκος Pi.*Pae.*3.26 ; νύμφαις . . ποταμοῦ παισὶν β. A.*Fr.*168 (hex.) ; αἶα S.*Ph.*1162 (lyr.) : in late Prose, γῆ Artem.2.39. **-δώτης**, ου, ὁ, = βιοδότης, of Apollo, *AP*9.525.3 ; voc. βιοδῶτα *IG*14.1015 :—fem. **-δῶτις**, ιδος, Orph.*H.*29.3. **-δώτωρ**, ορος, ὁ, = foreg., ib.73.2, *IG*3.

239. 2. *furnishing a livelihood*, [ναῦς] *AP*7.585 (Jul.). **-ζῠγής**, ές, *linking lives together*, ὑμέναιοι Nonn.*D*.33.179. ⊛ **-θάλμιος**, ον, (θάλλω) *strong, hale*, *h.Ven*.189. **-θᾰνᾰσία**, = βιαιο–, Ptol.*Tetr*. 85. **-θάνᾰτος** [θᾰ], = βιαιο–, *PMag.Par*.1.1950. **-θρέμμων**, ον, gen. ονος, *life-supporting*, πάντων Ar.*Nu*.570 (lyr.); φῦλα Orph.*H*.34.19. **-θρέπτειρα**, ἡ, fem. of foreg., ib.27.13. **-κλώστειρα**, ἡ, *spinning the thread of life*, of Fate, *Arch.Pap*.1.221 (ii B.C.). ⊛ **-κουρος**, ὁ, (*via, curo*), = IIIvir *viarum curandarum*, *IGRom*.4.1307 (Lydia). **-κωλύτης** [ῡ], ου, ὁ, *an officer to suppress violence* or *lawlessness*, Just.*Nov*.8.12, al. **-λογέομαι**, Pass., *to be sketched from life*, esp. *common life*, τὰ βιολογούμενα Longin.9.15. **-λογικός**, ή, όν, *of a* βιολόγος, κωμῳδίαι, = μῖμοι, Suid. s.v. Φιλιστίων. ⊛ **-λόγος**, ὁ, *one who represents to the life, player*, *IG*14.2342, *POxy*.1025.7 (iii A.D.). **-μήχᾰνος**, ον, *clever at getting a living*, Antipho Soph.41; of birds, Arist.*HA*$616^{b}$17, al. **-μορος**, ον, = βιαιοθάνατος, *PMag.Par*.1.1400. **-πλαγκτος**, ον, = sq., τύχη Nonn.*D*.3.356. **-πλᾰνής**, ές, *wandering to get one's living, a beggar*, βιοπλανές (poet. nom. pl. for -πλανέες) Call.*Fr*.497: neut. sg. βιόπλανες Hdn.Gr.ap.*Et.Gen*., A.D.*Pron*.93.8. **-πονητικός**, ή, όν, = sq., Hippodam.ap.Stob.4.1.94. **-πόνος**, ον, *living by labour*, ib.93. ⊛ **-πρᾱγος**, ον, *prosperous, successful*, Astramps. *Orac*.85, al. ⊛ **-πρᾱτος**, ὁ, *ne'er-do-weel*, *POxy*.1477.14 (iii/iv A.D.).

**βιορρός**· δουλεία, Hsch. (fort. εἴρερος).

⊛ **βίος** [ῐ], ὁ, *life*, i.e. not animal life (ζωή), but *mode of life* (cf. εἰ χρόνον τις λέγοι ψυχῆς ἐν κινήσει μεταβατικῇ ἐξ ἄλλου εἰς ἄλλον βίον ζωὴν εἶναι Plot.3.7.11), *manner of living* (mostly therefore of men, v. Ammon. p.32 V.; but also of animals, διεχώριζον ζῴων τε βίον δένδρων τε φύσιν Epicr.11.14, cf. X.*Mem*.3.11.6, etc.; also ζῆν φυτοῦ βίον Arist.*GA*$736^{b}$13); ζώεις δ' ἀγαθὸν βίον Od.15.491; ἐμὸν βίον ἀμφιπολεύειν 18.254; αἰῶνα βίοιο Hes.*Fr*.161; τὸν μακρὸν τείνειν βίον A.*Pr*.537 (lyr.); ὁ καθ' ἡμέραν β. S.*OC*1364; βίον διαγαγεῖν Ar.*Pax*439; τελεῖν S.*Ant*.1114; διατελεῖν Isoc.6.45; διέρχεσθαι βίου τέλος dub. in Pi.*I*.4(3).5; τελευτᾶν Isoc.4.84; ὑπ' ἄλλου τελευτῆσαι β. Pl.*Lg*.870e; ἐπειδὰν τοῦ ἀνθρωπίνου βίου τελευτήσω X.*Cyr*.8.7.17; τέρμα βίου περᾶν S.*OT*1530; ὁδὸς βίου Isoc.1.5, cf. X.*Mem*.2.1.21; διὰ βίου Arist.*Pol*.$1272^{a}$37; prov., ὁ ἐπὶ Κρόνου βίος 'the Golden Age', Id.*Ath*.16.7; so Ταρτησσοῦ β. Him.*Ecl*.10.11; β. ζωῆς Pl.*Epin*.982a (cf. βιοτή); ζῆν θαλάττιον β. Antiph.100; ἀμέριμνον ζῆν β. Philem.92.8; λαγὼ β. ζῆν δεδιὼς καὶ τρέμων D.18.263; σκληρὸς τῷ β. Men.*Georg*.66: rarely in pl., Alex.116.6 and 11, Men.855; τίνες καὶ πόσοι εἰσὶ β.; Pl.*Lg*.733d, cf. Arist.*EN*$1095^{b}$15, *Pol*.$1256^{a}$20. 2. in Poets sts. = ζωή, βίον ἐκπνέων A.*Ag*.1517 (lyr.); ἀποψύχειν S.*Aj*.1031; φείδεσθαι βίου Id.*Ph*.749; νοσφίζειν τινὰ βίου ib.1427, etc. 3. *lifetime*, ἐς τὸν ἅπαντα ἀνθρώπων β. Hdt.6.109; τῶν ἐπὶ τοῦ σοῦ β. γεγονότων λόγων Pl.*Phdr*. 242a, cf. *PMagd*.18.7 (iii B.C.), etc. II. *livelihood, means of living* (in Hom. βίοτος), βίος ἐπηετανός Hes.*Op*.31, Pi.*N*.6.10; τὸν βίον κτᾶσθαι, ποιεῖσθαι, ἔχειν ἀπό τινος, to make one's *living* off, to *live* by a thing, Hdt.8.106, Th.1.5, X.*Oec*.6.11; ἀπεστέρηκας τὸν βίον τὰ τόξ' ἑλών S.*Ph*.931, cf. 933,1282; κτᾶσθαι πλοῦτον καὶ βίον τέκνοις E.*Supp*.450; πλείον' ἐκμοχθεῖν β. ib.451; β. πολύς ib.861; ὀλίγος Ar.*Pl*.751; βίον κεκτημένος Philem.99.4; ὁ ἴδιος β. private *property*, *AJA*17.29 (i B.C.), cf. *SIG*762.40, Iamb.*VP*30.170; β. Δημήτριος, = *corn*, A.*Fr*.44. III. *the world we live in*, 'the world', οἱ ἀπὸ τοῦ β., opp. *the philosophers*, S.E.*M*.11.49; simply ὁ βίος Id.*P*.1.211; ὁ β. ὁ κοινός ib.237; μυθικὰς ὑποθέσεις ὧν μεστὸς ὁ β. ἐστί Ph.1.226; ἐκκαθαίρειν τὸν β., of Hercules, Luc.*DDeor*.13.1; τὸν βίον μιμούμενοι, of comic poets, Sch.Heph.p.115 C.; also, 'the public', ἵνα ὁ β. εἰδῇ τίνα δεῖ μετακαλεῖσθαι Sor.1.4. IV. *settled life*, almost, = *abode*, ἐν τῇ Θρακίᾳ νήσῳ βίους ἱδρύσαντο D.H.1.68, cf. 72. V. *a life, biography*, as those of Plu., *Thes*.1, cf. Ph.2.180. VI. *caste*, διεῖλε τὸ πλῆθος εἰς τέτταρας β. Str.8.7.1. VII. *wine made from partly dried unripe grapes*, Plin.*HN*14.77. VIII. Astrol., *the second region*, Paul.Al.*L*.2. (Cf. Skt. *jīvás* 'alive', *jīvati* 'live', Lat. *vīvus*, etc.)

**βῐός**, ὁ, *bow*, = τόξον, Il.1.49, Heraclit.48, etc. (Ambracian acc. to *AB*1095. Cf. Vedic *jiyā́* 'bow-string', Lith. *gijà* 'thread'.)

**βιόσσαο**· τὸ ζῆν ἔδωκας, βιῶσαι ἐποίησας, Hsch. (i.e. ἐβιώσαο).

**βῐοσσόος**, ον, *life-supporting* or *-preserving*, Nonn.*D*.33.109, 41.333, al.

**βῐοστερής**, ές, *reft of the means of life*, S.*OC*747.

⊛ **βῐοτεία**, ἡ, *way of life*, X.*Oec*.6.10, Plb.6.7.5.

**βῐο-τελής**, ές, dub. sens., *EM*198.11. **-τέρμων**, ον, gen. ονος, *marking the beginning of life*, ὥρη Man.4.77. II. *lasting till the close of life*, πλοῦτος Antioch.Astr. in *Cat.Cod.Astr*.1.110.

**βῐότ-ευμα**, ατος, τό, *manner of life*, Socr.*Ep*.29. **-εύω**, *live*, Pi.*N*.4.6; ἀβίωτον χρόνον β. E.*Alc*.243 (lyr.); β. ἀκρατῶς Arist.*EN*$1114^{a}$16; φαιδρῶς X.*Cyr*.4.6.6. 2. *get food*, αὐτόθεν πολεμοῦντα Th.1.11; *live* by or off a thing, ἀπὸ πολέμου X.*Cyr*.3.2.25; ἀπὸ τῶν ἀκανθῶν Arist.*HA*$610^{a}$5. 3. *reside*, ἐς θάλασσαν Aret.*CD*1.2; ἐν χώρῃσι θερμῇσι ib.4. **-ή**, ἡ, = βίοτος, βίος, Od.4.565, Phoc.10; ἑκατονταετὴς β. Pi.*P*.4.282: Trag. in lyr., A.*Pers*.853, S.*Ph*.690, E.*Andr*.785; rare in Prose, Hdt.7.47, Democr.200,297, X.*Cyr*.7.2.27, Ael.*NA*2.23: metaph. of foods, τὰ ἀσθενέστερα σιτία ὀλιγοχρόνιον β. ἔχει Hp.*Epid*.6.5.14. II. *living, sustenance*, S.*Ph*.164,1159, Ar.*V*.1452 (lyr.). **-ης**, ητος, ἡ, = foreg., *h.Hom*.8.10, *IG*14.1449. **-ήσιος**, ον, *supporting life*, ὦνος A.R.2.1006; ναυτιλίη β. voyage *of life*, *AP*9.208; ἴχνος ὅπου λήγει β. Benndorf-Niemann *Reisen in Lykien u. Karien* p.79. **-ιον**, τό, Dim. of βίοτος, *scant living*, Ar.*Pl*.1165. ⊛ **-ος**, ὁ, Ep., = βίος I, *life*, βιότοιο τελευτή Il.7.104, cf. Emp.15.2, A.*Pers*.360, al. II. = βίος II, *means of living, substance*, ναῖε δὲ δῶμα ἀφνειὸν βιότοιο Il.14.122; β. κατακείρετε πολλόν Od.4.686; γύαι φέρουσι β. ἄφθονον βροτοῖς A.*Fr*.196; βιότου κτῆσις Ar.*Av*.718, cf. *Ec*.669:—in late Prose, *PLond*.5.1889 (vi A.D.). III. = βίος III, *the world, mankind*, μνήμῃ βιότου παρέδωκεν *Epigr.Gr*.319 (Philadelphia).

**βῐοτοσκόπος**, ον, *of* or *for casting a nativity*, ὥρη Man.4.572.

**βῐο-τρόφος**, ον, *life-sustaining*, πνοή Aenigm. in *App.Anth*.7.69. **-φειδής**, ές, *penurious*, *AP*6.251 (Phil.). **-φθορία**, ἡ, *destruction of life*, Orph.*H*.73.8. ⊛ **-φθόρος**, ον, *destructive of life*, χρυσός Ps.-Phoc.44.

⊛ **βῐόω**, βιοῖ Arist.*HA*$558^{a}$20; βιοῦσι Democr.200, Arist.*HA*$576^{b}$2; βιοῦν E.*Fr*.238, etc.; part. βιοῦντες Arist.*HA*$566^{b}$24; subj. βιῶσι Emp.15.2: impf. ἐβίουν Hp.*Epid*.5.48: fut. βιώσομαι E.*Alc*.784, Ar.*Eq*.699, Pl.*R*.344e, Men.*Pk*.399; later βιώσω Id.*Mon*.270, App.*BC*4.119: aor. 1 ἐβίωσα Hdt.1.163, Pl.*Phd*.113d, X.*Oec*.4.18, Arist.*HA*$585^{a}$21; but in earlier writers aor. 2 is more used, ἐβίων Isoc.9.71, Is.3.1 codd.; 3 sg. imper. βιώτω Il.8.429; subj. βιῶ Pl.*Lg*.872c; opt. βιῴην Id.*Ti*.89c, v.l. for βιοίη in Id.*Grg*.512e; inf. βιῶναι Il.10.174, Aeschin.3.174, etc.; part. βιούς Hdt.9.10, Th.2.53, al.: pf. βεβίωκα Isoc.15.27 and 28, Pl.*Phd*.113d, etc.:—**Med.**, βιόομαι Hdt.2.177, Arist.*EN*$1180^{a}$17: for aor. Med. v. βιώσκομαι:—**Pass.**, fut. βιωθήσομαι M.Ant.9.30: pf. βεβίωμαι (v. infr.).—In early writers pres. and impf. are mostly supplied by ζάω: Hom. has only aor. 2:—*live, pass one's life* (opp. ζάω, *live, exist*), βέλτερον ἢ ἀπολέσθαι ἕνα χρόνον ἠὲ βιῶναι Il.15.511, cf. 10.174; ἄλλος μὲν ἀποφθίσθω, ἄλλος δὲ βιώτω 8.429; βίον βιοῦν Pl.*La*.188a, etc.; β. παρανόμως, μετρίως, ἐνδόξως, D.22.24, Lys.16.3, Plu.2.145f: with neut. Pron., ἀπ' αὐτῶν ὧν αὐτὸς βεβίωκεν ἄρξομαι.. from the very *actions of* his own *life*, D.18.130:—Pass., τὰ σοὶ κἀμοὶ βεβιωμένα *the actions of* our *life*, ib.265, cf. Isoc.15.7, Lys.16.1; τὰ πεπραγμένα καὶ βεβ. D.22.53; τοιούτων ὄντων ἃ τῷ βδελυρῷ τούτῳ..βεβίωται Id.21.151; ἐπιτηδευμάτων οἷα τούτῳ βεβίωται Id.22.78; ὅ γε βεβιωμένος [βίος] Id.19.200; impers., βεβίωταί [μοι] I *have lived*, Lat. *vixi*, Cic.*Att*.12.2.2, 14.21.3:—Med. in act. sense, Hdt.2.177, Arist.*EN*$1180^{a}$17. 2. *survive*, ἐβίω καυθείς Hp.*Epid*.5.16.—βιόμεσθα (as if from βίομαι) is found *h.Ap*.528 and 3 pl. βίονται Orac.ap.Phleg.*Mir*.2, cf. βέομαι.

**βιόωνται, -το**, v. βιάω.

⊛ **βιπίννιον**, τό, Dim. of Lat. *bipennis*, *Edict.Diocl.* in *IG*5(1).1406.9 (Asine).

**βιπτάζω**, for βαπτίζω, Epich.175, Sophr.114.

**βίρρη**· πυράγρα, οἱ δὲ δρέπανον, Hsch. **βίρροξ**· δασύ (Maced.), Id.

⊛ **βίρρος**, ὁ, Lat. *birrus*, a kind of *cloak*, Artem.2.3, *PGiss*.76.4 (ii A.D.), *Edict.Diocl*.19.26, al., Hierocl.*Facet*.99, Suid. (Cf. βύρρος.)

**βιρρωθῆναι**· ταπεινωθῆναι, Hsch.

**βίσβη**, ἡ, *pruning-hook* (Messap.), Hsch.:—hence **Βισβαῖα**, τά, a festival, = κλαδευτήρια, Id.

**βίσκαρις**· εἶδος βοτάνης, Hsch.

**βιστάκιον**, τό, = πιστ., Posidon.6, v.l. in Nic.*Th*.891, acc. to Ath.14.649d.

**βίσταξ**· βασιλεύς (Pers.), Hsch. **βιστήνη**· καρδία, Id.

**βίσχυν**, Adv. = σφόδρα ὀλίγον (Lacon.), Hsch., cf. Hdn.Gr.1.509.

**βίσων** [ῐ], ωνος, ὁ, *bison*, Paus.10.13.1, Opp.*C*.2.160.

**βίτος**, ὁ, *tyre*, *Edict.Diocl*.15.31a:—hence **βιτωτός**, ή, όν, *with tyres*, τροχοί ib.34; σαράγαρα, καροῦχον β., *with tyred wheels*, ib.36,37.

⊛ **βίττακος**, ου, ὁ, = ψίττακος, Eub.123, Ctes.*Fr*.57.3.

**βιῷ, βιῴην, ϝιῶναι, βιώτω**, v. βιόω. **βιῴατο**, v. βιάω.

**βιώλεθρος**, ον, *destructive of life*, Hdn.*Epim*.203, Zonar.

**βιώνης**, ου, ὁ, (ὠνέομαι) *one who buys food* on the public account, Hsch., Suid.

**βίωρ** (i.e. ϝίωρ)· ἴσως (Lacon.), Hsch.

**βιώσιμος**, ον, (βιόω) *to be lived*, χρόνος E.*Alc*.650; αἱ β. ἡμέραι Lib.*Decl*.2.34; esp. οὐ βιώσιμόν ἐστί τινι 'tis not *meet* for him to *live*, Hdt.1.45; τί γὰρ μόνῃ μοι τῆσδ' ἄτερ β.; S.*Ant*.566; οὐκ ἂν ἦν βιώσιμα ἀνθρώποισι Hdt.3.109. 2. *likely to live*, Thphr.*HP*9.12.1, Arr.*An*.2.4.8.

**βίωσις**, εως, ἡ, *way of life*, Lxx *Si.prol*.12, *Act.Ap*.26.4: in a Jewish Inscr., ἐνάρετος β. *IGRom*.4.655 (Acmonia, i A.D.); ἐν μιᾷ β. μετ' ἀλλήλων *PMasp*.158.26 (vi A.D.).

**βῐ-ώσκομαι**, causal of βιόω, *quicken, make* or *keep alive*, once in Hom. in aor., σὺ γάρ μ' ἐβιώσαο, κούρη Od.8.468; cf. βιόσσαο: the pres. occurs in the compd. ἀναβιώσκομαι. II. later in pass. sense, *revive*, ἕτεροι τόποι βιώσκονται Arist.*Mete*.$351^{a}$35; simply, *live*, βιωσαμένῳ *IG*14.2100; βιώσκεσθαι Arr.*Ind*.9. **-ωτέον**, *one must live*, Pl.*Grg*.500d, Lib.*Decl*.35.15. **-ωτικός**, ή, όν, *fit for life, lively*, τὴν διάνοιαν β. καὶ εὐμήχανος, = βιομήχανος, Arist.*HA*$616^{b}$27; acc. to Phryn.332 (who condemns the word), = χρήσιμος ἐν τῷ βίῳ, as in Sotad.6.12. II. *of* or *pertaining to life*, Plb.4.73.8, D.S.2.29, Ph.2.159; χάριτες Plu.2.142b; ἀηδίαι Artem.2.30; ἡ -κή (sc. τέχνη) M.Ant.7.61; τὰ β. κριτήρια, opp. λογικά, S.E.*P*.2.15; μέριμναι β. *Ev.Luc*.21.34; β. φροντίς Iamb.*Protr*.21.α'; β. σύμβολα *business documents*, *PTeb*.52.9 (ii B.C.); β. θρησκεία *popular* superstition (cf. βίος III), Sor.1.4; ὁ β. νόμος Arr.*Epict*.1.26 tit.; τὰ β. ib.3, cf. Plu.2.679d. Adv. **-κῶς** *in the tone of common life*, D.T.629; *in popular language*, Gal.10.269. 2. **βιωτικά**, τά, *victuals*, *PRyl*.125.11 (i A.D.); ἡ β. ἀγορά *BCH*44.74 (Lagina). **-ωτός**, όν, *to be lived, worth living*, mostly with neg., ἔμοιγ' ὁ μέλλων βίος οὐ β. S.*OC*1692 (lyr.), cf. Ar.*Pl*.197 (dub.), Pl.*Ap*.38a; οὐ βιωτὸν οὐδ' ἀνασχετόν Antiph.190.

10; οὐκ ἦν μοι β. τοῦτο ποιήσαντι D.21.120; ἆρ' οὖν β. ἡμῖν ἐστιν μετὰ μοχθηροῦ σώματος Pl.*Cri.*47e. ⊛ -ωφελής, ές, *useful for life*, Ph.2.88, al., Luc.*Am.*51; of persons, Ptol.*Tetr.*183: Comp., Ph.2.633: Sup., ib.480, Agath.1.7. Adv. -λῶς S.E.*M.*1.279.

**βλᾰβεραυγής**, ές, *baneful-gleaming*, Man.4.309.

**βλᾰβερός**, ά, όν, *harmful*, β. τὸ θύρηφιν Hes.*Op.*365 (= *h.Merc.*36); opp. συμφέρον, Democr.237; opp. ὠφέλιμος, X.*Cyr.*8.8.14; β. καὶ ζημιώδες Pl.*Cra.*417d. Adv. -ρῶς Id.*Phdr.*243c; opp. ὠφελίμως, Id.*Chrm.*164c, cf. Plu.2.599b.

⊛ **βλάβ-η** [ᾰ], ἡ, (v. βλάπτω) *harm, damage*, A.*Pr.*763, *IG*1$^{2}$.18, etc.; πεπονθέναι.. ἐς βλάβην φέρον S.*OT*517; τίς β.; c. inf., Id.*OC*1187; οἷς ἦν ἐν β. τειχισθέν Th.5.52; προσκαλοῦμαί σε.. βλάβης τῶν φορτίων Ar.*V.*1407; β. θεοῦ *mischief from* a god, E.*Ion*520, cf. S.*Ant.*1104; of a person, ἡ πᾶσα β. who is naught but *mischief*, Id.*El.*301, cf. 784, *Ph.*622: pl., ἐν ὄμμασιν βλάβας ἔχω A.*Ag.*889, cf. *Eu.*799; αἱματηρὰς θηγάνας, σπλάγχνων βλάβας νέων ib.859. 2. βλάβης δίκη an action *for damage done*, D.21.25; β. τετραπόδων *damage done by* cattle, Plu.*Sol.*24; β. τῶν θηρίων Id.2.642b (pl.); οἰκῆος καὶ δούλης τὴν β. εἶναι ὀφείλειν Sol.ap.Lys.10.19; οἱ περὶ τῆς β. νόμοι.. ἁπλοῦν τὸ βλάβος κελεύουσιν ἐκτίνειν D.21.43; διπλῆν τὴν β. ὀφείλειν (ὀφλεῖν Meier) Din.1.60, cf. *Foed.Delph.Pell.*1 B 7. -όεις, εσσα, εν, = βλαβερός, Nic.*Al.*186. -ομαι, = βλάπτομαι, only 3 sg., βλάβεται δέ τε γούνατ' ἰόντι Il.19.166; *stumble, hesitate*, of a speaker, ib.82; of a bowstring, *Anacreont.*31.26. -ος, gen. εος, contr. ους, τό, = βλάβη, Hdt.1.9, E.*Heracl.*255, *Ion*998, Ar.*Ra.*1151, Antipho 5.91, Pl.*Lg.*843c, *Foed.Delph.Pell.*2 A 12, Arist.*Pol.*1328$^{a}$14, *PRyl.*126.19 (i A.D.); distd. from βλάβη, D.21.43 (v. βλάβη 2). (More Attic than βλάβη acc. to Moer.103.)

**βλαβύρει**· πτερύσσεται, Hsch. **βλαβυρία**· εἰκαιολογία, Id. **βλαβύσσειν**· βλάπτεσθαι, Id. **βλαγίς**· κηλίς (Lacon.), Id. **βλαδάν**· νωθρῶς, Id.

⊛ **βλᾰδᾰρός**, ά, όν, = πλαδαρός, *flaccid*, cj. in Gal.19.88:—Hsch. has **βλᾰδός** and **βλᾰδύς** (which is prob. in Hp.*Aër.*20). (With βλαδύς cf. Skt. *mṛdús* 'soft', Lat. *mollis*; cf. μέλδομαι, ἀμαλδύνω.)

**βλάζειν**· μωραίνειν, Hsch. **βλάθρον**, = βλῆχνον, Id. **βλαί-βλητή** (leg. βληχή) (Lacon.), Id. **βλαῖκος**· ὁ δαλός, κλάδος, ὄζος, *EM*199.31.

**βλαισ-όομαι**, Pass., *to be crooked*, pf. ἐβλαίωται Arist.*HA*498$^{a}$21; but βεβλ- Id.*IA*713$^{b}$4, Gal.18(1).677. -ός, ή, όν, *bent, distorted*: hence, *splay-footed*, Hp.*Art.*53, cf. 82 (Comp.); ἐς τὸ β. ῥέπων ib.62, cf. Gal.18(1).674, al.; οἱ β. τῶν ἀνθρώπων X.*Eq.*1.3; also, *bandy*, β. καρκίνοι Batr.297, cf. Arist.*HA*526$^{a}$23; τὰ β. τῶν ὀπισθίων *the hollow* of the hind-leg in which bees carry the pollen, ib.624$^{b}$2: generally, *twisted, crooked*, πλατάνιστος *AP*4.1.17 (Mel.); κισσός ib.7.21 (Simm.). -ότης, ητος, ἡ, *crookedness, curvature*, τῶν σκελῶν Arist.*IA*713$^{b}$9; *curliness*, τῶν τριχῶν Id.*Pr.*909$^{a}$31. -ώδης, ες, = βλαισός, Gal.6.328. -ωσις, εως, ἡ, = βλαισότης, Gal.*UP*3.9. II. metaph., *retorting of a dilemma* on its proposer, Arist.*Rh.*1399$^{a}$26.

**βλαιτόνους**· ὁ βλαισόπους, *EM*199.32.

**βλᾰκ-εία** (-ία, Hsch.), ἡ, (βλάξ) *slackness*, X.*Cyr.*2.2.25, 7.5.84; *stupidity*, Pl.*Euthd.*287e, Phld.*Mus.*p.56 K., Hierocl.*in CA*17 p.457 M.; τὸ τῆς β. πεδίον Luc.*VH*2.33. -εννόμιον τέλος tax paid by astrologers at Alexandria (because *fools* consult them), *EM* 199.11. -ευμα, ατος, τό, *stupid trick*, Eust.1405.33. -εύω, *to be slack, lazy*, X.*An.*2.3.11, 5.8.15, Phld.*Hom.*p.39 O., etc.; ἐν τῇ κατατάσει Hp.*Fract.*17; β. καὶ ἀποδειλιᾶν D.H.9.31:—Med. (which is cited from X. by Eust.1405.32), = τρυφάω, Hld.7.27; but Act. in this sense, Procop.*Arc.*9. II. c. acc., *lose* or *waste through laziness*, Luc.*Ep.Sat.*26. -ίας· ἰχθύς ποιός, Hsch. -ικός, ή, όν, (βλάξ) *stupid*, Pl.*R.*432d, X.*Oec.*8.17, etc.; *lazy, sluggish*, δειλὰ καὶ β. Pl.*Plt.*307c; β. τὸ ἦθος Arist.*HA*618$^{b}$5. Adv. -κῶς Ar.*Av.*1323. -ότης, ητος, ἡ, = βλακεία, Steph.*in Hp.*1.63,97 D. -ώδης, ες, *lazy*, X.*Eq.*9.1 (Comp.); βλακωδῶς βαίνειν καὶ θρύπτεσθαι walk *mincingly*, of a coxcomb, Hld.4.7. Adv. -δῶς *indolently, stolidly*, Poll.3.123: Comp. -έστερον ibid.

**βλάμμα**, ατος, τό, = βλάβη, opp. ὠφέλημα, Chrysipp.*Stoic.*3.71 (pl.), Phld.*Rh.*1.215 S. (pl.); expl. of σίνος, Gal.18(2).445.

**βλάνος**· τυφλώδης, Hsch.

**βλάξ**, βλᾶκός, ὁ, ἡ, *stolid, stupid*, Pl.*Grg.*488a; β. καὶ ἠλίθιος X.*Cyr.*1.4.12; β. καὶ ἄφρων Arist.*EE*1247$^{a}$18; θεὸς κολάζει τοὺς βλᾶκας X.*Oec.*8.16, cf. Plb.16.22.5; β. ἄνθρωπος Heraclit.87: usually of persons, but β. ἵππος, opp. θυμοειδής, X.*Eq.*9.12: Comp. βλακότερος or -ώτερος Id.*Mem.*4.2.40: Sup. βλακότατος or -ώτατος (but -ίστατος ap.Ath.) ib.3.13.4. II. name of a *fish*, ὃς ἐν τῷ συνουσιάζειν δυσαπολύτως ἔχει, Erot. s. v. βλακεύειν. (Perh. βλᾱ- < μλᾱ-, cf. Skt. *mlāyati* 'become soft', μαλακός: Hsch., ἀπό τινος ἰχθύος δασώδους (leg. δυσώδους).)

**βλαπτ-ήριος**, ον, = sq., Opp.*H.*2.456. -ικός, ή, όν, *hurtful, mischievous*, δυνάμεις Ph.1.14, cf. S.E.*M.*6.4, etc.: c. gen., ἀνθρώπων Str.15.1.45, cf. Phld.*Piet.*99,100. Adv. -κῶς Arr.*Epict.*3.23.4, Ptol.*Tetr.*168.

**βλάπτω**, fut. -ψω E.*Heracl.*704, etc.: aor. ἔβλαψα, Ep. βλάψε Il.23.774: aor. 2 ἔβλᾰβον Q.S.5.509: pf. βέβλᾰφα D.19.180, Plb.12.26.2, ἔβλαφα (κατ-) *IG*7.303.51 (Oropus):—Pass., fut. βλᾰβήσομαι Isoc.1.25, Pl.*Men.*77e, *Grg.*475d, *Hp.Mi.*373a; βεβλάψομαι Hp.*Acut.*16: also fut. Med. βλάψομαι (in pass. signf.) Th.1.81, 6.64: aor. 1 ἐβλάφθην Il.16.331, etc.: aor. 2 ἐβλάβην [ᾰ], 3 pl. ἔβλαβεν, βλάβεν, 23.461, 545, part. βλᾰβείς A.*Ag.*120 (lyr.) (aor. Med. βλάψαντο only in Q.S.5.466): pf. βέβλαμμαι Il.16.660, etc.:—*disable, hinder*, μή τιν' ἑταίρων βλάπτοι ἐλαυνόντων Od.13.22; βλάψας δέ μοι ἵππους Il.23.571; β. πόδας *disable* the feet for running, *lame* them, ib.782:—Pass., ζωὸν ἕλε βλαφθέντα κατὰ κλόνον *entangled* in the mêlée, 16.331; ὄζῳ ἔνι βλαφθέντε μυρικίνῳ [the horses] *caught* in a branch, 6.39; βλάβεν ἅρματα καὶ ταχέ' ἵππω chariots and horses *were stopped*, 23.545; Διόθεν βλαφθέντα βέλεμνα *stopped, baffled* by Zeus, 15.489, cf. 484; βεβλαμμένος ἦτορ *stopped* in his life (s. v. l.), 16.660. 2. c. gen., *hinder from*, τόν γε θεοὶ βλάπτουσι κελεύθου Od.1.195; οὐδέ τις αὐτὸν βλάπτειν οὔτ' αἰδοῦς οὔτε δίκης ἐθέλει Tyrt.12.40 (repeated in Thgn. 938):—Pass., βλαβέντα λοισθίων δρόμων *arrested in* its last course, A.*Ag.*120 (lyr.). II. of the mind, *distract, pervert, mislead*, of the gods, τὸν δέ τις ἀθανάτων βλάψε φρένας Od.14.178, cf. *Trag.Adesp.* 455: c. acc. pers., Il.22.15, Od.23.14; so of Ate, φθάνει δέ τε πᾶσαν ἐπ' αἶαν βλάπτουσ' ἀνθρώπους Il.9.507; also of wine, Od.21.294; βλαφθείς, Lat. *mente captus*, Il.9.512: so c. gen., ἥ τε [Περσεφόνη].. βλάπτουσα νόοιο Thgn.705; νόου βεβλαμμένος ἐσθλοῦ Id.223. III. after Hom., *damage, hurt*, οἷσι μὴ βλάψῃ θεός (sc. τὰ τέκνα) A.*Eu.* 661, etc.: with neut. Adj., πλεῖω β. τινά Th.6.33; μείζω Pl.*Ap.*30c; ἄλλο τι X.*HG*1.1.22, etc.:—Pass., μεγάλα βεβλάφθαι Id.*Cyr.*5.3.30; βεβλαμμένος τὸν ὀφθαλμόν *PStrassb.*52.2 (ii A.D.), etc.: c. acc. cogn., β. τοὺς βίους μείζους βλάβας *do* greater *mischiefs to*.., Posidipp.12.4: c. dupl. acc., β. τὴν πόλιν τοὺς ὑπολοίπους *rob* her *of*.., App.*BC*2.131:—Pass., τοσούσδε βλαβῆναι τὴν πόλιν *lose* them, Id.*Hann.*28; τὸ βλαβέν, = βλάβη, Pl.*Lg.*933e. 2. c. acc. rei, β. λόγον *mar* the prophecy, Pi.*P.*9.94; τοὺς ὅρκους *violate* them, Arist.*Fr.*148. (βλαπ- < μλαπ- (*mlq$^{u}$*), cf. Skt. *marcáyati* 'injure', *mṛktás* 'wounded', Lat. *mulco* 'maltreat'.)

**βλάσαμον**, τό, metath. for βάλσαμον, v.l. in Nic.*Al.*64.

**βλάσκει**· λέγει, καπνίζει, Hsch. **βλασκίας**, ὁ, a *fish*, Id. **βλαστά**· πλαταγώνια (Sicel), Id. ⊛ **βλαστάζειν**· βλιμάζειν, Id.

**βλαστάνω**, S.*OC*611, etc. (later **βλαστέω**, Thphr.*CP*2.17.4 (interpol. in A.*Ch.*589, corrupt in Pass. -ουμένη S.*Fr.*255.7)); Ion. impf. βλαστάνεσκε (v.l. βλάστεσκεν) Id.*Fr.*546: fut. βλαστήσω Thphr.*HP* 2.7.2, βλαστήσομαι Alex.Trall.12: aor. 2 ἔβλαστον S.*Fr.*341, etc.: aor. 1 ἐβλάστησα Emp.21.10, Hp.*Nat.Puer.*26, etc. (not in Att.): pf. βεβλάστηκα Id.*Oss.*12, Hellanic.1(b) J., Plu.2.684c; ἐβλάστηκα E.*IA* 594 (lyr.), Eup.329: plpf. ἐβεβλαστήκει Th.3.26:—*bud, sprout, grow*, prop. of plants, A.*Th.*594, S.*OC*697 (lyr.), Th. l. c., Ar.*Nu.*1124, etc.; ἦ βλαστὸς οὐκ ἔβλαστεν; S.*Fr.*341; εἰς ἴα σου.., καὶ ἐς κρίνα βλαστήσειεν ὀστέα *IG*14.607 (Carales). 2. metaph. in Poets, *shoot forth, come to light*, βλάστε νᾶσος ἐξ ἁλός, of Rhodes, Pi.*O.*7.69; of children, *to be born*, Id.*N.*8.7; ἀνθρώπου φύσιν βλαστὼν *born* in man's nature, S.*Aj.*761, cf. *OT*1376, *El.*440; ἄργυρος κακὸν νόμισμ' ἔβλαστε Id.*Ant.* 296; β. δ' ἀπιστία Id.*OC*611; μέγιστ' ἔβλαστε νόμιμα Id.*El.*1095 (lyr.); not common in Prose, Th. l. c., Pl.*R.*498b, *Phdr.*251b, Iamb.*Myst.*3.28. II. causal, *make to grow, produce, propagate*, in pres., Hp.*Alim.*54: metaph., β. χάριτες εὔνοιαν Aristeas 230: mostly aor. 1 ἐβλάστησα A.R.1.1131; θεὸς.. ἄμπελον ἐβλάστησεν Nonn.*D.*36.356, cf. Lxx *Ge.*1.11, *Nu.*17.8:—Pass., βλαστηθείς Ph.1.667.

**βλασταρίζουσα**· ἐπικροτοῦσα, Hsch. **βλαστάριον**· ἕλιξ ἀμπέλου, *EM*330.30.

**βλαστ-άω**, late form of βλαστάνω, trans., *bring forth*, Lxx *Ec.*2.6: intr., Sch.Pi.*P.*4.113. -εῖον, τό, = βλάστη, Nic.*Al.*609 (pl.). -η, ἡ, = βλαστός, S.*Ichn.*276, Pl.*Lg.*765e, etc.; πετραία β. the *growth* of stone, S.*Ant.*827 (lyr.). II. of children, βλάσται γενέθλιοι πατρός *birth from* a father, Id.*OC*972; παιδὸς βλάσται Id.*OT*717, cf. *Tr.*382, *Trag.Adesp.*373. -ημα, ατος, τό, = βλάστη I, κισσίνοις β. E.*Ba.* 177, cf. Isoc.1.52, Thphr.*HP*1.1.9, *PLond.*1.131$^{r}$ix 191 (i A.D.). II. metaph., *offspring, offshoot*, μητρὸς β. A.*Th.*533; τέκνων γλυκερὸν β. E.*Med.*1099 (lyr.), cf. *IG*12(7).496.3 (Amorgos), etc.; also of animals, E.*Cyc.*206; ὦ χρυσέ β. χθονός *Trag.Adesp.*129.1: also in late Prose, Jul.*Or.*7.232d. III. *excrescence*, Hp.*Hum.*1; *eruption* on the skin, Aret.*CD*1.2. -ημός, ὁ, *growth*, βλαστημὸν ἀλδαίνοντα σώματος πολύν A.*Th.*12, cf. *Supp.*318. -ήμων, ον, gen. ονος, = βλαστικός, Nic.*Al.*548. -ησις, εως, ἡ, *budding, sprouting*, Arist.*HA*564$^{b}$2, Thphr.*HP*3.5.4 (pl.). -ητικός, ή, όν, *in active growth, sprouting*, Id.*CP*1.11.4; β. ὧραι *sprouting* season, Id.*Od.*63. -ικός, ή, όν, *budding, sprouting*, Id.*HP*3.12.8: Sup., dub. in Id.*CP*1.13.10; *furthering growth*, ὥρα *Gp.*9.9.3 (Comp.); κίνησις Herm.ap.Stob.1.41.7.

**βλαστο-δρεπής**, ές, *plucked as young shoots*, prob. in Nic.*Fr.*74.20. -κοπέω, *cut off young shoots*, in Pass., ὅταν ὑπὸ πνευμάτων -ηθῇ Thphr.*HP*4.14.6, cf. *CP*5.9.13. -λογέω, *pick off young shoots*, ib.3.16.1, Gal.6.619, *PLond.*1.131$^{r}$xxiii 507 (i A.D.):—Subst. -λογία, ἡ, Thphr. l. c., *POxy.*1631.13.

**βλαστόν**, τό, = sq., Nic.*Fr.*74.52.

**βλαστός**, ὁ, *shoot*, Hdt.6.37, 8.55, Thphr.*HP*3.6.3, Arist.*Col.*795$^{a}$4, *GA*731$^{a}$9, *POxy.*1692.20; *bud*, Thphr.*HP*1.8.4, *CP*1.11.4; *embryo, germ*, Id.*HP*8.2.2; ὁ τοῦ β. καιρός, i. e. Spring, D.S.17.82. 2. *blossom*, β. κρίνου Lxx 3*Ki.*7.24. II. *offspring*, S.*Fr.*341, *Epigr.Gr.*224 (Samos).

**βλαστοφυέω**, *put forth shoots*, prob. cj. in Thphr.*CP*1.11.7.

**βλαστόω**, = βλαστὸν παρατίθημι, *An.Ox.*1.96.

**βλασφημ-έω**, pf. βεβλασφήμηκα D.18.10:—*speak profanely of sacred things*, εἰς θεοὺς Pl.*R.*381e; *offer rash prayers*, Id.*Alc.*2.149c; β. κατά τινος *utter imprecations* against, Aeschin.1.180. 2. *speak ill* or *to the prejudice of* one, *slander*, περὶ τῆς ἐμῆς διατριβῆς Isoc.15.2, cf. D. l. c., ib.82; β. κατά τινος Isoc.12.65, cf. Arist.*Fr.*44; ὅσα εἰς ἡμᾶς ἐβλασφήμησαν D.51.3; β. τινά Babr.71.6, *Ev.Luc.*23.39, etc.:

abs., Phld.Lib.p.8O.:—Pass., to have evil spoken of one, βεβλασφημημένους Id.Vit.p.12J., cf. 1Ep.Cor.10.30. 3. speak impiously or irreverently of God, blaspheme, εἰς τὸν Κύριον LxxDa.3.29(96); εἰς τὸ πνεῦμα τὸ ἅγιον Ev.Marc.3.29; εἰς τὰ θεῖα Vett.Val.58.12; τοὺς θεούς Id.67.20: abs., Lxx 2Ma.10.34, al., Ev.Matt.9.3. **-ία**, ἡ, word of evil omen, profane speech, D.25.26; βλασφημίαν ἐφθέγξατο, at a sacrifice, E.Ion 1189; εἴ τις παραστὰς τοῖς βωμοῖς βλασφημοῖ β. πᾶσαν Pl.Lg.800c; πᾶσαν β. ἱερῶν καταχέουσι ib.d. 2. defamation, slander, Democr.177, D.10.36, 18.95; β. ποιεῖσθαι εἴς τινα Aeschin. 1.167, cf. Ep.Eph.4.31; ὅλας ἁμάξας βλασφημιῶν whole cart-loads of abuse, Luc.Eun.2. 3. irreverent speech against God, blasphemy, ἡ εἰς τὸ θεῖον β. Men.715: in pl., LxxEz.35.12, al.; τοῦ Πνεύματος against.., Ev.Matt.12.31; πρὸς τὸν θεόν Apoc.13.6. **-ος**, ον, speaking ill-omened words, evil-speaking, Arist.Rh.1398$^{b}$11: c. gen., against.., Plu.2.1100d, etc. 2. of words, slanderous, libellous, δέδοικα μὴ βλάσφημον μὲν εἰπεῖν ἀληθὲς δ' ᾖ D.9.1, cf. Luc.Alex.4 (Sup.). Adv. -μως Philostr.VA4.19, App.BC2.126. 3. blasphemous, ἔθνη Lxx 2Ma.10.4; ῥήματα Act.Ap.6.11; λαλεῖν βλάσφημα Apoc.13.5: Subst., blasphemer, Lxx 2Ma.9.28, 1Ep.Ti.1.13, etc.

**βλάττα**, ἡ, Lat. blatta, purple, Edict.Diocl.24.2:—Dim. **βλαττίον**, τό, Lyd.Mens.1.21.

**βλάτταν**· χόρτος, ἢ λάχανον, Hsch. **βλαττοῖ**· παιδαριεύεται, Id. **βλαῦδες**· ἐμβάδες, Id.

**βλαύτ-η**, ἡ, slipper, Hermipp.47.4, Lysipp.2, Herod.7.58: mostly in pl., βλαύτας σύρων Anaxil.18.2; β. ὑποδεδεμένος Pl.Smp. 174a. **-ίον**, τό, Dim. of foreg., Ar.Eq.889, Aristodem.8, AP6. 293 (Leon.); **βλαύρια** in Hsch., Cyr. **-όω**, beat with slippers, Hsch.; also, = ὑποδέω, Id.

⊛ **βλαχάν**· ὁ βάτραχος, Hsch.

**βλάχνον**, τό, = βλῆχνον, Phan.Hist.25, Sch.Nic.Th.39:—also **βλάθρον** and **βλάχρον**, Hsch.

**βλάψις**, εως, ἡ, harming, damage, Pl.Lg.932e (pl.).

⊛ **βλαψί-τᾰφος** [ῐ], ον, violating the grave, ἀτασθαλίη IG14.934.4. **-φρων**, ον, gen. ονος, (φρήν) maddening, φάρμακα Euph.14.2; ἄτη Tryph.411, cf. Orph.H.77.3, etc. II. = φρενοβλαβής, A.Th.725.

**βλεαίρει** (Boeot. for ἐλεαίρει)· οἰκτείρει, Hsch. (βλεερεῖ cod.).

⊛ **βλέθρα**, = πλέθρα, BCH9.382 (Thespiae, iii B.C.).

**βλεθράνασιν**· ἰχθῦν, Hsch. **βλεῖ**, = βλίσσει, v.l. in Id. **βλείης**, **βλεῖο**, v. βάλλω. **βλεκέμυξος**· βλακώδης, Id. **βλέκυξ**, v. βλέτυγες.

⊛ **βλεμεαίνω**, exult, σθένεϊ βλεμεαίνων, of a lion, Il.12.42; of Hector, 8.337; cf. ἀβλεμής.

⊛ **βλέμμα**, ατος, τό, look, glance, E.HF306, Ar.Pl.1022, D.21.72, Antiph.235, 2Ep.Pet.2.8, POxy.471.60 (ii A.D.); eyesight, AP9.159; βλεμμάτων βολή A.Fr.242.

**βλέννα**, ἡ, = μύξα, mucous discharge, Hp.Mul.1.58 (pl.); of the humour 'phlegm', Prodic.4, etc.

**βλέννος**, ους, τό, slime, Arist.HA591$^{a}$28. II. β., ὁ, fish allied to κωβιός, βαιών, Sophr.43, Opp.H.1.109.

**βλεννός**, ή, όν, drivelling, Epich.119, Sophr.51.

**βλεννώδης**, ες, slimy, mucous, Hp.Morb.2.12, Arist.HA591$^{a}$26.

**βλέορον** (prob. βλέθρον, cf. βέρεθρον, βέθρον)· βάθος, δεσμωτήριον, Hsch. **βλεπάζοντες**· βλέποντες, Id.

**βλεπεδαίμων**, ον, gen. ονος, ghostlike, Com.Adesp.85; a nickname of the Socratics, Paus.Gr.Fr.209.

**βλεπετύζει**· σκαρδαμύττει, βλέπει, Hsch.

**βλέπησις**, εως, ἡ, look, glance, Ar.Fr.757; πρὸς βλέπησιν by eye, βάπτειν PHolm.16.33.

**βλέπος**, ους, τό, = βλέμμα, look, Ἀττικὸν β. Ar.Nu.1176, cf. Theoc. 23.12.

**βλεπτ-έον**, one must look, εἴς τι Pl.Lg.965d, Arist.APr.44$^{a}$36, etc. **-ικός**, ή, όν, of or for sight, αἴσθησις App.Anth.3.158; sharp-seeing, Hdn.Epim.101 (Sup.). **-ός**, ή, όν, to be seen, S.OT1337.

⊛ **βλέπω**, Sol.11.8, etc.: impf. ἔβλεπον Batr.67: fut. βλέψομαι D. 25.98, Dor. inf. βλεψεῖσθαι IG4.951.75 (Epid.), later βλέψω Lxx Is. 6.9, Aristid.2.46J., etc.: aor. ἔβλεψα (v. infr.): pf. βέβλεφα (ἀπο-) Antip.Stoic.3.254 (codd. Stob.); βέβλοφα (ἐμ-) PLond.1.42.21 (ii A.D.):—Pass., aor. ἐβλέφθην (προσ-) Plu.2.680f: pf. βέβλεμμαι to be supplied in Ath.10.409c, cf. Eust.1401.16:—chiefly in pres. and aor. Act. in early writers: Med. (exc. fut.) and Pass. only late:—see, have the power of sight (dist. fr. ὁρῶ perceive, be aware of, cf. Plot.6.7.37), opp. τυφλός εἰμι, S.OT302, cf. 348, OC73, Ar. Pl.15, etc.; βλέποντες ἔβλεπον μάτην A.Pr.447; βλέποντας ἀθλιωτάτους Alex.234; μὴ βλέπων ὁ μάντις ᾖ lest he see too clearly, S.OT747; ὁ βλέπων the seer, Hebraism in Lxx 1Ki.9.9; ὀλίγον βλέπων short-sighted, POxy.39.9 (i A.D.). II. look, βλέφ' ὧδε S.Tr.402; ἐπὶ ἐμοί Id.Aj.345 (s.v.l.); εἴς τι A.Pers.802; ἐπί τι Th.7.71; εἰς τὰ τούτων πρόσωπα D.18.283; πῶς βλέπων; with what face? S.Ph.110; ὄμμασιν ποίοις β.; Id.OT1371; β. ἅμα πρόσσω καὶ ὀπίσσω Pl.Cra.428d: with Adv., φιλοφρόνως, ἐχθρῶς β. πρός τινας, X.Mem.3.10.4, Smp.4.58: freq. folld. by noun in acc., φόβον β. look terror, i.e. to look terrible, Θυιὰς ὣς φόβον βλέπων A.Th.498; Com., ἔβλεψε νᾶπυ looked mustard, Ar.Eq.631; ἀνδρεῖον..καὶ βλέποντ' ὀρίγανον Id.Ra.603; βλεπόντων κάρδαμα Id.V.455; πυρρίχην βλέπων looking like a war-dancer, Id.Av. 1169; αἰκείαν βλέπων looking like one disgraced, ib.1671; σκύτη β., of a slave, Eup.282, Ar.V.643; β. ἀπιστίαν Eup.309: also folld. by Adj., μέγα β. dub. in Semon.19; φθονερὰ β. Pi.N.4.39; γλίσχρον β. Euphro 10.16, cf. Men.Epit.479, Jul.Caes.309c: by inf., ἁρπάζειν β. Men.Epit.181; ὀρχεῖσθαι μόνον β. Alex.97: by part. neut., τί φροντικὸς βλέπεις; E.Alc.773. 2. β. ἐς look to, rely on, εἰς ἔργον οὐδὲν γιγνόμενον βλέπετε Sol.11.8; ἐς θεούς S.Ant.923; οὐκέτ' ἔστιν εἰς ὅ τι βλέπω Id.Aj.514; ἔς σε δὴ βλέπω, ὅπως.. in the hope that.., Id.El.954: metaph. also, have regard to, ἡ πολιτεία β. εἰς πλοῦτον Arist.Pol.1293$^{b}$14; of aspects, οἰκίαι πρὸς μεσημβρίαν βλέπουσαι.., X.Mem.3.8.9; πέτρα βλέπουσα πρὸς νότον Str.4.1.4; κάτω γὰρ οἱ ὀδόντες βλέπουσι Arist.HA502$^{a}$1; ὅταν τὸ οὖθαρ βλέπῃ κάτω ib.523$^{a}$ 2. 3. look longingly, expect, propose, c. inf., Ar.Ach.376, V. 847. 4. look to a thing, beware, ἀπό τινος Ev.Marc.8.15; τι Ep. Phil.3.2: c. acc. pers., β. ἑαυτούς Ev.Marc.13.9; βλέπε σα(υ)τὸν ἀπὸ τῶν Ἰουδαίων BGU1079.24 (i A.D.); β. ἵνα.. 1Ep.Cor.16.10; β. ἑαυτοὺς ἵνα μὴ.. 2Ep.Jo.8; βλέπετε τί ἀκούετε Ev.Marc.4.24. III. trans., see, behold, c. acc., S.Aj.1042, etc.; ἐξ αὑτοῦ βλεπόμενον self-evident, S.E.M.1.184; τὰ βλεπόμενα the visible universe, Lxx Wi.13. 7. 2. ζῇ τε καὶ β. φάος sees the light of day, A.Pers.299, cf. E.Hel. 60; νόστιμον β. φάος A.Pers.261; βλέποντα νῦν μὲν ὄρθ' ἔπειτα δὲ σκότον (i.e. being blind) S.OT419: hence, without φάος, to be alive, ζῶντα καὶ βλέποντα A.Ag.677; βλέποντα κἀμπνέοντα S.Ph.883, cf. 1349, Aj.962; of things, ἀληθῆ καὶ βλέποντα actually existing, A.Ch. 844. 3. look for, μεῖζόν τι β. Pl.Chrm.172c. 4. Astrol. of signs equidistant from the tropical points, to be in aspect, β. ἄλληλα Ptol.Tetr.36, Heph.Astr.1.9. (βλέφαρα occurs in Hom., but not βλέπω exc. in Batr. l.c.)

**βλέτενον**· βλιτάδη (βλητ- cod.), Hsch. **βλέτυγες**· φλυαρίαι: also **βλέκυγες**, Id.:—sg. **βλέκυξ**, Hdn.Gr.2.482. **βλέτυες**· αἱ βδέλλαι, Hsch.

⊛ **βλεφᾰρ-ίζω**, wink, Sch.Ar.Eq.292. **-ικός**, ή, όν, of or for the eyelids, collyria Cael.Aur.TP4.2.17. **-ίς**, ίδος, ἡ, eyelash, Ar.Ec. 402: mostly in pl., Id.Eq.373, X.Mem.1.4.6, Arist.PA658$^{a}$11. II. = βλέφαρον, eyelid, Id.HA504$^{a}$29. **-ῖτις**, ιδος, ἡ, of or on the eyelids, τρίχες Paul.Aeg.6.13.

**βλεφᾰροκάτοχος**, ον, holding the eyelid, μυδίον Paul.Aeg.6.8.

⊛ **βλέφᾰρον**, Dor. **γλέφᾰρον**, τό:—mostly in pl. (as always in Hom.), eyelids, βλέφαρ' ἀμφὶ καὶ ὀφρύας Od.9.389, al.; of sleep, φίλα βλέφαρ' ἀμφικαλύψας 5.493; ὕπνος ἀπὸ βλεφάροιϊν (dual) Il.10.187; ὕπνον ἐπὶ βλεφάροισιν ἔχευεν Od.20.54, al.; παῦρον ἐπὶ γλεφάροις ὕπνον ἀναλίσκοισα Pi.P.9.24; γλεφάρων ἁδὺ κλᾷστρον ib.1.8; βλέφαρα κέκληται S.Fr.711; β. συμβαλεῖν, κοιμᾶν ὕπνῳ, A.Ag.15, Th. 3; of weeping, δάκρυ χαμαὶ βάλεν ἐκ βλεφάροιϊν Od.17.490, cf. 23. 33; of death, λύειν β. S.Ant.1302: in Prose, Antipho Soph.81a, Pl. Ti.45d, PPetr.3p.23 (iii B.C.): rarely in sg., E.Or.302; β. τὸ ἄνω καὶ κάτω Arist.HA491$^{b}$19, cf. PA657$^{b}$14. II. in pl., eyes, βλεφάρων κυανεάων Hes.Sc.7 (where the fem. Adj. points to a nom. ἡ βλέφαρος); freq. in Trag., σκοτώσω β. καὶ δεδορκότα S.Aj.85, cf. Tr. 107 (lyr.): in sg., of the sun, ἁμέρας β. Id.Ant.104 (lyr.); of the curtain of darkness at nightfall, νυκτὸς ἀφεγγὲς β. E.Ph.543.

**βλεφᾰρό-ξυστον**, τό, an instrument for trimming the eyelids, Paul. Aeg.3.22.12. ⊛ **-σπάξ**, arching the eyebrows, Hdn.Gr.1.43. **-τόμον**, τό, surgical instrument, Hermes 38.280.

**βλεψίας**, ου, ὁ, a fish, = κεφαλῖνος, Dorio ap.Ath.7.306f.

**βλέψις**, εως, ἡ, act of sight, τὸ βλεπόμενον τὸ ὄν, οὐχ ἡ β. Plot.6.2. 8. II. sight (i.e. thing seen), πρὸς τὴν βλέψιν ἀναφλεχθείς Plu. Pel.32. III. metaph., contemplation, consideration, συμφερόντων Epicur.Ep.3p.63U.

**βλήδην**, Adv. by throwing, hurling, Hsch. **βλήεται**, v. βάλλω.

**βλήθα**, v. βλῆμα 4.

**βληθρήν**· τραχεῖαν, οἱ δὲ ⟨ἁ⟩παλήν, Hsch.

**βλῆμα**, ατος, τό, (βάλλω) throw, cast, of dice, ἄλλα βλήματ' ἐν κύβοις βαλεῖν E.Supp.330; of a missile, D.H.10.16; of the missile itself, Ph.2.431, Max.Tyr.9.8 (pl.). 2. shot, wound, Hdt.3.35, Hp.Prorrh.2.14 (pl.). 3. coverlet, AP7.413 (Antip.). 4. = ἄρτος ἐντεθρυμμένος καὶ θερμός, Seleuc.ap.Ath.3.114d (**βλήθα** in Hsch.).

**βλήμενος**, v. sub βάλλω. **βλῆναι**· ἀληθεῖς, Hsch.

**βλῆρ**, Aeol. for δέλεαρ, Alcm.130.

**βλῆραι**· αἱ κνίδαι, ἄλλοι χόρτον, οἱ δὲ τῶν ὀσπρίων τὴν καλάμην, Hsch.

**βλής**, ητός, ὁ, ἡ, thrown, prob. f.l. for ἀβλής, Call.Fr.anon.341.

**βλῆσθαι**, v. βάλλω. **βλήσσα⟨ν⟩**· βότρυν ἡμιπέ⟨πε⟩ιρον, Hsch. **βλήσσανον**· φυτὸν σχίνῳ ὅμοιον, Id. **βληστάς**· ὁ χερσαῖος σκορπίος, Id.

**βληστρ-ίζω**, toss about, ἑαυτὸν β., as a sick person on his bed, Hp. Morb.3.7; βληστρίζοντες ἐμὴν φροντίδ' ἀν' Ἑλλάδα γῆν Xenoph.8.2: metaph., ἐμαυτὸν πόλιν ἐκ πόλεως φέρων ἐβλήστριζον Id.45:—Pass., = βληστρίζειν ἑαυτόν, Aret.CA1.1. **-ισμός**, ὁ, tossing, restlessness, Hp.Epid.1.26.β'.

**βλήτ-ειρα**, ἡ, thrower, darter, ὀϊστῶν Alex.Aet.4.5. **-έον**, one must throw or put, Ev.Marc.2.22. **-ιεῖ**· καταβαλεῖ, νικήσει, Hsch. **-ικόν**, τό, = βλητόν (v. βλητός 2), Thphr.Fr.178. II. striking, β. ζῷα, opp. δάκετα (biting), prob. for βλητά in Ael.NA3.32.

**βλῆτο**, v. βάλλω. **βλῆτον**, v. βλίτον.

**βλητ-ός**, ή, όν, (βάλλω) stricken, palsy-stricken, Hp.Acut.17, Coac. 394; smitten by disease, λεχωΐδες Call.Dian.127, cf. Cer.102. 2. v. βλητικόν. **-ρον**, τό, fastening: band or hoop, ξυστὸν κολλητὸν βλήτροισι Il.15.678. II. = βλῆχνον, Nic.Th.39 (gen. sg., v.l. βλίτρου; Sch. gives nom. βλῆτρος). **-ρώσας**· ἐμβαλών, Hsch.

**βληχ-άζω**, = sq., Autocr.3. **-χάομαι**, aor. ἐβληχησάμην AP 7.657 (Leon.), Longus 3.13:—bleat, of sheep and goats, προβατίων βληχωμένων Ar.Pax 535, Fr.387.5; βληχώμενοι προβατίων αἰγῶν τε.. μέλη Id.*Pl.*293; of infants, τὰ δὲ συγκύψανθ' ἅμα βληχᾶται Id.*V.* 570: metaph. of men, c. acc. cogn., πάταγον Porph.*Chr.*35; βληχοῖντο (as if from βληχέομαι) is v.l. for βληχῷντο in Theoc.16. 92. **-άς**, άδος, ἡ, *bleater*, ὄϊας περὶ β. Opp.*C.*1.145. **-ή**, Dor. **βλᾱχά**, ἡ, *bleating*, οἰῶν Od.12.266; of lambs, E.*Cyc.*48 (lyr., pl.); *wailing* of infants, A.*Th.*348 (lyr., pl.). (Onomatop.) **-ηθμός**, ὁ, = foreg., Ael.*NA*5.51, Nonn.*D.*14.157. **-ημα**, ατος, τό, = βληχή, Hsch. (pl.): sg., = μωρός, προβατώδης, Id. **-ητά**, ῶν, τά, *bleaters*, i.e. *sheep*, Ael.*NA*2.54; β. τέκνα *sheepish* lads, Eup.103.

**βλῆχνον**, τό (v. l. **βλῆχρον**, as in Sch.Theoc.3.14, Cyr. (βλῆχρα Hsch.)), = πτέρις, *male fern*, *Aspidium Filix-mas*, Dsc.4.184.

**βληχρός**, ά, όν, *faint*, *gentle*, ἄνεμοι Alc.16; of the rivers of hell, *dull*, *sluggish*, Pi.*Fr.*130; πελάγη A.R.4.152; *gentle*, opp. ἀκράχολος, Phld.*Lib.*p.44 O.; β. πυρετοί *slight*, Hp.*Aph.*5.64, cf. Plu.*Per.*38; β. σφυγμοί Hp.*Mul.*1.37; νοῦσος -οτέρη ib.36; ὕπνου β. ὄνειαρ Q.S. 2.182. Adv. -ρῶς *slightly*, Hp.*Mul.*2.203; *weakly*, β. εἶχον καὶ οὐκ ἰσχυρῶς Ctes.*Fr.*29.42: Comp. -ότερον Hp.*Morb.*2.61. 2. metaph., *slight*, *small*, β. ἀπ' ἀρχᾶς B.10.65; χάριν οὐ β. Id.12.227.—Not in Hom. (who has ἀβληχρός), nor in Att.; η in all dialects.

**βλῆχρος**, ἡ, = γλήχων, Thphr.*CP*1.7.4, Ps.-Dsc.3.31.

**βλῆχρον**, v. βλῆχνον.

**βληχώδης**, ες, *bleating*, *sheepish*, Babr.93.5.

⊛ **βλήχων**, ἡ (later ὁ, *Gp.*8.7), gen. ωνος, also **βληχώ**, gen. οῦς; Ion. **γλήχων**, -ώ, Dor. **γλάχων**, -ώ (on the forms see Phryn.*PS* p.53 B., Sch.Ar.*Pax*711), dat. γλήχωνι *h.Cer.*209; βληχοῖ Thphr.*HP* 9.16.1: gen. γληχοῦς Hp.*Morb.*3.17; γλάχωνος Boeot.ap.Ar.*Ach.* 869: acc. γλάχωνα ib.861, Theoc.5.56; γλήχωνα Herod.9.13; γλαχώ Ar.*Ach.*874; βληχώ Id.*Lys.*89:—*pennyroyal*, *Mentha Pulegium*, ll. cc., Dsc.3.31, etc.

**βληχωνίας**, ου, ὁ, *prepared with pennyroyal*, κυκεών Ar.*Pax*712.

**βληχώνιον**, τό, = βλήχων, Sch.Theoc.5.56.

**βλιαρόν**· ἀβλεβές, Hsch.: βλιαρόν· λαῦρον, *EM*201.41. **βλιβρόν**· λαγ(α)ρόν, Hsch. **βλίδες**· ψεκάδες, Id. **βλίζω**, = βλίττω, Id. s.v. βλεῖ, cf. *EM*200.33. **βλιγχῶδες**· βλιχανῶδες (βλιχῶνες cod.), Hsch. **βλίκανος**, ὁ, = βάτραχος, Hsch., *EM*201. 42:—also **βλίχας**, Hsch.: **βλίκαρος**, Suid. **βλικάς** or **βλίκας**, *fig-leaf*, Hsch., *EM*201.41.

**βλῑμ-άζω**, Lacon. -άττω, *feel* hens to see if they are fat, Ar.*Av.* 530: hence sens. obsc., Cratin.302, Ar.*Lys.*1164, S.*Fr.*484:—Pass., *to be squeezed*, Hp.*Epid.*5.1. 2. *handle*, *treat*, β. τοὺς ἀξίους ἐπιεικέστερον Aristeas 188. II. = βλίττω, *EM*200.47. **-ἄσις**, εως, ἡ, *lewd handling*, Hsch.

**βλίμη**· προπηλακισμός, ὕβρις, Hsch., *EM*201.40. **βλινόν**· δαλόν, Hsch. **βλίξ**· συνεχῶς, Id. **βλίσσω**, v. βλίττω.

**βλιστηρίς**, ίδος, ἡ, (βλίττω) *honey-taking*, χείρ *AP*9.226 (Zon.).

**βλῑτάς**, άδος, ἡ, *worthless woman*, Men.955.

**βλιτάχεα**, τά, = κογχύλια or σελάχια, Epich.193: but **βλίταχος**· βάτραχος, Hsch.

⊛ **βλῖτο-μάμμας** or -μάμας, ου, ὁ, *booby*, Ar.*Nu.*1001, cf. Phryn. *PS* p.55 B.

⊛ **βλίτον**, τό, *blite*, *Amaranthus Blitum*, Hp.*Vict.*2.54, 3.75:—written **βλῆτον** Id.*Aff.*41, Thphr.*HP*1.14.2, Dsc.2.117: in pl., Theopomp.Com.62, Diph.14.

**βλίττω**, aor. ἔβλῐσα Pl.*R.*564e:—*cut out the comb of bees*, *take the honey*, l.c.; σφηκιὰν β. S.*Fr.*778: metaph., β. τὸν δῆμον *rob* the people *of their honey*, Ar.*Eq.*794, cf. *Lys.*475:—Pass., πλεῖστον δὴ.. τοῖς κηφῆσι μέλι βλίττεται prob. in Pl. l.c.; β. τὰ σμήνη the hives *have their honey taken*, Arist.*HA*554ª15, cf. 627ᵇ2. II. βλίσσειν· = μαλάσσειν, Erot.*Fr.*16. (For μλιτ-yω, cf. μέλι.)

**βλίτυρι**, τό, *twang of a harp-string*: hence of a *meaningless sound*, S.E.*M.*8.133, D.L.7.57, Artem.4.2, Gal.8.662.

**βλιτυρίζομαι**, Pass., *sound like a harp-string*, coined by Gal.8.662.

**βλίτυρον** ἐστὶ φυτὸν ἢ φάρμακον, ἢ χορδῆς μίμημα, *EM*201.43.

**βλίτωνας**· τοὺς εὐήθεις, Hsch.

⊛ **βλῑχ-ᾰνώδης**, ες, of fish, *clammy*, Diph.17.15. **-ώδης**, ες, *clammy*, *sticky*, of wounds or ulcers, Hp.*VC*19 ap.Erot. (γλισχρῶδες codd.), cf. Archig.ap.Orib.46.23.3.

**βλοσέμεν**· σκοτωθῆναι, Hsch.

**βλοσῠρόμμᾰτος**, ον, *grim-eyed*, prob. in Cerc.*Oxy.*1082 *Fr.*28.

**βλοσῠρός**, ά, όν, also ός, όν v.l. in Hes.*Sc.*250:—*hairy*, *shaggy*, *bristling*, μειδιόων βλοσυροῖσι προσώπασι Il.7.212; τὼ δέ οἱ ὄσσε λαμπέσθην βλοσυρῇσιν ὑπ' ὀφρύσιν 15.608, cf. Hes.*Sc.*147; of lions, ib. 175; of the Κῆρες, ib.250; ἡ δὲ συὸς βλοσυρῆς, to describe a woman, Phoc.3.3; β. χαίτη *Lyr.Alex.Adesp.*11.4; ἄρκτοι, φώκη, Opp.*H.*2.247, 5.38; πορδαλίων βλοσυρὰς δύσαντο καλύπτρας Nonn.*D.*14.131; later, *grim*, *fearful*, ἄγος A.*Eu.*167 (lyr.); ἄκρη A.R.2.740; κύματα *AP*9. 84 (Antiphan.), cf. 278 (Bianor); φάσματα ἀρχαγγέλων Iamb.*Myst.*2. 3. 2. *virile*, *burly*, γενναίους τε καὶ β. τὰ ἤθη Pl.*R.*535b; β. γε τὴν ψυχὴν ἔχεις Nicostr.35; of a woman, μαῖα γενναία καὶ β. *masculine*, Pl.*Tht.*149a; βλοσυρωτάτη τὸ εἶδος, of Boudicca, D.C.62.2; also, *coarse*, πίττα Thphr.*HP*9.2.3 (Comp.), cf. *CP*6.12.5 (Comp.). 3. *solemn*, *dignified*, σεμνὸν καὶ β. δρᾶν Ael.*VH*12.21; of persons, σεμνὴ καὶ β. Aristaenet.1.7, cf. Him.*Or.*23.12. Adv. -ῶς Hld.10.27.

⊛ **βλοσῠρό-της**, ητος, ἡ, *grimness*, Eust.1194.46. **-φρων**, ον, gen. ονος, *savage-minded*, A.*Supp.*833 (lyr.).

**βλοσῠρ-ώπης**, ου, ὁ, later masc. of sq., Opp.*C.*1.144. **-ῶπις**, ιδος, ἡ, (ὤψ) *grim-looking*, Γοργώ Il.11.36. **-ωπός**, όν, later form of foreg., D.P.123.

**βλόχον**, = βδέλλιον, Dsc.1.67. **βλύδιον**· ὑγρόν, ζέον, Hsch.

⊛ **βλύζω**, aor. ἔβλῠσα A.R.4.1446, Q.S.1.242, *AP*7.352, etc.; poet. opt. βλύσσειε *AP*11.58 (Maced.): aor. Pass. ἐβλύσθη Orac.ap.Eus.*PE* 5.16:—*bubble*, *gush forth*, of liquids, A.R. l. c., Orac. in Paus.5.7.3; ἐκ πηγῆς Philostr.*VA*3.45: c. dat., β. Λυαίῳ *with* wine, *AP*11.58 (Maced.): c. acc. cogn., μέθυ β. *spout* wine: metaph. of Anacreon, ib. 7.27 (Antip. Sid.); ὕδωρ Orph.*A.*599, cf. Nonn.*D.*17.125, al.; χρυσίον Lyd.*Mag.*3.45: metaph., αἰσχρὰ καθ' ἡμετέρης ἔβλυσε παρθενίης *AP* 7.352.

**βλύσις** [ῠ], εως, ἡ, *bubbling up*, *AP*9.819:—also **βλύσμα**, ατος, τό, Hdn.*Epim.*11: **βλυσμός**, ὁ, *Gloss.*

⊛ **βλυστάνω**, = sq., Procl.*in Cra.*p.80 P., Mich.*in PN*51.1, *Et.Gud.*

**βλυχάζω**, = μολύνω, in pf. part. Pass., Hsch.

⊛ **βλύω**, = βλύζω, c. dat., φόνῳ βλύουσαι Lyc.301: c. acc., δέμας οἱ ἔβλυεν ὕδωρ Nonn.*D.*19.287: c. gen., παρ' ὄρει θερμῶν ὑδάτων βλύοντι *OGI*199.11. [ῡ between two long syll. in Ep., ἀνα-βλύεσκε A.R. 3.223, cf. 4.1417.]

⊛ **βλωθρός**, ά, όν, *tall*, πίτυς β. Il.13.390; β. ὄγχνη Od.24.234, cf. A.R.4.1476, Q.S.8.204; βλωθρῇ ἐπὶ ποίῃ Arat.1089. (Perh. cf. Skt. *mūrdhā* 'head', OE. *molda* 'head'.)

**βλωμ-ός**, ὁ, = ψωμός, *morsel* of bread, Call.*Fr.*240; cf. ὀκτάβλωμος:—Dim. **-ίδιον**, τό, Eust.1817.55: **βλωμιαῖοι** ἄρτοι prob. l. in Philem.Gloss.ap.Ath.3.114e. II. **βλωμοί**· στραβοί, Hsch.

**βλωρός**, ὁ, *fig-leaf*, Hsch.

**βλῶσις**, εως, ἡ, *arrival*, *presence*, Hsch. II. *seat*, δίφρου β. *Trag.Adesp.*150.

⊛ **βλώσκω**, Nic.*Th.*450, (κατα-, προ-) Od.16.466, 21.239: fut. μολοῦμαι A.*Pr.*689 (lyr.), S.*OC*1742 (lyr.): aor. 2 ἔμολον Pi.*O.*14.18, etc., Ep. μόλον (ἐκ-, προ-) Il.11.604, Od.15.468, freq. in Trag., also Dor. (as aor. of pres. ἕρπω 'go') *IG*4.952.14 (Epid.), *SIG*558.26 (Ithaca), and sts. in Prose, X.*An.*7.1.33, Plb.30.9.5, Plu.*Cleom.*38; imper. μόλε Cratin.111: pf. μέμβλωκα Od.17.190, E.*Rh.*629; part. -κώς Call.*Aet.*1.1.7 (cf. βέβλωκεν· ἠρεμεῖ, φύεται, Hsch.): later fut. βλώξω (κατα-) Lyc.1068: aor. 1 ἔβλωξα Id.448, 1327: aor. 2 ἔβλω· ᾤχετο, Hsch., cf. μολέω:—*go* or *come*, mostly Poet. in aor. 2, δεῦρο μολόντες Od.3.44; μολοῦσα ποτὶ μέγαρ' Il.6.286; of Time, πρὶν δωδεκάτη μόλῃ ἠώς 24.781; μέμβλωκε μάλιστα ἦμαρ *has passed*, Od.17.190; ὅτε τὸ κύριον μόλῃ A.*Ag.*766 (lyr.): freq. with Preps., μολεῖν εἰς οἴκους, ἐπὶ δόμον, S.*OT*1010, E.*Or.*176 (lyr.); πρὸς χθόνα S.*Ph.*479; ἀπὸ Στρυμόνος, ἐκ Διός, A.*Ag.*192 (lyr.), *Pr.*667; κατὰ γαίας E.*Alc.*107 (lyr.): c. acc. only, ἔμολεν Ἥρας λαόν Pi.*N.*10.36; γῆν μολόντες Ἑλλάδα A. *Pers.*809, cf. *Ag.*968, *Supp.*239, S.*Ph.*1332, E.*Rh.*289; πρὶν φάος μολεῖν χθόνα ib.223; ἥβης τέλος μ. Id.*Med.*921, cf. *IT*1421: c. dat. pers., μηδέ μοι.. θάνατος μόλοι Sol.21, cf. S.*OC*70, *Ant.*233, etc.; δι' ἔχθρας μ. τινί, διὰ μάχης μολεῖν τινί, E.*Ph.*479, *IA*1392; εἰς ὕποπτα μ. τινί, = ὑποπτεύειν τινά, Id.*El.*345.—Rare in Prose (v. supr.); used by Ar. only in lyr. (*Av.*404, *Th.*1146, 1155, al.), or in the mouth of a Laconian, Id.*Lys.*984, cf. Plu.2.220e, 225d (both from *Apophth.Lac.*).

**βόα**, ἡ, a *fish*, = σάλπη, Pancrat.ap.Ath.7.321f.

**βο-ᾱγός**, ὁ, v. βουαγός:—hence **-ᾱγίδης**, ου, ὁ, of Heracles, Lyc. 652. **-άγριον**, τό, *shield of wild bull's hide*, Il.12.22, Od.16. 296, *AP*9.323 (Antip.). **-αγρος**, ὁ, (βοῦς) *wild bull*, Philostr. *VA*6.24.

**βοαδεῖ**· ὀκνεῖ, Hsch.

⊛ **βοᾱθόος**, Dor. for βοηθόος (q.v.); name of a Delphic month, *SIG* 672.78.

**βόᾱμα**, ατος, τό, (βοάω) Dor for βόημα (which occurs in D.C.51. 17), *shriek*, *cry*, χαμαιπετὲς β. A.*Ag.*920; *loud strain*, τηλέπορόν τι β. λύρας *Lyr.Adesp.*102.

**βο-άνθεμον**, τό, = βούφθαλμον, Hp.*Mul.*1.78, Nic.*Fr.*74.38. **-άνθρωπος**, ὁ, *bull-man*, of the Minotaur, Tz.*H.*1.489.

**βόαξ**, ᾱκος, ὁ, Ion. **βόηξ**, contr. **βῶξ**, Diph.Siph.ap.Ath.8.356a, Arist.*HA*610ᵇ4, *Gp.*20.7.1:—a *grunting fish*, sacred to Hermes, called from the sound it makes, *Box boops*, Epich.29, Ar.*Fr.*475, Numen.ap.Ath.7.286f, Speus.ibid.; cf. βόωψ.

**βοάριος**, α, ον, = Lat. *boarius*: ἀγορὰ βοαρία, = *forum boarium* at Rome, D.H.1.40, cf. D.C.78.25.

**βο-αρμία**, ἡ, (ἀραρίσκω) *ox-yoker*, epith. of Athena, Lyc.520. **-αρχος**, ον, *beginning with an ox*, of a sacrifice in which an ox is the first victim, τρίττοα *IG*1².5 (v B.C.). **-ᾶτις**, ιδος, ἡ, v. βοητής. ⊛ **-αύλιον**, τό, Dim. of sq., Epic. in *Arch.Pap.*7.7, Orph.*A.*438. **-αυλος**, ὁ, (βοῦς, αὐλή) *ox-stall*, Theoc.25.108:—also **-αυλον**, τό, A.R.3. 1290.

**βοάω**, Ep. 3 sg. βοάᾳ, 3 pl. βοόωσιν, part. βοόων, Il.14.394, 17.265, 15. 687: Ion. impf. βοάασκε A.R.2.588: fut. βοήσομαι Th.7.48, etc.; Dor. βοάσομαι Ar.*Nu.*1154 (lyr.); later βοήσω A.R.3.792, *AP*7.32 (Jul.), etc. (βοάσω E.*Ion* 1447 (lyr.) is aor. subj.): aor. ἐβόησα Il.11.15, S.*Tr.* 772, etc.; Ep. βόησα Il.23.847; Dor. βόασα B.16.14; Ion. ἔβωσα Il.12. 337, Hdt.1.146, Hippon.1, Herod.3.23; sts. in Com., Cratin.396, Ar. *Pax* 1155: pf. βεβόηκα Philostr.*VS*2.1.11:—**Med.**, βοώμενος Ar.*V.* 1228 (perh. Pass.): Ep. aor. βοήσατο Q.S.10.465, Ion. ἐβώσατο Theoc. 17.60; part. βοησάμενος Ant.Lib.25.3:—**Pass.**, Ion. aor. ἐβώσθην Hdt.6.131: pf. βεβόημαι *AP*7.138 (Aceratus), Ion. part. βεβωμένος Hdt.3.39: plpf. ἐβεβόητο Paus.6.11.3:—*cry aloud*, *shout*, ὀξὺ βοήσας Il.17.89; ὅσσον τε γέγωνε βοήσας Od.6.294; πᾶσα γὰρ πόλις βοᾷ A. *Ag.*1106 (lyr.); ὡς δράκων β. Id.*Th.*381; (β. γραμμάτων ἐν ξυλλαβαῖς ib.468; οἱ βοησόμενοι *men ready to shout* (in the ἐκκλησία), D.13. 20; ὁ δῆμος ἐβόησεν.., of acclamations, *POxy.*41.19 (iii/iv A.D.), cf. Charito 1.1, al., *IG*12(9).906 (Chalcis, iii A.D.). 2. of things, *roar, howl,* as the wind and waves, οὔτε..κῦμα τόσον βοάᾳ ποτὶ χέρσον Il.14.394; *resound, echo,* ἀμφὶ δέ τ' ἄκραι ἠϊόνες βοόωσιν 17.265; βοᾷ δὲ πόντιος κλύδων A.*Pr.*431 (lyr.), etc.; βοᾷ δ' ἐν ὠσὶ κέλαδος *rings,* Id.*Pers.*605; τὸ πρᾶγμα φανερόν ἐστιν, αὐτὸ γὰρ βοᾷ it *proclaims* itself, Ar.*V.*921; φαίνεται αὐτὰ τὰ στοιχεῖα βοᾶν ὡς ἑλκόμενα Arist.*Metaph.*1091$^{a}$10. II. c. acc. pers., *call to one, call on,* Pi.*P.*6.36, E.*Med.*205 (lyr.), Hdt.8.92, X.*Cyr.*7.2.5, Herod.4.41:—Med. βοησάμενοι δαίμονας Ant.Lib.l.c. 2. c. acc., *call for, shout out for,* S.*Tr.*772; β. τὴν βοήθειαν *Hell.Oxy.*10.2. 3. c. acc. cogn., β. βοάν Ar.*Nu.*1153 (lyr.); β. μέλος, ἰωάν, S.*Aj.*976, *Ph.*216 (lyr.); β. λοιγόν A.*Ch.*402 (lyr.); ἄλγος E.*Tr.*1310 (lyr.): c. dupl. acc., βοάσαθ' ὑμέναιον ἀοιδαῖς ἰαχαῖς τε νύμφαν *sound aloud* the bridal hymn in honour of the bride, ib.335 (lyr.); ἔλεγον ἰήϊον ἐβόα κίθαρις E.*Hyps.* *Fr.*3(1).iii 10. 4. *noise abroad, celebrate,* ἡ ῥάφανος ἣν ἐβοᾶτε Alex.15.7; πρήγματα βεβωμένα ἀνὰ Ἰωνίην Hdt.3.39; ἐβώσθησαν ἀνὰ τὴν Ἑλλάδα Id.6.131; οἱ βοηθέντες ἐπὶ χρήμασι Lib.*Or.*59.155; βεβοῆσθαι ἀπὸ τοῦ Μαραθῶνος, ἐκ τῶν ἀδικημάτων, Id.*Decl.*11.18, 5.53. 5. c. inf., *cry aloud* or *command in a loud voice* to do a thing, S.*OT*1287, E.*Andr.*297 (lyr.); βοᾶν τινι ἄγειν X.*An.*1.8.12; ἐβόων ἀλλήλοις μὴ θεῖν ib.19; also, *cry aloud* that.., Epicrat.11.31 (anap.); β. ὅτι.. X.*An.*1.8.1, Antiph.125.5. 6. Pass., *to be filled with sound,* πᾶσαν δὲ χρὴ γαῖαν βοᾶσθαι ὑμνῳδίαις E.*Hel.*1434; *to be deafened,* Ar.*V.*1228. (Cf. βοή.)

**βοει-ακός,** ή, όν, = sq., *EM*254.44. **-κός,** ή, όν, (βοῦς) = βόειος, *of* or *for oxen,* ζεύγη β. wagons *drawn by oxen,* Th.4.128, X.*An.*7.5.2, cf. Ar.*Fr.*109; κρέας β. Poll.6.55:—the form **βοϊκός,** freq. in codd. as in D.H.8.87, is censured by Hdn.Gr.2.416, but cf. ἱερεῖον βοϊκόν *Milet.*1(7).203*a* (i B.C.); θυσία βοϊκή *Inscr.Prien.*112.109 (i B.C.); βοϊκά, = *oxen, GDI*1158 (Elis); β. κτήνη *BGU*1189.12 (i A.D.). ❋ **-ος,** α, ον, Ep. and Ion. **βόεος,** η, ον (βόϝεον *Glotta*4.201 (Apulian vase) is dub.): (βοῦς):—*of an ox* or *oxen,* esp. *of ox-hide,* δέρμα βόειον Od.14.24; βοέοισιν ἱμᾶσιν Il.23.324; βοείας ἀσπίδας 5.452; βόεα κρέα Hdt.2.37, 168; τὰ β. κρέα Pl.*R.*338c; γάλα β. E.*Cyc.*218, Arist.*HA*521$^{b}$33, Dsc.4.83, Porph.*Abst.*4.17; ποδὶ βοείῳ τὸν θεὸν ἐλθεῖν, of Dionysus, Plu.2.364f: metaph., β. ῥήματα *bull*-words, Ar.*Ra.*924. II. **βοείη** or **βοέη** (sc. δορή), ἡ, *ox-hide,* ἀδέψητον βοέην Od.20.2, 142; βοὸς μεγάλοιο βοείην Il.17.389; *ox-hide shield,* βοέης εἰλυμένω ὤμους αὔησι στερεῇσι ib.492; βοῶν τ' εὖ ποιητάων (contr. for βοέων) 16.636. 2. = βοεύς, λύσαντε βοείας *h.Ap.*487, cf. 503 (s.v.l.).

❋ **βοεύς,** έως, ὁ, *rope of ox-hide,* ἐϋστρέπτοισι βοεῦσι Od.2.426.

**βοή,** Dor. **βοά,** ἡ, *loud cry, shout,* in Hom. mostly *battle-cry,* βοὴν ἀγαθός Il.2.408, al.; βοᾶς δ' ἔτι μηδ' ὄνομ' εἴη let there be not even the name *of war,* Theoc.16.97; later of prayer, Ἑλληνικὸν νόμισμα θυστάδος β. A.*Th.*269; κακοφάτιδα β. *cry* of mourning, Id.*Pers.*936 (lyr.); β. καὶ οἶκτος And.1.48; κραυγὴ καὶ β. D.54.9; also, *song* of joy, ἴτω ξύναυλος βοὰ χαρᾷ E.*El.*879 (lyr.), cf. Pi.*N.*3.67, Ar.*Ra.*212; of oracles, ἀείδουσα..βοὰς ἃς ἂν Ἀπόλλων κελαδήσῃ E.*Ion* 92 (lyr.); *shout, murmur* of a crowd, Pl.*Lg.*700c (pl.); θόρυβος καὶ β. Id.*Ti.*70e; of things, *roar* of the sea, Od.24.48; *sound* of musical instruments, αὐλοὶ φόρμιγγές τε βοὴν ἔχον Il.18.495, cf. Pi.*O.*3.8, *P.*10.39 (pl.); β. σάλπιγγος A.*Th.*394; *cry* of birds, S.*Ant.*1021; θηρίων β. E.*Ba.*1085; βοὴν θωΰσσειν, ἀΰτεῖν, S.*Aj.*335, E.*Hec.*1092 (lyr.); ἐφθέγξατο βοή τις Id.*IT*1386; βοάσομαι τὰν ὑπέρτονον βοάν Phryn.Com.46 (lyr.); βοὴν ἱστάναι Antiph.196.2; ὅσον καὶ ἀπὸ βοῆς ἕνεκα as far as *sound* went, only in appearance, Th.8.92, cf. X.*HG*2.4.31. II. = βοήθεια, *aid called for, succour,* A.*Supp.*730, *Ag.*1349, S.*OC*1057 (lyr.). (*g*ᵘ*o*ᵘ*ā,* cf. Skt. *jō-guvē* (intensive of *gávatē*) 'proclaim aloud'.)

**βοηγενής,** ές, *born of an ox,* of bees, *AP*9.363.13 (Mel.).

❋ **βο-ήγια,** τά, festival at Miletus, *SIG*577.71 (written **βοιη-**); but **-ηγία,** ἡ, a form of *contest,* perh., = ταυροκαθαψία, *Michel*838 (Didyma). ❋ **-ηγοί,** οἱ, *ox-drivers* in a procession, dub. in *Inscr.Prien.*112.108 (i B.C.).

**βοηδόν,** Adv. *like oxen,* πίνειν Agatharch.38.

**βοηδρομ-έω,** Dor. **βοᾱ-,** *run to a cry for aid, haste to help,* πρὸς δόμους E.*Or.*1356; ἐπ' ἐσχάραν Id.*Heracl.*121; πρὸς τὸ νικώμενον Plu.*Sert.*19; σὺν ἵπποις, Ἀρχ.Δελτ.1.57 (Thermon). 2. *run with a cry,* App.*Hann.*42: c. inf., τύραννον ἀνελεῖν Id.*BC*2.119. ❋ **-ια,** ων, τά, *games in memory of the succour given* by Theseus against the Amazons, Plu.*Thes.*27; B. πέμπειν lead a procession *at the B.,* D.3.31. **-ίη,** ἡ, *helping, aiding,* Max.381 (pl.). ❋ **-ιος,** ον, = βοηδρόμος, of Apollo, Call.*Ap.*69, Paus.9.17.2. II. Dor. **Βαδρόμιος** (sc. μήν), name of month at Rhodes, *SIG*644.19 (ii B.C.), etc. ❋ **-ιών,** ῶνος, ὁ, name of a month at Athens, etc., D.3.5, Arist.*HA*578$^{b}$13, *SIG*282.18 (Priene, iv B.C.), etc. (Written Βοι- *IG*2$^{2}$.657, al.) **-ος,** ον, *giving succour,* E.*Ph.*1432; β. ποδί Id.*Or.*1290 (lyr.).

**βοήθ-αρχος,** ὁ, *captain of auxiliaries,* name of a Carthaginian officer, Plb.1.79.2, App.*Pun.*70. ❋ **-εια,** ἡ (Dor. **βοάθοια** *SIG*421.36 (Thermon)), *help, aid,* Th.2.22, etc.; β. τῷ λόγῳ πρός τινα Pl.*Prm.*128c; ἡ ὑπὲρ τῶν δικαίων β. D.56.15; βοήθειαν ἔχειν πρὸς ὑγίειαν, πρὸς τὴν ἑκάστου ὑπερβολὴν μηχανᾶσθαι, Arist.*PA*651$^{b}$1, 652$^{a}$32: nom. sg., as exclamation *'help!',* Plb.13.8.5: pl., Gorg.*Pal.*33, D.18.302, Arist.*Rh.*1383$^{a}$29; αἱ πρὸς εὔπλοιαν β. Ph.2.46, cf. *Act.Ap.*27.17. 2. *medical aid, cure,* κίνδυνος ἰσχυρότερος πάσης β. Plu.*Alex.*19. II. *force of auxiliaries,* ἡ παρὰ Διονυσίου β. X.*HG*7.1.20; νεῶν β. Th.4.8: opp. regular forces, D.4.32. ❋ **-έω** (sts. written βοιηθέω, *IG*2$^{2}$.237 (iv B.C.), *BGU*1007.12 (iii B.C.)), Ion. **βωθέω,** only Hsch. βωθέοντες, not in Hdt. (but cf. Eust.812.59) or Hp., cf. βοηθήσω *Michel* 12.15 (Erythrae, iv B.C.); Dor. **βοᾱθοέω** *SIG*421.27 (Thermon); Aeol. **βᾱθόημι** (q.v.):—Med., fut. -ήσομαι Lib.*Or.*1.128:—*come to aid, succour, assist, aid,* c. dat., τῇ σφετέρῃ Hdt.1.82; τοῖσιν ἠδικημένοις E.*IA*79; πρὸς τοὺς αὑτῶν ψιλούς X.*HG*1.2.3; τινὶ ἀντία τινός Hdt.5.99; τινὶ πρὸς τὸ ἄναντες X.*HG*4.8.38; ναυσὶ β. τινὶ πολιορκουμένῳ ib.1.6.22; β. τοῖς φίλοις τὰ δίκαια Id.*Mem.*2.6.25; β. τοῖς τῶν προγόνων ἀτυχήμασιν Aeschin.3.169; β. τῷ λόγῳ Pl.*Phd.*88e; β. τῷ θεῷ *maintain* his *rights,* Epist.Philipp.ap.D.18.157; β. τοῖς νόμοις Aeschin.1.33: c. dat. et acc., πατρὶ βοηθῶν θάνατον Pl.*Lg.*874c; of a physician, β. τῷ θερμῷ ἐπὶ τὸ ψυχρόν Hp.*VM*13: abs., Plu.*Alex.*19. 2. abs., *come to the rescue,* Hdt.1.30, 7.158, A.*Supp.*613, etc.; β. παρά τινα Hdt.9.57; ἐπί τινα *against* one, Id.1.62, 4.125, Th.1.126, etc.; β. ἐς.. Hdt.6.103; ἐπὶ.. Th.3.97, 4.72; ἐπὶ τὰς ναῦς Id.8.11; ἐκεῖσε D.4.41; β. πρός τι *contribute* to an object, v.l. in Arist.*EN*1155$^{a}$14, cf. *Metaph.*1079$^{b}$16, or *keep* it *off,* Id.*Resp.*474$^{b}$24, *HA*621$^{a}$13; χρήμασι *with* money, Id.*EN*1130$^{a}$19: Medic., βοηθεῖ πρὸς τὸ κώνειον *it is an antidote* to.., Thphr.*HP*9.20.1; freq. in Dsc. as β. τοῖς φαγοῦσι 4.83. 3. Pass., *to be assisted, receive help,* παρά τινος Arist.*Rh.*1383$^{b}$28; βοηθήσομαι Lxx*Da.*11.34, but βοηθηθήσομαι *Is.*44.2; ἐβοήθην ib.10.3, 2 *Ch.*26.15 (v.l. ἐβοηθήθην); ἵν' ὦ βεβοηθημένη *PRyl.*122.12 (ii A.D.); esp. of patients, *derive benefit,* Dsc.4.82, Plu.2.687f: impers., ἐμοὶ βεβοήθηται τῷ τεθνεῶτι Antipho 1.31; ταύτῃ μοι βεβοηθημένον ἐγεγόνει φιλοσοφίᾳ Pl.*Ep.*347e. **-ημα,** ατος, τό, *resource,* Arist.*Rh.*1405$^{a}$7 (pl.); *assistance,* πρὸς τὴν μάχην Plb.1.22.3: in pl., *succours,* τὰ -ματα τοῦ συγγράμματος Diog.Oen.2. 2. *remedy,* Hp.*VM*13, D.S.1.25, Dsc.4.83, S.E.*P.*3.280. **-ημᾰτικός,** ή, όν, = βοηθητικός, Dsc.*Alex.Praef.*, Gal.19.395. **-ήσιμος,** ον, *curable,* Thphr.*HP*9.16.7. **-ησις,** εως, ἡ, *aid, succour,* Hp.*Praec.*8, dub. in Aen.Tact.16.4; πρὸς τὴν τῆς ὑγιείας β. Alex.Aphr.*in Sens.*98.22. **-ητέον,** *one must help,* X.*HG*6.5.10, D.1.17, etc. II. Adj. -ητέος, α, ον, Jul.*Or.*7.229a. ❋ **-ητικός,** ή, όν, *ready* or *able to help, serviceable,* τινί Arist.*Rh.*1374$^{a}$24; τοῖς πένησι Plu.*Sol.*29; τῶν δεομένων Diotog.ap.Stob.4.7.62; πρός τι so as to *keep it off,* Arist.*Pol.*1267$^{a}$16; or towards *promoting it,* Id.*HA*515$^{b}$9: Comp. -ώτερον, τὸ ἄρρεν τοῦ θήλεος ib.608$^{b}$15: Sup. -ώτατος Iamb.*VP*25.111. **-όος,** Dor. **βοᾱ-,** ον, (βοή, θέω, cf. βοη-δρόμος) *hasting to the cry for help* or *the call to arms,* Il.13.477; β. ἅρμα a chariot *hasting to the battle,* 17.481. II. *aiding, helping,* Pi.*N.*7.33, B.*Fr.*34:—Subst., *helper,* prob. Id.12.103, Theoc.22.23, Call.*Del.*27:—in Prose ❋ **βοηθός,** όν, *assisting, auxiliary,* νῆες Th.1.45: c. dat., ὁ τοῖς νόμοις β. Lys.*Fr.*53.1; freq. as Subst., *assistant,* Hdt.5.77, 6.100, Antipho 1.2, Pl.*R.*566b, al.; τῆς ἐπιτροπῆς *BGU*1047 iii 11 (ii A.D.); τοῦ στρατηγοῦ *POxy.*1469.10 (iii A.D.), etc. **-οῦρα,** ἡ, (with Lat. termination *-ura*) = βοήθεια, Lyd.*Mag.*3.6, 13.

**βοηλ-ᾰσία,** ἡ, *driving of oxen, cattle-lifting,* Il.11.672. II. *place where cattle are pastured, cattle-run, AP*7.626. III. *struggle with a bull,* Hld.10.31. ❋ **-ᾰτέω,** *drive away oxen,* Ar.*Fr.*758: generally, *urge on,* οὓς ἡ Κλεάνθους μωρία βοηλατεῖ Sosith.4; possibly, *drive with shouts,* Opp.*C.*4.64. 2. *tend oxen,* Lyc.816, Plu.*Phil.*4. **-άτης** [ᾰ], ου, ὁ, fem. **-άτις,** ιδος, ἡ: (βοῦς, ἐλαύνω):—*one that drives away oxen, cattle-lifter,* S.*Ichn.*117, *AP*11.176 (Lucill.). II. *ox-driving,* ῥάβδος *APl.*4.200 (Mosch.); *ox-tormenting,* μύωψ A.*Supp.*307. III. *cattle-driver,* Lys.7.19, Pl.*Plt.*261d, *PLond.*3.1177.112 (ii A.D.). IV. β. διθύραμβος the dithyramb *which gains a bull for the prize,* Pi.*O.*13.19. **-ᾰτικός,** ή, όν, *of* or *for cattle-driving*: -κή (sc. τέχνη), ἡ, *the herdsman's* art, Pl.*Euthphr.*13c.

**βόημα,** v. βόᾱμα.

**βοηνόμος,** ὁ, ἡ, *tending oxen,* Theoc.20.41.

**βόηξ,** v. βόαξ.

**βο-ήροτος,** ον, *ploughed by oxen,* Nic.*Fr.*43. ❋ **-ησις,** εως, ἡ, = βοή, *cry, shout for assistance,* Thd., Quint.*Ps.*21(22).2. **-ητής,** οῦ, ὁ, *clamorous,* Hp.*Ep.*19, prob. l. in *Morb.Sacr.*15, cf. Hsch. s. v. ἠπύτα: Dor. fem., **βοᾶτις** αὐδά A.*Pers.*575 (lyr.). **-ητικός,** ή, όν, gloss on foreg., Sch.A. l. c. **-ητός,** ή, όν, *shouted* or *sung aloud,* θρήνοισι βοητὸν ὑμήναον *Epigr.Gr.*418.7 (Cyrene). **-ητύς,** ύος, ἡ, Ep. for βόησις, Od.1.369.

**βοθρ-εύω,** *dig a trench* or *pit, Gp.*9.6.2:—also **-έω,** Nonn.*D.*47.69, and **-ίζω,** Heliod.ap.Orib.46.22.16. **-ίον,** τό, Dim. of βόθρος, *small trench,* to set plants in, *Gp.*8.18.2, Alciphr.3.13. II. *small ulcer,* Hp.*Liqu.*6. 2. in pl., *sockets* of the teeth, Gal.2.754.

**βοθροειδής,** ές, '*pitting*' on pressure, of tumours, Hp.*Mul.*2.118.

**βόθρ-ος,** ὁ, *hole, trench,* or *pit dug in the ground,* βόθρον ὀρύξαι Od.10.517; βόθρου τ' ἐξέστρεψε [τὴν ἐλαίαν] Il.17.58; *trough,* Od.6.92: generally, *hollow,* X.*An.*4.5.6; *grave, IG*14.238 (Acrae); ritual *pit* for offerings to ὑποχθόνιοι θεοί, β. καὶ μέγαρα Porph.*Antr.*6. **-όω,** = βοθρεύω, Gal.8.951 (Pass.); of caries, Heliod.ap.Orib.46.22.1; of a tumor '*pitting*' on pressure, Aët.15.1.

**βοθύν-ιον** [ῠ], τό, Dim. of sq., '*fossette*', Zos.Alch.p.222 B. ❋ **-ος,** ὁ, = βόθρος, Cratin.210, X.*Oec.*19.3, *BGU*1122.17 (i B.C.). II. a meteorological phenomenon, Arist.*Mete.*342$^{a}$36, *Mu.*392$^{b}$4. **-ωτής,** οῦ, ὁ, *ditcher,* Aq.4 *Ki.*25.12.

**βοιδ-άριον,** τό, Dim. of βοῦς, Ar.*Av.*585, *Fr.*82. **-ης,** ου, ὁ, *like an ox, quiet, stupid,* Men.1002. ❋ **-ιον,** τό, Dim. of βοῦς, Ar.*Ach.*1036, Arist.*HA*522$^{b}$14, *PSI*1.84 (iv/v A.D.):—also **βοΐδιον,** *AP*7.169; **βούδιον** (rejected by Phryn.69), Hermipp.35.2, *PFlor.*150.2 (iii A.D.).

**βοικεῖ·** γαμίσκει, Theognost.*Can.*19.4. **βοικία·** ἡ θεράπαινα, *AB*1354. 2. = ϝοικία, γᾶρ καὶ βοικίαρ ἔγκτησιν *Schwyzer* 425.24 (Elis, iii/ii B.C.).

**βοϊκός**, v. *βοεικός*. Adv. -**κῶς** Porph.*Abst*.3.3.

**βόϊνος**, η, ον, = βόειος, *Gloss.*; β. σάλπιγξ *having* βοὸς προτομή *as mouthpiece*, Eust.1139.58.

**βοιόν**, τό, *cycle of fifty years*, Hdn.Gr.1.376.

⊛ **βοϊστί**, Adv. *in ox-language*, λαλεῖν Porph.*VP*24.

**Βοιωτ-άρχης**, ου, ὁ, *Boeotarch*, one of the chief magistrates of the Boeotian league, Hdt.9.15, Th.4.91, *Hell.Oxy*.11.3, etc.:—also -**αρχος**, X.*HG*3.4.4: hence⊛-**αρχέω**, *to be a Boeotarch*, Th.4.91, D.59. 99. -**αρχία**, ἡ, *office of Boeotarch*, Ael.*VH*13.42, Plu.*Pel*.25: pl., Id.2.785c.

**Βοιωτ-ιάζω**, τῇ φωνῇ *speak Boeotian*, X.*An*.3.1.26, *Com.Adesp.* 677. II. *side with the Boeotians*, in politics, etc., X.*HG*5.4.34, Aeschin.3.139:—also -**ίζω**, Plu.2.575d codd. -**ίδιον** [τῐ], τό, Dim. of Βοιώτιος, Ar.*Ach*.872.

**Βοιωτιουργής**, ές, (ἔργον) *of Boeotian work*, κράνος X.*Eq*.12.3.

**Βοιωτός**, ὁ, *a Boeotian*, Il.2.494, etc.:—**Βοιωτία**, ἡ, *Boeotia*, so called from its *cattle-pastures*:—Adj.⊛**Βοιώτ-ιος**, α, ον, *Boeotian*, Hes. *Fr*.132, etc.; with a notion of *gluttonous*, οὕτω σφόδρ' ἐστὶ τοὺς τρόπους B. Eub.39, cf. 34; εἰμὶ γὰρ B. πολλὰ.. ἐσθίων Mnesim.2; ὀξύπεινον ἄνδρα καὶ B. Demonic.1; and of *dull, stupid*, Plu.2.995e: prov., ὗς Βοιωτία Pi.*O*.6.90, cf. *Fr*.83; also B. νόμος, melody used in κιθαρῳδία, S.*Fr*.966, Plu.2.1132d; Βοιώτιον μέλος Sch.Ar.*Ach*.13:—also -**ικός**, ή, όν, πόλεμος D.S.14.81, Plu.*Lys*.27, and -**ιακός**, ή, όν, *IG*11.161*B*122 (Delos, iii B.C.), Str.9.2.11. Adv. -ιακῶς (v.l. -ικῶς) ibid.; Βοιωτιακά, τά, title of work by Hellanicus, Sch.Il.2. 494:—fem. **Βοιωτίς**, ίδος, X.*HG*5.1.36.

**Βοκόπια** or **Βουκόπια**, τά, festival at Lindus, *IG*12(1).792, al.

⊛ **βολαῖος**, α, ον, (βολή) *violent*, θύννος *Trag.Adesp*.391, cf. Eust. 1404.52.

**βολαυγέω**, Astrol., = ἀκτινοβολέω, τινὰ ἀκτῖσι or ἐν ἀκτίνεσσι, Man. 4.272,431.

**βόλβα**, ἡ, = Lat. *vulva*, *AP*11.410 (Lucill.).

**βολβ-άριον**, τό, Dim. of βολβός, Epict.*Ench*.7. -**ίδιον**, τό, *small cuttle-fish*, with a strong smell, Hp.*Mul*.2.133: -**ίτιον**, Gal. 19.89.

**βόλβιθος**, ὁ, v. *βόλιτον*.

**βολβ-ίνη**, ἡ, *star-flower*, *Ornithogalum umbellatum*, Thphr.*HP*7. 3.9, Matro *Fr*.2.3. -**ίον**, τό, Dim. of βολβός, Hp.*Mul*.2.196. -**ίσκος**, ὁ, *AP*11.35 (Phld.). -**ιτίνη** (prob. l. for βολβοτύνη), ἡ, = βολβίδιον, Arist. and Speus.ap.Ath.7.318e:—also -**ιτίς**, ίδος, ἡ, Epich.61.

⊛ **βόλβῑτον**, τό, or **βόλβῑτος**, ὁ, Thphr.*HP*5.5.3, Dsc.2.167, Archig. ap.Gal.12.173, worse forms of *βόλιτον*, -τος, acc. to Phryn.335.

**βολβο-ειδής**, ές, *bulb-like, bulb-shaped*, Dsc.2.144, Aët.12.63. -**κάστᾰνον**, τό, *earth-nut*, = βούνιον, Alex.Trall.5.6.

**βολβός**, ὁ, *purse-tassels*, *Muscari comosum*, Ar.*Ec*.1092, Pl.*R*. 372c, Arist.*Pr*.926$^a$6, Thphr.*HP*7.13.8, Theoc.14.17, Dsc.2.170: freq. in Com., Pl.Com.173.9, etc.; identified with ὕδνον by Sch.Ar.*Nu*. 188; also of other bulbous plants, β. ἐμετικός, = *Narcissus Tazetta*, Dsc.4.156; β. ἄγριος, = κολχικόν, ib.4.83; β. ἐριοφόρος, = *Scilla hyacinthoides*, Thphr.*HP*7.13.8 (an Indian kind, perh. *Euodendron anfractuosum*, Phan.Hist.28); β., = νάρκισσος, Ps.-Dsc.4.158; = ἡμεροκαλλές, Id.3.122; βολβοί perh. = *eyes* on root-stock of κάλαμος, Dsc.1.85.

**βολβοτύνη**, v. βολβιτίνη.

**βολβοφάκη**, ἡ, *soup of bulbs and lentils*, *Com.Adesp*.367,368, Ath. 13.584d.

**βολβώδης**, ες, *bulbous*, Thphr.*HP*7.13.9.

**βολβωρῠχέω**, *dig* βολβοί, *Com.Adesp*.959.

**βολετισμός**, ὁ, *angling*, Orac. in *Ath.Mitt*.25.399 (Aezani).

**βολέω**, = βάλλω, *Theol.Ar*.37, Eust.1405.4; in early writers Ep. pf. Pass. βεβόλημαι *to be stricken* with grief and the like, ἄχεϊ.. βεβολημένος ἦτορ Il.9.9, cf. Od.10.247; πένθεϊ.. βεβολήατο πάντες Il.9.3; ἀμηχανίῃ βεβόλησαι A.R.4.1318; ἀμφασίῃ βεβόλητο Q.S.7. 726. II. in literal sense, μήτηρ ἀμφ' αὐτὸν βεβολημένη *falling* about his neck, A.R.1.262; Βοώτης.. ἀντέλλει βεβολημένος Ἀρκτούροιο *dominated by* Arcturus, Arat.609.

**βολεών**, ῶνος, ὁ, *dunghill*, Din.ap.Harp., Philem.221 codd., Nic. ap.Harp., Eust.1404 fin.

⊛ **βολή**, ἡ, *throw*: 1. *stroke* or *wound* of a missile (opp. πληγή, of sword or pike), Od.17.283, cf. 24.161; β. πέτρων E.*Or*.59; λίθων Phld.*Ir*.p.31 W. (pl.); μέχρι λίθου καὶ ἀκοντίου βολῆς Th.5.65; β. ἔρωτος *shafts of love*, *AP*12.160; βολαῖς.. σφόγγος ὤλεσεν γραφήν by its *stroke* or *touch*, A.*Ag*.1329; *swing* of ἁλτῆρες, Antyll.ap.Orib. 6.34.1. 2. κύβων βολαί *throws* or *casts* of dice, S.*Fr*.429. 3. metaph., β. ὀφθαλμῶν *quick glances*, Od.4.150; κάτω.. βλεμμάτων ῥέπει β. A.*Fr*.242, cf. Philostr.*VS*2.27.5. 4. β. κεραύνιοι *thunderbolts*, A.*Th*.430; βολαὶ ἡλίου *sun-beams*, S.*Aj*.877, cf. E.*Ion* 1134; χρυσοῦ.. βολαῖς *with* golden *rays*, of a statue, *IG*14.1026 (iii A.D.); βολαὶ χιόνος *radiance*, E.*Ba*.662; τὰς ψυχὰς οἷον βολὰς εἶναι λέγουσιν Plot.6.4.3. 5. βολαί, = ὠδῖνες, Procop.*Goth*.4.22. 6. *payment*, ἀποδώσω ἐπὶ βολαῖς δυσὶν *Stud.Pal*.20.139 (vi A.D.).

**βολίδιον**, τό, Dim. of βολίς 2, Olymp. *in Mete*.298.33.

⊛ **βολίζη**, ἡ, *female slave*, Cretan word in Seleuc.ap.Ath.6.267c.

**βολίζω**, (βολίς) *heave the lead, take soundings*, *Act.Ap*.27.28, Eust. 563.30:—Pass., *sink in water*, *Gp*.6.17.

**βόλῑμοι** δίκαι, = ἀναβόλιμοι δ., *deferred, adjourned* suits, Ἀρχ.Ἐφ. 1911.133 (Gonni): **βολῖμον**, τό, *period of delay*, *BCH*37.204 (Chios): hence **βολῑμοδῐκασταί**, οἱ, *judges who try* β. δίκαι, Ἀρχ.Ἐφ.1911.129 (Gonni).

⊛ **βόλιμος**, = μόλιβος, *SIG*241.28 (Delph., iv B.C.), *IG*4.1484.275 (Epid., iv B.C.): Syracusan acc. to *EM*204.40.

**βόλινθος**, ὁ, perh. = βόνασος, Arist.*Mir*.830$^a$7.

**βόλιον**, τό, *counter* used in the game of πεττοί, Hsch., *EM*666.16, Eust.1396.59. II. = πόλιον, Ps.-Dsc.3.110.

⊛ **βολίς**, ίδος, ἡ, *missile, javelin*, Plu.*Demetr*.3. 2. *sounding-lead*, Sch.Il.24.80. 3. ἀστραπῶν βολίδες *flashes* of lightning, Lxx *Wi*. 5.21; ἀστραπὴ βολίς (sic) ib.*Za*.9.14. 4. *cast of the dice*, *AP*9. 767 (Agath.). b. *die*, ib.768 (Id.).

**βολιστικός**, ή, όν, (βόλος) *to be caught by the casting-net*, Plu.2. 977f.

**βολίτ-αινα** [ῐ], ἡ, = βολβίδιον, Arist.*HA*525$^a$19, 621$^b$17; cf. ὄζολις. ⊛ -**ινος**, η, ον, *of cow-dung*, Ar.*Ra*.295; σκέλος Cratin.*inc*.17 Mein. -**ον**, τό (**βόλῐτος**, ὁ, acc. to Sch.Ar.*Ra*.295:—also **βόλβιθος**, ὁ, *PMag.Par*.1.1439), *cow-dung*, mostly in pl., Cratin.39, Ar. *Ach*.1026, *Eq*.658: prov., βολίτου δίκη vexatious action, Sch.Ar.*Eq*. 658.

**βόλλα**, Aeol. for βουλή, Plu.2.288b, *IG*12(2).6.38, etc.:—**βόλλαος**, = βουλαῖος, ib.68.8:—**βολλεύω**, for βουλεύω, ib.6.34.

**βόλλομαι**, Aeol., = βούλομαι, Sapph.*Supp*.5.17, Theoc.28.15.

**βολλωτός**, ή, όν, (Lat. *bulla*) *possessing knobs*, περονείδων ζεῦγος βολλωτῶν *CPR*12.4 (i A.D.).

**βολοί**, οἱ, shortening of ὀβολοί, Amphis 30.12, Hsch.

**βολοκτῠπία**, ἡ, *rattling of dice*, *AP*9.767 (Agath.).

⊛ **βόλομαι**, Ep., Ion. (*IG*12(9).189.31 (Eretria, iv B.C.)), Arc. (ib.5 (2).3.9 (Tegea, iv B.C.)), = βούλομαι, Τρωσὶν δὴ βόλεται δοῦναι κράτος Il.11.319; εἰ.. βόλεσθε αὐτόν τε ζώειν κτλ. Od.16.387; νῦν δ' ἑτέρως ἐβόλοντο θεοί (vulg. ἐβάλοντο) 1.234, cf. A.R.1.262; εἴ τι βόλεστε (2 pl.) *SIG*1259.5 (iv B.C.).

**βόλος**, ὁ, *throw with a casting-net*, Orac.ap.Hdt.1.62; μέγα δίκτυον ἐς β. ἕλκει draws it back for *a cast*, Theoc.1.40: metaph., εἰς β. καθίστασθαι, ἔρχεσθαι, fall within *the cast* of the net, E.*Ba*.848, *Rh*.730. b. *net*, Herod.7.75, Ael.*NA*8.3; for birds, *AP*6.184 (Zos.). 2. *thing caught*, ἰχθύων β. *draught, catch*, of fishes, A.*Pers*. 424, Plu.2.91c; βόλον ἀνασπάσασθαι land one's *catch*, E.*El*.582. II. *casting of teeth*, Arist.*HA*576$^b$13 (pl.), *GA*748$^b$9; καταμαθεῖν τὸν β. examine a horse's *teeth*, Hierocl.*Facet*.37. III. *cast of dice*, Poll.7.204, Plaut.*Rud*.360. IV. βόλος· θύρα, πηλός (i.e. βῶλος), Hsch.

**βόλυβδος**, ὁ, = μόλυβδος, *Tab.Defix*.107 (iv B.C.).

**βόλυνθον**, τό, = βόλιτον, Hsch.

**βομβάζω**, *jeer at*, Suid.

**βομβάξ**, interjection, *prodigious!* Ar.*Th*.45; intensified, **βομβᾰλοβομβάξ**, ib.48.

⊛ **βομβαύλιος**, ὁ, (βομβέω, αὐλός) comic compd. for ἀσκαύλης, *bagpiper*, with play on βομβυλιός, Ar.*Ach*.866.

**βομβ-έω**, (βόμβος) *make a booming noise*; in Hom. always of falling bodies, τρυφάλεια χαμαὶ βόμβησε πεσοῦσα Il.13.530; αἰχμὴ χαλκείη χαμάδις βόμβ. πεσ. 16.118, cf. Od.18.397; βόμβησαν.. κατὰ ῥόον the oars *fell with a loud noise*.., 12.204; βόμβησεν δὲ λίθος the stone *flew humming* through the air, 8.190; of the sea, *roar*, Simon. 1; of thunder, *roll, rumble*, Nonn.*D*.1.301; *hum*, of bees, etc., Arist.*HA*535$^b$6, 627$^a$24, Theoc.3.13, Pl.*R*.564d; βομβεῖ δὲ νεκρῶν σμῆνος S.*Fr*.879; of mosquitoes, *buzz*, Ar.*Pl*.538; of birds, λιγυρὸν βομβεῦσιν ἀκανθίδες *AP*5.291 (Agath.): generally of sound, *buzz in one's ears*, Pl.*Cri*.54d; but ὦτα βομβεῖ μοι Luc.*DMeretr*.9. 2: c. dat. instr., κόχλῳ β. Nonn.*D*.36.93. -**ηδόν**, Adv. *buzzing, with a hum*, A.R.2.133, Luc.*Pisc*.42. -**ήεις**, εσσα, εν, = βομβητικός, *APl*.4.74; κῦμα Nonn.*D*.3.32. -**ησις**, εως, ἡ, *buzzing*: *buzzing crowd*, Lxx *Ba*.2.29. -**ητής**, οῦ, ὁ, *buzzing*, ἑσμός *AP*6. 236 (Phil.):—fem. -**ήτρια**, Νύμφαι Orph.*H*.51.9. -**ητικός**, ή, όν, *humming*, Eust.945.23:—also -**ικός**, ή, όν, τὸ τῶν θρήνων β. Sch. metr.Pi.*O*.1.

**βομβοία**· κολυμβὰς ἐλαία (Cypr.), Hsch.: **βομβοιλαδόνας**· ἐνιαυτούς, Id.

⊛ **βόμβος**, ὁ, *booming, humming*, Pl.*Prt*.316a, Arist.*Resp*.475$^a$16; β. ἀνέμου κατιόντος its *booming sound*, Hld.5.27; of thunder, Epicur. *Ep*.2 p.46 U.; *buzzing in the ears*, Hp.*Coac*.189; *rumbling in the intestines*, Gal.7.241:—**βόμβο**, τό, barbarism in Ar.*Th*.1176. (Onomatop.)

**βομβόχυλον**, = μανδραγόρας, Dsc.4.75.

**βομβρύζων**· τονθορύζων, βοῶν, Hsch. **βομβρυνάζειν**· βρενθύεσθαι, Id.

⊛ **βομβῠκ-ίας** κάλαμος reed *used for making deep-toned flutes* (cf. βόμβυξ II), Thphr.*HP*4.11.3. -**ινος**, η, ον, *silken*, ἱμάτια Lib.*Decl*. 33.6; σινδών Ps.-Callisth.3.28.

**βομβύκιον** [ῠ], τό, species of *mason-bee*, *Chalicodoma muraria*, Arist.*HA*555$^a$13 (v.l. βομβυκοειδῶν). 2. *small buzzing insect*, Sch. Ar.*Nu*.158. II. *cocoon of silk-worm*, Arist.*HA*551$^b$14.

**βομβῠκοειδής**, ές, *like silk*, ὑφή Dsc.3.16.

**βομβῠλεύματα**, τά, *kickshaws*, *Com.Adesp*.960.

**βομβύλη**, ἡ, = λήκυθος, Hsch., Sch.A.R.2.569.

⊛ **Βομβυλία**, ἡ, title of Athena in Boeotia, Hsch.

⊛ **βομβῠλι-άζω**, (βομβέω) = βορβορύζω, Arist.*Pr*.949$^a$13 (v.l. -ίζουσιν). -**ον**, τό, = βολβίδιον, Gal.19.89. ⊛ -**ός** or -**ύλιος**, ὁ, *buzzing insect*: *humble-bee*, Ar.*V*.107, Isoc.10.12, Arist.*HA*623$^b$12, 629$^a$29; *gnat, mosquito*, Hsch. 2. *cocoon of the silk-worm* (v.l. βομβυλίς), Arist.*HA*551$^b$12. II. *narrow-necked vessel* that *gurgles* in pouring, Hp.*Morb*.3.16, *IG*11(2).154*A*68 (Delos, iii B.C.), Socr.ap.Ath. 11.784d, Luc.*Lex*.7. (On the accent v. Hdn.Gr.1.116, al.)

**βομβῠλίς**, ἴδος, ἡ, = πομφόλυξ, Hsch. II. cf. βομβυλιός I. 2.

❀ **βόμβυξ**, ῦκος, ὁ, *silk-worm*, Arist.*HA* ap.Ath.7.352f. b. insect like a wasp, Hsch. 2. *silk garment*, Alciphr.1.39. II. *deep-toned flute*, A.*Fr*.57.3, Arist.*Aud*.800$^b$25, Poll.4.82, Plu.2.713a. 2. *cap of a flute*, Poll.4.70. 3. *lowest note* on the flute, Arist.*Metaph*. 1093$^b$3:—hence Comp. **βομβυκέστερος**, *deeper in tone*, Nicom.*Harm*. 11. III. Lacon., = στάμνος, Hsch., *AB*1354.

**βομβώδης**, ες, = βομβητικός, Ael.*NA*6.37; of intestinal flatus, Gal.7.241.

**βομβών**, ῶνος, ὁ, late form for βουβών, Moeris94, Hdn.Gr.1.23, 2. 483.

**βόνασος** or **βόνασσος**, ὁ, *European bison, aurochs, Bos bonasus*, Arist.*HA*498$^b$31, 630$^a$18, *PA*663$^a$14, Str.15.1.69.

**βοο-βοσκός**, ὁ, *herdsman*, Suid. **-γληνος**, ον, *ox-eyed*, Nonn. *D*.7.260. **-δμητήρ**, ῆρος, ὁ, (δαμάω) *slaying oxen*, λέοντε Q.S. 1.524, cf. 587. **-ζύγιον** [ῠ], τό, *ox-yoke*, Lxx*Si*.26.7. **-θύτης** [ῠ], ου, ὁ, *slayer of oxen*, Suid. **-κλεψ**, contr. **βοῦκλεψ**, ὁ, *stealer of oxen*, S.*Fr*.318. **-κλόπος**, ον, *ox-stealing*, Orph.*A*.1057, Nonn.*D*.1.337; cf. βουκλόπος. **-κραιρος**, ον, *ox-horned*, ib.13. 314. ❀ **-κτᾰσία**, ἡ, (κτείνω) *slaying of oxen*, A.R.4.1724(pl.). **-κτῐτος**, ον, (κτίζω) of Thebes, *founded where the heifer lay*, Nonn.*D*.25. 415. **-νόμος**, ὁ, *herdsman*, Cyr., Suid. **-πρόσωπος**, ον, *ox-faced*, Porph.*Abst*.3.16codd. **-ρραίστης**, ου, ὁ, *slayer of oxen*, Tryph.361. **-σκόπος**, ον, *looking after oxen*, Nonn.*D*.31.225 (**βόοσκος**, Hsch. may be f.l. for this word). ❀ **-σσόος**, ον, (σεύω) *driving oxen wild*, of the gadfly, Nonn.*D*.11.191: contr., βουσσόον ὅν τε μύωπα..καλέουσιν Call.*Fr*.46, cf. Cerc.8.2. II. *ox-driving*, κέντρα Q.S.5.64, cf. Nonn.*D*.11.149, al. 2. = βοηλάτης I, epith. of Hermes, ib.4.31. **-στάσιον** [ᾰ], τό, = sq., *Stud.Pal*.20.74 (iii A.D.). **-στᾰσις**, εως, ἡ, = βούστασις, Call.*Del*.102. **-στικτος**, ον, dub. sens., θυηλή (of an offering *of bull's blood*) Nonn.*D*.5. 281. **-στολος**, ον, *riding on a bull*, νύμφη, of Europa, ib.1. 66. **-σφᾰγία**, Ion. -ίη, ἡ, *slaughter of oxen*, *APl*.4.101. **-τρόφος**, ον, = βουτρ-, D.P.558, Nonn.*D*.14.377, *PLond*.5.1654 (iv A.D.).

**βοόω**, *change into an ox*, Eust.70.28.

**βορά**, ἡ, *food*, prop. of carnivorous beasts, ποντίοις δάκεσι δὸς βοράν A.*Pr*.583(lyr.), cf. *Ch*.530; θηρσὶν ἄθλιον β. E.*Ph*.1603, cf. S.*Ant*.30; κυνὸς β. Ar.*Eq*.416; ὁ λέων..[χαίρει] ὅτι β. ἕξει Arist.*EN*1118$^a$23; of cannibal feasts, Hdt.1.119; κρεῶν.. οἰκείας βορᾶς of their own flesh *served as food*, of the children of Thyestes, A.*Ag*.1220, cf. 1597; βορᾶς τοῦ..Οἰδίπου γόνου *food* torn from the body of the son of Oedipus, S.*Ant*.1017, cf. 1040; βορᾷ χαίρουσιν ἀνθρωποκτόνῳ; E.*Cyc*.127; οὐ γὰρ ἐν γαστρὸς β. τὸ χρηστὸν εἶναι in *gluttony*, Id.*Supp*.865: less freq. of simple *food*, Pi.*Fr*.124.5, A.*Pers*.490, S.*Ph*.274, etc. (βορρά is prob. f.l. for φορβᾶ in *AP*3.14.) (Cf. βιβρώσκω: g$^w$erə-, cf. Skt. *-gara-* in compds. (cf. δημο-βόρος, Lat. *carni-vorus*) 'devouring', *giráti* 'swallow', Lat. *vorare*, Lith. *gérti* 'drink', etc.)

**βοράζω**, = τρέφω, *EM*205.6 (but -ᾴζω, 737.21).

**βόρασσος**, ὁ, *growing spadix of the date with immature fruit*, Dsc. 1.109.

❀ **βόρατον**, τό, *juniper, Juniperus foetidissima*, D.S.2.49. II. = βράθυ, Dsc.1.76.

**βοράω**, *eat*, *EM*216.14.

**βορβορ-ίζω**, (βόρβορος) *to be like mud*, ἐν γεύσει Dsc.5.75. II. βορβορίζει· γογγύζει, μολύνει (Cypr.), Hsch. **-ισμός**, ὁ, = βορβορυγμός, Cael.Aur.*CP*3.20.194. **-ῖται**, οἱ, name of a guild at Thera, *IG*12(3).6.

❀ **βορβορό-θῠμος**, ον, *muddy-minded*, Ar.*Pax*753. **-κοίτης**, ου, ὁ, *Mudcoucher*, name of a frog, Batr.230.

**βορβορόπη**, ἡ, *filthily lewd*, Hippon.110.

**βόρβορος**, ὁ, *mire, filth*, Asius1, Heraclit.13, A.*Eu*.694, Ar.*V*. 259, Pl.*Phd*.69c, Lxx*Je*.45.6, 2*Ep.Pet*.2.22, etc.: distd. fr. πηλός *clay, moist earth*, Luc.*Prom.Es*1; *sewer*, Hsch.: metaph., *foul abuse*, τοσοῦτον β. κατήντλησάς μου Luc.*Lex*.17.

**βορβορο-τάραξις**, ὁ, *mud-stirrer*, Ar.*Eq*.309. **-φόρβα**, ἡ, fem. Adj. *feeding on filth*, *PMag.Par*.1.1402.

**βορβορ-όω**, *make muddy*, Arist.*GA*763$^a$29 (Pass.). **-ὐγή**, ἡ, = sq., Hsch. ❀ **-υγμός**, ὁ, *intestinal rumbling*, Hp.*Prog*.11; *belching*, Suid. **-ώδης**, ες, *miry, filthy*, πηλὸς -έστερος Pl.*Phd*.111d; ἰλὺς Arist.*HA*547$^b$20; θάλαττα Men.25; of pus or pitch, *turbid*, Hp. *Aph*.7.44, Thphr.*HP*9.2.3: metaph., βίος Ph.1.322. **-ωπόν**· αἰσχρόν, βορβόρῳ ἐμφερές, Hsch. **-ωσις**, εως, ἡ, = βορβορυγμός, Archig.ap.Aët.9.40.

**βορβύλα**, ἡ, a *cake* made of poppy and sesame, Hsch. **βορδών**, ῶνος, ὁ, = βουρδών, Philagr.ap.Aët.12.51.

**Βορεάδης**, ου, ὁ, *son of Boreas*, D.S.4.44; Ep. **Βορηϊάδης** *AP*9. 550 (Antip.).

❀ **Βορέας**, ου, ὁ: Aeol. **Βορίαις** Alc.*Supp*.7.13; Ion. **Βορέης** Hom., or **Βορῆς**, έω, Hdt.7.189; Att. **Βορρᾶς**, ᾶ, Cratin.207, Th.6.2, al., Pl.*Criti*.112b, *PPetr*.1.21.11 (iii B.C.), *Ev.Luc*.13.29, etc.; but gen. Βορέου *IG*1$^2$.373.29:—*north wind*, personified as *Boreas*, Od.5.296, etc.: generally, opp. νότος, B. καὶ ἀπαρκτίας Arist.*Mete*.363$^b$14, cf. *Mu*.394$^b$20 (pl.), *HA*612$^b$5 (pl.); B. πνέουσιν ὀρνιθίαι *PHib*.1.27. 59 (iii B.C.). 2. *the north*, πρὸς Βορέην (v.l. -ρῆν) ἄνεμον towards *the north*, Hdt.2.101; πρὸς Βορέαν τοῦ ὄρους Th.2.96, cf. 6.2; Βορρᾷ *to the north*, *BGU*1127.12 (i B.C.), etc.; cf. Βορέην· τὴν φῦσαν, Hsch.

❀ **Βορεάς**, poet. **Βορειάς** and **Βορηϊάς**, άδος, ἡ, *Boread, daughter of Boreas*, S.*Ant*.985 (lyr.), Orph.*A*.738:—also **Βορηΐς**, ΐδος, Nonn.*D*. 33.211. II. as fem. Adj., *northern*, πνοαί A.*Fr*.195.

**Βορε-ασμός**, ὁ, *festival of Boreas* at Athens, Hsch. (pl.). **-ηθεν**, Adv. *from the north*, D.P.79. **-ηνδε**, Adv. *northwards*, Id. 137. **-ῆτις**, ιδος, ἡ, fem. of Βόρειος, Id.243.

**βορειαῖος**, α, ον, = βόρειος, *APl*.4.230 (Leon.).

**βορεινός**, ή, όν, = βόρειος, A.D.*Synt*.94.15, *CPHerm*.28.13 (iii A.D.): —also **βορινός**, ή, όν, *POxy*.498.8 (ii A.D.): **βορρινός**, ή, όν, ib.243. 21 (i A.D.), etc.

**Βορειόθεν**, poet. for Βορέηθεν, Nonn.*D*.6.127.

**βορεῖον**· γαστὴρ ἐσκευασμένη πως, Hsch.

❀ **βόρειος**, α, ον, also ος, ον S.*OC*1240 (lyr.): Ion. **βορήϊος**, η, ον:—*from the quarter of the north wind, northern*, opp νότιος, θάλασσα Hdt. 4.37, 6.31; β. ἀκτά *exposed to the north*, S. l. c.; τὸ β. τεῖχος Ar.*Fr*.556, And.3.5, Pl.*R*.439e; τῆς Πλειάδος βορείου γενομένης having appeared *in the north*, Arist.*HA*542$^b$11. 2. *of the north wind*, β. χειμών a winter *during which northerly winds prevail*, Hp.*Aph*.3.11, Arist.*Pr*. 859$^b$21; ἔαρ ib.862$^a$13; βόρεια, τά, *northerly winds*, ib.944$^a$1, etc. (rarely in sg., Ar.*V*.265; ὅταν ᾖ βόρειον X.*Cyn*.8.1); βορείοις *in the time of northerly winds*, Arist.*HA*574$^a$1, al.; βορείων ὄντων ib.592$^a$ 14: Comp. -ότερος Arat.247, Alex.Aphr.*in Metaph*.446.34: Sup. -ότατος Man.4.241. II. βόρειον, = ἐλλεβορίνη, Ps.-Dsc.4.108; βόρειος, = ἀείζωον τὸ μέγα, ib.88.

**βορεύς**, ὁ, = βορέας, in oblique cases βορῆος, -ῆι, -ῆα, Arat.430, 820, 882, etc.: nom. pl. βορεῖς Alciphr.1.1.

**βορεύω**, *blow from the north*, χειμῶνος βορεύοντος Thphr.*Sign*.53.

**βορηά**· βοτάνη πᾶσα (fort. ποιά), Hsch.

**Βορηϊάς, βορήϊος, Βορῆς**, v. Βορειάς, βόρειος, Βορέας.

**βορθαγορίσκεα**· τὰ χοίρεια κρέα: and **βορθαγορίσκοι**· μικροὶ χοῖροι (Lacon.), Hsch.; cf. ὀρθαγορίσκος.

**Βορθεία**, ἡ, = Ὀρθία, title of Artemis, *IG*5(1).864, al.

**βορι-αῖος**, α, ον, = βόρειος, Phlp.*in Ph*.894.19:—also **-ακός**, *IG Rom*.4.1603 (Chondriae).

**βόρμαξ**, = μύρμηξ, also **βύρμαξ**, Hsch.

**βόρμος**, ὁ, = βρόμος, Dieuch.ap.Orib.4.7.20, *EM*205.3, Hsch.

**βοροποιός**, όν, (ποιέω) *inducing appetite*, Eust.1538.30.

**βορός** (A), ά, όν, (βορά) *gluttonous*, Ar.*Pax*38, Arist.*Phgn*.810$^b$ 18: Sup., Mnesith.ap.Orib.21.7.7, Luc.*Tim*.46. Adv. -ῶς Ath.5. 186c. II. *inducing appetite*, Asclepiad.ap.Eust.1538.30.

**βορός** (B), οῦ, ὁ (for ϝορός), *juice of pressed grapes* (Lacon.), Hsch.

**βορράζων**· ψοφῶν, Hsch.

**Βορρ-ᾶθεν**, = Βορέηθεν, Thphr.*Sign*.11, *IG*2$^2$.1241, al., Hp.*Vict*.2. 37. **-αῖος**, α, ον, also ος, ον *AP*9.561 (Phil.), = βόρειος, A.*Th*.527, *AP*6.245 (Diod.), etc. **-απηλιώτης**, ου, ὁ, *north-east wind*, Ptol. *Tetr*.67:—Adj. **-απηλιωτικός**, ή, όν, *north-eastern*, ibid. **-ᾶς**, ᾶ, ὁ, v. Βορέας.

❀ **βορρό-λιψ**, λῖβος, ὁ, *north-west wind*, *PMag.Par*.1.1646, Ptol. *Tetr*.60:—hence Adj. **-λῐβῠκός**, ή, όν, *north-western*, ib.39.

**βορσόν**· σταυρόν (Elean), Hsch. **βόρταχος**· βάτραχος, Id.

**βόρυβος**, = ὄροβος, *Ostr.Strassb*.606 (i/ii A.D.).

❀ **βόρυες**, οἱ, = ὄρυες, Hdt.4.192.

**Βορυσθέν-ης**, ους, ὁ, *Borysthenes, Dnieper*, Hdt.4.18:—hence **-είτης** or **-ίτης**, ου, Ion. **-εΐτης**, εω, ὁ, *an inhabitant of its banks*, Hdt. 4.17, Men.883, etc.

**βόσις**, εως, ἡ, (βόσκω) *food, fodder*, ἰχθύσι Il.19.268; οἰωνοῖς καὶ θηρσί Q.S.1.329; β. καὶ τροφή Porph.*Antr*.15.

❀ **βοσκ-άδιος** [ᾰ], α, ον, *foddered, fatted*, χήν Nic.*Al*.228. ❀ **-άς**, άδος, ἡ, *feeding*, *fed*, νηδύς Id.*Th*.782; ὀρταλίς Id.*Al*.293. 2. of birds *which feed themselves, not artificially fed*, Aët.9.30 (cf. βοσκός). II. as Subst., kind of *duck*, perh. *teal, Anas crecca*, Arist. *HA*593$^b$17, Alex.Mynd.ap.Ath.9.395d. **-εών**, ῶνος, ὁ, *feeder*, Hsch. **-ή**, ἡ, *fodder, food, pasturage*, A.*Eu*.266 (lyr.); πέτεσθαι ἐπὶ βοσκήν Arist.*HA*624$^a$27, cf. *PLond*.5.1692 (vi A.D.): pl., μήλων τε βοσκάς A.*Fr*.44.5, cf. E.*Hel*.1331 (lyr.). ❀ **-ημα**, ατος, τό, *that which is fed* or *fatted*: in pl., *fatted beasts, cattle*, S.*Tr*.762, E.*Ba*.677, X.*HG*4.6.6; of sheep, E.*Alc*.576 (lyr.), *El*.494; ἐμῆς χερὸς β., of horses, Id.*Hipp*.1356 (lyr.); of dogs, X.*Cyr*.8.1.9; ζῆν ἀπὸ βοσκημάτων Arist.*Pol*.1319$^a$20: dual, of a couple of pigs, Ar.*Ach*.811: sg., of *a single beast*, ἄκανθα ποντίου β. A.*Fr*.275.3; ἐν τρόπῳ βοσκήματος πιαινόμενον ζῆν Pl.*Lg*.807a; opp. θηρίον, Arist.*MM*1204$^a$38, Str.16.4. 16. II. *food*, β. πημονῆς A.*Supp*.620, cf. S.*El*.364, Ar.*Ra*.892; ἀναίματον β. δαιμόνων *prey* drained of blood by the Erinyes, A.*Eu*. 302. **-ημᾰτώδης**, ες, *brutish, bestial*, θηριώδεις καὶ β. Str.5.2.7, cf. Ocell.4.14, M.Ant.4.28; ἀναίσθητος καὶ β. Aristid.Quint.2.6: coupled with ζῳώδης, Iamb.*Protr*.21.ιε'; β. ἔννοιαι Procl.*in Cra*.p.68P. **-ησις**, εως, ἡ, *feeding, pasture*, Sm.*Ec*.1.14, Hierocl.*Facet*.47. **-ητέον**, *one must feed*, τὸν πατέρα Ar.*Av*.1359. **-ήτωρ**, ορος, ὁ, *herdsman*, *EM*205.52, Sch.Il.12.302.

❀ **βοσκός**, ὁ, *herdsman*, Aesop.316, interpol. in *AP*7.703 (Myrin.); β. προβάτων *shepherd*, interpol. in Dsc.4.119. II. as Adj., *feeding itself* (= Lat. *agrestis, non pastus*), φασιανός, χήν, *Edict.Diocl*.4.18 (variant for ἄγριος), 22; cf. βοσκάς.

**βόσκω**, impf. ἔβοσκον, Ep. βόσκε Il.15.548: fut. -ήσω Od.17.559, Ar.*Ec*.590: aor. ἐβόσκησα *Gp*.18.7: pf. βεβόσκηκα *PMag*.6.13 (iii B.C.):—Pass. and Med. (v. infr. II): Ion. impf. βοσκέσκοντο Od.12. 355: fut. βοσκήσομαι Sarap. in Plu.2.398d, Dor. βοσκησεῦμαι Theoc. 5.103: aor. ἐβοσκήθην Nic.*Th*.34, Babr.89.7. I. prop. of herdsmen, *feed, tend*, αἰπόλια Od.14.102; ταῶς Stratt.27; ὁ βόσκων *the feeder*, Arist.*HA*540$^a$18. 2. generally, *feed, nourish*, βόσκει γαῖα

. . ἀνθρώπους Od.11.365, cf. 14.325; γαστέρα βοσκήσεις 17.559; πάντα βόσκουσαν φλόγα . . Ἡλίου S.*OT*1425; *maintain, keep*, ἐπικούρους Hdt.6.39; ναυτικόν Th.7.48; γυναῖκας Ar.*Lys*.260; οἰκέτας ib.1204, Herod.7.44: metaph., β. νόσον S.*Ph*.313; πράγματα β. troubles, i.e. children, Ar.*V*.313. **II.** Pass., of cattle, *feed, graze*, Od.21.49, etc.; ξύλοχον κάτα Il.5.162: c. acc., *feed on*, ποίην *h.Merc*.27,232, cf. A.*Ag*.1118 (lyr.), Arist.*HA*591ᵃ16, al.; τινί A.*Th*.244. **2.** metaph., *to be fed* or *nurtured*, λιγμοῖσι Id.*Ch*.26 (lyr.); κούφοις πνεύμασιν S.*Aj*. 558; ἐλπίσιν E.*Ba*.617; β. τινί or περί τι *run riot in* a thing, *AP* 5.271 (Paul. Sil.), prob. in 285 (Id.). (*gʷō*, cf. Lith. *guotas* 'herd'.)

**βόσμορον**, τό, an Indian *millet, ragi, Eleusine coracana*, Str.15.1.13 and 18:—also **βόσμορος**, ὁ, *Peripl.M.Rubr*.14,41.

**Βόσπορ-ος**, ὁ, (βοὸς πόρος Opp.*H*.1.617) wrongly expld. by the Greeks as *Ox-ford*, name of several straits, β. Κιμμέριος, Θρᾴκιος, Hdt.4.12,83, etc. (also applied to the Hellespont by A.*Pers*.723, 746, S.*Aj*.884, Sch.ad ll. cc.):—Adj. **-ειος**, ον, S.*Fr*.707:**-ιος**, α, ον, Id.*Aj*.l.c.: **-εῖον**, τό, name of a temple, Decr.Byz.ap.D.18.91: **-ίτης** [ῑ], ου, ὁ, *dweller on the Bosporus*, S.*Fr*.503: **-ανός** or **-ηνός**, ὁ, *inhabitant of the kingdom of Bosporus*, Str.7.4.7, 11.2.10, 16.2.39.

**βοστρῠχ-ηδόν**, Adv. *curly, like curls*, Luc.*Hist.Conscr*.19, *Philops*. 22. **-ιδῆ**· πολυκαμπῆ, Hsch. **-ίζω**, *curl* hair, Anaxil.42; ἄρρενες βεβοστρυχισμένοι D.H.7.9: metaph., *dress out*, διαλόγους κτενίζειν καὶ β. Id.*Comp*.25. **-ιον**, τό, Dim. of βόστρυχος, *AP* 11.66 (Antiphil.):—*vine-tendril*, Arist.*HA*549ᵇ30, cf. 544ᵃ9: in pl., = στέμφυλα, *pressed grapes*, Hsch. **-ίτης** [ῑ], οἶνος wine *made from pressed grapes*, Aët.15.21.

**βοστρῠχο-ειδής**, ές, *curly*, Adv. **-δῶς** Gal.2.900:—the Adj. may perh. be read in Hsch. for **βοστρυχιδῆ** and **βοστρυχῆνδες**. **-ομαι**, *to be curled*, Ach.Tat.1.19.

**βόστρῠχ-ος**, ὁ, heterocl. pl. βόστρυχα in *AP*5.259 (Paul. Sil.), 6.71 (Id.): acc. pl. βόστρυχας Dionys.*Av*.2.7:—*curl, lock of hair*, Archil. 58, A.*Ch*.178, Ar.*Nu*.536, etc.: in sg. collectively, *hair*, ἀμπέτασον β. ὤμοις E.*Hipp*.202 (lyr.). **2.** poet., *anything twisted* or *wreathed*, πυρὸς ἀμφήκης β. *thunderbolt*, A.*Pr*.1044: in pl., *tendrils*, Philostr. *VA*3.4. **3.** metaph., *ornament*, τῆς ἠπείρου, of Smyrna, Aristid. *Or*.18(20).9; of Nicomedia, Lib.*Or*.61.12; ἑστίας χρυσοῦς β., of a son, Him.*Or*.23.7. **II.** *winged insect*, perh. *male of the glow-worm*, Arist.*HA*551ᵇ26. **2.** in pl., *sea-weed*, Dionys.*Av*.l.c. **-ώδης**, ες, *curly*, γενειάς Philostr.*VS*2.5.1.

**βοτάμια**, τά, (βόσκω) *pastures*, dub. in Th.5.53.

**βοτάνη** [ᾰ], ἡ, (βόσκω) *pasture*, Il.13.493, Pl.*Prt*.321b, etc.; ἐκ βοτάνης ἀνιόντα Theoc.25.87; ἐν β. Id.28.12; ἔγρονται ἐς βοτάναν E.*Fr*.773.20; β. ὁ λέοντος the lion's *pasture*, i.e. Nemea, Pi.*N*.6.42: metaph., ὥσπερ ἐν κακῇ β. τρεφόμενοι Pl.*R*.401c. **2.** *fodder*, Od. 10.411. **3.** *herb*, Thphr.*HP*4.4.13, Dsc.1 *Praef*.1 (pl.), etc. **4.** in pl., *plants*, as material for making clothes, opp. δοραί, Diog.Oen. 10. **5.** *weeds*, Thphr.*HP*2.7.5, *POxy*.729.22 (ii A.D.): in pl., *Gp*. 2.46.2. **6.** ἱερὰ β., = περιστερεών, Dsc.4.60.

**βοτάνη-θεν** [ᾰ], Adv. *from the pasture*, Opp.*H*.4.293. **-φάγος** [φᾰ], ον, *herbivorous*, ib.3.424. **-φόρος**, ον, *herb-bearing*, Nonn. *D*.25.526.

**βοτᾰν-ίδιον**, τό, Dim. of βοτάνη, Sch.Pi.*N*.6.71. **-ίζω**, *root up weeds*, Thphr.*CP*3.20.9, *PLond*.1.131ʳii 42 (i A.D.), *Gp*.3.3.13:—Pass., ib.2.24.3. **-ικός**, ή, όν, *of herbs*, φάρμακα Plu.2.663c; ἡ β. παράδοσις the science *of herbal remedies*, Dsc.1 *Praef*.1:—τὰ **-κά** Id.2 *Praef*.; β. ἰατρός *herbalist*, Gal.*Thras*.24; **-κοί**, οἱ, *herb-gatherers*, Id.14.9. **-ιον**, τό, Dim. of βοτάνη, Thphr.*CP*2.17.3, Dsc.2.156: pl., Antiph.142.3 (s.v.l.). **2.** β. Ἑρμοῦ, = λινόζωστις, Dsc.4. 189. **-ισμός**, ὁ, *weeding*, *Gp*.2.24 tit., *BGU*197.17 (i A.D.), *PFlor*. 20.22 (ii A.D.).

**βοτᾰνο-λογέω**, *gather herbs*, Hp.*Ep*.16. **II.** *root up weeds*, *PGiss*.56.11 (vi A.D.). **-λογία**, ἡ, *weeding*, *POxy*.1631.26 (iii A.D.). **-λόγος**, ὁ, *gatherer of herbs*, Zonar.

**βοτᾰνώδης**, ες, *herbaceous*, Ath.2.62d: Comp., Dsc.4.173. **2.** *rich in herbs*, *Gp*.2.46.2.

**βότειος**, α, ον, (βοτόν) *of a sheep*, κώδια *PFay*.107.4.

**βοτέω**, = βόσκω, Ep. pres. part. βοτείων Call.*Fr*.7.5 P., cf. Hsch.:—Pass., Nic.*Th*.394.

**βοτ-ήρ**, ῆρος, ὁ, (βόσκω) *herdsman*, Od.15.504; οἰωνῶν β. *a soothsayer*, A.*Th*.24; κύων β. *herdsman's* dog, S.*Aj*.297: in later Prose, D.H.2.2, Plu.*Rom*.7, al.:—fem. **βότειρα**, epith. of Demeter, Eust. 1723.14. **-ηρικός**, ή, όν, *of* or *for a herdsman*, ἑορτή Plu.*Rom*.12; κύπελλα *AP*6.170 (Thyill.).

**βότης**, ου, ὁ, = βούτης, *EM*218.42.

**βότις**, ιος, ἡ (?), *a fish* or *plant* (dub.), Sophr.64:—βοτίς· βόλτιον, Hsch.

**βοτόν**, τό, (βόσκω) *beast*, A.*Ag*.1415, S.*Tr*.690: mostly in pl., *grazing beasts*, Il.18.521, S.*Aj*.145 (lyr.), etc.; opp. θηρία, Pl.*Mx*. 237d; but also of birds, Ar.*Nu*.1427; of the ostrich, Opp.*H*.4.630.

**βότρᾰχος**, v. βάτραχος.

**βοτρεύς**, έως, ὁ, *vintager*, *PLond*.2.189.58 (ii A.D.).

**βοτρ-ύδιον** [ῠ], τό, Dim. of βότρυς, *small cluster*, Alex.172.13, Dsc. 1.21, al., Longus 2.13. **II.** *an ear-ring of this pattern*, *Com.Adesp*. 962, Hsch. **-ῡδόν**, Adv. *like a bunch of grapes*: *in clusters*, β. πέτονται, of bees, Il.2.89, cf. *Gp*.15.2.29, Him.*Or*.28.1; τίκτει [ὁ πολύπους] ᾠὰ β. Arist.*Fr*.334, cf. Opp.*H*.1.550; τὰ ἄνθη πέφυκεν β. Thphr.*HP*3.16.4: metaph. of a crowd, Luc.*Pisc*.42.

**βοτρῠ-ηρός**, ά, όν, *of the grape kind*, Thphr.*HP*1.11.5. **-ηφόρος**, ον, *grape-bearing*, ἄμπελος Ph.1.681. **-ῖος**, α, ον, *of grapes*, φυτόν *AP*6.168 (Paul. Sil.). **-ίτης** [ῑ] (sc. λίθος), ου, ὁ, *calamine*, Dsc. 5.74:—also fem. **-ῖτις**, ιδος, ἡ, Plin.*HN*34.101, Gal.12.220.

**βοτρυμός**· τρυγητός, Hsch.

**βοτρῠό-δωρος**, ον, *grape-producing*, Ar.*Pax*520 (paratragoed.). **-ειδής**, ές, *like a bunch of grapes*, Dsc.4.189. Adv. **-δῶς** Orib.45.18. 23. **-εις**, εσσα, εν, *full of grapes, clustering*, οἰνάς Ion Eleg.1.4; κισσός *AP*9.363.12 (Mel.); πλοχμοί A.R.2.677; δένδρεα *IG*14.1389 ii 10. **-κοσμος**, ον, *decked with grapes*, Orph.*H*.52.11.

**βότρῠον**, τό, *cluster of berries*, Thphr.*HP*3.7.3; βότρυς, dub. in Luc.*Bacch*.2. **II.** = θλάσπι, Ps.-Dsc.2.156. **III.** a kind of *medicine*, Plin.*HN*28.44.

**βοτρῠόομαι**, of vines, *form clusters*, Thphr.*CP*1.18.4.

**βοτρῠό-παις**, παιδος, ὁ, ἡ, *grape-born, child of the grape*, χάρις *AP* 11.33 (Phil.). **2.** Act., *bearing grapes*, ἄμπελος Theoc.*Ep*.4. 8. **-σταγής**, ές, *dripping with grapes*, Archestr.*Fr*.60.3. **-στέφᾰνος**, ον, *grape-crowned*, of a vine-bearing district, Archyt.Amph.1; κωμῳδία dub. in *IG*3.3688. **-φορέω**, *bear grapes*, Ph.2.54. **-χαίτης**, ου, ὁ, *with clustering hair*, *AP*9.524.

**βότρυς**, υος, ὁ (heterocl. pl. βότρυα, τά, Euph.149), *bunch of grapes*, μέλανες δ' ἀνὰ βότρυες ἦσαν Il.18.562, etc.: pl., *grapes*, Hp.*Vict*.2.55: prov., βότρυς πρὸς βότρυν πεπαίνεται Jul.*Or*.7.225b. **2.** = sq. I, βότρυς κόμης *AP*5.286 (Agath.), cf. Nonn.*D*.1.528, etc. **3.** *clustered ear-ring*, Ar.*Fr*.320.10. **II.** = ἀμβροσία and ἀρτεμισία, Dsc.3. 114. **2.** *oak of Jerusalem, Chenopodium Botrys*, ib.115. **III.** *the Pleiades*, Sch.Il.18.486.

**βότρῠχος**, ὁ, = βόστρυχος, Pherecr.189, cj. in E.*Or*.1267 (lyr.). **II.** *peduncle of bunch of grapes*, Gal.6.577.

**βοτρῠχώδης**, ες, restored metri gr. for βοστρυχώδης, E.*Ph*.1485 (lyr.).

**βοτρυώδης**, ες, = βοτρυοειδής, E.*Ba*.12, Thphr.*HP*3.13.6, al.

**βου-**, prefix used in compos. (cf. βουγάϊος, etc.), *huge, monstrous*. (From βοῦς, cf. ἱππο-.)

**βοῦα**, ἡ, = ἀγέλη παίδων, at Sparta, Hsch.

**βουαγετόν**· ὑπὸ βοῶν εἱλκυσμένον ξύλον (Lacon.), Hsch. **βουᾱγόρ**, ὁ, (ἄγω) Lacon., *leader of a* βοῦα at Sparta, Id., *IG*5(1).257, al.:—also **βοᾱγόρ**, ib.292:—**βουᾱγός**, **βοᾱγός**, ib.283,523. **βουάκραι**, *palms* (Lacon.), Hsch. **βουάρχη**, gloss on βούπρωρος, Id.

**βουβάλειος** [ᾰ], α, ον, *of an antelope*, κέρας Hdn.Gr.2.438.

**βουβάλια** [βᾰ], ων, τά, a kind of *bracelets*, Nicostr.33, Diph.59, Lib. *Decl*.32.30, cf. *EM*206.16; Ἐρωτίων καὶ βουβαλίων ζεῦγος *IG*11(2). 161*B*118 (Delos, iii B.C.). **II.** sg., **βουβάλιον**, τό, = σίκυς ἄγριος, Ps.-Dsc.4.150, Hp.ap.Hsch. (but in masc. form **βουβάλιος**, ὁ, Id.ap. Gal.19.89).

**βούβᾰλις**, ιος, ἡ, an African *antelope*, *Bubalis mauretanica*, Hdt.4. 192, A.*Fr*.330: gen. βουβαλίδος Arist.*HA*515ᵇ34: gen. pl. **-ίδων** D.C. 48.23: also an Indian species, Ael.*NA*13.25. (On the accent v. Hdn.Gr.1.90: **-ίς**, Hsch.)

**βούβᾰλος**, ὁ, = foreg., Arist.*PA*663ᵃ11, Plb.12.3.5, D.S.2.51, Str. 17.3.4, Ph.2.352, J.*AJ*8.2.4, Opp.*C*.2.300. **II.** = ἀστράγαλος, Hsch. **III.** *buffalo*, Agath.1.4.

**βουβάρας**, = μέγας καὶ ἀναίσθητος, Hdn.Gr.1.57; cf. βουβάραι· μεγάλαι, Hsch.: also expld. as = μεγαλοναύτης (cf. βᾶρις), Id., cf. *EM* 206.18:—**βούβαρις**, Philist.56 (-βάρτις cod. Hsch.).

**Βούβαστ-ις**, ιος, ἡ, Egyptian divinity, Hdt.2.137, etc.:—hence **Βουβαστεία**, ἡ, Pythag. name for *five*, *Theol.Ar*.31. **-εῖον**, τό, *temple of Bubastis*, *BGU*820.18: **-ια**, τά, *festival of B.*, *OGI*56.37 (Canopus), *IG*9(1).86 (Phocis).

**βούβαστις**, ὁ, *groin*, Aët.4.21:—hence **βουβαστικά**, τά, *remedies for sores in the groin*, ibid.

**βουβαυκαλόσαυλος**, com. compd., prob. in Anaxandr.41.5.

**βούβελα**· κρέα βόεια, Hsch.

**βου-βῆτις**, ιος, ἡ, *stream for watering cattle*, *Tab.Herad*.2.13. **-βόσιον**, τό, (βόσκω) *cattle-pasture*, Call.*Ap*.49, Arat.1120: in pl., *grazing*, Str.12.4.7. **-βίλιξ**· σιταποχία, Hsch. **-βοσις**, εως, ἡ, (βόσκω) = βούβρωστις, *EM*206.24. **-βότης**, ου, ὁ, *giving pasture to cattle*, πρῶνες Pi.*N*.4.52. **2.** as Subst., *herdsman*, Id.*I*.6(5). 32. **-βοτος**, ον, *grazed by cattle*, Od.13.246, *AP*6.114 (Simm. or Phil.). **-βρωστις**, εως, ἡ, *ravenous appetite*, Opp.*H*.2.208, Call. *Cer*.103, *AP*11.379 (Agath.): *famine*, *Epigr.Gr*.793.3: in Hom. only metaph., *grinding poverty* or *misery*, Il.24.532 (but expld. by Sch. as = οἶστρος).

**βουβών**, ῶνος, ὁ, *groin*, Il.4.492, etc.; κοινὸν μέρος . . μηροῦ καὶ ἤτρου β. Arist.*HA*493ᵇ9: in pl., μέχρι βουβώνων Pherecr.23, cf. Luc.*Tim*. 56. **2.** in pl., *glands*, Hp.*Epid*.2.2.24. **3.** *swollen gland*, Id. *Aph*.4.55, Arist.*Pr*.883ᵇ21, Men.*Georg*.51, J.*Ap*.2.2. **II.** = Lat. *bubo*, *owl*, Id.*AJ*18.6.7, 19.8.2.

**βουβων-ιακός**, ή, όν, *for the groin*, of a bandage, Sor.*Fasc*.12.514C. (also **-ικός**). **-ιασκόπος**, ὁ, *one who treats* βουβῶνες *by magic*, Hsch., *EM*206.25. **-ιάω**, *suffer from swollen groins*, Ar.*V*.277, Call.Com.26, J.*Ap*.2.2: c. acc., τῷ νεφρῷ Ar.*Ra*.1280:—hence Subst. **-ίᾱσις**, εως, ἡ, Gal.19.566. **-ιον**, τό, = ἀστὴρ Ἀττικός, Dsc.4.119. **-ίσκος**, ὁ, *bandage for the groin*, Heliod.ap.Orib.48. 55 tit.

**βουβωνο-ειδής**, ές, *like a* βουβών, Poll.4.198. **-κήλη**, ἡ, *inguinal hernia*, Heliod.ap.Orib.48.57.5, Gal.7.730:—hence Adj. **-κηλικός**, ή, όν, *suffering from it*, Aët.4.26, Paul.Aeg.6.66. **-ομαι**, Pass., *swell to a* βουβών, Hp.*Gland*.8. **-φύλαξ** [ῠ], ακος, ὁ, *truss for hernia*, Heliod.ap.Orib.48.57 tit.

**βουβωνώδης**, ες, = βουβωνοειδής, Ruf.ap.Orib.44.17.3.

**βου-γάϊος** [ᾰ], ὁ, (γαίω) *bully, braggart*, only voc. as term of reproach, Il.13.824, Od.18.79; applied to those who lived on milk in Dulichion and Same, Nic.*Fr.*131. **-γενής**, ές, = βοηγενής, Emp.61.2, Call.*Fr.*230; of bees, Philet.22, *AP*9.548 (Bianor); Διόνυσος Plu.2.364f: metaph. of souls, Porph.*Antr.*18. **-γλωσσον**, τό (masc. form *buglossos* Plin.*HN*25.81), *bugloss, Anchusa italica*, Dsc.4.127, Opp.*H.*1.99. **2.** β. μέγα, = κρίσσιον, Ps.-Dsc.4.118. **3.** a surgical instrument, perh. *tongue-depressor, Hermes* 38.280. ✻ **-γλωσσος**, Att. -ττος, ὁ (Matro *Conv.*77) and ἡ (Archestr. *Fr.*32.2), a fish, *sole*, Epich.65, Xenarch.8.4, Speus.ap.Ath.7.329f, Dorio ib.330a; classed with σελάχη, Arist.*Fr.*280. **-γονής**, ές, *born of an ox*, of bees, *Gp.*15.2.14; βουγονή (nom.) ibid. tit. is perh. f.l. for βουγονῆ :—also **-γονία**, title of poem by Eumelus, Varro *RR* 2.5.5.

**βου-δάκη**· ἡ βούπρηστις, Hsch. **-δεψῆϊον**, τό, *tannery*, Id.

**βούδιον**, τό, v. βοΐδιον.

**βου-δόκος**, ον, *receiving oxen*, ἐχῖνος (i.e. λέβης) Call.*Fr.*250b. ✻ **-δόρος**, ον, (δέρω) *flaying oxen, galling*, Hes.*Op.*504 (βούδορα codd., βουδόρα Sch.T.Il.17.550, cf. Eust.1117.53). **II.** *for flaying*, μάχαιρα Babr.97.7: as Subst., Hsch., prob. in Tim.*Pers.*28. **2.** prov., β. νόμῳ of those who deserve flaying, Diogenian.3.66. **-δύτης** [ῠ], ου, ὁ, a bird, perh. *wagtail*, Dionys.*Av.*3.2.

**Βου-ζύγης** [ῠ], ὁ, epith. of an Attic hero *who first yoked oxen*, Arist.*Fr.*386, Hsch.; Heracles, acc. to Suid. **2.** *keeper of bullocks* at Eleusis, *IG*3.71; ἱερεὺς B. ib.3.294, cf. Eup.96,97. **-ζύγιος** [ῠ] (sc. ἄροτος), ὁ, *ritual ploughing*, at Athens, Plu.2.144b :—also Βουζύγια, τά, Ph.2.630. **-θερής**, ές, *affording summer-pasture*, λειμών S.*Tr.*188. **-θήλεια**, ἡ, = δάμαλις, *Gp.*17.2 tit. (pl.). ✻ **-θοίνης**, ου, ὁ, *beef-eater*, epith. of Hercules, *APl.*4.123, Eust.962.7. **-θόρος**, ον, *vaccas iniens*, ταῦρος A.*Supp.*301. **-θορος**, = βουθερής, Hsch. s.h.v. ✻ **-θουτον**, τό, a plant, = ἀμέμαρον (Lacon.), Hsch. **-θυσία**, Ion. -ίη, ἡ, *sacrifice of oxen*, *IG*14.830 (Puteoli), *AP*7.119, Porph. *Abst.*2.55; Ἥρας in her honour, Pi.*N.*10.23: in pl., Id.*O.*5.6, D.C.46.40. **-θύσιον** [ῠ], τό, = foreg., Sch.A.R.1.516. ✻ **-θυτέω**, *slay* or *sacrifice oxen*, S.*OC*888, E.*El.*785, Jul.*Mis.*362c, etc.: also in later Prose, Plb.32.15.2, D.C.42.28, al.: generally, *sacrifice, slaughter*, β. ὗν καὶ τράγον καὶ κριόν Ar.*Pl.*819; τὰς θυσίας τὰς καθηκούσας *IG*2.594.5; τῷ Ἀπόλλωνι ib.12(7).389.16, cf. *POxy.*1021.16 (i A.D.). **-θύτης** [ῠ], ου, ὁ, name given to Pythagoras, Procl.*in Euc.*p.426F. **-θύτος**, ον, *of* or *belonging to sacrifices*, esp. *of oxen*, τιμαί A.*Supp.*706 (lyr.); ἡδονή E.*Ion* 664; *accompanied by sacrifices*, ἑορταί B.3.15. **2.** *on which oxen are offered, sacrificial*, ἑστία S.*OC* 1495 (lyr.); ἐσχάρα Ar.*Av.*1232; ἦμαρ, ἁμέρα, A.*Ch.*261, E.*Hel.* 1474 (lyr.). **-θώνης**· βούχειλος, Hsch.

✻ **βουκαῖος**, ὁ, (βοῦκος) *cowherd*, Nic.*Th.*5. **II.** *one who ploughs with oxen*, Theoc.10.1,57 (prob. a pr. n.), Nic.*Fr.*90.

**βουκᾰνάω, βουκᾰνισμός**, v. sub βυκ-.

**βουκανή**, = ἀνεμώνη (Cypr.), Hsch.

**βου-κάπη** [ᾰ], ἡ, *ox-stall*, Hsch. **-κάπηλος** [ᾰ], ου, ὁ, *cattle-dealer*, Poll.7.185.

**βουκαρδία**, ἡ, a *gem*, Plin.*HN*37.150.

**Βουκάτιος**, ὁ, a month in west central Greece, *SIG*241.105 (Delph.), *IG*7.1777 (Thespiae), etc.: **Βουκάτια**, τά, festival held therein, *SIG*²438.42, al. (Delph.).

**βούκελλα**, ἡ, = Lat. *bucella, small loaf*, *PFlor.*74.13 (ii A.D.).

**βου-κέντης**, ου, ὁ, *goader of oxen, ox-driver*, Diogenian.7.86. **-κέντρον**, τό, *ox-goad*, Lxx *Ec.*12.11. **-κέραος**, ον, = βούκερως, Nonn. *D.*14.319. ✻ **-κερας**, αος (also **βούκερον**, τό, *Hippiatr.*117, dat. -ῳ Thphr.*HP*8.8.5), τό, = τῆλις, ll. cc., Nic.*Al.*424. **-κερως**, ων, gen. ω, *horned like an ox* or *cow*, ἄγαλμα Hdt.2.41; β. παρθένος, of Io, A. *Pr.*588 (lyr.); Ἴακχος S.*Fr.*959. **II.** = foreg., Dsc.2.102. **-κεφάλας**, α, ὁ, the horse of Alexander the Great, Str.15.1.29, Plu.*Alex.* 61, Arr.*An.*5.14.4.

**βουκεφάλιον** [ᾰ], τό, *ox-head*, used as an ornament, Lys.*Fr.*34, *SIG*695.71 (Magn. Mae.); β. χρυσᾶ *SIG*²588.199 (Delos, ii B.C.).

✻ **βουκέφᾰλος**, ον, *bull-headed*, epith. of Thessalian horses, τὸν βουκέφαλον καὶ κοππατίαν Ar.*Fr.*42, cf. 41. **2.** = τρίβολος, Ps.-Dsc. 4.15. **3.** βουκέφαλον, τό, = foreg., *IG*2.736 *B*11, *Chron.Lind.C.*114.

**βουκῑνίζω**, *blow the trumpet*, στρόμβοις S.E.*M.*6.24 :—also **βῡκᾰνίζω** or **-ῑνίζω**, Eust.1321.33, etc.: **βουκῑνάτωρ**, ὁ, = Lat. *buccinātor*, Lyd.*Mag.*1.46, etc.; cf. βυκάνη.

**βουκλόπος**, = βοοκλόπος, θεός Porph.*Antr.*18.

**βουκολ-εῖον**, τό, *residence of the* ἄρχων βασιλεύς at Athens, Arist. *Ath.*3.5. ✻ **-έω**, *tend cattle*, ἕλικας βοῦς βουκολέεσκες (Ep. impf.) Il.21.448, etc.: abs., Parth.4.1, Luc.*DDeor.*3 :—Med., βουκολεῖσθαι αἶγας Eup.18 :—Pass., of cattle, *graze*, ἕλος κάτα βουκολέοντο, of horses, Il.20.221, cf. Ar.*Pax* 153: metaph. of meteors, *range through the sky*, Call.*Del.*176. **b.** c. acc. rei, *graze on*, Τρηχινίδα Euph. 114. **2.** of persons, βουκολεῖς Σαβάζιον *you tend, serve him* (with allusion to his *tauriform* worship), Ar.*V.*10 :—Med., μὴ πρόκαμνε τόνδε βουκολούμενος πόνον *ruminating, pondering*, A.*Eu.*78. **II.** metaph., *cheat, beguile*, πάθος Id.*Ag.*669; τὸ δήμιον Ar.*Ec.*81, cf. Men.*Sam.*251; αἱ τίτθαι τοὺς παῖδας διὰ μυθολογίας βουκολοῦσιν Max.Tyr.10.3; β. λύπην Babr.19.7; ἀλλοτρίοις κόσμοις τὸ τῆς φύσεως ἀπρεπές β. Luc.*Am.*38 :—Med., ἐλπίσι βουκολοῦμαι *I feed myself* on hopes, *cheat myself* with them, Alciphr.3.5, cf. Luc.*Trag.*29; ἐπιθυμίαις Id.*Am.*2 :—Pass., *Stoic.*3.147; βουκολεῖσθαι ὑπὸ ἐνυπνίων Porph.*Marc.*6. **-ημα**, ατος, τό, *beguilement*, τῆς λύπης Babr.136. 9. **-ησις**, εως, ἡ, *tending of cattle*, Plu.2.802e. **-ητής**, οῦ, ὁ, *deceiver*, Hsch. **-ία**, ἡ, *herd of cattle*, *h.Merc.*498, Hes.*Th.*445, Hdt.1.114. **II.** *tending of cattle*, A.R.1.627 (pl.). **III.** perh. = βουκολεῖον, Crates Gramm.ap.Ath.6.235c. **IV.** = κακολογία, Hsch. **-ιάζομαι, -ιάσδομαι**, fut. -αξεῦμαι :—*sing* or *write pastorals*, Theoc.5.44, al., Mosch.3.120. ✻ **-ιασμός**, ὁ, *singing of pastorals*, Ath.14.619a (v.l. -ισμός). **-ιαστής**, οῦ, ὁ, *pastoral poet*, Theoc.5.68. **-ίζω**, = βουκολιάζομαι, Eust.1416.39. ✻ **-ικός**, ή, όν, *rustic, pastoral*, ἀοιδά Theoc.1.64,70, etc.; τὰ β. *pastoral poetry*, Hermog.*Id.*2.3. **2.** β. μέτρον metre *used by pastoral poets*, Plu. *Metr.*2; τομή '*bucolic*' caesura, ib.3. **II.** βουκολικός, ὁ, official in cult of Dionysus, *IG*2².1368.123. **2.** *bucolicon*, = πάνακες Ἀσκληπίειον, Plin.*HN*25.31. **-ίνη**, = κίγκλος, Hsch. ✻ **-ιον**, τό, *herd of cattle*, Hdt.1.126, X.*HG*4.6.6, Theoc.8.39, 25.12, etc. **2.** τὰ β. *district* of lower Egypt, *inhabited by shepherds*, Hld.1.5, *BGU*625. 6 (ii/iii A.D.), etc. **II.** *means of beguiling*, πενίης *AP*9.150 (Antip.), = ib.255 (Phil.); but with play on I. **-ίς** (sc. γῆ), ίδος, ἡ, *cattle-pasture*, D.H.1.37; β. πόα ib.39. **-ίσκος**, ὁ, a kind of *bandage*, Gal.18(1).777. ✻ **-ος**, ὁ, *tending kine*, βουκόλοι ἄνδρες, ἀγροιῶται, Il.13.571, Od.11.292, al.; β. δοῦλος Pl.*Ion* 540c; ποιμὴν αἰπόλος..καὶ β. Cratin.281: also abs., Hdt.1.110, *PGoodsp.Cair.*30 ix1 (ii A.D.), etc.; βέλει βουκόλου πτερόεντος, i.e. the gadfly, A. *Supp.*557 (lyr); β. ἵππων Ael.*NA*12.44. **II.** *worshipper of Dionysos in bull-form*, in pl., title of play by Cratinus, cf. E.*Fr.*203, *IG*12(9). 262 (Eretria, i B.C.), *IGRom.*4.386 (Pergam.), Luc.*Salt.*79, Hsch. s.v. πυρπερέγχει. **2.** β. τοῦ Ὀσοράπι *devotee* of Sarapis, *UPZ*57. 7. (βοῦς, $q^u$el-, cf. Lat. *colo*: in these words βωκολ- is found as v.l. for βουκολ- in some codd. of Theoc.)

✻ **βουκονιστήριον**, τό, *bullring*, *IGRom.*3.484 (Oenoanda, ii A.D.).

**βουκόπια**, τά, v. βοκόπια. ✻ **βουκόπος**, gloss on βουπλήξ, Hsch.

**βου-κόρυζα**, ης, ἡ, *severe cold in the head*, Men.1003. **-κόρυζος**, ον, *stupid* and *drivelling*, Hsch.

✻ **βοῦκος**, Dor. **βῶκος** (v.l.), ὁ, = βουκαῖος, Theoc.10.38. (Perh. a pr. n.)

✻ **βου-κράνιον** [ᾰ], τό, *ox-head*, *EM*207.55. **II.** = ἄμπελος μέλαινα, Ps.-Dsc.4.183. **2.** = ἀντίρρινον, ib.130, Gal.19.82. **III.** *machine for reducing dislocations*, Orib.49.4.74. ✻ **-κρᾶνος**, ον, *bull-headed*, Emp.61.3, Call.*Fr.*203, Plu.2.358d. **II. βούκρᾱνον**, τό, *ox-head*, Gem.3.3. **-κριος**, ὁ, *ox-ram*, fabulous monster, Ps.-Callisth.3.17.

**βούκτησις**· φυσητική, Hsch.; cf. βύκτης.

✻ **βουλαῖος**, α, ον, (βουλή) *of the council*, epith. of certain gods as having statues in the Council Chamber (Ἑστία βουλαία· ἡ ἐν τῇ βουλῇ ἱδρυμένη, Harp.), τὴν Ἑστίαν ἐπώμοσε τὴν β. Aeschin.2.45; of Zeus and Athena, Antipho 6.45, cf. *IG*3.272, *SIG*1011.6 (Chalcedon), Corn.*ND*9, Plu.2.789d; of Artemis, *IG*2².916, al.; Themis, Plu.2. 802b; θεοὶ β., name of thirty stars, D.S.2.30; of a man, θεῶν βουλαῖος ἀνάκτων, = imperatorum divorum *consiliarius*, *IG*4.1475 (Epidaurus). **II.** Subst. **βουλαία**, ἡ, = βουλεία, *Milet.*7.71; but **βουλαῖα**· τὰ βεβουλευμένα, and **βούλεον** (sic)· βούλευμα, Hsch.

**βούλακα**· βόλου ὄνομα, i.e. throw at dice, Hsch.

**βουλάπαθον**, τό, Lat. *bulapathum, Rumex scutatus*, Plin.*HN*20. 235.

**βουλαπτεροῦν**, etym. of βλαβερόν (βουλόμενον ἅπτειν ῥοῦν), Pl.*Cra.* 417e.

**βουλαρχ-έω**, *to be a* βούλαρχος, *IG*9(1).65 (Daulis), 226 (Drymaea), Arist.*Pol.*1295ᵇ12. **-ία**, ἡ, *office of* βούλαρχος, *IG*9(1).228 (Drymaea), 12(2).484.7 (Mytilene). **-ος**, ὁ, *president of the senate*, as at Thyateira, *IGRom.*4.1230; at Amorgos, *IG*12(7).287, cf. *Milet.*3. 230, 7.70. **II.** *adviser of a plan*, A.*Supp.*11,970.

**βουλᾱφόρος**, Dor. for βουληφ-.

**βουλαχ-εύς**, έως, ὁ, (perh. βοῦς, λαγχάνω) dub. sens. in *Milet.*1(7). p.323 (Didyma). **-έω**, *to be* βουλαχεύς, ib.3(2) Nos.168,171.

**βουλ-εία**, ἡ, (βουλεύω) *office of councillor*, Ar.*Th.*809, X.*HG*2.3. 38, Din.*Fr.*89.12; *membership of the Senate* at Rome, D.C.37.30, al.; of local βουλαί, *POxy.*1406.8 (iii A.D.). ✻ **-εῖον**, τό, = βουλευτήριον, *SIG*1011 (Chalcedon), 614.34 (Delph., ii B.C.), Ps.-Hdt.*Vit. Hom.*12. **-εκκλησία**, ἡ, *joint session of* βουλή *and* ἐκκλησία, *Inscr.Prien.*246.9 (iii A.D.) (pl.). **-ευμα**, ατος, τό, *resolution, purpose*, A.*Pr.*171 (lyr.), 619, Ar.*Av.*993, etc.: freq. in pl., Pi.*N.*5.28, Hdt.3.80, S.*OT*45, A.*Th.*594, Pl.*R.*334a, D.18.296: prov., τοῖς οἰκείοις β. ἁλίσκεσθαι 'to be hoist with one's own petard', Lib.*Or.*59. 20. **II.** *sitting of a* βουλή, φοιτᾶν εἰς τὰ β. Philostr.*Her.*19. 6. **-ευμάτιον**, τό, Dim. of foreg., Ar.*Eq.*100. ✻ **-εύς**, έως, ὁ, *Counsellor*, title of Zeus, *SIG*1024.17 (Myconos). ✻ **-ευσις**, εως, ἡ, *deliberation*, Arist.*EN*1112ᵇ22. **II.** as Att. law-term, **1.** *conspiracy* against life, Arist.*Ath.*57.3; against property, Hyp.*Ath.* 18. **2.** *wrongful retention on the list of state debtors of the name of one who has paid his debt*, D.25.28 and 73, Arist.*Ath.*59.3. **-ευτέον**, *one must take counsel*, ὅπως.. A.*Ag.*847; τί χρὴ δρᾶν S.*El.*16; περί τινος Isoc.6.90: pl., βουλευτέα Th.7.60. **-ευτήρ**, ῆρος, ὁ, = βουλευτής, Hsch. s.v. μάστροι. ✻ **-ευτήριον**, τό, *council-chamber*, seat of a βουλή, Hdt.1.170, A.*Eu.*570,684, E.*Andr.*1097, And.1.36, D.18. 169, Pl.*Grg.*452e, *Michel* 1203 (Iasos), etc.; = Lat. *curia*, Plu.*Cic.*31, Hdn.5.5.7. **II.** *Council, Senate*, D.H.2.12; of local βουλαί, *PLond.* 2.408.14 (iv A.D.), etc.; of individuals, δόλια βουλευτήρια *treacherous counsellor*, E.*Andr.*446; ῥυσὰ β. Theopomp Com.75 (paratrag.). ✻ **-ευτήριος**, ον, *giving advice*, κακῶν τ' Ἀδράστῳ τῶνδε βουλευτήριον A.*Th.*575. ✻ **-ευτής**, οῦ, ὁ, *councillor, senator*, Il.6.114, Hdt.9.5, Pl.*Ap.*25a, etc.; at Athens, *one of the* 500, Antipho 6.45, And.1.43, Ar.*Th.*808; at Rome, *senator*, D.H.2.12, Plu.*Rom.*13, etc. 2. *plotter, contriver*, θανάτου, πληγῆς, Antipho 4.3.4. ⊛ -ευτικός, ή, όν, *of* or *for the council*, β. ὅρκος oath *taken by the councillors*, X.*Mem.*1.1.18; νόμοι ap.D.24.20; β. τιμαί *CIG*1716 (Delph.); ἀρχὴ β. right *to sit in the* βουλή, Arist.*Pol.*1275b19; of the Roman Senate, τίμημα, ἐσθής, D.C.54.17, 40.46; -κά, τά, *funds at the disposal of a council*, *POxy.*1416.3 (iii A.D.). 2. *able to advise* or *deliberate*, ὁ β., opp. ὁ πολεμικός, Pl.*R.*434b, cf. 441a, Arist.*EN*1140a31, 1152a19; τὸ β. *the deliberative faculty*, Id.*Pol.*1260a12. II. Subst., -κόν, τό, in the Athen. theatre, *seats reserved for the Council*, Ar.*Av.*794, Hsch. 2. *the deliberative and judicial element* in the state, Arist.*Pol.*1329a31; at Rome, *senatorial order*, Plu.*Rom.*13. -ευτις, ιδος, ἡ, fem. of βουλευτής, A.*Fr.*172 (= Pl.Com.88). ⊛ -ευτός, ή, όν, *devised, plotted*, A.*Ch.*494. II. *matter for deliberation*, Arist.*EN*1113a2, etc. III. βουλευτός, = βουλευτής, Hsch. ⊛ -εύω, Il.2.379, etc., aor. ἐβούλευσα Od.5.23, etc., Ep. βούλ- Il.14.464: pf. βεβούλευκα S.*OT*701:—Med. and Pass., v. infr.: (βουλή):—*take counsel, deliberate*, in past tenses, *determine* or *resolve after deliberation*: 1. abs., ὡς βουλεύσαντε Il.1.531; βουλευέμεν ἠδὲ μάχεσθαι *in council* or in battle, Od.14.491; β. ὅπως ὄχ' ἄριστα γένοιτο 9.420, cf. 11.229; δυσμενέεσσι φόνον πέρι β. 16.234; ἔς γε μίαν βουλεύσομεν (sc. βουλήν) *we shall agree* to one plan, Il.2.379; θυμῷ β. Od.12.58; β. περί τινος Hdt.1.120, Th.3.28, 5.116: in Prose, chiefly Med. in this sense, v. infr. B. 2. c. acc. rei, *deliberate on, plan, devise*, β. βουλάς Il.24.652, al.; οὐ..τοῦτον μὲν ἐβούλευσας νόον αὐτή; Od.5.23; ὁδόν 1.444; φύξιν Il.10.311, 398; κέρδεα Od.23.217; ψεύδεα 14.296: c. dat. pers., τῷ γάρ ῥα θεοὶ βούλευσαν ὄλεθρον Il.14.464, cf. Hdt.9.110; θάνατόν τινι Pl.*Lg.*872a; β. πῆμά τινι Od.5.179, etc.; κέλευθον A.*Pers.*758; ποινάς Id.*Ag.*1223; νεώτερα β. περί τινος Hdt.1.210:—Pass. (with fut. Med., A.*Th.*198), aor. ἐβουλεύθην Hdt.7.157, Th.1.120, Pl.*R.*442b: pf. βεβούλευμαι (usu. in med. sense, v. infr. B):—*to be determined* or *planned*, ψῆφος κατ' αὐτῶν βουλεύσεται A.l.c.; βεβούλευται τάδε Id.*Pr.*998, cf. Hdt.7.10.δ'; τὰ βεβουλευμένα, = βουλεύματα, Id.4.128; τὰ βουλευόμενα X.*Cyr.*6.2.2; πῶς σφῷν βεβούλευται Pl.*Euthd.*274a. 3. c. inf., *take counsel, resolve* to do, τὸν μὲν ἐγὼ βούλευσα..οὐτάμεναι Od.9.299, cf. Hdt.1.73, 6.52, 61, etc.:—Pass., τοῖσι ἐβεβούλευτο τὸ παιδίον προσουδίσαι Id.5.92.γ'. II. *give counsel*, τὰ λῷστα β. A.*Pr.*206; β. δυνατός Pl.*Lg.*694b: c. dat. pers., *advise*, ἵνα σφίσι βουλεύησθα Il.9.99, cf. A.*Eu.*697. III. *sit in council*, of the Spartan γέροντες, Hdt.6.57; *to be a member of a* βουλή, Arist.*Pol.*1282a30; esp. *of the Council of* 500 at Athens, Antipho 6.45, And.1.75, X.*Mem.*1.1.18, Arist.*Ath.*62.3; ἡ βουλὴ ἡ βουλεύουσα Lys.13.19; βουλὴν β. *to be a member of the* β., ib.20; βουλεύειν λαχών Pl.*Grg.*473e.

B. Med., fut. -εύσομαι A.*Ag.*846, *Ch.*718, Th.1.43, Pl.*Smp.*174d: aor. ἐβουλευσάμην S.*OT*537, etc.; Ep. βουλ- Il.2.114; ἐβουλεύθην D.H.15.7: pf. βεβούλευμαι Hdt.3.134, S.*El.*385, Th.1.69, E.*Supp.*248, Pl.*Chrm.*176c (also in pass. sense, v. supr.):—more freq. in Att. Prose than Act., 1. abs., *take counsel with oneself, deliberate*, Hdt.7.10.δ', Arist.*EN*1112b11, 20; παραχρῆμα οὐδὲ -σάμενος D.37.13; ἅμα τινί Hdt.8.101; περὶ τοῦ μέλλοντος τῶν οἰκείων Th.3.44, cf. Pl.*Phdr.*231a; περί τι Id.*R.*604c; ὑπέρ τινος ib.428d; πρὸς τὴν γεγενημένην ξυμφοράν Th.7.47: c. acc. cogn., β. βούλευμα And.3.29; βουλήν Pl.*Plt.*298b, etc.; ἴσον τι ἢ δίκαιον Th.2.44:—also like Act., *take counsel*, πρός τινας Lxx 4*Ki.*6.8. 2. *act as member of council*, and so *originate measures*, β. καὶ κρίνειν Arist.*Pol.*1281b31; τὸ βουλευόμενον ib.1291a28. 3. c. acc. rei, *determine with oneself, resolve on*, κακὴν ἀπάτην βουλεύσατο Il.2.114 (Med. here only in Hom.); ἀλλοῖόν τι περί τινος Hdt.5.40, cf. Pl.*Ap.*32c. 4. c. inf., *resolve* to do, Hdt.3.134, Pl.*Chrm.*176c. 5. rarely folld. by Relat., β. ὅ τι ποιήσεις ibid.; β. ὅπως.. with subj., X.*Cyr.*1.4.13; β. πῶς τις, c. fut., Id.*An.*3.4.40; πῶς καὶ τί πρακτέον εἴη Plb.1.33.3; ἵνα *Ev.Jo.*12.10.

**βουλεψίη**, dub. sens. of the Amazons, Xanth.ap.Hsch.

⊛ **βουλή**, ἡ, Dor. **βωλά** Decr.Byz.ap.D.18.90, Aeol. **βόλλα** *Schwyzer* 623.1 (ii B.C.), Plu.2.288b: acc. pl. βουλᾶς Hes.*Th.*534: (βούλομαι):—*will, determination*, esp. of the gods, Il.1.5, etc. 2. *counsel, design*, βουλὰς βουλεύουσι Il.24.652, etc.: generally, *counsel, advice*, opp. μάχεσθαι, Il.1.258, cf. 2.202, etc.; κακὴ β. Hes.*Op.*266; πρᾶτος..καὶ βουλᾷ καὶ χερσὶν ἐς Ἄρεα *IG*9(1).658 (Ithaca); νυκτὶ βουλὴν διδόναι Hdt.7.12 (but ἐν νυκτὶ β. διδοὺς ἐμαυτῷ Men.*Epit.*35); ἐν β. ἔχειν τὰ γενόμενα Hdt.3.78; β. ποιεῖσθαι, = βουλεύεσθαι, Id.6.101, etc.; β. διδόναι X.*Cyr.*7.2.26; β. προτιθέναι περί τινος D.18.192; β. ἄγειν Polyaen.7.39; ἐν βουλῇ γενέσθαι πότερον.. D.H.2.44; τούτοις οὐκ ἔστι κοινὴ β. they have no common *ground of argument*, Pl.*Cri.*49d; βουλῆς ὀρθότης ἡ εὐβουλία Arist.*EN*1142b16: in pl., *counsels*, A.*Pr.*221, *Th.*842 (lyr.); ἐν βουλαῖς ἄριστος, ἐν βουλαῖσι κράτιστος, *Epigr.Gr.*854, *IG*3.716. 3. *deliberation*, Arist.*EN*1112a19, D.9.46. 4. *decree*, β. εἰσηγεῖσθαι And.1.61; β. ἄκυρον θεῖναι Id.2.28. II. *Council of elders, Senate*, βουλὴν ἷζε γερόντων Il.2.53, cf. Od.3.127, A.*Ag.*884; esp. at Athens, *Council* or *Senate of* 500 created by Cleisthenes, Hdt.9.5, Ar.*V.*590, Antipho 6.40, etc.; commonly called ἡ β. (or ἡ β. οἱ πεντακόσιοι Aeschin.3.20, to distinguish it from ἡ β. ἡ ἐν Ἀρείῳ πάγῳ ibid.; also β. ἀπὸ κυάμου Th.8.66); in other states, as at Argos, Hdt.7.149; at Thebes, X.*HG*5.2.29; of the Roman *Senate*, D.H.6.69, etc.; of local *senates*, *POxy.*58.14 (iii A.D.), etc.; βουλῆς εἶναι to be *of the Council, a member of it*, Th.3.70 (whence Sch. and Suid. made a Subst. βουλῆς, ὁ); ἀνὴρ βουλῆς τῆς Ῥωμαίων Paus.5.20.8; ἄνδρα ἐκ τῆς βουλῆς Id.7.11.1.

**βουλ-ηγορέω**, *speak in the Senate*, App.*BC*3.51. -ηγορία, ἡ, *speech in the Senate*, Poll.4.26. -ηγόρος, ὁ, *one who speaks in the Senate*, ib.25. -ήεις, εσσα, εν, *of good counsel, sage*, Sol.33.1. -ημα, ατος, τό, *purpose*, Gorg.*Hel.*6 (pl.), Ar.*Av.*993, Isoc.3.15, D.18.49 (pl.); *intent*, τοῦ νομοθέτου Pl.*Lg.*769d, 802c (pl.), al.; τὸ β. τῆς κρίσεως *intention* to judge, Id.*Phlb.*41e: pl., βουλήμασι Μοίρης *IG*12(7).303. 2. *meaning*, οὐδεὶς σαφῶς παρέδωκε τὸ β. Ael.*Tact.*18.1; τὸ β. τοῦ ποιητοῦ Hipparch.1.4.9, al. 3. *intention of a testator*, *BGU*361 ii 23 (ii A.D.): hence, *will, testament*, *POxy.*907.1 (iii A.D.), *PLips.*29.7 (iii A.D.). II. *express will, consent*, τῆς συγκλήτου Plb.6.15.4. -ημάτιον, τό, Dim. of foreg. 1.3, *will, testament*, *PMasp.*151.304 (vi A.D.). ⊛ -ησις, εως, ἡ, *willing*, Arist.*de An.*433a23; β. ἀγαθοῦ ὄρεξις Id.*Top.*146b5, cf. *EN*1111b19; τῶν ἀδυνάτων, τοῦ τέλους, ib.1111b22, 1113a15; *purpose*, πράσσειν β. E.*HF*1305; *wish, desire*, Th.3.39, Pl.*Grg.*509d, etc.; βούλησιν ἐλπίζει entertains a hope and *purpose*, Th.6.78; κατὰ τὴν β. Pl.*Cra.*420d, al.; παρὰ τὴν β. ibid., Arist.*EN*1136b24: pl., Pl.*Lg.*688b, Arist.*Rh.*1378b18; of the gods, Polystr.p.10 W. II. *purpose* or *meaning* of a poem, Pl.*Prt.*344b; *signification* of a word, Id.*Cra.*421b. III. *will, testament*, β. ἔγγραφος *PLips.*33 ii 10 (iv A.D.). -ητέος, α, ον, *to be wished for*, τὸ β. Arist.*MM*1208b38. 2. βουλητέον, *one must wish for*, Id.*Rh.Al.*1420b23. -ητός, ή, όν, *that is* or *should be willed*, οὔτε χρήσιμον οὔτε β. Phld.*Rh.*1.185 S.: τὸ β. *object of desire* or *will*, Pl.*Lg.*733d, Arist.*EN*1113a17. Adv. -τῶς Procl.*in Prm.*p.752 S.

**βουληφόρος**, ον, *counselling, advising*, in Il. a constant epith. of princes and leaders, β. ἄνδρα 2.24, al.; title of Artemis, *SIG*²660.3 (Milet.): also c. gen., β. Ἀχαιῶν, Τρώων, Il.24.651, 5.180; in Od.9.112 οὔτ' ἀγοραὶ β. οὔτε θέμιστες, cf. Pi.*O.*12.5: in later Prose, = βουλευτής, οἱ τοῦ μιάσματος β. Agath.3.5. Adv. -ρως *like a counsellor*, Men.123.

**βουλῑμ-ία**, ἡ, *ravenous hunger*, Timocl.13.3, Arist.*Pr.*887b39. -ίᾱσις, εως, ἡ, *suffering from* βουλιμία, Plu.2.695d. -ιάω, *suffer from* βουλιμία, Ar.*Pl.*873, X.*An.*4.5.7, Arist.*Pr.*887b38, Erasistr.ap.Gell.16.3.10, Plu.*Brut.*25. -ος, ὁ, = βουλιμία, Id.2.693f, Erasistr.ap.Gell.16.3.9, Sor.2.4, etc.; β. ἐσθ' ἄνθρωπος Alex.135.17. -ώδης, ες, *of the nature of* βούλιμος, Herod.Med.ap.Orib.5.30.15 (also -ιώδης, Gal.19.122). -ώττω, = βουλιμιάω, Suid.

**βούλιος**, ον, (βουλή) = βουλευτικός 1.2, *sage*, A.*Ch.*672 (in Comp. -ώτερος), prob. (for δούλιος) in Id.*Supp.*599 (lyr.).

**βουλλα**, ἡ, *tin*, *PHolm.*2.4, *PLeid.X.*6.

**βουλο-γρᾰφία**, ἡ, *registration of senatorial decrees*, *CIG*4015 (Ancyra):—hence ⊛ -γρᾰφέω, *Ostr.*1549. -κοπίδης, ου, ὁ, Com. name, on analogy of δημοκόπος, *AB*221.3.

⊛ **βούλομαι** (Ep. also **βόλομαι**, q. v.), Dor. **βώλ-** (q. v.), Aeol. **βόλλ-** (v. βόλομαι), Thess. **βέλλ-** *IG*9(2).517.20, Boeot. **βείλ-** ib.7.3080, **βήλ-** *SIG*1185.18 (Tanagra, iii B.C.), Locr. and Delph. **δείλ-** *IG*9(1).334.3, *GDI*2034.10, Coan, etc. **δήλ-** (q. v.), Ion. 2 sg. βούλεαι Od.18.364, Hdt.1.11: impf. ἐβουλόμην Il.11.79, etc.; ἠβουλόμην E.*Hel.*752, D.1.15, etc.; Ion. 3 pl. ἐβουλέατο codd. in Hdt.1.4, 3.143: fut. βουλήσομαι A.*Pr.*867, S.*OT*1077, etc.; later fut. βουληθήσομαι v.l. in Aristid.*Or.*48(24).8, Gal.13.636: aor. ἐβουλήθην, also ἠβ- (v. infr.), βουληθείς S.*OC*732, *IG*2².1236, etc., but Ep. aor. subj. 3 sg. βόληται (from *βόλσ-ε-ται) Il.1.67: pf. βεβούλημαι D.18.2; also βέβουλα (προ-) Il.1.113 (ἐβέβουλε dub. in Epigr. in *Berl.Sitzb.*1894.907):—forms with augm. ἠ- are found in Att. Inscrr. from 300 B.C. onwards, as *IG*2².657, al., and occur frequently in Mss. as ἠβούλοντο v.l. in Th.2.2, 6.79, ἠβούλου Hyp.*Lyc.*11; said to be Ionic in *An.Ox.*2.374.—An Act. βούλητε (= βούλησθε) Mitteis *Chr.*361.10 (iv A.D.):—*will, wish, be willing*, Hom., etc.: usu. implying choice or preference (cf. IV) opp. ἐθέλω 'consent', εἰ βούλει, ἐγὼ ἐθέλω Pl.*Grg.*522e, cf. *R.*347b, 437b; ἐὰν βούλῃ σύ.. ἐὰν θεὸς ἐθέλῃ Id.*Alc.*1.135d; ἂν οἵ τε θεοὶ 'θέλωσι καὶ ὑμεῖς βούλησθε D.2.20; οὔτ' ἀκούειν ἠθέλετ' οὔτε πιστεύειν ἐβούλεσθε Id.19.23; but ἐθέλω is also used = 'wish', λέξαι θέλω σοι, πρὶν θανεῖν, ἃ βούλομαι, E.*Alc.*281 (so ἐθέλω εἰπεῖν Pl.*Prt.*309b, but φράσαι τι βούλομαι Ar.*Pl.*1090): Hom. uses βούλομαι for ἐθέλω in the case of the gods, for with them *wish* is *will*: ἐθέλω is more general, and is sts. used where βούλομαι might have stood, e.g. Il.7.182.—Construct.: mostly c. inf., Τρώεσσιν ἐβούλετο κῦδος ὀρέξαι 11.79, etc.; sts. c. inf. fut., Thgn.184; c. acc. et inf., Od.4.353, and freq. in Prose: when βούλομαι is folld. by acc. only, an inf. may generally be supplied, as καί κε τὸ βουλοίμην (sc. γενέσθαι) Od.20.316; ἔτυχεν ὧν ἐβούλετο (sc. τυχεῖν) Antiph.18.6; πλακοῦντα β. (sc. σε λέγειν) Id.52.11; καὶ εἰ μάλα βούλεται ἄλλη [Ποσειδάων] (sc. τοῦτο γενέσθαι) Il.15.51; so εἰς τὸ βαλανεῖον βούλομαι (sc. ἰέναι) Ar.*Ra.*1279; βουλοίμην ἂν (sc. τόδε γενέσθαι) Pl.*Euthphr.*3a. 2. in Hom. of gods, c. acc. rei et dat. pers., Τρώεσσιν..ἐβούλετο νίκην he *willed* victory to the Trojans, Il.7.21, cf. 23.682: later c. acc., τὸ βουλόμενον τὴν πολιτείαν πλῆθος *that supports* the constitution, Arist.*Pol.*1309b17. II. Att. usages: 1. βούλει or βούλεσθε folld. by Verb in subj., βούλει λάβωμαι; *would you have* me take hold? S.*Ph.*761; βούλει φράσω; Ar.*Eq.*36, cf. Pl.*Phd.*79a, *R.*596a; ποῦ δὴ βούλει ἀναγνῶμεν; Id.*Phdr.*228e. 2. εἰ βούλει if *you please*, S.*Ant.*1168, X.*An.*3.4.41; also εἰ δὲ βούλει, ἐὰν δὲ βούλῃ, to express a concession, or if *you like*, Pl.*Smp.*201a, etc.; εἰ μὲν β., φρονήσει, εἰ δὲ β., ἰσχύι Id.*R.*432a. 3. ὁ βουλόμενος *any one who likes*, Hdt.1.54, Th.1.26, etc.; ἔδωκεν ἅπαντι τῷ βουλομένῳ D.21.45; ὁ β. the 'common informer', Ar.*Pl.*918 (whence, in jest, βούλομαι ib.908); ὅστις βούλει who or which ever *you like*, Pl.*Grg.*517b, *Cra.*432a. 4. βουλομένῳ μοί ἐστι, c. inf., it is *according to* my *wish* that.., Th.2.3; εἰ σοὶ β. ἐστὶν ἀποκρίνεσθαι Pl.*Grg.*448d; also τὰ θεῶν οὕτω βουλόμεν' ἔσται E.*IA*33; τὸ κείνου βουλόμενον his *wish*, ib.1270; but with pass. sense, τὸ β. the *object of desire*, Luc.*Am.*37, Plu.*Art.*28. 5. τί βουλόμενος; *with* what *purpose?* Pl.*Phd.*63a, D.18.172; τί βουληθεὶς πάρει; S.*El.*1100. III. *mean*, Pl.*R.*362e, 590e, etc.; τί ἡμῖν βούλεται οὗτος ὁ μῦθος; (folld. by β. λέγειν ὡς..) Id.*Tht.*156c; τί β. σημαίνειν τὸ τέρας D.H.4.59; βούλεται εἶναι *professes* or *pretends* to be, Pl.*R.*595c; β. τὸ ὄνομα ἐπικεῖσθαι Id.*Cra.*412c; freq. in Arist., τὸ ἀκούσιον βούλεται λέγεσθαι οὐκ εἰ.. *EN*1110b30; β. ἄσωτος εἶναι ὁ ἕν τι κακὸν ἔχων ib.1119b34; β. ὁ πρᾶος ἀτάραχος εἶναι ib.1125b33; *tend* to be, ἡ τοῦ ὕδατος φύσις β. εἶναι ἄχυμος Id.*Sens.*441a3; β. ἤδη τότε εἶναι πόλις ὅταν.. Id.*Pol.*1261b12, cf. 1293b40; ἡ φύσις β. μὲν τοῦτο ποιεῖν πολλάκις, οὐ μέντοι δύναται ib. 1255b3, cf. *GA*778a4, al. 2. *to be wont*, X.*An.*6.3.18. IV. folld. by ἤ.., *prefer*, for βούλομαι μᾶλλον (which is more usu. in Prose), βούλομ' ἐγὼ λαὸν σόον ἔμμεναι ἢ ἀπολέσθαι I *had rather*.., Il.1.117, cf. 23.594, Od.3.232, 11.489, 12.350; β. τὸ μέν τι εὐτυχέειν.. ἢ εὐτυχέειν τὰ πάντα Hdt.3.40; β. παρθενεύεσθαι πλέω χρόνον ἢ πατρὸς ἐστερῆσθαι (for πολὺν χρόνον, μᾶλλον ἤ..) ib.124, cf. E.*Andr.* 351; less freq. without ἤ.., πολὺ βούλομαι αὐτὴν οἴκοι ἔχειν I much *prefer*.., Il.1.112, cf. Od.15.88. (*gʷel-gʷol-*, cf. the dialectic forms.)

**βουλόμᾰχος**, ον, *strife-desiring*, Ar.*Pax* 1293 (hex.).

**βου-λύσιος** [ῠ] ὥρα the time *for unyoking*, Arat.825. **-λῡσις**, εως, ἡ, = sq., only in Cic.*Att.*15.27.3. ※ **-λῡτός** (sc. καιρός), ὁ, *time for unyoking oxen* (*early afternoon*, Hld.2.19, cf. Eust.1614.44, but *evening*, Ael.*NA*13.1, cf. Philostr.*Her.*19.20), Ar.*Av.*1500, A.R.3.1342, Luc.*Cat.*1, etc.; ὑπὸ.. ἀστέρα βουλυτοῖο *IG*14.2012.15 (Sulp. Max.): —Hom. only in Adv. **βουλῡτόνδε**, Il.16.779, Od.9.58. **-μᾰνές**, τό, a *plant*, Hsch. **-μασθος** or ※**-μαστος** (so in *PSI*4.429 (iii A.D.)) (sc. ἄμπελος), ἡ, *vine bearing large grapes*, Virg.*G.*2.102, Plin. *HN*14.15, Macr.*Sat.*3.20.7. **-μελία**, ἡ, *ash*, *Fraxinus excelsior*, Thphr.*HP*3.11.4, 4.8.2 (v.l. βουμέλιος, ὁ). **-μέτρης**, ου, ὁ, *official in charge of sacrifices* (Aetol.), Hsch. **-μολγός**, ὁ, (ἀμέλγω) *cow-milking*, *AP*6.255 (Eryc.). **-μῡκοι**, οἱ, *loud bellowings*, a kind of subterranean noise, Arist.*Pr.*937b39; in Hsch. βούμυκαι.

**βουναία**, ἡ, epith. of Hera, because her temple stood on a βουνός, Paus.2.4.7.

※ **βουνιάς**, άδος, ἡ, *French turnip*, *Brassica Napus*, Agatharch.51, Nic.*Fr.*70.3, J.*AJ*3.7.6, Dsc.2.111.

**βουνίζω**, (βουνός) *heap up*, *pile up*, Lxx *Ru.*2.14,16.

※ **βούνιον**, τό, *earth-nut*, *Bunium ferulaceum*, Dsc.4.123. 2. = περιστερεών, Ps.-Dsc.4.59. II. Dim. of βουνός I, *hill*, *Inscr.Prien.* 42.41 (ii B.C.).

**βοῦνις**, ιδος, ἡ, *hilly*, Ἀπίαν βοῦνιν A.*Supp.*117 (lyr.); voc. ἰὼ γᾶ βοῦνι, πάνδικον σέβας (prob. for βουνῖτι ἔνδικον) ib.776 (lyr.).

**βουνίτης** [ῑ], ου, ὁ, *dweller on the hills*, of Pan, *AP*6.106 (Zon.). II. cf. βωνίτης.

**βουνο-βᾰτέω**, *walk on* or *mount hills*, πρῶνας *AP*6.218 (Alc.). **-ειδής**, ές, *hill-like*, *hilly*, D.S.5.40, Str.11.8.4, Plu.*Thes.*36, etc.

**βου-νομέω**, *pasture cattle*, Str.13.1.7. **-νομία**, ἡ, *pasturage*, Pi.*Pae.*3.27. **-νομος**, ον, *grazed by cattle*, of pastures, A.*Fr.*249, S.*El.*181 (lyr.). 2. ἀγέλαι βουνόμοι (parox.) herds *of grazing oxen*, Id.*OT*26.

※ **βουνός**, ὁ, *hill*, *mound*, Cyrenaic word, acc. to Hdt.4.199; freq. in Syracusan poets, acc. to Phryn.333, cf. Philem.49,142, Lxx *Ex.* 17.9, al., Plb.3.83.1, *Schwyzer* 289.168 (Rhodian, ii B.C.), Str.3.2.9, *BGU*1129.14 (i B.C.), etc. 2. *heap* of stones, etc., Lxx *Ge.*31.46; σίτου *PFlor.*58.12. II. *clot* of blood, Cyr. s. v. θρόμβος, cf. Hsch. s. v. θρόμβοι. III. *altar*, Hsch. IV. = στιβάς (Cypr.), Id. (Barbarous word acc. to Ael.Dion.*Fr.*95.)

**βουνώδης**, ες, = βουνοειδής, *hilly*, Plb.2.15.8, etc.; θίς Plu.*Crass.* 25.

**βούπαις**, αιδος, ὁ, *big boy*, Ar.*V.*1206, Eup.402, A.R.1.760, *BCH* 47.85 (Philippi), Agath.2.14 (pl.). II. *child of the ox*, = βουγενής, of bees, in allusion to their fabulous origin, *AP*7.36 (Eryc.). III. a *fish* (nisi leg. ἰσχυρός), Hsch. IV. = βουκόλος, Suid.

**βουπάλινα**, τά, prob. = βουβάλια (v. βουβάλιον), *SIG*²588.171 (Delos, ii B.C.):—also **βουπαλίδες**· περισκελίδες, Hsch.

**βούπᾰλις**, εως, ὁ, ἡ, (πάλη) *wrestling like a bull*, i. e. *hard-struggling*, ἀεθλοσύνη *APl.*4.67.

**βου-πάμων** [ᾰ], ον, gen. ονος, (πάομαι) *rich in cattle*, *AP*6.263 (Leon.), 7.740 (Id.). **-πεινα**, ἡ, = βουλιμία, Lyc.581, Call.*Fr.*7.11 P. **-πελάτης** [ᾰ], ου, ὁ, *herdsman*, A.R.4.1342, Nic.*Al.*39, Opp.*C.*1.534, Androm.ap.Gal.14.37. **-πλᾰνόκτιστος**, ον, (βοῦς, πλάνη, κτίζω) *founded by the wandering cow*, of Troy, λόφος Lyc.29. **-πλάστης**, ου, ὁ, *cow-modeller*, of the sculptor Myron, *AP*9.734 (Diosc.). **-πλευρος**, ἡ, (cf. Sch.Nic.l.c.) *bishop's weed*, *Ammi majus*, Nic.*Th.*585. **-πληθής**, ές, *full of oxen*, Euph.52. **-πληκτρος**, ον, *goading oxen*, ἄκαινα *AP*6.41 (Agath.). **-πλήξ**, ῆγος, ὁ (also ἡ, Ps.-Luc.*Philopatr.*4, *EM*371.40), *ox-goad*, θεινόμεναι βουπλῆγι (gender undetermined) Il. 6.135. 2. *axe for felling an ox*, *AP*9.352 (Leon.), Timo 4.1, Q.S.1. 159. **-ποίητος**, ον, = βούπαις II, *AP*12.249 (Strat.). **-ποίμην**, ενος, ὁ, *herdsman*, ib.7.622 (Antiphil.). **-πόλος**, ον, *tending oxen*, Hsch.; cf. βουκόλος. **-πομπός**, όν, *celebrated with a procession of oxen*, ἑορτή Pi.*Fr.*193. ※ **-πόρος**, ον, (πείρω) *ox-piercing*, β. ὀβελός a spit *large enough for a whole ox*, Hdt.2.135, cf. E.*Cyc.*302; ἀμφώβολοι σφαγῆς.. βουπόροι spits *fit to pierce an ox's* throat, Id.*Andr.*1134; β. ὀβελίσκος X.*An.*7.8.14. **-πρηόνες**, *great precipices*, Hsch. **-πρηστις**, ιδος or εως, ἡ, (πρήθω) *poisonous beetle*, which being eaten by cattle in the grass causes them to swell up and die, Hp.*Nat.Mul.* 32, Arist.*Fr.*376, Nic.*Al.*346, Dsc.2.61. II. *hare's ear*, *Bupleurum protractum*, Thphr.*HP*7.7.3. **-πρόσωπος**, ον, *with the face of an ox* or *cow*, Porph.*Abst.*3.16 (βοο- codd.), Lyd.*Mens.*4.46, Phlp.*in GA*185.11. ※ **-πρῳρος**, ον, (πρῷρα) *with the forehead* or *face of an ox*, S.*Tr.*13 (ap.Str.10.2.19; Laur. Ms. βούκρανος); β. πρόσωπα Philostr. Jun.*Im.*4. II. β. ἑκατόμβη offering of 100 sheep *and one ox*, *SIG*604.8 (Delph., ii B.C.), Plu.2.668c, Hsch.; β. θυσία *Delph.*3(2). 66; ἔπεμψαν Κεῖοι δωδεκηΐδα β. ταῦρον Dürrbach *Choix d'Inscriptions de Délos* p.183 (ii A.D.). **-πρως**· ἀσθένεια, Hsch.

**βούπτινον**, = τρίφυλλον, Hsch.

**βουργάριος**, ὁ, = Lat. *burgarius*, *SIG*880.52 (Thrace).

※ **βουρδών**, ῶνος, ὁ, = βορδών, *mule*, *IG*5(1).1115 *B*137, *Edict.Diocl.* 14.10, *PLips.*87.1 (iv A.D.):—hence ※**βουρδωνάριος**, ὁ, *muleteer*, *Edict. Diocl.*7.17, Sch.Ar.*Th.*498: **βουρδωνάριον**, τό, Dim. of βουρδών, *PRyl.*238.11 (iii A.D.).

**βουρικυπάρισσος**· ἄμπελος (Perga), Hsch.

**βούρινον**, τό, = κυνοκεφάλιον, Ps.-Apul.*Herb.*86.

※ **βουριχάλλιον**, τό, senator's *ox-cart*, Lyd.*Mag.*1.18.

**βούρυγχος**, ὁ, a large *fish*, Hsch. **βούρυτος**, ὁ, *mighty river*, Id.

※ **βοῦς**, Dor. **βῶς** Theoc.9.7, *GDI*5005.5 (Gortyn), ὁ and ἡ: gen. βοός (written βοιός *GDI* iv p.883 No.62 (Erythrae)), poet. also βοῦ A. *Fr.*421, S.*Fr.*280: acc. βοῦν *IG*1².45 *A* 11, etc., βῶν Il.7.238 and Dor., *IG*4.914.18, al. (Epid.), *SIG*56.16 (Argos), Theoc.27.64, Ion. and poet. also βόα Pherecyd.162 J., *AP*9.255 (Phil.): dual βόε Hes.*Op.* 436: pl., nom. βόες, rarely contr. βοῦς Ar.*Fr.*760, Plu.*Aem.*33, etc.: gen. βοῶν, contr. βῶν Hes.*Th.*983; Boeot. βουῶν *IG*7.3171.45: dat. βουσί, Ep. βόεσσι, βοσί *AP*7.622 (Antiphil.); Boeot. βούεσσι *IG*7.3171. 38: acc. βόας Il.5.556, al., βοῦς 1.154, al., S.*Aj.*175 (lyr.), and Att., Antiph.172.5, etc. (but later βόας *Ev.Jo.*2.14, *POxy.*729.16 (ii A.D.), etc.):—*bullock*, *bull*, *ox*, or *cow*, in pl *cattle*, commonly fem.: to mark the male Hom. adds a word, β. ἄρσην Il.20.495; or ταῦρος β. 17.389; as a measure of value, βοὸς ἄξιον 23.885, cf. 7.474 and v. ἀλφεσίβοιος, ἑκατόμβοιος. b. βοῦς ἄγριος *buffalo*, Arist.*HA*499a4. c. βοῦς ἐν Συρίᾳ *zebu*, ib.606a15; β. ἐν Παιονίᾳ, perh. *urus*, Id.*Mir.*842b 33. d. βοὸς ὄμμα, = βούφθαλμος, *AP*4.1.52 (Mel.). 2. metaph. of any *dam* or *mother*, μία β. Κρηθεῖ τε μάτηρ καὶ Σαλμωνεῖ Pi.*P.*4.142; ἄπεχε τῆς β. τὸν ταῦρον A.*Ag.*1125. II. = βοείη or βοέη (always fem.), *ox-hide shield*, νωμῆσαι βῶν Il.7.238; τυκτῇσι βόεσσιν 12.105; βόας αὔας ib.137; γέρρα λευκῶν β. X.*An.*5.4. 12. III. a *fish*, perh. *Notidanus griseus*, Arist.*HA*540b17, *Fr.* 280. 2. a fish of the Nile, Str.17.2.4. IV. ἕβδομος β. *crescent loaf*, Clidem.16. V. *seam*, Poll.7.65. VI. *the constellation Taurus*, Max.162. VII. = μάστιξ, Hsch. VIII. prov., β. ἐπὶ γλώσσης ἐπιβαίνων Thgn.815; βοῦς ἐπὶ γλώσσῃ βέβηκε A.*Ag.*36; of people who keep silence from some weighty reason, τὸν βοῦν ἐπιτίθημι τῇ γλώττῃ Jul.*Or.*7.218a; βοῦς ἐμβαίνει μέγας Strattis 67 (wrongly expld. by Zen.2.70, etc., of bribery with coins bearing type of ox); β. ἐν πόλει 'bull in a china-shop', Diogenian.3.67; β. ἐν αὐλίῳ, of a useless person, Cratin.32; β. λύρας 'pearls before swine', Macho ap.Ath.8.349c. (βοῦς (from βωύς, Skt. *gaús*) acc. βῶν (Skt. *gắm*) are old forms: stem βωϝ- βοϝ-, cf. Lat. (Umbr.) *bos*, etc.)

**Βούσβατον**· τὴν Ἄρτεμιν (Thracian), Hsch.

**βουσέλῑνον**, τό, = σμύρνιον, Plin.*HN*20.118, Archig.ap.Gal.12. 406.

**βουσή**· δούλη, Hsch. **βουσία**· γογγυλίδι ὅμοιον (Thess.), Id.

**βουσκᾰφέω**, *undermine*, Lyc.434.

**βουσκητήριον**· εἰς εὐρύνην· εἴρηται κακοσχόλως ἐπὶ τοῦ γυναικείου αἰδοίου, Hsch.

**βου-σόη**, Lacon. **ϝουῆα**, ἡ, *herd*, *EM*208.6, 391.19. **-σόος**, v. βοοσσόος.

**ϝουσός**, ἡ, *pasture for oxen*, *Schwyzer* 664.15 (Orchom. Arc., iv B.C.).

**βούσταθμον**, τό, *ox-stall*, E.*Hel.*29, *IA*76, Lyc.92 (pl.): in masc. form, ἀμφὶ βουστάθμους E.*Hel.*359 (lyr.):—as Adj., βουστάθμου κάπης S.*Ichn.*8.

**βου-στάνη**· βοοστασία, Hsch.: also, = μάστιξ or πληγή, Id. **-στάς**, άδος, ἡ, *where oxen are stalled*, αὐλαί S.*Fr.*321. ※ **-στᾰσία**, ἡ, = βούσταθμον, Luc.*Alex.*1. **-στάσιον** [ᾰ], τό, = foreg., *PFlor.* 50.60 (iii A.D.), *Gp.*2.27.2, Olymp. *in Mete.*113.22. **-στᾰσις**, εως, ἡ, = foreg., A.*Pr.*653 (pl.), *IG*11(2).145.19 (Delos, iv B.C.), D.H.1. 79. **-στροφηδόν**, Adv. *turning like oxen in ploughing*; of writing from left to right and right to left alternately, Euph.ap.Harp. ὁ κάτωθεν νόμος, Paus 5.17.6, Hsch. **-στροφος**, ον, *ploughed by oxen*, Lyc.1438; but, II. parox. **-στρόφος**, ον, *ox-guiding*, δεσμά *AP*6.104 (Phil.); *ox-tormenting*, μύωψ ib.95 (Antiphil.). **-σῡκον**, τό, (βου-) *a large*, *coarse fig*, Hsch., cf. Varro *RR*2.5.4. **-σφᾰγέω**, *slaughter oxen*, E.*El.*627.

**βούτᾰλις**, ἡ, = ἀηδών, Aesop.85 (v.l. βώτ-). **βουτάνη**, *part of ship to which rudder was fastened*, Hsch.; also expld. as = μάστιξ, or μάχη, ἀηδία, Id.

**βούταρος**· ὁ παχύς, Hsch. **βουτελέστην**· θύτην, Id.

**βούτης**, ου, Dor. **βούτας** α, ὁ, (βοῦς) *herdsman*, A.*Pr.*568 (lyr.), E.*Andr.*280 (lyr.), Theoc.1.80, *AP*6.255 (Eryc.), etc.:—as Adj., β. φόνος the slaughter *of kine*, E.*Hipp.*537. II. = ὀρίγανος (Cydonia), Hsch.

**βούτῑμος**, ον, *worth an ox*, Hsch., *EM*207.5.

※ **ϝοῦτις** or **βοῦττις**, ἡ, *vessel in the shape of the frustum of a cone*, Hero *Stereom.*2.9; βούτη ib.1.52, Aët.3.133:—Dim. **βούτιον** *Hippiatr.*34.

**βού-τομον**, τό, or **-τομος**, ὁ, (τέμνω) *sedge*, *Carex riparia*, Ar.*Av.* 662, Theoc.13.35: masc., Thphr.*HP*1.10.5: neut., ib.4.10.4, Theoc.

l.c., *Gp*.2.6.28, Lxx *Jb*.8.11. **-τόρος**, *ον*, = *βουπόρος*, Suid.: *βούτορον ψάκαστρον· νιφάδ' ὑετοῦ*, Hsch.

**βουτόων·** *ὁδόν, ἀτραπόν*, Hsch. (fort. *βουδόν*, cf. *βουσόη*).

**Βουτράγιος**, *ὁ* (sc. *μήν*), name of month at Melitaea, *IG*9(2).206 i *b* 19.

**βού-τρᾰγος**, *ὁ*, *ox-goat*, fabulous animal, Philostr.*VA*6.24. **-τρᾰγοταυράνθρωπος**, *ὁ*, *a compound of ox, goat, bull, and man*, Tz.*H*.7.484. **-τροφία**, *ἡ*, *feeding of cattle*, Agatharch.7. ⊛ **-τρόφος**, *ον*, *ox-feeding*: *ὁ βουτρόφος*, = *βούτης*, Poll.1.249, *EM*209.54; cf. *βοοτρόφος*. **-τρωκτον**, *τό*, = *ὄροβος*, Hsch. **-τύπος** [ῠ], *ὁ*, *ox-butcher, slaughterer*, A.R.2.91, 4.468; esp. of the priest at the Dipolia (cf. *βουφόνια*), *IG*1$^{2}$.839, 3.1163.2, Clidem.17, Porph.*Abst*.2.30. **2.** = *οἶστρος*, *gadfly*, Opp.*H*.2.529; but = *ἐμπίς*, Hsch. **-τύρινος** [ῡ], *η, ον*, *of butter*, *μύρον* Dsc.1.54. ⊛ **-τῡρον**, *τό*, *butter*, *τὸ πῖον τοῦ γάλακτος* Hp.*Morb*.4.51, cf. Arist.*Fr*.636, Plu.2.1109b, Lxx *Ge*.18.8, Sor.1.86, Dsc.2.72, *Edict.Diocl*.4.50:—also **βούτῡρος**, *ὁ*, Gal.13.527. **II.** a *plant*, Hsch.; *ὄζει ὁ τόπος β.* Ath.9.395a. **-τῡροφάγος** [ᾰ], *ον*, *ὁ*, *butter-eater*, Anaxandr.41.8 (prob.). **-φάγος** [ᾰ], *ον*, *ox-eating*, Simon.179.4, *AP*7.426 (Antip. Sid.); of Hercules, Luc.*Am*.1, Porph.*Abst*.1.22, cf. *AP*9.59 (Antip.): expld. by *πολυφάγος*, Hsch.

**βουφάρας·** *γεφύρας*, Hsch.

**βούφαρον·** *τὴν εὐάροτον γῆν· φάρος γὰρ ἡ ἄροσις· καὶ ἐπίθετον βοός*, Hsch.

**βούφθαλμον**, *τό*, (*βοῦς, ὀφθαλμός*) *ox-eye*, *Anacyclus radiatus*, Dsc.3.139, Nic.*Fr*.74.59. **2.** = *χρυσάνθεμον*, Ps.-Dsc.4.58; = *ἀείζωον*, Dsc.4.88; = *βοάνθεμον*, Gal.19.87.

**βούφθαλμος**, *ὁ*, a *fish*, Marc.Sid.8.

**βουφον-έω**, *slaughter oxen*, Il.7.466. **-ια** (sc. *ἱερά*), *τά*, at Athens, ceremony at the Dipolia, at which *an ox was slain*, Ar.*Nu*.985, Androt.13, Paus.1.28.11, Ael.*VH*8.3. **-ιών**, *ῶνος*, *ὁ*, month at Delos, *IG*11.203*A*32,52 (iii B.C.); at Tenos, ib.12(5).824. **-ος**, *ον*, *ox-slaying*, *h.Merc*.436; *θεράπων* Simon.172.4; *πελέκεις* D.S.4.12:—as Subst., *priest*, Paus.1.28.10. **II.** *at* or *for which steers are slain*, *θοῖναι* A.*Pr*.531 (lyr.).

**βουφορβ-έω**, *tend cattle*, E.*Alc*.8. **-ια**, *τά*, *herd of oxen*, ib.1031, *IT*301. **-ός**, *όν* (fem. *-φορβή*, of Persephone, *Hymn.Mag*.3.26), *ox-feeding*:—as Subst., *herdsman*, E.*IT*237, Pl.*Plt*.268a.

**βού-φορτος**, *ον*, = *πολύφορτος*, *AP*6.222 (Theodorid.). **-χανδής**, *ές*, (*χανδάνω*) *holding an ox*, *λέβης* ib.153 (Anyte); expld. by *πολυχώρητος*, Hsch. **-χῑλος**, *ον*, *rich in fodder*, *λειμών* A.*Supp*.540 (lyr.); *Ἀρκαδίη* *AP*6.108 (Myrin.). **-χρώς** *τις· ἰσχυρός, ἢ ζηρος*, Hsch.

**βούχωμα·** *φρόνημα*, Hsch.

**βοώδης**, *ες*, *ox-like*, Adam.2.37; *stupid*, Apollon.*Lex*. s.v. *βουγάϊε*.

⊛ **βοών**, *ῶνος*, *ὁ*, *cow-house, byre*, *Tab.Heracl*.1.139, Phryn.*PS* p.52 B.

**βοῶνα·** *ὁδόν*, and **βοῶνας·** *ἀγροικίας*, Hsch.

**βο-ωνέω**, *buy oxen*, *IG*2.163.17. ⊛ **-ώνης**, *ου*, *ὁ*, (*ὠνέομαι*) at Athens, *an officer who bought oxen for the sacrifices*, D.21.171, *IG*2.163.18. **-ώνητος**, *ον*, *purchased with an ox*, Hsch.; *τὰ β.*, name of a place in Sparta, Paus.3.12.1. **-ωνία**, *ἡ*, *purchase of oxen*, *IG*2.741$^{a}$8. **II.** *βοωνία· αὔλιος θύρα* (Cret.), Hsch. **-ῶπις**, *ιδος*, *ἡ*, (*ὤψ*) *ox-eyed*, i.e. *having large, full eyes*, *βοῶπις πότνια Ἥρη* Il.1.551, al., cf. Eup.403; of Artemis, B.10.99; Amphitrite, Id.16.110; Harmonia, Pi.*P*.3.91; of women, Il.3.144, 7.10, 18.40:—masc. **βοώπης** Eust.768.43. **II.** (*ὄψ*) = *μεγαλόφωνος*, Hsch. ⊛ **-ωτέω**, *plough*, Hes.*Op*.391. **-ώτης**, *ου*, *ὁ*, *ploughman*, Lyc.268, Babr.52.3, *APl*.4.333 (Antiphil.). **II.** the constellation *Boötes*, Arat.92; but prob. = the star *Ἀρκτοῦρος* in Od.5.272. **-ωτία**, *ἡ*, *arable land* or *ploughing*, Crito Hist.3. **-ωψ**, *ωπος*, *ὁ*, small *fish* with large eyes, Ar.Byz.ap.Ath.7.287a. (Expld. as more correct than *βό-ωξ*, *βῶξ* (q.v.).)

⊛ **βρά·** *ἀδελφοί* (Elean), Hsch.

**βρᾷ**, Aeol. for *βρᾴδιον* (i.e. *ϝρᾴδιον*), A.D.*Adv*.163.21, Hdn.Gr.2.214.

**βρᾰβ-εία**, *ἡ*, *office of* *βραβεύς*: generally, *arbitration, judgement*, *ὅπως κλύοιμί σου κοινὰς βραβείας* E.*Ph*.450, cf. Lyc.1154. **-εῖον**, Ep. **-ήϊον**, *τό*, *prize in the games*, Men.*Mon*.653, 1*Ep.Cor*.9.24, Plu.2.742c, Opp.*C*.4.197. **II.** *wand, baton* given as a prize, *τιμηθεὶς χρυσείῳ β.* *CIG*3674 (Cyzicus, ii A.D.), cf. *IG*14.748 (Naples). ⊛ **-ευμα**, *ατος*, *τό*, *judge's award*, S.*Fr*.317. ⊛ **-εύς**, *έως*, *ὁ*, Att. pl. *βραβῆς*: acc. sg. *βραβῆ* (v. infr.):—*judge at the games*, S.*El*.690,709, Pl.*Lg*.949a: generally, *judge, arbitrator, umpire*, *δίκης* E.*Or*.1650; *λόγου* Id.*Med*.274, etc.; *Ἀΐδην κοινὸν ἔθεντο βραβῆ* Epigr.ap.D.18.289. **2.** generally, *chief, leader*, *μυρίας ἵππου β.* A.*Pers*.302; *φιλόμαχοι β.* Id.*Ag*.230 (lyr.); *author*, *μόχθων τῶν ἐν Ἰλίῳ*, of Helen, E.*Hel*.703. ⊛ **-ευτής**, *οῦ*, *ὁ*, = *βραβεύς*, Is.9.35, *POxy*.1050.11 (ii/iii A.D.); *β. τῶν λόγων* Pl.*Prt*.338b; *β. τοῦ δικαίου ὁ δικαστής* Arist.*Rh*.1376$^{b}$20, cf. Ph.2.346, al.; *αἱρεῖσθαί τινα β.* Plu.*Cat.Mi*.44. **II.** *official of a religious confraternity*, Buresch *Aus Lydien* 10, Ramsay *Eastern Provinces* 320. **-εύω**, *act as judge* or *umpire*, *ἐν τῇ κληρώσει τὴν τύχην βραβεύσειν* Isoc.7.23; *ὀρθῶς β.* Axiop.2.7; *preside* at an election, Plu.*Cat.Mi*.44. **II.** c. acc., *arbitrate, decide on*, *τὰ τῶν ἄλλων δίκαια* D.3.27, cf. Arist.*Ath*.9.2; *κρίσεις* Plu.*Cic*.35: *δικαστήριον* ib.9; *ἅμιλλαν* Id.2.960a, etc.: c. acc. et dat., *ἀγῶνα ἰσχυρὸν ἐβράβευσεν αὐτῷ* Lxx *Wi*.10.12; *προσήκει βασιλεῖ τὰ δίκαια β. τοῖς ὑπηκόοις* Muson.8 p.33 H.:—Pass., *βραβευθήσεται τὰ τοῦ πολέμου τῷ νενικηκότι* J.*AJ*6.9.1; *τὰ παρά τινι βραβευόμενα* Isoc.5.70; *συνέβη..τὴν κρίσιν βραβευθῆναι* *SIG*685.37 (Cret.). **2.** *direct, control*, *Michel* 163.10 (Delos), *AP*12.56 (Mel.); *νοῦς β. πάντα* Ph.1.94:—Pass., Plb.6.4.3, Plu.*Pel*.13; *πάντων ὑπὸ τοῦ δαιμονίου -ομένων* Phld.*Herc*.1251.7.

**βραβύλη**, = *ἀνεμώνη ἡ φοινικῆ*, Ps.-Dsc.2.176.

**βράβῠλον**, *τό*, *sloe*, *Prunus spinosa*, Theoc.7.146 (wrongly expld. by Sch. as *damson*), 12.3, Antyll.ap.Orib.10.20.4, Gal.6.621. **II.** = *κοκκύμηλον* (q.v.), Seleuc.ap.Ath.2.50a, Clearch.82.

**βράβῠλος**, *ἡ*, *the tree which bears* *βράβυλα*, Aret.*CA*2.2, *Gp*.10.39. **II.** = *βράβυλον*, *AP*9.377 (Pall.). **III.** *seedling peach*, *Gp*.10.13.5. (The forms *βράβιλος, βράβηλος* are found in codd. of *Gp*. and *AP*, *βράβηλον* *EM*211.3, *βράβιλον* codd. of Theoc. and Ath.)

**βράγος**, = *βράχος* (B), Hsch.

**βραγχ-ᾰλέος**, *α, ον*, (*βράγχος*) *hoarse*, Hp.*Acut*.(*Sp*.)55. **-άω**, *to have a sore throat*, Arist.*HA*603$^{b}$13, D.C.63.26, Porph.*Abst*.3.7. **-εία**, *ἡ*, = *βράγχος* I.1, Hsch. **-η**, *ἡ*, = *βράγχος* I.2, Xenocr.52. **-ιάζοισθε·** *πνίγοισθε*, Hsch. **-ιάω**, = *βραγχάω*, Arist.*Pr*.901$^{b}$5, *Aud*.804$^{a}$18, Lxx *Ps*.68(69).3; condemned by Phot. s.v. *λιθῶντας*. **-ιοειδής**, *ές*, = *βραγχοειδής*, Arist.*HA*526$^{b}$20. **-ιον**, *τό*, *fin*, dub. in Arion 1.4 (*βράγχιοι* codd. Ael.). **II.** in pl., *gills of fishes*, Arist.*HA*589$^{b}$19, *PA*696$^{b}$1, Theoc.11.54 (sg., Ael.*NA*16.12). **III.** = *βρόγχιον, βρόγχος*, dub.l. in Arist.*Spir*.483$^{a}$22, cf. *HA*603$^{a}$32. **IV.** *hull* of a ship, Hsch. **-ιώδης**, *ες*, = *βραγχοειδής*, Arist.*HA*526$^{a}$26.

**βραγχοειδής**, *ές*, *like fishes' gills*, Arist.*PA*684$^{a}$20.

**βράγχος**, *ὁ*, *hoarseness* or *sore throat causing hoarseness*, Hp.*VM*19 (pl.), al., Th.2.49: pl., Arist.*Pr*.860$^{a}$30,37. **2.** a *disease* in swine (either *anthrax* or *foot-and-mouth disease*), Id.*HA*603$^{a}$31. **II.** *βράγχος*, *τό*, in pl., = *βράγχια*, Opp.*H*.1.160; but *βράγχος*, *ὁ*, in Ptol.*Alm*.8.1.

**βραγχός**, *ή, όν*, *hoarse*, *βραγχὰ λαρυγγιόων* *AP*11.382.2 (Agath.).

⊛ **βραγχώδης**, *ες*, *subject to hoarseness*, Hp.*Aër*.6, *Epid*.1.1. Adv. *-δῶς* Gal.13.4. **2.** *causing it*, *ὕδατα -έστατα* Hp.*Aër*.7.

**βρᾰδᾰνίζω** (= *ϝραδ-*)· *ῥιπίζω, τινάσσω* (Aeol.), Hsch.

⊛ **βράδινος** [ᾰ], *α, ον*, Aeol. for *ῥαδινός*, Sapph.90,104.

**βρᾴδιον**, Aeol., = *ϝρᾴδιον*, *EM*210.43.

**βράδος** [ᾰ], *εος*, *τό*, = *βρᾰδυτής*, X.*Eq*.11.12, Epicur.*Ep*.1 p.10 U.

**βρᾰδῠ-ανάφορος**, *ον*, *slow-rising*, *τὰ β. τῶν ζῳδίων* Anon.*in Ptol.Tetr*.114. **-βάμων** [ᾱ], *ον*, gen. *ονος*, *slow-walking*, Arist.*Phgn*.813$^{a}$3. **-βουλία**, *ἡ*, *slowness of counsel*, Ph.2.662. **-γᾰμος**, *ον*, *late in marrying*, Ptol.*Tetr*.183. **-γενής**, *ές*, *late born*, Sch.Lyc.1276. **-γλωσσος**, Att. **-ττος**, *ον*, *slow of tongue*, Lxx *Ex*.4.10, *Cat.Cod.Astr*.2.167, Ps.-Luc.*Philopatr*.13. ⊛ **-δῑνής**, *ές*, *slow-eddying* or *whirling*, Nonn.*D*.37.482. **-ήκοος**, *ον*, (*ἀκούω*) *slow of hearing*, *EM*430.28. **-θάνᾰτος** [θᾰ], *ον*, *dying slowly*, Gal.16.631. **-καρπος**, *ον*, *late-fruiting*, Thphr.*CP*5.17.6. **-κατάφορος**, *ον*, *slow in setting*, *ζῴδια* Sch.Ptol.*Tetr*.114. **-κίνητος** [ῑ], *ον*, *slow-moving*, Gal.5.318, Adam.1.7: Comp. *-τότερος* Phlp.*in Ph*.680.31: Subst. **-κῑνησία**, *ἡ*, Aristid.Quint.2.9, Diog.Oen.71. **-κρίσῐμος** [ρῐ], *ον*, *slow in reaching a crisis*, Herod.Med. in *Rh.Mus*.58.95. **-λογία**, *ἡ*, *slowness of speech*, Poll.2.121:—Adj. ⊛ **-λόγος**, *ον*, Sch.Ven.Il.3.155. **-μᾰθής**, *ές*, *slow in learning*, Hsch. s.v. *ὀψιμαθής*:—Subst. **-μᾰθία**, *ἡ*, Zonar. **-νοια**, *ἡ*, *slowness of understanding*, D.L.7.93. **-νοος**, *ον*, contr. **-νους**, *ουν*, *slow of understanding*, Dam.*Isid*.81.

**βρᾰδύνω**, fut. *-ῠνῶ* Lxx *De*.7.10: aor. *ἐβράδῡνα* Luc.*Cont*.1, App.*BC*1.69: plpf. *ἐβεβραδύκειν* Luc.*Symp*.20: (*βραδύς*): **I.** trans., *make slow, delay*, Lxx *Is*.46.13:—Pass., *to be delayed*, *τἀπὸ σοῦ βραδύνεται* S.*OC*1628; *ἡ δ' ὁδὸς βραδύνεται* Id.*El*.1501. **II.** intr., *loiter, delay*, *εἰ βραδύνοιμεν βοῇ* A.*Supp*.730 (so in Med., *χεῖρα δ' οὐ βραδύνεται..ἁρπάσαι δόρυ* Id.*Th*.623); *μὴ βράδυνε* S.*Ph*.1400; *σπεύδων..βραδύνω* Pl.*R*.528d: c. inf., Polyaen.1.48.4; *βραδύνει σοι τοῦτο;* *are* you *slow, slack* in this? Philostr.*Im*.1.6.

⊛ **βρᾰδῠ-πειθής**, *ές*, (*πείθομαι*) *slow to be persuaded*, *AP*5.286 (Agath.). **II.** *reluctant*, Nonn.*D*.4.313. **-πεπτέω**, *digest slowly*, Dsc.5.39. **-πεπτος**, *ον*, *slow of digestion*, v.l. in Gal.6.770 (Comp.). **-πεψία**, *ἡ*, *slowness of digestion*, Sor.1.51, Dsc.5.38 (pl.), Gal.7.62. **-πλοέω**, *sail slowly*, *Act.Ap*.27.7, Artem.4.30, *AB*225. **-πνοος**, *ον*, *breathing slowly*, Aret.*SD*1.10. **-πορέω**, *proceed slowly*, of the sun, *Placit*.5.18.1. **-πόρος**, *ον*, *slow-passing*, of food, Hp.*Acut*.62, Ruf.ap.Orib.5.3.4, Philagr.ib.5.19.4; of humours, Gal.7.341: generally, *slow*, *ὅρασις* Plu.2.626a; *β. πέλαγος* *slow to pass*, ib.941b. **-πους**, *ὁ, ἡ*, *πουν*, *τό*, gen. *ποδος*, *slow of foot, slow*, *ἤλυσις* E.*Hec*.66 (anap.); *ὄνος* *AP*9.301 (Secund.), cf. 310 (Antiphil.); *βουλή* ib.10.37 (Luc.).

⊛ **βρᾰδύς**, *εῖα, ύ*: Comp. *βραδύτερος* Th.4.8; metath. *βαρδύτερος* Theoc.29.30; *βραδίων* Artem.1.70: Sup. *βραδύτατος* Ar.*Fr*.357, also *βράδιστος* (metath. *βάρδιστος* Il.23.310,530, Doroth(?).ap.Heph.*Astr*.3.30) Aret.*SD*1.6, *βραδίστατος* Ael.*Fr*.325:—*slow*, *κιχάνει τοι β. ὠκύν* Od.8.329, etc.: c. inf., *ἀλλά τοι ἵπποι βάρδιστοι θείειν* *slowest* at running, Il.23.310; *β. λέγειν* E.*HF*237, etc.; *τὸ β.* *delay*, Pl.*Lg*.766e. Adv. *βραδέως*, *χωρεῖν* Th.5.70; *θεῖν* Pl.*Prt*.336a, etc.: Comp. *-ύτερον* Hp.*Prog*.22, Pl.*Tht*.190a; *βραδυτέρως* Aen.Tact.16.12; *βράδῖον* Hes.*Op*.528, Sor.1.117 (condemned by Luc.*Sol*.7): Sup. *-ύτατα* Pl.*Ti*.39b. **2.** of the mind, *dull, sluggish*, *ἐπιλήσμων καὶ β.* Ar.*Nu*.129; opp. *ἀγχίνους*, Pl.*Phdr*.239a; *βράδιστοι τὴν γνώμην* Aret. l.c.: c. inf., *προνοῆσαι βραδεῖς* Th.3.38; *τὸ β. καὶ μέλλον* *slowness* and deliberation, Th.1.84. Adv. *βραδέως*, *βουλεύεσθαι* ib.78; *β. ὀλίγην ὀργὴν ποιεῖσθαι* Pl.*Phdr*.233c. **3.** in Egypt, of illiterates, βραδέως, βραδύτερον γράφειν, *PTeb.*316.101 (i A.D.), *PRyl.*173.13 (i A.D.); also βραδέα γράφουσα *BGU*446.19 (ii A.D.). II. of Time, *tardy, late,* σὺν χρόνῳ β. μολών S.*Tr.*395, cf. Th.7.43; βραδεῖαν.. ὁδὸν πέμπων S.*Aj.*738. Adv., ἕως βραδέως ἦν τῆς ἡμέρας D.L.2.139: neut. as Adv., ὀψὲ καὶ βραδὺ τῆς ἡλικίας Hld.2.29; βράδιον ἀπογαλακτίζειν Sor. l.c.

**βρᾰδῠ-σῑτέω,** *eat late in the day,* Alex.Trall.7.6:—Subst. **-σῑτία,** ἡ, Id.1.15, 11.1. **-σκελής,** ές, *slow of leg,* Ἥφαιστε *AP*6.101 (Phil.).

**βρᾰδυσμός,** ὁ, *making slow,* Sch.E.*Or.*426.

**βρᾰδῠτεκνία,** ἡ, *lateness in having offspring, Cat.Cod.Astr.*2.163.

**βρᾰδυτής,** ῆτος, ἡ, *slowness, sluggishness,* βραδυτῆτί τε νωχελίῃ τε Il.19.411; so of persons, S.*Ant.*932 (anap.), Th.1.71, 5.75, Pl.*Phd.*109d, Thphr.*Char.*14.1: in pl., Isoc.4.141, D.18.246: lit. *slowness,* opp. τάχος, Pl.*Ti.*39b, cf. Arist.*Ph.*228$^{b}$29.

**βρᾰδυ-τόκος,** ον, *slow in bringing to birth,* Arist.*Pr.*891$^{b}$28 (Comp.). **-χρόνιος,** ον, *late,* Sch.Il.2.325.

**βράδων·** ἀδύνατος, Hsch.

**βράζω,** *boil, froth up, ferment,* Call.Hist.3, Hld.5.16, Alex.Aphr.*Pr.*1.104. II. *growl,* of bears, Poll.5.88; of elephants, Juba ap. Poll. l.c.; but βράζειν· τὸ ἡσυχῇ ὀδύρεσθαι, Hsch.

⊛ **βράθυ,** υος, τό, *savin, Juniperus Sabina,* Dsc.1.76; also, = *J. foetidissima,* ibid. (Aram. *b^e rāt* 'cypress'.)

**βράκαι,** ῶν, αἱ, Lat. *braccae, breeches, trews, worn by the Gauls,* D.S.5.30 (**βράκες** (sic)· ἀναξυρίδες, Hsch.):—Dim. **βράκια,** τά, Sch.Ar.*V.*1082, *PGiss.*80.6 (iv A.D.), *IG*5(1).1406.23 (Edict. Diocl., Asine):—hence ⊛**βρακάριος,** ὁ, *breeches-maker,* ib.18, cf. *POxy.*1341 (iv A.D.):—but **βρακαρίαι,** αἱ, *breeches, PGiss.*90.6 (ii A.D.).

**βράκαλον·** ῥόπαλον, Hsch.

**βράκανα,** τά, *wild herbs,* Pherecr.13, Luc.*Lex.*2, Hsch.

**βρακεῖν, βρακείς,** Aeol., = συνιέναι, συνείς, Hsch.

**βρακέλλαι,** αἱ, = βράκαι, *BGU*814.29 (iii A.D.).

**βράκετ⟨ρ⟩ον,** τό, *pruning-hook,* Hsch.; also = πλῆθος, Id.

⊛ **βράκια,** τά, = βράκαι, *PGen.*80.6 (iv A.D.).

**βρακίας·** τραχεῖς τόπους, Hsch. (fort. βραχ-, cf. ῥαχία).

**βράκος** (i.e. Ϝράκος), εος, τό, *long robe,* Sapph.70; ὑδάτινα β. Theoc.28.11. II. = κάλαμος, Hsch.

⊛ **βράπτω,** aor. inf. βράψαι, = μάρπτω, Hsch. (βράξαι is f.l. for βράψαι).

⊛ **βράσις** [ᾰ], εως, ἡ, *boiling,* of water, Orib.5.33.3.

**βράσμα,** ατος, τό, *boiling,* μέχρι βρασμάτων ἑπτά Aët.6.80. II. v.l. for βρέγμα, Dsc.2.159. III. *shaking motion,* Herod.Med. in *Rh.Mus.*58.81.

**βρασμᾰτίας,** ου, ὁ, = βράστης, opp. σεισματίας, Posidon.ap.D.L.7.154, Amm.Marc.17.7.13 (pl.), Heraclit.*All.*38.

**βρασμός,** ὁ, *boiling up,* Aët.1.130, Hld.5.17; *fermentation,* τῆς ὕλης Corn.*ND*3: hence, *agitation, shaking,* γῆς Arist.ap.Ar.Did.*Fr.*13 (pl.), Orph.*H.*47.3 (pl.), Sor.1.65; *shivering* as if from cold, ib.80, Aret.*SD*2.3; *rigor,* Gal.7.607. 2. metaph., τοῦ πάθους, τῶν παθῶν, Ph.1.306,238. II. = βράστης, J.*BJ*1.19.4, D.C.68.24, Phlp. *in Mete.*7.23, Agath.5.3; of a tidal wave, Id.2.16.

**βρασσιότροχος·** κεραμικὸς ὁ μὴ ἐρρωγώς, Hsch.

**βράσσω,** Att. **-ττω,** aor. ἔβρᾰσα Hp.*Ep.*23, etc.:—Pass., aor. ἐβράσθην Aret.*SA*1.5: pf. βέβρασμαι (v. infr.):—*shake violently, throw up,* of the sea, σκολόπενδραν.. ἔβρασ' ἐπὶ σκοπέλους *AP*6.222 (Theodorid.); τὸν πρέσβυν.. ἔβρασε.. εἰς ἠϊόνα ib.7.294 (Tull.Laur.):—Pass., ὀστέα.. βέβρασται.. τῇδε παρ' ἠϊόνι ib.288 (Antip.), cf. Opp.*H.*1.779; *boil,* of surf, A.R.2.323, Opp.*H.*3.476; β. ὑπὸ γέλωτος *shake* with laughter, Luc.*Eun.*12. 2. *winnow* grain, Ar.*Fr.*271, Pl.*Sph.*226b. 3. abs., = βράζω, *boil,* interpol. in *Gp.*7.15.20; dub. sens. in Hp. l.c. 4. βρίττειν· πληθύνειν, βαρύνειν, Hsch.

**βράσσων,** ον, Homeric Comp. of βραχύς (q.v.).

**βραστέον,** *one must winnow, Gp.*3.7.1.

**βραστήρ,** ῆρος, ὁ, *winnowing-fan, Gloss.*

⊛ **βράστης,** ου, ὁ, (βράσσω) of an earthquake, *upheaving the earth vertically,* Arist.*Mu.*396$^{a}$3.

**βραστικός,** ή, όν, f.l. for βλαστικός, Herm.ap.Stob.1.41.7.

**βρατάναν·** τορύνην (Elean), Hsch. **βρατάνει·** ῥαΐζει ἀπὸ νόσου (Elean), Id. **βράταχος,** v. βάτραχος.

**βραυκᾰνάομαι,** v.l. for βρυχανάομαι, Nic.*Al.*221; *cry,* of infants, Hsch.

**βραύκη,** = ἀκρίς, Hsch.: **βραῦκος,** = μικρὰ ἀκρίς (Cret.), *AB*223; cf. βρεῦκος. **βραύλα·** φθείρ, Hsch. **βραῦλον·** κοῖλον, Id. **βραῦνα·** κήλη, κύστις, ἐντεροκήλη, Id. **βραυνία·** κοιλώματα γῆς, Id. **βραυῶσα·** κεκραγυῖα, Id.

**βράχαλον·** χρεμετισμόν, Hsch.

**βράχεα,** τά, as if from a nom. βράχος, τό (or **βραχέα,** neut. pl. of βραχύς, Arist.*HA*568$^{b}$28):—*shallows,* Hdt.2.102, 4.179, Th.2.91, Plb.1.39.3, etc.: sg. only late, Procop.*Pers.*1.19, *Goth.*1.1.

**βρᾰχεῖν,** aor. with no pres. in use, inf. only in Hsch., elsewh. in 3 sg. ἔβραχε or βράχε:—onomatop. Verb, *rattle, clash, ring,* mostly of arms and armour, δεινὸν ἔβραχε χαλκός Il.4.420; βράχε τεύχεα χαλκῷ 12.396, Hes.*Sc.*423, etc.; βράχε δ' εὐρεῖα χθών (with the din of battle) Il.21.387; μέγας ἔβραχεν αἰθήρ A.R.4.642; of a torrent, *roar,* βράχε δ' αἰπὰ ῥέεθρα Il.21.9; ἔβραχε δ' ἅλμη Q.S.14.527; *creak,* μέγα δ' ἔβραχε φήγινος ἄξων Il.5.838; *shriek* or *roar* with pain, ὁ δ' ἔβραχε χάλκεος Ἄρης ib.859; ὁ δ' ἔβραχε θυμὸν ἀΐσθων (of a wounded horse) 16.468; *shout* a command, c. inf., A.R.2.573.

**βρᾰχείς,** εῖσα, έν, v. βρέχω.

**βρᾰχῑάλιον,** τό, *bracelet,* Sm., Th.2*Ki.*1.10:—also **-άριον,** τό, Aq. ibid., and **βραχιόλιον,** τό, Alex.Trall.1.15.

**βρᾰχ-ῑόνιον,** τό, = sq., Roussel *Cultes Égyptiens* 235 (Delos, ii B.C.), Poll.5.99. **-ῑονιστήρ,** ῆρος, ὁ, *armlet,* Plu.*Rom.*17, Tz.*H.*13.48. ⊛**-ίων** [ῑ], ονος, ὁ, *arm* (opp. πῆχυς, Pl.*Ti.*75a, but = πῆχυς, Arist.*MA*698$^{b}$2), Il.13.529, Hdt.5.12, X.*Eq.*12.5, Arist.*HA*493$^{b}$26, etc.; πρυμνὸς βραχίων *the shoulder,* Il.13.532, 16.323; also, *shoulder of beasts,* ib.594$^{b}$13:—Poet. as a symbol of strength, ἐκ βραχιόνων *by force of arm,* E.*Supp.*478.

**βρᾰχίων** [Ion. ῐ, Att. ῑ], **βράχιστος,** Comp. and Sup. of βραχύς.

**βραχμάζουσαι·** χρεμετίζουσαι, Hsch.

**Βραχμᾶνες,** οἱ, *Brahmans,* D.Chr.49.7, Luc.*Fug.*6, etc.

**βράχος** (A) [ᾰ], ὁ, prob. f.l. for βάτραχος, Ephipp.13.

**βράχος** (B), εος, τό, v. βράχεα.

**βρᾰχῠ-βάμων** [ᾱ], ον, gen. ονος, *taking short steps,* Arist.*Phgn.*813$^{a}$5. **-βῐος,** ον, *short-lived,* Pl.*R.*546a, Arist.*HA*494$^{a}$1, etc.: Comp., Hp.*Art.*41, Arist.*HA*501$^{b}$23; of plants, Thphr.*HP*4.13.1 (= χελιδόνιον μέγα, Ps.-Dsc.2.180): Sup. **-ώτατος** Str.16.4.12. **-βῐότης,** ητος, ἡ, *shortness of life,* Arist.*Pr.*964$^{a}$35 (he also wrote περὶ μακρο- καὶ βραχυβιότητος); of plants, Thphr.*HP*4.13.1. **-βλᾰβής,** ές, *harming slightly,* Luc.*Trag.*323. **-βωλος,** ον, *with small* or *few clods,* β. χέρσος a *small* spot of ground, *AP*6.238 (Apollonid.): Ἶκος ib.7.2 (Antip. Sid.). **-γνώμων,** ον, gen. ονος, *of small understanding,* X.*Eq.Mag.*4.18 (Comp.). **-γρᾰφέω,** *write with a short syllable,* Tz.*H.*8.701. **-δάκτῠλος,** ον, *short-fingered,* Polem.*Phgn.*86. **-δρομος,** ον, *running a short way,* X.*Cyn.*5.21 (Sup.). **-έπεια,** ἡ, *laconic style,* dub.l. in Rutil.2.8. **-ῆλιξ,** -ῐκος, *youthful,* Eust.1554.2. **-θάλασσος** [θᾰ], ον, gloss on εὔφαλον (sic, i.e. ἔφαλον), Hsch. **-κατάληκτος,** ον, *ending in a short syllable,* A.D.*Pron.*50.24, Arc.192.20. Adv. **-τως** f.l. for -παραλήκτως (q.v.), Sch.Ar.*Pl.*1057, = Suid. s.v. παιδιά. II. β. μέτρον, *short by a foot,* Heph.4.4, Aristid.Quint.1.23:—hence **-καταληκτέω,** *to end so,* Sch.Ar.*Ra.*317:—Subst. **-καταληξία,** ἡ, *such an ending,* Heph.*Poëm.*5. **-κέφᾰλος,** ὁ, a *fish,* Xenocr.19. **-κίνητος** [ῑ], ον, *accompanied by slight motion,* ἐνέργεια Porph.*Gaur.*1.3. **-κομέω,** *wear short hair,* Str.11.11.8. **-κωλία,** ἡ, *use of short members,* Hermog.*Id.*1.12. **-κωλος,** ον, *with short strings,* of slings, Str.3.5.1. II. *consisting of short clauses,* περίοδοι Arist.*Rh.*1409$^{b}$31. **-λογέω,** *to be brief in speech,* Id.*Rh.Al.*1434$^{b}$10, Plu.2.193d, Demetr.*Eloc.*242; ὧδε ἐβραχυλόγησε, introducing a quotation, Philostr.*VA*4.33. **λόγημα,** ατος, τό, *pithy saying,* Tz.*H.*5.317. **-λογητέον,** *one must be brief in speech,* Arist.*Rh.Al.*1441$^{a}$18. **-λογία,** ἡ, *brevity in speech* or *writing,* Hp.*Decent.*12, Pl.*Grg.*449c; β. τις Λακωνική Id.*Prt.*343b, etc.; ἡ Πιττακοῦ β. Plu.2.153e, cf. Demetr.*Eloc.*243 (pl.); opp. μῆκος, Pl.*Lg.*887b. **-λογος,** ον, *short in speech, of few words,* Id.*Grg.*449c (Comp.), etc.; of the Spartans, Id.*Lg.*641e, Demetr.*Eloc.*7, etc. Adv. **-γως** Poll.4.24.

**βρᾰχῠλός,** = μικρός, dub. in Hsch.

**βρᾰχῠ-μέρεια,** ἡ, *aggregate of small elements,* νεφελοειδής, the 'Milky Way', Gem.5.68. **-μετρος,** ον, *short in measurement,* Aristeas 55. **-μογής,** ές, *losing one's breath rapidly,* Hp.*Epid.*2.2.24. **-μῡθία,** ἡ, = βραχυλογία, Suid.

⊛ **βρᾰχύνω,** *abridge, shorten,* i.e. *to be a sign of a brief attack,* Hp.*Aph.*1.12; *use as short,* συλλαβήν Pl.*Per.*4:—Pass., opp. μηκύνομαι, Luc.*Hist.Conscr.*55; **-όμενον** φωνῆεν Heph.1.1, D.T.633.

**βρᾰχύ-νωτος** [ῠ], ον, *short-backed,* Orac.ap.Str.6.1.12, Ruf.ap.Orib.7.26.9; στέρνον χθονός dub. in Pi.*Pae.*4.14. **-όνειρος,** ον, *with short* or *few dreams,* ὕπνος Pl.*Ti.*45e; φαντασίαι Plu.2.686b. **-παραλήκτως,** Adv. *with short penult.,* Sch.Ar.*Pl.*253. **-πνοέω,** *to be short of breath,* Antyll.ap.Orib.6.21.9. **-πνοια,** ἡ, *shortness of breath,* Gal.7.836. **-πνοος,** ον, contr. **-πνους,** ουν, *short of breath,* Hp.*Epid.*3.17.ιε'. **-πόρος,** ον, *with a short orbit,* of a cycle of births, Pl.*R.*546a; οἱ β. ὄρνιθες *of short flight,* Philostr.*VA*3.48: Comp., *completing an orbit in shorter time,* Procl.*Hyp.*1.24. 2. *with narrow passage,* εἴσπλους Plu.*Mar.*15 (dub. l.). **-πότης,** ου, ὁ, *one that drinks little,* Hp.*Prorrh.*1.16. ⊛ **-πότος,** ον, *drinking little,* Gal.17(1).755. **-πτερος,** ον, *short-winged,* Arist.*PA*644$^{a}$20. **-πτολις,** εως, ἡ, *little city,* Lyc.911:—also **-πολις,** Adj. *belonging to a small city,* Νιρεύς Eust.317.29. **-ρρεπής,** ές, *short in weight:* Comp. **-έστερον** *a smaller weight,* Damocr.ap.Gal.13.1004. **-ρρήμων,** ον, gen. ονος, (ῥῆμα) *brief of speech,* Them.*Or.*26.315a. **-ρρῑζία,** ἡ, *shortness of root,* Thphr.*CP*3.7.2. **-ρρῑζος,** ον, *with a short root,* ib.1.

⊛ **βρᾰχύς,** εῖα (Ion. έα Hdt.5.49), ύ, dat. pl. βραχέοις *JHS*33.317 (Thess.): Comp. βραχύτερος, βραχίων (cf. βράσσων): Sup. βραχύτατος, βράχιστος:—*short,* 1. of Space and Time, β. οἶμος, ὁδός, Pi.*P.*4.248, Pl.*Lg.*718e, etc.; [αἰών] prob. in B.3.74; βίος Hdt.7.46; καιρός Call.*Ep.*9; χρόνος A.*Pr.*939, *Pers.*713, etc.; μῦθος, λόγος, Id.*Pr.*505, v.l. in *Pers.*713; ἐν βραχεῖ (Ion. βραχέϊ) in *a short time,* Hdt.5.24, Pl.*Smp.*217a codd.; διὰ βραχέος Th.2.83; μακρὰν συνήθειαν βραχεῖ λῦσαι χρόνῳ Men.726; βραχὺ τηδὶ μεταστῶμεν *for a moment,* Id.*Georg.*32; of distance, β. ἀπόδοσις *short return* in ball-play, Antiph.234.6; ἐπὶ βραχὺ ἐξικνεῖσθαι X.*An.*3.3.17; πρὸ βραχέος Iamb.*VP*25.112: Comp., ἡ φάλαγξ -υτέρα ἐγένετο ἀναδιπλουμένη X.*Cyr.*7.5.5; τάξιν -υτέραν ἢ πρόσθεν, βαθυτέραν δὲ ποιήσαντες Plb.1.33.10; βραχύτερα τοξεύειν X.*An.*3.3.7. Adv. βραχέως, [πολέμους] ἐπ' ἀλλήλους ἐπιφέρειν *scantily, seldom,* Th.1.141. 2. of Size, *short, small,* μορφὰν β. Pi.*I.*4(3).53; βραχὺς ἐξικέσθαι θεῶν ἕδραν too *puny* to reach.., ib.7(6).44; β. τεῦχος S.*El.*1113, cf. 757; β. τεῖχος a *low* wall, Th.7.29; βραχύ μοι στόμα πάντ' ἀναγήσασθαι my mouth is *too small* to.., Pi.*N.*10.19; κατὰ β. προϊών *little by little*, Th.1.64, cf. Pl. *Sph.*241c; παρὰ βραχύ *scarcely, hardly*, φυγεῖν Alciphr.3.5; βραχύ τι λωφᾶν ἀπὸ νόσου καὶ πολέμου Th.6.12; ἁλὸς βραχύ *a small quantity* of salt, Bilabel'Οψαρτ.p.11. 3. of Number, *few*, ἐν βραχεῖ in *few words*, Pi.*P.*1.82, S.*El.*673; ἐν βραχίστοις Pi.*I.*6(5).59; ἐν βραχυτέροις Pl.*Grg.*449c; so διὰ βραχέων in *few words*, Id.*Prt.*336a; ὡς ἂν δύνωμαι διὰ βραχυτάτων D.27.3, Lys.16.9, cf. Pl.*Grg.*449c; ὡς ἐν βραχυτάτοις Antipho1.18. Adv. βραχέως, ἀπολογεῖσθαι *briefly, in few words*, X.*HG*1.7.5. 4. of Value or Importance, of persons, *humble, insignificant*, S.*OC*880; τὸν μὲν ἀφ' ὑψηλῶν βραχὺν ᾤκισε E. *Heracl.*613; β. τὴν διάνοιαν J.*AJ*12.4.1; of things, *petty, trifling*, ἀρχὴ β. ἐλπίδος S.*OT*121; χάρις Id.*Tr.*1217; πρόφασις E.*IA*1180; β. τις ἀσάφεια a *slight* obscurity, Gal.18(1).304; λυπεῖν τινὰ βραχύ, opp. μέγ' εὑρεῖν κέρδος, S.*El.*1304; οὐ περὶ βραχέων βουλεύεσθαι Th. 1.78, cf. 140; β. καὶ οὐδενὸς ἄξιον Id.8.76; β. κέρδους ἕνεκα Lys.7.17; οὐσία Is.10.25: neut. as Adv., βραχὺ φροντίζειν τινός think *lightly* of, D.17.4. 5. *short*, of vowels or syllables, Arist.*Cat.*4$^b$34, *Rh.* 1409$^a$18, *Po.*1458$^a$15, Heph.1.1, D.T.631, etc.; ἡ β. προσῳδία the sign ᵕ, S.E.*M.*1.113. (Cf. Avest. *mərəzu-* 'short', Goth. *ga-maurgjan* 'shorten', Lat. *brevis*.)

**βρᾰχύ-σημος** [ῠ], ον, in Comp., *containing fewer time-units*, πούς Aristid.Quint.1.24. **-σίδηρος** [ῐ], Dor. **-σίδᾱρος**, ον, ἄκων β. a dart *with a short, small head*, Pi.*N.*3.45. **-σκελής**, ές, *short-legged*, S.*Ichn.*297, Arist.*PA*692$^b$5, *IA*714$^a$13, Gal.*UP*3.3, *Gp.*19. 6.2. **-σκίος**, ον, *with a short shadow*, Ach.Tat.*Intr.Arat.* 31. **-στελέχης**, ες, *with a short stem*, Thphr.*HP*4.6.10. **-στῐχος**, ον, *of few verses*, Eust.ad D.P.1039. **-στομία**, ἡ, *smallness of mouth*, Eust.767.16. **-στομος**, ον, *with narrow mouth*, λιμήν Str.14.1.24; ἀγγεῖα Plu.2.47e. **-συλλᾰβία**, Ep. **-ίη**, ἡ, *fewness of syllables, brevity*, Call.*Ep.*10. **-σύλλᾰβος**, ον, *of short syllables*, D.H.*Comp.*17, Longin.41.3; χρόνος, *occupied by a 'short'*, Bacch. *Harm.*94. 2. of the pulse, *with rapid rhythm*, Ruf.*Syn.Puls.* 4.4. **-σύμβολος**, ον, *bringing a small contribution*, *AP*9.229 (Marc. Arg.). **-σώμᾰτος**, ον, *short of body*, Plu.*Fr.inc.* 149. **-τελής**, ές, *ending shortly, brief*, Lxx *Wi.*15.9.

❀ **βρᾰχύτης** [ῠ], ητος, ἡ, *shortness*, opp. μῆκος, Pl.*Plt.*283c; μελέτης βραχύτητι with *shortness* of practice, Th.1.138; *narrowness, deficiency*, μετὰ βραχύτητος γνώμης Id.3.42. 2. *smallness*, τοῦ βάθους Arist.*Mete.*354$^a$18. 3. *shortness* of a syllable, in prosody, Pl.*R.*400c (pl.), Arist.*Po.*1456$^b$32, Plu.2.947e, S.E.*M.*1.100. 4. *scantiness*, τῶν ὄντων Lib.*Or.*62.59. 5. *shallowness*, θαλάττης Scyl. 112. 6. Rhet., *use of a condensed* or *allusive expression*, Trypho *Trop.*p.202 S.

**βρᾰχύ-τομέω**, *prune close*, Thphr.*CP*3.14.2, *Gp.*5.32. **-τομος**, ον, *cut short, clipped*, Thphr.*CP*3.2.3. **-τονέω**, *have a short* τόνος (q.v.), of torsion-engines, Ph.*Bel.*53.30. **-τονος**, ον, *with a short* τόνος (q.v.), of torsion-engines, ib.53.34, Plu.*Marc.*15. **-τράχηλος** [τρᾰ], ον, *short-necked*, Pl.*Phdr.*253e, Arist.*HA*597$^b$26. **-ϋπνος**, ον, *of short* or *little sleep*, Id.*Somn.*454$^b$19, *HA*537$^a$2. **-φεγγίτης** [ῑ], ου, ὁ, *giving a feeble light*, λύχνος *AP*6.251 (Phil.). **-φυλλος**, ον, *with few leaves*, δένδρον ib.9.612. **-φωνία**, ἡ, *smallness, weakness of voice*, Polyaen.1.21.2. **-χειρ**, ὁ, ἡ, gen. χειρος, *short-handed*, opp. μακρόχειρ, Eust.610.32. **-χρόνιος**, ον, *of brief duration*, γένος Pl. *Ti.*75c (Comp.); τὸ β. τοῦ βίου Plu.2.107a. **-ωτος**, ον, (οὖς) *with short handles*, κώθων Henioch.1.

**βραχώδης**· τραχύς, Hsch. (Cf. βαχίς.)

❀ **βρέβιον**, τό, (Lat. *brevis*) *list, inventory*, *IG*12(9).907.15 (Chalcis, iv A.D.), *Cod.Just.*4.21.22 (pl.); βρέουιον *PLond.*2.414.9 (iv A.D.).

**βρέγκος**, ὁ, a sobriquet of doubtful meaning, Φίλιππος ὁ β. Herod. 2.73. (Perh. βρεῦκος should be read.)

❀ **βρέγμα**, ατος, τό, *front part of the head*, Batr.228, Hp.*VC*2, Stratt.34, Arist.*HA*491$^a$31, al., *PA*653$^a$35, Herod.4.51, 8.9, etc.:—also **βρεγμός** *EM*212.14; βρέχμα, βρεχμός, βροχμός (q.v.) (prob. from βρέχω, because this part of the bone is longest in hardening, Hp.l.c., Arist. *GA*744$^a$24). 2. in pl., *parietal bones*, Gal.17(2).3. 3. *substance found in peppercorns*, Dsc.2.159. II. = ἀπόβρεγμα, *infusion, extract*, D.S.3.32. III. *drenching* with rain, Erot. s.v. ὕσματα (pl.).

**βρεκάριος**, = βρακ-, *PLond.ined.*2176 (vi A.D.).

**βρεκεκεκέξ**, formed to imitate *the croaking of frogs*, Ar.*Ra.*209 sqq.

**βρέκται**· φυσᾶται, Hsch.

**βρεκτέον**, *one must soak*, *Gp.*3.8.

❀ **βρεκτός**, ή, όν, *soaked*, *Hippiatr.*129.

**βρέλλιον**, τό, perh. f.l. for βδέλλιον, *POxy.*1142.3 (iii A.D.).

**βρέμβος**· ἔμβρυον, Hsch. **βρεμεαίνων**· ἠχῶν, Id.

**βρέμω**, only pres. and impf. (aor. ἔβραμεν, vv.ll. ἔβραχεν, ἔβρεμεν, Call.*Del.*140):—*roar*, [κῦμα] ῥηγνύμενον μεγάλα βρέμει Il.4.425; δυσάνεμοι βρέμουσιν ἀκταί S.*Ant.*592 (lyr.):—Med., αἰγιαλῷ μεγάλῳ βρέμεται Il.2.210; of wind, μέγα βρέμεται χαλεπαίνων 14.399, cf. S.*Ant.*592 (lyr.), Ar.*Th.*998 (lyr.). II. after Hom., of arms, *clash, ring*, E.*Heracl.*832; of men, *clamour, rage*, β. ἐν αἰχμαῖς A. *Pr.*424 (lyr.), cf. *Th.*378; πολλοῖς μὲν ἵπποις, μυρίοις δ' ὅπλοις β. E.*Ph.*113; δεινὰ β. τινί *against* one, Id.*HF*962; of a mob, A.*Eu.* 978 (lyr.); *murmur, grumble*, ὁ χαμηλὰ πνέων ἄφαντον β. Pi.*P.*11. 30; *wail*, in Med., βλαχαὶ βρέμονται A.*Th.*350 (lyr.); but also of music, λύρα βρέμεται καὶ ἀοιδά Pi.*N.*11.7; λιγὺ λωτὸς βρέμων *Pae. Delph.*12; φθέγμα μηχανῇ βρέμον S.*Ichn.*278: c. acc., λωτὸς ὅταν ἱερὰ παίγματα βρέμῃ E.*Ba.*161 (lyr.). (*mrem-*, cf. Skt. *mármaras* 'noisy', Lat. *murmur*, Gk. μορμύρω, Lat. *fremo*, etc.)

**Βρέμων**, *Roarer*, name of a dog, X.*Cyn.*7.5.

**βρεναίαται**· δυσχεραίνει, προσποιεῖται, Hsch. **βρένδος**, = ἔλαφος, Id., *EM*212.47.

**βρένθειος**, α, ον, *costly*, μύρον Sapph.*Supp.*23.19; without μύρον, Pherecr.101.2.

**βρενθινά** (**βρενθία** Diogenian.ap.*EM*212.45), τά, roots used by women to make face-paint, Hsch.; cf. β⟨ρ⟩ενθινῷ· ἀνθινῷ, Id.

**βρένθις**, Cypr., = θρίδαξ, Nic.*Fr.*120 (-θιξ Hsch.).

**βρένθον**, τό, = βρένθειον μύρον, Hsch.

**βρένθος**, ὁ, an unknown *water-bird*, Arist.*HA*609$^a$23, Ael.*NA*5. 48, but in Arist.*HA*615$^a$16 (with v.l. βρίνθος) some kind of *singing-bird* (= κόσσυφος, Hsch.). II. *haughty carriage, arrogance*, Ath. 13.611e. III. *tomb*, Hsch.

**βρενθύομαι** [ῡ] (-ύνομαι *AP*11.305 (Pall.)), only pres. and impf., *bear oneself haughtily, hold one's head high, swagger*, ὑπὸ φρονήματος Ar.*Pax* 26, cf. *Nu.*362, Pl.*Smp.*221b, Luc.*DMort.*10.8; πρός τινα Ar. *Lys.*887; β. τι πρὸς αὐτόν Luc.*Tim.*54; β. ἐπί τινι *plume oneself* on.., Ath.14.625b; ἐβρενθύετο Lib.*Or.*56.17, Agath.1.14; also, *take umbrage*, β. καὶ ἀγανακτῶν Ael.*NA*5.36. (Either from βρένθος II or from βρένθειος, as Phld.*Vit.*p.37 J., Sch.Ar.*Lys.*887.)

**βρένθυς**, υος, ἡ, *perfume of* βρένθειον *μύρον*, Phld.*Vit.*p.37 J.

**βρενταί**· βρονταί, Hsch. **βρέουιον**, v. βρέβιον.

**βρέντιον**, Messap., = *stag's head*, Str.6.3.6; cf. βρένδος.

**βρέξις**, εως, ἡ, (βρέχω) = βροχή, *a wetting*, X.*Eq.*5.9.

❀ **Βρετᾰνικός** or **Βρεττᾰνικός**, ή, όν, *British*, νῆσοι Arist.*Mu.*393$^b$ 12. II. βρεττανική, ἡ, *scurvy-grass, Cochlearia anglica*, Dsc.4.2, Damocr.ap.Gal.14.197 (*herba Britannica*, Plin.*HN*25.20,99). 2. = ἅλιμος, Ps.-Dsc.1.91.

❀ **βρέτας**, τό, gen. βρέτεος, dat. βρέτει A.*Eu.*259 (lyr.): pl., nom. and acc. βρέτεα Id.*Supp.*463, but βρέτη Id.*Th.*95 (lyr.), 185, etc.; gen. βρετέων ib.97 (lyr.), *Supp.*429 (lyr.); Ep. dat. βρετάεσσιν Nic. *Fr.*74.68:—*wooden image* of a god, A.*Eu.*80, al., E.*Alc.*974 (lyr.), Ar.*Eq.*31, etc.; of a man, *IG*7.118 (Megara): in Prose, Str.8.7.2, Jul.*Or.*1.29d. 2. *mere image*, of a *blockhead*, Anaxandr.11.

**βρέττανα**· φοβερά, Hsch.

**Βρέττιος**, α, ον, *Bruttian*, γλῶσσα B, i.e. *barbarous*, Ar.*Fr.*629 (dub.); B., ὁ, = δραπέτης, D.S.16.15; Βρεττία· μέλαινα πίσσα, *AB* 223.

**βρεῦκος**, v. βροῦκος.

**βρεφικός**, ή, όν, *infantile*, Ph.2.84, Eust.767.16.

**βρεφόθεν**, Adv. *from a child*, Eust.14.20, etc.

**βρεφο-κομέω**, *nurse children*, Eust.565.40. **-κτόνος**, ον, *child-murdering*, Lyc.229.

❀ **βρέφος**, εος, τό, *babe in the womb, foetus*, β. ἡμίονον κυέουσαν, of a mare, Il.23.266, cf. Chrysipp.*Stoic.*2.222. II. *new-born babe*, Simon.37.15, Pi.*O.*6.33, A.*Ag.*1096 (lyr.); νέον β. E.*Ba.*289 [not in S.]: in later Prose, Lxx *Si.*19.11, *BGU*1104.24 (i B.C.), etc.; of beasts, *foal, whelp, cub*, etc., Hdt.3.153, Phylarch.36, Ael.*NA*3.8, Opp.*H.*5.464, etc.; *nestling*, Horap.2.99; ἐκ βρέφεος from *babyhood*, *AP*9.567 (Antip.); ἀπὸ β. 2*Ep.Ti.*3.15. (Cf. Slav. *žrěbę* 'foal'.)

**βρεφοτροφέω**, *rear infants*, Tz.*H.*9.513.

**βρεφ-όω**, *form into a foetus, engender*, Eust.1535.44:—Pass., *Theol.Ar.*6. **-ύλλιον**, τό, Dim. of βρέφος, Luc.*Fug.*19, Eust. 565.50. ❀ **-ώδης**, ες, *childish*, Ph.1.394, Diog.Oen.9, Procl.*Par. Ptol.*284.

**βρέχ-μα**, ατος, τό, = βρέγμα, Alciphr.3.5. **-μός**, ὁ, = foreg. I, Il.5.586, Nic.*Th.*219, Q.S.13.155.

❀ **βρέχω**, fut. -ξω Lxx *Am.*4.7, al., (ἀπο-) Gal.6.591, etc.: aor. ἔβρεξα Hp.*Mul.*1.78, Pl.*Phdr.*254c, X.*An.*4.3.12, etc.:—**Pass.**, fut. βραχήσομαι Lxx *Is.*34.3: aor. ἐβρέχθην E.*El.*326, X.*An.*1.4. 17, etc.: aor. 2 ἐβράχην [ᾰ] Hp.*Mul.*1.80, Arist.*Pr.*906$^b$26, Sotion p.190 W., Gal.6.270, *Anacreont.*31.26; but ἐβρέχην *PGiss.*160$^r$12 (ii A.D.), Wilcken*Chr.*341.6 (ii A.D.): pf. βέβρεγμαι Pi.*O.*6.55, Hp.*Acut.*(*Sp.*)47:—*wet*, of persons walking through water, τὸ γόνυ Hdt.1.189; τοὺς πόδας Pl.*Phdr.*229a; *steep* in water, Hp.*VM* 3; ἐν οἴνῳ Id.*Fract.*29; β. χρυσέαις νιφάδεσσι πόλιν *shower* wealth upon it, Pi.*O.*7.34; δακρύοισιν ἔβρεξαν ὅλον τάφον *IG*14.1422; β. ἐν δάκρυσι τὴν στρωμνήν Lxx *Ps.*6.7, cf. 77(78).27:—Pass., *get wet*, βρεχόμενοι πρὸς τὸν ὀμφαλόν X.*An.*4.5.2; βρέχεσθαι ἐν ὕδατι *to be bathed* in sweat or *drench themselves*, Hdt.3.104 (so ἱδρῶτι β. τὴν ψυχήν Pl.*Phdr.*254c); βεβρεγμένος *filled with water*, opp. διερός, Arist.*GC*330$^a$17; of sponges, Id.*Mete.*386$^b$5; ἄλφιτα β. ἐν ὕδατι Hp.*Mul.*2.110; *to be rained upon*, Plb.16.12.3; ὄμβροις Str. 15.1.13; esp. in Egypt of the inundation of the Nile, τὰ βρεχέντα πεδία *PFlor.*331.6 (ii A.D.); ἡ βεβρεγμένη (sc. γῆ) *PTeb.*71.2 (ii B.C.), *OGI*669.57 (i A.D.); γῆ οὐ βρεχομένη Lxx *Ez.*22.24:—but also intr. in Act., *to be inundated*, *PPetr.*3 p.119 (iii B.C.), *PTeb.*106.19 (ii B.C.): metaph., ἀκτῖσι βεβρεγμένος *steeped, bathed in* light, Pi.*O.* 6.55; σιγᾷ βρέχεσθαι Id.*Fr.*240; of hard drinkers, μέθῃ βρεχθείς E.*El.*326; βεβρεγμένος *tipsy*, Eub.126. II. *rain, send rain*, *Ev. Matt.*5.45; Ζεὺς ἔβρεχε *POxy.*1482.6 (ii A.D.): c. acc., ἔβρεξε Κύριος χάλαζαν Lxx *Ex.*9.23; θεῖον ib.*Ge.*19.24, cf. *Ev.Luc.*17.29; ἄρτους Al.*Ex.*16.4. 2. impers., βρέχει *it rains*, Telecl.54, *Ep.Jac.*5.17; ὅταν βρέχῃ Arr.*Epict.*1.6.26; also ἵνα ὑετὸς βρέχῃ *Apoc.*11.6.

**βρῆγμα**, ατος, τό, and **βρήσσω**, variants for βῆγμα, βήσσω, Gal.19. 89, Hp.ap.*AB*223, Hsch.

**Βρησαγενής**, title of Dionysus, *IG*12(2).478.2:—also **Βρησσαῖος** Hsch.; and **Βρησεύς** *CIG*3160 (Smyrna); cf. Βρισεύς.

**βρήσσω**, *bleat*, Hsch.

**βρητός**· ἀλεκτρυὼν ἐνιαύσιος, Hsch.

**βρῖ**, = βριθύ (for βριθέως), A.D.*Adv.*157.13, Hsch.; = βριαρόν, Hes.*Fr.*236.

❀ **βρία**, ἡ, = πόλις (Thracian), Str.7.6.1; but, = κώμη, Hsch.

**βριαγχόνη**, v. βάτραχος.

**Βρίακχος**, ἡ, = Βάκχη, S.*Fr.*779 (expld. by βριαρῶς ἰακχάζουσα, Hsch., *EM*213.26): name of a Satyr on vases, Berlin 2256, BMus. E.253.

**Βρῐάρεως** [ᾰ], ὁ, gen. Βριάρηο Ibyc.45, (βριαρός) a hundred-handed giant, *Aegaeon*, Il.1.403, Hes.*Th.*714: Βριάρεω στῆλαι, older name for the Pillars of Hercules, Arist.*Fr.*678; cf. ὄβριμος. (-ρεως is monosyll. in Ep.)

**βρῐᾰρός**, ά, όν, Ion. **βριερός**, ή, όν, Ep. Adj. *strong*, κόρυς, τρυφάλεια, Il.16.413, 19.381, cf. Coluth.30; δέμας Tryph.19; ῥίζα Nic.*Th.*659; δόμος Οὐλύμποιο Orph.*Fr.*248; of persons, Nonn.*D.*28.172, al.; στρατιή *Epigr.Gr.*448; λέων *IG*14.1293*C*.

**βρῐᾰρότης**, ητος, ἡ, *strength, might*, Eust.1289.14.

**βρῐᾰρόχειρ**, ειρος, ὁ, ἡ, *strong-handed*, Eust.586.2.

**βρῐάω**, (βρῖ) *make strong and mighty*, Hes.*Th.*447. II. intr., *to be strong*, βριάων Opp.*H.*5.96: in both senses, [Ζεὺς] ῥέα μὲν γὰρ βριάει, ῥέα δὲ βριάοντα χαλέπτει Hes.*Op.*5.

**βρίγκα**· μικρόν (Cypr.), Hsch.

**βρίγκος**, ὁ, a *sea-fish*, Ephipp.12.3, Mnesim.4.38.

**βριγκώμενον**· ὀργιζόμενον, θυμούμενον, Hsch. (leg. βριμώμενον).

**βριγχός**, όν, of taste, between δριμύς (*pungent*) and στρυφνός (*astringent*), Apollon.ap.Lyd.*Mens.*4.125.

**βριερός**, v. βριαρός.

❀ **βρίζα**, ἡ, *rye, Secale cereale*, in Thrace and Macedonia, Gal.6.514. (Probably a Thracian word, cognate with Lith. *rugiai* 'rye', Engl. *rye*, etc.) II. Aeol. for ῥίζα, A.D.*Adv.*157.20, Greg.Cor.p.576 S.

❀ **βρίζω**, aor. ἔβριξα E.*Rh.*826 (lyr.): —Pass., aor. βρισθείς· ὑπνώσας, Hsch.:—poet. Verb, *to be sleepy, nod*, οὐκ ἂν βρίζοντα ἴδοις Ἀγαμέμνονα Il.4.223; *slumber*, βρίζων A.*Ch.*897; δόξαν.. βριζούσης φρενός Id.*Ag.*275: metaph. of guilt, βρίζει γὰρ αἷμα Id.*Eu.*280. II. βρίζει· ἐσθίει, πιέζει, κύει, Hsch.

**βριζώ**, οῦς, ἡ, = ἐνυπνιόμαντις, Semus 5.

**βρῐήπυος**, ον, (ἠπύω) *loud-shouting*, of Ares, Il.13.521.

**βρίηρον**· μεγάλως κεχαρισμένον, Hsch. (Cf. ἦρα.)

**βρῖθος**, εος, τό, *weight*, Hp.*Mul.*1.48, E.*Tr.*1050, Plu.*Marc.*15; τῶν ἀτυχημάτων τὰ μὲν ἔχει τι β. καὶ ῥοπὴν πρὸς τὸν βίον Arist.*EN* $1101^a29$.

**βρῑθοσύνη**, ἡ, *weight*, Il.5.839, 12.460, Nonn.*D.*1.298.

**βρῑθύ-κερως**, ων, gen. ω, *with heavy horns*, Opp.*H.*2.290. **-νοος**, ον, *grave-minded, thoughtful*, *AP*9.525.3.

❀ **βρῑθύς**, εῖα, ύ, *heavy*, ἔγχος Il.5.746, etc.; once in Trag., βριθύτερος A.*Ag.*200 (lyr.), cf. Id.*Eleg.*5, Q.S.3.540 (Comp.).

❀ **βρίθω** [ῑ], Ep. subj. βρίθῃσι Od.19.112: Ep. impf. βρῖθον 9.219: fut. βρίσω B.9.47, Ep. inf. -έμεν *h.Cer.*456: aor. ἔβρῖσα Il.12.346, etc.: pf. βέβρῖθα 16.384, Hp.*Mul.*2.133, E.*El.*305: plpf. βεβρίθει Od.16.474:—Pass. (v. infr.):—poet. Verb (also in later Prose, v. infr.), *to be heavy* or *weighed down with*, c. dat., σταφυλῇσι βρίθουσαν ἀλωήν Il.18.561; βρίθῃσι δὲ δένδρεα καρπῷ Od.19.112, cf. 16.474; ὑπὸ λαίλαπι.. βέβριθε χθών (sc. ὕδατι) Il.16.384; βότρυσι, καρποῖς, Jul.*Or.*3.113a, 7.230d: metaph., ἀλάστωρ ξίφεσι βρίθων E.*Ph.*1557 (lyr.); ὄλβῳ β. Id.*Tr.*216 (lyr.); πίνῳ.. βέβριθα Id.*El.*305; κάτω β. περὶ τὴν ὕλην Iamb.*Myst.*5.11. 2. c. gen., *to be laden with* or *full of*, τράπεζαι σίτου καὶ κρειῶν ἠδ' οἴνου βεβρίθασι Od.15.334; πάντα δ' ἐρίθων ἀραχνᾶν βρίθει S.*Fr.*286; πεδιὰς βρίθουσα ζῴων καὶ φυτῶν Ph.2.217. 3. c. acc., βούβρωστις φόνον βρίθουσα *Epigr.Gr.*793.4. 4. abs., *to be heavy*, ἔρις.. βεβριθυῖα (= βαρεῖα) Il.21.385; εὔχεσθαι.. βρίθειν Δημήτερος ἱερὸν ἀκτήν Hes.*Op.*466; so in Hp. and later Prose, ᾗ ἂν.. βρίσῃ wherein *the weight is thrown*, Hp.*Flat.*10; βεβρίθασιν οἱ τιτθοί *are loaded*, Id.*Mul.*2.133, cf. Ph.1.330, etc.; ἐς γόνατα ἡ κεφαλὴ β. Philostr.*Im.*1.18: but rare in Att., βρίθει ὁ ἵππος bows or *sinks*, Pl.*Phdr.*247b; ὅταν βρίσῃ [ὁ κύκλος] ἐπὶ θάτερον μέρος *inclines* to one side, Arist.*Pr.*$915^b3$: metaph., πᾷ τύχα βρίσει how Fortune *will incline the scales*, B.9.47. II. of men, *outweigh, prevail*, ἑέδνοισι βρίσας Od.6.159: abs., *have the preponderance in fight, prevail*, ὧδε γὰρ ἔβρισαν Λυκίων ἀγοί Il.12.346; τῇ δὲ γὰρ ἔβρισαν.. Ἕκτωρ Αἰνείας τε 17.512; βρίσαντες ἔβησαν charged *with their might*, ib.233; later εὐδοξίᾳ β. *to be mighty* in.., Pi.*N.*3.40; εἰ.. χειρὶ βρίθεις ἢ πλούτου βάθει S.*Aj.*130. III. trans., *weigh down, load*, ὅσπερ Κινύραν ἔβρισε πλούτῳ Pi.*N.*8.18; τάλαντα βρίσας A.*Pers.*346. 2. Pass., *to be laden*, μήκων καρπῷ βριθομένη *laden* with fruit, Il.8.307; μόροισι βρίθεται [ἡ βάτος] A.*Fr.*116; τῷ δ' οὐ βρίθεται [ἡ τράπεζα] E.*Fr.*467; ἐβρίθοντο αἰόνες [σώμασι] Tim.*Pers.*108; πλοῦτον χρυσῷ καὶ ἀργύρῳ -όμενον Jul.*Or.*2.86b: c. gen., πέτηλα βριθόμενα σταχύων Hes.*Sc.*290; συμποσίων.. βρίθοντ' ἀγυιαί B.*Fr.*3.12; βριθομένης ἀγαθῶν τραπέζης Pherecr.190 (hex.); βριθομένη χαρίτων *AP*5.193 (Posidipp. or Asclep.): abs., ἄξονες βριθόμενοι A.*Th.*153 (lyr.). (Cf. βρῖ.)

**βρίκελος**, ὁ, a name of a *tragic mask*, Cratin.205, acc. to Did.ap.Hsch. also expld. as = ἱστοποδης or βάρβαρος (βριξὶν (leg. βρύξιν) ἴκελα· οὕτω δὲ ἔλεγον τοὺς βαρβάρους Paus.Gr.*Fr.*95).

**βρικίννη**· εἶδος βοτάνης, Hsch.

**βρικίσματα**, τά, name of a Phrygian *dance*, Hsch.

**βρικόν**· ὄνον (Cyren.), Hsch.: **βρικοί**· πονηροί, Id.

**βρῑμ-άζω**, *roar like a lion*, Suid., Hsch.: c. acc., *roar against*, *PMag.Par.*1.2247 (s. v. l.); also, = ὀργᾶν ἐς συνουσίαν (Cypr.), Hsch. **-αίνω**, = βριμάομαι, *EM*213.45: also in Med., Hsch. **-άομαι**, *snort with anger, to be indignant*, εἰ σὺ βριμήσαιο Ar.*Eq.*855, cf. Phld.*Ir.*p.49 W.:—Act. in Hsch. **-η**, ἡ, *strength, might*, *h.Hom.*28.10, A.R.4.1677. II. = ἀπειλή, Hsch. 2. *bellowing, roaring*, βρίμας ταυρείους ἀφιεὶς χαροποῦ τε λέοντος prob. in Orph.*Fr.*79. III. = γυναικεία ἀρρητοποιΐα, Hsch. **-ημα**, ατος, τό, = βρίμη, prob. l. *APl.*4.103 (Gem.), cf. Hsch. **-όομαι**, = βριμάομαι, ἐβριμοῦτο τῷ Κύρῳ *was indignant with* Cyrus, X.*Cyr.*4.5.9 (expld. by ἀπειλεῖ Ael.Dion.*Fr.*95): abs., Ph.1.681. ❀ **-ός**· μέγας, χαλεπός, Hsch. **-ώ**, οῦς, ἡ, epith. of Hecate and Persephone, *the Terrible one*, A.R.3.861, Orph.*Fr.*31, Luc.*Nec.*20. **-ώδης**, ες, *grim, stern*, dub. in Herm.ap.Stob.1.49.45 (Comp.). **-ωσις**, εως, ἡ, *indignation*, Phld.*Ir.*p.26 W.: pl., ib.p.52 W.

**βρινδεῖν**· θυμοῦσθαι, ἐρεθίζειν, Hsch. **βρίννια**, τά, *lamb's flesh*, Id. **βρίξ**· θριδακίνη, καὶ εἶδος ἄνθους, οἱ δὲ περιστερεῶνα, Id.

**βρῑσ-άρμᾰτος**, ον, (βρίθω) *chariot-pressing*, epith. of Ares, Hes.*Sc.*441, *h.Hom.*8.1: [Θῆβαι] Pi.*Dith.Oxy.*1604 *Fr.*1 ii 26. **-αύχην**, ενος, *neck-pressing*, i.e. *heavy*, Hsch. s. v. ὁ β.

**Βρῑσεύς**, έως, ὁ, title of Dionysus at Smyrna, *SIG*851 (written Βρεισ-, ii A. D.), Aristid.*Or.*41(4).5, Macr.*Sat.*1.18.9; cf. Βρησαγενής.

❀ **βρῑσόμᾰχος**, ον, *prevailing in fight*, *EM*668.55.

❀ **Βρῑτόμαρτις**, ἡ, acc. -ιν *SIG*527.29 (Dreros, iii B. C.; where B. is distd. fr. Artemis), name of Artemis in Crete, = *virgo dulcis*, acc. to Solin.11.8 (but a nymph in Call.*Dian.*190): gen. -εως, Str.10.4.14; -ιδος, *EM*214.23:—hence **Βρῑτομάρτια**, τά, festival at Delos, *IG*11(2).145.34. (Derived from βρίτον, = ἀγαθόν, acc. to *EM*214.29.)

**βρίτος**· ἔτος, Hsch. **βριτύ**· γλυκύ (Cret.), Id.

**βρογχ-εῖον**, τό, *bronchial cartilage*, S.E.*M.*8.252. **-ία**, Ion. **-ίη**, ἡ, imaginary *system of ducts* connecting heart with liver, Hp.*Anat.*1. **-ια**, ων, τά, *bronchial tubes*, Id.*Acut.*17, Ruf.*Anat.*25,27, cj. in Arist.*HA*$603^a32$: later in sg., Aret.*SD*1.10. 2. *cartilaginous rings of the trachea*, Gal.*UP*7.7: in sg., *one such ring*, Id.8.2. 3. *gills* of fish, Id.5.199. 4. *tubes passing through the ethmoid bone*, Hp.*Carn.*16. **-ιάζω**, *gulp down*, Hsch.

**βρογχο-κήλη**, ἡ, *tumour in the throat*, Sor.1.69, Gal.19.443, Act.15.6, Vett.Val.110.5. **-κηλικός**, όν, *suffering from* βρογχοκήλη, interpol. in Dsc.4.119. **-παράταξις**, εως, ἡ, *competition in gluttony*, Ath.7.298e.

**βρόγχος**, ὁ, *trachea, windpipe*, Hp.*Epid.*5.68, Arist.*Pr.*$900^a13$, Gal.*UP*7.11, etc. 2. generally, *throat*, Hp.*Aph.*6.37, Aret.*SA*1.6. II. *gulp, draught*, ψυχροῦ Apollon.ap.Arr.*Epict.*3.12.17. III. = βάτραχος, Hsch.

❀ **βρογχωτήρ**, ῆρος, ὁ, *neck-hole in a garment*, J.*AJ*3.7.2.

**βροδοδάκτυλος**, ον, = ῥοδο-, *rosy fingered*, μήνα (leg. σελάννα) Sapph.*Supp.*25.8.

**βρόδον**, i.e. ϝρ-, Aeol. for ῥόδον, Sapph.68.2, *Supp.*25.13, A.D.*Adv.*157.20.

**βροδόπᾱχυς**, = ῥοδόπηχυς, Sapph.65.

**βρόκος**, = βροῦκος, Hsch. II. = sq., in later Greek, Id.

**βρόκων**, ὁ, *boorish person*, Hsch.

**βρομέω**, = βρέμω, only used in pres. and impf. (exc. fut. βρομήσω *EM*214.36); of flies, *buzz*, Il.16.642; of wind, *roar*, θύελλαι β. A.R.4.787, cf. Nic.*Al.*596; of boiling broth, Id.*Fr.*68.5; also ἶσα Δὶ βρομέει, of a proud person, Rhian.1.13.

**βρομι-άζομαι**, = Βακχεύω, from Βρόμιος, *AP*9.774 (Glauc.). **-άς**, άδος, ἡ, fem. of sq. II, θοίνα Pi.*Dith.Oxy.*1604 *Fr.*1 i 11; πηγή Antiph.52.12. II. *large cup*, Ath.11.784d. **-ος**, α, ον, (βρόμος) *sounding*, φόρμιγξ Pi.*N.*9.8; *noisy, boisterous*, whence, II. **Βρόμιος**, ὁ, as a name of *Bacchus*, Id.*Fr.*75.10, A.*Eu.*24, E.*Ph.*649 (lyr.), al., Telecl.55; ὦ Διόνυσε Β. Ar.*Th.*991; Βρομίου πῶμα, i.e. wine, E.*Cyc.*123; ποδαπὸς ὁ Βρόμιος; whence comes the *wine*? Alex.230.3, cf. *APl.*4.309, *AP*9.368 (Jul. Imp., with play on βρόμος (B)). 2. Adj. Βρόμιος, α, ον, *Bacchic*, E.*HF*893 (lyr.), etc.; Β. χάρις, of the Dionysia, Ar.*Nu.*311:—also **Βρομιώδης**, ες, *Bacchic*, πηλός, of a drinking-cup, *AP*11.27 (Maced.): fem. **Βρομιῶτις**, ιδος, ἡ, Opp.*C.*4.340: as Subst., *Bacchante*, ib.300. III. βρόμιον, τό, name of a *plaster*, Orib.*Fr.*90.

❀ **βρόμος** (A), ὁ, (βρέμω) *any loud noise*, as the *crackling* of fire, Il.14.396, Thphr.*Fr.*165; *roaring* of thunder, Pi.*O.*2.27; of a storm, A.*Th.*213 (lyr.), *Fr.*195 codd.; of the drum, [Simon.]179.7; of horses, A.*Th.*476; ἐλάφῳ β. *belling*, Alc.97 (cf. *POxy.*1789.29); of the flute, *h.Merc.*452, cf. S.*Fr.*513; hence, *rage, fury*, E.*HF*1212:—rare in Prose, βρόμοι καὶ ὀλολυγμοί Epicur.*Fr.*143; of thunder, earthquake, or sea, Arist.*Mu.*$395^a13$, $396^a12$, *Mir.*$843^a8$; of a volcano, Id.*Fr.*634. II. τόπος εἰς ὃν ἔλαφοι οὐροῦσι καὶ ἀφοδεύουσι, Hsch.

❀ **βρόμος** (B), also **βόρμος** (Dieuch.ap.Orib.4.7.20, Hsch.), ὁ, *oats, Avena sativa*, Hp.*Vict.*2.43, Dsc.2.94, Polem.Hist.88. 2. *wild oats, Avena barbata*, Thphr.*HP*8.9.2, Ps.-Dsc.4.137: also, = αἰγίλωψ, ibid.

**βρομώδης**, freq. f. l. for βρωμ- (q. v.). Ath.3.88a, Plu.2.792b, etc.

**βροντ-αγωγός**, *bringing thunder*, *PMag.Par.*1.182. **-άζω**, = βροντῶ, ib.1039, Hsch. ❀ **-αῖος**, α, ον, *thundering*, Ζεύς Arist.*Mu.*$401^a17$, Orph.*H.*15.9; ὕδωρ β. thunder-*rain*, Hp.*Epid.*6.4.17. ❀ **-άω**, *thunder*, Ζεὺς δ' ἄμυδις βρόντησε Od.14.305, cf. Il.8.133; βροντᾶν οὐκ ἐμὸν ἀλλὰ Διός Call.*Fr.*490; so Βροντῶν, title of Zeus in Phrygia, *JHS*5.258, etc. (but βροντῶν θεός, = *Jupiter Tonans*, *IG*14.982, cf.

D.C.54.4): metaph. of Pericles, Ar.*Ach.*531, cf. *V.*624; of a seller asking too high a price, Herod.7.65. 2. impers., χειμέρια βροντᾷ *it thunders*, Ar.*Fr.*46; βροντήσαντος *if it thunders*, Arist.*HA*610$^{b}$35. II. Pass., *to be thunderstruck*, Id.*Div.Somn.*463$^{a}$13. **-εῖον,** τό, *engine for making stage-thunder*, Poll.4.130. **-ή,** ἡ, *thunder*, Διὸς μεγάλοιο κεραυνὸν δεινήν τε β. Il.21.199; ὑπὸ βροντῆς πατρὸς Διός 13.796; Ζηνός τε βροντῇ Od.20.121; ἀστραπὴ καὶ β. Hdt.3.86; β. στεροπῇ τε A.*Supp.*34 (anap.); β. καὶ κεραυνίᾳ φλογί Id.*Pr.*1017; βροντῆς μύκημα ib.1062 (anap.), cf. 1083 (anap.); β. δ' ἐρράγη δι' ἀστραπῆς S.*Fr.*578, etc.: in pl., Id.*OC*1514, X.*HG*1.6.28, Thphr.*Sign.*21, etc.; χθόνιαι β. Ar.*Av.*1745: metaph., τούτου τὰς β. οἶδ' ὅτι δείσεις Lib.*Ep.*98.4. II. *the state of one struck with thunder, astonishment*, ἐπεάν σφι θεὸς ἐμβάλῃ β. Hdt.7.10.ε'. (βρομτᾱ, cf. βρέμω.) **-ημα,** ατος, τό, *thunder-clap*, A.*Pr.*993. II. = ἐμβρόντητος, Hsch. **-ης,** ου, ὁ, *Thunderer*, one of the three Cyclopes, Hes.*Th.*140. **-ησικέραυνος,** ον, *sending thunder and lightning*, Νεφέλαι Ar.*Nu.*265 (anap.). **-ήσιος** Ζεύς, = *Jupiter Tonans*, *Mon.Anc.Gr.*18.21. **-ητικός,** *thundering*, epith. of Ζεύς, Eust. 141.27.

**βροντο-κεραυνοπάτωρ** [ᾰ], ορος, ὁ, *father of the thunderbolt*, epith. of Kronos, *PMag.Par.*1.3102. **-ποιός,** όν, *thunder-making*, Vett. Val.6.24, Ps.-Luc.*Philopatr.*4,24. **-σκοπία,** ἡ, *divination from thunder*, Lyd.*Ost.*27 tit., al.

**βροντώδης,** ες, *like thunder, thundering*, κτύποι Agath.5.8, cf. Lyd. *Ost.*42, al., Sch.Ar.*Ra.*826. II. *charged with thunder*, Vett.Val. 14.17, Ptol.*Tetr.*94.

**βρόξαι,** v. *βρόχω.

**βρόσσων,** Aeol., = βράσσων, Hsch.

**βρότᾰχος,** ὁ, Ion. for βάτραχος (q.v.), Xenoph.40.

⊛ **βρότειος,** ον, also α, ον Archil.15, Emp.2.9, E.*Hipp.*19, *Supp.*777:— poet. Adj. *mortal, human*, A.*Pr.*116 (lyr.), etc.; β. μῆτις Emp. l. c.; β. γένος E.*Fr.*898.13; ψυχὴν βροτείαν Id.*Supp.*777; β. πόνοι *of mortals*, Alex.240.9:—in Hom. only **βρότεος,** η, ον, φωνή Od.19.545; εὐνή *h.Ven.*47; also in Pi.*O.*9.34, Emp.100.17, A.*Eu.*171 (lyr.).

⊛ **βροτήσιος,** α, ον, = foreg., ἔργα Hes.*Op.*773; ἀνήρ Pi.*P.*5.3; δέμας Id.*Pae.*6.79; μορφή E.*Ba.*4, *Or.*271; φθογγή Lyc.1321: in late Prose, β. γένος *PMasp.*151.18 (vi A.D.).

⊛ **βροτο-βάμων** [ᾱ], ον, gen. ονος, *trampling on men*, *AP*15.21 (Theoc.). **-γηρυς,** υ, *with human voice*, ψιττακός ib.9.562 (Crin.). **-δαίμων,** ὁ, = ἡμίθεος, Hsch. **-ειδής,** ές, *like a man*, δείκηλον Man.6.446. ⊛ **-εις,** εσσα, εν, (βρότος) *gory*, ἔναρα Il.6.480, etc.; ἀνδράγρια 14.509. II. = βρότειος, Nonn.*D.*47.431 (s.v.l.). **-κέρτης,** ου, ὁ, (κείρω) *man-shaver*, pedantic word for *barber*, Alexarch.ap Heraclid.Lemb.5. **-κλώστειρα,** ἡ, *weaving the destiny of mortals*, κόσμοιο χορείη Man.4.11. **-κτονέω,** *murder men*, A.*Eu.*421. **-κτόνος,** ον, *man-slaying, homicidal*, θυσίαι E. *IT*384 (lyr.); κράνεια *AP*6.123 (Anyte): Ἄρης Orph.*H.*65.2; οὐ τὴν Οἰδιπόδαο βροτοκτόνον his *murderess*, i.e. the Sphinx, *Epigr.Gr.* 1015. ⊛ **-λοιγός,** όν, *plague of man, bane of men*, Ἄρης Il.5.31, al., Od.8.115; of Apollo, *Epigr.Gr.*1034.29; once in Trag., A.*Supp.* 665 (lyr.); ἔρως *AP*5.179 (Mel.).

**βροτόομαι,** Pass., (βρότος) *to be stained with gore*, βεβροτωμένα τεύχεα Od.11.41, Q.S.1.717; δράκων κάρα βεβρ. Stesich.42.

**βροτόπους** ἵππος horse *with human feet*, coin-legend in Head *Historia Numorum* p.517 (Nicaea).

**βροτός,** ὁ, poet. Noun, *mortal man*, opp. ἀθάνατος or θεός, in Hom. usu. Subst., οἳ νῦν βροτοί εἰσι Il.5.304, al.; βροτὸς εἰς θεόν E. *Andr.*1196 (lyr.); λόγος τις Ζῆνα μιχθῆναι βροτῷ A.*Supp.*295; θεοῦ δὲ πληγὴν οὐχ ὑπερπηδᾷ βροτός S.*Fr.*961; βροτοί, opp. νεκροί, Id.*Ant.* 850 (lyr.); but β. ἀνήρ Il.5.361; and so β. ἔθνος Pi.*P.*10.28: as fem., β. αὐδήεσσα Od.5.334; β. οὖσαν *AP*9.89 (Phil.); but βροταί· γυναῖκες, Hsch. (s.v.l.): freq. in gen. pl., after πολλοί B.1.42, S.*OT* 981, etc.; after τίς ib.437, etc.; βροτοί never takes the Art. in Trag. and Com., exc. when an Adj. or Pron. is added, τῶν πολυπόνων β. E.*Or.*175; ἡμεῖς οἱ β. Ar.*Eq.*601, *Pax*849, cf. Sannyr.1; οἱ ταλαίπωροι β. Alex.66; οἱ πάντες β. Men.538.8.—Rare in Prose, Pl. *R.*566d, Arist.*Top.*133$^{a}$31, 149$^{a}$7. II. of the *dead*, A.*Ch.*129 (v.l. νεκροῖς Sch.). (From *μροτός (cf. ἄ-μβροτος, μορτός), Skt. *mṛtás* 'dead', Lat. *morior*, etc.)

**βρότος,** ὁ, *blood that has run from a wound, gore*, in Il. always αἱματόεις, 7.425, al.; μέλας Od.24.189.

**βροτο-σκόπος,** ον, *taking note of man*, Ἐρινύες A.*Eu.*499 (lyr.). **-σσόος,** ον, (σαόω, σῴζω) *man-saving*, Orph.*L.*756. **-στόνος** κλύδων dub. in E.*Fr.*66). **-στῠγής,** ές, *hated by men*, Γοργόνες A.*Pr.*799; δνόφοι Id.*Ch.*51 (lyr.). **-φεγγής,** ές, *giving light to men*, αἴγλη *AP*9.399. **-φηλος,** ον, *deceiving men*, Hsch. **-φθόρος,** ον, *man-destroying*, A.*Eu.*787 (lyr.), *Supp.*264, etc. II. σκῦλα βροτοφθόρα *of slain men*, E.*Fr.*266.

**βροτωφελής,** ές, *helpful to men*, μελέτα B.12.191.

**βροῦ,** v. βρῦν.

⊛ **βροῦκος,** ὁ, *locust*, or its *wingless larva* (Ionic acc. to Hsch.), Thphr.*Fr.*174.4; **βροῦχος** Lxx *Le.*11.22, al., Ph.1.85, Lyd.*Ost.*56; collective in sg., Heph.Astr.1.20; Cypr. **βροῦκα,** Hsch.; **βρεῦκος** (Cret. acc. to Hsch.), prob. as sobriquet in Herod.2.73.

**βρουλλοκύπερος,** ἡ, a kind of κύπερος, Aët.1.132.

**βρουλός·** πονηρός, Hsch. ⊛ **βροῦνος·** ἐνεὸς ἢ μαινόμενος, Id. **βρούξ·** τράχηλος, βρόγχος, Id. **βρούτιδες·** γυναῖκες οὕτω καλούμεναι, Cyr., Suid. **βροῦτος,** = βρῦτος, Hsch. **βροῦχαλ·** θερμός, Id. **βρούχετος·** βάρβαρος: also, = βάτραχος (Cypr.), Id.

**βροχετός,** ὁ, (βρέχω) *wetting, rain*, *AP*6.21.3.

**βροχή,** ἡ, (βρέχω) *rain*, Democr.14.8, Lxx *Ps.*67(68).10, *Ev.Matt.* 7.25, Ph.1.48, *Gp.*2.39.7. II. *moistening*, Dsc.1.49, Philagr.ap. Orib.5.32.1, Mnesith.ib.8.35.11; *steeping*, in brewing, *PTeb.*401.27 (i A.D.). III. *inundation* of the Nile, in pl., *POxy.*280.5 (i A.D.), Heph.Astr.1.23. 2. *irrigation*, Thphr.*HP*9.6.3, *PPetr.*3 p.119 (iii B.C.).

**βροχθίζω,** *take a mouthful*, Arist.*Pr.*948$^{a}$5. II. *clear the throat*, τινί with.., Clearch.Com.2. III. *give to drink*, Aq.*Ge.*24.17.

**βρόχθος,** ὁ, *throat*, Theoc.3.54. II. *throatful* (as vomited), Hp.*Morb.*2.69,74. 2. *draught* (that which can be swallowed at a gulp, Sch.Nic.*Th.*366), *AP*11.298, Phld.*Mort.*33.

**βροχθώδης,** ες, *shallow* (acc. to Sch., cf. βρόχθος II. 2), λίμνη Nic. *Th.*366; τόπος τοῦ Νείλου *EM*206.28.

**βροχίζω,** *hang, strangle*, ἑαυτόν *POxy.*850.6; cf. Hsch. s.v. ἀλαῶν: —Pass., *to be ligatured*, Gal.4.679.

**βροχικός,** ή, όν, *rainy*, ζῴδια *Cat.Cod.Astr.*1.133.21,31.

**βρόχιον,** τό, *pot*, μέλανος *POxy.*326 (i A.D.).

⊛ **βροχίς,** ίδος, ἡ, Dim. of βρόχος, Opp.*H.*3.595; of a spider's *web*, *AP*9.372 (pl.). II. (βρέχω) *ink-horn*, ib.6.295 (Phan.). III. a measure of length, *IG*12(3).1232.10 (Melos).

**βροχ-μός,** = βρέγμα, Hsch.; from βρέχω, *EM*285.16. **-μώδης,** ες, *damp*, Democr.133.

**βρόχος,** ὁ, *noose, slip-knot*, Od.11.278, 22.472, Hdt.4.60, Democr. 134, S.*Ant.*1222, etc.; *snare for birds*, Ar.*Av.*527; θηρῶν β. E.*Hel.* 1169; ἁλοὺς βρόχων πλεκταῖς ἀνάγκαις Xenarch.1.8; *mesh* of a net, X.*Cyn.*2.5, etc.: metaph., β. ἀρκύων ξιφηφόροι E.*HF*729; ὡς ἂν ληφθῶσιν ἐν ταὐτῷ βρόχῳ A.*Ch.*557; ἐν βρόχῳ τὸν τράχηλον ἔχων νομοθετεῖν 'with *a halter* round one's neck', D.24.139. (βρόκχον shd. be written in Thgn.1099.)

⊛ **βρόχυς,** Thess. and Aeol., = βραχύς, Sapph.2.7, *IG*9(2).460.13 (as pr.n. Βρόχυς); cf. βρόσσων.

***βρόχω,** *gulp down*, only aor. 1 ἔβροξα *AP*9.1 (Polyaen.), subj. βρόξῃ (βρώξῃ codd.) ib.11.271, inf. βρόξαι· ῥοφῆσαι, Hsch.: used by Hom. only in compds., 1. ἀναβρόξαι, *swallow again, suck down again*, ἀλλ' ὅτ' ἀναβρόξειε.. ἁλμυρὸν ὕδωρ, opp. ὅτ' ἐξεμέσειε, of Charybdis, Od.12.240; πάντας ἀναβρόξασα A.R.4.826; ἅλις ἀναβέβροχεν (Zenod., -βέβρυχεν vulg.) ὕδωρ *has drunk up* water enough, Il.17.54:—Pass., ὕδωρ ἀπολέσκετ' ἀναβροχέν Od.11.586. 2. καταβρόξαι *gulp down* (καταβρόξαι· καταπιεῖν, Hsch.), ὃς τὸ καταβρόξειε whoever *swallowed* the potion, Od.4.222: aor. part. Pass. καταβροχθείς Lyc.55: misspelt κατα-βρώξῃ Id.742, -βρώξειε D.P.604, -βρώξας A.R.2.271.

⊛ **βροχωτός,** όν, *formed by a noose*, ἀγχόνη Neophr.3.2. 2. *twisted, corded*, of chain-work, β. ἔργον Aq., Sm.*Ex.*28.15.

**βρῦ,** v. βρῦν.

**βρύα,** ἡ, = μυρίκη, Plin.*HN*13.116.

⊛ **βρῠ-άζω,** fut. βρυάσομαι Hsch., aor. ἀν-εβρύαξα Ar.*Eq.*602, otherwise only pres. and impf.:—*swell, teem*, καρποῖσι β. Orph.*H.*53.10, cf. 33.7; ὁπόταν γε [Ζεὺς] βρυάζων οἶκον ἐσέλθῃ ib.73.4; of a lioness, *to be pregnant*, A.*Fr.*491; *bubble up*, δέπας ἀφρῷ βρυάζον Tim.*Fr.*7: metaph., *wax wanton*, A.*Supp.*878; ἁ λίθος οἶδε βρυάζειν *AP*9.756 (Aemil.): c. dat., *revel in*, Epicur.*Fr.*181; χαίρειν καὶ β. prob. l. Id. *Fr.*600, cf. 605; αἱ γυναῖκες ἐβρύαζον ταῖς Δωρίαις στολαῖς Duris 50; τοῦ ποτοῦ λαμπρῶς ἤδη -οντος Hld.5.16.

⊛ **βρύαθ⟨μ⟩ον·** βρυασμόν, Hsch., cf. *Hymn.Is.*89 (dub. sens.).

⊛ **βρυάκτης,** ου, ὁ, of Pan, *the jolly god*, Poet.ap.Stob.1.1.30.

**βρῠᾰλ-ιγμός,** ὁ, *noise*, Hsch. **-ίζων·** διαρρήσσων, Id. **-ίκτης** or **βρυαλλίκτης,** ου, ὁ, *one who performs in a kind of war-dance*, Stesich.79, Ibyc.53.

**βρυανιῶν** (-ίων cod.)· μετεωριζόμενος καὶ κορων⟨ι⟩ῶν, Hsch.

**βρύας,** ου, ὁ, v. βύας.

**βρυασμός,** ὁ, *voluptuousness*, Plu.2.1107a. **β⟨ρ⟩υατά·** βεβυσμένα αὕτη, Hsch.

**βρύγ-δην,** Adv., (βρύκω) properly, *with clenched teeth*: of a polypus, *tightly*, *AP*9.14 (Antiphil.). ⊛ **-μα,** ατος, τό, *a bite, gnawing*, Nic.*Th.*483. **-μός,** ὁ, *biting*, ib.716 (pl., v.l. βρυχμός); *gobbling*, Eup.347; *chattering, shivering*, Hp.*Vict.*3.84, *Steril.*214, Euryphon ap.Gal.17(1).888; β. ὀδόντων *gnashing* of teeth, *Ev.Matt.*8.12, al. II. *roaring* of a lion, Lxx *Pr.*19.12.

**βρυγκός·** ἄφωνος, νεκρός, Hsch. **βρυγχός,** = βρόχος, Id. ⊛ **βρυδαλίχα,** ἡ, *female mask*; also, *lewd woman* (Lacon.), Id.

⊛ **βρύζω,** dub. sens. in Archil.32.2. II. Pass., ἐβρύσθη· ἔπεσεν, Hsch. (Cf. Lith. *griúti* 'collapse'.)

**βρύθακες,** *silken tunics*, Hsch. **βρύκαι·** αἱ ἱεραί (leg. βρύκαιναι· ἱεραί) (Dorian), Id. **βρῡκᾰνάομαι,** = βρυχ-, Id. ⊛ **βρυκεδανός·** πολυφάγος, οἱ δὲ μακρός, Id. **βρυκετός,** = βρυγμός, Id. **βρύκος·** κῆρυξ (cf. βρύοχος), οἱ δὲ βάρβαρος (cf. βρούχετος), οἱ δὲ ἀττέλεβος (cf. βροῦκος), Id. **βρυκταία,** a kind of *plant*, Id.

⊛ **βρύκω** or **βρύχω** [ῡ] (the former Att. acc. to Moer. and Ammon.; the distn. βρύκω *bite*, βρύχω *gnash* does not hold good), mostly pres.: fut. βρύξω Hp.*Mul.*1.2, Lyc.678: aor. ἔβρυξα Hp. *Epid.*5.86, Nic.*Th.*207, al., *AP*7.624 (Diod.), (ἐπ-) Archipp.35: aor. 2 ἔβρῠχε *AP*9.252 (late, perh. impf.): for βέβρῡχα, v. βρυχάομαι:—Pass., v. infr.:—*eat greedily, gobble*, γνάθος ἱππείη βρύκει *champs* the bit, Hom.*Epigr.*14.13; ἑφθὰ καὶ ὀπτὰ [κρέα].. βρύκειν E. *Cyc.*358, cf. 372; πρὸς ταῦτα βρύκετ' Ar.*Pax*1315; *bite*, βρύκουσ' ἀπέδεσθαι.. τοὺς δακτύλους *biting*, Id.*Av.*26; of smoke, ὀδὰξ ἔβρυκε τὰς λήμας ἐμοῦ Id.*Lys.*301; later, simply, *devour, consume*, Nic.*Al.* 489, al.; βρύξας, of the sea, is perh. f. l. for βρόξας in *AP*7.624 (Diod.): metaph., *tear in pieces, devour*, of a gnawing disease, βρύκει S.*Tr.*987 (lyr.); βρύκει γὰρ ἅπαν τὸ παρόν Cratin.58; τὰ πατρῷα βρύκει Diph. 43.27:—Pass., ἀπόλωλα, τέκνον, βρύκομαι S.*Ph.*745; βρυχθεὶς ἁλὶ *AP*9.267 (Phil.). II. *gnash* or *grind* the teeth, τοὺς ὀδόντας βρύχει Hp.*Mul.*1.7, etc., cf. *AP*15.51 (Arch.); τὸ στόμα β. Babr.95. 45; β. τοὺς ὀδόντας ἐπί τινα *Act.Ap.*7.54; also βρύχει alone, Hp. *Mul.*2.120; also intr., οἱ ὀδόντες βρύχουσι ib.1.36; βρῦκον στόμα Nic. *Al.*226, cf. *Th.*207, al.:—Med., βρύχονται Hp.*Morb.Sacr.*1 (prob.).

⊛ **βρυλλιχίζειν**, *wear a female mask*, Hsch.; also, = ἀκταίνειν, Id.:—Subst. **-ιστής**, cf. βρυδαλίχα.

⊛ **βρύλλω**, *cry for drink*, of children (cf. βρῦν), Ar.*Eq.*1126, cf. Sch. II. βρύλλων· ὑποπίνων, Hsch.

**βρύματα**· μηρύματα, Hsch. (μυρήμ- cod.).

**βρῦν** εἰπεῖν cry for *drink*, of children, Ar.*Nu.*1382:—also **βρῦ** or **βροῦ**, Phryn.*PS* p.55 B., *AB*85 (βροῦς Hsch.).

**βρυνχόν**· κιθάραν (Thracian), Hsch.

***βρύξ**, in acc. βρύχα, *depth of the sea*, Opp.*H.*2.588: gen. βρυχός prob. l. in Orph.*A.*1066.

⊛ **βρυόεις**, εσσα, εν, *weedy*, ποταμός Nic.*Th.*208. II. *flourishing*, Id.*Al.*371,478.

⊛ **βρύον** [ῠ], τό, (βρύω) *oyster-green, Ulva Lactuca*, β. θαλάσσιον Hp. *Mul.*1.53, cf. Arist.*HA*591ᵇ12, Dsc.4.98: pl., Plu.*Caes.*52; β. alone, Nic.*Th.*792; also, a *marsh-plant*, ib.415. II. *tree-moss, Usnea barbata*, Theoc.21.7, Dsc.1.21. III. *liverwort, Marchantia polymorpha*, Id.4.53. IV. *clustering male blossom of the hazel*, Arist. *HA*624ᵃ34: generally, *catkin*, Thphr.*HP*3.7.3, Nic.*Th.*71,898. V. = καυκαλίς, Democr.ap.Ps.-Dsc.2.139.

**βρυόομαι**, aor. ἐβρυώθην, Pass., *to be grown over with* βρύον, Arist. *Col.*791ᵇ26, 792ᵃ1.

**βρυοφόρος**, ον, *catkin-bearing*, Thphr.*CP*2.11.4.

**βρύοχον**· κήρυκα, Hsch. **βρύσδην**· χύδην, Id. (cod. βρύγδην).

**βρύσις** [ῠ], εως, ἡ, *bubbling up*, Suid., Eust.1095.16: **βρυσμός**, ὁ, Arc.58.24.

⊛ **βρύσσος**, Att. **-ττος**, ὁ, a kind of *sea-urchin*, Arist.*HA*530ᵇ5, Hsch.

**βρύσται**· κρημνοί, also as place-name, Hsch.

**Βρῠσωνοθρᾰσῠμᾰχειοληψῐκέρμᾰτος**, ον, *taking coin like Bryso and Thrasymachus*, Ephipp.14.3.

**βρύτανα**, = βύτανα, Hdn.Gr.2.484.

**βρῠτᾰνεῖον, -εύω**, v. πρυτ-.

**βρύτεα** or **βρύτια** (so prob. in Cerc.4.34 [ῡ]), τά, = στέμφυλα, *refuse of olives* or *grapes after pressing*, Ath.2.56d, Hdn.Gr.2.484 (also expld. as εἶδος σκορόδου, Hsch.): metaph., τὰ δ' ἔσχατα β. Μυσῶν Cerc.l.c.; τὸ τῶν βρυτέων πόμα Aret.*SA*1.9, *SD*2.9.

**βρύτηρ** (i. e. Ϝρύ-), ηρος, ὁ, Aeol. for ῥυτήρ, A.D.*Adv.*157.20; = ῥόμβος, *EM*706.31.

**βρυτιγγοί**· χιτῶνες, Hsch.

**βρῡτ-ικός**, ή, όν, *drunken with beer*, Antiph.45 (codd. Ath.). **-ινος**, η, ον, *of* or *for* βρῦτον, Cratin.96 (παρὰ προσδοκίαν for βύσσινος).

**βρυτίς**, = ῥυτίς, *EM*214.32.

**βρύτιχοι**· βάτραχοι μικροὶ ἔχοντες οὐράς, Hsch.

**βρυτονία**· ῥίζα τις, Hsch.

**βρύτον**· ζῷον ὅμοιον κανθάρῳ, Hsch. s.v. βρυτίνη.

**βρῦτος**, ὁ (S.*Fr.*610), **βρῦτον**, τό (Ath.10.447c), elsewh. the gender is dub.:—*fermented liquor* made from barley, *beer*, Archil.32, Hecat.154 J., Hellanic.66 J., A.*Fr.*124.

**βρύττειν**· ἐσθίειν, Hsch.; also, = πυρέττειν, *EM*216.25; = ὀρύττειν, *Lex.Rhet.*ib.28. **βρύττιον**· πόμα ἐκ κριθῆς, Hsch.

**βρυχάνα**, = βυκάνη, Hsch.

**βρῡχάνάομαι**, rarer form of sq., Nic.*Al.*221.

**βρῡχ-άομαι**, aor. ἐβρυχησάμην, Ep. βρυχ- A.R.4.19, Max.Tyr. 31.3, D C.68.24, (ἀν-) Pl.*Phd.*117d; also ἐβρυχήθην (v. infr.): Ep. pf. βέβρῡχα Od.5.412, al.: plpf. ἐβεβρύχει 12.242:—onomatop. Verb, *roar, bellow*, prop. of lions, acc. to Hsch. and Ammon.; of a bull, ταῦρος ὣς βρυχώμενος S.*Aj.*322, cf. Ar.*Ra.*823; of wild beasts, δεινὸν δ' ἐβρυχῶντο Theoc.25.137; of the elephant, Plu.*Pyrrh.*33: in Il. mostly of the *death-cry* of wounded men, κεῖτο ταννσθείς, βεβρυχώς 13.393; so βρυχώμενον σπασμοῖσι, of Hercules, S.*Tr.*805, cf. 904; βέβρυχα κλαίων ib.1072; δεινὰ βρυχηθείς Id.*OT*1265; later, of an infant's *wail*, Men.1004; κλαίων καὶ β. Alciphr.1.35; also of *the roaring of waves*, ἀμφὶ δὲ κῦμα βέβρυχεν ῥόθιον Od.5.412, cf. Il.17. 264; ἀμφὶ δὲ πέτρη δεινὸν βεβρύχει Od.12.242, cf. Aristid.*Or.*17(15). 14; βρυχομένη (as if from βρύχομαι) is required by the metre in Q.S. 14.484, cf. βρύχεται· μαίνεται, Hsch.; but βρυχῶνται, -ώμενος shd. be read in Hp.*Morb.Sacr.*1, Luc.*DMar.*1.4. **-ετός**, ὁ, (βρύχω) *chattering of teeth, ague*, Hsch. ⊛ **-ή**, ἡ, (βρύχω) *gnashing* of teeth, ὀδόντων A.R.2.83, Q.S.5.392. II. (βρυχάομαι) *bellowing*, Opp. *H.*2.530. ⊛ **-ηδόν**, Adv., (βρύχω) *with gnashing of teeth*, *AP*9. 371. II. (βρυχάομαι) *with bellowing*, A.R.3.1374, Nonn.*D.*29. 311. **-ηθμός**, ὁ, *roaring*, of the sea or a river, Arist.*Mir.*843ᵃ22, Opp.*C.*4.171 (pl.); λέοντος Max.Tyr.31.3, cf. Aesop.226. 2. (βρύχω) *gnashing* of teeth, *lamentation*, Men.*Epit.*472. **-ημα**, ατος, τό, *roar, roaring*, λέοντος *APl.*4.94 (Arch.), cf. Opp.*C.*3.36; improperly of sheep (cf. βληχάομαι), A.*Fr.*158 (pl.); of men, Plu.*Mar.*20, *Alex.* 51. **-ητήρ**, ῆρος, ὁ, *roarer*, of the constellation *Leo*, Doroth.ap. Heph.Astr.3.36. **-ητής**, οῦ, ὁ, *roaring*, β. χόλος *AP*6.57 (Paul. Sil.). **-ητικός**, ή, όν, *roaring, bellowing*, Tz. ad Lyc.739.

**βρυχιάω**, *chatter* (?), of a defect of speech, *Cat.Cod.Astr.*2.167.

**βρύχιος** [ῠ], α, ον, also ος, ον A.*Pers.*397: (*βρύξ):—*from the depths of the sea, deep*, ἅλμη A. l.c., Tim.*Pers.*96; ἅλς A.R.1.1310; βρυχία ἠχὼ βροντῆς the sound of thunder *from the deep*, A.*Pr.*1082 (lyr.): metaph., βρύχιον ὑποστένειν heave a *deep* sigh, Hld.6.9.

**βρυχίς**· κλῆμα, Hsch.

**βρυχμή**, ἡ, f. l. for βρυχή, Q.S.4.241. **βρυχμός**, v. βρυγμός.

**βρυχός**, = βρύκος, Hsch. **βρύχω**, v. βρύκω; but **βρύχομαι**, v. βρυχάομαι.

⊛ **βρύω** [ῡ], mostly pres.: impf., Pherecyd.Syr.ap.D.L.1.122, Nicaenet.7: aor. part. βρύσας Procop. (v. infr.):—*to be full to bursting*: 1. c. dat., *swell* or *teem with*, esp. of plants, ἔρνος.. βρύει ἄνθεϊ λευκῷ *swells* with white bloom, Il.17.56, cf. E.*Ba.*107 (lyr.); κισσῷ κάρα βρύουσαν Eub.56.6; ἰούλῳ, θριξί, κόμαις, Philostr.*Her.*2.2, Alciphr.3.31, Luc.*Am.*12; γῇ φυτοῖς βρύουσα Arist.*Mu.*392ᵇ15; also βρύει ἱερὰ βουθύτοις ἑορταῖς B.3.15: metaph., βίος.. βρύων μελίτταις καὶ προβάτοις κτλ. Ar.*Nu.*45; of men, β. δόξᾳ B.12.179; παμμάχῳ θράσει βρύων A.*Ag.*169 (lyr.); ἀγαθοῖσι βρύοις Id.*Supp.*966 anap.); μαντικῇ β. τέχνῃ Id.*Fr.*350.6; ἄλλων ἰατρὸς αὐτὸς ἕλκεσι βρύων E.*Fr.*1086; β. ἄνθεσιν ἥβας Tim.*Pers.*221; βρύουσαν ἀοιδὰν σοφίᾳ *Lyr.Alex.Adesp.* 20.4; ἐμπόριον πλούτῳ βρύον Jul.*Or.*2.71d. 2. c. gen., *to be full of*, χῶρος.. βρύων δάφνης ἐλαίας ἀμπέλου S.*OC*16; βρύοντα στέφανον μύρτων Ar.*Ra.*329 (lyr.); στεφάνων δόμος ἔβρυεν prob. l. in Nicaenet. l. c.; τράπεζαν.. κόσμου βρύουσαν Alex.86.3; καρπόν.. βρύειν σμαράγδου λίθου Philostr.*VA*5.5; τόπος β. ὕλης J.*AJ*13.3.1; φθειρῶν ἔβρυον πᾶς Pherecyd.Syr. l. c.: metaph., νόσου β. A.*Ch.*70. 3. abs., *abound, grow luxuriantly*, S.*El.*422; of the earth, *teem with produce*, X.*Cyn.*5.12, cf. Philostr.*VA*3.56; of water, *burst forth*, ὕδωρ βρύσαν ἐξ ὑπονόμων Procop.*Arc.*19. 4. c. acc. cogn., *burst forth with, gush with*, γλυκύ, πικρὸν [ὕδωρ] *Ep.Jac.*3.11; τὴν γῆν τὰ οἰκεῖα βρύειν φησὶν ἀγαθά Ael.*Fr.*25; causal, Ὧραι β. λειμῶνας Him.*Or.*1.19; ῥόδα *Anacreont.*44.2.—Poet. and later Prose.

**βρυώδης**, ες, *full of seaweed*, Arist.*HA*543ᵇ1; τὰ β., = *seaweed*, *Gp.*2.22.2; of a ship, β. ἐπιπάγους προσάγεσθαι Plu.2.641e. 2. '*mossy*', *flabby*, σὰρξ πλαδαρὸς καὶ β. Alex.Aphr.*Pr.*2.62, cf. Gal.10. 195, Sor.1.82,95. II. *catkin-like*, ἄνθος Dsc.1.87, 4.181. III. = δυσώδης, Hsch.

**βρυ-ώνη**, ἡ, = ἄμπελος μέλαινα, Nic.*Th.*939:—also **-ωνίς**, ίδος, ἡ, ib.858; cf. sq. **-ωνία**, ἡ, prop. = ἄμπελος μέλαινα, Dsc.4.183; also, = ἄμπελος λευκή, *bryony*, ib.182, cf. Gal.11.827; β. ἀγρία, = χαμαίπιτυς, Ps.-Dsc.3.158; β., = φύλλον, ib.125. **-ωνιάς**, άδος, ἡ, = foreg., Colum.10.250.

**βρώζω**, = βιβρώσκω, Herod.7.63.

⊛ **βρῶμα**, ατος, τό, (βιβρώσκω) *that which is eaten, food, meat*, Hp. *VM*6, Th.4.26, al.: metaph., Ar.*Fr.*333: freq. in pl., Hp.*VM*3, Antiph.246, Pl.*Criti.*115b, etc.; opp. ὄψα, Sosip.1.30. II. *cavity* in a tooth, Hp.*Epid.*4.25, Dsc.1.105, Archig.ap.Gal.12.859. 2. *moth-eating*, in pl., Lxx *Ep.Je.*12. III. pl., *filth, ordure*, prob. in *Ev.Marc.*7.19; cf. βρῶμος (B).

⊛ **βρωμάομαι**, (βρέμω) *bray*, βρωμησάμενος Ar.*V.*618; *bellow*, of the stag or hart, Arist.*HA*579ᵃ1. III. *suffer hunger*, Hsch. (also aor. Act.).

⊛ **βρωμᾰτίζω**, *give to eat*, Aq.*De.*8.3.

⊛ **βρωμάτιον**, τό, Dim. of βρῶμα, Ath.3.111a.

**βρωμᾰτομιξᾰπάτη** [πᾰ], ἡ, *the false pleasure of eating made dishes*, *AP*9.642 (Agath.).

**βρωμ-έω**, (βρῶμος) *smell rank*, Al.*Ex.*7.18. **-η**, ἡ, (βιβρώσκω) = βρῶμα, Od.10.460, Nic.*Al.*499, A.R.3.1058, Opp.*C.*2.352. ⊛ **-ήεις**, εσσα, εν, (βρωμάομαι) *brayer*, i. e. *ass*, Nic.*Al.*409,486. **-ησις**, εως, ἡ, *braying of an ass*, Ael.*NA*3.7, Poll.5.88. **-ηστής**, οῦ, ὁ, = sq., *EM*215.57; also, = χορτοφάγος, ibid. **-ητής**, οῦ, ὁ, *brayer*, i. e. *ass*, Nic.*Fr.*74.30. **-ήτωρ**, ορος, ὁ, = foreg., Id.*Th.*357.

**βρωμολόγος**, ον, *foul-mouthed*, Luc.*Pseudol.*24.

**βρῶμος** (A), ὁ, (βιβρώσκω) = βρῶμα, Arat.1021.

**βρῶμος** (B), ὁ, *stink, noisome smell*, Lxx *Jb.*6.7, al., Gal.7.214, Sch.Nic.*Al.*519, Dsc.*Alex.Praef.* (Condemned by Phryn.133; βρόμος is freq. f. l.)

**βρωμώδης**, ες, *stinking, foul-smelling*, Str.5.4.6, Diph.Siph.ap. Ath.8.355f, Diocl.*Fr.*138, Dsc.1.7, etc.; cf. βρομώδης.

**βρωσείω**, Desiderat. of βιβρώσκω, *to be hungry*, Call.*Fr.*435.

**βρώσιμος**, ον, *eatable*, A.*Pr.*479, Diph.13, Lxx *Le.*19.23, *Ev.Luc.* 24.41; ἃ καὶ κυσὶν πεινῶσιν οὐχὶ βρώσιμα *Trag.Adesp.*118.4.

**βρῶσις**, εως, ἡ, Ep. **-ιος** Hes.*Th.*797: (βιβρώσκω):—*meat*, opp. πόσις, Od.15.490, cf. Hp.*Acut.*28, X.*Mem.*1.3.15, Pl.*Lg.*783c: in pl., opp. πόσεις, Democr.235; β. ἀναγκαία Th.2.70. 2. *pasture*, προβάτων *PLips.*118.15 (ii A.D.). II. *eating*, παίδων Pl.*R.*619c; ἐρινὸς ἀχρεῖος ὢν ἐς βρῶσιν S.*Fr.*181. 2. *taste, flavour*, Nic.*Al.* 377. 3. *corrosion, rust*, *Ev.Matt.*6.19; *decay*, Gal.6.422 (pl.), 12. 879.

**βρωστήρ**, ῆρος, ὁ, *moth*, Aq.*Ho.*5.12; cf. βρωτήρ.

**βρω-τέος**, α, ον, *to be eaten*, Luc.*Par.*9, Porph.*Abst.*2.10. 2. βρωτέον *one must eat*, Muson.*Fr.*18 B p.105 H.; ἀνθρώποις β. ταῦτα Porph.*Abst.*2.4. **-τήρ**, ῆρος, ὁ, *eating*, βρωτῆρας αἰχμὰς A.*Eu.* 803; ὀδόντες Nic.*Al.*421; ἱππάκης βρωτῆρες.. Σκύθαι A.*Fr.*198: as Subst. in pl., of insects, etc., Orph.*L.*599; *moth*, Aq.*Is.*50.9. **-τικός**, ή, όν, *inclined to eat, voracious*, Arist.*GA*745ᵃ29, *PA*682ᵃ17 (Comp.), *Fr.*231 (Sup.), Plu.2.352f (Comp.). Adv. **-κῶς**, ἔχειν *EM* 485.17, Eust.966.4, etc. II. *promoting this inclination*, δυνάμεις dub. l. in Chrysipp.*Stoic.*3.199 (ἐρωτικαί Coraes). III. *gnawing*, ἄλγημα Hp.*Epid*.7.52. ⊛ -τός, ή, όν, *to be eaten*, Archestr.*Fr*.28; φάρμακον, opp. ποτόν, Porph.*Abst*.1.27. II. βρωτόν, τό (τὸν β. *Bull.Soc.Alex*.6.45), *meat*, opp. ποτόν, X.*Mem*.2.1.1; βρωτοῖσι καὶ ποτοῖσι E.*Supp*.1110, cf. Lxx 1 *Es*.5.54, Aristeas 128, *PSI*1.64.21 (ii A.D.). -τύς, ἡ, Ion. for βρῶσις, *eating*, acc. βρωτὺν Il.19.205, Od. 18.407: gen. βρωτύος Philox.2.38. II. *food*, *AP*11.371 (Pall.).

**βῦ**, exclamation of admiration, *EM*216.55.

**βύας**, ου, ὁ, *eagle-owl*, *Strix bubo*, Arist.*HA*592$^b$9 (v.l. βρύας); βύας ἔβυξε *an owl* hooted, D.C.56.29, 72.24. (Onomatop.)

**βυβλάριον**, τό, Dim. of βύβλος, *PLille*7.7 (pl.); βιβλ-, *AP*11.78 (Lucill.).

**βυβλείδιον**, v. βιβλίδιον.

**βυβλία**, ἡ, *papyrus-bed*, *Tab.Heracl*.1.58; cf. βύβλινος.

**βυβλῖνοπέδῖλος**, ον, *with sandals of* βύβλος, Anon.ap.Eust.1913.44.

**βύβλινος**, η, ον, *made of* βύβλος (of various kinds), ὅπλον νεὸς ἀμφιελίσσης βύβλινον Od.21.391, cf. Hdt.7.25,36; ὑποδήματα, ἱστία, Id.2.37,96; τεύχη *Inscr.Prien*.114.11 (i B.C.); ἐπιστολαί Lxx *Is*.18.2 (βιβλ-); μασχάλα *papyrus*-marsh, *Tab.Heracl*.1.92; ζυγίδες *BGU* 544.4 (βιβλ-, ii A.D.).

**βυβλιοθήκη**, v. βιβλ-.

**βύβλιοι**· τάφων φύλακες (Cypr.), Hsch.

⊛ **βύβλος** and **βίβλος** (v. sub fin.), ἡ, *the Egyptian papyrus*, *Cyperus Papyrus*, Hdt.2.92, A.*Supp*.761, Str.17.1.15: in pl., *stalks of papyrus*, *PTeb*.308.7 (ii A.D.). 2. *rind* enclosing the pith of this plant, Thphr.*HP*4.8.4, etc.: generally, *bark*, φελλῶν καὶ βύβλων Pl.*Plt*. 288e, cf. Hdt.2.96, Plot.2.7.2. b. in pl., *slices of the pith* used as writing-material, Hdt.5.58, Hermipp.63.13: sg., *strip of* β., βύβλον εὐρύναντες ἀντὶ διαδήματος Ph.2.522. 3. *roll* of papyrus, *book*, Hdt.2.100, A.*Supp*.947, etc.: heterocl. pl., βύβλα, τά, *AP*9.98 (Stat. Flacc.); esp. of sacred or magical *writings*, βίβλων ὅμαδον Μουσαίου καὶ Ὀρφέως Pl.*R*.364e, cf. D.18.259, *Act.Ap*.19.19, *PPar*.19.1 (ii A.D.); ἱερὰ β. *OGI*56.70 (Canopus, iii B.C.); β. ἱερατική *PTeb*.291. 43 (ii A.D.); so of the Scriptures, ἡ β. γενέσεως οὐρανοῦ καὶ γῆς Lxx *Ge*.2.4, etc.; ἡ β. *the Sacred Writings*, Aristeas 316; β. Μωυσέως, ψαλμῶν, προφητῶν, *Ev.Marc*.12.26, *Act.Ap*.1.20, 7.42; β. ζωῆς *Ep. Phil*.4.3: pl., of magical *books*, *Act.Ap*.19.19. 4. a *division* of a book, Plb.4.87.12, D.S.1.4, etc.; αἱ β. the nine *books* of Hdt., Luc. *Herod*.1. II. β. στεφανωτρίς *flowering head of papyrus*, Theopomp.Hist.22c, Plu.*Ages*.36. [ῠ, A.*Supp*.761.] (βύβλος, βύβλινος, βυβλίον, etc., are the original forms: βιβλ- seems to have arisen in Attic by assimilation in βιβλίον, and is found in earlier Attic Inscrr., cf. *IG*2.1*b*, etc., and prevails in Ptolemaic papyri; Inscrr. vary, βυβλία *Test.Epict*.8.32 (iii/ii B.C.); βιβλία *IG*5(1).1390.12 (Andania, i B.C.); in Roman times βυβλ- was restored.)

**βυβός**, ή, όν, = μεστός, πλήρης, μέγας, Sophr.115.

**βυδοί**· οἱ μουσικοί, ἢ κρουμά τι, Hsch.; cf. βίδη.

**βῦζα**, ἡ, = βύας, Nic.*Fr*.55.

**βυζαντία**· εἶδος ὀρμιᾶς, Hsch.

**βύζην**, Adv. *close pressed*, *closely*, β. κλείειν Th.4.8, cf. Arr.*An*.2. 20.8, App.*Pun*.123, etc.; β. ὠστιζόμενοι Luc.*Lex*.4; τὰ β. συνεστηκότα στίφη Ph.2.382. II. = ἀθρόως (cf. Erot.), Hp.*Nat.Puer*.15, *Mul*.1.5.

**βυζόν**· πυκνόν, συνετόν, γαῦρον δὲ καὶ μέγα, Hsch.

**βύζω** (A), (βύω) *to be frequent*, ἡ πτύσις βύζεται Aret.*SA*2.2; cf. foreg., and βύζαντες· πλήθοντες, Hsch.

**βύζω** (B), *hoot*, βύας ἔβυξε D.C.56.29, 72.24.

**βύθαλον**· βύσμα, Hsch.

**βῦθ-άω**, (βυθός) *strike deep*, ῥίζα βυθόωσα Nic.*Th*.505. -ίζω, *sink* a ship, S.*Fr*.552; μίαν πεντήρη ἐβύθισαν Plb.2.10.5; *let down*, ἀγκύρας Them.*in Ph*.133.20; *bury*, *plunge*, ἑρπετόν.. ἐν μυχῷ τοῦ πηλοῦ Luc.*Alex*.13:—Pass., of a ship, etc., *sink*, D.S.11.18, Babr. 117.1, Plu.*Caes*.49, D.Chr.63.3; of a person, *to be plunged into the sea*, Plu.2.831d. II. *overwhelm*, *submerge*, of a flood, οἰκίας Plu. 2.306f:—Pass., Id.*Daed*.7. III. metaph., β. ἀνθρώπους εἰς ὄλεθρον 1*Ep.Ti*.6.9:—Pass., *to be ruined*, τοὺς διὰ φιλοκερδίαν βυθιζομένους Phld.*Mort*.33; τὸ νῆφον ὑπὸ τοῦ πάθους βυθίζεται Alciphr.1.13; νοῦς βυθισθεὶς θυμῷ ἢ ἐπιθυμίᾳ Simp.*in Ph*.273.11, cf. Hld.7.12. ⊛ -ιος, α, ον, also ος, ον Gal.2.634: —*in the deep*, *sunken*, Luc.*DMar*.3.1; κρηπῖδας β. πηξαμένη *AP*9.791 (Apollonid.); ἐκ β. ἰλύος from the mud *of the deep*, *Hymn.Is*.71. II. *in* or *of the sea*, τὰ β. (sc. ζῷα) *water-animals*, *AP*6.182 (Alex. Magn.); β. Κρονίδης *Poseidon*, Luc.*Epigr*. 34; τέχνη *fishery*, Opp.*H*.3.15. III. metaph., *deep*, βύθιόν τι καὶ δεινὸν φθέγγεσθαι Plu.*Crass*.23; β. διάνοια Ph.1.194 (but ἕως ἂν λογισμὸς β. οἴχηται vanishes *in the deep*, ib.639, cf. Nonn.*D*.2.55); *abysmal*, Dam.*Pr*.106. -ισμός, ὁ, *sinking*, *submersion*, Hld.9. 8. -ῖτις, ιδος, pecul. fem. of βύθιος, ψάμμος *AP*9.290 (Phil.). -μός· ἄντρον, πυθμήν, καὶ βυθμήν, Hsch.

**βῦθοκῦμᾰτοδρόμος**, ον, *traversing the depths of the sea*, ναῦται *Lyr. Alex.Adesp*.32.1.

⊛ **βῦθός**, ὁ, *the depth*, esp. of the sea, A.*Pr*.432 (lyr.), 2*Ep.Cor*.11. 25. b. generally, συνιζάνειν εἰς β. sink to the *bottom*, Thphr.*Od*.29: metaph., ἐξ οὐρίων δραμοῦσαν ἐς βυθὸν πεσεῖν S.*Aj*.1083; ἀνακουφίσαι κάρα βυθῶν Id.*OT*24; ἐκ βυθοῦ κηκίον αἷμα from the *deep wound*, Id. *Ph*.783; καταφέρεσθαι εἰς β. Arist.*HA*619$^a$7, etc.; τὴν ἀναφορὰν ποιησάμενος ἐκ τοῦ β. ib.622$^b$7; ἐν τῷ β. τῆς θαλάττης ib.537$^a$8: metaph., ἐν βυθῷ ἀτεχνίης in *the depth* of.., Hp.*Praec*.7; ἐν β. ἡ ἀλήθεια Democr.117; εἴς τινα β. φλυαρίας ἐμπεσών Pl.*Prm*.130d; ἀθεότητος Plu.2.757c; ὑπέρκοσμος β. *abyss*, Dam.*Pr*.106,205.

**βῦθο-τᾰραξοκίνησε** [ῐ] (sic, voc.), *stirring the deep to movement*, *PMag.Par*.1.184. -τρεφής, ές, *living in the deep*, Lxx 3*Ma*. 6.8.

**βῡκᾰν-άω** or **βουκᾰνάω**, *blow the trumpet*, Plb.6.35.12. -η, ἡ, *spiral trumpet*, *horn*, Id.15.12.2, al., D.H.2.8. (From Lat. *būcĭna*.) -ημα, ατος, τό, *sound of the trumpet*, App.*Pun*.21. ⊛ -ητής, οῦ, ὁ, *trumpeter*, Plb.2.29.6, App.*Hann*.41. -ισμός, ὁ, *deep note*, *bourdon*, Nicom.*Exc*.4 (**βουκανισμός** Ptol.*Harm*.1.4). ⊛ -ιστής, οῦ, ὁ, = βυκανητής, Plb.30.22.11, D.H.4.18.

**βυκής**· ὑπνηλός, Hsch. **βυκνισταί**· εἰκασταί, Id. **βυκός**· δασμοφόρος, Id. **βυκτά**· σχέτλια, δείλαια, Id.

⊛ **βύκτης**, ου, ὁ, *swelling*, *blustering*, βυκτάων ἀνέμων Od.10.20. II. Subst., *hurricane*, Lyc.738,756.

**βυλλά**· βεβυσμένα, Hsch.:—hence ⊛ **βυλλόω**, *stuff*, pf. Pass. βεβυλλῶσθαι, Id. **βυλλίχαι**, *dances at Sparta*, and **βυλλίχης**, *dancer*, Id. **βυλλιχίδες**· ῥαχίδες, Id. **βυνεύς**· σκεύασμά τι κρίθινον, Id.

**βῡνέω**, = βύω, χρυσίῳ.. ἐβύνουν τὸ στόμα Ar.*Pax*645.

**βύνη**, ἡ, *malt for brewing*, *PHolm*.15.33, *PLeid.X*.22, Aët.10. 29. II. = πεύκη, Hsch.

⊛ **Βύνη** [ῡ], ἡ, an old name of *the sea-goddess Ino* or *Leucothea*, Lyc. 107: hence, *the sea itself*, Euph.127.

**βύνητος**, ὁ, an Egyptian *garment*, Hdn.Gr.1.219.

⊛ **βύνις**, εως, dub. sens. in *PMag.Leid.V*.13.10,17.

**βυννεῖν**, *hold in the mouth*, Hsch.

**βῡνοκ[οπία]**, ἡ, *preparation of malt*, prob. in *PTeb*.401.30 (i A.D.).

**βύξ**· βυθός, Hsch. (Fort. βρύξ.)

**βύπτειν**· βαπτίζειν, Hsch. **βύρθακος**· βάτραχος, Id. **βυρικόμενος**· πνιγόμενος, τραχηλιζόμενος, Id. **βυριόθεν**, = βαυρ-, q. v., Id.: **βύριον**· οἴκημα, Id. **βύρμακας**· μύρμηκας, Id. **βυρμός**· σταθμός, Id. ⊛ **βυρρός**, = κάνθαρος (Tyrrhen.), Id. II. = βίρρος, *BGU*814.8 (iii A.D.).

**βύρσα**, ἡ, *skin stripped off*, *hide* (prop. *ox-hide*, β. καὶ ἄλλα δέρματα Hdt.3.110), Batr.127, Arist.*HA*531$^a$11, etc.; βύρσης ὄζειν smell *of leather*, Ar.*Eq*.892; βύρσης κτύπος *of the drum*, E.*Ba*.513; *wineskin*, Luc.*Lex*.6, Aristid.*Or*.26(14).18. 2. *skin* of a live animal, Theoc.25.238. 3. in contempt, of the human *skin*, ἡ κακὴ β. Herod.3.80. 4. *screen* or perh. *sail*, Luc.*Nav*.4.

**βυρσ-αίετος**, ὁ, *leather-eagle*, com. name of Cleon the tanner, Ar. *Eq*.197. -άτονος, = βυρσότονος, Hsch. ⊛ -εῖον, τό, *tan-pit*, Sch.Ar.*Ach*.724. -εύς, έως, ὁ, later word for βυρσοδέψης, Artem. 4.56, *Act.Ap*.9.43, *PFay*.121.15 (ii A.D.); guild of βυρσεῖς at Thyatira, *IGRom*.4.1216. -εύω, *dress hides*, *tan*, Hsch. s. v. σκυλοδέψιος. -ικός, ή, όν, *of hides* or *leather*, δυσωδία *Gp*.6.2.7. II. *used by tanners*, βοῦς *Hippiatr*.35. -ιμώλους· βυρσοδεψίμους, Hsch. -ίνη, ἡ, *leathern thong*, Ar.*Eq*.59,449 (with a play on μυρσίνη). -ινος, η, ον, *leathern*, πλοιάρια D.C.48.19. -ίς, ίδος, ἡ, Dim. of βύρσα, Hsch.

**βυρσοδεψ-εῖον**, τό, = βυρσεῖον, *EM*187.17. ⊛ -έω, *dress* or *tan hides*, Ar.*Pl*.167, Artem.1.51. -ης, ου, ὁ, (δέψω) *tanner*, Ar.*Eq*. 44, Pl.*Smp*.221e, Herod.6.88, *PPetr*.3 p.78 (iii B.C.), Artem.2. 20. -ησις, εως, ἡ, *tanning*, Eust.887.24. -ικός, ή, όν, *of* or *for tanning*, Hp.*Mul*.1.78, Thphr.*CP*3.9.3: hence -ική, ἡ, *art of tanning*, Socr.*Ep*.14.2. -ιμος, v. βυρσιμώλους. -ιον, τό, *tan-pit*, *IG*14.352i71 (Halaesa).

**βυρσό-καππος**, ὁ, dub. sens. (fort. -κάπηλος), sobriquet of Cleon, *Com.Adesp*.61. -παγής, ές, (πήγνυμι) *made of hides*, ῥόπτρα Plu. *Crass*.23. -παφλᾰγών, όνος, ὁ, *leather-Paphlagonian*, nickname of Cleon, Ar.*Eq*.47. -ποιός, όν, *tanning hides*, Din.*Fr*.89. 19. -πώλης, ου, ὁ, *leather-seller*, Ar.*Eq*.136. -τενής, ές, = βυρσότονος, τύμπανα E.*Hel*.1347 (lyr.). -τομέω, *cut leather*, Poll. 7.81. -τόμος, ον, (τέμνω) *leather-cutting*, Man.4.320, Hsch. s. v. ῥινοτόρος. -τονος, ον, *with skin stretched over it*, β. κύκλωμα, = τύμπανον, E.*Ba*.124 (lyr.).

**βυρσ-όω**, *cover with skins* or *leather*, Ath.Mech.12.10, al. -ώδης, ες, lit. *leathery*; of the pulse, *hard*, Gal.8.456 (Comp.).

**βύρτη**· λύρα, Hsch.

**βῡσαύχην**, ενος, ὁ, ἡ, (βύω) *short necked*, Ar.*Fr*.725 (v.l. for μεσαύχ-), Xenarch.1.4.

**Βύσιος**, ὁ, a Delphic month, *IG*2².1126.45, Plu.2.292e, etc.

**βύσμα**, ατος, τό, (βύω) *plug*, *bung*, Hp.*Mul*.2.114 (pl.), Ar.*Fr*. 299; Στίλπωνος βύσματα Stilpo's *stoppers*, i. e. arguments with which he stopped his opponents' mouths, Diph.23.

**βύσσα**, ἡ, = βυσσός, Opp.*H*.1.453. II. a *bird*, Ant.Lib.15.

**βύσσαλοι**· βόθροι, and **βυσσαλεύω**, *sink to the bottom*, Hsch.

⊛ **βύσσινος**, η, ον, *made of* βύσσος, σινδὼν β. *fine linen* bandage, used for mummy-cloths, Hdt.2.86; for wounds, Id.7.181; πέπλοι A.*Pers*. 125 (lyr.), E.*Ba*.821; φάρος S.*Fr*.373; ὀθόνια β. *OGI*90.17 (Rosetta), *PStrassb*.91.16 (i B.C.), Aristeas 320; β. περιβόλαια *PStrassb*.91.9 (i B.C.); βύσσινον, τό, Lxx *Es*.1.6 (pl.), al., *Apoc*.19.8; ὀθόνια καὶ βύσσινα *PHolm*.15.26. II. = πορφυροῦς, Hsch.

**βυσσοβαρῆ**· μεγάλα, and **βυσσοφαρεῖ**· μεγαλοφαρεῖ, Hsch.

**βυσσοδομεύω**, (δομέω) *build in the deep*: hence, *brood over* a thing *in the depth of one's soul*, *ponder deeply*; Hom. only in Od., always in bad sense, κακὰ φρεσὶ βυσσοδόμευον 17.66, al.; μύθους β. 4.676; δόλον φρεσὶ β. Hes.*Sc*.30: also in late Prose, ὀργὴν β. Luc.*Cal*.24; τὰ βυσσοδομευόμενα *secret designs*, Hld.7.11:—also ⊛ -δομέω, Eust. 1513.46, Suid.

⊛ **βυσσόθεν**, Adv. *from the bottom* of the sea, S.*Ant*.590; of a river, Call.*Del*.127; κινήσασα β. γνώμην Babr.95.49, cf. Eratosth.*Fr*.36.4:

metaph., *fundamentally*, Plot.6.5.12; *from the depths of the heart*, β. οἰμωγή Opp.*H*.4.17.

**βυσσομέτρης**, ου, ὁ, *measuring the deeps*, epith. of a fisherman, *AP*6.193 (Stat. Flacc.).

**βυσσός**, ὁ, = βυθός, *depth of the sea*, Il.24.80, Hdt.2.28,96, Arist. *HA*$547^{b}$15.

⊛ **βύσσος**, ἡ, *flax*, and *the linen made from it*, Emp.93, Theoc.2.73, etc.; used of *perennial flax, Linum angustifolium*, grown in Elis, Paus.6.26.6, and of *Linum usitatissimum*, = λίνον Ἑβραίων, Id.5.5.2; also, in later writers, of *Indian cotton, Gossypium herbaceum*, Poll. 7.76, Philostr.*VA*2.20; and of *silk*, τὰ Σηρικὰ ἔκ τινων φλοιῶν ξαινομένης βύσσου Str.15.1.20.

**βυσσ-ουργός**, ὁ, *byssus-weaver*, *PTeb*.5.239 (ii B.C.):—hence **-ουργικός**, ή, όν, ἐργαλεῖα ib.243. **-οφαρεῖ**, v. βυσσοβαρῆ. **-όφρων**, ον, gen. ονος, (φρήν) = βαθύφρων, *deep-thinking*, Ἐρινύς A.*Ch*.651 (lyr.). **-ωμα**, ατος, τό, *net woven of* βύσσος, *AP*6.33 (Maec.).

**βύσταξ**, ακος, ὁ, = μύσταξ, Antiph.44.4.

**βυστίχοις**· τοῖς ἐν θαλάττῃ βρόχοις, Hsch.

**βύστρα**, ἡ, = βύσμα, Antiph.180.

**βύτανα**· κόνδυλοι, Hsch. **βύτθαν**· τὸν ψᾶρα, Id. (fort. ψῆνα). **βυτθόν**· πλῆθος, Id. **βυτίνη**, ἡ, = πυτίνη (Tarent.); also, = ἀμίς, Id. **βύττος**· γυναικὸς αἰδοῖον, Id.

**βύω** Arist.*HA*$532^{a}$18: fut. βύσω [ῡ] Thalesap.D.L.1.35, (ἐπι-) Cratin.186.4, (προ-) Ar.*V*.250: aor. ἔβῡσα Hp.*Morb*.3.14, (ἐπι-) Ar. *Pl*.379:—**Med.**, only in compds.:—**Pass.**, aor. ἐβύσθην (παρ-) Luc. *Deor.Conc*.10: pf. βέβυσμαι, the tense chiefly in use (v. infr.):—*stuff*, 1. c. gen. rei, *stuff full of*, only in Pass., νήματος βεβυσμένος *stuffed full of* spun-work or spinning, Od.4.134; τὸ στόμα ἐβέβυστο (sc. χρυσοῦ) Hdt.6.125; ἀνάγκης βεβυσμένος οἶκος Nonn.*D*.9.298. 2. c. dat. rei, *stop* or *plug with*, βύσας τὴν ἕδρην σπόγγῳ Hp. l.c., cf. Arist. l.c.:—Pass., σπογγίῳ βεβυσμένος Ar.*Ach*.463; κηρίῳ Id.*Th*. 506; ῥαφίνοις τὴν ἕδραν βεβ. Alciphr.3.62; ἵππος ἀριστήεσσι βεβ. Tryph.308; ἀφραδίῃ τε βέβυστο [πόλις] Id.450. 3. abs., βεβυσμένος τὴν ῥῖνα *having* one's nose *stopped*, Hegesipp.1.26; βεβ. τὰ ὦτα *deaf*, Luc.*Cat*.5; εἷμα βεβ. a *close, thick-woven* robe, Hp.*Mul*.1. 1. 4. *stow* or *tuck away*, τι ὑπὸ τῇ πτέρυγι Ael.*NA*11.18. (Root βυτ-, cf. βύζην (<*βυσ-δην), βύσ-τρα; cf. ζέβυται· σέσακται, Hsch.)

**βυωτήν**· τὴν ἄρσιν, Hsch. **βῶ**· βοῦν, Id., cf. Sch.Il.7.238.

**βωβός**, ή, όν, *dumb*, ἐκ γενετῆς κωφοὶ καὶ β. Plu.*Fr.inc*.149, cf. Phlp.*in GA*223.32; also, = πηρός, χωλός, Hsch.

**βωβύζειν**· σαλπίζειν, Hsch. **βῴδιον**, τό, = βοΐδιον, Id. ⊛ **βωθέω**, Ion. contr. for βοηθέω, v.l. in Hdt.8.47.

⊛ **βωθύζειν**· βοᾶν, θωΰσσειν, Hsch. **βωκάριν**, prob. f.l. for σωκάριον, *Gp*.20.42. **βώκαρος**, = ἔαρ (Troezen.), *EM*217.40.

**βώκκαλις**, ίδος, ἡ, an Indian *bird*, Ael.*NA*13.25.

**βωκολ-ιάσδω, -ιαστής, -ικός, -ος**, Dor. for βουκ-. **βῶκος**, ὁ, Dor. for βοῦκος. II. βωκός· τρυφερὸς χιτών, Hsch. (fort. βράκος).

**βωλά**, Dor. for βουλή, *SIG*261.15 (Argos, iv B.C.), Decr.Byz.ap. D.18.90, etc.

**βωλάζω**, in pf. part. Pass. βεβωλασμένα πεδία *cloddy*, Onos.10.4.

⊛ **βωλ-άκιον** [ᾰ], τό, *loamy soil*, Hsch., Zonar. **-άκιος** [ᾰ], α, ον, *lumpy, loamy*, opp. dry sandy soil, γῆ Pi.*P*.4.228. ⊛ **-αξ**, ᾰκος, ἡ, = βῶλος, ib.37, Theoc.17.80, A.R.3.1334. **-άριον**, τό, Dim. of βῶλος, Str.16.4.18; λιβανωτοῦ M.Ant.4.15; Ἄθως β. τοῦ κόσμου Id. 6.36; ἁλός Aët.2.3. **-ηδόν**, Adv. *clod-like*, Dsc.5.106.

**βωληνή** (sc. ἄμπελος), ἡ, a kind of *vine* grown in Bithynia, *Gp*. 5.17.5.

**βωλητάρια** πινάκια *mushroom-shaped* dishes, *BGU*781 iii 8 (ii A.D.).

**βωλήτης**, = βωλίτης, Ath.3.113e:—hence **βωλητῖνος** ἄρτος a loaf *of this shape*, ibid.

**βωλήτιον**, τό, *saucepan*, *POxy*.1657.4 (iii A.D.).

**βώλινος**, η, ον, *made of clay*, i.e. *of brick*, Hsch.

**βωλίον**, τό, Dim. of βῶλος, Ar.*V*.203, Arist.*Mir*.$833^{b}$14.

**βωλίς**, ἡ, *cake* used in sacrifices, Hsch.

**βωλίτης** [ῑ], ου, ὁ, *terrestrial fungus*, Lat. *boletus*, *Gp*.12.17.8, Gal. 6.655. II. *root of* λυχνίς, Plin.*HN*21.171.

**βωλο-ειδής**, ές, *cloddy, lumpy*, Thphr.*Ign*.65, Erot. s.v. μώλυζα. Adv. -δῶς Dsc.1.73. ⊛**-κοπέω**, *break clods of earth*, Ar.*Fr*.761, Hp. *Ep*.17, Ael.*Ep*.19, *PLond*.1.131r iii 50 (i A.D.): pf. βεβωλοκόπηκα Ar.*Fr*.57 D.: metaph. in mal. part., Ἀρχ.Δελτ.2 *App*.47 (Thyrrheum). ⊛ **-κόπος**, ον, *clod-breaking*, Cratin.5. ⊛ **-κρῖθον**, τό, *barley-cake* for fodder, *PLond.ined*.2360 (iii B.C.). **-λογέω**, *sift out earth* from corn, *POxy*.708.7 (Pass., ii A.D.).

**βώλομαι**, Cret. for βούλομαι, *GDI*5042.16 (iii B.C.).

**βωλόναι**, αἱ, *mounds, barrows*, S.*Fr*.1035.

**βωλο-ποιέω**, *make into clods*, f.l. in Hp.*Ep*.17. **-πῡρος**, ὁ, *wheat-cake* for fodder, Wilcken *Chr*.198 (iii B.C.), *PLond.ined*.2360 (iii B.C.).

**βωλόρυχα** (βῶλος, ὀρύσσω)· τὴν σῦν (Lacon.), Hsch.

⊛ **βῶλος**, ἡ, less freq. ὁ (v. sub fin.), *lump, clod of earth*, εἴκοι δ' ὑπὸ βῶλος ἀρότρῳ Od.18.374; ὑγρᾶς ἀρούρας β. S.*Aj*.1286; ὡς βαλῶ ταύτῃ τῇ βώλῳ X.*Cyr*.8.3.27; β. ἀνιστάναι Plu.*Rom*.11; βῶλος ἄρουραν, prov. 'carrying coals to Newcastle', Zen.2.74; esp. of *earth* fraudulently mixed with corn, *POxy*.708.8 (ii A.D.); cf. ἄβωλος. 2. in Poets, *land, soil*, βαθεῖαν β. ἀροῦντες Mosch.4.37, cf. *AP*9.561 (Phil.), etc.; Λίβυσσα κρύψει β. Ἀννίβου δέμας Orac.ap.Plu.*Flam*.20, cf. Jul.*Or*.3.125b. 3. generally, *lump*, as of gold, *nugget*, Arist. *Mir*.$833^{b}$11, Str.3.2.8; χρυσέα βῶλος, of the sun, E.*Fr*.783, cf. *Or*.984 (lyr.); β. μολίβδου D.S.3.14. 4. = βωλίτης, Sch.Nic.*Al*.526. 5. = σπαργάνιον, Ps.-Dsc.4.21 (v.l.). (Fem. acc. to Phryn.37, Moer. 95; masc. in Arist. l.c., D.C.40.47, *PHolm*.2.31, etc.)

⊛ **βωλο-στροφέω**, *turn up clods in ploughing*, *Gp*.2.23.14 (Pass.), Eust.581.16:—hence **-στροφητέος**, α, ον, also ⊛**στροφία**, ἡ, *turning up of clods*, and **-στρόφιον**, τό, *dibble*, *Gloss*. **-τόμος**, ον, *clod-breaking*, μύρμηκες *AP*9.438 (Phil.).

**βωλ-ώδης**, ες, = βωλοειδής, Thphr.*Lap*.42, *PHolm*.24.38. **-ωσις**, εως, ἡ, *formation of lumps*, *PHolm*.8.[illegible].

**βωμαίνω**, aor. ἐβώμηνα, *swear*, Hsch.

**βωμάκευμα** [μᾱ], ατος, τό, = βωμολόχευμα, Apollod.Cyren.ap.Sch. Pl.*R*.606c (pl.), *EM*218.7.

**βώμαξ**, ᾱκος, ὁ, ἡ, = βωμολόχος, Agath.2.30, *EM*199.2, Suid. II. **βῶμαξ**, ᾰκος, ἡ, Dim. of βωμός, *AB*85. **βώμενος**· βωμός, Hsch.

**βώμευσις**, εως, ἡ, *erection of an altar*, Hsch.

**βωμιαῖος**, α, ον, = sq., S.*Fr*.[illegible]8.

⊛ **βωμικός**, ή, όν, = βώμιος, *BCH*2.600 (Cibyra).

**βωμίνας**· ἀναβάσεις, Hsch.

**βώμιος**, ον, also α, ον, v. infr.: (βωμός):—*of an altar*, ἀκτὰν πάρα βώμιον S.*OT*183 (lyr.); βώμιοι ἐσχάραι E.*Ph*.274; β. ἕδρη Orph.*A*. 992. 2. of a suppliant, βωμία ἐφημένη *at the altar*, E.*Supp*.93, cf. S.*Ant*.1301; ἀμφὶ βωμίους λιτάς E.*Ph*.1749 (lyr.).

**Βώμιος**, ὁ, name of a Lamian month, *IG*9(2).71.3, al.

⊛ **βωμ-ίς**, ίδος, ἡ, Dim. of βωμός, *step*, Hdt.2.125. **-ισκάριον**, τό, Dim. of βωμός, *IG*14.1030:—also **-ίσκιον**, τό, *BGU*162.12 (ii/iii A.D.). ⊛ **-ίσκος**, ὁ, Dim. of βωμός, *altar-shaped vessel*, Hero *Spir*. 1.38, al. 2. *bandage*, Gal.18(1).823. 3. Arith., *solid* or *solid number* with all its dimensions unequal bounded by rectangles and trapezia, Hero *Deff*.114, Theo Sm.p.41 H., Nicom.*Ar*.2.16, Syrian. *in Metaph*.143.7, al. b. Geom., *plane figure* resembling the solid β. in appearance, Papp.878. 4. name of a *constellation*, Ptol.*Alm*. 8.1. 5. *base* of molar teeth, Poll.2.93. **-ίστρια**, ἡ, *priestess*, Nic.*Al*.217. **-ῖτις** (sc. γῆ), ιδος, ἡ, *consecrated* land, *Inscr.Perg*. 157*D*17.

**βωμοειδής**, ές, *like an altar*, Plu.*Them*.32.

**βωμολόχ-ευμα**, ατος, τό, only in pl., *ribald jests*, Ar.*Eq*.902, *Pax* 748. ⊛ **-εύομαι**, *play the buffoon, indulge in ribaldry*, Ar.*Fr*.166; opp. σεμνύνομαι, Isoc.7.49; *play low tricks*, in Music, Ar.*Nu*.969, Phld.*Mus*.p.94 K.:—Act. in Hsch. s.v. Λέσβιος ᾠδός, Suid. **-έω**, *beg*, Poll.3.111. 2. = foreg., Plu.2.407c. **-ία**, ἡ, *mendicancy*, Poll. 3.111. 2. *coarse jesting, buffoonery, ribaldry*. Pl.*R*.606c, Arist. *EN*$1108^{a}$24, Plu.*Lyc*.12, etc. **-ικός**, ή, όν, *inclined to ribaldry*, Luc.*Herm*.58, Gal.6.228, al. Adv. -κῶς (Lat. -*ice*), Id.*Subf.Emp*. 11. **-ος**, ον, (λοχάω) prop. *one that waited about the altars, to beg or steal some of the meat offered thereon*, ἵνα μὴ πρὸς τοῖσι βωμοῖς ἀεὶ λοχῶντες βωμολόχοι καλώμεθα Pherecr.141; β. ἱερεῖς Man.5.119; expld. by ἱερόσυλος, Hsch., *Et.Gud*. 2. metaph., *ribald, coarse*, β. ξυνήγορος Ar.*Eq*.1358, cf. *Ra*.1085,1521, al., Arist.*EN*$1108^{a}$25, *Rh*.$1419^{b}$9, Luc.*Merc.Cond*.24, etc.; β. κόλαξ *AP*11.323 (Pall.): Sup. -ώτατος Phld.*Mus*.p.77 K.; βωμολόχον τι ἐξευρεῖν invent some *ribald trick*, Ar.*Eq*.1194; β. ἔπεσιν χαίρει Id.*Ra*.358; τὸ β., = βωμολοχία, Plu.2.68a sq. Adv. -χως Procop.*Arc*.9, Olymp.*in Phd*. p.70 N. 3. small *jackdaw*, Arist.*HA*$617^{b}$18.

**βωμονίκης** [ῑ], ου, ὁ, at Sparta, *the lad who won the prize for the endurance of the voluntary whipping at the altar of* Artemis Orthia, *IG* 5(1).554, al.:—hence **-νῑκέω**, ib.654.

⊛ **βωμός**, ὁ, (βαίνω) *raised platform, stand*, for chariots, Il.8.441; *base* of a statue, Od.7.100: but, 2. mostly, *altar with a base*, ἱερὸς β. Il.2.305, etc.; πρὸς βωμῷ σφαγείς A.*Eu*.305; βωμὸς ἀρῆς φυγάσιν ῥῦμα Id.*Supp*.84 (lyr.); βωμῶν ἀπείργειν τινά Id.*Ch*.293; ἀγυιεὺς β. S.*Fr*.370; of suppliants, ποτὶ βωμὸν ἵζεσθαι Od.22.334; βωμοῖσι προσῆσθαι, προσπεσόντα βωμῷ καθῆσθαι, S.*OT*16, *OC*1158; βωμὸν ἵζειν E.*Ion*1314: also in Prose, β. ἱδρύσασθαι Hdt.3.142, cf. Pl.*Prt*.322a; ἱζόμενοι ἐπὶ τὸν β. Hdt.6.108; ἐπὶ βωμῶν καθέζεσθαι Lys.2.11. 3. later, *tomb, cairn*, *Epigr.Gr*.319. 4. title of poems by Dosiades and Besantinus, *AP*15.26 and 25, cf. Luc.*Lex*.25. 5. *altar-shaped cake*, *IG*2.1651*B,C*, Poll.6.76. 6. Ζεὺς Βωμός, prob. a Syrian god, *Hermes*37.118 (Syria). 7. *central fire* in the system of Philolaus, acc. to *Placit*.2.7.7. 8. in pl., = ἔμβολοι, Hsch.

**βωμόσπειρον**, τό, *round base* or *torus* of a column *placed upon a square plinth*, *CIG*2782.31 (Aphrodisias), *Rev.Phil*.44.73 (Lydia).

**βῶν**, v. βοῦς.

**βώνημα**· εἴρημα (Lacon.), Hsch.

**βωνίτης**, ου, Dor. **-τας**, ὁ, = βουκόλος, Call.*Fr*.157, Choerob. in *An.Ox*.1.184, Hsch.; but βουνιτῇσι· τοῖς βουκόλοις, Suid.

**βῶξ**, βωκός, ὁ, contr. for βόαξ (q.v.).

**βωρεύς**, εως, ὁ, *pickled mullet*, Xenocr.76:—Dim. ⊛**βωρίδιον**, τό, Id. 78.

**Βωρθία**· Ὀρθία (q.v.), Hsch.; cf. Βορθεία.

**βώριμος** or **βῶρμος**, name of a Mariandynian *dirge*, Poll.4.54.

**βῶροι**· ὀφθαλμοί, Hsch.

**βῶς**, v. βοῦς.

**βωσαρή**, Indian name for an *elephant*, *Peripl.M.Rubr*.62.

**βώσας, βῶσον**, v. sub βοάω. ⊛ **βώσεσθε**, poet. for βιώσεσθε, A.R.1.685.

**βωσιδία**, ἡ, = sq., *Sammelb*.1160.4.

⊛ **βωσίον**, τό, dub. sens. of *a household utensil*, β. χαλκοῦν *Stud.Pal*. 20.67 (ii/iii A.D.).

**βωστήρ**, ῆρος, ὁ, = βοτήρ, Hsch.

**βωστρέω**, *call on*, esp. *call to aid*, βωστρεῖν δὲ Κραταιΐν Od.12.124, cf. Ar.*Pax*1146, al., Theoc.5.64; *cry after*, ἁ Κύπρις τὸν Ἔρωτα.. ἐβώστρει Mosch.1.1; β. τινὶ ποιεῖν τι Opp.*C*.4.293: abs., τὰ δ' ἐσίγα, τὰ δ' ἐβώστρει, of birds, *Lyr.Alex.Adesp*.7.8. (Formed from βοάω, cf. ἐλαστρέω, καλιστρέω.)

**βωτάριον**, *vessel for slow heating*, Zos.Alch.p.165B.; cf. βοῦτις.

**βωτάζειν**· βάλλειν, Hsch. **βωτῆρες**, gloss on βώτορες, Id.

⊛ **βωτιάνειρα** [ᾰν], ἡ, (βόσκω) *man-feeding, nurse of heroes*, epith. of fruitful countries, Il.1.155; χθών *h.Ap*.363, Hes.*Cat.Oxy*.1369*Fr*.1.16. **βωτίον**· σταμνίον, Hsch.

⊛ **βώτωρ**, ορος, ὁ, = βοτήρ, Il.12.302; βώτορες ἄνδρες Od.14.102, *AP*6.262 (Leon.).

**βώχ**· βοτάνης εἶδος, Hsch.

# Γ

**Γ** γ, third letter in Gr. alphabet; as Numeral γ' = *three, third, thrice*: also, with pr. n., Βάσσος γ' *B., son and grandson of B., IGRom*.4.1587 (ii A.D.), etc.: but ͵γ = 3,000. II. written for ϝ, freq. in Hsch., as γανδάνειν· ἀρέσκειν, etc.

⊛ **γᾶ**, Dor. for γε, Ar.*Ach*.775, etc.; cf. ἔγωγα, τύγα.

**γᾶ**, Dor. and Aeol. for γῆ.

⊛ **γαβαθόν**· τρύβλιον, Hsch.; cf. ζάβατος. **γαβαλάν**· ἐγκέφαλον ἢ κεφαλή, Id. ⊛ **γάβενα**· ὀξυβάφια ἤτοι τρύβλια, Id. ⊛ **γαβεργόρ** (= γα-ϝεργός), *labourer* (Lacon.), Id.

**Γαγάτης** (sc. λίθος), ου, ὁ, *lignite*, Orph.*L*.474, Plin.*HN*36.141, Dsc.5.128, Gal.12.203, *Gp*.15.1.32. 2. *jet*, Solin.22.11. II. = ἀστράγαλος, cj. in Ps.-Dsc.4.61. (From Γάγας or Γάγγαι, a town and river in Lycia.)

**γαγγαίνειν**· τὸ μετὰ γέλωτος προσπαίζειν, Hsch.

**γαγγᾰλ-ιάω**, = -ίζεσθαι, Hsch. ⊛ **-ίζω**, later form of Att. γαργαλίζω, Phryn.77, *Anacreont*.5.7 (but the contrary is stated in Phryn. *PS*p.56B.). **-ίδες**· γελασῖνοι, Hsch. ⊛ **-ος**, ὁ, *fickle person*, Id.

⊛ **γαγγᾰμ-εύς**, έως, ὁ, *fisher*, Hsch. **-ευτής**, οῦ, ὁ, = foreg., prob. in *EM*219.25. **-ον**, τό, *small round net*, esp. for oyster-catching, Opp.*H*.3.81: metaph., μέγα δουλείας γ. A.*Ag*.361 (anap.):—also ⊛ **γαγγάμη**, ἡ, Str.7.3.18. 2. *umbilical region*, Poll.2.169 (γαγγαμών is f.l.). **-ουλκός**, όν, (ἕλκω) *dragging an oyster-net*, *EM*219.23.

⊛ **Γαγγητικός**, ή, όν, *from the Ganges*, νάρδος, a fragrant medicinal grass, = *Cymbopogon Iwarancusa*, *Peripl.M.Rubr*.63; σινδόνες ibid.

**γαγγίας** ἢ **γαγγαλίας** (leg. γαγγαλίδας)· οἱ μὲν γελασῖνον, οἱ δὲ τὴν τῶν νεύρων (ἐρίων cod.) συστροφήν, ἄλλοι ὑποστάθμην, Hsch.

**Γαγγῖτις** or **Γαγγῆτις** λίθος, = Γαγάτης, Str.16.1.24: also Γ. νάρδος, = Γαγγητικὴ νάρδος, Dsc.1.7, Damocr.ap.Gal.13.1057.

**γαγγλίον**, τό, *encysted tumour on a tendon* or *aponeurosis*, Philagr. ap.Aët.15.9 (Ἀθηνᾶ 21.29), Heras ap.Gal.13.815, etc.; also on the head, Paul.Aeg.6.39; the nerve-knots now called *ganglia* are compared to such a tumour, Gal.*UP*16.5.

**γαγγλιώδης**, ες, *of the ganglion kind*, Hp.*Art*.40:—also **γαγγλιοειδής**, ές, Hsch.

⊛ **γάγγραιν-α**, ἡ, (γράω?) *gangrene*, Hp.*Mochl*.33, *2Ep.Ti*.2.17, Dsc.1.61, Plu.2.65d, Gal.18(1).687. ⊛ **-ικός**, ή, όν, *gangrenous*, νομαί Dsc.2.107: **-κά**, τά, Id.4.93. Adv. **-κῶς** Heliod.(?)ap.Orib. 47.16.1. **-όομαι**, Pass., *become gangrenous*, Hp.*Art*.63, Gal.18(1).156. **-ώδης**, ες, *of the gangrene kind*, Hp.*Epid*.7.110, Gal. 11.818. **-ωμα**, τό, = sq., Pall.*Febr*.7. **-ωσις**, εως, ἡ, *becoming gangrenous*: *gangrenous affection*, φλεβῶν Hp.*Fract*.11 (pl.), *Mochl*. 30 (pl.), Aret.*SA*2.10 (pl.).

**Γάδαρα** [Γᾰ], ων, τά, a town in Palestine, Str.16.2.29:—**Γᾰδᾰρεύς** or **Γᾰδᾰρηνός**, ὁ, an inhabitant, *Ev.Matt*.8.28:—**Γᾰδᾰρίς** (sc. γῆ), ἡ, the country, Str. l.c.

**γάδαρος**, = γαϊδάριον, Diogenian.5.36.

**γαδεῖν**, **γάδεσθαι**, = ϝαδ- (ϝηδ-), Hsch.:—also **γαδεδᾶν**· χαίρειν, and **γαδεώ**· χαρά, Id.

⊛ **Γάδειρα** [Γᾰ], ων, τά, *Cadiz*, Pi.*N*.4.69, etc.; Ion. **Γήδειρα** Hdt.4.8: **Γᾰδειρίτης** [ῑ], **Γᾰδειρεύς**, ὁ, *a man of Cadiz*, St.Byz.:—Adj. **Γᾰδειρικός**, ή, όν, τάριχος Eup.186, Pl.*Criti*.114b; or **Γᾰδειραῖος**, α, ον, as Γ. πορθμός the Straits *of Gibraltar*, Plu.*Sert*.8. Adv. **Γᾰδειρόθεν** *AP* 14.121 (Metrod.), Euthyd.ap Ath.3.116c.

**Γᾰδειτάνα**, ἡ, *woman of Cadiz, courtesan*, *PGrenf*.1.53.28 (iv A.D.: γαειτ- Pap.).

**γαδή**· κίβωτος, Hsch.

**γάδιξ(ις)**· ὁμολογία, Hsch. (ϝάδ-). **γᾶδος**· γάλα, ἄλλοι ὄξος, Id.

**γάδος**, a *fish*, = ὄνος, Dorio ap.Ath.7.315f. II. = γάνδος (q.v.).

**γαεών**, ῶνος, ὁ, v. γαιών.

**γάζα** [γᾰ], ἡ, *treasure*, Thphr.*HP*8.11.5, *OGI*54.22 (iii B.C.), Epigr. ap.Str.14.1.39, Lxx *2Es*.5.17, *Act.Ap*.8.27, etc.; ἐκ τῆς βασιλικῆς γ. D.S.17.35. II. *large sum of money*, Plb.11.34.12. (Persian word.)

**γάζας**, a *fish*, Hsch.

**Γαζίτιον**, τό, *Gaza measure*, *POxy*.1924.8 (v/vi A.D.).

**γᾱζο-φῠλᾰκέω**, *to be a treasurer*, D.S.17.74. **-φῠλάκιον** [λᾰ], τό, *treasury*, *OGI*225.16 (Didyma, iii B.C.), Lxx *4Ki*.23.11, Str.7.6.1, *Ev.Luc*.21.1, al. **-φύλαξ** [ῠ], ἄκος, ὁ, *treasurer*, Phylarch.29, Lxx *1Ch*.28.1, Str.16.2.40, J.*AJ*11.1.3, Plu.*Demetr*.25; written γαζζο-, *Syria* 5.347 (Dura).

**γάθευδον**· ἐκ γῆς ῥέον, Hsch.

**γᾱθέω**, **γάθω**, Dor. for γηθέω, γήθω. **γαθία**· ἀλλαντία, Hsch.

⊛ **γαῖα**, ἡ, gen. γαίης Hom. (and Antiph., v. infr.), Trag. γαίας, dat. γαίᾳ A.*Pers*.618, S.*Aj*.659, E.*Med*.736, etc., acc. γαῖαν: nom. γαίη only in late Poets, *IG*14.1935, etc.; Dor. γαίᾱ ib.803 (Naples): pl. γαῖαι Od. (v. infr.), Lxx *4Ki*.18.35, al.:—poet. for γῆ, *land, country*, φίλην ἐς πατρίδα γαῖαν to one's dear father*land*, Il.2.140, al.; γαῖάν τε τεὴν δῆμόν τε Od.8.555: pl., οὐδέ τις ἄλλη φαίνετο γαιάων 12.404, D.P.882. 2. *earth*, χυτὴ γ. *earth* thrown up to form a cairn, Il.23. 256; ὦ γ. κεραμί, of potters' *earth*, Eub.43, cf. Sannyr.4; κύτος πλαστὸν ἐκ γαίης Antiph.52.3; the forms γαιῶν, γαίαις, γαίας in codd. of Lxx are written for γεῶν, etc. 3. *earth*, as an element, ὑμεῖς.. ὕδωρ καὶ γ. γένοισθε Il.7.99; ἐμοῦ θανόντος γ. μειχθήτω πυρί *Trag. Adesp*.513; γαίης καὶ ὕδατος ἐκγενόμεσθα Xenoph.33, cf. Emp.17.18, 109.1, etc. II. *the earth*, Theoc.18.20: elsewh. Γαῖα, as pr. n., *Earth*, Hes.*Th*.45, A.*Eu*.2, etc. (The usu. form in Hom.; used in Trag. metri gr. and by Com. in paratrag., v. supr.)

**γαιάδας**· ὁ δῆμος (Lacon.), Hsch. ⊛ **γαιᾶται**· κερτομεῖ, Id. (leg. γλιᾶται).

**γαϊδάριον**, τό, *donkey*, *PAmh*.2.153 (vi/vii A.D.). (Arabic word.)

**γαιη-γενής**, ές, poet. for γηγενής, A.R.3.1186. **-θεν**, Adv. *from the land*, Opp.*H*.1.39. 2. *out of the earth*, ἐκφύεται γ. Orac. ap.Eus.*PE*6.2 (*App.Anth*.6.113); *from the earth*, ἀναστήσαντες Orac. ib.5.9 (*App.Anth*.6.162). ⊛ **-ῖος**, α, ον, *sprung from Gaia* or *Earth*, Τιτυόν, Γαιήϊον υἱόν Od.7.324, cf. *AP*14.23. II. *earthly*, βίου βροτέου γ. δεσμά Nonn.*D*.37.4; μελέων γ. ἄχθος *Eranos*13.88. **-οχος** (also **-οῦχος**, Hsch.), Dor. **γαιάοχος**, ον, **γαιάϝοχος** *IG*5(1).213 (Sparta, v B.C.):—epith. of Poseidon, *earth-moving, earth-carrying*, Il.13.43, al., A.*Th*.310 (lyr.), cf. S.*OC*1072 (lyr.): **Γαιάοχος**, abs., Il. 13.125, Pi.*O*.13.81, and so Γαιάϝοχος (v. supr.): also in pl., Γαάοχοι, name of a contest, *IG*5(1).296.11 (Sparta). 2. ὠκεανὸς γ. *App. Anth*.3.209. II. *protecting the country*, γαιάοχε παγκρατὲς Ζεῦ A.*Supp*.816 (lyr.); γαιάοχόν τ' Ἄρτεμιν S.*OT*160 (lyr.). 2. = ἠπειρώτης, Hsch. (In signf. 1 from γαῖα and ϝεχ-: ϝοχ-, cf. ὄχεα, Lat. *veho*, Skt. *vāhati*, Germ. *be-wegen*, etc. In signf. II from ἔχω (q.v.).) **-φάγος** [ᾰ], ον, *earth-eating*, of worms, Numen.ap.Ath. 7.305a; cf. γαφάγας.

**γαιθυλα** (δ supra scr.)· ἀμπελόπρασα, Hsch.; cf. γηθυλλίς.

**γαϊκός**, ή, όν, *concerning land*, κρίμα *SIG*421.44 (Thermon, iii B.C.).

**γαίνεται**· ἀνύει, Hsch.

**γάϊνος**, Dor. = γήϊνος (q.v.).

**γαιο-γράφος** [ᾰ], ὁ, = γεωγράφος, Hsch. **-δότης**, f.l. for γεωδαίτης in Call.*Fr*.158. **-μέτρης**, ου, ὁ, = γεωμ-, Man.4.210. **-νόμος**, ον, *dwelling in the land*: *inhabitant*, A.*Supp*.54 (anap.).

**γαῖος** [ᾱ], α, ον, Dor. for γήϊος, *on land*, A.*Supp*.826 (lyr.); *earthy*, γ. κόνις Id.*Th*.736; *of the land*, κόγχοι Epich.42.9; παῖς γ. child *of earth*, *terrae filius*, of a slave, prob. in *IG*14.1432 (cf. γάϊος παρὰ Ἰταλιώταις καὶ Ταραντίνοις ὁ μίσθιος Eust.188.30, cf. *EM*223.24); ἄνεμος a *land* wind, Hsch.; also, = ἐργάτης βοῦς, Id., *EM* l.c. II. τὸν γάϊον, = καταχθόνιον, prob. in A.*Supp*.156 (lyr.).

**γαιός**· μακροκέντης ἢ κόντος ἢ κολοβός, Cyr., cf. Hsch.

**γαιο-φάγος** [ᾰ], ον, = γαιηφάγος, Nic.*Th*.784. **-φανής**, ές, *earth-coloured*, in Comp., Archig.ap.Orib.8.2.4 (v.l. γεω-); τὸ γ. *the earthy appearance* of the moon, *Placit*.2.30.1 codd.

**γαιόω**, *make land, make solid*, Tz.*H*.1.907, al.

**γαῖσος**, ὁ (or **γαῖσον**, τό, Ph.*Bel*.99.16, cf. *AB*88), a sort of *javelin*, Lxx *Jo*.8.18, *Ju*.9.7, Plb.6.39.3, 18.18.4, *PTeb*.230 (ii B.C.), D.S.13. 57:—hence prob. Celtic pr. n. **Γαισάται** or **-οι**, οἱ, expld. by Plb. as *mercenaries*, 2.22.1. (Iberian word acc. to Ath.6.273f.)

**γαῖται**· γεωργοί, Hsch., *EM*223.29.

**γαϊτανά**, τά, *aseptic ligaments* made in Gaul, Gal.10.942, Marcell. Empir.8.27.

**γαίω**, impf. γαίεσκον Hsch.:—*rejoice, exult*, Hom. only in Il., in phrase, κύδεϊ γαίων Il.1.405, 5.906, 8.51; [Σφαῖρος] μονίῃ γαίων Emp. 27.4. (γάϝ-γω, v. γάνυμαι.)

⊛ **γαιώδης**, f.l. for γεώδης in Plb.2.15.8.

**γαιών**, ῶνος, ὁ, *heap of earth, boundary-heap*, *Tab.Heracl*.1.136: **γαεών** *IG*14.352ii83 (Halaesa, pl.).

**γάκα**· ἡδέως, **γακεῖαι**· γλυκεῖαι, **γάκον**· ἡδύ, γλυκύ, **γακούδια**· ἡδύσματα, and **γακουπώνης**· ἡδυπότης, Hsch. **γᾰκίνας** [ῑ], ὁ, *earthquake*, Id., Eust.890.38:—also **γᾰκῖνίας**, ὁ, Hsch., and **γάκῖνος**, ὁ, Att. acc. to *EM*219.41. **γακτός**· κλάσμα, Hsch. (ϝακ-, cf. ϝάγ-νυμι).

⊛ **γάλα** [⏑⏑], τό, gen. γάλακτος (also γάλακος, dat. γάλακι Call.*Hec*. 1.4.4, prob. in Pherecr.108.18, cf. *An.Ox*.4.338), also τοῦ γάλα indecl., Pl.Com.238: dat. pl. γάλαξι Pl.*Lg*.887d. (For γλακτ-, cf. Lat. *lac* for *glact*):—*milk*, ἀμελγόμενοι γ. λευκόν Il.4.434, cf. Od.4.88, etc.; εὔποτον γ., εὐτραφὲς γ., A.*Pers*.611, *Ch*.898; ἐν γάλακτι ὤν, τεθραμμένη, at *the breast*, E.*HF*1266, Pl.*Ti*.81c; ἐν γάλαξι τρέφεσθαι Id.*Lg*.l.c. (so metaph., ἐν σπαργάνοις καὶ γάλαξιν εἶναι, of art, Ael.*VH* 8.8); διδόναι γάλα X.*Cyn*.7.4; ἐμπλῆσαι γάλακτος to fill full of *milk*, Theoc.24.3: metaph., οἶνος, Ἀφροδίτης γ. Ar.*Fr*.596. 2. ὀρνίθων γ. (ὄρνιθος γάλα, = ὀρνιθόγαλον, Nic.*Fr*.71.5, Dsc.2.144), prov. of rare and dainty things, Ar.*V*.508, *Av*.734, Men.936; τὸ λεγόμενον, σπανιώτατον πάρεστιν ὀρνίθων γ. Mnesim.9, cf. Ach.Tat.*Intr.Arat*. 4 (expld. by Anaxag.22 as *white of egg*, cf. Sch.Luc.*Merc.Cond*. 13). 3. ἀγαθὸν γ. a good *wet-nurse*, Call.*Ep*.51; οὐδ' εἰ γ. λαγοῦ εἶχον..καὶ ταῶς, κατήσθιον Alex.123. II. *milky sap* of plants, Thphr.*HP*6.3.4, etc. III. *the milky way*, Parm.11, Arist.*Mete.* 345ᵃ12, Arat.476; but ὁ τοῦ γάλακτος κύκλος Euc.*Phaen.*p.4M., Gem.5.69.

**γάλαγγα**, *galingale, Alpinia officinarum*, Aët.1.131.

⊛ **γᾰλᾰθηνός**, ή, όν, *sucking, young, tender*, νεβροί Od.4.336, cf. Anacr.51; τέκος Simon.52; ἄρνες Theoc.18.41, J.*AJ*6.2.2; γαλαθηνά (sc. πρόβατα) Hdt.1.183; (sc. χοιρία) opp. τέλεια, Pherecr.44, cf. Hp.*Aff.*43, *SIG*1015.32 (Halic., written γαλαθεινός); ἀρνῶν καὶ χοίρων Crates Com.1; ὗς Pherecr.28, cf. Arist.*HA*603ᵇ25; βρέφη Clearch.17, cf. Theoc.24.31. (γάλα, θῆσθαι.)

**γαλαίριον**, τό, and **γαλάτιον**, τό, = γάλιον, Dsc.4.95.

**γαλακοθρέμμων**, ον, gen. ονος, (τρέφω) *milk-fed*, prob. in Antiph. 52.4 for γαλακτο-. **γαλακόχρως**, = γαλακτόχρως, nom. pl. -χροες Opp.*C*.3.478.

**γαλακτηφόρος**, ον, = γαλακτο-, *BCH*37.97 (ii/iii A.D.).

**γᾰλακτ-ίας**, ου, ὁ, with and without κύκλος, = γαλαξίας, Ptol.*Alm.* 8.2. **-ιάω**, *give no milk*, Poll.3.50; but γαλακτιῶντες· γάλακτος μεστοί, Hsch. **-ίζω**, *to be milky in appearance*, Dsc.2.144,175. 2. *form a milky way*, Phlp. *in Mete.*117.20. **-ινος**, η, ον, *milk-white*, στήθεα *AP*5.192 (Diosc.); χιτών *POxy.*267.7 (i A.D.); *milky*, χρώματα *PHolm.*24.31; v.l. for γαλακτίζον, Dsc.2.175. **-ιον**, τό, Dim. of γάλα, M.Ant.5.4: in pl., *fancy bread made with milk*, Alciphr.*Fr.* 6.10. **-ὶς** πέτρα, = -ίτης, Orph.*L.*201. II. γαλακτίς, ίδος, ἡ, = τιθύμαλλος, Aët.1.397. **-ισμός**, ὁ, *suckling*, παιδίου Mnesith.Cyz. ap.Orib.*inc.*15.17. ⊛**-ίτης** [ῑ] λίθος, stone *which makes water milky*, Dsc.5.132. II. γαλακτίτης, = γαλακτίς II, *Gloss.*

**γᾰλακτο-δόχος**, ον, *receiving, holding milk*, Sch.Theoc.1.25. **-ειδής**, ές, *like milk, milk-white*, χρῶμα *Placit.*3.1.4. **-θρέμμων**, v. γαλακοθρ-. **-κόμος**· ποιμήν, Hsch. **-κράς**, gen. -κρᾶτος, *mixed with milk*, Hdn.Gr.1.51,2.759.

**γᾰλακτόομαι**, Pass., *become milk* or *milky*, Thphr.*CP*1.7.3, Dsc. 3.48; τῇ χροίᾳ Antyll.ap.Orib.4.11.6, cf. Plu.2.968a.

**γᾰλακτο-πᾰγής**, ές, *like curdled milk*, χρώς *AP*5.59 (Rufin.); ἄρνα ib.12.204 (Strat.). **-ποιέω**, *convert into sap*, Tz.ad Hes.*Op.* 72. **-ποιητικός**, ή, όν, *milk-producing*, βοτάνη *EM*232.37. **-ποιΐα**, ἡ, *production of milk*, Sch.Vat.Nic.*Th.*944. **-ποσία**, ἡ, *drinking of milk*, Hp.*Int.*16. ⊛**-ποτέω**, *drink milk*, Id.*Morb.*2.51, *Int.* 16, Thphr.*HP*9.15.4, Str.17.3.8. (Written -πωτέω by Ammon. p.111 V.) **-πότης**, ου, ὁ, *milk-drinker*, Hdt.1.216,4.186, E.*El.*169 (lyr.). **-πώλης**, ου, ὁ, *milkseller*, *Gloss.* **-ρῦτος**, ον, *flowing with milk*, κρῆναι *Lyr.Alex.Adesp.*37.11. **-τροφέω**, *nourish with milk*, Lxx 4*Ma.*13.21, Ph.2.82 (Pass.), *PTeb.*399.4 (ii A.D.). **-τρόφησις**, εως, ἡ, *nourishment with milk*, Sch.rec.S.*Aj.*506. **-τροφία**, ἡ, = foreg., Lxx 4*Ma.*16.7, Ph.2.83, *BGU*297.14 (i A.D.).

**γᾰλακτ-ουργέω**, *make of milk*, as cheese, Poll.1.251. II. *make milk*, as a nursing woman, Sor.2.5. **-ουργός**, όν, *making milk-dishes*, Parmenion ap.Ath.13.608a. **-ουχέω**, *have* or *suck milk*, Poll.3.50; γαλακτουχούσης prob. in Plu.2.640f (γαλακτούσης codd.). **-οῦχος**, ον, (ἔχω) *having* or *sucking milk*, Poll.3.50.

**γᾰλακτο-φᾰγέω**, *live on milk*, Philostr.*VS*2.1.7. **φάγος** [φᾰ], ον, *milk fed*, Str.7.4.6, S.E.*P.*1.56. **-φορία**, ἡ, *giving milk*, *BGU* 297.14 (i A.D.). ⊛**-φόρος**, ον, *giving milk*, *PLond.*1.3.22 (ii B.C.), J.*BJ*3.3.4, Opp.*C.*1.443; of food, *causing an abundant flow of milk*, Sch.Nic.*Th.*553. **-χρως**, ωτος, ὁ, ἡ, *milk-coloured*, Philyll.4, Nausicr.2: neut. pl., γαλακτόχροα Dsc.3.47: nom. pl. γαλακτόχροες in Opp.*C.*3.478 is f.l. for γαλακόχροες.

**γᾰλακτ-ώδης**, ες, = γαλακτοειδής, ὑγρότης Arist.*HA*540ᵇ32; γ. τροφή Id.*PA*692ᵃ15; χυμός Thphr.*CP*6.4.1. 2. *milk-warm, tepid*, Herod.Med.ap.Orib.5.30.38, Antyll.ib.9.23.9, Alex.Trall.*Febr.* 4. 3. *mixed with milk*, οἶνος Hp.*Epid.*7.101. **-ωσις**, εως, ἡ, *changing into milk*, Thphr.*CP*4.4.7.

**γᾰλ-άνα**, **-ᾱνός**, Dor. for -ήνη, -ηνός. **γαλαός**, v. γάλις.

**γάλαξ**, ακος, ἡ, a kind of *shell-fish*, prob. *Mactra lactea*, Arist.*HA* 528ᵃ23.

**γαλαξ-αῖος**, α, ον, *milky, milk-white*, Nonn.*D.*6.338, al. **-ήεις**, εσσα, εν, = foreg., ῥέεθρα v.l. ib.22.18. **-ια**, τά, *festival at Athens* in honour of Cybele, *at which a kind of milk-frumenty* (γαλαξία, ἡ) *was eaten*, *IG*2².1011.13, Thphr.*Char.*21.11, Hsch. ⊛**-ίας**, ου, ὁ: 1. (sc. κύκλος) *the milky way*, D.S.5.23, Luc.*VH*1.16, Man.2. 116, etc.; in full, γ. κύκλος *Placit.*2.7.1, Sallust.4. II. (sc. λίθος) = λίθος μόροχθος, *tailor's chalk*, Dsc.5.134. III. = γαλεός I, Gal.6. 727 (v.l. γαλεξ-). **-ιών**, ῶνος, ὁ, name of a Delian month, *IG*11 (2).203*A*31, al. (Delos, iii B.C.).

⊛ **γαλαρίας**, ου, ὁ, = ὀνίσκος, Hsch.

**γάλας**· γῆ (Cypr.), Euclus ap.Hsch.: **γαλάσιον**· ἐνηρόσιον, Hsch.

⊛ **Γαλάται** [λᾰ], οἱ, = Κελτοί (but Κελτοὶ καὶ Γ. Arist.*Fr.*35), Plb.1.6. 2, etc.: fem. sg. **Γαλάτισσα**, *GDI*2154.7 (Delph., ii B.C.):—Adj. **Γᾰλᾰτικός**, ή, όν, πέλαγος Arist.*Mu.*393ᵃ27; χώρα *Act.Ap.*16.6; ἔργα βάρβαρα καὶ Γ. Plu.2.1049b. Adv. **-κῶς**, ἐνεσκευασμένος Id. *Oth.*6.

**Γᾰλᾰτάρχης**, ου, ὁ, *president of the provincial council of Galatia*, *OGI*547.11 (Ancyra), etc.

**γαλάτιον**, v. γαλαίριον. **γαλατμόν**· λάχανον ἄγριον, Hsch.

**γάλβινα** χρώματα, (Lat. *galbus*) *greenish-yellow* shades of colour, *PHolm.*25.2.

**γαλεάγκων**, v.l. for γαλιάγκων (q.v.).

⊛ **γᾰλεάγρα**, ἡ, *weasel-trap* or *weasel-cage*, Hyp.*Fr.*34,239: metaph., πλοῖον ἀνεῳγμένη γ. Secund.*Sent.*17: generally, *cage for beasts*, Lxx *Ez.*19.9, cf. Hierocl.p.59A.; θηρίων Str.6.2.6; used for prisoners, Plu.*Phoc.*33, App.*Pun.*4.

**γαλέαγρος**· *furo* (cod. *suro*), *Gloss.*

**γαλέη**, contr. **γαλῆ**, ῆς, ἡ, a name given to various animals of the *weasel* kind, *weasel, marten, polecat* or *foumart*, Batr.9, al., Ar.*Ach.* 255, *Pl.*693, Arist.*HA*609ᵃ17, al.; εἰ διάξειεν γαλῆ (a bad omen) Ar.*Ec.*792, cf. Thphr.*Char.*16.3: prov., θύρα δι' ἧς γαλῆ..οὐκ εἰσέρχεται Apollod.Car.6. 2. γ. ἀγρία wild *ferret* (found in Africa and Spain, Hdt.4.192), Arist.*HA*580ᵇ26, Ruf.*Fr.*79, Str.3.2.6; γ. Ταρτησσία Hdt. l.c., Diogenian.3.71. 3. γ. ἐνοικίδιος tame *weasel*, Plu.2.446e; γ. κατοικίδιος Philum.*Ven.*33.1, Dsc.2.25. 4. prov., γαλῆν ἔχεις, of bad luck, Diogenian.3.84; γαλῇ χιτώνιον κροκωτόν, of 'pearls before swine', Stratt.71, Zen.2.93; γαλῇ στέαρ, = βατράχῳ ὕδωρ (q.v.), Diogenian.3.83. II. a small *fish*, distd. from γαλεός by Ael.*NA*15.11. (From γαλεγᾱ, Adj. from *γαλις, cf. Skt. *girikā* 'mouse', Lat. *glīs*.)

**γᾰλεό-βδολον**, τό, = γαλήοψις, Dsc.4.94. **-ειδής**, ές, (γαλεός I) *of the shark kind*, οἱ γ. Arist.*HA*565ᵃ20:—more usu. **-ώδης** ib.505ᵃ 5, al.

⊛ **γᾰλεός**, ὁ, *dog-fish* or small *shark*, Pl.Com.137, Arist.*HA*489ᵇ6; γ. νεβρίας, *Scyllium stellare*, ib.565ᵃ26; γ. ἀστερίας ib.543ᵃ17, cf. Philyll. 1; γ. λεῖος, *Mustela laevis*, Arist.*HA*565ᵇ2. II. = γαλέη I. 3, οἱ ἐνοικάδιοι γ. Aret.*CD*1.4.

⊛ **γᾰλερός**, ά, όν, = γαληνός, *cheerful*, Hsch., *AB*229. Adv. **-ρῶς** cj. in *AP*12.50 (Asclep.).

**γαλερωπός**, όν, *with cheerful, happy face*, *AB*229.

**γαλεώδης**, v. γαλεοειδής.

⊛ **γαλεώνυμος**, ὁ, = γαλεός I, Philotim.ap.Gal.6.726.

**γᾰλεώτης**, ου, ὁ, *gecko lizard*, Ar.*Nu.*173, Arist.*Fr.*370. II. *sword-fish*, = ξιφίας, Plb.34.2.12, Str.1.2.15. III. *weasel*, Luc. *VH*1.35; γ. γέρων (transl. by *colore mustelino*, Ter.*Eun.*4.4.21) Men.188.

**γαλῆ**, ἡ, contr. for γαλέη (q.v.).

**γάλη**· ἐξέδρας εἶδος, καὶ ἐν ᾗ (leg. γαλῇ) γαλέα τὸ ζῷον, Hsch.

⊛ **γᾰλην-αίη**, ἡ, Ep. for γαλήνη, A.R.1.1156. **-αῖος**, α, ον, = γαληνός, *AP*10.21 (Phld.); ὄπωπαί *Epigr.Gr.*403.2 (Sebastopolis). Adv. **-αίως** Sch.Od.7.319. **-ειᾰ**, Dor. **γᾰλάνειᾰ**, ἡ, = γαλήνη, E.*IA* 546 (lyr.), *HF*402 (lyr.), *Hyps.Fr.*3iii4 (lyr.). **-η**, ἡ, *stillness of the sea, calm* (γ. μὲν ἐν θαλάσσῃ νηνεμία δ' ἐν ἀέρι Arist.*Top.*108ᵇ 25, but cf. Od.5.452,12.168), Hom. only in Od., λευκὴ δ' ἦν ἀμφὶ γαλήνη 10.94; οἱ δ' ἐλόωσι γαλήνην will sail the *calm sea*, 7.319; *stillness* of deep waters, Coluth.360; νηνεμίας τε καὶ γ. Pl.*Tht.*153c; ἐν ταῖς γ. καὶ εὐδίαις Arist.*HA*533ᵇ30: metaph. of the mind, *calmness, serenity*, φρόνημα νηνέμου γαλάνας A.*Ag.*740 (lyr.); ἐν γαλήνῃ in *calm, quiet*, S.*El.*899; γ. ἐν τῇ ψυχῇ Pl.*Lg.*791a. II. *lead sulphide, galena*, Plin.*HN*33.95, 34.159. III. name of an *antidote*, Androm.ap.Gal.14.32. (Aeol. γελήνη (sic) acc. to Jo.Gramm.*Comp.* 3.1; perh. akin to γελάω.) **-ής**, ές, = γαληνός, Arist.*Phgn.*811ᵇ 38. **-ιάζω**, = sq., Hp.*Vict.*2, Ph.1.276, Them.*Or.*1.17a:—Pass., aor. γαληνιασθῆναι Simp.*in Epict.*p.20 D. **-ιάω**, *to be calm, find peace*, χαίρει καὶ γ. Epicur.*Fr.*425, cf. Opp.*C.*1.115, Them.*Or.*15. 195a; Ep. part. γαληνιόων, -ωσα, *AP*9.208, 5.34.7 (Rufin.). **-ίδιον**, Dim. of γαλήνη, *Gloss.* **-ίζω**, *calm, still*, esp. waves or winds, Hp.*Vict.*3.71, E.*Fr.*1079. 2. intr., *become calm*, prob. in Hp. *Morb.Sacr.*13; *to be calm* or *tranquil*, Alex.178.6, Ph.1.354; τὸ γαληνίζον τῆς θαλάττης Arist.*Pr.*936ᵃ5:—so in Med., Xenocr.ap. Orib.2.58.98. **-ιος**, ον, = γαληνός, Luc.*Halc.*2. **-ισμός**, ὁ, *calming*, Epicur.*Ep.*1 p.32 U.; *calming* of the conscience, Arist. *Ep.*5.

**γᾰληνοβάτης** [βᾰ], ου, ὁ, in pl., epith. of demons, *PMag.Par.*1. 1364.

**γαληνός**, όν (ή, όν *Cat.Cod.Astr.*1.136), *calm*, esp. of the sea, γαλήν' ὁρῶ (neut. pl.) I see *a calm*, E.*Or.*279; of persons, *gentle*, Id. *IT*345; γ. προσφθέγματα Id.*Hec.*1160; γαληνὴ ἕξις μετώπου Arist. *Phgn.*812ᵃ1; βίος Pl.*Ax.*370d, Ph.1.411; τὸ γ. Them.*Or.*34 p.459 D.; as title, γαληνότατος δεσπότης *PGrenf.*1.60.16 (vi A.D.). Adv. **-νῶς** D.L.9.45: Comp. -νότερον J.*BJ*1.28.2.

⊛ **γᾰληνότης**, ητος, ἡ, = γαλήνη, S.E.*P.*1.10.

**γᾰληνώδης**, ες, *calm*, Sch.A.*Pr.*139.

**γαληόψις**, εως, ἡ, *brownwort, Scrofularia peregrina*, Dsc.4.94.

**γαληρός**, = γαλερός, Hsch. **γαληψός**, a *plant*, Id., *AB* 230. **γάλι**· ἱκανόν, Hsch.

**γαλία**· εἶδος πλοίου ληστρικοῦ, *EM*502.44.

**γαλιάγκων**, ωνος, ὁ, *weasel-armed*, i.e. *short-armed*, Hp.*Art.*12, al.:—more correctly written γαλεάγκων in Arist.*Phgn.*808ᵃ31, 813ᵃ 12, Plu.2.520c.

**γαλίαι**· οἱ ὀνίσκοι, Hsch.

**γαλιάω**, = ἀκολασταίνω, *Com.Adesp.*967.

**γᾰλῐδεύς**, έως, ὁ, *a young weasel*, Cratin.265.

**γάλινθοι** (or γέλινθοι)· ἐρέβινθοι, Hsch.

**γᾰλῐοβρᾰχίων** [χῑ], ονος, ὁ, = γαλιάγκων, coined by Gal.19.90.

**γάλιον**, τό, *bedstraw, Galium verum*, Dsc.4.95 (expld. by Dsc. from γάλα because used in place of rennet).

**γάλις**· γαλαός, Hsch.

**γαλλάζω**, *practise cult of Cybele*, *Schwyzer*633.12 (Eresus, ii/i B.C.).

**γαλλαῖος**, α, ον, *of a* Γάλλος, γ. Κυβέλης ὀλόλυγμα Rhian.67.

⊛ **γαλλερίας**, ου, ὁ, = ὀνίσκος, Dorio ap.Ath.7.315f.

**γάλλι**, τό, = δρῶπαξ, Aët.3.180.

**γάλλια**· ἔντερα, Hsch.

**γαλλῐαμβικὸν** *μέτρον*, variety of Ion. metre used in cult of Cybele, Heph.12.3.

**γαλλιάριος,** ὁ, *footpad, cutpurse, PLips.*40ii 10 (iv A.D.).

**γαλλικός,** ή, όν, perh. *gelded, POxy.*1836 (v/vi A.D.).

**γαλλιστὶ** *τεμεῖν*, prov. 'cut the Gordian knot', Macar.2.92.

**γαλλιώτας,** = *γαλεώτης* I (Lacon.), Hsch. **γάλλοι·** *ἧλοι*, Id. (Aeol. *ϝάλλοι*).

**γαλλομᾰνής,** ές, *frenzied like a Γάλλος*, Man.4.221.

**Γάλλος,** ὁ, *priest of Cybele, Schwyzer*633.11 (Eresus, ii/i B.C.), Arr. *Epict.*2.20.17, *AP*6.234 (Eryc.), 220 (Diosc.):—fem. form **Γαλλαί** *Lyr.Adesp.*121. II. *eunuch*, J.*AJ*4.8.40, *PGnom.*244, D.L.4.43.

**γάλμινος,** misspelling for *γάλβινος, Sammelb.*2251.

**γᾰλ-ουργέω,** *make of milk*, Poll.1.251. **-ουχέω,** *suckle*, Sor.1.88, J.*AJ*2.9.5, A.D.*Synt.*278.1 codd., Sm.1*Ki.*6.7: **-ουχία,** *suckling*, *Gp.*16.21.7: **-οῦχος,** ὁ, *wet-nurse*, Sor.1.89, Paul.Aeg.3.13. (Later forms for *γαλακτ-*.)

⊛ **γάλοως** [ᾰ], ἡ, gen. *γάλοω*, dat. sg. and nom. pl. *γαλόῳ* Il.3.122, 22.473: Att. **γάλως,** gen. *γάλω* Hdn.Gr.2.236 (also gen. *γάλωτος* acc. to *EM*220.18):—*husband's sister* or *brother's wife, sister-in-law*, Il.6.378, al. (Cf. Lat. *glōs*, Phryg. **γέλαρος·** *ἀδελφοῦ γυνή*, Hsch.)

**γαλωνές·** *χρῶμα ἵππων τὸ ὀνοειδές, EM*220.32.

**γαμάλη·** *κάμηλος* (Chald.), Hsch.

⊛ **γαμβρά,** ἡ, fem. of *γαμβρός, sister-in-law, BGU*827.29 (ii A.D.), *PLond.*2.403 (iv A.D.).

**γαμβρεύω,** *form connexions by marriage, πρός τινας* Lxx *De.*7.3; *τισί* 2*Es.*9.14:—Med., *marry*, v.l. ib.*Ge.*38.8:—Pass., *to be connected by marriage, τινί* J.*AJ*14.12.1.

**γάμβριον·** *τρύβλιον*, Hsch. **γάμβρια·** *δῶρα ἢ δεῖπνα γαμβροῦ*, Id.

**γαμβρο-κτόνος,** ον, *bridegroom-slaying*, Lyc.161. **-ποιέω,** *make a son-in-law of*, Tz.*H.*10.433.

⊛ **γαμβρός,** ὁ, *connexion by marriage*, Pi.*N.*5.37, A.*Ag.*708 (pl.): hence, I. *son-in-law*, Il.6.249, Hdt.5.30,67, Democr.272, E.*Ph.*427, etc. II. *brother-in-law*, i.e. *sister's husband*, Il.5.474, 13.464, Hdt.1.73, etc.; or, *wife's brother*, S.*OT*70. III. = *πενθερός*, *father-in-law*, E.*Hipp.*635, *Andr.*641, Lxx *Ex.*3.1. IV. Dor. and Aeol., *bridegroom, wooer*, Sapph.103, Pi.*P.*9.116, Theoc.18.49, 15.129, Arat.248. (Cf. Skt. *jārá-* (from *ĝm̥̄ró-*) 'lover'.)

**γαμβροτιδεύς,** έως, ὁ, *son of a γαμβρός*, Iamb.*Protr.*21.κζ'.

⊛ **γάμελα,** τά, *offerings made on the occasion of a marriage, Michel* 995*B*36 (Delph., v B.C.).

**γᾶμεν,** Dor. for *ἔγημεν*, aor. 1 of *γαμέω*, Pi.*P.*3.91, Theoc.8.93.

⊛ **γᾰμετ-ή,** ἡ, fem. of sq., *married woman, wife*, opp. concubine, [*γυναῖκα*] *κτητήν, οὐ γαμετήν* Hes.*Op.*406, cf. Pl.*Lg.*841d, Lys.1.31 (pl.), Men.*Pk.*237, *PTeb.*104.17 (i B.C.), etc.; *γαμετῇ ἀλόχῳ Epigr. Gr.*310 (Smyrna); so *γαμετή* alone, A.*Supp.*165 (lyr.), Arist.*Fr.*144, *POxy.*795.4 (i A.D.); *τέκνα καὶ γαμετάς* Phld.*Ir.*p.53 W., cf. *Herc.*1457.10, al. ⊛ **-ης,** ου, ὁ, *husband, spouse*, A.*Pr.*897 (lyr.), E.*Tr.*311 (lyr.), Euph.107.3; poet. word used by X.*Cyr.*4.6.3, and late, *PLond.*5.1711.53 (vi A.D.); Dor. gen. *γαμέτα* E.*Supp.*998 (lyr.):—fem. **γᾰμέτις,** ιδος, *a wife*, dub. in *AP*5.179 (Mel.), cf. *IPE*2.298.10 (Panticapaeum).

**γᾱμετρία,** = *γεωμετρία*, Archyt.1, Perict.ap.Stob.3.1.121:—so **γᾱμέτρας,** for *γεωμέτρης, Tab.Heracl.*1.187; **γᾱμετρικός** Archyt.2.

⊛ **γᾰμέω,** fut. *γαμέω* Il.9.388,391, contr. *γαμῶ* A.*Pr.*764, S.*OT*1500, *Ant.*750, E.*Or.*1655, X.*Cyr.*5.2.12, etc.; later *γαμήσω* Plu.2.386c, Luc.*Rh.Pr.*8 (for *γαμήσεις Tim.*52 leg. *γαμησείεις*): aor. 1 *ἔγημα* Il.14.121, etc.; later *ἐγάμησα* Lxx *Es.*10.3, *Ev.Marc.*6.17, Luc.*DDeor.*5.4, etc. (cf. infr. II. 2): pf. *γεγάμηκα* Ar.*Lys.*595, Pl.*Lg.*877e: plpf. *ἐγεγαμήκει* Th.1.126:—Med., fut. Ep. *γαμέσσεται* Il.9.394 codd., Att. *γαμοῦμαι* E.*Ph.*1673, Ar.*Th.*900, later *γαμήσομαι* Plu.*Art.*26, etc.: aor. *ἐγημάμην* Od.16.392, Anacr.86, Is.5.5, etc.:—Pass., fut. *γαμηθήσομαι* J.*AJ*6.13.8, Ant.Lib.1.2, D.C.58.3, Hld.5.30, etc.: aor. *ἐγαμήθην* D.H.11.34, Str.10.4.20, etc.: poet. shortd. *γαμεθεῖσα* v.l. in Theoc.8.91, cf. Eust.758.52: pf. *γεγάμημαι* X.*An.*4.5.24, D.36.32: plpf. *ἐγεγάμητο* App.*BC*4.23: (*γάμος*):—*marry*, i.e. *take to wife*, of the man, *Ἀδρήστοιο δ' ἔγημε θυγατρῶν* one of his daughters, Il.14.121; *ἔνθα δ' ἔγημε γυναῖκα* Od.15.241; *γ. γυναῖκα ἐς οἰκία*, like *ἄγεσθαι*, Hdt.4.78: c. acc. cogn., *γάμον γαμεῖν* A.*Pr.*764,909; *τὸν Ἑλένης γάμον..γῆμας* E.*IA*467; *γῆμαι λέκτρα βασιλέως* the king's daughter, Id.*Med.*594: rarely c. dupl. acc., *γάμους τοὺς πρώτους ἐγάμεε Κύρου δύο θυγατέρας* (for *πρῶτον ἐγάμεε .. θυγατέρας*) Hdt.3.88, cf. E.*Tr.*357; also *γάμῳ γ. marry* in lawful wedlock, D.39.26; *ἐκ κακοῦ, ἐξ ἀγαθοῦ γῆμαι, marry a wife* of mean or noble stock, Thgn.189,190; *ἐκ μειόνων* X.*Hier.*1.28; *ἐκ γενναίων* E.*Andr.*1279; *παρά τινος* ib.975, Pl.*Plt.*310c; *ἐπὶ θυγατρὶ γ. ἄλλην γυναῖκα* set a stepmother over one's daughter, Hdt.4.154, cf. E.*Alc.*372; *ἐπὶ δέκα ταλάντοις τινὰ γαμεῖν marry a wife* with a dowry of ten talents, And.4.13. 2. of mere sexual intercourse, *take for a paramour*, Od.1.36, Luc.*Asin.*32; *γ. βιαίως σκότιον λέχος* E.*Tr.*44. 3. later of the woman, *ἐὰν γαμήσῃ ἄλλον Ev.Marc.*10.12: abs., 1*Ep.Cor.*7.28. II. Med., *give oneself* or *one's* child *in marriage*: 1. of the woman, *give herself in marriage*, i.e. *wed*, c. dat., *γαμέεσθαι τῷ ὅτεῳ τε πατὴρ κέλεται* Od.2.113; *γημαμένη ᾧ υἷϊ· ὁ δ' ὃν πατέρ' ἐξεναρίξας γῆμεν* 11.273: abs., Hdt.4.117; *σοὶ μὲν γαμεῖσθαι μόρσιμον, γαμεῖν δ' ἐμοί* A.*Fr.*13; *εἰς τύρανν' ἐγημάμην* I *married* into a royal house, E.*Tr.*474; *γήματο δ' εἰς Μαραθῶνα*, i.e. she *married* Herodes of Marathon, *IG*14.1389 i 5 (*ἥν τ' ἐγήματο* is f.l. for *ἥ τ' ἐγ.* in E.*Med.*262): ironically of a henpecked husband, *κεῖνος οὐκ ἔγημεν ἀλλ' ἐγήματο* Anacr.86; so Medea to Jason, *μῶν γαμοῦσα..σέ;* did I *marry* you? E.*Med.*606; *ἐγημάμην*, of a man marrying a rich wife, Antiph.46; *γαμεῖται ἕκαστος* (sens. obsc.) Luc.*VH*1.22; *ὁ γαμηθεὶς ὡς παρθένος κἄπειτα γενόμενος ἀνήρ* Phld.*Sign.*2; incorrectly, in later writers, *γημάμενος* Apollod.3.12.6, cf. Q.S.1.728. 2. of parents, *get their children married, betroth* them, *get a wife for the son*, *Πηλεύς θήν μοι ἔπειτα γυναῖκα γαμέσσεται αὐτός* (where Aristarch. *γε μάσσεται will seek* or *make suit* for) Il.9.394:—Act. aor. 1 *ἐγάμησα* in this sense, Men.885. III. Pass., *to be taken to wife*: hence, *marry a husband*, ll.cc. ad init., *PGrenf.*2.76.11 (iv A.D.), etc.; rarely in correct authors, Poll.3.45.

**γᾰμήγῠρις,** εως, ἡ, *enrolment of youths in φρατρίαι, EM*221.4.

**γᾰμήλ-ευμα,** τό, = *γάμος*, A.*Ch.*624 (lyr.). **-ιος,** ον, *of* or *for a wedding, bridal, nuptial, κοίτη* Id.*Supp.*805 (lyr.); *τέλος* Id.*Eu.*835; *χοαί* Id.*Ch.*487; *λέκτρα* Id.*Fr.*242; *εὐνή* E.*Med.*673; *οὐχ ἧψαν φῶς τὸ γ. Epigr.Gr.*256.7 (Cyprus); *ζυγὸν γ. IG*14.2125; of divinities, *presiding over marriage*, Ath.5.185b, Poll.1.24; *Ἀφροδίτα* E.*Fr.*781.17 (lyr.). II. as Subst., *γαμήλιος* (sc. *πλακοῦς*), ὁ, *bride cake*, Philetaer.13.5. 2. *γαμηλία* (sc. *θυσία*), ἡ, *wedding-feast*, *γαμηλίαν εἰσφέρειν τοῖς φράτερσι* contribute *the wedding feast* for one's clansmen, D.57.69; *τοῖς φ. ὑπέρ τινος* ib.43, cf. Is.3.79: abs., ib.76. **-ιών,** ῶνος, ὁ, the seventh month of the Attic year, *IG*1$^{2}$.6.80, Arist.*Mete.*343$^{b}$5, Thphr.*HP*7.1.2, etc. (from *γαμέω*, because *it was the fashionable time for weddings*).

**γᾰμ-ησείω,** Desiderat. of *γαμέω, wish to marry*, Alciphr.1.13, 3.37. **-ήσιμος,** η, ον, *marriageable, Gloss.* **-ητέον,** *one must marry*, Plu.*Demetr.*14 (parody of E.*Ph.*395), Arr.*Epict.*3.7.10, Hermog.*Prog.*11. **-ητικῶς,** Adv. *with an inclination for marriage*, Hsch. s.v. *γαμησείειν*. ⊛ **-ίζω,** *give* a daughter *in marriage*, A.D.*Synt.*280.11, 1*Ep.Cor.*7.38. **-ικός,** ή, όν, *of* or *for marriage, νόμοι* Pl.*Lg.*721a; *γ. ὁμιλία connubial* intercourse, Arist.*Pol.*1334$^{b}$32; *γ. ὑμέναιος* Pherecr.12 D.; *γ. ὕμνος* a *bridal* song, Hippoloch.ap.Ath.4.130a, Porph.*Marc.*2; *συγγραφή POxy.*1473.25 (iii A.D.); *τὰ γ. bridal, wedding*, Th.2.15; *questions of marriage-rights*, Id.6.6, cf. Arist.*Pol.*1304$^{a}$14. Adv. *-κῶς ἑστιᾶν* feast *as at a wedding*, Id.*EN*1123$^{a}$22. 2. *γαμικόν*, τό, *marriage-contract, POxy.*903.17 (iv A.D.). II. of persons, *of marriageable age, Epigr.Gr.*288.7 (Cyprus): pr. n. in *IG*14.496.

⊛ **Γαμίλιος,** ου, ὁ (sc. *μήν*), name of month in Epirus, *GDI*1339 (Dodona).

**γάμ-ιος** [ᾰ], α, ον, = *γαμήλιος, μέλος* Mosch.2.124; *εὐνή* Opp.*C.*3.149, cf. Nonn.*D.*1.69, al.; *γαμίης ἐλπίδος ἐστέρεσεν IG*12(8).600 (Thasos). **-ίσκω,** = *γαμίζω*, Callicrat.ap.Stob.4.28.18:—Med. (or Pass.) in Arist.*Pol.*1335$^{a}$20; *ἀνδρί*, of a woman, *PLond.*5.1708 (vi A.D.):—Pass., *Ev.Marc.*12.25.

**γάμμα,** τό, indecl., *the letter γ*, X.*Cyr.*7.1.5, *Oec.*19.9, etc.:—also **γέμμα** Democr.19. (Aram. *gamlā'* 'camel'.)

⊛ **γαμμᾰτίσκιον,** τό, Dim. of *γάμμα, ornament on official dress*, Lyd.*Mag.*2.4.

**γαμμοειδής,** ές, *shaped like a Γ, οἰκία BGU*1037.8 (i A.D.); of the top of the thigh-bone, Heliod.ap.Orib.49.13.3, cf. Hero *Spir.*1.28. Adv. *-δῶς* Nicom.*Ar.*1.19.

**γᾰμο-δαίσια** (sc. *ἱερά*), τά, *wedding*, Ael.*NA*12.34. **-κλοπέω,** *have illicit intercourse*, Ps.-Phoc.3. ⊛ **-κλόπος,** ον, (*κλέπτω*) *adulterous, AP*9.475, Tryph.45, Nonn.*D.*3.377, al. **-ποιΐα,** ἡ, *celebration of a wedding*, Ath.5.180c.

**γᾱμόρος,** ὁ, Dor. for *γημόρος* (q.v.).

⊛ **γάμος** [ᾰ], ὁ, *wedding*, Il.5.429, al.; *γάμοι εἰλαπίναι τε* 18.491; *γάμον τεύχειν* furnish forth *a wedding*, Od.1.277; *γ. δαινύναι* 4.3; *ἀρτύειν* ib.770; *γάμον ποιεῖν* Herod.7.86, *Test.Epict.*2.19: pl., *γάμους διττοὺς ἑστιᾶν* Is.8.9; of a single wedding, *οἰκοσίτους τοὺς γ. ποιεῖσθαι* Men.450; *γάμους ποιεῖν* D.30.21, *Ev.Matt.*22.2; *ἐπιτελεῖν γ. τῆς θυγατρός* Arist.*Fr.*549, cf. D.S.13.84; *οἱ κεκλημένοι εἰς τοὺς γ.* Diph.17.2; *ἐν τοῖς γ. ἄκλητος εἰσδεδυκέναι* Apollod.Car.24. II. *marriage, wedlock*, Il.13.382, etc.; *ἄγειν* [*γυναῖκα*] *ἐπὶ γάμῳ* X.*An.*2.4.8; *ἀγαγέσθαι τινὰ πρὸς γάμον* Plu.*Cat.Ma.*24; *τὸν Οἰνέως γ.* the *marriage* granted by O., S.*Tr.*792; *γ. θεῶν τινος* E.*Tr.*979, cf. *IT*25; *εἰς γ. τινὸς ἐλθεῖν* Id.*IA*1041 (lyr.); more freq. in pl., A.*Pr.*558 (lyr.), 739 (lyr.), *Ag.*1156 (lyr.), etc.; cf. *γαμέω* I: also *τοῖς μεθημερινοῖς γάμοις*, i.e. *prostitution*, D.18.129; *Πανὸς ἀναβοᾷ γάμους*, i.e. *rape*, E.*Hel.*190 (lyr.); of *unlawful wedlock*, as of Paris and Helen, Id.*Tr.*932; *γάμοι ἄρρενες* Luc.*VH*1.22; *γ. ἀνδρεῖοι* Procop.*Arc.*16.23:—E.*Andr.*103, X.*Cyr.*8.4.19, do not establish the sense of *a wife*; for E.*Tr.*357, v. *γαμέω* I.1. III. *ἱερὸς γ. ritual marriage*, Men.320, Hsch., *EM*468.56; as a nickname, Anaxandr.34.2; name of play by Alc.Com. IV. Pythag. name for *three, Theol.Ar.*16; for *five*, Plu.2.388c; for *six*, Theo Sm.p.102 H., *Theol.Ar.*33. V. *Γάμος* personified, Philox.13, Lib.*Or.*5.27. VI. name of month at Epidaurus, *IG*4.1485,1492. (Perh. akin to Skt. *jāmis* 'brother or sister', Lat. *geminus*.)

**γᾰμο-στολέω,** *furnish forth a wedding*, Sch.Pi.*N.*3.97. **-στολικός,** ή, όν, *determining marriage*, Vett.Val.119.8; *τόπος Cat.Cod.Astr.*5(1).203. **-στόλος,** ον, *preparing a wedding*, epith. of Hera and Aphrodite, Pisand.ap.Sch.E.*Ph.*1760, *Epic.Alex.Adesp.*9 iii 5, Orph.*H.*55.8, *AP*6.207 (Arch.); *Ὑμέναιος* ib.7.188 (Ant. Thall.); *νύξ* Musae.282. 2. Astrol., name for the seventh house of the horoscope, Paul.Al.*M.*2. **-τελεῖν·** *γάμους ἐπιτελεῖν*, Hsch.

**γαμφαί,** αἱ, = sq., Lyc.152.

⊛ **γαμφηλαί,** ῶν, αἱ, *jaws* of animals, as of the lion, Il.16.489; of the horse, 19.394; of Typhon, A.*Pr.*357; *bill* or *beak* of birds, E.*Ion*

159 (lyr.), cf. Ps.-Orac. in Ar.*Eq.*198: as Adj., ὑπὸ γαμφηλῇσιν ὀδοῦσιν (sic) Man.5.187 (s. v. l.): once in sg., γαμφηλή· ἡ γνάθος ἢ σιαγών, *EM*221.13.

**γαμψ-ός**, ή, όν, *curved, crooked*, of the uterine κόλποι, Hp.*Nat.Puer.* 31; κέρατα Arist.*HA*630ᵃ31; ῥύγχος Id.*PA*662ᵇ2; ὄνυχες ib.662ᵇ5 (Comp.); ἅρπαι Lyc.358. 2. of birds of prey, = γαμψῶνυξ, Ar.*Nu.*337 (anap.). **-ότης**, ητος, ἡ, *crookedness*, of talons, Arist.*HA*619ᵇ9. **-όω**, *make curved*: only used in Pass., *to be* or *become so*, ib.619ᵃ17. **-ωλή**, ἡ, = γαμψότης, Hsch., *AB*1356. **-ῶνυξ**, υχος, ὁ, ἡ, (ὄνυξ) *with crooked talons*, of birds of prey, αἰγυπιοὶ γαμψώνυχες Il.16.428, Od.22.302; οἰωνοί A.*Pr.*488; τὰν γ. παρθένον, of the Sphinx, S.*OT*1199 (lyr.); γ. ἅρπη Nonn.*D.*12.336, etc.:—also **-ώνυχος**, ον, Arist.*HA*563ᵇ20, *GA*750ᵃ11, Plu.2.727c; τὸ γ. Plot. 6.7.9, Iamb.*Protr.*21.ιθ′: pl., γαμψώνυχοι ἀστακοί Epich.30; τὰ γ., of beasts of prey, Arist.*HA*517ᵇ1, cf. 503ᵃ30.

**γαμψωνυχοπαντοφιλάρπαγος**, ον, *snatcher of everything with curved talons*, Lyr. in *Philol.*80.336.

**γᾶν**· ἀγγεῖον σκύφῳ παραπλήσιον, Hsch.

**γάνα** (A) [ᾰ], Dor., esp. Sicil., for γυνή, Greg.Cor.p.345 S.

**γάνα** (B)· χέρσος, γῆ, Hsch. ⊛ **γανάεις**, cf. sq. II. 2.

**γαναπέας**· τελείας, and **γαναπέα**· πελία, Cyr. **γανάσσας**· καλῶς, Hsch. **γαναυγέας**· τέλειος ἐν τῷ δρᾶν, Id.

⊛ **γᾰνάω**, (γάνος) *glitter, gleam*, of metals; Hom. always in Ep. part., θώρηκες λαμπρὸν γανόωντες Il.13.265; κόρυθες λαμπρὸν γανόωσαι 19.359: hence, *look fresh and smiling*, πρασιαί.. ἐπηετανὸν γανόωσαι, of garden-beds, Od.7.128; νάρκισσον.. γανόωντα *h.Cer.*10; χαλκῷ γανάοντας ἐφήβους *Mus.Belg.*16.70 (Attica, ii A.D.); ὀφθαλμοὶ γανόωντες, in phthisis, Aret.*SD*1.8. 2. *exult, rejoice*, Opp.*H.*1. 659. II. trans., *make bright*, Arat.190; cf. γανάσσαι· σμῆξαι, ἡδῦναι, Hsch. 2. γανάοντες *glorifying*, Herm. for γανάεντες, A.*Supp.*1019 (lyr.).

**γανδάνειν**· ἀρέσκειν, Hsch. **γανδάω**· λάμπω, Id. **γάνδιον**· κιβώτιον, Id. **γάνδος**· ὁ πολλὰ εἰδὼς καὶ πανοῦργος· τινὲς δὲ γάδος, Id. **γάνδομα**· πυροί, ἄλευρα, Id. **γάνεα**· κῆπος, Id. (κόπους cod.). **γανεῖν**· λευκαίνειν, Id., *EM*223.44. **γανῖται**· δάπανοι, ἄσωτοι, Hsch. (cf. Lat. *ganeo*).

⊛ **γάννος**, = γλάνος (Ephes.), Phlp. *in GA*149.20.

**γάννυα**, perh. = γάνεα, Orph.*Fr.*47.5.

⊛ **γάνος** (A) [ᾰ], εος, τό, (γαίω, cf. γάνυμαι) *brightness, sheen*, Sapph. 127 (?), *Supp.*9.2. 2. *gladness, joy, pride*, λάφυρα.. ἀρχαῖον γάνος A.*Ag.*579. 3. of water and wine, from their *quickening* and *refreshing* qualities, χαίρουσαν οὐδὲν ἧσσον ἢ διοσδότῳ γάνει σπορητὸς (Pors. for Διὸς νότῳ γᾶν εἰ), i.e. rain, ib.1392; κρηναῖον γ. Id.*Pers.* 483; γ. ἀμπέλου, βότρυος, ib.615, E.*Ba.*261, 383 (lyr.); also of honey, γ. μελίσσης Id.*IT*634: abs., *water*, Lyc.1365; Ἀσωποῦ γ. E.*Supp.* 1150 (lyr.). 4. of a divine being, παγκρατὲς γ. *Hymn.Curet.*3.

⊛ **γάνος** (B)· παράδεισος (Cypr.), *EM*223.48, cf. γάνεα; dub. in *Ber. Sächs.Gesellsch.*1908.5 (Cypr.), *IG*12(2).58.17 (Mytilene). (Hebr. *gan* 'garden'.)

⊛ **γᾰνόω**, *make bright, polish*, Plu.2.74e: metaph., τὰ πράγματα τοῖς εὐπροσωποτάτοις τῶν ἐπιθέτων ib.683e:—metaph. in Pass., ἀληθείας φωτὶ γεγανωμένα Dam.*Pr.*33, cf. 26; ἀὴρ.. ζοφερὸς καὶ οἷον γεγανωμένος Agath.5.3; ἑοῖς ἐγάνωσεν ἰάκχοις *glorified*, *Epigr.Gr.*985 (Philae); *make glad, delight*, τὴν ψυχήν Ph.1.121:—Pass., *to be made glad, exult*, ταῦθ' ὡς ἐγανώθην Ar.*Ach.*7, Ph.l.c., al.:—esp. pf. part. Pass. γεγανωμένος *bright*, χλανίς Phld.*Vit.*p.21 J.; *glad-looking*, στίλβων καὶ γεγανωμένος Anacr.13 A; γεγ. ὑπὸ τῆς ᾠδῆς, *under the glamour* of song, Pl.*R.*411a, cf. Phld.*Mort.*13, Plu.2.42c; γεγ. καὶ ἀνθηρός, of oratorical style, Id.*TG*2. II. *tin, lacker*, ἀγγεῖον γεγανωμένον Crito ap.Gal.12.490; γ. τῷ κασσιτέρῳ Aët.12.55, cf. Eust.1188.61.

⊛ **γάνῠμαι** [ᾰ], mostly pres.; impf. ἐγάνυντο Q.S.5.652; ἐγάνυτο Jul.*Or.*1.8c: Ep. fut. γανύσσομαι Il.14.504: pf. part. γεγανυμένος *Anacreont.*35.3, Them.*Or.*13.177a: plpf. ἐγεγάνυσο ib.20.240d, al.:—*brighten up, be glad* or *happy*, γάνυται φρένα he *is glad* at heart, Il.13.493: c. dat., δάμαρ ἀνδρὶ φίλῳ ἐλθόντι γανύσσεται 14.504, cf. 20.405, Od.12.43, Ar.*V.*612; γ. ἐπί τινι E.*IT*1239 (lyr.); τινός A.*Eu.*970 (lyr.), cf. E.*Cyc.*504 (lyr.); ὑπὸ τοῦ λόγου Pl.*Phdr.*234d.—Freq. in later Prose, Ph.1.36, 56, Plu.2.1098f, Polyaen.1.18, Jul.*Or.*1.4b, al., Them. ll.cc.; ᾄδων καὶ γανύμενος Aristid.*Or.*50(26). 40; freq. written γανν- in codd. (γα-ν-υ- from root γαυ-, cf. γαίω, γαῦρος.)

**γανύματα**· ἀρτύματα, *AB*230 (γανύρμ- Hsch.). **γανυρόν**· λευκόν, ἡδύ, ἱλαρόν, Hsch.:—also **γανερόν**, *EM*223.46.

**γᾰνύσκομαι**, Dep., = γάνυμαι, Them.*Or.*2.26d, 21.254c: c. gen., γ. τοῦ τόπου Socr.*Ep.*18.

**γανυτελεῖν**· γανοπετεῖν, ἡδύσματα ποιεῖν, Hsch.

**γᾰν-ώδης**, ες, *bright*: of ground, *rich*, Thphr.*HP*6.5.4. **-ωμα**, ατος, τό, = γάνος, *brightness, brilliance*, prob. in *IG*4.1484.97 (Epid., iv B.C.), Plu.2.48d, 50a. II. *joy, gladness*, Ph.1.335, al. III. *lacker*, ἔστω τὸ γ. τοῦ χαλκοῦ μόλιβδος Aët.6.58. 2. metaph. of internal *membranes* or *coats*, τὸ γ. τῶν ἐντέρων Alex.Trall.9.3, cf. Sever.*Clyst.*p.34 D. ⊛ **-ωσις**, εως, ἡ, *polishing* (with oil or wax), ἀγάλματος Plu.2.287c, cf. Vitr.7.9.4; *varnishing, lackering*, Aq.*Am.* 7.7. 2. metaph., *making glad, brightening*, Phld.*Mus.*p.30 K. **-ωτής**, οῦ, ὁ, *tinsmith*, Gloss. ⊛ **-ωτός**, ή, όν, *tinned, polished, lackered*, ἀγγεῖον Aët.12.1.

⊛ **γᾱοδίκαι** [ῐ], οἱ, *arbitrators in territorial dispute*, *SIG*421.45 (Thermon, iii B.C.).

**γᾱοργέω**, Thess., = γεωργέω, *IG*9(2).1229.16 (Phalanna).

⊛ **γάπεδον**, τό, Dor. for γήπεδον, *IG*4.823.58 (Troezen).

**γαπελεῖν**· ἀμελεῖν, Hsch. **γάπος**· ὄχημα (Tyrrhen.), Id.

**γάποτος** [ᾱ], ον, *to be drunk up by Earth*, γ. χύσις, γ. χοαί, γ. τιμαί, of libations, A.*Ch.*97, 164, *Pers.*621.

**γάπτωμα** (sic), prob. γναμπτ-, *curvature*, *BCH*23.178 (Pisid.).

**γάρ** (γε, ἄρα), causal Conj., used alone or with other Particles.

I. introducing the reason or cause of what precedes, *for*, τῷ γὰρ ἐπὶ φρεσὶ θῆκε θεὰ λευκώλενος Ἥρη· κήδετο γ. Δαναῶν Il.1.56, etc.; but freq. in expl. of that wh. is implied in the preceding clause, πολλάων πολίων κατέλυσε κάρηνα.. τοῦ γὰρ κράτος ἐστὶ μέγιστον 2. 118, etc.: hence, b. in simple explanations, esp. after a Pronoun or demonstr. Adj., ἀλλὰ τόδ' αἰνὸν ἄχος κραδίην καὶ θυμὸν ἱκάνει· Ἕκτωρ γ. ποτε φήσει 8.148, cf. Od.2.163; ὁ δὲ δεινότατον.. ὁ Ζεὺς γ... Ar.*Av.*514; ὃ δὲ πάντων ἀδικώτατον ἔδοξε· τῶν γὰρ προγεγραμμένων ἠτίμωσε καὶ υἱοὺς Plu.*Sull.*31; freq. in introducing proofs or examples, μαρτύριον δέ· Δήλου γ. καθαιρομένης.. Th.1.8; τεκμήριον δέ· οὔτε γ. Λακεδαιμόνιοι.. Id.2.39, cf. D.20.10, etc.; in full, τεκμήριον δὲ τούτου τόδε· αἱ μὲν γ... Hdt.2.58; παράδειγμα τόδε τοῦ λόγου· ἐκ γ... Th.1.2; δηλοῖ δέ μοι τόδε· πρὸ γ... ib.3. c. to introduce a detailed description or narration already alluded to, ὅμως δὲ λεκτέα ἃ γιγνώσκω· ἔχει γ. [ἡ χώρα] πεδία κάλλιστα.. X.*An.* 5.6.6, etc. d. in answers to questions or statements challenging assent or denial, *yes*,.., *no*,.., οὐκουν.. ἀνάγκη ἐστί;—ἀνάγκη γ. οὖν, ἔφη, *ay doubtless* it is necessary, X.*Cyr.*2.1.7, cf. §§ 4 and 13; indicating assent, ἔχει γ. Pl.*Phdr.*268a; ἱκανὸς γ., ἔφη, συμβαίνει γ., ἔφη, Id.*R.*502b, c, cf. *Ap.*41a, etc.; οὔκουν δὴ τό γ' εἰκός.—οὐ γ.· Id.*Phdr.* 276c. 2. by inversion, preceding the fact explained, *since*, *as*, Ἀτρεΐδη, πολλοὶ γ. τεθνᾶσιν Ἀχαιοί.. τῷ σε χρὴ πόλεμον παῦσαι Il.7.328; χρόνου δὲ οὐ πολλοῦ διελθόντος (χρῆν γ. Κανδαύλῃ γενέσθαι κακῶς) ἔλεγε πρὸς τὸν Γύγην τοιάδε, Γύγη, οὐ γ. σε δοκέω πείθεσθαι.. (ὦτα γ. τυγχάνει κτλ.), ποίει ὅκως.. Hdt.1.8, cf. 6.102, al.; εἶεν, σὺ γ. τούτων ἐπιστήμων, τί χρὴ ποιεῖν; Pl.*Phd.*117a; the principal proposition is sts. b. blended with the causal one, τῇ δὲ κακῶς γ. ἔδεε γενέσθαι εἶπε, i.e. ἡ δέ (κακῶς γ. οἱ ἔδεε γενέσθαι) εἶπε Hdt. 9.109, cf. 1.24, 4.149, 200, Th.1.72, 8.30. c. attached to the hypothet. Particle instead of being joined to the apodosis, οὐδ' εἰ γ. ἦν τὸ πρᾶγμα μὴ θεήλατον, ἀκάθαρτον ὑμᾶς εἰκὸς ἦν οὕτως ἐᾶν, i.e. οὐδὲ γ. εἰ ἦν.., S.*OT*255. d. repeated, οὐ γ. οὖν σιγήσομαι· ἔτικτε γ... Id.*OC*980, cf. *Ant.*659 sq., 1255. 3. in elliptical phrases, where that of which γάρ gives the reason is omitted, and must be supplied, a. freq. in Trag. dialogue and Pl., when *yes* or *no* may be supplied from the context, καὶ δῆτ' ἐτόλμας τούσδ' ὑπερβαίνειν νόμους;—οὐ γ. τί μοι Ζεὺς ἦν ὁ κηρύξας τάδε [yes], *for* it was not Zeus, etc., S.*Ant.*450, cf. *OT*102, etc.; καλῶς γὰρ αὐτὸς ἠγάνισαι Pl. *Smp.*194a; freq. in phrase ἔστι γ. οὕτω [yes], *for* so it is, i.e. yes certainly: λέγεταί τι καινόν; γένοιτο γ. ἄν τι καινότερον ἢ..; [why,] could there be..? D.4.10; with negs., Ar.*Ra.*262 τούτῳ γ. οὐ νικήσετε [do so], *yet* shall ye never prevail by this means: for ἀλλὰ γ., v. infr. II. 1. b. to confirm or strengthen something said, οὐδ' οὐκέτ' εἰσί· τοῦτο γάρ σε δήξεται [I say this], *for* it will sting thee, E. *Med.*1370: after an Exclamation, ὦ πόποι· ἀνάριθμα γ. φέρω πήματα S.*OT*168 (lyr.), cf. E.*Hel.*857. c. in conditional propositions, where the condition is omitted, *else*, οὐ γ. ἄν με ἔπεμπον πάλιν (sc. εἰ μὴ ἐπίστευον) X.*An.*7.6.33; γίνεται γ. ἡ κοινωνία συμμαχία *for in that case*, Arist.*Pol.*1280ᵇ8. 4. in abrupt questions, *why, what*, τίς γ. σε θεῶν ἐμοὶ ἄγγελον ἧκεν; *why* who hath sent thee? Il.18.182; πῶς γ. νῦν.. εὕδουσι; 10.424; πατροκτονοῦσα γ. ξυνοικήσεις ἐμοί; *what*, wilt thou..? A.*Ch.*909: generally, after interrog. Particles, ἢ γ...; *what*, was it..? S.*OT*1000, 1039, etc.; τί γ.; *quid enim?* i.e. it must be so, Id.*OC*539, 542, 547, etc.; τί γ. δή ποτε; D.21.44; also πῶς γ.; πῶς γ. οὔ;, v. πῶς. 5. to strengthen a wish, c. opt., κακῶς γ. ἐξόλοιο O that you might perish! E.*Cyc.*261; cf. αἰ, εἰ, εἴθε, πῶς. II. joined with other Particles: 1. ἀλλὰ γ. where γάρ gives the reason of a clause to be supplied between ἀλλά and itself, as ἀλλ' ἐν γὰρ Τρώων πεδίῳ.. but [*far otherwise*], *for*.., Il.15.739; ἀλλὰ γὰρ ἤκουσ' αὐδ' ἐπὶ πράγος πικρόν but [*hush*], *for*.., A.*Th.*861; ἀλλ' οὐ γ. σ' ἐθέλω.. but [*look out*] *for*.., Il.7.242; in full, ἀλλ' οὐ γάρ σφιν ἐφαίνετο κέρδιον εἶναι μαίεσθαι προτέρω, τοὶ μὲν πάλιν αὖτις ἔβαινον Od.14.355; ἀλλ', οὐ γ. ἔπειθε, διδοῖ τὸ φᾶρος Hdt.9.109. 2. γ. ἄρα *for* indeed, Pl.*Prt.*315d, *Smp.*205b. 3. γ. δή *for* of course, *for* you know, Il.2.301, 23.607, Hdt.1.34, 114, etc.; φάμεν γ. δή *yes* certainly we say so, Pl.*Tht.*187e, cf. 164d; οὐ γ. δή S.*Ant.*46, etc. 4. γ. νυ Od.14.359. 5. γ. οὖν *for* indeed, to confirm or explain, Il.15.232, Hdt.5.34, S.*Ant.*489, 771, etc.; φησὶ γ. οὖν *yes* of course he says so, Pl.*Tht.*170a; γ. οὖν δή Id.*Prm.*148c, etc.; οὐ γ. οὖν ib.134b; cf. τοιγαροῦν. 6. γ. που *for* I suppose, esp. with negs., Id.*R.*381c, *Phd.*62d, etc.; οὐ γ. δήπου Id.*Prt.*309c. 7. γ. ῥα, = γὰρ ἄρα, Il.1.113, al. 8. γ. τε, 23.156; also τε γ. D.19.159, Arist.*Pol.*1333ᵃ2, al. 9. γ. τοι *for* surely.., E.*Hel.*93, *Supp.*564, etc.; οὐ γ. τοι Od.21.172, etc.; cf. τοιγάρτοι.

B. Position: γάρ prop. stands after the first word in a clause, but in Poets it freq. stands third or fourth, when the preceding words are closely connected, as ὁ μὲν γὰρ.. S.*Aj.*764; χὴ ναῦς γὰρ.. Id.*Ph.*527; τό τ' εἰκαθεῖν γὰρ.. Id.*Ant.*1096; τὸ μὴ θέμις γὰρ.. A.*Ch.*641, cf. 753: also in Prose, τὸ κατ' ἀξίαν γὰρ.. Arist. *EN*1163ᵇ11: sts. for metrical reasons, where there is no such connexion, as third (A.*Ag.*222, 729, S.*Ph.*219 (all lyr.)), fourth (Ar.*Av.*1545); in later Com. fifth (Men.462.2); sixth (Antiph.26. 22); seventh (Men.*Epit.*531, *Pk.*170, Athenio 1.5); once sixth in S., καιρὸς καὶ πλοῦς ὅδ' ἐπείγει γὰρ κατὰ πρύμναν *Ph.*1451. 2. inserted before the demonstr. -ί, as νυνγαρί for νυνὶ γάρ; cf. νυνί.

C. QUANTITY: γάρ is sts. long in Hom. metri gr., θήσειν γὰρ ἔτ' ἔμελλεν Il.2.39; φωνῆς γὰρ ἤκουσα *h.Cer.*57.—In Att. always short: Ar.*Eq.*366, *V.*217, *Lys.*20 are corrupt.

**γάραβος·** ὀλολυγών, Hsch.

⊛ **γᾰράριον,** τό, *jar for* γάρος, *BGU*781 iii 7 (i A.D.), etc.

**γάργα·** αἴγειρος, Hsch.

**γαργαίρω,** (γάργαρα) *swarm with*, ἀνδρῶν ἀρίστων πᾶσα γ. πόλις Cratin.290, cf. Ar.*Fr.*359; ἀργυρωμάτων ἐγάργαιρεν ἁ οἰκία Sophr.30 (ἐμάρμαιρεν codd. Ath.): c. dat., πόντος ἐγάργαιρε σώμασιν Tim.*Pers.* 107.

**γάργαλα,** = γάργαρα, Hsch.

**γαργάλη,** ἡ, = ἐρεθισμός, Erot. s.v. γαργαλισμός.

**γαργαλής,** ές, prob. f.l. for δυσγαργ-, Ael.*NA*16.9.

**γαργᾰλ-ίζω,** *tickle, titillate*, Pl.*Phlb.*47a, Epicur.*Fr.*411; αὐτὸς αὑτὸν οὐθεὶς γ. Arist.*Pr.*965$^{a}$11:—Pass., γαργαλίζεσθαι μόνον ἄνθρωπον Id.*PA*673$^{a}$6, cf. *EN*1150$^{b}$22: also, generally, *feel tickling* or *irritation*, Pl.*Phdr.*251c. 2. metaph., τὰ τὰς αἰσθήσεις γαργαλίζοντα ἡδέα Phld.*Mus.*p.33 K., cf. Ph.2.352; τὰ ὦτα γ. Aristid.*Or.*34(50). 16, cf. Luc.*Cal.*21; also of pain, ἀλγηδὼν -ουσα Plu.2.1088a:—Pass., γαργαλιζομένου τοῦ σώματος Plot.6.7.34. ⊛ **-ισμός,** ὁ, *tickling* (γέλως διὰ κινήσεως τοῦ μορίου τοῦ περὶ τὴν μασχάλην Arist.*PA*673$^{a}$8), Hp. *Alim.*26, Pl.*Smp.*189a (pl.), *Phdr.*253e, Epicur.*Fr.*412 (pl.); ἐν τῷ σώματι διέδραμε γ. Hegesipp.1.16; ἡδονὴ γαργαλισμοῦ ἐφίεται Ph.1. 118, cf. 212 (pl.), Plu.2.765c: **γάργαλος,** ὁ (more Att. acc. to Moer., cf. Ar.*Th.*133), and **γαργάλη,** ἡ, are cited by Erot. s.v. γαργαλισμός, fr. Ar.*Fr.*175 and Diph.25.

**γάργανον,** τό, v. τάργανον.

⊛ **γάργᾰρα,** τά, *heaps, lots, plenty*, ἀνδρῶν Aristomen.1; ἀνθρώπων Alc.Com.19.

**γαργᾰρεών,** ῶνος, ὁ, *uvula*, Hp.*Prog.*[23], Arist.*Resp.*474$^{a}$20; γ. ἀνεσπασμένος Hp.*Epid.*3.1.ς', cf. Gal.*UP*7.5. 2. a *morbid condition thereof*, = σταφυλή, Hp.*Aff.*4. 3. *trachea*, Arist.*HA*492$^{b}$11.

**γαργαρής·** θόρυβος, Hsch.

⊛ **γαργᾰρ-ίζω,** *gargle*, Sch.Il.8.48 (but f.l. for γαργαλ- in Gal.11. 352). **-ισμός,** ὁ, *gargling*, Alex.Trall.5.4. **-ιστέον,** *one must gargle*, Orib.*Fr.*19.

**γαργάρται·** λίθοι αὐτοφυεῖς, Hsch. **γάργασις·** γαργάλη ὑποσταθμοῦ, Id.

**γᾰρέλαιον,** τό, *paste made of* γάρος *and oil*, Gal.6.716.

**γᾰρηρόν,** τό, *pot of* γάρος, *POxy.*1299.8 (iv A.D.), etc.

**γαρῖνος,** ὁ, an unknown *fish*, Marcell.Sid.37.

**γάριον** [ᾰ], τό, Dim. of γάρος, Arr.*Epict.*2.20.29, *POxy.*1759.9 (ii A.D.).

**γᾰρίσκος,** ὁ, an unknown *fish*, Marcell.Sid.33.

**γᾰρῑτικός,** ή, όν, *made to hold* γάρος, βῖκος *PSI*5.535.36 (iii B.C.).

**γάρκα,** ἡ, *rod* (Maced.), Hsch.

**γάρκον,** τό, *axle-pin*, *EM*221.45: **γάρνον,** Poll.1.145, Hsch.

⊛ **γᾰροπώλης,** ὁ, *seller of* γάρος, *PBaden* 42.9 (ii A.D.), *Gloss.*

⊛ **γάρος** [ᾰ], ὁ, a kind of *sauce* or *paste, made of brine and small fish*, τὸν ἰχθύων γ. A.*Fr.*211; ταριχηρὸς γ. S.*Fr.*606, cf. Cratin.280, Pherecr.173, Pl.Com.198, Alciphr.1.18; of the *fish* itself, Ruf. *Podagr.*10 (Lat. version):—also **γάρον,** τό, Str.3.4.6, and **γάρος,** ους, τό, *POxy.*937.27 (iii A.D.).

**γᾱρότας,** α, ὁ, (γῆ, ἀρόω) Sicilian for a *bullock*, Athanis 1, = Dionys. Trag.12.

**γάρρα·** ῥάβδος, Hsch. **γάρρης·** ἄρρης (i.e. ϝάρρης, = ἄρρην), Id. **γαρρίαι·** γάμοι, Id. **γαρριώμεθα·** λοιδορούμεθα, Id. **γάρσανα·** φρύγανα (Cret.), Id. **γάσος,** ὁ, *cheat, rogue*, Id.

**γάσσα,** ἡ, acc. to Hsch., = ἡδονή. (Perh. akin to γηθέω.)

**γαστερο-πλήξ,** πλῆγος, ὁ, *glutton*, Eust.1837.39. **-χειρ,** χειρος, ὁ, ἡ, = γαστρόχειρ (q.v.), Str.8.6.11.

⊛ **γαστήρ,** ἡ, gen. έρος, γαστρός: dat. -έρι, γαστρί (the longer forms in Ep., Lyr., and once in Trag., E.*Cyc.*220): dat. pl. γαστῆρσι Hp. *Morb.*4.54, γαστράσι D.C.54.22:—*paunch, belly*, Il.13.372, etc.; γ. ἀσπίδος *the hollow* of a shield, Tyrt.11.24; *belly* or *wide part* of a bottle, Cratin.190. 2. *the belly*, as craving food, κέλεται δέ ἑ γ. Od.6. 133; βόσκειν ἣν γαστέρ' 17.228; γαστέρι δ' οὔ πως ἔστι νέκυν πενθῆσαι, i.e. by fasting, Il.19.225; ἐν γαστρὸς ἀνάγκαις A.*Ag.*726 (lyr.); to express *gluttony*, γαστέρες οἶον Hes.*Th.*26; γ. ἀργαί Epimenid.1; ἐγκράτεια γαστρὸς καὶ ποτοῦ X.*Cyr.*1.2.8, cf. *Oec.*9.11; γαστρὸς ἐγκρατής master of *his belly*, Id.*Mem.*1.2.1; opp. γαστρὸς ἥττων, ib.1.5. 1; γαστρὶ δουλεύειν, χαρίζεσθαι, to be the slave of *his belly*, ib.1.6.8, 2. 1.2; γ. δελεάζεσθαι ib.2.1.4; τῇ γ. μετρεῖν τὴν εὐδαιμονίαν D.18.296; τᾶς γαστρὸς φείδεσθαι, com. of one who has nothing to eat, Theoc. 21.41. 3. *paunch stuffed with mincemeat, sausage, haggis*, Od.18.44, 118, 20.25, Ar.*Nu.*409. II. *womb*, ὅντινα γαστέρι μήτηρ.. φέροι Il.6.58; ἐκ γαστρός from *the womb*, from *infancy*, Thgn.305; ἐν γαστρὶ ἔχουσα big with child, Hdt.3.32; ὗν ἔχουσαν ἐν γ. *PFlor.*130.3 (iii A.D.); ἐν γ. φέρουσα Pl.*Lg.*792e; ἐν γ. λαβεῖν *conceive*, Arist.*HA* 632$^{a}$28, *AP*11.18 (Nicarch.), Lxx *Ge.*30.41, al.; συλλαμβάνειν v.l. ib.*Ge.*25.21, cf. *Ev.Luc.*1.31; ἐς γ. βάλλεσθαι Hdt.3.28; κατὰ γαστρὸς ἔχειν Vett.Val.193.33; φέρειν *Gp.*16.1.3; also γυνὴ ἑπτὰ ἤδη γαστέρας δυστοκοῦσα Philostr.*VA*3.39. (Perh. for γραστήρ, cf. γράω.)

⊛ **γάστρα,** Ion. **-τρη,** ἡ, *the lower part* of a vessel *bulging out like a paunch*, τρίποδος Il.18.348, Callix.2, Hero *Spir.*2.16; *hull* of a ship, Sch.Th.1.50. II. a *vase with such a belly*, Aen.Tact.4.2 (prob. l.), *PSI*4.420.25 (iii B.C.), *IG*12(3).174.26 (Astypalaea), J.*BJ* 2.14.5, Dsc.5.89, *Gp.*14.8.2, etc. III. *architectural member* of similar shape, *Milet.*7.59, *BCH*29.460 (Delos). IV. = γαστήρ I, dub. in Eratosth.18. V. *back of the thigh*, Hsch. (pl.). VI. = γογγυλὶς ἢ κράμβη, Id.

**γαστραία,** ἡ, a kind of *turnip*, Lacon. word, Hsch.; restored in Ath.9.369a for γαστέρας or γαστέας.

⊛ **γαστρᾰφέτης,** ου, ὁ, *stomach-bow*, Hero *Bel.*81.2.

**γαστρήσιος,** = *castrensis*, *Edict.Diocl.*3.8 (Aegina).

**γαστρίαν·** στρόφον ἢ διάνοιαν, Hsch.

**γαστρίδιον,** τό, Dim. of γαστήρ, γαστρίον, Ar.*Nu.*392.

**γαστρίδουλος** [ῐ], ὁ, *a slave to one's belly*, D.S.8.18.

**γαστρίζω,** (γάστρις) *punch* a man *in the belly*, Ar.*Eq.*273 (Pass.), 454, *V.*1529. II. *stuff, gorge*, τὸν παιδαγωγόν D.Chr.66.11, cf. Luc. *DMeretr.*10.4 (Phryn.76 is incorrect):—Pass., *to be stuffed full, eat gluttonously*, Theopomp.Hist.187, Men.*Pk.*98, Posidon.18, Luc.*Rh. Pr.*24, Alciphr.3.45; ἱκανῶς γεγαστρίσμεθα Ath.3.96f. III. γαστρίζων σφυγμός, term invented by Archig., Gal.8.665.

**γαστρῐ-μαργέω,** *to be gluttonous*, Ph.2.22. **-μαργία,** ἡ, *gluttony*, Hp.*Int.*6, Pl.*Phd.*81e (pl.), Eus.Mynd.9, Andronic.Rhod.p.572 M.; pl., Luc.*Am.*42. ⊛ **-μαργος,** ον, *gluttonous* (cf. λαίμαργος), Pi.*O.* 1.52, Arist.*EN*1118$^{b}$19, Xanth.12, Cerc.16.2, Nic.Dam.p.22 D., etc.: Sup. -ότατα, θηρία Ph.2.22.

⊛ **γαστρίον,** τό, Dim. of γαστήρ, *paunch*, *SIG*1002.9 (Milet., v/iv B.C.); *sausage*, Archestr.*Fr.*47, *Com.Adesp.*394, *Milet.*6.21 (v B.C.). 2. *cake*, made with σήσαμον (Cret.), *EM*221.45. 3. Dim. of γάστρα II, Herm. *in Phdr.*p.202 A.

**γάστρις,** ιδος or εως, ὁ, ἡ, *pot-bellied*, πίθος Ael.*NA*14.26: as Subst., = γάστρα, *IG*11(2).154*A*69 (Delos, iii B.C.). 2. as Subst., *glutton*, Ar.*Av.*1604, *Th.*816, Jul.*Or.*5.176c: Comp. γαστρίστερος *more of a glutton*, Pl.Com.195: as Adj., γάστρις ἡδονή Ph.1.261. 3. *affected with tapeworm*, Hsch. II. *cake*, made in Crete, Chrysipp. Tyan.ap.Ath.14.647f.

**γαστρισμός,** ὁ, *gluttonous eating*, Sophil.6.

**γαστρο-βᾰρής,** ές, *heavy with child*, *AP*5.53 (Diosc.). **-βόρος,** ον, = γαστρίμαργος, Poll.2.168, 175. **-ειδής,** ές, *paunchlike, round*, ναῦς Plu.*Per.*26: in Eust.1684.28 **-οίδης** (leg. γαστροίδης).

**γαστροιΐς,** ίδος, ἡ, = foreg., Pherecr.143.5 (pl.).

**γαστρο-κνήμη,** *calf of the leg*, Gal.14.708, v.l. in Hp.*Off.*9:—also **-κνημία,** Ion. **-ίη,** ἡ, Hp.*Art.*60, Arist.*HA*494$^{a}$7, *BGU*183.3 (i A.D.), Luc.*VH*1.22, Gal.2.316; and ⊛ **-κνήμιον,** τό, Poll.2.190, *PFay.*90.8 (iii A.D.). **-λογία,** ἡ, the Greek *Almanach des Gourmands*, written by Archestratus, Ath.3.104b, 7.278b; also cited by the title of ἡ γαστρονομία, Id.1.4e, 2.56c. **-μαντεύομαι,** *divine by the belly*, Alciphr.2.4, 15. **-νομία,** v. γαστρολογία. **-πίων** [ῑ], ονος, ὁ, ἡ, *a pot-bellied person*, D.C.65.20.

⊛ **γαστρ-όπτης,** ου, ὁ, *vessel for cooking sausages*, *Demioprat.*ap. Poll.10.105:—fem. **-οπτίς** *IG*11(2).161*B*128 (Delos, iii B.C.), but **γαστροποτίς** ib.199*B*79.

**γαστρο-ρρᾰφία,** ἡ, (ῥάπτω) *sewing up of a belly-wound*, Scrib. Larg.206, Gal.10.416, Antyll.ap.Orib.44.23.46. **-ρροια,** ἡ, *diarrhoea*, Lyd.*Ost.*33, Steph. *in Hp.*1.87 D. **-τόμος,** ον, *opening bellies*, for embalming, Man.4.267. **-φορέω,** *bear in the belly*, of a bottle, *AP*9.232 (Phil.). **-φόρος,** ὁ, *bearer of* γάστρα II, *PLond.*1821. **-χάρυβδις** [χᾰ], ιος, ὁ, ἡ, *with a gulf of a belly*, Cratin.397. **-χειρ,** χειρος, ὁ, ἡ, *living by one's hands*, written γαστερόχειρ in Str.8.6.11, *EM*221; cf. χειρογάστωρ, ἐγχειρογάστωρ.

**γαστρώδης,** ες, = γαστροειδής, *pot-bellied*, Ar.*Pl.*560: generally, *convex, bulging*, Hp.*Medic.*7, Gal.19.120.

**γάστρων,** ωνος, ὁ, = γάστρις, *pot-belly*, Alc.37 B, Ar.*Ra.*200, Ph. 1.686.

**γατειλαί** (γατάλαι cod.)· οὐλαί, Hsch.; cf. ὠτειλή.

⊛ **γᾱτόμος,** ον, Dor. for γή-τομος, *cleaving the ground*, δίκελλα A.*Fr.* 196, cf. *AP*6.95 (Antiphil.), Hsch. s.v. τμήγας.

**γαυλικός,** ή, όν, *of* or *for a* γαῦλος II, χρήματα γ. *its* cargo, X.*An.*5. 8.1 (v.l. γαυλιτικά).

**γαυλίς,** ίδος, ἡ, = sq., Opp.*C.*1.126.

⊛ **γαυλός,** ὁ, *milk-pail*, Od.9.223, *AP*6.35 (Leon.); *water-bucket*, Hdt.6.119; *machine for raising water*, *IG*11.146*A*29 (Delos): generally, *any round vessel, beehive*, *AP*9.404 (Antiphil.); *drinking-bowl*, Antiph.224.5, Theoc.5.104, Longus 3.4. 2. = ὁ ἐξ ἀλλοτρίων ζῶν, Hsch., Cyr.; also, = εὐεξαπάτητος, Id. II. **γαῦλος** (on the accent cf. Hdn.Gr.1.156, Eust.1625.3), ὁ, *round-built Phoenician merchant vessel*, opp. μακρὰ ναῦς, γαύλοισιν ἐν Φοινικικοῖς Epich.54, cf. Hdt.3.136, 137, Ar.*Av.*602, Call.*Sos.*9.7, etc.

**γαυνάκη,** ἡ (in Lat. form *gaunaca*), and **γαυνάκης,** ὁ, *PSI*4.340. 22 (iii B.C.); = καυνάκης, *Gloss.*:—Dim. **γαυνάκιον** *PAmh.*2.144.22 (v A.D.).

**γαύρηξ,** ηκος, ὁ, (γαῦρος) *a braggart*, Alc.37 B, cf. Hsch. s.v.

**γαυρ-ίᾱμα,** ατος, τό, *arrogance, exultation*, Lxx *Ju.*10.8, Phld. *Mort.*18, Plu.*Aem.*27, etc. ⊛ **-ιάω,** mostly pres. Act. and Med., aor. 1 ἐγαυρίασα Lxx *Ju.*9.7:—*bear* oneself *proudly, prance*, prop. of horses, γαυριῶντες Plu.*Lyc.*22:—Med., φυσῶντα καὶ γαυριώμενον X.*Eq.*10.16; *to be splendid*, γαυριῶσαι.. τράπεζαι Cratin.301; *to be luxuriant*, ἡ γῆ θάλλει καὶ γ. Jul.*Or.*4.155c; of persons, Phld.*Vit.* p.27 J., Ph.1.152, al.: c. dat., *pride oneself on* a thing, εἰ ταύτῃ [τῇ ἥττῃ] γαυριᾷς D.18.244; so ἐπί σφισι γαυριόωντες (Meineke -όωντο) Theoc.25.133, cf. Plu.*Lyc.*30, Palaeph.1.8, Anon.*Oxy.*220 iii 3.

⊛ **γαῦρ-ος,** ον, *exulting in*, βοστρύχοισι Archil.58; ὄλβῳ E.*Supp.* 862: abs., *haughty, disdainful*, Id.*Fr.*788, Ar.*Ra.*282; γ. καὶ μετέωρος Luc.*Nigr.*5, cf. Jul.*Caes.*319d; in good sense, *splendid*, D.Chr. 67.5 (Comp.), D.C.68.31; epith. of ἔφηβοι, *IG*7.544,545 (Tanagra); also, *skittish*, μόσχω γαυροτέρα Theoc.11.21: τὸ γ., = γαυρότης, τὸ γ. ἐν φρεσὶν κεκτημένοι E.*Supp.*217; τὰ γαῦρα Babr.43.6. Adv. Sup. γαυρότατα, εἰπεῖν Max.Tyr.7.7. (Cf. γαίω.) **-ότης**, ητος, ἡ, *exultation*, Plu.*Marc.*6; of a horse or ass, Id.*Pel.*22, *Mar.*38. ※ **-όω**, *make proud*, only aor. ἐγαύρωσα Plu.*Cor.*15, D.C.55.6 (unless γαυρῶν 'overriding' (of χρόνος) is to be read in E.*Fr.*52.8): elsewh. Pass.

**γαυρόομαι**, = γαυριάω, *exult*, στῆ δὲ παρὰ λίμνην γαυρούμενος Batr. 262a; λέων γαυρούμενος Ph.2.125: c. dat., *pride oneself on*, μὴ γαυροῦ σοφίῃ Ps.-Phoc.53; πλούτῳ γαυρωθεὶς *PFlor.*367.11 (iii A.D.); ξανθοῖς βοστρύχοις γαυρούμενος E.*Or.*1532, cf. *Ba.*1144; ἐπὶ τῷ ἔργῳ γαυροῦνται X.*Hier.*2.15: impf. ἐγαυρούμην Babr.43.15, D.C.53.27: fut. -ωθήσομαι Lxx *Nu.*23.24 (v.l. γαυρι-): aor. ἐγαυρώθην *PFlor.*367.11 (iii A.D.), D.C.48.20: pf. γεγαύρωμαι Lxx *Wi.*6.2. **-ωμα**, ατος, τό, *subject for boasting*, E.*Tr.*1250, Aristid.*Or.*28(49).124.

**γαυσάδας**· ψευδής, Hsch. **γαυσαλίτης**, an Indian *bird*, Id.

**γαύσᾰπος**, ὁ, = Lat. *gausăpa*, Str.5.1.12: **γαυσάπης**, Varr.ap. Prisc.*Inst.*7.56.

**γαυσόομαι**, *to be bent*, pf. Pass. γεγαύσωται Sor.*Fract.*19:—Act., γαυσῶσαι, Hsch.

**γαυσός**, ἡ, όν, or **γαῦσος**, η, ον (accent uncertain, Gal.18(2).518; codd. of Hp. have γαῦσος but γαυσοί), *crooked, bent outwards*, μηρός Hp.*Fract.*20, *Art.*77.

**γᾱφάγας**, α, ὁ, Dor. word (Syrac., *EM*221.49), *earthworm*, Hsch., *AB*230.

**γάφυτον**· γηγενές, Hsch.

**γδοῦπος, γδουπέω**, poet. forms for δοῦπος, δουπέω (esp. in compds., e.g. ἐρίγδουπος, ἐριγδουπέω), ἐπὶ δ' ἐγδούπησαν Il.11.45.

**γε**, Dor. and Boeot. **γα**, enclitic Particle, giving emphasis to the word or words which it follows.

I. with single words, *at least, at any rate*, but often only to be rendered by italics in writing, or emphasis in pronunciation: τὸ γὰρ.. σιδήρου γε κράτος ἐστὶν such is the power of *iron*, Od.9.393; εἴ που πτωχῶν γε θεοὶ.. εἰσὶν if the poor *have* any gods to care for them, 17.475; μάλιστά γε 4.366; ὅ γ' ἐνθάδε λεώς *at any rate* the people here, S.*OC*42, etc.: with negs., οὐ δύο γε not *even* two, Il.5. 303, 20.286; οὔκουν φθόγγος γε not *the least* sound, E.*IA*9. 2. with Pronouns: with Pron. of 1st Pers. so closely joined, that the accent is changed, in ἔγωγε, ἔμοιγε (also ἔγωγα Lacon., but ἐγώνγα, ἰώνγα Boeot.): in Hom. freq. with Art. used as Pron., v. ὅ γε: with demonstr. Pronouns, κεῖνός γε, τοῦτό γε, etc.: in Com. coalescing with -ί final, αὐτηγί Ar.*Ach.*784; τουτογί, ταυταγί, etc., Id.*V.*781, *Pax*1057, etc. (but ἐνγεταυθί *Th.*646): after possess. Pronouns, ἐμόν γε θυμόν Il.20.425, etc.: freq. after relat. Pronouns, ὅς γε, οἵ γε, etc., οἵ γέ σου καθύβρισαν S.*Ph.*1364; ὅς γ' ἐξέλυσας δασμόν Id. *OT*35, etc.; ὅσον γε χρῄζεις *even* as much as.., ib.365; οἷόν γέ μοι φαίνεται Pl.*R.*329a: rarely with interrog. Pronouns, τίνα γε.. εἶπας; E.*Tr.*241; ποίου γε τούτου πλὴν γ' Ὀδυσσέως ἐρεῖς; S.*Ph.*441. 3. after Conjunctions, to emphasize the modification or condition introduced by the subjoined clause, πρίν γε, before *at least*, sts. repeated, οὐ μὲν.. οἴω πρίν γ' ἀποπαύσεσθαι, πρίν γε.. αἵματος ἆσαι Ἄρηα Il.5.288, cf. Od.2.127; πρὶν ἄν γε or πρίν γ' ἄν, Ar.*Eq.*961, *Ra.*78, etc.; ὅτε γε Pl.*Phd.*84e; ὁπότε γε S.*OC*1699; ἐπεί γε X.*An.*1.3.9; ἐπειδή γε Th.6.18; ὅπου γε X.*Cyr.*2.3.11; εἴ γε, ἐάν γε, if *that is to say*, if *really*, Th.6.18, Pl.*Phdr.*251c; also simply to lay stress on the condition, κἂν γε μὴ λέγω and *if* I do not.., Ar.*Ach.*317; εἴπερ γε if *at any rate*, Hdt.7.16.γ', 143, etc.; ὥστε γε (v.l. ὥς γε), with inf., so far *at least* as to.., Pl.*Phdr.*230b; ὥς γ' ἐμοὶ χρῆσθαι κριτῇ E.*Alc.*801; ὥς γε or ὥσπερ γε as *at least*, S.*Ant.*570, *OT*715, etc.:—γε may follow τε, when τε is closely attached to the preceding word, ὡς οἷόν τέ γε μάλιστα X.*Mem.*4.5.2, Pl.*R.*412b; ἐάντε γε Id.*Plt.*293d; οἵ τέ γε Id.*Grg.* 454e:—for its use in opposed or disjunctive clauses, v. infr. II. 3. 4. after other Particles, καὶ μὴν.. γε, οὐ μὴν.. γε, with words intervening, X.*Mem.*1.4.12, E.*Alc.*518, etc.; after ἄν in apodosi, when preceded by οὐ or καί, Id.*Ph.*1215, *Or.*784; ἄταρ.. γε but *yet*, Ar.*Ach.* 448; καίτοι γε, v. καίτοι; ἀλλά γε (without intervening words) is f.l. in Pl.*Hp.Ma.*287b (leg. ἀλλ' ἄγε), *R.*331b (ἀλλά γε ἓν codd., ἀλλὰ ἕν γε Stob.); ἀλλά γε δή dub. in Id.*Phdr.*262a; later, Plu.2.394c, Ael.*NA*10.49 codd.: but, 5. when preceding other Particles, γε commonly refers to the preceding word, while the Particle retains its own force: but sts. modifies the sense of the following Particle, γε μὴν *nevertheless*, πάντως γε μὴν Ar.*Eq.*232, cf. E.*El.*754, X., etc.; Ep. and Ion. γε μέν Il.2.703, Od.4.195, Hdt.7.152; γε μὲν δή A.*Ag.* 661, S.*Tr.*484; γε μέντοι Pl.*Tht.*164a, X.*An.*2.3.9, etc.: γε δή freq. strengthens an assertion, A.*Pr.*42, Th.2.62, etc.; οἰόμεθά γε δή Pl.*Euthd.*275a (cf. also II. 1); γέ τοι, implying that the assertion is *the least* that one can say, Ar.*V.*934, *Pl.*424,1041, etc.; γέ τοι Pl. *Grg.*447b; γέ τοι δή S.*OT*1171, Pl.*Phdr.*264b; γέ τοί που Id.*Lg.* 888e; γε δήπου Id.*Phd.*94a, etc.; γέ που *at all events, any how*, Ar. *Ach.*896, Pl.*R.*607d, 478a, etc.; for γε οὖν, v. γοῦν. II. exercising an influence over the whole clause: 1. epexegetic, *namely, that is*, Διός γε διδόντος *that is* if God grant it, Od.1.390; κλῦθι, Ποσείδαον.., εἰ ἐτεόν γε σός εἰμι if *indeed* I am really thine, 9.529: hence to limit, strengthen or amplify a general assertion, ἀνὴρ.. ὅστις πινυτός γε any man—*at least* any wise man, 1.229; freq. preceded by καί, usu. with words intervening, ἦ μὴν κελεύσω κἀπιθωΰξω γε πρὸς *ay and* besides that.., A.*Pr.*73; παρῆσάν τινες καὶ πολλοί γε some, *ay and* a great many, Pl.*Phd.*58d; καὶ γελοίως γε Id.*R.*531a; freq. with the last term in an enumeration, ταύτῃ ἄρα.. πρακτέον καὶ γυμναστέον καὶ ἐδεστέον γε καὶ ποτέον Id.*Cri.* 47b; ὄψεις τε καὶ ἀκοαὶ καὶ.. καὶ ἡδοναί γε δή Id.*Tht.*156b; repeated, συνήγαγόν μοι καί γε ἀργύριον καί γε χρυσίον Lxx *Ec.*2.8; rarely without intervening words, καί γε ὁ θάνατος διὰ τὴν μοίρην ἔλαχεν Hp.*Septim.*9, cf. Lys.11.7 codd.; καί γε.. ἐκχεῶ *Act.Ap.*2.18: hence, 2. in dialogue, in answers where something is added to the statement of the previous speaker, as ἔπεμψέ τίς σοι.. κρέα; Answ. καλῶς γε ποιῶν *yes and* quite right too, Ar.*Ach.*1049; κενὸν τόδ' ἄγγος, ἢ στέγει τι; Answ. σά γ' ἔνδυτα.. *yes indeed*, your clothes, E.*Ion*1412; οὕτω γὰρ ἂν μάλιστα δηχθείη πόσις. Answ. σὺ δ' ἂν γένοιο γ' ἀθλιωτάτη γυνή *yes truly*, and you.., Id.*Med.*817, cf. S.*OT* 680, etc.; πάνυ γε *yes* certainly, Pl.*Euthphr.*8e, etc.; οὕτω γέ πως *yes* somehow so, Id.*Tht.*165c; sts. preceded by καί, καὶ οὐδέν γ' ἄτοπον *yes* and no wonder, ib.142b, cf. d, 147e; sts. ironically, εὖ γε κηδεύεις πόλιν E.*IT*1212. 3. to heighten a contrast or opposition, a. after conditional clauses, εἰ μὲν δὴ σύ γ'.., τῷ κε Ποσειδάων γε.. if *you* do so, then *at all events* Poseidon will.., Il.15.49 sq.; ἐπεὶ πρὸς τοῦτο σιωπᾶν ἥδιόν σοι.. τόδε γε εἰπέ *at any rate* tell me this, X.*Cyr.* 5.5.20; εἰ μὴ τὸ ὅλον, μέρος γ' ἐπιβάλλει D.18.272:—sts. in the protasis, εἰ γὰρ μὴ ἑκόντες γε.. ἀλλ' ἀέκοντας.. Hdt.4.120. b. in disjunctive sentences to emphasize an alternative, ἤτοι κεῖνόν γε.. δεῖ ἀπόλλυσθαι ἢ σέ.. Id.1.11; ἤτοι κρινόμεν γε ἢ ἐνθυμούμεθα ὀρθῶς τὰ πράγματα Th.2.40; πατὴρ δ' ἐμός.. ζώει ὅ γ' ἢ τέθνηκε Od.2.131, cf. Il.10.504: also in the second clause, εἰπέ μοι, ἠὲ ἑκὼν ὑποδάμνασαι ἦ σέ γε λαοὶ ἐχθαίρουσι Od.3.214, cf. Hdt.7.10.θ', S.*OT*1098 sq. 4. in exclamations, etc., ὥς γε μή ποτ' ὤφελον λαβεῖν dub. in E.*IA*70, cf. S.*OC*977, *Ph.*1003, Ar.*Ach.*93,836, etc.; in oaths, οὔτοι μὰ τὴν Δήμητρά γ' v.l. in Ar.*Eq.*698; μὰ τὸν Ποσειδῶ γ' οὐδέποτ' Id.*Ec.*748; καὶ ναὶ μὰ Δία γε X.*Ap.*20; καὶ νὴ Δία γε Ar.*Eq.*1350, D.Chr.17.4, Luc. *Merc.Cond.*28, Lib.*Or.*11.59, etc.: with words intervening, καὶ νὴ Δί', ὦ ἄνδρες Ἀθηναῖοι, ἕτεροί γε.. D.13.16; νὴ Δία, ὦ Ἀθηναῖοι, ἄρα γε ὑμῖν X.*HG*7.1.37; merely in strong assertions, τίς ἂν φιλέοντι μάχοιτο; ἄφρων δὴ κεῖνός γέ.. Od.8.209, etc. 5. implying concession, εἶμί γε *well then* I will go (in apodosi), E.*HF*861; δρᾶ γ' εἴ τι δράσεις Id.*IA*817, cf. *Andr.*239. III. γε freq. repeated in protasis and apodosis, as πρίν γε.., πρίν γε, v. supr. I. 3; εἰ μή γε.. τινὶ μείζονι, τῇ γε παρούσῃ ἀτιμίᾳ Lys.31.29; even in the same clause, οὐδέν γ' ἄλλο πλὴν γε καρκίνους Ar.*V.*1507, cf. Hdt.1.187, E.*Ph.*554, Pl.*R.*335b, *Grg.*502a. IV. Position: γε normally follows the word which it limits; but is freq. placed immediately after the Article, as ὅ γε πόλεμος Th.1.66, etc.; or the Prep., κατά γε τὸν σὸν λόγον X.*Cyr.*3.1.15; ἔν γε ταῖς Θήβαις S.*OT*1380; or δέ, νῦν δέ γε Pl.*Tht.*144e; τὸ δέ γε ib.164b; δοῖμεν δέ γέ που ἂν Id.*R.*607d, cf. *Phd.*94a, etc.; freq. in retorts, ἀμές ποκ' ἦμες ἄλκιμοι νεανίαι. Answ. ἀμὲς δέ γ' εἰμές *Carm.Pop.*18; οὐκ οἶδ' ὅτι λέγεις. Answ. ἡ γραῦς δέ γε οἶδ', ὡς ἐγᾦμαι Men.*Epit.*577, cf. A.*Th.*1031, etc.

**γέα**, v. γῆ. **γέαρ**· ἔαρ, Hsch. (γ = ϝ). **γέβους**· ζυγά, Id. **γέβουτον**· ψόφον, Id. **γεγάᾱτε, γεγάᾱσι**, v. γίγνομαι. **γεγάθει**, v. sub γηθέω.

**γεγάκειν** [ᾱ], Dor. for γεγακέναι, = γεγονέναι, Pi.*O.*6.49.

**γεγάλημαι**· γεγαλήνισμαι, διακέχυται, Hsch. **γεγάμεν, γεγαώς**, v. γίγνομαι. **γέγγει**· βρέχει, Id. (leg. τέγγει).

※ **γέγειος**, ον, *earth-born*, ἄνθεα Call.*Fr.*252b: hence, *ancient*, Hecat. 362 J.; λόγος Call.*Fr.*252: Comp. -ότερον ib.103.

**γεγηθότως**, Adv. pf. of γηθέω, *with joy*, Hld.7.5, Ph.2.295.

**γέγλανται**· κεκοίλανται, Hsch.; cf. γλάφω. **γεγλύπωνται**· ἀντεγκλείονται, Id. **γεγριφώς**· ὁ ταῖς χερσὶν ἀλοῶν, Id.

**γεγυμνωμένως**, *defencelessly*, J.*Ap.*1.22. **γεγυναικωμένα**· πέμματά τινα, Hsch.

※ **γέγων-α**, Ep. pf. with pres. and past signf., used by Hom. in 3 sg. γέγωνε and part. γεγωνώς Il.11.275, al.: 3 sg. plpf. (with impf. signf.) ἐγεγώνειν 22.34, 23.425, Od.21.368: later, imper. γέγωνε A.*Pr.*195, S.*Ph.*238, E.*Or.*1220; subj. γεγώνω S.*OC*213; part. γεγωνώς Arist.*Pr.*904$^b$35, cf. γεγωνός:—from pres. *γεγώνω Hom. has inf. γεγωνέμεν Il.8.223, 11.6, 3 sg. impf. ἐγέγωνεν (v.l. γέγωνεν) 14.469:—from pres. *γεγωνέω come inf. γεγωνεῖν 12.337, Pi.*P.*9.3, A.*Pr.*523, Pl.*Hp.Ma.*292d: impf. ἐγεγώνευν Od.17.161, γεγώνευν 9.47: after Hom., 3 sg. γεγωνεῖ Arist.*deAn.*420$^a$1, *Pr.* 917$^b$21: impf. -είτω X.*Cyn.*6.24; part. γεγωνέοντες *Michel*1383*B* (Chios): fut. γεγωνήσω E.*Ion*696 (lyr.): aor. inf. γεγωνῆσαι A.*Pr.*990, part. -ήσας D.C.68.3; cf. γεγωνητέον, γεγωνίσκω:—*shout so as to make oneself heard*, κώκυσεν.. γέγωνέ τε πᾶν κατὰ ἄστυ Il.24.703; ἐβόησε, γέγωνέ τε πᾶσι θεοῖσι Od.8.305: in pres. sense, ὅσσον τε γέγωνε βοήσας as far as [a man] *can make himself heard* by shouting, Od.6.294 (also in past sense, 5.400, al.); οὔ πώς οἱ ἔην βώσαντι γεγωνεῖν Il.12. 337; ἀδηνέως γεγωνέοντες *Michel* l.c.; *make one's voice carry*, πολλῷ πλέον γεγωνεῖν (Cobet for ἢ ἀγνοεῖν) ἔστι νύκτωρ ἢ μεθ' ἡμέραν Antipho 5.44; πορρωτέρω ὁ αὐτὸς τῇ αὐτῇ φωνῇ γεγωνεῖ μετ' ἄλλων ᾄδων καὶ βοῶν ἢ μόνος Arist.*Pr.*917$^b$21: c. dat. pers., *cry out to*, ἐγεγώνει.. Πουλυδάμαντι Il.14.469, etc.; θεοῖσι μετ' ἀθανάτοισι γεγώνευν Od.12.370; *make oneself heard by* a person, οὐδὲν σοι μᾶλλον γεγωνεῖν δύναμαι ἢ εἴ μοι παρεκάθησο λίθος Pl.*Hp.Ma.*292d. b. *speak articulately*, opp. to mere sound, ὁ ἀὴρ οὐ γεγωνεῖ Arist. *de An.*420$^a$1; οὐ δύνανται γεγωνεῖν.. ἀλλὰ μόνον φωνοῦσιν Id.*Aud.*804$^b$24. 2. c. acc. pers., *sing, celebrate*, Pi.*P.*9.3. 3. c. acc. rei, *tell out, proclaim*, A.*Pr.* 523, al.; τινί τι ib.195,784, S.*Ph.*238; τινί τι ἐς οὖς γ. E.*Ion*696; τὰ γεγωνᾱμένα the *proclamation*, *IG*5(1).1111.12 (Geronthrae); also οὐκ ἔχω.. γεγωνεῖν ὅπα I cannot *tell* where [it is], E.*Hipp.*586 codd.—For part. γεγωνώς as Adj., v. γεγωνός 2. **-αί**· ὁμιλίαι, Hsch. **-ησις**, εως, ἡ, *loud talking, hallooing*, Plu.2.722f (pl.). **-ητέον**, *one must proclaim*, Pi.O.2.6. **-ίσκω**, lengthd. pres. for γέγωνα, *cry aloud, shout*, ὡς ἐπὶ πλεῖστον Th.7.76: impf. ἐγεγώνισκον D.C.56.14. 2. c. acc. rei, *tell out, proclaim*, A.Pr. 627, E.El.809.

**γεγωνοκώμη**, ἡ, *filling the village with clamour*, Com.Adesp.1354.

**γεγωνός**, όν, Adj. (from part. γεγωνώς, as ἀραρός, όν, from ἀραρώς) *loud-sounding, sonorous*, πέμπει γεγωνὰ..ἔπη A.Th.443; ὄντα δ' ἄφωνα βοὴν ἵστησι γεγωνόν Antiph.196.2; *loud of voice*, ἀνήρ AP7. 428.15 (Mel.): in later Prose, φωνή D.H.8.56, Ph.1.348, Corn.ND 16; λόγος Ph.1.95, al.; οὐ λόγῳ γ. ἀλλὰ τῇ ψυχῇ ἐκτείνασιν ἑαυτοὺς εἰς εὐχήν Plot.5.1.6: Comp. γεγωνότερος, κύκνων AP9.92 (Antip. Thess.), cf. D.H.5.24, Hld.10.32; γ. φθέγγεσθαι Ath.14.622e, etc. 2. γεγωνός as neut., γ. μέλος Ael.VH2.44; γεγωνὸς ἀναβοᾶν Luc.Gall.1; φθέγγεσθαι Philostr.VA5.9, cf. Her.2.2; τὸ γ. τῆς ὀγκήσεως Corn.ND21: also masc. and fem. as Adj., γεγωνότος λόγου Ph.1.133; πλήξεις γεγωνυίας *resounding* blows, ib.123. 3. Adv. Comp. γεγωνότερον ἐκβοήσας J.AJ4.3.2, cf. Porph.Chr.23.

**γεγώς**, ῶσα, ώς, v. γίγνομαι.

**γέεννα**, ης, ἡ, Hebr. *gê-hinnôm*, the *valley of Hinnom*, which represented *the place of future punishment*, Ev.Matt.5.22, al.

✱ **γέη**, ἡ, = γῆ, Orac.ap.Eus.PE4.9: **γέηθεν**, *from the earth*, Orac.ib. 5.9.

**γεη-πόνος, -πονικός, -πονία**, ἡ, v. γεωπ-.

**γεήοχος**, ὁ, = γαιήοχος, v.l. in Hes.Th.15.

**γεηρός**, όν, (γέα) *of earth, earthy*, Arist.GA743$^{a}$12, etc.; γ. καὶ πετρώδη Pl.R.612a, cf. Hp.Aër.7; τὸ γ., opp. τὸ οὐράνιον, Them.Or. 32.359a.

**γειαρότης**, ου, ὁ, *plougher of earth*, AP9.23 (Antip.), APl.4.94 (Arch.), etc.; of oxen, Epigr.Gr.793 (Phrygia, ii A.D.).

**γειδάριον**, τό, = γαϊδάριον, BGU377.

**γεῖθρον**· ἔνδυμα, Hsch.

**γεϊκός**, ή, όν, *of land*, γ. πόδες, in land-surveying, Hero Geom.23. 67, al.

✱ **γείνομαι** (γέν-yομαι, cf. γί-γν-ομαι): I. as Pass., only pres. and impf., *to be born*, cf. γίγνομαι (which is a constant v.l. in Hom.), γεινομένῳ *at one's birth*, Il.20.128, 24.210, Od.4.208, cf. Hes.Th.82, Alc.Supp.14: impf. γεινόμεθ' Il.22.477, Hes.Sc.88. II. as Med., aor. 1 ἐγεινάμην (Aeol. 3 sg. γέννατ' Alc.Supp.8.13), in causal sense, *beget*, ἐγείναο παῖδ' ἀΐδηλον Il.5.880, cf. S.Aj.1172, etc.; more freq. of the mother, *bring forth*, θεὰ δέ σε γείνατο μήτηρ Il.1.280, cf. 6.26, Od.6.25, etc.; οἱ γεινάμενοι the *parents*, Hdt.1.120, X.Ap.20; ὁ γεινάμενος the *father*, Ph.2.171; ἡ γειναμένη the *mother*, Hdt.4.10, 6.52, E.Tr.825 (lyr.); αἱ γ. *women in childbed*, Arist.HA582$^{b}$15; μήτηρ ἥ μ' ἐγείνατο she who *bare* me, A.Eu.736, cf. Fr.175, Supp.581 (lyr.), S. OT1020; πατρὶς ἥ μ' ἐγείνατο E.Ph.996. 2. of Zeus, *bring into life*, οὐκ ἐλεαίρεις ἄνδρας, ἐπὴν δὴ γείνεαι αὐτός Od.20.202. 3. metaph., ἐγείνατο μόρον αὐτῷ A.Th.751 (lyr.). III. aor. 1, in later Poets, in pass. sense, = ἐγενόμην, Call.Cer.58. (Sts. written by itacism for γίνομαι, as IG2$^{2}$.786.7 (iii B.C.).)

✱ **γειόθεν**, Adv. = γῆθεν, Call.Fr.35c, A.D.Adv.188.19.

**γειο-κόμος**, ον, *cultivating land*, Hsch. **-μόρος**, = γεωμόρος, A.R.3.1387, AP9.438 (Phil.), D.P.190. **-πόνος**, = γεωπόνος, AP6.41 (Agath.), Nonn.D.42.329, etc. **-τόμος**, = γητόμος, A.R. 1.687, Opp.C.1.137, Nonn.D.21.97, al. **-φόρος**, ον, *earth-bearing*, σκαφίδες AP6.297 (Phan.).

**γεῖσα**, ἡ, = γεῖσον, AB227.

✱ **γεισήπους**, ποδος, ὁ, *projecting end of rafter*, IG2$^{2}$.463.51:—hence ✱ **γεισηπόδισμα**, ατος, τό, ib.114: the spellings **γεισίποδες** (Poll.1.81, AB227), ✱ **γεισιπόδ-ισμα** and ✱ **-ίζω** (*support the cornice*, Is.Fr.113) are less correct.

**γείσιον**, τό, Dim. of γεῖσον, *low parapet*, J.BJ5.5.6.

**γεισόλογχος**, ον, *with a cornice of spear-heads*, γ. ὄγκωμα ὀδόντων, metaph. of thole-pins, prob. in Tim.Pers.4.

**γεῖσ-ον** (in codd. freq. written **γεῖσσον**), τό, *projecting part of the roof, cornice*, IG2$^{2}$.463.51, Thphr.Sign.18 (pl.), Demetr.Eloc.108 (pl.): in pl., of the stones composing it, IG1$^{2}$.372.152; γ. καταιέτια ib.2. 1054.39. 2. *coping* of a wall, E.Or.1570, 1620, Ph.1158, 1180. 3. metaph., *hem* or *border of a garment*, Ar.Fr.762; γεῖσα ὀφρύων Poll. 2.49. **-ος**, ους, τό, = foreg., LxxEz.43.17: pl., γείση BCH35.76 (ii B.C.); dat. pl. γείσεσι OGI483.127 (Pergam., ii B.C.):—also γεῖσος, ὁ, Gloss. (Carian word, acc. to St.Byz. s.v. Μονόγισσα.) **-όω**, *protect with a* γεῖσον, EM229.40. **-ωμα**, ατος, τό, *pent-house*, Poll.1.76. **-ωσις**, εως, ἡ, *eaves*, Hsch., EM229.41.

**γείταινα**, ἡ, fem. of γείτων, as τέκταινα of τέκτων, AB1199.

**γείτη**· βάμματα ἐξ ἐρίων, Hsch.

**γειτνέω**, = γειτνιάω, BGU775.15 (iii A.D.).

✱ **γειτνί-α**, ἡ, = γειτονία 1, Hp.Ep.23, OGI383.98 (Commagene): in pl., *adjoining areas*, PTeb.14.10 (ii B.C.), PAvrom.2 A 8 (i B.C.), PAmh.2.68.4 (i A.D.), etc. **-άζω**, = γειτνιάω, Aesop.75. **-ακός**, ή, όν, *neighbouring*, J.AJ2.14.6. **-αμα**, ατος, τό, gloss on γειτόνημα, Hsch. ✱ **-ασις**, εως, ἡ, = γειτονία, *neighbourhood, proximity*, Arist.PA672$^{b}$28, etc. 2. *a neighbourhood, district*, OGI483.28, 32 (Pergam., ii B.C.), Ph.2.475 (pl.), Plu.Cor.24; βαρβαρικαὶ γ. Id. Per.19. II. *proximity, resemblance*, κατὰ τὴν γ. καὶ ὁμοιότητα Arist.EE1232$^{a}$21, cf. Pol.1257$^{a}$2, J.AJ12.2.9. **-άω**, pres. (3 sg. impf. ἐγειτνία S.Ichn.232, and v. sub fin.), *to be a neighbour, be adjacent*, Ar.Ec.327, D.55.3, PTeb.105.19 (ii B.C.), Plb.6.33.10, Jul. Or.5.168a, etc.:—chiefly in Prose, but Ep. part., γειτνιόωσαν πόντῳ IG14.889 (Sinuessa). II. *border on, resemble*, γ. τῇ πολιτείᾳ Arist. Pol.1295$^{a}$33; [τῷ καλῷ] Id.Rh.1367$^{b}$12; νόσος γειτνιῶσα θανάτῳ Ph.2.548; τινὶ κακῷ Metrod.Herc.831.3: later fut. -άσω Gal.3.690: aor. ἐγειτνίασα Ps.-Luc.Philopatr.1. ✱ **-ος**, α, ον, *neighbouring, adjacent*, BGU94.

**γειτον-εία**, ἡ, = γειτονία, IG5(2).443.13 (Megalop., ii/i B.C.), Plot. 5.8.7; *nearness*, Phld.D.3.9. **-εύω**, = sq., c. dat., X.Vect.1.8, Str. 3.3.8, al.: abs., Id.4.6.8, al., Phld.Ir.p.48 W., etc.:—Med., τὸ ἄλλο ἥμισυ τοῦ σώματος γειτονεύεται ταύτῃ τῇ ἴξει Hp.Fract.18. **-έω**, = γειτνιάω, c. dat., A.Pers.311, Supp.780 (lyr.), v.l. in S.OC1525, SIG 685.38 (ii B.C.), Procop.Aed.4.1; γειτονεῦσ' ἀποπνίγεις Call.Iamb.1. 300: metaph., τὸ σῶμα γειτονῆσαν μετέλαβεν αὐτῆς (sc. ψυχῆς) Plot.3. 9.2, cf. 1.2.5. **-ημα**, ατος, τό, *neighbourhood, neighbouring place*, Alcm.116; ἁλμυρὸν καὶ πικρὸν γ. Pl.Lg.705a, cf. Ael.Ep.13, Procop. Aed.1.11, al., Agath.3.6; τῆς καρδίης καίριον γ. ὁ στόμαχος Aret. CA2.3, cf. CD2.6; *proximity*, τὸ ψυχῆς πρὸς τὸ ἄνω γ. Plot.5.1. 3. **-ησις**, εως, ἡ, = sq., Luc.Symp.33, Plot.1.2.5. ✱ **-ία**, ἡ, *neighbourship*, πικρὰ γ. Pl.Lg.843c, cf. Arist.Rh.1395$^{b}$9; *neighbouring region*, Plot.4.4.19. 2. *quarter, ward*, in a city, J.BJ7.4.1:—hence **-ίαρχος**, ὁ, *chief official of a ward*, Hsch. s.v. ῥεγεονάριος. **-ιάω**, = γειτνιάω, Theopomp.Hist.253.

✱ **γειτο-σύνη**, ἡ, = γειτονία, Str.13.1.22. ✱ **-συνος**, ον, *neighbouring*, AP9.407 (Antip.).

✱ **γείτων**, ονος, ὁ, ἡ, *neighbour, borderer*, γείτονες ἠδὲ ἔται Μενελάου Od.4.16, cf. 9.48, Hes.Op.346, etc.; opp. σύνοικος, Pl.Lg.696b; γ. τινός E.IT1451, X.An.3.2.4; τινί ib.2.3.18; ἐκ τῶν γ. or ἐκ γειτόνων *from* or *in the neighbourhood*, Ar.Pl.435, etc.; οἷον ἐκ γ. φωνὴν θηρευόμενοι Pl.R.531a; λύχνον ἐκ τῶν γ. ἐνάψασθαι Lys.1.14; ἐκ γ. τῆς πατρίδος μετοικεῖν Lycurg.21, cf. Str.10.4.12; rarely ἀπὸ γ. D.S.13. 84; ἐν γειτόνων (sc. οἴκοις) οἰκεῖν Men.Pk.27, Luc.Philops.25, etc.; τὸ χωρίον τὸ ἐν γ. D.53.10: metaph., ἐν γ. εἶναι to be *of like kind*, Luc.Icar.8: prov., μέγα γείτονι γείτων Alcm.5c, cf. Pi.N.7.87. II. as Adj., *neighbouring, bordering*, πόλις, πόντος, Id.P.1.32, N.9.43; χώρα, πύλαι, ῥοαί, A.Pers 67 (lyr.), Th.486, S.Aj.418 (lyr.): c. dat., Ἀθήναις γ. πόλις E.Ion294; νεκροῖσι γ. θᾶκοι Id.HF1097; also in Prose, ἡ γ. πόλις Pl.Lg.877b; οἱ γ. βάρβαροι Jul.Or.2.72c: neut. γεῖτον Hsch.: neut. pl. γείτω IG2.814$^{a}$B36. III. γίτονας (sic)· τὰ δύο αἰδοῖα, Hsch.

**γειωπείνης**, ὁ, = γεωπείνης, Hdn.Epim.15.

**γειώρας**, ου, ὁ, *sojourner*, LxxIs.14.1, Ph.1.417. 2. *proselyte*, Hsch.

**γεκαθά**· ἑκοῦσα, Hsch. (Prob. Cret. ϝέκαθθα < ϝεκητ-yᾰ.) **γέκαλον** (i.e. ϝέκηλον)· ἥσυχον, Id. **γεκᾶσα** (γ = ϝ)· ἑκοῦσα, Id. **γελαιώς**· ὁ γέλως, Id. **γέλαν**· αὐγὴν ἡλίου, Id. (ϝελ-, cf. εἵλη); cf. γελεῖν. **γελανδρόν**· ψυχρόν, Id.

**γελᾱνής**, ές, (γελάω) *cheerful*, καρδία, θυμός, Pi.O.5.2, P.4.181.

**γέλανοι**, οἱ, *an inferior breed of horses*, Hsch.

**γελᾱνόω**, *brighten, cheer*: hence, *calm*, θυμόν B.5.80.

**γελαρής**· γαλήνη (Lacon.), Hsch. **γελαρίης**, = γαλλερίας, Euthyd.ap.Ath.7.315f. **γέλαρος**, v. γαλόως. **γέλας**· ναύτας, Hsch.

**γελᾰσ-είω**, Desiderat. of γελάω, *to be ready to laugh*, Pl.Phd. 64b. **-ιμος**, ον, *laughable*, Stratt.77, Luc.Somn.5: less correct than γέλοιος, Phryn.206. **-ῖνος**, ὁ, *laugher*, of Democritus, Ael. VH4.20: fem. γελασίνη Anaxandr.25. II. οἱ γ. (sc. ὀδόντες) *the grinners*, i.e. *the front teeth*, which show when one laughs, Poll.2. 91. 2. mostly pl., *dimples*, which appear in the cheeks when persons laugh, Mart.7.25 (sg.), Choerob.in An.Ox.2.188; also of *dimples in the hinder parts*, Alciphr.1.39, AP5.34 (Rufin.). **-ις**, εως, ἡ, *laughing*, EM801.13. **-κω**, = γελάω, AP7.621. **-μα**, ατος, τό, *smile*, κυμάτων ἀνήριθμον γέλασμα A.Pr.90. II. *cause of laughter*, γῆρας πολυχρόνιον γ. Secund.Sent.12. **-τής**, οῦ, ὁ, *laugher, sneerer*, S.OT1422:—fem. **-τρια**, Sch.Ar.Th.1068. **-τικός**, ή, όν, *able to laugh*, S.E.P.2.211, Simp.in Ph.104.27; τό γ. Antig.Mir. 175, Iamb.Protr.21.κϛ'; ἄνθρωπος γελαστικόν Luc.Vit.Auct.26. Adv. -κῶς Suid. **-τός**, ή, όν, *laughable*, ἔργα Od.8.307; of persons, Babr.45.12. **-τύς**, ύος, ἡ, Ion. for γέλως, Call.Del.324.

✱ **γελάω**, Ep. γελόω Od.21.105, Aeol. γέλαιμι Hdn.Gr.2.463, al.; Ep. part. γελόωντες Od.18.40, γελώοντες, -ώωντες, or -οίωντες ib.111, cf. 20.390; Ep. impf. γελώων or -οίων 20.347; Dor. part. γελᾶσα, 3 pl. γελᾶντι, Theoc.1.36, 90; Aeol. γελαίσας Sapph.2.5: Att. fut. γελάσομαι Pl.Phdr.252b, X.Smp.1.16, etc.; later γελάσω AP5.178 (Mel.), 11.29 (Autom.), Anacreont.38.8, etc.: aor. ἐγέλασα E.IT.276, etc.; Ep. ἐγέλασσα Il.15.101; Dor. ἐγέλαξα Theoc.20.1, v.l. ib.7.42; 3 pl. γέλαν for ἐγέλασαν Poet.ap.EM255.6:—Pass., fut. -ασθήσομαι D.L.1.78, Luc.Am.2: aor. ἐγελάσθην D.2.10, (κατ-) Th.3.83, Pl. Euthphr.3c, etc.: pf. γεγέλασται (κατα-) Luc.DMort.1.1. I. abs., *laugh*, ἁπαλὸν γελάσαι Od.14.465; ἀχρεῖον γ. 18.163; γναθμοῖσι γελοίων ἀλλοτρίοισιν 20.347; δακρυόεν γ. Il.6.484; μηδὲν ἵλεων γ. S.Aj. 1011; ἡ δ' ἐγέλασσε χείλεσιν, of feigned laughter, Il.15.101; ἐγέλασσε δέ οἱ φίλον ἦτορ his heart *laughed* within him, 21.389; γελῶ ὁρῶν Hdt.4.36:—Pass., εἵνεκα τοῦ γελασθῆναι for the sake of *a laugh being raised*, D.2.19. 2. of things, γέλασσε δὲ πᾶσα περὶ χθὼν Il. 19.362; γαῖά τε πᾶσ' ἐγέλασσε h.Cer.14; γελᾷ δέ τε δώματα πατρὸς Hes.Th.40; γελῶντα ὕδατη Lyr.Alex.Adesp.32.4. II. *laugh* at, ἐπ' αὐτῷ ἡδὺ γέλασσαν Il.2.270, 23.784; ἐπ' ἀλλήλοισι γελῶσιν Thgn. 1113; γελᾷ δὲ δαίμων ἐπ' ἀνδρὶ θερμῷ *laughs scornfully* at.., A.Eu. 560 (lyr.); ἐπί τινι at a thing, X.Mem.4.2.5, Pl.Phlb.50a: freq. c. dat., γελᾷ δὲ τοῖσδε.. ἄχεσιν πολὺν γέλωτα S.Aj.957 (lyr.), cf. 1043, Ar. Nu.560; ἐγέλασα ψολοκομπίαις *was amused* at them, Id.Eq.696;

ὅταν ποτ' ἀνθρώποισιν ἡ τύχη γελᾷ Philem.110; εἰς ἐχθροὺς γ. S.*Aj.*79; ἐν κακοῖσι τοῖς ἐμοῖς A.*Ch.*222: rarely c. gen. pers., γελᾷ μου S.*Ph.*1125 (lyr.), cf. Pl.*Tht.*175b, Luc.*Dem.Enc.*16, Procop.*Goth.*4.28 (v.l.). **2.** c. acc., *deride*, τινά Theoc.20.1; ἢ τόδε γελᾶτε, εἰ..; X.*Smp.*2.19; τί δὲ τοῦτ' ἐγέλασας ἐτεόν; what is this you *are laughing at?* Ar.*Nu.*820:—Pass., *to be derided*, A.*Eu.*789 (lyr.), S.*Ant.*839 (lyr.); πρός τινος Id.*Ph.*1023; παρά τινος Id.*OC*1423.

**γέλγει·** βαπτίζει, χρωματίζει, Hsch.

**γέλγη,** έων, τά, = ῥῶπος, *frippery*: *the market where they are sold*, Eup.304, Luc.*Lex.*3. (γέλγη, ἡ, Ael.Dion.*Fr.*295, is prob. an error due to Eust.)

**γελγηθεύειν·** ἀπατηλογεῖν, Hsch. **γέλγια·** πήνη, σπάθη, κουράλια, Id.

**γελγῑδόομαι,** Pass., *form a compound bulb*, of garlic, Thphr.*HP* 7.4.11.

**γέλγις,** ἡ, gen. γέλγῑθος, also γέλγιος and -ιδος (in codd. freq. with false accent γελγίς, γελγῖθος, etc., but cf. Hdn.Gr.1.87): pl. γέλγεις Thphr.*HP*7.4.11, *CP*1.4.5:—*head of garlic*, and in pl., the *cloves* which compose it, ἡ γέλγις διαιρεῖται εἰς τὰς γέλγεις Id.*HP*7.4.12, cf. Hp.*Nat.Mul.*77; πότιμοι γέλγῑθες *AP*6.232 (Crin.).

⊕ **γελγο-πωλέω,** *sell garlic*, Hermipp.13. **II.** *sell* γέλγη, Hsch.

⊕ **-πώλης,** ου, ὁ, *dealer in garlic*, Poll.7.198:—fem. **-πωλις,** ιδος, Cratin.48.

**γέλεα·** τέλεα, Hsch. **γελεῖν·** λάμπειν, ἀνθεῖν, Id. **γέλενος·** ἀσφόδελος, νάρκισσος, Id.

⊕ **Γελέοντες,** οἱ, one of the four Ionic tribes, Plu.*Sol.*23, *CIG*3078 (Teos), 3664 (Cyzicus), etc.: **Γελέων,** οντος, ὁ, epith. of Zeus, *IG*2².1072.

**γελίκη·** ἕλιξ, Hsch. **γέλιν·** ὀρκιᾶν (leg. ὀρμιάν), Id. **γέλινθοι·** ἐρέβινθοι, Id. ⊕ **γέλλαι·** τῖλαι (cf. Lat. *vello*), Id. **γελλίζειν·** γαργαλίζειν, Id. **γελλίξαι** (Aeol. for ϝειλίξαι)· συνειλῆσαι, Id. (In the above lemmata. exc. γελλίζειν, γ stands for ϝ.)

**Γελλώ,** οῦς, Aeol. **Γέλλω,** ως, ἡ, a kind of *vampire* or *goblin*, supposed to carry off young children, Sapph.47.

**γελοδυτία·** ἡλιοδυσία, Hsch.; cf. γέλαν.

⊕ **γελοι-άζω,** only pres., *jest*, Lxx *Ge.*19.14, Aristarch.ap.Ath.2.39e, Plu.2.231c, Arr.*Epict.*3.16.4, Jul.*Caes.*306b, Procop.*Arc.*9. **-ασμός,** ὁ, *jesting*, Lxx *Je.*3 (48).27. **-αστής,** οῦ, ὁ, *jester, buffoon*, Ptol. Megalop.2, Lxx *Jb.*31.5, Poll.5.128, prob. in Luc.*Merc.Cond.*4. **-αστικός,** ή, όν, *mirth-provoking*, Eust.1837.8. **-άω,** Ep. for γελάω, in aor. part. γελοιήσασα *h.Ven.*49.

**γελοιομελέω,** *write comic songs*, *AP*7.719 (Leon.).

⊕ **γέλοιος** or **γελοῖος,** α, ον, *mirth-provoking*, *amusing*, once in Hom., Il.2.215 (in Ep. form γελοίιος); χρῆμα Archil.70, cf. Hdt.8.25; Αἰσώπου τι γ. Ar.*V.*566, cf. 1259; γελοῖα *jests*, Thgn.311; γέλοια λέγειν Anaxandr.10, Alex.183; opp. σπουδαῖος, X.*Cyr.*2.3.1, Pl.*Lg.*816d; τοῦ ἀληθοῦς ἕνεκα, οὐ τοῦ γ. Id.*Smp.*215a; τὸ γ. *the comic*, Arist.*Po.*1449ᵃ34, al.; τὰ γ. ἡδέα Id.*Rh.*1371ᵇ35; of persons, *facetious*, μισῶ γελοίους E.*Fr.*492; ἡδὺς καὶ γ. Aeschin.1.126; γ. ἐστι καὶ βούλεται Pl.*Smp.*213c. Adv. -οίως Id.*Cri.*53d. **II.** *ludicrous, absurd*, Ζεὺς γ. ὀμνύμενος τοῖς εἰδόσιν Ar.*Nu.*1241; γ. ἔσομαι αὐτοσχεδιάζων Pl.*Phdr.*236d; γ. ἰατρός, διδάσκαλος, Id.*Prt.*340e, *R.*392d; ἐπὶ τὸ -ότερον ὅμοιος a *caricature*, Arist.*Top.*117ᵇ17, cf. *Po.*1449ᵃ36; of arguments, etc., *paradoxical*, Pl.*Prt.*355a, *Tht.*158e, etc. Adv. -οίως, ἔχειν Id.*R.*528d, cf. Arist.*Mete.*362ᵇ12.—In *Smp.*189b, Pl. confines γ. to signf. I, γ. εἰπεῖν ἀλλὰ μὴ καταγέλαστα. (Att. γέλοιος A.D.*Pron.*50.5, but γελοῖος Ael.Dion.*Fr.*101, and so cod. R in Ar.*Ach.*1058, *Nu.*1241. Some Gramm. expl. γέλοιος, = γέλωτος ἄξιος, γελοῖος, = γελωτοποιός, Ammon.p.38V., *EM*224.43; others reversely, *Et.Gud.*, etc.: Suid. gives both views. Phlp.ap.Eust. 906.53 wrote γελοιός, = γελωτοποιός.)

**γελοιότης,** ητος, ἡ, *absurdity*, Ath.11.497f.

**γελοιώδης,** ες, = γέλοιος II, Porph.*Chr.*55, Procop.*Arc.*22, *Goth.*4.21, Sch.Ar.*V.*564. Adv. -δῶς Id.*Pl.*681, Hsch. s. v. ἀστείως.

**γελοίων, γελοίωντες, γελόω, γελόωντες,** v. sub γελάω.

**γέλουτρον·** ἔλυτρον, Hsch. (ϝελ-).

**γελωμῑλία,** ἡ, *fellowship in laughing*, *AP*9.573 (Ammian.).

**γελσόν·** ἀτυχές, Hsch. **γελυνμάξαι·** γελοιάσαι, Id.

**Γελχάνος** (i.e. ϝελχ-), title of Zeus in Crete, Hsch.

⊕ **γέλως,** Aeol. **γέλος,** ὁ, gen. γέλωτος, Att. γέλω: dat. γέλωτι, Ep. γέλῳ or γέλῳ Od.18.100: acc. γέλωτα, poet. (and late Prose, Polyaen.1.34.2, f.l. in Palaeph.30) γέλων, v. infr. (acc. γέλω is v.l. in Od 18.350, cf. infr.): gen. pl. γελώτων Pl *Lg.*732c: dat. γέλωσιν Ph. 2.167, *PGiss.*1.3.6 (ii A.D.): (γελάω):—*laughter*, γέλῳ ἔκθανον Od. 18.100; γέλω.. παρέχουσαι 20.8; ἄσβεστον γέλω (v.l. γέλον) ὦρσεν ib.346; ἄσβεστος δ' ἄρ' ἐνῶρτο γέλως.. θεοῖσι Il.1.599; γέλων δ' ἑτάροισιν ἔτευχε Od.18.350; γέλων δ' ἔθηκε συνδείπνοις E.*Ion* 1172; γέλωτα ποιεῖν, μηχανᾶσθαι, κινεῖν, X.*Cyr.*2.2.11 and 14, *Smp.*1.14; παρασκευάζειν Pl.*Lg.*669d; γέλων ξυντιθέναι, γέλωτα ἄγειν, S.*Aj.*303,382; γ. ἔχει τινά Od.8.344; γ. ἂν γίγνοιτο Pl.*Plt.*295e; γέλωτος καταρραγέντος Ath.5.211c (so in Act., πολλοὺς κατέρρηξεν ἡμῶν γέλωτας Hipploch.ib.130c); καταχεῖν γέλωτα X.*Cyr.*2.2.5, etc.; οὐ γέλωτα δεῖ σ' ὀφλεῖν E.*Med.*404, cf. Ar.*Fr.*898; ἐπὶ γέλωτι to provoke *laughter*, Hdt.9.82, Ar.*Ra.*405; γέλωτος ἄξια *ridiculous*, E.*Heracl.*507; ἅμα or σὺν γέλωτι, Pl.*Lg.*789d, X.*An.*1.2.18; μετὰ γέλωτος Antiph.144.6; ἐν γέλωτι προφέρειν in *joke*, Plu.2.124d; πολὺς γ. loud *laughter*, X.*Cyr.*2.3.18, etc. (πλατὺς γ., which Thom.Mag.p.293R. recommends, is not classical); μέγιστος, ἰσχυρὸς γ., Pl.*Plt.*l.c., *R.*388e; Σαρδόνιος γ. (v. Σαρδόνιος); Αἰάντειος γ. a maniac's *laugh*, Diogenian.1.17. **2.** metaph. of waves, = γέλασμα, Opp.*H.*4.334. **II.** *occasion of laughter, food for laughter*, γ. γίγνομαί τινι S.*OC*902; ταῦτ' οὐ γ. κλύειν ἐμοῦ; E.*Ion* 528; γέλωτά τινα τίθεσθαι Hdt.3.29, 7.209; ἀποδεῖξαι Pl.*Tht.*166a; εἰς γ. τρέπειν, ἐμβάλλειν, Th.6.35, D.10.75; ἐν γέλωτι ποιεῖσθαί τι Luc.*Hist.Conscr.*32, etc.; γ. ἔσθ' ὡς χρώμεθα τοῖς πράγμασι D.4.25; ὅσα γὰρ.., πλείων ἐστὶ γ. τοῦ μηδενός Id.14.26. **III.** *dimple* in the hinder parts, Luc.*Am.*14.

**γελωτῖνος·** καταγέλαστος, Hsch.

**γελωτο-ποιέω,** *to create, make laughter*, esp. by buffoonery, X.*Smp.*3.11, Pl.*R.*606c, Hyp.*Phil.*2. **-ποιΐα,** ἡ, *buffoonery*, X.*Smp.*4.50, Luc.*Salt.*68, Procop.*Arc.*15. **-ποιϊκῶς,** Adv. *ridiculously*, Poll.9.149. **-ποιός,** όν, *exciting laughter, ridiculous*, A.*Fr.*180.2; βωμολοχίαι Procop.*Arc.*9. **II.** as Subst., *jester, buffoon*, X.*An.*7.3.33, *Smp.*1.11, Pl.*R.*620c. **2.** = βατράχιον II (because it produced a wry face), Ps.-Dsc.2.175. **-φυή,** ἡ, = foreg. II.2, Apul.*Herb.*8. **-φυλλίς,** ίδος, ἡ, *Indian hemp, Cannabis sativa*, Plin.*HN*24.164.

**γελωτός,** ή, όν, prob. f.l. for γελοῖος, Olymp. *in Alc.*p.10C.

**γελώων, γελώωντες,** v. γελάω.

**γεμ-ίζω,** (γέμω) *fill full of, load, freight* or *charge with*, prop. of a ship, τινός Th.7.53, X.*HG*6.2.25, etc.; γεμίσας τὴν ναῦν ξύλων Test. ap.D.21.168; ναῦν σίτου D.34.36; θηρίων τὰς ναῦς Plb.1.18.8; τραπέζας θοίνης *OGI*383.146 (Commagene); of animals, *load*, κτήνη *PFay.*117.14 (ii A.D.), cf. *PTeb.*419.17 (iii A.D.): c. dupl. acc., *PFlor.*195.4 (iii A.D.); σποδοῦ γ. λέβητας *charging* them *with* ashes, A.*Ag.*443; γεμίσω σε *let me fill* you, addressed to a cup, Theopomp.Com. 32; αὐτόν *stuff, gorge*, Men.*Pk.*296; τὴν κοιλίαν ἀπό τινος v.l. in *Ev.Luc.*15.16:—Med., D.20.31; ἐγεμιζόμην ἀνθρωπείου τροφῆς Luc.*Asin.*46:—Pass., metaph. of the Cyclops, E.*Cyc.*505 (lyr.); of bees, γεμισθεῖσαι ἀποπέτονται Arist.*HA*624ᵇ2: c. gen., γ. ἀλαζονείας, εὐσεβείας, Ph.2.186,357. **II.** later, c. acc. rei, γεμίζειν ὕδωρ (sc. τὴν ὑδρίαν) *to fill* it *full of* water, Paus.3.13.3:—Pass., οἶνον, πῦρ γεμισθείς, *AP*12.85 (Mel.). **-ισμα,** ατος, τό, gloss on γέμος, Hsch. **-ιστός,** ή, όν, *laden, full*, Ath.9.381a.

**γέμμα,** Ion., = γάμμα, Democr.19.

**γέμματα·** ἱμάτια, Hsch. (ϝέμμ-, cf. εἷμα).

**γέμος,** ους, τό, *load*, σπλάγχν', ἐποίκτιστον γέμος A.*Ag.*1221.

**γεμόω,** = γεμίζω, *PRein.*53.4 (iii A.D.).

**γεμπός·** κοῖλος, Hsch. **γεμπύλος,** ὁ, = πηλαμύς, Id.

⊕ **γέμω,** used only in pres. and impf., *to be full*, prop. of a ship, Hdt. 8.118, X.*HG*5.1.21: generally, πάντα γ. Jul.*Mis.*368c. **b.** = κύειν, Hsch. **2.** c. gen. rei, *to be full of*, πλοῖα γέμοντα χρημάτων Th.7.25; λιμὴν ἔγεμεν πλοίων Pl.*Criti.*117e; κώμας πολλῶν καὶ ἀγαθῶν γεμούσας X.*An.*4.6.27; of animals, *to be laden*, ὄνοι γέμοντες οἴνου καὶ βρωμάτων Posidon.5: metaph., κόμπος τῆς ἀληθείας γ. A.*Ag.*613, cf. S.*OT*4; γέμω κακῶν δή E.*HF*1245; γ. θρασύτητος Pl.*Lg.*649d; ἀσυμμετρίας καὶ αἰσχρότητος γέμουσα ψυχή Id.*Grg.*525a; πικρίας Phld.*Ir.*p.56W.: c. dat., *to be filled with*, ἰτρίοισι, πέμμασι, Archipp.9, Antiph.174.2; γῆν πυρὸς γέμουσαν ῥεύμασιν Carc.5; γ. ἐξ ἁρπαγῆς *Ev.Matt.*23.25.

**γεναρχ-έω,** *to be the ancestor of the human race*, ὁ γεναρχῶν ἄνθρωπος (of the Gnostic πρωτάνθρωπος) Iamb.*Myst.*10.5. ⊕ **-ης,** ου, ὁ, *founder* or *first ancestor of a family*, Call.*Fr.*36, Lyc.1307; of Julius Caesar, Ph.2.528; of Abraham, Id.1.513; epith. of Heracles, *IG* 5(1).497 (Sparta), al. **II.** *ruler of created beings*, γενάρχα τῆς γενεσιουργίας *Corp.Herm.*13.21, cf. Orph.*H.*13.8.

⊕ **γενεά,** ᾶς, Ion. **γενεή,** ῆς, ἡ, Ep. dat. γενεῆφι Il.14.112: (γενέσθαι): **I.** of the persons in a family, **1.** *race, family*, Πριάμου γ. Il.20.306, cf. Od.1.222, 16.117; γενεήν τε τόκον τε Il.15.141; ἴδμεν.. γενεήν, ἴδμεν δὲ τοκῆας 20.203, cf. 214; γενεῇ ὑπέρτερος higher *by birth* or *blood*, 11.786 (but *younger* in Archil.ap.Sch.ad l.); ταύτης εἶναι γ. καὶ αἵματος *of* this *race* and blood, Il.6.211; πατρόθεν ἐκ γενεῆς ὀνομάζειν 10.68; γενεῇ *by birthright*, Od.1.387; Αἰτωλὸς γενεήν *by descent*, Il.23.471; γενεὴν Διός 21.187; γενεὴ ἔκ τινος *descent* from.., ib.157; γενεὴν ἀπὸ Θρηΐκης Hdt.2.134; of horses, *breed, stock*, Il.5.265, 268: pl., χρήματα καὶ γενεὰς *families*, Plu.*Tim.*34; γενεὰς ποιεῖσθαι to have *issue*, *GDI*1798 (Delph.); πατριὰ καὶ γ., = φρατρία καὶ γένος, ib.1152 (Elis): hence, *tribe, nation*, Περσῶν γ., Τυρρηνῶν γ., A.*Pers.*912 (lyr.), *Eleg.*2:—rare in Prose, τίς ὢν γενεάν; X.*Cyr.*1.1.6; καὶ αὐτὸν καὶ τὰν γ. ἀπολέσθαι *SIG*306.8 (Tegea, iv B.C.). **2.** *race, generation*, οἵηπερ φύλλων γ. τοιήδε καὶ ἀνδρῶν Il.6.146; δύο γ. μερόπων ἀνθρώπων 1.250, etc., cf. Hdt.2.142, Th.1.14, Heraclit.ap.Plu.2.415e (but, = μήν, Id.ap.Lyd.*Mens.*3.14); ἀστὴν ἐξ ἀστῶν ἀμφοτέρων ἐπὶ τρεῖς γ. γεγενημένην *SIG*1015.6 (Halic.); *age*, γ. ἀνθρωπηΐη the historical, opp. to the mythical, age, Hdt.3.122; ἐπὶ τῆς ἡμετέρας γ. D.H.3.15. **3.** *offspring*, Il.21.191, Orac.ap.Hdt.6.86, S.*Aj.*189 (lyr.); of a single person, Τυροῦς γ. (i.e. Pelias) Pi.*P.*4.136, cf. *I.*8(7).71. **4.** metaph., *class, kind*, τὸ σύμμετρον καὶ καλὸν καὶ ὁπόσα τῆς γ. ταύτης ἐστίν Pl.*Phlb.*66b; ταύτης τοι γενεᾶς ὁ νοῦς οὗτος Plot.5.1.7. **II.** of Time or Place, **1.** *birthplace*, γ. ἐπὶ λίμνῃ Γυγαίῃ Il.20.390, cf. Od.1.407; of an eagle's *eyrie*, 15.175. **2.** *age, time of life*, γενεῆφι νεώτατος Il.14.112; γενεῇ πρεσβύτατος, προγενέστερος, ὁπλότερος, 6.24, 9.161, Od.19.184. **3.** after Hom., *time of birth*, ἐκ γενεῆς Hdt.3.33, 4.23; ἀπὸ γ. X.*Cyr.*1.2.8.

**γενεᾱλογ-έω,** Ion. γενεη-, *trace a pedigree*, γ. γένεσιν Hdt.2.146; γ. ἑωυτόν *draw out* one's pedigree, ib.143; γ. τὴν συγγένειαν X.*Smp.*4.51; γ. τινά τινος Plu.2.894b; γ. τινὰ γενέσθαι, εἶναι.., Id.*Lyc.*1, Paus.5.14.9; περί τινος Luc.*Salt.*7: abs., οἱ -λογοῦντες Isoc.15.180, Thphr.*Char.*28.2:—Pass., Hp.*Sept.*4; ταῦτα μέν νυν γεγενεηλόγηται Hdt.6.54; τὰ νυνδὴ γενεαλογηθέντα Pl.*Ti.*23b; γενεαλογούμενος ἐκ τινος *Ep.Hebr.*7.6; ἐγενεαλογήθη (impers.) *the genealogy was reckoned*, Lxx 1*Ch.*5.1. **-ημα**, ατος, τό, *pedigree*, Eust.18.29. ® **-ία**, ἡ, *tracing a pedigree*, Pl.*Cra.*396c, al.: in pl., Isoc.11.8; title of work by Hecataeus; γ. καὶ μῦθοι Plb.9.2.1, cf. 1*Ep.Ti.*1.4, Jul.*Or.*7. 205c. **-ικός**, ή, όν, *genealogical*, Plb.9.1.4, Ph.2.141, S.E.*M.*1. 253. **-ος**, ὁ, *genealogist*, D.H.1.13, D.L.1.115.

**γενεάρχ-ης**, ου, ὁ, = ἄρχων τοῦ γένους, *IG*3.1278, cf. *OGI*531 (Bith.); = γενάρχης (which is freq. v.l.), Apollod.2.1.4, Heraclit. *All.*22, Jul.*Ep.*89, etc.; πόλεως γ. *chief, sheikh*, *CRAcad.Inscr.*1924. 28 (Dura). ® **-ικός**, ή, όν, *patrimonial*, χωρία Just.*Edict.*3.1.1.

**γενεῆθεν**, Adv. *from birth, by descent*, Arat.260; ἀγραυλοι γ. *AP* 7.415 (Pers.).

® **γενέθλ-η**, Dor. **-θλα**, ἡ: I. of persons, *race, stock, family*, c. gen. pers., Παιήονός εἰσι γενέθλης Od.4.232, cf. 13.130; σῆς ἐξ αἵματός εἰσι γενέθλης of thy *race* by blood, Il.19.111; γενέθλην *by birth* or *origin*, ἦν δὲ γ. Ἴκιος Call.*Aet.*1.1.7; of horses, *breed, stock*, Il.5. 270; θηρῶν γ. *h.Hom.*27.10; τῶν ἀλιθίων ἀπείρων [ἐστὶ] γενέθλα Simon.5.6. 2. *offspring*, *h.Ap.*136, S.*El.*129 (lyr.), 226 (lyr.), etc. 3. *birth*, γενέθλας ἀρχά *Hymn.Is.*36. II. *birthplace*, ὅθι ἀργύρου ἐστὶ γ. Il.2.857. 2. *generation, age*, οὔ τι παλαιόν, ἐφ' ἡμετέρῃ δὲ γενέθλῃ Opp.*H.*5.459. 3. *time of birth*, ἐκ γενέθλης D.P.1044. **-ήϊος**, ον, = γενέθλιος, Orac.ap.Eus.*PE*6.2. **-ια**, τά, v. γενέθλιος. **-ιάζω**, *keep a birthday*, App.*BC*4.134. **-ιᾰκός**, ή, όν, *belonging to a birthday*, ὧραι *AP*6.321 (Leon.); ἡμέρα Vett.Val.26.14, al., cf. Ph.2.529. II. = γενεθλιαλόγος, Gal.15.441, cf. Gell.14.1.1.

**γενεθλιᾰλογ-έω**, *cast nativities, practise astrology*, Str.16.1.6:— Med., *Cat.Cod.Astr.*1.170. **-ία**, ἡ, *casting of nativities, astrology*, J.*AJ*18.6.9, Ptol.*Tetr.*7, Iamb.*Myst.*9.1, Hierocl.*Prov.*ap.Phot. p.172 B. **-ικός**, ή, όν, *of* or *for nativity-casting*, Ptol.*Tetr.*54: ἡ -κή (sub. τέχνη), = foreg., Ph.1.464. **-ος**, ὁ, *caster of nativities*, Ptol.*Tetr.*13, Hierocl.*Prov.*ap.Phot.p.172 B., Iamb.*Myst.*1.18.

**γενεθλίδιος**, ον, = γενέθλιος, δῶρα *AP*6.325 (Leon.), cf. 243 (Diod.).

**γενεθλιολόγος**, = γενεθλιαλ-, Hsch. s.v. ἀστρολόγος.

® **γενέθλιος**, ον, also α, ον Lyc.1194:—*of* or *belonging to one's birth*, γ. δόσις a *birthday* gift, A.*Eu.*7; ἡ γενέθλιος ἡμέρα *birthday*, Epicur. *Fr.*217, *OGI*111.29 (ii B.C.), etc.; γενεθλία ἡμέρα ib.222.6 (iii B.C.): pl., ib.493.20 (ii A.D.); τῇ γενεθλίᾳ *POxy.*494.24 (ii A.D.); and ἡ γενέθλιος, without ἡμέρα, *CIG*3957*b*, Luc.*Dem.Enc.*2; γενέθλιον ἦμαρ *AP*6.261 (Crin.); also ἀγὼν γ. τοῦ θεάτρου *to celebrate a birthday*, *CIG* 4342*d* (Aspendus); τὰ γ. *birthday feast*, *SIG*461.11; γ. θύειν offer *birthday offerings*, E.*Ion*653, Pl.*Alc.*1.121c; ἑστιᾶν Luc.*Herm.*11, cf. *BGU*362x9 (iii A.D.), etc. II. *of one's race* or *family*, esp. of tutelary gods, Ζεὺς γ. Pi.*O.*8.16, *P.*4.167; γ. δαίμων Id.*O.*13.105; γ. θεοί A.*Th.*639 (but in Pl.*Lg.*729c, 879d, *presiding over generation*, and in D.H.1.67, = *Penates*); αἷμα γ. *kindred* blood, E.*Or.*89; γ. ἀραί a *parent's* curse, A.*Ch.*912. III. *giving birth, generative*, γενέθλιος ἀκτίνων πατήρ, i.e. the Sun, Pi.*O.*7.70; γ. πόρος thy *natal* stream, A.*Eu.*293; βλάσται γ. S.*OC*972; ἀνέλυσα γενέθλιον.. [δελφύν], of her first child, *Hymn.Is.*17.

**γενεθλίωμα**, ατος, τό, = γενέθλη, Iamb.ap.Sch.Hes.*Th.*459.

**γένεθλον**, τό, = γενέθλη, *race, descent*, A.*Supp.*290. 2. *offspring*, Id.*Ag.*784 (lyr.), 914, etc.; γ. Οἰταίου πατρός S.*Ph.*453; τὰ θνητῶν γ. the *sons* of men, Id.*OT*1425.

**γενει-άζω**, Dor. **-άσδω**, (γένειον) *get a beard, come to man's estate*, D.H.1.76, *AP*12.12 (Flacc.); ἄρτι γενειάσδων Theoc.11.9, cf. *CIG* 3715 (Apamea Bith.): pf. γεγενείακα Philem.15. **-άς**, άδος, ἡ, *beard*, κυάνεαι.. γενειάδες ἀμφὶ γένειον (pl. for sg.) Od.16.176; δάσκιον γενειάδα A.*Pers.*316, cf. S.*Tr.*13, Theoc.2.78; πρός (σε) γενειάδος.. ἅπτομαι E.*Supp.*277. 2. pl., *cheeks*, E.*Ion*1460, *Ph.* 1381, *IT*1366; of horses, χαλινὰ γενειάσιν ἀφρίζοντες δάπτον Q.S.4. 548. II. *bandage for the chin*, Heliod.ap.Orib.48.20.9, Gal.18 (1).786. **-ᾰσις**, εως, ἡ, *growth of the beard*, in pl., Plot.4.3. 13. **-άσκω**, *begin to get a beard*, Pl.*Smp.*181d, X.*Cyr.*4.6.5; ἄρτι γενειάσκων *IG*3.1314. **-αστήρ**, ῆρος, ὁ, *chin-strap* of a bridle, Poll. 1.147. **-άτης** [ᾱ], Ep. and Ion. **-ήτης**, ου, ὁ, *bearded*, Theoc. 17.33, Luc.*BisAcc.*28, Jul.*Or.*4.131a, Call.*Dian.*90:—fem. **-ᾶτις**, τρίγλα Sophr.31; Ion. γενειῆτις τρίγλη Eratosth.12. **-άω**, = γενειάζω, *grow a beard, get a beard*, ἐπὴν δὴ παῖδα γενειήσαντα ἴδηαι Od.18.269, cf. 176, Hp.*Nat.Puer.*20, X.*An.*2.6.28, etc.; εἰς ἄνδρα γενειῶν Theoc.14.28. 2. *have a beard*, Ar.*Ec.*145, Pl.*Plt.*270e, Arist.*GA*745b24, D.C.68.15. ® **-όλης**, ου, ὁ, = γενειάτης, Hdn.Gr. 2.638. ® **-ον**, τό, (γένυς) *part covered by the beard, chin*, Od.16.176; πολιόν γ. Il.22.74; esp. in supplication, ἔλλαβε χειρὶ γενείου 8.371; γ. χειρὶ παχείῃ ἀψάμενος 10.454; γενείου λευκήρη τρίχα A.*Pers.*1056 (lyr.), cf. *Th.*666, Hdt.2.36: in pl., S.*OT*1277, Plu.*Ant.*1; κείρασθαι τὰ γ. Id.*Cat.Mi.*53: prov. of a lean animal, οὐδὲν ἄλλο πλὴν γ. τε καὶ κέρατα nothing but *chin* and horns, Ar.*Av.*902. 2. *beard*, Hdt.6. 117: pl., Theoc.6.36, J.*AJ*11.5.3, Paus.2.10.3, Theo Sm.p.104 H. b. a lion's *mane*, Luc.*Cyn.*14. 3. *chaps*, Arist.*HA*518b17; *jaws*, *AP*7.531 (Antip.Thess.). 4. pl., *teeth* of a saw, Nic.*Th.*53. 5. dub. sens. in *IG*11(2).165.11, 28 (Delos, iii B.C.).

**γενειοσυλλεκτάδαι**, οἱ, *beard-gatherers*, Ath.4.157b.

**γενεός· εἶδός τι πελέκεος**, Hsch.

® **γενεσιακός**, ή, όν, = γενεθλ-, ἡμέρα Vett.Val.19.27.

**γενεσιᾰλόγος** (**-ολόγος**, *Gloss.*), ὁ, = γενεθλιαλόγος, Ach.Tat.*Intr. Arat.*23, v.l. in Artem.2.69.

**γενεσι-άρχης**, ου, ὁ, *creator*, τοῦ κάλλους Lxx *Wi.*13.3; of the Sun, Jul.Astr. in *Cat.Cod.Astr.*1.136.2. **-αρχικός**, ή, ον, = γεναρχικός, χωρία Just.*Nov.*21.2. ® **-ος**, ον, = γενέθλιος, θεός Plu.2. 402a; epith. of Posidon, Paus.2.38.4. II. Γενέσιον, τό, shrine of Posidon Γ., Paus.l.c. III. γενέσια, τά, *day kept in memory of the birthday of the dead*, Hdt.4.26, cf. Ammon.p.36 V., Phryn.83; to be distinguished from γενέθλια *birthday-feast*, though used for it in Pl.*Lg.*784d (s.v.l.) and later Gk., *POxy.*736.56 (i B.C./i A.D.), *PFay.*114.20 (i/ii A.D.), etc., Alciphr.3.18 and 55, *Ev.Matt.*14.6, *Ev.Marc.*6.21, D.C.47.18; so ἡ γ. ἡμέρα, = ἡ γενέθλιος, *CIG*2883c (Branchidae); ἡ γ. alone, *OGI*583.14 (Cyprus); τῇ τοῦ Σεβαστοῦ ἐμμήνῳ γ. *IGRom.*4.353*b* (Pergam., ii A.D.). ® **-ουργέω**, *bring into being*, μυριάδας ψυχῶν Herm.ap.Stob.1.49.44. **-ουργία**, ἡ, *generation*, *Corp.Herm.*13.21, Iamb.*Comm.Math.*9; τοῦ κόσμου Id. *Myst.*1.11. **-ουργός**, όν, *concerned with* or *incident to generation*, φύσις ibid.; δαίμονες ib.2.7; παθήματα Id.*VP*32.228; ἀστήρ Porph.ap.Eus.*PE*3.11; ὁρμαί Procl.*in Cra.*p.105 P.; δυνάμεις Id.*Inst.* 209; θεοί Dam.*Pr.*381, al.; τὸ γ. ib.349:—Subst. γ., ὁ, *author of existence*, c. gen., Lxx *Wi.*13.5; τῆς παλιγγενεσίας *Corp.Herm.*13. 4; *fashioner, creator*, Herm.ap.Stob.1.49.44; παντὸς κόσμου Jul.*Gal.* 100c.

® **γένεσις**, εως, ἡ, (γενέσθαι) *origin, source*, Ὠκεανόν τε θεῶν γένεσιν Il.14.201; Ὠκεανοῦ, ὅς περ γ. πάντεσσι τέτυκται ib.246, cf. Pl.*Tht.* 180d; *beginning*, in dual, τοῖν γενεσέοιν ἡ ἑτέρα Id.*Phd.*71e. II. *manner of birth*, Hdt.1.204, 6.69, etc.; *race, descent*, Id.2.146; πατρὸς οὖσα γένεσιν Εὐρύτου S.*Tr.*380; κατὰ γένεσιν, opp. καθ' υἱοθεσίαν, *IG*12(1).181 (Rhodes). 2. Astrol., *nativity, geniture*, *AP* 11.164 (Lucill.), 183 (Id.), *Epigr.Gr.*314.21 (Smyrna), *PLond.*1. 98r60 (i A.D.), Vett.Val.216.6: hence, *lot, fortune*, Astramps.*Orac.* 16.8, 23.7. III. *production, generation, coming into being*, opp. ὄλεθρος, Parm.8.21; more usu. opp. φθορά, Pl.*Phlb.*55a, etc.; περὶ γενέσεως καὶ φθορᾶς, title of work by Arist.: generally, *formation*, νόσου Hp.*Aph.*2.47; *origination, making*, ἱματίων, περὶ τὰ ἀμφιέσματα, Pl. *Plt.*281b,e; γ. καὶ οὐσία δικαιοσύνης Id.*R.*359a. 2. = τὸ γίγνεσθαι, *becoming*, opp. οὐσία, ib.525b, *Ti.*29c, Procl.*Inst.*45, al. IV. concrete, *creation*, i.e. *all created things*, Pl.*Phdr.*245e; γ. καὶ κόσμος Id. *Ti* 29e, freq. in Ph., as 1.3, al., cf. Plot.6.3.2, etc. V. *race, kind* or *sort* of animals, Pl.*Plt.*265b, etc.; *family*, δίδυμος γ. of the Spartan kings, Id.*Lg.*691d. VI. *generation, age*, Id.*Phdr.*252d: pl., Id. *Plt.*310d; κατὰ περίστασιν τῆς γ. according to the circumstances of his *time*, Porph.*Sent.*32. VII. παιδοπόρος γ. *genitalia muliebria*, *AP*9.311 (Phil.). VIII. Math., *generation* of a figure, Papp.234. 4, al. b. *origin* of a spiral, Id.272.7; ἡ ἐν γ. εὐθεῖα the *initial* line, Id.286.22.

**Γενεσιών**, ῶνος, ὁ (sc. μήν), name of month at Magnesia on the Maeander, *Inscr.Magn.*116.

® **γενέτ-ειρα**, fem. of γενετήρ, *mother*, Pi.*N.*7.2, *CIG*4132 (Galatia); late Prose, τροφὸς πάντων καὶ γ. ἡ γῆ Artem.1.79; ἀλήθεια γ. Plot.5. 8.4. II. *daughter*, Euph.84.4. **-ή**, ἡ, = γενεά II. 3, ἐκ γενετῆς from *the hour of birth*, Il.24.535, Od.18.6; εὐθὺς ἐκ γ. Arist.*EN*1144b6; opp. δι' ἔθος, ib.1154a33; later ἀπὸ γενετῆς Iamb.*VP*30.171. **-ήρ**, ῆρος, ὁ, = γενέτης, *Epic.Alex.Adesp.*2.10, Arist.*Mu.*397a4, *IG*7.716, Coluth.373, Tryph.294: in pl., *parents*, *IG*7.2543, Nonn.*D.*4.61, al. ® **-ης**, ου, ὁ, *begetter, ancestor*, E.*Or.*1011 (anap.), Call.*Epigr.* 23.2; *father*, *IG*3.1335, 12(7).115 (Amorgos); γενέται καὶ πατρὶς ἔχουσιν ὀστέα, i.e. *the tomb of my fathers*, *BMus.Inscr.*2.179, al.: in pl., *parents*, *IG*4.682 (Hermione): generally, *author*, *Epigr.Gr.*979. 4 (Philae). 2. *son*, ὁ Διὸς γ. S.*OT*472; ὁ ἐμὸς γ. E.*Ion*916 (lyr.). II. as Adj., = γενέθλιος, θεοί A.*Supp.*77 (lyr.), E.*Ion* 1130. 2. *produced*, ὁ Νεῖλος θέρει γ. Olymp.*in Mete.*94.9. **-ήσιος**, ον, *sexual*, ὁρμή *AP*15.12.12 (Leo Phil.). **-ικός**, ή, όν:—fem. -κή (sc. πτῶσις), ἡ, *genitive case*, Sch.D.P.449. **-ιος**, ὁ (sc. μήν), name of month at Halos, *IG*9(2).109*a*74. **-ις**, ἡ, fem. of γενέτης, Lxx *Wi.*7.12: acc. -τιν Aglaïas 10.

**Γενετυλλίς**, ίδος, ἡ, *goddess of one's birth-hour*, Ar.*Nu.*52: in pl., Id.*Th.*130, Luc.*Pseudol.*11.

**γενέτωρ**, ορος, ὁ, = γενέτης, πόντος γ. νεφέων ἀνέμων τε Xenoph. 30.5, cf. Hdt.8.137; γ. πατήρ E.*Ion*136 (lyr.), cf. *IG*5(1).540 (Lacon.), 14.1565, Arist.*Mu.*397b21, 399a31; Ἀπόλλων ὁ γ. Id.*Fr.*489; Ἁδριανῷ γενέτορι *IGRom.*4.562 (Aezani).

**γενή**, ἡ, poet. for γενεά, Call.*Fr.*241, Herod.2.1, 4.84.

**γενῆς**, -ῆδος, Att. γενής, ῆδος, ἡ, *pickaxe, mattock*, S.*Ant.*249.

® **γένημα**, ατος, τό, *produce*, of the fruits of the earth (cf. γέννημα), *PRev.Laws*24.15, al. (iii B.C.), Lxx *Ge.*40.17, al.; γ. τῆς ἀμπέλου *Ev. Marc.*14.25: pl., τοῦ ἐνεστῶτος ἔτους *OGI*262.9 (Syria), cf. *BGU* 188.9 (ii A.D.), *POxy.*277.6 (i B.C.); γ. καὶ ἐπιγενήματα *PRyl.*154.22 (i A.D.), etc. **γενημάτιον**, τό, Dim. of foreg., *PEdgar*41.9.

**γενημᾰτο-γρᾰφέω**, *sequester produce of land* for non-payment of taxes, in Pass., *PFay.*23.14, 26.8, al., *BGU*291, 599. **-γρᾰφία**, ἡ, *sequestration*, prob. in Wilcken *Chr.*363 (ii A.D.). ® **-φύλαξ** [ῠ], ακος, ὁ, *custodian of crops*, *PMagd.*1.10 (iii B.C.), etc.:—hence **-φῠλᾰκέω**, τὸν σπόρον *PTeb.ined.*, and **-φῠλᾰκία**, ἡ, *PTeb.*27.4 (pl.), al. (ii B.C.), *PRyl.*90.50 (iii A.D.).

**γενητικός**, v.l. for γενν-, Arist.*Top.*124a24.

**γενητός**, ή, όν, (γενέσθαι) *originated* or *originable*, Arist.*Cael.*280b 15 sqq., v.l. in Pl.*Ti.*28b,c, cf. Ph.1.3, al. (Freq. confused with γεννητός in codd.)

**γενιᾶς· ἔκγονος**, Hsch.

® **γενικός**, ή, όν, *belonging to* or *connected with the γένος*, Arist.*Top.* 102a36; ἡ διαφορὰ γ. ib.101b18; *generic*, Chrysipp.*Stoic.*2.28, Phld. *Sign.*18, 19, etc.: Comp., *Stoic.*2.117, Ptol.*Phas.*p.5 H.: Sup., Diog. Bab.*Stoic.*3.214, *BGU*282.19 (ii A.D.), etc. Adv. **-κῶς** M.Ant.8.55,

Plot.6.1.9, Iamb.*in Nic.*p.22 P., etc. **2.** *principal, typical*, ὀρχήσεις Luc.*Salt.*34(Comp.), cf. 22(Sup.). **II.** *consisting of families*, φυλαί D.H.4.14, etc.; *of the family*, νόμος *CIG*3467.54 (Sardis), cf. 2712 (Mylasa). **III.** *sexual*, ἁμάρτημα Hdn.6.1.5 (dub.). **IV.** *in kind*, opp. ἀργυρικός, λόγος *PFlor.*77.7 (iii A.D.). **V.** Gramm., ἡ γενική (sc. πτῶσις) *genitive case*, *Stoic.*2.59, D.T.636, etc.

**γενισμός**, ὁ, *arrangement according to* γένη, *classification of rents according to* (1) *hypothetical estimate* and (2) *actual method of collection*, *PTeb.*67.5, al. (ii B.C.).

⊛ **γένν-ᾰ** Emp.17.27, 22.9, A.*Pr.*853 (but γέννᾱ in lyr. passages of E., as *Hec.*159), ης, ἡ:—poet. for γένος, *descent, birth, origin*, γέννᾳ μεγαλυνομένων A.*Pr.*892, cf. *Ag.*760 (lyr.). **2.** *origin*, [τοῦ ὄντος] Parm. 8.6; διέχειν γέννη τε κρήσει τε Emp.22.7; γῆ γ. πάντων Secund. *Sent.*15; *production*, πύου Aret.*SD*1.14; ὑγρῶν ib.15. **II.** *offspring, son*, Pi.*O.*7.23; θνάσκοντα γέννας ἄτερ A.*Th.*748; λαγίνα γ. Id.*Ag.*119; *generation*, πέμπτη δ' ἀπ' αὐτοῦ γέννα Id.*Pr.*853, cf. 774. **2.** *race, family*, οὐρανία γ. ib.165; ἀρσένων γ. E.*Med.*428 (lyr.): rare in Prose, ἡ τοῦ πέρατος γ. Pl.*Phlb.*25d, cf. Is.*Fr.* 136. **3.** *creation, creature*, *PMag.Leid.V.*7.14. **4.** personified, *Creative Force*, ib.*W.*5.3. **III.** of the Moon, *coming forth*, Ach.Tat.*Intr.Arat.*21, Sch.Arat.735, Paul.Al.*G.*4. ⊛ **-άδας** [νᾰ], ου, ὁ, (Dor. word) *noble, generous*, χρηστὸς καὶ γ. Ar.*Ra.*179; γ. καὶ πρᾷος Pl.*Phdr.*243c, cf. Arist.*EN*1100$^{b}$32; *highly bred*, ἐπὶ τῶν γενναδῶν ἵππων Polem.*Phgn.*78; *notable*, c. inf., Luc.*Hist.Conscr.* 33. **-αιάζω**, *to be brave*, Sch.E.*Hipp.*206:—also **-αΐζομαι**, Suid. s.v. τὴν λεοντῆν ἐνδύου. **-αιοπρεπής**, ές, *befitting a noble*: only in Adv. -πῶς Ar.*Pax*988. ⊛ **-αῖος**, α, ον, also ος, ον E.*Hec.*592: (γέννα):—*true to one's birth* or *descent* (εὐγενὲς μέν ἐστι τὸ ἐξ ἀγαθοῦ γένους, γενναῖον δὲ τὸ μὴ ἐξιστάμενον ἐκ τῆς αὑτοῦ φύσεως Arist.*HA*488$^{b}$19, cf. *Rh.*1390$^{b}$22), οὔ μοι γενναῖον ἀλυσκάζοντι μάχεσθαι Il.5.253 (nowhere else in Hom.); γενναῖον δέ σοι ταχέως ὑπακούειν Ar.*Fr.*28 D.: hence, **I.** of persons, *high-born, noble*, Archil.107, etc.; τέκνα Hdt.1.173; ὦ γονῇ γενναῖε S.*OT*1469; ἐσθλοὺς ἔκ τε γενναίων γεγῶτας Id.*Fr.*107.3; γενναῖός τις ἑπτὰ πάππους ἔχων ἀποφῆναι Pl.*Tht.*174e; οἱ γ., opp. οἱ ἀγεννεῖς, Arist.*Pol.* 1296$^{b}$22; so of animals, *well-bred*, σκύλαξ Pl.*R.*375a, X.*Cyr.*1.4.15; opp. ἀγεννής, Arist.*HA*558$^{b}$16. **2.** *noble in mind, high-minded*, Hdt.3.140 (Sup.), S.*El.*129 (lyr.), etc.; τὸ γ., = γενναιότης, Id.*OC* 569; of actions, *noble*, Hdt.1.37; λῆμα γ. Pi.*P.*8.44; τλάσας τὸ γ. S. *OC*1640, cf. E.*Alc.*624; γ. ἔπος, λόγοι, πόνοι, S.*Ph.*1402, E.*Heracl.* 537, *HF*357 (lyr.). **3.** as a form of polite speech, γενναῖος εἶ you are *very good*, Ar.*Th.*220. **b.** ὦ γενναῖε, common form of address in Pl., as *Grg.*494e, cf. S.*Ph.*801; ironical, D.H.7.46. **II.** of things, *good of their kind, excellent*, μέλος A.*Fr.*281.5; σταφυλή, σῦκα, Pl. *Lg.*844e; γενναίου.. ἄξιον οὐθενός of no *great* use, Ath.Mech.31.2; ironical, γένει γ. σοφιστική Pl.*Sph.*231b (cf. I.1), etc.; *genuine, intense*, δύη S.*Aj.*938, etc.; *violent*, σεισμός Philostr.*VA*6.38; θάλπη Jul.*Or.* 2.101d. **b.** γενναῖον· τὸ τῆς γενέσεως ἀρχηγόν, Hsch. **III.** Adv. -αίως *nobly*, Hdt.7.139, Th.2.41, Pl.*La.*196b, Men.672; ὅρκος, πῆγμα γ. παγέν A.*Ag.*1198; ironical, μάλα γ. ἐπιλαθόμενον ὧν εὖ πάθοι Jul.*Or.*3.125c: Comp. -οτέρως Pl.*Tht.*166c, Ps.-Callisth.1.38: Sup. -ότατα E.*Cyc.*657 (lyr.). **2.** irreg. Sup. γενναιέστατος Dinol. 10. **-αιότης**, ητος, ἡ, *the character of a* γενναῖος, *nobility*, E.*Ph.* 1680, Th.3.82; of land, *fertility*, X.*Cyr.*8.3.38, Plb.3.44.8; *noble birth*, J.*AJ*19.3.1; *high spirit*, of colts, Max.Tyr.7.8. **-ας**, ὁ, *mother's brother, uncle*, Hsch. **-άω**, fut. Med. γεννήσομαι in pass. sense, D.S.19.2 (but -ηθήσομαι Id.4.9): (γέννα):—causal of γίγνομαι (cf. γείνομαι), mostly of the father, *beget*, ὁ γεννήσας πατήρ S.*El.*1412; οἱ γεννήσαντές σε your *parents*, X.*Mem.*2.1.27; τὸ γεννώμενον ἔκ τινος Hdt.1.108, etc.; ὅθεν γεγενναμένοι *sprung*, Pi.*P.*5.74; of the mother, *bring forth, bear*, A.*Supp.*48, Arist.*GA*716$^{a}$22, X. *Lac.*1.3, etc.:—Med., *produce from oneself, create*, Pl.*Ti.*34b, *Mx.* 238a. **2.** *produce, grow, get*, κἂν σῶμα γεννήσῃ μέγα S.*Aj.*1077. **3.** metaph., *engender, produce*, λήθη τῶν ἰδίων κακῶν θρασύτητα γεννᾷ Democr.196; παντοίαν ἀρετήν Pl.*Smp.*209e; διανοήματά τε καὶ δόξας Id.*R.*496a, etc.; γεννῶσι τὸν οὐρανὸν [οἱ φιλόσοφοι] *call* it *into existence*, Arist.*Cael.*283$^{b}$31; ὁ ἐξ ἀσωμάτου γεννῶν λόγος ib.305$^{a}$16, cf. Plot.6.6.9; of numbers, *produce* a total, Ph.1.347. **-ήεις**, εσσα, εν, *generative*, μήδεα Emp.29.2. ⊛ **-ημα**, ατος, τό, *that which is produced* or *born, child*, S.*Tr.*315; παίδων τῶν σῶν νέατον γ. Id. *Ant.*627; τῶν Λαΐου.. τις ἦν γεννημάτων Id.*OT*1167: generally, any *product* or *work*, Pl.*R.*597e, etc.: in pl., *fruits* of the earth, Plb.1.71.1, etc.; τῶν στοιχείων Phld.*Sign.*37. **2.** *breeding*, δηλοῖ τὸ γ. ὠμὸν (sc. ὄν).. παιδός S.*Ant.*471. **II.** Act., *begetting*, A.*Pr.* 850 (pl., s.v.l.). **2.** *producing*, Pl.*Sph.*266d. **-ημᾰτίζω**, *produce offspring*, Aq.*Is.*55.10, al. **-ημᾰτικός**, ή, όν, = γεννητικός, J.*BJ*4. 8.3. **-ησιουργός**, = γενεσιουργός, Hsch. **-ησις**, Dor. **-ᾱσις**, εως, ἡ, *engendering, producing*, E.*IA*1065 (lyr., codd.); γ. καὶ τόκος Pl.*Smp.*206e; *birth*, *IG*2$^{2}$.1368.130, v.l. in *Ev.Luc.*1.14. **2.** *production*, ἀγαθῶν Arist.*Pol.*1332$^{a}$18 (pl.). **-ήτειρα**, ἡ, fem. of γεννητήρ, Pl.*Cra.*410c. **-ητέον**, *one must produce, grow*, Gal.10. 198. **-ητήρ**, ῆρος, ὁ, = sq. I, *App.Anth.*6.128. **-ητής**, οῦ, ὁ, *begetter, parent*, S.*OT*1015, *Fr.*752, Pl.*Cri.*51e, *Lg.*717e; τῶν πράξεων ὥσπερ καὶ τέκνων Arist.*EN*1113$^{b}$18: generally, *producer*, Plot.3.3.3. **II.** ⊛ **γεννῆται**, οἱ, (γέννα) at Athens, *members of* γένη, Pl.*Lg.*878d, Philoch.94; εἰς τοὺς γ. ἐγγράφειν, ἄγειν, Is.7. 13,15, cf. Arist.*Ath.Fr.*3, *IG*2$^{2}$.1229.5; Ἀπόλλωνος Πατρῴου καὶ Διὸς Ἑρκείου γ. D.57.67. **-ητικός**, ή, όν, *generative, productive*, ἡ πρᾶξις ἡ γ. Arist.*HA*539$^{b}$21; ψυχὴ γ. Id.*de An.*416$^{b}$25: c. gen., *generative* or *productive of*.., τινός Epicur.*Ep.*1 p.11 U., Arist.*GA*726$^{b}$21, etc.; ὕλην σπέρματος -κήν Epicur.*Nat.Herc.*908.1. **2.** of men or animals, *able to procreate*, Arist.*HA*544$^{b}$26, *de An.*432$^{b}$24. **-ητός**, ή, όν, *begotten*, υἱὸς γ., opp. ποιητός, Pl.*Lg.*923e; *mortal*, Luc.*Icar.*2; γεννητοὶ γυναικῶν *born of* women, *Ev.Matt.*11.11, *Ev.Luc.*7.28. **II.** *generable*, opp. φθαρτός, Arist.*Metaph.*1027$^{a}$29 (v.l.); ὕλη γ. matter *for generation*, ib.1042$^{b}$6. Adv. -τῶς *by means of generation*, Iamb. *Myst.*1.18. **-ήτρια**, ἡ, = γεννήτειρα, δικῶν Phryn.*PS*p.62 B. ⊛ **-ήτωρ**, Dor. **-άτωρ**, ορος, ὁ, = γενέτωρ, Ζεύς A.*Supp.*206, E.*Hipp.*683, Jul.*Or.*2.51d, v.l. in Arist.*Mu.*397$^{b}$21; γ. καὶ ἑστιοῦχον Pl.*Lg.*878a: pl., ib.869a; θεῷ γεννήτορι πάντων *IG*3.636: metaph. of numbers, ἐὰν πυθμενικοὶ ὦσιν οἱ γ. Iamb.*in Nic.*p.56 P., al. **-ικός**, ή, όν, = γενναῖος, *noble*, Ar.*Eq.*457 (Sup.), Pl.*Phdr.*279a (Comp.); γ. καὶ κοσμία γύναι Men.*Georg.*42; of things, λεπαστή Antiph.45; δεῖπνον Alciphr.3.5. Adv. -ῶς Ar.*Lys.*1070, Antiph.192, Luc.*Somn.*7, Max.Tyr.31.1; *vigorously, drastically*, of the action of medicines, Gal.11.864, al.

**γεννοδότειρα**, ἡ, *the giver of heirs*, Ἀφροδίτη Orph.*H.*55.12.

**γεννόν**· ἀρχαῖον, Hsch. (perh. for ἕνον); also, = κοῖλον, Id. **γέννου**· καὶ λάβε (cf. γέντο) καὶ κάθιζε (Cypr.), Id.

⊛ **γένος**, εος or ους, τό, *race, stock, kin*, ἀμφοτέροισιν ὁμὸν γ. ἠδ' ἴα πάτρη Il.13.354; αἷμά τε καὶ γ. Od.8.583; ὑμετέρου δ' οὐκ ἔστι γένεος βασιλεύτερον 15.533; γένος πατέρων αἰσχυνέμεν Il.6.209; γ. ἀπόλωλε τοκήων Od.4.62; ὅθι τοι γένος ἐστὶ καὶ αὐτῇ 6.35: freq. abs. in acc., ἐξ Ἰθάκης γένος εἰμί from Ithaca I am *by race*, 15.267, cf. Il. 5.544,896, S.*Ph.*239, etc.; in Att. freq. with the Art., ποδαπὸς τὸ γένος εἶ; Ar.*Pax*186, cf. Pl.*Sph.*216a: so in dat., γένει πολῖται D.23.24; γένει υἱός, opp. an adopted son, Id.44.2; οἱ ἐν γένει, = συγγενεῖς, S.*OT*1430; οἱ ἔξω γένους Id.*Ant.*660; οὐδὲν ἐν γένει Id. *OT*1016; γένει προσήκειν τινί X.*An.*1.6.1; γένει ἀπωτέρω εἶναι D. 44.13: in gen., γένους εἶναί τινος to be of his *race*, ἄναγνος καὶ γένους τοῦ Λαΐου S.*OT*1383, cf. X.*HG*4.2.9; ἐγγυτέρω, ἐγγύτατα γένους, nearer, next *of kin*, Is.8.33, A.*Supp.*388. **2.** *direct descent*, opp. *collateral relationship*, γένος γάρ, ἀλλ' οὐχὶ συγγένεια Is.8.33; αἱ κατὰ γένος βασιλεῖαι *hereditary* monarchies, Arist.*Pol.*1285$^{a}$16, 1313$^{a}$ 10. **II.** *offspring*, even of *a single descendant*, σὸν γ. Il.19.124, 21.186; ἡ δ' ἄρ' ἔην θεῖον γ. οὐδ' ἀνθρώπων 6.180; ἁμὸν Οἰδίπου γ. A. *Th.*654; Διὸς γ., of Bacchus, S.*Ant.*1117 (lyr.); Τέκμησσα, δύσμορον γ. Id.*Aj.*784. **2.** collectively, *offspring, posterity*, ἐκεῖνοι καὶ τὸ γ. τὸ ἀπ' ἐκείνων Th.1.126; ἐξώλη ποιεῖν αὑτὸν καὶ γ. καὶ οἰκίαν D.19. 71. **III.** generally, *race*, of beings, θεῶν Ar.*Th.*960; ἡμιθέων γ. ἀνδρῶν Il.12.23; ἡμιόνων, βοῶν γ., Il.2.852, Od.20.212; ἵππειον γ., i.e. *mules*, S.*Ant.*342; ἰχθύων πλωτὸν γ. Id.*Fr.*941.9. **b.** *clan, house, family*, Hdt.1.125, etc.; Φρὺξ μὲν γενεῇ, γένεος δὲ τοῦ βασιληΐου ib.35; τοὺς ἀπὸ γένους men *of noble family*, Plu.*Rom.*21; ἱερεὺς κατὰ γ. *IG* 5(1).497, al.; also ἱέρεια ἀπὸ γένους, διὰ γένους, ib.607.29,602; esp. at Athens and elsewhere as a subdivision of the φρατρία, Arist.*Ath. Fr.*3, Pl.*Alc.*1.120e, etc.; = Lat. *gens*, D.S.4.21, Plu.*Num.*1. **c.** *tribe*, as a subdivision of ἔθνος, Hdt.1.56,101. **d.** *caste*, Id.2.164. **e.** of animals, *breed*, Id.4.29. **2.** *age, generation*, Od.3.245; γ. χρύσεον, etc., Hes.*Op.*109: hence, *age, time of life*, γένει ὕστερος Il.3. 215, cf. Arist.*Rh.*1408$^{a}$27. **IV.** *sex*, Epich.172.1, Pl.*Smp.*189d; *gender*, Arist.*Rh.*1407$^{b}$7, Diog.Bab.*Stoic.*3.214, etc. **V.** *class, sort, kind*, τὰ γ. τῶν κυνῶν ἐστι δισσά X.*Cyn.*3.1; τὸ φιλόσοφον γ. Pl. *R.*501e; τὸ τῶν γεωργῶν [γ.] Id.*Ti.*17c, cf. *R.*434b, Arist.*Pol.*1329$^{a}$ 27; τῶν ἰχθυοπωλῶν γ. Xenarch.7.4; τὸ τῶν παρασίτων γ. Nicol. Com.1.1, etc. **2.** in Logic, opp. εἶδος (species), Pl.*Prm.*129c, al., Arist.*Top.*102$^{a}$31, 102$^{b}$12, al.; τὰ γ. εἰς εἴδη πλείω καὶ διαφέροντα διαιρεῖται Id.*Metaph.*1059$^{b}$36. **3.** in the animal kingdom, τὰ μέγιστα γ., = the modern *Classes*, such as birds, fishes, Id.*HA*490$^{b}$7, cf. 505$^{b}$26; so in the vegetable kingdom, γένη τὰ μέγιστα, = σιτώδη, χεδροπά and ἀνώνυμα, Thphr.*HP*8.1.1. **b.** *genus*, τὸ τῶν καρκίνων γ., τὸ τῶν περιστερῶν γ., etc., Arist.*HA*487$^{b}$17, 488$^{a}$4; τῶν δένδρων καὶ τῶν φυτῶν εἴδη πλείω τυγχάνει καθ' ἕκαστον γένος Thphr.*HP*1.14.3; τοῦ αὐτοῦ γένους [πίτυς] καὶ πεύκη Dsc.1.69, al. **c.** γένος τι a *species* of plant, Thphr.*HP*4.8.13; so later, γένη, = *crops*, ἄλλοις γένεσι τοῖς πρὸς πυρὸν διοικουμένοις *PTeb.*66.43, al. (ii B.C.); οἷς ἐὰν αἱρῶμαι γένεσι πλὴν κνήκου *PAmh.*2.91.15 (ii A.D.); *produce*, *POxy.*727.20 (ii A.D.); *materials*, ib.54.16 (iii A.D.); ἐν γένεσιν in *kind*, opp. ἐν ἀργυρίῳ, *PFay.*21.10 (ii A.D.). **4.** τὰ γ. the *elements*, Pl.*Ti.*54b. (Cf. Skt. *jánas*, gen. *jánasas*; Lat. *genus*, *-eris*, v. γίγνομαι.)

**γενούστης**, ου, ὁ, misread for γένους τῆς in Pl.*Phlb.*30d, cf. Hsch.

⊛ **γέντα**, τά, = ἔντερα, Call.*Fr.*309, Nic.*Al.*62,557; = κρέα, σπλάγχνα, Hsch.

**γεντιᾱνή**, ἡ, *gentian*, Hp.*Ep.*19, Dsc.3.3. [-ᾱνή Damocr.ap.Gal. 13.822, 14.97, but -ᾰνή ib.14.123.]

**γεντιὰς** ῥίζα, = foreg., Androm.ap.Gal.14.41. **2.** = γλυκύρριζα, Dsc.3.5; = κενταύρειον τὸ μέγα ib.6.

**γέντιμος**· ἄκρον τοῦ ἁλιευτικοῦ καλάμου, Hsch.; cf. γέρσυμον. **γέντινοι**· οἰκεῖοι, and **γέντινος**· ὕπνος, Id.

**γέντο**, *he grasped*, = ἔλαβεν, 3 sg. of Verb found only in this form, Il.8.43, al. (Cf. ἀπόγεμε· ἄφελκε, and ὕγγεμος· συλλαβή (Cypr.), Hsch.) **II.** shortd. form for ἐγένετο, v. γίγνομαι.

**γένυξ**· πέλεκυς, Hsch.

**γένῠς**, υος, ἡ, dat. γένυι Pi.*O.*13.85: pl., gen. γενύων *P.*4.225 (disyll.), A.*Th.*122 (lyr.): dat. γένυσι S.*Ant.*121 (lyr.), Ep. γένυσσι Il.11.416, γενύεσσι Nic. (v. infr.): acc. γένυας, contr. γένῡς:—*jaw*, πυκάσαι τε γένυς εὐανθέϊ λάχνῃ Od.11.320; ἡ ἄνω γ., ἡ κάτωθεν, Arist.*HA*492$^{b}$ 23, sq.: pl., γένυες *both jaws, the mouth with the teeth*, Il.23.688, 11.

416, Pi.P.4.225, S.Ant.121: in sg., Thgn.1327, E.Ph.1380, al.: generally, *side of the face, cheek*, φίλον φίλημα παρὰ γένυν τιθέντα E. Supp.1154. II. *edge of an axe, axe*, S.Ph.1205 (lyr.), El.196 (lyr.); of a fishing-hook, Opp.H.3.539; πυράγρης Nic.Al.50 (pl.). (Cf. Skr. *hanus*, Lat. *gena*, etc.) [ῠ twice in E., El.1214 (lyr.), Fr. 530.6.]

**γεο-ειδής**, ές, = γεώδης, Ti.Locr.101a, Arist.GA731b13, HA555b28. ⊛-**θαλπής**, ές, *earth-cherishing*, CIG3769 (Nicomedia). -**κτείτης**, ου, = γεωμόρος (?) (add.), ib.3695b (Mysia).

**γεόομαι**, Pass., *to become earth*, D.S.3.40.

**γεοῦχος**, ὁ, *landowner*, Agatharch.95, PAmh.88.30 (ii A.D.), POxy.910.16, etc. (γαιοῦχος Paul.Al.N.2): hence **γεουχέω** PFay.23.6, BGU18.19 (ii A.D.), etc.; **γεουχικός**, ή, όν, POxy.1638.15 (iii A.D.).

**γέραδος**· αἰγιαλός, Hsch.; cf. χέραδος. **γεράζω**, *honour*, EM 8.5, 227.43:—Pass., Hsch.

**γεραίομαι**, dub. l. in Nic.Al.396.

**γεραιός**, ά, όν, (γέρων, γῆρας) = γηραιός, *old*: in Hom. (who never has γηραιός) always of men, with notion of dignity (v. infr.), cf. Pi. N.4.89; ὁ γεραιός *that reverend sire*, Il.1.35, etc.; γεραιέ 10.164, etc.; but γεραιάς (acc. pl. fem.) 6.87 (cf. 270,287) is f.l. for γεραίρας, v. γεραρός: Comp. γεραίτερος Od.3.24, A.Eu.848, Hdt.6.52; γονῇ πεφυκὼς γ. (-τέρᾳ codd.) S.OC1294; freq. in political sense, οἱ γ. *the elders, senators*, X.Cyr.1.5.5, Pl.Lg.952a, IG14.2445 (Massilia): Sup. γεραίτατος Ar.Ach.286, Pl.Lg.855e, etc.; rarely, = πρεσβύτατος, *eldest*, Theoc.15.139. II. of things, *ancient*, πόλις A.Ag.710 (lyr.); χείρ E.Hec.64 (lyr.). (γεραῐὸς Tyrt.10.20, E.HF446 (lyr.); cf. γεραός.)

**γεραιότης**, ητος, ἡ, *advanced age*, PMasp.279.26 (vi A.D.), etc.

**γεραιό-φλοιος**, ον, *with old, wrinkled skin*, σῦκα AP6.102 (Phil.). -**φρων**, ονος, ὁ, ἡ, (φρήν) *old of mind, sage*, A.Supp.361 (lyr., Burges for γεραφρόνων).

**γέραιρα**, ἡ, v. γεραρός. **γεραιράδες** or **γεραράδες**, αἱ, = γεραραί, AB228; priestesses of Athena at Argos, ib.231.10; γερηράδες, Hsch.

**γεραίρω**, Ep. impf. γέραιρον Il.7.321: fut. γεραρῶ Jusj.ap.D.59.78, Epigr.Gr.992 (Balbilla): aor. 1 ἐγέρηρα CIG2936 (Tralles), APl. 4.183.7, Orph.A.507, γέρηρα IG4.1475 (Epid.); ἐγέραρα Pi.O.5.5, N.5.8: (γεραρός):—*honour, reward* with a gift, νώτοισιν δ' Αἴαντα διηνεκέεσσι γέραιρεν Il.7.321, cf. Od.14.437,441, etc.: generally, *honour*, τινά Pi.O.3.2: c. dat. modi, βωμοὺς ἑορταῖς ib.5.5; τινὰ ἐπινικίοις B.2.8; γένος θεῶν γ. φωνῇ Ar.Th.961 (lyr.); δώροις καὶ ἀρχαῖς καὶ ἕδραις καὶ πάσαις τιμαῖς X.Cyr.8.1.39; στεφάνοις τοὺς νικῶντας Id. HG1.7.33; ὃν.. ἐπεστεφάνωσε γεραίρων IG3.713:—Pass., τίμιος γεραίρεται E.Supp.553; τιμαῖς X.Cyr.8.8.4. 2. γεραίρει· τέρπει, Hsch.:—Pass., γεραιρόμενα μυλοισι prob. in Nic.Al.396. 3. reversely, γ. τινί τι *present as an honorary gift*, τὰ Ἰοβάκχεια τῷ Διονύσῳ Jusj.ap.D. l.c. II. *celebrate*, τὰ πάθεα τραγικοῖσι χοροῖσι Hdt. 5.67; χορείαις θυσίαν Pl.Lg.799a, cf. Epin.980b.—Not in early Prose, exc. Hdt., X., and Pl.: in later Prose, Ph.1.186, Arr.Ind.8.5 (Pass.), Porph.Abst.2.16, etc.

**Γεραίστιος**, v. Γεράστιος.

**γεραίτερος**, **γεραίτατος**, Comp. and Sup. of γεραιός (q.v.).

**γερᾰλέος**, = γηρ-, Hsch.

**γεράνδρυον**, τό, (δρῦς) *an old tree* or *stump*, Ph.2.437, Plu.2.796b, etc.: hence of an old person, Aristaen.2.1: heterocl. pl., γεράνδρυες, Hsch. 2. as Adj., *old, withered*, Thphr.HP2.7.2, A.R.1.1118, Jul.Ep.98; γ. πρέμνα Dsc.4.186. (ῠ A.R. l.c., ῡ AP9.233 (Eryc.).)

**γεράν-ειον** [ᾰ], τό, a kind of *truffle*, Eust.1017.19; = ὕδνον, Thphr. HP1.6.9, ap.Ath.2.62a (om.codd. Thphr.); but dist. from ὕ. ib.1.6.5, ap.Ath.2.61f. -**ίας**, ου, ὁ, (γέρανος) *crane-necked, long-necked*, Phryn.PSp.55B. -**ίζω**, *utter the crane's note*, Gloss. -**ιον**, τό, (γέρᾰνος) *Geranium tuberosum*, a plant, Dsc.3.116; ἕτερον γ. *crane's-bill, Erodium malacoides*, ibid.; also γεράνιος, Hsch. (but ἡ γεράνιος a *plaster*, Aët.15.15). II. substance used in Alchemy, Pelag.Alch.p.256B. -**ίς**, ίδος, ἡ, a kind of *surgical bandage*, Heliod.ap.Orib.48.47 tit., Gal.18(1).814. -**ίτης** (sc. λίθος), ου, ὁ, *a precious stone*, Plin.37.187. [ῐ]

**γερᾰνο-βοσία**, ἡ, = sq., Poll.9.16. -**βωτία**, ἡ, *feeding of cranes*, Pl.Plt.264c (pl.). -**γέρων**, = γεράνιον, Ps.-Dsc.3.116. -**μᾰχία**, ἡ, *battle with cranes*, Ὁμηρικὴ τῶν Πυγμαίων γ. Str.2.1.9. -**πόδιον**, = λυχνίς, Ps.-Dsc.3.100.

⊛ **γέρᾰνος**, ἡ, also ὁ, Thphr.Sign.38:—*crane, Grus cinerea*, Il.3.3, Hes.Op.448, Alc.Supp.9, Ar.Av.710, Arist.HA614b18, al. II. *crane for lifting weights*, esp. used in the theatre, Poll.4.130. 2. *quern*, Hsch. III. *dance resembling the movements of the crane*, Luc.Salt.34, Plu.Thes.21, Poll.4.101. IV. (masc.) a *fish*, Ael. NA15.9. V. = ὄμβρος (Cyren.), EM227.51. (Cf. OHG. *chranuh*, OE. *cran* 'crane', Lith. *garnỹs* 'stork', etc.)

**γερᾰνουλκός**, ὁ, *leader of the dance called* γέρανος at Delos, Hsch.

**γερᾰνόφθαλμος**, ον, *crane-eyed*, Sch.Opp.H.1.386.

**γερᾰνώδης**, ες, *crane like*, τράχηλος Phryn.PSp.55B.

**γεραός**, ή, όν, = γεραιός, S.OC200, Tim.Pers.227, Nic.Fr.74.71, IG3.779.

**γεραόχος**, ον, *holder of privilege*, gloss on ἀγέρωχος, Sch.Il.10.430.

⊛ **γερᾰρός**, ά, όν, *of reverend bearing, majestic*, Il.3.170; γεραρώτερος ἦεν Ὀδυσσεύς ib.211; γεραρὴ τράπεζα a table *of honour*, Xenoph.1.9; γεραραῖς χερσί IG14.818; ἀνὴρ γ. τὸ εἶδος Plu.Alex.26; τὸ γ. τοῦ ἤθους M.Ant.1.15. Adv. -ρῶς, μέλπουσιν AP9.692. 2. later, = γεραιός, A.Ag.722 (lyr); γ. τοκῆες IG3.1335, Q.S.9.90. 3. γεραραί, αἱ, *elders*, A.Supp.667 (lyr.); but γεραραί *priestesses of Dionysus* is f. l. for **γέραιραι** in D.59.73, al.; cf. Μητρὸς.. πρόπολος σεμνή τε γέραιρα IG2.2116, and γεραίρας (acc. pl.) is prob. l. in Il.6.270, cf. 87,287 (cf. Sch. BT); cf. EM227.35. (γέραιρα old fem. of γεραρός; cf. χίμαιρα: χίμαρος.)

⊛ **γέρᾰς**, αος (in Prose -ως X.Ag.1.5, Luc.Tyr.9), τό: nom. pl. γέρᾰ, apoc. for γέραα, Il.2.237, 9.334, Od.4.66; γέρᾱ E.Ph.874; γέρεα Hdt.2.168, SIG1037 (Milet.); γέρη ib.1025 (Cos); γέρᾱτα IG14.1389 i 29: gen. pl. γερῶν Th.3.58, etc.; Ep. dat. γεράεσσι Hes.Th. 449, Theoc.17.109:—*gift of honour*, μοῖραν καὶ γ. ἐσθλὸν ἔχων Od.11.534; τὸ γὰρ γ. ἐστὶ θανόντων *the last honours* of the dead, Il.16.457; *privilege, prerogative* conferred on kings or nobles, γ. θ' ὅ τι δῆμος ἔδωκεν Od.7.150, cf. Il.20.182; τὰς ἀγγελίας ἐσφέρειν ἐδίδου γ. Hdt. 1.114, etc.; πρότερον δὲ ἦσαν ἐπὶ ῥητοῖς γέρασι πατρικαὶ βασιλεῖαι Th. 1.13; τιμαὶ καὶ ἔπαινοι καὶ γ. Pl.R.516c; γ. καὶ ἆθλα ib.460b; freq. of priests (cf. 3), Aeschin.3.18; δαίμοσιν νέμει γέρα ἄλλοισιν ἄλλα A.Pr.231; so later, γ. ἀλειτουργησίας PFlor.382.3 (iii A.D.). 2. generally, *gift, present*, Od.20.297, etc. 3. esp. *perquisite* received by priests at sacrifices, τὰ δέρματα καὶ τὰ ἄλλα γέρεα SIG1037 (Milet., iv/iii B.C.); γέρη λαμβάνει τὸ δέρμα καὶ τὸ σκέλος ib.1025.22 (Cos, iv/iii B.C.); ὁ πριάμενος τῶν γερῶν λήψεται τὰς γενομένας καρπείας PEleph.14.13 (iii B.C.). 4. *reward*, POxy.1408.16 (iii A.D.). (If akin to γέρων, prop. *privilege of age*.)

⊛ **γεράσμιος**, ον, (γέρας) *honouring*, h.Merc.122. II. = γεραρός, *honoured*, E.Ph.923; μάντις Nic.Th.613; *aged*, ὄσσων E.Supp.95.

⊛ **Γεράστιος**, ὁ, *a month* at Sparta and Cos, Th.4.119, SIG1012.15; at Troezen and Calaurea (in form Γεραίστ-), Caryst.13, SIG993.

**γεραστός**, ή, όν, *honoured*, EM227.43.

**γερασφόρος**, ον, *winning honour*, Pi.P.2.43.

**γεράτης**, name of a breed of horses, POxy.922.7 (vi/vii A.D.).

**γεργαθός**, = γυργ-, POxy.741.5 (ii A.D.). **γέργανα** (i.e. ϝεργ-)· ἐργαλεῖα, Hsch.

**γέργερα**· πολλά, Hsch. (γέργενα cod., cf. Varr.LL5.11).

**γεργέριμος** (sc. ἐλαία), = δρυπεπής, Call.Fr.50, cf. Suid., Hsch.; also of figs, Didym.ap.Ath.2.56d.

**γεργέρινος**, = γεργῖνος, Hsch. **γέργερος**· βρόγχος, Id.; cf. γαργαρεών. **γεργέροψ**· ζῷον, Id. (γεργέλ- cod.). **γεργῖνος**, ὁ, = διάβολος, Id. **γέργυπες**· νεκροί, Id.

**γέργυρα**, v. γόργυρα.

**γερδιοραβδιστής**, ὁ, *worker who beat the web* in a weaving-shed, PTeb.305.5 (ii A.D.).

**γερδιός** or **γέρδιος**, ὁ, *weaver*, Hsch., Rev.Épigr.1.146, PTeb.116.48 (ii B.C.), POxy.39.8 (i A.D.), etc.:—also **γέρδις**, BGU426.19, etc.:—fem. **γερδία**, Edict.Diocl.20.12, ⊛ **γερδίαινα**, BGU617.4 (but **γέρδιος**, ἡ, EM228.40):—Adj. ⊛ **γερδιακός**, ή, όν, τέχνη PGrenf.2.59.10; ἱστός POxy.646: -**κόν** (sc. τέλος), τό, *tax on weaving*, ib.288.2 (i A.D.).

**γερδιών**, ῶνος, ὁ, *weaving-shed*, PFlor.50.70 (iii A.D.).

**γερδοποιόν**, τό, = *textrinum*, Gloss.

⊛ **γερεᾰφόρος**, *one who enjoys perquisites*, title of priest at Cos (cf. γέρας 3), γ. βασιλέων SIG1025.21.

**γέρην**, ἡ, fem. of γέρανος, Ael.Dion.Fr.104, Hsch.; also, = ἔντιμος, Id.

**Γερήνιος**, ὁ, Homeric epith. of Nestor, Γερήνιος ἱππότα Νέστωρ, *from Gerena* or *Gerenon*, a city of Messenia; ξεῖνος ἐὼν.. παρ' ἱπποδάμοισι Γερήνοις Hes.Fr.15.3.

**γερη-φορία**, ἡ, *enjoyment of privileges*, D.H.2.10 (pl.). -**φόρος**, = γερεαφόρος, BCH12.282 (Myndos).

**γερθυρέον**· ἱλαρόν, Hsch. **γέρινθοι**· ἐρέβινθοι, Id.

**γεροάκται**· δήμαρχοι (Lacon.), Hsch. (for γερωιακταί, = γερουσιασταί).

⊛ **γεροῖα**, τά, *tales of old time*, Corinn.20: as title of poems by her, Ant.Lib.25 (prob.).

**γεροίταν**· πάππον (Cypr.), Hsch.; cf. **γέρυς**, **γερύτας**, = γέρων, Id.

**γεροντ-ᾰγωγέω**, (ἀγωγός) *guide an old man*, S.OC348: c.acc., Πηλέα γ. Id.Fr.487, parodied by Com.Adesp.11, cf. Ar.Eq.1099. -**άριον**, τό, = γερόντιον, Gloss. -**εία**, ἡ, *membership of a* γερουσία, OGI 534 (Ephesus). ⊛ -**ειος**, α, ον, *belonging to an old man* or *old age*, Ar.Fr.715. -**εύω**, *to be a senator*, γεροντεύσας IG5(1).254 (Sparta, i B.C.), al.:—Med., Hsch.s.v. γηρωπίζεται. ⊛ -**ία**, ἡ, Lacon., = γερουσία, X.Lac.10.1. -**ίας**, ου, ὁ, *father's father* (Lacon.), Sch.Il.14.118, Eust.971.23. -**ιάω**, *grow old* or *childish*, D.L.3.18. ⊛ -**ικός**, ή, όν, *of* or *for old men*, λουτρὰ Pl.Lg.761c; κρᾶσις Ath.Med.ap.Orib. inc.23.6: -**κόν**, τό, *senate-house*, Str.14.1.43; cf. sq. Adv. -**κῶς** *like an old man*, v.l. in Ar.V.1132, cf. Plu.2.639d: Comp. -**κώτερον** Cic. Att.12.1.2. -**ιον**, τό, Dim. of γέρων, *little old man*, Hp.Ep.13, Ar.Ach.993, X.An.6.3.22, Theoc.4.58, Luc.Bacch.3. II. the Carthaginian *Senate*, Plb.6.51.2 (v.l. γεροντικόν).

**γεροντο-γράδιο** [ᾰ], τό, (γραῦς) *old man-woman*, barbarism in Ar. Th.1199 (sed divisim leg.). ⊛ -**δῐδάσκᾰλος**, ὁ, ἡ, *old man's master*, Pl.Euthd.272c. -**ειδής**, ές, *like an old man*, Eust.1923.63. -**κομεῖον**, τό, (κομέω) *hospital for the old*, Cod.Just.1.3.45.1:—also Subst. -**κόμος**, ὁ, *warden of such a hospital*, Just.Nov.7.1: -**κομικά**, τά, Sch. Pl.Phdr.240c. -**μανία**, ἡ, *craze* or *dotage of old men*, name of a play by Anaxandrides, Arist.Rh.1413b26.

⊛ **γερουσί-α**, ἡ, *Council of Elders, senate*, E.Rh.401: esp. at Sparta, D.20.107, Arist.Pol.1270b24, IG5(2).345.10 (Orchom. Arc., ii/i B.C.); cf. γερωΐα and γεροντία; also of the Carthaginian *Senate*,

Arist.*Pol.*1272$^{b}$37; and the Roman, Plu.2.789e, Jul.*Or.*2.97b; of the Jewish *Sanhedrin*, *Act.Ap.*5.21, cf. Lxx *Ex.*3.16. 2. *sacred college*, ἱερὰ γ. *IG*3.702 (Eleusis), cf. 7.2808 (Hyettus, iii B.C.), etc. II. = πρεσβεία, E.*Rh.*936. ⊛ **-ακός**, ά, όν, *of* or *belonging to the senate*, χρήματα *CIG*3080 (Teos). ⊛ **-άρχης**, ου, ὁ, *president of Jewish elders*, ib.9902 (Rome). **-ας**, ου, ὁ, *member of the γερουσία* at Sparta, *IG*5(1).31, al.: pl., ib.62.19; also, *official* of a guild, ib.206, 209. ⊛ **-αστής**, οῦ, ὁ, *member of a γερουσία*, Plb.7.9.1, *IG*7.2808.17 (Hyettus, iii B.C.). **-ος**, α, ον, *for* or *befitting the γέροντες*, γ. οἶνος *wine drunk only by the chiefs*, Il.4.259, Od.13.8; γ. ὅρκος an oath *taken by them*, Il.22.119; γερούσιον, τό, *perquisite of chiefs*, Hsch.

**γερράδια**, τά, *mats of plaited work*, Hsch.

**γέρρον**, τό, *anything made of wicker-work*: I. *oblong shield*, covered with ox-hide, Hdt.7.61, X.*Cyr.*7.1.33, etc.; Θρᾴκια γ. Plu. *Aem.*32. II. γέρρα, τά, *wattled screens* or *booths*, used in the Athen. market-place, τὰ γ. ἐνεπίμπρασαν D.18.169; τὰ γ. ἀναιρεῖν Id.59.90: generally, *wattles*, Str.4.4.3, Jul.*Or.*1.29d: metaph. of the eyelashes, Gal.*UP*10.6. III. *wicker body of a cart*, Str.7.2.3. IV. = γερροχελώνη, Plb.8.3.3 (pl.), D.H.6.92, Arr.*An.*1.21.5. V. *stake*, Eup.405; *dart*, dub. in Alcm.133. 2. = αἰδοῖον (Sicel) (or prob., = ὄλισβος, cf. Orion 43.24), Epich.235.

**γερρο-φόροι**, οἱ, *troops that used wicker shields*, X.*An.*1.8.9, Pl.*La.*191c, Str.7.3.17. **-φύλαξ** [ῠ], ακος, ὁ, *defender of wicker-work barrier*, *Sammelb.*1918, prob. in *OGI*11 (nisi leg. δροφύλαξ). **-χελώνη**, ἡ, *penthouse, mantlet*, used in siege-works, Ph.*Bel.*98.19.

**γέρρω**· ἀπόλωλα, Hsch. (i.e. ϝέρρω).

**γέρσυμον**, τό, *end of a fishing-rod*, Hsch.

**γέρῡνος**, ὁ, = γύρινος, Nic.*Th.*620, *Al.*563.

**γερωΐα** (i.e. γερωΐα), ἡ, Lacon. form of γερουσία, Ar.*Lys.*980 (γερωχία codd.); cf. **γερωνία**, Hsch.

⊛ **γέρων**, οντος, ὁ, *old man*, Il.1.33, etc.: pleon., παλαιοὶ γέροντες Ar. *Ach.*676; ἄνους τε καὶ γ. S.*Ant.*281, cf. Ar.*Eq.*1349; ἀεὶ γὰρ ἡβᾷ τοῖς γέρουσιν εὖ μαθεῖν A.*Ag.*584; καλὸν δὲ καὶ γέροντα μανθάνειν σοφά Id.*Fr.*396. 2. γέροντες, οἱ, *Elders, Chiefs*, κίκλησκεν δὲ γέροντας ἀριστῆας Παναχαιῶν Il.2.404 sq., cf. 9.574, Od.2.14; later, *Senators*, esp. at Sparta, Hdt.1.65, 6.57, Pl.*Lg.*692a, *IG*2$^{2}$.687, Arist.*Pol.*1265$^{b}$38 (sg. γέροντι *IG*5(1).1346, but usu. γερουσίας, q.v.); in other states, as at Elis, Arist.*Pol.*1306$^{a}$17, cf. 1272$^{a}$7, *OGI*479.11 (Dorylaeum). II. as Adj., *old*, γέρον σάκος Od.22.184; γ. γράμμα A.*Fr.*331; more freq. in masc., γ. πατήρ Il.1.358, Od.18.53; ἀνὴρ γ. Thgn. 1351; γ. χαλκός Simon.144; γ. λόγος A.*Ag.*750 (lyr.); ἵππος S.*El.*25; πόνος Id.*OC*1258 (codd. but πίνος Scaliger, edd.); οἶνος Alex. 167.5, cf. Eub.124; πέπλος, λέμβος, Theoc.7.17, 21.12: rarely in Prose, οἱ γέροντες τῶν ἰχθύων Arist.*HA*607$^{b}$28; of stags, ib.611$^{b}$3; Ἀντίγονος ὁ γ. Antigonus *the Elder*, Plu.*Pel.*2: neut. pl., γέροντα βουλεύεις (for ἀρχαῖα) S.*Fr.*794. III. *part of the spinning-wheel*, Pherecr.114. (Skt. *járant-* 'old', *járati* 'render infirm'; cf. γέρας.)

**γερωνία** and **γερωχία**, v. γερωΐα. **γερώνιον**· κοῖλον, κενόν, Hsch. **γέσμα**· γεῦμα, Id. **γέστα**· γογγυλίς, Id.:—also **γεστία**· ἔνδυσις, and **γέστρα**· στολή, Id. **γέτορ**· ἔτος, and **γέτος**· ἐνιαυτός, Id. (γ = ϝ). **γεῦ**· γυνὴν τί ἄρα, Id.

**γευθμός**, ὁ, = γεῦσις, Nic.*Al.*399.

**γεύλοφα**, = γεώλοφα, Hsch.

⊛ **γεῦμα**, ατος, τό, (γεύω) *taste, smack* of a thing, E.*Cyc.*150; τρία γ. Ar.*Ach.*187; γεύματος χάριν Arist.*HA*491$^{a}$8. II. *food*, σιτηρὰ γ. Hp.*Acut.*10: metaph., ἄγευστοι τοῦ παντρόφου γ. σοφίας Ph.1.544.

**γευματικός**, ή, όν, dub. sens., χιτών *Schwyzer*462*B*29 (Tanagra, iii B.C.).

**γευνῶν**· γονάτων, Hsch. (leg. γεύνων, cf. γόνυ).

**γεῦος**, τό, in pl. γεύη, perh. *ass*, *POxy.*1675.12 (iii A.D.).

**γεῦσ-ις**, εως, ἡ, *sense of taste*, Democr.11, Arist.*EN*1118$^{a}$26, *de An.*422$^{a}$29, etc. II. *a tasting*, Lxx *Da.*5.2. III. *food*, Lxx *Wi.*16.2, al. IV. *taste, flavour*, Dsc.1.12, *Gp.*5.7.3. V. *back of the tongue*, Poll.2.104. **-τέον**, *one must make to taste*, τινὰ αἵματος Pl.*R.*537a. **-τήριον**, τό, *cup for tasting with*, Ar.*Fr.*299, Pherecr. 143.3. **-της**, ου, ὁ, *taster*, *CIG*2214.8 (Chios). **-τικός**, ή, όν, *of* or *for taste*, γ. αἰσθητήριον the seat of the sense *of taste*, Arist.*de An.*422$^{b}$5; αἴσθησις D.H.*Comp.*12; δύναμις Alex.Aphr.*Pr.*2.60; τὸ γ. Plu.2.990a. Adv. **-κῶς** Sch.Ven.Il.5.661. **-τός**, ή, όν, *that may be tasted*, τὸ γ. Arist.*Rh.*1370$^{a}$23, *de An.*422$^{a}$8, Plu.2.38a, Porph.*Abst.*1.33.

**Γευστός**, ὁ, name of a month at Lamia, *IG*9(2).66, al.

**γευστρίνην**· γαυλόν, Hsch.

**γεύστριον**, **γευστρίδιον**, and **γευστρίς**, = γευστήριον, *Gloss.*

⊛ **γεύω**, fut. γεύσω Anaxipp.1.27: aor. ἔγευσα Hdt.7.46, E.*Cyc.*149: —Med., fut. γεύσομαι Od.17.413, etc.: aor. ἐγευσάμην 20.181, etc.; γεύσεται, -σόμεθα, Ep. for -ηται, -ώμεθα, Il.21.61, 20.258: 3 pl. opt. γευσαίατο E.*IA*423: pf. γέγευμαι A. v. infr., etc. (γεύμεθα Theoc.14.51): plpf. ἐγέγευντο Th.2.70:—*give a taste* of, γλυκὺν γεύσας τὸν αἰῶνα Hdt.7.46; τινά τι E.*Cyc.*149, Theopomp.Com.65, Polyaen. 1.1.1; τινά τινος Anaxipp. l.c., Alex.179, Pl.*Lg.*634a: metaph., τινὰ ἀγαθῶν λόγων dub. in Men.*Georg.*45; σ' ἔγευσ' ἂν τῶν ἐμῶν χειρῶν Herod.6.11: but, II. Med., γεύομαι, with pf. and plpf. Pass., *taste*, c. gen., προικὸς γεύσεσθαι Ἀχαιῶν Od.17.413; ἀλλήλων ἐγέγευντο *they had tasted, eaten of..*, Th.2.70; μέλιτος Pl.*R.*559d, etc. 2. *take food*, Hp.*Epid.*3.1.β', *Act.Ap.*10.10; *dine*, *PLond. ined.*2487 (iv A.D.). 3. metaph., *taste, make proof of, feel*, δουρὸς ἀκωκῆς ἡμετέροιο γεύσεται Il.21.60; ὀϊστοῦ Od.21.98; χειρῶν 20.181; ἀλλ' ἄγε.. γευσόμεθ' ἀλλήλων ἐγχείῃσιν *let us try* one another with the spear, Il.20.258; *taste the sweets of*, ἀρχῆς, ἐλευθερίης, Hdt. 4.147, 6.5; ὕμνων Pi.*I.*5(4).20; ἀλκᾶς, στεφάνων, Id.*P.*9.35, *I.*1.21; εἰ δὲ γεύεται ἀνδρὸς ἀνήρ τι Id.*N.*7.86; of a married woman, ἀνδρὸς γεγευμένη A.*Fr.*243; γ. πόνων *to have experience of* them, Pi. *N.*6.24; μόχθων S.*Tr.*1101; πένθους E.*Alc.*1069; νόμων Pl.*Lg.*752c; ἀμφοτέρων Id.*R.*358e; γ. ἐμπύρων *make trial of* them, S.*Ant.*1005: rarely c. acc., ἔρσης ἰκμάδα γευόμενος *AP*6.120 (Leon.); κάππαριν Plu.2.687d: abs., S.*Aj.*844. (Cf. Skt. *juṣáte* 'enjoy', Lat. *gusto*.)

⊛ **γέφυρα** (Boeot. **βέφυρα** Stratt.47.5), Lacon. **δίφουρα** Hsch., Cret. **δέφυρα** *GDI*5000 ii *b* 6 (Gortyn), ἡ (used by Hom. only in Il., always in pl.):—*dyke, dam*, ποταμῷ πλήθοντι ἐοικὼς χειμάρρῳ, ὅς τ' ὦκα ῥέων ἐκέδασσε γεφύρας· τὸν δ' οὔτ' ἄρ τε γέφυραι ἐεργμέναι ἰσχανόωσι Il.5.88; cf. γεφυρόω: metaph., πολέμοιο γέφυραι, expld. by Sch.Il. as αἱ δίοδοι τῶν φαλάγγων, i.e. the *open space* between hostile armies, but more prob. *limits* of the battlefield, Il.4.371, 11.160, etc.; πόντου γ. of the Isthmus of Corinth, *causeway* through the sea, Pi.*N.*6.39, cf. *I.*4(3).20; so, of the *causeway* between Athens and Eleusis, *Carm. Pop.*9; at the Euripus, Str.9.2.2. II. after Hom., in sg., *bridge*, γέφυραν ζευγνύναι Hdt.4.97, cf. 1.75 (pl.); γ. γαῖν δυοῖν ζευκτηρίαν A. *Pers.*736; γ. λῦσαι X.*An.*2.4.17; πόρον ὑπὲρ γεφυρῶν ἄγοντες Lib. *Or.*11.243; also, *of a tunnel*, ὑποστεῖχει γ. Philostr.*VA*1.25.

**γεφῡρ-εργάτης** [ᾰ], ου, ὁ, = γεφυροποιός, Tz.*H.*2.82. **-ίζω**, *abuse from the causeway*, in the procession from Athens to Eleusis, Hsch., Suid.: hence, *abuse freely*, Plu.*Sull.*6, 13. **-ιον**, τό, Dim. of γέφῡρα, Ael.*VH*8.14. **-ισμός**, ὁ, *gross abuse*, Str.9.1.24 (pl.). **-ιστής**, οῦ, ὁ, *abuser, reviler*, οἱ Ἀθήνησι γ. Plu.*Sull.*2.

**γεφῡρο-ποιέω**, *make a bridge*, Plb.3.64.1. **-ποιός**, ὁ, *bridge-maker*, = Lat. *pontifex*, Plu.*Num.*9.

**γεφῡρ-ουργία**, ἡ, *bridge-making*, Tz.*H.*1.931. **-όω**, (γέφυρα) *dam up* (cf. γέφυρα I), γεφύρωσεν δέ μιν (sc. τὸν ποταμὸν ἡ πτελέη) Il.21.245; but in Prose, γ. τὸν ποταμόν *throw a bridge over* it, Hdt.4.118; Βόσπορον ib.88; τοὺς τῆς θαλάττης τροχοὺς Pl.*Criti.*115c; ἐγεφυρώθη ὁ πόρος Hdt.7.36; πλοίοις τὴν διάβασιν γ. Plb.3.66.6; also, *dam*, ποταμοὺς νεκροῖς Luc.*DMort.*12.2; τὰ δύσπορα Id.*Demon.*1, cf. Nonn. *D.*27.185. 2. *make into a causeway* or *embankment*, γεφύρωσεν δὲ κέλευθον Il.15.357. 3. metaph., νόστον Ἀτρείδαις γ. Pi.*I.*8(7).51. **-ωμα**, ατος, τό, *bridge*, J.*BJ*3.7.28 (pl.). **-ωσις**, εως, ἡ, *furnishing with a causeway* or *bridge*, Str.1.3.18 (pl.); γ. ἡ διὰ τῶν νεῶν Arr.*An.*5.7.3; in concrete sense, διέβη τὰς γ. Ctes.*Fr.*29.17. **-ωτής**, οῦ, ὁ, *bridge-builder*, Plu.*Luc.*26 (pl.).

**γεωγρᾰφ-έω**, *describe the earth's surface*, Str.1.1.16, Arist.*Mu.*393$^{b}$20:—Pass., τὰ γεωγραφούμενα *geographic description*, title of Strabo's work, Ath.14.657f. **-ία**, ἡ, *geography*, Phld.*Po.*5.1425.2, Str. l.c. II. *geographical work*, Democr.14$^{c}$, Plu.*Thes.*1 (pl.), Porph. *Antr.*4. 2. *map*, στρογγύλας γράφοντες τὰς γ. Gem.16.4. **-ικός**, ή, όν, *geographical*, γ. ἐμπειρία, γ. πίναξ, Str.1.1.2, 11. Adv. **-κῶς** Id.2.1.41, etc.: τὰ -κά *geographical treatise*, ib.1; of Strabo's work, Ath.3.121a. ⊛ **-ος**, ον, *earth-describing*: Subst., *geographer*, Str.1.1.16, al.; ὁ γ., i.e. Strabo, Eust.ad D.P.11, al.

⊛ **γεω-δαισία**, ἡ, (δαίω) *land-dividing*: *mensuration*, opp. the science of geometry, Arist.*Metaph.*997$^{b}$26, Jul.*Gal.*178b, Procl.*in Euc.* p.25 F. **-δαίστης**, ου, ὁ, *land-surveyor*, Hero *Def.*138.3:—also **-δαίτης**, Call.*Oxy.incd.* (= *Fr.*158), Iamb.*Comm.Math.*26. **-δαιτέομαι**, *divide, parcel out land*, Eust.1619.2.

⊛ **γεώδης**, ες, *earth-like, earthy*, Pl.*Phd.*81c, Hierocl.*in CA Praef.* p.417 M.; γ. καὶ ἄλιθον *with deep soil*, X.*An.*6.4.5, al.; τὸ γ. Arist. *GA*753$^{a}$25, 782$^{b}$22; τὸ -έστερον ib.751$^{b}$3; γ. φῦλον Aristid.*Or.*43(1).14; ἄνθρακες -έστατοι Thphr.*HP*5.9.1. II. epith. of certain ζῴδια, Vett.Val.10.11.

**γεω-λοφία**, ἡ, *hill of earth*, Str.5.4.3, *AP*6.98 (Zon.). **-λοφος**, ον, *crested with earth*, ὄρη Str.16.2.16; χωρία Id.12.7.1. II. Subst. γεώλοφος, ὁ, *hill, hillock*, X.*Cyr.*3.3.28 codd., Plb.1.75.4, Ph.1.191; γεώλοφον, τό, Theoc.1.13, Numen.ap.Ath.7.305a. 2. γεώλοφος, ὁ, *boor, clod-hopper*, Ael.Dion.*Fr.*107.

**γεωμαντ-εία**, ἡ, *geomancy*, Varr.ap.Isid.8.9.13: Subst. **-ις**, εως, ὁ, Id.ap.Serv.Virg.*A.*3.359.

**γεωμετρ-έω**, prop., *measure, survey land*, *BGU*12.27 (ii A.D.):—but usu., *practise* or *profess geometry*, Pl.*Tht.*162e, *Men.*85e, Arist. *Rh.*1406$^{b}$30. II. generally, *measure*, c. acc., τὸν ἀέρα Ar.*Av.*995; τὰ ἐπίπεδα Pl.*Tht.*173e, cf. X.*Smp.*6.8, *BGU*12.27 (ii A.D.), Luc. *Icar.*21 (Pass.). ⊛ **-ης**, ου, ὁ, *land measurer*, ib.28 (ii A.D.):—but usu., *geometer*, Pl.*Tht.*143b, al., cf. Men.495, *CIG*3544 (Perg.). **-ητος**, ον, *geometrical*, λόγοι Procl.*in Euc.*p.201 F.; τὰ -τα ib.p.185 F. **-ία**, Ion. -ίη, ἡ, *geometry*, Hdt.2.109, Ar.*Nu.*202: pl., τὰ ἐν ταῖς γ. Pl. *Men* 76a, cf. Man.4.129. II. *land-survey*, τῶν ἀμπελώνων καὶ παραδείσων *PTeb.*24.42 (ii B.C.), cf. *POxy.*499.27 (ii A.D.). III. *land tax*, *PLips.*67.2 (ii A.D.), *PFay.*55.11 (ii A.D.), etc. 2. *tax for surveying*, *PTeb.*93.2, al. (ii B.C.). **-ικός**, ή, όν, *of* or *for geometry, geometrical*, ἀριθμός Pl.*R.*546c, etc.; ἰσότης Id.*Grg.*508a; ἀναλογία Arist.*EN*1131$^{b}$13; μεσότης Theo Sm.p.106 H., etc. (cf. γαμετρικός); ἁρμονία Nicom.*Ar.*2.26; θεωρήματα Plu.2.720a (Sup.); γεωμετρική (sc. τέχνη), *geometry*, Pl.*Grg.*450d, Nicom.Com.1.18; τὰ -κά title of work on *geometry*, Democr.11$^{n}$, cf. Arist.*APo.*79$^{a}$9. Adv. **-κῶς** *by a rigidly deductive proof*, Procl.*in Prm.*p.897 S., Id.*in Ti.*1.345 D.: γ. *refellere*, prove wrong *to demonstration*, Cic.*Att.*12.5.3. II. *skilled in geometry*, Pl.*R.*511d, Plu.2.579b, Arist.*Pol.*1282$^{a}$9; γ. Βριάρεως, of Archimedes, Id.*Marc.*17: Comp. -ώτερος Ph.1.621. Adv. **-κῶς** Arist.*Top.*161$^{a}$35, Str.2.1.41, Plu.2.643c.

**γεωμῐγής**, ές, *mixed with earth*, Str.12.7.3, *Placit.*3.2.6.

**γεωμορ-έω**, *till* or *farm the land*, Alex.ap.Eus.*PE*9.22. ❋ **-ία**, ἡ, *portion of land*, Nic.*Al.*10: pl., *farms, cultivated lands*, Opp.*C.*4.434. II. = γεωργία, Alciphr.1.4, *AP*7.532 (Isid.). III. *harvest*, λιπαρὰ γ. *AP*6.258 (Addaeus). IV. *division of land*, Nicom.*Ar.*1.3. **-ικός**, ή, όν, *concerning* γεωμορία, γ. νόμος an *agrarian* law, D.H.10.39. **-ος**, v. **γημόρος**. II. = γεωργός, Hsch.

**γεώνιον**, τό, *price of earth*, *SIG*$^2$.587.57.

**γεω-νόμος**, ον, (νέμω) *one who distributes land*, *IG*1$^2$.45 (pl.). 2. *receiving a portion of distributed lands, colonist*, D.C.38.1:—also **-νόμης**, ου, ὁ, Phryn.*PS*p.57 B.

❋ **γεώπεδον**, τό, *portion* or *plot of ground, garden*, esp. within a town, Hdt.7.28 (v.l. γεοπέδων, γεωπεδίων); cf. γήπεδον.

**γεωπείνης**, ου, ὁ, *poor in land*, Hdt.2.6, 8.111, Aristid.1.191 J.

**γεωπον-έω**, *till the ground*, Ph.1.212; **γᾱπ-** E.*Rh.*75; **γεη-** Heph.Astr.2.28. **-ία**, Ion. **-ίη**, ἡ, *tillage*, Orph.*Fr.*280, *Epigr.Gr.*446 (Arabia), Max.Tyr.27.5:—also **γεη-** Ps.-Phoc.161, **γη-** Them.*Or.*30.350a, Hld.10.6. **-ικός**, ή, όν, *of* or *for agriculture*, Gal.6.311; τὰ γ. title of treatise on the subject compiled by Cassianus Bassus. **-ος**, ὁ, *husbandman*, *AP*7.175 (Antiphil.), 281 (Heraclid.); *labourer*, opp. γεωργός, Ph.1.211:—also **γεηπόνος** Democr. ap.Gal.13.40, Agath.2.17 (pl.), Babr.108.14: **γᾱπ-** E.*Supp.*420: **γηπ-** Them.*Or.*30.350c, Hld.5.23.

❋ **γεωργ-έω**, *to be a husbandman, farmer*, Pl.*Lg.*805e, X.*Oec.*14.2, etc.; γ. ἐν τῇ γῇ And.1.92; ἐν τῇ Νάξῳ Pl.*Euthphr.*4c, etc.; γεωργεῖς ἐκ τούτων you *have become a landed proprietor* by these means (i.e. the fruits of treason), D.19.314: c. acc. cogn., γεωργίαν ζῶσαν γ. of pastoral nomads, Arist.*Pol.*1256a35:—Med., οἱ γεωργούμενοι Aristeas 112. II. c. acc., *till, plough, cultivate*, πολλήν (sc. γῆν) Ar.*Ec.*592; τὰς ἄλλας [νήσους] Th.3.88; γεωργῶν τὰ ἐκείνων D.18.41:—Pass., of land, *IG*9(1).61 (Daulis); χώρας γεγεωργημένης καὶ γεωργηθησομένης *SIG*685.80 (Crete); τὰ γεωργούμενα φυτά Arist.*Pr.*896a10. 2. generally, *cultivate*, ἐλαίαν *Gp.*9.2.6: hence, γ. ἔλαιον, οἶνον, *produce* it, D.C.49.36, cf. *IG*2$^2$.1100; τοῦ γεωργουμένου οἴνου *Gp.*6.7.2. 3. metaph., *work at* a thing, *practise* or *exploit* it, D.25.82; φιλίαν Plu.2.776b; τέχνην Hld.6.6; τὸν ἱππόδρομον Lib.*Or.*35.13; *cultivate*, ψυχὰς δόγμασι Ph.2.348. 4. of a river, *fertilize*, Philostr.*Im.*1.11, *Ep.*59, Hld.2.28. **-ημα**, ατος, τό, in pl., *operations of husbandry*, Pl.*Lg.*674c. **-ήσιμος**, ον, *tilled* or *fit for tillage*, Arist.*Pr.*924a22, Str.16.4.18, Plb.1.56.4. **-ητέον**, *one must till the soil*, Them.*Or.*30 tit. ❋ **-ία**, ἡ, *tillage*, τῆς Χερσονήσου Th.1.11, etc.; *agriculture, farming*, Pl.*Smp.*187a, etc.; γ. ψιλή *tillage* of arable land and pasture, opp. πεφυτευμένη, of vineyards and orchards, Arist.*Pol.*1258b17. 2. in pl., *farms, tilled land*, τοῖς μὲν γεωργίας ἐπὶ μισθώσεσι παραδιδόντες Isoc.7.32, cf. Pl.*Lg.*806d, Luc.*Prom.*14, etc.; rarely in sg., D.30.30. II. metaph., *source of income*, Lib.*Or.*39.12. **-ικός**, ή, όν, *agricultural*, σκεύη Ar.*Pax* 552; κόποι γ. *CIG*4659 (Palestine, iii A.D.); ὑπηρεσία *BGU* 197.17 (i A.D.); βιβλίον γ. a book *on rural economy*, Plu.*Cato Ma.*25; ἡ γ. (sc. τέχνη) *agriculture, farming*, Pl.*Lg.*889d, etc.; τὰ γ. *lands*, Chrysipp.*Stoic.*3.180; also, *treatise on agriculture*, Democr.26b, Ath.14.649d; esp. that of Nicander, Id.3.92c. II. *occupied* or *skilled in farming*, Arist.*Pol.*1317a25; δῆμος ib.1318b9; λεώς Ar.*Pax*920:—as Subst., *a good farmer*, Pl.*Ap.*20b, etc.; *fond of rural pursuits*, Plu.2.268c. Adv. **-κῶς** Poll.7.141. ❋ **-ιον**, τό, *field*, Ph.*Bel.*96.49 (pl.), Theagen.17 (pl.), *BGU*1092.10 (iv A.D.); *orchard*, Str.14.5.6: metaph., Θεοῦ γ. 1 *Ep.Cor.*3.9. II. *husbandry*, Lxx *Si.*27.6. III. *crop*, ib.*Pr.*24.5. IV. in pl., *tax* on land, dub. in *SIG*311.9 (Lagina, iv B.C.). ❋ **-ισσα**, ης, ἡ, fem. of γεωργός, Just.*Nov.*156 *Praef.* (pl.). **-ίτης**, ὁ, = γεωργός, Proll.Hermog.in *Rh.*7.45 W. ❋ **-ός**, όν, (γῆ, ἔργον) *tilling the ground*, βοίδιον Ar.*Ach.*1036; *fertilizing*, Νεῖλος Lib.*Or.*13.39:—as Subst., γεωργός, ὁ, *husbandman*, Hdt.4.18, Ar.*Pax*296, Pl.*Phdr.*276b, etc.; οἱ γ., opp. οἱ μισθαρνοῦντες, Arist.*Pol.*1296b28; but γ., opp. ὁ δεσπότης τοῦ χωρίου, *IG*2$^2$.1100; so of vine-dressers, gardeners, etc., Pl.*Tht.*178d, Ael.*NA*7.28; γ. ὄχλος *the peasantry*, D.H.10.53; γ. βίος prob. in Ar.*Pax*589; δένδρων ὧν γ. αἵδε αἱ χεῖρες Philostr.*VA*2.26. **-ώδης**, ες, *agricultural*, Plu.2.8b.

**γεῶρες**· γεωφύλακες, Suid. (Cf. γειώρας.)

**γεωρῠχ-έω**, *dig in the earth, dig a mine*, Hdt.4.200, Ael.*NA*16.15. **-ία**, *excavation*, *IG*2.1055.27, Ael.*NA*6.43. **-ος**, ον, (γῆ, ὀρύσσω) *burrowing*, λαγιδεῖς Str.3.2.6, cf. Hsch. s.v. σκάλοψ:—fem. **γεωρῠχίς**, ἡ, *mole*, prob. cj. in *Gloss.* (pl.).

**γεωτομ-ία**, ἡ, *turning up the earth, ploughing*, *Eleg.Alex.Adesp.*1.1, Max.499. ❋ **-ος**, ον, *cutting the ground*, ὅπλον *AP*10.101 (Bian.).

**γεωτρᾰγία**, ἡ, *an eating of earthy substances*, Hp.*Morb.*4.55.

**γεωφᾰν-ής**, ές, *looking like earth*, ἐπικλίνων ἐπὶ τὸ -έστερον Archig. ap.Orib.8.2.4: esp. in pl., γ. *a spot where a kind of ochre was dug*, at Samos, Thphr.*Lap.*61:—so **-ιον** or **-ειον**, τό, περὶ τοῦ γ. title of speech by Din., D.H.*Din.*10, cf. Sch.Nic.*Al.*149, Poll.7.99, *EM* 229.21.

**γεωφύλαξ**, v. γεῶρες.

**γεωχᾰρής**, ές, *fond of the earth*, of *creeping* plants, Jul.*Or.*5.175d.

❋ **γῆ**, ἡ, occasionally in Hom., freq. in Hes., and the only form in Att. Prose for γαῖα: dual γαῖν A.*Pers.*736: pl. rare, γαῖ Arist.*Pr.*934b9, γέαι *SIG*279.40 (Zelea), etc., *AP*9.430 (Crin.): gen. γεῶν Hdt.4.198, *GDI*5755.14 (Mylasa); γῶν *BGU*993 iii 10 (ii B.C.): acc. γέας [Democr.]299, *SIG*46.3 (Halic.), γᾶς *PTeb.*6.31 (ii B.C.), Str.2.5.26; Cypr. ζᾶς *Inscr.Cypr.*135.30 H.: dat. pl. γέαις prob. in *CIG* 2693f9 (Mylasa), *LW*415.9 (ibid.):—*earth* (including land and sea, Sapph.*Supp.*5.2) opp. *heaven*, or *land* opp. *sea*, Γῆ τε καὶ Ἥλιος καὶ Ἐρινύες Il.19.259, cf. 3.104; τίς γῆ; Od.13.233; γῆς περίοδοι Hdt.4.36, Arist.*Mete.*362b12, title of work by Hecat.: personified, Il. l.c., A.*Th.*69, *Pers.*629, etc.; κατὰ γῆν on *land*, by *land*, opp. ναυσί, Th.1.18; opp. ἐκ θαλάσσης, Id.2.81; κατὰ γῆν στέλλεσθαι X.*An.*5.6.5, etc.; ἐπὶ γῆς on *earth*, opp. νέρθε, S.*OT*416; κατὰ γῆς below *the earth*, A.*Ch.*377, 475, etc.; κάτω γῆς S.*OT*968; ὑπὸ γῆς Id.*Fr.*572; γᾶς ὑπένερθε Pi.*Fr.*292: gen. with local Adverbs, ἵνα γῆς E.*Andr.*168; ποῦ, ποῖ, ὅποι γ., S.*OT*108, *Ph.*1211, *El.*922; ὅπου γ. Ar.*Av.*9. 2. *earth*, as an element, Xenoph.27, Anaxag.4, Pl.*Prt.*320d, *Lg.*889b, Arist.*Metaph.*989a5, *Cael.*306a18, etc. b. γῆν καὶ ὕδωρ αἰτεῖν, as tokens of submission, Hdt.5.18, Lycurg.71; γῆν καὶ ὕδωρ διδόναι Hdt.5.18, al. II. *land, country*, καὶ γῆν καὶ πόλιν A.*Eu.*993; γῆν πρὸ γῆς ἐλαύνεσθαι, διώκειν, from *land to land*, Id.*Pr.*682, Ar.*Ach.*235; ἡ ἁγία γῆ Lxx *Wi.*12.3; one's *native land*, Thgn.1213, Tyrt.12.33, A.*Supp.*890 (lyr.), S.*OC*44, E.*Ph.*1090; freq. omitted with art., ἐκ τῆς ἐμαυτοῦ (sc. γῆς) δραπέτας Id.*Heracl.*140, etc. 2. freq. in Trag., *city*, αὐτός τε καὶ γῆ δορὶ πεσοῦσ' Ἑλληνικῷ Id.*Tr.*868. III. *the earth* or *ground* as tilled, ἄροτον γῆς S.*OT*270; γᾶ φθίνουσα ib.665, etc.; τὴν γῆν ἐργάζεσθαι, θεραπεύειν, till *the ground*, Pl.*R.*420e, X.*Oec.*5.12; τὰ ἐκ τῆς γῆς φυόμενα Id.*Mem.*4.3.10. 2. *estate, farm*, γῆν πρίασθαι Lys.32.23; ἐπὶ γῇ δανείζειν lend on mortgage, D.36.6. IV. of particular *kinds of earth* or *minerals*, e.g. *fuller's earth*, Thphr.*Char.*10.14, cf. Gal.12.168; Κιμωλία γ. Ar.*Ra.*712, cf. Hp.*Mul.*2.189.

**γηγεν-έτης**, ου, ὁ, = sq., ἄργυρος Tim.*Fr.*26; γίγας E.*Ph.*128 (lyr.). ❋ **-ής**, ές, Dor. **γᾱγενής** Hdn.Gr.2.419:—*earthborn*, βολβός Xenarch.1.5; of a potter's vessel, Antiph.182.3; *indigenous*, βούβαλις S.*Fr.*792. 2. *earthborn*, of primeval men, Ἐρεχθεύς Hdt.8.55; Παλαίχθων A.*Supp.*250; τοὺς ἔμπροσθεν φύεσθαι γηγενεῖς καὶ μὴ ἐξ ἀλλήλων γεννᾶσθαι Pl.*Plt.*269b, cf. Arist.*GA*762b29; of the Thebans, *Trag.Adesp.*84; γ. πρωτοπλάστης Lxx *Wi.*7.1; of body, opp. soul, Pl.*Lg.*727e. 3. οἱ γ. *the dead, the shades*, ib.*Pr.*2.18, 9.18. II. *born of Gaia*, of Titans and Giants, Batr.7, A.*Pr.*353, E.*Ba.*996 (lyr.); ὁ γ. στρατὸς Γιγάντων S.*Tr.*1058; τὴν ἐπὶ τῶν γηγενῶν (sc. ἀναστροφήν), opp. civilized life, Phld.*Sto.Herc.*339.10: in Com. with an insinuation of impiety, Ar.*Nu.*853; (but also *boorish*, βῶλος, ἄροτρον, γ. ἄνθρωπος Alex.108.5); of things, *Titanic*, i.e. *portentous*, γηγενεῖ φυσήματι Ar.*Ra.*825: Sup. **-έστατος** *most earthy*, i.e. limited in intelligence, Procl.*in Prm.*p.763 S.

**γηγῆλιξ**, ὁ, *field-mouse*, Hsch.:—also **γήλιγρος**, ὁ, Id. **γηγυρίδαι**· οἰκτροί, Id.

**γήδιον**, τό, Dim. of γῆ, *little farm, piece of land*, Ar.*Pax*570, *Fr.*387.2, Arist.*Pol.*1320a39, Ph.2.541, *POxy.*1559.11 (pl., iv A.D.); μικρὸν γ. X.*Cyr.*8.3.38.

**γηθᾰλάσσιος**, ον, *amphibious*, ζῷον *Cat.Cod.Astr.*7.208.14.

**γηθᾰλέος**, α, ον, (γηθέω) *joyous*, Androm.ap.Gal.14.36.

❋ **γῆθεν**, Adv. *out of* or *from the earth*, A.*Th.*247, *Eu.*904, S.*OC*1591; *from beneath*, Id.*El.*453: in late Prose, τὰ γ. J.*AJ*4.3.2; γ. ἥκεις Luc.*Icar.*4.

❋ **γηθέω**, 3 sg. γηθεῖ (contr.) Il.14.140, Dor. γᾱθεῖ Theoc.1.54 (but pf. is always used for pres. in Trag., unless γηθούσῃ φρενί be read in A.*Ch.*772, and impf. ἐπ-εγήθει (v. infr.) in Id.*Pr.*157 (lyr.)): impf. ἐγήθεον Il.7.127, 214: fut. γηθήσω 8.378, etc.: aor. ἐγήθησα, Ep. γήθησα Hes.*Sc.*116, Dor. γάθησα Pi.*P.*4.122, cf. Limen.7: pf. γέγηθα (in pres. sense, v. supr.), Dor. γέγᾱθα with 3 sg. γεγάθει Epich.109 (imper. γέγᾱθι *Hymn.Curet.*6), Il.8.559, etc.: plpf. ἐγεγήθειν restored by Elmsl. in A.*Pr.*157, Ep. γεγήθειν Il.11.683, 13.494, Boeot. 3 sg. γεγάθι Corinn.*Supp.*1.27. A collat. form **γήθω**, Dor. **γάθω**, mentioned by Hsch., is found in *CIG*3632 (Ilium), Orph.*H.*16.10, al.:—Med., γήθομαι Q.S.14.92, *AP*6.261 (Crin.), S.E.*M.*11.107: (v. γαίω):—*rejoice*, c. acc. rei, τίς ἂν τάδε γηθήσειεν Il.9.77; γ. κατὰ θυμόν 13.416; νῶι γηθήσει προφανέντε *will rejoice* at our appearing, 8.378: freq. c. part., *rejoice in doing* .., γέγηθας ζῶν S.*Ph.*1021; πίνων E.*Cyc.*168: γεγήθει φρένα Il.11.683 (but Ἀχιλλῆος κῆρ γηθεῖ 14.140); θυμῷ γηθήσας Hes.*Sc.*116; ἂν περὶ ψυχὰν γάθησεν Pi.*P.*4.122; παλαιαῖσιν ἐν ἀρεταῖς γ. Id.*N.*3.33; γεγηθέναι ἐπί τινι S.*El.*1231, Hierocl.*in CA*5p.427 M.: c. dat., ἄλλος ἄλλῳ γέγαθε Axiop.1.23; τοῖς μεγάλοις ἀεὶ κακοῖς γέγηθ' ὁ κόσμος Sotad.15.4: part. γεγηθώς, like χαίρων, Lat. *impune*, ἦ καὶ γ. ταῦτ' ἀεὶ λέξειν δοκεῖς; S.*OT*368; but simply, *cheerful*, φαιδρὸς καὶ γ. D.18.323.

**γηθία**· ἤθη, Hsch. (For ϝήθεα.)

**γῆθος**, εος, τό, = sq., Epicur.*Fr.*423, Plu.*Ages.*29, Luc.*Am.*9, etc.

**γηθο-σύνη**, ἡ, *joy, delight*, Il.13.29, 21.390, Ph.1.354; = Φιλία (q.v.), Emp.17.24: in pl., *h.Cer.*437, A.R.2.878. **-συνος**, η, ον, also ος, ον Orph.*H.*27.14, *AP*6.235 (Thall.):—*joyful, glad*, Il.7.122; χάρμῃ 13.82. Adv. **-νως** Hp.*Ep.*17, Suid.

**γηθυλλίς**, Dor. **γᾱθ-** Epich.134, ίδος, ἡ, Dim. of γήθυον:—*spring onion* (acc. to Moer.115, the Att. equivalent for ἀμπελόπρασον), Epich. l.c., Eub.89.3, Nic.*Al.*431, Epaenet.ap.Ath.9.371e, *IG*5(1).1511 (Sparta, prob.).

**γήθυον**, τό, = γήτειον, Ar.*Fr.*5, Phryn.Com.12, Thphr.7.1.2, etc.

❋ **γή-ινος**, η, ον, *of earth*, τὴν δὲ..πλάσαντες γηίνην Semon.7.21; πλίνθοι X.*An.*7.8.14; τείχη Pl.*Lg.*778e; σῶμα Id.*Phdr.*246c, cf. Hierocl.*in CA*4p.425 M.; οὐδὲ τὸ ξύλον γῆ, ἀλλὰ γήινον Arist.*Metaph.*1049a20; νόος *App.Anth.*3.146 (Theon.): Sup. **-ώτατος**, ἀριθμός Lyd.*Ost.*45. ❋ **-ίτης** [ῑ], ου, ὁ, *husbandman*, S.*Tr.*32 (in contr. form γήτης). **-λεχής**, ές, *sleeping on the earth*, Call.*Del.*286.

**γηλιᾶσθαι·** κατέχεσθαι, Hsch. **γηλουμένους·** συνειλημμένους, Id.

**γήλοφος,** ὁ, = γεώλοφος, *hill*, X.*An*.1.5.8, Pl.*Criti*.111d; γ. χειροποίητος artificial *mound*, Jul.*Or*.2.63b; γήλοφον, τό, J.*BJ*1.21.10: as Adj., *Gp*.3.1.9; (in Dor. form) γαλόφῳ πρῶνι Limen.12.

**γῆμα·** ἱμάτιον, Hsch. (γ = ϝ).

* **γη-μόριον,** τό, *burial plot*, *IG*7.2183 (Thespiae). * **-μόρος,** ὁ, Dor. and Trag. **γᾱμόρος,** *Trag.Adesp*.208 (s. v. l.), A.*Supp*.613, *PLond.ined*.2134 (ii A.D.); cf. τῆσδε γαμόρῳ χθονός (Dobree for τῇ δέ γ' ἀμοίρου) A.*Eu*.890; Att. **γεωμόρος** (γῆ, μείρομαι):—*one who has a share of land, landowner*: οἱ γαμόροι, in Sicily, *the wealthy landowners*, Hdt.7.155: at Argos, A.*Supp*. l.c.; at Athens, γεωμόροι *landowners*, large or small, opp. εὐπατρίδαι, δημιουργοί, Arist.*Ath*. *Fr*.2, Pl.*Lg*.737e, etc. 2. γεωμόροι, οἱ, = Lat. *tresviri agris dividundis*, D.H.9.52. 3. metaph. of Ἅιδης, *Trag.Adesp*. l.c. II. as Adj., *dividing earth*, i.e. *ploughing*, βοῦς A.R.1.1214; γεωμόρος τέχνα *IG*9(1).880 (Corc.).

**γήνεια·** ὅσα ἐκ τῆς γῆς ὠφέλιμα, Hsch. (Fort. γήινα.) **γήνεσθαι·** κατέχεσθαι, Id. (Cf. ϝηλέω, = εἰλέω).

**γη-οῦχος,** ον, (ἔχω) *land-holding*, Eust.1392.23; cf. γαιήοχος. **-οχέω,** *hold land*, Hdt.7.190. **-πάτταλος,** ὁ, *oblong radish*, com. word in Luc.*Lex*.2. * **-πεδον,** τό, = γεώπεδον, *plot of ground*, Pl.*Lg* 741c, Arist.*Pol*.1263ᵃ3. II. Trag. used Dor. form γάπεδον acc. to St. Byz.: hence γ. for δάπεδον (metri gr.), A.*Pr*.829 (Pors.). **-πετής,** ές, (πίπτω) *falling* or *fallen to earth*, E.*Ph*.668 (lyr.). **-πονέω, -πονία, -πονικός, -πόνος,** = γεωπ-, qq.v. **-ποτος,** ον, v. γάποτος.

**γηράεις,** εσσα, εν, = sq., Alc.*Oxy*.1233.16.

**γηρ-αιός,** ά, όν (also ός, όν Antipho4.1.2): (γῆρας):—longer form of γεραιός, *aged, old*, γηραιὸς δὲ θάνοις Hes.*Op*.378, cf. Hdt.3.64, Pi.*P*.4.157, A.*Pers*.854 (lyr.), *Supp*.606, Th.6.54; γ. τελευτᾶν X.*Ages*.11.15, Pl.*Smp*.179e; τὸν μὲν ἄρ' αἰὼν γ. κατέπεφνε Maiist. 12. **-ᾰλέος,** α, ον (also **γηράλιος,** Hsch., **γηράλειος,** *IG*12(7). 113 (Amorg.)), = foreg., Xenoph.1.18, Pi.*P*.4.121, A.*Pers*.171, Cratin.126, J.*BJ*1.2.2; γ. ὀδόντες, ῥυτίδες, Anacr.43.2, *AP*5.128 (Autom.); σανίς ib.9.242 (Antiphil.); ἀπὸ κροτάφων πελόμεσθα πάντες γηραλέοι Theoc.14.69. **-ᾱμα,** ατος, τό, = γήρειον, Sch.Arat. 921. **-άμων·** γράζα, Hsch. **-άναι,** v. γηράσκω. **-άνιον·** γήραν, Hsch. **-ανσις,** εως, ἡ, *a growing old*, Arist.*Metaph*.1065ᵇ20, *Ph*.201ᵃ19. **-ᾰός,** όν, = γηραιός, *IG*14.1721.

**γηράς,** v. γηράσκω.

* **γῆρας,** τό, gen. γήραος Il.22.60, al., Archil.116, Mimn.2.6, Pi.*O*.8.71, etc.; γήρως Thgn.174, Att. (v. infr.): dat. γήραϊ Pi.*N*.7.99, Hdt.6.24, contr. γήρᾳ S.*Aj*.507, etc., γήρατι v.l. in Adam.*Phgn*.1.14 (cf. γῆρος):—*old age*, γ. λυγρόν Od.24.250; στυγερόν Il.19.336; ἐπὶ γήραος οὐδῷ (v. οὐδός) 22.60; opp. γ. λιπαρόν, Od.19.368, Pi. l.c.; γ. πολιόν Thgn.174; γῆρας ἐκδῦναι, ἀποσείσασθαι, Ar.*Pax*336, Lys. 670 (with play on signf. II); ἐπὶ γήρως *in old age*, Id.*Eq*.524; ἐν τῷ γήρᾳ Pl.*R*.329c, Lys.2.73; σὺν γήρᾳ, ἐν γ. βαρύς, S.*OT*17, *Aj*.1017; διανοίας γ. Arist.*Pol*.1271ᵃ1: metaph., οὐκ ἔστι γῆρας τοῦδε τοῦ μιάσματος, i.e. it never wears out, A.*Th*.682. II. *cast skin, slough of a serpent*, γῆρας ἐκδύνειν Arist.*HA*549ᵇ26, Nic.*Th*.31, Antig.*Mir*. 20, Antyll.ap.Orib.10.35.4; of crabs, Arist.*HA*600ᵇ20, Thphr.*Fr*. 177.

**γηράσιμος,** η, ον, = γηραιός, *JHS*34.12 (Teos).

* **γηράσκω,** fut. γηράσομαι [ᾰ] Critias1.5 (and in compds., ἐγ-, κατα-, συγ-, Th.6.18, Ar.*Eq*.1308, E.*Fr*.1058); γηράσω Pl.*R*.393e: poet. inf. γηρᾰσέμεν Simon.85.9: aor. ἐγήρᾱσα (κατ-) Hdt.2.146, Pl.*Tht*.202d (also causal, cf. infr. II): acc. fem. part. γηράσασαν (v.l. γηρᾶσαν) Hdt.7.114: pf. γεγήρᾱκα S.*OC*727, etc.:—also **γηράω** X.*Cyr*.4.1.15, Arist.*EN*1135ᵇ2, Men 481.14, Plu.2.911b, part. γηρῶν Epict.*Fr*.3: aor. 2 (as if from γήρημι or γήρᾱμι) ἐγήρα Il.7.148, 17.197, Od.14.67, (κατ-) Hdt.6.72; inf. γηράναι [ᾰ] A.*Ch*.908 (cum Sch.), S.*OC*870 (so *EM*230.53, but γηρᾶναι Moer.115), part. γηράς Il.17.197, dat. pl. γηράντεσσι Hes.*Op*.188, gen. pl. (ὑπερ-) γηράντων dub. in Ael.*NA*7.17; also γηρείς, έντος, Xenoph.9:—Med., γηράσκομαι Hes.*Fr*.171:—Pass., (ὑπερ-) γηραθείς Ps.-Callisth.1.25:—*grow old*, and in aor. and pf., *to be so*, κηρύσσων γήρασκε *grew old* in his office of herald, Il.17.325, cf. 2.663, etc.; of things, ὄγχνη ἐπ' ὄγχνῃ γ. Od.7.120; χρόνος γηράσκων A.*Pr*.981; πάλιν γὰρ αὖθις παῖς ὁ γ. ἀνήρ S.*Fr*.487; μετὰ τὴν δόσιν γ. χάρις Men.*Mon*.347; τὸ τῆσδε χώρας οὐ γεγήρακε σθένος S.*OC*727: c. acc. cogn., βίον τοιοῦτον γηράναι ib.870:—so in Med., Hes.*Fr*.171. II. causal in aor. 1 ἐγήρᾱσα, *bring to old age*, ἐγήρασάν με τροφῇ A.*Supp*.894; γηράσας πόδα (but perh. acc. cogn.) *AP*6.94 (Phil.). (Akin to γέρων, γῆρας.)

**γήρειον,** τό, *thistledown*, Arat.921, Nic.*Al*.126, *Th*.329.

**γηροβοσκ-έω,** *to feed* or *cherish in old age*, esp. one's parents, E. *Med*.1033, *Alc*.663; also τέκνα Demoph.*Sent*.43:—Pass., *to be cherished when old*, Ar.*Ach*.678 (γηρωβοσκήσει is read in Lib.*Decl*. 49.22; γηρωβοσκήσαντα is v.l. in Stob.3.1.38; cf. γηρο-κομεῖον, -κομέω, -κομία, -κόμος: such forms might be due to contr. of γηραο-, but are more prob. misspellings). **-ία,** ἡ, *care of the aged*, Alex. 312, Plu.2.111e; esp. of parents, *POxy*.1210.5 (i A.D.). * **-ός,** όν, (βόσκω) *nourishing* or *taking care of in old age*, esp. one's parents, S.*Aj*.570, Hyp.*Fr*.233; γηροβοσκὸν οὐκ ἔχω.. παῖδα E.*Supp*.923 (lyr.); γ. ἀποδιδόναι χάριτας D.H.8.47; γ. ἐλπίδες hopes *of such nurture*, ib.51: Subst., X.*Oec*.7.12.

* **γηροκομ-εῖον,** τό, *alms-house for the aged*, Suid. (γηρωκ- Hdn. *Epim*.205), Zonar. **-έω,** = γηροβοσκέω, abs., *Trag.Adesp*.25: c. acc., Call.*Ep*.51, J.*AJ*4.8.24, Ael.*NA*10.16, Luc.*Tox*.22, Max. Tyr.5.7:—Pass., ἐν θυγατράσιν γ. Agath.2.14 (γηρωκ- J. l.c., Luc. l.c., Max.Tyr. l.c.). **-ία,** = γηροβοσκία, J.*AJ*5.9.4 (γηρωκ-), Plu. *Cat.Ma*.5 (pl., γηρωκ-), 2.583c. **-ικός,** ή, όν, *belonging to* γηροκομία, Gal.6.330. * **-ος,** ον, (κομέω) *tending old age*, χήτει γηροκόμοιο for want *of one to tend one's age*, Hes.*Th*.605; ἃς δαίμων ἀντ' ἐμέθεν ὤπασε γηροκόμους, i.e. daughters, *Epigr.Gr*.536 (Tomi); χείρ γ. *IG*3.1335; φροντίδες γ. Opp.*H*.5.85: in later Prose (written γηρωκόμος), J.*AJ*1.13.3, Alciphr.3.16, Lib.*Decl*.49.25.

**γῆρος,** τό, = γῆρας, not found in nom., gen. γήρους Hp.*Int*.6, *Rev. Arch*.1913.247 (Selymbria), dat. γήρει Lxx *Ge*.15.15, al., *Ev.Luc*.1. 36; γήρεϊ v.l. ap.Sch.Il.3.150. (These forms are also found as vv.ll. for γήραος, γήραϊ.)

**γηροτροφ-έω,** = γηροβοσκέω, Is.1.39, Pl.*Mx*.248d:—Pass., γηροτροφούμενοι Isoc.14.48: fut. Med. in pass. sense, γηροτροφήσονται D.60.32; ὑπὸ τῶν.. παίδων γηροτροφηθέντες Lys.13.45, cf. Lycurg. 144. **-ία,** ἡ, = γηροβοσκία, Antipho Soph.66, *PFlor*.382.39 (iii A.D.); τὰς γ. ἀποτίνειν Plu.2.579e. **-ιον** or **-εῖον,** τό, *alms-house for the aged*, Suid. s. v. γηροκομεῖον. * **-ος,** ον, (τρέφω) = γηροβοσκός, E.*Alc*.668; γ. ἐλπίς Pi.*Fr*.214, cf. *CIG*2240 (Chios); χάριν οὐ δυνάμην γ. τελέσαι *Supp.Epigr*.1.567.10 (Karanis).

**γηροφορέω,** *carry an old person*, Plu.2.983b.

**γηρόω,** v. γυρόω.

**γηρυγόνος,** η, ον, *born of sound*, κούρας γηρυγόνας, i.e. echoes, Theoc.*Syrinx*6.

* **γήρῡμα,** ατος, τό, (γηρύω) *sound*, of a trumpet, A.*Eu*.569 (lyr.): pl., ἀδίδακτα γ. Plu.2.973a.

**Γηρῠόνης,** ου, ὁ, (γηρύω) the three-bodied Giant *Geryon*, Pi.*I*.1. 13, etc.: **Γηρῠονεύς,** έως, Ep. ῆος, Hes.*Th*.287: **Γηρῠών,** όνος, A. *Ag*.870:—hence **Γηρῠονίς** or **-ηΐς,** ίδος, ἡ, *a poem on Geryon* by Stesichorus, Ath.11.499e, Paus.8.3.2.

**γῆρυς,** Dor. **γᾶρυς,** B.5.15, S.*Ichn*.65, υος, ἡ, *voice, speech*, Il.4. 437; στονόεσσα γ. S.*OT*186 (lyr.); Ὀρφεία γ., i.e. Orpheus, E.*Alc*. 969; Κολχίδα γῆρυν ἰεῖσα A.R.4.731: in later Prose, Plu.2.397c: metaph. of the *voice* of passion, Ph.1.373. (Cf. OIr. *gāir, gairm* 'shout', Welsh *gawr, garm*.)

**γηρύω,** Dor. and Aeol. **γᾱρύω,** Sapph.*Supp*.25.20, etc.; inf. γαρύεν, -έμεν Pi.*O*.1.3, *N*.3.32: fut. -ύσω: aor. ἐγήρυσα Ar.*Pax*805; Dor. ἐγάρυσα S.*Ichn*.244:—Med., fut. -ύσομαι Pi.*I*.1.34, E.*Hipp*. 213: aor. ἐγηρυσάμην Id.*El*.1327 (lyr.); Dor. opt. γαρύσαιντο Theoc. 1.136, etc.; also ἐγηρύθην (v. infr.):—*sing* or *say, speak, cry*, Sapph. l.c., dub. in Simon.31: c. acc., *utter*, ἄκραντα Pi.*O*.2.96; φρονέοντι συνετὰ γ. B.3.85; γ. εὖχος Pi.*N*.6.58; ὕπα Ar.*Pax*805; θέσπιν αὐδὰν S. l.c. 2. trans., *sing of, celebrate*, τινά Pi.*N*.7.83; τι Id.*O*. 13.50, etc. II. Med., abs., *sing*, h.*Merc*.426; τοὶ σκῶπες ἀηδόσι γαρύσαιντο let the owls *sing against* the nightingales, Theoc.1.136 (perh. f.l. for δηρίσαιντο): c. acc. cogn., γηρύετ' ἀνθρώπων νόον Hes. *Op*.260; γαρύσομαι αἶσαν Pi.*I*.1.34, cf. *P*.5.72; οὐ μὴ τάδε γηρύσῃ E.*Hipp*.213 (lyr.), cf. 1074; αὐδὴν τήνδε γηρυθεῖσ' ἔσει A.*Supp*.460. (ῠ in pres. Hes., Pi., etc.; ῡ A.*Pr*.78, Theoc.9.7, Orph.*A*.432, *AP*7. 201 (Pamph.): ῡ always in fut. and aor.)

**γηρωβοσκέω, γηρωκομέω,** etc., v. γηρο-. **γηρωπίζεται·** γεροντεύεται, Hsch. **γήρως,** v. γῆρας.

**γήτειον,** τό, = γήθυον, *horn onion, Allium Cepa*, var., Ar.*Eq*.677, al., Anaxandr.41.57, Alex.127.7, Call.*Aet*.1.1.25: pl., Ph.1.665.

**γήτης,** ὁ, contr. for γηΐτης (q.v.).

**γητικά,** τά, a kind of *cup*, Epist.Alex.ap.Hsch.

* **γη-τομέω,** *cleave the ground*, A.R.2.1005, Lyc.268. **-φᾰγέω,** *eat earth*, Arist.ap.*EM*222.9. **-φάγος** [ᾰ], ον, = γαιηφάγος, *herb-eating*, i.e. *poor*, Call.*Fr*.58. **-φοριών,** ῶνος, ὁ (sc. μήν), name of month at Iasus, *GDI*3750.

**γήχῠτον,** τό, (χέω) *the soft mould* or *soil* on the earth's surface, Gal.19.91.

**γία·** ἄνθη (i.e. ϝία), Hsch. **γίαι·** ὀδύναι, Id. **γίαρ[ες]·** ἔαρ, Id. **γιγαλία·** ἡ γῆ, Id.

**Γῐγάντ-ειος,** α, ον, *gigantic*, *AP*9.708 (Phil.), Luc.*Philops*.23:—also **Γῐγανταῖος,** α, ον, Aesop.53, Hsch. s. v. Ἀβραμιαῖος: **Γιγαντιαῖος,** σώματα Pall.*in Hp*.2.143 D.: **Γιγαντικός,** ή, όν, *of* or *for the Giants*, τὰ -κά Plu.2.360f; *monstrous*, θρασύτης Simp.*in Ph*.1145. 4, cf. Procl.*in Prm*.p.659 S. **-ία,** ἡ, = Γιγαντομαχία, Philostr. *VS*1.21.5. **-ιάς,** άδος, ἡ, title of Epic by Dionysius, St.Byz. s. v. Δωδώνη. **-ιος,** ὁ (sc. μήν), name of month at Amphissa, *GDI* 2091; at Triteia, ib.1813. **-ολέτης,** ου, *giantkiller*, name of Dionysus and Apollo, *AP*9.524, 525, Ps.-Luc.*Philopatr*.4; of Zeus, prob. in Pancrat.*Oxy*.1085.25; **-ολέτωρ,** ορος, ὁ, Luc.*Tim*.4:—fem. **-ολέτειρα** and **-ολέτις,** ιδος, Suid., Ps.-Luc.*Philopatr*.8.

**Γῐγαντο-μᾰχία,** ἡ, *battle of the gods and giants*, Pl.*R*.378c (pl.), *Sph*.246a, Plu.*Ant*.60, etc. **-ραιστος,** ὁ, *giant-quelling*, Lyc. 63. **-φθόρος,** ον, = sq., Sch.Lyc.63. **-φόνος,** ον, *giant-killing*, E. *HF*1193, Nonn.*D*.1.516. **-φόντις,** ιδος, ἡ, fem. of foreg., Corn.*ND*20.

**Γιγαντώδης,** ες, *gigantic*, Ph.2.117, Eun.*Hist*.p.218 D.

**γιγαρτίς·** σταφίς, Hsch.

**γίγαρτ-ον** [ῐ], *grape-stone*, Simon.88, Ar.*Pax*634, Thphr.*HP*1.11. 6, Lxx *Nu*.6.4, Apollon.*Mir*.15, etc.; *olive-stone*, *PSI*4.430.1 (iii B.C.), Phlp.*in Ph*.629.16. **-ώδης,** ες, *like grape-stones*, Thphr.*HP* 3.17.6, Thd.*Is*.1.25. **-ώνιον,** τό, expld. by *unripe grapes*, *PLond. ined*.1821.

**Γίγας** [ῐ], αντος, ὁ, mostly in pl., *Giants*, ὑπέρθυμοι Od.7.59; Κύκλωπές τε καὶ ἄγρια φῦλα Γιγάντων ib.206; οὐκ ἄνδρεσσιν ἐοικότες ἀλλὰ Γίγασιν 10.120; γ. γηγενέται Hes.*Th.*185, cf. E.*Ph.*128 (lyr.); of Capaneus, A.*Th.*424. II. as Adj., *mighty* (γίγαντος· μεγάλου, ἰσχυροῦ, ὑπερφυοῦς, Hsch.), Ζεφύρου γίγαντος αὔρᾳ Id.*Ag.*692 (lyr.), cf. Eurytus (*PLG*3.639).

**γιγγίδιον,** τό, *a plant, Daucus Gingidium,* Dsc.2.137, 3.52: **γιγγικίδιον,** Sch.Nic.*Al.*432. II. = λεπίδιον, Dsc.2.174.

**γιγγίς,** ίδος, ἡ, kind of *turnip, French carrot,* Alex.Trall.1.15.

⊛ **γίγγλᾰρος,** ὁ, a kind of *flute* or *fife,* Poll.4.82:—Dim. **γιγγλάριον,** τό, *AB*88; cf. γίγγρας.

**γιγγλίαν·** κάλυμμα κεφαλῆς ἐρεοῦν, Hsch.

**γιγγλισμός,** ὁ, *tickling,* Suid. II. = γίγγλυμος 5, Paus.Gr.*Fr.* 108.

**γίγγλος·** νᾶνος, Hsch.

**γιγγλύμιον** [ῠ], τό, Dim. of γίγγλυμος, Anthem.p.155 W. (γιγλ- codd.).

**γιγγλῠμο-ειδής,** ές, *like a hinge,* τοῦ βραχίονος τὸ γ. Hp.*Fract.*2, Gal.2.735. Adv. -δῶς Gal.18(1).513. **-ομαι,** *to be hinge-jointed,* γεγιγγλύμωνται πρὸς ἀλλήλους οἱ σφόνδυλοι Hp.*Art.*45.

**γίγγλῠμος** (**γιγγλυμός,** Hsch.), ὁ, *hinge,* οἷον εἰ γ. Hp.*Loc.Hom.*6, cf. Apollod.*Poliorc.*190.1: hence a species of *joint,* Arist. *de An.*$433^{b}$ 22, Gal.2.735. 2. metal *pivot* or *gudgeon* on which a door turns, = στρόφιγξ, *IG*4.1484.74 (Epid.), 11(2).165.15 (Delos, iii B.C.):—written **γλυμός,** ib.142.49 (an engraver's error). 3. *joint in a coat of mail,* X.*Eq.*12.6. 4. *clasp, buckle,* J.*AJ*3.6.3,4. 5. *mode of kissing,* Hsch.

**γιγγλῠμ-ώδης,** ες, = γιγγλυμοειδής, Arist.*HA*$529^{a}$32. **-ωτός,** όν, *hinged,* σανίδες Ph.*Bel.*91.29, Apollod.*Poliorc.*189.9. II. γ. φίλημα, = γίγγλυμος 5, Telecl.13.

**γιγγρ-άϊνος,** ον, *like the* γίγγρας, αὐλοί Ath.4.174f. **-αντός,** ή, όν, *composed for the* γίγγρας, μέλη γ. of 'scrannel pipes', Ath.4.175b. **-ας,** ου, ὁ, *small Phoenician flute* or *fife,* of a high pitch and plaintive tone, Amphis 14 (from Γίγγρης, Phoenician name for Adonis, Ath.4.174f):—also **γίγγρος** αὐλός Antiph.108, Men.259: **γίγγρον,** Hsch. 2. *its music,* Trypho *Fr.*109 V.; *dance to its tune,* Poll.4.102. **-ασμός,** ὁ, *the tone of the* γίγγρας, Hsch.

⊛ **γιγγρί,** an abusive interjection, Hsch. **γιγγρίας,** = γίγγρας, Id.

⊛ **γίγνομαι,** Ion. and after Arist. **γίνομαι** [ῑ], (Att. Inscrr. have γιγν- in fifth and fourth cent., cf. *IG*2.11.9, 1055.25, etc.); Thess. **γίνυμαι** *IG*9(2).517.22; Boeot. **γίνιουμαι** ib.7.3303: fut. γενήσομαι: aor. ἐγενόμην (ἐγενάμην Lxx *Je.*14.1, al. (προ-) Decr.Byz.ap.D.18.90), Ion. 2 sg. γένευ Il.5.897, 3 sg. γενέσκετο Od.11.208, ἔγεντο Hes.*Th.*705, Sapph.16, Pi.*P.*3.87, Parm.8.20, *IG*4.492 (Mycenae), prob. in *Scol.* 19; Ep. γέντο Hes.*Th.*199, Emp.98.5, Call.*Jov.*1.50, Theoc.14.27, etc. (γn̥-το): pf. γέγονα Il.19.122, etc.: 3 pl. γέγοναν *Apoc.*21.6: plpf. ἐγεγόνει Lys.31.17, etc.; Ion. ἐγεγόνεε Hdt.2.2; Ep. forms (as if from pf. γέγᾰα), 2 pl. γεγάᾱτε Batr.143; γεγάᾱσι Il.4.325, freq. in Od.: 3 pl. γεγάκᾰσιν cj. in Emp.23.10: 3 dual plpf. ἐκ-γεγάτην [ᾰ] Od.10.138; inf. γεγάμεν [ᾰ] Pi.*O.*9.110, (ἐκ) Il.5.248, etc.; part. γεγᾰώς -ᾰυῖα, pl. -ᾰῶτες, -ᾰυῖαι Hom., etc., contr. γεγώς, -ῶσα S.*Aj.*472, E.*Med.*406; inf. γεγάκειν Pi.*O.*6.49: Med. forms ἐκγεγάασθε Epigr.Hom.16, ἐκ-γεγάονται (in fut. sense) *h.Ven.*197 (s.v.l.):—Pass. forms, fut. γενηθήσομαι (only in Pl.*Prm.*141e, οὔτε γενήσεται, οὔτε γενηθήσεται, cf. Procl.*in Prm.*p.963 S.): aor. ἐγενήθην Epich.209, Archyt.1, Hp.*Epid.*6.8.32, 7.3, later Att., Philem. 95.2 and 167, *IG*2.630*b*10 (i B.C.) and Hellenistic Gk., Plb.2.67.8, D.S.13.51: pf. γεγένημαι Simon.69, freq. in Att. Poets and Prose, in Att. inscr. first in cent. iv, *IG*2.555: 3 pl. γεγενέανται Philet. ap.Eust.1885.51: plpf. ἐγεγένητο Th.7.18, al.; cf. γείνομαι:—*come into a new state of being*: hence, I. abs., *come into being* opp. εἶναι, Emp.17.11, Pl.*Phd.*102e, cf. *Ti.*29a; and so, 1. of persons, *to be born,* νέον γεγαώς new *born,* Od.19.400; ὑπὸ Τμώλῳ γεγαῶτας *born* (and so *living*) under Tmolus, Il.2.866; ἢ πρόσθε θανεῖν ἢ ἔπειτα γ. Hes.*Op.*175; γιγνομέναισι λάχη τάδ'.. ἐκράνθη *at our birth,* A.*Eu.*347; γ. ἔκ τινος Il.5.548, Hdt.7.11; πατρὸς ἐκ ταὐτοῦ E.*IA* 406, cf. Isoc.5.136; σέθεν .. ἐξ αἵματος A.*Th.* 142; less freq. ἀπό τινος Hdt.8.22, etc.; ἐσθλῶν E.*Hec.*380, etc.; γεγονέναι κακῶς, καλῶς, Ar.*Eq.*218, Isoc.7.37, etc.; κάλλιον, εὖ, Hdt. 1.146, 3.69; τὸ μὴ γενέσθαι not *to have been born,* A.*Fr.*401: freq. with Numerals, ἔτεα τρία καὶ δέκα γεγονώς Hdt.1.119; ἀμφὶ τὰ πέντε ἢ ἑκκαίδεκα ἔτη γενόμενος X.*Cyr.*1.4.16; γεγονὼς ἔτη περὶ πεντήκοντα D. 21.154; οἱ ὑπὲρ τὰ στρατεύσιμα ἔτη γεγονότες *those of an age* beyond .., X.*Cyr.*1.2.4: c. gen., γεγονὼς πλειόνων ἐτῶν ἢ πεντήκοντα Pl.*Lg.* 951c, etc.: rarely with ordinals, ὀγδοηκοστὸν ἔτος γεγονώς Luc.*Macr.* 22, cf. Plu.*Phil.*18. 2. of things, *to be produced,* ὅσα φύλλα καὶ ἄνθεα γίγνεται ὥρῃ Od.9.51; opp. ὄλλυσθαι, Parm.8.13,40; opp. ἀπόλλυσθαι, Anaxag.17, cf. Pl.*R.*527b, etc.; opp. ἀπολείπειν, Diog. Apoll.7; opp. ἀπολήγειν, Emp.17.30; τὰ γιγνόμενα καὶ ἐξ ὧν γίγνεται Pl.*Phlb.*27a; ἁπλῇ διηγήσει ἢ διὰ μιμήσεως γ. Id.*R.*392d; ὁ ἐκ τῆς χώρας γιγνόμενος σῖτος X.*Mem.*3.6.13; τὰ ἐν ἀγρῷ γιγνόμενα ib.2.9.4; of profits, καρποὶ οἱ ἐξ ἀγελῶν γ. Id.*Cyr.*1.1.2, etc.; τὰ ἆθλα ἀπὸ τεττάρων ταλάντων ἐγένοντο *were the produce of,* i.e. *were worth,* 4 talents, Id.*HG*4.2.7; τὸ ἀπὸ τῶν αἰχμαλώτων γενόμενον ἀργύριον *produced by* [the ransom of] .., Id.*An.*5.3.4; of sums, ὁ γεγονὼς ἀριθμὸς τῶν ψήφων the *total* of the votes, Pl.*Ap.*36a; ἕκατον εἴκοσι στατήρων γίγνονται τρισχίλιαι τριακόσιαι ἑξήκοντα [δραχμαί] 120 staters *amount to* 3,360 drachmae, D.34.24; so in Math., of *products,* ὁ ἐξ αὐτῶν γενόμενος ἀριθμός Euc.7.24; ἀριθμὸς γενόμενος ἑκατοντάκις *multiplied* by 100, Papp.10.13; of times of day, ὡς ἡ ἡμέρα ἐγένετο Th.7.81, etc.; ἕως ἂν φῶς γένηται Pl.*Prt.*311a; ἅμα ἕῳ γιγνομένῃ Th.4.32; of Time in general, *elapse,* διέτης χρόνος ἐγεγόνεε ταῦτα πρήσσουσι Hdt.2.2; χρόνου γενομένου D.S.20.109. b. *fall due,* οἱ γιγνόμενοι δασμοί X.*An.*1.1. 8; τοὺς τόκους τοὺς γ. Isoc.17.37; τὸ τίμημα τὸ γ., τὸ γ. ἀργύριον, D.24. 82, Syngr.ap.eund.35.11; τὸ γ. μέρος X.*HG*7.4.33; τὸ γ. τοῖ πλήθι τᾶς ζαμίαν *IG*5(2).6*A*20 (Tegea, iv B.C.): c. dat., τὸ γ. τινὶ ἔλαιον *UPZ* 19.32 (ii B.C.); τοῖς γείτοσι τὸ γ. Thphr.*Fr.*97; τὰ γ. *dues, PHib.*1.92 and 111 (iii B.C.): hence γιγνόμενος *regular, normal,* τίμημα, χάρις, D. 38.25; ἐν ταῖς γ. ἡμέραις in the *usual number* of days, X.*Cyr.*5.4.51; freq. in later Gk., as Luc.*Tox.*18, etc. 3. of events, *take place, come to pass,* and in past tenses *to be,* καί σφιν ἄχος κατὰ θυμὸν ἐγίγνετο Il.13. 86, etc.; μάχη ἐγεγόνει Pl.*Chrm.*153b, etc.; ἐκεχειρία γίγνεταί τισι πρὸς ἀλλήλους Th.4.58; ἡ νόσος ἤρξατο γίγνεσθαι Id.2.47; πνεῦμα εἰώθει γ. ib.84; τὰ Ὀλύμπια γίγνεται, τραγῳδοὶ γίγνονται, *are held,* X.*HG*7. 4.28, Aeschin.3.41, etc.; ψήφισμα γ. *is passed,* X.*Cyr.*2.2.21; πιστὰ γ., ὅρκοι γ., pledges *are given,* oaths *taken,* ib.7.4.3, D.19.158; γίγνεταί τι ὑπό τινος (masc.), X.*An.*7.1.30, (neut.) Pl.*Tht.*200e; τὰ γιγνόμενα ὑπὸ τῶν Ἀθηναίων Th.6.88; τὰ γενόμενα ἐξ ἀνθρώπων Hdt.*Praef.*; ὕβρισμα ἐκ τῶν Σαμίων γενόμενον Id.3.48; ἀπό τινος γ. X.*An.*5.6.30; παρά τινος Pl.*R.*614a; ὃ μὴ γένοιτο which *God forbid,* D.10.27, 28. 21; but γένοιτο, = *Amen,* Lxx *Is.*25.1; γένοιτο γένοιτο ib.*Ps.*71(72). 19: Math., γεγονέτω *suppose it done,* Euc.6.23, etc.; γέγονε *it is done, Apoc.*16.17: c. dat. et part., γίγνεταί τί μοι βουλομένῳ, ἀσμένῳ (v. βούλομαι, ἄσμενος); οὐκ ἂν ἐμοί γε ἐλπομένῳ τὰ γένοιτο, i.e. I could not hope to see these things *take place,* Od.3.228; ἡδομένοισι ἡμῖν οἱ λόγοι γεγόνασι Hdt.9.46, etc.; of sacrifices, omens, etc., οὐ γάρ σφι ἐγίνετο τὰ σφάγια χρηστά ib.61, cf. 62; τὰ ἱερὰ καλὰ ἐγένετο X.*An.*6.4.9: abs., τὰ διαβατήρια ἐγ. *were favourable,* Th.5.55; θυομένῳ οὐκ ἐγίγνετο τὰ ἱερά X.*HG*3.1.17: in neut. part., τὸ γενόμενον *the event, the fact,* Th.6.54; τὰ γενόμενα *the facts,* X.*Cyr.*3.1.9, etc.; τὸ γιγνόμενον Pl.*Tht.*161b, etc.; τὰ γεγενημένα *the past,* X.*An.*6.2. 14; τὸ γενησόμενον *the future,* Th.1.138; τὰ γεγονότα, opp. ὄντα, μέλλοντα, Pl.*R.*392d, cf. *Lg.*896a: of Time, ὡς τρίτη ἡμέρη τῷ παιδίῳ ἐκκειμένῳ ἐγένετο Hdt.1.113; ἕως ἄν τινες χρόνοι γένωνται Pl.*Phd.* 108c; but in pf. and plpf., *to have passed,* ὡς διετὴς χρόνος ἐγεγόνεε Hdt.2.2; πρὶν ἓξ μῆνας γεγονέναι Pl.*Prt.*320a: impers., ἐγένετο or γέγονεν ὥστε.. *it happened, came to pass* that.., X.*HG*5.3.10, Isoc. 6.40, etc.; ἐγένετο, ὡς ἤκουσεν..καὶ ἐθυμώθη *it came to pass,* when he heard..that.., Lxx *Ge.*39.19; ἐγένετο ἐν τῷ πορεύεσθαι..καὶ διήρχετο *Ev.Luc.*17.11: c. inf., γίνεται εὑρεῖν *it is possible* to find, Thgn.639; ἐγένετο, c. acc. et inf., *it came to pass* that, *Act.Ap.*9.3, al., *PAmh.*2. 135.10 (ii A.D.): c. dat. et inf., ἐάν σοι γένηται στραφῆναι Epict.*Ench.* 23. II. folld. by a Predicate, *come into* a certain state, *become,* and (in past tenses), *to be,* 1. folld. by Nouns and Adjs., δηΐοισι δὲ χάρμα γ. Il.6.82, cf. 8.282; σωτὴρ γενοῦ μοι A.*Ch.*2; κωλυτὴς γ. τινός Th.3.23; [οὖροι] νηῶν πομπῆες γ. Od.4.362, etc.; πάντα δὲ γιγνόμενος πειρήσεται *turning* every way, ib.417; παντοῖος γ., folld. by μή, c. inf., Hdt.3.124; παντοῖος γ. δεόμενος Id.7.10.γ′; ἐκ πλουσίου πένης γ. X.*An.*7.7.28; δημοτικὸς ἐξ ὀλιγαρχικοῦ γ. Pl.*R.*572d: rarely c. part., μὴ προδοὺς ἡμᾶς γένῃ, i.e. προδότης ἡμῶν, S.*Aj.*588, cf. *Ph.* 773; μὴ ἀπαρνηθεὶς γένῃ Pl.*Sph.*217c; ἀποτετραμμένοι ἐγένοντο Th. 3.68, etc.: with Pron., τί γένωμαι; what *am I to become,* i.e. what is to become of me? A.*Th.*297, cf. Theoc.15.51; οὐκ ἔχοντες ὅτι γένωνται Th.2.52; less freq. with masc., οὐδ' ἔχω τίς ἂν γενοίμαν A.*Pr.*905; γίγνονται πάνθ' ὅτι βούλονται Ar.*Nu.*348. b. in past tenses, *having ceased to be,* ὁ γενόμενος στρατηγός the *ex*-strategus, *POxy.*38.11 (i A.D.); ἡ γ. γυνή τινος the *former* wife, *PFlor.*99.4 (i/ii A.D.). 2. with Advbs., κακῶς χρῆν Κανδαύλῃ γενέσθαι Hdt.1.8; εὖ, καλῶς, ἡδέως γ., *it goes* well, etc., X.*An.*1.7.5, Arr.*Epict.*3.24.97, Lxx *To.* 7.9; with personal construction, οἱ παρὰ Πλάτωνι δειπνήσαντες ἐς αὔριον ἡδέως γίγνονται Plu.2.127b; δίχα γ. τοῦ σώματος *to be parted from..,* X.*Cyr.*8.7.20; τριχῇ γ. *to be* in three divisions, Id.*An.*6.2. 16; γ. ἐμποδών, ἐκποδών, E.*Hec.*372, X.*HG*6.5.38, etc. 3. folld. by oblique cases of Nouns, a. c. gen., γ. τῶν δικαστέων, τῶν γεραιτέρων, *become one of..,* Hdt.5.25, X.*Cyr.*1.2.15, cf. Ar.*Nu.*107, etc.; βουλῆς γεγονώς D.C.36.28 (cf. supr. I.b); *fall to, belong to,* ἡ νίκη Ἀγησιλάου ἐγεγένητο X.*HG*4.3.20; *to be under control of,* ὁ νοῦς ὅταν αὐτοῦ γένηται S.*OC*660, cf. Pl.*Phdr.*250a (s.v.l.); ὑμῶν αὐτῶν γενέσθαι D.4.7 (also ἐντὸς ἑωυτοῦ γ. Hdt.1.119; ἐν ἑαυτῷ γ. X.*An.*1. 5.17; ἐν σαυτοῦ γενοῦ S.*Ph.*950); τὴν πόλιν ἐλπίδος μεγάλης γινομένην Plu.*Phoc.*23: of things, *to be at,* i.e. *cost,* so much, αἱ τριχίδες εἰ γενοίαθ' ἑκατὸν τοὐβολοῦ Ar.*Eq.*662, cf. X.*Oec.*20.23. b. c. dat., *fall to,* i.e. as wife, Lxx *Nu.*36.11. c. with Preps., γ. ἀπὸ δείπνου, ἐκ θυσίας, *have done..,* Hdt.2.78, 1.50; πολὺν χρόνον γ. ἀπό τινος *to be separated* from.., X.*Mem.*1.2.25; γ. εἴς τι *turn* into, τὸ κακὸν γ. εἰς ἀγαθόν Thgn.162; freq. in Lxx, ἐγενήθη μοι εἰς γυναῖκα *Ge.*20.12; εἰς βρῶσιν ib.*La.*4.10; εἰς οὐδέν, εἰς κενόν, *Act.Ap.*5.36, 1 *Ep.Thess.* 3.5; ἐς Λακεδαίμονα Hdt.5.38 (in Hom. even without Prep., ἐμὲ χρεὼ γ. Od.4.634); γ. τι εἴς τινα *comes* to him, of a dowry, Is.3. 36; of a ward, And.1.117; γ. ἐξ ὀφθαλμῶν τινι *to be* out of sight, Hdt.5.24; ἐξ ἀνθρώπων γ. *disappear* from.., Paus.4.26.6; γ. ἐν Χίῳ Hdt.5.33, etc.; γ. ἐν.., *to be engaged* in.., οἱ ἐν ποιήσει γινόμενοι in poetry, Id.2.82; ἐν [πολέμῳ] Th.1.78; ἐν πείρᾳ γ. τινος X.*An.*1.9.1; ἐν ὀργῇ, ἐν αἰτίᾳ πρός τινα γ., Plu.*Flam.*16, *Rom.*7; of things, ἐν καιρῷ γ. *to be* in season, X.*HG*4.3.2; ἐν τύχῃ γ. τινί τι Th.4.73; γ. διὰ γηλόφων, of a road, X.*An.*3.4.24; but δι' ἔχθρας γ. τινί *to be* at enmity with, Ar.*Ra.*1412; γ. ἐπὶ ποταμῷ *arrive* or *be* at.., Hdt.1. 189, etc.; γ. ἐπί τινι *fall into* or *be in* one's power, X.*An.*3.1.13, etc.; ἐπὶ συμφοραῖς γ. D.21.58 codd. (-ᾶς Schaefer); γ. ἐπί τινι, also, *to be set* over.., X.*Cyr.*3.3.53; γ. ἐφ' ἡμῶν αὐτῶν *to be* alone, Aeschin.2.

36; γ. ἐπὶ τῆς διοικήσεως D.C.43.48; γ. ἐπ' ἐλπίδος *to be* in hope, Plu.*Sol.*14: Math., γ. ἐπὶ ἀριθμόν *to be multiplied* into a number, *Theol.Ar.*3; γ. κατά τινα or τι *to be* near .. or *opposite to* .., in battle, X.*Cyr.*7.1.14, *HG*4.2.18; but κατὰ ξυστάσεις γ. *to be formed* into groups, Th.2.21; καθ' ἓν γ. Id.3.10; καθ' αὑτοὺς γ. *to be* alone, D.10.52; γ. μετὰ τοῦ θείου *to be* with God, X.*Cyr.*8.7.27, etc.; ἡ νίκη γ. σύν τινι Id.*Ages.*2.13; γ. παρ' ἀμφοτέροις τοῖς πράγμασι *to be present* on both sides, Th.5.26; γ. παρά τι *to depend* upon .., D.18.232; γ. περὶ τὸ συμβουλεύειν *to be engaged* in.., Isoc.3.12; γενοῦ πρός τινα *go* to So-and-so, *PFay.*128, etc.; γ. πρὸς τῇ καρδίᾳ *to be at* or *near* .., Pl.*Phd.*118, etc.; γ. πρός τινι *to be engaged* in.., Isoc.12.270, D.18.176; αὐτὸς πρὸς αὑτῷ *meditate*, Plu.2.151c; so γ. πρὸς τὸ ἰᾶσθαι Pl.*R.*604d; πρὸς παρασκευήν Plb.1.22.2: impers., ἐπεὶ πρὸς ἡμέραν ἐγίγνετο X.*HG*2.4.6; γενέσθαι πρός τινων *to be* inclined towards them, Hdt.7.22; γ. πρὸ ὁδοῦ *to be* forward on the way, Il.4.382; γ. ὑπό τινι *to be* subject to.., Hdt.7.11, Th.7.64; γ. ὑπὸ ταῖς μηχαναῖς *to be* under the protection of.., X.*Cyr.*7.1.34. 4. γίγνεται folld. by pl. nouns, ἵνα γίγνηται.. ἀρχαί τε καὶ γάμοι Pl.*R.*563a, cf. *Smp.*188b; ἐγένετο.. ἡμέραι ὀκτώ *Ev.Luc*9.28. (Cf. *jánati* 'procreate', *jánas* (= γένος), Lat. *gigno*, *gnatus*.)

✱ **γιγνώσκω**, Dor. (Epich.9, Pi.*O.*6.97), Aeol., Ion., and after Arist. **γινώσκω**, but γιγνώσκω in early Att. Inscrr., as *IG*1².127.19 (κατα-), etc.: fut. γνώσομαι Il.23.497, etc., Dor. 3 sg. γνωσεῖται Call.*Lav. Pall.*123 (γνώσω is f.l. in Hp.*Steril.*215); Cret. form ἀνα-γνώοντι dub. in *GDI*5075 (for aor. 1, v. ἀναγιγνώσκω): pf. ἔγνωκα Pi.*P.*4.287, etc.: aor. 2 ἔγνων Il.13.72, etc., Ep. dual γνώτην Od.21.36, Dor. 3 pl. ἔγνον Pi.*P.*4.120; imper. γνῶθι Epich.[264], etc.; subj. γνῶ, γνῷς, γνῷ Il.1.411, etc., Ep. also γνώω, γνώομεν Od.16.304, γνώωσι Il.23.610; opt. γνοίην Il.18.125, etc.; pl. γνοῖμεν Pl.*Alc.*1.129a; inf. γνῶναι Od.13.312, etc., Ep. γνώμεναι Il.21.266; part. γνούς S.*El.*731, etc.:—Med., aor. 1 γνώσασθαι Man.2 51:—Pass., fut. γνωσθήσομαι Ar.*Nu.*918, Th.1.124, etc.: aor. ἐγνώσθην A.*Supp.*7 (lyr.), E.*El.*852, Th.2.65: pf. ἔγνωσμαι E.*HF*1287, Th.3.38:—*come to know, perceive*, and in past tenses, *know*, c. acc., Il.12.272, etc.; as dist. fr. οἶδα *know by reflection*, γιγνώσκω, = *know by observation*, γνόντες δὲ εἰδότας περιορᾶν Th.1.69; ἐγὼ δ' οἶδ' ὅτι γιγνώσκετε τοῦτον ἅπαντες D.18.276; χαλεπὸν ἐστι τὸ γνῶναι εἰ οἶδεν ἢ μή it is hard to *perceive* whether one knows or not, Arist.*APo.*76ª26; *discern, distinguish, recognize*, ὄφρ' εὖ γιγνώσκῃς ἠμὲν θεὸν ἠδὲ καὶ ἄνδρα Il.5.128; ἀσπίδι γιγνώσκων by his shield, ib.182; ironically, εὖ νύ τις αὐτὸν γνώσεται he will *learn* him to his cost, 18.270; νῦν ἔγνων τὸν Ἔρωτα Theoc.3.15: sts. c. gen., γνώτην ἀλλήλων *were aware of*.., Od.21.36, cf. 23.109. 2. folld. by relat. clauses, γιγνώσκω δ' ὡς .. I *perceive* that.., 21.209; ἔγνως ὡς θεός εἰμι Il.22.10; ἔγνωκας ὡς οὐδὲν λέγεις Ar.*Nu.*1095; γ. ὅτι.. Heraclit.108, A.*Pr.*104,379, etc.; ἵν' εἰδῆτε ὑμεῖς καὶ γνῶτε ὅτι.. D.21.143; γνώμεναι εἴ μιν.. φοβέουσι Il.21.266; γ. τί πέπονθε πάθος Pl.*Phlb.*60d: c. acc. and relat. clause, Τυδεΐδην δ' οὐκ ἂν γνοίης, ποτέροισι μετείη Il.5.85; γ. θεοὺς οἵτινές εἰσι Heraclit.5; Σωκράτην γ. οἷος ἦν X.*Mem.*4.8.11; τοὺς Πέρσας γ. ὅτι.. Id.*Cyr.*2.1.11; also ἀλλοτρίας γῆς γ. ὅτι δύναται φέρειν Id.*Oec.*16.3: c. part., ἔγνων μιν.. οἰωνὸν ἐόντα *perceived* that he was.., Od.15.532; γνόντες οὐδεμίαν σφίσι τιμωρίαν οὖσαν Th.1.25; ἔγνωκα.. ἠπατημένη S.*Aj.*807; ἔγνων ἡττημένος I *felt that* I was beaten, Ar.*Eq.*658; χρυσῷ πάττων μ' οὐ γιγνώσκεις Id.*Nu.*912, cf. Antipho5.33, X.*Cyr.*7.2.17: c. gen., ὡς γνῶ χωομένοιο when *he was aware of*.., Il.4.357, cf. Pl.*Ap.*27a: c. inf., ἵνα γνῷ τρέφειν τὴν γλῶσσαν ἡσυχεστέραν S.*Ant.*1089: c. acc. et inf., *recognize* that.., Th.1.43, etc.; *take* a thing *to mean* that.., Hdt.1.78: c. dupl. acc., *perceive* or *know* another to be.., οἵους γνώσεσθε τοὺς ἀνθρώπους X.*An.*1.7.4: abs., ὁ γιγνώσκων *the perceiver*, opp. τὰ γιγνωσκόμενα *the objects perceived*, Pl.*R.*508e; also ὁ γ. *one who knows, a prudent person*, ib.347d:—Pass., εἰ γνωσθεῖεν ᾧ.. if *it were known of them* in what.., Id.*Prt.*342b. II. *form a judgement, think*, ταὐτὰ Hdt.9.2; τἀναντία τούτοις γ. X.*HG*2.3.38; οὕτω γ. Id.*An.*6.1.19; τὰ δίκαια γ. Lys.22.2; ἃ γιγνώσκω λέγειν (= τὴν γνώμην λ.) D.4.1; περὶ τῆς βοηθείας ταῦτα γιγνώσκω Id.1.19; τοῦτο γιγνώσκων, ὅτι.. Men.572, cf. 648; ὡς ἐμοῦ ἀγωνιουμένου οὕτω γίγνωσκε X.*Cyr.*2.3.15: abs., αὐτὸς γνώσῃ *see* thou to that, Pl.*Grg.*505c; esp. in dialogue, ἔγνων *I understand*, S.*Aj.*36; ἔγνως *you are right*, Id.*Tr.*1221, E.*Andr.*883; ἔγνωκας; Lat. *tenes?* Nausicr.1.5; *judge, determine, decree that*.., c. acc. et inf., Hdt.1.74, 6.85, Isoc.17.16: c. inf., *determine to*.., And.1.107:—Pass., *to be pronounced*, of a sentence or judgement, Th.3.36; παρανόμως γνωσθεῖσα δίαιτα D.33.33, cf. 59.47; κρίσις ἐγνωσμένη ὑπό τινος Isoc.6.30. 2. Pass., of persons, *to be judged guilty*, A.*Supp.*7; γνωσθέντα ζημιοῦσιν οἱ νόμοι Arist.*Rh.Al.*1431ᵇ30; τεθνάτω ἐὰν γνωσθῇ, ἐὰν δὲ φυγῇ γνωσθῇ, φευγέτω *IG*1².10.29. 3. pf. Pass. with act. sense, ὡμολόγηκεν ὑμᾶς ὑπάρχειν ἐγνωσμένους are *determined*, D.18.228 (sed leg. ἡμᾶς). III. *know carnally*, Men.558.5, Heraclid.*Pol.*64, Lxx *Ge.*4.1, al., *Ev.Matt.*1.25, Plu.*Galb.*9, etc. IV. γ. χάριν, = εἰδέναι χάριν, D.C.39.9.

B. causal, *make known, celebrate*, γνώσομαι τὰν ὀλβίαν Κόρινθον Pi.*O.*13.3 acc. to Sch. ad loc., v. dub. (Root γνω-, cf. Skt. *jānāmi*, *jñātas*, Lat. *gnosco*, *gnotus*, etc.)

**γιζί**, ἡ, a kind of *cassia*, Gal.14.67; **γίζιρ** (v.l. ζίγιρ) Dsc.1.13; **γίζειρ** *Peripl.M.Rubr.*12; **γιζηρά**, Orib.*Syn.*2.56.17.

**γιλός**· ἑτερόφθαλμος, Hsch. **γιμάσαι**· σιαγόνες, Id. **γιμβάναι**· ζεύγανα, Id. **γίν**· σοί (leg. τίν), Id. **γινιπτήριον**, τό, perh. f.l. for γινιστ-, = Lat. *genista*, *broom*, *PLeid.X.*19.

✱ **γίννος** or **γιννός**, ὁ, alleged offspring of mare by mule, Arist.*HA*577ᵇ25, cf. *GA*748ᵇ34; *small mule*, Str.4.6.2; *hinny*, Hsch.; **γῖνος** *IG*12(1).677.23 (Ialysus).

**γίνομαι, γινώσκω**, v. γιγν-.

**γίξαι**· χωρῆσαι, Hsch. **γίο**· αὐτοῦ, Id. **γῖπον**· εἶπον, Id. **γίς**· ἱμὰς καὶ γῆ καὶ ἰσχύς (i.e. ϝίς), Id. **γισάμεναι**· εἰδέναι, Id. **γίσας**· φθείρας, Id.: inf., γίσαι *deflower*, *App.Anth.*4.73 (perh. Strat.). **γίσγον**· ἴσον, Hsch. (ϝίσϝον). **γίσιον**· μικρὸν τεῖχος, Id. (leg. γείσ-). **γιστία**· ἐσχάρα (ἐσχάτη cod.), Id. **γιστίαι**· ἱστουργοί, Id. **γιστιῶ**· παύσομαι, Id. **γισχύν**· ἰσχύν, Id. **γιτέα**· ἰτέα (ἐτέα cod.), Id. (In the above words, γ freq. = ϝ.) **γῖτον**, τό, dub. sens. in *UPZ*89.14 (pl., ii B.C.). **γίτονας**, v. γείτων.

**γλᾰγ-άω**, *to be milky, juicy*, γλαγόωντι σπέρματι *AP*9.384.23. **-έας**· γεγαλακτωμένας, Hsch. ✱ **-ερός**, ά, όν, *full of milk*, *AP*6.154 (Leon. or Gaet.). 2. *soft, plump*, Opp.*C.*1.200, 332.

**γλᾰγό-εις**, εσσα, εν, = foreg., μαζοί *AP*5.55 (Diosc.). 2. *milky, milk-white*, Nic.*Th.*923, Opp.*H.*4.113. **-πήξ**, ῆγος, ὁ, ἡ, *curdling milk*, γαυλοὶ γ. bowls *for the purpose*, *AP*6.35 (Leon.).

**γλάγος** [ᾰ], εος, τό, poet. for γάλα (q.v.), *milk*, Il.2.471, Pi.*Fr.*106, Nic.*Al.*385.

**γλᾰγότροφος**, ον, *milk-fed*, Lyc.1260.

✱ **γλάζω**, = κλάζω, *sing aloud*, μέλος Pi.*Fr.*97. ✱ **γλᾶθις**, ιος, ἡ, name of a *sacrifice* or *festival*, dub. sens. in *Riv.Fil.*53.208 (Crete, pl.).

**γλαινοί** or **γλαῖνοι**, οἱ, *star-shaped ornaments*, Hsch., *EM*232.40. **γλαισμοί**· λόφοι, Hsch. **γλακάω**, = γλαγάω, Id. **γλακκόν**· γαλαθηνόν, Id.

✱ **γλακτο-πᾰγής**, ές, *full of milk*, μαστός *Jahrb.*19.*Anz.*186 (Smyrna). **-φάγος** [ᾰ], ον, shortd. for γαλακτ-, *living on milk*, Il.13.6: Γλακτοφάγοι, οἱ, Scythian people, Hes.*Fr.*54. **-φόρος**, ον, *milk-producing*, prob. in Marc.Sid.100.

**γλάματα**· ἀστράγαλοι, Hsch.

**γλᾰμάω**, = λημάω, Poll.4.185, Moer.111.

**γλᾰμός**· μύξα, Hsch. **γλάμπτειν**· πίνειν, Id.

**γλᾰμυξιάω**, = γλαμάω, and **γλάμυξος** [ᾰ], ον, = sq., *EM*232.42.

**γλᾰμῠρός**, ά, όν, *blear-eyed*, ὀφθαλμοί Hp.*Mul.*2.116,119; prov., ἐν τυφλῶν πόλεϊ γ. βασιλεύει 'dans le royaume des aveugles le borgne est roi', Sch.Il.24.192. II. of birds, perh. = λαμυρός, S.*Fr.*396 (but ἐνυγροβίους *EM*232.44). (With γλαμάω, γλάμυξος (<γλαμο-ā-), γλαμυρός, γλαμώδης, cf. Lett. *glums* 'mucus', *glumt* 'become viscous', Engl. *clammy*.)

**γλαμψοί**· χαλινοὶ στόματος, Hsch.

**γλᾰμώδης**, ες, = γλαμυρός, *EM*232.44.

**γλάμων** [ᾰ], ον, = γλᾰμυρός, Ar.*Ra.*588, *Ec.*254, Eup.9, Lys.14.25.

**γλάνις** [ᾰ], ὁ (ἡ Paus.4.34.2), or **γλᾶνις** (Hsch., also expld. as, = ἀργός), gen. ιδος Ephipp.12.1, Mnesim.4.32; γλάνιος (v.l. γλάνεως) Arist.*HA*568ᵇ22, al.: acc. γλάνιν *AB*88: pl. γλάνεις, οἱ, Arist.*HA*602ᵇ24; γλάνιδες Archipp.26; γλάνιες Matro *Conv.*80:—*sheat-fish, Silurus*, esp. *Parasilurus Aristotelis*, Arist.*HA*568ª25, etc.:—also **γλάνιος**, ὁ, Hdn.Gr.1.94, *Gloss.*

**γλανοί**· ἀχρεῖοι, Hsch.

**γλάνος**, ὁ, *hyena*, Arist.*HA*594ª31.

**γλάξ**, v. γλαύξ III. **γλάπτω**, = γλάφω, *EM*233.7.

✱ **γλᾰρίς**, ίδος, ἡ, *chisel*, whether for wood or stone work, S.*Fr.*529, *IG*11(2).161*A*87 (Delos, iii B.C.), Call.*Fr.*159 (pl.), Poll.7.118, 10.147. II. = ὅρος, Hsch.

**γλάσσα**, v. γλῶσσα:—hence **γλάσσων**· μωρός, Zonar.

**γλαυκειοῦς**, οῦν, = γλαύκινος, *IG*2.759 ii 11 (iv B.C.).

**γλαυκηπόρος**, ον, *blue-rolling*, κλύδων [Emp.]*Sphaer.*143.

**γλαυκ-ία** ἢ **γλαυκόν**· βοτάνη τις (cf. γλαύκιον), Hsch. **-ιάω**, Hom. only in Ep. part. γλαυκιόων, *glaring fiercely*, of a lion, Il.20.172; γ. ὄσσοις δεινόν Hes.*Sc.*430; of a sparkling stone, D.P.1121; γλαυκιόωσα σελήνη Man.5.250: 3 pl. γλαυκιόωσι Opp.*C.*3.70; late Prose, γλαυκιῶν τὸ βλέμμα Hld.7.10. 2. *have a* γλαύκωμα, *glare blindly*, ὀφθαλμοί.. δυσαλθέα γλαυκιόωντες Q.S.12.408. **-ίδανον**, τό, name of an *eyesalve*, Gal.12.746. **-ίδιον**, τό, Dim. of γλαῦκος, Antiph.222.1. 2. Dim. of γλαύξ, *IG*2.735.33. **-ίζω**, *to be bluish-grey*, of marble, Str.5.2.5; χρῶμα -ίζον Sch.Arat.367, cf. *PLeid.X.*100, al. II. = ἀμβλυωπέω, Hsch. ✱ **-ινίδιον** [νῐ], τό, = γλαυκίδιον, Amphis35. ✱ **-ῖνος**, η, ον, *bluish-grey*, ἱμάτιον Plu.2.821e, cf. 565c. II. γ. ἔλαιον oil *flavoured with* γλαύκιον, *Edict. Diocl.*32.67. **-ιον**, τό, *juice of the horned poppy*, *Glaucium corniculatum*, Dsc.3.86, cf. 1.64, Gal.11.857. II. kind of *duck*, perh. *white-eyed duck*, *Anas leucophthalmus*, Ath.9.395c. **-ίσκος**, ὁ, a fish so called from its colour, Philem.79.21, Damox.2.18, *PEdgar*15.4 (iii B.C.), *AP*5.184 (Asclep.). II. a *plant*, Hegesand.35. **-ισμός**, ὁ, *dyeing blue-grey*, *PHolm.*21.42.

**γλαυκοειδής**, ές, *grey*, Sch.Il.16.34.

✱ **γλαυκόμματος**, ον, *grey-eyed*, Pl.*Phdr.*253e.

✱ **γλαυκός**, ή, όν, orig. without any notion of colour, *gleaming* (cf. γλαύσσω, γλαυσός), once in Hom., γλαυκὴ δέ σε τίκτε θάλασσα Il.16.34 (hence γλαυκὴ δυσπέμφελος, = the sea, Hes.*Th.*440): so in Trag. (not A.), γ. λίμνα S.*Fr.*371,476; ἅλς E.*Cyc.*16; οἶδμα Id.*Hel.*1501 (lyr.); later γ. σελάνα Mesom.*h.Sol.*21; πλήθοντα πυρὸς γλαυκοῖο σελήνη Tryph.514; ἀστέρες Him.*Ecl.*13.37; γ. ἠώς Theoc.16.5; also γ. δράκων Pi.*O.*8.37 (expld. by Sch. as, = γλαύκωψ, γλαυκῶπις). II. later, of colour (κυανοῦς λευκῷ κεραννύμενος Pl.*Ti.*68c; cf. γλαυκότερον κυάνοιο φαείνεται Hegesianax 1), *bluish green* or *grey*, of the olive, S.*OC*701, E.*IT*1101, *Tr.*802 (all lyr.), etc.; of the elder,

Pmp.93; ὀπώρα, of grapes, S.*Tr.*703; of vine leaves, *AP*9.87 (Marc. Arg.); of the beryl and topaz, D.P.1119 sq.; μάραγδος Nonn.*D.*5.178. 2. freq. of the eye, *light blue, grey*, opp. μέλας, χαροπός, Arist.*GA*779ᵇ13, *HA*492ᵃ3, cf. Paus.1.14.6; ἔθνος γ. ἰσχυρῶς καὶ πυρρόν Hdt.4.108, cf. Hp.*Aër.*14, Arist.*Pr.*892ᵃ3, etc.; γ. Ἀθάνα E.*Heracl.*754 (lyr.), Theoc.28.1, cf. Plot.4.4.19; cf. γλαυκῶπις:—this colour was not admired, Luc.*DMeretr.*2.1, Philostr. *VA*7.42.

**γλαῦκος**, ὁ, an eatable *fish of grey colour*, Epich.49,50, Cratin.161, Antiph.7.6, Arist.*HA*607ᵇ27, Numen.ap.Ath.7.295c, etc. II. as pr. n., esp. of a Chian inventor: hence prov., οὐχ ἡ Γλαύκου τέχνη, c. inf., 'it does not need a genius to..', Pl.*Phd.*108d, etc.

**γλαυκότης**, ητος, ἡ, *greyness*, of the eyes, Arist.*GA*778ᵃ18; ὀμμάτων γ. δεινῶς πικρά Plu.*Sull.*2; also γ. ἀέρος Corn.*ND*35.

**γλαυκόφθαλμος**, ον, = γλαυκόμματος, Dsc.1.125, Gal.12.740.

**γλαυκοφόρβιδας**· ἵππους εὐγενεστάτας, Hsch.

⊛ **γλαυκο-χαίτης**, ου, ὁ, *with greyish hair* or *mane*, Choerob.in *Cod. Barocc.*50f.200. **-χροος**, ὁ, ἡ, acc. γλαυκόχροα, *grey-coloured*, of the olive, Pi.*O.*3.13.

**γλαυκόω**, *dye blue-grey*, ἔρια *PHolm.*19.28, 26.30, cf. *EM*233.24. II. Pass., *to be affected with* γλαύκωμα, Hp.*Prorrh.*2.20, *Epid.*4.30; τὰς ὄψεις γλαυκωθῆναι J.*AJ*12.2.14.

**Γλαυκώ**, οῦς, name for the *moon*, Sch.Pi.*O.*6.76.

**γλαυκ-ώδης**, ες, *of the owl kind*, Arist.*HA*504ᵃ26. **-ώλενος**, ον, of Tethys, *with sea-grey arms*, *Hymn.Is.*148. **-ωμα**, ατος, τό, *opacity of the crystalline lens, cataract*, Arist.*GA*780ᵃ17; esp. of the supposedly incurable forms of this affection, opp. ὑπόχυμα, Ruf.ap. Orib.*Syn.*8.49, cf. Paul.Aeg.3.22, Gal.19.435. **-ώπιον**, τό, *temple of Athena Glaucopis*, prob. in Alc.32. ⊛ **-ῶπις**, ἡ, gen. ιδος: acc. ιδα, also ιν Od.1.156:—in Hom., epith. of Athena, prob., *with gleaming eyes*, Il.1.206, al., cf. *IG*1².418, Sch.Ven.ad 5.458, Hsch. II. = γλαυκός, of the olive, Euph.150; of the moon, Emp.42.3, E.*Fr.* 1009. **-ωπός**, όν, = foreg., Corn.*ND*20, Ael.*NA*17.23, Eust.86.46:—also **-ώπης**, ὁ, Eust.1389.2. **-ωσις**, εως, ἡ, *blindness from* γλαύκωμα, Hp.*Aph.*3.31 (pl.), Gal.*UP*10.6, etc. **-ώψ**, ῶπος, ὁ, ἡ, = γλαυκῶπις, δράκοντες Pi.*O.*6.45; ὄφις Id.*P.*4.249; Προνοίη Euph.2.

**γλαυνός**, ὁ, a kind of *tunic*, Poll.7.48.

⊛ **γλαύξ**, Att. **γλαῦξ**, γλαυκός, ἡ, Euphronius ap.Sch.Ar.*V.*1081, cf. Hdn.Gr.2.947:—*the little owl, Athene noctua*, so called from its *glaring eyes*, Epich.166, Arist.*HA*488ᵃ26, al.; freq. as emblem of Athena, Ar.*Av.*516, *Eq.*1093, etc.: prov., γλαῦκ' Ἀθήναζε, γλαῦκ' εἰς Ἀθήνας, 'carry coals to Newcastle', Ar.*Av.*301, Antiph.175.2; γλαῦξ ἐν πόλει 'Jack's as good as his master', Hsch., etc.; γλαῦκες Λαυρειωτικαί, of Athenian coins, from the type, Ar.*Av.*1106; so of figures of owls, *IG*2.678*B*76. 2. γ. θαλαττία, an unknown *bird*, Thphr. *Sign.*52. II. a kind of *dance*, Ath.14.629f. III. *wart cress*, *Coronopus procumbens*, Dsc.4.138, Gal.11.857:—also **γλάξ**, Hdn. Gr.1.395, al.

**γλαυρόν**· σεμνόν, Hsch. **γλαυσόν**· λαμπρόν, θρασύ, ἰταμόν, Id.

**γλαύσσω**, *shine, glitter*, Hsch.: aor. imper. γλαῦξον *EM*234.15. (Denom fr. γλαυκός, cf. δια-γλαύσσω.)

**γλᾰφίς**, = γλυφίς, *EM*235.10.

**γλάφῠ** [ᾰ], τό, (γλάφω) *hollow, cavern*, Hes.*Op.*533.

**γλᾰφῠρ-ία**, ἡ, *elegance*, Plu.*Pyrrh.*8 (pl.); of mathematical demonstrations, *neatness*, Iamb.*in Nic.*p.38P., al.: metaph., *smoothness* of manner, γ. καὶ πιθανότης Plu.2.1065d. ⊛ **-ός**, ά, όν, (γλάφω) *hollow, hollowed*, νῆες Il.2.454, al.; γ. πέτρη, σπέος 2.88, 18.402; ἄντρον Agath.1.10 (Sup.); τὰ γ. τῆς γῆς Id.2.15; γ. φόρμιγξ Od. 17.262; γ. ἅρματα Pi.*N.*9.12; γ. λιμήν *a deep* harbour or cove, Od. 12.305.—In this sense Ep. and Lyr. (not in Trag.); twice in Com., Hermipp.63.11 (mock-Epic); [ποτήρια] ταπεινὰ καὶ γ. Epigen.4.3; later πόδες *arched*, Arist.*H* 1538ᵇ11 (Comp.). II. *polished*: hence, 1. *hairless, smooth*, of spiders, Arist.*HA*555ᵇ11. 2. *neat, delicate*, ῥύγχος Id.*PA*662ᵇ8; κηρίον Id.*HA*.554ᵇ28 (Comp.); of dishes, *dainty*, δειπνάριον Diph.64.1; ἐμβαμμάτια Anaxipp.1.35. III. metaph., *subtle, exact*, of persons and things, ὦ σοφώτατ', ὦ γλαφυρώτατε Ar.*Av.*1272; γ. ἀστεῖός θ' ἅμα Macho ap.Ath.13.579ᵇ; γλαφυρώτερος τῶν νῦν νομοθετῶν Arist.*Pol.*1274ᵇ8; γλαφυρωτέραν ἔχειν τὴν διάνοιαν Id.*PA*650ᵇ19; εἴ τι κομψὸν ἢ σοφὸν ἢ γ. οἶσθα Dionys.Com. 3.1, cf. Plot.4.8.6; τὸ γ. *subtlety*, ποικίλλοντες τῷ γ. γεωμετρίαν Plu. *Marc.*14, cf. Iamb.*in Nic.*p.20P.; γ. τέχναι, θεωρία, Ph.1.270,566: Sup., Id.2.262. Adv., Comp. -οτέρως *more subtly*, Arist.*de An.*405ᵃ 8. 2. *skilful, neat*, χείρ Theoc.*Ep.*8.5; [ἀράχνιον] σοφώτατον καὶ -ώτατον Arist.*HA*623ᵃ8. Adv. -ρῶς, ἧττον γ. ἔχειν with less *finish*, Id.*Pol.*1271ᵇ21, cf. Alex.110.20. 3. *refined*, γλαφυρόν τι καὶ προσαγωγὸν ἐμειδίασεν Luc.*DDeor.*20.11; γ. διατριβαί Plu.*Cim.*13. Adv. -ρῶς, γ. καὶ περιττῶς διάγειν Id.2.989c; γ. βιώσας *CIG*2004 (Maced.). 4. of literary style, *polished, elegant*, γ. ἁρμονία D.H.*Dem.* 36; ῥυθμός Id.*Comp.*13; σύνθεσις, opp. αὐστηρά, ib.21. Adv. -ρῶς, λέγειν Id.*Isoc.*2; of music, ἐμελῴδει πάνυ γλαφυρὸν καὶ ἐναρμόνιον Luc. *DDeor.*7.4.

**γλᾰφῠρότης**, ητος, ἡ, *subtlety*, θεωρίας Ph.1.521, cf. 530 (pl.); *elegance*, ἔργων J.*AJ*12.2.9; παραβολῶν Luc.*Dem.Enc.*6, cf. Phld. *Rh.*1.165S.

**γλάφω** [ᾰ], *scrape up, dig up, hollow*, ποσσὶ γλάφει, of a lion, Hes. *Sc.*431. II. *engrave*, *CR*12.282 (ii A.D.).

**γλάχων** [ᾱ], Dor. for γλήχων, v. βλήχων.

**γλέβα**· ἀξίωμα συγκλήτου, Hsch. **γλεῖνος**, ὁ, v. γλῖνος.

⊛ **γλευκ-ᾰγωγός**, όν, *for carrying new wine*, βύρσα Pherecr.16. ⊛ **-άω**, in aor. part. -ήσας, of *oversweetened* wine, Hsch. **-η**, ης, ἡ, = γλυκύτης, Sch.Nic.*Al.*171. ⊛ **-ινος**, η, ον, *made with* γλεῦκος *as a vehicle*, μύρον, a special kind of confection or oil, Dsc.1.57, Androm. ap.Gal.13.1039, Aët.12.55; also γ. ἔλαιον Colum.12.53, Plin.*HN*23. 46. 2. *partly fermented*, οἶνος Gal.*UP*4.3. **-ίτης** [ῑ] (sc. οἶνος), ου, ὁ, = γλεῦκος 1.1, Olymp.*in Mete.*311.13.

⊛ **γλευκοπότης**, ου, ὁ, *drinker of new wine*, Σάτυροι *AP*6.44 (Leon. (?)); Πάν *APl.*4.235 (Apollonid.).

⊛ **γλεῦκος**, εος (Dor. gen. γλεύκιος *GDI*4993 (Gortyn)), τό, *sweet new wine*, Arist.*Mete.*380ᵇ32, Nic.*Al.*184,299, *PPetr.*3p.149 (iii B.C.), *Act.Ap.*2.13, Dsc.5.6; οἴνου γλεύκους *PGrenf.*2.24.12 (ii B.C.), *PFlor.*65.8 (vi A.D.). 2. *grape-juice*, Gal.6.575. II. *sweetness*, Arist.*Pr.*931ᵃ18.

**γλεῦξις**, v. γλύξις. ⊛ **γλέφαρον**, τό, Aeol. for βλέφαρον, Pi.*O.* 3.12, etc.

**γλημώδης**, ες, = γλαμυρός, Gal.19.91.

**γλήν**, ἡ, = sq., Hermesian.1.

**γλήνη**, ἡ, *eyeball*, Il.14.494, Od.9.390; τὸ εἴδωλον τὸ ἐν τῇ ὄψει, Ruf. *Onom.*24, cf. Poll.2.70; poet. *eye*, S.*OT*1277; Φαέθων μονάδι γλήνᾳ παραυγεῖ Cerc.4.18. II. ἔρρε, κακὴ γ. Il.8.164, perh. *doll, plaything* (since figures are reflected small in the pupil, cf. κόρη). III. *socket of a joint*, distd. from κοτύλη as being not so deep, Gal.2. 736. IV. *honeycomb*, *AB*233, Hsch. V. = γλίνη (q.v.), Hdn. Gr.1.330.

**γληνίς** (or **γλῆνις**), ἡ, perh. a measure of capacity, ἐλαίω κοτύλα γληνίς *IG*5(1).1447 (Messene, iii/ii B.C.).

**γληνοειδής**, ές, *like a* γλήνη III, opp. κοτυλοειδής, Hp.*Art.*79; κοιλότης Gal.*UP*2.11: ἀποφύσεις Id.2.760.

**γλῆνος**, εος, τό, in pl., *gaudy things, playthings, trinkets*, Il.24.192, A.R.4.428 (expld. from γληνόν, = ποικίλον by Hsch.). II. = γλήνη I, Nic.*Th.*228. III. = φάος, Hsch., prob. in A.*Fr.*300.4: in pl., *stars*, Arat.318. IV. pl., = χρήματα (Elean), Sch.Il. l.c.

**γληνῶσαι**· διαφθεῖραι, Cyr., and **γληνωτά** (γλήνωσα cod.)· πονηρά, Hsch. **γληχυλίς**· πονηρά, Cyr. (**γληχυρίς**, Zonar.).

**γλήχων**, Dor. γλάχων, ἡ, v. βλήχων. II. γ. ἀγρία, = καλαμίνθη II, Ps.-Dsc.3.35; = δίκταμνον, ib.32.

**γληχωνίτης** οἶνος, ὁ, wine *prepared with* γλήχων, Dsc.5.52, *Gp.* 8.7.

**γληχωνοειδές**, τό, = δίκταμνον, Hsch.

**γλία**, ἡ, *glue*, *EM*234.24, Suid.; cf. γλοιός.

**γλιᾶται**· παίζει, Hsch.:—but **γλιῶσαι**· τὸ παίζειν, *EM*234.24.

**γλίνη**, ἡ, = γλοιός, Suid.: **γλίνα** *EM*234.26: **γλήνη** Hdn.Gr.1. 330:—Adj. **γλινώδης**, ες, = γλοιώδης, Arist.*Fr.*311 codd. Ath., Sch. Nic.*Al.*471, Dsc.4.82:—written **γληνώδης**, *Gp.*2.6.35,41.

**γλῖνος** or **γλεῖνος**, ὁ, *Cretan maple, Acer creticum*, Thphr.*HP*3.3. 1, 3.11.2.

**γλίον**, = εὔτονον or ἰσχυρόν, Hsch., *EM*234.24, Eust.1560.32.

**γλισχρ-αίνομαι**, Pass., *to be sticky, lubricated*, Hp.*Art.*55; *become tenacious*, of sputum, Gal.7.918. **-αντιλογεξεπίτριπτος**, ον, Com. word in Ar.*Nu.*1004, *hair-splitting-pettifogging-barefaced-knavish*. ⊛ **-ασμα**, ατος, τό, *gluten*, Hp.*Acut.*10; *thick mucilage*, Aret.*CA*1.9; ἕως γλισχράσματος ἕψειν Dsc.*Eup.*1.1. **-εύομαι**, *to be close, stingy*, M.Ant.5.5. **-ία**, ἡ, = γλισχρότης, *stinginess*, Sch.Ar.*Pax*193 (but expld. by ἀτυχία).

**γλισχρο-λογέομαι**, *squabble about trifles*, Ph.1.526. **-λογία**, ἡ, *straw-splitting*, ib.698, D.L.2.30.

⊛ **γλίσχρος**, α, ον, *sticky*, Hp.*VC*14; γῆ Thphr.6.5.4; joined with λιπαρός, Pl.*Ti.*82d,84a; γ. τὸ σίαλον Pherecr.69.3; of oil, Arist.*Mete.* 383ᵇ34; opp. ψαθυρός (q.v.), ib.385ᵃ17; *tough*, ξύλον Thphr.3.17. 5. II. metaph., 1. *sticking close, importunate*, γ. προσαιτῶν λιπαρῶν τε Ar.*Ach.*452: metaph., *clinging*, γ. ἡ ὁλκὴ τῆς ὁμοιότητος Pl.*Cra.*435c. Adv. -ρως, ἐπιθυμεῖν Id.*Cri.*53e; εἰκάζειν make a *close* comparison, Id.*R.*488a, cf. *Cra.*414c: Sup. -ότατα, σαρκάζοντες Ar. *Pax*482. 2. *penurious, niggardly*, Arist.*EN*1121ᵇ22; γλίσχρον βλέπειν Euphro10.16. Adv. -ρως καὶ κατὰ σμικρὸν φειδόμενος Pl.*R.*553c, cf. X.*Cyr.*8.3.37; φαύλως καὶ γ. παρείχοντο χρήματα *Hell.Oxy.*14.2; γ. ζῆν, opp. τρυφᾶν, Arist.*Pol.*1266ᵇ26; γ. λαμβάνειν, opp. ἀφθόνως διδόναι, ib.1314ᵇ3: hence, *with difficulty, hardly*, γ. καὶ μόλις λαμβάνειν D.37.38, cf. App.*Mith.*72; ἢ τὸ παράπαν οὐδέν.., ἢ γ. Arist.*Pol.*1275ᵃ 38; also τρόπον τινὰ γλίσχρον but *scantily*, Id.*PA*660ᵇ14. 3. of things, *mean, shabby*, of buildings, D.23.208; γ. δεῖπνον Plu.*Lyc.*17; of land, *poor*, Id.*Flam.*4; γ. τέχναι Luc.*Fug.*13; Χρύσιππος πολλαχοῦ γ. ἐστίν Plu.2.31e. 4. Adv. -ρως, of painting, *carefully, with elaborate detail*, Philostr.*Im.*2.12 and 28. (Cf. γλοιός.)

**γλισχρότης**, ητος, ἡ, *stickiness*, Arist.*HA*517ᵇ28, Thphr.*CP*1.6.4, etc.; *slipperiness*, Plb.26.1.14, Luc.*Anach.*29. II. metaph., *parsimony, stinginess*, opp. τρυφή, Arist.*Pol.*1326ᵇ38; *meanness*, Plu. *Them.*5,2.125e. 2. γ. ὀνομάτων the 'birdlime' of verbiage (as *clogging* the intelligence), Ph.1.146.

**γλισχρόχολος**, ον, *viscous from bile*, Hp.*Epid.*4.26 (-χροος f.l. ap. Erot.).

**γλισχρώδης**, ες, *glutinous*, f.l. for βλιχ-, Hp.*VC*19.

⊛ **γλίσχρων**, ονος, ὁ, *niggard*, Ar.*Pax*193.

**γλίττον**, τό, = γλοιός, Hsch.; = ἀπόλυμα, Eust.1560.32.

⊛ **γλίχομαι**, only pres. and impf., exc. aor. 1 ἐγλιξάμην Pl.Com. 241:—*cling to, strive after, long for*, τινός Hdt.3.72; Αἰγύπτου Id. 4.152 (but γ. περὶ ἐλευθερίης Id.1.102 (s.v.l.)); ταῦτ' ἦν ὧν μάλιστ' ἐγλίχετο D.5.22; γ. τοῦ ζῆν Pl.*Phd.*117a, Charond.ap.Stob.4.2.24; κράτους Thphr.*Char.*26.1: c. acc., Hp.*Ep.*17 (dub.), Pl.*Hipparch.*

226e : folld. by a relat. clause, γλιχόμεθα τὴν μᾶζαν ἵνα λευκὴ παρῇ Alex.141.7; ὡς στρατηγήσεις γλίχεαι how thou shalt become general, Hdt.7.161 : c. inf., ὧν ἐγλίχοντο μὴ ἅψασθαι Th.8 15; εἰδέναι Pl.Grg. 489d; λέγειν D.6.11; ἀποστερῆσαι Id.18.207; ζῆν Antiph.86.3; θιγεῖν Phld.D.3.1.—Not in Ep. or Trag. (γλῐ-: γλίχων [ῑ] is f.l. for γλήχων in Hdn.Gr.1.37.)

γλιχός, = γλίσχρος 2, Hsch.; also, = περίεργος, Id.:—fem. **γλιχώ**, similarly expld. by *EM*234.26; = φειδωλία, Zonar.

**γλιχύτης**· ἀτυχὴς ἢ ἐπίπονος ἢ ἐρωτική, Hsch., cf. *EM*234.25.

**γλοηρὸν** χαλκοῦν, dub. sens. in *IG*2.716$^{b}$6.

**γλοία** or **γλοιά**, ἡ, = γλία, *glue*, Hsch.

**γλοιάζω**, *wink, twinkle with the eyes*, Hp.ap.Gal.19.91, *EM*234.45.

**γλοιάς**, άδος, ἡ, *vicious*, of mares, S.*Fr*.1037:—masc. **γλοίης**, ητος, of horses, Hdn.Gr.2.680; also of persons, *slippery, shifty*, *EM* 234.44.

**γλοιό-ομαι**, *become sticky*, Dsc.5.79. **-ποιέομαι**, = foreg., Id. *Eup*.1.2. **-πότις**, ιδος, ἡ, *sucking up grease*, χλαμύς *AP*6.282 (Theodor.).

⊛ **γλοιός**, ὁ, *any glutinous substance, gum*, Hdt.3.112; ὁ γλισχρότατος γ. Arist.*Mir*.844$^{a}$14, cf. Sor.2.11, *Gp*.20.13, *POxy*.1220.16 (iii A.D.; γλυοῦ Pap.); esp. *oil and dirt* scraped off the wrestler's skin with the στλεγγίς, Sch.Ar.*Nu*.449: generally, *oily sediment* in baths, Semon.8, Telesp.41 H.; γ. παιδικός substitute for butter in ointments, *Hippiatr*.69. II. as Adj. **γλοιός**, ά, όν, *slippery, knavish*, Ar.*Nu*. l.c. 2. = νωθρός, ἀσθενής, Hsch. Adv. **-ῶς**, = νυσταλτικῶς, Id. 3. *thick*, παλλίολον *CPR*27.9 (ii A.D.). (For γλοι-ϝός, cf. γλία, γλίνη, etc., Lat. *glūs, glūten*.)

**γλοιώδης**, ες, *glutinous*, Pl.*Cra*.427b, Arist.*Fr*.311 (γλιν- codd. Ath.); τὸ γ. Thphr.*HP*5.4.1. Adv. **-δῶς** Sor.2.13, Gal.19.91. 2. *full of oily sediment*, ὕδωρ M.Ant.8.24.

⊛ **γλουρός**, οῦ, ὁ, *gold*, *AP*15.25.7 (Besant.), Hsch.:—hence **γλούρεα**· χρύσεα (Phryg.), Id.

⊛ **γλούτια**, τά, *medullary tubercles near the pineal gland of the brain*, Gal.*UP*8.14. II. *the great trochanter*, Id.2.773.

⊛ **γλουτός**, ὁ, *buttock*, γ. δεξιός Il.5.66, cf. Hp.*Fract*.13, Arist.*HA* 493$^{a}$23: pl., Il.8.340, Hdt.4.9: dual, τὼ γλουτὼ X.*Eq*.7.2: heterocl. pl., γλουτά, τά, Sch.Theoc.6.30. II. = σφαίρωμα τῆς κοτύλης, Hsch. (Cf. Skt. *glaús* 'round lump', Engl. *clot*.)

⊛ **γλῠκ-άδιον**, τό, *sweetmeat*, Hsch. 2. *vinegar*, Orus ap.*EM*626.58, Choerob.*Rh*.p.251 S. **-άζω**, *sweeten*, τὴν κατάποσιν Epict. *Gnom*.22; *affect with a sensation of sweetness*, τοὺς ὑγιαίνοντας S.E. *P*.1.211:—Pass., *receive a taste of sweetness*, Hierocl.p.29 A., S.E. *P*.1.20; but, *taste sweet*, *Gp*.2.39.4, and so intr. in Act. of wine, Ath. 1.26c; μέλι γλυκάζον LXX *Ez*.3.3, cf. Plot.4.3.26. ⊛ **-αίνω**, fut. -ᾰνῶ LXX *Si*.12.16: aor. ἐγλύκᾰνα D.L.8.70:—*sweeten*, LXX *Si*.27.23; opp. πικραίνω, D.L. l.c.; *affect with a sensation of sweetness*, τὴν ἀκοήν D.H.*Comp*.15: abs., *produce an effect of sweetness*, in Music, Aristox.*Harm*.p.23 M.:—more freq. in Pass., fut. γλυκανθήσομαι LXX *Si*.49.1: aor. ἐγλυκάνθην Hp.*Morb*.3.17, Mosch.3.110: pf. γεγλύκασμαι Ath.9.384d, but ἀπ-εγλ. Diph.Siph.ib.2.55f:—*to be sweetened, turn sweet*, Hp.*Aër*.8, Arist.*Ph*.244$^{b}$23; *to be affected with a sensation of sweetness*, D.H.*Comp*.12, Ph.1.121. **-άνισον**, τό, = ἄνισον (= ἄνηθον), Sch.Theoc.7.63. **-ανσις**, εως, ἡ, *sweetening*, Thphr.*CP* 4.4.5. **-αντικός**, ή, όν, *of* or *for sweetening*, Ocell.1.9. Adv. **-κῶς** S.E.*M*.7.344; γ. διατίθεσθαι ib.367. **-ασμα**, ατος, τό, *sweetness*, LXX *Pr*.16.24, al.; *sweet wine*, ib.*Ne*.8.10, al. **-ασμός**, ὁ, *sweetness*, Dsc.*Alex*.7, LXX *Ca*.5.16 (pl.); *sweet wine*, ib.*Am*.9.13. **-είδιον**, τό, Dim. of γλυκύς II, *BGU*417.18 (ii/iii A.D.). **-ειος**, α, ον, = γλυκύς, τῆς..οὔτι γλυκειότερον *IG*14.1935. ⊛ **-έλαιον**, τό, *sweet oil*, Xenocr.55, *Sammelb*.5747.8 (γλυκνέλ-), Gal.14.793. ⊛ **-ερός**, ά, όν, = γλυκύς, Od.14.194, 17.41, Pi.*P*.4.32, E.*Med*.1099 (anap.), Arist. *PA*677$^{a}$23; opp. ὠφέλιμος, Crates Theb.10.5: Comp. -ώτερος Od.9.28, Them.*Or*.21.262c.

**γλῠκερο-στάφῡλος** [ᾰ], ον, *with sweet grapes*, Opp.*C*.1.465. **-χρως**, ωτος, ὁ, ἡ, *with sweet skin*, *AP*7.207 (Mel.).

**γλυκή**· βοτάνη τις ἐδώδιμος, Hsch. (Perh., = sq.)

**γλῠκήρατον**, τό, = γλυκύρριζα, Ps.-Dsc.3.5.

⊛ **γλῠκ-ίζω**, *treat with sweetmeats*, τοὺς πολίτας *IG*7.190.17 (Pagae). II. intr., *have a sweet flavour*, ὄξος -ίζον *Gp*.6.15.1, cf. 5.26.10:—also in Pass., *become sweet, form lead acetate*, Zos.Alch. p.248 B. **-ίνας**, ου, ὁ, in Crete, *cake made with sweet wine*, Seleuc. ap.Ath.14.645d, Hsch. **-ιος**, α, ον, *sugary, sickly*, Arist.*EE*1238$^{a}$ 28; v.l. for Λύκιον in S.*Ph*.1461. **-ισμός**, ὁ, *distribution of sweetmeats* or *sweet wine*, Callix.2, *Inscr.Prien*.108.257 (ii B.C.), *IG*7.2712.68 (Acraeph.).

**γλύκκα**, = γλυκύτης, and **γλυκκός**· γλυκύς, Hsch.

**γλῠκόεις**, εσσα, εν, = γλυκύς, ποτόν Nic.*Al*.444.

**γλῠκύ-δακρυς**, υ, *shedding sweet tears*, Ἔρως *AP*7.419 (Mel.), 12.167 (Id.). **-δερκής**, ές, *with a sweet glance*, Hsch., Cyr. **-διον**, τό, = γλυκείδιον, *PLond*.2.239.13 (iv A.D.: -οίδιον Pap.). **-δρόμος**, ον, *faring pleasantly*, Νειλῶται *Lyr.Alex.Adesp*.32.3. **-δωρος**, ον, *with sweet gifts*, Κλειώ B.3.3; Νίκα Id.10.1; Ἔρως *AP*5.21 (Rufin.). II. γ. ἄγαλμα *sweet gift* brought in thy honour, B. 5.4. **-ηχής**, Dor. **-ᾱχής**, ές, *sweet-voiced*, *AP*9.26 (Antip. Thess.). **-θῡμέω**, *to be pleasant*, Hierocl. *in CA*26 p.479 M. **-θῡμία**, ἡ, *sweetness of mind*, γ. πρὸς τὰς ἡδονάς *readiness to indulge*.., opp. τὸ καρτερεῖν, Pl.*Lg*.635c, cf. Plu.2.476d. II. *kindly disposition*, Id.*Them*.10, Id.2.970b; πρός τινα *Sammelb*.4630.8 (ii A.D.). III. *pleasantness*, Iamb.*Myst*.5.11. **-θῡμος**, ον, *sweet of mood*, Il.20.467; of the Epicureans, Luc.*Herm*.16. II. Act., *charming the mind, delightful*, ἔρως, ὕπνος, Ar.*Lys*.551, *Nu*.705. **-κάλᾰμον** [κᾰ], τό, *scented lotus*, Zonar. **-καρπέω**, *bear sweet fruit*, Thphr.*CP*2.3.7. **-καρπος**, ον, *bearing sweet fruit*, ἄμπελος Theoc. 11.46, cf. Corn.*ND*14. **-κρεος**, ον, *of sweet flesh*, κογχύλιον Sophr. 24. **-λᾰλος**, ον, = sq., *Cat.Cod.Astr*.2.209. **-λογος**, ον, *sweet-speaking*, Sch.E.*Hec*.134. **-μαρίδες**, αἱ, *a kind of cockle*, Xenocr. 60,61, prob. in Gal.13.174. **-μήχᾰνος**, Dor. **-μάχᾰνος**, ον, *having pleasant devices*, Pi.*Pae*.2.80. ⊛ **-μείλῐχος**, ον, *sweetly winning*, *h.Hom*.5.19.

**γλυκυμή**, = γλυκύρριζα, Hp.ap.Gal.19.91.

⊛ **γλῠκύ-μηλον** [κῠ], Aeol. and Dor. **γλῠκύ-μᾱλον**, τό, = μελίμηλον, *sweet-apple*, Sapph.93, Call.*Cer*.29, Dsc.1.115, Orib.5.31.3; as a term of endearment, Theoc.11.39. **-μῡθέω**, *speak sweetly*, *AP* 12.122 (Mel.). **-μῡθος**, ον, *sweetly-spoken*, ἔπος ib.5.194 (Id.). ⊛ **-νους**, ουν, gen. ου, = γλυκύθυμος, Polem.*Phgn*.22. **-παις**, παιδος, ὁ, ἡ, *full of sweet boys*, Ῥόδος *AP*12.52 (Mel.). **-πάρθενος**, ἡ, *sweet maid*, in pl., Ὧραι ib.9.16 (Id.). ⊛ **-πῑκρος**, ον, *sweetly bitter*, Ἔρος.. γ. ὄρπετον Sapph.40, cf. *AP*5.133 (Posid.), 12.109 (Mel.), Plu.2.681b; of news, 'a gilded pill', Cic.*Att*.5.21.4; ἡδονή Ph.1.678: later in literal sense, Gal.11.586. **-πότης**, ου, ὁ (γλυκο- codd.), *drinker of sweet wine*, Philagr.ap.Orib.5.19.6. **-πράτιον** [ᾰ], τό, *shop where sweetmeats are sold*, *Gloss*.:—also **γλυκεοπράτης** (sic), ου, ὁ, *dealer in sweetmeats*, ib. **-πῡρος**, ὁ, a kind of *wheat*, *BGU*1067.16 (ii A.D.). **-ρριζα**, ἡ, *sweet-root*, i.e. *liquorice*, *Glycyrrhiza glabra*, Dsc.3.5, Antyll.ap.Orib.10.24.4:—also **-ρριζον**, τό, *Gp*.7.24.4, and **-ρριζος**, ἡ, Hsch.

⊛ **γλῠκύς**, εῖα (-ῆα Herod.4.2), ύ (-ύν *IG*14.1890), *sweet to the taste* or *smell*, νέκταρ Il.1.598; οἶνος Epich.124, etc.; γλυκὺ ὄζειν Cratin.Jun. 1, prob. in Crates Com.2; opp. ὀξύς, Hp.*Vict*.2.55; opp. δριμύς, Plu. 2.708e: mostly metaph., even in Hom., *pleasant, delightful*, ἵμερος, ὕπνος, Il.3.139, Od.2.395; γ. αἰών 5.152, Hdt.7.46; πόλεμος γλυκίων γένετ' ἠὲ νέεσθαι Il.2.453; οὐδὲν γλύκιον ἧς πατρίδος οὐδὲ τοκήων Od.9. 34, cf. Pi.*N*.5.2, E.*Med*.1036, etc.; γλυκὺ [ἐστι], c. inf., A.*Pr*.698, Alex. 210; θανεῖν γλύκιστον B.3.47; ὅτῳ..μηδὲν ἦν ἰδεῖν γλυκύ S.*OT*1335 (lyr.), cf. 1390. b. of water, *sweet, fresh*, Xenoph.1.8, etc.; opp. πικρός, Hdt.4.52; opp. ἁλμυρός, Arist.*Mete*.355$^{a}$33, etc. 2. after Hom. (but v. supr.), of persons, *sweet, dear*, γλυκεῖα (v.l. -ῆα) μᾶτερ Sapph. 90; γλυκεῖαι παῖδες ἀρχαίου Σκότου S.*OC*106: c. inf., γ. φρὴν συμπόταισιν ὁμιλεῖν Pi.*P*.6.52; freq. in epitaphs, *IG*14.1472 (Sup.), etc.; also ὑπὲρ τῆς γλυκυτάτης πατρίδος τελευτῆσαι *POxy*.33 i 13 (ii A.D.); ὦ γλυκύτατε *my dear fellow*, Ar.*Ach*.462, cf. *Ec*.124; sts. in bad sense, *simple, silly*, ὡς γ. εἶ! Pl.*Hp.Ma*.288b; also applied κατ' ἀντίφρασιν to a swine, Gal.18(2).611; γλυκὺ πνεῖον, of mustard, Matro *Conv*.90. II. as Subst., ὁ γ. (sc. οἶνος) *grape-syrup*, Alex. 59, 172.14, Arist.*Pr*.875$^{b}$2, Herod.6.77, *POxy*.1088.51; also τὸ γ. Nic.*Al*.386, *POxy*.234 ii 6 (ii/iii A.D.). b. of the eye of Polyphemus, Theoc.6.22. 2. ἡ γ., = γλυκύρριζα, Thphr.*HP*9.13. 2. 3. ἡ γ., = χολή, Sch.Nic.*Th*.594. III. Comp. and Sup. γλυκίων Od.9.34; γλύκιστος B.3.47, Ael.*NA*12.46, etc.; also γλυκύτερος, -τατος Pi.*O*.1.109, 19, etc.; γλύσσων Xenoph.38.2. IV. Adv. -κέως Poll.4.24. (Perh. fr. *δλυκύς, cf. Lat. *dulcis*.)

**γλῠκυσίδη** [ῐ], ἡ, *peony* (γ. ἄρρην, = *Paeonia officinalis*, γ. θήλεια, = *P. corallina*, Dsc.3.140), Hp.*Superf*.33, *Mul*.2.136, Pl.Com.61, Thphr.*HP*9.8.6.

**γλύκυσμα**, ατος, τό, *sweetness*, Lib.*Descr*.30.15. II. *sweetmeat*, Sch.Ar.*Pl*.660.

**γλῠκύστρυφνος**, ον, *sweet with an astringent taste*, Thphr.*HP*9. 20.5.

**γλῠκύτης**, ητος, ἡ, *sweetness of taste*, Hdt.4.177, Thphr.*CP*6.9.4; ὑδάτων D.S.4.84, cf. Arr.*Peripl.M.Eux*.49. 2. *sweetness, pleasantness*, γ. φυσική, of life, Arist.*Pol*.1278$^{b}$30; τῆς λέξεως D.H.*Comp*.11; μέλος καὶ γ. Phld.*Mus*.p.49 K.; of persons, Plu.2.67b: in pl., *delights*, ἐπιθυμίαι πονηραὶ καὶ γλυκύτητες Phld.*Lib*.p.61 O.

**γλῠκῠ-φᾰγία**, ἡ, *the use of sweet food*, Alex.Trall.1.15. **-φαιον**, = ἐρυθρόδανον (Cret.), Hsch. **-φθογγος**, ον, *sweet-toned*, Sch. Pi.*O*.6.162. **-φρουροι**, οἱ, *those who love staying at home*, Hsch. **-φυλλον**, τό, dub. in Gal.19.730. **-φῦτον**, τό, = γλυκύρριζα, Ps.-Dsc.3.5. **-φωνέω**, *speak sweetly*, Theoc.15.146 (sed leg. γλυκὺ φωνεῖ). **-φωνία**, ἡ, *sweet voice* or *speech*, D.S.3.69, Heraclit.*Incred*.14. **-φωνος**, ον, *sweet-voiced, sweet-sounding*, Sch.Pi.*O*.4.4; rejected by Poll.2.113. **-χῡλος**, ον, *with sweet juices*, Hp.*Ep*.16, Xenocr.24,30. **-χῡμος**, ον, = foreg., Gal.11. 494; δίαιτα Paul.Aeg.2.15:—Subst. **-χῡμία**, ἡ, Gal.14.749.

**γλύκων**, ωνος, ὁ, *sweet one*: ὦ γλύκων *you dear silly creature!* Ar. *Ec*.985.

**Γλῠκώνειος**, α, ον, *Glyconic*, a kind of verse, so called from its inventor Glycon, Heph.10.2, Sch.Metr.Pi.*O*.1, etc.

**γλύμμα**, ατος, τό, (γλύφω) *engraved figure, signet*, Eup.406, Str. 14.1.16, *BGU*86.45 (ii A.D.); *inscription*, *AP*11.38 (Polemo Rex), Gal.12.773.

**γλυμός**, ὁ, prob. misspelt for γιγγλυμός, *IG*11(2).142.49 (Delos, iv B.C.).

**γλύξις**, εως, ἡ, *sweet insipid wine*, Phryn.Com.65, Polyzel.12 (pl.), cf. Ath.1.31e:—also written **γλεῦξις** in Hsch.

**γλυπτ-ήρ**, ῆρος, ὁ, (γλύφω) *graving tool, chisel*, *AP*6.68 (Jul.). ⊛ **-ης**, Dor. **-ας**, ου, ὁ, *carver, sculptor*, *APl*.4.142, 145. **-ικός**, ή, όν, *of engraving*, γλυπτικὴ σφραγίδων (sc. τέχνη) Poll.7.209.

⊛ **γλυπτός**, ή, όν, *fit for carving*, of wood or stone, Thphr.*Lap*.5. 2.

*carved*, λύγδου γ. *AP*5.193 (Posidipp. or Ascl.); γ. ὁμοίωμα Lxx *De.* 4.25; πρόσοψις Iamb.*Protr.*21.κγ´; γλυπτόν, τό, *carved image*, Lxx *Is.*44.10, al.: but γλυπτά, τά, *quarries*, ib.*Jd.*3.19.

**γλύφ-ᾰνος** [ῠ], ὁ, (γλύφω) *tool for carving, knife, chisel*, *h.Merc.*41, Theoc.1.28; γ. καλάμου pen-*knife*, *AP*6.63 (Damoch.). **-εῖον**, τό, = γλύφανος, Luc.*Somn.*13. **-εύς**, έως, ὁ, *carver*, J.*AJ*8.5.2, *IG*5(1).209 (Sparta); σφρηγίδων Man.6.344 (pl.). **-ευτής**, οῦ, ὁ, *stone-mason* or *sculptor*, *PMasp.*147.8 (vi A. D.). **-ή**, ἡ, *carving*: *carved work*, D.S.5.44, *CPHerm.*127 (iii A. D.); γ. τῇ σφραγῖδι ποιεῖν its *emblem, device*, Plu.2.985b, cf. Iamb.*Protr.*21.κγ´; Δημητρίου γ. *the work* of D., under a carving, *IG*5(1).540 (Mistrá), cf. *CIG*4558 (Acre). II. *hole cut* in a beam, Anon.ap.Suid. v. καινοπρεπές. ❋ **-ικός**, ή, όν, *of* or *for carving*: γλυφική (sc. τέχνη) *Epigr.Gr.* 841 (Thrace). **-ίς**, ίδος, ἡ, in early writers always pl. γλυφίδες (but sg., opp. ἀκίς, of the constellation Sagitta, Hipparch.2.5.12), *notched end* of the arrow, ἕλκε δ' ὁμοῦ γλυφίδας τε λαβὼν καὶ νεῦρα Il. 4.122; ἕλκεν νευρὴν γλυφίδας τε Od.21.419; γλυφίδες μέσσῃ ἐγκάτθετο νευρῇ A.R.3.282; but perh. of *notches* or *grooves* for the fingers, παρὰ τὰς γλυφίδας περιειλίξαντες καὶ πτερώσαντες τὸ βυβλίον Hdt.8. 128, cf. Aen.Tact.31.26; τόξων πτερωταὶ γλυφίδες, poet. for *the arrow itself*, E.*Or.*274, cf. *AP*5.57 (Arch., sg.): also in pl., *notches in the arrow-head*, Paul.Aeg.6.88. II. *pen-knife*, *AP*6.62 (Phil.), 64 (Paul. Sil., pl.). 2. *chisel*, J.*BJ*5.5.2. III. in Architecture, *capitals* of columns, θριγκὸς.. λαΐνεος χαλκέῃσιν ἐπὶ γλυφίδεσσιν ἀρήρει A.R.3.218, cf. Sch. ad loc., *EM*235.13. IV. in pl., = θαλάμαι, Hsch.

❋ **γλύφω** [ῡ], fut. γλύψω Lxx *Ex.*28.9: aor. ἔγλυψα Str.9.2.25:— Med., aor. ἐγλυψάμην Theoc.*Epigr.*8, Plu.2.806d:—Pass., aor. 1 part. γλυφθέν *AP*6.229 (Crin.), but aor. 2 γλυφέν [ῠ] *App.Anth.*3. 79 (Posidipp.), Ps.-Callisth.3.22, (δια-) Ael.*VH*14.7: pf. γέγλυμμαι *AP*9.752 (Ascl. or Antip. Thess.), Pl.*Smp.*216d, (ἐγ-) Hdt.2.106, but ἐξ-έγλ- Eup.331, Pl.*R.*616d:—*carve, cut out with a knife*, ναῦς τ' ἔγλυφεν Ar.*Nu.*879; γ. σφρηγῖδας *engrave* them, Hdt.7.69, cf. Pl. *Hp.Mi.*368c; of sculptors, opp. γράφω, Hdt.2.46, Str. l.c.; ἔγλυψέν με σίδηρος, written under a statue, *IG*14.973:—Med., *cause to be engraved*, Theoc. l.c., Plu. l.c. II. *note down* or *write* [on waxen tablets], τόκους *AP*11.289 (Pall.). III. Pass., *to be hatched*, ἕως γλυφῆναι τὰ ᾠά Antig.*Mir.*97. (Cf. Lat. *glūbo* 'peel', *glūma* 'husk', OHG. *klioban* 'cleave'.)

**γλώνη**· οὐδενὸς ἄξιον, Hsch.

❋ **γλώξ**, ἡ, only pl. γλῶχες, *beard of corn*, Hes.*Sc.*398. (Cf. γλωχίν.)

**γλωρεῖν**· χρονίζειν, Hsch. **γλωρόν**· νομόν, Id.

❋ **γλῶσσα**, Ion. **γλάσσα**, Herod.3.84, al., *SIG*1002.7 (Milet.), *Schwyzer* 692 (Chios), Att. **γλῶττα**, ης, ἡ, *tongue*, Od.3.332, etc. b. γ. λάρυγγος, = γλωττίς, *larynx*, Gal.*UP*7.13. 2. *tongue*, as the organ of speech, γλώσσης χάριν through love *of talking*, Hes.*Op.*709, A.*Ch.* 266; γλώσσῃ ματαίᾳ Id.*Pr.*331, cf. *Eu.*830; γλώσσης ἀκρατής Id.*Pr.*884 (lyr.); μεγάλης γ. κόμποι S.*Ant.*128; γλώσσῃ δεινός, θρασύς, Id.*OC*806, *Aj.*1142; ἡ γ. ὀμώμοχ' ἡ δὲ φρὴν ἀνώμοτος E.*Hipp.*612: with Preps., ἀπὸ γλώσσης by *frankness of speech*, Thgn.63; φθέγγεσθαι Pi.*O.*6.13 (but ἀπὸ γ. ληΐσσεται, opp. χερσὶ βίῃ, of fraud opp. violence, Hes. *Op.*322); also, by *word of mouth*, Hdt.1.123, Th.7.10, Arr.*An.*2. 14.1; τῷ νῷ θ' ὁμοίως κἀπὸ τῆς γ. λέγω S.*OC*936; τὰ γλώσσης ἄπο, i.e. *our words*, E.*Ba.*1049; ἀπὸ γ. φράσω by *heart*, opp. γράμμασιν, Cratin.122; οὐκ ἀπὸ γλώσσης not from *mere word of mouth*, but after full argument, A.*Ag.*813; μὴ διὰ γλώσσης without using *the tongue*, E.*Supp.*112; ἐν ὄμμασιν.. δεδορκὼς κοὐ κατὰ γλῶσσαν κλύων S.*Tr.* 747:—phrases: πᾶσαν γλῶτταν βασάνιζε try every *art of tongue*, Ar. *V.*547; πᾶσαν ἱέναι γλῶσσαν let loose one's whole *tongue*, speak without restraint, S.*El.*596; πολλὴν γ. ἐγχέας μάτην Id.*Fr.*929; κακὰ γ. slander, Pi.*P.*4.283: pl., ἐν κερτομίοις γλώσσαις, i.e. with blasphemies, S.*Ant.*962 (lyr.), cf. *Aj.*199 (lyr.): βοῦς, κλῇς ἐπὶ γλώσσῃ, v. βοῦς, κλείς. 3. of persons, *one who is all tongue, speaker*, of Pericles, μεγίστη γ. τῶν Ἑλληνίδων Cratin.293, cf. Ar.*Fr.*629 (s.v.l.). 4. ἡ γ. τοῦ ταμιείου the *advocacy* of the fiscus, Philostr.*VS*2.29. II. *language*, ἄλλη δ' ἄλλων γ. μεμιγμένη Od.19.175, cf. Il.2.804; γλῶσσαν ἱέναι speak a *language* or *dialect*, Hdt.1.57; γ. Ἑλληνίδα, Δωρίδα ἱέναι, Id.9.16, Th.3.112, cf. A.*Pers.*406, *Ch.*564; γλῶσσαν νομίζειν Hdt.1.142, 4.183; γλώσσῃ χρῆσθαι Id.4.109; κατὰ τὴν ἀρχαίαν γ. Arist.*Rh.*1357ᵇ10; *dialect*, ἡ Ἀττικὴ γ. Demetr.*Eloc.*177; but also Δωρὶς διάλεκτος μία ὑφ' ἥν εἰσι γ. πολλαί Tryph.ap.Sch.D.T.p.320 H. 2. *obsolete* or *foreign word*, which needs explanation, Arist. *Rh.*1410ᵇ12, *Po.*1457ᵇ4, Plu.2.406f: hence Γλῶσσαι, title of works by Philemon and others. 3. *people speaking a distinct language*, Lxx *Ju.*3.8 (pl.), interpol. in Scyl.15. III. *anything shaped like the tongue* (cf. γλῶσσαι ὡσεὶ πυρός *Act.Ap.*2.3). 1. in Music, *reed* or *tongue of a pipe*, Aeschin.3.229, Arist.*HA*565ᵃ24, Thphr.*HP*4.11. 4, etc. 2. *tongue* or *thong of leather, shoe-latchet*, Pl.Com.51, Aeschin.Socr.57. 3. *tongue of land*, App.*Pun.*121, cf. 95. 4. *ingot*, γ. χρυσῆ Lxx *Jo.*7.21. 5. *marking* on the liver, in divination, Hsch. (γλῶσσα from γλωχ-yᾰ, cf. γλώξ, γλωχίς; γλάσσα from *γλᾰχ-yᾰ, weak grade of same root.)

**γλωσσ-αλγέω** or (by dissimilation) **-αργέω**, *talk till one's tongue aches*, Poll.4.185. **-αλγία**, ἡ, *endless talking, wordiness*, E.*Med.* 525, *Andr.*689, Ph.2.165; but **γλωτταργία**, *idleness of the tongue*, σιωπὴν καὶ γ. ἡμῖν ἐπιβάλλει Luc.*Lex.*19. ❋ **-αλγος**, ον, (ἄλγος) *talking till one's tongue aches, garrulous*, Poll.6.119, Demoph.*Sent.* 7 (Sup.); *itching to speak*, Plu.2.510a:—also **-αργος**, [τέχνα] Pi. *Parth.Fr.*13ᵇ67; ἡδονή J.*AJ*18.6.7; ἀηδών D.Chr.47.16: Sup., Ph. 2.571. ❋ **-άομαι**, pf. part. γεγλωσσαμένος, *tuneful*, στόμα κακκαβίδων prob. in Alcm.25. **-άριον**, τό, Dim. of γλῶσσα, Dsc.3.144, Gal.12.149. II. kind of *spoon* or *spatula*, *BGU*162.2 (ii/iii A. D.). **-ασπις**, ιδος, ὁ, *one who uses his tongue as his shield and defence*, *EM*235.39. ❋ **-ημα**, ατος, τό, = γλῶσσα II. 2, Quint.*Inst.*1.8. 15, M.Ant.4.33. II. *tongue* or *point of a dart*, A.*Fr.*152. **-ηματικός**, ή, όν, (γλῶσσα II. 2) *interlarded with* γλῶσσαι, λέξις, φράσις, D.H.*Amm.*2.2, *Th.*50, etc. Adv. **-κῶς** Tim.*Lex.Praef.* ❋ **-ίδιον**, Att. **γλωττ-**, τό, Dim. of γλῶσσα, Zen.5.65 (pl.). II. Dim. of γλωττίς II, Porph.*in Harm.*p.273. ❋ **ίδος**, ἡ, *inflammation of the tongue*, in horses, *Hippiatr.*130.

**γλωσσο-γάστωρ**, ορος, ὁ, ἡ, *living by one's tongue*, Com.ap.Poll. 2.108. **-γράφος** [ᾰ], ον, *writer on* γλῶσσαι, Str.13.1.19, Ath. 3.114b, 15.699e, Gal.19.106. **-ειδής**, ές, v. γλωττ-. **-κάτοχον**, τό, *tongue-depressor*, Heliod.ap.Orib.44.14.13. **-κηλόκομπος**, ον, *soothing with boastful tongue*, *Com.Adesp.*86. ❋ **-κομεῖον**, τό, (κομέω) *case to keep the reeds* or *tongues of musical instruments*, Lysipp.5: generally, *casket*, *BGU*824.9 (i A. D.), *PLond.*2.191.14 (ii A. D.): more freq. in form ❋**-κομον**, τό, *case, casket*, *Test.Epict.*8.25, Apollod.Caryst.7, *PTeb.*414.21 (ii A. D.), *PMag.Lond.*122.55, etc.; = κιβωτός, *chest* (*Ark*), Lxx 2*Ki.*6.11 (v.l.); *money-box*, *Ev.Jo.*12.6, Plu. *Galb.*16; *compartment* in a water-organ, Hero *Spir.*1.42, cf. *Aut.*12. 1; *cage*, Longin.44.5; *coffin*, prob. in *AP*11.3; rejected by Phryn. 79:—also masc. **-κομος**, ὁ, *sarcophagus*, *BSA*17.235 (Pamphylia). II. *surgical instrument*, used for reducing fractures and dislocations, Heliod.ap.Orib.49.20. b. *box-splint*, Gal.10.442, *UP*7.14. III. *pudenda muliebria*, Eub.142. **-ποιΐα**, ἡ, *making of mouth-pieces* (γλῶσσα III. 1), and ❋**-ποιός**, όν, *making them*, Poll.2. 108, 7.153. **-πωγώνιον**, τό, *half a head with the tongue*, *POxy.* 108.14 (ii/iii A. D.).

**γλωσσός**, ή, όν, *talking, chattering*, Hdn.Gr.1.208.

❋ **γλωσσο-στροφεῖν**· περιλαλεῖν καὶ στωμύλλεσθαι, Hsch. **-τέχνης**, ου, ὁ, *tongue-artificer*, opp. χειροτέχνης, D.Chr.7.124 (pl.). **-τμητος**, ον, *with the tongue cut out*, Lxx *Le.*22.22. **-τομέω**, *cut out the tongue*, ib.2*Ma.*7.4:—Pass., Plu.2.849b. **-χᾰρῐτέω**, = χαριτογλωσσέω, *flatter*, Lxx *Pr.*28.23.

**γλωσσώδης**, ες, = γλωσσοειδής: *talkative, babbling*, Lxx *Ps.*139 (140).11, Sext.*Sent.*13 M.

**γλῶττα**, ἡ, Att. for γλῶσσα.

**γλωττήν**, dub. in Pl.Com.239: perh. f.l. for γλωττ⟨οδέψ⟩ην.

**γλωττ-ίζω**, *kiss lasciviously, bill*, *AP*5.128 (Autom.). **-ικός**, ή, όν, *of the tongue*, τὸ γ. (sc. ὄργανον) Arist.*PA*683ᵃ21. ❋ **-ίς**, ίδος, ἡ, *glottis, mouth of the windpipe*, Gal.*UP*7.13, al. II. *mouthpiece of a pipe, in which the reed was inserted*, Luc.*Harm.*1, Theo Sm.p.61 H.; of a trumpet, Hero *Spir.*1.16. III. *shoe-string*, Phryn.208; *latchet*, Lyd.*Mag.*2.13. IV. a bird, perh. *landrail*, Arist.*HA*597ᵇ 16. **-ισμός**, ὁ, *lascivious kiss*, *AP*5.131 (Philod., pl.).

**γλωττο-δεψέω**, = Lat. *fellare*, *Com.Adesp.*32 D. **-ειδής**, ές, *tongue-shaped*, Arist.*HA*528ᵇ30; γλωσσ-, v.l. in Dsc.4.88. **-ποιέω**, = γλωττοδεψέω, Ar.*V.*1283. ❋ **-στροφέω**, *ply the tongue*, Ar.*Nu.* 792.

❋ **γλωχίν** [ῑ] or **γλωχίς** (cf. Hdn.Gr.2.431, 437), ἡ, gen. ῖνος:—*projecting point*: hence, 1. *end of the yoke-strap*, Il.24.274. 2. *barb* of an arrow, S.*Tr.*681, cf. Sch. ad loc., Gal.5.548; *point* of a penknife, *AP*6.63 (Damoch.); τριαίνης Nonn.*D.*36.111; κεραίας ib. 1.193; of the moon's horns, ib.40.314. 3. Pythagorean name for *an angle*, Hero *Deff.*15. 4. *extremity*, πυμάτη γ. D.P.184; *inlet*, θαλάττης γ. Agath.5.22. 5. *stigma* of saffron, *Gp.*11.261.

**γλωχῑνωτός**, ή, όν, *barbed*, βέλη Paul.Aeg.6.88.

**γναθ-μός**, ὁ, *jaw*, poet. form of sq., Il.17.617, al.: also in pl., Od. 18.29; γναθμοῖς ἀδήλοις φαρμάκων E.*Med.*1201; for ἀλλοτρίοις γναθμοῖσι γελᾶν, v. ἀλλότριος; also γναθμόν· τομώτατον καὶ αἱρετικώτατον, Hsch. ❋ **-ος** [ᾰ], ἡ, *jaw*, Prose form of γναθμός, also freq. in Poets, γ. ἱππείη Hom.*Epigr.*14.13; ἡ ἄνω, ἡ κάτω γ., Hp.*Art.*30, cf. Hdt. 2.68; καὶ γ. καὶ τὸ ἄνω τῆς γ. (where γνάθος, = *lower jaw*) Id.9.83; ἔπαγε γνάθον take your *teeth* to it! Ar.*V.*370; γνάθου δοῦλος a greedy fellow, E.*Fr.*282.5; also ὄνου γ. Eup.434: freq. in pl., Pl.*Phdr.* 254e, Arist.*PA*664ᵃ11. 2. *cheek*, in pl., Hp.*VM*19, Gal.2.424, etc.; τὰς γ. φυσῶν D.19.314, cf. Ruf.*Onom.*47, Gal.18(1).423. 3. metaph., ποταμοὶ πυρὸς δάπτοντες ἀγρίαις γνάθοις A.*Pr.*370, cf. *Ch.* 280; also τραχεῖα πόντου Σαλμυδησσία γ., of jagged rocks, Id.*Pr.* 726. II. *point* of a wedge, ib.64. **-όω**, *hit on the cheek*, Phryn.Com.28. **-ων**, ωνος, ὁ, *full-mouth*, pr. n. of a parasite, Plu.2.707e, Longus4.16:—also **Γναθωνάριον**, ibid.: **Γναθωνίδης** Luc.*Tim.*45. **-ώνειος**, ον, *like a* Γνάθων, Plu.2.707e.

**γναμπ-τήρ**, ῆρος, ὁ, *jaw*, ἰοβόλων Androm.ap.Gal.14.36. **-τός**, ή, όν, *curved, bent*, ἰχθυάασκον γναμπτοῖς ἀγκίστροισιν Od.4.369; μετὰ γναμπτῇσι γένυσσιν Il.11.416; πόρπας τε γναμπτάς θ' ἕλικας 18.401; ὄνυχες γ. Hes.*Op.*204; γ. δρόμοι, of the diaulos, Pi.*I.*1.57; γ. χαλινούς, Hsch. 2. *supple, pliant*, of the limbs of living men (opp. to the stark and stiff ones of the dead), ἐνὶ γναμπτοῖσι μέλεσσι Il.11. 669, 24.359, Od.11.394, etc. 3. metaph., *pliable*, οὔτε νόημα γναμπτὸν ἐνὶ στήθεσσι (of Achilles), Il.24.41. ❋ **-τω** (in codd. freq. κνάμπτω), fut. **-ψω** A.*Pr.*995, *Paean Oxy.*660.8, Lyc.1247: aor. ἔγναμψα, Ep. γνάμψα A.R.2.965:—poet. form of κάμπτω used by Hom. only in compds. in tmesi, ἐν δὲ γόνυ γνάμψεν Il.23.731; γ. τινά *bend* his will, A. l.c.; νόον Orph.*L.*195; in literal sense, δόρυ γ. Lyc. l.c.; ἄκρην *round* a headland, A.R. l.c., al.:—Pass., Nic.*Th.*423, Plu.*Arat.*13.

**γναμφαί**, = γνάθοι, Hsch. **γνάμψις**, εως, ἡ, *bending*, *EM*235.55.

**γνα(π)ταὶ** ἀκταί, *curving* beach, Hsch.; γναπτὰς ἕλικας· τὰ καμφθέντα ψελλία, Id.; cf. γναμπτός. ⊛ **γνάπτω**, = γνάμπτω, Id.

**γνάπτωρ**, ορος, ὁ, = γναφεύς, Man.4.422.

**γνά-φαλον** or **-φαλλον**, **-φεῖον**, **-φεύς**, **-φευτικός**, **-φεύω**, **-φικός**, **-φισσα**, **-φος**, **-φω**, v. κν–.

**γνᾰφάδιον**, τό, = sq., Hsch.

**γνᾰφάλλιον**, τό, *cotton-weed*, *Diotis maritima*, Dsc.3.117, Plin. *HN*27.88 :—also **γνᾰφαλλίς**, ίδος, ἡ, Ps.-Dsc.3.117.

⊛ **γνάφαλλον** [ᾰ], τό, *flock of wool*, *Jahresh*.14*Beibl*.52, *PMagd*.8.7 (iii B. C.) :—hence Subst. ⊛ **γναφαλλολόγος**, ὁ, *flock-picker*, *Ostr*.1081; more freq. by haplology **γναφαλλόγος**, ib.1082,1086, *PPetr*.2*Intr*. p.44 (iii B. C.).

**γνάφαλος**, ὁ, an unknown *bird*, Arist.*HA*616ᵇ16.

⊛ **γνάψις**, εως, ἡ, *dressing* of cloth, Pl.*Plt*.282e, Sch.Ar.*Pl*.166.

⊛ **γνήσι-ος**, α, ον, (γένος) *belonging to the race*, i. e. *lawfully begotten, born in wedlock*, νόθον καὶ γνήσιον Il.11.102, cf. Od.14.202, Hdt.3.2, *Leg.Gort*.10.41, Ar.*Av*.1665, And.1.127, D.44.49, etc.; παίδων ἐπ' ἀρότῳ γνησίων Men.*Pk*.435; ἀδελφός Ar.*Av*.1659; νόθος.. γνησίοις ἴσως σθένει S.*Fr*.87; φρονοῦντα γνήσια E.*Hipp*.309; γ. φρόνημα S.*Fr*. 307. 2. generally, *genuine, legitimate*, φίλος Phoc.2 A; γ. γυναῖκες *lawful* wives, opp. παλλακίδες, X.*Cyr*.4.3.1; πολῖται Arist.*Pol*.1278ᵃ 30, cf. 1319ᵇ9; γ. τῆς Ἑλλάδος *true* Greeks, D.9.30; ἀκουστής D.H. *Isoc*.18 (Sup.); μήτηρ τῶν ἐρωτικῶν λόγων, of Aphrodite, Luc.*Am*.19; γ. ἀρεταί *real, unfeigned* virtues, Pi.*O*.2.11; γ. ὕμνοι *inspired* song, B.8.83; of fevers, γ. τριταῖος a *genuine* tertian, Hp.*Progn*.24; γ. ὄξος *genuine* vinegar, Eub.65; of writings, *genuine*, Gal.15.748, Harp.s.v. Ἀλκιβιάδης. Adv. **-ίως** *genuinely, truly*, E.*Alc*.678, Lys.2.76, D.*Ep*. 3.32, etc.; γ. φέρειν bear *nobly*, Antiph.281, Men.205; *lawfully*, τοῖς γ. συμβιώσασιν Phld.*Piet*.93. II. γνήσια, τά, *charges on land*, γ. δημόσια *PAmh*.86.15 (i A. D.), cf. *PLond*.3.1157.4 (ii A. D.). ⊛ **-ότης**, ητος, ἡ, *legitimate birth*, ἀπ' ἀμφοῖν Arist.*Rh*.1360ᵇ35, cf. Phld.*Hom*. p.50 O. II. *genuineness, sincerity*, μετὰ πάσης γ. *POxy*.140.16 (vi A. D.).

**γνίς**· γέρανος (Tyrrhen.), Hsch.

**Γνίφων**, ωνος, ὁ, *niggard*, as pr. n., Luc.*Vit.Auct*.23; prob. in Alciphr.3.34.

**γνοιῦσαι**· γνοῦσαι, Hsch. **γνοτέρα**, = βαλλωτή, Ps.-Dsc.3. 103. ⊛ **γνόφεον**· μέλαν, Id.; cf. sq.

**γνοφ-ίας**, ου, ὁ, name of a wind, Lyd.*Mens*.4.119. ⊛ **-ος**, later form for δνόφος, *darkness*, *Chron.Lind*.D.28, *Ep.Hebr*.12.18, D.Chr. 34.37 (pl.), Luc.*Per*.43: pl., *storm-clouds*, Arist.*Mu*.391ᵇ12. **-όω**, *darken*, Lxx*La*.2.1. ⊛ **-ώδης**, ες, *dark, gloomy*, ib.*Pr*.7.9, Ph.2. 109, Plu.2.949a.

**γνύθος** [ῠ], εος, τό, *pit*, Lyc.485: but γνύθος, ὁ, *hollow*, Hsch.

⊛ **γνύξ**, Adv., (γόνυ) *with bent knee*, Il., always in phrase γνὺξ ἐριπών falling *on the knee*, 5.309,357, al.; later γ. ἥμενος Arat.921; σφῆλεν γ. ἐπιόντα A.R.3.1310; γ. ἑδριόωσαι Orac.ap.Zos.2.6: in later Prose, Gal.*UP*3.15.

**γνυπεσόν**· ἀργόν, οἱ δὲ ἔκλυτον, Hsch.

**γνύπετος**, ον, (γόνυ, πίπτω) *falling on the knee* :—hence ⊛ **γνυπτέω** (leg. γνυπετέω), *to be weak*, Hsch. **γνύποντι** (leg. -οῦντι)· ἀσθενοῦντι, Id., and **γνύπων**, ωνος, *depressed* or *weak*, Id.

**γνυφαί**· νάπαι, Hsch. **γνύων**· νωθραίνων, Id.

⊛ **γνῶμα**, ατος, τό, (γνῶναι) *mark, token*, Hdt.7.52; *test*, S.*Tr*.593; of an ass's teeth, Arist.*HA*577ᵇ3. II. *opinion, judgement*, A. *Ag*.1352, E.*Heracl*.407. III. = Lat. *groma*, Suid.

**γνωμανάδοχος**, ὁ, *surety for performance of a service*, *PMonac*.14. 63 (vi A. D.).

**γνωμᾰτ-ευτής**, οῦ, ὁ, *a dealer in maxims*, Sch.Il.10.31. **-εύω**, *discriminate, discern*, σκιὰς γ. Pl.*R*.516e (v. γνωμονεύω), cf. Philostr. *VA*2.30, Plot.5.8.11, v.l. in S.E.*M*.7.332; τὰ βουλεύματα τῶν πολεμίων Agath.1.14; γ. πήχει καὶ μέτρῳ τὴν ἀρετήν Them.*Or*.2.36b: abs., *exercise discrimination*, Plot.5.8.11; *decide*, c. acc. et inf., Men. Prot.p.47 D.

⊛ **γνωμεισηγητής**, οῦ, ὁ, *proposer of a motion*, *BGU*362 xv 8 (iii A. D.).

⊛ **γνώμ-η**, ἡ, *means of knowing*: hence, *mark, token*, Thgn.60 (pl.); of the teeth (cf. γνώμων III), Arist.*HA*576ᵇ15. II. *organ by which one perceives or knows, intelligence*, 1. *thought, judgement* (τῆς ψυχῆς ἢ γ. Pl.*Lg*.672b), ἐκμαθεῖν ψυχήν τε καὶ φρόνημα καὶ γ. S. *Ant*.176: acc. abs., γνώμην ἱκανός *intelligent*, Hdt.3.4; γ. ἀγαθός, κακός, S.*OT*687, *Ph*.910; τοιάδε τὴν γ. Id.*El*.1021; κατὰ γ. ἴδρις Id. *OT*1087 (lyr.); γνώμᾳ διπλόαν θέτο βουλάν Pi.*N*.10.89; γνώμῃ μαθεῖν τι S.*OC*403; γνώμῃ κυρήσας Id.*OT*398; γνώμη φρενῶν, opp. ῥύμη, ib. 524; γνώμης ξύνεσις Th.1.75; γνώμης μᾶλλον ἐφόδῳ ἢ ἰσχύος Id.3.11; ταῖς γ. καὶ τοῖς σώμασι σφάλλεσθαι X.*Cyr*.1.3.10, cf. Th.1.70; γνώμη, opp. τύχη, σωφρονοῦντες Isoc.3.47; γνώμης ἅπτεσθαι affect *the head*, of wine or fever, Hp.*Acut*.63, *Fract*.11; γνώμην ἔχειν *understand*, S. *El*.214 (lyr.), Ar.*Ach*.396; πάντων γ. ἴσχειν S.*Ph*.837 (lyr.); προσέχειν γνώμην give *heed, attend*, δεῦρο τὴν γ. προσίσχετε Eup.37; πρὸς ἑτέρον γνώμην ἔχειν Aeschin.3.192; to be on one's *guard*, Th.1.95; δηλοῦν τὴν γ. ἔν τινι to show one's *wit* in.., Id 3.37; ἐν γνώμῃ τι παραστῆσαι D.4.17; ἀπὸ γνώμης φέρειν ψῆφον δικαίαν with a good *conscience*, A.*Eu*.674; but οὐκ ἀπὸ γ. λέγεις not without *judgement*, with good *sense*, S.*Tr*.389; ἄτερ γνώμης A.*Pr*.456; ἄνευ γ. S.*OC*594; γνώμῃ κολάζειν *with good reason*, X.*An*.2.6.10; γνώμῃ τῇ ἀρίστῃ (sc. κρίνειν or δικάζειν) *to* the best of *one's judgement*, in the dicasts' oath, Arist.*Rh*. 1375ᵃ29; ἡ καλουμένη γ. τοῦ ἐπιεικοῦς κρίσις ὀρθή Id.*EN*1143ᵃ19; so περὶ ὧν ἂν νόμοι μὴ ὦσι, γνώμῃ τῇ δικαιοτάτῃ κρινεῖν D.20.118; γ. τῇ δ. δικάσειν ὀμωμόκασιν Id.23.96, cf. 39.40; τῇ δ. γ. Arist.*Pol*.1287ᵃ 26; ὅστις γνώμῃ μὴ καθαρεύει has not a clear *conscience*, Ar.*Ra*. 355. 2. *will, disposition, inclination*, εὐσεβεῖ γνώμᾳ Pi.*O*.3.41; γ. Διός A.*Pr*.1003; ἐν γνώμῃ γεγονέναι τινί to stand *high in his favour*, Hdt.6.37; πάσῃ τῇ γ. with all *one's zeal*, Th.6.45; τίνα αὐτοὺς οἴεσθε γ. ἕξειν περὶ σφῶν αὐτῶν And.1.104; γ. ἔ. περί τινα Lys.10.21; πρὸς τοὺς Ἀθηναίους τὴν γ. ἔχειν *to be inclined* towards.., Th.5.44; ἐμπιμπλάναι τὴν γ. τινός satisfy his *wishes*, X.*An*.1.7.8, cf. *HG*6.1. 15 (pl.); ἀφ' ἑαυτοῦ γνώμης on his own *initiative*, Th.4.68; ἐκ μιᾶς γ. of one *accord*, with one *consent*, D.10.59; μιᾷ γνώμῃ Th.1.122, 6.17; διὰ μιᾶς γ. γίγνεσθαι Isoc.4.139; κατὰ γνώμην according to one's *mind* or *wishes*, ὅταν τάκει θῶ κατὰ γνώμην ἐμήν E.*Andr*.737; ἄν τι μὴ κατὰ γ. ἐκβῇ D.1.16: in pl., φίλιαι γνῶμαι friendly *sentiments*, Hdt. 9.4. III. *judgement, opinion*, βροτῶν γ. Parm.8.61; ταύτῃ.. τῇ γνώμῃ πλεῖστός εἰμι I incline mostly *to this view*, Hdt.7.220 (s. v. l.); also ταύτῃ πλεῖστος τὴν γνώμην εἰμί Id.1.120; ἡ πλείστη γ. ἐστί τινι Id.5.126; πλέον φέρει ἡ γ. τινί Id.8.100; τὸ πλεῖστον τῆς γ. εἶχεν.. προσμεῖξαι Th.3.31; γνώμην τίθεσθαι Hdt.3.80; οὕτως τὴν γ. ἔχειν to be of this *opinion*, Th.7.15, cf. X.*Cyr*.6.2.8, Ar.*Nu*.157; εἴ τινι γ. τοιαύτη παρειστήκει περὶ ἐμοῦ And.1.54; τὴν αὐτὴν γ. ἔχειν Th.2.55; τῆς αὐτῆς γ. εἶναι, ἔχεσθαι, Id.1.113,140; ὁ αὐτὸς εἰμὶ τῇ γ. Id.3.38; κατὰ γ. τὴν ἐμήν in my *judgement* or *opinion*, Hdt.2.26, 5.3; ellipt., κατά γε τὴν ἐμήν Ar.*Ec*.153, cf. Plb.18.1.18, D.H.*Isoc*.3: abs., γνώμην ἐμήν Ar.*V*.983, *Pax* 232; παρὰ γνώμην τοῖς Ἕλλησιν ἐγένετο contrary to *general opinion*, Th.4.40; but παρὰ γ. κινδυνευταί *reckless* venturers, Id.1.70, cf. 4.19; εἰπὲ μὴ παρὰ γ. ἐμοί either contrary to *my wish*, or contrary to *your true opinion*, A.*Ag*.931, cf. *Supp*.454: freq. of *opinions* delivered publicly, ἑστάναι πρὸς τὴν γ. τινός Th.4. 56; Θεμιστοκλέους γνώμῃ *by the advice* of Th., Id.1.90,93; γνώμην ἀποφαίνειν deliver *an opinion*, Hdt.1.40; ἀποδείκνυσθαι ib.207; ἐκφαίνειν Id.5.36; τίθεσθαι S.*Ph*.1448 (anap.), Ar.*Ec*.658; ἀποφαίνεσθαι E.*Supp*.336; ποιεῖσθαι περί τινων Th.3.36; γνώμας κατέθεντο have made up their *minds*, Parm.8.53. b. *verdict*, ἡ τοῦ δικαστοῦ γ. *IG*4.364 (Corinth, iv A. D.), cf. 685.32 (pl., Cret., ii B. C.). 2. *proposition, motion*, γνώμην εἰσφέρειν Hdt.3.80,81; εἰπεῖν Th.8.68, etc.; (but γνώμας προτιθέναι hold a debate, Th.3.36); γνῶμαι τρεῖς προεκέατο Hdt.3.83: freq. in Inscrr., *resolution*, *IG*1².118.28, etc.; γ. στρατηγῶν ib.2².27; Κλεισόφου καὶ συμπρυτάνεων ib.1; ἡ ἐκφερομένη γ. ib.1051ᶜ26; γνώμην νικᾶν carry *a motion*, Ar.*V*.594, *Nu*.432; κρατεῖν τῇ γ. Plu.*Cor*.17. 3. γνῶμαι, αἱ, *practical maxims*, Heraclit. 78, S.*Aj*.1091, X.*Mem*.4.2.9, Arist.*Rh*.1395ᵃ11 (sg., 1394ᵃ22). 4. in pl., *fancies, illusions*, S.*Aj*.52. 5. *intention, purpose, resolve*, ἀπὸ τοιᾶσδε γνώμης with some such *purpose* as this, Th.3.92; γνώμην ποιεῖσθαι, c. inf., *propose* to do, Id.1.128; κατὰ γνώμην of *set purpose*, D.H. 6.81 (so also γνώμης Lib.*Or*.33.13, 50.12); τίνα ἔχουσα γνώμην; with what *purpose?* Hdt.3.119; οἶδα δ' οὐ γνώμῃ τίνι; with what *intent?* S.*OT*527, cf. *Aj*.448; ἡ ξύμπασα γ. τῶν λεχθέντων the general *purport*.., Th.1.22; ἦν τοῦ τείχους ἡ γνώμη.., ἵνα.. *the purpose* of it was.., that.., Id.8.90. **-ηδόν**, Adv. (γνώμη III. 2) *vote by vote*, πυνθάνεσθαι D.H.8.43. **-ηστός**, ὁ, *knowledge*, ἀφ' οὗ γ. as far as my *memory* goes, Hsch. s. h. v. **-ίδιον**, τό, Dim. of γνώμη, Ar. *Eq*.100, *Nu*.321, Luc.*Par*.42. **-ικός**, ή, όν, *normative* (nisi leg. γνωμονικά), γ. ἁ φύσις ἁ τοῦ ἀριθμοῦ Philol.11. 2. (γνώμη III. 3), *dealing in* or *suited to maxims, didactic*, περίοδος Hermog.*Inv*.4.3; τὰ γ. S.E.*M*.1.278; τὸ γ. D.Chr.52.17; σχῆμα γ. Sch.Od.15.74. Adv. **-κῶς** Phld.*Hom*.p.15 O., Ath.5.191e.

**γνωμο-δοτέω**, *give advice*, *IG*12(7).p.1 (Amorgos). **-λογέω**, *speak in maxims*, Arist.*Rh*.1394ᵃ21, *Rh.Al*.1439ᵃ3, Plu.2.481b, D.L. 8.78, Procop.Gaz.*Ep*.21. **-λογητέον**, *one must speak in maxims*, Arist.*Rh.Al*.1439ᵃ3. ⊛ **-λογία**, ἡ, *sententious style*, Pl.*Phdr*.267c; *theory of maxims*, Arist.*Rh*.1394ᵃ19. 2. *collection of maxims*, Plu. *Cat.Ma*.2 (pl.), Suid. Θέογνις: pl., Plb.12.28.1c, D.H.*Dem*.46, Plu. *Fab*.1, etc. **-λογικός**, ή, όν, *sententious*, τὰς τελευτὰς γ. ποιεῖσθαι Arist.*Rh.Al*.1439ᵃ5, Demetr.*Eloc*.9. Adv. **-κῶς** Theon*Prog*.5.

**γνωμον-εύω**, *measure as on a sun-dial, test*, v.l. in Pl.*R*.516e (ap. Tim.*Lex*.). ⊛ **-ικός**, ή, όν, (γνώμων I) *judging by rule*, X.*Mem*.4. 2.10; *fit to judge of, skilled in* a thing, τινός Pl.*R*.467c, Iamb.*Myst*. 3.27. II. (γνώμων II. 2. a) *of* or *concerning sun-dials*, θεωρήματα Hipparch.1.9.8, cf. Str.1.1.20: **-κός**, ὁ, *expert in sun-dials*, *AP*14.139, Gal.5.652, Procl.*Hyp*.5.54: ἡ -κή (sc. τέχνη), *the art of making them*, Vitr.1.3. Adv. **-κῶς** Str.2.1.35. 2. *forming a γνώμων* (II. 2. c), τρίγωνα Iamb.*in Nic*.p.71 P. Adv. **-κῶς** ib.p.77 P. **-ιον**, τό, Dim. of γνώμων II. 2. a, *pointer* or *dial-hand*, Hero *Dioptr*.5, Procl.*Hyp*.3.26 (pl.).

**γνωμο-σύνη**, ἡ, *prudence, judgement*, Sol.16. **-τῠπέω**, *coin maxims*, Ar.*Th*.55. **-τῠπία**, ἡ, *coining of maxims*, Hsch. **-τῠπικός**, ή, όν, *clever at coining maxims*, Ar.*Eq*.1379. **-τύπος** [ῠ], ον, (τύπτω) *maxim-coining, sententious*, Id.*Ra*.877, *Nu*.952 (lyr.); γ. μάλιστα οἱ ἀγροῖκοι Arist.*Rh*.1395ᵃ7. **-φλυᾱκέω**, *babble of 'saws and instances'*, dub. cj. in Cerc.9.5.

⊛ **γνώμων**, ονος, ὁ, (γι-γνώ-σκω) *one that knows* or *examines, an interpreter, discerner*, θεσφάτων A.*Ag*.1130; τῶν παραχρῆμα Th.1.138; γλῶττα γ. (sc. γλυκέων καὶ δριμέων) X.*Mem*.1.4.5: γνώμονες, οἱ, *inspectors* of the sacred olives at Athens, Lys.7.25. 2. *expert witness* or *valuer*, *SIG*169.52 (Iasus, iv B. C.). 3. as Adj., *discerning*, νόος *Hymn.Is*.141. II. *carpenter's square*, Polyaen.4.3.21; [ὁ δημιουργὸς τῇ δεκάδι] ὥσπερ γνώμονι καὶ εὐθυντηρίῳ ἐχρήσατο *Theol. Ar*.59. 2. *pointer* of the sun-dial, Hdt.2.109, Phld.*Sign*.30, Plu. *Per*.6 (pl.), D.L.2.1. b. Geom., *gnomon*, Euc.2*Def*.2, etc. c.

Arith., number added to a figurate number to obtain the next number of the same figure, Iamb.*in Nic.*p.58 P.: esp. of the odd integers, Arist.*Ph.*203$^a$14, Theo Sm.p.32 H.; also of the original figurate number, *Theol.Ar.*9 (dub. l.) **3.** = κλεψύδρα, Thphr.*Fr.* 159. **4.** *point* of a drill, Apollod.*Poliorc.*149.4. **5.** generally, *index*, τινός Plu.2.968f, Ael.*NA*6.34, al., Vett.Val.305.10; simply, *mark*, *POxy.*1409.18 iii A.D.). **6.** in pl., *teeth that mark* a horse's age, X.*Eq.*3.1. **7.** metaph., *rule* of life, Thgn.543, cf. Luc.*Herm.* 76. **8.** sens. obsc., ὁ γ. ἀνίσταται Diog.*Ep.*35. **V.** *tariff*, *OGI* 674.5 (Coptos), *BGU* 1118.45 (i B.C.), *AB* 233. **2.** *code of regulations*, *PGnom.*1, *OGI* 669.44 (i A.D.).

⊛ **γνωρ-ίζω**, fut. Att. -ιῶ: pf. ἐγνώρικα Pl.*Phdr.*262b:—*make known, point out*, A.*Pr.*487, Lxx 1 *Ki.*10.8, al., *Ep.Rom.*9.22:—in this sense mostly Pass., *become known*, Pl.*R.*428a, Arist.*APr.*64$^b$35; τὰ γνωριζόμενα μέρη τῆς οἰκουμένης Plb.2.37.4. **2.** c. acc. pers., *make known*, τινά τινι Plu.*Fab.*21; *commend*, τινὰ τῇ βουλῇ ἰσχυρῶς App. *Mac.*9.6. **3.** *certify* a person's *identity*, *BGU* 581.13 (ii A.D.), *POxy.* 1024.18 (ii A.D.). **II.** *gain knowledge of, become acquainted with, discover*, c. part., τοὔργον ὡς οὐ γνωριοῖμί σου τόδε δόλῳ προσέρπον S. *OT* 538; τὰ καλὰ γ. οἱ εὐφυέες πρὸς αὐτά Democr.56, cf. E.*Alc.*564, Th.7.44, Arist.*Ph.*184$^a$12:—Pass., Th.5.103, Men.72; γ. περί τι or περί τινος Arist.*Metaph.*1005$^b$8, 1037$^a$16. **2.** *become acquainted with*, τινά Pl.*La.*181c, D.25.6; τινὰς ὁποῖοί τινές εἰσι Isoc.2.28:—Pass., ἐγνωρισμένοι αὐτῷ *being made acquainted with* him, ibid.; πρός τινος Luc.*Tim.*5. ⊛ **-ιμος**, ον, rarely η, ον, Pl.*R.*614e, Luc. *Somn.*9:—*well-known*, γνώριμα λέγεις Pl.*R.*558c; φίλα τε καὶ συνήθη καὶ γ. Id.*Lg.*798e; λόγος γ. τινι D.7.23; ὀνόματα γ. *familiar*, Arist.*Po.*1451$^b$20, *Top.*149$^a$18 (Sup.); opp. ἄγνωστον, ibid.: γ. ἡμῖν, opp. ἁπλῶς, Id.*EN* 1095$^b$3: more freq. in Comp. -ώτερον, ἁπλῶς, opp. γ. ἡμῖν, Id.*APo.*72$^a$3, al.; -ώτερα τεκμήρια Iamb.*Myst.*5.13. **2.** of persons, γνωριμώτερον ποιεῖν τινά τινι X.*Cyr.*5.5.28. **3.** Subst., *acquaintance*, ἑταῖρος ἢ καὶ γ. ἄλλος Od.16.9; less than φίλος, D.18. 284; τοῖς οἰκείοις καὶ τοῖς γ. Pl.*R.*343e, cf. X.*Mem.*2.3.1, D.21.73, etc. **b.** *pupil*, Ἰσοκράτους καὶ τῶν ἐκείνου γ. D.H.*Comp.*19, cf. Philostr.*VS*1.24.2, al., Plu.2.448e, *IG*3.774. **c.** *kinsman*, Lxx *Ru.*3.2. **II.** *notable, distinguished*, οἱ γνώριμοι *the notables* or *wealthy class*, X.*HG*2.2.6; opp. δῆμος, Arist.*Pol.*1291$^b$18, Plu. *Nic.*2, etc.: Sup. οἱ ἐν ταῖς πόλεσι -ώτατοι D.19.259; less freq. of things, *remarkable*, Luc.*Herm.*21. **III.** Adv. -μως *intelligibly*, γ. αἰνίξομαι E.*El.*946; γ. μοι πάνυ φράσεις Antiph.52.6; ἁπλῶς καὶ πᾶσι γ. γεγράφθαι D.24.68; γ. μᾶλλον λέγειν, opp. οὐ σαφῶς, Arist.*GA*747$^a$27. **2.** *familiarly*, γ. ἔχειν τινί to be on *friendly terms* with one, D.53.4.—Rare in poetry. **-ιμότης**, ητος, ἡ, *acquaintance*, Stob.2.7.5[l]. **-ισις**, εως, ἡ, *making known*, Pl.*Plt.*257a. **2.** οἰκειότης καὶ γ. ἀλλήλων Id.*Lg.*771d, etc. **3.** *getting to know*, γνωρίσεως ἕνεκα τῶν τόπων ib.763b; *cognition*, Id.*Sph.*219c. **-ισμα**, τό, *that by which a thing is made known, mark, token*, X.*Cyr.*2.1.27 (pl.), Arist.*Phgn.*806$^a$15, etc.; ἴχνη καὶ γ. Plu.2.855b: in pl., *tokens by which* a lost child *is recognized*, Men.*Epit.*86, Plu.*Thes.*4, etc.: also in sg., Parth.1. 5. **2.** in criminal trials, *corpus delicti*, *PMasp.*143.16, al. (vi A.D.). **-ισμός**, ὁ, *making known*, Arist.*APo.*90$^b$16. **2.** *identification*, *PTeb.*288.15 (iii A.D.). **II.** *recognition*, *EM* 735.25, Suid. **-ιστέον**, *one must know*, Arist.*EN* 1180$^b$22; *one may recognize*, Alex.Trall.1.15. ⊛ **-ιστής**, οῦ, ὁ, *one that takes cognizance of*, δίκης Antipho 5.94. **II.** *diviner*, Lxx 4 *Ki.*23.24. **-ιστικός**, ή, όν, *capable of apprehending, cognitive*, Pl.*Def.*414c; κινητικὸν ἔδοξει ἡ ψυχὴ εἶναι καὶ γ. Arist.*de An.*404$^b$28; τοῦ εἴδους Id.*Ph.*194$^b$4; ἡ διαλεκτικὴ πειραστικὴ περὶ ὧν ἡ φιλοσοφία γ. Id.*Metaph.*1004$^b$26; ἡ τῆς γ. γραμμῆς τομή title of work ascribed to Archytas, Iamb.*Comm. Math.*2; *capable of knowing*, Plu.2.79d, Arr.*Epict.*2.20.21; γ. τοῦ μέλλοντος Max.Tyr.1.5. Adv. -κῶς, ζῆν Porph.*Gaur.*16.3. **II.** *corresponding with knowledge*, ἰδιότητες τοῦ ὄντος Porph.*Sent.*38.

**γνωσῐ-γρᾰφία**, ἡ, *picturing of the effect* of a verdict, as a Rhetorical device, Aps.p.304 H. ⊛ **-δίκα** [ῐ], ἡ, *judicial decision*, *IG*5(2).262. 15 (Mantinea, v B.C.). **-μᾰχέω**, *fight with one's own opinion* (τῇ προτέρᾳ γνώμῃ μάχεσθαι Phryn.*PS*p.59 B.), or *recognize one's own fighting power* (as compared with the enemy): hence, *give way, submit*, Hdt.3.25, 7.130, E.*Heracl.*706 (anap.), Ar.*Av.*555, D.H.3.57; γ. μὴ εἶναι ὁμοῖοι *give way and confess* that.., Hdt.8.29. **b.** *admit one's error*, Isoc.5.7, *POxy.*1119.20 (iii A.D.), 71 ii 14 (iv A.D.). **II.** in later Prose, *contend obstinately*, in argument, Ph.1.526, al.; γνωσιμαχήσαντες πρὸς ἀλλήλους D.H.9.1 (s.v.l.): abs., *to be at variance*, Hp.*Ep.*27. **-μᾰχία**, ἡ, *obstinate contention*, Ph.1.693 (pl.).

⊛ **γνῶσις**, εως, ἡ, *seeking to know, inquiry, investigation*, esp. judicial, τὰς τῶν δικαστηρίων γ. D.18.224; τὴν κατὰ τοῦ διαιτητοῦ γ. Id.21.92, cf. 7.9, Lycurg.141; γ. περὶ τῆς δίκης *PHib.*1.92.13 (iii B.C.). **2.** *result of investigation, decision*, *PPetr.*3 p.118 (iii B.C.). **II.** *knowing, knowledge*, Heraclit.56; opp. ἀγνωσίη, Hp.*Vict.*1.23 (dub.); opp. ἄγνοια, Pl.*R.*478c; ἡ αἴσθησις γ. τις Arist.*GA*731$^a$33: pl., Θεὸς γνώσεων κύριος Lxx 1 *Ki.*2.3. **b.** *higher, esoteric knowledge*, 1 *Ep. Cor.*8.7, 10, *Ep.Eph.*3.19, etc.; χαρισάμενος ἡμῖν νοῦν, λόγον, γνῶσιν *PMag.Par.*2.290. **2.** *acquaintance with* a person, πρός τινα Test. ap.Aeschin.1.50; τῶν Σεβαστῶν *IPE*1.47.6 (Olbia). **3.** *recognizing*, Th.7.44. **4.** *means of knowing*, [αἱ αἰσθήσεις] κυριώταται τῶν καθ' ἕκαστα γ. Arist.*Metaph.*981$^b$11. **III.** *being known*, γνῶσιν ἔχει τι, = γνωστόν ἐστι, Pl.*Tht.*206b. **2.** *fame, credit*, Hdn.7.5.5, Luc.*Herod.*3. **IV.** *means of knowing*: hence, *statement in writing*, *PLond.*5.1708, etc. (vi A.D.). **V.** = γνῶμα, Hsch. s.h.v.

**γνῶσμα**, ατος, τό, *knowable object*, Dam.*Pr.*81.

⊛ **γνωστ-εία**, ἡ, *certification of identity*, *PFay.*65.5 (ii A.D.). **-έον**, *one must know*, Pl.*R.*396a. Adj. γνωστέα, τά, *things that must be known*, Gal.17(2).1. ⊛ **-εύω**, *to be witness to identity* for a person, *BGU* 895 (ii A.D.):—Pass., *to be certified*, ὑπό τινος *PFlor.*382.80 (iii A.D.). **-ήρ**, ῆρος, ὁ, *one that knows*: *surety*, X.*Cyr.*6.2.39, *BGU* 1032.11: *witness to identity*, *POxy.*496.16 (ii A.D.). **2.** *inspector*, *PAmh.*2.139.23 (iv A.D.), *PLond.*3.1249.3 (iv A.D.). ⊛ **-ης**, ου, ὁ, *one that knows*, τῶν ἐθῶν *Act.Ap.*26.3; τοῦ εὐαγγελίου Sammelb 421. 1 (iii A.D.): esp. *one who knows the future, diviner*, Lxx 1 *Ki.*28.3. **II.** = γνωστήρ, *surety*, γ. τῆς πίστεως Plu.*Flam.*4; *expert witness* or *valuer*, *PLips.*106.10 (i A.D.). **-ικός**, ή, όν, *of* or *for knowing, cognitive*: ἡ -κή (sc. ἐπιστήμη), *theoretical* science (opp. πρακτική), Pl.*Plt.*258e, etc.; τὸ γ. ib.261b; ἕξεις γ. Arist.*APo.*100$^a$11 (Comp.); γ. εἰκόνες Hierocl.*in CA*25 p.475 M.: c. gen., *able to discern*, Ocell. 2.7. Adv. -κῶς Procl.*Inst.*39, Dam.*Pr.*79, Phlp.*in Ph.*241.22.

**γνωστοποιός**, όν, *creating the knowable*, Dam.*Pr.*80.

**γνωστός**, ή, όν, collat. form of γνωτός (q.v.), *known*, A.*Ch.*702, S. *OT*361, *Fr.*203, Pl.*Tht.*205d, X.*HG*2.3.44, etc.; γνωστόν, τό, *common knowledge*, τινός *PAmh.*145.9 (iv/v A.D.). Adv. -τῶς *clearly*, Lxx *Pr.*27.23, Eust.1540.1. **2.** *knowable*, Arist.*Metaph.*1016$^b$20, *APo.*64$^b$37, etc.; γνωστὰ σαρκὸς bodily *symptoms* (of anger), Phld. *Ir.*p.24 W. **II.** pl., as Subst., = γνώριμοι, *notables*, Sm.*Pr.*31. 23; *acquaintance, friend*, *Ev.Luc.*2.44, al. **III.** Act., *knowing*, dub. in Lxx *Ge.*2.9 (γνωστικός ap.Ph.1.37).

**γνωτέρα**, = βαλλωτή, Ps.-Dsc.3.103 (γνοτέρα Wellm.).

**γνωτός** (A), ή, όν (ός, όν S.*OT*396), older and more correct form of γνωστός (Eust.400.26, 1450.62):—of things, *perceived, understood, known*, Il.7.401, Od.24.182; γνωτὰ κοὐκ ἄγνωτά μοι S.*OT*58; [μαντεῖαν] ἐκ θεῶν του γνωτόν ib.396. **2.** of persons, *well-known*, ἐκ κάρτα βαιῶν γ. ἂν γένοιτ' ἀνήρ Id.*Fr.*282.

**γνωτός** (B), ἡ, *kinsman, kinswoman*, γνωτοί τε γνωταί τε *brothers* and *sisters*, Il.15.350; θάλαμον γνωτούς τε λιποῦσα 3.174, cf. 22.234; γνωτὸν μητρυιῆς 13.697; *brother*, A.R.1.53; *sister*, αὐτὴ.. γνωτή Nicaenet.1.9, cf. Nonn.*D.*2.313, al.; also, = ἐρωμένη, Hsch. (Cf. Lett. *znuots* 'son-in-law, brother-in-law', Skt. *jñātis* 'relative'.)

⊛ **γνωτο-φόνος**, ον, *murderer of another's brother*, Nonn.*D.*26.82:—fem. **-φόντις**, ιδος, ἡ, *murderess of a brother*, Lyc.1318.

⊛ **γοάω**, γοάει Mosch.3.88, -άουσι A.R.3.995, γοόωσι Q.S.2.648: Dor. 3 pl. -άοντι Mosch.3.24; opt. γοάοιμεν Il.24.664; γοόωεν Od. 24.190; Ep. inf. γοήμεναι Il.14.502; part. γοόων, -όωσα 6.373, etc.: Ep impf. γόων Od.10.567 (γόον Il.6.500 may be aor.), Ion. γοάασκεν Od.8.92: Ep. fut. γοήσομαι Il.21.124, later γοήσω *AP*7. 638 (Crin.), Nonn.*D.*2.137: aor. 1 ἐγόησα *IG*12(7).445 (Amorgos), *AP*7.599 (Jul.), 611 (Eutolm.):—Med., Trag. (v. infr.) and once in Prose, X.*Cyr.*4.6.9:—Pass., v. infr.:—*groan, weep*, Od.8.92, etc.: c acc., *bewail*, Il.16.857, etc.; ὑπέρ τινος Mosch.4.83:—Med. (never in Hom. exc. in fut.), γοᾶσθε A.*Pers.*1072, cf. *Ch.*632; ὀδύρματα τὴν Ἡράκλειον ἔξοδον γοωμένην S.*Tr.*51; ἀμφί νιν γοώμενος ib.937:—Pass., γοᾶται A.*Ch.*632; μακρὰ γοηθεὶς *AP*7.371 (Crin.).

**γοβρίαι**· φανοί, λαμπτῆρες, Hsch.; cf. γράβιον.

**γογγρίον**, τό, Dim. of γόγγρος, Sch.Opp.*H.*1.113.

**γογγρο-ειδής**, ές, *like a conger*, Arist.*HA*505$^b$9 (Comp.). **-κτόνος**, ον, *conger-killing*, Plu.2.966a.

⊛ **γόγγρος**, ὁ, *conger-eel*, Antiph.26.12, Alex.15.15, Arist.*HA*571$^a$ 28, etc. **II.** *tubercular disease in olive-trees*, Thphr.*HP*1.8.6.

**γογγρύζω**, *grunt*, Hsch., *EM* 237.40.

**γογγρώδης**, ες, *like an excrescence*, ἔκφυσις Hsch. s.v. γόγγρος.

**γογγρώνη**, ἡ, *excrescence on the neck*, Hp.*Epid.*6.3.6, Gal.17(2).38. (Cf. γόγγρος II.)

**γογγύζω**, Ion. (Phryn.336) and later Gr. for Att. τονθορύζω, *mutter, murmur, grumble*, ἐπί τινι Lxx *Nu.*14.29, cf. 17.5; κατά τινος *Ev.Matt.*20.11; περί τινος *Ev.Jo.*6.41, etc.: abs., *PPetr.*3 p.130 (iii B.C.), Lxx *Nu.*11.1, *POxy.*33 iii 14 (ii A.D.), Arr.*Epict.*1.29.55. **2.** of doves, *coo*, Poll.5.89. (Cf. Skt. *gañgūyati* 'utter cries of joy'.)

**γογγῠλάτης** [ᾰ], ου, ὁ, of Zeus, *hurling balls of fire*, Lyc.435.

**γογγύλη** [ῠ], ἡ, = γογγυλίς, Poll.6.54; rejected by the Atticists, Phryn.81, but used in the jargon of a Scythian in Ar.*Th.*1185, also by Diocl.*Frr.*125, 141, Dsc.2.110, Gal.11.861, Str.5.4.10, *POxy.*1212. 6 (ii A.D.). **II.** γ. ἀγρία, *Eastern cress*, *Erucaria aleppica*, Dsc.l.c.

⊛ **γογγῠλίδιον**, τό, = καταπότιον, Hp.ap.Erot. (γογγυλίδα codd.), Gal.19.91.

**γογγῠλίζω**, v. γογγύλλω.

⊛ **γογγῠλίς**, ίδος, ἡ, *turnip*, *Brassica Rapa*, Ar.*Fr.*569.6, Eub.4 (pl., Id.74), Speus.ap.Ath.9.369b, Thphr.*HP*7.4.3, *PPetr.*3 p.152 (iii B.C.), Dsc.5.20, *POxy.*736.5 (i A.D.).

⊛ **γογγύλλω**, *round* (μεταστρέφει Suid.), Ar.*Th.*56 (Pors. for γογγυλίζει); cf. γογγυλεῖν· συστρέφειν (perh. συστρέψειν), Hsch.

**γογγῠλοειδής**, ές, *roundish*, Sch.Nic.*Th.*855. Adv. -δῶς Dsc.5.18.

**γογγῠλό-ρυγχος**, ον, *with round nozzle*, *PMag.Par.*1.2183. **-σπᾰρᾰγον** [πᾰ], τό, *turnip-tops*, *Gp.*12.1.8.

⊛ **γογγύλος** [ῠ], η, ον, = στρογγύλος, *round*, A.*Fr.*199.7, S.*Ichn.*297, Pl.*Cra.*427c; [μᾶζα] Ar.*Pax* 28; λίθος ἄθετος *IG*1$^2$.372.22; ἐλαῖαι Plb. 12.2.4: Comp. -ώτερος Ath.4.139a. **2.** = σκληρός, Hsch. **II.** Subst. γόγγῠλος, ὁ, (proparox. acc. to Hdn.Gr.1.164) = κόνδυλος, Sch.Lyc.435. **2.** = ὄλυνθος, Nic.*Th.*855. (Redupl. form from root of γαυλός, γύλιος, etc.)

**γογγυλόσκηνος**, ον, *having a round body* (cf. σκῆνος), Hsch., *EM* 238.44; *having a round house*, Hsch. (Perh. epith. of a mollusc.)

**γογγῠλ-ώδης**, ες, *roundish*, Sch.Ar.*Pax* 788. **-ώματα**· στρογγυλεύματα, Hsch. **-ωπός**, όν, *round-faced, stout-looking*, Id. **-ωτόν**· *rapatum*, *Gloss.*

**γόγγ-ῠσις**, εως, ἡ, = sq., Lxx *Nu.*14.27. **-υσμός**, ὁ, *murmuring, muttering, grumbling*, Anaxandr.31, M.Ant.9.37, Lxx *Ex.*16.7–9, *Act.Ap.*6.1, *Cat.Cod.Astr.*7.139. **-ῠσος**, ὁ, = γογγυστής, Thd.*Pr.*16.28, Hdn.Gr.1.213. **-υστής**, οῦ, ὁ, *murmurer, mutterer, grumbler*, *Ep.Jud.*16, Thd.*Pr.*26.20. **-υστικός**, ή, όν, *inclined to murmur*, in Adv. -κῶς Erot. s. v. τρύζειν, *EM*771.11.

**γόγγων**· μωρός, Hsch. **γόδα**, τά, = ἔντερα (Maced.), Id. **γοδᾶν**· κλαίειν (Cypr.), Id. **γόδατος**· θήρα, Id. **γοδόν**· γόητα, Id. **γοδοῦλος**, v. γοιδοῦλος.

**γο-εδνός**, ή, όν, = sq. I, A.*Pers.*1057 (lyr.), *Supp.*73 (lyr.), 194. II. = sq. II, Id.*Pers.*1039 (lyr.). **-ερός**, ά, όν, (γόος) of things, *mournful, distressful*, θρῆνοι Erinna 6.8 codd.; πάθη A.*Ag.*1176 (lyr.); δάκρυα E.*Ph.*1567 (lyr.); τὸ γ. καὶ ἡσύχιον μέλος Arist.*Pr.*922$^{b}$19. II. of persons, *wailing, lamenting*, ἥξει τι μέλος γοερὸν γοεραῖς E.*Hec.*84; of the nightingale, Call.*Lav.Pall.*94. Adv. -ρῶς D.T.629.21, Eust. 1147.9. **-εροστ....ηνολαλήμων**, ονος, *uttering plaintive... notes*, ἀηδών Lyr. in *Philol.*80.336. **-ήμεναι**, v. γοάω. **-ήμων**, ον, gen. ονος, = γοερός I, φωνή *APl.*4.101, Nonn.*D.*11.196. II. = γ. II, ib.20.162; κύνες ib.5.454. **-ηρός**, ά, όν, poet. for γοερός, Lyc. 1057, *Epigr.Gr.*790.7 (Dyme).

**γόης**, ητος, ὁ, *sorcerer, wizard*, Phoronis 2, Hdt.2.33, 4.105, Pl.*R.* 380d, Phld.*Ir.*p.29 W.; γ. ἐπῳδὸς Λυδίας ἀπὸ χθονός E.*Ba.*234, cf. *Hipp.*1038; prob. f.l. for βοῆσι Hdt.7.191. 2. *juggler, cheat*, δεινὸς γ. καὶ φαρμακεὺς καὶ σοφιστής Pl.*Smp.*203d; δεινὸν καὶ γ. καὶ σοφιστὴν..ὀνομάζων D.18.276; ἄπιστος γ. πονηρός Id.19.109; μάγος καὶ γ. Aeschin.3.137: Comp. γοητότερος Ach.Tat.6.7 (s.v.l.). (Cf. Lith. *žavēti* 'incantare'.)

**γοησίοδος**· ᾠδός (leg. γοησιῳδός), ἀπατεών, Hsch.

**γοητ-εία**, ἡ, *witchcraft, jugglery*, γ. καὶ μαγεία Gorg.*Hel.*10, cf. Pl. *Smp.*203a: metaph., οὐδὲν ὑγιές, ἀλλὰ γ. τις Id.*R.*584a, Andronic. Rhod.p.573 M., etc.; ἀπάτη καὶ γ. Plb.4.20.5, cf. Luc.*Nigr.*15; γ. τῆς ὑποκρίσεως D.S.1.76; ἡδονῆς δι' ὀμμάτων Plu.2.961d; in a milder sense, '*finesse*', Cic.*Att.*9.13.4; ἡ τῆς φύσεως γ. the *magic* of Nature, Plot.4. 4.44. **-ευμα**, ατος, τό, *spell, charm*, Pl.*Phlb.*44c, Alciphr.3.17, Ael. *NA*3.17, Agath.*Praef.*; τὸ γ. τῆς φύσεως Porph.*Abst.*1.43. **-ευσις**, εως, ἡ, *sorcery*, Plot.4.4.43. **-ευτικός**, ή, όν, = γοητικός, Porph.*VP* 39, Poll.4.48. Adv. -κῶς ib.51. **-εύτρια**, ἡ, *sorceress*, Eust.881. 62. **-εύω**, *bewitch, beguile*, Pl.*Grg.*483e, etc.:—Pass., Id.*R.*412e, 413b, D.19.102, etc.; *fascinate*, as a snake, Plot.4.4.40. 2. abs., *play the wizard*, D.L.8.59. **-ής**, οῦ, ὁ, *wailer*, γοητῶν νόμον A.*Ch.* 822 codd. (γοατᾶν Herm.), cf. Tim.*Pers.*112. **-ικός**, ή, όν, (γόης) *skilled in witchcraft, juggling*, ἡ γ. μαγεία Arist.*Fr.*36. Adv. -κῶς Poll.4.51:—pecul. fem. γοῆτις μορφή *bewitching*, *AP*12.192 (Strat.). **γοητός** (sic) is prob. f.l. for foreg. in *PHib.*52.18 (iii B.C.).

❋ **γοῖ, γοῖ**, to imitate the sound of pigs *grunting*, *AP*11.327 (Antip. Thess.). II. γοί (i.e. ϝοί)· αὐτῷ, Hsch.

**γοῖδα** (i.e. ϝοῖδα)· οἶδα, Hsch. (prob. l.). **γοίδημι**· ἐπίσταμαι, Id. **γοιδοῦλος**· λαλιός, οἱ δὲ γοδοῦλος, Id. **γοιδύες**· δυτῆρες, Id. **γοίνακες**· βλαστοί, Id. **γοινά(ρ)υτις** (ϝοῖνος, ἀρύτω)· οἰνοχόη, Id. **γοινέες**· κόρακες, Id. **γοῖνος**· οἶνος, Id. **γοῖσος**· μέλαν, πλατύ, Id., cf. *EM*238.45: **γοισοῦται**· πλατύνεται κτλ., *EM*237.51. ❋ **γοῖτα**· οἷς (leg. ὗς), Hsch.; cf. γοῖ. ❋ **γοιταί**· κριθαί, γράστις, Id. **γοῖτος**· βίοτος, πάθος, Id., cf. *EM*51.17. **Γοιτόσυρος**, = Οἰτόσυρος (q.v.), Hsch. **γόλαμος**· διωγμός, Id. **γόλανα**· ἀγκύλη, ἀντιλαβεύς, Id. **γόλησις**· κακοδαιμονία, Id. **γόλλακα**· λάκκον, Id. **γόλμις**, = ψάρος, Id. **γολμοί**· στολμοί, Id. **γολοινά**· χλωρά, ἡ γολονά, Id. **γολομένη**, name of a *plant*, Id. **γολύριον**· κέλυφος (Tarent.), Id.

**γομάριον**, τό, Dim. of γόμος 2, *PFlor.*274.5 (iii A.D.).

**γόμνη**· ὀρίγανον, Hsch.

❋ **γόμος**, ὁ, (γέμω) *ship's freight, cargo*, A.*Supp.*444 (dub.), D.32. 4; πεντακισχιλίων ταλάντων γόμον ἔχειν to be of 5,000 talents *burden*, Hdt.1.194. 2. *beast's load*, Babr.7.11, Lxx *Ex.*23.5, al., *PAmh.*2.138.11 (pl., iv A.D.); γ. καμηλικός *OGI*629.87, al. (Palmyra, ii A.D.); γ. καρρικός ib.16. 3. *guild of transport-agents* in Nubia, *CIG*4980, al. II. γόμος· ζωμός, Hsch.

**γομοφόρος**, ον, *bearing loads*, *Gloss.*

**γομόω**, *load*, γομώσων τὸν ὄνον Babr.111.9, cf. *PFlor.*129.5 (iii A.D.), etc.:—Pass., ἅμαξα ξύλων γεγομωμένη *Edict.Diocl.*14.8.

**γομφ-αλγία**, ἡ, *toothache*, Dsc.4.164 (pl.). **-άριον**, τό, = κεστρεύς, Tz. ad Lyc.664, Sch.Opp.*H.*1.112, 3.339.

❋ **γομφι-άζω**, *have pain in the back teeth* or *gnash* them, γ. τοὺς ὀδόντας Lxx *Si.*30.10. 2. of the teeth, *suffer pain*, ib.*Ez.*18.2. **-ᾰσις**, εως, ἡ, *toothache* or *gnashing of teeth*, Dsc.2.59 (pl.). ❋ **-ασμός**, ὁ, Lxx *Am.*4.6.

**γομφιόδουπος**, ον, *rattling in the teeth*, χαλινός *AP*6.233 (Maec.).

**γομφ-ίος** (sc. ὀδούς), ὁ, more Att. than μύλος, Moer.111: (γόμφος): —*grinder-tooth, molar*, chiefly in pl., Hp.*Epid.*5.100, Hdt.9.83, Ar. *Pax* 34, etc.; ψοφεῖ δ' ὁ γ. Epich.21; γομφίους συγκρούων with his *teeth* chattering, Babr.92.8; opp. προσθίος, X.*Mem.*1.4.6, Arist.*PA* 661$^{b}$8. II. *tooth of a key*, Ar.*Th.*423. **-ίτης** [ῑ], ου, ὁ (fort. sc. νάρδος), a kind of στύραξ, Aet.1.131, Steph. *in Hp.*2.460 D.

**γομφό-δετος**, ον, *nail-bound*, δόρει A.*Supp.*846 (lyr.). **-παγής**, ές, *fastened with bolts*: metaph., *creaky*, ῥήματα γομφοπαγῆ, of the long compound words of Aeschylus, Ar.*Ra.*824.

❋ **γόμφος**, ὁ, *bolt*, for ship-building, Od.5.248; for other uses, Hes. *Op.*431, A.*Th.*542; *dowel*, *SIG*246 ii 40 (Delph., iv B.C.); γόμφοις καὶ περόνησιν ἀρηρότε Parm.1.20; γόμφῳ ἢ κόλλῃ ἢ ἁφῇ Arist.*Ph.*227$^{a}$17, cf. *Metaph.*1052$^{a}$24: generally, *bond, fastening*, as of the *cross-ribs* of Egyptian canoes, Hdt.2.96; of the ankle-joint, Arist.*PA*654$^{b}$21; of the invisible *bonds* uniting the particles of the body, Pl.*Ti.*43a: metaph., γ. κατάστοργοι, of love, Emp.87; τῶνδ' ἐφήλωται..γόμφος διαμπάξ these things are *determined*, A.*Supp.*945:—acc. to *EM*238. 4, γ. were prop. of wood; but cf. γ. χαλκοί *IG*9(1).691 (Corc.), γ. σιδηροῖ Plb.13.7.9. 2. *instrument for cautery*, *Hippiatr.*97. 3. = γόμφιος, Hsch. II. *sea-fish*, = γομφάριον, *Gloss.* (Cf. Skt. *jámbhas* 'tooth', Lith. *žam̃bas* 'edge of a beam', etc.)

❋ **γομφ-όω**, *fasten with bolts* or *nails*, esp. of ships, ἴκρια γομφώσαντες Nonn.*D.*40.447:—mostly in Pass., γεγόμφωται σκάφος the ship's hull *is ready built*, A.*Supp.*440, cf. Ar.*Eq.*463, *AP*11.248 (Bianor). II. metaph., *curdle*, γάλα λευκὸν ἐγόμφωσεν Emp.33. **-ωμα**, ατος, τό, *that which is fastened by bolts, frame-work*, Plu.*Marc.*15. 2. = γόμφος, Id.2.321d, Longus 2.26. 3. metaph., κλειδῶν ἀχαλκεύτων γ. Vett.Val.334.11 (pl.). **-ωσις**, εως, ἡ, *bolting together*, Sch. Theoc.7.105. II. a mode of *articulation*, Gal.2.738. 2. *framework* of the body, Eun.*VS* p.474 B. **-ωτήρ**, ῆρος, ὁ, *a ship-builder*, *AP*9.31 (Zelot.). II. *surgical instrument for excising bone*, Antyll.ap.Orib.44.23.15. **-ωτήριον**, τό, *tenon*, *IG*11(2).163*A* 14 (Delos, iii B.C.), Hero *Aut.*27.1; gloss on τέρετρα, Sch.Od.5. 246. **-ωτικός**, ή, όν, *of* or *fastening with nails*: ἡ -κή (sc. τέχνη), *the joiner's art, carpentry*, Pl.*Plt.*28cd. **-ωτός**, ή, όν, *fastened with bolts*: πλοῖα γ. ships *slightly put together*, so that they could be taken to pieces, Str.16.1.11, cf. Aristeas 71.

**γόμωσις**, εως, ἡ, *loading*, ξύλων *PFlor.*203.4 (iii A.D.).

**γονάρ**· μήτρα (Lacon.), Hsch.: **γονάδες**· μῆτραι, Id.

**γονᾰτ-ίζω**, *thrust with the knee*, Cratin.399. II. *bend the knee*, Aq.*Ge.*24.11, 41.43. III. σφυγμὸς γονατίζων, term coined by Archig.ap.Gal.8.665. **-ιον**, τό, Dim. of γόνυ, Heliod.ap.Orib. 48.66.3, Ruf.ap.eund.49.34.1, *POxy.*52.17 (iv A.D.). 2. *hip-joint, groin*, Luc.*Asin.*10, cf. Ph.2.479, Sch.Nic.*Th.*541, Ptol.*Alm.*8.1, etc. II. = γύης I, Procl. ad Hes.*Op.*425, *Et.Gud.* III. *knot* or *joint* of a reed, Tz.*H.*7.741.

**γονᾰτόδεσμος**, ὁ, *knee-band*, *Gloss.*

**γονᾰτ-όομαι**, Pass., *become* or *be jointed*, of grasses, reeds, etc., Thphr.*HP*8.2.4, Dsc.3.51. **-ώδης**, ες, *with joints*, Thphr.*HP* 1.5.3, Dsc.1.1, 4.29.

**γονάω**, = γεννάω, Hsch.

**γον-εά**, Cret. = γενεά, *GDI*5112 (Phaestus). **-εία**, ἡ, *generation*, Hdn.*Epim.*16. **-εύς**, έως, ὁ, *begetter, father*, mostly in pl., *parents*, *h.Cer.*240, Hes.*Op.*235, Pi.*P.*6.27, Pl.*Smp.*178b, etc.: in sg., of a serpent, Hdt.3.109; of a man, Pl.*R.*457d; φράζε τίνος γονέως *IG*12 (5).310: generally, *progenitor, ancestor*, πέμπτος γ. *ancestor* in the fifth generation, Hdt.1.91, cf. Is.8.32; οἱ ἄνωθεν γ. Arist.*GA*722$^{a}$8. (Nom. pl. γονεῖες *Histria* 7.27: acc. pl. γονέας Antiph.261: dat. pl. γονεῖσι *SIG*1267.24 (Ios, iii A.D.).) **-εύω**, *produce*, καρπούς Thphr. *CP*1.14.1; ἀὴρ [σκώληκας] γονεύων Id.*HP*8.10.5; of animals, Plu. 2.980d:—Pass., ib.981d.

❋ **γονή**, ἡ, (γενέσθαι) *offspring*, οἱ οὔ τι παίδων γ. γένετο κρειόντων Il. 24.539; γ. Ἀρκεισιάδαο Od.4.755; τέκνων δίπτυχος γ. two *children*, E.*Med.*1136: pl., εἰσὶ χἀτέροις γοναὶ κακαί S.*OC*1192; γ. κατηκόους φύσαντες Id.*Ant.*641; of animals, ταύρων γοναί A.*Fr.*194; ἐν..τετρασκελεῖ γ., i.e. among quadrupeds, S.*Fr.*941.10; *fruits* of the earth, Pl.*Ax.*371c. 2. *race, stock, family*, A.*Ag.*1565 (lyr.); ὦ γονὴ γενναῖε S.*OT*1469, cf. *El.*156 (lyr.); ἁ Δαρδάνου γ. E.*Tr.*1290: pl., μηδὲν ὢν γοναῖσι S.*Aj.*1094; *parentage*, ἐξευρεῖν γονάς E.*Ion*328. 3. *generation*, τριταισιν ἐν γ. Pi.*P.*4.143; τρίτος..πρὸς δέκ' ἄλλαισιν γ. A.*Pr.*774; τριτοσπόρῳ γονῇ Id.*Pers.*818. II. *that which engenders, seed*, Hes.*Op.*733, Hdt.3.101, 109, Hp.*Genit.*3, Arist.*GA*726$^{a}$18, etc.: pl., Pi.*N.*7.84, S.*Ant.*950 (lyr.). 2. *organs of generation*, generally, Hp.*Art.*45, *Mochl.*1 (also restricted to the *womb*, Ruf.*Onom.*193, Gal.2.889); πρὶν..μητρὸς ἐκ γονῆς μολεῖν E.*Ph.*1597. III. *act of generation*, Pi.*I.*7(6).7; κατὰ φύσιν γονὰς ποιεῖσθαι Aeschin.3. 111. 2. of the mother, *child-birth*, E.*Ph.*355, Theoc.17.44. 3. of the child, *birth*, ἐκ γονῆς Hp.*Epid.*4.31; γονῇ φῦναι γεραιτέρα S. *OC*1294; γοναὶ ζῴων Arist.*Mu.*399$^{a}$28. 4. cure for sterility, Paul. Aeg.3.74. IV. Pythag. name for *unity*, *Theol.Ar.*6.

**γόνημα**, ατος, τό, = γένημα, *PLond.*1.125.17.

**γονής**· νάρκισσος, Hsch.

**γόνθος**, = κόγχος, Hdn.Gr.1.144.

**γονιαῖος**, *molaris*, *Gloss.* (leg. γομφ-).

**γονίας** χειμών, in A.*Ch.*1067 (anap.), acc. to Hsch. εὐχερής, *a fair wind*; but, acc. to the Sch., ὅταν ἐξ εὐδίας κινηθῇ χαλεπὸν πνεῦμα.

**γονικόθεν**, Adv. *by inheritance from parents*, *PMasp.*151.182 (vi A.D.).

**γονικός**, ή, όν, (γονή II.1) *of the seed*, γ. ἔκκρισις Arist.*Pr.*879$^{b}$28. 2. *ancestral*, νόμοι Tim.*Lex.* s. v. πατρονομούμενοι.

❋ **γόνιμος**, ον, also η, ον Hp.*Vict.*1.25, Isyll.53:—*productive, fertile, fruitful*, σπέρμα γ., opp. ἄγονον, Arist.*HA*523$^{a}$25; κύημα γ. Id.*GA*736$^{a}$35; ᾠὰ γ., opp. ὑπηνέμια, ib.730$^{a}$6; of women, Id.*Pr.*876$^{b}$12; of the male, Id.*HA*546$^{a}$2, al.; ἐν τῇσι ἡλικίῃσι τῇσι γονίμῃσι εἶναι Hp.l.c.; γ. μέλεα a *parent's* limbs, E.*El.*1209 (lyr.); γ. φλέψ *AP*6.218 (Alc.); γ. μέρεα *generative* organs, Aret.*SD*2.5: hence (metaph.), ἀπὸ τίκτειν γ. τε καὶ ἀληθές Pl.*Tht.*150c; γ. ἢ ἀνεμιαῖον ib.151e; Νεῖλος γ., opp. πέλαγος, *Lyr.Alex.Adesp.*32.6, cf. *Sammelb.*2074 (Sup.). Adv. -μως, σπέρμα ἐν τῇ μήτρᾳ γ. κρατηθῆναι Porph.*Gaur.*2.2. 2. c. gen. rei, νέφος γ. ὕδατος Arist.*Mu.*394ᵃ27, cf. Thphr.*Ign.*44, Ael.*NA*7.5: metaph., πηγαὶ τῆς ὑψηγορίας γονιμώταται Longin.8.1. 3. metaph. of persons, ποιητὴς γ. poet *of true genius*, Ar.*Ra.*96; γονιμωτέρα γενέσθω ἡ γλῶσσα Luc.*Rh.Pr.*23. b. *born in lawful wedlock*, Man.6.56: metaph., ἀγαθὰ γ. τῇ αὐτῶν φύσει Pl.*R.*367d; γ. ὕδωρ ποταμῶν, opp. νόθον, *AP*9.277 (Antiph.). 4. = βιώσιμος, *viable*, παιδίον Hp. *Superf.*4; ἔμβρυον Arist.*HA*583ᵇ31; βρέφη Ph.1.45. 5. *favourable to generation*, of uneven days, Pythagorean term, Plu.2.288c; of days in illness (because critical for life or death, Erot.s.v.), Hp. *Epid.*2.6.8, 2.5.12; γ. μήν, ἔτος, ib.6.10.

**γονιμότης**, ητος, ἡ, *vitality*, of the embryo, *Theol.Ar.*47, Simp.*in Ph.*503.31. 2. *generative power*, Dam.*Pr.*108.

**γονιμώδης**, ες, *fruitful*, Orph.*H.*55.19.

**γονο-ειδής**, ές, *like seed*, Hp.*Epid.*2.3.11, Aret.*SA*2.12, *SD*2.11. **-εις**, εσσα, εν, *fruitful*, Nic.*Al.*101, *Hymn.Is* 1. **-κτονέω**, *murder one's child*, Ps.-Plu.*Fluv.*22.1. **-κτονία**, ἡ, *murder of parents*, *Gloss.* **-ποιέω**, *impregnate*, Aët.16.17; *make fruitful*, Al.*Le.*26.9, *Gp.*19.4, Sch.Lyc.899. **-ποιΐα**, *production of offspring*, Alex.Aphr.*Pr.*2.68. **-πώτης**, ου, ὁ, *qui semen bibit*, Man.4.311 (pl.). **-ρροια**, ἡ, (ῥέω) *spermatorrhoea*, Antyll.ap.Orib.6.1.5, Aret. *SD*2.5, Sor.ap.Cael.Aur.*CP*3.18. II. in women, *blennorrhagia*, Aret.*SD*2.11. **-ρροϊκός**, ή, όν, *suffering from* or *subject to*, Antyll.ap.Orib.6.22.3, J.*BJ*5.9.3 (v.l. -οιοις); πάθος Ruf.*Sat.Gon.*15. **-ρρυέω**, *to be subject to spermatorrhoea*, Lxx *Le* 22.4 (v.l.), Sch. Nic.*Th.*721. **-ρρυής**, ές, = γονορροϊκός, Lxx *Le.*15.4, al., Ph.1.88.

**γόνον**· μίτον, Hsch. (leg. τόνον).

**γόνος**, ὁ, and (in signf. I) ἡ, E.*IA*793: late Ion. **γοῦνος** Aret.*CD*2.5:—*that which is begotten, child*, Il.5.635, 6.191; *offspring*, 20.409, Hes. *Th.*919, etc; ἄπαις ἔρσενος γόνου Hdt.1.109; πρεσβύτατος παντὸς τοῦ γ. Id.7.2; αὐτὸν καὶ γόνον *Schwyzer*415 (Elis); ὁ Πηλέως γ. his *son*, S *Ph.*333, cf. 366, 416, etc.; of animals, γ. ὀρταλίχων Id.*Fr.*793; of fish, *roe*, Hegem.1, Archestr.*Fr.*9; of bees, Arist.*HA*554ᵃ18. 2. *product*, of plants, γ. ἀμπέλου *Anacreont.*54.7; γ. πλουτόχθων, of the silver mines at Laureion, A.*Eu* 946 (lyr.); τοῦ φόρου τὸν γ. Ar.*V.*1116 codd. 3. ἐς ἔρσενα γόνον to any of the male *sex*, Hdt.6.135. II. *race, stock, descent*, οὔ πώ τις ἑὸν γ. αὐτὸς ἀνέγνω Od.1.216, cf. 11.234. III. *begetting, procreation*, A.*Supp.*172 (lyr.); γόνῳ πατήρ, opp. ποιητός, Lys.13.91; γόνῳ γεγονώς D.44.49; γ. υἱός Men.*Sam.*131, D.C.40.51, cf. *IG*3.1445, al. 2. of plants, *bearing*, Thphr.*CP*3.15.3. IV. *seed*, Hp.*Genit.*7, Arist.*GA*748ᵃ22, Lxx *Le.*15.3; σπέρμα καὶ γ. Ti.Locr.100b, cf. Gal.19.450. 2. *genitals*, Hp.*Liqu.*2. V. γ. Ἑρμοῦ, = βούφθαλμος, Ps.-Dsc.3.139.

**γονοτύλη** [ῠ], ἡ, *callus on the knee*, Hsch.

* **γόνυ**, τό, gen. γόνατος, Ep. and Ion. γούνατος (for γόνϝατος) Il.21.591, Hdt.2.80: pl. nom. γούνατα Il.5.176, Hes.*Op.*587, Hdt.1.199, *Schwyzer*694.7 (Chios, iv B.C.), gen. γουνάτων Hdt.9.76, dat. γούνασι Il.9.455, Hdt.4.152 (also Pi.*I.*2.26), γονάτεσσι Theoc.16.11, *Epigr.Gr.*782 (Halic.); also Ep. gen. γουνός (expl. as for γόνυος by Hdn.Gr.2.768, A.D.*Synt.*342.9) Il.11.547: pl. γοῦνα 6.511; γούνων 1.407, al.: dat. γούνεσσι 9.488, al. (v.l. γούνασσι):—Aeol. acc. pl. γόνα Alc.39.7 (prob.), but γόννα acc. to St.Byz. s.v. Γόννοι, Eust.335.39: gen. pl. γόνων Alc.*Supp.*10: E. has γουνάτων *Hec.*752, 839, γούνασι *Supp.*285 (lyr.), *Andr.*529 (lyr.), but not γουνός (γοῦν' acc. pl. was read by Sch. in *Ph.*852): gen. pl. γεύνων, Hsch.:—*knee*, γόνυ γουνὸς ἀμείβων Il.11.547, etc.: freq. of *clasping the knees* in earnest supplication, ἥψατο γούνων 1.512; ἑλεῖν, λαβεῖν γούνων 21.71, 1.407, etc.; τῶν γουνάτων λαβέσθαι Hdt.9.76; ποτὶ (v.l. περὶ) or ἀμφὶ γούνασί τινος χεῖρας βαλεῖν Od.6.310, 7.142; περὶ γόνυ χέρας ἱκεσίους ἔβαλον E.*Or.*1414, cf. *Ph.*1622, etc.; τὰ σὰ γούναθ' ἱκάνομαι Il.18.457, cf. Od.7.147, etc.; κιχανόμενοι τὰ σὰ γοῦνα ἱκόμεθ' 9.266; ἀντίος ἤλυθε γούνων Il.20.463; γόνυ σὸν ἀμπίσχειν χερὶ E.*Supp.*165; σοῖς προστίθημι γόνασιν ὠλένας Id.*Andr.*895; ἐς γούνατά τινι or τινος πεσεῖν Hdt.5.86, S.*OC*1607; ἀμφὶ γόνυ τινὸς πίπτειν E.*Hec.*787; γόνυ τινός or πρὸς γόνυ προσπίπτειν ib.339, *HF*79; γόνασί τινος προσπίπτειν Id. *Or.*1332 (but προσπίτνω σε γόνασιν *on my knees*, S.*Ph.*485); πίπτειν πρὸς τὰ γ. τινος, τινι, Lys.1.19, D.19.198; also γούνων λίσσεσθαι Il.9.451; ἐλλιτανεύειν Od.10.481; γουνάζεσθαι Il.22.345; ἅντεσθαι πρὸς τῶν γονάτων E.*Med.*710; ἱκετεῦσαι πρὸς τ. γ. D.58.70. 2. of a sitting posture, φησί μιν ἀσπασίως γ. κάμψειν will be glad to bend *the knee* so as to sit down and rest, Il.7.118, cf. 19.72; but also, bow *the knee* in submission, ἐμοὶ κάμψει (intr.) πᾶν γ. Lxx *Is.*45.23; γ. ὀκλάζειν τινί ib.3*Ki.*19.18, v. sub κάμπτω: ἐπὶ γούνασι *on* one's *knees*, ἐπὶ γούνασι πατρός Il.22.500; ποτὶ γ. 5.408; γούνασιν ἐφέσσεσθαι φίλον υἱόν 9.455; σ' ἐπ' ἐμοῖσι..γούνεσσι καθίσσας 9.488; τόν ῥά οἱ.. ἐπὶ γούνασι θῆκεν Od.19.401; ἐν τοῖς γόνασί τινος στρέφεσθαι Pl.*R.*617b; πέπλον..θεῖναι Ἀθηναίης ἐπὶ γούνασιν to lay it on her *lap* (as an offering), Il.6.92, cf. *Schwyzer* l.c.: hence metaph., θεῶν ἐν γούνασι κεῖται it rests *in the lap of*.., Il.17.514, Od.1.267, etc.; but ἐν γούνασιν πίτνοντα Νίκας victorious, Pi.*I.*2.26. 3. of the knees as the seat of strength, ἐν δὲ βίην ὤμοισι καὶ ἐν γούνεσσιν ἔθηκε Il.17.569; of swiftness, λαιψηρὰ γ. 22.204, etc.; γούνατά τινος λύειν disable, kill him, 5.176, etc.; ὑπὸ γούνατ' ἔλυσεν 11.579; βλάπτειν γ. τινι, κάματος δ' ὑπὸ γ. ἐδάμνα, 7.271, 21.52:—Pass., αὐτοῦ λύτο γούνατα 21.114, etc. 4. metaph., ἐς γόνυ βάλλειν bring down upon *the knee*, i.e. humble, conquer, Hdt.6.27; ἐς γ. ῥίπτειν, κλίνειν, App.*BC*3.20, 30; ἐς γ. ἐλθεῖν Procop.*Arc.*14, *Pers.*1.17; Ἀσία δὲ χθών..ἐπὶ γόνυ κέκλιται A.*Pers.*931 (lyr.). 5. prov., ἀπωτέρω ἢ γόνυ κνάμα 'blood is thicker than water', 'charity begins at home', Theoc.16.18; γ. κνήμης ἔγγιον Arist.*EN*1168ᵇ8, Ath.9.383b. II. *joint* of grasses or plants, Hdt.3.98, X.*An.*4.5.26, Thphr.*HP*8.2.4, Porph.*Antr.*19. (Cf. Skt. *jānu*, Lat. *genu*, etc.)

* **γονῠ-αλγής**, ές, *suffering pain in the knee*, Hp.*Epid.*6.4.11. **-καμψεπίκυρτος**, ον, *twisting the knee awry*, of the gout, Luc.*Trag.*203. **-κανσαγρύπνα**, ἡ, *keeping awake by inflammation of the knee*, ib.201. **-κλῐνέω**, *bend the knee*, Eust.669.32. **-κλῐνής**, ές, *on bended knee*, γ. ἐχόμενός τινος *POxy.*1089.31 (iii A.D.). **-κλῐτέω**, = γονυκλινέω, Simp.*in Epict.*p.107 D. **-κροτος**, ον, *knocking the knees together*, of the gait of women, Arist.*HA*538ᵇ10 (Comp.); of effeminate men, Anacr.144, Arist.*Phgn.*808ᵃ13, 810ᵃ34. **-πετέω**, *fall on the knee*, Plb.15.29.9, etc. 2. *fall down before* one, τινά *Ev. Matt.*17.14, cf. *Ev.Marc.*1.40: abs., Corn.*ND*12. **-πετής**, ές, (πεσεῖν) *falling on the knee*, Tim.*Pers.*189; ἕδραι γ. a *kneeling* posture, E.*Ph.*293. **-πλήξ**, *ruscus*, *Gloss.*

**γονώδης**, ες, = γονοειδής, Hp.*Coac.*446.

**γονώνη**· ὀρίγανος, Hsch.

**γόον**, v. γοάω.

**γόος**, ὁ, *weeping, wailing*, σχέθε δ' ὄσσε γόοιο Od.4.758; also of *louder signs of grief*, ib.103; ἐρικλάγκταν γόον Pi.*P.*12.21; ἀρίδακρυς γ., πολύδακρυς γ., A.*Pers.*949 (lyr.), *Ch.*449 (lyr.); γόους δακρύειν S. *Aj.*579; οἰκτρὰς γ. ὄρνιθος, of the nightingale, ib.629 (lyr.); γ. τινός *grief for* one, Q.S.3.644; so γόους πρὸς αὐτὴν [τούτων] θησόμεσθ', ἃ πάσχομεν *for* our sufferings, E.*Or.*1121: in late Prose, Lxx 3*Ma.*1.18 (pl.), al.

**γοράπιες**· ῥάφανοι, Hsch.

**γοράτου**· ἠφινόν, οἱ δὲ ῥανῶ, Id.

**Γοργάς**, άδος, ἡ, = Γοργώ, Phot. s.v. πλόκιον Γοργάδος: pl., E. *Hyps.Fr.*41(64).77. 2. ἡ παλίμφρων Γ., of Hera, Lyc.1349. II. in pl., *sea-nymphs*, S.*Fr.*163:—also **Γοργίδες**, Hsch.

**Γόργειος**, α, ον, *of* or *belonging to the Gorgon*, Γοργείη κεφαλή Il.5.741, Od.11.634; Γόργειον, τό, *a Tragic mask*, *EM*238.46, Poll.10.167, etc.

* **γοργεύω**, *move rapidly, hasten*, Sm.*Ec.*10.10, Hsch. 2. *busy oneself*, τινί or μετά τινος *PPar.*18.6.12 (ii A.D.).

**γοργία**, *agilitas*, *Gloss.*

**Γοργῐ-άζω**, *speak like Gorgias*, Philostr.*VS*1.16.2. * **-ειος**, ον, *of Gorgias, Gorgias-like*, ῥήματα X.*Smp.*2.26; σχήματα D.H.*Dem.*5; of vases, *called after one Gorgias*, *IG*11(2).128.31, al. (Delos, iii B.C.).

**Γοργολόφας**, ου, ὁ, *he of the Gorgon-crest*, Ar.*Ach.*567:—fem. **Γοργολόφα**, ης, ἡ, Id.*Eq.*1181.

**Γοργονεία** (sc. λίθος), ἡ, *coral*, Plin.*HN*37.164: **Γοργονιὰς** βοτάνη, *Gorgon-like plant*, Dam.*Isid.*68.

**Γοργόνειος**, ον, = Γοργεῖος, πεδία A.*Pr.*793; τὸ Γ. *a Gorgon-mask*, *IG*2.654, al., cf. Plu.*Them.*10; *the Gorgon's head*, a group of stars in Perseus, Gem.3.11, Ptol.*Alm.*7.5, etc., Plu.*Them.*10; but also, the constellation *Medusa*, Hipparch.2.3.27, al.; *bogey*, Ruf.ap.Orib. *inc.*20.27; Orphic name for the *moon*, because of the face in it, Orph.*Fr.*33. II. Γ., τό, = λιθόσπερμον, Ps.-Dsc.3.141.

**Γοργόνη**, ἡ, = Γοργώ, Hdn.*Epim.*17, Suid.

**Γοργόνιον**, τό, = ἠρύγγη, Ps.-Dsc.3.21.

**Γοργονώδης**, ες, *Gorgon-like*, Sch.E.*Ph.*146.

**Γοργόνωτος** ἀσπίδος κύκλος, ἡ, a shield *with the Gorgon on it*, Ar. *Ach.*1124.

**γοργόομαι**, Pass., *to be spirited*, of a horse, X.*Eq.*10.4.

* **γοργός**, ή, όν, *grim, fierce, terrible*, γ. ὄμμ' ἔχων, of Parthenopaeus, A.*Th.*537; ὄμμασι γοργὸς E.*Ph.*146 (lyr.); τοῖς κερτομοῦσι γοργὸν ὡς ἀναβλέπει looks *fiercely* at.., dub. l. in Id.*Supp.*322; γοργότεροι ἰδεῖν, δρᾶσθαι, *terrible* to behold, X.*Cyr.*4.4.3, *Smp.*1.10; γοργὸν βλέπειν look *terrible*, Ael.*VH*2.44; of horses, γ. ἰδεῖν X.*Eq.*10.17; ἵππου γ. βλέμμα Poll.1.192; in Ephebic Inscrr., φίλοι, γοργοί, γνήσιοι, *IG*3.1079. 2. *spirited, vigorous*, of persons, Luc.*DDeor.*7.3, *Asin.*8; of animals, *PRyl.*238.9 (iii A.D.); *quick*, c. inf., γ. ἐπινοεῖν Procop. *Arc.*16. Adv. -γῶς, τρέχειν Choerob.Rh.p.247 S. 3. of literary style, *vehement, vigorous*, v.l. in D.H.*Comp.*19 (Comp.), Hermog. *Id.*1.11, 2.1 (Comp.). Adv. -γῶς Syrian. *in Metaph.*130.6, Eust.1082.5, etc.

**γοργότης**, ητος, ἡ, *rapidity*, Sm.*Ec.*2.21, *Gloss.* II. of style, *vehemence, vigour*, Hermog.*Id.*2.1, Procl.*in Prm.*p.509 S., Sch.Od.1.110, etc.

* **Γοργοτομία**, ἡ, (τέμνω) *cutting off the Gorgon's head*, Str.8.6.2.

**γοργόφθαλμος**, ον, = γοργωπός, Suid. s.v. γοργῶπις.

**Γοργοφόνος**, ον, *Gorgon-killing*, E.*Fr.*985: fem. Γοργοφόνα, as a name of Athena, Id.*Ion* 1478 (lyr.).

* **γόργῡρα** (Dor. γέργ-), ἡ, *underground drain* or *sewer*, Alcm.132, cf. *AB*233, Hsch.: used as *a dungeon*, Hdt.3.145, cf. Harp., etc.

**Γοργώ**, ἡ, *the Gorgon*, i.e. *the Grim One* (cf. γοργός), Hes.*Sc.*224, 230: acc. pl., Γοργούς Id.*Th.*276.—Sg. Γοργώ Il.11.36: gen. Γοργοῦς 8.349, Hes.*Sc.*224, E.*Or.*1521, *Ion*1003, etc.; also Γοργών Id.*Rh.*306: gen. Γοργόνος Id.*Fr.*360.46, *Ph.*456 (s.v.l.): acc. Γοργόνα Id. *Or.*1520: pl. Γοργόνες, acc. -ας, are the regul. forms (but v. supr.), Hes.*Sc.*230, A.*Pr.*799, al.: gen. Γοργόνων Pi.*P.*12.7, E.*Ba.*990 (lyr.).

* **γοργ-ωπός**, όν, *fierce-eyed, grim-eyed*, σέλας A.*Pr.*358; κόραι E.*HF* 868; ἴτυς Id.*Ion*210 (lyr.); γοργωπὰ λεύσσων Id.*Hyps.Fr.*16(18); ἀλέκτωρ *AP*7.428 (Mel.); τὸ γ. Corn.*ND*20. **-ώψ**, ῶπος, ὁ, ἡ, = foreg., E.*El.*1257, *Or.*261:—fem. * **-ῶπις**, ιδος, of Athena, S.*Aj.*450, *Fr.*844.

**γοργώψατο**· πικρὸν ἔβλεψε, Hsch.

**γορδελίζειν**· ἀδολεσχεῖν, Id.

**Γόριλλαι**, αἱ, name of a tribe of hairy women (but prob. *gorilla*), Hanno *Peripl.*18.

**γορός**· κυρτός, Hsch., Cyr., Zonar. (Perh. f. l. for γυρός.)

**Γορπιαῖος**, ὁ (sc. μήν), name of a Macedonian month, J.*BJ*2.17.8, Plu.*Thes.*20, etc.; at Nysa, *SIG*781.4 (i B.C.).

**γόρτυξ**· ὄρτυξ, Hsch. **γόρυνος**· μῦς, βάτραχος, Id.; ὁ μικρὸς βάτραχος, Zonar. (Cf. γύρινος.)

**γορυνίας**, Boeotian name for μυρσίνη ἀγρία, Ps.-Dsc.2.110.

**γορφ΄α**, τά, *stocks from which olive-trees are struck* (Aram. *g*ᵉ*rōphith*), *Gp* 9.5.12.

**γοτάν**· ὗν (Maced.), Hsch.

**γουβενάριον**, τό, dub. in *POxy.*921 *Intr.* (iii A.D.).

**γουβικός**, f. l. for κυβικός, Hero *Stereom.*1.48.

**γοῦν** or γ' οὖν, Ion. and Dor. **γῶν** (γε οὖν); restrictive Particle with an inferential force, *at least then*, freq. scarcely distinguishable from simple γε: twice in Hom. (with a second γε added), εἴ γ' οὖν ἕτερός γε φύγῃσιν Il.5.258; μή ἐμέ γ' οὖν οὗτός γε 16.30 (so ἔοικα γοῦν τούτου γε..σοφώτερος εἶναι Pl.*Ap.*21d); freq. later, δοκέων πάγχυ δευτερεῖα γῶν οἴσεσθαι Hdt.1.31; γνώσει..ὄψὲ γοῦν τὸ σωφρονεῖν A.*Ag.*1425, cf. 432 (lyr.), etc.; freq. in adducing an instance, or a fact giving rise to a presumption, Heraclit.58, Th.1.2, X.*Cyr.*1.5.8; τὸν γοῦν ἄλλον χρόνον in past time *at all events*, D.20.16; emphasizing a personal or possessive pronoun, τὸ γ. ἐμόν S.*OT*626, cf. *Ant.*45; introducing an apodosis, Pl.*Alc.*1.112b; simply emphatic, *why yes*, E.*Ph.*618, Pl.*Sph.*219d, etc.; each Particle has its full force in τὰς γοῦν Ἀθήνας οἶδα *well* (οὖν), I know *Athens* (γε), S.*OC*24:—freq. separated by a word, πάνυ γ' ἂν οὖν Ar.*Ec.*806, cf. Th.1.76, etc.:—rarely γε οὖν in full, D.H.2.56 codd. (The negat. form is οὔκουν..γε.)

**γοῦνα, γούνων**, poet. pl. of γόνυ (q. v.).

**γουνάζομαι**, fut. -σομαι: aor. 1 γουνασάμεσθα Orph.*A.*618, subj. γουνάσσηαι A.R.4.747, cf. Orph.*A.*943: (γόνυ):—Ep. Verb, *clasp* another's *knees* (v. sub γόνυ I. 2): hence, *implore, entreat*, abs., Il. 11.130: c. inf., τῶν ὕπερ..γουνάζομαι οὐ παρεόντων ἑστάμεναι κρατερῶς in whose name..I *implore* you to stand your ground, 15.665; νῦν δέ σε πρὸς πατρὸς γουνάζομαι Od.13.324; νῦν δέ σε τῶν ὄπιθεν γ., ..πρός τ' ἀλόχου καὶ πατρός 11.66; μή με..γούνων γουνάζεο *entreat* me not by [clasping] my knees, Il.22.345.

**γούν-ασμα**, ατος, τό, *supplication*, Lyc.1243:—also **-ασμός**, ὁ, Eust.627.9.

**γούνατα, γούνασι**, Ep. **γούνεσσι**, etc., v. γόνυ.

**γουνιαῖος** τόπος, sine expl., Hsch. **γουννοννία**· σάμψυχος, Id.

**γουνόομαι** (also -έομαι, Hsch.), contr. -οῦμαι, = γουνάζομαι, only pres. and impf., γουνοῦμαι Il.21.74, Od.6.149, Archil.75, Anacr.1.1, etc.; γουνούμην Od.11.29; γουνοῦσθαι 10.521; γουνούμενος 4.433, etc.

**γουνο-πᾰχής**, ές, *thick-kneed*, v. l. **γουνο-πᾰγής**, *cramping the knees*, Ἀχλύς Hes.*Sc.*266.

**γουνός**, ὁ, *high ground*, φυτὸν ὣς γουνῷ ἀλωῆς Il.18.57; ἀνὰ γουνὸν ἀλωῆς οἰνοπέδοιο Od.1.193, etc.; ἐκ Κρήτης ἐς γουνὸν Ἀθηνάων 11.323; τῆς Ἀττικῆς..τὸν γ. τὸν Σουνιακόν Hdt.4.99: pl., γουνοῖσιν Ἐλευθῆρος μεδέουσα Hes.*Th.*54; γουνοῖσιν κατένασσε Νεμείης ib.329; ἐν γουνοῖς Ἀθανᾶν Pi.*I.*4(3).25. (Expld. as τόπος γονιμώτατος by Sch.Il. l.c., but better as ὑψηλὸς τόπος (cf. γόνυ) Orion 38, *EM*239.5.)

✻ **γούντη**, ἡ (Lydian word), *tomb*, Keil-Premerstein *Zweiter Bericht* 255 (iii A.D.):—also **γουτάριον**, τό, Ramsay *Cities and Bishoprics* No. 566.

**γοῦρος**, ὁ, a kind of *cake*, Sol.38.3.

**γουττᾶτον**, τό, a kind of *cake*, Chrysipp.Tyan.ap.Ath.14.647c.

**γοώδης**, ες, *mournful*, ἁρμονίαι Pl.*Lg.*800d (Sup.); φωνή Arist. *HA*615ᵇ5.

**γρᾶ**, v. γράω.

✻ **γράα**, ἡ, a kind of *serpent*, *Peripl.M.Rubr.*38.

**γραβάν**· σκάφιον, βόθρον, Hsch. ✻ **γράβατος**, v. κράβατος.

**γράβδην**, Adv., (γράφω) *grazing, scraping*, Eust.852.8, *EM*781. 27.

**γραβδίς**, ἡ, = sq., *EM*239.28 (acc. γράβδις, Sch.D.T.p.197 H.).

**γράβιον**, τό, *torch*, Strattis 50, Amerias ap.Ath.15.699e, prob. in S.*Fr.*177 (pl.).

**γράζα**, v. γηράσκω. **γράθμα**, v. γράμμα.

✻ **γραῖα**, late Poet. nom **γραίη**, Dor. **γραία** (only gen. sg. in Hom.), ἡ, *old woman*, Od.1.438, S.*Tr.*870, E.*Tr.*465, al.: as Adj., γραῖαι δαίμονες, of the Eumenides, A.*Eu.*150 (lyr.), cf. 69. 2. as Adj., of things, *old*, γραίας ἐρείκης Id.*Ag.*295; γραίας ἀκάνθης S.*Fr.*868; γραῖαν ὠλένην E.*Ion*1213; γραίῃ χερὶ Id.*Hec.*877; γραῖαν πηρᾶν Theoc.15.19; σταφυλὴ γραίη *raisins*, *AP*6.231 (Phil.). 3. Γραῖαι, αἱ, *the Graiae*, with hair grey from their birth, Hes.*Th.*270, prob. in A.*Fr.*262. II. = γραῦς II, *scum* or *skin which forms over boiled milk*, etc., Arist.*Pr.*893ᵇ32. III. *folds of skin below the navel*, Ruf. *Onom.*99, Poll.2.170. IV. = γραῦς III, *sea-crab*, Epich.61. V. = κάρδοπος, Hsch.

**γραιβία** or **γραιτία** (i. e. γραιϝία)· πανηγυρίς (Tarent.), Hsch.

**γρᾱΐδιον**, τό, Dim. of γραῦς, *old hag*, Ar.*Pl.*536:—elsewh. contr. **γρᾴδιον**, ib.674, Philyll.5, X.*An.*6.3.22, D.18.260, Men.*Georg.*54, etc.: barbarous form γρᾴδιο Ar.*Th.*1194.

**γραΐζω** (γραῦς II), *skim milk*, etc., Ar.*Fr.*446.

✻ **Γραικός**, ὁ, *Greek*, Ἕλληνες ὠνομάσθησαν τὸ πρότερον Γραικοὶ καλούμενοι *Marm.Par.*11 (iv B.C.), cf. Arist.*Mete.*352ᵇ2, Apollod.1.7.3, Call.*Fr.*104, Lyc.532, etc.; Γραῖκες Alcm.134, S.*Fr.*518 is of doubtful meaning, cf. also Ῥαικός:—hence ✻ **Γραικ-ίτης**, ου, ὁ, Lyc.605: **-ίζω**, *speak Greek*, Hdn.*Epim.*12: **-ιστί**, *in Greek*, *EM*239.19. (Local name for a tribe in West Greece, applied by the Italians to Greeks in general.)

**γραίνω**, = γράω, *gnaw*, Hsch. **γραιολέας**· πονηρὰς ἢ ὀλεθρίας γραίας, Id.

**γραιόομαι**, Pass., *become aged, withered*, of a vine, *AP*9.261 (Epigon.).

**γραΐς**, ΐδος, ἡ, = γραῦς, γραῖα, Charito 6.1, *PMag.Lond.*125.21 (v A.D.), Palch. in *Cat.Cod.Astr.*1.95.

**γραιωπίας**, ου, ὁ, *man like an old woman*, Hsch. **γραμαιτιτά**, γραμματευτά, Hsch.

✻ **γράμμα**, ατος, τό, Dor. **γράθμα**, prob. in *IG*4.506 (Heraeum, vi/v B.C.), cf. *An.Ox.*1.102, but **γράσσμα**, *IG*4.554 (Argos, v B.C.): late Aeol. pl. **γρόππατα**, *Epigr.Gr.*990.11 (Balbilla): (γράφω):—*that which is drawn*: pl., *lines of a drawing, picture*, etc., E.*Ion*1146 (of tapestry), Theoc.15.81; *picture*, Ἀπέλλεω γ. Herod.4.73, cf. *AP* 6.352 (Erinna): sg., *drawing, picture*, Pl.*R.*472d, *Cra.*430e, cf. 431c: pl., *figures* in a picture, Procop.Gaz.*Ecphr.*p.157 B. II. *written character, letter*, Hdt.1.139, 148, etc.: in pl., *letters, characters*, γραμμάτων τε συνθέσεις A.*Pr.*460; πηλίκοις γ. *Ep.Gal.*6.11; *the letters, the alphabet*, Hdt.5.58; τὰ γ. καὶ τὰς συλλαβάς Pl.*Cra.*390e; γ. Φοινίκια S.*Fr.*514; Ἀσσύρια, Ἑλληνικά, Hdt.4.87; γράμματα ἐπίστασθαι Pl.*Lg.*689d; μαθεῖν to have learnt *to read*, Id.*Prt* 325e; γ. μὴ εἰδέναι *SIG*²844.6; ἐδίδασκες γράμματα, ἐγὼ δ' ἐφοίτων you *kept school*—I went there, D.18.265; ἤτοι τέθνηκεν ἢ διδάσκει γ. *Com. Adesp.*20; παιδεύειν γράμματα Arist.*Pol.*1337ᵇ24; τέχνη ἡμῶν γ. our profession is that of the *scribe*, *PTeb.*316.16 (i A.D.). b. *articulate sound, letter*, Pl.*Phlb.*18c; τὰ γ. πάθη ἐστὶ τῆς φωνῆς Arist.*Pr.*895ᵃ 12; γράμματα φθέγγεσθαι ib.8, cf. *PA*660ᵃ5. c. παρὰ γράμμα λέγοντα..σκοπεῖν *etymologically*, Id.*MM*1185ᵇ39; τὰ παρὰ γ. σκώμματα puns, Id.*Rh.*1412ᵃ28; but ἀρετὴν παρὰ γ. διώκοντες, with ref. to Νικαρέτη, the mistress of Stilpo, Crates Theb.1. d. *inscription*, τὸ Δελφικὸν γ. Pl.*Phdr.*229e, cf. *Chrm.*164d, X.*Mem.*4.2.24, etc., *IG* 2.2876, al.: prov., εἰς πέλαγος..γράμματα γράψαι *Epigr.Gr.*1038.8 (Attalia). 2. in pl., *notes* in music, *AP*11.78 (Lucill.). 3. mathematical *diagram*, Epigr.ap.D.L.8.12. 4. *letter* inscribed on the lots which the δικασταί drew, Ar.*Pl.*277, al., Arist.*Ath.*64.4; practically, = *division* of dicasts, ἐν ὁποίῳ γ. δειπνεῖ Ar.*Ec.*683; ὁ κατὰ γράμμα φυλακά the *roster* of guards, *SIG*569.21 (Cos, iii B.C.). b. *quarters* of a town, *PRein.*49.2; *accent*, *EM*240.42, Zonar. 5. a small weight, $\frac{1}{24}$ *ounce, scruple*, Androm.ap.Gal.13.114, *Gp.*7.13.2, *PLips.*62 ii 27 (iv A.D.). III. in pl., *set of written characters, piece of writing*, Hdt.1.124: hence, *letter*, Id.5.14, *IG*2².103.8, etc.; γραμμάτων πτυχαί S.*Fr.*144, cf. E.*IT*594, al., Pl.*Ep.*347c; *inscription, epitaph*, etc., ἐκόλαψε ἐς τὸν τάφον γράμματα λέγοντα τάδε Hdt. 1.187, cf. 4.91, And.3.12, Theoc.18.47, *IG*3.751. 2. *papers, documents*, Antipho 1.30, D.36.21, etc. (sg., D.Chr.65.14); τούτων τὰ γ. the *documents to prove* this, Lys.32.14; τὰ γ. τῆς δίκης Ar.*Nu.*772; τὰ δημόσια γ. the public *records*, Decr.ap.D.18.55; *title-deeds*, D.C.65. 14; *account* of loans, D.49.59; ἐπικαρπίαν ἐν γράμμασιν ἀποφέρειν Pl. *Lg.*955d; *contract* or *estimate*, *BCH*46.323 (Teos); *catalogue*, X.*Cyr.*7. 4.12: in sg., *bond*, *Ev.Luc.*16.7; *note of hand*, J.*AJ*18.6.3. 3. a man's *writings*, i. e. *book, treatise*, τὰ τοῦ Ζήνωνος γ. Pl.*Prm.*127c (but sg., ib.128a): pl., *books*, X.*Mem.*4.2.1; Πλάτωνος τὸ περὶ ψυχῆς γ. Call.*Ep.*25, cf. *AP*9.63 (Asclep.), Gal.18(2).928; τὰ ἱερὰ γ. the Holy *Scriptures*, *OGI*56.36 (iii B.C.), Ph.2.574, *2Ep.Ti.*3.15, J.*Ap.*1.10; ἱερὰ γ., = Imperial *rescripts*, *IG*12(5).132 (Paros, iii A.D.); = *hieroglyphics*, *OGI*90.54 (Rosetta, ii B.C.): in sg., the *Law* of Moses, *Ep. Rom.*2.27, al.; opp. πνεῦμα, ib.29: sg., *article* of a treaty, Th. 5.29. 4. *laws* or *rules*, Pl.*R.*425b, *Plt.*292a, al., Ar.*Ec.*1050; κατὰ γράμματα ἄρχειν, opp. ἄνευ γραμμάτων, Pl.*Plt.*293a; ἡ κατὰ γ. καὶ νόμους πολιτεία Arist.*Pol.*1286ᵃ15, cf. 1272ᵃ38: οἱ κατὰ γ. νόμοι, opp. οἱ κατὰ τὰ ἔθη, ib.1287ᵇ5, cf. Pl.*Plt.*299d; κατὰ γράμματα ἰατρεύεσθαι Arist.*Pol.*1287ᵃ34; ἡ ἐκ τῶν γ. θεραπεία ib.40. IV. in pl., also, *letters, learning*, ἀπείρους γραμμάτων Pl.*Ap.*26d, etc.

**γραμμαθέπτα**· δραπέτα, Hsch. (leg. γράμμαθ' ἑπτά).

✻ **γραμμάριον**, τό, *weight of two obols*, Aët.7.117.

**γραμμᾰτ-εία**, ἡ, *office of* γραμματεύς, *PTeb.*30.18 (ii B.C.), Plu. *Comp.Sert.Eum.*1, *BGU*587.11 (ii A.D.); the *term* of such office, *JRS*2.243 (Phrygia). II. *learning*, Lxx *Si.*44.4. **-είδιον**, τό, Dim. of γραμματεῖον, *small tablet*, Antipho 5.53, D.54.37, Thphr. *Char.*6.8, Plu.*Brut.*5, etc.; γ. δίθυρον Men.327; *menu*, Ath.2.49d; *memorandum*, Jul. *ad Ath.*277b. (γραμματίδιον which is freq. found in codd., cf. *PLips.*111.5 (iv A.D.), is expl. as Dim. of γράμματα by Gramm., cf. Hdn.Gr.2.488.) **-ειδιοποιός**, ὁ, *a maker of tablets*, title of plays by Apollodorus of Carystus (Ath.7.280d) and Apollodorus of Gela (Poll.4.19). ✻ **-εῖον**, τό, *that on which one writes, tablets*, Ar.*Fr.*157, Antipho 1.10, Pl.*Prt.*326d, prob. in Gorg.*Pal.*6; *tablet* on which names, etc., are recorded, λελευκωμένα γ. Arist.*Ath.* 47.2, cf. D.46.11, *IG*2.91.11, etc. 2. *bond, document, contract*, Lys. 32.7; κατὰ γραμματεῖον ᾑταιρηκέναι Aeschin.1.165, cf. *POxy.*101.*Fr.* 9 ii 15; *account-book, ledger*, Ar.*Nu.*19, D.45.33: freq. written γραμμάτιον. 3. τὸ ληξιαρχικὸν γ. *list in which* Athenian citizens *were enrolled*, *IG*2.79, Is.7.27, D.57.26. 4. *will, testament*, Is.6.29. 5. *pass* (?), *PPetr.*3p.130. 6. *memorandum*, D.22.23, Jul. *ad Ath.* 283b; *petition*, Luc.*Peregr.*16. II. *place where* γράμματα *were taught, a school*, Anon.ap.Suid. III. *office of* γραμματεύς, Plb.4.87. 8, Poll.9.41. IV. *public dining-hall* in Syria, Posidon.18. ✻ **-εύς**, έως, ὁ, *secretary, registrar*, title of officials at Athens and elsewhere,

*IG*1².15, etc.; ὁ γ. ὁ τῆς πόλεως Th.7.10; γ. τοῦ δήμου *OGI*493.10 (Ephesus, ii A.D.), *Act.Ap.*19.35; γ. ἀνδραπόδων *PHib.*29.7; γ. τῶν μαχίμων *UPZ*110.145 (ii B.C.); γ. τοῦ θεοῦ *IG*9(2).1109.21 (Magn. Thess.); also of subordinate officials, *clerk*, sts. a term of contempt, ὄλεθρος γ. D.18.127; θεοῖς ἐχθρὸς καὶ γ. Id.19.95; ἡ γ., in joke, Ar. *Th.*432. 2. metaph., *recorder*, of memory, Pl.*Phlb.*39a. 3. *scholar*, γ. σαφής A.*Fr.*358 (s.v.l.). 4. *one who traces* or *marks out*, of Egyptian embalmers, D.S.1.91. -ευτά, v. γραμματιτά. -εύω, *to be secretary, hold his office*, *IG*1².392, Th.4.118, etc.: c. dat., *IG*1².352, etc.; later, c. gen., γ. τοῦ συνεδρίου *IG*3.752. -ηφόρος, ὁ, *letter-carrier*, D.H.20.4, Plu.*Galb.*8, al., *PFlor.*39.6 (iv A.D.), etc. -ίας (sc. λίθος), ου, ὁ, precious stone like an emerald, v.l. in Plin.*HN*37.118:—Hsch. has γραμματίας· περιεσπασμένους. -ίδιον, v. γραμματεῖδιον. -ίζω, *teach the spelling of a word*, Herod.3.24:—Pass., pf. *to be skilled in* γράμματα, Hsch.; γραμματισμένος (sic) *man of education*, *Cat.Cod.Astr.*6.65.8. II. *to be a secretary*, συνέδροις *IG*5(1).1432.19 (Messene); Boeot. γραμματίδδοντος *IG*7.1739 (Thespiae), al. -ικεύομαι, Dep., *to be a grammarian*, *AP*9.169 (Pall.).

**γραμματικομάστιξ**, ῖγος, ὁ, *scourge of critics*, title of Aus.*Idyll.*14.

⊛ **γραμμᾰτ-ικός**, ή, όν, *knowing one's letters, a good scholar*, X.*Mem.*4.2.20, Pl.*Tht.*207b, Arist.*EN*1105ᵃ21: Comp., Pl.*Plt.*285d, Ph.1.621; opp. ἀγράμματος, Arr.*Epict.*3.19.6; ἀνὴρ γ. Plu.2.582a. Adv. -κῶς Pl.*Tht.* l.c., etc. 2. γ. ἔκπωμα a cup *engraved with the alphabet* or *an inscription*, Eub.69, cf. Ath.11.466d, Luc.*Lex.*7. 3. γ. ἀνάγκαι f.l. for γραμμικαί, Alex.Aphr.*Pr.*2.46. II. Subst., γραμματικός, ὁ, *teacher of the rudiments*, Hp.*Epid.*4.37, Plu.2.59f:—fem. -κή, *Sammelb.*5753. 2. *one who occupies himself with literary texts, grammarian, critic*, Plb.32.2.5, D.L.3.61, D.Chr.53.1, *IG*14.1183, etc.; first used of Apollodorus of Cyrene, acc. to Clem.Al.*Strom.*1.16.79:—fem. -κή, ἡ, Ath.1.14d. 3. *concerned with textual criticism*, ἐξήγησις D.H.*Th.*51; γραμματικά, title of work by Eratosthenes, Clem.Al. l.c. III. ἡ -κή (with or without τέχνη) *grammar*, Pl.*Cra.*431e, *Sph.*253a, etc.; ἡ γ. ἐπιστήμη Arist.*Top.*142ᵇ31. b. *faculty of scholarship*, γ. ἐστιν ἕξις παντελὴς ἐν γράμμασι Eratosth.ap.Sch.D.T.p.160H., cf. Ph.1.502, *AP*7.588 (Paul. Sil.). 2. *alphabet, script*, Str.3.1.6, Plu.*Arist.*1, etc.; ἡ ἱερὰ γ. hieroglyphic *writing*, *OGI*56.64 (iii B.C.). IV. γραμματικόν, τό, *fee paid to scribes* in Egypt, *PHib.*1.110 (iii B.C.), *PTeb.*61ᵇ.89 (ii B.C.), etc. -ιον, τό, Dim. of γράμμα, Luc.*Merc.Cond.*36. II. = γραμματεῖον, *bond, contract*, *POxy.*71.5 (iv A.D.). -ισμός· *limpidus* (sic), *Gloss.* (Perh. *plinthium.*) ⊛ -ιστής, οῦ, ὁ, = γραμματεύς, *clerk, registrar*, Hdt.2.28, 3.123, *IG*7.1745 (Thespiae), *SIG*529.4 (Dyme, iii B.C.), etc.: metaph., *recorder*, of memory (cf. γραμματεύς 2), Pl.*Phlb.*39b. II. *one who teaches* γράμματα, *elementary schoolmaster*, X.*Smp.*4.27, Pl.*Prt.*312b, al., D.19.281, D.H.11.28, Diog.Oen.11, etc. -ιστική, ἡ, *elementary teaching*, Phld.*Rh.*1.70S., S.E.*M.*1.44, Them.*Or.*23.297d (also -κά, τά, Id.*Or.*21.251a): but distd. fr. γραμματική as more elementary, Ph.1.540.

**γραμμᾰτο-δῐδασκᾰλεῖον**, τό, = γραμματεῖον II, Plu.2.712a, al. -δῐδάσκᾰλος, ὁ, *schoolmaster*, *SIG*578.8 (Teos), Teles p.50H., Phld. *Acad.Ind.*p.24M., Plu.*Alc.*7, Porph.*Plot.*3, *BGU*1214.4; cf. γραμμοδιδασκαλίδης. -ειδής, ές, *line-like*, διαφύσεις Sch.Il.21.169. -εις, εσσα, εν, *inscribed*, στήλη *Rev.Phil.*46.127 (Miscamus). ⊛ -εισαγωγεύς, ὁ, *schoolmaster*: *governor*, Lxx *De.*1.15, al. -κύφων [ῠ], ωνος, nickname of a γραμματεύς, *porer over records*, D.18.209, Ph.2.536: pl., ib.520. -λικρῐφίς, ίδος, ὁ, *puzzle-headed grammarian*, *AP*11.140 (Lucill.). -πίναξ [ῐ], ακος, ὁ, *map-maker*, Sch.D.P.5. -φορέω, *carry* or *deliver letters*, Str.5.4.13. -φόρος, ὁ, *letter-carrier*, Plb.2.61.4, al., Plu.*Pel.*10. ⊛ -φῠλᾰκεῖον, τό, = sq. I, J.*BJ*2.17.6, Plu.2.520c, S.E.*M.*2.27. -φῠλάκιον [ᾰκ], τό, *a place for keeping records*, Plu.*Arist.*21, *OGI*669.23 (i A.D.), *IG*5(2).516 (Lycosura, i A.D.), 5(1).20 (Sparta, ii A.D.): in pl., τὰ τῆς πόλεως γ. *BGU*913.4 (iii A.D.). II. *deed-box*, *EM*412.38. -φύλαξ [ῠ], ακος, ὁ, *recorder, registrar*, *IG*5(1).32*B*17 (Sparta), *OGI*229.51 (Smyrna), *Test.Epict.*8.27.

⊛ **γραμμή**, ἡ, (γράφω) *stroke* or *line* of a pen, *line*, as in mathematical figures, γραμμῆς λόγος ὁ τῶν δύο Pythagorei ap.Arist.*Metaph.*1036ᵇ12, cf. Pl.*Men.*82c, *R.*509d, etc.; περὶ ἀλόγων γ. title of work by Democritus, περὶ ἀτόμων γ., title of work ascribed to Arist.: hence γραμμαί, αἱ, *astronomy*, *AP*9.344 (Leon.); also in forming letters, *line* traced by teacher, Pl.*Prt.*326d; *outline*, opp. σκιά, Metop.ap.Stob.3.1.116, cf. Plb.2.14.8; ἡ ἐκτὸς γ. Hero *Aut.*27.2. II. = βαλβίς, *line across the course, starting-* or *winning-point*, Pi.*P.*9.118, cf. Ar.*Ach.*483; εὐθὺς ἀπὸ γ. Lib.*Or.*59.13: metaph. of life, πέλας γραμμῆς ἱκέσθαι E.*El.*956; ἐπ' ἄκραν ἥκομεν γ. κακῶν Id.*Fr.*169; ἡ ἐσχάτη τοῦ βίου γ. D.S.17.118: hence, *boundary-line, edge*, dub. l. in Hp.*Art.*80; *cutting edge* of a knife, Gal.2.673. III. *line* or *square on a chequer-board*: hence prov., τὸν ἀπὸ γραμμᾶς κινεῖν λίθον to move a piece from this line, i.e. try one's last chance, Theoc.6.18 (usu. called ἡ ἱερά (sc. γραμμή), cf. ἱερός); αἱ γ. *the board* itself, Poll.9.99. 2. διὰ γραμμῆς παίζειν to play at *tug-of-war* (διελκυστίνδα), Pl.Com.153.1, Pl.*Tht.*181a. IV. ἡ μακρά (sc. γραμμή), v. τιμάω III.1. V. Medic., *linea alba*, Gal.2.514. 2. = ζέα, *Hippiatr.*1.

**γραμμ-ιαῖος**, α, ον, *linear*, σχῆμα Dam.*Pr.*262. -ίζω, prob. f.l. for δια-, of a game (cf. γραμμή III.1), Eust.633.63. -ικός, ή, όν, *linear, geometrical*, θεωρία Gal.*UP*10.12; ἀπόδειξις Plu.*Marc.*14, *Theol.Ar.*26; ἀνάγκαι Olymp.*in Grg.*p.260J. Adv. -κῶς *by means of lines, geometrically*, ἀποδείκνυσθαι S.E.*M.*3.92, cf. Ptol.*Alm.*2.12, Procl.*in R.*2.27K. 2. γ. ἀριθμός *linear* number, Nicom.*Ar.*2.7, cf. Speus. ap.*Theol.Ar.*61. II. = γραμματικός, Plu.2.606c (s.v.l.). -ιστήρ, ῆρος, ὁ, *a surgical instrument*, *Hermes* 38.281. -ιστός, ή, όν, *chequered*, Eust.852.11.

**γραμμο-δῐδασκᾰλίδης**, = γραμματοδιδάσκαλος, in contempt, Timo 51. ⊛ -ειδής, ές, *slender as a line*, φῶς Paul.Al.*G.*4. Adv. -δῶς *in wavy lines*, Arist.*Mu.*395ᵃ27. -ποίκῐλος, ον, *striped*, Arist.*Fr.*295.

**γραμμός**, ὁ, *act of writing*, Hdn.Gr.1.168.

**γραμμοτόκος**, ον, *mother of lines*, μέλασμα, of the leaden plummet, *AP*6.63 (Damoch.).

**γραμμώδης**, ες, = γραμμοειδής, *wiry*, Thphr.*HP*4.12.2; *with linear markings*, ib.7.3.2.

**γρανθέωνα**· γέροντα, Hsch.

**γρᾱολογία**, ἡ, *old wife's talk, gossip*, γραμματικὴ γ. S.E.*M.*1.141: pl., Porph.*Chr.*34.

**γρᾱο-σόβης**, ου, ὁ, *lover of old women*, Ar.*Pax*812; cf. Sch.ad loc., and v. σοβάς. -συλλέκτρια, ἡ, *gossip-monger*, Suid. s. v. Τίμαιος. -τρεφής, ές, *reared by an old woman, coddled*, Eust.971.41. -φῐλος, ὁ, *lover of old women*, Sch.Ar.*Pax*812.

**γρατίνης**· οἶνος τραχύς, Hsch., *EM*239.32.

**γράπις**, ιδος, ἡ, *cast slough* of serpents, etc., Hsch. 2. *wrinkled*, S.*Ichn.*177, *EM*239.31. 3. kind of *bird*, Hsch.

**γραπτ-έον**, *one must write* or *describe*, ὅπως.. X.*Eq.*2.1; *one must write, spell*, Str.9.4.5, Gal.15.720. 2. γραπτέος, α, ον, *to be written, described*, Pl.*Ep.*341d, Luc.*Im.*17. -εύς, έως, ὁ, = γραφεύς, Sch. Ar.*Th.*1103. -ήρ, ῆρος, ὁ, *writer*, *AP*6.66 (Paul. Sil.), Man.1.132 (pl.). -ης, ου, ὁ, *wrinkled*, Eust.633.56. ⊛ -ός, ή, όν, *painted*, ζῷα Emp.128.5; τύποι E.*Fr.*764; κύρβις Achae.19; εἰκών *SIG*1068.21 (Patmos): γραπτά, τά, *paintings*, opp. γλυπτά, D.H.*Comp.*25. 2. *marked as with letters*, ἁ γραπτὰ ὑάκινθος Theoc.10.28; γ. λίθος *IG*14.1089. II. *written*, νόμοι γ. Gorg.*Pal.*30, cf. Pl.*Lg.*773e, etc.; ἀσφάλεια *PAmh.*78.17 (ii A.D.): γραπτά, τά, *rescripts, proclamations*, Lxx *2Ma.*11.15; *legal documents, bonds*, Man.3.214. ⊛ -ρα, τά, *fee for writing* or *copying*, *PLond.ined.*2110 (ii A.D.), *BGU*1062.20 (iii A.D.), *POxy.*895.12 (iv A.D.). -ύς, ύος, ἡ, *scratching, tearing*, Od.24.229 (pl.). II. in pl., *writings*, A.R.4.279.

**γράσθι**, v. γράω.

**γράσος**, ὁ, prop., *smell of a goat*: hence, of men, A. or Ar.ap. Phot. s. v. ψό, Eup.242, Arist.*Pr.*879ᵃ23, Plu.2.180c, M.Ant.9.36.

**γράσσμα**, ατος, τό, Argive, = γράμμα, *IG*4.554 (pl.).

⊛ **γραστ-ίζω**, *feed at grass*, ἵππους *Gp.*16.1.11 (Pass.), *Hippiatr.*98. -ισμός, ὁ, *feeding at grass*, ib.10. -ις, εως, ἡ, (γράω) *grass, green fodder*, *PPetr.*2p.113 (corr. in 3p.333) (iii B.C.), etc.; γ. πυρίνη, κριθίνη, *Hippiatr.*68, 98, cf. Eust.633.47, Hsch.:—also **γράσσις**, *PHamb.*39 ii (ii A.D.); cf. κράστις.

**γράσων**, ωνος, ὁ, ἡ, (γράσος) *smelling like a goat*, M.Ant.11.15, Ath.13.585e; a term of abuse, Hsch. II. = γράσος, M.Ant.8.37 (s.v.l.).

**γρασωνία**, ἡ, = γράσος, Archig.ap.Aët.8.7 (pl.).

**γραῦις**, ιδος, ἡ, Dor. for γρηῦς, γραῦς, Call.*Fr.*326.

**γραύκαλας**· ὄρνις τεφρός, Hsch.

⊛ **γραῦς**, gen. γρᾱός, ἡ: Ion. **γρηῦς**, γρηός, voc. γρηῦ: poet. also **γρηΰς**, voc. γρηΰ: barbarous voc. γρᾱο in Ar.*Th.*1222: nom. pl. γρᾶες Ar.*Fr.*350, Timocl.25: acc. γραῦς E.*Andr.*612, etc.:—*old woman*, Hom., esp. in Od., 1.191, al., A.*Eu.*38, etc.; γ. παλαιή Od.19.346: prov., γραῶν ὕθλος *old wives'* fables, Pl.*Tht.*176b: with Subst., γ. γυνή E.*Tr.*490, Ar.*Th.*345, D.19.283: Com., ὁ γραῦς of *an old man*, Ar.*Th.*1214 cod. R. II. *scum* of boiled milk, Id.*Pl.*1206, Arist.*GA*743ᵇ7. III. *sea-crab*, Arist.*HA*601ᵃ18 (as v.l.), Artem.2.14. IV. kind of *locust*, γ. σέριφος Zen.2.94.

**γρᾰφ-είδιον** (or -ίδιον), τό, Dim. of sq., Isoc.ap.Theon.*Prog.*5, *EM*240.16, Suid. -εῖον, τό, *pencil*, Hp.*Superf.*8 (f.l.), Arist.*Ph.*248ᵇ8, Macho ap.Ath.13.582c. 2. *paint-brush*, Plu.2.859e, S.E.*P.*1.28; *graving tool, chisel*, *Epigr.Gr.*980.4 (Philae). II. *registry, record-office*, *Michel* 595.12 (Halic.), *PRyl.*65.4 (i B.C.), *PAmh.*110.21 (i A.D.), etc.:—written **γράφιον**, *PPetr.*3p.155. III. *tax on writing-materials*, *BGU*277 ii 11: but in pl., *fees for copying*, ib.1214.12. -εύς, έως, ὁ, *painter*, Emp.23.1, E.*Hec.*807 (s.v.l.), And.4.17, Pl.*Phd.*110b, etc. II. = γραμματεύς, X.*HG*4.1.39, Plu.*Ages.*13; *private secretary*, τοῦ Δημοκρίτου Epicur.*Fr.*172. III. *writer*, D.S.21.17; *scribe, scrivener*, X.*Ages.*1.26; *copyist*, Arist.*Rh.*1409ᵃ20, Plb.12.4ᵃ.4, Str.13.1.54 (pl.): τὰ τῶν γραφέων πταίσματα Porph.*Plot.*19; cf. γραφής, γροφεύς. -ή, ἡ, *representation by means of lines*: hence, I. *drawing, delineation*, Hdt.4.36; κατὰ γραφήν in *outline*, cj. in Pl.*Smp.*193a; also of *painting*, γραφῇ κοσμέειν Hdt.3.24; εἰκὼν γραφῇ εἰκασμένη Id.2.182; *the art of drawing* or *painting*, Pl.*Plt.*277c, *Ti.*19b. 2. *that which is drawn* or *painted, drawing, picture*, ὅσον γραφῇ only *in a picture*, Hdt.2.73; πρέπουσά θ' ὡς ἐν γραφαῖς A.*Ag.*242 (lyr.); σπόγγος ὤλεσεν γραφήν ib.1329; μήτε ἄγαλμα μήτε γ. Arist.*Pol.*1336ᵇ15; also of embroidery, A.*Ch.*232; γραφαὶ ἀπὸ κερκίδος Philostr.*Im.*2.5. 3. γ. παρειῶν *painting, rouging* the cheeks, Id.*Ep.*22. II. *writing* or *the art of writing*, Pl.*Phdr.*274b, etc.: pl., αἱ γ. τῶν δικῶν *the registration of*.., Arist.*Pol.*1321ᵇ36; γραφαὶ περὶ συμμαχίας, of treaties, ib.1280ᵃ40. 2. *that which is written, writing*, S.*Tr.*683, Agatho 4: hence, of various written documents, *letter*, Th.1.129: also in pl., E.*IT*735; ψευδεῖς γ. spurious *documents*, ap.D.18.55 (but in E.*Hipp.*1311 false *statements*); of published *writings*, τῶν φιλοσόφων Phld.*Ir*.p.73W., cf. D.H.*Orat.Vett*.4; ἐν τῇ πρώτῃ γ. in the first *book*, Epicur.*Nat.Herc*.1431.16; *written law*, Pl.*Lg*.934c; *contract*, *PAmh*.2.43.13 (ii B.C.): pl., *copies* of judgements delivered in court, *IG*12(2).526$^{d}$8 (Eresos). b. *catalogue*, *list*, *return*, ἱερῶν *PTeb*.88.2 (ii B.C.); τοῦ κατ' ἄνδρα *OGI*179.21 (Egypt, i B.C.); τὰς κατ' ἄνδρα γραφάς *PTeb*.27.7 (ii B.C.), etc.; *price-list*, D.S.1.91. c. *inscription*, Th.1.134, *IG*12(5).679 (Syros), *Epigr.Gr*.347 (Cios), D.C.37.21. d. *MS. reading*, Str.1.2.25, Gal.15.430, Alex.Aphr.*inSens*.9.29, Herm.*inPhdr*.p.154A., etc. 3. *the Holy Scripture*, Aristeas155, 2*Ep.Pet*.1.20: pl., Ph.1.18, J.*Ap*.2.4, *Ev.Matt*.21.42, al.: also in sg., of a particular passage, *Act.Ap*.8.32, al. 4. γ. φαρμάκου medical *prescription*, Gal.12.293, 13.638, 15.918. 5. *record-office*, *archive*, *IG*11(2).203*B*101 (Delos, iii B.C.). III. (γράφομαι) as law-term, 1. *bill of indictment* in a public prosecution, λέγε, τὴν γ. αὐτὴν λαβών D.18.53. 2. *criminal prosecution* in the interest of the state (cf. Poll.8.41), γραφὴν ὕβρεως καὶ δίκην κακηγορίας ἰδίαν φεύξεται Id.21.32, cf. Lys.1.44, Is.11.28, etc.; γραφὴν γράφεσθαι Pl.*Lg*.929e, etc.; γρ. γ. τινά Id.*Euthphr*.2b, etc.; γ. ἀπενεγκεῖν Aeschin.3.217; γραφήν τινος διώκειν τινά D.19.293; πολλὰς γ. διώξας οὐδεμίαν εἷλεν Antipho 2.1.5; γραφὴν ἁλῶναι Id.2.2.9; γ. κατασκευάζειν κατά τινος, ἐπί τινα, D.21.103, 22.2; γ. εἰσέρχεσθαι, εἰσιέναι, appear before the court *in a public prosecution*, either as prosecutor or prosecuted, Id.18.105. 3. generally, *an ordinary public action*, opp. to special forms (such as εἰσαγγελία, εὔθυναι, etc.), γραφάς, εὐθύνας, εἰσαγγελίας, πάντα ταῦτ' ἐπαγόντων μοι D.18.249, cf. X.*Ath*.3.2, Lys.16.12. **-ημα**, ατος, τό, = γράμμα, *AB*787. **-ής**, ὁ, = γραφεύς II, *IG*5(2).8 (Tegea, iv B.C.), al. **-ία**, ἡ, = γραφή, *Gloss*. ❋ **-ικός**, ή, όν, *capable of drawing* or *painting*, Pl.*Tht*.144e, Ael.*VH*14.37: Comp., *a better judge of painting*, ib.2.3: -κή (sc. τέχνη), ἡ, *the art of painting*, Pl.*Grg*.450c, etc. 2. of things, *as if painted*, Ἔρωτες Plu.*Ant*.26 (so Adv. -κῶς ibid., 2.747c, Luc.*Im*.15); *picturesque*, πρόσοψις D.S.2.53. II. *of* or *for writing*, *suited for writing*: -κή, ἡ, *the art of writing*, Hp.*VM*20; γ.λέξις, opp. ἀγωνιστική, Arist.*Rh*.1413$^{b}$8; δύναμις Alcid.*Soph*.29; γ. ῥέεθρον, i.e. ink, *AP*6.63 (Damoch.); κάλαμος *Gp*.10.75.8, *PGrenf*.2.38.7 (i A.D.); μέλαν Gal.6.565; *in writing*, γ. ἁμάρτημα a *clerical* error, Plb.34.3.11. 2. *skilled in writing*, Arr.*Epict*.2.18.2; *shorthand writer*, *IG*14.1528. 3. *able to describe*, Plu.2.874b, Luc.*Alex*.3; of style, *graphic*, *lively*, D.H.*Amm*.1.4; ὑπόθεσις γ. a subject *for description*, Plu.*Alex*.17.

**γρᾰφιο-ειδής**, ές, *like a stylus*, γ. ἔκφυσις *styloid* process of the temporal bone, Gal.*UP*7.19, 11.4. **-θήκη**, ἡ, *case for* γραφεῖα, *Gloss*.

❋ **γρᾰφίς**, ίδος, ἡ, = γραφεῖον I, *AP*6.63 (Damoch.), 65 (Paul. Sil.), 67 (Jul.): esp. *stilus for writing* on waxen tablets, Pl.*Prt*.326d; *paint-brush*, *APl*.4.178 (Antip.); *graving tool*, Lxx *Ex*.32.4; σύμβολα.. γραφίδεσσι κατέξυσα *Hymn.Is*.11, cf. *AP*4.3b.72 (Agath.); *needle for embroidering*, *APl*.4.324. II. *embroidery*, *AP*5.275 (Agath.): but in pl., = *paintings*, Nonn.*D*.25.433.

**γρᾰφίσκος**, ὁ, *surgical instrument* for extracting arrows, etc., *Cels*.7.5.3.

**γρᾰφοειδής**, ές, ἀπόφυσις, of the *styloid* process of the ulna, Gal.2.252,271.

**γρᾰφος** [ᾰ], εος, τό, = γράμμα, τὰ γράφεα *SIG*9 (Olympia, vi B.C.), *IG*5(2).343 (Orchom. Arc., iv B.C.).

❋ **γρᾰφω** [ᾰ], fut. -ψω Hdt.1.95, etc.: aor. ἔγραψα, Ep. γράψα Il.17.599: pf. γέγραφα Cratin.124, Th.5.26, etc.; later γεγράφηκα *PHib*.1.78.2 (iii B.C.):—Med., fut. γράψομαι Ar.*Pax* 107, etc. (but in pass. sense, Gal.*Protr*.13): aor. ἐγραψάμην Ar.*V*.894, etc.:—Pass., fut. γρᾰφήσομαι Hp.*Acut*.26, Nicom.Com.1.39, (μετεγ-) Ar.*Eq* 1370; more freq. γεγράψομαι S.*OT*411, Theoc.18.47, etc.: aor. ἐγράφην [ᾰ], Hdt.4.91, Pl.*Prm*.128c, etc.; ἐγράφθην *SIG*57.5 (Milet., v B.C.), Archim.*Fluit*.2.4: pf. γέγραμμαι (also in med. sense, v. fin.), 3 sg. ἔγραπται Opp.*C*.3.274; part. ἐγραμμένος or ἠγρ- *SIG*9 (Elis, dub.), *Leg.Gort*.1.45, al.; later γεγράφηται Ph.2.637: 3 pl. γεγράφαται *IG* 1$^{2}$.57.10, Dor. γεγράβανται *Schwyzer*90.12 (Argos): plpf. ἐγέγραπτο X.*Mem*.1.2.64: 3 pl. ἐγεγράφατο D.C.56.32. Used by Hom. only in aor. Act.:—*scratch*, *graze*, αἰχμὴ γράψεν οἱ ὀστέον ἄχρις Il.17.599; γράψας ἐν πίνακι πτυκτῷ θυμοφθόρα πολλά *having marked* or *drawn* signs thereon, 6.169: hence, later, *represent by lines*, *draw*, *paint*, Hdt.2.41, A.*Eu*.50, Pl.*R*.377e; γῆς περιόδους γ. *draw* maps, Hdt.4.36; γ. Ἔρωθ' ὑπόπτερον Eub.41.1; προσπεπατταλευμένον γ. τὸν Προμηθέα Men.535.2; ἀνδριάντα γ. Pl.*R*.420c; ζῷα γ., = ζωγραφεῖν (q.v.), Id.*Grg*.453c: metaph., ὁπόσα τοὺς λειμῶνας αἱ ὧραι γράφουσι Philostr.*Im.Praef*.:—Med., ζῷα γράφεσθαι Hdt.4.88:—Pass., εἰκὼν γεγραμμένη Ar.*Ra*.537; πίνακες γεγραμμένοι τὰ Ἀλεξάνδρου ἔργα Philostr.*VA*2.20. 2. Math., *describe* a figure, Euc.*Post*.3, al., Archim.*Sph.Cyl*.1.23, al., Gal.1.47. b. of a point or line in motion, *generate* a figure, Arist.*Mech*.848$^{b}$10, al.; τὸ σαμεῖον ἕλικα γράφει Archim.*Sph.Cyl.Def*.1, cf. Apollon.Perg.*Con*.1.2, Hero *Aut*.8.1. 3. *brand*, *mark*, Opp.*C*.1.326:—Pass. in form γεγράφαται, ib.322. II. *express by written characters*, *write*, τι Hdt.1.125, etc.; γ. διαθήκην Pl.*Lg*.923c, cf. X.*Cyr*.4.5.34 (Pass.); γ. τινὶ ὅτι.. Th.7.14; γ. τινί, c. inf., *SIG*552.13 (Abae, iii B.C.); γ. τι εἰς διφθέρας Hdt.5.58: prov., ὅρκους.. γυναικὸς εἰς ὕδωρ γράφω S.*Fr*.811, cf. Xenarch.6; εἰς τέφραν γ. Philonid.7; εἰς ὕδωρ, ἐν ὕδατι, Men.*Mon*.25, Pl.*Phdr*.276c; ἐν χρυσῷ πίνακι Id.*Criti*.120c; ἐν φλοιῷ Theoc.18.47; καθ' ὕδατος Luc.*Cat*.21; εἰς πέλαγος γράμματα γράψαι *Epigr.Gr*.1038.8 (Attalia):—Pass., πόθι φρενὸς γέγραπται in what leaf of memory *it is written*, Pi.*O*.10(11).3. 2. *inscribe*, γ. εἰς σκῦλα, εἰς στήλην, E.*Ph*.574, D.9.41:—Pass., γράφεσθαί τι *to be inscribed with* a thing, S.*Tr*.157; ὧδε γέγραμμαι *have my name inscribed*, *IG*12(7).3* (dub.); ἐν τῷ προσώπῳ γραφεὶς τὴν συμφορὰν *having* it *branded* on his forehead, Pl.*Lg*.854d; γεγραμμένα κωκύουσαν, of the hyacinth, Euph.40. 3. *write down*, γ. τινὰ αἴτιον *set* him *down* as the cause, Hdt.7.214; γ. τι ἱερόν τινι *register* as.., Pi.*O*.3.30; in magic, *invoke a curse upon*, *Tab.Defix.Aud*.14*A*1; γ. τινὰ κληρονόμον, ἐπίτροπον, *institute by a written document*, Pl.*Lg*.923c, 924a; *register*, *enrol*, ἐμὲ γράφε τῶν ἱππεύειν ὑπερεπιθυμούντων X.*Cyr*.4.3.21; οὐ Κρέοντος προστάτου γεγράψομαι, as a dependent of Cr., S.*OT*411. 4. γ. τινί *write a letter to* one, γ. σοὶ ἵνα εἰδῇς *PGrenf*.1.11ii21 (ii B.C.), etc.; εἴς τινα Luc.*Syr.D*.23. 5. γ. περί τινος *write on* a subject, X.*Cyn*.13.2, etc.; ὑπέρ τινος Plb.1.1.4, etc.; εἴς τινα *against*.., Longin.4.3; πρός τινα *address a work* to.., Id.1.3; *describe*, οἱ ὑφ' ἡμῶν γραφόμενοι καιροί Plb.2.56.4; esp. of Prose, opp. ποιεῖν, Isoc.2.48: c. dupl. acc., τί.. γράψειεν ἄν σε μουσοποιὸς ἐν τάφῳ; E.*Tr*.1189. 6. *write down* a law to be proposed: hence, *propose*, *move*, γνώμην, νόμον, ψήφισμα, etc., X.*HG*1.7.34, Ar.*Nu*.1429, etc.: abs. (sc. νόμον), D.18.179; γ. καὶ νομοθετεῖν περί τινος Id.24.48; γ. πόλεμον, εἰρήνην, Id.10.55, 19.55: c. inf., σὺ γράφεις ταῦτ' εἶναι στρατιωτικά Id.1.19; ἔγραψα.. ἀποπλεῖν.. τοὺς πρέσβεις Id.18.25; *enact*, νόμοι οὓς τὸ πλῆθος συνελθὸν ἔγραψε X.*Mem*.1.2.42:—Pass., παρὰ τὰ γραφέντα δρᾶν Pl.*Plt*.295d; τὸ γεγραμμένον ὑπὸ σοῦ ψήφισμα Din.1.70. 7. *prescribe*, *ordain*, πότμος ἔγραψε Pi.*N*.6.7. 8. ὁ γράφων τὸν Ὀξυρυγχίτην (sc. νομόν) the *secretary for* the nome of Oxyrhynchus, *POxy*.239.1 (i A.D.); τῷ ἰδίῳ λόγῳ γράφοντι τὸν νομὸν *PFlor*.358.5 (ii A.D.).

B. Med., *write for oneself* or *for one's own use*, *note down*, Hdt.2.82, *IG*1$^{2}$.57.39, etc.; γ. τι ἐν φρεσίν A.*Ch*.450 (lyr.); φρενῶν ἔσω S.*Ph*.1325; ἐγραψάμην ὑπομνήματα I *wrote me down* some memoranda, Pl.*Tht*.143a; *cause to be written*, συγγραφήν D.56.6, etc.; γ. πρόσοδον πρὸς τὴν βουλήν *petition for* a hearing before the Council, Id.24.48. 2. *enrol oneself*, γράψασθαι φυλῆς καὶ δήμου καὶ φρατρίας *IG*1$^{2}$.374.16, ib.2.115$^{b}$21: abs., of colonists, Pl.*Lg*.850b; but also (cf. A.II.3), ἕνα τῶν μαθητῶν ἐμὲ γράφου *enrol* me as one of *your* disciples, Id.*Cra*.428b. 3. as law-term, γ. τινά *to indict* one, τινός *for* some public offence, e.g. τῆς αἰσχροκερδείας, Pl.*Lg*.754e; γ. [τινὰ] παρανόμων D.18.13; in full, γραφὴν γράψασθαί τινα Ar.*Nu*.1482 (but in Pass., εἴ σοι γράφοιτο δίκη ib.758); γράψασθαι δίκας *SIG*344.38 (Teos): c. acc. et inf., γ. τινὰ ἀδικεῖν Ar.*V*.894, cf. *Pax*107: abs., οἱ γραψάμενοι *the prosecutors*, Id.*V*.881; ἑτέροις οὐκ ἦν γράψασθαι And.1.75; also γράφεσθαί τι *indict* an act, i.e. the doer of it, as criminal, ἐγράψατο τὴν Χαβρίου δωρεάν he *brought a* γραφὴ παρανόμων *against* the person who proposed the grant to Chabrias, D.20.146, cf. 95; τὸ χάριν τούτων ἀποδοῦναι παρανόμων γράφει (2 sg.) Id.18.119. b. Pass., *to be indicted*, γραφεὶς ἀπέφυγον D.18.103; τοῦτο τὸ ψήφισμα ἐγράφη παρανόμων *was indicted* as illegal, Aeschin.3.62; ψηφίσματα ὑπὸ τούτου οὐδὲ γραφέντα not even *indicted*, D.18.222 (but in 18.28, εἰ μὴ τοῦτ' ἐγράφη if this decree *had not been proposed*, as Pass. of A.II.6); τὰ γεγραμμένα *the articles of the indictment*, Id.18.56; τὸ γεγραμμένον *the penalty named in the indictment*, Id.24.83:—but γέγραμμαι usu. takes the sense of the Med., *indict*, Id.18.59,119, cf. Pl.*Euthphr*.2b, *Tht*.210d.

**γραψαῖος**, ὁ, *crab*, Diph.Siph.ap.Ath.3.106d.

**γραψείω**, Desiderat. of γράφω, *Gloss*.

❋ **γράω**, *gnaw*, *eat*, Call.*Fr*.200: hence γρά· φάγε (Cypr.), Hsch.; γράσθι (imper.), *Inscr.Cypr*.144H. (Golgoi). (Cf. γράστις, Skt. *grásati* 'devour'?)

❋ **γρᾱώδης**, ες, = γραϊκός, ἀδολεσχία Chrysipp.*Stoic*.2.255; μυθολογία Str.1.2.3; μυθάριον Cleom.2.1, cf. Iamb.*VP*23,105, 1*Ep.Ti*.4.7: Comp. -έστερος Gal.5.315.

**γρεῦς**, ἡ, collat. form of γραῦς, Hdn.Gr.1.401.

**γρηγορ-έω**, late pres., formed from pf. ἐγρήγορα (q.v.), *to be* or *become fully awake*, *watch*, Lxx *Ne*.7.3, *Ev.Matt*.24.43, al., Ach.Tat.4.17; ἐπί τισι Lxx *Ba*.2.9; ἐπὶ τὰς πόλεις ib.*Je*.5.6:—Pass., ἐγρηγορήθη ἐπὶ τὰ ἀσεβήματά μου ib.*La*.1.14; opp. καθεύδω, of life opp. death, 1*Ep.Thess*.5.10. **-ησις**, εως, ἡ, *wakefulness*, Lxx *Da*.5.11. **-ία**, ἡ, = foreg., *Gloss*. **-ικός**, ή, όν, *wakeful*, *watchful*, Id. **-σις**, εως, ἡ, = γρηγόρησις, Ph.1.510.

❋ **γρήϊος**, ον, Ion. for γραῖος, Call.*Fr*.511.

**γρήνη**· ἄνθη σύμμικτα, *EM*241.14, Hsch.

**γρῆνος** or **γρήνυς**, = ἀγρηνόν, Eratosth.*Fr*.33.

**γρηῦς**, **γρηΰς**, Ion. and Ep. for γραῦς.

**γρῖνος**, ὁ and ἡ, Aeol. for ῥινός (i.e. ϝρῖνος), acc. to Eust.1926.56; cf. γρῖνος· δέρμα, Hsch., *EM*241.47.

**γρῑ́ντης**, ου, ὁ, *tanner*, Hdn.Gr.2.429 (γρηντις cod., Hsch.). 2. = ὑβριστής, Cyr., Zonar. 3. = οὐρανός Cyr. (γρίντις *EM*241.48).

**γρῑπάομαι**, *to be contracted* or *convulsed*, Hsch.

**γρῑπ-εύς**, έως, ὁ, *fisher*, Sapph.120, Theoc.1.39, Mosch.*Fr*.1.9, *AP*7.305 (Addaeus), Procop.*Pers*.1.4. 2. *maker of fishing-nets*, Hsch. **-εύω**, *fish*, Zonar. **-έω**, *catch*: metaph., *gain*, οὐδὲν ἐγρίπησαν *LW*2261 (Syria): pf. part. γεγριφώς, Hsch. **-ηΐς** τέχνη, ἡ, art *of fishing*, *AP*6.223 (Antip.). **-ίζω**, = γριπεύω, Hsch.: metaph., of *netting* a profit, Lib.et Bas.*Epp*.14.1, cf. *Et. Gud.d* s.v. γρυμεία. **-ισμα**, ατος, τό, *that which is caught*, *gain*, *EM*241.22, Zonar.

❋ **γρῖπος**, ὁ, = γρῖφος, *AP*6.23, Artem.2.14. II. *haul* or *take of fish*, D.L.1.32.

**γρίπων** [ῐ], ὁ, (γρῖπος) *fisherman*, γρίπωνος γριπεύς..ἔχωσε τάφον *AP*7.504.12 (Leon). (Prob. a pr. n.)

**γρίσων**, ωνος, ὁ, *pig*, Hdn.Gr.2.429.

**γριτή**, ἡ, dub. sens. in Lib.et Bas.*Epp*.15.1, 16.2 (perh. f.l. for γρύτη).

**γρῑφᾶσθαι**, Lacon. = γράφειν, Hsch.; also, *scratch*, Id.: ἀλγήματα γριφόμενα (prob. -ώμενα) *lancinating* pains, Hp.*Prorrh*.1.100, cf. Gal.ad loc.

**γρῑφεύω**, *ask riddles*, Ath.10.451b (cf. Diph.50), Eust.884.10.

**γρῑφο-ειδής**, ές, *enigmatical*, Hsch. **-πλόκος**, ον, *weaving riddles*, Tz.ad Hes.*Op*.588.

⊛ **γρῖφ-ος**, ὁ, = γρῖπος, *fishing-basket, creel*, Plu.2.471d, Opp.*H*.3.80, *PTeb*.486 (ii/iii A.D.). 2. metaph., *anything intricate, dark saying, riddle*, Ar.*V*.20, Demetr.*Eloc*.153, Ath.10.448b sqq.; γ. προβάλλειν Antiph.74.5; λέγειν γρίφους παρὰ πότον Id.124.2; distd. fr. αἴνιγμα, Poll.6.19. b. *forfeit paid* for failing to guess a riddle, Hsch. **-ότης**, ητος, ἡ, *obscurity*, Hdn.*Epim*.6. **-ώδης**, ες, *like a riddle*, Luc.*JTr*.28, Ath.10.456c.

**γρομφάζω**, *grunt*, *Gloss*.:—from **γρόμφαινα**, ἡ, *old sow*, Id.:—also **γρομφάς**, άδος, ἡ, Hsch., and **γρόμφις**, ιος, ἡ, acc. γρόμφιν, Hippon.69.

**γρονθάριον**, τό, Dim. of γρόνθος II, marginal gloss on χελώνιον, Apollod.*Poliorc*.178.4 codd.

**γρονθοκοπῶ**, *beat with fists*, *Gloss*.

⊛ **γρονθονεύεται**· θυμοῦται, βρενθύεται, Hsch.

**γρόνθος**, ὁ, = πυγμή, *fist*, Gloss.*Oxy*.1099.18, Hsch., etc.; κατέκτειναν γρόνθοις καὶ λακτίσμασι *PAmh*.2.141.10 (iv A.D.); γρόνθῳ παίσας Sch.Il.2.220; γ. παλαστιαῖος, = σπιθαμή, Aq.*Jd*.3.16, al., cf. Hero *Geom*.4.11. II. *spoke* on a machine, Ps.-Apollod.*Poliorc*. p.46 Thévenot.

⊛ **γρόνθων**, ωνος, ὁ, *first lessons on the flute*, Poll.4.83, Hsch.

**γρόππα**, v. γράμμα.

**γρόπτος**, Aeol. for γραπτός, *Epigr.Gr*.991.14 (Balbilla).

**γρόσυνον**· τάραξον, Hsch. (cf. δροθύνω).

**γροσφομάχος**, ον, *fighting with the* γρόσφος, οἱ γ., = Lat. *velites*, Plb.1.33.9, 6.21.7.

**γρόσφος**, ὁ, a kind of *javelin*, Plb.6.22.4, Str.4.4.3, Plu.*Sull*.18.

**γροσφοφόρος**, ον, = γροσφομάχος, Plb.6.21.9.

**γροῦμος**· στρόβιλος, Hsch.

⊛ **γρουνός**, ὁ, = γρυνός, Call.*Fr.anon*.84.

**γρούσσεται**· μηρύεται, ἐκτείνεται, Hsch.

**γροφά**, Dor. for γραφή, *painting*, *IG*4.1484.271 (Epid.).

**γροφ-εύς**, έως, ὁ, Dor. and Arc. for γραμματεύς, *IG*4.498 (Mycenae); γ. βωλᾶς ib.12(3).1259.16 (Cimolus), 5(2).357.20 (Stymphalus). 2. = ζωγράφος, Hsch. **-εύω**, Dor. = γραμματεύω, *IG* 4.609.8 (Argos).

**γροφίς**, Dor. = γραφίς, *IG*4.1484.292 (Epid.).

**γρόφω**, Dor. = γράφω, *IG*12(3).1075 (Melos), *Schwyzer* 209 (Melian, from Olympia).

**γρῦ**, used with negs., ἀποκρινομένῳ..οὐδὲ γρῦ not *a syllable*, Ar.*Pl*. 17, cf. D.19.39; μηδὲ γ. λέγε Men.521; ὄψου μηδὲν..μηδὲ γ. not *a morsel*, not *a bit*, Antiph.190.13; διαφέρει Χαιρεφῶντος οὐδὲ γ. Men. 364, cf. *Sam*.310, Aristaenet.1.17, Jul.*ad Ath*.273b. (Expld. of the noise of swine, not even *a grunt*, by Sch.Ar.l.c.; also, *a small coin*, Suid.; but prop., = *dirt under the nail*, Hsch., who also explains it as = γρύτη, cf. γρύξ.)

**γρυβός**, ὁ, = γρύψ, Hsch., *EM*242.2.

⊛ **γρύζω**, fut. γρύξω, Ar.*Eq*.294 codd., Lxx *Ex*.11.7, γρύξομαι Alc. Com.22: aor. ἔγρυξα (v. infr.):—*say* γρῦ (v. sub voc.), *grumble, mutter*, γρύζειν δὲ καὶ τολμᾶτον..; Ar.*Pl*.454; παιδὸς φωνὴν γρύξαντος Id.*Nu*.963; εἴ τι γρύξει Id.*Eq*.294; μὴ φλαῦρον μηδὲν γρύζειν Id. *Pax* 97 (anap.); γρύζοντας οὐδὲ τουτί Id.*Ra*.913; οὐκ ἐτόλμα γρύξαι τὸ παράπαν prob. in Is.8.27: c. dupl. acc., ἐγὼ μὲν οὔτε χρηστὸν οὔτε σε γρύζω ἀπηνὲς οὐδέν Call.*Iamb*.1.257; later, *growl*, of a dog, Lxx l.c.; *grunt*, of a pig, Alciphr.3.73; *grumble, murmur*, πρός τινα Porph. *Abst*.1.27. II. fut. γρύσει, = τήξει *will liquefy*, Arist.*Pr*.876$^b$18.

⊛ **γρυήλιον**· ῥωσμὴν δρυός, Hsch.

**γρυκτός**, ή, όν, (γρύζω) ἆρα γρυκτόν ἐστιν ὑμῖν; will ye *dare to grumble*? Ar.*Lys*.656.

**γρῡλ-ίζω** (**γρυλλίζω** is incorrect acc. to Phryn.*PS*p.58 B.), Dor. fut. γρυλιξεῖτε Ar.*Ach*.746:—*grunt*, of swine, Ar.l.c., *Pl*.307, D. Chr.7.74; of a person, Procop.*Arc*.17. **-ισμός**, ὁ, *grunting*, Arist.*HA*535$^b$17 (written γρυλλ- in Poll.). **-ίων**· χοῖρος, Hsch.

**γρύλλη**· ὑῶν φωνή, Hsch.

**γρυλλισμός**, ὁ, *Egyptian dance*, Phryn.*PS*p.58 B.

**γρυλλογράφέω** (γρύλλος 2), *draw caricatures*, opp. καλοὺς δημιουργεῖν πίνακας, Phld.*Rh*.2.297 S.

⊛ **γρύλλος**, ὁ, = γρυλλισμός, Phryn.*PS*p.58 B.; *performer in such a dance*, ibid. 2. *comic figure, caricature*, in painting, Plin.*HN*35. 114.

**γρῦλος**, later **γρύλλος**, Hsch., ὁ, *pig, porker*, Plu.2.986b, Zonar. 2. = γόγγρος, Diph.Siph.ap.Ath.8.356a, Nic.*Fr*.122.

**γρῡμέα** (in codd. freq. written γρυμαία), ἡ, *bag* or *chest* for old clothes, etc., Diph.127, Poll.10.160, Phryn.*PS*p.60 B.:—also **γρυμεία** or **-εία**, ibid., *Et.Gud.d.* II. = γρύτη I (Hsch.), *trash, trumpery*, Sotad.Com.1.3; of persons, *riff-raff*, ῥήτορας καὶ ποιητὰς καὶ πᾶσαν τὴν τοιαύτην γ. Phld.*Ir*.p.65 W., cf. Them.*Or*.21.257a; γ. παντοδαπῶν βιβλίων Dam.*Isid*.293:—hence **γρῡμεοπώλης**, ου, ὁ, Luc. *Lex*.3.

**γρυμπάνειν**, = γρύπτειν, Hsch.

**γρύνη**· λιβανωτός, Theognost.*Can*.108.

**γρυνόν**, = σίκυς ἄγριος, Ps.-Dsc.4.150.

⊛ **γρῡνός**, ὁ, *fagot, firebrand*, Hom.*Fr*.18, Lyc.86, 294.

**γρῦνος**, ὁ, = γρύψ, Hsch.

**γρύξ**· ὁ τόπος (leg. ῥύπος) τοῦ ὄνυχος, Hsch.

**γρῡπάετος** [ᾱ], ὁ, *a kind of griffin* or *wyvern*, Ar.*Ra*.929.

**γρῡπαίνω**, = γρυπόομαι, Dionys.ap.Harp., Hsch.

**γρῡπᾰλώπηξ**, ἡ, *griffin-fox*, nickname in Hp.*Epid*.6.8.29.

**γρῡπᾰνίζω**, *become wrinkled*, of the earth in earthquake, Antipho Soph.31.

⊛ **γρῡπ-άνιος**, ον, *wrinkled*, of the earth, Antipho Soph.30:—also **-άνιον** or **-άλιον**, τό, *old woman*, Hsch.

**γρυπή**, ἡ, in pl., *vulture's nests*, Hsch.

**γρῡπ-νόν**· στυγνόν, κατηφές, Hsch.; cf. γνύπων. **-όομαι**, Pass., *to become hooked*, of the nails, Hp.*Prog*.17, Alex.Aphr.*Pr*.2. 18, Gal.8.47. **-ός**, ή, όν, *hook-nosed, aquiline*, opp. σιμός, X.*Cyr*. 8.4.21, Pl.*R*.474d, etc.: generally, *hooked*, ὄνυχες Aret.*SA*2.1, *SD* 1.8; *curved*, γρυπὴ γαστήρ a *round* paunch, X.l.c.; γ. στέφανος Eub.105 (Sup.); τὸ γρυπόν, = γρυπότης, Arist.*Pol*.1309$^b$24. **-ότης**, ητος, ἡ, *hookedness*, of the nose, opp. σιμότης, X.*Cyr*.8.4.21, Arist. *Rh*.1360$^a$27; of a beak, Plu.2.994f; of talons, ib.641d. **-τω**, *become bent* or *wrinkled*, Hsch.: aor. 2 ἔγρυπον, *become wrinkled*: metaph. of the earth in an earthquake, Melanth.Hist.1: in pf. part. Pass., γᾶν ἐγρυμμέναν *Annuario* 3.195 (Gortyn). **-ωσις**, εως, ἡ, *crooking, hooking*, of the nails, Cael.Aur.*CP*2.32, Steph.*in Hp*.1. 187 D.

**γρυσμός**, ὁ, (γρύζω) *a grunting*, Agathocl.2.

**γρῡτάριον**, τό, Dim. of γρύτη, Zen.5.54, *CPHerm*.9.5 (pl., iii A.D.).

**γρυτεύεται**· παρασκευάζεται, Hsch.

⊛ **γρύτη** [ῡ], ἡ (also **γρῦτα**, ἡ, *Gloss*.), *woman's dressing-case* or *vanity-bag*, Sapph.156; σκευῶν γ. prob. a workman's *tool-bag*, *PPetr*.3 p.78. 2. *frippery*, Phryn.209, *PS*p.60 B.; cf. γριτή: pl., = σκεύη, Hsch. 3. of fish, λεπτὴ γ. small *fry*, *Gp*.20.12.2.

⊛ **γρῡτο-δόκη**, ἡ, = γρυμέα I, *AP*6.254 (Myrin.). **-πωλεῖον**, τό, *small-ware shop*, *Gloss*. ⊛ **-πώλης**, ου, ὁ, *seller of small wares*, Sch.Ar.*Pl*.17: written κρυτ-, *BGU*9112 (iii A.D.).

⊛ **γρύψ**, gen. γρῡπός, ὁ, *griffin*, Aristeas ap.Hdt.3.116, cf. 4.13, A. *Pr*.804, *IG*1$^2$.280.80; τράπεζα ἔχουσα πόδας ἀναγλύπτους γρῦπας *SIG* 996.10 (Smyrna). II. a bird, prob. the *Lämmergeier*, Lxx *Le*. 11.13, *De*.14.13. III. pl., part of a ship's *tackle*, or *anchor*, Hsch.

**γρωθύλοι**· γωλιοί, σπήλαια, Hsch. **γρωθώνη**· σαπρὰ γραῦς, οἱ δὲ τὴν παλαιὰν ὄνησιν, Id. **γρώνα** (s.v.l.), ἡ, *sow* (Lacon.), and pl. **γρωνάδες**, Id.

⊛ **γρῶνος**, η, ον, (γράω) *eaten out, cavernous*, Lyc.631, 1280; *hollow*, πελλίδες Nic.*Al*.77. 2. in pl., *those who listen and do not speak*, Hsch. II. as Subst. **γρώνη** (sc. πέτρα), ἡ, *hole*, γ. μυοδόχοι Nic.*Th*.794 (pl.). 2. *hollow vessel, kneading-trough*, *AP*7.736 (Leon.).

**γύαια**, τά, (γύης II) = πρυμνήσια, *AP*10.1 (Leon.), Hsch.

⊛ **γυᾰλας** [ᾰ], ὁ, *a* Megarian *cup*, Philet.ap.Ath.11.467c, Parth.ibid.

**γυᾰλοθώραξ**, ᾶκος, ὁ, *cuirass composed of front- and back-piece*, Paus.10.26.2.

**γύᾰλον** [ῠ], τό, *hollow*, in Il. always of the *breast-* or *back-piece* of the cuirass, [θώρηκα] γυάλοισιν ἀρηρότα Il.15.530: sg., usu. of the *front-piece*, 5.99, al. 2. *hollow* of a vessel, κρατήρων γ. E.*IA* 1052 (lyr.); *hollow vessel*, χρυσοῦ γέμοντα γύαλα θησαυροὺς βροτῶν Id. *Andr*.1093 (v. infr. 4). 3. κοίλας πέτρας γ. *hollow* of a rock, S.*Ph*. 1081 (lyr.); *cavern*, πέτρινα [μύχατα] γύαλα E.*Hel*.189 (lyr.). 4. pl., of *hollow ground, vales, dells*, γυάλοις ὕπο Παρνησοῖο Hes.*Th*. 499, cf. *h.Ap*.396; Νύσης *h.Hom*.26.5; γ. Θεράπνας Pi.*N*.10.56 (but γ. Πυθῶνος, Φοίβου Id.*P*.8.63, E.*Ph*.237 (lyr.), cf. *Ion* 245, S.*Fr*.460, may perh. refer to the rock-chambers of Delphi, cf. γύαλα· θησαυροί, ταμιεῖα, Hsch., and so perh. in E.*Andr*.1093 (v. supr.)); Λυδιά τ' ἀγ γύαλα throughout *the vales* of Lydia, A.*Supp*.550 (lyr.); γύαλα χώρας Ar.*Th*.110 (lyr.); αἰθέρια γύαλα *the vault* of heaven, Opp.*C*. 1.281, cf. Orph.*H*.19.16.

**γύᾰλος** [ῠ], ὁ, *cubical stone*, *EM*243.12; also oxyt. as Adj., γυαλὸν λίθον ἀγκάσσασθαι Call.*Fr.anon*.331.

**γυβᾷ**· κολυμβᾷ, Hsch.

**γῠβερνήτης**, ὁ, = κυβ–, *PGrenf*.1.49.21 (iii A.D.).

**γυγαί**· πάπποι, Hsch. **γυγαίη** νύξ· ἡ σκοτεινή, Id.

**γύγης**, ου, ὁ, *a bird*, Dionys.*Av*.2.16.

**γυέλιον**· κόλπον, Hsch.

⊛ **γύης** [ῠ], ου, ὁ, *the curved piece of wood* in a plough, to which the share was fitted, *the tree*, Hes.*Op*.427, 436. II. *a measure of land*, rarely in sg., E.*Heracl*.839, v.l. in S.*Fr*.601; *field*, *PTeb*.105. 15 (ii B.C.); γ. ἄνυδρος *POxy*.918 ii 10 (ii A.D.): more freq. in pl., *lands*, Σικελίας λευροὺς γύας A.*Pr*.371; ἀνηρότους γύας ib.708; αὐτόσποροι γ. Id.*Fr*.196.5; οἱ πλησίοι γ. S.*OC*58, cf. *Tab.Heracl*.2.13. 2. metaph. of a wife, ἀρώσιμοι γ. S.*Ant*.569. 3. = ἀστραγάλων, σύνθεσις, Hsch. 4. γύαι· ὁδοί, Id. (Fem. (cf. γύη· μέτρον πλέθρου, Hsch.), E.*Hel*.89, *Ba*.13 codd.: but τούς, τούσδε Elmsl.)

⊛ **γυήτης**· χωλός, Hsch.; cf. ἀμφιγυήεις.

**γυθίσσων** (prob. γυνθ–)· διορύσσων, Hsch.

**γυι-αλθής**, ές, *nourishing the limbs*, Nic.*Th*.529. **-αλκής**, ές, *strong of limb*, σώματα B.8.38, cf. 11.8; ἥβη Opp.*H*.5.465; παλαισμοσύνη ib.2.277. **-αρκής**, ές, *strengthening the limbs*, νωδυνία Pi.*P*.3.6.

**γυΐζω,** *take in the hand*, coined by *EM*309.31, cf. Eust.250.36.

**γυιο-βᾰρής,** ές, *weighing down the limbs*, παλαίσματα, κάματος, A. *Ag.*63 (lyr.), *AP*10.12. **-βόρος,** ον, *gnawing the limbs, eating*, μελεδῶναι (v.l. γυιοκόρος, dub. sens.) Hes.*Op.*66; πῦρ *AP*9.443 (Paul. Sil.). **-δᾰμος,** η, ον, *taming limbs, conquering*, ἐν γυιοδάμαις.. χερσίν Pi.*I.*5(4).59: unless from Subst. -δάμας, ὁ, *athlete.* **-δόνητος,** ον, *with bruised limbs*, Phryn.Trag.2. **-κολλος,** ον, *binding the limbs*, Lyc.1202.

**γυῖον,** τό, *limb*, Hom., always pl., in phrases such as γυῖα λέλυντο Il.13.85; ὑπὸ τρόμος ἔλλαβε γυῖα 14.506; ὅπποτέ κέν μιν γυῖα λάβῃ κάματος 4.230, etc., cf. A.*Pers.*913 (lyr.), Id.*Eleg.*3; γυῖα ποδῶν *the feet*, Il.13.512; μητρὸς γυῖα *womb*, *h.Merc.*20; γυῖα *hands*, Theoc. 22.81; γυῖον, sg., *the hand*, ib.121 (so prob. as device on signet, *Tab. Heracl.*1.183); but γυῖον *the whole body*, Pi.*N.*7.73, Hp.*Epid.*6.4.26.—Not in Att. Prose: later, opp. στέρνα καὶ κεφαλή, Plu.*Arist.*14.

**γυιο-πᾰγής,** ές, *stiffening the limbs*, νιφάς *AP*6.219 (Antip.); κάματοι *IG*3.779.6. ⊛ **-πέδη,** ἡ, *fetter*: in pl., Pi.*P.*2.41, A.*Pr.*169 (lyr.).

**γυιός,** ή, όν, *lame*, Call.*Dian.*177, Lyc.144, Aret.*SD*2.12; γ. πόδας *AP*6.203 (Lacon. or Phil.).

**γυιοτᾰκής,** ές, *melting* or *wasting the limbs*, πενίη *AP*6.30 (Maced.). II. Pass., *with pining limbs*, ib.71 (Paul. Sil.).

**γυιοῦχος,** ον, *fettering the limbs*, Lyc.1076.

**γυιόχαλκος,** ον, *of brasen limb*, Dosiad.*Ara*6.

⊛ **γυιόω,** (γυιός) *lame*, γυιώσω..ὑφ' ἅρμασιν ὠκέας ἵππους Il.8.402, cf. 416; *wound*, Nic.*Th.*731; γυιωθείς *lame*, Hes.*Th.*858, cf. Hp. *Art.*52; *weaken, reduce*, Id.*Acut.*59; γ. βίης *deprive* of strength, Orph.*Fr.*135.

**γυλάριον,** τό, = μυξῖνος, Sch.Opp.*H.*1.111.

**γῠλιαύχην,** ενος, ὁ, ἡ, *long-necked, scraggy-necked*, Ar.*Pax*789.

⊛ **γυλιός** (*AB*228, *EM*244.21; also **γύλιος, γύλλιον,** Hsch.), ὁ, *long-shaped wallet*, Ar.*Ach.*1097, *Pax*527 (ubi v. Sch.), Critias 34 D., Philem.35, *IG*4.951.80 (Epid.), Lib.*Decl.*33.41. II. *hedgehog*, Sophr.73.

**γυλίσκος,** ὁ, a *fish* (cf. γυλάριον), Hsch. ⊛ **γύλλινα·** ἐρείσματα, γεῖσοι, Id.

**γυλλάς,** ἡ, kind of *cup* (Maced.), Hsch.; cf. γυάλας.

⊛ **γυλλός,** ὁ, *block of stone*, *Schwyzer* 725 (Milet., vi B.C.), *SIG*57.25 (Milet., v B.C.); also γυλλοί· στολμοί, Hsch.

**γυμν-άδδομαι,** Dor. for γυμνάζομαι, Ar.*Lys.*82. ⊛ **-άζω,** fut. -άσω: aor. ἐγύμνατα A.*Ag.*540: pf. γεγύμνακα Id.*Pr.*586 (lyr.):—**Med.,** (v. infr.):—**Pass.,** aor. ἐγυμνάσθην [D.]61.43: pf. γεγύμνασμαι (v. infr.): (γυμνός):—*train naked, train in gymnastic exercise*: generally, *train, exercise*, τὸ σῶμα, τὴν ψυχήν, Isoc.2.11; ἑαυτὸν καὶ τοὺς ἵππους X.*An.*1.2.7; ἑαυτὸν πρός τι Arr.*Epict.*2.18.27: c. inf., γ. τοὺς παῖδάς τι ποιεῖν *train* or *accustom* them *to* do a thing, X.*Cyr.*1.6.32; γ. τινά τινι *accustom* him *to* it, ib.1.2.10; τινὰ περί τι Isoc.10.5; *teach rhetoric*, Phld.*Rh.*2.50 S.:—Med., *exercise for oneself, practise*, γυμνάσασθαι τέχνην Pl.*Grg.*514e; τὰ περὶ τὰς διαίτας Str.14.2.19; γυμνάσιον τὸ εἰωθός Ael.*VH*5.6; *practise gymnastic exercises*, Thgn. 1335, Hdt.7.208, Th.1.6, etc.; δρόμῳ *IG*4.955.8 (ii A.D.), etc.; generally, *practise*, ναῦς -ομένας X.*HG*1.1.16; of a disputer, Arist.*Top.* 108$^{a}$13, etc.:—Pass., ὁ γεγυμνασμένος *the trained* or *practised* orator, opp. ὁ εὐφυής, Id.*Rh.*1410$^{b}$8; γεγυμνάσθαι πρός τι, ἔν τινι, *be trained* or *practised for* or *in* a thing, Pl.*Lg.*626b, 635c; περὶ τὰ ὅπλα γυμνάζεσθαι X.*HG*6.5.23: c. acc., τὰ πρὸς τὰς πολεμικὰς πράξεις γεγυμνασμένοι τὰς ἕξεις.. Arist.*Pol.*1319$^{a}$22; θήραν Philostr.*VA*3.9: c. gen., γεγ. θαλάττης, πολέμων, σοφίας, Id.*Her.*2.15, 3.1, 10.1; καρδία γεγ. πλεονεξίας τινί 2*Ep.Pet.*2.14; also ὕδωρ ὑπὸ συνεχῶν πληγῶν γεγ. καὶ κεκαθαρμένον J.*AJ*3.1.2. 2. *prepare*, βιβλίδιον *PFlor.*338.4 (iii A.D.). II. metaph., *wear out, harass*, ἄδην με..πλάναι γεγυμνάκασι A.*Pr.*586; ἔρως πατρῴας τῆσδε γῆς σ' ἐγύμνασε Id.*Ag.*540; κρυμὸς..πλευρὰ γυμνάζει χολῆς, of pleurisy, E.*Fr.*682:—Pass., τοὺς ὑπερμήκεις δρόμους..γυμνάζεται A.*Pr.*592. 2. *investigate*, *Sammelb.*5941.12 (Pass., vi A.D.). III. = γυμνόω, *PSI*1.70 (Pass., vi A.D.). **-άς,** άδος, prop. fem. of γυμνός, *naked*, E.*Tr.*448: also with masc. Subst., γ. στόλος ἀνδρῶν Id.*Fr.*105. II. *trained, exercised*, ποδὶ γυμνάδος ἵππου (restored for γυμνάδας ἵππους) E.*Hipp.* 1134 (lyr.): masc., *trained, practised*, ἀμφ' ἀρετήν *IG*3.1322. III. Subst., = γυμνασία or γυμνάσιον, γυμνάδος ἐν τεμένει *IG*12(7).447 (Amorg.), cf. 12(3).202 (Astypalaea); γυμνάδος..πόνον ἐκτελέσαντα *Inscr.Cos*419.5: pl., Orph.*H.*28.5. **-ᾰσία,** ἡ, *right to use* γυμνάσιον, Arist.*Pol.*1297$^{a}$17 (s.v.l.); *exercise*, σωματικὴ γ. 1*Ep.Ti.*4.8: pl., *IG*2$^{2}$.1006.65, *SIG*1073.19 (Olympia, ii A.D.); of *military exercises*, ἡ ἐν τοῖς ὅπλοις γ. Plb.4.7.6; generally, *struggle*, Str.3.2.7; αἱ καθ' ἡμέραν γ. *lessons*, D.H.*Comp.*20: metaph. of *mental exercise*, Iamb.*Comm.Math.*24; freq. of disputation, Pl.*Tht.*169c, Arist. *Top.*101$^{a}$27, al.; *training*, γ. πρὸς τὰς πολιτικὰς πράξεις Plb.1.1.2. 2. Rhet., *practice*: hence, *arrangement, disposition*, τοῦ διηγήματος Theo *Prog.*4, cf. Aphth.*Prog.*6.

⊛ **γυμνᾰσιαρχ-έω,** *to be gymnasiarch*, at Athens and elsewhere, *IG* 3.1104, al., 5(1).481, al. (Sparta), 7.1669 (Plataea), *BGU*184.3 (i A.D.), etc.; εἰς Προμήθεια Lys.21.3, Is.7.36; γ. λαμπάδι (cf. λαμπαδηφορία) Id.6.60:—Med., γυμνασιαρχεῖσθαι ἐν ταῖς λαμπάσι X.*Vect.* 4.52. II. trans., *provide for, supply as gymnasiarch*, πάντα τὰ γυμνάσια Keil-Premerstein *Zweiter Bericht* No.69:—Pass., *to be supplied with gymnasiarchs*, γυμνασιαρχοῦσιν οἱ πλούσιοι.., ὁ δὲ δῆμος γυμνασιαρχεῖται X.*Ath.*1.13. **-ης,** ου, ὁ, = -αρχος, *IG*3.1104, Lex ap.Aeschin.1.39. 2. name of a throw at dice, Hsch. ⊛ **-ία,** ἡ, *office of gymnasiarch*, X.*Ath.*1.13 (pl.), Arist.*Pol.*1323$^{a}$1, Pl.*Ax.* 367a, *IG*12(2).82 (Mytilene), 5(1).531 (Sparta), *PAmh.*70.3 (ii A.D.), etc. ⊛ **-ικός,** ή, όν, *of* or *for a gymnasiarch*, ῥάβδοι Plu.*Ant.*33; πολιτεία Iamb.*VP*27.130; νόμος *IG*12(7).515.82 (Amorg.); ἔκλογος *CPHerm.*53.7 (iii A.D.). ⊛ **-ίς,** ίδος, ἡ, fem. of -άρχης, *CIG*5132 (Cyren.), *PAmh.*64.6 (ii A.D.). ⊛ **-ος,** ὁ, *gymnasiarch, superintendent of athletic training* at Athens and elsewhere, And.1.132, D. 35.48, *IG*2$^{2}$.1227.4, 5(1).20 *A* 5 (Sparta), *PAmh.*2.130.1 (i A.D.), etc.: fem. ἡ -αρχος, *IGRom.*3.802 (Pamphyl.). 2. *director of a* γυμνάσιον, Pl.*Erx.*399a, Phld.*Herc.*1040.

**γυμνᾰσ-ίδιον,** τό, Dim. of sq., Arr.*Epict.*2.16.29. **-ιον** [ᾰ], τό, I. in pl., *bodily exercises*, Pi.*Fr.*129.4, Hdt.9.33, Hp.*Art.*58, Pl.*R.*539d, etc. 2. metaph., γυμνάσιον γράφειν write *an exercise* or *essay*, Gal.19.17. II. *gymnastic school*, E.*Ph.*368, Antipho 3.2.3, Pl.*Criti.*117c (pl.), etc.; ἐκ θἠμετέρου γυμνασίου from our *school*, Ar.*V.* 526: pl., γ. τὰ ἱππόκροτα the *hippodrome*, E.*Hipp.*229 (anap.). b. οἱ ἀπὸ γ. in Egypt, *those who have received training as* ἔφηβοι, i.e. the Hellenized inhabitants of the μητροπόλεις, *PFlor.*179.24 (i A.D.), etc. 2. generally, *school*, ἐν γυμνασίοις Ἀκαδημίας Epicr.11.11; ἐν Ὁμηρείῳ γ. *Epigr.Gr.*860 (Chios); γ. ἀρετῆς Luc.*Nigr.*19; of a philosophic *school*, ἐκ τοῦ αὐτοῦ γ. Pl.*Grg.*493d, cf. ὁ ἀπὸ τοῦ αὐτοῦ γ. Dam.*Pr.*399: metaph., γῆ γ. ζωῆς Secund.*Sent.*15. 3. in collective sense, *the youths who attend the school*, *IPE*2.299.8 (Panticapaeum). **-ις,** εως, ἡ, *exercise*, Poll.3.153. **-ιώδης,** ες, *fit for a* γυμνάσιον, *ornamenta* Cic.*Att.*1.6.2. **-μα,** ατος, τό, *an exercise*, γ. καὶ ἀσκήματα τῆς ῥητορικῆς D.H.*Rh.*2.1, cf. J.*Ap.*1.10, Plu.2.1119d; γ. τῆς ψυχῆς Ph.1.590: in pl., rhetorical *text-books*, Theo *Prog.* 1. 2. physical *exercises*, Ruf.ap.Orib.*inc.*2.15, Luc.*Anach.*8, Ath. 10.413c. **-τέον,** *one must train*, τὸ σῶμα X.*Mem.*2.1.28; of disputation, Arist.*Top.*164$^{b}$9. II. Adj. -τέος, α, ον, Philostr.*Gym.*29, al. **-τήριον,** τό, = γυμνάσιον, Gal.6.186: metaph., δικῶν Aristaenet. 2.3. **-τής,** οῦ, ὁ, *trainer of professional athletes*, X.*Mem.*2.1.20, Pl.*Lg.*720e, etc.; ἰατρὸς καὶ γ. Arist.*EN*1180$^{b}$14. ⊛ **-τικός,** ή, όν, *fond of athletic exercises, skilled in them*, Hp.*Aph.*1.3; γ. ἢ ἰατρός Pl. *Prt.*313d: Comp., Philostr.*Gym.*35: Sup., ib.11; *of the gymnastic master* (opp. παιδοτρίβης, q.v.), Arist.*Pol.*1288$^{b}$18; γ. [θεραπεία] Pl. *Grg.*464b: ἡ -κή (with or without τέχνη), *gymnastics*, Id.*Smp.*187a, etc. Adv. -κῶς Ar.*V.*1212. II. γ. λῆμμα (opp. ῥητορικόν) *suited for dialectical discussion*, *Stoic.*2.76. Adv. -κῶς *by means of testing*, Simp.*in Ph.*139.3.

**γυμν-ηλός,** ή, όν, *poor, needy*, Hsch., *EM*243.14. **-ής,** ῆτος, ὁ, = γυμνός, βίος D.S.?.8. II. Subst., *light-armed foot-soldier*, Tyrt.11.35, Hdt.9.63, E.*Ph.*1147, X.*An.*4.1.28, *Hell.Oxy.*6.5. 2. in pl., γυμνῆτες, οἱ, *Argive serfs*, Poll.3.83, *Et.Gud.*; also γυμνήσιοι, οἱ, St.Byz. s.v. Χίος, Eust. ad D.P.533. 3. = Γυμνοσοφισταί, Str.15. 1.70. **-ήσιαι** νῆσοι, αἱ, (γυμνής) the Balearic islands, from the skill of the inhabitants *as light-armed troops*, esp. slingers, Arist. *Mir.*837$^{a}$30, Str.3.5.1, D.S.5.17, etc.

**γυμνήσιοι,** v. γυμνής.

**γυμνητ-εία** (v.l. -ητία), ἡ, *light-armed troops*, Th.7.37. II. *nakedness*, Corn.*ND*15; *going unclothed*, as a symptom of insanity, Ptol.*Tetr.*170. **-εύω,** *to be naked*, 1*Ep.Cor.*4.11, Demoph.*Sent.* 8. 2. *to be lightly clad*, D.Chr.25.3. 3. *to be light-armed*, Plu. *Aem.*16. ⊛ **-ης,** ου, ὁ, = f.l. for γυμνής II. 1, X.*An.*4.1.6. II. Adj., *naked*, Lyc.388, Luc.*Bacch.*3. **-ικός,** ή, όν, *of* or *for a* γυμνής, ὅπλα X.*Cyr.*1.2.4, Plu.*Flam.*4; τὸ γ., = γυμνητεία, Str.7.3.17. **-ις,** ιδος, ἡ, fem. of γυμνήτης, in signf. of γυμνής II. 3, σοφία, Plu.2.332b.

⊛ **γυμνικός,** ή, όν, *of* or *for gymnastic exercises*, γ. ἀγών *a gymnastic contest*, Hdt.2.91, etc., opp. ἱππικός, Id.1.167; opp. μουσικός, Th. 3.104, Pl.*Lg.*658a; τὰ γ. ἐπιδείκνυσθαι *POxy.*42.5 (iv A.D.): Sup., Luc.*Ner.*2.

**γυμνο-δερκέομαι,** Pass., *show oneself naked*, Luc.*Cyn.*1. **-καρπος,** ον, *huskless*, of fruits, Thphr.*CP*1.17.8. **-κοχλίας,** *snail*, *Gloss.* **-παιδίαι,** αἱ, *festival* at Sparta, *at which naked boys danced and went through gymnastic exercises*, Hdt.6.67, Th.5.82, etc.: later in sg., Plu.2.208d; ἡ τῶν Λυκαίων γ., = *Lupercalia*, D.C. 44.11. **-παιδική** (sc. ὄρχησις), ἡ, *dance of naked boys*, Ath.14. 630d: pl., Phld *Mus.*p.15 K. ⊛ **-περίβολος,** ον, *bare of coverings*, epith. of Γυμνοσοφισταί, Ps.-Callisth.3.5. **-ποδέω,** *go barefoot*, Socr.*Ep.*13. **-πόδης,** ου, ὁ, = γυμνόπους, Suid. **-πόδιον,** τό, *kind of sandal* or *slipper*, Poll.7.94. **-πους,** ὁ, ἡ, gen. ποδος, *barefooted*, Str.7.2.3, J.*BJ*2.15.1. **-ρρύπᾰρος** [ῠ], ον, *naked and dirty*, of Zeno, D.L.7.16.

⊛ **γυμνός,** ή, όν, *naked, unclad*, γ. περ ἐών Od.6.136, etc.; τὰ γ. Thphr.*Char.*4.4: Comp., Ἴρου γυμνότερος Procop.Gaz.*Ep.*122; γυμνὸν στάδιον, opp. ὁπλιτοδρόμος, Pi.*P.*11.49. 2. *unarmed*, οὐδ' ὑπέμεινε Πάτροκλον, γυμνόν περ ἐόντ' ἐν δηϊοτῆτι Il.16.815, etc.; γυμνὰ τὰ νῶτα παρέχειν Plu.*Fab.*11; τὰ γυμνά *parts not covered by armour, exposed parts*, Th.3.23, X.*HG*4.4.12; esp. *right side* (the left being covered by the shields), Th.5.10.71. 3. of things *bare*, γ. τόξον an *uncovered* bow, i.e. taken out of the case, Od.11.607; γ. ὀϊστός 21.417; γ. μάχαιραι Theoc.22.146; ξίφος A.R.1.1254; γ. τῇ κεφαλῇ Pl.*Phdr.*243b. 4. c. gen., *stripped of* a thing, κολεοῦ γ. φάσγανον Pi. *N.*1.52, cf. X.*Ages.*2.14; κᾶπος [δένδρων] γ. Pi.*O.*3.24; γ. ὀστράκων A.*Fr.*337; γ. προπομπῶν Id.*Pers.*1036 (lyr.); (but also γ. τῶν ἀριστείων ἄτερ S.*Aj.*464): in Prose, γ. ὅπλων Hdt.2.141 (v.l.); ἡ ψυχὴ γ. τοῦ σώματος Pl.*Cra.*403b, cf. *R.*577b, *Grg.*523d: Comp. ἀνδριάντων -ότερος D.Chr.34.3. 5. *lightly clad*, i.e. *in the undergarment only*, Hes.*Op.*391, Ar.*Nu.*498, Pl.*R.*474a, Luc.*Herm.*23;

μικροῦ γ. ἐν τῷ χιτωνίσκῳ D.21.216; of horses, *without harness*, Arr. *Cyn*.24.3. **6.** of facts, *naked, bald*, γυμνῶν τῶν πραγμάτων θεωρουμένων D.S.1.76; γ. τὸ ἔργον διηγήσασθαι Luc.*Tox*.42; γυμνοτέροις χρήσασθαι τοῖς ὀνόμασιν Ph.1.5; γ. χρῆσθαι τῇ μιμήσει Demetr.*Eloc*. 112. Adv. -ῶς *baldly*, Sch.A.*Pers*.740. **7.** *destitute*, *PSI*6.605. 4 (iii B.C.), etc. **8.** *bare, mere*, κόκκος 1*Ep.Cor*.15.37. **9.** *beardless*, A.R.2.707. **10.** *scalped*, Archil.161. **11.** γυμνή· ἄνηβος, Hsch. **12.** prov. of impossibilities, γυμνῷ φυλακὴν ἐπιτάττεις Pherecr.144, Philem.12. (Akin to Skt. *nagnás*, Lat. *nūdus*, etc.; cf. λυγνός.)

**γυμνο-σάνδᾰλος**, ον, *without sandals, barefooted*, *PMag.Par*.1. 2481. **-σοφισταί**, ῶν, οἱ, *naked philosophers* of India, Arist.*Fr*.35, Str.16.2.39, Ph.2.27, Plu.*Alex*.64, Luc.*Fug*.7, Porph.*Abst*.4.17:—hence **-σοφιστεία**, ἡ, *their philosophy*, Suid. s.v. Ἀδάμ. **-σπέρματος** and **-σπερμος**, ον, *having the seed with no apparent pericarp*, Thphr.*HP*1.11.2 and 3.

**γυμνότης**, ητος, ἡ, *nakedness*, Lxx *De*.28.48, *Ep.Rom*.8.35, M.Ant. 10.27; γ. ψυχική Ph.1.77. **2.** *bare statement*, τῶν προτάσεων D.H. *Rh*.10.6.

**γυμνο-φᾰνής**, ές, *appearing naked*, πόρναι Lyd.*Mag*.3.65. **-χρους**, ὁ, ἡ, *having the body naked*, Nonn.*D*.7.124.

⊛ **γυμν-όω**, *strip naked*, τὰ ὀστέα τῶν κρεῶν γ. *strip* the bones of their flesh, Hdt.4.61; σῶμα γυμνώσαντες εὖ S.*Ant*.410:—Hom. only Med. and Pass., *strip oneself* or *be stripped naked*, αἰδέομαι γὰρ γυμνοῦσθαι Od.6.222; mostly of warriors, *to be exposed*, ὅτεῳ στρεφθέντι μετάφρενα γυμνωθείη Il.12.428; οὖτα Θόαντα στέρνον γυμνωθέντα παρ' ἀσπίδα 16.312, cf. Od.10.341, Call.*Iamb*.1.219; τεῖχος ἐγυμνώθη the wall *was left bare*, i.e. *defenceless*, Il.12.399: c. gen., γυμνώθη ῥακέων he *stripped himself* of his rags, Od.22.1; later γυμνωθὲν ξίφος, δόρυ, Hdt.3.64, A.*Th*.624: metaph., *to be stripped* or *deprived of* a thing, Pl.*R*.601b; ἀφορμῆς Antipho Soph.14. **2.** metaph., *lay bare*, φύσιν τῷ λόγῳ Ph.1.118:—Pass., Dam.*Pr*.400. **3.** *lay aside*, σάκκον Lxx *Ju*.9.1. **-ωσις**, εως, ἡ, *stripping*, παρθένων Plu. *Lyc*.14, cf. *Cat.Ma*.20, Dsc.2.173. **II.** *exposure*, Lxx *Ge*.9.22; ἐξαλλάσσειν τὴν ἑαυτοῦ γ. his *defenceless side* (cf. γυμνός 2), Th.5. 71. **-ωτέος**, α, ον, *to be stripped of*, τινός Pl.*R*.361c. **II.** γυμνωτέον *one must strip*, Gal.10.448: pl., -τέα Them.*Or*.23.294c.

⊛ **γῠναικ-άδελφος** [ᾰ], ὁ, *wife's brother*, *PMasp*.95.14 (vi A.D.), Sch. S.*OT*70, Sch.E.*Hec*.833. **-άνηρ** [ᾰ], ανδρος, ὁ, *woman-man*: dat. pl., γυναικάνδρεσσι Epich.218, cf. Eust.1132.32. **-άνθη**, ἡ, = ἄμπελος μέλαινα, Plin.*HN*23.27. **-άριον**, τό, Dim. of γυνή, Diocl. Com.11, Epict.*Ench*.7, 2*Ep.Ti*.3.6, M.Ant.5.11. ⊛ **-εῖος**, α, ον A. *Ch*.630 (lyr.), also ος, ον ib.878, E.*IA*233 (lyr.): Ion. **-ήιος**, η, ον: (γυνή):—*of* or *belonging to women, feminine*, γυναικεῖαι βουλαί *a woman's* designs, Od.11.437; λουτρόν Hes.*Op*.753; ἔργα Hdt.4.114; κόσμος Pl.*R*.373c; σκεῦος (i.e. *woman*) 1*Ep.Pet*.3.7; γ. αἰδοῖον, τόποι, χῶροι, Gal.*UP*15.3, Aret.*SA*2.11, *CA*2.10; κόλπος (= αἰδοῖον) Sor.1. 16; ῥοῦς *leucorrhoea*, Id.2.43; γονόρροια Aret.*SD*2.11; ἰατρός Sor.2.3; γ. ἀγορά Thphr.*Char*.2.9; ἡ γ. θεός, = Lat. *bona dea*, Plu.*Caes*.9, *Cic*. 19; γ. πόλεμος war *with women*, *AP*7.352 (Mel.(?)). **2.** in bad sense, *womanish, effeminate*, πένθος Archil.9.10; δράματα Ar.*Th*. 151; μαθήματα Pl.*Alc*.1.127a; γ. καὶ σμικρὰ διάνοια Id.*R*.469d. Adv. -είως, πικραίνεσθαι Id.*Lg*.731d; ἐμπικραίνεσθαι Eus.Mynd.54; διακεῖσθαι D.C.38.18. **II.** as Subst., **1.** ἡ γυναικεία, Ion. -ηίη, = γυναικών, *part of the house reserved for the women*, Hdt.5.20, Lxx *To*.2.11. **b.** ἡ γ. (sc. ἀγορά), Thphr.*Char*.22.10. **2.** τὰ γυναικεῖα *partes muliebres*, Hp.*Epid*.1.26 ε', Aret.*SA*2.11. **b.** = τὰ καταμήνια, Hp.*Aph*.5.28, Arist.*PA*648$^{a}$31, al., Lxx *Ge*.18.11. **c.** *lochia*, Gal.17(2).817. **d.** *female disorders*, title of works by Hp. and Sor., cf. Thphr.*HP*4.8.6, Aret.*CA*1.3. **e.** (sc. φάρμακα) *remedies for female complaints*, Hp.*Mul*.1.64. **f.** *women's garments*, *PSI* 4.341.7 (iii B.C.). **3.** γυναικεῖον, τό, = στίβι, Dsc.5.84. **-εραστέω**, *to be a lover of women*, and **-εραστής**, οῦ, ὁ, *woman-lover*, Poll. 3.68,70. **-ήιος**, η, ον, Ion. for γυναικεῖος (q.v.). **-ηρός**, ά, όν, = γυναικεῖος, Diocl.Com.4; γ. τρόπος Phryn.*PS*p.55 B. **-ίας**, ου, ὁ, = γύννις, *weakling*, Eup.124 (dub.), Luc.*Pisc*.31, Lib.*Or*.64. 64. **-ίζω**, *to be womanish, play the woman*, Hp.*Aër*.22, Ar.*Th*. 268:—Med., Plb.32.15.7, J.*BJ*4.9.10. **II.** *muliebria pati*, Luc. *Gall*.19: = ἀφροδισιάζεσθαι, Hsch. **-ικός**, ή, όν, *womanish*, Arist. *Pr*.895$^{a}$32, *GA*766$^{b}$32 (Comp.); γυναικικώτεροι γίνονται οἱ μαστοί *more like those of women*, Id.*HA*582$^{a}$13. Adv. -κῶς Suid. **-ιον**, τό, Dim. of γυνή, Longus 3.6.15 (v.l. γύναιον). **-ισις**, εως, ἡ, *womanish behaviour*, Ar.*Th*.863, Lib.*Or*.64.74. **-ίσκιον**, τό, *young girl*, Hsch. **-ισμός**, ὁ, *womanish weakness*, Plb.30.18.5, cf. Phld.*Mus*.p.16 K., D.S.31.15, Plu.*Caes*.63. **-ιστί**, Adv. *like a woman*, Ath.12.528f.

**γῠναικό-βουλος**, ον, *devised by a woman*, μήτιδες A.*Ch*.626 (lyr.). **-γήρῡτος**, ον, *proclaimed by a woman*, κλέος Id.*Ag*.487 (lyr.). **-δίδακτος** [ῐ], ον, *taught by a woman*, Olymp.*in Alc*. p.136 C. **-ειδής**, ές, = γυναικώδης, Sch.Ar.*Nu*.289. **-ήθης**, ες, *of womanish disposition*, Hsch. s.v. μαλακός. **-θοίνας**, ὁ, *feasted by the women* or *feaster of women*, epith. of Ares at Tegea, Paus.8.48.4. **-θῡμος**, ον, *of womanish mind*, Ptol.*Tetr*.162. Adv. -μως Plb.2.8.12; χειρίζειν τι, of a man, Id.32.15.9. **-ἵέραξ**, ᾱκος, ὁ, *woman-hunter*, Anon.ap.Suid. **-κλωψ**, ωπος, ὁ, *stealer of women*, Lyc.771. **-κοσμοι**, οἱ, = γυναικονόμοι, Poll.8. 112. **-κρᾱσία**, ἡ, (κρᾶσις) *womanish temper*, Str.3.4.18, Plu. *Cleom*.33 (s.v.l.), 2.20a. ⊛ **-κρᾰτέομαι**, Pass., *to be ruled by women*, Arist.*Pol*.1269$^{b}$24, D.S.2.45, Plu.2.755c. **-κράτητος** [ᾰ], ον, *ruled by women*, Sch.E.*Or*.742. **-κρᾰτία** (-κράτεια Procop.*Arc*.5), ἡ, *dominion of women*, Arist.*Pol*.1313$^{b}$33, Plu.*Cat. Ma*.8: title of plays by Amphis and Alexis. **-κτόνος**, ον, *murdering women*, Ph.2.581, *Cat.Cod.Astr*.8(4).128. **-μᾰνέω**, *to be mad for women*, Ar.*Th*.576, J.*BJ*1.22.3. **-μᾰνής**, ές, *mad for women*, Chrysipp.*Stoic*.3.167, Ph.2.312, Gal.5.396, *AP*12.86 (Mel.), Luc.*Alex*.11. **-μᾰνία**, ἡ, *madness for women*, Chrysipp.*Stoic*.3. 167. **-μασθος** or **-μαστος**, ον, *having breasts like a woman*: -μασθον, τό, abnormal development of the mamma, Gal.19.444, cf. Paul.Aeg.6.46. **-μῖμος**, ον, *aping women*, γυναικομίμοις ὑπτιάσμασιν χερῶν A.*Pr*.1005; ἐσθήματα S.*Fr*.769; μόρφωμα E.*Antiop*. ii *A* 7 A.; στολά Id.*Ba*.980 (lyr.). **-μορφος**, ον, *in woman's shape*, ib.855, Ph.2.280. **-νομέω**, *to be a* γυναικονόμος, *BCH*47. 376 (Notium), Artem.2.31. **-νομία**, ἡ, *office of* γυναικονόμος, Arist.*Pol*.1322$^{b}$39. ⊛ **-νόμος**, ὁ, *supervisor of women*, title of magistrate at Athens and elsewhere, Timocl.32.3, Men.272, Arist.*Pol*. 1299$^{a}$22, Philoch.103, *IG*5(1).170 (Sparta, iii A.D.), 1390.26 (Andania, i B.C.), *SIG*1219.17 (Gambreion).

**γῠναικο-πᾰθέω**, *to be effeminate*, Ath.12.523c. ⊛ **-πίπης** [ῑ], ου, ὁ, (ὀπιπτεύω) *one who ogles women*, Eust.851.54. **-πληθής**, ές, *composed of women*, ὅμιλος A.*Pers*.122 (lyr.); ξύλλογοι E.*Alc*.952. **-ποινος**, ον, *woman-avenging*, πόλεμοι A.*Ag*.225 (lyr.). **-πρεπής**, ές, *befitting women, womanish*, Plu.2.102e: Comp., Procl.*Par.Ptol*.203. **-πρεπώδης**, ες, = foreg., Ptol.*Tetr*.144 (Comp.). **-πρόσωπος**, ον, *with woman's face*, *Mim.Oxy*.465.203, Sch.Il.1.131. **-τροφος**, ον, *reared by a woman*, Suid. s.v. τηθαλλαδοῦς. **-ῠφή**, ἡ, *women's weaving*, τεχνῖται τῆς κατὰ τὴν ἐρέαν πᾶσαν γυναικυφη (sic), *PSI*4. 341.2 (iii B.C.). ⊛ **-φίλης** [ῐ], ου, Dor. **-ας**, α, ὁ, *woman loving*, Polyzel.10, Theoc.8.[60]: voc. -φίλα *AP*6.78 (Eratosth.). **-φόνος**, ον, *slaying women*, ἰχώρ Orph.*L*.488 (s.v.l.). **-φρων**, ον, gen. ονος, *of woman's mind*, E.*Fr*.362.34. **-φῠής**, ές, *female by nature*, Emp.61.4. **-φωνος**, ον, '*speaking small like a woman*', Ar.*Th*.192. **-ψῡχος**, ον, *of womanish soul*, Procl.*Par.Ptol*. 228.

⊛ **γῠναικόω**, *make effeminate*, Ph.2.21:—Pass., Hp.*Epid*.6.8.32; παρθένος οὐδέποτε γυναικουμένη Ph.1.682.

**γῠναικ-ώδης**, ες, *woman-like, womanish*, τὸ ἀγεννὲς καὶ γ. Plb.2. 56.9, cf. D.S.2.24, Ph.1.366; ἄνανδρα καὶ γ. πάθη Plu.*Sol*.21: -ῶδες φθέγγεσθαι Luc.*Nigr*.11. Adv. -δῶς Sch.Ar.*Th*.575. **-ών**, ῶνος, ὁ, = sq., X.*Cyr*.5.5.2. **-ωνῖτις**, ιδος, ἡ, *women's apartments* in a house, opp. ἀνδρών (cf. γυναικών), Lys.1.9, Men.519, Ph.1.107, etc.; *harem* of an eastern prince, i.e. *the women*, Plu.*Cat.Mi*.30, 2. 819d; at Jerusalem, the *women's court* in the Temple, J.*BJ*5.5. 2. **2.** as Adj., ἡ γ. αὐλή the court *of the women's apartments*, D.S.17.50; ἑστία Ph.1.312.

**γῠναι-μᾰνής**, ές, = γυναικομανής, *mad for women*, Il.3.39, *h.Bacch*. 17, Ael.*NA*15.14, Q.S.1.726:—in late Ep. **-μανέων**, as if a part., ib. 735, Nonn.*D*.2.125, al. **II.** *making women mad*, Hsch.

⊛ **γύναιος** [ῠ], α, ον, = γυναικεῖος, γ. δῶρα presents *made to a woman*, Od.11.521, 15.247; φυὴ γυναίη Mosch.2.45. **II.** Subst. **γύναιον**, τό, *little woman*, term of endearment for a wife, Ar.*V*.610, *Th*.792: more freq. in a contemptuous sense, *weak woman*, And.1.130, etc.; γυναίου πρᾶγμ' ἐποίει D.25.57, cf. Arist.*EN*1171$^{b}$10: but simply, = γυνή, Aen.Tact.2.6, D.S.17.24, J.*AJ*1.12.4, al., Ph.1.99, al., Plu. *Pel*.9.

⊛ **γύνανδρος** [ῠ], ον, *of doubtful sex, womanish*, S.*Fr*.963, Ael.*Fr*.10, 290. **2.** of a woman, *virago*, Ph.1.183, 2.379.

**γῠνή**, Dor. **γυνά**, Boeot. **βανά** (v. sub voce), ἡ, gen. γυναικός, acc. γυναῖκα, voc. γύναι (γυνή Alc.Com.32): dual γυναῖκε S.*Ant*.61: pl. γυναῖκες, γυναικῶν, etc. (as if from γύναιξ wh. is only found in Gramm., cf. Hdn.Gr.2.643): gen. γυναικείων Phoc.3 (s.v.l.): Aeol. dat. pl. γυναίκεσσι Sapph.*Supp*.7.6: Com. acc. γυνήν Pherecr.91: pl. nom. γυναί Philippid.2, Men.484, acc. γυνάς *Com.Adesp*.1336, cf. *EM*243.24, *AB*86:—*woman*, opp. *man*, Il.15.683, etc.: with a second Subst., γ. ταμίη housekeeper, 6.390; δέσποινα Od.7.347; γρηῦς (q.v.), ἀλετρίς (q.v.), δμῳαὶ γυναῖκες Il.9.477, al.; Περσίδες γ. Hdt.3.3: voc., as a term of respect or affection, *mistress, lady*, E.*Med*.290, Theoc.15.12, etc.; φαντὶ γυναῖκες *the lasses* say, Id.20.30; πρὸς γυναικός like *a woman*, A.*Ag*.592: prov., γ. μονωθεῖσ' οὐδέν Id.*Supp*. 749; ὅρκους γυναικὸς εἰς ὕδωρ γράφω (cf. γράφω II) S.*Fr*.811; γυναιξὶ κόσμον ἡ σιγὴ φέρει Id.*Aj*.293. **II.** *wife, spouse*, Il.6.160, Od.8. 523, Hdt.1.34, etc.; γ. καὶ παρθένοι X.*An*.3.2.25; opp. ἑταίρα, Is.3. 13; γ. γνησία, *PEleph*.1.3 (iv B.C.); also, *concubine*, Il.24.497. **III.** *mortal woman*, opp. *goddess*, 14.315, Od.10.228, etc. **IV.** *female, mate* of animals, Arist.*Pol*.1262$^{a}$22 (dub. sens.), Xenarch.14, etc.—Not to be taken as Adj. in γυναῖκα θήσατο μαζόν Il.24.58. (Cf. Ved. *gnā*- (freq. disyll.), Skt. *janis*.)

**γύννις**, ιδος, ὁ, *a womanish man*, ποδαπὸς ὁ γ.; of Bacchus, A.*Fr*. 61, cf. Theoc.22.69 (s.v.l.), Ael.*VH*12.12, Lib.*Or*.64.49. **2.** = ἵππουρις, Ps.-Dsc.4.46,47.

**γύον**, τό, = γύης, Sch.Od.18.374.

**γύος**, ὁ, = γύης II, *PLips*.106.16 (i A.D.), *PTeb*.373.7 (ii A.D.), etc.

**γῡπ-αιεύς**, έως, ὁ, title of Apollo, Conon 35.5. **-ᾰλέκτωρ**, ορος, ὁ, *vulture-cock*, fabulous bird, *PMag.Berol*.2.18. **-άριον**, τό, Dim. of sq., *nest, cranny*, Ar.*Eq*.793.

⊛ **γύπη** [ῡ], ἡ, *vulture's nest*, Hsch.; κοίλωμα γῆς, θαλάμη, γωνία, Id.

**γῡπιαῖος**, α, ον, = γύπινος, Tz.*H*.12 No.430 tit.

⊛ **γῡπ-ιάς**, άδος, ἡ, *vulture-haunted*, πέτρα A.*Supp*.796 (lyr.). ⊛ **-ινος**, η, ον, *of a vulture*, πτέρυξ Luc.*Icar*.11.

**γῡπο-γίγας** [ῐ], αντος, ὁ, in pl., 'men of prey', Marin.*Procl.* 15. **-ειδής**, ές, *vulture-like*: τὸ γ. Porph.ap.Eus.*PE*3.12.

**γυπόν**· μακρόν, Hsch.

**γῡπώδης**, ες, = γυποειδής, *hooknosed*, Arist.*Phgn.*$808^{b}7$.

⊛ **γύπωνες**, οἱ, dancers at Sparta, Poll.4.104.

**γῡράλεος** [ᾰ], α, ον, = γυρός, *rounded, curved*, Opp.*C.*1.57.

⊛ **γυργᾰθίον**, τό, Dim. of sq., in Alchemy, *net* for suspending substances in fluids, *PHolm.*18.17.

⊛ **γυργᾰθός** (on the accent v. Hdn.Gr.1.145, but γύργαθος in Mss.), ὁ, *wicker-basket, creel*, Ar.*Fr.*217, Aen.Tact.18.6, Timo38, Luc.*DMeretr.*14.2; of the *net* woven by phalangia, Arist.*HA*$555^{b}10$; *cage* for insane patients, Paul.Aeg.3.14: prov., γυργαθὸν φυσᾶν, of labour in vain, Aristaen.2.20:—also **γυργαθόν**, τό, *BGU*1092.29 (iv A.D.); cf. γεργαθός.

**γῡρεύω**, *run round in a circle*, Str.6.1.8: c. acc. cogn., καμπτῆρας Babr.29.4.

⊛ **γῡρητόμος**, ον, *tracing a circle*, αὖλαξ *AP*9.274 (Phil.).

**γῡρίνη**, ἡ, a kind of *cake*, Luc.*Trag.*158.

⊛ **γῦρῖνος** (so Hdn.Gr.1.183) or **γύρῖνος**, ὁ, *tadpole*, [βάτραχος] γ. Pl.*Tht.*161d, cf. Arat.947; χείρους γυρίνων οἱ ῥήτορες Lib.*Decl.*26.36.

**γῠρῖνώδης**, ες, *like a tadpole*, Arist.*HA*$568^{a}1$.

**γύριος** [ῡ], α, ον, (γυρός) *circular, round*, λίμνη Anon.ap.Suid.

**γῦρις**, εως, ἡ, *the finest meal*, Dsc.2.85, Sor.1.118, Ath.3.115d, *POxy.*520.12 (ii A.D.):—also **γύριος**, prob. in *PSI*4.428.44 (iii B.C.), cf. *girius*, = *farina, pollen, Gloss.*

**γῡρ-ιστήριον** κόσκινον, *sieve for* γῦρις, *Gloss.* **-ιστός**, ή, όν, *rounded, curved*, Sch.Philostr.p.579 B. **-ίτης** [ῑ] (sc. ἄρτος), ου, ὁ, *bread of the finest meal*, *Gp.*20.41, Hsch.

**γῡρο-δρόμος**, ον, *running round in a circle*, πέτρος a millstone, *AP*9.20. ⊛ **-ειδής**, ές, *like a circle, round.* Adv. -δῶς Dsc.2.173.

**γῡρόθεν**, Adv. *in a circle*, [Lib.] *Descr.*30.14.

**γῡρόμαντις**, εως, ὁ, (γῦρις) = ἀλευρόμαντις, dub. l. in Artem.2.69.

⊛ **γῡρός**, ά, όν, *rounded, curved, crooked*, γυρὸς ἐν ὤμοισι *round-shouldered*, Od.19.246, cf. D.H.14.10, *Hymn.Is.*29; κέρας, ἄγκιστρα, *AP*6.255 (Eryc.), 28 (Jul.); κόνις, of a tomb, ib.7.180 (Apollonid.); γ. πάλη, i.e. wrestling, Philostr.*Gym.*11: Comp. -ότερος Ael.*NA*4.34.

**γῦρ-ος**, ὁ, *ring, circle*, Plb.29.11.5; γ. οὐρανοῦ, γῆς, Lxx *Jb.*22.14, *Is.*40.22; perh. an *ornament, bangle*, Men.334. 2. *trench* made round a tree, Thphr.*CP*3.4.1, Orph.*Fr.*280.4; γύρους περισκάψας Alciphr.3.13. ⊛ **-όω**, *make round*, οὐρανόν Lxx *Si.*43.12; *bend*, Opp.*H.*2.333; *wind*, τρίχα ἵππου *PHolm.*3.42 (γήρ- Pap.); *bind up*, Opp.*H.*4.419; ἐπ' αὐχένι δεσμὰ βραχίοσι γ. of a bride, ib. 150:—Pass., *to be bent*: hence of the aged, *to be weak* in body, *Com.Adesp.*969. II. *plant in a* γῦρος, Arat.9, Ph.2.294; *make a* γῦρος *round* a tree, ib.402, *Gp.*4.3.1:—Med., *dig, trench*, βώλακα γαίης Nic.*Al.*514. III. intr., *coil oneself up*, of the ichneumon, Opp.*C.*3.440.

**γυρτεύς**· ἀνακρωτόφονος, Hsch. ⊛ **γυρτόν**· σκύφον, Id.

⊛ **γύρ-ωσις** [ῡ], εως, ἡ, *making of a* γῦρος, *POxy.*1631.11 (iii A.D.), *Gp.*2.46.4. **-ωτέον**, *one must surround with a* γῦρος, τοὺς ὀφθαλμούς ib.5.21.2.

**γῦς**, written for γύος, *PLond.*1.131r.82, al. (i A.D.).

⊛ **γύψ**, γῡπός, ὁ (ἡ only as v.l. in Porph.ap.Eus.*PE*3.12), Ep. dat. γύπεσσι Il.11.162:—*vulture*, prob. including several species, 22.42, E.*Tr.*599, Arist.*HA*$563^{a}5$, etc.

**γυψ-εμπλαστής**, οῦ, ὁ, = γυψωτής, Zonar. **-εμπλαστικός**, ή, όν, *belonging to plasterers*, Phlp.*in APo.*382.16. ⊛ **-ίζω**, *plaster with gypsum*, *PMag.Lond.*46.360. **-ική**, ἡ, *tax on plasterers*, *BGU*471.15, *PFay.*23a. ⊛ **-ινος**, η, ον, *made of gypsum*, ἀγαλμάτιον *EM*530.15. II. γ., τό, *room plastered with gypsum*, *BGU*1028.88 (ii A.D.). **-ίον**, τό, = γύψος, *Stud.Pal.*10.259 (vi A.D.). **-ισμός**, ὁ, *plastering with gypsum*, *BGU*952.8 (pl., ii/iii A.D.).

**γυψοειδής**, ές, = γυψώδης, Paul.Aeg.6.21.

⊛ **γύψος**, ἡ, *chalk*, Hdt.7.69, Pl.*Phd.*110c. II. *gypsum*, Thphr.*Lap.*64, *BGU*952.8 (ii/iii A.D.). III. *cement*, Thphr.*Lap.*65, Ph.*Bel.*79.5; ἐν γύψῳ κείμενος embedded in *cement*, D.S.2.10, Arr.*An.*2.21.4.

**γυψ-όω**, *rub with chalk, chalk over*, Hdt.3.24, 8.27, Polyaen.6.18.1. 2. *plaster with gypsum*, *Gp.*4.15.13. **-ώδης**, ες, *chalky*, γάλα Sor.1.91, cf. Eust.1304.27. **-ωσις**, εως, ἡ, *plastering*, *Gp.*6 *Arg.*18. **-ωτής**, οῦ, ὁ, *plasterer*, *EM*811.36. **-ωτός**, ή, όν, *plastered*, Hsch. s.v. τιτανωτή.

**γῶ**, coined by Gramm., as etym. of χωρῶ, γαστήρ, γυνή, γωρυτός, etc., *Et.Gud.* s.v. γεγῶσα, cf. *EM*244.6, Philox.ap.Orion 39.

**γωγγάμη**, = γαγγάμη, Hsch. **γωγώνη**· φάρυγξ, Id.

**γωλεός**, ὁ, *a hole*, Arist.*HA*$603^{a}6$ (v.l. φωλεός); **γωλιός**, Hsch.: heterocl. pl., φωλειοῦ ὑπὸ γωλεά Nic.*Th.*125; γωλειά Lyc.376. (Cf. Lith. *guõlis* 'lair'.)

**γῶν**, Ion. for γοῦν,

⊛ **γωνία**, ἡ, *corner, angle*, Hdt.1.51, Pl.*Men.*84d, etc.; γ. ἐπίπεδος, στερεά, *plane, solid angle*, Euc.1 *Def.*8, 11 *Def.*11; αἱ πρὸς τῇ βάσει γ. *the angles* at the base, Id.1.5; ἡ ὑπὸ ΒΑΓ or ὑπὸ τῶν ΒΑΓ γ. *the angle* ΒΑΓ, Id.1.9, al. 2. metaph., *corner, secluded spot*, ἐν γωνίᾳ ψιθυρίζειν Pl.*Grg.*485d; ἐν γ. πεπραγμένον *Act.Ap.*26.26. 3. of the four *quarters* of the compass, Ptol.*Tetr.*29. 4. *joint*, Arist.*PA*$690^{a}13$. II. *joiner's square*, Pl.*Phlb.*51c, Plu.*Marc.*19. III. *cutwater* of a bridge, D.S.2.8. IV. of persons, *leader, chief*, Lxx 1 *Ki.*14.38. (Akin to γόνυ.)

**γωνι-άζω**, *place at an angle*, Porph.*in Cat.*132.31. ⊛ **-αῖος**, α, ον, *on* or *at the angle*, λίθος Lxx *Jb.*38.6, cf. *IG*$1^2$.372.19; στυλίς D.H.3.22; μέρος τείχους J.*BJ*5.3.5; also γωνιήϊος *BCH*26.64 (Delph.). II. *angular*, γ. ῥῆμα, i.e. hard to pronounce, Pl.Com.67. **-ακός**, ή, όν, *angular, of, in* or *at angles*, συμβολαί Procl. *in Euc.*p.129 F.; κόσμοι Id.*in Ti.*1.454 D.; ὀδούς Sch.Ar.*Pl.*1059. Adv. -κῶς, γ. καὶ ἐπιπέδως Procl.*in Ti.*2.217 D. **-ασμός**, ὁ, *squaring off corners*, Lys.*Fr.*61; name of a *proposition in geometry*, Hsch.: metaph., ἐπῶν γωνιασμοί *finishing* of verses *by square and rule*, Ar.*Ra.*956.

**γωνίδιον**, τό, Dim. of γωνία, Luc.*Nec.*17, M.Ant.3.10.

**γωνιο-βόμβυξ**, ῡκος, ὁ, *one that buzzes in a corner*, nickname of Grammarians, Herodic.ap.Ath.5.222a. **-ειδής**, ές, *angular*, Arist.*GC*$319^{b}14$, Thphr.*HP*1.10.1, al. (γωνο- codd.), *PHib.*1.16.42 (Thphr.(?)). ⊛ **-ομαι**, Pass., *become angular*, Dsc.3.7; γεγωνιωμένα σχήματα Procl. *in Euc.*p.163 F. **-ποιέομαι**, *form into an angle*:—Pass., Erot. s.v. ἐγγώνιος πῆχυς. **-πους**, ὁ, ἡ, **-πουν**, τό, gen. ποδος, *crook-footed*, D.L.9.116.

**γώνιος**, = γωνιακός, εἴδη *Theol.Ar.*3 (s.v.l.); *angular*, σφυρίδια *PKlein.Form.*321.4 (vi A.D.).

**γωνιόφυλλος**, ον, *with pointed leaves*, Thphr.*HP*1.10.5.

**γωνι-ώδης**, ες, *angular*, Th.8.104; *at a sharp angle*, διαστροφή Hp.*Art.*47. **-ωμα**, ατος, τό, = γωνία, Eust.1082.28. ⊛ **-ωσις**, εως, ἡ, name for a pulse, coined by Archig.ap.Gal.9.324. **-ωτός**, ή, όν, *angular*, Paul.Aeg.6.88.

**γωνοειδής**, ές, = γωνιο-, Democr.ap.Thphr.*Sens.*65, freq. written in codd. of Thphr.

**γῶνορ**, = γωνία (Lacon.), Hsch. **γωνορίσματα**· γνωρίσματα, τοποθεσίαι, Id. ⊛ **γῶνος**· γουνός, ἕδος, καὶ παιδιά τις παλαιστρική, οἱ δὲ κώπη, Id. **γώνυμος**· φερώνυμος, Id. **γῶος**· μνημεῖον, Id. **γωροῦται**· σαρκοῖ (Lacon.), Id.

⊛ **γωρῡτός**, ὁ (ἡ *AP*6.34 (Rhian.)), *quiver*, ἀπὸ πασσάλου αἴνυτο τόξον αὐτῷ γωρυτῷ Od.21.54, cf. Lyc.458, *AP*6.34 (Rhian.), J.*AJ*3.5.5, Luc.*Herc.*1, Q.S.3.35; γ. πλήρεις ὀϊστῶν Anon.ap.Suid., cf. *EM*244.7; wrongly expld. as *bow-case*, Apollon.*Lex.*, Eust.1898.21.

**γώψ**· κολοιός (Maced.), Hsch.

# Δ

**Δ δ, δέλτα** (q.v.), fourth letter of the Gr. alphabet: as numeral, δʹ, = τέσσαρες and τέταρτος, but ͵δ, = 4,000.

**δᾰ-**, intens. Prefix, = ζα-, as in δάσκιος, δαφοινός.

**δᾶ**, expld. by the Sch.A.*Ag.*1072, *EM*60.8 as Dor. for γᾶ, γῆ, in Trag. (lyr.) φεῦ δᾶ, E.*Ph.*1296, Ar.*Lys.*198; οἰοῖ δᾶ φεῦ A.*Eu.*874; ἄλευ' ἆ δᾶ Id.*Pr.*567; ὀτοτοτοτοτοῖ ποποῖ δᾶ Id.*Ag.*1072; οὐ δᾶν no *by earth*, Theoc.4.17 (v.l. γᾶν):—prob. an exclamation of horror.

**δαάναι**· δύεσθαι, ὅσον εἰς τὴν χρείαν τοῦ στήμονος μεριζόμενον καθάπτεσθαι, Hsch. **δαβελός** [i.e. δαϝ], = δαλός (Lacon.), Id. **δαβῆ**· καυθῇ (Lacon.), Id.

**δαγκάνω**, = δάκνω, cf. Heraclid.ap.Eust.28.42, Hdn.Gr.1.451, etc.

**δάγκολον**, τό, = δρέπανον, Hsch.; cf. ζάγκλη.

**δάγμα**, ατος, τό, v. δάχμα.

**δάγμνος** (sic)· οἰκτρός, πένης, ἐλεεινός, Hsch.

**δαγμός**, ὁ, = δηγμός, Ruf.*Fr.*64.20.

⊛ **δαγνόν**· πυκνόν, Hsch. (leg. ἀδινόν). **δαγόμενον**· ἐρρωμένον, Id.

⊛ **δᾱγύς**, ῦδος, ἡ, *wax doll*, used in magic rites, *puppet*, Theoc.2.110.

**δαδαίνω**, = δανδαίνω, Hsch.

**Δᾳδᾱφόριος**, ὁ (sc. μήν), name of a month at Delphi, *SIG*729.1, etc.: ⊛ **-φόρια**, τά, *torchlight festival held in this month*, *Michel* 995 *D* 4.

**δᾳδηφόρος**, ον, *torch-bearing*, epith. of κόρη, *App.Anth.*1.266c (Eleusis).

⊛ **δᾴδ-ινος**, η, ον, (δᾴς) *of pine wood*, Gal.19.738, Aët.3.141. ⊛ **-ίον**, τό, Dim. of δαΐς, δᾴς, *splinter of pine wood*, Dsc.1.69, 2.73; *little torch*, Iamb.*Protr.*21.ιϛʹ, Procop.*Goth.*2.20, Poll.10.111; used of *firewood*, Ar.*Eq.*921. 2. *dilator* (cf. δαΐς 4), Hp.*Mul.*1.13, 2.133. **-ίς**, ίδος, ἡ, *a torch-feast*, Luc.*Alex.*39.

**δᾳδοκοπέω** πεύκην, *cut out the resin-glut* from it, Thphr.*CP*5.16.2 (Pass.).

**δᾳδόομαι**, Pass., (δᾴς) *become afflicted with resin-glut*, Thphr.*CP*5.11.3.

**δᾳδουργ-έω**, = δᾳδοκοπέω, Thphr.*CP*5.16.2:—Pass., Id.*HP*4.16.1. **-ός**, ὁ, *one who cuts pines for torches*, ib.3.9.3.

**δᾳδουχ-έω**, *carry a torch*, esp. in pageants, E.*Tr.*343, Luc.*Cat.*22. 2. *hold the office of* δᾳδοῦχος 1.1, *IG*2.1413, 1414. II. c. acc., *celebrate*, τὰ μυστήρια Them.*Or.*5.71a:—Med., γόον οὐχ ὑμέναιον ἐδᾳδουχήσατο *Epigr.Gr.*413:—Pass., *to be illuminated*, Socr.Rhod.1. ⊛ **-ία**, ἡ, *torch-bearing*, Lxx 2 *Ma.*4.22, Plu.2.621c, Luc.*Alex.*38. ⊛ **-ιον**, τό, *office of the* δᾳδοῦχος, *IG*$1^2$.6.99 (prob.). ⊛ **-ος**, ὁ, (ἔχω) *torch-bearer*, App.*BC*2.17: but usu. of the holder of a hereditary office at the mysteries of the Eleusinian Demeter, X.*HG*6.3.3, Arist.*Rh.*$1405^{a}20$, *IG*$1^2$.76.25, *SIG*$^2$587.305; δ. Κόρης *IG*3.172.9. 2. metaph., δᾳδοῦχοι τῆς σοφίας Plu.2.10e. 3. of the Sun, Cleanth.*Stoic.*1.123. II. *torch-stand, candelabrum*, *CIG*4647 (Bostra): also in Lacon. form **δᾳδῶχορ**, Hsch.

**δᾳδο-φορέω**, *carry torches*, Luc.*Peregr*.36. **II.** *produce* δαΐς, Thphr.*HP*9.2.8. ⊛ **-φόρος**, ον, *torch-bearing*, Ἑκάτα B.*Fr*.23.1.

**δαδύσσομαι**, *to be distracted*, ἐν ὅσσῳ δέει δαδύσσεσθε Sophr.117.

**δᾳδ-ώδης**, ες, *resinous*, Thphr.*HP*3.9.7, 9.2.5 (Comp.), Plu.2.648d. **-ωσις**, εως, ἡ, *the disease of resin-glut*, Thphr.*CP*5.11.3.

**δαεγώ**· οἶδα, ἐπίσταμαι, Hsch. **δαεινόν**· κλαύσιμον, Id. (leg. καυσ-).

⊛ **Δάειρα** [ᾰ], ἡ, *Knowing one*, epith. of Persephone at Athens, Pherecyd.45 J., Lyc.710, *IG*2.741 *Ab*2 : **Δαῖρα**, A.*Fr*.277, *IG*2².1358.12 : —**Δαειρίτης**, ου, ὁ, *her priest*, Poll.1.35.

**δαείω, δαήμεναι**, v. *δάω.

⊛ **δαελός**, Syracusan form of δαλός, Sophr.116 ; but, = δῆλος, Hsch.

**δᾰερός**, (δαίω A) *hot*, cj. in Emp.90 ; also, *black*, or *burnt*, Hsch.

**δαηθμόν**· ἐμπρησμόν, Hsch. **δαήμεναι**· ἔμπειροι γυναῖκες, Id.

⊛ **δαημ-οσύνη**, ἡ, *skill, knowledge*, A.R.2.175 (pl.), 4.1273, Orph.*A*.728 (pl.), Them.*Or*.33.366a. ⊛ **-ων**, ον, gen. ονος, (δαῆναι) *knowing, experienced in* a thing, τέκτονος ἐν παλάμῃσι δαήμονος Il.15.411 ; ἐν πάντεσσ' ἔργοισι δαήμονα 23.671 : c. gen. rei, δαήμονι φωτὶ ἐΐσκω ἄθλων Od.8.159, cf. Democr.197 : c. inf., κοσμῆσαι δ. *knowing best how to*.., Arr.*An*.7.28.2 ; χρήματα φυλάττειν δ. Them.*Or*.2.25c : Comp. -έστερος Eun.*VS*p.499 B., Procop.*Arc.Praef*. : Sup. -έστατος X.*Cyr*.1.2.12, Agath.5.6. Adv. Sup. -έστατα Id.3.25.

**δαῆναι**, v. *δάω.

⊛ **δᾱήρ**, έρος, ὁ, voc. δᾶερ, Il.3.180, 6.344, Men.135 : dat. written τῷ δαιρι (sic) *JHS*37.105, cf. *BCH*8.382, Buresch *Aus Lydien* 116 :—*husband's brother, brother-in-law* : gen. pl. as disyll., δαέρων ἢ γαλόων Il.24.769. (Cf. Skt. *devár-*, Lith. gen. sg. *dieverš*, Slav. *děverĭ*, Lat. *lēvir*.)

**δαηρόν**· θερμόν, λαμπρόν, καυματηρόν, *EM*244.42, cf. Hsch. ; perh. to be read in Emp.90, cf. δαερός. **δάης**· μάχης μεγάλης, Hsch. **δάησις** [ᾰ], εως, ἡ, *learning, understanding*, δ. καὶ ἐμπειρία *EM*250.53.

**δάθεα**· ἅρπη, φρεάτια (Tarent.), Hsch.

**δαί**, colloquial form of δή, used after interrogatives, to express wonder or curiosity, τίς δ. ὅμιλος ὅδ' ἔπλετο ; Od.1.225 ; ποῦ δ. νηῦς ἕστηκε ; 24.299, cf. A.D.*Synt*.78.2 (but wrongly read by Aristarch. for δ' αἱ Il.10.408) : freq. in Com., τί δ. σύ..πεποίηκας ; Ar.*Eq*.351 ; mostly in a separate clause, τί δ. ; *what? how?* Pherecr.93, Ar.*Eq*.171, al. ; τί δ. σύ ; Id.*Av*.136 ; πῶς δ. ; Id.*V*.1212 ; dub. l. in A.*Pr*.933, *Ch*.900, S.*Ant*.318, but prob. to be read E.*Med*.1012, *Ion* 275, al. : freq. in codd. of Pl., but prob. f.l. for δέ, as in Ar.*Ach*.912.

**δαΐ** [ῐ], Ep. dat. of δαΐς.

**δαϊγμός**, ὁ, *division, partition*, *EM*613.45.

**δαιδάλεόδμος**, ον, *with artificial fragrance*, μύρα Emp.128.5.

**δαιδάλ-εος** [ᾰ] (not -έος, Hdn.Gr.1.114), α, ον : (δαιδάλλω) :—*cunningly* or *curiously wrought*, in Hom. always of metal or wood, ζωστήρ, θώρηξ, σάκος, θρόνος, Il.4.135, 8.195, 19.380, Od.1.131 ; λάρναξ Simon.37.1, B.5.140 ; also of embroidery, Hes.*Th*.575, E.*Hec*.470 (lyr.), Theopomp.Com.33. **2.** of natural objects, *dappled, spotted*, etc., of fish, Alex.17 ; of deer, Nonn.*D*.5.391 ; *shot with light, sheeny*, Opp.*C*.1.218. **II.** *cunning*, χείρ Pl.*Epigr*.22 : Ἥφαιστος *AP*9.755. **-εύομαι**, = δαιδάλλω, Ph.1.666. **-εύτρια**, ἡ, *skilful workwoman*, Lyc.578.

**δαιδάλλω**, Act. only in pres. and impf. :—*work cunningly, embellish*, σάκος..πάντοσε δαιδάλλων Il.18.479 ; λέχος ἔξεον..δαιδάλλων χρυσῷ τε καὶ ἀργύρῳ ἠδ' ἐλέφαντι Od.23.200 ; of a *painter* or *sculptor*, Opp.*C*.1.335, *IG*14.967 :—Pass., to be *spotted, marked*, σφραγῖσι Opp.*C*.1.324. **2.** metaph., δ. πόλιν εὐανορίαισι Pi.*O*.5.21 ; δ. ἔπεσιν Id.*Parth*.2.32 :—Pass., δεδαιδαλμένοι ψεύδεσι μῦθοι Id.*O*.1.29 ; πλοῦτος ἀρεταῖς δεδ. ib.2.53 ; [μέλη] δαιδαλθέντ' ἀοιδαῖς Id.*N*.11.18.

**δαίδαλ-μα**, ατος, τό, *work of art*, θεῶν Theoc.1.32, cf. Luc.*Am*.13 ; τὰ τῆς οἰκοδομίας δ. Agath.2.15. **-όεις**, εσσα, εν, = δαιδάλεος, τεύχεα Q.S.1.141 ; βρέτας χρυσῷ δ. *AP*9.332 (Nossis). ⊛ **-ος**, ον, *cunningly* or *curiously wrought*, μάχαιρα Pi.*N*.4.59 (Did., Δαιδάλου codd.) ; πέπλος A.*Eu*.635 : in Hom. only neut. as Subst., ὃς χερσὶν ἐπίστατο δαίδαλα πάντα τεύχειν..*to frame all cunning works*, Il.5.60, al. ; τεκτόνων δ. Pi.*P*.5.36, cf. Opp.*C*.1.355 : also in sg., Od.19.227. **2.** *spotted, speckled*, or perh. rather, *sheeny, shot with light*, of fish, Opp.*C*.1.58. **II.** as pr. n., Δαίδαλος, ὁ, *Daedalus*, i. e. *the Cunning Worker, the Artist*, traditional name for the first sculptor, Il.18.592, Pl.*Men*.97d : hence δαίδαλα, τά, = *statues*, Paus.9.3.2 : also Δαίδαλα, τά, festival of Hera at Argos, ib., Plu.*Daed*.tit.

**δαιδαλούργ-ημα**, ατος, τό, = δαίδαλμα, δ. χάλκειον Vett.Val.275.4. **-ία**, ἡ, *cunning workmanship*, *Corp.Herm*.3.3.1. **-ός**, όν, *cunningly wrought*, ἀνδριάντες Zen.3.7.

**δαιδᾰλόχειρ**, ὁ, ἡ, gen. χειρος, *cunning of hand*, *AP*6.204 (Leon.).

**δαιδαλόω**, = δαιδάλλω, poet. inf. fut. -ωσέμεν Pi.*O*.1.105.

**δαιδήσσουσι**· βασανίζουσι, Hsch. **δαιδύσσεσθαι**· ἕλκεσθαι, Id. ; cf. δαδύσσομαι. **δαιέλιξι**· τοῖς πεπυρακτωμένοις ξύλοις μετὰ προσβολῆς πυρσῶν (Arg.), Id. **δαιημός**, ὁ, *division*, Id. (leg. δαιθμός). **δαιῆσαι**· διδάξαι, Id. ; cf. *δάω.

**δαΐζω**, aor. ἐδάϊξα (v. infr.) :—Med. fut. δαΐσονται Man.4.615 :—Pass. (v. infr., cf. δαίω B) :—poet. (Trag. in lyr.), *cleave asunder*, πάντα διεμοιρᾶτο δαΐζων Od.14.434 ; χιτῶνα περὶ στήθεσσι δαΐξαι Il.2.416, cf. 7.247 ; δαΐζων ὀξέϊ χαλκῷ 24.393 ; κάρανα δαΐξας A.*Ch*.396. **2.** *slay*, δαΐζων ἵππους τε καὶ ἀνέρας Il.11.497 ; τέκνον δαΐξω A.*Ag*.208 : freq. in Pass., χαλκῷ δεδαϊγμένος Il.22.72, etc. ; δεδαϊγμένος ἦτορ *pierced through* the heart, 17.535 ; δεδαϊγμένον ἦτορ a heart *torn* by misery, Od.13.320 ; ἐκ βελέων δαϊχθεὶς Pi.*P*.6.33 ; ἐξ ἐμᾶν χερῶν E.*IT*872. **3.** *rend*, χερσὶ κόμην ᾔσχυνε δαΐζων Il.18.27 (so in Med. fut., Man. l. c.) ; δαΐζειν πόλιν *destroy* it *utterly*, A.*Supp*.680, cf. *Ch*.396. **4.** *divide*, ἐδαΐζετο θυμὸς ἐνὶ στήθεσσιν Ἀχαιῶν their soul *was divided* within them, Il.9.8 ; δαϊζόμενος κατὰ θυμὸν διχθάδια *divided* or *doubting* between two opinions, 14.20 ; δαΐζειν ἐννέα μοίρας *to divide into*.., Orph.*L*.712. **5.** = δαινύναι (q. v.), θυσίας ἃς δαΐζοι ἁ πόλις *IG*7.207 (Aegosthena). [δᾰ- ; but δᾱ- Il.11.497, A.*Ch*.396.] (Prob. δαϝίζω from *δα-ϝο-s '*cut*' ; cf. δᾰ-τέομαι.)

⊛ **δαιθμός**, ὁ, (δαίω B) *allotment* of land, *IG*14.352ii23 (Halaesa). **II.** *rule of distribution*, *IG*12(5).50 (Naxos).

**δᾰϊκτάμενος**, η, ον, *slain in battle*, Il.21.146, 301.

⊛ **δᾰϊκτ-ήρ**, ῆρος, ὁ, *slayer, murderer*, of Ares, Alc.28. **2.** as Adj., *heart-rending*, γόος A.*Th*.916 (lyr.). **-ής**, οῦ, ὁ, = foreg. 2, φθόνος *Anacreont*.40.10 (prob.). **-ός**, ή, όν, *to be slain*, Orph.*A*.976. **-ωρ**, ορος, ὁ, = δαϊκτήρ 2, γάμος A.*Supp*.798 (lyr.).

**δαῖμα**· σπιθαμήν, καὶ τὸ ἔγκωλον τοῦ σχοινίου, στήμονα δὲ (i. e. δίασμα) Ταραντῖνοι, Hsch. **δαιμοδία**· ἡ τῶν ἀρίστων ἐπιβολή, Id. **δαιμοί**· οἱ καταδικασθέντες τὰς οὐσίας εἰς βασιλέως, Id.

**δαιμονάω**, *to be under the power of a* δαίμων, *to suffer by a divine visitation*, δαιμονᾷ δόμος κακοῖς A.*Ch*.566 ; δαιμονῶντες ἐν ἄτᾳ Id.*Th*.1008 (lyr.) : abs., *to be possessed, to be mad*, E.*Ph*.888, X.*Mem*.1.1.9, Plu.*Marc*.20, etc. ; δαιμονᾷς Men.140.

**δαιμονητιᾷ**· δαιμονίζεται (Cret.), Hsch.

**δαιμονι-άζομαι**, = δαιμονίζομαι III, *PMag.Par*.1.3007. **-ακός**, = δαιμονικός, *PMag.Osl*.1.143 (-ων-). **-άω**, *to be possessed of a God*, Phld.*D*.1.18. **-άρχης**, ου, ὁ, *ruler of demons*, Lact.*Inst*.2.14.6.

**δαιμον-ίζομαι**, Med., = δαιμονάω, ἄλλος κατ' ἄλλην δαιμονίζεται τύχην each one hath his own *fate appointed*, Philem.191. **II.** as Pass., *to be deified*, S.*Fr*.173 (so expld. by *AB*90 ; Act. in Hsch.). **III.** *to be possessed by a demon* or *evil spirit*, *Ev.Matt*.4.24, al., Plu.2.706d. **-ικός**, ή, όν, of persons or animals, *possessed by a demon*, ζῷον Plu.2.362f : of things, *sent by a demon*, οὐ θεῖον, ἀλλὰ δ. ib.996c, cf. 458c ; δ. δύναμις ib.363a.

**δαιμόνιον**, τό, *divine Power, Divinity*, Hdt.5.87, E.*Ba*.894 (lyr.), Isoc.1.13, Pl.*R*.382e, etc. ; τὸ δαιμόνιον ἄρ' ἢ θεὸς ἢ θεοῦ ἔργον Arist.*Rh*.1398ᵃ15, cf. 1419ᵃ9 ; οἱ θεοὶ εἴσονται καὶ τὸ δ. D.19.239 ; φοβεῖσθαι μή τι δ. πρᾶγμ' ἐλαύνῃ some *fatality*, Id.9.54 ; τὰ τοῦ δ. the favours of *fortune*, Pl.*Epin*.992d. **II.** *inferior divine being*, μεταξὺ θεοῦ τε καὶ θνητοῦ Id.*Smp*.202e ; καινὰ δ. εἰσφέρειν X.*Mem*.1.1.2, Pl.*Ap*.24c, cf. Vett.Val.67.5, etc. ; applied to the '*genius*' of Socrates, X.*Mem*.1.1.2, Pl.*Ap*.40a, *Tht*.151a, *Euthphr*.3b. **2.** *evil spirit*, δ. φαῦλα Chrysipp.*Stoic*.2.338, cf. Lxx *De*.32.17, *To*.3.8, *Ev.Matt*.7.22, al., *PMag.Lond*.1.46.120 (iv A. D.).

⊛ **δαιμονιό-πληκτος**, ον, = δαιμονιόληπτος, *PMag.Leid.V*.9.1, Ptol.*Tetr*.169 : Subst. **-πληξία**, ἡ, ib.170, Petas.ap.Olymp.Alch.p.95 B.

**δαιμόνιος**, α, ον : also ος, ον A.*Th*.892, Lys.6.32, *OGI*383.175 (Commagene) :—*of* or *belonging to a* δαίμων : properly *miraculous, marvellous*, but : **I.** in Hom. only in voc., δαιμόνιε, -ίη, *good sir*, or *lady*, addressed to chiefs or commoners, Il.2.190, 200, al., Hes.*Th*.655 : pl., Od.4.774 : esp. in addressing strangers, 23.166, 174 ; used by husbands and wives, Il.6.407, 486 (Hector and Andromache), 24.194 (Priam to Hecuba) : later c. gen., δαιμόνιε ἀνδρῶν Hdt.4.126, 7.48, 8.84 : freq. in Com., in an iron. sense, ὦ δαιμόνι' ἀνδρῶν Ar.*Ec*.564, 784, etc. ; ὦ δαιμόνι' Id.*Ra*.44, 175 ; ὦ δαιμόνι' ἀνθρώπων Id.*Av*.1638, cf. Pl.*R*.344d, 522b, *Grg*.489d, etc. **II.** from Hdt. and Pi. downwds. (Trag. in lyr.), *heaven-sent, miraculous, marvellous*, βῶλαξ Pi.*P*.4.37 ; τέρας B.15.35, S.*Ant*.376 ; ὁρμή Hdt.7.18 ; ἀραί, ἄχη, A.*Th*.892, *Pers*.581 ; ἡ φύσις δ. ἀλλ' οὐ θεία Arist.*Div.Somn*.463ᵇ14 ; εὐεργεσία D.2.1 ; εἰ μή τι δ. εἴη were it not *a divine intervention*, X.*Mem*.1.3.5, cf. S.*El*.1270 ; τὰ δαιμόνια *visitations of heaven, ways of God*, Th.2.64, X.*Mem*.1.1.12 ; πολλαὶ μορφαὶ τῶν δ. E.*Alc*.1159, al. ; δ. ἀνάγκη Lys. l. c. ; δ. τύχη of *ill* fortune, Pl.*Hp.Ma*.304b ; Ἄπολλον, ἔφη, δαιμονίας ὑπερβολῆς ! Id.*R*.509c. **2.** of persons, τῷ δ. ὡς ἀληθῶς καὶ θαυμαστῷ Id.*Smp*.219b ; ὁ περὶ τοιαῦτα σοφὸς δ. ἀνήρ ib.203a ; δαιμόνιος τὴν σοφίαν Luc.*Philops*.32 : Comp. -ώτερος D.C.53.8. **III.** Adv. -ίως *by Divine power*, opp. ἀνθρωπίνως, Aeschin.3.133, cf. Pl.*Ti*.25e ; *marvellously*, Ar.*Nu*.76 ; δ. περί τι ἐσπουδακώς Aeschin.1.41 ; δ. ποιεῖ, of remedies, Aët.15.14, al. ; [οἶνος] δ. γέρων Alex.167.5 ; δ. καὶ μεγαλοπρεπῶς prob. in Epicur.*Fr*.183 (cf. δαῖος) : neut. pl. as Adv., δαιμόνια Ar.*Pax*585 ; δαιμονιώτατα ἀποθνήσκει *most clearly by the hand of the gods*, X.*HG*7.4.3 : also in fem. dat., δαιμονίᾳ, formed like κοινῇ, θεσπεσίῃ, etc., Pi.*O*.9.110.

**δαιμονιοῦχος** αἰτία, *spiritual* cause, Procl.*in Prm*.p.513 S.

**δαιμον-ίς**, ίδος, ἡ, fem. of δαίμων, Procl.*in Ti*.1.47 D., *in Prm*.p.643 S., Herm.*in Phdr*.p.87 A. :—also **-ισσα**, ἡ, *PMag.Leid.W*.16.48. **-ισμός**, ὁ, *demoniac possession*, Vett.Val.2.18.

**δαιμονιώδης**, ες, *like a demon*, Sch.Ar.*Ra*.293 ; *demoniacal, devilish*, *Ep.Jac*.3.15 ; *like a* δαίμων, Procl.*in Ti*.1.113 D.

**δαιμονο-βλάβεια** [ᾰ], ἡ, *heaven-sent visitation*, Plb.28.9.4. **-μᾰχέω**, *fight against heaven*, Eust.1097.6. **-πλήξ**, ῆγος, *smitten of heaven*, cj. in S.*Fr*.221.13. **-πληξία**, ἡ, = δαιμονιοπλ-, Petas.ap.Olymp.Alch.p.97 B. **-τάκτης**, ου, ὁ, *ruler of demons*, *PMag.Par*.1.1374 (pl., written δαιμονατ.).

⊛ **δαίμων**, ονος, voc. δαῖμον S.*OC*1480 (lyr.), δαῖμον Theoc.2.11, ὁ, ἡ, *god, goddess*, of individual gods or goddesses, Il.1.222, 3.420, etc. ; δαίμονι ἶσος 5.438 ; ἐμίσγετο δαίμονι δαίμων, of Φιλίη and Νεῖκος, Emp.59.1 :—but more freq. of *the Divine power* (while θεός denotes a God in person), *the Deity*, cf. Od.3.27 ; πρὸς δαίμονα against *the Divine power*, Il.17.98 ; σὺν δαίμονι by its grace, 11.792 ; κατὰ δαίμονα, almost, = τύχῃ, by *chance*, Hdt.1.111 ; τύχᾳ δαίμονος Pi.*O*.8.67 ; ἄμαχος δ., i.e. Destiny, B.15.23: in pl., ὅτι δαίμονες θέλωσιν, what *the Gods* ordain, Id.16.117; ταῦτα δ' ἐν τῷ δ. S.*OC*1443; ἡ τύχη καὶ ὁ δ. Lys. 13.63, cf. Aeschin.3.111; κατὰ δαίμονα καὶ συντυχίαν Ar.*Av.*544. 2. *the power controlling the destiny of individuals*: hence, one's *lot* or *fortune*, στυγερὸς δέ οἱ ἔχραε δ. Od.5.396, cf. 10.64; δαίμονος αἶσα κακή 11.61; δαίμονα δώσω I will deal thee *fate*, i.e. kill thee, Il.8.166; freq. in Trag. of *good* or *ill fortune*, ὅταν ὁ δ. εὐροῇ A.*Pers.*601; δ. ἀσινής Id.*Ag.*1342 (lyr.); κοινός Id.*Th.*812; γενναῖος πλὴν τοῦ δαίμονος S.*OC*76; δαίμονος σκληρότης Antipho 3.3.4; τὸν οἴακα στρέφει δ. ἑκάστῳ Anaxandr.4.6; personified as *the good* or *evil genius* of a family or person, δ. τῷ Πλεισθενιδῶν A.*Ag.*1569, cf. S.*OT*1194 (lyr.); ὁ ἑκάστου δ. Pl.*Phd.*107d, cf. *PMag.Lond.*121.505, Iamb.*Myst.*9.1; δ δ. ὁ τὴν ἡμετέραν μοῖραν λελογχώς Lys.2.78; ἅπαντι δ. ἀνδρὶ συμπαρίσταται εὐθὺς γενομένῳ μυσταγωγὸς τοῦ βίου Men.16.2 D.; δ. ἀλάστορες Id. 8 D.; ὁ μέγας [τοῦ Καίσαρος] δ. Plu.*Caes.*69; ὁ σὸς δ. κακός ibid.; ὁ βασιλέως δ. Id.*Art.*15; ἦθος ἀνθρώπῳ δ. Heraclit.119; Ξενοκράτης φησὶ τὴν ψυχὴν ἑκάστου εἶναι δ. Arist.*Top.*112ᵃ37. II. δαίμονες, οἱ, *souls of men of the golden age*, acting as tutelary deities, Hes.*Op.* 122, Thgn.1348, Phoc.15, Emp.115.5, etc.; θεῶν, δ., ἡρώων, τῶν ἐν Ἅιδου Pl.*R.*392a: less freq. in sg., δαίμονι δ' οἷος ἔησθα τὸ ἐργάζεσθαι ἄμεινον Hes.*Op.*314; τὸν τε δ. Δαρεῖον ἀγκαλεῖσθε, of the deified Darius, A.*Pers.*620; νῦν δ' ἐστὶ μάκαιρα δ., of Alcestis, E.*Alc.*1003 (lyr.), cf. *IG*12(5).305.5 (Paros): later, of *departed souls*, Luc.*Luct.*24; δαίμοσιν εὐσεβέσιν, = *Dis Manibus*, *IG*14.1683; so θεοὶ δ., ib.938, al.: also, *ghost*, Paus.6.6.8. 2. generally, *spiritual* or *semi-divine being* inferior to the Gods, Plu.2.415a, al., Sallust.12, Dam.*Pr.*183, etc.; esp. *evil spirit*, *demon*, *Ev.Matt.*8.31, *JAJ*8.2.5; φαῦλοι δ. Alex.Aphr.*Pr.*2.46; δαίμονος ἔσοδος εἰς τὸν ἄνθρωπον, Aret.*SD*1. 4; πρᾶξις ἐκβάλλουσα δαίμονας *PMag.Par.*1227. 3. ἀγαθὸς δ. *the Good Genius* to whom a toast was drunk after dinner, Ar.*V.*525, Nicostr.Com.20, D.S.4.3, Plu.2.655e, Philonid.ap.Ath.15.675b, Paus.9.39.5, *IG*12(3).436 (Thera), etc.; of Nero, ἀ. δ. τῆς οἰκουμένης *OGI*666.3; of the Nile, ἀ. δ. ποταμός ib.672.7 (i A.D.); of the tutelary genius of individuals (supr. 1), ἀ. δ. Ποσειδωνίου *SIG*1044.9 (Halic.): pl., δαίμονες ἀ., = Lat. *Di Manes*, *SIG*1246 (Mylasa): Astrol., ἀγαθός, κακός δ., names of celestial κλῆροι, Paul.Al.*N.*4, *O.*1, etc. (Less correctly written Ἀγαθοδαίμων, q.v.).

B. = δαήμων, *knowing*, δ. μάχης *skilled in* fight, Archil.3.4. (Pl. *Cra.*398b, suggests this as the orig. sense; while others would write δαήμονες in Archil., and get rid of this sense altogether; cf. however αἴμων. More probably the Root of δαίμων (*deity*) is δαίω *to distribute destinies*; cf. Alcm.48.)

**δαίνῡμι**, imper. δαίνῡ Il.9.70, part. -ύντα Od.4.3: Ep. impf. δαίνῡ Il.23.29; δαίνυεν (from δαινύω) Call.*Cer.*84: fut. δαίσω Il.19.299, A.*Eu.*305: aor. ἔδαισα Pi.*N.*9.24, Hdt.1.162, E.*Or.*15:—Med., δαίνῡται Il.15.99: 2 sg. subj. δαινύῃ Od.19.328; Ep. 3 sg. opt. δαινῦτο Il.24.665; 3 pl. opt. δαινύατο Od.18.248; part. -ύμενος Cratin. 142; 2 sg. impf. δαίνυ' (i.e. -υο) Il.24.63: fut. δαίσομαι Lyc.668, Herod.4.93, etc., (μετα-) Od.18.48: aor. ἐδαισάμην Archil.99, Pi.*P.*10.31, etc.; δαισάμενοι Od.18.408; [δαινῦῃ Od.19.328; but δαινῦῃ 8.243 (for wh. δαινύεαι shd. be read)]. (V. δαίω B.):—poet. Verb (used by Hdt.), *give a banquet* or *feast*, δαίνυ δαῖτα γέρουσι Il.9. 70; ἔφασκες.. δαίσειν γάμον didst promise *to give* me a marriage-*feast*, 19.299, cf. Od.4.3, *h.Ven.*141, Pi.*N.*1.72; ὁ τοῖσι τάφον μενοεικέα δαίνυ Il.23.29, cf. Od.3.309; δ. ὑμεναίους, γάμους, E.*IA*123 (lyr.), 707. 2. c. acc. pers., *feast* one *on* a thing, τὸν..Ἀστυάγης ἀνόμῳ τραπέζῃ ἔδαισε Hdt.1.162, cf. E.*Or.*15; ζῶν με δαίσεις *thou shalt be* my living *feast*, A.*Eu.*305. II. Med., *have a feast given one*, *feast*, in Hom. more freq. than Act., Il.15.99, al., cf. Pi.*I.*6(5).36, Hdt.1. 211; δαίσασθαι γάμον Archil. l.c. 2. c. acc., *feast on*, *eat*, δαῖτα, ἑκατόμβας, κρέα, Od.3.66, Il.9.535, Od.12.30; κρέα δαίνυσθαι Hdt.3. 18, Ant.Lib.18.2 (but c. gen., Id.11.7); ἐδαίσατο παῖδα S.*Fr.*771.5, cf. *El.*543; μίαν δ. τράπεζαν *eat* at a common table, Theoc.13.38: of fire, *consume*, Pi.*N.*9.24, S.*Tr.*765; of poison, ib.1088.

⊛ **δαΐξανδρος**, ον, *man-destroying*, χεῖρες *Hymn.Is.*45, cf. *Sammelb.* 5829.

⊛ **δάϊος**, contr. **δᾷος**, α, ον, Dor. for Ep. **δήιος** (contr. **δῇος** Thgn. 552b), η, ον: also **δάϊος**, ον, E.*Tr.*1301 (lyr.), *HF*915 (lyr.) (Trag. always use the Dor. form): (δαίω A):—*hostile*, *destructive*, Hom. only in Il., δηΐου ἐκ πολέμου 7.119; δ. ἄνδρα 6.481: esp. as epith. of πῦρ, *burning*, *consuming*, 8.181, al.; δάϊοι *enemies*, Pi.*N.*8.28, A.*Ag.*559; λάφυρα δᾴων Id.*Th.*278 (dub. l.); φόβημα δαΐων S.*OC*699 (lyr.): in sg., *fighting man*, Ar.*Ra.*1022; also δᾴου μάχας S.*Ichn.*239; δαΐον δρμάν *hostile*, Ar.*Nu.*335 (= [Philox.] 18 (anap.)); ἔπιτε δαΐαν ὁδὸν Ar.*Ra.* 897 (lyr.). 2 *unhappy*, *wretched*, A.*Pers.*282 (lyr.), etc., S.*Aj.*784, E.*Andr.*838 (lyr.). II. (δαῆναι) *knowing*, *cunning*, τεχνίτης *APl.* 4.119 (Posid.). Adv. δαΐως Epicur.*Fr.*183 codd. Plu. (δαιμονίως Usener). [δάϊος: but disyll. in Hom. where the last syll. is long; Trag., when disyll., written δᾷος, A.*Pers.*282; δηΐων at the end of a pentam., *AP*6.123 (Anyte).]

**δαϊόφρων**, ονος, ὁ, ἡ, (φρήν) *unhappy in mind*, *miserable*, A.*Th.*918 (lyr.).

**δαϊόω**, v. δηιόω.

⊛ **δαΐς**, δαΐδος, Att. contr. **δᾴς**, δᾳδός, ἡ: (δαίω A):—*fire-brand*, *pine-torch*, δαΐδων ὕπο λαμπομενάων Il.18.492; δαΐδας μετὰ χερσὶν ἔχοντες Od.7.101; δᾷδες, = λαμπάδες, Philyll.29; ἀραμένη δαΐδας *IG*12(5).229. 8; ἔλαχεν μυστιπόλους δ., of a δᾳδοῦχος, ib.3.172: in sg., Ar.*Nu.* 1494, Antiph.199, 272: collective in sg., metaph., ἐπὶ τὴν δᾷδα προελθεῖν to come to the *funeral-torch*, i.e. end of life, Plu.2.789a. 2. as collective noun, *pine-wood*, such as torches were made of, *SIG* 57.32 (Milet., v B.C.), Ar.*Nu.*612, Th.7.53, X.*Cyr.*7.5.23, Arist.*Col.* 791ᵇ24, *Supp.Epigr.*1.329.24. 3. *a disease in pines*, *resin-glut*, Thphr.*HP*3.9.5. 4. = δᾳδίον 2, Hp.*Mul.*2.133.

⊛ **δαΐς** (δαίω A), *war*, *battle*, mostly in apoc. dat. δαΐ, as always in Hom., Il.13.286, al., cf. Hes.*Th.*650, A.*Th.*925: acc. δάϊν Call.*Fr.* 243.

**δαίς**, δαιτός, ἡ, (δαίω B) *meal*, *banquet*, δαὶς ἐΐση, *duly shared*, Il.15.95, etc.; δαὶς πίειρα sumptuous *banquet*, 19.179; *sacrificial feast*, βωμὸς ἐδεύετο δαιτὸς ἐΐσης 24.69; δαῖτα θάλειαν Hom.*Fr.inc.* 4 Kinkel (cf. Od.17.382); Θυέστου δαῖτα παιδείων κρεῶν *the feast* of Th. on.., A.*Ag.*1242, cf. 1593: pl., Od.20.182, A.*Ch.*483: of beasts of prey, Il.24.43; [τούτοις] παρέξω δαῖθ' ὑφ' ὧν ἐφερβόμην S.*Ph.* 957. 2. *meat*, *food*, E.*Cyc.*245, cf. Od.18.279. 3 personified, S.*Fr.*605. Rare in Prose (exc. in Homeric allusions, Pl.*Phdr.*247a, etc.) as Hdt.1.133, 211.

**δαισάνη**· πτισάνη, *EM*251.47.

**δαίσιμος** or **δαίσιος**, *eatable*, Hsch., *EM*352.29.

**Δαίσιος**, ὁ, a Macedonian month, *SIG*700.39 (ii B.C.), Plu.*Alex.*16, *Cam.*19, *Arat.*53, etc.

**δαῖσις**, εως, ἡ, *division of property*, *Leg.Gort.*4.25, 5.47.

**δαΐσφαλτος**, ον, *in which one is overthrown*, πάλη Lyc.170.

**δαιτ-αλ-άομαι**, *feast*, Lyc.654. **-εύς**, έως, ὁ, *banqueter*, ἄκλητος δ., of the eagle eating Prometheus' liver, A.*Pr.*1024: pl., *Com.Adesp.*30 D; Δαιταλῆς, play by Aristophanes. **-ουργία**, ἡ, *cookery*, Lyc.199.

**δαίτη**, ἡ, poet. for δαίς, *feast*, *banquet*, Il.10.217 (pl.), Od.3.44, A.R.2.761, Call.*Act.*1.1.5; of beasts, Opp.*H.*2.251, Nic.*Al.*380.

**δαιτηθεν**, Adv. *from a feast*, Od.10.216, Theoc.17.28.

⊛ **δαιτήριον**, τό, *place of distribution*, *EM*251.52, Zonar.

⊛ **δαίτης**, ου, ὁ, *priest who divided the victims*, E.*Fr.*472.12.

⊛ **δαῖτις**, v. δέτις. II. epith. of Aphrodite at Ephesus, *Jahresh.* 17.146.

**δαιτρ-εία**, ἡ, *place where meat is cut up*, Hdn.*Epim.*19. **-ευτῶς**, Adv. *by dividing* or *distributing*, Zonar. **-εύω**, *divide*, esp. *cut up* meat, δαιτρεῦσαί τε καὶ ὀπτῆσαι *to cut up* and roast it, Od.15. 323; ἂν δὲ.. ἵστατο δαιτρεύσων *to carve*, 14.433; τὰ δ' ἄλλ' ἐς δῆμον ἔδωκε δαιτρεύειν *to cut up for distribution* among the people, Il.11.705, cf. 688; ἵππους δαίτρευον, of the Amazons, A.R.2.1176; τὰ πιότερα τῶν προβάτων Them.*Or.*13.171c; of animals, *devour* prey, Opp.*H.*2. 294: —Med., ib.656, Nonn.*D.*5.363, al.:—Pass., Lyc.160, etc. **-όν**, τό, *one's portion*, δαιτρὸν πίνειν Il.4.262.

**δαιτροπόνος**, = σιτοπόνος, σιτοποιός, Hsch., *EM*252.4.

**δαιτρός**, ὁ, (δαίω) *one that carves and portions out*, esp. meat at table, Od.1.141, 17.331, Lyc.35, Nic.*Al.*258, Ath.1.12d. II. hereditary priest who officiated at the Dipolia, Porph.*Abst.*2.30.

**δαιτροσύνη**, ἡ, *art of carving meat into portions*, Od.16.253 (pl.).

**δαιτῡμ-ονεύς**, Ep. gen. ῆος, ὁ, = sq., Nonn.*D.*2.666. ⊛ **-ών**, όνος, ὁ, (δαίς) *one that is entertained*, *guest*, (but in Od.4.621 of *those who bring each his portion*) Hom. only in pl., Od.7.102, 148, al., cf. Hdt. 1.73, etc.: in sg., Pl.*R.*345c, Arist.*Pol.*1282ᵃ22.

**δαιτύς**, ύος, ἡ, Ep. for δαίς, *a meal*, Il.22.496.

**δαΐφρων**, ον, gen. ονος, 1. (δάϊς) *warlike*, *fiery*, Il.2.23, al. (not in Od.); Λατοῦς θυγάτηρ B.5.122, cf. 137, Q.S.1.47; δ. ἀλκή Id.1. 218. 2. (δαῆναι) *wise*, *prudent*, Ὀδυσῆα δ. ποικιλομήτην Il.11.482, cf. Od.1.48, al.; of a charioteer, Il.24.325; *craftsman*, Od.8.373; of a woman, 15.356: hence δ. Περσεφόνεια *h.Cer.*359, cf. Pi.*P.*9.84. (Δα(σ)ι-, cf. Skt. *dasrás* 'working miracles'.)

⊛ **δαίω** (A), Act. only pres. and impf. (but ἔδευσε may be for ἔδαυσε aor. 1, cf. infr. II, *Berl.Sitzb.*1902.1098):—Pass., pres. and impf., Hom.: aor. 2 subj. δάηται Il.20.316: also intr. in pf. 2 Act. δέδηα, plpf. δεδήειν (v. infr.); Ep. part. fem. δεδαΐα Nonn.*D.*6.305: aor. part. δαισθείς E.*Heracl.*914 (if not from δαίνυμι): also aor. 2 subj. δαβῇ, ἐκδαβῇ, Hsch.: pf. Pass. δέδαυμαι (v. infr. II). (*δαϝ-yω, cf. δε-δαυ-μένος, δαβελός, Skt. *dunóti* 'burn'):—poet. Verb, *light up*, *kindle*, δαῖέ οἱ ἐκ κόρυθός τε καὶ ἀσπίδος ἀκάματον πῦρ *she made* fire *burn* from.., Il.5.4, cf. 7; ἐκ δ' αὐτοῦ δαῖε φλόγα 18.206, cf. 227; so πῦρ καὶ φῶς δ. A.*Ch.*864 (lyr.); φλόγα Id.*Ag.*496: metaph., δαῖε δ' ἐν ὀφθαλμοῖς.. πόθον A.R.4.1147:—Pass., *blaze*, *burn fiercely*, ἐν πεδίῳ πῦρ δαίετο καῖε δὲ νεκρούς Il.21.343; πυρὶ ὄσσε δεδήει *blazed* with fire, 12.466; ἐν δέ οἱ ὄσσε δαίεται *blaze like fire*, Od.6.132; σεμνῶν ὀργίων ἐδαίετο φλόξ S.*Tr.*765: mostly metaph. sense, μάχη πόλεμός τε δέδηεν Il.20.18, al., cf. 12.35, 17.253; Ὄσσα δεδήει Rumour *spread like wild-fire*, 2.93; φιλοφροσύνη δεδήει *glowed*, Emp.130.2. II. *burn up*, μηρ' ἐπὶ βωμῶν *Epigr.Gr.*1035. 20 (Pergam.); σάρκας ἔδευσε (sic) πυρὶ *Berl.Sitzb.* l.c.; τὰν χώραν δ. Decr.Byz.ap.D.18.90; *use cautery*, Hp.*Haem.*2 (very rare in Prose):—Pass., φλογὶ σῶμα δαισθείς E. l.c.; μηρίων δεδαυμένων Semon.30; ἐν ἔρωτι δεδ., prob. in Call.*Epigr.*50 (cf. δάκνω III).

**δαίω** (B), *divide*:—Act. is not found in this sense (for aor. ἔδαισα v. δαίνυμι), δαΐζω being used:—Pass., δαίεται ἦτορ my heart *is torn*, *distracted*, Od.1.48: Ep. 3 pl. pf., Αἰθίοπας, τοὶ διχθὰ δεδαίαται ib.23: —more freq. in Med., *distribute*, κρέα δαίετο 15.140; κρέα πολλὰ δαιόμενος 17.332; πήματα..δαίονται βροτοῖς ἀθάνατοι Pi.*P.*3.81; cf. δατέομαι. II. aor. ἔδαισα, *feast*, from Hdt. downwards, though formed from δαίω, belongs in sense to δαίνυμι (q.v.):—Med., *feast on*, [ἀμβροσίην] δαίονται Matro *Conv.*72. (δαι- also in δαίς, δαίνυμι, etc.: prob. akin to δα- in δατέομαι.)

**δάκαρ**, v.l. for δάρκα, Dsc.1.13.

**δᾰκέθῡμος**, ον, *heart-eating, heart vexing*, ἴδρώς Simon.58.5; ἄτη S.*Ph*.705 (lyr.).

**δᾰκετόν** or **δάκετον**, τό, = δάκος 1, Ar.*Av*.1069, Thphr.*HP*9.19.3, Ph.1.399, etc.: as Adj., δ. θηρία D.S.1.87, 20.42, Vett.Val.126.29.

**δάκια**· τὰ ἄγρια ὀρνιθάρια, Hsch.; but, = τὰ μικρὰ θηρία, *EM*245.33.

**δακκύλιος**, v. δάκτυλος.

**δακν-άζω**, = δάκνω, *AP*7.504 (Leon.). II. metaph. in Pass., *to be afflicted, mournful*, imper. δακνάζου A.*Pers*.571. **-ηρός**, ά, όν, *biting*, ἔπη Phld.*Ir*.p.31 W.; δακνηρόν, τό, ib.p.75 W., Herm.ap. Stob.1.49.44. **-ίς**, ἡ, a *bird*, Hsch. **-ιστήρ**, ῆρος, ὁ, *biter, stinger*, v. μακιστήρ. **-ω**, Hippon.49.6 (cj.), A.*Th*.399, etc.: fut. δήξομαι Hp.*Nat.Mul*.16, *Mul*.1.18 (v.l. δάξεται): pf. δέδηχα Babr. 77: aor. 1 ἔδηξα late, Luc.*Asin*.9: aor. 2 (the only tense in Hom.) ἔδᾰκον Batr.181, Tyrt.10.32, etc., Ep. δάκε Il.5.493, etc., Ep. δάκε *AP*12.15 (Strat.): Ep. inf. δακέειν Il.17.572:—**Pass.**, δάκνομαι Thgn.910: fut. δηχθήσομαι E.*Alc*.1100: aor. ἐδήχθην S.*Tr*.254, Ar. *Ach*.18, etc.; later ἐδάκην Aret.*SD*2.2: pf. δέδηγμαι Ar.*Ach*.1, etc.; Dor. δεδαγμένος Pi.*P*.8.87, Call.*Ep*.50 codd.:—*bite*, of dogs, δακέειν μὲν ἀπετρωπῶντο λεόντων Il.18.585; of a gnat, ἰσχανάᾳ δακέειν 17.572; στόμιον δ. *champ* the bit, A.*Pr*.1009; χεῖλος ὀδοῦσι δακών, as a mark of stern determination, Tyrt.l.c.: abs., δακὼν ἀνάσχου Men. *Sam*.141; δ. στόμα *bite* one's tongue, so as to refrain from speaking, πρὸ τῶν τοιούτων χρὴ λόγων δ. στόμα A.*Fr*.397, cf. S.*Tr*.976; δ. ἑαυτόν *to bite* one's lips for fear of laughing, Ar.*Ra*.43; so (by a joke παρὰ προσδοκίαν) δ. θυμόν Id.*Nu*.1369; δ. χόλον A.R.3.1170. II. metaph. of pungent smoke and dust, *sting*, Ar.*Ach*.18, *Lys*.298, *Pl*. 822; δ. ὄμματα, of dry winds, Hp.*Aph*.3.17. III. of the mind, *bite, sting*, δάκε δὲ φρένας Ἕκτορι μῦθος Il.5.493, cf. Hes.*Th*.567; ἔδακε λύπη Hdt.7.16.α΄; συμφορὰ δ. A.*Pers*.846; λόφοι δὲ κώδων τ' οὐ δάκνουσ' ἄνευ δορός *have* no *sting*, Id.*Th*.399; σαίνουσα δάκνεις S.*Fr*. 885; τὸ δάκνον τῆς συμβουλῆς Jul.*Or*.7.207d; of love, πάντες οἱ ἐν ὥρᾳ τὸν φιλόπαιδα δάκνουσι Pl.*R*.474d:—freq. in Pass., δηχθεῖσα κέντροις .. ἠράσθη E.*Hipp*.1303; ἔρωτι δεδαγμένος Call. l.c.; of vexation, δάκνομαι ψυχήν Thgn.910; συμφορᾷ δεδαγμένοι Pi.l.c.; δέδηγμαι καρδίαν Ar.*Ach*.1; ὑπὸ τῆς δαπάνης Id.*Nu*.12; πρός τι, ἐπί τινι, at a thing, S.*Ph*.378, X.*Cyr*.4.3.3; ὑπὸ τῶν ἐν φιλοσοφίᾳ λόγων Pl.*Smp*.218a: c. part., ἐδήχθη ἀκούσας X.*Cyr*.1.4.13. (Cf. Skt. *daśati* 'bite', Goth. *tahjan* 'tear'.) **-ώδης**, ες, *biting, pungent*, Hp. *Aph*.5.20, Gal.6.237; *painful*, Mich.*in EN*499.3.

⊛ **δάκος** [ᾰ], εος, τό, (δάκνω) *animal of which the bite is dangerous, noxious beast*, A.*Pr*.583 (lyr.), *Th*.558; Ἀργεῖον δ., of the Trojan horse, Id.*Ag*.824; δάκη θηρῶν *ravenous* beasts, E.*Hipp*.646; θήρειον δ. Id.*Cyc*.325; generally, β. δάκος, of a whale, Opp.*H*.5.333. II. *bite, sting*, δ. κακαγοριᾶν Pi.*P*.2.53, cf. Opp.*H*.2.454, 5.30.

**δακόσσαι**· πορθῆσαι, Hsch.

**δάκρυ**, τό, used by Poets metri gr. for δάκρυον in sg. δάκρυ and dat. pl. δάκρυσι Il.9.570, etc.: dat. pl. sts. in Prose, Th.7.75, D.30. 32, *Ev.Luc*.7.38: pl., δάκρη *An.Ox*.1.121 (cj. Bgk. in Pi.*Fr*.122.3, cf. δάκρυον 2):—*tear*, Il.2.266, Od.4.114, A.*Pr*.638, etc.; τοῦ δ' γε δ. χέων Od.2.24. II. generally, *drop*, λιβάνου Pi.l.c.; δ. πεύκινον E.*Med*.1200. (Cf. Lat. *lacruma*, Goth. *tagr*, OE. *tear*.)

**δακρ-ύδιον**, τό, Dim. of δάκρυ, = σκαμμωνία, Ps.-Dsc.4.170, cf. Alex. Trall.*Febr*.5. **-ῡμα**, ατος, τό, *that which is wept for, a subject for tears*, Orac.ap.Hdt.7.169. II. *tear*, A.*Pers*.134 (lyr.), E.*Andr*. 92 (pl.).

**δακρυο-γόνος**, ον, *author of tears*, Ἄρης A.*Supp*.682 (lyr.). ⊛ **-εις**, εσσα, εν, neut. -όειν A.R.4.1291: 1. of persons, *tearful*, Il.21. 506, etc.; γόος Od.24.323; δακρυόεν γελάσασα smiling *through tears*, Il.6.484. 2. of things, *causing tears*, πόλεμος, ἄλγεα, θάνατος, 5. 737, Hes.*Th*.227, etc.

**δάκρυον**, τό, used in sg. δάκρυον, pl. δάκρυα, -ύων, -ύοις, Ep. gen. pl. δακρυόφι (-φιν) Il.17.696, Od.5.152, etc.: (v. δάκρυ):—*tear*, δ. θερμὰ χέων Il.16.3; δ. λείβειν, εἴβειν, 13.88, Od.4.153; βλεφάρων ἄπο δ. ἧκεν 23.33; ἐς δάκρυα πεσεῖν Hdt.6.21; ἴσχειν πηγὰς δακρύων S.*Ant*.803 (lyr.), etc.; μετὰ πολλῶν δ. ἱκετεύειν Pl.*Ap*.34c. 2. *that which drops like tears, gum, sap*, τῆς ἀκάνθης Hdt.2.96; κρομμύου Hp.*Mul*.2.201; τῶν δένδρων Arist.*HA*553$^b$28; ἀμπέλου *AP*11.298; τὸ ἤλεκτρον καὶ ὅσα λέγεται ὡς δάκρυα Arist.*Mete*.388$^b$19; δ. καμώνος, = σκαμμωνία, Nic.*Al*.484; of the bulbils of κρίνον (q.v.), Thphr. *HP*2.2.1, al. II. = δάκρυμα 1, *AP*7.527 (Theodorid.).

**δακρῡο-πετής**, ές, *making tears fall*, πάθεα A.*Supp*.113 (lyr.). **-ποιός**, όν, *inducing tears*, Dsc.1.1. **-τῖμος**, ον, *honoured with tears*, Orph.*H*.56.6.

**δακρυ-πλώω**, (πλέω) *swim with tears*, of drunken men, Od.19. 122. ⊛ **-ρροέω**, *melt into tears, shed tears*, S.*Tr*.326, Ph.2.179; χαρᾷ S.*El*.1313; ἐπὶ παισί E.*HF*1181; of the eyes, *run with tears*, Hp.*Epid*.4.25; ὄμμα δακρυρροοῦν E.*Alc*.826, cf. *Ph*.370 codd., Alex. 313. 2. of vines, '*weep*', Thphr.*CP*3.13.2, *Gp*.5.38. **-ρροια**, ἡ, *shedding of tears*, Ps.-Callisth.3.3, Sch.E.*Or*.788. **-ρροος**, ον, *flowing with tears*, E.*Supp*.773; τέκνων πηγαί Id.*HF*98.

**δακρῡσίστακτος**, ον, *in floods of tears*, neut. pl. as Adv., A.*Pr*. 400 (lyr.).

⊛ **δακρῡτός**, όν (ή, όν J.*AJ*4.8.48), *wept over, tearful*, ἐλπίς A.*Ch*. 236; μόρος *AP*7.495 (Alc.); ἀπαλλαγή J. l.c.: irreg. Sup. δακρυώτατος, Hsch.

**δακρῡ-χάρής**, ές, *delighting in tears*, Πλούτων *IG*14.769 (Naples); Λάθας κευθμὼν *Mon.Ant*.11.477 (Cret.); κνίσματα prob. l. in *AP*5.165 (Mel.). **-χέων**, ουσα, wrongly written for δάκρυ χέων in Hom., etc.: hence Nonn. formed δακρυχέειν in trans. sense, *bewail*, *D*.5. 532.

⊛ **δακρύω**, first in A.*Ch*.81: fut. -ύσω E.*El*.658, later -ύσομαι Tryph. 404: aor. ἐδάκρῡσα Hdt.1.112, etc., Ep. δάκρῡσα Od.11.55: pf. δεδάκρῡκα Alciphr.2.3.14:—**Med.**, δακρύεσθαι A.*Th*.815: aor. δακρύσατο Tryph.431:—**Pass.**, pres., E.*Hel*.1226: pf. δεδάκρῡμαι Il.16.7, etc.: [ῡ long in all tenses, except in late Poets, as *AP*9.148]: (for the Root, v. δάκρυ). I. intr., *weep, shed tears*, Od. l.c., etc.: c. acc. cogn., δ. γόους to lament *with tears*, S.*Aj*.580: c. gen. causae, δ. συμφορᾶς E.*HF*528 (dub. l.); δ. βλέφαρα *to flood* them *with tears*, Id.*Hel*.948; δ. χαρᾷ X.*HG*7.2.9; ἐπὶ ταῖς συμφοραῖς Isoc.4.168:—Pass., pf. δεδάκρυμαι *to be in tears*, τίπτε δεδάκρυσαι, Πατρόκλεες; Il. 16.7; δεδάκρυνται δὲ παρειαί 22.491; δεδακρυμένος *in tears*, Pl.*Ax*. 364b, Plu.*Publ*.6, etc. 2. of the eyes, *run*, Arist.*HA*620$^a$5. 3. of trees, *exude gum*, Thphr.*Fr*.121; ἤλεκτρον δακρύειν Luc.*Salt*. 55. II. c. acc., *weep for*, τινά A.*Ag*.1490 (lyr.), S.*OT*1486, Ar. *Ach*.1027, etc.:—Pass., *to be wept for*, συμφορὰ δακρύεται E.*Hel*.1226 (prob. Med. in A.*Th*.815).

**δακρυώδης**, ες, *exuding a watery fluid*, ἕλκος δ. καὶ ἀνεκπύητον Hp. *Fract*.25; *running* at the eyes, *Hippiatr*.1, al. 2. *tear-like*, συρροή, of the bulbils of κρίνον (cf. δάκρυον 1.2), Thphr.*HP*6.6.8. II. *tearful, lamentable*, Luc.*Vit.Auct*.14.

**δακτῠλ-ήθρα**, ἡ, (δάκτυλος) *finger-sheath*, X.*Cyr*.8.8.17, Clearch. 21; *thumb-screw*, Lxx 4*Ma*.8.13. **-ηθρον**, τό, *ring*, Them.*Or*. 21.253a. **-ιαῖος**, α, ον, *of a finger's length, breadth* or *thickness*, ῥάβδοι Hp.*Fract*.30; κάραβοι Arist.*HA*549$^b$10; τομοὶ δ. τῷ τε μήκει καὶ πάχει Democr.ap.Gal.13.1000: Astron., *a digit in extent*, Cleom. 2.3. II. *possessing* δάκτυλοι, δ. μέρη τοῦ σώματος, i.e. hands and feet, D.S.1.77. **-ίδιον** [λῐ], τό, Dim. of δακτύλιος, *ring*, *IG*11(2). 161*B*119 (Delos, iii B.C.), *BGU*1104.13 (8 B.C.), *PAmh*.126.55 (ii A.D.), Poll.2.155, 5.100, *BGU*843.8, etc., but rejected by Atticists, cf. *AB*88. II. ⊛ **δακτυλίδιον** [λῐ], τό, Dim. of δάκτυλος, *toe*, Ar. *Lys*.417. **-ίδρυον**, τό, late spelling of δακτυλίδιον 1, *BGU*1036. 14 (ii A.D.):—also **δακτυριτριω(ν)** (sic, gen. pl.), *PLond*.2.193$^v$4 (ii A.D.), cf. ib.44. **-ίζω**, = δακτυλοδεικτέω (in bad sense), Hsch. s.vv. ἐδακτύλιζον, σκινδαρεύεσθαι. II. Pass. in metre, *to be made a dactyl*, Eust.874.8. ⊛ **-ικός**, ή, όν, *of* or *for the finger*: αὐλὸς δ. a flute *played with the fingers*, Ath.4.176f; δ. ψῆφος a stone *for calculating*, *AP*11.290 (Pall.). 2. *for the anus*, ἔμπλαστρος Orib.*Fr*.83, Cass.Fel.74. II. *dactylic*, ῥυθμός Longin.39.4, Heph.4. Adv. -κῶς, ποδίζεσθαι Eust.11.25. III. = δακτυλιαῖος, διάστημα Theo Sm.p.125 H.

**δακτῠλιο-γλῠφία**, ἡ, *art of cutting gems*, Pl.*Alc*.1.128c. **-γλύφος**, ὁ, *engraver of gems*, Critias 66 D., Phld.*Po.Herc*.1676.5, D.L. 1.57, Gal.12.205. **-θήκη**, ἡ, *collection of gems*, Plin.*HN*37.11. II. *ring-case*, Mart.11.59.

**δακτύλιον**, τό, = sq. 1, *BGU*781 ii 15: = sq. II. 2, Aët.2.185 (s.v.l.); also v.l. for δακρύδιον Ps.-Dsc.4.170.

⊛ **δακτύλιος** [ῠ], Boeot. **δακκύλιος** (v. δάκτυλος), ὁ, *ring, signet*, Sapph.35, Hdt.2.38, Ar.*Pl*.884, Pl.*R*.359e; ὁ ἐπὶ τοῦ δ. keeper of the *signet*, Lxx *To*.1.22; ὁ τῆς πόλεως δ. *OGI*229.88 (Smyrna, iii B.C.); δ. φαρμακίτης Eup.87, cf. Antiph.177. II. *anything ring-shaped*, as, 1. *felloe* of a wheel, Poll.1.145. 2. *anus*, Dsc.1.70, Luc.*Demon*.17, *PRyl*.28.68 (iv A.D.). 3. pl., *movable rings* on a bit, X.*Eq*.10.9. 4. *stone* to which mooring-cables were attached, Hsch. 5. *door-handle*, Id. 6. *end of the steering-paddle*, Id.

**δακτῠλιουργός**, ὁ, *ring maker*, Philyll.15, Pherecr.207.

**δακτῠλ-ίς**, ίδος, ἡ, name of a kind of *grape*, Plin.*HN*14.40. II. = δάκτυλος, Steph.*in Hp.Aph*.2.294 D. **-ίσκος**, ὁ, Dim. of δάκτυλος II, *IG*7.3073.115 (Lebad.). **-ιστής**, οῦ, ὁ, (δάκτυλος II) *measurer, surveyor*, *PFay*.112.11 (i A.D.), *PAmh*.126.32 (ii A.D.).

**δακτῠλῖτις**, ἡ, = ἀριστολοχεία μακρά, Dsc.3.4, Isid.*Etym*.17.9.52.

**δακτῠλο-δεικτέω**, *point with the finger*, D.25.68: c. acc., D.C.61. 17:—Pass., D.H.*Rh*.7.4, Ph.2.539. ⊛ **-δεικτος**, ον, *pointed at with the finger*, μέλαθρα A.*Ag*.1332 (lyr.), cf. *PLond.ined*.1821. **-δικτος**, ον, (δικεῖν) *thrown from the fingers*, δ. μέλος, of the humming of a top, A.*Fr*.57 codd. Str. (-δεικτον edd.). **-δόχμη**, ἡ, *four fingers' breadth*, = παλαιστή, Poll.2.157. **-ειδής**, ές, *like a finger*, Philem. Gloss.ap.Ath.11.468f, Ruf.*Oss*.22. **-καμψόδῠνος**, ον, *wearying the fingers by keeping them bent*, *APl*.1.18. **-κοιλογλύφος** [λῠ], ὁ, = δακτυλιογλύφος, *IGRom*.4.1648 (Philadelphia). **-ποιητικός**, ή, όν, *finger-making*, δύναμις Phlp.*in GA*193.11. **-πους**, ὁ, gen. ποδος, *first phalanx*, δ. ἡ ῥιζοδάκτυλος *Cat.Cod.Astr*.7.238.25.

⊛ **δάκτῠλος**, ὁ, poet. pl. δάκτυλα Theoc.19.3, *AP*9.365 (Jul. Imp.), also Arist.*Phgn*.810$^a$22:—*finger*, ἐπὶ δακτύλων συμβάλλεσθαι τοὺς μῆνας to reckon on *the fingers*, Hdt.6.63; ὁ μέγας δ. *the thumb*, Id. 3.8, Diog.Apoll.6; ὁ μέσος Arist.*PA*687$^b$18; οἱ λιχανοί Hp.*Art*.37; ὁ ἔσχατος Id.*PA*687$^b$17: prov., ἄκρῳ δ. γεύεσθαι Procop.Gaz.*Ep*. 31; οὐκ ἄξια ψόφου δακτύλων Clearch.5. 2. οἱ δ. τῶν ποδῶν *the toes*, X.*An*.4.5.12; and, without ποδῶν, Batr.45, Ar.*Eq*.874, Arist. *HA*494$^a$12; τὸ τῶν δ. μέγεθος ἐναντίως ἔχει ἐπί τε τῶν ποδῶν καὶ τῶν χειρῶν Id.*PA*690$^a$30; ὁ μέσος δ. of a monkey, Id.*HA*502$^b$3; ὁ μείζων δ. the great *toe*, Plu.*Pyrrh*.3. b. of *the toes* of beasts, Arist.*HA*498$^a$34; of birds, Id.*PA*695$^a$22. II. a measure of length, *finger's breadth*, = about $\frac{7}{10}$ of an inch, Hdt.1.60, al.; πώνωμεν, δάκτυλος ἀμέρα Alc.41; δάκτυλος ἀώς *AP*12.50 (Asclep.): Astron., *digit*, i.e. twelfth part of the sun's or moon's apparent diameter, Cleom.2.3. III. metrical foot, *dactyl*, – ⏑ ⏑, Pl.*R*.400b; ῥυθμὸς κατὰ δάκτυλον Ar.*Nu*.651; δ. κατ' ἴαμβον, *diiambus*, Aristid.

Quint.1.17. 2. δάκτυλοι, οἱ, a *dance*, Ath.14.629d. IV. *date*, fruit of the φοῖνιξ, Arist.*Mete*.342ᵃ10, Artem.5.89. 2. kind of *grape*, Plin.*HN*14.15, Colum.3.2.1. 3. = ἄγρωστις, Plin.*HN*24.182. V. Δάκτυλοι Ἰδαῖοι mythical *wizards* and *craftsmen* in Crete (or Phrygia, D.S.17.7), attached to the cult of Rhea Cybele, Hes.*Fr.*176, Pherecyd.47 J., S.*Fr*.364, Str.8.3.30, D.S.5.64, *IG*12(9).259.22 (Eretria). 2. δ. Ἰδαῖοι, = γλυκυσίδη, Dsc.3.140. b. fossil found in Crete, Plin.*HN*37.170. VI. δ. θεοῦ the *hand* of God, Lxx *Ex*.8.19, cf. *Ev.Luc.*11.20. (Orig. *δάτκυλος, cf. Boeot. δακκύλιος *Schwyzer* 462 *B* 51; δατ- = *dn̥t*, cf. Skt. *a-datkas* 'toothless'.)

**δακτῠλότριπτος**, ον, *worn by the fingers*, ἄτρακτος *AP*6.247.3 (Phil.).

**δακτῠλωτός**, ή, όν, *with finger-like handles*, ἔκπωμα Ion Trag.1, Didym.ap.Ath.11.468e.

**δάλα**· ἄμπελος, Hsch. **δάλαν**· λύμην, Id. (Cf. δηλέομαι.) **δαλάγχαν**· θάλασσαν (Maced.), Id. **δάλεμον**· κηδεμόνα, Id.

**δᾰλέομαι**, Dor. for δηλέομαι.

**δᾰλερός**, ά, όν, *burning, hot*, dub. l. in Emp.90.2.

**δάλιδας**· τὰς μεμνηστευμένας, Hsch. (leg. τάλιδας).

**δᾰλίον**, τό, Dim. of δαλός, Ar.*Pax*959.

**Δάλιος**, Dor. for Δήλιος (q. v.).

**δαλιοχεῖν**, = παιδὶ συνεῖναι (Ambrac.); also, = μοιχεύειν, Hsch.: **δαλιοχός**· μοιχός, Id. **δαλίς**· μωρός, Id. **δάλκιον**· πινάκιον, Id. **δάλλει**· κακουργεῖ, Id. (Cf. δηλέομαι.) **δαλλώ** or **δαλώ**, *old woman* (cf. δαλός II), Id. **δαλμᾶναι**· εἰκάσαι, Id.

⊛ **Δαλμᾰτεῖς**, οἱ, *Dalmatians*, Plb.12.5.2, Str.7.5.5:—also **Δαλμάται**, App.*Ill*.11: **Δαλμᾰτία**, ἡ, Str.7.5.3:—Adj. **-τικός**, ή, όν, Id. 7.5.5:—hence **Δαλμᾰτική**, ἡ, *a robe*, *CPR*21.16 (iii A. D.):—more freq. **Δελμ-**, *Edict.Diocl.*19.9, al., *BGU*93.7 (ii/iii A. D.):—Dim. **Δελματίκιον**, τό, *Sammelb*.1988, *POxy*.1026.10 (v A. D.):—also **δερματική**, *PTeb*.405.10 (iii A. D.):—Dim. **δερματίκιν**, *PTeb*.413.8 (ii/iii A. D.).

⊛ **δαλμᾰτικομᾰφόρτης**, ου, ὁ, *Dalmatian cloak with a hood*, *POxy*.1273.14 (iii A. D.) (δελμ-):—Dim. **δερμᾰτικομᾰφόρτιν**, ib.114.5 (ii/iii A. D.).

**Δᾰλογενής**, ές, Dor. for Δηλογενής.

⊛ **δᾱλός**, ὁ, (δαίω) *fire-brand*, Il.15.421, Od.5.488, E.*Cyc*.471,472, A.*Ch*.608 (lyr.), Arist.*Mete*.344ᵃ26; *beacon-light*, *AP*9.675; of the thunderbolt, Il.13.320, cf. Luc.*Tim*.2. 2. a kind of *meteor*, Arist. *Mete*.341ᵇ28. II. *burnt-out torch*: metaph. of an old man, *AP*12.41 (Mel.). (Contr. fr. δᾱϝελός, cf. δαβελός.)

**δαλός**· μελάνουρος ἰχθύς, Hsch. **δαλοῦν**· σύντομον, Id.

**δάλτος**, Cypr. = δέλτος, *Inscr.Cypr.*135.26 H. (Idalium).

⊛ **δαμάζω** A.*Ch*.324 (lyr.), etc.: fut. δαμάσω *AP*6.329 (Leon.); Ep. δαμάσσω Il.22.176, also δαμᾷ, δαμάᾳ, 1.61, 22.271; 3 pl. δαμόωσι 6.368 (v. δαμάω): aor. 1 ἐδάμασα Pi.*N*.7.90 (part. δαμάσσαις *O*.9.92), Ep. ἐδάμασσα, δάμασσα, Il.5.191, Od.14.367: pf. δεδάμακα Stob. *Flor.Monac.*82:—**Med.**, fut. Ep. δαμάσσομαι Il.21.226: aor. ἐδαμάσσατο, δαμάσαντο, δαμασσάμενος, Od.9.516, Il.10.210, Od.9.454; aor. 1 opt. δαμάσαιτο *Leg.Gort*.2.11: aor. 2 opt. δάμοιτο *CIG*4000.18 (Iconium):—**Pass.**, fut. 3 δεδμήσομαι *h.Ap*.543; irreg. δαμοῦμαι *PMag.Par.*1.2906: aor. ἐδαμάσθην Od.8.231, Pi.*O*.2.20, A.*Pers.*279 (lyr.), E.*Ph*.563; Ep. δαμάσθην Il.19.9, cf. 16.816; ἐδμήθην, imper. δμηθήτω 9.158, δμηθεὶς 4.99, Hes.*Th*.1000, Dor. δμᾱθεὶς A. *Pers*.907 (lyr.), E. (lyr., v. infr.), Cerc.7.1: ἐδάμην [ᾰ] Il.13.812, Parm.7.1, etc.; Ep. δάμην Od.3.90; 3 pl. δάμεν Il.8.344; Ep. subj. δαμείω Od.18.54, 2 and 3 sg. δαμήῃς -ήῃ Il.3.436, 22.246, 2 pl. δαμήετε 7.72; opt. δαμείην Il.3.301, E.*Med*.648; inf. δαμῆναι Il.15.522, A.*Ch*.368 (lyr.), S.*Ph*.200, Ep. inf. δᾰμήμεναι Il.20.312; part. δαμείς 22.40, Sapph.90, etc. (only form of aor. used by S., and preferred by A. and E.): pf. δέδμημαι Il.5.878, etc., -ημένος 14.482, etc.; later δεδαμασμένος Nic.*Al*.29, *Epigr.Gr.*550.9: plpf. δέδμητο Od.3.305; 3 pl. -ήατο Il.3.183.—Poet. Verb, used by X. in pres. part. δαμάζων *Mem*.4.3.10: aor. Pass. δαμασθεῖεν ib.4.1.3; also inf. δαμασθῆναι is f. l. in Isoc.7.4:—*overpower*: I. of animals, *tame, break in*, twice in Hom., in Med., ἡμίονον.. ἥτ' ἀλγίστη δαμάσασθαι Il.23.655; τῶν κέν τιν'.. δαμασαίμην Od.4.637:—later in Act., X.*Mem*.4.3.10:—Pass., ib.4.1.3. 2. of metals, *work*, σίδαρον E.*Alc*.980 (lyr.); of land, *clear*, *PSI*4.316 (iv(?) A. D.). II. of maidens, *make subject* to a husband, ἀνδρὶ δάμασσεν Il.18.432:—Med., *force, seduce*, *Leg.Gort.* l. c.:—Pass., Il.3.301, Od.3.269. III. *subdue, conquer*, Od.9.59, al.; βίῃ καὶ χερσὶ δ. Hes.*Th*.490:—Pass., *to be subject to* another, σοί τ' ἐπιπείθονται καὶ δεδμήμεσθα ἕκαστος Il.5.878; δέδμητο δὲ λαὸς ὑπ' αὐτῷ Od.3.305. b. of the gods, *bring low*, Il.9.118, 16.845, al. c. *subdue, gain the mastery over*, ἐπιθυμίαν Stob. l. c. 2. *lay low, kill*, esp. in fight, εἴ χ' ὑπ' ἐμοί γε θεὸς δαμάσῃ μνηστῆρας Od.21.213:—Pass., ὑπ' ἐμοὶ δμηθέντα Il.5.646; ὑπὸ δουρὶ δαμέντα ib.653. 3. of the powers of nature, etc., *overcome, overpower*, ἔρος.. θυμὸν ἐνὶ στήθεσσιν.. ἐδάμασσεν 14.316:—Med., δαμασσάμενος φρένας οἴνῳ Od.9.454, cf. 516:—Pass., *to be overcome*, αἴθρῳ καὶ καμάτῳ δεδμημένον 14.318; μαλακῷ δεδμημένοι ὕπνῳ Il.10.2; ὕπνῳ καὶ φιλότητι δαμείς 14.353; ἀλλ' δέδμητο φίλον κῆρ Od.5.454, cf. 8.231; δμαθέντες *dead*, E.*Alc*.127 (lyr.). IV. ἀγῶνα δαμάσσαι ἔργῳ *win* it, Pi.*P*.8.80. V. οὐ μήποτε τοῦτο δαμῇ, εἶναι μὴ ἐόντα it shall never be *proved* that.., Parm.7.1. (δᾰμᾰ- : δμη- underlies δάμνημι, ἐδάμα(σ)σα, δέδμημαι; δαμάζω is a post-Homeric form of pres.; cf. Skt. *dā́myati* 'to be tamed', *damitar-* 'tamer', etc.)

**Δᾰμαῖος**, ὁ, (δαμάζω) *Horse-Tamer*, epith. of Poseidon, Pi.*O*.13.69.

**δᾰμάλη** [μᾰ], ἡ, = δάμαλις, E.*Ba*.739, Theoc.4.12, *POxy*.1734.2, etc.

**δᾰμᾰλήβοτος**, ον, *browsed by heifers*, *APl*.4.230 (Leon.).

**δᾰμάλης** [μᾰ], ου, ὁ, (δαμάζω) *subduer*, Ἔρως Anacr.2.1. II. *young steer*, Arist.*HA*632ᵃ15, *AP*6.96 (Eryc.).

**δᾰμᾰληφάγος** [φᾰ], ον, *beef-eating*, Ἀλκείδης *AP*9.237 (Eryc.).

⊛ **δᾰμᾰλ-ίζω**, poet. = δαμάζω, *to subdue*, Pi.*P*.5.121 codd.:—Med., πώλους δαμαλιζομένα E.*Hipp*.231 (lyr.). **-ιον**, τό, Dim. of δάμαλις, *PFlor*.150.2 (iii A. D.). **-ις**, εως, ἡ (ὁ D.H.1.39), (δαμάζω) *young cow, heifer*, A.*Supp*.351 (lyr.), Aen.Tact.27.1, D.H.1.35; of Io, B.18.24, Nic.*Al*.344; also masc., Hellanic.111 J. 2. δ. σῦς *IG*5(1).1390.34,69 (Andania, i B. C.). II. *girl*, Epicr.9, *AP*5.291 (Agath.).

**δαμάλλοντες**· δαρδάπτοντες, Hsch.

**δᾰμᾰλοπόδια**, ων, τά, *calves' feet*, Alex.Trall.7.8.

**δᾰμᾰλος**, ὁ, perh. *calf*, Hdn.Gr.1.159.

**δᾰμαντήρ**, ῆρος, ὁ, *tamer*, v. l. in Alcm.9.

⊛ **δάμᾰρ** [ᾰ], αρτος, ἡ, (δαμάζω II) *wife, spouse*, Il.3.122, Pi.*N*.4.57, A.*Pr*.834, etc.

**δᾰμαρίππεως**, ω, a kind of *fig*, Eup.407.

**δαμαρούσιος**· ὀχετὸς δημόσιος, Hsch.

**δᾰμᾰσ-άνδρα**, ἡ, *subduer of men*, of the moon, *Hymn.Mag.*5.43. **-ήνωρ**, ορος, *man-slaying*, λέων Pancrat.*Oxy*.1085.3.

**δᾰμᾰσι-κόνδυλος**, ον, *conquering with the knuckles*, Eup.408. **-μβροτος**, ον, *taming mortals, man-slaying*, Σπάρτη Simon.218; αἰχμή Pi.*O*.9.79; χαλκός B.12.50.

**δᾰμάσιππος** [μᾰ], ον, *horse-taming*, of Athena, Lamprocl.1.4 (perh. Stes., cf. Sch.Aristid.3.537 D.), cf. Corn.*ND*20; Λυδία B.3.23.

**δᾰμᾰσις** [δᾰ], εως, ἡ, *taming, subduing*, Sch.Pi.*O*.13.98.

**δᾰμᾰσί-φρων**, ον, gen. ονος, *heart-subduing* χρυσός Pi.*O*.13.78. **-φως**, ωτος, ὁ, ἡ, = δαμασίμβροτος, ὕπνος Simon.232; of Ares, prob. in Tim.*Pers*.22.

**δᾰμᾰσίχθων**, ονος, ὁ, *earth-subduer*, epith. of Poseidon, B.15.19.

⊛ **Δαμασκηνόν**, τό, *Damascus-plum, damson*, Ath.2.49d, Gal.6.353.

**δᾰμασ-τέον**, *one must break in*, τριετῆ πῶλον *Gp*.16.1.11. II. Adj. -τέος, α, ον, Hsch. s. v. δματέα. **-τής**, οῦ, ὁ, *subduer*, *Gloss.*, prob. epith. of Ἔρως, [Epich.]301. ⊛ **-τικός**, ή, όν, gloss on Δαμαῖος, Sch.Pi.*O*.13.98.

⊛ **δαμασώνιον**, τό, = ἄλισμα, Dsc.3.152; = ἄλιμος, Ps.-Dsc.1.91. II. a diuretic, Pall.*in Hp*.2.18 D.

⊛ **δᾰμάτειρα** [μᾰ], ἡ, fem. of δαμαντήρ, *AP*11.403 (Luc.).

**Δαμάτηρ**, v. Δημήτηρ.

**δᾰμᾱτρίζειν** (Δημήτηρ) *gather in the fruits of the earth* (Cypr.), Hsch.

**δαμάτριον**· ἄνθος ὅμοιον ναρκίσσῳ, Hsch.

⊛ **Δᾰμάτριος**, ὁ, Boeotian month, *IG*7.296, al., Plu.2.378e.

**δᾰμάω**, a form assumed as the 1st pers. of δαμᾷ, δαμάᾳ, δαμόωσι, which in Hom. are fut. of δαμάζω or δάμνημι: but δαμόωσι, δαμόωνται, are pres. in late Ep., Q.S.5.247,249.

**Δάμεια**, τά, festival at Tarentum, Hsch.

**δᾰμείω, δᾰμήμεναι**, v. δαμάζω.

**δᾱμέτας**, α, ὁ, = δημότης, *IG*12(1).1032.13 (Carpathus).

⊛ **δᾱμία**, Cret. for ζημία. ⊛ **Δαμία**, ἡ, fertility-Goddess at Aegina, Hdt.5.82, Paus.2.30.4: also **Δαμοία**, *IG*5(1).363 (Sparta), 1314 (Thalamae).

⊛ **δᾱμεύω**, = δημοσιόω, *IG*4.554 (Argos), cf. Hsch.

**δᾰμι-εργός, -οεργός, -οργός**, Dor. for δημιουργός: **δᾱμιόργιον**, τό, *office of* δαμιοργοί, *LW*1572ᵇ (Cnidus): **δάμιος**, Dor. for δήμιος: **δαμιόω**, Boeot. and Cret. for ζημιόω.

**δαμναμένη**, = κατανάγκη, Ps.-Dsc.4.131; = κῆμος, ib.133.

**δαμνάω**, = δαμάζω, Hom. only in 3 sg. pres. δαμνᾷ Od.11.221: impf. ἐδάμνα Il.21.52, Sapph.*Supp*.1.12; δάμνα Il.16.103, al.; Ion. δάμνασκε *h.Ven*.251: 2 sg. pres. δαμνᾷς Thgn.1388 (s. v. l.); imper. δάμνα Sapph.1.3. (These forms may belong orig. to δαμνᾶμι, Aeol. for sq.; Hsch. also gives pres. δάμνει and fut. δαμνήσει.)

**δάμνημι** (v. also foreg.), = δαμάζω, τὴν μὲν.. δάμνημ' ἐπέεσσι Il.5.893; δάμνησι στίχας ἀνδρῶν ib.746, etc.; ἄνδρ' ἀγαθὸν πενίη δάμνησι Thgn.173; πενία.. δ. λαόν Alc.92:—Med., ἵμερον, ᾧ τε σὺ πάντας δαμνᾷ ἀθανάτους Il.14.199; ἀλλά με χεῖμα δάμναται Od.14.488; Ἔρος δ. νόον Hes.*Th*.122, cf. Archil.85, A.*Pr*.165, Q.S.11.25:—Pass., πυκνὰ καρῆαθ' ὑφ' Ἕκτορι δάμνατο Il.11.309; μηδ' οὕτω Τρώεσσιν ἔα δάμνασθαι Ἀχαιούς 8.244; Ἀχαιοὺς Τρωσὶν δαμναμένους 13.16; δάμναμαι A.*Supp*.904 (lyr.); imper. μηκέτι δάμναο θυμόν Maiist.51: pf. part. δεδαμναμένα *forced, seduced*, *Leg.Gort*.2.13.

**δαμνῆτις**, ιδος, ἡ, *she that subdues*, Hsch. ⊛ **δάμνια**· θύματα, σφάγια, Id.

**δάμνιππος**, ον, *horse-taming*, Orph.*A*.740.

**δαμνογόνη, δαμνοδάμεια, δαμνώ**, *she that subdues*, epiths. of the Moon, *Hymn.Mag.*5.43.

**δαμνόν**· δεινόν, Hsch. **δάμνος**· ἵππος (Tyrrhen.), Id.

**δᾰμογέρων, δαμόθεν, δαμόομαι, δᾱμόσιος, δᾶμος, δαμότης**, Dor. for δημ-.

**δᾱμοθοινία**, Dor. = δημο-, *public feast*, *SIG*671 *A* 2, al. (Delph., ii B. C.).

**Δαμοία**, v. Δαμία.

**δαμοσιομάστας**, ὁ, official title, prob. = μαστρός (q. v.), *IG*5(1).47 (Sparta, ii A. D.); -μαστης, ib.554.

⊛ **δᾱμοσιοργία**, ἡ, = δημιουργία, *GDI*3052.10.

**δᾱμοσιοφύλᾰκες** [ῠ], οἱ, title of board of magistrates at Dyme, *GDI*1615, *SIG*529.4 (iii B. C.).

**δαμοσόνιος**, a plant, Hsch.; cf. δαμασώνιον. **δαμοῦαι**· οἱ ἐπὶ

Μελαντίας πεμπόμενοι (Lacon.), Id. **δαμοῦχοι**, οἱ, Dor. for δημ–, title of a board of magistrates, Id. **δαμοφανής**, = ἱμάτιον (Lacon.), Id. **δαμπόν**, = πυρίεφθον (Cret.), Id.

* **δᾱμώματα**, τά, = τὰ δημοσίᾳ ᾀδόμενα, Ar.*Pax*797, from Stes.(*Fr.* 37): expld. by κοινώματα, δημοσιώματα, Hsch. **δαμώμενος**· ἀγαλλόμενος, οἱ δὲ παίζων, Id. **δαμώσεις**· δημόται, ἢ οἱ ἐντελεῖς (Lacon.), Id. **δαμώσικτον**· δεδοκιμασμένον (Lacon.), Id. **δᾶν**, v. δᾶ.

**Δάν**, = Ζεύς, *BphW*31.1578 (Delph.), Hdn.Gr.1.394.

**δάν, δαναιός**, Dor. for δήν, δηναιός.

**Δανάη**, ἡ, = δάφνη, Ps.-Dsc.4.145.

**δάναιε**· δαιδοῦλαι (Tarent.), Hsch.

**Δαναΐς**, ἡ, = κόνυζα πλατύφυλλος, Ps.-Dsc.3.121.

* **δᾰνάκη** [νᾰ], ἡ, *Persian coin*, worth rather more than an obol: hence, *the coin buried with a corpse* as Charon's fee, Call.*Fr.*110, Poll. 9.82, Hsch., *EM*247.41: Dim. **δανάκιον**, τό, prob. in Suid. (Pers. *dānak*.)

**Δᾰναοί**, οἱ, *the Danaäns*, subjects of Δάναος, king of Argos, but in Il.1.42, al., for *the Greeks* generally (but expl. as = νεκροί (cf. δάνος (B)), *EM*247.49): Com. Sup. Δαναώτατος Ar.*Fr.*259.—**Δαναΐδαι**, ῶν, οἱ, *the sons* or *descendants of Danaus*, E.*Ph.*466:—**Δαναΐδες**, αἱ, *his daughters*, name of a play of A.

**δάνας**· μερίδας (Caryst.), Hsch. **δανδαίνειν**· ἀτενίζειν, φροντίζειν, μεριμνᾶν, Id.

**δανδαλίς**, ίδος, ἡ, = δενδαλίς, Poll.6.77, Hsch.

**δάνδαλος**, ὁ, = ἐριθακός, Hsch. **δανδαρίκαι**· οἱ βολευταί, Id.

**δᾰν-ειακός**, ή, όν, *concerning loans*, *Cod.Just.*1.3.45, Just.*Nov.* 134.8. * **–είζω**, fut. -είσω D.35.52: aor. ἐδάνεισα X.*Cyr.*3.1.34, etc.: pf. δεδάνεικα D.35.52:—**Med.**, ibid.: fut. δανείσομαι Id.32.15: aor. ἐδανεισάμην Lys.12.59, etc.: pf. δεδάνεισμαι in med. sense, X. *HG*6.5.19, D.37.53:—**Pass.**, aor. ἐδανείσθην X.*HG*2.4.28, D.33. 12: pf. δεδάνεισμαι Id.36.5, 49.53: (δάνος):—*put out money at usury, lend*, *IG*1².302.56, Ar.*Th.*842, al.; more fully, δ. ἐπὶ τόκῳ Pl.*Lg.* 742c; ἐπὶ ὀκτὼ ὀβολοῖς τὴν μνᾶν δ. τοῦ μηνὸς ἑκάστου D.53. 13, cf. Aeschin.1.107; δ. ἐπὶ τούτοις τοῖς ἀνδραπόδοις on the security of.., D.27.27; ἐπὶ τοῖς σώμασι Arist.*Ath.*9.1; εἰς τὰ ἡμέτερα D.27.28; δανεῖσαι χρήματα εἰς τὸν Πόντον καὶ πάλιν Ἀθήναζε Id.35.3. 2. Med., *have lent to one, borrow*, Ar.*Nu.*1306, etc.; ἀπό τινος Lys.17.2; ἐπὶ τοῖς μεγάλοις [τόκοις] D.1.15; δ. ἐγγείων τόκων 34.23:—Act. and Med. opposed, ἀποδώσουσι οἱ δανεισάμενοι τοῖς δανείσασι τὸ γιγνόμενον ἀργύριον ap.D.35.11:—Pass., of the money, *to be lent out*, Ar.*Nu.*756, X.*HG*2.4.28, D.33.12. 3. metaph. in Med., μόρια ἀπὸ τοῦ κόσμου Pl.*Ti.*42e; ἀποδώσετέ μοι ἃ ἐδανείσασθε ἐν τῷ λόγῳ Pl.*R.*612c.

**δανειοκόπος**, ὁ, *usurer*, prob. in Mitteis *Chr.*80.27 (i A.D.).

* **δάν-ειον** [ᾰ], τό, *loan*, δ. ἀπαιτεῖν D.34.12; ἀποδοτέον Arist.*EN* 1164ᵇ32: pl., Men.*Mon.*97; σπέρματα δάνεια *POxy.*1262.16 (ii A.D.): —written **δάνιον**, Lxx *De.*15.8, al. * **–εισμα**, ατος, τό, = δάνειον, δ. ποιεῖσθαι, = δανείζεσθαι, Th.1.121; τῶν μαρτύρων τῶν παραγιγνομένων τῷ δ. D.35.9: metaph., οἷον δάνεισμα καὶ μόρια τοῦ μεγάλου κόσμου Gal.19.159. **–εισμός**, ὁ, *money-lending*, *IG*2².1172, Pl.*Lg.*842d (pl.), Arist.*EN*1131ᵃ3, etc. II. *borrowing*, Pl.*R.*573e (pl.), *POxy.*799 (i A.D.), Plu.2.706b: metaph., αἷμα δ' αἵματος πικρὸς δ. ἦλθε E.*El.* 858. **–ειστέον**, *one must lend money*, Plu.2.408c. **–ειστής**, οῦ, ὁ, *money-lender* or *creditor*, *IPE*1².32 *B*84 (Olbia), Lxx 4*Ki.*4.1, *Ev. Luc.*7.41, Ph.2.284, al., Hierocl.p.57 A., *POxy.*68.25 (ii A.D.). II. *borrower*, *IG*12(7).67.41, 68.4 (Amorg.), Plu.*Sol.*13. * **–ειστικός**, ή, όν, *concerning loans*, *BGU*1149.23 (i B.C.), Plu.*Agis*13, etc.; ὁ δ., = δανειστής, Luc.*Smp.*5.

**δανές**· ἀληθὲς ἢ δῶρον ἢ μερίδα ἢ ἰσχύν, γέρας ἢ δάνειον, Hsch. **δανήλοφα**, = μακροτράχηλα or ὑψηλοτράχηλα, Id. (i.e. ταν–).

* **δανίζω**, Hellenistic form for δανείζω, Lxx *Pr.*19.14: fut. Act. δανιῶ and Med. δανιοῦμαι ib.*De.*28.12: aor. part. δανίσας *AP*11.309 (Lucill.), *Lyr.Alex.Adesp.*37.27.

* **δᾰνός**, ή, όν, *burnt, dry, parched*, ξύλα δ. Od.15.322: Sup. ξύλα δανότατα Ar.*Pax*1134. (Prob. from *δᾰϝεσ-νός, cf. δαίω.)

* **δάνος** (A), [ᾰ], εος, τό, *gift, present*, Euph.42. II. *loan, debt*, Call. *Ep.*48, *PMasp.*126.11 (vi A.D.): metaph., ὁ χρόνος ἐστὶ δ. *Lyr.Alex. Adesp.*37.27; πνεῦμα λαβὼν δ. οὐρανόθεν.. αὔτ' ἀπέδωκα *IG*14.2000.

**δάνος** (B), [ᾰ], ὁ, Maced. for θάνατος, Plu.2.22c.

**δᾰνοτής**, ῆτος, ἡ, perh. f.l. for δαϊοτῆτος (cf. δηι–), ἀμερίων μόχθων καὶ δανοτῆτος S.*Fr.*369.

**δάντα**· ζυγά, Hsch. **δανῶν**· κακοποιῶν, κτείνων (Maced.), Id.

**δάξ**, Adv., = ὀδάξ, Opp.*H.*4.60.

**δάξα**· θάλασσα (Epir.), Hsch.

**δαξασμός**, ὁ, = ὀδαγμός, ὀδαξησμός, Ti.Locr.103a.

* **δαόν**· πολυχρόνιον, Hsch.

**δάος** [ᾰ], εος, τό, (δαίω) = δαΐς, δαλός, *firebrand, torch*, Il.24.647, Od.4.300, Q.S.9.454:—also **δάος**, ὁ, *JHS*32.163 (iii A.D.). II. Phryg., = λύκος, Hsch.

**Δᾶος**, ὁ, as the name of a slave, Lat. *Davus* (Δᾶϝος), Men.*Georg.* 32; from the name of a barbarous people, cf. Hdt.1.125.

**δάοχος**· μοιχός, Hsch.; cf. δαλιοχός.

**δάπακες** (cod. δαρπ–)· θυμάλωπες, Hsch.; cf. δαύακες.

* **δᾰπᾰν-άω**:—**Pass.**, pres. part. δαπανούμενα (as if from δαπανέω) *IG*5(1).1390.55 (Andania, i B.C.): fut. δαπανηθήσομαι Satyr.20, Plu.2.218d: aor. ἐδαπανήθην X.*Cyr.*2.4.11: pf. δεδαπάνημαι Hdt.2. 125, Lys.21.5, etc.: plpf. δεδαπάνητο (κατα–) Hdt.5.34:—Pass., also Med. δαπανάομαι Id.2.37, Ar.*Pl.*588, Pl., etc.; impf., Ar.*Fr.* 569.10, Lys.25.13: aor., Isoc.15.225, Is.5.43 (but –ήσας ib.45) (aor. Med. ἐδαπανησάμην Eun.*Hist.*p.271 D.): pf., Isoc.18.63:—*spend*, Th.7.29, etc.; ὑπὲρ τὴν οὐσίαν δ. Diph.32.7; δ. τὰ προσταττόμενα And.4.42; δ. εἴς τι *to spend* upon a thing, Th.8.45, X.*Mem.* 1.3.11, prob. in Arist.*Pol.*1307ᵇ34; δ. ἐκ τῶν αὑτοῦ Is.7.38; τἀναλώματα πάντα ἐκ τῶν ἰδίων ἐδαπανῶμεν *defrayed* all expenses, interpol. in D.21.154:—Pass., Hdt.2.125; τὰ λαμβανόμενα καὶ δαπανώμενα Arist.*Pol.*1314ᵇ5: also Med. (v. supr.), *spend*, Hdt.2.37; δ. μεγάλα And.4.32, cf. Lys.33.5: c. acc. cogn., τοσαύτας δαπάνας δαπανώμενος Id.21.3; ὅσα δεδαπάνησθε εἰς τὸν πόλεμον D.1.27, cf. Isoc.18.63; δαπανηθεὶς οὐδέν dub. l. in Is.5.43. 2. *consume, use up*, ἡ φύσις δ. τὸν θορόν Arist.*GA*757ᵃ25; χρόνον εἴς τι Onos.1.5:—Pass., Arist.*GA* 745ᵃ13; of time, App.*Pun.*130; *destroy, consume*, φλὸξ δ. πάντα Ph. 2.208; ἄνεμος [πόλιν] ἐδαπάνησεν App.*BC*1.94; of persons, *to be destroyed*, ὑπὸ θηρίων Ph.2.43; καθάπερ ὑπὸ πυρὸς ib.433; πρὸς θηρίων App. *BC*5.79; ἐν ταρτάροις καὶ βαράθροις δαπανωμένους D.H.4.81; ὑπὸ νόσου or νόσῳ δαπανᾶσθαι Plu.*Galb.*17, Lib.*Or.*55.27:—Med., πυρὶ καὶ φόνῳ καὶ σιδήρῳ πάντα δαπανήσασθαι Eun.l.c. II. causal, τὴν πόλιν δαπανᾶν *to put* it *to expense, exhaust* it, Th.4.3, cf. Ph.2.642. * **–η**, ἡ, *cost, expenditure*, Hes.*Op.*723, al.; δ. χρυσοῦ καὶ ἀργύρου, χρημάτων, Th.1. 129, 3.13; δ. κοῦφα *the cost* is little, c. inf., E.*Ba.*893 (lyr.); εἰς κενὸν ἡ δ. *IG*14.1746.10: also in pl., Th.6.15; δαπάναι ἐλπίδων Pi.*I.*4 (5).57. II. *money spent*, ἵππων *on* horses, ib.3(4).47; δαπάνην παρέχειν *money for spending*, Hdt.1.41; ξυμφέρειν Th.1.99; ὅπως μὴ ἡ εἰς τὸν ἐνιαυτὸν κειμένη δ. εἰς τὸν μῆνα δαπανᾶται X.*Oec.*7. 36. III. *extravagance*, ἡ ἐν τῇ φύσει δ. Aeschin.3.218. * **–ημα**, ατος, τό, *cost, expense*, mostly in pl., X.*Cyr.*8.1.9, Philem.96.6, *IG*7. 2712.32 (Acraeph.); τοῖς ἰδίοις δ. *BGU*1130.21 (i B.C.), etc.; δαπανημάτων ἔνδεια want *of necessaries*, Plb.9.42.4: sg. in Arist.*EN*1122ᵃ 24, *CIG*3600 (Ilium), etc. **–ηρία**, ἡ, *extravagance*, Arist.*EE* 1221ᵃ11. **–ηρός**, ά, όν, of men, *lavish, extravagant*, Pl.*R.*564b, X.*Mem.*2.6.2; εἰς ἑαυτόν, εἰς ἀκολασίαν, Arist.*EN*1123ᵃ4, 1119ᵇ 31. II. of things, *expensive*, πόλεμος D.5.5; λειτουργία Arist. *Pol.*1309ᵃ18, cf. *EN*1122ᵃ21: Comp. -ότερα, λειτουργήματα Jul. *Or.*1.21d. Adv. -ρῶς X.*HG*6.5.4. III. *consuming*, πῦρ Ph.2. 91. * **–ησις**, εως, ἡ, *consuming, devouring*, Aristeas 146. * **–ητής**, οῦ, ὁ, *spendthrift*, *EM*40.44. **–ητικός**, ή, όν, *consuming*, δύναμις Philagr.ap.Aët.12.67, cf. Iamb.*Myst.*2.5. Adv. -κῶς *extravagantly*, βιοῦν S.E.*P.*1.230.

**δᾰπᾰνοθήκη**, ἡ, *penuarium*, *Gloss.*

* **δᾰπᾰν-ος** [δᾰ], ον, = δαπανηρός, ἐλπίς Th.5.103; ῥαθυμία cj. in Longin.44.11: c. gen., Plu.2.624d. **–όω**, = δαπανάω, *expend*, *IG* 5(1).1390.55 (Pass., Andania, i B.C.). **–ύλλα**, ἡ, Dim. of δαπάνη, Cerc.4.18

* **δάπεδον** [δᾰ], τό, *level surface*, ἐν τυκτῷ δαπέδῳ Od.4.627; *floor of a chamber*, 10.227, al., X.*Cyr.*8.8.16, *IG*4.952.44 (Epid.); *ground, soil*, γῆς ἀρότροις ῥήξας δ. Ar.*Pl.*515; πόλιος δ. Hdt.4.200; Συρίης δ. *AP*12.131 (Posidipp.): abs., *ground*, κείμενον ἐν δαπέδῳ Od.11.577: in pl., a ship's *decks* (fore and aft), A.*Ap.*416; but, *plain*, Pi.*N.*7.34, E.*Hipp.*230 (anap.); Βοιωτῶν δ. *AP*7.245 (Gaet.).—Mostly poet.; in later Prose, Luc.*Sacr.*8 alludes to Il.4.2. (From *dm̥-pedo- [dem-, dom-, dm̥-, = house; expld. by οἶκος, ἐρείπιον, Hsch.]; cf. ζάπεδον.)

**δάπης**, = δάπις, Hsch.

**δᾰπίδιον**, τό, Dim. of δάπις, Hipparch.Com.1.3.

**δᾰπῐδῠφάντης**, ου, ὁ, *carpet-weaver*, prob. in *Ostr.*1395.

**δάπις** [ᾰ], ιδος, ἡ, = τάπης, *carpet, rug*, Ar.*Pl.*528, Pherecr.185, v.l. in X.*Cyr.*8.8.16, in pl.; Καρχηδὼν δάπιδας καὶ ποικίλα προσκεφάλαια Hermipp.63.23, cf. Ar.*V.*676.

**δάπτης**, ου, ὁ, *eater, bloodsucker*, δάπταις αἱμοπώταισιν, of gnats, Lyc.1403.

**δάπτω**, fut. δάψω Il.13.831: aor. ἔδαψα, poet. δάψα Pi.*N.*8.23, Opp. *H.*3.333:—*devour*, as wild beasts, Il.16.159, etc.; ἀλλήλους δάπτοντες Emp.136; of fire, δώσω Πριαμίδην πυρὶ δαπτέμεν Il.23.183; of a spear, *rend*, χρόα λειριόεντα δάψει 13.831, cf. A.*Pr.*370; of moths and worms, [χρυσὸν] οὐ σὴς οὐδὲ κὶς δ. Pi.*Fr.*222; δ. τὰν παρειάν *tear* with the nails, A.*Supp.*70 (lyr.); *corrode*, ὑγρὸν δάπτον Aret.*SD*1.9; metaph., *consume*, δ. πόλιν, of a tyrant, Alc.*Supp.*23.7; of envy, Pi.*N.* 8.23; δάπτει τὸ μὴ 'νδικον S.*OT*682 (lyr.); οἰκτρὰ συμφορὰ δ. φρένας *Trag.Adesp.Oxy.*213(*a*).10:—Pass., συννοίᾳ δάπτομαι κέαρ A.*Pr.*437.

* **δάρατος**, ὁ, a Thessalian kind of *bread*, Maced. δράμις, Seleuc.ap. Ath.3.114b: neut. **δάρατον**, τό, prob. in *IG*9(2).1202 (Coropa, vi/v B.C.). II. *unleavened bread*, Nic.*Fr.*184:—also fem. pl. **δαράται**, αἱ, *cakes* offered at marriage and registration ceremonies by a φρατρία, *Michel*995 *A*5, al. (Delph., v/iv B.C.).

**δάρδα**, = μέλισσα, Hsch. **δαρδαίνει**· μολύνει, Id.

**Δάρδᾰνος**, ὁ, *Dardanus*, son of Zeus, founder of Dardania or Troy, Il.20.215: Adj. Δάρδανος ἀνήρ *Trojan*, 2.701, 16.807: mostly pl., Τρῶες καὶ Δάρδανοι 3.456, al.:—Adj. **Δαρδάνιος**, α, ον, *Trojan*, 2.819; **Δαρδάνειος**, E.*Tr.*840 (lyr.):—fem. **Δαρδανίς**, ίδος, ἡ, *Trojan woman*, Il.18.122; also, = κώνειον, Ps.-Dsc.4.78: **Δαρδανία** (sc. γῆ), ἡ, *Troy*, Il.20.216:—**Δαρδανίδης**, ου, ὁ, *son* or *descendant of Dardanus*, 3.303, al.: **Δαρδανίωνες**, οἱ, *sons of Dardanus*, 7.414.

**δαρδάπτω**, aor. subj. δαρδάψῃ Opp.*H.*4.628; inf. δαρδάψαι, Hsch.: pf. δεδάρδαφα, Id.:—*devour*, of wild beasts, Il.11.479, Hp.*Ep.*17, etc.; κτήματα, χρήματα δαρδάπτουσιν, *they devour* one's patrimony, Od.14.92, 16.315, cf. Ar.*Nu.*711; δ. με πόθος Εὐριπίδου Id.*Ra.*66: in late Prose, Luc.*Nec.*14. (Perh. dissim. from *δαρ-δϝπτω, cf. δρέπω.)

* **Δᾱρεικός**, ὁ, a Persian gold coin (but Δ. ἀργύρειοι Plu.*Cim.*10),

prop. Adj. agreeing with στατήρ (in full, Th.8.28, Hdt.7.28), Ar.*Ec.* 602, X.*An.*1.1.9, Herod.7.122, etc.; so χρυσὸς χαρακτῆρα Δαρεικὸν ἔχων D.S.17.66; χρυσὸς Δαρεικός Alciphr.1.5:—written **Δαρικός** and **Δαριχός**, *IG*5(1).1 (Sparta). (From Δαρεῖος, cf. Poll.3.87, acc. to some not D. Nothus, Harp.; the connection with Bab. *dariku* (dub. sens.) is v. doubtful.)

**Δᾱρειογενής**, ές, *born from Darius*, A.*Pers.*6,145 (anap.).

**Δᾱρεῖος**, ὁ, *Darius* (OPers. *Dārayavauš* '*upholder of the Good*'), name of several kings of Persia; acc. to Hdt.6.98, = Gr. ἐρξίης (q.v.):—also **Δαρειαῖος**, X.*HG*2.1.8 and 9, Ctes.*Fr.*29.49: **Δαρῖάν** A.*Pers.*651 (lyr.): **Δαριήκης** Str.16.4.27. II. a throw of the dice, Hsch.

**δάρειρ**, = σπιθαμή, Hsch.: **δάριν**· σπιθαμήν (Arc.), Id.

**δαρθάνω**, *sleep*, Hierocl.*in CA* 19 p.461 M.: aor. 2 ἔδρᾰθον, ἔδραθ' ἐνὶ προδόμῳ Od.20.143. (Prob. akin to Lat. *dormio*, Slav. *drěmati*, Skt. *drāti* 'sleep'.)

**Δαρικός**, v. Δαρεικός.

**δάρκα**, a kind of κασσία, Dsc.1.13 (v.l. δάκαρ).

**δάρκανος**, = ἐρυθρόδανον, Ps.-Dsc.3.143.

**δάρκες**· δέσμαι, Hsch.

**✱ δαρκνά** (for δαρχνά), Cret., = δραχμή, *GDI*4985, *Leg.Gort.*1.32, al.: —also **δαρκμά**, *GDI*5071 (Cnossus), al.: **δαρχμά** ib.1154 (Elis), *IG* 5(2).3 (Tegea).

**δάρμα**, ατος, τό, Delph., = δέρμα, *Michel* 995 *D*35 (ca. 400 B.C.).

**δᾱρός**, **δᾱρό-βιος**, Dor. for δηρός, δηρό-βιος: δαρόν also expld. by ἑορτή, and ἄρτος ἄζυμος (cf. δάρατος), Hsch.

**✱ δάροσος**, = βουτύπιον, Hsch. **δάρπη**· σαργάνη, κόφινος, Id.

**δάρσις**, εως, ἡ, (δέρω) *separation of parts united by cellular tissue by tearing*, Herophil.ap.Gal.2.349, cf. Gal.2.483, etc.

**δάρτης**, ου, ὁ, *one who flogs*, *Gloss.* **δάρτινον**· πέπλον λινοῦν, Hsch.

**✱ δαρτός**, ή, όν, (δέρω) *flayed*, ἵππων δ. πρόσωπα the skin *flayed from* horses' heads, Choeril.4.5; δ. χιτών, of skin *stripped off*, Paul.Aeg. 6.61. II. τὰ δ. *fish which must be skinned before dressing*, Mnesith. ap.Ath.8.357c; of animals, ἔν τι τῶν δ. ὀνομαζομένων Gal.2.644, cf. *IG*1².190, *SIG*57.31 (Milet., v B.C.).

**δάρυλλος**, ἡ, Maced., = δρῦς, Hsch. **δαρχμά**, v. δαρκνά.

**δάς**· ἐπὶ τοῦ πολλοῦ καὶ μεγάλου, Hsch. **δᾴς**, v. δαΐς (A). **δάσασθαι**, **δασάσκετο**, **δασαίμεθα**, v. δατέομαι.

**δασκάζει**· ὑποφεύγει, Hsch.

**δάσκιλλος**, ὁ, name of *a fish*, Arist.*HA*591ᵃ14.

**δάσκῐος**, ον, (δα-, σκιά) *thick-shaded, bushy*, ὕλη Od.5.470, B.10.93, etc.; ὄρη E.*Ba.*218; γενειάς A.*Pers.*316, S.*Tr.*13.

**δασκόν**· δασύ, Hsch.

**δάσμα**, ατος, τό, (δάσασθαι) *share, portion*, Hsch.

**δάσμευσις**, εως, ἡ, *dividing, distributing*, X.*An.*7.1.37.

**δασμο-λογέω**, fut. -ήσω Isoc.*Ep.*7.4:—*collect as tribute*, ἀργύριον παρὰ τῶν ἐραστῶν D.59.31. 2. c. acc. pers., *subject* one *to tribute*, τοὺς νησιώτας δ. Isoc.4.132; δ. τοὺς ἐκλογεῖς Hyp.*Eux.*36:—Pass., Isoc.4.123. **-λογία**, ἡ, *collection of tribute*, Plu.*Ant.*23. **-λόγος**, ὁ, *exactor of tribute*, βίαιος καὶ δ. Str.10.4.8.

**✱ δασμός**, ὁ, (δάσασθαι) *division of spoil*, ἤν ποτε δ. ἵκηται Il.1.166; διάτριχα δ. ἐτύχθη *h.Cer.*86. II. *tribute*, Isoc.10.27; σκληρᾶς ἀοιδοῦ δ. *tribute paid* to her, S.*OT*36; δ. τίνειν Id.*OC*635; δ. φέρειν X.*An.*5.5.10; ἀποφέρειν, ἀποδιδόναι, Id.*Cyr.*4.6.9, 2.4.14: pl., Id.*An.*1.1.8.

**✱ δασμο-φορέω**, *to be subject to tribute*, A.*Pers.*586 (lyr.):—Pass., δασμοφορεῖταί τινι *tribute is paid* one, X.*Cyr.*8.6.4. **-φορία**, ἡ, *payment of tribute*, Agath.5.2. **-φόρος**, ον, *tributary*, Hdt.3.97, etc.; δ. εἶναί τινι Id.7.51, X.*Cyr.*7.5.79.

**δάσομαι**, v. δατέομαι.

**δάσος** [ᾰ], εος, τό, (δᾰσύς) *thicket, copse*, Men.*Epit.*25, Str.9.3.13, 17.2.2 (pl.), Ael.*NA*7.2, etc. II. *shagginess*, τοῦ σώματος Alciphr. 3.28; *roughness*, *PLeid.X.*74.

**δάσοφρυς** [ᾰ], υ, *with shaggy brows*, Adam.2.26.

**δασπέτᾰλον**· πολύφυλλον, Hsch.

**✱ δασπλῆτις**, ἡ (voc. -πλῆτα *AP*5.240 (Paul. Sil.)), *horrid, frightful*, θεὰ δ. Ἐρινύς Od.15.234; of Hecate, Theoc.2.14:—also **✱ δασπλής**, ῆτος, ὁ, ἡ, sc. δασπλῆτα Χάρυβδιν Simon.38; δασπλῆτες Εὐμενίδες Euph.94; δασπλῆτε δράκοντε Nic.*Th.*609; freq. in Nonn., γυναῖκες 46.210; μάχαιρα 22.219, al.:—nom. **δασπλῆτα**, Call.*Fr.*534: **δασπλήτης** *An.Ox.*1.149: **δάσπλη** (sic), Hsch.

**δάσσα**· λάχανα, Hsch. **δάσσασθαι**, v. δατέομαι.

**✱ δάσσω**, = δατέομαι, *divide*, ἀνώμαλα δ. Call.*Fr.anon.*145.

**δαστός**, **δαστῶ**, etym. of δατέομαι, coined by *EM*249.37.

**δᾰσῠ-γένειος**, ον, *with thick beard*, v.l. for βαθυ-, Tz. ad Lyc. 307. **✱ -γρᾰφέω**, *write with the rough breathing*, Hdn.*Epim.* 25. **✱ -θριξ**, ὁ, ἡ, gen. τρῐχος, *hairy*, αἴξ *AP*6.113 (Simm.), Nonn. *D.*48.673; μῆλα *AP*9.136 (Cyr.); of a person, ib.11.345, cf. Polem. *Phgn.*5. **-κερκος**, ον, *bushy-tailed*, ἀλώπηξ Theoc.5.112. **-κλωνον**, τό, = πτερίς, Ps.-Dsc.4.184. **✱ -κνῆμις**, ῖδος, = sq., Nonn.*D.* 14.81. **-κνημος**, Dor. **-κναμος**, ον, *shaggy-legged*, Πάν *AP*6.32 (Agath.); γέρων Nonn.*D.*13.45. **-κνήμων**, Dor. **-κνάμων**, ον, gen. ονος, = foreg., *APl.*4.233 (Theaet.).

**Δᾰσύλλιος**, ον, epith. of Bacchus, Paus.1.43.5 (παρὰ τὸ δασύνειν τὰς ἀμπέλους, acc. to *EM*248.54).

**δᾰσυλλις**, ῖδος, ἡ, *bear*, *EM*248.55.

**δάσῡμα** [ᾰ], ατος, τό, = τράχωμα, Sever.ap.Aët.7.45.

**δᾰσύ-μαλλος**, ον, *thick-fleeced, woolly*, ὄϊες, αἰγίς, Od.9.425, E. *Cyc.*360. **-μέτωπος**, ον, *with hairy forehead*, κριός *Gp.*18.1.3.

**δᾰσυν-τέον**, *one must aspirate*, Ath.3.107f, Sch.Il.*Oxy.*221 xiv 2. **-τής**, οῦ, ὁ, *fond of the aspirate*, Ἀττικοί Moer.179,245. **✱ -ω**, pf. Pass., δεδάσυμμαι or -υσμαι Hp.*Coac.*172: inf. -ύνθαι Adam. *Phgn.*2.26:—*make rough* or *hairy*, δ. τὰς ἀλωπεκίας *bring back the hair on* them, Dsc.1.125, *Gp.*12.22.12:—Pass., *become* or *be hairy*, Ar.*Ec.*66, Hp.*Epid.*6.8.32; opp. φαλακρόομαι, Arist.*HA*518ᵇ27; *become bushy*, Thphr.*HP*2.6.12. II. *make thick and cloudy, overcast*, οὐρανόν Id.*Vent.*51, *Sign.*36. III. *aspirate*, Trypho *Fr.* 5, D.H.*Comp.*14, A.D.*Pron.*12.21, Seleuc.ap.Ath.9.398a. IV. Pass., of urine, *become cloudy*, Hp.*Prorrh.*1.95. 2. of breathing, *become rapid*, Agathin.ap.Orib.10.7.22. 3. of the voice, *become hoarse*, Dsc.3.80.

**✱ δᾰσῠ-πόδειος**, α, ον, *of a hare*: τὸ δ. *the species hare*, Arist.*HA*574ᵇ13. **-πόδιον**, = ἴον πορφυροῦν, Ps.-Dsc.4.121. **-πους**, ποδος, ὁ, *rough-foot*, i.e. *hare*, *Lepus timidus*, Cratin.400, Alc.Com.17, Antiph.133.6, Arist.*HA*511ᵃ31, Lxx *Le.*11.5, etc.; λαγωὸς δ. Babr. 69.1: prov., χελώνη παραδραμεῖται δασύποδα, Suid. II. in Plin., prob. *rabbit*, *Lepus cuniculus*, *HN*8.219, 10.173. **-πρωκτος**, ον, *rough-bottomed*, Pl.Com.3. **-πῡγος**, ον, = foreg., Sch.Theoc.5. 112. **-πώγων**, ωνος, ὁ, ἡ, *shaggy-bearded*, Ar.*Th.*33.

**✱ δᾰσύς**, εῖα, ύ, Ion. fem. δασέα Hdt.3.32; opp. ψιλός in all senses: I. *with a shaggy surface*, 1. *hairy, shaggy*, δέρμα.. μέγα καὶ δ. Od.14.51; ὁ δ. γενέσθαι, of the bald, *recover their hair*, Hp. *Aph.*6.34; of young hares, *downy*, Hdt.3.108; γέρρα δ. βοῶν, βοῶν δασειῶν ὠμοβόεινα shields of skin *with the hair on*, X.*An.*5.4.12, 4.7. 22; ὀσφὺν δασέαν *SIG*1037.6 (Milet., iv/iii B.C.); of birds, Thphr. *Fr.*180; τὰ σώματα δασεῖς Arr.*Ind.*24: Sup., Arist.*Phgn.*812ᵇ17. Adv. δασέως, ἔχειν περὶ τὴν κοιλίαν ib.15. 2. *thick with leaves*, Od.14.49; θρίδαξ δασεῖα, opp. παρατετιλμένη, Hdt.3.32; of places, *thickly wooded, bushy*, abs., Id.4.191, cf. Hp.*Aër.*1; διὰ.. τῶν δασέων through *the thickets*, Ar.*Nu.*325: c. dat. modi, δ. ὕλῃ παντοίῃ Hdt.4. 21; ἴδῃσι παντοίῃσι ib.109; ἐλαίαις Lys.7.7: rarely c. gen., δ. παντοίων δένδρων X.*An.*2.4.14; τὸ δ. *bushy country*, ib.4.7.7; δ. γῆ *Schwyzer* 734 (Zelea). 3. generally, *rough, thick*, μαλακαὶ καὶ δ. νεφέλαι D.S. 3.45. 4. δ. οὖρα *cloudy*, Hp.*Epid.*7.112. II. *hoarse*, ἀναπνοή Gal.18(1).574. 2. *aspirated*, Arist.*Aud.*804ᵇ8, Ph.1.29, D.T.631. 22, etc.; ἡ δασεῖα (sc. προσῳδία) Seleuc.ap.Ath.9.398a, A.D.*Synt.*319. 20; δ. τὸ θ καὶ τὸ φ καὶ τὸ χ D.H.*Comp.*14. Adv. -έως, ἀναγνῶναι, ἐκφέρειν, A.D.*Pron.*78.16, S.E.*M.*1.59. III. δ. παράγωγος, Hsch. (Perh. for δη-σύς, cf. Lat. *densus*.)

**δασυσμός**, ὁ, *making rough*, δ. φωνῆς *hoarseness*, Dsc.1.64 (pl.).

**δᾰσύ-στερνος**, ον, *shaggy-breasted*, Hes.*Op.*514; of Nessus, S. *Tr.*557; ὑμέναιοι, of a Satyr, Nonn.*D.*28.90. **-στηθος**, ον, = foreg., Procl.*Par.Ptol.*202. **-στομος**, ον, *with hoarse voice*, Gal. 16.509.

**δᾰσύτης**, ητος, ἡ, *roughness, hairiness*, opp. ψιλότης, Arist.*HA* 499ᵃ11; γῆς Corn.*ND*27: in pl., D.S.3.35. II. in pronunciation, *aspiration*, opp. ψιλότης, Arist.*Po.*1456ᵇ32, Plb.10.47.10, Phld.*Po. Herc.*994.33, D.H.*Comp.*14.

**δασύ-τρωγλος**, ον, = δασύπρωκτος, *AP*12.41 (Mel.). **-φλοιος**, ον, *with rough rind*, v.l. for λαχυ-, Nic.*Al.*269. **-χαίτης**, ου, ὁ, *shaggy-haired*, τράγος *AP*6.32 (Agath.).

**δατεῖν**· ζητεῖν, Hsch.

**✱ δᾰτ-έομαι**, Il.18.264, etc., irreg. inf. δατέασθαι (v.l. -έεσθαι) Hes. *Op.*767: fut. δάσομαι (κατα-) Il.22.354 (tm.): aor. ἐδασάμην, δασσάμην Od.14.208, Il.1.368, etc.; Ion. δασάσκετο 9.333 (δια-, tm.): pf. δέδασμαι Diog.Apoll.3, Q.S.2.57 in pass. sense (v. infr. II): aor. inf. δασθῆναι, Hsch.:—*divide among themselves*, ὅτε κεν δατεώμεθα ληΐδ' Ἀχαιοί Il.9.138; τὰ μὲν εὖ δάσσαντο μετὰ σφίσιν υἷες Ἀχαιῶν 1.368; ἄνδιχα πάντα δάσασθαι 18.511, cf. Od.2.335, etc.; χθόνα δατέοντο Ζεύς τε καὶ ἀθάνατοι Pi.*O.*7.55; μένος Ἄρηος δατέονται *they share*, i.e. *are alike filled with*, the fury of Ares, Il.18.264: freq. of banqueters, κρέα πολλὰ δατεῦντο Od.1.112; μοίρας δασσάμενοι δαίνυντ' 3.66; ὑπέστην Ἕκτορα.. δώσειν κυσὶν ὠμὰ δάσασθαι *tear* in pieces, Il.23.21, cf. Od.18.87, E.*Tr.*450. 2. [ἡμίονοι] χθόνα ποσσὶ δατεῦντο *measured* the ground with their feet, Il.23. 121. 3. *cut in two*, τὸν μὲν.. ἵπποι ἐπισσώτροις δατέοντο 20. 394. II. in act. sense, simply, *divide*, τρεῖς μοίρας δασάμενοι τὸν πεζόν *having divided into*.., Hdt.7.121; *divide* or *give* to others, τῶν θεῶν τῷ ταχίστῳ.. τῶν θνητῶν τὸ τάχιστον δατέονται Id.1.216; τοῖς παισὶ τὰ χρήματα Democr.279; μεῖον, πλέον δ. X.*Cyr.*4.2.43, *Oec.* 7.24; τὸ ἐπιβάλλον Corn.*ND*27: pf. in pass. sense, *to be divided, distributed*, Il.1.125, 15.189, Hdt.2.84, Diog.Apoll. l.c., E.*HF*1329.—Ep. and Ion., also Cret., *Leg.Gort.*4.28, al., and Arc., *IG*5(2).262 (Mantinea, v B.C.); rare in Trag., never in correct Att. Prose, exc. Lys.*Fr.*7 S. (Cf. δαίω (B).) **✱ -ήριος**, α, ον, *dividing, distributing*, χρημάτων A.*Th.*711. **-ησις**, εως, ἡ, *division*, condemned by Poll. 8.136. **-ητής**, οῦ, ὁ, *distributer*, πικρὸς χρημάτων δ. Ἄρης A.*Th.* 943 (lyr.). II. in Att. law, *liquidator* of estates or partnerships, Arist.*Ath.*56.6, etc.

**✱ Δᾱτισμός**, ὁ, *a speaking like Datis* (the Median commander at Marathon), i.e. *speaking broken Greek*, Hdn.*Philet.*p.443, Suid. s.v. Δᾶτις.

**δατύς**, = κουράλλιον; also νύμφη λευκόκηρος, Hsch.

**δᾰτύσσω**, *devour*, Hsch.; *swallow*, dub. l. in Aret.*SD*2.13.

**δαύακες**· θυμάλωπες, Hsch. **δαυάς**· μέλαινα, καὶ πονηρά, Id. **δαῦγος**· δασύς, Id.

**δαυκίτης** οἶνος, wine flavoured with δαῦκος Κρητικός, Dsc.5.60.

**✱ δαῦκος**, ὁ, an umbelliferous plant growing in Crete, *Athamanta*

*Cretensis*, Hp.*Acut.*23, Dsc.3.72 (who applies the name to two other species, *Peucedanum Cervaria* and *Psychotis Amnis*), *POxy.*1088.65, Gal.6.654; also, = σταφυλῖνος, *wild carrot*, *Daucus Carota*, Id.11.862, which is called **δαῦκον**, τό, by Thphr.*HP*9.15.5 (but, = *Malabaila aurea*, ib.9.15.8, 9.20.2): **δαύκειον**, τό, Nic.*Th.*858,939: **δαυκίν** (i.e. δαυκίον), *Gp.*12.1.2 :—also **δαυχμός**, Nic.*Th.*94 (cf. Sch. ad loc.), *Al.*199.

* **δαῦκος**· ὁ θρασύς, Hsch.

**Δαυλιάς**, ἡ, *woman of Daulis*, epith. of Procne, who was changed into *the nightingale*, Th.2.29 (Δαυλία κορώνη, Suid.); so her sister Philomela, changed into *the swallow*, was **Δαυλίς**, Plu.2.727d.

**Δαυλίς**, ίδος, ἡ, *Daulis*, a city of Phocis, Il.2.520, etc.; also name of a festival at Argos, Hsch. (Δαῦλις cod.), etc.: **Δαύλιος**, ὁ, *a Daulian*, Hdt.8.35, or **Δαυλιεύς**, έως, A.*Ch.*674: **Δαυλία** (sc. χώρα), ἡ, *the country of Daulis, Phocis*, S.*OT*734.

**δαῦλον**· ἡμίφλεκτον ξύλον, Hsch.; cf. δαελός.

**δαυλός** (Hdn.Gr.1.156, but δαῦλος Paus.Gr.*Fr.*117), όν, *thick, shaggy*, ὑπήνη A.*Fr.*27; γένεια Nonn.*D.*6.160: metaph., δαυλοὶ πραπίδων δάσκιοί τε πόροι *dark* devices, A.*Supp.*93 (lyr.).

**δαυμάσαι** (leg. δαῦσαι)· ἐκκαῦσαι, Hsch. **δαυνίς**, dub. sens. in Hdn.Gr.1.96. **δαύξ**, dub. sens. in *An.Ox.*3.243. **δαῦτα**· λάχανα, Hsch. * **δαυχμός**, v. δαῦκος. II. **δαυχμόν**· εὔκαυστον ξύλον δάφνης, Hsch., cf. *EM*250.20.

* **δαύχνα**, Thess., = δάφνη, found only in compds. (cf. ἀρχιδαυχναφορέω) :—hence **δαυχνοφόρος**, = δαφνηφόρος, cj. in Alcm.17 :***Δαυχναφόριος**, ὁ, prob. epith. of Apollo in Cyprus, *Ber.Sächs.Ges.*1908.3; cf. **Δαυχναῖος**, patron. fr. Δαύχνας, *IG*9(2).1228.26. (Perh. akin not to δάφνη, but to δαῦκος.)

**δαύω**, = ἰαύω, *sleep*, Sapph.83: aor. ἔδαυσεν, Hsch. (Cf. δαίω (A).)

**δαφν-αία**, ἡ, a precious stone, Plin.*HN*37.157. **-αῖος**, α, ον, = δαφνικός, *of bay*, πέταλα Nonn.*D.*19.73. II. epith. of Apollo, *AP*9.477, Nonn.*D.*13.82. **-έλαιον**, τό, *oil of bay*, Dsc.1.40 tit. (v.l.), Sch.Nic.*Al.*198. **-εών**, = δαφνών, *Gloss.*

**δάφνη**, ἡ, *sweet bay*, *Laurus nobilis*, Od.9.183, Hes.*Th.*30, prob. in Men.*Georg.*36; τὸ τῆς δ. (sc. τρύπανον) ἄριστον Thphr.*HP*5.9.7; δάφναν μὴ δρέπε *Supp.Epigr.*2.185 (Boeot., v B.C.); ['Απόλλων] χρείων ἐκ δάφνης γυάλων ὕπο Παρνησοῖο *h.Ap.*396; ἐξ ὧν εἶπέ μοι ὁ Φοῖβος..Πυθικὴν σείσας δάφνην Ar.*Pl.*213; ἐρέω τι τορώτερον ἢ ἀπὸ δάφνης Call.*Del.*94; στεφανῶσαι δάφνης στεφάνῳ *GDI*2507 (Delph.), cf. *Epigr.Gr.*786 (Halic.), *CIG*3641*b* 20 (add., Lampsacus). II. δ. Ἀλεξανδρεία, *Ruscus Hypoglossum*, Thphr.*HP*1.10.8, 3.17.4, Dsc.4.145. 2. = χαμαιδάφνη, Ps.-Dsc.4.147. III. *white mangrove*, *Avicennia officinalis*, Thphr.*HP*4.7.2. IV. a kind of *coral*, ibid. (ᾰ Theoc.11.45.)

* **δαφνή-εις**, εσσα, εν, *abounding in bay*, Nonn.*D.*13.76. **-φᾰγία**, *eating of bay*, Tz.*Proll.Hes.*p.14. * **-φάγος** [ᾰ], ον, *bay-eating*: hence, *inspired*, Lyc.6. **-φορεῖον**, τό, *temple of Apollo* δαφνηφόρος, Thphr.*Fr.*119. * **-φορέω**, *bear boughs* or *crowns of bay*, Paus.9.10.4, Plu.*Aem.*34, *IG*14.1293*B*, Hdn.2.2.10; of the Roman *fasces laureati*, Id.7.6.2; to be read for δαφνοφορέω in D.C.37.21. **-φορία**, ἡ, *bay-bearing*, Boeotian festival in honour of Apollo, Procl.ap.Phot.*Bibl.*p.321 B. **-φορικός**, ή, όν, *of* or *for Apollo* δαφνηφόρος: τὰ -κά *songs in his honour*, Poll.4.53, Suid. s.v. Πίνδαρος, Procl.ap.Phot.*Bibl.*p.321 B. * **-φόριος**, = δαφνηφόρος II, title of Apollo, *IG*7.3407 (Chaeronea). * **-φόρος**, ον, *bay-bearing*, δ. τιμαῖς A.*Supp.*706; δ. κλῶνες branches *of bay borne in worship* of Apollo, E.*Ion*422; δ. ἄλση groves *of bay-trees*, Hdn.1.12.2. 2. Subst., *bearer of bays*, at Eleusis, *IG*2².1092*B*25. II. epith. of Apollo at Thebes, Paus.9.10.4; at Eretria, *IG*12(9).210.

**δαφν-ιακός**, ή, όν, *belonging to a bay*: δ. βίβλοι, = δαφνιακά, a poem by Agathias, *AP*6.80. **-ῖνος**, η, ον, *made of bay*, ἔλαιον Thphr.*Od.*28, Dsc.1.40; *of bay-wood*, ὅρπηξ Call.*h.Ap.*1. II. δάφνινον (sc. χρῶμα) *PLond.*3.928.13 (ii A.D.). **-ιος**, α, ον, f.l. for foreg., Hp.*Morb.*2.13; epith. of Artemis, Str.8.3.12. * **-ίς**, ίδος, ἡ, *bay-berry*, Hp.*Morb.*2.13, *Nat.Mul.*33, Thphr.*HP*1.11.3. 2. *bay-tree*, *PEdgar* 21.3 (iii B.C.). **-ίτης** [ῑ], ου, ὁ, *laureate*, epith. of Apollo at Syracuse, Hsch. II. *of bay*, οἶνος *Gp.*8.8.

**δαφνῖτις**, ιδος, ἡ, = ἄχυ, Dsc.1.13, Gal.14.72. II. = χαμαιδάφνη, Ps.-Dsc.4.147. III. = δαφνοειδές, ib.146.

**δαφνο-γηθής**, ές, *delighting in the bay*, of Apollo, *AP*9.525.5. **-ειδής**, ές, *like bay*, δαῦκον Thphr *HP*9.15.5 (s. v. l.); of certain corals, ib.4.7.1. II. τὸ δ. *spurge-laurel*, *Daphne Laureola*, Hp.*Nat.Mul.*33, Dsc.4.146. 2. = κληματίς, Dsc.4.7. * **-κοκκον**, τό, = δαφνίς, Alex.Trall.8.2. **-κόμης**, ου, ὁ, = sq., Opp.*C.*1.365. **-κομος**, ον, *bay-crowned*, τρίποδες *AP*9.505.11. **-πώλης**, ου, ὁ, *bay-seller*, Com. epith. of Apollo, Ar.*Fr.*764.

**δάφνος** Σαμοθρᾳκική, = δάφνη Ἀλεξανδρεία, Ps.-Dsc.4.145.

**δαφνόσκιος**, ον, *bay-shaded*, ἄλσος Diog.Trag.1.

**δαφν-ώδης**, ες, *bay-wooded*, γύαλα E.*Ion*76. II. *like bay*, Thphr.*HP*9.10.1. * **-ών**, ῶνος, ὁ, *laurel grove*, Str.16.4.14 (pl.), Petron.126, Gell.2.20.9 (pl.), *Peripl.M.Rubr.*11. **-ωτός**, ή, όν, *laurelized*, κινάραι, prob. in *Gp.*12.39.6 (δαφνάτους codd.).

**δᾰφοινεός**, όν, = δαφοινός, εἷμα δαφοινεὸν αἵματι *dark* with blood, Il.18.538, cf. Hes.*Sc.*159.

**δᾰφοινήεις**, εσσα, εν, later form of sq., Nonn.*D.*1.425.

**δᾰφοινός**, όν (ή, όν Opp.*C.*3.440; δαφοινή as etym. of δάφνη in Corn.*ND*32), epith. of savage animals, *tawny* (as expld. by most Gramm., though some also give *blood-reeking*), δαφοινὸν δέρμα λέοντος Il.10.23; δράκων ἐπὶ νῶτα δαφοινός 2.308; θῶες δ. 11.474; λαῖφος δ' ἐπὶ νῶτα δαφοινὸν λυγκὸς ἔχει *h.Pan.*23; πῆμα δ., of the dragon Python, *h.Ap.*304; δ. αἰετός A.*Pr.*1022; λεόντων ἃ δ. ἴλα E.*Alc.*581 (lyr.); δ. ἄγρα *tawny*, Pi.*N.*3.81. 2. metaph., δ. Κῆρες Hes.*Sc.*250; δαλός A.*Ch.*607 (lyr.).

**δάχανος**, ὁ, = νότος, *Peripl.M.Rubr.*50.

**δαψίλ-εια** [ῐ], ἡ, *abundance, plenty*, τροφῆς Arist.*HA*572ᵃ3; τοῦ ὑγροῦ Id.*GA*782ᵇ18; εὐωνία καὶ δ. Plb.2.15.4; μετάλλου D.S.5.13, cf. Agatharch.95; χρημάτων Onos.35.2: metaph., δ. τύφου Metrod.31. **-εύομαι**, *abound*, ἀγέλαις ἐλεφάντων Ph.Byz.*Mir.*3.2. 2. *to be anxious, careworn*, διά τινα Lxx 1*Ki.*10.2. 3. Pass., *spend lavishly*, *SIG*708.34 (Istropolis), Andronic.Rhod.p.577 M.; *bestow lavishly*, τοῖς αἰτοῦσι τὸ ἔλεος Ph.*Fr.*104 H., cf. Eustr.*in EN*91.20. **-ής**, ές, *abundant, plentiful*, ὕδωρ Hp.*Acut.*65; ποτόν Hdt.2.121.δ'; δωρεή Id.3.130; τροφή Arist.*GA*774ᵇ26; τῷ ἁλὶ -εστέρῳ χρῆσθαι *in too great quantity*, Id.*HA*585ᵃ27; ἔπαινοι Phld.*Lib.*p.32 O.; ἔργα Herod.7.84; πλῆθος σωμάτων Plb.4.38.4 (Sup.); πηγαί Plu.*Num.*15; χώρα ib.16 (Comp.); ἑβένου τάλαντον δ. a *full* talent, *BCH* 35.286 (Delos, ii B.C.). Adv. -έως *in abundance*, Theoc.7.145; δαψιλῶς τοὺς φαγόντας βρέχειν Antiph.286; παρέχεσθαι πάντα D.S.5.14, cf. 19.3: neut. as Adv. δαψιλὲς ἠπείλησεν Call.*Del.*125: Comp. -έστερον J.*BJ*4.11.4; -εστέρως ib.8.3, Ptol.*Tetr.*56. 2. of space, *ample, wide*, ἐρημία Lyc.957. II. of persons, *liberal, profuse*, Arist.*VV*1280ᵇ25, Axiop.4.4; δ. χορηγός Plu.*Per.*16; so κακία δ. τοῖς πάθεσιν Id.2.500e. Adv. -ῶς, ζῆν X.*Mem.*2.7.6: Sup. -έστατα, χρῆσθαι Id.*Cyr.*1.6.17, cf. Ph.*Bel.*101.4. **-ός**, ή, όν, = foreg. I. 2, αἰθήρ Emp.39.1.

* ***δάω** [ᾰ], *learn* (also causal, *teach*, v. infr. II and cf. διδάσκω): I. intr., aor. ἐδάην Il.3.208, Trag. (in lyr.), A.*Ag.*123, S.*El.*169; subj. δαῶμεν Il.2.299, Ep. δαείω 16.423, Od.9.280; opt. δαείην A.R.2.415; inf. δαῆναι Od.4.493, *IG*4.760 (Troezen), Ep. δαήμεναι Il.21.487; part. δαείς Sol.13.50, A.*Ch.*603, Pi.*O.*7.91 (for aor. δέδαον, ἔδαον, v. infr. II): fut. δαήσομαι Od.3.187: pf. δεδάηκα 8.134,146, part. δεδαώς 17.519; also δεδάημαι *h.Merc.*483, Theoc.8.4, etc.:—*learn*, and in pf., *know*, ll. cc.: c. gen. pers., ἐμεῦ δαήσεαι *wilt learn* from me, Od.19.325: c. gen. rei, πολέμοιο δαήμεναι Il.21.487; Ἄρεος εὖ δεδαῶτες D.P.1004; σοφίης δεδαημένο Epic.*Oxy.*1015.20: c. acc. rei, φάρμακα Theoc.28.19; ἄξια Μοισᾶν *IG*3.771; ἀλεξητήρια νούσων ib.9(1).881 (Corc.); ἄκεσμα νόσου ib.14.1750; ἔργα Ἀθηναίης ib.12(5).30 (Sicinus); *perceive*, ἐδά ψυχάς B.5.64; δάεν ῥιπὰν μελιαδέος οἴνου *felt* the impulse of.., Pi.*Fr.*166: abs., δαέντι *to one who knows*, Id.*O.*7.53.—Hom. has also inf. δεδάασθαι (perh. for δεδαέσθαι) *search out*, c. acc., Od.16.316.—The pres. in this sense is supplied by διδάσκομαι. II. causal, *teach*, Hom. only in redupl. aor. 2 δέδαε *he taught*, c. dupl. acc., ὃν Ἥφαιστος δέδαεν..παντοίην τέχνην Od.6.233, cf. 8.448, 23.160; ἔργα δ' Ἀθηναίη δέδαε κλυτὰ ἐργάζεσθαι 20.72, cf. Theoc.24.129 (v.l. ἔδαεν); 3 pl. δέδαον Hsch.; also δάε, ἔδαε, A.R.1.724, 4.989.—The pres. in this sense is supplied by διδάσκω.

* **δέ**, *but*: adversative and copulative Particle, I. answering to μέν (q. v.), τὴν νῦν μὲν Βοιωτίαν, πρότερον δὲ Καδμηίδα γῆν καλουμένην Th.1.12, etc. II. without preceding μέν, 1. adversative, expressing dist. opposition, αἰεί τοι τὰ κάκ' ἐστὶ φίλα..μαντεύεσθαι, ἐσθλὸν δ' οὔτε τί πω εἶπας Il.1.108; ὀρθῶς ἔλεξας, οὐ φίλως δέ μοι λέγεις E.*Or.*100, cf. S.*Ant.*85, etc.; τέθνηκεν ἀνδρὸς οὐδενός, θεοῦ δ' ὕπο Id.*Ph.*334; so in Prose, οὐκ ἐπὶ κακῷ, ἐλευθερώσει δέ.. Th.4.86; οἱ αἰχμάλωτοι..ᾤχοντο εἰς Δεκέλειαν, οἱ δ' εἰς Μέγαρα X.*HG*1.2.14, cf. *Cyr.*4.5.46; ἡ δ' ἑτέρα *IG*2.652*A*45. 2. copulative, a. in explanatory clauses, ξυνέβησαν..τὰ μακρὰ τείχη ἑλεῖν (ἦν δὲ σταδίων μάλιστα ὀκτώ) Th.4.66, cf. Il.7.48: when a Subst. is folld. by words in apposition, Ἀρισταγόρῃ τῷ Μιλησίῳ, δούλῳ δὲ ἡμετέρῳ Hdt.7.8.β'; μήτηρ βασιλέως βασίλεια δ' ἐμή A.*Pers.*152; so in answers, διπλᾶ λέγειν.—Answ. διπλᾶ δ' ὁρᾶν Id.*Th.*974. b. in enumerations or transitions, Il.1.43–49,345–351, X.*Cyr.*1.2.1, etc.; with repetition of a word in different relations, ὡς Ἀχιλεὺς θάμβησεν.., θάμβησαν δὲ καὶ ἄλλοι Il.24.483; σάκος εἷλε.., εἵλετο δ' ἔγχος 14.9 sq.; Ζεύς ἐστιν αἰθήρ, Ζεὺς δὲ γῆ, Ζεὺς δ' οὐρανός A.*Fr.*70; κινεῖ κραδίαν, κινεῖ δὲ χόλον E.*Med.*99; ὄζει ἴων, ὄζει δὲ ῥόδων, ὄζει δ' ὑακίνθου Hermipp.82.8; in rhetorical outbursts, οὐκ ἂν εὐθέως εἴποιεν· τὸν δὲ βάσκανον, τὸν δὲ ὄλεθρον, τοῦτον δὲ ὑβρίζειν,—ἀναπνεῖν δέ! D.21.209; in a climax, πᾶν γύναιον καὶ παιδίον καὶ θηρίον δέ *nay* even beast, Pl.*Tht.*171e, cf. X.*HG*5.2.37; in the combination καὶ δέ Il.23.80, al., καὶ .. δέ A.*Pr.*973, E.*El.*1117, etc., each particle retains its force. c. answering to τε (q. v.), ἅ τῶν τε ἀποβαινόντων ἕνεκα ἄξια κεκτῆσθαι, πολὺ δὲ μᾶλλον αὐτὰ αὑτῶν Pl.*R.*367c. 3. implying causal connexion, less direct than γάρ, Il.6.160, Od.1.433. 4. in questions, with implied opposition, ἑόρακας δ', ἔφη, τὴν γυναῖκα; X.*Cyr.*5.1.4; καὶ ὁ Σωκράτης, εἰπέ μοι, ἔφη, κύνας δὲ τρέφεις; Id.*Mem.*2.9.2, cf. 2.1.26, S.*Ant.*1172: in Trag. (not in Com. or Oratt.), when the speaker turns from one person to another, the voc. stands first, then the pers. Pron. folld. by δέ, as Μενέλαε, σοὶ δὲ τάδε λέγω.. E.*Or.*622, etc.; also in Hdt., ὦ δέσποτα, ἐγὼ δὲ ταῦτα ἐποίησα 1.115. b. τί δέ; what *then*? to mark a transition in dialogue; v. τίς. II. in apodosi: 1. after hypothetical clauses, εἰ δέ κε μὴ δώωσιν, ἐγὼ δέ κεν αὐτὸς ἕλωμαι if they will not give it, *then* I.., Il.1.137, cf. Od.12.54; εἰ μηδὲ τοῦτο βούλει ἀποκρίνασθαι, σὺ δὲ τοὐντεῦθεν λέγε X.*Cyr.*5.5.21, cf. Pi.*O.*3.43 (v.l.), A.*Ag.*1060, Hdt.5.1, etc. b. after temporal or relative clauses, with ἐπεί, ἕως, etc., Il.24.255, Hdt.9.70, etc.; μέχρι .. εἶχον τὰ βέλη, οἱ δὲ ἀντεῖχον Th.3.98; with demonstr. Pronouns or Advbs. answering to a preceding relative, οἵηπερ φύλλων γενεή,

τοίη δὲ καὶ ἀνδρῶν Il.6.146, etc.; ἆθλα οἷς κεῖται ἀρετῆς μέγιστα, τοῖς δὲ καὶ ἄνδρες ἄριστοι πολιτεύουσιν Th.2.46; τοὺς δ' ἔλαβε τυράννους.. τούτους δὲ.. ἐξεδίδου Hdt.5.37, cf. Isoc.4.98, Pl.*La.*194d; οἷα μὲν ἕκαστα ἐμοὶ φαίνεται τοιαῦτα μὲν ἔστιν ἐμοί, οἷα δὲ σοί, τοιαῦτα δὲ αὖ σοί Id.*Tht.*152a: sts. after a participle, οἰόμενοι.. τιμῆς τεύξεσθαι, ἀντὶ δὲ τούτων οὐδ' ὅμοιοι.. ἐσόμεθα X.*An.*6.6.16, cf. Isoc.15.71 (v.l.). **2.** to resume after an interruption or parenthesis, χρόνου δὲ ἐπιγινομένου καὶ κατεστραμμένων σχεδὸν πάντων..,—κατεστραμμένων δὲ τούτων.. Hdt.1.28,29; νῦν δ' αὖ πάλιν ὑπό τε πλούτου διαθρυπτόμενος.. καὶ ὑπ' ἀνθρώπων.. ὑπὸ τοιούτων δέ.. X.*Cyr.*7.2.23; with an anacoluthon, ἡ δὲ ψυχὴ ἄρα,—οἷ ἂν θεὸς θέλῃ.. τῇ ἐμῇ ψυχῇ ἰτέον, αὕτη δὲ δή.. Pl.*Phd.*80d: for δ' οὖν, v. οὖν. **3.** to begin a story, ἦμος δ' ἠέλιος.. *well,* when the sun.., Od.4.400. **4.** to introduce a proof, τεκμήριον δέ, σημεῖον δέ, v. sub vocc.

**B.** Position of δέ. It usu. stands second: hence freq. between Art. and Subst. or Prep. and case; but also after Subst., or words forming a connected notion, hence it may stand third, γυναῖκα πιστὴν δ' ἐν δόμοις εὕροι A.*Ag.*606, cf. *Th.*411, *Eu.*531, S.*Ph.*959, etc.; fourth, Id.*OT*485, E.*Hel.*688, A.*Pr.*323,383, etc.; fifth, ib.401 codd.; even sixth, Epigen.7 (codd. Poll.); so in Prose after a neg., οὐχ ὑπ' ἐραστοῦ δέ, to avoid confusion between οὐ δέ and οὐδέ, Pl.*Phdr.*227c.

⊛**–δε,** an enclitic post-position: joined, **I.** to names of Places in the acc., to denote *motion towards* that place, οἶκόνδε (Att. οἴκαδε) home-*wards,* ἅλαδε sea-*wards,* Οὔλυμπόνδε *to* Olympus, Αἴγυπτόνδε to the Nile, θύραζε (for θύρασδε) *to* the door (v. sub vocc.); repeated with the possess. Pron., ὅνδε δόμονδε Il.16.445; sts. after εἰς, εἰς ἅλαδε Od.10.351; after the gen. Ἄϊδόσδε. **b.** to names of persons, Πηλεΐωνάδε Il.24.338; to Prons., ἡμέτερόνδε, ὑμ–, Od.8.39, Il.23.86; ὅνδε, v. supr. In Att. mostly joined to the names of places, Ἐλευσῖνάδε, etc.; also Ἀθήναζε, Θήβαζε (for Ἀθήνασδε, Θήβασδε); rarely, in Att., with appellatives, as οἴκαδε. **c.** to time-words, βουλυτόνδε (v. βουλυτός). **2.** to denote *purpose* only, μήτι φόβονδ' ἀγόρευε Il.5.252. **II.** to the demonstr. Pron., to give it greater force, ὅδε, τοιόσδε, τοσόσδε, etc., such a man *as this* (v. sub vocc.).

**δεά,** = θεά (Tyrrhen.), Hsch.

**δέᾰτο,** *seemed,* ἀεικέλιος δέατ' εἶναι *methought* he was a pitiful fellow, Od.6.242; εἰκ ἂν δέατοι, = ἣν δοκῇ, ὅσᾳ ἂν δ., = ὅσῃ ἂν δοκῇ, *IG*5(2).6.10,18 (Tegea); ὀπόθ' ἂν δεάσητοι ἀμφοτέροις ib.343.24 (Orchom. Arc.); cf. δέαται· δοκεῖ, δεάμην· ἐδοκίμαζον, ἐδόξαζον, δέασθεν (prob.)· ἐδόκουν, Hsch. (Root δεyᾰ, cf. δῆλος, δοάσσατο, Skt. *dī́deti* 'appear'.)

**δέατος,** v. δέος.

**δέγμενος,** v. δέχομαι. ⊛ **δέγμον·** ὁδόν, Hsch. **δεγμών·** χρόνος, Id. **δεδάασθαι, δέδαε, δεδάηκα, δεδαημένος,** v. *δάω. **δεδαίαται,** v. δαίω (B). **δεδάλας·** δέσμας, Id. **δέδαλοι·** προμαχῶνες, Id. **δέδασται,** v. δατέομαι. **δεδαώς,** v. *δάω. **δεδέαται·** δέδενται, Id. **δέδεια·** φοβοῦ, and **δεδειαί·** δειλίαι, Id. **δεδείκελος,** *timorous,* Id. **δεδειπνάναι,** v. δειπνέω. **δεδεῖσαι·** φοβῆσαι, Id. **δεδεῖσθαι·** εὐλαβεῖσθαι, φοβεῖσθαι, Id. **δεδέχαται,** v. δέχομαι. ⊛ **δέδηε, δεδήει,** v. δαίω (A).

**δεδημευμένως,** *in a popular manner,* Procl.*in Prm.*p.880S.

**δεδηνῶσθαι·** ἐνεχυράσασθαι, ἐνδήσασθαι ἐνεχύροις, Hsch.

**δέδια,** poet. **δείδια,** v. δείδω.

**δεδιότως,** Adv. of part. pf. δεδιώς, *in fear,* D.C.42.17, Vett.Val. 238.32, prob. in D.H.11.47.

**δεδίσκηται·** ἔρριπται, Hsch. (fort. –ευται).

⊛ **δεδίσκομαι,** v. δειδίσκομαι. **II.** v. δειδίσσομαι.

**δεδιττέον,** *one must fear,* ὑπέρ τινος Themist.*Ep.*8.

**δεδίττομαι,** v. δειδίσσομαι. **δεδμάων·** κριὸς ἡγεμών, Hsch.

**δέδμημαι,** pf. Pass. of δαμάζω and δέμω.

**δεδοικότως,** Adv. part. pf. of δείδω, = δεδιότως, Ruf.*Interrog.*2, Philostr.*VA*4.20.

**δεδοίκω,** Dor. pres., = δείδω, δέδια, Theoc.15.58: fut. δεδοικήσω Macr.*Diff.*p.610K. (Syrac.).

**δεδοκημένος,** irreg. part. pf. of δέχομαι (Ion. δέκομαι), in act. sense, *waiting, watching,* Il.15.730, Hes.*Sc.*214, A.R.4.900; δ. ἥντινα ῥέξει μῆτιν *waiting to see..,* ib.1660: c. acc., *observing,* φάσιας Nic.*Th.*122; *watching,* Nonn.*D.*30.88, al.: c. gen., ἤματος Arat.559.

**δέδορκα,** v. δέρκομαι. **δεδρίομεν·** ῥέξομεν, Hsch. **δεδροικώς·** δοικώς, Id. (leg. δεδϝοικώς· δεδοικώς).

**δεείλη,** = δείλη, Phryn.Trag.ap.Sch.Il.*Oxy.*221 iii 6.

**δέελος,** η, ον, resolved form of δῆλος, Il.10.466. **II.** = δεσμός, ἅμμα, Hsch. **δεήλαδες·** φύλακες, Id.

**δέ-ημα,** ατος, τό, (δέομαι) *entreaty,* δέημα δεῖσθαι Ar.*Ach.*1059. **–ησίδιον,** τό, Dim. of sq. I. 2, *Gloss.* **–ημος·** νόμος ἢ δεσμός, Hsch. ⊛ **–ησις,** εως, ἡ, *entreaty,* Lys.2.15 (pl.), Isoc.8.138 (pl.), Pl.*Ep.*329d (pl.), etc.; δέομαι δ' ὑμῶν.. δικαίαν δέησιν D.29.4; δεήσεις ποιεῖσθαι *Ev.Luc.*5.33, cf. Wilcken *Chr.*41 ii 12 (iii A.D.). **2.** written *petition, CPHerm.*6.10, J.*BJ*7.5.2, Ph.2.586, *PGen.*16.10 (iii A.D.). **II.** *want, need,* Antipho Soph.11; ἐν ἐπιθυμίαις τε καὶ δεήσεσιν Pl.*Erx.*405e; κατὰ τὰς δεήσεις according to their *needs,* Arist.*Pol.*1257$^{a}$23; δεήσεις εἰσὶν αἱ ὀρέξεις Id.*Rh.*1385$^{a}$22. **–ητέον,** *one must entreat,* Aristid.Quint.3.9. **–ητικός,** ή, όν, *disposed to ask,* Arist.*EN*1125$^{a}$10; *suppliant,* φωνή D.S.17.44; λόγος Plu.*Cor.*18; ἐπιστολαί Ph.2.590 (Sup.); εὐχαί Id.2.206 (Sup.).

⊛ **δεῖ:** subj. δέῃ, sts. contr. δῇ (in codd. of Com., as Ar.*Ra.*265); ὁπόσου κα δῇ *IG*4.1484.65 (Epid.), cf. *SIG*245 *G*47 (Delph.); opt. δέοι Th.4.4; inf. δεῖν; part. δέον (v. infr. IV): impf. ἔδει, Ion. ἔδεε: fut. δεήσει E.*Hipp.*941, etc.: aor. 1 ἐδέησε Th.2.77, etc.—Impers. from δέω (A), *there is need* (the sense of moral obligation, prop. belonging to χρή, is later, S.*Ph.*583, etc.): **I.** c. acc. pers. et inf., *it is needful for* one to do, *one must,* once in Hom., τί δὲ δεῖ πολεμιζέμεναι.. Ἀργείους why *need* the Argives fight? Il.9.337; δ. ⟨μ'⟩ ἐλθεῖν Pi.*O.*6.28, etc.: with nom. of the Pron., ἡγούμην.. δεῖν.. μεγαλοψυχότερος φαίνεσθαι D.19.235: rarely δεῖ σ' ὅπως δείξεις, = δεῖ σε δεῖξαι, S.*Aj.*556, cf. *Ph.*54; δεῖ σ' ὅπως μηδὲν διοίσεις Cratin.108; (the full constr. in S.*Ph.*77 τοῦτο δεῖ σοφισθῆναι.. ὅπως γενήσῃ): rarely c. dat. pers., *there is need of..* for.., θεοῖσι προσβαλεῖν χθονὶ ἄλλην δεήσει γαῖαν E.*Hipp.*941, cf. X.*An.*3.4.35, *Oec.*7.20: the acc. pers. is often omitted, ἐκ τῶν μανθάνειν δεῖ (sc. ἡμᾶς) Hdt.1.8, cf. A.*Ag.*567, *Eu.*826, etc. **2.** c. acc. rei et inf., δεῖ τι γενέσθαι Th.5.26; παραδείγματα, καθ' ἃ δέοι ἀποκρίνεσθαι Pl.*Men.*79a, etc.; also ἐπεὶ δέ οἱ ἔδεε κακῶς γενέσθαι since *it was fated* for him.., since he *was doomed..,* Hdt.2.161, cf. 8.53, 9.109, S.*OT*825; for οἴομαι δεῖν, v. οἴομαι. **3.** abs. with inf. understood, μὴ πεῖθ' ἃ μὴ δεῖ (sc. πείθειν) S.*OC*1442, cf. *OT*1273; εἴ τι δέοι, ἤν τι δέῃ (sc. γενέσθαι), X.*Mem.*1.2.59, Th.1.44; κἂν δέῃ (sc. τροχάζειν), τροχάζω Philetaer.3. **II.** c. gen. rei, *there is need of,* freq. with neg., οὐδὲν ἂν δέοι πολλοῦ ἀργυρίου Pl.*Cri.*45a, etc.; τί δεῖ τῆς ἀρετῆς; Arist.*Pol.*1309$^{b}$10; sts. with inf. added, μακροῦ λόγου δεῖ ταῦτ' ἐπεξελθεῖν A.*Pr.*870, cf. 875, *Supp.*407. **b.** freq. in phrases, πολλοῦ δεῖ *there wants much, far from it,* ὀλίγου δεῖ *there wants little, all but*; in full c. inf., πολλοῦ δεῖ οὕτως ἔχειν Pl.*Ap.*35d; τοὺς Πλαταιέας ἐλαχίστου ἐδέησε διαφθεῖραι [τὸ πῦρ] Th.2.77; πολλοῦ γε δεῖ, πολλοῦ γε καὶ δεῖ Ar.*Ach.*543, D.18.300, 21.71; τοῦ πλεῦνος αἰεὶ ἔδεε *there was* always further *to travel,* Hdt.4.43; τοῦ παντὸς δεῖ Luc.*Merc.Cond.*13: also ὀλίγου δεῖν abs., in same sense, Pl.*Ap.*22a, etc.; μικροῦ δεῖν D.27.29. **2.** with dat. pers. added, δεῖ μοί τινος A.*Ag.*848, E.*Med.*565, Th.1.71, etc. **3.** with acc. pers. added, αὐτὸν γάρ σε δεῖ προμηθέως A.*Pr.*86, cf. E.*Rh.*837, *Hipp.*23. **4.** rarely with Subj. in nom., δεῖ μοί τι something *is needful* to me, ἓν δεῖ μόνον μοι E.*Supp.*594; εἴ τι δέοι τῷ χορῷ Antipho 6.12; πρῶτον μὲν τοῦτο δεῖ, ὑπειληφέναι.. D.10.15. **III.** Med., δεῖται *there is need,* c. gen., δεῖταί σοι τῆς αὐτῆς ἐρωτήσεως Pl.*Men.*79c; ὅσων δέοιτο Aen.Tact.13.1; ἑτέρου δεῖσθαι στρατηγοῦ νομίζων Plu.*Pel.*26: c. inf., ὥστε βραχέ' ἐμοὶ δεῖσθαι φράσαι S.*OC*570 (codd.); δεήσεται.. ἀναγράφεσθαι Aen.Tact.31.9; τὴν μεν γλῶσσαν ἐκτεμεῖν δεῖται Herod.6.41. **IV.** neut. part. **δέον** (**δεῖν** is dub. in Ar.*Fr.*220, Lys.14.7, cf. A.D.*Adv.*132.30, Hdn.Gr.2.328, al., Hsch.): abs., *it being needful* or *fitting,* Pl.*Prt.*355d, etc.; οὐκ ἀπήντα, δέον, he did not appear in court, *though he ought to have done so,* D.21.90: c. inf., Ar.*Nu.*988; οὐδὲν δέον *there being* no *need,* Hdt.3.65, etc.: fut. ὡς αὐτίκα δεῆσον διώκειν X.*Cyr.*3.2.8: aor. δεῆσαν Plu.*Fab.*9, etc.: also δέον ἂν εἴη, = δέοι ἄν, Plb.2.37.5, etc.: less freq. gen. abs. δέοντος, c. acc. inf., Corn.*ND*17. **2.** Subst. δέον, τό (v. sub voc.).

⊛ **Δεῖα,** τά, = Δῖα, *games in honour of Zeus, JHS*37.89 (Philadelphia, iii A.D.).

**δεία·** ἔνδεια, Hsch.

⊛ **δεῖγμα,** ατος, τό, (δείκνυμι) *sample, pattern,* καρπῶν Isoc.15.54, cf. *POxy.*113.5 (ii A.D.); τοῦ βίου Ar.*Ach.*988; λαβὼν δ' Ἄδραστον δεῖγμα τῶν ἐμῶν λόγων taking him *as evidence* of.., E.*Supp.*354; μὴ.. αὐτοὶ καθ' ὑμῶν αὐτῶν δ. τοιοῦτον ἐξενέγκητε D.21.183; τοῦτο τὸ δ. ἐξενηνοχὼς περὶ αὐτοῦ Id.19.12, cf. Pl.*Lg.*788c; δείγματος εἵνεκα by way *of sample,* D.23.65; δείγματος χάριν S.E.*M.*11.40; δ. προφέρειν, ἐκτίθεσθαι, παρασχεῖν, Pl.*Lg.*718b, Plb.4.24.9, D.H.*Rh.*6.5; δ. μικροψυχίας Men.*Georg.Fr.*3; δ. ψυχῆς *sign* of life, Luc.*Prom.Es* 2 (s.v.l.); δ. φιλοσοφίας Ἀττικῆς Id.*Scyth.*7; [ἀνδριάντα] δ. ἀρετᾶς θεμένα *Epigr.Gr.*860.6, cf. *IG*14.967, etc. **b.** *plan, sketch, PGiss.*15.3. **c.** *sense-evidence,* τὰ ἐπὶ τοῦ ὀργάνου δείγματα Epicur.*Nat.*11.7. **2.** *mart, bazaar,* in the Piraeus, X.*HG*5.1.21, Lys.*Fr.*75.6; περιεπάτουν ἐν τῷ δ. τῷ ἡμετέρῳ D.35.29; elsewh., *IPE*1.16$^{B}$49 (Olbia), Aen.Tact.30.2, Plb.5.88.8, D.S.19.45. **b.** metaph., δ. δικῶν Ar.*Eq.*979.

**δειγμᾰτ-ίζω,** *make a show of, Ep.Col.*2.15; *make an example of, Ev.Matt.*1.19; *furnish a sample,* in Pass., *PTeb.*576 (i B.C./i A.D.); δειγματισθήσεται.. ἀπολέσθαι *will be proved to..,* *PRyl.*1.28.32 (iv A.D.). **2.** *make trial of, test, PHolm.*18.20, 22.29. **II.** intr., *appear,* Ar.Byz.*Epit.*41.19, Hp.*Ep.*19 (in *Hermes* 53.67). **–ισμός,** οῦ, ὁ, *public inspection, verification, PSI*4.358.8 (iii B.C.), *OGI*90.30 (Rosetta), *BGU*246.6 (ii/iii A.D.), al. **III.** *putting to shame, exposure,* in pl., Vett.Val.43.26, Heph.Astr.2.32,34, *PRyl.*1.28.70 (iv A.D.).

**δειγμᾰτο-άρτης,** ου, ὁ, *inspector of the market, POxy.*63.8 (ii/iii A.D.), *PLond.*3.1159.39 (ii A.D.). **–κατᾰγωγία,** ἡ, *conveyance of samples, POxy.*1254.5 (iii A.D.). **–κατᾰγωγός,** ὁ, *official who delivered samples* of corn, *PStrassb.*31.6 (iii A.D.).

**δείδεκτο, δειδέχαται, δειδέχατο,** v. δειδίσκομαι; **δειδέχθαι,** v. δέχομαι.

**δειδήμων,** ονος, (δείδω) *fearful, cowardly,* Il.3.56, Nonn.*D.*15.199, al.

**δείδια, δείδιμεν** and **δειδέμεν,** v. δείδω.

⊛ **δειδίσκομαι,** (cf. δέχομαι) *greet, welcome,* δεξιτερῇ δειδίσκετο χειρί Od.20.197; δέπαϊ χρυσέῳ δειδίσκετο 18.121; δεδισκόμενος 15.150:—to the same verb the following forms probably belong, πλησάμενος δ' οἴνοιο δέπας δείδεκτ' Ἀχιλῆα *pledged* him, Il.9.224; τοὺς μὲν ἄρα χρυσέοισι κυπέλλοις.. δειδέχατο ib.671, cf. 4.4; δειδέχαται μύθοισι Od.7.72; δεικνύμενος *welcoming,* 4.59, Il.9.196; *pledging, h.Ap.*11; so, δεδεγμένος Panyas.12. **II.** (δείκνυμι) *show,* A.R.1.558.

* **δειδίσσομαι**, later **δεδίσσομαι**, Att. **-ττομαι**: impf. ἐδεδίσκετο Ar.*Lys.*564: fut. -ίξομαι Il.20.201: aor. 1 inf. δειδίξασθαι (v. infr.), δεδίξασθαι Hsch.; part. δεδιξάμενος D.19.291:—causal of δείδω, *frighten, alarm*, μὴ.. δειδίσσεο λαὸν Ἀχαιῶν Il.4.184, cf. 13.810, Pl.*Phdr.*245b, Luc.*BisAcc.*7, etc.; μὴ δή μ' ἐπέεσσι.. ἔλπεο δειδίξεσθαι Il.20.201, cf. Hes.*Sc.*111; Ἕκτορα.. ἀπὸ νεκροῦ δειδίξασθαι *to scare him away* from the corpse, Il.18.164 (in 2.190 οὔ σε ἔοικε, κακὸν ὥς, δειδίσσεσθαι it may be taken in either sense, cf. 15.196): c. inf., φευγέμεν ἂψ ὀπίσω δειδίσσετο Theoc.25.74, D.19.291, *Prooem.*43, D.H.1.71, al.; cf. δεδίσκομαι II. **II.** intr., *fear*, ἢν ἡ γυνὴ.. δειδίσσηται (v.l. διδ-) Hp.*Mul.*1.25; μὴ.. λίην δειδίσσεο θυμῷ A.R.2.1219, cf. Plu.*Dio* 57: c. acc., *to be afraid of*, Orph.*A.*56, etc.: aor. δειδισάμενος App.*BC*5.79; τὴν αὐγὴν Aret.*CA*1.1; τὸν ἄνδρα Luc.*Sol.*5.

* **δείδω**, (for δε-δϝοy-α) 1st sg. pf. in pres. sense, Il.14.44, Od.5.300 (δείδιτε should prob. be restored for δείδετε in *AP*9.147 (Antag.)): fut. δείσομαι Il.15.299, etc.; later δείσω Q.S.4.36, etc.: aor. ἔδεισα, in Hom. ἔδδεισα (i.e. ἔδϝεισα, cf. ὑποδδείσας, = ὑποδϝείσας): aor. 2 δίον Il.22.251 (v. infr. 7), 3 sg. δίε 5.566; pf. δέδοικα, ας, ε, (in pres. sense), freq. in sg., Thgn.39, A.*Pers.*751, Ar.*Eq.*38, etc.; rare in pl., δεδοίκαμεν Men.534.11, Luc.*Charid.*24, -κατε Ar.*Ec.*181; Ep. δείδοικα (i.e. δε-δϝ-) Il.1.555, al.; subj. δεδοίκωσι Hp.*Art.*37; inf. δεδοικέναι E.*Supp.*548, Ar.*V.*1091, Pl.*Ax.*372, etc.; part. -κώς Anacr.43, Ar.*Pax*607, Hdt.1.107, etc.: plpf. in impf. sense, Ar.*Pl.*684, Pl.*R.*472a, etc.; 3 pl. -οίκεσαν Th.4.27, X.*An.*3.5.18:—also δέδια A.*Pr.*184 (lyr.), S.*OC*1469 (lyr.), commonly used in Prose, D.14.4, Luc.*Prom.Es*5, etc.; δέδιε Amphis 33.6, Men.223.13; pl. δέδιμεν, δέδιτε, Th.3.53,56, 4.126, etc.; δεδίασι Ar.*Eq.*224, Pl.*Ap.*29a, etc. (once in Hom., Il.24.663); Ep. δείδια ib.13.49, al., 3 sg. δείδιε Od.16.306; pl. δείδιμεν Il.9.230, etc.; δείδιτε *AP* l.c. (v. supr.); imper. δέδιθι Ar.*Eq.*230, *V.*273, Ep. δείδιθι Il.5.827, etc.; later δείδιχι Nic.*Al.*443 (δείδιχθι cod. opt.), δέδιθι Babr.75.2 codd.; subj. δεδίῃ X.*Ath.*1.11; δεδίωσι Isoc.4.156, etc.; inf. δεδιέναι Th.1.136, Pl.*Phd.*88b, etc., Ep. δειδίμεν (to be distd. from 1 pl. indic. δείδιμεν) Od.9.274, 10.381; part. δεδιώς Ar.*Ec.*643, *Pl.*448, Th.6.24, etc., fem. δεδιυῖα prob. in Pl.*Phdr.*254e, Ep. acc. δειδιότα, pl. -ιότες, -ιότων, -ιότας, Il 6.137, etc.: plpf. ἐδεδίειν, εις, ει, Hyp.*Lyc.*6, D.34.27, etc.; Ep. 3 sg. δείδιε Il.18.34; 3 pl. ἐδεδίεσαν Th.4.55 codd., X.*An.*5.7.36, ἐδέδισαν Pl.*Lg.*685c; Ep. 1 pl. ἐδείδιμεν Il.6.99, 3 pl. ἐδείδισαν 5.790, al., δείδισαν 15.652 (hence in late Ep., impf. ἐδείδιον, -ιες, -ιε, Q.S.10.450, Nonn.*D.*2.608, 35.30):—in Prose the shorter forms are generally preferred:—*fear*, distd. from φοβέομαι (v. δέος): Construct.: 1. abs., Hom., etc. 2. folld. by a Prep., δ. περί τινι *to be alarmed, anxious* about.., Il.17.242, 5.566, etc.; ἀμφί τινι A.*Pr.*184 (lyr.); τῆς τυραννίδος πέρι E.*Supp.*446; ὑπέρ τινος Th.1.74; δ. ἐκ τῶν ὕπνων Plb.5.52.13; θορύβῳ Plu.*Dem.*9. 3. folld. by a relat. clause, mostly with μή.., and folld. by subj., Il.1.555, etc.; rarely by indic., δείδω μὴ.. νημερτέα εἶπεν Od.5.300; ὃν δέδοικ' ἐγὼ μή μοι βεβήκῃ S.*Ph.*493, cf. *OT*767, Th.6.88; δέδοιχ' ὅπως μὴ.. ἀναρρήξει κακά, = δέδοικα μή.., S.*OT*1074, cf. D.8.53, 9.75, Ar.*Eq.*112; μὴ δείσῃς ποθ' ὡς.. ὄψεται S.*El.*1309; δ. μὴ οὐ, folld. by subj., δέδιμεν μὴ οὐ βέβαιοι ἦτε Th.3.57, cf. Hdt.7.163, X.*Mem.*2.3.10, E.*Andr.*626, etc.; also δ. ὅπως λάθω E.*IT*995; μὴ δείσητε ὡς οὐχ ἡδέως καθευδήσετε X.*Cyr.*6.2.30. 4. c. inf., *fear to do*, δεῖσαν δ' ὑποδέχθαι Il.7.93, Th.1.136: c. acc. et inf., δ. νέμεσιν ἔσεσθαι Od.22.40; θανεῖν σε δείσας E.*Ion*1564: c. inf. Pass., οὐκ ἐδεδίεσαν βασανισθῆναι Lys.13.27. 5. c. acc., *fear, dread*, Δία Od.14.389; σημάντορας ib.4.431, etc.; τὸ σὸν πρόσωπον S.*OT*448; τοὺς γονέας Pl.*R.*562e; coupled with φοβοῦμαι, τοὺς Ἀθηναίους ἡγούμενοι ἅπερ ἐδεδίεσαν φοβεῖσθαι Th.4.117; οὐδὲ δέδοικα οὐδὲ φοβοῦμαι τὸν μέλλοντα ἀγῶνα D.21.200, cf. Isoc.12.48, Pl.*Euthphr.*12b,c. 6. part. pf., τὸ δεδιός *one's fearing*, much like δέος, Th.1.36. 7. *flee from*, c. acc. (by assimilation to φοβήσομαι), Il.22.251.

**δειελιάω**, (δείελος) *take an afternoon meal*, σὺ δ' ἔρχεο δειελιήσας Od.17.599, cf. Ath.5.193a.

**δειελίη**, ἡ, (δείελος) f.l. for δείελον, Call.*Fr.*190.

**δειελινός**, ή, όν, = δείελος, *at evening*, Theoc.13.33; δειελινὴν τὴν δ' εἷλε κακὸς χλόος Call.*Aet.*3.1.12.

**δείελος**, ον, *of* or *belonging to* δείλη (q.v.), δ. ἦμαρ *the evening part of* day, *eventide*, Od.17.606, Theoc.25.86; δ. ὥρη A.R.3.417. **II.** Subst. (sc. ἡμέρα), *late evening*, εἰσόκεν ἔλθῃ δ. ὀψὲ δύων Il.21.232, cf. Call.*Hec.*1.4.1; ποτὶ or ὑπὸ δείελον *at even*, *AP*9.650 (Leont.), A.R.1.1160. 2. δείελον, τό, *afternoon meal*, Call.*Fr.*190 (perh. = *Oxy.*1362 ii *Fr.*4). (δειελός Hdn.Gr.1.161.)

**δείεμα**· βρῶμα, Hsch.

* **δεικᾰνάω**, (δείκνυμι) *point out, show*, in Ion. and Ep. impf. δεικανάασκεν Theoc.24.57; Ep. 3 pl. pres. δεικανόωσι Arat.209: but **II.** Med., (cf. δειδίσκομαι) *salute, pledge*, δεικανόωντο δέπασσιν Il.15.86; δεικανόωντ' ἐπέεσσιν Od.18.111; cf. δεκανᾶται.

**δείκᾰνον**, τό, = δείκηλον, of *embroidered figures* in tapestry, *EM* 260.43 (pl.).

* **δείκελον**, τό, = δείκηλον II.1, Democr.123, Hegesianax 2. 2. = δείκηλον II.2, Nonn.*D.*48.697, *AP*9.153 (Agath.).

**δεικές**· λαμπρόν, κτλ., Hsch.

* **δεικηλίκτας**, α, ὁ, Dor. for δεικηλίστης, *one who represents*; esp. Lacon., = ὑποκριτής, *actor who played burlesque parts*, Plu.*Ages.*21, 2.212f, Ath.14.621e (δικ- codd.).

**δείκηλον**, τό, *representation, exhibition*, παθέων Hdt.2.171. **II.** *reflection, image*, A.R.1.746; *phantom*, Id.4.1672 (pl.). 2. *sculptured figure*, *IG*14.1301, Lyc.1179 (pl.), J.*BJ*2.10.4, Porph.ap.Eus.*PE*3.9.

* **δείκνυμι** (also **δεικνύω** Hes.*Op.*451, Men.562; Ion. **δέκνυμι** *GDI* 5653*b* 14 (ἀπο-, Chios), 5493*b* 25 (ἀπο-, Milet.), freq. in Hdt.; Cret. **δίκνυμι** (προ-) *GDI*5112); 3 sg. δείκνυ Hes.*Op.*526; imper. δείκνυε ib.502, Pl.*Phdr.*228e, 3 sg. δεικνύτω S.*OC*1532: impf. 3 pl. ἐδείκνυσαν X.*An.*4.5.33, D.18.213, also -νον Hdt.4.150, Antipho 5.76, etc.; 3 sg. δείκνυεν Pi.*P.*4.220: fut. δείξω Od.12.25, etc., Ion. δέξω Hdt.4.179, al.: aor. 1 ἔδειξα, Ep. δεῖξα Od.3.174, etc., Ion. ἔδεξα Hdt.2.30, al.: pf. δέδειχα Alex.268, (ἐπι-) D.26.16, (ἀνα-) Plb.4.48.3:—Med., with pf. Pass., for Ep. forms δεικνύμενος, δείδεκτο, δειδέχαται, δειδέχατο, v. δειδίσκομαι:—Pass., fut. δειχθήσομαι Isoc.5.1, 12.4; δεδείξομαι Plu.2.416d, A.D.*Synt.*23.26, al.: aor. ἐδείχθην E.*Supp.*1209, etc., Ion. ἐδέχθην (ἀπ-) Hdt.1 *Prooem.*: pf. δέδειγμαι S.*Fr.*432, Ion. δέδεκται Hp.*de Arte* 10:—*bring to light, show forth*, [θεὸς] ἡμῖν δεῖξε [τέρας] Od.3.178; δεικνὺς σῆμα βροτοῖσιν Il.13.244; ἄγος δ. S.*OT*1427; τὸν κτανόντα ib.278; ἵν' ἐλαίας.. ἔδειξε κλάδον Ἀθάνα E.*Tr.*802; of artists, *portray, represent*, Luc.*Im.*5; *cause*, δυσθέατα πήματα ἐδείξατ' A.*Th.*982 codd.; *render* so and so, τυφλοὺς τοὺς ἐμβλέποντας δεικνύει Men.83; τινὰ ὑπὸ τῶν τραυμάτων δείξας νεκρόν D.S.34.2.21:—Med., δείκνυμαι *set before one*, ἄεθλα Il.23.701. 2. *show, point out*, δ. Ἀλέξανδρον Μενελάῳ Il.3.452; δέσμιον.. ἔδειξ' Ἀχαιοῖς (sc. αὐτόν) S.*Ph.*609, cf. 492,630; αὐτὸ δ. experiment *will show*, Cratin.177, cf. Pl.*Tht.*200e, *Hp.Ma.*288b; δείξει δὴ τάχα alone, *time will show*, Ar.*Ra.*1261; δ. εἴς τινα *point* towards, Hdt.4.150:—Med., δείξατο δ' εἰς Κρονίωνα *h.Merc.*367. 3. *show, make known*, esp. by words, *explain*, ὁδόν Od.12.25, etc.; ἀντολὰς ἐγὼ ἄστρων ἔδειξα A.*Pr.*458, cf. 482. 4. *show, prove*, with part., ποῦ γὰρ ὢν δείξω φίλος; E.*Or.*802; ἔδειξαν ἕτοιμοι ὄντες Th.4.73, cf. 5.72; δεικνύω ἐσπουδακώς Men.562; δείξω αὐτὸν πολλῶν θανάτων ὄντ' ἄξιον D.21.21; εἰ.. δειχθήσεται τοῦτο πεποιηκώς ib.160; ἱκανώτατα δέδεικται ψυχὴ τῶν πάντων πρεσβυτάτη Pl.*Lg.*896b: folld. by a relat. clause with ὡς.., ὅτι.., εἰ.., etc., A.*Th.*176, Th.1.76,143, etc.; πᾶσα ἀπόδειξίς τι κατά τινος δείκνυσι Arist.*APo.*90[b]34: ὅπερ ἔδει δεῖξαι, = Q.E.D., Luc.1.4, al.: abs., δέδεικται *it is clear* or *proven*, Pl.*Phd.*66d, etc.; δεδείξεται A.D. l.c. 5. of accusers, *inform against*, τινά Ar.*Eq.*278 (Dobree ex Sch. ἐγὼ ἐνδείκνυμι). 6. *display, exhibit*, ἀγλαΐαν Pi.*P.*6.46; ἀρετήν, προθυμίαν, Th.1.37, 6.11. 7. *offer, proffer*, καὶ τὰ πίστ' ἐδειξάτην A.*Ag.*651. (Cf. Lat. *dīco*, Goth. *gateihan* 'announce', OHG. *zeigōn* 'show'.)

**δεικ-τέον**, *one must show, prove*, X.*Mem.*3.5.8; περί τινος Thphr.*CP*3.7.5; τοὺς νόμους δεικτέον μοι it is my *duty to point out*.., D.18.58, cf. Porph.*Abst.*3.7. **-τηριάς**, άδος, ἡ, = Lat. *mima*, Plb.14.11.4. * **-τήριον**, τό, *place for showing*; at Samos, *place where* Athena *showed* Perseus *a representation of the Gorgon*, *EM*261.9. **II.** = δεῖγμα, *PPetr.*3p.333. **-της**, ου, ὁ, *exhibitor*, Orph.*H.*8.16; τῶν ἱερῶν ἀγώνων prob. in *CIG*2932 (Tralles); ὁ λόγος δ. ἐστὶ πάντων τῶν ἀγαθῶν Zos.Alch.p.191B. * **-τικός**, ή, όν, *able to show*: in Logic, of syllogisms, *those which can be directly reduced*, Arist.*APr.*45[a]24; δ. ἐνθύμημα, opp. ἐλεγκτικόν, Id.*Rh.*1396[b]24. Adv. -κῶς Id.*APr.*29[a]31. 2. *categorical*, πρότασις *Stoic.*2.85. **II.** Gramm., *demonstrative*, τὸ "τοῦτο" δεικτικόν Chrysipp.*Stoic.*2.65; δ. ὄνομα D.T.636.12; ἄρθρα Apollod.Ath. and D.T.ap.A.D.*Pron.*5.19; ἀντωνυμία ib.9.17: -ώτεραι γιγνόμεναι (sc. ἀντωνυμίαι) προσλαμβάνουσι τὸ ῑ ib.59.16: -κόν, τό, Demetr.*Eloc.*289. Adv. -κῶς Chrysipp.*Stoic.*2.245, Plu.2.747d, S.E.*M.*7.267. * **-τός**, ή, όν, *capable of proof*, Arist.*APo.*76[b]27. 2. *perceptible*, Phlp.*in Cat.*88.21.

**δειλαινομένως**, Adv. *with trepidation*, Gloss.

* **δειλαίνω**, *to be a coward* or *cowardly*, Arist.*EN*1107[a]18, 1137[a]22, Plot.1.4.15:—Med., Luc.*Ocyp.*153, *PTeb.*58.27:—Pass., aor. δειλανθείς· κλεφθείς, ἀπατηθείς, Hsch.; δειλάσαι· δειλιάσαι, Id.

* **δείλαιος**, α, ον (ος, ον *IG*14.1722.7), lengthd. form of δειλός (q.v.): —*wretched, sorry, paltry*, not in Hom., freq. in Trag., esp. of persons, A.*Pr.*580 (lyr.), etc.; δείλαιε τοῦ νοῦ S.*OT*1347 (lyr.); δ. χάρις a *sorry* kindness, A.*Ch.*517; δ. σποδός *paltry* dust, S.*El.*758; δ. ἄχεα, ἀλγηδών, δύα, Emp.145, S.*OC*513 (lyr.), *Ant.*1311 (lyr.); γῆρας E.*Hec.*156 (lyr.): sts. found in Com. (v. infr.) and Prose, Lys.24.23 (Sup.), Aeschin.1.172: in later Prose, Jul.*Or.*1.29b. (The penult. is short in S.*Ant.*1311, *El.*849 (lyr.), E.*Supp.*279 (lyr.), Ar.*Eq.*139, *V.*165, etc.)

**δειλαιότης**, ητος, ἡ, *misery*, Sch.Ar.*Eq.*1148.

**δειλ-ακρίνας**, = sq., *EM*261.38. **-ακρίων**, ωνος, ὁ, *pitiable creature*; in Com., *poor fellow!* Ar.*Pax*193, *Av.*143. **-ακρος**, α, ον, *pitiable*, Ar.*Pl.*973, Carm.*Pop.*27. **-ανδρέω**, *to be cowardly*, Lxx 2*Ma.*8.13, 4*Ma.*10.14. **-ανδρος**, ον, *cowardly*, Hdn.Gr.1.204.

* **δεῖλαρ**, ατος, τό, = δέλεαρ, Call.*Fr.*458 (pl.).

**δείλη**, ἡ, *afternoon* (δ. ἡμέρας τελευτή Pl.*Def.*411b), ἔσσεται ἢ ἠὼς ἢ δείλη ἢ μέσον ἦμαρ Il.21.111: divided into *early* and *late* (πρωΐα and ὀψία), περὶ δείλην πρωΐην γενομένην Hdt.8.6 (opp. δ. ὀψίην, ib.9); δείλης ὀψίης Id.7.167, cf. D.57.9; περὶ δείλην ἤδη ὀψίαν Th.8.26; later περὶ δ. ἑσπέραν Ph.2.533, Hdn.3.12.7. **II.** δ. alone, 1. *early afternoon*, δείλη δὲ τέμνεται ὀπώρα S.*Fr.*255; ἤδη ἦν μέσον ἡμέρας.., ἡνίκα δὲ δείλη ἐγένετο X.*An.*1.8.8; ἀμφὶ δείλην ib.2.2.14 (opp. ὀψέ, ib.16); περὶ δείλην Hdt.9.101, Th.4.69,103; ἀπὸ δείλης from *the hour of afternoon*, Arist.*HA*564[a]19; τῆς δείλης *in the course of the afternoon*, X.*An.*7.3.10; but also, b. *late afternoon*, τῆς ἡμέρας ὅλης διῆλθον.. ἀπὸ δείλης ἀφίκοντο ib.3.3.11; ἡνίκα ἦν δ., opp. τῆς νυκτός, ib.3.4.34, cf. 4.2.1, 7.2.16; μέχρι δείλης ἐξ ἑωθινοῦ Id.*HG*1.1.5, cf. 4.1.22; ἀπ' ἠοῦς μέχρι δείλης Pl.*Def.*411a; ἕωθεν καὶ δείλης early in the morning and *late in the evening*, Arist.*Fr.*531; πρὸς τὴν δείλην Id.*HA*596ᵃ23; δείλαν alone, Theoc.10.5. 2. in late Prose, *any time of day*, περὶ μεσημβρίαν δ. about mid-*day*, Ach.Tat.3.2. b. apparently, *day*, opp. *night*, δείλ(η)ς ἐργ(άταις) *PLond.*1.131ʳ44 (ii A.D.), cf. 244.

**δείληθι·** φοβοῦ, Hsch. (leg. δείδιθι). **δειλήμων,** = δειδήμων (εἰδήμονες cod.), Id.

**δειλία,** ἡ, *timidity, cowardice*, Hdt.1.37, S.*OT*536, etc.; δειλίην ὀφλεῖν to be charged with *cowardice*, Hdt.8.26; δειλίας ὀφλεῖν (sc. δίκην) And.1.74; ἔνοχος δειλίας (sc. δίκῃ) Lys.1.45; opp. ἀνδρεία, θρασύτης, Pl.*Lg.*648b, *Ti.*87a. II. *misery*, Procop.*Goth.*4.32.

**δειλι-αίνω,** *make afraid*, Lxx *De.*20.8. **-ᾰσις,** εως, ἡ, *fright, faintheartedness*, Plu.*Fab.*17.

**δειλίασμα, δειλινισμός,** and **δείλισμα,** = Lat. *merenda*, *Gloss.*

* **δειλιάω,** *to be afraid*, Lxx *De.*1.28, al., D.S.20.78, Paul.Aeg.3.76. (Later Gr. for ἀποδειλ-.)

**δειλινός,** ή, όν, (δείλη) = δειελινός, *in the afternoon*, δ. ἤρξατο *Com.Adesp.*609, cf. Luc.*Dem.Enc.*31, Secund.*Sent.*4, *BGU*513.3 (ii A.D.); τὸ δ., as Adv., *at even*, Lxx *Ge.*3.8, Luc.*Lex.*2; δ. ὁλοκαύτωμα Lxx 1*Es.*5.50; ὧραι Str.17.3.8; ἑσπέρα Ph.1.505 (s.v.l.); διατριβή Plu.2.70e. 2. *western*, κλίμα Str.9.2.41. II. τὸ δ. (sc. δεῖπνον) *evening meal*, f.l. in Ath.10.418b (quoting Plb.20.6.6), cf. Ath.1.11e.

**δειλοκατα-φρονητής,** οῦ, or **-φρόνητος,** ον, *cowardly and insolent*, Ptol.*Tetr.*66.

**δειλοκοπέω,** *cheat* or *terrify*, Hermipp.88.

**δείλομαι** (A), (δείλη) *verge towards afternoon*, δείλετό τ' ἠέλιος the sun *was westering*, Od.7.289 (Aristarch. and others for δύσετο).

**δείλομαι** (B), Delph. and Locr., = βούλομαι.

**δειλόομαι,** Pass., *to be afraid*, read by Nicanor in S.*Ichn.*150, cf. Lxx 1*Ma.*16.6, D.S.20.78.

**δειλοποιός,** όν, *making cowardly*, Sch.S.*Tr.*1028.

**δειλός,** ή, όν, (δέος): I. of persons, *cowardly*, opp. ἄλκιμος, Il.13.278; opp. ἀνδρεῖος, Pl.*Phdr.*239a, etc.: hence, *vile, worthless*, Il.1.293; δειλαί τοι δειλῶν γε καὶ ἐγγύαι Od.8.351; opp. ἐσθλός, *lowborn, mean*, Hes.*Fr.*164; πλοῦτος καὶ δειλοῖσιν ἀνθρώπων ὁμιλεῖ B.1.50; ἀγαθοὶ δειλῶν ἐπὶ δαῖτας ἴασιν Eup.289; of animals, Hdt.3.108: c. gen., δειλὸς μυάγρης *afraid of*.., *AP*9.410 (Tull. Sab.): c. inf., ib.6.232 (Crin.). Adv. -λῶς Theoc.*Adon.*15, Plu.2.26b. 2. more commonly, *miserable, wretched*, with a compassionate sense, δειλοὶ βροτοί *poor* mortals! Il.22.31, al.; ἆ δειλέ *poor wretch!* ἆ δειλοί *poor wretches!* 17.201, Od.20.351; ἆ δειλὲ ξείνων 14.361; Πατροκλῆος δειλοῖο Il.17.670. II. of things, *miserable, wretched*, γῆρας Hes.*Op.*113; δ. δ' ἐνὶ πυθμένι φειδώ ib.369; τὰ δ. κέρδη S.*Ant.*326; ἔργα, λόγος, etc., Thgn.307, E.*Andr.*757, etc.: Comp., Longin.2.1: Sup., Ar.*Pl.*123: neut. pl. as Adv., ὀχλεῖ μοι δειλὰ ὁ Τρωΐλος *PIand.*11.4 (iii A.D.).—Trag. use δειλός chiefly in former sense, δείλαιος in latter.

**δειλότης,** ητος, ἡ, = δειλία, *cowardice*, Hsch. s.v. δειλίην.

**δειλόψῡχος,** ον, *fainthearted*, Lxx 4*Ma.*8.16.

**δεῖμα,** ατος, τό, (δέος) *fear*, δεῖμα φέρων Δαναοῖσι Il.5.682; φρένα δείματι πάλλων S.*OT*153 (lyr.); δ. ἔλαβέ τινα Hdt.6.74; ἐς δ. πεσεῖν, ἐν δείματι καθεστάναι, Id.8.118, 36; opp. θάρσος, Aen.Tact.16.3: pl., S.*El.*636; φόβοι καὶ δ. Th.7.80, Phld.*D.*1.22, etc. II. *object of fear, terror*, ὦ πῦρ σὺ καὶ πᾶν δ. S.*Ph.*927; ἐκ δ. του νυκτέρου Id.*El.*410; ἀντιπάλοις δ. *a terror* to them, *Epigr.Gr.*343 (Germa): esp. in pl., A.*Pr.*691 (lyr.), *Ch.*524, A.R.4.735; δειμάτων ἄχη *fearful* plagues or monsters, A.*Ch.*586 (lyr.); δ. θηρῶν E.*HF*700 (lyr.).

* **δειμ-αίνω,** only pres. and impf. (Ep. δειμαίνεσκε Q.S.2.439):—*to be afraid*, *h.Ap.*404, Hdt.3.51, etc., S.*OC*492, Pl.*R.*330c, etc.; δ. περὶ ἑωυτῷ, ὑπέρ τινος, Hdt.3.35, 8.140.β'; ἀμφί τινι S.*OC*492; ἐπί τινι Jul.*Or.*2.82a:—Pass., *to be frightened*, Q.S.2.499. 2. folld. by a relat. clause with μή.., Thgn.541, Hdt.1.165, S.*Tr.*481. 3. c. inf., Mosch.3.56, Opp.*H.*5.320. 4. c. acc., *fear*, τὴν Περσέων δύναμιν Hdt.1.159; πάντα δ. A.*Pers.*600, cf. *Pr.*41: c. acc. cogn., δεῖμ' ὃ δειμαίνεις E.*Andr.*868. **-ᾰλέος,** α, ον, *timid*, Arist.*Phgn.*810ᵃ23, Mosch.2.20, Opp.*C.*1.165. II. *horrible, fearful*, Batr.287, cj. in Thgn.1128.

**δειμαλέτα·** τὰ λεπτὰ τῶν βοσκημάτων, οἱ δὲ Λάκωνες νεκρά, Hsch.

**δειμᾰτ-ηρός,** ά, όν, *fearful, timid*, A.D.*Synt.*189.25. **-ίας,** ου, ὁ, epith. of Zeus, *the Scarer*, D.H.6.90. **-όεις,** εσσα, εν, *frightened, scared*, *AP*9.244 (Apollonid.).

**δειμᾰτο-ποιός,** όν, *terrifying*, Sch.E.*Hec.*70. **-σταγής,** ές, (στάζω) *reeking with horror*, A.*Ch.*842 (leg. αἱματοσταγές).

**δειμᾰτ-όω,** *frighten*, Hdt.6.3, Ar.*Ra.*144, Ph.2.204:—Pass., A.*Ch.*845, S.*Ichn.*142, E.*Andr.*42, Pl.*Ax.*370a, etc. **-ώδης,** ες, *terrible, frightful*, Aret.*SD*1.5, al., Hsch. **-ωσις,** εως, ἡ, *scaring*, Sch.Lyc.1182.

* **δειμός,** ὁ, (δέος) *fear, terror*, δειμόν τινα ἀναπλάσσειν J.*Ap.*2.34. II. Δεῖμος, ὁ, personified as accompanying Φόβος, Ἔρις, Γοργώ, etc., Il.4.440, cf. 11.37, 15.119, Hes.*Th.*934.

**δειμώδης,** = φοβερός, Erot. (dub. l.).

**δεῖν,** v. δεῖ.

* **δεῖνα,** ὁ, ἡ, τό, gen. δεῖνος, dat. δεῖνι, acc. δεῖνα: sts. indecl. (v. infr.): nom. δεῖν, ὁ, Sophr.58: gen. and dat. τοῦ δείνατος, τῷ δείνατι, A.D.*Pron.*60.12, *EM*614.51:—*such an one, so-and-so*, always with Art., ὁ δεῖνα Ar.*Ra.*918, etc.; τὸν δεῖνα τὸν τοῦ δεῖνα Id.*Th.*622; ὁ δεῖνα τοῦ δεῖνος τὸν δεῖν' εἰσήγγειλεν D.13.5; ἃ ἂν ὁ δ. ἢ ὁ δ. εἴπῃ Id.2.31; ὁ δ. καὶ ὁ δ. Arist.*Rh.*1416ᵃ23; ἡ δεῖνα Ant.Lib.22; τὸ δ., euphem. for τὸ πέος, Ar.*Ach.*1149, cf. Sch.Luc.*BisAcc.*23; τὸ δ. δ' ἐσθίεις; do you eat *such a fish?* Antiph.129.6: in gen., ἐμὸς ἢ τοῦ δεῖνος mine or *some other's*, Arist.*Pol.*1262ᵃ3: dat., τῷ δεῖνι μεμφόμενος D.20.104, cf. 37.56: pl., οἱ δεῖνες Id.24.180; τῶν δείνων Id.20.106. II. τὸ δ. in Com. as an interjection to express an idea which suddenly strikes one, *by the way, mark you*, Ar.*V.*524, *Pax* 268, etc.: in later Prose, Luc.*Vit.Auct.*19.

**δεινάζω,** *to be in straits*, Lxx 2*Ma.*4.35.

**δειναυξῆσαι,** *exaggerate*, *Gloss.*

**δεινιάς** (sc. ἐμβάς), άδος, ἡ, *shoe called after Dinias* (D.20.146), Cleanth.*Stoic.*1.133.

**δεινο-βίης** [ῐ], ου, ὁ, (βία) *terribly strong*, Orph.*A.*65. **-επής,** gloss on ἀπτοεπές, Sch.Il.8.209, *EM*133.45. **-θέτης,** Dor. **-ας,** ου, ὁ, (τίθημι) *knave*, Mosch.*Fr.*3.7. **-κάθεκτος,** ον, *hard to be repressed*, Orph.*H.*10.6. **-λεχής,** ές, *dreadfully married*, Id.*A.*906.

**δεινόλινος·** ὁ δεινῇ εἱμαρμένῃ ἐφθαρμένος, *EM*264.28.

**δεινο-λογέομαι,** *complain loudly*, ὅτι.. Hdt.1.44; εἰ.. Plu.*Sert.*6: abs., Hdt.4.68, Eus.Mynd.59. **-λογία,** ἡ, *exaggerated complaint*, Plb.33.11.3. **-πάθεια** [πᾰ], ἡ, *exaggerated complaint*, condemned by Poll.6.201, cf. Suid. s.v. τραγῳδία. **-πᾰθέω,** *complain loudly of sufferings*, D.40.53, Teles p.58 H., Plb.12.16.9, Luc.*Syr.D.*24; ἐπί τινι D.S.19.75, Plu.2.781a. **-πενθής,** ές, gloss on στονόεσσα, Sch.Il.24.721. **-ποιέω,** in Rhet., *amplify*, D.H.*Th.*23, Nicol.*Prog.*p.42 F.; *use terrifying expressions*, Porph.*Chr.*30. **-πους,** ὁ, ἡ, **-πουν,** τό, gen. ποδος, *with terrible foot*, Ἀρά (as if she were a hound upon the track), S.*OT*418. * **-προσωπέω,** *to be stern of countenance*, περὶ τῆς τυραννίδος Arg.E.*Ph.*

**δεινός,** ή, όν, (δέος, cf. Pl.*La.*198b) *fearful, terrible*; in Hom., of persons and things, Χάρυβδις Od.12.260; κλαγγή Il.1.49; ὅπλα 10.254: freq. in neut., δεινὸν ἄϋσαι 11.10; βροντᾶν 20.56; δεινὸν δέρκεσθαι 3.342; παπταίνειν Od.11.608; δεινὰ δ' ὑπόδρα ἰδών Il.15.13; δ. ἰδέσθαι *fearful* to behold, Od.22.405; δ. μὲν δρᾶν, δ. δὲ κλύειν S.*OC*141; εἰ καὶ δεινόν τῳ ἀκοῦσαι Th.1.122; δεινὴ παρὰ τοῖς εἰδόσιν ἡ βάσανος And.1.30; in milder sense, *awful*, δεινή τε καὶ αἰδοίη θεός Il.18.394, cf. 3.172, Od.8.22, etc.; τὸ δεινόν *danger, suffering, horror*, A.*Ch.*634, etc.; *awe, terror*, Id.*Eu.*517; ὅπου τὸ δ. ἐλπὶς οὐδὲν ὠφελεῖ S.*Fr.*196; πρὸς τὸ δ. ἔρχεσθαι ib.351: in pl., ἐκτὸς ὄντα πημάτων τὰ δείν' ὁρᾶν Id.*Ph.*504; εἰ δείν' ἔδρασας, δεινὰ καὶ παθεῖν σε δεῖ Id.*Fr.*962, etc.; δεινὸν γίγνεται μή.. there is *danger* that.., Hdt.7.157; οὐδὲν δεινοὶ ἔσονται μὴ ἀποστέωσιν no *fear* of their revolting, Id.1.155, etc.; δεινότατον μή.. the *greatest danger* lest.., And.3.1; δεινόν ἐστι, c. inf., it is *dangerous* to do, Lys.12.87; δεινὸν ποιεῖσθαι *take ill, complain of, be indignant at* a thing: abs., Th.1.102, etc.: c. inf., ὑπὸ Μήδων ἄρχεσθαι Hdt.1.127, etc.; also δεινὰ ποιεῖν *make complaints*, Id.3.14, 5.41; ἐν δεινῷ τίθεσθαι J.*AJ*18.9.8; δεινόν τι ἔσχε αὐτὸν ἀτιμάζεσθαι Hdt.1.61; δεινὸν or δεινὰ παθεῖν suffer *illegal, arbitrary* treatment, Ar.*Ra.*252, cf. Pl.*Prt.*317b, etc.; δεινότερα π. Th.3.13; τὸ δ. τὸ πείσομαι Hdt.7.11: in Oratt., δεινὸν ἂν εἴη εἰ.. And.1.30, Lys.12.88, etc. Adv. -νῶς, φέρειν Hdt.2.121.γ'; δ. καὶ ἀπόρως ἔχει μοι I am in *dire* straits, Antipho 1.1; δ. ἔχειν τῇ ἐνδείᾳ X.*An.*6.4.23; δ. διατεθῆναι τυπτόμενος Lys.3.27. II. *marvellously strong, powerful*: δ. σάκος the *mighty* shield, Il.7.245; simply, *wondrous, marvellous, strange*, τὸ συγγενές τοι δεινὸν ἥ θ' ὁμιλία kin and social ties *have strange power*, A.*Pr.*39; δ. τὸ κοινὸν σπλάγχνον Id.*Th.*1036; δ. τὸ τίκτειν S.*El.*770; πολλὰ τὰ δ. κοὐδὲν ἀνθρώπου -ότερον πέλει Id.*Ant.*333; δ. ἵμερος, ἔρως, Hdt.9.3, Pl.*Tht.*169c; οἶκτος S.*Tr.*298, etc.; δ. λέγεις πρᾶγμα Pl.*Euthd.*298c; δ. γ' εἶπας, εἰ καὶ ζῇς θανὼν S.*Aj.*1127; freq. δεινὸν ἂν εἴη εἰ.. it were *strange* that.., as E.*Hec.*592. Adv. -νῶς *marvellously, exceedingly*, δ. μέλαινα, ἄνυδρος, Hdt.2.76, 149; δ. ἐν φυλακῇσι εἶναι Id.3.152; δ. πῶς εἰμ' ἐπιλήσμων Metag.2, etc.: Comp. -οτέρως Sch.Min.Il.7.97. III. *clever, skilful*, first in Hdt.5.23 ἀνὴρ δ. τε καὶ σοφός; of Odysseus, γλώσσῃ.. δεινοῦ καὶ σοφοῦ S.*Ph.*440, cf. *OC*806, Antipho 2.2.3, Lys.7.12; σοφὸς καὶ δ. Pl.*Prt.*341a; opp. σοφός, of *practical ability*, Id.*Phdr.*245c, *Tht.*164d; opp. ἰδιώτης, D.4.35: c. inf., δεινὸς εὑρεῖν A.*Pr.*59; δεινοὶ πλέκειν τοι μηχανὰς Αἰγύπτιοι Id.*Fr.*373; δ. λέγειν *clever* at speaking, S.*OT*545, etc.; δ. εἰπεῖν is rare, D.20.150; νόσος δ. φαγεῖν Ar.*Nu.*243; δ. πράγμασι χρῆσθαι D.1.3; αἱ εὐπραξίαι δ. συγκρύψαι τὰ ὀνείδη are *wonderfully liable* to.., Id.2.20: c. acc., δ. τὴν τέχνην Ar.*Ec.*364; δ. περὶ τοὺς λόγους τοὺς εἰς τὰ δικαστήρια Pl.*Euthd.*304d; ἐς τὰ πάντα Ar.*Ra.*968; δ. περὶ τὸ ἀδικεῖν, περὶ Ὁμήρου, Pl.*R.*405c, *Ion* 531a; δ. ἀμφί τι Arr.*Tact.*9.5; δ. κατὰ χειρουργίαν Ael.*VH*3.1; ἐν λόγοισι δ. Ὑπερείδης Timocl.4.7 (but also of the *forcible, vehement*, style in oratory, Demetr.*Eloc.*240, al.); in bad sense, *over-clever*, Pl.*Euthphr.*3c; δ. ὑπὸ πανουργίας Id.*Tht.*176d, cf. Arist.*EN*1144ᵃ27. (For δϝεινός, cf. Δϝενία, gen. of pr.n. Δεινίας, *IG*4.858.)

**δεῖνος** (A), gen. of δεῖνα (q.v.).

**δεῖνος** (B), ὁ, = δῖνος, a name for *different round vessels*, Stratt.34, Dionys.Com.5, etc.: Cyren., = ποδανιπτήρ, Philet.ap.Ath.11.467d. II. a *dance*, Apolloph.1. III. *threshing-floor*, Telesilla 7. IV. *instrument for making* or *gilding pills*, *Schwyzer* 182a.3 (Gortyn, v/iv B.C.).

**δείνοσμος** (i.e. *evil-smelling*), = κόνυζα πλατύφυλλος, Ps.-Dsc.3.121.

**δεινότης,** ητος, ἡ, *terribleness*, Th.3.59, 4.10; *harshness, severity*, νόμων Id.3.46. II. *cleverness, shrewdness*, D.18.144, Arist.

*EN*1144ᵃ23; opp. ἀλήθεια, Antipho 5.5; esp. in an orator, Th.3.37, D.18.242,277; ἡ ἐν τοῖς λόγοις δ. Isoc.1.4; δεινότητα λόγου ἐπιδείκνυσθαι Plu.*Pomp.*77. III. Rhet., *intensity, forcefulness,* D.H.*Comp.*18, *Th.*53, al., Longin.34.4, Hermog.*Id.*2.9, al.: pl., Demetr.*Eloc.*243.

**δειν-όω,** *make terrible*: *exaggerate,* ἐπὶ τὸ μεῖζον πάντα δεινώσας Th.8.74; δεινῶσαι τὰς συμφοράς Plu.*Per.*28. **-ωμα,** ατος, τό, *exaggerated view,* τὸ δ. τῶν κριτῶν Phld.*Rh.*1.286S. **-ωπός,** όν, = δεινώψ, Hes.*Sc.*250. **-ωσις,** εως, ἡ, *exaggeration* or *exacerbation,* Pl.*Phdr.*272a, Quint.*Inst.*6.2.24, Longin.11.2, 12.5 (pl.), Demetr.*Eloc.*130; αὔξησις καὶ δ. D.H.*Vett.Cens.*2.5, cf. *Lys.*19 (pl.). II. *indignation,* Arist.*Rh.*1417ᵃ13, 1419ᵇ26. 2. *frowning,* ὀφρύες δεινώσιος μετέχουσαι Hp.*Acut.*42. **-ωτικός,** ή, όν, Rhet., *pertaining to* δείνωσις 1, ὕλαι Corn.*Rh.*p.394H. **-ώψ,** ῶπος, ὁ, ἡ, *fierce-eyed,* of the Erinyes, S.*OC*84.

**δειομένη·** δεισομένη, Hsch.

⊛ **δεῖξις,** εως, ἡ, (δείκνυμι) *mode of proof,* ἐκ τῶν σημείων Arist.*Rh.*1408ᵃ26, cf. *APr.*34ᵃ4. 2. *proof, specimen,* δ. ἀνδρείας παρέχεσθαι, δ. εὐνοίας, Hdn.1.15.2, 2.3.5. II. *display, exhibition,* Macho ap.Ath.6.245e; δεῖξιν λόγων ποιεῖσθαι Ath.3.98c; anatomical *demonstration,* Gal.14.627. 2. *calling up,* θεῶν Alciphr.2.4.15, cf. *PMag.Leid.W.*6.42. 3. Gramm., *demonstrative force* or *reference,* Chrysipp.*Stoic.*2.65, al., A.D.*Pron.*9.8, al.

**δείους,** Ep. gen. of δέος (q.v.).

**Δειπάτυρος·** θεὸς παρὰ Στυμφαίοις, Hsch.

**δειπν-άριον,** τό, Dim. of δεῖπνον, Diph.64.1, *AP*11.10 (Lucill.). **-εύς,** έως, ὁ, divinity worshipped by cooks in Achaia, Ath.2.39d. **-εύω,** = δειπνίζω, prob. in *CIG*2719 (Stratonicea). **-έω,** fut. -ήσω Ar.*Pax* 1084, X.*Cyr.*5.3.35, -ήσομαι D.S.11.9, Gal.11.6: aor. ἐδείπνησα, Ep. δεῖπνησα Od.14.111, etc.: pf. δεδείπνηκα Ar.*Ec.*1133, etc.; Att. 1 pl. δεδείπναμεν Alex.109, Eub.91; inf. δεδειπνάναι Ar.*Fr.*464,249, Pl.Com.144: plpf. ἐδεδειπνήκεσαν Antipho 1.18; Ep. δεδειπνήκειν Od.17.359:—*make a meal,* Hom. (v. δεῖπνον): in Att. always, *take the chief meal, dine,* once in Trag., δειπνεῖν E.*Fr.*894 (dub. l.); δ. τὸ ἄριστον *make* breakfast *serve as dinner,* X.*Cyr.*1.2.11; δ. παρά τινι *with* one, Antipho 1.18; [ἐν πρυτανείῳ] And.1.45. 2. c. acc., δ. ἄρτον *make a meal on* bread, Hes.*Op.*442; δ. μοσχίον Ephipp.15.13; κοτύλην μίαν Alex.221.17; ξίφη Mnesim.7; δ. τἀλλότρια, of parasites, freq. in Com., Theopomp.34, Eub.72, etc.; also δ. ἀπό τινος Ar.*Pl.*890. II. Act., *entertain,* τινάς *Milet.*7.68, *Inscr.Cos* 131. **-ήεντα·** δειπνοφόρα, οὐ δυνάμενα φέρειν ἡμᾶς, Hsch. **-ηστος,** ὁ, *meal-time,* Od.17.170; δ. ἀκρόνυχος Nic.*Th.*761 (v.l. -ηστός). (Acc. to some Gramm., δειπνηστός (sc. καιρός) = *meal-time,* δείπνηστος = *meal,* Eust.1814.36.) **-ηστύς,** ύος, ἡ, *meal-time,* Hsch. **-ητήριον,** τό, *dining-room,* Plu.*Luc.*41, Inscr. ap.*PFay.*p.33, J.*BJ*2.8.5. **-ητής,** οῦ, ὁ, *diner, guest,* Plb.3.57.7. **-ητικός,** ή, όν, *fond of dinner,* Anaxipp.1.36; ἐπιστολαὶ δ. letters *on cookery,* Ath.4.128a. Adv. -κῶς *like a cook, artistically,* Ar.*Ach.*1016. **-ίζω,** Att. fut. -ιῶ Diph.62: aor. ἐδείπνισα X.*Cyr.*4.5.5 (v. Od. infr. cit.):—*entertain at dinner,* κατέπεφνεν δειπνίσσας Od.4.535; δειπνίζοντες Ξέρξεα Hdt.7.118; δ. τὴν πόλιν ὅλην *IG*5(1).1346: also c. acc. cogn., δ. τινὰ δεῖπνον *give* one *a* dinner, Matro *Conv.*2:—Pass., βοὰς δεδειπνισμένων θεάτρων the applause of spectators *bribed by dinners,* Plu.2.92e. **-ίον,** ου, τό, Dim. of δεῖπνον, Ar.*Fr.*483. **-ιστήριον,** τό, = δειπνητήριον, *IG*5(2).268.36 (Mantinea, i B.C.), 12(9).906.10 (Chalcis, iii A.D.), *Mon.Ant.*23.124 (Side). **-ιστός,** ὁ, = δείπνηστος, Orus ap.*EM*262.45. **-ῖτις,** ιδος, ἡ, = fem. of δειπνητικός, στολή D.C.69.18.

**δειπνο-θήρας,** ου, ὁ, = δειπνολόχος, Ph.1.665. ⊛ **-κλήτωρ,** ορος, ὁ, *one who invites to dinner,* v.l. in *Ev.Matt.*20.27. II = ἐδέατρος, Artem.ap.Ath.4.171b:—hence **-κλητόριον,** τό, Eust.766.58. **-κρίτης** [ῐ], ου, ὁ, *judge of the feasts,* of a religious official, Epigr. in *CRAcad.Inscr.*1907.141 (Janiculum). **-λογία,** ἡ, *poem on dining* by Archestratus, Ath.1.4e:—hence **-λόγος,** ὁ, *dinner-bard,* of Archestratus, ib.29a. ⊛ **-λόχος,** η, ον, *laying traps, fishing for invitations to dinner, parasitic,* Hes.*Op.*704. **-μανής,** ές, *mad after eating,* Timo 16.1.

⊛ **δεῖπνον,** τό, *meal*: in Hom. sts. *noonday meal,* Il.11.86; sts. = ἄριστον, *morning meal,* 2.381, 10.578, 19.171 sq., Od.15.94 sq., 500; sts. = δόρπον, *evening meal,* 17.176, 20.390 sq.; later, *the midday meal,* σῖτον εἰδέναι διώρισα, ἄριστα, δεῖπνα, δόρπα θ' αἱρεῖσθαι τρίτα A.*Fr.*182; later, *the afternoon meal, dinner* or *supper,* σοὶ δὲ μελήσει, ὅταν ᾖ δεκάπουν τὸ στοιχεῖον, λιπαρῷ χωρεῖν ἐπὶ δ. Ar.*Ec.*652: freq. in pl., S.*OT*779, *El.*203 (lyr.); δ. Θυέστου E.*Or.*1008 (lyr.); ἀπὸ δείπνου straightway after *the meal,* ἀπὸ δ. αὐτοῦ θωρήσσοντο Il.8.54, cf. Antipho 1.17; καλεῖν ἐπὶ δεῖπνον, κεκλῆσθαι ἐπὶ δ., Eub.72,119.2; δ. παρασκευάζειν Pherecr.45,172; παραθεῖναι Id.184; ποιεῖν Dionys.Com.2.4; of animals, etc., Hom.*Epigr.*11, Ael.*VH*1.12, 12.27. 2. generally, *food, provender,* ἵπποισιν δεῖπνον δόντε Il.2.383; ὄρνισι δεῖπνον A.*Supp.*801; κοράκεσσιν Epigr.ap.Philostr.*Her.*19.17.

**δειπνο-πίθηκος** [ῐ], ὁ, Com. name for a *parasite, Com.Adesp.*321. ⊛ **-ποιέω,** *prepare a dinner,* X.*Cyr.*5.2.6 (v.l. -οῦντο), Alciphr.2.1:—Med., *dine,* Th.4.103, Plu.2.225d. **-ποιΐα,** ἡ, *preparing* or *taking dinner,* D.S.17.37. ⊛ **-ποιός,** ὁ, *dinner-preparer, caterer,* Arist.*MM*1206ᵃ27.

**δεῖπνος,** ὁ, late form of δεῖπνον, v.l. in D.S.4.3, Sch.Ar.*Pax* 564.

⊛ **δειπνοσοφιστής,** οῦ, ὁ, *one learned in the mysteries of the kitchen*: in pl., title of work by Athenaeus.

**δειπνοσύνη,** ἡ, Com. for δεῖπνον, Matro *Conv.*10 (pl.).

⊛ **δειπνο-φορία,** ἡ, *solemn procession with meat-offerings* to Herse, Pandrosos, and Aglauros, Is.*Fr.*151. **-φόρος,** ον, *carrying meals,* of birds, Arist.*HA*616ᵇ34, 619ᵇ24. II. *carrying meat-offerings,* Lys.*Fr.*311S., Hyp.*Fr.*88, Plu.*Thes.*23, *IG*3.371.

**δεῖρα·** δείμοιρα (leg. διμοιρία, cf. δεισιάδα), τράχηλος, διαίρεσις, Hsch.

**δειράδιον,** τό, Dim. of δειρή I.2, Poll.2.235.

**δειράζειν·** κλέπτειν, Hsch.

**δειραῖος,** α, ον, *hilly, craggy,* Lyc.994.

**δειράρ·** κορυφή, Hsch. (Lacon. = sq.)

**δειράς** (Cret. **δηράς** *GDI*5024.19), άδος, ἡ, *ridge of a chain of hills, h.Ap.*281, S.*Aj.*697 (lyr.), Limen.22; of the isthmus of Corinth, Pi.*O.*8.52, *I.*1.10; of Trachis, S.*Ph.*491: in pl., E.*Ph.*206 (lyr.): metaph., τέγγει δ' ὑπ' ὀφρύσι δειράδας, of the petrified form of Niobe on Mt. Sipylus, which poured tears under the brow of the hill over its *ridges,* S.*Ant.*832 (lyr.). (δερσ-, cf. Skt. *dṛṣad-* 'rock'.)

⊛ **δειρ-αχθής,** ές, *heavy on the neck,* ἅμμα *AP*6.179 (Arch.): **-αγχής** (cf. Hsch.), cj. Brunck, which is dub. l. in *AP*7.473 (Aristodic.).

⊛ **δειρή,** ἡ, Att. **δέρη** A.*Ag.*329,875, etc.; Aeol. **δέρα** Sapph.*Supp.*23.16 (v. infr.):—*neck, throat,* Il.11.26, etc.; τὰ ἀπὸ τῆς δ. *ornaments,* Hdt.1.51. 2. *collar,* Poll.2.235. II. in pl., *gully, glen,* Pi.*O.*3.27, 9.59: but in sg., = δειράς, prob. in Hermesian.7.54. (The original form is preserved in Arc. **δερϝά** *BCH*39.55 (Orchom.): Aeol. **δέρρη** is coined by *EM*262.57 as etym. of δέρρις: Hsch. has δέρα· ὑπερβολὴ ὄρους, οἱ δὲ τὰ σιμὰ τῶν ὀρῶν by confusion with δειράς. Κοῖλα δέρα, place-name in *Inscr.Olymp.*46.30. Prob. from root of ζέρεθρον, βιβρώσκω.)

**δειρητής,** ὁ, Elean, = στρουθός, Nic.*Fr.*123.

**δειριᾶν·** λοιδορεῖσθαι (Lacon.), Hsch.: also **δειρεῖοι·** λοίδοροι (Lacon.), Id., cf. δερίαι.

**δειρο-κύπελλον** [ῠ], τό, *long-necked cup,* Luc.*Lex.*7. ⊛ **-παις,** αιδος, ὁ, ἡ, *producing young by the neck,* as weasels were supposed to do, Lyc.843.

**δεῖρος,** εος, τό, = δειρή, Euph.38 (pl.). II. = δειράς, Hsch.

**δειροτομέω,** fut. -ήσω, *cut the throat* of a person, σὺ δ' ἄμφω δειροτομήσεις Il.21.89, cf. 555, Od.22.349.

**δείρω,** v. δέρω.

⊛ **δείς,** δενός, *no one* or *thing,* Alc.76. II. *something,* μὴ μᾶλλον τὸ δὲν ἢ τὸ μηδὲν εἶναι (expld. as = σῶμα, opp. κενόν), Democr.156. (Abstracted from οὐδείς.)

**δεῖσα,** ἡ, *slime, filth, PTeb.*105.27,60, 106.26 (ii B.C.), *BGU*1119.31 (i B.C.), Suid. II. = ἡ τῶν βοτανῶν συλλογή, *EM*651.48.

**δεισαλία,** ἡ, = foreg., Thd.*Is.*28.12.

**δεισήνωρ,** ορος, ὁ, ἡ, *fearing man,* A.*Ag.*154 (lyr.).

**δεισία,** ἡ, *distribution,* κρεῶν *IG*2².1356: cf. **δεισιάδα·** τὴν μοῖραν, οἱ δὲ διμοιρίαν, Hsch.

**δεισιδαιμ-ονέω,** *have superstitious fears,* Plb.9.19.1, D.S.12.59, Polystr.9, etc.: rare in good sense, *to be religious,* Zaleuc.ap.Stob.4.2.19. ⊛ **-ονία,** ἡ, *fear of the gods, religious feeling,* Plb.6.56.7, Phld.*Herc.*1251.10, *CIG*2737*b*11 (Aphrodisias), D.S.1.70, etc.; ἡ τῶν θεῶν δ. Id.11.89. 2. in bad sense, *superstition,* Thphr.*Char.*16, Plb.12.24.5; ἡ πρὸς τὰ ζῷα δ. D.S.1.83; περὶ Δεισιδαιμονίας, title of work by Plu. **-ων,** ον, gen. ονος, (δείδω) *fearing the gods,* 1. in good sense, *pious, religious,* X.*Cyr.*3.3.58, *Ages.*11.8; δ. εἶναι καὶ φροντίζειν τῶν θεῶν Arist.*Pol.*1315ᵃ1; φίλος θνητοῖς εἴς τ' ἀθανάτους δ. *IG*14.1683: Comp. -έστερος *Act.Ap.*17.22. 2. in bad sense, *superstitious,* Thphr.*Char.*16, Phld.*Piet.*105; δ. διάθεσις, = δεισιδαιμονία, D.S.1.62: Comp. -έστερος D.L.2.132: Sup. -έστατος Luc.*Pr.Im.*27. Adv. -όνως Aristeas 129, Ph.1.195, Corn.*ND*27.

**δεισίθεος,** ον, = foreg., Poll.1.21.

**δεισιλός·** δειλός, Hsch.

**δείσοζος,** ον, (δεῖσα) *smelling of filth, AP*6.305 (Leon.).

⊛ **δέκᾰ,** οἱ, αἱ, τά, indecl., *ten,* Il.2.372, Od.9.160, etc.; οἱ δ. *the Ten,* Isoc.18.6; ἡ τῶν δ. τυραννίς Arist.*Ath.*41.2; also οἱ δ. the *Attic Orators,* Philostr.*VS*2.1.14; τὰ δέκα [ἔτη] ἀφ' ἥβης those who are *ten* years past 20 (the age of military service), X.*HG*3.4.23; δ. ἄνδρες, = Lat. *decemviri,* App.*Hann.*56: compds. (not in early writers, but usu. in Hellenistic Gr.) **δεκᾰ-είς,** *Tab.Heracl.*2.34, Plu.*Num.*3: ⊛ **-δύο,** *PSI*5.509.10 (iii B.C.), *IG*2².1013.31 (ii/i B.C.), Plu.*Cat.Mi.*44, *Act.Ap.*19.7: **-τρεῖς,** D.47.77,81, *BGU*644.5 (i A.D.): **-τέσσᾰρες,** α, Plb.1.36.11, etc.; Delph. **-τέτορες** *SIG*241 *A* 2 (iv B.C.): ⊛ **-πέντε,** *PRev.Laws* 12.17 (iii B.C., prob.), D.S 2.13 codd.; Thess. **-πέμπε** *IG*9(2).553.13 (Larisa, i B.C.): ⊛ **-ἕξ,** *Tab.Heracl.*2.40, *PSI*4.379.6 (iii B.C.), Lxx *Ge.*46.18, Str.2.5.42: ⊛ **-επτά,** *PSI*5.509.13 (iii B.C.), v.l. in D.S.12.36, J.*BJ*5.11.4, S.E.*M.*1.114, etc.: **-οκτώ,** *IG*2.1054.47, Cleonid.*Harm.*2, *Ev.Luc.*13.11: **-εννέα,** *PSI*4.396.12 (iii B.C.), D.S.12.71, Plu.2.932b:—hence **-έννατος,** *nineteenth,* ἡμέρα Lyd.*Ost.*18.

**δεκά-βαθμος** [κᾰ], ον, *with ten steps,* κρηπίς Ph.Byz.*Mir.*6.2. **-βάμων** [βᾱ], ονος, ὁ, ἡ, *with ten steps* or *intervals,* ἐνδεκάχορδε λύρα, δεκαβάμονα τάξιν ἔχουσα Ion Lyr.3.1. **-βοιος,** ον, (βοῦς) *worth ten oxen,* τὸ δ. a coin attributed to Theseus, Plu.*Thes.*25; δεκάβοιον ἀποτίνειν, from a law of Draco, Poll.2.61. **-γονία,** ἡ, *the tenth generation,* Luc.*Herm.*77. **-γράμμᾰτος,** f.l. for ἐνδεκα-, Ath.10.455b. **-γώνιον,** τό, and **-γωνον,** τό, *decagon,* Hero *Geom.*21.21, *Stereom.*2.63, Ptol.*Alm.*1.10. 2. Adj. δεκάγωνος, ον, ἀριθμοί Theo Sm.p.40H. **-δακτῠλιαῖος,** ον, = sq., Heliod.ap.Orib.49.7.4. **-δάκτῠλος,** ον, *ten fingers long* or *broad,* βάλανος Hp.*Morb.*3.14, cf. Ath.Mech.16.6. 2. *ten-fingered,* χεῖρες D.C.47.40.

® **δεκᾰδαρχ-έω**, *to be a* δεκάδαρχος, Hsch. s.h.v. ® **-ης**, ου, ὁ, later form for δεκάδαρχος, = Lat. *decurio*, J.*BJ*2.20.7, Arr.*An*.7.23.3, *IGRom*.4.1221 (Thyatira), *BGU*81.2 (ii A.D.), *PHamb*.10.1 (ii A.D.). II. -άρχαι, οἱ, with or without θεοί, name of an order of divine beings, Herm. *in Phdr*.p.134A., Dam.*Pr*.351. **-ία**, ἡ, *government of ten*, v.l. in Isoc.4.110, cf. D.6.22; = Lat. *decemviratus*, D.H.11.27. II. *decuria of cavalry*, Arr.*Tact*.42.1. ® **-ος**, ὁ, = δεκάρχης, *commander of ten men*, X.*Cyr*.8.1.14, Plb.6.25.2, Arr.*Tact*.42.1, Lxx*Ex*.18.21,25, *De*.1.15, 1*Ma*.3.55. II. = Lat. *decemvir*, D.H.10.60. III. = τελώνης, Hsch. (Cf. δεκατ-.)

**δεκᾰδ-εύς**, έως, ὁ, *one of a decury*, X.*Cyr*.2.2.30. II. *chairman of a board of ten*, in acc. sg. δεκαδῆ, *IG*4.748.21 (Troezen). **-ικός**, ή, όν, *of the* δεκάς, Herm. *in Phdr*.p.137A. Adv. **-κῶς** Syrian. *in Metaph*.106.15. ® **-ιστής**, οῦ, ὁ, *one who celebrates the tenth day of the month*, cj. in Thphr.*Char*.27.11, cf. *IG*11(4).1227 (Delos), 2.1139*b*:—fem. **-ίστρια**, ibid. **-οῦχος**, ὁ, *one of the ten*, Harp.

**δεκά-δραχμος** [κᾰ], ον, *at the price of ten drachmae*, Arist.*Oec*.1352$^b$15, *BGU*1134.7 (i B.C.). II. Subst. δ., ὁ, *taxpayer assessed at ten* δραχμαί, ib.1118ii9 (ii A.D.). **-δρομοι**, οἱ, *adults* (i.e. *those who have taken part in ten contests*) (Cret.), Hsch. **-δωρος**, ον, (δῶρον II) *ten palms long or broad*, Hes.*Op*.426. ® **-έτηρος**, ον, (ἔτος) *ten-yearly*: χρόνος δ. a space *of ten years*. Pl.*Lg*.772b codd.:—fem. **-ετηρὶς** πανήγυρις D.C.57.24: more freq. as Subst., *period of ten years*, prob. in Pl. l. c., Vett.Val.252.9, *OGI*722 (Egypt, iv A.D.):—also ® **-ετηρία**, ἡ, title of Orphic work, Suid. **-ετής**, ές, or **-έτης**, ες, *ten years old*, Hdt.1.114, Hp.*Epid*.1.10. II. *of or lasting ten years*, πόλεμος Th.5.25,26 codd., Jul.*Or*.2.74b. (Cf. δεκέτης.)—The statements of Gramm. as to the accentuation of this and similar words are confused, cf. Poll.1.54, *EM*765.21, Choerob. *in Thd*.1.167, 2.385: they were prob. parox. in Attic, oxyt. in the κοινή. **-ετία**, ἡ, *space of ten years*, δεκαετίαν (-έτειαν Pap.) ἄρχειν Arist.*Ath*.3.1, cf. D.H.1.71, Str.15.1.43, Ph.1.531, Plu.*Num*.10.

® **δεκάζω**, *bribe, corrupt*, esp. judges, Isoc.8.50, Aeschin.1.87, Arist.*Ath*.27.5:—Pass., *to be bribed*, Lys.29.12, Plu.*Cat.Mi*.44. II. metaph. in Pass., *to be subject to allurements*, δεδεκασμέναι ἀκοαί Ph.1.523, cf. Plot.6.8.13; ὑπὸ τῶν ἡδονῶν Porph.*Abst*.4.1. III. δεκάζων· ὁ εἰς δέκατον ἀριθμὸν ἥκων, Hsch.

**δεκάκις**, Adv. *ten-times*, Il.9.379, etc. 2. *tenfold*, *AP*5.117 (Marc. Arg.); in hyperbole, Men.*Sam*.131.

**δεκά-κλῑνος**, ον, (κλίνη) *holding ten dinner-couches*, στέγη X.*Oec*.8.13. II. *ten* κλῖναι *long*, κρήνη Arist.*Mir*.834$^b$8. **-κότῠλος**, ον, *holding ten* κοτύλαι, Str.3.2.7. **-κῡμία**, ἡ, (κῦμα) *tenth* (i.e. *overwhelming*) *wave*, Luc.*Merc.Cond*.2. **-λιτρος**, ον, *weighing or worth ten* λίτραι, στατήρ Epich.10, Arist.*Fr*.510: as Subst., δεκάλιτρον, τό, *coin worth ten* λίτραι, ὁ μισθὸς δ. Sophr.37, cf. Poll.9.81. **-λογος**, ου, ἡ, *Decalogue*, Jul.*Gal*.152b. **-μαζος**, ον, *with ten breasts*, of Ephesian Artemis, *Epigr.Gr*.406.10. **-μετρος**, *of ten metrical units*: Subst. -μετρον (sc. κῶλον), τό, *decameter*, Sch.Ar.*Eq*.496, etc. **-μηναῖος**, α, ον, *in the tenth month*, Tz.*H*.2.192. ® **-μηνιαῖος**, α, ον, = sq., χρόνος Plu.*Num*.12; βρέφη Alex. Aphr.*Pr*.1.40. ® **-μηνος**, ον, *ten months old*, σκύλαξ X.*Cyn*.7.6, cf. Theoc.24.1. 2. *in the tenth month*, ἡ αἵρεσις ἐγένετο ἔς τι δ. Hdt.9.3; τὰ δ. (sc. παιδία) Hp.*Septim*.7; γυνὴ κυεῖ δ. prob. l. in Men.413; τόκος δ. Arist.*GA*777$^b$14: neut. pl. as Adv., ib.772$^b$9. 3. *consisting of ten months*, ἡ δ. (sc. περίοδος) *Placit*.5.18.1: Subst. δεκάμηνον, τό, *Schwyzer* 195.12 (Delos, ii B.C.), *PRyl*.88.17 (ii A.D.). **-μναῖος** or **-μναιαῖος**, α, ον, = sq., Plb.13.2.3; πετροβόλος throwing a projectile *weighing ten minae*, Ph.*Bel*.51.49. ® **-μνους**, μνουν, (μνᾶ) *weighing or worth ten minae*, Ar.*Pax* 1224, 1235; δεκάμνουν, τό, *weight of ten minae*, *IG*2$^2$.1013.55; written δεκάμνων in ib.11.203*B*99 (Delos, iii B.C.). **-μοιρία**, ἡ, *space of ten degrees of the zodiac*, J.*AJ*3.7.7, Ptol.*Alm*.2.7, Anon.ap.Lyd.*Ost*.p.174 W.:—hence Adj. **-μοιριαῖος**, Heph.Astr.1.1. **-μοιρον**, τό, name of an *ointment*, Orib.ap.Aët.12.62: perh. f.l. for **δεκά-μῦρον**, τό, a similar remedy, Alex.Trall.7.8. **-μυξος**, ον, *with ten wicks*, λύχνος Roussel *Cultes Égyptiens* 235 (Delos, ii B.C.).

**δεκάμφορος**, ον, *holding ten* ἀμφορεῖς, κρατήρ E.*Cyc*.388; πίθος Sosith.2.8.

® **δεκᾰνᾱΐα**, ἡ, (ναῦς) *squadron of ten ships*, Plb.22.7.4, D.S.14.103, prob. in Str.7.7.6.

**δεκανᾶται**· ἀσπάζεται, Hsch.; cf. δεικανάω II.

**δέκανδρος**, ὁ, = Lat. *decemvir*, *OGI*482 (Acmonia):—hence **δεκανδρικός**, ή, όν, = Lat. *decemviralis*, ἀρχή Lyd.*Mag*.1.34.

**δεκᾰνία**, ἡ, = Lat. *decuria*, Arr.*Tact*.6.1. 2. *measure* or *division* of land, ἀμπέλων δ., δ. Κολπηνή, *IGRom*.4.1675 (Lydia), cf. *PFay*.156 (ii A.D.), *POxy*.1512 (iv A.D.); also δ. πυροῦ *BGU*894.11. 3. *guard-house of a decuria*, *IGRom*.3.1286 (Arabia), *Princeton Exp. Inscr*.636.

**δεκᾰνικός**, ή, όν, *of* or *for a* δεκανός I, *PHib*.1.30.13 (iii B.C.), 96.21; δεκανικόν, τό, *tax for maintenance of* δεκανοί, δ. πλοίων *BGU*1.1 (ii/iii A.D.); δ. ἰχθυομεταβόλων *PRyl*.196.6 (ii A.D.). II. *of a* δεκανός II, Paul.Al.*C*.2.

**δεκᾰνός**, ὁ, = Lat. *decurio*, *IGRom*.1.1046 (Alexandria); *police officer* in Egypt, *PTeb*.27.31 (ii B.C.), *POxy*.387 (i A.D.), etc. II. Astrol., δεκανοί, οἱ, *decans*, thirty-six divinities each of whom presided over ten degrees of the zodiac, Nech.ap.Firm.4.22.2, Herm.ap. Stob.1.21.9, Heph.Astr.1.1, Gal.11.797, *PMag.Par*.1.1203, Leont. *in Arat*.p.569 M., Ps.-Callisth.1.4, etc.

**δεκᾰ-ολυμπῑονίκης** [νῑ], ου, ὁ, *winner of ten victories at Olympia*, *Sammelb*.5225 (iii A.D.). **-πᾰλαι** [κᾰ], Adv. *a very long time ago*, Com. form of πάλαι (cf. δωδεκάπαλαι), Ar.*Eq*.1154, Philonid.8, Henioch.2.1. ® **-πεδον**, τό, *distance of ten feet*, *Klio* 16.170 (Delph., ii B.C.). **-πηχυαῖος**, α, ον, = sq., *Gp*.9.9.10, 15.2.22. **-πηχυς**, υ, *ten cubits long*, Hdt.9.81, Plb.18.16.2, *IG*11.161*D*122 (Delos, iii B.C.), Luc.*Tim*.4. **-πλᾰσιάζω**, *multiply by ten*, Lxx*Ba*.4.28, Ph.1.462. **-πλάσιος** [πλᾰ], ον, *tenfold*, Hp.*VM*16; δ. τὸ ἔκτεισμα τοῦ ἀδικήματος ἐκτίνειν Pl.*R*.615b: c. gen., *ten times greater than*, Plb.21.22.15; τὴν δεκαπλασίαν (sc. τιμήν) καταδικάζειν mulct in *ten times the amount*, Lex ap.D.24.105 (dub.); δ. ὀφρῆσθαι rob the state of *a tenfold penalty*, D.24.82. Adv. **-ως** Hp.*VM*6. **-πλᾰσίων**, ον, gen. ονος, = foreg., Sch.Il.2.488, Thd.*Da*.1.20. ® **-πλεθρος**, ον, *enclosing ten* πλέθρα, προτείχισμα Th.6.102. **-πλευρος**, ον, *ten-sided*, Procl. *in Euc*.p.422 F. **-πληγος**, ἡ, *the ten plagues* of Egypt, *PMag. Par*.1.3037. **-πλοκος**, ον, *folded ten times*, Paul.Aeg.6.65. **-πλόος**, ον, contr. **-πλοῦς**, οῦν, = δεκαπλάσιος, D.24.83; τὸ γνωσθὲν ἀποτίνεται δ. Arist.*Ath*.54.2, cf. Hyp.*Dem.Fr*.7: also in fem. ἀποτεισάτω δεκαπλόαν *IG*5(1).1421.13 (Cyparissia, iv/iii B.C.). **-πολις**, εως, ἡ, *district with ten cities*, *Decapolis*, Ev.*Matt*.4.25, J.*BJ*3.9.7, *IGRom*.3.1057 (ii A.D.). ® **-πους**, ὁ, ἡ, -πουν, τό, *ten feet long*, Ar.*Ec*.652; ἄκαινα Call.*Aet.Fr*.7.6P. ® **-πρωτεία**, ἡ, *office of* δεκάπρωτοι, *IGRom*.3.802 (Syllaeum), *POxy*.1204.4 (iii A.D.), etc. ® **-πρωτεύω**, *serve as member of* δεκάπρωτοι, *JHS*37.108 (Thyatira), *CIG*2929 (Tralles), etc. ® **-πρωτοι**, οἱ, = Lat. *decemprimi*, the chief municipal authorities of a city, γνώμη στρατηγῶν καὶ δεκαπρώτων *IG*12(7).395.4 (Amorgos), etc.: sg., ib.239.12, *Rev.Phil*.37.311 (Thyatira), *POxy*.1204.4 (iii A.D.): fem. **-πρώτη**, ἡ, *PFlor*.76.11 (iii A.D.). II. = Lat. *decemviri*, Lyd.*Mag*.1.34tit. **-πτῠχος**, ον, *with ten folds*: metaph., *comprised in ten tablets*, Orph.*Fr*.247.21.

**δεκ-άρουρος** [ᾰ], ον, *of ten arurae*, *PTeb*.5.44 (ii B.C.), *PLond*.3.604*B*244 (i A.D.). ® **-ἀρτᾰβος**, ον, *of ten* ἀρτάβαι, *PRyl*.119.22 (i A.D.).

**δεκάρχ-ης**, ου, ὁ, = δεκαδάρχης, *decurion*, Hdt.7.81; = Lat. *decurio* (in form **δέκαρχος**), Arr.*Alan*.22, D.C.71.27. II. = Lat. *decemvir*, f.l. in D.H.2.14. **-ία**, ἡ, = δεκαδαρχία, X.*HG*3.4.2, Isoc.4.110, al.

® **δεκάς**, άδος, ἡ, *company of ten*, Il.2.126, Hdt.3.25; of ships, A.*Pers*.340, etc.: generally, *company*, ἧς καὶ σὺ φαίνει δεκάδος E.*Supp*.219; *number, tale*, τῶν ἐτέων ἡ δ. οὐκ ὀλίγη Call.*Fr*.489; ἡ Ἀττικὴ δ., the *ten Attic Orators*, Luc.*Scyth*.10. 2. Λύκου δ. *the company of* Lycus, a name given to bribed dicasts at Athens, because the bribers were to be found near the statue of Lycus in the law-courts, Eratosth.ap.Harp.s.v. II. the number *ten*, περὶ τῆς δ., title of work by Archytas, cf. Philol.11, Arist.*Metaph*.1084$^a$12; τέλειον ἡ δ., Pythag., ib.986$^a$8, cf. *Fr*.203. III. = δεκάτη I, Hsch. s.v. δεκατευταί.

® **δεκά-σημος** [κᾰ], ον, *of ten time-units* in Music, Aristid.Quint.1.14. **-σκαλμος** ναῦς *with ten banks of oars*, Suid.

**δεκασμός**, ὁ, (δεκάζω) *bribery*, D.H.7.64, Plu.*Cat.Mi*.44: in pl., Id.*Cic*.29.

**δεκά-σπορος** χρόνος, ὁ, lapse *of ten seed-times*, i.e. *ten years*, E.*Tr*.20, cf. *El*.1154. **-στᾰδιαῖος**, α, ον, *ten stadia high*, Theo Sm.p.125 H., al. ® **-στάδιον** [στᾰ], τό, *race-course of ten stadia*, *IG*4.951.79 (Epid.), Herzog *Koische Forschungen* p.55. **-στάτηρος** [στᾰ], ον, *in receipt of ten staters*, Arr.*An*.7.23.3: Subst. -στάτηρον, τό, *sum of ten staters*, *Leg.Gort*.9.49, *Schwyzer* 179a5 (Crete); *weight of ten staters*, *IG*1$^2$.918. **-στεγος**, ον, *ten stories high*, πύργος Str.15.3.7, Ath.Mech.11.8. **-στῐχος**, ον, *containing ten lines*, βίβλος Sch.Il.4.101. **-στῡλος**, ον, *with ten columns in front*, Vitr.3.2.8. **-σχημος**, ον, *with ten forms*, of certain verses, Ps.-Plu.*Metr*.p.471 B.

® **δεκᾰταῖος**, α, ον, *for ten days*, δ. τῶν νεκρῶν διεφθαρμένων Pl.*R*.614b. II. *ten days old*, δεκαταίου δ' ἤδη ὄντος τοῦ ᾠοῦ Arist.*HA*561$^a$26; βρέφος Luc.*Halc*.5.

**δεκᾰτάλαντ-ία**, ἡ, *sum of ten talents*, Poll.9.52. ® **-ος**, ον, *weighing or worth ten talents*, λίθος Ar.*Fr*.276; δίκη δ. an action *in which the damages were laid at ten talents*, Aeschin.2.99.

**δεκᾰτάρχ-ης**, ου, ὁ, = δεκάταρχος, Lat. *decurio*, in the Roman fleet, *IG*5(1).818.5 (Sparta, iii A.D.), *Supp.Epigr*.1.345 (Paros, i A.D.). **-ία**, ἡ (for δεκαδαρχία), *group of ten*, e.g. cultivators, Wilcken *Chr*.304 (iii B.C.). ® **-ος**, ὁ, *head of a* δεκαταρχία, *PSI* 4.337.4 (iii B.C.); τῶν λατόμων *PPetr*.2 p.6; v.l. for δεκαδάρχης, Lxx 1*Ma*.3.55.

**δεκάτεια**, ἡ, = δεκάτευσις, Plu.*Ant*.39.

® **δεκᾰτέσσᾰρες**, α, v. δέκα.

® **δεκάτ-ευμα** [κᾰ], ατος, τό, *tenth, tithe*, Call.*Ep*.40 (pl.). ® **-ευσις**, εως, ἡ, *decimation*, D.H.1.24. **-ευτήριον**, τό, *office for collection of* δεκάτη, *custom-house*, X.*HG*1.1.22. ®**-ευτής**, οῦ, ὁ, *tithe-farmer*, Harp. ® **-εύω**, *exact tithe from*, τινά D.22.77; τὰς πόλεις Jusj.ap. Lycurg.81; τούτους δεκατεῦσαι τῷ ἐν Δελφοῖσι θεῷ *make them pay a tithe* to Apollo, Hdt.7.132; of things, δ. τὰ ἐξ ἀγροῦ ὡραῖα *tithe* them (as an offering).., X.*An*.5.3.9; δ. τοὺς Θηβαίους τοῖς θεοῖς Plb.9.39.5:—Pass., ἀναγκαίως ἔχει [τὰ χρήματα] δεκατευθῆναι τῷ Διί Hdt.1.89; ἐλπὶς ἦν δεκατευθῆναι τὰς Θήβας, i.e. *that it would be taken and tithed*, X.*HG*6.3.20, 5.35. 2. abs., *to be a* δεκατευτής, Ar.*Fr*.455. II. in war, *take out the tenth man for execution, decimate*, D.C.48.42, etc. 2. *divide into ten sections*, τινάς App.*BC*1.49. III. = ἀρκτεύω, Lys.*Fr*.250S., D.ap.Harp. IV. metaph. in Astrol., *to be superior to*, Man.6.279.

**δεκάτη**, ἡ, v. δέκατος.

**δεκάτη-λογία**, ἡ, *collection of tithe*, Poll.1.169. **-λόγιον**, τό, =

δεκατευτήριον, Id.9.28. **-λόγος**, ὁ, (λέγω) = δεκατευτής, D.23.177. **-μοιρία**, ἡ, *tenth part*, Just.*Edict*.7.5. **-μόριον**, τό, (μέρος) *tenth part*, Pl.*Lg*.924a. ⊛ **-φόρος**, ον, *tithe-paying*, ἀπαρχαί Call.*Del*.278. II. *receiving tithe*, epith. of Apollo at Megara, Paus. 1.42.5: Dor. **δεκατᾱφόρος** *GDI*5045 (Crete), etc.

⊛ **δεκᾰτ-ισμός**, ὁ, *formation of decuriae*, Them.*Or*.5.65d. **-ισταί**, οἱ, perh. = δεκαδισταί, *BCH*24.367 (Bithyn.).

**δεκᾰτοκύριοι** [ῡ], οἱ, prob. = δεκάταρχοι, *PPetr*.2 p.33.

⊛ **δέκᾰτος** (Arc. **δέκοτος** *IG*5(2).282 (Mantinea, v B.C.), also Aeol. in *Epigr.Gr*.988.5 (Balbilla)), η, ον: (δέκα):—*tenth*, Ἠὼς Il.6.175, etc.; as a round number, Od.16.18, etc. II. **δεκάτη** (sc. μερίς), ἡ, *tenth part, tithe*, τᾶς δεκάτας δεκάταν Simon.141.4, cf. Hdt.2.135, etc.; τῇ θεῷ τὰς δ. ἐξαιρεθῆναι Lys.20.24; τὰ ἐκ τῆς δ. the produce *of the tenth*, *IG*1².91, cf. *Tab.Defix*.99.14: esp. as a customs-duty, D.20.60; δεκάτη μόσχων *PTeb*.307.8 (iii A.D.). 2. δεκάτη (sc. ἡμέρα), ἡ, *the tenth day*, Od.9.83, al. b. δ. προτέρα· ἡ πρὸ εἰκάδος, ὡς ὑστέρα· ἡ μετ' εἰκάδα, Hsch. 3. *festival on the tenth day after birth*, when the child has a name given it, τὴν δ. θύειν to give a *naming-day feast*, Ar.*Av*.922, cf. 494: δ. ὑπέρ τινος ἑστιᾶσαι D.40.28, cf. 39.22. 4. δεκάτα· τάξις, ἄθροισμα, καὶ ἡ τῶν εἴκοσιν ἁρμάτων τάξις, Hsch. 5. δέκατον, τό, *tenth part*, Lxx *Le*.23.13,17 (pl.).

**δεκᾰτόσπορος**, ον, *in the tenth generation*, Epigr.ap.Str.10.3.2.

⊛ **δεκᾰτόω**, *take tithe of* a person, τινά *Ep.Hebr*.7.6:—Pass., *pay tithe*, ib.9.

**δεκα-τρεῖς**, **-τρια**, v. sub δέκα.

⊛ **δεκᾰτ-ώνης**, ου, ὁ, *tithe-farmer*, Anaxil.8. **-ώνιον**, τό, *office of the* δεκατῶναι, Antiph.27.

**δεκά-φυιος** [κᾰ], ον, (φυή) *tenfold*, Call.*Fr*.162. **-φῡλος**, ον, *consisting of ten tribes*, Hdt.5.66. **-χαλκον**, τό, *coin worth ten* χαλκοῖ, = Lat. *denarius* (*worth ten asses*), Plu.*Cam*.13. **-χειλε·** πρὸς ἀποδοχὴν ἐπιτήδειον, Hsch. **-χειλοι·** δεκα(κι)σχίλιοι, Id.; cf. δεκάχιλοι.

**δεκᾰχῆ**, Adv. *in ten parts*, D.C.55.24, prob. in Hdt.5.69: Att. **δέκᾰχᾰ** *IG*2².1.34.

**δεκά-χῑλοι** [κᾰ], αι, α, *ten thousand*, Il.5.860, 14.148; cf. ἐννεάχιλοι. (Aristarch. read the true Ion. form -χειλοι (from *ghezl-*) which he mistranslated "ἐννέα χείλη ἔχοντες", Sch.T.Il.14.148.) **-χοια·** δεκαπλαῖ, Hsch. **-χορδος**, ον, *ten-stringed*, λύρα Ion Lyr.3 (fort. ἐνδεκάχορδος), Lxx *Ps*.32(33).2, al.

**δεκάω**, dub. l. et sens., *Ath.Mitt*.18.225 (Attica, viii B.C.(?)).

**Δεκέλεια**, Ion. **-έη**, ἡ, a place in Attica, Hdt., etc.:—**Δεκελεύς**, έως, ὁ, *a Decelean*, Hdt.9.73; but **Δεκελειεύς** Inscrr. Att., as *IG*2.660, al.; **-εεύς** ib.2.1247, al.: Adj. **Δεκελεικός**, ή, όν, *Decelean*, ὁ Δ. πόλεμος, name given to the latter part of the Pelop. war, Isoc.8.37, etc. Advbs. **Δεκελειῆθεν** *from D.*, Hdt. l. c.; **-ειόθεν** Lys.23.2: **Δεκελειᾶσιν** *at D.*, Isoc.8.84: **-ειᾶζε** *to D.*, St.Byz.

**δεκ-έμβολος**, ον, *with ten beaks*, ναῦς A.*Fr*.133. **-ετηρικός** (sc. λόγος), *for the Decennalia* of an Emperor, Them.*Or*.11 tit. **-ετηρίς**, ίδος, ἡ, *space of ten years*, D.C.53.16 (pl.); = Lat. *Decennalia*, *BGU*362 iii 24 (iii A.D.). **-έτηρος**, ον, = sq., *AP*9.474. ⊛ **-έτης**, ου, ὁ, *lasting ten years*, χρόνος S.*Ph*.715 (lyr.), Pl.*Lg*.682d; δεκέτεις ἀλάληντο *for a space of ten years*, E.*Andr*.306 (lyr.): fem. δεκέτις, ιδος, παιδοποιΐα Pl.*Lg*.784b; προστασία D.C.56.28. II. *ten years old*, fem. δεκέτις Ar.*Lys*.644.

⊛ **δεκήρης**, ες, *with ten banks of oars*, ναῦς Plb.16.3.3, Plu.*Ant*.64.

**δέκομαι**, v. δέχομαι. **δέκοτος**, v. δέκατος.

**δεκ-τέος**, α, ον, (δέχομαι) *to be received*, Luc.*Herm*.74. II. **δεκτέον**, *one must take* or *understand*, Str.10.2.22, Sch.Th.*Oxy*.853 vii 9. **-τή·** χλαῖνα, χλανίς, Hsch. ⊛ **-τήρ**, ῆρος, ὁ, title of an official *receiver*, *IG*5(2).274 (Mantinea, ii/i B.C.), cf. Hsch., Suid. ⊛ **-της**, ου, ὁ, (δέχομαι) *receiver, beggar*, Od.4.248. ⊛ **-τικός**, ή, όν, *fit for receiving*, τὸ τῆς τροφῆς δ. *the part that receives* the food (sc. ἡ κοιλία), Arist.*Pol*.1290ᵇ27, cf. *HA*489ᵃ3; αἰσθητήριον δ. τῶν αἰσθητῶν Id.*PA*647ᵃ7; [τοῦ εἴδους] Id.*Metaph*.1023ᵃ12: Comp., Id.*Pr*.966ᵃ12. 2. *capable of*, ἐπιστήμης Pl.*Def*.415a; ἐναντιώσεων Arist.*GC*320ᵃ4; τῆς ἕξεως Id.*Cat*.12ᵃ30; διατάξεως Porph.*Abst*.1.7; παθημάτων Hierocl.*in CA*24 p.470M.; θυμοῦ Phld.*Ir*.p.87W.; πόνων Demetr.Lac.*Herc*.1012.45F., cf. Phld.*D*.1.2. 3. abs., *capable of receiving, recipient*, Arist.*de An*.414ᵃ10, *Ph*.249ᵃ2. **-το**, v. δέχομαι. **-τός**, ή, όν, *to be received* or *accepted, acceptable*, Lxx *Is*.61.2, al., *Ev.Luc*.4.24; δεκτόν [ἐστι] it is *an accepted principle*, c. inf., Erot.*Praef*. 2. *to be grasped*, χείρ Iamb.*Protr*.21.ιθ'. II. *to be taken, understood*, Phld.*Rh*.2.269S. ⊛ **-τρια**, ἡ, fem. of δεκτήρ, Archil.19, *AP*11.400 (Luc.). **-τωρ**, ορος, ὁ, *one who takes upon himself* or *on his own head*, αἵματος δ. νέου A.*Eu*.204.

**δεκῠρεύω**, *to be a decurio*, *IG*14.575 (Centuripa).

⊛ **δεκώβολον**, τό, *sum of ten obols*, *IG*2.837.23.

**δέκων·** ὁ δεκαζόμενος, Hsch.

**δεκώρυγος**, ον, (ὀργυιά) *ten fathoms long*, X.*Cyn*.2.5.

**δελαστρεύς**, έως, ὁ, *using bait*, ἰχθυβολῆες Nic.*Th*.793.

**δελε-άζω**, (δέλεαρ) *entice* or *catch by a bait*, τὴν γραῦν δ. λεπαστῇ Antiph.45, cf. Hdn.2.15.3; δ. τινὰς ἐπὶ πλεονεξίαν Onos.6.10:—Pass., γαστρὶ δελεάζεσθαι X.*Mem*.2.1.4, cf. Isoc.8.34, Epicur.*Sent.Vat*.16, Phld.*Lib*.p.14O.; ῥᾳστώνῃ καὶ σχολῇ D.18.45; ὑπὸ χρημάτων, ὑπὸ τῆς ἡδονῆς, Luc.*Apol*.9, Jul.*Or*.6.185a. II. c. acc. cogn., νῶτον ὑὸς περὶ ἄγκιστρον δ. *put* it on the hook *as a bait*, Hdt.2.70; but δ. ἄγκιστρον ἰσχάδι *bait* it with a fig, Luc.*Pisc*.47; δ. ἄγκιστρον ἐπ' ἄλλους to catch others, ib.48. **-ᾱμα**, ατος, τό, = sq., Anon.ap.Suid. s.v. ἔγκειται (fort. δελέασμα). ⊛ **-αρ**, ατος, τό, Ep. **δεῖλαρ** (q.v.); Ep. gen. δελείατος Numen.ap.Ath.7.305a; dat. pl. δελέασσιν Opp.*H*.3.437: contr. in dat. δέλητι Hsch.; neut. pl. δέλητα cj. in Theoc.21.10:—*bait*, X.*Mem*.2.1.4, Plb.15.21.6 (pl.): metaph., δ. τινος *bait* for a person, E.*Andr*.264, cf. *Fr*.981.5, Luc.*Rh.Pr*.25 (pl.), etc.; τιμαὶ γάρ, ἆθλα, δ. ἃ ὁ θεὸς ἔδωκεν ἀνθρώποις Antipho Soph.49: c. gen. rei, *an incitement to* . ., ἡδονὴ κακοῦ δέλεαρ Pl.*Ti*.69d, cf. J.*Ap*.2.39; δ. σοφίης *Epigr.Gr*.880.6 (Cyzicus). **-άρπαξ**, αγος, ὁ, ἡ, *snapping at the bait*, πέρκη *AP*7.504.3 (Leon.). **-ασμα**, ατος, τό, = δελέαμα, δέλεαρ, Ar.*Eq*.789. **-ασμάτιον**, τό, Dim. of foreg., Philox.2.5. **-ασμός**, ὁ, *catching with a bait*, Arist.*HA*535ᵃ7 (pl.); *enticement, allurement*, τινός A.D.*Pron*.41.1. **-άστρα**, ἡ, *baited trap* or *noose*, Cratin.216. **-αστρον**, τό, = foreg., Nicopho 4. **-τρον**, τό, = δέλεαρ, Numen.ap.Ath.7.287c, 306c, Opp.*H*.2.431, 3.185. 2. *torch*, Timach.ap.Ath.15.699e, Hsch.

**δελήτιον**, τό, Dim. of δέλεαρ, Sophr.118 (= [S.]*Fr*.1124).

**δελία·** δάφνη, Hsch. **δέλιχρα·** τὰ ἡμίχοιρα, Id.

**δελκανός**, ὁ, a kind of *fish*, Euthyd.ap.Ath.3.118b.

⊛ **δέλλει·** καλεῖ, Hsch. (leg. βάλλει).

**δελλίθιον** [λῐ], τό, *the nest of the* δέλλις, Hsch.

**δέλλῑς** (A), ἴθος, ἡ, kind of *wasp*, Hdn.Gr.1.89, Hsch.

⊛ **δέλλις** (B), acc. δέλλιν, = δέλφαξ, *Annuario* 3.144 (Pisidia).

**Δελματία**, **Δελματ-ική**, **-ίκιον**, **-ιον**, v. Δαλμ-.

**δέλος**, εος, τό, = δέλεαρ, Eust.235.7: gen. pl. δελέων *PMag.Par*.1.939.

⊛ **δέλτα**, τό, indecl., *the letter* δέλτα: gen. δέλτατος Democr.20. (Hebr. *dāleth* 'door'.) II. *anything shaped like a* Δ, esp. *island formed by the mouths of a large river*, as the Nile, Hdt.2.13, etc.; of the Indus, Str.15.1.33, Arr.*An*.5.4.1, etc. 2. adverbially, δ. παρατετιλμέναι Ar.*Lys*.151. III. = δελτωτόν, Ptol.*Tetr*.27.

**δελτάριον**, τό, Dim. of δέλτος, Plb.29.27.2, Plu.*Cat.Mi*.24. II. a surgical instrument, *Hermes* 38.284.

**δελτίον**, τό, Dim. of δέλτος, Hdt.7.239, *PLond*.5.1674 (vi A.D.).

⊛ **δελτο-γράφημα** [γρᾰ], ατος, τό, *official rescript*, τοῦ ἀνθυπάτου *OGI* 458.62 (i B.C./i A.D.). **-γράφος** [ᾰ], ον, *writing on a tablet, recording*, δελτογράφῳ δὲ πάντ' ἐπωπᾷ φρενί A.*Eu*.275. **-ειδής**, ές, *delta-shaped, triangular*, Hsch. s.v. καρχήσιον; of the *deltoid* muscle, Gal.2.354. Adv. **-δῶς** Ruf.*Oss*.10. **-ομαι**, Med., *note down on tablets for oneself*, τἄμ' ἔπη δελτουμένας A.*Supp*.179. **-ποιός**, *tabellarius*, *Gloss*.

**δέλτος** (A)· ἀγαθός, Phot.

⊛ **δέλτος** (B) (Cypr. **δάλτος** *Inscr.Cypr*.135.26H.), ἡ, *writing-tablet*, Batr.3 (pl.), Hdt.8.135, etc.; ἐν . . δέλτου πτυχαῖς γράψας E.*IA*98; χαλκῆς . . δύσνιπτον ἐκ δέλτου γραφήν S.*Tr*.683; δέλτον ἐγγεγραμμένην ξυνθήματα inscribed with . ., ib.157; δέλτον ἀναθεῖναι *IG*12(2).58 *b* 17 (Mytilene): esp. pl., E.*IA*116,798 (both lyr.); πινάκων ξεστῶν δέλτοι Ar.*Th*.778: metaph., ἣν ἐγγράφου σὺ μνήμοσιν δέλτοις φρενῶν *on the tablets* of the heart, A.*Pr*.789; θὲς (cj. for σὲ δ') ἐν φρενὸς δέλτοισι τοὺς ἐμοὺς λόγους S.*Fr*.597. II. any *writing*: *letter*, Pl.*Ep*.312d; *will*, Luc.*Tim*.22, etc.; δέλτον χαλκῆν ἐκσφραγισθεῖσαν *BGU*265.21 (ii A.D.), cf. 780.15, 1032.3; Ὁμήρου δέλτον *the books* of Homer, *IG*9(1).880.10 (Corc.), cf. *AP*12.2 (Strato); αἱ δώδεκα δ. the Twelve *Tables*, D.H.2.27.

**δελτωτός**, ή, όν, *in the shape of the letter* Δ: τὸ δ. *the constellation Triangle*, Arat.235, Eratosth.*Cat*.20 tit.

**δελφάκ-ειος** [ᾰ], ον, *of a* δέλφαξ, πλευρὰ δ. ribs *of pork*, Pherecr.108.16, cf. Alex.124.2; ζωμὸς Dieuch.ap.Orib.4.6.1. **-ίνη** [ῑ], ἡ, = δέλφαξ, Epich.124.2. **-ιον**, τό, Dim. of δέλφαξ, *sucking-pig*, Ar.*Th*.237, *Lys*.1061, Aeschin.Socr.4, *BGU*949.8 (iii/iv A.D.), etc. II. *pudenda muliebria*, Hsch. **-ίς**, ίδος, ἡ, = foreg. 1, *Ostr*.1031 (i A.D.), *PGiss*.49.17 (iii A.D.). **-όομαι**, Pass., *grow up to pighood*, Ar.*Ach*.786.

⊛ **δέλφαξ**, ᾰκος, ἡ (cf. Ath.9.375a, ὁ, Epich.100.4, Sopat.5, Pl.Com.110), Hippon.70B, Hdt.2.70, Ar.*Fr*.506.4, Eup.281, Theopomp.Com.48, Arist.*HA*573ᵇ13:—*pig*, ll. cc., etc.; full-grown, opp. χοῖρος, Ar.Byz.ap.Ath. l. c.; sacrificed to Persephone, *IG*3.77.7.

**Δελφίδιος**, Dor., = Δελφίνιος, *SIG*712.13 (Cnossus).

**δελφίν**, ῖνος, ὁ, later form of δελφίς (q. v.).

**δελφῑν-άριον**, τό, *small dolphin*, Hero *Aut*.27.2. **-ιάς**, άδος, ἡ, = δελφίνιον II, Ps.-Dsc.3.73. **-ίζω**, *duck like a dolphin*, τὸ κάρα Luc.*Lex*.5. **-ιον** [φῐ], τό, *temple of Apollo Delphinios*, esp. at Athens, τὸ ἐπὶ Δελφινίῳ δικαστήριον the law-court *there*, Decr.ap.And.1.78, Arist.*Ath*.57.3, Plu.*Thes*.12.18, etc.: also at Chalcis, etc., Id.*Flam*.16, etc. II. *larkspur, Delphinium Ajacis*, Ps.-Dsc.3.73, *Gp*.20.2.2. b. *dolphin-flower, Delphinium Consolida*, Ps.-Dsc. l. c.

**Δελφίνιος** [φῐ], ὁ, epith. of Apollo, *h.Ap*.495, *SIG*57.11 (Milet., v B.C.), *IG*12(3).537 (Thera), Plu.2.984a, etc. II. (sc. μήν), name of month at Thera, Aegina, etc., *Test.Epict*.2.31, Sch.Pi.*N*.5.81, etc. 2. = δελφίνιον II, Hsch. III. Δελφίνια, τά, *festival of Apollo D.*, Sch.Pi.*O*.13.155, etc.

**δελφῑνίς**, ίδος, ἡ, τράπεζα, prob. *with dolphins for a base*, Luc.*Lex*.7.

**δελφῑνίσκος**, ὁ, Dim. of δελφίς, Arist.*HA*631ᵃ17.

**δελφῑνο-ειδής**, ές, *like a dolphin*, φυλλάρια Ps.-Dsc.3.73. **-σημος**, ον, *bearing a dolphin as a device*, Lyc.658. ⊛ **-φόρος**, ον, *bearing dolphins*, A.*Fr*.150. II. *carrying* δελφῖνες II, κεραίαι Th.7.41, cf. Pherecr.12.

**δελφιξ**, ῖκος, ὁ, *tripod*, δέλφικας ἀργυροῦς Plu.*TG*2 (prob. for δελφῖνας); δέλφικα· τὸν τρίποδα *EM*255.10.

⊛ **δελφίς** (later **δελφίν**, Mosch.3.37 (dub.l.), Man.5.157), ῖνος, ὁ:—

*dolphin*, Il.21.22, Od.12.96, Archil.74.7, Pi.*P*.2.51, Hdt.1.24, Arist. *HA*489ᵇ2, Opp.*H*.1.648, etc.; as an ornament, *IG*2.678ᴮ37; cf. βελφίν. II. *mass of lead shaped like a dolphin*, hung at the yard-arm, and let down on the decks of the enemy's ships, τοὺς δ. μετεωρίζου Ar.*Eq*.762, cf. Sch. ad loc.; δ. κεροῦχος Pherecr.12. 2. = κερκέτης, Paus.Gr.*Fr*.118, Opp.*H*.3.290. 3. *stops* in a machine, Orib.48. 4.44. III. *the constellation Dolphin*, Democr.14, Arist.*Mete*.345ᵇ 22, Arat.316, Eratosth.*Cat*.31 tit., etc.

**Δελφοί**, ῶν, οἱ, *Delphi*, Δελφῶν ἐς πίονα δῆμον *h.Hom*.27.14, cf. S. *OT*734; Δελφοῖς *at Delphi*, Th.1.143: also **Δαλφοί** *Schwyzer* 324. 13, **Δερφοί** *Delph*.3(2).238, **Δολφοί** *GDI*5607.5; Aeol. **Βέλφοι** *EM* 200.27; Boeot. **Βελφός, Βελφίς**, etc., *IG*7.2385,619, etc. II. *the Delphians*, Hdt.1.54, etc.: sg., Δελφός, pr.n. of king of Delphi, A.*Eu*.16; Δ. ἀνήρ E.*Andr*.1151, etc.: fem. **Δελφίς** S.*OT*464 (lyr.), etc.; Δελφίς, ίδος, ἡ, *territory of Delphi*, *SIG*534.16 (Delph., iii B.C.); Δελφίδες (sc. δραχμαί) *Schwyzer* 322 (Delph., v/iv B.C.):—Adj. **Δελφικός**, ή, όν, *Delphic, Delphian*, S.*OC*413, Pl.*Lg*.686a, etc.; **Δέλφιος** is dub. in Call.*Aet*.3.1.20.

**δέλφος**, ους, τό, *pig*, dub. in *SIG*1039.15.

**δελφύς**, ύος, ἡ, *womb*, Hp.*Steril*.222, Arist.*HA*510ᵇ13, Ath.9. 375a:—Dor. **δελφύα**, ἡ, acc. in Greg.Cor.p.344 S.

**δέμα**, ατος, τό, (δέω A) *band*, Plb.6.33.11; = σχοινίον, Hsch. II. Archit., *clamp, dowel*, *IG*7.3073.70 (Lebad.). III. *tow-rope*, Ph. *Bel*.73.24.

**δέμας**, τό, (δέμω) *bodily frame*, usu. of man, Hom. (v. infr.); rarely of other animals, Od.10.240, Pi.*O*.1.20; prop. *the living body*, but also of a corpse, νεκρὸν δ. Batr.106, cf. S.*Ant*.205, E.*Or*.40,1066, Sch.Ven.Il.1.115.—Hom. uses it only in acc. sg., usu. abs., μικρὸς δ. small *in stature*, Il.5.801; ἄριστος εἶδός τε δ. τε Od.8.116; δέμας εἴκυῖα θεῇσιν Il.8.305; δέμας ἀθανάτοισιν ὁμοῖος Od.8.14; οὐ.. ἐστι χερείων οὐ δέμας οὐδὲ φυήν Il.1.115, cf. Od.5.212; δέμας καὶ εἶδος ἀγητός Il.24.376, cf. Od.18.251; χαρίεσσα δέμας Hes.*Th*.260; Κλύμενον ..ἀμώμητον δ. B.5.147: nom. in later poets, as S.*OC*110,501, etc.: dat. δέμαϊ Pi.*Pae*.6.80. 2. in Lyr. and Trag. as a periphrasis, Ἀστερίας δ., the island of Delos, ib.5.42; κτανεῖν μητρῷον δ. A. *Eu*.84; οἰκετῶν δ. S.*Tr*.908; Ἡράκλειον δ. E.*HF*1037 (lyr.); οἰνάνθης δ., i.e. the vine-*shoot*, S.*Fr*.255.4; ἀστερωπὸν οὐρανοῦ δ. v.l. in Critias 25.33 D.; Δάματρος ἀκτᾶς..δ., i.e. bread, E.*Hipp*.138: in later Ep., ὕλης δ. Orph.*L*.238. 3. Com., = πόσθη, Pl.Com.173. 10. II. as Adv., δέμας πυρὸς αἰθομένοιο *in form* or *fashion like* burning fire, Il.11.596, cf. 17.366.

**δεμάτιον**, τό, Dim. of δέμα, *Hippiatr*.22, Sch.Theoc.4.18.

**Δέματρος**, ὁ (sc. μήν), month at Halos, *IG*9(2).109ᴮ47.

**δέμει**· ὁδός, Hsch.

**δεμελέας**, τάς, acc. pl., *leeches*, *IG*4.951.98 (Epid.); cf. **δεμβλεῖς**· βδέλλαι, Hsch. (Nom. sg. unknown.)

**δέμνιον**, τό, (δέμω) mostly in pl. δέμνια, *bedstead, mattress*, Il.24. 644, Od.4.297, etc. 2. generally, *bed*, freq. in pl., Od.6.20, 8. 282, S.*Tr*.901,915: also in sg., Pi.*N*.1.3, E.*Or*.229, *Alc*.183 (δεμνίων 186), Call.*Del*.248.

**δεμνιοτήρης**, ες, *keeping one to one's bed*: μοῖρα δ. *a lingering* fate, A.*Ag*.1449 (lyr.); δ. πόνος δρακόντων ib.53 (anap.).

**δέμω**, rare in pres. and impf., Ep. impf. δέμον Od.23.192, part. δέμων *h.Merc*.87: aor. ἔδειμα Il.21.446, Hdt.2.124, Ep. δεῖμα A.R. 3.37, subj. δείμομεν for δείμωμεν Il.7.337:—Med., aor. (v. infr.):—Pass., pf. δέδμημαι 6.249, etc., Dor. 3 pl. δέδμανθ' Theoc.15.120: plpf. ἐδέδμητο Hdt.7.59,176:—*build*, τεῖχος ἔδειμαν Il.7.436, etc.; τείχη παλαιὰ δείμας E.*Rh*.232:—Med., ἐδείματο οἴκους he *built him* houses, Od.6.9; ἄστη Pl.*Ax*.370b. 2. generally, *construct, prepare*, δ. ἀλωήν *h.Merc*.87; δ. ὁδόν, Lat. *munire viam*, Hdt.2.124:—Pass., ἁμαξιτὸς δέδμηται Id.7.200: metaph. of persons, δέδμηνται πάσῃ κόσμος Ἰαονίῃ Haussoullier *Milet* p.141.

**δεμών**· χρόνος, Hsch. **δέν**, v. δείς.

**δενδαλίς**, ίδος, ὁ, a kind of *barley-cake*, Nicopho 15, Eratosth.10; cf. δανδαλίς.

**δενδίλλω**, *turn the eyes* or *glance quickly*, πόλλ' ἐπέτελλε..δενδίλλων ἐς ἕκαστον Il.9.180; ὀξέα δενδίλλων A.R.3.281.—Ep. word, also S.*Fr*.1039.

**δενδρ-αῖος**, α, ον, *produced by trees*, ἐέρση *tree*-honey, Nonn.*D*.26. 198. **-άς**, άδος, ἡ, *wooded*, λόχμη ib.13.399; χαίτη ib.11. 514. **-ειος**, α, ον, = δενδρικός, prob. in Str.15.1.60, cf. Nonn.*D*. 12.57.

**δενδρεόθρεπτος**, ον, *nourishing trees*, ῥεύματα Emp.111.8.

**δένδρεον, δένδρον**, and **δένδρος**, τό (late δένδρος, ὁ, Ath.Med.ap. Orib.*inc*.7.4), δένδρεον always in Ep. (δενδρέῳ, δενδρέων, disyll., Il. 3.152, Od.19.520), also Ion., Hdt.4.22, and Dor., *IG*4.951.90 (Epid., iii B.C.); Aeol. **δένδριον** Theoc.29.12; later Ep. **δένδρειον**, τό, Arat. 1008, Nic.*Th*.832: δένδρος, τό, nom., *IG*14.1934i3; acc., Hdt.6.79; gen. δένδρεος *IG*4.951.91, δένδρους Meno*Iatr*.32.53; dat. δένδρει, Ion. -εῖ Hp.*Nat.Puer*.26, Meno*Iatr*.33.4, Arr.*Ind*.7.11: nom. pl. δένδρη E.*Fr*.484.5, Pherecr.130.9, *IG*4.951.121, *PHal*.1.99 (iii B.C.), Ant.Lib.31.5; dat. pl. δένδρεσι Hdt.2.138, Hp.*Nat.Puer*.26 (and so usu. in Att. Prose, as Th.2.75, Pl.*Lg*.625b, cf. Moer.131, and later, as *BCH*12.27 (Mylasa), Str.2.1.14), late δενδρᾶσι v.l. in J.*BJ*6.1.1: indeterminate forms, nom. pl. δένδρεα Hecat.292(a) J., Hdt.1.17, al., E.*Ba*.563 (lyr.); gen. δενδρέων Hdt.1.202, al., *Tab.Heracl*.1.129, al.: δένδρον, τό, first in Hdt.1.193, 3.107, regul. in Att., Lys.7.28, etc., and later Gr. (exc. in dat. pl., v. supr.), cf. Ael.Dion.*Fr*.119:—*tree*: δένδρον ἐλάας an olive-*tree*, Ar.*Av*.617; δ. ἄρκτου, = ἀκτῆ, Ps.-Dsc.4.173; δένδρα *fruit-* or *mast-bearing trees*, opp. ὕλη, timber, Th.4.69; δ. ἥμερα καὶ ἄγρια Hdt.8.115; δένδρα *tall plants*, Id.1.193 (so of rattan, Thphr.*HP*5.4.7; mustard, *Ev.Matt*.13.32); αὖον δ. *stick*, Call.*Fr*.49.

**δενδρ-ήεις**, εσσα, εν, *wooded*, νῆσος, ἄλσος, Od.1.51, 9.200; ἀλωαί Theoc.25.30; νῆσος Jul.*Mis*.352a. 2. *with tree-like markings*, ἀχάτης Orph.*L*.236. II. = δενδρικός, *of* or *for a tree*, πόθος Opp.*H*. 4.270. **-ιακός**, ή, όν, = δενδρικός, *AP*6.22 (Zon.). **-ίζω**, *to be like a tree*, δενδρίζον κουράλιον Dsc.5.122. **-ικός**, ή, όν, *of a tree*, σπέρματα Thphr.*CP*5.18.1; καρπός Heph.Astr.1.22. II. *wooded*, ἄρουρα *BGU*328 i 17 (ii A.D.); ἐδάφη *Stud.Pal*.20.65.13 (ii A.D.). **-ινος**, η, ον, = foreg., *Gloss*. **-ίον**, τό, Dim. of δένδρον, Agathocl.6. II. Aeol. form of δένδρεον, prob. in Alc.44, Theoc.29.12. **-ίτης** [ῑ], ου, ὁ, *of a tree*, καρπός Thphr.*Vent*.13; ὑάκινθος, a gem, Mart.Cap.1. 75; name of Dionysus, Plu.2.675f; Δενδρῖται, οἱ, a fabulous people, Luc.*VH*1.22:—fem. **δενδρῖτις** γῆ soil *suited for planting*, D.H.1.37; opp. ψιλή, *Inscr.Prien*.12.23 (iii B.C.); ἄμπελος δ., = ἀναδενδράς, Str. 5.3.5; νύμφη δ. *wood*-nymph, *AP*9.665 (Agath.): epith. of Helen at Rhodes, Paus.3.19.10. II. δενδρίτης· κροκόδειλος, f.l. in Hsch.

**δενδρο-βατέω**, *climb trees*, *AP*11.348 (Antiphan.). **-γάληνος** οἶνος, a Bithynian wine made from the μερσίτης ἄμπελος, *Gp*.5.2. 10. **-έθειρα**, ἡ, *wooded*, πτυχαί Tim.*Pers*.116. **-ειδής**, ές, *tree-like*, Dsc.4.164.9, *Gloss*. **-κολάπτης**, ου, ὁ, *woodpecker*, *Gloss*. **-κόμης**, ου, ὁ, = δενδρόκομος I, *AP*5.18 (Rufin.). **-κομικός**, ή, όν, *of* or *like a woodman*, Ael.*NA*13.18. **-κομος**, ον, *grown with wood*, ἐναύλεια E.*Hel*.1107 (lyr.); ὀρέων κορυφαί Ar.*Nu*. 280 (lyr.). II. δενδροκόμος, ον, *tree-tending*, Nonn.*D*.47.182, 199. **-κοπέω**, *cut down trees*, esp. *vines and fruit trees*, X.*Mem*. 2.1.13; δ. χώραν *to waste* a country *by cutting down the trees*, Decr. Byz.ap.D.18.90:—Pass., Corn.*ND*30. **-κόπιον**, τό, *tree-cutting*, name of a festival, Herzog *Koische Forschungen* p.133. **-κόπος**, ὁ, *woodcutter*, *Gloss*. **-λάχανα** [λᾰ], τά, *tall-growing potherbs*, etc., Thphr.*HP*1.3.4. **-λίβανον** [ῐ], τό, *rosemary, Rosmarinus officinalis*, Gal.12.67, Aët.1.130, *Gp*.11.15 tit. **-μαλάχη** [λᾰ], ἡ, *tree-mallow, Lavatera arborea*, ib.15.5.6, etc.

**δένδρον**, v. δένδρεον.

**δενδροπήμων**, ον, gen. ονος, *blasting trees*, βλάβα A.*Eu*.938 (lyr.).

**δένδρος**, εος, τό, v. δένδρεον.

**δενδρότης**, ητος, ἡ, *growth of trees*, Suid.

**δενδρο-τομέω**, *cut down trees*, πρὸς καῦσιν Str.14.6.5, cf. S.E.*M*. 5.69: but usu., 2. *lay waste* a country, Th.1.108: metaph., δ. τὸ νῶτον Ar.*Pax*747. **-τομία**, ἡ, *laying waste*, Ph.2.401,548 (pl.). **-τόμος**, ον, *cutting down trees*, Sch.rec.S.*El*.98. **-τρόφος**, ον, *rearing trees*, ὄρη Max.Tyr.31.7. **-φορέω**, *to bear trees* in procession, Artem.2.37. **-φορία**, ἡ, *carrying of trees*, as a religious ceremony, Str.10.3.10 (pl.). II. *bearing, production of trees*, *Gp*. 2.9.3. **-φόρος**, ον, *bearing trees*, φάραγξ Theodor.ap.Ath.14.621b; ἄρουρα *BGU*328 i 17 (ii A.D.): Sup. -ώτατος Plu.*Sull*.12; ἡ δ. (sc. γῆ) Ph.2.582. II. in pl., *tree-bearers*, a guild in the cult of Cybele, μήτηρ δενδροφόρων *IGRom*.1.614 (Tomi, iii A.D.); freq. in Lat. Inscrr., cf. Lyd.*Mens*.4.59. **-φυέω**, *produce trees*, Porph.*Abst*. 2.5. **-φυής**, ές, *tree-like*, *Lyr.Adesp*.84.7. **-φυτος**, ον, *planted with trees*, χώρα Plu.*Cam*.16, cf. *PRyl*.427. II. πέτρα δ. a kind of *agate, with tree-like marks*, Orph.*L*.232.

**δενδρόω**, *turn into a tree*, γυῖα Nonn.*D*.43.234:—Med., ἑὴν δενδρώσατο μορφήν ib.12.190. II. Pass., *grow into a tree*, Thphr.*HP* 1.9.4. 2. *to be turned into a tree*, Plot.3.4.1.

**δενδρ-υάζω**, *lurk, hide in the wood*, Paus.Gr.*Fr*.119, Hsch. II. *dive and remain under water*, *EM*256.4. **-ύφιον**, τό, Dim. of δένδρον, M.Ant.4.20, Dsc.1.108; *toy tree*, Hero *Spir*.1.41, al.; of corals, Thphr.*HP*4.7.2. **-ύω**, = δενδρυάζω II, *IG*4.952.20 (Epid.); cf. δρυάσαι, δρύεται. **-ώδης**, ες, = δενδροειδής, *tree-like*, Arist.*Long*. 467ᵇ1, Dsc.4.164,173, Heraclit.*Incred*.23. 2. δ. Νύμφαι *wood*-nymphs, *AP*7.196 (Mel.). 3. *wooded*, ὄρη Hp.*Aër*.13. **-ωμα**, ατος, τό, = sq., Aq.1*Ki*.22.6. **-ών**, ῶνος, ὁ, *thicket*, Id.*Ge*.21.33, 1*Ki*.31.13. **-ωσις**, εως, ἡ, *growth into a tree*, Thphr.*CP*2.15. 5. **-ῶτις**, ιδος, ἡ, *wooded*, πέτρα E.*HF*790; ὥρα f.l. in A.*Fr*.44.6.

**δενέμωρ**· κροκόδειλος, prob. in Hsch. **Δένθις**· οἶνος (Lacon.), Id. (Pr. n., cf. Alcm.117.)

**δενν-άζω**, (δέννος) *abuse, revile*, τινά Thgn.1211; τέχνην E.*Rh*. 925; ἐπὶ ψόγοισι δεννάσεις ἐμέ S.*Ant*.759: c. acc. cogn., κακὰ ῥήματα δ. *to utter* words *of foul reproach*, Id.*Aj*.243 (lyr.). **-αστός**, ή, όν, *reviled*, Hsch.

**δέννος**, ὁ, *reproach*, prob. in Archil.65 (pl.), Hdt.9.107, Lyc.777 (pl.), Herod.7.104. II. δεννόν· κακολόγον, Hsch.

**δέννω**, = δέω (A), *PMag.Osl*.5.2, *POxy*.2061.

**δεντή**· δέλεαρ, Hsch.

**δεξαμενή**, ἡ, (aor. 1 part. of δέχομαι, with different accent) *receptacle* for water, *tank, cistern*, Hdt.3.9, 6.119, *PSI*1.66 (v A.D.); of the *veins*, Democr.135; *vehicle*, as matter of form, Pl.*Ti*.53a, Aen.Gaz. *Thphr*.p.66 B.; generally, *receptacle*, Ph.1.647, D.C.76.1.

**δεξιά**, Ion. -ιή (fem. of δεξιός), ἡ, *right hand*, opp. ἀριστερά (*left*), δεξιῇ ἠσπάζοντο Il.10.542; ἐκ δεξιᾶς on *the right*, Ar.*Eq*.639; δεξιᾶς abs., *IG*2.733*A*,835; ἐν δεξιῇ ἔχειν τὰ οὔρεα keep them on *the right* as you go, Hdt.7.217, cf. Th.2.19,98, etc.; ἐν δ. λαβεῖν τὴν Σικελίαν Id.7. 1; so Ἐπίδαμνός ἐστι πόλις ἐν δ. ἐσπλέοντι.. on *your right* as you sail in.., Id.1.24; πορεύεσθαι τὴν εἰς δ. sc. ὁδόν) Pl.*R*.614c; ἐπὶ δεξιᾷ τοῦ βήματος Plu.2.192f. 2. in welcoming or saluting (as we shake *hands*), δεξιὰν διδόναι Ar.*Nu*.81; προτείνειν, ἐμβάλλειν, etc. (v. sub vocc.); esp. as a sign of *assurance, pledge* or *treaty*, σπονδαὶ.. καὶ δεξιαὶ ᾗς ἐπέπιθμεν Il.2.341; δεξιὰς δόντες καὶ λαβόντες having exchanged *assurances*, X.*An*.7.3.1, cf. 1.1.6; δεξιὰς παρὰ βασιλέως φέρειν μὴ μνησικακήσειν bring *pledges* that he would not.., ib.2.4.1; δεξιᾶς πίστις μεγίστη E.*Med*.21; φυλάσσειν, τηρεῖν τὴν δ., *PFay*.124.13, *POxy*.533.18:—χείρ is never expressed in Hom., but is used later, χεῖρα δ. S.*Ph*.912, 1254, etc.; φεῦ δ. χείρ E.*Med*.496; χειρὸς δ. ib.899, etc.; τὴν χεῖρα δὸς τὴν δ. Ar.*Nu*.81.

**δεξῐ-άζω**, in Pass., = δεξιόομαι Lxx *2Ma*.4.34. II. Med., *approve*, γάμον *PLips*.41.5 (iv A.D.). **-δωρος**, ον, (δέχομαι) = δωροδόκος, Suid. **-μηλος**, ον, *receiving sheep*, i.e. *rich in sacrifices*, δόμος, ἐσχάρα, ἀγάλματα, E.*Andr*.129 (lyr.), 1138, *Ph*.632.

**δέξιμος**, η, ον, *acceptable, satisfactory* in quality, πυρός *PFlor*.368.9 (i A.D.).

**δεξιο-βόλος**, v. δεξιολάβος. **-γυιος**, ον, (δεξιός IV) *ready of limb*, Pi.*O*.9.111. **-λάβος** [ᾰ], ὁ, *spearman*: in pl., *guards*, *Act.Ap*.23.23 (v.l. δεξιοβόλους).

✱ **δεξιόομαι**, impf. ἐδεξιούμην X.*Cyr*.7.5.38, Ep. 3 pl. δεξιόωντο *h.Hom*.6.16, A.R.2.756: fut. -ώσομαι A.*Ag*.852, S.*El*.976: aor. ἐδεξιωσάμην Lys.2.37, X.*Cyr*.7.5.53, etc.:—Pass., aor. ἐδεξιώθην Pl.*R*.468b: (δεξιά, δεξιός):—*greet with the right hand, welcome*, c. acc. pers., Ar.*Pl*.753, Lys.2.37, X.*Cyr*.7.5.53; *canvass*, τὸν δῆμον Plu.*Cat.Mi*.49: but also c. dat. pers., δεξιοῦσθαι θεοῖς *to raise one's right hand* to the gods, *pay greeting* or *honour to* them, A.*Ag*.852: also c. dat. modi, δ. χερσί *h.Hom*. l.c.; ἐπαίνοις S.*El*.976; δώροις Arist.*Mu*.391b8; λόγοις χρηστοῖς καὶ ἔργοις Paus.2.16.2; στόματι Luc.*Alex*.41; ὀφθαλμοῖς Lib.*Decl*.4.18: c. acc. rei, πυκνὴν ἄμυστιν δεξιούμενοι *pledging one in* many a bumper, E.*Rh*.419:—Pass., Pl. l.c.; ζῷα δεξιούμενα *with right hands joined*, *IG*2.754.33. II. δεξιώσασθαι· ἐγγίσασθαι γυναικί, Hsch.

**δεξιόπηρος**, ον, *blind of the right eye*, Hierocl.*Facet*.63.

✱ **δεξιός**, ά, όν, *on the right hand* or *side*, opp. ἀριστερός, δ. μαζός, γλουτός, ὦμος, Il.4.481, 5.66, Od.17.462; τὸ δ. (sc. κέρας) *the right* of an army, X.*Ages*.2.9, etc.: freq. in adverb. usages, ἐπὶ δεξιά on or to *the right*, νωμῆσαι βῶν Il.7.238, cf. Hdt.1.51; ἐν τῷ ἐπὶ δ. τοῦ ὀπισθοδόμου *IG*$1^2$.92.55; ἐπὶ δεξιόφιν (Ep. gen.) towards *the right*, Il.13.308; χειρὸς εἰς τὰ δ. S.*Fr*.598, cf. Arist.*Pr*.943b29; ἀπὸ τῶν δ. Id.*Cael*.284b28; ἐν τοῖς δ. *Ev.Marc*.16.5; ἐκ δεξιῶν Hero *Aut*.26.4, *Ev.Matt*.20.21, al.; ἐπὶ δ. χειρός Theoc.25.18; κατὰ δ. χειρός Arat.707; πρὸς δ. Hdt.7.69; εἰς δεξιά Pl.*Ti*.43b; δεξιά as Adv., Plb.3.82.9 (s.v.l.). II. *fortunate*, esp. of the flight of birds and other omens, δ. ὄρνις Il.13.821, cf. Od.2.154, A.*Pr*.489, *Michel*727 (Ephesus); ἀοιδὰν.. δεξιωτάταν ὀπαδόν Pi.*N*.3.8; βροντή X.*Cyr*.7.1.3. Adv. -ῶς Hdn.3.9.12. III. Astron., *northerly*, Cleom.1.1. IV. metaph., *dexterous, ready, skilful, clever*, Pi.*I*.5(4).61, Ar.*Nu*.428, 834, al., Th.3.82, etc.; δεξιὸν ποιεῖν *a clever thing*, Antipho 1.19; Εὐριπίδου δρᾶμα δεξιώτατον Stratt.1; δ. περὶ τὰς δίκας Pl.*Hipparch*.225c. Adv. -ιῶς Antiph.229.2; δ. ἔχειν πρός τι Plu.2.660a; δ. φέρειν *in the right spirit*, Phld.*Lib*.pp.18,41 O.: Sup. δεξιώτατα Ar.*Nu*.148. V. *courteous, kindly*, Luc.*Nec*.13, *Alex*.57; τὸ δ. καὶ ἐπιεικές Gal.14.296. Adv. -ιῶς ib.211. (Cf. Skt. *dákṣiṇas*, Lat. *dexter*, etc.)

**δεξιό-σειρος** ἵππος, ὁ, *right-hand trace*-horse in team of four, which did the hardest work: hence, generally, *vigorous, impetuous*, S.*Ant*.140 (lyr.). **-στάτης** [ᾰ], ου, ὁ, *one who stands in the right file of* the Chorus, Poll.2.161, 4.106.

**δεξιότης**, ητος, ἡ, *dexterity*, esp. of mind, *sharpness, cleverness*, σοφίη καὶ δ. Hdt.8.124, cf. Ar.*Eq*.719, al.; opp. ἀμαθία, Th.3.37. II. = δεξίωσις, δ. καὶ φιλία Paus.7.7.5. III. *courtesy, kindliness* (cf. δεξιός v), Ph.2.30. IV. *fortune, felicity*, καιροῦ Lyd.*Mag*.1.3.

**δεξιό-τοιχος**, ον, *on the starboard side of a ship*, *AB*91, Hsch. **-φᾰνής**, ές, *not reversed* (of images in a mirror), Plu.2.930b; *not producing a reversed image*, κάτοπτρα Phlp. *in Mete*.28.17. **-φιν**, v. δεξιός. **-φύλαξ** [ῠ], ακος, ὁ, *right rear flank man*, Hsch. s.v. οὐραγός.

**δεξίπῠρος** [ῐ], ον, *receiving fire*, θυμέλαι E.*Supp*.64 (lyr.).

✱ **δέξις**, εως, ἡ, *reception*, E.*IA*1182. II. δεξίς, *part of the liver* observed in divination, Hsch.

**δεξίστρᾰτος**, ον, *receiving the host*, ἀγορά B.14.43.

**δεξῐτερός**, ά, όν, (δεξιός) *right-hand of two*, δ. κατὰ μαζόν Il.5.393; δ. χειρί Od.20.197; ποδί Pi.*P*.4.96; δεξιτερά (sc. χείρ), ἡ, *the right hand*, Il.1.501; Ep. dat. δεξιτερῆφι 24.284; rare in Com., Antiph.174.6.

✱ **δεξί-ωμα**, ατος, τό, *acceptable thing*, ὦ χρυσέ, δ. κάλλιστον βροτοῖς E.*Fr*.324.1. II. *pledge* or *mark of friendship*, S.*OC*619 (pl.), D.C.58.5 (pl.). **-ώνυμος**, ον, prop. *right* or *lucky in name*; but simply. = δεξιός, χερσὶ δεξιωνύμοις A.*Supp*.607. **-ωσις**, εως, ἡ, *offer of the right hand, greeting*, Ph.1.478, 2.124 (pl.), Plu.*Alex*.9 (pl.), *Pomp*.79; *canvassing*, φιλονεικίαι καὶ δ. ib.67 (pl.): metaph., *greeting*, τῶν διαστάντων Dam.*Pr*.83. **-ωτικός**, ή, όν, *welcoming, hospitable*, φιλοφροσύνη Eust.782.56.

**δέξο**, v. δέχομαι.

**Δεξώ**, οῦς, ὁ, *Receiver*, Com. name of a corrupt person, Cratin.401.

**δεόμενος**· νόμος, δεσμός, Hsch.

✱ **δέον** (written δεῖον *PSI*4.361.4 (iii B.C.), etc.), οντος, τό, neut. Subst., prop. part. of impers. δεῖ (q.v.):—*that which is binding, needful, right*, μᾶλλον τοῦ δ. X.*Mem*.4.3.8; τὰ δ. Th.1.22, etc.; οὐδὲν τῶν δ. πράττοντες Isoc.3.25; πρὸ τοῦ δ. before *it be needful*, S.*Ph*.891; ἐν δέοντι (sc. καιρῷ) *in good time*, E.*Med*.1277, Plu.*Cim*.17; ἐν τῷ δ. Hdt.2.159; ἐς δέον ἐγεγόνεε Id.1.119, cf. 186; ἐς δ. πάρεστι S.*OT*1416, cf. *Ant*.386; εἰς δ. λέγειν D.4.14; εἰς τὸ δ. for *needful purposes*, or *in case of need*, ἐς τὸ δ. χρῆσθαι Hdt.2.173: hence of *secret service*, εἰς τὸ δ. ἀπώλεσα Ar.*Nu*.859 (parody of Pericles' εἰς τὸ δ. ἀνήλωσα Sch. ad loc.); εἰς οὐδὲν δ. ἀναλίσκειν D.3.28: so in pl., εἰς δέοντα ἀναλωθῆναι Andronic.Rhod.p.577 M.

**δεόντως**, Adv. of δέον, *as it ought*, Pl.*Clit*.409c, Epicur.*Ep*.2 p.36 U., *SIG*615.6 (Delph., ii B.C.), Plb.1.12.7, al., Phld.*Sign*.17,18, Hero *Aut*.11.6, *BGU*1013.29 (ii A.D.), etc.; δ. ἔχειν Plb.9.7.3; *suitably*, χρῆσθαι Orib.*Eup*.2.1, al.

**Δεονῦς**, Ion., = Διόνυσος, gen. Δεονῦσος *IG*12(8).270 (Thasos), also Δεονῦσος *GDI*5644 (Abdera), 5694 (Erythrae).

**δεός**, = θεός, Hsch.

✱ **δέος**, gen. δέους (also δέᾰτος S.*Fr*.328, Cerc.*Fr*.18 ii 4; δείους (written for δέϝεος) Il.10.376, 15.4), τό: pl., v. infr. II:—*fear, alarm*, χλωρὸν δέος *pale fear*, ib.7.479, etc.: distd. by Ammon. from φόβος, as being more lasting (δέος.. κακοῦ ὑπόνοια, φόβος δὲ ἡ παραυτίκα πτόησις), cf. Prodic.ap.Pl.*Prt*.358d; φόβος τε καὶ δ. Hdt.4.115; τὸ δ. καὶ ὁ φ. Lys.20.8; δέει καὶ φόβῳ D.21.124, cf. 23.103; also δέος.. αἰσχύνη θ' ὁμοῦ S.*Aj*.1079; ἵνα γὰρ δ., ἔνθα καὶ αἰδώς Poet.ap.Pl.*Euthphr*.12b; δ. τινός *fear of* a person or thing, Ar.*Ach*.581; δέει τῶν Κερκυραίων μή.. Th.1.26; τεθνᾶσι τῷ δέει τοὺς τοιούτους ἀποστόλους (τεθνᾶσι τῷ δέει = δεδίασι) D.4.45; τρέμειν τῷ δέει τί πείσεται Alex.110.6: c. inf., σοὶ δ' οὐ δ. ἔστ' ἀπολέσθαι Il.12.246: folld. by μή with subj., οὐχὶ δ. μή σε φιλήσῃ Ar.*Ec*.650; μέγα τὸ δ. ἐγένετο μή.. Th.3.33; δέος ἴσχετε μηδέν, ὅσ' αὐδῶ S.*OC*223; ἀδεὲς δ. δεδιέναι *to fear* where no fear is, Pl.*Smp*.198a; πρὸς δέους λαβεῖν τι Plu.*Flam*.7; of *reverence*, A.*Pers*.703. II. *reason for fear*, Il.1.515; *means of inspiring fear*, δ. δεινότερον Th.3.45: rarely in pl., δέη ἐπιπέμπει πολλὰ ὁ θεός Lys.6.20; δέα ποικίλα Ael.*NA*8.10; also δέατα Hecat.364 J. (δϝεγ-ος, cf. δεινός, Skt. *dveṣṭi* 'hate'.)

**δεπάζω**, etym. of δέπαστρον, *EM*443.56.

✱ **δέπας**, αος, τό, dat. δέπᾳ Od.10.316: pl. nom. δέπᾰ 15.466, etc.; δέπατα dub. in *IG*12(3).450a1 (Thera): Ep. dat. δεπάεσσι Il.1.471, δέπασσι 15.86:—*beaker, goblet*, Od.10.316, etc.; δ. ἀμφικύπελλον Il.1.584, al.; δ. χρυσείοις ἤλοισι πεπαρμένον 11.632; δ. σκύπφειον Stes.7; δ. ἐκ κεράμοιο *APl*.4.333 (Antiphil.); of the golden *bowl* in which the sun floated back from West to East during the night, Stes.8.1, Pherecyd.18(a) J.; δ. Ἡφαιστοτυκές A.*Fr*.69 (lyr.).

**δεπαστραῖος**, α, ον, *in* or *of a cup*, Lyc.489.

**δέπαστρον**, τό, = δέπας, Antim.21, cf. 15 (pl.), *Carm.Pop*.41.8.

**δέρα**, v. δειρή.

**δερ-άγχη**, ἡ, (δέρη) *collar*, *AP*6.109.3 (Antip.). ✱ **-αγχής**, ές, *throttling*, πάγαι ib.107 (Phil.).

✱ **δέραιον**, τό, *necklace*, E.*Ion*1431 (pl.), Men.*Epit*.86 (pl.), Satyr.*Vit.Eur.Fr*.39 vii 14 (pl.); *collar*, X.*Cyn*.6:—the form **δεραιοί** is given by Hsch.

✱ **δεραιοπέδη**, ἡ, *collar*, *AP*6.14 (Antip. Sid.), 9.76 (Antip.).

**Δεραμῖτις**, ἡ, epith. of Athena, *Schwyzer* 196 (Crete).

**δέρας**, ατος, τό, = δέρος (q.v.).

✱ **δερβιστήρ**, = δέρος, *EM*257.52 (δερϝ-, cf. δειρή).

**δέργ-μα**, ατος, τό, (δέρκομαι) *look, glance*, κυανοῦν λεύσσων δέργμα δράκοντος looking the *look* of.., A.*Pers*.82, cf. E.*Med*.187, etc. II. *thing seen, sight*, Orph.*L*.339. **-μός**, ὁ, = foreg., Hsch.

**δέρεθρον**· λίμνη ἀποχώρησιν ἔχουσα, Hsch.; cf. βάραθρον, ζέρεθρον.

**δέρϝα**, δέρη, v. δειρή.

**δερίαι**· λοιδορίαι, Hsch. **δερίπιον**· φλοιόν, Id.

**δέρις**, ιος, ἡ, = δέρη, Alciphr.1.28, Hsch. II. = δέρρις, Poll.2.235.

✱ **δεριστήρ**, ῆρος, ὁ, *horse-collar*, Hsch.: **δεριστής**· κυνάγχης περιαυχένιος, Id. (δερρ- cod.)

**δερκευνής**, ές, *sleeping with the eyes open*, Nic.*Al*.67.

**δερκιάομαι**, poet. for δέρκομαι, Hes.*Th*.911.

✱ **δέρκομαι** (Act. only in Hsch.), Il.11.37, etc.: impf. ἐδερκόμην, Ep. δερκέσκετο Od.5.158: fut. δέρξομαι Androm.ap.Gal.6.37: pf. in pres. sense δέδορκα Il.22.95, Pi.*O*.1.94, A.*Th*.103 (lyr.), etc.; also later Prose, Arist.*Phgn*.808a4, Luc.*Herm*.20, *Icar*.6, 14: aor. ἔδρᾰκον Od.10.197, A.*Eu*.34, E.*HF*951 (never in S.): aor. part. Pass. δρακείς Pi.*P*.2.20, *N*.7.3; ἐδέρχθην A.*Pr*.547 (lyr.); δέρχθη S.*Aj*.425 (lyr.), imper. δέρχθητε A.*Pr*.93 (lyr.), part. δερχθείς S.*Fr*.837; later in med. forms δέρξατο *APl*.4.166 (Even.), ἐδρακόμην *AP*7.224:—*see clearly, see*, Il.17.675; part. δερκόμενος *having sight*, opp. τυφλός, S.*OT*454, cf. *El*.66: hence, *alive, living*, ζῶντος καὶ ἐπὶ χθονὶ δερκομένοιο Il.1.88, cf. Od.16.439; δρακεῖσ' ἀσφαλές *since she lives* in safety, Pi.*P*.2.20; ἀλαοῖσι καὶ δεδορκόσι A.*Eu*.322 (lyr.); δεδορκότ' S.*El*.66: freq. with neut. Adj., δεινόν, σμερδαλέον δ., *look* terrible, Il.3.342, 22.95, etc.; δεινὰ.. ὀφθαλμοῖς δρακεῖν A.*Eu*.34; φόνια δ. Ar.*Ra*.1337 (lyr.): c. acc. cogn., πῦρ ὀφθαλμοῖσι δεδορκώς *flashing* fire from his eyes, Od.19.446; Ἄρη δεδορκότων A.*Th*.53; but σκότον δεδ. *blind*, E.*Ph*.377. 2. c. acc. objecti, *look on* or *at*, Il.13.86, etc.; τί.. ἥδιον δρ.; A.*Ag*.602; ἐδέρχθης ὀλιγοδρανίαν Id.*Pr*.547; so δ. εἴς τινα Hes.*Sc*.169, E.*HF*951; κατά τι A.*Pr*.679; *descry, perceive*, Od.10.197, E.*Andr*.545; κτύπον δέδορκα A.*Th*.103 (lyr.). b. *look with favour on*, of Destiny, Pi.*P*.3.85. II. of light, *flash, gleam*, like the eye, δέδορκεν φάος, φέγγος, Id.*N*.3.84, 9.41; δεδορκὸς βλέπειν to be *keen-eyed*, Chrysipp.*Stoic*.3.198; τὸ σφοδρὸν καὶ δεδορκός Plu.2.15b. (Cf. Skt. *dadárśa* 'have seen', *dṛṣṭás* 'seen'; prop. not merely of *sight*, but of *sharp sight*, cf. A.*Supp*.409, S.*Aj*.85.—Poet. and later Prose.)

**δερκύλλειν**· αἱμοποτεῖν, ἄλλοι **δερμύλλειν**, Hsch.

✱ **δέρμα**, ατος, τό, (δέρω) *skin, hide*, συὸς Il.9.548, al.; κριοῦ Pi.*P*.4

161; δ. αἴγειον *PEdgar* 11.8 (iii B.C.), etc.; λέοντος a lion's *skin* for a cloak, Il.10.23; κελαινόν, of a shield, 6.117; of *skins prepared for bags, bottles*, etc., Od.2.291; of *a man's skin*, Il.16.341, Od.13.431, Pl.*Phd*.98d, etc.; of *a man's skin* stripped off, Hdt.4.64, 5.25; παλαιὸν δ. A.*Fr*.275.4; περὶ τῷ δ. δέδοικα Ar.*Eq*.27, cf. *Pax* 746; ἀνὴρ κατὰ δέρμα θαυμαστὸς οἷος Aristid.*Or*.51(27).38; of *the shell* of a tortoise, Ar.*V*.429, 1292. 2. *skin* of fruits, Thphr.*HP* 4.14.10; περικαρπίων δέρματα *outer coverings* of seed-vessels, ib.1.2.6. 3. *wallet, scrip*, Hsch.

⊕ **δερμᾰτ-ηρά**, ἡ, *tax on hides*, *PPetr*.3 p.66 (iii B.C.). ⊕ **-ίκιον**, τό, prob. written for δελμ-, *PTeb*.413 (ii/iii A.D.), etc. **-ικός**, ή, όν, *of skin, like skin*, ὑμήν Arist.*HA* 495$^{a}$8; of the wings of insects, Id.*PA* 682$^{b}$19; σκέπη Id.*GA* 719$^{b}$5. II. δερματικόν (sc. ἀργύριον), τό, the *money received for the sale of the hides* of sacrificial animals, *IG* 2.741, Lycurg.*Fr*.1. III. v. δαλματικόν. **-ινος**, η, ον, *of skin, leathern*, ἠρτύναντο δ' ἐρετμὰ τροποῖς ἐν δ. Od.4.782; ἀσπίς Hdt. 7.79; ὑμήν Arist.*Fr*.335; πλοῖα Str.16.4.19; ζώνη *Ev.Marc*.1.6; ὑποδήματα *IG* 5(1).1390.23 (Andania, i B.C.); τεύχη *Inscr.Prien*.114. 11,30 (i B.C.); ὄγκος Ph.1.100; χιτών (of the human skin), Porph. *Abst*.2.46. ⊕ **-ιον**, τό, Dim. of δέρμα, Pl.*Erx*.400a, Arist.*Phgn*. 807$^{b}$18.

**δερμᾰτο-μᾰλάκτης**, ου, ὁ, *currier*, Sch.Pl.*Grg*.517e. **-πτερος**, ον, *with wings of skin*, of the bat, Ar.Byz.*Epit*.120.7.

**δερμᾰτουργικός**, ή, όν, *of* or *for tanning*, Pl.*Plt*.280c.

**δερμᾰτο-φᾰγέω**, *eat skin and all*, Str.16.4.17. **-φορέω**, *wear a skin* or *hide*, Sch.A.R.1.324. **-φόρος**, ον, *clothed in skins*, Str.16. 4.17. **-χίτων** [ῐ], ωνος, ὁ, *wearing a leathern jerkin*, Sch.Lyc.634.

**δερμᾰτόω**, in Pass., *to be turned into hide*, Hsch. s.v. ἰσχαλωμέναι.

**δερμᾰτώδης**, ες, *like skin*, κάλυμμα, φλέψ, Arist.*HA* 505$^{a}$7, 513$^{b}$8; opp. σαρκώδης, Thphr.*HP* 4.3.4 (Comp.); ἐπιφύσεις Gal.2.615, cf. Aët.16.1; *leathery*, Xenocr.29.

**δέρμη**· ὁδός, Hsch.

**δερμηστής** (-ιστής Hsch.), οῦ, ὁ, (δέρμα, ἔδω) *worm which eats skin* or *leather*, S.*Fr*.449, Lys.*Fr*.104S., Aristid.Mil.29; = ὄφις, Aristarch. ap.Harp.

**δέρμητες**· οἱ ἐξ ἐφήβων (ἐφ' ἡμῶν cod.) περισσοί, Hsch.

**δερμό-πτερος**, ον, *with membranous wings*, as a bat, τὰ δ. Arist. *HA* 487$^{b}$22, 490$^{a}$7, Ael.*NA* 11.37. **-τῠλον**, τό (-τοιλον Pap.), *leather cushion*, *PLond*.5.1790 (v/vi A.D.).

**δερμύλλω**, = φλάω, Sch.Ar.*Nu*.734; cf. δερκύλλειν.

**δέρξις**, εως, ἡ, *sense of sight*, Orac.ap.Plu.2.432b, Hsch.

**δεροεργής**, ές, *tanning*, Man.4.320.

**δέρον**, v. δέρω.

**δέρος** and **δέρας**, τό, poet. and Ion. (δέρας *GDI* iv p.875 (Chios)) for δέρμα, only nom. and acc. (exc. gen. δέρατος or δέρους in D.S.4.56): δέρος S.*Fr*.11, E.*Med*.5 cod. L, *Ph*.1120, *Ion* 995, A.R.1.245, al., Epic. in *Arch.Pap*.7.3; δέρας E.*Med*.480 codd. plures, *Ba*.835.

**δέρρη**, v. δειρή.

**δερρῐδόγομφος**, ον, *with screens fastened upon them*, πύλαι Com. *Adesp*.858.

**δέρριον**· τρίχινον σακίον, Hsch.

⊕ **δέρρις**, εως, ἡ, (Att. form of *δέρσις, cf. δέρω) *skin*, δ. τριχίνη Lxx *Za*.13.4, cf. *AP* 12.33 (Mel.). II. *leathern covering*, of a jerkin, Eup.328; of a curtain, Pl.Com.240, Myrtil.1. III. in pl. (sg., Ph.*Bel*.95.34), *screens of skin* or *hide*, hung before fortifications to deaden the enemy's missiles, Th.2.75, Cic.*Att*.4.19.1, D.S.20.9, Apollod.*Poliorc*.142.2, Polyaen.3.11.13: generally, *curtain*, Lxx *Ex*. 26.7, al., *IG* 5(1).1390.35 (Andania, i B.C.).

**δερρίσκος**, ὁ, Dim. of foreg., *IG* 2.678*B* 73.

**δερτόν**, τό, *flayed sheep*, *SIG* 1024.25 (Myconos); cf. δαρτός.

**δέρτρον**, τό, (δέρω) = ἐπίπλους, *caul* or *membrane which contains the bowels*, χολάδας δέρτροισι καλύψεις Antim.45, cf. Hp.*Epid*.5.26; γῦπε ..δέρτρον ἔσω δύνοντες even to *the bowels*, Od.11.579. II. in Od. l.c., δέρτρον is expld. by Gramm., as *EM* 257.31, etc., of the vulture's *beak*: hence, of *a sharp point*, Lyc.880. III. pl., = τύμπανα, Hsch.

⊕ **δέρω** Ar.*V*.485, Pl.*Euthd*.285c, etc.:—also **δείρω** Hdt.2.39, Ar. *Nu*.442, *Av*.365, Cratin.361: impf. ἔδερον Il.23.167, Ep. δέρον Od. 8.61: fut. δερῶ Ar.*Eq*.370: aor. ἔδειρα Il.2.422, (ἀπ-) Hdt.5.25, (ἐκ-) Pl.*R*.616a:—Med., v. ἀναδέρω:—Pass., fut. δαρήσομαι *Ev.Marc*.13. 9, *POxy*.653*b* (ii A.D.): aor. ἐδάρην [ᾰ] Men.*Mon*.422, (ἀπ-) X.*An*. 3.5.9, (ἐκ-) Hdt.7.26; part. δαρθείς Nicoch.8: pf. δέδαρμαι (v. infr.):— *skin, flay*, of animals, δ. βοῦς Il.23.167: prov., κύνα δ. δεδαρμένην 'flog a dead horse', Pherecr.179; ἀσκὸς δεδάρθαι *to have one's* skin *flayed off*, Sol.33.7; δερῶ σε θύλακον κλοπῆς I *will make* a thief's purse *of* your *skin*, Ar.*Eq*.370: prov., πρὶν ἐσφάχθαι δέρεις 'first catch your hare, then cook it', Eust.1792.45; ἀέρα δέρειν 'plough the sands', Id. 1215.50, Suid. 2. Anat., *separate by avulsion*, Herophil.ap.Gal. 2.349. II. colloquially, *cudgel, thrash*, δέδοκταί μοι δέρεσθαι καὶ δέρειν δι' ἡμέρας Ar.*V*.485, cf. *Nu*.442, *POxy*. l.c. (ii A.D., Pass.): prov., ὁ μὴ δαρεὶς ἄνθρωπος οὐ παιδεύεται 'spare the rod and spoil the child', Men. l.c., cf. *SIG* 1109.91 (ii A.D.): metaph., εἰς πρόσωπόν τινα δ. 2*Ep.Cor*.11.20. (Cf. Lith. *derù* 'flay', Skt. *dṛṇā́ti* 'split'.)

**δεσαύχενες**· οἱ ἀσκοί, Hsch., *EM* 258.28.

⊕ **δέσις**, εως, ἡ, (δέω A) *binding together*, Pl.*Cra*.418e; *setting* of stones, Lxx *Si*.45.11; *tying in bundles*, Hdn.8.4.5; ποδῶν δ., = ὑπόδημα, Ezek.*Exag*.97. II. *complication of a dramatic plot*, opp. λύσις, Arist.*Po*.1455$^{b}$26. III. = δέσμη (prob. of a belt-purse), *UPZ* 121.9 (cf. δεσμός II). IV. Botan., *joint*, Sch.Orib.2 p.743 D.

⊕ **δέσκαλος**, ἡ, dub. sens., ἀσπάζεταί ἡμᾶς..'Αθηναῒς ἡ δέσκαλος *BGU* 332.9 (ii/iii A.D.).

**δέσμα**, ατος, τό, (δέω A) poet. for δεσμός, *bond, fetter*, σιδήρεα δέσματ' Od.1.204, cf. 8.278. II. *head-band*, ἀπὸ κρατὸς βάλε δέσματα Il. 22.468.

**δεσμ-άτιον**, τό, Dim. of δέσμα, Sch.Theoc.4.18. **-ευτήριον**, τό, = δεσμωτήριον, *PTeb*.567 (i A.D.). **-ευτής**, οῦ, ὁ, *one who binds*, Sch.Opp.*H*.3.373. **-ευτικός**, ή, όν, *of* or *for fetters*, Pl.*Lg*.847d. ⊕ **-εύω**, *fetter, put in chains*, *h.Bacch*.17, E.*Ba*.616, Pl.*Lg*.808e; *tie together*, as corn in the sheaf, Hes.*Op*.481; δ. ἀγκάλας *PLond*.1.131$^{r}$426 (ii A.D.); χόρτον *PFlor*.322.31 (iii A.D.); δ. ἔκ τινος *bind fast to*.., Plb.3.93.4, Apollod.2.1.3. II. *lay snares for*, Lxx 1*Ki*.24.12. **-έω**, = δεσμεύω (un-Attic, Moer.122), *Ev. Luc*.8.29, Hld.8.9:—Pass., Diog.Oen.39, Luc.*JTr*.20, Alex.Aphr. *Pr*.1.75, 106; of joints, *undergo ankylosis*, Gal.15.410. ⊕ **-η**, ἡ, *package, bundle*, Test.ap.D.35.34, Alex.117, Arist.*Fr*.140, D.H.3. 61. 2. a *measure* in Egypt, φοινίκων *PFay*.119.4, al.; ἀσπαράγου *POxy*.1212.4 (ii A.D.). b. in Medicine, *handful*, Androm.ap. Gal.13.1033; ὑσσώπου κόμης Ezek.*Exag*.185. **-ή**· ὁδός, Hsch.; cf. δέρμη. **-ημα**, ατος, τό, = δεσμίς, Tz. ad Hes.*Op*.479. **-ίας**, ου, ὁ, *worthy of bonds*, Hsch. (-ίης cod.). **-ίδιον**, τό, Dim. of δεσμίς (= δέσμη 2b), Dsc.*Eup*.2.65, Aët.3.79, *POxy*.1288.9 (iv A.D.), 1130. 29 (v A.D.). 2. *small bandage*, Antyll.ap.Orib.44.23.74. **-ιον**, τό, = δεσμός, *AP* 9.479 (pl.). **-ιος**, ον, *binding*: metaph., *binding as with a spell, enchaining*, c. gen., ὕμνος ἐξ 'Ερινύων δ. φρενῶν A.*Eu*. 332 (lyr.), cf. 306. II. Pass., *bound, captive*, S.*Aj*.299, *Ph*.608, E.*Ba*.226, *POxy*.580 (ii A.D.), etc.; *on leash*, [κύων] prob. in Aen. Tact.31.32; δ. φυγών, = ἐκ δεσμῶν, E.*Ba*.792. **-ίς**, ίδος, ἡ, = δέσμη, Hp.*Mul*.1.78, Thphr.*HP* 9.16.2.

**δεσμόβροχος**, ὁ, *noose*, Man.5.133.

**δεσμός**, ὁ, pl. δεσμά *h.Merc*.157, al., Thgn.459, Hdt 6.91, and so mostly in Trag., A.*Pr*.513, etc., and Pl.*Euthphr*.9a; but δεσμοί A.*Pr*. 525, E.*Ba*.518, 634, usu. in Pl., as *Lg*.793b, al.: both forms in Att. Inscrr., δεσμοί *IG* 2.678*B* 48, δεσμά ib.791.31, the latter preferred by Thom.Mag.p.79 R. (sg. δεσμόν *SIG* 246 ii 36 (Delph.), Att. acc. to Hsch.): (δέω A):—*band, bond, anything for tying and fastening*, as *halter*, Il.6.507; *mooring-cable*, Od.13.100, etc.; *door-latch*, 21. 241; *yoke-strap*, X.*An*.3.5.10: metaph., any *bond of union* or *connexion*, Pl.*Ti*.31c, etc.; of the vowels, Id.*Sph*.253a; δεσμοὶ πολιτείας, of the laws, Id.*Lg*.793b; εἰς τὰ δεσμοῦ *for binding material*, *PTeb*.120.70 (i B.C.). 2. in pl. (never δεσμά in this sense), *bonds, chains*, ἐκ δεσμῶν λυθῆναι A.*Pr*.509, 770; πρὶν ἂν ἐξ ἀγρίων δ. χαλάσῃ ib.177; ἐν δεσμοῖσι S.*Fr*.63; εἰς δεσμοὺς ἄγειν E.*Ba*.518; δεσμοῖς Th.7.82; ὁ ἐπὶ τῶν δ., = δεσμοφύλαξ, Luc.*Tox*.29: in sg., collectively, *bonds, imprisonment*, δ. ἀχλυόεις Epigr.ap.Hdt.5.77 (= *IG* 1$^{2}$.394); οὐδὲν ἄξιον δεσμοῦ Hdt.3.145; ἐν. δ. S.*Ant*.958; ἐν δημοσίῳ δ. δεθείς Pl.*Lg*.864e; ἔδησεν ἑαυτὸν τιμησάμενος δεσμοῦ Lys.6.21: metaph. of moral *bondage*, Porph.*Abst*.1.38, al. 3. *ligature*, Arist.*HA* 495$^{b}$13, al. 4. δ. ἄρθρου in Hp.*Fract*.37 is expld. by Gal. ad loc. as *ankylosis*. 5. *spell, charm*, Iamb.*Myst*.3.27. II. = δέσμη, Pap. in *Philol*.80.341, Poll.2.135, Eust.862.27; ἀσπαράγου δ. *BGU* 1120. 14 (i B.C.); δ. ἀργυρίου Lxx *Ge*.42.27; cf. δέσις III.

**δεσμό-τρῐχον**, τό, gloss on κεκρύφαλος, Hsch. **-φῠλᾰκεία**, ἡ, *tax for maintenance of prisons*, *PFay*.53.6; *service as warder*, *PFlor*. 253 (iii A.D.), al. **-φῠλάκειον** [ᾰ], τό, *prison*, ib.2.100 (iii A.D.). ⊕ **-φύλαξ** [ῠ], ακος, ὁ, *gaoler*, *BGU* 1138.12 (i B.C.), *Act.Ap*. 16.23, Luc.*Tox*.30, Artem.2.60.

**δεσμ-ωμα**, ατος, τό, *bond, fetter*, A.*Pers*.745, S.*Fr*.29 (both pl.). **-ωτήριον**, τό, *prison*, Th.6.60, Pl.*Grg*.486a, D.9.60, etc.; δ. ἀνδρῶν Hdt.3.23: pl., = Lat. *ergastula*, Plu.*TG* 8. **-ώτης**, ου, ὁ, *prisoner, captive*, Hdt.3.143, Th.5.35, etc.:—fem. **-ῶτις**, Hld.8.8: metaph. of the soul, Ph.1.289. II. as Adj., *in chains, fettered*, A.*Pr*.119 (the play is called Προμηθεὺς δ.): fem. δεσμῶτις ποίμνη S.*Aj*.234 (lyr.); Μελανίππη δ., name of a play by E. III. *gaoler*, Cratin.189.

**δεσπόζω**, mostly pres. and impf.: fut. -όσω A.*Pr*.210, al., Ep. -όσσω *h.Cer*.365: aor. inf. δεσπόσαι E.*Alc*.486: 1. abs., *to be lord* or *master, gain the mastery*, πρὸς βίαν δ. A.*Pr*.210; ἄρχειν καὶ δ. Pl.*Phd*.80a, al.: as law-term, *to be the legal proprietor*, opp. κρατεῖν, *PTheb.Bank* 1.15, cf. *BGU* 1187.9 (i B.C.), *PLond*.3.977.32 (iv A.D.). b. Astrol., of planets, *to be dominant* in a nativity, Vett. Val.72.5. 2. c. gen., *to be lord* or *master of*, *h.Cer*.365, Hdt.3. 142, etc.; Ζηνὸς (or Διὸς) δεσπόσαι A.*Pr*.930; δεσπόζοντ' ἐμοῦ E. *Supp*.518; δ. τινός, opp. δουλεύειν ἄλλῳ, Pl.*R*.576a; δεσπόζειν φόβης *own* it, A.*Ch*.188; *make oneself master of*, λέκτροις ὧν ἐδέσποζον E.*Andr*.928: metaph., τοῦδε δ. λόγου A.*Ag*.543. 3. c. acc., *lord it over*, δ. πόλιν E.*HF* 28:—Pass., δεσπόζονται Hp.*Aër*.16; δεσποζόμεναι πόλεις Pl.*Lg*.712e; δ. ὑπό τινος D.S.18.60; πρός τινος Ph.1.337.

⊕ **δέσποινα**, ἡ, fem. of δεσπότης, *mistress, lady of the house*, of Penelope, Od.14.127; ἄλοχος δ., of the wife of Nestor, 3.403; γυνὴ δ., of Arete, 7.347; *mistress* of a slave, *POxy*.49.4 (i/ii A.D.), *BGU* 55 ii 5 (ii A.D.). 2. *princess, queen*, δ. Κόλχων Pi.*P*.4.11; Κύπρου Id. *Fr*.122.14; δέσποιν' ἁπασῶν, πότνι' 'Αθηναίων πόλι Com.*Adesp*.340. 1. 3. coupled with the names of goddesses, δ. 'Εκάτη A.*Fr*.388; Ἄρτεμις S.*El*.626, cf. B.10.117, etc.; δ. νύμφη A.*Fr*.342; esp. as a name of Persephone, Pl.*Lg*.796b; in Arcadia, *IG* 5(2).514 (Lycosura), Paus.8.37.1–10; of Κύπρις, Xenarch.4.21. 4. in Thessaly, simply, = γυνή, Hsch. 5. at Rome, *Empress*, *PSI* 1.76.1 (vi A.D.), etc.

**δεσποινικός**, ή, όν, *belonging to the Imperial household*, *PMasp*.88. 10 (vi A.D.).

**Δεσποσιοναῦται**, ῶν, οἱ, Helots at Sparta *who were freed on condition of serving at sea*, Myro 2.

**δεσπ-όσιος**, ον, = δεσπόσυνος, ὕβρις A.*Supp*.845 (lyr.). II. Subst., = *verna*, Eust.846.13. **-οσμα**, ατος, τό, *act of authority*: pl., δ. Μοιρῶν *decrees* of fate, Man.4.38. **-οστός**, ή, όν, *suited to despotic rule*, of persons, cj. in Arist.*Pol*.1287^b38 (v.l. δεσποτικόν), 1324^b39. **-οσύνη**, ἡ, *absolute rule, despotism*, Hdt.7.102. ⊛ **-όσυνος**, ον, also η, ον Pi.*P*.4.267:—*of* or *belonging to the master* or *lord*, λέχος *h.Cer*.144; δόμοι δ. A.*Ch*.942 (lyr.); μέλαθρα Ar.*Th*.42 (anap.); τὰ δ. χρήματα *the master's* property, X.*Oec*.9.16 (δεσπόσυνα, τά, ib.14.2, Phld.*Oec*.p.24 J.); δ. ἀνάγκαι *arbitrary rule*, A.*Pers*.587 (lyr.); also, = τῆς δεσποίνης, γόνατα Tim.*Pers*.136. II. Subst., = δεσπότης, Tyrt.6.2 (cf. Plu.*Lyc*.28), Anaxandr.41.33 (anap.), *GDI*4334 (Megiste). 2. = *verna*, Eust.846.13.

**δεσποτ-εία**, ἡ, *the power of a master* over slaves, or *the relation of master* to slaves, Pl.*Prm*.133e, Arist.*Pol*.1253^b18, 1278^b32; *of husband* over wife, Ph.1.40, cf. 151. 2. *absolute rule, despotism*, Pl.*Lg*. 698a, Luc.*Luct*.6; δ. βαρβαρική Isoc.5.154. II. *ownership*, *BGU* 1187.32 (i B.C.), *POxy*.67.10 (iv A.D.), Just.*Nov*.2.2*Pr*. **-ειος**, α, ον, = δεσπόσυνος, Lyc.1183. **-ειρα**, ἡ, fem. of δεσπότης, *mistress*, S.*Fr*.1040. ⊛ **-εύω**, = δεσπόζω, Lxx 3*Ma*.5.28, *CIG*3702 (Lopadium), D.C.60.28: c. gen., *enjoy ownership of*.., *PGen*.60.1 (iv A.D.). **-έω**, = δεσπόζω, c. gen., Pl.*Ti*.44d:—Pass., *to be despotically ruled*, πρὸς ἄλλης χερός A.*Ch*.104; σῇ χερί E.*Heracl*.884; δεσποτούμενος βίος, opp. ἀνάρχετος, A.*Eu*.527 (lyr.), cf. 696.

⊛ **δεσπότ-ης**, ου, ὁ; voc. δέσποτα: Ion. acc. δεσπότεα Hdt.1.91, al., Luc.*Syr.D*.25:—*master, lord*, prop. *the master of the house*, δόμων A.*Eu*.60, etc.; ὄμμα γὰρ δόμων νομίζω δεσπότου παρουσίαν Id.*Pers*.169: pl., of a family, Id.*Ag*.32, *Ch*.53, 82 (lyr.); in respect of slaves, Pl.*Prm*.133d; δοῦλοι καὶ δ. οὐκ ἄν ποτε γένοιντο φίλοι Id.*Lg*. 757a, etc.; δ. καὶ δοῦλος Arist.*Pol*.1253^b6, cf. 1278^b35; ὦ δέσποτ' ἄναξ Ar.*Pax*90 (anap.); ὦναξ δέσποτα ib.389, *Fr*.598; δέσποτ' ἄναξ Men. 312.5. 2. *despot, absolute ruler*, Hdt.3.89, Th.6.77; τύραννος καὶ δ. Pl.*Lg*.859a; of the Roman *Emperors*, Ph.2.568, D.C.55.12, Hdn.1.6.4; γᾶς καὶ θαλάσσας δ. *IG*12(2).216 (Mytilene). 3. of the gods, S.*Fr*.535, E.*Hipp*.88, Ar.*V*.875, X.*An*.3.2.13. 4. *dominant planet*, Vett.Val.5.16. II. generally, *master, lord, owner*, κώμου, ναῶν, Pi.*O*.6.18, *P*.4.207; μαντευμάτων A.*Th*.27; τῶν Ἡρακλείων ὅπλων S.*Ph*.262; ἑπτὰ δεσποτῶν, of the seven *Chiefs* against Thebes, E.*Supp*.636; τοῦ ὄρτυγος Poll.9.108.—Not in Hom. (for metrical reasons), though he uses δέσποινα in Od. (Prob. for δεμσ-ποτ- 'lord of the house', cf. δόμος.) **-ίδιον**, τό, Dim. of δεσπότης, Aristaenet.1.24. ⊛ **-ικός**, ή, όν, *of* or *for a master*, συμφοραὶ misfortunes *that befall one's master*, X.*Cyr*.7.5.64; δίκαιον a *master's* right, Arist.*EN*1134^b8; ὑπομένειν τὴν δ. ἀρχήν Id.*Pol*.1285^a22; ἡ δ., = δεσποτεία, ib.1259^a37; τὸ δ. Pl.*Lg*.697c. 2. *Imperial*, νομισμάτια *PFlor*.95.10; κτήσεις *PLond*.2.234.1 (iv A.D.); νοτάριος ib.416.3 (iv A.D.). II. *fitted to rule*, ἀδικία -ώτερον δικαιοσύνης Pl.*R*.344c, etc.; *inclined to tyranny, despotic*, ὀλιγαρχία δ. Arist.*Pol*.1306^b3; δῆμος ib.1292^a16; of persons, *tyrannical*, Phld.*Ir*.p.59 W. Adv. -κῶς, βουλεύεσθαι Isoc.4.104; ἄρχειν Arist.*Pol*.1295^a16: Comp. -ωτέρως Id.*Ath*.24.2. 2. c. gen., *exercising despotic power over*, τινός X. *Oec*.13.5; ἐστὶ δὲ τυραννὶς μοναρχία δ. τῆς πολιτικῆς κοινωνίας Arist. *Pol*.1279^b16; δ. τῶν βελτιόνων ib.1292^a19. ⊛ **-ις**, ἡ, = δέσποινα, voc. δεσπότι Limen.39; acc. δεσπότιν S.*Tr*.407, *El*.597, E.*Med*.17, Pl.*Ti*.34c, Epicur.*Ep*.3 p.65 U.; gen. δεσπότιδος *POxy*.48.7 (i A.D.); dat. δεσπότιδι *AP*6.160.8 (Antip. Sid.). **-ίσκος**, ὁ, Dim. of δεσπότης, E.*Cyc*.267. **-ρια**, ἡ, = δέσποινα, Sch.E.*Hec*.397.

**δέστρον**, τό, part of an axle, Poll.1.145.

**δετέον**, *one must bind*, *Gp*.4.12.16.

**δέτις**, ιδος, ἡ, *torch*, Hp.ap.Erot. (dub.l.), Gal.19.92. 2. *head of garlic* (from being *bound up* like a faggot), Id. l.c. 3. = παλάθη (-άνθη cod.), Hsch.

**δετός**, ή, όν, *that may be bound*, παλάμαι Opp.*C*.4.289. II. δετή, ἡ, *faggot*, καιόμεναι δεταί Il.11.554; *torch*, Ar.*V*.1361; also, *fetter*, and *sheaf*, Hsch.

**δέτρον**, τό, = δέρτρον, Hsch., *Et.Gud*. **δετρός**· μάγειρος, Hsch. (leg. δαιτρός). **δεύασθαι**· γεύσασθαι, Id.

**δευκής**, ές, = γλυκύς, dub. in Nic.*Al*.328; cf. δευκές· λαμπρόν, ὅμοιον, Hsch.

**δεῦκος**, εος, τό, = γλεῦκος, Sch.A.R.1.1037; Aetol. acc. to Sch.Nic. *Th*.625.

**δεύκω**· βλέπω, *EM*260.54; cf. δεύκει· φροντίζει, Hsch. **δευλόν**· πονηρόν, ἀχρεῖον, Id.

⊛ **δεῦμα**, ατος, τό, (δεύω A) *that which is steeped, seethed*, δεύματα κρεῶν *boiled* flesh, dub. in Pi.*O*.1.50; cf. δεύτατος.

**δεῦμαι, δεύμενον**, v. δέομαι.

**Δεύνῡσος**, ὁ, Ion. for Διόνυσος, Anacr.2.11:—from **δεῦνος**, Indian for βασιλεύς, acc. to *EM*259.32: v. Δεονῦς.

**δεύομαι**, Ep. for δέομαι; cf. δεύω (B).

⊛ **δεῦρο** (Aeol. **δεῦρυ** Hdn.Gr.2.933, who read δεύρω in Il.3.240), strengthd. in Att. **δευρί** Ar.*Nu*.323, And.2.10: sts. written **δεῦρε** in Att. Inscrr., as *IG*1².900: late **δευρεί** *Stud.Pal*.10.7.6 (iv/v A.D.). Adv.: I. of Place, *hither*, with all Verbs of motion, Il.1.153, etc.: strengthd., δ. τόδ' ἵκω Od.17.444, cf. Il.14.309; in pregn. sense with Verbs of rest, *to* [*have come hither and*] *be here*, δ. παρέστης 3. 405; πάρεστι δ... ὅδε S.*OC*1253; τὰ τῇδε καὶ τὰ δεῦρο πάντ' ἀνασκόπει Ar.*Th*.666: with Art., μακρὸν τὸ δ. πέλαγος S.*OC*663; τῆς δ. ὁδοῦ ib.1165; τὸ τῇδε καὶ τὸ κεῖσε καὶ τὸ δ. Ar.*Av*.426, cf. E.*Ph*. 266, [315]; δ. ἐλθών Pl.*Tht*.143a. b. later, *here*, τὰ δ., = *sensible objects*, Arist.*Metaph*.991^b30; τὰ σώματα τὰ δ. Id.*Cael*.269^b15; τὰ δ. κακά Max.Tyr.14.7. 2. used as Interjection, *come on!* in Hom. with 2 sg. imper. (δεῦτε (q.v.) being used with pl.), ἄγε δ. Il.11.314; δ. ἄγε Od.8.145; δ. ἴθι Il.3.130; δ. ἴτω 7.75; δ. ὄρσο Od.22.395: later with 2 pl. imper., δ. ἴτε A.*Eu*.1041 (lyr.); δ. ἕπεσθε E.*HF* 724. b. with 1 pl. subj., δεῦρο, φίλη, λέκτρονδε τραπείομεν *come* let us.., Od.8.292, cf. Il.17.120, al.; later in this sense with imper., καί μοι δ. εἰπέ *here now*, tell me, Pl.*Ap*.24c; δεῦρό σου στέψω κάρα *come* let me.., E.*Ba*.341. c. without a Verb, δ. δηὖτε Μοῖσαι Sapph.84; δεῦρο, σύ *here*, you! Ar.*Pax* 881; δ. παρὰ Σωκράτη (sc. καθίζου) Pl.*Tht*.144d; δ. δὴ πάλιν (sc. βλέπε) Id.*R*.477d. d. later, *go away!* Lxx 4*Ki*.3.13. 3. in arguments, μέχρι δ. τοῦ λόγου up *to this point* of the argument, Pl.*Smp*.217e; τὸ μέχρι δ. ἡμῖν εἰρήσθω Id.*Lg*.814d; δεῦρ' ἀεὶ προεληλύθαμεν Id.*Plt*.292c; ἄχρι δ. Gal.15.453. II. of Time, *until now, hitherto*, Trag. (v. infr.) and Prose, Pl.*Ti*.21d; μέχρι τοῦ δ. Th.3.64, Onos.*Praef*.7, *PLond*. 2.358.16 (ii A.D.); μέχρι δεύρου (sic) *PGen*.47.8 (iv A.D.); εἰς τὴν δ. Hld.1.19; ἐξ ἔω μέχρι δ. Pl.*Lg*.811c; δεῦρ' ἀεί E.*Med*.670, *Ion* 56, etc.; paratrag. in Ar.*Lys*.1135; δεῦρό γ' ἀεί A.*Eu*.596.

**δευρόλας**· ὁ ἐξ ἐφήβων Ἀθηναίων, Hsch.

**Δεύς**, Boeot. for Ζεύς, Corinn.*Supp*.2, Ar.*Ach*.911, Hdn.Gr.1.400, al.; also Lacon., *GDI*4417, *An.Ox*.4.325, Hsch.; on a Rhodian vase, *Schwyzer*276a. (Expld. ἀπὸ τοῦ δεύειν τὴν γῆν Corn.*ND*2.)

**δεύσιμος**, η, ον, *fit for watering*, τόπος Sch.Il.12.21.

**δευσοποι-έω**, *dye, stain*, τὰς παρειάς Alciphr.3.11: metaph., Dam. *Pr*.427. **-ία**, ἡ, *dyeing*, Poll.1.49. ⊛ **-ός**, όν, (δεύω A) *deeply dyed, fast*, of colours, δ. γίγνεται τὸ βαφέν Pl.*R*.429e, cf. Alex.141.9, D.Chr. 77.4; δ. σπάργανα Diph.72.2; δ. φάρμακα Luc.*Im*.16; δ. καὶ δυσέκνιπτος Ael.*NA*16.1: metaph., δόξα δ. Pl.*R*.430a; πονηρία Din.2.4; δέος Plu.*Alex*.74. Adv. -ῶς Simp.*in Cat*.253.28. 2. title of play by Apollod.Gel., Suid. 3. = βαφεύς, Hsch.

**δευσορούσιος**, α, ον, (δεύω A, ῥοῦς) *dyed red*, prob. in *PMasp*.6 ii 81 (vi A.D.).

**δευτάτιος** [ᾰ], α, ον, poet. for δεύτατος, Max.350.

⊛ **δεύτατος**, η, ον, Sup. of δεύτερος, = ὕστατος, *the last*, Il.19.51, Mosch.4.65, *Schwyzer*90.3, 92.2 (Argos, iii B.C.), etc.:—prob. f.l. in Pi.*O*.1.50.

⊛ **δεῦτε**, Adv., as pl. of δεῦρο, *come hither!* in Hom. with pl. imper. (exc. δεῦτ' ἄγε Φαιήκων ἡγήτορες Od.8.11), either expressed, δεῦτ' ἄγετ' Il.7.350, al.; or understood, δεῦτε, φίλοι 13.481; δεῦθ', ἵνα.. ἴδησθε Od.8.30: rarely in Lyr., Sapph.60, 65, and Trag., δεῦτε, λείπετε στέγος E.*Med*.894: in later Prose, δ. οἰκοδομήσωμεν Lxx *Ge*. 11.4; δ. ἴδετε *Ev.Matt*.28.6; δ. καὶ ἀκούσατε Arr.*Epict*.3.23.6; δ. πρός τινα Plu.*Cor*.33.

⊛ **δευτερᾰγωνιστ-έω**, *play second-class parts*, Poll.4.124. ⊛ **-ής**, οῦ, ὁ, *actor who takes second-class parts*, Hsch. 2. metaph., *seconder, supporter*, D.19.10, Luc.*Peregr*.36.

**δευτερ-αῖος**, α, ον, *on the second day*, usu. agreeing with the subject of the Verb, δ. ἐκ τοῦ Ἀθηναίων ἄστεος ἦν ἐν Σπάρτῃ Hdt.6.106, cf. X.*Cyr*.5.2.2, etc.; also τῇ δ. (sc. ἡμέρᾳ) Hdt.4.113. **-εῖος**, α, ον, *of second quality*, Dsc.1.49; ἄρτοι *Gp*.2.32.3; βίρρος *Edict.Diocl*. 7.43. II. neut. pl. δευτερεῖα (sc. ἆθλα), τά, *second prize* in a contest, hence *second place* or *rank*, δ. νέμειν τινί Hdt.1.32; δευτερείοισι ὑπερβάλλειν *votes for second place*, Id.8.123, cf. Pl.*Phlb*.22c, etc.:—later in sg., *CIG*2360.29 (Delos), 2759 (Aphrodisias), D.L.2. 133. 2. *secondary action*, Arist.*Pr*.921^b36. **-έσχᾰτος**, ον, *last but one*, Heliod.ap.Orib.46.11.23. ⊛ **-εύω**, *to be second*, οὐδενὸς Plb. 18.55.5; δ. μετὰ τὸν βασιλέα D.S.1.73, cf. Str.8.6.18; δ. τινός *to be next best to* it, Dsc.3.39, cf. Herod.Med.ap.Orib.10.11.3; δ. τινί *to play second to*.., Plu.*Eum*.13, cf. Lxx *Es*.4.8. **-έω**, = foreg., v.l. in ib.*Je*.52.24, cf. Hld.10.6. **-ιάζω**, *play the second part*, Ar.*Ec*. 634. **-ίας** (sc. οἶνος), ὁ, *seconds*, a poor wine made from στέμφυλα, Dsc.5.6, Poll.1.248, 6.17, Hsch.; prob. l. in Nicopho 20. **-ίναρ**, = foreg., Hsch. **-ιος**, α, ον, *of inferior quality*, οἶνος Nicoph.20 codd.; cf. δευτερίας. 2. τὸ δ. or τὰ δ. *afterbirth*, Aq.*De*.28.57, prob. in Paul.Aeg.6.75. 3. = χόριον, Steph.*in Hp*.2.463 D.

⊛ **δευτερο-βόλος**, ον, *shedding the teeth a second time*, ἵππος Hierocl. *Facet*.4, cf. *Hippiatr*.20, *POxy*.1708.10 (iv A.D.); of camels, *BGU* 1088.4 (ii A.D.), etc. **-γενής**, ές, *produced later*, τρίχες Antig.*Mir*. 109. **-γονος**, ον, *second-born*, Aq.*Ge*.30.42.

**δευτερ-οδέομαι** (better -ῳδέομαι), Pass., *to be secondary, produced by repetition*, of numbers, *Theol.Ar*.22; μονάδες Nicom.*Ar*.1.19, cf. Syrian.*in Metaph*.149.23:—hence Subst. **-οδία** (better -ῳδία), ἡ, *secondary series*, *Theol.Ar*.34.

**δευτερο-κοιτέω**, *to have a bedfellow*, Ath.13.584b. **-λεπτον**, τό, Astron., *second of a minute of degree*, Rhetor. in *Cat.Cod.Astr*.7. 194.22. **-λογέω**, *speak a second time*, Lxx 2*Ma*.13.22. **-λογία**, *second speech*, Hermog.*Meth*.27, *Stat*.3 (pl.), Aphth.*Prog*.7, etc. **-λόγος**, ὁ, *second speaker*, Teles p.5 H. **-νόμιον**, τό, *second* or *repeated Law*, the fifth book of the Pentateuch, Lxx, cf. *De*.17.18, *Jo*.9.5(8.32). **-πάθεια** [πᾰ], ἡ, *secondary affection*, Gal. 8.31:—**πᾰθέω**, *have a secondary affection*, ibid. **-ποτμος**, ον, = ὑστερόποτμος, Hsch. **-πρωτον σάββατον**, τό, prob. corrupt in *Ev.Luc*.6.1 (no expl. is satisfactory).

⊛ **δεύτερος**, α, ον, *second*, (perh. from δύο with Comp. termination): I. *next* in Order (with a notion of Time), in Il. (not in Od.) of one who *comes in second* in a race, 23.265; δ. ἐλθεῖν 22. 207; δ. αὖτ'.. προΐει.. ἔγχος *next*, 20.273, etc.; οὔ μ' ἔτι δ. ὧδε ἵξετ' ἄχος no *second* grief, i.e. none *hereafter* like this, 23.46; as Comp., c. gen., ἐμεῖο δεύτεροι *after* my *time*, ib.248; σοὶ δ' οὐκέτι δ. ἔσται no *second choice* will be allowed thee, Hes.*Op.*34; in Att. and Trag. with Art., ὁ δ. S.*OC*1315, etc.; αἱ δ. πως φροντίδες σοφώτεραι *second* thoughts are wisest, E.*Hipp.*436: prov., δ. πλοῦς the *next best* way, Pl.*Phd.*99d, etc.; ὁ δ. πλοῦς ἐστι δήπου λεγόμενος, ἂν ἀποτύχῃ τις οὐρίου, κώπαισι πλεῖν Men.241. 2. of Time, *next, later*, δ. χρόνῳ in *after* time, Pi.*O.*1.43; δ. ἡμέρῃ on the *next* day, Hdt.1.82; δ. ἔτεϊ τούτων in the year *after* this, Id.6.46: neut. as Adv., δεύτερον αὖ, αὖτε, αὖτις, *a second time*, Il.3.332,191, Od.9.354; ἐν τᾷ δ. ἐκκλησίᾳ *SIG*544.20: with the Art., τὸ δ. Sapph.*Supp.*4.11, Hdt.1.79, A.*Ag.*1082, X.*Cyr.*2.2.1: also pl., Hdt.3.53, 9.3; τὰ δ. κινδυνεύσοντας about to run the *next* dangers, Th.6.78; later, ἐκ δευτέρου for *the second time*, *Ev.Marc.*14.72, Dsc.5.87.10; ἐκ δευτέρης Babr. 114.5, cf. *PStrassb.*100.22 (ii B.C.): regul. Adv. δευτέρως Pl.*Lg.* 955e, Sallust.18, etc. b. ὁ δ. the *younger*, *BGU*592.10 (ii A.D.). II. in Order or Rank (without any notion of Time), *second*, δ. μετ' ἐκεῖνον Hdt.1.31, cf. S.*Ph.*1442, etc.; πολὺ δ. Id.*OC.* 228 (lyr.); πολὺ δ. μετά τι very much *behind*, Th.2.97; μετὰ τὸ πλουτεῖν δ. Antiph.144.9: c. gen., δ. οὐδενός *second* to none, Hdt.1.23, Plb.31. 27.16; δ. παιδὸς σῆς E.*Tr.*618; πάντα τἄλλα δεύτερ' ἦν τῶν προσδοκιῶν D.19.24; πρὸς τὰ χρήματα θνητοῖσι τἄλλα δεύτερ' S.*Fr.*354.5; τὰ ἄλλα πάντα δ. τε καὶ ὕστερα λεκτέον Pl.*Phlb.*59c; logically or metaphysically *posterior*, πᾶν πλῆθος δ. ἐστι τοῦ ἑνός Procl.*Inst.*5, cf. 36, Dam.*Pr.*126, al.; δεύτερ' ἡγεῖσθαι think *quite secondary*, S.*OC* 351; δεύτερον ἄγειν, δεύτερα ποιεῖσθαι, Luc.*Symp.*9, Plu.2.162e; ἐν δευτέρῳ τίθεσθαι Id.*Fab.*24, cf. Jul.*Or.*8.242b; ἱερὸν δ. *of the second class*, *OGI*56.59 (iii B.C.), etc. 2. *the second of two*, δ. αὐτή herself *with another*, Hdt.4.113, cf. *AB*89; ἑπτὰ δ. σοφοί a *second* seven sages, Euphro 1.12; εἷς καὶ δ. *unus et alter*, Hdn.Gr.2.934; εἷς ἢ δ. Jul.*Or.*6.190d; ἕν τι.. ἢ δεύτερον D.Chr.33.7; δ. καὶ τρίτος *two* or three, Plb.26.1.1; neut. as Adv., ἅπαξ καὶ δεύτερον once or *twice*, Jul. *ad Ath.*278c. 3. δ. ἀριθμός number *whose prime factors are odd*, Nicom.*Ar.*1.12. III. as Subst., τὰ δ., = δευτερεῖα, *the second prize* or *place*, Il.23.538; τὰ δ. φέρεσθαι Hdt.8.104. 2. *after-birth*, Dsc.1.48,50. 3. δευτέρα σαββάτου (sc. ἡμέρα) *second day of the week*, Lxx*Ps.*47(48) tit.

**δευτερο-στάτης** [ᾰ], ου, ὁ, *one who stands in the rear file of the Chorus*, Them.*Or.*13.175b. 2. in pl., *soldiers in the rear rank*, Arr.*Alan.*17. **-στολιστής**, οῦ, ὁ, στολιστής (q. v.) *of the second class*, *PTeb.*313.5 (iii A.D.).

**δευτεροστρᾰτηλᾰτιανοί**, οἱ, = Lat. *Comitatenses*, Lyd.*Mag.*2.7.

**δευτερο-τᾰγής**, ές, *in the second series*, Nicom.*Ar.*1.13. **-τόκος**, ον, *bearing a second time*, Arist.*HA*546ᵃ12.

**δευτερ-ουργής**, ές, *vamped up, second-hand*, χλαῖνα Poll.7. 77. **-ουργός**, όν, *working in the second place, secondary*, opp. πρωτουργός, κινήσεις Pl.*Lg.*897a, cf. Iamb.*Myst.*3.1: but, II. Subst. δευτερουργός, ὁ, *one who vamps up old clothes*, Poll.7.77. **-οῦχος**, ον, = τὰ δευτερεῖα ἔχων, Lyc.204.

**δευτερό-φωνος**, ον, *speaking after one*, of Echo, Nonn.*D.*2.119. **-χύται** [ῠ], αἱ, *wine from the second pressing*, *PFlor.*178.2 (iii A.D.).

⊛ **δευτερ-όω**, *do the second time*: *repeat*, λόγον Lxx*Si.*7.14, al. 2. *change*, ὁδόν ib.*Je.*2.36. II. δ. τινί *to give* one *a second blow*, ib. 1*Ki.*26.8: c. acc., τινά *slay*, ib.3*Ki.*21(20).20. III. intr., *occur twice*, ib.*Ge.*41.32. **-ωδέομαι, -ωδία**, v. δευτεροδέομαι, -οδία. **-ωμα**, ατος, τό, *repetition*, Eust.80.10. **-ωσις**, εως, ἡ, *second rank* or *course*, Lxx4*Ki.*23.4. II. *Jewish traditions*, Just.*Nov.*146.1.2.

⊛ **δευτήρ**, ῆρος, ὁ, *kettle, cauldron*, Demiopr.ap.Poll.10.105; cf. δεῦμα.

⊛ **δεύω** (A), impf. ἔδευον, Ep. δεῦον, Ion. δεύεσκον, Od.8.522, Il.13. 655, Od.7.260: fut. δεύσω Eub.90.4: aor. ἔδευσα Eup.332, Pl.Com. 173.9, S.*Aj.*376 (lyr.):—Med., Od.5.53:—Pass., ib.6.44, etc.: fut. δεύσομαι (ἀνα-) Gal.10.867: aor. ἐδεύθην Hp.*Ulc.*11, Thphr.*HP*9.9. 1: pf. δέδευμαι E.*Fr.*467.5, Pl.*Lg.*782c, X.*Cyr.*6.2.28:—*wet, drench*, δεῦε δὲ γαῖαν (sc. αἷμα) Il.13.655, cf. 23.220; γλάγος ἄγγεα δεύει 2. 471; δάκρυ δ' ἔδευε.. παρειάς Od.8.522; σπογγιὰν δεύων Hp.*Loc. Hom.*12: c. dat. modi, εἵματα δ' αἰεὶ δάκρυσι δεύεσκον Od.7.260:—Pass., δεύοντο δὲ δάκρυσι κόλποι Il.9.570; αἵματι δὲ χθὼν δεύετο 17. 361; χρίμασι δευόμενοι Xenoph.3.6; μέλιτι καρποὶ δεδευμένοι Pl.*Lg.* l. c.; *to be flooded* with light, ἀργεῖ δεύεται αὐγῇ Emp.21.4; ῥίζα ὄξει δευθεῖσα *steeped* in.., Thphr. l. c.:—Med., πυκινὰ πτερὰ δεύεται ἅλμῃ *wets his* wings in the brine, Od.5.53, cf. E.*Alc.*184: rarely c. gen. modi, αἵματος ἔδευσε γαῖαν Id.*Ph.*674 (lyr.). 2. *mix* a dry mass *with liquid*, so as to make it fit to knead, Ar.*Fr.*271; δεῦσαι καὶ μάξαι X.*Oec.*10.11; ἄρτον ὕδατι δεδευμένον Id.*Cyr.*6.2.28; ἀλφίτοις δ. *knead up* with meal, D.H 7.72. 3. *smear*, δᾶδας πίττῃ δεδευμένας Hdn.8. 4.11:—Med., ἀμφὶ μελαίνῃ δευόμεναι σποδιῇ πλόκαμον *AP*7.10. II. causal, *make to flow, shed*, ἐρεμνὸν αἷμ' ἔδευσα S.*Aj.*376 (lyr.).

⊛ **δεύω** (B), Aeol. and Ep. form of δέω (B), *miss, want*, Act. used by Hom. only in aor., ἐδεύησεν δ' οἰήϊον ἄκρον ἱκέσθαι *he missed, failed* in reaching it, Od.9.483,540: δεύει, = δεῖ, *IG*12(2).526*A* 19 (Eresus); δεύοντος Alc.*Oxy.*1788.15 ii 3. II. Dep. **δεύομαι**, fut. δευήσομαι Od.6.192, = Att. δέομαι, *feel the want* or *loss of, be without*, θυμοῦ δευόμενος *reft of* life, Il.3.294, 20.472; *stand in need of*, βάκτρου E.*Tr.* 276; ἐν καιροῖς ἐπιμελήτας δευομένοις *IG*12(2).243 (Mytilene); αἴ κέ τινος δεύωνται ib.15.26; ἐδεύετο ἤματος ὥρη.. νέεσθαι the time of day *required* her to return, A.R.3.1138. 2. *to be wanting, deficient in*, δ. πολέμοιο Il.13.310 μάχης ἄρα πολλὸν ἐδεύεο 17.142: abs., δευόμενος *in need*, 22.492; τετράκις εἰς ἑκατὸν δεύοιτό κεν *it would fall short*.., A.R.2.974. 3. c. gen. pers., *to be inferior to*, ἄλλα τε πάντα δεύεαι Ἀργείων Il.23.484; οὔ τευ δευόμενον Od.4.264.

**δεφιδασταί**, οἱ, guild of fullers, *IG*4.608 (Argos).

**δέφῡρα**, ἡ, Cret., = γέφυρα, *GDI*5000 (Gortyn).

**δέφω**, *soften* by working with the hand: δ. ἑαυτόν, sens. obsc., = Lat. *masturbari*, Eub.120.5:—Med., Ar.*Eq.*24, *Pax*290.

**δεχάμμᾰτος**, ον, (δέκα, ἅμμα) *with ten meshes*, X.*Cyn.*10.2.

**δεχάς**, άδος, ἡ, *receptacle*, coined by Pythag. to expl. δεκάς, Ph.2. 184, *Theol.Ar.*59, Ascl.*in Metaph.*38.31, etc.

**δέχαται**, v. δέχομαι.

⊛ **δεχεπτά**, *seventeen*, J.*BJ*5.11.4.

**δεχήμερος**, ον, *for ten days, lasting ten days*, θυσία Pl.*Ep.*349d; ἐκεχειρία δ. truce *terminable at ten days' notice* (or, *renewable every ten days*), Th.5.26; ἀνοχαί Plb.20.9.5; σπονδαί Th.6.7,10; written δεκ- *BGU*312 i 1 (ii/iii A.D.). II. δεχήμερον, τό, *a space of ten days*, Poll.1.63.

**δέχνῠμαι**, poet. for δέχομαι, Orph.*A.*564, Parth.*Fr.*4, *AP*9.553, Epic.in*Arch.Pap.*7.5, *IG*3.1347, Coluth.159, Q.S.12.585: in late Prose, Hld.3.2.

**δεχοκτώ**, *eighteen*, *IG*14.1648.

⊛ **δέχομαι**, Ion., Aeol., Cret. **δέκομαι**, Hdt.9.91, Sapph.1.22, Pi.*O.*2. 69, impf. ἐδεκόμην Hdt.3.135: fut. δέξομαι, Ep. also δεδέξομαι Il.5. 238, also in *AP*5.8 (Rufin.), Aristid.*Or.*28(49).24; δεξοῦμαι *SIG* 360.29 (Chersonesus); δεχθήσομαι (in pass. sense) Lxx*Le.*22.25: aor. ἐδεξάμην Il.18.238, etc., δεξάμην Pi.*P.*4.70; also ἐδέχθην (ὑπ-) E.*Heracl.*757 (lyr., δεχθείς in pass. sense), J.*AJ*18.6.4, (εἰσ-) D.40.14 (Pass.): pf. δέδεγμαι Il.4.107, Pi.*P.*1.100, etc.; imper. δέδεξο Il.5. 228, pl. δέδεχθε *h.Ap.*538; Ion. 3 pl. ἀπο-δεδέχαται Hdt.2.43, al.:—Hom. also has Ep. impf. ἐδέγμην Od.9.513, 3 sg. δέκτο Il.15.88, al., later ἔδεκτο Pi.*O.*2.54, Simon.184; imper. δέξο Il.19.10, pl. δέχθε A.R.4.1554; inf. δέχθαι E.*R.*525; part. δέγμενος Il.18.524 (also δέχμενος Hsch.); also a 3 pl. pres. δέχαται Il.12.147; cf. προτίδεγμαι, and v. δεδοκημένος:— I. of things as the object, *take, accept, receive*, etc., ἄποινα 1.20, etc.; μισθὸν τῆς φυλακῆς Pl.*R.*416e; φόρον Th.1.96; δ. τι χείρεσσι Od.19.355; τὸ διδόμενον παρά τινος Pl.*Grg.*499c; τι ἐν παρακαταθήκῃ παρά τινος Plb.33.6.2, etc.; δ. τί τινι *receive* something *at the hand of* another, δέξατό οἱ σκῆπτρον πατρώϊον Il.2.186, cf.*IG*12(3).1075 (Melos, vi B.C.), etc.; *accept* as legal tender, ὀδελὸς *GDI*5011 (Gortyn); τι παρά τινος Il.24.429; τι ἔκ τινος S. *OT*1107 (lyr.); τί τινος Il.1.596, 24.305, S.*OT*1163; also δ. τί τινος *receive in exchange for*.., χρυσὸν φίλου ἀνδρὸς ἐδέξατο Od.11.327; *choose*, τι δ. πρό τινος Pl.*Lg.*729d; μᾶλλον δ. τι ἀντί τινος Id.*Grg.* 475d: c. inf., *prefer*, δεξαίμην ἂν πάσας τὰς ἀσπίδας ἐρριφέναι ἢ.. Lys. 10.21, cf. Pl.*Phlb.*63b; δ. μᾶλλον.. X.*HG*5.1.14, *Smp.*4.12; οὐδεὶς ἂν δέξαιτο φεύγειν Th.1.143; Ὀρφεῖ συγγενέσθαι ἐπὶ πόσῳ ἄν τις δέξαιτ' ἂν ὑμῶν; Pl.*Ap.*41a; οὐκ ἂν δεξαίμην τι ἔχειν And.1.5. b. *catch*, as in a vessel, ὀπὸν.. κάδοις δ. S.*Fr.*534.7. 2. of mental reception, *take, accept* without complaint, χαλεπόν περ ἐόντα δεχώμεθα μῦθον Od.20.271; κῆρα δ' ἐγὼ τότε δέξομαι Il.18.115. b. *accept* graciously, τοῦτο δ' ἐγὼ πρόφρων δ. 23.647; of the gods, ἀλλ' ὅ γε δέκτο μὲν ἱρά 2.420; προσφιλῶς γέρα δ., of one dead, S.*El.*443; τὰ σφάγια δ. Ar.*Lys.*204, cf. Pi.*P.*5.86; τὸ χρησθέν, τὸν οἰωνὸν δ., *accept, hail* the oracle, the omen, Hdt.1.63, 9.91; δέχου τὸν ἄνδρα καὶ τὸν ὄρνιν Ar.*Pl.*63; δ. τὰ ἀγαθά *IG*2².410, al.; ἐδεξάμην τὸ ῥηθέν S.*El.*668: abs., δεχομένοις λέγεις θανεῖν σε A.*Ag.*1653, cf. X.*An.*1.8.17; *accept, approve*, τὸν λόγον, ξυμμαχίαν, Hdt.9.5, Th.1.37; τοὺς λόγους ib.95; διδόναι καὶ δέχεσθαι τὰ δίκαια ib.37, cf. *h.Merc.*312; δέχεσθαι ὅρκον, v. ὅρκος; *accept* a confession, and so *forgive*, ἀδικίαν Lxx*Ge.*50.17. c. simply, *give ear to, hear*, ὠσὶν ἠχήν E.*Ba.*1086; δ. ὀμφάν Id.*Med.*175 (lyr.); τὰ παραγγελλόμενα ὀξέως δ. Th.2.11,89. d. *take* or *regard* as so and so, μηδὲ συμφορὰν δέχου τὸν ἄνδρα S.*Aj.*68; *understand* in a certain sense, ὅπῃ βούλει δέξασθαι ταύτῃ δέχου Pl.*Ep.*315c: c. inf., κωλά με δέξαι νυνὶ λέγειν D.H.*Comp.*22, cf. Str.1.3.13, etc. e. *cap* verses, σκόλια δ. Ar.*V.*1222. 3. *take upon oneself*, τὴν δαπάνην Plb.31.28.5: c. inf., *undertake*, *SIG*245.34. II. of persons as the object, *welcome*, κύλπῳ Il.6.483; ἀγαθῷ νόῳ Hdt.1.60; ἐν μεγάροισι, ἐν δόμοισιν, Il.18.331, Od.17.110; δόμοις δ. τινά S.*OT*818; στέγαις, πυρὶ δ. τινά, E.*Or.*47; δ. χώρᾳ Id.*Med.*713; τῇ πόλει δ. *to admit* into the city, Th.4.103; ἀγορᾷ, ἄστει δ., Id.6.44; ἔσω ibid.; εἰς τὸ τεῖχος X.*An.*5.5.6; δ. τινὰ ξύμμαχον *accept* or *admit* as an ally, Th.1.43, etc.; *accept as security*, *PGrenf.*1.33.4, etc.: metaph. of places, τόποι τοὺς κατοικιζομένους ἵλεῳ δεχόμενοι Pl.*Lg.*747e; *entertain*, δείπνοις Anaxandr.41.2 (anap.); δωρήμασιν S.*OC*4. 2. *receive as an enemy, await the attack of*, ἐπιόντα δ. δουρί Il.5.238, cf. 15.745; of a hunter *waiting for* game, 4.107; of a wild boar *waiting for* the hunters, 12.147; of troops, εἰς χεῖρας δ. X.*An.*4.3.31; τοὺς Λακεδαιμονίους δ. Hdt.3.54, cf. 8.28, Th.4.43; ἐπιόντας δ. Id.7.77; δ. τὴν πρώτην ἔφοδον Id.4.126; ἐδέξατο πόλις πόνον E.*Supp.*393. 3. *expect, wait*, c. acc. et fut. inf., ἀλλ' αἰεί τινα φῶτα.. ἐδέγμην ἐνθάδ' ἐλεύσεσθαι Od.9.513, cf. 12.230; also δέγμενος Αἰακίδην, ὁπότε λήξειεν Il.9.191; δεδεγμένος εἰσόκεν ἔλθῃς 10.62.—In these two last senses, Hom. always uses fut. δεδέξομαι, pf. δέδεγμαι, and δεδεγμένος, cf. δεδεγμένος ὁππόθ' ἵκοιτο Theoc.25. 228; δέγμενος is used in sense 3 only, exc. in *h.Cer.*29, *Merc.*477: inf. δειδέχθαι as imper., *expect*, c. gen., βορέω Arat.795, cf. 907, 928. III. rarely with a thing as the subject, *occupy, engage* one, τίς ἀρχὰ δέξατο ναυτιλίας [αὐτούς]; Pi.*P.*4.70. 2. *receive, hold*, τὴν τροφήν Arist.*HA*531ᵃ23, al.; οἰκίαι ἱκαναὶ δέξασθαι ὑμᾶς *SIG*344. 10. 3. *admit of*, ψεῦδος οὐδὲν δ. ἃ τῷ ἀριθμῷ φύσις Philol.11; τὸ μᾶλλον Arist.*Top.*146ᵃ3, cf. D.H.*Isoc.*2. 4. Geom., *contain, circum-*

*scribe*, γωνίας ἴσας Euc.3 *Def.* 11; πενταγώνον Papp.422.34. IV. intr., *succeed, come next*, ὥς μοι δέχεται κακὸν ἐκ κακοῦ αἰεί Il.19.290; ἄλλος γ' ἐξ ἄλλου δέχεται χαλεπώτερος ἆθλος Hes. *Th.* 800; ἄλλος ἐξ ἄλλου δ. Emp.115.12; of places, ἐκ τοῦ στεινοῦ τὸ Ἀρτεμίσιον δέκεται Hdt.7.176. (δέκομαι is prob. the original form, cf. Slav. *desiti, dositi* 'find'.)

**δέψα**, ἡ, *skin, hide*, Suid.

**δέψω**, aor. ἐδέψησα, *work* or *knead* a thing *till it is soft*, κηρὸν δεψήσας μελιηδέα Od.12.48; δέψει χερσὶ [τὸ δέρμα] Hdt.4.64.

**δέω** (A), imper. 3 pl. δεόντων Od.12.54 codd. (v. δίδημι): fut. δήσω: aor. ἔδησα, Ep. δῆσα Il.21.30: pf. δέδεκα D.24.207, v.l. δεδηκότας in Aeschin.2.134: plpf. ἐδεδήκει And.4.17 (prob.):—Med., Ep. impf. δέοντο Il.18.553: aor. ἐδησάμην 24.340, al.; Ep. 3 sg. δησάσκετο ib.15:—Pass., fut. δεθήσομαι D.24.126,131, etc., δεδήσομαι Pl. *R.* 361e, X. *Cyr.* 4.3.18; δεδέσομαι f.l. in Aristid. *Or.* 41(4).7: aor. ἐδέθην D.24.132, etc.: pf. δέδεμαι (v. infr.): plpf. ἐδεδέμην And.1.48; Ep. δέδετο Il.5.387; Ion. 3 pl. ἐδεδέατο Hdt.1.66, etc.—In this Verb, though a disyll., εο and εω are occas. contr. τὸ δοῦν, τῷ δοῦντι, Pl. *Cra.* 419b, 421c; δοῦσα Din. *Fr.* 89.15:—*bind, tie, fetter*, δεσμῷ τινα δῆσαι Il.10.443, etc.; ἐνὶ δεσμῷ 5.386, etc.; ἐν πέδαις (v.l. ἐς πέδας) Hdt.5.77; δῆσε δ' ὀπίσσω χεῖρας.. ἱμᾶσιν Il.21.30; δ. τινὰ χεῖράς τε πόδας τε Od.12.50; δ. ἔκ τινος *to bind* from (i.e. to) a thing, ἐκ ἐπιδιφριάδος ἱμᾶσι δέδεντο Il.10.475, cf. Hdt.4.72; δῆσαί τινα ξύλῳ or ἐν ξύλῳ (cf. ξύλον II.2); ἐν κλίμακι Ar. *Ra.* 619; δ. κύνα κλοιῷ *tie* a clog to a dog, Lex Solonis ap. Plu. *Sol.* 24, cf. E. *Cyc.* 234; δ. τινὰ πρὸς φάραγγι A. *Pr.* 15; πρὸς κίονα, κίονι, S. *Aj.* 108, 240 (lyr.); δεδεμένοι πρὸς ἀλλήλους Th.4.47; δεδέσθαι ἐν τῇ ποδοκάκκῃ Lex Solonis ap. D.24.105. 2. alone, *bind, keep in bonds*, πῶς ἂν ἐγώ σε δέοιμι; says Hephaistos, pointing to the nets in which he had caught Ares, Od.8.352; αὐτὸς δ' ἔδησε πατέρα A. *Eu.* 641; δήσαντες ἔχειν τινάς Th.1.30; δησάντων αὐτὸν οἱ ἕνδεκα Lex ap. D.24.105, etc. 3. metaph., *bind, enchain*, γλῶσσα δέ οἱ δέδεται Thgn.178; κέρδει καὶ σοφία δέδεται Pi. *P.* 3.54; ψυχὰ δ. λύπῃ E. *Hipp.* 160 (lyr.); later, *bind by spells*, τὸ στόμα *AP* 11.138 (Lucill.), cf. *Tab. Defix.* 96, 108. 4. c. gen., *hinder from* a thing, ἔδησε κελεύθου Od.4.380, 469. 5. Medic., *harden, brace up*, Hp. *Off.* 17, etc. II. Med., *bind, tie, put on oneself*, ποσσὶ δ' ὑπὸ λιπαροῖσιν ἐδήσατο καλὰ πέδιλα *tied* them on *his* feet, Il.2.44, etc.:—Pass., περὶ δὲ κνήμησι βοείας κνημῖδας.. δέδετο he *had* greaves *bound* round his legs, Od.24.228. (Cf. Skt. *ditás* 'bound', *dāma* 'bond'.)

**δέω** (B), A. *Pr.* 1006, etc.: fut. δεήσω Pl. *R.* 395e: aor. ἐδέησα Lys.30.8, Ep. δῆσα only Il.18.100: pf. δεδέηκα Pl. *Plt.* 277d:—Med., fut. δεήσομαι Th.1.32, etc., Dor. δεοῦμαι Epich.120; later -θήσομαι Lxx *Jb.* 5.8, Plu.2.213c, etc.: aor. ἐδεήθην Hdt.4.84, Ar. *Pl.* 986, etc.: pf. δεδέημαι X. *An.* 7.7.14, Is.8.22 (the forms δεήσω, etc., compared with the Ep. ἐδεύησα, δεύομαι, point to √δεϝ):—*lack, miss, stand in need of*, c. gen., ἐμεῖο δὲ δῆσε.. ἀλκτῆρα γενέσθαι Il. l.c. (elsewh. Hom. uses δεύω, q.v.); παραδείγματος τὸ παράδειγμα αὐτὸ δεδέηκεν Pl. *Plt.* 277d, cf. X. *Mem.* 4.2.10. 2. freq. in Att., πολλοῦ δέω I *want* much, i.e. *am* far *from*, mostly c. inf. pres., πολλοῦ δ. ἀπολογεῖσθαι I *am* far *from* defending myself, Pl. *Ap.* 30d; πολλοῦ δεῖς εἰπεῖν Id. *Men.* 79b; π. δ. ἀγνοεῖν Id. *Ly.* 204e; π. γε δέουσι μαίνεσθαι Id. *Men.* 92a; also μικροῦ ἔδεον ἐν χερσὶν εἶναι X. *HG* 4.6.11, cf. Men. *Georg.* 25; τοσούτου δέω ἱκανὸς εἶναι λέγειν ὥστε.. Lys.17.1; τοσούτου δέουσι μιμεῖσθαι Isoc.14.17 (also τοσοῦτον δέω εἰδέναι Pl. *Men.* 71a); παρὰ μικρὸν ἐδέησα ἀποθανεῖν v.l. in Isoc.17.42; simply ἐδέησα κινδύνῳ περιπεσεῖν Alciphr.3.5: abs., πολλοῦ γε δέω I *am* far *from* it, Pl. *Phdr.* 228a; τοῦ παντὸς δέω A. *Pr.* 1006; παντὸς δεῖ τοιούτος εἶναι Pl. *Sph.* 221d (impers. πολλοῦ δεῖ, etc., v. δεῖ II.1.b): in part., παλαστῆς δεόντων τεττάρων ποδῶν *IG* 1².373.8; μικροῦ δέοντα τέτταρα τάλαντα D.27.35; the part. is freq. used to express numerals compounded with 8 or 9, ἀνδράσιν ἑνὸς δέουσι τριάκοντα *IG* 1².374.413; δυοῖν δέοντα τεσσεράκοντα forty *lacking* two, thirty-eight, Hdt.1.14; πεντήκοντα δυοῖν δέοντα ἔτη Th.2.2; ἑνὸς δέον εἰκοστὸν ἔτος the 20th year *save* one, the 19th, Id.8.6; δυοῖν δεούσαις εἴκοσι ναυσίν X. *HG* 1.1.5: later, the inf. stands abs., περὶ τὰ ἑνὸς δεῖν πεντήκοντα fifty *save* one, Arist. *Rh.* 1390ᵇ11: part. in gen., τροφαλίδες μιᾶς δεούσης εἴκοσιν Id. *HA* 522ᵃ31; πόλεων δυοῖν δεούσαιν ἑξήκοντα D.L.5.27; ἑξήκοντα ἑνὸς δέοντα ἔτη Plu. *Pomp.* 79. 3. part. δέων, δέουσα, as Adj., *fit, proper*, ὁ καιρὸς οὐκ ἔστι χρόνος δέων Arist. *APr.* 48ᵇ36; τοῖς δέουσι χρόνοις *IG* 12(3).247.11 (Anaphe); ἡ δέουσα ἑκάστων χρῆσις Hierocl. p.61 A., etc.: esp. freq. in neut., v. δέον. 4. δεῖ impers., v. h. v. II. Dep. **δέομαι**: contr. δῆσθε Sophr.46, part. δεύμενος Id.36: fut. δεήσομαι Pl. *Phlb.* 53b: aor. ἐδεήθην: always personal, and used by Hom. only in form δεύομαι (v. δεύω B): 1. abs., *to be in want* or *need, require*, mostly in part., κάρτα δεόμενος Hdt.8.59; οἱ δεόμενοι the *needy*, opp. οἱ κεκτημένοι τὰς οὐσίας, Isoc.6.67. b. *stand in need of, want*, c. gen., Hdt.1.36, etc.; τὰ σὰ δεῖται κολαστοῦ.. ἔπη S. *OT* 1148; ῥώμης τινὸς δ. ib.1293; οὐδὲν δεῖσθαι τροφῆς *have* no *need of*.., Th.8.43; ἤν τι δέωνται βασιλέως if *they have* any *need* of him, ib.37: c. inf., τοῦτο ἔτι δέομαι μαθεῖν Pl. *R.* 392d, cf. *Euthd.* 275d, etc.; τὰ πράττεσθαι δεόμενα *things needing* to be done, X. *Cyr.* 2.3.3; τὰ δεόμενα *necessaries*, *IG* 2.573.4; ἐπισκευάσαι τὰ δεόμενα parts *needing* repair, ib.2².1176.15; τὸ δεόμενον *the point threatened*, Plb.15.15.7; δεῖται impers., v. δεῖ. 2. *beg* a thing *from* a person, c. dupl. gen. rei et pers., τῶν ἐδέετο σφέων Hdt.3.157, cf. Th.1.32, etc.; μή μου δεηθῇς. ΘΗ. πράγματος ποίου; S. *OC* 1170: freq. with neut. Pron. in acc., τοῦτο ὑμῶν δέομαι Pl. *Ap.* 17c, cf. *Smp.* 173e, etc.: c. acc. cogn., δέημα, or oftener δέησιν, δεῖσθαί τινος, Ar. *Ach.* 1059, Aeschin.2.43, etc.: also c. acc. rei only, ξύμφορα δ. Th.1.32; δυνατά τινος Pl. *Prt.* 335e; δίκαια καὶ μέτρια ὑμῶν D.38.2; διαπράξωμαι ἃ δέομαι X. *An.* 2.3.29: with gen. pers. only, δεηθεὶς ὑμῶν *having begged a favour* of you, D.21.108: c. gen. pers. et inf., ἐδέετο τοῦ δήμου φυλακῆς πρὸς αὐτοῦ κυρῆσαι Hdt.1.59, cf. Pl. *Prt.* 336a, etc.; δ. τινὸς ὥστε.. Th.1.119; ὅπως.. Plu. *Ant.* 84: rarely c. acc. pers., ἐδέοντο Βοιωτοὺς ὅπως παραδώσουσι Th.5.36: parenthetic, δέομαι *I pray*, Lxx *Ge.* 44.18.

**δέω** (C), = δήω (A), Alc.102.

**δή**, prop. a temporal Particle (cf. ἤδη), *at this* or *that point*: hence, *now, then, already*, or *at length*: I. in Ep. (rarely Lyr.) sts. at the beginning of a sentence or clause, Τεῦκρε πέπον, δὴ νῶϊν ἀπέκτατο πιστὸς ἑταῖρος Il.15.437; δὴ πάμπαν ἀποίχεαι ἀνδρὸς ἑῆος 19.342; δὴ γὰρ μέγα νεῖκος ὄρωρεν 13.122; δὴ τότε, δή ῥα τότε, 1.476, 13.719, al., cf. Pi. *O.* 3.25, A. *Th.* 214 (lyr.): but usu. second (or nearly so), freq. with Numerals and temporal Particles, ὀκτὼ δὴ προέηκα.. ὀϊστούς Il.8.297; ἐννέα δὴ βεβάασι.. ἐνιαυτοί *full* nine years, 2.134; ἕκτον δὲ δὴ τόδ' ἦμαρ this is *just* the sixth day, E. *Or.* 39, cf. Il.24.107, etc.: also after Advbs. of Time, πολλάκι δή many a time *and oft*, often *ere now*, 19.85; ὀψὲ δὲ δή 7.94; τρὶς δή Pi. *P.* 9.91; πάλαι δή, Lat. *jamdudum*, S. *Ph.* 806; νῦν δή *just* now, Ar. *Av.* 923 (freq. written νυνδή, Pl. *Tht.* 145b, etc.); νῦν τε καὶ ἄλλοτε δή ib.187d; now *at length*, Id. *R.* 353a, etc.; τότε δή at that *very* time, Th.1.49, etc.; αὐτίκα δὴ μάλα this *very* instant, Pl. *R.* 338b, etc.; ὕστερον δή *yet* later, Th.2.17: freq. with temporal Conjunctions, ἐπεὶ δή (written ἐπειδή, q.v.), etc. II. without temporal significance, as a Particle of emphasis, *in fact, of course, certainly*, ναὶ δή, ἢ δή, Il.1.286, 518, etc.; οὐ δή *surely* not, S. *Ph.* 246, cf. E. *Or.* 1069, etc.; δῆλα δή, v. δῆλος; with Verbs, δὴ γὰρ ἴδον ὀφθαλμοῖσι Il.15.488; νῦν δὲ ὁρᾶτε δὴ X. *Cyr.* 3.2.12; καὶ ἴστε δὴ οἷος.. Pl. *Ap.* 21a: less freq. with Substs., σοφιστὴν δή τοι ὀνομάζουσι τὸν ἄνδρα εἶναι they call the man a sophist *as you know*, Id. *Prt.* 311e: with Conjunctions, ἵνα δή, ὡς δή, Il.23.207, 5.24, etc.; ὅπως δή Th.5.85; γὰρ δή for *manifestly*, A. *Ch.* 874, 891, Pl. *Tht.* 156c; οὐ γὰρ δή S. *OC* 265: hence with a part. representing Conjunction and Verb, ἅτε δὴ ἐόντες since they *evidently* are, Hdt.8.90; but ὡς φόνον νίζουσα δή *as though* she were.., E. *IT* 1338, cf. Hdt.1.66, X. *Cyr.* 5.4.4, etc.; and so, ironically, ὡς δή Il.1.110, Ar. *V.* 1315, *Eq.* 693, Pl. *Prt.* 342c, al.; freq. with σύ, ὡς δὴ σύ μοι τύραννος Ἀργείων ἔσῃ A. *Ag.* 1633, cf. S. *OC* 809, E. *Andr.* 235, etc.; also ἵνα δὴ .. Pl. *R.* 420e, *Men.* 86d; ὅτι δή.. Id. *Phdr.* 268d; also εἰσήγαγε τὰς ἑταιρίδας δή the *pretended* courtesans, X. *HG* 5.4.6, cf. E. *Ion* 1181, Th.4.67, 6.80. 2. freq. placed immediately after Pronouns, ἐμὲ δή me *of all persons*, Hdt.3.155; σὺ δή you *of all persons*, Id.1.115, S. *Aj.* 1226; οὗτος δή this *and no other*, Hdt.1.43; ὑμεῖς δὲ κεῖνοι δὴ οἱ.. S. *Tr.* 1091; οὗτος δὴ ὁ Σωκράτης, ironically, Pl. *Tht.* 166a; τὸ λεγόμενον δὴ τοῦτο as the *well-known* saying goes, Id. *Grg.* 514e, cf. E. *Hipp.* 962; δή τις some one *you know of*, Pl. *Phd.* 108c, al.: with possess. Pronouns, τὸ σὸν δὴ τοῦτο Pl. *Smp.* 221b, cf. *Grg.* 508d, etc.: with relatives, ὃς δὴ νῦν κρατέει Il.21.315; τὰ δὴ καὶ ἐγένετο Hdt.1.22; οἷος δὴ σύ *just* such as thou, Il.24.376, cf. Od.1.32, S. *Aj.* 995, etc.; ὅσα δή Ar. *Ach.* 1, etc.: with Adjs., οἴη δή, μοῦνος δή, Od.12.69, Hdt.1.25; ἐν πολλῇ δὴ ἀπορίᾳ ἦσαν X. *An.* 3.1.2: freq. with Superlatives, μάχη ἐγένετο πλείστου δὴ χρόνου μεγίστη δὴ τῶν Ἑλληνικῶν Th.5.74; ἁπάντων δὴ ἄλγιστον S. *Aj.* 992, etc. III. to mark a transition, with or without inference, *so, then*, νίκη μὲν δὴ φαίνετ'.. Il.3.457; τὴν μὲν δὴ τυραννίδα οὕτω ἔσχον Hdt.1.14; τοῦτο δὴ τὸ ἄγος οἱ Λακεδαιμόνιοι ἐκέλευον ἐλαύνειν Th.1.127. IV. with Indef. Particles, v. δήποθεν, δήποτε, δήπω, δήπουθεν: with interrogatives, τοῦ δὴ ἕνεκα; Pl. *Grg.* 457e; τί δὲ δή..; Id. *Phd.* 58c (simply τί δή; what *then?* *R.* 357d); πότερα δή; S. *Ph.* 1235 (and with Advbs., ποῖ δὴ καὶ πόθεν; Pl. *Phdr.* init.; ποῦ δή; πῇ δή; ib.228e, Il.2.339, etc.): with Indef. Pronouns, δή strengthens the indef. notion, ἄλλοισιν δὴ ταῦτ' ἐπιτέλλεο others *be they who they may*, Il.1.295; μηδεὶς δή no one *at all*, Pl. *Tht.* 170e; δή τις some one *or other*, Id. *R.* 498a (pl.), etc. (rarely τις δή E. *IT* 946); the neut. δή τι is common, ἦ ἄρα δή τι εἴσκομεν ἄξιον εἶναι; in any way, *whatever it be*, Il.13.446; τὸ ἱππικόν, τῷ δή τι καὶ ἐπεῖχε ἐλλάμψεσθαι Hdt.1.80; οὕτω δή τι Id.3.108, etc.; θεῶν ὅτεῳ δή *whosoever it be*, Id.1.86; ἐπὶ μισθῷ ὅσῳ δή, Lat. *quantocumque*, ib.160, etc.; οἷα δή γε.. E. *Heracl.* 632, cf. *Supp.* 162; but θαυμαστὰ δὴ ὅσα Pl. *Smp.* 220b; ὡς δή Il.5.24, etc.; so almost, = ἤδη, ἀναπέτομαι δὴ πρὸς Ὄλυμπον Anacr.24; καὶ δή φίλον τις ἔκταν' ἀγνοίας ὕπο A. *Supp.* 499; ἤκουσα δή S. *Ant.* 823; πάθη μὲν οὖν δὴ πόλλ' ἔγωγ' ἐκλαυσάμην Id. *Tr.* 153; οἶσθα μὲν δή ib.627; so καὶ δή *already, in fact*, freq. not at the beginning of the sentence, κεῖται καὶ δὴ πάνθ' ἅπερ εἶπας Ar. *Ec.* 514, cf. *Nu.* 906, Theoc.5.83; but καὶ δή σφε λείπω A. *Supp.* 507. 2. to continue a narrative, freq. after μέν, *then, so*, τότε μὲν δὴ.. ἡσυχίην εἶχε Hdt.1.11; Σόλων μὲν δὴ ἔνεμε ib.32; τὸν μὲν δὴ πέμπει ib.116; alone, εἷς δὴ τούτων.. so one of these.., ib.114, etc.: freq. in summing up, τοιαῦτα μὲν δὴ ταῦτα, Lat. *haec hactenus*, A. *Pr.* 500, cf. Hdt.1.14, Th.2.4; τούτων δὴ ἕνεκα X. *Cyr.* 3.2.28, etc.; in summing up numbers, γίγνονται δὴ οὗτοι χίλιοι these *then* amount to 1,000, ib.1.5.5; in resuming after a parenthesis, Ἀνδρομάχη, θυγάτηρ μεγαλήτορος Ἠετίωνος.., τοῦ περ δὴ θυγάτηρ Il.6.395; οὗτος δή.., ὁ μὲν δή Hdt.1.43. b. with imper. and subj., μὴ δή.. ἐπιέλπεο Il.1.545, cf. 5.684, etc.; χωρῶμεν δὴ πάντες S. *Ph.* 1469; ἐννοεῖτε γὰρ δή for do *but* consider, X. *Cyr.* 4.3.5; ἄγε δή, φέρε δή, ἴθι δή, σκόπει δή, λέγε δή, Pl. *Sph.* 235a, *Phd.* 63b, *Sph.* 224c, *Phd.* 80a, *Prt.* 312c. 3. to express what follows *a fortiori*, καὶ μετὰ ὅπλων γε δή *above all* with arms, Th.4.78; μή τί γε δή not to mention, D.2.23; εἰ δὲ δὴ πόλεμος ἥξει Id.

1.27. 4. καὶ δή and *what is more*, adding an emphatic statement, Il.1.161, 15.251, Hdt.5.67, Lys.13.4; in Prose, freq. καὶ δὴ καί.., ἐς Αἴγυπτον ἀπίκετο.., καὶ δὴ καὶ ἐς Σάρδις Hdt.1.30, etc.; καὶ δὴ καὶ νῦν τί φής; and *now* what do you say? Pl.*Tht.*187c; καὶ δὴ μὲν οὖν παρόντα yes, and *actually* here present, S.*OC*31; esp. in a series, ὑγίεια καὶ ἰσχὺς καὶ κάλλος καὶ πλοῦτος δή and *of course* riches, Pl.*Men.*87e, cf. *Tht.*159c, *R.*367d; εἴτ'.. εἴτ'.. εἴτε δή ib.493d. b. καὶ δή is also used in answers, ἦ καὶ παρέστη κἀπὶ τέρμ' ἀφίκετο; Answ. καὶ δὴ 'πὶ δισσαῖς ἦν.. πύλαις *yes*, he was *even* so far as.., S.*Aj.*49; βλέψον κάτω. Answ. καὶ δὴ βλέπω *well*, I am looking, Ar. *Av.*175, cf. *Pax*327, *Pl.*227 sq., S.*El.*317 sq., 1436, etc.; πρόσθιγέ νύν μου. Answ. ψαύω καὶ δή S.*OC*173; without καί, ἀποκρίνου περὶ ὧν ἂν ἐρωτῶ. Answ. ἐρώτα δή Pl.*Tht.*157d; ἐρώτα. Answ. ἐρωτῶ δή Id. *Grg.*448b. c. in assumptions or suppositions, καὶ δὴ δέδεγμαι and *now suppose* I have accepted, A.*Eu.*894, cf. *Ch.*565, E.*Med.*386, *Hel.* 1059, not found in S., once in Ar.*V.*1224. 5. δή in apodosi, after εἰ or ἐάν, Il.5.898, Hdt.1.108, Pl.*R.*524e, etc.; after ὅτε, ἡνίκα, *even then*, S.*Ant.*170 sq., *El.*954; after ἐπεί, ἐπειδάν, X.*Cyr.*1.6.14, Pl. *Cra.*435e, etc.; after ὡς, X.*Cyr.*7.2.4; ἐν ᾧ δὲ ταῦτα ἐβουλεύοντο, καὶ δὴ ὁ βασιλεύς.. *already*, Id.*An.*1.10.10.

**δῆ·** γῆ, καὶ σιωπᾷ, Hsch. **δηαί,** = κριθαί (Cret.), *EM*264.13; cf. δητταί. **δηάλωτος,** ον, contr. for δηϊάλωτος (q.v.). **δηατάχα·** καὶ φθορὰ δένδρων, Hsch. **δηβοιλοί·** κιθαρῳδοί, Id. **δηγῆρες,** = στρουθοί, Id., Suid., *Et.Gud.*

⊛ **δῆγμα,** ατος, τό, *bite, sting*, X.*Mem.*1.3.12, Arist.*HA*604$^b$21, etc.: metaph., δ. λύπης A.*Ag.*791 (lyr.); ἔρωτος S.*Fr.*841; ψυχῆς cj. in Luc.*Prom.Es* 2. II. = σπάραγμα ὀδόντων, Hsch.

⊛ **δηγμός,** ὁ, *bite, sting*, μυίας Chrysipp.*Stoic.*3.51. 2. *gnawing pain*, Hp.*Coac.*626, Thphr.*HP*4.4.5; of mental *suffering*, *Stoic.*3. 107, Phld.*Mort.*25,35, *Lib.*p.48 O., Ph.1.212 (pl.); of a speech, δ. προσάγειν Plu.2.69a, cf. *Alc.*4: in pl., *painful operations*, Id.*Per.*15.

**δηγοῖ·** πληροῖ, Hsch.

⊛ **δηθά,** Ep. Adv. = δήν, *for a long time*, δηθά τε καὶ δολιχόν Il.10.52; δ. μάλα ib.5.587; οὐ μετὰ δ. not *long* after, A.R.2.651.

**δηθαγόρος,** ον, *prolix*, Hsch. **δηθαίων,** ωνος, ὁ, ἡ, *long-lived*, Id.

**δηθάκι** and **δηθάκις,** Adv. *often*, Nic.*Al.*215, Man.3.22, Opp.*C.* 1.27, etc.

⊛ **δῆθεν** (δῆθε E.*El.*268, cj. in Eup.7.1 D.), Adv., a strengthd. form of δή, ὡς Ζεὺς ἀνάσσοι δ. A.*Pr.*204; ὡς παῖδα δ. μὴ τέκοις E.*El.*268, cf. *Ion*831; τί δὴ ἀνδρωθέντες δ. ποιήσουσι; Hdt.6.138; ἄρτι δ. *I suppose*, Pl.*Plt.*297c. 2. more freq. ironically, *forsooth*, οἵ μιν ἠθέλησαν ἀπολέσαι δ.. *as he pretended*, Hdt.1.59; δ. οὐδὲν ἱστορῶν S. *Tr.*382; οὐκ ἐπὶ κωλύμῃ ἀλλὰ γνώμης παραινέσει δ. Th.1.92, cf. 127, 3.111: freq. after ὡς, mostly with a word interposed, φέροντες ὡς ἄγρην δ. Hdt.1.73; ὡς κατασκόπους δ. ἐόντας Id.3.136, cf. 6.39, 8.5; also κέντρον δ. ὡς ἔχων χερί E.*HF*949; εἴσιμεν.. δ. ὡς θανούμενοι Id. *Or.*1119; θεατὴν δ., ὡς οὐκ ὄντ' ἐμόν Id.*Ion*656. II. *from that time, thenceforth*, *Anacreont.*1.16, Hsch.

**δηθύνω,** pres. and impf. only, Ep. subj. δηθύνῃσθα Od.12.121: (δηθά):—*tarry, delay*, Il.6.503, *AP*5.222.6 (Maced.); of disease, *to be prolonged*, Aret.*SD*1.2; δ. οὔασι *to be slow* of hearing, Orph.*L.* 467.

**δηθυρεῖν·** σχολάζειν, διατρίβειν, Hsch.

**δηϊάλωτος** [ᾰ], ον, (δήϊος, ἁλῶναι) *taken by the enemy, captive*, E. *Andr.*105 (lyr.); contr. **δηάλωτος,** A.*Th.*72.

**Δηϊάνειρα** [ᾰν], ἡ, *destroying her spouse*, the wife of Heracles—her name expressing the legend of his death, S., etc.

**δήϊος,** η, ον, Ep. for δάϊος (q.v.).

**δηϊοτής,** ῆτος, ἡ, *battle-strife, the battle*, Il.3.20, etc.; *mortal struggle, death*, Od.12.257; cf. δανοτής.

**δηϊοῦσα,** = κώνειον, Ps.-Dsc.4.78.

⊛ **δηϊόω,** Ep. opt. δηϊόῳεν Od.4.226, part. δηϊόων Il.17.566; Att. pres. **δηῶ,** δηοῦμεν, -οῦτε, X.*Cyr.*3.3.18, Ar.*Lys.*1146, part. δηῶν Il.17.65: impf. ἐδῄουν Th.1.65, X.*Cyr.*5.4.23, ἐδήϊουν Hdt.8.33,50 (ἐδήευν v.l. in 5.89); Ep. δῄουν Il.11.71, al., δηϊάασκον (as if from δηϊάω) A.R. 2.142: fut. δῃώσω Il.9.243, etc.: aor. ἐδῄωσα Th.1.114, subj. δῃώσῃ, -ωσιν, Il.16.650, 4.416, part. δῃώσας 8.534, al., Ion. δηϊώσας Hdt.6. 135: pf. δεδῄωκα Rh.8.193 W. (Sopat.):—Med., fut. δῃώσεσθαι (in pass. sense) A.R.2.117: aor.1 δῃώσασθαι v.l. in *J.BJ*2.13.2, cf. Q.S.5. 567, Opp.*H.*5.350:—Pass., aor. ἐδηϊώθην Hdt.7.133, δῃωθείς Il.4.417: pf., Hsch., part. δεδῃωμένος Luc.*DMort.*10.11.—Hom. has δῃ-, when ι is folld. by a long syll.: A.R. forms impf. ἐδήϊον (as if from δηϊω) 3. 1374, said by Sch. to be taken from Eumel. (*Fr.*9), cf. δηϊεῖν· πολεμεῖν, φονεύειν, Hsch. (δηεῖν cod.), Cyr., δηΐων· διακόπτων, Hsch., Cyr.: this is perh. a difft. Verb, and δήϊον, δήϊων might be read in Hom.:—*cut down, slay*, χαλκῷ δηϊόων Il.17.566, etc.; ἔγχεϊ δηϊόων περὶ Πατρόκλοιο θανόντος *slaying* [men].., 18.195: abs., δῄουν *were slaying*, 16. 771; δηϊόωντο *were being slain*, 13.675; Ἕκτορα δῃώσαντε 22.218; Κικόνων ὕπο δῃωθέντες Od.9.66. 2. *rend, tear, cleave*, δῄουν.. βοείας ἀσπίδας *were cleaving* shields, Il.5.452, etc.; of a spear, *cut asunder*, 14.518; of savage beasts, ἔγκατα πάντα λαφύσσει δηῶν 17. 65, cf. 16.158; τὸν πώγωνα δεδῃωμένος *having had* his beard *cut off*, Luc.*DMort.*10.11. II. after Hom., *waste, ravage* a country, Sol.13. 21, Hdt.5.89, 7.133, etc.; δ. χώραν Ar.*Lys.*1146, Th.1.81, etc.; ἄστυ δῃώσειν πυρί S.*OC*1319.

**δηϊφόβος** [ῐ], Dor. **δαϊφ-,** ον, *scaring the foe*, dub. in Alc.28:—in Hom. only pr. n.

**δηΐω,** v. δηϊόω.

**δηκτ-ήριος,** ον, *biting, torturing*, καρδίας E.*Hec.*235. **-ης,** ου, ὁ, *biter*, E.*Fr.*555: metaph. as Adj., δ. λόγος Plu.2.55b: with neut. Subst., δήκτᾳ στόματι *APl.*4.266.7. **-ικός,** ή, όν, *biting, stinging*, φαλάγγια Arist.*HA*622$^b$28; τῶν ἰχθύων οἱ δ. Id.*PA*662$^a$31; *pungent*, Diph.Siph.ap.Ath.3.121a (Comp.), Diocl.*Fr.*138, Ruf.*Fr.*68.3, Dsc. 1.105; φάρμακον Luc.*Nigr.*37, etc.: metaph., of anger, Phld.*Ir.* p.77 W.; -κόν, τό, Ph.1.684; ἀστεῖον καὶ δ. Luc.*Demon.*50. Adv. -κῶς Sch.Ar.*V.*937.

**δήκω,** = δάκνω, cj. in Hippon.49.6.

⊛ **δηλαδή** (cf. δῆλος II.4), Adv. *clearly, manifestly*, Epich.149, S.*OT* 1501, E.*IA*1366, Timocl.3 D., etc.: ironically, προφάσιος τῆσδε δηλαδή on this pretext *forsooth*, Hdt.4.135: freq. in answers, οὐ πόλλ' ἔνεστι δεινὰ τῷ γήρᾳ κακά;—δηλαδή *yes plainly, of course*, Ar. *V.*441: but better written divisim in such phrases as ἦ δῆλα δὴ ὅτι..; Pl.*Prt.*309a, etc.; cf. δῆλα δὴ καὶ ταῦτα Id.*Cri.*48b.

**δηλαίνουσι·** παίζουσι, Hsch.

**δηλαϊστός,** v.l. for δείλαιος, LXX*Ez.*5.15, cf. Hsch.

**δηλαυγῶς·** ἄγαν φανερῶς, Hsch.

**δηλ-έομαι** (A), Dor. **δᾱλ-** Theoc.15.48: fut. -ήσομαι: aor. ἐδηλησάμην: pf. δεδήλημαι, prob. in act. sense, E.*Hipp.*175 (in pass. sense, Hdt.4.198, 8.100): I. mostly of persons, *hurt, do a mischief to*, μήπως [ἵππους] δηλήσεαι, by accident, Il.23.428; also on purpose, Ἀχαιοὺς ὑπὲρ ὅρκια δηλήσασθαι 4.67; ἥ σε.. ἄνδρες ἐδηλήσαντο *did* thee *a mischief*, i.e. *slew* thee, Od.11.401; μή με.. δηλήσεται ὀξέϊ χαλκῷ (Ep. subj.) 22.368; of the sword, ῥινὸν δηλήσατο χαλκός ib. 278; ἄλλον δηλήσομαι, ἄλλον ὀνήσω *h.Merc.*541; δ. τινὰ ἔργμασι λυγροῖς Mimn.7, = Thgn.795: in Ion. Prose, ἵνα μὴ ἔχοιέν σφεας δηλέεσθαι Hdt.6.36, cf. 7.51; πλεῖστόν σφεας ἐδηλέετο ἡ ἐσθής Id.9.63; τούς.. ποτῷ δαλήσατο Κίρκα Theoc.9.36. II. of things, *damage, spoil*, καρπὸν ἐδηλήσαντ' Il.1.156; so in Hdt., γῆν δ. πολλά 4.115; ἅλμην ἐπανθέουσαν, ὥστε καὶ τὰς πυραμίδας δηλέεσθαι Id.2.12: freq. in Hom. in the phrase, ὅρκια δηλήσασθαι *violate* a truce, Il.3.107, al.; of thieves, μή τις.. δηλήσεται (Ep. subj.) *should steal them*, Od.8. 444, cf. 13.124. 2. abs., *to do mischief, be hurtful*, ἔνθα κε σὴ βουλὴ δηλήσεται Il.14.102: c. acc. cogn., ἠδ' ὅσα.. ἄνδρες ἐδηλήσαντο all *the mischief* they *did*, Od.10.459. (Ep., Ion., and rarely Dor., Theoc. ll. cc.; cf. δάλλει, πανδάλητος, and perh. ἀδαλές.)

**δηλέομαι** (B), only in fut. Pass., δηληθήσονται· θεωρηθήσονται, Hsch.

⊛ **δηληγατεύω,** *assign* as tax to be paid, μέτρον ἐλαίου *PLips.*64.3 (iv A.D.). **δηληγατίων,** ωνος, ἡ, *delegatio, annual declaration by the state of the amount of taxes to be paid*, *BGU*836.3 (vi A.D.), 974.7 (iv A.D.), cf. Suid.

**δηλ-ήεις,** εσσα, εν, = δηλήμων, Orph.*A.*923: neut. sg. δηλῆειν prob. in Nic.*Al.*42. **-ημα,** ατος, τό, *mischief, bane*, ἄνεμοι χαλεποί, δηλήματα νηῶν Od.12.286; ὁδοιπόρων A.*Fr.*123; βροτοῖσιν *h.Ap.*364, cf. S.*OT*1495; τύχης δηλήμασι *IPE*2.197 (Panticapaeum). **-ήμων,** ον, gen. ονος, *baneful, noxious*, βροτῶν δηλήμονα πάντων Od.18.85, al.; ὄφιες ἀνθρώπων οὐδαμῶς δηλήμονες *doing* men *no hurt*, Hdt.2.74, cf. 3.109: abs., of the gods, σχέτλιοί ἐστε, θεοί, δηλήμονες Il.24.33 (in Od.5.118 nearly all codd. give ζηλήμονες): in late Prose, Jul.*Or.*2.87a. **-ησις,** εως, ἡ, *mischief*, μὴ κλῶπες ἐπὶ δηλήσι φανέωσι Hdt.1.41, cf. 4.112; ἀλεξητήριον τῆς δ. Thphr.*HP*7. 13.4; *injury of health*, ἐπὶ δηλήσι Hp.*Jusj.* **-ητήρ,** ῆρος, ὁ, *a destroyer*, Hom.*Epigr.*14.8. ⊛ **-ητήριος,** ον, *noxious*, φάρμακα *SIG* 37 (Teos, v B.C.), cf. *J.BJ*1.13.10, Gal.*Nat.Fac.*3.7, Hdn.3.5.5. 2. δηλητήριον (sc. φάρμακον), τό, *poison*, Hp.*Ep.*19 (*Hermes* 53.69), Plu. 2.662c, Hdn.1.17.10, Lib.*Or.*64.33; τὰ ὑγιεινὰ καὶ τὰ νοσερὰ καὶ τὰ δ. Porph.*Abst.*3.8. ⊛ **-ητηριώδης,** ες, *noxious*, Dav.*Proll.*32. 26.

**δήλιοι·** οἱ ἀδελφὰς γεγαμηκότες, Hsch.; cf. ἀέλιοι.

⊛ **Δήλιος,** Dor. **Δάλιος,** α, ον, also ος, ον E.*Tr.*89:—*Delian*, A.*Eu.* 9, etc.: ὁ Δ., name of Apollo, S.*Aj.*704, Th.1.13; τοῖς Δηλίοις καὶ ταῖσι Δηλίαισι, the gods and goddesses *worshipped at Delos*, Ar.*Th.* 334:—**Δήλιος,** ὁ, *a Delian*, Hdt.4.33, etc.:—also **Δηλιεύς,** *IG*12(7). 50 (Amorgos):—fem. **Δηλιάς,** άδος, ἡ, *Delian woman*, κοῦραι Δ. *h. Ap.*157, cf. E.*HF*687: with neut. Subst., Δηλιάσιν γυάλοις cj. in Id. *IT*1235:—Adj. **Δηλιακός,** ή, όν, χορός Th.3.104; πλοῖον Plu.2. 786f. II. **Δηλιὰς** θεωρία mission *sent to Delos* every fourth year, Philoch.158:—hence **Δηλιασταί,** οἱ, *members of this* θεωρία, Lycurg. *Fr.*80, Herodicus ap.Ath.6.234e, Harp., Hsch. III. Δήλιον, τό, *precinct of Apollo* Δ., Herodicus l.c., *Schwyzer*688 *A* 7 (Chios, v B.C.), etc. IV. Δήλια (sc. ἱερά), τά, *festival of Apollo at Delos*, Th.3. 104, X.*Mem.*4.8.2; also at Tanagra, etc., *SIG*319.16, etc.

**Δηλογενής,** Dor. **Δᾱλ-,** ές, *Delos-born*, Simon.26 B, B.3.58, 10.15.

**δήλομαι,** Dor. for βούλομαι, Theoc.5.27, Ti.Locr.94d, Archyt.ap. Stob.3.1.105, Plu.2.219d, *Tab.Heracl.*1.146, *Chron.Lind.D.*66, *GDI* 3585.18 (Calymna): also Elean **δηλόμηρ,** = βουλόμενος, *Michel* 1334.5.

**δηλονότι,** i.e. δῆλόν [ἐστιν] ὅτι (cf. δῆλος II.3), used adverbially, *clearly, manifestly*, Pl.*Cri.*53a, *Grg.*487d, etc.; once in *NT*, 1*Ep. Cor.*15.27. II. freq. epexegetically, *that is to say, namely*, Pl. *Smp.*199a, X.*Cyr.*5.4.6, etc.: in Gramm. the common form for introducing an explanation, Sch.Ar.*Ach.*11, etc.

**Δηλόπτης,** ου, ὁ, a Thracian divinity associated with Bendis, *IG* 2$^2$.1324 (Piraeus), *Ath.Mitt.*25.172 (Samos).

**Δῆλος,** Dor. **Δᾶλος,** ἡ, *Delos*, Od.6.162, Pi.*Fr.*87, etc.: prov., ᾄδεις ὥσπερ εἰς Δ. πλέων, from the careless joviality of the Δηλιασταί (q.v.), Zen.2.37. (Expld. from δῆλος, because of the legend that it became *visible* on a sudden, Arist.*Fr.*488, *EM*264.22; but cf. sq.)

❀ **δῆλος** (also Dor., Archyt.1, Theoc.11.79, etc., and Aeol., cf. πρόδηλος), η, ον, also ος, ον E.*Med.*1197: Ep. **δέελος**: I. prop. *visible, conspicuous*, δέελον δ' ἐπὶ σῆμά τ' ἔθηκε Il.10.466, but: II. commonly, *clear* to the mind, *manifest*, νῦν δ' ἤδη τόδε δ. Od.20.333, etc. 2. δ. εἰμι is freq. used c. part., δ. ἐστιν ἀλγεινῶς φέρων i.e. *it is clear* that he takes it ill, S.*Ph.*1011, cf. *OT*673,1008, etc; οἱ ἂν δ. ὦσι μὴ ἐπιτρέψοντες who are *clearly* not going to permit, Th.1.71; with ὡς, δ. ἐστιν ὥς τι δρασείων κακόν S.*Aj.*326; δ. ἔσεσθε ὡς ὀργιζόμενοι Lys.12.90, cf. X.*An.*1.5.9; δ. δρᾶσθαι..ὢν being as was *plainly* to be seen, E.*Or.*350: with ὅτι and a Verb, δ. ἐστιν ὅτι.. ἀκήκοεν Ar.*Pl.*333; δ. ἡ οἰκοδομία ὅτι κατὰ σπουδὴν ἐγένετο Th.1.9; δ. ἔσται ὅτι.. Lys.12.50: sts. the part. or relat. clause must be supplied, καταγελᾷς μου, δ. εἶ (sc. καταγελῶν) Ar.*Av.*1407, cf. Id.*Lys.*919; δῆλοι δέ (sc. οὐ μένοντες) Th.5.10. 3. δῆλον ποιεῖν *show plainly*, τινὶ ὅτι.. Id.6.34, etc.: c. part., δῆλον ἐποιήσατε..μηδίσαντες Id.3.64. 4. δῆλον (sc. ἐστί) *it is manifest*, αὐτὸς πρὸς αὑτοῦ· δῆλον S.*Aj.*906; ἀλγεινά, Πρόκνη, δῆλον Id.*Fr.*585; ἐκ πίθω ἀντλεῖς, δῆλον Theoc.10.13; δῆλον δέ, to introduce a proof, folld. by γάρ, Th.1.11, Arist.*Col.*799ᵃ5, etc.; δῆλον γάρ S.*Fr.*63; δῆλον ὅτι Th.3.38, etc.; τὰ Κύρου δῆλον ὅτι οὕτως ἔχει X.*An.*1.3.9, cf. *Cyr.*2.4.24, etc., v. δηλονότι: in pl., δῆλα δή, δ. δ. καὶ ταῦτα Pl.*Cri.*48b; ἢ δ. δ. ὅτι..; Id. *Prt.*309a, etc.: hence as Adv., usu. written δηλαδή (q.v.). 5. Adv. δήλως is rejected by Att., Poll.6.207. III. δῆλοι, οἱ, *Urim*, Lxx 1*Ki.*28.6, al. (Cf. δέατο.)

**δηλοφᾰνής**, ές, *manifest*, f.l. in Polus ap.Stob.3.9.51 (Comp.).

❀ **δηλ-όω**:—Pass., fut. δηλωθήσομαι Th.1.144; δηλώσομαι in pass. sense, S.*OC*581; δεδηλώσομαι Hp.*Art.*45, Diog.Apoll.4:—*make visible* or *manifest, show, exhibit*, τὸν ἄνδρ' Ἀχαιοῖς δ. S.*Ph.*616; ποῖον ὄμμα πατρὶ δηλώσω; Id.*Aj.*462: with inf. added, ὡς γένος ἄτλητον ἀνθρώποισι δηλώσοιμ' ὁρᾶν Id.*OT*792, etc.:—Pass., *to be* or *become manifest*, Id.*OC*581, etc. 2. *make known, disclose, reveal*, A.*Pers.*519, S.*OT*77, etc.; *prove*, Id.*OC*146, Th.1.3; δηλοῖ ὁ λόγος ὅτι.. Democr.7; αὐτὸ δηλώσει D.19.157; *explain, set forth*, Th.2.62; *signify*, ἐδήλουν οὐδὲν ὅτι ἴσασιν *gave* no *sign* of knowing, Id.4.68: *indicate*, τὰς μεγίστας καὶ ἐλαχίστας Id.1.10, etc. Construct.: mostly δ. τινί τι Antipho 1.30; δ. τι πρός or εἴς τινα, S.*Tr.*369, Th.1.9; δ. περί τινος Lys.10.7; τινὶ περί τι Isoc.11.9: c. acc. et inf., *SIG*888.52 (Scaptopara, iii A.D.): folld. by a relat. clause, δ. ὅτι S.*El.*1106, Hdt.2.149, cf. 1.57, etc.; οἷα φρονῶ S.*El.*334; δ. περί τινος, ὡς.. Th.1.72,73: c. acc. et part., σκευή τε γάρ σε καὶ τὸ δύστηνον κάρα δηλοῦτον..ὅθ' ὃς εἶ S.*OC*555; ὥς σε δηλώσω κακὸν [ὄντα] ib.783, cf. *Ant.*471: c. part. nom., referring to the subject, δηλώσω πατρὶ μή τοι ἄσπλαγχνος γεγώς I *will show* my father that I am no dastard, Id.*Aj.*472; δηλοῖς..τι καλχαίνουσ' ἔπος thou *showest* that thou art pondering.., Id *Ant.*20; δηλοῖς ὥς τι σημανῶν ib.242; δηλώσω οὐ παραγενόμενος I *will show* that I was not present, Antipho 2.4.8; δηλώσει μείζων γεγενημένος Th.1.21; also Λιβύη δηλοῖ ἑωυτὴν ἐοῦσα περίρρυτος Hdt.4.42: ἑαυτὸν ἐδήλωσεν ὅστις ἦν D.H.3.48. II. intr., *to be clear* or *plain*, δηλοῖ ὅτι οὐκ Ὁμήρου τὰ Κύπρια ἔπεά ἐστι Hdt.2.117; δηλοῖ δὲ ταῦτα.. ὅτι οὕτως ἔχει Pl.*Grg.*483d; δηλώσει ἡ ἔχθρα ὅταν πρῶτον.. And.4.12; *to be significant, possess a meaning*, c. dat., Pl.*Cra.*434c. 2. impers. δηλοῖ, = δῆλόν ἐστι, δηλοῖ μοι ὅτι.., Hdt.9.68, cf. Arist.*Pol.*1296ᵃ20; δηλώσει Lys.10.20, Pl.*R.*497c; ἐδήλωσε X.*Mem.*1.2.32, cf. *Cyr* 7.1.30. **-ωμα**, ατος, τό, *a means of making known*, τινός Pl.*Lg.*792a, Plu.2.78e, etc.: pl., ib. 62d. ❀ **-ωσις**, εως, ἡ, *pointing out, explanation*, Th.1.73; αἰσθήσει ἢ δηλώσει Pl.*Min* 314a; ἡ τῶν ὄντων λόγῳ δ. Id.*Plt.*287a; δ. ποιεῖσθαι, = δηλοῦν, Th.4.40. 2. *direction, order*, ἡ τῶν ἀρχόντων δ. Pl.*Lg.*942c. 3. *Urim*, Lxx *Le.*8.8. 4. *interpretation*, ib.*Da.*2.27. **-ωτέον**, *one must set forth*, Pl.*Ti.*48e, Ph.1.15. **-ωτικός**, ή, όν, *indicative*, τινός Hp.*Acut.*42, Arist.*Phgn.*808ᵇ30, D.H. *Comp.*16: abs., *notificatory*, *PMonac.*2.15 (vi A.D.). Adv. **-κῶς** Aen. Tact.14.2. 2. *expressive*, of dancing, Poll 4.96. 3. *visible*, *PMag.Berol.*1.259. **-ωτός**, ή, όν, *able to be shown*, Arist.*Xen.* 979ᵃ13.

**δῆμα**, ατος, τό, = δέμα, Sch.A.R.2.535.

**δημᾰγωγ-έω**, *to be a leader of the people*, καλῶς δ. Isoc.2.16; τῇ μὲν ἐξουσίᾳ τυραννῶν, ταῖς δ' εὐεργεσίαις δημαγωγῶν Id.10.37; cf. δημαγωγεῖ· στρατηγεῖ, Hsch.: usu. in bad sense, Ar.*Ra.*423, etc. 2. c. acc. pers., δ. ἄνδρας *curry favour with*, X.*An.*7.6.4, cf. Arist.*Pol.* 1305ᵃ26, al.:—Pass., *to be won over, conciliated by popular arts*, J.*AJ* 16.2.5. b. = ψυχαγωγέω, τὸν πόθον, of a work of art, Him.*Ecl.*31. 6; τὸ θέατρον, of Homer, Id.*Or.*20.3. 3. c. acc. rei, *introduce* measures *so as to win popularity*, τὰ πρὸς ἡδονὴν τῷ πλήθει D.H.*Dem.* 17; βουλὰς δ. Lxx 1*Es.*5.70(73). II. in causal sense, δ. τινά *make* him *popular*, App.*BC*5.53, *Pun.*133. **-ία**, ἡ, *control* or *leadership of the people*, Ar.*Eq.*191, Th.8.65, Arist.*Pol.*1305ᵇ23, *Ath.*28.4, Luc.*Dem.Enc.*19; *demagogic method*, Plb.2.21.8. **-ικός**, ή, όν, *fit for* or *like a demagogue*, τὰ -κά *arts of a demagogue*, Ar.*Eq.*217, cf. Plb.15.21.1: generally, *popular*, of a dancer, Poll.4.96. Adv. **-κῶς** ib.4.26. **-ός**, ὁ, *popular leader*, as Cleon or Pericles, Th. 4.21, Isoc.8.126; δ. ἀγαθοί Lys.27.10; ὁ δίκαιος δ. Hyp.*Dem.Fr.* 5. 2. more freq. in bad sense, *leader of the mob, demagogue*, X. *HG*2.3.27; ὀχλοκόπος καὶ δ. Plb.3.80.3; λόγοι δημαγωγοῦ, opp. ἔργα τυράννου, And.4.27; ἔστι γὰρ ὁ δ. τοῦ δήμου κόλαξ Arist.*Pol.*1313ᵇ 40, cf. 1292ᵃ20, etc.

**δημᾰκίδιον** [κῐ], τό, Com. Dim. of *δῆμαξ, 'magnificative' of δῆμος, Ar.*Eq.*823; cf. δημίδιον.

**δημᾰ́ρᾱτος** [μᾰ], ον, (ἀράομαι) *prayed for by the people*: hence as pr. n. of a king of Sparta, Hdt.5.75 (in Ion. form -άρητος), etc., cf. Eust.1093.57.

**δημαρχ-έω**, *to be* δήμαρχος at Athens, Is.12.11, D.57.26; at Chios, *Schwyzer*687*A* 3; or *tribune* at Rome, App.*BC*1.2: pf. δεδημάρχηκα Arr.*Epict.*3.14.12. ❀ **-ία**, ἡ, *the office* or *rank of* δήμαρχος, D.57.63; at Rome, *tribunate*, Plu.*Fab.*9, etc. II. *office* in general, Ph.*Fr.* 33 H. (pl.). 2. = δημοκρατία, Hsch. **-ικός**, ή, όν, *tribunician*, δέλτοι Plu.*Cat.Mi.*40; δ. ἐξουσία, = Lat. *tribunicia potestas*, D.H.6.89, *Mon.Anc.Gr.*5.18, D.C.54.28: freq. in Inscrr. and Pap., *IG*3. 40, *BGU*74.3, etc. ❀ **-ος**, ὁ, at Athens, *chief official of a* δῆμος, Ar. *Nu.*37, Lys.*Fr.*184S., D.50.6, Lex ap.eund.43.58, Arist.*Ath.*21.5; also at Cos, *Inscr.Cos*344, al.; at Chios, *Schwyzer*687*C*1. b. at Naples, one of the *chief magistrates* of the city, Str.5.4.7; at Eretria, *IG*12(9).189.24(iv B.C.). 2. at Rome, = Lat. *tribunus plebis*, Plb. 6.12.2, D.H.6.89, Plu.*Cor.*7, etc.

❀ **δηματρεύεσθαι**· ἐπὶ πολὺ ὑπερτίθεσθαι, Hsch. **δημεῖαι**· αἱ τῶν δήμων συστάσεις, Id. **δημελέητος**, ον, *object of general pity*, Id., Suid.

**δημεραστ-έω**, *to be a friend of the people*, Olymp.*in Grg.*p.385 J. **-ής**, οῦ, ὁ, *friend of the people*, Pl.*Alc.*1.132a, D.C.47.38:— hence Subst. **-ία**, ἡ, Poll.3.65, and Adj. **-ικός**, ή, όν, *friendly to the people*, Procl.*in Alc.*p.146C.

**δήμ-ευσις**, εως, ἡ, *confiscation of property*, θάνατον ἢ φυγὴν ἢ δ. χρημάτων *IG*1².101.7, cf. Pl.*Prt.*325c (pl.), D.17.15; δ. alone, Arist. *Pol.*1298ᵃ6; δημεύσει τῶν ὑπαρχόντων ζημιοῦν D.21.43; τῆς οὐσίης *SIG*167.26 (Mylasa, iv B.C.). ❀ **-εύω**, (δῆμος) *seize as public property*, esp. of a citizen's goods, *confiscate*, Th.5.60, And.1:51; πολλὰ δ. διὰ τῶν δικαστηρίων Arist.*Pol.*1320ᵃ5: abs., D.8.69,71:—Pass., τὰ δημευόμενα Arist.*Ath.*43.4; τῶν ἐκ προνοίας δεδήμευται τὰ ὄντα D.23.45; later of persons, ἐδημεύθη τὴν οὐσίαν Philostr.*VS*2.1.2; δημευθήσεσθαι Hdn.2.14.3. II. generally, *make public*, δεδήμευται κράτος the power *is in the hands of the people*, E.*Cyc.*119:—Pass., also, *to be published*, Pl.*Phlb.*14d,e. III. δεδημευμένα ὀνόματα *vulgarized, hackneyed* words, Ammon.*in Int.*66.3. IV. = ἐνδημέω, and also, = δημαγωγέω, Hsch.

**δημεχθηλός**, όν, = sq., Hsch.

❀ **δημεχθής**, ές, (ἔχθος) *hated by the people*, Call.*Fr.*472.

**δημηγερσία**, ἡ, *sedition, agitation*, *PFlor.*295.5 (vi A.D.); cf. δημοεγερτής.

**δημηγορ-έω**, *practise speaking in the assembly*, Ar.*Eq.*956, etc.; πρὸ τοῦ πολιτεύεσθαι καὶ δ. ἐμέ D.18.60; δ. περί τινος Lys.14.45; δ. πρός τινας Pl.*Lg.*817c; ἐν τοῖς ὄχλοις Arist.*Fr.*83: c. acc. cogn., δ. καὶ συνηγορεῖν λόγους D.19.15; δ. λόγον παρά τισι Id.23.110:—Pass., τὰ δεδημηγορημένα *public speeches*, Id.19.9. II. esp. *make popular speeches, use clap-trap*, ταῦτα δημηγορεῖς Pl.*Grg.*482c: abs., ib.503b, *Tht.*162d, *R.*350e; τῶν δημηγοριῶν ὧν δ. D.21.202; δ. πρὸς χάριν, πρὸς ἡδονήν, Id.3.3,4.38, cf. Hermog.*Meth.*1. **-ία**, ἡ, *deliberative speaking*, opp. forensic (δικανική), Arist.*Rh.*1354ᵇ28. 2. *speech in the public assembly*, Aeschin.2.243, Jul.*Or.*2.75b (pl.). 3. *position of a public speaker*, Pl.*Ap.*36b (pl.). II. esp. *popular oratory, claptrap*, Id.*Tht.*162d. ❀ **-ικός**, ή, όν, *suited to public speaking*, opp. δικανικός, X.*Mem.*1.2.48; προοίμια, title of work by Critias, Hermog. *Id.*2.11; *popular*, Pl.*Grg.*482e; δ. καὶ δικανικὴ σοφία Id.*R.*365d, etc.; λέξις Arist.*Rh.*1413ᵇ4: Comp. or Sup., ib.1418ᵃ1:—ἡ -κή (sc. τέχνη), = δημηγορία, Pl.*Sph.*222c; τὰ -κά Arist.*Rh.*1354ᵇ28. Adv. **-κῶς** Poll.4.26. **-ος**, ὁ, (ἀγορεύω) *popular orator*, mostly in a bad sense, Pl.*Grg.*520b, *Lg.*908d, etc.; ὅρκος ἑταίρας ταὐτὸ καὶ δημηγόρου Diph.101; but δ. ἀγαθοί, opp. ῥήτορες φαῦλοι, X.*Mem.*2.6.15: as Adj., δημηγόρος, ον, τιμαὶ δ. *a speaker's* honours, E.*Hec.*254; στροφαὶ δημηγόροι *rhetorical* tricks, A.*Supp.*623.

**δημ-ηλᾰσία**, ἡ, *banishment decreed by the people, exile*, A.*Supp.* 6 (anap.). **-ήλᾰτος** φυγή, = foreg., ib.614.

❀ **Δημήτηρ**, τερος and τρος, ἡ: Dor., Arc., Boeot. **Δαμάτηρ**; also **Δημήτρα** Buresch *Aus Lydien*69: acc. Δημήτραν Epigr.ap.Paus.1. 37.2: gen. Δαμάτρας *IG*7.2793 (Copae); Aeol. **Δωμάτηρ** Hoffmann *Griechische Dialekte* 2.153 (Aegae); Thess. dat. Δαμμάτερι *IG*9(2). 1235:—*Demeter*, Il.2.696, al., once in Od., 5.125, *h.Cer.*, etc. 2. appell., as a name for *bread*, Opp.*H.*3.463; cf. ἀκτή, καρπός. (Variously expld. by Gramm. as, = Γημήτηρ, δημομήτηρ, or from δηαί, = κριθαί, cf. *EM*265.54.)

**Δημήτρειοι**, οἱ, *the dead*, Plu.2.943b.

**Δημητριακός**, ή, όν, *of* or *belonging to Demeter*, καρποί D.S.2.36, cf. Corn.*ND*28, Alex.Aphr.*Pr.*2.68; σπέρματα Orib.3.2.5. II. Δημητριακόν (sc. βιβλίον), τό, work by Demetrius Lacon, Phld. *Sign.*28.

**Δημητριάς**, άδος, ἡ, fem. Adj.: I. (sc. φυλή) tribe *named in honour of Demetrius Poliorcetes*, Plu.*Demetr.*10. II. city founded by him, Plb.3.6.4, etc.:—hence **Δημητριεῖς**, οἱ, its citizens, Id.5.99. 3. III. as Subst., *six-rowed barley*, Hsch. 2. = περιστερεὼν ὕπτιος, Ps.-Dsc.4.60.

**Δημητριασταί**, οἱ, guild of *worshippers of Demeter* at Ephesus, *BMus.Inscr.*3.595, Ἀρχ.Δελτ.7.200.

**Δημήτριος**, ον (also Δημήτρειος, v. Δημήτρειοι), *of* or *belonging to Demeter*, βίος A.*Fr.*44.5; καρπὸς Δ. corn, Thphr.*CP*2.4.5; also Δ. σπέρματα, of leguminous plants, Gal.15.454: Δημήτριος (sc. μήν), ὁ, month in Bithynia, *Hemerolog.Flor.*: Boeot. **Δαμάτριος**, *IG*7.296, al., Plu.2.378e. II. τὸ Δημήτριον *the temple of D.*, Str.9.5. 14. III. τὰ Δημήτρια *her festival*, Poll.1.37, etc.; but later, *in honour of Demetrius*, Plu.*Demetr.*12:—also **Δημητρίεια**, τά, *Supp. Epigr.*1.362.8 (Samos, iv B.C.).

⊛ **Δημητριών**, *ῶνος, ὁ*, name of a month at Cassandrea, *SIG*380; at Athens, new name given to the month Μουνυχιών, in honour of *Demetrius*, Plu.*Demetr.*12.

**δημίδιον** [μῐ], *τό*, Com. Dim. of δῆμος, Ar.*Eq.*726,1199; cf. δημακίδιον.

**δημίζω**, *pose as 'friend of the people'*, Ar.*V.*699.

**δημιο-εργείη**, *ἡ*, = δημιουργία, Procl.*H.*7.20. **-εργός**, *όν*, poet. for δημιουργός (q.v.). **-πληθής**, *ές*, *abounding for public use*, κτήνη δ. cattle *of which the people have large store*, A.*Ag.*129 (lyr.). ⊛ **-πρᾶτα**, *τά*, *goods seized by public authority, and put up for sale*, Ar.*V.*659, Poll.10.96, Ath.11.476e, Phalar.*Ep.*95; περὶ τῶν δ. πρὸς Εὐθίαν, title of speech by Lys.

⊛ **δήμιος**, Dor. **δάμ-**, *ον* (*α, ον* A.*Ch.*57 (lyr.), δημίην· πόρνην (Cypr.), Hsch.): (δῆμος):—*belonging to the people*, οἶκος Od.20.264; αἰσυμνῆται δ. judges *elected by the people*, 8.259; πρῆξις δ' ἥδ' ἰδίη, οὐ δήμιος not *public*, 3.82; δήμιον ἢ ἴδιον; 4.314, cf. 2.32: epith. of Hestia at Paros, *IG*12(5).238 (v B.C.): neut. pl. as Adv., δήμια πίνειν *at the public cost*, Il.17.250; τὸ δ. *the sovereign people*, A.*Supp.*370,699 (lyr.). **II.** ὁ δ. (sc. δοῦλος) *public executioner*, Ar.*Ec.*81, Pl.*R.*439e, Lys.13.56, Aeschin.2.126, etc. (δάμιος μαστίκτωρ in A.*Eu.*160 (lyr.)); ὁ κοινὸς δ. Pl.*Lg.*872b. **2.** *public physician*, πτωχὸς ἦν καὶ δ. Phoenicid.4.13. **III.** δημίαι πύλαι, perh. a mistake for Διομῆσι, Hsch.

**δημιουργ-εῖον**, *τό*, *work-place*, App.*Pun.*93. ⊛ **-έω** (cf. II. infr.), *practise a handicraft*, Pl.*Plt.*288d, etc.; τινί *for* one, Id.*Lg.*846e, *R.*342e: metaph., ἡ δημιουργήσασα φύσις Arist.*PA*645$^{a}$9. **2.** c. acc. rei, *work at, fabricate*, Pl.*Plt.*288e; ἡ φύσις οὐδὲν δ. μάτην Arist.*IA*711$^{a}$18, cf. *PA*647$^{b}$5; δ. τὸν υἱὸν εἰς ἀρετήν *to train* him to.., Plu.*Cat.Ma.*20:—Pass., *to be wrought* or *fabricated*, Pl.*R.*414d, al.; τὰ δημιουργούμενα *products of arts and crafts*, Arist.*EN*1094$^{b}$14. **3.** of divine power, *create*, τὸν ὁρατὸν κόσμον Ph.1.4; ὁ δημιουργῶν θεός Numen.ap.Eus.*PE*11.18.6, cf. Dam.*Pr.*304, etc.:—Pass., Procl.*Inst.*207. **II.** *hold office of* δημιουργός, *CIG*4415*b* (Iotapata), etc.; of a woman, *Supp.Epigr.*1.393 (Samos, i B.C.); δαμιοργέοντος Μίκκωνος *IG*9(1).330 (Locr.); *to be a civil official*, opp. στρατηγέω, Artem.2.22. **b.** c. acc., *administer*, δαμιουργεόντων τὰ ἱερά *IG*9(1).32.44 (Stiris). ⊛ **-ημα**, *ατος, τό*, *a work of art, piece of workmanship*, Longin.13.4 (pl.), Ath.11.497c, Herm.*in Phdr.* p.202 A.; δ. χειρῶν D.H.*Comp.*1; τὰ δ. Φειδίου Jul.*Or.*2.54b; οὐ τύχης οὐδ' ἀνθρώπων δ., of the universe, Zaleuc.ap.Stob.4.2.19, cf. Dam.*Pr.*175; θεοειδὲς δ. ᾧ λογιζόμεθα Ph.1.208; *creature*, πρὸς ἀπότεξιν εὐτρεπὲς δ. Hierocl.p.7 A.; also of actions, Iamb.*Myst.*1.5, 2.7. ⊛ **-ία**, *ἡ*, *workmanship, handicraft*, Pl.*R.*401a; τέχναι καὶ δ. ib.495d; *piece of mechanism*, Arist.*Mu.*400$^{a}$1. **2.** *making, creating*, ζῴων Pl.*Ti.*41c, etc.; δ. ἔκ τινος Id.*Plt.*280c; *creative activity*, μεριστὴ δ. Jul.*Or.*5.179b, al.; *the creation*, ἡ φανερὰ δ. ib.4.144b; ὁ κόσμος ὅδε καὶ ἁπλῶς ἡ δ. Dam.*Pr.*283. **3.** *physical function*, Arist.*HA*489$^{a}$13. **4.** δ. τῶν τεχνῶν *handling* or *practising* them, Pl.*Smp.*197a. **II.** *the office of* δημιουργός, *OGI*578.12 (pl., Tarsus), etc.: generally, *magistracy, office*, Arist.*Pol.*1310$^{b}$22 (pl.). **-ικός**, *ή, όν*, *of a craftsman*, βίος Pl.*Phdr.*248e; ἀρετή Id.*Prt.*322d; τεχνήματα *craftsmen's* works, Id.*Lg.*846d; τιμαί, of cooks, Clidem.2. Adv. *-κῶς in a workmanlike manner*, Ar.*Pax* 429. **2.** *creative*, θεός Numen.ap.Eus.*PE*11.18; τετρακτύς Hierocl.*in CA*20 p.466 M.; αἴτια, δυνάμεις, Iamb.*Myst.*5.26, 10.6; νοῦς Phlp.*in Mete.*12.25; *-κόν, τό*, opp. πατρικόν (as οὐσιοποιόν to εἰδοποιόν), Procl.*Inst.*157, cf. Dam.*Pr.*184. Adv. *-κῶς* Syrian.*in Metaph.*82.31. **II.** *of* or *for the magistrates*, τὸ δ. *the official class*, Arist.*Pol.*1291$^{a}$34. **-ιον**, Dor. **δαμιόργιον** or **-ούργιον**, *τό*, *office of the* δημιουργοί, *GDI*3502 (Cnidus, also **-εῖον**, *τό*, ib.3501). **II.** *meeting of the* δ., ἐν ἐννόμῳ δαμιουργίῳ *SIG*830.3 (Delph., ii A.D.). **-ίς**, *ίδος, ἡ*, *office of* δημιουργός II, *IGRom.*3.800 (Pamphyl.), *Jahresh.*18 *Beibl.*55 (Anazarba). ⊛ **-ός**, Ep. **δημιοεργός** (also Hdt.7.31 codd.), *ὁ*, *one who works for the people, skilled workman, handicraftsman* (opp. ἰδιώτης, Pl.*Plt.*298c, *Prt.*327c, *Ion* 531c), Od.17.383, 19.135; ἐχάλκευσε ξίφος.. Αιδης δ. ἄγριος S.*Aj.*1035; of medical *practitioners*, Hp.*VM*1, Pl.*Smp.*186d; but opp. scientific physicians (ἀρχιτεκτονικοί), Arist.*Pol.*1282$^{a}$3; of sculptors, Pl.*R.*529e; of confectioners and cooks, Hdt.7.31, Men.518.12 (fem.), Antiph.225, Alexandr.Com.3; μέλιτος δ., of the bee, Jul.*Or.*8.241a; οἱ δ. *the artisan class* at Athens, Arist.*Ath.*13.2, Plu.*Thes.*25; opp. πολιτικοί, Pl.*Ap.*23e; δαμιουργοί, = πόρναι, Hsch. **2.** metaph., *maker*, ἡ μαντικὴ φιλίας θεῶν καὶ ἀνθρώπων δ. Pl.*Smp.*188d; νόμων, πολιτείας, Arist.*Pol.*1273$^{b}$32; λόγων Aeschin.3.215; δ. κακῶν *author* of ill, E.*Fr.*1059.7; πειθοῦς δ. ἡ ῥητορική Pl.*Grg.*453a; ἀρετῆς Id.*R.*500d, Arist.*Pol.*1329$^{a}$21; ἐναργείας Demetr.*Eloc.*215; ὄρθρος δημιοεργός morn *that calls man to work*, *h.Merc.*98. **3.** *creator, producer*, νυκτός τε καὶ ἡμέρας Pl.*Ti.*40c; οὐρανοῦ Id.*R.*530a; esp. in later philosophy, *the Creator* of the visible world, *Demiurge*, [Philol.]21, Hp.*Ep.*23, Ph.1.632, etc.; ὁ νοῦς ἀπεκύησε ἕτερον νοῦν δ. *Corp.Herm.*1.9; also name for μονάς, *Theol.Ar.*5.24: as Adj., δ. λόγος *creative* reason, Syrian.*in Metaph.*7.27. **II.** in many Greek states, title of *a magistrate*, Th.5.47 (Mantinea), Epist. Philipp.ap.D.18.157 (Peloponnesus), Plb.23.5.16 (Achaean League), etc.:—Dor. **δαμιωργός**, *IG*12(3).174 (Astypalaea); **δαμιουργός**, ib.4.679 (Hermione); **δαμιοργός**, ib.5(1).1390.116 (Andania, i B.C.); **δαμιεργός**, ib.12(3).168 (Astypalaea):—Ion. **δημιοργός**, ib.12(7).241 (Amorgos), *Michel* 368.1 (Samos).—In Arist.*Pol.*1275$^{b}$29 there is a play upon the double meaning. **III.** as a priestly title, δ. θεᾶς Ῥώμης *BGU*937.9 (iii A.D.).

**δημιώδης**, *ες*, = δημώδης, Phld.*Mus.*p.27 K. (s.v.l.).

**δημιῶν**· τὸν δῆμον διοικῶν, Hsch.

**δημοαλῆ**· περιβόητον, Hsch. (leg. -λαλῆ, cf. δημολάλητος).

**δημο-βόητος**, gloss on δημολάλητος, *notorious*, Hsch. **-βορέω**, *devour the people*, Eust.1143.46. **-βόρος**, *ον*, *devourer of the common stock*, δ. βασιλεύς Il.1.231; of Caligula, Ph.2.561. **-γέρων**, *οντος, ὁ*, *elder of the people*, Il.11.372: in pl., *nobles, chiefs*, 3.149, E.*Andr.*300 (lyr.), Plot.6.4.15; of the Jewish *elders*, δ. τοῦ ἔθνους Ph.2.94; δ. θεός, = Lat. *deus minorum gentium*, dub. l. in *AP*9.334 (Pers.). **-δίωκτος** [ῐ], gloss on δημόσσοος, Hsch. ⊛ **-εγερτής**, *οῦ, ὁ*, *sedition-monger, agitator*, Suid. **-ειδής**, *ές*, *vulgar*, κιβδηλίη Hp.*Art.*78. **-θεές**· θεωρόν, Hsch., and **-θέσεση** (sic)· ἐθεώρει, Id.

⊛ **δημόθεν**, Adv. *at the public cost*, δημόθεν ἄλφιτα δῶκα Od.19.197. **2.** *from among the people*, A.R.1.7. **II.** δ. Εὐπυρίδης an Eupyrian *by deme*, *IG*3.121.

⊛ **δημοθοιν-έω**, *give a public feast*, *IG*12(7).389 (Amorgos), *Ath.Mitt.*36.159. ⊛ **-ία**, *ἡ*, *public feast*, Arist.*Mu.*400$^{b}$21 (pl.), Luc.*Dem.Enc.*16, *CIG*2880 (Branchidae), Ph.2.55, *OGI*533.9 (Ancyra):—Delph. **δᾱμο-**, *SIG*672.53.

**δημό-θροος**, *οον*, contr. **-θρους**, *ουν*, *uttered by the people*, φήμη, ἀρὰ δ., A.*Ag.*938,1409; δ. ἀναρχία lawlessness *of popular clamour*, ib.883. **-καλλίας** (-κας cod., but cf. καλλίας, = πίθηκος)· τοὺς περὶ τὰ δημόσια ἀναστρέφοντας, Hsch. **-κηδής**, *ὁ*, *caring for, friendly to the people* or *to democracy*, Str.14.2.5; = Lat. *Publicola*, D.H.5.19, Plu.*Publ.*10. **-κλίναρχος** [ῑ], *ὁ*, *president of a municipal religious association*, *Arch.Pap.*1.417 (Talmis). ⊛ **-κοινος** (sc. δοῦλος), *ὁ*, = δήμιος II, *executioner*, S.*Fr.*780, Antipho 1.20, Isoc.17.15. **2.** = πόρνος, Hsch. **II.** as Adj., δημόκοινος, *ον*, *vile, common*, of coarse food, Lyc.Trag.2.4. **-κόλαξ**, *ακος, ὁ*, *mob-flatterer*, D.H.6.60, Luc.*Dem.Enc.*31.

**δημοκοπ-έω**, *court the mob*, Plu.*CG*9, Charito 1.5; opp. δημαγωγέω, Plu.2.802d; δ. ἔς τινας App.*Syr.*16; δ. τὸ πλῆθος ἐπί τισι Id.*BC*4.94:—Med., Phld.*Rh.*1.380 S. **-ημα**, *ατος, τό*, *attempt to gain mob-favour*, App.*BC*1.24. **-ία**, *ἡ*, *courting the mob*, D.H.6.60, *IG*4.1153 (Epid.); *bribery*, Plu.*Dio* 47: pl., Str.14.5.14, Ph.*Fr.*33 H., App.*BC*1.34. **-ικός**, *ή, όν*, *of* or *suited to a* δημοκόπος, βίος δ. Pl.*Phdr.*248e; τὸ περὶ ἀνθρώπους δ. M.Ant.1.16: Sup., App.*Hisp.*4. ⊛ **-ος**, *ὁ*, *demagogue*, D.H.5.65, D.S.18.10, Ph.2.47, etc.

**δημόκραντος**, *ον*, *ratified by the people*, ἀρὰ δ. A.*Ag.*457 (lyr.).

**δημοκρᾰτ-έομαι**, Pass. with fut. Med. -κρατήσομαι Th.8.48, Lys.34.4, D.24.99, but -κρατηθήσομαι v.l. in Th.8.75: pf. δεδημοκράτημαι D.C.52.13:—*have a democratic constitution*, Hdt.6.43, Ar.*Ach.*642, Lys.12.4, etc.; πόλις δημοκρατουμένη Lex ap.And.1.88, cf. Th.5.29. **2.** impers., δημοκρατεῖται *democratic principles prevail*, Arist.*Pol.*1265$^{b}$38. ⊛ **-ία** (Dor. **δᾱμο-** *SIG*360.14 (Chersonesus)), *ἡ*, *democracy, popular government*, Hdt.6.43, Antipho 6.45, etc.; ἐν δ. D.18.132; δ. καταλυθείσης And.1.95, cf. Th.6.89, Arist.*Pol.*1279$^{b}$18, al. **II.** personified, Paus.1.3.2; θυσία τῇ Δ. *IG*2.741.67; ἄγαλμα τῆς Δ. *SIG*694.31 (Elaea). **-ίζω**, *to be on the democratic side*, App.*Pun.*70. **-ικός**, *ή, όν*, *of* or *for a democracy*, νόμοι Pl.*R.*338e; δημοκρατικόν τι δρᾶν to do a *popular* act, Ar.*Ra.*952; τὸ δίκαιον τὸ δ. Arist.*Pol.*1280$^{a}$9. Adv. *-κῶς* D.S.2.32, Str.6.3.4. **II.** of persons (δημοτικός is more usu. in this sense), *favouring democracy* or *suited to democracy*, Lys.25.8, Pl.*R.*571a, Arist.*EN*1131$^{a}$27.

⊛ **Δημοκρίτειοι**, *οἱ*, *followers of Democritus* of Abdera, Ael.*VH*12.25, Plu.2.1108e; ἡ Δ. φιλοσοφία S.E.*P.*1.213.

**δημο-κώκῡτος** (-τυτος cod.)· ἀθρήνητος, ἀνελεήμων, Hsch. **-λάλητος** [ᾰ], *ον*, *notorious*, Id., *EM*265.19. **-λευστος**, *ον*, *publicly stoned*, δ. φόνος death *by public stoning*, S.*Ant.*36; of a person, Lyc.331. **-λογέω**, = δημόομαι, μείλιχα δ. *AP*7.440 (Leon.). **-λογικός**, *ή, όν*, *suited to public speaking*: *popular, superficial*, Pl.*Sph.*268b:—hence **Δημολογοκλέων**, *ὁ*, a nickname given by the Chorus to Bdelycleon in Ar.*V.*342.

**δημόομαι**, Dor. **δαμ-**, *sing a popular song* (cf. δάμωμα), γλυκύ τι δαμωσόμεθα Pi.*I.*8(7).9; δημούμενον λέγειν talk *ad captandum*, Pl.*Tht.*161e; also δ. ἱερὰς ἐσθῆτας *display*, Jul.*Ep.*89b (s.v.l.). **II.** Pass., *to be made public*, D.C.53.19, *Fr.*57.80.

**δημο-πίθηκος** [ῐ], *ὁ*, *mob-jackanapes, charlatan*, Ar.*Ra.*1085. ⊛ **-ποίητος**, *ον*, *made a citizen*, but not one by birth, Plu.*Sol.*24, Luc.*Scyth.*8, Aristid.1.103 J. **-πρακτος**, *ον*, *resolved by the people*, ψῆφος A.*Supp.*942. ⊛ **-πράτης** [ᾱ], *ου, ὁ*, *auctioneer of public goods*, Poll.9.10. **-ρρῐφής**, *ές*, *hurled by the people*, ἀραί A.*Ag.*1616.

⊛ **δῆμος**, Dor. **δᾶμος** (cf. infr. IV), *ὁ*, *district, country, land*, Βοιωτοὶ μάλα πίονα δ. ἔχοντες Il.5.710; Λυκίης ἐν πίονι δ. 16.437, cf. Od.13.322, etc.; Ἰθάκης ἐνὶ δ. 1.103; δήμῳ ἔνι Τρώων 13.266; λαοὶ ἀνὰ δῆμον 16.95: metaph., δῆμος ὀνείρων *the land* of dreams, 24.12. **2.** the *people, inhabitants* of such a district, πόληΐ τε παντί τε δήμῳ Il.3.50, cf. *h.Cer.*271; Βακτρίων ἔρρει πανώλης δ. A.*Pers.*732. **II.** hence (since the common people lived in the country, the chiefs in the city), *the commons, common people*, δήμου ἀνήρ, opp. βασιλεύς, ἔξοχος ἀνήρ, etc., Il.2.198,188, cf. 11.328, Hes.*Op.*261, Hdt.5.66, *Act.Ap.*12.22, etc. (rarely of a single person, δῆμον ἐόντα being *a commoner*, Il.12.213); opp. οἱ εὐδαίμονες, Hdt.1.196; opp. οἱ παχέες, Id.5.30; opp. οἱ δυνατοί, Th.5.4; οἱ..ἐπαναστάντες τοῖς δυνατοῖς καὶ ὄντες δῆμος Id.8.73; = Lat. *plebs*, D.H.6.88, etc.; τοῦ πολλοῦ δ. εἷς *unus de plebe*, Luc.*Sat.*2; τοῦ δ. ὤν Id.*Gall.*22; in an army, *rank and file*, opp. officers, ὁ δ. τῶν στρατιωτῶν X.*Cyr.*6.1.14. **2.** metaph., δ. ἰχθύων Antiph.206.7; τυράννων Philostr.*VS*1.15.1; πιθήκων Id.*VA*3.4; ὀρνέων

Alciphr.3.30. **III.** in a political sense, *the sovereign people*, *the free citizens*, A.*Th.*199,1011, etc.; ὁ δ. ὁ Ἀθηναίων *IG*1$^2$.10.37, etc.; προστάτης τοῦ δήμου Th.6.35, etc.; personified, Ar.*Eq.*42, al.; ἱερεὺς τοῦ Δ. καὶ τῶν Χαρίτων *IG*2$^2$.1028. **2.** *popular government*, *democracy*, opp. ὀλιγαρχίη, Hdt.3.82; opp. οἱ τύραννοι, And.1.106; πολίτευμα εἶναι ἐν Χίῳ δ. *SIG*283.4 (iv B.C.); δήμου κατάλυσις X.*HG*2.3.28, Arist.*Ath.*8.4; ταῦτα καταλύει δῆμον, οὐ κωμῳδία Philippid.25.7; δ. καταστῆσαι, καταπαύειν, X.*HG*7.3.3, Th.1.107: in pl., *democracies*, Id.3.82, D.20.15; δ. ὁ ἔσχατος Arist.*Pol.*1277$^b$3. **3.** *the popular assembly*, λέγειν ἐν τῷ δ. Pl.*R.*565b; ἡ βουλὴ καὶ ὁ δ., formula in Inscrr., as *IG*1$^2$.39, etc.; of the *assembly* of Oxyrhynchus, *POxy.*41.19 (iii/iv A.D.), 1407.19 (iii A.D.). **IV.** *township*, *commune* ( = Dor. κώμη acc. to Arist.*Po.*1448$^a$37; but διελόμενοι τὴν μὲν πόλιν κατὰ κώμας, τὴν δὲ χώραν κατὰ δήμους Isoc.7.46, cf. Pl.*Lg.*746d, and v. infr.), in Attica, Hdt.5.69, Arist.*Ath.*21.5, Str.9.1.16, *IG*1$^2$.76.9, al.; elsewh., ib.12(5).594 (Ceos), *PHib.*1.28.13 (iii A.D.), *OGI*49.14 (Ptolemais), etc.:—Dor. **δᾶμος,** *Michel*418.34 (Calymna), *IG*12(1).58.23 (Lindos): in indications of origin, Σωφάνης ἐκ δ. Δεκελεῆθεν Hdt.9.73; δήμου Ἁλαιεύς Antiph.211; τῶν δήμων Πιτθεύς Pl.*Euthphr.*2b; τῶν δ. Θορίκιος D.39.30, cf. Arist.*Ath.*21.4; ἐπιγράψαι τοὺς βουλευτὰς πατρόθεν καὶ τοῦ δ. *IG*2$^2$.223*B*4: metaph., οἱ τῆς θαλάσσης δ. Philostr.*Gym.*44. **V.** name for a prostitute, Archil.184. **VI.** *faction* in the circus, *Tab.Defix.Aud.*15.8 (Syria, iii A.D.). **VII.** = κατανάγκη, Ps.-Dsc.4.131. (Perh. cognate with Skt. *dā́ti* 'reap', δαίομαι, δατέομαι.)

**δημός,** ὁ, *fat*, βοῦν..πίονα δημῷ Il.23.750, cf. Hes.*Th.*538, Ar.*V.*40, etc.; δίπλακι δημῷ (of sacrificial meat) *with fat* above *and fat* below, Il.23.243; of men, κορέει κύνας ἠδ' οἰωνοὺς δημῷ 8.380.

**Δημοσθέν-ειος,** α, ον, *Demosthenic*, Longin.34.2:—also **-ικός,** ή, όν, D.H.*Rh.*11.10, Luc.*Dem.Enc.*15. Adv. -κῶς Aristid.*Rh.*1 p.510 S. **-ίζω,** *imitate Demosthenes*, Plu.*Cic.*24.

**δημοσίᾳ,** Adv., v. δημόσιος.

⊛ **δημοσιεύω,** Dor. **δᾱμ-,** *make public* or *common*, *confiscate*, τὰ χρήματα X.*HG*1.7.10. **2.** *publish* a book, J.*Vit.*65, Gal.14.62; κοινοῦν καὶ δ. τὴν χρείαν [λόγου] Plu.2.34c:—Pass., τὰ δεδημοσιευμένα *sayings that have become public property*, Arist.*Rh.*1395$^a$19. **3.** δ. τὴν τοῦ σώματος ὥραν *prostitute* it, D.H.1.84. **4.** Pass., *to be manifested*, *displayed*, -εύεται ἡ θερμότης τινός Steph.*in Hp.*1.186 D. **5.** Pass., *to be produced as evidence*, *PLond.*1.77.5 (vi A.D.), etc. **II.** intr., *to be in the public service*, esp. of physicians *in receipt of a salary from the state*, Ar.*Ach.*1030, Pl.*Grg.*514d, *POxy.*40.9 (ii/iii A.D.); οἱ ἰατροὶ οἱ δαμοσιεύοντες ἐν τᾷ πόλει *SIG*943.7 (Cos); δ. δωρεάν *IG*2$^2$.483.17: generally, *to be a public man*, opp. ἰδιωτεύω, Pl.*Grg.*515b, *Ap.*32a; φροντίσι δ. *devote oneself* in every thought *to the common good*, Plu.2.823c; but ἐπὶ μισθῷ δ. *to be a* paid *official*, Id.*Comp.Arist.Cat.*6; also of things, ἐν βαλανείῳ δημοσιεύοντι Id.*Phoc.*4.

**δημοσιο-μάστης,** v. δαμοσιομάστας. **-πρακτος,** ον, *engaged in public business*, *Cat.Cod.Astr.*1.150.

⊛ **δημόσιος,** Dor. **δᾱμ-,** α, ον (ος, ον Hp. (v. infr.)), *belonging to the people* or *state*, κτέανα Xenoph.2.8; τὰ δ. Hdt.5.29, Ar.*V.*554; δ. χρήματα Cratin.171; πλοῦτος Th.1.80; χώρα, opp. ἱερά, ἰδία, Arist.*Pol.*1267$^b$34; ἡ δ. τράπεζα *IG*2$^2$.1013; τὰ ἱερὰ τὰ δ., opp. ἰδιωτικά, *SIG*1015.9 (Halic.); ἀγῶνες, δίκαι, Aeschin.1.2, Arist.*Pol.*1320$^a$12; δ. λόγος, = Lat. *fiscus*, *BGU*193.27, *OGI*669.21; δημόσιον εἶναι, γίγνεσθαι, to be, become *state-property*, be *confiscated*, Th.2.13, *IG*2$^2$.1100.40 (Hadr.), Pl.*Lg.*742b, etc.; γῆν δ. ποιεῖν Lys.18.14. **b.** *used by the public*, βαλανεῖα, λουτρόν, Plb.26.1.12, Hdn.1.12.4. **2.** *common*, δημοσιώτατος τρόπος, τόπος, Arist.*Top.*162$^a$35, *SE*165$^a$5; δημόσιος κακίη *epidemic*, Hp.*Ep.*19 (*Hermes* 53.67). **II.** as Subst.: **a.** δημόσιος (sc. δοῦλος), ὁ, *any public slave* or *servant*, as, *the public crier*, Hdt.6.121; *policeman*, Ar.*Lys.*436; *public notary*, = γραμματεύς, D.19.129, etc.; *public executioner*, D.S.13.102: generally, *public official*, τὸν ἀρχέφοδον καὶ τοὺς ἄλλους δημοσίους *POxy.*69.13 (ii A.D.). **b.** *public victim*, = φάρμακος, Ar.*Eq.*1136, cf. Sch. ad loc. **c.** *harlot*, *prostitute*, Procop.*Arc.*9 (cf. Sapph.148). **III.** neut., δημόσιον, τό, *the state*, Hdt.1.14, Aeschin.3.58; οἱ ἐκ δ. *public officials*, X.*Lac.*3.3. **b.** *public building*, *hall*, Hdt.6.52. **c.** *treasury*, = τὸ κοινόν, ἀργύριον ὀφείλοντες τῷ δ. And.1.73, cf. D.21.182, Din.2.2; ὁ ἐκ δ. μισθός Th.6.31; ἡ ἐκ τοῦ δ. τροφή Pl.*R.*465d; τελεῖν εἰς τὸ δ. *BGU*1188.12 (Aug.), 1158.18 (i B.C.). **d.** *the public prison*, Th.5.18. **2.** τὰ δ. *public archives*, *OGI*229.108 (Smyrna). **b.** *public dues*, *taxes*, in pl., *PLond.*3.938.11 (iii A.D.), *BGU*1018.21 (iii A.D.). **IV.** fem., δαμοσία (sc. σκηνή), ἡ, *tent of the Spartan kings*: hence οἱ περὶ δαμοσίαν the *king's council*, X.*HG*4.5.8, *Lac.*13.7. **V.** as Adv.: **1.** dat. δημοσίᾳ, Ion. -ίῃ, *at the public expense*, Hdt.1.30, Ar.*Av.*396, etc.; *by public consent*, D.21.50; *on public service*, δ. ἀποδημεῖν Id.45.3; δ. κρίνειν try *in the public courts*, And.1.105; δ. τεθνάναι to die *by the hands of the public executioner*, D.45.81. **2.** *as a community*, opp. ἰδίᾳ, Pl.*Ap.*30b. **3.** *commonly*, *popularly*, τὰ δ. νομιζόμενα ἀγαθά Luc.*Nigr.*4. **4.** regul. Adv. -ίως A.D.*Adv.*151.12; *on public business*, καταπλεῦσαι *SIG*520.7 (Naxos, iii B.C.).

⊛ **δημοσιουργία,** Dor. **δᾱμοσιοργία,** ἡ, *eligibility for public office*, *SIG*1009.10 (Chalcedon).

**δημοσιοφύλαξ** [ῠ], Dor. **δᾱμοσιο-,** ακος, ὁ, *treasury official*, *SIG*529.4, 531.26 (Dyme, iii B.C.).

⊛ **δημοσι-όω,** *confiscate*, Th.3.68, Procop.*Arc.*11:—Pass., of the Ager Publicus at Rome, *to be converted to public use*, D.H.8.74; also δεδημοσιωμέναι γυναῖκες *prostitutes*, Plu.2.519e. **II.** *publish*, D.L.8.55:—usu. Pass., Pl.*Sph.*232d, Plu.2.507f. **2.** *register* a deed, παρὰ τῷ ἀρχιδικαστῇ *Sammelb.*4651.6 (iii A.D.):—usu. Pass., *BGU*50.5 (ii A.D.), etc. **-ωμα,** gloss on δάμωμα, Hsch. **-ώνης,** ου, ὁ, *farmer of the revenue*, Str.12.3.40, D.S.34.38, al., *OGI*629.25 (Palmyra), *IG*7.413 (Oropus), *POxy.*44.8 (i A.D.), etc. **-ωνία,** ἡ, *leasing of the revenues*, Memn.38.2, *OGI*440.9 (Ilium). ⊛ **-ώνιον,** τό, *office of revenue-leases*, Plu.2.820c. ⊛ **-ωσις,** εως, ἡ, *registration* of a deed in the record office, *POxy.*906.9 (ii/iii A.D.), 1200.7 (iii A.D.), etc.

**δημοσσόος,** ον, (σῴζω) *saving the people*: but, **II.** δημόσσοος, (σεύω) *driven away by the people*:—both in Hsch.

**δημο-στροφέω,** *go about amongst the people*, Hsch. ⊛ **-σώστης,** ου, ὁ, *saviour of the people*, *IGRom.*3.67 (Prusias): fem. **-σῶστις,** βουλή prob. l. in *Bayr.Sitzb.*1863.220. ⊛ **-τελής,** ές, (τέλος) *at the public cost*, θυσίη Hdt.6.57, cf. Pl.*Lg.*935b, Plb.6.53.6, *CIG*3493.7 (Thyatira); ἑορτή Th.2.15, cf. *OGI*56.41 (iii B.C.); πανάγυριν δαμοτέλην (sic) *IG*12(2).645.44 (Nesus); δ. ἱερὰ τελεῖν Orac.ap.D.21.53. **2.** *with public authority*, *sovereign*, ἐκκλησία *AJA*18.324 (Sardis). Adv. -λῶς Suid. **II.** epith. of Demeter, *IG*12(7).4.5 (Amorgos).

⊛ **δημότερος,** α, ον, poet. for δημοτικός II, A.R.3.606. **II.** = δημόσιος I.1, χρήματα *AP*9.693. **III.** = δημόσιος I.2, *common*, *vulgar*, Κύπρις ib.415.2 (Antiphil.).

**δημοτερπής,** ές, *popular*, *attractive*, Pl.*Min.*321a (Sup.), D.H.*Rh.*1.8 (Comp.), Max.Tyr.10.6.

⊛ **δημοτεύομαι,** Pass., *to be a* δημότης, ἠρόμην ὁπόθεν δημοτεύοιτο Lys.23.2, cf. Antipho *Fr.*65, D.57.49.

⊛ **δημότης,** ου, ὁ, Dor. **δᾱμότας,** also **δᾱμέτας** (q.v.), *one of the people*, *commoner*, opp. a man of rank, Tyrt.4.5, Hdt.2.172, 5.11, X.*Cyr.*2.3.7; ἄνδρα δ. S.*Aj.*1071; δ. ὅμιλος Ar.*Pax*921; δ. τε καὶ ξένος E.*Supp.*895; δημόται καὶ πένητες X.*Mem.*1.2.58:—fem. **δημότις,** ιδος, opp. βασίλισσα, Plb.22.20.2: pl., opp. εὐγενέσταται, D.C.62.15. **2.** = ἰδιώτης, γνωστὰ λέγειν δημότῃσι speak *popularly*, Hp.*VM* 2, cf. *Acut.*8; ἀμαθίη τῶν δ. Id.*Art.*67. **II.** *one of the same people*, *fellow-citizen*, Pi.*N.*7.65, E.*Alc.*1057. **III.** at Athens and elsewhere, *member of a deme* or *of the same deme*, S.*OC*78, Susario 1, Pl.*Ap.*33e, D.18.261, *IG*2$^2$.1172, etc.; φράτερας καὶ δ. Cratin.Jun.9:—so fem. **δημότις,** ιδος, Ar.*Lys.*333, Theoc.28.22. ⊛ **-ικός,** ή, όν, *of* or *for the people*, *in common use*, δ. γράμματα in Egypt, opp. ἱρά, Hdt.2.36; οἶνος Plu.*Mar.*44; of opinions and the like, ὑπόληψις *popular*, Arist.*Metaph.*989$^a$11; *common*, *ordinary*, ὀνόματα Luc.*Hist.Conscr.*22; ὕλη Max.Tyr.10.7; πράγματα μικρὰ καὶ δ. Plu.2.408c. **2.** = δημόσιος, τὰ -κά *public affairs*, Alciphr.1.4; δ. λειτουργία *PSI*1.86 (iv A.D.). **II.** *of the populace*, *one of them*, D.21.209. Adv. -κῶς, ἐσταλμένος Luc.*Scyth.*5. **2.** *on the popular* or *democratic side*, τὸ σόφισμα δ. Ar.*Nu.*205; ὄρνεα δ. Id.*Av.*1584; τὴν οὐ δ. παρανομίαν Th.6.28; opp. ὀλιγαρχικός, Isoc.16.37; λέγεις πόσα δεῖ προσεῖναι τῷ δ. D.18.122; οὐδὲν δ. πράττειν to do nothing *for the people*, X.*HG*2.3.39; δ. συκοφάνται Isoc.8.133: generally, *popular*, δ. καὶ φιλάνθρωπος X.*Mem.*1.2.60; τῶν μετρίων τινὰ καὶ δ. D.21.183; δημοτικὸν τοῦτο δρᾷ Antiph.190.19: hence, *generous*, *kindly*, *affable*, X.*Mem.*1.2.60; δ. τι καὶ πρᾶον Pl.*Euthd.*303d; πρᾶός τις καὶ δ. Plb.10.26.1; δ. καὶ φιλάνθρωπα Plu.*Oth.*1. Adv. -κῶς *affably*, *kindly*, καλῶς καὶ δ. D.24.59; φιλανθρώπως καὶ δ. ib.24: Comp. -ώτερον Plu.*Demetr.*42. **3.** of governments, *popular*, *democratic*, πολιτεία Arist.*Pol.*1292$^b$13: Comp. -ώτερα Id.*Ath.*22.1. **4.** δ. δικαστήριον *trying suits between citizens*, *SIG*286.17 (Milet., iv B.C.). **5.** Adv. χρῆσθαι ἀλλήλοις δ. *in a spirit of equality*, Arist.*Pol.*1308$^a$11; δ. πεπαιδευμένοι ib.1310$^a$17; δ. ἐρίζειν *like a free and independent citizen*, Luc.*Ner.*9. **III.** *of* or *belonging to a deme*, opp. δημόσιος, Lex ap. D.43.71; ἱερά Hsch. s.v. δημοτελῆ.

**δημοῦχος,** Dor. **δᾱμ-,** ον, (ἔχω) *protectors* or *possessors of the land*, epith. of guardian deities, S.*OC*458; δαμοῦχοι γᾶς ib.1087 (lyr.); ἄνδρες δ. χθονός ib.1348; title of the Heraclidae at Thespiae, D.S.4.29.

**δημο-φάγος** [ᾰ], ον, = δημοβόρος, τύραννος Thgn.1181. **-φᾰνής,** ές, (φαίνω) *public*, *solemn*, ἑορτή Ph.2.169. **II.** *notorious*, πρᾶγμα Phryn.*PS*p.64 B. **-φαντος,** ον, = foreg., Hsch. **-φθόρος,** ον, *ruining the people*, f.l. for θυμο-, Callistr.*Stat.*14. **-φῐλής,** ές, = φιλόδημος, Sch.Ar.*Pl.*550.

**Δημοφῶν,** = θλάσπι, prob. l. in Ps.-Dsc.2.156 (Wellm.).

⊛ **δημο-χᾰρής,** ές, *pleasing the people*, *popular*, Paul.Al.*N.*2. **-χᾰριστής,** οῦ, ὁ, *mob-courtier*, E.*Hec.*132 (anap.). **-χᾰριστικῶς,** *like a* δημοχαριστής, Sch.Il.2.350.

**δημ-όω,** v. δημόομαι. **-ώδης,** ες, *popular*: μουσική, σωφροσύνη, *in the popular sense*, Pl.*Phd.*61a, *Lg.*710a; ἀρεταὶ καὶ κακίαι Phld.*Rh.*1.217 S.; *hackneyed*, κοινὰ καὶ δ. ὀνόματα Longin.40.2; στιχίδια Plu.*Per.*30, cf. Ael.*VH*3.3; λόγος ib.3.45; τὸ δ. πλῆθος, of civilians, opp. στρατιωτικοί, Hdn.1.4.8, cf. 1.15.7; of a prostitute, *common*, *AP*7.345. Adv. -δῶς Apollon.Cit.1. **-ώλης,** ες, *having lost membership of a* δῆμος, *IG*1$^2$.913. ⊛ **-ωμα,** v. δάμωμα. ⊛ **-ωφελής,** ές, *of public use*, λόγοι Pl.*Phdr.*227d; πολιτεύματα Plu.2.784d; δ. τι πραχθέν D.C.72.7, cf. Luc.*Bis Acc.*11; τὸ δ. *the common good*, Hdn.2.3.8: Sup. τὸ -έστατον Ph.2.177. **2.** of persons, Democr.282, Phld.*Rh.*2.92 S.; ἡγεμών Plu.*Sull.*30. **3.** Adv. -λῶς *CIG*4415*b* (Iotapata), *IPE*1$^2$.39.36 (Olbia), *IGRom.*4.860 (Laodicea ad Lycum): Sup. -έστατα D.C.56.37. **-ωφελῶν·** δῆμον ὠφελῶν, Hsch.

⊛ **Δήν,** Δῆνος, Cret., = Ζεύς, *SIG*527.18 (iii B.C.).

⊛ **δήν,** Dor. **δάν** (or **δοάν** Alcm.135, cf. A.D.*Adv.*160.18), Adv. *for a long while*, Il.5.412; οὐδὲ γὰρ..δ. ἦν nor was he *long-lived*, 6.131, cf. 16.736; δ. δὴ . . φίλοι ὦμεν Thgn.1243; ἐπὶ δ. μετέπειτα A.R.1.516, cf. Euph.9.8; once in Trag., A.*Pers.*584 (lyr.). 2. *long ago*, δ. οἴχεσθαι Od.18.313. (δοάν, = δϝάν, cf. Lat. *dudum*: hence οὐδὲ δ(ϝ)ὴν Il.16.736.)

**δηναιός**, ή, όν, Dor. **δᾱναιός**, ά, όν, *long-lived*, Il.5.407; δ. κλέος Theoc.16.54; *long-continued*, ὁδοιπορίη *IG*14.1780; χρόνος A.R.4.1547; βίος *AP*6.39.7 (Arch.): neut. as Adv., Man.3.143. 2. *aged*, κόραι A.*Pr.*794; *ancient*, θρόνοι ib.912 (and in *Eu.*846 (lyr.), δαναιὰν should be restored with Dindorf for δαμαίων, cf. Call.*Fr.*105); ἀοιδοί Id.*Jov.*60; *worn out*, δένδρα Hsch. II. *after a long time*, δ. εἰσαφίκοντο A.R.4.645; *late come, long absent*, ἀδελφεός Opp.*H.*4.154: neut. δηναιόν, as Adv., A.R.3.590: so pl., δηναιά Maiist.8. III. personified, Θόωσα and Δηναιή, *Overspeed* and *Loitering*, Emp.122.3.

**δηναιότης**, ητος, ἡ, *long life*, Democr.201.

**Δηναιών**, ῶνος, ὁ (sc. μήν), name of month at Erythrae, *SIG*1014.24 (iii B.C.).

**δηνάριον**, τό, = Lat. *denarius* (usu. represented by δραχμή (q.v.)), Arr.*Epict.*1.4.16, *Placit.*4.11.5, etc.; = *one tetradrachm*, *PLond.*2.248.20 (iv A.D.), *POxy.*1431.3 (iv A.D.).

**δήνεα**, τά, only in pl., *counsels, plans, arts*, whether good or bad, δ. θεῶν Od.23.82; ἤπια δ. οἶδε Il.4.361, Hes.*Th.*236; ὀλοφώϊα Od.10.289; δ. πάντα καὶ τρόπους ἐπίσταται Semon.7.78; δ. Κίρκης A.R.4.559; δ. τέχνης Opp.*H.*1.7.—Sg. nom. **δῆνος**, εος, τό, Hsch.: **δήνεον** (sic), Suid.

**δήξ**, gen. δηκός, ὁ or ἡ, *worm in wood*, Tz. ad Hes.*Op.*418.

**δηξίθῡμος** [ῐ], ον, = δακέθυμος, ἔρωτος ἄνθος A.*Ag.*743 (lyr.); comically, δ. ὀξάλμη Sopat.21.

**δῆξις**, εως, ἡ, (δάκνω) *bite, biting*, Arist.*HA*623ᵃ1; δήξιες σπλάγχνων *gnawings*, Hp.*VM*19: metaph., of mental anguish, *pangs*, Zeno *Stoic.*1.51 (pl.), Chrysipp.ib.3.119, Phld.*D.*3*Fr.*22; also, *biting jokes*, Plu.*Lycurg.*14.

**δῆος**· βωβός (Cret.), Hsch.

**δηόω**, contr. for δηϊόω.

**δήποθεν**, indef. Adv. (better written **δή ποθεν**) *from any quarter*, Pl.*Ep.*331e; dub. l. in A.*Ch.*632 (lyr.); perh. = δήπου, as in Orac. ap. Phleg.*Olymp.Fr.*1, Iamb.*Myst.*5.20.

**δήποτε**, indef. Adv. (better written **δή ποτε**), Ion. **δήκοτε**, Dor. **δήποκα**, *at some time, once upon a time*, Od.6.162, E.*Supp.*1131 (lyr.); αἰεὶ δ. Th.8.73; *at length*, A.*Ag.*577. 2. εἰ δή ποτε if *ever*, Il.1.40. 3. with interrog., τί δή ποτε; what *in the world?* what or why *now?* καίτοι τί δή ποτε; D.4.35; πόσοι δή ποτ' εἰσὶν οἱ . .; how many *do you suppose?* Id.20.21. 4. esp. freq. with relatives, ὅτι δή κοτε πρήξαντα Hdt.6.134; ὅστις δ. ὤν Pl.*Phdr.*273c; ὅτι δή ποτε whatever *it may be*, '*so-and-so*', D.21.32; ὁπόθεν δ. Id.35.6: strengthd. by οὖν, ὅντινα δή ποτ' οὖν τρόπον Id.40.8; οἷος δή ποτ' οὖν v.l. in Dsc.5.10; also δή ποτ' οὖν without relat., κατὰ πρεσβείαν ἢ κατ' ἄλλην δ. χρείαν *Arch.Pap.*6.9 (Delos).

**δήπου**, indef. Adv. (better written **δή που**) *perhaps, it may be*, ᾧ δή που ἀδελφεὸν ἔκτανε Il.24.736: in Trag. and Att. usu. *doubtless, I presume*, οὐ δήπου τλητόν A.*Pr.*1064; τῶν Λαΐου δ. τις ὠνομάζετο S.*OT*1042, cf. Ar.*Pl.*491, 582, Th.1.121, etc.; ἴστε γὰρ δή που, μέμνησθε γὰρ δή που, D.2.25, 19.113, cf. 18.249; σχεδὸν ἴσμεν ἅπαντες δή που Id.3.9; οὐδεὶς ἀγνοεῖ δή που Id.21.156. II. as interrog. implying an affirm. answer, τὴν αἰχμάλωτον κάτοισθα δή που; i.e. *I presume* you know, S.*Tr.*418; ἀνόμοιον δή που Pl.*Tht.*159b; οὐ δή που; *surely it is* not *so?* implying a neg. answer, as Ar.*Ra.*526, Pl.*Men.*73c.

**δήπουθεν** (-θε before a consonant, Bato 7.3), indef. Adv. = δήπου, chiefly used before a vowel (before a consonant, Pl.*Ion* 534a, etc.), freq. in Com., Ar.*V.*296, *Pl.*140, etc.; in answer to a rhetorical question, οὐ δ., ἀλλά. Lys.6.36, cf. D.27.59, Pl.*Phlb.*62e, etc.

**δηράς**, ἡ, Cret., = δειράς (q.v.). **δηρή**, = δειρή, Hsch.: but **δήρη**· μάχη, Id.

[**δηρ**]**ιάζομαι**, = sq., περί τινος Pi.*Pae.*6.119 (prob.).

**δηρῑάομαι**, (δῆρις) *contend*, περὶ νεκροῦ δηριάασθαι (v.l. δηρίσασθαι) Il.17.734; ὥστ' ἀμφ' οὔροισι δύ' ἀνέρε δηριάασθον *wrangle* about boundaries, 12.421: abs., ὅ τ' ἄριστοι . . δηριόωντο Od.8.78; οἱ δ' αὐτοὶ δηριαάσθων Il.21.467; δ. τινί *contend with* one, A.R.4.1729.—Later Act. **δηρῑάω**, *contest a prize*, Pi.*N.*11.26; δίφροι δηριόωντες A.R.1.752, cf. Opp.*C.*1.230.—From **δηρίομαι** (used by Pi.*O.*13.44) Hom. has aor. 1 Med. δηρίσαντο Od.8.76: 3 dual aor. 1 Pass. δηρινθήτην (as if from δηρίνομαι) Il.16.756 (later δηρινθῆναι A.R.2.16, -θέντες Euph.98.3): fut. δηρίσομαι Theoc.22.70: also in aor. Act., δηρισάντοιν Thgn.995; οὐκ ἄν τοί τις ἐδήρισεν περὶ τιμῆς Theoc.25.82, cf. Lyc.1306. ῐ in pres.; ῑ in fut. and aor.]

**δῆρις**, ἡ, *battle, contest*, Il.17.158, al. (only in acc.): nom. in A.*Supp.*412 (lyr.), Emp.122.2 (personified), *Epigr.Gr.*343 (Germa); gen. δήριος A.*Ag.*942, δήρεως Suid.

**δηρίττειν**· ἐρίζειν, Hsch.

**δηρίφᾰτος** [ῐ], ον, = ἀρείφατος, prob. in *AP*7.722 (Theodorid.).

**δηρόβῐος**, Dor. **δᾱρ-**, ον, *long-lived*, θεοί A.*Th.*524 (lyr.).

**δηρός**, Dor. **δᾱρός**, ά, όν, (cf. δήν) *long, too long*, δηρὸν χρόνον Il.14.206, *h.Cer.*282: more freq. δηρόν (sc. χρόνον) as Adv., *all too long*, Il.2.298, etc.; also ἐπὶ δηρὸν δέ μοι αἰὼν ἔσσεται 9.415, cf. Musae.291: freq. with neg., οὐδέ σέ φημι δ. . . ἀλύξειν Il.10.371, cf. 2.435, etc.: Trag. use only Dor. form, πολὺν δαρόν τε χρόνον S.*Aj.*414 (lyr.), cf. A.*Supp.*516, E.*IT*1339; δαρόν alone, A.*Pr.*648, 940, S., etc.; also δαρὸν χρόνου πόδα time's *lingering* foot, E.*Ba.*889 (lyr.).

**δηρότη(ς)**· κακουργία, Hsch. (leg. δηϊότης).

**δησάσκετο**, v. δέω (A). **δῆσε**, aor. of δέω (A): also for ἐδέησε, aor. of δέω (B).

**δῆτα**, Adv., lengthd. and more emphatic form of δή, first as v.l. in Hdt.4.69, mostly used by Trag. and Pl. (v. infr.).—Never placed at the beginning of a sentence or verse, exc. in S.*Aj.*986. 1. in answers, mostly added to a word which echoes a statement or question, as ἴσασιν ὅστις ἦρξε . . Answ. ἴσασι δ. *aye* they know, E.*Med.*1373; γιγνώσκεθ' ὑμεῖς . .; Answ. γιγνώσκομεν δ. *yes* we know her, Ar.*Th.*606, cf. *Eq.*6, al.; ἰὼ δὴ κατ' ἄστυ. Answ. ἰὼ δ. A.*Pers.*1071, cf. S.*OC*536 (lyr.), Pl.*R.*333a, *Phd.*90d, al. (with a word repeated in the same speech, ὥς μ' ἀπώλεσας· ἀπώλεσας δ. how hast thou destroyed me! — *aye*, destroyed *indeed*, S.*El.*1164; ἰὼ δύστηνε σύ, δύστηνε δῆτα Id.*Ph.*760); also to correct the previous speaker, οἴκτιρέ θ' ἡμᾶς . . Answ. οἴκτιρε δ . . ἐκγόνους *nay rather* pity . ., E.*El.*673, cf. 676; without repeating the word, αὐτὸς δ' ἀναλοῖ δ. *yes truly* . ., A.*Th.*814; ἐκεῖνος αὐτὸς δ. Ar.*Ra.*552: freq. with a neg., not so, οὐ δῆτα μὰ τὸν Ἀπόλλω Id.*Eq.*870; οὐ δῆτ' ἔγωγε *faith* not I, Id.*Av.*1391, E.*Med.*1048; οὐ δ. Lacon. ap. Arist.*Rh.*1419ᵃ34, cf. *Pol.*1313ᵃ33. 2. in questions, to mark an inference or consequence (cf. δή), τί δ.; what *then?* A.*Pr.*627; τί δ. ἐρεῖς, ἦν . .; Ar.*Nu.*1087; τί δ. ἐπειδὰν . .; Id.*Ach.*1011; πῶς δ.; A.*Ag.*1211, Ar.*Nu.*79; ἆρ' οἶσθα δ.; S.*OT*1014; ἀλλὰ δ . . .; as the last of several questions, Id.*Aj.*466, etc.; ποῦ δῆθ' ὁ τῖμος; A.*Ch.*916; ποῖ δ. κρανεῖ; ib.1075, etc.; sts. expressing indignation, καὶ δῆτ' ἐτόλμας; and *so* thou hast dared? S.*Ant.*449; ταῦτα δῆτ' ἀνασχετά; Id.*Ph.*987; ἢ ταῦτα δῆτ' ἀνεκτά; Id.*OT*429; ἔγνωκας οὖν δῆτ' . .; Ar.*Eq.*871; ironical, τῷ σῷ δικαίῳ δ. ἐπισπέσθαι με δεῖ; your principle of justice *forsooth*, S.*El.*1037, cf. *OT*364; in implied questions, esp. after ἀλλά, ἀλλ' ἡ τέκνων δῆτ' ὄψις ἦν ἐφίμερος ib.1375, cf. Ar.*Av.*375, Pl.*Hp.Ma.*283c; τὴν Εὐρυτείαν οἶσθα δ. παρθένον; *of course* you know . ., S.*Tr.*1219. 3. in prayers or wishes, ἀπόλοιο δ. *now* a murrain take thee! Ar.*Nu.*6; λαβοῦ, λαβοῦ δ. take, *oh* take hold, E.*Or.*219, cf. 1231, etc.; σκόπει δ. *just* think, Pl.*Grg.*452c: with μή, it strengthens the deprecatory force, μὴ δ. τοῦτό γ' S.*Ph.*762, cf. 1367; μὴ δ. μὴ δ. ἴδοιμι Id.*OT*830, cf. 1153. 4. in resuming after a parenthesis, ἑσπέρας γε .—ἑσπέρας δ. Pl.*Prt.*310c. 5. καὶ δ., = καὶ δή, ibid., Ar.*Av.*511, Th.6.38. II. rarely, like δή I, to emphasize single words, ἅπασι δ. Ar.*Ec.*1144.

**δητός** (A), οῦ, ὁ, (δέω A) *bundle*, σχοινίων *Sammelb.*1.5 (pl., iii A.D.).

**δητός** (B)· ὕστερος, Hsch.

**δηταί**· αἱ ἐπτισμέναι κριθαί, Hsch.; cf. δηαί.

**δηὖτε**, contr. for δὴ αὖτε, freq. in Lyr.; v. αὖτε.

**δήω** (A), *find, meet with*, always in pres. (exc. impf. ἔδηεν Hsch.) with fut. sense, δήεις Il.13.260, Od.7.49, *AP*7.370 (Diod.); δήομεν Od.4.544; δήετε Il.9.418; δήουσι A.R.4.591; δήωμεν, δήοιμεν, ib.1336, 1460. (Poet. exc. as etym. of Δηώ in Corn.*ND*28.)

**δήω** (B), *burn*, *EM*265.7.

**Δηώ**, όος, contr. οῦς, ἡ, = Δημήτηρ, *Demeter*, first in *h.Cer.*47, al.; Ἐλευσινίας Δηοῦς ἐν κόλποις S.*Ant.*1121 (lyr.); Δηοῦς ἐσχάραι, καρπός, E.*Supp.*290, Ar.*Pl.*515; dat. Δηοῖ Call.*Ap.*110, *IG*3.900.3:—Adj. **Δηῷος**, α, ον, *sacred to Demeter*, ib.14.1389 ii 5:—**Δηωΐνη**, ἡ, *daughter of Demeter, Persephone*, Call.*Fr.*48.

**δῃώω**, v. δηϊόω.

**δῄωσις**, εως, ἡ, *ravaging*, Ph.2.548 (pl.), Polyaen.1.36.2.

**Δί, Δία**, v. Ζεύς.

**διά**, poet. **διαί** (Aeol. ζά, q.v.), Prep. governing gen. and acc.—Rad. sense, *through*; never anastroph. [Prop. δῐᾰ: but Hom. uses ῑ at the beginning of a line, Il.3.357, 4.135, al.: also ᾱ, metri gr., freq. in Hom., for which A. uses διαί in lyr., *Ag.*448, al.]

A. With Gen. I. of Place or Space: 1. of motion *in a line*, from one end to the other, *right through*, in Hom. freq. of the effect of weapons, διὰ μὲν ἀσπίδος ἦλθε . . ἔγχος καὶ διὰ θώρηκος . . Il.3.357; δουρὶ βάλεν Δάμασον κυνέης διά 12.183; δι' ὤμου . . ἔγχος ἦλθεν 4.481; in Prose, τιτρώσκειν διὰ τοῦ θώρακος X.*An.*1.8.26; διὰ τοῦ ὀρόφου ἐφαίνετο πῦρ ib.7.4.16: also of persons, διὰ Σκαιῶν πεδίονδ' ἔχον ὠκέας ἵππους *out through* the Scaean gate, Il.3.263; δι' ἠέρος αἰθέρ' ἵκανεν *quite through* the lower air even to the ether, Il.14.288, cf. 2.458; διὰ Τρώων πέτετο *straight through* them, 13.755; δι' ὀμμάτος . . λείβων δάκρυον S.*OC*1250, etc.: also in Compos. with πρό and ἐκ, v. διαπρό, διέκ: in adverbial phrases, διὰ πασῶν (sc. χορδῶν), v. διαπασῶν: διὰ πάσης *throughout*, Th.1.14; διὰ κενῆς *idly*, Id.4.126, etc. (cf. III.1.c). 2. of motion *through* a space, but *not in a line, throughout, over*, ἐπόμεσθα διὰ πεδίοιο Il.11.754; δι' ὄρεσφι 10.185, al.; ὀδύνη διὰ χροὸς ἦλθε *through all* his frame, 11.398; τεῦχε βοὴν διὰ ἄστεος Od.10.118; δι' ὁμίλου Il.6.226, etc.; θορύβου διὰ τῶν τάξεων ἰόντος X.*An.*1.8.16, cf. 2.4.26, etc.; later, in quoting an authority, ἱστορεῖ δ. τῆς δευτέρας *in the course of* . ., Ath.10.438b. 3. *in the midst of*, Il.9.468; κεῖτο τανυσσάμενος δ. μήλων Od.9.298; *between*, δ. τῶν πλευρέων ταμόντα Hp.*Morb.*2.61: hence, of *pre-eminence*, ἔπρεπε καὶ δ. πάντων Il.12.104; τετίμακε δι' ἀνθρώπων Pi.*I.*4(3).37; εὐδοκιμέοντι δ. πάντων Hdt.6.63, cf. 1.25, etc. 4. in Prose, sts. of extension, *along*, παρήκει δ. τῆσδε τῆς θαλάσσης ἡ ἀκτή Id.4.39 (but πέταται δ. θαλάσσας *across* the sea, Pi.*N.*6.48); λόφος, δι' οὗ τὸ σταύρωμα περιεβέβλητο X.*HG*7.4.22. 5. in Prose, of Intervals of Space, δ. τριήκοντα δόμων *at intervals of* thirty layers, i.e. *after every* thirtieth layer, Hdt.1.179; δ. δέκα ἐπάλξεων *at every* tenth battlement, Th.3.21; cf. infr. II.3: of a single interval, δ. πέντε σταδίων *at a distance of* five stades, Hdt.7.30, cf. 198; δ. τοσούτου μᾶλλον ἢ δ. πολλῶν ἡμερῶν ὁδοῦ *at* so short *a distance*, etc., Th.2.29; δ. πολλοῦ *at* a great *distance apart*, Id.3.94; δ. πλείστου Id.2.97; δι' ἐλάσσονος Id.3.51; ὕδατα δ. μακροῦ ἀγόμενα Hp.*Aër.*9, etc. II. of Time, 1. of *duration* from one end of a period to the other, *throughout*, δ. παντὸς [τοῦ χρόνου] Hdt.9.13; δι' ὅλου τοῦ αἰῶνος Th.1.70; δι' αἰῶνος S.*El.*1024; δι' ἡμέρας ὅλης Ar.*Pax* 27; δι' ὅλης τῆς νυκτός X.*An.*4.2.4, etc.: without an Adj., δι' ἡμέρης *all* day *long*, Hdt.1.97; δ. νυκτός Th.2.4, X.*An.*4.6.22 (but δ. νυκτός *in the course of* the night, *by* night, *Act.Ap.*5.19, *PRyl.*138.15 (i A.D.), etc.); δ. νυκτὸς καὶ ἡμέρας Pl.*R.*343b; δι' ἐνιαυτοῦ, δι' ἔτους, Ar.*Fr.*569.8, *V.*1058; δ. βίου Pl.*Smp.*183e, etc.; δ. τέλους *from beginning to end*, A.*Pr.*275, Pl.*R.*519c, etc.: with Adjs. alone, δ. παντός *continually*, A.*Ch.*862 (lyr.), etc.; δι' ὀλίγου *for* a short time, Th.1.77; δ. μακροῦ E.*Hec.*320; ὁ δ. μέσου χρόνος Hdt. 8.27. 2. of the interval which has passed *between* two points of Time, δ. χρόνου πολλοῦ or δ. πολλοῦ χρ. *after* a long time, Id.3.27, Ar.*Pl.*1045; δ. μακρῶν χρόνων Pl.*Ti.*22d: without an Adj., δ. χρόνου *after* a time, S.*Ph.*758, X.*Cyr.*1.4.28, etc.; δι' ἡμερῶν *after* several days, *Ev.Marc.*2.1; and with Adjs. alone, δι' ὀλίγου Th.5.14; οὐ δ. μακροῦ Id.6.15,91; δ. πολλοῦ Luc.*Nigr.*2, etc.: with Numerals, δι' ἐτέων εἴκοσι Hdt.6.118, cf. *OGI*56.38 (iii B.C.), etc.: but δ. τῆς ἑβδόμης *till* the seventh day, Luc.*Hist.Conscr.*21: also distributively, χρόνος δ. χρόνου προὔβαινε time *after* time, S.*Ph.*285; ἄλλος δι' ἄλλου E.*Andr.*1248. 3. of successive Intervals, δ. τρίτης ἡμέρης every other day, Hdt.2.37; δ. τρίτου ἔτεος ib.4, etc.; δ. πεντετηρίδος every four years (with inclusive reckoning), Id.3.97; δι' ἔτους πέμπτου, of the Olympic games, Ar.*Pl.*584 (but δι' ἑνδεκάτου ἔτεος *in the course of* the eleventh year, Hdt.1.62). III. causal, *through*, *by*, a. of the Agent, δι' ἀγγέλων or -ου ἐπικηρυκεύεσθαι, ποιεῖσθαι, *by the mouth of*.. Id.1.69,6.4, cf. 1.113; δι' ἑρμηνέως λέγειν X.*An.*2.3.17, etc.; τὸ ῥηθὲν ὑπὸ Κυρίου δ. τοῦ προφήτου *Ev.Matt.*1.22; δι' ἑκόντων ἀλλ' οὐ δ. βίας ποιεῖσθαι Pl.*Phlb.*58b; πεσόντ' ἀλλοτρίας διαὶ γυναικός *by* her *doing*, A.*Ag.*448 (lyr.); ἐκ θεῶν γεγονὼς δ. βασιλέων πεφυκώς X.*Cyr.*7.2.24; δι' ἑαυτοῦ ποιεῖν τι *of oneself*, *not by another's agency*, ib.1.1.4, etc.; but also, *by oneself alone*, *unassisted*, D.15.14, cf. 22.38. b. of the Instrument or Means, δ. χειρῶν *by* hand (prop. *by holding between* the hands), δι' ὁσίων χ. θιγών S.*OC*470; also δ. χερῶν λαβεῖν, δ. χειρὸς ἔχειν *in* the hand, Id.*Ant.*916,1258 (but τὰ τῶν ξυμμάχων δ. χειρὸς ἔχειν to keep a *firm* hand on, Th.2.13); δ. στέρνων ἔχειν S.*Ant.*639; ἡ ἀκούουσα πηγὴ δι' ὤτων Id.*OT*1387; δ. στόματος ἔχειν X.*Cyr.*1.4.25; δ. μνήμης ἔχειν Luc.*Cat.*9; αἱ δ. τοῦ σώματος ἡδοναί X.*Mem.*1.5.6; δ. λόγων συγγίγνεσθαι to hold intercourse *by* word, Pl.*Plt.*272b; δ. λόγου ἀπαγγέλλειν *Act.Ap.*15.27; δι' ἐπιστολῶν 2*Ep.Cor.*10.9, *POxy.*1070.15 (iii A.D.). c. of Manner (where διά with its Noun freq. serves as an Adv.), δ. μέθης ποιήσασθαι τὴν συνουσίαν Pl.*Smp.*176e; παίω δι' ὀργῆς *through* passion, *in* passion, S.*OT*807; δ. τάχους, = ταχέως, Id.*Aj.*822, Th.1.63 (but δ. ταχέων ib.80, al.); δ. σπουδῆς *in* haste, hastily, E.*Ba.*212; δι' αἰδοῦς *with* reverence, respectfully, ib.441; δ. ψευδῶν ἔπη lying words, Id.*Hel.*309; αἱ δ. καρτερίας ἐπιμέλειαι *long-continued* exertions, X.*Mem.*2.1.20; δι' ἀκριβείας, δ. πάσης ἀκρ., Pl.*Ti.*23d, *Lg.*876c; δ. σιγῆς Id.*Grg.*450c; δ. ξυμφορῶν ἡ ξύμβασις ἐγένετο Th.6.10; οὐ δι' αἰνιγμάτων, ἀλλ' ἐναργῶς γέγραπται Aeschin.3.121; δι' αἵματος, οὐ δ. μέλανος τοὺς νόμους ὁ Δράκων ἔγραψεν Plu.*Sol.*17: also with Adjs., δ. βραχέων, δ. μακρῶν τοὺς λόγους ποιεῖσθαι, Isoc.14.3, Pl.*Grg.*449b; ἀποκρίνεσθαι δ. βραχυτάτων ibid. d; cf. infr. IV. 2. in later Prose, of Material *out of* which a thing is made, κατασκευάζειν εἴδωλα δι' ἐλέφαντος καὶ χρυσοῦ D.S.17.115; θυσίαι δι' ἀλφίτου καὶ σπονδῆς πεποιημέναι Plu.*Num.*8; βρώματα δ. μέλιτος κ. γάλακτος γιγνόμενα Ath.14.646e; οἶνος δ. βουνίου Dsc.5.46. IV. διά τινος ἔχειν, εἶναι, γίγνεσθαι, to express conditions or states, ἀγὼν διὰ πάσης ἀγωνίης ἔχων extending *through* every kind of contest, Hdt.2.91; δι' ἡσυχίης εἶναι Id.1.206; δι' ὄχλου εἶναι to be trouble*some*, Ar.*Ec.*888; δ. φόβου εἶναι Th.6.59; δι' ἀπεχθείας γίγνεσθαι X.*Hier.*9.2; ἡ ἐπιμέλεια δ. χάριτος γίγνεται ibid.; δ. μιᾶς γνώμης γίγνεσθαι Isoc.4.138. b. with Verbs of motion, δ. μάχης ἐλεύσονται will engage *in* battle, Hdt.6.9; ἐλθεῖν Th.4.92; δ. παντὸς πολέμου, δ. φιλίας ἰέναι τινί, X.*An.*3.2.8; δ. δίκης ἰέναι τινί go *to* law with.., S.*Ant.*742, cf. Th.6.60; δ. τύχης ἰέναι S.*OT*773; δι' ὀργῆς ἥκειν Id.*OC*905; ἐμαυτῷ δ. λόγων ἀφικόμην I held converse with myself, E.*Med.*872; δ. λόγων, δ. γλώσσης ἰέναι come *to* open speech, Id.*Tr.*916, *Supp.*112; δ. φιλημάτων ἰέναι come *to* kissing, Id.*Andr.*416; δ. δικαιοσύνης ἰέναι καὶ σωφροσύνης Pl.*Prt.*323a, etc.; δ. πυρὸς ἰέναι (v. πῦρ): in pass. sense, δι' ἀπεχθείας ἐλθεῖν τινι to be *hated* by.., A.*Pr.*121 (anap.). c. with trans. Verbs, δι' αἰτίας ἔχειν or ἄγειν τινά hold *in* fault, Th.2.60, Ael.*VH*9.32; δι' ὀργῆς ἔχειν τινά Th.2.37, etc.; δ. φυλακῆς ἔχειν τι Id.7.8; δι' οἴκτου ἔχειν τινά, δι' αἰσχύνης ἔχειν τι, E.*Hec.*851, *IT*683; δ. πένθους τὸ γῆρας διάγειν X.*Cyr.*4.6.6; δι' οὐδενὸς ποιεῖσθαί τι S.*OC*584.

B. WITH ACC. I. of Place, only Poet., in same sense as διά c. gen.: 1. *through*, ἐξ δὲ δ. πτύχας ἦλθε.. χαλκός Il.7.247; ἤϊξε δ. δρυμὰ.. καὶ ὕλην 11.118, cf. 23.122, etc.; δ. τάφρον ἐλαύνειν *across* it, 12.62; δ. δώματα ποιπνύοντα 1.600; ἐπὶ χθόνα καὶ δ. πόντον βέβακεν Pi.*I.*4(3).41; φεύγειν δ. κῦμ' ἅλιον A.*Supp.*14 (anap.). 2. *through*, *among*, in, οἴκεον δι' ἄκριας Od.9.400; ἄραβος δὲ δ. στόμα γίγνετ' ὀδόντων Il.10.375 (but μῦθον, ὃν.. δ. στόμα.. ἄγοιτο *through* his mouth, 14.91; so δ. στόμα ὄσσαν ἱεῖσαι Hes.*Th.*65; ἀεὶ γὰρ ἡ γυνή σ' ἔχει δ. στόμα Ar.*Lys.*855); δ. κρατερὰς ὑσμίνας Hes.*Th.*631; νόμοι δι' αἰθέρα τεκνωθέντες S.*OT*867 (lyr.). II. of Time, also Poet., δ. νύκτα Il.2.57, etc.; δ. γλυκὺν ὕπνον *during* sweet sleep, Mosch.4.91. III. causal: 1. of persons, *thanks to*, *by aid of*, νικῆσαι δ.. Ἀθήνην Od.8.520, cf. 13.121; δ. δμῳὰς.. εἷλον 19.154; δ. σε *by* thy *fault* or *service*, S.*OC*1129, Ar.*Pl.*145, cf. 160,170: in Prose, *by reason of*, *on account of*, δι' ἡμᾶς Th.1.41, cf. X.*An.*7.6.33, D.18.249; οὐ δι' ἐμαυτόν And.1.144; so εἰ μὴ διά τινα if it had not been *for*.., εἰ μὴ δι' ἄνδρας ἀγαθοὺς Lys.12.60; Μιλτιάδην εἰς τὸ βάραθρον ἐμβαλεῖν ἐψηφίσαντο, καὶ εἰ μὴ δ. τὸν πρύτανιν ἐνέπεσεν ἄν Pl.*Grg.*516e, cf. D.19.74; εἰ μὴ δ. τὴν ἐκείνου μέλλησιν Th.2.18, cf. Ar.*V.*558; πλέον' ἔλπομαι λόγον Ὀδυσσέος ἢ πάθαν γενέσθαι δι' Ὅμηρον Pi.*N.*7.21. 2. of things, to express the Cause, Occasion, or Purpose, δι' ἐμὴν ἰότητα *because of* my will, Il.15.41; Διὸς μεγάλου δ. βουλάς Od.8.82; δι' ἀφραδίας *for*, *through* want of thought, 19.523; δι' ἀτασθαλίας 23.67; δι' ἔνδειαν *by reason of* poverty, X.*An.*7.8.6; δ. καῦμα, δ. χειμῶνα, ib.1.7.6; δι' ἄγνοιαν καὶ ἀμαθίαν Pl.*Prt.*360b, etc.: freq. also with neut. Adjs., δ. τί; *wherefore?*; δ. τοῦτο, δ. ταῦτα *on* this *account*; δι' ὅ, δι' ἅ *on* which *account*; δ. πολλά *for* many *reasons*, etc. 3. = ἕνεκα, to express Purpose, δι' ἀχθηδόνα *for the sake of* vexing, Th.4.40, cf. 5.53; δ. τὴν τούτου σαφήνειαν *with a view to* clearing this up, Pl.*R.*524c, cf. Arist.*EN* $1172^b21$; αὐτὴ δι' αὑτὴν *for* its own *sake*, Pl.*R.*367b, etc.

C. WITHOUT CASE as Adv. *throughout*, δ. πρό (v. supr. A. I. 1); δ. δ' ἀμπερές Il.11.377.

D. IN COMPOS.: I. *through*, *right through*, of Space, διαβαίνω, διέχω, διιπνέω. II. *in different directions*, as in διαπέμπω, διαφορέω; of separation, *asunder*, διαιρέω, διαλύω; of difference or disagreement, *at variance*, διαφωνέω, διαφέρω; or simply mutual relation, *one with another*, διαγωνίζομαι, διᾴδω, διαθέω, διαπίνω, διαφιλοτιμέομαι. III. pre-eminence, διαπρέπω, διαφέρω. IV. completion, *to the end*, *utterly*, διεργάζομαι, δ. αμάχομαι, διαπράττω, διαφθείρω: of Time, διαβιόω. V. to add strength, *thoroughly*, *out and out*, διαγαληνίζω, etc.; cf. ζα. VI. of mixture, *between*, *partly*, esp. in Adj., as διάλευκος, διάχρυσος, διάχλωρος, etc. VII. of leaving an *interval* or *breach*, διαλείπω, διαναπαύω. (Cogn. with δύο, δίς.)

**δῖα**, ἡ, fem. of δῖος. **Δία**, acc. of Ζεύς.

**Δῖα** (sc. ἱερά), τά, = Διάσια, *SIG*38.34 (Teos, v B.C.); cf. Δεῖα.

**διαβᾰδίζω**, fut. -ιοῦμαι, later -ιῶ Luc.*Dem.Enc.*1, -βαδίσω D.C.37.53:—*go across*, Th.6.101, Gal.6.185. 2. *walk to and fro*, App.*BC*1.25, Luc. l.c.: in pres. Med., Them.*Or.*21.253a.

**δια-βάθρα**, ἡ, *ladder*, Aristeas 106, Str.16.2.40, D.H.5.41, etc.: esp. *ship's gangway*, *PPetr.*2p.38 (iii B.C.). II. *drawbridge*, Apollod.*Poliorc.*170.1, al.: generally, *bridge*, *PSI*5.543 (iii B.C.). **-βαθρον**, τό, a kind of *slipper*, Alex.98.8, Herod.7.61, Alciphr.3.46; cf. Lat. *diabathrarii*, Plaut.*Aul.*513.

**διαβαίνω**, fut. -βήσομαι: aor. -έβην, Aeol. part. ζάβαις Alc.*Supp.*7.3: I. intr., *stride*, *walk* or *stand with legs apart*, εὖ διαβάς, of a man *planting himself firmly* for fighting, Il.12.458, Tyrt.11.21; ἀδὶ διαβὰς Ar.*V.*688; τοσόνδε βῆμα διαβεβηκότος Id.*Eq.*77; opp. συμβεβηκώς, X.*Eq.*1.14; πόδας μὴ -βεβῶτας Hp.*Art.*43, cf. D.S.4.76; κολοσσοὶ -βεβηκότες Plu.2.779f; simply, *spacious*, δόμοι Corn.*ND* 15: metaph., μεγάλα δ. ἐπί τινα *to go with* huge *strides* against.., Luc.*Anach.*32; ὀνόματα -βεβηκότα εἰς πλάτος *great straddling* words, D.H.*Comp.*22; [ποὺς] -βεβηκὼς *with a mighty stride*, ib.17: c. acc. cogn., αἱ ἁρμονίαι διαβεβήκασι εὐμεγέθεις διαβάσεις ib.20; also ἐξερείσματα χρόνων πρὸς ἑδραῖον -βεβηκότα μέγεθος Longin.40.4. II. c. acc., *step across*, *pass over*, τάφρον Il.12.50; πόρον Ὠκεανοῖο Hes.*Th.*292, cf. A.*Pers.*865 (lyr.); Ἀχέροντα Alc. l.c.; ποταμόν Hdt.1.75, etc., cf. 7.35; also διὰ ποταμοῦ X.*An.*4.8.2. 2. abs. (θάλασσαν or ποταμόν being omitted), *cross over*, Ἤλιδ' ἐς εὐρύχορον διαβήμεναι Od.4.635; ⟨ἐς⟩ τήνδε τὴν ἤπειρον Hdt.4.118; πλοίῳ Id.1.186, cf. Th.1.114, Pl.*Phdr.*229c, etc.: metaph., τῷ λόγῳ διέβαινε ἐς Εὐρυβιάδεα *he went over* to him, Hdt.8.62; δ. ἐπὶ τὰ μείζω Arr.*Epict.*1.18.18. b. πόθεν.. διαβέβηκε τὸ ἀργύριον from what sources the money *has mounted up*, Plu.2.829e. 3. *bestride*, *AP*7.74 (Diosc.). 4. *decide*, δίκας *SIG*426.7 (Teos, iii B.C.). 5. *come home to*, *affect*, εἴς τινα Diog.Oen.2, Steph. *in Rh.*281.5.

⊛ **διαβάλλω**, fut. -βᾰλῶ: pf. -βέβληκα:—*throw* or *carry over* or *across*, νέας Hdt.5.33,34; in wrestling, Ar.*Eq.*262 codd. 2. more freq. intr., *pass over*, *cross*, ἐκ.. ἐς.. Hdt.9.114; φυγῇ πρὸς Ἄργος E.*Supp.*931; πρὸς τὴν ἤπειρον Th.2.83: c. acc. spatii, δ. πόρον A.*Fr.*69 (dub.); γεφύρας E.*Rh.*117; τὸν Ἰόνιον Th.6.30; τὸ πέλαγος εἰς Μεσσαπίους Demetr.Com.Vet.1. 3. *put through*, τῆς θύρας δάκτυλον D.L.1.118; τύλος διαβεβλημένος διὰ τοῦ ῥυμοῦ Arr.*An.*2.3.7 (= Aristobul.*Fr.*4); κρίκων δι' ἀλλήλων διαβεβλημένων D.Chr.30.20; διαβληθέντων τῶν ἀγκώνων διὰ μέσων τῶν τόνων Hero *Bel.*101.12, cf. 108.6. II. in Ar.*Pax* 643 ἅττα διαβάλοι τις αὐτῷ, ταῦτ' ἂν ἥδιστ' ἤσθιεν, for παραβάλοι, whatever scraps *they threw to* him, with a play on signf. v. III. *set at variance*, ἐμὲ καὶ Ἀγάθωνα Pl.*Smp.*222c,d, cf. *R.*498c; δ. τινὰς ἀλλήλοις Arist.*Pol.*$1313^b16$; *set against*, τινὰς πρὸς τὰ πάθη, πρὸς τὴν βρῶσιν, Plu.2.727d,73cf; *bring into discredit*, μή με διαβάλῃς στρατῷ S.*Ph.*582; δ. [τινὰ] τῇ πόλει Pl.*R.*566b:—Pass., *to be at variance with*, τινί Id.*Phd.*67e; *to be filled with suspicion and resentment against* another, Hdt.5.35, 6.64, Th.8.81,83; οὐδὲν ὑπολείπεται ὅτῳ ἄν μοι δικαίως διαβεβλῆσθε And.2.24; πρός τινα Hdt.8.22, Arist.*Rh.*$1404^b21$, Plb.30.19.2; τοὺς -βεβλημένους πρὸς τὴν φιλοσοφίαν Isoc.15.175; *to be brought into discredit*, ἐς τοὺς ξυμμάχους Th.4.22; διαβεβλημένος *discredited*, Lys.7.27,8.7. IV. *put off with evasions*, δ. τινὰ μίαν (sc. ἡμέραν) ἐκ μιᾶς *Sammelb.*5343.41 (ii A.D.), cf. *PFlor.*36.23 (iv A.D.). V. *attack* a man's character, *calumniate*, δ. τοὺς Ἀθηναίους πρὸς τὸν Ἀρταφρένεα Hdt.5.96; Πελοποννησίους ἐς τοὺς Ἕλληνας Th.3.109; διέβαλλον τοὺς Ἴωνας ὡς δι' ἐκείνους ἀπολοίατο αἱ νέες Hdt.8.90; διαβαλὼν αὐτοὺς ὡς οὐδὲν ἀληθὲς ἐν νῷ ἔχουσι Th.5.45; *accuse, complain of*, without implied malice or falsehood, *PTeb*.23.4 (ii B.C.): c. dat. rei, *reproach* a man *with*.., τῇ ἀτυχίᾳ Antipho 2.4.4; δ. τινὰ εἴς or πρός τι, Luc.*Demon*. 50, *Macr*.14:—Pass., διεβλήθη ὡς *Ev.Luc*.16.1; ἐπὶ βίῳ μὴ σώφρονι διαβεβλημένος Hdn.2.6.6. 2. c. acc. rei, *misrepresent*, D.18.225, 28.1, etc.: *speak* or *state slanderously*, ὡς οὗτος διέβαλλεν Id.18.20, cf. ib.14; τοῦτό μου διαβάλλει ib.28: generally, *give hostile information*, without any insinuation of falsehood, Th.3.4. 3. δ. τι εἴς τινα *lay the blame for* a thing on.., Procop.*Arc*.22.19. 4. *disprove* a scientific or philosophical doctrine, Gal.5.289:—Pass., Id.5.480, Plu.2.930b. 5. δ. ἔπος *declare it spurious*, Id.*Thes*. 34. VI. *deceive by false accounts, impose upon, mislead*, τινά Hdt.3.1, 5.50, 8.110, E.*Fr*.435:—Med., Hdt.9.116, Ar.*Av*.1648 (ubi v. Sch.), *Th*.1214:—Pass., Hp.*Nat.Puer*.30, Pl.*Phdr*.255a, Plu.2.563d. VII. *divert* from a course of action, πρὸς τὴν κακίαν τινάς ib.809f:—Pass., ψυχὴ -βέβληται πρὸς μάχην Arr.*Epict*.2.26.3. VIII. Med., *contract an obligation* (?), *Leg.Gort*.9.26. IX. διαβάλλεσθαι ἀστραγάλοις πρός τινα *throw* against him, Plu.2.148d, 272f.

**διαβαπτίζομαι**, *dive for a match*, πρός τινα Polyaen.4.2.6. 2. metaph., *contend in foul language with*, τινί D.25.41.

**διάβαρος** λίθος, a volcanic stone, dub. in Thphr.*Lap*.20 (leg. διάβορος, *porous*).

**διαβᾰσᾰνίζω**, *test thoroughly*, Pl.*Lg*.736c, J.*AJ*5.7.10, Arr.*Epict*. 3.26.13.

**διαβᾰσείω**, Desiderat. of διαβαίνω, D.C.40.32.

**διαβᾰσῐλίζομαι**, *to be a pretender to a kingdom*, *Com.Adesp*.322.

⊛ **διάβᾰσις**, εως, ἡ, *crossing over, passage*, δ. ποιεῖσθαι Hdt.1.186, etc.; *act of crossing*, αἱ δ. τῶν ὀχετῶν διασπῶσι τὰς φάλαγγας Arist. *Pol*.1303$^b$12. 2. *means* or *place of crossing*, Hdt.1.205; δ. ποταμῶν *fords*, Th.7.74, cf. X.*An*.1.5.12, etc.; *bridge*, ib.2.3.10; *passage along a ship's deck, gangway*, Hp.*Ep*.14, Plu.*Cim*.12; *ferry-boat*, Lxx 2*Ki*.19.18. II. the Jewish *Passover*, Ph.1.117. III. ἡ τῶν ὡρῶν δ. *transition* of the seasons, Ael.*NA*9.46. IV. in Gramm., *transitive force* of Verbs, τὰ ἐν δ. τοῦ προσώπου ῥήματα A.D. *Synt*.202.7, al. V. in Rhet. of *intervals* or *pauses* in pronunciation caused by long syllables and the like, ῥυθμοὶ πλείστην ἔχοντες δ. D.H.*Comp*.20; cf. διαβαίνω I.

**διαβάσκω**, = διαβαίνω, *strut*, διαβάσκει Ar.*Av*.486; cf. διαβιβάσκω.

**διαβαστ-αγμός**· *cunctatio*, *Gloss*. -**άζω**, *carry over*, Aq.*Is*.51.18, Sm.*Ex*.15.13:—Pass., Vett.Val.162.28. II. *weigh in the hand, estimate*, Plu.*Dem*.25, Luc.*Ep.Sat*.33. 2. *contain*, Vett. Val.222.1.

**διαβᾰτ-έος**, α, ον, *that must be crossed* or *passed through*, ποταμός X.*An*.2.4.6; νάπος ib.6.5.12. II. διαβατέον *one must cross*, Plb. 5.51.5, Plu.*Luc*.31, etc. -**ήρια** (sc. ἱερά), τά, *offerings before crossing the border*, τὰ δ. προὐχώρει, τὰ δ. ἐγένετο, they were favourable, Th.5.54, 55, cf. X.*HG*4.7.2; also, *for crossing a river*, ἔθυσε τῷ Εὐφράτῃ ταῦρον δ. Plu.*Luc*.24; τὰ δ. δυσχερέστατα ἐγένετο D.C.40.18: also masc., Ζεὺς διαβατήριος Ctes.*Fr*.29.17. II. Jewish *Passover*, Ph.2.292, al. ⊛ -**ης**, ου, ὁ, *one who ferries over* or *crosses*, Ar.*Fr*.765. II. = διαβήτης, Hsch. -**ικός**, ή, όν, of Verbs, *transitive*, A.D.*Synt*.43.18. II. *slipping through* the fingers, Sch.Ar.*Nu*. 448. -**ός**, ή, όν, *to be crossed* or *passed, fordable*, Hdt.1.75, Th. 2.5, etc.; νῆσον δ. ἐξ ἠπείρου *easily got at* from the main land, Hdt. 4.195:—Aeol. **ζάβατος**, Sapph.158. II. **διάβατον**, τό, *passage for water*, *PIand*.52.14 (i A.D.).

**διαβεβαι-όω**, *confirm*, ὑπόληψιν D.L.8.70:—usu. Med. -**όομαι**, *maintain strongly, affirm, confirm*, D.17.30; οἱ πρεσβύτεροι δ. οὐδέν Arist.*Rh*.1389$^b$16; δ. γεγονέναι τι D.S.13.90, cf. Aristeas 99, D.H. 2.39, *BGU*1917 (ii A.D.), *POxy*.67.10 (iv A.D.); *to be positive*, περί τινος Plb.12.12.6, S.E.*P*.1.191:—Pass., Phld.*Rh*.1.226S., *Sign*. 17. -**ωσις**, εως, ἡ, *assurance*, δοῦναι, ἐργάζεσθαι, ib.24, 35; *asseveration*, Hdn.*Fig*.p.96S. -**ωτικός**, ή, όν, *affirmative*, δ. σύνδεσμος A.D.*Conj*.235.26, al., *EM*415.42; θεωρία Ptol.*Tetr*.7. Adv. -κῶς A.D.*Synt*.318.28, S.E.*P*.1.233.

**διαβέτης**, εος, ὁ, (perh. for δια-ϝέτης, cf. ἔτης) title of *official* at Sparta, *IG*5(1).32*A*2, al.

**διά-βημα**, ατος, τό, *a step across, a step*, Lxx *Jb*.31.4: metaph. in pl., *successive moments*, ἡ διακόσμησις τρισὶ διώρισται δ. Dam.*Pr*. 423. -**βημᾰτίζω**, *step out, pace out*, Aq.2*Ki*.6.13. -**βησείω**, later form, = -βασείω, Agath.2.4. -**βήτης**, ου, ὁ, (διαβαίνω) *compass*, so called from its outstretched legs, Ar.*Nu*.178, *Av*.1003. 2. *carpenter's* or *stonemason's rule*, ξύσας ὀρθὸν πρὸς διαβήτην *IG*12(2).11.20 (Lesbos), cf. ib.2.1054.10, Pl.*Phlb*.56b, Plu.2.802f, Sch.Il.2. 765. II. *siphon*, Colum.3.10, Hero *Spir*.1.29. III. Medic., the disease *diabetes*, Aret.*SD*2.2, Philagr.ap.Orib.5.19.9, Gal.8. 394. -**βητίζομαι**, Med., *make straight by rule*, *IG*7.3073.186 (Lebad.). ⊛ -**βήτινος**, η, ον, *made by rule*, ἐκτομάς *Stud.Pal*.20. 211.9 (v/vi A.D.).

⊛ **διαβῐάζομαι**, strengthd. for βιάζομαι, E.*IT*1365, Lxx *Nu*.14.44; δ. τὴν ἀσθένειαν τῇ συνηθείᾳ τῇ πρὸ τοῦ Plb.23.12.2; of plants, *penetrate* the soil in germination, Thphr.*CP*2.17.7.

**διαβῐβ-άζω**, causal of διαβαίνω, *carry over* or *across, transport, lead over*, δ. τὸν στρατὸν κατὰ γεφύρας Hdt.1.75; ἐς τὴν νῆσον ὁπλίτας Th.4.8: also c. acc. loci, ποταμὸν δ. [τινά] *take* one *across* a river, Pl. *Lg*.900c, Plu.*Pel*.24: metaph., δ. ἐπὶ τὰ ὁμοειδῆ τὸ χρήσιμον Chrysipp. *Stoic*.2.31, cf. Apollon.Cit.1 (Pass.), Aristid.*Or*.28(49).29; *lead* to a conclusion, τινὰ εἰς πέρας τῷ λόγῳ Hld.2.24: in Music, *cause* the melody *to pass*, ἐπὶ τὴν παρυπάτην Plu.2.1134f. 2. δ. κλήρους *pass through* the heats or rounds of an athletic contest, *JRS*3.282 (Antioch in Pisidia). 3. Pass., of Verbs, *have a transitive force*, A.D.*Synt*.277.10, al. 4. later, *pass time*, Sch.Ar.*Pl*.847. -**άσκω**, = foreg., Hp.*Fract*.4, cf. Erot. (διέβασκον codd.). -**ασμός**, ὁ, Gramm., *transitive force*, A.D.*Pron*.113.21. -**αστικός**, ή, όν, of Verbs, *transitive*, Id.*Synt*.298.15.

⊛ **διαβιβρώσκω** Gal.13.553: fut. Pass. -βρωθήσομαι ib.466: mostly in pf. Pass. -βέβρωμαι:—*eat up, consume, corrode*, Hp.*Morb*.2.24, Pl.*Ti*.83a, etc., Luc.*Ind*.1: metaph., διαβιβρώσκονται ὑπὸ [λόγων] Plu.2.508d; ψυχὴ -βεβρωμένη Max.Tyr.6.7.

**διαβῐ-όω**, fut. -ώσομαι: aor. 2 -εβίων, inf. -βιῶναι (also -βιῶσαι· ζῆσαι, Hsch.): pf. -βεβίωκα Isoc.9.70:—*live through, pass*, χρόνον Pl.*Lg*.730c; τὸν βίον Id.*Men*.81b; τὸν ἐνθάδε χρόνον Isoc.l.c.: abs., *spend one's whole life*, δ. δικαίως Pl.*Grg*.526a: c. part., μελετῶν διαβεβιωκέναι X.*Ap*.3, *Mem*.4.8.4. 2. *survive*, Procop.*Pers*.2.5, al. 3. δ. ἀπὸ χρημάτων *live* on, Plu.*Publ*.3. -**ώσκω**, = foreg. 2, Agath.*Praef*. -**ωτέον**, *one must spend one's life*, δ. παίζοντα Pl. *Lg*.803e.

**διαβλαστ-άνω**, *sprout*, Thphr.*CP*4.8.1, Plu.*Crass*.22. -**ησις**, εως, ἡ, *germination*, Thphr.*CP*2.17.10.

**διαβλέπω**, *stare with eyes wide open*, Pl.*Phd*.86d, Arist.*Insomn*. 462$^a$13; δ. εἴς τινα, πρός τινα, Plu.*Alex*.14, 2.548b. 2. *see clearly*, Dionys.Com.2.13; ἐν τοῖς σκοτεινοῖς Phld.*Rh*.1.252S., cf. Luc.*Merc. Cond*.22: c. inf., διαβλέψεις ἐκβαλεῖν τὸ κάρφος *Ev.Matt*.7.5.

**διά-βλημα**, ατος, τό, *strap passing through* a shoe-buckle, Lyd. *Mag*.2.13. -**βλητικός**, ή, όν, = διαβολικός, Poll.5.118: -κή, ἡ, *art of calumny*, Phld.*Vit*.p.42J. Adv. -κῶς Poll.l.c. -**βλήτωρ**, ορος, ὁ, *slanderer*, Man.4.236.

**διαβλύζω**, *gush forth*, κολώνης Nonn.*D*.22.21.

⊛ **διαβο-άω**, late fut. -βοήσω Hdn.2.2.2:—*proclaim, publish*, aor. subj. -βοάσω A.*Pers*.638 (lyr.): c. acc. et inf., ἐκεῖσε χωρεῖν τινὰς διεβόησαν Corn.*ND*35:—Pass., *to be the common talk*, ταῦτα δὴ διαβεβόηται Pl.*Ep*.312b; *to be celebrated*, of persons or things, Plu.*Sol*.11, *Them*.3; πρός τινα Id.*Per*.9; ἐπί τινι Luc.*Nec*.6, Ant.Lib.12.4. II. *cry aloud*, δ. ὡς.. Th.8.53, 78: abs., Luc.*Am*.17. III. Med., *contend in shouting*, D.26.19. -**ησις**, εως, ἡ, *crying out* or *aloud*, Plu.2.455b. -**ητος**, ον, *noised abroad, famous*, Plu.*Lyc*.5, Hdn. 4.4.8; ἐφ' ὥρᾳ καὶ λαμυρίᾳ Plu.*Luc*.6, cf. X.Eph.1.2, D.Chr.3.72, Luc. *Alex*.4.

**διαβολ-ή**, ἡ, (διαβάλλω v) *false accusation, slander*, Epich.148; ἐπὶ διαβολῇ εἰπεῖν Hdt.3.66, 73; δ. λόγου Th.8.91; διαβολὰς ἐνδέχεσθαι, προσίεσθαι, to give ear to *them*, Hdt.3.80, 6.123; διαβολὰς ἔχειν ὡς.. to have *it slanderously said* that.., Isoc.8.125; ὀνείδους καὶ δ. τυγχάνειν Lys.25.6; ἐν δ. καθεστηκέναι ibid.; διαλύσειν τὴν δ. Th.1.131: of *charges* not necessarily false or malicious, δ. ταῖς ἐμαῖς *the accusations* which I bring, E.*Andr*.1005, cf. Isoc.1.17; τὰ πρὸς διαβολὴν κυροῦντα tending *to discredit*, Plb.12.15.9, cf. 2.11.4; ἐμὴ δ. *prejudice against* me, Pl. *Ap*.19b; δ. εἰς ἐμέ And.1.30; δ. καθ' αὑτοῦ παρέσχεν Plu.*Them*.4, cf. Phryn.Com.58; opp. δόξα, *ill-repute*, Men.723; δ. λῦσαι καὶ ποιῆσαι remove, create *prejudice* against an antagonist, Arist.*Rh*.1415$^a$27; δ. ἀπολύεσθαι D.H.6.59. II. (διαβάλλω III) *quarrel, enmity*, κατὰ τὰς ἰδίας δ. Th.2.65; ἡ πρὸς τὸ συγγενὲς δ. Plu.2.479b; ἡ πρὸς θάνατον δ. *fear, aversion* from it, ib.110a: c. gen., δ. τοῦ πάθους ib.456b; εἰς διαβολήν τινος to *withstand* them, Lxx *Nu*.22.32. III. (διαβάλλω VIII) *legal obligation* (?), *Leg.Gort*.9.35. IV. *fraud*, Sch.Ar.*Pl*. 373. -**ία**, Ion. -ίη, ἡ, = διαβολή, Thgn.324; δεινόν ἐστιν ἡ δ. Hippias *Fr*.17D.: in pl., Pi.*P*.2.76. (Perh. to be written διαι- metri gr. in poetry.) -**ικός**, ή, όν, *slanderous*, κακοτεχνία Ph. *Fr*.98H. II. *devilish*, δ. καὶ σατανικὴ ἐνέργεια *PLond*.5.1731. 11 (vi A.D.). -**ος**, ον, *slanderous, backbiting*, γραῦς Men.878, cf. Phld.*Lib*.p.24O.: Sup. -ώτατος Ar.*Eq*.45; διάβολόν τι, *aliquid invidiae*, And.2.24; τὸ δ. Plu.2.61d. II. Subst., *slanderer*, Pi. *Fr*.297, Arist.*Top*.126$^a$31, Ath.11.508d; *enemy*, Lxx *Es*.7.4, 8.1: hence, = *Sātān*, ib.1*Chr*.21.1; *the Devil*, *Ev.Matt*.4.1, etc. III. Adv. -λως *injuriously, invidiously*, Th.6.15; χρῆσθαί τινι Procop. *Arc*.2.

**διαβορβορύζω**, strengthd. for βορβορύζω, Hp.*Aph*.4.73.

**διαβόρειος**, ον, *stretching northwards*, Str.2.1.33 (s.v.l.).

**διαβόρος**, ον, (βιβρώσκω) *devouring*, νόσος S.*Tr*.1084, *Ph*.7. II. διάβορος, ον, Pass., *eaten up, consumed*, Id.*Tr*.676; cf. διάβαρος.

**διαβόσκω**, fut. -ήσω Socr.*Ep*.19:—*feed*, ὄροβοι καὶ τὰ ἐς βρῶσιν ἀναγκαῖα διέβοσκεν αὐτοὺς Philostr.*VA*1.15; τὴν γαστέρα ἐπί τινι Alciphr.3.7; *pasture*, *PMasp*.112.15 (vi A.D.).

**διαβοστρῠχόομαι**, Pass., *to be curled*, διαβεβοστρυχωμένος Archil. 162.

**διαβουκολέω**, *cheat with false hopes*, Luc.*DMort*.5.2:—Med., διαβουκολεῖσθαί τινι *beguile oneself with*.., Them.*Or*.21.255d.

**διαβουλ-ευείρ**· ὁ ἐν τοῖς ἱστοῖς πρόβολος (Lacon.), Hsch. -**εύω**, of a Council, *complete its term*, Arist.*Ath*.32.1. II. mostly in Med. (Dor. διαβωλ- *IG*5(2).343), *deliberate, discuss thoroughly*, And. 2.19, Th.2.5, 7.50; δ. εἴτε.. εἴτε Pl.*Plt*.304e, cf. Luc.*Hist.Conscr*. 31; *decide*, c. inf., Id.*Pisc*.24. ⊛ -**ία**, ἡ, = sq., Lxx *Ps*.5.10, *Ho*. 11.6. -**ιον**, τό, *debate, deliberation*, ib.*Wi*.1.9 (pl.), al.; δ. ἄγειν Plb.3.20.1, etc. II. *resolution, decree*, Id.4.24.2, etc. III. *meeting for debate*, Id.29.10.2, *IG*5(1).1390.172 (Andania, i B.C.). -**οι**· δίπλοι, δίβουλοι, Hsch.

**διαβουνίν,** *sweetmeat eaten at dessert,* Hsch.

**διαβρᾰβεύω,** *bestow,* Aesop.24(v.l.).

**διάβραγχος,** ὁ, *windpipe* (?), *Hippiatr.*20.

**διά-βρεγμα,** ατος, τό, *extract prepared by maceration,* Dieuch.ap. Orib.4.7.11(pl.). **-βρεκτέον,** *one must macerate,* τυρὸν ὠμῇ λύσει *Gp.*18.19.9. **-βρεξις,** εως, ἡ, *soaking,* Erot. s.v. τέγξις. ❋ **-βρεχής,** ές, *wet through, soaked,* Luc.*Trag.*304. **-βρέχω,** *soak,* τἀρτύματα A.*Fr.*306: abs., Arist.*Pr.*866$^{a}$10:—Pass., ἄλφιτα ζωμῷ διαβραχέντα Ael.*NA*1.23, cf. *Gp.*17.17.2; διαβεβρεγμένος, of a person, *soaked in liquor,* Hld.5.31; πρὶν διαβραχῆναι πικροτάτους εἶναι Zeno *Stoic.*1.65; ἐν οἴνῳ καὶ μέθῃ διαβραχείς Porph.*Chr.*30.

**διαβρίθει·** βαρύνει, Hsch., and **διαβρῑθής·** ἰσχυρός, Id.

**διαβρῑμάομαι,** strengthd. for βριμάομαι, Them.*Or.*21.261c.

**διαβροχή,** ἡ, *maceration,* v.l. in Dsc.2.107, cf. Antyll.ap.Orib.4.11.2; *soaking, wetting,* σωμάτων ib.9.23.1.

**διαβροχισμός,** ὁ, *catching in a noose,* Antyll.ap.Orib.45.24.5, Gal.18(2).679.

**διάβροχος,** ον, (διαβρέχω) *very wet, moist,* ὄμμα E.*El.*503; ἄγκος ὕδασι δ. Id.*Ba.*1051, cf. Call.*Del.*48; γῆ Hp.*Aër.*10, Arist.*SE*167$^{b}$7. **2.** *soaked, sodden,* ναῦς δ. *leaky,* Th.7.12; σάρξ Arist.*Pr.*870$^{a}$11: metaph., ἔρωτι, μέθῃ δ., Luc.*Tox.*15, *Bis Acc.*17. **3.** *tearful,* δ. δάκρυσι Hld.1.26.

**διά-βρωμα,** ατος, τό, (διαβιβρώσκω) *that which is eaten through; worm-eaten wood, parchment,* etc., Str.13.1.54. **-βρωσις,** εως, ἡ, *eating through,* τινός Plu.2.967f(pl.); *chewing,* Dsc.5.74. **II.** Medic., *erosion* of the coats of a vessel, Aret.*SA*2.2, *SD*2.9(pl.), J.*BJ*7.11.4, Gal.8.262; of the tissues generally, ib.81; also βλεφάρων Dsc.1.105(pl.). **-βρωτικός,** ή, όν, *corrosive,* Alex.Aphr.*Pr.*1.99, Gal.1.280(Sup.).

**δια-βυνέω, -βύνω,** v. διαβύω.

**διαβύσσει·** διακαμύσσει, Hsch.

**διαβύω,** *thrust through,* ἐς τὸ στόμα Hp.*Superf.*5:—Med. (from -**βυνέω**), διαβυνέονται ὀϊστοὺς διὰ τῆς ἀριστερῆς they *pass* arrows *through their* left hand, Hdt.4.71:—Pass. (from -**βύνω**), πηδάλιον διὰ τῆς τρόπιος διαβύνεται is *passed through* the keel, Id.2.96.

**διαγᾰληνίζω,** *make quite calm,* τὰ πρόσωπα Ar.*Eq.*646.

**διᾰγᾰνακτ-έω,** *to be full of indignation,* Lys.*Oxy.*1606.84, D.27.63, Plu.2.74b, D.S.14.1; πρός τι J.*BJ*4.4.4. **II.** Medic., *to be severely affected,* Antyll.ap.Orib.44.8.1; *to be irritated,* Sor.1.81, 118. **-ησις,** εως, ἡ, *great indignation,* Ph.2.178, Plu.*Mar.*16(pl.).

**διᾰγᾰπάω,** strengthd. for ἀγαπάω, *love,* τὸν αὑτῆς ἄνδρα *PMasp.*112.15(vi A.D.).

**διαγαυριάω,** *plume oneself, strut about,* *EM*270.38. **διάγγαρον·** δικέφαλον, Hsch.

**διαγγ-ελία,** ἡ, *notification,* J.*BJ*3.8.5. **-έλλω,** fut. -ελῶ: aor. διήγγειλα X.*An.*1.6.2:—*give notice by a messenger,* c. dat., Th.7.73, X. l.c., etc.; δ. εἰς.. Id.*Mem.*3.11.3; πρός τινα Philipp.ap.D.12.16: generally, *noise abroad, proclaim,* δ. ὅτι.. Pi.*N.*5.3; τι E.*Hel.*436, Pl.*Prt.*317a: c. inf., *order* to do, E.*IA*353:—Med., *pass* the word of command *from man to man,* X.*An.*3.4.36. ❋ **-ελμα,** ατος, τό, *a message, notice,* Lxx 3*Ki.*4.20(7). ❋ **-ελος,** ὁ, *messenger, negotiator,* esp. *secret informant, go-between,* Th.7.73. **2.** military term, *adjutant,* Plu.2.678d; but, = Lat. *speculator,* Plu.*Galb.*24. **-ελτέον,** *one must notify,* τὰς παραινέσεις πᾶσι Ph.2.259.

❋ **διαγ[ειτ]ονία,** ἡ, *local group,* prob. in *IG*12(1).922.4 (Lindus).

❋ **διαγελάω,** *laugh at, mock,* τινά E.*Ba.*272,322, X.*An.*2.6.26, J.*AJ*16.7.6, Phld.*Piet.*110, Plu.2.1118c; τῶν ἰαμάτων τινὰ δ. ὡς ἀπίθανα ἐόντα *IG*4.951.35 (Epid.): abs., Luc.*Pseudol.*16. **2.** intr., *look bright,* of the weather, Thphr.*HP*8.2.4, *CP*1.2.8; δ. ἡ ἡμέρα Procop.*Aed.*1.1; of water, Plu.2.950b, cf. *Caes.*4.

**διαγέλως,** ωτος, ὁ, *derision,* prob. in Phld.*Herc.*1251.17.

**διαγενής·** εὐγενής, Hsch. (fort. διογενής).

**διά-γευσις,** εως, ἡ, *tasting,* *Gp.*7.7 tit. **-γεύω,** *give a taste of,* τινὰ τῆς φωνῆς καὶ τοῦ μέλους Eun.*Hist.*p.247 D. **II.** Med., *taste,* Plu.2.469c, *Gp.*7.7.1.

**διαγιγγράζω,** lit. *tune up*: metaph. of a cook, Athenio 1.31 (cj. Dobr.).

❋ **διαγίγνομαι,** Ion. and later Att. **-γίνομαι** [γῑ], fut. -γενήσομαι: aor. διεγενόμην, also διεγενήθην Phld.*Piet.*37:—*go through, pass,* τοσάδε ἔτη Pl.*Ap.*32e; τὴν νύκτα X.*An.*1.10.19; δ. ἀπραγμόνως τὴν ἡμέραν Nicom.Com.1.42: abs., *go through life, live,* Ar.*Av.*45, Th.5.16; *survive,* v.l. in Hp.*Epid.*1.2; ἐὰν ἄρα διαγιγνώμεθα if we *live long enough,* Aeschin.1.51; ἂν διαγένωμαι Diog.Oen.66; δ. ἀπὸ τῆς τέχνης *to subsist* by it, Arist.*Pol.*1268$^{a}$31; γενναίως δ. ἔν τινι *behave* nobly in.., Plu.2.119d: freq. c. part., διαγενέσθαι ἄρχων *continue in* the government, X.*Cyr.*1.1.1; οὐδὲν ἄλλο ποιῶν διαγεγένηται ἢ διασκοπῶν he *was never anything* but a theorist, Id.*Mem.*4.8.4; δ. κολακεύων D.23.179. **II.** *intervene, elapse,* χρόνου μεταξὺ διαγενομένου Lys.1.15; χρόνων διαγενομένων Is.11.9, cf. Plu.*Rom.*22, etc.; οἴδαμεν..ἤδη τῇ κρίσει ἐκείνῃ διαγεγονότα ἔτη ὀκτώ Test.ap.D.21.82, cf. Plu.2.162c, Phld.*Piet.*37, *POxy.*68.18(ii A.D.).

**διαγιγνώσκω,** Ion. and later Att. **-γῑνώσκω,** fut. -γνώσομαι D.50.1:—*know one from the other, distinguish, discern,* εὖ διαγιγνώσκοντες Il.23.240; ἔνθα διαγνῶναι χαλεπῶς ἦν ἄνδρα ἕκαστον 7.424, cf. Ar.*Pl.*91; δ. εἰ ὅμοιοί εἰσι *to distinguish* whether they are equals or no, Hdt.1.134; οὐδ' ἂν..διαγνοίη, λίνου ἢ καννάβιός ἐστι Id.4.74; δ. τὴν βοὴν ὁποτέρα μείζων Th.1.87; δ. διότι.. Arist.*Pol.*1266$^{b}$16; δ. πότερον.., ἢ.. Id.*Mete.*389$^{a}$5; δ. τὸν καλόν τε καὶ αἰσχρὸν ἔρωτα Pl.*Smp.*186c; δ. τὸ ὀρθὸν καὶ μή Aeschin.3.199; δ. τὴν θήλειαν καὶ τὸν ἄρρενα Arist.*HA*613$^{a}$16; δ. τοὺς νεωτέρους καὶ πρεσβυτέρους ἐκ τῶν ὀδόντων ib.501$^{b}$11; δ. ὑμᾶς ὄντας.., i.e. δ. ὑμῶν οἵτινές εἰσιν.., Ar.*Eq.*518:—Pass., τὸν χαλκὸν μὴ διαγινώσκεσθαι τῇ χροᾷ πρὸς τὸν χρυσόν Arist.*Mir.*834$^{a}$2, cf. Thphr.*HP*5.3.2; *to be distinguished, celebrated,* ἀρεταῖς Pi.*Pae.*4.21. **2.** *discern exactly, perceive, descry,* τι S.*El.*1186; δ. ὅτι.. Isoc.3.47. **3.** Medic., *form a diagnosis,* Erasistr.ap.Gal.8.14. **II.** *determine* by vote or otherwise, c. inf., Hdt.6.138, Luc.*Am.*9, Hdn.4.4.2:—Pass., impers. διέγνωστο αὐτοῖς λελύσθαι τὰς σπονδάς Th.1.118. **2.** law-term, *determine* or *decide* a suit, δίκην A.*Eu.*709, cf. *IG*5(2).159 (Tegea, v B.C.), Antipho 6.3; τὰ ἀμφισβητήσιμα Id.2.1.1; *give judgement,* περί τινος Th.4.46, Lys.7.22, D.28.10; *take cognizance of* an action, *PPetr.*3p.118 (iii B.C.), etc.:—Pass., διεγνωσμένη κρίσις Th.3.53; μενέτωσαν ἐν τοῖς διαγνωσθεῖσι Lexap.D.21.94. **III.** = διαναγιγνώσκω (which shd. perh. be read), *read through,* Plb.3.32.2, Ph.2.555, al.

❋ **διαγκῠλόομαι,** Dep., (ἀγκύλη) *hold a javelin by the thong*:—only pf. part. Pass. διηγκυλωμένος *ready to throw* or *shoot,* X.*An.*4.3.28 (v.l. -ισμένος), 5.2.12: later in form -ημένος (as if from -άομαι), τόξον, κεραυνόν, δ. *ready to shoot with..,* Hdn.1.14.9, Luc.*Jup.Conf.*15.

**διάγκῠλος,** ον, *with two loops,* βρόχος Heraclas ap.Orib.48.16.1: Subst. διάγκῠλον, τό, *double loop,* Sor.*Fasc.*7.

**διαγκων-ίζομαι,** *lean on one's elbow,* Dam.*Isid.*134. **II.** διηγκωνισμένος σφυγμός, term coined by Archig., Gal.8.651. **-ισμός,** ὁ, *jostling with the elbow,* Plu.2.644a.

**διαγλαίνειν·** διαλυμαίνεσθαι, Hsch.

**διαγλαύσσω,** *shine brightly,* ἀταρποί A.R.1.1281.

**διαγλάφω** [ᾰ], *scoop out,* εὐνὰς ἐν ψαμάθοισι διαγλάψασ' (v.l. -γνάψ-) Od.4.438.

**διά-γλυμμα,** ατος, τό, in pl., *scrapings,* Sch.Ar.*Ra.*835, Hsch. s.v. σμιλεύματα. **-γλυπτος,** ον, *divided,* of a quill-pen, *AP*6.227 (Crin.). **-γλῠφή,** ἡ, *scooping out,* Orib.49.4.28. **-γλῠφος,** ον, *hollowed out, coffered,* of ceilings, *EM*789.18, Suid. ❋ **-γλύφω** [ῠ], *scoop out,* pf. Pass. διέγλυπται Androsth.ap.Ath.3.93b; *carve, engrave,* ἄγαλμα Ael.*VH*2.33; δακτυλίους ib.12.30:—Pass., διαγλυφέντες καὶ διατορευθέντες, metaph. of athletes, ib.14.7; ὀροφὴ φάτναις διαγεγλυμμένη D.S.1.66. **2.** Medic., *shape, trim,* Gal.12.348, etc.

**διάγματα·** διασκευάσματα, Hsch.

**διαγνοέω,** *to be ignorant of*:—Pass., dub. in Philostr.*Her.Prooem.*

**διάγνοια,** ἡ, *deliberation,* dub. in J.*AJ*17.9.5.

**δια-γνώμη,** ἡ, *decree, resolution,* Th.1.87; διαγνώμας ποιεῖσθαι Id.3.67; δ. προθεῖναι περί τινος ib.42. **-γνωμονέω,** *consider, reflect, deliberate,* Eust.1237.21. ❋ **-γνώμων,** ον, gen. ονος, *distinguishing,* and so *rewarding,* ὁσίων Antipho 3.3.3.

**διαγνωρ-ίζω,** *make known,* τί τινι *Ev.Luc.*2.15 (v.l.); *speak publicly,* περί τινος ib.17. **-ισμός,** ὁ, = διάγνωσις, Gal.17(1).141.

❋ **διά-γνωσις,** εως, ἡ, *distinguishing,* τὴν δ. ποιεῖσθαι ὁποῖοι ἐκράτουν ἢ ἐκρατοῦντο Th.1.50; *means of distinguishing* or *discerning,* E.*Hipp.*926; καλῶν ἢ μὴ τοιούτων τίς δ.; D.18.128; δ. φωνῆς καὶ σιγῆς Arist.*Cael.*290$^{b}$27; of medical *diagnosis,* δ. ποιεῖσθαι Hp.*VC*10, Gal.8.766, etc. **2.** *power of discernment,* E.*Hipp.*696. **II.** *resolving, deciding,* δ. ποιεῖσθαι Antipho 6.18; περί τινος D.18.7; ταχίστην ἔχει δ. Isoc.1.34; τοῦ ὃ πρακτέον ἐστίν Metrod.*Fr.*27; δ. τῆς ἀξίας ποιεῖσθαι to *determine* the value, Pl.*Lg.*865c; = Lat. *cognitio,* *Act.Ap.*25.21, *BGU*19 i 20 (ii A.D.), 891$^{r}$24 (ii A.D.); ἐπὶ διαγνώσεων τοῦ Σεβαστοῦ, = Lat. *a cognitionibus Augusti,* *IG*14.1072, cf. *Ephes.*3 No.51 (iii A.D.). **-γνωστέον,** *one must distinguish,* Luc.*Herm.*16. **-γνώστης,** ου, ὁ, *examining magistrate,* = Lat. *cognitor,* *Gloss.* **-γνωστικός,** ή, όν, *able to distinguish,* ἀληθῶν καὶ ψευδῶν λόγων S.E.*P.*2.229, cf. Luc.*Salt.*74; δ. καὶ διακριτικός Id.*Herm.*69, cf. Gal.*UP*5.10; δ. θεωρία Id.1.271; δ. σημεῖα, opp. προγνωστικά, ib.313. **II.** *belonging to a* διάγνωσις II, ὑπομνήματα *PLips.*34.15 (iv A.D.). **-γνωστός,** ή, όν, *to be distinguished,* Gal.8.940.

❋ **διαγογγύζω,** *mutter* or *murmur among themselves,* κατά τινος Lxx *Ex.*16.7; ἐπί τινι ib.*Nu.*14.2: abs., *Ev.Luc.*15.2, 19.7, Hld.7.27.

**διαγόρ-ευσις,** εως, ἡ, *declaration,* Porph.ap.Stob.2.8.42. ❋ **-εύω,** *declare, state explicitly,* συγγραφῆς -ούσης *PMagd.*3.4 (iii B.C.); ὡς ὁ νόμος δ. Lxx *Su.*61, cf. D.H.1.78 (v.l.), Jul.*Or.*1.3d; *give orders, command,* Ph.1.437; τι Id.2.291: c. inf., Id.2.324, al.: τινί, c. inf., Plu.*CG*16; so μή.. *forbid,* App.*BC*1.54:—Pass., *to be declared* or *established,* Pl.*Lg.*757a; τὰ διηγορευμένα *PTeb.*105.30 (ii B.C.), *PStrassb.*115.6 (ii B.C.). **II.** *relate in detail,* D.H.11.19. **III.** *speak of,* κακῶς δ. τινά Luc.*Pisc.*26 (v.l.). **IV.** = τὰ διάφορα καὶ οὐ τὰ αὐτὰ λέγειν, Is.*Fr.*18.

❋ **διάγραμμα,** ατος, τό, *figure marked out by lines, plan,* Pl.*R.*529e: esp. *geometrical figure,* X.*Mem.*4.7.3, Pl.*Phd.*73b, Arist.*Cael.*280$^{a}$1, etc. **b.** *geometrical proposition,* Id.*EN*1112$^{b}$21, *APr.*41$^{b}$14, Ascl. *in Metaph.*174.9. **2.** in Music, *scale,* Phan.Hist.17; but ἀφ' ἑνὸς δ. ὑποκρέκειν on one *note,* Plu.2.55d, cf. *Dem.*13. **3.** *horoscope, nativity,* Id.*Mar.*42. **4.** *map,* Jul.*Ep.*10. **II.** *list, register,* D.14.21; *inventory,* σκευῶν Id.47.36; *register* of taxable property, *PRev.Laws* 39.17, al. (iii B.C.). Harp., Suid. **III.** *ordinance, regulation,* *GDI*5040.64 (Cret.), *PEleph.*14.27 (iii B.C.), D.S.18.57; τὸ δ. τῷ Ἀντιγόνῳ *OGI*7 (Cyme); = Lat. *edictum,* Plb.22.10.6, Plu.*Marc.*24.

**διαγραμμ-ίζω,** *divide by lines*: hence, *play at chequers,* Philem.209. **-ισμός,** ὁ, *game of chequers,* Poll.9.99, Eust.633.65.

**διαγραπ-τέον,** (διαγράφω IV) *one must strike out, erase,* Phryn.368. **-τος,** ον, *struck out of the list,* δίκη Hsch.

❋ **διαγρᾰφ-άριος·** ὁ ἀπαιτῶν δημόσια, Hsch. **-εύς,** έως, ὁ, *one who makes a* διάγραμμα: at Athens, *one who drew up a register* of taxable properties, Harp. s.v. διάγραμμα. **2.** *describer*, ἠθῶν δ. Marcellin.*Vit.Thuc.*51. ❀ -ή, ἡ, *delineation*, Pl.*R.*501a; *diagram*, Plu.*Phil.*4; ἡ δ. τῶν φύλλων *outline*, Thphr.*HP*3.13.1; *delimitation* of land, *PAmh.*2.40.11 (ii B.C.): in pl., *plans, specifications* of a building, *OGI*46.3 (Halic.). **II.** *outline, scheme*, τὰς δ. ποιεῖσθαι Arist.*Top.*105ᵇ13; *table, syllabus*, Id.*EN*1107ᵃ33, cf. *EE*1228ᵃ28 (cf. ὑπογραφή); *description* of goods sold, *PTheb.Bank*2.6; *register*, ἁπάντων τῶν γενῶν Diph.43.7, cf. *CIG*3060 (Teos), etc.; *list* of articles, *Sammelb.*3924.21. **III.** *decree, ordinance*, esp. of Alexander, *IG*12(2).526.35, al.; αἱ περὶ τῶν ἱερῶν δ. D.H.3.36. **IV.** *crossing out, cancelling*, of a debt: hence, *payment*, ποιεῖν τὴν δ. τινὶ τῶν εἴκοσι πέντε ταλάντων Plb.31.27.7, cf. *PTeb.*121.3 (i B.C.), al.; *payment by draft*, *SIG*742.52 (Ephesus, pl.); *certificate that such payment has been made*, *BGU*281.15 (ii A.D.). **V.** *contract*, *PTeb.*88.9 (ii B.C.). **VI.** *levy, tax*, Just.*Nov.*131.5, al. -ον, τό, dub. in *POxy.*127.2 (vi A.D.). ❀ -ω, *mark out by lines, delineate*, τὴν πόλιν Pl.*R.*500e; δ. λόγῳ *map out*, Id.*Lg.*778a; δ. τινά *describe* a person, Philostr.*VS*2.2.7, *Her.*2.1: abs., Plu.*Nic.*23, etc. **b.** δ. γραμμήν *draw* a line *between*, Pl.Com.153.2. **2.** *draft* a law, etc., D.H.6.88:—Pass., συνθηκῶν διαγραφεισῶν Plb.1.62.7. **II.** *draw out a list of*, προτάσεις Arist.*APr.*46ᵃ8 (Pass.), *Rh.*1378ᵃ28, cf. *PRev.Laws*13.2. **III.** *enroll, levy*, στρατιώτας Plb.6.12.6. **b.** of things, *fix by written ordinance*, τὸ πλῆθος τὸ διαγραφὲν ἀποτινέτω *PRev.Laws*43.7 (iii B.C.). **IV.** *draw a line through, cross out, erase*, Pl.*R.*387b; δ. τινά *strike off* a person's name, E.*El.*1073; δ. δίκην, of the magistrates, *strike* a cause *out of the list*, Ar.*Nu.*774 (Pass.), cf. Lys.17.5 codd., D.48.26 (but in *SIG*².511.28,47 (Pass.), prob. *to be entered in the list*):—Med., διαγράψασθαι δίκην, of the plaintiff, *give up* a cause, *withdraw* it, Lys.*Fr.*195 S., D.20.145. **2.** *cancel, rescind*, δόγμα Plu.*Mar.*4; *rule out, exclude*, τὰ ἄλογα τῶν ζῴων Porph.*Abst.*3.1. **3.** *reduce, degrade*, θεοὺς εἰς ὀνόματα στρατηγῶν Plu.2.360a, cf. 377d, 757b. **V.** *write an order for*, ὀψωνισμοὺς τοῖς στρατιώταις D.H.5.28, cf. *SIG*410.16 (Pass.); *pay by banker's draft*, *UPZ*114, *IG*11(2).287*A*135 (Delos, iii B.C.), etc.; simply, *pay*, στατῆρας ἑκατὸν *Milet.*3.147.12, cf. *SIG*577.9, *PRev.Laws*32.11 (iii B.C.), *PTeb.*100.3 (ii B.C.), Lxx 2*Ma.*4.9. **VI.** *distribute*, χώρας Plu.*Pomp.*31; σατραπείας D.S.18.50.

**διαγρηγορέω**, *start into full wakefulness*, *Ev.Luc.*9.32; *keep awake*, πάσης τῆς νυκτὸς ἐν φροντίσιν καὶ δέει δ. Hdn.3.4.4.

**διαγριαίνω**, strengthd. for ἀγριαίνω, Plu.*Ant.*86, *Brut.*20 (Pass.).

**διαγρυπν-έω**, *lie awake*, ἐν μακρῷ χρόνῳ νυκτὸς δ. Ar.*Ra.*931, cf. Luc.*Nec.*6, Porph.*Abst.*1.27; τὴν νύκτα D.S.14.105. **-ητής**, οῦ, ὁ, *one who lies awake*, Sch.Ar.*Eq.*277.

**διάγυιος** παιών, *the foot* – ∪ –, Aristid.Quint.1.16. (Perh. *two-limbed*.)

**διαγυμν-άζω**, *keep in hard exercise*, Polyaen.6.1.7; *continue exercise*, Gal.6.163:—Med., *take hard exercise*, Id.*Parv.Pil.*4. **-όω**, *strip naked, lay bare*, τὴν ἀλήθειαν δ. Eun.*Hist.*p.250 D.

**διάγχω**, strengthd. for ἄγχω, Luc.*Anach.*31.

❀ **διάγω** [ᾰ], *carry over* or *across*, πορθμῆες δ' ἄρα τούς γε διήγαγον Od.20.187, cf. Th.4.78; δ. ἐπὶ σχεδίας ἄρτους X.*Cyr.*2.4.28. **b.** intr., *cross over*, Id.*An.*7.2.12. **2.** *draw through*, τὴν προβοσκίδα Plu.2.968d. **3.** Geom., *draw through* or *across, produce* a line, Euc.1.21, al. **4.** *draw apart*, τὰ ὄμματα *IG*4.951.121 (Epid.). **II.** of Time, *pass, spend*, αἰῶνα *h.Hom.*20.7; βίοτον, βίον, A.*Pers.*711, S.*OC*1619, Ar.*Nu.*464; δ. τὸν βίον μαχόμενος Pl.*R.*579d; ἡσύχιον βίον δ. ἐν εὐσεβείᾳ 1*Ep.Tim.*2.2; γῆρας, νύκτα, X.*Cyr.*4.6.6, *An.*6.5.1; χρόνον Plu.*Tim.*10 (but χρόνος διῆγέ με, = χρόνον διῆγον, S.*El.*782); δ. ἑορτὴν *celebrate* it, Ath.8.363f: hence, **2.** intr., without βίον, *pass life, live*, Democr.191, D.18.254, 25.82; = διαιτῶμαι, διατρίβω, Thom.Mag.pp.90,98 R.; δ. ἐν φιλοσοφίᾳ Pl.*Tht.*174b; *tarry*, ἐν τῷ δικαστηρίῳ Id.*Euthphr.*3e; ἐν προαστείῳ Hdn.1.12.5:—Med., διαγόμενος Pl.*R.*344e, etc.; τὰ πρὸς τοὺς θεοὺς εὐσεβῶς δ. *Michel*352.15 (Iasus). **b.** *delay*, Th.1.90, D.C.57.3: c. acc., *spin out, protract*, τοὺς λόγους Philostr.*VA*1.17. **c.** c. acc. pers., *divert, fob off*, ἐλπίδας λέγων διῆγε [τοὺς στρατιώτας] X.*An.*1.2.11, cf. D.*Prooem.*53, Luc.*Phal.*1.3. **d.** *continue*, δ. σιωπῇ X.*Cyr.*4.4.14: freq. c. part., *continue doing* so and so, δ. λιπαρέοντας Hdt.1.94; δ. μανθάνων, ἐπιμελόμενος, X.*Cyr.*1.2.6, 7.5.85. **e.** with Advbs., ἐν τοῖς χαλεπώτατα δ. Th.7.71; ἄριστα X.*Mem.*4.4.15; εὖ Arist.*HA*625ᵇ23; ἀκινδύνως Id.*Pol.*1295ᵇ33; also εὐσεβῆ δ. τρόπον περί τινα *conduct oneself piously*, Ar.*Ra.*457. **III.** *cause to continue, keep* in a certain state, πόλιν ὀρθοδίκαιον δ. A.*Eu.*995 (lyr.); πόλεις ἐν ὁμονοίᾳ Isoc.3.41; ἐν πᾶσι τοῖς κατὰ βίον .. διῆγεν ὑμᾶς D.18.89; τὸ ὑπήκοον ἐν ἡσυχίᾳ δ. D.C.40.30. **IV.** *entertain, feed*, τραγήμασι καὶ λαχάνοις τὸν στρατόν Philostr.*Her.*10.4:—Pass., [λέων] μελιτούτταις διήγετο Id.*VA*5.42. **V.** *manage*, κάλλιστα πάντα δ. Pl.*Plt.*273c; πανηγυρικώτερον δ. τὰ κατὰ τὴν ἀρχὴν Plb.5.34.3. **VI.** *separate, force apart*, τὰ σκέλεα Hp.*Ster.*230, Lxx *Ez.*16.25; τοὺς ὀδόντας Aret.*SA*1.6. **2.** *divert*, τινὰ ἀπό τινος Philostr.*Her.Prooem.*3; simply, *divert*, τὰς βασιλείους φροντίδας Id.*VS*1.8.2.

**διᾰγωγ-εύς**, έως, ὁ, *conductor*, ψυχῶν, of Hermes, *EM*268.24. ❀ -ή, ἡ, *carrying across*, τριήρων Polyaen.5.2.6. **2.** lit. *carrying through*: hence metaph., ἡ διὰ πάντων αὐτῶν δ. *taking a person through* a subject by instruction, Pl.*Ep.*343e; so, *course of instruction, lectures*, ἐν τῇ ἐνεστώσῃ δ. prob. in Phld.*Piet.*25. **II.** *passing of life, way* or *course of life*, δ. βίου Pl.*R.*344e: abs., Id.*Tht.*177a, etc. **2.** *way of passing time, amusement*, δ. μετὰ παιδιᾶς Arist.*EN*1127ᵇ34, cf. 1177ᵃ27; δ. ἐλευθέριος Id.*Pol.*1339ᵇ5; διαγωγαὶ τοῦ συζῆν public *pastimes*, ib.1280ᵇ37, cf. Plu.126b (pl.). **3.** *delay*, D.C.57.3. **III.** *management*, τῶν πραγμάτων δ. *dispatch* of business, Id.48.5. **IV.** *station* for ships, f.l. in Hdn.4.2.8. **V.** διαγωγάν· διαίρεσιν, διανομήν, διέλευσιν, Hsch. **-ικός**, ή, όν, *of* or *for a passage*: τέλος δ., = sq., Str.4.3.2. **-ιον**, τό, *transit-duty, toll*, Plb.4.52.5.

**διᾰγων-ία**, ἡ, *struggle*, Max.Tyr.1.1. (Fort. διαφωνία.) **-ιάω**, pf. διηγωνιακα *IPE*1².32*B*22 (Olbia):—strengthd. for ἀγωνιάω, Aristeas 124, Lxx 2*Ma.*3.21; δ. μὴ σφαλῶσιν Plb.3.105.5: c. acc., *stand in dread of*, ib.102.10. ❀ **-ίζομαι**, *contend, struggle against*, τινί, πρός τινα, X.*Mem.*3.9.2, *Cyr.*1.6.26; ταῦτα δ. πρὸς ἀλλήλους ib.1.2.12; τῷ Διὶ ὑπὲρ εὐδαιμονίας Epicur.*Fr.*602; ὑπὲρ τῆς ἀρχῆς D.H.3.17; περί τινος Luc.*VH*2.8: abs., μάχῃ δ. Th.5.10; λόγῳ δ. Pl.*Grg.*456b, cf. 464e, D.7.8; *finish a contest*, of the Chorus, X.*HG*6.4.16; but, *decide a contest*, περί τινος Aeschin.3.132:—Pass., διηγώνισται Plu.2.556e; πράξεις διαγωνισθεῖσαι Socr.*Ep.*30.9, etc.

**διαγώνιος**, ον, *from angle to angle, diagonal*, Str.2.1.36, Vitr.9.1.5, Aristid.Quint.3.3, Antyll.ap.Orib.6.29.3, Procl.*Hyp.*3.16; δ. πάσσαλος Nicom.*Harm.*6. Adv. -ίως Id.*Ar.*2.12.

**διᾰγων-ισμός**, ὁ, *a great straining*, τῆς κοιλίας Aët.9.30. **-ιστέον**, *one must make a great effort*, Ph.2.471.

**διᾰγωνοθετέω**, *set at variance*, Plb.25.4.7.

**διαδάκνω**, fut. -δήξομαι, *bite hard*, Max.Tyr.6.2: metaph. of calumny, δ. τινά Plb.4.87.5; of sarcasm, Iamb.*Protr.*21.λα':—Med., *have a biting-match with*, τῷ Κερβέρῳ Plu.2.1105a; *bite each other*, κυνίδια διαδακνόμενα M.Ant.5.33.

**διαδακρύω** [ῡ], *weep*, D.H.10.17 (s.v.l.).

**διαδάπτω**, *tear asunder, rend*, διὰ δὲ χρόα καλὸν ἔδαψεν Il.5.858, cf. 21.398.

**διαδᾰτέομαι**, aor. διεδασάμην Pi. (v. infr.): **1.** in reciprocal sense, *divide among themselves*, διὰ κτῆσιν δατέοντο Il.5.158, Hes.*Th.*606, cf. Pi.*O.*1.51; δ. τὴν ληΐην Hdt.8.121. **2.** in act. sense, *divide, distribute*, διὰ παῖρα δασάσκετο (Ion. iterative form) Il.9.333; ἐς φυλὰς διεδάσαντο *distributed* them among the tribes, Hdt.4.145:—Pass., *to be divided*, γῆς διαδατουμένης App.*BC*1.1.

**διαδείκνῡμι**, fut. -δείξω, Ion. -δέξω, strengthd. for δείκνυμι, *show plainly*, Hdt.2.162, al.; φρόνημα καὶ μέγεθος ἀρετῆς Plu.2.96d: folld. by a relat. clause with ὅτι, Hdt.7.172, 9.58: also c. part., διαδεξάτω τις βασιλέος κηδόμενος Id.8.118; δ. τὴν Ἑλλήνων ἀλκὴν ἀπρόσμαχον οὖσαν Plu.*Arat.*9:—Med., *display*, ἐπιμέλειαν *BGU*778.6 (ii A.D.):—Pass., διαδεικνύσθω ἐὼν πολέμιος *let him be declared* the king's enemy, Hdt.3.72; ἀγαθοὶ διεδείχθησαν Lib.*Or.*11.105, cf. Hermog.*Inv.*3.4, Aen.Gaz.*Thphr.*p.56 B. **II.** sts. intr. in forms διέδεξε and ὡς διέδεξε, *it was clear, manifest*, Hdt.2.134, 3.82.

**διαδεκ-τήρ**, ῆρος, ὁ, (διαδέχομαι) *transmitter*, σημείων Aen.Tact.6.4, 7.2. **-τωρ**, ορος, ὁ, *inheritor*, καμάτου Man.4.223. **II.** Pass. as Adj., πλοῦτος δ. *inherited* wealth, E.*Ion*478.

**διαδέλλειν**· διασπᾶν, Hsch.; cf. διαδηλέομαι.

**διαδέξιος**, ον, *of right good omen*, Hdt.7.180.

**διαδέξις**, εως, ἡ, *passage*, ὑποχονδρίων Hp.*Epid.*6.2.14; δ. ἐκ πατέρων hereditary *transmission*, Aret.*CD*2.12; δ. γένεος *procreation*, ib.2.5. **II.** *transition* from one disease to another, ib.1.1.

**διαδέρκομαι**, aor. -έδρᾰκον, *see* one thing *through* another, οὐδ' ἂν νῶϊ διαδράκοι *would not see us through* [the cloud], Il.14.344. **2.** *look about*, πάντῃ δὲ διέδρακεν ὀφθαλμοῖσι Theoc.25.230. **II.** *see over*, νῆσον Cypr.11.3.

**διαδέρω**, *strip off*, δέρμα Paul.Aeg.6.50:—Pass., ib.68.

**διά-δεσις**, εως, ἡ, (διαδέω) *bandaging*, Antyll.ap.Orib.7.9.7, Heliod.ib.10.18.3 (pl.). **-δεσμα**, ατος, τό, *tree-mallow, Lavatera arborea*, Zoroaster ap.Ps.-Dsc.2.118. **-δεσμεύω**, = sq., Sor.1.50. **-δεσμέω**, *bind*, τὴν κεφαλὴν δ. ταινίᾳ Lyd.*Mens.*1.20. ❀ **-δεσμος**, ὁ, *connecting band*, Hp.*Nat.Puer.*14; *bandage*, Aret.*CA*1.9; *ligature*, διαδέσμοις σφίγγων τὰ ἄκρα Philum.ap.Aët.9.12. **-δετέον**, *one must bind round*, Archig.ap.Orib.47.13.5, Gal.17(1).434. **-δετος**, ον, *bound fast*, χαλινοὶ διάδετοι γενύων ἱππίων bits *firm bound through* the horse's mouth, A.*Th.*122 (lyr.); δακτύλιος ἠλέκτρῳ δ. τὸν κύκλον *adorned with* a strip of amber *set in* .., Hld.5.13; δ. ταινίαις τὰς κόμας Lib.*Decl.*12.27.

**διαδέχομαι**, fut. -ξομαι, *receive one from another*, δ. τὸν λόγον *take up* the word, i.e. *speak next*, Pl.*R.*576b; λόγον παρά τινος D.H.*Rh.*8.14: abs., διαδεξάμενοι ἔλεγον Hdt.8.142; ἀποκρινόμενοι διαδέχεσθε Pl.*Lg.*900c; δ. νόμους παρὰ τῶν θεῶν, τέχνην, Antipho 1.3, Lys.24.6; τὴν διατριβήν, leadership of a school of philosophy, Phld.*Acad.Ind.*p.58 M. **2.** δ. βασιλείαν *succeed to* the kingdom, Plb.2.4.7; ἀρχὴν παρά τινος Id.9.28.8; τὴν ναῦν δ. τινί, of a trierarch (cf. διαδοχή I), D.50.38; πλοῦτον παρά τινος Luc.*DMort.*11.3. **II.** διαδέχεσθαί τινι *succeed* one, *take* his *place, relieve* him on guard, etc., Pl.*Lg.*758b, X.*Cyr.*8.6.18: later, δ. τινά Arist.*Pol.*1299ᵃ4, Plb.28.3.6; δ. τὰ κατὰ τὴν στρατηγίαν *act for* the στρατηγός, *BGU*18.3 (ii A.D.), etc.; τοὺς προφήτας στολισταὶ δ. *represent*, *PGnom.*193. **b.** *appoint a successor to*, τινά Eun.*Hist.*p.231 D.:—Pass., διεδέχθη τῆς στρατηγίας *was relieved of* his command, Id.p.243 D. **2.** abs., *relieve one another*, τοῖς ἵπποις *with fresh* horses, X.*An.*1.5.2 (wrongly expld. as *closing in from both sides* by Demetr.*Eloc.*93); *succeed*, οἱ διαδεχόμενοι στρατηγοί Lys.13.62, cf. Arist.*Pol.*1293ᵃ29; οἱ διαδεξάμενοι *the successors* (of Alexander), Plb.9.34.11; οἱ τὰ Πύρρου δ. App.*Ill.*7: pf. part. Pass., νὺξ εἰσάγει καὶ νὺξ ἀπωθεῖ διαδεδεγμένη *in turns, by turns*, S.*Tr.*30; διαδεξάμενοι *Act.Ap.*7.45; οἱ διαδεχόμενοι καιροί Herod.Med.ap.Orib.7.8.3. **III.** *supersede*, τὸν ὕπατον D.S.24.1.

**διαδέω**, *bind on either side*, δ. τὸ πλοῖον ἀμφοτέρωθεν Hdt.2.29, cf. 4.154; δ. τὰ χαλκεῖα ταινίᾳ Arist.*Aud.*802$^a$40; *bandage*, Herod.Med. ap.Orib.10.18.2; *put in chains*, δοῦλον *POxy.*1423.9 (iv A.D.); ψυχὴ διαδεδεμένη ἐν τῷ σώματι *fast-bound*, Pl.*Phd.*82e:—Med., δ. ἱμάτια ταῖς λαιαῖς *bind, wrap them* round *their* left arms, App.*Mith.*86: abs., διαδεῖσθαι καυσίαις *bind one's head* (with a diadem), Plu.*Demetr.*41; ὁ διαδούμενος *the boy binding his hair*, a famous statue by Polyclitus, Plin.*HN*34.55; διαδησάμενος Plu.2.489f:—Pass., διαδέδεσθαι τὴν κεφαλὴν διαδήματι, μίτρᾳ, *have one's* head *bound* with.., D.S.4.4, Luc.*DMort.*12.3.

**διαδηλέομαι**, *do great harm to, rend in pieces*, ὀλίγου σε κύνες διεδηλήσαντο Od.14.37, cf. Theoc.24.85, A.R.2.284, Agath.5.7.

⊛ **διάδηλ-ος**, ον, also η, ον Arist.*HA*613$^b$1:—*distinguishable among others*, Th.4.68, Pl.*R.*474b, Plb.6.22.3; δ. παρὰ τοὺς ἄλλους D.H. 72; of a person, *distinguished*, *OGI*504.9 (Aezani): c. part., δ. εἶναι εὐτακτῶν X.*Mem.*4.4.1: c. dat., δ. τῇσι μελεδώνῃσι Aret.*SD*2.4. **-όω**, *make manifest, indicate clearly*, *PRev.Laws* 16.17 (iii B.C.), J.*BJ*5.9.3, Plu.*Caes.*6, D.L.4.46, S.E.*M.*7.87, D.C.40.17.

⊛ **διάδημα**, ατος, τό, (διαδέω) *band* or *fillet*: esp. *band round the* τιάρα worn by the Persian king, X.*Cyr.*8.3.13, Plu.2.488d; by Alexander, Arr.*An.*7.22.2; by his successors, *OGI*248.17 (Pergam., Antiochus IV), Hdn.1.3.3; by kings generally, Plu.2.753d, D.S.20.54; δ. τῆς Ἀσίας LXX 1 *Ma.*13.32. II. Ὀσίριδος δ., = ἄλιμος, Ps.-Dsc.1.91.

**διαδηματίζομαι**, *wear the* διάδημα, Aq.*Ps.*21(22).13.

**διαδηματοφόρος**, ον, *bearing a diadem*, καυσία Plu.*Ant.*54.

⊛ **διαδιδράσκω**, Ion. **διαδιδρήσκω**, aor. 2 part. -δράντας Hdt.8.75: pf. -δέδρακα Ar.*Ach.*601:—*run away, escape*, Hdt. l.c., Th.7.85, *PPetr.*3 p.101 (iii B.C.), etc.; διαδεδρακότες *shirkers*, Ar. l.c. 2. c. acc., *escape from*, τινά Hdt.3.135, etc.; τὸ πάθος, τὸν ὄλεθρον, Aret.*SA*1.10, 2.8:—Pass., Hsch. 3. *fly in all directions*, LXX 2 *Ma.*8.13.

**διαδίδωμι**, fut. -δώσω Pl.*R.*328a:—*pass on, hand over*, ἐμοὶ τοῦτον διέδωκαν (sc. Μοῖσαι) ἀθάνατον πόνον Pi.*Pae.*9 *Fr.*16.16; λαμπάδια ἔχοντες διαδώσουσιν ἀλλήλοις Pl. l.c.; *propound* for consideration, Pall.*in Hp.Fract.*12.277C.; *spread abroad*, λόγον Plu.*Them.*19:—Pass., λόγος διεδόθη v.l. in X.*Cyr.*4.2.10, cf. Plu.*Sol.*8; διαδοθέντος τοῦ λόγου Isoc.5.7, cf. 9.74; περὶ τῶν ἀρχαίων δ. *to be handed down* by tradition, Arist.*Cael.*270$^b$17; ἐν παροιμίᾳ διαδοθῆναι Str.6.2.4. 2. *distribute*, τινί τι X.*An.*1.10.18, Th.4.38, D.49.14:—Pass., τῇ σάλπιγγι σιωπῆς εἰς ἅπαντας διαδοθείσης Plu.*Flam.*10; τὸ διαδιδόμενον εἰς τὰς φλέβας, of food, Arist.*PA*678$^a$18; of the bowels, *secrete*, τῆς κοιλίης ὑδατόχολα πολλὰ διαδιδούσης Hp.*Coac.*67. 3. δ. κόρας *cast* one's eyes *around*, E.*Ph.*1371, cj. in *Or.*1267. 4. διαδοῦναι δίκας *give* satisfaction to injured party, Hsch. II. intr., *spread about*, Arist.*HA*495$^b$8. 2. *remit*, Hp.*Acut.*(*Sp.*)5.

**διαδικ-άζω**, *give judgement*, And.1.28, Pl.*R.*614c, *Lg.*916b (Pass.); χορηγοῖς, ἀρχαῖς δ., X.*Ath.*3.4; διεδίκαζον δίκας *IG*7.21 (Megara); τὰς ἀμφισβητήσεις τισί Arist.*Ath.*57.2: c. gen., δ. ἀστρατείας X.*Ath.*3.5 (prob. l.). 2. *hold inquiry*, esp. at Athens, of naval matters, δ. εἴ τις τὴν ναῦν μὴ ἐπισκευάζει X.*Ath.*3.4; ἀριθμὸς τριήρων καὶ σκευῶν τῶν -δεδικασμένων *IG*2.795 f 60. 3. Med., *go to law, dispute*, διαδικαζόμενος τῇ βουλῇ περὶ ἀληθείας Din.2.1; ταύτῃ διαδικασόμεθα περὶ τῆς σοφίας Pl.*Smp.*175e, etc.; διαδικάσασθαι ἐν φίλοις τὰ πρὸς ἐμέ *to settle* by friendly arbitration, D.30.2; Διαδικαζόμενοι, title of play by Dioxippus, Suid., cf. *IG*2.975 iii 21, *BGU*1914 (ii A.D.). b. *submit oneself to trial*, Pl.*Phd.*107d, 113d, X.*HG*5.3.10: later, aor. Pass. διαδικασθῆναι, = διαδικάσασθαι, D.L.1.74, D.C.48.12. II. = διὰ ὅλου τοῦ ἔτους δικάζω, Critias *Fr.*71 D. **-αιόω**, *justify* an action, Th.4.106; *defend as matter of right*, ὑπέρ τινος, D.C.39.60; *defend* a person's *right*, τὰ τοῦ Καίσαρος Id.40.62. **-ασία**, ἡ, *suit to decide between claimants*, e.g. to an estate, δ. κλήρου D.44.7; to a wardship, δ. ἐπιτροπῆς Arist.*Ath.*56.6; to exemption from a λειτουργία, D.28.17, cf. Lys.17.1, D.24.13, etc.; τὴν δ. ποιεῖσθαι *IG*12(5).722.48 (Andros); esp. of *judicial inquiries* relating to naval matters, D.47.26, Arist.*Ath.*61.1. 2. *judicial decision* or *settlement*, X.*Cyr.*8.1.18, *OGI* 437.78. 3. metaph., δ. τῷ βήματι πρὸς τὸ στρατήγιον *dispute* between the orators and the board of generals, Aeschin.3.146; generally, τὴν τῶν ἀριστείων δ. *the competition for* public honours, Pl.*Lg.*952d, cf. Polem.*Call.*53. 4. διαδικασίαν προθεῖναι ταῖς γνώμαις put *the question* to the vote, D.H.11.21. **-ασμα**, ατος, τό, *object of litigation in a* διαδικασία, Lys.17.10. **-ασμός**, ὁ, *lawsuit: contention*, Aq.*Ez.*48.28.

⊛ **δια-δικέω** (A), *contend at law*, πρός τινα *PRein.*19.16 (ii B.C.); οἱ διαδικοῦντες *the contending parties*, Plu.2.196c, *POxy.*1101.8 (iv A.D.). 2. *decide a suit*, οἱ διαδικοῦντες *the jurors*, D.C.40.55 (s. v. l.).

**δι-ᾰδικέω** (B), *do wrong, injure*, D.C.58.16.

⊛ **διάδικος**· τὸ εἰς δίκην καλεῖν (Att.), Hsch.

**διαδιφρεύω**, *drive horses as in a chariot-race*, E.*Or.*990 (lyr.).

**διαδοιδῠκίζω**, (δοίδυξ) *make a closed fist like a pestle*, *Com.Adesp.*973. II. = ὀρχεῖσθαι ἀσχημόνως, ibid.

**διαδοκέω**, plpf. Pass. διεδέδοκτο *it had been determined*, v.l. in J.*Vit.*11.

**διαδοκῐμάζω**, *distinguish by testing*, τὰ καλὰ καὶ κίβδηλα ἀργύρια X.*Oec.*19.16.

**διαδοκίς**, ίδος, ἡ, (δοκός) *cross-beam*, Hsch.

⊛ **διάδομα**, ατος, τό, (διαδίδωμι) *distribution of money*, *IG*7.2715.64 (Acraeph.), Ἀρχ.Δελτ.2.148 (pl.), *UPZ*2.8 (ii B.C.).

⊛ **διαδοξάζω**, *form a definite opinion*, Pl.*Phlb.*38b, Iamb.*Myst.*4.6:—Med., ib.8.5.

**διαδορᾰτ-ίζομαι**, *fight with spears*, and generally, *contend in battle*, Plb.5.84.2, J.*BJ*5.3.3, M.Ant.4.3: metaph., '*break a lance*', *contend*, Longin.13.4 (and so perh. in M.Ant. l.c.). **-ισμός**, ὁ, *fighting with the spear*, M.Ant.7.3 (pl.).

**διά-δοσις**, εως, ἡ, *distribution*, D.44.37; χώρας Plb.2.23.1; ἀννώνης *POxy.*1115.9 (iii A.D.): pl., *IGRom.*3.739. II. Medic., δ. οὔρων an *evacuation*, Hp.*Epid.*3.4; ἡ τῆς τροφῆς δ. its *distribution* through the body, Arist.*IA*705$^a$32. III. *exchange*, μειδιαμάτων Plu.*Sull.*35 (pl.). IV. *communication*, κινήσεως Epicur.*Ep.*2 p.48U.; δ. ἐκ θεῶν εἰς ἀνθρώπους Arr.*Epict.*1.12.6; ταῖς ἀρίσταις διαδόσεσι κινεῖσθαι (of just men) Phld.*Piet.*68, cf. M.Ant.1.17.6 (pl.); ἐκ -δόσεως τῆς ἁφῆς γινώσκειν τι Heliod.ap.Orib.44.23.59: Astrol., of celestial influence, Ptol.*Tetr.*5 (pl.), 105. **-δοτέος**, έα, έον, *to be published*, Isoc.12.233. II. διαδοτέον *one must distribute*, Pl.*Ti.*19a. **-δότης**, ου, ὁ, an official, *distributor* of provisions to the soldiers, οἴνου *PRein.*56.9 (iv A.D.), *PLond.*3.1245.3 (iv A.D.), *BGU* 1025 xvi 15 (iv/v A.D.).

⊛ **διαδοχ-ή**, ἡ, (διαδέχομαι) *taking over from* another, νεώς, of a trierarch, D.50.1. 2. *succession*, ἄλλος παρ' ἄλλου διαδοχαῖς πληρούμενοι by *successions* or *reliefs*, A.*Ag.*313; διαδοχῇ τῶν ἐπιγιγνομένων Th.2.36; ἡ τῶν τέκνων δ. Arist.*Pol.*1334$^b$39: freq. in dat. pl., ἀνάσσειν διαδοχαῖσιν ἐν μέρει ἐνιαυσίαισιν E.*Supp.*406; διαδοχαῖς Ἐρινύων (apparently) *by successive attacks* of the Furies, Id.*IT*79; γένους μακραῖς δ. by long *pedigrees*, Hdn.1.2.2: with Preps., ἐκ διαδοχῆς ἀλλήλοις in *turns*, D.4.21, cf. Antiph.8 (but, in *succession*, Arist.*Ph.*228$^a$28); κατὰ διαδοχὴν χρόνου or κατὰ δ., Th.7.27,28; κατὰ διαδοχάς Arist.*Mu.*398$^a$33; τὰ κατὰ διαδοχὴν κληρονομηθέντα *POxy.*1201.7 (iii A.D.), cf. *BGU*907.13 (iii A.D.). II. concrete in military sense, *relief, relay*, ἡ δ. τῇ πρόσθεν φυλακῇ ἔρχεται X.*Cyr.*1.4.17, cf. D.21.164: metaph., σελήνη ἡλίου δ. Secund.*Sent.*6. 2. *the succession* (i.e. *successors*), Luc.*Nigr.*38; ἡ περὶ τὸν Πλάτωνα δ. the *school* of Plato, S.E.*M.*7.190; Στωϊκὴ δ. Plu.2.605b; ἡ Ἐπικούρου δ. *IG*2$^2$.1009 (Epist. Plotinae); αἱ Διαδοχαί, title of work by Sotion on *the Successions* or *successive heads* of the Philosophic Schools, Ath.4.162e, cf. D.L.*Prooem.*1, 2.12. **-ικός**, ή, όν, *belonging to a philosophic school*, τὰ δ. *endowments*, Olymp.*in Alc.*p.141C., Suid. s.v. Πλάτων. ⊛ **-ος**, ον, *succeeding* a person *in* a thing: 1. c. dat. pers. et gen. rei, δ. Μεγαβάζῳ τῆς στρατηγίης his *successor in* the command, Hdt.5.26, cf. 1.162, etc.; θνητοῖς.. διάδοχοι μοχθημάτων *succeeding* them *in*, i.e. *relieving* them *from*, toils, A.*Pr.*464, cf. 1027; σοὶ τῶνδε διάδοχος δόμων E.*Alc.*655. 2. c. gen. rei only, δ. τῆς Ἀστυόχου ναυαρχίας *succeeding to* his command, Th.8.85; δ. τῆς κληρονομίας Isoc.19.43; τῆς φιλοσοφίας Epicur.*Fr.*217. 3. c. gen. pers. only, φέγγος ὕπνου δ. sleep's *successor* light, S.*Ph.*867. 4. c. dat. pers. only, δ. Κλεάνδρῳ X.*An.*7.2.5: c. dat. rei, ἔργοισι δ' ἔργα διάδοχα E.*Andr.*743; κακὸν κακῷ δ. ib.803; quasi-act., λύπη.. δ. κακῶν κακοῖς *bringing a succession* of evils *after* evils, *Hec.*588; ἀγὼν.. γόων γόοις (γόων bis codd.) δ. *Supp.*72 (lyr.). 5. abs., διάδοχοι ἐφοίτων they went to work *in relays* or *gangs*, Hdt.7.22, cf. Th.1.110: neut. pl. as Adv., *in turn*, E.*Andr.*1200 (lyr.). 6. as Subst., οἱ Δ. the *Successors* of Alexander, D.S.18.42. b. the lowest grade of court officials at Alexandria, *OGI*100.4, *PAmh.*2.36.5, *PRyl.*67.2 (both ii B.C.). c. *substitute, deputy*, *BGU*852.4 (ii A.D.), *POxy.*54.7 (iii A.D.). d. *head of a school of philosophers*, τῆς σχολῆς Phld.*Ind.Sto.*53; δ. Στωικός *IG*3.661, cf. 2$^2$.1009 (Epist. Plotinae). e. a kind of *gem*, Plin.*HN*37.157.

**διαδρᾱμᾰτίζω**, *finish acting a play*, M.Ant.3.8, D.L.3.56.

**διαδρᾱσῐπολῖται**, οἱ, *citizens who shirk all state burdens*, Ar.*Ra.*1014.

**διάδρᾱσις**, εως, ἡ, (διαδιδράσκω) *an escape from*, ἀναγκῶν, πυρός, J.*AJ*17.4.2 and 10.2.

**διαδράσσομαι**, *seize hold of*, ἀλλήλων Plb.1.58.8, Ph.2.328.

**διαδρηστεύω** or **διαδρηπετεύω**, *run off, go over to*, suggested emendations for διεπρήστευσε in Hdt.4.79.

⊛ **διαδρομ-ή**, ἡ, (διαδραμεῖν) *running to and fro through* a city, A.*Th.*351 (pl.), cf. Hp.*Epid.*7.122, Plb.15.30.2; αἱ δ. τῶν ἀστέρων *shooting*, Arist.*Mete.*341$^a$33, al.; διαδρομὰς ὀξείας ἔχειν *spread* rapidly, of disease, Plu.2.825d. 2. *running across*, Antipho 3.4.4; *passage through*, σπιλάδος Plu.2.476a. 3. *race* (perh. *team-race*) or *parade*, *OGI* 339.36 (Sestos), 764.24 (Pergam.), *SIG*694.56 (Elaea, ii B.C.). 4. *a cavalry manœuvre*, Anon.ap.Suid. 5. Medic., δ. πνευμάτων, = βορβορυγμός, Dsc.5.45; *sensation*, δ. νυγματώδης, φρικώδης, Sor.2.17, Philum.*Ven.*17.1. 6. *course*, ἡμέρα δωδεκάωρος δ. Secund.*Sent.*4. II. *place for running through, passage*, X.*Cyn.*10.8; of fish ponds, δ. ἰχθυοτρόφοι Plu.*Luc.*39. **-ος**, ον, *running through* or *about, wandering*, φυγαί A.*Th.*191; λέχος δ. *stray, lawless* love, E.*El.*1156 (lyr.); ἔμβολα κίοσι δ. the architrave *reeling, ready to fall*, Id.*Ba.*592 (lyr.). II. Subst. διάδρομος, ὁ, = διαδρομή II, Luc.*Hipp.*6.

**διαδῠναστεύω**, *prevail*, f.l. for δυναστεύω, Arist.*Mu.*395$^a$2.

**δια-δύνω** Hp.*Flat.*13, Arist.*de An.*404$^a$7: **διαδύω** Hdt.2.66 codd.; more freq. Dep. **διαδύομαι**, fut. -δύσομαι: aor. 2 διέδυν:—*slip through* a hole or gap, διαδύντες διὰ τοῦ τείχους Th.4.110; διὰ τούτων ἡ φιλία διαδυομένη X.*Mem.*2.6.22: abs., *slip through, slip away*, Hdt. l.c.; διαδὺς Ar.*V.*212; μῶν ὁ γέρων πῃ διαδύεται; ib.396. 2. c. acc., *evade, shirk*, τοῖς διαδυομένοις τὰς λειτουργίας Lys.21.12, cf. D.42.23; ᾗ.. διαδύσεται τὸν λόγον Pl.*Sph.*231c, etc.; τὸ δίκην δοῦναι διαδὺς D.18.133. **-δῠσις**, εως, ἡ, *passing through, passage*, ἐς τὼς πόρως Ti.Locr.100e, cf. Thphr.*Od.*50: metaph. in pl., *evasions*, τῶν ἀδικη-

μάτων, i.e. *escape from* the consequences of crimes, D.24.139, cf. 94, Plu.*Dem.*6: abs., Lib.*Or.*18.32. II. in pl., *passages, galleries,* in mines, etc., D.S.5.36: sg., prob. l. in Aen.Tact.24.5; *subterranean channel,* Demetr.Sceps.ap.Str.13.1.43. **-δῠτικός**, ή, όν, *penetrating,* ἀήρ Thphr.*CP*5.14.1 (Comp.).

**διάδωμα**, ατος, τό, prob. = διάζωμα, *IGRom.*4.914 (fort. διάδομα).

**διαδωρέομαι**, *distribute in presents,* X.*Cyr.*3.3.6, Posidon.24. 2. generally, *distribute, assign,* τινὰς εἰς τὰς ἐπαρχίας J.*BJ*6.9.2.

**διαειδής**, ές, *transparent,* ὕδωρ Theoc.16.62.

**δια-είδω** (i.e. δια- εἴδω) (A), fut. -είσομαι, *discern, distinguish,* αὔριον ἣν ἀρετὴν διαείσεται *will test* his manhood, Il.8.535:—Pass., ἔνθα μάλιστ' ἀρετὴ διαείδεται *is discerned,* 13.277, cf. Aret.*SD*1.1; simply, *appear between,* A.R.2.579 (tm.).

**δι-ᾱείδω** (B), fut. -ᾱείσομαι: Att. **δι-ᾴδω**, -ᾴσομαι:—Med., aor. διᾴσασθαι Phryn.*PS*p.65B.:—*contend in singing,* τινί *with* one, Theoc.5.22: abs., *contend in song, sing for the prize,* Arist.*Po.*1462ᵃ7, Phryn. l. c. II. *to be dissonant,* opp. συνᾴδω, Heraclit.10.

**διαειμένος**, pf. part. Pass. of διΐημι. **διαειπέμεν, διαϝειπάμενος**, v. διεῖπον.

**διαείρω**, = διαιρέω, *divide,* τριχῇ θυσίας Orac.ap.Eus.*PE*4.9.2.

**διαέριος**, v. sub διηέριος.

**διαζάω**, Ion. **-ζώω**, inf. διαζῆν, *live through, pass,* ὀρθῶς τὸν βίον E.*IA*923; τὸ καθ' ἡμέραν Pl.*R.*561c, etc.: abs., καλῶς δ. X.*HG*7.1.8. 2. c. part., *live* by doing so and so, ποιηφαγέοντες διέζωον they *supported life* by.., Hdt.3.25; δ. ἀπό τινος *live* off or by a thing, S.*Ph.*535, Ar.*Av.*1434, etc.; ἔκ τινος *Stoic.*3.187; πῶς οὖν διέζης ἢ πόθεν μηδὲν ποιῶν; Ar.*Pl.*906; δ. νομῇ of pastoral *life,* Pl.*Lg.*679a.

⊛ **διά-ζευγμα**, ατος, τό, dub. sens., perh. *bridge* over or *branch* of a canal, *PLond.*1.131.205 (i A.D.). **-ζευγμός**, ὁ, = διάζευξις, Plb.10.7.1. ⊛ **-ζεύγνῡμι**, *part, separate,* διὰ γὰρ ζευγνῦσ' ἡμᾶς πατρίων μελάθρων μητρὸς κατάραι E.*El.*1323 (anap.), cf. Charito8.16; λίθους ἀλλήλων Lib.*Or.*30.38; *open* sluices, *PPetr.*3p.121 (iii B.C.); *take to pieces,* σκάφη Polyaen.3.11.3; *dissolve,* θάνατος δ. γάμον Ph.2.311; *disjoin, distinguish,* τί τινος ib.298, al.:—but more freq. Pass., *to be disjoined, parted,* τινός *from* one, Aeschin.2.179; ἀπό τινος X.*An.*4.2.10: abs., ὅπως αἱ πρότερον συνήθειαι διαζευχθῶσιν Arist.*Pol.*1319ᵇ26; *to be divorced,* Pl.*Lg.*784b; διεζευγμένον (sc. ἀξίωμα) *disjunctive proposition,* Chrysipp.*Stoic.*2.5.71, etc. (with ἀξίωμα in full, Gell.16.8.12); λῆμμα Gal.*Nat.Fac.*2.7. 2. τὸ διεζ. σύστημα the *disjunct* scale, in which two tetrachords were so combined that the first note of one was a tone lower than the last note of the other, opp. συνημμένον, Cleonid.*Harm.*10; νήτη διεζευγμένων Euc.*Sect.Can.*15; [τετράχορδον] διεζευγμένων Plu.2.1029b. 3. Math., διεζευγμένη μεσότης, ἀναλογία, *discrete* mean, proportion, Nicom.*Ar.*2.21. 4. Medic., *reckon* periods *exclusively,* opp. συνάπτεσθαι, Gal.9.901. **-ζευκτικός**, ή, όν, *disjunctive,* σύνδεσμος Chrysipp.*Stoic.*2.68, A.D.*Conj.*216.10; συλλογισμός Chrysipp.*Stoic.*2.88; πρὸς τοὺς Ἀμεινίου -κούς (sc. λόγους), title of work by Chrysipp., *Stoic.*2.7. Adv. -κῶς A.D.*Synt.*9.27. ⊛ **-ζευξις**, εως, ἡ, *disjoining, parting,* τοῦ σώματος Pl.*Phd.*88b; δ. τε καὶ σύζευξιν ποιεῖσθαι Id.*Lg.*930b; ἡ δ. τῶν γυναικῶν, in Crete, Arist.*Pol.*1272ᵃ23. 2. Musical term, *disjunction* of two tetrachords, Plu.2.491a, Cleonid.*Harm.*10, etc. 3. Gramm., *disjunction,* κατὰ διάζευξιν παραλαμβάνεσθαι A.D.*Synt.*125.12: in Logic, συμπλοκαὶ καὶ διαζεύξεις Plu.2.1011a. 4. Medic., κατὰ διάζευξιν by *exclusive reckoning,* Gal.18(2).232, al.

**διαζέω**, *boil through,* Suid., cf. Hsch. s. v. διασμύχων.

**διαζηλεύομαι**, *to be lost in admiration,* Hp.*Praec.*13.

**διαζηλοτῠπέομαι**, *engage in rivalry,* τινί Ath.13.588e; πρός τινα Plb.36.8.2.

**διάζησις**, εως, ἡ, *way of living,* Hierocl.p.15A., Porph.ap.Stob.2.8.40.

**διαζητ-έω**, *search through, examine,* Ar.*Eq.*1292, Pl.*Plt.*258b, etc. II. *seek out, invent,* λόγους εὖ διεζητημένους Ar.*Th.*439. **-ησις**, εως, ἡ, *inquiry, inquisition, Gloss.*

⊛ **διάζομαι**, *set the warp in the loom,* i.e. *begin the web,* Nicopho5; opp. προφορεῖσθαι τὸν στήμονα, Sch.Ar.*Av.*4; cf. δίασμα: διέζετο (post διαείδεται)· διεσχίζετο, Hsch.

**διαζῠγή**, ἡ, *division, Corp.Herm.*13.12 (pl.).

**διαζῠγία**, ἡ, = διάζευξις, *AP*5.8 (Rufin.).

**διαζύγιον** [ῠ], τό, *divorce,* Eust.893.51, 1667.33: pl. **διαζύγια**, τά, *differences, quarrels* between man and wife, Just.*Nov.*140.1 *Intr.*

**διαζωγρᾰφ-έω**, *paint in divers colours,* Pl.*Ti.*55c, Plu.2.1003d, Ael.*VH*12.41, Dam.*Isid.*70:—Subst. **-ησις**, εως, ἡ, Sch.D.T.p.490H.

⊛ **διάζωμα**, ατος, τό, *that which is put round as a girdle*: hence, 1. *a girdle, drawers,* δ. ἔχειν περὶ τὰ αἰδοῖα Th.1.6. b. *bandage,* Hp.*Fist.*9. 2. φρενῶν δ., = διάφραγμα II, Arist.*PA*672ᵇ10; τὸ δ. τὸ τοῦ θώρακος Id.*HA*497ᵃ23: of the *pelvis,* ib.493ᵃ22; *partition,* Id.*PA*681ᵃ3. 3. *cornice* or *frieze* in Architecture, Thphr.*Lap.*7. 4. *gangway,* giving access to the seats in a theatre, *CIG*(add.)2755 (Aphrodisias), Vitr.5.6.7. 5. *vein, layer, marking,* in stone, Dsc.5.126. 6. *isthmus,* Plu.*Phoc.*13. 7. *layer, stratum* of atmosphere, Herm.ap.Stob.1.49.69; *vein,* of copper ore, Dsc.5.74 (pl.).

**διαζωμάτιον**, τό, Dim. of foreg. 1, *Gloss.*

**διαζωμεύω**, (ζωμός) *make into soup,* τὰ κρέα v.l. in Hp.*Int.*9.

**δια-ζώνη**, ἡ, *girdle,* Aq.*Ex.*29.9. ⊛ **-ζώννῡμι** or -ύω, fut. -ζώσω: pf. Pass. διέζωμαι *IG*2.736B19, ib.11(2).161.35 (Delos, iii B.C.):—*gird round, encircle, embrace,* Gal.14.715: metaph., τὸν ὅλον ἄνθρωπον διέζωσεν [ἡ ψυχή] Diog.Oen.39:—Med., *undergird one's* ship, App.*BC*5.91; but usu. *gird oneself with,* διαζωσάμενοι τὸ τριβώνιον Luc.*Hist.Conscr.*3:—Pass., διαζώννυσθαι ἐσθῆτα, ἀκινάκην, Id.*Somn.*6, *Anach.*6: abs., διεζωσμένοι *wearing the* διάζωμα 1, Th.1.6 codd. (-ζωμένοι Phot., Suid.): metaph., ἀρχὴν διεζωσμένος *invested with* office, J.*AJ*14.9.3. II. metaph., *engirdle, encompass,* of fire, Plu.*Brut.*31; τὸν αὐχένα (i.e. the Chersonese) δ. ἐρύμασι Id.*Per.*19; νήσους Id.*Them.*12:—Pass., [ἡ Ἀττικὴ] μέση διέζωσται ὄρεσιν X.*Mem.*3.5.25; ῥάχει διεζῶσθαι Plb.5.69.1; also *pass like a girdle,* διὰ τῶν τροπικῶν Arist.*Mu.*392ᵃ12. **-ζωσις**, εως, ἡ, *cincture,* ἡ τοῦ ζῳδιακοῦ δ. Eudem.ap.Theon.Sm.p.198H., cf. Hero*Deff.*138.11. **-ζωσμα**, ατος, τό, = διάζωμα 1, Hp.*Haem.*2, Plu.2.132a. II. = διάζωμα 3, Callix.1. **-ζωστήρ**, ῆρος, ὁ, *twelfth vertebra in the spine,* Poll.2.179. **-ζώστρα**, ἡ, = διάζωμα 1, Pers.*Stoic.*1.100; condemned by Hermog.*Meth.*3.

**διαζωτικός**, ή, όν, *vital,* ἰδίωμα Procl.*in Prm.*p.576S.

**διαζώω**, v. διαζάω.

⊛ **διάημι** [ᾰ], impf. διάην, Ep. Verb, *blow through,* c. acc., τοὺς [θάμνους]..οὔτ' ἀνέμων διάη μένος Od.5.478; πώεα..οὐ διάησι ἲς ἀνέμου Hes.*Op.*517: c. gen., τῶν [οὐρῶν] ψυχρὸς ἐὼν διάησι [Βορέας] ib.514.

**διαθᾰλασσεύω**, in Pass., *to be parted by the sea,* Alciphr.2.3.

**διαθάλπω**, *warm through,* Plu.2.799b.

**διαθαρρέω**, *take heart,* Ael.*NA*4.14.

**διαθε-άομαι**, *look through, look into, examine,* τι Pl.*Prt.*316a, *Cra.*424d; δ. ὅσην χώραν ἔχοιεν X.*An.*3.1.19. **-ατέον**, *one must examine,* λογισμῷ Pl.*R.*611c.

**διαθειόω**, *fumigate thoroughly,* εὖ διεθείωσεν μέγαρον Od.22.494.

**διαθέλγω**, *soothe thoroughly,* Anon.ap.Suid. s.v. κατεπᾴδουσα.

**διάθεμα**, ατος, τό, *disposition* of the stars at one's nativity, Thrasyll.in *Cat.Cod.Astr.*8(3).101, S.E.*M.*5.53, Vett.Val.78.25, etc.

**διαθερίζω**, *pass the summer,* Lyd.*Mag.*1.46. II. *cut asunder,* Hsch. s. v. διαμῆσαι.

**διαθερμ-αίνω**, *warm through,* Pl.*Ti.*65e, Arist.*Pr.*880ᵇ11, etc.:—Pass., *to be heated,* Thphr.*CP*6.9.3; *to be overheated,* Hp.*Art.*50; by drinking, D.19.197, Plu.2.622c. **-ᾰσία**, ἡ, *warming effect,* Epicur.*Fr.*58. **-ος**, ον, *thoroughly warm* or *hot,* Hp.*VM*16, Antig.*Mir.*82. II. *of a hot temperament,* Arist.*Rh.*1389ᵃ19; δ. καὶ θαρραλέοι Id.*Pr.*947ᵇ24.

**διαθέρομαι**, *to be heated,* Agath.5.7.

⊛ **διάθεσις**, εως, ἡ, (διατίθημι) *placing in order, arrangement* (ἡ τοῦ ἔχοντος μέρη τάξις Arist.*Metaph.*1022ᵇ1), Antipho Soph.24a; πολιτείας Pl.*Lg.*710b; τῶν ξενίων Id.*Ti.*27a. 2. *disposition* or *composition* in a work of art (opp. εὕρεσις), Id.*Phdr.*236a; opp. ἱστορία, μῦθος, Plb.34.4.1, Plu.*Arat.*32, etc.; δ. ᾠδῆς Eup.303; τῶν ἐπῶν Phryn.Com.55; *plan* of a building, Plu.*Per.*13; *subject* of a picture, etc., Polem.ap.Ath.5.210b; δ. μυθολογίας Plu.2.16b; *representation* in a play, Hero *Aut.*20.2: in pl., *word-painting,* Plu.2.17b; of geographical *description,* Str.1.1.16; *rhetorical art,* μετ' αὐξήσεως καὶ διαθέσεως Plb.2.61.1. b. in oratory, *delivery,* Plu.*Dem.*7; δ. σώματός τε καὶ τόνου φωνῆς Longin.*Rh.*p.194H. 3. *disposition* of property, *will, testament,* = διαθήκη, Lys.*Fr.*44, Pl.*Lg.*922b. 4. *disposing of, sale,* τῶν περιόντων Isoc.11.14, cf. *PTeb.*38.10 (ii B.C.), Str.11.2.12, Plu.*Sol.*24; οἷς δ. εὔπορος, perh. *means of disposing of* it, *of making away with* it, Arist.*Rh.*1372ᵃ33 (possibly, *inventive disposition*). 5. δ. ἔγγραφος written *report, POxy.*52.13 (iv A.D.). 6. = διάθεμα, Procl.*in Cra.*p.10P. (pl.). II. (from Pass.) *bodily state, condition,* Hp.*VM*7, Arist.*GA*778ᵇ34; δ. τοῦ σώματος Philem.95.4; δ. ὑγιεινή, νοσώδης, Gal.5.826, 17(2).238; ἕξις defined as δ. μόνιμος Id.5.826; νευρικὴ δ. *OGI*331.11 (Pergam.); of the mind, Antipho Soph.24a; ἕξις ψυχῆς καὶ δ. Pl.*Phlb.*11d; distd. from ἕξις, Arist.*Cat.*8ᵇ28, *de An.*417ᵇ15, Zeno and Chrysipp.*Stoic.*1.50, 3.111; δ. ἁμαρτωλός Phld.*Lib.*p.56O., al.; δ. σωματική, ψυχική, A.D.*Synt.*278.10: pl., Diotog.ap.Stob.4.7.62. b. *disposition* towards persons, Pl.*R.*489a; *propensity,* Cic.*Att.*14.3.2; πρός τινα Sch.E.*Hec.*8. 2. generally, *state, condition,* τὴν βασιλείαν εἰς τὴν ἀρχαίαν δ. κατέστησεν *OGI*219.11 (Sigeum, iv/iii B.C.). 3. Gramm., *force, function,* τοῦ ὀνόματος δ. εἰσὶ δύο, ἐνέργεια καὶ πάθος (e.g. κριτής, κριτός) D.T.637.29; esp. of the *voices* of the verb, δ. εἰσὶ τρεῖς, ἐνέργεια, πάθος, μεσότης Id.638.8; δ. παθητική, μέση, A.D.*Synt.*210.19, 226.10; also of tense, χρονικὴ δ. ib.251.1 (s.v.l.); διαβατικὴ δ. transitive *force,* ib.43.18.

**διαθεσμοθετ-έω**, *prescribe severally, ordain,* πάντα αὐτοῖς ταῦτα Pl.*Ti.*42d, cf. Iamb.*VP*16.68, Hierocl.*in CA*19p.460M., Procl.*in Cra.*p.49P. **-ησις**, εως, ἡ, in pl., *ordinances,* Herm.*in Phdr.*p.149A.

**διαθετ-ήρ**, ῆρος, ὁ, = sq., Pl.*Lg.*765a, Them.*Or.*26.321d. **-ης**, ου, ὁ, (διατίθημι) *one who arranges, sets in order,* χρησμῶν τῶν Μουσαίου Hdt.7.6; οἴκου Dam.*Isid.*24; συνουσίας Procl.*in Prm.*p.479S. ⊛ **-ικός**, ή, όν, *affecting,* πάθος δ. ψυχῆς Anon.Lond.2.14.

**διαθέω**, aor. 1 part. διαθεύσας Vett.Val.345.35:—*run about, run to and fro,* Th.8.92, Jul.*Mis.*338c, etc.; of reports, *spread,* X.*Oec.*20.3; of a panic, Id.*Cyr.*6.2.13; ἀστέρες διαθέοντες *shooting* stars, Arist.*Mete.*342ᵇ21. II. *run a race,* Pl.*Tht.*148c; τινί *with* or *against*.., Id.*Prt.*335e; πρός τινα Plu.2.58f: c. acc. cogn., δ. τὴν λαμπάδα *run* the torch-*race,* Id.*Sol.*1.

**διαθεωρέω**, *examine closely,* ὅθεν ἂν τὸ πλεῖον αὔξοιτο Phld.*Oec.*p.55J., cf. S.E.*M.*7.438.

**διαθηγή**, v. διαθιγή.

**διαθήκη**, ἡ, (διατίθημι) *disposition* of property by will, *testament,* Ar.*V.*584, 589, D.27.13, etc.; κατὰ διαθήκην by *will, OGI*753.8 (Cilicia), *Test.Epict.*4.8, *BGU*1113.5 (i B.C.), etc.: in pl., διαθήκας διαθέσθαι Lys.19.39; θέσθαι *CIG*2690 (Iasus). II. αἱ ἀπόρρητοι δ. mystic *deposits* on which the common weal depended, prob. oracles

(cf. διαθέτης), Din.1.9 codd. 2. name of an eyesalve, because the recipe was *deposited* in a temple, Aët.7.118. III. *compact, covenant*, ἣν μὴ διαθῶνται διαθήκην ἐμοί Ar.*Av*.440; freq. in Lxx, *Ge*.6.18, al.; καινή, παλαιὰ δ., *Ev.Luc*.22.20, *2Ep.Cor*.3.14; *disposition* (with allusion to I), *Ep.Gal*.3.15, cf. *Ep.Hebr*.9.15. IV. = διάθεσις II, σώματος δ. Democr.9.

**δια-θηκημιαῖος**, α, *testamentary*, *Sammelb*.5294 (iii A.D.):—also **-θηκιμαῖος**, *PMasp*.15.1.9, al. (vi A.D.).

**διαθηκογράφος** [γρᾰ], ον, *notary who drafts wills*, *Gloss*.

**διαθηλύνω**, strengthd. for θηλύνω, Thphr.*CP*1.16.6.

**διάθημα**, ατος, τό, = διάθεμα, Ptol.ap.Heph.Astr.2.11.

**διαθηράω**, *hunt*, θηρίον Philostr.*Im*.1.6: metaph., ὥραν μειρακίου ib.28.

**διαθηριόω**, strengthd. for θηριόω, Plu.2.330b.

**διαθιγή**, ἡ, (διαθιγγάνω) *mutual contact*, Leucipp. and Democr.ap. Arist.*Metaph*.985b15, al.; v.l. **διαθηγή**, perh. = διάθεσις (cf. θήγη· θήκη, θέσις, τάξις, Hsch.).

**διαθλάω**, *break in pieces*, Ael.*NA*4.21, Nonn.*D*.17.167:—Pass., Antyll.ap.Orib.45.10.5.

**διαθλ-εύω**, = sq. II, δ. πολλοὺς ἀγῶνας Vett.Val.359.29, cf. 248.27. **-έω**, *struggle desperately*, πρός τινα Ael.*VH*5.6; ὑπὲρ τοῦ γάμου Conon 10. II. *struggle through*, βίον Hld.7.5; ἀγῶνας Hierocl. *in CA* 14 p.450 M. **-ητέον**, verb. Adj., *one must fight it out*, Ph.2.471.

**διαθλίβω** [λῑ], *break in pieces*, Call.*Fr*.67.

**διαθολόω**, *darken*, ἡ σκιὰ τῆς γῆς δ. τὸ φέγγος Plu.*Daed*.4:—Pass., τῆς θαλάσσης διαθολωθείσης Id.2.978b.

**διάθονται**, sine expl., Hsch.

**διαθορῠβέω**, *render uneasy, disquiet*, τινά Th.5.29, Luc.*Alex*.31, Eun.*Hist*.p.222 D.: abs., *make a great noise*, Plu.*Galb*.18.

**διά-θραυστος**, ον, *easily broken*, Thphr.*Lap*.11. **-θραύω**, *break in small pieces*, in Pass., Pl.*Ti*.57b, Arist.*HA*616a27; τῇ μασήσει Thphr.*CP*6.9.3.

**διαθρ-έω**, *look closely into, examine closely*, Ar.*Eq*.543, *Th*.658, Ael.*VH*3.28, Luc.*Am*.13; *peruse*, βύβλους Epicur.*Ep*.1 p.3 U.: abs., Ar.*Nu*.700. **-ησις**, εως, ἡ, *perspicacity*, ψυχῆς Eun.*VS*p.476 B.

**διαθριαμβεύω**, strengthd. for θριαμβεύω, θρίαμβον App.*Pun*.135.

**διαθρίζω**, shortd. from διαθερίζω, Q.S.8.322.

**διαθροέω**, *spread a report, give out*, ὡς Th.6.46; δ. ἐν ταῖς πόλεσιν ὅτι.., X.*HG*1.6.4:—Pass., D.C.53.19, 61.8.

**διαθροίζω**, *collect*, Gal.12.185.

⊛ **διαθρῠλέω**, *spread abroad*, mostly in pf. and plpf. Pass., *to be commonly reported*, διετεθρύλητο ὡς.. X.*Mem*.1.1.2; *to be hackneyed*, of a quotation, Plu.*Cim*.15. II. Pass., *to be talked deaf*, διαθρυλουμένους ὑπό σου X.*Mem*.1.2.37; διατεθρύλημαι ἀκούων Pl.*Ly*.205b; διατεθρυλημένος τὰ ὦτα Id.*R*.358c.

**διαθρυμμᾰτίς**, ίδος, ἡ, = θρυμματίς, Antiph.90.

⊛ **διαθρύπτω**:—Pass., aor. διετρύφην [ῠ] Il.3.363, διεθρύφθην D.L.7.153, διεθρύβην [ῠ] Lxx *Na*.1.6: *break in pieces*, τὸ κρανίον Luc.*DMort*.20.2; φλὸξ δ. τὴν τῶν λίθων ἰσχύν Procop.*Pers*.2.17:—Pass., once in Hom., τριχθά τε καὶ τετραχθὰ διατρυφὲν [τὸ ξίφος] Il.l.c.; of a drug, *to be crushed*, Hp.*Mul*.1.74; ἀσπίδες διατεθρυμμέναι X.*Ages*.2.14, cf. D.H.9.21. II. metaph., *break down* by profligate living and indulgence, *enervate, pamper*, τινά Pl.*Ly*.210e; σώματα X.*Lac*.2.1:—Pass., *to be enervated*, πλούτῳ A.*Pr*.891 (lyr.); διὰ τὸν πλοῦτον X.*Mem*.4.2.35; ὑπὸ πολλῶν ἀνθρώπων ib.1.2.24; διατεθρύφθαι τὸν βίον Ael.*VH*13.8; τῷ βίῳ Plu.*Pomp*.18; διατεθρυμμένος τὰ ὦτα κολακείαις Id.*Dio*8. Adv. διατεθρυμμένως, ἔχειν Pl.*Lg*.922c. 2. Med., *give oneself airs*; of a prudish girl, *to be coy*, Theoc.6.15; of a singer, διαθρύπτεται ἤδη *is beginning her airs and graces*, Id.15.99; of a doctor, *have an affected 'bedside manner'*, Gal.17(2).148.

**διαθρῴσκω**, *shoot forth, flash through*, φῶς ἔξω διαθρῷσκον Emp.84.5, cf. Dam.*Pr*.81, Epic. in *Arch.Pap*.7.3; of eggs, *slip through*, Opp.*H*.1.549: c. gen., κόλπου Nonn.*D*.8.397.

**διάθῠρα**, ων, τά, *lattice across the doorway* of a Greek house, Vitr.6.7.5.

**διαθωκέω**, pf. Pass. διατεθώκηται:—*separate*, Hsch.

**διαί, διαιβολία**, v. διά, διαβολία.

**διαῐγδην**, Adv., (διαΐσσω) *bursting through*, Opp.*H*.3.119.

**διαίθομαι**, Pass., *to be kept warm*, ἐρίοισι Aret.*SD*1.11.

**διαιθριάζω**, *become clear and fine*, ἐδόκει διαιθριάζειν it seemed likely *to be fine*, X.*An*.4.4.10 (or, it seemed best *to bivouac*).

**δίαιθρος**, ον, *clear and fine*, Plu.*Sull*.7; also, = δίυγρος, Hsch.

⊛ **διαιθύσσω**, *move rapidly in different directions*, διαιθύσσοισιν αὖραι *change rapidly*, Pi.*O*.7.95. II. c. acc., ἐλπὶς διαιθύσσει φρένας causes the heart *to flutter*, B.*Fr*.16.4; *shake out*, Nonn.*D*.11.498, 20.190.

**δίαιμος**, ον, *bloody*, Hp.*Dent*.17; ὄνυξ E.*Hec*.656 (lyr.); δίαιμον ἀναπτύειν spit blood, Plu.*Arat*.52, cf. Plb.8.12.5; δίαιμα ἐκκρινόμενα Antyll.ap.Aët.9.40.

⊛ **διαινέω**, (αἶνος III) *decree, resolve*, τὸ διαινεθὲν ἄκυρον ἔστω *GDI* 2642.23 (Delph., ii B.C.).

⊛ **δῐαίνω**, aor. ἐδίηνα, *wet, moisten*, ὑπερῴην δ' οὐκ ἐδίηνε Il.22.495; ὄμμα διῆναι Heliod.Med(?).ap.Stob.4.36.8 (hex.); διαίνετο.. ἄξων Il.13.30; οἴνῳ διαίνων ἔντερ' Axionic.8.3:—Med., διαίνεσθαι ὄσσε *wet one's* eyes, A.*Pers*.1064 (lyr.): and abs., *weep*, ib.258 (lyr.); δίαινε πῆμα. Ans. διαίνομαι *weep for* the woe—I *weep*, ib.1038 (lyr.), cf. Sch. ad loc., S *Fr*.210.35.—Rare in Prose, Arist.*Mete*.387a28.

**διαιολάω**, *cajole, deceive*, Hsch.

**διαιρ-έσιμος**, ον, *divisible*, *Gloss*. ⊛ **-εσις**, εως, ἡ, *divisibility*, Arist.*Metaph*.1016b4, al. 2. Medic., *dissection*, ζῴων Gal.4.664. b. *venesection*, Antyll.ap.Orib.7.9.2. c. *surgical operation*, Phld.*Lib*.p.56 O. d. pl., *wounds*, Diod.Rh.p.53 H. II. *dividing, distribution*, of money, Hdt.7.144; of spoil, X.*Cyr*.4.5.55; ἐν διαιρέσει [ψήφων] *in the reckoning* of the votes *on either side*, A.*Eu*.749; ἀντίγραφον διαιρέσεως *BGU*1013.1 (i A.D.). III. *distinction*, ἀγνωσίας τε καὶ γνώσεως Pl.*Sph*.267b; [τῆς δημοκρατίας καὶ τῆς ὀλιγαρχίας] Arist.*Pol*.1294a34. IV. in Logic, *division* of genus into species, τῶν γενῶν κατ' εἴδη δ. Pl.*Sph*.267d; ἡ διὰ τῶν γενῶν δ. Arist.*APr*.46a31; opp. συναγωγαί, Pl.*Phdr*.266b. b. *separation* of subject and predicate, περὶ σύνθεσιν καὶ δ. ἐστι τὸ ψεῦδος καὶ τὸ ἀληθές Arist.*Int*.16a12. 2. ὁ παρὰ τὴν δ. [λόγος] the fallacy of *division* (cf. σύνθεσις), Id.*SE*177a33. V. Rhet., *division* or *distribution* into heads, Hermog.*Prog*.7, *Stat*.1, Onos.2 tit., etc. VI. Gramm., *resolution* of a diphthong into two syllables, A.D.*Pron*.87.2, al.; of one word into two, κατὰ διαίρεσιν ἀναγνωστέον Ath.11.492a, cf. Trypho *Trop*.1.8. VII. in Metric, *division of a line at the close of a foot, diaeresis*, Aristid.Quint.1.24. VIII. Math., δ. λόγου *transformation* of a ratio *dividendo*, Euc.5 *Def*.15; κατὰ διαίρεσιν Archim.*Sph.Cyl*.2.6. IX. *division* of troops, of the Roman *cohors*, J.*AJ*7.14.9. **-ετέον**, *one must divide* or *distinguish*, Pl.*R*.412b, *Lg*.874e, Porph.*Abst*.2.38; δίχα δ. Pl.*Sph*.265a; τινὰς ἀπ' ἀλλήλων Id.*Plt*.287b; διαιρετέον πόσαι διαφοραί Arist.*Pol*.1289b12. 2. *one must open* a vein, Antyll.ap.Orib.7.2 tit., Aët.16.90. **-ετήρ**, ῆρος, ὁ, = δατητής, *EM*249.46. **-έτης**, ου, ὁ, *divider, distributor*, Dam.*Pr*.273 (pl.). **-ετικός**, ή, όν, *logically distinguishable*, Pl.*Sph*.226c. 2. *able to divide, separative*, Arist.*Pr*.884b35; δ. δύναμις Plu.2.1026d, cf. 952b. 3. *given to resolving diphthongs*, -κώτατοι οἱ Ἴωνες A.D.*Pron*.95.4. 4. *suited for breaking up*, λίθων Gal.19.694. II. in Logic, *by means of division*, ὅροι Arist.*APo*.91b39; διαιρετική, ἡ, as a branch of Dialectic, Ammon. *in APr*.7.31, cf. Iamb.*Comm.Math*.20; δ. μέθοδος Gal.10.115; δ. συλλογισμός *disjunctive* syllogism, with contradictory alternatives, *Stoic*.2.87. Adv. -κῶς Plu.2.802f. III. Rhet., *concerned with distribution under heads*, τέχνη Hermog.*Inv*.3.4, cf. *Stat*.6, Lib.*Decl*.49 *Intr*.2. ⊛ **-ετός**, ή, όν (ός, όν S.*Tr*.163), *divided, separated*, opp. σύνθετος, X.*Cyr*.4.3.20; δ. τυραννίδες, of extreme oligarchies and pure democracies, Arist.*Pol*.1312b37. b. *having divisions*, ἀμφορεῖς Id.*Ath*.68.3. 2. *divisible*, Parm.8.22; πᾶν συνεχὲς δ. εἰς ἀεὶ διαιρετὰ Arist.*Ph*.231b16, cf. *EN*1106a26; opp. ἀδιαίρετος, Id.*APo*.92a23; δ. ψυχή Id.*de An*.411b27; δ. πλοῖα *which can be taken to pieces*, D.S.2.16. Adv. -τῶς Dam.*Pr*.174. II. *divided, distributed*, μοῖραν γῆς διαιρετὸν νέμειν S.l.c. III. *distinguishable*, τύχας οὐ λόγῳ δ. not *to be determined* by argument, Th.1.84. ⊛ **-έω**, *take apart, cleave in twain, divide*, διὰ δ' ἀμφοτέρους ἕλε κύκλους ἀσπίδος Il.20.280; παῖδα κατὰ μέλεα διελών Hdt.1.119; δ. λαγὸν *cut it open*, ib.123; δ. πυλίδα *break it open*, Th.4.110, 6.51; δ. τὴν ὀροφὴν *tear away, pull down*, Id.4.48; τοὺς σταυροὺς X.*An*.5.2.21; δ. τοῦ τείχους *take down* part of the wall, *make a breach* in it, Th.2.75; τὸ διῃρημένον *the breach*, ib.76, 5.3; διῃρημένοι τὸ ὑπόζωμα, of insects, Arist.*HA*556a18; διαιρουμένος τὴν καρδίαν Phld.*Sign*.1. II. *divide*, δύο μοίρας Λυδῶν the Lydians *into* two parts, Hdt.1.94, cf. 4.148; δύο μερίδας D.48.12; δ. τριχῇ ψυχήν Pl.*Phdr*.253c; δ. εἰς τὸ ἐλάχιστον Arist.*Sens*.440b5; εἰς ὁμοιομερῆ Id.*HA*486a5 (Pass.):—Med., *divide for themselves*, κατ' ὀλίγας ναῦς διελόμενοι *distributing* their ships in small divisions, Th.4.11; τοῖς δικάζουσι δ. τὰ ὦτα *lending* an ear *to both* parties, Lib.*Or*.52.4; *divide among themselves*, τιμάς Hes.*Th*.112; τὴν λῃΐην Hdt.9.85; κατὰ πόλεις τὸ ἔργον Th.7.19; τἀδικήματα D.45.38: abs., δ. κατὰ πόλεις Th.5.114:—Pass., διῃρημένοι κατ' ἀναπαύλας *divided* into relays, Id.2.75; διαιρήσομαι as fut. Pass., Pl.*Plt*.261c; διῄρητο τὰ τῶν Ἑλλήνων εἰς δύο D.10.51. 2. *break up*, opp. συντιθέναι, Pl.*Phd*.78c, etc. 3. *dispense*, φάρμακον Plu.2.73b. III. *distinguish*, τυραννίδος εἴδη δύο διείλομεν Arist.*Pol*.1295a8, etc.; δ. πότερα.. X.*Oec*.7.26: abs., Ar.*Nu*.742:—Med., Pl.*Tht*.182c; δ. τοὺς ἀμείνους καὶ τοὺς χείρονας Id.*Lg*.950c; δ. περί τινος Id.*Chrm*.163d. 2. *determine, decide*, διαφορὰς διαιρέοντες Hdt.4.23; δίκας A.*Eu*.472; τοῦτο πρᾶγμα ib.488; ψήφῳ δ. τοῦδε πράγματος πέρι ib.630; τὰ ἀμφίλογα X.*Vect*.3.3, cf. Pl.*R*.571a, *Prt*.314b, al.; κλήρῳ δ. τὸν νικῶντα Id.*Lg*.946b; δ. περί τινος Arist.*Ph*.239b13, etc.; διαιρείσθω πόσα εἴδη, etc., Id.*Pol*.1300b18, etc.: abs., Ar.*Ra*.1100; also δ. εἴτε E.*Ba*.206 codd. 3. *define expressly*, Hdt.7.16.γ' and 103:—Med., c. acc. et inf., Id.7.47. 4. Med., *interpret*, τέρας, σημεῖον, D.H.4.60, 9.6. IV. in Logic, *divide*, δ. κατ' εἴδη τὰ ὄντα Pl.*Phdr*.273e; *divide* a genus into its species, Arist.*APo*.96b15, al.:—Med., Id.*PA*642b5. V. Math., *divide*, Pl.*Lg*.895e (Pass.); διελόντι, *dividendo*, Archim.*Sph.Cyl*.1.6, al. VI. *divide words, punctuate* in reading, Isoc.12.17, Arist.*Rh*.1401a24 (Pass.); Gramm., *resolve* a diphthong or contracted form, διῃρῆσθαι Ἰακῶς A.D.*Pron*.38.17, cf. Corn.*ND*5, Hdn.*Philet*.p.456 P. (Pass.). VII. *allocate* revenues, *OGI*573.24 (Cilicia). **-ημα**, ατος, τό, *part divided, division*, Dam.*Pr*.201. 2. *logical division*, Simp. *in Cat*.425.1. 3. in pl., gloss on φακῶν ἐρέγματα, Erot.

⊛ **διαίρω**, aor. διῆρα D.H.1.35:—*raise up, lift up*, δ. ἄνω τὸν αὐχένα X.*Eq*.10.3: metaph., *exaggerate*, τὰ πράγματα Ph.2.575:—Med., *rise, become prominent*, of the breasts, Hp.*Gland*.16; *lift up oneself*, πρὸς τὴν τῶν ὅλων θέαν Arist.*Mu*.391a3: c. acc., *lift up what is one's own*, δ. τὴν βακτηρίαν Plu.*Lys*.15; τοὺς ἄκοντας Luc.*Tox*.40; τόσον δ. *take* so much *on oneself*, dub. l. in Pl.*Ax*.370b:—Pass., δ. πρός, εἰς ὕψος, Ph.2.510, 619: metaph., πρὸς ἀλαζονείαν Plu.2.

116e. **II.** *separate, remove*, τὸν πόλεμον ἀπό.. Plu.*Ages.*15 :—Med., διαράμενος (sc. τοὺς πόδας) *with long strides*, Thphr.*Char.*3.6. **2.** δ. τὸ στόμα *open* one's mouth, D.19.112,207: hence Rhet., διηρμένος *lofty, sublime*, D.H.*Rh.*6.6, *Vett.Cens.*5.3, Longin.2.2, Hermog.*Id.*2.9; λέξις ib.1.1; ποιητική Luc.*Hist.Conscr.*45. **III.** intr. (sc. ἑαυτόν, etc.), *lift oneself over, cross*, τὸ πέλαγος, of swans, Arist.*Fr.*344; τὸν πόρον Plb.1.37.1; εἰς Σαρδόνα ib.24.5, etc.; τὴν ἀκτήν D.H. l.c.

**διαισθ-άνομαι**, *perceive distinctly, distinguish*, τι Pl.*Sph.*253d; τὰς διαφοράς Arist.*GA*780ᵇ17, al.; διάστημα Aristox.*Harm.*p.14 M.: abs., Pl.*Phdr.*250b. **-ησις**, εως, ἡ, *clear perception*, Apolloph. *Stoic.*1.90, Numen.ap.Eus.*PE*14.9.

**διαίσιον**, τό, = Lat. *repudium, notice of divorce*, Just.*Nov.*22.6, al., *Cod.Just.*1.3.52.15.

⊛ **διᾱΐσσω**, Att. -ᾴσσω or -ᾴττω (wrongly written διάττω in codd., Arist.*Mete.*341ᵇ35, etc.), aor. 1 διῇξα (v. infr.):—*rush* or *dart through* or *across*, πυρὸς λαμπρὸν διαΐσσεν μένος B.3.54; λαγὸς ἐς τὸ μέσον διήϊξε Hdt.4.134: also c. acc., Λύκι' ὄρεα διάσσει S.*OT*208 (lyr.); of sound, ἀχὼ..διῇξεν ἄντρων μυχόν A.*Pr.*133 (lyr.) (but φήμη διῇξε *spread abroad*, E.*IA*426); of pain, σπασμὸς διῇξε πλευρῶν S.*Tr.*1083, cf. Hp.*Morb.*1.22; φρῖκαι διὰ τοῦ σώματος δ. Id.*Mul.*1.35; διάττοντες [ἀστέρες] *shooting* stars, Anaxag.ap.D.L.2.9, Arist.*Cael.*395ᵃ32, Gem.17.47.

**διᾱϊστόω**, *make an end of*, Πέργαμον Pi.*Pae.*6.96 (dub.); αὐτήν S.*Tr.*881.

**διαισχύνομαι**, strengthd. for αἰσχύνομαι, Luc.*Electr.*3.

⊛ **δίαιτα** [ῐ], ἡ, *way of living, mode of life*, τὰ τῆς οἴκοι δ. S.*OC*352; πτωχῷ δ. ib.751; σκληρὰς δ. ἐκπονεῖν E.*Fr.*525.5; δ. εὐτελέστεραι X.*Cyr.*1.3.2; δ. ἔχειν A.*Pr.*490; δίαιταν ἔχειν ἐν Κροίσου, παρὰ τῇσι γυναιξί, Hdt.1.36,136; ξυνήθη τὴν δ. μεθ' ὅπλων ποιεῖσθαι Th.1.6; δ. ποιεῖσθαι ἐν ὕδατι pass *one's life*, Hdt.2.68 (but δ. ἐποιήσατο τῶν παίδων he made them *live*, Id.2.2); δ. τῆς ζόης μεταβάλλειν Id.1.157, cf. Th.2.16; παρὰ τὴν δ. at *table*, Ath.12.519b. **2.** δίαιτα τοῦ οὐρανοῦ· τὸ φαγεῖν, τὸ πιεῖν, Hsch. **II.** *dwelling, abode*, Arist.*EN*1096ᵃ27; κοινὴ θεῶν ἁπάντων δ. *OGI*383.27 (i B.C.); δ. πολιτικαί public *buildings*, J.*AJ* 5.9.6; *room* (or, more often, *suite* of rooms), Ar.*Ra.*114, *CIG*3268 (prob. Smyrna), Plu.*Publ.*15; τὰς τῶν θεραπόντων δ. Id.2.515f; sailors' *quarters* in a ship, Moschion ap.Ath.5.207c; of fishes, Arist.*Mu.*398ᵇ32. **2.** Medic., *prescribed manner of life, regimen*, Hp.*Vict.*1.1, Pl.*R.*404a, etc.; esp. of *diet*, Hp.*Fract.*36, Gal.*Thras.*35, etc. **b.** *state, condition*, ἕλκεος Aret.*SD* 2.4. **III.** at Athens and elsewhere, *arbitration*, S.*El.*1073 (lyr.), Lex ap.And.1.87; opp. δίκη, Arist.*Rh.*1374ᵇ20; ἐμμένειν τῇ δ. Ar.*V.*524; δίαιταν ἐπιτρέψαι τινί Lys.32.2, Isoc.18.10, Is.5.31 (prob. l.); ὀφλεῖν τὴν δ. to have *judgement* against one, D.29.58. **2.** *the office of arbiter*, δ. λαβεῖν Hyp.*Eux.*31. **IV.** *discussion, investigation*, ταῦτα μακροτέρας ἐστὶ δ. Str.1.1.7; δ. ποιήσασθαι περί τινος 15.1.10. (Cf. διαιτάω.)

**δῐαιτ-άριος**, ὁ, (δίαιτα II. 1) Lat. *diaetarius, house-steward*, *Dig.*33.7.12.42, *Gloss.*; title of a subordinate official, Lyd.*Mag.*3.21. **-άρχης**, ου, ὁ, = foreg., *Dig.* l. c., *Gloss.* **2.** *ship's steward*, *Dig.*4.9.1.3. ⊛ **-άω**, impf. διῄτων D.H.2.75, also ἐδιαίτων A*B*91, in compos. κατ-εδιῄτα D.49.19: fut. διαιτήσω Id.29.58: aor. 1 διῄτησα Is.2.31, Plu.*Pomp.*12, etc.; ἀπ-εδιῄτησα Is.12.12, D.40.17; κατεδ- Id.21.84,96; μετεδ- Luc.*DMort.*12.3; Dor. διαίτāσα Pi.*P.*9.68: pf. δεδιῄτηκα D.33.31: plpf. κατ-εδεδιῃτήκει Id.21.85:—Med. and Pass., impf. διῃτώμην Pl.Com.168, Lys.32.8, etc., but 2 sg. ἐδιῃτῶ Lib.*Or.*64.93; Ion διαιτώμην, -ᾶτο, Hdt.3.65, 4.95, part. διαιτεύμενος Hp.*Ep.*19 (*Hermes*53.64): fut. διαιτήσομαι Lys.16.4:—pass. forms, aor. διῃτήθην Th.7.87, Is.6.15; διαιτήθην Hdt.2.112 (aor. Med. only κατα-): pf. δεδιῄτημαι Th.7.77, later διῄτημαι Hdn.6.9.5, Gal.6.249: plpf. ἐξεδεδιῄτητο Th.1.132.—The double augm. and redupl. is the rule in compds., but in the simple Verb occurs only in pf. (but δεδιαίτ- in Arist.*Ath.*53.4 Pap.) and plpf.:—*treat*, τινά πως Hp.*Aph.*1.7; δ. τοὺς νοσοῦντας οἴκοι Plu.*Cat.Ma.*23; κατὰ τωὐτὸ δ. Hp.*Epid.*2.9:—Pass., διαιτᾶται σκέλος Id.*Art.*58, cf. Porph. *Abst.*1.2. **2.** Med. and Pass., *lead one's life, live*, ἐπ' ἀγροῦ Hdt.1.120, cf. 123, Th.1.6; παρά τινι Hdt.2.112, S.*OC*928; τοὺν δόμοισιν ἣν διαιτᾶσθαι γλυκύ ib.769; ἄνω, κάτω, *live up* or down-stairs, Lys.1.9; ἐν Πειραιεῖ Id.32.8; ἐν πύργῳ Aen.Tact.11.3; πολλὰ ἐς θεοὺς νόμιμα δ. *live in the observance of*.., Th.7.77; ἐν ὅπλοις ἀεὶ καὶ πολεμικοῖς ἔργοις διῃτημένος Hdn. l.c.; δ. ἀκριβῶς And.4.32; ἀνειμένως Th.2.39, cf. 1.6, etc.; δίαιταν δ. μοχθηράν Pl.*Ep.*330c. **II.** *to be arbiter* or *umpire*, Is.2.29: c. inf., διῄτησαν ἡμᾶς ἀποστῆναι ib.31; οὗτος διαιτῶν ἡμῖν D.21.84: c. acc. cogn., δ. δίαιταν Arist.*Ath.*53.5; also οἱ τὴν Οἰνηΐδα διαιτῶντες *the panel of arbitrators for* the tribe Oeneis, D.47.12. **2.** c. acc. rei, *arbitrate on*, παισὶ φιλήματα Theoc.12.34; νείκη D.H.7.52. **b.** *decide, prove* a thing, Pi.*P.*9.68. **c.** *investigate, discuss*, τι Str.2.2.1, al.; περί τινος ib.3.8; *criticize*, τινάς Id.1.2.1. **3.** generally, *regulate, govern*, πόλιν Pi.*O.*9.66: abs., αὐτοτελῶς Phld.*D.*1.22, cf. 24. **4.** *reconcile*, τινά τινι App.*BC*5.93. **5.** *moderate, regulate*, Hld.3.10, al.; *administer*, τὰ ἐκ τῶν διαθηκῶν Luc.*Tox.*23. (Perh. formed from δια-ιτάω from διά and *ἰτάω (εἶμι 'ibo'); for sense II cf. διαβαίνω II. 4: δίαιτα is a post-verbal creation.)

**διαιτέω**, *turn by entreaty*, Lxx *Ju.*8.16 (Pass.).

**δῐαίτ-ημα**, ατος, τό, mostly in pl., *food, diet*, Hp.*VM*13; *sustenance, provisions*, X.*Mem.*1.6.5: in sg., δ. τὸ καθ' ἡμέραν Arist.*Pr.*866ᵇ3. **2.** pl., *rules of life, regimen*, esp. in regard of *diet*, Hp. *VM*3: generally, *institutions, customs*, Th.1.6, X.*Ath.*1.8. **3.** *abode*, Hld.2.26; ὁ νοῦς ἐμόν ἐστιν δ. (v.l. ἐνδ-) Ph.1.160. **-ημᾰτώδης**, ες, *to be treated by dieting*, of disease, Hp.*Ep.*19 (*Hermes*53.64).

**δῐαιτ-ήσιμος**, ον, *belonging to a* διαιτητής, Is.*Fr.*153. ⊛ **-ησις**, εως, ἡ, *way of life*, *PLips.*64.58 (iv A.D.). ⊛ **-ητέον**, *one must treat*, v.l. in Hp.*Vict.*1.27, cf. Agath.4.4. **2.** c. acc., δ. τὴν τροφόν Sor.1.93. **-ητήριον**, τό, (δίαιτα II. 1) in pl., *dwelling-rooms*, X.*Oec.*9.4: sg., *dwelling-place*, Procop.*Aed.*1.9. **-ητής**, οῦ, ὁ, *arbitrator, umpire*, Hdt.5.95, Pl.*Lg.*956c, etc.; τῆς γὰρ δίκης..γίγνεταί μοι δ. Στράτων D.21.83; δ. ὁ μέσος Arist.*Pol.*1297ᵃ6; esp. at Athens, Id.*Ath.*53, etc. **II.** in later Law, = *judex pedaneus*, *Cod.Just.*4.20.15, etc. ⊛ **-ητικός**, ή, όν, *of* or *for diet*: ἡ δ. (sc. τέχνη) *dietetics*, Hp.*Acut.*(*Sp.*)54; τὸ δ. μέρος τῆς ἰατρικῆς Plb.12.25ᵈ.3, Gal.*Thras.*33; also of persons, δ. ἰατρός ib.24. **II.** (δίαιτα IV) λόγος δ. *critical* discussion, Str.10.2.24. **III.** -κόν, τό, *decision of an arbitrator*, *PLips.*43.5 (iv A.D.). **-ητός**· ὁ μὴ κατὰ κλῆρον δικαστής, Hsch.

⊛ **διαιτός**· κριτής, Hsch.

**διαιτοχορηγία**, ἡ, *maintenance*, *PMasp.*151.185 (vi A.D.).

**δίαιτρον**· δίοπτρον διαφανές, Hsch.

**διαίτωμα**, ατος, τό, = δίαιτα III, *BCH*25.350 (Delph., ii B.C.).

**διαιων-ίζω**, *perpetuate*, τὸ γένος Ph.2.318:—Pass., Id.*Fr.*64 H.; but usu. intr., *to be eternal*, Id.2.19c, al. **-ιος**, α, ον (also ος, ον Phld.*Piet.*80, Ph.2.569), *everlasting*, φύσις Pl.*Ti.*39e; εὐδαιμονία Phld. l.c., cf. Ph. l.c., Jul.*Or.*4.144c; ζῷα Phld.*Piet.*111. Adv. -ίως Procl.*Theol.Plat.*5.37, Syrian.*in Metaph.*103.28, Jul.*Or.*4.145a.

**διαιωρέομαι**, Pass., *float about, move to and fro*, Pl.*Ti.*78e.

⊛ **διακαής**, ές, (διακαίω) *burnt through, very hot*, cj. in Thphr.*Vent.*21, cf. Gal.11.21, etc.; ἀήρ Luc.*Anach.*16; πυρετοί Simp.*in Cael.*602.9: metaph., τῷ ζήλῳ δ. Luc.*Dom.*31. Adv. -ῶς Alciphr.1.27, Alex.Trall.*Febr.*2.

**διακᾰθ-αίρω**, aor. part. -άρας *IG*1²(2).287 *A*79:—*purge thoroughly*, Ar.*Ec.*847, Pl.*R.*399e, Apollod.3.6.7; κρουνούς *IG* l.c.; ἅλωνα *Ev. Luc.*3.17: metaph., [φιλοσοφία] τέχνας δ. Iamb.*Comm.Math.*16; τινὰ τοῦ αἰσχροῦ ὀνόματος Procop.*Goth.*1.4:—Med., of *one's own* stock, Pl.*Lg.*735c. **II.** *prune*, Thphr.*HP*2.7.2 (Pass.); δένδρα Ph.2.207. **-ᾰρίζω**, = foreg., *Ev.Matt.*3.12 (s.v.l.). ⊛ **-αρσις**, εως, ἡ, *thorough cleansing* or *purging*, Pl.*Lg.*735d; ὦτων Erot. s. v. διαπτερώσιες. **II.** *pruning*, Thphr.*HP*2.7.2, *CP*3.7.5, dub. l. in Corn.*ND* 27. **-αρτέον**, *one must purge, purify, clear* from incongruous associations, Dam.*Pr.*39.

**διακαθ-έζομαι**, Med., *take up position*, of an army, ἐπὶ τῶν ὀρῶν J.*BJ*1.15.6; *take each his own seat*, Plu.2.412f. **-ημαι**, = foreg., of an army, *take up position*, J.*AJ*14.16.1, Arr.*Epict.*3.4.4; of birds, *perch*, Plu.*Cic.*47. **-ιζάνω**, *sit down apart*, i. e. *alvum solvere*, Lxx *De.*23.13(14): metaph., *hold aloof*, δ. ὁ νοῦς Ph.1.72. ⊛ **-ίζω**, *cause to sit apart*, X.*Oec.*6.6. **II.** intr., = foreg., Lxx 2*Ki.*11.1.

**διακαινίζομαι**, Med., *surrender, hand over*, τὰ ἱερὰ τοῖς βαρβάροις *PMasp.*4.9 (vi A.D.).

**διακαίνω**· *interneco*, *Gloss.*

**διακαίω**, *burn through, heat to excess*, Hdt.2.26: freq. in pf. part. Pass., γῆ διάθερμος καὶ διακεκαυμένη Arist.*Pr.*906ᵇ13, cf. *Mete.*345ᵃ17; ἀὴρ δ. Thphr.*Vent.*21; δ. εἰς τὸ μελάντατον Luc.*Herc.*1; ἡ δ. ζώνη the *torrid* zone, Str.2.1.13, al.; κύκλος *Placit.*2.30.1; ὥρα ἔτους Ar.Did.*Epit.*26; δ. ὑπ. ὀργῆς πρόσωπον *flushed* with anger, J.*AJ*11.6.9. **2.** *inflame*, ἄνεμοι δ. τὰς κόρας *Gp.*2.26.2: metaph., *inflame, excite*, τινά Plu.*Thes.*6, al.: c. acc. cogn., δ. φιλοτιμίαν Theopomp. Hist.300:—Pass., Luc.*Cal.*14. **3.** in Surgery, *brand, apply cautery across* or *throughout*, ἐς τὸ πέρην Hp.*Art.*11; πέρην ib.40 (Pass.); καυτῆρι τὸ πρόσωπον *Gp.*17.20.4.

**διακᾰλᾰμάσαρκες**, epith. of ἔριφοι, Lex Rhod.ap.Hsch. (expld. as feeding on καλάμη σπερμάτων.

**διακᾰλέομαι**, *urge on from all quarters*, κυνορτικὸν σύριγμα δ. by means of.., S *Ichn.*167.

⊛ **διακᾰλ-ινδω**, aor. διεκάλισα, *transport by means of rollers*, ξύλα prob. in *SIG*²587.158. **-ῑσις**, εως, ἡ, *transportation by means of rollers*, *IG*4.742.12 (Hermione).

**διακαλλωπίζω**, *adorn*, Hsch. s. v. πρῷρα (Pass.).

**διακᾰλοκᾰγᾰθίζομαι**, (καλοκἀγαθία) *vie with another in virtue*, τινί Diog.ap.Stob.3.4.111.

**διακᾰλύπτω**:—Pass., fut. -καλυφθήσομαι D.11.13:—*reveal*, βουλεύματα D.H.5.54, cf. J.*BJ*6.3.4, Plu.2.764b:—Med., διακαλύψασθαι τὸ ἱμάτιον *throw aside* one's cloak, Ael.*VH*5.19:—Pass., D. l.c.

**διακάμπτω**, *bend* or *turn about*, Lxx 4*Ki.*4.34, dub. in Gal.16.137.

**διακαμπῠλόω**, *bend*, Suid. s. v. διεκιρνῶντο.

**διάκαμψις**, εως, ἡ, *bending*, of the body, in exercise, Archig.ap. Aët.12.1.

**διακᾰνάσσω**, only aor. 1, μῶν τὸν λάρυγγα διεκάναξέ σου; has aught *run gurgling through* thy throat? E.*Cyc.*157.

**διακᾰπηλεύω**, *sell by retail*, ὅτι τύχοιεν ἕκαστος D.Chr.8.9.

**διακᾰρᾰδοκέω**, *expect anxiously*, νύκτα Diph.35; πόλεμον Plu.*Ant.*56.

**διακάρδιος**, ον, *heart-piercing*, ὀδύνη J.*AJ*16.8.2.

**διακαρτερ-έω**, *endure to the end*, Hdt.3.52; ἐς τὸ ἔσχατον Id.7.107; εἰς τὴν πατρίδα δ. *stand by* one's country, Lycurg.85; ἐν τῇ συμμαχίᾳ X.*HG*7.1.1: c. part., δ. πολεμῶν ib.4.8, cf. Plu.*Sert.*7: c. inf., δ. μὴ λέγειν τἀληθῆ *to be obstinate* in refusing to speak the truth, Arist.*Rh.*

1377ᵃ4. 2. c. acc., *bear patiently*, δ. τηλικαύτην ἡμέραν Alex.233; κακοπάθειαν δ. Plb.36.16.4. -ησις, εως, ἡ, *endurance, perseverance*, Marin.*Procl.*26 (pl.).

**διακατελέγχομαι**, Med., *confute thoroughly*, τισί *Act.Ap.*18.28.

**διακατέχω**, *hold fast*, Apollon.Cit.1, Ruf.*Anat.*4; *hold* in the mouth, Heraclid.Tarent.ap.Gal.12.958; of splinters of bone, Aët.15.14; *keep in check*, ἐπιβολάς Plb.2.51.2, etc. II. *hold in possession*, ib.70.3; *inhabit*, ib.17.5; *occupy, hold*, Lxx*Ju.*4.7(6), Onos.18; ξενικοῖς ὅπλοις τὴν πόλιν D.S.14.32; δ. ἐπαρχείαν, = Lat. *obtinere provinciam*, *OGI*441.108; ἱερωσύνην Decr.ap.J.*AJ*14.10.4: of the head of a school, [σχολὴν] δι' ἔτη Phld.*Acad.Ind.*p.100M., cf. p.108M. III. *keep on foot*, τὸν πόλεμον D.S.15.82.

⊕ **διακάτιοι**, αι, α, = διακόσιοι, *IG*5(2).159 (Tegea), 2².1126.29 (Lex Amphictyonum), etc.

⊕ **διακατ-οχή**, ἡ, *holding in possession*, *SIG*742.54 (Ephesus, pl.); = Lat. *bonorum possessio*, *POxy.*1201.15 (iii A.D.), etc. -οχος, ον, *holding, possessing*, *Gloss.*, = Lat. *bonorum possessor*, *PSI*3.183 (v A.D.), etc.

**διακαυλέω**, *run to stalk*, Thphr.*CP*2.12.4.

**διάκαυμα**, ατος, τό, *burning heat*, f.l. in *AP*6.291.

**διακαυνιάζω**, (καῦνος) *determine by lot*, Ar.*Pax*1081 (hex.).

**διάκαυσις**, εως, ἡ, (διακαίω) *the use of cautery*, ἡ πέρην δ. Hp.*Art.*40, cf. Antyll.ap.Aët.12.1. II. *burnt-up remains*, ἀστέρος *Placit.*3.1.2.

**διακαυτέον**, *one must burn through*, *Gp.*17.25.

⊕ **διακεάζω**, *cleave asunder*, διὰ ξύλα δανὰ κεάσσαι Od.15.322, cf. A.R.4.392.

**διακεδάννῡμι**, *scatter abroad*, δούρατα A.R.2.1126 (tm.); *shed abroad*, κῶμα Nic.*Al.*458 (tm.).

⊕ **διάκειμαι**, 3sg. subj. διάκηται Sapph.*Supp.*2.9; inf. -κεῖσθαι: fut. -κείσομαι: first in Hes.*Sc.*20:—serving as Pass. to διατίθημι, δ. ὑπό τινος X.*HG*4.5.1, 33, cf. 6.5.1; *to be served at table*, Philostr.*VA*2.28; of troops, *to be stationed*, *POxy.*1204.7 (iii A.D.), etc.: but mostly, II. *to be in a* certain *state* of mind, body, or circumstances, *to be disposed* or *affected* in a certain manner, Hdt.2.83, etc.: freq. with Adv., ὡς διάκειμαι what *a state I am in!* E.*Tr.*113 (lyr.); ὁρᾶτε ὡς δ. ὑπὸ τῆς νόσου Th.7.77, etc.; σχεδόν τι οὕτω διεκείμεθα, τοτὲ μὲν γελῶντες κτλ. Pl.*Phd.*59a; μοχθηρῶς, φαυλότατα δ., *to be in a* sorry *plight*, Id.*Grg.*504e, *Erx.*405d; οὕτω δ. τὴν γνώμην ὡς.. Isoc.2.13; εὖ δ. τινί, *to be* well *disposed* towards him, Is.4.18; πρός τινα κακῶς δ. Lys.16.2; πρὸς τοὺς ἄρχοντας Isoc.3.10; φιλικῶς τινί, οἰκείως πρός τινα, X.*An.*2.5.27, 7.5.16: abs., *to be well-disposed*, πρός τινα Philostr.*VA*1.7 (cf. ἀπὸ τοῦ διακειμένου ἀκροασάμενος Id.*VS*2.10.1); ἐπιφθόνως δ. τινί *to be* envied *by* him, Th.1.75; ὑπόπτως τῷ πλήθει δ. *to be* suspected *by* the people, Id.8.68; ἐρωτικῶς δ. τῶν καλῶν *to be* in love *with*.., Pl.*Smp.*216d; ἀπλήστως δ. πρὸς ἡδονήν X.*Cyr.*4.1.14; λύμῃ δ., = λυμαίνεσθαι, Hdt.2.162; τὸ διακείμενον, of the *intransitive* Verb, opp. τὸ ποιοῦν, Arist.*SE*166ᵇ14. 2. of things, *to be settled, fixed*, or *ordered*, τώς οἱ διέκειτο Hes.l.c.; τὰ διακείμενα *conditions, terms*, ἐπὶ διακειμένοισι μουνομαχῆσαι Hdt.9.26; of a gift, ἄμεινον διακείσεται *it will be* better *disposed of*, X.*An.*7.3.17. 3. of property, etc., *to be situated*, *PGiss.*119.3 (v A.D.), etc.

**διακείρω**, Ep. aor. διέκερσα (v. infr.), prop. *cut through*, τένοντας A.R.1.430; νεῦρα D.H.14.10: metaph., μή τις..πειράτω διακέρσαι ἐμὸν ἔπος *make* it *null, frustrate* it, Il.8.8:—Pass., σκευάρια διακεκαρμένος *shorn of* his trappings, Ar.*V.*1313.

**διακεκρῐμένως**, Adv., (διακρίνω) *differently*, Arist.*HA*600ᵃ18. II. *specially*, δ. ἀρίστη Paus.10.33.7. III. *separately, distinctly*, Procl.*Inst.*176, Jul.*Or.*5.164d.

**διακέλ-ευμα** (better than -ευσμα), ατος, τό, *an exhortation, command*, Pl.*Lg.*805c. -εύομαι, *exhort, give orders, direct*, δ. τινὶ εἶναι, ποιεῖν, etc., Hdt.1.36, Lys.25.28, etc.; οὐ τοῦτό σοι διεκελευόμην, c. inf., Pl.*Euthphr.*6d; so δ. ὅπως.. Id.*R.*549e; also δ. τινί τι (sc. ποιεῖν) Id.*Sph.*218a, etc.: abs., Id.*Tht.*148e, etc. 2. *encourage one another*, Hdt.1.1, 3.77; freq. with ἀλλήλοις added, *cheer one another on*, X.*An.*4.8.3; δ. ἑαυτῷ Id.*Cyr.*1.4.13; δ. τοῖς θέουσι Pl.*Phd.*61a. 3. *admonish, inform*, τινὶ περί τινος Isoc.9.78.—The Act. only in Suid. -ευσμός, ὁ, *exhortation, cheering on*, Th.7.71, J.*AJ*3.2.4. -ευστέον, *one must direct*, προστάξεις τισί Pl.*Lg.*631d.

**δια-κενῆς** or better **διὰ κενῆς** (sc. πράξεως), Adv. *in vain, idly, to no purpose*, Hp.*Epid.*7.5, E.*Tr.*758, Th.4.126; δ. ἄλλως Ar.*V.*929; μάτην δ. Pl.Com.174.21. -κενος, ον, *empty, hollow*, σφαῖρα Sor.1.93; τὸ δ. *gap, breach*, Th.4.135, 5.71; τὸ δ. τοῦ ὀδόντος Antyll.ap.Orib.10.36.3; *interval*, Aristox.*Harm.*p.26M.; τὰ δ. *hollows*, Pl.*Ti.*58b, 60e; διάκενον δεδορκότα with *a vacant* stare, of skeletons, Luc.*Nec.*15. II. *empty* or *vain*, Pl.*Lg.*820e; δ. ἑλκυσμός, of *idle* fancies, Chrysipp.*Stoic.*2.22. Adv. -νως, ἕλκειν τὴν διάνοιαν Iamb.*Myst.*2.10; κοπιᾶν Macar.1.99. III. *thin, lank*, Plu.*Lyc.*17; δ. καὶ λαγαροί Id.*Publ.*15; δ. τοὺς βουβῶνας Philostr.*Gym.*37. IV. *porous*, Gal.8.672; δ. ἄρτοι *light* bread, Lxx*Nu.*21.5. V. Adv. διακένως, ζώνη δ. ὑφασμένη of *a gauzy* texture, J.*AJ*3.7.2. -κενόω, *empty outright*, Hp.*Nat.Puer.*30 (Pass.).

**διακεντ-έω**, *pierce through, make a puncture*, Hp.*Acut.*(*Sp.*)61:—Pass., *to be adorned with openwork*, Corn.*ND*24. ⊕ -ησις, εως, ἡ, *piercing through*, of the teeth, Hp.*Dent.*11. -ητέον, *one must pierce, puncture*, Herod.Med. in *Rh.Mus.*58.85, *Gp.*17.19.2.

**διακέν-ωμα**, ατος, τό, *space, interval*, Pall. in *Hp.Fract.*12.282C. -ωσις, εως, ἡ, *emptying out*, Hsch. s.v. διελάφυξας.

**διᾰκέομαι**, *repair*, *IG*11.154*A*10, 199*A*69, 103 (Delos, iii B.C.).

**διακεράννῡμαι**, Pass., *to be mixed up with*, τοῦ λόγου Philostr.*VS*2.12.2.

**διακερμᾰτίζομαι**, *get changed into small coin*, δραχμήν Ar.*V.*789.

**διακερτομέω**, strengthd. for κερτομέω, *to mock at*, D.C.43.20.

**διακεφᾰλαιῶσαι**, gloss on διαπηνηκίσαι, Hsch. **διακεχλῐδέναι**· θρύπτεσθαι, and -κεχλιδώς (-οιδῶς cod.)· διαρρέων ὑπὸ τρυφῆς, Id.; cf. χλιδή.

**διακεχῠμένως**, Adv., (διαχέω) *immoderately*, δ. γελᾶν Suid. s.v. ἀπασκαρίζειν.

**διακεχωρισμένως**, Adv., (διαχωρίζω) *distinctly*, Suid. s.v. διακεκριμένως, Sch.Opp.*H.*1.498.

**διακηρῡκεύομαι**, *negotiate by herald*, πρός τινας Th.4.38.

**διακήρυξις**, εως, ἡ, *sale by auction*, and Adj. **διακηρυκτικός**, ή, όν, *pertaining to such a sale*, *Gloss.*

**διακηρύσσω**, *proclaim by herald*, ἐν διακεκηρυγμένοις in *declared war*, Plu.*Arat.*10: metaph., ἀσεβὲς εἶναι.. Phld.*Herc.*862.12. 2. Med., = διακηρυκεύομαι, D.S.18.7. 3. *sell by auction*, τὴν οὐσίαν Philostr.*VS*2.21.1 (Pass.); τὴν οὐσίαν Plu.*Cic.*33. 4. *celebrate*, ἡ παροιμία δ. τινά Iamb.*VP*6.30.

**διακιβδηλεύω**, *corrupt*, Suid. s.v. Ἀδάμ.

**διακιγκλίζω**, strengthd. for κιγκλίζω, Hp.*Art.*70, Ar.*Fr.*29.

**διακινδῡν-ευτέον**, *one must risk*, τὸ φάναι Pl.*Ti.*72d: abs. in pl., ἐδόκει -ευτέα εἶναι Arr.*An.*1.1.8. -εύω, *run all risks, make a desperate attempt*, abs., ἀλόγως δ. Th.8.27; δ. τῷ σώματι Antipho 5.63; ἐς τὰς Ἐπιπολάς Th.7.47; πρὸς ὀλίγας [ναῦς] Id.1.142: c. inf., Id.7.1; δ. ὑπὲρ τῆς Ἑλλάδος Lys.2.20; πρὸ βασιλέως X.*Cyr.*8.8.4; περὶ τῶν ὅλων D.*Ep.*3.12 (simply, *run the risk*, c. acc. et inf., δ. ἢ χ. ηστὸν [τὸ σῶμα] γενέσθαι ἢ πονηρόν Pl.*Prt.*313a):—Pass., διακεκινδυνευμένα φάρμακα *desperate* remedies, Isoc.11.22.

⊕ **διακῑν-έω**, *move slightly*, ἄρθρον Hp.*Art.*9:—Pass., *to be put in motion, move*, Hdt.3.108, Hp.*Art.*30; of *mincing* gait, Ar.*V.*688, Luc.*Merc.Cond.*16. 2. *throw into disorder, confound*, τὰ πεπραγμένα Th.5.25; *agitate*, τὰ συμμαχικά Plu.*CG*10; τὴν γνώμην Philostr.*VA*2.36. II. *sift thoroughly, scrutinize*, τὸν νοῦν Ar.*Nu.*477; τινὰ περί τινος Sosip.1.22. -ημα, ατος, τό, *displacement of a bone, partial dislocation*, Hp.*Fract.*37 (pl.), Gal.19.461, Id.ap.Orib.47.5.1. -ησις, εως, ἡ, *slight movement*, Gal.18(1).742.

**διάκινον**· δυσκίνητον (Cret.), Hsch.; cf. διακόνιν.

**διακιρνάω**, *mix well*, τί τινι or ἔν τινι, Hp.*Vict.*2.56, *Int.*45.

**διακίχρημι**, *lend to various persons*:—Pass., διακεχρημένον τάλαντον D.27.11.

**διά-κλᾰσις**, εως, ἡ, *breaking-up* of light-rays, Procl.*Hyp.*7.14. -κλάω, *break in twain*, τόξα..χερσὶ διακλάσσας (Ep. for -κλάσας) Il.5.216. II. Pass., = διαθρύπτομαι, διακλᾶσθαι Ἰωνικῶς *practise soft* Ionian airs, cj. in Ar.*Th.*163; διακεκλασμένος *enervated*, Luc.*Demon.*18; δ. ὄμμα prob. in Zeno *Stoic.*1.58; διακλώμενοι ῥυθμοί, opp. ἀνδρώδεις, D.H.*Dem.*43, cf. *Comp.*17.

**διά-κλεισις**, εως, ἡ, *closing*, εἰσόδων τῶν πρός τινα J.*AJ*18.6.4. -κλείω, *shut out* or *off*, χορηγίας τινί Plb.1.82.13; τινὰ ἀπὸ τῆς χώρας ib.73.6; τινὰ τῆς εἰσόδου D.H.11.14: c. inf., διεκλείσθη συμμετασχεῖν J.*BJ*1.19.1. II. *close*, τὸ στόμα τοῦ Πόντου App.*Mith.*12.

⊕ **διακλέπτω**, *steal at different times*, ὅσα δὲ διακέκλεπται D.27.12; τὸ δὲ διακλαπὲν πολὺ *the number stolen* [by the soldiers] *and dispersed* was great, Th.7.85, cf. Plu.*Nic.*27:—Med., *steal away*, Lxx*2Ki.*19.3(4). II. *keep alive* or *save by stealth*, τινά Hdt.1.38; ἑαυτὴν Plu.*Sull.*22. III. *evade*, τῇ ἀπολογίᾳ δ. τὴν κατηγορίαν Lys.26.3; δ. τοῖς ἑαυτοῦ λόγοις τὴν ἀλήθειαν D.29.5; *disguise*, τῇ χάριτι τῆς συνθέσεως τὴν ἀνάγκην D.H.*Comp.*18; *pass in evasion of duty*, τὸν λοιπὸν χρόνον τῆς ὑπατείας Id.10.54.

**διακληρονομέω**, *disperse*, Longin.12.4 (Pass.).

⊕ **διακληρ-όω**, Dor. -κλᾱρόω, *assign by lot, allot*, ἐφ' ἑκάστῃ..φερνήν A.*Supp.*978 (anap.), cf. Arist.*Ath.*30.3, 50.2; ἐπὶ τὰς φυλάς *SIG*531.29 (Dyme, iii B.C.):—Med., *have allotted to one*, τῦφον ἐκ νόμων Diog.*Ep.*28.1, cf. Procop.*Goth.*4.20, al.:—Pass., Pl.*Lg.*760c. 2. *choose by lot*, X.*Cyr.*6.3.36; τὸ δέκατον δ. θανεῖν, of decimating soldiers, App.*BC*2.47:—Med. c. acc., ib.18, Iamb.*Myst.*1.5, al.: but usu. abs., *cast lots*, Th.8.30, X.*Cyr.*6.3.34; πρὸς σφᾶς αὐτούς D.59.103. ⊕ -ωσις, εως, ἡ, *allotment, apportionment*, App.*BC*1.14, Iamb.*Myst.*2.3. 2. perh. f.l. for ἀποκλήρωσις, Porph.*Abst.*1.41.

**διακλῑμακίζω**, strengthd. for κλιμακίζω, Pl.Com.124.

**δια-κλίνω** [ῑ], *turn away, retreat from*, τῆς ἀγορᾶς Plb.11.9.8; ἀπό τινος Id.6.41.11. 2. c. acc., *evade, shun*, Id.35.4.6; φίλημα Plu.*Alex.*54. 3. *bend*, πῆχυν Philostr.*Im.*2.18. -κλῐσις, εως, ἡ, *avoidance of battle, retreat*, Plu.*Pyrrh.*21.

⊕ **διακλονέω**, *shake violently*, Hsch.

**δια-κλύζω**, *wash, wash out*, ἄντρ' ἃ πόντος νοτίδι δ. E.*IT*107; οἴνῳ τι Ath.9.381b:—Med., *wash out one's mouth*, Hp.*Epid.*7.2, Arist.*Pr.*948ᵃ2; *use a clyster*, Hp.*Aff.*27:—Pass., *to be washed out*, θερμῷ with hot water, Arist.*GA*739ᵇ12. -κλυσμα, ατος, τό, *lotion for washing out the mouth*, Gal.11.839; ὀδονταλγίας δ. to prevent toothache, Dsc.1.43, cf. 96, Apollonius ap.Gal.12.864, cf. Id.11.879. -κλυσμός, ὁ, *clyster*, Dsc.2.156. -κλυστήριον, τό, = ψυκτήρ, Suid. s.v. κύλιξ ῥοπαλωτή.

⊕ **διακναίω**, *scrape* or *grate away*, ὄψιν δ. *gouge out* his eye, E.*Cyc.*487 (lyr.):—Pass., *to be lacerated*, Hp.*Mul.*2.120; διακναιομένης κάμακος the spear *being shivered*, A.*Ag.*65 (anap.). 2. *wear out, wear away*, ἡ ἀσιτίη δ. Hp.*Morb.*1.13; πόθος μ' ἔχει διακναίσας Ar.*Ec.*957, cf. E.*IA*27 (lyr.), *Heracl.*296 (lyr.); δ. Ὀρέστην *murder* Orestes (i.e.

the character, by bad acting), Stratt.1:—Pass., *to be worn quite away, destroyed*, αἰκίαις, μόχθοις, A.*Pr.*94,541 (lyr.), cf. E.*Med.*164 (lyr.), *Alc.*109 (lyr.); πόλις διακναισθήσεται Ar.*Pax*251; τὸ χρῶμα διακεκναισμένος *with all one's* colour *scraped off*, Id.*Nu.*120.

❋ **διακνημόομαι**, = διακναίω, in aor. 1 διεκνημώσατο, Hsch.

**διακνίζω**, *pull to pieces*, ἄνθεα *AP*4.1.32 (Mel.), cf. Dsc.1.44, al.; *make incisions in*, Orib.9.40.2:—Pass., Arist.*HA*570$^{a}$18, 583$^{b}$16. 2. metaph., *pick to pieces* (by attacking), δ. καὶ συκοφαντεῖ D.H.*Dem.*35, cf. Phld.*Ir.*p.4 W. (dub.).

**διακοιλαίνω**, *hollow out*, Sch.Od.4.438.

**διάκοιλος**, ον, *quite hollow*, D.S.17.115.

**διακοινοποιέω**, *use interchangeably*, ὀνόματα Sch.Pi.*P.*4.25.

❋ **διακοιρᾰνέοντα**· βασιλικῶς ἐπερχόμενον, ἢ ὡς κοίρανον διαπορευόμενον, διέποντα, Hsch.

**διακολᾰκεύομαι**, *vie with each other in flattery*, Isoc.12.159:—Act. only as v.l. in Sch.E.*Or.*714.

❋ **διακολάπτω**, *dress stone with a chisel*, Agath.2.19:—also **διακολαπτηρίζω**, *IG*7.3073.185 (Lebad.).

❋ **διᾰκολλ-άω**, *glue together*, Luc.*Ind.*16:—Pass., λίθῳ διακεκολλημένος *formed* of stones *morticed together*, Id.*Hipp.*6. **-ημα**, ατος, τό, *stuffing*, Eup.409. **-ησις**, εως, ἡ, *joining together*, σωλήνων *PLond.*3.1177.305 (ii A.D.). **-ητικός**, prob. f.l. for διακωλυτικός, ἔργα Poll.7.209.

**διᾰκολουθέω**, strengthd. for ἀκολουθέω, v.l. in S.E.*M.*7.275.

**διακολυμβάω**, *dive and swim across*, ἀπὸ τῶν πειρατῶν *IG*12(5).653.29 (Syros); πρός τινα Plb.5.46.8, cf. Lxx 1*Ma.*9.48, Palaeph.27; τὸν Τίβεριν D.S.14.116.

❋ **διακομ-ῐδή**, Dor. **-ῐδά**, ἡ, *carrying over*, τῶν ἀνδρῶν ἐς τὴν νῆσον Th.3.76. II. (from Pass.) *passage, voyage*, ἐκ Κρήτας εἰς Ῥόδον *SIG*581.23 (Crete, ii B.C.). **-ίζω**, *carry over* or *across*, ἐς τὴν νῆσον Th.3.75; πέντε σταδίους δ. τινά Hdt.1.31; simply, *convey*, Luc.*Merc.Cond.*27, *PLips.*34.5 (iv A.D.):—Med., *carry over what is one's own*, δ. παῖδας Th.1.89:—Pass., *to be carried over*, ib.136, Pl.*Lg.*905b; *pass over, cross*, Th.3.23, And.3.30. II. *recover, revive*, τινὰ σιτίοισι Hp.*Morb.*2.51.

**διάκομμα**, ατος, τό, *cut, gash*, Hp.*Prorrh.*2.15, Gal.12.816. II. *breach* in an embankment, *PPetr.*3p.80, al.

**διακομπάζω**, *boast one against the other*, πολλὰ δὴ διεκόμπασας σὺ κἀγώ Ar.*V.*1248 (Burges for -κομίσας).

❋ **διακομπέω**, strengthd. for κομπέω, Pi.*Fr.*157, Posidon.41.

❋ **διᾱκον-έω**, Ion. **διηκ-**, impf. ἐδιακόνουν E.*Cyc.*406 (dub.), Alc. Com.13, Nicostr.Com.36; later διηκόνουν *Ev.Matt.*4.11: fut. -ήσω Hdt.4.154, Pl.*Grg.*521a: aor. διηκόνησα Aristid.2.198 J.; inf. -ῆσαι Antipho 1.16: pf. δεδιακόνηκα Arched.3.8:—Med., impf. διηκονούμην Luc.*Philops.*35: fut. -ήσομαι Id.*DDeor.*4.4: aor. διηκονησάμην Id. *Tyr.*22:—Pass., fut. δεδιακονήσομαι J.*AJ*18.8.7: aor. ἐδιακονήθην D.50.2: pf. δεδιακόνημαι, v. infr. II: (διάκονος):—*minister, do service*, abs., E.*Ion* 396, Ar.*Av.*1323, *POxy.*275.10 (i A.D.): c. dat. pers., *serve*, D.19.69, etc.; δ. διακονικὰ ἔργα Arist.*Pol.*1333$^{a}$8; δ. ὑποθήκαις τινός Antipho 1.17; δ. παρὰ τῷ δεσπότῃ Posidipp.2; δ. πρὸς ὠνήν τε καὶ πρᾶσιν Pl.*R.*371d:—Med., *minister to one's own needs, serve oneself*, S.*Ph.*287; αὑτῷ διακονεῖται Ar.*Ach.*1017; διακονοῦντες καὶ διακονούμενοι ἑαυτοῖς *acting as servants* and *serving themselves*, Pl.*Lg.*763a: also simply like Act., οἶνον ἡμῖν χρυσίῳ διακονούμενοι Luc.*Asin.*53, cf. Lib.*Or.*53.9:—Pass., *to be served*, οὐκ ἦλθε διακονηθῆναι ἀλλὰ διακονῆσαι *Ev.Matt.*20.28. 2. *to be a deacon*, 1*Ep.Ti.*3.10,13. II. c. acc. rei, *render a service*, τινὶ ὅ τι ἂν δεηθῇ Hdt.4.154, cf. Pl.*Plt.*290a; δ. γάμους Posidipp.26.19:—Pass., *to be supplied*, τῇ πόλει ἐδιακονήθησαν [αἱ πράξεις] D.50.2; τῶν καλῶς δεδιακονημένων Id.51.7: c. dat. instr., ἐκπώμασι διακονείσθωσαν *OGI*383.159 (i B.C.). **-ημα**, ατος, τό, *servants' business, service*, δουλικὰ δ. Pl.*Tht.*175e; δ. ἐγκύκλια Arist.*Pol.*1255$^{b}$25, cf. *CIG*2811 *b*24 (Aphrodisias, prob.). 2. *service* rendered to a god, Jul.*Or.*2.68c. II. pl., *instruments* or *utensils of service*, Ath.6.274b, Diog.*Ep.*37.3. **-ησις**, εως, ἡ, *serving, doing service*, Pl.*Lg.*633c. **-ητικός**, ή, όν, *pertaining to service*, Alex. Aphr.*de An.*59.14. **-ία**, ἡ, *service*, Th.1.133 (pl.), Pl.*R.*371c, etc.; οὐκ ἔστι ταῦτ' ἀρχή, ἀλλ' ἐπιμέλειά τις καὶ δ. Aeschin.3.13. 2. *attendance on a duty, ministration*, D.18.206; ἡ δ. ἡ καθημερινή, of *ministering* to external wants, *Act.Ap.*6.1; but also ἡ δ. τοῦ λόγου ib.4, cf. 1.17, etc. II. *body of servants* or *attendants*, Plb.15.25.21. III. *instruments of service*, = διακόνημα II, Moschio ap.Ath. 5.208b. **-ικός**, ή, όν, *serviceable*, Ar.*Pl.*1170, etc.; -κή (sc. τέχνη), ἡ, Pl.*Plt.*299d; δ. φύσις Id.ap.Plu.2.416f: Comp. -ώτερος Id. *Grg.*517b; αἱ δ. πράξεις, τὰ δ. ἔργα *servants'* business, *menial* work, Arist.*Pol.*1277$^{a}$36, 1333$^{a}$7; δ. ἀρεταί ib.1259$^{b}$23. Adv. -κῶς *in the course of service*, Men.113; *serviceably*, Sor.1.80.

**διακόνιν**· δυσκίνητον (Cret.), Hsch.; cf. διάκινον.

**διᾱκονίομαι** [νῑ], Pass., *roll in the dust*, Hp.*Ep.*27 (Oratio Thessali): hence, *prepare for combat*, Plu.2.970f.

**διακόνιον**, τό, a sort of *cake*, Pherecr.156.

**διακονίς**, ίδος, ἡ, a kind of coarsely woven *tunic*, Hsch.; also ἄνθρωπος ὁ μὴ πυκνὸς δ., Id.

❋ **διᾱκόνισσα**, ἡ, *deaconess*, *IG*3.3527.

❋ **διάκονος** [ᾱ], Ion. **διήκονος**, ὁ, later **διάκων** (q.v.):—*servant*, Hdt.4.71,72, *PFlor.*121.3 (iii A.D.), etc.; *messenger*, A.*Pr.*942, S.*Ph.*497; ὄρνιθα καὶ κήρυκα καὶ δ. Id.*Fr.*133:—as fem., Ar.*Ec.*1116, D.24.197. 2. *attendant* or *official* in a temple or religious guild, *Inscr.Magn.*109,217, *IG*9(1).486 (Acarnania, ii/i B.C.), 4.774.12 (Troezen, iii B.C.): fem., *CIG*3037 (Metropolis in Lydia):—esp. in the Christian church, *deacon*, 1*Ep.Ti.*3.8, etc., *POxy.*1162.3 (iv A.D.): fem., *deaconess*, *Ep.Rom.*16.1. II. as Adj., *servile, menial*, ἐπιστήμη Pl.*Plt.*290c: irreg. Comp. διᾱκονέστερος Epich.159 Ahr. (Cf. ἐγ-κονέω, ἀ-κονιτί.)

**διᾰκοντ-ίζομαι**, Att. fut. -ιοῦμαι, *contend with others at throwing the javelin*, X.*Cyr.*1.4.4; τινί Thphr.*Char.*27.13; simply, *hurl darts*, J.*BJ*4.3.12, 5.7.3. **-ισμός**, ὁ, *competition in javelin-throwing*, *OGI*339.68.

**διακόντωσις**, εως, ἡ, = κόντωσις, Ael.*NA*12.43.

❋ **διακοπή**, ἡ, *gash, cleft*, as in the skull, Hp.*VC*7, Gal.7.38; *deep-seated wound*, Id.18(1).27; διακοπαὶ σωμάτων Plu.*Mar.*19; *severance* of a musical string, Theo Sm.p.71 H. b. *rupture* of a blood-vessel, Gal.19.457. II. *cutting* or *canal* through an isthmus or mountain, Str.1.3.18 (pl.); through a wall or dam, *BGU*1188.8 (i B.C.); *narrow channel* or *passage*, Lxx *Jb.*28.4, al., cf. J.*AJ*7.4.2. III. *divorce*, Sm.*De.*24.3(1). IV. metaph., *breach, rupture, quarrel*, Lxx *Jd.*21.15: pl., δ. φίλων Vett.Val.3.2. V. *refutation*, λόγων Phld.*Rh.*1.11 S., al. VI. *intermission*, Herod.Med.ap.Orib. 6.20.19. VII. Gramm., *tmesis*, Charis.p.275 K.

**διάκοπος**, ὁ, *breach* in a dyke, *POxy.*1409.16 (iii A.D.), Ulp.ap. *Dig.*47.11.10. II. *chopping up* of firewood, *PGoodsp.Cair.*30.4, al. (ii A.D.). III. (sc. λόγος) *formula* or *spell for producing breach* or *separation*, esp. between husband and wife, *PMag.Leid.V.*11.15.

**διάκοπρος**, ον, *well-manured*, Thphr.*CP*4.12.3.

**δια-κοπτέον**, *one must cut short*, πρεσβείας ἀκαίρους Plu.2.819a. ❋ **-κόπτω**, *cut in two, cut through*, διὰ δέρην ἔκοψε μέσσην Anacr.80, cf. Th.2.4, X.*An.*7.1.17, etc.; χῶμα Wilcken *Chr.*11 *B*6 (ii B.C.); ἰσθμόν Str.1.3.18; *gash*, σκέλος Men.*Georg.*48:—Pass., *receive a gash*, Hp.*Aph.*6.18, al., Plb.2.30.7; so διακέκοπται of base coin which *had a hole drilled* in it, Suid. 2. *break through* the enemy's line, δ. τάξιν X.*An.*1.8.10; τὴν φάλαγγα Plu.*Pyrrh.*7; τεῖχος Aen. Tact.32.7: abs., *break through* the enemy's line, X.*HG*7.5.23, etc.; διακεκοφότας πρὸς τὰς εἰσόδους Id.*Cyr.*3.3.66; so, of a weapon, δ. ἄχρι τοῦ διελθεῖν Luc.*Nigr.*37: metaph. of a remedy, *have decisive effect*, *SIG*1170.16 (Epid.). 3. *break off, interrupt*, τὴν περίοδον Arist.*Rh.*1409$^{b}$9 (Pass.); δ. τὰς διαλύσεις Plb.1.69.5; συνθήκας Id. 18.42.3; ἑορτήν, ῥῆσιν, Luc.*Lex.*11, *Dom.*14; ὕπνον Ael.*NA*3.37:—Pass., of the pulse, Gal.8.459; also, *to be checked*, τὰ πρὸς ἑταίρας δ. σωφρονισμοῖς Plu.2.712c; διακέκομμαι τὸ στόμα *I am struck dumb*, Men.*Sam.*334. 4. *refute*, in Pass., Phld.*Sign.*11.

❋ **διακόρ-ευσις**, εως, ἡ, = διακόρησις, Sor.1.25, al. **-εύω**, (κόρη I) *deflower*, Ar.*Th.*480, Ephor.164, Sor.1.8, Luc.*DMeretr.*11.2, Artem. 2.65. ❋ **-έω**, = foreg., Luc.*Tox.*25:—Pass., Ael.*NA*11.16. **-ής**, ές, = διάκορος, τινός Pl.*Lg.*629b, Max.Tyr.7.6, D.C.61.13, Jul.*Or.*2.65d: abs., Plu.*Lyc.*15. **-ησις**, εως, ἡ, *deflowering*, prob.l. in J.*AJ*7.8.1, Sor.1.33, Sch.Il.18.493. **-ίζω**, = διακορέω, Hsch. s.v. δια⟨κε⟩κόρισται. II. Med., (κόρη III) *gaze intently*, Id.

**διακορκορῠγέω**, *rumble through*, τὴν γαστέρα Ar.*Nu.*387.

**διάκορος**, ον, *satiated*, c. gen., ἀλλήλων X.*Lac.*1.5: abs., σῶμα δ. Plu.2.996a; *saturated* with rain, Hdt.3.117; δ. ἤδη τοῦτο this is *quite enough*, Gal.7.498. Adv. -ρως *immoderately*, πίνειν D.C.68.7.

**διᾱκοσι-άκις**, Adv. *two hundred times*, Herod.Med.ap.Orib.6.20.11. **-άπρωτοι**, οἱ, *highest class of tax-payers* at Aphrodisias, *Rev. Ét.Gr.*19.242. ❋ **-οι**, Ion. **διηκ-**, αι, α, *two hundred*, Hdt.1.193, etc.: sg. with Noun of multitude, δ. ἵππος *two hundred* horse, Th.1.62; v. διακάτιοι. ❋ **-οντάχους**, ουν, *two-hundred-fold*, Str.15.3.11. ❋ **-οντάκις**, *two hundred times*, Suid.

❋ **διᾱκοσιο-και-τεσσᾰρᾰκοντά-χους**, ουν, *two-hundred-and-forty-fold*, Str.17.3.11.

❋ **διᾱκοσιοστός**, ή, όν, *two-hundredth*, D.H.8.83; -στή, ἡ, *tax of* ½% in Ptolemaic Egypt, *PHib.*1.66.1. (Written διακοσσιαστοῦ (gen.) in *Princeton Exp.Inscr.*797[2] (iv A.D.).)

**διακοσκῑν⟨εύ⟩ω**, *riddle, sift thoroughly*, Gal.10.355 (Pass.).

❋ **διακοσμ-έω**, *divide and marshal, muster, array*, ὡς τοὺς ἡγεμόνες διεκόσμεον Il.2.476; πομπήν Th.1.20:—Pass., εἴ περ..ἐς δεκάδας διακοσμηθεῖμεν Ἀχαιοί Il.2.126; διὰ τρίχα κοσμηθέντες ib.655. 2. *order, regulate*, Anaxag.12, Hdt.1.100, Th.2.100, Pl.*Lg.*864a, al., etc.:—Med., πᾶν μέγαρον διεκοσμήσαντο *got* it all *set in order*, Od.22.457; δ. τὸ σῶμα Hp.*Vict.*1.9. 3. Stoic t. t., *re-establish the world-order* after ἐκπύρωσις, εἶτ' αὖθις πάλιν -εῖσθαι [τὸν κόσμον] Zeno *Stoic.*1.27. II. *adorn variously*, τινί τι Crobyl.10:—Pass., στιγμαῖς Philum.*Ven.*21.1. **-ησις** (hyperdor. -ᾱσις Ocell.1.8), εως, ἡ, *setting in order, regulation*, ἡ περί τι δ. Pl.*Smp.*209a; τῶν νόμων Id.*Lg.*853a; θριάμβου Plb.2.31.6, cf. Phld.*Oec.*p.35 J., Corn.*ND*17, al.; τοῦ πόλου *OGI*56.46 (iii B.C.). 2. *the orderly arrangement* of the Universe, esp. in the Pythagorean system, Arist.*Metaph.*986$^{a}$6, Plu.*Per.*4, D.S.12.20, S.E.*M.*9.27, Porph.*Antr.*6, etc. 3. Stoic t. t., of the *new order* after ἐκπύρωσις, Zeno *Stoic.*1.28, etc. 4. *order, class* of beings, Procl.*Inst.*144, Dam.*Pr.*301, al. **-ητικός**, ή, όν, *regulative*, δύναμις Iamb.*Myst.*10.6. **-ος**, ὁ, = διακόσμησις, Parm.8.60; ὁ τοῦ βίου δ. Arist.*Mu.*399$^{b}$16; δ. οὐρανοῦ καὶ γῆς ib.400$^{b}$32; ὁ λογικὸς δ. εἰκὼν ὅλου τοῦ δημιουργοῦ Hierocl.*in CA* 1 p.419 M., cf. Orph.*H.*34.18; θεῶν, νοεροὶ δ., Procl.*Inst.*145, Dam.*Pr.*81; μέγας, μικρὸς Διάκοσμος, titles of works by Leucippus and Democritus, D.L. 9.13; ὁ Ἀναξαγόρειος δ. Satyr.*Vit.Eur.Fr.*37 iii 18. 2. *battle-order*, Th.4.93. II. *the Catalogue of ships* in Il.2, Str.12.3.5, Sch.Il. *Oxy.*221 vi 22.

**διακουράζομαι**· τὸ ἀτενὲς βλέπειν, *EM*267.27, Suid.

**διακουστής**, οῦ, ὁ, *hearer*, θεῶν καὶ ἀνθρώπων *PMag.Leid.V.*7.8.

**δφίζω**, intr., *become lighter for an interval, remit*, σμικρὰ δ. Hp.1.7. 2. trans., *relieve*, σπλῆνα Ruf.ap.Orib.45.30.69.

**δω**, fut. -ακούσομαι *Act.Ap.*23.35 :—*hear out* or *to the end*, τι X.C1 ; πάντα Men.*Epit.*471 : abs., of a court, *try out* a case, *OG*.1 (Pergam.); *hear* or *learn* from another, τινὸς ἄττα Pl.*Ep.* 338ὁά τινος Theopomp.Hist.244 ; δ. τά δόξαντα τοῖς ἄρχουσιν Aris1273$^{a}$10 : c. gen. rei, [λόγων] Pl.*Prm.*126c ; τῶν λεγομένων .58.8 ; περί τινος Id.3.15.4 : c. gen. pers., of parties to a disp*IG*599.20(Priene), 685.29(Crete), *PGrenf.*1.11i8(ii B.C.), *Act.*c., etc.; δ. μου πρὸς αὐτούς *BGU*168.28(ii A.D.), cf. *PLond.* 3.92ii A.D.) ; also, *to be a hearer* or *disciple of*, Phld.*Rh.*1.96 S., Plu; τὰ γεωμετρικά τινος D.L.8.86 : abs., Phld.*Herc.*862.3.

**δις**, εως, ἡ, = διακοπή, Thphr.*CP*5.9.11 (pl.).

**δδαίνω**, *shake violently*, σῶμα Tim.*Pers.*25, cf. Ar.Did.*Epit.* 13.

**δζω**, pf. διακέκρᾱγα, *have a screaming-match*, Ar.*Av.*306 ; δ. τινί*self against* another *at screaming*, Id.*Eq.*1403.

⊛ **δτ-έω**, *hold fast, control*, τὰ ὅπλα Phylarch.24 ; τὸν ὅλον κόσerm.ap.Stob.1.15.16, cf. Iamb.*Myst.*4.12 ; ὀργάδα D.H.1. 79 ; ἐν τῷ στόματι Dsc.2.152 (Pass.), cf. *Gp.*12.30.3 (Pass.), etc.2. *hold in possession*, *BGU*1047 ii 6 (ii A.D., Pass.). 3. *ma establish*, λόγον Stob.1.1.9 ; *retain, preserve*, in argument, Da439. 4. *hold up, support*, ἱστόν Erot. s.v. ὅπλα ; δέπας Ath2b (Pass.) : metaph., *support, keep alive*, αὐτόν D.L.9.43. 5. *hol detain*, in Pass., πρὸς τῶν χρηστῶν App.*BC*2.8. **-ημα**, ατο*remedy to be held in the mouth*, Gal.12.268. II. *that whield together*, Secund.*Sent.*1. **-ησις**, εως, ἡ, *holding fast*, *rete* σπέρματος Sor.1.36, cf. Dsc.*Ther.Praef.* ; *control*, Iamb. *My*; *possession*, Sch.Th.1.139, Suid. v. ἀόριστος : dub. in Eun. *His*2 D. **-ητέον**, *one must hold fast*, Archig.ap.Gal.13. 176 **-ητικός**, ή, όν, *able to hold fast*, τινός S.E.*M.*9. 72. **-υντικός**, ή, όν, *making firm*, τῶν ὀδόντων Dsc.1.30.

**Δις**, Att. **-κρῆς**, οἱ, *inhabitants of* Διακρία in Euboea, *IG*1$^{2}$. 211., Hsch., *EM*268.3 ; cf. Διάκριοι.

⊛ **δω**, *strike the strings* of the lyre, χέλυν *APl.*4.307 (Leon.).

**δμνίζω**, v.l. for κατακρημνίζω, J.*BJ*1.2.4.

⊛ **δνόω**, Dor. **-κρᾱνόω**, *make to flow*, πῶμα Theoc.7.154 (v.l.).

**δ-εία**, ἡ, *minute observance* of the law, Lxx 3*Ki.*11.33 (pl. **-ολογέομαι**, *inquire minutely*, Pl.*Sph.*245e ; ὑπέρ τινος He*All.*49. **-όω**, *portray exactly*, Ἔρωτα *APl.*4.204 (Praxitele 2. *examine* or *discuss minutely* or *with precision*, τὰς τάξεις X.C.27 ; τὸν ὅρον Arist.*SE*169$^{b}$15, cf. *EN*1178$^{a}$23 :—Med., Pl. *Th*; περί τινος Isoc.4.18 :—Pass., διηκρίβωται *the subject has been*ined minutely, Arist.*Rh.*1366$^{a}$21, cf. Phld.*Herc.*862.13 ; *to be* it *to exactness* or *perfection*, Arist.*EN*1112$^{b}$6, etc.; διηκριβω*ccomplished* persons, Pl.*Lg.*965a ; διηκρ. ἑρμηνεία Aristox. *H*a16 M. ; διηκρ. τέχναι Ath.12.511d. **-ωσις**, εως, ἡ, acc*nvestigation*, Ptol.*Geog.*8.1. **-ωτέον**, *one must examine* mi Plu.*Lys.*12.

**δδά**, Adv. = sq., Opp.*C.*2.496. ⊛ **-κρῐδόν**, Adv., (διακρίνω) *em*, δ. εἶναι ἄριστοι Il.12.103, cf. 15.108, Hdt.4.53 ; δ. ἠσκημέν Luc.*Am.*3. 2. *precisely*, of measurement, Nic.*Th.*955 ; *in* A.R.4.721 ; *distinctly*, *Hymn.Is.*14. 3. *separately*, A.R. 1.5 ; ἔνθα καὶ ἔνθα δ. Nonn.*D.*34.349, cf. Opp.*C.*2.130, Agath. 5.7. without *distinction*, περὶ τῶν ὁσίων ἢ δικαίων App.*BC*5.9.

**δα**, ατος, τό, *discrete condition*, opp. σύγκριμα, συναίρεμα, ἕνam.*Pr.*53,56.

**δω** [ρῑ], fut. -κρῐνῶ, Ep. and Delph. -κρῐνέω Il.2.387, *SIG*614. 8 (i :—*separate one from another*, ὥς τ' αἰπόλια . . αἰπόλοι ἄνδρες ῥεῖινωσιν Il.2.475, cf. Hdt.8.114 ; *part* combatants, εἰς ὅ κε δαίμε διακρίνῃ Il.7.292, etc. ; εἰ μὴ νὺξ . . διακρινέει μένος ἀνδρῶν 2.3φιλέοντε Od.4.179 ; κρόκην καὶ στήμονας συγκεχυμένους δ. Pl. *Cr* :—Pass., *to be parted*, of hair, Plu.*Rom.*15 : more freq. of conts, διακρινθήμεναι (Ep. inf. aor. 1 Pass.) ἤδη Ἀργείους καὶ Τρ4.98, cf. 102, 7.306, etc. : also in fut. Med., διακρινέεσθαι Od. 180.180 ; διακριθέντες ἐκ τῆς ναυμαχίης Hdt.8.18 ; διακριθῆναι ἀπίων Th.1.105, cf. 3.9 ; διακρίνεσθαι πρός . . *part and join differents*, Id.1.18. b. Pass., *to be divorced*, *Leg.Gort.*2.46. 2. in ophy, *separate, decompose into elemental parts*, opp. συγκρίνω, ch Pass., Anaxag.12, cf. Arist.*Metaph.*985$^{a}$28, [Epich.]245, Pl.1b, *Prm.*157a, etc. 3. ἄστρων διακρίνει φάη σελάνα prob. *set*, *removes*, i.e. *outshines*, B.8.28. II. *distinguish*, καί κ' ἀλκρίνειε τὸ σῆμα Od.8.195 ; οὐδένα δ. without *distinction* of perso t.3.39 ; οὐχὶ δ. τὴν πενιχρὰν ἢ πλουσίαν Diod.Com.2.8 : pf. Pamed. sense, διακεκρίμεθα τάς τε καθαρὰς ἡδονὰς καὶ . . Pl.*Phlb.* 52f. in pass. sense, διεκέκριτο οὐδέν no *distinction was made*, Th διακεκριμέναι *distinct, varied*, B.*Fr.*24. III. *decide*, of juφθᾷ δ. φρενί Pi.*O.*8.24 ; δ. δίκας Hdt.1.100 ; διὰ δὲ κρίνουσι θέ Theoc.25.46 ; also, *determine* a fever, *mark* its *crisis*, Hp. *C*c ; ἡ νοῦσος μάλιστα διακρίνει ἐν οὐδενί *has* usually no *crisis* inatient, Id.*Morb.*2.71 ; δ. αἵρεσιν Hdt.1.11 ; δ. εἰ . . Id.7.54 ; δ. νος Ar.*Av.*719 :—Med., νεῖκος δ. *get* it *decided*, Hes.*Op.*35 ; τὸμενον Pl.*Phlb.*46b ; *decide among yourselves*, ταῦτα . . ὅπως πο δ. D.32.28 :—Pass., *bring an issue to decision*, ἐπέεσσί γε νηι ὧδε διακρινθέντε Il.20.212 ; αἴ τινι τᾶν πολίων ᾖ ἀμφίλλογα, διμεν Foed.Dor.ap.Th.5.79 ; διακριθεῖμεν περί τινος Pl.*Euthphr.* 7combatants, μάχῃ διακριθῆναι πρός τινα Hdt.9.58 ; πρός τινα ὑπs Lxx *Jl.*3(4).2 ; ὅπλοις ἢ λόγοις διακρίνεσθαι Philipp.ap.D. 1ακρίνεσθαι περὶ τῶν ὅλων Plb.3.111.2 ; τινί *with* one, *Ep. Jud.*9 : abs., *PMagd.*1.15 (iii B.C.), etc. ; also πόλεμος διακριθήσεται Hdt.7.206 ; of a person, *to be judged*, Polem.*Call.*18. IV. *set* [a place] *apart for holy purposes*, Pi.*O.*10(11).46. V. *interpret* a dream, etc., Ph.2.54, Junc.ap.Stob.4.50.95. VI. *question*, τοὺς ἰατρούς Arr.*Epict.*4.1.148. VII. *doubt, hesitate, waver*, *Act.Ap.* 11.12 (s.v.l.) : usu. in Med. and Pass., μηδὲν διακρινόμενος ib.10.20 ; μὴ διακριθῆτε *Ev.Matt.*21.21, cf. *Ep.Rom.*4.20.

**Διάκριοι**, οἱ, = Διακρεῖς, *IG*1$^{2}$.63.93 : esp. at Athens, *the Mountaineers*, one of the three political parties at Athens, after Solon's time, Ar.*V.*1223, Arist.*Ath.*13.4, Plu.*Sol.*13 ; cf. ὑπεράκριοι.

⊛ **διά-κρῐσις**, εως, ἡ, *separation, dissolution*, opp. σύγκρισις, Emp. 58, Anaxag.10, Pl.*Sph.*243b, al. ; *segregation*, τῶν ἡμαρτηκότων J.*BJ* 2.14.8 ; *discrimination*, καλοῦ τε καὶ κακοῦ *Ep.Hebr.*5.14 ; πνευμάτων 1*Ep.Cor.*12.10 ; *differentiation*, Dam.*Pr.*1. 2. in concrete sense, *resolved form*, ἡ ἀτμὶς ὕδατος δ. ἐστιν Arist.*Mete.*340$^{b}$3, 341$^{b}$15. II. *decision, determination*, Pl.*Lg.*765a, X.*Cyr.*8.2.27, A.R.4.1169 ; *judicial decision*, *PLond.*2.476.9 (i A.D.) : metaph., *Ep.Rom.*14.1 (pl.) ; *interpretation* of dreams or omens, Ph.2.55, Paus.1.34.5 ; δ. σημειώσεως medical *diagnosis*, Sor.2.23 : but in pl., αἱ ἐκ νούσων δ. *determinations, crises*, Hp.*Genit.*3. 2. *examination* or *revision of accounts*, δ. πρακτόρων Wilcken *Chr.*41 iii 6 (iii A.D.). III. *decision by battle*, τάξεων πρὸς ἀλλήλους Plb.18.28.3 ; *quarrel, dispute*, Epicur. *Ep.*1 p.29 U., Arat.109, *Milet.*3.149.39. IV. in X.*Cyn.*4.1, *space between the eyes* in dogs. V. *separation* of tumour from blood-vessels, Antyll.ap.Orib.45.2.9. 2. *secretion*, οὔρων Aret.*SA*1. 9, cf. Gal.6.382. VI. *a bandage*, Id.18(1).777. **-κρῐτέον**, *one must decide*, D.L.9.92 : pl. -έα Th.1.86. 2. *one must distinguish*, Dsc.5.106, Porph.*Abst.*2.50, Iamb.*Myst.*2.2 : Adj. -κριτέος, α, ον, *to be distinguished*, Philostr.*Gym.*33. 3. *one must separate*, Sor.2.89. **-κρῐτής**, οῦ, ὁ, *official in charge of revision of arrears of taxation*, δ. ἐχθέσεων ὅλου νομοῦ *PGiss.*58 ii 11 (ii A.D.) : pl., *BGU*734 ii 6 (iii A.D.). **-κρῐτικός**, ή, όν, *piercing, penetrating*, opp. *compressing* (συγκριτικός), Pl.*Ti.*67e ; χρῶμα Arist.*Metaph.* 1057$^{b}$8. 2. *separative*, ἡ -κή, opp. ἡ συγκριτική (q.v.), Pl.*Plt.* 282b sqq. Adv. -κῶς Democr.164. II. *able to distinguish*, τῆς οὐσίας Pl.*Cra.*388c ; ὄψις ἕξις δ. σωμάτων Id.*Def.*411c : abs., Luc. *Herm.*69. **-κρῐτικότης**, ητος, ἡ, *power of discrimination*, Procl. *in Prm.*p.793 S. **-κρῐτος**, ον, *separated* : hence, *choice, excellent*, Theoc.22.163.

**διακροβολ-ίζομαι**, *skirmish*, J.*BJ*4.7.1, Onos.14.3. **-ισμός**, ὁ, *skirmishing, mock-fight*, Str.3.3.7.

**διάκροκος**, ον, *containing saffron*, κολλύρια Gal.12.608.

**διακροτέω**, *pierce through*, sens. obsc., E.*Cyc.*180. II. *resolve into components*, as words into their elements, opp. συγκροτέω, Pl. *Cra.*421c. III. *knock off*, κρίκους Plu.2.304b.

**διακρότως**, Adv. = ἀποκρότως, Hsch.

**διά-κρουσις**, εως, ἡ, *putting off*, ἐπὶ διακρούσει, *to gain time*, D.54. 27 ; *delay, evasion*, Plu.*Cor.*19 : pl., δ. καὶ ὑπερθέσεις Id.*Cic.*7 ; *escape from*, βασάνων Lib.*Or.*14.19. **-κρουστικός**, ή, όν, *expressive of deception*, ῥήματα A.D.*Synt.*284.20. ⊛ **-κρούω**, *knock* or *drive through*, ὅταν οἱ σφῆνες διακρουσθῶσιν Thphr.*CP*2.15.4 ; *knock off*, δεσμά Paus.4.17.1. 2. *prove by knocking* or *ringing*, as one does an earthen vessel, δ. εἴτε ὑγιὲς εἴτε σαθρὸν φθέγγεται Pl.*Tht.*179d, cf. Luc.*Par.*4 :—perh. in a similar sense in *IG*7.3073.164 (Lebad.). II. Med., *drive from oneself, get rid of*, τοὺς Ἕλληνας Hdt.7.168 ; πρόσοδον [πρέσβεων] D.H.3.3 ; μακρὰς στρατηγίας Plu.*Nic.*6 ; *evade*, διακρούεσθαι τὸ δίκην δοῦναι D.21.128 ; διακρούεται τὰ χρήματα ἐκτῖσαι *POxy.*71 i 13 (iv A.D.) ; δ. τινά *evade* his creditor *by delays*, of a debtor, D.34.13 ; δ. τοὺς λοιδοροῦντας Plu.2.70d ; δ. τοὺς κυρίους μὴ καταθεῖναι D.38.12 ; so δ. τὸν παρόντα χρόνον Id.19.33 ; *evade, slur over* a difficult question, ψιλῇ παρατηρήσει A.D.*Pron.*41.8 ; *evade* an argument, Sor.1.58 : abs., *practise evasions and delays*, D.21.186, 201, *POxy.*237 viii 10 (ii A.D.) :—Pass., διακρουσθῆναι τῆς τιμωρίας *escape from* punishment, D.24.132. III. *hinder, entangle*, ἑαυτὸν διακρούειν ἐν τοῖς πράγμασι Plu.2.80d. IV. intr., *break away, escape*, Numen.ap.Eus.*PE*11.18. V. Med., *put aside for oneself, conceal, embezzle*, χόρτον *PSI*4.354.7 (iii B.C.).

⊛ **διακρύπτω**, strengthd. for κρύπτω, D.L.4.16 :—Med., Poll.6.209.

**διακτενίζω**, *comb well*, διεκτενισμένα μειράκια Philostr.*VA*8.7.

**διακτέον**, (διάγω) *one must treat* a patient, Hp.*Vict.*1.27.

**διακτορία**, *office of a* διάκτορος, *service*, Musae.6, *AP*6.68 (Jul.).

⊛ **διάκτορος**, ὁ, epith. of Hermes in Hom., δ. Ἀργεϊφόντης Il.2. 103, Od.5.43, etc. ; δ. alone, ib.12.390, 15.319 ; Ζηνὸς δ. *AP*13.2 (Phaedim.) : variously expld. by ancient writers, cf. Nessas 2, Corn. *ND*16, *EM*268.10, Eust.182.8, etc. : apptly. taken as *minister*, = διάκονος, by A.*Pr.*941 ; as *messenger* (διάγων ἀγγελίας), by later poets, ὄρνι Διὸς δ., of the eagle, *AP*7.161 (Antip. Sid.) ; applied to Iris by Nonn.*D.*31.107 ; to Athena, ib.30.250 (so perh. of Athena's owl, Call. *Fr.*164 ; πολέμων δ., of a poet, Luc.*Alex.*33) ; cf. συνδιάκτορος : used as neut. Adj., διάκτορα δηϊοτῆτος ἔγχεα Nonn.*D.*39.82 : cf. διάκτωρ.

⊛ **δίακτος**, ον, *carried through pipes*, of oils or unguents used at the bath, *CIG*2820 (Aphrodisias), 3871*b* (add., Sebaste) ; τὰ κατ' ἄνδρα δ. *IGRom.*4.860 (Laodicea ad Lycum).

**διάκτωρ**, ορος, ὁ, = διάκτορος, βούταν δ. *AP*10.101 (Bianor) ; διάκτορσι· ἡγεμόσι, βασιλεῦσιν, Hsch.

**διακῠβερνάω**, *steer through, pilot*, τὸ θνητὸν ζῷον, τἀνθρώπινα, Pl. *Ti.*42e, *Lg.*709b ; τὸν κόσμον Plu.2.1026f ; τὸν πότον ib.712b ; ἐμαυτήν τε καὶ τὸ παιδίον σοῦ *PLond.*1.42.16 (ii B.C.) ; of a physician, Arist.*Pr.*859$^{a}$18 :—Pass., Iamb.*Myst.*8.3.

⊛ **διακῠβεύω**, *play at dice* with another, πρός τινα Plu.*Rom.*5 : abs., Id.2.128a ; περί τινος ib.70d.

**διακῠβιστάω**, *throw head over heels*, Suid.

**διακυδόμεναι**· διαχεόμεναι, Hsch.

**διακῠκάω**, *mix one with another, jumble*, ἄνω καὶ κάτω δ. D.18.111, cf. Agath.5.5 :—Pass., Id.4.17.

**διακῠλινδέω**, *to roll about*, Arist.*HA*613ᵇ26.

**διακῡμαίνω**, *raise into waves*, τὸ πέλαγος Luc.*DMar.*15.4, cf. *Icar.* 26.

**διακῡνοφθαλμίζομαι**, Med., *to look askance one at another*, *Com. Adesp.*975, cf. Ael.Dion.*Fr.*124.

**διακύπτω**, *stoop and creep through* a narrow place, Hdt.3.145, Ar. *Ec.*930. 2. *stoop so as to peep in*, Id.*Pax*78 ; διὰ τῆς κεραμίδος Diph.84, cf. Men.*Epit.*463. 3. *look out*, διὰ τῆς θυρίδος Lxx4*Ki.* 9.30, cf. *PMagd.*24.4 (iii B.C.), Luc.*Asin.*45.

**διακῡρίττεσθαι**, *fight*, prop. of rams, Hsch.

**διακῡρόω**, *confirm, ratify*, Phryn.*PS*p.62 B.

**διακωδωνίζω**, strengthd. for κωδωνίζω, Lys.*Fr.*313S. (Pass.), D. 19.167, Porph.*Abst.*4.17 (Pass.), Harp. II. *bruit abroad*, Str. 2.3.4. III. *dismiss by the sound of a bell*, Philostr.*VS*2.27.5.

**διακώλ-ῡμα**, ατος, τό, *hindrance, obstacle*, ἔργων Pl.*Lg.*807d. **-ῡσις**, εως, ἡ, *hindering, preventing*, αἱ τῶν ἀναιρέσεων δ. Id.*R.*469e ; ἀπὸ προαιρέσεων Arist.*Rh.Al.*1421ᵇ22. **-ῡτέον**, *one must prevent*, Pl.*R.*401b, Agath.2.6. **-ῡτής**, οῦ, ὁ, *a hinderer*, Hdt.6.56, Pl. *Phdr.*240a. **-ῡτικός**, ή, όν, *preventive*, Id.*Plt.*280d, prob. l. in Poll.7.209. **-ύω** [ῡ], *hinder, prevent*, τινὰ μὴ ποιεῖν Hdt.8.144, cf. Lys.20.36 ; δ. σε ὀρφανὸν εἶναι E.*Hec.*148 ; δ. τὰ ἱερὰ μὴ γίγνεσθαι Antipho5.82 ; δ. ἄδικα γίγνεσθαι Pl.*Ap.*31e ; δ. τινά Th.8.92, *Ev. Matt.*3.14 ; δ. τινά τι (sc. ποιεῖν) Pl.*Ep.*315d ; δ. τινά τινος D.S.20. 79 ; δ. φόνον S.*OC*1771 (lyr.) ; δ. τὸ πρᾶγμα Alc.Com.3, cf. Arist. *EN*1159ᵇ6 :—Pass., Th.1.101 ; διακωλυθεὶς τοῦ σκοποῦ τυχεῖν Antipho3.2.7 : ἃ διεκωλύθη (sc. ποιεῖν) D.18.60.

**διακωμῳδέω**, *satirize*, Pl.*Grg.*462e, Arist.*Po.*1458ᵇ6, Jul.*Or.*6.203a: abs., D.H.*Dem.*57.

⊛ **διάκων**, = διάκονος, *BGU*597.4 (i A.D.) ; pr. n., ib.1046.24 (ii A.D.).

**διακωνέω**, *daub with pitch*, Hsch.

**διακωπηλᾰτέω**, gloss on διερέττοντα, Suid. **διακωχή**, v. διοκωχή.

**διαλᾰβή**, ἡ, *seizing by the middle*, δόρατα ἐκ διαλαβῆς κρατούμενα D.H.20.11.

**διαλαγχάνω**, *divide* or *part by lot*, Hdt.4.68, A.*Th.*789 (lyr.), 816 (tm.), X.*Cyr.*7.3.1, etc. ; θηκτῷ σιδήρῳ δῶμα δ. E.*Ph.*68 : metaph., *tear in pieces*, Id.*Ba.*1291. II. *obtain a share by inheritance*, *Leg. Gort.*8.4,24 ; *obtain by lot*, D.H.3.48. III. *share with*, τινὶ λείας Procop.*Goth.*4.18.

**διαλαιμοτομέομαι**, Pass., *have one's throat cut*, Mnesim.4.16.

**διαλᾰκέω**, *crack asunder, burst*, Ar.*Nu.*410, *Hippiatr.*130.121.

**διαλακτίζω**, *kick away, spurn*, Theoc.24.25, Plu.2.648b.

**διαλᾰλ-έω**, *talk with*, τινὶ περί τινος Plb.1.85.2, cf. *POxy.*1417.24 (iv A.D.) ; ἐν ἑαυτοῖς ὑπέρ τινος Plb.9.32.1 ; κατὰ συμμορίας D.H.6. 57 ; πρὸς ἀλλήλους τί ἂν ποιήσειαν *Ev.Luc.*6.11 ; αὐτὴν ἐν αὐτῇ δ. Plu.2.141d. II. δ. τινί τι *talk over* a thing *with* another, E.*Cyc.* 175 :—Pass., *to be much talked of*, *Ev.Luc.*1.65. **-ησις**, εως, ἡ, *talking, discourse*, Sch.Pi.*O.*7.17 (pl.). **-ία**, ἡ, *verbal order*, Lyd. *Mag.*3.67. II. = Lat. *interlocutio*, Just.*Nov.*126.1, *Cod.Just.*4.20. 16, *PLond.*5.1674.45 (vi A.D.). III. *language*, Αἰγυπτιακὴ δ. ib. 1.77.69 (vi A.D.), *POxy.*1836 (vi A.D.).

⊛ **διαλαμβάνω**, fut. -λήψομαι : aor. διέλᾰβον : pf. διείληφα : pf. Pass. διείλημμαι, also διαλέλημμαι Ar.*Ec.*1090, Ion. -λέλαμμαι Hdt.4.68 :—*take* or *receive severally*, i.e. *each his own share*, ἵνα διαλαμβάνοιεν ἕκαστοι τὰ ἄξια X.*Cyr.*7.3.1, cf. *An.*5.3.4 ; δ. οἰκίας Lys.12.8. II. *grasp* or *lay hold of separately*, διαλαβόντες..τὰς χεῖρας καὶ τοὺς πόδας Hdt.4.94 : hence, *seize, arrest*, τινά Id.1.114, Pl.*R.*615e ; διαλελαμμένος ἄγεται Hdt.4.68, cf. Ar.*Ec.*1090 (v. Sch. ad loc.). 2. in wrestling, *grasp round the waist, seize by the middle*, διαλαβὼν ἀγκυρίσας cj. Casaub. in Ar.*Eq.*262 ; διαλαμβάνων τοὺς νεανίσκους ἐτραχήλιζεν Plu.*Ant.*33 ; in full, μέσον δ. τινά Ach.Tat.3.13 ; also, *tie up*, σπάρτῳ *PHolm.*12.13 : metaph. of the soul, διειλημμένη ὑπὸ τοῦ σωματοειδοῦς Pl.*Phd.*81c. 3. *treat, handle*, ταύτῃ τοὺς νόμους Lys. 14.4 ; τὸν ἡγεμόνα ὡς ἀνδράποδον Philostr.*VA*5.36. 4. metaph., *embrace*, ὡς ἐπὶ τὸ πᾶν δ. *comprehend* in a general statement, Thphr. *HP*8.1.6. III. *divide*, τὸν ποταμὸν ἐς τριηκοσίας διώρυχας δ. Hdt.1.190, cf. 202, 5.52 ; τριχῇ δώδεκα μέρη δ. *divide* 12 parts into 3 (i.e. of 4 each), Pl.*Lg.*763c ; ἵνα χωρὶς ἡμᾶς διαλάβῃ, of a person taking his seat between two others, Id.*Smp.*222e ; δ. εἰς δύο πάντας *divide* them into two parties, Arist.*Pol.*1296ᵃ11 ; δ. τὸν δῆμον, τοὺς ἀπόρους, ib.1272ᵇ11, 1320ᵇ8 ; τὴν σύμπασαν ἀρχὴν κατὰ ἔθνη Id. *Mu.*398ᵃ29 :—Pass., ποταμὸς διαλελαμμένος πενταχοῦ *divided* into five channels, Hdt.3.117 ; of troops, Aen.Tact.10.25 ; θώρακες διειλημμένοι τὸ βάρος ὑπὸ τῶν ὤμων, στήθους κτλ. coat-armour *having* its weight *distributed* so as to be borne by.., X.*Mem.*3.10.13. 2. *mark at intervals*, στήλαις δ. τοὺς ὅρους Decr.ap.D.18.154 ; τὰ τείχη δ. φυλακτηρίοις καὶ πύργοις *provide* them *at intervals with*.., Arist.*Pol.* 1331ᵃ20 (Pass.), cf. *OGI*701.13 (Egypt) : of Time, τὰ τῶν ὡρῶν ἐνιαυτοῖς διειλημμένα Pl.*Lg.*886a. b. *make a pause*, δ. λέγοντα Id.*Prt.*346e : abs., διαλαβὼν *at intervals*, Hp.*Mul.*1.68. c. *give relief, make a break*, Arist.*Pr.*880ᵇ22. 3. *cut off, intercept*, τὰ στενόπορα Th.7. 73 codd. ; ὁ πορθμὸς ὁ δ. τὴν Σικελίαν Arist.*Mir.*840ᵃ2 ; δ. τάφρῳ Plb. 5.99.9 ; δ. φυλακαῖς διαστήματα Id.1.18.4, etc. 4. *mark off, distinguish*, αἱ πολιτεῖαι .. τοὺς πλείστους διειλήφασιν Isoc.4.16. 5. *diversify, intersperse*, ἐπεισοδίοις δ. τὴν ποίησιν Arist.*Po.*14 ; λόγον περιόδοις D.H.*Comp.*2 ; παραπληρώμασι ib.16 ; ποιήσεις s ib.26 :—Pass., γῆ χρώμασι διειλημμένη *marked with various* c, Pl.*Phd.*110b ; λειμῶνες παντοδαποῖς φυτοῖς διειλ. Luc.*Pr.* 10. b. in pf. part. Pass., διειλημμένος *distinct*, Phld.*D.*1.2 ; οὐ δ. δόξας ibid. ; cf. διειλημμένως. 6. *divide* or *distingu*[ish in] thought, ταῦτα δ. τοῖς διανοήμασι Pl.*Lg.*777a ; δ. δίχα [αὐτῷ] παίζειν καὶ μή ib.935d, cf. E.*El.*373 ; διὰ τῶν ἔργων δ. τὴν *draw distinctive* arguments from facts, dub. l. in Arist.*Pol.*13 ; περί τινος Id.*PA*665ᵃ31, *PAmh.*2.35.44 (ii B.C.) : ὑπέρ τιν. 2.42.7 ; δ. τί δεῖ ποιεῖν Id.4.25.1, cf. *PRyl.*68.23 (i B.C.) : *determine, define*, τὸν καιρόν Plb.15.5.2 : c. inf., Id.30.9.2 ; *apprehend*, Epicur.*Ep.*1 p.5 U., al. ; *perceive*, ὅτι.. Phld.*Si*; *give a judicial decision*, *BGU*195.36 (ii A.D.), 1511 6 (ii A.D.) later Prose, simply, *think, believe*, J.*AJ*2.16.5, Anon.Lond. etc. 7. *state distinctly*, Philipp.ap.D.12.23 ; περί τινος A.H. 22.8, etc. :—Med., ib.162.27. 8. *to be pre-eminent thro*[ugh] ἀρεταῖς πᾶσαν τὴν ὑφ' ἡλίῳ *OGI*520.5 (Iasus).

**δια-λαμπής**, ές, *white-hot*, *EM*109.33. **-λαμπρος**, ον, *white*, ἐσθῆτες Demoph.*Sim.*25. **-λαμπρύνω**, *make splendi*[d, illus]*trate*, λόγον παλαιόν Plu.2.734f ; *illuminate*, Dsc.*Ther.Praef.* (v.l.). **-λάμπω**, *shine through*, Arist.*HA*503ᵇ20, 536ᵃ1 2.390b ; φῶς ἀληθείᾳ -λάμπον Porph.*Marc.*13 : metaph., δ. τὸ (sc. ἐν ταῖς ἀτυχίαις) Arist.*EN*1100ᵇ30 ; ὥσπερ ἀστραπὴ -λα τῆς ψυχῆς Plu.2.382d. 2. *dawn*, διέλαμψεν ἡμέρα Ar.*Pl.*744, διαλάμποντος (sc. τοῦ ἡλίου) Plu.*Pyrrh.*32. 3. metaph., *be conspicuous* in a composition, δ. ἰδέαι Isoc.12.2 ; of me[n], *conspicuous*, πίνακες τῶν ἐν πάσῃ παιδείᾳ διαλαμψάντων, title o[f work] by Callimachus, Suid. II. of a singer, *to be conspicuous* [in] a chorus, Arist.*Pr.*922ᵃ36. III. Act., *cause to shine fo*[rth] ἀνείδεον ἐν εἴδεσι Iamb.*Myst.*1.5, cf. Plu.2.393e. **-λαμψι**[ς], ἡ, *shining through*, Arist.*Mete.*369ᵇ15, Paul.Al.*T.*1. II. and Dor. form of Hellenistic διάλημψις, = -ληψις, *repute*. ἔχ[ει] ἐν τᾷ καλλίστᾳ διαλάμψει *Schwyzer* 647.28 (Chyme) ; *appreciatio*[n] 721.25 (Crete, found at Delos).

**διαλανθάνω**, fut. -λήσω Isoc.3.16, and as v.l. in Hp.*Acut.* 21 -λήσομαι : aor. διέλαθον : pf. διαλέληθα Pl.*Euthd.*278a :—[*escape*] *notice*, with part., διαλήσει χρηστὸς ὤν Isoc.l.c. ; but also δ[ιαλανθάνει] ἐσέρχεται Th.3.25 : c. acc. pers., *escape the notice of*, θεοὺς X.*H.* 4.19 ; σὲ τοῦτο διαλέληθε Pl. l.c., Isoc.1.44 ; ὁ διαλεληθὼς (sc. λόγος), *a fallacy*, Chrysipp.*Stoic.*2.8. II. *abscond*, *BGU*1187.23 ( ), *PSI*4.285.11 (iv A.D.).

⊛ **διάλαυρος** (sc. οἰκία), ἡ, *block of houses surrounded by* [lanes], Hsch.

**διαλᾰφύσσω**, aor. 1 διελάφυξα, *waste, squander*, Hsch.

**διαλᾰχαίνω**, *cut asunder as with a plough*, διὰ κῦμα λ. Op[p.H.2.] 264.

**διαλγ-έω**, strengthd. for ἀλγέω, Plb.4.4.2 ; ἐπί τινι Id. 10. **-ής**, ές, *grievous*, ἄτα A.*Ch.*68 (lyr.). II. *sufferin*[g] *pain*, Plu.*Alex.*75. Adv. -γῶς, ἔχει *is pained*, Phld.*D.*3*Fr.*77.

⊛ **διαλεαίνω**, *triturate*, Archig.ap.Gal.13.169 (Pass.) ; *grind*, Gal.13.169. II. *plane, smooth* : hence metaph. in Me[d.] Boeot. διαλιάνασθη, = διαλεάνασθαι, *cancel* a debt, *IG*7.3172.15 (Orchom. Boeot.).

**διαλεγδόν**· διαφερόντως, Hsch.

⊛ **διαλέγω**, *pick out*, Hdt.8.107, 113, X.*Oec.*8.9, etc. ; πτῶμα[τα] fallen olives, *PFay.*102.20 ; cf. διαλέγειν· ἀνακαθαίρειν, [Hsch.] *select, separate*, Pl.*Lg.*735b ; *examine, check* documents, *P*[…] 26 (ii B.C.), etc. II. διαλέγων τὴν ὀπήν *picking open* the h[ole to] escape, Ar.*Lys.*720 ; cf. διαλέξαι· διορύξαι, Hsch.

B. as Dep., διαλέγομαι : fut. διαλέξομαι Isoc.12.5 and 112 -λεχθήσομαι Id.9.34, D.18.252 ; -λεγήσομαι *Inscr.Perg.*5 (iii aor. διελεξάμην Hom., Ar.*Fr.*343 ; Aeol. imper. ζάλεξαι Sapph. 16.3 ; also διελέχθην Hdt.3.51, and always in Att. Inscrr., *IG*2 etc. : less freq. aor. 2 διελέγην Arist.*Top.*154ᵃ34, 159ᵃ5, Scy *IG*5(1).5.5 (Lacon.), *GDI*5163ᵃ2 (Crete), *PPetr.*3 p.130 (iii B.C. 2².1236 ; 3 pl. διέλεγεν *CIG*3656.7 (Cyzic.) : pf. διείλεγμαι P 158c, Isoc.5.81 : plpf. διείλεκτο D.21.119, but in pass. sense, 5 :—*hold converse with*, c. dat. pers., μοι ταῦτα φίλος διελέξατο Il.11.407, cf. Archil.80, Hdt.3.50,51, Ar.*Nu.*425, etc. ; πρὸς [ἀλ]λους Pl.*Plt.*272c, etc. ; δ. τί τινι or πρός τινα, *discuss* a questio[n with] another, X.*Mem.*2.10.1, 1.6.1 ; δ. ὅρους *talk in* definitions, Arist 92ᵇ32 ; δ. περί τινος Isoc.3.8, D.18.252 ; ἀνὴρ ἀνδρὶ δ. Th.8.93 ; μὴ ποιεῖν *argue with* one against doing, Id.5.59 ; εἰ τουτὶ τὸ ἀλλὰ μὴ τουτὶ διελέχθην ἐγώ D.18.232 ; οἱ νόμοι οὐδὲν τούτῳ δ nothing to *say* to him, *concern* him not, Id.43.59 ; ὁ νομ οὕτω τινὶ δ. Aeschin.1.17 ; δ. πρός τι *to argue on*.., Arist.*To* 7 ; or *against*.., Id.*Ph.*185ᵃ6 : abs., *to discourse, reason*, X.*M* 5.12 ; δ. περί τινος Isoc.5.109, etc., freq. in Pl., *Ap.*33a, al. ; γλ εὔτροχος ἐν τῷ δ. Plu.*Per.*7 ; *reason, calculate*, = διαλογίζομ *Marc.*18 :—the Act. in med. sense, Hermipp.40 ; οἱ διαλεγό[μενοι] of logicians, Polystr.p.6 W., al. 2. in Philosophy, *practis*[e dia]*lectic, elicit conclusions by discussion*, οὐκ ἐρίζειν ἀλλὰ δ. Pl.*R.*45[4a], 511c, *Tht.*167e, etc. 3. later, *discourse, lecture*, Philostr. 21.3. 4. *use a dialect* or *language*, κατὰ ταὐτά τισι δ. Hdt.1 Φοινικιστί Plb.1.80.6 ; *write in prose*, opp. ποιεῖν, D.H.*Comp.*20. *speak articulately*, Arist.*HA*535ᵇ2. 5. in Att., euphem. for [ὁμιλεῖν, συνου]σιάζω, *have intercourse*, Ar.*Ec.*890, *Pl.*1082, Hyp.*Fr.*171, Pl 20, Hierocl.p.64A. 6. *have dealings with*, *OGI*484.23 (Perg

**διάλειμμα**, ατος, τό, (διαλείπω) *interstice, gap*, Pl.*Ti.*59b, Arist.*PA* 680b34, *BGU*12.31 (ii A.D.); in Music, *interval*, Arist.*Pr.*921b10; of Time, Plb.1.66.2; *pause*, τὰ δ. τῆς ἐνεργείας D.H.*Comp.*20; ἐκ διαλειμμάτων at *intervals*, Epicur.*Ep.*3p.64 U., Plu.*Per.*7; esp. of *intervals* between attacks of fever, Gal.7.414, cf. 427.

**διᾰλειπτόν**, τό, (διαλείφω) *liniment*, Hp.*Mul.*1.97.

**διαλείπω**, aor. διέλῐπον Ar.*Nu.*496: pf. -λέλοιπα Isoc.12.5:—*leave an interval between*, τὸ ὀλίγιστον Arist.*Ph.*226b28:—Pass., διελέλειπτο *a gap had been left*, Hdt.7.40,41; διαλέλειπται μικρὰ χώρα Arist.*HA*503a34. 2. *intermit*, τὴν ὀχείαν Id.*GA*757b4: esp. of Time, διαλιπὼν ἡμέρας τὰς συγκειμένας, ἐνιαυτόν, *having left an interval of*.., Hdt.3.157, D.20.8; ἀκαρῆ διαλιπών *having waited* an instant, Ar.*Nu.*496; χρόνον ὀλίγον Isoc.5.8; πολὺν χρόνον Arist.*Pol.*1299a 37; later in gen., μιᾶς ἡμέρας δ. Hdn.7.8.9; so οὐ πολὺ διαλιπὼν *after* a short *time*, Th.5.10: abs., opp. εὐθύς, Men.*Sam.*198, cf. Hyp. *Eux.*32. II. intr., *stand at intervals*, δ. δύο πλέθρα ἀπ' ἀλλήλων Th.7.38; πίτυες διαλείπουσαι μεγάλαι X.*An.*4.7.6; τὸ δέρμα ταύτῃ δ. *is discontinuous* at this point, opp. συνεχές ἐστι, Arist.*HA*518a3; τὸ -λεῖπον *an interval* or *gap*, X.*An.*4.8.13: impers., διαλείπει *there are intervals*, of the heavens, opp. πλήρη ἀστέρων εἶναι, Arist.*Mete.*346a 36. 2. c. part., mostly with neg., οὐ πώποτε διέλειπον ζητῶν X. *Ap.*16, etc.; οὐδένα διαλέλοιπα χρόνον διαβαλλόμενος I *have* never *ceased* to be slandered. Isoc.12.5; οὐ διέλιπον..παραινῶν πείθεσθαι.. *BGU*747i 7 (ii A.D.), cf. *POxy.*281.16 (i A.D.): without a neg., Luc. *Vit.Auct.*13, *D.Meretr.*11.1. 3. of Time, διαλιπόντων ἐτῶν τριῶν, διαλιπούσης ἡμέρας, *after an interval* of.., Th.1.112, 3.74; τὸ διαλεῖπον *the interval of time*, Arist.*Ph.*228b4. 4. in part., *intermittent*, διαλείποντες πνέουσιν οἱ ἄνεμοι Id.*Mete.*362a28, cf. *GA*748a19; δ. πυρετός Hp.*Aph.*4.43, *Coac.*139. 5. *die*, *GDI*1920.9, 2082.5 (Delph.).

**διαλείφω**, *anoint*, Hp.*Mul.*1.64. II. *plaster*, *SIG*2587.107. III. *erase, strike out*, Plu.*Arat.*12; δίκην Chamael.ap.Ath.9.407c.

**διαλείχω**, *lick clean*, Ar.*Eq.*1034, *V.*904.

**διάλειψις**, εως, ἡ, *an interval, interstice*, v.l. in Hp.*Art.*35, cf. Arist. *Aud.*803b37; δ. τῶν πλινθίδων *IG*2.1054.93; δ. φυλλική, *internode*, Thphr.*HP*3.18.11; *intermission*, Erot. s.v. τριταιοφυεῖς.

**διαλεκτ-έον**, (διαλέγομαι) *one must discourse*, Isoc.12.134, Pl.*Ly.* 211c: esp philosophically, Arist.*APo.*77b13, *Metaph.*1012b7. **-ικεύομαι**, '*chop logic*', M.Ant.8.13, Gal.13.573. **-ικός**, ή, όν, *conversational*, χορός Demetr.*Eloc.*167. 2. δ. ὄργανα organs *of articulate speech*, opp. φωνητικά, Gal.16.204. II. *skilled in dialectic*, ὁ ἐρωτᾶν καὶ ἀποκρίνεσθαι ἐπιστάμενος Pl.*Cra.*390c; ἦ καὶ δ. καλεῖς τὸν λόγον ἑκάστου λαμβάνοντα τῆς οὐσίας; Id.*R.*534b; *dialectical*, Arist. *Metaph.*995b23; δ. συλλογισμός Id.*Top.*100a22; πρὸς τοὺς δ., title of work by Metrodorus, D.L.10.24, cf. Phld.*Rh.*1.279S., al. III. ἡ διαλεκτική (sc. τέχνη) *dialectic, discussion by question and answer*, invented by Zeno of Elea, Arist.*Fr.*65; *philosophical method*, ὥσπερ θριγκὸς τοῖς μαθήμασιν ἡ δ. ἐπάνω κεῖται Pl.*R.*534e: τὸ -κόν Id.*Sph.* 253e; περὶ -κῆς, title of work by Cleanthes, D.L.7.174. 2. *the logic of probabilities*, ἡ δ. πειραστικὴ περὶ ὧν ἡ φιλοσοφία γνωριστική Arist.*Metaph.*1004b25, cf. *Rh.*1354a1. IV. Adv. -κῶς *dialectically*, Pl.*Phlb.*17a, etc.; *for the sake of argument*, opp. κατ' ἀλήθειαν, Arist. *Top.*105b31, cf. *de An.*403a2; *by argument on general principles*, opp. scientifically, Phld.*Rh.*2.134 S., *Mus.*p.89 K.: Comp. -ώτερον Pl.*Men.* 75d; *more logically*, Dam.*Pr.*97. **-ος**, ἡ, *discourse, conversation*, Hp.*Art.*30; θεοῖς πρὸς ἀνθρώπους Pl.*Smp.*203a; *discussion, debate, argument*, Id.*Tht.*146b; opp. ἔρις, Id.*R.*454a. 2. *common language, talk*, δ. ἡ πρὸς ἀλλήλους Arist.*Po.*1449a26; ἡ εἰωθυῖα δ. Id.*Rh.* 1404b24. II. *speech, language*, Ar.*Fr.*685; καινὴν δ. λαλῶν Antiph. 171; δ. ἀμνίου, opp. τὰ ἔνδον δράκοντος, Hermipp.3; *articulate speech, language*, opp. φωνή, Arist.*HA*535a28; τοῦ ἀνθρώπου μία φωνή, ἀλλὰ διάλεκτοι πολλαί Id.*Pr.*895a6; but also, *spoken*, opp. written *language*, D.H.*Comp.*11. 2. *the language of a country*, Plb.1.80.6, D.S.5.6, etc.: esp. *dialect*, as Ionic, Attic, etc., Diog.Bab.*Stoic.*3.213, D.H.*Comp.*3, S.E.*M.*1.59, Hdn.Gr.2.932; also, *local word* or *expression*, Plu.*Alex.*31. III. *way of speaking, accent*, D.37.55. 2. pl., *modes of expression*, Epicur.*Ep.*1 p.24 U. IV. *style*, πανηγυρική, ποιητικὴ δ., D.H.*Comp.*23,21: esp. *poetical diction*, Phld.*Po.* 2 *Fr.*33, al. V. of musical instruments, *quality*, '*idiom*', Arist. *de An.*420b8.

**διαλελῠμένως**, Adv., (διαλύω) *laxly*, Arist.*Pr.*900a24. II. *not in composition*, Ath.15.676f; e.g. πόδας ὠκύς, as compared with ποδώκης, Eust.64.22. b. *in an uncontracted form*, e.g. χαλκέα, opp. χαλκῆ, Moer.414. c. *without conjunctions, in asyndeton*, Ph. 1.500. III. *in conversational style*, opp. ἐμμέτρως, Sch.Heph. p.115 C., cf. Sch.Ar.*Eq.*937.

**διάλεξις**, εως, ἡ, *discourse, argument*, Ar.*Nu.*317, Jul.*ad Them.* 255b (pl.), f.l. in Pl.*Ep.*350d, Philostr.*VA*4.40; *conversation, interview*, Wilcken *Chr.*155.17 (iii A.D.). II. = διάλεκτος II. 2, D.C. 60.17. III. *passage* in a book, *specimen of style*, D.H.*Dem.* 21; *phrase*, Ἀττικαὶ δ., title of work by Aristophanes of Byzantium. IV. *popular discourse, lecture*, Philostr.*VS*1.24.1, al., Diog.Oen.18, etc.; of the *discourses* of Epictetus, Gell.19.1.14.

**διαλεπίζω**, *strip of bark*, δένδρον Gloss.

**διαλεπτολογέομαι**, *discourse subtly*, '*chop logic*', τινὶ *with* one, Ar. *Nu.*1496.

**διάλεπτ-ος**, ον, *very small* or *narrow*, ὑμήν Eust.1157.18. **-ύνω**, *make thin, pare away, fine down*, Hp.*Fract.*11; *grind small*, Sch.E. *Ph.*1159:—Pass., *become thin, watery*, of a fluid, Ruf.*Sat.Gon.*15:—hence Subst. **-υνσις**, εως, ἡ, Aët.16.55.

**διαλεσχαίνω**, *prate, chatter*, Phryn.*PS* p.36 B.

**διαλευκαίνω**, *whiten*, Philostr.Jun.*Im.*12. 2. *illustrate, elucidate*, v.l. in Dsc.*Ther.Praef.*

※ **διάλευκος**, ον, *quite white*, Arist.*Pr.*894a39, Lxx *Ge.*30.32, Str.17. 1.31, Plu.*Alex.*51, Aret.*SD*2.13; αἱ λίμναι -ότεραι τῆς θαλάττης Arist. *Pr.*932a29.

**διαληκάομαι**, *laugh at*, Ael.Dion.*Fr.*125:—hence **διαληκίνδα**, a game, Theognost. in *AB*1353a.

**διάλημμα**, ατος, τό, *windings* of a chain, Ath.Mech.24.6. II. *gap*, *PPetr.*3 p.290 (iii B.C.).

※ **διάληξις**, εως, ἡ, (διαλαγχάνω) *division* of an inheritance, Antipho *Fr.*64, Hsch., Suid.

**διαληπτ-έον**, *one must divide*, τὰς ἐπιστήμας Pl.*Plt.*258b; δ. ὡς.. *we must distinguish and say* that.., Arist.*Pol.*1290b9. II. *one must hold an opinion, form a judgement*, τὸ παραπλήσιον δ. περί τινος Plb.6.44.1, 11.25.3. III. *one must discuss, treat*, Porph.*Abst.* 1.57. **-ικός**, ή, όν, *forming a judgement*. ἐπίστασις M Ant.10.8, cf. Epicur.*Nat.*50 G. **-ός**, ή, όν, *distinguishable*, Id.*Ep.*1 p.16 U.

**διαληρέω**, *speak foolishly*, Eun.*Hist.*p.265 D.

※ **διάληψις**, later **διάλημψις**, in Doricized form **διάλᾱμψις** (q.v.), εως, ἡ, (διαλαμβάνω) *grasping with both hands*: ἐκ διαλήψεως, opp. ἐκ καταφορᾶς, as *thrusting* to cutting, Plb.2.33.6. 2. ἡ δ. τῆς χώρας *power of holding, capacity*, D.S.3.37. 3. *containing, storage*, *PPetr.* 3 p.141 (iii B.C.). II. *separating* or *distinguishing* in thought, Epicur.*Ep.*1 p.13 U., Phld.*D.*3.8; κατὰ διάληψιν *separately*, Id.*Ir.* p.76 W., *Rh.*1.91 S. III. *judgement, opinion*, Epicur.*Nat.*28.7; ἡ περὶ θεῶν δ. Plb.6.56.6; αἱ ὑπὲρ τῶν ἐν Ἅιδου δ. ib.12, cf. Lxx 2*Ma.* 3.32; ἐγέννησε τὴν περὶ αὐτοῦ δ. ὡς.. D.S.18.54: esp. in good sense, τῆς προαιρέσεως ἐπ' ἀγαθῷ τὴν δ. ἐχούσης *Inscr.Prien.*117.60 (i B.C.); ἀρετὴ καὶ δ. *BCH*37.125 (Abdera, ii B.C.). 2. *sentence, punishment*, ἐνέχεσθαι ἱεροσυλίᾳ καὶ πίπτειν ὑπὸ πικροτέραν δ. *Annales du Service* 19.40, cf. 42 (Egypt, i B.C.). IV. *division*, Porph.*Sent.*36 (pl.); *distinction* of parts, Arist.*IA*705a25: pl., *points of division* or *ramification*, Id.*PA*647b2; of the *divisions* of the vertebrae, ib. 652a17. 2. *interval*, = διάλειμμα, v.l. in Aret.*SD*1.12. V. *digression* in a narrative, Iamb.*Bab.*17.

※ **διαλῐθος**, ον, *set with precious stones*, *IG*2.652 *B*13, Men.503, *Epit.*169, *OGI*56.59 (iii B.C.), Lxx *To.*10.7, Aristeas 62; ὅρμος ῥόδων δ. *IG*12.289; κόσμος Str.15.1.54; στέφανος D.C.44.6.

**διαλιμπάνω**, = διαλείπω, *intermit*, Gal.17(1).220, Mich.*in EN*560. 1, v.l. in *Act.Ap.*8.24.

**διαλῑνάω**, *slip through a net*, Phryn.*PS* p.64 B.:—Med., Eust.574. 31.

**Διάλιος** ἱερεύς, ὁ, = Lat. *flamen Dialis*, D.C.44.6.

**διαλιχμάομαι**, = διαλείχω, Iamb.*Bab.*3, Agath.2.3.

**διαλλ-ἀγή**, ἡ, (διαλλάσσω) *interchange*, ὡς διαλλαγὰς ἔχοιμεν ἀλλήλοισιν ὧν πένοιτο γῆ E.*Supp.*209. II. *change*, δυναστειῶν, ἀρχόντων, D.C.47.5, 48.53; ἀριθμοῦ A.D.*Synt.*259.25: but esp. 2. *change* from enmity *to friendship, reconciliation*, Hdt.1.22, Is.7. 44; Δ. personified, Ar.*Ach.*989: in pl., E.*Ph.*375, Ar.*V.*472, etc.; διαλλαγαὶ πρός τινα Isoc.4.94, cf. D.2.1. III. *difference*, D.H.*Isoc.*11. **-αγμα**, ατος, τό, *substitute, changeling*, E.*Hel.* 586. II. *difference*, D.H.7.64. III. *renewal*, *PLips.*97 xxvi 13 (iv A.D.). **-ακτήρ**, ῆρος, ὁ, *mediator*, A.*Th.*908 (lyr.), *OGI* 43.2 (iii B.C.), D.H.2.76, App.*Mac.*4, Poll.1.153. **-ακτήριος**, ον, *mediating, conciliating*, λόγοι D.H.5.31. **-ακτής**, οῦ, ὁ, = διαλλακτήρ, E.*Ph.*468, Th.4.60, *IG*12(7).3.31 (Amorgos), Arist. *Ath.*38.4, etc. **-ακτικός**, ή, όν, *inclined to mediate*, D.H.7. 34. **-αξις**, εως, ἡ, *separation*, μιγέντων Emp.8.3, cf. Hp.*Vict.*1. 10. 2. pl., *attempts at reconciliation*, Pl.*Ep.*35cd. ※ **-άσσω**, Att. **-ττω**, fut. -ξω: pf. διήλλαχα Dionys.Com. (v. infr.), A.D.*Synt.*70. 11. I. Med., *interchange*, τὰς τάξεις Hdt.9.47, cf. Pi.*O.*11(10).21: abs., *make an exchange*, X.*Cyr.*8.3.32, *Test.Epict.*2.14. II. *exchange*, i.e., 1. *give in exchange*, τί τινι E.*Alc.*14; τί τινι ἀντὶ ἀργυρίου Pl. *R.*371d; τινὰ ὑπέρ τινος one for another, D.H.10.24; τὴν σκευὴν πρὸς τὸν δεσπότην D.C.47.10; or, 2. *take in exchange*, δ. ἀετοῦ βίον *take* an eagle's life *for* one's own, Pl.*R.*620b; ἐσθῆτα τῇ συμφορᾷ πρέπουσαν Plu.*Cic.*19; δ. Μακεδονίαν *change* one land *for* another, i.e. *pass through* a land, X.*HG*4.3.3 (also abs., ἐξ ἄλλης εἰς ἄλλην πόλιν δ. Pl. *Sph.*223d):—Med., τι ἀντί τινος D.H.2.3. 3. simply, *change, alter*, κελεύθους Emp.35.15; τοὺς ναυάρχους X.*HG*1.6.4; τοὺς λόγους Arist. *Rh.Al.*1434a38. 4. abs., *change, alter*, Emp.17.12; δ. ἀπ' ἀλλήλων *to be discordant*, Hp.*Vict.*1.6; διαλλάττοντας *different*, opp. ὁμοίους, Phld.*Sign.*3, al. b. *depart this life, die*, Lycurg.*Fr.*33, Corn.*ND* 35. 5. *change money*, δ. τὸ δηνάριον *OGI*484.10 (ii A.D.). III. esp. *change enmity for friendship, reconcile* one to another, τινά τινι Th.2.95, 6.47, etc.; πόλεις πρὸς ἀλλήλας Isoc.5.111: most freq. c. acc. pl. only, E.*Ph.*436, Antipho 6.39, Test.ap.D.59.47, D.24.91: rarely c. acc. sg., *make it up with* one, διαλλάξεις με φιλάσας Theoc.23. 42:—Pass. with fut. διαλλαχθήσομαι Ar.*V.*1395, etc.; διαλλαγήσομαι Pl.*R.*471a: pf. διήλλαγμαι A.*Th.*885 (lyr.): aor. -ηλλάχθην Ar.*Lys.* 900, -ηλλάγην ib.1161:—*to be reconciled, to be made friends*, A.l.c., Pl. *Prt.*346b, etc.; τοῖς ἀποστᾶσι Isoc.9.63; πρός τινα περί τινος Id.3.33; τῆς πρόσθεν ἔχθρας ἐς φίλους E.*Med.*896, cf. And.2.26. IV. intr., c. dat. pers. et acc. rei, *differ from* one *in* a thing, εἴδει δ. οὐδὲν τοῖσι ἑτέροισι Hdt.7.70; δ. ταῖς ἡλικίαις Arist.*EN*1161a5; κλήσει, οὐ φύσει D.H.1.29; πρός τινα Aristid.*Or.*36(48).16: also c. gen. pers., δ. τινός τινι Plb.2.37.11; ἔν τινι Luc.*Pisc.*23: abs., πολὺ διήλλαχεν Dionys.Com.2.10; τὸ διαλλάσσον τῆς γνώμης Th.3.10: pf. part.

διηλλαχώς *differing*, τῇ ἐγκλίσει A.D. l. c. 2. *excel*, πολὺ δ. τῇ ἀρετῇ Arist.*EN*1165$^{b}$24; τινῶν τῷ μεγέθει D.S.1.35, D.H.*Th.*51:—so, V. Pass., *to be different*, τοῖς εἴδεσι διηλλαγμένα Th.3.82; πρὸς τὸν καιρόν Luc.*Salt.*19. **-ηλος**, ον, *reciprocating*, λόγος *Stoic.*2.90; *interchangeable*, of the order of words, A.D.*Adv.*126.2; *confused*, of argument, Id.*Pron.*50.20; δ. τρόπος argument *in a circle*, S.E.*P.*1.117, 2.68; δ. δεῖξις Dam.*Pr.*290. II. *interrelated, interdependent*, Plot.6.8.14. **-οιόω**, strengthd. for ἀλλοιόω, Thphr. *CP*5.6.12 (Pass.), *Od.*59.

**διάλλομαι**, *leap across*, τάφρον X.*Eq.*8.8, Plu.*Rom.*10.

**διάλλῠδις**, Adv. = ἄλλυδις (q.v.) ἄλλῃ, Epic. in *Arch.Pap.*7.4.

**διαλλύος**· ὁ ἀντὶ ἄλλου διακονῶν, Hsch. (Perh. f.l. for διάμοιος.)

**δίαλμα**, ατος, τό, as gymnastic term, = ἅλμα, Sch.Pi.*O.*13.39.

**διᾰλοάω**, strengthd. for ἀλοάω, Ael.*NA*1.9.

⊛ **διαλογ-ή**, ἡ, (διαλέγω) *estimate, enumeration*, τῶν ψήφων Arist.*Pol.*1268$^{b}$17; ἡ δ. τῶν ἕξεων καθ' ἕκαστα τὰ πάθη Id.*EE*1222$^{b}$5. 2. = διάλογος or διάλεξις, Ps.-Hdt.*Vit.Hom.*36. 3. *account*, *BGU*584.4, 578.4 (ii A.D.). 4. οἱ ἐπὶ τῆς δ. or πρὸς τῇ δ., officials in charge of *checking and transmission of documents* to the archives, *POxy.*34$^{v}$ ii 3 (ii A.D.), *PLips.*10 ii 33 (iii A.D.). ⊛ **-ίζομαι**, pf. -λελόγισμαι Amphis 33.9:—*balance accounts*, πρός τινα D.52.3; τινί *PSI*5.510.10 (iii B.C.):—Pass., *SIG*241 C 127 (Delph., iv B.C.). 2. *calculate exactly*, ὁπόσον.. Diph.43.15, cf. Amphis l. c.; *consider*, ἀεί τι δ. καλόν Democr.112, cf. Isoc.6.90, Men.*Epit.*36; κενὰ δ. ib.347; πρὸς ὑμᾶς αὐτούς Is.7.45; *stop to consider*, D.18.98; *distinguish between*, τὰ καλὰ καὶ τὰ μή Aeschin.1.18. II. *debate, argue*, περί τινος X.*Mem.*3.5.1. III. *impute*, τί τινι Lxx *2Ki.*19.19(20). IV. c. acc. loci, *hold a circuit court* (Lat. *conventus*) *for* a district, *PRyl.*74.8 (ii A.D.), *POxy.*484.24 (ii A.D.); ἐν Ἰουλιοπόλει *BGU*903.18 (ii A.D.). **-ικός**, ή, όν, *belonging to dialogue*, or *in dialogue form*, περίοδος Demetr.*Eloc.*19, 21; εἶδος συγγραφῆς Porph.*Plot.*9, 17; συγγράμματα Phlp. *in Cat.*3.15, cf. Dex. *in Cat.*4.2. Adv. -κῶς, ἀπαγγέλλειν Theon *Prog.*4. **-ισμα**, ατος, τό, = sq. II, in pl., Epicur.*Ep.*1 p.22, 2 p.35 U. **-ισμός**, ὁ, *balancing of accounts*, D.36.23, *PRev.Laws* 17.17 (pl.), *IG*5(1).1432.6 (Messene), etc.: hence, II. *calculation, consideration*, Pl.*Ax.*367a; δ. λαβεῖν περὶ σφῶν αὐτῶν Str.5.3.7; ὁ δ. οὗτος this *consideration*, Phld.*D.*1.15. III. *debate, argument, discussion*, Epicur.*Fr.*138 (pl.), Metrod.37, Plu.2.180c. IV. *circuit court*, τοῦ νομοῦ δ. ποιῆσαι *PLond.*2.358.19, cf. *BGU*19 i 13 (ii A.D.). V. *judicial inquiry*, *PTeb.*27.35 (ii B.C.), *PFay.*66.2 (ii A.D.). **-ιστέον**, *one must calculate*, Sor.1.96. **-ιστικός**, ή, όν, *of* or *for discourse*: ἡ -κή *the reasoning faculty*, Plu.2.1004d. **-ος**, ὁ, (διαλέγομαι) *conversation, dialogue*, Pl.*Prt.*335d, Demetr.*Eloc.*223; δ. τῆς ψυχῆς πρὸς αὑτήν Pl.*Sph.*263e; οἱ Σωκρατικοὶ δ. Arist.*Fr.*72; τὰ ἐν τοῖς δ. *debating arguments*, Id.*APo.*78$^{a}$12: generally, *talk, chat*, Cic.*Att.*5.5.2. II. perh. *speech* or *series of speeches, debate* (cf. διάλεξις), *IG*3.1128, al. III. = διαλογισμός I, *PHib.*1.122 (iii B.C.), *PTeb.*58.31 (ii B.C.).

**διαλοιδορ-έομαι**, *rail furiously at*, τινί Hdt.2.121.δ'; ἀπειλήσας καὶ διαλοιδορηθείς D.21.86.—Act. only in late authors, v.l. in Lib.*Decl.*40.11. **-ησις**, εως, ἡ, *railing, abuse*, Lxx *Si.*27.15.

⊛ **δίαλον**· φανερόν, and **διάλας**· τὰς δήλας καὶ φανεράς, Hsch.

**διαλοξ-εύω**, *turn aside* or *askance*, ὄμμα Lib.*Descr.*30.16. **-ος**, ον, *sidelong*, στροφαί ib.12.

**διαλουφῶν**· διατίλλων, Hsch.

**δίαλσις**, εως, ἡ, perh. *nourishing*, *GDI*5125 (Crete).

**διαλῠγ-ίζω**, *twist about*, and **-ισμα**, ατος, τό, *bend*, both in Hsch.

⊛ **διαλῡμαίνομαι**, aor. 1 διελυμηνάμην E.*Or.*1515:—*maltreat shamefully*, τινά Hdt.9.112; Ἑλλάδα δ. E. l. c.; ἵμερός με δ. Ar.*Ra.*59, etc. 2. *cheat grossly*, δ. τινὰ ταῖς κοτύλαις Id.*Pl.*436. 3. *falsify, corrupt*, τὸ νόμισμα Id.*Th.*348; of poetry, Id.*Ra.*1062. 4. *ruin, spoil*, τὰ πολλὰ Plu.*Ant.*24: c. dat., Jul.*Or.*2.54b. II. Pass., Orib.7.20.5: pf. part. διαλελυμασμένος in Hdt.9.112: aor. διελυμάνθην E.*Hipp.*1349 (lyr.).

**διαλῡπέω**, *grieve sorely*, Plu.2.578c (Pass.).

⊛ **διά-λῠσις**, εως, ἡ, (διαλύω) *separating, parting*, δ. τῆς ψυχῆς καὶ τοῦ σώματος Pl.*Grg.*524b; δ. τοῦ σώματος its *dissolution*, Id.*Phd.*88b, cf. Democr.297; τὴν τῶν γεφυρῶν οὐ δ. the failure to *break* the bridges, Th.1.137; *disbanding* of troops, X.*Cyr.*6.1.3; *breaking up* of an assembly, opp. συλλογή, Pl.*Lg.*758d; δ. ἀγορῆς *the time of* its *breaking up*, Hdt.3.104; τὴν δ. ἐποιήσαντο *broke off* the action, Th.1.51; χρεῶν δ. *liquidation* of debts, Pl.*Lg.*684d, cf. *POxy.*104.20 (i A.D.), etc.; δ. γάμου *divorce*, Plu.*Sull.*35, etc.; ἡ φθορὰ δ. οὐσίας Arist.*Top.*153$^{b}$31: hence abs., *dissolution*, opp. σύνθεσις, Id.*Cael.*304$^{b}$29, cf. Thphr.*Ign.*37; διάκρισις καὶ δ. Pl.*Phlb.*32a; opp. γένεσις, Phld.*D.*3.6; *resolution* into elements, e.g. of words into letters, D.H.*Comp.*14; *dissolution* of friendship, Arist.*EN*1164$^{a}$9, 1165$^{b}$36; of partnerships, κοινωνίαι καὶ -σεις Pl.*Lg.*632b; συμμαχία καὶ δ. Arist.*Pol.*1298$^{a}$5. 2. *ending, cessation*, κακῶν E.*Ph.*435; πολέμου Th.4.19, v.l. in Isoc.6.51: abs., *cessation of hostilities*, *Com.Adesp.*21.23 D.; *settlement, compromise*, *IG*12(2).6.20 (Mytilene, iv B.C.), *PAmh.*2.63.9 (iii A.D.), etc.: in pl., *settlement* of a dispute, ἠξίου δὲ καὶ πρὸς ἔμ' αὐτῷ..γίγνεσθαι τὰς διαλύσεις D.21.119, cf. Phoenicid.1. 3. *solution* of a problem, A.D.*Synt.*243.11; χρησμῶν Luc.*Alex.*49. 4. *refutation* of an argument, S.E.*P.*2.238. 5. *resolution of a diphthong*: ἐν διαλύσει, = διαλελυμένως, A.D.*Pron.*29.13. 6. Rhet., *asyndeton*, Alex.*Fig.*2.12, etc. 7. *discharge*, χορηγιῶν *PRyl.*181.10 (iii A.D.); τῶν χρεωστουμένων *POxy.*71.13 (iv A.D.). 8. *deed of separation* or *divorce*, *PLips.*39.10 (iv A.D.); ἔγγραφος δ. *PMasp.*153.16 (vi A.D.). 9. *division* of inheritance, *Sammelb.*6000.22 (vi A.D.), etc. ⊛ **-λῡσίφῐλος** [σῐ], ον, *love-dissolving*, *AP*5.20 (Rufin.). **-λῡσος**, ὁ, *releaser*, coined as expl. of Διόνυσος, Corn.*ND*30. **-λῠτέον**, *one must dissolve*, φιλίαν Arist.*EN*1165$^{b}$17. ⊛ **-λύτης** [ῠ], ου, ὁ, *dissolver, breaker-up*, τῆς ἑταιρίας Th.3.82; εἰρήνης Procop.*Pers.*1.14. ⊛ **-λῠτικός**, ή, όν, *able to sever*, τινός (sc. τέχνη) Pl.*Plt.*281a; *destructive*, Id.*Ti.*60b; opp. γεννητικός, Phld.*D.*3.9. Adv. -κῶς Arist.*Top.*153$^{b}$32. II. Medic., *relaxing*, νότοι Hp.*Aph.*3.5. III. *embodying a settlement* or *compromise*, ὁμολογία *PMasp.*154.1 (vi A.D.). ⊛ **-λῠτος**, ον, *relaxed*, Plu.2.136b; ἁρμογαί Luc.*Trag.*222. II. διαλῠτός, ή, όν, *capable of dissolution*, Pl.*Phd.*80b, v.l. in *Ti.*57b, Ph.1.495; = φθαρτός, Phld.*D.*3.9.

**διαλύτρωσις**, εως, ἡ, *ransom*, ἀνδρῶν, αἰχμαλώτων, Plb.6.58.11, 27.14.1.

⊛ **διαλύω**, fut. -λύσω, etc., *loose one from another, part asunder*, διαπλέκων καὶ διαλύων twining and *untwining*, Hdt.4.67; νὺξ δ. τοὺς ἀγωνιζομένους Id.8.11; δ. τὸν σύλλογον, τὴν συνουσίαν, τὴν πανήγυριν, etc., *break* it *up*, *dismiss* it, Id.7.10.δ', Pl.*Ly.*223b, X.*Cyr.*6.1.10, etc.; τὴν σκηνὴν εἰς κοίτην δ. *break up* the party and go to bed, ib.2.3.1; δ. τὴν στρατιάν ib.6.1.6; τὸ ναυτικὸν *disband* it, Th.2.93:—Med., συνουσίας Pl.*Grg.*457d:—Pass., of an army, assembly, etc., *disperse*, Hdt.1.128, etc.; ἐκ τοῦ συλλόγου Id.3.73, cf. 8.56: in fut. Med., *part* from one's escort, Th.2.12; of a man, *die*, X.*Cyr.*8.7.20. 2. *dissolve* into its elements, *break up, destroy*, δ. καὶ ἀπολλύναι Pl.*R.*609a sq.; ἐξ ἑνὸς εἰς πολλὰ δ. Id.*Ti.*68d; *disperse, break up* a herd of sheep, *BGU*1012.12 (ii B.C.); *break up* a ship, παλαιὰν τριήρη δ. *IG*2.804, cf. *PSI*4.382 (iii B.C.); τρίπους, ὅρμος διαλελυμένος, *SIG*$^{2}$588.169, 198 (Delos, ii B.C.); τὰς οἰκήσεις Plb.4.65.4; *dissolve*, κοινόν *Test.Epict.*8.6; σῴζεσθαι καὶ διαλυθεῖσαν οἴχεσθαι πολιτείαν Pl.*Lg.*945c; of the sun, *thaw* frozen things, X.*Cyn.*5.2:—Pass., ἐξ ὧν σύγκειται καὶ εἰς ἃ διαλύεται Arist.*GC*325$^{b}$19, cf. *Ph.*204$^{b}$33, etc. 3. *break off, put an end to* friendship, ὁμολογίας Isoc.4.175; φιλίαν Arist.*EN*1157$^{b}$10:—Pass., of married persons, *separate, be divorced*, *SIG*364.59 (Ephesus): Med., διαλύσασθαι ξεινίην Hdt.4.154: abs., *dissolve friendship*, Arist.*EN*1162$^{b}$25:—Pass., αἱ σπονδαὶ διελέλυντο Th.5.1. 4. *put an end to* enmity, ἔχθραν, πόλεμον, Id.8.46:—Med., δ. ἔχθρας Is.7.11; διαφοράς Isoc.12.160; πολέμους Id.4.172, cf. D.4.15: in plpf. Pass. (with Med. signf.), διελέλυσθε τὸν πόλεμον Isoc.14.27 (v.l. διελύεσθε):—Pass., τὰς ἔχθρας διαλύεσθαι Th.4.19: hence, b. c. acc. pers., *reconcile*, πρὸς ἔμ' αὐτὸν διαλύειν ἠξίου D.21.122, cf. 41.14; δ. τινὰς ἐκ διαφορᾶς Plb.1.87.4; οὐ γὰρ ἦν ὁ διαλύσων οὔτε λόγος οὔτε ὅρκος Th.3.83; esp. in legal proceedings, *PHamb.*25.5 (iii B.C.), etc.:—Pass. and Med., c. gen. rei, διαλύεσθαι νείκους *to be parted from* quarrel, i.e. be reconciled, E.*Or.*1679 (v.l. νείκας); so διαλυθείσης τῆς διαφορᾶς prob. in D.S.14.110: also abs., *to be reconciled, make up a quarrel*, X.*HG*7.4.25, cf. Test.ap.Aeschin.1.66, Thphr.*Char.*12.14; πρός τινας D.38.24; περί τινος Lys.4.1: in fut. Med., ὅπως..μὴ διαλύσει D.21.216. 5. generally, *put an end to, do away with*, χρήμασι τὴν διαβολήν Th.1.131; πάσας αὐτοῦ διαλύσω τὰς ἀπολογίας D.27.58; τὸν ἐχόμενον φόβον δ. τῶν Ἑλλήνων Pl.*Mx.*241b:—so in Med., ἐγκλήματα δ. Th.1.140; δ. περὶ τῶν ἐγκλημάτων ib.145; διαβολάς Isoc.11.37, 15.16; τι τῶν κατηγορημένων Id.12.218; δ. ἃ ἐψηφίσασθε *cancel* your vote, Lys.18.15; διαλύσασθαι τὰ πρὸς ἀλλήλους *settle* mutual claims, Isoc.4.40. 6. *solve* a difficulty, Pl.*Sph.*252d; τὴν ἀπορίαν Arist.*Metaph.*1062$^{b}$31:—Med., διαλύσεσθαι σόφισμα S.E.*P.*2.238. 7. δ. τὰς τιμάς *pay the full* value, D.29.7; *pay, discharge*, τὴν δαπάνην Hdt.5.30; χρήματα D.20.12; τὰ συμβόλαια Arist.*Pol.*1276$^{a}$11; χρέος τινί Plb.31.27.4; πάντα διελέλυτο D.28.2: also c. acc. pers., δ. τὸν ναύκληρον *satisfy* him, i.e. *pay* him *off*, D.49.29, cf. 34.40, 36.50:—Med., *order* debts *to be paid*, διαλέλυμαι ταῦτα Arr.*An.*7.10.3; but also, *to have* them *paid to oneself*, D.Chr.46.6. II. *relax, weaken*, τὸ σῶμα Hp.*Aph.*3.17; esp. of the result of hunger, διαλύεσθαι τῷ λιμῷ *UPZ*11.27 (ii B.C.), cf. 42.9 (also in Act. intr., ὑπὸ τῆς λιμοῦ δ. ib.122.23 (ii B.C.)); *make supple and pliant*, Ar.*Pax*85:—Pass., δ. καὶ ἀδυνατεῖν Arist.*HA*585$^{a}$33; ἀνάπλους διαλελυμένος a sailing out *in loose order*, Plb.16.2.6; διαλελυμένη λέξις a *lax* style, D.H.*Lys.*9. 2. abs., *slacken one's hold, undo*, Theoc.24.32.

**διαλφῑτόω**, *to fill full of barley meal*, Ar.*Nu.*669.

**διαλωβάομαι**, Dep. strengthd. for λωβάομαι, Plb.11.7.2: pf. part. Pass., in pass. sense, Plu.*Caes.*68: metaph., δόξαι διαλελωβημέναι Id.2.986e.—Act. -λωβάω only late, Mich. *in EN*503.21.

**διαμᾰγεύω**, *charm with magic arts*, Luc.*Am.*41 (Pass.).

**διᾰμᾰθύνω**, *grind to powder, utterly destroy*, πόλιν διημάθυνεν A.*Ag.*824; κύνες διημάθυνον ἄνδρα δεσπότην (sc. Actaeon) Id.*Fr.*244.

**διαμάλαξις** [μᾰ], εως, ἡ, *softening*, Gal.11.714.

**διαμᾰλάττω**, strengthd. for μαλάττω, Sor.1.118, Luc.*Prom.*13:—Med., Hp.*Steril.*221.

⊛ **διαμανθάνω**, *learn by inquiry*, Philostr.*VA*1.16.

**διαμαντ-εία**, ἡ, *oracular response*, prob. in *SIG*987.39 (Chios, pl.). **-εύομαι**, *determine by an oracle*, τι Pl.*Lg.*696a; *make divinations*, Id.*Sis.*387e; ὄρνισι or ἐπ' ὄρνισι, Plu.*TG*17, *Cam.*32. II. *consult an oracle*, περί τινος D.H.3.69, Plu.2.302d.

**διάμαξος** [ᾰμ], ον, *for a chariot*, ὁδὸς δ. *carriage*-road, *GDI*5075.56 (Crete).

**διαμάρανσις** [μᾰ], εως, ἡ, *wasting away*, Alex.Aphr. *in Mete.*121.28.

⊛ **διᾰμαρτ-άνω**, fut. -αμαρτήσομαι D.19.151:—strengthd. for ἁμαρτάνω, *miss entirely, go quite astray from*, τῆς ὁδοῦ Th.1.106; τοῦ πράγματος D.21.192, 51.2; τοῦ ἑταίρου Pl.*Phdr.*257d; τῆς ὀρθοτάτης

πολιτείας Arist.*Pol.*1293$^b$25. 2. *fail utterly of, fail of obtaining,* τινός Th.2.78; τῶν ἐλπίδων Isoc.4.93; τοῦ ἀγῶνος Is.6.52; τῆς εἰρήνης D.18.30; δυοῖν χρησίμοιν οὐ δ. not *to miss both of* two good things, Id.19.151. 3. abs., *fail utterly*, opp. τυγχάνω, Pl.*Tht.*178a; *to be quite wrong,* Macho 2.6; γνώμῃ in judgement, D.24.48,110; δ. τοῖς ὅλοις Arist.*EN*1098$^b$28; ἐν τῇ ἀρχῇ ib.1163$^a$3; περί τι Id.*Oec.* 1345$^b$10:—Pass., τὰ πολλὰ..διημαρτημένα *utter failures,* Pl.*Lg.*639e; διημαρτημένας δόξας Diogenian.Epicur.2.32; διημαρτημένος *faulty,* of style, Phld.*Rh.*1.8S., Longin.33.1, Demetr.*Eloc.*114 (also in act. sense, πολλαχῇ διημαρτημένου τοῦ Πλάτωνος Longin.32.8, cf. Plu.2.41e). Adv. διημαρτημένως Poll.6.205. **-ημα,** ατος, τό, *mistake,* *POxy.*1235.64 (Arg. Men.). **-ητέον,** οὐ δ. *one must* not *miss,* Agath.1.5. ❀ **-ία,** ἡ, *total mistake,* τοῦ Ἀννίβου Plu.*Fab.*6; τοῦ τόπου ibid.; δ. τῶν ἡμερῶν *wrong reckoning* of the days, Th.4.89; δ. τῆς γλώττης, *lapsus linguae*, Luc.*Laps.*1. 2. *gross fault,* ἄγνοιαι καὶ δ. Ph.1.345, cf. Plu.2.153b; δ. ἐρωτικὴ *guilty passion,* Philostr. *VA*1.13: pl., *faults,* δ. καὶ .. ἐλαττώσεις Phld.*Lib.*p.19O. II. *failure in obtaining, disappointment in,* τινός Luc.*Sacr.*1, cf. D.C. 49.28.

**διαμαρτῠρ-έω,** as Att. law-term, *use a* διαμαρτυρία (q.v.), πρός τινα D.44.27. 2. c. inf., *affirm by a* διαμαρτυρία *that..*, δ. μὴ ἐπίδικον.. τὸν κλῆρον εἶναι Is.3.3, cf. D.44.48:—Pass., aor. διεμαρτυρήθην, *to be affirmed in a* διαμαρτυρία to be so and so, διεμαρτυρήθη μὴ Πλαταιεὺς εἶναι Lys.23.13, cf. Is.3.5; τὰ διαμαρτυρηθέντα Isoc.18.15. 3. Med., *testify against,* τὰ πραττόμενα J.*AJ*9.8.3. 4. *attest,* -ουμένην τὴν παρὰ τῶν θεῶν εὐμένειαν *Inscr.Prien.*108.20, 110.15 (ii B.C.). ❀ **-ία,** ἡ, as Att. law-term, *obstructive plea,* put forward at the preliminary investigation to prevent a case from coming to trial, D.44.58, Is.3.5, Harp.; καθάπερ διαμαρτυρίαν θέμενος Satyr.*Vit.Eur.Fr.*39xvii21. 2. generally, *affidavit, CPR*232.6 (ii/iii A.D.). etc. II. generally, *testifying, solemn protest,* τοῦ ἔθνους Lxx 4*Ma.*16.16.

**διαμαρτύρομαι** [ῡ], aor. 1 -μαρτῡράμην: pf. -μεμαρτύρημαι [ῠ], Dep.:—abs., *call gods and men to witness, protest solemnly,* esp in case of falsehood or wrong, βοᾶν καὶ δ. D.18.23,143; δ. μή.., c. inf., Id.33.20; δ. ὅπως μή.., c. fut., Id.42.28; δ. τινὶ μὴ ποιεῖν *protest* against his doing, Aeschin.2.89: c. inf., Plb.1.33.5, al.; *call to witness,* ὑμῖν τὸν οὐρανόν Lxx *Ju.*7.28. 2. generally, *protest, asseverate,* Pl.*Phd.*101a, etc., *PSI*4.422 (iii B.C.): c. acc., *bear witness to,* τὸ εὐαγγέλιον *Act.Ap.*20.24; *testify,* Lxx *De.*32.46, al.; τῇ Ἱερουσαλὴμ τὰς ἀνομίας αὐτῆς ib.*Ez.*16.2. 3. abs., *beg earnestly of* one, *conjure* him, X.*Cyr.*7.1.9; δ. καὶ παρακαλεῖν *Act.Ap.*2.40; δ. τινὰ ἵνα .. 1*Ep.Ti.*5.21.

❀ **διαμᾰσ-άομαι,** *chew up,* Arist.*HA*612$^a$1, Thphr.*CP*6.9.1, Apolloph.5, Lxx *Si.*34(31).16, Luc.*Alex.*12; δ. τὴν γλῶτταν, for ἐνδακεῖν, Alciphr.3.57:—Pass., *to be chewed,* Arist.*Pr.*890$^a$25, *Gp.*12.33. II. metaph., *carp at,* τι Philostr.*VS Praef.* **-ημα,** ατος, τό, *that which is chewed,* Hp.*Aff.*4, Dsc.1.96. **-ησις,** εως, ἡ, *chewing up,* Dsc.1.18. **-ητέον,** *one must chew,* Apollon.ap.Gal.12.999. **-ητός,** ή, όν, *fit for chewing,* Hp.*Aff.*4.

**διαμάσσω,** Att. -ττω, *bake to a turn,* μαζίσκας -μεμαγμένας Ar.*Eq.* 1105: metaph., λόγον δ. Id.*Av.*463.

❀ **διαμαστῑγ-όω,** *scourge severely,* Phld.*Rh.*2.298 S.:—Pass., *bear marks of scourging,* Pl.*Grg.*524c. **-ωσις,** εως, ἡ, *severe scourging,* esp. of the Spartan boys, Plu.2.239d.

**διάμαστος**· θεός, Hsch. (Perh. of Artemis Ephesia.)

**διαμαστροπεύω,** *pander*: metaph. in Pass., -ομένης τῆς ἡγεμονίας γάμοις *bargained away* by a marriage, Plu.*Caes.*14.

**διαμασχᾰλίζω,** *stick under one's arm,* τι Ar.*Fr.*253.

**διαμᾰχ-ετέον,** *one must strive earnestly,* Pl.*Sph.*241d (v.l. διαμαχητέον), *R.*380b; *one must contend,* πρός τι D.Chr.8.35 (-ητέον). **-έω,** = διαμάχομαι, πρὸς τὴν ἀνάγκην J.*BJ*6.9.4. **-η,** ἡ, *a fight, struggle,* πρὸς φόβους καὶ λύπας Pl.*Lg.*633d, cf. J.*BJ*6.2.8 (pl.), Ph.1.7, al., Plu.2.74c, etc. ❀ **-ησις,** εως, ἡ, *struggle,* Gal.9.921 (ap.Aët.5.24). **-ομαι,** fut. -μαχέσομαι (v.l. for -μαχεσώμεθα aor. subj.) Hdt.9.48:—*fight, contend,* σιδήρῳ E.*Supp.*678; εἷς πρὸς ἕνα Pl.*Lg.*833e; opp. λανθάνειν, Id.*R.*345a; πρός τι v.l. in D.17.18; περὶ τῆς χώρης τοῖς ἐπιοῦσιν Hdt.4.11; περὶ τοῦ πρότερος εἰπεῖν Ar.*Eq.*339, cf. Pl.*Men.*86c; περὶ τούτου ὡς οὐκ.. Lys.4.1; ὑπέρ τινος Pl.*Smp.*207b; δ. μὴ μεταγνῶναι ὑμᾶς I *resist to the uttermost* your change of opinion, Th.3.40; δ. τὸ μὴ θανεῖν E.*Alc.*694. 2. *exert oneself, strive earnestly,* περὶ τούτου ὅπως.. Pl.*Prt.*325d; ὅπως μή.. Id.*Grg.*502b. 3. in argument, *contend* or *maintain* that.., c. acc. et inf., Id.*Tht.*158d: with a neg., δ. τι μὴ εἶναι Th.3.42; δ. ὅτι οὐκ ἀπόλλυται Pl.*Phd.* 106c; ὡς οὐ.. Id.*Prm.*127e, etc.; also δ. τι *carry* a point, Id.*Sph.* 261a.

**διαμαψαμένη**· διασμηξαμένη, διαψησαμένη, Hsch.

**διᾰμάω,** fut. -ήσω, *to cut through,* χιτῶνα Il.3.359; λευκὴν παρηΐδα E.*El.*1023; διὰ λαιμὸν ἀμῆσαι A.R.4.374 (tm.). II. *scrape* or *clear away,* δακτύλοις δ. χθόνα E.*Ba.*709:—also in Med., διαμᾶσθαι τὸν κάχληκα Th.4.26; τὴν χιόνα Plb.3.55.6; τὴν ψάμμον J.*AJ*3.1.3.

**διαμβλώττω,** *procure abortion, Et.Gud.*

**διαμεθίημι,** *leave off,* μόχθον E.*Ba.*627; *give up,* τι Id.*El.*978.

❀ **διᾰμείβω,** *exchange,* τι πρός τι one thing *with* another, Pl.*Plt.*289e; τὰς οἰκίας J.*BJ*1.6.1:—Med., τισὶ τῆς ἀρετῆς τὸν πλοῦτον Sol.15.2; τινί τι ἀντί τινος Pl.*Lg.*915e; τὰ ἱμάτια πρός τινα Plu.*Cim.*10; διαμεῖψαι Ἀσίαν Εὐρώπης *change* Asia *for* Europe, i.e. *pass into* Asia, E.*IT*397 (lyr.); δ. μεταβολήν Dam.*Pr.*392; δ. τὴν φύσιν πρός τι ib. 396. 2. δ. ὁδόν *finish* a journey, A.*Th.*334 (lyr.):—Med., δολιχῆς τέρμα κελεύθου διαμειψάμενος Id.*Pr.*287 (anap.); but in Med. also, *pass through,* πολλὰ φῦλα Id.*Supp.*543 (lyr.); πόντου πεδίον Id.*Fr.*150 (lyr.). b. *cross, traverse,* ὄρη Procop.*Goth.*3.40. 3. *change,* χρόα Parm.8.41 (tm.):—abs. in Med., *alter,* Hdt.9.108. 4. Med., ἀγορὰς διαποντίους δ. *trade in* foreign markets, D.H.5.66. 5. Med., *requite,* D.C.56.6.

**διαμειδιάω,** *smile,* Pl.*Ti.*21c, Plu.2.152c, D.C.71.32.

**διάμειπτος** [ᾰ], ον, *communicable,* Sapph.14.

**διαμειρᾰκιεύομαι,** *strive hotly with,* τινί Plu.*Comp.Dem.Cic.*2.

**διάμειψις** [ᾰ], εως, ἡ, *exchange* of prisoners, Plu.*Fab.*7; of arms, Id.*Pyrrh.*17. II. *change,* τῆς μορφῆς Iamb.*Myst.*7.3.

**διαμελαίνω,** *make quite dark,* τὸν ἀέρα Plu.*Flam.*4. II. intr., *to be* or *become so,* Id.2.921f.

**διαμελεοί**· οἰκέται, Hsch.

**διαμελετάω,** *practise diligently,* Pl.*Prm.*126c:—Med., Max.Tyr. 7.7:—Pass., Pl.*Lg.*830b, cf. Sm.*Ps.*76(77).13: c. inf., δ. τοῦ θανάτου καταφρονεῖν Iamb.*Protr.*20.

**διαμελλ-ίζομαι,** *rival in singing,* Plu.2.973b. **-ίζω,** *dismember,* D.S.3.65:—Pass., Lxx *Da.*3.29(96), Plu.2.993b. **-ισμός,** ὁ, *dismemberment,* ib.996c: pl., ib.355b.

**διαμέλλ-ησις,** εως, ἡ, *postponement, procrastination,* πολλὴν δ. φυλακῆς long *postponement* of precautionary measures, Th.5.99, cf. D.C.*Fr.*40.21. **-ησμός,** ὁ, = foreg., *Gloss.* **-ω,** fut. -μελλήσω, *to be always going* to do, *to make a show* of doing: hence, *delay, put off,* Th.1.71,142, Ph.1.353, Luc.*Nigr.*10, al.:—Pass., Th.8.54.

**διαμεμερισμένως,** (διαμερίζω) *separately,* γράφειν Sch.D.T.p.191 H.

**διαμέμφομαι,** *blame greatly,* τι Th.8.89; τοὺς φιλοσοφοῦντας Isoc. 3.1; τινὰ ἐπί τινι D.C.46.51; τινὰ ὅτι.. Arist.*PA*663$^a$35.

❀ **διαμένω,** fut. -μενῶ Epich.[265] (prob.), Men.*Epit.*513: aor. -έμεινα D.4.15: pf. -μεμένηκα Plb.3.55.1:—*continue, persist,* of disease, τοῖσι παιδίοισι Hp.*Aph.*3.28; διαμένει ἔτι καὶ νῦν τοῖς βασιλεῦσιν ἡ πολυδωρία X.*Cyr.*8.2.7: abs., *keep,* of seeds, Thphr.*HP*7.5.5; *persevere,* ἐν τῇ ἕξει Pl.*Prt.*344b; ἐπὶ τῇ διατριβῇ X.*Ap.*30; δ. ἐν ἑαυτῷ *maintain* his *purpose,* Plb.10.40.6: c. dat., τῇ φιλίᾳ D.S.14.48 codd.: abs., *hold out,* D.21.216; δ. ἕως.. Id.4.15; παρθένος δ. D.S.4.16; *to last, remain, live on,* Epich. l.c.; *endure, be strong,* Isoc.8.51; of form, colour, and the like, ταὐτὸν δ. *continue* the same, *be permanent,* Alex.34; χρῶμα διαμένον Nicol.1.28, cf. Antiph.232.2: c. part., δ. λέγων D.8. 71; δ. ὅμοιοι ὄντες Arist.*EN*1159$^b$8: c. inf., *continue to..,* D.H.1.23.

**διαμερ-ίζω,** *divide,* Pl.*Phlb.*15e; *distribute,* τὸ ἐπιβάλλον Corn. *ND*27; τοὺς πόνους εἰς ἅπαν τὸ σῶμα Arist.*Pr.*885$^a$18:—Pass., *to be cut up,* Pl.*Lg.*849d. II. *part, separate,* Men.883:—Med., *divide* or *part among themselves, Ev.Matt.*27.35; πρὸς ἑαυτούς *PAmh.*2.152. 18 (v/vi A.D.):—Pass., *to be set at variance, Ev.Luc.*12.52,53. **-ισις,** εως, ἡ, = sq., *Gloss.* **-ισμός,** ὁ, *division,* Pl.*Lg.*771d, *POxy.*12vi 17, D.S.11.47, Lxx *Ez.*48.29 (pl.), J.*AJ*10.11.7. II. *dissension, Ev.Luc.*12.51. **-ιστής,** οῦ, ὁ, *a divider, Gloss.*

**διάμεσος,** ον, *midway between*: οἱ δ. *the middle class,* Hsch.

**διαμέσταν**· ἀλαζόνα, ἐξαλλάκτην, Hsch.; cf. διαμευστής.

**διάμεστ-ος,** ον, *brim-full,* Antiph.246; δ. εἰς τὸ ἥμισυ *exactly* half *full,* Arist.*Pr.*922$^b$36. **-όω,** *fill full,* ib.939$^a$4.

**διαμετρ-έω,** *measure through, measure out* or *off,* χῶρον δ. *measure* lists for combat, Il.3.315; *survey,* χώραν *OGI*502.12 (Aezani): abs., μετρῶν καὶ δ. καὶ λογιζόμενος D.Chr.40.7:—Med., Plb.6.41.3, Max. Tyr.6.3:—Pass., ἡμέρα διαμεμετρημένη *measured by the clepsydra,* D.19.120, Arist.*Ath.*67.3. 2. *measure out in portions, distribute,* μεδίμνους δ. τισὶ τῆς καθεστηκυίας τιμῆς D.34.39; οὐδὲν δ. τοῖς στρατιώταις *give out* no *rations,* X.*An.*7.1.40, cf. 41, etc.:—Med., *divide amongst themselves,* Orac.ap.Hdt.1.66, X.*Cyr.*7.5.9; *receive as one's share,* D.34.37:—Med. in act. sense, Call.*Ap.*55, *Dian.* 36. 3. Med., δ. τὸν βίον *die,* Procop.*Aed.*3.1. 4. *measure with the eye, scan,* Nonn.*D.*5.306, al. 5. *pass over, traverse,* Ὑδάσπην ib.23.149, cf. 22.42. II. Astron., δ. φάεσιν φάος ἀντικέλευθον *to be in opposition,* Man.4.74, cf. 296, Gal.19.557: c. acc., *to be diametrically opposite to,* τὸν ἥλιον Cleom.1.11: abs., ibid., Simp.*in Cael.*480.6; ὁκόταν ὁ χειμὼν διαμετρέῃ τῷ κατὰ λόγον Hp. *Ep.*19 (*Hermes* 53.70). **-ησις,** εως, ἡ, *measuring out,* Lxx 2*Ch.*3.3, J.*AJ*3.6.4, Plu.2.785d; *distribution* of corn, *SIG*976.55 (Samos, ii B.C.). II. Astron., *diametrical opposition,* Ptol.*Tetr.* 195, etc. **-ητός,** ή, όν, *measured out* or *off,* δ. ἐνὶ χώρῳ Il.3. 344. II. *diametrical,* τὴν δ. (sc. ὁδὸν) διεξεληλυθέναι Dam.*Pr.* 87. **-ικός,** ή, όν, *diagonal*: [ἀριθμοί] *the numerators of the successive convergents to* $\sqrt{2}$ *expressed as a continued fraction,* *Theol.Ar.*3.59; cf. πλευρικός. ❀ **-ον,** τό, *measured allowance, soldiers' rations,* Plu. *Demetr.*40. **-ος,** ον, *diametrical*: Astrol., *diametrically opposed,* Ptol.*Tetr.*115, Man.1.89. II. Subst. δ. (sc. γραμμή), ἡ, *diagonal* of a parallelogram, Pl.*Men.*85b, al.; κατὰ δ. συντίθεσθαι, of triangles, *by the hypotenuses,* Id.*Ti.*54d; *diameter* of a circle, Arist.*Cael.*271$^a$ 12, etc.; *axis* of a sphere, Id.*MA*699$^a$29; *diameter* of other curves, Apollon.Perg.*Con.*1 *Def.*1; *axis* of a conic, Archim.*Aequil.*2.10; ἡ κατὰ διάμετρον σύζευξις, of circles, Arist.*EN*1133$^a$6; τὰ κατὰ δ. Id. *Cael.*277$^a$24; κεῖσθαι κατὰ δ. Id.*Mete.*363$^a$34, al.; κατὰ δ. κινεῖσθαι, of quadrupeds, which move the legs *cross-corner-wise,* as horses when *trotting* (opp. κατὰ πλευρὰν κινεῖσθαι ambling, in which the legs on either side move together), Id.*HA*490$^b$4, *IA*712$^a$25, cf. Plu. 2.43a; ἐκ διαμέτρου ἀντικείμενος, of planets, *in opposition, PMag. Par.*1.2221; ἐκ διαμέτρου ἡμῖν οἱ βίοι Luc.*Cat.*14. 2. prob. *mitre-square,* Ar.*Ra.*801.

**διαμευστής,** οῦ, ὁ, = ἀλαζών, Hsch.: also **διαμευτής** (-μέττης cod.), οῦ, ὁ, *cheat,* Id.

**διαμήδομαι**, = μήδομαι, Hom.*Epigr.*4.12.
**διαμηκίζω**, (μῆκος) *to be in direct opposition*, Ptol.*Tetr.*125,151.
**διάμηκος**, ον, *broad*, dub. in *Hippiatr.*14.
**διαμηκύνω**, *last out, live through*, ἡμέρας τέσσαρας *PMag.Leid.V.* 11.29.
**διαμηνύω**, *point out clearly*, Str.11.14.4.
® **διαμηρ-ίζω**, *femora diducere, inire*, Ar.*Av.*669, Zeno *Stoic.*1.59. ® **-ισμός**, ὁ, *femorum diductio*, ibid. (pl.).
**διαμηρύω** [ῡ], *arrange in kinks* (cf. μήρυμα), Hero *Aut.*10.3.
**διαμηχᾰν-άομαι**, *bring about, contrive*, δ. ὅπως.. Ar.*Eq.*917; δ. ζῶν εἰσιέναι ἐς Ἅιδου Pl.*Smp.*179d. **-ητέον**, *one must contrive*, Plu.2.131e.
® **διαμίγνῡμι** or -ύω (Plu.2.1131e), fut. -μίξω, *to mix up*, l.c.:—Pass., διαμεμιγμένα; Pl.Com.174.9 codd. Ath.; cf. διαμίσγω.
**διαμῑκρολογέομαι**, *deal grudgingly*, πρός τινα Plu.*Sol.*30.
**διάμιλλ-α** [ᾰμ], ἡ, *fight*, of animals, Hierocl.pp.11,17A. (pl.). **-άομαι**, fut. -ήσομαι Str.17.1.11:—*contend hotly, strive earnestly*, δέκα πρὸς δέκα ἀλλήλοις Pl.*Lg.*833e; τινί *with* one, Id.*R.*516e; πρός τινα Plb.16.21.6; δ. περί τινος about a thing, Pl.*R.*517d; τινὶ ἐν λόγοις καὶ ἐν ἔργοις ib.563a: c. gen. rei, δ. λειοτέρας ὁδοῦ Id.*Lg.*833b; τινὶ περὶ δεῖπνα Plu.*Them.*5: pf. διημίλληται in pass. sense, Luc.*Par.*58. **-ητέον**, *one must contend*, Plu.2.817d.
**διαμιμνήσκομαι**, only pf. Pass. διαμέμνημαι, *keep in memory*, X.*Mem.*1.4.13, D.H.4.9. II. *make mention of*, Ph.1.509, Lyd.*Mag.*1.7.
**διαμῑνύρομαι** [ῡ], *warble a plaintive ditty*, Ar.*Th.*100.
**διαμίσγω**, = διαμίγνυμι, Hp.*Mul.*1.64, Ph.*Bel.*88.13.
**διαμῑσέω**, *hate bitterly*, Arist.*Pol.*1274$^a$34, Ph.1.396, J.*BJ*4.5.4, Plu.*Tim.*35 (Pass.), Ant.Lib.12.2 (Pass.).
**διαμισθ-όω**, *farm out*, *PAmh.*2.95.7, al., *OGI*669.14 (i A.D.), etc.:—Med., App.*BC*2.10. **-ωσις**, εως, ἡ, *farming out* of state land, *PTeb.*72.450 (ii B.C.), 376.15 (ii A.D.). ® **-ωτικόν**, τό, *rent* of state land, *BGU*475.1.
**διαμιστύλλω**, aor. 1 -εμίστυλα, *cut up piecemeal*, Hdt.1.132.
**διάμιτρος**, ον, *veiled with a μίτρα*, Poll.4.151,154.
**διαμμᾰτίζω**, *knot* (a cord): pf. Pass., διημματισμένος κῶλος Orib.49.22.8.
**διαμμοιρηδά**, Adv. *dividing in twain*, μέσσην νύκτα δ. φυλάξας A.R.3.1029.
**δίαμμος**, ον, *very sandy*, Plb.34.10.2, Str.1.3.7.
**διαμνημον-ευτέον**, *one must remember*, Aen.Tact.31.35. ® **-εύω**, *remember distinctly*, abs., Hdt.3.3, Lys.23.16, Antipho 5.54; c. gen. pers., Pl.*Smp.*180c; τι X.*Mem.*1.3.1, Phld.*Mort.*30, Plu.*Sol.*3, etc.:—Pass., διὰ τούτων διαμνημονεύονται D.S.12.13. 2. *mention, record*, Ph.1.22; διαμνημονεύεται ἔχων he *is mentioned* as having, X.*Cyr.*1.1.2. 3. *call to mind*, τι Pl.*Epin.*976c.
**διαμνημον-ικός**, ή, όν, *having a good memory*, Suid. s. v. ἀνελέγετο:—also in form **-ητικός**, Id. s. v. Ἀπολλώνιος Τυανεύς.
**διάμοιος**· ὁ ἀντ' ἄλλου διακονῶν, Hsch. (fort. διαμοιβός).
**διαμοιρ-άζω**, *divide into equal portions, cut up*, κόστον Aët.1.138. **-ασία**, ἡ, *division into equal portions*, βοὸς Tz. ad Hes.*Op.*56. **-άω**, *divide, rend asunder*, E.*Hipp.*1376 (lyr.):—Med., E.*Hec.*717, Orph.*Fr.*210:—Pass., Ath.1.12e. 2. Med., also, *portion out, distribute*, ἕπταχα πάντα διεμοιρᾶτο [ε͂] Od.14.434.
**διαμολύνω** [ῡ], *befoul with writing*, παλίμψηστα Plu.2.504d.
® **διαμονή**, ἡ, (διαμένω) *continuance, permanence*, Arist.*Spir.*481$^a$1, Epicur.*Ep.*2 p.38 U., Phld.*D.*3.8, *IG*12(5).659.5 (Syros), Ocell.1.9, Ph.1.2, al., Procl.*Inst.*129, *BGU*362 iv 11 (iii A.D.), etc.; of seeds or corn, *keeping*, Thphr.*HP*7.5.5, J.*BJ*7.8.4.
**διαμόνῐμος**, ον, *steadfast*, πιστὸν καὶ δ. Porph.*Abst.*1.52. Adv. -μως *permanently*, Phld.*Mus.*p.67 K.
**διαμονομᾰχέω**, *fight a single combat*, πρὸς ἀδελφούς Plu.2.482c, cf. Hld.7.16.
® **διάμονος**, ον, *permanent*, ζωή Sammelb.4678.9 (vi A.D.).
**διάμορφος**, ον, *endued with various forms*, Emp.21.7. II. διάμορφον, = μανδραγόρας, prob. in Ps.-Dsc.4.75.
**διαμορφοσκοπέομαι**, *vie in beauty with*, τινί Ath.5.188d.
**διαμορφ-όω**, *give form to, shape*, ψυχὴν πρὸς εἶδος Ph.2.368; δοῦν ὥσπερ τρόπαιον Plu.*Rom.*16:—Pass., διαμεμορφωμένος *articulate*, Id.2.722c, cf. Ath.Med.ap.Orib.22.9.4. **-ωσις**, εως, ἡ, *forming, shaping*, τῆς ὕλης Plu.2.1023c; ἐμβρύων Ath.Med.ap.Orib.22.9.1. II. *gesture*, '*business*', in acting, Demetr.*Eloc.*195. **-ωτικός**, ή, όν, *formative*, φύσις Ptol.*Tetr.*142.
**διάμοτ-ον**, τό, *tent*, Paul.Aeg.4.54. **-όω**, (μότος) *put lint into* a wound, so as to keep it open, δ. ἕλκος Hp.*VC*14, Gal.13.752: hence **-ωσις**, εως, ἡ, Heliod.ap.Orib.44.14.14, Leonidas ap.Aët.6.1.
**διαμ-πάξ** (for δι-ανα-πάξ), Adv. *right through, through and through*, c. gen., στέρνων δ. A.*Pr.*65, cf. *Supp.*945, E.*Ba.*991 (lyr.); δι' αἴας Φρυγίας δ. A.*Supp.*548 (lyr.); ἐτέτρωτο τὸν μηρὸν δ. X.*HG*7.4.23: δ. ἄχρις Luc.*DMort.*27.4; πόδες δ. προσεληλαμένοι πρὸς τοὔδαφος Plu.*Crass.*25. **-πείρω**, poet. for διαναπ-, Q.S.1.614, Hsch. ® **-περές**, Adv., I. of Place, *through and through, right through*, c. gen., δ. ἀσπίδος Il.12.429, cf. 20.362; δ. στέρνων S.*Ph.*791: c. acc., βέβληαι κενεῶνα δ. Il.5.284; δ. οὖς prob. in A.*Ch.*380 (lyr.); δ. διὰ μέσου τοῦ [σφονδύλου] Pl.*R.*616e. 2. abs., *without break, continuously*, ἐκ κεφαλῆς.. δ. ἐς πόδας ἄκρους Il.16.640; πέτρη ἠλίβατος .. δ. ἀμφοτέρωθεν Od.10.88; σταυροὺς.. ἔλασσε δ. ἔνθα καὶ ἔνθα 14.11; ἡ δ' [the wall] ἕσπετο πᾶσα δ. all *in a piece*, Il.12.398. II. of Time, *throughout, for ever*, Od.8.245, Hes.*Th.*402, Emp.17.6; pleon., ἤματα πάντα δ. Il.16.499, cf. *Supp.Epigr.*1.409 (Eretria); αἰὲν διαμπερές *for ever and aye*, Il.15.70. (Found in tmesi διὰ δ' ἀμπερές 11.377, 17.309; cf. ἀμπερέως: poet. for δι-ανα-περές (πείρω).) **-περέως**, = foreg., *through and through*, of piercing pains, Hp.*Int.*8; also, διείσομαι πάντα δ. Nic.*Th.*495. **-περής**, ές, *piercing*, ὀδύνη Hp.*Mul.*2.125. **-περονάω** and **-πραθέειν**, perh. ff. ll. for διαπ-, Hsch.
**διαμῠδαίνω**, *putrefy*, A.*Fr.*54A, cf. *AB*238, *EM*269.1.
**διαμῠδᾰλέος**, α, ον, *drenching*, δάκρυα A.*Pers.*539 (lyr.). (ῡ for ῠ metri gr.)
**διαμῠδάω**, *become fungoid*, of diseased bone, membrane, etc., Hp.*VC*21.
**διαμύδησις** [ῠ], εως, ἡ, *decay, mortification*, Sor.1.73.
**διαμύθησις** [ῠ], εως, ἡ, *deception, cajolery*, Hsch.
**διαμῡθολογέω**, *communicate by word of mouth, express in speech*, γλώσσᾳ A.*Pr.*889 (lyr.); τι Pl.*Lg.*632e; δ. πρὸς ἀλλήλους *converse*, Id.*Ap.*39e; περί τινος Id.*Phd.*70b; *tell a story*, Max.Tyr.16.1.
**διαμυκτηρίζω**, strengthd. for μυκτηρίζω, D.L.9.113.
**διαμυλλαίνω**, *make mouths* (in scorn), Ar.*V.*1315.
**διαμύσσω**, *stimulate*, Paul.Aeg.3.9.
**διαμφάδην** [ᾰ], Adv., strengthd. for ἀμφάδην, Poll.2.129.
**διαμφιβάλλω**, *doubt*, ὅτι οὐ.. but that.., Simp.*in Cat.*417.5.
**διαμφίδιος** [φῐ], ον, *utterly different*, A.*Pr.*555 (lyr.; Hsch. also has -άδιον).
**διαμφίς**, Adv. *separately*, D.P.907.
**διαμφισβητ-έω**, *dispute, disagree*, πρὸς ἀλλήλους περί τινος Decr. ap.D.18.185, cf. Arist.*MM*1211$^a$14; τινὶ περὶ μουσικῆς Ath.8.351a; ἀρετῆς κτλ. Plu.2.787d; δ. περί τινος *lay claim to*, Arist.*Pol.*1283$^b$14; πρός τι ib.1287$^b$35; δ. ποῖα θερμὰ τῶν ζῴων Id.*PA*648$^a$24: abs., Id.*Pol.*1283$^a$30, *CPR*1.20 (i A.D.), etc.:—Pass., διαμφισβητεῖται περὶ φιλίας οὐκ ὀλίγα not a few *questions are debateable*, Arist.*EN*1155$^a$32; τὰ διαμφισβητούμενα the *points at issue*, D.44.57. **-ησις**, εως, ἡ, *disputing*, δ. ἔχει πότερον.. it admits of *dispute* whether.., Arist.*Pol.*1256$^a$14; διαμφισβητήσεις ἔχειν contain *ambiguous points*, of Solon's laws, Id.*Ath.*35.2; χώρα ὑπὸ τὴν δ. ἠγμένη *disputed* territory, *SIG*685.55 (Crete); δ. παρέξειν πότερον.. Plu.*Tim.Praef.*: pl., Iamb.*Myst.*4.1.
**διαμφοδ-έω**, *miss the right* ἄμφοδος, Eust.780.54: metaph., *miss the right way* (in a question), S.E.*M.*9.31, cf. Hsch. s. v. ἀμφαλλάξαι. **-ησις**, εως, ἡ, *missing of the right* ἄμφοδος, Eust.789.51.
**διαμωκ-άομαι**, *mock* or *laugh at*, Phld.*Rh.*2.59 S., D.C.59.25, Iamb.*VP*33.234: abs., Aristaenet.1.27. ® **-ησις**, εως, ἡ, *mocking, raillery*, τινός Ath.5.20cb.
**διαμωλύω**, *soften, mollify*, *BGU*1200.21 (i B.C.).
® **διανα-βάλλω**, *delay, procrastinate*, *PTeb.*50.27 (ii B.C.):—Med., Hsch. s. v. διακρούεσθαι. **-βολή**, ἡ, *postponement, delay*, *EM*80.23 (pl.). **-γιγνώσκω**, *read through*, Isoc.12.201, Plb.31.21.9; Δημόκριτον πάντα δ. Damox.2.13:—Pass., D.C.58.10.
**διᾰναγκ-άζω**, *drill, train*, Pl.*Lg.*836a (Pass.); *reduce* dislocation, Hp.*Mochl.*38; δ. πόρους *force open* the pores, Id.*Vict.*2.64:—Pass., *to be dilated*, Id.*Fist.*4. **-ᾰσις**, εως, ἡ, *reduction* of dislocations, Id.*Mochl.*38. **-ασμός**, ὁ, = foreg.; *machine for this purpose*, Id.*Art.*47.
**διανάγω**, *bring back into its place*, Gal.18(1).421.
**διανα-κᾰθίζω**, = ἀνακαθίζω, Hp.*Mul.*2.201. **-κλάομαι**, Pass., *to be reflected*, Arist.*Pr.*934$^a$22. **-κόπτω**, *pound up*, Sor.1.82. **-κύπτω**, *raise the head*, Aristeas 18; *look carefully into*, Ph.1.383.
**διανᾱλίσκω**, *consume*, dub. in D.C.*Fr.*55.1.
**διανά-παυμα**, ατος, τό, *intermission*, *AB*1167. **-παυσις**, εως, ἡ, *resting at intervals*, Arist.*Spir.*485$^a$20, Diocl.*Fr.*142. **-παύω**, *allow to rest awhile*, Hp.*Aph.*2.48, Arist.*Pol.*1339$^b$30, Plu.*Flam.*4; *interrupt*, τὸ συνεχές Luc.*Am.*7; δ. τὴν ταυτότητα *relieve* the monotony, D.H.*Comp.*12:—Med., *rest awhile*, Pl.*Lg.*625b, Ph.2.197, Porph.*Marc.*4:—also intr. in Act., Aristid.*Or.*51(27).17. **-πηδάω**, f.l. for ἀνα-, X.*Cyr.*1.4.4. **-πνοή**, ἡ, *breathing through*, Gal.18(2).899.
**διαναρκάω**, *grow stiff* or *numb*, Corn.*ND*35. 2. *remain torpid through* the winter, *hibernate*, f.l. in Thphr.*Fr.*171.7; cf. διαρκέω.
**διαναρμοστέω**, *to be out of time*, Poll.4.63.
**διαναρτάομαι**, f.l. in Iamb.*Protr.*13 (leg. δὴ ἀναρτᾶσθαι).
**διανάσσω**, *stop chinks*: *caulk ships*, Str.4.4.1:—Pass., pf. part. διανεναγμένος σφυγμός, name coined by Archig.ap.Gal.8.662.
**διανά-στᾰσις**, εως, ἡ, *rising up*, Hp.*Epid.*7.11 (of going to stool), Plb.5.70.8: pl., X.*Cyn.*10.18. **-στᾰτέον**, *one must make to get up*, τινά Sor.1.69. **-στρέφομαι**, *to be distorted, roll*, of the eyes, Herod.Med. in *Rh.Mus.*58.78.
® **διαναυμᾰχέω**, *maintain a sea-fight*, Hdt.8.63, Th.8.27; πρός τινα Isoc.4.97.
**διαναψύχω**· *perfrigesco*, *Gloss.*
® **διανάω**, *flow through, percolate*, Plu.*Aem.*14; cf. ® **διαναῦσαι**· διαπλεῦσαι, Hsch.
**διανδής**· πολυχρόνιος (Cret.), Hsch.
**διάνδῐχα**, Adv. = ἄνδιχα, *two ways*, δ. μερμηρίζειν halt *between two opinions*, Il.1.189; σοὶ δὲ δ. δῶκε endowed thee *by halves*, 9.37; in tmesi, διὰ δ' ἄνδιχα θυμὸν ἔχουσιν Hes.*Op.*13; διὰ δ' ἄνδιχα ἔαξα broke it *in twain*, Theoc.25.256, cf. A.R.2.1109; once in Trag., δ. κλῆθρα κλίνεται E.*HF*1029 (lyr.); also δ. νηὸς ἰούσης, perh. *with sails and oars*, A.R.1.934.
**διανδρᾰγᾰθέω**, *continue to behave honourably*, Wilcken *Chr.*10.3 (ii B.C.), *BGU*1204.6 (i B.C.).

**διᾶνεκής**, ές, v. διηνεκής.

⊛ **διανέμ-ησις**, εως, ἡ, *distribution*, Arist.*Mu*.401$^{b}$13, J.*AJ*4.8.22, Corn.*ND*13, Plu.*Ant*.54. **-ητέον**, *one must distribute*, X.*Oec*. 7.36, Iamb.*in Nic*.p.64P. **-ητής**, οῦ, ὁ, *distributor*, gloss on δατητής, *EM*249.43. **-ητικός**, ή, όν, *distributive*, τινὸς εἰς ἴσα μέρη Pl.*Ti*.55a, cf. Andronic.Rhod.p.576M.; τὸ δ. δίκαιον Arist.*EN*1131$^{b}$27; of persons, ib.1134$^{a}$3. **II.** Pass., *divisible*, εἰς ἴσα δ. Plu.2.1003c.

**διᾶνεμόομαι**, (ἄνεμος) Pass., *flutter in the wind*, Luc.*Im*.7, *AP*9.777 (Phil.); *to be blown away by the wind*, Eun.*Hist*.p.269D.

**διανέμω**, late fut. -νεμήσω App.*BC*5.3: aor. διένειμα X.*Cyr*.4.5.45, etc.; aor. regul. -ένειμα, but inf. διανεμῆσαι Did.*in D*.9.21: pf. -νενέμηκα X.*Cyr*.4.5.45:—*distribute, apportion*, τοῖς μὲν τιμάς, τοῖς δὲ ἀτιμίας Pl.*Lg*.830e, etc.; ἐπὶ τὰ αὑτῶν ἕκαστα ἐκμαγεῖα Id.*Tht*.194d; δ. μέρη *divide into* portions, Id.*Lg*.756c, cf. *Ti*.35b; ἡ χώρα κατὰ δώδεκα μέρη διανενέμηται Id.*Lg*.758e; δ. ἑαυτόν *distribute* oneself among friends, Arist.*EN*1171$^{a}$3; δ. ἴσον αὐτόν [ὁ Πλοῦτος] Ar.*Pl*. 510; ὁ διανέμων *the distributor*, Arist.*EN*1136$^{b}$26; *assign*, Pl.*Cra*. 430b, Arist.*Cael*.306$^{b}$31:—Med., *divide among themselves*, τὰ κοινά And.1.135; τὴν ἀρχήν Pl.*Grg*.523a; δ. τὰ τῶν πλουσίων Arist.*Pol*. 1281$^{a}$15; also διανειμάμενοι δίχ' ἑαυτούς Pl.Com.153.2:—Pass., δ. εἰς τὸν λαόν *to be spread abroad*, *Act.Ap*.4.17. **II.** *set in order, govern*, ἄστυ Pi.*P*.4.261, cf. 8.62.

**διανενοημένως**, Adv., (διανοέω) *circumspectly*, Sch.A.R.1.1336.

⊛ **διανεύω**, *nod, beckon*, ταῖς κεφαλαῖς D.S.3.18; τινί to a person, Alex.261.12, *Ev.Luc*.1.22, Luc.*VH*2.25. **II.** *bend away from, avoid*, τὰς τῶν ὀργάνων ἐπιβολάς τι Plb.1.23.8; ὀργάς Plu.*Fr*.27.

**διανέω**, *swim across*, ἐς Σαλαμῖνα Hdt.8.89; τὸν Τίγρητα Luc.*Hist. Conscr*.19. **II.** c. acc., *swim through*, i.e. *get safe through*, δ. πέλαγος λόγων Pl.*Prm*.137a, cf. *R*.441c; ποταμόν Ael.*NA*3.6. **III.** metaph. in Med., *filter through*, c. gen., Marc.Sid.76.

**διανήθω**, in pf. part. Pass. -νενησμένος, *spin out*, Lxx *Ex*35.6.

**διάνημα**, ατος, τό, *that which is spun, a thread*, Pl.*Plt*.309b.

**διάνηξις**, εως, ἡ, *swimming through*, Herm.ap.Stob.1.49.44.

**διανηστ-εύω**, *remain fasting*, Hp.*Aff*.27, J.*AJ*3.10.3. **-ισμός**, ὁ, *breakfast*, Philem.Gloss.ap.Ath.1.11d.

**διανήχομαι**, = διανέω, Hellanic.111J., J.*AJ*13.1.3, Plu.*Luc*.10, Ael.*NA*9.15, Palaeph.30, Porph.*Abst*.2.5; of sound, *penetrate*, Erinna 3: metaph., δ. τὸν βίον Vett.Val.68.12.

**διάνηψις**, εως, ἡ, *clearing off*, τῶν χυμῶν Aret.*CD*2.2 (perh. f.l. for -νιψις).

**διανθ-έω**, *flower again*, Plu.*in Arat*.7. ⊛ **-ής**, ές, *double-flowering*, i.e. *twofold*, with outer (corolla) and inner (stamens and pistil) flower, Thphr.*HP*1.13.2. **II.** *flowering in succession*, ἀσφόδελος Nic.*Th*.534. **-ίζω**, *adorn with flowers*, δ. τὴν κεφαλὴν στεφάνοις Luc.*Bis Acc*.16 (Pass.); also with jewels, J.*AJ*8.5.2:—Pass., *to be picked out, decorated*, χλαμύδες διηνθισμέναι Plu.*Phil*.9; κέδρου ζῴδια χρυσῷ διηνθισμένα Paus.6.19.12; ξόανον χρυσῷ δ. Id.7.26.4, cf. Hdn. 5.3.6; μηκέτι διηνθισμένος ποικιλίᾳ χρωμάτων, ὅλον δὲ λευκωθείς, of a leper, Ph.1.346.

**διᾶνιάομαι**, Pass., *grieve sorely*, Ael.*VH*1.24.

**διανίζω**, *wash out* or *thoroughly*, κύλικα, σκεῦος, λοπάδας, Crates Com.14.7, Eub.31, Damox.2.44; τὴν κοιλίαν Diocl.*Fr*.139:—Med., διανιψάσθω τὸ αἰδοῖον Hp.*Mul*.2.112.

**διανίημι**, *dissolve*, οἴνῳ *Hippiatr*.22.

**διάνιον**· κονία, Hsch.

**διανίσσομαι**, *go through*, τινός Pi.*P*.12.25, Opp.*H*.1.550: Ep. Subj. -νίσσεται Orph.*Fr*.285.56.

⊛ **διανίστημι**, fut. -στήσω, *awaken, rouse*, D.H.4.2, J.*AJ*6.13.9; *raise up*, opp. καταβάλλω, Ph.1.669:—Med., fut. -στήσομαι, *restore*, D.H.3.20. **II.** Pass., with aor. 2 and pf. Act., *stand up, rise*, νύκτωρ Arist.*Oec*.1345$^{a}$16; *spring up* from ambush, Plb.3.74.1, cf. *PPetr*.2p.59 iii B.C.), D.S 10.1, Plu.2.596a, etc. **2.** *stand aloof from, depart from*, τινός Th.4.128. **3.** *form factions*, περὶ σπουδὰς ὀρχηστῶν Plu.2.487f.

**διάνιψις**, εως, ἡ, (διανίζω) *ablution*, Hp.*Hum*.1; cf. διάνηψις.

⊛ **διανο-έω**, *have in mind*, Philostr.*Im*.2.1:—but in early writers always **-έομαι**, fut. -νοήσομαι: aor. διενοήθην, part. διανοηθεὶς in pass. sense, Pl.*Lg*.654c: aor. Med. -ησάμην D.S.20.3: pf. διανενόημαι Pl.*Alc*.1.106a: (νοέω):—*to be minded, intend, purpose*, c. inf. pres., fut., or aor., Hdt.2.121.δ' and 126, Ar.*Lys*.724, Pl.*R*. 504e, etc.; μηδὲ δ. περὶ παραθήκης ἄλλο γε ἢ ἀποδιδόναι Hdt.6.86.δ'; διανενοημένοι βοηθεῖν Th.4.72, cf. 7.56; δ. τὴν ἀπόβασιν Id.4.29; διανοήθητε ἢ ὑπακούειν ἢ μὴ εἴξοντες Id.1.141; ὑπουργεῖν ἃ διανοούμεθα (sc. ὑπουργεῖν) Antipho 4.3.4. **II.** *have in mind*, τι Hp.*VM*7; τί διανοούμενος εἶπε what he really *meant* by his words, Pl.*Tht*.184a; περί τινος δ. οὑτωσί, ὀρθῶς περί τι, Id.*Lg*.644d, 686d: c. acc. et inf., *think* or *suppose* that.., Id.*Prt*.324b, etc.: c. gen. abs., διανοεῖσθαί τινων ὡς διαλλαγησομένων Id.*R*.470e: abs., *think*, λέγω νοῦν ᾧ δ... ἡ ψυχή Arist.*de An*.429$^{a}$23; τὸ διανοεῖσθαι *the process of thought*, Pl. *Tht*.189e; opp. νοεῖν, Arist.*de An*.408$^{b}$25. **2.** *bethink oneself*, Lxx *Ge*.6.6. **III.** with Advbs., *to be minded* or *disposed* so and so, ἄλλως πως πρός τινας, Pl.*R*.343b; κακῶς δ. περὶ τῶν οἰκείων Isoc. 1.35: with ὡς and part., ὅταν ὡς πετόμενοι διανοῶνται when they *are affected* as if flying, Pl.*Tht*.158b. **-ημα**, ατος, τό, *thought, notion*, X.*HG*7.5.19, Isoc.3.9, Pl.*Smp*.210d; διανοήματος εὐτέλεια Plu.2.40c; *thought*, opp. words, Pl.*Prt*.348d, Phld.*Po*.2.30,40: pl., *meanings* of words, Id.*Rh*.2.190S.; esp. *whim, sick fancy*, Hp.*Epid*.1.23; *intention*, *PLond*.5.1724.15, etc. ⊛ **-ησις**, εως, ἡ, *process of thinking, thought*, Pl.*Plt*.306e; opp. βούλευσις, Plot.5.8.6: in pl., Pl.*Ti*.87c, Phld.*Herc*.1003, *Vit.Philonid*.p.4C., Plu.2.961d; διανοήσεως ἐκπίπτοντα πάσης, i.e. absurd, Phld.*Rh*.1.223S.; *cunning, skill*, Lxx 2*Ch*. 2.14(13). **II.** *way of thinking*, Pl.*Lg*.888c. **-ητέον**, *one must think*, ib.626d, Plu.2.434b, etc. **-ητής**, οῦ, ὁ, *one who thinks*, gloss on φρόνιμος, Hsch. **-ητικός**, ή, όν, *of* or *for thinking, intellectual*, ἡ δ. κίνησις Pl.*Ti*.89a; ἀρετὴ δ., opp. ἠθική, Arist.*EN*1103$^{a}$ 14, etc.; ἐπιστήμη δ. Id.*Metaph*.1025$^{b}$6; δ. μέρη, of a play, parts *which display thought*, Id.*Po*.1460$^{b}$4; δ. σύγκρισις Epicur.*Nat*.14.20; δ. φαντασίαι *mental* images, Cic.*Fam*.15.16.1; *discursive*, opp. νοερός, Dam.*Pr*.415: Comp. -ώτερος ib.219. Adv. -κῶς Arr.*Epict*.1.14. 7. **-ητός**, ή, όν, *that which is* or *can be thought about*, τὸ δ. καὶ νοητόν Arist.*Metaph*.1012$^{a}$2, cf. 1021$^{a}$30; οὐδὲ δ. not even *thinkable*, Plu.2.1081a, cf. Procl.*Inst*.123.

**διάνοιᾰ**, ἡ, Aeol. **διανοΐα** Alc.*Supp*.1a.1 (nisi leg. δι' ἀνοΐα[ν]), poet. also **διανοΐᾱ** acc. to Eust.1679.29:—*thought*, i.e. *intention, purpose*, Hdt.1.46,90, And.4.35, etc.; τῇ διανοίᾳ in the *spirit* of his action, D.21.219; ὤλοντ' ἀσεβεῖ διανοίᾳ A.*Th*.831 (lyr.); μαινόλις δ. Id.*Supp*.109 (lyr.); εὔφρονος ἐκ δ. Id.*Ag*.797 (lyr.), cf. *Eu*.1013 (anap.); τοῦ ὑπαπιέναι τὴν διάνοιαν ἔχειν Th.5.9; ἐπί τινι Isoc.5. 14; πρός τινι Anaxipp.1.37; ἐπ' ἄλλο τι.. τρέψαι τινὸς τὴν δ. Pl. *Euthd*.275b; ἐξ ὅλης τῆς δ. with all one's *heart*, Arr.*Epict*.2.2.13; ἐχθροὺς τῇ δ. *Ep.Col*.1.21. **2.** *thought, notion*, Hdt.2.169, Pl. *Phd*.63d, Arist.*Metaph*.986$^{b}$10; ἀπὸ τῆς αὐτῆς δ. D.18.210. **II.** *process of thinking, thought*, ὁ ἐντὸς τῆς ψυχῆς πρὸς αὑτὴν διάλογος.. ἐπωνομάσθη δ. Pl.*Sph*.263d; πᾶσα δ. ἢ πρακτικὴ ἢ ποιητικὴ ἢ θεωρητική Arist.*Metaph*.1025$^{b}$25; ταχίστη ἡ διανοίας κίνησις Id.*LI*968$^{a}$ 25; esp. *discursive thought*, opp. νόησις, Procl.*Inst*.123. **III.** *thinking faculty, intelligence, understanding*, ὡς μεταξύ τι δόξης τε καὶ νοῦ τὴν δ. οὖσαν Pl.*R*.511d, al.; opp. σῶμα, Id.*Lg*.916a, cf. *R*.395b; ἔστιν ὥσπερ τοῦ σώματος καὶ τῆς δ. γῆρας Arist.*Pol*.1270$^{b}$40; ἐπιτάττοντος τοῦ νοῦ καὶ λεγούσης τῆς δ. φεύγειν τι ἢ διώκειν Id.*de An*.433$^{a}$ 2; ἔκστασις διανοίας Lxx *De*.28.28. **IV.** *thought expressed, meaning of* a word or passage, Pl.*Ly*.205b, *Phdr*.228d; τὰς τῶν ὀνομάτων δ. Id.*Cra*.418a; τὴν αὐτὴν ἔχει δ. Arist.*de An*.404$^{a}$17; ἡ φυσικὴ δ. τοῦ νόμου Aristeas 171; so δ., opp. ῥητόν, *spirit*, opp. letter, Hermog.*Stat*.2. **V.** *intellectual capacity* revealed in speech or action by the characters in drama, Arist.*Po*.1450$^{a}$6, $^{b}$11, 1456$^{a}$34, *Rh*.1404$^{a}$19, al. (Rare in Poetry.)

**διαν-οίγω**, *lay open*, τοὺς ὀφθαλμούς Pl.*Ly*.210a; μήτραν *Ev. Luc*.2.23:—Pass., Lxx *Ge*.3.5, al., Sor.1.86; of a dead body, Arist. *HA*507$^{a}$21. **II.** *open so as to connect*, τὸν Ἰνδικὸν καὶ Περσικὸν κόλπον Id.*Mu*.393$^{b}$3. **III.** *reveal, explain*, τὰς γραφάς *Ev.Luc*. 24.32, cf. *Act.Ap*.17.3; τὰ τῶν παλαιῶν ἀπόρρητα Aen.Gaz.*Thphr*. p.5B. **-οικίζω**, *build up, restore*, Philostr.*VS*2.9.2 codd. (Pass.). **-οιξις**, εως, ἡ, *opening*, Ruf.*Anat*.23, Thd.*Is*.61.1.

**διανομ-εύς**, έως, ὁ, *distributor*, Ph.*Fr*.15H., Plu.*Cim*.9, Polyaen. 1.34.2. **-ή**, ἡ, *distribution*, Pl.*R*.535a, Arist.*Pol*.1329$^{b}$41, etc.; παλαιᾶς δ. καταφθίσας A.*Eu*.727; μισθῶν διανομαί Plu.*Per*.9; esp. of *doles* or *largess*, *IG*12(5).663.22 (Syros), 951.13 (Tenos), M.Ant. 1.16, Luc.*Pisc*.41, App.*BC*1.27. **2.** *division* or *factorization* of numbers, Pl.*Lg*.747a, 771c, al. **II.** *regulation*, τῇ δ. τῶν πραγμάτων ἕπεσθαι Plu.2.102e; τὴν τοῦ νοῦ δ. ἐπονομάζοντας νόμον Pl.*Lg*. 714a.

**διανομοθετέω**, *get* a motion *carried and made law*, νόμους Pl.*Lg*. 628a, cf. D.C.56.40: abs., Id.37.50. **II.** *regulate by law*, τι Id. 38.7:—Med., διενομοθετήσαντο τί τίνος ἔργον Pl.*Lg*.832e.

**διάνομος**, ὁ, = ὑπόνομος, *IG*1$^{2}$.325.10, *BCH*33.461 (Argos).

**διανοσέω**, in aor. διενόσησα *fall ill*, Hp *Epid*.3.6, Gal.*Thras* 7.

**διανοσφίζω**, *separate, part asunder*, D.P.19 (tm.):—Med., *put aside for oneself, peculate*, D.S.19.71.

**δίανσις** [δῐ], εως, ἡ, *moistening*. Gal.11.740.

**δίαντα**, Adv. *right through*, τετρήατο prob. in Emp.84.9.

**διανταῖος**, α, ον (ος, ον E.*Ion*766 (lyr.)), *extending throughout*, of ligaments *running the whole length of* the spine, Hp.*Art*.45; *right through*, διανταίαν πλαγὰν πεπλαγμένος A.*Th*.895 (lyr.); διανταίαν οὐτᾶν Id.*Ch*.640 (lyr.); δ. βέλει ib.184; ὀδύνα E.*Ion*766 (lyr.); μοῖρα δ. *relentless* destiny, A.*Eu*.334 (lyr.). Adv. -αίως, παθεῖν Antyll.ap. Orib.44.23.14.

**διανταίρω**, *make war against*, πρός τινα prob. in Phld.*Acad.Ind*. p.57M.

**δῐαντικός**, ή, όν, (διαίνω) *able to wet*, ἔκκρισις Arist.*Mete* 387$^{a}$26.

**διαντλ-έω**, *drain, exhaust*: only metaph., *drink to the dregs, endure to the end*, νοῦσον Pi.*P*.4.293; πόνους E.*Andr*.1217 (lyr.); οἰκουρίας Id.*HF*1373; βίου χρόνον Ph.1.161; ὕθλους καὶ λήρους Luc.*Pseudol*. 25: abs., Heraclit.*Incred*.21:—Pass., πόλεμος διηντλήθη Pl.*Mx*. 241e, cf. Lib.*Or*.59.94. **-ίζομαι**, Pass., *exhaust oneself*, *to be worried* or *troubled*, περὶ μισθαρίων Hp.*Praec*.7.

**δῐαντός**, ή, όν, *capable of being wetted*, Arist.*Mete*.385$^{b}$10.

**διανυκτερεύω**, *pass the night*, νύκτα X.*HG*5.4.3, cf. *PTeb*.268.73 (iii A.D.): abs., Ph.2.488, Plu.*Aem*.16, al.; ἐν τῇ προσευχῇ *Ev.Luc*. 6.12, cf. Hdn.1.16.5.

**διάνῠσ-ις** [ᾰ], εως, ἡ, *distance traversed*, δ. ἡμερήσιαι day's *journeys*, Ptol.*Geog*.1.8.1, cf. 1.9.5. **II.** *accomplishment*, ἔργων Iamb.*Myst*. 4.3. **-μα**, ατος, τό, foreg. 1, δ. ἡμερήσιον Plb.9.14.8: pl., ib. 15.3.

**Διάνυσος**, ὁ, (διαίνω) coined as etym. of Διόνυσος, Corn.*ND*30.

**διᾰνυστ-έον**, *one must accomplish*, Agath.2.2. **-ικῶς**, Adv. *discursively*, γιγνώσκειν Ammon.*in APr*.25.24.

**διανύττω**, strengthd. for νύττω, Aristaenet.1.19, Paul.Aeg.3.70.

**διανύχιος** [ῠ], ον, *nocturnal*, read by Theon in S.*Ichn*.66 (lyr.).

⊛ **διᾰνύω** (also **διᾰνύτω** S.*Ichn*.64, X.*Mem*.2.4.7) [ῠ], pf. -ήνυκα Plb.4.11.7 :—*bring quite to an end, accomplish, finish*, κέλευθα δ. *finish* a journey, *h.Cer*.380, cf. *h.Ap*.108 ; δίαυλον E.*El*.825 ; τὸ ἑξῆς τῆς ὁδοῦ X. l. c. ; τὸν πλοῦν ἀπὸ Τύρου *Act.Ap*.21.7 ; πόνους Vett.Val. 330.9 ; τὰ προσήκοντα *POxy*.1469.4 (iii A.D.): c. acc. loci, πολὺν διὰ πόντον ἀνύσσας *having finished one's course over* the sea, Hes.*Op*.635 ; πλεῖον δ. *traverse*, of a point moving along a line, Arist.*LI*968ᵃ25, cf. Archim.*Sph.Cyl.Praef*., al. ; τόπους Plb.4.11.7 : abs., δ. εἰς τὰς ὑπερβολάς *arrive* at a place, Id.3.53.9 :—Pass., ὁδὸς διηνυσμένη ib.63.7 : aor. inf. διανυσθῆναι Hsch. : c. part., *finish doing* a thing, οὔ πω κακότητα διήνυσεν ἣν ἀγορεύων Od.17.517 ; but πόνοις σε διδοῦσα διήνυσεν *continued* giving . . , E.*Or*.1663 : abs., *live*, Vett.Val.58.17.

**διαομῑλῶ**, gloss on διαθρυλλῶ, Hsch.

**διαξαίνω**, aor. -έξᾱνα *Gp*.2.6.42, but inf. -ξῆναι Ar.*Lys*.578 : pf. part. Pass. -εξαμμένος Gal.8.415, -εξασμένος Dsc.5.106, Simp.*in Cael*.571.6, Paul.Aeg.3.61 :—*card, shred*, Ar.*Lys*.578 ; ἐσθῆτας Str. 11.14.8 ; ἔριον Paul.Aeg. l. c. ; νεῦρον εἰς ἶνας Alex.Aphr.*Pr*.2.52, cf. Gal. l.c. ; ἔντερον Ruf.ap.Orib.7.26.170 ; of flesh, Paul.Aeg.6. 77,88 :—Pass., of alum, Dsc. l. c., *to be dispersed, broken up*, Simp. l. c. 2. metaph., κόμην, of the wind, Hld.3.3 ; δ. θάλασσαν πτερύγεσσι Opp.*H*.5.306 ; as a punishment, δ. τινά Ael.*Fr*.131 :—Pass., ὑπὸ Ῥωμαίων ἐκτριβέντες διεξάνθησαν ib.130.

⊛ **διαξέω**, *smooth, polish off*, *IG*7.3073.138 (Lebad.), Poll.1.13. II. *erode*, Aët.5.41 (Pass.).

**διαξηραίνω**, *dry quite up*, D.S.1.10.

**διάξηρος**, ον, *quite dry*, *Gp*.6.2.4, v.l. in Arist.*Mete*.352ᵇ19, cf. Olymp. ad loc.

**διάξιμος**, ον, *to be transferred*, *Cod.Just*.1.15.2.

**διαξῐφ-ίζομαι**, *fight to the death*, τινὶ περί τινος Ar.*Eq*.781. **-ισμός**, ὁ, *fighting with swords*, Plu.2.597f.

**διαξόος**, ὁ, *stone-dresser*, *SIG*247 *K*¹ii 55 (Delph.).

**διάξῠλον**, τό, *cross-piece*, Apollod.*Poliorc*.177.12. II. = ἀσπάλαθος I, Dsc.1.20.

**διαξῠράομαι**, Med., *shave oneself*, Arr.*Epict*.1.2.29.

**διά-ξυσμα**, ατος, τό, *filings* : metaph., ἰσοτιμίας δ., of εὐγένεια, Chrysipp.*Stoic*.3.85. II. *flute* of a column, D.S.13.82. ⊛ **-ξύω**, *cut into wrinkles*, τὰ περὶ τὸ πρόσωπον διεξυσμένα Arist.*Phgn*.808ᵃ18 and 35 : generally, *cut up*, Ael.*Fr*.85.

**διαπαγκρᾰτιάζω**, *contend in the* παγκράτιον, Plu.2.811d.

**διαπαιγμός**, ὁ, *jesting*, *Gloss*.

**διαπαιδᾰγωγέω**, *attend children* : generally, *guide*, Pl.*Ti*.89d ; *entertain, amuse*, ἡδοναῖς τὴν πόλιν Plu.*Per*.11 ; δ. τὸν καιρόν *while away* the time, Id.*Sert*.16.

**διαπαιδεύομαι**, Pass., *take a course of education*, X.*Cyr*.1.2.15.

**διαπαίζω**, late fut. -ξω Gal.8.569 : pf. -πέπαιχα Plu. (v. infr.) :—*jest*, Gal. l. c. ; διαπαίζων *in jest*, J.*Ap*.2.37 (dub.), D.L.8.6 :—Pass., παιδιὰ καλῶς διαπεπαισμένη a sport well *kept up*, Pl.*Lg*.769a. II. *laugh, jest at*, c. acc., J.*BJ*5.7.4, Arr.*Epict*.2.18.22, Demetr.*Eloc*.147, D.L.4.53 : abs., Phld.*Lib*.p.57 O. III. perh. *imitate playfully*, [ὁ Σοφοκλῆς] διαπεπαιχὼς τὸν Αἰσχύλου ὄγκον Plu.2.79b.

**διαπαίκτης**, ου, ὁ, *jester, deceiver*. *Gloss*.

**διαπᾰλαίω**, *continue wrestling*, Ar.*Eq*.573, Ph.2.544, J.*AJ*1.20.2 ; πρός τινα Ach.Tat.4.19 : c. dat., νοσήματι *struggle with*, Gal.17(1). 569.

**διαπάλη** [πᾰ], ἡ, *hard struggle*, διαπάλαι πολέμου Plu.*Cor*.2, cf. 2.50f.

**διαπάλλω**, fut. -παλῶ A.*Fr*.304.4 :—*brandish*, A. l. c. :—but in Pass., *to be driven to and fro*, of a hunted deer, Opp.*H*.2.620. II. *distribute by lot*, χθόνα ναίειν διαπήλας A.*Th*.731 (lyr.).

**διαπᾰλύνω** [ῡ], *grind to powder*, E.*Ph*.1159.

**διαπαννῠχ-ίζω**, *pass the whole night*, Plu.2.775d. **-ισμός**, ὁ, *complete vigil*, D.H.2.19.

**διαπαντάω**, *meet*, Porph.*Abst*.3.10.

**διαπαντός**, Adv., later spelling of διὰ παντός, v. διά A. II. 1.

**διαπαπταίνω**, *look timidly round*, Plu.*Fab*.11.

**διαπαρα-δίδωμι**, *hand over* to a successor, *IG*9(2).1109.64,91 (Magn. Thess.). **-τηρέομαι**, *lie in wait for continually*, τινά Lxx 2*Ki*.3.30. **-τρῐβή**, ἡ, *constant wrangling*, 1*Ep.Ti*.6.5.

**διαπαρθέν-ευσις**, εως, ἡ, *deflowering of a maiden*, Hdn.*Epim*. 20. **-ευτής**, οῦ, ὁ, *one who deflowers*, *Gloss*. **-εύω**, *deflower a maiden*, Hdt.4.168 (Pass.), Diocl.Com.16, Antiph.75, Alex.314. **-ια** δῶρα, τά, presents *made to the bride on the morning after the wedding*, Amphis 49.

**διαπαρίστημι**, *set up statue of*, τινί *JHS*10.71 (Lydae).

**διάπαρ-μα**, ατος, τό, *transfixion*, *Gloss*. **-σις**, εως, ἡ, = foreg., Aret.*SA*1.7 (pl.).

**διάπασμα**, ατος, τό, (διαπάσσω) *scented powder to sprinkle over the person*, Dsc.1.7, Antyll.ap.Orib.10.31.1 : freq. in pl., Thphr.*Od*.8, Plu.2.990c, Plin.*HN*13.19, Luc.*Am*.39.

**διαπασσᾰλεύω**, Att. **διαπαττ-**, *stretch out by nailing the extremities*, πρὸς σανίδα Hdt.7.33 ; of a hide *pegged out for tanning*, Ar.*Eq*. 371, cf. Plu.*Art*.17.

**δια-πάσσω**, Att. **-ττω**, *sprinkle*, -πάσας τοῦ ψήγματος ἐς τὰς τρίχας Hdt.6.125 ; σμύρνῃ δ. τὴν ὁδόν Eub.128 ; δασύποδας ἁλσὶ δ. Alc.Com. 17 ; μέλανι διαπεπασμένον χρῶμα Arist.*HA*526ᵃ12 ; πυρρὰ διαπεπασμένα *with* red *spots*, ib.527ᵇ30. **-παστέον**, *one must powder*, prob. in Philum.ap.Aët.5.128.

**διαπάσχω**, *endure, sustain*, χλεύην *POxy*.904.2 (v A.D.).

⊛ **διαπᾱσῶν**, ἡ, i. e. ἡ διὰ πασῶν χορδῶν συμφωνία, *concord of the first and last notes, octave* ; more correctly divisim, τέταται διὰ πασῶν (sc. χορδῶν) Pl.*R*.432a ; τὸ δὶς διὰ πασῶν Plu.2.1019b.

**διᾰπᾰτάω**, *deceive utterly*, Pl.*Lg*.738e, Ph.2.92 :—Pass., Arist. *HA*496ᵇ5.

**διαπᾰτέω**, *tread through*, τὴν χιόνα Plb.3.55.2 ; dub. in Ph.1.354 codd.

**διάπαυ-μα**, ατος, τό, *cessation, rest*, πόνων Pl.*Lg*.824a. 2. *gap*, *IG*14.352ii 48 (Halaesa). **-σις**, εως, ἡ, *pause*, Arist.*Pr*. 894ᵃ26. **-ω**, *bring to an end, conclude*, τὸν βίον, i. e. *die*, prob. in *SIG*494.4 (Delph., iii B.C.) :—Med., *rest between times, pause*, Pl. *Smp*.191c, *R*.336b :—Pass., αἱ στρατιαὶ διεπέπαυντο *had ceased for the time being*, X.*HG*4.4.14.

**διαπαφλάζω**, *boil up, effervesce*, of anger, Nonn.*D*.31.24.

**διάπεζος**, ον, of women's robes, either *reaching to the feet* or *having a border* (πέζα), Callix.2.

**διαπείθω**, *convince*, ὁ διαπείθων λόγος dub. in Phld.*Ir*.p.80 W. :— Pass., *BGU*1062.19 (iii A.D.).

⊛ **διᾰπειλέω**, *threaten violently*, Hdt.7.15 ; δ. ὡς μηνύσει Id.2.121.γ' : c. inf. fut., Plu.*Oth*.16 :—Med., διαπειλεῖσθαί τινι Aeschin.1.43, Alex. 306, *PPetr*.2 p.1 : c. inf., *forbid with threats*, μηθένα φέρειν ὅπλον Plb. 1.78.15 ; ἄλλα τε δ. καὶ ὡς . . Conon 50.3.

**διαπεινάω**, inf. -πεινῆν, *hunger one against the other, have a starving-match*, διαπεινᾶμες (Dor.), with a play on διαπίνομεν, Ar.*Ach*. 751.

⊛ **διά-πειρα**, ἡ, *crucial experiment, trial, proof*, ἐς διάπειράν τινος ἀπικέσθαι Hdt.2.28,77 ; ἀποπέμπειν ἐς τὴν δ. τινός Id.1.47 ; δ. βροτῶν ἔλεγχος Pi.*O*.4.18. **-πειράζω**, *tempt, make trial of*, τινά Lxx 3*Ma*. 5.40. II. *attempt, try*, c. inf., J.*AJ*15.4.2.

⊛ **διαπειραίνω**, *pierce through*, Man.2.106 (Pass.).

⊛ **διαπειράομαι**, aor. -επειράθην Antipho 5.34 : pf. -πεπείραμαι Th. 6.91 :—*make trial* or *proof of*, τῶν Περσέων Hdt.5.109, cf. 3.14, Cratin. Jun.7.2 ; *try to impose on* a man, Pl.*Lg*.921b : c. gen. rei, *have experience* of a thing, Th.6.91 : abs., ὥσπερ αἴνιγμα συντιθέντι διαπειρωμένῳ Pl.*Ap*.27a, cf. *Lg*. l. c. 2. *attempt obstinately*, τὰ ψευδῆ λέγειν Antipho l. c. II. late in Act., διαπειρῶν δωροδοκίαις Plu. *Pomp*.51.

**διαπείρω**, *drive through*, σφυρῶν κέντρα E.*Ph*.26, cf. Il.16.405 (tm.); δ. ὀβελούς Iamb.*Myst*.3.4. 2. *pierce, transfix*, ἥλῳ τὰ στελέχη *Gp*. 5.36.3 ; βελόναις τὴν γλῶτταν Plu.*Art*.14 ; λίνῳ Dsc.2.61 :—Pass., διαπεπαρμένος ἥλοις Plu.2.567f ; τὴν χεῖρα διαπᾰρείς J.*AJ*10.1.2 ; *to be interpenetrated*, of muscle and flesh, Gal.8.74.

**διαπείσμα** (freq. misspelt **-πισμα**), ατος, τό, (διαπείθω) *present*, '*douceur*', *PTeb*.311.29 (ii A.D.), *POxy*.133.14 (vi A.D.), etc. ; 'King's shilling' given to recruits, ib.1103.8 (iv A.D.).

**διαπελάζω**, *approach*, etym. of δασπλῆτις, Sch.Theoc.2.14.

**διαπεμπτος**, ἡ, *period of five days*, Gal.19.551, *Cat.Cod.Astr*.1. 119.9, 121.19 ; cf. διάτριτος.

**διαπέμπω**, *send off in different directions*, Hdt.1.48,84, etc. ; ἄλλους ἄλλῃ δ. Th.8.64 ; φρουρὰς κατὰ χώραν Id.4.55 ; δ. τὴν ἰκμάδα (through the body), Arist.*PA*681ᵃ30 ; τὸ πνεῦμα Id.*HA*496ᵃ32 ; τὴν φωνὴν εἰς τὸ πρόσω Id.*PA*662ᵇ22 :—Med., *send out expeditions*, *OGI*199.35 (Adule). II. *send over* or *across*, τινὰ πρός τινα Ar.*Pl*.398 ; τινά τινι Th.4.123 ; *transmit*, *BGU*5ii 19 (ii A.D.), etc. ; ἐπιστολήν Th.1. 129 :—Med., Id.3.75 (possibly Pass.), *SIG*741.33 (Nysa, i B.C.) ; ἐσθῆτά τινι Ph.2.43. III. Med., *send messages*, περὶ βοηθείας πρός τινα Plb.5.72.1 ; πρὸς τοὺς φίλους Plu.*Arat*.8. **-πεμψις**, εως, ἡ, *distribution* of nourishment in the body, Hp.*Vict*.1.9. 2. *transmission* of a letter, Themist.*Ep*.16.

**διαπενθέω**, *mourn throughout*, ἐνιαυτόν Plu.*Publ*.23.

**διαπενταθλέω**, *contend in the* πένταθλον, Tz. ad Lyc.860.

**διαπεπονημένως**, Adv., (διαπονέω) *elaborately*, Isoc.*Ep*.6.6.

**διαπεραίνω**, *bring to a conclusion*, λόγους E.*Andr*.333 ; *describe thoroughly*, τι Pl.*Phlb*.47b, etc. ; διαπέρανέ μοι *tell* me *all*, E.*Andr*. 1056 ; δ. ὁδόν Pl.*Lg*.625b :—Med., μορφῆς διαπεράνασθαι κρίσιν *to get* the trial of beauty *decided*, E.*Hel*.26 ; διαπεράνασθαι λόγον Pl.*Phdr*. 263e, etc. :—Pass., Iamb.*Myst*.7.4. II. *traverse, pass through*, λοβὸν Aret.*SA*2.8 (cf. διαπεράω).

**διαπεραι-όω**, *take across, ferry over*, Plu.*Sull*.27 :—Pass., *to be carried over, cross*, ἐνθεῦτεν διαπεραιωθεὶς Hdt.5.23 ; δ. τὸν ποταμόν Id.2.124 ; ἐπεὶ πάντες διεπεπεραίωντο Th.3.23 : in aor. Med., Pl. *Ax*.370b. 2. κολεῶν διεπεραιώθη ξίφη swords *were unsheathed*, S.*Aj*.730. **-ωσις**, εως, ἡ, *carrying over*, Sch.Th.3.76. II. *crossing over*, Marcian.*Peripl*.1.44 (pl.).

⊛ **διαπέρᾱμα**, ατος, τό, (διαπεράω) *strait of the sea, ferry*, Str.6.1.5, *Peripl.M.Rubr*.32, Ptol.*Geog*.1.13.8.

**διαπερᾰντέον**, *one must carry to its conclusion*, λόγον Pl.*Lg*.715e.

**διαπεράσιμος** [ρᾱ], ον, *penetrating*, Sch.Il.12.439, Eust.709.48.

**διαπεράω**, *go over* or *across*, ῥοάς E.*Tr*.1151 ; πελάγη Isoc.1.19 ; δ. ἐπ' οἶδμα E.*IT*395 (lyr.) ; δ. πόλιν *pass through* it, Ar.*Av*.1264 ; δ. Ἑλλάδα E.*Supp*.117 ; δ. εἰς Ἰταλίαν Arist.*Fr*.485 ; of Time, δ. τὸν βίον *pass through* life, X.*Oec*.11.7. b. διαπερᾶν Μολοσσίαν *reign through all* Molossia, E.*Andr*.1248 codd. 2. *pass through, pierce*, κνήμην διεπέρασεν Ἀργεῖον δόρυ Id.*Ph*.1394 ; *traverse*, ἧπαρ, of a vein, Aret. *SA*2.8 (cf. διαπεραίνω). 3. οἶσθα διαπερῶν *by traversing*, i. e. *by experience*, A.*Th*.994 (lyr.), cf. Sch. II. *reach, arrive at* a place, *PFlor*.247.9 (iii A.D.). III. trans., *carry over*, ὕδωρ ποταμοῦ σῶμα δ. Eub.151, cf. Luc.*DMort*.20.1.

**διαπερδῑκίζω**, *slip through like a partridge*, *Com.Adesp.*87.

⊛ **διαπέρθω**, aor. 1 -έπερσα Pi.*Pae.*6.104: aor. 2 -έπρᾰθον Il.1.367, Ep. inf. -πραθέειν 7.32: aor. Med. -επράθετο in pass. sense, Od.15.384:—*destroy utterly*, *sack*, *waste*, always of cities, ll.cc.

**διαπεριπᾰτέω**, *keep walking about*, Ath.4.157e, 12.539c.

**διαπερονάω**, *pin* or *pierce through*, σφυρὰ σιδήρῳ D.S.4.64; τινὰ διαμπάξ Agath.1.9:—Pass., Id.2.9, al., Luc.*Gall.*24; σαυνίῳ διὰ τοῦ θυρεοῦ διαπερονηθείς D.H.9.64.

**διαπέρχομαι**, *slip away one by one*, of soldiers deserting, D.49.14, 50.

**διαπετάννῡμι**, pf. -πεπέτακα D.S.17.115, Pass. -πεπέτασμαι ib. 10:—*open and spread out*, Ar.*Lys.*732,733; τὰς πλεκτάνας, of the polypus, Arist.*HA*541$^b$5; ἀετοὺς διαπεπετακότας τοὺς πτέρυγας D.S. 17.115:—Pass., pf. διαπέπ[τ]α[νται] πύλαι prob. in Pi.*Dith.Oxy.*2.4.

**διαπέτεια**, ἡ, *opening*, πόρων Eust.1842.48.

**διαπετής**, ές, *spread out*, *unfolded*, *open*, Hp.*Cord.*10.

**διαπέτομαι** (**δῐίπταμαι** Hdn.,v.infr.), aor.-επτάμην (v.infr.): aor. Act. -έπτην Luc.*DMeretr.*9.4: pres. διαπέταται S.*OT*1310 (lyr.) is f.l. for διαπωτᾶται:—*fly through*, διὰ δ' ἔπτατο πικρὸς ὀϊστός Il.5.99; δρᾷς τὸν ἁβρὸν οὗ βέλος διέπτατο E.*Supp.*860; δ. διὰ τῆς πόλεως Ar.*Av.* 1217: c. acc., E.*Med.*1, Ar.*V.*1086. II. *fly away*, *vanish*, διαπτομένη οἴχεσθαι Pl.*Phd.*70a,84b, etc.; of Time, E.*HF*507. III. of a report, *fly in all directions*, διϊπταμένη ἡ φήμη Hdn.2.8.7.

⊛ **διαπεττεύω**, *gamble*, δ. τὴν ἐλπίδα *try* one's luck *at play*, Luc.*Am.* 16.

**διαπέττω**, *digest*, τροφήν Arist *GA*766$^b$13.

**διαπεύθομαι**, poet. for διαπυνθάνομαι, A.*Ag.*807 (anap.).

**διαπέφλοιδεν**· διακέχυται, and **διαπέφρυδεν**· χαίρει, διακέχυται, Hsch. **διαπεφρυκέναι**· διεσκέφθαι, καὶ καθεωρακέναι, Id.

⊛ **διά-πηγα**, τά, *panels*, Lxx 3*Ki.*7.31,32. **-πήγιον**, τό, = sq., *BGU*781 iii 8 (i A.D.). ⊛ **-πηγμα**, ατος, τό, (διαπήγνυμι) *cross-bar*, Ph. *Bel.*54.19, Hero *Bel.*83.8, *Dioptr.*34, Heliod.ap.Orib.49.7.1; *partition*, Hero *Aut.*11.9. **-πηγμάτιον**, τό, Dim. of foreg., *small cross-bar*, Ph.*Bel.*64.7. **-πήγνῡμι**, *fix* or *thrust through*, ἀκόντιον διὰ πλευρῶν Antipho 3.3.5; *transfix*, διέπαξε σιδάρῳ Epigr. in *PTeb.*3.29 (i B.C.). II. *freeze hard*, Thphr.*Vent.*54: pf. -πέπηγα, intr., *to be frozen*, Arist.*Mir.*835$^a$30. III. Med., δ. σχεδίας *get* them *put together*, Luc.*DMort.*12.5.

⊛ **διαπηδ-άω**, fut. -πηδήσομαι, *leap across*, τάφρον Ar.*Ach.*1178, cf. X.*Eq.*3.7: metaph., *pass over lightly*, Philostr.*Her.*2.10: abs., *take a leap*, of a horse, X.*Cyr.*1.4.8. 2. Medic., *ooze through*, perh. f.l. for -πιδύω, Hp.*Hum.*11. 3. *leap apart*, *form a chasm*, of the earth, Lyd.*Ost.*53. **-ησις**, εως, ἡ, *leaping* or *starting through*: metaph. in Medic., of blood, etc., *transudation through the tissues*, Sor.1.23, v.l. in Hp.*Nat.Puer.*21.

**διαπηνηκίζω** λόγον *trick out deceitfully*, Cratin.282 (prob. l., cf. πήνηξ).

**διάπηξ**, ηγος, ὁ, = διάπηγμα, Apollod.*Poliorc.*172.7: as Adj., διάπηγες μοχλοί Ph.Byz.*Mir.*4.2.

**διάπηξις**, εως, ἡ, *fastening together*, *structure*, δ. σωματική bodily *frame*, Herm.ap.Stob.1.49.69.

**διαπῑαίνω**, *make very fat*, in Pass., Thphr.*CP*6.11.7, Theoc.16.91.

**διαπῑδάω** ὕδωρ *let* water *ooze through*, Arist.*Mete.*350$^a$8.

**διαπῑδ-ύω**, *ooze through*, διὰ τῶν πόρων Arist.*GA*743$^a$9, cf. Hp.*Nat. Puer.*21. **-ῡσις**, εως, ἡ, *transudation*, ibid.

**διαπιέζω**, *press together*, Luc.*Lex.*11.

**διαπῐθᾰνεύομαι**, *oppose by probable argument*, ἄλλου ἄλλως εἰκάζοντος καὶ διαπιθανευομένου S.E.*M.*8.324.

**διαπῐθηκίζω**, strengthd. for πιθηκίζω, *EM*269.38, Suid.

**διαπικραίνομαι**, Pass., *to be greatly embittered*, πρός τινα Plu.2. 457a.

**διάπικρος**, ον, *very bitter*, ὕδωρ D.S.2.48, 19.98.

**διαπίμελος** [ῐ], ον, *obese*, *adipose*, Ruf.*Onom.*175.

**διαπίμπλημι**, aor. inf. -πλῆσαι, *fill full*, οἰκίας Philostr.*Im.*2.27; λόγων τὴν οἰκουμένην Eun.*VS* p.493 D., cf. Nonn.*D.*5.194; in early writers in Pass., *to be filled with*, τινός Th.7.85; *to be satiated* or *tired*, διαπεπλησμένος τινός *of* one, And.1.125.

**διαπίμπρημι**, *burn*, ναῦς Plb.21.44.30; μοχλὸν διαπρήσας Aen. Tact.4.2 (nisi leg. -πρίσας):—Pass., *swell up* (cf. πρήθω), Nic.*Al.* 341; οἱ μυκτῆρες διαπέπρηνται *Hippiatr.*27.

⊛ **διαπίνω** [ῑ], *drink one against another*, Hdt.5.18, 9.16, Pl.*R.*420e; = προπίνειν, Epig.8:—Med., δ. ἀνδράσι Hedyl.ap.Ath.11.486c. II. *drink at intervals*, Anaxandr.57:—but Pass., *to be swallowed at a draught*, διαπινόμενοι Arist.*Pr.*872$^b$27.

**διαπιπράσκω**, *sell off*, *PTeb.*5.192 (ii B.C.), etc.; οὐσίαν Plu.*Comp. Lys.Sull.*3.

⊛ **διαπίπτω**, *fall through*, Arist.*Cael.*313$^b$1. II. *fall away*, *slip away*, *escape*, ἐν τῇ μάχῃ X.*HG*3.2.4; πρός τινα ib.4.3.18; εἰς τὴν Ἀσπίδα Plb.1.34.11, etc. 2. of reports and rumours, *spread abroad*, εἰς τὰ στρατεύματα Plu.*Galb.*22. 3. of Time, *elapse*, Arist.*Ath.*35. 4. III. *fall asunder*, *crumble in pieces*, διαπέσοιμι πανταχῇ Ar. *Eq.*695, cf. Pl.*Phd.*80c, Arist.*Mete.*365$^b$12; *burst*, of bubbles, Id.*Pr.* 936$^b$5; *rot*, Lxx *Nu.*5.21; *perish*, διέπεσε πᾶσα γενεὰ ἀνδρῶν ib.*De.* 2.14; *to be missing*, *lost*, of moneys, etc., *PEleph.*21.19 (iii B.C.), etc.; of books, *to be imperfect*, J.*AJ*12.2.4. b. of an *intermittent* pulse, Gal.19.636. 2. of things, *turn out ill*, *be useless*, τὸ συκοφάντημα διέπιπτεν αὐτῷ Aeschin.2.39, cf. Plb.5.26.16, *PAmh.*2.33.26 (ii B.C.), etc. 3. of persons, *make mistakes*, ἐν τοῖς σημαινομένοις Chrysipp.*Stoic.*3.33, cf. Phld.*Ir.*p.73 W.: c. gen., *fail of*, *miss*, Epicur.*Ep.*2 p.43 U., Phld.*Rh.*1.49 S.; δ. περὶ τῆς δόξης Socr *Ep.*22; περὶ τῶν μεγίστων Arr.*Epict.*2.22.36: abs., *err*, Phld.*Ir.*p.91 W.; οὐ διαπεσούμεθα Iamb.*in Nic.*p.63 P.; *to be cheated*, ἐν χρήσει νομίσματος Arr.*Epict.*1.7.6. IV. ἡ διαπίπτουσα or ὁ τόπος ὁ διαπίπτων, *Tophet*, Lxx *Je.*19.12,13.

**διαπιστεύω**, *entrust to* one *in confidence*, τινὶ τὴν πόλιν, τὴν δυναστείαν, Aeschin.3.8, Plb.5.40.7; τῷ θεῷ τὰν ὠνάν Rüsch *Grammatik der delph.Inschr.*p.326 (ii B.C.); also δ. τινὶ περί τινος Aeschin.1. 188. II. *believe thoroughly*, τι Arist.*PA*673$^a$17, cf. Max.Tyr.10. 7. 2. c. dat., *have confidence in*, *believe*, *PHib.*1.147 (iii B.C.):—Pass., *to be trusted* or *believed*, D.10.51, Aen.Gaz.*Thphr.*p.18 B.

**διᾰπιστέω**, *distrust utterly*, τινί D.19.324, Arist.*Pol.*1314$^a$17: abs., *disbelieve*, *PSI*4.377.9 (iii B.C.), Aps.*Rh.*p.287 H.:—Med., *mistrust oneself*, Plb.18.46.7.

**διαπλᾰνάω**, *lead quite astray*, Plu.2.917e, Arr.*Epict.*1.20.10; *deceive*, *cheat*, *BGU*36.7 (ii A.D.):—Pass., *go astray*, *wander*, D.S.17. 116, Plu.*Fr.inc.*11 (v.l.).

**διά-πλᾰσις**, εως, ἡ, *putting into shape*: *setting of a dislocated limb*, Gal.18(2).332. II. *formation*, *modelling*, νεύρου Alex.Aphr.*Pr.*2.72; *conformation*, Gal.7.26; σώματος Hierocl. *in CA* 10 p.437 M. III. *deformation* by mirrors, Phlp. *in Mete.*28.19. ⊛ **-πλασμα**, ατος, τό, *model*, *shape*, or perh. *modelled jug*, Sch.Ar.*V.*614. **-πλασμός**, ὁ, v.l. for διάπλασις, *Placit.*1.3.18. 2. *massage* of infants, Sor.1. 101. **-πλάσσω**, Att. -ττω, *form*, *mould*, ζῷα Ph.1.15; ὕλην, ἄρτον, σῶμα, Plu.2.427b, 401f, Him.*Or.*14.13; διανοήματα ῥυθμοῖς Jul.*Or.*2.78d: metaph., ἐπίνοια J.*BJ*7.8.1; δ. τῷ λόγῳ Ael.*VH*3.1:—Pass., τέτταρσι διαπλασθέντα προσώποις μῦθον *AP*9.542 (Crin.); δ. τὰ μόρια [τοῦ ἐμβρύου] Arist.*GA*740$^a$36, cf. Epicur.*Ep.*2 p.38 U.: metaph., *to be concocted*, *invented*, *PMonac.*6.47 (vi A.D.). II. *plaster*, πηλῷ Thphr.*HP*4.15.2. III. Medic., *reshape* a broken nose, Heliod.ap.Orib.48.23.5, Gal.18(1).479. ⊛ **-πλαστικός**, ή, όν, *formative*, δύναμις Alex.Aphr.*Pr.*1.47, Gal.*Nat.Fac.*1.6.

⊛ **διαπλᾰτύνω**, *dilate*, X.*Lac.*2.5; *flatten out*, Chrysipp.Tyan.ap. Ath.14.648a.

**διάπλεγμα**, ατος, τό, *woof* or *web*, Eust.1571.56.

**διαπλέκω**, *weave*, *plait*, σάνδαλα *h.Merc.*80; opp. **διαλύω**, Hdt.4. 67; τὰ τὸν ὄσχεον διαπλέκοντα σώματα Paul.Aeg.6.62: metaph., θρῆνον δ. Pi.*P.*12.8; ἀγὰν πάγχυ δ. *to try* every *twist*, *wind* all ways, ib.2.82:—Med., διαπλέξασθαι κόμας *plait one's* hair, Aristaenet.1.25:—Pass., ψυχὴ διαπλακεῖσα *interwoven* [with matter]., Pl.*Ti.*36e, cf. Plot.1.1.3. II. metaph., διαπλέξαντος τὸν βίον εὖ *finish the web of* one's life, Hdt.5.92.ζ'; δ. βίοτον λιπαρῷ γήραϊ **Pi.*N.*7.99**; ἀμέραν prob. in Alcm.23.38; ἀσκητικόν τινα βίον Pl.*Lg.*806a, cf. *Com.Adesp.*231: without βίον, δ. ζῶν ἡδέως Ar.*Av.*754.

**διαπλευρισμός**, ὁ, *cross-dyke*, *PLille* 1 16 (iii B.C.).

**διαπλέω**, Ion. -πλώω (q.v.), *sail through* a strait or gap, Th.4.24, Plb.14.10.12; sail *across*, Μέγαράδε Lys.12.17; εἰς Αἴγιναν Ar.*V.* 122, etc.: c. acc., δ. τὸ πέλαγος Plu.2.206d, *IG*14.1976: metaph., δ. βίον *sail through* life, *make* life's *voyage*, Pl.*Phd.*85d. 2. *flow through*, *pass*, τὰ ψαμμία σὺν τοῖσι οὔροισι δ. Aret.*SD*2.3.

**διάπλεως**, ων, *brim-full*, τινός Cratin.280, Plu.2.551a: pl., διάπλεα Thphr.*CP*2.1.4: fem. διάπλεαι Plu.*Tim.*11.

⊛ **διαπληκτ-ίζομαι**, *spar*, Lxx *Ex.*2.13; τινί Luc.*Anach.*11: generally, *skirmish with*, ἱππεῦσι Plu.*Luc.*31: metaph., *wrangle*, δ. τοῖς γυναίοις Id.*Tim.*14; πρὸς γύναιον Id.2.76ca, cf. Agath.2.29: c. dat. modi, δ. τοῖς σκώμμασι Plu.*Sull.*2:—late in Act., Horap.1.70. **-ισις**, εως, ἡ, = sq., Sch Il.1.138. **-ισμός**, ὁ, *sparring*, *disputing*, *wrangling*, πρὸς Σωκράτην περί τινος Plu.2.711cc (pl.); δ. τε καὶ ὀργαί Porph. *Marc.*2.

**διαπληρόω**, strengthd. for πληρόω:—Pass., -πεπληρωμένοι λαφύρων Aen.Tact.16.8.

**διαπλήσσω**, *break in pieces*, *split*, *cleave*, δρῦς Il.23.120 (v.l. διαπλίσσοντες): aor. inf. -πλῆξαι read by Aristarch. in Od.8.507.

**διαπλίσσομαι**, *stand* or *walk with the legs apart*, διαπεπλιγμένος *long-shanked*, *straddling*, Archil.58: so in pf. part. Act., στόμα διαπεπλιχὸς *wide open*, Hp.*Mul.*2.167, cf. Hsch., and v. foreg.

⊛ **δια-πλοκή**, ἡ, *intermixture*, Hp.*Alim.*11. II. in pl., *crooked ways*, Aq.*Ps.*124(125).5. **-πλόκινος**, ον, = sq., σκάφιον Str.17.1. 50. ⊛ **-πλοκος**, ον, *interwoven*, *plaited*, Hld.2.3.

⊛ **διάπλοος**, ον, contr. -πλους, ουν, I. Adj., *sailing across* or *sailing continually*, δ. καθίστασαν λεών they kept them *at the oar*, A. *Pers.*382. II. as Subst., **διάπλους**, ὁ, *a voyage across*, *passage*, πρὸς τὸ Κήναιον Th.3.93; ἀπὸ τῆς οἰκείας Id.6.31. 2. *room for sailing through*, *passage*, δυοῖν νεοῖν for two ships abreast, Id.4.8. 3. *cross-channel*, Pl.*Criti.*118e.

**διάπλουτος**, = ζάπλουτος (q.v.), *EM*407.8.

**διαπλόω**, *unfold*, Heb.*Ge.*38.29; διαπλοῦσθαι v.l. for διαπνεῖσθαι, X.*Smp.*2.25 as quoted by Ath.11.504d.

**διαπλύνω**, strengthd. for πλύνω, Ar.*Fr.*686.

**διαπλώω**, Ion. = -πλέω, A.R.2.629, Nic.*Al.*559, *AP*7.23 (Antip. Sid.).

**δια-πνείω**, poet. for διαπνέω, Nonn.*D.*29.201. **-πνευμα**, ατος, τό, *breeze*, dub.l. in Hp.*Aër.*19 (pl.). **-πνευσις**, εως, ἡ, = διαπνοή, *exhaling*, *Gp.*5.28.1. **-πνεύστας**· παραλογιστικός, prob. in Hsch. **-πνευστία**, ἡ, = διαπνοή, Gal.19.514. **-πνευστικός**, ή, όν, *promoting exhalation*, Aret.*CA*1.1. **-πνευστός**, όν, *easily dissipated*, *volatile*, ἀήρ Alex.Aphr. *in Sens.*36.4. ⊛ **-πνέω**, Ep. -πνείω, fut. -πνεύσομαι, *blow through*, of air, δ. τὸ σῶμα Arist.*Pr.*967$^a$2, cf. *Mete.*370$^b$ 6, etc.:—Pass., αὔραις διαπνεῖσθαι X.*Smp.*2.25, cf Arist.*HA*518$^a$16,

D.S.5.82. 2. intr., *admit air*, ἀπόφραξον ἅπαντα ὡς μὴ διαπνέειν Hero*Spir.*2.21. II. *breathe between times, get breath*, Plb.27.9.10, Plu.*Cim.*12, Ph.1.90,al.; ἐκ δυσχερείας Plu.31.4.1. III. intr., *disperse in vapour, evaporate*, Arist.*Resp.*479$^a$17, *PA*671$^a$20, cf. Ph. 2.42: so, IV. Pass., διαπίπτειν καὶ διαπνεῖσθαι Pl.*Phd.*80c; δ. καὶ σήπεται τὸ σῶμα Arist.*de An.*411$^b$9. 2. Medic., *dissipate by exhalation*, Aret.*SA*1.7:—Pass., Gal.15.377 (also intr. in pass. sense, διέπνευσε τὸ ἄλγος Aret.*CA*1.10). 3. Pass., of plants, *exhale*, διαπνεῖται καὶ ἐξατμίζεται Thphr.*CP*1.1.3, cf. M.Ant.6.16; of human beings, *perspire*, Id.3.1, Gal.15.377:—so Med., Hp.*Alim.*28.

**δια-πνοή**, ἡ, *outlet, vent for the wind*, Arist.*Mete.*368$^b$9: pl., *gap, interstice*, Erot. s.v. διαρόγχας; *pores*, Aret.*CA*2.7; *organs of respiration*, Id.*SA*1.5. II. *exhalation*, Thphr.*CP*6.16.6. III. *transpiration*, Hp.*Alim.*28, Alex.Aphr.*Pr.*2.60, Gal.15.180, Aret. *SA*1.10; of *vapours* or *humours*, Id.*CA*1.1, *CD*2.13. IV. *expulsion of flatus*, Id.*SD*2.8. **-πνοια**, ἡ, = foreg. I. Poll.2.219, *Gp.* 7.6.10, Simp.*in Cael.*524.10. II. *opening, gap*, Pall.*in Hp.Fract.* 12.283C.

**διαποδ-ίζω**, *measure with the foot*, Hsch., *EM*269.25. **-ισμός**, ὁ, *jumping about*: a kind of *dance*, Poll.4.99.

**διαπο-ζεύγνυμαι**, Pass., *to be utterly separated, depart*, Ph.1. 255. **-θνήσκω**, *keep dying*, διαμάχεσθαι καὶ δ. Plb.16.31.8.

⊕ **διαποιέω**, *complete a transaction*, *BGU*1261.13 (i B.C.), *PTheb. Bank* 126.4.

**διαποικίλλω**, *variegate, adorn with variety*, mostly metaph., τοῖς διαιτήμασι Hp.*Vict.*3.68; ποίησιν Isoc.9.9; literally, δ. τι ἀργύρῳ καὶ χρυσῷ Plu.*Sert.*14:—Pass., μέλανι δ. *to be dappled*, Arist.*HA*503$^b$5: metaph., δ. ἐκ.. *to be blended of various sorts*, Pl.*Lg.*693d, cf. 863a; ἀπάταις τὰ πολλὰ δ. τοῦ πολέμου Plu.*Lys.*7, cf. Iamb.*Myst.*7.3.

**διαποίκῐλος**, ον, *variegated*, Hp.*Coac.*603; ἄκανθα δ. τὴν χρόαν Arist.*Fr.*269; δ. ῥάβδοις *striated*, Id.*HA*525$^a$12; δ. ψῆφοι Str.5.2. 6. 2. metaph., ἀοιδά *Lyr.Alex.Adesp.*20.6. II. of persons, *clad in embroidered robes*, Luc.*Nec.*12.

**διαποιμαίνω**, *feed*: metaph. of educators, βίον Man.4.419.

**διαπολεμ-έω**, *carry a war through*, Hdt.7.158; δ. τὸν πόλεμον Pl. *Criti.*108e; δ. τινί *fight it out with* one, X.*An.*3.3.3, Plb.3.2.3, Plu. *Fab.*19; πρός τινα D.S.14.99:—Pass., διαπεπολεμήσεται [ὁ πόλεμος] the war *will be at an end*, Th.7.14, cf. 25, Jul.*Or.*2.55c. II. *carry on the war*, Th.6.37. **-ησις**, εως, ἡ, *finishing of a war*, Id.7.42.

**διαπολῐορκέω**, *carry a siege to its conclusion*, Th.3.17.

⊕ **διαπολῑτ-εία**, ἡ, *party strife*, Plu.2.510c (pl.); αἱ πρός τινας δ. Cic. *Att.*9.4.2. **-εύομαι**, *to be a political rival*, Aeschin.3.194, Harp. s.v. διαγορεύων; δ. Περικλεῖ, of Thucydides son of Melesias, Marcellin.*Vit.Thuc.*28. **-ευτής**, οῦ, ὁ, *political opponent*, prob. in App. *Hisp.*8 (-πολῖται codd.).

**διαπόλλῡμι**, *destroy utterly*, Thphr.*HP*8.10.3.

**διαπομπ-εύω**, *carry the procession to an end*, Luc.*Nec.*16; Ῥάριον ὀργειῶνα νόμῳ -πομπεύουσα prob. in Hermesian.7.19. II. *carry all round*, ὕδωρ Critias 1.7 D. **-ή**, ἡ, *interchange of messages, negotiation*, πρὸς τὰς πόλεις Th.6.41 (pl.); φίλων, ἐραστῶν, App.*BC*5.71, *POxy.*471.61 (pl.): sg., App.*Hisp.*91. **-ησις**, εως, ἡ, = ἀποδιοπόμπησις, Sch.Ar.*Pl.*651. **-ιμος**, ον, *exported*, D.S.2.49, Opp. *C.*3.47.

**διαπονδαρίζει** (leg. -πυδ-)· διαναβάλλεται, διαναρρίπτεται, Hsch.

⊕ **διαπον-έω**, *work out with labour, elaborate*, Isoc.5.85; *cultivate, practise*, δ. γράμματα Pl.*Lg.*810b, cf. *R.*535c; τὰ πρὸς ἀγῶνας συντείνοντα Arist.*Pol.*1341$^a$11; *exercise*, σώματα X.*Cyn.*4.10; σώματα δρόμοις καὶ πάλαις Plu.*Lyc.*14; αὐτὸν Id.*Dem.*6; στρατόν App.*Syr.*43; τοὺς νέους Luc.*Anach.*18:—Med., διαπονεῖσθαι ἐπιτηδεύματα, τέχνας, Pl.*Lg.*846d, cf. *Phdr.*273e, X.*Mem.*2.1.33:—Pass., Pl.*Criti.*118c, *Ep.* 326d, etc.; οἴκου.. οὐχ ὡς τὰ πρόσθ' ἄριστα διαπονουμένου *managed, governed*, A.*Ag.*19; διαπονηθῆναι τὴν μουσικήν *to be taught* it *thoroughly*, Plu.*Per.*4; διαπεπονημένοι *veterans*, D.S.11.7; ὄψων.. περιττῶς διαπεπονημένων Plu.*Luc.*40. 2. *till* or *cultivate completely*, χώραν Plb.4.45.7:—Pass., *Hell.Oxy.*12.5. 3. Pass., *to be worn out, troubled*, *Act.Ap.*4.2, 16.18, *POxy.*743.22 (i B.C.). II. intr., *to work hard*, δ. τῇ διανοίᾳ καὶ τῷ σώματι Arist.*Pol.*1339$^a$8, cf. Aristeas 92; περὶ τὸ σῶμα Arist.*EN*1178$^a$26; περὶ τὰ δημιουργικὰ τεχνήματα Pl.*Lg.*846d: c. inf., δ. πᾶν ἰσόρροπον ποιεῖν X.*Smp.*2.17:—Med., δ. τὸ πᾶσαν πίστιν λαβεῖν Pl.*Lg.*966c; δ. περὶ τὸν γόνον Arist. *GA*759$^b$1; οἱ διαπονούμενοι *the hard-working, hardy*, opp. ἄπονοι, X. *Lac.*5.8; *to be hard-worked*, of hounds, Arr.*Cyn.*32.1, al. **-ημα**, ατος, τό, *hard labour, exercise*, τὰ περὶ τὸν πόλεμον δ. Pl.*Lg.*813d. II. concrete, *work*, τὰ τῶν τεκτόνων δ. Id.*Criti.*114e; *achievement, work done*, βασιλέως Procop.*Aed.*2.7; *thing achieved, reward of toil*, Id. *Goth.*4.19.

**διαπονηρεύομαι**, *deal unfairly*, πρός τινα D.H.*Is.*3.

**διαπόν-ησις**, εως, ἡ, *working at, preparing*, πυροῦ Plu.2.693d. **-ητέον**, *one must work hard at*, Ph.2.235. **-ητότατα**, Adv. Sup., *most elaborately*, dub. l. in Id.2.20. **-ος**, ον, of persons, *exercised, hardy*, δ. τὰ σώματα Plu.*Mar.*26, al., cf. Onos.1.1. 2. *worn out*, σῶμα δ. πρός τι Plu.2.135f. II. Adv. -νως *with labour* or *toil*, Id. *Fab.*1.

**διαπόντιος**, ον, *beyond sea*, γᾶ A.*Ch.*352 (lyr.); στράτευμα Hermipp.58; πόλεμοι Th.1.141; λήμματα *revenues*, Antiph.196.8; πρεσβεία *IGRom.*4.881 (Tacina). II. *across the sea*, δ. πέτεσθαι Alex. 210; ναύτης δ. μονόμαχος Secund.*Sent.*18.

[**διαπο**]**ντοπλᾰνής**, ές, *wandering over the sea*, dub. in *Lyr.Alex. Adesp.*20.13.

**διαπορ-εία**, ἡ, *procession* of heavenly bodies, Pl.*Epin.*982c. II. *journey*, metaph., ἡ τοῦ λόγου δ. Id.*Criti.*106a. III. *mediation*, Id.*Epin.*984e. **-εύσιμος**, gloss on διαπρύσιος, Sch.Il.8.227, Hsch. **-ευσις**, εως, ἡ, gloss on διαπορεία, Suid. **-ευτός**, όν, *which may be traversed*, Apollon.*Lex.* s.v. ἀμαξιτός, Sch.X.*An.*1.2. 21. **-εύω**, *carry over, conduct through*, X.*An.*2.5.18. II. mostly Med., with aor. Pass. διεπορεύθην:—*pass across*, ἐς Εὔβοιαν Hdt.4.33: c. acc., *go through*, Πελοπόννησον Th.5.52; χώραν X. *An.*3.3.3; δ. τὰς ὁδούς Pl.*Lg.*845a; στόμα δι' οὗ μέλη τε καὶ ἔπη δ. Satyr.*Vit.Eur.Fr.*39 xx 14; δ. γραμμήν *travel along* a line, Arist.*EN* 1174$^b$1, cf. Archim.*Spir.*12: abs., Th.1.107, Pl.*Phd.*85d, Arist.*PA* 640$^b$15; οἱ δ. απορευόμενοι *the passers-by*, Aen.Tact.32.10. 2. *go through, detail*, εὐεργεσίας Plb.16.26.2; *perform*, τὰς κρούσεις Id.30. 22.5. 3. of Time, *elapse*, *BGU*1116.11, al. (i B.C.).

⊕ **διᾱπορ-έω**, *to be quite at a loss, to be in doubt* or *difficulty*, τί χρὴ δρᾶν Pl.*Lg.*777c; ἐπὶ τοῖς συμβαίνουσι Plb.4.71.5: in aor. Pass., διηπορήθη Aeschin.2.34: pf. Pass., διηπορημένος Plu.*Alex.*25:—Med., δ. ὑπ' αἰσχύνης Pl.*Phdr.*237a. 2. *to be in want*, Arist.*Oec.*1353$^a$ 26. II. *go through all the* ἀπορίαι, Id.*Pol.*1276$^b$36, al.: but, 2. commonly only a stronger form of ἀπορέω, *raise an* ἀπορία, *start a difficulty*, Id.*EN*1096$^a$11; ἔστι δὲ τοῖς εὐπορῆσαι βουλομένοις προὔργου τὸ διαπορῆσαι καλῶς Id.*Metaph.*995$^a$28; περί τινος Plb.4.20.2, Phld. *Sign.*21; εἰ.. Epicur.*Fr.*21:—Med., διαπορεῖσθαί τι περί τινος Pl. *Sph.*217a:—Pass., *to be matter of doubt* or *discussion*, Pl.*Sph.*250e, Arist.*Metaph.*1086$^a$19, al.; τὸ διαπορούμενον Pl.*Lg.*799e; τὸ διαπορεῖσθαι Arist.*EN*1101$^a$35; τὸ διαπορηθέν Id.*Pol.*1282$^b$8: impers., διαπορεῖται περί τινος *a question arises* about.., Id.*HA*631$^b$2. **-ημα**, ατος, τό, *vexed question*, Id.*APo.*93$^b$20 (pl.), al. II. *restlessness*, Hp.*Acut.*42. **-ησις**, εως, ἡ, *doubting, perplexity*, ὑπέρ τινος Plb. 28.3.6; εἰ δεῖ.. Id.35.5.1. **-ητέον**, *one must raise questions*, Id. 36.17.12, Ph.1.288, Longin.2.1. **-ητικός**, ή, όν, *at a loss, hesitating*, Plu.2.395a. II. Adv. -κῶς *in the form of a question*, περιοδεῦσαι Hermog.*Inv.*4.3.

**διαπορθέω**, = διαπέρθω, Il.2.691, Th.6.102, D.H.8.50, etc.:—Pass., *to be utterly ruined*, A.*Pers.*714, S.*Aj.*896 (lyr.), E.*Hel.*111, Paus.7. 17.1, D.C.47.45.

⊕ **διαπορθμ-εύω**, *carry over* or *across* a river or strait, Hdt.4.141, Acus.29 J., etc.; *carry a message from one to another*, Hdt.9.4:—Pass., *to be ferried across*, *BGU*1188.10 (i B.C.). 2. metaph., *transmit*, θεοῖς τὰ παρ' ἀνθρώπων καὶ ἀνθρώποις τὰ παρὰ θεῶν Pl.*Smp.* 202e, cf. Procl.*Inst.*148, Iamb.*Myst.*1.5; κλῆρον εἰς τοὺς ἐκγόνους Jul. *Or.*2.81c. II. δ. ποταμόν, of ferry-boats, *ply across* a river, Hdt. 1.205, 5.52: abs., *cross over*, Iamb.*VP*2.11. **-ιος**, ον, *transmitting, mediating*, of certain spiritual beings, Orac.ap.Dam.*Pr.*339; τὸ ὄνομα τῶν ἰύγγων Procl.*in Cra.*33 P., cf. eund. *in Alc.*p.69 C.

**διαπορίαι**, αἱ, *Questions, Problems*, title of work by Epicurus, D.L.10.27; διαπορίας τοῖς ἰατροῖς παρέχειν Gal.5.721.

**διαπορίζω**, *furnish, render*, *POxy.*971 (iii A.D.).

**διαπορπᾰκίζω**, aor. inf. -κίξαι, *put the hand through the* πόρπαξ, Hsch.

**διαπόρφῠρος**, ον, *shot with purple*, ἄνθη Dsc.1.11; ἐσθάς Melissa *Ep.*1.

**διαπο-στέλλω**, *dispatch*, χρήματα εἰς Χίον D.35.54, cf. Plb.5.17.9, D.S.19.30; κήρυκας *Supp.Epigr.*2.261.6 (Delph., iii B.C.):—Pass., τοῦ παρ' ἡμῶν -ομένου παιδαρίου *UPZ*39.18 (ii B.C.); of a letter, Plb. 5.42.7; of scouts, Id.18.22.2:—Med. in act. sense, *IG*12(7).32.15 (Amorgos), *SIG*692.56 (Delph., ii B.C.); *send as a representative*, *POxy.*286.26 (i A.D.), etc. **-στολή**, ἡ, *sending of messages*, Plb. 5.37.3 (pl.), *OGI*248.58 (ii B.C.); πρεσβειῶν D.H.7.12.

**διαποσῴζω**, *carry safe through*, Arr.*Ind.*37.5.

**διαπραγμᾰτεύομαι**, *discuss* or *examine thoroughly*, τοῦτον τὸν λόγον Pl.*Phd.*77d; τὴν αἰτίαν ib.95e. II. *gain by trading*, *Ev.Luc.* 19.15. III. *accomplish*, τι πρὸς τοὺς θεούς Iamb.*Myst.*5.16.

**διαπρακτ-έος**, α, ον, *practicable*, Isoc.*Ep.*6.8. **-ικός**, ή, όν, *effective, operative*, Dam.*Pr.*34.

**διάπραξις**, εως, ἡ, *accomplishment of ends*, δ. πολιτικαί Pl.*Smp.* 184b, cf. Ph.1.429; *action, agency*, J.*AJ*17.1.1, Iamb.*Myst.*4.3.

⊕ **διάπρᾱσις**, εως, ἡ, *sale to various purchasers*, D.H.7.29, Plu.*Sull.* 33, *POxy.*83.8 (iv A.D.). II. *farming out*, προσόδων, τῶν τελωνικῶν, *PTeb.*8.15 (iii B.C.), *POxy.*44.4 (i A.D.).

⊕ **διαπράσσω**, Att. -ττω, Ion. -πρήσσω, *pass over*, c. gen., διέπρησσον πεδίοιο they *made their way over* the plain, Il.2.785, 3.14; also οἱ κε.. διαπρήσσωσι κέλευθον *may finish* their journey, Od.2.213, cf. 429: of Time, c. part., ἤματα.. διέπρησσον πολεμίζων I *went through* days in fighting, Il.9.326; κεν.. εἰς ἐνιαυτὸν ἅπαντα οὔ τι διαπρήξαιμι λέγων I *should* not *finish* speaking.., Od.14.197:—Med., διαπραξάμενος βίον Alex.262.2 (dub.). II. *bring about, accomplish*, Hdt.9.94; δ. τινί τι *get* a thing *done* for a man, Id.3.61, cf. A.*Eu.*953 (lyr.): c. inf., X.*Smp.*5.9: abs., Ar.*Eq.*93:—Pass., ἐπ' ἔργοις διαπεπραγμένοις καλῶς A.*Ch.*739:—freq. in Med., Hdt.1.2, 2.2, Ar.*Lys.*518, etc.; δι' ἑρμηνέων Hdt.4.24; οὐδὲν καινὸν διαπράττονται D.35.1: pf. Pass. in med. sense, τὸ αὐτὸ διαπεπραγμένοι εἰσὶν ὥσπερ ἂν εἰ.. Pl.*Grg.*479a; πολλοῖς πολλὰ παρὰ τοῦ πάππου ἀγαθὰ διεπέπρακτο X.*Cyr.*4.2.10, cf. *An.*2.3.25; ὃ οὗτοι διαπεπραγμένοι εἰσί D.35.26, cf. Din.1.97, Isoc. 4.137; τοὺς ἀνήκεστα δ. Theodect.ap.Arist.*Rh.*1399$^b$4, cf. Men. *Per.Fr.*1: also strictly in sense of Med., *effect for oneself, gain one's point*, Hdt.9.41; τὸ ἴδιον Antipho 5.61; φιλίαν δ. πρός τινα X.*An.*7. 3.16; πλοῖα παρά τινος ib.6.2.17: c. inf., δ. τῶν ἀγγέλων γενέσθαι Pl.*R.*360a; δ. ὥστε folld. by inf., Lys.16.15, Pl.*Grg.*478e, by ind.,

X.*An*.4.2.23; δ. μὴ καίειν ib.3.5.5. 2. Med., *get for oneself, obtain*, πλοῖα ib.6.2.17, cf. 3.2.29. III. *make an end of, destroy*, in Pass., A.*Pers*.260(lyr.), al., S.*Tr*.784, E.*Hel*.858; διαπέπρακται τὰ Καρχηδονίων Plu.*Fab*.5. IV. Med., *intrigue successfully*, Aeschin. 3.232 (so in Act., διαπρήσσει· ἀπατᾷ, ψεύδεται, Hsch.).

⊛ **διαπρᾱΰνω**, *soothe*, Philostr.*VA*6.14, *VS*1.21.5.

**διαπρέπ-εια**, ἡ, *magnificence*, Aq.*Ps*.28(29).2, al. **-ής**, ές, *distinguished*, νᾶσος Pi.*I*.5(4).44; ἀρετή Th.2.34; ἐσθῆτι καὶ κόσμῳ δ. Democr.195, cf. E.*Supp*.841, *IA*1588; γυναικομίμῳ μορφώματι Id. *Antiop*.ii A7A.; τὸ δ. *magnificence*, Th.6.16. Adv. **-πῶς** *magnificently*, σκηνὴ δ. κεκοσμημένη Plu.*Alc*.12; δ. ἀγωνίσασθαι Id.*Mar*.28, J.*BJ*7.1.2 (Comp.): Sup. -πέστατα D.50.7. **-όντως**, *remarkably*, Sch.E.*Or*.1483. ⊛ **-ω**, *appear prominent* or *conspicuous, strike the eye*, h.*Merc*.351, Pi.*O*.1.2; διαπρέπον κακόν A.*Pers*.1007 (lyr.). 2. *to be eminent*, ἔν τινι *AP*9.513 (Crin.); ἐπί τινι Luc.*Salt*.9, cf. D.C. 68.6; κάλλει, ὥρας ἀκμῇ, Plu.2.771e, D.C.42.34: c. gen., δ. πάντων ἀψυχίᾳ E.*Alc*.642. 3. *to be suitable*, κτητικὴ λεχθεῖσα ἂν διαπρέψειεν Pl.*Sph*.219c. II. c. acc. rei, *adorn*, E.*Fr*.185.

**διαπρεσβ-εία**, ἡ, *reciprocal embassy*, Plb.5.67.11. **-εύομαι**, *send embassies*, εἰς τὰς πόλεις X.*HG*3.2.24, cf. *SIG*633.121 (Milet., ii B.C.), Plb.1.11.11, D.S.11.68, Plu.*Sert*.23; τισί D.C.45.43:—later in Act., *serve as envoy*, *PPetr*.3 p.150. **-ευσις**, εως, ἡ, = διαπρεσβεία, App.*Gall*.18 (pl.); ἐς ἀλλήλους Id.*Syr*.2.

**διαπρηστεύω**, v. διαδρηστεύω.

**δια-πρίζω**, = -πρίω, Paul.Aeg.6.18:—Pass., Sor.1.80; cf. διαπρίζει· διαπερᾷ, Hsch. ⊛ **-πριστος**, ον, *sawn through*, θύρα Demioprat. ap.Poll.10.24. ⊛ **-πρίω** [ῑ], *saw through, saw asunder*, Ar.*Eq*.768, cj. in Aen.Tact.4.2 (cf. διαπίμπρημι); *split*, κύμινον Jul.*Caes*.312a:—Pass., Hp.*VC*21; -πεπρισμένα [ξύλα] *SIG*²587.304; διαπεπρισμένα ἡμίσε'.. ὡσπερεὶ τὰ σύμβολα Eub.70: metaph., διεπρίοντο ταῖς καρδίαις *Act.Ap*.7.54, cf. 5.33; also εἰς πλείω δ. τὴν Παλαιστίνην Lib.*Ep*. 334. II. δ. τοὺς ὀδόντας *gnash* the teeth, Luc.*Cal*.24. III. διαπρίεται· διαγοράζει, μαίνεται, Hsch.

**διαπρί-ωσις** [ῑ], εως, ἡ, *sawing up* into planks, *SIG*248*N*8 (Delph., iv B.C.). **-ωτός**, ή, όν, = διάπριστος, Hp.*VC*21.

⊛ **διαπρό**, v. διά. **διάπροθι**, Adv. = foreg., Nic.*Al*.3.

**διαπροστᾰτεύω**, *continue to propose*, τι Plb.4.13.7.

**διαπρύσιος** [ῠ], α, ον, *going through, piercing*, in Hom. only as Adv., πρῶν πεδίοιο διαπρύσιον τετυχηκώς a hill *piercing into, running out into*, the plain, Il.17.748. 2. of sound, *piercing, thrilling*, ἤϋσεν δὲ διαπρύσιον he gave a *piercing* cry, 8.227; δ. κιθαρίζων h.*Ven*. 80: in late Prose, τορόν τι βοῶν καὶ δ. Agath.4.11. II. later as Adj., Ἀπείρῳ διαπρυσίᾳ *far-stretching*, Pi.*N*.4.51. 2. freq. of sound, *piercing*, ὀλολυγαί h.*Ven*.19; ὄτοβος S.*OC*1479 (lyr.); κέλαδος E.*Hel*. 1308 (lyr.): in late Prose, οἰμωγαί J.*BJ*2.1.2. 3. δ. κεραϊστής a *downright* thief, h.*Merc*.336; δ. πόλεμος *open* war, D.L.2.143. 4. Adv. **-ίως** *loudly*, ἱστορίας μαρτυρία κηρύττουσα δ. D.S.11.38: metaph., *intensely*, μισεῖσθαι ὑπό τινος Sch.Ar.*Pax* 481.

**διαπταίω**, *stutter much*, Luc.*Somn*.8.

⊛ **διαπτερ-όω**, *clean with* or *as with a feather*, Hp.*Acut*.58, Aret.*CD* 1.8. **-ύσσομαι**, *flutter about*, Ps.-Plu.*Fluv*.6.4. **-ωσις**, εως, ἡ, *cleaning with a feather*, v.l. in Hp.*Acut*.58, cf. Erot.

**διαπτίσσω**, aor. inf. -πτίσαι, *winnow, sift*, *EM*125.43.

**διαπτο-έω**, fut. -ήσω: Ep. aor. διεπτοίησα:—*scare away, startle and scatter*, ἐπέεσσι διεπτοίησε γυναῖκας Od.18.340; *strike with panic*, στρατὸν.. φόβος διεπτόησε E.*Ba*.304; with personal subject, Plu. *Cleom*.5; τοὺς ἀντιπάλους Them.*Or*.21.257b:—Pass., *to be panic-stricken*, δείσαντες διεπτοήθημεν Pl.*R*.336b, cf. Plu.*Caes*.10, etc.; of horses, Plb.3.51.5. II. in Pass., = πτοέω II, διεπτόηντο ταῖς ὁρμαῖς πρὸς τὸν Τίτον Plu.*Flam*.5. **-ησις**, εως, ἡ, *violent excitement*, Pl.*Lg*.783c.

**διά-πτυξις**, εως, ἡ, *spreading out fanwise*, τῶν ἐπιπέδων Procl.*Hyp*. 5.110; *explication*, Gal.1.305. **-πτύσσω**, Att. -ττω, *open and spread out, unfold, disclose*: metaph., διαπτυχθέντες ὤφθησαν κενοί S.*Ant*.709, cf. E.*Hipp*.985, Pl.*Lg*.858e (Pass.); σύμβολα Iamb.*Protr*. 21; λόγῳ δ. Moschio Trag.6. 2. *split open*, κράνος D.S.17.20; *open up*, τὸ ἐπιγάστριον Gal.2.520. II. *fold one with another, intertwine*, Arist.*GA*720$^{b}$17. **-πτῠχή**, ἡ, *fold, folding leaf*, δέλτου διαπτυχαί, γραμμάτων δ., E.*IT*727,793.

**διαπτύω**, *spit upon*, τινός Ael.*NA*4.22: abs., Gal.13.46: metaph., c. acc., ὁ σεμνὸς ἀνὴρ καὶ διαπτύων τοὺς ἄλλους D.18.258, cf. Lib.*Or*. 57.53, al.; of food, Plu.2.101c; δ. τὸν χαλινόν, Lat. *frenum respuere*, Philostr.*Im*.2.5:—Pass., D.Chr.38.38.

**διά-πτωμα**, ατος, τό, *stumble, slip*, Philem.60; *error*, Chrysipp. *Stoic*.2.215, Phld.*Herc*.1251.5; *failure*, opp. ἐπίτευγμα, Id.*Po*.5.21; μεγάλοις δ. περιπίπτειν fall in with great *losses*, *IPE*1².32.55 (Olbia), cf. *SIG*364.62 (Ephesus); *loss, deficiency* in accounts, *PHib*.1.52.9 (iii B.C.), etc. **-πτωσις**, εως, ἡ, *fall*, Gal.18(1).506: chiefly metaph., *failure*, Epicur.*Fr*.556; ἀγωνία φόβος διαπτώσεως *Stoic*. 3.98, cf. Phld.*Lib*.p.28 O., *Herc*.1251.7, S.E.*M*.7.423, Plu.2.800a, etc.

**διαπῡδαρίζω**, v. πυδαρίζω.

**διαπῡ-έω**, *suppurate*, Hp.*Aph*.4.82, etc. **-ημα**, ατος, τό, *collection of pus*, Id.*Prog*.7 (pl.). **-ησις**, εως, ἡ, *suppuration*, ibid., Sor.1. 76. **-ητικός**, ή, όν, *promoting suppuration*, Gal.11.118. **-ΐσκομαι**, Pass., *suppurate throughout*, Hp *VC*2, M.Ant.4.39:—later in Act., Aret.*SD*1.9.

**διάπυκνος**, ον, v.l. for διάκοιλος in Dsc.4.114.

**διαπυκτεύω**, *spar, fight with*, τινί X.*Cyr*.7.5.53, Arr.*Epict*.2.21.11, etc.: abs., of cocks, Luc.*Anach*.37: metaph., Id.*Gall*.22.

**διαπύλιον** [ῠ], τό, (πύλη) *gate-toll*, Arist.*Oec*.1348$^{a}$26, *PTeb*.8.19 (iii/ii B.C.).

**διαπυνθάνομαι** (poet. διαπεύθομαι (q.v.)), *search out by questioning, find out*, τὴν τινων συνουσίαν.. περὶ τῶν λόγων τίνες ἦσαν Pl.*Smp*.172a, etc.; τί τινος something *from* one, Plu.*Cat.Mi*.16; δ. τοῦ θεοῦ, πῶς χρή.. Pl.*R*.469a: abs., Id.*Hp.Mi*.369d.

**διά-πῡος**, ον, (πῦον) *suppurating*, Hp.*Aph*.7.45. **-πῡόω**, intr., *suppurate*, *Hippiatr*.16,20.

**διαπῠρ-ιάομαι**, Pass., *to be thoroughly heated*, Hp.*Steril*.234. **-ίζω**, *heat thoroughly*:—Pass., metaph., *glow with anger*, Hsch. **-ινα**, τά, *cautery irons*, Gal.18(1).376. **-όομαι**, *set on fire*, E.*Cyc*.694: Pass., metaph., τῷ θυμῷ διεπυροῦτο Plu.*Phoc*.6; *to be consumed with thirst*, Lxx 4*Ma*.3.15. ⊛ **-ος**, ον, *red-hot*, Anaxag.A.1, al., Hp.*Aër*. 17, E.*Cyc*.631, Arist.*Pr*.954$^{a}$18; σίδηρος Epicur.*Fr*.346b; διάπυρα, τά, *embers*, Pl.*Ti*.58c; *extremely hot*, πέτραι δ. ὑπὸ τοῦ ἡλίου Porph. *Abst*.1.13. 2. *inflamed*, Hp.*VM*18. 3. metaph., *ardent, fiery*, Pl.*R*.615e, *Lg*.783a (Sup.); δ. πρὸς ὀργήν, πρὸς δόξαν, Plu.2. 577a, *Luc*.4; ἐραστής Procop.*Pers*.2.12; δ. μῖσος Plu.*Arat*.3. Adv. **-ρως** *ardently*, προσέχειν σχολῇ εὐσεβείας Jul.*Ep*.89a; ἐρασθῆναί τινος Ael.*VH*2.4. 4. *using fire*, χρεία Max.Tyr.10.8.

**διαπυρπᾰλᾰμάω**, aor. -ησα, *juggle*, h.*Merc*.357.

**διάπυρρος**, ον, *bright red*, Xenocr.15.

**διαπυρσεύω**, *communicate by beacon*, τινί App.*Mith*.79: metaph., *blazon abroad as by beacon-fires*, τὰς πράξεις τῇ δόξῃ εἰς ἅπαντας τοὺς ἀνθρώπους Plu.*Demetr*.8: c. gen., Philostr.*VA*2.22 (v.l. -πυρσαίνω):—Med., *make signals by beacons*, Plb.1.19.7.

**διαπύρσιος**· μέγας, διαβόητος, Hsch.:—also **διαπύρσιον**· μέγα, διαπορεύσιμον, ἐξάκουστον (i.e. διαπρύσιον), κτλ., Cyr.

⊛ **διαπύρωσις** [ῠ], εως, ἡ, *severe inflammation*, Sor.1.82. II. *thorough heating*, *PHolm*.2.7.

**διάπυστος**, ον, *heard of, well-known*, δ. γίγνεσθαι Hdn.2.12.2.

**διαπῠτίζω**, Att. fut. -ιῶ, *spit* or *spirt out*, Arched.3.12.

**διαπωλέω**, *sell publicly*, X.*HG*4.6.6, Plu.*Oth*.4; *sell entirely*, πάντα τά τινος *PLips*.35.17 (iv A.D.):—Pass., *SIG*695.62 (Magn. Mae.).

**διαπωρόομαι**, Pass., *form a callus thoroughly*, of a broken bone, Hp.*Art*.21.

**διᾰράομαι**, *curse*, Aristeas311.

**διαρᾰπισμός**, ὁ, *scourging*, prob. in *POxy*.1873 (v A.D.).

**διαράσσω**, *strike through*, διὰ σαρκὸς ἄραξε Hes.*Sc*.364; *smash in pieces*, τινὰ τῷ ῥοπάλῳ ὥσπερ πίθον παλαιόν D.Chr.8.31.

**διάργεμος**, ον, *flecked with white*, Babr.85.15.

**διάρδω**, *water, irrigate*, J.*BJ*3.10.8 (Pass.).

⊛ **διάρημα**, ατος, τό, = λέμβος, Procop.*Aed*.6.1 (pl.).

**διαρθρ-έω**, = ἐξαρθρέω, dub. in Gal.18(1).626. **-όω**, *divide by joints, articulate*, τὰ στήθη διήρθρου Pl.*Smp*.191a:—Pass., διηρθρωμένος *well-jointed, well-knit*, Hp.*Aër*.24, Pl.*Phdr*.253d (metaph., πρὸς σωφροσύνην πεπηγὸς καὶ δ. Eun.*Hist*.p.246 D.); πόδες, δάκτυλοι, Arist.*Phgn*.810$^{a}$16, *HA*504$^{a}$7; *to be differentiated*, of the embryo, ib.489$^{b}$9, cf. Hp.*Nat.Puer*.17; *to be movable-jointed*, Id.*Art*. 30; esp. *to be jointed by* διάρθρωσις (q.v.), Gal.2.656, 18(1).433; also διηρθρωμένον γράμμα a *distinct* birth-mark (opp. συγκεχυμένον), Arist.*GA*721$^{b}$34. 2. *endue with articulate speech*, τὴν γλῶτταν Luc.*Enc.Dem*.14, cf. Plu.*Dem*.11:—Med., φωνὴν καὶ ὀνόματα διηρθρώσατο τῇ τέχνῃ *invented articulate* speech and names, Pl.*Prt*. 322a. 3. *describe distinctly*, Id.*Lg*.963b, 645c (Pass.), Porph. *Plot*.18, Iamb.*VP*23.103, etc.; *perceive clearly, distinguish*, Phld.*D*. 1.22, *Mus*.p.39 K., *Vit.Philonid*.p.9 C.; διηρθρωμένη διάληψις Porph. *Abst*.2.43; opp. συγκεχυμένος, Id.*Marc*.10. 4. *complete in detail, fill up so as to form an organic whole*, lit., πρὶν διηρθρῶσθαι τὸ σῶμα Arist.*HA*521$^{a}$10 (Act. δ. σάρκα τῇ γλώττῃ of a bear *licking* its cub *into shape*, Ael.*NA*6.3): metaph., Arist.*EN*1098$^{a}$22:—Pass., Id. *Metaph*.986$^{b}$6; ἂν διαρθροῖτο ὁ συλλογισμός Id.*Top*.156$^{a}$20. 5. *distinguish*, τὸ γένος A.D.*Synt*.138.24. ⊛ **-ωσις**, εως, ἡ, *articulation*, τῶν μελέων Hp.*Nat.Puer*.18; *differentiation*, δ. λαμβάνειν, of the embryo, Arist.*HA*583$^{b}$23, cf. *GA*744$^{b}$11; of the Universe, Epicur.*Ep*.2 p.38 U. (pl.). b. esp. *movable articulation, diarthrosis* (opp. συνάρθρωσις), Gal.2.735, 18(1).433. 2. of the voice, *articulate utterance*, Arist.*HA*535$^{a}$31; ἡ τῶν γραμμάτων δ. Id.*PA*660$^{a}$22. 3. *distinct statement*, ἠθικῶν ἐννοιῶν, title of work by Chrysipp., *Stoic*.2. 8, cf. Iamb.*Myst*.5.13; *distinctness*, λόγου Longin.ap.Porph.*Plot*.20, cf. Alex.Aphr.*in Metaph*.3.14. **-ωτέον**, *one must define precisely*, Arist.*EE*1248$^{a}$10, Porph.*Abst*.1.31, Simp.*in Epict*.p.2 D. **-ωτικός**, ή, όν, *explanatory*, Epict.*Ench*.52; δ. τέχνη S.E.*M*.1.300; *giving shape or form*, Sch.Hes.*Th*.130.

**διᾰριθμ-έω**, *reckon up one by one, enumerate*, ψήφους E.*IT*966, cf. Ar.*Av*.1622; τάργύριον Phld.*Ir*.p.37 W.; ὑπολείποι ἂν ὁ αἰὼν διαριθμοῦντα Arist.*Rh*.1374$^{a}$33:—more freq. in Med., as Pl.*Cra*.437d, *Phdr*.273e, al.; *count and classify*, Id.*Grg*.501a; διαριθμήσασθαι περί τινος Id.*Lg*.633a:—Pass., Aeschin.3.207, Arist.*Ph*.322$^{b}$30. 2. *count out, pay*, δωρεάν τισι App.*BC*4.101. ⊛ **-ησις**, εως, ἡ, *reckoning up*, χρημάτων Plu.2.27c; χρόνου Theo Sm.p.148 H. **-ητικός**, v.l. for διαρθρωτικός, Epict.*Ench*.52.

**διάρῑνον**, τό, *mustard*, Hsch., prob. in Polyaen.4.3.32.

⊛ **διάριον**, τό, = Lat. *diarium, day-wage*, *POxy*.1729 (iv A.D.), etc.

**διαρίπτω**, poet. for διαρρίπτω, dub. l. in Ar.*Th*.665 (lyr.).

**διᾰριστάομαι**, *eat at breakfast for a wager*, βοῦν αὐτῷ δ. *eat* an ox *against* another, Ath.9.412f.

**διᾰριστεύομαι**, *strive for the pre-eminence*, πρός τινα Longin.13.4.

**διάρκ-εια**, ἡ, *sufficiency*, τῆς τροφῆς Thphr.*CP*1.11.6. ⊛ **-έω**,

*suffice*, τρία ἔπεα διαρκέσει Pi.*N.*7.48, cf. X.*Cyr.*6.2.26, Phld.*Herc.* 1251.19, etc.; πρός τι Thphr.*CP*1.16.4; *endure, hold out*, Isoc.2.19; δ. πρός τινα *hold out* against.., Luc.*Luct.*24, etc. 2. in point of Time, *endure, last*, A.*Th.*842 (lyr.); οὐ διήρκεσε δεῦρο ὁ λόγος Pl.*Ti.* 21d: c. part., δ. πολιορκούμενος X.*HG*5.3.21; δ. ἐπὶ πολὺν χρόνον Arist. *Mete.*352b4; οὐ διήρκεσε τῷ βίῳ πρὸς τὸ τοῦ πολέμου τέλος Plu.*Fab.*27; ἀπόσιτος [ὢν] ἐς ἑβδόμην δ. Luc.*Hist.Conscr.*21. II. *supply nourishment*, τινί Plu.*Sol.*22; *sustain*, τινάς Aeschin.*Ep.*5.3. ❋ -ής, ές, *sufficient*, χώρα Th.1.15; τροφή Arist.*HA*626a2, Thphr.*CP*1.11.6; δυνάμεις D.H.4.23, etc. 2. *lasting*, ὠφέλεια D.3.33; ἐπὶ πολύ D.H.6.54: Comp., Luc.*Anach.*24: Sup., *with staying power*, of an athlete, Paus.6.13.3; ἵπποι Them.*Or.*11.146a. Adv. -κῶς S.E.*P.* 3.115, Eun.*Hist.*p.209 D., Demoph.*Sent.*10, etc.; δ. ἔχειν τι to be *amply* provided with, Procop.*Pers.*1.21, al.: Sup. διαρκέστατα ζῆν *in complete competence*, X.*Mem.*2.8.6. -ούντως, Adv. *sufficiently*, dub. l. in J.*AJ*14.13.9.

❋ **διάρμα**, ατος, τό, (διαίρω) *passage by sea*, Plb.10.8.2, Agathem.3. 13; *crossing of a channel*, Str.4.5.2. II. *elevation* of style, ὄγκος καὶ δ. Plu.2.853c, Longin.12.1; δ. ψυχῆς λαβεῖν D.L.9.7. III. = κούφισμα, Hsch.

❋ **διαρμόζω** or -ττω, fut. -σω, *distribute in various places*, E.*Or.*1451 (lyr.): hence, 2. Med., *arrange, dispose*, ταῦτα πρὸς τὸ μέλλον Plb.8.25.5:—Pass., τὸν τρόπον τοῦτον διηρμοσμένοι ib.7.1; *regulate*, τὸν βίον Plu.2.88a.

**διαρνέομαι**, *deny*, Petr.Patr.p.434 D., Just.*Nov.*18.10.

**διαρόγχαι**, αἱ, *gaps left in applying a bandage*, Hp.ap.Erot. (-ρωχαί codd.); cf. διαρωχμίας.

**διάρουρον**, τό, *plot of two* ἄρουραι, *PBas.*17.3 (i A.D.).

**διᾰρόω**, *plough*, A.R.3.1053 (tm.).

❋ **διαρπ-ᾰγή**, ἡ, *plundering*, Hdt.9.42, Plb.10.16.6, *PMasp.*4.13 (vi A.D.). ❋ -άζω, fut. -άσομαι Pl.*R.*336b, later -άσω App.*Pun.*55: — *tear in pieces*, [λύκοι] αἶψα διαρπάζουσι [ἄρνας] Il.16.355; of the wind, *carry away, efface*, τὰ ἴχνη X.*Cyn.*6.2; τείχη διηρπασμένα *dismantled*, Jul.*ad Ath.*279a. II. *spoil, plunder*, πόλιν Hdt.1.88, etc.:—Med., Συρίαν J.*AJ*1.9.1. 2. *seize as plunder*, χρήματα Hdt. l. c., cf. Lys. 7.6, 19.40, *Hell.Oxy.*13.3, Arist.*Pol.*1281a25, etc.:—Pass., Pl.*Plt.* 274b; τὰν τῇ Βοιωτίᾳ διαρπασθησόμεν' ὑπὸ τοῦ πολέμου D.18.213, cf. Lys.19.41, Th.8.36. 3. *snatch from*, θηρείων παῖδα γενείων Nonn. *D.*48.290. -ᾰσις, εως, ἡ, = διαρπαγή, *AB*438.4.

**διαρρᾰγή**, ἡ, *tearing apart*, ὀστέων Hp.*Coac.*184.

❋ **διαρραίνω**, pf. διέρραγκα Lxx *Pr.*7.17:—*sprinkle*, κόνιν Philostr. *Gym.*56; *shed*, ἀκτῖνας Lyd.*Ost.*10a; *besprinkle*, Lxx l. c.; *purify by lustration*, οἰκίην *IG*12(5).593A17 (Ceos, Pass.):—Pass., ἀφρῷ ἡ γῆ διέρρανται Philostr.*Im.*7.27:—also intr. in Act., Lyd.*Ost.*9b. II. Pass., *to be diffused, dissipated*, S.*Tr.*14, Arist.*Mete.*341a30.

❋ **διαρραίω**, *dash in pieces, destroy*, διαρραῖσαι μεμαῶτες Il.2.473, etc.; οἶκον Od.2.49:—Pass., c. fut. Med., *to be destroyed, perish*, τάχα δ' ἄμμε διαρραίσεσθαι ὀΐω Il.24.355; διαρραισθέντας εἰς Ἀΐδου μολεῖν A. *Pr.*238. II. ῥωχμαὶ σάρκα διαρραίουσι dub. in Marc.Sid.80.

**διάρραμμα**, ατος, τό, (διαρράπτω) *seam*, Plu.2.978a.

**διαρρᾰπίζω**, *cuff soundly*, Hld.7.7, 8.9 (Pass.).

**διαρραπτέον**, *one must insert a suture*, Archig.ap.Orib.47.13.5.

**διαρράπτω**, *sew through* or *together*, Str.15.1.67, Plu.2.978a; *insert a suture*, Gal.18(2).746.

❋ **διαρρᾰφή**, ἡ, *sewing up*, Sor.2.40.

**διαρρᾰχίζω**, *carve*, Eub.15.4 (Pass.).

**διαρρέμβομαι**, *dawdle*, Anon.ap.Suid. s. v. ῥεμβώδης.

❋ **διαρρέπω**, *oscillate*: *halt in one's gait*, Hp.*Art.*55.

❋ **διαρρέω**, *flow through*, διὰ μέσου Hdt.7.108; δ. μέσου αὐτοῦ Ael. *VH*3.1: c. acc., τὴν χώραν Isoc.11.14; δ. εἰς τὴν θάλατταν, of rivers, Arist.*HA*569a20:—Pass., Epicur.*Ep.*2p.47 U.; *to be drenched*, ἱδρῶτι Hld.10.13; of a country, ποταμοῖς διαρρεῖσθαι Plu.2.951f: also intr. in Act., τὸ ἔδαφος διαρρέον καὶ τὴν ἰκμάδα παρέχον Thphr.*Ign.* 41. 2. *slip through*, τῶν χειρῶν Luc.*Anach.*28; διὰ τῶν δακτύλων Id.*DMort.*17.1. 3. of a vessel, *leak*, ib.10.1. 4. of a report, *fade away, die away*, Plu.*Aem.*24. 5. χείλη διερρυηκότα *gaping* lips, Ar.*Nu.*873. II. *fall away like water, die* or *waste away*, χάρις διαρρεῖ S.*Aj.*1267; of the moon, *wane*, πάλιν διαρρεῖ κἀπὶ μηδὲν ἔρχεται Id.*Fr.*871.8; to be 'boiled to rags', Ar.*V.*1156; of money, μὴ λαθεῖν διαρρυὲν τἀργύριον D.37.54; of soldiers, δ. ἐκ τῆς στρατοπεδείας Plb.1.74.10; δ. κατὰ πόλεις Plu.*Sull.*27, etc.; also δ. ὑπὸ πλούτου καὶ μαλακίας, Lat. *diffluere luxuria*, Id.2.32f, cf. *Ages.*14, Luc.*DMort.*11.4, etc.; δ. τῷ βίῳ *lead a loose* life, Ael.*VH*9.24.

**διάρρηγμα**, ατος, τό, *fragment*, prob. in Hsch. s. v. κεάσματα.

❋ **διαρρήγνῡμι**, *break through*, Hom. only in Med., διά τε ῥήξασθαι ἐπάλξεις Il.12.308; διαρρήξασα χαλινόν *having broken* the bridle *asunder*, Thgn.259; μόγις ἂν.. διαρρήξειας [τὴν κεφαλήν] Hdt.3.12; πλευρὰν διαρρήξαντα.. φασγάνῳ *having cloven* it, S.*Aj.*834; δ. τὰς χορδάς Pl.*Phd.*86a:—Pass., *burst*, as with eating, X.*Cyr.*8.2.21, Anaxil.25, Phoenicid.3, etc.; δ. μυρίων ἀγαθῶν Men.10 D.; with passion, διαρραγήσομαι Ar.*Eq.*340; ὑπὸ φθόνου Luc.*Tim.*40; οὐδ' ἂν σὺ διαρραγῇς ψευδόμενος D.18.21, cf. 87; διαρραγείης, as a curse, '*split you!*' Ar.*Av.*2, etc.: pf. διέρρωγα *to be broken* or *torn*, διερρωγυιῶν τῶν χορδῶν Pl.*Phd.* l. c.; ἀκεσαμένη τὸ διερρωγός Arist.*HA*623a18; ὑπόδημα δ. Plu.2.82b: later pf. part. Pass. διερρηγμένος Jul.*Or.*2.64c.

❋ **διαρρήδην**, Adv., (διαρρηθῆναι) *expressly, explicitly*, *h.Merc.*313, Plb.3.26.5; esp. of legal enactments or treaties, δ. γέγραπται Foed. ap.And.2.14; δ. εἴρηται μή.. Lys.1.20: ὁ νόμος δ. λέγει Is.3.68; δ. ψηφίσασθαι D.19.6; δ. πέμπειν Pl.*Lg.*698c; νομοθετεῖν ib.876c.

**διαρρήκτης**, ου, ὁ, *plotter*, Hsch.

**διάρρηξις**, εως, ἡ, = διαρραγή, Epicur.*Ep.*2p.49 U., J.*AJ*18.9.1, Herod.Med.in *Rh.Mus.*49.552.

❋ **διάρρησις**, εως, ἡ, *explicit enactment*, Pl.*Lg.*932e, dub. in *Leg. Gort.*9.36.

**διαρρήσσω**, = διαρρήγνυμι, Babr.38.7, *Ev.Luc.*8.29, Artem.4 *Praef.*:—Pass., Ps.-Callisth.1.46.

**διαρρικνόομαι**, *draw up and twist the body*, of an unseemly kind of dance, Cratin.219.

**διάρριμμα**, ατος, τό, *casting about, questing*, of a hound, X.*Cyn.*4. 4 (pl.).

**διαρρῑν-άω**, *file through* or *perforate*, Hero *Aut.*25.5, Sor.2.63: pf. part. Pass. διερρινημένος *perforated*, ἐπίθημα Arist.*Ath.*68.3, cf. Dsc. 4.114: metaph., *fine, critical*, ἀνὴρ λεπτὸς καὶ δ. τὴν γαστέρα Max. Tyr.36.4. -ησις, εως, ἡ, *filing through, perforation*, Heliod.ap. Orib.47.17.4.

**διαρρῑπίζω**, *blow away, disperse*, Hld.3.7: metaph. in Pass., Id. 9.14. II. *expose to draughts*, Hp.*Ep.*16 (Pass.).

❋ **διαρρίπτω**, poet. **διαρίπτω**, also pres. **διαρριπτέω** Ar.*V.*59, X. *Cyn.*5.8, Aeschin.1.59, etc.:—*shoot through*, διαρρίπτασκεν ὀϊστόν Od.19.575. 2. *cast* or *throw about*, διάριψον ὄμμα πανταχῇ *fling* glances *round*, dub. in Ar.*Th.*665; τὰς ὄψιας πυκνὰ δ. Hp.*Coac.*214; δ. σκέλεα Id.*Prog.*3 (Pass.); δ. τὴν οὐράν, of a dog, *wag* the tail, X. *Cyn.*6.23. 3. *throw about*, as nuts, etc., among a crowd, Ar.*V.* 59; χρήματά τισι Plb.16.21.8: metaph., *toss about*, Pl.*Ep.*343d; *squander*, τὸν βίον Lib.*Or.*12.33: pf. part. Pass., *indiscriminate*, Pl. *Lg.*860c; *scattered, dispersed*, δ. κατὰ πόλεις Plu.*Phil.*8; διερριμμένην μνήμην ποιήσασθαι mention *here and there*, Plb.2.57.5. 4. *throw down*, τὸν περίβολον Id.16.1.6. II. intr., *plunge*, ἐν τῇ θαλάττῃ X.*Cyn.*5.8.

❋ **διαρρῐφή**, Dor. -φά, ἡ, *casting about*, ποδός Pratin.Lyr.1.16.

**διάρριψις**, εως, ἡ, *scattering*, X.*An.*5.8.7, Thphr.*HP*6.3.4.

**διάρροδος**, ον, *compounded of roses*, κολλούριον Gal.12.765.

**διαρροή**, ἡ, *channel, pipe*, πνεύματος διαρροαί the wind-*pipe*, E.*Hec.* 567; of a stream, αἱ δ. τοῦ Ῥειτοῦ *SIG*86.15 (Eleusis, v B.C.). II. *flowing through*, ἡ ἄνω τε καὶ κάτω τοῦ ὠκεανοῦ διαρροή, ebb and flow, D.C.39.41.

**διαρροθέω**, *to roar* or *rustle through*, διαρροθῆσαι κάκην τινί *to inspire* fear *by clamour*, A.*Th.*192. II. διαροθεῦντα· διασοβοῦντα, Hsch.

**διάρροια**, ἡ, *flowing through, diarrhoea*, Hp.*Aph.*3.21 (pl.), Ar. *Fr.*150, Th.2.49, Pl.*Ti.*85e (pl.), Arist.*HA*605a27; δ. κοιλίας Plu. *Mar.*30; δ. εἰς οὖρα *diabetes*, Gal.7.81.

**διαρροιζέω**, *to whizz through*, διερροίζησε στέρνων [ὁ ἰός] S.*Tr.* 568.

**διαρροῐζομαι**, *suffer from diarrhoea*, Dsc.4.88, Arr.*Epict.*4.10.11, Alex.Aphr.*Pr.*1.98.

**διαρροϊκός**, ή, όν, *suffering from diarrhoea*, Ruf.ap.Orib.7.26.6.

**διαρρομβέομαι**, *assume the figure of a rhombus*, Hero *Metr.*1.16.

**διάρρομβος**, ον, *rhomboid*, of a bandage, *Hippiatr.*74.

❋ **διάρρους**, ου, ὁ, *passage, channel*, D.S.13.47, Str.4.1.2, Sch.Il. *Oxy.*221 ii 7.

**διαρρύδαν** [ῠ], Dor. for -ρύδην, Adv. *flowing away, vanishing*, φόνος πέπηγεν οὐ δ. A.*Ch.*67 (lyr.).

**διαρρυθμίζω**, *adjust*, κανόνα *IG*1².373.70; *arrange in order*, Lxx 2*Ma.*7.22.

**διαρρυμβονάω**, *scatter, dissipate*, in aor. 1, Hsch.

**διαρρύομαι**, *deliver*, τινὰ ἐκ τοῦ δεσμωτηρίου Ph.1.95.

**διαρρυπτικός**, ή, όν, *cleansing*, φάρμακα Gal.11.744.

**διαρρύπτω**, *cleanse thoroughly*, τοὺς πόρους Gal.6.261; κηλῖδα Lib.*Decl.*33.31.

**διάρρῠσις**, εως, ἡ, = διάρρους, Hero *Spir.*1.1, al.

**διάρρῠτος**, ον, *intersected by streams*, Str.5.1.7, Epic. in *Arch.Pap.* 7.7; διαρρύτους· διηντλημένους, Hsch.

**διαρρωγή**, ἡ, *gap, interstice*, left in applying a bandage, Hp.*Art.* 35.

**διαρρώξ**, ῶγος, ὁ, ἡ, (διαρρήγνυμι) *rent asunder*, δ. κυμάτων σάλῳ ἀγμός a broken cliff *rent asunder* by the waves, E.*IT*262; πέτραι Opp.*H.*5.211. II. as Subst., *rent*, of the Straits of Messina, ib. 5.216.

**διάρσις**, εως, ἡ, *raising up*, ἱστίων D.S.3.40; ἡ ἐκ διάρσεως μάχη fight *with broadswords*, Plb.2.33.5. II. = διάρμα II, Longin.8.1.

**διαρτᾰβ-ία**, ἡ, *tax of two* ἀρτάβαι, *PTeb.*2p.178. ❋ -ος, ον, *paying two* ἀρτάβαι *of rent*, *POxy.*1031.12 (iii A.D.).

**διαρτάζω**, *speak fitly*, dub. l. in A.*Fr.*318 (fort. διάρτισον).

**διαρτᾰμέω**, strengthd. for ἀρταμέω, *cut limb-meal*, A.*Pr.*1023, Anaxandr.6; διαρταμῶντες (as if from -αρταμάω) [σώματα] κατὰ μέλη is cj. in Ph.2.564.

**διαρτ-άω**, *suspend*, Hsch., dub. l. for διαττᾶσθαι, Plb.34.9.10. 2. *keep in suspense, keep engaged*, τινί in or by.., D.H.1.46; *mislead, deceive*, Men.1006. II. *to separate*, διδύμους Ph.2.302, al., cf. Heliod. ap.Orib.44.10.5; τὴν δύναμιν ἀπὸ Συρακουσῶν Plu.*Tim.*25; διηρτημένα ἀπ' ἀλλήλων Str.5.3.7: c. gen., σῶμα τοῦ ὅλου διαρτηθέν Ph.2. 509; *dismember*, Plot.6.9.5; *interrupt*, τὰς ἀκολουθίας D.H.*Dem.* 40; διηρτημένων τῶν λέξεων *forced apart*, Id.*Comp.*20; διηρτημένων .. φωνῶν Demetr.Lac.1014.48 F.; διηρτῆσθαι, of argument, *to lack connexion, be incoherent*, διηρτημένα τινὰ καὶ ψευδῆ ib.46 F., cf. S.E. *P.*2.153. III. = καταρτίζω, Hsch. (Pass.). -ησις, εως, ἡ, *incoherence, irrelevance*, κατὰ διάρτησιν λόγος *a non-sequitur*, *Stoic.*2.79

(perh. Chrysipp.). -ίζω, *mould, form*, Lxx*Jb.*33.6; *speak fitly*, Hsch. -ισις, εως, ἡ, *moulding, shaping*, *EM*361.8, Suid.; *composition*, prob. l. for διάρτησις, Gal.15.102. -ισμός, ὁ, = foreg., Sm.*Ez.*4.12.

**διαρτύω**, *dress, prepare*: metaph., πλάσις εἰς τὴν τῶν πολεμίων ἀπάτην διηρτυμένη Eun.*Hist.*p.248 D.

**διαρύτω**, strengthd. for ἀρύτω, Hsch., *EM*270.3.

**Δίαρχοι**, οἱ, *the Hellenodicae*, Hsch.

**διάρχω**, *hold office to the end*, Lys.*Fr.*177 S., D.C.40.66: c. acc. cogn., στρατηγίαν τὴν οἴκοι Id.36.41.

**διαρωχμίας**· διαστάτεις, Hsch.; cf. διαρόγχαι.

**διασαικωνίζω**, v. διασαλακωνίζω.

**διασαίνω**, strengthd. for σαίνω, ταῖς οὐραῖς X.*Cyn.*4.3.

**διασαίρω**, pf. part. -σεσηρώς, *grin, sneer*, Plu.*Mar.*12.

⊛ **διασᾰλᾰκωνίζω**, strengthd. for σαλακωνίζω, Ar.*V.*1169; but perh. better διασαικωνίζω, cf. Id.*Fr.*849.

**διασάλ-ευσις** [σᾰ], εως, ἡ, *agitated motion*, Marcellin.*Puls.*500. ⊛-εύω, *shake violently*, Plb.1.48.2, Luc.*VH*2.5; of missiles, Plb.16.30.4; κλεῖθρα Corn.*ND*30. 2. *confuse*, τὰς ἁρμονίας, τοὺς ἤχους, D.H.*Comp.*22,23; *cause excitement in*, πόλιν Luc.*Alex.*31; διασεσαλευμένος τὸ βάδισμα *negligent, easy* in gait, Id.*Rh.Pr.*11; δ. τὸ βλέμμα, of an ogler, Id.*Merc.Cond.*35. II. intr., = σαλεύω II. 3, Arist.*Phgn.*809ᵇ32. 2. = σαλεύω II. 2, ἐπ' ἀγκυρῶν App.*BC*5.89.

**διασαρδᾰνόω**, = διαγελάω, *EM*273.46.

**διασαρκων-ίζω**, = foreg., Hsch. (also -σαρωνίζω); but -ισμα· ἀσελγές τι σχῆμα, Id.

**διασάτηρ**· διαπαίζειν (Lacon.), Hsch.

**διασάττω**, *stuff with* a thing, αἵματι καὶ σαρξίν Gal.1.32: pf. part. Pass. διασεσαγμένος Archig.ap.eund.8.931; δ. ὑπό, c. gen., *gorged with*.., Macho ap.Ath.6.244c: c. gen., *Gp.*19.9.5: c. dat., σκυβάλοις Ruf.ap.Orib.8.24.13.

**διασαυλόομαι**, strengthd. for σαυλόομαι, Ar.*Fr.*621.

⊛ **διασᾰφ-έω**, *make quite clear, show plainly*, ἐλπίδας οὔσας κενάς E.*Ph.*398; τι Pl.*Lg.*916e, Phld.*Lib.*p.13 O., etc.; δ. εἴτε.. εἴτε μή Pl.*Prt.*348b, cf. Phld.*Po.*5.13; also δ. περί τινος *make a clear statement about*.., Arist.*de An.*404ᵇ1; δ. εἰς Καρχηδόνα περί τινος *send clear information*.., Plb.3.87.4; δ. ὑπέρ τινος Id.2.19.13; *instruct plainly*, ἵνα.. Id.4.26.3, Lxx 2*Ma.*1.18; ὅπως *PEleph.*18.3 (iii B.C.):—Med., dub. in *PPar.*70 p.413:—Pass., Arist.*EN*1094ᵇ12, etc. -ηνίζω, *make clear*, X.*Mem.*3.1.11, *Ap.*1; τινὶ τὰ πεπραγμένα D.H.11.33, cf. Aët.13.15:—Pass., Hero *Bel.*98.6: -ηνέω, = foreg., dub. in Hp.*Ep.*12. -ησις, εως, ἡ, *explanation, interpretation*, Lxx*Ge.*40.8. -ητέον, *one must make quite clear*, Arist.*de An.*416ᵇ30; ὑπέρ τινος Thphr.*CP*6.14.5. ⊛ -ητικός, ή, όν, *affirmative*, σύνδεσμος A.D.*Conj.*221.23; *explanatory*, Sch.Ar.*Av.*825, *An.Ox.*1.188; *declaratory*, *EM*415.27. -ίζω, = διασαφέω, Lxx 2*Ma.*1.21.

⊛ **διά-σεισις**, εως, ἡ, *succussion*, of the spine, Gal.18(1).520. II. = διασεισμός, *PTeb.*41.30 (ii B.C.). -σεισμα, ατος, τό, *extortion*, *BGU*1138.11 (i B.C.). -σεισμός, ὁ, *abuse of power, extortion*, συκοφαντία καὶ δ. *PTaur.*1ᵛ1 (ii B.C.), cf. *PTeb.*43.36 (ii B.C.), *POxy.*1252ʳ33 (iii A.D.). -σειστος, ον, *shaken about*, ἀστράγαλοι Aeschin.1.59, cf. Men.423; κύβοι Poll.7.203. -σείω, *shake violently*, Hp.*Morb.*1.6, dub. in Arist.*Ath.*64.2; τι εἰς ἀταξίαν Pl.*Ti.*85e, cf. 88a; τὴν κεφαλήν Plu.2.435c: c. dat., δ. τοῖν χεροῖν Aeschin.*Socr.*50; δ. τῇ οὐρᾷ *to keep wagging* the tail, X.*Cyn.*6.15:—Med., *shake* people *off, shake oneself free*, D.H.1.56. 2. *confound, throw into confusion*, τὰ τῶν Ἀθηναίων φρονήματα Hdt.6.109; τοὺς ἀκούοντας Plb.18.45.2; *intimidate, oppress*, Id.10.26.4, cf. *OGI*519.14 (Pass.); *browbeat*, *PTaur.*1ᵛiii 13 (ii B.C.); *extort money by intimidation from* a person, *PPar.*15.37 (ii B.C.), *Ev.Luc.*3.14, etc.: c. gen., *PTeb.*41.10 (ii B.C.):—Pass., *POxy.*284.5 (i A.D.). 3. of political affairs, *throw into confusion*, Plu.*Cic.*10. 4. *stir up*, in Pass., Dam.*Pr.*29. 5. *sound, take the measure of*, Plu.2.580d, 704d.

**διασεύομαι**, *dart through*, used by Hom. only in 3 sg. Ep. aor. Pass. διέσσυτο, c. gen., τάφροιο δ. Il.10.194; αἰχμὴ δὲ στέρνοιο δ. 15.542; ἐκ μεγάροιο δ. Od.4.37: less freq. c. acc., δ. λαὸν Ἀχαιῶν Il.2.450: abs., αἰχμὴ δὲ δ. [μηροῦ or μηρόν] 5.661: later in part. διεσσύμενος Q.S.3.641: pf. διέσσυται Opp.*H.*2.259.

**διασήθω**, aor. -έσησα, *sift*, Hp.*VM*3, Dsc.5.75; prob. for διασείσας, Diocl.ap.Orib.8.41.3:—Pass., Aret.*CA*2.3.

**διασηκόω**, *weigh*, Suid. s.v. βαστάσας.

**διασημ-αίνω**, *mark out, point out clearly*, τι Hdt.5.86, X.*An.*2.1.23; τινί τι Id.*Oec.*12.11. 2. *indicate by a signal*, σάλπιγγι τὸν καιρὸν τῆς προσβολῆς Plb.10.12.4. II. Med., *note the bearings of*, τόπους Arist.*HA*549ᵇ17. 2. *approve*, D.S.19.15. 3. *signify*, Str.17.1.6, Plu.*Dem.*19. III. intr., *show its symptoms, appear*, Hp.*Aph.*6.41. -ᾰσία, ἡ, *method of marking*, Ptol.*Alm.*7.4, 8.3 (pl.). -ειόομαι, *cause to be placed on record*, *Inscr.Magn.*117.3 (ii A.D.). ⊛ -ος, ον, (σῆμα) *clear, distinct*: neut. pl. as Adv., διάσημα θροεῖ S.*Ph.*209 (lyr.). II. *conspicuous, eminent*, Hippias Soph.4 (Sup.), Plu.*Dio*54; δ. κράνος Id.*TG*17; γένει καὶ ἀξίᾳ *BMus.Inscr.*481*.15 (ii A.D.): esp. in Sup., διασημοτάτη πόλις *Epigr.Gr.*904 (Erythrae); διασημότατος, = Lat. *clarissimus*, *IG*3.635; = *perfectissimus*, δ. ἡγεμών *BGU*198.5 (ii A.D.), al., *Epigr.Gr.*1078.10 (Adana); ἐπίτροπος *Sammelb.*4421.5 (iii A.D.).

**διασήπω**, *cause to putrefy*, χρῶτα Str.15.1.37, cf. Dsc.2.173, Gal.18(2).455; τοῦ κακοῦ -σήψαντος τὰ οὖλα Ael.*NA*9.62:—freq. in Pass., with pf. διασέσηπα, *putrefy*, Thphr.*HP*5.7.5, Luc.*Luct.*18; διασαπεὶς τὸν πόδα Id.*Alex.*59.

**διασθενέω**, *to be exhausted*, of soil, *POxy.*1502ᵛ6 (iii A.D.).

⊛ **Δῑάσια**, τά, *the festival of Zeus* μειλίχιος, at Athens, Ar.*Nu.*408, Th.1.126, etc. [ᾰσ Ar. l. c., cf. Sch. ad v. 862.]

**διασίζω**, *kiss* or *whistle violently*, Aeschin.*Socr.*50.

**διασιλλ-αίνω**, *mock, jeer at*, c. acc., Luc.*Lex.*24; πράγματα καὶ δόγματα Iamb.*Protr.*21.λα'; τινὰ ἐπί τινι Alciphr.3.62. -όω, = foreg., *Com.Adesp.*978, D.C.59.25, 77.11.

**διασῑωπάω**, fut. -ήσομαι, *remain silent*, E.*Hel.*1551, X.*Mem.*3.6.4. 2. *pause* in reading, Gal.16.742, al. II. trans., *pass over in silence*, E.*Ion* 1566; also in Dor. fut., διασωπάσομαί οἱ μόρον Pi.*O.*13.91.

**διασκαίρω**, *bound through, dart along*, A.R.1.574.

**διασκᾰλεύω**, = sq., Plu.2.98e, Hsch. s. v. διαγλάψασ'.

**διασκάλλω**, *pick over*, τὸν ὄνθον Arist.*Fr.*354.

**διασκάλων**, v. διασκελίδα.

**διασκανδῑκίζω**, prop. *feed on chervil* (σκάνδιξ), Telecl.38: hence Com. for διευριπιδίζω, *to come Euripides over one* (his mother was said to be a λαχανόπωλις), Ar.*Eq.*19.

⊛ **διασκάπτω**, Dor. 3 pl. fut. -σκάψοντι *Tab.Heracl.*1.131:—*dig through*, ἰσθμόν Paus.2.1.5; δ. τὰ τείχη *make a breach in* them, Lys.13.14; ῥόως τῷ ὕδατι *make a breach* for water *in* the canals, *Tab.Heracl.* l. c., cf. Ph.*Bel.*98.27: also c. gen., τοῦ τείχους Plu.*Pyrrh.*33; *excavate*, τάφον Charito 8.7.

⊛ **διασκᾰρῑφάομαι**, *sketch in outline*: hence, *slur over*, τὰς εὐτυχίας ..διεσκαριφησάμεθα καὶ διελύσαμεν Isoc.7.12. II. Act., *scratch the ground*, of birds, Hsch.

**διασκᾰτόομαι**, Pass., *to be befouled* or *filthy*, ἄνανδρος καὶ διεσκατωμένη τρυφή, of the Epicureans, Diog.Sinop.1.

**διασκεδ-άζω**, = sq., Lxx *Ps.*32(33).10; *disperse* a tumour, Aët.15.15. -άννῡμι, Att. fut. -σκεδῶ S.*Ant.*287, Ar.*V.*229, etc.:—*scatter abroad, scatter to the winds*, δούρατα Od.5.370; τῷ κέ τοι ἀγλαΐας γε διασκεδάσειεν 17.244; γῆν ἐκείνων καὶ νόμους διασκεδῶν S. l. c.; τὰ νῦν ξύμφωνα δεξιώματα δόρει διασκεδῶσιν Id.*OC*620; διασκεδᾶτε τὸ προσὸν νῦν νέφος Anaxandr.58; of the wind, διεσκέδασεν αὐτὰ (sc. ναυάγια καὶ νεκρούς) πανταχῇ Th.1.54: metaph., *BGU*1253.12 (ii B.C.):—Pass., Eus.Mynd.63. 2. in Hdt., τὸν στρατὸν διεσκέδασε *disbanded* it, 1.77, cf. 79:—Pass., 1.63, 5.15, Th.3.98, D.C.47.38; δ. κατ' ἑωυτοὺς ἕκαστοι Hdt.8.57 (but also of an enemy, *scatter*, 8.68.β'). 3. *disperse* the soul, when it leaves the body, Pl.*Phd.*77e, cf. 70a, 78b. 4. in Pass., of reports, *to be spread abroad*, Hdn.7.6.9. 5. *reject*, βουλήν Lxx 3*Ki.*12.24. -ᾰσις, εως, ἡ, *scattering*, Thd.*Is.*24.19. -ασμός, ὁ, *scattering*, Hsch. s. v. Φαραδ. -αστής, οῦ, ὁ, *scatterer*, as Adj., *extravagant, reckless*, τρόπος Ph.1.89. -αστικός, ή, όν, *fitted for dispersing* or *digesting*, ἀρχομένης ὑποχύσεως Dsc.3.80, cf. 5.115.

**διασκελίδα**· σπυρίδα ἣν ἔνιοι **διασκάλων**, Hsch.

**διασκελίζομαι**, in pf. part. Pass., *having the legs parted*, σῶμα διεσκελισμένον *PMag.Par.*1.2309; δ. καθῆσθαι Eust.1038.10, cf. *EM*502.39.

**διάσκεμμα**, ατος, τό, *observation*, Gal.1.293 (pl.).

**διασκεπάζω**, *screen, hide*, αὐγήν D.C.60.26.

**διασκεπ-τέον**, *one must consider*, Pl.*Lg.*859b, Arist.*Pol.*1324ᵃ3, etc. -τικός, ή, όν, *cautious, considerate*, Poll.1.178. -τομαι, = διασκοπέω, Luc.*Vit.Auct.*27, *VH*2.18.

⊛ **διασκευ-άζω**, *get ready, set in order*, τι Plb.15.27.9:—Pass., *PTeb.*24.32 (ii B.C.). II. *equip*, τινὰ βασιλικῶς Luc.*Nec.*16:—Pass., εἰς Σατύρους διεσκευασμένοι *dressed* as.., Plu.*Ant.*24; ὅπλοις Aen.Tact.26.1:—Med., *prepare for oneself, provide*, τἆλλα ὡς ἐς πλοῦν Th.4.38; *arm, equip* or *prepare oneself*, ὡς εἰς μάχην X.*HG*4.2.19; διεσκευάσθαι πρὸς τὸν δῆμον Din.1.70; διασκευάσασθαι πρὸς τοὺς δικαστάς *prepare all one's tricks* for a trial, X.*Ath.*3.7. III. Med., διασκευασάμενος τὴν οὐσίαν *having disposed of one's* property, D.29.3. IV. *revise* or *edit* a work *for publication*, Aristeas 311, D.S.1.5. 2. *compile*, ἐκ πολλῶν [βιβλίων Gal.15.10. 3. *elaborate* with rhetorical devices, αἰτία μὲν κατασκευάζει, τρόπος δὲ δ. Hermog.*Inv.*2.7. -ασμα, gloss on διάγματα, Hsch. ⊛ -αστής, οῦ, ὁ, *reviser, editor* of a poem, Sch.Il.6.441. -αστικός, ή, όν, *descriptive of dress*, σχῆμα Eust.169.31. -ή, ἡ, *construction*, Aristeas 64, al. II. *equipment*, δ. νομαδική Plb.8.29.7; δ. πολεμική D.S.4.38; *furniture* or *vessels*, τῆς σκηνῆς Lxx*Ex.*31.7, cf. Plb.30.26.3, Agatharch.8 (pl.). III. *rhetorical elaboration* of a topic, Hermog.*Inv.*3.15; ποιεῖσθαι τὰς δ. τῶν μύθων Jul.*Or.*7.205b. 2. διασκευαί *set phrases*, Plb.15.34.1. IV. *new edition* or *recension* of a work, Aristeas 310, Ath.3.110b (pl.). V. = ἀνασκευή, δ. καὶ χλευασμὸς τοῦ διδασκαλείου Porph.*VP*53. VI. *theatrical performance*, κωμῳδίαι καὶ δ. D.Chr.32.94. -ωρέω, *revise, rehandle*, τι Pl.*Ep.*316a:—Med., *set in order*, τὴν πόλιν Id.*R.*540e.

**διάσκεψις**, εως, ἡ, *inspection, examination*, περί τινος Pl.*Lg.*697c, Luc.*Anach.*21, Posidon.ap.Gal.5.469, cf. Lyd.*Mag.*1.45: in pl., *questions for decision*, Plu.*Tim.*38.

**διασκέω**, *deck out*, in Pass., διησκημένοι τὰς κόμας χρυσῷ Phylarch.62. II. *train*, τινὰ Luc.*Vit.Auct.*9:—Pass., Id.*Peregr.*17. III. *practise*, ῥητορικά D.L.4.49.

⊛ **διασκην-έω**, *separate and retire each to his billet* (σκηναί), *take up one's quarters*, διασκηνῆσαι κατὰ τὰς κώμας X.*An.*4.4.8: abs., *go into billets*, ib.4.5.29, *Lac.*5.3. II. *leave* another's *tent*, διασκηνούντων μετὰ δεῖπνον Id.*Cyr.*3.1.38, dub. in Id.*HG*4.8.18. III. Act., *shade*, Lyd.*Mag.*3.70. -ητέον, *one must take up one's quarters*, εἰς στέγας X.*An.*4.4.14.

**διασκηνίπτω,** *crush, destroy,* ὤεα Nic.*Th.*193.

**διασκηνόω,** *pitch like tents at intervals,* καπηλεῖα Ael.*VH*3.14 (Pass.). II. intr., = διασκηνέω I, X.*An.*4.4.10.

**διασκηρίπτω,** *prop on each side, prop up, AP*6.203 (Laco or Phil.).

**διασκίδνημι,** poet. for -σκεδάννυμι, Il.5.526, Hes.*Th.*875, Emp. 84.4, Hdt.2.25:—Pass., Luc.*DDeor.*20.5, *Sacr.*13.

**διασκιρτάω,** *leap about,* Lxx *Wi.*19.9, Plu.*Eum.*11, Philostr.Jun. *Im.*10.

⊛ **διασκοπέω** (cf. διασκέπτομαι), fut. διασκέψομαι: aor. διεσκεψάμην: pf. διέσκεμμαι Ar.*Ra.*836, but διεσκέφθαι in pass. sense, Id.*Th.*687:—*look at in different ways, examine* or *consider well,* Hdt.3.38, E.*Cyc.* 557, etc.; ἑξῆς δ. τὸν λόγον Pl.*R.*350e, cf. *Tht.*168e; also δ. πρὸς ἑαυτόν Id.*Chrm.*160e; περὶ σφᾶς αὐτούς, περί τινος, Th.7.71, Pl.*Phd.* 61e; δ. περί τινος εἰ.. Arist.*Pol.*1272$^a$26: c. gen., τῆς ἑαυτῶν ἀσφαλείας D.C.58.7:—Med., πρὸς τὰ ἔξω διασκοπεῖσθαι Th.6.59: impf., Pl.*Plt.*259c. II. abs., *look round one, keep watching,* μὴ δρῶνται X.*Cyn.*9.3.

**διασκοπιάομαι,** *watch as from a* σκοπιά: hence, *spy out,* σε.. προέηκε διασκοπιᾶσθαι ἕκαστα, of Dolon, Il.10.388; *discern, distinguish,* ἀργαλέον..διασκοπιᾶσθαι ἕκαστον 17.252.

⊛ **διασκορπ-ίζω,** *scatter abroad,* Lxx *Ge.*49.7 (v.l.), al.:—Pass., *Ev. Jo.*11.52, Plb.1.47.5, *BGU*1049.7 (iv A.D.); *squander,* οὐσίαν *Ev. Luc.*15.13; *confound,* ib.1.51; *winnow,* συνάγων ὅθεν οὐ διεσκόρπισας *Ev.Matt.*25.24. **-ῐσις,** εως, ἡ, *scattering abroad,* Zos.Alch.p.178 B. **-ισμός,** ὁ, *scattering, dispersal,* Lxx *Ez.*6.8, al.; *confusion,* τῆς φορολογίας *PTeb.*24.55 (ii B.C.). **-ιστικός,** ή, όν, *dissipative,* of waste-products, Antyll.ap.Orib.6.21.30.

**διασκώπτω,** *jest upon,* τινά dub. l. in Plu.2.82b; δεῖπνα Ath.2. 55d:—Med., *jest one with another, bandy jests,* X.*Cyr.*8.4.23.

**δίασμα,** ατος, τό, (διάζομαι) *warp,* διάσματα, φάρεος ἀρχήν Call.*Fr.* 244, cf. Lxx *Jd.*16.13, *Ostr.*1155, Nonn.*D.*6.151.

**διασμάω,** *wipe* or *rinse out,* ποτήρια Hdt.2.37.

**διασμήχω,** *rub well,* ψυχὴ πρὸς ὀξυωπίαν ἑαυτὴν διασμήξασα Hierocl. *in CA*21 p.467 M.:—Pass., ἅλσιν διασμηχθεὶς ὄναιτ' ἂν οὑτοσί Ar.*Nu.* 1237: pf. διέσμηκται Plu.2.693d. 2. *rub off,* λύματα τρυφαλείης Nonn.*D.*30.92.

**διασμῑλεύω,** *polish off with the chisel*: metaph., δ. βίβλους *AP*15. 38 (Cometas); διεσμιλευμέναι φροντίδες *refined, subtle* theories, Alex. 221.8. Adv. διεσμιλευμένως Poll.6.150, Hsch.

**διάσμυρνον,** τό, name for various *eyesalves,* Gal.12.257,806; for a *plaster,* Asclep.ap.eund.13.967.

**διασμύχομαι** [ῡ], *smoulder,* πῦρ διασμυχόμενον Ph.2.143.

**διασοβ-έω,** *scare away,* Plu.2.133a; διασεσόβηται ὁ γάμος Hld.7. 26. II. *agitate, excite,* Alciphr.*Fr.*5, Agath.3.11:—Pass., *to be excited, puffed up,* Plu.2.32d. **-ησις,** εως, ἡ, *trepidation,* M.Ant. 11.22.

**διασοφίζομαι,** *quibble like a sophist,* Ar.*Av.*1619.

**διάσοφος,** ον, *very wise,* dub. l. in *Lyr.Adesp.*135.

⊛ **διασπᾰθ-άω,** *squander away,* Plu.*Cic.*27. II. Med., *plunder, rob, POxy.*71 ii 12 (iv A.D.). **-ίζω,** = foreg. 1, Lyd.*Mag.*2.19:—Pass., ib.1.36.

**διασπᾰρ-ακτός,** ή, όν, *torn to pieces,* E.*Ba.*1220, Ael.*NA*12. 7. ⊛ **-άσσω,** Att. **-ττω,** *rend in pieces,* A.*Pers.*195:—Pass., Eub. 15.3. 2. metaph., δ. τινὰ τῷ λόγῳ Luc.*Icar.*21. II. *dilate forcibly,* Sor.2.59.

⊛ **διά-σπᾰσις,** εως, ἡ, *tearing asunder, forcible separation,* Arist.*Cael.* 313$^b$20, *Mete.*372$^b$19, Thphr.*Lass.*18, cj. in Epicur.*Ep.*2 p.44 U. II. *gap,* Plu.2.721a. **-σπασμα,** ατος, τό, = foreg. II, Id.*Aem.*20, Polyaen.4.3.17. **-σπασμός,** ὁ, *tearing in pieces,* Lxx *Je.*15.3, Phld.*Piet.*96. II. *interruption, interval,* in pl., Plu.2.129b, etc.; παντελὴς δ. complete *severance,* Dam.*Pr.*74: metaph., *distraction,* τῆς ψυχῆς Phld.*Ir.*p.29 W. **-σπαστέον,** *one must break up,* Arist. *PA*642$^b$17. ⊛ **-σπαστος,** ον, *incoherent, disconnected,* ἐπιστολαί Alciphr.2.2. ⊛ **-σπάω,** fut. -σπάσομαι [ᾰ] Ar.*Ra.*477, *Ec.*1076, also -σπάσω Hdt.7.236: aor. -έσπᾰσα, Med. -εσπασάμην E.*Hec.*1126, *Ba.*339, Plu.*Caes.*68: pf. -έσπᾰκα Sch.Th.*Oxy.*853 i 15:—**Pass.,** aor. -εσπάσθην: pf. -έσπασμαι (v. infr.):—*tear asunder,* τοὺς ἄνδρας κρεοργηδὸν δ. Hdt.3.13, cf. E. and Ar. ll. cc., etc.; ἐμὲ καὶ τὸν ἄνδρα δ. X.*Cyr.*6.1.45; δ. τὸ σταύρωμα *to break through* or *tear down* the palisade, Id.*HG*4.4.10; δ. τὴν γέφυραν, τὸ ἔδαφος, Plb.6.55.1, Plu. *Cam.*5; *break up, SIG*364.10 (Ephesus, iii B.C.): metaph., διασπᾶν τὴν σύμπνοιαν τοῦ παντός Iamb.*Protr.*21.λ':—Pass., διέσπασται μελέων φύσις Emp.63; τὸ Ἀττικὸν [ἔθνος]..διεσπασμένον ὑπὸ Πεισιστράτου Hdt.1.59; μόνον οὐ διεσπάσθην D.5.5; δ. ἀπὸ τῶν φίλων *to be torn away* from.., Arist.*Rh.*1386$^a$10. 2. in military sense, *separate* part of an army from the rest, X.*Cyr.*5.4.19; of army and fleet, Hdt.7.236; δ. τὰς φάλαγγας *break* them *up,* Arist.*Pol.*1303$^b$13:—Pass., στράτευμα διεσπασμένον an army *scattered and in disorder,* Th.6.98, cf. 7.44; of a fleet, Id.8.104; τῷ διεσπάσθαι τὰς δυνάμεις *to be widely scattered,* X.*An.*1.5.9. 3. metaph., *pull different ways,* πόλεις *distract* states, Pl.*Lg.*875a; τὰς πολιτείας D.4.48; τοὺς νόμους X.*Cyr.*8.5.25; διέσπακε τὴν ἱστορίαν *has broken the continuity of* the narrative, Sch.Th. l. c.:—Pass., διασπώμενος *distracted,* πρὸς τοσαύτας ὑπηρεσίας Luc.*DDeor.*24.1; ὑπὸ τῶν λόγων Id.*Icar.*23.

⊛ **διασπείρω,** aor. 2 Pass. -εσπάρην [ᾰ] S.*El.*748, etc.:—*scatter* or *spread about,* [τὰς μνέας].. αὐτοχειρίῃ διέσπειρε τῇ στρατιῇ Hdt.3. 13; διέσπειρε ἡμέας ἄλλην ἄλλῃ τάξας *dispersed* us, ib.68; δ. λόγον X.*HG*5.1.25; τοὔνομα εἰς τὴν Ἀσίαν Isoc.5.104; *squander,* S.*El.* 1291:—Pass., *to be scattered,* κρατὸς διασπαρέντος αἵματός θ' ὁμοῦ Id. *Tr.*782; πῶλοι διεσπάρησαν ἐς μέσον δρόμον Id.*El.*748; of troops, διεσπαρμένοι Th.1.11, X.*HG*5.3.1, etc.; φύσεις ὁμοίως διεσπαρμέναι equally *distributed,* Pl.*R.*455d, cf. *Sph.*260b, etc.; ἡ ψυχὴ διασπείρεται *is dissipated,* Epicur.*Ep.*1 p.21 U.; τὸ διεσπαρμένον δόγμα the *current* opinion, Id.*Nat.*14.7; τῶν χρωμάτων διεσπαρμένων Ael.*NA* 11.21.

**διασπεύδω,** *work zealously,* Plb.4.33.9:—Med., Is.*Fr.*56 S.; of political factions, D.C.*Fr.*83.5, cf. 52.7. II. *incite,* c. acc. et inf., Plb.*Fr.*126.

**διάσπῐλος,** ον, *all rocky, Peripl.M.Rubr.*43.

**διασπλεκόω,** strengthd. for σπλεκόω, Ar.*Pl.*1082.

**διασποδέω,** sens. obsc., = Lat. *subigitare,* Ar.*Ec.*939, cf. Hsch. s.v. διεσποδημένη; διεσποδήσατο· διέσεισε, διετίναξε, Id.

**διασπορ-ά,** ἡ, (διασπείρω) *scattering, dispersion,* Plu.2.1105a, Lxx *Je.*15.7; δ. ψυχική Ph.2.426. 2. collectively, = οἱ διεσπαρμένοι, Lxx *De.*28.25, *Ev.Jo.*7.35: pl., Lxx *Ps.*146(147).2. **-εύς,** έως, ὁ, *disperser,* Poll.3.129.

**διασπουδάζω,** *do zealously*:—and Pass., *to be anxiously done* or *looked to,* τί μάλιστα ἐν ἅπασι διεσπούδασται τοῖς νόμοις; D.20.157, cf. 23.78: c. inf., δ. μὴ λαβεῖν ὑμᾶς ib.182; διεσπούδαστο ἐλθεῖν J.*AJ* 15.8.1; διεσπουδάζετο abs., Arr.*An.*7.22.8. 2. *to be zealous,* περί τι D.H.*Lys.*14. II. *employ electoral corruption,* D.C.36.38: in fut. Med., Id.52.20.

**διασσάω,** v. διαττάω.

**διᾴσσω,** Att. **διᾴττω,** v. sub διαΐσσω.

**διαστᾰδόν,** Adv. *standing apart,* A.R.2.67; δ. ἀλλήλῃσι *apart from..,* Id.4.942, cf. Opp.*H.*1.502.

**διαστάζω,** *leak, Gp.*7.8.4; *pour off,* ἱδρὼς δ. μετώπων Nonn.*D.*37. 463. 2. trans., *pour,* ποτὸν κυπέλλῳ ib.44.136.

**διασταθμ-άομαι,** *separate,* αἰνῶ δ' ὃς βίοτον ἐκ πεφυρμένου θεῶν διεσταθμήσατο E.*Supp.*202:—Act. -σταθμῆσαι· διελεῖν, Hsch. **-ησις,** εως, ἡ, *standard,* κατὰ τὴν δ. Phld.*D.*3 *Fr.*89. **-ίζω,** = διασταθμάομαι, Sm.*Is.*33.18.

**διαστᾰλάσσω,** *shed,* δάκρυον Lib.*Descr.*30.16.

**διάσταλ-μα,** ατος, τό, *ordinance, regulation, BGU*913.9 (iii A.D.). ⊛**-μός,** ὁ, *assessment for taxation, PLond.*5.1686.17 (vi A.D.). **-σις,** εως, ἡ, *arrangement, compact,* Lxx 2 *Ma.*13.25. II. = διαστολή, perh. to be read in Gal.8.736 for διάστασις. **-τέον,** *one must distinguish,* Plot.1.3.1, Nicom.*Ar.*2.18, Sch.Il.2.3. ⊛ **-τικός,** ή, όν, *serving to distinguish,* προσώπων A.D.*Adv.*185.10, cf. D.L.4.33, Eust. 1610.3; *antithetic,* A.D.*Pron.*24.12. Adv. -κῶς ib.49.24, Eust.72. 31. II. of Music, *exciting, exalting,* Aristid.Quint.1.12, Cleonid. *Harm.*13.

**διαστᾰσιάζω,** *form into separate factions,* πάντας Arist.*Pol.*1303$^b$ 26; τοὺς ἐποίκους..πρὸς τοὺς εὐπόρους ib.1306$^a$3; τὸ πλῆθος, τὴν πόλιν, J.*BJ*1.11.5, Plu.*Cam.*36; *set at variance,* σῶμα καὶ ψυχήν J. *BJ*3.8.5. II. *to be at variance,* πρὸς σφᾶς, πρὸς ἀλλήλους, Plb. 1.82.4, etc.; τινί D.C.54.17; τοῖς ἀληθέσι Iamb.*Myst.*9.4: abs., ib. 4.9.

⊛ **διά-στᾰσις,** εως, ἡ, (διΐστημι) *parting, separation* (opp. ἕνωσις, Dam.*Pr.*273), ὀρέων Hdt.7.129; ὀστέων Hp.*Art.*20, cf. Gal.19.461; φάραγγες καὶ δ. τῆς γῆς *fissures,* Arist.*Mete.*350$^b$36; *breach* in a barrier, Ph.*Bel.*98.31; *opening,* τῆς γέννος Aret.*CD*1.3. b. κεφαλῆς δ. *splitting headache,* ibid. (pl.), v.l. in Pl.*R.*407c. c. *distension,* Arist.*PA*681$^b$24; φλεβῶν Aret.*SA*2.2. d. δ. κενεή *retching,* ib. 2.7. e. = διαστολή, of the pulse, Zeno ap.Gal.8.736. f. *expansion* of air, opp. πίλησις, Ph.*Bel.*77.23. 2. *setting at variance,* τοὺς νέους ἐς τοὺς πρεσβυτέρους Th.6.18, cf. Plu.*Cor.*16; *cause of breach,* Arist.*Pol.*1303$^b$15. b. *contrasting,* Pl.*R.*360e. 3. *difference, contrast,* Arist.*Cael.*312$^a$13. 4. *disagreement,* δ. ἢ στάσις Pl. *Lg.*744d, cf. Arist.*Pol.*1296$^a$8, 1300$^b$37. 5. *divorce,* Plu.*Aem.*5, etc. II. Gramm., of vowels, διαίρεσις κατὰ διάστασιν (as in πάϊς) A.D.*Pron.*87.4. b. τὰ κατὰ δ. forms *written as two words,* e.g. ἐμέθεν αὐτῆς ib.114.11. III. *interval,* Pl.*Ti.*36a, etc.; in Music, Aristox.*Harm.*p.4 M., al.; of space, *extension,* Arist.*Top.*142$^b$5, al.; *dimension,* τὰς αὐτὰς διαστάσεις εἰς βάθος εἰληφός Epicur.*Nat.*2.7, cf. Gal.11.503, S.E.*M.*3.19; ἡ δ. ἡ τριχῇ *tridimensionality,* Plot.1.2.6, cf. 6.6.17, Porph.*Sent.*35, Dam.*Pr.*375. IV. = διακόσμησις, Antipho Soph.23. (Freq. confused with διάτασις, wh. shd. perh. be read in I. 1. b, c, d.) **-στάτης,** gloss on δίοπος, Hsch. ⊛ **-στᾰτικός,** ή, όν, *disintegrating,* Ti.Locr.100e, Plu.2.952b; τινός Corn.*ND* 21. 2. *causing discord,* λόγοι Plu.*Pomp.*53, cf. Ph.*Fr.*101 H. 3. Adv. -κῶς *separately,* of vowels, -ώτερόν φαμεν τὸ γρηύς A.D.*Adv.* 150.7; *in extension,* v.l. for διαστατῶς, Porph.*Sent.*2. **-στᾰτός,** όν, also ή, όν Lyd.*Mens.*4.76:—*torn by faction,* πόλις Men.515. II. *having extension* or *dimension,* σῶμα δ. τριχῇ Apollodor.*Stoic.*3.259, cf. Ph.1.8, etc.; opp. ἀμερής, Procl.*Inst.*176; τὸ πάντῃ δ. Plu.2. 1023b; δ. πράγματα Dam.*Pr.*375. Adv. -τῶς *dimensionally* or *in extension,* Porph.*Sent.*33, Syrian. *in Metaph.*85.14; opp. νοερῶς, Procl. *in Cra.*p.55 P.

**διασταυρόω,** *cut off and fortify with a palisade,* D.C.41.50:—Med., διασταυρώσασθαι τὸν ἰσθμόν *to have* it *fortified,* Th.6.97.

**διαστείβω,** *go through, across,* ἐπ' οἶδμα ναῒ θοᾷ Pi.*Fr.*221.4. II. *trample on,* τινά Nonn.*D.*36.239.

**διαστείχω,** aor. -έστῐχον (v. infr.), *go through* or *across,* πόλιν, γύαλα, E.*Andr.*1090, 1092. 2. c. gen., δ. πλούτου *walk in ways* of wealth, Pi.*I.*3.17. 3. *go one's way,* ἀνεγρομένη γε διέστιχε Theoc. 27.69; *walk, AP*12.85 (Mel.), Coluth.215.

⊛ **διαστέλλω,** *put asunder, expand, separate,* συνεσταλμένα δ. Hp.

Off.11; τὸν ἀέρα ταῖς πτέρυξιν Arist.*IA*713a12; τινὰς ξίφει J.*BJ*5.2.2; δ. τι ταῖς ὄνυξι *to tear* it *open*, Plu.*Thes*.36:—Pass., *to be dilated*, of the lungs or heart, Arist.*Aud*.800b2, Gal.2.657,al.; διασταλέντα τὰ ὑγρὰ *being dispersed*, Arist.*Pr*.891a2; διασταλήτω πᾶσα σκοτία *let* all darkness *be dispelled*, *PMag.Par*.1.2472. 2. *divide*, δίχα Pl.*Plt*.265e; *distinguish*, τοὺς Τρῶας τῶν Δαρδάνων Sch.Il.*Oxy*.1086.115; τῷ τόνῳ *POxy*.1012*Fr*.16.5 (Pass.). b. *define precisely*, τὰ λεγόμενα Pl.*Euthd*.295d, cf. Arist.*Top*.134b22, Phld.*Rh*.1.50S.; intr., ὅρασις διαστέλλουσα *distinct* vision, Lxx 1*Ki*.3.1; also, *to be distinctive*, opp. ἀπόλυτον εἶναι, A.D.*Pron*.39.1:—Med., δ. περί τινος Arist.*Pol*.1268b32, Phld.*D*.3*Fr*.8: c. acc., Pl.*R*.535b:—Pass., διεσταλμένος *definite, determinate*, A.D.*Synt*.37.7,al. 3. *command expressly, give express orders*, ῥητῶς ὑπέρ τινος Plb.3.23.5; ἐπιτακτικῶς δ. περί τινων D.S.28.15:—Med., Lxx *Jd*.1.19,al., *PHal*.7.6 (iii B.C.), *Ev.Marc*.5.43, etc. 4. *pronounce*, χείλεσι Lxx *Le*.5.4. 5. *give orders in writing*, *UPZ*111.6 (ii B.C.):—more freq. in Med., ib.11.23 (ii B.C.),al. 6. *pay, render*, esp. in kind, *POxy*.88.5 (ii A.D.),al.; *make an order for payment*, *Ostr*.1164 (ii/iii A.D.); *discharge* a vow, Lxx *Le*.22.21. 7. *set apart*, τινὰ ἑαυτῷ ib.3*Ki*.8.53; τὴν ἱερὰν γῆν *PRev.Laws*36.7 (iii B.C.), cf. *PTeb*.74.2 (ii B.C.). II. intr., *differ*, πρός τινα Plb.18.47.11.

⊛ **διάστεμα**, = διάστημα, *PRyl*.207a27 (ii A.D.).

**διάστενος**, ον, *very narrow*, Gal.19.444.

**διάστερος**, ον, *starred, jewelled*, δ. λίθοις Luc.*Am*.41.

⊛ **διάστημα**, ατος, τό, (διαστῆναι) *interval*, freq. in Music, Archyt.2, Pl.*R*.531a, Aristox.*Harm*.p.4M., al., Arist.*Pr*.922b6, Damox.2.57; of Time, δ. τετραετές Plb.9.1.1: generally, ἐκ μεγάλων δ. κινεῖσθαι Democr.191; δ. μεταξὺ κόσμων Epicur.*Ep*.2p.37U.; *distance*, Phld.*D*.3.8,9. b. Geom., *radius*, κέντρῳ τῷ Α, διαστήματι τῷ ΑΒ, γεγράφθω κύκλος Euc.1.1, cf. Ph.*Bel*.52.14; of a sphere, Autol.6. c. *aperture*, ἀγγεῖον ἔχον δ. μέγα Arist.*GA*787b4; ἐκ πολλοῦ δ. Id.*Aud*.800a36; τὰ δ. τῆς χειρὸς τῶν δακτύλων *the spaces* between the fingers, Aen.Tact.31.35. 2. Medic., *diastasis*, of bones, Hp.*Off*.23 (pl.), cf. Gal.18(2).887. 3. *difference*, τῶν ἡδονῶν μεγάλα τὰ δ. Nicom.Com.1.22. 4. *ratio*, Archyt.2, Arist.*Ph*.202a18. 5. in Aristotle's symbolism, *conjunction of two terms*, *APr*.42b10, *APo*.82b7, al. 6. *extension, dimension*, χρόνος κινήσεως δ. Zeno *Stoic*.1.26, cf. Chrysipp.ib.2.164, Dam.*Pr*.389; of Space, Arist.*Ph*.209a4, Plot.6.4.2; ὧν πρότερον διάστημα ἐνειστήκει whose *extension* (i.e. *surface*) it (the εἴδωλον) formerly occupied, Epicur.*Nat*.2.3. II. *distinction* of style, Longin.40.2.

**διαστηματικός**, ή, όν, *proceeding by intervals*, of musical progressions, δ. κίνησις Archyt.1, Aristox.*Harm*.p.9M., etc.; of Time, *measured by intervals*, Porph.*Sent*.44. II. *indicating distance*, of the pronoun ἐκεῖνος, A.D.*Pron*.57.10. III. *dimensional*, opp. ἀδιάστατος, φύσις Ph.2.184, cf. Dam.*Pr*.110; δ. φαντασία *spatial* representation, Procl.*in R*.2.249K. IV. Adv. -κῶς, = διαστατικῶς, Simp.*in Epict*.p.5D., Procl.*in Prm*.p.663S., Syrian.*in Metaph*.24.22; τοπικῶς καὶ δ. Procl.*in Ti*.2.10D.

**διαστήρ**, ῆρος, ὁ, dub. sens. in *PLond*.3.1164.9 (iii A.D.).

**διαστηρίζω**, *make firm, strengthen*, *AP*6.203 (Laco or Phil.):—Pass., *prop oneself up, secure one's footing*, Hp.*Ep*.17. II. *fix firmly*, Nonn.*D*.2.659, 36.369.

⊛ **διάστησις**, εως, ἡ, = διάστασις, τοῖν ποδοῖν Hld.3.13.

**Διαστί**, *in the language of Zeus*, prob. in D.Chr.11.23.

**δια-στιγμή**, ἡ, *punctuation*, Gloss. ⊛ **-στίζω**, *distinguish by a mark, punctuate*, [οὐ] ῥᾴδιον διαστίξαι τὰ Ἡρακλείτου Arist.*Rh*.1407b13: generally, *distinguish*, Stob.2.7.3c. 2. *spot, mottle*, Nonn.*D*.28.130. 3. *brand*, Just.*Nov*.115.4. **-στικτέον**, *one must punctuate*, Sch.S.*El*.878. **-στίκτης**, ου, ὁ, *one who punctuates*, Gloss.

**διαστίλβω**, *gleam*, Ar.*Pax*567, Nonn.*D*.42.420; *gleam through*, Ar.*Fr*.8, *AP*5.47 (Rufin.), Plu.2.497e.

⊛ **διάστιξις**, εως, ἡ, *branding*, Just.*Nov*.115.4.

**διαστοιβάζω**, *stuff in between*, Hdt.1.179.

**διαστοιχίζομαι**, Med., *arrange for oneself regularly, regulate exactly*, ἀρχήν A.*Pr*.232.

⊛ **διαστολ-εύς**, έως, ὁ, *instrument for examining cavities, dilator*, Gal.19.110, Paul.Aeg.6.78; for opening a horse's mouth, *Hippiatr*.2. II. *cashier*, title of official, *BGU*1064.19 (iii A.D.), *Cod.Just*.10.71.4. ⊛ **-ή**, ἡ, (διαστέλλω) *drawing asunder, dilatation*, of the lungs, Arist.*Aud*.800a35; of the heart, Gal.2.597; of the pulse, Id.8.736, al.; δ. χειλέων *parting* of the lips, i.e. *utterance*, Lxx *Nu*.30.7. b. *separation*, Thphr.*CP*3.16.3; *notch* or *nick*, Plu.*Cic*.1; *boundary, fence*, *Tab.Heracl*.2.46; *fencing off*, τῆς γῆς *PAmh*.2.40.25 (ii B.C.). 2. *distinction*, Chrysipp.*Stoic*.2.158, Lxx *Ex*.8.23, Epicur.*Nat*.28.7, Phld.*Piet*.123, *Ep.Rom*.3.22; ἁγίων καὶ βεβήλων Ph.2.159; μετὰ διαστολῆς προενεχθέντα with *discrimination*, Demetr.Lac.1014.48F.; *detailed statement* or *explanation*, Plb.1.15.6; ἀξίους μνήμης καὶ δ. Id.16.14.2, cf. *SIG*284.11 (Chios), Apollon.Cit.3; *specification* of items in an account, *PRyl*.65.17 (i B.C.); *article* in a contract, etc., *PTheb.Bank*6.8, 7.7. 3. *command, injunction, order*, Lxx *Nu*.19.2, al., *PTeb*.24.45 (ii B.C.), etc. 4. *payment*, *BGU*485.26, *PTeb*.363.1 (ii A.D.). II. Gramm., *comma* (as in ὅ, τι), D.T.629. b. *distinction*, γενῶν A.D.*Pron*.11.28, al. c. *opposition*, πρός τι ib.41.24. 2. in Music, *distinctness*, of notes, 1*Ep.Cor*.14.7. **-ικόν**, τό, *official notification of payment due, writ*, *POxy*.68.33 (ii A.D.), al.; in full, δ. ὑπόμνημα *BGU*513.18. **-ιον**, τό, = διαστολεύς I, *Hippiatr*.16. **-ον**, τό, in pl., *dispositions of a deed*, *PLond*.1727.58 (vi A.D.).

**διαστομᾰλίζομαι**· λοιδορέω, in impf., Hsch.

**διαστόμ-ωσις**, εως, ἡ, *expansion*, Alex.Aphr.*Pr*.1.93. **-ωτρίς** (with or without μήλη), εως, ἡ, = διαστολεύς I, Hp.ap.Gal.19.122,92.

**διαστοχάζομαι**, *guess*, Hsch. s. v. διατεκμαίρομαι.

**διάστρα**, ἡ, (διάζω) *warp set up in a loom*, *Gloss*.

**διαστράπτω**, *glance like lightning*, Lxx *Wi*.16.22.

**διαστρᾰτεύομαι**, Med., *serve through one's campaigns*: διαστρατευσάμενος *a veteran*, D.C.58.18.

**διαστρᾰτηγέω**, *assume the position of general*, Plu.*Phoc*.25, *Aem*.13, al. II. trans., *to out-general*, τοὺς Ῥωμαίους Plb.21.39.9; τοὺς βαρβάρους Dion.Byz.53. 2. δ. τι *practise stratagems*, Plb.16.37.1. 3. δ. πόλεμον *conduct* a war *to its close*, Plu.*Sull*.23; δ. τὰν ἀρχάν Polus ap.Stob.3.9.51. 4. at Rome, *come to the end of one's praetorship*, D.C.54.33.

**διαστρεβλόω**, strengthd. for στρεβλόω, Aeschin.3.224.

**διάστρεμμα**, ατος, τό, *wrench, dislocation*, Hp.*Off*.23.

⊛ **διαστρέφω**, *turn different ways, twist about*, τὰ σώματα, as in the dance, X.*Smp*.7.3; δ. τὸ πρόσωπον *to distort* it, Plu.2.535a:—mostly Pass., *to be distorted* or *twisted*, of the eyes, limbs, etc., Hp.*Aph*.4.49; ἡ ῥὶς δ. Id.*Art*.38; μέλη διεστρομμένα Pl.*Grg*.524c; *to be warped*, τὰ διεστραμμένα τῶν ξύλων Arist.*EN*1109b6: also of persons, *to have one's eyes distorted*, or *to have one's neck twisted* (Scholl. give both interprr.), εὐδαιμονίζω δ' εἰ διαστραφήσομαι; Ar.*Eq*.175; so ἀπολαύσομαί τί γ' εἰ δ. Id.*Av*.177; of the eyes, διεστράφην ἰδὼν Id.*Ach*.15; τὰ ὄμματα διαστρέφεσθαι Arist.*Pr*.960a13; without ὄμματα, ib.9, cf. 957b7; ὁ διεστραμμένος, opp. ὁ τυφλός, Eup.276.3; διεστρ. τοὺς πόδας *with the feet twisted*, Paus.5.18.1, cf. Arist.*Pr*.896b5: of torture, τῇ κλίμακι διαστρέφονται *Com.Adesp*.422; διεστράφησαν τὸν στόμαχον *had* their stomachs *turned*, Jul.*Or*.6.190d. 2. metaph., *distort, pervert*, [τρόπον χρηστόν] E.*Fr*.597; τοὺς νόμους Is.11.4; τὸν δικαστήν Arist.*Rh*.1354a24; ὑπόληψιν Id.*EN*1114b14; τῶν διαστρεφόντων (sc. παθῶν) Phld.*Lib*.p.32O.; διαστρέψαντες τἀληθῆ *having misrepresented* it, D.*Prooem*.46.2:—Pass., διαστραφῆναι τὴν διάνοιαν Luc.*Vit.Auct*.24; γενεὰ διεστραμμένη *perverse*, Lxx *De*.32.5. II. *turn aside, divert*, ἴχνος τὸ πρόσθεν φρενῶν A.*Supp*.1017. III. sens. obsc., = βινεῖν, Eup.7D.

**διαστροβέω**, *stir up*, πέλαγος *Trag.Adesp*.391. 2. = διασοβέω, Alciphr.3.9.

**διαστροφ-εύς**, gloss on παραχαράκτης, Hsch., etc. ⊛ **-ή**, ἡ, *twisting*, of a fractured limb, Hp.*Fract*.16; *distortion*, Id.*Art*.46; τῶν ὀμμάτων Arist.*Pr*.958a6, cf. 960a20: abs., of limbs, Sor.1.111. 2. metaph., *perversion*, Arist.*EE*1227a21; τοῦ δήμου ἐπὶ τὸ χεῖρον Plb.2.21.8, Porph.*Abst*.1.1?, etc.; γενῶν Plu.2.520c; δ. κακή Lxx *Pr*.2.14. 3. *distraction*, Metrod.*Herc*.831.7; *madness*, D.L.2.89. 4. *tergiversation*, Just.*Nov*.17.8.1 (pl.). **-ος**, ον, *twisted, distorted*, δ. καὶ ἔμπηρα καὶ ἀπόπληκτα Hdt.1.167; μορφὴ καὶ φρένες δ. A.*Pr*.673, cf. S.*Aj*.447; ὀφθαλμός Id.*Tr*.794; δ. κόρας ἑλίσσουσ' E.*Ba*.1122, cf. 1166 (lyr.); of a person, δ. τοὺς ὀφθαλμούς, τὸ σῶμα, Ath.8.339f, Luc.*Ind*.7. Adv. -φως *incorrectly*, λέγειν S.E.*M*.1.152.

**διάστρωμα**, ατος, τό, *abstract of title-deeds* in land registry, *POxy*.237 viii 39 (ii A.D.), etc. II. = *digestum*, *Gloss*.

**διαστρώννυμι**, *spread* a couch, etc., κλισίαν Luc.*DDeor*.24.1: abs., *spread*, Lxx 1*Ki*.9.25:—Pass., Phylarch.43. II. Pass., of titles to property, *to be registered*, *POxy*.1725.17 (iii A.D.), etc.

**διαστρωφάομαι**, = διαστρέφομαι, Sm.*Ps*.54(55).5.

**διαστυγνάζω**, *make stern*, τὰ πρόσωπα Eun.*VS*p.503D.

**διαστύλ-ιον** [ῠ], τό, in Architecture, *space between the columns*, Lat. *intercolumnium*, Bito 54.3. 2. ἀνέστησε δ. δύο perh. *a monument with three pillars*, Keil-Premerstein *Dritter Bericht* No.107. ⊛ **-ος**, ον, *diastyle*, i.e. *having a space of three diameters between the columns*, Vitr.3.3.1. II. διάστυλον, τό, = foreg. I, *IG*4.1484.63 (Epid.), *Ephes*.2.76, al. **-όω**, *support by pillars set at intervals*, Plb.5.100.4:—Pass., ib.4.8; διεστύλωτο δοκοῖς D.S.20.23.

**διαστύρακοι**, οἱ, *those with dark pupil and light iris*, Hsch.

**διαστύφομαι** [ῠ], aor. -εστύφθην, *become constipated*, *Hippiatr*.35.

**διασυγ-χέω**, *confuse utterly*, Plu.2.1078a. **-χύνω**, = foreg., A.D.*Adv*.202.15.

**διασυκάξαι**· διασκεδάσαι (Tarent.), Hsch.

**διασυν-ιστάνω**, = sq., τὸ μέλλον ἀγαθὸν δ. τῇ ψυχῇ Ph.1.603. **-ίστημι**, *set forth, signify clearly*, ib.237, al., D.L.3.79. II. *introduce, bring forward*, τινὰ λέγοντα Ph.1.368, al.:—Pass., *to be presented to the mind*, M.Ant.3.2. 2. *designate a successor to*, ἱερητείαν *SIG*1014.155 (Erythrae, iii B.C.). **-τρέχω**, *revolve with*, τοῖς ἄλλοις, of heavenly bodies, Anon.*in Ptol.Tetr*.119.

**διασῡριγμός**, ὁ, f.l. for διασυρμός, D.S.14.109.

⊛ **διασῡρίζω**, *whistle*, of the wind, Lxx *Da*.3.50; f.l. in Theopomp.Hist.76:—also **-συρίττω**, c. acc. metaph., τὸ τῆς φήμης πτερὸν τὴν ὕβριν ἁπανταχῇ δ. Lib.*Decl*.40.59; also, *whistle away, waste idly*, τὴν μέχρι τῆς αὐλῆς (sc. ὁδόν) Lyd.*Mag*.2.26.

**διασυρ-μός**, ὁ, *disparagement, ridicule*, Phld.*Vit*.p.37J., D.S.14.109, Longin.38.6, Ph.2.571 (pl.), Artem.3.25. **-σις**, εως, ἡ, *drawing through* a surgical dressing, Paul.Aeg.6.62. II. metaph., = foreg., Ptol.*Tetr*.160. **-τέον**, *one must ridicule*, Arist.*Rh.Al*.1443a9. **-της**, ου, ὁ, *detractor*, Ptol.*Tetr*.164. **-τικός**, ή, όν, *disparaging*, Phld.*Lib*.p.18O., Ptol.*Tetr*.160; λόγος Trypho *Trop*.p.206S. Adv. -κῶς Sch.E.*Hec*.925. **-τος**, ον, *drawn through*, λημνίσκος Paul.Aeg.6.34. ⊛ **-ω** [ῡ], pf. -σέσυρκα Diph.75:—Pass., pf. -σεσύρθαι Arist.*Rh.Al*.1433b6:—*tear in pieces*, κρέα prob. in Theopomp.Hist.76: metaph., *pull to pieces*, i.e. *to disparage, ridi-*

*cule*, Alex.141.11,237; διεσύρε τὰ παρόντα D.13.12, al.; λοιδορούμενος καὶ διασύρων Id.18.180, cf. Plb.4.3.13, Phld.*Ir*.p.59 W., etc. II. *break up, disperse*, σύνοδον Plb.10.42.4. III. *draw through*, Paul. Aeg.6.25:—Pass., *to be drawn to one side*, *Hippiatr*.26.

**διασύστᾰσις**, εως, ἡ, *commending*, τοῦ ζητουμένου Ph.2.154; *introduction*, Id.1.26. II. *designation of a successor*, δ. ἱερητειῶν *SIG*1014.13 (pl., Erythrae, iii B.C.).

**διασφᾰγ-ή**, ἡ, *gap*, Lxx *Ne*.4.7(1); v. διασφάξ. 2. *sluice-gate*, Wilcken *Chr*.11 *B*6 (ii B.C.). **-μα**, ατος, τό, = διασφάξ II. 2, Hippon.68 A.

**διασφαιρ-ίζω**, *throw about like a ball*, σάρκα E.*Ba*.1136. **-όομαι**, *to be rolled up into a ball*, plpf. διεσφαίρωτο Nonn.*D*.7.137.

**διασφακτήρ**, ῆρος, ὁ, *murderous*, σίδηρος *AP*7.493 (Antip. Thess.).

⊛ **διασφᾰλίζομαι**, *secure firmly*, Plb.5.69.2, Ph.Byz.*Mir*.4.2, Herod. Med.ap.Orib.8.7.3:—Pass., σιδήρῳ διησφαλισμένα J.*AJ*15.11.3.

⊛ **διασφάλλω**, *overturn utterly*, τὴν τέχνην Luc.*Abd*.17:—Pass., *to fail of, be disappointed of*, τινός Aeschin.2.35, 3.91, D.S.20.10; τῇ προνοίᾳ, ἐν πράξεσι, Plb.5.81.7, 4.14.3, cf. Arist.*Ath*.19.3; πάντα δ. Vett.Val.116.34.

**διασφάξ**, ᾱγος, ἡ, (διασφάζω) *any opening made by violence, rent*, esp. *gorge*, through which a river runs, Hdt.2.158 (pl.), 3.117, etc.; *cleft* in the earth, Lyc.317. 2. Medic., of *divisions* of blood-vessels, Hp.*Loc.Hom*.3; *fissure* in the liver, Herophil.ap.Gal.2.570. 3. *sluice*, *POxy*.1188.24 (i A.D.). II. *gill-cavity*, in fishes, Opp.*H*. 1.744. 2. = τὸ θῆλυ μόριον, Eust.897.60.

**διάσφαξις**, εως, ἡ, = διασφάξ, Hp.*Epid*.2.1.8 (dub. l.).

**διασφάττω**, *slaughter*, f.l. in Lib.*Loc*.1.8.

**διασφενδονάω**, *scatter as by a sling*, D.S.17.83:—Pass., *to be hurled from slings*, Agath.3.25, 5.3; *to be scattered in all directions*, X.*An*. 4.2.3, Plu.*Marc*.15, D.C.56.14. II. *dismember*, Plu.*Alex*.43.

⊛ **διασφετερίζομαι**, f. l. for σφετερίζομαι, Ph.2.130.

**διασφηκόομαι**, Pass., *to be made like a wasp, be pinched in at the waist*, μέσος διεσφηκωμένος Ar.*V*.1072. II. later in Act., *bind tight*, Nonn.*D*.25.189, al.

**διασφην-όω**, *dilate as with a wedge*, Meges ap.Orib.44.24.2:—Pass., Antyll.ib.10.23.7; in literal sense, Apollod.*Poliorc*.180. 14. **-ωσις**, εως, ἡ, *plugging*, μοτῶν Sor.2.40 (pl.).

**δια-σφίγγω**, *bind tight*, ζώναις τὴν κοιλίαν Erasistr.ap.Gell.16.3.8, cf. Antyll.ap.Orib.7.9.3, Aret.*SA*1.5:—Pass., [σώματα] κατὰ τὸ μέσον διεσφιγμένα *narrow-waisted*, Eun.*Hist*.p.234D.; also σφραγῖσι χρυσοδέτοις δ. ib.p.255D.; dub. l. ib.p.261D. **-σφιγκτέον**, *one must bind tightly*, Paul.Aeg.3.44. **-σφιγξις**, εως, ἡ, *binding tight, ligature*, Sor.2.41, Heliod.ap.Orib.10.18, Antyll.ib.7.9.3, Aret. *CA*2.2.

**διασφρᾱγ-ίζομαι**, *seal up*, Lxx *Je*.39(32).10.

**διασφῠδόω**, *cause to swell up*, Hsch.; cf. σφυδόω.

**διάσφυξις**, εως, ἡ, (σφύζω) *pulsation*, φλεβῶν Hp.*Alim*.48; ἀρτηρίης Aret.*SA*2.2; *throbbing*, ἐγκεφάλου Id.*CD*1.3.

**διασχάζω**, *open a vein*, Aret.*CA*2.10.

**διάσχεσις**, εως, ἡ, prob. = διάσχισμα II, Hsch., *EM*340.6.

**διασχημᾰτ-ίζω**, *shape, form variously*, Str.17.1.4, Plu.2.499e:—Med., of God, *mould as Creator*, Pl.*Ti*.53b:—Pass., ib.50c. 2. simply, *shape, model*, Luc.*Icar*.6, v.l. in *Prom*.11 (Pass.). 3. *shape oneself, prepare*, ἐπὶ πρᾶγμα Eun.*Hist*.p.269D. **-ισις**, εως, ἡ, *formation*, i.e. *dimensions*, of a groove, Procl.*Hyp*.3.19: generally, Id. *in Ti*.3.261D.

**δια-σχῐδής**, ές, *cloven, split, parted*, Ath.11.488e. **-σχίζω**, *cleave asunder, sever*, ἱστία δέ σφιν..διέσχισεν ἲς ἀνέμοιο Od.9.71; ἐάν τις ἓν δ. Pl.*Phd*.97a, etc.:—Pass., *to be cloven asunder*, νεῦρα διεσχίσθη Il.16.316; opp. συγκρίνεσθαι, Pl.*Lg*.893e; θοἰμάτιον δ. Id.*Grg*. 469d; of soldiers, *to be separated, parted*, X.*Cyr*.4.5.13; *to be set at variance*, διέσχιστο ἡ πόλις Charito 6.1: impers., τούτοις διέσχισται they *have a cleft*, Arist.*Resp*.475$^{a}$2. **-σχίς**, ἴδος, ἡ, *division*, φλεβός Hp.*Fract*.44, cf. Gal.14.706. **-σχῐσις**, εως, ἡ, *division, cleft*, Ath.11.488e; of roads, Them.*Or*.20.236b (pl.). **-σχισμα**, ατος, τό, *interval*, Sch.D.T.p.191 H. (Dind. for διάσχημα). II. in Music, *interval of half the* δίεσις, Philol.6. **-σχισμός**, ὁ, = διάσχισις, Sch.A.*Supp*.131. II. metaph., *dissension*, *BGU*923. 21 (i/ii A.D.).

**διασχοινίζω**, *scatter*, in pf. part. Pass., Hsch. (-σχην- cod.).

**διασχολέω**, strengthd. for ἀσχολέω, περί τι Hdn.7.6.7 (Med.).

**διασῴζω**, *preserve through* a danger, of persons, Ἀπόλλωνα δ. κατακρύψατα Hdt.2.156; δ. πόλιν E.*Ph*.783; δ. τινὰ ἐκ κινδύνων Isoc. 1.23:—Med., *save for oneself*, τὰ πλείστου ἄξια X.*Cyr*.4.2.28:—Pass., Pl.*Ti*.22d; *come safe through*, τοὺς διασωθέντας Id.*R*.540a, cf. 1*Ep. Pet*.3.20, etc.; διασῴζεσθαι ἐς.. or πρός.. *to come safe* to a place, Th.4.113, X.*An*.5.4.5, etc.; *recover* from illness, Id.*Mem*.2.10. 2. II. of things, *preserve, maintain*, ἀνδρὶ τἀμὰ δ. λέχη.. E.*Hel*. 65; *keep in memory*, X.*Mem*.3.5.22; δ. πίστιν τινί Id.*HG*7.2.17; δ. τὸν πρῶτον λόγον Pl.*R*.395b, cf. Arist.*Ph*.189$^{b}$1; τὰ παλαιά Isoc.10. 63:—Med., *preserve for oneself, retain*, εὐδαιμονίαν, εὐτυχίαν, Th.3.39, 5.16; δόξαν Lys.2.69; τὴν τῶν Μήδων μαλακίαν X.*Cyr*.8.8.15.

**διασωμᾰτίζω**, *dismember*, gloss on διατκηνίψαι, Hsch.

**διασωπάσομαι**, v. διασιωπάω.

**διασωσ-τέον**, *one must maintain*, Pl.*Ep*.360b, *Com.Adesp*.25.41 D. ⊛ **-τής**, οῦ, ὁ, *policeman*, Just.*Nov*.130.1. ⊛ **-τικός**, ή, όν, *preservative*, Max.Tyr.20.5, al.; δύναμις Gal.*Nat.Fac*.1.14; θεὸς δ. καὶ τῶν φύσεων τηρητικός *Theol.Ar*.5.

**διασώχω**, *rub to pieces*, Nic.*Th*.696 (tm.).

**διατᾱγεύω**, *arrange*, v.l. for διατάξαι in X.*Cyr*.8.3.33.

⊛ **δια-τᾰγή**, ἡ, *command, ordinance*, Lxx 2*Es*.4.11, *Ep.Rom*.13.2; ἐκ διαταγῆς *CIG*3465, *POxy*.92.3 (iv A.D.); *testamentary disposition*, *IGRom*.4.840.3, etc.; δ. τῆς τρύγης ποιήσασθαι make *arrangements* for.., *PFay*.133.4 (iv A.D.); πόλεως Ps.-Callisth.1.23; εἰς διαταγὰς ἀγγέλων *Act.Ap*.7.53; *medical regimen*, Ruf.ap.Orib.6.38. 13; = τάξις, *Placit*.1.15.8. **-ταγμα**, ατος, τό, *ordinance, edict*, Phld.*Rh*.2.289S., D.S.18.64, Ph.1.180, *Ep.Hebr*.11.23, Plu.*Pomp*.6, *IG*2$^{2}$.1077.34; κατὰ τὸ δ. (sc. τῆς συγκλήτου) ib.12(3).173.10; = Lat. *edictum*, *OGI*458.81 (i B.C.), *BGU*1074.3 (iii A.D.), etc.; = Lat. *formula*, *IG*14.951.24,25 (Rome); *testamentary disposition*, *POxy*.1282. 27 (i A.D.). **-ταγματικός**, ή, όν, *edictalis*, *Gloss*. **-ταγμός**, ὁ, = διάταξις II, ib. **-τακτα**, τά, *miscellaneous treatises*, Anon.*Vit.Arist*. p.14.3 W. **-τακτέον**, *one must assign*, τὰ πρόσφορα χαρακτῆρι ἑκάστῳ Demetr.*Eloc*.59. **-τακτέω**, *issue a decree*, *Gloss*. ⊛ **-τάκτης**, ου, ὁ, *assigner of posts*, Herm.ap.Stob.1.49.69. ⊛ **-τακτικός**, ή, όν, *capable of ordering, arranging*, Phld.*Oec*.p.52 J., Ptol.*Tetr*.82. Adv. -κῶς *Gloss*. **-τάκτωρ**, ορος, ὁ, = -τάκτης, Orph.*Fr*.54, Sch.Il.1.16.

**διατᾰλαντόομαι**, Pass., *swing to and fro*, of a ship, Ach.Tat.3.1.

**διατᾰμιεύω**, *manage, dispense*, Pl.*Lg*.805e:—Med., *store, husband*, Id.*Criti*.111d.

**διατάμνω**, Ion. and Dor. for διατέμνω, Hdt.2.139, *Tab.Heracl*.1.12.

**διατᾰνύω**, = διατείνω, διὰ πτερὰ..τανύσσας A.R.4.601.

⊛ **διαταξίαρχος**, ὁ, *assigner of offices, official of guild of* βουκόλοι, *IG Rom*.4.386 (Pergam.).

⊛ **διάταξις**, εως, ἡ, (διατάσσω) *disposition, arrangement*, of troops, Hdt.9.26; ἡ δ. τῶν φυλάκων D.18.248; *disposition* of the elements, Pl.*Ti*.53b; ταύτην ὁ κόσμος ἔχει τὴν δ. Arist.*Cael*.300$^{b}$25; of a treatise, Ph.*Bel*.49.4; Rhet., *arrangement of topics*, Luc.*Hist.Conscr*. 24. II. *command*, Lxx *Ps*.118(119).91, Plb.4.19.10, Phld.*Herc*. 1251.20, *Po*.2.48 (pl.); *testamentary disposition*, Plb.4.87.5; *compact*, Id.8.16.12. 2. *imperial constitution*, θεῖαι δ. Wilcken *Chr*.41 iii 20 (iii A.D.); κατὰ διάταξιν τοῦ Ἁδριανοῦ *BGU*1022.9 (ii A.D.); νεαραὶ δ., title of Justinian's Novels; of the *decree* of the *praefectus Aegypti*, Wilcken *Chr*.27.10 (ii A.D.).

**διατᾰράσσω**, Att. -ττω, *throw into confusion*, X.*Mem*.4.2.40, Pl. *Lg*.693c, Plb.11.1.9, Phld.*Piet*.108:—Pass., δ. ἐν ταῖς τοῦ βίου μεταβολαῖς Isoc.2.39, cf. Epicur.*Ep*.3 p.66 U., D.S.18.7, Jul.*Or*.3.116d.

**διατᾰρᾰχή**, ἡ, *disturbance*, Plu.2.317b (pl.).

**διάτᾰσις**, εως, ἡ, *tension, dilatation*, ἔχειν δ. to have the *power of dilatation*, Arist.*PA*664$^{a}$33 (v.l.); κεφαλῆς διατάσεις καὶ ἰλίγγους Pl. *R*.407c (prob.). 2. *extension*, of a fractured or dislocated limb, Hp.*Off*.15, cf. Heliod.ap.Orib.49.8.33; σπαρτῶν Alciphr.2.4. 3. *stretching across*: hence Medic., δ. φρενῶν *diaphragm*, Hp.*VM*22; δ. alone, Id.*Coac*.394; also of vaginal *obstruction*, Paul.Aeg.6.72. II. *tension, exertion*, πνεύματος Thphr.*Sud*.32; of athletes and the like, Arist.*Pr*.885$^{b}$23, *IA*705$^{a}$18; διατάσεις καὶ κλαυθμοί, of infants, Id. *Pol*.1336$^{a}$34: metaph., ἡ εὔνοια..οὐκ ἔχει δ. Id.*EN*1166$^{b}$33; ἐν δ. γενομένης τῆς ψυχῆς Plu.*Cor*.21; ἡ πρὸς τὸν ἥλιον δ., of plants, Iamb. *Protr*.21.λη'. 2. *contention, quarrel*, εἰς μεγάλην ἐλθεῖν δ. πρός τινα D.S.38/9.2 (s.v.l.).

⊛ **διατάσσω**, Att. -ττω, pf. διατέτᾰχα *BGU*1151.6 (i B.C.), prob. in *OGI*326.27 (Teos):—*appoint* or *ordain severally, dispose*, εὖ δὲ ἕκαστα ἀθανάτοις διέταξε Hes.*Th*.74; ἀνθρώποισι νόμον δ. Id.*Op*.276; *appoint to separate offices*, δ. τοὺς μὲν οἰκίας οἰκοδομέειν, τοὺς δὲ δορυφόρους εἶναι Hdt.1.114; δ. τι εἶναι Pl.*Ti*.45b; τίνας εἶναι χρεὼν τῶν ἐπιστημῶν.. ἡ πολιτικὴ δ. Arist.*EN*1094$^{b}$1: abs., *make arrangements*, πρὸς τὸ συμπῖπτον ἀεὶ δ. X.*Cyr*.8.5.16:—Med., *arrange for oneself, classify*, Pl.*Phdr*.271b; τινὶ περί τινος Plb.5.21.1; *undertake, pledge oneself*, πρός τινα c. fut. inf., ib.14.11; also in act. sense, περὶ θυσιῶν *OGI*331.53 (Pergam.):—Pass., *to be appointed, constituted*, Pl.*Lg*.932a; παρὰ τὰ -τεταγμένα contrary to *orders*, *BGU*1022.17 (ii A.D.): c. inf., v.l. in Hdt.1.110: c. acc., δ. γῆν *to be appointed to cultivate*, *POxy*.899.22 (200 A.D.). 2. esp. *draw up* an army, *set in array*, Hdt.6.107, Th.4.103; διέταξε χωρὶς ἑκάστους εἶναι Hdt.1. 103:—Med., διαταξάμενοι *posting themselves in battle-order*, Ar.*V*. 360, Th.8.104, X.*HG*7.1.20:—pf. Pass., διατετάχθαι *to be in battle-order*, Hdt.7.178, Th.4.31; διετέτακτο Hdt.6.112 (but in med. sense, J.*AJ*12.5.4). II. Med., *make testamentary dispositions*, περί τινος Plu.2.1129a; *order by will*, c. inf., *AP*11.133 (Lucill.); *bequeath*, *BGU*1151.6 (i B.C.):—Pass., *to be bequeathed*, *PFay*.97.13 (i A.D.).

**διατᾰτικός**, ή, όν, *on the stretch, urgent*, Plb.*Fr*.29 (Comp.). Adv. Comp. -ώτερον *by an extension of meaning*, S.E.*M*.1.45 codd.

**διαταφρεύω**, *cut off* or *fortify by a ditch*, Plb.3.105.11, Plu.*Pomp*. 62:—Pass., J.*BJ*5.4.2.

**διατεθρυμμένως**, Adv., (διαθρύπτω) *weakly*, Pl.*Lg*.922c.

⊛ **διατείνω**, *stretch to the uttermost*, δ. τὸ τόξον Hdt.3.35; *keep stretched out*, τὴν χεῖρα Hp.*Fract*.8; δ. τὰς χεῖρας ἐπί τι X.*Cyr*.1.3.4; ἀράχνιον δ. πρὸς τὰ πέρατα Arist.*HA*623$^{a}$9; τινὰ ὑπὲρ λεχέων *AP*5.54 (Diosc.):—Pass., *extend*, μία ἰδέα πάντῃ διατεταμένη Pl.*Sph*. 253d. II. intr., *extend*, Diog.Apoll.6; διὰ παντὸς τοῦ βίου Arist.*EN* 1172$^{a}$23; καθ' ἅπαν τὸ σῶμα Id.*HA*503$^{b}$21; κατὰ τὸ συνεχὲς ἕως εἰς .. Plb.3.37.9; *to continue*, γένος διέτεινε λαμπρόν Plu.*Marc*.30. 2. δ. εἰς, ποτί τι, *extend* or *relate to, concern*, *SIG*569.11,38 (Halasarna, iii B.C.), cf. Plb.8.29.6; πρὸς τὰ ὅλα Id.9.5.4. 3. *reach, arrive at, extend as far as*, πρός.. Epicur.*Ep*.1 p.13 U., Plb.5.86.4, D.S.12.70, etc.; *live until the time of*, εἴς τινα Plu.*Cat.Ma*.15.

B. Med. and Pass., *exert oneself*, τί οὖν..διετεινάμην οὑτωσὶ σφοδρῶς; D.18.142; διατεινάμενος φεύγειν *at full speed*, X.*Mem*.4.2.23;

θεῖν διατεταμένους Pl.*R*.474a; ἱέναι ib.501c; πὺξ διατεινάμενος Theoc. 22.67; *strain, exert the voice*, Arist.*Pol*.1336a39; διατείνεσθαι πρός τι *exert oneself* for a purpose, X.*Mem*.3.7.9; διετείναντο αὐτὸν μὴ εἰσελθεῖν *prevented* him from going in, Antipho 5.46; δ. τὰ κάλλιστα πράττειν Arist.*EN*1169a9. 2. *maintain earnestly, contend*, δ. ὡς.. *maintain stoutly* that.., Pl.*Sph*.247c, Thphr.*HP*3.18.7, *CP*4.6.1, etc. b. *oppose*, opp. συναποφήνασθαι, Gal.4.759; πρός τινα ib. 773. II. in strict sense of Med., *stretch oneself*, Anaxandr.41. 67. 2. *to stretch out for oneself* or *what is one's own*, δ. τὸ τόξον Hdt.4.9; τὰ βέλεα ὡς ἀπήσοντες *to have their lances poised* as if they were about to throw, Id.9.18; διατεινάμενοι οἱ μὲν τὰ παλτὰ οἱ δὲ τὰ τόξα X.*Cyr*.1.4.23; διατεταμένοι τὰς μάστιγας Plb.15.28.2.

**διατειχ-ίζω**, *cut off and fortify by a wall*, Ar.*Eq*.818; τὸν Ἰσθμὸν Lys.2.44; τὴν πόλιν ἀπὸ τῆς ἄκρας Plb.8.32.2. 2. *divide as by a wall*, ἡ ῥὶς διατετείχικε τὰ ὄμματα X.*Smp*.5.6: metaph., *keep apart*, φῶς καὶ σκότος Ph.1.632, al.; διατετείχισται ἡ ἱστορία πρὸς τὸ ἐγκώμιον *is separated* from it, Luc.*Hist.Conscr*.7. **—ιον**, τό, = sq., D.S.16. 12 (s.v.l.). **—ισμα**, ατος, τό, *place walled off and fortified*, Th.3. 34; *cross-wall*, Id.7.60. 2. *wall between two places*, *SIG*421.46 (Thermon, iii B.C.), Plb.8.34.9: metaph., *wall of partition*, Luc. *DMeretr*.11.4. ⊛ **—ισμός**, ὁ, *fortifying*, τᾶς πόλιος *IG*4.757 *B* 25 (Troezen).

**διατεκμαίρομαι**, only aor. 1 —τεκμηράμην, *mark out, assign*, ἔργα ἀνθρώποισι Hes.*Op*.398, cf. D.P.1172; *mark, trace out*, A.R.4.284; *determine*, γενέθλην Μοῖραι δ. Man.6.750.

**διατελευτάω**, *bring to fulfilment*, θεὸς διὰ πάντα τ. Il.10.90.

⊛ **διατελ-έω**, fut. —τελέσω, Att. —τελῶ: pf. διατετέλεκα X.*Cyr*.1.5.4, *IG*2$^2$.223 *A* 5:—*bring quite to an end, accomplish*, ἐπεί περ ἠρξάμην, διατελέσαι βούλομαι X.*HG*7.3.4; δ. χάριν E.*Heracl*.434; so of Time, διατετελεκὼς τὰ ἐν τοῖς ἐφήβοις δέκα ἔτη X.*Cyr*. l.c. II. abs., 1. mostly c. part., *continue being* or *doing* so and so, τὸ λοιπὸν τῆς ζόης δ. ἐόντα τυφλὸν Hdt.6.117; δ. ἐόντες ἐλεύθεροι Id. 7.111, cf. 1.32, etc.; δ. τὸν λοιπὸν βίον δουλεύοντες And.1.38; δ. καθεύδοντες Pl.*Ap*.31a; μινυρίζων δ. τὸν βίον ὅλον Id.*R*.411a; διετέλεσας πειρώμενος you *have been* trying *all along*, Id.*Tht*.206a: with Adjs., δ. πρόθυμος *continue* zealous, Th.6.89, cf. 1.34; δ. ἀχίτων X. *Mem*.1.6.2; ἡδὺς δ. Alex.45.9. 2. with no part. or Adj., *continue, live*, δ. μετ' ἀλλήλων διὰ βίου Pl.*Smp*.192c; δ. χαριέντως Id.*R*. 426a; ἐν ἀγρῷ Men.*Georg*.4. b. generally, *continue, persevere*, διατέλει ὥσπερ ἦρξω Pl.*Grg*.494c; δ. ἐν ὕπνῳ Arist.*GA*779a24; ἐν τῇ θαλάττῃ Id.*Pr*.933a14; of things, *continue*, ἐὰν αἱ μιμήσεις ἐκ νέων πόρρω δ. Pl.*R*.395d. **—ής**, ές, *continuous, incessant*, βρονταί S.*OC* 1514; *ever-flowing*, ὕδατα Ael.*VH*13.1; *permanent*, τυραννίδες Pl.*R*. 618a; *perpetual*, ἀρετή *IG*7.2509 (Thebes). (διὰ τέλους serves as the Adv.)

⊛ **διατέμνω**, Ion. and Dor. —τάμνω (q.v.), fut. —τεμῶ, *cut through, cut in twain, dissever*, διὰ δὲ γλῶσσαν τάμε μέσσην Il.17.618, cf. 522 (tm.), Hdt.2.139; διὰ κάρα τεμών S.*Fr*.799.6; διὰ κῦμα τεμών *cleaving* the wave, ib.271.5 (anap.); διχῇ γαῖαν δ. *part* it asunder, A.*Supp*.545 (lyr.); δίχα δ. Pl.*Smp*.190d; τι ἀπό τινος Id.*Plt*.280b: metaph., *disunite*, διατετμηκότα τὴν πολιτείαν Aeschin.3.207. 2. *cut up*, Hdt.2.41.

⊛ **διατενής**, ές, *tending*, πρὸς τὴν τελείωσιν Thphr.*CP*2.15.2.

**διατέρπομαι**, *take one's pleasure with*, γυναικί App.*Mith*.27.

**διατερσαίνω**, strengthd. for τερσαίνω, Prisc.p.301 D., Hsch.

**διατετᾰμένως**, Adv., (διατείνω) *with might and main, earnestly*, δ. φεύγειν Arist.*EN*1166b28; ἐνεργεῖν ib.1175a8, cf. Plu.*Cat.Mi*.26, Iamb.*Protr*.19, Hierocl.*in CA*20p.464M.

**διατετηρημένως**, *carefully*, prob. in Sch.D.P.1.

**διατετραίνω**, fut. (Ion.) —τετρανέω Hdt. (v. infr.), or —τρήσω Apollod.*Poliorc*.148.3: aor. —έτρησα Plu.2.370b, App.*Mith*.26:—Med., —τρήσαιο Gal.4.708:—Pass., aor. part. —τρηθείς *BGU*321.13: pf. part. —τετρημένος Apollod.*Poliorc*.152.2:—*bore through*, κεφαλὰς Hdt. 3.12; ᾠὸν Plu. l.c.:—Med., aor., ὦτα διετετρήνατο Ar.*Th*.18:—διατιτραίνω Thphr.*CP*1.17.9 (Pass.); also (as if from διατίτρημι) part. διατιτράντες D.C.69.12, impf. διετίτρη App.*Pun*.122:—late pres. διατιτράω Suid.: impf. διετίτρων App.*Hisp*.77; διετίτρα Gal.14.18.

**διατήκω**, *melt, soften by heat*, κηρὸν Ar.*Nu*.149; *relax* the bowels, Hp.*Aër*.7. 2. *soak*, ἐν ἐλαίῳ Thphr.*Od*.29, Aët.15.13:—Pass., aor. —ετήχθην Ph.*Bel*.89.20. II. Pass., with pf. —τέτηκα, *melt away, thaw*, X.*An*.4.5.6; *waste away*, Arist.*Mete*.385a28, Agath.2.14.

**διάτηξις**· *tabes*, *Gloss*.

**διατηρ-έω**, Boeot. —τᾱρέω *Supp.Epigr*.1.132.8 (ii B.C.), but Dor. —τηρέω *SIG*541 *A* 4:—*watch closely, observe*, Pl.*Lg*.836d (v.l.), Arist. *HA*612b28; δ. μή τι πάθωσι D.9.20. 2. *maintain*, τὴν ἐλευθερίαν Decr.ap.D.18.184; τὴν τάξιν Decr.ib.37; τὸ πρέπον Arist.*EN*1178a 13; τὰ τοῦ βίου δίκαια Men.637; τὴν πόλιν καὶ τὴν ἑαυτῶν πίστιν Plb.1.7.7; τὴν εὔνοιαν *IG*12(7).506; τὴν ἀφθαρσίαν Phld.*D*.3*Fr*.19, etc.:—Med., —εῖται τὸν καιρὸν *observes*, ib.*Fr*.77:—Pass., ὅταν διατηρηθῶσιν οἱ νόμοι τῇ πόλει Aeschin.3.6; ἀλειτούργητος —τηρείσθω ἡ θεία φύσις Epicur.*Ep*.2p.42 U. 3. with predicates, βοῦς ἐννέα ἔτη δ. ἀνοχεύτους Arist.*HA*595b18; ἀβλαβές δ. Plb.7.8.7; ἀφλυκταίνωτα δ. τὰ μέρη Dsc.5.156; δ. τὸν πόλεμον Plu.*Dio*33. 4. δ. ἑαυτὸν ἔκ τινος *keep* oneself from.., *Act.Ap*.15.29. **—ησις**, εως, ἡ, *preservation*, Lxx *Ex*.16.33, al.; ἑαυτῶν D.S.2.50; τῶν ἁγίων Ph. 1.203; γένους J.*AJ*1.3.2, etc. **—ητέον**, *one must preserve*, *Gp*. 9.11.10; *one must keep*, ἐν ἀγρυπνίᾳ Aët.13.12. **—ητικός**, ή, όν, *disposed for keeping*, φίλων M.Ant.1.16; ὑγιείας Porph.*Abst*.1.53, cf. Asp.*in EN*14.2.

⊛ **διατίθημι**, 3 pl. impf. διετίθουν Antipho Trag.1:—*arrange* each *in their several places, distribute*, τὰ κρέα, in sacrificing, Hdt.1.132; τὸ μὲν ἐπὶ δεξιά, τὸ δ' ἐπ' ἀριστερά Id.7.39; ᾗπερ οἱ θεοὶ διέθεσαν τὰ ὄντα X.*Mem*.2.1.27; δ. οἶνον εἰς ὀστράκια Arist.*HA*594a11. II. *manage* well or ill, usu. with Adv., κράτιστα δ. τὰ τοῦ πολέμου Th.6.15; καλὸν πρᾶγμα κακῶς δ. D.19.88; of persons, δ. ἑωυτὸν ἀνηκέστως *treat himself barbarously*, Hdt.3.155:—Pass., οὐ ῥᾳδίως διετέθη he *was* not very gently *handled*, Th.6.57; ἀπόρως διατεθέντας *reduced to* helplessness, Lys.18.23; ἀθλίως διατιθέμενος Pl.*Criti*.121b; σῶμα διατεθειμένῳ κακῶς Men.591. 2. c. acc. pers., with Advbs., *dispose* one so or so, ὅταν οὕτω διαθῇς τοὺς Ἕλληνας Isoc.5.80; οὕτω διαθεὶς.. τὰς πόλεις πρὸς ἀλλήλας D.18.168; δ. τινὰς ἀπίστως πρὸς ἡμᾶς αὐτούς Id.20.22; τὸν ἀκροατὴν δ. πως Arist.*Rh*.1356a3:—Pass., *to be disposed* in a certain manner, πρός τινα Pl.*Tht*.151c, Isoc.8.14; οἰκειότερον διατεθῆναί τινι Id.12.160; τὸν εἰρημένον τρόπον Arist.*Pol*.1302a35; ἐρωτικῶς δ., of animals, Pl.*Smp*.207c, cf. Longus 1.15 (διάκειμαι is more usu. as Pass. in this sense). III. *set forth*, of speakers, minstrels, etc., *recite*, κακῶς ποιήματα Pl.*Chrm*.162d, cf. *Lg*.658d; cf. B.6. 2. *describe*, Str.1.1.16, etc.

B. Med., *arrange as one likes, dispose of*, τὴν θυγατέρα X.*Cyr*. 5.2.7; τὰ σώματα ἐπονειδίστως δ. Isoc.12.140; οὐδ' ὅσ' ἂν πορίσωσι.. ταῦτ' ἔχοντες διαθέσθαι D.2.16; εἰς καλὸν δ. τὰ πεπραγμένα Luc.*Hist. Conscr*.51, cf. *Merc.Cond*.25; *spend*, δ. τὰς οὐσίας εἴς τι Plb.20.6.5: metaph., τὸ πλεῖον τῆς ὀργῆς εἴς τινα Id.16.1.2. 2. *dispose of one's* property, *devise* it *by will*, Is.3.68; τὴν οὐσίαν ἑτέρῳ Id.7.1; δ. διαθήκας, διαθήκην, *make* a will, Lys.19.39, Pl.*Lg*.922c: abs., ibid., Lys. 6.41; κἂν ἀποθάνῃ μὴ διαθέμενος *intestate*, Arist.*Pol*.1270a28; ὁ δ. *the testator*, *Ep.Hebr*.9.16. 3. *dispose of* merchandise, φόρτον Hdt. 1.1,194, cf. X.*An*.7.3.10, *Ath*.2.11; τισί Pl.*Lg*.849d; ἔλαιον καὶ κίκι *PRev.Laws*48.4 (iii B.C.); δ. τὴν ὥραν καὶ τὴν σοφίαν X.*Mem*.1.6.13; δ. τι τριπλασίας τιμῆς ἢ πρότερον D.42.31. 4. *arrange* or *settle mutually*, δ. διαθήκην τινί *make a covenant with* one, Ar.*Av*.439; δ. διαθήκην πρός τινα *Act.Ap*.3.25; ἔριν δ. ἀλλήλοις *settle* a quarrel, X. *Mem*.2.6.23; ὡμολόγησαν καὶ διέθεντο ὀφείλειν *IG*12(7).67.58 (Amorgos). 5. *compose, make*, νόμους Pl.*Lg*.834a. 6. *set forth, recite*, λόγους, δημηγορίαν, etc., Plb.3.108.2, D.H.11.7, cf. D.S.12.17; πολλοὺς ἐπαίνους τινῶν D.H.3.17; δ. ῥῆσιν ἐφ' ἑαυτοῦ Luc.*Herm*. 1. b. Gramm., διατιθέναι and —τίθεσθαι *to act* and *be acted upon*, A.D.*Synt*.12.15; τὸ διατιθέν and τὸ διατιθέμενον *subject* and *object*, ib.127.22.

**διατῑλάω**, *pass excrements*, *Hippiatr*.31, al.

⊛ **διατίλλω**, lit., *pluck*, κουραῖς.. διατετιλμένη φόβην *having had its* mane *clipped*, S.*Fr*.659.7.

**διάτιλμα**, ατος, τό, *portion plucked off*, φύλλων *AP*6.71 (Paul. Sil.).

**διατῑμ-άω**, *finish honouring, honour no longer*, τὰ τοῦδε διατετίμηται θεοῖς A.*Th*.1052 Sch. (τοῦδ' οὐ codd.). 2. Med., *get* a thing *estimated* or *valued*, τὴν οὐσίαν D.S.4.21; τὸ ἀδίκημα ταλάντων πεντακοσίων Id.16.29; τὴν χώραν J.*AJ*19.9.2, cf. *CIG*2266.8 (Delos), *SIG*679.60 (ii B.C.):—also in Act., *PRev.Laws* 26.10, Sm. *Le*.27.14. ⊛ **—ησις**, εως, ἡ, *valuation*, δ. ποιεῖσθαι Ath.6.274e, cf. D.S.29.10, *POxy*.267.18 (i A.D.); *assessed value*, *PRev.Laws* 55. 24. **—ητής**, οῦ, ὁ, *appraiser, valuer*, Just.*Nov*.64.1: pl., Id.*Edict*. 9.4. **—ητικός**, gloss on δοκιμαστικός, Suid.

⊛ **διατῑνάσσω**, *shake asunder, shake to pieces*, ἐπὴν σχεδίην.. διὰ κῦμα τινάξῃ Od.5.363; τὰ δώματα E.*Ba*.606: fut. Med. in pass. sense, ib.587 (lyr.). II. *shake violently*, κάρα δ. ἄνω κάτω Id.*IT*282; *shake out*, στρώματα Hierocl.p.63A.

**διατινθαλέος**, α, ον, = τινθαλέος, Ar.*V*.329.

**διατιτραίνω, διατιτράω, διατίτρημι**, v. διατετραίνω.

**διατιτρώσκω**, *pierce through, transfix*, δέρμα Hp.*Fract*.11; ταύρους D.C.63.3:—Pass., J.*BJ*6.3.1.

**διατλῆναι**, part. διατλάς, *endure, suffer*, Hsch.

**διατμέω**, (ἀτμός) *evaporate*, Hp.*Morb*.4.45.

⊛ **δια-τμήγω**, aor. 1 διέτμηξα: aor. 2 διέτμᾰγον:—Pass., aor. 2 —τμάγην [μᾰ] (v. infr.):—Ep. for διατέμνω, *cut in twain*, ἔνθα διατμήξας.. then *having cut* [the Trojan host] *in twain*.., Il.21.3; νηχόμενος.. λαῖτμα διέτμαγον Od.7.276, cf. 5.409; ὦλκα δ., of ploughing, Mosch.2. 81 (Med., ἀρούρας διατμήξασθαι A.R.1.628); Ἀπόλλωνα ἠελίοιο χωρὶ δ. *distinguish* him from the Sun, Call.*Fr*.48:—Pass., διέτμαγεν (3 pl. aor. 2 for —τμάγησαν) ἐν φιλότητι they *parted* friends, Il.7.302: abs., they *parted*, 1.531, Od.13.439; also, they *were scattered abroad*, Il. 16.354. **—τμημα**, ατος, τό, *space partitioned off*, Lyd.*Mag*.3. 37. **—τμητέον**· *decidendum*, *Gloss*.

**διατμίζω**, *evaporate*, Arist.*Mete*.344b23, 353b8, Sor.1.106, Corn. *ND*32, etc.: c. acc. cogn., ἱδρῶτα δ. Plu.2.695c:—Pass., in same sense, Arist.*Cael*.305b14; of perspiration, τὸ σύμπαν σκῆνος διητμίσθη Aret.*CA*1.1.

**διατοιχέω**, = ἀνατοιχέω (q.v.), Eub.51, Aristid.1.462 J.

**διάτοιχος**, ον, *extending through the width of the wall*, ὑπερτόναια ξύλινα δ. *IG*2$^2$.463.57. II. Subst. διάτοιχος (sc. λίθος), ὁ, *bonding course* or *stone*, ib.11(2).144 *A* 57,97 (Delos, iv B.C.), 199 *C* 32 (iii B.C.), *Milet*.7.56,57 (pl.), cf. Hsch.

**διατομή**, ἡ, *cutting through, severance*, A.*Th*.934 (lyr., pl., dub.), Ael.*NA*13.20. II. *sharp edge*, ὀδόντων ib.1.31. III. *hole, perforation*, in a pipe, D.S.2.10.

⊛ **διάτομος**, ον, = δίχοτομος, Mart.Cap.8.864.

⊛ **διατόναιον**, τό, *joist*, *PPetr*.2 p.14 (iii B.C.); *curtain-rod*, Callix. 1:—so **—τόνιον**, *curtain-hook* or *-ring*, Lxx *Ex*.35.11.

**διατονθορύζω**, strengthd. for τονθορύζω, φοβερόν τι D.C.73.8.

**διατονικός**, ή, όν, = διάτονος II, εἶδος, γένος, Ph.1.321, Aristid. Quint.2.19; διάστημα Cleonid.*Harm*.5. Adv. -κῶς Nicom.*Harm*. 11.2.

**διατονόομαι**, *to be in a state of tension*, Pall.*Febr*.12.

⊛ **διάτονος**, ον, (διατείνω) *on the stretch, vehement*, αὖραι Thphr.*CP* 2.3.1. 2. *extending from front to back*, of *bonding courses* in a wall, Vitr.2.8.7. II. in Music, διάτονον (sc. γένος), τό, *the diatonic scale*, opp. χρωματικόν, ἐναρμόνιον, Aristox.*Harm*.p.19 M., etc.; δ. μέλος Alciphr.1.18; δ. μελῳδία D.H.*Comp*.19.

**διατοξ-εία**, ἡ, *contest in archery*, *OGI*339.82 (Sestos). **-εύσιμος**, ον, *that can be shot across*, χώρα a place *within bowshot*, Plu.*Luc*. 28. ⊛ **-εύω**, *shoot through*: metaph., δ. λόγον τινί *shoot* it *across* to him, Hld.5.32. II. Med., *contend with others in archery*, X. *Cyr*.1.4.4; τινί Parth.4.4.

**διατόρ-ευμα**, ατος, τό, *graven work*, Lxx 3*Ki*.7.17(30). **-εύω**, *engrave, chase*, S.*Fr*.315; δ. χρυσᾶς φιάλας στεφάνοις ἀμπέλου Aristeas 79; ὁ θεὸς ἐπίσταται τὰ ἑαυτοῦ δημιουργήματα δ. Ph.1.105; δ. ἐν σησάμῳ γράμμασιν ἔπη Plu.2.1083e:—Pass., Ael.*VH*14.7, Hierocl. p.37 A. **-έω**, *strike through, pierce*, Anon.ap.Suid. **-ία**, ἡ, *shrill, high-pitched music*, prob. in Thphr.*HP*4.11.4. **-νεύω**, *round off*, Lib.*Descr*.30.6. ⊛ **-ος**, ον, (τείρω) *piercing*, πέδαι A.*Pr*. 76; δ. φόβος *thrilling* fear, ib.181 (lyr.); of sound, δ. Τυρσηνικὴ σάλπιγξ Id.*Eu*.567: neut. as Adv., διάτορον φθέγγεσθαι Plu.2.303e; ἀναβοᾶν Luc.*Gall*.1. II. Pass., *pierced, bored through*, ποδοῖν ἀκμαί S.*OT*1034.

**διατρᾰγεῖν**, v. διατρώγω.

**διατρᾰγῳδέω**, = τραγῳδέω, interpol. in D.18.22; also gloss on διακωμῳδέω, Hsch. (corrupt).

**διάτρᾰμις**, εως, ὁ, ἡ, = λισπόπυγος, Stratt.74.

**διατρᾱνόω**, *articulate clearly*, χρωματικὸν γένος Nicom.*Harm*.7; βρέφος διατετρανωμένον *Theol.Ar*.47: metaph., Iamb.*in Nic*.p.72 P.

**διατρᾱνῶς**, Adv. *clearly*, δ. [ὁρῶσι] Phld.*Lib*.p.58 O.

⊛ **διατρᾰχηλίζομαι**, *put one's neck under the yoke*, Telesp.10 H. II. *fall head over heels*, Plu.2.501e.

**διατρᾱχύνω**, *make quite rough*, Plu.2.979b (Pass.).

**διατρεμέω**, *to be very still*, Arr.*Peripl.M.Eux*.6.

**διατρεπτικός**, ή, όν, *dissuasive*, λόγος Plu.2.788f.

⊛ **διατρέπω**, fut. -τρέψω Plb.2.47.8:—*turn away, deter from* a thing, δ. τινὰ τοῦ μή.. Id.5.4.10; τινά τινος Plu.2.87f; τινὰ πρὸς τὸ μὴ ἀπολιπεῖν Arr.*Epict*.1.6.10:—Pass., fut. διατρᾰπήσομαι Epicur. (v. infr.), etc.: aor. διετράπην [ᾰ] D.25.95, etc.:—*turn aside from one's purpose*, Epicur.p.xxviii U.; *to be confounded* or *perplexed*, Hp.*Epid*.5.81, D. l. c., Plb.3.86.6, al.; ὑπὸ παντὸς δ. καὶ διαρρεῖν D.Chr.66.19: c. acc., *to be overawed by*, ὄχλον.., Epict.*Gnom*.65; *avoid, refuse to face*, τινάς Plu.2.532e, etc. II. *pervert*, Critias *Fr*.22 D. 2. *overthrow, do away with*, ὅρους S.E.*P*.2.212:—Pass., ib.194, al.

⊛ **διατρέφω**, fut. -θρέψω D.C.63.27:—*breed up, support*, dub. l. in Arar.16; τὸ τέκνιον ἡμᾶς -θρέψει D.C. l. c.; τινὰ ἀπό τινος X.*Mem*. 2.7.6; δ. σπουδαίως *keep* patient well *nourished*, Aët.16.36:—Pass., *to be sustained continually*, Th.4.39; *to be maintained*, *BGU*1024 viii 14 (iv A. D.), etc.

⊛ **διατρέχω**, aor. -έδρᾰμον Od.3.177, etc., also -έθρεξα Call.*Lav. Pall*.23, *AP*5.225 (Paul. Sil.):—*run across* or *over*, ἰχθυόεντα κέλευθα διέδραμον Od. l. c.; τίς δ' ἂν ἑκὼν τοσσόνδε διαδράμοι ἁλμυρὸν ὕδωρ; 5.100; ἀτρεμίζων καὶ μὴ διατρέχων Antipho 3.2.5; *pass through*, διὰ τῆς πόλεως *Sammelb*.3924.26 (i A. D.). 2. metaph., *run through*, τὸν βίον Pl.*Lg*.802a; τὰ ἡδέα X.*Mem*.2.1.31; δ. τὸν λόγον *get to the end of* it, Pl.*Phdr*.237a. II. abs., *run about*, δ. εἰς ἀγρόν Ar.*Pax* 536, cf. Men.*Epit*.245; διατρέχοντες ἀστέρες Ar.*Pax*838; νεφέλαι διέδραμον Theoc.22.20: metaph., *run through, spread*, ἐν τῷ σώματι διέδραμε γαργαλισμός Hegesipp.Com.1.16; δ. σάλος ἁπάντων καὶ νεωτερισμός Plu.*Alex*.68; θροῦς δ. τῆς ἐκκλησίας Id.*Pyrrh*.13. 2. of Time, *pass away*, Hdn.2.6.3. 3. δ. εἰς.. *come quite to*.., Hp.*Int*. 39; δ. μέχρι *penetrate to*.., Plu.*Pyrrh*.24; πρὸς τὴν οἰκονομίαν *PGiss*. 79 ii 4 (ii A. D.).

**διατρέω**, *run trembling about, flee all ways*, διέτρεσαν ἄλλυδις ἄλλος Il.11.486, cf. 17.729, Plu.*Marc*.29, *Bru*.18.

**διά-τρημα**, ατος, τό, *foramen* for spinal nerves, Gal.2.848. II. *dug out, canoe*, Procop.*Aed*.6.1. ⊛**-τρησις**, εως, ἡ, *perforation*: *pore*, Hp.*Loc.Hom*.10, Gal.*UP*8.6. 2. *hole* in bone, ib.9. 5. **-τρητάριος**, ὁ, *maker of diatreta*, *Cod.Just*.10.66.1. **-τρητος**, ον, *bored through, pierced*, Gal.5.668. II. Lat. *diatreta, glass vessels with open-work decoration*, Mart.12.70.9.

⊛ **διατρῑβή**, ἡ, *wearing away*, esp. of Time, *way* or *manner of spending*, χρόνου τε διατριβὰς .. ἐφηῦρε .. πεσσοὺς κύβους τε *pastimes*, S. *Fr*.479.2: hence, abs., 1. *pastime, amusement*, Ar.*Pl*.923, Alex. 219.4, etc.; ἐν συνουσίᾳ τινὶ καὶ δ. D.21.71; γέλωτα καὶ δ. παρέχειν τινί Aeschin.1.175, cf. Plu.*Tim*.11; τοῦ συμποσίου δ. Alex.185; παρέσχε τοῖς κωμικοῖς δ. *materiem jocandi*, Plu.*Per*.4, cf. Jul.*Or*.2.52b; *place of amusement*, Men.481.10, Bato 2.4. 2. *serious occupation, study*, etc., τοὺς ἐν φιλοσοφίᾳ καὶ τῇ τοιᾷδε δ. τεθραμμένους Pl.*Tht*. 172c; διατριβὰς ποιεῖσθαι περί τι Lys.16.11, cf. Is.11.37; πρός τι Aeschin.2.38; ἐπί τινι Ar.*Ra*.1498; ἡ δ. τὰ πολλὰ ἐν λόγοις Pl.*Ly*. 204a. b. *discourse*, τὰς ἐμὰς δ. καὶ τοὺς λόγους Id.*Ap*.37d, cf. *Grg*. 484e, Isoc.12.19, etc.; αἱ πολιτικαὶ δ. D.H.10.15. c. *short ethical treatise* or *lecture*, δ. βραχέος διανοήματος ἠθικοῦ ἔκτασις Hermog. *Meth*.5, cf. Suid.: title of works by Zeno, Cleanthes, etc. d. *school* of philosophy, Ath.5.211d, al., Luc.*Alex*.5; Μωυσοῦ καὶ Χριστοῦ Gal. 8.579; Ἐπικούρου δ. Numen.ap.Eus.*PE*14.5; also, *a place of teaching, school*, ἡ ἐν τῷ κήπῳ δ. Epicur.*Fr*.217, cf. Phld.*Acad.Ind*.p.39 M., Luc.*Nigr*.25, Ath.8.350b. 3. *way of life, passing of time*, δ. ἐν ἀγορᾷ Ar.*Nu*.1055; δ. νέων ἐν δικαστηρίοις And.4.32; ἡ ἐν Σικελίᾳ δ. *stay* there, Pl.*Ep*.337e; ποιεῖσθαι ἐν τῷ ὑγρῷ τὴν δ., ἐν τῇ γῇ, Arist. *HA*487ᵃ20, *Resp*.474ᵇ26; διατριβὰς μετ' ἀλλήλων διατρίβειν Aeschin. 1.147. 4. *place of resort, haunt*, τὰς ἐν Λυκείῳ δ. Pl.*Euthphr*.2a; ᾗα ἐπὶ τὰς συνήθεις δ. Id.*Chrm*.153a. II. in bad sense, *waste of time, loss of time, delay*, with or without χρόνου, E.*Ph*.751, etc.; δ. ποιεῖσθαι Isoc.4.164: pl., δ. καὶ μελλήσεις Th.5.82; χρόνου δ. ἐμποιεῖν, παρέχειν, Id.3.38, X.*Oec*.8.13, etc.; ἐμβαλεῖν Plu.*Nic*.20; διατριβὴν ποτῷ ποιεῖν *prolong* a carouse, Alex.226.4. III. Rhet., *occasion for dwelling on a subject*, Arist.*Rh*.1418ᵃ27 (pl.). IV. *continuance, permanence*, Id.*Mete*.374ᵃ12. V. sens. obsc., = συνουσία, Procop. *Arc*.2.

**διατρῐβικός**, ή, όν, *scholastic, pedantic*, of persons, Plb.12.26ᵈ.6; λόγοι ib.25ᵏ.2; ῥητορική Phld.*Rh*.2.65 S.; οἱ δ. ib.1.32 S.

⊛ **διατρίβω** [ρῑ], pf. -τέτρῐφα Plb.4.57.3:—Pass., aor. 2 διετρίβην [ῐ] (v. infr.):—*rub hard*, χερσὶ διατρίψας Il.11.847: more freq., *wear away, consume*, πάντα διατρίβουσιν Ἀχαιοί Od.2.265; χρήματα Thgn. 921; τὰ τῶν Πελοποννησίων Th.8.87; εἰς αἰτίας ἀλόγους δ. τὸ θεῖον *to fritter away* Providence into unreasoning causes, Plu.*Nic*.23:—Pass., κάκιστα διατριβῆναι *perish* utterly, Hdt.7.120 (v. l. ἐκ-), cf. Th. 8.78. II. *spend*, of Time, θερείην Hdt.1.189; freq. χρόνον δ. Lys. 3.11; παρά τινι Hdt.1.24, etc.; δ. τινὰς ἡμέρας X.*HG*6.5.49; ἓξ ἔτη Isoc.4.141 (later c. gen., ἐτῶν οὐκ ὀλίγων ἐν Ῥώμῃ δ. Hdn.3.10.2):—Pass., ἐνιαυτὸς διετρίβη Th.1.125. 2. abs. (without χρόνον), *waste time*, οὐ μὴ διατρίψεις..; *make* no more *delay*, Ar.*Ra*.462; δ. ἐν γυμνασίοις *pass all one's time* there, Id.*Nu*.1002; ἐν ἄστει Antipho 1.14; ἐν ἀγρῷ Philem.71.6; αὐτοῦ, ἔνδον, Pl.*Prt*.311a; δ. μετ' ἀλλήλων *go on talking*, Id.*Phd*.59d, etc.: hence, *busy, employ oneself*, ἐν ζητήσει Id. *Ap*.29c; ἐν φιλοσοφίᾳ Id.*Tht*.173c; ἐπί τινι Id.*Euthd*.305a, Isoc.3.19, D.2.16; ἀμφί τι X.*Eq*.2.1; περί τι Pl.*Phd*.90c, Isoc.1.4; πρὸς ἱππικῇ Pl.*Prm*.126c; πρὸς τοῖς ἔργοις Arist.*Pol*.1309ᵃ8; πρὸς φιλοσοφίᾳ (prob. l. for -ίαν) Pl.*R*.540b: c. part., δ. μελετῶσαι X.*Cyr*.1.2.12. b. abs., *lose time, delay*, Il.19.150, Hp.*VC*19, Ar.*Eq*.515, etc.; λέγε καὶ μὴ διάτριβε Pl.*R*.472b; διατέτρῐφα *I have let the time slip by*.., Id. *Tht*.143a: c. part., καθ' ἕκαστα λέγων δ. *to waste time* in speaking, Isoc.7.35, cf. D.1.9. 3. *reside*, *PHal*.1.182 (iii B. C.), *PStrassb*. 22.6 (ii A. D.), etc. III. *put off by delay, thwart, hinder*, μή τι διατρίβειν ἐμὸν χόλον Il.4.42; οὔ τι διατρίβω μητρὸς γάμον Od.20.341; τἄριστον Ar.*Fr*.503: c. dupl. acc. pers. et rei, ὄφρα κεν ἥ γε διατρίβησιν Ἀχαιοὺς ὃν γάμον *put* them *off* in the matter of her wedding, Od. 2.204: c. gen. rei, μὴ δηθὰ διατρίβωμεν ὁδοῖο *let us* not *lose time* on the way, ib.404:—Med., μή τι διατριβώμεθα πείρης A.R.2.883.

**διατρίζω**, pf. -τέτρῑγα, *squeak, creak*, Agath.5.7: c. acc. cogn., φωνάς prob. in Plu.2.994e.

**διάτριμμα**, ατος, τό, *a sore from the skin being rubbed off* in riding, *Gloss*.

**διατριπ-τέον**, *one must spend time*, Arist.*Rh*.1417ᵃ10, Men.*Rh*. p.359 S. II. *one must rub*, *Hippiatr*.1. **-τικός**, ή, όν, *fit for bruising*, μύρον Ar.*Lys*.943.

**διατρῑταῖος**, α, ον, = διάτριτος, in Lat. form, Cael.Aur.*CP*1.3.

**διατρῑτάριος** ἰατρός physician *who prescribes three days' fast*, Gal. 10.582.

**διάτρῑτος**, ον, *tertian*, opp. ἀμφημερινός, περίοδοι Ph.1.427: but more freq., II. δ. (sc. περίοδος), ἡ, *period of three days*, τὴν ἀπὸ ταύτης φυλακτέον δ. Herod.Med.ap.Orib.5.27.23; ἡ πρώτη δ. Thessal.ap.Gal.10.264; πρὸ τῆς πρώτης δ. S.E.*P*.2.237.

**διάτριψις**, εως, ἡ, *grinding*, Dsc.4.45; *trituration*, Sor.1.93.

**διάτρῐχα**, Adv. = τρίχα, *in three divisions, three ways*, usu. written divisim in Hom., as Il.2.655; as one word, *h.Cer*.86, A.R.2.997.

⊛ **δια-τροπή**, ἡ, *confusion, agitation*, *PTeb*.27.104 (ii B. C.), Plb.1.16. 4, al., Onos.42.2 (pl.); *fiasco, débâcle*, Cic.*Att*.9.13.7. 2. *disgust*, Metrod.*Herc*.831.7,19, cf. Phld.*Rh*.1.219 S.; δ. καὶ φόβος D.S.17. 41. 3. *pity, sympathy*, Anon.ap.Suid. 4. δ. τοῖς ἀδικοῦσι γίνεσθαι *divert* them *from* wrongdoing, J.*BJ*2.16.4. **-τρόπιος**, ον, dub. sens., χροία Paul.Aeg.5.19. **-τροπος**, ον, *various in dispositions*, τρόποις E.*IA*559 codd.

⊛ **διατροφή**, ἡ, *sustenance and support*, X.*Vect*.4.49, Men.14, *Epit*. 88, D.S.1.74, *BGU*321.7 (iii A. D.); τῷ τέρατι [the Minotaur] πρὸς διατροφὴν κατασκευάσαι λαβύρινθον D.S.4.77: pl., *means of subsistence*, 1*Ep.Ti*.6.8.

**διατροχάδες**, αἱ, title of a poetical form, Praxiph.ap.Hsch.

**διατροχάζω**, of a horse, *trot*, X.*Eq*.7.11; of a person, *ride to and fro*, App.*BC*4.125; also, *hasten*, ἐπί, ἐς.., ib.1.69, 5.105: abs., *bustle about*, Eun.*VS*p.463 B.

**διατρύγιος** [ῡ], ον, (τρύγη), διατρύγιος δὲ ἕκαστος [ὄρχος] ἦην each row *bore grapes in succession*, Od.24.342, cf. Eust. ad loc.

**διατρῡπάω**, *bore through, pierce*, Arist.*HA*528ᵇ33:—Pass., Luc. *Sat*.24.

**διατρῡφάω**, strengthd. for τρυφάω, Pl.*Lg*.695c.

**διατρῡφέν**, v. sub διαθρύπτω.

**διατρώγω**, fut. -τρώξομαι Ar.*V*.164: aor. -έτρᾰγον ib.367:—*gnaw through*, τὸ δίκτυον ll. cc., cf. *Com.Adesp*.757; τὰς νευράς Arist. *Rh*.1401ᵇ16; *keep munching*, Pl.Com.173.10:—Pass., Hp.*Mul*.1. 107. 2. c. gen. rei, *eat of*, Ael.*VH*1.10.

**διαττ-άω**, *sift, riddle*, Hp.*Ulc*.21, Pl.*Sph*.226b, al., *SIG*²587.60, Ruf.ap.Orib.7.26.97:—Pass., Pl.*Cra*.402c, *IG*2².463.83, Thphr.

*HP*3.18.5. (The form διασσάω is given as etym. in *EM*271.37; διασσηθέντος dub. cj. in Emp.5.3; prop. δια-ττάω, cf. ἀλευρό-ττησις, ἐττημένα: hence pf. part. Pass. διεττημένης *IG*2².463.83 (but διηττ- codd. Thphr. l.c.).) **–ησις**, εως, ἡ, *sifting*, prob. in Plu.2.693e. **–ος**, ὁ, *sieve*, Hsch.

**διάττω**, v. διαΐσσω.

⊛ **διατυγχάνω**, *go wrong, make a mistake*, *PMasp.*76.15 (vi A.D.).

**διατῠλίσσω**, Att. **–ττω**, *unroll*, S.E.*M.*1.281.

**διάτῠλος**, ον, *callous*, of a fistula, Megesap.Orib.44.24.8.

⊛ **διατῠπόω**, *form*, χαρακτῆρας D.S.3.67; δ. νόμους *give* them *a lasting form*, Luc.*Jud.Voc.*5:—Pass., Lxx *Wi.*19.6, D.S.4.11, al., Sor.1.59; of seals, *to be engraved*, Arist.*Aud.*801b5. 2. metaph., *imagine, conceive*, Act., Luc.*Alex.*4; δ. τῇ φαντασίᾳ Chor.p.213 B., cf. Hdn.4.3.8; *represent, portray*, Plu.2.83a; χρώμασί τι Lib.*Eth.* 27.2. 3. *make dispositions*, of a testator, Just.*Nov.*1.2.2; of a legislator, ib.3 *Praef.*:—Pass., ib.6.1.1; *to be arranged, regulated by agreement*, μεταξὺ τῶν Ἑλληνίδων πόλεων..ὁπόσα χρὴ ἑκάστην..λύειν *IG*7.24.4.

**διατύπτομαι**, = πληκτίζομαι, Sch.Ar.*Ec.*958.

⊛ **διατύπ-ωσις** [ῠ], εως, ἡ, *full and perfect shape*, Arist.*HA*551b2; *configuration*, δ. ἀνδρείκελος Plu.*Alex.*72. 2. *system*, μηχανικῶν Hero *Mens.*23. 3. *vivid description*, Longin.20.1, Alex.*Fig.*3.25, etc. II. *regulation, apportionment*, *IG*12(9).907.9 (Chalcis, iv A.D.), 14.455 (Catana, v A.D.), *Ostr.Fay.*23 (iii A.D.), *PLips.*63.6 (iv A.D.); *disposition* made by a legislator, Just.*Nov.*117.13; by a testator, ib.1.1.2. **–ωτέον**, *one must represent*, λόγῳ ὁποῖος ἂν ὁ βίος γένοιτο D.H.*Rh.*2.6. **–ωτικός**, ή, όν, *descriptive, vivid*, Sch.A.R. 1.834. II. *formative*, *Theol.Ar.*34.

**διατύφω** [ῡ], pf. part. Pass. διατεθυμμένη *dazed*, Lib.*Or.*1.95 (nisi leg. –τεθρυμμένη).

**διατωθάζω**, *tease*, Alciphr.2.4.

⊛ **διαυγ-άζω**, *glance, shine through*, τῷ σχισμῷ *Placit.*3.3.3; ἕως οὗ ἡμέρα διαυγάσῃ 2*Ep.Pet.*1.19: impers., ἅμα τῷ διαυγάζειν (sc. τὴν ἡμέραν) Plb.3.104.5; *to be transparent*, Mnesith.ap.Orib.*inc.*15.11. II. = φωτίζω, Hsch.: and so metaph., διαυγασθεὶς *being enlightened, perceiving the truth*, J.*AJ*5.10.4. III. Astrol., *influence by its rays* (= ἐπιθεωρέω), *PLond.*1.130.70 (i A.D.). IV. Pass., *to be glazed*, of pottery, prob. in *BGU*1143.15 (i B.C.). **–ασμα**, ατος, τό, = sq., Aq.*Hb.*3.4. **–ασμός**, ὁ, *splendour bursting forth*, of lightning, *Placit.*3.3.1. **–εια**, ἡ, = foreg., Philostr.*Im.*2.1, Them. *Or.*13.175a, etc. 2. *translucency*, Plu.2.914b, Hierocl.*CA*26 p.480M.: metaph. of sayings, *clarity*, Plu.2.408e. II. *hole to admit light*, D.S.17.82; *peephole*, Procl.*Hyp.*3.25. **–έω**, *dawn*, ἡμέρας –ούσης Plu.*Arat.*22, D.H.5.49. II. ἧττον δ. *to be less obvious*, of a tumour, Antyll.ap.Orib.46.27.4. III. Pass., *to be transparent*, Gal.7.88, Hsch. ⊛ **–ής**, ές, *translucent*, of water, Arist. *Mir.*840b34, *AP*9.227 (Bianor), 277 (Antiphil.): Sup., v.l. in Arist. *Mu.*397a16; τὰ ὑγρὰ τῶν ὀφθαλμῶν –έστατα Alex.Aphr.*Pr.*1.68, cf. Ecphant.ap.Stob.4.7.64; *radiant*, of metal, Call.*Lav.Pall.*21; of stars, A.R.2.1104; of gems, ἀμέθυστος *AP*5.204; ὀφθαλμοί Aristaenet.1.1. **–ίζω**, = –άζω, Aq.*Jb.*25.5. **–ιον**, τό, *vent*, Hero*Spir.*1.18, al.; *peephole*, Procl.*Hyp.*3.16.

**διαυθεντέω**, *to be certainly informed*, S.E.*M.*7.425.

**διαυλ-έω**, *accompany with a* διαύλιον, μάθησιν *BGU*1125.20 (i B.C.). ⊛ **–ία**, ἡ, *duet on the flute*, Hsch., *EM*269.30. **–ίζω**· βαθύνω ἢ μηκύνω, Suid.:—Pass., διηυλίσθη· διεφθάρη, Hsch. **–ικός**, ή, όν, *of the* δίαυλος, τρόπος Iamb.*in Nic.*p.89P. ⊛ **–ιον**, τό, (αὐλός) *an air on the flute in the interval of the choral song*, Sch.Ar.*Ra.*1282, Hsch.: **–ειον**, Suid.

**δῐαυλοδρομ-έω**, *to run the* δίαυλος, Sch.Ar.*Av.*293; *return to the starting-point*, Arist.*GA*741b21; of the moon, Ph.1.24; of evils, *recur*, Id.2.350. **–ης**, ου, ὁ, *runner in the* δίαυλος, Pi.*P.*10.9. **–ία**, ἡ, *running forwards and backwards*, Lyd.*Mens.*1.12. **–ος**, *running the* δίαυλος, *IG*7.1772 (Thespiae), *Liv.Ann.*3.146 (Thessaly): written **–αδρόμος** *CIG*2758 (Aphrodisias): metaph. of the cock, διὰ γὰρ τῆς αὐλῆς τρέχει interpol. in Artem.4.22.

⊛ **δίαυλος** [ῐ], ὁ, *double pipe* or *channel*: usu. in the race, *double course*, Pi.*O.*13.37, E.*El.*825, *IG*2².957, al.: compared with *recurrent* nerves, Gal.*UP*7.14. b. δ. ἵππος, Hp.*Vict.*2.63. 2. metaph., κάμψαι διαύλου θάτερον κῶλον πάλιν *to run the homeward course, retrace one's steps*, A.*Ag.*344; δίαυλοι κυμάτων *ebb and flow, rise and fall* of the waves, E.*Hec.*29; εἰς αὐγὰς πάλιν ἁλίου δισσοὺς ἂν ἔβαν διαύλους they would twice *return*, Id.*HF*662 (lyr.), cf. 1102; τὸν ὕστατον τρέχων δ. τοῦ βίου Alex.235; ἐκπεριτρέχειν διαύλους *to run to and fro*, Aristaenet.1.27; of a wife's *return* to her husband, Anaxandr.56.4. II. *strait*, E.*Tr.*435. 2. in pl., of *air-passages*, Opp.*C.* 2.181.

**διαυλων-ία**, ἡ, (αὐλών) *narrow passage*, Eust.1917.32. **–ίζω**, *pass through a narrow channel*, Arist.*Resp.*478b12, *Mete.*366a27. 2. *admit a thorough draught*, Ath.5.189c. **–ισμός**, οῦ, ὁ, *passage of wind through a narrow opening*, Eust.1107.63.

**διαυξάνω**, *spread out*, Aët.7.1.

**δίαυρος**· δαλὸς διάπυρος, Hsch.

**διαυχενίζομαι**, *hold the neck erect*, Eun.*Hist.*pp.263,272 D.

**διαυχένιος**, ον, *running through the neck*, μυελός Pl.*Ti.*74a.

**διαύχην**· εὐεξίαν, Hsch.

**διαύω**, f.l. for ἰαύω, E.*HF*1049 (lyr.).

**διαφᾰγεῖν**, aor. 2 inf. of διεσθίω, *eat through*, Hdt.3.109, Hp.*Mul.* 1.2.

**διαφάδην**, Dor. **–άδαν** [φᾰ], Adv. *openly*, ὀνειδίσαι Sol.ap.Arist. *Ath.*12.5, cf. Alcm.23.56.

**διαφαίκωσι**· διαφαίνειν, Hsch.

**διαφαίνω**, *show through, let* a thing *be seen through*, τὴν λευκότητα δ. Arist.*GA*735b20; Ἀὼς καλὸν διέφαινε πρόσωπον Theoc.18.26; δ. τὰς ἑαυτῶν φύσεις Plb.12.24.1. 2. *allow light to pass*, Hero *Aut.* 27.1. 3. *convey* (to the reader), κατασκευὴν Phld.*Po.*2.35. II. Pass., *show through*, νεκύων δ. χῶρος *showed clear* of dead bodies, Il. 8.491; *to be seen through* a transparent substance, Hdt.3.24; μέλαν τὸ μὴ διαφαινόμενον *impervious to light*, Arist.*GA*780a34, cf. *Pr.*936a8; λίθος διαφαινόμενος *transparent* stone, Agatharch.82. 2. *to glow, to be red-hot*, μοχλὸς διεφαίνετο αἰνῶς Od.9.379. 3. metaph., *to be proved, show itself*, ἐν πείρᾳ τέλος –εται Pi.*N.*3.71, cf. Th.2.51; *to be conspicuous*, δυνάμει ταῦτα μέγιστα διεφάνη Id.1.18; *stand out, excel*, πάνθ' ἁπλῶς ἃ διαφαίνεται prob. in Phld.*Po.*5.4. III. intr., *show light through, to be transparent*, ἱμάτια –οντα Philem.81; *dawn*, ἡμέρης –ούσης Hdt.7.219, cf. 8.83: metaph., *shine through*, τὸ μεγαλοπρεπὲς διὰ τοῦ προσώπου διαφαίνει X.*Mem.*3.10.5. 2. πυρὰ διέφᾶνε (Dor. aor. 1) the pyre *parted its flames*, so as to allow a passage, Pi.*P.*3.44 (v.l. –φαινε).

**διαφαιρέω**, *take quite away*: aor. Med. διαφειλόμην v.l. in Paul. Aeg.6.35, prob.l. in Lxx 1*Ki.*17.39.

**διαφάν-εια** [φᾰ], ἡ, *transparency*, Pl.*Phd.*110d. ⊛ **–ής**, ές, (φαίνω) *translucent, transparent*, [ὕαλος] Ar.*Nu.*767; οὖρα Hp.*Aph.* 4.72, *Epid.*1.26.β'; ὦτα Id.*Coac.*188; ὑδάτια Pl.*Phdr.*229b; χιτώνια Ar.*Lys.*48; χιτωνάριον Men.727, cf. *IG*5(1).1390.16,21; τὸ δ. Arist. *de An.*418b4, al. 2. *red-hot*, Hdt.2.9, 4.73,75, Hp.*Art.*11. II. metaph., *manifest*, τάδ' ἤδη διαφανῆ S.*OT*754; *distinct, distinctly seen*, φλέβες Hp.*Epid.*6.3.17; εἶδος δ. Pl.*R.*544c, 548c (Sup.). Adv. –νῶς Th.2.65, X.*An.*6.1.24: Sup. –έστατα D.C.37.46. 2. *conspicuous*, ἐν τοῖς ἄλλοις Pl.*R.*600b; εἰς ἅπαντας ἀνθρώπους ἀρετῇ Id. *Ti.*25b. III. Subst. δ., τό, *talc*, Gal.13.663, Orib.*Fr.*99.

**διαφαρμᾰκεύω**, *give medicine to*, τινάς v.l. in Plu.2.157c.

**διάφαρος** χιτὼν *made in two pieces*, *EM*175.39.

⊛ **διάφᾰσις**, εως, ἡ, (διαφαίνω) *view through*, opp. ἔμφασις, Thphr. *Lap.*30: metaph., ἐκφάσεις καὶ δ. τῆς ἀληθείας Plu.2.354b, cf. Cic. *Att.*2.3.2.

**διαφάσσειν**· διασιλλαίνειν, Hsch.

**διαφαυλίζω**, *hold cheap, depreciate*, Pl.*Lg.*804b, Hierocl.p.59A., Lib.*Decl.*50.48.

⊛ **διά-φαυμα**, ατος, τό, *daybreak*, *PLond.*5.1684.4 (vi A.D.). **–φαυσις**, εως, ἡ, *shining through*, Plu.2.929b.

**διαφαύσκω**, Ion. (and later Prose, D.H.9.63) **–φώσκω**, aor. –έφαυσα Lxx *Ge.*44.3, al.:—*show light through, dawn*, ἅμ' ἡμέρῃ διαφωσκούσῃ as soon as day *began to dawn*, Hdt.3.86, 9.45; ἄρτι διαφαύσκοντος (abs.) Plb.31.14.13.

**διαφεγγής**, ές, *pellucid*: Adv. Comp., ὑέλου –έστερον ἀπαστράπτειν Luc.*Am.*26.

⊛ **διαφερόντως**, Adv. pres. part. Act. of διαφέρω, *differently from*, δ. ἤ.., Lys.31.20, Pl.*R.*538b, *Phd.*85b. 2. c. gen., δ. τῶν ἄλλων *above* all others, Id.*Cri.*52b; πάντων δ. προθυμότατος Th.8.68. II. abs., *differently, in different ways* or *degrees*, Arist.*EN*1098a29, *Pol.* 1260a11, Hierocl.*in CA*7 p.430M. 2. *especially, pre-eminently*, Th.1.38, etc.; δ. ἧττον πολύ Pl.*Lg.*862d.

⊛ **διαφέρω**, fut. διοίσω S.*OT*321, διοίσομαι *h.Merc.*255, etc.: aor. 1 διήνεγκα, Ion. διήνεικα: aor. 2 διήνεγκον:—*carry over* or *across*, δ. ναῦς τὸν Ἰσθμόν Th.8.8; *carry from one to another*, διαφέρεις κηρύγματα E.*Supp.*382; [τὸ ἤλεκτρον] διαφέρεται εἰς τοὺς Ἕλληνας Arist. *Mir.*836b6: metaph., γλῶσσαν διοίσει *will put* the tongue *in motion*, will speak, S.*Tr.*323 codd. 2. of Time, δ. τὸν αἰῶνα, τὸν βίον, *go through* life, Hdt.3.40, E.*Hel.*[10]; νύκτα Id.*Rh.*600: abs., ἄπαις διοίσει ib.982:—Med., *live, continue*, ὑγιηροὶ τἄλλα διαφέρονται Hp. *Art.*56; σοῦ διοίσεται μόνος *will pass his life* apart from thee, S.*Aj.* 511; σκοπούμενος διοίσει X.*Mem.*2.1.24 (cj. Dind. for διέσῃ). 3. *bear through, bear to the end*, σκῆπτρα E.*IA*1195; γαστρὸς ὄγκον δ., of a woman, Id.*Ion*15, cf. X.*Mem.*2.2.5: hence, 4. *bear to the end, go through with*, πόλεμον Hdt.1.25, Th.1.11; but also, *bear the burden of* war, Id.6.54; *endure, support*, with an Adv., ῥᾷστα γὰρ τὸ σόν τε σὺ κἀγὼ διοίσω τοὐμόν S.*OT*321; δ. πότμον δάκρυσι E.*Hipp.*1143 (lyr.): abs., of patients in disease, δ. ἕως τῶν εἰκοσιτεσσάρων ἡμερέων Hp.*Int.*40; δ. φθειρόμενος ib.12 (also ἡ νοῦσος δ. ἐννέα ἔτεα ibid.). II. *carry different ways*, Ar.*Lys.*570, etc.; δ. ἕκαστα εἰς τὰς χώρας τὰς προσηκούσας X.*Oec.*9.8; *toss about*, ὅπλισμα.. διαφέρων ἐσφενδόνα E.*Supp.*715; δ. τὰς κόρας *to turn* the eyes *about*, Id.*Ba.*1087, *Or.* 1261 (lyr.):—Pass., *to be drawn apart, disrupted*, opp. συμφέρεσθαι, Heraclit.10, Pl.*Sph.*242e, Epicur.*Nat.*908.2; *to be tossed about*, dub. in Str.3.2.5; δ. ἐν τῷ Ἀδρίᾳ *Act.Ap.*27.27, cf. Plu.*Galb.*26. 2. δ. τινά *spread* his *fame abroad*, Pi.*P.*11.60; εἰς ἅπαντας τὴν ἐκείνου μνήμην δ. D.61.46:—Pass., φήμη διηνέχθη Plu.2.163c. 3. *tear asunder*, E.*Ba.*754; *disjoin*, Arist.*Po.*1451a34 (Pass.): metaph., *distract*, τὰς ψυχὰς φροντίσιν Plu.2.133d, cf. 97f (Pass.), D.Chr.32.46 (Pass.). 4. δ. τὴν ψῆφον *give* one's vote *a different way*, i.e. against another, Hdt.4.138, etc.; but also, *give each man* his vote, E.*Or.*49, Th.4.74, X.*Smp.*5.8. 5. ἐράνους δ., = διαλύεσθαι, *pay* them *up, discharge* them, Lycurg.22. 6. *defer, reserve* for judgement, τὸν αἴτιον A.*Ch.*68 (lyr., διασπαράσσει Sch.). 7. *plunder*, Herod.7.90:—Pass., τῶν ἀπὸ [τῆς οἰκίας] φορτίων διενηνεγμένων *PLond.*1.45.9 (ii B.C.). 8. *excel*, ἀρετῇ τοὺς ἄλλους D.S.11.67, cf. 2.5; καλλιτεκνίᾳ πάσας γυναῖκας *Stud.Pont.*3.123 (Amasia). III.

intr., *differ*, φυᾷ δ. Pi.*N*.7.54; ἆρ' οἱ τεκόντες διαφέρουσιν ἢ τροφαί; is it one's parents or nurture *that make the difference?* E.*Hec*.599: c. gen., *to be different from*, Id.*Or*.251, Th.5.86, etc.; οὐδὲν διοίσεις Χαιρεφῶντος τὴν φύσιν Ar.*Nu*.503, cf. Pl.*Prt*.329d; τὸ δ'.. ἀφανίζειν ἱερὰ ἔσθ' ὅτι τοῦ κόπτειν διαφέρει; D.21.147; δ. τὰς μορφάς Arist.*HA* 497$^b$15; δ. εἴς τι, ἔν τινι, X.*Hier*.1.2,7; παρὰ τὴν Βεβρυκίαν App.*Mith*. 1; καθ' ὑπεροχὴν καὶ ἔλλειψιν Arist.*HA*486$^a$22; κατὰ τὴν θέσιν Id. *Mete*.341$^b$24; πρός τι Id.*HA*505$^a$21; τίνι δ. τὰ ἄρρενα τῶν θηλειῶν.. θεωρείσθω Id.*PA*684$^b$3: c. inf., μόνῃ τῇ μορφῇ μὴ οὐχὶ πρόβατα εἶναι δ. Luc.*Alex*.15: with Art., τρεῖς μόναι ψῆφοι διήνεγκαν τὸ μὴ θανάτου τιμῆσαι three votes *made the difference* (i.e. majority) against capital punishment, D.23.167; also διαφέρει τὸ ἥμισυ τοῦ ἔργου *makes a difference* equal to half the effort expended, X.*Oec*.20.17. **2.** impers., διαφέρει *it makes a difference*, πλεῖστον δ. Hp.*Aph*.5.22; βραχὺ δ. τοῖς θανοῦσιν εἰ.. E.*Tr*.1248, etc.; οὐδὲν δ. *it makes* no *odds*, Pl.*Phd*.89c, cf. Men.*Epit*.193; σμικρὸν οἴει διαφέρειν; Pl.*R*. 467c: c. dat. pers., δ. μοι *it makes a difference* to me, Antipho 5.13, Pl.*Prt*.316b, etc.; ἰδίᾳ τι αὐτῷ δ. he *has* some private *interest at stake*, Th.3.42; εἰ ὑμῖν μή τι δ. if you *see* no *objection*, Pl.*La*.187d; τί δέ σοι τοῦτο δ. εἴτε.. εἴτε μή; Id.*R*.349a, cf. *Grg*.497b, etc.: c. inf., οὐδέ τί οἱ διέφερεν ἀποθανεῖν Hdt.1.85: with personal constr., πράγματά τινι διαφέροντα Plu.*Caes*.65; *to be of importance*, πρός or εἴς τι, Gal.15.420,428; τῷ ζῴῳ Id.*UP*9.5. **3.** τὸ δ. *the difference, the odds*, Pl.*Phlb*.45d; = τὸ συμφέρον Antiph.31; περὶ μεγίστων δὴ τῶν -όντων βουλεύεσθαι Th.6.92, cf. Lys.31.5, Is.4.12; τὰ ἀναγκαιότερα τῷ ταμιείῳ δ. vital *interests*, *PThead*.15.17 (iii A.D.); τὸ δ. μέρος τῶν ἀποφάσεων the *essential* part, *POxy*.1204.11 (iii A.D.); τὰ δ. *vital* matters, *Ep.Rom*.2.18; ἐπιστάμενος τὰ δ. παραβαίνειν τολμᾷ And. 3.19 (but τὰ δ. also simply, *points of difference*, in character and the like, Th.1.70, etc.). **4.** *to be different from* a person: generally, *in point of excess, surpass, excel* him (cf. supr. II.8), τινός v.l. for -όντως in Th.3.39; τινί *in* a thing, Id.2.39, Alex.36.6; ἔν τινι Isoc.3. 39; εἴς τι Pl.*Ap*.35b; κατὰ μέγεθος X.*Lac*.1.10; πρός τι Aeschin.1. 181: c. inf., δ. τινὸς μεταβιβάζειν τινά Pl.*Grg*.517b: sts. folld. by ἤ, πολὺ διέφερεν ἀλέξασθαι ἤ.. *it was far better..than..*, X.*An*.3.4.33, cf. *Mem*.3.11.14, *Vect*.4.25 (where it means *to differ in point of diminution*); also δ. μέγα τι παρὰ τὰς ἄλλας πόλεις Plb.10.27.5: abs., *excel*, ἐπί τινι Isoc.10.12; τάχει Jul.*Or*.2.53c; οἱ τόποι διαφέρουσι Thphr.*CP*5.14.9; διαφέρον τι πεπραχέναι *a remarkable achievement*, Plb.6.39.2. **5.** *prevail*, ἐπὶ πολὺ διήνεγκε Th.3.83. **6.** *quarrel, struggle*, Telecl.20; οἱ διαφέροντες *the parties, litigants*, *PPar*.69B 10 (iii A.D.). **7.** *come between, intervene*, ὁ διαφέρων χρόνος Antipho 5.94. **8.** *belong to*, τινί, as property, Ph.1.207, *PLond*. 3.940.23 (iii A.D.); of persons, *belong to* a household, *PStrassb*.26.5 (iv A.D.); οἱ -φέροντες *kinsfolk*, *Annuario* 4/5.476 (Bargylia); *appertain to*, τῇ ὠνῇ *BGU*1062.21 (iii A.D.); τὰ εἰς τοῦτο -φέροντα πράγματα Mitteis *Chr*.372 v 3 (ii A.D.). **IV.** Med. and Pass., *be at variance, quarrel*, τινί Heraclit.72, cf. Amphis 32, etc.; περί τινος Hdt.1.173, Pl.*Euthphr*.7b; δ. ἀλλήλοις *differ with*, ibid., cf. Antipho 5.42; τινὶ περί τινος Th.5.31, cf. X.*Oec*.17.4; πρὸς ἀλλήλους Lys.18. 17, cf. Hyp.*Oxy*.1607 *Fr*.1 iii 60, etc.; τὰ πρὸς ἀλλήλους *Supp.Epigr*. 1.363.5 (Samos, iii B.C.); ἀμφί τινος X.*An*.4.5.17; διενεχθέντας γνώμῃ Hdt.7.220; δ. ὡς.. *maintain on the contrary* that.., D.56.46; οὐ διαφέρομαι, = οὔ μοι διαφέρει, Id.9.8; μηδὲν διὰ τοῦτο διαφέρου *let there be* no *dispute* on this ground, Lys.10.17; οἱ -φερόμενοι *the litigants*, *SIG*685.29 (Crete, ii B.C.).—Not in Ep.

**διάφεσις**, εως, ἡ, *IG*2$^2$.1036.4 (dub. sens.).

⊕ **δια-φεύγω**, fut. -φεύξομαι Pl.*Prm*.135d:—*get away from, escape*, τινά or τι, Hdt.1.204, 3.19, Antipho 5.90, etc.; θάνατον Pl.*Ap*.39a; κίνδυνον Isoc.2.6; *survive*, [νόσημα] Arist.*HA*603$^b$11; γάμον Men. *Georg*.21: abs., Democr.239, Hdt.1.10, etc.; μὴ.. ἀθῷος διαφύγῃ *PTeb*.44.28 (ii B.C.); ἐκ τῆς Μήλου Th.8.39; δ. ἐκ πόνων εἰς ἀγαθά Pl.*Lg*.815e; διαφεύγει δ' οὐδὲ νῦν but *it is* not even now *too late*, D.10. 31:—Pass., διεφεύχθη ὁ κίνδυνος J.*AJ*18.8.9. **2.** *escape one's notice* or *memory*, Pl.*Phd*.95e, *Men*.96e; σὲ διαφεύξεται ἡ ἀλήθεια Id.*Prm*. 135d; δ. τὰ πολλὰ τῶν νοσημάτων αὐτούς Jul.*Or*.7.228a; πολλά με διαπέφευγε Isoc.4.187. **-φευκτέον**, *one must avoid*, Gal.13. 27. **-φευκτικός**, ή, όν, *able to escape*, Luc.*Tim*.29. **-φευξις**, εως, ἡ, *escaping, means of escape*, Th.3.23, J.*AJ*17.10.7, Plu.*TG*5 (v.l. -φυξις), D.C.40.32; *avoidance*, Phld.*Rh*.1.192S.

**διαφημέω**, *bring discredit on*, τὴν εὐγένειαν dub. in Plu.*Nob*.19.

⊕ **διαφημίζω**, *make known, spread abroad*, D.H.11.46, *Ev.Marc*.1. 45; ὡς.. Palaeph.13:—Pass., c. inf., διεφημίσθη θνήσκειν ὁ βασιλεὺς J.*BJ*1.33.3: abs., *to be celebrated*, ἐπὶ ταῖς καλοκἀγαθίαις Vett.Val. 250.5:—Med., aor. 1 διεφημίξαντο D.P.26. **II.** *call, name*, Arat. 221:—Med., Id.442 (v.l.), D.P.50.

**διαφθαρτικός**, ή, όν, *destructive, fatal*, Arist.*Pr*.865$^a$8, Poll.5.132.

**διαφθέγγομαι**, *utter, speak*, Porph.*Chr*.63, al.

⊕ **διαφθείρω**, fut. -φθερῶ S.*OT*438, etc., Ep. -φθέρσω Il.13.625: pf. διέφθαρκα E.*Med*.226, Pl.*Ap*.30d, etc.; also διέφθορα (v. infr. III):—Pass., fut. διαφθαρήσομαι Th.4.37; Ion. διαφθερέομαι Hdt.8.108, 9.42: 3 pl. plpf. διεφθάρατο Id.8.90:—*destroy utterly*, πόλιν Il.13.625; ἔργα διαφθείρεσκε Hdt.1.36; *make away with, kill*, τινά Id.9.88, etc.; *destroy, ruin*, ἥδ' ἡμέρα φύσει σε καὶ διαφθερεῖ S. l. c.; τὴν τύχην Id. *Ph*.1069; δ. χεῖρα *weaken, slacken* one's hand, E.*Med*.1055; *spoil, break*, ὑγιῆ λίθον *IG*7.3073.33 (Lebad., ii B.C.); τὰ θυρώματα διεφθάρθαι *IG*2$^2$.1046.11; δ. τὴν συνουσίαν *break up* the party, Pl.*Prt*. 338d. **2.** in moral sense, *corrupt, ruin*, γνώμην A.*Ag*.932; δ. τοὺς νέους, τοὺς νεωτέρους, Pl.*Ap*.30b, 25a; νεανίσκον συνὼν δ. Eup. 337; esp. *corrupt by bribes*, Hdt.5.51; ἀργυρίῳ δ. τινά Lys.28.9; διαφθειρομένων ἐπὶ χρήμασι D.18.45; δ. γυναῖκα *seduce* a woman, Lys.1.16, etc., cf. E.*Ba*.318 (Pass.); δ. τοὺς νόμους *falsify, counterfeit* them, Isoc.18.11; γραμματεῖον Id.17.33 (Pass., ib.24); τὰ ϝεϝαδηκότα *IG*9(1).334.37 (Locr., v B.C.). **3.** οὐδὲν διαφθείρας τοῦ χρώματος *having changed* nothing of his colour, Pl.*Phd*.117b. **4.** of a woman, *to lose by miscarriage* or *premature birth*, ἔμβρυα, βρέφος, Hp.*Aph*.5.53, Plu.2.242c: abs., *miscarry*, Hp.*Epid*.7.73, Is.8. 36:—Pass., τῶν διαφθαρεισῶν τὰ ἔμβρυα Hp.*Mul*.1.72. **5.** *lose, forget*, E.*Hipp*.389. **6.** = διάγω, dub. in Id.*Fr*.280. **II.** Pass., *to be destroyed*, δ. ἐπὶ τοῖς ἱματίοις *to be murdered* for the clothes he wore, Antipho 2.2.5; of animals, freq. in Pap., *POxy*.74.14 (ii A.D.), etc.; esp. *to be crippled, disabled*, Hdt.1.34; of ships, ib.166, And.1. 142; *to be spoilt*, γάλα *BGU*1109.11 (i B.C.), cf. Th.7.84; *to be corrupted*, αἷμα Gal.15.297, al.; τὴν ἀκοὴν διεφθαρμένος *deaf*, Hdt.1.38; τὰ σκέλεα διεφθάρησαν *had* their legs *broken*, Id.8.28; διέφθαρμαι δέμας τὸ πᾶν S.*Tr*.1056; τὰ ὄμματα δ. *blinded*, Pl.*R*.517a; σὰς φρένας E.*Hel*.1192; τὸ φρενῶν διαφθαρέν, = φρενοβλάβεια, Id.*Or*.297, cf. X.*Cyr*.4.1.8: abs., διεφθαρμένος *decomposed*, of a corpse, Pl.*R*. 614b. **III.** pf. διέφθορα intr., *to have lost one's wits*, διέφθορας Il. 15.128; also in Hp., διεφθορὸς αἷμα *corrupted* blood, *Mul*.2.134; freq. in later Prose, γάλα δ. ἤδη J.*AJ*5.5.4; τὰ δ. σώματα Plu.2.87c, cf. 128e, Luc.*Sol*.3, etc.; but, **2.** in Trag. and Com. always trans. (cf. Ammon.42, Moer.127), τὰς.. ἐλπίδας διέφθορεν S.*El*.306; τὰς φρένας διέφθορε.. μοναρχία E.*Hipp*.1014; τὸν λόγον δ. Cratin. 292, cf. Eup. l. c., Pherecr.145.15, Ar.*Fr*.490, Men.3. **IV.** aor. διέφθειρα intr., *became corrupt*, Lxx *Jd*.2.19.

**διαφθίνω**, pf. part. διεφθινηκώς *wasted away*, Sch.Theoc.10.18.

**διαφθονέω**, *envy*, τινί Lxx *Es*.6.3 (v.l.):—Pass., *to be grudged, deprived of* one's good fortune, J.*AJ*2.6.7; *to be envied*, Agath.1. 16.

⊕ **διαφθορ-ά**, Ion. -ρή, ἡ, (διαφθείρω) *destruction, ruin*, ἐπὶ -φθορᾷ τῆς πόλεως Th.8.86; ἀπέστειλε ἐπὶ διαφθορῇ Hdt.4.164; μέχρι διαφθορᾶς Pl.*Mx*.242d: pl., S.*OT*573, etc. **2.** *destruction, blight*, of things, ὀμμάτων διαφθοραί Id.*OC*552; διαφθορὰ μορφῆς A.*Pr*.643. **3.** in moral sense, *corruption, seduction*, νέων X.*Ap*.19; κριτῶν Arist. *Rh*.1372$^a$34 (pl.). **4.** *miscarriage, abortion*, Hp.*Mul*.1.3, *Coac*. 505, *Mélanges Holleaux* 265 (ii/i B.C.). **5.** stomachic *disorder*, Aret.*CA*1.5. **II.** concrete, ἰχθύσιν δ. *a prey* for fishes, of a corpse, S.*Aj*.1297; πολεμίοις ὕβρισμα καὶ δ. E.*HF*459. **-εύς**, έως, ὁ, *corrupter*, νόμων, ἀνθρώπων, Pl.*Cri*.53c; τῶν νέων Them.*Or*.23.296b: as fem., E.*Hipp*.682. **-έω**, = διαφθείρω, dub. in Procop.*Aed*.6.5.

**διαφίημι**, aor. διαφῆκα X. and Plb. (v. infr.): inf. διαφεῖναι D.23. 171: fut. διαφήσουσι is f.l. in Th.7.32:—*dismiss, disband*, τὸ στράτευμα ἐκ τῆς χώρας X.*HG*3.2.24; τὴν δύναμιν D. l. c.; an assembly, Plb.3.63.14, al.

**διαφῐλο-νῑκέω**, *dispute earnestly*, Arist.*SE*165$^b$13, Plu.*Alex*.29, D.L.3.34. **-τεκνέω**, *persist in philoprogenitiveness*, Phld.*Sto*.339. 9. **-τῑμέομαι**, *strive emulously* or *earnestly*, Thphr.*HP*4.4.1; τινὶ ὑπέρ τινος Plu.*Arist*.16.

**διαφλέγω**, *burn up*, Lxx *Ps*.82(83).15:—Pass., Plu.*Alc*.39: metaph., *inflame*, τὰς ψυχάς Id.*Mar*.16; οἱ διαφλέξαντες Ἀχιλλέα θυμοί Heraclit.*All*.20.

**διάφλοισβοι**· τεταραγμένοι, Hsch.

**διαφλύω**, in Pass., *to be permeated*, ὑπὸ θερμοῦ Hp.*Mul*.1.77.

**δια-φλύζω** and -φλύω, *to be in exuberant health*:—also Subst. -φλυξις, εως, ἡ, = ὑπέρβλυσις, Gal.19.92.

**διάφοβος**, ον, *timorous*, Tz. ad Lyc.1242.

**διαφοιβάζω**, *drive mad*, διαπεφοιβάσθαι κακοῖς S.*Aj*.332.

**διαφοιγυομόρ**· ἐπὶ πάσῃ ἡμέρᾳ τῆς τῶν φιδιτίων σιτήσεως (Lacon.), Hsch.

**διαφοινίσσομαι**, *become quite red*, Hp.*Coac*.458.

⊕ **διαφοιτάω**, Aeol. part. ζαφοίταισ' Sapph.*Supp*.25.15:—*wander, roam*, l.c., Hdt.1.60; *go backwards and forwards*, ib.186; of hounds on the scent, X.*Cyn*.3.3; δ. διὰ τῆς χώρας Ar.*Av*.557; ἀν' ἐρῆμον δρίος prob. in *Lyr.Alex.Adesp*.7.2; δ. τῆς Ἰταλίας Plu.*Caes*.33: c. acc., διαφοιτῶντες [τὸ ζεῦγμα] Philostr.*Im*.2.17; οἰμωγὴ δ. τὸν στρατόν Id.*Her*.19.12; of a report, *spread*, εἰς Ῥώμην Plu.*Fab*.8, cf. Luc.*Alex*.7, Hdn.1.4.8, etc. **II.** *permeate*, ψυχὴ διαπεφοιτηκυῖα (sc. σώματος) Plot.1.1.4, cf. M.Ant.8.54; [δημιουργὸς] τῆς ὕλης [τῆς ὕλης] διαπεφοιτηκώς Gal.4.561.

⊕ **διαφορ-ά**, ἡ, (διαφέρω) *moving hither and thither*, πεσσῶν διαφοραί *moves*, E.*Fr*.360.9. **2.** *dislocation*, τοῦ ὤμου Heliod.ap.Orib.49. 8.4, 49.9 tit. **II.** *difference*, Th.3.10 (pl.), etc.; περί τι D.H. *Comp*.15; θεοῦ πρὸς ἄνθρωπον Plu.2.1075c; διαφορὰν ἔχειν to *differ*, Men.426. **2.** in Logic, *the differentia* of a species, ἐκ τοῦ γένους καὶ τῶν διαφορῶν τὰ εἴδη Arist.*Metaph*.1057$^b$7, cf. *Top*.139$^a$29: hence in pl. of *species* or *kinds*, Id.*Pol*.1285$^a$1, 1289$^a$20, Thphr. *HP*6.4.5; εἴδη καὶ δ. Plu.2.719e; also κατὰ διαφορὰν ποιός *Stoic*.2. 128, al. **III.** *variance, disagreement*, Hdt.1.1; δ. ἔχειν τινί E. *Med*.75: pl., τὰς διαφορὰς διαιρέειν, καταλαμβάνειν, *settle the differences*, Hdt.4.23, 7.9.β'; δ. θέσθαι καλῶς And.1.140; διαφοραὶ πρός τινας Pl.*Phdr*.231b; δ. πρὸς ἀλλήλους περί τινος Lys.25.10; ἐν δ. καταστῆναί τινι Antipho 1.1; δ. φιλοσοφίᾳ καὶ ποιητικῇ Pl.*R*. 607b. **IV.** *distinction, excellence*, Id.*Ti*.23a; ναυπηγίας Plb.1.51. 4. **V.** *advantage, profit*, Antipho 2.3.3; πᾶν τὸ πῖπτον εἰς διαφορᾶς λόγον, *valuables*, Agatharch.102. **VI.** *vote, division*, in an assembly, δ. ποιήσασθαι *IG*12(2).526$^a$18 (Eresus). **VII.** *delay*, *PMagd*.11.10 (iii B.C.). **VIII.** δ. διανοίας *being beside oneself*, Dsc.

*Ther.*7. ⊛ **-έω**, = διαφέρω, *spread abroad, disperse*, κλέος εὐρὺ διὰ ξεῖνοι φορέουσι Od.19.333; σωρὸν . . διαφορῆσαι ῥάδιον Diph.100; τὴν ὑγρότητα Plu.2.366c, etc.; πολλὰ τῆς οὐσίας ib.484a; δ. κραιπάλη τὴν κραιπάλην ib.127f:—Pass., διαπεφορῆσθαι Critias *Fr.*62 D.; τὰ διαπεφορημένα τῶν εἰδώλων Arist.*Div.Somn.*464$^b$13. **2.** *carry away*, τοὺς σταυρούς Th.6.100; esp. as plunder, χρήματα τὰ σὰ διαφορέει Hdt.1.88; ὧν κοινῇ διαπεφορημένων D.27.29. **3.** *plunder*, ἐπαρχίας Plu.*Brut.*6, etc.:—Med., *PSI*5.522.5 (iii B.C.):—most freq. in Pass., οἶκον διαφορηθέντα Hdt.3.53; διαφορουμένης τῆς χώρας ὑπὸ λῃστῶν D.19.315; διαφορεῖσθαι τὴν γνώμην *to be robbed* of one's wits, Pl. *Lg.*672b. **4.** *tear in pieces*, ἄλλαι δὲ δαμάλας διεφόρουν E.*Ba.*739; τινὰς τοξεύμασι Id.*HF*571; ὑπὸ κυνῶν τε καὶ ὀρνίθων διαφορεύμενος Hdt. 7.10.θ', cf. Ar.*Av.*338. **5.** Pass., of ice, *break up*, *Gp.*19.6.4. **II.** = διαφέρω I.1, *carry across from one place to another*, ἀπὸ τῶν ξυμμάχων προσόδου διαφορουμένης Th.6.91. **III.** Medic. (cf. διαφόρησις, -ητικός): **1.** *dissipate* by evaporation, perspiration, etc., in Pass., Aret.*SD*2.1, Alex.Aphr.*Pr.*1.68, Gal.10.657, al. **2.** '*discuss*', *disperse* by drugs or treatment, φύματα Dsc.5.156, cf. Gal.10. 392: abs., Dsc.1.30. **3.** *exhaust by dissipating, weaken*, καρδιακὸν με διαφορεῖ πάθος Diog.Oen.66: metaph., ὁ μερισμὸς δ. καὶ ἐκλύει τὴν ἑκάστου δύναμιν Procl.*Inst.*86:—Pass., Gal.14.735. **IV.** Pass., *dispute, debate*, S.E.*M.*1.205. **V.** διαφορούμενον ἀξίωμα, v. διφορέω. **-ημα**, ατος, τό, *thing thrown to and fro*; *the game of ball*, Hsch., Suid. **II.** *thing torn to pieces, prey*, Lxx *Je.*37.16. **-ησις**, εως, ἡ, *plundering, stealing*, προβάτων *PTeb.*72.239 (ii B.C.): pl., Plu. *Cor.*9, *Cic.*14. **II.** *evaporation, dissipation*, Sor.1.22, Olymp.*in Mete.*145.14; *perspiration*, Cic.*Fam.*16.18.1; δ. τῶν ἱδρώτων Plu.*Fr. inc.*149. **2.** *dispersion, discussion*, Gal.10.919. **3.** *exhaustion*, Cael.Aur.*CP*1.15, al. **III.** *dubitation, perplexity*, Plu.2. 389a. **-ητικός**, ή, όν, *promoting perspiration*, etc., Antyll.ap. Orib.6.21.30: Comp., Dsc.1.30. **2.** *capable of dispersing, discutient*, δύναμις δ. οἰδημάτων Id.4.112, cf. Gal.13.925. **3.** *perspiring*, Cael.Aur.*CP*2.36. **-ητος**, ον, *torn in pieces*, σάρξ prob. in E. *Cyc.*344. **-ία**, ἡ, = διαφορά I, f.l. in D.H.*Rh.*11.10. ⊛ **-ος**, ον, *different, unlike*, Hdt.2.83, 4.81, Pl.*Lg.*964a, etc.; παρά τι Iamb. *Myst.*3.30: c. gen., *differing from*, Pl.*Phlb.*61d, etc. **b.** *several, various*, κατὰ τὰς δ. ὕλας Phld.*Sign.*24; δ. πρόσωπα *POxy.*1033. 88 (iv A.D.), cf. *Ep.Hebr.*9.13. **c.** *ambiguous*, Hsch. **2.** *differing* or *disagreeing with* another, πολλοῖς δ. εἰμι E.*Med.*579; esp. in hostile sense, *at variance with*, Κλεομένεϊ Hdt.5.75; τοῖς οἰκείοις Lys.14.44; ἀλλήλοις, ἑαυτοῖς, Pl.*Prt.*337b, *Lg.*679b; ἀνώμαλος καὶ δ. πρὸς ἑαυτόν Plu.*Sull.*6: c. gen., δ. τινος one's *adversary*, D.29.15, cf. Antiph.209.1, Philem.162. **3.** *excellent, distinguished, remarkable*, Antiph.175.3; δ. γλυκύτητι D.S.2.57; πρὸς ἀρετήν Plu.*Cleom.*16: Comp., ὄνομα *Ep.Hebr.*1.4. **4.** *making a difference to one*, **a.** in good sense, *advantageous, profitable, important*, δ. ἑτέρου μᾶλλον Th.4.3; πρὸς σωτηρίαν Pl.*Lg.*779b. **b.** rarely in bad sense, *disagreeable*, γείτονα γείτονι μηδὲν ποιεῖν δ. ib. 843c. **II.** as Subst., διάφορον, τό, **1.** *difference*, σμικρόν τι τὸ δ. εὕροι τις ἄν Hdt.2.7; διάφορα πολλὰ θεῶν βροτοῖσιν εἰσορῶ I see many *differences* between gods and men, E.*Supp.*612 (lyr.); μέγα τὸ δ. ἐστι (v.l. διαφέρον) Hp.*Art.*14; ἆρα μικρὰ τὰ δ. ἑκατέροις τῆς οὐσίας; Is.11.47; ἡλίκα γ' ἐστὶν τὰ διάφορ' ἐνθάδ' ἢ ἐκεῖ πολεμεῖν D.1.27. **2.** *what concerns one*, τῶν ἡμῖν ἐς τὰ μέγιστα διαφόρων *matters of* the greatest *concern* to us, Th.4.87; τηλικούτων ὄντων αὐτῷ τῶν δ. D.19. 68, cf. Arist.*Oec.*1352$^b$2. **3.** *difference, disagreement*, ἕνεκα τῶν αὐτοῖς ἰδίᾳ δ. on account of their private *differences*, Th.1.68, cf. 2.37; τὸ Ἀθηναίων δ. *difference with* the A., Id.2.27. **4.** in reference to money-matters, *difference, balance*, Hyp.*Eux.*17, cf. Epict.*Ench.*25. 4; *expenditure*, Arist.*VV*1251$^b$10; ἡ μικρολογία ἐστὶ φειδωλία τοῦ δ. Thphr.*Char.*10.1: in pl., *expenses*, D.32.18, *IG*5(1).1390.45 (Andania, i B.C.); *losses*, *OGI*90.30 (ii B.C.), Wilcken *Chr.*11 *B*8 (ii B.C.). **b.** *ready money, cash*, χρείας γενομένης ἀναγκαίας τῷ δήμῳ διαφόρου *IG*12(7).388.7 (Amorgos); *sum of money*, *PSI*4.330.8 (iii B.C.), *UPZ*3.7 (ii B.C.), Plb.4.18.8, *IG*12(5).653.56 (Syros, i B.C.), etc.: pl., Plb.31.27.13, *CIG*2695 (Iasus); *interest*, ἐπὶ διαφόρῳ ἡμιολίας *POxy.*1040.8 (iii A.D.); *price*, Luc.*Herm.*81, D.L.6.9. **5.** *expenses of carriage*, *PAmh.*2.69.12 (ii A.D.), *PFay.*86a11 (ii A.D.). **III.** Adv. -ρως *with a difference*, τοῖς παροῦσιν ἤθεσι δ. πολιτεύειν Th.6.18, cf. Pl.*Ion*531b: c. gen., δ. τῶν λοιπῶν δένδρων *Gp.*10.37.1; *in a variety of ways*, Phld.*D.*3.9: Comp. -ώτερον Id.*Mus.*p.109 K. **2.** δ. ἔχειν *differ*, Pl.*Phlb.*25e, etc.; δ. ἔχειν τινί *to differ with*.., D.33. 18. **3.** *pre-eminently*, πρᾶος καὶ φιλάνθρωπος τῶν ἄλλων δ. ὤν Id. 24.196, cf. J.*BJ*2.8.9 (Sup.); δ. συναρέσκει Men.*Epit.*333, cf. *Pk.*72; *excellently, with distinction*, ἀγωνίσασθαι Sosyl.p.30 B.; δ. ἀπειργασμένος Plb.13.7.2: Comp. -ώτερον Hsch.

⊛ **διαφορότης**, ητος, ἡ, *difference*, Pl.*R.*587e, Ph.2.370, J.*AJ*18.1.5, Ael.*NA*1.12, Iamb.*Comm.Math.*14.

**διαφουλλαί**· διακοπαί, διαλογαί, Hsch. **διαφράγιον**· ἀλλοῖον καὶ διάφορον, Id.

⊛ **διάφραγμα**, ατος, τό, *partition* or *barrier*, Th.1.133, Hero *Spir.*1.8; στοᾶς *Inscr.Prien.*99.19; *lock* in a canal, *PPetr.*3p.343 (iii B.C.), D.S.1.33. **II.** *muscle which divides the thorax from the abdomen, midriff, diaphragm*, Pl.*Ti.*70a, 84d, Gal.*UP*4.14, etc. **b.** δ. [τοῦ μυκτῆρος] *cartilage which divides* the nostrils, Arist.*HA*492$^b$16, cf. Ruf.*Onom.*34, Gal.17(1).824. **c.** the *velum palati*, Hp.*Epid.*2.2. 24. **d.** *septum lucidum* of the brain, Gal.2.719.

**διαφραγμάτιον**, τό, Dim. of foreg., *small partition*, *IG*11(2).199*A* 15, 45 (Delos, iii B.C.).

**διαφράγνῡμι**, *barricade*, Plu.*Cam.*34 (Med.):—Pass., *to be barricaded*, ἐρύμασι καὶ προτειχίσμασι Id.*Aem.*13.

**διαφρᾰδής**, ές, *distinct*, of sound: in Adv. -έως Hp.*Loc.Hom.*2.

⊛ **διαφράζω**, only in pf. διαπέφρᾰδε, *show plainly*, ὡς .. μοι μήτηρ διεπέφραδε Il.18.9; διεπέφραδε κούρῃ Od.6.47, cf. 17.590, A.R.1.848, Opp.*C.*4.378, Q.S.3.80.

**διαφρακτέον**, *one must partition off*, Ph.*Bel.*95.34.

**διάφραξις**, εως, ἡ, *midriff*, Hp.*Virg.*1.

**διαφράσσω**, Att. -ττω, = διαφράγνυμι, διαφάρξαντι τὰ μετακιόνια *IG*1$^2$.373.251; δ. μεταστύλιον ib.2.1054.63, cf. D.S.17.96, Them. *Or.*20.235d:—Pass., *to be divided off*, δ. ὑμέσι Dsc.2.24; μήνιγξι Erasistr.ap.Gal.5.603, cf. Hdn.3.1.4; διαφρᾰγείς *obstructed*, Ruf. *Anat.*30; but ἔλλοβα διαπεφραγμένα *with divisions*, Thphr.*HP*8.5.2.

**διαφρέω**, *let through, let pass*, διὰ τῆς πόλεως . . τὴν κνῖσαν οὐ διαφρήσετε Ar.*Av.*193; ὅπως μὴ διαφρήσωσι τοὺς πολεμίους Th.7.32.

**διαφρίσσω**, strengthd. for φρίσσω, Poll.1.107.

**διαφρονέω**, *meditate*, Hsch. (-φορέων cod.). **II.** *quarrel*, Id., *Lyr.Alex.Adesp.*37.2 (s. v. l.).

**διαφροντίζω**, *meditate on, consider*, τι Hp.*Aër.*1; δ. δρᾶμα *compose*, Ael.*VH*2.21: abs., *meditate*, Epicr.11.22. **2.** c. gen., *take care of, pay regard to*, Arist.*Pol.*1262$^b$20.

**διάφρος**, ον, *foamy*, Gal.19.93.

**διαφρουρέω**, *to keep one's post*: metaph., διαπεφρούρηται βίος A.*Fr.* 265.

**δια-φρύγω** [ῡ], *bake*, *Hippiatr.*103, Lyd.*Ost.*27. **-φρυκτος**, ον, *parched*, of beans used in voting, Hsch.:—hence **-φρυκτόω**, *vote* or *cast lots*, Id., *EM*271.50, Suid.

**διαφυάς**, άδος, ἡ, = διαφυή, D.S.1.47.

**διαφυγγάνω**, = διαφεύγω, Heraclit.86, Th.7.44, Aeschin.3.10, J. *AJ*19.1.15.

**διαφῠγετεῖν**· παρ' ἐλπίδα σωθῆναι, Hsch.

**διαφῠγή**, ἡ, *refuge, means of escape*, Th.8.11; τινός from a thing, Pl.*Prt.*321a (pl.), al.; ἔκ τινος Plu.*Alc.*25.

⊛ **διαφῠή**, ἡ, (διαφύω) *natural break, joint, suture*, τὰ ὀστᾶ . . διαφυὰς ἔχει χωρὶς ἀπ' ἀλλήλων Pl.*Phd.*98c, cf. Philostr.*VA*4.28; *distinction*, Pl.*Plt.*259d; *dissepiment*, as in chestnuts, X.*An.*5.4.29, cf. Plu.*Cic.*1; *joint* in reeds or grasses, Longus 1.10; *divisions* between the teeth, Plu.*Pyrrh.*3; *cleft* in rocks, D.S.5.22. **II.** *stratum* or *vein* of earth, stone, metal, Thphr.*Lap.*63; δ. καὶ φλέβες D.S.3.12. **III.** *string-basket*, *PRyl.*97.7 (ii B.C.).

**διαφῠλακ-τέος**, α, ον, *to be watched, preserved*, v.l. for φυλακτέα, X.*Cyr.*5.3.43. **2.** διαφυλακτέον *one must preserve*, Arist.*Rh.Al.* 1423$^a$31. **-τικός**, ή, όν, *fit for preserving*, ἕξις Pl.*Def.*412a, cf. Plu.2.276a; τριχῶν Crito ap.Gal.12.438.

**διαφῠλάσσω**, Att. -ττω, Cret. -δδω (written -δω), *GDI*5169.11, al.:—*watch closely, guard carefully*, τὰ τείχεα, τὴν πόλιν, Hdt.6.101, 133; τὴν πάροδον Lys.2.30; τὰ ἀγαθά Isoc.2.6, cf. *SIG*577.15 (Milet., iii/ii B.C.); esp. of providential care, Lxx *Ps.*90(91).11, al., cf. *PGiss.* 17.7 (Hadr.), etc.:—Med., *guard for oneself*, πόλιν E.*IA*369. **2.** *observe closely*, τὰ μέτρα Hdt.2.121.α'. **3.** *observe, maintain*, τοὺς νόμους Pl.*Lg.*951b, cf. *SIG*1044.10 (Halic., iv/iii B.C.), *PTeb.*25.3 (ii B.C., Pass.); εἰρήνην Philipp.ap.D.18.78; τὴν πρός τινα πίστιν Plb. 1.78.8; εὔνοιαν *IG*12(7).241.22 (Amorgos, iii B.C.); δ. τὸ μὴ σπουδάζειν *guard against* being too particular.., Pl.*Plt.*261e; πλῆθος δ. ὅτι μάλιστα ταὐτὸν αὐτῶν εἶναι *take care* that.., Id.*Criti.*112d. **4.** *remember, retain*, Luc.*Tim.*1, *Cont.*7.

**διάφυξις**, εως, ἡ, v.l. for -φευξις (q. v.).

⊛ **διαφύομαι**, Pass., fut. -φύσομαι Philostr.Jun.*Im.*13: with aor. 2 Act. διέφῡν: pf. διαπέφῡκα:—*germinate*, of seeds, Thphr.*CP*2.17. 7. **II.** *to be disjoined*, διαφύντος ἑνός Emp.17.10. **III.** *grow between*, Arist.*Fr.*335, Thphr.*CP*3.7.9; *intervene*, χρόνος διέφυ καὶ πάντα ἐξήρτυτο Hdt.1.61; βαθὺς δ. αὐλών Eratosth.8. **IV.** *to be different from*, ἀπ' ἀλλήλων Philostr.*Im.*2.32. **V.** *to be inseparably connected with*, τινός Philostr.Jun. l. c.; *to identify oneself with*, τυραννίδος Plu.*Dio* 12; *to be intimately acquainted with*, τῶν Ἑλληνικῶν D.C.72.6, cf. 77.13; δι' ὅλης τῆς Ἰταλίας *to pervade, leaven* all Italy (of Sulla's veterans), Plu.*Cic.*14. [ῠ only metri gr., Eratosth. l. c.]

**διαφῡσ-άω**, *blow in different directions, disperse*, μὴ . . ὁ ἄνεμος αὐτὴν (sc. τὴν ψυχὴν) διαφυσᾷ Pl.*Phd.*77d:—Pass., ib.8cd, 84b. **II.** *blow* or *breathe through*, Luc.*Herm.*68; ἐκ τοῦ στόματος Plu.2.950c (Pass.). **III.** *inflate, fill with air*, μήτραν Hp.*Steril.*228, cf. Gal. 1.605. **-ησις**, εως, ἡ, *exhalation* from the body, Arist.*Pr.*908$^a$17 (pl.). **II.** *distension* by πνεῦμα, αἰδοίου Gal.7.266.

**διαφῠσικεύομαι**, *study natural philosophy*, Julian.ap.Gal.18(1). 256.

⊛ **διάφῠσις**, εως, ἡ, (διαφύω) *germination*, Thphr.*HP*8.1.6. **II.** *division*, Arist.*HA*495$^b$9 (pl.), Hp.*Mochl.*1 (pl.); *partition*, Arist.*HA* 562$^a$26, Hp. *de Arte* 10; *crack, crevice* in rocks, Ph.*Bel.*102.21 (pl.); *gorge*, Ph.2.117 (pl.); *point* or *line of separation between* the stalk and branch, Hp.*Oct.*12. **III.** *spinous process of the tibia*, Id.*Fract.* 12, Gal.18(2).475.

**διάφυσον**· φασκίς, Hsch.

**διᾰφύσσω**, aor. -ήφῠσα, *draw continually*, οἶνον διαφυσσόμενον Od. 16.110. **II.** *draw away, tear away*, πολλὸν δὲ διήφυσε σαρκὸς ὀδόντι 19.450; διὰ δ' ἔντερα χαλκὸς ἤφυσ' Il.13.508. **III.** *draw out*, χίμετλα Nic.*Th.*682.

**διαφῠτεύω**, *transplant*, Thphr.*HP*4.4.3 (Pass.); *plant*, πλάτανον Ar.*Fr.*111; νῆσον δένδρεσι Philostr.*VA*7.25.

⊛ **διαφων-έω**, *to be a discord*, in Music, Aristox.*Harm.*p.45 M.; *to be*

*out of tune*, Pl.Grg.482b. 2. generally, *disagree*, Id.Lg.860a, etc.; δ. περί τινος Arist.Metaph.1085b36; διαφωνεῖ τι τῶν χρημάτων *there is a discrepancy* in the accounts, Plb.21.43.23; τῷ ῥηθέντι Pl.Plt.292b, etc.; ἀλλήλοις συμφωνεῖν ἢ δ. Id.Phd.101d; τῷ ψευδεῖ δ. τἀληθές Arist. EN1098b12, al.; πρὸς τὴν ἀλήθειαν Iamb.Myst.9.3:—Pass., διαπεφώνηται *it has been disputed*, D.H.1.45. 3. *fail to answer roll-calls, desert*, LXX Ex.24.11, al.; δ. ἐν μηδενὶ τῶν ἀγαθῶν *fail*, Ph.Fr.59 H.: metaph. of promises, *fail, be found wanting*, LXX 3Ki.8.56. b. *to be lost, perish*, SIG521.25 (Amorgos, iii B.C.), 611.10 (Delph., ii B.C.), Agatharch.84, S.E.M.1.267; of plants or animals, BGU530.31 (i B.C.), Hippiatr.2; διαπεφωνήκαμεν we are lost, LXX Ez.37.11; *to be lost*, of things, PSI5.527.15 (iii B.C.); of books, D.S.16.3:—in pf. Pass., PRein.17.14 (ii B.C.). -ία, ἡ, *discord, disagreement*, Pl.Lg.689a, 691a, Str.2.1.7, Plu.2.861a, etc.; δ. πρὸς ἑαυτόν *inconsistency*, Phld. Po.994.4; esp. in Music, *discord*, Bacch.Harm.59, prob. in Cleonid. Harm.5. -ος, ον, *discordant, inconsistent*, ἱστορίαι D.S.4.55, cf. Plu.2.1039d, etc.; τινί *with* one, Luc.Cyn.16; esp. in Music, διάφωνον ἕλκειν strike a *false note*, Damox.2.61, cf. Hp.Vict.1.18 (metaph. of tastes), etc.; opp. σύμφωνος, Euc.Sect.Can.Praef., Theo Sm.p.49 H. Adv. -νως Plu.2.1137c: c. dat., S.E.M.7.170: metaph., δ. ἵστασθαι πρός τινα Phld.Rh.1.90 S.

**διαφώσκω**, Ion. for διαφαύσκω.

**διαφωτ-ίζω**, *enlighten*, τὴν ψυχήν Plu.2.76b; βίᾳ διαφωτίσαι τόπον *clear* a place by force, Id.Cat.Ma.20; *throw light upon*, νυκτερινὰς διατριβάς Luc.Icar.21: abs., *dawn*, LXX Ne.8.3. -ισις, εως, ἡ, *clearing up, explanation*, PGiss.67.14 (ii A.D.).

**διαχάζομαι**, *withdraw*, X.Cyr.7.1.31; cf. διχάζω II.

**διαχάλ-ᾰσις** [χᾰ], εως, ἡ, *disjoining* in the sutures of the skull, Hp. VC12. -ασμα, ατος, τό, *loosening*, τῶν ἁρμονιῶν D.H.Comp. 22. -αστέον, *one must relax*, Sor.1.56. -άω, *loosen, relax*, τὸ πῦρ δ. τὸ πεπηγός Arist.Pr.886b2; τὰς ἁρμονίας τοῦ σώματος Epicr. 3.19; δ. μέλαθρα *unbar*, E.IA1340. II. *make supple by exercise*, X.Eq.7.11. III. intr., *to be disjointed, gape*, ὀστέον Hp.VC12 (v.l. διαχαλασθῇ).

**διαχᾰρακτηρίζω**· *persono*, Gloss.

**διαχάραξις** [χᾰ], εως, ἡ, *cleaving*, αὖλαξ.. δ. τοῦ ἀρότρου EM170.33.

**διαχᾰράσσω**, Att. -ττω, *sever, divide*, D.H.Dem.43 (Pass.); *strip off*, ἐκ τοῦ αὐχένος τὸ δέρμα Agath.4.23; *carve, give shape to*, Plu. 2.636c (Pass.), cf. Ph.1.649 (Pass.); *sharpen*, τὸν ὀφθαλμόν Plu.2. 974b:—Med., *scrape*, S.Ichn.255:—Pass., πέτραις -κεχαραγμένοι τὰ σκέλη Agath.4.20.

**διαχᾰρίζομαι**, *distribute as presents*, D.S.19.20.

**διαχάσκω**, aor. 2 -έχᾰνον: pf. -κέχηνα:—*gape, yawn*, Ar.Eq.533, Thphr.HP3.9.1, Plu.2.976b, 980b; ἀμφί, πρός τι, Agath.2.32, 5.3.

**διαχεθῆ**· διαχεσθῇ, Hsch.

**διαχειμάζω**, *pass the winter*, Th.7.42, X.An.7.6.31.

**διαχειρ-έω**, = -ίζω, χρήματα IG2.574e24. -ησις, v. διαχείρισις. -ίζω, *have in hand, conduct, manage*, χρήματα, πράγματα, And.1.147, 2.17, cf. Lys.9.12, Pl.Grg.526b, etc.; αἱ ἀρχαὶ δ. πολλὰ τῶν κοινῶν Arist.Pol.1322b8; χρήματα OGI218.74 (Ilium, iii B.C.), etc.:—so in Med., fut. part. -ιούμενος Hp.Mul.2.111, etc.:—Pass., X.An.1.9.17. II. Med., *lay hands on, slay*, Plb.8.21.8, Act.Ap.5.30, Plu.2.220b, D.C.72.14. -ισις, εως, ἡ, *management, administration*, πραγμάτων Th.1.97, cf. Lib.Ep.245. 2. in Rhet., *treatment*, prob. for διαχείρησις, Aristid.Rh.1p.501 S. -ισμός, ὁ, *manipulation*, φαρμάκων Hp.Epid.2.3.2. ⊕ -ιστικόν, τό, *commission paid for handling* grain, PLond.ined.2093 (iii B.C.).

**διαχειροτον-έω**, *choose between two* persons or proposals *by show of hands*, εἴτε.. ἤ, εἴτε.. εἴτε, IG1².57,98, cf. D.47.43, etc.:—Pass., X.HG1.7.34; *to be selected*, Pl.Lg.755d. 2. *vote on* a person's case, δ. τινὰ πότερον ἐπιτήδειός ἐστιν ἢ οὔ Arist.Ath.49.2. -ία, ἡ, *choice between two* persons or things, *election*, δ. ποιεῖν, = διαχειροτονεῖν, D. 24.25, IG12(7).237.19 (Amorgos, ii/i B.C.); δ. διδόναι to allow *a right of election*, Aeschin.3.39.

**διαχείρως**, Adv. *in the appropriate manner* (?), κατακαίειν Zos.Alch. p.108 B.

⊕ **διαχέω**, fut. -χεῶ, later -χύσω Gp.7.8.4: aor. -έχεα, Ep. -έχευα (the only tense used by Hom.):—*pour different ways, scatter*, τὸν χοῦν Hdt.2.150. b. in Hom., *cut up* a victim into joints, αἶψ' ἄρα μιν διέχευαν Od.3.456, cf. Il.7.316, al.; χαλκὸς ἔγκατα διέχευεν Theoc.22.203. 2. *disperse*, τὰ συγκεκριμένα Pl.Phlb.46e; ἡ θερμότης δ. τὸ ὑγρόν Arist.Pr.869a15; *melt, fuse*, χαλκόν Paus.9.41.1; *liquefy*, opp. πηγνύναι, Pl.Ti.46d; νῆα.. διέχευαν ἄελλαι A.R.3.320; δ. ἀποστήματα *disperse* abscesses, Thphr.Od.59(61); δ. ἴχνη *to destroy* the scent, X.Cyn.5.3:—Pass., ib.8.1:—also Med., *dissolve*, Nic. Al.373. 3. metaph., *confound*, τὰ βεβουλευμένα Hdt.8.57. 4. *put in a good humour*, τινὰ ὁμιλίαις καὶ λόγοις Plu.2.74d, cf. Philostr. VS2.10.1, Hermog.Id.2.9. II. more freq. in Pass., *to be poured from one vessel into another*, Hdt.6.119. 2. *run through, spread*, Th.2.75,76, Arist.Fr.243. 3. *to be dissolved, liquefied*, X.Cyn. 8.1, Arist.Pr.890b17, etc.; of a corpse, Hdt.3.16; *disperse*, of soldiers, X.HG7.4.34; of humours, Hp.Epid.4.45. 4. metaph., *to be* or *become diffused* or *relaxed*, εὐφραινόμενον -χεῖται, opp. λυπούμενον συσπειρᾶται, Pl.Smp.206d; ὑπὸ μέθης διακεχυμένος Id.Lg.775c, cf. Plb.8.27.4; [αἱ ἐπιθυμίαι] οὐ διαχέονται Epicur.Sent.30; μαλακὸν καὶ διακεχυμένον βλέπειν Arist.Phgn.813a26; φαιδρὸν καὶ δ. πρόσωπον Plu.Alex.19; τῆς ψυχῆς τὸ παθητικὸν διακεχυμένον ὑπὸ τοῦ λόγου Zeno ap.eund.2.82f, cf. Tryph.Trop.p.205 S.

**διαχλαινόω**, strengthd. for χλαινόω, τινά τινι Nonn.D.2.166.

**διαχλευάζω**, strengthd. for χλευάζω, c. acc., D.50.49, Pl.Ax.364b: abs., Plb.30.22.12. 2. *deceive*, τοὺς ὠνουμένους Gp.7.7.5.

**διαχλιαίνω**, v.l. for χλιαίνω, Hp.Mul.2.208.

*διαχλίδω, = θρύπτομαι, only pf. part. διακεχλιδώς Archipp.45 (-οιδώς Hsch.).

⊕ **διάχλωρος**, ον, *of translucent green*, λίθος Ph.Byz.Mir.2.3, dub. in Gal.18(1).495; of a garment, CPR24.6 (ii A.D.).

**διάχολος**, ον, *bilious*, Hp.Hebd. in Hermes 46.439.

**διαχόω**, *bank up*: διαχοῦν τὸ χῶμα *complete* the mound, Hdt.8. 97. 2. *block with a mole*, πορθμόν Str.9.1.13, cf. 7.4.7.

**διαχράομαι**, fut. -ήσομαι, Dor. 3sg. διαχρησεῖται Theoc.15.54. I. Dep., c. dat. rei, *use constantly* or *habitually*, chiefly in Hdt., τῇ αὐτῇ γλώσσῃ 1.58; τῷ αὐτῷ τρόπῳ 2.127; οὐκ οἴνῳ διαχρέωνται 1.71, cf. 2.77; ἐσθῆτι φοινικηίῃ 4.43; τῇ ἀληθείῃ δ. speak the truth, 3.72; οἰμωγῇ ἀφθόνῳ 3.66, cf. 6.58; ἀρετῇ 7.102; ἀγνωμοσύνῃ 6.10; ἀναιδείῃ τε καὶ ἀβουλίῃ 7.210; νόμοις τοῖς προτέροισιν Ar.Ec.609; λιμῷ ὥσπερ ὄψῳ δ. *use* hunger as a sauce, X.Cyr.1.5.12. b. of passive states, *meet with, suffer under*, συμφορῇ μεγάλῃ, τοιούτῳ μόρῳ, Hdt. 3.117, 1.167; αὐχμῷ δ. Id.2.13. 2. *treat, handle*, ἀνομώτατα Str. 6.1.8: c. acc., *destroy, kill*, Hdt.1.24,110, Antipho 1.23, Th.3.36, etc. II. Pass., *to be lent out to different persons*, v. διακίχρημι. 2. *to be killed*, D.L.1.102. III. later in Act., διαχράω *reveal by oracle*, τελετήν Orac.ap.Phleg.Olymp.Fr.1.

⊕ **διαχρέμπτομαι**, strengthd. for χρέμπτομαι, Phryn.PSp.126 B.

**διαχρέομαι**, subj. διαχρέωμαι, Ion. for διαχράομαι (q.v.).

**διάχρηστος**, ον, dub. in Hsch. s.v. λαβροστομία.

**διά-χρῖσις**, εως, ἡ, *anointing*, Archig.ap.Aët.6.39; *smearing with pitch*, Gp.6.9.2. -χρισμα, ατος, τό, *unguent, salve*, Archig.ap. Aët.6.27. II. *preparation for smearing, pitching*, πίθων Gp.6.9 tit. -χρισμός, ὁ, v.l. for -χρῖσις, Paul.Aeg.1.46 tit. -χριστέον, *one must anoint*, Sor.2.16. -χριστος, ον, *anointed*: hence δ. ἐσχαρίτης, a *rich* cake, Lynceus ap.Ath.3.109e: -χριστα, τά, *salves, ointments*, Dsc.1.30, Antyll.ap.Orib.10.34 tit., Aret.CA1.1.

**διαχρίω** [ῑ], *smear all over*, Hp.Fist.3,9, Gp.6.9.1; τινί with a thing, Arist.HA623b30.

**διαχρόν**· χλιαρόν, Hsch.

⊕ **διάχρῡσος**, ον, *interwoven with gold*, ἱμάτιον Test.ap.D.21.22; ἐσθῆτες Plb.6.53.7; σκηναί D.S.14.109; ὑποδήματα Plu.2.142c.

**διάχῠλ-ος**, ον, *juicy, succulent*, σάρξ Arist.HA603b20. -όομαι, *to be made into a syrup*, σεμίδαλις -κεχυλωμένη ὕδατι Hippiatr.32.

**διάχῠμα**, ατος, τό, gloss on γέλασμα, Sch.A.Pr.90.

**διάχῠσις**, εως, ἡ, *diffusion*, Hp.Vict.2.60, Pl.Cra.419c; *extension*, Plu.2.771b; *spreading*, γῆς Gp.5.25.2; δ. λιμνώδη λαμβάνειν to *spread out* like a lake, Plu.Mar.37. 2. *waste, loss*, σπέρματος Thphr.CP4.4.7. 3. *softening*, ib.4.12.2. II. *dissolution, liquefaction*, opp. πῆξις, Arist.Mete.382a30. III. *relaxation*, συστολαὶ καὶ δ. Epicur.Fr.410, cf. Chrysipp.Stoic.3.119; τὰς ἐπὶ σαρκὶ τῆς ψυχῆς δ. Epicur. l.c., cf. Aret.SD1.5; *cheerfulness*, ψυχῆς Sor.1. 97; *merriment*, Plu.Cat.Mi.46, Hierocl.p.54 A., Hdn.Fig.p.9 S.; *ridicule*, Phld.Lib.p.37 O.; *cheerful expression*, Plu.Dem.25. IV. δ. ὀμμάτων '*melting*' look, Id.2.335c. V. = δελφίνιον, Ps.-Dsc. 3.73.

**διαχῠτικός**, ή, όν, *able to dissolve*, Pl.Ti.60a, Thphr.Sens.84, Dsc. 1.71 (dub. l.).

**διαχυτλάζω**, *besprinkle*, Hsch.

**διάχῠτον**, τό, *wine made from partly dried grapes*, Plin.HN14.84.

**διαχωλεύω**, *limp*, Hsch.

**διάχωμα**, ατος, τό, *embankment*, PSI4.337.6 (iii B.C.), etc. II. *tax for maintenance of embankments*, PHib.1.104.4 (iii B.C.).

**διαχωρ-έω**, *pass through*, Pl.Ti.78a, PFlor.200.4 (iii A.D.). 2. *abscond*, PSI4.359.7 (iii B.C.). 3. of food, *to be excreted*, Hp.Vict. 2.45 (also Pass., ibid.): impers., κάτω διεχώρει αὐτοῖς they suffered from *diarrhoea*, X.An.4.8.20, cf. Pl.Phdr.268b; of a person, Anon. Lond.Fr.1.1; δ. ἄπεπτα *pass* food, Arist.PA675a20, cf. Hp.Morb.4. 44. 4. of coins, *to be current*, Luc.Luct.10. 5. metaph., *pass muster, obtain credence*, Plb.18.43.3. II. *part asunder, divide*, Arr. An.1.1.8; δ. εἰς πλάτος or εἰς βάθος, of a mountain-range, *part* so as to leave a plain *between*, ib.2.8.2,7. 2. *depart*, PSI4.359.7 (iii B.C.), Gal.18(2).40. -ημα, ατος, τό, *excrement*, Hp.Aph.2.14, Str. 14.5.14, Aret.SA2.5, etc. -ησις, εως, ἡ, *excretion*, Hp.Aph.2.18, Arist.PA675a22, Phld.D.3.14 (pl.), Porph.Abst.1.45; δ. αἵματος Hp.Aph.5.64. -ητικός, ή, όν, *laxative*, Id.Aër.7, prob. in Aristox. Fr.Hist.7: Comp., Hp.Acut.50, Arist.Pr.928a18: Sup., Hp.Int.13, etc. -ίζω, *separate*, X.Oec.9.7; τι ἀπό τινος Pl.Plt.262b; τι καί τι Epicr.11.14:—Med., Ar.Th.14:—Pass., Pl.Ti.59c, Phlb.17a; γυνὴ -χωρισθεῖσα *divorced*, J.AJ15.7.10. -ισις, εως, ἡ, *separation*, Arist.GA723b15. -ισμα, ατος, τό, *cleft, division*, Luc.VH2. 43. ⊕ -ισμός, ὁ, = διαχώρισις, J.AJ6.11.10, Gal.1.249. -ιστέον, gloss on διοριστέον, Hsch. -ιστής, οῦ, ὁ, *separator*, Gloss. -οι, οἱ, *intervals* in order of battle, Suid.

**διάχωσις**, εως, ἡ, *the making of a mound*, D.S.13.47.

**διαψᾰθάλλω**, *feel with the fingers, scratch*, Hsch.

**διαψαίρω**, *brush away, blow away*, θυμιαμάτων αὖραι διαψαίρουσι πλεκτάνην καπνοῦ Ar.Av.1717; διαψαίρουσα πέπλους (sc. αὔρα) Hermipp.6; *cleanse*, γλώσσῃ διαψαίρουσα μυκτήρων πόρους E.Fr.926; *scratch through*, of birds, Opp.H.2.115. II. intr., *flutter* in the wind, Nic.Al.127.

**διαψᾰλάττομαι**, = διαψαθάλλω, Hsch.

**διαψᾰλίζω**, *clip with scissors*, Paul.Aeg.4.48:—Pass., Gal.11.130.

**διαψάλλω**, strengthd. for ψάλλω, abs., Eup.77: c. acc., πρὶν διαψήλῃ τὴν λύραν Him.*Or.*17.2.

**διάψαλμα**, ατος, τό, *musical interlude*, used by the Lxx, in the Psalms, for the Hebr. *Selah*.

**διαψαμμόω**, *polish with sand*, *IG*12(2).11 (Lesbos).

**διαψαύω**, strengthd. for ψαύω, in Med., Hp.*Art.*57.

❋ **διαψάω**, *cleanse* nostrils or ears, Dsc.*Eup.*1.7, Archig.ap.Gal.12.621. II. *massage*, Max.Tyr.12.2. III. *scratch through*, ἄμμον Anon.ap.Suid. (s. v. l.).

**διαψέγω**, strengthd. for ψέγω, Pl.*Lg.*639a, Ael.*VH*2.2.

**δια-ψεύδω**, *deceive*, D.*Ep.*3.34:—Med., abs., And.1.42: c. acc., Plu.*Fab.*7. 2. Med., *deny, disclaim*, A.D.*Synt.*115.24, *Pron.*81.17. II. *cheat*, [πατρίδα ἐλπίδων] Plb.3.109.12:—usu. Pass.: pf. διέψευσμαι: aor. διεψεύσθην:—*to be deceived, mistaken*, Isoc.5.1, D.1.22; τινός *to be cheated of, deceived in* a person or thing, X.*Mem.*4.2.27, D.23.19; τῆς ψυχῆς τινῶν πέρι Pl.*Ep.*351d; περί τι Arist.*EN* 1144$^a$35; τι *in* a thing, Id.*Pol.*1323$^a$33; ὑπολήψει καὶ δόξῃ Id.*EN* 1139$^b$17; λογισμοῖς Plb.3.16.5: abs., μηδὲν διεψεῦσθαι *BGU*2113 (iv A.D.). -**ψευσις**, εως, ἡ, *deceit*, Stob.2.7.11$^l$. -**ψευσμα**, ατος, τό, *falsehood*, Aq.*Ps.*61(62).5. -**ψευστῶς**, Adv. *with fraudulent purpose*, Stob.2.7.11$^m$.

**διαψηλᾰφ-άω**, *handle* a thing, Herod.Med.ap.Orib.6.20.10, Sor.1.100, Aq.*Ge.*31.34, Sm.*Is.*59.10. -**ητέον**, *one must handle*, Paul.Aeg.2.43.

**διαψηφ-ίζω**, Dor. aor. inf. διαψᾱφίξαι, *put to the vote*, τὰν γνώμαν *IG*12(3).249.38 (Anaphe); δ. τοὺς φόρους *keep account of* tribute, of the *rationales*, Lyd.*Mag.*3.46. II. more freq. Dep. διαψηφίζομαι, Att. fut. -ιοῦμαι, *vote by ballot*, Antipho 5.8, Hyp.*Eux.*40, etc.; δ. περὶ δίκης Pl.*Lg.*937a; δ. κρύβδην, κρύφα, And.4.3, Th.4.88. 2. *decide by vote*, τι Lys.26.1; ταύτῃ διαψηφίσασθε v.l. in D.28.23. III. Pass., διαψηφισθεὶς εἰ γνήσιός ἐστι Lib.*Decl.*16.29. ❋ -**ισις**, εως, ἡ, *voting by ballot*, Pl.*Lg.*855d; esp. of a *vote* on claims to registration of citizens, Aeschin.1.77, D.57.26 (pl.); προτιθέναι τὴν δ. X.*HG*1.7.14; ῥᾳδίαν τὴν δ. ποιεῖν, of a criminal confessing his guilt, Lys.12.34. -**ισμός**, ὁ, = foreg., Arist.*Ath.*13.5, Ath.5.218a. II. *reckoning, assessment*, τᾶς ὀκτωβόλου εἰσφορᾶς *IG*5(1).1432 (Messene, i B.C.). -**ιστής**, οῦ, ὁ, = Lat. *rationalis*, Lyd.*Mag.*3.7, cf. *PLips.*34.4. -**ιστός**, ή, όν, *elected*, ἀρχαὶ κρυπτῇ ψήφῳ δ. Arist.*Rh.Al.*1424$^b$2.

**διαψηφοφορέομαι**, of candidates for office, *to be submitted to a ballot*, *Ath.Mitt.*32.294 (Pergam.).

**διαψήχω**, *wear down, fritter away*, δύναμιν Plu.*Lys.*23.

❋ **διαψῐθῠρίζω**, *whisper*, πρὸς τὸ οὖς προσπίπτων δ. Thphr.*Char.*2.10. II. *whisper among themselves*, Lxx *Si.*12.18, Plb.15.26.8, Luc.*Gall.*25.

❋ **διάψῑλος**, ον, *uncultivated*, γῆ *POxy.*707.23 (ii A.D.), *CPR*34.6 (ii A.D.).

**διαψοφέω**, = παραψοφέω, Hsch.

**διά-ψυγμα**, ατος, τό, *dry*, i.e. *unfruitful land*, *BGU*277 ii 5 (ii A.D.). -**ψυκτικός**, ή, όν, *cooling, refreshing*, Hp.*Vict.*2.65. -**ψυξις**, εως, ἡ, *cooling*, Plu.2.967f (pl.), Aët.5.44. -**ψύχω**, *cool*, σῶμα Hp.*VM*16:—Pass., *to be chilly*, τὰ ἄκρα Id.*Acut.*30. 2. *air, dry and clean*, ναῦς Th.7.12, cf. Luc.*Cont.*23, etc.: metaph. of misers bringing out their hoards, X.*Cyr.*8.2.21. 3. Pass., *become dry*, i.e. *unfruitful*, ἵνα μὴ ἡ γῆ διαψυγῇ *PSI*6.603.11 (iii B.C.). 4. f.l. for διαψήχω in Plu.*Lys.*23.

**διάω**, v. διάημι.

**διβάλανα**· κάρυα Ποντικά, Hsch. (διαβ- cod.). **δίβαλον**· μέλι καὶ μελίκρατον, Id. (διαβ- cod.).

**δίβᾱμος**, ον, (βῆμα) *on two legs*, E.*Rh.*215.

**δίβαν**· ὄφιν (Cret.), Hsch.

**διβᾰφ-ής**, ές, = sq., Sm., Thd.*Ex.*25.4. -**ος**, ον, *double-dyed*, of purple cloth, Sm.*Ex.*28.5, *Edict.Diocl.*24.6; ἡ δ. (sc. ἐσθής) Cic.*Att.*2.9.2.

**δῐβολ-έω**, *harrow*, *PSI*4.422 (iii B.C.), *PFay.*112.5 (i A.D.). -**ητός**, ὁ, *harrowing*, *PAmh.*2.91.11 (ii A.D.), *PTeb.*378.19 (iii A.D.). -**ητρος**, ὁ, = foreg., *PFay.*112.4 (i A.D.). -**ία**, ἡ, = δίβολος χλαῖνα, Plu.2.754f. II. *double-pointed lance, halbert*, Ar.*Fr.*476, Men.*Kol.*30, Hdn.2.13.4; of a German weapon, Plu.*Mar.*25. -**ος**, ον, (βάλλω) *twice-thrown*. δ. χλαῖνα a garment *doubled and thrown over* the shoulders, Poll.7.47, Hsch. II. *two-pointed*, ἄκων E.*Rh.*374 (lyr.); περόνα *AP*6.282 (Theod.); *in two pieces*, ξύλον *SIG*$^2$587.307: generally, *redoubled*, v. διόβολος. III. δίβολον· φᾶρος διπλοῦν, Hsch.

❋ **δίβος** [ῐ], ὁ, name of a *square on the draught-board*, *AP*9.482 (Agath.).

**δίβουλος**, ον, *of two minds*, Hsch. s.v. διάβουλοι.

**δίβρᾰχυς**, εια, υ, *of two short syllables*, Arc.92.7, Ter.Maur.1365, etc.

**δίβροχος**, ον, (βρέχω) *prepared with a double infusion*, Dsc.1.55.

❋ **δίγαμμα**, τό, indecl., Priscian.*Inst.*1.12, Donat.ad Ter.*Andr.*173:—also **δίγαμμος** *littera*, Ter.Maur.163, cf. 645, and **δίγαμμον** (sc. στοιχεῖον) Quint.*Inst.*1.4.7, Prob.ad Verg.*G.*1.70:—*digamma*, Trypho *Pass.*11; δ. Αἰολικόν A.D.*Pron.*76.32, al.; described, though not named, by D.H.1.20: ὥσπερ γάμμα διτταῖς ἐπὶ μίαν ὀρθὴν ἐπιζευγνύμενον ταῖς πλαγίοις, ὡς Ϝελένη καὶ Ϝάναξ καὶ Ϝοῖκος καὶ Ϝαήρ.

**δί-γᾰμος** [ῐ], ον, *married to two people, adulterous*, Stes.26, Man.5.291. -**γενής**, ές, *of doubtful sex*, Eust.150.27.

**δίγηρες**· στρουθοί, Hsch.

**δί-γληνος**, ον, *with two eye-balls*, Theoc.*Ep.*6. ❋ -**γλωσσος**, Att. -ττος, ον, *speaking two languages*, Th.8.85, 4.109, Gal.8.585:—as Subst., δίγλωσσος, ὁ, *interpreter, dragoman*, Plu.*Them.*6. II. *double-tongued, deceitful*, Lxx *Si.*5.9, al. -**γνωμος**, ον, *of two minds, vacillating*, Simp.*in Epict.*p.134 D., Diogenian.4.32. -**γνώμων**, ὁ, ἡ, gen. ονος, = foreg., Sch.E.*Or.*633. -**γομία**, ἡ, *double burden, load*, Lxx *Jd.*5.16. -**γόνᾰτος**, ον, *with two joints*, κλωνία Dsc.4.189. -**γονέω**, = διισσογονέω, Phlp.*in GA*17.24. ❋ -**γονία**, ἡ, *double parturition*, Arist.*GA*719$^a$24. -**γονος**, ον, *twice-born*, Βάκχος E.*Hipp.*560 (lyr.), cf. *AP*9.524.5. 2. *twin*: *double*, μάσθλης δ. S.*Fr.*129 (nisi leg. δίτονον); δ. σώματα *two* bodies, E.*El.*1178 (lyr.); but, II. parox., διγόνος, ον, *bearing twice*, Emp.69; *bearing twins*, Man.5.291. III. δίγονος· περιστερά, Hsch. -**γυιος**, ον, (γυῖον) *of two members*, Mart.Cap.9.989, 990. II. as expl. of διάγυιος, Aristid.Quint.1.16. -**γωνία**, ἡ, *angle half-way between cardinal points*, Adam.ap.Aët.3.163.

**δίδαγμα** [ῐ], ατος, τό, *lesson, instruction*, Hp.*Fract.*1, Ar.*Nu.*668, X.*Eq.*9.10, Pl.*Clit.*409b, Mosch.*Fr.*2.7, etc.; χρόνος δ. ποικιλώτατον E.*Fr.*291; *evidence, proof*, τινός Plu.*Galb.*17.

**δῐδαγμοσύνη**, ἡ, = διδασκαλία, Doroth.ap.Heph.Astr.2.19.

**δῐδακ-τέον**, *one must teach*, Pl.*R.*451e, D.S.1.89, Jul.*Ep.*89b. -**τήρ**, ῆρος, ὁ, *ox-goad*, Aq.*Jd.*3.31. -**τήριος**, ον, = sq.: τὸ δ. *proof*, Hp.*Acut.*39. ❋ -**τικός**, ή, όν, *apt at teaching*, Ph.2.412, 1*Ep.Ti.*3.2, 2*Ep.Ti.*2.24. -**τός**, ή, όν, also ός, όν Pl.*Erx.*398d: I. of things, *taught, learnt*, ἅπαντα γάρ σοι τἀμὰ νουθετήματα κείνης διδακτά *of* her *teaching*, S.*El.*344; δ. ἀνθρωπίνης σοφίας λόγοι 1*Ep.Cor.*2.13; ὅσοις δ. μηδέν, ἀλλ' ἐν τῇ φύσει τὸ σωφρονεῖν εἴληχεν E.*Hipp.*79. 2. *that can be taught* or *learnt*, τὰ δ. *things which may be taught by study and experience*, Pi.*N.*3.41; opp. ἄρρητα, S.*OT*300; δίδαξον.. εἰ διδακτά μοι if I *may learn* them, Id.*Tr.*64, cf. 671; τὰ μὲν δ. μανθάνω, τὰ δ' εὑρετὰ ζητῶ Id.*Fr.*843; κἄστ' οὐ διδακτόν (sc. τὸ τῆς τύχης) E.*Alc.*786, cf. *Supp.*914; καθ' ὅσον δ. Isoc.13.20; ἀρετὴ.. εἴτε δ. εἴτε μὴ δ. Pl.*Men.*71a, cf. *Prt.*328c, *Euthd.*274e; ἐπιστήμη Arist.*EN*1139$^b$25. II. of persons, *taught, instructed*, πολέμου Lxx 1*Ma.*4.7; also δ. θεοῦ *taught* by God, ib.*Is.*54.13 (= *Ev.Jo.*6.45). -**τρα**, τά, *teacher's fee*, Theoc.8.86, Poll.6.186.

**δῐδακτῠλ-ιαῖος**, α, ον, *two fingers long* or *broad*, διάστημα S.E.*M.*10.156, cf. Heliod.ap.Orib.48.23.2, etc.:—so -**ος**, ον, Hp.*Art.*7, Thphr.*HP*9.5.3, *IG*2$^2$.463.78.

**δίδαξις** [δῐ], εως, ἡ, *teaching, instruction*, E.*Hec.*601, Arist.*Ph.*202$^a$32, Phld.*Rh.*2.249 S. (pl., dub.), *PRyl.*62.21 (iii A.D.).

**δῐδασκᾰλ-εῖον**, τό, *teaching-place, school*, [S.]*Fr.*1120.3, Antipho 6.11, Th.7.29, prob. in Pl.*Lg.*764c; εἰς τὸ δ. ἰέναι Aeschin.1.9; τὰ παιδία τὰ ἐκ τῶν διδασκαλείων Hyp.*Eux.*22; τὰ δ. τῶν ῥητορικῶν Epicur.*Fr.*50; τὸ Σωκρατικὸν δ. D.H.*Dem.*2. II. in pl., = δίδακτρα, Ps.-Hdt.*Vit.Hom.*26. ❋ -**ία**, ἡ, *teaching, instruction*, Pi.*P.*4.102, Even.1, Hp.*Lex*2, X.*Cyr.*8.7.24, Pl.*R.*493b, etc.; δ. ποιεῖσθαι, c. acc. et inf., Th.2.42; δ. παρέχειν serve as a *lesson*, ib.87; ἐκ δ., opp. ἐξ ἔθους, Arist.*EN*1103$^a$15. 2. *elucidation*, Id.*Po.*1456$^b$5. 3. *official instructions*, *PLips.*64.24 (iv A.D.); πρὸς διδασκαλίαν for *information*, *POxy.*1101.4 (iv A.D.). II. *training, rehearsing* of a chorus, etc., δ. τῶν χορῶν Pl.*Grg.*501e, cf. Simon.147.5, Plu.2.1096a, etc.; also, *the dramas produced*, Id.2.839d, *Cim.*8, *Per.*5, *AP*7.37 (Diosc.). 2. διδασκαλίαι, αἱ, *Catalogues of the Dramas*, their writers, dates, and success, title of compilation by Arist. and others, D.L.5.26, cf. Sch.Ar.*Ra.*1155, etc. ❋ -**ικός**, ή, όν, *of* or *for teaching*, τινός Philol.11; ὄργανον Pl.*Cra.*388b; λόγοι X.*Mem.*1.2.21; πειθὼ δ. περί τι Pl.*Grg.*453e, cf. 455a: ἡ -κή (sc. τέχνη) *the faculty of giving instruction*, Id.*Sph.*231b; τὸ -κόν Id.*Lg.*813b; so, in disparagement, τὸ πρεσβυτικὸν καὶ δ. *the didactic manner* of old age, of Isocrates, Hermog.*Id.*2.11: Comp. -ώτερος Arist.*Metaph.*982$^a$13. Adv. -κῶς Pl.*Cra.*388c, Plb.6.3.5: Comp. -ώτερον Dioph.1 p.474 T., Hermog.*Inv.*1.1. 2. -κή (sc. ὁμολογία), ἡ, *contract of apprenticeship*, *POxy.*275.34 (i A.D.). 3. Gramm., τόπος δ., *locus classicus*, Sch.Il.5.857. ❋ -**ιον**, τό, *thing taught, science* or *art* (= αὐτὸ τὸ μάθημα, Suid.), Hdt.5.58; *lesson*, X.*Eq.*11.5. II. in pl., = δίδακτρα, Plu.*Lyc.*14, *Alex.*7, al. ❋ -**ος**, ὁ (but fem., *h.Merc.*556, A.*Pr.*110, cf. ξυμφορὴ γίνεται δ. Democr.76; πενία ἐπινοιῶν δ. Secund.*Sent.*10), *teacher, master*, μαντείης *h.Merc.* l.c.; δ. τέχνης πάσης βροτοῖς A.*Pr.* l.c.; δεινῶν ἔργων Lys.12.78; πόλεμος βίαιος δ. Th.3.82; διδάσκαλον λαβεῖν get *a master*, [S.]*Fr.*1120.8; εἰς διδασκάλου (sc. οἶκον) φοιτᾶν go to *school*, Pl.*Alc.*1.109d, etc.; διδασκάλων or ἐκ διδασκάλων ἀπαλλαγῆναι leave *school*, Id.*Grg.*514c, *Prt.*326c; ἐν διδασκάλων at *school*, Id.*Alc.*1.110b. II. *trainer* of a dithyrambic or dramatic chorus, *producer* of a play, etc., ἵτω δὲ καὶ τραγῳδίας ὁ Κλεομάχου δ. Cratin.256, cf. Ar.*Av.*912, *Ach.*628, Antipho 6.13, etc.; δ. τοῦ μεγάλου χοροῦ *SIG*698.8 (Delph., ii B.C.).

❋ **δῐδάσκω**, Ep. inf. -έμεναι and -έμεν, Il.9.442, 23.308: fut. διδάξω A.*Supp.*519, etc.: aor. ἐδίδαξα Il.23.307, etc.; poet. ἐδιδάσκησα *h.Cer.*144 (prob.), Hes.*Op.*64, Pi.*P.*4.217: pf. δεδίδαχα X.*Cyr.*1.3.18, Pl.*Men.*85e:—Med., fut. διδάξομαι: aor. ἐδιδαξάμην:—Pass., fut. διδαχθήσομαι D.H.3.70, etc.: aor. ἐδιδάχθην Sol.13.51, Hdt.3.81, Ar.*Nu.*637, etc.: pf. δεδίδαγμαι Il.11.831, Pl.*Phdr.*269c, etc. Redupl. form of δάω (q.v.) in causal sense:—*instruct* a person, or *teach* a thing, Il.11.832, 9.442: c. dupl. acc., σε.. ἱπποσύνας ἐδίδαξαν they *taught* thee riding, 23.307, cf. Od.8.481; πολλὰ διδάσκει μ' ὁ πολὺς βίοτος E.*Hipp.*252 (lyr.), etc.; also δ. τινὰ περί τινος Ar.*Nu.*382; δ. τῶν γενομένων τισὶ τὴν ἀλήθειαν Pl.*Tht.*201b: c. acc. pers. et inf., σε διδάσκουσιν θεοὶ αὐτοὶ ὑψαγόρην ἔμεναι *teach* thee to be.., Od.1.384: c. inf. only, δίδαξε γὰρ Ἄρτεμις αὐτὴ βάλλειν ἄγρια πάντα she *taught how* to shoot, Il.5.51, etc.: without inf., πολλοὶ τοὺς υἱοὺς ῥήτορας διδάσκουσιν Aristonym.ap.Stob.3.4.105; δ. πολλοὺς αὐλητάς Charon

9; τούτους ἱππέας ἐδίδαξεν οὐδενὸς χείρους Pl.*Men.*94b; also δ. τινὰ σοφόν E.*Heracl.*575: with an abstract subject, πολυμαθίη νόον οὐ διδάσκει Heraclit.40; ξενιτείη αὐτάρκειαν δ. Democr.246:—Med., *teach oneself, learn*, φθέγμα καὶ ἀστυνόμους ὀργὰς ἐδιδάξατο S.*Ant.*356 (lyr.); but usu., *have* one *taught* or *educated*, esp. of a father, τὰ ἄλλα.. διδάσκεσθαι τοὺς υἱεῖς Pl.*Prt.*325b; δ. τοὺς υἱεῖς τὰς κούφας ἐργασίας Arist.*Pol.*1321ᵃ24: c. inf., δ. τινὰ ἱππεύειν Pl.*R.*467e; δ. τινα ἱππέα Id.*Men.*93d, cf. X.*Mem.*4.4.5 (this distn. between Act. and Med. was neglected by some Poets and late Prose writers, Med. being used like Act. in Pi.*O.*8.59, Luc.*Somn.*10, etc.; but in Ar.*Nu.*783 Elmsl. restored διδάξαιμ' ἄν σ' ἔτι for διδαξαίμην σ' ἔτι, and in Pl.*R.*421e Cobet cj. διδάξει for -εται: Med. is used of gods, [θεοί].. ὅπλων χρῆσιν διδαξάμενοι Id.*Mx.*238b):—Pass., *to be taught, learn*, c. gen., διδασκόμενος πολέμοιο *trained, skilled* in war, Il.16.811: c. acc., τά σε προτί φασιν Ἀχιλλῆος δεδιδάχθαι which [medicines] they say thou *wert taught* by Achilles, 11.831, cf. Arat.529; ὃς οὔτ' ἐδιδάχθη οὔτε εἶδε καλὸν οὐδέν Hdt.3.81; διδάξω καὶ διδάξομαι λόγους E.*Andr.*739: freq. c. inf., δεδιδαγμένον εἶναι χειροήθεα Hdt.2.69; βρέφος διδάσκεται λέγειν ἀκούειν θ' E.*Supp.*914; διδάσκεσθαι ὡς.. X.*HG*2.3.45. **2.** c. gen., *indicate, give sign of*, χειμῶνος συναγειρομένοιο Arat.793, cf. 734. **II.** abs., *explain*, πῶς δή; δίδαξον A.*Eu.*431; σαφῶς δ. Th.2.60, etc.; *show by argument, prove*, λέγων διδασκέτω X.*An.*5.7.11, etc.; δ. περί τινος ὡς.. Th.3.71; ἡλίκον ἐστὶ τὸ ἀλαζόνευμα..πειράσομαι..διδάξαι Aeschin.3.238; ποιητὴς δ. ὅτι.. Jul.*Or.*2.50b. **III.** of dithyrambic and dramatic Poets (cf. διδάσκαλος II), δ. διθύραμβον, δρᾶμα, *produce* a piece, Hdt.1.23, 6.21; Πέρσας Ar.*Ra.*1026, cf. Pl.*Prt.*327d, *IG*1².770, al.:—Med., διδάξασθαι χορόν *train one's own* chorus, Simon.145.

**δῐδᾰχή**, ἡ, *teaching*, Democr.33, Th.1.120, Pl.*R.*536d; ἐκ διδαχῆς λέγειν Hdt.3.134; δ. ποιεῖσθαι Th.4.126.—Poet. only late, Ps.-Phoc. 89. **2.** military *regulations* or *discipline*, τοὐναντίον αὐτῶν τῆς στρατιωτικῆς δ. πεποιηκότων *BGU*140.16 (ii A.D.). **II.** = διδασκαλία II. 2, *IG*14.2124.

**δίδημι**, Aeol. inf. δίδην and pres. ind. δίδει Hsch., part. διδείς, εῖσα, έν, *GDI*2156, al. (Delph.), fem. δ[ιδέ]ουσα *Delph.*3(2).131: redupl. form of δέω (A):—*bind, fetter*, ὣ ποτ' Ἀχιλλεὺς..δίδη μόσχοισι λύγοισιν (Ep. 3 impf. for ἐδίδη) Il.11.105; οἱ δέ σ'..ἐν δεσμοῖσι διδέντων (Aristarch. for δεόντων) *let them bind* thee, Od.12.54: 3 pl. ind. διδέασι X.*An.*5.8.24 (v.l. δεσμεύουσι).

**δίδραγμον**, τό, *weight of two* δραγμαί, Hero *Mens.*60.4; cf. δίδραχμον.

⊛ **διδράσκω**, *run away*, Hsch.: pf., δέδρᾱκα τοῦ καπηλείου Eun.*Hist.* p.255 D.: aor. imper. δράντων prob. l. in *Tab.Defix.Aud.*26 (Crete, iii B.C.); part. δράσαντα *POxy.*1423.6 (iv A.D.); but mostly found in compds., esp. ἀπο-.

⊛ **δῐδραχμ-ία**, ἡ, *tax of two* δραχμαί in Roman Egypt, δ. τοῦ Σούχου θεοῦ *BGU*741 iii 3 (i A.D.). ⊛ **-ιαῖος**, α, ον, = sq.1, Critias 58 D. ⊛ **-ος**, ον, *priced at two drachms*, Arist.*Oec.*1353ᵃ17; δ. ὁπλῖται soldiers *with pay of two drachms a day*, Th.3.[17]. **II.** *weighing two drachms*, ὁλκή Eudem.ap.Gal.14.185. **III.** δ. τόκος interest *at two drachms* per mina per month (24 %), *IG*5(1).1146.38 (Gythium, i B.C.), *BGU*1126.17 (i B.C.). **IV.** δίδραχμον, τό, *coin of two drachms*, *IG*1².79, Arist.*Ath.*10.7, etc.: esp. *half-shekel*, paid to the temple-treasury at Jerusalem, Lxx *Nu.*3.47, al. (freq. with v.l. δίδραγμον, q.v.), *Ev.Matt.*17.24.

**δῐδῠμᾱγενεῖς**, οἱ, *twins*, *BGU*447.10 (ii A.D.), *POxy.*1119.26 (iii A.D.).

**δῐδῠμαῖον**, τό, = ὄρχις, Hp.*Int.*30 (διδύμη, Gal.19.93).

⊛ **Δῐδῠμαῖος**, ὁ, a name of Zeus as worshipped at Didyma in Miletus jointly with Apollo, Nic.*Fr.*1; of Apollo, *SIG*906 A (so ⊛ **Δῐδῠμεύς**, ὁ, of Apollo, Orph.*H.*34.7); τὸ Διδυμαῖον, *their temple* at Miletus, Plu.*Pomp.*24:—**Δῐδύμεια**, τά, *their festival* there, *CIG*2881, al. (Branchidae), *IG*3.129.8.

**δῐδῠμάνωρ** [ᾱ], ορος, ὁ, ἡ, τό, *touching both the men*, κακά A.*Th.*849 (lyr.).

**δῐδῠμ-άων** [ᾱ], ονος, ὁ, ἡ, poet. for δίδυμος, used by Hom. only in dual nom. and pl. dat., *twins*, Il.5.548: later of things, μαζοί Nonn. *D.*3.390; simply, *two*, δούρατα ib.23.33: sg., *double*, κεραίη ib.15.30; βουλή ib.4.179. **-εύω**, *bear twins*, Lxx *Ca.*4.2.

**διδύμη**, v. διδυμαῖον.

**δῐδῠμη-τοκέω**, *bear twins*, Scymn.379. ⊛ **-τόκος**, Dor. **διδυμᾱτόκος**, ον, = διδυμοτόκος, Theoc.1.25, Call.*Ap.*54, *AP*6.99 (Phil.), etc. **2.** *twin-born*, Man.4.455.

**δῐδύμια** [ῠ], τά, *small convexities near the pineal gland of the brain*, Gal.*UP*8.14, al. **II.** Dim. of δίδυμος III. 2, Paul.Aeg.6.68. **III.** διδυμίου ῥίζα, = ὄρχις, Hsch.

**δῐδύμιος** [ῠ], = δίδυμος, *Sammelb.*1068.

**δίδυμνος** [ῐ], poet. for δίδυμος (cf. νώνυμνος for νώνυμος), to be read metri gr. in Pi.*O.*3.35.

**δῐδῠμο-γενής**, ές, *twin-born*, E.*Hel.*206 (lyr.); cf. διδυμᾱγενεῖς. **-γονος**, ον, = foreg., Ptol.*Tetr.*110, Vett.Val.299.9. ⊛ **-ζῠγος**, ον, *with a pair of horses*; *twofold*, ὕδωρ Nonn.*D.*15.21; μόρος ib.34.240. **-ζυξ**, ῠγος, ὁ, ἡ, = foreg., δίφρος ib.21.212; αὐλός ib.23.211. **-θροος**, ον, *double-voiced*, αὐλός ib.10.234, al. **-κτῠπος**, ον, *double-sounding*, ib.20.307; ἠχώ ib.36.12.

⊛ **δίδῠμος** [ῐ], η, ον, also ος, ον v.l. in Pi.*P.*4.209, E.*HF*656 (lyr.), Pl.*Criti.*113e:—redupl. from δύο, *double, twofold*, Od.19.227, etc.; διδύμαιν χεροῖν S.*El.*206 (lyr.): also in sg., χερὶ διδύμᾳ with *both* hands, Pi.*P.*2.9; δ. ἅλς, i.e. the Pontus and Bosporus, S.*Ant.*967 (lyr.); δ. γένος *AP*7.72 (Men.); δ. ξύλον *forked*, Lxx *Jo.*8.29; τὸ γλυκύ μοι δ., of a wife, *IG*14.1974. **II.** *twin*, δ. κασίγνητος Pi.*N.*1.36; δ. τέκνων ἄριστα S.*OC*1693 (lyr.); δ. τέκεα E.*Hel.*220 (lyr.). **III.** Subst., δίδυμοι *twins*, Il.23.641, Hdt.5.41: of *the Twins* in the zodiac, Eudox.ap.Hipparch.1.2.8, Arat.147, *IG*14.1307; also δίδυμα, τά, Hdt. 6.52; δύο διδύμω E.*Or.*1401 (lyr.). **2.** *the testicles*, Lxx *De.*25.11, *AP*5.125 (Phld.): sg., Herophil.ap.Gal.*UP*14.11. **3.** *ovaries*, Herophil. l.c., Sor.1.12.

**δῐδῠμόστροφος**, ον, *turning this way and that*, Man.4.590.

**δῐδῠμότης**, ητος, ἡ, *duality*, Pl.*Phlb.*57d, Aristid.Quint.2.26, Gal. *UP*8.10.

**δῐδῠμο-τοκέω**, *to bear twins*, Arist.*HA*573ᵇ30. **-τοκία**, ἡ, *a bearing of twins*, Id.*GA*772ᵇ14. **-τόκος**, ον, *producing twins*, Id. *HA*573ᵇ32. **-χροος**, ον, *two-coloured*, Musae.59: heterocl. dat. sg. διδυμόχροϊ Nonn.*D.*11.378, acc. pl. -χροας ib.21.216.

**Δῐδῠμών**, ῶνος, ὁ (sc. μήν), name of month at Alexandria, Ptol. *Alm.*9.7.

**δίδυξ** (leg. δοῖδυξ)· τὸ τριβήδιν (leg. τριβίδιον) τοῦ ὅλμ[ί]ου, Hsch.

⊛ **δίδωμι**, Il.23.620, etc. (late δίδω *POxy.*121 (iii A.D.)); late forms, 1 pl. δίδομεν v.l. in J.*BJ*3.8.5, etc., 3 pl. δίδωσι (παρα-) Id.*AJ*10.4.1, etc.; but thematic forms are freq. used, esp. in Ep. and Ion., διδοῖς, διδοῖσθα, Il.9.164, 19.270, διδοῖ Od.17.350, Mimn.2.16, Hdt.2.48, Hp.*Aër.*12 (ἀνα-), A.*Supp.*1010, etc., διδοῦσι Il.19.265 (always in Hom.), dub. in Att., Antiph.156; imper. δίδου Thgn.1303, Hdt.3.140, E.*Or.*642, δίδοι Pi.*O.*1.85, Epigr. in *Class.Phil.*4.78, Ep. δίδωθι Od.3.380; inf. διδόναι, also διδοῦν Thgn.1329, Ep. διδοῦναι Il.24.425, Aeol. δίδων Theoc.29.9; part. διδούς, Aeol. δίδοις Alc.*Supp.*23.13: impf. ἐδίδουν -ους -ου, Ar.*Eq.*678, Od.19.367, 11.289 (Ep. δίδου Il. 5.165), etc.; 3 pl. ἐδίδοσαν Hdt.8.9, etc., ἐδίδουν (v.l. ἐδίδων) Hes. *Op.*139, D.H.5.6 codd. (ἀπ-), also ἔδιδον prob. in *h.Cer.*437, δίδον ib.328; Ep. iter. δόσκον Il.14.382: fut. δώσω 14.268, etc., Ep. διδώσω Od.13.358, 24.314; inf. δωσέμεναι Il.13.369: aor. 1 ἔδωκα, used only in ind., Od.9.361, etc., Ep. δῶκα Il.4.43: aor. 2 ἔδων, used in pl. ind. ἔδομεν ἔδοτε ἔδοσαν (Lacon. ἔδον *IG*5(1).1*B*1), and in moods, δός, δῶ, δοίην, δοῦναι, δούς; Ep. forms of aor., subj. 3 sg. δώῃ, δώῃσι, δῷσι, Il.16.725, 1.324, Od.2.144; 3 sg. δώη, Boeot. δώει *SIG*²858.17 (Delph.), *IG*7.3054 (Lebad.), δοῖ *PPetr.*2 p.24; 1 pl. δώομεν Il.7.299, Od.16.184, 3 pl. δώωσι Il.1.137; 3 sg. opt. is written δόη *UPZ*1.4, δοῖ *IG* 4.1488, etc.; inf. δόμεναι Il.1.116, δόμεν 4.379 (also Dor., Ar.*Lys.*1163 (ἀπο-), δόμειν *SIG*942 (Dodona)); Cypr. inf. δοϜέναι *Inscr.Cypr.*135.5 H. (also opt. δυϜάνοι ib. 6); Arc. part. ἀπυ-δόας *IG*5(2).6.13 (Tegea); inf. δῶναι *Schwyzer* 666.2 (Orchom., iii B.C.), also in later Greek, *BGU*38.13 (ii A.D.): pf. δέδωκα Pi.*N.*2.8, etc.; Boeot. 3 pl. ἀπο-δεδόανθι *IG*7.3171.35 (Orchom.): plpf. ἐδεδώκει X.*Cyr.*1.4.26:—Med. only in compds.:—Pass., fut. δοθήσομαι E.*Ph.*1650, Is.3.39, etc.: aor. ἐδόθην Od.2.78, etc.: pf. δέδομαι Il.5.428, A.*Supp.*1041, Th.1.26, etc.; 3 pl. δέδονται E.*Supp.*757: plpf. ἐδέδοτο Th.3.109:—*give freely*, τινί τι Od.24.274, etc.: in pres. and impf., *to be ready to give, offer*, Il.9.519, Hdt.5.94, 9.109, Ar.*Fr.*100, X.*An.*6.3.9, etc.; τὰ διδόμενα *things offered*, D.18. 119. **2.** of the gods, *grant, assign*, κῦδος, νίκην, etc., Il.19.204, 11.397, etc.; of evils, δ. ἄλγεα, ἄτας, κήδεα, etc., 1.96, 19.270, Od.9. 15, etc.; twice in Hom. in Pass., οὔ τοι δέδοται πολεμήϊα ἔργα not to thee *have* deeds of war *been granted*, Il.5.428, cf. Od.2.78; later εὖ διδόναι τινί *give* good fortune, *provide* well *for*.., S.*OT*1081, *OC*642, E.*Andr.*750: abs., of the laws, *grant permission*, δόντων αὐτῷ τῶν νόμων Is.7.2, cf. Pl.*Lg.*813c. **3.** *offer* to the gods, ἑκατόμβας, ἱρὰ θεοῖσιν, Il.12.6, Od.1.67, etc. **4.** with inf. added, ξεῖνος γάρ οἱ ἔδωκεν.. ἐς πόλεμον φορέειν *gave* it him to wear in war, Il.15.532, cf. 23.183; δῶκε [τεύχεα] θεράποντι φορῆναι 7.149: later freq. of *giving* to eat or drink, ἐκ χειρὸς διδοῖ πιεῖν Hdt.4.172, cf. Cratin.124, Pherecr.69, etc.; ἐδίδου ῥοφεῖν Ar.*Fr.*203; δίδου μασᾶσθαι Eup. 253; δὸς καταφαγεῖν Hegem.1; τὴν κύλικα δὸς ἐμπιεῖν Pherecr.41; δὸς τὴν μεγάλην σπάσαι Diph.17.7; with inf. omitted, φιάλην ἔδωκε κεράσας Ephipp.10; εὐζωρότερον δός Diph.58; also of *giving* water to wash with, δίδου κατὰ χειρός (sc. νίψασθαι) Arched.2.3, cf. Alex.261. 2. **5.** Prose phrases, δ. ὅρκον, opp. λαμβάνειν, *tender* an oath, δοκεῖ κἂν ὀμόσαι εἴ τις αὐτῷ ὅρκον διδοίη Is.9.24, cf. D.39.3, Arist. *Rh.*1377ᵃ8; δ. ψῆφον, γνώμην, *put* a proposal to the vote, *propose* a resolution, D.21.87, 24.13: δ. χάριν, = χαρίζεσθαι, S.*Aj.*1354, Cratin. 317; ὀργῇ χάριν δοὺς *having indulged*.., S.*OC*855; λόγον τινὶ δ. *give* one leave to speak, X.*HG*5.2.20; δ. λόγον σφίσι *deliberate*, Hdt. 1.97; οὐκ, εἰ δ. διδοίης..σαυτῷ λόγον S.*OT*583; δοῦναι, λαβεῖν λόγον, Arist.*SE*165ᵃ27 (but δ. λόγον, εὐθύνας, *render* accounts, *IG*1².91, al.): δ. δίκην or δίκας, v. δίκη: ἀκοὴν δ. λόγοις *lend* an ear to.., S.*El.*30, etc.; δ. ἐργασίαν *give* diligence, = Lat. *dare operam*, *OGI*441. 109 (Lagina, i B.C.), *POxy.*742.11: c. inf., *Ev.Luc.*12.58: abs., sc. πληγήν, λίθῳ δ. τινί *PLips.*13 iii 3; ἐμβολὰς διδόναι, *ram*, of ships, D.S.13.10. **II.** c. acc. pers., *hand over, deliver up*, ἀχέεσσί με δώσεις Od.19.167; μιν..ὀδύνῃσιν ἔδωκεν Il.5.397; Ἕκτορα κυσὶν 23. 21; πυρί τινα Od.24.65; πληγαῖς τινά Pl.*R.*574c; ἔδωκε θῆρας φόβῳ Pi.*P.*5.60. **2.** of parents, *give* their daughter *to wife*, θυγατέρα ἀνδρί Il.6.192, Od.4.7; also of Telemachus, ἀνέρι μητέρα δώσω 2. 223; τὴν..Σάμηνδε ἔδοσαν *gave* her *in marriage* to go to Samé, 15. 367, cf. 17.442; with inf. added, δώσω σοι Χαρίτων μίαν ὀπυιέμεναι Il. 14.268: in Prose and Trag., θυγατέρα δ. τινὶ γυναῖκα Hdt.1.107, cf. Th.6.59, X.*HG*4.1.4, etc.: abs., ἐδίδοσαν καὶ ἤγοντο ἐξ ἀλλήλων Hdt. 5.92.β', cf. E.*Med.*288; also δ. κόρᾳ ἄνδρα Pi.*P.*9.117. **3.** διδόναι τινά τινι *grant* another to one's entreaties, *pardon* him at one's

request, X.*An.*6.6.31; διδόναι τινί τι *forgive* one a thing, *condone* it, E.*Cyc.*296 (s.v.l.). 4. δ. ἑαυτόν τινι *give* oneself *up*, δ. σφέας αὐτοὺς τοῖσι Ἀθηναίοισι Hdt.6.108, cf. S.*Ph.*84, Th.2.68; τινὶ εἰς χεῖρας S.*El.*1348; δ. ἑαυτὸν τοῖς δεινοῖς D.18.97; εἰς τοὺς κινδύνους Plb.3.17.8; εἰς ἔντευξιν Id.3.15.4; εἰς τρυφήν, εἰς λῃστείας, D.S.17.108, 18.47: c. inf., δίδωσ' ἑκὼν κτείνειν ἑαυτόν S.*Ph.*1341. 5. *appoint, establish,* of a priest, Lxx*Ex.*31.6; δῶμεν ἀρχηγόν ib.*Nu.*14.4; δ. τινὰ εἰς ἔθνος μέγα ib.*Ge.*17.20; *place,* τινὰ ὑπεράνω πάντα τὰ ἔθνη ib.*De.*28.1:—Pass., οἱ δεδομένοι, = *Nethinim, ministers* of the Temple, ib.*Ne.*5.3; ἐδόθη αὐτοῖς ἵνα.. *orders were given* them that.., *Apoc.*9.5. III. in vows and prayers, c. acc. pers. et inf., *grant, allow, bring about that..*, esp. in prayers, δὸς ἀποφθίμενον δῦναι δόμον Ἄϊδος εἴσω *grant that* he may go.., Il.3.322; τὸν κασίγνητον δότε τυίδ' ἵκεσθαι Sapph.*Supp.*1.2; δός με τείσασθαι *give* me *to..*, A.*Ch.*18, cf. *Eu.*31; also c. dat. pers., τούτῳ.. εὐτυχεῖν δοῖεν θεοί Id.*Th.*422; θεοὶ δοῖέν ποτ' αὐτοῖς.. παθεῖν S.*Ph.*316, cf. *OC*1101, 1287, Pl.*Lg.*737b. 2. *grant, concede* in argument, δ. καὶ συγχωρεῖν Id.*Phd.*100b, cf. Arist.*Metaph.*990a12, al.: c. inf., Id.*Ph.*239b29; δ. εἶναι θεούς Iamb.*Myst.*1.3; ἑνὸς ἀτόπου δοθέντος τἆλλα συμβαίνει Arist.*Ph.*186a9; δεδομένα, τά, *data,* title of work by Euclid; ἡ δοθεῖσα γραμμή, γωνία, etc., Pl.*Men.*87a, Euc.1.9, etc.; δεδόσθω κύκλος Archim.*Sph.Cyl.*1.6, al.; also in Alchemy, δός *take* certain substances, *PLeid.X.*69. IV. Gramm., *describe, record,* Sch.Pi.*P.*5.93, Sch.Il.16.207. V. seemingly intr., *give oneself up, devote oneself,* c. dat., esp. ἡδονῇ E.*Ph.*21, Plu.*Publ.*13; ἡδοναῖς Philostr.*VS*1.12; ἐλπίδι J.*AJ*17.12.2; εἰς δημοκοπίαν D.S.25.8; δρόμῳ δοὺς φέρεσθαι *at full speed,* Alciphr.3.47.

**δῖε**, v. δῖος. II. δίε, v. δίω. III. ⊛ διέ, Thess., = διά, *IG*9(2).517.16 (Larisa).

**διεγγελάω**, gloss on γλοιάζω, Hsch.

**διεγγύ-α**, ἡ, (ἐγγύη) *surety, bail,* Sch.Th.3.70. ⊛ **-άω**, I. *give bail to produce,* σώματα D.H.7.12:—Med., *to take bail for,* κατεγγυῶντος (v.l. δι-) Μενεξένου τὸν παῖδα, Πασίων αὐτὸν ἑπτὰ ταλάντων διεγγυήσατο Isoc.17.14, cf. Plu.*Caes.*11:—Pass., *to be bailed* by any one, ὀκτακοσίων ταλάντων τοῖς προξένοις διηγγυημένοι *bailed* by their Proxeni for eight hundred talents, Th.3.70. 2. *give security,* *SIG*976.49 (Samos, ii B.C.). II. *take pledges, distrain,* ib.629.20 (ii B.C.). III. abs., *mortgage* one's property, Lxx*Ne.*5.3. **-ημα**, ατος, τό, *pledge, security,* *PTeb.*5.12 (ii B.C.), *BGU*1112.12 (i A.D.), etc. **-ησις**, εως, ἡ, *giving bail* or *security,* D.24.73, *IG*11(2).287*A*136 (Delos, iii B.C.), D.Chr.11.18 (pl.). II. *giving bail for production,* τοῦ σώματος D.H.11.32.

⊛ **διεγ-είρω**, *wake up,* Anaxipp.1.47, J.*AJ*8.13.7, Hdn.2.1.5; *stir up, arouse,* Lxx2*Ma.*7.21; *excite, promote,* αὔξησιν φυτοῦ *Gp.*9.3.7:—Pass., Hp.*Ep.*15, Arist.*Pr.*876a22, Lxx*Es.*11.11, Ph.2.485, Longus 2.35; *to be raised up* from a sick-bed, *AP*11.171 (Lucill.); Ep. aor. διέγρετο ib.5.274 (Paul. Sil.). II. *raise,* τὸν αὐχένα Hld.4.4; χώματα J.*BJ*6.1.1, 6.2.7:—Pass., πύλας διεγειρομένας εἰς ὕψος πηχῶν ἑβδομήκοντα Lxx*Ju.*1.4; τοῖς πηδήμασι πρὸς οὐρανὸν διεγείρεσθε μέσον Procop.Gaz.ἠθοπ.ποιμένος p.137 B. **-ερσις**, εως, ἡ, *arousing,* σώματος *Hippiatr.*128. **-ερτέον**, *one must arouse,* Ath.Med.ap.Orib.*inc.*23.19, Archig.ap.Gal.13.176. **-ερτικός**, ή, όν, *exciting, stimulant,* S.E.*M.*6.19; ἀφροδισίων Diph.Siph.ap.Ath.2.64b, cf. Philum.ap.Orib.*Syn.*8.6.4.

**διεγκόπτω**, strengthd. for ἐγκόπτω, Stob.1.36.2.

**διέδεξε**, v. διαδείκνυμι.

**διέδην**, Adv., (διίημι) *throughout, to the end,* Hsch.

**διεδρεία**, ἡ, *sitting apart,* of birds whose position was ominous of strife, opp. συνεδρία, Arist.*HA*608b27 (pl.), Id.*EE*1236b10 (pl.).

**διέδριον**, τό, (ἕδρα) *seat for two persons,* Anon.ap.Suid.

⊛ **δίεδρος**, ον, (ἕδρα) *sitting apart,* opp. σύνεδρος, Arist.*HA*608b28. 2. = διαφανής, Hsch. II. δίεδρον, τό, *tripod-stand,* Callix.2. 2. *chaise-longue,* Antyll.ap.Orib.10.37.5, Erot. (pl.), Suid. s.v. ζεῦγος ἡμιονικόν.

**διεζευγμένως**, Adv., (διαζεύγνυμι) *discretely,* of ratios, Nicom.*Ar.*2.24.

**διεθίζω**, *become chronic,* Aret.*CD*1.2. II. of persons, *become habituated,* ἐμέτῳ Archig.ap.Orib.8.23.1.

**διειδής**, ές, (διεῖδον) *transparent, clear,* Thphr.*CP*6.19.2, Ael.*NA*4.30, Philostr.*Ep.*33; ποταμοί Max.Tyr.36.1: Sup., Luc.*Bacch.*6.

**διεῖδον**, inf. διϊδεῖν, aor. 2 with no pres. in use (διοράω being used), *see thoroughly, discern* (on the Homeric usage v. δια-είδω), τι Ar.*Nu.*168, Pl.*Phdr.*264c; λόγος οὐ ῥᾴδιος διϊδεῖν Id.*Phd.*62b. 2. *see through*:—Pass., διειδομένη ἐν ὕδατι νῆσος Call.*Del.*191; ἀτραπὸς.. διειδομένη πεδίοιο *seen through* or *across* the plain, A.R.1.546. II. pf. δίοιδα, inf. διειδέναι, Ep. διΐδμεναι Id.4.1360, *distinguish, discern,* ἀνδρῶν.. τὸν κακὸν διειδέναι E.*Med.*518, cf. Ar.*Ra.*975, Pl.*Phdr.*262a: fut., διείσεται ἡ χείρ Orib.8.36.6; *decide,* S.*OC*295.

**διεικάζομαι**, Pass., pf. inf. διεικάσθαι *to be like,* c. dat., Philostr.*Im.*1.19.

**διειλέω**, *unroll* a book, Plu.2.1039e, dub. in Phld.*Rh.*1.340 S.

**διειλημμένως**, Adv., (διαλαμβάνω) *distinctly, precisely,* X.*Oec.*11.25, Ptol.*Tetr.*11; opp. ἀδιαλήπτως, Phld.*Ir.*p.83 W., *Rh.*1.158 S.

**διειλοκομπάσας**· σκιᾷ καὶ κόμπῳ ἐξαπατήσας, Hsch.

⊛ **διειλύομαι**, Pass., *slip out of,* διειλυσθεῖσα δόμοιο A.R.4.35.

**δίειμι**, serving as fut. to διέρχομαι, impf. διῄειν: fut. διείσομαι Nic.*Th.*494, 837, cf. Hsch.:—*go to and fro, roam about,* Ar.*Ach.*845; of a report, *spread,* λόγος διῄει Plu.*Ant.*56. 2. *pass through,* δι' αὐτῶν μέσων Th.3.21; *get through, escape,* διὰ τῶν πόρων Arist.*Cael.*307b13; ἔξω Thphr.*CP*5.9.12: abs., Arist.*Ph.*204a4. 3. *pass,* ἡμέρα χειμέριος δίεισιν Thphr.*Sign.*46; *proceed,* of a play, Ar.*Ra.*920. II. c. acc., *go through, traverse,* Id.*Av.*1392: c. acc. cogn., δ. τὸν θεῖον δρόμον Pl.*Ax.*370e. b. *go through a subject* in speaking or writing, *narrate, describe, discuss,* Id.*Cri.*47c; δ. τῷ λόγῳ Id.*Grg.*505e, cf. Nic. ll.cc., Luc.*Icar.*3.

**διειξις**· διάστασις, Hsch. **Διειπετής**, v. Διϊπετής.

⊛ **διεῖπον**, in Hom. also διαεῖπον (v. infr.), serving as aor. 2 to διαγορεύω:—*tell fully* or *distinctly,* μεμιγμένοι.. ἢ ἀπάνευθε; δίειπέ μοι, ὄφρα δαείω Il.10.425; τρόπον πόνων S.*Tr.*22; *declare,* of an oracle, Id.*OT*854; *interpret* a riddle, ib.394, cf. Pl.*Plt.*275a. 2. *speak one with another, converse,* διαειπέμεν ἀλλήλοισιν Od.4.215. II. Med., *fix upon, agree,* διειπάμενος ἐν ᾧ [χρόνῳ] ἀποδώσει Arist.*Oec.*1351b5: abs., Id.*EE*1243a31, *Leg.Gort.*9.27.

**διειργασμένως**, Adv. *elaborately,* Men.Rh.p.387 S.

⊛ **διείργω**, Ep. and Ion. **διέργω**, Ep. also **διεέργω**:—*keep asunder, separate,* τοὺς διέεργον ἐπάλξιες Il.12.424, cf. Hdt.1.180, Pi.*N.*6.2, Th.3.107, E.*Fr.*382.6, *PTeb.*50.6 (ii B.C.); δ. τινὰ τοῦ μὴ συγκεχύσθαι Arist.*HA*562a25; ποταμοὶ δ. [τινὰς] τῆς οἴκαδε ὁδοῦ X.*An.*3.1.2:—Pass., πόρῳ διείργεται τῆς Ἀττικῆς ἡ νῆσος Plu.*Them.*13; χώρα ἰσθμῷ δ. μὴ νῆσον εἶναι Polyaen.2.2.4: c. inf., *to be prevented from..*, Porph.*Abst.*2.47. 2. *ward off,* Pl.*Criti.*115e; *exclude,* τινὰς παντὸς λόγου Philostr.*VA*3.31.

**διείρηκα**, v. διερῶ. **διείρομαι**, v. διέρομαι.

**διεῖρον**, τό, dub. sens. in *PFay.*117.21 (ii A.D.).

**διειρύω**, Ep. and Ion. for διερύω, *draw across,* τὰς νέας τὸν ἰσθμόν Hdt.7.24; *draw through,* νειοῖο ἄροτρον A.R.1.687.

**διείρω**, aor. inf. διέρσαι Hp.*Art.*11, al., but διεῖραι Id.*Morb.*2.5; imper. δίειρον Aen.Tact.31.18; part. διείρας Luc.*Alex.*26, Ael.*VH*4.28: pf. διεῖρκα X.*Cyr.*8.3.10: pf. part. Pass. διηρμένη Hp.*Art.*70, but διειρμένα *PHolm.*3.14:—*pass* or *draw through,* ὑπάλειπτρον διὰ καυμάτων Hp.*Art.*11; χεῖρας διὰ τῶν κανδύων X. l.c.; τὸν δάκτυλον διὰ τῆς ὀπῆς Ael. l.c.; βελόνας Aeschin.3.166; *insert,* παττάλους Thphr.*CP*2.14.4; λίνον Aen.Tact. l.c.; βελόνην διὰ τῶν ὀφθαλμῶν *PMag.Par.*1.2949: intr., δάκτυλοι οἷον διείροντες Philostr.*VA*4.28. 2. *string* upon, κάνθαρον χρυσῷ *PMag.Lond.*46.229:—Pass., *PHolm.* l.c. II. *string together in order, weave* a story, Philostr.*VA*8.12:—Pass., λόγος διειρόμενος, = εἰρόμενος, f.l. in D.H.*Comp.*26.

**διειρωνόξενος**, ον, (εἴρων) *dissembling with one's guests, treacherous under the mask of hospitality,* Ar.*Pax* 623.

**διείς**, v. διίημι.

**διεισ-δύνω** or **-δύω**, *go into and through,* [τὴν γῆν] Alex.Aphr.*Pr.*1.127; εἰς τοὺς πόρους ib.2.76, cf. Phlp.*in Mete.*93.37, al. **-δυσις**, εως, ἡ, *passing through,* Id.*in Cat.*5.33.

**διεισέρχομαι**, Medic., *effect an entrance through* pores or membranes, Steph.*in Hp.*1.165 D., al.; also **διεισκρίνομαι**, ibid.

⊛ **διέκ**, before a vowel **διέξ** (but διὲξ σωλῆνος Archil.5), *out through,* δ. προθύρου, μεγάροιο, Il.15.124, Od.10.388, etc.; cf. παρέκ.

**διεκ-βαίνω**, *go through and out of,* τὰ ὄρη Str.12.2.4. **-βάλλω**, *pass* a needle, string, etc., *through, thread,* Hero*Bel.*98.10, Heliod.ap.Orib.44.10.4, Gal.10.417. 2. *subtract from* ζῴδια *in succession,* Vett.Val.175.35. 3. *pay through a bank,* *BGU*1200.23 (Pass., i B.C.). II. intr. (sc. στρατόν), *march through,* Στυμφαλίαν Plb.4.68.5, prob. in Plu.*Pel.*17. 2. of rivers, boundaries, etc., δ. τὰ ὅρια εἰς.. Lxx*Jo.*15.8; ὁ Εὐφράτης δ. διὰ τοῦ Ταύρου Str.16.1.13; δ. εἰς νότον καὶ βορρᾶ(ν) *PLond.*2.154.9 (i A.D.). **-βλητέον**, *one must pass a needle through,* Antyll.ap.Orib.45.24.9. ⊛ **-βολή**, ἡ, *mountain-pass,* in pl., Plb.1.75.4, 3.40.1: sg., D.S.17.68. II. *estuary,* Str.9.5.22. III. *way out* of a city, J.*AJ*15.7.10 (pl.). IV. *traversing,* Onos.7.1; *passing through,* of needle, Heliod.ap.Orib.44.14.14. V. *acknowledgement of payment received* by a bank, *PTeb.*389.3 (ii A.D.), *BGU*445.8 (ii A.D.). **-βόλιον**, τό, *medicine to eject a dead foetus,* Hp.*Mul.*1.91. **-δίδωμι**, = διαδίδωμι, ibid. **-δικέω**, strengthd. for ἐκδικέω, ἑαυτήν Zos.Alch.p.112 B., cf. *PMasp.*299.14 (vi A.D.), Arg.3 Hes.*Sc.*, Sch.E.*Hec.*1027. II. *claim,* = Lat. *vindicare,* *Cod.Just.*10.16.1 (Pass.). **-δικητής**, οῦ, ὁ, = Lat *defensor,* ib.10.11.8.7a (pl.). ⊛ **-δρομή**, ἡ, *darting forth,* ἀστέρων Ptol.*Tetr.*102; *passing through,* Ezek.*Exag.*199 (pl.). **-δύομαι**, aor. διεξέδυν (but διεκδῦσαι· ἀποδρᾶσαι, Hsch.), *slip out through,* Hp.*Morb.Sacr.*7; δ. τὸν ὄχλον Plu.*Tim.*10: abs., prob. in Id.*Pel.*17. **-δυσις**, εως, ἡ, *means of escape,* δ. μυῶν *mouse-holes,* Ath.3.98d, cf. Plu.*Sert.*13. **-θέστερον**· ἀκριβέστερον, Hsch.; cf. διεκτελέστερον. **-θέω**, *run through, extend,* ἄχρι τῆς γῆς Arist.*Mu.*395a22; διά τινος Plu.2.666b: c. gen., ib.589d: abs., Id.*Dio* 30; ἐς ἔμετον, of bile, Aret.*SA*2.5. **-θρώσκω**, aor. inf. -θορέειν, *leap through,* Opp.*H.*4.674.

**διεκί**, Thess., = διότι, *IG*9(2).517.11 (Larisa), 1229.36 (Phalanna).

**διεκ-κύπτω**, *peep out,* Lxx 2*Ma.*3.19, Eust.1754.44. **-λαμβάνω**, *rent, hire,* *PSI*6.584.12 (iii B.C.). **-λάμπω**, *shine out through,* Hld.2.31. **-λανθάνομαι**, Med., *forget utterly,* Q.S.13.380 (tm.). **-λύω**, *dissolve, relax,* Gal.19.70; *remove* hindrances, Vett.Val.183.2:—Pass., Alex.Aphr.*Pr.*1.135. **-μηρύομαι**, *unwind,* Ph.*Bel.*57.44. **-μυζάω**, *suck out,* *Gp.*7.15.2. **-νέομαι**, *depart from among,* A.R.4.409 (tm.); διὲξ ἁλὸς οἶδμα νέοντο they *crossed* the sea, ib.659. **-παίω**, *break* or *burst through,* τῆς ἵππου J.*BJ*5.2.2, cf. Philostr.*Her.*19.4, *Im.*2.23; διά τινος Paus.7.16.5: c. acc., στοάν Diox.3, cf. App.*BC*5.34, etc., Luc.*Tox.*61:—Med., δ. τὰς πύλας D.H.11.37; τοὺς πολεμίους Plu.*Sert.*21: abs., J.*BJ*7.6.4, Polyaen.4.2.14; δ. ἔξω Iamb.*VP*35.249. **-παυσις**, εως, ἡ, *intermission,* τοῦ κακοῦ Vett.Val.209.25. **-περαίνω**, *go through with,* τὰ τούτων ἐχόμενα

δ. X.*Oec.*6.1 :—Pass., πρὶν . . βίος διεκπερανθῇ S.*Fr.*646. ® **-περαιόομαι**, Pass., *pass out through*, Str.12.2.3. **-περάω**, *pass out through*, c. acc., τὰς Ἡρακλέας στήλας Hdt.4.152; δ. τὴν ἄνυδρον *pass quite through* it, Id.3.4; τὸν ποταμόν Id.5.52; βίον E.*Supp.*954; *traverse*, ἀταρπόν Orac.ap.Jul.*Ep.*89b. **2.** abs., δ. ἐς χθόνα A.*Pers.*485; of food, like διαχωρέω, Pl.*Ti.*73a. **II.** *pass by, overlook*, Ar.*Pl.*283, v. Sch. **-περδικίζω**, = διαπερδικίζω, Suid. **-πηδάω**, *jump, run about*, Antyll.ap.Orib.6.26.6; *bound violently*, καρδία Aristaenet.2.13. ® **-πίπτω**, *issue, escape through*, φωτὸς -πίπτοντος διὰ τῶν νεφῶν Epicur.*Ep.*2 p.45 U., cf. Ph.*Bel.*57.3: abs., *escape*, Arist.*Pr.*910ᵃ17; *exude*, τῶν πόρων Plu.2.51a, Gal.10.948; τι Onos.21.1, Hld.10.28; διὰ τῆς πόλεως Arr.*An.*1.8.7. **2.** *escape*, εἰς Θήβας D.S.4.54, cf. 12.56. **II.** *spread abroad*, of a proverbial saying, Eust.ad D.P.809. **-πλέκω**, dub. sens. in Alex.*Fig.*2.20. **-πλέω**, Ion. **-πλώω**, aor. -έπλωσα :—*sail out through*, τὸν Ἑλλήσποντον Hdt.7.147; τὰς Κυανέας Id.4.89; τὴν διώρυχα Id.7.122; σχοίνους δυώδεκα Id.2.29; Ἡρακλέων στηλέων Id.4.42: abs., *sail out*, ib.43. **II.** in naval tactics, *break the enemy's line by sailing through it*, so as to be able to charge their ships in flank or rear, Hdt.6.15, Th.1.50, 7.36, Sosyl.p.31 B., Plb.1.51.9. **-πλοος**, contr. **διέκπλους**, ὁ, *passage*, τῶν βραχέων *through* the shallows, Hdt.4.179; δ. ὑπόφαυσιν καταλιπεῖν Id.7.36, cf. Pl.*Criti.*115e. **II.** *breaking the enemy's line* in a sea-fight, δ. ποιεύμενος Hdt.6.12, cf. Th.1.49, 7.36. **-πλώω**, v. διεκπλέω. **-πνέω**, *blow from start to finish*, of winds, Arist.*Mu.*394ᵇ35. **-πνοή**, ἡ, *exhalation*, Thphr.*CP*4.12.12; πυρός *Placit.*2.24.2. **II.** *ventilation-hole*, Ph.*Bel.*87.4 (pl.). **-πονέω**, *work out, calculate*, Gal.19.520; prob. for -ποιέω, ib.531. **-πορεύομαι**, *go out through*, D.H.9.26; *pass through, traverse*, διὰ τῆς τῶν ὅλων οὐσίας M.Ant.7.19. **-πτύω**, *spit all about*, Philostr.*Im.*2.23. **-πτωσις**, εως, ἡ, *issue*, of nerves from the spine, Gal.8.57. **II.** *passage through* a sieve, of powders, Id.11.134. **-ρέω**, *flow out*, ὅκως ἀθρόως δ. τὸ αἷμα Aret.*CA*1.5. **-ροος**, ὁ, *passage for the stream to escape*, Hdt.7.129. **-σεύω**, *drive through*, νῆα διὲκ πέλαγος σεύεν A.R.2.620. **-τείνω**, *stretch out, extend*, v.l. in Hp.*Mochl.*38 for δεῖ ἐκτ-, cf. Hero *Bel.*99.1:—Pass., fut. -ταθήσομαι Iamb.*in Nic.*p.71 P. **-τελέστερον**· ἀκριβέστερον, Hsch. **-τελέω**, *accomplish*, τὴν οἰκονομίαν *PMag.Par.*1.2107. **-τέλλω**, *arise, grow from*, Nic.*Fr.*74.30. **-τέμνω**, *divide through the midst*, v.l. in J.*BJ*3.10.7. **-τετραίνω**, gloss on διεκπαίω, Hsch.; -τετρημένος v.l. for διατετρ-, Heliod.ap.Orib.49.23.15. **-τρέχω**, aor. -έδρᾰμον, *traverse*, Ph.*Bel.*77.36; ὁππότ' ἂν . . ἠέλιος Κριὸν . . διεκτρέχῃ Orph.*Fr.*285.5: abs., *sally, rush out*, J.*AJ*5.2.11; κυνὸς διεκδραμόντος Plu.2.490d. **-τρησις**, εως, ἡ, *hole bored quite through*, Gal.*UP*10.5 (pl.). **-τρῡπάω**, gloss on διεκπαίω, Suid. **-τῡλόω**, *remove a callus*, Sor.1.46. **-τύλωσις**, εως, ἡ, *removal of a callus*, ibid. **-φαίνω**, strengthd. for ἐκφαίνω, Eust.1538.17:—Pass., Philostr.*Im.*1.14. **-φέρω**, strengthd. for ἐκφέρω, Hsch. s.v. διεξαγάγη, A.R.3.73 (tm.). **-φεύγω**, strengthd. for ἐκφεύγω, Plu.*Cam.*27 (v.l.); κινδ(υ)ν *Corp.Herm.*12.7; διὲκ πέτρας φ. A.R.2.616. **-φύω**, *spring from*, of veins and muscles, Gal.2.786, 18(1).446. **-χέω**, strengthd. for ἐκχέω, Aret.*CA*2.5.

**διέλᾰσις**, εως, ἡ, *driving through*, of a nail, Plu.2.659d. **II.** *charge* or *exercise of cavalry*, ἡ εἰς τάχος δ. X.*Eq.Mag.*3.4.

**διελαύνω**, Att. fut. διελῶ: aor. 1 διήλᾰσα :—*drive through* or *across*, τάφροιο διήλασε μώνυχας ἵππους Il.10.564, cf. 12.120, E.*Supp.*676. **b.** ἥδε σ' ἡμέρα διήλασε *has brought* you *to the end* (sc. of servitude), Id.*Heracl.*788. **2.** *thrust through*, λαπάρης δὲ διήλασε χάλκεον ἔγχος Il.16.318, cf. 13.161; νεκροῦ περὶ τὴν ἄκανθαν ξύλον . . δ. Hdt.4.72. **3.** δ. τινὰ λόγχῃ *thrust* one *through* with a lance, Plu.*Marc.*29, cf. Luc.*DMort.*27.4 (Pass.). **II.** intr., *ride through*, X.*An.*1.5.12, etc.; *charge through*, ib.1.10.7, al.: c. acc. cogn., δ. ὁδόν Id.*Cyr.*4.4.4. **III.** Pass., *to be driven through*, *IG*1².81.12. **2.** *dart through*, of a shooting pain, Aret.*SA*2.7. **3.** *to be distributed*, of the branches of an artery, ib.2.1. **IV.** Med., διηλάσω· διηγήσω, διῆλθες, Hsch.

**διελεγκτέον**, *one must refute*, Plu.2.450b.

**διελέγχω**, *refute*, Pl.*Grg.*457e, Arist.*Fr.*94, Plb.7.3.3, Luc.*Prom.*6, etc. **II.** *convict, expose*, Ph.1.265, al., Plu.2.437b, *PLips.*40iii23 (iv A.D.):—Pass., Philostr.Jun.*Im.*1, *BGU*321.14 (iii A.D.). **III.** *prove, try*, Philostr.*Gym.*17; *investigate*, Jul.*Or.*3.111b:—Pass., πάντα δ. φωτὶ Ph.2.345. **IV.** Med. or Pass., *dispute*, Lxx *Is.*1.18, *Mi.*6.2. **2.** Pass., *to be distinguished*, Phlp. *in Mete.*128.30.

**διελευθερόω**, *liberate*, εἱργμῶν τὸν νοῦν Porph.*VP*46.

**διέλευσις**, εως, ἡ, *transit*, Ptol.*Tetr.*135.

**διέλθυρις**· διάμφοδος, Hsch.

**διελινήσατο**· ἐξέφυγε, Hsch.

**διελῑνύω**, *to cease entirely from labour* or *exercise*, Hp.*Acut.*45.

® **διελίσσω**, Att. -ττω, *unfold*: *deploy*, of military evolutions, D.C.74.5: metaph., *expose*, Plu.2.411b:—Med., *roll over*, Q.S.6.565.

**διελίτην**· δόλιον, κακοῦργον· καὶ πανταχοῦ διερχόμενον (i.e. διηλύτην), Hsch.; cf. διηλίτης.

**διελκ-υσμός**, ὁ, *pushing about*, D.H.*Comp.*20. **2.** *delay*, *PTeb.*25.2 (ii B.C.). **3.** *brawl*, Arg.1 Ar.*Ach.* **-υστίνδα** παίζειν, *tug-of-war*, Poll.9.112. **-ω**, fut. διελκύσω: aor. -είλκυσα Ar.*Pl.*1036, Pl.*R.*440a:—*tear asunder, open wide*, τοὺς ὀφθαλμούς Pl.l.c.; τὸ στόμα D.L.7.20. **2.** metaph. in Pass., *diverge, vary*, of Ms. readings, τὸ . . "παντὸς" διέλκεται κατὰ τὰ ἀντίγραφα Demetr.Lac.1012.23 F. **II.** *pull through*, διὰ δακτυλίου Ar.l.c.; βρόχῳ Hp.*Aff.*5. **2.** *haul* ships *across* an isthmus, D.S.4.56. **III.** of Time, in Pass., *to be protracted*, Plb.31.18.4:—Act., δ. βίον *drag on* life, Plu.2.1033d; δ. τὸν φόρον *postpone payment of* a tax, *BGU*1116.21 (i B.C.), cf. 1120.35 (i B.C.):—Med., *procrastinate*, 2 dual aor. διηλκύσασθον Hsch. **IV.** *continue drinking*, Ar.*Pax*1131 (where others supply τὸν βίον), cf. *Fr.*109 (dub.).

® **δίεμαι**, Pass., *speed*, ἵπποι πεδίοιο δίενται *speed* over the plain, Il.23.475; οὐ . . μέμονε . . δίεσθαι he is not minded *to hasten away*, 12.304. **II.** *fear*, c. inf., A.*Pers.*701 (lyr., δείομαι cod. Med.). (Cf. δίω.)

**διεμβάλλω**, *put in through*, Lxx *Nu.*4.6, al., Gal.2.574, Aët.15.12.

**διέμενος**, v. δίημι.

**διεμ-μένω**, *keep in place*, Gal.18(1).828. **-πῖλος**, ον, *well-capped, well-hatted*, κεφαλή Luc.*Lex.*13. **-πίμπλημι**, *fill completely*, Lxx 2*Ma.*4.40, Hsch. **-πίπτω**, *fall quite into*, εἴς τι Plb.38.9.4. **-πολάω**, *sell to different buyers* or *sell in lots*, E.*Ba.*512; ἐμπορικὰ χρήματα δ. Ar.*Ach.*973. **2.** metaph., τί με . . διεμπολᾷ λόγοισι πρός σε; what *bargain* is he *driving*? S.*Ph.*579; of a mercenary marriage, ὠθούμεθ' ἔξω καὶ διεμπολώμεθα Id.*Fr.*583.7. **-φαίνω**, *show through*, ὀφθαλμοὶ . . γοργὸν δ. Luc.*Alex.*3 (dub. l.). **-φᾰνίζω**, *let* a thing *be seen*, Aristaenet.2.16.

**διεμφύομαι**, *breed in*, τερηδόνων, ἃ διεμφύεται τοῖς δένδρεσι Procl. ad Hes.*Op.*412.

**διενέγκαι**, Ion. **-ενεῖκαι**, v. διαφέρω.

**διεν-ειλέω**, *involve*, λόγος διενειλημένος Ps.-Luc.*Philopatr.*1. **-είργω**, *shut quite up*, Gal.17(1).453 (Pass.).

**διενεκτέον**, (διαφέρω) *one must excel*, Luc.*Astr.*1.

**διεν-εργέω**, strengthd. for ἐνεργέω, Crito ap.Stob.3.3.64. **-εργητικός**, ή, όν, strengthd. for ἐνεργητικός, δύναμις Herod.Med. in *Rh. Mus.*58.76. **-θῡμέομαι**, *consider, reflect*, περί τινος *Act.Ap.*10.19.

**διενῐαυτίζω**, *live out the year*, Hdt.4.7. **II.** *spend a whole year*, *POxy.*899.11 (ii/iii A.D.).

**διενίημι**, *insert*, Orib.10.24.3, Ruf.ap.eund.8.24.29.

**δίενος** [ĭ], ον, *two years old*, Thphr.*HP*7.5.5, 8.11.5.

® **διενοχλέω**, *annoy*, τινί Ph.2.590, J.*AJ*9.3.1 (v.l.), Aristaenet.1.5: abs., Luc.*Symp.*14:—Pass., ὑπὸ τῶν πρακτόρων *BGU*830.8 (i A.D.).

**διεντέρευμα**, ατος, τό, (ἔντερον) *looking through entrails*, Com. word for *sharp-sightedness*, coined by Ar.*Nu.*166.

**διέξ**, v. διέκ.

**διεξ-αγνέω**, = sq., *IG*5(1).26.9 (Sparta, ii B.C.). **-άγω** [ᾰ], Aeol. aor. 1 Pass. διεξάχθην *Milet.*3 No.152.25 (ii B.C.):—*lead through*, δύναμιν διὰ τειχῶν D.S.14.20. **b.** τροφὴ διεξάγουσα *laxative* diet, Aret.*CA*2.5. **2.** *bring to an end, settle*, λόγῳ ἀμφισβήτησιν Plb.5.1.5, etc.; *try* a cause, *GDI*5040.69 (Crete):—Pass., *PTeb.*5.219 (ii B.C.), al., *PSI*2.173.15 (ii B.C.); τὸ δίκαιον διεξάγεται Plb.4.73.8. **3.** *arrange, manage*, Chrysipp.*Stoic.*3.185; *administer, conduct*, ἀσφαλῶς τὰ κατὰ τὴν ἀρχήν Plb.1.9.6, cf. *PLond.*3.1221.2 (ii A.D.); ταμιεῖαν *IG*2².1326.38:—Pass., ὁ τῆς φύσεως νόμος καθ' ὃν διεξάγεται τὰ γιγνόμενα Plu.2.568d. **4.** *treat*, τινὰς ἐν τῇ πάσῃ φιλανθρωπίᾳ Plb.3.77.4. **II.** δ. τοὺς βίους ἀπό τινος *support* life, Id.1.71.1: abs., Plu.109cb. **-αγωγή**, ἡ, *settlement* of a dispute, Plb.5.102.3. **II.** *inquiry, inquest*, *PTeb.*14.6 (ii B.C.), *PRyl.*65.10 (i B.C.). **2.** *trial*, δ. ποιήσασθαι *GDI*5040.59 (Crete). **III.** δ. τοῦ βίου *a way of living*, D.S.4.30, cf. Hierocl.p.53 A., S.E.*M.*7.158, al.: abs., Phld.*Sto.*339.19, Arr.*Epict.*1.6.21, Ecphant.ap.Stob.4.7.64; τὰς δ. ποιεῖσθαι S.E.*M.*1.178. **-αγωγός**, ὁ, *steward, manager*, Sch.Pi.*O.*14.13. **-αιρέω**, strengthd. for ἐξαιρέω, Demetr.*Eloc.*299. **-ᾱΐσσω**, Att. -άττω, *rush forth*, Theoc.13.23, Arist.*Mu.*394ᵇ15, 397ᵃ31. **-αμείβομαι**, Pass., *to be passed*, ἐτῶν διεξάμειπτο διπλὰ δεκὰς *IG*12(8).441.11 (Thasos). **-άνθημα**, ατος, τό, *pustule*, Aret.*SA*1.9. **-ανθίζω**, *variegate with flowers*, cj. Pors. in Eub.99. **-ανίσταμαι**, *rise up, prepare to deal with*, ἐπὶ τὰ λειπόμενα τῶν πραγμάτων Eun.*Hist.*p.263 D. **-ανύω**, *complete*, πλοῦν Iamb.*VP*3.16. ® **-αρκέω**, *suffice*, πρὸς τὸ παρόν Ph.1.607; εἰς ἑκάστην ἡμέραν Id.2.297, cf. Anon.Lond.37.47. **-αρτάομαι**, *depend on*, τῆς λογικῆς φύσεως Ph.1.446. **-ατμίζω**, strengthd. for ἐξατμίζω, Hp.*Morb.*4.47. **-άττω**, v. διεξαΐσσω. ® **-ειμι**, (εἶμι *ibo*) *go out through*, δ. ἐξίμεναι πεδίονδε Il.6.393; ἐξ αὐλῆς ἐς . . Hdt.2.148. **2.** *go through, pass through* a country, δ. τῆς Λιβύης τὰ ἄνω ib.25; τὴν Μιλησίην Id.5.29; διὰ πάσης Εὐρώπης Id.2.36; διὰ παντὸς τοῦ σώματος Th.2.49, cf. 3.45; χώραν, τόπον, Plb.4.25.4, Plu.2.149a. **3.** *traverse the whole length of* a line, Arist.*EN*1174ᵃ34. **II.** in counting or recounting, *go through in detail, relate circumstantially*, Hdt.1.116, 7.77, etc.; περί τινος Isoc.5.4, Pl.*Prt.*361e, etc.; *go through*, by way of examining, E.*Hipp.*1024; *expound*, Epicur.*Nat.*2.11; *deliver*, ἐγκώμιον Plu.*Ant.*14. **-έλᾰσις**, εως, ἡ, = διέλασις, Id.*Sull.*18, Hld.9.18. ® **-ελαύνω**, Att. fut. -ελῶ: intr., *drive, ride, march through*, abs., Hdt.1.187: c. acc. loci, δ. τὴν ἄνυδρον Id.3.11; τὰς πύλας Id.5.52, etc.; also κατὰ τὸ προάστειον Id.3.86; δ. ἐπὶ ἅρματος Id.7.100; δ. ἵππῳ τὸν πόρον Plu.*Publ.*19: c. gen. loci, δ. τῆς Ῥώμης Id.*Cam.*7. **-ελέγχω**, *refute utterly*, Luc.*Alex.*61, Plu.2.922e, Gal.4.518:—Pass., ὅταν ἀμαθέστεροι διεξελέγχωνται when they *are convicted of* ignorance, Them.*Or.*21.259b. **-έλευσις**, εως, ἡ, = διέξοδος, Sch.A.R.4.1573. **-ελίσσω**, Ion. -ειλίσσω, *unroll, untie*, Hdt.4.67. **-εργάζομαι**, *work out, effect*, κακά Pl.*Lg.*798d. **II.** *make away with*, v.l. in Hdt.5.92.γ' and D.H.6.35. **-ερέομαι**, *question closely*, c. dupl. acc., ἐμὲ ταῦτα Il.10.432, cf. A.R.1.327. **-ερευνάω**, *examine* or *survey closely*, Pi.*N.*3.24 (tm.):—Med., χώραν Pl.*Lg.*763a, cf. *Phlb.*58d. **-έρπω**, *run his course*, of the sun, Arist.*Mu.*399ᵃ24: fut. διεξερπύσει ib.398ᵇ33. **-ερύγησις** [ῠ], εως, ἡ, *power of belching forth*, Orac.ap.Porph.

ap.Eus.*PE*6.3. **-έρχομαι**, fut. -ελεύσομαι, = διέξειμι:—*go through, pass through*, τὸ χωρίον Hdt.2.29, cf. 5.29; πεδίον *Hell.Oxy.*7.3, etc. 2. *go completely through*, νόμον τὸν ὄρθιον Hdt.1.24; πάντας φίλους E.*Alc.*15; τὴν ὁδόν Pl.*Lg.*822a; τὴν δίκην ib.856a; δ. πόνους S.*Ph.*1419: c. part., δ. πωλέων *be done* selling, Hdt.1.196. 3. folld. by διά, *go through in succession*, διὰ πάντων δ. τῶν παίδων, i.e. killing them one after another, Id.3.11; διὰ τῶν δέκα Id.5.92.γ'; διὰ τῶν πόλεων Pl.*Prt.*315a. 4. *go through in detail, relate circumstantially*, Hdt.3.75, 7.18, D.18.21; λόγον Pl.*Lg.*893a; ἡ ψυχὴ δ. λόγον πρὸς αὑτήν Id.*Tht.*189e; τῷ λόγῳ Polystr.p.30 W.; περὶ νόμων Pl.*Lg.*857e. II. intr., *to be past, gone by*, of time, Hdt.2.52; ἡμέρα διεξῆλθεν ἀργή Plu.*Arist.*16. 2. *to be gone through*, of legal formalities, πάντα δ' ἤδη διεξεληλύθει D.21.84, cf. Pl.*Lg.*805b. **-ετάζω**, strengthd. for ἐξετάζω, Iamb.*in Nic.*p.88 P., Asp.*in EN*114.22; διεξητασμένος, of a surgeon, Eun.*VS*p.499 B. **-ηγέομαι**, strengthd. for ἐξηγέομαι, v.l. in X.*Mem.*4.2.12. **-ίημι**, strengthd. for ἐξίημι, *let pass through*, διεξῆκαν αὐτοὺς διὰ τῆς πόλεως Hdt.4.203. II. intr., of a river, *empty itself*, ἐς θάλασσαν Th.2.102 (s.v.l.). **-ικνέομαι**, *arrive at*, εἰς.. Plb.10.29.3. **-ιππάζομαι**, *ride out through*, dub. for διεξεπαίσατο (cf. διεκπαίω), Polyaen.5.16.5. **-ιτέον**, *one must narrate, describe*, Pl.*Ti.*44d, Arist.*Rh.Al.*1425$^b$2, Agath. *Praef.* **-ιχνεύω**, *search through*, δικαιώματα *PMasp.*167.35 (vi A.D.). **-οδευτικός**, ή, όν, *giving issue*, ποταμῶν δ. ἀφέσεις εἰς θάλατταν *EM*692.52. **-οδεύω**, *have a way out, escape*, Hp.*Epid.*2.3.8; *march out*, J.*BJ*7.5.4. II. c. acc., *go through*, λόγον S.E.*M.*2.9, al. III. Pass., *to be regularized*, διεξωδευμένη φαντασία ib.7.166, al. **-οδικός**, ή, όν, *of* or *for going through*: τὸ δ. *fundament*, Arist. *HA*493$^a$23. 2. Math., *produced by traversing*, of loci (e.g. line by point or surface by line), Papp.662.2. II. *detailed*, λόγος Plb.12.25$^b$4; ἱστορία Plu.*Fab.*16. Adv. -κῶς *in detail*, δ. ἀποκρίνεσθαι, of an answer *involving a statement* (opp. 'yes' or 'no'), *Stoic.* 2.62, etc.: Comp., J.*BJProoem.*6, Phlp.*in GA*101.36; *verbatim*, ἀναγραφῆναι *SIG*694.38 (Pergam., ii B.C.); also, *by discursive reasoning*, Ammon.*in APr.*25.2; opp. συμβολικῶς, Porph.*VP*36. ⊛ **-οδος**, ἡ, *outlet, passage*, Hp.*Aph.*7.51, Arist.*PA*684$^b$26, etc.; ἀποκεκληϊμένου τοῦ ὕδατος τῆς δ. Hdt.3.117, cf. 4.140; διέξοδοι δδῶν *passage*-ways, Id.1.199; ἀνέμων διέξοδοι (through the body), S.*Fr.*477; ὅταν πλευμων μὴ καθαρὰς παρέχῃ τὰς δ. Pl.*Ti.*84d, cf. 91c; *way out from*, Th. 3.98; αἱ δ. τῶν ὁδῶν *Ev.Matt.*22.9; of the main *roads out of* a town, Aristeas 105; δ. ὑδάτων, of a spring, Lxx 4*Ki.*2.21; of tears, ib.*Ps.* 118(119).136. 2. *pathway, orbit*, of the sun, Hdt.2.24; τρεῖς ἡλίου διέξοδοι three *days*, E.*Andr.*1086; of planets, Arist.*Mu.*399$^a$3: metaph., πολλὰς φροντίδων δ. Henioch.4.5; δ. τῶν βουλευμάτων the *paths* of his counsels, Hdt.3.156; δ. τῆς φύσεως, τῆς οὐσίας, Ocell. 1.5,12; [ὁ νοῦς] ἔχων τὴν αὐτὴν διὰ τῶν οὐκ αὐτῶν δ. Plot.6.7.13. 3. *issue, event*, δ. λαβεῖν Plb.2.1.3, etc. 4. *means of escape*, πάσας δ. διεξελθών Pl.*R.*405c; δ. πραγμάτων *way out of* difficulties, Chrysipp. *Stoic.*3.66. 5. Medic., *evacuation*, Hp.*Prog.*11, Gal.17(1).132 (pl.). II. *detailed narrative* or *description*, ἡ τοῦ λόγου δ. *the course* of the narrative or argument, Pl.*Criti.*109a, cf. *Prt.*361d, Chrysipp.*Stoic.*2.250, Ph.1.407; *exposition*, Phld.*Sign.*38, *Mus.* p.110 K., al.; ἡ διὰ στοιχείου δ. *description* by resolving into elements, Pl.*Tht.*207c; κατὰ διέξοδον *in detail*, Aristid.*Rh.*1 p.505 S.; δ. καὶ ἔπαινοι *narratives, tales*, Pl.*Prt.*326a, etc. III. *military evolution*, δ. τακτικαί Id.*Lg.*813e, cf. D.C.74.5. 2. *excursion*, Pl.*Phdr.* 247a. 3. *repeated experiment*, Gal.10.169. **-οιγνῦμι**, *lay quite open*, πλευρὰ διεξῴξεν Q.S.13.41. **-οιδάω** or **-έω**, pf. part. διεξῳδηκώς, *to swell out*, Philostr.*Im.*1.13. **-ουρέω**, strengthd. for ἐξουρέω, Hp.*Int.*14, Gal.19.652.

**διεξωδέστερον**, Adv. = διεξοδικώτερον, *more fully, in greater detail*, incorrect formation in Wilcken *Chr.*238.4 (ii A.D.).

**διεορτάζω**, *keep the feast throughout*, τὰ Ἴσθμια Th.8.9, cf. Plu. *Pyrrh.*20: plpf. διεωρτάκει D.C.47.20:—Pass., ταῦτα διεωρτάσθη these *festivities were kept*, Id.51.21.

**διεπαχήσατο**· διεπράξατο, Hsch. **διεπέμφρακτο**· διέφθαρτο, Id.

**διεπέφραδε**, v. διαφράζω.

**διεπι-βαίνω**, *overlap*, Gal.2.564. **-στέλλω**, *dispatch*, *PLips.* 101 ii 32. **-φώσκω**, strengthd. for ἐπιφώσκω, D.H.9.63 (prob. f.l. for διέφωσκε).

**διέπραθ-ον**, **-όμην**, v. διαπέρθω. **διέπτατο**, v. διαπέτομαι.

⊛ **διέπω**, *manage, conduct*, τὸ πλεῖον πολέμοιο Il.1.166; στρατόν 2. 207; ἕκαστα 11.706; σκηπανίῳ δίεπ' ἀνέρας *drove* them *away*, 24.247; δ. πόλιν, ἄλσος, Pi.*O.*6.93, B.3.21; μάχας Xenoph.1.21; δ. τὰ πρήγματα, τὸν ἀγῶνα, Hdt.3.53, 5.22: rare in Trag. (lyr.), A.*Pers.*105, *Eu.*931: abs., ἀνὰ στρατιὴν διέπουσαν Sulla ap.App.*BC*1.97: in Prose, Arist.*Mu.*399$^a$18, Ecphant.ap.Stob.4.7.64; δ. ἀρχήν Plu.*Lyc.* 3; ἐπάρχειον *IPE*1$^2$.174.8 (Olbia, ii A.D.); τὴν τῶν στεμμάτων διοίκησιν *PRyl.*77.30 (ii A.D.); esp. as deputy or substitute, δ. τὰ κατὰ τὴν στρατηγίαν, τὴν ἀρχιδικαστείαν, *PTeb.*522 (ii A.D.), *PLond.*3. 908.19 (ii A.D.). b. Astrol., τὸν πολεύοντα καὶ διέποντα [ἀστέρα] Serapio in *Cat.Cod.Astr.*1.99, cf. Paul.Al.*C.*2. 2. *traverse*, ἅλα *AP*10.24 (Crin.). II. Med., *to be ever engaged in*, γόοις E.*El.* 146 (lyr.).

⊛ **διέρ-ᾱμα**, ατος, τό, *funnel, strainer*, Plu.2.1088e. II. *hopper for lading corn in bulk*, *PThead.*26,27 (pl., iii A.D.): hence, **-ᾱμάτίτης**, ου, ὁ, *contractor for use of* διέραμα 11, *POxy.*1197.4 (iii A.D.).

**διεράμαι**, *love passionately*, c. gen., f.l. in Pl.*Ax.*370b (cf. διεράω).

⊛ **διέρᾱσις**, εως, ἡ, *lading of corn in bulk* (cf. διέραμα), *PTeb.*328 (ii A.D.), *POxy.*1197.11 (iii A.D.).

**διεραυνάω**, later form of διερευνάω, *PMasp.*166.22 (vi A.D.).

**διεράω**, *strain through*, Plu.2.692c (Pass.).

**διεργάζομαι**, *work thoroughly, cultivate*, but pf. part. with pass. sense, γῆ διειργασμένη Thphr.*CP*5.13.10, al.; διεργασθὲν *dressed*, of wool, Arist.*Pr.*931$^a$14. 2. *work out*, Isoc.10.69; πολλὰ καὶ κακὰ δ. Plb.3.73.7. II. *make an end of, kill, destroy*, ἑωυτόν Hdt.1.213; τινά E.*Hec.*369, cf. Pl.*Lg.*865c (Pass.), Ant.Lib.21.3; μὴ.. πόλιν διεργάσῃ S.*OC*1417: plpf. in pass. sense, διέργαστο ἂν τὰ πρήγματα Hdt.7.10.γ'; also aor. διεργασθεῖτ' ἂν E.*Heracl.*174.

**διεργάτινος** [ᾰ], η, ον, *busy, laborious*, παλάμαι *IG*12(2).129.7 (Mytilene).

**διέργω**, v. διείργω.

**διερεθ-ίζω**, *provoke greatly*, Plb.9.18.9, Phld.*Ir.*p.48 W., al., Ph.1. 602, Aesop.250:—Pass., δ. πρὸς ἀλλήλους Arist.*Mir.*837$^b$17; ἔκ τινος Plu.*Oth.*4. 2. *stimulate*, τὰς ἐκκρίσεις Herod.Med.ap.Orib.8.4. 1. **-ισις**, εως, ἡ, *excitation*, Phlp.*in GA*196.23. **-ισμα**, ατος, τό, *provocation*, App.*BC*5.53. **-ισμός**, ὁ, *provocation*, Phld.*Ir.*p.26 W.: pl., ib.p.29 W.; *irritation*, Paul.Aeg.3.66. **-ιστέον**, *one must provoke, stimulate*, Herod.Med.ap.Orib.5.30.27. **-ιστικός**, ή, όν, *provocative*, τῶν συμπτωμάτων ib.23; δ. σημεῖον Phlp.*in GA*197.18.

⊛ **διερείδω**, *prop up*, Plu.2.529c, Luc.*VH*2.1. 2. *hold apart*, as the collar-bones do the shoulders, Sor.2.63: so metaph., of vowels, *thrust apart*, D.H.*Comp.*22. II. Med., *lean upon*, τινί E.*Hec.*66: c. acc., σχῆμα βακτηρίᾳ δ. *lean one's body on*.., Ar.*Ec.*150. 2. δ. πρός τι *set oneself firmly, struggle against*.., Plb.21.24.14, Plu.*Phil.* 17, prob. in Phld.*D.*3*Fr.*32; περί τινος for a thing, Plb.5.84.3.

**διερείκω**, aor. -ήρῖκον (also aor. 1 part. -ερείξας Hsch.), *cleave*, πλευρὰ καὶ θώρηκα Euph.41, Alex.Aet.3.21 (tm.).

**διέρ-εισμα**, ατος, τό, *supporting beam*, *IG*2.1054.68, 11(2).287 *A* 84 (Delos, iii B.C.); also δ. χαλκᾶ ib.2.652 *A* 25. **-εισμός**, ὁ, *thrusting apart, separation*, D.H.*Comp.*22. **-ειστέον**, *one must prop up*, Sor.1.114.

⊛ **διερέσσω**, aor. -ήρεσα, poet. -ήρεσσα Od.14.351:—*row about*, χερσὶ δ. *to swim*, 12.444, 14.351. 2. c. acc., δ. χέρας *wave* them *about*, E.*Tr.*1258 (lyr.).

⊛ **διερευν-άω**, *track down*, Pl.*Sph.*241b; *search, examine*, *CPHerm.* 8 ii 5 (ii A.D.), Jul.*Or.*7.222c, etc.:—freq. in Med., Pl.*Phd.*78a, *Mx.* 246b, Onos.6.7, Plu.*Them.*10, etc.; δ. τί ἐστιν ἑκάτερον Pl.*R.*368c:—Pass., Plb.14.2.1. **-ησις**, εως, ἡ, *investigation*, Str.16.4.5, Iamb. *Comm.Math.*22, dub. in Epicur.*Nat.*135 G. **-ητέον**, *one must track down*, Pl.*Sph.*260e, *Lg.*654e. **-ητής**, οῦ, ὁ, *scout* or *vedette*, X. *Cyr.*5.4.4, 6.3.2. II. *spy*, D.H.4.43. **-ητικός**, ή, όν, Ptol. *Tetr.*57. Adv. -κῶς ib.7.

**διερέω**, (διερός) *wet, moisten*, prob. l. in Arist.*Pr.*939$^a$28.

**διερίζω**, *strive with one another*, interpol. in Epigr. in Gell.3.11; περί τι Iamb.*Bab.*4:—Med., *contend with*, τινί Plu.*Cat.Ma.*15.

**διερμήν-ευσις**, εως, ἡ, *parleying*, Pl.*Ti.*19c; *interpretation*, Iamb. *Myst.*5.5. **-ευτέον**, *one must interpret*, Ph.1.481. ⊛ **-ευτής**, οῦ, ὁ, *interpreter*, v.l. in 1*Ep.Cor.*14.28. **-ευτικός**, ή, όν, *interpretative*, τοῖς τῇδε τῶν ἀπὸ τῶν θεῶν Olymp.*in Alc.*p.17 C. **-εύω**, *interpret, expound*, Plb.3.22.3, Epicur.*Nat.*1431.17, Phld.*Rh.*1.84 S., 1*Ep.Cor.* 14.27; *translate*, Aristeas 15:—Pass., Lxx 2*Ma.*1.36, *PTaur.*1$^v$4, Ph.1.226.

**διέρομαι**, Ep. **διείρομαι**, *ask* or *question closely*, τί με ταῦτα διείρεαι; Od.4.492; μὴ ταῦτα διείρεο Il.1.550, etc.: aor. inf., διερέσθαι τινὰ ἐρώτησιν Pl.*Phlb.*42e; διήρετο D.C.38.4.

⊛ **διερός**, ά, όν, *active, alive*, twice in Hom., οὐκ ἔσθ' οὗτος ἀνὴρ διερὸς βροτός Od.6.201, cf. Aristarch. ad loc. (but perh. for δϝι-ερός, 'to be feared'); διερῷ ποδί with *nimble* foot, 9.43; διερῇ φλογί *AP*7. 123 (Diog. Laert.). II. after Hom., *wet, liquid*, ὕδατι διερόν cj. in Pi.*Fr.*107.14; αἷμα τὸ δ. A.*Eu.*263; τὸ δ., opp. ξηρόν, Anaxag. 4,12; of the air, opp. λαμπρός, v.l. in Hp.*Aër.*15; of birds, which *float* through the air, Ar.*Nu.*337; δ. μέλεα, of the nightingale's notes, dub. l. in Id.*Av.*213; δ. καὶ βαρεῖα γῆ Thphr.*CP*3.23.2; δ. φῦκος Ph. *Bel.*99.24; τοῦ δ. παγέντος Alciphr.1.23; δ. κέλευθος, of the sea, A.R.1.184; πώγων δ. [ὀστρέου] *AP*9.86 (Antiphil.); διερὰς χαίτας εὐώδεας Orph.*Fr.*142; δ. μόρος death *by drowning*, Opp.*H.*5.345; δ. πῦρ the *watery* star, i.e. the constellation Eridanus, Nonn.*D.*23.301. (Prop., acc. to Arist.*GC*330$^a$16 διερὸν μέν ἐστι τὸ ἔχον ἀλλοτρίαν ὑγρότητα ἐπιπολῆς, opp. βεβρεγμένον (*soaked through*), but cf. σπόγγος ὄζει διερός Dsc.*Eup.*1.141; διερά, = σεσηπότα, Hsch.) (In signf. I, perh. cogn. with δίεμαι (but not with βίος): in signf. II, prob. connected with διαίνω.)

**διερπύζω**, = sq., c. acc., Opp.*H.*2.261, Hld.6.1: c. gen., Nonn.*D.* 13.565, al.

**διέρπω**, *creep* or *pass through*, πῦρ δ., of the ordeal of fire, S.*Ant.* 265; διὰ τινος Plu.2.517a: metaph., τὸ διέρπον τῶν μηχανημάτων Eun.*Hist.*p.254 D.: abs., of disease, *spread*, Ph.2.349.

**διερριμμένως**, Adv. *in a disjointed way*, Plb.3.58.3.

**διέρρωγα**, v. διαρρήγνυμι.

⊛ **διέρσις**, εως, ἡ, (διείρω) *drawing through*, dub. cj. in Arist.*Pr.*915$^a$ 9 for διαιρέσει: δ. λίνου Aen.Tact.31.18, cf. Gal.19.134.

**διέρυθρος**, ον, *shot with red*, Dsc.3.9.

**διερύκω** [ῡ], *keep off*, Arat.299 (tm.); *hinder*, ἀψιμαχίαν Plu. *Lyc.*2.

**διερύω**, v. διειρύω.

⊛ **διέρχομαι**, fut. διελεύσομαι (but δίειμι is used in Att. as fut., and διῄειν as impf.): aor. διῆλθον:—*go through, pass through*, abs., ἀντικρὺ δὲ διῆλθε βέλος Il.23.876, etc.: c. gen., φάτο.. ἔγχος ῥέα διελεύ-

σεσθαι..Αἰνείαο 20.263, cf. 100; σφαγῶν διελθὼν ἰός S.*Tr.*717; δ. διὰ τῆς νήσου Hdt.6.31; διέρχεται ἅπαντα διὰ τούτου Ar.*Av.*181; δ. διὰ πάντων *Act.Ap.*9.32; εἰ σῶμα οὖσα ἡ ψυχὴ..διῆλθε διὰ παντός Plot. 4.7.8: c. acc., δ. πῶϋ, ἄστυ, Il.3.198, 6.392; θύρας (pl.) Lys.12.16; τὴν πολεμίαν Th.5.64; τρεῖς σταθμούς X.*An.*3.3.8. **2.** *pass through, complete*, τὸ πέμπτον μέρος τῆς ὁδοῦ Hdt.3.25; τὸν βίον Pl. *R.*365b, etc.; παιδείαν X.*Cyr.*1.5.1. **3.** of reports, βάξις διῆλθ' Ἀχαιούς S.*Aj.*999: abs., διῆλθεν ὁ λόγος *went abroad, spread*, Th.6.46, cf. X.*An.*1.4.7; κληδὼν γῆς διῆλθε S.*Ph.*256. **4.** of pain, *shoot through* one, ib.743; of passion, ἵμερος δ. Ἡρακλῆ Id.*Tr.*477; ἐμὲ διῆλθέ τι a thought *shot through* me, E.*Supp.*288. **5.** *pass through and reach, arrive at*, βίου τέλος Pi.*I.*4(3).5. **6.** *go through in detail, recount*, λόγον Id.*N.*4.72; χρησμόν A.*Pr.*874; ἃ διῆλθον the details I *have gone through*, Th.1.21; ὀλίγα διελθών a little *further on*, Pl.*Prt.*344b; δ. περί τινος Isoc.4.66, 9.12, Pl.*Prt.*347a; ὑπέρ τινος Plb.1.13.10; πάντα μετὰ φρεσί *h.Ven.*276; πρὸς αὐτόν Isoc.11.47; δ. τίς πολιτεία..συμφέρει Arist.*Pol.*1296$^b$14. **II.** intr. of Time, *pass, elapse*, χρόνου οὐ πολλοῦ διελθόντος Hdt.1.8, cf. 3.152, D.23. 153, Plb.20.10.17; τοῦ διεληλυθότος ἔτους the *past* year, *BGU*410.7 (ii A.D.), etc.; διελθουσῶν τῶν σπονδῶν Th.4.115; διελθὼν ἐς βραχὺν χρόνον *having waited*, E.*HF*957 codd. (fort. ὡς).

**διερῶ** serving as fut., **διείρηκα** as pf., of διαγορεύω (διεῖπον (q.v.), being aor.):—*say fully, distinctly, expressly*, Pl.*Lg.*809e, etc.; διείρηκεν ὁ νόμος D.20.28, cf. 23.72:—Pass., aor. διερρήθην Pl.*Lg.*932e: pf. διείρημαι ib.813a, etc.; διειρημένον *it having been expressly stated*, D.17.28.

**διερωτ-άω**, *cross-question*, τινά Pl.*Ap.*22b, *Grg.*458a, etc.; δ. τινά τι Id.*Prt.*315c. **II.** *ask constantly* or *continually*, οἱ διερωτῶντες ὑμᾶς..τί βούλεσθε; D.3.22. **-ητέον**, *one must cross-question*, Gal.18(2).638.

**διεσθίω**, fut. -έδομαι Plu.2.170a: aor. διέφαγον Hp.*Mul.*1.2:—*eat through*, δ. τὴν μητέρα (v.l. μήτραν), of young vipers, Hdt.3.109, cf. Arist.*HA*558$^a$30. **II.** *consume, corrode*, Hp. l.c., Plu. l.c.: metaph., D.L.5.76:—Med., τὴν ψυχήν Ph.2.541.

**διεσιαῖος**, α, ον, (δίεσις III) *consisting of quarter-tones*, διαστήματα Aristid.Quint.3.11; τόπος Cleonid.*Harm.*6; λεῖμμα Theo Sm. p.91 H.

⊛ **δίεσις**, εως, ἡ, (δίημι) *sending through, discharge*, of a liquid, f.l. for δέξις, Hp.*Superf.*29; *putting through*, τῆς πλεκτάνης διὰ τοῦ αὐλοῦ Arist.*GA*720$^b$33; *letting through*, opp. σύλληψις, Plu.*Art.*3. **2.** *release, discharge*, *Sammelb.*4638.21 (ii B.C.). **3.** *dismissal* of a wife, *divorce*, *PMasp.*153.17 (vi A.D.), etc. **II.** *moistening, wetting*, Hp.*Ulc.*14, Dsc.1.26. **III.** in Music, the *smallest interval* in the scale, [ἡ ἀρχὴ] ἐν μέλει δ. Arist.*APo.*84$^b$39, cf. *Metaph.*1053$^a$12, D.H.*Comp.*11, etc.; *semi-tone* in the diatonic scale, Philol.6, Arist.*Pr.*917$^b$36; in enharmonic, *quarter-tone*, Aristox.*Harm.*p.21 M., etc., cf. Theo Sm.p.55 H.

⊛ **διεσκεμμένως**, Adv. *prudently*, X.*Oec.*7.18.

**διεσκευασμένως** (-σκεδ- cod.)· διατετυπωμένως, Hsch.

**διεσμιλευμένως**, Adv. *in polished style*, Poll.6.150, Hsch.

**διεσπαρμένως**, Adv., (διασπείρω) *in a disjointed manner*, Aristid. Quint.1.2, v.l. for sq. in Gal.*UP*16.1.

**διεσπασμένως**, Adv. *intermittently*, δ. πνεῖν (al. διεσπαρμένως) Hp. *Epid.*1.1, 3.2; *in a disjointed manner*, Gal.*UP*16.1.

**διεσπουδασμένως**, Adv. *diligently*, D.H.1.6 codd.

**διέσσυτο**, v. sub διασεύομαι.

**διεστραμμένως**, Adv., (διαστρέφω) *perversely*, Lxx *Si.*4.17; *distortedly*, τῶν ὄψεων δ. ἔχειν Hld.2.19.

**διεσφαλμένως**, Adv. *wrongly*, Arr.*Epict.*3.23.3.

**διετᾰρίστρια**, ἡ, = τριβάς, Hsch.

**δι-ετηρίς**, ίδος, ἡ, (διετής) *space of two years*, Lxx *2Ki.*13.23, *IG Rom.*4.850 (Laodicea ad Lycum). **-ετήρων**, ον, gen. ονος, = sq., μόσχος *Epigr.Gr.*1035.21 (Pergam.). **-ετής**, ές, or **διέτης**, ες, *of* or *lasting two years*, χρόνος Hdt.2.2, etc.; κύησις Arist.*GA*777$^b$15, etc.; ἀρξάμενος ἀπὸ διετοῦς Id.*HA*500$^a$11; ἐπὶ διετὲς ἡβᾶν to be *two years* past puberty, Is.10.12, Aeschin.3.122, Lexap.D.46.20. **II.** *two years old*, Arist.*HA*545$^b$11. **III.** = sq., Hsch. **-ετήσιος**, ον, *lasting through the year*, θυσίαι Th.2.38, cf. *Inscr.Prien.*112.69 (i B.C.). Adv. -ίως Ar.*Fr.*766. **-ετία**, ἡ, = διετηρίς, Ph.2.536, *Act. Ap.*24.27, 28.30; διετίᾳ Cleom.1.3, *CIG*5033 (Nubia), *Inscr.Magn.* 164.12, *POxy.*707.24 (ii A.D.), Theo Sm.p.136 H.; ἐκ διετίας βήσσοντα *SIG*1171.4 (Lebena). **-ετίζω**, (ἔτος) *live the year through*, i.e. *live more than a year*, of wasps, Arist.*HA*627$^b$29; of plants, *to be biennial*, Thphr.*HP*1.2.2.

**διέτμᾰγεν, διέτμᾰγον**, v. διατμήγω.

**διευεργετέω**, *to be a firm friend to*, τινά Sch.A.*Pers.*854 (prob.).

**διευθετ-έω**, *set in order*, Cic.*Att.*6.5.2 (prob.), Sch.A.*Pers.*854. **-ησις**, εως, ἡ, *good order*, Eust.26.27.

**διευθηνέω**, *continue in prosperity*, οὐκ ἐπὶ πολὺ δ. Ptol.*Tetr.*194.

**διευθυδρομέω**, *persevere with*, τὰς πράξεις *Cat.Cod.Astr.*7.218.23.

**διευθ-υντήρ**, ῆρος, ὁ, *pilot, governor*, Man.4.106. **II.** δ. ψήφων *accountant, auditor*, *Cat.Cod.Astr.*2.172 (pl.). ⊛ **-ύνω**, *make* or *keep straight*, δρόμον Ph.1.327. **II.** *set right, amend*, Luc.*Prom.* 19, Man.4.90. **III.** *settle* an account, *PLond.*3.924.8.

⊛ **διευκρῖν-έω**, pf. διευκρίνηκα Phld.*Rh.*2.47 S.:—*arrange carefully*, διηυκρινημένοι ὁπλῖται X.*Oec.*8.6. **II.** *examine thoroughly, elucidate*, ὑπέρ τινος Plb.2.56.4; περί τινος πότεροις.. Id.3.28.5; τὰ ἀπορούμενα D.H.*Comp.*20, cf. Phld. l.c., Porph.*Abst.*2.4, etc.:—Pass., ὁ περί τινος λόγος -εῖται Plb.6.5.1, cf. Iamb.*Myst.*8.4, al.:—Att., only in Med., as Pl.*Prm.*135b, D.27.15. **2.** *judge rightly*, τὰ διαφέροντα Plb.31.8.1, al. **-ημένως**, *distinctly*, Vett.Val.309.12; *in careful order*, Simp. *in Cat.*301.20. **-ής**, ές, *clear, distinct*, Suid. **-ησις**, εως, ἡ, *analysis, discussion, elucidation*, Ptol.*Alm.*12.3, Simp.*in Cael.*194.2.

⊛ **διευλᾰβ-έομαι**, aor. -ηυλαβήθην Pl.*Lg.*843e:—*take good heed to, beware of, be on one's guard against*, c. acc., Id.*Phd.*81e, *Lg.*797a, Lxx *De.*28.60, Plb.14.2.7, etc.: c. gen., Pl.*Lg.*843e; δ. μή.. ib.789e; but δ. μὴ παθεῖν Id.*Ep.*351c. **2.** *reverence*, τινά Id.*Lg.*879c. **-ητέον**, *one must take heed to*, τὰ τοιαῦτα Id.*R.*536a.

**διευλῠτ-έω**, *pay off, liquidate* debts, etc., *BGU*1151.42 (i B.C.), J. *AJ*16.9.3:—Pass., *POxy.*268.15 (i A.D.). ⊛ **-ησις**, εως, ἡ, *discharge* of a debt, *PLips.*120.12 (i A.D.). **-όω**, = διευλυτέω, *pay off* a debt, *PTeb.*381.18 (ii A.D.). **II.** αἰτιῶν ἑαυτοὺς δ. *clear* themselves from charges, Just.*Nov.*123.22. ⊛ **-ωσις**, εως, ἡ, *discharge* of a debt, *Gloss.*, prob. in Petersen-Luschan *Reisen in Lykien* p.12 No.19.

⊛ **διευημερέω**, *enjoy good success throughout*, Paul.Al.*N.*4.

**διευνάω**, *lay asleep*, τὸν βίοτον E.*Hipp.*1377 (lyr.).

**διευπρᾱγέω**, *continue fortunate*, J.*AJ*6.10.2.

**διευρῑπῐδίζω**, *play the part of Euripides*, Sch.Ar.*Eq.*19.

**διευρῑπίζω**, *to be constantly changing like the tide of the Euripus*, Arist.*Pr.*940$^a$3 (διαρριπίζω cj. Dind.).

**διευρύνω**, *dilate*, in Pass., Hp.*Morb.*4.52, Aen.Tact.31.12, Arist. *de An.*422$^a$3.

**διευστοχέω**, strengthd. for εὐστοχέω, D.H.*Comp.*11.

**διευσχημονέω**, *preserve decorum*, Plu.*Ages.*29, *PSI*6.571.12.

**διευτακτέω**, *pay interest regularly*, *BSA*22.205 (Mylasa, i B.C.). **II.** Pass., *to be regularly arranged in sequence*, Iamb. *in Nic.*p.46 P., al.

⊛ **διευτελίζω**, *hold very cheap*, Ael.*VH*14.49.

**διευτονέω**, *make one's way through, win through*, Thphr.*Sens.*7; πρὸς χώραν Plb.4.43.8. **II.** *acquire strength*, Sor.1.95.

**διευτρεπίζω**, *prepare*, Suid. s.v. Σεμίραμις.

**διευτῠχέω**, *continue prosperous*, τῇ οὐσίᾳ D.42.4; λήξεως Ael.*NA* 17.27; περί τι Theopomp.Hist.111: abs., Men.531.3, etc.; διευτύχει *fare thee well*, *CIG*4076 (Ancyra), cf. *PMag.Berol.*1.194, *BGU* 1197.23 (i B.C.).

**διεφθάρᾰτο**, v. διαφθείρω.

**δίεφθος**, ον, *well-boiled*, opp. ὀπτός, Hp.*Aff.*40 (Comp.), Antig.*Mir.* 82, prob.l. in Dsc.2.120, etc.; ἀκροκώλια Pherecr.108.14, Telecl.48.

**διεφικνέομαι**, pf. διέφιγμαι dub. sens. in Eun.*Hist.*p.361 D. (leg. διέσφιγκται).

⊛ **διέχ-εια**, ἡ, *breach of continuity*, Aristid.Quint.3.10, Sch.Ar.*Pax* 938; κατὰ διέχειαν ἀριθμεῖσθαι to be reckoned *exclusively*, Steph. *in Hp.*1.198 D. **-ής**, ές, *discontinuous*, opp. συνεχής, Plu.2.115f, Aristid.Quint.3.10; σπεῖρα Procl.*in Euc.*p.119 F.

⊛ **διεχθρ-αίνω**, strengthd. for ἐχθραίνω, τινί S.E.*M.*1.49. **-εύω**, strengthd. for ἐχθρεύω, τινί D.H.4.70, Arr.*Cyn.*12.5; τὸ -εῦον *enmity*, Alciphr.2.3.

**διέχω**: **I.** trans., *keep apart* or *separate*, ὁ ποταμὸς δ. τὰ ῥέεθρα Hdt.9.51; δ. τὴν φάλαγγα *leave gaps in* it, Arr.*An.*1.1.10 (so abs., διασχεῖν *make way for* a person, Plu.*TG*18); δ. τοὺς μαχομένους Id. *Caes.*20; δ. τὰς χεῖρας *spread* them *out*, esp. for the purpose *of parting* combatants, Plb.4.52.1; τὰς χεῖρας ἐν μέσῳ δ. Plu.*Cim.*19; διασχοῦσα τὰς χεῖρας Id.*Ant.*20: c. gen., τῆς ἐσθῆτος διασχών Id.*Aem.* 31. **2.** *hold fast*, κόντους Paus.10.25.2. **II.** intr., *go through, hold its way*, ἀντικρὺ δὲ διέσχε [ὀϊστός] Il.5.100, 11.253; δι' ὤμου δ' ὄβριμον ἔγχος ἔσχεν 13.520; διά τινος δ. Arist.*HA*496$^b$31; *extend, reach*, ἐς τὸν Ἀράβιον κόλπον Hdt.4.42, cf. 7.122; ἀπὸ τῶν νεύρων πρὸς τὰς φλέβας Arist.*HA*515$^b$28. **2.** *stand apart, be separated, distant*, ἐκὰς δ. Thgn.970; ὅταν διάσχῃ τὰ κέρατα X.*An.*3.4.20, cf. Th. 8.95 (v.l.); δ. πολὺ ἀπ' ἀλλήλων Id.2.81; δ. ἀλλήλων ὡς τεσσαράκοντα στάδια X.*An.*1.10.4; διέχοντες πολὺ ἦσαν they marched *with* broad *intervals*, Th.3.22; ὁ Ἑλλήσποντος ταύτῃ σταδίους ὡς πεντήκοντα διεῖχε *was* about fifty stades *wide* at this point, X.*HG*2.1. 21. **3.** of Time, παιδὸς δὲ βλάστας οὐ διέσχον ἡμέραι τρεῖς not three days *parted* the birth (sc. from what followed), S.*OT*717. **4.** of the earth, *open*, σεισμῷ Philostr.*Her.*1.2; of a river, *broaden out*, Arr.*An.*6.5.3. **5.** *differ*, γέννῃ τε κρήσει τε Emp.22.6, cf. Arist. *Rh.*1412$^a$12; οὐδὲν ἂν διέχοι φαγεῖν ἢ μὴ φαγεῖν Id.*Metaph.*1063$^a$ 31. **b.** *excel*, τόλμῃ καὶ προθυμίᾳ App.*Pun.*132.

**διεψευσμένως**, Adv. *falsely* or *mistakenly*, Str.1.3.1 codd., M.Ant. 2.17.

**διέψω**, *scorch thoroughly*, δ. ἀνθρώπους, of the effect of the westering sun, in Hp.*Aër.*6.

**δίζα**· αἴξ (Lacon.), Hsch.

⊛ **δίζημαι**, Hdt.7.103, Anacr.4, Theoc.16.68: 2 sg. δίζηαι Od.11. 100: 3 pl. δίζηνται B.1.67, once in Trag., A.*Supp.*821 (lyr.); part. διζήμενος Od.16.391, al., Hdt.7.142, al.: impf. διζήντο Id.3.41, Phoen.1.4: fut. διζήσομαι Od.16.239, Lyc.682; 2 sg. διζήσεαι Parm. 8.6: aor. ἐδιζησάμην Heraclit.101. (Ep., Ion., Lyr., = Att. ζητέω (which occurs only once in Hom.); cf. δίζω II):—*seek out, look for* among many, Πάνδαρον.. διζημένη εἴ που ἐφεύροι Il.4.88, cf. 5.168, Anacr.4; ἐδιζησάμην ἐμεωυτόν Heraclit. l.c. **II.** *seek for*, ἢ καὶ διζησόμεθ' ἄλλους Od.16.239; νόστον δίζηαι; 11.100; νόστον ἑταίροισιν διζήμενος ἠδ' ἐμοὶ αὐτῷ *devising means for* a return, 23.253; μνάσθω ἐέδνοισιν διζήμενος *seeking to win her* by gifts, 16.391; γύην.. κατ' ὄρος δ. ἢ κατ' ἄρουραν Hes.*Op.*428; δ. τὸ μαντήϊον *to seek out, seek the meaning of*, Hdt.7.142; ἀγγέλους δ. εἰ.. *to inquire of* them whether.., Id.4.151; δ. ἐπ' ᾧ ἄν.. Id.3.41; ὅτινι.. Theoc.16.68.

abs., Democr.108. **III.** c. inf., *seek, desire* to do, πλέον δ. ἔχειν Hdt.2.147, cf. A. l. c., B. l. c., and later Ep., Tryph.525, etc.: c. acc. et inf., *demand, require that..*, σὲ δ. εἴκοσι εἶναι ἀντάξιον Hdt.7.103. (Perh. redupl. fr. root of ζητέω.)

**δίζησις**, εως, ἡ, *inquiry*, Parm.1.33, 4.2, Orph.*Fr.*333 (pl.).

**δι-ζῠγής**, ές, = δίζυξ, πῆχυς *containing two bones*, Heliod.ap. Orib.44.23.26. **-ζῠγία**, ἡ, *double yoke of draught-cattle*, *Gp.* 2.23.14. **-ζῠγος**, ον, = δίζυξ, μέλος, οὐρή, Nonn.*D.*15.55, 39. 330. **-ζυξ**, ζῠγος, *double-yoked*, ἵπποι Il.5.195, 10.473; *double*, δίζυγος ἠπείροιο *AP*4.3b.40 (Agath.); δ. χαλκός *castanets*, ib.9.139 (Claudian): neut. pl., δίζυγα ξύλα *IG*12(9).907.30 (Chalcis); δίζυγι πυρί Nonn.*D.*22.352; δ. κῶλα *having two bones* (cf. διζυγής), Paul. Aeg.6.107.

⊕ **δίζῠφον**, τό, = ζίζυφον, *POxy.*920.1 (pl., ii/iii A.D.).

**δίζω**, Ep. impf. δίζον Il.16.713:—*to be in doubt, at a loss*, δίζε γὰρ ἠὲ μάχοιτο.., ἦ λαοὺς ὁμοκλήσειε l. c.; δίζω ἤ σε θεὸν μαντεύσομαι ἢ ἄνθρωπον Orac.ap.Hdt.1.65:—Med., δ. ὅτι.., μή.., Eus.Mynd.58, Tryph.240. **II.** Med., = δίζημαι II, ἄτεκνον ἔριθον δίζεσθαι Hes.*Op.* 603 codd.; δίζεαι Theoc.25.37; δίζετο Bion *Fr.*14.2, Coluth.81, Epic. in *Arch.Pap.*7.9, etc.; διζόμεσθα Herod.8.12; δίζοντο Q.S.4.16; opt. δίζοιτο Ecphant.ap.Stob.4.7.64; part. διζόμενος *APl.*4.146, *Epigr. Gr.*226.10. (Perh. fr. δίς, cf. διστάζω.)

**δίζῳδος**, ον, (ζῴδιον) *bearing two figures*, of coins, *PLips.*13.10 (iv A.D.), *BGU*316.16 (iv A.D.).

**δίζωος**, ον, (ζωή) *with two lives*, φὼρ δίζωος, i.e. Sisyphus, who returned from Hades, Dosiad *Ara*17.

**δίζως**, ων, *of double form*, of Pan, Theoc.*Syrinx*5.

**διηγανές**· λαμπρόν, Hsch.

**διηγ-έομαι**, *set out in detail, describe*, [ἔργα] Heraclit.1; πρᾶγμα Ar. *Av.*198; τὴν ἀλήθειαν περί τινος Antipho1.13, cf. Th.6.54, Pl.*Prt.* 310a, al.; περὶ ταύτης εἰπεῖν καὶ διηγήσασθαι D.21.77: c. acc. pers., οἷον.. σὺ τοῦτον διηγῇ such as you *describe* him, Pl.*Tht.*144c. **-ημα**, ατος, τό, *tale*, λέγειν Phoenicid.4.15; δ. ἀνωφελές Plb.1.14.6, cf. Lxx *De.*28.37, Polem.*Call.*42, Porph.*Antr.*4, etc. ⊕ **-ηματικός**, ή, όν, *descriptive, narrative*, δ. ποίησις, μίμησις, Arist.*Po.*1459$^{a}$17, $^{b}$36; παρεκβάσεις Plb.38.6.1; διάλογοι Plu.2.711c; ποιητής Sch.Il.*Oxy.*1086. 59. Adv. -κῶς Corn.*Rh.*p.371 H., D.L.9.103. **II.** *fond of narrating*, τινός Plu.2.631a, cf. 513d. **-ημάτιον**, τό, Dim. of διήγημα, Str.14.2.3. ⊕ **-ησις**, εως, ἡ, *narration, narrative*, Pl.*R.*392d, *Phdr.* 246a, Aristeas 1, *Ev.Luc.*1.1, etc.; in a speech, *statement of the case*, Arist.*Rh.*1416$^{b}$29, Zeno *Stoic.*1.23. **-ητέον**, *one must narrate*, Aps.*Rh.*p.250 H., Trypho *Trop.*4, etc. **-ητής**, οῦ, ὁ, *narrator*, Ach.Tat.4.15. **-ητικός**, ή, όν, = διηγηματικός I, Arist.*Po.*1459$^{b}$ 33. **II.** = δ. II, Id.*EN*1117$^{b}$34.

**διήέριος**, α, ον, also ος, ον, *through the air*, δ. ποτέονται A.R.2.227, etc.:—in Prose, **διάέριος**, ον, Luc.*Salt.*42, etc.; διαέρια λέγειν, = μετέωρα λ., Id.*Icar.*1.

⊕ **διηθ-έω**, *strain through, filter*, Hp.*Acut.*7, Pl.*Sph.*226b, *Ti.*45c; οἶνον δ. πυρέττοντι Plu.2.101c, cf. *Mim.Oxy.*413.161:—Pass., Arist. *Mete.*368$^{a}$22, Plb.34.9.10; of air in the lungs, Gal.2.705; καθαρὸν καὶ διηθημένον [γένος], opp. μικτόν, Ph.2.3. **2.** *wash out, cleanse*, τὴν κοιλίην οἴνῳ, θυμιήμασι, Hdt.2.86. **II.** intr., of liquid, *filter through, percolate*, Id.2.93. **-ημα**, ατος, τό, *product of sifting*: δ. γῆς *riddled* earth, Sor.2.88; δ. αἵματος, of urine, Steph.*Urin.* 1. **-ησις**, εως, ἡ, *straining, percolation*, Epicur.*Ep.*2 p.45 U., Thphr.*CP*6.1.1, Plu.*Ant.*3: pl., D.Chr.33.6; *filtering* of urine in kidneys, Aret.*SD*2.3; *haemorrhage*, κατὰ δ. Aët.15.10. **-ητέον**, *one must strain*, Dsc.2.76.6. **-μεύω**, = διηθέω, Hsch. s. v. διυλίζοντες.

**διηκονέω, διήκονος, διηκόσιοι**, Ion. for διακ-.

**διηκρῑβωμένως**, Adv., (διακριβόω) *exactly, carefully*, Arist.*Rh.Al.* 1420$^{a}$10, Ph.1.92, cj. in Pl.*Lg.*965a.

⊕ **διήκω**, fut. -ξω Gal.*Anim.Pass.*1:—*extend* or *reach* from one place to another, ἐκ.. εἰς or ἐπί.., Hdt.2.106, 6.31; μέχρι.. Id.4.185; ἄχρις.. Ti.Locr.101a; δ. ἔς τε τὸ ἔσω.. καὶ ἐς τὸ ἔξω, i.e. *right through*, Th.3.21; ἀπό.. πρός.. Luc.*VH*1.19; διὰ πάντων Corn.*ND* 11; κατά, περί τι, Iamb.*Comm.Math.*4, 15. **II.** c. acc., *pervade*, πόλιν διήκει.. βάξις A.*Ag.*476 (lyr.), cf. *Th.*900 (lyr.); τὸ σὸν ὄνομα δ. πάντας, *volitat per ora*, S.*OC*306 (but in an inverted constr. σῶφρον γὰρ ὄμμα τοὐμὸν Ἑλλήνων λόγος πολὺς διήκει E.*Hyps.Fr.*34(60).45); διὰ πάντων διήκουσα δύναμις Arist.*Mu.*396$^{b}$29; κατὰ στενὸν δ. ib.393$^{b}$ 5; αἱ κοιναὶ καὶ διήκουσαι κακίαι *pervading* faults, Phld.*Sign.*28: c. gen., φρόνημα δ. λόγου Philostr.*VS*1.17.3; ἡδονὴ δ. [ποιημάτων] Id.*Her.*18.1. **2.** *pass over*, ἡλίου κύκλος μέσον πόρον διῆκε A.*Pers.* 505. **3.** *discuss in detail*, Gal. l. c.

**διήλᾰσε**, v. διελαύνω. **διηλάσίην**· δίοδον, Hsch.

**διηλιόω**, *expose to the sun's heat*, Thphr.*CP*4.12.12 (Pass.).

**διηλίτης**· κακοῦργος, ἀπατεών, Hsch.; cf. διελίτην.

**διηλῐφής**, ές, (ἀλείφω) *sleek with unguents*, γένειον S.*Fr.*564.

**διηλλαγμένως**, Adv. *differently*, Str.13.1.3, D.S.2.31.

**διηλόω**, *drive a nail through, nail fast*, Lxx *Jd.*5.26:—Pass., τεῖχος πασσάλοις δ. Jul.*Or.*2.76a.

**διήλῠσις**, εως, ἡ, *passage through*, πόντοιο A.R.4.1573.

**διημαρτημένως**, Adv. *erroneously*, Hipparch.1.1.4, al., Alex.Aphr. *in Metaph.*172.5.

**διημερεύω**, *pass the day*, μετά τινος Pl.*Phd.*59d, X.*Cyr.*7.5.53; ἔν τινι in a thing, ib.86, Isoc.7.48, D.S.16.46: c. dat., Thphr.*Char.*8. 14 codd.; ψυχαὶ ἐν τῷ τοῦ παντὸς θεάτρῳ δ. Ph.1.266: c. part., *pass the whole day* in doing, Arist.*HA*540$^{a}$16; δ. ἀνάριστον καὶ ἄδειπνον Plu.2.157d. **2.** of things, *continue all day*, Arist.*Pr.*947$^{a}$25.

**διήμερον**, τό, *period of twenty-four hours* (?), Lyd.*Ost.*66.

**διημερόω**, *cultivate thoroughly*, γῆς -ωθείσης Thphr.*CP*3.20.6.

⊕ **διηνεκής**, Dor. **διᾱνεκής** (v. infr.) *Supp.Epigr.*1.327.10 (Callatis, i A.D.), ές:—*continuous, unbroken*, ἀτραπιτοί τε διηνεκέες Od.13.195; νώτοισι.. διηνεκέεσσι with slices *cut the whole length* of the chine, Il.7.321; ῥίζαι, ῥάβδοι, 12.134, 297; εἰ ὦλκα διηνεκέα προταμοίμην Od. 18.375; so δ. σώματα Pl.*Hp.Ma.*301b, cf. Anaxandr.6, *BGU*646.22 (ii A.D.); ὅρος δ. Str.3.1.3; κανών *IG*7.3073.108 (Lebad., ii B.C.); τὸ δ. *regularity*, Gal.2.355; of Time, *perpetual*, δ. νυκτί Luc.*VH*1.19; δικτάτωρ εἰς τὸ δ. App.*BC*1.4. Adv. διηνεκέως in phrase δ. ἀγορεύειν to tell *from beginning to end*, Od.7.241, 12.56 (*distinctly, positively*, 4.836); ἅπαντα δ. κατέλεξε Hes.*Th.*627; cf. τὰ ἕκαστα διηνεκὲς ἐξενέποντα A.R.2.391; Boeot. and Dor. διανεκῶς *without ceasing*, εὕδειν Corinn.9 (dub.), cf. *SIG*793.3 (Cos, i A.D.); διηνεκῶς once in Trag., A.*Ag.*319, *Com.Adesp.*382, M.Ant.2.17, *OGI*194.12 (Egypt, i B.C.), D.Chr.49.8, etc.; so διηνεκές *h.Ap.*255, Call.*Fr.*158; also εἰς τὸ διηνεκὲς *in perpetuity*, *Ep.Hebr.*7.3, *PRyl.*2.427 (ii A.D.), *JHS*33.338 (Macedonia, ii A.D.); -κῶς *invariably*, opp. πλεονάκις, Gal.18(2). 315.—The Aeol. and Dor. form διᾱνεκής is used also in Att., as Pl.*Hp.Ma.*301b,e (cf. Diogenian.ap.Sch. ad loc.), Anaxandr. l. c., *IG*2.1054.81; but νόμος διηνεκής a *perpetual* law is read in Pl.*Lg.* 839a.

⊕ **διήνεμος**, ον, *blown through, wind-swept*, πέτρα S.*Tr.*327.

**διηπειρόω**, *make dry land of*, θάλασσαν *AP*9.708 (Phil.).

**διήρεσα**, v. διερέσσω.

**διηρεφής**, ές, (ἐρέφω) *all covered*, Q.S.6.325.

**διῃρημένως**, Adv., (διαιρέω) *separately*, M.Ant.11.6, Alex.Aphr. *in Metaph.*296.4, Hld.10.23.

**διηρθρωμένως**, Adv. *articulately, distinctly*, Gal.17(2).160, Alex. Aphr. *in Metaph.*61.3, *Theol.Ar.*49.

⊕ **διήρης**, ες, (ἀραρίσκω) *double*, διῆρες ὑπερῷον *upper* story, *upper chamber*, Pl.Com.112: μελάθρων διῆρες ἔσχατον (sc. ὑπερῷον) E.*Ph.* 90, cf. Plu.2.77e. **II.** ἡ δ. (sc. ναῦς) *bireme, ship with two banks of oars*, Poll.1.82.

**διητανές**· λιτόν, διατεταμένον, Hsch.

**διηυκρῑνημένως**, Adv., (διευκρινέω) *carefully, exactly*, v.l. in D.S. 1.93.

**διηχ-έω**, *ring with*, τὸ μέγεθος τοῦ κατορθώματος Plu.*Tim.*21: abs., *resound*, *Placit.*4.16.2:—Pass., pf. part. διηχημένος *commonly spoken of*, ποιότητες Archig.ap.Gal.8.578. **-ής**, ές, *conducting sound*, Ar.Did.*Epit.*17, Plu.2.721e, Phlp. *in de An.*353.12, al. **II.** *loud*, βρονταί Lyd.*Ost.*22 (Sup.). **-ήτας**· ἄρτου εἶδος, Hsch. **-ητικός**, ή, όν, *sonorous*, Prisc.Lyd.16.6.

**δῐ-θάλασσος**, Att. -ττος [θᾰ], ον, *divided into two seas*, of the Euxine, Str.2.5.22, cf. D.P.156; of the Atlantic, Str.1.1.8. **II.** *between two seas, where two seas meet*, as is often the case off a headland, *Act.Ap.*27.41; βραχέα καὶ διθάλαττα shallows and *meetings of currents*, in the Syrtes, D.Chr.5.9. **-θαλλος**, ον, *feeding on two kinds of food*, Arist.*HA*616$^{b}$27 (dub.). **-θηκτος**, ον, *two-edged*, ξίφος A.*Pr.*863. **-θρονος**, ον, *two-throned*, Ἀχαιῶν δ. κράτος the *two-throned* might of the Achaeans, i.e. the brother-kings, Id.*Ag.* 109 (lyr.), cf. 43 (anap.). **-θροος**, ον, of sound, *redoubled*, Nonn. *D.*47.26. **-θῡμία**, ἡ, *dissension*, Hsch., *EM*275.5, Eust.936. 36. **-θῡμος**, ον, *at variance*, Lxx *Pr.*26.20.

**δῑθῠραμβ-έω**, *sing a dithyramb*, Philoch.21. **-ικός**, ή, όν, *dithyrambic*, D.H.*Th.*29; τὰ δ. *dithyrambic poems*, Arist.*Po.*1447$^{b}$ 26. Adv. -κῶς Demetr.*Eloc.*91. **-ιος**, ὁ (sc. μήν), name of a month at Gonni, Ἀρχ.Ἐφ.1911.130, al.

**Δῑθυραμβο-γενής**, v. διθύραμβος II.

**δῑθυραμβο-γράφος** [γρᾰ], ὁ, *writer of dithyrambs*, Tz.*H.*10.839. **-διδάσκᾰλος**, ὁ, *dithyrambic poet who trained his own chorus*, Ar. *Pax*829. **-ποιητική** (sc. ποίησις), ἡ, *writing of dithyrambic poetry*, Arist.*Po.*1447$^{a}$14. **-ποιός**, ὁ, *dithyrambic poet*, Id.*Rh.* 1406$^{b}$21, D.S.15.6, Plu.2.952f.

⊕ **δῑθύραμβος** [ῠ], ὁ, metapl. acc. sg. διθύραμβα Pi.*Fr.*86:—*dithyramb*, Archil.77, Epich.132, Hdt.1.23, Pi.*O.*13.19, Pherecr.145.11, Pl.*Lg.*700b, Arist.*Pol.*1342$^{b}$7, *Pr.*918$^{b}$18, etc.; μιξοβόας δ. A.*Fr.* 355: metaph. of *bombastic language*, τοσουτονὶ δ. ᾆσας Pl.*Hp.Ma.* 292c; οὐκέτι πόρρω διθυράμβων φθέγγομαι Id.*Phdr.*238d. **II.** a name of Dionysus, E.*Ba.*526 (lyr.), Philod.Scarph.1:—hence **Δῑθυραμβογενής**, *AP*9.524. (Pi. is said to have written it λυθίραμβος (*Fr.*85)—as if from λῦθι ῥάμμα, the cry of Bacchus when sewn up in his father's thigh.)

**δῑθῠραμβοχώνα**, ἡ, *funnel of dithyrambs*, Μοῦσα prob. in *AP*13. 21 (Theodorid.) (-χανα cod.).

**δῑθῠραμβώδης**, ες, *fitted for the dithyramb*, ὄνομα Pl.*Cra.*409c, cf. D.H.*Dem.*29, Demetr.*Eloc.*116.

⊕ **δί-θῠρος** [ῐ], ον, *with two doors* or *entrances*, νεώς, ἄντρον, Plu.*Num.* 20, Porph.*Antr.*3; *bivalve*, of shell-fish, Arist.*HA*528$^{a}$12; of the mouth, Corn.*ND*30, etc.; *of two leaves*, δ. γραμματείδιον *a diptych*, Men.327, cf. Lib.*Or.*51.11, *Ep.*1021.1; of seeds, *which split in germinating*, Arist.*Juv.*468$^{b}$19, Thphr.*HP*8.2.2; δίθυρον, τό, *door with two leaves*, *Annales du Service* 19.63, 64 (ii B.C.), *BGU*1028.9 (ii A.D.). **II.** τὰ δ. *seat of honour*, = Lat. *tribunal*, Plb.27.1.6. **-θυρσον**, τό, *a double thyrsus*, *AP*6.172 (Agath.(?)). **-ίαμβος**, ὁ, *syzygy of two iambic feet*, Heph.3.3, D.T.p.120 U., Aristid.Quint.1.22.

**διιδεῖν**, v. διεῖδον.

**δῐΐδρ-ος**, ον, (ἱδρώς) *perspiring*, Gal.19.93. **-όω**, *transude*, Hp. *Loc.Hom.*27, Gal.8.644 (Pass.), Hsch. s. v. κηκίειν.

**διΐημι** (3 sg. fut. διαήσει Hsch.), *drive, thrust* or *pass through*, διὰ δ' ἧκε σιδήρου (sc. τὸν ὀϊστόν) Od.21.328; δ. ξίφος λαιμῶν E.*Ph.*1092; δίεs στυπτηρίαν ὄξους *PHolm.*12.45: c. dupl. acc., στέρνα δ. λόγχην E.*Ph.*1398. **2.** *let* people *go through* a country, *give* them *a passage through*, εἰ μήτε οἱ ποταμοὶ διήσουσιν.. X.*An.*3.2.23, etc.; διέντες αὐτοὺς ἐφ' ὑμᾶς D.18.213, cf. ib.146: c. gen., ξυμφορὰς τοῦ σοῦ διῆκας στόματος *didst let* them *pass through* thy mouth, *gavest utterance to* them, S.*OC*963, cf. διαφέρω I. 1:—Pass., *pass through*, Arist.*Mir.*835b20: Ep. pf. part. διαειμένος A.R.2.372. **II.** *dismiss, disband*, στράτευμα X.*HG*2.4.39, etc.; τοὺς ὀδόντας δ. *unclose* them, D.S.10.17. **2.** *soak*, Hp.*Acut.*21; ἐλαδίῳ διείς Sotad.Com. 1.27, cf. Arist.*HA*583a24:—Med., διέμενος ὄξει *having diluted* it with vinegar, Ar.*Pl.*720:—Pass., Alex.188.3. **3.** *release* prisoners, *PGoodsp.Cair.*5.2 (ii B.C.), J.*AJ*15.10.3; διειμένος *set free*, Plu. *Demetr.*39.

**διϊθ-υντήρ**, ῆρος, ὁ, = διευθυντήρ, Man.4.40:—also **-υντής**, οῦ, ὁ, Hsch. **-ύνω**, *direct by steering*, εὔπλοιην *AP*9.107 (Leon.(?)); τὸν πλοῦν Them.*Or.*4.50b, cf. Numen.ap.Eus.*PE*11.18.

**διϊκαδία**· ἐπὶ ὁμοίων καὶ ἀπαραλλάκτων, Hsch.

**διϊκμάζω**, *moisten*, Thphr.*CP*3.4.3 (Pass.).

**διϊκμάω**, *winnow thoroughly*, Thphr.*CP*4.12.9 (Pass.).

❀ **διϊκνέομαι**, fut. -ίξομαι: aor. -ικόμην:—*go through, penetrate*, ποτὶ τὰν ψυχάν δι' ὤτων Ti.Locr.101a; ἐφ' ὅσον—εἶναι τὸ ὕδωρ Thphr. *CP*3.20.4; διῖκτο ἡ δόξα μέχρι βασιλέως Plu.*Dem.*20, cf. D.Chr.12. 35; *reach*, with missiles, Th.7.79; βραδέως τοῦ παραγγέλματος διικνουμένου Plu.*Nic.*27. **2.** in speaking, *go through, tell of*, πάντα δ. Il.9.61, 19.186, A.R.2.411. **3.** of Time, *intervene*, διετοῦς χρόνου διικνουμένου Longus 1.4.

**Διίκτυννα**, coined (ἀπὸ τοῦ διικνεῖσθαι) as etym. of Δίκτυννα by Corn.*ND*34.

**διΐξις**, εως, ἡ, *interpenetration*, δι' ἀλλήλων Procl. *in Ti.*2.88 D., cf. Olymp. *in Alc.*p.215 C.; *penetration* of sensations to consciousness, Prisc.Lyd.14.22.

**Δῖος**, ον, *of Zeus*, v.l. in Pl.*Phdr.*252e, cf. Plu.2.421e, Them.*Or.* 13.165c.

❀ **Διϊπετής** (better **Διειπετής**, cf. Zenodor.ap.Sch.Od.4.477), ές, (πίπτω) *fallen from Zeus*, i.e. *from heaven*, Ep. epith. of streams, *fed* or *swollen by rain*, Il.16.174, Od.4.477, Hes.*Fr.*217; νάματ' οὐ δ., of stagnant water, E.*Hyps.Fr.*5(3).31; δ. ὕδατα, of rain, Plu.*Mar.* 21. **2.** generally, *divine, bright*, χαλκός Emp.100.9; αἰθὴρ διϊπετὴς *divine, holy*, E.*Ba.*1267; δ. πυρσοῖς *gleaming* with fires, Id.*Rh.*43 (lyr.). **3.** *in continual flow*, Hp.*Mul.*1.24 (expld. as = διαυγής, καθαρός, Erot.). **4.** διϊπετέες οἰωνοί, prob. *hovering in the sky*, *h.Ven.*4.

**Διιπόλεια, Διιπόλια, Διιπολιώδης**, v. sub Διπολ-.

**διϊππ-ᾰσία**, ἡ, *riding through*, Suid., *EM*274.55. **-ευσις**, εως, ἡ, *charging through* the enemy's ranks, Ascl.*Tact.*7.3, al. ❀ **-εύω**, *ride through*, D.S.19.30; διὰ τῆς θαλάσσης D.C.59.17; *traverse*, τὴν ὠκεάνιον ζώνην ἐν κύκλῳ Porph.*Chr.*69: metaph. of Time, *elapse*, ib.60.

❀ **διίπταμαι**, late pres., = διαπέτομαι, Arist.*Mir.*839a23, Hdn.2.8.7, Luc.*Am.*6, Max.Tyr.22.6; impf. διιπτάμην J.*BJ*3.7.20.

**διϊσθμίζω**, (ἰσθμός) *draw ships across the Isthmus*, Plb.4.19.7.

**διϊστάνω**, = διΐστημι, Phld.*Mort.*27; τὴν φιλίαν D.S.19.46; τὸ πλῆθος App.*Hisp.*36:—also ❀ **διϊστάω**, D.T.642.31, Lyd.*Mag.*3.54.

**διϊστέον**, (δίοιδα) *one must learn*, v.l. for διοιστέον, E.*Hipp.*491.

❀ **διΐστημι**, fut. διαστήσω, *set apart, separate*, τοὺς λόχους Th.4.74; κατ' εἴδη Pl.*Phlb.*23d; διέστησεν [αὐτοὺς] εἰς μέρη πολλά D.18.61; ζῶντας ἡμᾶς οὐθὲν ἀλλήλων διέστησε Plu.*Ant.*84:—Pass., κίονες διεστάθησαν Callix.2. **2.** *set* one *at variance with* another, τινά τινος Ar. *V.*41, Th.6.77; δ. τὴν Ἑλλάδα *divide* it *into factions*, Hdt.9.2; δ. τοὺς πένητας ἀπὸ τῶν εὐπόρων D.H.9.17. **3.** μέσας διαστήσας ἡμέρας δύο *having left an interval of* two days, *Epigr.Gr.*996.7, cf. *BKT*3.20. **4.** *distinguish*, τί τινος Ath.7.305d, cf. Aret.*SA*2.2. **5.** *inflate*, κενοὺς ἀσκούς Demoph.*Sim.*57. **II.** more freq. in Pass., with aor. 2, pf., and plpf. Act.:—*stand apart, be divided*, Il., mostly in aor. 2, 24. 718, al.: once in impf. Med., θάλασσα διΐστατο the sea *made way, opened*, 13.29; διαστὰν γῆς βάθρον *yawning wide*, S.*OC*1662; τὰ διεστεῶτα ὑπὸ σεισμοῦ Hdt.7.129; διεστῶτα, opp. ἡνωμένα, Chrysipp. *Stoic.*2.124, al.; ἔτους διεστῶτος *after an interval of* a year, *SIG*344. 119 (Teos). **b.** *stand with legs apart*, Luc.*Ner.*7. **2.** of persons, *stand apart, be at variance*, διαστήτην ἐρίσαντε Il.1.6; εἴ τινές που διασταῖεν Th.1.18; διέστη ἐς ξυμμαχίαν ἑκατέρων *sided* with one or the other party, ib.15; κατὰ πόλεις διέσταμεν Id.4.61; διεστηκότες εἰς δύο D.10.4, cf. 18.18; ἐρίζειν καὶ διεστάναι Id.2.29; simply, *differ, be different*, πλούτου ἀρετὴ διέστηκεν Pl.*R.*550e; πρὸς ἄλληλα Arist.*Pol.*1256a29, cf. *Po.*1448a17; ἡ ἀριστοκρατία διέστηκεν ἀπὸ ταύτης πολὺ τῆς πολιτείας Id.*Pol.*1289b3; οὖρα διεστηκότα *not homogeneous*, Hp.*Aph.*7.33. **3.** *part* after fighting, Hdt.1.76, 8.16, 18: hence, *to be reconciled*, Isoc.5.38. **b.** of an army, *retire*, Plb.10.3. 6. **4.** *stand at certain distances* or *intervals*, Hdt.2.66; of guards in a row, Id.3.72; of post-stations, Id.8.98; of soldiers, δ. κατὰ διακοσίους Th.4.32; διάστηθι *mark distances!* a word of command, Ael. *Tact.*12.11: Geom., ἴσα ἀπ' ἀλλάλων διέστακεν *are equidistant* from one another, Archim.*Aequil.*1.6. **III.** Med., sts. trans., *separate*, γεώδη γένη διϊστάμενοι Pl.*Ti.*63c: chiefly in aor. 1, δ. τόν τε δικαιότατον καὶ τὸν ἀδικώτατον *contrast*, Id.*R.*360e; ἀράχνια, of spiders, *spread*, Theoc.16.97.

**διϊστορέω**, *relate*, Phld.*Rh.*2.150 S.

**διΐσχανω**, poet. for διέχω, *cleave*, νύκτ' ὀλοὴν οὐκ ἄστρα διΐσχανεν οὐκ ἀμαρυγαὶ μήνης A.R.4.1696.

**διϊσχναίνω**, *make very lean*, f.l. in Hp.*Loc.Hom.*38.

**διϊσχῡρ-ίζω**, *wish* or *mean to affirm*, Hp.*Art.*1. ❀ **-ίζομαι**, *lean upon, rely on*, τῷ λόγῳ Antipho 5.33, cf. Aeschin.1.1. **II.** *affirm confidently*, τι Pl.*Phd.*63c, etc.; δ. ταῦτα οὕτως ἔχειν ib.114d; δ. ὡς.. Id.*Tht.*154a; δ. περί τινος And.2.4, Lys.13.85; τι ὑπέρ τινος Pl.*Men.* 86b; περὶ σοῦ ὡς.. Id.*Ep.*317c: abs., ὁμοίως ἐφ' ἑκατέροις δ. Id.*Tht.* 158d, etc. **-ιστέον**, *one must affirm*, Str.6.3.8.

**διϊσχύω**, strengthd. for ἰσχύω, Ph.2.627.

❀ **Διϊσωτήρια**, τά, *festival of Zeus Soter* at Athens, *IG*2².1008. 21, al.

**διϊτέον** [ῐτ], (δίειμι) *one must go through*, Pl.*R.*545a.

**διϊτικός** [ῐτ], ή, όν, (δίειμι) *penetrable*, in Comp., Arist.*Pr.*905b13.

**διΐφῐλος** [ῐφ], ον, *dear to Zeus*, usu. written divisim, Il.1.74, etc., but cf. *EM*275.6, etc.

**διϊχνεύω**, *track out*, Plb.4.68.3, Opp.*H.*3.37.

❀ **δῐκᾰδία**, ἡ, *vessel containing two* κάδοι, *IG*2.856.

❀ **δῐκάζω**, fut. δικάσω Il.23.579, Ar.*Eq.*1080, *V.*689, 801, Pl.*Criti.* 120a, etc.; Ion. δικῶ Hdt.1.97; inf. δικᾶν *GDI* iv p.880 (Chios), *SIG* 134b23 (Milet.): aor. ἐδίκασα, Ep. δίκασα, δίκασσα, Od.11.547, Il.23. 574: pf. δεδίκακα Heraclid.Cum.1:—**Med.** (v. infr. II), fut. -άσομαι Hdt.1.96, D.37.37: aor. ἐδικασάμην Lys.12.4, D.38.17, etc.: plpf. ἐδεδίκαστο (v. infr. II):—**Pass.**, fut. δικασθήσομαι D.H.5.61, δεδικάσομαι Luc.*Bis Acc.*14: aor. ἐδικάσθην Th.1.28, Pl.*Cri.*50b: pf. δεδίκασμαι Lys.21.18: plpf. ἐδεδίκαστο D.33.27: (δίκη):—*judge, sit in judgement*, Il.23.579, Hdt.1.14, Antipho 5.90, etc.; *sit as a juror*, D.21.75; δ. καὶ ἐκκλησιάζειν Lys.26.2, cf. Arist.*Pol.*1293a9, etc. **2.** c. acc. rei, *give judgement on, decide, determine*, Il.1. 542; δ. δίκην Hes.*Op.*39, etc.; ἀλιτρά Pi.*O.*2.65; πρᾶγμα A.*Eu.* 471, cf. 601; τἀμπλακήματα Id.*Supp.*230; δ. δίκην ἄδικον *give* an unjust *judgement*, Hdt.5.25; δ. ἐμπορικὰς δίκας D.35.46; less freq., γραφὰς δ. Lycurg.7; εὐθύνας D.19.132; ἀγῶνα Din.1.46: c. acc. cogn., δίκας δ. *adjudge* a penalty, Hdt.6.139; δ. φυγήν τινι *decree* it *as* his *punishment*, A.*Ag.*1412; δ. φόνον ματέρος *ordain* her slaughter, E.*Or.*164 (lyr.): c. gen., δικάζειν τοὺς βασιλέας αἰτιῶν φόνου Lex Draconis ap.*IG*1².115.11; δ. τοῦ ἐγκλήματος (sc. δίκην) X.*Cyr.*1.2. 7:—Pass., δίκαι δικασθεῖσαι Pl.*Cri.*50b, cf. Lys.17.3; ὁποτέρων ἂν δικασθῇ εἶναι τὴν ἀποικίαν *it may be decided*.., Th.1.28. **b.** *pass judgement on, condemn*, γάμον ἄγαμον S.*OT*1214 (lyr.). **3.** φόνον δ. *plead in a case of* murder, E.*Or.*580: abs., *plead*, D.C.69.18. **4.** c. dat. pers., *decide between* persons, *judge their cause*, Τρωσί τε καὶ Δαναοῖσι δικαζέτω ὡς ἐπιεικές Il.8.431; ἐς μέσον ἀμφοτέροισι δικάσσατε 23.574, cf. Hdt.1.97; τοῖσι Πέρσῃσι δίκας δ. Id.3.31; ἑκάστῳ κατὰ τὸ μέγαθος τοῦ ἀδικήματος *passed judgement* on each, Id.2.137. **5.** c. inf., δικαξάτω λαγάσαι *Leg.Gort.*1.5; ἐδίκασαν δέκα ἀνταπόλλυσθαι Hdt.3.14; δ. ὡς.. Id.1.84. **6.** Pass., αἰσχρὰς δίκας δ. *to have actions brought against one*, Lys.21.18. **II.** Med., of the party, *plead one's cause, go to law*, Od.11.545, 12.440, Hdt.1.96, Th.1.77; πρὸς τοὺς ἀστυνόμους Pl.*Lg.*845e; δίκην δικάζεσθαί τινι *go to law with* one, Lys.12.4, D.55.31; simply, δ. τινί Pl.*Euthphr.*4e; πρός τινας Th. 3.44; prop. of a private suit, opp. a public prosecution, D.21.26: with gen. added, δ. τινὶ κακηγορίας Lys.10.12; κλοπῆς D.22.27, etc.; ἐδεδίκαστο ἄν μοι τῆς ἐγγύης Id.33.27; δ. τινὶ περί τινος ib.26. **2.** τὸ δ. *forensic speaking*, Arist.*Rh.*1354b26, cf. Antipho 2.2.12.

**δῐκαία**, Ion. -αίη, ἡ, poet. for δίκη, like Σεληναίη for Σελήνη, Cerc.18.5, cf. *EM*24.48.

**δῐκαιάδῐκος** [ᾰ], ὁ, *one neither just nor unjust*, Ph.2.346.

**δῐκαιαρχία**· ἀρχὴ δικαία, Hsch.

**δῐκαῐκός**, ή, όν, *inclined to justice*, διάθεσις M.Ant.5.34.

**δῐκαιο-δοσία**, ἡ, *jurisdiction*, Plb.20.6.2, etc.; *trial*, ἑλκομένης δ. Id. 22.4.2: pl., εἰς δ. προκαλεῖσθαί τινα Id.4.16.4; ἡ πρὸς ἀλλήλους δ. *Milet.* 3 No.154.5 (ii B.C.), cf. *IG*12(9).903 (Chalcis, ii B.C.); *administration of justice*, Str.13.1.55, al., D.S.37.8, al., *BGU*226.11 (i A.D.). **II.** *international compact for trying suits in the forum rei*, Plb.23.1.2, 32. 17.4. ❀ **-δοτέω**, *administer justice*, Str.11.3.6, Plu.2.779b, Epist.ap. J.*AJ*16.6.7, *POxy.*484.25 (ii A.D.): c. acc., *administer as juridicus*, ἐπαρχίαν *IGRom.*4.401 (Pergam., i B.C.). ❀ **-δότης**, ου, ὁ, = Lat. *juridicus*, at Alexandria, Str.17.1.12, *POxy.*237 vii 39 (ii A.D.), etc.: generally, δ. τοῦ ἔθνους *governor* of the province, J.*AJ*18.1.1; = Lat. *legatus juridicus*, δ. Σπανίας Dessau *Inscr.Lat.Sel.*8842. **-θέτης**, ου, ὁ, = foreg., Baillet *Inscr. des tombeaux des rois* 1836 (s.v.l.). **-κρῐσία**, ἡ, *righteous judgement*, *Ep.Rom.*2.5, Heph.Astr.3.34, *POxy.*71 i 4 (iv A.D.). ❀ **-κρίτης** [ῑ], ου, ὁ, *righteous judge*, Lxx 2*Ma.*12.41, *PRyl.*113.35 (ii A.D.). **-λογέομαι**, fut. -ήσομαι Plb.4.3.12: aor. ἐδικαιολογησάμην Luc.*Prom.*4, or Pass. ἐδικαιολογήθην Plb.31.12.8: —*plead one's cause before the judge, come to issue with* a person. abs., Aeschin.2.21; περί τινος Lys.*Fr.*34; πρός τινα Hyp.*Eux.*20, Plb.4.3. 12, D.Chr.48.10: metaph., Iamb *Myst.*2.19. **2.** *remonstrate*, Luc. *Alex.*55. **II.** later in Act., δ. ὑπὲρ τῆς πόλεως *Inscr.Prien.*111.126 (i B.C.), cf. 108.105; οἱ δικαιολογοῦντες *advocates*, Luc.*Tim.*11, cf. *Apol.*12. **-λόγητον**, *allegandum*, Gloss. **-λογία**, ἡ, *plea in justification*, Demad.7, Arist.*Rh.Al.*1438a25, Lxx 2*Ma.*4.44, *PFlor.*6. 13 (iii A.D.): generally, *pleading*, Plb.3.21.3, al. **II.** pl., *forensic speeches*, Arist.*Rh.Al.*1421b13, 1432b33. **-λογίζομαι**, = -λογέομαι, Sch.Ar.*Ach.*361. ❀ **-λογικός**, ή, όν, *of* or *for pleading, judicial*, Sch.S.*OC*237. Adv. **-κῶς**, Comp. **-κώτερον** ibid. **-λόγος**, ὁ, *advocate*, Arc.89.19, Sch.Ar.*Av.*1702. **-μετρον** (sc. ἀγγεῖον), τό, *vessel which pours out an equal volume of liquid each time*, Hero *Spir.* 2.1. **-νομέω**, = δικαιοδοτέω, Ph.1.126. **-νομία**, ἡ, = δικαιοδοσία, Id.2.365, *IG*7.21.21 (Megara). **-νόμος**, ον, = *juridicus*,

D.C.78.22. **-ποιέω,** *act honestly*, Simp.*in Epict.*p.129 D. **-πολις,** εως, ὁ, ἡ, *strict in public faith*, Pi.*P.*8.22.

⊛ **δῐκαιοπρᾱγ-έω,** *act honestly*, Arist.*EN*1135ᵃ16, *PTeb.*183 (ii B.C.), Ceb.41, Plu.*Sol.*5, Sallust.19, etc.; τὰ μεγάλα Jason ap.Plu.2.135f; πρός τινα Arist.*Rh.*1373ᵇ22. **-ημα,** ατος, τό, *just* or *righteous act*, Id.*EN*1135ᵃ12, Chrysipp.*Stoic.*3.73. **-ής,** ές, *acting justly*, *PSI*1.76.5 (vi A.D.), Sch.Ar.*Av.*1354, Suid. s.v. ἀντιπελαργεῖν. **-ητέον,** *one must deal justly*, Iamb.*Protr.*21.ιθ'. **-ία,** ἡ, *just* or *righteous dealing*, Arist.*EN*1133ᵇ30, Phld.*Rh.*1.266S., Porph.*Marc.*11, Jul. *Ep.*89; περὶ δ., title of work by Epicurus. **-μοσύνη,** ἡ, = foreg., Heraclit.*Ep.*2 (v.l.).

⊛ **δίκαιος** [ῐ], α, ον, also ος, ον E.*Heracl.*901 (lyr.), *IT*1202, D.S.5.72: (δίκη): A. in Hom. and all writers, of persons, *observant of custom* or *rule*, Od.3.52; esp. *of social rule, well-ordered, civilized*, ὑβρισταί τε καὶ ἄγριοι οὐδὲ δ. 9.175, cf. 8.575; [Γαλακτοφάγοι] δικαιότατοι Il.13.6; [Χείρων] δικαιότατος Κενταύρων 11.832, cf. Thgn.314, 794; δ. πολίτης a *good* citizen, D.3.21, etc.: metaph. of the sea, Sol.12.2 (Sup.); δικαίη ζόη a *civilized* way of living, Hdt.2.177. Adv. δικαίως, μνᾶσθαι woo *in due form, decently*, Od.14.90; ὑπὸ ζυγῷ λόφον δ. εἶχον *loyally*, S.*Ant.*292. 2. *observant of duty* to gods and men, *righteous*, Od.13.209, etc.; δ. πρὸς πᾶσαν ὁμιλίην Hp.*Medic.* 2; ἰθὺς καὶ δ. Hdt.1.96; opp. δυσσεβής, A.*Th.*598, cf. 610; δ. καὶ ὅσιος Pl.*Grg.*507b; δικαίων ἀδίκους φρένας παρασπᾷς S.*Ant.*791 (lyr.); also of actions, etc., *righteous*, ἐπὶ ῥηθέντι δικαίῳ a thing *rightly* said, Od.18.414, etc. 3. ὁ δίκαιος, euphem. of a sacred snake, *GDI* 5056 (Crete).

B. later: I. *equal, even, well-balanced*, ἅρμα δίκαιον *even-going* chariot, X.*Cyr.*2.2.26: so metaph., νωμᾷ δικαίῳ πηδαλίῳ στρατόν Pi.*P.*1.86; δικαιόταται ἀντιρροπαί Hp.*Art.*7; δικαιότατα μοχλεύειν ibid.: hence, *fair, impartial*, βάσανος Antipho 1.8; συγγραφεύς Luc.*Hist.Conscr.*39. b. *legally exact, precise*, τῷ δικαιοτάτῳ τῶν λόγων to speak *quite exactly*, Hdt.7.108, cf. Th.3.44; of Numbers, αἱ ἑκατὸν ὀργυιαὶ δίκαιαι Hdt.2.149. Adv. -αίως, πάντα δ. ὑμῖν τετήρηται D.21.3; δ. ἐξετάζειν ib.154. 2. *lawful, just*, esp. τὸ δ. *right*, opp. τὸ ἄδικον, Hdt.1.96, A.*Pr.*189 (lyr.), etc.; τὸ δ. τὸ νόμιμον καὶ τὸ ἴσον Arist.*EN*1129ᵃ34; δ. διορθωτικόν, διανεμητικόν, ib.1131ᵇ25, 27; τὸ πολιτικὸν δ. ib.1134ᵇ18; ἔστι ἐπιεικὲς τὸ παρὰ τὸν γεγραμμένον νόμον δ. Id.*Rh.*1374ᵃ27, cf. *EN*1137ᵇ12; καὶ δίκαια κἄδικα Ar. *Nu.*99; τὰ ἴσα καὶ τὰ δ. D.21.67; τοὐμὸν δ. my own *right*, E.*IA*810; ἐλθεῖν ἐπὶ τοῦτο τὸ δ. bring the case to this *issue*, Antipho 6.24; οὐδὲν τῶν δ. ποιεῖν τινί not to do *what is just and right* by a man, X.*HG*5.3. 10; τὰ δ. ἔχειν, λαμβάνειν, receive *one's due*, Id.*An.*7.7.14, 17; τὰ δ. πράττεσθαι πόλιν give a city its *deserts*, A.*Ag.*812; ἐκ τοῦ δικαίου, = δικαίως, Ar.*Av.*1435, cf. Th.2.89; so ἀπὸ τοῦ δικαίου, τῶν δικαίων, *Inscr.Prien.*50.8 (ii B.C.), 123.8 (i B.C.); μετὰ τοῦ δ. Lys.2.12, D.21. 177; τὸ δίκαιον *lawful claim*, ἃ ἔχομεν δίκαια πρός.. Th.3.54, cf. D. 21.179, Plu.*Luc.*3, etc.; τὰ πρὸς ἀλλήλους δ. mutual *obligations* or *contracts*, Plb.3.21.10; ἐπὶ συγκειμένοις τισὶ δικαίοις on certain agreed *terms*, D.H.3.51. Adv. -αίως *rightly, justly*, Hdt.6.137; μεῖζον ἢ δ. A.*Ag.*376 (lyr.); καὶ δ. καὶ ἀδίκως And.1.135. II. of persons and things, *meet and right, fitting*, δ. τοῦδε τοῦ φόνου ῥαφεύς A.*Ag.*1604; κόσμος οὐ φέρειν δ. Id.*Eu.*55; ἵππον δ. ποιεῖσθαί τινι make a horse *fit for* another's *use*, X.*Mem.*4.4.5, cf. *Cyn.*7.4 (ἵππος δ. τὴν σιαγόνα having a *good* mouth, Poll.1.196). b. *normal*, σχήματα Hp.*Art.*69; φύσις Id.*Fract.*1 (Sup.). 2. *real, genuine*, γόνος S.*Fr.*[1119]; ποιῶν τὰ ἐν τῇ τέχνῃ δ. *Supp.Epigr.*2.184.7 (Tanagra, ii B.C.). Adv., εἴπερ δικαίως ἔστ' ἐμὸς *really and truly* mine, S.*Aj.*547, cf. Pl.*Cra.*418e. 3. ὁ δ. λόγος the plea *of equity*, Th.1.76. Adv. -αίως *with reason*, Id.6. 34, cf. S.*OT*675: Comp. -ότερον Ar.*V.*1149, etc.; also -οτέρως Isoc. 15.170: Sup. -ότατα Ar.*Av.*1222; Aeol. δικαίτατα *IG*12(2).526c17 (Eresus). III. ψυχὴ ἐς τὸ δ. ἔβη 'the land of the leal', *IG*7. 2543.3 (Thebes).

C. in Prose, δίκαιός εἰμι, c. inf., δίκαιοί ἐστε ἰέναι you *are bound* to come, Hdt.9.60, cf. 8.137; δ. εἶμεν ἔχειν Id.9.27; δ. εἰμι κολάζειν *I have a right* to punish, Ar.*Nu.*1434, cf. S.*Ant.*400; δ. ἐστι περιπεσεῖν κακοῖς Antipho 3.3.7; δ. εἰσι ἀπιστότατοι εἶναι they *have most reason* to distrust, Th.4.17; δ. βλάπτεσθαι Lys.20.12; δ. ἐστιν ἀπολωλέναι *dignus est qui pereat*, D.6.37; ὁ σπουδαῖος ἄρχειν δ. *has a right* to.., Arist.*Pol.*1287ᵇ12; with a non-personal subject, ἔλεος δ. ἀντιδίδοσθαι Th.3.40: less freq. in Comp. and Sup., δικαιότεροι χαρίσασθαι Lys.20.34; δικαιότατος εἶ ἀπαγγέλλειν Pl.*Smp.*172b; but δίκαιόν ἐστι is also found, Hdt.1.39, A.*Pr.*611, etc.: pl., δίκαια γὰρ τὸνδ' εὐτυχεῖν S.*Aj.*1126, cf. *Tr.*495, 1116; δικαίως ἄν, c. opt., Pl. *Phdr.*276a. [δικαίων with penult. short in Orph.*Fr.*247.2; cf. οὐ δίκαον· οὐ δίκαιον, Hsch.]

⊛ **δῐκαι-οσύνη,** ἡ, *righteousness, justice*, Thgn.147, Hdt.1.96, al., Pl. *R.*433a, Lxx *Ge.*15.6, etc.; δ. δικαστική legal *justice*, Arist.*Pol.*1291ᵃ 27; opp. ἐπιείκεια, Id.*EN*1137ᵃ32. 2. *fulfilment of the Law*, Lxx *Is.*26.2, al., *Ev.Matt.*3.15, al. II. *justice, the business of a judge*, Pl.*Grg.*464b,c (v.l. δικαστική), *Clit.*408b. III. Δ., personified, *AP*9.164; Ἶσις Δ. *SIG*1131 (Delos), *IG*3.203. IV. Pythag. name for *four*, *Theol.Ar.*23. V. δικαιοσύνη· ἡ χοῖνιξ, μυστικῶς, Hsch. **-όσυνος,** ὁ, *Guardian of justice*, of Zeus, *AJA*1905.302 (Sinope), *Com.Adesp.*752, Eust.918.47: generally, *just*, Simp.*in Cat.*264.24. ⊛ **-ότης,** ητος, ἡ, = δικαιοσύνη, X.*An.*2.6.26, Pl.*Prt.* 331b, Ph.2.641, Plot.4.7.8. ⊛ **-οφᾰνής,** ές, *having an appearance of justice*, Sch.Th.6.80. ⊛ **-όω,** Ion. impf. ἐδικαίευν Hdt.1.100: fut. -ώσω Orac.ap.eund.5.92.β', Th.5.26; -ώσομαι Id.3.40: aor. ἐδικαίωσα Id.2.71:—Pass., fut. -ωθήσομαι Lxx *Si.*18.2: aor. ἐδικαιώθην A.*Ag.* 393 (lyr.): pf. δεδικαίωμαι Lxx *Ez.*21.13(18). I. *set right*, νόμος.. δικαιῶν τὸ βιαιότατον Pi.*Fr.*169.3; δικαιωθεὶς *proved, tested*, A. l.c. II. *hold* or *deem right, claim* or *demand as a right*, c. inf., Hdt.1.89, 133, Hp.*Fract.*31; δεινά με δικαιοῖ δρᾶν S.*OT*640, cf. 575; δικαιοῦντες μὴ ἀφαιρεθῆναι αὐτήν Th.2.41: with inf. omitted, οὕτω δ. (sc. γενέσθαι) Hdt.9.42; δίκας δ. (sc. γενέσθαι) ib.93; ὅποι ποτὲ θεὸς δικαιοῖ S.*Ph.*781; οὐκ ὀρθῶς δ. Th.5.26; *pronounce judgement*, Id. 2.71: c. inf., ἐδικαίωσεν ἀποδοῦναι ἡμᾶς τὸ κεφάλαιον *PRyl.*119.14 (i A.D.); *consent*, δουλεύειν Hdt.2.172, cf. 6.86; οὐκ ἐδικαίου οὐδένα οἱ ἐσαγγεῖλαι he *would* not *allow*.. Id.3.118:—Pass., τὸ δικαιωθὲν ὑπό τινος *that which is ordained*, D.H.10.1. III. *do a man right* or *justice*: hence, 1. *chastise, punish*, Hdt.1.100:—Pass., Id.3. 29, Pl.*Lg.*934b, D.C.*Fr.*57.47; *pass sentence on*, ὑμᾶς αὐτοὺς δικαιώσεσθε Th.3.40. 2. Pass., also, *have right done one*, opp. ἀδικεῖσθαι, Arist.*EN*1136ᵃ18. 3. *pronounce and treat as righteous, justify, vindicate*, Lxx *Ex.*23.7, *Je.*3.11; ἑαυτούς *Ev.Luc.*16.15, etc.:—freq. in Pass., ib.7.35, etc.

**δίκαιρον,** τό, an Indian *bird*, Ctes.*Fr.*57.17, Ael.*NA*4.41. (The properties of opium are ascribed to its dung, ll. cc.)

⊛ **δῐκαί-ωμα,** ατος, τό, *act of right*, opp. ἀδίκημα, Arist.*Rh.*1359ᵃ25; *duty*, τὰ πρὸς ἀνθρώπους δ. Ph.2.199; prop. *amendment of a wrong*, opp. δικαιοπράγημα, Arist.*EN*1135ᵃ13: hence, a. *judgement, penalty*, Pl.*Lg.*864e. b. *justification, plea of right*, Th.1.41, Isoc. 6.25, Arist.*Cael.*279ᵇ9, Lxx *2Ki.*19.28(29), *PLond.*2.360.8 (ii A.D.), etc.; δικαιώματα Ἑλληνίδων πόλεων, compiled by Arist. for Philip, Harp. s.v. Δρύμος. c. pl., *pleadings, documents* in a suit, *OGI*13. 13 (Samos), *PLille* 29.25 (iii B.C.), etc.; also, *credentials*, *BGU*113.10 (ii A.D.), al. d. *act of* δικαίωσις I. 3, *Ep.Rom.*5.16. II. *ordinance, decree*, Lxx *Ge.*26.5, *Ex.*15.26 (pl.), al., *Ep.Rom.*1.32, 2.26 (pl.), al. **-ωσις,** εως, ἡ, *setting right, doing justice to*: hence, 1. *condemnation, punishment*, Th.8.66, D.C.40.43 (pl.), cj. in Plu.2.421d. 2. *plea of legal right, justification*, Lys.9.8, cf. Harp. 3. *making* or *accounting righteous, justification*, *Ep.Rom.*4.25, etc. II. *demand of right* or *as of right, just claim*, Th.1.141, Plu.*Demetr.*18. III. *judgement of what is right*, ἀντήλλαξαν τῇ δικαιώσει altered *at their will and pleasure*, Th.3.82. **-ωτήριον,** τό, *place of punishment*, Pl. *Phdr.*249a (pl.); *place of judgement*, Junc.ap.Stob.4.53.35 (pl.). II. = κριτήριον, Hsch. **-ωτής,** οῦ, ὁ, *judge*, αἰσχρῶν καὶ καλῶν Plu. *Art.*23, cf. 2.549d.

**δῐκαμπ-ής,** ές, *with a double twist*, ψέλια *BGU*1065.8 (i A.D.). **-ίας** οἶνος wine *which has undergone two* τροπαί, *Com.Adesp.*983.

**δίκανα·** ποικίλα ἱμάτια, Hsch.

⊛ **δῐκᾰνικός,** ή, όν, I. of persons, *skilled in pleading*, Pl.*Grg.*512b, *Tht.*201a, X.*Mem.*1.2.48, etc.: in bad sense, *lawyer-like, pettifogging*, σμικρὸς τὴν ψυχὴν καὶ δ. Pl.*Tht.*175d. II. *belonging to trials, judicial*, λόγοι Isoc.13.20; ῥημάτιον δ. *law*-term, Ar.*Pax*534; ἡ -κή (sc. τέχνη) *forensic oratory*, Pl.*R.*405a, Arist.*Rh.*1371ᵃ7; μετὰ δικανικὴν after *serving as advocate*, *Epigr.Gr.*919; τὸ δ. S.E.*M.*2.89; τὰ δικανικὰ Arist.*Rh.*1354ᵇ23. 2. in bad sense, *savouring of the law-courts*, φορτικὰ μὲν καὶ δ. Pl.*Ap.*32a; ὡς μακρὸν τὸ ἐνύπνιον καὶ δ. Luc.*Somn.*17. Adv. -κῶς Charito 5.4.

**δῐκανούς·** τοὺς περὶ τὰς δίκας διατρίβοντας, Hsch.

**δῐ-κάρδιος,** ον, *with two hearts*, Ar.Byz.*Epit.*28.16, Ael.*NA*11.40; τὸ δ. a kind of *lettuce*, *Gp.*12.1.2. **-κάρηνος,** Dor. -ᾱνος [κᾰ], ον, *two-headed*, Batr.298, *AP*6.306 (Aristo). **-καρπέω,** *bear two crops*, Thphr.*CP*1.13.9. **-καρπος,** ον, *bearing two crops*, γῆ Str. 17.3.11.

**δῐκᾰσ-ία,** ἡ, *lawsuit*, Aq.*De.*1.12, al., Sm., Thd.*Pr.*25.9. ⊛ **-ιμος,** ον, *judicial*, δ. ἡμέρα *when the courts are open*, Men.969; τῇ ἑξῆς δ. (sc. ἡμέρᾳ) *PLips.*32.13 (iii A.D.); δ. μῆνες Pl.*Lg.*958b. **-ις,** εως, ἡ, *exercise of the function of a* δικαστής, Sch.Ar.*Pl.*277.

**δῐκασκόποι,** οἱ, title of *judges* at Mytilene, *IG*12(2).6.12 (iv B.C.); at Cyme, *BCH*37.157 (iii B.C.).

**δῐκασμός,** ὁ, *giving judgement*, Ph.1.133.

**δῐκασ-πολέω,** *judge*, Diotog.ap.Stob.4.7.61. **-πολία,** ἡ, *judgement*, *Hymn.Is.*36, Man.2.261, Coluth.12, *AP*11.376 (Agath.): pl., *IG*14.1363, *Inscr.Magn.*202.2. II. *office of a judge*, Orph.*A.* 381, Q.S.5.172. **-πόλος,** ὁ, (qᵘel, cf. τελέω) *one who gives law, judge*, Il.1.238, Phoen.1.7; fem., Orph.*H.*69.11: as Adj., δ. ἄνδρα Od.11.186; σκῆπτρον δ. A.R.4.1178; δ. χρόνος Maiist.52.

⊛ **δῐκαστ-ᾰγωγός,** ὁ, *official who escorted foreign* δικασταί *to their homes*, *Milet.*3.152.94 (ii B.C.); δ. ἀπὸ Ἀσίας ἐπὶ Ἀγητορίδα *IG*5(1). 39 (Sparta, ii A.D.). **-εία,** ἡ, *function of a* δικαστής, ib.12(9).4.8 (Carystus), *CIG*3184 (Smyrna), Ἀρχ.Ἐφ.1911.134 (Gonni). **-έον,** *one must sue at law*, Ph.1.90. **-ήρ,** ῆρος, ὁ, = δικαστής, *Foed.Delph. Pell.*1 A 7, *IG*9(1).334.33 (Locr., v B.C.), Rhet.*Oxy.*410.11, Babr. 118.3. **-ηριακός,** ή, όν, *connected with law-courts*, Phld.*Rh.*1. 212S. **-ηρίδιον** [ρῐ], τό, Dim. of sq., Ar.*V.*803. ⊛ **-ήριον,** τό, *court of justice*, δ. συνάγειν Hdt.6.85; συγκλῄειν Ar.*Eq.*1317; ὑπὸ δ. ὑπαχθεὶς Hdt.6.72, cf. 104; εἰς δ. ἄγεσθαι Pl.*Phdr.*273b; ἀναβὰς ἐς τὸ δ. Antipho 6.21; παραδιδόναι τῷ δ. And.1.17; ἐπὶ δ. ἐλθεῖν Is.1.1; ἐπὶ τοῦ δ. Id.5.29; πρὸ τῶν δικαστηρίων κληροῦσθαι Isoc.7. 54; in Egypt, *office of the governor*, *PLips.*64.24 (iv A.D.). 2. *the court*, i.e. *the judges*, Ar.*V.*624, Pl.*Lg.*880d, etc.; ἐπειδὰν ἀναστῇ τὸ δ. D.21.221. **-ής,** οῦ, ὁ, *a judge*, Hdt.1.96, 3.14, 31, A.*Ch.*120, *Eu.*81, etc. 2. of stars, δ. τῶν βίων D.S.2.31. 3. at Athens and elsewh., *juror*, S.*Aj.*1136, etc.; opp. νομοθέτης, Lys.14.4, cf. Antipho 1.23, X.*Smp.*5.10. II. δ. αἵματος *avenger*, E.*HF* 1150. **-ικός,** ή, όν, *of* or *for law* or *trials, practised in them*, X.

*Mem.*2.6.38; νόμος δ. Plu.*CG*5; μισθός Sch.Ar.*V.*299; ἡ -κή (sc. τέχνη) *business of a judge* or *juryman*, Pl.*Plt.*303e, etc.; τὸ δ. *juror's fee*, Arist.*Pol.*1320a26 (but τὸ δ. the *judicial element* in the state, 1300b13). Adv. -κῶς Luc.*Herm.*47.

**δῐκαστοφῠλᾰκέω**, *to be a member of the bodyguard of a jury*, *Inscr. Magn.*93a.23.

**δῐκάστρια**, ἡ, fem. of δικαστής, Luc.*Pisc.*9.

**δῐκαστύς**, ύος, ἡ, *judgement*, Μίνως.. δικαστύας ἔξοχα κρίνων Epigr. in *Abh.Berl.Akad.*1909.62.

**δῐκατάληκτος**, ον, *having two* καταλήξεις, Heph.15.23 and 24: hence **δῐκαταληξία**, ἡ, Mar.Vict.p.62 K.

**δικάτωρ**· ὁ διπλασίαν τὴν ἀρχὴν ἔχων, Hsch.

**δῐκαυλέω**, *have two stems*, Thphr.*HP*6.6.8.

⊛ **δῐκεῖν**, inf. of ἔδῐκον, an aor. used by Pi. and Trag. (the pres. δίκει Aristaenet.2.1 is prob. f.l. for δίεπει):—*throw*, *cast*, τι Pi.*P.*9.123, A.*Ch.*99; πεδόσε σώματα E.*Ba.*600; χεῖρ' ἐς οὐρανὸν Id.*HF* 498. 2. *strike*, δ. πέτρῳ Pi.*O.*10(11).72; κρᾶτα φόνιον.. ὠλένας δικὼν βολαῖς E.*Ph.*664.

⊛ **δί-κελλα** [ῐ], ης, ἡ, (κέλλω) *two-pronged fork*, Ps.-Phoc.158, A.*Fr.*196, S.*Ant.*250, E.*Ph.*1155, *IG*11.159*A*57 (Delos, iii B.C.), etc.; ἀπαλλαγεὶς δικέλλης καὶ κακῶν Men.*Georg.*65. -**κελλίτης** [λῐ], ου, ὁ, *a digger*, Luc.*Tim.*8. ⊛ -**κελλον**· δικράδεστος· ξένος δύο κλάδους ἔχων, Hsch. ⊛ -**κέντητον**, τό, name of an *eyesalve*, Dem. Ophth.ap.Aët.7.117. -**κεντρος**, ον, *with two stings*, Ael.*NA*6.20, 16.42. -**κέντρων**, a *throw at dice*, Hsch. ⊛ -**κέραιος**, ον, *two-horned*, *two-pointed*, στρόφυγξ *AP*6.111 (Antip.(?)). ⊛ -**κερας**, ατος, τό, *double horn*, Callix.2. -**κέρᾰτος**, ον, *two-horned*, *PMag. Lond.*121.757, Antig.*Mir.*53. -**κερκος**, ον, *with two tails*, Ael. *NA*12.3. -**κερως**, ωτος, ὁ, ἡ, *two-horned*, *h.Hom.*19.2, *AP*6.32 (Agath.), etc.: also δίκερως, ων, Orph.*Fr.*274, Arist.*HA*499b18. -**κέφᾰλος**, ον, *two-headed*, ib.540b3, *GA*770a24, Paul.Aeg.3.76; δράκων D.C.50.8.

**δῐκέω**, *mulct*, prob. an error in *IG*2².1092*B*17 (Pass.).

⊛ **δίκη** [ῐ], ἡ, *custom*, *usage*, αὕτη δ. ἐστὶ βροτῶν this is the *way* of mortals, Od.11.218; ἡ γὰρ δ. ἐστὶ γερόντων 24.255, etc.; ἥ τ' ἐστὶ δ. θείων βασιλήων 4.691; ἡ γὰρ δμώων δ. ἐστίν 14.59, etc.; ἡ γὰρ δ., ὁππότε.. this is always *the way*, when.., 19.168 (so in late Prose, ἥπερ ἱππομαχίας δ. Arr.*An.*3.15.2); δίκαν ἐφέπειν τινός to imitate him, Pi.*P.*1.50; δ. ἐπέχειν τινός to be *like*.., Anon.Lond.6.18; *normal course of nature*, ἐκ τουτέων ὁ θάνατος οὐ γίνεται κατά γε δίκην, οὐδ' ἣν γένηται Hp.*VC*3: hence, 2. adverb. in acc. δίκην, *in the way of*, *after the manner of*, c. gen., λύκοιο Pi.*P.*2.84; πώλου S.*Fr.*659; τοξότου Pl.*Lg.*705e; in later Prose, Arist.*Mu.*395b22, Luc. *Dem.Enc.*31, Alciphr.1.6, etc.: mostly of living creatures or persons, but also of things, as δίκην ὕδατος, ἀγγείου, A.*Th.*85 (lyr.), Pl. *Phdr.*235d. II. *order*, *right*, μή τι δίκης ἐπιδευές nothing short of *what is fit*, Il.19.180; opp. βία, might, 16.388; opp. σχέτλια ἔργα, Od.14.84; personified, Hes.*Th.*902, A.*Th.*662, etc.; Δίκης βωμός Id. *Ag.*383 (lyr.), *Eu.*539 (lyr.); *Truth*, Pi.*P.*8.71. 2. δίκη ἐστί, = δίκαιόν ἐστι, A.*Ag.*259, cf. 811, *Eu.*277. 3. Adverb. usages, δίκῃ *duly*, *rightly*, Il.23.542, Pl.*Criti.*112e; ἐν δίκᾳ Pi.*O.*6.12, cf. S.*Tr.*1069, etc.; σὺν δίκῃ Thgn.197, Pi.*P.*9.96, A.*Th.*444, etc.; κατὰ δίκην Hdt. 7.35, E.*Tr.*888, etc.; μετὰ δίκης Pl.*Lg.*643e; πρὸς δίκης S.*OT*1014, *El.*1211 (but πρὸς δίκας on the score *of justice*, Id.*OC*546 (lyr.)); διαὶ δίκας A.*Ch.*641; ἐκ δίκης Herod.4.77: opp. παρὰ δίκαν Pi.*O.*2.18, etc.; ἄνευ δίκης A.*Eu.*554; πέρα δίκης Id.*Pr.*30; βίᾳ δίκης Id. *Supp.*430 (lyr.); δίχα δίκης without *trial*, Plu.*Ages.*32; πρὸ δίκης in preference to *legal proceedings*, Th.1.141. III. *judgement*, δίκην ἰθύντατα εἰπεῖν give *judgement* most righteously (cf. ἰθύς), Il.18.508: esp. in pl., Λυκίην εἴρυτο δίκῃσί τε καὶ σθένεϊ ᾧ 16.542; περὶ οἶδε δίκας Od.3.244, etc.; δίκαι σκολιαί Hes.*Op.*219,250; κρῖνε εὐθεῖαν δίκην A.*Eu.*433. IV. after Hom., of *proceedings instituted to determine legal rights*, hence, 1. *lawsuit*, Pl.*Euthphr.*2a, D.18.210, etc.; prop. *private suit* or *action*, opp. γραφή (q.v.), Lys.1.44, etc.; ἐκαλοῦντο αἱ γραφαὶ δίκαι, οὐ μέντοι αἱ δίκαι καὶ γραφαί Poll.8.41; οἱ δίκην ἔχοντες the parties to *a suit*, *IG*7.21.8 (Megara), cf. Plu.*Cic.* 17. 2. *trial* of the case, πρὸ δίκης Is.5.10, etc.; μέχρι τοῦ δίκην γενέσθαι Th.2.53; *court* by which it was tried, ἐν ὑμῖν ἐστι καὶ τῇ δίκῃ Antipho 6.6. b. δίκην εἰπεῖν to plead a *cause*, X.*Mem.*4.8.1; δ. μακρὰν λέγειν Ar.*V.*776, cf. Men.*Epit.*12. 3. *the object* or *consequence of the action*, *atonement*, *satisfaction*, *penalty*, δίκην ἐκτίνειν, τίνειν, Hdt.9.94, S.*Aj.*113: adverbially in acc., τοῦ δίκην πάσχεις τάδε; A.*Pr.*614; freq. δίκην or δίκας διδόναι suffer *punishment*, i.e. make *amends* (but δίκας δ., in A.*Supp.*703 (lyr.), to grant *arbitration*); δίκας διδόναι τινί τινος Hdt.1.2, cf. 5.106; ἔμελλε τῶνδέ μοι δώσειν δίκην S.*El.*538, etc.; also ἀντί or ὑπέρ τινος, Ar.*Pl.* 433, Lys.3.42; also δίκην διδόναι ὑπὸ θεῶν *to be punished* by.., Pl. *Grg.*525b; but δίκας ἤθελον δοῦναι they consented to submit to *trial*, Th.1.28; δίκας λαμβάνειν sts. = δ. διδόναι, Hdt.1.115; δίκην ἀξίαν ἐλάμβανες E.*Ba.*1312, *Heracl.*852; more freq. its correlative, inflict *punishment*, take *vengeance*, Lys.1.29, etc.; λαβεῖν δίκην παρά τινος D.21.92, cf. 9.2, etc.; so δίκην ἔχειν to have *one's punishment*, Antipho 3.4.9, Pl.*R.*529c (but ἔχω τὴν δ. have *satisfaction*, Id.*Ep.*319e; παρά τινος Hdt.1.45); δίκας or δίκην ὑπέχειν stand *trial*, Id.2.118, cf. S. *OT*552; δίκην παρασχεῖν E.*Hipp.*50; θανάτου δίκην ὀφλεῖν ὑπό τινος to incur the death *penalty*, Pl.*Ap.*39b; δίκας λαγχάνειν τινί D.21.78; δίκης τυχεῖν παρά τινος ib.142; δίκην ὀφείλειν, ὀφλεῖν, Id.21.77, 47.63; ἐρήμην ὀφλεῖν τὴν δ. Antipho 5.13; δίκην φεύγειν *to escape it*, be the defendant in *the trial* (opp. διώκειν prosecute), D. 38.2; δίκας αἰτέειν demand *satisfaction*, τινός *for* a thing, Hdt.8.114; δ. ἐπιτιθέναι τινί Id.1.120; τινός *for* a thing, Antipho 4.1.5; δίκαι ἐπιφερόμεναι Arist.*Pol.*1302b24; δίκας ἀφιέναι τινί D.21.79; δίκας ἑλεῖν, v. ἔρημος II; δίκην τείσασθαι, v. τίνω II; δὸς δὲ δίκην καὶ δέξο παρὰ Ζηνὶ *h.Merc.*312; δίκας διδόναι καὶ λαμβάνειν παρ' ἀλλήλων, of communities, submit *causes* to trial, Hdt.5.83; δίκην δοῦναι καὶ λαβεῖν ἐν τῷ δήμῳ X.*Ath.*1.18, etc.; δίκας δοῦναι καὶ δέξασθαι submit differences to a peaceful settlement, Th.5.59. V. Pythag. name for *three*, Plu.2.381f, *Theol.Ar.*12; for *five*, ib.31. (Cf. Skt. *diś-*, *diśā* 'direction', 'quarter of the heavens'.)

**δῐκήγορος**, ὁ, *advocate*, Lyd.*Mag.*3.66, Agath.5.7, Suid. s.v. Ἀλέξανδρος Αἰγαῖος, Eust.131.2.

**δίκηλον**, written for δείκηλον, Hsch.

**δίκηλος** [ῑ], ον, (κήλη) *with double hernia*, Heliod.ap.Orib.50.42.3. II. *with double hydrocele*, Paul.Aeg.6.62.

**δίκησις** [ῐ], εως, ἡ, *vengeance*, = ἐκδίκησις, Lxx *Si.*47.25 (v.l.).

**δῐκη-τροπεῖ**· φυγαδεύει, Suid. -**φόρος**, ον, *bringing justice*, *avenging*, Ζεύς A.*Ag.*525; ἡμέρα δ. the day of *vengeance*, ib.1577; ὁ δ. *avenger*, opp. δικαστής, Id.*Ch.*120.

**δῐκίδιον** [ῐδ], τό, Dim. of δίκη, *little trial*, Ar.*Eq.*347, *V.*511.

**δίκληρος**, Dor. **δίκλᾱρος**, ον, *occupying the space of two* κλῆροι, ἐλαιοκόμιον *IG*14.352 i 69 (Halaesa).

**δῐκλίς**, ίδος, ἡ, (κλίνω) *double-folding*, epith. of doors or gates, mostly in pl. with σανίδες, θύραι, πύλαι, Od.2.345, 17.268, Il.12.455; later δικλίδες alone, *folding-doors*, *AP*7.182 (Mel.), 5.144 (Asclep.), 255 (Paul. Sil.), etc.: rarely in sg., Theoc.14.42, *AP*5.241 (Eratosth.); δ. θύρη Arat.193:—written **δίκλεις**, ειδος, as if from κλείς, *double-fastened*, Hp.*Art.*7 (cf. Gal. ad loc.).

**δῐκο-γρᾰφία**, ἡ, *composition of forensic speeches*, Isoc.15.2. -**γρᾰφικῶς**, Adv. *like a writer of forensic speeches*, Id.ap.Poll.8.24. -**γράφος** [ᾰ], ὁ, (γράφω) *composer of forensic speeches*, Hyp.*Fr.*234, D.L.6.15. -**δίφης** [δῐφ], ου, ὁ, *one who grubs for lawsuits*, Luc.*Lex.*9.

**δίκοκκος** [ῐ], ον, *with two grains*, ζέα, of rice-wheat, Dsc.2.89. 2. δίκοκκον, τό, = χόνδρος, Ps.-Dsc.2.96.

**δῐκολέκτης**, ου, ὁ, = δικολόγος, *AP*10.48 (Pall.), *APl.*4.313.

⊛ **δῐκόλλῠβος**, *sum of two* κόλλυβοι, Ar.*Fr.*3.

⊛ **δῐκο-λογέω**, *plead causes*, Arist.*Rh.*1355a20. -**λογία**, ἡ, *pleading*, ib.1354b29. ⊛ -**λόγος**, ὁ, *pleader*, *advocate*, Plu.*Luc.*1, Ptol. *Tetr.*180, *Edict.Diocl.*7.72, *PFlor.*71.692 (iv A.D.), Artem.2.29 (pl.).

**δῐ-κόλουρος**, ον, *doubly truncated*, πυραμίδες Nicom.*Ar.*2.14. -**κολπος**, ον, *with two sinuses*, Gal.2.890.

**δῐκο-λύμης** [ῡ], ου, ὁ, *one who destroys by lawsuits*, *Com.Adesp.* 859. -**μᾰχέω**, *carry on a lawsuit*, Alciphr.3.29 (vulg. ἀδικ-). -**μήτρα**, ἡ, *mother of lawsuits*, *Com.Adesp.*984.

**δῐ-κόνδῠλος**, ον, *double-knuckled*, δάκτυλοι Arist.*HA*493b30. 2. *provided with two knobs* (?), *Sammelb.*1958. ⊛ -**κορίασις**, εως, ἡ, (κόρη) *possession of double pupil*, Dem.Ophth.ap.Simon.Januens. -**κορμος**, ον, *with two trunks*, δένδρον v.l. in Artem.5.74. -**κορος**, ον, *having a double pupil*, Ptol.Chenn.p.192 W., Suid., Eust.295.44.

**δῐκο-ρράπτης**, ου, ὁ, = δικορράφος, Phryn.*PS*p.62 B. -**ρρᾰφέω**, *stitch*, i.e. *get up*, *a lawsuit*, Ar.*Nu.*1483, Apollod.Com.13.12. -**ρρᾰφία**, ἡ, *getting up a lawsuit*, Man.2.296, Sch.Ar.*Nu.* 1015. -**ρράφος** [ᾰ], ὁ, (ῥάπτω) *pettifogger*, D.Chr.7.123, Aristaenet.2.3, Phryn.*PS*p.62 B.

**δί-κορσος** [ῐ], ον, *two-headed*, *Lex.Rh.*ap.Eust.947.28, Hsch. ⊛ -**κόρυμβος**, ον, *twin-peaked*, ἕδρανα, of Parnassus, *Pae.Delph.*4, cf. Luc. *Cont.*5.

**δῐ-κόρῠφος**, ον, *two-peaked*, δ. πλάξ, of Parnassus, E.*Ba.*307; λάμπουσα πέτρα.. δ. σέλας Id.*Ph.*227 (lyr.); κλειτύς Limen.2. 2. *with two crowns*, of the hair on the head, Arist.*HA*491b7, Poll.2.43. 3. *with two tops*, ἐνθέματα *Gp.*10.75.7.

**δῐκοτέχνης**, ου, ὁ, *professional advocate*, D.Chr.7.124.

**δικοτροπεῖ**· φυγαδεύει, Hsch.

**δῐ-κοτύλιον** [ῠ], τό, *measure of two* κοτύλαι, Orib.*Fr.*83. -**κότῠλος**, ον, *with two rows of tentacula*, like the poulp, Arist.*HA*525a19, *PA*685b12. II. *holding two* κοτύλαι, Hp.*Int.*12, Sotad.Com. 1.33, Polyaen.8.16.2. 2. Subst. δικότυλον, τό, *measure of two* κοτύλαι, *POxy.*937.27 (iii A.D.). -**κραιόομαι**, *branch*, *fork*, prob. in Hp.*Epid.*2.4.1 (but cf. *Oss.*10); cf. Erot. -**κραιος**, ον, *forked*, *cleft*, Hp.*Loc.Hom.*6, al. -**κραιότης**, ητος, ἡ, *division*, ibid. -**κραιρος**, ον, *two-horned*, *AP*6.32 (Agath.). II. *forked*, δίκραιρα.. κήτεος ὁλκαία A.R.4.1613. -**κρᾰνίζω**, *fork up earth*, *PFay.*110.17 (Pass.). -**κρᾶνος**, ον, *two-headed*, Parm.6.5. II. Subst. **δίκρᾱνον**, τό, *pitchfork*, δικράνοις ἐξωθεῖν Luc.*Tim.*12. III. δικράνους· τὰς τριόδους, Hsch. -**κρᾱνοφόρος**, *furcifer*, *Gloss.* -**κρᾰτής**, ές, *holding joint authority*, δικρατεῖς Ἀτρεῖδαι S.*Aj.*252 (lyr.); δικρατεῖς λόγχας στήσαντε *double-slaying* spears, of Eteocles and Polynices, Id.*Ant.*145 (lyr.). -**κρατον** νόμισμα ἢ δίκρανον, Hsch. -**κρεας**, τό, *double portion of meat*, νώτου *SIG*1025.53 (Cos); also **δίκρεως** μερίς ib.1013.5 (Chios); δύο μοίρας δίκρεως *BCH*37.195 (Chios, iv B.C.).

⊛ **δικράδεστος**, v. δίκελλον.

⊛ **δί-κροος**, α, ον, contr. **δίκρους**, α, ουν; or **δικρόος**, contr. **δικροῦς**, ᾶ, οῦν; also written **δίκρος**, α, ον:—*forked*, *cloven*, γλώσσημα A.*Fr.*152, cf. X.*Cyn.*10.7; ξύλον Timocl.9.6; χηλή Arist.*HA*590b25, etc.; of a serpent's tongue, Id.*PA*660b6, al.; of the womb, in selachians, Id.*HA*511a6; of muscles and tendons, Gal.2.369; δίκρα ῥίζα Thphr. *HP*9.11.3; δικροῖς ἔωθουν τὴν θεόν—κεκράγμασιν (παρὰ προσδοκίαν for ξύλοις) Ar.*Pax* 637; δίκρουν or δικροῦν, τό, *bifurcation*, Hp.*Coac.*

225, cf. Pl.*Ti.*78b; also **δικρόα**, ἡ, X.*Cyn.*9.19, Thphr.*HP*2.6. 9. **–κρόσσιον**, τό, *double-fringed cloth*, *Peripl.M.Rubr.*6. **–κροσσος**, ον, *double-bordered* or *fringed*, Poll.7.72, *EM*430.30. **–κροτίζω**, *beat double*, of the pulse, Gal.19.640. ⊛ **–κροτος**, ον, *double-beating*, ῥόθια κώπας E.*IT*408 (lyr.); of the pulse, Archig.ap.Gal.8.537, al., Ruf.*Syn.Puls.*8.5. 2. of ships, *with only two banks of oars manned*, X.*HG*2.1.28; later, = διήρης, Arr.*An.*6.5.2, Luc.*Am.*6: Subst. δίκροτον, τό, Plb.5.62.3, App.*Mith.*17; δίκροτος, ἡ, *AP*7.640 (Antip.). II. δ. ἁμαξιτός a road *for two carriages*, E.*El.*775. ⊛ **–κρουνος**, ον, *with two springs*, ῥυτὸν δ. a vase *from which two kinds of wine could be poured*, Damox.1.3; δ., τό, Haussoullier *Milet* p.199.

⊛ **Δικταῖος**, ὁ, epith. of Zeus, from the Cretan mountain *Dicté*, Str. 10.4.12.

**δικταμνίτης** [νῖ] οἶνος wine *flavoured with dittany*, Dsc.5.47.

**δικταμνοειδές**, name of a *plant*, prob. = ψευδοδίκταμνον, Hsch.

**δίκταμνον**, τό, Arist.*HA*612ᵃ4, Thphr.*HP*9.16.1: **δίκταμον**, Arist. *Mir.*830ᵇ21:—*dittany of Crete*, *Origanum Dictamnus*. 2. *bastard dittany*, *Ballota acetabulosa*, Dsc.3.32.

**δικτάτωρ** [ᾰ], ορος or ωρος, ὁ, Lat. *dictator*, Plb.3.87.7, etc.: hence **δικτᾱτωρ-εία**, ἡ, *the dictatorship*, D.H.6.22 (–ία, Plu.*Fab.*3): **–εύω**, *to be dictator*, D.C.43.1.

**δίκτον**, τό, = δίκταμνον, Arat.33 (Zenod.ap.Sch., but prob. pr.n.).

**δίκτυ**, = δίκτυον, *EM*275.27.

**δικτῠ-ἄγωγός**, ὁ, *drawer of nets*, Poll.5.17. ⊛ **–αρχέω**, *hold office in the cult of Isis*, or (less prob.) *in a fishery guild*, *IGRom.*1.817 (Callipolis). **–βολέω**, *cast the net*, dub. l. in *AP*6.186 (Diocles). ⊛**–βόλος**, ον, *a fisherman*, ib.105 (Apollonid.), Opp.*H.*4. 578. **–διον**, τό, Dim. of δίκτυον, Poll.7.179. **–εία** or **–ία**, ἡ, *net-fishing*, Ael.*NA*12.43. **–εύς**, έως, ὁ, *one who fishes with nets*, Str.8.7.2, Ael.*NA*1.12.

⊛ **Δίκτυννα**, ἡ, (δίκτυον) epith. of Artemis as *goddess of the chase*, Hdt.3.59, E.*Hipp.*145 (lyr.), etc.:—hence **Δικτυνναῖος**, ὁ (sc. μήν), name of month in Crete, *GDI*5173.

**δικτῠο-βόλος**, ον, = δικτυβόλος, Poll.7.137. **–ειδής**, ές, *net-like*, δ. πλέγμα *rete mirabile Galeni*, Herophil.ap.Gal.5.155, Gal.*UP*9. 4. **–θήρας**, ου, ὁ, *net-fisher*, Sch.Theoc.1.40. **–θηρευτική** (sc. τέχνη), ἡ, *net-fishing*, Poll.7.139. **–κλωστος**, ον, (κλώθω) *woven in meshes*, σπεῖραι δ. *the net's meshy* coils, S.*Ant.*347 (lyr.).

⊛ **δίκτῠον**, τό, (δικεῖν) *net*: 1. *fishing-net*, δικτύῳ ἐξέρυσαν πολυωπῷ (sc. ἰχθύας) Od.22.386; φελλοὶ δ' ὣς ἄγουσι δ. A.*Ch.*506; μολυβδὶς ὥστε δ. κατέσπασεν S.*Fr.*840; δ. καθιέναι, ἀναιρεῖσθαι, Arist. *HA*533ᵇ19, 602ᵇ8. 2. *hunting-net*, Hdt.1.123, Ar.*Av.*1083, etc.; larger than ἄρκυς, X.*Cyn.*2.5, cf. Poll.5.26, 27. 3. metaph., δ. ἄτης, Ἅιδου, A.*Pr.*1078 (anap.), *Ag.*1115 (lyr.), cf. S.*Fr.*932. 4. *lattice-work*, *IG*11(2).165.4, 13 (Delos, iii B.C.). 5. *bottom of a sieve*, Hsch.

**δικτῠόομαι**, Pass., *to be wrought in net-work*, Lxx 3*Ki.*7.18(6). II. *to be caught in a net*, Babr.107.11.

⊛ **δικτῠοπλόκος**, ον, *weaving nets*, Poll.7.139.

**δικτῠουλκός**, όν, *drawing nets*, Poll.7.137. II. Subst., *fisher*, Iamb.*VP*8.36: Δικτυουλκοί, οἱ, title of play by A.

**δικτῠοῦχος**, ὁ, = *retiarius*, *Gloss.*; also **δικτυοφόρος**, ὁ, Id.

**δίκτῠπος**, ον, *double-sounding*, ἠχώ Nonn.*D.*10.225.

**δίκτυς**, υος, ὁ, an unknown Libyan animal, Hdt.4.192. II. = ἰκτῖνος (Lacon.), Hsch.

**δικτῠ-ώδης**, ες, = δικτυοειδής, Sch.Ar.*V.*99, Poll.4.116. II. Subst. –ῶδες, τό, = δ. πλέγμα, Hp.*Ep.*19 (*Hermes* 53.69). ⊛ **–ωτός**, ἡ, όν, *made in net-fashion*, D.S.18.26; *latticed*, *trellised*, θύραι Plb.15.30.8; θυρὶς δ. *lattice*-window, Lxx *Ez.*41.16: Subst. δικτυωτόν, τό, = θυρὶς δ., ib.4*Ki.*1.2.

**δί-κυκλος** [ῐ], ον, *two-wheeled*, ὄχημα Lib.*Or.*1.33; δ. [ἅρμα] *two-wheeled* car, D.C.76.7. **–κῡμος**, ον, *bearing twins*, πρόβατα Suid. **–κύπελλος** [ῠ], ον, gloss on ἀμφικύπελλος, Eust.159. 4. **–κυρτος**, ον, *two-humped*, of the Bactrian camel, *An.Ox.*4. 264, *Gp.*16.22.4.

*δίκω, v. δικεῖν.

**δῐ-κωλία**, ἡ, *period of two members*, Mar.Vict.p.182 K. **–κωλος**, ον, *with two limbs* or *legs*, Lyc.636; ἀκρίδια Dsc.2.94; of a crane, μηχανή *Milet.*7.60; *in two sections*, σύριγγες Nicom.*Harm.*10. II. in Rhet., *with two members*, περίοδος Demetr.*Eloc.*34, Hermog.*Inv.*4.3, Hdn.*Fig.*p.98 S.:—also in metre, Sch.Ar.*Ach.*1212, etc. **–κωπέω**, *ply a pair of sculls*, sens. obsc., ἀμφοτέρας δ. Ar.*Ec.*1091. **–κωπία**, ἡ, *pair of sculls*, Luc.*Cont.*1, Sch.Th.4.67. **–κωπος**, ον, *two-oared*, σκάφος E.*Alc.*252 (lyr.), cf. 444 (lyr.), Plb.34.3.2.

**δίλαξ**· ἀρία (Lacon.), Hsch.

⊛ **δίλασσον**, τό, a kind of *garment*, dub. sens. in *BGU*814.25, 816.17 (ii A.D.); cf. τετράλασσον.

**δῐλέκῐθος**, ον, *with two yolks*, ᾠόν Sch.E.*Or.*463.

**διλέσβιος**, ον, dub. sens., διλέσβια λευκά (sc. κεράμια?) *PSI*5.535.28.

**δῐ-λήκῠθον**, τό, *double* λήκυθος, Hippoloch.ap.Ath.4.129c. ⊛ **–λημμα**, ατος, τό, *ambiguous proposition*, Roman.2, Suid. **–λήμμᾰτος**, ον, *involving two propositions*, συλλογισμός Gal.*Inst.Log.*6.5: **–τον**, τό, *dilemma*, Hermog.*Inv.*4.6. Adv. **–τως** Ulp.ad D.3.13. II. *ambiguous*, λέξεις Sch.Ar.*Nu.*480. III. *two-handled*, gloss on περιδέξιος, *EM*699.41. **–λήμνιον**, τό, *double lemniscus*, *IG*12(1).155.56 (Rhodes), *BCH*11.308 (Caria, written διλεμνίσκι). **–ληπτος**, ον, *ambiguous*, Sch.Il.2.642. **–λιτραῖος**, ον, *weighing two pounds*, μῆλα Tz.*H.*9.342:—also **–λιτρόμηλα**, ib.347. ⊛ **–λιτρον**, τό, *weight of two pounds*, *Gloss.* **–λογέω**, *repeat*, X.*Eq.*8.2; περὶ τῶν αὐτῶν D.S. 16.46:—Pass., διλογηθὲν ὄνομα Demetr.*Eloc.*267: **–τέον**, *one must repeat*, ib.197. **–λογία**, ἡ, *repetition*, X.*Eq.*8.2: as a rhetorical figure, Demetr.*Eloc.*211. **–λογος**, ον, *double-tongued*, *doubtful*, 1*Ep.Ti.*3. 8. **–λογχος**, ον, *double-pointed*, *twofold*, ἄτη A.*Ag.*643; epith. of Βενδῖς (i.e. Artemis) from her *twofold* attributes, Cratin.80. **–λοφος**, ον, *double-crested*, πέτρα, of Parnassus, S.*Ant.*1126 (lyr.); ἀλέκτωρ *PMag.Leid.V.*9.21. **–λοχία**, ἡ, *double company*, Aen.Tact. 15.3, Plb.10.23.4; *body of thirty-two men*, Ascl.*Tact.*2.8, Arr.*Tact.* 10.1. **–λοχίτης** [χῑ], ου, ὁ, *commander of a* διλοχία, Ascl. and Arr. ll. cc. ⊛ **–λωρος**, ον, dub. sens., *BGU*620.9 (iii A.D.). ⊛ **–μαλλος**, ον, *with double fleece*, *Gloss.* **–μάχαιρος** [μᾰ], ον, *with two swords*, of gladiators, Artem.2.32. **–μάχης** [ᾰ], ου, ὁ, *mounted infantryman*, D.S.5.33 (with vv.ll.), Poll.1.132. **–μέδιμνον**, τό, *measure holding two* μέδιμνοι, Hsch. **–μελος** (?), *two-membered*, *Gloss.* **–μερής**, ές, *bipartite*, of the human body, the brain, etc., Arist.*PA*667ᵇ32, al.; δ. ψυχή Ph.1.523; δ. κλισία J.*AJ*12.2.12; φιλοσοφία Jul.*Or.*6.190a. Adv. **–ρῶς** *in two instalments*, *Jahresh.*18 *Beibl.*23 (Seleucia in Cilicia, ii A.D.). **–μέτρητος**, ον, *holding two* μετρηταί, κώδων Callix.2, cf. *CIG*3071 (Teos). **–μετρος**, ον, of a verse, *having two metres*, Heph.5.3, etc. II. δίμετρον, τό, *double measure*, Lxx 4*Ki.*7.1, al. **–μέτωπος**, ον, *with two fronts*, App. *BC*5.33. ⊛ **–μηνία**, ἡ, *period of two months*, prob. in *SIG*344.107 (Teos). **–μηνιαῖος**, α, ον, *two months old*, Hp.*Nat.Mul.*19, *Mul.* 1.47; *of two months*, χρόνος Cleom.1.7, Gem.6.14, *Gp.*17.3.3 (v.l. –μηναῖος). **–μηνος**, ον, *of* or *for two months*, δ. πυρός *maturing in two months*, Thphr.*HP*8.4.4; ἀνοχαί Plb.18.10.4; δίμηνα ἐκτιτρώσκειν Hp.*Aph.*5.45; δίμηνος, ἡ, *space of two months*, Arist.*HA*573ᵃ 12; εἰς δ. Id.*Oec.*1353ᵃ22; ἐντὸς διμήνου *POxy.*1032.22 (ii A.D.); τὴν δ. ἄρχειν Plb.6.34.3. **–μηρον**, *bicoxum*, *Gloss.* **–μήτωρ**, Dor. **–μάτωρ**, ορος, ὁ, ἡ, *twice-born*, of Bacchus, Alex.283, Orph.*H.*52.9, D.S.3.62:—also **–μήτριος**, *Et.Gud.*, Hdn.*Epim.*265. ⊛ **–μῖτος**, ον, *of double thread*, καυσία Eust.393.4. ⊛ **–μιτρος**, ον, *with double mitre*, Plu.*Demetr.*41. **–μνααῖος**, α, ον, *paid at the rate of two minae*, ὁμιληταί Them.*Or.*23.290c. **–μναῖος**, α, ον, Ion. **–μνεως**, (μνᾶ) *worth* or *costing two minae*, δίμνεως (v.l. διμναίας) ἀποτιμήσασθαι to value at *two minae*, Hdt.5.77; δ. τιμήσασθαί τι Arist.*Oec.* 1347ᵃ23; μισθώματα διμναῖα Luc.*DMeretr.*14.4:—also ⊛ **–μνους**, ουν, Ph.*Bel.*69.13: Subst. δίμνουν, τό, *weight of two minae*, *IG*2².1013. 55. **–μνῳος** χόρτος, dub. sens. in *PRyl.*183.17, etc.

⊛ **δῐμοιρ-αῖος**, gloss on διμοιρίτης, Hsch. II. δ. τόκος interest *at two-thirds of the legal maximum*, Just.*Nov.*136.4, *PMasp.*126.23 (vi A.D.). ⊛ **–ία**, ἡ, *double share*, X.*An.*7.2.36, *Lac.*15.4; δ. βασιλέως Antiph.81.5; *double pay*, X.*HG*6.1.6 (pl.). 2. *two-thirds*, D.H.8. 77, *BGU*136.8 (pl., ii A.D.). II. = ἡμιλόχιον, Ascl.*Tact.*2.2, Ael. *Tact.*5.2, Arr.*Tact.*6.2. ⊛ **–ιαῖος**, α, ον, *of two-thirds*, μῆκος Apollod. *Poliorc.*162.7. ⊛ **–ίτης** [ρῑ], ου, ὁ, *one who receives double pay*, *PLille* 27.3 (iii B.C.), Men.*Kol.*28 (v. Sch.), Arr.*An.*7.23.3. 2. = Lat. *duplarius*, Id.*Tact.*42.1. II. *leader of a* διμοιρία, Ascl.*Tact.*2.2, Luc.*DMeretr.*9.5; *mate* of a ship, Id.*JTr.*48. **–ος**, ον, *two-thirds*, esp. in neut., δίμοιρον, τό, A.*Supp.*1070 (lyr.), Euc.1.3, *BGU*661. 22 (i A.D.), Nicom.*Harm.*10, etc.; διμοίρου ὀρθῆς ἐστιν ἡ γωνία the angle measures *two-thirds* of a right angle, Papp.178.23; δ. σπιθαμῆς Hero *Mens.*60.14, cf. *Gp.*8.36.3. 2. *half a drachma*, Pl.*Ax.* 366c: at Rome, *half a libra*, Plu.*CG*17. II. in A.*Th.*850 (lyr.), Herm. restored **δίμορα τέλεα** (for δίμοιρα τέλεια) metri gr.

⊛ **δί-μορφος** [ῐ], ον, *two-formed*, Lyc.111, 892; *of twin form*, Vett. Val.13.3; *androgynous*, D.S.32.12. **–μόρφωτος**, ον, *of twin form*, ζῴδια, i.e. Gemini and Pisces, Man.4.452. **–μυξος**, ον, *with two wicks*, Philyll.26, Philonid.4, Pl.Com.84, Metagen.12, *CIG*3071.9 (Teos).

⊛ **δινάζω**, = δινέω, Artem.ap.Ath.8.333f: aor. Med. δινάσσατο in Pi. *Fr.*101.3 is corrupt.

**δῑνάκω**, *change*, *amend*, dub. in *Schwyzer*412.4 (Elis).

⊛ **δίν-ευμα** [ῑ], τό, *whirling round*, esp. in dancing, prob. in Ar.*Th.* 122; *wheeling*, of a horse, X.*Eq.*3.11; *rotation*, ῥόμβου Orph.*H.*8.7 (pl.). ⊛ **–εύω**, mostly in pres. and impf. (iter. δινεύεσκον Il.24.12), but aor. part. δινεύσας A.R.3.310:—also **δῑνέω**, A.*Th.*462: impf. ἐδίνεον, Ep. δίνεον Il.18.494, Od.9.384: aor. ἐδίνησα Il.23.840, A. *Th.*490: Aeol. **δίννημι** Sapph.1.11:—Med. (v. περιδ-):—Pass., δινεύομαι Arat.455, Opp.*H.*1.376: aor. ἐδινήθην Od.22.85 (as v.l.), E. *Rh.*353 (lyr.): pf. δεδίνημαι (ἀμφι-) Il.23.562: also impf. or plpf. δίνηντο from δίνημι, B.16.107.—Poet. Verbs, also in X. and Pl. and later Prose (v. infr.): (δίνη):—*whirl*, *spin round*, ἧκε δὲ δινήσας [τὸν σόλον] *after whirling* it, Il.23.840; ζεύγεα δινεύοντες *driving* them *round a circle*, 18.543; μοχλὸν ἑλόντες δινέομεν *twirled* the stake *round* in the Cyclops' eye, Od.9.388; δ. πτέρα Sapph.1.11; ἵππους, [ἀσπίδα], A.*Th.*462, 490; ὄμμα E.*Or.*1459 (lyr.):—Pass., *whirl*, *roll about*, ὅσσε .. πάντοσε δινείσθην Il.17.680; κάππεσε δινηθεὶς v.l. for ἰδνωθείς, Od.22.85; of a river, *eddy*, E.*Rh.*353 (lyr.); *whirl round* in the dance, X.*An.*6.1.9, prob. for δον- in Id.*Smp.*2.8; of tumblers, ἐπὶ τροχοῦ δινεῖσθαι Pl.*Euthd.*294e; *writhe*, ἐκ τῶν ἀλγηδόνων J.*BJ*6. 2.10. 2. Pass., *roam about*, ἐδινεόμεσθα κατ' αὐτήν [νῆσον] Od.9. 153; βροτῶν ἐπὶ ἄστεα δινηθῆναι 16.63; κατ' ἀμευσίπορον τριόδον ἐδινήθην Pi.*P.*11.38. 3. ἀμφὶ χαίταις δίνηντο ταινίαι were *twined*, B. 16.107. II. intr. in Act., *whirl about*, ὀρχηστῆρες ἐδίνεον Il.18. 494; of tumblers, ἐδίνευον κατὰ μέσσους ib.606; of a warrior, ὅστις .. δινεύοι κατὰ μέσσον 4.541; δινεύουσαν ὑπὸ πτέρυγος βάλε *as it was circling in its flight*, of a pigeon, 23.875: generally, δ. ἐν ἅρμασιν A.R.3.310; *roam about*, δινεύεσκ' ἀλύων παρὰ θῖν' ἁλὸς Il.24.12; δινεύων κατὰ οἶκον Od.19.67; ἀνὰ νῆσον ἐδίνεον A.R.2.695; δινεύων

βλεφάροις look wildly about, E.*Or*.837 (dub.). ⊛ **-η**, ἡ, *whirlpool*, *eddy*, Il.21.213, A.*Eu*.559, E.*Tr*.210, Pl.*Cra*.439c, etc.: pl., Il. 21.353, Hes.*Th*.791, Hdt.2.28, etc.; ἐπὶ Κυανέας δ. *CIG*3797 (Chalcedon): generally, of the sea, Τυρσηνὶς δ. *AP*9.308 (Bianor). 2. of the *rotating heaven*, Emp.35.4; αἰθέρος δῖναι Id.115.11, cf. Pl.*Phd*. 99b, Arist.*Cael*.295$^a$13, *Ph*.196$^a$26. 3. *whirlwind*, Ar.*Av*.697; δῖναι νεφέλας E.*Alc*.244 (lyr.). 4. generally, *circular motion*, *rotation*, Ar.*Av*.1198; ἀτράκτου Pl.*R*.620e, cf. Epicur.*Ep*.2 p.40 U., al. 5. metaph., ἀνάγκης στερραῖς δ. A.*Pr*.1052 (anap.); τελεσφόροις δίναις κυκλούμενον κέαρ Id.*Ag*.997 (lyr.). **-ήεις**, Dor. **-άεις**, Aeol. **διννάεις** Alc.*Supp*.7.2, εσσα, εν, gen. contr. δινᾶντος B.12.78:—*whirling*, *eddying*, Ξάνθῳ ἐπὶ δινήεντι Il.5.479, cf. Od.6.89, Simon.53. 2, E.*Cyc*.46, etc. II. *rounded*, ταλάροιο Mosch.2.55. **-ημα**, ατος, τό, *rotation*, κόσμου Man.4.553. **-ησις**, εως, ἡ, *whirling motion*, *rotation*, Arist.*Cael*.295$^a$10, *Ph*.243$^a$17, Epicur.*Ep*.2 p.38 U. (pl.); *vertigo*, Aret.*SD*1.4. **-ητός**, ή, όν, *whirled round*, *AP*7.394 (Phil.).

**δίνομον** [ῐ], τό, *coin worth two νοῦμμοι*, *SIG*$^2$588.215 (Delos, ii B.C.), *BCH*35.260 (ibid.).

**δῖνος**, ὁ, like δίνη, *whirling*, *rotation*, such as Anaxagoras held to be the effect of νοῦς as the regulator of the Universe, Clem.Al.*Str*.2. 14 (pl.); personified, Δῖνος βασιλεύει τὸν Δί᾽ ἐξεληλακώς Ar.*Nu*.828: generally, ὁ τοῦ κοσκίνου δ. Democr.164; σφενδόνης δ. Onos.17. 2. *eddy*, *whirlpool*, Epicur.*Ep*.2 pp.38,47 U., Arist.*Pr*.932$^a$5, Plu.2.404f; δ. ἀπὸ τοῦ παντὸς ἀποκριθῆναι παντοίων εἰδέων Democr.167: metaph., δῖνοι ἡδυλόγου σοφίης cj. in Timo 67.4. 3. a *dance*, Hdn.Gr.2.492, Eust.1166.10. II. *vertigo*, Hp.*VC*11. III. *round threshing-floor*, Telesill.7, cj. in X.*Oec*.18.5. IV. *round goblet*, Ar.*V*.618, *IG*11(2).110 (Delos, iii B.C.), al. (cf. δεῖνος, which is freq. v.l. and is found in puns with δεινός, Apolloph.1, Arched.1.4).

**δίνουμμον** [ῐ], τό, *coin of the value of two νοῦμμοι* (q.v.), *Gloss.*

**δῑνόω**, *turn with a lathe*, Eust.412.31, etc.

**Δίνυσος**, v. Διόνυσος.

⊛ **δίν-ω** [ῑ], used only in pres., *thresh out on the δῖνος* III, ἱερὸν ἀκτὴν δινέμεν Hes.*Op*.598:—Pass., δινομένην ὑπὸ (v.l. περὶ) βουσὶν..ἅλωα *trodden by the circling* oxen, Call.*Fr*.51:—Aeol. **δίννω** Hdn.Gr.2.492: Dor. 3 pl. ἀπο-δίνωντι *Tab.Heracl*.1.102. **-ώδης**, ες, *eddying*, D.C. 68.13; τὰ δινώδη *eddies*, Plu.*Cat.Ma*.20.

**Δινών**, ῶνος, ὁ (sc. μήν), name of month in Locris, *GDI*1908.

**δῑνωτός**, ή, όν, *turned*, *rounded*, λέχη, κλισίη, Il.3.391, Od.19.56; ῥινοῖσι βοῶν καὶ νώροπι χαλκῷ δινωτήν (sc. ἀσπίδα) *covered with..circular plates* (or *adorned with spirals*), Il.13.407; θρόνος A.R.3. 44. II. *whirling*, κύκλοι Parm.1.7; πτέρυγες *Epic.Alex.Adesp*. 4.14 Pap.

**διξᾶται**, *pandat*, *Gloss.*

**δίξεστον**, τό, *measure of two ξέσται*, Sch.Ar.*Th*.354.

**δίξοος**, ον, (ξέω) *cleft*, *forked*, Thphr.*HP*5.1.9,10.

**διξός**, ή, όν, Ion., = δισσός, Anacr.88, Hdt.2.44, etc.

**δίξῠλος**, ον, *with two blocks*, τροχιλίαι Heliod.ap.Orib.49.8.9.

⊛ **Δῐο-** (in Ep. **Δῑο-** metri gr.), in compds., both *sprung from Zeus* or *the gods*, and *godlike*.

⊛ **διό**, Conj., for δι᾽ ὅ, *wherefore*, *on which account*, Pl.*R*.358d, etc.; διὸ δή Th.2.21, Pl.*Cra*.412a, al.; διὸ καί, διὸ δὴ καί, Id.*Phdr*.258e, *Smp*. 203c; διόπερ Th.1.71,120, 8.92, etc.

**διοβελία**, ἡ, = διωβελία, *IG*2$^2$.1103.

⊛ **Διο-βλής**, ῆτος, ὁ, ἡ, *hurled by Zeus*, Sch.Pi.*P*.8.23. **-βλητος**, ον, = foreg., Democr.152, Nonn.*D*.2.511. 2. *smitten by Zeus*, ib.21. 223, Ael.*NA*6.62, *Fr*.250, Anon.*Incred*.17. **-βολος**, ον, = foreg. 1, of the thunderbolt, κτύπος S.*OC*1464 (lyr.), E.*Alc*.128 (lyr.).

**Διογένειον**, τό, *the school of Diogenes*, *IG*3.1133.170. II. Διογένεια, τά, festival at Athens *in honour of Diogenes* the Macedonian, *IG*2$^2$.1028.24.

**Διο-γενέτωρ**, ορος, ὁ, *giving birth to Zeus*, Διογενέτορες ἔναυλοι *natal* cave *of Zeus*, E.*Ba*.122 (lyr.). **-γενής**, ές, *sprung from Zeus*, in Hom. epith. of kings, *ordained and upheld by Zeus*, Il.1.337, al.; δ. Ὀδυσσεύς Od.2.352; later, Δ. θεοί A.*Th*.301 (lyr.), *Supp*.631 (lyr.), Ar.*Av*.1263; Διογενὲς κράτος, of Pallas, A.*Th*.127 (lyr.); δ. τέκνον S.*Aj*.91; Ἀμφίων A.*Th*.528; αἷμα τὸ δ., of Achilles, E.*Andr*. 1195 (lyr.): generally, *divine*, φάος Id.*Med*.1258 (lyr.). II. parox., Διογένης, ους, ὁ, pr. n. [Δῑ- in Ep., ῐ̄ in Trag.]

**Διογενισμός**, ὁ, *life after the manner of Diogenes*, Jul.*Or*.6. 186c.

**διογκ-όω**, *distend*, *blow out*, πυρόν Plu.2.676b; λέξις δ. τὸ στόμα Hermog.*Id*.1.6; τὸ ω̄ καὶ τὸ ᾱ δ. τὸν λόγον ibid., cf. Alex.Aphr.*Pr*. 1.59:—Pass., *swell* or *be distended*, Hp.*Acut*.10,28, Plu.*Ages*.27, Sor.2.37: metaph., *to be lifted up*, *raised to a higher position*, Artem. 1.14; *to be puffed up*, Eun.*VS* p.478 B.; λέξεις διωγκωμέναι (cf. supra) Hermog. l.c.; of a lake, *rise*, *overflow*, Plu.*Cam*.3. **-ύλλομαι**, *to be puffed up with pride*, Eun.*VS* p.502 B. **-ωσις**, εως, ἡ, *swelling*, Sor.1.55, Plu.2.771b; *tumour*, Gal.1.185. II. *diastole*, Marcellin. *Puls*.478.

⊛ **Διόγνητος**, ον, contr. for Διογένητος, = Διογενής, Hes.*Sc*.340.

**Διόγονος**, ον, f.l. for δίγονος, Βάκχος E.*Hipp*.560 (lyr.).

**διοδ-εία**, ἡ, *passage through*, τῶν στρατευμάτων *BSA*23.73 (Macedonia, ii A.D.), cf. Suid. **-ευσις**, εως, ἡ, = foreg., Hp.*Flat*.9. ⊛ **-εύω**, *travel through*, τὴν χώραν Plb.2.15.5; *march through*, Plu.*Ages*.17; πανδοκεῖον Arr.*Epict*.2.23,26; διὰ τῶν νομῶν *OGI*665.22 (Oasis Magna): c. gen., διοδεύσει πάντων ἡ τύχη J.*BJ*3.8.7: abs., X.Eph.4.1; *pass away*, of the cause of disease, Gal.8.20:—Pass., Sor.2.59, *AP* 9.708 (Phil.). **-ία**, *bivium*, *Gloss.* **-ιον**, τό, *passage through*, τὸ δ. τῆς λιθοτομίας *IG*2$^2$.1035.49 (i B.C.).

**διοδοιπορέω**, = διοδεύω, τὰς δύο μοίρας [τῆς ὁδοῦ] Hdt.8.129, cf. J. *Ap*.2.16.

**διοδοποιέω**, = foreg., dub. l. in Thphr.*Ign*.59.

⊛ **δίοδος**, ἡ, *way through*, *passage*, *pass*, of Thermopylae, Hdt.7. 201, cf. 9.99, Ar.*Th*.658, *IG*2$^2$.463.122, etc.; δ. ὕδατος Th.2.102; ἄστρων δίοδοι their *pathways*, *orbits*, A.*Pr*.1050 (lyr.); δ. ἔχειν to command *the road*, Th.7.32; αἱ δ. τῶν πτερῶν Pl.*Phdr*.255d; δ. αἰτεῖσθαι, αἰτεῖν, ask *leave to pass*, demand *a safe-conduct*, Ar.*Av*.189, Aeschin.3.151. II. *passing* through the bowels, μελάνων Hp. *Prorrh*.1.127.

**Διόδοτος**, ον, v. Διόσδοτος.

⊛ **δῐόδους**, *bidens*, *Gloss.*

**διοζόομαι**, Pass., *branch out*, Hp.*Nat.Puer*.19.

**δίοζος** [ῐ], ον, *with two knots* or *eyes*, Thphr.*HP*1.8.3.

⊛ **Δῐόθεν**, Adv. *sent from Zeus*, *according to his will*, Δ. βλαφθέντα βέλεμνα Il.15.489; Δ. ἄγγελος ἦλθε 24.194, cf. A.*Ag*.43 (anap.); ἐκ Δ. Hes.*Op*.765.

**διοίγνῡμι**, *open*, τὰς γνάθους διοίγνυτε Ar.*Ec*.852: metaph., τὸ τῆς ψυχῆς ὄμμα Ph.1.442:—Pass., Id.2.414:—also **διοίγω**, S.*Aj*.346, *OT*1287, 1295 (Pass.), Pl.*Smp*.222a (Pass.), etc.; ᾗ δ᾽ ἂν διοίξῃς σφάγια (sc. τῇ μαχαίρᾳ) E.*Supp*.1205.

**δίοιδα**, v. διεῖδον.

**διοιδ-αίνω**, = sq., Aët.3.34: metaph., διοίδαινον τῶν ὄχλων αἱ ψυχαί Hdn.7.3.6; also οἱ στρατιῶται δ. τὰς ψυχάς Id.8.8.1. **-έω**, pf. and plpf., διῴδηκα, -ειν, Luc.*Gall*.10, *Nec*.18:—strengthd. for οἰδέω, Hp. *Art*.79 (prob.), J.*BJ*5.12.3, Luc. ll. cc.; of the sea, Str.3.5.8: metaph. of a person, *swell with anger*, Ph.2.583; of a city, *to be in a ferment*, D.H.9.48:—Med., metaph., διοιδουμένη καὶ οὐκ ἄνευ ζηλοτυπίας Hld. 7.7. **-ής**, ές, *swollen*, *turgid*, μαζός Nic.*Al*.90. **-ησις**, εως, ἡ, *swelling*, Heliod.ap.Orib.50.52.1. II. *ebullition* of temper, Phld.*Ir*.p.26 W. **-ίσκομαι**, = διοιδέω, Gal.5.523.

**διοικ-εία**, ἡ, = διοίκησις, dub. in Eustr. *in EN*179.8. **-εσις**, εως, ἡ, = διοίκησις, *IG*12(2).15.34 (Mytilene). ⊛ **-έω**, impf. διῴκουν Th.8. 21, etc.: fut. -ήσω Pl.*Men*.73b: aor. διῴκησα Isoc.1.35, etc.: pf. διῴκηκα Pl.*Ti*.19e, D.24.202:—**Med.**, fut. -ήσομαι Id.8.13 (also in pass. sense, Hdn.8.7.6): aor. διῳκησάμην D.18.247: pf. (in med. sense) διῴκημαι (v. infr.):—**Pass.**, aor. διῳκήθην Luc.*Nec*.19: pf. διῴκημαι Arist.*Ath*.25.2, dub. l. in Antiph.191.18, D.22.74: plpf. διῴκητο (προ-) Id.23.14; but with both augm. and redupl., pf. δεδιῴκημαι Antiph.155, Macho ap.Ath.8.341c, Phld.*Rh*.2.266 S.:—*keep house*: hence, generally, *control*, *manage*, *administer*, τὴν πόλιν Th.8.21, etc.; τὰ τῆς πόλεως Ar.*Ec*.305; τάς τε οἰκίας καὶ τὰς πόλεις Pl.*Men*. 91a; τὸν κόσμον Id.*Phdr*.246c; τὸν οὐρανόν Id.*Lg*.896e; τὰ ἀνθρώπινα ib.713c; τὸν ἑαυτοῦ βίον Isoc.1.10; τὴν οὐσίαν D.27.50, etc.; τὰ κοινά Id.1.22; τὴν ἀρχήν Arist.*Pol*.1313$^a$35; τὰ μέγιστα ὁ λογισμὸς διῴκηκε Epicur.*Sent*.16; δ. πάντα ἀκριβῶς, of a housekeeper, Lys. 1.7; πολέμους Din.1.69; of a financier, δ. τὰ πρὸς τὴν πόλιν, ἐπὶ τῇ τραπέζῃ, D.27.60, 45.33; πεντεκαίδεκα τάλαντα, ἃ Καλλισθένης διῴκησεν Id.20.33; *administer as deputy*, τὴν λογιστείαν *Stud.Pal*.8.1010.1 (iii/iv A.D.):—Pass., *to be ordered*, *managed*, etc., τύχῃ δ. Hp.*VM*1, Aeschin.1.4; ἅπας ὁ βίος φύσει καὶ νόμοις δ. D.25.15:—Med., *manage after one's own will and pleasure*, τὰ πράγματα διοικήσασθαι Id.4.12: pf. Pass. (in med. sense), ἵν᾽ ἃ βουλόμεθα ὦμεν διῳκημένοι Id.18.178; διοικούμενος οὕτως ἀδίκους πλεονεξίας *managing to make* such iniquitous profits, Id.44.38, cf. 40; διοικεῖσθαι πρὸς ἀλλήλους *act collusively with..*, Id.58.20, cf. 19. b. abs., *exercise authority*, *govern*, τυραννικώτερον Arist.*Pol*.1313$^a$2, cf. 1298$^b$12. 2. *provide*, *furnish*, ἀπορῶ τἆλλα ὁπόθεν διοικῶ D.27.66, cf. Decr.ap.eund.24.27 (Pass.); δ. τὴν ἀδελφήν *provide for*, *settle* her, D.24.202:—Pass., *to be nourished* or *supported*, ὑπό τινος Str.14.2.24; γάλακτι Ath.2.46e (dub. l.). 3. *rent*, *farm*, νομῶν τῶν πρὸς χαλκὸν διοικουμένων *PTeb*.79.8 (ii B.C.), al. 4. *digest* food, D.L.6.34. 5. Rhet., Med., *distribute*, *arrange in a discourse*, D.H.*Rh*.9.4. II. *inhabit distinct places*, Pl.*Ti*.19e:—Med., *live apart*, κατὰ κώμας X.*HG*5.2.5 (s.v.l.; διοικ⟨ι⟩οῖντο Cobet). ⊛ **-ημα**, ατος, τό, *sum of money administered*, Hsch., Suid.s.v. ἀλογίου δίκη. ⊛ **-ησις**, εως, ἡ, prop. *housekeeping*: hence, generally, *internal administration*, τῆς πόλεως Pl.*Prt*.319d, cf. Arist. *Pol*.1287$^a$6, Lys.30.22, etc.; ἐγκύκλιος δ. Arist.*Ath*.43.1; κοινὴ δ. Aeschin.2.149; esp. of *financial administration*, δ. ἱερὰ καὶ ὅσια D. 24.96, cf. X.*HG*6.1.2; *department of finance* in Egypt, *PTeb*.7.4 (ii B.C.), al.; ὅπως .. ἡ δ. γένηται ἱκανή Decr.ap.D.24.27; ὁ ἐπὶ τῇ δ. *treasurer*, *IG*2.251, al., Poll.8.113; ὁ ἐπὶ τῆς διοικήσεως *IG*2$^2$.677, Decr.ap.D.18.38 (in Egypt, = διοικητής, *PRev.Laws*19.7); τὰ περιόντα χρήματα τῆς δ. D.59.4. 2. *farming*, *renting*, [χλωρῶν] *PTeb*.61(*a*).206 (ii B.C.), etc. II. = Lat. *conventus*, *assize-district*, Str.13.4.12, Cic.*Fam*.13.53.2, 67.1, *OGI*458.65 (Eumenia); later, *group of provinces*, *CIL*3.352 (iv A.D.), etc. **-ητής**, οῦ, ὁ, *administrator*, *governor*, στρατοπέδων Men.*Pk*.90, cf. *Kol*.6, Plb.27.13. 2; esp. *treasurer*, Lxx 2*Es*.8.36, al., *IG*9(1).694.144 (Corc.), Plu.2. 179f; *chief financial official* in Egypt, *OGI*53.7 (iii B.C.), *PTeb*.5. 27 (ii B.C.), etc.; = Lat. *procurator*, Str.17.3.25, Plu.*Ant*.67, etc.: Astrol., *controller*, of the Seven Planets, *Corp.Herm*.1.9. **-ητικός**, ή, όν, *controlling*, δύναμις Chrysipp.*Stoic*.2.264, cf. Ptol.*Tetr*.160: c. gen., πολέμων Corn.*ND*20. II. *digestive*, Orib.45.29.17. III. *pertaining to the chief financial officer*, χρηματισμοί *PTeb*.24.61 (ii B.C.), al.; ὑπηρέτης *PFlor*.312.7 (i A.D.). **-ήτρια**, ἡ, *housekeeper*, Sch.Ar. *Ec*.212. **-ήτωρ**, τορος, ὁ, = διοικητής, of the planets, *Corp.Herm.*

1.14. -ίζω, Att. fut. -ιῶ D.5.10:—*cause to live apart, disperse*, opp. συνοικίζω, δ. τὰς πόλεις *break* them *up* into villages (κῶμαι), Isoc. 5.43, cf. Arist.*Pol.*1311ᵃ14; τὴν Θηβαίων πόλιν διοικιεῖν D.l.c.; δ. Μαντινεῖς ἐκ μιᾶς πόλεως εἰς πλείους Plb.4.27.6:—Pass., διῳκίσθη ἡ Μαντίνεια τετραχῇ X.*HG*5.2.7; διῳκισμένοι κατὰ κώμας D.19.81: generally, *to be scattered abroad*, Pl.*Smp.*193a; *remove, migrate*, ἐκ Κολλυτοῦ εἰς.. Lys.32.14; διῳκισμένοι τινός *separated from*.., Luc. *Charid.*19: metaph. of rich and poor, διῳκίσμεθα καὶ δύο πόλεις ἔχομεν D.H.6.36. -ισις, εως, ἡ, *removal, change of abode*, Lys. 32.14. -ισμός, ὁ, = foreg., Ph.1.459, Plu.*Cam.*9; *living apart* (cf. διοικίζω fin.), D.H.6.81.

**διοικο-δομέω**, *build across, wall off*, Th.4.69, 8.90. 2. *to set a partition-wall between*: metaph., ἰσθμὸν καὶ ὅρον δ. τῆς τε κεφαλῆς καὶ τοῦ στήθους Pl.*Ti.*69e; δ. τοῦ θώρακος .. τὸ κύτος ibid. II. *barricade*, ὁδούς D.S.13.56. -δομή, ἡ, *construction*, Aristeas 87. -δόμησις, εως, ἡ, *fortification*, *IG*4.757*A*42, *B*33 (Troezen, ii B.C.). -νομέω, strengthd. for οἰκονομέω, Phld.*Oec.*p.9 J. (dub.), Anon.Lond.22.49, Poll.5.156:—Pass., Arist.*Mu.*400ᵇ32.

**διοινόομαι**, Pass., *to be quite full of wine*, pf. part. διῳνωμένος Pl. *Lg.*775c.

**διοινοχοέω**, *mix wine for drinking*, Posidon.1 J. (Pass.).

**δίοιξις**, εως, ἡ, (διοίγνυμι) *opening*, ἀνθῶν Thphr.*CP*2.19.3.

**διοιστέον**, (διαφέρω) *one must move round*, ὄμμα πανταχῇ E.*Ph.* 265.

**διοϊστεύω**, *shoot an arrow between*, ὅς κε..διοϊστεύσῃ πελέκεων Od. 19.578, al. II. abs., καί κεν διοϊστεύσειας thou mightest *reach it with an arrow*, i.e. thou art but a bow-shot from it, 12.102.

**διοιστρέω**, strengthd. for οἰστρέω, D.S.4.12, Philostr.*VA*1.33 (Pass.).

**διοίσω, διοίσομαι**, v. διαφέρω.

**διοιχνέω**, *go through*, ἀσινὴς δ' αἰῶνα διοιχνεῖ A.*Eu.*315 (anap.), cf. Lyc.10. II. abs., *wander about*, ἐν πέτρῃσιν *h.Hom.*19.10.

**διοίχομαι**, fut. -οιχήσομαι: pf. -οίχημαι Hdt.4.136:—*to be quite gone by*, ἡμέραι διοίχηνται Id.l.c.; of persons and things, *to be clean gone, to have perished*, τἀμὰ γὰρ διοίχεται A.*Fr.*138, cf. S.*Aj.*973, E. *Or.*181 (lyr.), Ar.*Th.*609, etc.; rare in Prose, Hdt.l.c., Pl.*Phd.* 87e. II. *to be gone through, ended*, ὁ λόγος διοίχεται S.*OC*574 (codd. recc. for διέρχεται); χἠ δίκη δ. E.*Supp.*530.

**διοκνέω**, *to be much afraid*, Antig.Car.ap.Ath.13.607e.

**διοκωχή**, ἡ, = διοχή, *cessation*, Th.3.87; esp. *armistice*, D.C.39. 47, etc.

**διολισθάνω** (in Pl.*Ly.*216d codd. -αίνω, cf. Luc.*Cont.*1, al., Lib. *Or.*11.225), Ion. aor. -ωλίσθησα Hp.*Art.*63: aor. 2 inf. διολισθεῖν Ar.*Nu.*434:—*slip through*, ὑπὸ τοὺς δακτύλους Hp.*Art.*40; of a bone put out, ib.63; δ. τοὺς χρήστας *to give* them *the slip*, Ar.l.c.; δ. καὶ διαδύεται ἡμᾶς Pl.l.c.; ἐπ' ἄκρων δ. κυμάτων, of a ship, Luc.*Dom.* 12: abs., *slip away*, Id.*Anach.*28,29; δ. τὴν γλῶσσαν *slipping* with his tongue, of one drunken, Id.*Vit.Auct.*12.

❀ **διολκή**, ἡ, (διέλκω) *drawing away*, διολκὴν εἰς τἀναντία γίνεσθαι Phld.*Mus.*p.35 K.; *extraction* of the foetus, Sor.2.62 (pl.). II. *diversity of opinion*, S.E.*M.*8.322, Numen.ap.Eus.*PE*14.5.

❀ **δίολκος**, ὁ, *slipway* for passage of ships across the Isthmus of Corinth, Str.7.2.1.

**διόλλυμι** or -ύω (Them.*Or.*32.356a), fut. -ολέσω, Att. -ολῶ S.*Tr.* (v. infr.):—*destroy utterly, bring to naught*, Emp.139, S.*OT*442, *Tr.* 1028 (lyr.), Pl.*Cri.*47c, etc.; δ. γυναῖκα *ruin* a woman, E.*El.*921:—Pass., with fut. -ολοῦμαι, pf. -όλωλα, *perish utterly, come to naught*, Th.3.40, etc.; διώλετο ἔκ τινος by some one's hand, S.*OT*225. II. *blot out of one's mind, forget*, εἰδὼς διώλεσα ib.318.

**διόλου**, Adv. for δι' ὅλου (cf. καθόλου), *altogether*, Phoc.2A, Arist.*Po.*1459ᵇ16, etc.; of Time, *always*, Lxx 1 *Ma.*6.18, *AP*5.157 (Asclep.), *Lyr.Alex.Adesp.*37.5, *Ev.Jo.*19.23, etc.

**διολούφειν**· διατίλλειν ἢ διασιλλαίνειν, Hsch.

**διολοφύρομαι** [ῠ], strengthd. for ὀλοφύρομαι, πρὸς αὐτόν Plb.21. 26.11.

**δίομαι**, v. δίω.

**διομᾰλ-ίζω**, pf. διωμάλικα Phld.*Po.Herc.*1425.34:—*maintain a standard*, ἀρετὴ διομαλίζουσα Id.*Rh.*1.264S., cf. Longin.33.4, Plu. *Cat.Ma.*4, S.E.*M.*11.207; *to be consistent*, of observations, ib.5. 103. -ισμός, ὁ, *consistency, steadiness*, τῶν πράξεων S.E.*P.*3.244, cf. *M.*11.206: pl., *uniform periods*, in illness, Herod.Med.ap.Orib. 7.8.5. -ύνω, *distribute evenly*, Plu.2.130d.

❀ **Διομᾰνής**, ές, *driven mad by Zeus* or *raging against Zeus*, Hsch.

**διομβρ-έω**, *soak through*, τὰ χώματα *PPetr.*2p.17. -ος, ον, *wet through*, Arist.*Pr.*870ᵇ25; *rainy*, χώρα Ath.Med.ap.Orib.9.12. 13.

**Διομειᾰλαζών**, όνος, ὁ, *a braggart of the deme Diomea*, Ar.*Ach.*605.

**Διομήδεια** ἀνάγκη *absolute, dire* necessity; -εία Pl.*R.*493d codd.; -ειος Hsch., Ar.*Ec.*1029, Zen.3.8; proverbial expression variously expld.

**Διομήδης**, εος, ὁ, *Jove-counselled*; only as a pr. n. *Diomedes*.

**Διομηνία**, Ep. -ίη, ἡ, *wrath of Zeus*, Orph.*Fr.*285.21 (dub.).

**διομήτωρ**, ορος, ὁ, Pythag. name for δυάς, *Theol.Ar.*12.

**διόμνῡμι** or -ύω (*BGU*647.22 (ii A.D.)), *swear solemnly, declare on oath*, esp. in courts of justice, c. fut. inf., ὅρκον αὐτῷ προσβαλὼν διώμοσεν, ἦ μὴν.. δουλώσειν S.*Tr.*255; δ. κτείνειν (κτενεῖν Cobet) Lycurg.127:—more freq. in Med., διόμνῠμαι, fut. -ομοῦμαι: aor. -ωμοσάμην, *vow, asseverate*, S.*Aj.*1233, *Tr.*378: c. inf., Ῥωμύλον ἰδεῖν Plu.*Num.*2; ζημιώσειν Id.*Cam.*39: esp. of the διωμοσία (q.v.), δ. ὅρκον Antipho 5.12; ταῦτα διωμόσω ἐν τῇ ἀντιγραφῇ *you swore to* this *in the oath* you took in support of the indictment, Pl.*Ap.*27c, cf. Lys.3.4; δ. ὑπέρ τινος Antipho 1.28; ἠρνεῖσθε διομνύμενοι *on oath*, D.18.286; διομόσασθαι τὸν υἱόν *swear by* his head, Id.47.73; τοὺς θεούς Din.1.47.

❀ **διομολογ-έω**, *make an agreement*, ἀποστήσεσθαι X.*Ages.*3.5; *agree, concede*, c. acc. et inf., Luc.*Nigr.*26:—Pass., *to be agreed on*, mostly in pf., διωμολογημένον ἐμοί τε καὶ σοί Pl.*Euthd.*282c, cf. *BGU*350.17 (ii A.D.), etc.; ἡ Ἀσία διωμολόγηται παρ' ἡμῶν βασιλέως εἶναι Isoc.4.137; also τὰ διομολογούμενα Plb.31.19.1: aor., δεῖ διομολογηθῆναι ὅτι.. Pl.*R.*456c. II. more freq. in Med., aor. -ωμολογησάμην, *agree mutually, agree upon* certain points, *take* them *as granted, concede, grant*, δ. τὴν δικαιοσύνην ἀρετὴν εἶναι ib.350d; τι ib.507a, al.; δ. τοὺς τόκους *agree on* the interest to be paid, D.56.5; δ. περί τινος Pl.*Tht* 169e, Is.7.39; ἅπαντα διωμολογημένος πρὸς τὸν πατέρα *having agreed* with my father to do everything, D.28.14: c inf. pres., Is.3.28, fut., ibid., aor., 8.23; folld. by a relat. Conj., δ. πότερον.. Pl.*R.*394d; δ. εἰ.. Id.*Grg.*500e; τί ποτ' ἔστιν Id.*Sph.*260a. -ησις, εως, ἡ, *convention*, πρός τινα Plb.3.27.9 (pl.), D.S.9.10 (pl.). -ητέον, *one must agree on* or *concede*, Pl.*R.*527b, al. II. -έος, α, ον, *to be conceded*, Id.*Prm.*14 b. -ία, ἡ, *agreement, contract*, δ. ποιεῖν περί τινος Is.11.21,23; γίνεται δ. τῆς ὑπουργίας Arist.*EN*1164ᵃ34.

**δῖον**, v. δῖος. **δίον**, v. δείδω.

**διονομάζω**, *distinguish by a name*, Pl.*Plt.*263d:—Pass., διωνόμασται *have received a name*, Arist.*HA*494ᵇ20, cf. *Mete.*350ᵇ12. II. Pass., *to be widely known*, Isoc.20.19, Str.2.5.17, D.H.*Th.*4; ἐπ' ἀνδρείᾳ Id.5.25.

**Δῐόνῡ**, as voc. of Διόνυσος in Phryn.Com.10 (Meineke); cf. διονῦς· ὁ γυναικίας καὶ παράθηλυς, Hsch.; διοννύς· ἡ γυναικεία καὶ θῆλυς ἐσθής, Eust.629.42.

**δῐόνυξ**, -ῠχος, ὁ, *double nail*, as a superficial measure, Hero *Stereom.*1.95.

**Δῐόνυξος**, coined as etym. of Διόνυσος, Corn.*ND*30, *EM*277.35 (νύττω, from the legend of his birth).

**Δῐονῡσ-ᾰλέξανδρος**, ὁ, *Dionysus masquerading as Paris*, title of play by Cratinus, *POxy.*663, etc. -ια (sc. ἱερά), τά, *festival of Dionysus*, *IG*1².57, Foed.ap.Th.5.23, etc.; τὰ ἐν ἄστει *IG*2².1299.31; τὰ ἀστικά Th.5.20; τὰ μεγάλα *IG*2².654.41; τὰ κατ' ἀγρούς Ar.*Ach.*202, Aeschin.1.157; τὰ ἐπὶ Ληναίῳ *IG*2.741.10; elsewh., *SIG*285.14 (Erythrae), *IG*12(1).6.3 (Rhodes, from Erythrae), etc.; Δ. παίδων ib.11 (2).105 (Delos, iii B.C.), al. -ιάζω, *keep the Dionysia*: Διονυσιάζουσαι, αἱ, title of play by Timocles, Ath.6.223b: hence, *live festively* or *extravagantly*, Luc.*Dem.Enc.*25, Philomnest.2. -ιακός, ή, όν, *belonging to the Dionysia* or *to Dionysus*, Δ. θέατρον Th.8.93; ἀγών Arist.*Rh.*1416ᵃ32, cf. *Pol.*1323ᵃ2: Διονυσιακά, τά, *poems on the legend of Bacchus*, e.g. by Nonnus: -κόν, τό, prob., = Διονύσιος III, Gal.12. 423. ❀ -ιάς, άδος, ἡ, pecul. fem. of Διονυσιακός, θυμέλα Pratin.1.2; λοιβά E.*HF*894 (lyr.); Πηγή Paus.4.36.5. 2. as Subst., *Bacchante*, Id.3.13.7. 3. a plaster, Orib.*Fr.*96, Philum.ap.Aët.16.38. 4. name of Naxos, Call.*Aet.*3.1.41. II. = ἀνδρόσαιμον, Dsc.3.156; = κατανάγκη, Ps.-Dsc.4.131. -ιασταί, οἱ, guild of *worshippers of D.*, *IG*2².1325.20, 12(1).155.43, 12(3).104.17 (Nisyros), etc. -ιον (sc. ἱερόν), τό, *the temple of Dionysus*, Th.8.93, Ar.*Fr.*131, Paus.1.43. 5, etc. ❀ -ιος, α, ον, *of Dionysus*, ὄρβα B.*Scol.Oxy.Fr.*1.9. II. Δ., ὁ (sc. μήν), name of month in Aetolia, *IG*9(1).374, cf. *SIG*524.14 (Crete), 1009.20 (Chalcedon), etc. III. Διονύσιον, τό, fruit of κισσός, Dsc.2.179. -ίσκος, ὁ, Dim. of Διόνυσος, *person who has bony excrescences on the temples*, Heliod.ap.Orib.46.28.2, Gal.19.443.

**Δῐονῡσο-δότης**, ου, ὁ, *bestower of Dionysus*, Olymp.*in Phd.*p.111 N. -κόλᾰκες, οἱ, nickname of the τεχνῖται Διονυσιακοί, Theopomp. Hist.267, Arist.*Rh.*1405ᵃ23, Chares ap.Ath.12.538f, Alciphr.3.48: hence, II. *flatterers of Dionysius* the Tyrant, and the school of Plato, Epicur.*Fr.*238, Thphr.ap.Ath.8.249f, 10.435e. -κουροπυρώνων, Comic compd., corrupt in Cratin.208. -μᾰνέω, *to be full of Bacchic frenzy*, Philostr.*VA*5.32. -νυμφάς, άδος, ἡ, *burnet, Poterium Sanguisorba*, Plin.*HN*24.165. -πλάτων [ᾰ], ωνος, ὁ, *double herm of Dionysus and Plato* as a signet, *POxy.*105. 20. -φόροι· ἀρχή τις ἐν Συρακούσαις, Hsch.

❀ **Δῐόνῡσος**, ὁ, Od.11.325, S.*Ant.*957, etc.:—Ep. also **Διώνῡσος**, Il. 6.132, 14.325, Od.24.74, Hes.*Th.*947, Archil.77, Thgn.976:—Boeot. **Διώνουσος**, *IG*7.2468a, al., and **Δεύνυσος** (q.v.):—also **Δίνυσος**, Ἀρχ.Ἐφ.1913.221 (Mytilene): **Διένυσος**, *IG*12(7).78 (Amorgos):—*Dionysus*, Διονύσου γοναί, name of comedies by Polyzelus and Anaxandrides, *IG*14.1098.

**δῐόνῠχος**, ον, *with cloven hoof*, ζῷα *EM*811.16.

**διοξειῶν**, v. ὀξύς.

**Δῐό-παις**, παιδος, ὁ, *son of Zeus*, *AP*9.525. -πᾱν, πᾶνος, ὁ, *Zeus-Pan*, *Epigr.Gr.*827b (Caesarea Panias). -πεμπτος, ον, *sent from Zeus*, ὄνειροι Eust.48.29.

**διόπερ** or δι' ὅπερ, v. διό.

❀ **Διοπετής**, ές, *that fell from Zeus*, ἄγαλμα E.*IT*977; Παλλάδιον D.H.2.66; πέλτη Plu.*Num.*13, cf. D.H.2.71; ὄρνις Alciphr.3.59; Μένιππος Luc.*Icar.*2; οἰκίαι, i.e. 'taboo', Aristopho 3; διοπετές (sc. ἄγαλμα), τό, *Act.Ap.*19.35.

❀ **διοπεύω**, *to be captain of* a ship, δ. τὴν ναῦν (Harp., διοπτεύων codd.) Test.ap.D.35.20,34.

❀ **διόπη**, ἡ, (διά, ὀπή) kind of *ear-ring*, Ar.*Fr.*320.10, *IG*1².291, 2.652*B*26. 2. kind of *shoe*, Hsch.

**διοπλήκταν** (prob. l.)· ἰσχυροπλήκτην, Hsch.

**διοπομπ-έομαι**, = ἀποδιοπ. (q.v.), Hsch., Suid., *EM*125.33. **-ή**, = πέμψις, *Et.Gud.*147.54.

⊛ **δίοπος** (A) [ῐ], ὁ, (διέπω) *ruler, commander*, A.*Pers.*44 (anap.), E. *Rh.*741 (anap.); θεὸς δ. πάντων Ph.2.369, cf. 1.145. II. *captain of a ship*, Hp.*Epid.*7.36, 5.74, *EM*18.28.

**δίοπος** (B) [ῐ], ον, (ὀπή) *with two holes*, φῶτες *IG*4.1488.46 (Epid.); αὐλοί Ath.4.176f.

**διοπτάω**, *roast thoroughly*, Zos.Alch.p.247 B.

**διοπτ-εία**, ἡ, *seeing through*, τὴν δ. ἀκώλυτον παρέχειν Procl.*Hyp.* 3.17. II. *use of the* διόπτρα, Hero *Deff.*135.8. **-ευσις**, εως, ἡ, *examination with the* διόπτρα, Ptol.*Alm.*5.1, al. **-ευτήριον**, τό, dub. sens. in Petos.*Fr.*24 R. **-εύω**, *watch accurately, spy about*, ἠὲ διοπτεύσων Il.10.451; *look into*, στέγος S.*Aj.*307, cf. Antipho Soph.6, Critias *Fr.*53 D.; δ. τί.. X.*Cyr.*8.2.10: c. acc., D.C. 52.37:—Pass., *to be overlooked* by a neighbour, Agath.5.6. II. *take a sight*, διὰ τοῦ μήκους τῆς σύριγγος Hero *Bel.*86.7; esp. *through the* διόπτρα, Id.*Dioptr.*4. ⊛**-ήρ**, ῆρος, ὁ, *spy, scout*, στρατοῦ Il.10. 562: in late Prose, Agath.2.2. II. διάγγελοι καὶ διοπτῆρες, the *optiones* and *tesserarii* of the Romans, Plu.*Galb.*24. III. = διόπτρα III, Aët.16.105. **-ης**, ου, ὁ, *looker through*, ὦ Ζεῦ διόπτα! says Dicaeopolis in Ar.*Ach.*435, holding up a ragged garment to the light. II. = foreg. I, E.*Rh.*234 (lyr.). III. = διόπτρα I, Hsch. **-ιον**, τό, *sighting instrument for the* ἑλέπολις, Bito 53. 1. **-ος**, ον, *transparent*, Alex.Aphr.*in Sens.*46.17; τὰ δ. ib.45.12.

**διόπτρ-α**, ἡ, *optical instrument* for measuring angles, altitudes, etc., Euc.*Phaen.*p.10 M., Plb.10.46.1, Attal.ap.Hipparch.1.10.24, Gem. 1.4, Ptol.*Alm.*5.14, etc.; ἡ τῶν δ. θεωρία Gem.5.11. 2. *aperture-sight* in a torsion-engine, Ph.*Bel.*64.9, 76.48. II. *plate of talc* for glazing windows, Str.12.2.10. III. = διαστολεύς, Aët.16.89, Paul.Aeg.6.73. IV. σημεῖον ἐν θυτικῇ, Hsch. **-ίζω**, *use the speculum*, Paul.Aeg.3.75. **-ικός**, ή, όν, *of, belonging to the use of the* διόπτρα, ὄργανον δ., = διόπτρα, Str.2.1.35; τὰ δ. *the science of dioptrics*, Plu.2.1093e: also **-κή**, ἡ, Procl.*in Euc.*p.42 F. **-ιον**, τό, *small speculum*, Leonid.ap.Paul.Aeg.6.78. **-ισμός**, ὁ, *use of the speculum*, Sor.2.40, Paul.Aeg.6.73. **-ίτης** [ρῑ] λίθος *talc*, *PHolm.* 3.39. **-ον**, τό, *means for seeing through*, οἶνος γὰρ ἀνθρώπῳ δ. Alc. 53. II. = διόπτρα I, Hsch. s. v. ἀστραβιστήρ.

**διοπωπ-έας**· τοὺς βασιλεῖς, *EM*278.12. **-εύω**, = διέπω, *AB* 237.

**διορ-ᾱτικός**, ή, όν, *clear-sighted*, Ph.1.478: c. gen., Luc.*Salt.*4 (Comp.); τῶν ὄντων Max.Tyr.16.3, cf. Asp.*in EN*79.28. **-άω**, *see through, see clearly*, X.*An.*5.2.30; δ. τὸ ἀληθές Pl.*Prm.*136c, etc. II. *distinguish*, τοὺς.. κολακεύοντας καὶ τοὺς.. θεραπεύοντας Isoc.2.28; τὰς φύσεις τῶν ἀνθρώπων Id.3.16; πότε ὑπάρχει καὶ πότε οὐ οὐ ῥᾴδιον διιδεῖν Arist.*Mete.*390a20; δόξας διορᾶν Epicur.*Nat.*15. 24, cf. 11.8.

**διοργᾰν-ίζω**, *dispose suitably*, in Pass., Zos.Alch.p.251 B., Syn. Alch.p.62 B. **-όομαι**, *to be provided with organs*, Iamb.*VP*15.66; of the foetus, Agath.4.25. ⊛ **-ωσις**, εως, ἡ, *formation, fashioning*, Iamb.*VP*15.67; *structural differentiation*, Procl.*in Prm.*p.616 S., Simp.*in Cael.*389.19.

**διοργίζομαι**, *to be very angry*, Plb.2.8.13; τινί Lxx 3*Ma.*3.1 (v.l.), Plu.*Ages.*6; διωργισμένος Phld.*Ir.*p.9 W.; διοργισθείς D.S.14.14.

**διοργυι-όομαι**, *stretch out the arms*: διωργυιωμένος *with arms akimbo*, Hipparch.1.7.22: metaph., Ἀνάγκην -ωμένην ἐν παντὶ τῷ κόσμῳ Dam.*Pr.*123 bis. **-ος**, ον, *two fathoms deep, high*, etc., Hdt. 4.195, X.*Cyn.*2.5.

**διορθ-εύω**, = sq., only in E.*Supp.*417 μὴ διορθεύων λόγους not *judging rightly of* words. ⊛ **-όω**, *make straight*, Hp.*Art.*38. 2. δ. λόγον *tell* my tale *aright*, Pi.*O.*7.21. II. *set right, restore to order*, Isoc.9.47; δ. λόγοις ἔριν *make up* a quarrel, E.*Hel.*1159 (lyr.); δ. ἀδικήματα *amend* them, Plb.4.24.4; δ. τὴν Ἰλιάδα *correct* or *revise* it, Plu.*Alex.*8, cf. *Alc.*7 (Pass.), Porph.*Plot.*7, al.:—Med., *amend for oneself*, διορθοῦσθαι τὰ μέλλοντα Isoc.4.181; τἀγνοούμενα D.*Ep.*1.3; σφᾶς αὐτοὺς Plb.24.10.12; δ. πίστιν *make good, redeem* it, Id.1.7.12; τὰ προσοφειλόμενα *pay off*, Id.12.28.5 (cf. III); *maintain in argument*, Aeschin.2.112:—but freq. like Act., ἐξέστω διορθώσασθαι τὰς συνθήκας *SIG*581.85 (Crete, ii B.C.); δ. τὴν Ἰλλυριῶν ἄγνοιαν Plb.3.16.4, etc.; also διορθοῦσθαι ὑπέρ τινος *take full security* for.., D.33. 11. III. *pay*, τὸ λοιπόν *PHib.*1.63.13 (iii B.C.); τόκον *POxy.*483. 16 (ii A.D.):—Med., *PRev.Laws* 18.14, al. (iii B.C.); φόρους *PEleph.* 14.1 (iii B.C.), cf. *PSI*5.509.13 (iii B.C.), etc.; ἀργύριον *BCH*46.420 (Caria, i B.C.). IV. *reconcile*, τινά τινι Philostr.*VS*1.17.2.

**διορθρίζω**, *rise early*, v.l. in Lxx 1*Ki.*29.10.

⊛ **διόρθ-ωμα**, ατος, τό, *making straight, setting right*, Hp.*Art.*33 (pl.); *instrument* or *means of setting right*, δ. τι ἐντιθέναι εἰς.. ib.37; *means of correction*, Arist.*Pol.*1284b20. II. *amendment*, Plu.*Num.*17; *revision*, νόμου *PRev.Laws* 57.1 (iii B.C.). **-ωσις**, εως, ἡ, *making straight*, as in the setting of a limb, Hp.*Off.*16, cf. *Mochl.*38; *setting straight, restoration*, οἰκοδομημάτων καὶ ὁδῶν Arist.*Pol.*1321b21. 2. *correction, chastisement*, ἐπὶ διορθώσει Plb.2.56.14; διορθώσεως σφίσι δεῖν D.H.6.20. II. generally, *amendment, correction*, of men, Plb.7.11.2: pl., Arist.*Pol.*1317a35, Plb.3.118.12; τῶν νόμων *IG*9(1). 694.137 (Corc.); *correction*, ἐρωτημάτων Arist.*SE*176b34, cf. *Pol.* 1275a20; εἰς δ. ἄγειν Plb.3.58.4; δ., opp. βλάβη, Id.5.88.2; ὑδάτων Orib.5.4 tit. 2. *right treatment*, τινός Pl.*Lg.*642a. III. *recension, revised edition of* a work, Sch.Il.10.397: in pl., *emendations*, D.L.3.66. IV. *payment*, ὀψωνίων Plb.5.50.7, cf. *PTeb.*61(*a*). 33 (ii B.C.). **-ωτέος**, α, ον, *to be set*, of joints, Hp.*Mochl.*38. II. **-τέον**, *one must correct*, Ath.Med.ap.Orib.*inc.*5.1; δόγματα Simp.*in Epict.*p.28 D. **-ωτήρ**, ῆρος, ὁ, = sq., *IG*9(1).694.138 (pl.). ⊛**-ωτής**, οῦ, ὁ, *a corrector*, τῶν σοφῶν Lxx *Wi.*7.15; τῆς πολιτείας Plu.*Sol.*16; = Lat. *corrector civitatium*, Arr.*Epict.*3.7.1. 2. esp. *of books, editor, reviser*, D.S.15.6, Gal.8.758. **-ωτικός**, ή, όν, *corrective*, Arist.*EN*1131a1; τὰ -κά, title of works on textual criticism by Seleucus and Crates, Sch.Il.*Oxy.*221 xv 25, xvii 31. Adv. **-κῶς** Eust. 936.43.

⊛ **διορία**, v. διωρία.

⊛ **διορ-ίζω**, Ion. **διουρίζω**, Att. fut. -ιῶ Pl.*Lg.*860e: fut. Med. in pass. sense (v. infr. I. 3):—*draw a boundary through, delimit, separate*, Hdt.4.42; τὴν Εὐρώπην ἀπὸ τῆς Ἀσίης D.S.1.55; δίχα δ. Pl.*Sph.* 267a: metaph., οὐ στενῷ τῷ ἰσθμῷ διώρισται ἡ ἱστορία πρὸς τὸ ἐγκώμιον Luc.*Hist.Conscr.*7. 2. *distinguish, determine, define*, τὰ οὐνόματα Hdt.4.45; θεοῖσι.. γέρα τίς ἄλλος ἢ 'γὼ.. διώρισεν; A.*Pr.* 440; πτῆσιν οἰωνῶν.. διώρισα, of auguries, ib.489; σῖτον δ' εἰδέναι δ. so as to know it, Id.*Fr.*182; γλυκὺν οἶνον καὶ οἰνώδεα Hp.*Acut.*50; δ. ἀκούσιά τε καὶ ἑκούσια Pl.*Lg.*860e, cf. *Cra.*391d; δ. περὶ ἐνεργείας τί ἐστιν Arist.*Metaph.*1048a26; *define* logically, δ. κατὰ τὰς διαφορὰς Id.*Top.*146b20, cf. *EN*1103a3 (Pass.), etc.:—Med., διορίζεσθαι τῷ στόματι τὰ γράμματα *pronounce clearly*, Alex.301. 3. *determine, declare*, τοιαῦτα φῆμαι μαντικαὶ διώρισαν S.*OT*723: c. inf., *determine* one to be so and so, καθαρὸν διώρισεν εἶναι D.20.158: with inf. omitted, οἱ συγγενεῖς μῆνές με μικρὸν καὶ μέγαν διώρισαν S.*OT*1083:—Med., δηλοῖ καὶ δ. ὅτι.. D.18.40; διορισαμένων ὅπως.. Id.56.11; διορίσασθαι τίς αἱρετώτατος βίος Arist.*Pol.*1323a15: pf. Pass. in med. sense, ἃ χρὴ ποιεῖν διωρίσμεθα D.24.192:—Pass., διώρισται ὁπότερον .. And.4.8; διωρισμένον *it being prescribed*, Lys.30.4; τὸν νόμον ὡς ἐτέθη καὶ πρὸς οὓς διωρίσθη D.59.93; ἐν τῷ διωρισμένῳ χρόνῳ *PTeb.* 105.33 (ii B.C.), etc.: impers., διοριεῖται περί τινος we *will give precepts* about.., Hp.*Art.*9; ἐν οἷς [λόγοις] διώρισται περὶ τῶν ἠθικῶν Arist.*Pol.*1282b20, cf. *EN*1136a10. 4. *draw distinctions, lay down definitions*, οὐδ' ὁτιοῦν διορίζων D.21.104; τοῦτό μοι.. διόρισον Pl. *Grg.*488d:—mostly in Med., δ. περί τινος And.3.12, Isoc.3.5, Arist. *Ph.*200b15; πρὸς ἀλλήλους Pl.*Grg.*457c; δίκην διωρίσω *didst settle the conditions of* the trial, Ar.*Ach.*364. II. *remove across the frontier, banish*, ἔξω τῶν ὅρων Pl.*Lg.*873e; τὸν ἐνθένδε πόλεμον εἰς τὴν ἤπειρον Isoc.4.174; τινὰ ὑπὲρ θυμέλας E.*Ion* 46: generally, *carry abroad*, στράτευμα Τροίαν ἔπι Id.*Hel.*394; δ. πόδα to depart, ib.828. III. *send out a branch*, of the Bosporus, Plb.4.43.7. IV. Pass., *to be discontinuous*, opp. συνάπτω, Arist.*Cat.*4b28; διωρισμένος, opp. συνεχής, ib.20. **-ισις**, εως, ἡ, *distinction*, Pl.*Lg.*777b; *separation*, Arist. *Ph.*213b26. **-ισμα**, ατος, τό, *ordinance*, Porph.*Abst.*1.7. **-ισμός**, ὁ, *division, distinction*, Pl.*Ti.*38c, Arist.*EN*1134b33, Porph.*Abst.*3. 20. II. *logical distinction*, Pl.*Plt.*282c; *definition*, Arist.*SE*168a 23, al. III. Math., *particular enunciation* of a problem, Procl.*in Euc.*p.203 F. 2. *statement of limits of possibility* of a problem, Apollon.Perg.*Con.Praef.*, Archim.*Sph.Cyl.*2.4, Phld.*Acad.Ind.*p.17 M. **-ιστέον**, *one must distinguish*, Pl.*Lg.*874d, Arist.*Ph.*204a 2, Longin.11.3, etc. **-ιστικός**, ή, όν, *capable of distinguishing*, S.E.*M.*10.128: -ιστική (sc. τέχνη), ἡ, Syrian.*in Metaph.*56.3. 2. *limiting*, Iamb.*in Nic.*pp.88, 89 P.

**διορκ-ίζω**, *adjure*, *Sammelb.*4324.13:—Pass., of an oath, *to be sworn*, dub. in Wilcken *Chr.*110 *A* 27 (ii B.C.). **-ισμός**, ὁ, *assurance on oath*, Plb.16.26.6.

**διορμάομαι**, *to be impelled*, c. inf., θεῖν Max.Tyr.41.5.

⊛ **διορμίζω**, strengthd. for ὁρμίζω, τὰς ναῦς Longus 2.25:—Pass., D.S.20.88: metaph., διορμίζεται ὁ βίος Hierocl.p.56 A.

**διόρνῡμαι**, *hurry through*, A.*Supp.*552 (lyr.).

**δίορος**, = διαστάτης, Hsch.; *stone used in the game* ἐφεδρισμός, Poll.9.119.

**διορόω**, *turn into serum*, Hp.*Morb.*1.30, Gal.19.93:—Pass., *become serous*, of the blood, Hp.*Steril.*213, Arist.*HA*521a13; of milk, ib.521b34.

**διορρωδέω**, f. l. in D.Chr.3.69.

**διορ-ῠγή**, ἡ, = διωρυχή, Lxx *Je.*38(31).9. **-υγμα**, ατος, τό, *cut, canal*, as that across the isthmus of Mount Athos, Th.4.109. II. *digging through, house-breaking*, Lxx *Ex.*22.2(1), *Je.*2.34. III. *hole made in wall by* χελώνη, Aen.Tact.32.12. IV. *siege-mine*, D.S.20.94. **-υκτρὶς** χελώνη *battering*-ram, Apollod.*Poliorc.*138. 19. **-υξις**, εως, ἡ, *digging through*, Sch.Theoc.1.67. **-ύσσω**, Att. -ττω, *dig through*, διὰ τάφρον ὀρύξας *having dug* a trench *across* or *along*, Od.21.120; τοῖχον δ., = τοιχωρυχέω, Hdt.9.37, cf. Ar.*Pl.* 565, Th.2.3, D.54.37; δεσμωτήριον Id.25.56; οἰκίαν X.*Smp.*4.30, *PPetr.*3 p.60: c. acc. loci, τὸν Ἄθω Lys.2.29, cf. Pl.*Lg.*699a, D.6.30:—Pass., *Ev.Matt.*24.43. 2. metaph., *undermine, ruin*, D.45.30; φιλίαν Lib.*Or.*1.123; δημοκρατίαν Id.*Decl.*1.41:—Pass., διορωρυγμένα δωροδοκίαις Plu.*Phoc.*12, cf. Him.*Ecl.*5.6 (but *to be entrenched* in our *several* cities, D.9.28). II. *worm out*, ἀπόρρητα Bato 6; τὰ βουλευόμενα Plu.2.87c. III. Pass., *to be shut up in a funeral vault*, D.S.4.43. **-ῠχή**, ἡ, = διωρυχή, Χερσονήσου D.7.40; φρεάτων Ph.1.626; τοίχων Lib.*Decl.*8.19: metaph., *undermining*, νόμων, δικαστηρίων, Id.*Or.*63.21.

**διορχέομαι**, *dance across* or *along*, Opp.*H.*5.440. II. *dance a match*, Ar.*V.*1481.

**διόρωσις**, εως, ἡ, *becoming* or *making serous*, Hp.*Morb.*1.30.

⊛ **δῖος**, δῖα (Hom., v. infr.), δῖον, fem. δία in E.*Rh.*226 (lyr.), *IT*404 (lyr.) (δίη Hes.*Th.*260 codd.); fem. δῖος E.*Ba.*599 (anap.):—in Ep., *heavenly*, δ. γένος Il.9.538, etc., used by Hom., 1. of goddesses,

δῖα θεά 10.290; more freq. δῖα θεάων, with superl. force, 18.388, 19.6, etc.; δαίμονα δῖον Hes.*Th.*991. **2.** of illustrious men or women, *noble*, Il.2.221, etc.; δῖα γυναικῶν *noblest* of women, Od.4.305; *excellent*, δ. ὑφορβός 16.20, al. **3.** of nations, etc., δῖοι Ἀχαιοί Il. 5.451; δ. Πελασγοί Od.19.177; δ. ἑταῖροι Il.5.692; of cities, as Elis, 2.615; Lacedaemon, Od.3.326. **4.** of a *noble* horse, Il.8.185, 23. 346. **5.** of things, esp. of the powers of nature, *divine, awful, marvellous*, αἰθέρος ἐκ δίης, εἰς ἅλα δῖαν, χθὼν δῖα, Il.16.365, 1.141, 14.347, cf. Emp.109.2; δῖον πῦρ E.*Alc.*5, etc.; δῖα Χάρυβδις Od.12. 104. **II.** first in Trag. as Adj. of Ζεύς, Δ. βούλευμα A.*Pr.*619; Δ. ὄμμα, στόμα, ib.654, 1033, etc. (For dῑv-ἴyos, cf. Skt. *div-yá-* 'heavenly' (freq. trisyll.), but fem. δῖα for *div-ya.*)

⊛ **Δῖος**, ὁ (sc. μήν), the first month of the Maced. year, *PEleph.*1.2 (iv B.C.), *J.BJ*2.19.9, etc.; in Aetolia, *SIG*$^2$845.1; in Thessaly, *IG* 9(1).689.8 (found in Corc.).

**Διός** [ῐ], gen. of Ζεύς.

**δῖοσ-**, the first element in various compound names of plants: **διόσ-ανθος**, ὁ, *carnation, Dianthus inodorus*, Thphr.*HP*6.1.1, al., Nic.*Fr.*74.59. **-βάλᾰνος** [βᾰ], *sweet chestnut, Castanea vesca*, Thphr.*HP*4.5.1, al., Dsc.1.106. **-ηλᾰκάτη** [κᾰ], ἡ, = πολύκνημον, Ps.-Dsc.3.94; = περιστερεὼν ὕπτιος, Id.4.60. **-κύᾰμος** [ῠ], ὁ, = ὕοσκ., ib.68. **πῡρον**, τό, *fruit of nettle-tree, Celtis australis*, Thphr. *HP*3.13.3:—but **-πυρος**, ὁ, = λιθόσπερμον, Dsc.3.141. **-πώγων**, ωνος, ὁ, = χρυσοκόμη, Ps.-Dsc.4.55.

**Δῖοσ-ᾰτᾱβῠρῐασταί**, οἱ, *worshippers of Zeus Atabyrios*, *IG*12(1). 161 (Rhodes):—also **Διοσ-ξεινιασταί** or **-ξενιασταί**, *worshippers of Zeus Xenios*, ibid.: **Διοσσωτηριασταί**, οἱ, *worshippers of Zeus Soter*, ib.162: **Διοσμειλῐχιασταί**, οἱ, *worshippers of Zeus Meilichios*, *IG*12 (3).104 (Nisyros).

⊛ **Δῐόσδοτος**, ον, (δίδωμι) *given by Zeus, heaven-sent*, αἴγλα Pi.*P.*8. 96; σκῆπτρα A.*Eu.*626; γάνος Id.*Ag.*1391 (Porson): in Id.*Th.*946 the metre requires Διοδότων.

**Διοσηλακάτη**, v. διοσ-.

**Δῐοσημ-ᾰσία**, ἡ, = Διοσημία, Lyd.*Ost.*47. **-ειακός**, ή, όν, *portent-bearing*, ἀστέρες ib.15. **-ία**, ἡ, *a sign from Zeus, an omen from the sky*, esp. of thunder, lightning, rain, διοσημία 'στί Ar.*Ach.* 171: pl., *Stoic.*2.203, D.S.2.19, Plu.2.419e, Philostr.*VA*2.33, Jul. *Or.*7.212b. (Freq. written -εία in codd.)

**Διοσθεών**, ὁ, name of a month at Stratonicea, *BCH*44.71.

**Διόσθυος**, ὁ, name of a month in Rhodes, *IG*12(1).155.1; Thera, *Test.Epict.*4.1, cf. Call.ap.*EM*278.28.

⊛ **διοσκέω**, *look earnestly at*, Anacr.3; also expld. by διαφορεῖσθαι τῷ σώματι καὶ τῇ ψυχῇ, διαπολέσαι, διαφθεῖραι, Hsch.

**Δῐοσ-κόρειον**, τό, *temple of the Dioscuri*, Th.4.110 (-κουρ- codd.), D.19.158, etc.:—also **Διοσκούριον**, *PPetr.*3p.295 (iii B.C.), *IG*11(2). 154*A*37 (Delos, iii B.C.): **Διοσκούρειον**, Plu.*Sull.*33, etc. **II.** **Διοσκούρεια**, τά, *festival of the Dioscuri*, *IG*5(1).559 (Sparta): -κορήϊα *SIG*$^2$438.175 (Delph.): -κούρια *SIG*1067.15 (Rhodes). **-κόριος**, ὁ, name of a month in Syria, cj. in Lxx 2*Ma.*11.21; in Crete, *Hemerolog.Flor.* ⊛ **-κοροι** (the Att. form, Phryn.212), Ion. and later **Διόσ-κουροι**, οἱ, *the sons of Zeus*, i.e. *the twins of Leda*, Castor and Polydeuces, *h.Hom.*33.1, etc.: dual Διοσκόρω, τώ, Ar.*Pax*285, *Ec.*1069, E.*Or.*465, Amphis9, Men.846, Them.*Or.*21.253d: sg. dub. in Hippon.120, cf. Varro *LL*5.66: Διόσκοροι is required by metre in E.*Hel.*1643, *El.*1239: -κούρων Pl.*Euthd.*293a; -κόρων Id.*Lg.*796b, cod. Laur. in Th.3.75: both forms in codd. of Hdt.2.43, 6.127. **II.** constellation named from them *the Twins*, Eratosth.*Cat.*10. **III.** = παρωτίδες, Gal.19.440, Eust.410.17. ⊛ **-κουριασταί**, οἱ, *guild of worshippers of Dioscuri*, *Arch.Pap.*5.158 (iii B.C.).

**Διοσκύαμος**, v. διοσ-.

**δίοσμος**, ον, (ὄζω) *transmitting smells*, ἀήρ *EM*136.23, cf. Alex. Aphr. *in Sens.*89.2, Them. *in de An.*62.32.

**Διόσ-πυρος** and **-πώγων**, v. διοσ-.

**δῐόστεος**, ον, *double-boned*, Arist.*HA*494$^a$5.

**διοσφραίνω**, *give a smell to, perfume*, Sch.Ar.*Ra.*1107.

⊛ **διοτήρ**· κατάσκοπος, Hsch. (leg. διοπτήρ).

⊛ **δῐότι**, Conj. for διὰ τοῦτο ὅτι.. (cf. A.D.*Conj.*242.1), *because, for the reason that, since*, Hdt.1.44, 3.55, Th.1.52, Thphr.*Char.*17.4; οὐδὲ δι' ἓν ἄλλο ἢ διότι.. Pl.*Phd.*100c; answering to διὰ τί; Id.*Plt.*310d, Amphis14.6, Timocl.2.4 D., etc. **2.** indirect, *wherefore, for what reason*, φράσω διότι.. Hdt.2.24; σκοπεῖν διότι.. Th.1.77; ἐρωτᾶν διότι.. Henioch.4.7. **II.** = ὅτι, *that*, Hdt.2.43, 50, Isoc.4.48, D.12. 18, Is.3.50, Arist.*Metaph.*1062$^a$6, al., Phld.*Ir.*p.84 W.; τὸ δ. Arist. *APr.*53$^b$9: folld. by inf., Plb.31.12.4, v.l. in D.S.4.76.

**διοτιδήποτε**, *for whatever reason*, Simp. *in Ph.*50.20.

**διότιπερ**, strengthd. for διότι, *because*, Iamb. *in Nic.*p.83 P.

**Διο-τρεφής**, ές, *fostered, cherished by Zeus*, βασιλῆες Il.2.196, Hes. *Th.*82, etc.; αἰζηοί Il.2.660; also of the Scamander, *fed by rain*, 21. 223. (Cf. Διειτρεφής.)

**Διοτρόφος**, ον, *nurse of Zeus*, Κρήτα E.*Hyps.Fr.*3 iii 23 (lyr.).

⊛ **διού**, Boeot., = δύο, *IG*7.3193.

⊛ **δῐούγκιον**, τό, *weight of two ounces*, *IGRom.*1.668 (Tomi): written διούγγιον, Orib.*Fr.*88.

⊛ **διουργέω**, *cultivate* (metaph.), *Klio* 18.302 (Delph.).

**διουρ-έω**, *pass in urine*, τι Dsc.*Eup.*2.65:—Pass., Hp.*Aër.*7: hence, *to have diuretic properties*, Id.*Aff.*48. **II.** intr., *pass urine*, Id.*Aer.* 9. **-ητικός**, ή, όν, *diuretic*, Id.*Acut.*50, Diocl.*Fr.*112, Aret.*CA*1.1, etc. **-ίζω**, Ion. for διορίζω, Hdt. **II.** *percolate*, Orib.*Fr.*97.

**διοφανής**, dub. l. (for δια-), Them.*Or.*4.60d.

**διοχετ-εία**, ἡ, in pl., *irrigation-works*, Str.10.2.19. **-εύω**, *furnish with channels*, σῶμα Pl.*Ti.*77c. **2.** *distribute by conduits*, Luc.*VH*1.33:—Pass., διωχετευμένων ὑδάτων D.S.20.8: metaph. of the spinal cord, δ. διὰ τῶν σφονδύλων Ruf.*Anat.*7. **II.** in Pass., of a country, *to be irrigated*, Str.5.1.5.

**διοχεύομαι**, *to be impregnated*, διὰ φωτός Plu. *in Hes.*84 (prob. for διοιχηθείσῃ).

**διοχή**, ἡ, (διέχω) *distance, interval*, Ph.*Bel.*75.6.

**διοχλ-έω**, *annoy exceedingly*, πόλεις Lys.6.6; *weary, bore*, D.19. 329: pf. διώχληκα Jul.*Or.*2.78b; *press for payment*, *POxy.*286.13 (i A.D.); later, τινί Aeschin.*Ep.*2.2, Plu.*Cim.*18, Longus 3.20: abs., Ph.1.356:—Pass., Luc.*Am.*50, *IG*3.48 (iii A.D.); ὑπὸ ῥυθμῶν D.H. *Comp.*11. **-ησις**, εως, ἡ, *annoyance*, *IG*3.48 (iii A.D.). ⊛ **-ίζω**, *move asunder, open*, Nic.*Al.*226 (tm.).

**διοχῡρόω**, strengthd. for ὀχυρόω, Plb.5.46.3 (Pass.).

**δίοψ**· οἰκονόμος (cf. δίοπος A). Hsch.

**δίοψις**, εως, ἡ, *a view through*, Plu.2.915a; *transparency*, ib.408e: metaph., ἤθους Id.*Comp.Dem.Cic.*1. **II.** metaph., *consideration*, Pl.*Ti.*40d codd. (δι' ὄψεως Procl.).

**διόψομαι**, v. διοράω.

⊛ **δίπαις** [ῐ], παιδος, ὁ, ἡ, *with two children*, A.*Supp.*319: Cypr. **δίπας**, *Inscr.Cypr.*93 H. **2.** δ. θρῆνος a dirge *chanted by one's two children*, A.*Ch.*334 (lyr.).

**δῐ-πάλαιστος** [πᾰ], ον, *two palms broad* or *long*, X.*Cyn.*2.4, Plb. 27.11.2:—also **δῐπᾰλαιστιαῖος**, α, ον, Heliod.ap.Orib.49.8.6, *Gp.* 9.10.2. ⊛ **-παλτος**, ον, *brandished with both hands*, ξίφη E.*IT*323; δ. πῦρ lightning *hurled* by Zeus *with both hands*, i.e. *with all his might*, Id.*Tr.*1103 (lyr.); πᾶς.. στρατὸς δίπαλτος ἄν με χειρὶ φονεύοι all the host would kill me *with sword brandished in both hands*, i.e. *with all their might*, S.*Aj.*408 (lyr.).

**διπάνας**· τοὺς διδύμους γεγενημένους, Hsch.

**δί-πελμος** [ῐ], ον, *with double soles*, *Edict.Diocl.*9.12a, 15. **-πενθημῐμερής**, ές, *consisting of two members of* $2\frac{1}{2}$ *feet* (sc. μέτρον), Heph. 15.10; κῶλα Sch.Ar.*Pax*775:—also **-μερικός**, ή, όν, Sacerd.p.512 K. **-πηχῠαῖος**, α, ον, = sq., Dsc.1.28, S.E.*M.*8.459. **-πηχυς**, υ, *two cubits long, broad*, etc., Hdt.2.78, Hp.*Art.*7, etc.

⊛ **διπλάδιος** [ᾰ], ον, *double*, poet. for διπλάσιος, *AP*11.158 (Antip. (?)). **II.** Subst. δ., τό, *a measure* of wine, *Sammelb.*4425 ii 9, al.

⊛ **διπλάζω**, = διπλασιάζω, *double*, φόρον And.4.11 (s.v.l.), Alex.122: —Pass., *to be doubled*, στρατηλάταις δορὸς διπλάζεται τιμά E.*Supp.* 781 (lyr.), cf. Men.319.10. **II.** intr., *to be twofold* or *double*, τό τοι διπλάζον μεῖζον κακόν S.*Aj.*268.

⊛ **δίπλαξ**, ᾰκος, ὁ, ἡ, *in double folds* or *layers*, δημός Il.23.243: generally, *twofold, double*, θεσμὸς Orph.*Fr.*247.37. **II.** as Subst., δίπλαξ, ἡ, *double-folded mantle*, Il.3.126, Od.19.241, Lyd.*Mag.*1.17: dat. pl. διπλάκεσσιν dub. l. in A.*Pers.*277 (lyr.).

**διπλᾰσι-άζω**, *double*, Pl.*Lg.*920a, Hierocl. *in CA* 20 p.465 M., etc.: —Pass., Prodic.7, X.*Ages.*5.1, Ph.2.534; δ. λέγεται διχῶς· ἢ γὰρ τόπον.. μένοντος τοῦ πλήθους τῶν ἀνδρῶν, ἢ τὸν ἀριθμόν Ascl.*Tact.*10. 17; so δ. τὸ βάθος Plb.18.24.8. **2.** Gramm., *reduplicate*, A.D. *Pron.*62.23, al.:—Pass., Id.*Synt.*237.23. **b.** *double* a consonant, Hdn.Gr.2.932, etc. **3.** *repeat* a metrical phrase, in Pass., Aristid. Quint.1.24. **II.** intr., *to be twice the size of*, τινός D.S.4.84; *to be doubled in value*, Lys.32.25. **-ᾰσις**, εως, ἡ, = sq., τῶν ἀνδρῶν Ascl. *Tact.*10.17; τῆς χώρας Nicom.*Ar.*1.13. **-ασμός**, ὁ, *doubling*, Antipho Soph.75; τοῦ κύβου Pl.*Sis.*388e; τοῦ στερεοῦ Plu.2.718f. **II.** Gramm., *the Ionic doubling of consonants*, as in τόσσος, *EM*68.47, Eust.73.3, etc. **b.** *reduplication*, A.D.*Synt.*323.6. **III.** in Tactics, *doubling of front*, Ascl.*Tact.*10.18, etc.; of Numbers, ib.17, etc. **IV.** in Anatomy, *cross-action* of muscles, Gal.18(2).974. **V.** = δίπλωσις II, *PHolm.*1.39. **-αστικός**, ή, όν, *of* or *for doubling*, Alex.Aphr. *in Metaph.*756.24. **-επιδίμοιρος** [δῐμ], ον, Gaud.*Harm.* 10, and **-επιδῐμερής**, ές, Nicom.*Ar.*1.23, $2\frac{2}{3}$ *times as great*: **-επιδίτρῑτος**, ον, ibid., Domnin. in *Rev.Phil.*7.90, $2\frac{2}{3}$ *times as great*: **-επιέκτος**, ον, Nicom.*Ar.*1.22, $2\frac{1}{6}$ *times as great*: **-επίπεμπτος**, ον, ibid., $2\frac{1}{5}$ *times as great*: **-επιτέταρτος**, ον, ibid., $2\frac{1}{4}$ *times as great*: **-επιτετραμερής**, ές, ib.23, and **-επιτετράπεμπτος**, ον, ibid., $2\frac{4}{5}$ *times as great*: **-επιτρῐμερής**, ές, ibid., $2\frac{3}{4}$ *times as great*: **-επιτρῑτέταρτος**, $2\frac{3}{4}$ *times as great*, ibid.: **-επίτρῑτος**, ον, ib.22, Theo Sm.p.110 H., $2\frac{1}{3}$ *times as great*: **-εφήμῐσυς**, υ, Nicom.*Ar.*1.22, $2\frac{1}{2}$ *times as great*. **-ημιόλιος**, ον, ἀναλογία *ratio of* $\frac{5}{2}$, Theo Sm.p.110 H.

**διπλᾰσιο-λογία**, ἡ, *repetition of words*, Pl.*Phdr.*267c. **-ομαι**, Pass., *to be doubled*, Th.1.69, *PLeid.X.*87. **-πλευρος**, ον, *with two sides twice as long as the other two*, κλίνη Arist.*Mech.*856$^a$39.

⊛ **διπλ-άσιος** [ᾰ], α, ον, Ion. **-ήσιος**, η, ον, *twofold, double*, Hdt 4.68, etc.: never in Trag. (δίκρουν is prob. in A.*Fr.*152): freq. as Comp. folld. by ἤ.. Hdt.6.57, Th.1.10, etc.; also διπλήσιον ἢ ὅσον.. Hdt. 7.23: or c. gen., *twice the size of*, Id.6.133; δ. ἐγίνετο αὐτὸς ἑωυτοῦ Id.8.137; διπλάσια τῶν ἄλλων D.18.238; δ. τῆς ἀληθείας Philem.160; διπλασίοις ἐλάττω (sc. τὰ χρήματα) D.27.52. **2.** Subst. διπλήσιον, τό, *as much again*, Hdt.7.103: as Adv., διπλάσιον σπεύδουσι Thgn. 229. **3.** διπλασίαν (sc. ζημίαν), πράττεσθαι Pl.*Lg.*762b; τὴν δ. καταδικάζειν Lex ap.D.24.105. **4.** Adv. **-ως** Th.8.1, Men.645; δ. ἄμεινον Aeschin.2.122, *AP*7.611 (Eutolm.). **-ᾰσίων**, ον, gen. ονος, later form for διπλάσιος, Arist.*Pr.*923$^a$3, *Mu.*399$^a$9, Arr.*Tact.* 16.11, *PLips.*64.31 (iv A.D.), etc.; δ. λόγος *duplicate* ratio, Ph.1.22, Plu.2.1138e. **-ασμός**, ὁ, = διπλασιασμός, Eust.1396.52, prob. l. in Plot.6.1.9.

⊛ **διπλεθρ-ία**, ἡ, *a measure of two* πλέθρα, *IG*9(1).693.20 (Corc.).

**-ος**, *ον*, *two* πλέθρα *long* or *broad*, Theopomp.Hist.350, Luc.*VH*1.16. **2.** Subst. δίπλεθρον, τό, *space of two* πλέθρα, Plb.34.12.4.

**διπλεία** or **-ηΐα**, ἡ, *double*, τὰν διπλείαν τᾶς τιμᾶς *Leg.Gort.*6.42, cf. *GDI*4982. ⊛ **δίπλειον**, τό, *PPetr.*2p.42.

**δίπλευρος**, ον, *with two fronts*, Ael.*Tact.*36.4, Arr.*Tact.*28.4.

**διπλῆ**, ἡ, (διπλοῦς) a marg. mark used by Gramm. (⊱ >, < ⊰), to indicate vv. ll., rejected verses, etc., and, in dramatic poetry, a new speaker, Cic.*Att.*8.2.4, Heph.*Poëm.*p.74C., Sch.Il.*Oxy.*1086 ii 55, etc. **II.** *a dance*, Poll.4.105, Hsch. **III.** διπλαῖ, αἱ, = δίπλωμα, *IG*14.1054*b*: also sg., *PSI*5.446 (ii A.D.). **IV.** = διπλοΐς, Ap.Ty.*Ep.*3.

⊛ **διπλῇ** (Dor. **διπλεῖ** *Tab.Heracl.*1.109, *Leg.Gort.*2.7), Adv. *twice*, E.*Ion*760, cj. in S.*Ant.*725. **II.** *twice as much*, opp. ἁπλῇ, *IG*1$^{2}$.6.47; folld. by ἤ, Pl.*R.*330c.

**διπληγίς**, ίδος, ὁ, = διπλοΐς, Poll.7.47.

**διπλήθης**, ες, *double in quantity*, Nic.*Al.*153 (v.l. διπλήρης).

**διπλήσιος**, η, ον, Ion. for διπλάσιος.

**δίπλινθος**, ον, *of two bricks in height*, θυρίδας διπλίνθους *IG*2$^{2}$.463.55.

**διπλοειμάτος**, ον, *with double cloak*, Cerc.1.3.

⊛ **διπλόη**, ἡ, *fold, doubling*, Gal.2.710: but usu., **II.** *porous substance between the double plates in the bones in the skull*, Hp.*VC*1,17, Heliod.ap.Orib.46.9.4, Ruf.*Onom.*135: generally, *spongy core* of bone, Paul.Aeg.6.77; also, *tissue between layers* of intestine, Aret.*SD*2.9: hence, **2.** *weak spot, flaw* in metal, Pl.*Sph.*267e, Ph.*Bel.*71.28, Plu.2.802b: metaph., αἱ δ. τῆς ψυχῆς ib.715f, cf. 441d; 'patchiness', Plot.5.2.1; also, *concealed sense*, in oracles, Plu.2.407c. **III.** *hollow sting* of the scorpion, Ael.*NA*9.4.

**διπλόθριξ**, ὁ, ἡ, gen. τριχος, *with geminate leaves*, of the stone-pine, Dionys.*Av.*1.27.

**διπλοΐδιον**, τό, Dim. of διπλοΐς I, Poll.7.49.

**διπλοΐζω**, = διπλασιάζω, A.*Ag.*835; cf. ἐπιδιπλοΐζω.

⊛ **διπλοΐς**, ΐδος, ἡ, *double cloak*, Lxx 1*Ki.*2.19, J.*AJ*6.14.2, etc.; worn by Cynics, *AP*7.65 (Antip. (?)). **II.** = διπλόη I, Hp.*Morb.*2.23. **2.** *abscess* in horse's ear, *Hippiatr.*17.

**διπλο-ϊσότης**, ητος, ἡ, *double equation*, Dioph.p.96T. ⊛ **-κάριος**, ὁ, = Lat. *duplicarius, receiving double pay*, *PGrenf.*2.51.5 (ii A.D., -κάρις Pap.). **-κεράμιον** [ᾰ], τό, *measure of wine in Egypt*, *Ostr.*1166, al., *POxy.*1751.3 (iv A.D., -μον Pap.).

⊛ **διπλόος**, η, ον, contr. **διπλοῦς**, ῆ, οῦν, Ion. fem. διπλέη Hdt.3.42 codd., but διπλήν or -ῆν Id.5.90, διπλάς or -ᾶς Id.3.28: contr. always in Trag., exc. διπλόοι A.*Fr.*39: (cf. ἁπλόος):—*twofold, double*, prop. of cloaks and articles of dress, χλαῖνα διπλῆ, = δίπλαξ or διπλοΐς, Il.10.134, Od.19.226; ὅθι.. διπλόος ἤντετο θώρηξ where the cuirass met [the buckle] *so as to be double*, Il.4.133; τὴν ἐπωμίδα πτύξας διπλῆν having folded it *double*, Apollod.Car.4: generally, καλύβη διπλῆ διαφράγματι Th.1.133; διπλόος θάνατος Hdt.6.104; παῖσον διπλῆν (sc. πληγήν) S.*El.*1415; δ. οἰκίδιον *of two stories*, Lys.1.9; διπλῆ ἄκανθα spine *bent double* by age, E.*El.*492; διπλῆ ⟨ῥάχις⟩ X.*Eq.*1.11; σύμβολον δ. *executed in duplicate*, *PHib.*1.29 (iii B.C.). **2.** διπλῇ χερὶ θανεῖν by *mutual* slaughter, S.*Ant.*14. **3.** δ. ὀνόματα *compound* words, Arist.*Po.*1459$^{a}$9, *Rh.*1404$^{b}$29, etc. **4.** of fevers in which two paroxysms took place in a given time, δ. ἀμφημερινός, τριταῖος, Gal.7.472, 9.677. **5.** δ. ἰσότης, = διπλοϊσότης (q.v.), Dioph.p.98T., etc. **6.** δ. ἄνδρας· τὰ δισύλλαβα ἀνδρῶν ὀνόματα, Hsch. **II.** as Comp., *twice as much, large*, etc., βίος Pl.*Ti.*75b; δίκη Id.*Lg.*865c; δ. ἤ.. *twice as much as*.. (v. διπλῇ): c. gen., Id.*Ti.*35b; διπλοῦν ὀφείλειν ὅσον.. Lex ap.D.23.28; διπλῷ, = διπλῇ, Pl.*Lg.*722b. **III.** pl., in Trag., = δύο, A.*Pr.*950, *Ch.*761, S.*Aj.*960, *OT*20, *Ant.*51. **IV.** *double, doubtful*, οὐ γνώμᾳ διπλόαν θέτο βουλάν Pi.*N.*10.89; διπλᾶς καὶ ἀμφιβόλους λέξεις Ph.1.302. **2.** *double-minded, treacherous*, E.*Rh.*395, etc.; οὐδὲν δ. X.*HG*4.1.32; δ. καὶ ποικίλος D.H.*Rh.*11.5; also, *playing two parts*, Pl.*R.*397e; *at variance with oneself*, ib.554d. **V.** διπλοῦν, τό, = δίπλωμα III, Androm.ap.Gal.13.29, al.

**διπλόρους**, ουν, *spelt with ρρ*, Tz.*H.*12.636.

⊛ **διπλός**, ή, όν, poet. for διπλόος (cf. ἁπλός), Opp.*C.*2.449, *AP*10.101 (Bianor): Comp. διπλότερος, = διπλάσιος, App.*Praef.*10, *Ev.Matt.*23.15.

**διπλο-σήμαντος**, ον, *with double meaning*, Sch.Ar.*Nu.*225:—also **-σημος**, ον, Eust.1356.60.

⊛ **διπλ-όω**, *repeat* a process, Arist.*APo.*91$^{a}$21; *double*, τρίβωνα, of philosophers, D.L.6.22; *multiply by two*, Vett.Val.159.27:—Pass., ἐδεδίπλωτο ἡ φάλαγξ X.*HG*6.5.19; of swords, *to be bent double*, Plu.*Cam.*41; of a bow-string, Ach.Tat.3.8; of fevers (cf. διπλοῦς), Gal.7.472; δεδιπλωμένον ἔμβρυον, of position of foetus at birth, Aspasia ap.Aët.16.22, cf. Sor.2.55. **II.** *repay twofold*, δ. διπλᾶ κατὰ τὰ ἔργα αὐτῆς *Apoc.*18.6. **-ῳδέομαι**, *recur*, τῶν διατόνων καθ' ἕκαστον τετράχορδον διπλῳδουμένων Theo Sm.p.93H. ⊛ **-ωμα**, ατος, τό, *anything double*: hence of the parallel streams of the 'milky way', Arist.*Mete.*346$^{a}$24; of 'doubled' position of foetus at birth, Sor.2.60, Philum.ap.Aët.16.23. **II.** *folded paper*: hence, *letter of recommendation*, esp. *passport*, Cic.*Att.*10.17.4, *Fam.*6.12.3; later, *order enabling a traveller to use the public post*, Plu.*Galb.*8, *OGI*665.25 (Egypt, i A.D.), etc.; *receipt* for payment of licences or taxes, *PAmh.*2.92 (ii A.D.), etc. **2.** *duplicate, counterpart*, *CIG*3276 (Smyrna). **3.** δ. ὄνων, tax in Egypt, *BGU*213 (ii A.D.); δ. ἵππων *PAmh.*2.92.21 (ii A.D.). **III.** *double pot* for boiling unguents, etc., Dsc.2.77, Crito ap.Gal.13.37. **-ωσις**, εως, ἡ, *compounding of words*, Arist.*Rh.*1406$^{a}$6. **II.** *doubling*, μήνιγγος Gal.*UP*9.6 (pl.); esp. in Alch., δ. ἀργύρου Zos.Alch.p.183B., cf. *PHolm.*2.18, al. **III.** *folding*, Eust.633.20, Hsch. s.v. πτύξις.

**δί-πνοος**, ον, *with two breathing apertures*, Gal.19.93 (δίπνος codd.); cf. **δίπνοια** τρώματα· εἰς κενὰ τραύματα, Hsch. **-πόδης** [ῐ], gen. -πόδου, *two feet long, broad*, etc., X.*Oec.*19.3. **-ποδία**, ἡ, *two-footedness*, Arist.*PA*643$^{a}$3, Plot.6.3.5. **II.** *a Lacedaemonian dance*, Cratin.162. **III.** in Metric, *combination of two feet*, Anon.*Oxy.*220 viii 1, Heph.4.3, Aristid.Quint.1.24, etc. ⊛ **-ποδιάζω**, fut. -άξω, *dance the* διποδία, Ar.*Lys.*1243. **-ποδισμός**, ὁ, = διποδία II, Hsch.

**δῑπολητς**, ΐδος, ἡ, *of* or *through two cities*, φήμη Man.4.376.

**Δῑπολίεια**, τά, contr. from Διιπ-, an ancient *festival of Zeus Polieus* at Athens, *IG*1$^{2}$.188, 843; Διιπόλεια codd. in Ar.*Pax*420, Antipho 2.4.8, cf. Sch.Ar. l.c.; Διπόλεια Hdn.Gr.2.493.

**δῐ-πολις**, εως, ὁ, ἡ, *of* or *divided into two cities*, Str.3.4.8, 14.2.15. **-πολίτης** [λῑ], ου, ὁ, *citizen of two cities*, Man.5.291.

**Δῑπολιώδης**, ες, *like the feast of Dipolia, old-world*, Ar.*Nu.*984.

**δί-πολος** [ῐ], ον, (πολέω) *twice-ploughed*, Procl.ad Hes.*Op.*460. **II.** = διπλόος, A.*Fr.*209 (dub.). **-πορος**, ον, *with two roads* or *openings*, δ. κορυφὰν ἴσθμιον E.*Tr.*1097 (lyr.). **-πος**, = δίπους, Pythag.ap.Iamb.*VP*25.144. **-πότᾰμος**, ον, *between two rivers*, πόλις E.*Supp.*621 (lyr.). **-πους**, ποδος (acc. δίπουν *IG*2.1054.24, etc.), ὁ, ἡ, neut. πουν, *two-footed*, A.*Ag.*1258, *Supp.*895 (lyr.), Pl.*Plt.*276c, etc.: δίποδα, τά, *two-footed animals*, Plu.2.636e. **2.** δίπους, ὁ, *jerboa*, which springs *from its two hind feet*, Hdt.4.192. **II.** *two feet long*, γραμμή Pl.*Men.*83d; διάμετρος δυνάμει δ. Id.*Plt.*266b. ⊛ **-πρόσωπος**, ον, *two-faced*, ἄγαλμα Hdn.1.16.2; ποτήριον, σκάφιον, *IG*11(4).1308, 1309 (Delos, ii B.C.). **2.** *ambiguous*, Luc.*JTr.*43. **3.** Gramm., *denoting two persons*, A.D.*Pron.*17.1, 110.24. **4.** διπρόσωπος, ἡ, name of a *plaster*, Gal.11.127. **-πρυμνος**, ον, v. sq. **-πρῳρος**, ον, ναῦς δ. καὶ δίπρυμνος a ship *double-prowed* and *double-sterned*, i.e. a *twin* ship, Callix.1, Promathidas ap.Ath.11.489b (here perh., = ἀμφίπρῳρος). **-πτερος**, ον, *two-winged*, of insects, opp. τετράπτερος, Arist.*HA*490$^{a}$16, al. **II.** ὁ δ. (sc. ναός) temple *with double peristyle*, Vitr.3.2.7. **-πτέρῠγος**, ον, = foreg. I, *AP*5.150 (Mel.), cf. 9.570 (Phld.). **II.** δ., τό, *mantle with two* πτερά (cf. πτερόν III.10), *IG*2.754.38, *Jahresh.*16 *Beibl.*53. **-πτυον**, τό, a Cyprian *measure* (perh., = ½ μέδιμνος), Hsch. **-πτῠχής**, ές, = δίπτυχος, Arist.*HA*515$^{b}$8. **-πτῠχίζω**, Dor. aor. imper. -ιξον, *fold, double*, Hsch. (-διξον cod.). ⊛ **-πτῠχος**, ον, (πτύσσω) *double-folded, doubled*, δίπτυχον ἀμφ' ὤμοισιν ἔχων.. λώπην Od.13.224 (so δίπτυχα λώπην, metaplast. acc. as if from δίπτυξ, A.R.2.32); δ. δελτίον *a pair of* tablets, Hdt.7.239; δ. κάτοπτρον *folding* mirror, *BGU*717.12; κωδίκιλλοι δ. ib.326 ii 15 (ii A.D.):—in the Homeric phrase δίπτυχα ποιήσαντες [τὴν κνίσην], δίπτυχα is interpr. by Sch.BT as an Adv., *having doubled* the fat, i.e. putting one layer of fat under the thighs (μηροί) and another over them, but may be acc., = *fold*, Il.1.461, al. **II.** *twofold*, δ. δῶρον E.*Ion*1010; γλῶσσα Id.*Tr.*286: in pl., = δισσοί, *two*, δ. ὀδύναι S.*Fr.*152; νεανίαι E.*IT*242, cf. *Or.*633, *Andr.*578, Ar.*Fr.*558. **III.** δίπτυχα, τά, = Lat. *tabulae*, *SIG*827 i 9 (Delph., ii A.D.). **-πτωτος**, ον, *having one form for two cases*, A.D.*Pron.*91.7. **-πῠλος**, ον, *double-gated, with two entrances*, S.*Ph.*952. **II.** δίπυλον, τό, a name for the Θριάσιαι πύλαι at Athens, Plb.16.25.7, Plu.*Per.*30; at Rome for the temple of Janus, Id.2.322a. **2.** = ὑπερῷον, Hsch. **-πυργία** οἰκία house *with two wings*, *POxy.*247.23 (i A.D.), *PLond.*2.348 (iii A.D.), etc.:—also **-πυργιαία**, *POxy.*1703.12 (iii A.D.). **-πύρηνος**, ον, (πῡρήν) *with two knobs*: Subst. -πύρηνον, τό, *probe*, Herophil.ap.Sor.2.85, Cael.Aur.*CP*3.3, Gal.2.574, al. **-πῡρίτης** [ρῑ] (sc. ἄρτος), ὁ, *twice-baked bread, biscuit*, Hp.*Int.*25. **-πῡρος** (sc. ἄρτος), ον, *twice fired*, i.e. *baked*, = foreg., Eub.18, Alex.172.10: pl., Alc.Com.5; δ. σῖτος *JHS*32.154. **II.** διπύρους ἀνέχουσα λαμπάδας.. Ἑκάτα Hecate holding up *two flaming* torches, Ar.*Ra.*1361. **-πωλος**, ον, *with two horses*, ἅρμα (Ἄρης cod.) Hsch. s.v. συνωρίδα.

**δίρηγες**· στρουθοί, Hsch.; cf. δίγηρες.

**διρκαία**, ἡ, = κιρκαία, Dsc.3.119: **δίρκαιον**, τό, = δαῦκος, Ps.-Dsc.3.72; = στρύχνον ὑπνωτικόν, Id.4.72. ⊛ **δίρκος**, ὁ, = φθείρ III, Paus.Gr.*Fr.*131.

**δί-ρραβδος**, ον, *with two stripes*, Arist.*Fr.*294. **-ρρυθμος**, ον, = δίμετρος, in paeonic metre, Sch.Ar.*Eq.*613, etc. **-ρρῡμία**, ἡ, *double pole*, A.*Fr.*324. **-ρρῡμος**, ον, *with two poles*, i.e. three horses, Id.*Pers.*47 (anap.).

⊛ **δίς** [ῐ], Adv. *twice, doubly*, with Nouns, δ. τόσσον *twice* as much, Od.9.491, cf. Th.6.57, etc.; ἀληθὴς ὁ λόγος ὡς δ. παῖς γέρων Cratin.24; δ. παῖδες οἱ γέροντες Theopomp.Com.69: more freq. with Verbs, τοῦτο δ. ἤδη ἐγένετο Hdt.8.104; δ. φράσαι A.*Pers.*173, cf. *Ag.*1384; δ. αἰάζειν καὶ τρίς S.*Aj.*432; δ. καὶ τρίς φασι καλὸν εἶναι τὰ καλὰ λέγειν Pl.*Grg.*498e, cf. *Phlb.*60a, Emp.25; δ. βιῶναι *twice over*, Men.223.4; δειπνεῖν.. δ. τῆς ἡμέρας Pl.Com.207; ἐς δ. App.*Mith.*78: ὁ δ. Νέωνος, = *son and grandson* of N., *GDI*3092.18 (Aegosthena); Αὐρήλιος Αὐξάνων δ. *BCH*17.249 (Apamea); Αὐρ. Δοῦ⟨ρ⟩λος δ. *JHS*19.301 (Selmea [Lycaonia]).—In compds. δι-, but δισ- in δισμύριοι, δισχίλιοι, δισθανής, δίσαβος, δισάρπαγος, δίσευνος, etc. (Cf. Skt. *dvis* 'twice', Lat. *bis*.)

**-δις**, inseparable Suffix, signifying motion to a place, like -δε, but only used in a few words, as ἄλλυδις, οἴκαδις, χαμάδις.

**Δίς**, ὁ, = Ζεύς, Rhinth.14; otherwise only in oblique cases, Διός, Διΐ, Δία (pl. Δίες, Δίας, Plu.2.425e): the contr. dat. Δί *SIG*35, Pi.*N.*1.72, etc.: apocop. acc. Δί in νηδί, v. Ζεύς.

**δίσᾱβος** [ῐ], ον, hyperdor. for δίσηβος, *twice young*, *AP*15.26 (Dosiad.).

**δῐσάκκ-ιον**, τό, *saddle-bag, panniers*, *PFay.*347 (ii A. D.), *PStrassb.* 37.17 (iii A. D.):—Dim. **-ίδιον**, τό, *POxy.*741.2 (ii A. D.).

**δίσαλα**· ἀκαθαρσία, and **δισαλέος**· ῥυπαρός, Hsch. (cf. δεῖσα, etc.).

**δῐσ-άρπᾰγος**, ον, *twice ravished*, Lyc.513. **-εβδομηκοντάπηχυς**, υ, 140 *cubits long*, Tz.*H.*3.942. **-έβδομος**, ον, *fourteenth*, ib.9. 781. **-έκγονοι**, οἱ, *second cousins*, Asp.*in EN*184.26. **-έκτωρ**, dub. sens. in *Stud.Pal.*20.75 i 22 (iii/iv A. D.). **-εξάδελφος** [ᾰ], ον, ὁ, *great-nephew*, Sch.A.R.3.359. **-ευνος**, ον, *with two wives*, *AP* 15.26 (Dosiad.).

✱ **δί-σημος** [ῐ], ον, *of two times*, πούς Aristid.Quint.1.14 (but in Music, *of four times*, acc. to Elias *in Cat.*189.9). II. *of doubtful quantity*, Sch.D.T.p.38 H. III. in Rhythm, *of two time-units*, χρόνος, μέγεθος, Aristox.*Rhyth.*2.10,31, cf. Aristid.Quint.1.14. IV. of a garment, *with double border*, *PTeb.*406.17 (iii A. D.), *POxy.*1051. 5 (iii A. D.).

✱ **δισθᾰνής**, ές, *twice dead*, Od.12.22.

**δῐσῑτέομαι**, *eat two meals a day*, Herod.Med.ap.Aët.9.13.

**δισκ-άζομαι**, = διαφέρομαι, Hsch. **-άριον**, τό, Dim. of δίσκος, Orib.*Syn.*7.44.1. **-έλλα**· σπυρίς, Hsch. **-εύς**, έως, ὁ, a kind of *comet*, Lyd.*Ost.*10ᵃ, 15ᵃ. **-ευτής**, οῦ, ὁ, *one who pitches quoits*, Mich.*in EN*487.31. ✱ **-εύω**, = δισκέω, Sosith.3, Philostr.*Ep.*7; δ. αὐτόν D.L.1.118, Porph.*Chr.*48:—Pass., *to be pitched* or *thrown*, *AP*9.14 (Antiphil.), v.l. in E.*Ion*1268; cf. sq. ✱ **-έω**, *pitch the quoit*, δίσκον.. στιβαρώτερον οὐκ ὀλίγον περ ἢ οἵῳ.. ἐδίσκεον ἀλλήλοισιν Od. 8.188; μακρὰ δισκήσαις *having made a* long *throw*, Pi.*I.*2.35; αἵ τις δισκίοι *IG*5(1).828 (Sparta):—Pass., *to be hurled*, of a person, E.*Ion* 1268 (v.l. -ευθήσεται); of a squid, *AP*9.227 (Bianor). **-ημα**, ατος, τό, *a thing thrown*, δ. πικρόν, of Astyanax, E.*Tr.*1121. II. *quoit-throw*, S.*Fr.*380.

**δί-σκηπτρος**, ον, *two-sceptred*, τιμή, of the Atridae, A.*Ag.*43 (anap.).

**δισκο-βολέω**, *pitch the quoit*, Gal.*Thras.*33, Hsch. s. v. δισκεύει: *throw down like a quoit*, *Epigr.Gr.*336 (Alexandria Troas). **-βολία**, ἡ, *quoit-throwing*, Gal.6.325. **-βόλος**, ὁ, *quoit-thrower*, subject of statues, by Myron, Luc.*Philops.*18; by Naucydes, Plin.*HN*34. 80. **-ειδής**, ές, *quoit-shaped*, Agatharch.105, Dsc.2.156, *Placit.*2. 27.3, Ruf.*Anat.*16. **-ομαι**, Pass., *to be made in the form of a disk*, Lyd.*Ost.*6.

**δισκόραξ**, ακος, ὁ, *double-dyed Korax* (with play on κόραξ), Luc. *Pseudol.*30.

✱ **δίσκος**, ὁ, (δικεῖν) *quoit*, Il.2.774, Od.8.186, E.*IA*200, al., Arist. *Fr.*533, etc.; δίσκου οὖρα *quoit's* cast, Il.23.431; λιθίνοις ἐν δ. Pi.*I.* 1.25. II. *anything quoit-shaped*: 1. *dish, trencher*, *AP*11.371 (Pall.), Lib.*Decl.*30.24; *salver*, *BGU*388 ii 22 (ii/iii A. D.). 2. *round mirror*, *AP*6.18 (Jul.). 3. the sun's *disk*, Alex.Aphr.*Pr.* 2.46, *Placit.*2.24.1, al. 4. *gong*, S.E.*M.*5.28, al. 5. *reliquary*, Procop.*Aed.*1.7. III. *marigold*, *Calendula arvensis*, Alex.Trall. 12. (Cf. δικεῖν.)

**δίσκ-ουρα**, τά, (οὖρος) *quoit's cast*, as a measure of distance, ἐς δίσκουρα λέλειπτο Il.23.523:—also **-ούρια**, Hsch.

✱ **δισκοφόρος**, ον, *bringing the discus*, Luc.*Philops.*18.

**δισ-μῡρίανδρος** πόλις a city *of twenty thousand inhabitants*, Str.12. 7.3. **-μύριοι** [ῡ], αι, α, *twenty thousand*, Hdt.1.32, Pl.*Ion*535d: sg., δισμύριος, α, ον, with collective Nouns, ἵππος δισμυρία Luc.*Zeux.*8.

✱ **δισπερίοδος**, ὁ, *twice a* περιοδονίκης (q. v.), κῆρυξ *IG*3.129 (iii A. D.).

**δι-σπῐθᾰμαῖος**, α, ον, = sq., Dsc.2.144. **-σπίθᾰμος**, ον, *of two spans' length*, ib.156. **-σπόνδειος**, ὁ, *double spondee*, Heph.3.3, Aristid.Quint.1.22, Hermog.*Id.*1.6. **-σπορέω**, (σπόρος) *sow twice*, *PEdgar*27.2 (iii B. C.), Str.16.4.2 (Pass.).

**δισσ-άκις** [ᾰ], poet. -ι, Adv. *twice over*, Arat.968, Q.S.2.56, *AP* 6.223 (Antip.). **-άρχης**, ου, ὁ, *joint-ruling*, δισσάρχαι βασιλεῖς S.*Aj.*390 (lyr.). **-ᾰχῆ**, Adv. *at two points*, Arist.*de An.*406ᵇ 32. **-ᾰχοῦ**, Att. διττ-, Adv. = foreg., Thphr.*Lap.*25.

**δισσο-γονέω**, Att. διττ-, *bear doubly*, i. e. to be both viviparous and oviparous, Arist.*GA*719ᵃ14. **-γρᾰφία**, ἡ, *dittography, repetition of words* by copyist, Simp.*in Cat.*88.24. **-λογέω**, Att. διττ-, *say twice, repeat*, as in phrases like ἄπιστ' ἄπιστα, καινὰ καινά, Sch.E. *Hec.*688; *go over again*, Vett.Val.249.20. II. *call in question, leave doubtful*, Simp.*in Cael.*194.17. **-λογία**, ἡ, *repetition of words*, Sch.Od.1.406. **-λόγος**, ον, *speaking two languages*, Man.5.291. **-ποιός**, όν, *making doubtful, perplexing*, Sch.S.*El.* 645.

✱ **δισσός**, Att. διττός, Ion. διξός (q. v.), ή, όν, (δίς) *twofold, double*, Hdt.2.44, 7.70, Pl.*Tht.*198d, etc. Adv. διττῶς, opp. ἁπλῶς, *doubly, in two ways*, δ. [γνώριμα] Arist.*EN*1095ᵇ2; δ. λέγεσθαι ib.1096ᵇ13, al. 2. *executed in duplicate*, ἀποχή *POxy.*1024.39 (ii A. D.), etc. II. pl., *two*, Pi.*N.*1.44, Hdt.5.40,52, A.*Pr.*957, S.*Aj.*57, etc.: with a dual, δισσοὶ προάγοντε μάλιστα Iamb.*Comm.Math.* 25. III. metaph., *divided, disagreeing* in mind, λήμασι δισσούς (λήμασιν ἴσους Dind.) A.*Ag.*122 (lyr.). 2. *doubtful, ambiguous*, ὄνειροι S.*El.*645; τὸ δ. *ambiguity*, Arist.*Pol.*1261ᵇ29. Adv. διττῶς Id.*SE*180ᵃ15.

**δισσο-τόκος**, ον, *bearing twice*, Nonn.*D.*5.199. II. proparox., δισσότοκος, ον, *twice-born*, of Bacchus, ib.1.4. **-φυής**, ές, *of double nature*, ib.14.97, etc.

**δίστ-αγμα**, ατος, τό, *doubt, uncertainty*, Phld.*Rh.*1.111 S.:—also **-αγμός**, ὁ, Agatharch.21, Plu.2.214f, Steph.*in Hp.*1.59 D.

**δι-στάδιος** [ᾰ], ον, *two stadia long*, διάστημα App.*Hann.*37.

✱ **διστ-άζω**, fut. -άσω Phld.*Sign.*1, al.: (δίς):—*doubt, hesitate*, abs., Pl.*Tht.*190a, *Ion*534e, etc.; δ. εἰ.. Id.*Lg.*897b, *BGU*388 i 17 (ii/iii A. D.); μή.. Pl.*Sph.*235a; μή ποτε, c. ind., Phld.*Sign.*13,21; πῶς.. Arist.*EN*1112ᵇ2; πότερον.. Id.*Metaph.*1091ᵃ14; περί τι Id.*EN*1112ᵇ 8; περί τινος Plu.2.62a:—Pass., *to be in doubt*, D.S.17.9; τὰ -όμενα *OGI*315.66 (Pessinus), Phld.*Lib.*p.23 O. **-ακτικός**, ή, όν, *expressive of doubt*, ἔγκλισις, of the subjunctive, Sch.D.T.p.245 H., cf. A.D. *Synt.*264.18. Adv. **-κῶς** Sch.E.*Or.*632, Sch.Il.1.100.

**διστάσιος** [ᾰ], ον, *of twice the value*, Pl.*Hipparch.*231d, Aglaïas 19.

**διστασμός**, ὁ, = δισταγμός, Thphr.*Metaph.*31, Sch.Od.2.276.

**δι-στεγής**, ές, = δίστεγος, *EM*274.27. **-στεγία**, ἡ, *second story*, Poll.4.130. ✱ **-στεγος**, ον, *of two stories*, οἰκία, πύργος, *Sammelb.* 5246 (i B. C.), *POxy.*243.15 (i A. D.), cf. Str.15.3.8, J.*BJ*5.4.3, Sor. 1.70, etc. 2. *of two chambers* on the same floor, J.*BJ*5.5.4. 3. δίστεγον, τό, *room on the upper floor*, *Gp.*8.25.1. **-στεφής**, ές, *twice-crowned*, Call.*Sos.*7.2. **-στῐχής**, ές, = δίστιχος, ὀδόντες Ar. Byz.*Epit.*120.9. **-στῐχία**, ἡ, *double row* or *line*, of fruit, J.*AJ*8.3. 4; of ships, Sch.Il.14.31. 2. *couplet, distich*, Heph.*Poëm.*1, Sch. Ar.*Nu.*1348. II. Medic., *growth of a second row* of eyelashes, Gal. 14.767. **-στῐχίασις**, εως, ἡ, = διστιχία II, Sever.ap.Aët.7.68, Paul. Aeg.6.8. **-στῐχος**, ον, *with two rows*, κριθαί *Placit.*5.10.2. 2. *of two verses*, ἐπίγραμμα *AP*9.369 (Cyrill.); δίστιχον, τό, *distich*, *AP* 6.329 (Leon.); '*a couple of lines*', of a brief letter, *FGiss.*20.23 (ii A. D.). 3. *doubly woven*, μαφόρια *PMasp.*6 ii 80 (vi A. D.). **-στοιχία**, ἡ, *double row*, Thphr.*HP*4.8.6, Ael.*NA*9.40. ✱ **-στοιχος**, ον, *in two rows*, ὀδόντες Arist.*HA*501ᵃ24; [βράγχια] ib.505ᵃ16; κριθὴ δ. *two-rowed* barley, Thphr.*HP*8.4.2; *in two courses*, ὑπερτόναια *SIG* 969.32. **-στολος**, ον, *in pairs, two together*, or simply, *two*, ἀδελφαί S.*OC*1055 (lyr.). ✱ **-στομος**, ον, (στόμα) *double-mouthed, with two entrances*, πέτρα S.*Ph.*16; δ. ὁδοί *double-branching* roads, Id.*OC* 900; so of rivers *with two mouths*, Plb.34.10.5; *with two harbours*, Hsch. II. of a weapon, *two-edged*, ξίφος E.*Hel.*983; πελέκεως γένυς Id.*Fr.*530.5.

**διστραλίον**, τό, *single-bladed axe*, Sch.Il.23.851 (Lat. *dextrale*).

**δίστροπον**, τό, *vessel for libations*, *BGU*590 (ii A. D.).

**δίστροφος**, ον, *doubly twisted*, of cords, Meges ap.Orib.44.24. 12. II. *of two turns*, ἕλιξ Papp.1110.15.

**δῐσυλλᾰβ-έω**, *to be of two syllables*, Hdn Gr.2.908, A.D.*Pron.*78. 24. **-ία**, ἡ, *pair of syllables*, καταληκτικὸν εἰς δ. Sch.Ar.*Av.*904, etc. **-ος**, ον, *of two syllables*, Demetr.Poliorc ap.Phylarch.12 J. (of slave-names), D.H.*Comp.*11, A.D.*Pron.*49.14, Luc.*Gall.*29; δισυλλάβῳ περιττεύειν Heph.4.4. Adv. **-βως** A.D.*Pron.*35.25, Ath.10. 446e, Sch.Th.*Oxy.*853 v 12.

**δῐσύν-απτος**, ον, *double-plaited*, στέφανος Philox.1. **-εγγύάω**, *become joint surety twice*, *Sammelb.*4369 ii 6 (iii B. C.).

**δῐσύπᾰτος** [ῠ], ὁ, *twice consul*, Plu.2.777b, Arr.*Epict.*4.1.6, Philostr. *VS*2.1.1 (pl.).

**δισχέλιοι**, οἱ, Aeol. for δισχίλιοι.

**δισχῐδ-ής**, ές, (σχίζω) *cloven-hoofed*, opp. ἀσχιδής, πολυσχιδής, Arist.*HA*499ᵇ9. 2. *cloven*, ποδότης Id.*PA*642ᵇ29. 3. *divided, parted*, κόμη Callistr.*Stat.*7; ὁδός *Trag.Adesp.*338. Adv. **-δῶς** Dosith.p.412 K. 4. *branching*, of arteries, etc., Gal.*UP*16. 10, etc. **-όν**, Adv. of foreg., *in double columns*, of writing, Sch. D.T.p.191 H., al. (wrongly expld. as = στιχηδόν).

**δισχῑλιάς**, άδος, ἡ, *number of twenty thousand*, Lxx 1 *Ma.*9.4.

**δισχίλιοι** [χῑ], αι, α, Aeol. **δισχέλιοι** Alc.*Supp.*22.2:—*two thousand*, Hdt.2.44, Ar.*V.*660, Pl.*Criti.*118a, etc.: poet. dat. pl., δισχίλλοις ἀνδραπόδοισιν *IG*1².1085: sg., δισχίλιος, α, ον, with collective Nouns, e. g. ἵππος Hdt.7.158.

✱ **δί-σχοινος**, ον, *measuring two* σχοῖνοι (i. e. 60 *stades*), χώρα δ. κύκλῳ Str.12.3.34. **-σώματος**, ον, *double-bodied*, D.S.4.12, Orph. *H.*71.5, *Fr.*57, Ph.2.481; *with two chambers*, εἰσάστης *CIG*2842 (Aphrodisias). ✱ **-σωμος**, ον, applied to certain constellations, Serapio in *Cat.Cod.Astr.*1.100, S.E.*M.*5.6, Vett.Val.7.25, etc.

**δισώνῠμος**, ον, *with two names*, Sch.Od.12.22.

**Δισωτήριον**, τό, contr. for Διοσ-, *the temple of* Ζεὺς Σωτήρ on the Acropolis at Athens, *AB*91; cf. Διισωτήρια.

✱ **δῐ-τάλαντος** [τᾰ], ον, *weighing two talents*, σταθμός Hdt.1.50, 2. 96; *worth two talents*, δ. εἶχες ἔρανον D.18.312; οἶκοι δ. Id.27.64: neut. as Subst., δ. ἀργυρίου Lxx 4 *Ki.*5.23. **-τοιχος**· ἀναίσθητος, Hsch. ✱ **-τοκέω**, *bear two at a birth*, Arist.*HA*558ᵇ23, *GA*772ᵃ 35:—also **δῐτοκεύω**, Nic.*Fr.*72.1. **-τόκος**, ον, *having borne two at a birth*, Anacr.145: opp. μονοτόκος, Arist.*GA*774ᵇ9; but perh. *having borne two children*, *AJA*17.162 (Cyrene). ✱ **-τομία**, *second cutting* of reeds, *POxy.*1631.14 (iii A. D.). **-τονέω**, *have a double accent*, A.D.*Synt.*307.15; or *two accents*, Id.*Pron.*60.16. **-τονιαῖος**, α, ον, = δίτονος, Aristox.*Harm* p.66 M. **-τονίζω**, *accent in two ways*, Sch.rec.S.*Aj.*733. **-τονος**, ον, *of two tones*, διάστημα Gaud.*Harm.*3; δίτονον, τό, *the major third*, Aristox.*Harm.*p.65 M., Cleonid *Harm.*5, Plu.2.430a; also, περισπώμενον, prob. in *Gramm. Lat.*4.527 K. **-τορμία**, ἡ, *double socket* or *tenon*, Ph.*Bel.*63.24, Hero *Bel.*92.9, *Spir.*1.42. **-τρῐχιάω**, *have double eyelashes*, Gal.14. 771. **-τροπος**, ον, expl. of δίχολος, Diogenian.4.32. **-τρόχαιος**, ὁ, *double trochee*, Heph.3.2, Aristid.Quint.1.22. **-τροχία**, ἡ, *windlass with two wheels*, Bito 63.10. **-τροχος**, ον, *two-wheeled*, ἅμαξα *Edict.Diocl.*15.40; καθέδρα Men.Prot.p.51 D.

✱ **διττάμενον**· ἀρνούμενον (Cret.), Hsch.

✱ **διτταχῶς**· διχῶς, Hsch. **διττός**, etc., v. δισσ-.

**δῐτῠλος**, ον, *with two humps*, κάμηλοι D.S.2.54.

**διῠγῐαίνω**, *to be healthy throughout*, Plu.2.135c, Iamb.*VP*22.102.

**διυγραίνω**, *soak thoroughly*, Thphr.*CP*2.9.3 :—Pass., Hp.*Aph*.7.51.

**δίυγρος**, ον, *washed out, pale*, δ. τὴν εἴδεην Hp.*Int*.43 (A.*Th*.990 is corrupt). 2. of a *melting* glance, νεῦμα δ. *AP*12.68.7 (Mel.). II. *liquid, moist*, Arist.*Pr*.887b25 ; ἀναθυμίασις Porph.*Sent*.29 ; στοιχεῖον δ., of the sea, Id.ap.Eus.*PE*3.11 ; τὸ δ. τῆς ὕλης Jul.*Or*.5.165d ; πνεῦμα Iamb.*Myst*.4.13 ; *watery*, αἷμα Steph.*in Hp*.1.132 D.

⊕ **διῠδᾰτίζω**, *give water to drink*, Sch.Il.6.307.

**δίυδρος**, ον, (ὕδωρ) *full of water*, γαστήρ Hp.*Int*.26.

**διῡλ-ίζω**, *strain, filter thoroughly*, οἶνον Mim.*Oxy*.413.154, Dsc.5.72, Artem.4.48 :—Pass., διυλισμένος οἶνος Lxx *Am*.6.6 : metaph., διυλισμένα ἀρετὰ ἀπὸ παντὸς τῶ θνατῶ πάθεος Archyt.ap.Stob.3.1.108, cf. Pl.*Ti*.69a. II. *strain off*, κώνωπα *Ev.Matt*.23.24. **-ῐσις**, εως, ἡ, *filtering, refining, purifying*, Suid. ⊕ **-ισμα**, ατος, τό, *filtered* or *clarified liquor*, Gal.12.836. **-ιστήρ**, ῆρος, ὁ, *filter, strainer*, Sch. Ar.*Pax* 534. **-ιστήριον**, τό, gloss on ἠθμάριον, Hsch. **-ιστός**, ή, όν, *filtered, strained*, ἔλαιον *PRyl*.97.3, cf. Gal.19.688.

**διυπερτίθημι**, *postpone*, *POxy*.1479.6 (i B.C.).

**διυπηρετέομαι**, *serve*, Sch.E.*Ph*.1435.

**διυπνίζω**, (ὕπνος) *awake from sleep*, trans., Ael.*NA*7.46 : intr., Luc.*Ocyp*.108 : —Pass., Diocl.*Fr*.141, J.*AJ*5.10.4 (v.l.), Zos.Alch. p.117 B., *AP*9.378 (Pall.) : but, II. *fall asleep*, Simp. *in Ph*. 1258.25.

**διυπο-βάλλω**, in Pass., of wrestlers in a *clinch*, Theo Sm.p.122 H. **-βλέπω**, gloss on διακυνοφθαλμίζομαι, Hsch.

**διυποπτεύω**, *dissimulate* (?), Zos.Alch.p.208 B.

**δι-ῡφαίνω**, *fill up by weaving*, τὰς διαστάσεις Gal.2.904, cf. Luc. *VH*1.15 :—Pass. ἀράχνιον μήπω διυφασμένον Gal.2.569. 2. *interweave*, in Pass., Ael.*NA*9.17 ; ζώνη διυφασμένη καλλίστοις χρώμασιν Aristeas 97, cf. Lxx *Ex*.36.31 (39.23). **-ύφαντος** [ῠ], ον, *doubly woven*, *PMasp*.6 ii 98 (vi A.D.). ⊕ **-υφή**, ἡ, *woven fabric*, Aristeas 86.

**διυφίημι**, *let fall, drop*, of offspring, in Pass., Ph.2.319 (s.v.l.).

**διφαδεύει**· ἐξελεῖται, Hsch. **δίφακος**, a *plant*, Id.

**δῐφᾰλαγγ-άρχης**, ου, ὁ, *leader of a* διφαλαγγαρχία, Suid. **-αρχία**, ἡ, *corps of two* φαλαγγαρχίαι or 8,192 men (half a phalanx), Ael.*Tact*. 9.9, Arr.*Tact*.10.7. **-ία**, ἡ, *phalanx marching in two divisions*, Plb.2.66.9, 12.20.7, Ael.*Tact*.36.3, Arr.*Tact*.28.6. 2. = διφαλαγγαρχία, Ascl.*Tact*.2.10, Ael.*Tact*.33.5.

**δῐφᾰλέος**, α, ον, (διφάω) *searching, sagacious*, *Hymn.Is*.10.

**διφάνινος** λύχνος, dub. sens. in *PLond*.2.193.29 (ii A.D.).

**δίφας**, ἡ, a kind of *serpent*, Artem.2.13 ; cf. δίβαν, δίφατον.

**δῐφᾰσία**, ἡ, (δίφατος) = διλογία, Hsch.

**δῐφάσιος** [ᾰ], α, ον, Ion. Adj., *of two kinds*, γράμματα Hdt.2.36 ; αἰτίαι Id.3.122, cf. *Schwyzer* 725 (Milet.), Eus.Mynd.63. II. in pl., = δύο, Hdt.1.18, 2.17, al.

**δίφατον**· ὄφιν (Cret.), Hsch.

**δῐφᾰτος** [ῐ], ον, *ambiguous*, Hsch.

⊕ **δῐφ-άω**, only pres., *search after*, πόντῳ ἐν ἰχθυόεντι.. τήθεα διφῶν Il.16.747 ; τεὴν διφῶσα καλιήν Hes.*Op*.374 ; ἐν οὔρεσι πάντα λαγωὸν διφᾷ Call.*Epigr*.33, cf. *Fr*.165 ; διφᾷ τὰ καλύμματα (or καλλύσματα, q.v.) *search* them *well*, Thphr.*Char*.10.6 : abs., Herod.6.73 ; εἴ ποθι διφώωσα.. ἀθρήσειεν Nonn.*D*.48.592 :—Ion. διφέω, *AP*9.559 (Crin.). **-ήτωρ**, ορος, ὁ, *a searcher*, βυθῶν διφήτορες Opp.*H*.2.435.

⊕ **διφθέρα**, ἡ, *prepared hide, piece of leather*, Hdt.1.194 ; ἐκ διφθερέων πεποιημέναι κυνέαι Id.7.77 ; διφθέραι, opp. δέρρεις (hides), Th.2.75 ; of a *drum*, Hero *Aut*.20.4 ; esp. as writing-material, τὰς βύβλους διφθέρας καλέουσι ἀπὸ τοῦ παλαιοῦ οἱ Ἴωνες Hdt.5.58 ; δ. μελαγγραφεῖς E.*Fr*.627 ; δ. βασιλικαί, of Persian records, Ctes.ap.D.S.2.32 ; δ. ἱεραί, at Carthage, Plu.2.942c ; χαλκαῖ δ., ib.297a, cf. Sch.Il.1.175 : prov., ἀρχαιότερα τῆς διφθέρας λέγεις Diogenian.2.2 ; used for bindings, διφθέρας περιβάλλειν sc. βιβλίοις Luc.*Ind*.16. II. *anything made of leather, leathern jerkin*, Ar.*Nu*.72, Pl.*Cri*.53d, *SIG* 1259.6 (iv B.C.), Men.*Epit*.12, Luc.*Tim*.6,38, Arr.*An*.7.9.2, etc.; properly, *of goatskin*, opp. μηλωτή, Ammon.*Diff*.p.44 V. 2. *wallet, bag*, X.*An*.5.2.12, Lib.*Or*.58.5. 3. pl., *skins used as tents*, X.*An*. 1.5.10, Phylarch.41 J.

⊕ **διφθερ-άλοιφος** [ᾰ], ὁ, Cypr. for *a schoolmaster*, *JHS*12.330, Hsch. **-άριος**, ὁ, *parchment-maker*, *Edict.Diocl.Asin*.7.38. ⊕ **-ίας**, ου, ὁ, *clad in a leathern jerkin* ; the dress of old men in Tragedy, of boors in Comedy, Posidipp.ap.Ath.10.414e, Luc.*Tim*.8, Poll.4.137. **-ινος**, η, ον, *of tanned leather*, σχεδίαι X.*An*.2.4.28 ; πλοῖα Str.3.3.7. ⊕ **-ιον**, τό, Dim. of διφθέρα, Theognost.*Can*.125.25. **-ίς**, ίδος, ἡ, = διφθέρα, *AP*9.546 (Antiphil.). **-ῖτις**, ιδος, fem. of διφθερίας, Poll.4.138. **-όομαι**, Pass., *to be clad in leather*, Str.17.3.11.

**διφθεροπώλης**, ου, ὁ, *leather-seller*, Nicoph.19.

**διφθέρωμα**, ατος, τό, = διφθέρα, Thd.*Is*.8.1.

**διφθογγ-ίζω**, *write with a diphthong*, Eust.1571.29. **-ιστέον**, *one must write with a diphthong*, Tz.*H*.5.690.

**διφθογγογρᾰφέω**, = διφθογγίζω, Sch.rec.S.*Aj*.715, etc.

**διφθογγόομαι**, *to be written with a diphthong*, Hdn.*Epim*.276.

**δίφθογγος**, ον, *with two sounds*, γραφή Tz.*H*.5.694 : δίφθογγος, ἡ, *diphthong*, D.T.639.15, A.D.*Adv*.128.8, al. : later δίφθογγον, τό, Hdn.*Epim*.245.

⊕ **δῐφορ-έω**, *to bear double*, esp. of fruit, Thphr.*CP*1.14.1. II. Pass., *to be spelt* or *pronounced in two ways*, Hdn.*Gr*.2.543, *EM*197.51, al. III. διφορούμενος συλλογισμός syllogism with an identical proposition as premise, *Stoic*.2.87, al. **-ησις**, εως, ἡ, *double mode of writing*, Eust.74.1. ⊕ **-ος**, ον, *bearing fruit twice in the year*, Ar.*Ec*.708, Pherecr.97, Antiph.198, Thphr.*HP*1.14.1. 2. *bearing two kinds of fruit*, Ph.2.369. II. metaph., *paying twice over*, of Ephorus, Hsch.

**διφοῦρα**, = γέφυρα (Lacon.), Hsch. **διφράγες**, name of a corps of Parthian soldiers, Id.

**δίφρ-ακον**, ου, τό, = δίφρος, *seat*, *Michel* 832.46 (Samos, iv B.C.). ⊕ **-αξ**, ᾰκος, ἡ, poet. for δίφρος, *seat, chair*, Theoc.14.41 :—also **-άς**, άδος, ἡ, Hom.*Epigr*.15.8 (v.l. δίφρακα). **-εία**, ἡ, *chariot-driving*, X.*Cyr*.6.1.27, Procl.*H*.1.11 (pl.), Lib.*Decl*.12.14 ; δ. ἁρμάτων, ἵππων, Arr.*Tact*.19.4. **-ελάτειρα** [ᾰ], ἡ, pecul. fem. of διφρηλάτης, *APl*. 4.359. **-ευτής**, οῦ, ὁ, *charioteer*, S.*Aj*.857. **-ευτικός**, ή, όν, *concerned with chariot-driving*, ἐπιστήμη Ephor.97 J. **-εύω**, *drive a chariot*, E.*Andr*.108 (eleg.), Heraclit.*Incred*.22. 2. c. acc., *drive over*, δ. ἅλιον πέλαγος E.*Andr*.1010 (lyr.) ; νύξ.. νῶτα διφρεύουσ' αἰθέρος Id.*Fr*.114. 3. c. acc. cogn., αἴγλαν ἐδίφρευ' Ἅλιος.. κατ' αἰθέρα Id.*Supp*.991 (lyr.) ; ὅταν Φαέθων πυμάτην ἁψῖδα διφρεύῃ Archestr.*Fr*.33. 4. = διακαθίζω, Hsch. **-ηλᾰσία**, ἡ, *chariot-driving*, Pi.*O*.3.38. ⊕ **-ηλᾰτέω**, *drive a chariot*, τὸν οὐρανὸν δ., of the Sun, S.*Aj*.845 ; δ. ἵππους E.*Rh*.781 : in late Prose, Phlp. *in Mete*. 101.27. **-ηλάτης** [ᾰ], ου, ὁ, *charioteer*, Pi.*P*.9.81, A.*Eu*.156 (lyr.), S.*El*.753, E.*IA*216 (lyr.), etc.—Poet. and later Prose, Luc.*DDeor*. 25.1. **-ήλᾰτος**, ον, *car-borne*, E.*Fr*.1108. **-ίδιον**, τό, Dim. of δίφρος, *EM*718.45 (pl.). ⊕ **-ίον**, τό, Dim. of δίφρος, Tim.*Lex*. s.v. σκολύθρια. **-ιος**, α, ον, *of a chariot* : neut. pl. as Adv., δίφρια συρόμενος dragged *at the chariot wheels*, *AP*7.152. **-ις**, ὁ, *sedentary person*, Hsch. (fort. διφρίας). **-ίσκος**, ὁ, Dim. of δίφρος, Ar.*Nu*.31.

**δί-φροντις**, ιδος, ὁ, ἡ, *divided in mind, doubting*, A.*Ch*.196.

**διφροπηγία**, ἡ, *cart-building*, Thphr.*HP*5.7.6.

⊕ **δίφρος**, ὁ, heterocl. pl. δίφρα, τά, Call.*Dian*.135, Nonn.*D*.27.238 : (perh. for διφόρος) :—*chariot-board*, on which *two* could stand, the driver (ἡνίοχος) and the combatant (παραιβάτης), Il.5.160, 11.748, Hes.*Sc*.61 : metaph., ἕστηκεν ἐν τῷ δ. τῆς πόλεως Pl.*R*.566d. 2. *chariot*, Il.10.305, al., Pi.*P*.2.10, al., Arr.*Tact*.19.3, etc. ; ἐϋπλέκτῳ ἐνὶ δίφρῳ Il.23.335 ; μεταμείβοντος δίφρον ἐκ δίφρου Jul.*Or*.3.122b ; of the Sun's *chariot*, E.*Ph*.2, Call.*Dian*.111 ; Μοισᾶν δ. Pi.*O*.9.81 ; *travelling-car*, Od.3.324 ; *litter*, δ. κατάστεγος D.C.60.2. II. *seat, couch, stool*, Il.3.424, 6.354, Od.19.97, Ar.*Eq*.1164, Pl.*R*.328c, etc. ; δ. Θετταλικός Eup.58 ; = Lat. *sella curulis*, Plb.6.53.9, etc. ; judge's *seat of office*, Lxx 1*Ki*.1.9, al. ; royal *throne*, *OGI*199.38 (i A.D.) ; *night-stool*, Aristid.*Or*.49(25).19.

**διφρ-ουλκέω**, (ἕλκω) *draw a chariot*, *AP*9.285 (Phil.). **-ουργία**, ἡ, (ἔργον) *making chairs*, Thphr.*HP*3.10.1. **-οῦχος**, ον, (ἔχω) *with a seat*, ἅρμα Melanipp.1.

**διφρο-φορέω**, *carry in a chair* or *litter*, D.C.47.10 :—Pass., *travel in one*, οἱ διφροφορούμενοι, of the Persian princes, Hdt.3.146, cf. D.C.60.2, Lib.*Or*.25.32. II. *carry a camp-stool* (cf. sq.), Ar.*Av*. 1552. **-φόρος**, ον, *carrying a camp-stool* ; esp. of the female μέτοικοι, who had to carry seats for the use of the κανηφόροι, Id.*Ec*. 734, Hermipp.26, Nicoph.16, Strattis 8 ; also ὁ βασιλέως δ. Dinon 18.

⊕ **δι-φρῠγής**, ές, (φρύγω) *twice roasted* : διφρυγές, τό, *baked clay* or *pyrites from copper-mines*, Dsc.5.103,125, Gal.12.214. ⊕ **-φυής**, ές : neut. pl. διφυῆ, also διφυᾶ Arist.*PA*669b18 (s.v.l.) :—*of double nature* or *form*, ἔχιδνα μειξοπάρθενος δ. Hdt.4.9 ; of Centaurs, S.*Tr*. 1095, Pherecyd.50 J. ; of Pan, Pl.*Cra*.408d ; Κέκροψ, i.e. man and serpent, but expld. as *of double sex* (Suid.), or *of double race* (Egyptian and Greek), D.S.1.28 ; δ. Ἔρως *sexual intercourse*, Orph.*A*. 14. 2. generally, *twofold, double*, κόραι Ion Lyr.16 ; ὀφρύες Arist. *HA*491b14 ; στῆθος διφυὲς μαστοῖς ib.493a12 ; ἡ τῶν μυκτήρων δύναμις Id.*PA*657a4 ; μῦς, of the biceps, Gal.*UP*13.13 ; αὐλὸς Aret.*SD*2. 13. **-φυΐα**, ἡ, *bipartition*, τῶν κώλων Arist.*PA*668b22. ⊕ **-φυιος** [ῐ], ον, = διφυής, Antag.1.7. II. = δύο, A.*Ag*.1469 (lyr.). III. = διπλοῦς, *Schwyzer* 411.5, 419.8 (Elis) : ζίφ- prob. in ib.410.1 (ibid.). ⊕ **-φωνος**, ον, *speaking two languages*, Philist.62, D.S.17. 110.

**δίχᾰ** [ῐ], (δίς), I. Adv. *in two, asunder*, δ. πάντας.. ἠρίθμεον Od.10.203 ; δ. πάντα δέδασται 15.412 ; πλευροκοπῶν δ. ἀνερρήγνυ S. *Aj*.236 ; δ. πρίσαντες Th.4.100 ; τέμνειν δ. Pl.*Sph*.265e ; δ. διαλαβεῖν Id.*Tht*.147e ; δ. τὸ στράτευμα ποιεῖν X.*An*.6.4.11 ; δ. τὴν δύναμιν λαβεῖν catch the force *divided*, Th.6.10 ; ὅτι δ. πέφυκε (sc. ἡ Σικελία) is *divided against itself*, Id.4.61 : generally, *apart, aloof*, διαστῆναι Hdt.4.180 ; κεῖσθαι Pi.*P*.5.93 ; οἰκεῖν S.*OC*602. 2. metaph., *at two, two ways*, whether with others or oneself, *at variance* or *in doubt*, δ. δέ σφισι ἥνδανε βουλή Il.18.510 ; δίχα θυμὸν ἔχοντες 20. 32 ; δ. δέ σφιν ἐνὶ φρεσὶ θυμὸς ἄητο 21.386 ; δ. θυμὸς ἐνὶ φρεσὶ μερμηρίζει Od.16.73 ; δ. θυμὸς ὀρώρεται ἔνθα καὶ ἔνθα 19.524 ; δίχα βάζομεν 3.127 ; δ. μοι τὰ νοήματα prob. in Sapph.36 ; μὴ γλώσσῃ δ. ἔχειν νόον Thgn.91, etc. ; ἐγίνοντο δ. αἱ γνῶμαι Hdt.6.109 ; δόξα δ' ἐχώρει δίχα E.*Hec*.117 ; μαθήσεται ὅσον τό τ' ἄρχειν καὶ τὸ δουλεύειν δίχα *differ*, A.*Pr*.927 ; τὸ γὰρ τοπάζειν τοῦ σάφ' εἰδέναι δ. Id.*Ag*.1369 ; δ. ψηφίζεσθαι *on different sides*, X.*Mem*.4.4.8 ; ἐὰν δ. γένηται τὸ δικαστήριον Arist.*Pol*.1318a40. II. Prep., c. gen., *apart from*, Emp.21.19 ; *without*, πυρός, ἄρσενος, A.*Th*.25, *Ag*.861 ; ἀνθρώπων δ. S.*Ph*.31 ; οἷος Ἀτρειδῶν δ. Id.*Aj*.750 ; μόνη.. φασγάνου δ. Id.*Tr*.1063 ; δ. τέλους *Supp.Epigr*.1.329.25 (Istros, i A.D.) ; δ. γνώμης ἐμῆς καὶ συγκαταθέσεως *PFlor*.58.8 (iii A.D.) ; δ. πραγμάτων Jul.*Or*.7.212a, etc. 2. *differently from, unlike*, δ. ἄλλων A.*Ag*.757 ; σῆς δ. γνώμης λέγω S.*El*.

547. 3. πόλεως δ. *against the will of*, Id.*OC*48, cf. *Aj*.768. 4. *except*, δ. γε Διός A.*Pr*.163; τῶν λελεγμένων δ. Id.*Ch*.778. 5. *besides*, dub. in D.H.7.19.—As a Prep. it commonly follows its case in Trag., but precedes it in A.*Pr*. l. c., S.*Ph*.195, al., E.*IT*185.

**δῐχάδε**, Adv. = δίχα, διοιχθέντες Pl.*Smp*.215b.

**δῐχάδεια**, = δίχα (?), Theognost.*Can*.164.26.

**δῐχάζω**, fut. -άσω Plot.5.3.10:—*divide in two*, Pl.*Plt*.264d (of logical dichotomy):—Pass., Nonn.*D*.3.33, al.; αἴγειρος.. διισσοῖσι κλάδοις δεδιχασμένη ἑνὸς ἐκ στελέχους Lyr.in *Philol*.80.334; δεδιχασμένον διχασμῷ Aq.*De*.14.6. b. *divide by two*, Nicom.*Ar*.1.7, al. (Pass.). 2. δ. τινὰ κατά τινος *divide* one against another, *Ev.Matt*.10.35. II. intr., *to be divided*, interpol. in X.*An*.4.8.18; διχαζούσης ἡμέρας at *mid*-day, Anon.ap.Suid.

**δίχαιος**, coined to expl. δίκαιος, Arist.*EN*1132ᵃ32.

**δῐχαίτης**, *disulcis*, *Gloss*.

**δῐχαίω**, = διχάζω, in Pass., Arat.495,807.

**δῐ-χάλα**, ἡ, Dor. for διχήλη, the *fork* of the legs, Medici ap.Gal. 14.707. -**χαλκον**, τό, *double chalcus*, a copper coin, = ¼ of an obol, *AP*11.165 (Lucill.), Poll.9.65; as a weight (variously expld.), Dsc.4.150, etc. -**χᾱλος**, Dor. for δίχηλος (q. v.). II. δίχαλον ζυγόν· τὸν ἑκατέρωθεν κεκοιλασμένον, Hsch.

**δῐχάμετρος**, ον, to explain διάμετρος, Arist.*Pr*.910ᵇ20.

**δίχανον**· κεχωρισμένον, Hsch.

**δῐχάρακτος** [χᾰ], ον, [νόμισμα] *doubly stamped*, i. e. in mint condition, *IGRom*.4.595 (Phrygia).

**δῐχ-άς**, άδος, ἡ, *the half*, *middle*, Arat.807. -**ᾰσις**, εως, ἡ, *division*, *halving*, Id.737. -**ασμός**, ὁ, *division into two parts*, Aq.*De*.14.6. 2. *division by two*, Nicom.*Ar*.1.10. II. *payment in two instalments*, dub. in Ἀρχ.Ἐφ.1917.133 (Perrhaebia). -**αστής**, οῦ, ὁ, *divider*, to explain δικαστής, Arist.*EN*1132ᵃ32. -**αστῆρες** ὀδόντες, οἱ, *the incisors*, Poll.2.91. ※ -**αστός**, ή, όν, *divisible by two*, *Theol.Ar*.35. -**άω**, poet. for διχάζω, Ep. part. διχόωντι, -όωσα, Arat.512,605:—Med., διχόωνται Id.856:—Pass., διχόωντο A.R.4.1616.

**δίχειλον**, *bilabrum*, *Gloss*.

**δῐχή**, ἡ, *bisection*, Ascl.*in Metaph*.34.19.

**δῐχῇ**, Adv. = δίχα, *in two*, *asunder*, A.*Supp*.544 (lyr.), Pl.*Ti*.62c, etc. 2. *in two ways*, δ. ἐπονομασθῆναι Id.*R*.445d; δεῖ δ. τὴν βοήθειαν εἶναι D.1.18.

**δῐχηλ-έω**, ὁπλὴν δ. *divide* the hoof, Arist.*PA*695ᵃ18 (v.l.), Aristeas150, Lxx *Le*.11.3, al., Ph.2.353 (**διχηλεύω** is v.l. in Lxx *De*.14.6). -**ησις**, εως, ἡ, *dividing of the hoofs*, Ph.1.321: -**ία**, ἡ, = foreg., Aristeas161. -**ος**, ον, *cloven-hoofed*, Hdt.2.71; δ. ἔμβασις E.*Ba*.740:—freq. in Dor. form **δίχᾱλος**, Arist.*PA*663ᵃ31, al. II. *with two pincers*, *prongs*, or *claws*, πυραγρέτης *AP*6.92 (Phil.); πάγουρος ib.196 (Stat. Flacc.), cf. Hero *Bel*.76.10; δίχιλα (sic) ξύλα *BGU*37.4 (i A.D.); εἰς δίχηλον διεσχισμένος Hero *Spir*.1.28. III. Subst., δίχηλα ὕεια pigs' *trotters*, Luc.*Lex*.6; cf. διχάλα.

**δῐχήρης**, ες, *dividing in twain*, κύκλος.. μηνὸς διχήρης, of the moon, E.*Ion*1156.

**δῐχθά**, Adv., Ep. for δίχα, δ. δεδαίαται they are parted *in twain*, Od.1.23; δ. δέ μοι κραδίη μέμονε my heart is *divided*, Il.16.435.

※ **δῐχθάδιος** [ᾰ], α, ον, *twofold*, *double*, κῆρες Il.9.411, 14.21; δ. κατὰ κῶλον in *either* leg, *APl*.1.15; simply, *two*, *AP*6.4 (Leon.), al.

**δῐχθάς**, άδος, ἡ, fem. of foreg., Musae.298.

**δῐχίτων** [χῐ], ωνος, ὁ, ἡ, *with two coats*, ἀρτηρίαι Gal.4.728:—also **δῐχίτωνος**, ον, Id.19.366.

**δῐχό-βουλος**, ον, *of different counsel*, *adverse*, Νέμεσις Pi.*O*.8.86. -**γνωμέω**, = sq., Poll.2.229. -**γνωμονέω**, *to differ in opinion*, X.*Mem*.2.6.21, D.C.44.25; δ. πρὸς ἑαυτόν Iamb.ap.Stob.2.33.15. 2. *doubt*, Lib.*Decl*.43.43. -**γνωμος**, ον, *ambiguous*, Sch.E.*Or*.890. -**γνωμοσύνη**, ἡ, *discord*, Poll.8.153. -**γνώμων**, ὁ, ἡ, gen. ονος, *divided between two opinions*, Plu.2.11c. Adv. -γνωμόνως Poll.8.154. -**γρᾰφέω**, *write in two ways*, St.Byz. s.v. Δώτιον (Pass.). -**ζωνος**, ον, = διχόμηνος, Doroth. in *Cat.Cod.Astr*.2.82. -**θεν**, Adv. *from both sides*, *both ways*, A.*Pers*.76 (lyr.), Ar.*Pax*477, Th.2.44, etc.; δ. μισθοφορεῖν D.24.123; *from two sources*, τὸ δίκαιον δ. συνίσταται Aps.*Rh*.p.294 H. -**θῦμος**, ον, *wavering*, cj. in Pittac.1 Bgk.

**δῐχοινῖκ-ία**, ἡ, *tax of two* χοίνικες *per* ἄρουρα, *PLond*.372.25 (ap. *PTeb*.ii p.339) (ii A.D.), etc. -**ιος**, ον, = sq., *PSI*1.33.18 (iii A.D.). ※ -**ος**, ον, *holding two* χοίνικες, Ar.*Nu*.640. II. Subst. διχοίνικον, τό, *measure of two* χ., *SIG*945.4 (pl., Assos, iv B.C.).

**δῐ-χολος** [ῐ], ον, *with double gall*, Ael.*NA*11.29. II. *at variance*, πόλις cj. in Alc.37 A; δ. γνῶμαι, = διάφοροι, Achae.39. -**χόλωτος**, ον, *doubly furious*, v.l. for τριχόλωτος, ἀνάγκη *AP*9.168 (Pall.).

**δῐχό-μην**, ηνος, ὁ, ἡ, = διχόμηνος, σελήνη Arat.78, cf. 737. -**μηνία**, ἡ, *full moon*, *IG*1².6.62, *PRev.Laws*56.18 (iii B.C.), Lxx *Si*.39.12, Gem.8.1, etc.; δ. μηνὸς Μεταγειτνιῶνος *Inscr.Prien*.4.45 (iv B.C.); ἡ σελήνη δ. ἦγεν Plu.*Dio*23. 2. *mid-menstrual period*, Hp.*Oct*.13. -**μηνιαία** (sc. ἡμέρα), ἡ, *day of full moon*, Gal.9.908; also, = Lat. *Idus*, Suid. -**μηνιάς**, άδος, ἡ, = διχόμηνις, Max.454. -**μηνις**, ιδος, ὁ, ἡ, = sq., Μήνα Pi.*O*.3.19, cf. A.R.4.167; δ. ἑσπέραι evenings *at the full of the moon*, Pi.*I*.8(7).47; νύξ B.8.29. II. ἡμέρα, = Lat. *Idus*, D.H.1.38, etc. -**μηνος**, ον, (μήν) *dividing the month*, i. e. *at* or *of the full moon*, ἑσπερίη *h.Hom*.32.11; δ. σελήνη *Gp*.10.48.2, cf. Plu.*Flam*.4; διχόμηνος, ἡ, Arat.808, Ph.2.293; διχομήνη, ἡ, *Gp*.2.14.7, *Cat.Cod.Astr*.1.173. -**μῡθος**, ον, *double-speaking*, νόημα Pittac.1 Bgk.; γλῶσσα Sol.42.4; *double-dealing*, *deceptive*, Ant.Lib.23; λέγειν διχόμυθα speak *ambiguously*, E.*Or*.890.

**διχόνδις**· ἀπύγων, Hsch.

※ **δῐχο-νοέω**, = διχογνωμονέω, condemned by Poll.2.228. -**νοητικός**, ή, όν, *indicating doubt*, Eust.166.28. Adv. -κῶς *discordantly*, *Gloss*. -**νοια**, ἡ, *discord*, *disagreement*, Pl.*Alc*.1.126c, Plu.2.70c; δ. περὶ τοῦ ἀρίστου Ph.2.181: c. gen., *disagreement with*, τῆς Ἀντωνίου γνώμης App.*BC*5.33. -**νοος**, ον, contr. -**νους**, ουν, *double-minded*, Ph.2.269, cf. 663. -**ποιός**, όν, *productive of division*, opp. ἑνοποιός, Alex.Aphr.*in Metaph*.58.11.

**δῐ-χορδος** [ῐ], ον, *two-stringed*, πηκτίς Sopat.11:—Subst. -**χορδον**, τό, Euphro1.34. -**χόρειος** (sc. πούς), ὁ, *ditrochaeus*, Longin.41.1. -**χορία**, ἡ, *division of a chorus into two parts*, Poll.4.107, Arg.Ar.*Lys*.1. -**χοριάζω**, *sing in two halves*, of a chorus, Hsch.

**δῐχο-ρρᾰγής**, ές, (ῥήγνυμι) *broken in twain*, E.*HF*1008 (lyr.). -**ρροπος**, ον, *oscillating*, γνώμη *Trag.Adesp*.341. Adv. -πως *waveringly*, *doubtfully*, used only by A., and always with a neg., οὐ or μὴ δ. *Ag*.349,815,1272, *Supp*.605,982. -**στᾰσία**, ἡ, *dissension*, B.10.67 (pl.), Hdt.5.75, Eus.Mynd.45, Plu.2.2cc; *sedition*, Sol.4.38, Thgn.78, Lxx 1 *Ma*.3.29. -**στᾰτέω**, (στῆναι) *stand apart*, *disagree*, ὄξος τ' ἄλειφά τ'.. διχοστατοῦντ' ἂν οὐ φίλως προσεννέποις A.*Ag*.323; δ. λάχη Id.*Eu*.386 (lyr.); λόγος S.*Fr*.867; δ. πρός τινα E.*Med*.15, Pl.*R*.465b. II. *feel doubts*, Alex.Aphr.*Fr.Praef*. -**στομος**, ον, = δίστομος II, δορὸς πλᾶκτρον S.*Fr*.152. ※ -**τομέω**, *cut in twain*: *bisect* a line, Plb.6.28.2:—Pass., Arist.*Pr*.913ᵇ31; σώματος -ηθέντος Plu.*Pyrrh*.24: metaph. of the medial raphe of the perineum, Paul.Aeg.6.62, etc. 2. *punish with the last severity*, *Ev.Matt*.24.51. 3. *divide into two* (logically), Pl.*Plt*.302e, Arist.*PA*642ᵇ22, 644ᵇ19. 4. intr., of the moon, dub. in Plu.2.929f. -**τόμημα**, ατος, τό, *half of a thing cut in two*: hence, generally, *any portion of a thing cut up*, Lxx *Ez*.29.17, *Le*.1.8, Ph.1.503 (pl.). -**τόμησις**, εως, ἡ, = sq., κύκλου S.E.*M*.9.284. -**τομία**, ἡ, *dividing in two*, of the moon's quarters, Arist.*GA*777ᵇ22, Gem.9.3, Simp.*in Ph*.455.22; *bisection*, Theo Sm.p.184 H. 2. *point of bisection*, Archim.*Aequil*.1.6, al. b. *point of division* between wings of army, Ascl.*Tact*.2.6. II. *division into two parts* (logically), *dichotomy*, Arist.*PA*644ᵃ9, Iamb.*Comm.Math*.1. -**τομιαῖος**, α, ον, = sq., Paul.Al.*G*.4. -**τόμος**, ον, *cutting in two*, Ammon.p.44 V.: but, II. proparox., διχότομος, ον, *cut in half*, *divided equally*, μυκτήρ Arist.*HA*492ᵇ17; δ. σελήνη the *half*-moon, Id.*Pr*.911ᵇ36, Aristarch.Sam.*Hyp*.3, Gem.9.8, prob. in Plu.2.929f; σελήνης σύμβολον τὸ δ. Porph. ap.Eus.*PE*3.11; μέχρι διχοτόμου till *the second quarter*, Antyll.ap. Orib.9.3.2; κατ' ἀμφοτέρας τὰς διχοτόμους (sc. φάσεις) at *the first and third quarters*, Ptol.*Alm*.5.1.

**δῐχοῦ**, Adv. = δίχα, δ. σφέας διελόντες Hdt.4.120, Choer.*in Theod*.1.388.

**δῐ-χους** [ῐ], ουν, neut. pl. δίχοα, *holding two* χόες, Posidon.25 J., Arist.*Ath*.67.2; δίχουν, τό, Dsc.5.57.

**δῐχο-φορέω**, = sq., Plu.2.447d. -**φρονέω**, *to hold different opinions*, ib.763e. -**φροσύνη**, ἡ, *discord*, *faction*, ib.824d (pl.), Ocell.4.6, D.Chr.44.10, Anon.ap.Iamb.*VP*7.34. -**φρων**, ον, gen. ονος, (φρήν) *at variance*, πότμος δ. a destiny *full of discord*, A.*Th*.899 (lyr.). -**φυής**, ές, *forked*, Gal.14.707. -**φῠΐα**, ἡ, *a disease of the hair, when it splits*, Id.19.430. -**φωνέω**, *disagree*, Pythagorei ap.Iamb.*in Nic*.p.73 P. -**φωνία**, ἡ, (φωνή) *discord*, Id.*VP*7.34.

**δῐχόω**, f. l. for δικραιόω in Hp.*Oss*.10.

**δῐ-χροια**, ἡ, *double colour*, Arist.*GA*751ᵃ32. -**χρονία**, ἡ, in Metric, *two short syllables*, Sch.Heph.p.110 C. II. Pythag. name for *six*, *Theol.Ar*.37. -**χρονος**, ον, in Metre, *of two quantities*, *common*, D.H.*Comp*.14, Plu.2.737e, S.E.*M*.1.100; περὶ διχρόνων, title of treatise by Hdn.Gr. II. *consisting of two short syllables*, [πούς] Heph.3.1, cf. Arc.139.20: metaph. of the pulse, Ruf.*Syn.Puls*.4.4. III. *equivalent to two time-units*, Longin.*Proll.Heph*.p.87 C. -**χροος**, ον, contr. -**χρους**, ουν, *two-coloured*, ᾠά Arist.*HA*489ᵇ14, *GA*749ᵃ18. -**χρωμος**, ον, = foreg., Luc.*Prom.Es*4, Gal.13.460. II. Subst. δίχρωμος, ἡ, name of a *plaster*, Aët.15.13. 2. δίχρωμον, τό, = περιστερεῶν ὕπτιος, Ps.-Dsc.4.60. -**χρως**, ων, = foreg., Arist.*HA*564ᵇ24. -**χρωτος**, ον, = foreg., *Gloss*.

**δίχωρον**, τό, a *measure of wine* in Egypt, = eight χόες, *BGU*531 ii 5 (i A.D.), etc.

**δῐχῶς**, Adv. *doubly*, *in two ways*, A.*Ch*.915 (dub.), Arist.*Mu*.393ᵃ24, Ascl.*Tact*.10.10; *in two senses*, Arist.*Po*.1457ᵃ28.

**δίψα**, ης, ἡ, *thirst*, δ. τε καὶ λιμός Il.19.166; πεῖνα καὶ δ. Pl.*R*.585a; δίψῃ ξυνέχεσθαι Th.2.49, etc.; of trees, Antiph.231.6, *PFlor*.176.12 (iii A.D.): pl., Arist.*EN*1154ᵇ3. 2. c. gen., *thirst for*, ποτοῦ Pl.*R*.437d: metaph., ἀοιδᾶν δ. Pi.*P*.9.104.—The form **δίψη** occurs in Opp.*C*.4.339, and in codd. of A.*Ch*.756; cf. δίψος.

**δίψαι**· βλάψαι, Hsch.; cf. δίψιος I. fin.

**δῐψ-ᾰκερός**, ά, όν, *thirsty*, *EM*801.48; expld. by ταλαίπωρον, Hsch. -**ᾰκος**, ὁ, prob. a kind of *diabetes*, *attended with violent thirst*, Gal.8.394, Alex.Trall.11.6. II. *teasel*, *Dipsacus fullonum*, Dsc.3.11, Gal.11.864. -**ᾰλέος**, α, ον, *thirsty*, μῦς Batr.9; ἀνήρ Call.*Jov*.27, cf. *AP*9.128; ἐπιθυμία Ph.1.116; δ. θρυαλλίδιον *wanting oil*, Luc.*Tim*.14; ὀδύνη δ. the pain *of thirst*, Id.*Dips*.6; ὄργανα δ. *subject to thirst*, Aret.*SA*2.4. 2. *dry*, *parched*, ἀήρ A.R.4.678, Nonn.*D*.22.260, al. II. *thirst-provoking*, χοῖρος *AP*9.487 (Pall.). -**άρα**· δέλτος, οἱ δὲ διφθέρα, Hsch. ※ -**άς**, άδος, used as fem. of δίψιος, βοτάναι Euph.141; χῶραι J.*BJ*3.3.1, cf. Opp.*C*.4.322, etc. II. Subst., *venomous serpent*, *whose bite caused intense thirst*, Nic.*Th*.334, Ael

*NA*6.51; δ. ἔχιδνα *AP*7.172 (Antip. Sid.), *IG*4.620.4 (Argos). 2. δ. ἄκανθα a desert *thorn*, *Acacia tortilis*, Thphr.*HP*4.7.1. ⊛ -άω, late Ep. -ώω Tryph.548, *AP*11.57 (Agath.): Ion. -έω Archil.68; part. διψεῦσα *AP*6.21; contr. 3 sg. διψῇ Pi.*N*.3.6, Pl.*Phlb*.35b; inf. διψῆν Hdt.2.24, S.*Fr*.735, Ar.*Nu*.441, etc.: impf. 3 sg. ἐδίψη Hp. *Epid*.3.1.β',γ' (διψᾷς, -ᾷ, -ᾶν only in later writers, *APl*.4.137 (Phil.), Pl.*Ax*.366a, Lxx *Is*.29.8, Gal.5.837): fut. -ήσω X.*Mem*.2.1.17: aor. ἐδίψησα Pl.*R*.562c: pf. δεδίψηκα Hp.*Cord*.2, Plu.*Pomp*.73:—Med. (v. infr.):—*thirst*, στεῦτο δὲ διψάων [ᾰ] Od.11.584, etc.; of the ground, *to be thirsty, parched*, Hdt.2.24; δ. ὑπὸ καύματος Alc.39.2; of trees, Thphr.*CP*3.22.5:—Med., διψώμεθα Hermipp.25. 2. metaph., δ. τινός *thirst after* a thing, Pi.*N*.3.6; ἐλευθερίας Pl.*R*.562c: later c. acc., δ. Χῖον Teles p.8 H.; φόνον *APl*.4.137 (Phil.); δικαιοσύνην *Ev.Matt*. 5.6; αἷμα J.*BJ*1.32.2; also δ. πρὸς τὸν θεόν Lxx *Ps*.41(42).2: c. dat., ὕδατι ib.*Ex*.17.3: c. inf., διψῶ χαρίζεσθαι ὑμῖν X.*Cyr*.5.1.1; ἀκρατῶς ἐδίψη οἴνου πίνειν Ael.*VH*2.41, etc. -ηρός, ά, όν, = δίψιος, Hp.*Aër*.7; [οἶνος] Posidipp.34 (s. v.l.):—also -ήρης, ες, Nic.*Th*. 371. ⊛ -ησις, εως, ἡ, *a thirst, longing*, Ath.1.10b; cf. δίψα. -ητικός, ή, όν, *thirsty*, Arist.*PA*671ᵃ2. 2. *provoking thirst*, ὁ φόβος -κόν Id.*Pr*.947ᵇ39: Comp., Dsc.1.128. ⊛ -ιος, α, ον, also ος, ον A.*Ch*. 185, Nic.*Th*.147: (δίψα):—*thirsty*, and of things, *dry, parched*, δ. κόνις A.*Ag*.495, S.*Ant*.246; χθών E.*Alc*.560; πῦρ θεοῦ Id.*Rh*.417; ἐξ ὀμμάτων δὲ δίψιοι πίπτουσι σταγόνες, perh. *tears checked in their flow*, A.*Ch*.185; δίψιον, expld. by βεβλαμμένον, S.*Fr*.296, by βλαπτικόν, Hsch.; cf. δῖψαι. II. *causing thirst*, ὕδατα Hermipp.ap.J.*Ap*.1. 22; δ. σήψ Nic.*Th*.147; cf. διψάς II.

**διψοποιός**, όν, *provoking thirst*, Dsc.5.6, Sch.Theoc.7.66.

**δίψος**, εος, τό, = δίψα, Th.7.87 codd., X.*Cyr*.8.1.36, Pl.*Phd*.94b, Nic.*Th*.774, Luc.*Hist.Conscr*.28, etc., v.l. for δίψα in Ar.*Eq*.534, Th. 4.35. (Sch.Il.19.166 calls δίψος Attic, δίψα Ionic; both forms in Lxx, cf. *Wi*.11.4,8; δίψος 2*Ep.Cor*.11.27.)

**διψοσύνη** [ῠ], ἡ, = δίψα, Orac.ap.Porph.ap.Eus.*PE*6.2.

**διψῡχ-ία**· ἀπορία, Hsch. -ος, ον, *double-minded*, Ph.2.663, *Ep.Jac*.1.8.

**διψώδης**, ες, *thirsty*, Hp.*Aph*.4.54, Plu.2.129b, Aret.*SA*2.4; τοῦ πάθους τὸ μανικὸν καὶ δ. Plu.2.555e. II. *exciting thirst*, Hp.*Acut*. 59, Diph.Siph.ap.Ath.2.71e.

⊛ **δίω** [ῑ], Ep. Verb (used also by A. in lyr. passages, v. sub fin.), only pres. and impf. Med. (of which Hom. has subj. δίωμαι, δίηται, δίωνται, opt. δίοιτο Od.17.317, but mostly inf. δίεσθαι; for δίον v. δείδω):—*put to flight*, δηΐους προτὶ ἄστυ δίεσθαι Il.12.276; [μητέρα] ἀπὸ μεγάροιο δίεσθαι Od.20.343; μή σε.. ἀγρόνδε δίωμαι βάλλων χερμαδίοισι 21.370; ὡς δ' ὅτε νεβρὸν.. κύων.. δίηται Il.22.189; ἐπεί κ' ἀπὸ ναῦφι μάχην.. δίηται 16.246; rarely, *drive*, ὅς τ'.. ἵππους.. προτὶ ἄστυ δίηται 15.681; also in A., ἀτίετα διόμεναι λάχη *pursuing* a dishonoured office, *Eu*.385 (lyr.); and intr. folld. by Prep., *give chase, hunt*, ἐπὶ τὸν ᾧ διόμεναι ib.357 codd. (ὧδ' ἱέμεναι Ahrens); μετά με δρόμοισι διόμενοι Id.*Supp*.819; f.l. for δίεμαι, Id.*Pers*.700.

**δῑ-ωβελία**, ἡ, (ὀβολός) at Athens, *a daily allowance of two obols* to needy citizens, *IG*1².304, al., prob. for Δεκελείας in X.*HG*1.7.2, cf. Arist.*Pol*.1267ᵇ2 (-βολία codd.). ⊛ -ωβολιαῖος, α, ον, *weighing two obols*, Archig.ap.Gal.13.264, etc. ⊛ -ώβολον, τό, *double obol*, Ar.*Fr*.3, Alex.186, Theopomp.Com.55, Arist.*Ath*.41.3.

**δίωγ-μα**, ατος, τό, *pursuit, chase*, A.*Eu*.139 (pl.), Plb.1.34.9, Onos. 10.6 (pl.); δ. πώλων, = τοὺς διώκοντας πώλους, E.*Or*.988; ὑπ' αἰετοῦ δ. φεύγων Id.*Hel*.20; δ. ξιφοκτόνον, i.e. the sword, ib.354; τὰ πλούτου δ. *eager pursuit* of wealth, Pl.*Plt*.310b. II. *that which is chased*, X. *Cyn*.3.9. III. a secret rite in the Thesmophoria, *from which men were driven away*, Hsch. ⊛ -μείτης, ου, ὁ, *mounted policeman*, *CIG*3831a8 (Aezani). -μητικά, τά, *fees*, = Lat. *persecutiones*, *Cod.Just*.10.30.4.4. -μός, ὁ, *the chase*, X.*Cyr*.1.4.21, etc. 2. *pursuit*, D.S.4.13, al., Ael.*Tact*.34.4, Iamb.*VP*31.191. II. *persecution, harassing*, in pl., A.*Supp*.148, 1046, E.*Or*.412; also in later Prose, Plu.2.483a: sg., *Ev.Matt*.13.21, *Act.Ap*.8.1.

**διώδῡνος**, ον, (ὀδύνη) *with thrilling anguish*, σπαραγμός S.*Tr*. 777.

⊛ **διωθ-έω**, aor. διῶσα Hom. (v. infr.), διέωσα X.*HG*2.1.8, ἐδίωσα codd. in Hero *Aut*.24.3:—*push asunder, tear away*, [πτελέη] ἐκ ῥιζέων ἐριποῦσα κρημνὸν.. διῶσε the elm as it fell uprooted *tore* the bank *away*, Il.21.244; διώσας καὶ κατακτείνας ἐχθροὺς E.*Heracl*.995; *drive apart*, τῶν ὀφθαλμῶν τὰς διεξόδους Pl.*Ti*.67e. 2. *thrust through*, τι διά τινος X.*HG*2.1.8, Plb.21.28.14. II. more freq. in Med. (fut. διώσομαι Democr.191), *force one's way through, break through*, τὰ γέρρα Hdt.9.102; τὸν ὄχλον X.*Cyr*.7.5.39; τὰς τάξεις Plb.11.1. 12; δ. τὴν ὕλην, of roots, Thphr.*HP*8.11.8; τὴν θάλατταν, of a river, Plb.4.41.4. 2. *push from oneself, push away*, τοῖς κοντοῖς διεωθοῦντο, of sailors, Th.2.84; ἡ γαστὴρ δ. τὸ περιττὸν εἰς τὴν νῆστιν Gal. 5.567; *repulse*, στρατὸν ἰθυμαχίῃ Hdt.4.102; οἷς [πέτροις].. διώσει στρατόν A.*Fr*.199.9 (Dobr.); κῆρας Democr. l.c.; τὰς τύχας E.*HF* 315; ψευδῆ λόγον καὶ συκοφαντίαν *repel* it, D.21.124; τὴν ἐπιβουλὴν Id.58.65: abs., *get rid of danger*, Hdt.9.88. 3. *reject*, τὴν εὔνοιαν Id.7.104; ὁ μὴ προσίενται Th.4.108; τὴν ἐπικουρίαν Arist.*EN*1163ᵇ 25; of bribes, D.19.139: abs., *refuse*, Hdt.6.86.β', Plu.*Brut*.52: so pf. Pass. διῶσμαι cj. for δίωμαι in this sense, Thgn.1311. -ησις, εως, ἡ, *thrusting*, Hero *Spir*.1.11. -ίζομαι, *scuffle, jostle*, App.*BC* 2.117. -ισμός, ὁ, *pushing about, scuffle*, Plu.*Cam*.29 (pl.).

**διωκ-άθω** [ᾰ], pres. assumed by Gramm. as lengthd. form of διώκω and read in Pl.*Euthphr*.15d, E.*Fr*.362.25 codd. Stob.: the remaining forms may be referred to an aor. **διωκαθεῖν**: Subj. διωκάθω Ar. *Nu*.1482: 2 sg. ἐδιώκαθες Pl.*Grg*.483a, etc. -τέος, α, ον, verb. Adj. of διώκω, *to be pursued*, Hdt.9.58, Ar.*Ach*.221. 2. of objects, *to be pursued*, Pl.*Tht*.167d, etc. II. διωκτέον *one must pursue*, Id.*Grg*.507d, al.: pl., διωκτέα ἐφαίνετο Arr.*An*.3.21.6. -τήρ, ῆρος, ὁ, *pursuer*, Babr.128.14. -της, ου, ὁ, = foreg., 1*Ep.Ti*.1. 13. -τικός, ή, όν, *apt to pursue, follow* a course [χρυσὸς] δ. τῆς ἐπὶ τὸ μέσον φορᾶς Iamb.*Protr*.21.λε'; *swift in pursuit*, *EM*468. 23. -τός, ή, όν, *driven into exile, banished*, S.*Fr*.1041. 2. of objects, *to be pursued*, Chrysipp.ap.Ath.1.8d, Arist.*EN*1097ᵃ31. -τρια, ἡ, fem. of διωκτήρ, Sch.A.*Eu*.206. -τύς, ύος, ἡ, Ion. for δίωξις, *persecution*, Call.*Dian*.194. -τωρ, ορος, ὁ, = διωκτήρ, cj. for διάκτορα, *APl*.101 (Bianor).

⊛ **διώκω**, Ep. inf. διωκέμεναι, -έμεν (v. infr.): fut. -ξω Sapph.1.21, Pi.*O*.3.45, X.*Cyr*.6.3.13 (s. v.l.), *An*.1.4.8, D.38.16 codd.; but διώξομαι Ar.*Eq*.368 (and Elmsl. restored διώξει for -εις in *Eq*.969, *Nu*.1296, *Th*.1224), Pl.*Tht*.168a: aor. ἐδίωξα: aor. 2 ἐδιώκαθον (v. διωκάθω): pf. δεδίωχα Hyp.*Lyc*.16:—Med. (v. infr.):—Pass., fut. διωχθήσομαι D.S.19.95, Polyaen.2.13; but διώξομαι in pass. sense, Lxx *Am*.2.16, D.H.3.20: aor. ἐδιώχθην Hdt 5.73, Antipho 2.1.3,6, (ἐπ-, κατ-) Th.3.69, 3.4: pf. δεδίωγμαι *Ev.Matt*.5.10: (cf. ϝιώκω *GDI*3153 (Corinthian vase); v. δίω):—*cause to run, set in quick motion*, opp. φεύγω: 1. *pursue, chase*, in war or hunting, φεύγοντα διώκειν Il.22.199, etc.: abs., πεδίοιο διωκέμεν ἠδὲ φέβεσθαι 5.223, cf. Hdt.9.11:—Med., διώκεσθαί τινα πεδίοιο, δόμοιο, *chase* one over or across.., Il.21.602, Od.18.8. b. c. acc. pers., of a lover, Sapph. l.c.; *follow*, X.*HG*1.1.13; τοὺς εὐγνώμονας Id.*Mem*.2.8.6; δ. καὶ φιλεῖν τινα Pl.*Tht*.168a, cf. *Ev.Luc*.17.23. 2. *pursue* an object, *seek after*, ἀκίχητα διώκειν Il.17.75; σὸν μόρον δ. S.*Aj*.997; τιμὰς δ. Th.2.63; ἡδονήν, τὸ ἀγαθὸν καὶ καλόν, Pl.*Phdr*.251a, *Grg*.482e; ἀλήθειαν ib.482e; δικαιοσύνην *Ep.Rom*.9.30; λαθραίαν Κύπριν Eub. 67.9: prov., τὰ πετόμενα δ. Arist.*Metaph*.1009ᵇ38; κατὰ σκοπὸν δ. *Ep.Phil*.3.14; of plants, δ. τοὺς ξηροὺς τόπους *seek* them, Thphr. *HP*1.4.2; δ. τὰ συμβάντα or τὸ συμβαῖνον *follow* or *wait for* the event, D.4.39, 10.21:—Med., διώκεσθαι τὸ πλέον ἔχειν D.H.1.87 (s. v.l.); μοῖρα διωξαμένη [αὐτούς] *IG*5(1).1355 (Messenia). 3. *pursue* an argument, τὴν ἐναντίωσιν Pl.*R*.454a; also, *describe*, ὕμνῳ ἀρετάς Pi.*I*.4(3).21; τὴν Ἡρακλέους παίδευσιν X.*Mem*.2.1.34; *recite*, λόγον *PMag.Par*.1.958, cf. 335 (Pass.). II. *drive* or *chase away*, διώκω οὔτιν' ἔγωγε I don't *force* any one *away*, Od.18.409; ἐκ γῆς Hdt.9.77; *banish*, Id.5.92.ε': metaph., διώκεις μ' ᾗ μάλιστ' ἐγὼ 'σφάλην you *push* or *press* me.., E.*Supp*.156. III. of the wind, *drive* a ship, Od.5.332; of rowers, *impel, speed on her way*, ῥίμφα διώκοντες (sc. τὴν νῆα) 12.182; νηῦς ῥίμφα διωκομένη 13.162; Συρηγενὲς ἅρμα διώκων *driving* it, Orac.ap.Hdt.7.140, cf. A.*Pers*.84; ἄτρυτον δ. πόδα Id.*Eu*.403, cf. *Th*.371. 2. seemingly intr., *drive, drive on*, Il.23.344,424; *gallop, run*, etc., dub. in A.*Th*.91 (lyr.); ἀναπηδήσαντες ἐδίωκον X.*An*.7.2.20; ἅμα διώκοντος *on the march*, Plu. *Caes*.17: c. acc. spatii, διώξας περὶ ὀκτακοσίους σταδίους Chares 17. 3. *urge, impel*, βέλος χερί Pi.*I*.8(7).35; φόρμιγγα πλάκτρῳ Id.*N*.5.24; esp. of music, δ. μοῦσαν Pratin.Lyr.5; δ. μέλος Simon. 29:—Pass., ὑφ' ἡδονῆς διώκομαι.. σὺν τάχει μολεῖν S.*El*.871. 4. of work, *urge on, carry forward*, σκαφήτρους *PFay*.112.2 (i A.D.). 5. pf. part. Pass. δεδιωγμένος *hurried, rapid*, σφυγμοί Aret.*SA*2. 8. IV. as law-term, *prosecute*, ὁ διώκων *the prosecutor*, opp. ὁ φεύγων, the defendant, Hdt.6.82 (pl.), A.*Eu*.583, etc.; ὁ διώκων τοῦ ψηφίσματος τὸ λέγειν.., *he who impeaches* the clause in the decree.., D.18.59; γραφὰς δ. Antipho 2.1.5; γραφὴν δ. τινά *indict*, D. 59.69; δ. εἰσαγγελίαν Hyp.*Eux*.9; δ. τινὰ περὶ θανάτου X.*HG*7.3.6: c. gen. criminis, *accuse of.., prosecute for..*, δ. τινὰ τυραννίδος Hdt. 6.104; δειλίας Ar.*Eq*.368; παρανόμων And.1.22, cf. διωκάθειν; ψευδομαρτυριῶν D.29.13, etc.; δ. ἀπάτης εἵνεκεν Hdt.6.136; φόνον τινὸς δ. *avenge* another's murder, E.*Or*.1534 (anap.), cf. Arist.*Pol*.1269ᵃ2; δίκην δ. *pursue* one's rights at law, D.54.41; δίκας μὴ οὔσας δ. Lys. 32.2: c. acc. et inf., *accuse* one of doing, App.*BC*4.50:—Pass., ὁ διωκόμενος Antipho 2.1.5; θανάτου ὑπό τινος -εσθαι X.*Ap*.21; with play on 1.1, Ar.*Ach*.698 sq. V. *persecute*, *Ev.Jo*.5.16, al.; δεδιωγμένοι ἕνεκα δικαιοσύνης *Ev.Matt*.5.10.

⊛ **διωλένιος**, ον, *AP*7.711 (Antip.(?)); also η, ον Arat.202:—*with stretched out arms*, Id. l.c.; δ. φλόγα πεύκας, of torches, *upheld in both arms*, *AP*l.c.

**διωλύγιος** [ῠ], ον, *immense, enormous*, μήκη δ. Pl.*Lg*.890e; μακρὰ.. καὶ δ. φλυαρία Id.*Tht*.162a (Sch. expl. both by περιβόητος and σκοτεινός); πράγματα Is.*Fr*.123; μακρὸς ὁ λόγος καὶ δ. Jul.*Or*.2.101d; κῦμα δ. Call.*Fr*.111; ἤπειρος δ. A.R.4.1258; σκότος Dam.*Isid*.303; τιμαί Them.*Or*.11.146b; πνεῦμα δ., of a water-clock striking, perh. *far-sounding*, *AP*7.641 (Antiphil.); *loud, piercing*, φθέγμα θρηνῶδες καὶ δ. Agath.1.12: neut. as Adv., δ. ἀνῴμωζον J.*BJ*7.6.4; δ. ἀνεβόησεν Charito 3.3, Lib.*Decl*.26.47. (Etym. unknown: expld. by ἠχοῦν ἐπὶ πολύ, μέγα καὶ σφοδρόν, διατεταμένον, Hsch.; by μέγα καὶ ἐπὶ πολὺ διῆκον, Suid.)

⊛ **διωμοσία**, ἡ, *an oath taken by both parties at the* ἀνάκρισις *before the trial came on*, Antipho 5.88 (pl.), D.23.69; τὰς δ. ποιεῖσθαι Lys.10.11.

**διώμοτος**, ον, *bound by oath*, c. inf., S.*Ph*.593: abs., Aristid.*Or*. 34(50).42. Adv. -τως, ὁμαιχμίαν ποιεῖσθαι Procop.*Goth*.4.25.

**διωνέομαι**, *buy up*, *PPar*.21.38.

⊛ **Διώνη**, ἡ, *Dione*, mother of Aphrodite by Zeus, Il.5.370, Hes.*Th*. 17, Str.7.7.12. II. later, as a Metronymic, *daughter of Dione*, i.e. *Aphrodite*, Theoc.7.116, dub. l. in Bion 1.93:—Adj. **Διωναῖος**, α, ον, Κύπρι Δ. Theoc.15.106; Διωναίη alone, D.P.853.

**δῐωνῠμ-έω,** *use two names,* Eust.288.20. ⊛ **-ία,** ἡ, *pair of names* or *double name,* Vett.Val.187.25, Man.4.376, Hdn.*Fig*.p.103 S. **-ος,** ον, (δίς, ὄνυμα, ὄνομα) *with two names,* D.T.636.11 (s. v.l.); or, of two persons, *named together,* θεαί E.*Ph*.683 (lyr.). II. (διά) *far-famed,* εὐτυχία Plu.*Tim*.30; στρατηγός App.*BC*4.54; χῶρος J.*BJ* 5.1.3.

**Διώνῡσος,** etc., Ep. for Διον-.

**δῑωξῐκέλευθος,** ον, *urging on the way,* κέντρα *AP*6.246 (Phld. or Marc. Arg.).

**δῑώξιππος,** ον, *horse-driving,* Κυράνα Pi.*P*.9.4; Ἄρης B.8.44, *AP* 9.322.9 (Leon.); μύωψ ib.6.233 (Maec.).

**δίωξις** [ῐ], εως, ἡ, (διώκω) *chase, pursuit,* esp. of soldiers or ships, Th.3.33, etc.; δ. ποιεῖσθαι Id.8.102. 2. *pursuit* of an object, τοῦ ὅλου Pl.*Smp*.192e; opp. φυγή, Arist.*EN*1139ᵃ22, Epicur.*Sent*.25; δ. τῶν καλῶν Plu.2.550e. II. as law-term, *prosecution,* δίωξιν εἶναι κατὰ τῶν ἐλεγχθέντων *IG*1².10.10; δ. ποιεῖσθαι Antipho6.7, cf. D.45.50; δ. τῶν ἀδικούντων Plu.*Per*.10.

**διωργισμένως,** Adv. *angrily,* Phld.*Rh*.1.200S.

⊛ **διωρία,** ἡ, either (ὅρος) *fixed space* or *interval,* or (ὥρα) *appointed time,* J.*BJ*5.9.1.

**διωρισμένως,** Adv. pf. part. Pass. of διορίζω, *distinctly, separately,* Arist.*HA*521ᵃ15, Iamb.*Protr*.4; *definitely,* Plu.2.415b.

**δίωρος** [ῐ], ον, (ὅρος) *having two boundary stones,* λόφος *Schwyzer* 664.20 (Orchom. Arc., iv B.C.). II. δίωρον· ἀσύμφωνον, οἱ δὲ ἀνόμοιον, διάφωνον, Hsch.

⊛ **δῐώροφος,** ον, (ὀροφος) *with two roofs* or *stories,* Lxx *Ge*.6.16, App. *Pun*.95:—written **διώρυφος,** *PPetr*.3p.39.

**διωρῠγή,** ἡ, v.l. for διωρυχή.

**διωρύγιον** [ῠ], τό, Dim. of διῶρυξ, *PLond*.1.131ʳ633 (i A.D.).

**δῐώρῠγος,** ον, = διόργυιος, X.*Cyn*.2.5.

**διῶρυξ,** ῠχος (sts. in Pap., *BGU*543.7 (i B.C.), etc.; later Gr. more freq. ῠγος *PPetr*.3p.60 (iii B.C.), *Tab.Herad*.1.59, *PTeb*.72.72 (ii B.C.), J.*Vit*.31, etc.), ἡ (ὁ, *PRyl*.154.18):—*trench, conduit, canal,* Hdt.1.75, Hp.*Aër*.15, Th.1.109, etc.; κρυπτὴ δ. an underground *passage,* Hdt.3.146; = *fossa,* Plu.*Fab*.1 (pl.).

**διωρῠχή,** ἡ, *digging* or *cutting through,* Χερρονήσου v.l. for διορυχή in D.7.40, cf. Polyaen.4.18.1, Aristid.*Or*.17(15).14. (διορυγή is f.l. in Plu.*Fab*.1 (cf. foreg.), Them.*Or*.2.36d.)

**δίωσ-ις,** εως, ἡ, *pushing asunder, forcing open,* Arist.*Pr*.964ᵃ22, *Ph*. 243ᵇ4. II. *putting off 'sine die',* δίκης Id.*Rh*.1372ᵃ33. **-μός,** ὁ, = foreg. I, χειρῶν, in gymnastics, Aret.*CD*1.3. 2. in surgery, *pushing through* of embedded weapons, Paul.Aeg.6.88. **-τήρ,** ῆρος, ὁ, *instrument for pushing out* embedded weapons, ibid. II. *pole running through rings,* for carrying the ark, Lxx *Ex*.38.10 (37.13). **-τρα,** ἡ, *projector* or *barrel* of a torsion-engine, Ph.*Bel*.74.22, Hero *Bel*.77.9, al.

⊛ **δίωτος** [ῐ], ον, (οὖς, ὠτός) *two-eared;* of vessels, *two-handled,* Pl. *Hp.Ma*.288d; καδίσκος Anticlid.13; ψυκτὴρ *OGI*214.57 (Branchidae, iii B.C.); πίναξ *IG*2².120.44.

**διώττας·** ἐργοδιώκτας, Hsch. **διωφέλλειν·** διορύσσειν, Id.

**δῐωχής,** ές, (ἔχω) *that will hold two,* δίφρος Pherecr.3, Paus.Gr.*Fr*. 132.

**δίωχμος,** ὁ, Aeol. for διωγμός, *EM*371.21.

**δμηθείς, δμηθήτω,** v. δαμάζω.

**δμῆσις,** εως, ἡ, (δαμάζω) *taming, breaking,* ἵππων Il.17.476.

**δμητέος,** Dor. **δματέος,** = δαμαστέος, Hsch.

**δμητήρ,** ῆρος, ὁ, *tamer,* ἵππων *h.Hom*.22.5, cf. Alcm.9: fem., νὺξ δμήτειρα θεῶν Il.14.259.

**δμητός,** ή, όν, *tamed,* Hsch., *EM*389.46.

**δμῳ-ή** (Choerob.*in Theod*.1.405) or **δμω-ή** (both spellings freq. in codd.), ἡ, (δαμάω) prop. *female slave taken in war,* δμῳαὶ δ' ἃς Ἀχιλεὺς ληΐσσατο (cf. δμώς) Il.18.28, cf. 9.658, 24.643: generally, *female slave, serving-woman,* only in pl. in Hom., mostly joined with γυναῖκες: δμῳαί A.*Ag*.908, S.*Ant*.1189; δ. γυναῖκες A.*Ch*.84; rare in Prose, X.*Cyr*.5.1.6, Philostr.*VA*1.5: later in sg., Q.S.5.561; of things, δμωὴν..Αἴδος..μάκελλαν *IG*14.1389ii25. **-ιάς,** άδος, ἡ, = foreg., Q.S.3.684, 9.341: also as disyll., **δμῳάς** Man.2.276. **-ιος,** ον, *in servile condition,* βρέφος *AP*9.407 (Antip. Sid. (but prob. Thess.)). ⊛ **-ίς,** ίδος, ἡ, = δμωή, A.*Th*.363 (lyr.), *Supp*.335, E.*Ba*. 514, Lyc.1123, A.R.1.285.

⊛ **δμῶος,** ὁ, = sq., Hes.*Op*.430, Leucon ap.Sch.Il.*Oxy*.1087.55, Call. *Hec*.1.4.15 (pl.).

**δμώς,** ωός, ὁ, (δαμάω) *slave taken in war,* δμώων οὗς..ληΐσσατο δῖος Ὀδυσσεύς (cf. δμωή) Od.1.398: generally, *slave,* τεῦ δμὼς εἷς ἀνδρῶν; 24.257: mostly in pl., κτῆσιν ἐμὴν δμῶάς τε Il.19.333: dat. pl. δμώεσσι Od.6.71, etc.—Once in S.*Ant*.578; freq. in E., *Med*.188 (lyr.), al., but not found in Prose.

**δνοπᾰλ-ίζω,** *shake violently, fling down,* ἀν' ἄρ ἄνδρ' ἐδνοπάλιζεν Il. 4.472; τὰ σὰ ῥάκεα δνοπαλίξεις *'wrap* thy old cloak *about thee',* Od. 14.512:—Pass., γυῖα δνοπαλίζεται, of the polypus, its arms *wave about,* Opp.*H*.2.295. **-ιξις,** εως, ἡ, *shaking, fluttering,* Sch.Opp. *H*.2.295.

⊛ **δνοφ-έος,** α, ον, = sq., κάλυμμα B.15.32, cf. Hsch. ⊛ **-ερός,** ά, όν, *dark, murky,* νύξ Od.13.269; ὕδωρ Il.9.15, cf. Thgn.243; ἀχλύς A. *Eu*.379 (lyr.); κατὰ δ. γᾶς E.*IT*1266 (lyr.), etc.: metaph., δ. κᾶδος Pi.*P*.4.112; πένθος A.*Pers*.536 (lyr.).—Poet. word; but τὸ δνοφερόν *gloom,* Hp.*Morb.Sacr*.16. **-ερώδης,** ες, v.l. for δνοφώδης, Id. l.c. **-όεις,** εσσα, εν, = δνοφερός, ὄμβρος Emp.21.5. **-ος,** ὁ, *darkness, dusk, gloom,* Simon.37.8: pl., A.*Ch*.52 (lyr.).—Poet. word, though its collat. form γνόφος (q.v.) occurs in later Prose. **-ώδης,** ες, = δνοφερός, E.*Tr*.79 (as Dind. for γνοφώδη), Hp.*Morb.Sacr*.16; later γνοφ- (q.v.).

**δνόψ·** χιτῶνος εἶδος, βάθος, Hsch.

**δοάν,** Dor. for δήν (q.v.), Alcm.135.

**δοάσσατο,** Homeric aor. form, mostly impers., = Att. ἔδοξε, *it seemed,* in phrase ὧδε δέ (or ὡς ἄρα) οἱ φρονέοντι δοάσσατο κέρδιον εἶναι so *it seemed* to him to be best, Il.13.458, Od.5.474, al.; also ὡς ἂν τοι πλήμνη γε δοάσσεται (Ep. for δοάσσηται) ἄκρον ἱκέσθαι till the nave *appear* even to graze, Il.23.339. II. for δοάσσαι, δοάσσατο, as used by A.R., v. δοιάζω. (For δο-άσσατο: δέ-ατο cf. τροχ-άζω: τρέχω.)

⊛ **δόγμα,** ατος, τό, (δοκέω) *that which seems to one, opinion* or *belief,* Pl.*R*.538c; δ. πόλεως κοινόν Id.*Lg*.644d, etc.; esp. of philosophical *doctrines,* Epicur.*Nat*.14.7, 15.28, Str.15.1.59, Ph.1.204, etc.; *notion,* Pl.*Tht*.158d, al. 2. *decision, judgement,* Id.*Lg*.926d (pl.); *public decree, ordinance,* And.4.6; τὰ τῶν Ἀμφικτυόνων δ. D.5.19, cf. 18. 154; δόγμα ποιήσασθαι, c. inf., X.*An*.3.3.5; esp. of Roman *Senatus-consulta,* δ. συγκλήτου Plb.6.13.2, *IG*12(3).173.22; δ. τῆς βουλῆς D.H.8.87.

**δογμᾰτ-ίας,** ου, ὁ, *sententious person,* Philostr.*VS*1.16.4. **-ίζω,** *lay down as an opinion,* ἀϊδίους εἶναι Phld.*Piet*.19; τὰ αἰσχρά Arr.*Epict*. 3.7.18: abs., S.E.*P*.1.13, al.; οἱ -οντες, = οἱ δογματικοί, Gal.18(1). 270:—Pass., τὰ -όμενα S.E.*P*.1.18. 2. *decree by ordinance,* c. inf., D.S.4.83, Lxx 1*Es*.6.34; of the Roman Senate, J.*AJ*14.10.22; δ. τινὰ καλήν *declare* her beautiful, *AP*9.576 (Nicarch.):—Pass., τὰ δογματισθέντα *IG*12(3).173.53 (Astypalaea), cf. ib.14.759.13 (Naples). 3. in Pass., of persons, *submit to ordinances, Ep.Col*.2.20. **-ικός,** ή, όν, *of* or *for doctrines, didactic,* [διάλογοι] Quint.*Inst*.2.15.26. II. of persons, δ. ἰατροί physicians *who go by general principles,* opp. ἐμπειρικοί and μεθοδικοί, Dsc.*Ther.Praef*., Gal.1.65; in Philosophy, S.E.*M*.7.1, D.L.9.70, etc.; δ. ὑπολήψεις Id.9.83; δ. φιλοσοφία S.E. *P*.1.4. Adv. -κῶς D.L.9.74, S.E.*P*.1.197: Comp. -κώτερον Id.*M*. 6.4.

⊛ **δογμᾰτο-γρᾰφέω,** *draft decrees, Ephes*.2.20 (ii A.D.). **-γράφος** [γρᾰ], ὁ, *drafter of decrees, IG*5(1).26 (Amyclae), *IGRom*.4.259 (Assos), 661 (Acmonia), etc. **-λογία,** ἡ, *expounding of a doctrine,* S.E.*M*.8.367 (pl.). **-ποιέω,** *make a decree,* c. inf., Plb.1.81.4:—also Med., *IG*5(1).1390.57 (Andania). ⊛ **-ποιΐα,** ἡ, *maintenance of* δόγματα, Aristob.ap.Eus.*PE*13.12.

**δοειδές·** διαφανές, Hsch.

**δοθιήν,** ῆνος, ὁ, *small abscess, boil,* Hp.*Hum*.20, Hermipp.30, Ar. *V*.1172, Telecl.43, Dsc.1.128.6, etc.

**δοθιηνικόν,** τό, *remedy for boils,* Paul.Aeg.4.23.

**δοθιών,** όνος, ὁ, = δοθιήν, Anon.Lond.19.31, Hdn.Gr.2.923.

**δοιάζω** or **δοάζω,** *consider in two ways, be in two minds:* hence, *have a mind to,* aor., δοίαξε φάσγανον ἐν στέρνοισι πᾶξαι B.10.87; also βουλὰς δοιάζεσκε *was hesitating between*.., A.R.3.819; ὁππότε δοῦπον ..δοάσσαι (poet. aor. opt.) when she *imagined* a noise, ib.955:—Med., δοάσσατο she *doubted,* ib.770; δοιάζοντο λεύσσειν *imagined* they saw, Id.4.576. (The forms in δοα- and some meanings are due to confusion with δοάσσατο.)

**δοιάς,** άδος, ἡ, *duality, Gloss*.

**δοιδῡκο-ποιός,** ὁ, *pestle-maker,* Plu.*Phoc*.4. **-φόβα,** ἡ, *pestle-fearing,* Luc.*Trag*.201.

⊛ **δοῖδυξ,** ῡκος, ὁ, *pestle,* Ar.*Eq*.984, Gal.12.189, etc.

**δοιέτης,** ου, *two years old, TAM*2.369 (Xanthus).

**δοιή,** ἡ, *doubt, perplexity,* ἐν δοιῇ Il.9.230, Call.*Jov*.5, Antag.1.1. (Cf. Skt. dat. sg. *dvayyái* (*dvayí* 'duality').)

⊛ **δοιοί,** αί, ά, Ep. for δύο, *two, both,* Il.5.206, Hes.*Op*.432, etc.: neut. pl. δοιά as Adv., *in two ways, in two points,* Od.2.46. 2. sg., δοιός, ή, όν, *twofold, double,* Emp.17.3, Call.*Ep*.1.3, *AP*9.46 (Antip. Thess.), etc.—Ep. word, also Dor., *IG*12(3).378 (Thera), and Aret. *SD*2.9,11.

**δοιοτόκος,** ον, *bearing twins,* prob. in *AP*7.742 (Apollonid.).

**δοῖτρον·** πύελον, σκάφην, Hsch. (Perh. for δροῖτρον, cf. δροίτη.)

**δοιώ,** = δοιοί (of which it is properly the dual), = δύο, indecl., Hom.; commonly masc., Il.3.236, al.; but neut. in 24.648.

**δοκάζω,** *wait for,* πλόον Sophr.52, cf. S.*Fr*.221.23.

**δοκᾰνα,** τά, (δοκός) at Sparta, *two upright parallel bars* joined towards each end (as symbols of the Dioscuri), Plu.2.478a.

**δοκάνη** [ᾰ], ἡ, (δοκή, δέχομαι) = στάλιξ, *forked pole* on which hunting-nets are fixed, Hsch.

**δοκεύς,** έως, ὁ, = δοκός II, Heph.Astr.1.24.

⊛ **δοκεύω,** *keep an eye upon, watch narrowly,* ἑλισσόμενόν τε δοκεύει [the hound] *watches* [the boar] turning to bay, Il.8.340; Θόωνα μεταστρεφθέντα δοκεύσας *having watched for* his turning round, 13.545; Ἀμφίκλον ἐφορμηθέντα δοκεύσας 16.313; τὸν προὔχοντα δοκεύει *watches* him that is before [in the race], 23.325; of the Great Bear, ἥ τ'.. Ὠρίωνα δοκεύει *watches* the hunter Orion, 18.488; λόχμαισι δ. *lie in wait for* [them] in.., Pi.*O*.10(11).30, cf. *AP*6.45, Theoc.9.26; νιν.. ὄψεται δοκεύοντα will see him *playing the spy,* E.*Ba*.984 (lyr.); ἃ μὴ θέμις οὐκ ἐδόκευσα *sought* not for, *IG*14.2068. 2. *expect,* c. acc., Arat.987, al.: c. gen., ἀνέμοιο γαληναίης τε δ. Id.813. 3. in later Poets, *observe, see,* Nonn.*D*.1.530, al., *AP*5.252 (Iren.), Man.6.142; also, *think,* Orph.*A*.891, 1083.

⊛ **δοκέω** Il.7.192, Att. impf. ἐδόκουν, Ep. δοκέεσκον *AP*5.298 (Agath.):—Med., δοκέοντο Opp.*C*.4.296: part. δοκεύμενος ib.109: the fut. and other tenses are twofold: 1. fut. δόξω and aor. 1 ἔδοξα

Pi.N.4.37, h.Merc.208, etc.: pf. δέδοχα inferred from plpf. ἐδεδόχεσαν D.C.44.26 :—Pass., aor. ἐδόχθην Plb.21.10.8, etc., (κατ–) Antipho 2.2.2: pf. δέδογμαι Hdt.8.100, etc.: plpf. ἐδέδοκτο Id.9.74. 2. regul. forms (chiefly Trag., Com., and late Prose), fut. δοκήσω A.Pr.388, Ar.Nu.562, etc. (once in Hdt., 4.74); Dor. δοκησῶ or -ασῶ Theoc.1.150: aor. ἐδόκησα, Ep. δόκ- Od.10.415, Pi.O.13.56, A.Th.1041, Ar.Ra.1485, etc.: pf. δεδόκηκα A.Eu.309 (lyr.):—Pass., aor. ἐδοκήθην E.Med.1417 (anap.): pf. δεδόκημαι Pi.N.5.19, E.Med.763 (anap.), Ar.V.726, also in Hdt.7.16.γ'; but δεδοκημένος (q.v.) belongs to δέχομαι.

I. *expect* (Iterat. of δέκομαι, cf. δέχομαι II. 3): hence, *think, suppose, imagine*, (opp. φρονέω, S.Aj.942 (lyr.), Pherecr.146.4): 1. c. acc. et inf., δοκέω νικησέμεν Ἕκτορα Il.7.192; οὔ σε δοκέω πείθεσθαι Hdt.1.8, cf. 11,27, al., Antipho 2.4.5, etc.: rarely with inf. omitted, δοκῶ.. οὐδὲν ῥῆμα.. κακὸν [εἶναι] S.El.61; τούτους τι δοκεῖτε [εἶναι] X.An.5.7.26; freq. in relating a dream or vision, τεκεῖν δράκοντ' ἔδοξεν she *thought* a serpent produced young, A.Ch.527; ἐδόκουν αἰετὸν.. φέρειν *methought* an eagle was carrying, Ar.V.15; ὁρᾷς γὰρ οὐδὲν ὢν δοκεῖς σάφ' εἰδέναι E.Or.259: with inf. only, ἔδοξ' ἰδεῖν *methought* I saw, ib.408; ἔδοξ' ἀκοῦσαι Pl.Prt.315e: ἔδοξ' ἐν ὕπνῳ.. οἰκεῖν ἐν Ἄργει E.IT44 (sts. also, as in signf. II, ἐδοξάτην μοι δύο γυναῖκε.. μολεῖν A.Pers.181; ἐν τῷ σταδίῳ.. μέ τις ἐδόκει στεφανοῦν Alex.272.4). b. *think* to do, *purpose*, ὅταν δ' ἀείδειν.. δοκῶ A.Ag.16. 2. abs., *have* or *form an opinion*, περί τινος Hdt.9.65; mostly in parenthetic phrases, ὡς δοκῶ Pl.Phdr.264e; δοκῶ alone, Hdt.9.65, Ar.Pax47, Pl.Prm.126b; πῶς δοκεῖς; to call attention to something remarked, τοῦτον, πῶς δοκεῖς; καθύβρισεν E.Hipp.446, cf. Hec.1160, Diph.96, etc.; πόσον δοκεῖς; Ar.Ec.399. 3. δοκῶ μοι I *seem to myself, methinks*, c. inf., ἐγώ μοι δοκέω κατανοέειν τοῦτο Hdt.2.93, etc.; ἡδέως ἄν μοι δοκῶ κοινωνῆσαί τινος X.Cyr.8.7.25, cf. Oec.6.11; οὔ μοι δοκῶ I *think* not.., Pl.Tht.158e; δοκῶ μοι parenthetic, Id.Thg.121d. b. δοκῶ μοι I *am determined, resolved*, c. inf. pres., Ar.V.177, etc.: c. inf. fut., Aeschin.3.53, etc.: c. inf. aor., dub. in Ar.Av.671, etc.: rarely without μοι, *think fit*, σὺ δ' αὐτὸς ἤδη γνῶθι τίνα πέμπειν δοκεῖς A.Th.650. 4. *seem, pretend*, c. inf. (with or without neg.), ὁρέων μὲν οὐδέν, δοκέων δὲ [ὁρᾶν] dub. l. in Alcm.87; οὔτε ἔδοξε μαθέειν Hdt.1.10; οὐδὲ γιγνώσκειν δοκῶν Pherecr.163; τὰ μὲν ποιεῖν, τὰ δὲ δοκεῖν Arist.Pol.1314ᵃ39; ἤκουσά του λέγοντος, οὐ δοκῶν κλύειν E.Med.67; πόσους δοκεῖς.. ὁρῶντας.. μὴ δοκεῖν ὁρᾶν; Id.Hipp.462, cf. Ar.Eq.1146, X.HG4.5.6. 5. Pass., *to be considered*, δοκεῖσθαι οὕτω Pl.R.612d; τὰ νῦν δοκούμενα περί τινος the *current opinions*, ib.490a. 6. Med., Opp.C.4.296; δοκεύμενος.. ἀλύξειν ib.109.

II. of an Object, *seem*, c. dat. pers. et inf. pres., δοκέεις δέ μοι οὐκ ἀπινύσσειν Od.5.342; δόκησε δ' ἄρα σφίσι θυμὸς ὣς ἔμεν ὡς εἰ.. their heart *seemed* just as if.., *felt* as though.., 10.415: c. inf. fut., *seem likely*, δοκέει δέ μοι ὧδε λώϊον ἔσσεσθαι Il.6.338: c. inf. aor. (never in Hom.), τί δ' ἂν δοκεῖ σοι Πρίαμος (sc. ποιῆσαι); A.Ag.935; *seem* or *be thought* to have done, esp. of suspected persons, Th.2.21; *to be convicted*, ἂν ἁλῷ καὶ δοκῇ τοὔργον εἰργάσθαι D.23.71. 2. abs., *seem*, as opp. to reality, τὸ δοκεῖν καὶ τὰν ἀλάθειαν βιᾶται Simon.76; οὐ δοκεῖν ἄριστος ἀλλ' εἶναι θέλει A.Th.592, cf. Pl.Grg.527b; in full, τὸ δοκεῖν εἶναι A.Ag.788 (anap.). 3. *seem good, be resolved on*, εἰ δοκεῖ σοι ταῦτα ib.944; τοιαῦτ' ἔδοξε τῷδε Καδμείων τέλει Id.Th.1030. 4. freq. impers., δοκεῖ μοι *it seems* to me, *methinks*, ὥς μοι δοκεῖ εἶναι ἄριστα Il.12.215; ὡς ἐμοὶ δοκεῖ as I *think*, A.Th.369, etc.; τὸ σοὶ δοκοῦν your *opinion*, Pl.R.487d: freq. in inf. in parenth. clause, ὡς ἐμοὶ δοκέειν *to* my *thinking*, Hdt.9.113; δοκέειν ἐμοί Id.1.172; ἀλλ', ἐμοὶ δοκεῖν, τάχ' εἴσει A.Pers.246, etc.; without μοι, X.An.4.5.1. b. *it seems good* to me, *it is* my *pleasure*, δοκεῖ ἡμῖν χρῆσθαι Th.4.118, cf. A.Ag.1350: freq. of a public resolution, τοῖσι Ἕλλησι δόξαι.. ἀπαιτέειν Hdt.1.3, etc.; ἔδοξεν Ἀργείοισιν A.Supp.605, cf. Th.1010; esp. in decrees and the like, ἔδοξε τῇ βουλῇ, τῷ δήμῳ, Ar.Th.372, Th.4.118, cf. IG1.32, etc.; τὰ δόξαντα S.El.29, D.3.14; παρὰ τὸ δοκοῦν ἡμῖν Th.1.84, etc.:—Pass., δέδοκται Hdt.4.68; οὕτω δέδοκται; S.Ph.1277, etc.; εἰ ἐπαινῆσαι δεδόκηται Pi.N.5.19; δεδόχθω τὸ ἄτοπον τοῦτο Pl.Lg.799e, etc.; τοῦτ' ἔστ' ἐμοὶ δεδογμένον E.Heracl.1; δεδογμέν' [ἐστί].. τῆνδε καθανεῖν S.Ant.576, cf. OC1431; τὰ δεδογμένα Hdt.3.76; δεδόχθαι τῇ βουλῇ καὶ τῷ δήμῳ IG2².1.12, etc. c. acc. abs., δόξαν *when it was decreed* or *resolved*, δόξαν αὐτοῖς ὥστε διαναυμαχεῖν Th.8.79; δόξαν δέ σφι (sc. λιπέσθαι) Hdt.2.148; δόξαν ἡμῖν ταῦτα Pl.Prt.314c, cf. X.An.4.1.13; ἰδίᾳ δοκῆσάν σοι τόδ'..; E.Supp.129; also δεδογμένον αὐτοῖς Th.1.125, etc.; but also δόξαντος τούτου X.HG1.1.36; δόξαντα ταῦτα καὶ περανθέντα ib.3.2.19. 5. *to be reputed*, c. inf., Pi.O.13.56, P.6.40; ἄξιοι ὑμῖν δοκοῦντες Th.1.76; δοκοῦντες εἶναί τι *men who are held* to be something, *men of repute*, Pl.Grg.472a; τὸ δοκεῖν τινὲς εἶναι.. προσειληφότες D.21.213; τὸ φρονεῖν ἐδόκει τις εἶναι περιττός Plu.Arist.1; οἱ δοκοῦντες Heraclit.28 (dub.), E.Hec.295; τὰ δοκοῦντα, opp. τὰ μηδὲν ὄντα, Id.Tr.613; μετ' ἀρετῆς δοκούσης ἐς ἀλλήλους γίγνεσθαι Th.3.10; *to be an established, current opinion*, Arist.APo.76ᵇ24, al.; τὰ δοκοῦντα Id.Metaph.1088ᵃ16, al.:—Pass., οἱ δεδογμένοι ἀνδροφόνοι *those who have been found guilty* of homicide, D.23.28; also αἱ δοκούμεναι Πέρσαις τέχναι Polem.Call.60. (The two senses of δοκέω are sts. contrasted, τὰ ἀεὶ δοκοῦντα.. τῷ δοκοῦντι εἶναι ἀληθῆ that which *seems* true is true *to him who thinks* it, Pl.Tht.158e; τὸ δοκοῦν ἑκάστῳ τοῦτο καὶ εἶναι τῷ δοκοῦντι ib.162c.)

⊛ **δοκή**, ἡ, *vision, fancy*, Hdn.Gr.1.313. II. = δοχή, Hsch.

**δόκημα**, ατος, τό, *vision, fancy*, δ. ὀνείρων E.HF111 (lyr.); τὰ δοκήμασιν σοφά Id.Tr.411; δοκήματα *make-believes*, of adopted sons, Id.Fr.359. 2. *opinion, expectation*, δοκημάτων ἐκτός Id.HF771 (lyr.). II. = δόγμα, δ. τοῦ συνεδρίου IG12(3).1259.3 (Cimolus), Schwyzer91.27 (Argos, iii B.C.).

**δοκησῐ-δέξιος**, ον, *clever in one's own conceit*, Pherecr.154, Callias Com.27. **-νους**, ουν, = foreg., ibid.

**δόκησις**, εως, ἡ, (δοκέω) *opinion, fancy*, δ. δὲ δεῖ λέγειν Hdt.7.185, cf. Chrysipp.Stoic.2.22, etc.; δ. εἰπεῖν, opp. ἐξακριβῶσαι λόγον, S.Tr.426; δ. ἀγνὼς λόγων ἦλθε a vague *suspicion* was thrown out, Id.OT681 (lyr.); δ. τῆς ἀληθείας Th.2.35; δώρων δ. *suspicion* of bribery, Id.5.16; δ. παρέχειν ὡς.. Plu.Pomp.54. 2. *apparition, phantom*, κενὴν δ. E.Hel.36; σκοπεῖτε μὴ δόκησιν εἶχετ' ἐκ θεῶν ib.119; οὕτω δοκεῖτε τὴν δ. ἀσφαλῆ ib.121. 3. *appearance*, opp. reality, Ph.1.222; φάσμα καὶ δ. ἑαυτῆς παρέχειν Plu.2.392a; δ. ἰσχίου Aret.SD2.12. II. *repute, credit*, Th.4.18, Stoic.3.38; ὁ στρατηγὸς τὴν δ. ἄρνυται E.Andr.696.

**δοκησῐ-σοφία**, ἡ, *conceit of wisdom*, Pl.(?)ap.Poll.4.9. **-σοφος**, ον, *wise in one's own conceit*, Ar.Pax44, Antipho Soph.105, Ph.1.122; δ. φρόνημα ib.605.

**δοκίας**, ου, ὁ, = δοκός II, Phlp.in Mete.92.24, Suid.s.v. κομῆται. **δοκίδιον**, τό, Dim. of δοκός, Harp.

**δοκικῶ**, com. barbarism for δοκέω, Hermipp.12.

⊛ **δοκῐμάζω**, (δόκιμος) *assay, test*, πορφύραν καὶ χρυσόν Isoc.12.39; τοὺς οἴνους Arist.EN1118ᵃ28; τὰ νομίσματα Id.HA491ᵃ21 :—Med., *prove for oneself, choose*, χώραν X.Oec.8.10, cf. Men.532.11 (dub.):—Pass., ἐπειδὰν τὸ ἔργον.. δοκιμασθῇ CIG2266.15 (Delos). 2. of persons, δ. αὐτοὺς *put* them *to the test, make trial of* them, Isoc.2.50; δ. τοὺς μηνυτάς Th.6.53; φίλους X.Mem.2.6.1, cf. PEleph.1.8 (iv B.C.), etc.; also of Apis-bulls, Hdt.2.38. II. *approve, sanction*, μετὰ δεδοκιμασμένου [λόγου] μὴ ξυνέπεσθαι Th.2.38; ἐψηφίσασθε δοκιμάσαντες τοὺς νόμους, εἶτ' ἀναγράψαι τούτους οἳ ἂν δοκιμασθῶσι And.1.82; ἄρρενας ἔρωτας Plu.2.11e; ὅπῃ ταύτῃ ἀρετὴ δοκιμάζεται Pl.R.407c: c. inf., ἐκπονεῖν ἐδοκίμαζε he *approved of* their working, X.Mem.1.2.4; ἐπειδὴ.. ἐδοκιμάσθη ταῦτα καλῶς ἔχειν Th.2.35. 2. as a political term, a. *approve after scrutiny as fit* for an office, Lys.16.3, Pl.Lg.759d, Arist.Ath.45.3 :—Pass., *to be approved as fit*, Lys.15.6, etc.; δοκιμασθεὶς ἀρχέτω Pl.Lg.765b; μου δοκιμαζομένου *when I was undergoing a scrutiny*, D.21.111; δεδοκιμασμένος [ἰατρός] PFay.106.24 (ii A.D.), cf. PGnom.201 (ii A.D.): metaph., ὃν ὁ Ἥφαιστος ἐδοκίμασεν OGI90.3 (ii B.C.); ὑπὲρ τοῦ στεφανωθῆναι δοκιμάζομαι D.18.266. b. *pass as fit to serve*, ἱππεύειν δεδοκιμασμένος Lys.14.22, cf. X.An.3.3.20, IG2².1126.15,1369. c. *examine and admit* boys *to the class of* ἔφηβοι or ἔφηβοι *to the rights of manhood*, Ar.V.578 (Pass.), Arist.Ath.42.2, etc.; ἕως ἐγὼ ἀνὴρ εἶναι δοκιμασθείην D.27.5; εἰς ἄνδρας δεδοκιμασμένοι Isoc.12.28. d. *test* an orator's *right to speak* (cf. δοκιμασία 4), AB310. 3. c. inf., *think fit* to do, Luc.BisAcc.31, J.AJ2.7.4, etc.: with neg., *refuse* to do, Ep.Rom.1.28: abs., BGU248.19 (i A.D.), etc.

**δοκῐμαίνονται**· δοκιμάζουσι, Hsch.

**δοκῐμ-ασία**, ἡ, *examination, scrutiny*: 1. of magistrates after election, to see if they fulfil the legal requirements of legitimacy, full citizenship, etc., ἡ δ. τῶν στρατηγῶν Lys.15.2, cf. 16.9 (pl.); τῶν ἱερέων Pl.Lg.759d; δ. εἰσάγειν ταῖς ἀρχαῖς Arist.Ath.59.4 (pl.), cf. IG2².856,980. 2. δ. τῶν ἱππέων *passing muster*, X.Eq.Mag.3.9 (pl.). 3. δ. (sc. ἐφήβων), before admission to the rights of manhood, D.44.41, v.l. in 57.62. 4. δ. τῶν ῥητόρων a judicial *process to determine the right* of a man *to speak* in the ἐκκλησία or in the law-courts, Aeschin.1.2. 5. *examination* of recruits, PLond.3.982.6 (iv A.D.). 6. generally, *test*, δ. ἱκανὴν [τινος] λαβεῖν make full *trial of*, Is.7.34 (but, receive *assurance* of.., Plb.3.31.8); ἡ κατὰ τὸν χρόνον δ. Arist.EN1162ᵃ14; κρίσιν καὶ δ. τινῶν ποιεῖν Plu.Cleom.10; λίθος δοκιμασίας LxxSi.6.21; δ. οἰκοδόμων PSI3.176 (v A.D.). **-αστέος**, α, ον, *to be approved after scrutiny*, Luc.Eun.8. II. impers., δοκιμαστέον, *one must approve after scrutiny*, Lys.21.25, Epicur.Sent.Vat.28, Plu.2.3d, Max.Tyr.7.9. **-αστήρ**, ῆρος, ὁ, = δοκιμαστής, τῶν κοινῶν Plb.24.7.5, cf. 6.8. **-αστήριον**, τό, *test, means of trial*, Men.Mon.537, Arr.Epict.3.6.10; μύρων, of the nose, Artem.4.27. ⊛ **-αστής**, οῦ, ὁ, *examiner, scrutineer*, Lys.26.16, Pl.Lg.802b; πράγματος D.48.3; διαίτης Aeschin.2.146 (pl.); *money-changer*, Men.532.8. II. *approver, panegyrist*, D.21.127; δ. καὶ ἐπαινηταί D.C.38.4. **-αστικός**, ή, όν, *of* or *for scrutiny*, δύναμις Arr.Epict.1.1.1, cf. S.E.M.1.64, Theol.Ar.52, v.l. in Diog.Bab.Stoic.3.219. Adv. -κῶς *approvingly*, διακεῖσθαι Stoic.3.160. II. -κόν, τό, *commission paid to an assayer*, PHib.29.24, al. **-αστός**, ή, όν, *approved*, Diog.Bab.Stoic.3.219, cf. 49, D.L.7.105. **-άω**, = -άζω, PTeb.24.78 (ii B.C.). ⊛ **-εῖον**, τό, *test, means of testing*, Pl.Ti.65c (v.l. **δοκίμιον**, as in D.H.Rh.11.1, Ep.Jac.1.3, 1Ep.Pet.1.7, S.E.M.7.430, Lib.Decl.16.55), IG7.303.31 (Orop.); *proof*, εὐσεβείας OGI308.16 (Hierapolis), cf. Zos.3.13. **-εῖος** (freq. written **δοκίμιος**), α, ον, = δόκιμος, χρυσίον BGU717.8, cf. IG2.684.5, etc. ⊛ **-ή**, ἡ, *proof, test*, interpol. in Dsc.4.184. 2. *tried* or *approved character*, Ep.Phil.2.22, cf. 2Ep.Cor.2.9. ⊛ **-ος**, ον (Dor. α, ον Tab.Heracl.1.103), (δέχομαι) *acceptable*: hence, 1. of persons, *trustworthy*, Heraclit.28 (Sup.), Democr.67; *approved, esteemed*, Hdt.1.65, al.; δ. παρά τινι Id.7.117; δοκιμώτατος Ἑλλάδι *most approved* by Hellas, her *noblest* son, E.Supp.277 (anap.): c. inf., *of approved ability* to do.., δόκιμος δ' οὔτις.. εἴργειν A.Pers.87 (lyr.). 2. of things, *excellent*, τὸ ἔαρ -ώτατον Hdt.7.162; *notable, considerable*, ποταμός Id.7.129; *approved*, κριθὰ καθαρὰ δ. Tab.Heracl. l.c.; δ. ἀργύριον *legal* tender, D.35.24, cf. PLond.3.938.6 (iii A.D.); ὕμνος *acceptable*, Pi.N.3.11. 3. Adv. -μως *really, genuinely*, A.Pers.547 (lyr.), X.Cyr.1.6.7. ⊛ **-όω**, = δοκιμάζω,

Parm.1.32, Pherecyd.ap.D.L.1.122, Theoc.30.25, Hsch. ⊛ **-ωμι,** Aeol. form of δοκιμόω, = δοκέω, Sapph.69, cf. 37 (dub.), *Epigr.Gr.* 991.7 (Balbilla).

**δοκίον,** τό, = δοκίς, Arist.*HA*532$^{b}$21, *IG*11.146*A*68 (Delos, iv B.C.), D.S.18.42.

⊛ **δοκίς,** ίδος, ἡ, *plank*, Hp.*Fract.*13, X.*Cyn.*9.15, *IG*11.287*A*24 (Delos, iii B.C.). 2. *screen* or *shield* used by sappers, = χελώνη ὀρυκτρίς, Ph.*Bel.*81.28, al. II. = δοκός II, Arist.*Mu.*392$^{b}$4, Ptol. *Tetr.*90; πυρίνη δ. D.S.15.50, cf. Nonn.*D.*2.199. III. *number of the form mn*$^{2}$ (*m*>*n*), Theo Sm.p.42 H., Nicom.*Ar.*2.17.

**δοκίτης,** ου, ὁ, = δοκός II, Suid.

**δοκοθήκη,** ἡ, *stone with hole for insertion of roof-beam*, *IG*11(2).161$^{A}$55 (Delos, iii B.C.). **δοκόν,** τό, = δοκός, *PLond.*3.1259.13 (iv A.D.). **δοκοποιός,** *tignarius*, *Gloss.*

⊛ **δοκός,** ἡ, later also ὁ, Luc.*VH*2.1: (δέχομαι):—*bearing-beam, main beam*, esp. in the roof or floor of a house, Od.22.176, Ar.*Nu.*1496; any *balk* or *beam*, Il.17.744, Th.4.112; *bar* of a gate or door, Ar.*V.*201: also, in pl., *firewood*, *PFlor.*127.5 (iii A.D.): prov., ὁ τὴν δοκὸν φέρων *one who has 'swallowed a poker'*, Ar.*Rh.*1413$^{b}$28; ἐν δοκοῖσι is prob. f.l. for ἐνδόκοισι in Archil.66.?, cf. Hsch. s.v. ἔνδοκος. II. a kind of *meteor*, Plin.*HN*2.96, Lyd.*Ost.*10$^{b}$, Hsch.; cf. δοκεύς, δοκίας, δοκίς II.

⊛ **δόκος,** ὁ, = δόκησις, Xenoph.34.4, Call.*Fr.*100; περὶ τοῦ δ., title of work by Demetrius of Phalerum, D.L.5.81. II. = ἀγχονή, Ar.*Fr.*515.

**δοκοτέκτων,** ονος, ὁ, *carpenter*, *Gloss.*

**δοκόω,** *furnish with rafters*, in Pass., S.E.*P.*3.99; οἰκία δεδοκωμένη *Sammelb.*5105.3 (ii B.C.), *PGrenf.*2.35 (i B.C.).

**δοκώ,** όος, contr. οῦς, ἡ, = δόκησις, E.*El.*747.

**δοκ-ώδης,** ες, *beam-like*, *Gloss.* **-ωσις,** εως, ἡ, *furnishing with rafters, roofing*, Lxx*Ec.*10.18, Plu.2.1112e (pl.), S.E.*P.*3.99, *M.*9.343, *POxy.*1648.60 (ii A.D.).

**δολάν** (leg. δοάν)· ἀντὶ τοῦ δήν, Hsch. **δολάνα·** μαστροπός, Id. (cf. δολομάν). **δολβαί·** θύματα, οἱ δὲ μικρὰ (μικτὰ cod.) πλακούντια, Id.; cf. δόλπαι.

**δολερός,** ά, όν, (δόλος) *deceitful, treacherous*, νόος Hdt.2.151; ἄνθρωποι, εἵματα, Id.3.22; φρήν S.*Ph.*1112 (lyr.), cf. X.*Cyr.*1.6.27, Ant.Lib.29.3; δολερὸν πέφυκεν ἄνθρωπος Arr.*An.*4.5.1; δ. ἔρως Pl.*Smp.*205d. Adv. -ρῶς Ph.2.314, J.*AJ*14.13.6, Poll.3.132.

**δόλευμα,** ατος, τό, *stratagem, ruse*, Aen.Tact.39 tit.

**δολέων·** δοθιήν, Hsch.

**δολία,** ἡ, = κώνειον, Ps.-Dsc.4.78.

**δολῐεύομαι,** *deal treacherously*, Aq., Sm.*Ge.*37.18. 2. λόγος δεδολιευμένος a *sophism*, S.E.*P.*2.229.

**δολίζω,** *adulterate*, Dsc.1.64, al.

**δολῐό-βουλος,** ον, gloss on δολόμητις, Suid. **-γνωμος,** ον, gloss on δολιομῆτα, Hsch. **-μήτης,** voc. -μῆτα, ὁ, = sq., Id. **-μητις,** ιδος, ὁ, ἡ, *crafty-minded*, A.*Supp.*750 (lyr.). **-μῦθος,** ον, *crafty of speech*, prob. for δολό-, S.*Tr.*839 (lyr.). **-πους,** ὁ, ἡ, πουν, τό, *stealthy of foot*, Id.*El.*1392 (lyr.).

⊛ **δόλιος,** α, ον (ος, ον E.*Alc.*33, *Tr.*530), Lxx*Ps.*51(52).6, etc. (lyr.):—*crafty, deceitful, treacherous*, in Od. always of things, ἔπεα, τέχνη, 9.282, 4.455; ὁππότε..δόλιον περὶ κύκλον ἄγωσιν the *treacherous* circle, i.e. the net, 4.792; μῆνις A.*Ag.*155 (lyr.); of persons, Pi.*P.*2.82, etc.; δόλιον ὄμμ' ἔχων A.*Pr.*569; epith. of Aphrodite, B.16.116, E.*Hel.*238 (lyr.); of Hermes, S.*Ph.*133, Ar.*Pl.*1157; in later Prose, Plb.21.34.1; δ. χείλη Lxx*Pr.*26.23; ἀνελεύθερος καὶ δ. Phld.*Ir.* p.60 W. Adv. -ίως Batr.93, *Epigr.Gr.*387.7 (Apamea), Lxx*Je.*9.4(3), D.L.9.35.

**δολιότης,** ητος, ἡ, *deceit, subtlety*, Lxx*Nu.*25.17, al.

**δολιό-τροπος,** ον, *crafty*, γνώμη Tz.*H.*3.443. **-φρων,** ὁ, ἡ, gen. ονος, *crafty of mind, wily*, ποινά A.*Ch.*947 (lyr.); Κύπρις E.*IA*1300.

**δολιόω,** 3 pl. impf. ἐδολιοῦσαν, *deal treacherously with* one, Lxx*Ps.*5.10, al.: abs., *to be treacherous*, Sm.*Pr.*26.19.

**δολίσκος,** ὁ, Dim. of δόλων II, Hsch. **δολίφονον·** πέπαικται δὲ τοῦ δολοφονίου, Id.

**δολῐχ-αίων,** ὁ, ἡ, gen. ωνος, *long-lived, immortal*, θεοί Emp.21.12, 23.8. **-άορος** [ᾱ], ον, *with long sword*, Ἀθηναίη Philet.23. ⊛ **-αυλος,** ον, *with a long tube*, δ. αἰγανέη a spear *with a long iron socket* for the shaft, Od.9.156. **-αύχην,** ενος, ὁ, ἡ, *long-necked*, πταναί E.*Hel.*1487 (lyr.); κύκνος B.15.6, E.*IA*793 (lyr.). **-εγχής,** ές, *with tall spear*, Παίονες Il.21.155. ⊛ **-εύω,** = δολιχοδρομέω, *AP*11.82 (Nicarch.): generally, δρόμον δ. *go through a long* course, Ph.1.331; δ. τὴν φύσιν *prolong* its existence, ib.9; δ. πολλοὺς πλοῦς Ael.*Fr.*71.

**δολῐχήπους,** ὁ, ἡ, gen. ποδος, *with long feet*, Numen.ap.Ath.7.305a.

**δολῐχ-ήρετμος,** ον, (ἐρετμός) *long-oared*, of a ship, Od.4.499, etc.; of the Phaeacians, *using long oars*, 8.191; δ. Αἴγινα Pi.*O.*8.20. **-ήρης,** ες, = δολιχός, *long*, Nic.*Th.*183, Opp.*C.*1.408.

**δολῐχο-γρᾰφία,** ἡ, *prolix writing*, *AP*6.327 (Leon.). II. *long-continued writing*, ib.65 (Paul. Sil.). **-δειρος,** Ep. **δουλ-,** ον, *long-necked*, κύκνοι Il.2.460. **-δρομέω,** *run the* δόλιχος, Aeschin.3.91. **-δρόμος,** ον, *running the* δόλιχος, Pl.*Prt.*335e, X.*Smp.*2.17:—Aeol. and Dor. **δολιχαδρόμος,** *IG*12(2).383 (Mytilene), *CIG*2758 (Aphrodisias), *IG*5(1).19 (Sparta). **-εις,** εσσα, εν, Ion. **δουλ-,** = δολιχός, *AP*6.4 (Leon.). **-κρότᾰφος,** ον, *long-headed*, *IG*3.1310.

**δολῐχό-ουρος** or **δολίχ-ουρος,** ον, *long-tailed*: metaph. of verses with a syll. redundant (as Od.5.231), Sch.Heph.p.290C., Eust.12.33.

⊛ **δολῐχό-πους,** ὁ, ἡ, πουν, τό, = δολιχήπους.

⊛ **δολῐχός,** ή, όν, *long*, ἔγχεα, δόρυ, Il.4.533, al.; also of Time, νύξ, νοῦσος, Od.23.243, 11.172; δολιχόν, as Adv., Il.10.52; σχελίδες Archipp.11.3 (lyr.); ἐλάται A.R.1.914; πρυμνήσια *AP*10.4 (Marc. Arg.); some phrases, as δ. πλόος, δ. ὁδός, unite both senses, Od.3.169, 4.393. (Cf. Skt. *dīrghas* 'long'.)

⊛ **δόλιχος,** ὁ, *the long course*, in racing, opp. στάδιον, *IG*2$^{2}$.956, etc.; τὸν δ. ἁμιλλᾶσθαι Pl.*Lg.*833b; θεῖν X.*An.*4.8.27; νικᾶν Luc.*Hist. Conscr.*30; δολίχῳ κρατεῖν Paus.3.21.1: metaph., δ. κατατείνουσι τοῦ λόγου Pl.*Prt.*329a; δόλιχον τοῖς ἔτεσι..τρέχειν Epicr.3.18; δόλιχον βιότου σταδιεύσας *Epigr.Gr.*311; γήρως δ. ib.231. 2. a *measure of length*, = 12 *stades*, Hero *Geom.*4.13. II. *calavance, Vigna sinensis*, Thphr.*HP*8.3.2, Diocl.*Fr.*117.

**δολῐχ-όσκῐος,** ον, (σκιά) *casting a long shadow*, Homeric epith. of ἔγχος, Il.3.346, etc.: in later Ep. as a general epith., *long*, οὐρή Opp.*C.*1.411; αὐχήν Nonn.*D.*12.181; *far-reaching*, ἰός Id.2.612, etc. **-ούᾰτος,** ον, (οὖας) *long-eared*, Opp.*C.*3.186.

**δολῐχόφρων,** ὁ, ἡ, gen. ονος, *far-reaching*, μέριμναι Emp.11.1.

**δολιχωπά·** μακρά, Hsch.

**δολό-εις,** εσσα, εν, (δόλος) *subtle, wily*, Καλυψώ, Κίρκη, Od.7.245, 9.32. II. of things, *craftily contrived, artful*, δέσματα 8.281; θάνατος Hellanic.69(a) J.; Τροίας ἕδη E.*IA*1527 (lyr.). **-εργής,** ές, *working by fraud*, Man.4.394:—also **-εργός,** όν, ib.57, al. **-κτᾰσία,** ἡ, (κτείνω) *murder by treachery*, A.R.4.479 (pl.).

**δολομάν·** μαστροπόν (Lacon.), Hsch.

⊛ **δολο-μήδης,** ες, gen. εος, *wily, crafty*, f.l. in Simon.43. **-μήτης,** ου, ὁ, voc. δολομῆτα, = sq., Il.1.540. **-μητις,** ι, *crafty of counsel, wily*, of persons, Od.1.300; Ἀφροδίτα prob. in Simon.43; ἀπάτα A.*Pers.*93 (lyr.). **-μήχᾰνος,** ον, *contriving wiles*, Ἄρης Simon.43 (codd. of Sch.A.R.), Theoc.30.25. **-μῦθος,** ον, *subtle-speaking*, f.l. in S.*Tr.*839 (lyr.).

**δολοπεύω,** *plot*, Hsch. (cf. δόλοψ).

**δολο-πλᾰνής,** ές, *treacherous*, Nonn.*D.*8.126. **-πλοκία,** ἡ, *subtlety, craft*, in pl., Thgn.226, Hp.*Ep.*17. ⊛ **-πλόκος,** ον (α, ον v.l. in *Lyr.Adesp.*129), *weaving wiles*, Ἀφροδίτα Sapph.1.2; μῦθος Tryph.264. **-ποιός,** όν, *treacherous, ensnaring*, ἀνάγκα S.*Tr.*832 (lyr.).

**δολορρᾰφ-έω,** *lay snares*, Ctes.*Fr.*29.4. **-ής,** ές, *treacherously wrought*, of nets, Opp.*H.*3.84. II. *weaving treacherously*, Nonn.*D.*20.182, al. **-ία,** ἡ, *artful contrivance*, *AP*5.285 (Paul. Sil.). **-ος,** ον, (ῥάπτω) *treacherous*, Tz.*H.*8.925.

⊛ **δόλος** (A), ὁ, prop. *bait* for fish, Od.12.252: hence, *any cunning contrivance for deceiving* or *catching*, as the net in which Hephaestus catches Ares, 8.276; the Trojan horse, ib.494; Ixion's bride, Pi.*P.*2.39; the robe of Penelope, Od.19.137 (pl.); ξύλινος δ. mouse-*trap*, Batr.116. b. generally, *any trick* or *stratagem*, πυκινὸν δ. ἄλλον ὕφαινε Il.6.187, etc.: in pl., *wiles*, δόλοι καὶ μήδεα 3.202; δόλοισι κεκασμένε 4.339, etc. 2. in the abstract, *craft, cunning, treachery*, δόλῳ ἠὲ βίηφι Od.9.406; ἔπεφνε δόλῳ, οὔ τι κράτεΐ γε Il.7.142; οὐ κατ' ἰσχὺν..δόλῳ δέ.. A.*Pr.*215, cf. *Ch.*556, etc.; δόλοις ib.888, S.*OT*960, etc.; ἐκ δόλου Id.*El.*279; ἐν δόλῳ Id.*Ph.*102; σὺν δόλῳ A.*Pers.*775; μετὰ δόλου καὶ τέχνης Isoc.9.36; δόλῳ πονηρῷ, = Lat. *dolo malo*, *Supp.Epigr.*1.161.53; μετὰ δόλου πονηροῦ *IG*12(2).510.9 (Methymna); χωρὶς δ. π. *OGI*629.112 (Palmyra). 3. *spy*, Hsch.

**δόλος** (B)· πάσσαλος, Hsch.

**δολοσχερής,** ές, neut. pl. τὰ δολοσχερέα, of parts of a bier, *IG*12(5).593 (Ceos); cf. foreg. (Perh. τὰ δ' ὁλοσχερέα.)

**δολοφον-έω,** *slay by treachery*, Str.5.3.2, al., Ph.1.412:—Pass., Plb.32.5.11; but freq. simply, *murder* (with no implication of treachery), Ph.1.205, al., App.*Syr.*69:—Pass., D.19.194, Arist.*Mir.*836$^{a}$16, *POxy.*12$^{r}$v8, *BGU*388 i 23 (ii/iii A.D.), etc. **-ησις,** εως, ἡ, = sq., App.*Syr.*69. **-ία,** ἡ, *slaying by treachery*, Arist.*EN*1131$^{a}$7; *murder*, Plb.6.13.4 (pl.). **-ος,** ον, *slaying by treachery, privy to treacherous murder*, λέβης δ. A.*Ag.*1129 (lyr.).

**δολο-φρᾰδής,** ές, *wily-minded*, *h.Merc.*282, Pi.*N.*8.33. **-φράδμων,** ον, gen. ονος, = foreg., Ἀφροδίτη Nonn.*D.*4.68, 32.1. **-φρονέων,** ουσα, ον, *planning craft, wily-minded*, Il.3.405, Od.10.339, Archil.93. ⊛ **-φροσύνη,** ἡ, *craft, subtlety*, Il.19.97, 112. **-φρων,** ον, gen. ονος, = δολοφραδής, f.l. in A.*Supp.*750 (lyr.); Ἀπάτα *AP*7.145 (Asclep.).

⊛ **δόλοψ,** οπος, ὁ, *lurker in ambush*, Hsch.

⊛ **δολόω,** *beguile, ensnare, take by craft*, A.*Ag.*273, 1636; φαρμάκῳ δ. Hdt.1.212; ὗς πλέγμασι δ. X.*Cyr.*1.6.28; δολοῦν τινὰ γάμοις *beguile* by the anticipation of.., E.*IA*898 (anap.):—Med., *Leg.Gort.*2.36, 44:—Pass., Hes.*Th.*494, S.*Ph.*1288. II. *disguise*, μορφήν ib.129; *adulterate* incense, wine, etc., Dsc.1.81, Luc.*Herm.*59; *alloy*, Gal.14.48 (Pass.); *dye*, τὰ ἔρια Poll.7.169.

**δόλπαι,** αἱ, *small cakes* (Cos), Hsch.; cf. δολβαί. **Δολφοί,** v. Δελφοί. **δολφός,** ὁ, (cf. δελφύς) *womb*, Id.

**δόλωμα,** ατος, τό, *trick, deceit*, A.*Ch.*1003; *stratagem, ruse*, Aen.Tact.8.2 (pl.).

**δόλων,** ωνος, ὁ, *flying jib*, Plb.16.15.2, D.S.20.61. 2. *spar which carries such a sail*, Poll.1.91. II. *secret weapon, poniard, stiletto*, Plu.*TG*10. III. *fishing-rod* (?), Artem.2.14.

**δολωνικός,** ή, όν, *pertaining to a top-sail*, ξύλον εἰς τράπεζαν δολωνικήν *PLond.ined.*2305 (iii B.C.).

**δολ-ῶπις,** ιδος, ἡ, *artful-looking, treacherous*, S.*Tr.*1050. **-ωσις,** εως, ἡ, *tricking*, X.*Cyr.*1.6.28 (pl.). 2. *alloying*, Gal.14.48.

* **δόμα** (A), ατος, τό, (δίδωμι) *gift*, Pl.*Def.*415b, Lxx *Ge.*25.6 (pl.), Plu.2.182e. **2.** *payment*, *PPetr.*2 p.11 (iii B.C.).

**δόμα** (B), ατος, τό, = δῶμα, Max.448, = τειχίον, Hsch.

**δομαῖος**, α, ον, (δομή) *for building*: δομαῖοι (sc. λίθοι) *foundation-stones*, A.R.1.737; δ. λᾶα *APl.*4.279.

**δομᾰτίζω**, *bestow presents on*, Sm.*Ez.*16.33:—Pass., Ps.-Callisth. 1.11 (cod. A).

**δομ-άω**, = δέμω:—Pass., λίθοι εὖ δεδομημένοι Aristid.1.821 J., cf. J.*BJ*5.4.2, al., Arr.*An.*7.22.2.

**δόμεναι, δόμεν**, v. sub δίδωμι.

**δομ-έοντι**· οἰκοδομοῦντι, Hsch. **-ή**, ἡ, (δέμω) *building*, dub. l. in J.*AJ*15.11.3, cf. Hsch. **II.** Alex. word for δέμας, A.R.3.1395, Nic.*Th.*153, Lyc.334,597,783.

**δόμημα**, ατος, τό, *building*, J.*BJ*5.5.1.

**δόμ-ησις**, εως, ἡ, = δομή I, J.*BJ*1.21.6, al. **-ήτωρ**, ορος, ὁ, *builder*, Anon.*Prog.* in Rh.1.642 W.

**δόμονδε**, Adv. *homeward*, Hom.; ὅνδε δόμονδε *to* his own *house*, Od.1.83; also δόμον Archestr.*Fr.*26.

**δόμορτις**· γυνή, Hsch.

**δόμος**, ὁ, (δέμω, cf. Lat. *domus*): **1.** *house*, Il.2.513, Sapph.1.7, etc.; also, *part of a house*, *room*, *chamber*, Od.8.57, 22.204: freq. in pl. for *a house*, Hes.*Op.*96, etc.; freq. in Trag., A.*Supp.*433, etc.: chiefly poet., οἶκος or οἰκία being used in Prose. **2.** *house* of a god, *temple*, Διὸς δόμος Il.8.375; δ. Ἀρτέμιδος Ar.*Ra.*1273; Ἐρεχθῆος πυκινὸν δόμον *the building* of Erechtheus, i.e. *the temple* of Athena, Od.7.81; Ἄϊδος δ., of the nether world, Il.3.322, etc.; δ. δίκας A.*Eu.*516 (lyr.); μυστοδόκος δ., of the *temple* at Eleusis, Ar.*Nu.*303: so in pl., εἰν Ἀΐδαο δόμοισι Il.22.52; δόμων τῶν Λοξίου A.*Eu.*35, cf. E.*Ion* 249; *chamber* in a temple, χρύσεος δ. ἐν Διὸς οἴκῳ Theoc.17.17. **3.** *abode* of animals, e.g. sheep*fold*, Il.12.301; κοῖλος δ. wasps' or bees' *nest*, ib.169; serpent's *hole*, Ael.*NA*2.9. **4.** ξύλινος δ. *pyre*, B.3.49. **5.** κέδρινοι δόμοι *closet* or *chest* of cedar, E.*Alc.*160. **II.** in Trag., *household*, *family*, A.*Ch.*263, S.*OC*370, E.*Or.*70, *Med.*114 (anap.); *one's father's house*, ἔξω δόμων τε καὶ πάτρας ὠθεῖν ἐμέ A.*Pr.*665, etc. **III.** *course* of stone or bricks in a building, ὑποδείμας τὸν πρῶτον δ. λίθου Αἰθιοπικοῦ Hdt.2.127; διὰ τριήκοντα δόμων πλίνθου at every thirtieth *layer* of bricks, Id.1.179, cf. Lxx 1*Es.*6.24, D.S.1.64; καθ' ἕνα δόμον Plb.10.22.7. **2.** *ply* or *strand* of gut in the τόνοι of a torsion-engine, Ph.*Bel.*65.42, Hero *Bel.*82.1.

**δομο-σφᾰλής**, ές, *shaking the house*, κτύπος A.*Ag.*1533 (lyr.). ***-τέκτων**, ονος, ὁ, = *valvarius*, *Gloss.*; *carpenter*, *Ath.Mitt.*25.123 (Philadelphia).

**δομόω**, *provide with lodging*, *PMasp.*96.29 (Pass., vi A.D.).

**δονᾰκ-εύομαι**, *fowl with reed and birdlime*, *AP*9.264 (Apollonid. or Phil.). **-εύς**, ῆος or έως, ὁ, (δόναξ) *thicket of reeds*, Il.18.576: pl., Opp.*H.*4.507. **II.** *fowler*, Id.*C.*1.73. **III.** = δόναξ, *AP* 6.64 (Paul. Sil.). **-ηδόν**, Adv. *like a reed*, A.D.*Adv.*197.19. **-ήματα**· ἀναλήμματα, Hsch. **-ινος**, η, ον, *made of reeds*, κερκίδες Hsch. s. h. v. **-ῖτις**, ιδος, ἡ, *of reed*, ψήκτρα *AP*6.307 (Phan.). **II.** Subst., = λευκὴ ἄκανθα, Ps.-Dsc.3.12.

**δονᾰκο-γλύφος** [ῠ], ον, *reed-cutting*, *pen-making*, σμίλα *AP*6.295 (Phan.). **-δίφης** [ῐ], poet. **δουν-**, ου, ὁ, *one who searches among reeds*, prob. in ib.10.22 (Bianor). **-εις**, εσσα, εν, *reedy*, δονακόεντος Εὐρώτα E.*Hel.*210 (lyr.); δόλος δ. a reed covered with birdlime, *AP* 9.273 (Bianor). **-τρόφος**, ον, *producing reeds*, Εὐρώτας Thgn.785, E.*IA*179 (lyr.); Λάδων Corinn.12. * **-φοίτης**, v. δουν-. **-χλοος**, ον, contr. **-χλους**, ουν, *green with reeds*, E.*IT*400.

**Δονάκτας**, ου, ὁ, epith. of Apollo, prob. in Theopomp.Hist.281.

**δονᾰκ-ώδης**, ες, *reedy*, Νεῖλος B.*Fr.*22, cf. A.R.2.818; *reed-like*, μορφή Nonn.*D.*42.385; *made by a reed*, μέλος ib.1.440. **-ών**, ῶνος, ὁ, *a thicket of reeds*, Paus.9.31.7 (as pr. n.), Epic. in *Arch.Pap.*7.7.

* **δόναξ**, ᾰκος, ὁ, poet. gen. δούνακος *AP* (v. infr.), dat. δώνακι Theoc. (v. infr.): (δονέω, 'a reed *shaken with the wind*'):—*pole-reed*, *Arundo Donax*, smaller than the κάλαμος (Eust.Il.1165.23), Il.10.467, Od.14.474, Thphr.*HP*4.11.11, etc.; δόνακες καλάμοιο reed-*stalks*, *h.Merc.*47. **2.** *bed of reeds*, App.*BC*3.67, al. **II.** *anything made of reed*, **1.** *shaft of an arrow*, Il.11.584. **2.** *shepherd's pipe*, Pi.*P.*12.25 (pl.), A.*Pr.*574 (lyr.), Theoc.20.29. **3.** *fishing-rod* or *limed reed*, *AP*7.702 (Apollonid.). **4.** *bridge* of the lyre, Ar.*Ra.*232. **III.** shell-fish, = σωλήν, Diph.Siph.ap.Ath.3.90d.

* **δον-έω**, *shake*, of the effects of the wind, τὸ δέ τε πνοιαὶ δονέουσιν they *shake* the young tree, Il.17.55; ἄνεμος..νέφεα σκιόεντα δονήσας *having driven* them, 12.157; ἀνέμῳ δεδονημένον αὖον ἄχερδον Theoc.24.90: generally, *shake*, δ. γάλα, in order to make butter, Hdt.4.2; δ. ἄκοντα Pi.*P.*1.44:—Pass., δονοῦνται τὸ νευρῶδες *have twitchings in* the tendons, Paul.Aeg.6.74. **2.** *drive about*, τὰς..οἶστρος..ἐδόνησεν (sc. τὰς βόας) Od.22.300; *disturb*, *terrify*, Tim.*Pers.*222: hence of love, *agitate*, *excite*, Sapph.40, Ar.*Ec.*954 (lyr.); ποθεινὰ Ἑλλὰς αὐτὰν δ. μάστιγι πειθοῦς Pi.*P.*4.219, cf. 6.36 (Pass.); θυμὸν δονέουσι μέριμναι B.1.69 (but δ. καρδίαν *to agitate* one's mind, *Fr.*8); ὀσμὴ.. μυκτῆρα δονεῖ Mnesim.4.60; ἡμᾶς ἐδόνησεν ἡ μουσική Alciphr.*Fr.*6.12:—Pass., ἡ Ἀσίη ἐδονέετο Asia *was in commotion*, Hdt.7.1; τὰ ὑπερόρια πολέμοις ἐδονεῖτο App.*BC*4.52; πελέκεσσι δονεῖσθαι Corinn.18; Ἔρωτι δονεύμενος Bion *Fr.*6.5; παῖδα ποθῶν δεδόνητο Theoc.13.65: fut. Med. in pass. sense, ἅρματα καλὰ δονήσεται *h.Ap.*270. **3.** Pass., *wheel*, of troops, Arist.*Mu.*399$^{b}$9. **II.** of sound, *murmur*, *buzz*, of bees, prob. in *h.Merc.*563; δ. θρόον ὕμνων *rouse* the voice of song, Pi.*N.*7.81:—also in Med. or Pass., λυρᾶν τε βοαὶ καναχαί τ' αὐλῶν δονέονται Id.*P.*10.39; of bees, Choeril.2; ῥοιζήμασιν αἰθὴρ δονεῖται Ar.*Av.*1183.—Poet. word, used in Ion., X.*Smp.*2.8, and late Prose; of medical *percussion*, Aret.*SD*2.1. **-ημα**, ατος, τό, *agitation*, *waving*, δένδρου Luc.*Salt.*19.

* **δόξᾰ**, ἡ, (δοκέω, δέκομαι) *expectation*, οὐδ' ἀπὸ δόξης not otherwise than *one expects*, Il.10.324, Od.11.344; in Prose, παρὰ δόξαν ἢ ὡς κατεδόκεε Hdt.1.79, etc.; ἐν δόξᾳ θέμενος εὖχος *hoping for*.., Pi.*O.*10(11).63; δόξαν παρέχειν τινὶ μὴ ποιήσεσθαι.. to make one *expect* that.., X.*HG*7.5.21; δόξαν παρέχεσθαί τινι ὡς.., c. part., Pl.*Sph.*216d; ἀπὸ τῆς δ. πεσέειν, = Lat. *spe excidere*, Hdt.7.203. **II.** after Hom., *notion*, *opinion*, *judgement*, whether well grounded or not, βροτῶν δόξαι Parm.1.30, cf. 8.51; ψυχῆς εὐτλήμονι δόξῃ A.*Pers.*28 (anap.); ἃ δόξῃ τοπάζω S.*Fr.*235; δόξῃ γοῦν ἐμῇ Id.*Tr.*718; κατά γε τὴν ἐμήν, with or without δόξαν, Pl.*Grg.*472e, *Phlb.*41b: opp. ἐπιστήμη, Id.*Tht.*187b sq., *R.*506c, Hp.*Lex* 4, Arist.*Metaph.*1074$^{b}$36; φάσεις καὶ δ. Id.*EN*1143$^{b}$13; opp. νόησις, Pl.*R.*534a; ἀληθεῖ δόξῃ δοξασταί capable of being subjects of true *opinion*, Id.*Tht.*202b; δ. ἀληθεῖς ἢ ψευδεῖς Id.*Phlb.*36c; δόξης ὀρθότης ἀλήθεια Arist.*EN*1142$^{b}$11; δ. ἐμποιεῖν περί τινος Id.*Pol.*1314$^{b}$22; κύριαι δ. philosophical *maxims*, title of work by Epicurus, Phld.*Ir.*p.86 W., etc.; αἱ κοιναὶ δ. *axioms*, Arist.*Metaph.*996$^{b}$28. **2.** *mere opinion*, *conjecture*, δόξῃ ἐπίστασθαι, ἡγεῖσθαι, *imagine*, *suppose* (wrongly), Hdt.8.132, Th.5.105; δόξης ἁμαρτία Id.1.32; δόξαι joined with φαντασίαι, Pl.*Tht.*161e, cf. Arist.*Ph.*254$^{a}$29 (but distd. fr. φαντασίαι, Id. *de An.*428$^{a}$20); κατὰ δόξαν, opp. κατ' οὐσίαν, Pl.*R.*534c; ὡς δόξῃ χρώμενοι speaking *by guess*, Isoc.8.8, cf. 13.8. **3.** *fancy*, *vision*, δ. ἀκόνας λιγυρᾶς Pi.*O.*6.82; δ. βριζούσης φρενός A.*Ag.*275; οὐκ εἰσὶ δόξαι τῶνδε πημάτων Id.*Ch.*1053, cf. 1051; of a dream, E.*Rh.*780; δ. ἐνυπνίου Philostr.*VA* ..23: pl., *hallucinations*, Alex.Trall.1.17. **III.** *the opinion which others have of one*, *estimation*, *repute*, first in Sol.13.4 ἀνθρώπων δόξαν ἔχειν ἀγαθήν, cf. 34; δ. ἐπ' ἀμφότερα φέρεσθαι Th.2.11. **2.** mostly, *good repute*, *honour*, *glory*, Alc.*Supp.*25.11, A.*Eu.*373 (lyr., pl.), Pi.*O.*8.64, etc.; δόξαν φύσας Hdt.5.91; δόξαν σχεῖν τινός *for* a thing, E.*HF*157; ἐπὶ σοφίᾳ δ. εἰληφώς Isoc.13.2; ἐπὶ καλοκἀγαθίᾳ καὶ σωφροσύνῃ δ. ὁμολογουμένην πεποιημένος Plb.35.4.8; δόξαν ἀντὶ τοῦ ζῆν ᾑρημένος D.2.15; δόξαν εἶχον ἄμαχοι εἶναι Pl.*Mx.*241b; δ. ἔχειν ὥς εἰσι..D.2.17; δ. καταλιπεῖν Id.3.24: in pl., οἱ ἐν ταῖς μεγίσταις δόξαις ὄντες Isoc.4.51. **3.** rarely of *ill repute*, [δ.] ἀντὶ καλῆς αἰσχρὰν τῇ πόλει περιάπτειν D.20.10; λαμβάνειν δ. φαύλην Id.*Ep.*3.5; κληρονομήσειν τὴν ἐπ' ἀσεβείᾳ δ. Plb.15.22.3. **4.** *popular repute* or *estimate*, εἰσφέρων οὐκ ἀφ' ὑπαρχούσης οὐσίας..ἀλλ' ἀπὸ τῆς δόξης ὧν ὁ πατήρ μοι κατέλιπεν D.21.157. **IV.** of external appearance, *glory*, *splendour*, esp. of the *Shechinah*, Lxx *Ex.*16.10, al.; δ. τοῦ φωτός *Act.Ap.*22.11: generally, *magnificence*, πλοῦτον καὶ δ. Lxx *Ge.*31.16, cf. *Ev.Matt.*4.8, al.; esp. of *celestial beatitude*, 2*Ep.Cor.*4.17: pl., 1*Ep.Pet.*1.11; also of *illustrious persons*, *dignities*, δόξας οὐ τρέμουσιν 2*Ep.Pet.*2.10; δ. βλασφημεῖν *Ep.Jud.*8.

* **δοξ-άζω**, *think*, *imagine*, c. acc. et inf., A.*Ag.*673, E.*Supp.*1043, etc.; c. dupl. acc., πῶς ταῦτ' ἀληθῆ..δοξάσω; how *can I suppose* this to be true? A.*Ch.*844; δ. βελτίους ἑαυτούς Pl.*Phlb.*48e; τὰ εὔχρηστα τῶν ζῴων θεοὺς ἐδόξασαν D.L.1.11; also abs., μετ' ἀσφαλείας δ. Th.1.120; δοξάζων μὲν οὔ not *expecting* it, S.*Ph.*545:—Pass., δ. εἶναι *to be supposed* to be, Pl.*Ti.*46d, al.; ὅση δοξάζεται (sc. εἶναι) Id.*Phd.*108c; δ. κακοί Id.*Lg.*646e; δ. δίκαιος Id.*R.*588b; τὰ δοξαζόμενα Id.*Plt.*278b. **2.** c. part., δοξάσει τις ἀκούων *will suppose that* he hears, A.*Supp.*60 (lyr.). **3.** c. acc. cogn., δόξας δ. *entertain* opinions, Pl.*Cri.*46d; δ. ψευδῆ *hold* false *opinions*, Id.*Tht.*189c; ψευδῶς δοξαζόμενα Polystr.p.26 W. **4.** abs., *form* or *hold an opinion*, Pl.*Tht.*187a, al.; περί τινος Id.*Grg.*461b; κακῶς δ. Id.*R.*327c; παρὰ τὰ ὄντα Id.*Phdr.*262b; opp. γιγνώσκω, Id.*R.*476d; opp. ἐπίσταμαι, Arist.*APo.*89$^{a}$7; δ. ἄνευ ἐπιστήμης Pl.*Tht.*201c. **5.** Pass., *to be matter of opinion*, ταῦτα δεδοξάσθαι Xenoph.35, cf. Epicur.*Sent.*22. **II.** *magnify*, *extol*, ἐπὶ πλέον τι αὐτὸν δ. Th.3.45, cf. Lxx *Ex.*15.2, al.; τὸν θεόν *Ep.Rom.*1.21, al.:—Pass., *to be distinguished*, *held in honour*, *magnified*, Dionys.Com.2.24; δεδοξασμένος ἐπ' ἀρετῇ Plb.6.53.10, cf. Lxx *Ex.*15.1, al., *Ev.Jo.*7.39, al.; ἱερὸν δεδοξασμένον ἐξ ἀρχαίων *OGI* 168.56 (ii B.C.). **-άριον**, τό, Dim. of δόξα, Arr.*Epict.*2.22.11, Luc.*Peregr.*8. **-ᾰσία**, ἡ, *opinion*, D.C.53.19. **-ασις**, εως, ἡ, *formation of opinion*, Simp. *in Ph.*268.16 (pl.). **-ασμα**, ατος, τό, *opinion*, *notion*, *conjecture*, Th.1.141, Pl.*Phdr.*274c, etc.; *fancy*, E.*El.*383; *idea*, *presentation*, Pl.*Tht.*158e. **II.** *glory*, Lxx *Is.*46.13, *La.*2.1. **-ασμός**, ὁ, *formation of opinions*, κατὰ δοξασμόν Chrysipp.*Stoic.*2.107. **II.** *glorification*, Sm.*Is.*13.?, Al.2*Ki.*22.25. **-αστέον**, *one must opine*, τὰ παραπλήσια Ph.1.4; ὡς.. Epicur.*Ep.*1 p.23 U. * **-αστής**, οῦ, ὁ, *one who forms opinions* or *conjectures*, opp. κριτής, Antipho 5.94, cf. S.E.*M.*7.157; opp. ἐπιστήμων, Pl.*Tht.*208e. **II.** δοξασταί· δικασταί, Hsch. **-αστικός**, ή, όν, *forming opinions*, *conjecturing*, opp. ἐπιστήμων, Pl.*Tht.*207c; δ. ἐπιστήμη *conjectural* knowledge, Id.*Sph.*233c, cf. 268c; δ. ἔννοιαι *pertaining to judgement*, Epicur.*Sent.*24; τὰς δοξαστικὰς (sc. φαντασίας) *belonging to opinion*, Phld.*Herc.*1003; τὸ δ. [μέρος τῆς ψυχῆς], opp. τὸ ἐπιστημονικόν, Arist.*EN*1140$^{b}$26. **2.** in good sense, *original*, *full of ideas*, ψυχὴ ἀνδρικὴ καὶ δ. Isoc.13.17: τὸ -κόν Antig.Nic.ap.Heph.Astr.2.18. **II.** Adv. -κῶς, opp. κατ' ἀλήθειαν, Arist.*APr.*43$^{b}$8, cf. Phld.*Oec.*p.14 J., S.E.*M.*11.156, Procl. *in Prm.*p.609 S. **-αστός**, ή, όν, *matter of opinion*, *conjectural*, opp. νοητός, Pl.*R.*534a, Plu.2.1114c; opp. γνωστός, Pl.*R.*478b, etc.; opp. ἐπιστητός, Arist.*APo.*88$^{b}$30; opp. ὁρατός, δ. θεός Plu.2.756d; συλλαβὰς .. ἀληθεῖ δόξῃ δοξαστάς Pl.*Tht.*202b; τροφὴ δοξαστή food *of opinion*, Id.*Phdr.*248b. Adv. -τῶς S.E.*M.*2.53. **II.** *glorified*, Lxx *De.*26.19; *held in honour*, prob. in Hp.*Decent.*18.

**δόξις**, εως, ἡ, = δόξα, Democr.7.

**δοξο-καθαιρετικός**, ή, όν, *clever at removing suspicion*, Paul.Aeg. 2.12. **-κᾰλία**, ἡ, *conceit of beauty*, Pl.*Phlb*.49d. **-κομπέω**, = sq., Simp.*in Epict*.p.86 D. (s. v. l.). **-κοπέω**, *court popularity*, Plb.12.25ᵉ.3, D.Chr.66.1, Plu.*Per*.5. **2.** *strike, impress the imagination*, τῷ ὄχλῳ τοῦ ἀριθμοῦ Longin.23.2. **-κοπία**, ἡ, *thirst for fame* or *popularity*, Phld.*Lib*.p.57 O., Heraclit.*Ep*.2, Plu.*Per*.5, M.Ant.11.18, Luc.*Peregr*.2, App.*BC*2.44, *Hann*.9, etc.; δ. ἄκρατος Epicur.*Fr*.120. **-κοπικός**, ή, όν, *popularity-hunting*, Apollon.ap. Stob.*App*.p.14 Gaisf. **-κόπος**, ον, = *thirsting for notoriety*, Teles p.39 H., Ph.2.269, Muson.*Fr*.7 p.29 H., D.Chr.32.24. **-λογία**, ἡ, *laudation*, Iamb.*Myst*.2.10. **-μᾰνέω**, *to be mad after fame*, Ph. 1.550. **-μᾰνής**, ές, *mad after fame*, Chrysipp.*Stoic*.3.167, Ph. 1.564, Iamb.*VP*12.58. **-μᾰνία**, ἡ, *mad thirst for fame*, Plu.*Sull*. 7. **-μᾰταιόσοφος**, ον, *would-be philosopher*, Epigr.ap.Hegesand. 1. **-μῑμητής**, οῦ, ὁ, *one who imitates mere semblance* (and not reality), Pl.*Sph*.267e. **-μῑμητική** (sc. τέχνη), ἡ, *his art*, ibid. **-παιδευτικός**, ή, όν, *having the semblance of education*, τέχνη ib.223b. **-ποιέω**, *glorify*, *praise* a god, *PMag.Berol*.2. 176. **II.** Pass., *possess the power of judgement*, τὸ τῶν ἀνθρώπων γένος δεδοξοποιημένον Plb.18.15.16. **-σοφία**, ἡ, *conceit of wisdom*, Pl.*Sph*.231b, *Phlb*.49a,d, Plu.2.999f. **-σοφος**, ον, *wise in one's own conceit*, Pl.*Phdr*.275b; *pretending to wisdom*, Arist.*Rh*.1387ᵇ 32. **-φᾰγία**, ἡ, *hunger after fame*, Plb.6.9.7. **-φαυλος**, ον, *apparently bad*, γάλα Sor.1.92. **-φόρος**, ον, *winning fame*, Man. 4.514.

**δοξόω**, only Pass., **δοξόομαι**, *have the character* or *credit* of being, ἐδοξώθη εἶναι σοφώτατος Hdt.8.124; δεδόξωσθε εἶναι ἀγαθοί Id.7.135, cf. 9.48.

**δορά** (A), ἡ, (δέρω) *skin when taken off*, *hide*, of beasts, δ. αἰγῶν Thgn.55; θηρῶν E.*Cyc*.330, cf. Diog.Oen.10; of birds, Hdt.4.175; of men, Pl.*Euthd*.285c; σατύρου Id.*Smp*.221e; grape-*skin*, Ruf. *Anat*.12. **2.** rarely, *skin* on the living body, Ph.2.100, Hld.9. 18. **II.** *flaying*, Gal.2.423.

**δορά** (B), = δορός (Cret.), *EM*284.12; cf. δόρυ.

**δοράζει**· κολάζει, *EM*284.15; but λογχάζει, Hsch.

**δόραντον**, τό, *horn for glue*, Hsch.

**δορᾰτ-ίζομαι**, *fight with spears*, Hsch., *EM*284.15. **-ιον**, τό, Dim. of δόρυ, Hdt.1.34, Th.4.34, Aen.Tact.29.6, Onos.26.1. **-ισμός**, ὁ, *fighting with spears*, Plu.*Pyrrh*.7, *Tim*.28, cj. in Lib.*Descr*.1.6.

**δορᾰτο-θήκη**, ἡ, *spear-case*, *EM*736.29. **-μᾰχέω**, *to fight with spears*, *AB*357, Suid. s. v. αἰχμάσσουσι. **-ξόος**, ον, = δορυξόος, τέκτων Nic.*Th*.170. **-πᾰχής**, ές, *of a spear-shaft's thickness*, X. *Cyn*.10.3. **-φόρος**, ον, = δορυφόρος, *Lyr.Adesp*.108, Lxx 1 *Ch*.12. 24. Ascl.*Tact*.1.3, etc.

**δορεύς**, έως, ὁ, *flayer*, prob. in Herod.8.64; name of a *throw of the dice*, Eub.57.5.

**δορήϊος**, α, ον, (δόρυ) *wooden*, *AP*15.14 (Theophanes).

**δορίαλλος**, ὁ, *pudendum muliebre*, Ar.*Fr*.367.

**δορῐ-ᾰλωσία**, ἡ, *a being taken by storm*, App.*BC*4.52. ❋ **-άλωτος** [ᾰ], ον, *captive of the spear*, *taken in war*, χώρα Hdt.8.74, 9.4; of persons, *captive*, E.*Tr*.518 (lyr.), Isoc.4.177; πόλεις Decr.ap.D.18. 181, cf. Plb.23.10.6; Ion. δουριάλωτον λέχος, of Tecmessa, S.*Aj*. 211 (lyr.): -δορυάλωτος is a freq. v. l., as in Hp.*Ep*.27, X.*Cyr*.7.5. 35, *HG*5.2.5, Ph.2.526, etc., cf. *IG*14.1293.57. **-γαμβρος**, ον, *bride of battles*, i. e. *causing war by marriage*, or *wooed by battle*, of Helen, A.*Ag*.686 (lyr.). **-δμητος**, ον, *subdued by the spear*, Sammelb. 5829.6. **-θήρᾱτος**, ον, *hunted and taken by the spear*, E.*Hec*.103 (anap.), *Tr*.574 (lyr.). **-θρασής**, ές, v. δορυθαρσής. **-κανής**, ές, *slain by the spear*, δ. μόρος A.*Supp*.987. **-κμής**, ῆτος, ὁ, ἡ, Ion. δουρ-, = foreg., λαὸς Id.*Ch*.365 (lyr.). **-κός**, ή, όν, *of skin* or *hide*, ἱμάτια Hp.*Nat.Puer*.24. ❋ **-κρᾶνος**, ον, *spear-headed*, λόγχη A.*Pers*. 148 (lyr., δορυκρ- cod. Med.). **-κτητος**, ον, *won by the spear*, γυνή E.*Andr*.155, cf. Lyc.933, etc.: in Hom., also the Ion. fem. δουρικτήτη Il.9.343, cf. A.R.1.806: **δορύκτητος** Tryph.553; fem. -τη Id.630, Plu.2.232a. **-κτῠπος**, ον, *spear-clashing*, Pi.*N*.3.60. **-ληπτος**, ον, *won by the spear*, S.*Aj*.146 (anap.), E.*Hec*.478 (lyr.), etc.; Ion. δουρίλ- S.*Aj*.894; = κατηγορούμενος, Hsch. **-λύμαντος** [ῠ], ον, *destroyed by the spear*, A.*Fr*.131.2 (anap.). **-μᾰνής**, ές, *raging with the spear*, E.*Supp*.485. **-μαργος**, ον, *raging with the spear*, A.*Th*.687 (lyr.). ❋ **-μᾰχος**, ον, *fighting with the spear*, ἀρετά Tim.*Fr*. 14; Ion. **δουρίμᾰχος** Orac.ap.Sch.Il.2.543. **-μήστωρ**, ορος, ὁ, *master of the spear*, E.*Andr*.1016 (lyr.). **-παλτος**, ον, (πάλλω) *wielding the spear*, ἐκ χερὸς δοριπάλτου on the *right* hand, A.*Ag*.117 (lyr., δορυ- cod. Med.). **-πετής**, ές, (πίπτω) *fallen by the spear*, πεσήματα, ἀγωνία δ., *death by the spear*, E.*Andr*.653, *Tr*.1003. ❋ **-πληκτος**, ον, *smitten by the spear*, Sch.E.*Andr*.653. **-πονος**, ον, *toiling with the spear*, *bearing the brunt of war*, πόλις A.*Th*.169 (lyr.); ἄνδρες E.*El*.479 (lyr.); δ. κακά A.*Th*.628 (lyr.); δ. ἀσπίδες E.*IA*771 (lyr.). **-πτοίητος**, ον, *scattered by the spear*, *AP*7.297 (Polystr.).

❋ **δορίς**, ίδος, ἡ, *sacrificial knife*, Anaxipp.6.3, Call.*Aet*.3.1.11.

**δορι-σθενής**, ές, *mighty with the spear*, A.*Ch*.158 (δορυσθενὴς cod. Med., as in *h.Hom*.8.3); βασιλῆες *AP*9.475. **-στέφᾰνος**, ον, *crowned for bravery*, Σπάρτα ib.596. **-τίνακτος** [τῐ], ον, *shaken by battle*, αἰθὴρ A.*Th*.155 (lyr.). **-τμητος**, ον, *pierced by the spear*, Id. *Ch*.347 (lyr.). **-τολμος**, ον, *bold in war*, *APl*.4.46.

**δορκάδ-ειος** [ᾰ], α, ον, (δορκάς) *of an antelope* or *gazelle*, ἀστράγαλοι Thphr.*Char*.5.9, Plb.26.1.8:—also written **δορκάδεοι**, ἀστράγαλοι *IG*2.766.23, cf. *PSI*4.331.2, 444.2 (iii B. C.). **-ίζω**, *bound like an antelope*, of the pulse, Herophil.ap.Gal.8.556, al. ❋ **-ιον**, τό, Dim. of δορκάς, Lxx *Is*.13.14, Hsch. s. v. βούβαλος; *silver ornament in that shape*, *IG*11(2).203*A* 10 (Delos, iii B. C.). **II.** = δίκταμνον, Ps.-Dsc.3.32.

**δορκάζω**, = περιβλέπω, Hsch. **δόρκαι**· κονίδες, Id.

**δορκᾰλίς**, ίδος, ἡ, = δορκάς, Call.*Ep*.33.2, *AP*7.578 (Agath.), Opp. *C*.1.165; of a girl, *AP*5.291.12 (Agath.). **II. δορκαλῖδες**, ων, αἱ, = δορκάδειοι ἀστράγαλοι, Herod.3.19.

**δόρκανα**, Adv., (δέρκομαι) *quick-sightedly*, *accurately* (Crete), Hsch.

❋ **δορκάς**, άδος [ᾰ], ἡ, (δέρκομαι, δέδορκα) *an animal of the deer kind* (so called from its large bright eyes), in Greece, *roe*, *Cervus capreolus*, E.*Ba*.699, X.*Cyr*.1.4.7; in Syria and Africa, *gazelle*, *Antilope dorcas*, Hdt.4.192 (in form ζορκάς), 7.69.—Other forms:—**δόρξ**, δορκός, ἡ, E.*HF*376 (prob.), Call.*Lav.Pall*.91, Luc.*Am*.16: **δόρκος**, ὁ, Dsc.2.75, Opp.*C*.2.315, 3.3: **δόρκων**, ωνος, ὁ, Palamed.ap.Ath.11. 397a, Lxx *Ca*.2.17, Ar.Byz.*Epit*.3.15: **ζορκάς** (v. supr.): **ζόρξ**, Call. *Dian*.97, *Fr*.239, Nic.*Th*.42: **ἴορκος**, Opp.*C*.2.296, 3.3. (δόρκος and ἴορκος are distd. fr. δορκάς.)

**δόρκειος**, α, ον, *of a deer*, Theognost.*Can*.185.29: **δόρκιος**, *Edict. Diocl*.8.21.

❋ **δόρκων**, ωνος, v. δορκάς. **II.** a kind of *ship*, David *Proll*.22.2.

**δοροεργής**, ές, *tanning* or *currying hides*, Man.4.320.

**δορός**, ὁ, (δέρω) *leathern bag* or *wallet*, Od.2.354, 380.

**δορόω**, *coat*, *plaster*, πηλῷ ἠχυρωμένῳ *IG*2².463.68, cf. 2.1054.58, dub. in ib.11(2).287*A* 121 (Delos, iii B. C.).

**δορπέω**, *take supper*, Il.23.11, Od.8.539.

**δορπήϊον**, τό, *food*, *a meal*, Nic.*Al*.166 (pl.).

**δορπηστός**, ὁ, *supper-time*, *evening*, Hp.*Epid*.5.22, Ar.*V*.103, X. *An*.1.10.17: acc. to Philem.ap.Ath.1.11d, some made it = ἄριστον.

**Δορπία**, ἡ, *the first day of the feast Apaturia*, celebrated by public suppers in each phratria, personified in Philyll.8.2: πρόπεμπτα τῆς Δ. *IG*2.841*b*62; but τῆς ὀρτῆς τῇ δορπίῃ on the *eve* of the feast, Hdt. 2.48.

**δορπιάζω**, *take an evening meal*, Hsch.

**δόρπιος**, ον, *belonging to the feast*, ἁρμονίη Nonn.*D*.12.148. **II.** Subst. **δόρπιον**, τό, *supper-time*, v. l. (Erot.*Fr*.18) in Hp.*Epid*.5. 24.

❋ **δόρπον**, τό, in Hom., *evening meal*, Od.12.439; taken at sunset, Il.19.208, Od.4.429, Pi.*O*.1c(11).47; ἄριστα, δεῖπνα, δόρπα θ' αἱρεῖσθαι τρίτα A.*Fr*.182.3, cf. Sch.Od.2.20.—In later Ep., generally, *meal*, *food*, *h.Ap*.511, A.R.2.304, Q.S.4.278, Opp.*H*.1.26 (pl.); δόρποιο ποτοῦ θ' ἅλις Orph.*A*.406.

**δόρπος**, ὁ, = foreg., Nic.*Al*.66, *AP*9.551 (Antiphil.), Q.S.9.431.

❋ **δορποφόρος**, ον, *offering supper*, βωμὸς *IG*12(5).244 (Paros).

❋ **δόρυ**, τό, Att. gen. δόρατος, rare in Poets, as Ar.*Ach*.1120, late Ep. dat. pl. δοράτεσσι Q.S.6.363: Ep. and Ion. decl., gen. δούρατος (also in Pi.*P*.4.38); dat. δούρατι (also in S.*Ph*.721 (lyr.)); pl. δούρατα, δούρασι (but codd. of Hdt. usu. have δόρατα, δόρασι): more commonly δουρός, δουρί (but δορί Archil.2.1); dual δοῦρε; pl. δοῦρα, δούρων, δούρεσσι; dat. pl. δούροις Opp.*H*.3.573: Trag., gen. δορός; dat. δορί or δόρει, the former required by metre in A.*Th*.347, 456, 958, *Ag*.111, E.*Hec*. 909, *Ph*.186, etc. (all lyr.), also in Id.*Hec*.5; δόρει is required in S.*OC*620, 1314, 1386; ξὺν δορὶ ξὺν ἀσπίδι Ar.*V*.1081, but σὺν δόρει σὺν ἀσπίδι Achae.29, cf. Choerob.*in Theod*.1.346; δορί occurs in Prose in the phrases δορὶ ἑλεῖν, λαβεῖν (v. infr. II. 2): nom. pl. δόρη E. *Rh*.274, Theopomp.Com.25; gen. δορῶν Hsch.: nom. δοῦρας *AP*6. 97 (Antiphil.). Exc. sg. δόρυ, Hom. uses only the Ion. forms: **I.** *stem*, *tree*, οὔπω τοῖον ἀνήλυθεν ἐκ δόρυ γαίης Od.6.167; but commonly, *plank* or *beam*, δοῦρ' ἐλάτης κέρσαντες Il.24.450; δούρατα μακρὰ ταμών Od.5.162, cf. Il.3.61; δούρατα πύργων 12.36; δούρατ' ἁμάξης Hes.*Op*.456; mostly of ships, δόρυ νήϊον ship's *plank*, Il.15.410, etc.; νήϊα δοῦρα Od.9.498; also, *mast*, E.*Tr*.1148: hence, **2.** δ. εἰνάλιον, ἀμφῆρες, of a *ship*, Pi.*P*.4.27, E.*Cyc*.15; δ. ποντοπόρον S.*Ph*. 721 (lyr.); also δόρυ alone, A.*Pers*.411, *Ag*.1618, E.*Hel*.1611; ἐπ' Ἀργῴου δορὸς Id.*Andr*.793; also δούρων, of *oars*, *Hymn.Is*.152. **3.** *pillory*, *stocks*, ἐν δουρὶ δεθεὶς αὐχένα Anacr.21.9. **II.** *shaft of a spear*, δόρυ μείλινον the ashen *shaft*, Il.5.666, al.: hence, generally, *spear itself*, δ. χάλκεον 13.247; ἀσπίδα καὶ δύο δοῦρε Od.1.256, etc.; *hunting-spear*, Il.12.303; δόρατα ναύμαχα boarding-*pikes*, Hdt.7.89: freq. in military phrases, v. πέλεκυς I; εἰς δόρατος πληγὴν within *spear's* throw, X.*Eq*.8.10; εἰς δόρυ ἀφικόμενοι Id.*HG*4.3.17; ἐπὶ δόρυ to *the right hand*, in which the spear was held, opp. ἐπ' ἀσπίδα, Id. *An*.4.3.29 (cf. κλίνω IV. 3, κλίσις III); παρὰ δόρυ Id.*Lac*.11.10; εἰς δόρυ Id.*HG*6.5.18; τὴν ἐμβολὴν ἐκ δόρατος ποιεῖσθαι Plb.3.115.9:— ὑπὸ δόρυ πωλεῖσθαι, = Lat. *sub hasta venire*, D.H.4.24, cf. Str.4.6. 7. **b.** *pole* of a standard, X.*Cyr*.7.1.4. **c.** *sceptre*, E.*Hec*. 9. **d.** *stick* used as tourniquet, Hp.*Nat.Puer*.24. **2.** metaph., δουρὶ κτεατίζειν win wealth *by the spear*, i. e. *in war*, Il.16.57; ὑπὸ δουρὶ πόλιν πέρθαι ib.708; in Prose, δορὶ ἑλεῖν, λαβεῖν, Th.1.128, App. *BC*4.8; *an armed force*, συμμάχῳ δ. A.*Eu*.773; δ. ἐπακτοῦ S.*OC* 1525; καὶ τὸ δ. καὶ τὸ κηρύκειον πέμπειν to offer *war* or peace, Plb. 4.52.4. (Cf. Skt. *dāru* 'piece of wood', δορά (B), δρῦς.)

**δορύαλλος**, = δορίαλλος, Hsch.

**δορῠ-άλωτος**, v. δοριάλωτος. **-βόλος**, ον, *hurling spears*, μηχάνημα J.*AJ*9.10.3; δορυβόλον alone, Ph.*Bel*.95.20.

**δορύδιον**, τό, Dim. of δόρυ, *shaft* of a hook or probe, Heliod.(?)ap. Orib.47.17.5.

**δορυ-δρέπᾰνον**, τό, a kind of *halbert*, Pl.*La*.183d; esp. a large

kind *used for cutting off* halyards in sea-fights, Str.4.4.1; in sieges, *for pulling down* battlements, Plb.21.27.4. ✻ -θαρσής, ές, = δορίτολμος, *Epigr.Gr.*1035.18 (Pergam.), *APl.*4.170 (Hermodor.):—also -θρᾰσής, ές, Nonn.*D.*17.100, 21.164, al.

**δορύκαι**· δουροδόκαι, Hsch.

**δορῠκέντειρα**, ἡ, *piercing with the spear*, v.l. in Corn.*ND*20.

**δορυκνίδιον**, τό, Dim. of sq. 1, Gal.11.864.

✻ **δορύκνιον**, τό, *Convolvulus oleaefolius*, Dsc.4.74, Plu.*Demetr.*20. 2. = μελισσόφυλλον, Nic.*Al.*376 (cf. Sch. ad loc.). 3. = πύρεθρον, Ps.-Dsc.3.73. 4. = στρύχνον μανικόν, ib.4.72.

**δορύκρᾱνος, δορύκτητος, δορύμᾰχος**, v. δορι-.

**δορύλλιον**, τό, Dim. of δόρυ, Suid. s.v. ξυστόν. **δορυμήστωρ**, ορος, ὁ, *skilled with the spear*, Hsch. **δορυμόλπης**· ὁ προηγούμενος τοῦ θυομένου βοὸς τῷ Διί, Id. **δορυξε⟨ί⟩ον**, τό, *workshop where spear-shafts are made*, Id.

**δορύ-ξενος**, ὁ, ἡ, *spear-friend*, i.e. *war-friend, ally* (wrongly expld. as ἐκ δορυαλώτου δ. προσαγορευόμενος by Plu.2.295b), A.*Ag.*880; ξένος τε καὶ δ. δόμων Id.*Ch.*562, cf. S.*El.*46, etc.: as Adj., δόμοι δορύξενοι A.*Ch.*914; ἑστία S.*OC*632. -ξόος, ον, contr. -ξοῦς, ουν, (ξέω) *spear-polishing*: *maker of spears*, Plu.*Pel.*12:—also -ξός, ὁ, Ar.*Pax* 447, 1213; -ξύς, *PTeb.*278.4 (i A.D.). -πᾰγής [ῠ], ές, *compact of beams*, νῆας A.*Supp.*743 (lyr.):—Ion. δουροπ– Opp.*H.*1.358. -πῡρος, ον, *with fiery spears*, ἄστρων στρατὸς *Lyr.Adesp.*128.

**δορυσθενής**, v. δορι-.

**δορυσ-σόητος**, ον, = sq., μόχθων δορυσσοήτων *of the toils of battle*, S.*Aj.*1188. ✻ -σόος, ον, contr. -σοῦς, οῦν (v. infr.): (σεύω):—*brandishing the lance*, of persons, Hes.*Sc.*54, A.*Supp.*182, 985; πόνος δ. Thgn.987: contr. -σοῦς S.*OC*1313, A.*Th.*125, prob. in E.*Heracl.* 774 (lyr.).

**δορυφία**· καρποφορία ἀγαθή, Hsch.

**δορῠφόνος**, ον, *slaying with the spear*, Ar.*Fr.*196, Telecl.29 (s.v.l.).

**δορῠφορ-έω**, *attend as a body-guard*, τινά Hdt.2.168, 3.127, Th.1.130; τὸν ἔπαρχον *PAmh.*2.79.52 (ii A.D.): generally, *keep guard over*, τὴν ἑκάστου σωτηρίαν D.23.123:—Med., ψυχὴν λογισμῷ Them.*Or.*1.5b:—Pass., *to be guarded*, στρατοπέδοις D.17.12; δορυφορεῖσθαι τῇ τῶν πολιτῶν εὐνοίᾳ Isoc.10.37: metaph., ὑπὸ μανίας Pl.*R.*573a, cf. Ph.2.239, al. b. Astrol., of planets, *attend*, i.e. *flank*, the Sun, etc., Ptol.*Tetr.*114, al., S.E.*M.*5.38 (Pass.). 2. c. dat., *attend as guard*, ἡμῖν αὐτοῖς X.*Cyr.*7.5.84; πειθαρχοῦντας αὐτῷ καὶ -φοροῦντας Plb.32.8.6. 3. metaph. of numbers in a series, *flank*, Iamb.*in Nic.* p.77 P.:—Pass., ib.p.40 P. -ημα, ατος, τό, *body-guard*: used of the κωφὰ πρόσωπα or *mute characters* on the stage, Luc.*Hist.Conscr.*4, Jul.*Caes.*316c: hence of Aridaeus, who was put up as the successor of Alexander, ὁ δέ, ὥσπερ ἐπὶ σκηνῆς δ., κωφὸν ἦν ὄνομα βασιλείας Plu.2.791e, cf. Id.*Alex.*77. -ησις, εως, ἡ, *protection of body-guard*, M.Ant.1.17 (pl.). -ία, ἡ, *guard kept over*, τῆς ἐπιστολῆς X.*Cyr.*2.2.10: abs., Iamb.*Myst.*2.7; concrete, *body-guard*, Lxx 2*Ma.*3.28. II. Astron., κατὰ δορυφορίαν τῶν τροπικῶν κύκλων *Placit.*2.23.6. -ικός, ή, όν, *of or for the guard*, οἴκησις Pl.*Ti.*70b, *Criti.*117c; δ. σημεῖα, = Lat. *signa praetoria*, standards *of the praetorian guard*, D.C.60.35; τὸ δ. *the guard*, Id.42.52. -ος, ον, *spear-bearing*, ὀπάονες A.*Ch.*769. II. Subst., *spearman*, X.*An.*5.2.4. 2. esp. *one of the body-guard* of kings and tyrants, Hdt.1.59, etc.; [ὁ Περίανδρος] πρῶτος -φόρους ἔσχε Arist.*Fr.*516. b. at Rome, of *the praetorians*, Plu.*Galb.*13, Hdn.5.4.8. 3. metaph., ἡδοναὶ δ. *mere satellite* pleasures, Pl.*R.*587c, cf. 573e; δ. τῶν ἐπιθυμιῶν τινος *pandering to* his lusts, Luc.*Tyr.*4. 4. in Drama, *mute character*, Hsch., *EM*284.21.

**δορχελοί**· ἀστράγαλοι, Hsch.

**δορ-ώσιμος**, η, ον, (δορόω) *for plastering*, *PPetr.*3 p.139 (iii B.C.). ✻-ωσις, εως, ἡ, *plastering*, ibid.

**δός, δόθι**, v. δίδωμι.

**δοσείδιον**, τό, Dim. of δόσις II. 5, *IG*14.956*A* 22.

**δοσείω**, Desiderat., *to be inclined to give*, Hsch.

**δοσίδῐκος**, ον, f.l. for δωσίδικος, Hdt.6.42, Plb.4.4.3.

✻ **δόσιμος**, η, ον, of houses, *liable to be surrendered as billets*, *PTeb.*5.176 (ii B.C.).

**δοσίπῡγος**, v. δωσίπυγος.

✻ **δόσις**, εως, ἡ, (δίδωμι) *giving*, φαρμάκου Antipho 1.18; χρημάτων Hdt.1.61; μισθοῦ Th.1.143; opp. αἴτησις, Pl.*Euthphr.*14d; δ. χρημάτων καὶ λῆψις Arist.*EN*1107$^{b}$8; λήψεις καὶ δόσεις Arr.*Epict.*2.9.12, cf. Lxx *Si.*41.19, *Ep.Phil.*4.15. b. *licence, permission*, *SIG* 987.33 (Chios, iv B.C.). 2. ἐμβολῶν δ. *ramming* in naval tactics, D.S.13.10. II. *gift*, καί οἱ δ. ἔσσεται ἐσθλή Il.10.213; δ. ὀλίγη τε φίλη τε Od.6.208, 14.58, cf. Hdt.1.90, 9.93, S.*OT*1518, etc.; δόσιν κακὰν κακῶν κακοῖς A.*Pers.*1041 (lyr.); θεῶν εἰς ἀνθρώπους Pl.*Phlb.*16c. 2. *bequest, legacy*: κατὰ δόσιν by *will* (opp. κατὰ γένος, as heir-at-law), Is.4.7, Isoc.19.45, cf. Harp. 3. *largess*, = Lat. *congiarium*, Hdn.6.8.8 (pl.). 4. *contribution* towards the fulfilment of a purpose, Chrysipp.(?)*Stoic.*3.30. 5. *payment on account, instalment*, *IG*1$^{2}$.296, 7.303.35 (Orop.), etc.; *payment in kind*, *PMasp.*146.4 (vi A.D.), al. 6. *portion*, Lxx *Ge.*47.22, al., *BGU*1122.12 (i B.C.); διελὼν εἰς δόσεις Plu.*Arat.*13. 7. *dose of medicine*, Dsc.2.171; δ. τελεία full *dose*, Ruf.ap.Orib.8.57.5, etc., cf. Luc.*Abd.*4. 8. τῆς οἰκονομίας πολλὴν ποιεῖσθαι δ. lay great *stress* on an arrangement, D.H.*Dem.*51; οὐ τοσαύτην ποιούμενοι τῆς ἡδονῆς δ. ὅσην τῆς ἀληθείας ib.18. 9. *destiny, fate* of an individual, ἡ ἀνθρωπίνη δ. Iamb.*Myst.*1.3; esp. of planetary *influence*, Plot.2.3.2, al.

**δόσκον**, Ep. iterative of δίδωμι (q.v.).

✻ **δοσοληψία**, ἡ, *give-and-take, exchange, barter*, Orph.*Fr.*278 (pl.), Vett.Val. in *Cat.Cod.Astr.*2.163.

✻ **δότ-ειρα**, ἡ, fem. of δοτήρ, Hes.*Op.*356, Nic.*Al.*612. -έος, α, ον, (δίδωμι) *to be given*, Hdt.8.111. II. δοτέον *one must give*, Pl.*R.*452e, Alex.250, etc.; *one must allow*, c. inf., Luc.*Abd.*9. -ήρ, ῆρος, ὁ, *giver, dispenser*, ταμίαι.. σίτοιο δοτῆρες Il.19.44; δισσοὶ θανάτοιο δ. Hes.*Sc.*131; esp. of the gods, δ. εὐθηλέος ἥβης *h.Hom.*8.9; μαντευμάτων Pi.*Pae.*7.1; πυρὸς βροτοῖς δοτῆρα A.*Pr.*612.—Poet. form used by X.*Cyr.*8.1.9, and in later Prose, θεὸς δ. παντὸς ἀγαθοῦ D.H.2.62, cf. J.*AJ*18.6, Iamb.*Myst.*3.31. -ης, ου, ὁ, later form of δοτήρ, Lxx *Pr.*22.8, 2*Ep.Cor.*9.7. -ικός, ή, όν, *inclined to give, giving freely*, Arist.*EN*1121$^{b}$16. Adv. -κῶς Hsch. s.v. δοσείειν. II. ἡ -κή (sc. πτῶσις), *the dative case*, *Stoic.*2.59, Str.14.1.41, D.T.636.4, A.D.*Synt.*28.23, etc. -ός, ή, όν, (δίδωμι) *granted*, Lxx 1*Ki.*1.11, Ph.1.273; *that may* or *must be granted*, Max.Tyr.11.7.

✻ **δουκηνάριος**, ὁ, = Lat. *ducenarius*, *official receiving salary of* 200,000 *sesterces*, *IG*14.1347, *POxy.*1711.4 (iii A.D.), etc. II. fem. **δουκηναρία**, ἡ, *assessment of* 200,000 *sesterces*, ib.1274.14 (iii A.D.).

✻ **δουκικός**, ή, όν, = Lat. *ducianus*, Just.*Edict.*13.2.

**δουλᾰγωγ-έω**, *make a slave, treat as such*, dub. in D.S.12.24, cf. Arr.*Epict.*3.24.76. 2. metaph. of pleasure, etc., δ. τοὺς βίους Longin.44.6, cf. Charito 2.7; τὸ σῶμα *bring it into subjection*, 1*Ep.Cor.*9.27. -ία, ἡ, *enslavement*, *IG*9(1).39,42 (Stiris), *POxy.*38.10 (i A.D.). ✻ -ός, όν, *enslaving*, δ. θηρίον ἡ ἡδονή Plu.*Volupt.Fr.*2.

**δουλ-ᾰπᾰτία**, ἡ, *enticement of slaves from their master*, Arist.*EN* 1131$^{a}$7. -άριον, τό, Dim. of δούλη, Ar.*Th.*537, Metag.19, etc.; not used of male slaves, acc. to Luc.*Lex.*25, but cf. Arr.*Epict.*2.21.11. ✻ -εία, ἡ, Ion. -ηΐη Anacr.114, Hdt.6.12: also δουλία Pi.*P.*1.75:—*slavery, bondage*, Il.cc., A.*Th.*253; δουλείας γάγγαμον, ζυγά, Id.*Ag.*360 (anap.), S.*Aj.*944 (lyr.); δ. καὶ ὑπηρεσία Ar.*V.*602; ἡ τῶν κρεισσόνων δ. *imposed by* them, Th.1.8; ἡ ὑπὸ τῶν βαρβάρων δ. Pl.*R.*469c; applied to the condition of the subject allies of Athens, Th.5.9. II. collectively, *slaves*, δουλεύοντα δουλείαις ἐμαῖς E.*Ba.*803; ἤν.. ἡ δ. ἐπανιστῆται if *the slave-class* rise in rebellion, Th.5.23; ἡ Ἡρακλεωτῶν δ. Pl.*Lg.*776d; τὰς.. Εἱλωτείας καὶ Πενεστείας καὶ δουλείας Arist.*Pol.*1264$^{a}$36. III. *service for hire*, μισθὸν δουλείας Lxx 3*Ki.*5.6. ✻ -ειος, α, ον, also ος, ον Pi.*Fr.*223, E.*Tr.*1330 (lyr.):—*slavish, servile*, εἶδος Od.24.252; κεφαλή Thgn.535; τύχα Pi.l.c.; δούλειον ἦμαρ E.*Hec.*56, *Andr.*99, cf. *Tr.*1330; ζυγόν Pl.*Lg.*770e; ἤθη ib.790a. -έκδουλος, ὁ, *a born slave*, Seleuc.ap.Ath.6.267c, D.S.10 *Fr.*1. ✻ -ελεύθερος, ὁ, *freedman*, Vett.Val.7.8, al. -εος, α, ον, poet. for δούλειος, δ. δεσμὰ γυναικῶν A.R.*Fr.*12.13. -ευμα, ατος, τό, *a service*, E.*Or.*221. II. *a slave*, S.*Ant.*756, cf. E.*Ion* 748. -ευσις, εως, ἡ, *slavery*, prob. f.l. for δούλωσις, Porph.*Abst.*1.8. -ευτέον, *one must be a slave*, τινί E.*Ph.*395, *Ba.*366; οὐ μὴν δουλευτέον τοὺς νοῦν ἔχοντας τοῖς κακῶς φρονοῦσιν Isoc.9.7. -ευτός, ή, όν, *servile*, Al.*Le.*23.7. -εύτρια, ἡ, *female attendant*, Eust.1661.47. ✻ -εύω, (δοῦλος) *to be a slave*, Hdt.2.56, And.1.138, Pl.*Lg.*777d, etc.; παρά τινι D.18.129: c. acc. cogn., δουλείαν δ. X.*Mem.*2.12.2, Pl.*Smp.*183a, al. 2. *serve, be subject*, τό τ' ἄρχειν καὶ τὸ δ. δίχα A.*Pr.*927, etc.; δ. ζεύγλαις ib.463; τοῖς ἄρχουσι καὶ τοῖς νόμοις Pl.*Lg.*698b; ἡδονῇ Id.*Phdr.*238e, etc.; δ. γαστρί, ὕπνῳ, λαγνείᾳ, X.*Mem.*1.6.8; κεναῖς δόξαις Polystr.p.29 W.; τῇ γῇ δ. *make oneself a slave* to one's land, i.e. give up rights that one may keep it, Th.1.81; so δ. τῇ κτήσει αὐτοῦ Pl.*R.*494d; δουλεύομεν δόξαισιν Philem.93.8; δ. τῷ καιρῷ *accommodate oneself* to the occasion, *AP*9.441 (Pall.); θυμῷ Hdn.1.17.6. 3. *render a service*, τινά *PLond.*5.1727.11 (vi A.D.). -ία, v. δουλεία. -ίδιον, τό, Dim. of δουλίς, Hsch. s.v. θεράπνιον. ✻ -ικός, ή, όν, = sq. 1, ὅπλον X.*Cyr.*7.4.15 (Sup.); διακονήματα Pl.*Tht.*175e; ἔργον Araros 18; δ. καὶ ταπεινὰ πράγματα ποιεῖν D.57.45; -ώτεροι τὰ ἤθη Arist.*Pol.*1285$^{a}$20; δ. πόλεμος *slave-war*, Plu.*Crass.*10. Adv. -κῶς Phryn.Com.2 D., X.*Oec.*10.10: Comp. -ώτερον Arr.*Epict.*4.1.25. 2. = sq. 2, παιδίον, σώματα, *BGU*1120.10 (i B.C.), 26.23 (i A.D.). -ιος, α, ον (ος, ον *AP*7.401 (Crin.)), *slavish, servile*, in Hom. only δούλιον ἦμαρ the day *of slavery*, Il.6.463, al., cf. *IG*1$^{2}$.763; ἐσθῆτι δουλίῃ (δουληΐῃ is f.l.) Hdt.3.14; δ. ζυγόν Id.7.8.γ', A.*Ag.*953, *Th.*471; δ. τροφή S.*Aj.*499. 2. *of a slave*, δ. φρήν a *slave's* mind, A.*Ag.*1084 (lyr.); ἔργον (prob.) *PGrenf.*2.78.11 (iv A.D.).—In a few places the Med. Ms. of A. gives δούλειος (*Th.*75, 471, 793), but the metre freq. requires δούλιος (*Pers.*50 (anap.), *Ag.* 953, 1041, al., so in S.*Aj.*499), never δούλειος: in E., however, δούλειος is certainly required (v. sub v.). The common form in Att. Prose is δουλικός, and δοῦλος is used as Adj. in same sense. -ίς, ίδος, ἡ, = δούλη, Hyp.*Fr.*235, *AP*5.17 (Rufin.), *IG*14.1839.8: condemned by Poll.3.74.

**δουλῐχό-δειρος**, ον, Ion. for δολιχόδ–. -εις, εσσα, εν, Ion. for δολιχόεις.

**δουλό-βοτος**, ον, *eaten up by slaves*, τὰ αὐτοῦ Philostr.*VS*1.21.4. -γάμος [ᾰ], ον, = δουλομίκτης, *Cat.Cod.Astr.*8(4).127. -γνώμων, ον, gen. ονος, *of slavish mind*, *AB*393, Suid. s.v. ἀνδραποδώδεις. -δῐδάσκᾰλος, ὁ, *teacher of slaves*, title of play by Pherecr., cf. Ath.6.262b; of Theodora, Procop.*Arc.*15. ✻ -κοίτης, ου, ὁ, *consorting with slaves*, Paul.Al.*O.*2. -κρᾰτέομαι, Pass., *to be ruled by slaves*, D.C.60.2; or, *like slaves*, Lib.*Decl.*43.35. -κρᾰτία, ἡ, *slave-government*, J.*AJ*19.4.4. -μᾰχία, ἡ, *servile war*, Lyd.*Ost.*34. -μίκτης, ου, ὁ, *one who consorts with slaves*, Tz.*H.*6.466. -μιξία, ἡ, *consorting with slaves*, ib.467. -ποιέω, *enslave*, Herm.ap.Stob.1.49.45. -ποιός, όν, *enslaving*, Sch.E.*Or.*488. -πόνηρος, ον, *bad like a slave's*, κόλυθρον Telecl.3. -πρέ-

πεια, ἡ, *slavish spirit*, Pl.*Alc.*1.135c, Theopomp.Com.87. **-πρεπής,** ές, *befitting a slave, servile*, πόνος Hdt.1.126; opp. ἐλευθέριος, X.*Mem.* 2.8.4 (Comp.), cf. Pl.*Grg.*485b,518a, etc.: Sup., Phld.*Herc.*1457.3. Adv. -πῶς, φθαρῆναι D.C.61.15, cf. Gal.17(2).146: Sup. -έστατα Cratin.403.

* **δοῦλος** (A), Cret. δῶλος *Leg.Gort.*1.1, al., ὁ:—prop. *born bondman* or *slave*, opp. *one made a slave*, τὰ ἀνδράποδα πάντα καὶ δοῦλα καὶ ἐλεύθερα Th.8.28, cf. E.*IA*330: then, generally, *bondman, slave*, opp. δεσπότης (q.v.): not in Hom., who twice has fem. **δούλη,** ἡ, *bondwoman*, Il.3.409, Od.4.12, cf. A.*Ag.*1326, X.*Cyr.*5.1.4, Pl.*R.* 395e, etc.: freq. of Persians and other nations subject to a despot, Hdt., etc.; οὔ τινος δοῦλοι κέκληνται, of the Greeks, A.*Pers.*242: metaph., χρημάτων δ. *slaves to* money, E.*Hec.*865; so γνάθου δ. Id.*Fr.* 282.5; τῶν αἰεὶ ἀτόπων Th.3.38; λιχνειῶν, λαγνειῶν, X.*Oec.*1.22, cf. *Mem.*1.3.11. II. Adj. (not in A.), δοῦλος, η, ον, *slavish, servile, subject*, δ. πόλις S.*OC*917, X.*Mem.*4.2.29; γνώμαισι δούλαις S.*Tr.*53; δ. ἔχειν βίον ib.302; σῶμα δ., opp. νοῦς ἐλεύθερος, Id.*Fr.*940; τοὺς τρόπους δούλους παρασχεῖν E.*Supp.*877; δ. θάνατος, ζυγόν, πούς, Id.*Or.* 1170, *Tr.*678,507; δ. καὶ τυραννουμένη πόλις Pl.*R.*577d; δ. ἡδοναί, = δουλοπρεπεῖς, ib.587c, etc.: Comp. δουλότερος *more enslaved*, Αἴγυπτον δ. ποιεῖν Hdt.7.7. 2. τὸ δ., = οἱ δοῦλοι, E.*Ion*983, etc.; also, *slavery, a slavish life*, ib.556 (troch.). 3. *ancillary*, δ. ἐπιστῆμαι Arist.*Metaph.*996ᵇ11.

* **δοῦλος** (B)· ἡ οἰκία ἢ τὴν ἐπὶ τὸ αὐτὸ συνέλευσιν τῶν γυναικῶν, Hsch.; cf. δωλοδομεῖς, δωλέννετος.

**δουλό-σύνη,** ἡ, poet. and Ion. for δουλεία, *slavery*, Od.22.423, Pi. *P.*12.15, A.*Th.*112, E.*Ph.*192 (anap.), Hdt.1.129, al. **-συνος,** ον, = δοῦλος (A) II, *enslaved*, τινί E.*Hec.*448 (lyr.). **-φᾰνής,** ές, *slave-like, slavish to look on*, σῶμα J.*BJ*2.7.2. **-ψῡχος,** ον, = foreg., Ptol.*Tetr.*66.

**δουλ-όω,** *enslave*, Hdt.1.27; δουλοῖς καὶ σὲ καὶ πᾶσαν πόλιν A.*Th.* 254, cf. S.*Tr.*467; δ. φρόνημα Th.2.61:—mostly in Pass., *to be enslaved*, ὑπὸ Πέρσῃσι, ὑπὸ Ἁρπάγου, Hdt.1.94,174, cf. Th.1.98; αἱ ψυχαὶ δεδούλωνται Hp.*Aër.*23; δεδουλωμένοι τῇ γνώμῃ, τὴν γνώμην ἐδουλοῦντο, Th.4.34, 7.71; ἐλεύθερος πᾶς ἑνὶ δεδούλωται, νόμῳ Men.699, cf *Sam.*280:—Med. (with pf. δεδουλῶσθαι Th.6.82), *make subject to oneself, enslave*, Id.1.18, 5.29, 7.68,75, Pl.*Mx.*239d; τὸν ἥσσονα δουλούμεθ' ἄνδρα E.*Supp.*493; ἐπιθυμίαν Pl.*Lg.*838d; τὸ ἑαυτοῦ θειότατον ὑπὸ τῷ ἀθεωτάτῳ.. δουλοῦται Id.*R.*589e. **-ωσις,** εως, ἡ, *enslavement*, Th.3.10, Plu.*Publ.*21, D.C.53.7. 2. *constraint*, opp. τρυφή, Pl. *Lg.*791d. **-ωτικός,** ή, όν, *pertaining to service*, πρᾶγμα Plu.*Nob.*2.

**δοῦναξ, δουνακόεις,** poet. for δον-.

* **δούξ,** δουκός, ὁ, = Lat. *dux*, *PLond.*2.141.18 (iv A.D.), Just.*Edict.* 13.18 *Intr.*, etc.

**δουπέω,** fut. -ήσω *AP*9.427 (s.v.l., Barb.): Ep. aor. δούπησα Il.4.504, al.; also ἐγδούπησα (from γδουπέω) 11.45: pf. δέδουπα 23. 679, Nic.*Al.*15, A.R.1.1304, Euph.40; not freq. exc. in Ep.: (δοῦπος):—*sound heavy* or *dead*; in Hom., of *the heavy thud of a corpse*, opp. the clashing of the armour, δούπησεν δὲ πεσών, ἀράβησε δὲ τεύχε' ἐπ' αὐτῷ Il.4.504, al.; ἢ αὐτὸς δουπῆσαι ἀμύνων λοιγὸν Ἀχαιοῖς 13.426; δεδουπότος Οἰδιπόδαο 23.679, cf. A.R.1.1304, Euph.40; δουπεῖ χεὶρ γυναικῶν *falls with heavy sound* upon their breasts, E.*Alc.*104 (lyr.); of rowers, κώπῃ δουπεῖν dub. in *AP*9.427 (Barb.); of soldiers, *strike heavily*, ταῖς ἀσπίσι πρὸς τὰ δόρατα ἐδούπησαν X.*An.*1.8.18; τοῖς δόρασι δ. πρὸς τὰς ἀσπίδας Arr.*An.*1.6.4:—Pass., aor. δουπήθησαν *AP* 9.283 (Crin.).—Rare in Prose, cf. Luc.*Hist.Conscr.*22. (Said to be Cypr., *AB*1095.)

**δουπήτωρ,** ορος, ὁ, *clattering*, χαλκός *AP*4.3b.13 (Agath.).

* **δοῦπος,** ὁ, *any dead, heavy sound, thud*, δ. ἀκόντων Il.11.364.16. 361; δ. ὀρώρει πύργων βαλλομένων 9.573, cf. 12.289; of the distant *din* of battle, 16.635; of the *sound* of footsteps, 10.354, Od.16.10; of *the measured tread* of infantry, Il.23.234, Hes.*Th.*70; ὅμαδον καὶ δ., of a multitude, Od.10.556; of the *roar* of the sea dashing against rocks or of a distant torrent, 5.401, Il.4.455.—Rare in Trag., δ. μαράγνης A.*Ch.*376 (lyr.); χερόπλακτοι δ' ἐν στέρνοισι πεσοῦνται δοῦποι the *loud* beating of breasts, S.*Aj.*634, cf. E.*Ba.*513; ἀκούομεν πυλῶν δ. *the noise* of opening gates, Id.*Ion*516. Rare in Prose, Th. 3.22 (v.l. ψόφον); θόρυβος καὶ δ. X.*An.*2.2.19.

**δοῦρας,** τό, a nom. sg. formed from the Homeric pl. δούρατα (v. sub δόρυ), *AP*6.97 (Antiphil.).

**δουράτεος** [ᾰ], α, ον, *of planks* or *beams of wood*, ἵππος δ. the *wooden* horse, Od.8.493,512; ὀβελοί *h.Merc.*121; πύργοι A.R.2.381.

**δουρᾰτόγλῠφος,** ον, *carved from wood*, Lyc.361.

* **δούρειος,** α, ον, = δουράτεος, E.*Tr.*14, Pl.*Tht.*184d.

**δουρεμηκές·** δόρατος μῆκος, Hsch.

**δουρηνεκής,** ές, (ἐνεγκεῖν) *a spear's throw off* or *distant*, only neut. as Adv., Il.10.357.

**δουρῐ-ᾰλής** (-άλης cod.)· αἰχμάλωτος, Hsch. **-άλωτος,** ον, Ion. for δοριάλ-. **-βᾰρής** κάματος burden *of a heavy spear*, *Wien.Stud.* 25.3 (Crete). **-κλειτός,** όν, *famed for the spear*, Homeric epith. of heroes, Il.5.55, Od.15.52. **-κλῠτός,** όν, = foreg., Il.2.645, Od. 15.544, Archil.3: dat. pl. δουρικλύτοις (sic) A.*Pers.*85 (lyr.).

**δουρι-κμής, -κτητος, -ληπτος, -μανής, -μαχος,** Ion. for δορι-.

* **δούριος,** α, ον, = δούρειος, Ar.*Av.*1128.

* **δουρί-πηκτος,** ον, *fixed on spears*, λάφυρα δάων δουρίπηχθ' A.*Th.* 278. **-τῠπής,** ές, *wood-splitting*, σφῦρα *AP*6.103 (Phil.). II. *smitten with the spear*, *IPE*2.298.8 (Panticapaeum, ii A.D.). **-φᾰτος,** ον, *slain by the spear*, Opp.*H.*4.556.

**δουρο-δόκη,** ἡ, (δέχομαι) *case* or *stand for spears*, Od.1.128. **-δόκος,** ὁ, *one of the principal beams* of the roof, Harp. s. v. στρωτήρ, *EM* 731.10. **-μᾰνής,** ές, poet. for δοριμανής, πόλεμος *AP*9.553. **-πᾰγής,** ές, poet. for δορυπαγής, Opp.*H.*1.358, Nonn.*D.*4.230. **-τόμος,** poet. for δρυτόμος, Opp.*H.*5.198; πελέκεις *AP*7.445 (Pers.).

* **δοχ-αῖος,** α, ον, *fit for holding*, σκαφίδες Nic.*Th.*618; κραδίην Id. *Al.*21 (s.v.l., Sch. δοχεῖον). * **-εῖον,** Ion. -ήϊον, τό, *holder*, μέλανος δ. ink-*horn*, *AP*6.66 (Paul. Sil.), cf. 63 (Damoch.), Gal.14.719; τὸ θῆλυ ὥσπερ γονῆς τι δ. Luc.*Am.*19. * **-εύς,** έως, ὁ, *recipient*, esp. of oracles or inspiration, Orac.ap.Porph.ap.Eus.*PE*5.9, Herm. *in Phdr.*pp.105,111A. **-ή,** ἡ, = δοχεῖον, *receptacle*, E.*El.*828, Pl. *Ti.*71c. II. *reception, entertainment*, Macho ap.Ath.8.348f, Lxx *Ge.*21.8, al., *PTeb.*112.89 (ii B.C.), *Ev.Luc.*5.29, etc.; = ἄριστον, Hsch. III. σημεῖον ἐν θυτικῇ, Id.

**δοχικός,** ή, όν, δ. μέτρον *receiving* measure (officially prescribed for use by revenue officials), opp. ἀνηλωτικόν, *PHib.*1.74 (iii B.C.), al., cf. *PTeb.*11.6, *PPar.*66.26, etc.

**δοχμαϊκός,** v. δόχμιος. **δοχμαλόν·** χαμαίζηλον, ταπεινόν, Hsch.

**δοχμή** or **δόχμη,** ἡ, (δέχομαι) *space contained in a hand's breadth*, Cratin.350, Ar.*Eq.*318, *Com.Adesp.*571, Scyl.112: expld. as, = παλαιστή, Sch.Ar. ad loc.; but also as, = σπιθαμή, Phot. s. h. v.; Hsch. and Suid. give both senses. (On the accent, v. Ael.Dion.*Fr.*136, Poll.2.157.)

**δοχμιάζω,** *use the dochmiac metre*, Sch.E.*Or.*140.

* **δόχμιος,** α, ον, *across, aslant*, δόχμια.. ἦλθον Il.23.116, cf. E *Or.* 1261 (lyr.); δ. κέλευθον ἐμβάνειν Id.*Alc.*1000 (lyr.), cf. 575 (lyr.); πέσε δ. A.R.1.1169. II. in Prosody, πούς δ. *the dochmiac measure*, Choerob. *in Heph.*p.219 C.; ῥυθμὸς δ. Aristid.Quint.1.17, Bacch. *Harm.*100:—hence Adj. forms, **δοχμιακός** Aristid.Quint. l. c.: **δοχμικός, -αϊκός,** Sch.A.*Th.*128, Sch.Ar.*Av.*937. (Perh. cf. Skt. *jihmá-* 'oblique'.)

**δοχμό-κορσοι·** πλαγιοχαῖται, Hsch. **-λοφος,** ον, *with slanting, nodding plume*, A.*Th.*114 (lyr.). **-ομαι,** *turn sideways*, δοχμωθείς, of a boar *turning himself* to whet his tusks or rip up his enemy, Hes. *Sc.*389; of Hermes *turning himself* to dart through the keyhole, *h.Merc.*146.—Later in aor. Act. δόχμωσε, Med. δοχμώσατο, Nonn.*D.* 42.193, 37.254.

**δοχμός,** όν (Delph. ά, όν, v. infr.), = δόχμιος I, δοχμὼ ἀΐσσοντε rushing on *slantwise*, Il.12.148; δοχμοὶ μῆτραι *lying obliquely*, Hp.*Mul.* 2.141; δ. ἀπὸ προβολῆς κλινθείς Theoc.22.120; δ. ἀνακρούων θηρὸς πάτον Nic.*Th.*479; ἁ ὁδὸς ἁ δοχμά the *cross*-road, *Klio* 16.170 (Delph., ii B.C.). II. = δόχμιος II, συζυγία Sch.Ar.*Ach.*283.

**δοχός,** όν, (δέχομαι) *containing, able to hold*, θερμοῦ καὶ ὑγροῦ Thphr. *CP*2.4.11. II. Subst. δοχός, ὁ, *receptacle*, Hsch.; also, = λουτήρ, Id.

**δράβη,** ἡ, *Arabian mustard, Lepidium Draba*, Dsc.2.157.

**δραγατεύω,** *to be a watcher of a field* or *vineyard* (cf. Mod. Gr. δραγάτης), Ἀρχ.Ἐφ.1913.27 (Thess.).

**δράγδην,** Adv. *in the grasp, with the hand*, Plu.2.418e, Q.S.13.91.

**δραγκάζειν·** κρύπτειν, Hsch. **δραγκαλακτᾶν·** βριμοῦσθαι, Id.

**δράγ-λη,** ἡ, a kind of *javelin*, *PLond.*2.191.12 (ii A.D.). (Cf. Lat. *tragula.*) * **-μα,** ατος, τό, (δράσσομαι) *handful*; esp. *as many stalks of corn as the reaper can grasp* in his left hand, *truss*, Il.11.69, 18.552; also, *sheaf*, = ἄμαλλα, X.*HG*7.2.8, Theoc.10.44, Ph.*Bel.*86.24, *BGU* 757.16 (i A.D.), Plu.*Publ.*8. II. later, *uncut corn*. *AP*11.365.10 (Agath.), Luc.*Hes.*7: metaph., πρώτης δράγματα φυταλιῆς *first-fruits*, *AP*6.44 (Leon. (?)), cf. Lxx *Le.*23.12. III. ἐποίησεν ἡ γῆ δράγματα brought forth *by handfuls*, i. e. *plenty*, ib.*Ge.*41.47.

**δραγμᾶναι·** αἱ ἐν ταῖς τοῦ ἐγκεφάλου κοιλότησι.., Hsch.

**δραγμᾰτ-εύω,** = δραγμεύω, Eust.1162.17. * **-ηγέω,** *convey sheaves*, *BGU*698.14 (ii A.D.). * **-ηγία,** ἡ, *conveyance of sheaves*, ib.831.13, *PFlor.*2.185.17 (iii A.D.). **-ηγός,** ὁ, *labourer who conveys sheaves*, *BGU*698.24 (ii A.D.). **-ηφόρος,** ον, *carrying sheaves*, Babr.88.16.

**δραγμᾰτο-κλεπτέω,** *steal sheaves*, *PPetr.*3p.60 (iii B.C.). * **-λόγος,** ον, *gleaning*, Hsch.

**δραγ-μεύω,** *collect the corn into sheaves*, Il.18.555. **-μή,** ἡ, *handful*, *EM*285.52. II. = δραχμή (q.v.). **-μίς,** ίδος, ἡ, *small handful, pinch*, v.l. for δραχμίς, Hp.*Morb.*2.55. **-μός,** ὁ, *grasping*, E.*Cyc.*170, dub. l. in Q.S.1.350.

* **δραϝεός,** ἡ, uncertain object dedicated to Athena, *GDI*1537 (Phocis, pl.).

**δραθεῖν,** v. δαρθάνω.

**δραίνω,** *to be ready to do*, Il.10.96. II. *have strength*, δ. μοῦ ὅσον Herod.1.15, cf. 2.95.

**δραιόν·** μακρόν· πυλεόν (fort. l. μάκτραν, πύελον), Hsch. **δραιώμη·** ὠφέλεια, Id.

* **δράκαινα,** ης, ἡ, fem. of δράκων, *she-dragon*, *h.Ap.*300; of the Erinyes, A.*Eu.*128; Ἅιδου δ., of the Erinys of Clytaemnestra, E.*IT* 286; compared with a courtesan, δ. ἄμεικτος Anaxil.22.3, cf. Secund. *Sent.*8. II. *scourge*, Ar.*Fr.*767.

**δρᾰκαινίς,** ίδος, ἡ, = δράκων III, Ephipp.12.6, Mnesim.4.42.

**δράκαυλος** [ᾰ], ον, prob. *living with a snake*, epith. of the daughters of Cecrops, S.*Fr.*643.

**δρᾰκείς, δρακῆναι, δράκον,** v. δέρκομαι:—but **δράκεν·** ἐνεργεῖ, πράσσει, is prob. f. l. for δέδρακεν, Hsch.

**δρακ-ίζω,** *play the buffoon*, Gloss. **-ις,** ὁ, dub. sens. in S.*Ichn.* 177. **-ιστής,** οῦ, ὁ, *buffoon*, Gloss.

* **δρᾰκονθόμῑλος,** ον, *of dragon brood*, A.*Supp.*267.

* **δρᾰκόντειος,** ον, *of a dragon*, κρημνοί E.*Ph.*1315; νῶτα *AP*12.257 (Mel.); δειραί *APl.*4.90; πούς Luc.*Philops.*4.

**δρᾰκοντία** μεγάλη, = δρακόντιον III, Ps.-Dsc.2.166; δ. μικρά, = ἄρον, ib.167.

**δρᾰκοντίας** πυρός, ὁ, a wheat *with coarse straw*, Thphr.*CP*3.21.2. 2. δ. πελειάς, ἡ, a kind of *pigeon*, Nic.*Fr*.73. 3. δ. σίκυς, = σ. ἄγριος, Euthyd.ap.Ath.3.74b. 4. *stone found in a serpent's head*, Plin.*HN*37.158.

**δρακοντίασις**, εως, ἡ, *guinea-worm disease*, Gal.14.790.

**δρᾰκόντ-ιον**, τό, Dim. of δράκων I, δ. ἀργυροῦν *IG*11(2).203*B*44 (Delos, iii B.C.). II. a kind of *fish* (v. l. for δράκων III), Hp.*Int*.21. III. *edder-wort, Dracunculus vulgaris*, ib.1, Thphr.*HP*7.12.2, Dsc.2.166 (where δρακοντία, ἡ, Ps.-Dsc.: -εία βοτάνη *Gp*.13.8.7). IV. *guinea-worm, Filaria medinensis*, Plu.2.733b, Sor.ap.Paul.Aeg.4.58, Gal.19.449. V. a kind of *fig*, Ath.3.78a. VI. a pigment, *dragon's-blood*, Alex.Aphr.*in Mete*.161.5 (but δρακόντιον αἷμα *cinnabar*, *PHolm*.10.32). **-ίς**, ίδος, ἡ, a kind of *bird*, Ant. Lib.9.3. II. in pl., certain *vessels* near the heart, Hp.ap.Ruf. *Onom*.202. **-ίτης** [ῑ] (sc. λίθος), ου, ὁ, *dragon-stone*, conferring sharp vision, Ptol.Chenn.p.192 W.

**δρᾰκοντο-βόλος**, ον, *dragon-hurling* (?), Nonn.*D*.36.177. **-βότος**, ον, *feeding dragons*, ib.4.356, al. **-γενής**, ές, *dragon-gendered*, of Thebans, Sch.S.*Ant*.126. **-έθειρα**, ἡ, *with snaky locks*, Γοργών Orph.*L*.542. **-ειδής**, ές, *snake-like*, ὄφεις δ. τὴν κεφαλήν *Peripl.M.Rubr*.55. Adv. -δῶς, ῥεῖν to have a *serpentine* course, Str.9.3.16. **-ζωνες**, dub. in Poet.Magic.ap.Afric.*Cest.Oxy*.412 i 29. **-κέφᾰλος**, ον, *with a serpent's head*, *BGU*1065.9 (i A.D.), Suid. s. v. Ἑκάτην. **-κομος**, ον, *with snaky locks*, Nonn.*D*.1.18, 47.552. **-κτονία**, ἡ, *slaying of a serpent*, Arg.Pi.*P*.

**δρᾰκοντ-ολέτης**, ου, ὁ, *serpent-slayer*, of Apollo, *AP*9.525.

**δρᾰκοντό-μαλλος**, ον, *with snaky locks*, Γοργόνες A.*Pr*.799. **-μῑμος**, ον, *serpent-like*, τορεύματα Sopat.19. **-μορφος**, ον, *of serpent-form*, Lyc.1042, *POxy*.490.12 (ii A.D.). **-πους**, ὁ, ἡ, gen. ποδος, *snake-footed, with serpents for feet*, Tz. ad Lyc.63, *EM*371.46. **-τρῐχέω**, *have snaky hair*, Tz.*H*.5.720. **-φόνος**, ον, *serpent-slaying*, Orph.*L*.158, Nonn.*D*.25.453. **-φόροι**, οἱ, = Lat. *draconarii*, Lyd.*Mag*.1.46. II. Adj. **-φόρος**, ον, *snaky*, κόμαι Nonn.*D*.25.221 (s.v.l.). **-φρουρος**, ον, *watched by a dragon*, Lyc.1311.

**δρᾰκοντώδης**, ες, = δρακοντοειδής, κόραι, τύραννος, E.*Or*.256, Plu.2.551e; *vermiform*, κάθισμα, worm of a still, Zos.Alch.p.224 B.

⊛ **δράκος** [ᾰ], εος, τό, (δέρκομαι) *eye*, Nic.*Al*.481. II. (δράσσομαι) = δράγμα, Lxx 3*Ma*.5.2.

⊛ **δρακτόν**, τό, *small vase* (cf. δράξ), *OGI*479.10 (Dorylaeum), *BCH*11.385 (Panamara), etc.

**δρᾰκών, δρᾰκόμενος**, v. δέρκομαι.

⊛ **δράκων** [ᾰ], οντος, ὁ: (prob. from δέρκομαι, δρᾰκεῖν, cf. Porph.*Abst*.3.8):—*dragon, serpent*, Il.11.39, al.; interchangeable with ὄφις, 12.202, 208, cf. Hes.*Th*.322, 825, Pi.*N*.1.40, A.*Th*.292 (lyr.); ἀετὸς καὶ δ. πολέμια Arist.*HA*609$^{a}$4; perh. a *water-snake*, ib.602$^{b}$25. II. the constellation *Draco*, Arat.46, al., Man.2.69. III. a sea-fish, *the great weever*, Epich.60, Arist.*HA*598$^{a}$11, Hp.*Vict*.2.48. IV. = κηρύκειον, prob. *a wand with a serpent coiled round* it, S.*Fr*.700 (cf. 701). 2. *serpent-shaped bracelet* or *necklace*, Luc.*Am*.41. 3. a *noose* or *crossed bandage* for the ankle, Heraclas ap.Orib.48.5.1. 4. *dragon-standard*, Lib.*Or*.1.144, Them.*Or*.18.219a, cf. *Or*.1.2a: hence, *corps of* 1,000 *men* in the Parthian army, Luc.*Hist. Conscr*.29.

**δράλαινα**· λαμυρά (Cos), Hsch.

**δρᾶμα**, ατος, τό, (δράω) *deed, act*, opp. πάθος, A.*Ag*.533; *office, business, duty*, Pl.*Tht*.150a, *R*.451c; τὸ δ. δρᾶν to go about one's *business*, Id.*Tht*.169b. II. *action* represented on the stage, *drama, play*, Ar.*Ra*.920, Arist.*Po*.1448$^{a}$28, etc.; μὴ ἐν τῷ δ. not in *the action on the stage*, ib.1460$^{a}$31; ἔξω τοῦ δ. ib.1453$^{b}$32; δ. ποιεῖν Ar.*Ra*.1021; σατυρικὸν δ. Pl.*Smp*.222d (with play on I): metaph., *stage effect* of any kind, τὰ ἐλεινὰ ταῦτα δ. εἰσάγειν Id.*Ap*.35b: also, *tragical event*, Plb.23.10.12, Him.*Ecl*.1.12, etc.

**δρᾱμᾰτ-ικός**, ή, όν, *dramatic*, μιμήσεις Arist.*Po*.1448$^{b}$35; μῦθοι ib.1459$^{a}$19; δ. ἀτοπία *such as is found in plays*, D.H.1.84. Adv. -κῶς Ammon.*in Cat*.14.15, Eust.6.11. **-ιον**, τό, Dim. of δρᾶμα, Plu.*Dem*.4; δ. σατυρικόν Ath.13.595e.

**δρᾱμᾰτοποι-έω**, *put into dramatic form*, τὸ γελοῖον Arist.*Po*.1448$^{b}$37. **-ΐα**, ἡ, *dramatic composition*, Ph.2.597. **-ός**, οῦ, ὁ, *dramatic poet*, Heph.8.1, Ps.-Luc.*Philopatr*.13: metaph., *melodramatic*, δ. καὶ ποτνιαστής Phld.*Herc*.1457.12.

**δρᾱμᾰτουργ-έω**, = δραματοποιέω, τὸν διάλογον Ath.*Epit*.1.1f, cf. Max.Tyr.7.1; '*act a part*', πάντα δ. J.*BJ*1.24.1, Alciphr.2.3. II. = πανουργέω, Hsch. **-ημα**, ατος, τό, *dramatic composition*, Id. **-ία**, ἡ, = δραματοποιΐα, Luc.*Salt*.68: metaph. of life, Sopat. ap.Stob.4.5.52, Max.Tyr.7.10; the *action* of a play, Str.1.2.27. **-ός**, όν, *contriver*, μύσους J.*BJ*1.26.4.

**δρᾰμεῖν**, v. τρέχω.

**δράμ-ημα** [ᾰ], ατος, τό (cf. *EM*316.50), *running, course*, Hdt.8.98, A.*Pers*.247 (anap.), S.*OT*193 (lyr.), *Ichn*.74, Ion Trag.1, E.*Ba*.872 (lyr.), al.; κυμάτων δ. Id.*Tr*.693 (pl.): the later form δρόμημα is found in codd. of Id.*Med*.1180, al., cf. *APl*.5.385 (pl.), Ar.Byz.*Epit*.73.14. **-ητέον**, *one must run*, S.E.*M*.8.271.

**δράμις**, ἡ, a kind of *loaf*, Maced. word, Seleuc.ap.Ath.3.114b.

**δρᾱμοσύνη**, ἡ, *ceremony*, *IG*2$^{2}$.1358 ii 34, 40 (iv B.C.).

**δρᾰμοῦμαι**, v. τρέχω.

**δρανεῖς**· δραστικοί, Hsch.

**δρᾶνος**, εος, τό, (δράω) *doing, deed, power*; also, = ὄργανον, ἄγαλμα, κατασκεύασμα, Hsch. (δρανός cod.).

⊛ **δράξ**, ᾰκός, ἡ, *handful*, πηλοῦ Batr.237; ἀλφίτων Porph.*Abst*.2.17. II. *the hand*, τίς ἐμέτρησε τὴν γῆν δρακί; Lxx *Is*.40.12 (so δράξ· παλάμη, Hsch.); τὰς δράκας καρτερῶς σφίγξαι Herm.ap.Stob.1.49.44; the *claw* of the constellation Leo, Ptol.*Alm*.7.5. III. a *measure*, Dsc.5.87, Hero *Mens*.61.9, Hsch. IV. βακχικαὶ δ., = θύρσοι, Sch.Il.6.134.

**δραξών**, a temple in Sicily, Hsch. II. *thief*, *EM*.86.32. 2. = πορνοβοσκός, Hsch.

⊛ **δράπᾰνον** [δρᾰ], τό, = δρέπανον, Epigr. in *BKT*5(1) p.77.

**δραπενίδες**· εἶδος ὀρνέου, Hsch.

**δρᾱπετ-ᾰγωγός**, όν, *recovering a runaway slave*: Δ., ὁ, a comedy by Antiphanes, Ath.4.161d. **-εία**, ἡ, *running away*, Hsch. s. v. δράσκασις. **-ευμα**, ατος, τό, = foreg., Diocl.Com.12. ⊛ **-εύω**, *run away*, X.*Mem*.2.1.16; τινά *from* one, Pl.*Smp*.216b; παρά τινος Luc.*Somn*.12; δραπετεύσουσι ὑπὸ ταῖς ἀσπίσιν *will skulk* behind.., X.*HG*2.4.16; δραπετεύοντα πολεμεῖν Id.*Ages*.1.23: metaph., *shirk public service*, D.42.25; [αἱ δόξαι] δ. ἐκ τῆς ψυχῆς Pl.*Men*.98a; ἐκ τοῦ βίου Luc.*Peregr*.21; ἐκ φιλοσοφίας Plu.2.46e; *slip away*, εἰς τὸ βάθος, of fluids, Paul.Aeg.6.3. **-ης**, ου, Ion. **δρηπέτης**, εω, ὁ, (διδράσκω, δρᾶναι) *runaway*, βασιλέος *from* the king, Hdt.3.137; esp. *runaway slave*, δούλοισι, καὶ τοῦτο δρηπέτῃσι Id.6.11, cf. Ar.*Ach*.1187, Herod.2.13, etc.; δ. ἀνήρ S.*Fr*.63. 2. Adj., πούς δ. E.*Or*.1498 (lyr.), cf. Aeschin.3.152; βίος δ. *fugitive* life, *AP*10.87 (Pall.); οὐ δραπέτην τὸν κλῆρον.. μεθείς no *skulker's* lot, i. e. not a lump of earth which would fall in pieces, of the lot of Cresphontes, S.*Aj*.1285. II. fem. **δρᾱπέτις**, ιδος, Luc.*Asin*.25: as Adj., στέγη a home *whose occupants are shifting*, S.*Fr*.174; ψυχή *AP*12.80 (Mel.); μέλισσαι Ael.*Ep*.5; Δραπέτιδες, title of play by Cratinus. **-ίδης**, ου, Dor. **-δᾶς**, ὁ, = foreg., δ. ἐμός ἐστιν Mosch.1.3. **-ικός**, ή, όν, *of* or *for a* δραπέτης, δ. θρίαμβος a triumph *over runaway slaves*, Plu.*Pomp*.31; δ. σώματα *CIG*2554.102 (Crete); δραπετικοί, οἱ, *IG*5(1).1390.83 (Andania); of a slave, *likely to run away*, *BGU*887.3 (ii A.D.). **-ίνδα** (Adv.) παίζειν, a game *where one chased the rest*, *EM*286.48; expld. by δραπετικῶς, Hsch. **-ις**, ιδος, ἡ, fem. of δραπέτης (q. v.). **-ίσκος**, ὁ, Dim. of δραπέτης, Luc.*Fug*.33.

**δράπων**, ὁ, = δραπέτης, Hdn.Gr.1.34, al.

⊛ **δρᾱσείω**, Desiderat. of δράω, *have a mind to do*, S.*Aj*.326, 585, E.*Ph*.1208, *Med*.93, Ar.*Pax*62.

⊛ **δράσῐμος** [ᾱ], ον, = δραστήριος: τὸ δ. *activity, vigour*, A.*Th*.554.

**δρᾶσις**, εως, ἡ, *strength, efficacy*, Luc.*Trag*.276. 2. *sacrifice*, Hsch. 3. Gramm., *active force* of a verb, A.D.*Pron*.44.1, *Synt*.283.23: generally, *action*, opp. *passivity*, Mich.*in EN*275.8. II. (δράω B) *vision*, *EM*287.8.

**δρασκ-άζω**, (διδράσκω) *attempt an escape*, Lex ap.Lys.10.17: prov., ἐν ἅλῳ δρασκάζεις, of those who 'bury their head in the sand', Zen.3.74. **-ᾰσις**, εως, ἡ, *running away, escape*, Hsch.

**δρασματικός**, ή, όν, = δραστήριος, *Cat.Cod.Astr*.2.165.

**δρασμάτων**· πανουργημάτων, Hsch.

**δρασμός**, Ion. **δρησμός**, ὁ, (διδράσκω) *running away, flight*, δρησμὸν βουλεύειν Hdt.5.124; δρησμῷ ἐπιχειρέειν Id.6.70; δρασμῷ κρυφαίῳ A.*Pers*.360; δρασμὸν εὑρεῖν ib.370: in pl., E.*Or*.1374 (lyr.), etc.: not freq. in Prose, δρασμῷ χρῆσθαι Aeschin.3.21, cf. Plb.5.26.14, *BGU*987.23 (i A.D.), Jul.*Or*.2.57b.

⊛ **δράσσομαι**, Att. **δράττομαι**, Hdt.3.13; impf. ἐδραττόμην Ar.*Ra*.545: fut. δράξομαι *APl*.4.275.10 (Posidipp.), Lxx *Nu*.5.26: aor. ἐδραξάμην Pl.*Ly*.209e, etc.: pf. δέδραγμαι, 2 pers. δέδραξαι E.*Tr*.750, part. δεδραγμένος Il.13.393:—the Act., δράσσω only in Poll.3.155, *EM*285.43, prob. in *PLond*.3.1170$^{v}$113 (iii A.D.), cf. δράξαι· κρατῆσαι, Hsch.: (cf. δράξ, δράγμα, δραχμή):—*grasp* with the hand, c. gen. rei, κόνιος δεδραγμένος αἱματοέσσης *clutching handfuls* of gory dust, Il. l. c.: metaph., ἐλπίδος δεδραγμένος S.*Ant*.235 (vv. ll. πεπρ-, πεφρ-), cf. Plb.36.15.7; δραξάμενοι τῶν ἁλῶν *taking a handful* of salt, Pl. l. c., etc. 2. *lay hold of*, τί μου δέδραξαι χερσί; E.*Tr*.750; δραξάμενος φάρυγος *having seized* [them] by the throat, Theoc.24.28, cf. 25.145, *POxy*.1298.10 (iv A.D.): metaph., δράξασθαι καιροῦ D.S.12.67; μείζονος οἴκου (i.e. by marriage), Call.*Epigr*.1.14; μεγάλης ἀπήνης *AP*11.238 (Demod.); τᾶς κραδίας Theoc.30.9; [ὧν χρ]ὴ δράξασθαι τὸ στόμα sounds the mouth has to *grip*, i.e. *make*, dub. in Phld.*Po*.2.41. II. c. acc., *take by handfuls*, ταύτας [τὰς μνέας] δ. Hdt.3.13; also, *catch*, τοὺς σοφοὺς ἐν τῇ πανουργίᾳ αὐτῶν 1 *Ep.Cor*.3.20.

⊛ **δραστ-έος**, α, ον, *to be done*, S.*Tr*.1204. II. δραστέον *one must do*, Id.*OT*1443, E.*IA*1024, D.Chr.12.16. **-ην**· κόφινον, Hsch. **-ήρ**, ῆρος, ὁ, *cook*, Id.; cf. δρηστήρ. **-ηρά**· δραστικά, Id. **-ήριος**, ον, *active, efficacious*, μηχανή A.*Th*.1046; φάρμακον E.*Ion*1185; ἀνὴρ δ. ἐς τὰ πάντα Th.4.81; τὸ δ. *activity, energy*, Id.2.63. Adv. -ίως Ph.1.104, Jul.*Ep*.10, Hierocl.*in CA*26 p.479 M. 2. rarely in bad sense, τὰ δεινὰ καὶ δ. *audacious deeds*, E.*Or*.1554. 3. *active*, opp. *passive*, Plot.6.1.29: esp. in Gramm., of verbs, D.H.*Th*.24. Adv. -ίως Syrian.*in Metaph*.82.31. **-ηριότης**, ητος, ἡ, *activity, energy*, Eust.123.46. **-ηριώδης**, ες, = δραστήριος, Gal.12.123 (Comp.).

**δράστης** and **δράστας**, ὁ, Att. and Dor. for δρήστης.

**δραστικός**, ή, όν, = δραστήριος, σχήματα *representing attack*, in a war-dance, Pl.*Lg*.815a; *efficient* (cause), δ. αἴτιον ὀργῆς Phld.*Ir*.p.98 W., cf. *D*.1.14; δραστικοὺς τῶν κακῶν (τοὺς θεούς) ib.19, cf. Max.Tyr.18.2; παχυμεροῦς ὕλης δ., of river fish, Xenocr.9; of persons, Plu.*Cor*.21: Comp. διάνοια -ώτερον χειρός Ph.1.542: Sup., Onos.22.4. 2. *active*, opp. *passive*, δ. ποιότητες, ἀρχαί, *Stoic*.2.133, 134;

-ώτατον τὸ θερμόν ib.135; -ώτατα στοιχεῖα Ph.2.142. 3. as Medic. term, *drastic*, Dsc.1.19.4 (Sup.); φάρμακον *Gp*.13.14.5, cf. Xenocr.ap.Orib.2.58.50. Adv. -κῶς Gal.10.368. 4. Gramm., δ. διάβασις, = δρᾶσις 1.3, A.D.*Pron*.115.6.

**δράστις**, = βύσσος, and **δραστιουργοί**, *flax-* or *linen-workers*, Hsch.

**δραστοσύνη**, v. δρηστοσύνη.

**δρᾱτός**, ή, όν, = δαρτός, (δέρω) *skinned, flayed*, δρατὰ σώματα Il.23.169 (v.l. δρετά).

**δραύκιον**, τό, *necklace, Gloss.*

**δραχμ-αῖος**, α, ον, = δραχμιαῖος, Nic.*Th*.519. ⊛ **-ή**, ή, (δράσσομαι, prop. *as much as one can hold in the hand*, cf. Plu.*Lys*.17): I. a weight, *drachm*, [κρεῶν] prob. in *IG*1².10.4, Thphr.*Od*.17, etc. 2. a silver coin, *drachma*, worth six obols, Hdt.7.144, And.4.18, *IG*7.3171.52 (Orchom. Boeot.), 9(1).694.54 (Corc.), etc. [The penult. is long in Simon.157, and sts. in Com., Ar.*V*.691 (anap.), *Pax* 1201, *Pl*.1019, Pl.Com.174.17: **δαρχμή** is found in Hsch.; cf. δαρκνά.] **-ῆιος**, α, ον, Ion. for δραχμαῖος, *weighing a drachm*, ἄχθος Nic.*Th*.604. ⊛ **-ιαῖος**, α, ον, *worth* or *costing a drachma*, Ar.*Fr*.425; [ἐπίδειξις] Pl.*Cra*.384b; δ. συναλλάγματα Arist.*Pol*.1300ᵇ33; δ. τόκος interest *at the rate of 1 dr. per 100 denarii per month, IGRom*.4.788 (Apamea), cf. *BGU*1038.20 (ii A.D.). 2. *weighing one drachm*, Archig.ap.Gal.12.876, etc. ⊛ **-ίον**, τό, Dim. of δραχμή, Aristeas 5. **-ός**, ὁ, = δραγμός, v.l. in Q.S.1.350.

⊛ **δράω** (A), Aeol. 3 pl. δραῖσι Alc.*Supp*.27.11, subj. δρῶ, δρᾷς, δρᾷ, opt. δρῴην, Ep. δρώοιμι Od.15.317; παρα-δρώωσι ib.324: impf. ἔδρων: fut. δράσω: aor. 1 ἔδρᾱσα, Ion. ἔδρησα Thgn.954: pf. δέδρᾱκα:—Pass., aor. 1 ἐδράσθην, δρασθείς, Th.3.38, 6.53: pf. δέδρᾱμαι (δεδρασμένων is f.l. in Id.3.54):—*do, accomplish*, esp. *do some great thing*, good or bad (acc. to some δ. was the equiv. Dor. Verb for Att. πράττειν, Arist.*Po*.1448ᵇ1), αἶψά κεν εὖ δρώοιμι μετὰ σφίσιν ἅσσ' ἐθέλοιεν Od.15.317 (where the Sch. interprets it διακονοίην, δουλεύοιμι I *would serve*.., cf. δρήστης); ἄνδρες δραῖσιν ἀτάσθαλοι Alc. l.c.; opp. πάσχω, freq. in Trag., εὖ δρῶσαν, εὖ πάσχουσαν A.*Eu*.868; ἄξια δράσας ἄξια πάσχων Id.*Ag*.1527; κακῶς δράσαντες οὐκ ἐλάσσονα πάσχουσι Id.*Pers*.813; of one in extreme perplexity, τί πάθω; τί δὲ δρῶ; Id.*Th*.1062, cf. *Ch*.899; δρῶν ἀντιπάσχω χρηστά S.*Ph*.584; prov., "δράσαντι παθεῖν" τριγέρων μῦθος τάδε φωνεῖ A.*Ch*.313; δράσαντι γάρ τοι καὶ παθεῖν ὀφείλεται Id.*Fr*.456, cf. S.*OT*1272; τά γ' ἔργα μου πεπονθότα.. μᾶλλον ἢ δεδρακότα acts of suffering rather than of *doing*, Id.*OC*267; ὁ δρῶν the *doer*, whoever he be, A.*Ag*.1359, etc.; ὁ δράσας the *culprit*, Pl.*Lg*.879a, cf. S.*Tr*.1108; ὁ δεδρακώς Id.*OT*246, D.23.40; used to avoid repetition of a verb, Th.2.49, al.: c. dupl. acc., οἷ' ἔργ' ὁ παῖς μ' ἔδρασεν S.*Ph*.940, cf. *OC*854, etc.: with Adv., εὖ, κακῶς δρᾶν τινά, *do* one a good or ill turn, Thgn.108, S.*Aj*.1154; δρᾶν τι εἴς τινα Id.*OC*976; τί τινι Id.*OT*1402; πάντα δρᾶν *try* every way, cj. in E.*Hipp*.284; παντὸς εἶχε δρωντος ἡδονήν was satisfied with *the doing*, S.*OC*1604; τὰ δρώμενα *what is doing* or *being done*, ib.1644, cf. D.C.37.57: sg., τὸ δρώμενον S.*El*.40, Th.5.102; τί δράσω; to express helplessness or despair, S.*Aj*.920, etc.; for οἶσθ' οὖν ὃ δρᾶσον; v. *εἴδω fin. 2. of things, τουτὶ τί δρᾷ τὸ ποτήριον; Ar.*Eq*.237; ὅπερ ἡ λίθος δρᾷ τὸν σίδηρον Luc.*Im*.1: so, generally, *to be active*, εἰς ἄλληλα πάσχειν καὶ δ. Chrysipp.*Stoic*.2.135, cf. Prisc.Lyd.4.10. II. *offer sacrifice* or *perform mystical rites*, δ. τὰ ἱερὰ *IG*1².4, cf. 188, Ath.14.660a, Paus.1.43.2, Iamb.*Myst*.1.21, etc.:—Pass., τὰ δρώμενα Gal.*UP*7.14, Sopat.in Rh.8.1 W., etc.; τὰ δημοσίᾳ δρώμενα Plu.*Num*.9.

**δράω** (B), = ὁράω, A.D.*Adv*.139.8, *EM*287.7.

**δρέμμα**· κλέμμα (fort. κλῆμα), οἱ δὲ κλάσμα, Hsch.

**δρεπάνη** [ᾰ], ἡ, (δρέπω) *sickle, reaping-hook*, ἤμων ὀξείας δρεπάνας ἐν χερσὶν ἔχοντες Il.18.551, cf. *AP*9.383.9; *pruning-hook*, ἐτρύγων.. δρεπάνας ἐν χ. ἔχ. Hes.*Sc*.292: rare in Prose, Plu.*Cleom*.26, Alciphr.3.19.

⊛ **δρεπᾰνηΐς**, ΐδος, ἡ, poet. for foreg., Nic.*Fr*.21.

**δρεπᾰνηφόρος**, ον, *bearing a scythe* or *hook*, ἅρμα δ. *scythed* car, X.*An*.1.7.10, Plb.5.53.10, D.S.17.53, Ascl.*Tact*.8, Ph.2.107.

**δρεπάνιον** [ᾰ], τό, Dim. of δρέπανον, Seleuc.ap.Ath.4.155e.

**δρεπᾰνίς**, ίδος, ἡ (also **δραπενίς** Hsch.), a kind of *bird*, so called from the shape of its wings, prob. the *Alpine swift, Cypselus melba*, Arist.*HA*487ᵇ27; = κεγχρίς (κέγχρος cod.), Hsch.

**δρεπᾰνο-ειδής**, ές, *sickle-shaped*, Th.6.4, Str.8.2.3. **-μάχαιρα** [μᾰ], ἡ, *scimitar*, Sch.Ar.*Th*.1138. **-ποιός**, ὁ, *sickle-maker, Gloss.*

⊛ **δρέπᾰνον**, τό, also **δράπανον** (q.v.), (δρέπω) = δρεπάνη, δ. εὐκαμπές Od.18.368; χαλκέοις ἧμα δ. S.*Fr*.534; the usual form in Prose and Com., Hdt.1.125, etc.; δ. θεριστικόν *PMagd*.8.6 (iii B.C.). 2. *pruning-knife*, Pl.*R*.333d. 3. *scythe*, X.*Cyr*.6.1.30. 4. *curved sword, scimitar*, Hdt.5.112, 7.93, Ar.*Ra*.576.

⊛ **δρεπᾰνουργός**, ὁ, *sword-maker, armourer*, Pherecr.130.2, Ar.*Pax* 548.

**δρεπᾰνοφόρος**, ον, = δρεπανηφόρος, τέθριππα Anon.Hist. in *Rev. Ét.Gr*.5.323.

**δρεπᾰνώδης**, ες, = δρεπανοειδής, αἰχμαί Agath.5.22, cf. *EM*219.2.

**δρεπ-τεύς**, έως, ὁ, *vintager*, Hsch. (but **δρεπεύς** *EM*287.30). **-τικῶς**, Adv. *carptim, Gloss.*, Dosith.p.412 K. **-τός**, ή, όν, *plucked*: δρεπτόν, a name for a kiss, Teleclid.13. **-τω**, poet. for sq., *pluck*, Ep. impf. δρέπτον Mosch.2.69:—more freq. in Med., Opp.*C*.2.38, *APl*.4.231 (Anyte), etc. **-ω**, Ep. impf. δρέπον *h.Cer*.425: aor. 1 ἔδρεψα Hdt.2.92, (ἀπο-) Pi.*P*.9.110: aor. 2 ἔδρᾰπον ib.4.130: Aeol. subj. δρόπωσιν Alc.*Oxy*.1788 *Fr*.15 ii 23:—Med., Dor. fut. δρεψεῦμαι Theoc.18.40: aor. ἐδρεψάμην Od.12.357, etc.:—**Pass.**, aor. ἐδρέφθην Philostr.*VA*8.7.5:—*pluck*, ἄνθεα *h.Cer*.425, Hdt.2.92, cf. E.*El*.778, *Ion*889 (lyr.); καρπόν Hdt.3.110: metaph., *gain possession* or *enjoyment of*, δ. τιμάν, ἥβαν, Pi.*P*.1.49, 6.48, etc.; δραπὼν εὐζώας ἄωτον ib.4.130; δ. κορυφὰς ἀρετᾶν ἄπο Id.*O*.1.13; σοφίας καρπὸν δ. Id.*Fr*.209; λειμῶνα Μουσῶν δ., of a poet, Ar.*Ra*.1300. II. Med., *pluck for oneself, cull*, φύλλα δρεψάμεναι.. δρυὸς Od.12.357; νάρκισσον.. δρεπόμην *h.Cer*.429; Ἰσθμιάδων δρέπεσθαι ἄωτον Pi.*N*.2.9; ἀπὸ κρηνῶν μελιρρύτων δρεπόμενοι τὰ μέλη Pl.*Ion*534b; στεφάνως δρεψεύμεναι Theoc.18.40; κενεὰς ἐλπίδας ἐδρεπόμαν *AP*12.125 (Mel.); ἡδύσματα παρὰ τῆς ποιητικῆς Μούσης Jul.*Or*.7.207c; ψυχὴν θείαν Orph.*Fr*.228; αἷμα δρέψασθαι *cull the fruits of* murder, A.*Th*.718, cf. Bion 1.22: abs., E.*Hipp*.81: c. gen., κατὰ καιρὸν ἐρώτων δ. Pi.*Fr*.123.1.

**δρέχμονες**· νεφροί, Hsch. **δρῆγες**· στρουθοί (Maced.), Id.; cf. δίγηρες, δρίξ. **δρηλοί**· φοβεῖται, Id. (Fort. δϝηλοῖ.)

**Δρηνεία**, ἡ, title of Artemis, Ἀρχ.Ἐφ.1913.227 (Lesbos).

**δρηπέτης, δρησμός**, Ion. for δραπέτης, δρασμός.

**δρησμοσύνη**, ἡ, = δρηστοσύνη, δ. ἱερῶν *care* of the holy rites, *h.Cer*.476. II. = δρασμός, Max.351.

**δρηστ-εύω**, *perform rites*, θεοῖς Ἀρχ.Ἐφ.1913.223 (Lesbos). ⊛ **-ήρ**, ῆρος, ὁ, (δράω A) *labourer, working man*, Od.16.248: fem. δρήστειρα *workwoman*, 10.349, 19.345. II. (διδράσκω) *runaway*, λῃστής Babr.128.14. **-ης**, Att. **δράστης**, ου, Dor. **δράστας**, α, ὁ, *worker*, Archil.72; θεράπων, οὐ δράστας as an attendant, not *a slave*, Pi.*P*.4.287; *doer, actor*, αὐτουργὸς καὶ δράστης Plb.12.25ʰ.6. 2. as Adj., *energetic*, Man.5.85. II. = δραπέτης, Hsch. **-ις**, ιος, ἡ, (διδράσκω) = δραπέτις, Call.*Ep*.42. **-οσύνη**, ἡ, Ep. for δραστ-, *service*, Od.15.321; δμωὶς δρηστοσύνῃσι κεκασμένη *IG*3.1310.

**δριάεντα**· χλωρά, Hsch.; **δριάουσαν**· θάλλουσαν, Id. **δριαλεῖν**· ποιεῖν, Id. **δρικηαί**, in pl., a kind of *bird*, Id.: cf. δρίξ. **δρίλαξ**, ακος, *leech* (Elean), Id.

⊛ **δρῖλος**, ὁ, expld. by Lat. *verpus*, sens. obsc., *AP*11.197 (Lucill.); **δρεῖλος**, *Supp.Epigr*.2.353 (Amphissa).

**δρίμαι**· ψῦχος, Hsch.

**δρῑμεύω**, *itch*, Anon. in *EN*448.3.

**δρῑμυγμός**, ὁ, *pungency*, θύμου Tz.*H*.11.374.

**δρῑμῠλέων**, οντος, ὁ, epith. applied by Menodotus the Empiric to the dogmatic physicians, Gal.*Subf.Emp*.11 p.63 Bonnet.

⊛ **δρῑμύλος** [ῠ], ον, Dim., ὄμμα δ. *a piercing little* eye, Mosch.1.8.

**δρῑμύμωρος** [ῠ], ον, = ὀξύμωρος, used of the dogmatic physicians by Menodotus the Empiric, Gal.*Subf.Emp*.11 p.63 Bonnet.

**δρίμυξις** [ῐ], εως, ἡ, *smarting*, Orib.*Fr*.64, Sor.(?)ap.Aët.16.77.

**δρῑμῠποιέω**, *make pungent*, Herod.Med. in *Rh.Mus*.58.82.

⊛ **δρῑμύς**, εῖα, ύ, *piercing, sharp, keen*, βέλος Il.11.270: metaph., δριμεῖα μάχη 15.696, Hes.*Sc*.261; δ. χόλος Il.18.322; μένος Od.24.319; ἄχος Hes.*Sc*.457; θυμὸς A.*Ch*.391 (lyr.). II. of things which affect the eyes or taste, *keen, pungent, acrid*, of smoke, δριμύτατος καπνῶν Ar.*V*.146; of radish, etc., opp. γλυκύς, X.*Mem*.1.4.5, cf. Pl.Com.154 (Sup.); χυμός Arist.*de An*.422ᵇ13; ὀσμαί ib.421ᵃ30; δριμέσιν ἰητρεύειν *with pungent drugs*, Hp.*Fract*.27; δ. οἶνος Luc.*Merc.Cond*.18. Adv. -έως: Comp. δριμύτερον, ὄζειν Arist.*Pr*.907ᵃ13; ῥεύματος δριμύτερον γενομένου Hp.*VM*18. III. metaph., of persons, *bitter, fierce*, ἀλάστωρ A.*Ag*.1501 (lyr.); ἄγροικος Ar.*Eq*.808, etc.; also, *keen, shrewd*, κρόταλον E.*Cyc*.104; ἔντονοι καὶ δ. Pl.*Tht*.173a; δ. καὶ δικανικός ib.175d; δ. ἐν τῷ ἀποκρίνεσθαι Arist.*Top*.156ᵇ37; λόγος δριμύτατος Id.*SE*182ᵇ37 (but λέξις and λόγος δ. of *striking* turns of phrase, Hermog.*Id*.1.2, 2.5): neut. as Adv., δριμὺ βλέπειν look *bitter*, Ar.*Ra*.562; but also to look *sharply, keenly*, Pl.*R*.519a, Luc.*Symp*.16; ἐνορᾶν Id.*Cat*.3, Ael.*VH*14.22, D.C.59.26:—regul. Adv. δριμέως, Anaxandr.15.3; ἐρασθῆναι Ael.*NA*7.15; δριμύτατα ἀλγεῖν Id.*VH*12.1.

**δρῑμύσσω**, *cause to smart*, ὀφθαλμούς Alex.Trall.2:—Pass., οἱ δριμυττόμενοι τὰ βλέφαρα Aët.7.15. II. *treat severely*, Eust.201.23; δριμύξεται τὰ ἐναγώνια Lib.*Decl*.43 *Intr*.4.

**δρῑμύτης**, ητος, ἡ, *acridness* of humours, Hp.*VM*18 (pl.); *pungency* of taste, etc., Anaxipp.1.46, Alex.Aphr.*Pr*.2.70: pl., Arched.2.7, Thphr.*CP*1.16.9; *itches*, Agatharch.58; of smoke, Plb.21.28.16. II. metaph., *keenness, eagerness*, Pl.*Plt*.311a; δ. πρὸς τὰ μαθήματα Id.*R*.535b; *keenness* of wit or satire, Plu.2.48a, Luc.*Alex*.4; πανουργία καὶ δ. ib.483f; ποικιλία καὶ δ. Arr.*Epict*.2.23.40; *bitterness* in controversy, Phld.*Ir*.p.22 W. 2. esp. in Lit. Crit., *use of striking words and turns of phrase*, Id.*Piet*.15, Hermog.*Id*.2.5, *Inv*.3.13, Aristid.*Rh*.2 pp.513, 524 S. 3. *fierceness, grimness*, τοῦ προσώπου App.*BC*1.70.

**δρῑμῠφᾰγ-έω**, *live on acrid food*, Sor.1.64, Paul.Aeg.4.1. **-ία**, ἡ, *acrid diet*, Dsc.2.31 (pl.), Philum.ap.Orib.45.29.13, Aët.16.75.

**δρίξ**· στρουθός, Cyr.; cf. δρῆγες.

**δρίος** [ῐ], εος, τό, *copse, thicket*, δρίος ὕλης *copse*-wood, Od.14.353; δ. εὔδενδρον, ὑλῆεν, *AP*7.193 (Simm.), 203 (Id.); ἅπαν Opp.*H*.4.588; ἀν' ἐρῆμον δ. *Lyr.Alex.Adesp*.7.3: heterocl. pl. δρία, τά, Hes.*Op*.530, S.*Tr*.1012 (hex.), E.*Hel*.1326 (lyr.): also dat. pl. δρισί (as if from δρίες) dub. in *IG*14.217.43.

**δρίς**· δύναμις, Hsch. **δρίφακτος**· κράββατος, Id.

⊛ **δρίφος**, = δίφρος, Sophr.10.

**δροιόν**· καλόν (Cret.), Hsch. (Fort. κᾶλον.)

**δροίτη**, ἡ, *bathing-tub, bath*, A.*Ag*.1540 (lyr.), *Ch*.999(985), *Eu*.633, Nic.*Al*.462, Lyc.1108. 2. *cradle*, Alex.Aet.16. 3. *bier*, Parth.*Fr*.44, cf. *EM*288.4. 4. *a dance*, Hsch. (The form δρύτη cited from Hermipp. in *EM* is due to a false derivation from δρῦς.)

**δρομάασκε,** v. δρομάω.

**δρομ-ᾱγετέω,** *act as clerk of the course*, *IG*12(2).134,258 (Mytil.). **-αδάριος** or **-εδάριος,** ὁ, = Lat. *dromedarius*, *POxy.*1652 *a* 6, *BGU* 827ʳ, etc. **-άδην** [ᾰ], Adv., (δρόμος) *in running*, Hsch. **-αῖος,** α, ον, also ος, ον E.*Alc.*245 (lyr.) :—*running at full speed*, *swift*, κἀγὼ δρομαίᾳ βᾶσα S.*Tr.*927 ; οὐχ ὡς δ. πῶλος E.*Hel.*543 ; νεφέλας δρομαίου Id.*Alc.* l. c. ; χωρεῖ δρομαίαν Id.*Fr.*495.4 ; δρομαίαν πτέρυγ' ἐκτείνων Ar.*Pax* 160 : in Prose, λαγὼς δ. a hare *run by hounds*, opp. εὐναῖος, X.*Cyn.*5.9 ; ἴχνη δ., opp. εὐναῖα, the track *of a running hare*, ib.3. 8 : metaph., δ. τῆς ψυχῆς ὁρμή Alcid.ap.Arist.*Rh.*1406ᵃ23. Adv. -ως Sch.E.*Or.*1416. II. epith. of Apollo, as patron of racing, Plu.2.724c, *IG*5(1).497, al. (Sparta). **-αξ,** ακος, ὁ, *good at running*, κάμηλος *Gp.*16.22.7. *-άς, άδος, ὁ, ἡ, *running*, πρός σ' ἔβαν δρομὰς ἐξ οἴκων E.*Supp.*1000 (lyr.) ; ἄντυξ δ. the *whirling* wheel, S.*Ph.*678 (lyr.) ; ὁλκάδες Ar.*Fr.*420 ; δ. κάμηλος *dromedary*, D.S.19. 37, Str.15.2.10, J.*AJ*6.14.6, Plu.*Alex.*31 : also with a neut., δρομάδι κώλῳ E.*Hel.*1301 (lyr.) ; δρομάσι βλεφάροις Id.*Or.*837 (lyr.). 2. *wildly roaming*, *frantic*, Ναΐς, παρθένος, Id.*Hipp.*549 (lyr.), *Tr.*42 ; Γαλλαὶ μητρὸς ὀρείης φιλόθυρσοι δρομάδες *Lyr.Adesp.*121. II. of certain fish, *migratory*, Arist.*HA*488ᵃ6. III. *street-walker*, Phryn. Com.33. **-άσσειν·** τρέχειν, Hsch.

**δρομ-άω (not found in pres.), = τρέχω : Ep. iter. δρομάασκε Hes.*Fr.*117 (v.l. φοίτασκε) : aor. 1 part. δρομήσασα Vett.Val.345.33 (but inf. δρομῆσαι dub. in Hp.*Fract.*4) : pf. ὑπα-δεδρόμακε Sapph.2. 10. **-εδάριος,** v. δρομαδ-. * **-εύς,** έως, ὁ, *runner*, E.*El.*824, Ar. *V.*1206, Pl.*Lg.*822b, Lxx *Jb.*9.25, *BGU*141 ii 11 (iii A.D.), etc.: pl., δρομῆς Eup.94, Pl.*R.*613b; later dat. δρομέσι Call.*Fr.*555. 2. in Crete, = ἔφηβος, *Leg.Gort.*1.40 ; cf. δρόμος II. 3. 3. *race-horse* (?), *PMag.Lond.*121.390. **-ή,** ἡ, = δρόμος, Hdn.Gr.1.325. **-ήϊος,** ὁ (sc. μήν), name of month in Crete, *GDI*5040. **-ημα,** v. δράμημα.

* **δρομιάφιον** ἦμαρ, = ἀμφιδρόμια, Hsch.

**δρομ-ίας,** ου, ὁ, a kind of *fish*, Eratosth.*Fr.*12. II. *horseman-crab*, Ael.*NA*7.24. * **-ικός,** ή, όν, *good at running*, *swift*, Pl.*Tht.* 148c, Arist.*EN*1101ᵇ16 : Comp., Philostr.*Her.*3.4 : Sup., Polyaen.3. 11.10. 2. *belonging to the foot-race*, τὰ δ. τοῦ πεντάθλου X.*HG*7.4. 29 ; τὰ δ. γυμνάζεσθαι D.61.24 ; τῷ δρομικῷ ἀγωνίσασθαι D.C.67.8. Adv. -κῶς, ἀποχωρεῖν Pl.*Lg.*706c. II. *set up in race-courses*, οἱ δ. τῶν Ἑρμῶν Philostr.*Her.*2.21. * **-ικότης,** ητος, ἡ, *fleetness of foot*, Simp. *in Cat.*24.18. **-ιον,** τό, *race-course*, *Tab.Defix.Aud.*163.80 (Rome, iv/v A.D.).

**Δρόμιος,** ὁ, *god of the race-course*, epith. of Hermes in Crete, *GDI* 5115. II. in Metric, δρόμιος (sc. πούς), ὁ, the foot ⏑ ⏑ – ⏑, Choerob. *in Heph.*p.218 C.

**δρομοκήρυξ,** ῦκος, ὁ, *runner*, *postman*, Aeschin.2.130, Aen.Tact. 22.3, Polyaen.5.26 (pl.), Philostr.*Gym.*4, D.C.78.35.

* **δρόμος,** ὁ, (δραμεῖν) *course*, *race*, in Il. mostly of horses, ἵπποισι τάθη δρόμος 23.375 ; also of men, τέτατο δρόμος ib.758 ; οὐρίῳ δρόμῳ with prosperous *course*, S.*Aj.*889 (lyr.) ; ἅπαντι χρῆσθαι τῷ δρόμῳ at full *speed*, Luc.*Dom.*10 : of *any quick movement*, e. g. *flight*, A.*Pers.*207 : of Time, ἡμέρης δ. a day's *running*, i. e. the distance one can go in a day, Hdt.2.5 ; κατανύσαι τὸν προκείμενον δ. Id.8.98 ; ἵππου δ. ἡμέρας D.19.273 : of Things, δ. νεφέλης, ἡλίου τε καὶ σελήνης, E.*Ph.*163, Pl. *Ax.*370b (pl.), etc. ; οἱ δ. τῶν ἀστέρων Procl.*Par.Ptol.*136 ; δρόμῳ *at a run*, freq. with Verbs of motion, δρόμῳ διαβάντας τὸν Ἀσωπὸν Hdt.9. 59 ; ἰέναι Id.3.77 ; χρῆσθαι Id.6.112 ; χωρεῖν Th.4.31 ; δ. ξυνῆψαν E. *Ph.*1101 ; βοηθῆσαι δ. Ar.*Fr.*551 : in pl., δρόμοις A.*Pr.*838, *Supp.* 819. 2. *foot-race*, as a contest, *IG*2.594.11, al. : prov., περὶ τοῦ παντὸς δρόμου (-μου codd.) θεῖν to *run* for one's life, Hdt.8.74 ; τὸν περὶ ψυχῆς δρόμον δραμεῖν Ar.*V.*375 ; περὶ ψυχῆς δ δ. Pl.*Tht.*173a : generally, *contest*, πλαγᾶν δρόμος, i. e. a pugilistic *contest*, Pi.*I.*5(4).60. 3. *lap* in a race, S.*El.*726 (interpol. ib.691) ; ἐν τῷ δευτέρῳ δ. Arist.*HA* 579ᵃ8. 4. in speaking, *rapid delivery*, Longin.*Rh.*p.312 S. II. *place for running*, δρόμοι εὐρέες *runs* for cattle, Od.4.605. 2. *race-course*, Hdt.6.126, E.*Andr.*599. 3. *public walk*, ἐν εὐσκίοις δ. Ἀκαδήμου Eup.32, cf. *IG*2².1126.36, etc. ; *colonnade*, Pl.*Tht.*144c ; κατάστεγος δ. *cloister*, Id.*Euthd.*273a ; δ. ξυστός Aristias 5 ; in Crete, = γυμνάσιον, Suid., cf. *SIG*463.14 (Itanos, iii B.C.) ; δύ' ἢ τρεῖς δρόμους περιεληλυθότε having taken two or three *turns in the cloister*, Pl.*Euthd.* l. c. ; in Egypt, *avenue* of Sphinxes at entrance of temples, *OGI*56.52 (Canopus, Ptol. III), Str.17.1.28, etc. ; δ. τοῦ ἱεροῦ *BGU* 1130.10 (i B.C.). 4. *orchestra* in the theatre (Tarent.), Hsch. 5. metaph., ἔξω δρόμου or ἐκτὸς δρόμου φέρεσθαι get off the *course*, i. e. wander from the point, A.*Pr.*883 (anap.), Pl.*Cra.*414b ; ἐκ δρόμου πεσεῖν A.*Ag.*1245 ; οὐδέν ἐστ' ἔξω δρόμου 'tis not foreign to the purpose, Id.*Ch.*514. III. δ. δημόσιος, = Lat. *cursus publicus*, Procop. *Vand.*1.16, *Arc.*30, Lyd.*Mag.*2.10 ; δ. ὀξύς, = Lat. *cursus velox*, ib.3. 61, *POxy.*900.7 (iv A.D.), etc.

**δρομόω,** *hasten*, Aq.*Ps.*67(68).32.

* **δρόμων,** ωνος, ὁ, *a light vessel*, Procop.*Vand.*1.11, Lyd.*Mag.*2.14, etc. II. = δρομίας II, Hsch.

**δρόξιμα,** τά, late form for τρώξιμα, *uncooked fruit*, *PLond.*5.1674 (v A.D.), *PMasp.*2 iii 10 (vi A.D.).

**δροόν·** ἰσχυρόν (Argive), Hsch.

**δροπά,** = δρεπτά, S.*Fr.*481. (Perh. due to wrong division of a compd., e. g. ἀρτίδροπος.)

**δρόπις·** τρυγητός, Hsch. **δροπίσκος,** ὁ, *flower-basket*, Id.

**δρόσαλλις,** ιδος, ἡ, a kind of *vine*, *Gp.*5.17.3 (Bithynian).

* **δροσ-ερός,** ά, όν, (δρόσος) *dewy*, *watery*, αἰθήρ, πηγαί, E.*Ba.*865 (lyr.), *Hel.*1335 ; νεφέλαι Ar.*Nu.*338 (anap.) ; *dewy*, *fresh*, λάχανα Id. *Pl.*298. 2. *tender*, *soft*, στόματα *AP*5.243 (Paul. Sil.). **-ία,** poet. -ίη, ἡ, *foam* of a horse's mouth, Orac.ap.Luc.*Alex.*53 ; *dew*, *Cat.Cod. Astr.*1.172. * **-ίζω,** *bedew*, *besprinkle*, in Med., Ar.*Ra.*1312 (lyr.), prob. in E.*Hyps.Fr.*9.4 : — later in Act., Posidon.20 J., Babr.12.16 :— Pass., Hp.*Ulc.*12 ; δεδροσισμένον νέφος *dewy*, D.L.7.152 : metaph., ἡνίκ' ἂν ὑπὸ τοῦ οἴνου δροσισθῇ ἡ ψυχή Epict.*Gnom.*26. II. intr., *form dew*, Arist.*Pr.*939ᵇ38 ; δροσίζων ἱδρώς Herod.Med. in *Rh.Mus.* 58.99 ; *to be in a flaccid condition*, of the body, Philostr.*Gym.*48, cf. Archig.ap.Aët.6.3. **-ιμος,** ον, = sq., Plu.2.918a. **-ινός,** ή, όν, = δροσερός, *AP*9.570 (Phld.). **-ισμός,** ὁ, *exposure to dew*, Olymp.Alch.p.87 B.

**δροσο-βολέω,** *to shed dew*, ὁ ἀὴρ δροσοβολεῖ Plu.2.659b. **-βόλος,** ον, *dewy*, χῶραι Thphr.*CP*3.24.4 ; ἀήρ ib.6.18.3 ; πανσέληνοι Plu.2. 917f. **-γόνος,** ον, *dew-producing*, of the sign Aquarius, *Cat.Cod. Astr.*7.209. **-ειδής,** ές, *dew-like*, Adv. -ειδῶς Gal.*Nat.Fac.*2.3, al., Paul.Aeg.4.17. **-είμων,** ον, gen. ονος, *dew-clad*, νεφέλαι Orph.*H.* 21.6, 51.6. **-εις,** εσσα, εν, *dewy*, Sapph.*Supp.*24.12, etc. ; πεδία A.R. 1.1282, cf. Coluth.343 ; *shedding dew*, Σελήνη Nonn.*D.*40.376 ; *fresh*, λουτρά E.*Tr.*833 ; χείλεα *AP*5.269 (Paul. Sil.). **-λιθος,** ὁ, a *gem*, Isid.*Etym.*16.12.2. **-μελι,** ιτος, τό, = ἀερόμελι, Gal.6.739. **-ομαι,** Pass., *to be wet with dew*, *Anacreont.*53.31. **-παγής,** ές, *dew-nourished*, Ph.Byz.*Mir.*1. **-πάχνη,** ἡ, *hoar-frost*, *rime*, Arist. *Mu.*394ᵃ26.

* **δρόσος,** ἡ, *dew*, Hdt.2.68, Pl.*Ti.*59e : pl., A.*Ag.*336, S.*Aj.*1208 (lyr.), etc. 2. in Poets, *pure water*, ποντία δ. A.*Eu.*904 ; δρόσῳ ἐναλίᾳ, θαλασσίᾳ, E.*IT*255, 1192 ; ποταμίᾳ δ. Id.*Hipp.*127 (lyr.) ; ποταμίαισι δρόσοις ib.78 ; ἐπὶ κρηναίαισι δρόσοις Id.*IA*182 (lyr.) ; δρόσος alone, Ἀχελῴου δ. Id.*Andr.*167 ; καθαραῖς δρόσοις Id.*Ion* 96 (lyr.) ; ἐκ ποταμῶν δρόσον ἄρατε Ar.*Ra.*1339. 3. of other liquids, δ. ἀμπέλου Pi.*O.*7.2 ; δ. φοινία A.*Ag.*1390, etc. ; ἀπόπτυστος Ar.*Eq.* 1285 ; of oil, *AP*5.3 (Phld.) ; of honey, Philostr.*Her.*19.19 ; δ. καλάμου *sugar*, Antyll.ap.Orib.10.27.18 : metaph., δρόσος κώμων Pi.*P.* 5.99. 4. *down* on the cheek, δ. καὶ χνοῦς Ar.*Nu.*978, cf. Plu.2. 79d. II. metaph., *the young of animals*, A.*Ag.*141 (lyr., pl.) : in sg., δ. Ἡφαίστοιο Call.*Hec.*1.2.3.

**δροσώδης,** ες, *dewy*, *moist*, κύπειρος Pherecr.109 ; λιβάς Antiph. 52.13 ; κρεάδια Alex.124.12 ; ἱδρώς Plu.2.695c ; δ. ὕδατος νοτίς a spring of *fresh* water, E.*Ba.*705.

**Δρουίδης,** = Δρυΐδης, prob. in D.S.5.31.

**δροῦνα·** ἡ ἀρχή (Tyrrhen.), Hsch.

**δρυάζειν·** φλυαρεῖν, Hsch. : — also **δρυάσαι·** κατακολυμβῆσαι, Id. ; cf. δενδρυάζω II. **δρύακες,** = δρύοχοι, Id.

**δρυάριον,** τό, Dim. of δρῦς, Eust.1715.52.

* **Δρυάς,** άδος, ἡ, (δρῦς) *a Dryad*, nymph whose life was bound up with that of her tree, Plu.*Caes.*9. II. a *snake*, Androm.ap.Gal. 14.33.

**δρυαταί·** ἄδιψοι, ψεῦσται, Hsch.

**δρυαχαρνεύς,** έως, ὁ, *tough Acharnian*, *Com.Adesp.*75.

**δρύεται·** κρύπτεται, Hsch.

**δρυηκόπος,** ον, (κόπτω) *wood-cutting*, Lyc.1378.

**Δρυΐδης,** ου, ὁ, *Druid*, Arist.*Fr.*35, Str.4.4.4.

**δρυ-ΐνας,** ου, ὁ, *serpent living in hollow oaks*, Nic.*Th.*411, Dsc. *Ther.*11. * **-ϊνος,** η, ον, (δρῦς) *oaken*, Od.21.43, Hp.*Fract.*13, E.*Ba.* 1103, etc. ; δ. πῦρ a fire *of oak-wood*, Theoc.9.19 ; μέλι δ. honey *from the hollow of an oak*, *AP*9.72 (Antip.(?)) ; ὁ δ. στέφανος *Mon.Anc. Gr.*17.24. **-ϊνών,** ῶνος, ὁ, *oak-coppice*, *IG*1².328 (dub.). **-ίτης** [ῑ], ου, ὁ, in Thphr.*CP*1.2.2, said to be a kind of *cypress*. II. δ. λίθος a *precious stone*, Plin.37.188. **-καρπον,** τό, *acorn* or *similar fruit*, Lyc.83, Eust.773.49 (in pl.). **-κολάπτης,** v. δρυοκολάπτης.

**δρυμάζω** or **-σσω,** = δρύπτω ; fut. δρυμάξω *Com.Adesp.*986.

**δρυμεῖτις** (sc. γῆ), ιδος, ἡ, *woodland*, *Stud.Pal.*22.159 (ii A.D.).

**δρύμιος,** α, ον, *passing through a copse*, ῥόϝος *Inscr.Cypr.*135.19 H.

**δρυμίους·** τοὺς κατὰ τὴν χώραν κακοποιοῦντας, Hsch.

**δρυμίς,** ίδος, ἡ, = δρυάς, δ. Νύμφαι *An.Ox.*1.225.

**δρυμόνιος,** α, ον, *haunting the woods*, epith. of Artemis, Orph.*H.* 36.12.

* **δρυμός,** ὁ, *copse*, *thicket*, S.*OT*1399, *SIG*57.28 (Milet., v B.C.), E. *Hipp.*1127 (lyr.), *Tab.Heracl.*1.19, *PLille* 5.13 (iii B.C.), Lxx *Ec.*2.6, Plb.2.15.2, *AP*7.544, etc. : pl., A.*Fr.*304.10, Theoc.1.117, *AP*6.13 (Leon.), 9.4 (Cyllen.), 84 (Antiphan.), Plu.*Comp.Per.Fab.*1. II. Hom. has only pl., δρυμά, τά, Il.11.118, Od.10.150, 197, 251, also in Simm.15 (prob.) ; δρυμά in late Ep., D.P.492, Opp.*C.*1.64. III. δρυμός· φρούριον, Hsch., perh. in this sense in *PPetr.*2 p.140. (Cf. Skt. *drumá-* 'tree', Slav. *drŭmŭ* 'thicket' : ῠ is original, ῡ borrowed from δρῦς.)

**δρυμο-φύλαξ,** *saltuarius*, *Gloss.* **-χαρής,** ές, *delighting in the woods*, Orph.*H.*51.13.

**δρυμ-ώδης,** ες, *woody*, τόποι D.S.3.26, cf. Str.8.3.25 ; λόφος *Inscr. Prien.*42.46 (ii/i B.C.). **-ών,** ῶνος, ὁ, = δρυμός, J.*AJ*8.6.5, al., Babr.45.11, Opp.*C.*2.78.

**δρυο-βάλανος** [βᾰ], ἡ, *acorn*, Str.15.3.18 : sg. in collect. sense, Id.3.3.7. **-βαφής,** ές, *dyed with oak-bark*, ἱμάτια Hsch. **-γόνος,** ον, (γενέσθαι) *oak-grown*, ὄρη Ar.*Th.*114. **-εις,** εσσα, εν, *full of oaks*, *woody*, Il.2.783ᵃ, Nonn.*D.*5.60. II. *made of oak-wood*, ib. 17.322, al. **-κοίτης,** ου, ὁ, *dweller on the oak*, τέττιξ *AP*7.190 (Anyte or Leon.). **-κολάπτης,** ου, ὁ, *woodpecker*, of which Arist. distinguishes four species, the *great black*, *Picus martius*, the *green*, *Picus viridis*, and the *spotted* (both *greater* and *less*), *Picus major* and *minor*, *HA*593ᵃ5, cf. 614ᵇ7, Str.5.4.2 ; = Lat. *picus*, D.H.1.14 :—also

**δρῠκολάπτης**, Ar.*Av.*480,979; **δρῠοκόλαψ**, Hsch. s.v. ἵππα (prob. l.); **δρῠοκόπος**, Arist.*PA*662ᵇ7. **-πᾰγής** στόλος, in S.*Fr* 702, expld. by Eust.1726.16 as ὁ δρύϊνος πάσσαλος, the *oak-fastening* instrument, an *oaken* bolt. (Cf. στόλος, = ἔμβολον, A.*Pers.*408.) **-πετής**, ές, = δρυπεπής (v. δρυπεπής), Gal.6.608; **δαφνίδες** Dsc.1.40 (s.v.l.). **-πτερίς**, έως, ὁ, *black oak-fern*, *Asplenium onopteris*, Dsc. 4.187.

※ **δρύος**, ὁ, *woodland*, *POxy.*1044.8, al. (ii/iii A.D.).

**δρῠο-τομία**, ἡ, *felling of trees for timber*, Pl.*Lg.*678d. **-τομική** (sc. τέχνη), ἡ, = foreg., Id.*Plt.*288d. **-τόμος**, ὁ, = δρυτόμος, Aesop. 35, Gal.13.573, etc. [δρῡ- v.l. in Q.S.1.250.] **-φακτος**, coined as etym. of δρύφακτος, Sch.Ar.*Eq.*672.

※ **δρύοχοι** [ῠ], οἱ, (δρυ- 'wooden structure', 'ship' (cf. δόρυ), ἔχω) *props* or *shores* upon which is laid the frame of a new ship, Od.19.574, cf. Eust. et Sch. ad loc.; κατὰ δρυόχων ἐπάγη σανίς Epigr.ap.Moschion. ap.Ath.5.209c; ἐκ δρυόχων ναυπηγεῖσθαι to build a ship from *the keel*, Plb.1.38.5; δρυόχους ἐπεβάλλετο νηός A.R.1.723: metaph., δρυόχους τιθέναι δράματος ἀρχάς to lay *the keel* of a new play, Ar.*Th.*52: οἷον ἐκ δρυόχων Pl.*Ti.*81b, cf. Plu.2.321e: sg. only in Poll.1.85. II. = δρυμά, *woods*, *AP*6.16 (Arch.): heterocl. pl. δρύοχα E.*El.*1163 (lyr.).

**δρύοψ** [ῠ], οπος, ὁ, a kind of *woodpecker*, Ar.*Av.*304.

**δρῠπεπής**, ές, *ripened on the tree, quite ripe*, ἐλάα Chionid.7, Eup. 312; αἱ δρυπεπεῖς (sc. ἰσχάδες) Ar.*Lys.*564, Callias Com.21: by a com. metaph., μᾶζαι δ. Cratin.165, Telecl.38; δ. ἑταῖραι Ar.*Fr.* 141: heterocl. acc. sg., τὴν ἀλίπαστον δρύπεπα, as Subst., *AP*6.191 (Longus):—**δρυπετής** or **-πέτης** (πίπτω), *ready to fall, over-ripe*, is a constant v.l., cf. Sch.Orib.2 p.746 D., Hsch.

**δρυπίς**, ίδος, ἡ, (δρύπτω) *knot-wort*, *Drypis spinosa*, Thphr.*HP*1. 10.6.

**δρυπολεῖ**· ταλαιπωρεῖ, ὀρειβατεῖ, πυρὶ πολιορκεῖ, Hsch.

**δρύππᾱ**, ἡ, *olive*, *AP*6.299 (Phan.), Ath.2.56a.

**δρύππιος**, α, ον, perh. *planted with olives*, ἀγρός *IG*9(1).61.20 (Daulis).

**δρυπτερίς**, = δρυοπτερίς, Hsch.

**δρύπτην**· ἀλήτην, Hsch.; cf. δρώπτης.

**δρύπτω**, E.*El.*150: fut. δρύψω (κατα-) v.l. in *AP*5.42 (Rufin.): aor. ἔδρυψα, Ep. δρύψα Il.16.324:—**Med.**, Hes.*Sc.*243 (κατα-, tm.), E.*Hec.* 655 (lyr.): aor. δρυψάμενος Od.2.153:—**Pass.**, *AP*7.2 (Antip. Sid.): plpf. δέδρυπτο Q.S.14.391:—*tear, strip*, βραχίονα δουρὸς ἀκωκὴ δρύψ' ἀπὸ μυώνων Il. l.c.:—Med., δρυψαμένω δ' ὀνύχεσσι παρειὰς ἀμφί τε δειράς *tearing each other's* cheeks and necks all round, Od. l.c.: mostly in sign of mourning, δρύπτεν κάρα E.*El.*150 (lyr.); ἑκάτερθε παρειάς A.R.3.672; also δρύπτεσθαι παρειάν *to tear one's* cheek, E. *Hec.*655; without παρειάν, X.*Cyr.*3.1.13. 2. metaph., τὴν δὲ χοῖρον αὐονὴ δρύπτει Herod.8.2.—Poet., X. and later Prose, as Philostr. *VA*3.38.

※ **δρῦς**, ἡ (Pelop. ὁ, acc. to Sch.Ar.*Nu.*401, cf. *IG*9(1).485.5 (Thyrrheum), but fem. in Arc., *Schwyzer* 664.23): gen. δρυός: acc. δρῦν (δρύα Q.S.3.280): nom. pl. δρύες Il.12.132, A.*Pr.*832, etc., δρῦς Thphr.*CP*2.9.2, Paus.8.12.1: acc. pl. δρῦς Ar.*Eq.*528, *Nu.*402, δρύας S.*Fr.*403, Call.*Del.*84, *AP*7.8 (Antip. Sid.): gen. δρυῶν Hdt.7.218: dual δρύε Hdn.Gr.1.420. [ῠ, exc. in δρῦς, δρῦν: gen. δρῡός at the beginning of a verse, Hes.*Op.*436]:—originally, *tree* (δρῦν ἐκάλουν οἱ παλαιοὶ.. πᾶν δένδρον Sch.Il.11.86, cf. Hsch.); including various trees, Thphr.*HP*3.8.2; esp. *Quercus Aegilops* (φηγός) and *Quercus Ilex* (πρῖνος), cf. ἡ φηγὸς καὶ ἡ πρῖνος εἴδη δρυός Dsc.1.106; opp. πεύκη, Il.11.494; opp. πίτυς, Od.9.186, cf. Il.13.389, 23.328, etc.; στέφανος δρυός crown *of oak leaves*, *SIG*²588.7 (Delos, ii B.C.); commonly, *the oak*, δ. ὑψικάρηνοι, ὑψίκομοι, Il.12.132, 14.398, cf. 13. 389, 23.328, etc.; sacred to Zeus, who gave his oracles from the oaks of Dodona, Od.14.328; αἱ προσήγοροι δρύες A.*Pr.*832; πολύγλωσσος δ. S.*Tr.*1168, cf. Pl.*Phdr.*275b: prov., οὐ γὰρ ἀπὸ δρυός ἐσσι.. οὐδ' ἀπὸ πέτρης thou art no foundling from *the woods* or rocks, i.e. thou hast parents and a country, Od.19.163, cf. Pl.*Ap.*34d, *R.* 544d, *AP*10.55 (Pall.); but οὐ μέν πως νῦν ἔστιν ἀπὸ δρυὸς οὐδ' ἀπὸ πέτρης.. ὀαριζέμεν 'tis no time now to talk at ease from *tree* or rock, like lovers, Il.22.126; ἀλλὰ τί ἦ μοι ταῦτα περὶ δρῦν ἢ περὶ πέτρην; why all this about *trees* and rocks (i.e. things we have nothing to do with)? Hes.*Th.*35; also διὰ πέτρας καὶ διὰ δρυὸς ὁρᾶν 'to see through a brick wall', Plu.2.1083d. II. of other trees bearing acorns or mast (Paus.8.1.6), πίειρα δρῦς the resinous *wood* (of the pine), S.*Tr.*766; of the olive, E.*Cyc.*615 (lyr.); δ. θαλασσία, = ἁλίφλοιος, Ps.-Democr.*Symp.Ant.*p.5 G. III. δ. ποντία, *gulf-weed*, *Sargassum vulgare*, Thphr.*HP*4.6.9. IV. metaph., *worn-out old man*, *AP*6.254 (Myrin.), Artem.2.25. (Cogn. with δόρυ; cf. Skt. *dru-* 'wood', in compds.)

※ **δρύσσομαι**, aor. part. δρυξάμενος, perh. = δρυφάσσω, δ. τῆς γῆς ἀπὸ τῶν ὁρίων *PGrenf.*1.11.14 (ii B.C.).

※ **δρῠτόμος**, ον, *wood-cutter*, Il.11.86, Theoc.5.64, Philostr.*Im.*2.33, al.; cf. δρυοτόμος. [δρῡ- Q.S.9.163,453, 13.56.]

**δρῠφάδες**, αἱ, *nail-parings*, Hsch.; also, = λῦπαι, ὀδύναι, i.e. *lancinating pains* or *weals, bruises*, Id.

**δρυφάζω**, aor. inf. δρυφάξαι· δακεῖν, Hsch. **δρυφαίνηκα**· τὸν οὐ μέγαν (Elean), Id.

※ **δρύφακτ-ος** [ῠ], ὁ, later **τρύφακτος** *BCH*35.23 (Delos, iv B.C.), *OGI*598.3 (Jerusalem), Hdn.Gr.2.595:—*railing* or *latticed partition*, serving as *the bar* of the courts of law, the council-chamber, etc., Ar. *V.*380: mostly in pl., ὑπερεπήδων τοὺς δ. Id.*Eq.*675; ὑπὸ τοῖς δ. Id.*V.* 386; ἐπὶ τοῖς δ. ib.552, X.*HG*2.3.55: sg., δρυφάκτου τρόπῳ Apollod. *Poliorc.*172.1. 2. *hand-rail*, Plb.1.22.6,10. 3. *balcony*, Arist. *Ath.*50.2:—written **δρύφρακτοι**, Lib.*Or.*11.217. (By dissim. for δρύ-φρακτος (φράσσω), cf. Lib. l.c., Hellad.ap.Sch.Orib.2 p.746 D., Sch.Ar.*Eq.* l.c.) **-όω**, *fence, fortify*, Plb.8.4.4. **-ωμα**, ατος, τό, *enclosure*, Str.13.4.14.

**δρῠφάσσω**, *fence round, guard by a fence*, Lyc.758 (Pass.).

※ **δρύφειν**· περαίνειν, and **δρυφόμενοι**· φθειρόμενοι, Hsch.

**δρυφή** [ῠ], τό, (δρύπτω) *tearing*, and **δρυφοί**, οἱ, *scrapings*, Hsch.:—also **δρύφη**, = κλάσματα, Id. s.v. πύρνα, cf. Suid.

**δρῠφόροι**, οἱ, religious guild at Thessalonica (cf. δενδροφόρος), *BCH*38.41 (δροι- lapis).

※ **δρύψελον**, τό, lit. *bark*: of a *leaf*, Parth.*Fr.*26: **δρύψαλα**, Hsch.

※ **δρύψια**, τά, = foreg., δ. τυρῶν *AP*6.299 (Phan.).

**δρυψο-γέρων**, οντος, ὁ, (δρύπτω) *worn-out old man*, and **-παις**, παιδος, ὁ, ἡ, *coquette*, Hsch.; also, = ἐλεεινός, Id.

**δρυώδης**, ες, gloss on δρυόεις, Hsch.

**δρωκτάζεις** (δροκτ- cod.)· περιβλέπεις, Hsch.; cf. δρωπάζω, δρώπτω. **δρωμᾷ**· τρέχει, and **δρωμίσσουσα**· τρέχουσα, Id.

**δρωπάζω** (δράω B), *gaze at*, A.D.*Adv.*139.8, Hsch.

**δρωπᾰκ-ίζω**, *apply a depilatory*, δ. μέλιτι Orib.*Eup.*4.7:—Med., Arr.*Epict.*3.22.10, Hierocl.*Facet.*64:—Pass., Luc.*Demon.*50. **-ισμός**, ὁ, *the application of a pitch-plaster*, as a counter-irritant, Dsc. *Ther.*3. **-ιστέον**, *one must apply a pitch-plaster*, Orib.*Fr.* 75. ※ **-ιστής**, οῦ, ὁ, = *depilator*, *Gloss.* **-ιστός**, ή, όν, *serving as a counter-irritant*, Gal.18(2).894. **-ίστρια**, ἡ, = παρατίλτρια, Phot.

**δρῶπαξ**, ἄκος, ὁ, (δρέπω) *pitch-plaster*, Hp.*Ep.*19 (*Hermes* 53.71), Gal.6.416, Dsc.*Eup.*1.233, Archig.ap.Aët.3.180:—also neut. pl. **δρώπακα** (sc. φάρμακα), Gal.18(2).894. [ᾰ in Lat. gen., Mart.3.74, 10.65.]

**δρώπτης**· πλανήτης, πτωχός, Hsch.

**δρώπτω**, = διακόπτω ἢ διασκοπῶ, A.*Fr.*278.

※ **δρώψ**· ἄνθρωπος, Hsch. **δύα**, Dor. for δύη. II. **δύαν**· κρήνην, Id.

**δῠᾰδ-ίζω**, *make into a dyad*, in Pass., ἡ δυαδιζομένη μονάς Dam.*Pr.* 147. **-ικός**, ή, όν, (δύο) *of* or *for the number two*, Plu.2.1025d; opp. μοναδικός, Dam.*Pr.*119; δ. πᾶσα πρόοδος ib.47. Adv. **-κῶς** Procl.*in Prm.*p.915 S., Herm.*in Phdr.*p.151 A. **-ισμός**, ὁ, *making into a dyad*, Dam.*Pr.*193.

**δῠ-άζω**, *express in the dual number*, Eust.47.28. 2. Pass., *to be impressed with the sense of a thing's being double, see double*, etc., S.E.*M.*7.193. II. *make into two*, Ascl.*in Metaph.*432.12 (Pass.):—Pass., *to be halved*, of the moon, *Theol.Ar.*12. 2. *double*, Theo Sm.p.29 H., Iamb.*in Nic.*p.60 P. III. δυάζει· φλυαρεῖ, Hsch., Cyr. (cf. δρυάζω); also δυαεῖ Hsch. **-άκις**, Adv. *twice*, Ar.*Fr.* 769. **-άνδρες**, οἱ, = Lat. *duumviri*, *Wien.Stud.*24.288 (Olbasa). **-ανδρικός**, ή, όν, = *duumviralis*, ib.289. **-ᾰνερικός**, ή, όν, = foreg., *CIG*3979 (Antioch. Pisid.). **-άς**, άδος, ἡ, *the number two*, Pl.*Phd.*101c, *Prm.*149c, Arist.*Ph.*220ᵃ27, etc. 2. *dyad*, ἡ ἀόριστος δ. Arist.*Metaph.*1081ᵃ14, Alex.Aphr.*in Metaph.*58.12. 3. *pair*, Philostr.*Im.*1.6, Lib.*Or.*61.7.

**δῠάω**, (δύη) *plunge in misery*, δυόωσιν.. ἀνθρώπους Od.20.195:—Pass., pf. part. δεδυημένη Hsch.

**δυγός**, Dor. for ζυγός, *Schwyzer* 180 (Crete), 317 (Delph.), *EM* 316.57; Aeol., ib.466.36; Boeot., Choerob.*in Theod.*2.390.

**δῠ-ειδής**, ές, *of the class of the dyad*, μεσότης Dam.*Pr.*189. **-ενιαυσίως**, Adv. *twice yearly*, *PAmh.*2.148.8 (v A.D.).

※ **δῠερός**, ά, όν, (δύη) *miserable*, δυεροῦ θανάτοιο τυχεῖν *IG*3.1337, cf. Max.65,182.

**δυϝάνοι**, v. δίδωμι.

**δύη** [ῠ], ἡ, Dor. (not in Trag.) **δύα**, poet. Noun, *misery, anguish*, Od.14.215, etc.; πῆμα δύης height *of woe*, ib.338; πέλαγος ἀτηρᾶς δύης A.*Pr.*746; γενναία δ. S.*Aj.*938 (lyr.): pl., πημοναῖς δύαις τε A. *Pr.*513, cf. 181 (lyr.), 525, etc.: also in late Prose, App.*BC*4.42; Pythag. name for *two* (by false etym.), *Theol.Ar.*12.

**δῠη-πᾰθέω**, *endure misery*, Nonn.*D.*26.113. **-πᾰθής**, ές, *much-suffering*, A.R.4.1165, Opp.*H.*2.436; *painful*, τοκετός Nonn.*D.*41. 411. **-πᾰθία**, poet. -ίη, ἡ, *misery*, A.R.4.1395, *APl.*4.113 (Jul.), Hsch.:—written **-πάθεια**, *EM*291.10. **-πᾰθος**, ον, = δυηπαθής, *h.Merc.*486.

**δυθμή**, = δυσμή (q.v.).

**δῠϊκός**, ή, όν, *dual*, D.T.635.30; τὸ δ. *the dual number*, A.D. *Pron.*10.28, S.E.*M.*1.142. Adv. **-κῶς** *in the dual number*, Phoeb. *Fig.*1.4, Anon.*in Tht.*73.4; = διττῶς, Suid.

**δῠϊος** [ῠ], α, ον, = δυερός, A.*Supp.*829 (lyr.).

**δῦμα**, ατος, τό, = ἔνδυμα, *POxy.*929.8,15 (ii/iii A.D.).

**δύμεναι** [ῡ], Ep. aor. 2 inf. Act. of δύω.

※ **δύνᾰμαι** [ῠ], 2 sg. δύνασαι Il.1.393, Od.4.374, S.*Aj.*1164 (anap.), Ar.*Nu.*811 (lyr.), *Pl.*574, X.*An.*7.7.8, etc.; δύνῃ *Carm.Aur.*19, also in codd. of S.*Ph.*798, E.*Hec.*253, *Andr.*239, and later Prose, Plb. 7.11.5, Ael.*VH*13.32; Aeol. and Dor. δύνᾳ Alc.*Oxy.*1788 *Fr.*15 ii 16, Theoc.10.2, also S.*Ph.*849 (lyr.), dub. in *OT*696 (lyr.); δύνῃ is subj., Ar.*Eq.*491, cf. Phryn.337; Ion. 3 pl. δυνέαται Hdt.2.142; subj. δύνωμαι, Ion. 2 sg. δύνηαι Il.6.229 (δυνεώμεθα -ωνται as vv.ll. in Hdt.4.97, 7.163); also δύνᾱμαι Sapph.*Supp.*3.3, *GDI*4952 *A* 42 (Crete): impf. 2 sg. ἐδύνω *h.Merc.*405, X.*An.*1.6.7; later ἐδύνασο Hp.*Ep.*16 (v.l. ἠδ.), Luc.*DMort.*9.1; Ion. 3 pl. ἐδυνέατο Hdt.4.110, al. (ἠδ- codd.): fut. δυνήσομαι Od.16.238, etc.; Dor. δυνᾱσοῦμαι Archyt.3; later δυνηθήσομαι D.C.52.37: aor. ἐδυνησάμην Il.14.33, Ep. δυν- 5.621; subj. δυνήσωνται Semon.1.17, never in good Att., f.l. in

D.19.323: Pass. forms, Ep., Ion., Lyr., ἐδυνάσθην or δυνάσθην Il.23.465, al., Hdt.2.19, al., Pi.*O*.1.56, Hp.*Art*.48 (v. l. δυνηθείη), also in X.*Mem*.1.2.24, *An*.7.6.20; Trag. and Att. Prose ἐδυνήθην S.*Aj*.1067, *OT*1212 (lyr.), E.*Ion*867 (anap.), D.21.80,186: pf. δεδύνημαι D.4.30, Din.2.14, Phld.*Rh*.1.261 S.—The double augment ἠδυνάμην is Att. acc. to Moer.175, but Ion. acc. to *An.Ox*.2.374, and is found in codd. of Hdt.4.110, al., Hp.*Epid*.1.26.β', al.; ἠδύνω is required by metre in Philippid.16; but is not found in Att. Inscrr. before 300 B.C., *IG*2².678.12, al., cf. ἠδύνασθε ib.7.2711 (Acraeph., i A.D.); both forms occur in later writers: ἠδυνήθην occurs in A.*Pr*.208, and codd. of Th.4.33, Lys.3.42, etc.: δύνομαι is a late form freq. in Pap. as *UPZ*9 (ii B.C.), al. [ῠ, exc. in δῡναμένοιο Od.1.276, 11.414, Hom. *Epigr*.15.1, and pr. n. Δῡναμένη, metri gr.]

I. *to be able, strong enough* to do, c. inf. pres. et aor., Il.19.163, 1.562, etc.: fut. inf. is f.l. (πείσειν for πείθειν) in S.*Ph*.1394, (κωλύσειν for κωλῦσαι) Plb.21.11.13, etc.: freq. abs., with inf. supplied from the context, εἰ δύνασαί γε if at least thou *canst* (sc. περισχέσθαι), Il.1.393: also c. acc. Pron. or Adj., ὅσσον δύναμαι χερσίν τε ποσίν τε 20.360; [Ζεὺς] δύναται ἅπαντα Od.4.237; μέγα δυνάμενος very *powerful, mighty*, 1.276, cf. 11.414; δ. μέγιστον ξείνων Hdt.9.9, etc.; μέγα δύναται, *multum valet*, A.*Eu*.950 (lyr.); δ. Διὸς ἄγχιστα Id.*Supp*.1035; οἱ δυνάμενοι *men of power, rank, and influence*, E.*Or*.889, Th.6.39, etc.; οἱ δυνάμενοι, opp. οἱ μὴ ἔχοντες, Democr.255; opp. οἱ πένητες, Archyt.3; δυνάμενος παρά τινι *having influence* with him, Hdt.7.5, And.4.26, etc.; δύνασθαι ἐν τοῖς πρώτοις Th.4.105; δ. τοῖς χρήμασι, τῷ σώματι, Lys.6.48, 24.4; ὁ δυνάμενος *one that can maintain himself*, Id.24.12; of things, [διαφέρει] οἷς δύνανται differ in their *potentialities*, Plot.6.3.17. 2. of moral possibility, *to be able, dare, bear* to do a thing, mostly with neg., οὔτε τελευτὴν ποιῆσαι δύναται Od.1.250; σε ..οὐ δύναμαι προλιπεῖν 13.331, cf. S.*Ant*.455; οὐκέτι ἐδύνατο ἐν τῷ καθεστῶτι τρόπῳ βιοτεύειν Th.1.130; οὐδὲ σθένειν τοσοῦτον ᾠόμην τὰ σὰ κηρύγμαθ' ὥστε.. θεῶν νόμιμα δύνασθαι.. ὑπερδραμεῖν S.*Ant*.455. b. *enjoy a legal right*, δ. τῆς γεωργίας ἀπηλλάχθαι *POxy*.899.31 (ii/iii A.D.), etc. 3. with ὡς and Sup., ὡς ἐδύνατο ἀδηλότατα as secretly as they *could*, Th.7.50; ὡς δύναμαι μάλιστα κατατείνας as forcibly as I *possibly can*, Pl.*R*.367b; ὡς δύναιτο κάλλιστον Id.*Smp*.214c; ὡς ἂν δύνωμαι διὰ βραχυτάτων D.27.3, etc.; simply ὡς ἐδύνατο in the best way he *could*, X.*An*.2.6.2: with relat., ὅσους ἐδύνατο πλείστους ἀθροίσας Id.*HG*2.2.9; λαβεῖν.. οὓς ἂν σοφωτάτους δύνωμαι Alex.213. II. *to be equivalent to*, λόγοι ἔργα δυνάμενοι words *that are as good as* deeds, Th.6.40: hence, 1. of money, *to be worth*, c. acc., ὁ σίγλος δύναται ἑπτὰ ὀβολοὺς X.*An*.1.5.6, cf. D.34.23: abs., *pass, be current*, Luc.*Luct*.10. 2. of Number, etc., *to be equal* or *equivalent to*, τριηκόσιαι γενεαὶ δυνέαται μύρια ἔτεα Hdt.2.142; δυνήσεται τὴν ὑποτείνουσαν *will be equivalent to* the hypotenuse, Arist.*IA* 709ᵃ19. 3. of words, *signify, mean*, Hdt.4.110, al.; τὸ πειρηθῆναι καὶ τὸ ποιεῖν ἴσον δύναται Id.6.86.γ'; δύναται ἴσον τῷ δρᾶν τὸ νοεῖν Ar.*Fr*.691; δύναται τὸ νεοδαμῶδες ἤδη ἐλεύθερον εἶναι Th.7.58: in later Greek, δύναται τὸ "μνασθέντι" ἀντὶ τοῦ "μνασθέντος" *is equivalent to*.., Sch.Pi.*O*.7.110. b. *avail to produce*, οὐδένα καιρὸν δύναται *brings* no advantage, E.*Med*.128 (anap.), cf. Pl.*Phlb*.23d. c. of things, *mean*, '*spell*', τὸ τριβώνιον τί δύναται; Ar.*Pl*.842; αἱ ἀγγελίαι τοῦτο δύνανται they *mean* this much, Th.6.36; τὴν αὐτὴν δ. δούλωσιν Id.1.141, cf. Arist.*Pol*.1313ᵇ25. 4. Math., δύνασθαί τι *to be equivalent when squared to* a number or area, τοῖς ἐπιπέδοις ἃ δύνανται in the areas of which they [the lines] *are the roots*, Pl.*Tht*.148b; ἡ ΒΓ τῆς Α μεῖζον δύναται τῇ ΔΖ *the square on* ΒΓ *is greater* than *the square on* Α by the *square on* ΔΖ, Euc.10.17; αἱ δυνάμεναι αὐτὰ [τὰ μεγέθη] the lines *representing* their *square roots*, ib.*Def*.4, cf. *Prop*.22; αὐξήσεις δυνάμεναί τε καὶ δυναστευόμεναι increments both *in the roots* and *powers* of numbers, Pl.*R*.546b; τὴν ὑποτείνουσαν ταῖς περὶ τὴν ὀρθὴν ἴσον δυναμένην Plu.2.720a, cf. Iamb.*Comm.Math*.17; ἡ δυναμένη, Pythag. name for the *hypotenuse* of a right-angled triangle, Alex.Aphr.*in Metaph*.75.31. b. of numbers multiplied together, *come to*, Papp.1.24,27. III. impers., οὐ δύναται, c. aor. inf., *it cannot be, is not to be*, τοῖσι Σπαρτιήτῃσι καλλιερῆσαι οὐκ ἐδύνατο Hdt.7.134, cf. 9.45; δύναται *it is possible*, Plu.2.440e (s. v. l.).

**δῠνᾰμερός**, ά, όν, *potent*, of drugs: hence as Subst., φυσικὰ δυναμερά, title of work by Ps.-Bolus, Suid. s. v. Βῶλος, cf. Archig.ap.Aët.3.114.

**δῠνᾰμικός**, ή, όν, *powerful, efficacious*, ἐρωτήματα Chrysipp.*Stoic*.2.90 (Comp.); τὸ τοῦ λόγου δ. Phld.*Rh*.1.378S. (Sup.); λόγος, of a magician's spell, Ps.-Callisth.1.3; πρός τι Plb.22.21.4, Onos.12.2 (Comp.); κατὰ τὴν σωματικὴν ἕξιν Plb.36.16.3 (Sup.); of wine, *potent*, Ath.1.26b (Sup.). 2. *potential*, τὸ δ., opp. τὸ ὑποστατικόν, τὸ ἐνεργητικόν, Dam.*Pr*.61. b. Gramm., *expressing possibility*, δ. σύνδεσμος (of κα) Sch.Theoc.1.4.

✻ **δύνᾰμις** [ῠ], ἡ, gen. εως, Ion. ιος, Ion. dat. δυνάμι: (δύναμαι):—*power, might*, in Hom., esp. of *bodily strength*, εἴ μοι δ. γε παρείη Od.2.62, cf. Il.8.294; οἵη ἐμὴ δ. καὶ χεῖρες Od.20.237; ἡ δ. τῶν νέων Antipho 4.3.2, etc.: generally, *strength, power, ability* to do anything, πὰρ δύναμιν beyond one's *strength*, Il.13.787; in Prose, παρὰ δ. τολμηταί Th.1.70, etc.; ὑπὲρ δ. D.18.193; opp. κατὰ δ. as far as *lies in one*, Hdt.3.142, etc. (κὰδ δ. Hes.*Op*.336); εἰς δύναμιν Cratin.172, Pl.*R*.458e, etc.; πρὸς τὴν δ. Id.*Phdr*.231a. 2. *outward power, influence, authority*, A.*Pers*.174 (anap.), *Ag*.779 (lyr.); καταπαύσαντα τὴν Κύρου δ. Hdt.1.90; δυνάμει προὔχοντες Th.7.21, etc.; ἐν δ. εἶναι, γενέσθαι, X.*HG*4.4.5, D.13.29. 3. *force for war, forces*, δ. ἀνδρῶν Hdt.5.100, cf. Pl.*Mx*.240d, Plb.1.41.2, Lxx *Ge*.21.22, *OGI*139.8 (ii B.C.); μετὰ δυνάμεων ἱκανῶν Wilcken *Chr*.10 (ii B.C.), etc.; δ. καὶ πεζὴ καὶ ἱππικὴ καὶ ναυτικὴ X.*An*.1.3.12; πέντε δυνάμεσι πεφρουρημένον, of the five projecting rows of sarissae in the phalanx, Ascl.*Tact*.5.2, al. 4. *a power, quantity*, χρημάτων δ. Hdt.7.9.α'. 5. *means*, κατὰ δύναμιν Arist.*EE*1243ᵇ12; opp. παρὰ δ., 2*Ep.Cor*.8.3; κατὰ δ. τῶν ὑπαρχόντων *BGU*1051.17 (Aug.). II. *power, faculty, capacity*, αἱ ἀμφὶ τὸ σῶμα δ. Hp.*VM*14; αἱ τοῦ σώματος δυνάμεις Pl.*Tht*.185e; ἡ τῆς ὄψεως δ. Id.*R*.532a; ἡ τῶν λεγόντων δ. D.22.11: c. gen. rei, *capacity for*, τῶν ἔργων Arist.*Pol*.1309ᵃ35; τοῦ λέγειν Id.*Rh*.1362ᵇ22; τοῦ λόγου, τῶν λόγων, Men.578, Alex.94; δ. στρατηγική Plb.1.84.6; δ. ἐν πραγματείᾳ Id.2.56.5; δ. συνθετική D.H.*Comp*.2: abs., any *natural capacity* or *faculty*, that may be improved and may be used for good or ill, Arist.*Top*.126ᵃ37, cf. *MM*1183ᵇ28. 2. *elementary force*, such as heat, cold, etc., Hp.*VM*16, Arist.*PA*646ᵃ14; ἡ τοῦ θερμοῦ δ. ib.650ᵃ5; θερμαντικὴ δ. Epicur.*Fr*.60, cf. Polystr.p.23W. b. *property, quality*, ἰδίην δύναμιν καὶ φύσιν ἔχειν Hp.*VM*13, cf. *Nat.Hom*.5, *Vict*.1.10; esp. of the *natural properties* of plants, etc., αἱ δ. τῶν φυομένων, τῶν σπερμάτων, X.*Cyr*.8.8.14, Thphr.*HP*8.11.1; *productive power*, τῆς γῆς Id.*Oec*.16.4; μετάλλων Id.*Vect*.4.1: generally, *function, faculty*, δύναμις φυσική, ζωική, ψυχική, Gal.10.635; περὶ φυσικῶν δ., title of work by Galen. c. in pl., *agencies*, ὑπάρχειν ἐν τῇ φύσει τὰς τοιαύτας δυνάμεις (sc. the gods) Polystr.p.10W. d. *function, meaning*, of part in whole, Id.p.17W. e. in Music, *function, value*, of a note in the scale, δ. ἐστὶ τάξις φθόγγου ἐν συστήματι Cleonid.*Harm*.14, cf. Aristox.*Harm*.p.69M.; μέση κατὰ δύναμιν, opp. κατὰ θέσιν, Ptol.*Harm*.2.5. 3. *faculty, art*, or *craft*, Pl.*R*.532d, Arist.*Metaph*.1018ᵃ30, *EN*1094ᵃ10, Arr.*Epict*.1.1.1; δ. σκεπτική the *doctrine* of the Sceptics, S.E.*M*.7.1. 4. *a medicine*, Timostr.7, etc.; δ. ἁπλαῖ Hp.*Decent*.9, Aret.*CD*1.4, etc.; δ. πολυφάρμακοι Plu.2.403c, Gal.13.365: in pl., *collection of formulae* or *prescriptions*, Orib.10.33. b. *action* of medicines, περὶ τῆς ἁπλῶν φαρμάκων δ., title of work by Galen; also, *potency*, δυνάμει θερμά, ψυχρά, Id.1.672, al. 5. *magically potent substance* or *object*, *PMag.Leid.V*.8.12: in pl., *magical powers*, Hld.4.7. III. *force* or *meaning* of a word, Lys.10.7, Pl.*Cra*.394b, Diog.Oen.12, Phld.*Sign*.31, etc. b. phonetic *value* of sounds or letters, Plb.10.47.8, D.H.*Comp*.12, Luc.*Jud.Voc*.5, etc. 2. *worth* or *value* of money, Th.6.46, 2.97, Plu.*Lyc*.9, *Sol*.15. IV. *capability of existing or acting, potentiality*, opp. *actuality* (ἐνέργεια), Arist.*Metaph*.1047ᵇ31, 1051ᵃ5, etc.: hence δυνάμει as Adv., *virtually*, ὕστερον ὂν τῇ τάξει, πρότερον τῇ δυνάμει.. ἐστί D.3.15; opp. ἐνεργείᾳ, Arist.*APo*.86ᵃ28, al.; opp. ἐντελεχείᾳ, Id.*Ph*.193ᵇ8, al. V. Math., *power*, κατὰ μεταφορὰν ἡ ἐν γεωμετρίᾳ λέγεται δ. Id.*Metaph*.1019ᵇ33; usu. *second power, square*, κατὰ δύναμιν *in square*, Pl.*Ti*.54b, cf. *Theol.Ar*.11, etc.: chiefly in dat., [εὐθεῖα] δυνάμει ἴση a line *the square* on which is equal to an area, ἡ ΒΑ ἐλάσσων ἐστὶν ἢ διπλασίων δυνάμει τῆς ΑΚ the *square* on ΒΑ is less than double of the *square* on ΑΚ, Archim.*Sph.Cyl*.2.9: εὐθεῖαι δ. σύμμετροι commensurable *in square*, Euc.10*Def*.2; ἡ δυνάμει δεκάς the series $1^2 + 2^2 .. + 10^2$, *Theol.Ar*.64. b. *square number*, Pl.*Ti*.32a. c. *square* of an unknown quantity ($x^2$), Dioph.*Def*.2, al. 2. *square root* of a number which is not a perfect square, *surd*, opp. μῆκος, Pl.*Tht*.147d. 3. *product* of two numbers, ἡ ἀμφοῖν (sc. τριάδος καὶ δυάδος) δ. ἑξάς Ph.1.3, cf. Iamb.*in Nic*.p.108P.; δυνάμει *in product*, Hero *Metr*.1.15, *Theol.Ar*.33. VI. concrete, *powers*, esp. of divine beings, αἱ δ. τῶν οὐρανῶν Lxx *Is*.34.4, cf. 1*Ep.Pet*.3.22, al., Ph.1.587, *Corp.Herm*.1.26, Porph.*Abst*.2.34: sg., *Act.Ap*.8.10, *PMag.Par*.1.1275; πολυώνυμος δ., of God, Secund.*Sent*.3. VII. *manifestation of divine power, miracle*, *Ev.Matt*.11.21, al., Buresch *Aus Lydien* 113, etc.

**δῠνᾰμο-δύνᾰμις**, εως, ἡ, *square multiplied by square, fourth power*, Hero *Metr*.1.17; *fourth power of unknown quantity* ($x^4$), Dioph.*Def*.1 (pl.), al.: – hence **–δυνᾰμοστόν**, τό, *the fraction* $1/x^4$, Id.*Def*.3, al. **–κῠβος**, ὁ, *square multiplied by cube, fifth power*, Hippol.*Haer*.1.2.10; *fifth power of unknown quantity* ($x^5$), Dioph.*Def*.1 (pl.), al.:—hence **–κυβοστόν**, τό, *the fraction* $1/x^5$, Id.*Def*.3, al.

**δῠνᾰμοστόν**, τό, *the fraction* $1/x^2$, Dioph.*Def*.3, al.

**δῠνᾰμ-όω**, *strengthen*, Lxx *Ec*.10.10, Thd.*Da*.9.27, Polem.*Call*.30, Porph.*Sent*.35, Sall.16, Procl.*Inst*.70, al.:—Pass., *Ep.Col*.1.11, etc. 2. in magic, *put power into*, σῶμα *PMag.Leid.W*.7.16; πρᾶγμα ib.*V*.8.19; τινά *PMag.Par*.1.197:—Pass., *PMag.Berol*.2.121. **–ωσις**, εως, ἡ, *strengthening, fortifying, invigoration*, ψυχῆς Plot.4.6.3. **–ωτικός**, ή, όν, *strengthening*, ἡ δύναμις τῶν πάντων -ωτάτων (sc. αἴτιον) Dam.*Pr*.61.

**δύνᾰσις** [ῠ], εως, ἡ, poet. for δύναμις, Pi.*P*.4.238, B.9.49, S.*Ant*.604 (lyr.), 952 (lyr.), E.*Ion*1012; ἐν (i. e. ἐς) δύνασιν *pro virili parte*, *IG*2².1126.5 (Amphict. Delph.).

✻ **δυναστ-εία**, ἡ, *power, lordship, domination*, S.*OT*593, D.18.67; δ. ὀλίγων ἀνδρῶν Th.3.62; πολιτικαὶ δ. *the exercise of* political *power*, Pl.*Tht*.176c; οἱ τὰς δ. ἔχοντες Isoc.2.8, cf. 9.19, Plb.3.18.1. II. *close oligarchy*, opp. ἰσονομία, Th.4.78, cf. And.2.27, X.*HG*5.4.46, etc.; ὑπὸ τῶν ὀλίγων δ. Pl.*Plt*.291d; opp. πολιτεία, Arist.*Pol*.1272ᵇ10; distd. fr. ὀλιγαρχία, ib.1292ᵇ10, cf. 1293ᵃ31: in pl., of the Roman Senate, D.C.52.1. III. in pl., *mighty deeds*, Lxx 4*Ki*.13.12, al. **–ειρα**, ἡ, fem. of δυναστήρ, *Tab.Defix.Aud* 38.11 (Alexandria, iii A.D.). **–ευμα**, ατος, τό, in pl., *natural resources*, τὰ δ. τοῦ Λιβάνου Lxx 3*Ki*.2.46c. ✻ **–ευτικός**, ή, όν, *arbitrary*, ὀλιγαρχία Arist.*Pol*.1298ᵃ32; *oligarchical*, αἵρεσις ib.1306ᵃ18; ἰατρεία (opp. πολιτική) ib.1272ᵇ3; πόλεις καὶ χῶραι Phld.*Rh*.2.145 S.; λόγος Plu.2.818a; *tyrannical*, δούλωσις Porph.*Abst*.1.8. ✻ **–εύω**, *hold power* or *lordship, be powerful* or *influential*, Hdt.9.2, Isoc.12.82, *OGI*56.12, etc.; τὸ -εῦον, opp.

δῆμος, Th.6.89; ἡ πόλις τῶν λοιπέων ἐδυνάστευε μέγιστον Hdt.5.97: c. gen., *to be lord over*, Οἰχαλίας D.S.4.31: metaph., αἱ ἄλογοι ἡδοναὶ δ. ψυχῆς Ph.1.19: c. dat., Ath.14.624d: generally, *prevail, be prevalent*, of a wind, of climate, Hp.*Aph*.3.5, *Aër*.12; *to be influential, potent*, ἐν τῷ σώματι Id.*VM*16, cf. Herophil.ap.Gal.12.619:—Pass., *to be ruled*, πρὸς μυρίων Ph.2.503. **II.** Math., in Pass., *to be concerned with powers* of numbers, Pl.*R*.546b. **-ης**, ου, ὁ, *lord, master, ruler*, of Zeus, S.*Ant*.608 (lyr.); ἄνδρες δ. *the chief men* in a state, Hdt.2.32, cf. Pl.*R*.473d, etc.; *petty chief, princelet*, Th.7.33, etc.; ἡγεμόσι καὶ δ. καὶ βασιλεῦσιν Plb.9.23.5, cf. 10.34.2, Posidon.50J., Str. 17.3.25; λαμπροὶ δυνάσται, of the stars, A.*Ag*.6. **-ικός**, ή, όν, *of* or *for a* δυνάστης, *arbitrary*, Arist.*Pol*.1320$^b$31 (Sup.): Comp., *more potent*, Gal.6.396. **-ις**, ιδος, ἡ, fem. of δυνάστης, Demetr.*Eloc*. 292; τύχη ἡ πάντων δ. ἀνθρώπων dub. in Phld.*Mort*.24. **-ωρ**, ορος, ὁ, = δυνάστης, E.*IA*280 (lyr.).

⊛ **δῠνᾰτ-έω**, = δύναμαι, δυνατήσει τὸ συμβαῖνον ἴσχειν Phld.*Sign*. 11. **2.** *to be mighty*, 2*Ep.Cor*.13.3. **-ης**, ου, ὁ, poet. for δυνάστης, ὦ δυνάτα A.*Pers*.674 (lyr., cod. Med.). ⊛ **-ός**, ή, όν, also ός, όν Pi.*N*.2.14, Apollon.Cit.2:—*strong, mighty*, in body or mind, ὅ τι ἦν αὐτῶν δυνατώτατον *the ablest-bodied men*, Hdt.9.31; *sound in limb*, opp. ἀδύνατος, Lys.24.12; σῶμα δ. πρός τι X.*Oec*.7.23; χερσὶ καὶ ψυχᾷ δ. Pi.*N*.9.39; τοῖς σώμασι καὶ ταῖς ψυχαῖς X.*Mem*.2.1.19; εἴς τι Pl.*Hp.Mi*.366a; κατά τι ib.366d (Sup.): c. acc., ibid. (Sup.); of ships, *fit for service*, Th.7.60; of things, δυνατώτερον ἀδικία δικαιοσύνης Pl.*R*.351a; λόγος a *powerful* argument, Epicur.*Ep*.1 p.31 U.; δ. προτείχισμα Plb.10.31.8. **2.** c. inf., *able* to do, Hdt.1.97, etc.; δ. λῦσαι *mighty* to loose, Pi.*O*.10(11).9; λέγειν τε καὶ πράσσειν -ώτατος Th.1.139, Pl.*Prt*.319a; -ώτατοι καὶ τοῖς σώμασιν καὶ τοῖς χρήμασιν λητουργεῖν Decr.ap.Arist.*Ath*.29.5; ἐὰν τοὺς δ. ἄρχειν X.*Ath*.1.3; ὅσονπερ δ. εἰμι, with inf. omitted, E.*Or*.523. **3.** of outward power, *powerful, influential*, S.*El*.219; τῶν Ἑλλήνων δυνατώτατοι Hdt.1.53; οἱ δ. *the chief men of rank and influence*, Th.2.65; χρήμασι δ. Id.1.13, etc., cf. *OGI*669.13 (i A.D.). **4.** *able to produce, productive*, χώρα -ωτέρα εἰς τὴν καρπῶν ἔκφυσιν *Gp*.2.21.5. **5.** *potential*, Arist.*Metaph*.1048$^a$27. **II.** Pass., of things, *possible*, οὐ δύνατον γένεσθαι Sapph.*Supp*.5.21, cf. Hdt.9.111, A.*Ag*.97 (lyr.), etc.; ὁδὸς δυνατὴ καὶ τοῖς ὑποζυγίοις πορεύεσθαι *practicable*, X.*An*.4.1.24; λόγου δ. κατανοῆσαι Pl.*Phd*.90c; βίον τοῖς πλείστοις κοινωνῆσαι δ. Arist.*Pol*.1295$^a$30; κατὰ τὸ δυνατόν, *quantum fieri possit*, Pl.*Cra*.422d, D.3.6, etc.; ἐς τὸ δ. Hdt.3.24; εἰς ὅσον ἀνθρώπῳ δ. μάλιστα Pl.*Phdr*.277a; ἐκ τῶν δυνατῶν X.*An*.4.2.23; ἐπὶ τὸ δ. Id.*Cyn*.5.8; ἐν δυνατῷ εἶναι *BCH*29.172 (Delos, ii B.C.); also ὅσον δυνατόν E.*IA*997; ὅσον καθ' ἡμᾶς δ. Id.*Ba*.183; esp. with Sup., ὡς δ. πλεῖστον Isoc.12.278; ὡς δ. κακίστους X.*Mem*.4.5.5; γνώμη ὡς δ. δικαιοτάτη D.24.13; τὰ δ. things *which are practicable*, Th.5.89, cf. Arist.*Rh*.1359$^b$1. **III.** Adv. -τῶς *strongly, powerfully*, εἰπεῖν δ. Aeschin. 2.48: Sup. -ώτατα *most ably*, Pl.*R*.516d. **2.** δ. ἔχει it is *possible*, Hdt.7.11.

**δῠνᾰτοτερέω** (sic), *to be more capable* of financial burdens, τινός *PFlor*.296.37 (vi A.D.).

**δυνδεκάτη**· ἡμέρᾳ δωδεκάτῃ, Hsch.

**δῠνητικός**, ή, όν, *potential*, of the particle ἄν, κεν, A.D.*Synt*.205.5, 265.15, cf. Sch.E.*Or*.379.

⊛ **δύο** [ῠ], also **δύω** in Ep., Eleg. and late, *SIG*1231 (Nicomedia, iii/iv A.D.), not in Ion. Inscrr. nor in Trag. (δύο ῥοπάς shd. be read in E.*Hel*.1090), nor in Att. Prose or Inscrr.: Lacon. acc. δύε *IG*5(1).1; Thess. fem. δύας ib.9(2).517: gen. and dat. δυοῖν Hp.*Vict*.1.3, but f.l. in Hdt.1.11,91 [used as monos. in S.*OT*640, cf. δώδεκα for δυώδ-]; later Att. also δυεῖν (esp. in fem. gen.) found in codd. of E.*El*. 536, cited fr. Th. by Ael.Dion.(?)*Fr*.372, cf. 1.20 (cod. Laur.); Boeot. δουῖν Corinn.*Supp*.2.54; later δυσί, δυσὶν ἡμέραις Th.8.101 codd., δυσὶν ἡμέρῃσι v.l. in Hp.*Acut*.(*Sp*.)67; δυοῖν ὄμμασι καὶ δυσὶν ἀκοαῖς Arist.*Pol*.1287$^b$27, cf. Men.699, *SIG*344.26 (Teos, iv B.C.), etc.: early Att. Inscrr. have δυοῖν *IG*1$^2$.3.10, al., later δυεῖν *SIG*$^2$587.286, *IG*2$^2$.463.78, al., from cent. iii on δυσί ib.1028.27, al.; Ion. gen. δυῶν *GDI*5653*d*9 (Chios), Hdt.1.94,130, etc., dat. δυοῖσι ib.32, 7.104; δυῶν also Dor., *Leg.Gort*.1.40, *Tab.Heracl*.1.139; δυοῖς *Leg.Gort*.7.46.—Used indecl., like ἄμφω, by Hom. (who has no gen. or dat. δυοῖν), τῶν δύο μοιράων Il.10.253; δύω κανόνεσσι 13.407, etc.; so in Hdt. and Att., δύο νεῶν Hdt.8.82; δύο ζεύγεσι Id.3.130; δύο νεῶν Th.3. 89; δύο πλέθρων X.*An*.3.4.9; with dual, δύο μναῖν dub. l. Id.*Mem*. 2.5.2; but not in Trag. and rare in Com., ἔτεσιν δύο Alex.105; δύ' ἔτεσιν Damox.2.3: not in Att. Inscrr. before the Roman period, *IG*3.1443, al.:—*two*, Il.1.16, etc.; in Hom., δύο and δύω are sts. joined with plural Nouns, δύο δ' ἄνδρες 18.498, al.; also in Trag., δύο κριούς S.*Aj*.237 (lyr.); in Att. Prose, δύο τέχνας Pl.*Grg*.464b; but δυοῖν is rare with plural Nouns, ὀρθοστάταις δυοῖν *IG*2.1054.64; ἕνα καὶ δύο one or *two*, a few, Il.2.346; δύ' ἢ τρεῖς Ar.*Pax*829, cf. X.*HG* 3.5.20; εἰς δύο *two and two*, Id.*Cyr*.7.5.17; σὺν δύο *two* together, Il. 10.224, Hdt.4.66; δύο ποιεῖν τὴν πόλιν to split the state into *two*, divide it, Arist.*Pol*.1310$^a$4.

**δυογόν**, coined as etym. of ζυγόν, Pl.*Cra*.418d.

**δῠοδεκάς**, **δεκᾰδικός**, v. δυω-. **δῠοδεκαπλάσιος**, = δωδ-, Bito 59.8. **δῠοδεκᾰτημόριον**, τό, = δωδεκ-, Paul.Al.*K*.1. **δυόδεκο**, v. δυώδεκα.

**δῠοειδής**, ές, *of two forms, double, dual*, λόγος Porph.*VP*50; τὸ δ. τῆς ψυχῆς Herm.*in Phdr* p.167 A. Adv. -δῶς Dam.*Pr*.55.

⊛ **δῠοκαίδεκα**, οἱ, αἱ, τά, *twelve*, Il.2.557, etc.

⊛ **δῠοκαιδεκά-δελτος**, ὁ, or **-δελτον**, τό, *the Laws of the Twelve Tables*, Lyd.*Mag*.1.26,42. **-ζῳδος** κύκλος *zodiac*, Vett.Val.172. 32. **-μηνος**, ον, = δωδεκάμηνος, χρόνοι S.*Tr*.648 (lyr.). **-τος**, ον, *twelfth*, Hp.*Morb*.3.16, *Epid*.7.5.

**δῠοκαι-εβδομηκοστός**, ή, όν, *seventy-second*, *SIG*1011.21 (Chalcedon, iii/ii B.C.). **-εικοσίπηχυς** [σῐ], υ, *of two and twenty cubits*, Eust.644.39. **-εικοστός**, ή, όν, *twenty-second*, *IG*1$^2$.212, Archim.*Aren*.4. **-πεντηκοστός**, ή, όν, Dor. **-πεντᾱ-**, *fifty-second*, ib.14.

**δῠόμῐσυ**, (δύο, ἥμισυ) *two and a half*, *Supp.Epigr*.2.705 (Perga).

**δῠοποιός**, όν, *making two*, Arist.*Metaph*.1083$^b$36, Procl.*in Prm*. p.548 S.

**δῠοστός**, ή, όν, *second*, τὸ δ. (sc. μόριον) answering the question ποστημόριον, i.e. *half*, Sch.E.*Hec*.32.

**δυοχοῖ**, = πωματίζει, Democr.136; δυοχῶσαι· πωμάσαι, Hsch.

⊛ **δύπτης**, ου, ὁ, *diver*, Call.*Fr*.167, Opp.*H*.2.436: as Adj., κηρύλος Lyc.387; of persons, Id.73.

**δύπτω** (lengthd. from δύω), *duck, dive*, ἠΰτε τις καύηξ δύπτῃσιν ἐς ἁλμυρὸν ὕδωρ Antim.*Eleg*.6 (nisi leg. δύπτης); πρὸς κῦμα δυπτούσας Lyc.715: without a Prep., ἔδυψε Νηρέως τάφους Id.164; νειόθι δύψας A.R.1.1326: c. acc., δύπτοντες κεφαλάς ib.1008.

**δύρομαι** [ῡ], poet. for ὀδύρομαι (q.v.).

**δῠσ-**, insepar. Prefix, opp. εὖ, *un-*, *mis-*, with notion of *hard, bad, unlucky*, etc., as δυσήλιος, δύσαγνος; *destroying the good sense* of a word, or *increasing its bad sense*: hence, joined even to words expressing negation, as δυσάμμορος, δυσανάσχετος; poet. in strong contrasts, as Πάρις Δύσπαρις, γάμος δύσγαμος. Before στ, σθ, σπ, σφ, σχ, the final σ was omitted, v. δυστ-. (Cf. Skt. *duṣ-*, *dur-*, e.g. *durmanās*, = δυσμενής; ONorse *tor-*, e.g. *torsóttligr* (δύσμαχος); OIr. *du-*, *do-*, e.g. *dochruth* 'misshapen'.)

⊛ **δῠσ-άγγελος**, ον, *messenger of ill*, Nonn.*D*.20.184. **-ᾰγέω**, *to be impious*, *IG*14.432 (Tauromenium). **-ᾰγής**, ές, (ἄγος) *impious*, opp. εὐαγής, Man.5.180, Poll.1.33. **-αγκόμιστος**, **-άγκρῖτος**, poet. for δυσανακ-. **-αγνος**, ον, *unchaste*, A.*Supp*.751 (lyr.), Orac.ap Luc. *Alex*.54. **-αγρέω**, *have bad sport in fishing*, Plu.*Ant*.29. **-αγρής**, ές, *unluckily caught*, of fish, Opp.*H*.3.272. **-αγρία**, ἡ, *bad sport*, Poll.5.13. **-άγωγος** [ᾰ], ον, *hard to guide*, D.H.2.28, Luc.*Abd*. 3,17; ἐπὶ τὸ καλόν D.H.9.8; of horses, *Hippiatr.Praef*. **-άγων** [ᾰ], ωνος, ὁ, ἡ, *having seen hard service*, Plu.*Tim*.36. **-ᾰγώνιστος**, ον, *impregnable*, Poll.3.141, 5.79,105. **-άδελφος** [ᾰ], ον, *unhappy in one's brothers*, A.*Th*.871 (lyr., Sup.), Vett.Val.18.5. **-άεθλος** [ᾰ], ον, *laborious*, Eust.740.54. **-ᾱερία**, ἡ, *badness of air*, Str. 5.1.7, *Cat.Cod.Astr*.2.161: pl., *fogs*, Str.4.1.8. **-άερος** [ᾱ], ον, *having bad air*, δεσμωτήριον (sc. ὁ κόσμος) D.Chr.30.11; *unwholesome*, of the atmosphere, Procl.*Par.Ptol*.122, cf. Sabin.ap.Orib.9. 20.8. **-ᾱής**, ές, (ἄημι) *ill-blowing, stormy*, ἀνέμοιο δυσαέος Il.5. 865; Ζεφύροιο δ. 23.200, al.: poet. gen. pl. δυσαήων for δυσαέων, Od.13.99. **2.** generally, *excessive*, δ. κρυμός Call.*Dian*.115; καῦμα Q.S.13.134; κῦμα *AP*7.739 (Phaedim.). **II.** *ill-smelling*, of a seal, Opp.*C*.3.114; φάρμακα Id.*H*.4.662. ⊛ **-άθλιος**, ον, *most miserable*, τροφαί S.*OC*330, Lxx 3*Ma*.4.4. **-αίακτος**, ον, *most mournful, miserable*, ib.6.31. **-αιᾱνής**, ές, *most melancholy*, βοά A.*Pers*.281 (lyr.). **-αίθριος**, ον, *not clear, murky*, ὄρφνη E.*Heracl*. 857. **-αιμορράγητος** [ρᾰ], ον, *bleeding with difficulty*, Aët.8. 44. **-αίνητος**, ον, *of ill fame*, Orph.*A*.1340. **-αίνιγμα**, ατος, τό, *riddle of woe*, Sch.E.*Ph*.45. **-αίρετος**, ον, *hard to take, impregnable*, Poll.1.170. **-αισθησία**, ἡ, *low degree of sensibility*, Ti. Locr.102e, Gal.7.55 (pl.), prob. in Phld.*Piet*.67. **-αισθητέω**, *to be hardly sensible*, Alex.Trall.1.13. **-αίσθητος**, ον, *insensible*, σώματα Alex.Aphr.*Pr*.1.72, cf. Adam.1.7; τὸ δυσαίσθητον, = ἀναισθησία, Gal.4.784. **II.** Pass., *scarcely perceptible*, Alex.Aphr.*in Sens*.85. 24; *hard to trace*, Poll.5.12. **-αιτῐολόγητος**, ον, *hard to account for*, Ph.2.644, Gal.13.605. **-αίων**, ωνος, ὁ, ἡ, *most miserable*, Trag. only lyr., A.*Th*.926 (prob.), S.*OC*151; αἰὼν δ. a life *that is no life*, E.*Hel*.213; δ. ὁ βίος Id.*Supp*.960. **-άκεστος** [ᾰ], ον, *hard to heal*, ἐκτρίμματα Hp.*Fract*.29. **-ᾰκής**, ές, = foreg., Hsch. s.v. δυσηκῆ. **-άλγημα**, ατος, τό, *severe pain*, Herod.Med. in *Rh.Mus*. 58.82. **-αλγής**, ές, *very painful*, A.*Ag*.1165, Plu.2.106d, Q.S. 14.68. **-άλγητος**, ον, *hard to be borne, most painful*, Eup. 410. **II.** *unfeeling, hard hearted*, S.*OT*12; δειλὸς ἢ δ. φρένας Id.*Fr*.952. **-αλθής**, ές, = sq., Hp.*Art*.41, Cass.*Probl*.1 (Comp.); τὸ τῆς φύσεως δ. Pl.*Ax*.367b. Adv. -θῶς Philum.ap.Orib.45.29.36. **2.** *deadly*, Nic.*Al*.12,157, Luc.*Dem.Enc*.13: neut. pl. as Adv., Q.S.12. 408. **-άλθητος**, ον, *hard to cure, inveterate*, Id.9.388 (-άλθετος Hsch.). **-άλιος** [ᾱ], ον, Dor. for δυσήλιος. **-αλλοίωτος**, ον, *hard to alter*, Gal.*Protr*.11; *hard to digest*, Hp.*Alim*.49; χυμός Alex.Aphr. *Pr*.1.83. ⊛ **-άλυκτος** [ᾰ], ον, *hard to escape*, Nic.*Al*.251,537, Lxx *Wi*.17.17, Man.3.247. **-άλωτος** [ᾰ], ον, *hard to catch* or *take*, ἄγρα Pl.*Ly*.206a (Comp.); of birds and fish, Arist.*HA*615$^a$17, 599$^b$25; ἐρύματα Ph.2.133. **2.** *hard to conquer*, ἀρχά A.*Pr*.167 (lyr.); πάθος Luc.*Abd*.18 (Sup.); *immune*, τοῖς ἔξωθεν αἰτίοις δ. σῶμα Gal.4.742; πρὸς νόσους Sor.1.32 (Comp.): c. gen., δ. κακῶν *beyond reach* of ills, S.*OC*1723 (lyr.). **3.** *hard to comprehend*, Pl.*Ti*.51a (Sup.). **-ᾰμάρτητος**, ον, *making unfortunate mistakes*, Vett.Val.11.16. **-άμβᾰτος**, ον, poet. for δυσανάβατος, πέτραι Simon.58.2. **-ᾱμερία**, Dor. for δυσημ-. **-άμμορος**, ον, *most miserable*, Il.19.315, 22.428,485, A.R. 2.218. **-ανάβᾰτος**, ον, *hard to climb*, Corn.*ND*14. **-αναβλαστέω**, prob. f.l. for δυσαναβλυστέω, *well up with difficulty*, Plu.2. 688e. **-⟨ανά⟩γνωστος**, ον, *hard to read*, prob. for δύσγνωστος, Plb.3.32.1. **-ανάγωγος** [ᾰγ], ον, *hard to throw up*, ὑγρά Dsc.1.1, cf. Androm.ap.Gal.13.28.

**δῠσανά-δοτος**, ον, *hard to assimilate*, Diph.Siph.ap.Ath.3.91e, Gal. 19.364, *Hippiatr.*1. **-θῡμίᾱτος**, ον, *hard to evaporate*, Artem. 1.1. **-κάθαρτος** [κᾰ], ον, *hard to cleanse*, ἕλκωσις Gal.ap.Orib. *Syn.*9.3.8. **-κλητος**, ον, *hard to call back*, Plu.2.74e; J.*BJ*2.18.8 (but simply, *hard to summon, call together*, Plu.*Thes.*24), etc. 2. *hard to restore*, of hysterics, Sor.2.29 (Comp.), cf. Herod.Med. in *Rh.Mus.*58.74; or to good spirits, Max.Tyr.33.6. Adv. -τως, ἔχειν to be *hard to restore* to one's senses, Dsc.*Alex.*16. ⊛ **-κόμιστος**, ον, *hard to carry upwards*, ψυχή Plu.*Rom.*28 :—poet. **δυσαγκόμιστος**, *hard to recall*, αἷμα A.*Eu.*262 (lyr.). **-κρᾶτος**, ον, *hard to mix* or *temper*, κοινωνία Plu.2.1024d. **-κρῖτος**, ον, *hard to determine*: poet. **-άγκρῖτος**, πόνοι A.*Supp.*126 (lyr.). ⊛ **-ληπτος**, ον, *hard to recover*, μνήμη Alcid.*Soph.*19. II. *hard to recover from*, ἀρρωστία Jul.*Or.*6.181a. Adv. -λήπτως, ἔχειν to be *in a bad way for recovery*, Ruf.ap.Orib.8.47.4. 2. of an athlete, *unable to return to ordinary habits*, Ath.Med.ap.Orib.*inc.*1.6. **-ληψία**, ἡ, *difficult convalescence*, Vett.Val.236.17. **-λῠτος**, ον, *hard to analyse*, Porph. *in Cat.*132.9. Adv. -τως Simp. *in Cat.*212.16.

**δῠσανάλωτος** [ᾰλ], ον, *hard to destroy, consume*, στοιχεῖον Ph.2. 505.

**δῠσανά-παυστος**, ον, *restless*, Eust.1296.58. **-πειστος**, ον, *hard to convince*, Pl.*Prm.*135a. **-πλους**, ουν, *hard to sail up*, ὁ Ῥοδανός Str.4.1.14. **-πλωτος**, ον, = foreg., Id.5.2.5. **-πνευστος**, ον, *offensive to inhalation*, Arist.*Sens.*443ᵇ12. 2. *transpiring with difficulty*, Gal.7.287. **-πόρευτος**, ον, *hard to pass*, Ph. 1.672, 2.118. **-σκεύαστος**, ον, *hard to restore*, Alex.Trall.*Febr.* 7. **-σφαλτος**, ον, *hardly recovering from an illness*, Hp.*Alim.* 28. **-σχετέω**, *bear ill*, Th.7.71; *to be greatly vexed*, ἐπί τινι, πρός τι, Plu.*Cam.*35, Plb.16.12.5; περί τινος Phalar.*Ep.*37; τοῖς γενομένοις J.*AJ*13.16.2: abs., Eus.Mynd.59, Aët.8.44. **-σχετος**, ον, *hard to bear, intolerable*, ὕβρεις Ph.2.92; κήδη Phleg.*Macr.*4, cf. Dsc. *Eup.*1.235, Porph.*Abst.*3.20: poet. **-άνσχετος** A.R.2.272. II. Act., *bearing hardly*, in Adv. -τως, ἔχειν A.D.*Synt.*218.9, cf. Poll.3. 130. **-τρεπτος**, ον, *hard to overthrow*, δύναμις Plu.*Caes.*4, cf. Gal. 18(1).604. **-φορικός**· δυσκόλως ἀναφερόμενος, Hsch.

**δῠσ-ανδρία**, ἡ, (ἀνήρ) *want of men*, App.*BC*1.7. **-άνεκτος**, ον, = δυσανάσχετος I, interpol. in X.*Mem.*2.2.8, cf. Gal.7.181. Adv. -τως Poll.3.130. ⊛ **-άνεμος** [ᾰ], ον, Dor. for δυσήνεμος, S.*Ant.*591 (lyr.). **-ανθής**, ές, *shy of flowering*, Poll.1.231. **-άνῐος** [ᾰ], ον, (ἀνία) *soon vexed, ill to please*, Antipho Soph.89, Critias *Fr.*42 D., Men.803 (but better -ήνιον (q.v.)); opp. εὔθυμος, Arist.*Phgn.*805ᵇ6; *vexed, annoyed*, in Comp. -ιώτερος Phld.*Acad.Ind.*p.50 M. ⊛ **-ᾰνιῶν**, ῶσα, ῶν, (ἀνιάω) *much vexing*, Plu.2.106d. **-άνοικτος**, ον, *hard to open*, πυξίδες Diog.*Ep.*50. **-άνολβος**, ον, strengthd. for ἄνολβος, E.Hp.124. **-άνσχετος**, ον, poet. for δυσανάσχετος. **-αντᾰγώνιστος**, ον, *hard to struggle against*, Paus.1.17.6, D.L.2.134, Jul.*Or.*1. 34b. **-άντης** or **-αντής**, ές, = sq. I, φῦλα Opp.*C.*3.262; μῆνις Nonn. *D.*42.380. II. = sq. II, κύματα ib.6.310, cf. Musae.324. III. *hard to climb*, ὁδός Ph.1.255; κολῶναι Opp.*C.*4.432. **-άντητος**, ον, *disagreeable to meet, boding of ill*, opp. εὐάντητος, Luc.*Tim.*5, etc. II. *hard to withstand*, πάθη Plu.2.118c; ὀδύναι Procl.*H.*3. 5; κακά Max.Tyr.5.3.

**δῠσαντί-βλεπτος**, ον, *hard to look in the face*, Plu.*Marc.*23; -βλεπτον στίλβειν ἀπὸ τῶν ὀμμάτων Corn.*ND*20; *hard to face*, ἀπορία χαλεπωτάτη καὶ δ. Syrian. *in Metaph.*178.30; *hard to vie with*, Philostr. Jun.*Im.Praef.*; ὠφέλεια Agathin.ap.Orib.10.7.6. **-λεκτος**, ον, *hard to gainsay*, D.H.5.18: metaph., ἐπιθυμία J.*AJ*18.9.5. **-ρρητος**, ον, = foreg., gloss on ἐχυρόν, Hsch., *EM*406.7. Adv. -τως Plb. 9.31.7.

**δῠσ-αντοφθάλμητος**, ον, *hard to resist*, Plb.22.8.13. **-άνωρ** [ᾰ] γάμος marriage *with a bad husband*, A.*Supp.*1064. **-αξίωτος**, ον, *inexorable*, Sch.S.*OT*334.

**δῠσαπ-άλειπτος** [ᾰλ], ον, *hard to wipe out*, Sch.S.*Tr.*682. **-αλλακτία**, ἡ, *the quality of being difficult to get rid of, persistency*, Pl. *Phlb.*46c. ⊛ **-άλλακτος**, ον, *hard to get rid of*, νοῦσος Hp.*Nat.Mul.* 40; ὀδύναι S.*Tr.*959 (lyr.); πρόσταγμα Isoc.10.28; ἀρρώστημα Arist. *PA*671ᵇ9, cf. *Cat.*10ᵃ4: c. gen., -ότεραι τῶν ἐμβρύων *having difficulty in bringing forth*, Id.*HA*587ᵇ1; δ. ἀπὸ λόγου a person *hard to draw away* from.., Pl.*Tht.*195c. Adv. -τως, ἔχειν τινός Eust.1389.46, cf. Eustr. *in EN*140.18. **-άντητος**, ον, = δυσάντητος, Eust.1054.30, Suid.

**δῠσάπιστος**, ον, *very disobedient*, *AP*12.179 (Strato):—hence **-απιστέω**, *AB*1285.

**δῠσαπο-βίβαστος** [ῐ], v.l. for δυσυπο-, Gal.6.535. **-βλητος**, ον, *hard to get rid of*, πυρετός Alex.Aphr.*Febr.*19; *hard to cast away*, Olymp. *in Alc.*p.51C.; *hard to lose*, Id. *in Cat.*116.25, cf. Ammon. *in Cat.*82.8, Simp. *in Cat.*228.23. **-δεικτος**, ον, *hard to demonstrate*, Pl.*R.*488a. **-δίδακτος** [ῐ], ον, *hard to unlearn*, J.*AJ*16.2. 4. **-δίωκτος** [ῐ], ον, *hard to drive away*, Sch.Theoc.10.11. **-δοτος**, ον, *hard to render* or *define*, S.E.*M.*7.242, Bacch.*Harm.*95. **-θετος**, ον, *hard to put aside*, πάθος Olymp. *in Alc.*p.101C. **-κατάστᾰσις**, εως, ἡ, *difficulty of recovering, mortal sickness*, Erot. s.v. δυσθεσίην. **-κατάστᾰτος**, ον, *hard to restore*, M.Ant.11.8, Gal.14. 792. II. *hard to recover from*, ὀργαί Phld.*Ir.*p.63 W. **-κλίτως** [ῐ], Adv. *with difficulty in bending*, Herod.Med. in *Rh.Mus.*58. 90. **-κρῖτος**, ον, *hard to answer*, Luc.*Vit.Auct.*22. Adv. -τως, ἔχειν, of a letter, Mithr.*Ep.*1. II. Act., *hardly answering*, Paul. Aeg.3.9. **-ληπτος**, ον, *hard to catch*, Alex.Aphr. *in Sens.*26.18; *irreparable*, *Gloss.* **-λόγητος**, ον, *hard to defend* or *excuse*, Plb. 1.10.4, cf. Ph.1.562, J.*AJ*16.4.2; *hard to answer*, Aristeas 213; *hard to explain*, Str.4.1.7. Adv. -τως, ἔχειν Eust.147.23. **-λῠτος**, ον, *hard to get free of*, δ. πάθος τὸ φιλότιμον Olymp. *in Alc.*p.51 C. Adv. -τως Erot. s. v. βλακεύειν, Gal.8.284. **-νιπτος**, ον, *hard to wash off* or *out*, Zen.1.47, Sch.E.*Ph.*63: Comp., *Theol.Ar.*22. **-πτωτος**, ον, *not apt to fall off*, καρπός Thphr.*CP*1.11.8. **-σπαστος**, ον, *hard to tear away*, Posidon.15 J., Secund.*Sent.*10, Dsc.3.14. Adv. δυσαποσπάστως, ἔχειν Pl.*Ax.*365b, Aristeas 123, D.S.20.51. II. *from which it is hard to tear oneself away*, Ph.2.11,14; κάλλος Charito 5.8. **-σχετος**, ον, *hard to abstain from*, S.E.*M.*9.152. **-τέλεστος**, ον, *hard to accomplish*, Eust.1956.18. **-τρεπτος**, ον, *hard to dissuade, refractory*, X.*Mem.*4.1.4, Aristaenet.1.28. **-τριπτος**, ον, *hard to rub off* and so *get rid of*, ὀνείδη Macar.8.47, cf. Ph.1.459,615 (Sup.), Thessal.ap.Gal.10.252; of persons, Plu.2.55e. ⊛ **-τροπος**, ον, *difficult to avert*, ἄτη *IG*2.1660.22.

⊛ **δῠσαπούλωτος**, ον, *hard to cicatrize*, Dsc.4.41, Aët.1.243, *Hippiatr.* 26: Comp., Phlp. *in APo.*182.13.

**δυσαρεεῖ**· δυσφροντίστῳ, Hsch.

**δυσαρεσκόμενος**, incorrect form for δυσαρεστούμενος, Hsch.

⊛ **δῠσᾰρεστ-έω**, *suffer annoyance*, Arist.*HA*560ᵇ24; *to be displeased*, τινί *at* a thing, Plb.4.22.9, D.S.5.9, J.*AJ*5.5.3, Aq., Sm., Thd.*Ps.*94 (95).10; δ. ὅτι D.H.*Comp.*11: Medic., *suffer malaise*, Gal.10.551, Aët.5.5:—also Med., τινί Plb.5.94.2; ἐπί τινι 11.28.11. II. c. dat. pers., *to be displeasing to*, Id.7.5.6, D.S.18.62; τῷ θεῷ Ph.2.6:—also Med. -ουμένη φιλία Plu.2.94d, cf. Iamb.*VP*35.255. **-ημα**, ατος, τό, Medic., *malaise, distress*, Antyll.ap.Stob.4.37.15, Sor.1.26. **-ησις**, εως, ἡ, *distress*, Pl.*Ax.*366d; *dissatisfaction*, τινί or ἐπί τινι, Plb.4.21. 7, 23.7.5. II. Medic., *malaise*, Cael.Aur.*TP*3.6, Sor.1.56. **-ία**, ἡ, *distress, malaise*, Herod.Med. in *Hermes* 40.584, prob. in Aët.16. 18 (for -ησίαι), Hierocl. *in CA*11 p.442 M. **-ικός**, ή, όν, *distressing*, σύμπτωμα Herod.Med.ap.Orib.6.20.21. **-ος**, ον, *hard to appease, implacable*, δαίμονες A.*Eu.*928; *ill-pleased*, τι *at* a thing, Luc.*Nav.*46; *ill to please, fastidious, peevish*, δυσάρεστον οἱ νοσοῦντες E.*Or.*232, cf. Isoc.1.31, 12.8, X.*Mem.*3.13.3 (Comp.), Diph.63, Nicostr.31 (Comp.), Plu.2.128d; ἀνοίας νόσημα δυσάρεστον Polystr.*Herc.*1520.1; τὸ δ. *displeasure*, Plu.*Sol.*25. Adv. -τως, ἔχειν πρός τι Id.2.476b.

**δῠσ-ᾰρίθμητος**, ον, *hard to count up*, App.*BC*2.73. **-ἀριστοτόκεια**, ἡ, *unhappy mother of the noblest son*, as Thetis calls herself, Il.18.54. **-αρκτος**, ον, *hard to govern*, φρένες A.*Ch.*1024; στρατόπεδα J.*AJ*4.2.1; οὐδὲν ἀνθρώπου -ότερον Plu.*Luc.*2; ἔθνος -ότατον App.*BC*2.149. **-αρμοστία**, ἡ, *disharmony*, ἠθῶν Plu.*Aem.* 5. **-άρμοστος**, ον, *ill-united*, Id.*Eum.*13; *insecure*, πύργος App. *Mith.*34. **-αρχία**, ἡ, *ill discipline*, App.*BC*5.17. **-αυγής**, ές, *blinding*, Poet. *de herb.*65. **-αύλητος**· δυσεγκλήμων, Hsch. ⊛ **-αυλία**, ἡ, *ill* or *hard lodging*, A.*Ag.*555 (pl.), Ph.1.195 (pl.). **-αυλις**, ἡ, dub. sens., St.Byz. s. v. αὐλή (expld. as compd. of Αὖλις). **-αύλιστος**, gloss on sq., Hsch. **-αυλος**, ον, (αὐλή) *bad for lodging, inhospitable*, of frost, S.*Ant.*356 (lyr.). **-αυλος** ἔρις *an unhappy contest with the flute* (αὐλός), *AP*9.266 (Antip.). **-αυξής**, ές, *hardly* or *slowly growing*, Arist.*Aud.*802ᵃ25, Thphr.*CP*1.8.4, J.*AJ*3.1.3:—also **-αύξητος**, ον, Thphr.*CP*1.8.2. **-αυρία**, ἡ, *stormy wind*, Ar. Byz.*Epit.*24.18 (s. v. l.). ⊛ **-αυχής**, ές, *idly boasting, vain-glorious*, A.R.3.976. **-αφαίρετος**, ον, *hard to take away*, Arist.*EN*1095ᵇ 26; *hard to remove*, of an application, Gal.12.356. **-ᾰφής**, ές, *hard to the touch*, σάρξ Id.6.100. **-ᾱχής**, ές, Dor. for δυσηχής, πόλεμος Anacr.107. **-ᾰχής**, ές, (ἄχος) *most painful*, πάθος A.*Eu.*145 (lyr.). **-αχθής**, ές, *very grievous*, Tryph.42, Max. 308. **-βάρνακος**· δυσκατανόητος, βάρνακα γὰρ ἄγρια λάχανα δύσπλυτα *EM*291.45. **-βᾰσᾰνίστως**, gloss on ἀβασανίστως, Hsch. **-βάστακτος**, ον, *intolerable, grievous to be borne*, Lxx *Pr.* 27.3, *Ev.Matt.*23.4, Plu.2.915f, etc.; of persons, Antisth.ap.Ph.2. 449. **-βᾰτοποιέομαι**, *make impassable*, dub. l. in X.*Eq.Mag.*8.9 (prob. for δύσβατα ποιούμενον). **-βᾰτος**, ον, *hard to traverse, impassable*, ἀμαχανίαι Pi.*N.*7.97; τόπος Pl.*R.*432c; τὰ δ., = δυσχωρίαι, X.*Cyr.*2.4.27: metaph., δ. καὶ μακρὰ διερμήνευσις Iamb.*Myst.*5. 5. II. *trodden in sorrow*, Περσὶς αἶα A.*Pers.*1069 (lyr.). **-βήρης** or **-βηρής**, ές, = δύσβατος, Hsch., *EM*291.42. **-βίοτος**, ον, = sq., *AB*323. **-βίοτος** [ῐ], ον, *making life wretched*, πενίη *AP*7.648 (Leon.). **-βλεπτέω**, *see badly*, Hsch. s.v. κικυμώττειν. **-βοήθητος**, ον, *hard to help* or *cure*, Hp.*Coac.*491, D.S.3.47, 11.15, Paul. Aeg.5.29: Comp., Dsc.*Eup.*2.159. Adv. -τως Gal.5.122. **-βολος**, ον, *throwing badly*, esp. with dice, Poll.9.94. **-βούλευτος**, ον, *ill-advised*, *EM*3.51. **-βουλία**, ἡ, *ill counsel*, A.*Th.*802, *Ag.*1609, S.*Ant.*95: pl., ib.1269 (lyr.). **-βράκᾰνος** [ρᾰ], ον, *hard to deal with*, Cratin.404; cf. βρακεῖν. **-βωλος**, ον, *of ill soil, unfruitful*, γῆ Hom.*Epigr.*7; χθών *AP*7.401 (Crin.).

**δυσγᾰμ-έω**, *to be unhappily married*, Heph.Astr.1.1. **-ία**, ἡ, *an ill marriage*, Man.1.19. **-ος**, ον, *ill-wedded*, γάμοι δ. E.*Ph.*1047 (lyr.); ῥυστάγματα Lyc.1089, cf. Paul.Al.*N.*2; δύσγαμον αἶσχος ἑλών, of Menelaus, E.*Tr.*1114; χελιδών Luc.*Trag.*49.

**δυσ-γάργᾰλις**, ι, *very ticklish, skittish*, ἵππος X.*Eq.*3.10, cf. Ar.*Fr.* 43, Ael.*NA*16.9:—also **-γαργάλιστος**, ον, prob. l. in *Gp.*16.2.1, cf. Tim.Gaz.148.3: **-γάργᾰλος**, ον, Lib.*Ep.*234.1 codd., Phryn.*PS* p.65 B. **-γένεια**, ἡ, *low birth*, S.*OT*1079, E.*IA*446, Pl.*R.*618d (pl.), Cerc.17.36, Plu.2.1b, etc. II. *meanness*, E.*HF*663 (lyr.), Plu.*Alex.* 62. ⊛ **-γενής**, ές, *low-born*, E.*Ion* 1477, Ar.*Ra.*1219, etc.: Comp., Men.533.10. II. *low-minded, mean*, E.*El.*363, etc.; δ. ὢν τῷ τρόπῳ Com.ap.Stob.4.30.6a. **-γεφύρωτος** [ῡ], ον, *hard to make a bridge over*, Str.4.3.3. **-γεώργητος**, ον, *hard to till* or *cultivate*, Id.17.3.

25. **-γνοια,** ἡ, *ignorance, doubt*, E.*HF* 1107. **-γνώμων,** gloss on δυσέκτων (sic), Suid. **-γνώριστος,** ον, *hard to recognize*, Gal.7.804, al., Poll.5.150. Adv. -τως ib.160. **-γνωσία,** ἡ, *difficulty of knowing*, δυσγνωσίαν εἶχον προσώπου I did *not know* thy face, E.*El*.767. **-γνωστος,** ον, *hard to understand*, Pl.*Alc*.2.147c. 2. *hard to recognize*, τισί Plb.3.78.4: Sup., Aen.Tact.25.2. **-γοήτευτος,** ον, *hard to seduce by enchantments*, Pl.*R*.413e. **-γονος,** ον, *conceiving with difficulty*, Vett.Val.18.24, *Cat.Cod.Astr*.2.207. **-γράμμᾰτος,** ον, *hard to write*, Aristid.2.360 J. II. *unlearned*, Philostr.*VS*2.1.10. ⊛ **-γρίπιστος** [ῐπ], ον, *very grasping*, Lib.Bas.*Ep*.13.

**δύσγω·** ἀποδύω, Hsch.

**δυσδαιμ-ονέω,** *to be wretched*, Longin.9.7. **-ονία,** ἡ, *misery*, E.*IT*1120(lyr.), And.2.7. **-ων,** ον, gen. ονος, *ill-starred, unhappy*, πότμος Emp.9.4, A.*Th*.827, S.*Ant*.274; μοῖρα Id.*OT*1302 (anap.); τύχη Pl.*Lg*.905c; νέρτεροι Ti.Locr.104d; of a person, *BGU*1024 vii 24 (iv A.D.): Comp. -έστερος And.2.9. Adv. -νως Eust.1064.44.

**δυσ-δάκρῡτος,** ον, *sorely wept*, A.*Ag*.442 (lyr.). II. Act., *sorely weeping*, *AP*12.80 (Mel.); δάκρυα δ. tears *of anguish*, ib.7.476 (Id.). **-δᾰμαρ,** αρτος, ὁ, ἡ, *ill-wedded*, A.*Ag*.1319. **-δάμαστος** [δᾰ], ον, *hard to subdue*: hence, *hard to work*, σίδηρος Sch.Hes.*Sc*.122. **-δεικτος,** ον, *hard to prove*, θεωρήματα Gal.15.139. **-δέρκετος,** ον, = sq., Opp.*C*.2.607. **-δερκής,** ές, *ill to look upon, grim, ugly*, ib.3.263, *H*.1.47. II. *hard to see, faint*, ἴχνη Id.*C*.1.102, cf. 451. **-δηλις,** ιδος, ὁ, ἡ, (δηλέομαι) *baneful*, Hsch. **-δηνίας·** δύσνους, κακὰ βουλευομένους, Id. **-δηρις,** ι, gen. ιος, *hard to fight with*, Nic.*Th*.738.

**δυσδιά-βᾰτος,** ον, *hard to get through*, ποταμός Aen.Tact.8.1, cf. X.*An*.6.5.19; τόποι Plb.1.39.13; ῥεῦμα D.S.17.93. **-γνω⟨σ⟩τικός,** ή, όν, τὸ δ. *the difficulty in diagnosis*, Alex.Trall.8.2. **-γνωστος,** ον, *hard to distinguish*, Cic.*Att*.5.4.1, D.H.2.71, Gal.9.433, etc.

**δυσδιάγωγος** [ᾰ], ον, *unpleasant to live in*, πόλις Str.16.2.23: Comp., Ptol.*Tetr*.168.

**δυσδιάθετος,** ον, *hard to dispose of* (in marriage), χαλεπόν γε θυγάτηρ κτῆμα καὶ δυσδιάθετον Men.18. 2. *hard to manage* or *settle*, Plu.*Caes*.11, D.C.73.15, Hierocl. *in CA*11 p.438 M.

**δυσδιαίρετος,** ον, *hard to divide* or *split*, Arist.*Pr*.928ᵃ29, Thphr. *HP*7.11.3, Sor.1.118, *Theol.Ar*.5.

**δυσδιαίτητος,** ον, *hard to decide*, Plu.*Comp.Cim.Luc*.3; λόγος Porph.*Abst*.2.1.

**δυσδιακόμιστος,** ον, *hard to carry through*, Hsch.

**δυσδιᾰκόντιστος,** ον, *hard to pierce*, Ael.*NA*17.44.

**δυσδιάκρῐτος,** ον, *hard to distinguish*, Str.13.4.12, Clytus 1; ἀξίαι Plu.2.617d; δ. ἀπό.. Corn.*ND*31. II. of litigants, *whose case is hard to decide*, D.S.33.28a. III. *hard to digest*, Xenocr.9.

**δυσδιάλλακτος,** ον, *hard to reconcile*, Suid. Adv. -τως Ammon.63.

**δυσδιά-λῠτος,** ον, *hard to dissolve*, Arist.*Pr*.870ᵇ31 (Comp.): σχῆμα τῆς τάξεως Plb.1.26.16. 2. *hard to digest*, Philotim.ap.Ath.2.53f, Gal.16.760. II. *hard to reconcile*, Arist.*EN*1126ᵃ20. **-νόητος,** ον, *hard to understand*, Sch.E.*Ph*.30.

**δυσδιάνοικτος,** ον, *hard to open*, ὀφθαλμός *Hippiatr*.1.

**δυσδιά-πνευστος,** ον, *slow to evaporate*, Thphr.*CP*1.2.4, Dsc.5.6. II. *slow to perspire*, Herod.Med.ap.Orib.5.27.3. **-σπαστος,** ον, *hard to break*, τάξις Plb.15.15.7; *hard to pull up*, of a palisade, Ph.*Bel*.82.35. **-στᾰτέω,** *to be unstable*, dub. in Plu.2.993e. **-στᾰτος,** ον, *hard to separate*, Herod.Med. in *Rh.Mus*.58.90. **-τηκτος,** ον, *hard to soften*, prob. l., Thphr.*CP*2.15.2. **-φευκτος** or **-φυκτος,** ον, *hard to escape*, Suid., Hsch. (-διαφύ[λα]κτον cod.). **-φθαρτος,** ον, *hard to break up*, τὰ δ. βραδυπεψίας ἐργάζεται Gal.7.209. ⊛ **-φορησία,** ἡ, *difficulty of dissipation*, Cass.*Pr*.66. **-φόρητος,** ον, *hard to disperse* or *dissipate*, Gal.11.119. II. *hardly evaporating*, Id.10.657; *not excreting readily*, Id.17(1).188; διάθεσις Alex.Trall.8.2; cf. δυσδιαχώρητος. **-φύλακτος,** v. δυσδιάφευκτος. ⊛ **-χώρητος,** ον, *indigestible*, Arist.*Pr*.927ᵇ21 (Comp.); *hard to pass*, prob. for -φόρητος, Xenocr.34. II. Act., *costive*, Alex.Aphr.*Pr*.1.90, Sever.p.6 D.

**δυσδίδακτος** [ῐ], ον, *hard to instruct*, Hp.*Ep*.17.

**δυσδι-έγερτος,** ον, *hard to be roused from*, καταφορά Gal.19.413, cf. Herod.(?)Med. in *Rh.Mus*.58.77. **-έξακτος,** ον, *hard to pass*, βίος Porph.*Abst*.4.18. **-εξίτητος** [ῐτ], ον, *hard to get through*, v.l. in D.S.3.44. **-εξόδευτος,** ον, = sq. II, *Hippiatr*.69. **-έξοδος,** ον, *hard to get through, traverse*, D.S.5.34, D.C.60.20. II. *hard to pass*, Gal.6.535. **-ερεύνητος,** ον, *hard to search thoroughly*, Pl.*R*.432c, D.C.51.26, Them.*Or*.21.254d. **-ήγητος,** ον, *hard to narrate*, Lxx *Wi*.17.1. **-όδευτος,** ον, = -ήλῠτος, Hsch.; of a child's tissues, Sor.1.95. **-οδος,** ον, *hard to pass through*, Plb.3.61.3, etc. **-οίκητος,** ον, *hard to manage*, J.*BJ*2.16.4, Poll.5.105 (vulg. -ητικός). II. *hard to digest*, Xenocr.31, Sor.1.93. **-όρᾱτος,** ον, *hard to see one's way in*, τόπος διὰ τὸ σκοτεινόν Alcin.*Intr*.35. **-όρθωτος,** ον, *hard to set right*, Hsch. **-όριστος,** ον, *hard to delimit*, ἀπ' ἀλλήλων S.E.*M*.5.74; *hard to distinguish*, φαντασία ib.7.416.

**δυσδίωκτος** [ῐ], ον, gloss on δύσσοα, Sch.Theoc.4.45.

**δυσδοκίμαστος** [ῐ], ον, *hard to test*, τῇ γεύσει Dsc.3.82.

**δύσδωρος,** ον, = ἄδωρος, Opp.*H*.3.303.

**δύσεα·** τοῦ τοίχου τὰ πέριξ (Cypr.), Hsch.

**δυσέγερτος,** ον, *hard to wake*, Gal.16.645, Paul.Aeg.3.9.

⊛ **δυσεγ-καρτέρητος,** ον, *hard to sustain*, S.E.*M*.9.152. **-κλήμων,** v. δυσαύλητος. **-χείρητος,** ον, *hard to take in hand*, J.*AJ*15.11.2. **-χωστος,** ον, *hard to dam up*, prob. in Str.16.1.10.

**δυσ-έδρος** [ῠ], ον, *bringing evil in one's abode*, A.*Ag*.746 (lyr.). 2. *fitting ill, awry*, D.H.*Comp*.6. **-είδεια,** ἡ, *ugliness*, D.L.2.33. ⊛ **-ειδής,** ές, *unshapely, ugly*, Hdt.6.61, S.*Fr*.88.9, Pl.*Sph*.228a, Agatharch.74; of sounds, ἧττον δ. τοῦ ε̄ τὸ ο̄ D.H.*Comp*.14. II. *difficult to discern*, τὸ δ. τῆς οὐσίας Procl.*Theol.Plat*.5.23. **-είκαστος,** ον, *hard to make out*, of Thucydides' style, D.H.*Lys*.4, cf. Luc.*Icar*.4. ⊛ **-εικτος,** ον, *unyielding, stiff*, Paul.Aeg.2.11.21.

**δυσειμ-ᾰτέω,** *to wear mean clothes*, Plu.2.299e. **-ᾰτος,** ον, *meanly clad*, E.*El*.1107. **-ονία,** ἡ, *mean clothing*, Sch.E.*Hec*.240. **-ων,** ον, gen. ονος, *ill-clad*, Ps.-Hes.ap.Ath.3.116a.

**δυσειρεσία,** ἡ, *difficulty in rowing*, Suid.

**δυσεισ-βολος,** ον, *hard to enter* or *invade*, of Laconia, E.*Fr*.1083, cf. Aen.Tact.16.17; of a river, Str.4.1.8: Sup. -ώτατος, ον, *least accessible*, of Locris, Th.3.101. **-οδος,** ον, *difficult to enter*, σπήλαιον *TAM*2(1).174*C*13 (Sidyma). **-πλους,** ουν, gen. ου, *hard to sail into*, Str.4.1.8. **-πλωτος,** ον, = foreg., prob. l. for δυσεκ-, Sch.Th.3.2.

**δυσέκ-βᾰτος,** ον, *hard to get out of*, D.C.56.19, Nonn.*D*.45.269 (but f.l. for δυσέμβ-, φλόξ 2.487). **-βίαστος** [ῐ], ον, *hard to overpower*, ἐπιθυμίαι Plu.2.127a, cf. *Cor*.2, Eun.*VS* p.500 B. **-δεκτος,** ον, *hard to endure, intolerable*, Gal.19.2. **-δρομος,** ον, *hard to escape*, Nic.*Al*.14. **-δῠτος,** ον, *hard to shake off*, Hsch. s. v. νήδυμον. **-θέρμαντος,** ον, *hard to warm*, Plu.2.625a, Gal.6.608, Antyll.ap.Orib.10.13.9. Adv. -τως Id.ib.10.29.3, Gal.10.674. **-θῦτος,** ον, *hard to avert by sacrifice*, σημεῖα Plu.*Crass*.18. **-κάθαρτος** [κᾰ], ον, *hard to wash away*, D.H.4.24. ⊛ **-καρτέρητος,** ον, *hard to endure*, κακόν Phld.*D*.1.12. **-κένωτος,** ον, *hard to evacuate*, Gal.8.192. **-κόμιστος,** ον, *hard to carry out*, Hsch. and Suid. s. v. δυσέξοιστον. **-κρῐτος,** ον, *hard to digest and pass*, Diph.Siph.ap.Ath.2.69e, Xenocr.38. Adv. -τως, ἀθροίζεσθαι Gal.*UP*10.10. 2. Act., *excreting with difficulty*, γαστέρες Id.6.462. **-κρουστος,** ον, *hard to disturb, shake*, φυλακή S.E.*M*.7.23. **-λάλητος** [ᾰ], ον, *hard to express*, Cic.*Att*.5.10.3 (prob.), D.H.*Lys*.11. ⊛ **-λειπτος,** ον, *hard to escape from*, Plu.2.829b. ⊛ **-ληπτως,** Adv. dub. in Gal.*Anim.Pass*.1.5 (leg. δυσεξάλειπτον). **-λόγιστος,** ον, *hard to calculate*, Suid. **-λῠτος,** ον, *hard to undo*, τέχνημα A.*Fr*.375 (Dind. δυσέκδυτον *hard to escape from*); δόξα Ph.1.192, cf. Vett.Val.71.23, al. Adv. -τως *indissolubly*, A.*Pr*.60. **-μόχλευτος,** ον, *hard to dislodge*, of disease, Antyll.ap.Orib.10.29.3. **-μύζητος,** ον, *hard to suck out*, Sor.1.87. **-νευστος,** ον, *hard to swim out of*, Max.Tyr.17.10. **-νιπτος,** ον, *hard to wash out*, Pl.*R*.378d, *Trag.Adesp.* in *Gött.Nachr*.1922.26, Cerc.3, Ach.Tat.6.11, Porph.*Abst*.4.20; μῖσος Them.*Or*.21.249c. Adv. -τως Gal.8.36, al. 2. *hard to cleanse*, ὀδόντες Ael.*NA*1.48. **-πέρᾱτος,** ον, *hard to pass out from, hard to escape*, E.*Hipp*.678 (lyr.), 883 (lyr., v.l. δυσεκπέραντος). **-πληκτος,** ον, *hard to terrify*, ὑπὸ φόβων Arist.*VV*1250ᵃ7. **-πλήρωτος,** ον, *hardly realizable*, Phld.*D*.1.12. **-πλοκος,** ον, *tangled, inextricable*, Gloss. **-πλους,** ουν, *hard to sail out of*, Plb.34.2.5, Str.1.2.15. **-πλῦτος,** ον, *hard to wash out*, Ph.2.182,487, Plu.2.488b. II. *hard to cleanse*, ὀδόντες Ael.*NA*1.48: metaph., ψυχαί Ph.1.558. **-πνευστος,** ον, *hard to breathe out*, Sch.E.*Ph*.1438. **-πόνητος,** ον, τιμωρίας καὶ πόνους δυσ[εκπο]νήτους *hard to endure*, Phld.*Herc*.1251.12 (dub. rest.). **-πόρευτος,** ον, *hard to get out of*, πύλαι Ph.*Bel*.79.25; τέλμα J.*AJ*13.2.4. **-πτωτος,** ον, *not easily dislocated*, Paul.Aeg.6.114. **-πύητος** [ῠ], ον, *hard to bring to suppuration*, Gal.11.119, Paul.Aeg.4.18. **-ρίζωτος** [ῐ], ον, *hard to extirpate*, πλάνη Ph.*Fr*.105 H. **-ρίπτος,** ον, *not easily displaced*. Adv. -τως Orib.49.22.17. **-ρυπτος,** ον, *hard to wash out*, Xenocr.58. **-τηκτος,** ον, *hard to melt*, dub. in Hp.*Alim*.51. ⊛ **-φευκτος,** ον, *hard to escape from*, Tim.*Pers*.130, Theodect.10, Plb.1.77.7, Man.4.477; *hardly escaping*, Tim.*Pers*.140. Adv. δυσεκφύκτως *APl*.4.198 (Maec.).

**δυσεκ-φόρητος,** ον, = sq., D.H.*Comp*.22. **-φορος,** ον, *hard to pronounce* or *utter*, Phld.*Po*.994 *Fr*.22, 1676.8, D.H.*Comp*.12,16 (Sup.); λαλιά *Cat.Cod.Astr*.2.167. Adv. -ρως, δ. καὶ τραχέως λαλεῖν Str.14.2.28. **-φώνητος,** ον, *hard to pronounce*, Eust.76.33.

**δυσέλεγκτος,** ον, *hard to refute*, of persons or arguments, Str.1.2.1 (Comp.), 11.6.4, Luc.*Pisc*.17.

⊛ **Δυσελένα,** ἡ, *ill-starred Helen*, E.*Or*.1388 (lyr.); cf. Δύσπαρις.

**δυσ-έλικτος,** ον, *hard to undo*, Eust.229.38; *hard to unroll* and read, βίβλοι Jul.*Or*.7.227b. **-ελκής,** ές, *unfavourable for the healing of sores*, of a constitution, opp. εὐελκής, Hp.*Acut*.46, cf. *Morb*.2.52, Gal.10.387. **-ελκία,** ἡ, *the constitution of a* δυσελκής, Hp.*Epid*.2.10 (pl.).

**δυσελπ-ίζω,** incorrect spelling for δυσελπιστέω, Plb.16.33.1, 21.13.2. **-ις,** ι, gen. ιδος, *hardly hoping, despondent*, A.*Ch*.412 (lyr.), Hp.*Nat.Mul*.41 (prob.), X.*HG*5.4.31, Arist.*Rh*.1390ᵃ4; δ. τι ἐρεῖν Luc.*Herm*.69. II. Pass., *hardly hoped for*, νίκη Onos.38.2. **-ιστέω,** *to have scarce a hope*, τοῖς ὅλοις, ἐπὶ ταῖς βοηθείαις, Plb.2.10.8, 4.60.4:—Pass., *to be despaired of*, Epicur.*Sent.Vat*.17. **-ιστία,** ἡ, *despondency*, Arist.*VV*1251ᵇ25, Plb.1.39.14, Teles p.35 H., Ph.1.119, App.*BC*4.12. **-ιστος,** ον, = δύσελπις, *Lyr.Adesp*.138, Epicur.*Fr*.470, Plu.*Fab*.17. Adv. δυσελπίστως, ἔχειν Plb.1.87.1. II. *unhoped for*, ἐκ δυσελπίστων *unexpectedly*, X.*Cyr*.6.1.47, cf. Vett.Val.124.25.

**δυσέμ-βᾰτος,** ον, *hard to walk on, rugged*, τοῦ χωρίου τὸ δ. Th.4.10;

*inaccessible*, οἰωνοῖσι D.P.1150. **-βλητος**, ον, *hard to set*, of dislocations, Hp.*Art.*71. * **-βολος**, ον, = foreg., Id.*Fract.*38 (Comp.). II. *hard to enter*, δυσεμβολωτάτη ἡ Λακωνική X.*HG*6.5.24; δ. τοῖς πολεμίοις [χώρα] Arist.*Pol.*1326b41; ὄρη Plb.3.49.7, cf. J.*AJ*17.2.1.

**δῠσεμ-έω**, *not to vomit easily*, Philum.ap.Aët.9.23. **-ής**, ές, *hard to make to vomit*, Gal.17(2).329, prob. l. in Dsc.4.153; cf. δυσημής.

**δῠσέμπρηστος**, ον, *hard to burn*, Ph.*Bel.*82.23.

**δῠσέμπτωτος**, ον, *not easily falling into* a thing, Nicom.*Harm.*11, Gal.5.433. Adv. -τως Nicom.*Harm.*4.

**δῠσενέδρευτος**, ον, *hard to way-lay*, App.*Hisp.*88.

**δῠσενέργ-εια**, ἡ, *lassitude*, Dsc.5.49. **-ητος**, ον, *sluggish*, Sch. Ar.*Pl.*313. II. of food, *badly digested*, Sor.1.34.

* **δῠσεντερ-ία**, ἡ, *dysentery*, Hp.*Aph.*3.12 (pl.), al., Hdt.8.115, Pl. *Ti.*86a (pl.), Arist.*Pr.*861b16, etc. **-ιάω**, *suffer from dysentery*, *Hippiatr.*39, Alex.Trall.9.3. **-ικός**, ή, όν, *afflicted with dysentery*, Hp.*Coac.*451, Arr.*Epict.*2.21.22, Mnesith.ap.Orib.4.4.4; *liable to it*, Plu.2.101c; δ. πάθη Epicur.*Fr.*138; τὰ δ. Dsc.1.51. **-ιον**, τό, late form of δυσεντερία, *Act.Ap.*28.8, Moeris 129. **-ιώδης**, ες, *ill with dysentery*, Hp.*Epid.*1.5, 3.8; *symptomatic of* or *belonging to it*, ib.3.17.θ'; τρόπος Aret.*SD*2.9. **-ος**, ον, *suffering from dysentery*, Nic.*Al.*382.

**δῠσέν-τευκτος**, ον, *unpleasant to meet, physically repulsive*, δ. καὶ ἀηδής Thphr.*Char.*19; but more usu. *unpleasant to deal with*, Plb. 5.34.4, Plu.2.27e; τὸ δ. Ph.2.520, J.*AJ*13.2.1. **-τευξία**, ἡ, *repulsive demeanour*, D.S.19.9, Cass.*Pr.*80 (pl.).

**δῠσένωτος**, ον, (ἑνόω) *hard to unite*, M.Ant.11.8.

**δῠσεξ-άγωγος** [ᾰ], ον, *difficult to carry off* or *get rid of*, Hp.*Insomn.*89, Arist.*Pr.*871a19 (Comp.). **-άκουστος** [ᾰ], ον, *difficult to hear*, τὰ διὰ φωνῆς (sc. παραγγέλματα) Ael.*Tact.*35.3. **-άλειπτος** [ᾰ], ον, *hard to wipe out*, εὔνοια Plb.39.3.1; συνήθεια D.S.3.6; μνήμη Longin.7.3; ψυχῆς διάθεσις Corn.*Rh.*p.353 H. *-**άλυκτος** [ᾰ], ον, *hard to avoid*, Hsch. **-ανάλωτος** [ᾰλ], ον, = δυσανάλωτος, Hp. *Alim.*49. **-ᾰπάτητος** [πᾰ], ον, *hard to deceive*, Pl.*R.*413c, X.*Ages.*11.12. **-απτος**, ον, *hard to unbind*, ψυχὴ δ. *hard to loose from* the bonds of the body, Plu.*Rom.*28. II. *hard to kindle*, χυμός Gal. 7.341, cf. Steph.*in Hp.*1.284 D. **-ᾰρίθμητος**, ον, *hard to count*, Plb.3.58.6, Plu.2.667e. **-ατμιστος**, ον, *hard to evaporate*, Gal. 14.776. **-ειλήτως**, v. -ίλλητος. **-έλεγκτος**, ον, *hard to refute*, Pl.*Phd.*85c (Sup.), Ptol.*Tetr.*164. II. *hard to discover*, φάρμακα D.H.3.5. **-έλευστος**, ον, *hard to get out of*, Tz.*H.*11.556. **-έλικτος**, ον, *hard to unfold, involved*, πλοκή D.H.*Thuc.*29, cf. *Amm.*2.2, Plu.*Brut.*13; δυσεξέλικτα κυματούμενος κλύδων Luc.*Trag.*25; *twisted, contorted*, ὀδόντες Ael.*NA*14.8. **-έργαστος**, ον, *hard to work out*, Eust.1394.7. **-ερεύνητος**, ον, *hard to explore*, Arist.*Pol.*1330b26. **-εύρετος**, ον, *hard to find out*, Id.*HA*611a26, Plu.2.407f. **-ήγητος**, ον, *hard to explain*, Darius ap.D.L.9.13, Gal.17(2).71. **-ημέρωτος**, ον, *hard to tame*, Plu.*Art.*25. **-ήνυστος**, ον, *indissoluble*, δεσμός E.*Hipp.*1237. **-ίλαστος** [ῑ], ον, *hard to appease*, πένθη Plu.2.609f. **-ίλλητος**, ον, *hard to unravel*, Cic. *Att.*5.10.3 (s.v.l.). Adv., in form δυσεξειλήτως, v.l. in Sch.Theoc. 14.51. **-ίτηλος** [ῑ], ον, *not easily perishing*, ἄνθος φαρμάκων Str. 11.8.7, cf. Plu.2.696d, Philum.*Ven.*4.3. **-ίτητος** [ῑ], ον, = sq., Hsch., *EM*238.42. **-ῖτος**, ον, *hard to get out of*, D.S.3.44 (v.l. δυσδιεξίτητος). **-όδευτος**, ον, = δυσδιέξοδος, Procl.*Par.Ptol.*153. **-οδος**, ον, *hard to get out of*, Arist.*Pol.*1330b26, Lyc.1099, Paus.2.31.1: metaph., ἐρώτησις Luc.*Fug.*10. 2. *hard to remedy*, Hp.*Epid.*4.30. **-οιστος**, ον, *hard to explain*: τὸ δ. Porph.*VP*48, cf. Hsch. II. = δυσεκκόμιστος, Id. **-οχος**, ον, *craggy, rugged*, Eust.ad D.P.389. * **-ῡβωτός**, ον, *not easily displaced outwards*, Sor.1.102. **-ώθητος**, ον, *hard to dislodge*, Simp.*in Ph.*677.29.

**δῠσέπ-ακτος**, ον, *hard to draw back*, of overwound strands of gut, Ph.*Bel.*58.23. **-ανόρθωτος**, ον, *hard to correct* or *reform*, Vett. Val.77.6; πολιτεία Theo *Prog.*12. **-έκτᾰτος**, ον, *hard to extend* or *distend*, Gal.8.288, al. **-ήβολος**, ον, *hard to master*, Suid. s.v. Ἀγάπιος.

**δῠσεπί-βᾰτος**, ον, *hard to get at*, D.S.1.69. **-βλητος**, ον, *hard to attain to*, παράδειγμα *OGI*764.17 (Pergam.). **-βολος**, ον, *hard to assail*, χώρα Aen.Tact.8.1 codd.; *risky to undertake*, πλοῦς *Peripl. M.Rubr.*39; *unsuccessful*, Paul.Al.*N.*4. **-βούλευτος**, ον, *hard to attack secretly*, X.*Eq.Mag.*4.11 (Comp.), *Ages.*6.7 (Sup.). 2. *hard to damage*, Apollod.*Poliorc.*139.7. **-γνωστος**, ον, *hard to identify* or *find out*, *SIG*1023.9 (Cos, iii/ii B.C.), App.*BC*1.18. **-θετος**, ον, *hard to attack*, Aen.Tact.*Praef.*2. **-κούρητος**, ον, *hard to meet*, ἀπορία Alcid.*Soph.*21. **-κρῐτος**, ον, *hard to decide*, Ap.Ty. *Ep.*19, Gal.13.789. **-λόγιστος**, ον, *hard to conceive*, Diog.Oen. 38. **-μικτος**, ον, *disinclined for intercourse*, τινί Str.11.2.2: abs., *unsociable*, Id.3.3.8; τὸ ἄστοργον καὶ δ. Plu.2.917c, Porph.*Abst.*4.6. **-νόητος**, ον, *hard to understand*, M.Ant.6.17; *hard to devise* or *plan out*, Jul.*Or.*1.12b. **-στροφος**, ον, *hard to turn* or *guide*, ἅρματα App.*Mith.*42. **-σχετος**, ον, *hard to check*, of bleeding, Gal.19.457, Aret.*CA*2.6. Adv. -τως Gal.7.725, Herod.Med.in *Rh. Mus.*58.99. **-τευκτος**, ον, *hard to accomplish*, στρατεία D.S.17.93; *ineffective*, Vett.Val.43.12, al., *Cat.Cod.Astr.*1.164. Adv. -τως Vett.Val.194.27. 2. *hard to treat*, *Hippiatr.*26. **-τίμητος** [τῑ], ον, *hard to criticize*, Alex.Aphr.*in Top.*543.5. **-χείρητος**, ον, *hard to prove*, πρόβλημα Arist.*APr.*42b31. 2. *hard to attack*, θέσις Id.*Top.*159a3; πρόβλημα ib.158b16: Sup. -ότατοι τῶν ὅρων ib. 158b8; of a person, J.*BJ*4.3.10, Plu.2.281a, App.*Pun.*118.

**δῠσεπούλωτος**, ον, *hard to cicatrize*, Gal.6.751, v.l. in Dsc.4.41.

**δῠσέραστος**, ον, *unhappy in love*, Max.Tyr.3.5 (Comp., wrongly spelt δυσερασίστερος). II. *unfavourable to love*, ὄρθρος *AP*5.171 (Mel.), 172 (Id.).

**δῠσεργ-ᾰσία**, ἡ, *difficulty of performing*, Artem.1.67. **-αστος**, ον, *difficult to construct*, χώματα J.*BJ*5.9.2. **-εια**, ἡ, *difficulty*, Sor.2.53, Orib.45.18.14; *functional defect*, Paul.Aeg.6.42, al. **-έω**, *to be sluggish*, καταμήνια -γοῦντα, of dysmenorrhoea, Hp.*Ep.*21. **-ημα**, ατος, τό, *difficulty, hindrance*, Dsc.*Ther.Praef.* **-ής**, ές, *difficult*, App.*Hisp.*73, al.; τὸ δ. *OGI*502.6 (Aezani): Comp., of an operation, Antyll.(?)ap.Orib.44.23.23; *making it hard to work*, βαρύτητες Plu.2.1129d. **-ία**, ἡ, *difficulty in working* or *construction*, δυσεργίαν παρέχειν Ph.*Bel.*56.42, cf. Hero *Aut.*23.8 (in form -έργεια), Plu.*Aem.*16; *difficulty* in pronouncing, ἡ ἐν τῇ προφορᾷ δ. Phld.*Po.*2.42; *inability to exert oneself*, Hp.*VM*10 (v.l. δυσοργίη); *inability to act*, App.*Syr.*19. **-ος**, ον, *hard to work*, ὕλη Thphr.*HP* 5.1.1; λίθοι Paus.3.21.4; *unfit to be worked*, σίδηρος Plu.*Lyc.*9; *hard to manage*, ὁπλισμός Id.*Flam.*8; δ. χρῆσθαι Id.*Tim.*28; πόλις -οτέρα *harder to besiege*, Id.*Nic.*17. 2. *hard to effect, difficult*, Plb.28.8.3, Ph.1.272 (Sup.); πόλεμος App.*Hisp.*63 (Sup.); τὸ παραφυλάττειν τὰς ἐξόδους -ότερον J.*BJ*5.12.1. Adv. -γως, κινηθῆναι Plu.*Demetr.*43. II. Act., *incapable of work, useless*, πρός τι App.*Syr.*16; χεῖμα δ., *hiems ignava*, Bion *Fr.*15.5; *idle*, νωθρὸς καὶ δ. Plu.*Alex.*33.

**δῠσ-ερεύνητος**, ον, *hard to search*, χωρία J.*BJ*1.16.5. **-έρημος**, ον, *very lonely, desolate*, πάγος *AP*9.561 (Phil.). **-ερις**, ι, gen. ιδος, *quarrelsome, contentious*, Isoc.1.31, Arist.*Rh.*1381a32, *EN*1108a30, al.; δ. λόγος Pl.*Lg.*864a. II. Act., *producing unhappy strife*, φθόνος Plu.*Pel.*4; τὸ δανείζειν δ. App.*BC*1.54. **-εριστία**, ἡ, *contentious disposition*, Procl.*in Prm.*p.539 S.; *irreconcilability*, Iamb. *Myst.*1.2. **-έριστος**, ον, *pertaining to unholy strife*, αἷμα S.*El.* 1385 (lyr.); σπουδή Cleanth.*Stoic.*1.122. **-ερμήνευτος**, ον, *hard to interpret*, *Ep.Hebr.*5.11, Gal.11.454, *Cat.Cod.Astr.*1.114.26; *hard to describe*, χρόα D.S.2.52; θέα Ph.1.649. **-ερμος**, ον, *not favoured by Hermes, unlucky*, Suid.:—hence **-ερμία**, ἡ, *ill luck*, Hsch., *EM*291.49. **-ερνής**, ές, *hardly shooting* or *sprouting*, Poll.1.231. **-ερως**, ωτος, ὁ, ἡ, *madly* or *disastrously loving*, τινός E.*Hipp.*193; τῶν ἀπόντων Th.6.13; τῶν ἀφροδισίων X.*Oec.*11.13; *mali cupidus*, Max. Tyr.36.4; εἰς χρήματα Jul.*Or.*2.85c: abs., Lys.4.8 (s.v.l.), Call.*Ep.*42.6, *AP*5.244 (Maced.), al.; of bees, *Lyr.Alex.Adesp.*7.16; δ. ἔρως Plu.*Per.*20. II. *laggard in love*, Theoc.1.85, 6.7. **-ερωτιάω**, *to be desperately in love*, Ach.Tat.5.1, Plu.*Fr.*21.2. **-ετηρία**, ἡ, (ἔτος) *bad season*, Poll.1.52. **-ετῠμολόγητος**, ον, *hard to derive*, ὄνομα Corn.*ND*20. **-ευνήτωρ**, Dor. -άτωρ, ορος, ὁ, *ill bedfellow*, A.*Th.*293 (lyr.):—expld. by **-εύνητος**, *ill-bedded*, in Sch.ad loc. **-ευπόριστος**, ον, *hard to procure*, Alex.Trall.1.15. * **-εύρετος**, ον, *hard to find out*, A.*Pr.*816; λόγος Porph.ap.Eus.*PE*3.11; δ. τό τινων γένος Ph.1.234. 2. *hard to find* or *get*, X.*Mem.*3.14.7, Secund.*Sent.*11; σπάνιον καὶ δ. Plu.2.97b. 3. *hard to find one's way through, impenetrable*, ὕλη E.*Ba.*1221. **-έφικτος**, ον, *hard to come at*, Plb.31.25.3, Plu.2.65e, Phld.*Rh.*2.119 S.; ἀνθρώπῳ Ecphant.ap. Stob.4.7.64; *hard to understand*, Vett.Val.272.8, al. **-έφοδος**, ον, *hard to get at, inaccessible*, D.S.1.57 (Sup.); τὸ δ. Phld.*Rh.*1.325 S. (nisi leg. δυσέφικτον). **-έψᾰνος** [ᾰ], ον, *hard to digest*, Suid. s.vv. ἕψανον, τέραμνον. **-έψητος**, ον, = foreg., Phryn *PS*p.33 B.; *hard to cook*, Gal.6.541 (Comp.). **-ζηλία**, ἡ, *jealousy*, Ath.13.589a. * **-ζηλος**, ον, *exceeding jealous*, Od.7.307; ἐπί τινι A.R.4.1081; γυνή Plu.*Alex.*9; τὸ δ. Id.2.471a. Adv. -λως, ἔχειν πρός τινα Id.*Alex.*77. 2. *eager*, ὁρμή Emp.114.3. II. *rivalling in hardship*, αἰθυίῃσι βίον δύσζηλον ἔχοντες Hom.*Epigr.*8. **-ζήτητος**, ον, *hard to seek* or *track*, X.*Cyn.*8.1, Poll.5.50. **-ζωΐα**, v.l. for δυσοδία, Ps.-Callisth.3.9. **-ζωος**, ον, *wretched*, βίοτος δ. *AP*9.574. **-ήβολον**· δυσάν(τ)ητον, Hsch. **-ήκεστος**, ον, *hard to heal* or *cure*, Hp.*Fract.*29, *AP*3.19 (Cyzicus). **-ηκής**, ές, = foreg., Hsch.

**δῠσηκο-έω**, *to be hard of hearing*, Antyll.ap.Orib.10.13.5. * **-ΐα**, ἡ, *hardness of hearing*, Dsc.5.17, Plu.2.1073d, Vett.Val.109.31; *disobedience*, Plu.2.794d. **-ος**, ον, *hard of hearing*, ὦτα Ph.2.35; δυσήκοος ὦ Στρατονίκη, epitaph in *Inscr.Mus.Alex.*299 (iii B.C.); *disobedient*, Plu.2.13f. II. *ill-sounding, terrible to hear*, prob. in S. *Fr.*220; *unpleasant to the ear*, Demetr.*Eloc.*48, Poll.2.117, Philostr. *VS*1.12; of an orator, Eun.*VS*p.456 B.

**δῠσ-ηλάκᾰτος** [λᾰ], ον, *spinner of ill*, Μοῖρα Nonn.*D.*1.367; Φιλομήλη ib.4.321. **-ήλᾰτος**, ον, *hard to drive through* or *over*, Poll. 1.186. * **-ηλεγής**, ές, (ἄλγος, ἀλεγ-εινός) Homeric epith. of death and war, *bringing bitter grief, cruel, ruthless*, θάνατος, πόλεμος, Od.22.325, Il.20.154; πηγάδες .. δυσηλεγέες *cruel* frosts, Hes *Op.*506; δυσηλεγέος ἀπὸ δεσμοῦ Id.*Th.*652; also of men, πολῖται Thgn.795; γείτονες Max.87. * **-ήλιος**, Dor. -άλιος, ον, *ill-sunned, sunless*, κνέφας A.*Eu.*396 (lyr.), cf. E.*Rh.*247 (lyr.), Plu.*Mar.*11, etc. II. *too much sunned, parched*, θέρος *Trag.Adesp.*340.

**δῠσημερ-έω**, *have an unlucky day, be unlucky*, Pherecr.98; κατὰ τὰς μάχας D.H.1.57. **-ημα**, ατος, τό, *ill luck*, Sch.Il.6.336. * **-ία**, Dor. -ᾱμερία, ἡ, *unlucky day*: *mishap, misery*, δυσαμερίαν πρύτανιν A.*Fr.*236; μοῖρα δυσαμερίας S.*Fr.*591, cf. Plu.*Eum.*9.

**δῠσ-ήμερος**, ον, (ἥμερος) *hard to tame, restive*, Str.3.3.8, Ptol.*Tetr.*56. **-ήμετος**, ον, = sq., Hp.*Epid.*6.8.26. **-ημής**, ές, = δυσεμής, Id.*Aph.*4.7. * **-ήνεμον**· δυστάραχον, τὸ κακοὺς ἀνέμους ἔχον, Hsch. **-ηνίαστος**, ον, *hard to bridle*, Tim.Gaz.124.11. **-ήνιος**, ον, (ἡνία) = foreg., *refractory*, Epict.*Gnom.*63; γυνὴ δυσήνιόν ἐστι

(v. l. -ἀνιόν) Men.803. B. (ἀνία) = δυσάνιος, *ill at ease, uneasy*, Hp.*Epid.*3.17.ια' codd. **-ηνίοχητος**, ον, *hard to hold in, ungovernable*, Luc.*Abd.*17. ❀ **-ήνυτος**, ον, (ἀνύω) *hard to accomplish*, J.*BJ*5.12.1; also **-ήνυκτος**, Hsch. **-ήρης**, ες, *difficult*, opp. εὐήρης, Suid. **-ηρις**, ιδος, ὁ, ἡ, = δύσερις I, Pi.*O.*6.19, Axiop.1.4: Att. form of δύσερις acc. to Moer.126. **-ήριστος**, ον, = foreg., Hsch.; also, = ἀμφίβολος, Id. **-ήροτος**, ον, (ἀρόω) *hard to plough*, Call.*Del.*268, Poll.1.227. **-ήττητος**, ον, *hard to conquer*, ib. 157. **-ήτωρ**, ορος, ὁ, ἡ, *heavy at heart*, Hsch. **-ηχής**, Dor. **-ᾱχής**, ές, (ἠχέω) *ill-sounding*, Phld.*Po.*2.16, v.l. in D.H.*Comp.*14; *giving a dull sound*, of metals, Plu.2.721c; ἰσθμοῖο δ. Emp.100.19:— in Hom., epith. of πόλεμος, Il.2.686 (cf. Anacr.107), al.; and of θάνατος, Il.16.442, al. (where it should perh. be taken, = *bringer of great woe* (ἄχος), cf. Apollon.*Lex.*), of φόνος Emp.136.1; *of ill-repute*, δ. ἀνδράσιν *h.Ap.*64. **-ηχία**, ἡ, *unpleasantness of sound*, Phld.*Po.*2.24, *Po.Herc.*994.23. **-ηχος**, ον, *ill-sounding*, ῥυθμός Hermog.*Id.*1.7; συνθήκη ibid. **-θάλασσος** [θᾰ], ον, *subject to sea-sickness*, Sor.1.109. **-θᾰλής**, ές, *hardly growing*, Cratin.405, Alex.Mynd.ap.Ath.9.393a. **-θᾰλία**, ας, ἡ, *a misfortune*, Sophr. 83 (pl.). **-θαλπής**, ές, *hard to warm: chilly*, χειμών Il.17.549. II. *over-warm, burning hot*, Q.S.11.156 codd.

**δυσθᾰνᾰτ-άω**, strengthd. for θανατάω, *long for death*, J.*BJ*5.9.3, 6.6.2, Agath.3.22, cf. *EM*442.48; but freq. confused with sq., as in Ph.2.390. 2. δυσθανατῶσα γραῦς 'with one foot in the grave', Chrysipp.*Stoic.*3.50. **-έω**, *to be loath to die*, Hdt.9.72; *struggle against death, die hard*, Pl.*R.*406b, Thphr.*HP*3.11.3, Plu.*Ant.*77, etc.; also, *to be sick to death with desire*, περί τι Ph.2.167; *to be deadly obstinate*, περί τι ib.100: abs., *to be in deadly terror*, ib.173. **-ος**, ον, *bringing a hard death*, Hp.*Prorrh.*1.55; κρατῆρες E.*Ion* 1051 (lyr.).

**δυσ-θᾰνής**, ές, *unhappy in death*, *AP*9.81 (Crin.). **-θέᾱτος**, ον, *ill to look on*, A.*Pr.*69 (lyr.), S.*Aj.*1004. II. *hard to see*, ἀμαυρὸν αἴθυγμα καὶ δ. Plu.2.966b, cf. Ael.*NA*9.61. **-θενέω**, (σθένος) *to be weak and powerless*, Hp.*Morb.*2.54, al. **-θεος**, ον, *godless, ungodly*, A.*Ag.*1590, *Ch.*46 (lyr.); ὦ δ. μίσημα S.*El.*289. 2. *miserable, wretched*, μισθὸς εὐσεβίης *AJA*17.170 (Cyrene, written δύσθιον). **-θερᾰπευσία**, ἡ, *difficulty of treatment*, Cass.*Pr.* 1. **-θεράπευτος** [ᾰ], ον, *hard to cure*, Hp.*Medic.*10, S.*Aj.*609 (lyr.); εὐήθεια Ph.1.334. **-θερέας**· δυσαλθήτους, Hsch. **-θέρμαντος**, ον, *cold*, Sch.Il.17.549. **-θερος**, ον, *over-hot, parched*, Poll.5. 110. **-θεσία**, ἡ, *bad condition*: *fretfulness, peevishness*, Hp.*Fract.* 33 (v.l. δυσαισθησίη). ❀ **-θετέω**, *to be dissatisfied*, ταῖς συνθήκαις Plb.*Fr.*128; *to be in distress*, D.S.14.113. II. mostly in Med., abs., *to be vexed*, X.*Cyr.*2.2.5; τινί Plb.33.17.1; *to be in straits*, Id. 8.5.4. **-θετος**, ον, (τίθημι) *in bad case*, κακόν Ph.1.97; τὸ δ. *bad condition*, J.*AJ*15.9.6. II. *hard to set right*, Hp.*Fract.*38 (Comp.). **-θεώρητος**, ον, *hard to observe*, Arist.*HA*511ᵇ13; *scarcely visible*, τρύπημα HeroSpir.1.31, cf. Philum.*Ven.*15.6. II. *hard to understand or reduce to theory*, τέχνη Ph.*Bel.*49.19, cf. Plb.3. 31.7, Phld.*Rh.*1.141 S., Ph.2.84. **-θήρᾱτος**, ον, *hard to catch*, Arist.*HA*615ᵃ22, Plu.*Pomp.*38: metaph., τὸ δ. [τῆς φιλοσοφίας] Ph.1.234; δ. τἀληθές Plu.*Per.*13, cf. Ph.2.217, al. **-θήρευτος**, ον, = foreg., Pl.*Sph.*218d, 261a. **-θηρία**, ἡ, *bad hunting*, Poll.5.13. **-θηρος**, ον, *having bad sport*, Opp.*H.*3.431, Poll.5. 13. **-θησαύριστος**, ον, *hard to store*, καρπός Pl.*Criti.*115b, cf. Arist.*Mu.*401ᵃ5. **-θιος**, v. δύσθεος. **-θλαστος**, ον, *hard to crush, tough*, Thphr.*HP*3.4.1 (Comp.), Gal.*UP*11.17. **-θνήσκω**, = δυσθανατέω, only in part., E.*El.*843, *Rh.*791. **-θνητέω**, = foreg., Nic.Dam.p.36 D. **-θραυστος**, ον, *hard to break*, Dsc.4.154, Gal. *UP*11.17. **-θρήνητος**, ον, *loud-wailing, most mournful*, ἔπος S. *Ant.*1211; θρῆνοι E.*IT*144 (anap.):—also **-θρηνος**, gloss on δυσηχής, Apollon.*Lex.* **-θροος**, ον, *ill-sounding*, φωνά Pi.*P.*4.63; βάγματα, αὐδά, γόοι, A.*Pers.*637 (lyr.), 942 (anap.), 1076 (lyr.). **-θρυπτος**, ον, *hard to break in pieces*, στερρότης Plu.ap.*EM*104.1 (dub. l.).

**δυσθῡμ-αίνω**, *to be dispirited, despond*, *h.Cer.*362. **-έω**, = foreg., Hdt.8.100, Onos.10.26; δ. ταῖς ἐλπίσιν Plu.*Tim.*34:—Med., *to be melancholy, angry*, Democr.286, E.*Med.*91. **-ία**, ἡ, *despondency, despair*, Hp.*VM*10, Pl.*Lg.*666b, etc.; πρὶν ἐλθεῖν ξυμμάχους δυσθυμίαν E.*Supp.*696: pl., Id.*Med.*691, S.*Fr.*663, Arist.*Pr.*954ᵇ35, Ph.2. 99. II. *ill-temper*, Them.*Or.*13.172c. **-ικός**, ή, όν, *melancholy*, Arist.*Phgn.*813ᵃ33. **-ος**, ον, *desponding, melancholy*, S.*El.* 218 (lyr.), X.*Cyr.*5.2.34, Arist.*Pr.*955ᵃ17 (Comp.), Phld.*Herc.*1251. 10; τοῖς πεπραγμένοις S.*El.*550; τὸ δ., = δυσθυμία, Plu.*Per.*15. Adv. **-μως**, ἔχειν Plb.1.87.1, Phld.*Mort.*27: Comp. **-ότερον** Pl.*Phd.*85b.

**δῠσ-ῑᾱτέω**, *to be hard to heal*, Paul.Aeg.3.18. **-ίᾱτος**, Ion. **-ίητος** [ῐ], ον, *hard to heal*, κλητίς Hp.*Art.*14 (Comp.), cf. Cass.*Pr.*1 (Comp.); κακὸν δ. an ill *that none can cure*, A.*Ag.*1103 (lyr.); ὀργή E.*Med.*520; νόσημα Pl.*Lg.*916a, cf. Ph.1.40, al.; of persons, *implacable*, Them.*Or.*15.192c. Adv. **-τως**, μόριον πεπονθὸς δ. Gal.18(2). 273. **-ίδρως**, ωτος, ὁ, ἡ, *hardly perspiring*, Thphr.*Sud.*18. **-ῑερέω**, *to have bad omens in a sacrifice*, Plu.*Caes.*63, 2.587c.

**δῡσῑθάλασσος** [θᾰ], Att. **-ττος**, ον, (δύω) *dipped in the sea*, *AP*6.38 (Phil.).

**δύσικμος** [ῠ], ον, (ἰκμάς) *with scanty secretions*, Hp.*Mul.*1.34; δ. πάθος Orib.*Fr.*78.

**δῠσικός**, ή, όν, = δυτικός, *PLond.*1.98.51.

**δῠσ-ίμερος** [ῑ], ον, κάματος, πῆμα, of the *torments of love*, A.R.3. 961, 4.4. II. *tormented by love*, Nonn.*D.*42.202, al. **-ίππαστος**, ον, = sq., τόπος Anon.Hist.in *Rev.Ét.Gr.*5.320, Sch.Pl.*Mx.* 240c, cf. Poll.1.186 (v.l.). **-ιππος**, ον, *hard to ride in*: τὰ δ. *parts unfit for cavalry-service*, X.*HG*3.4.12; δ. χώρα Plu.*Phil.*14.

**δύσις** [ῠ], εως, ἡ, (δύω) *setting of the sun* or *stars*, opp. ἀνατολή, Heraclit.120, A.*Pr.*458; ἀμφὶ Πλειάδων δύσιν (cf. Πλειάδες) Id.*Ag.* 826; περὶ δύσιν Πλειάδος Damox.2.19; δ. χειμερινή, θερινή, ἰσημερινή, Cleom.1.9; δ. τροπική Str.2.4.7; ἄχρι ἡλίου δύσεως *IG*4.597 (Argos); ἁλίου ἄχρι δ. ib.606 (ibid.); Κυνὸς ψυχρὰν δ. S.*Fr.*432.11; personified, *PMag.Berol.*2.94: pl., δύσιες, opp. ἀντολαί, A.R.1.85: metaph., δ. τοῦ λογισμοῦ Ph.1.511. 2. *quarter in which the sun sets, west*, πρὸς ἡλίου δύσιν Th.2.96; πρὸς δύσεις Arist.*Mu.*393ᵃ18; ἀπὸ δύσεως *CIG*1755 (Opus); πρὸς δύσει Plb.1.42.5; πρὸς τὰς δύσεις βλέπειν Id. 5.104.7. II. *hiding-place*, Opp.*H.*1.330.

**δῠσ-ίχνευτος**, ον, *hard to track*, Sch.S.*Aj.*32. **-ίωτος** [ῑ], ον, *not easily rusted*, in Comp., Orib.49.3.5. **-κᾰής**, ές, *hard to burn, burning badly*, Plu.2.952c. **-καθαίρετος**, ον, *hard to overthrow*, Ph.1.61; στάσις J.*BJ*2.17.4. ❀ **-κάθαρτος** [κᾰ], ον, *hard to purify*, Ph.1.239, al.; *hard to purge*, πνεύματα Plu.2.991b, cf. Dsc.5.69. II. *hard to satisfy by purification* or *atonement*, δ. Ἅιδου λιμήν, of the house of the Labdacidae in which murders never ceased, S.*Ant.* 1284 (lyr.); δαίμων Ar.*Pax*1250. **-κάθεκτος**, ον, *hard to hold in*, ἵπποι X.*Mem.*4.1.3 (Sup.); πλήθη Plu.*Num.*4: metaph., Corn.*ND*30; πλοῦτος Luc.*Tim.*29 (s.v.l., al. δυσκάτοχος); *hard to keep in mind, retain*, Plu.2.408b. **-κάθοδος**, ον, *hard to go down into*, σπήλαιον Conon35.1. **-καμπής**, ές, *hard to bend*, Plu.2.650d, Aret.*SD*2.3: Comp., Sabin.ap.Orib.9.19.2. **-καμπτος**, ον, = foreg., Cass. *Pr.*61, Sch.Ar.*Th.*74. Adv. **-τως**, ἔχειν Aët.16.8. **-καπνος**, ον, *noisome from smoke*, δώματα A.*Ag.*774 (lyr.). II. *producing an unpleasant smoke*, Thphr.*Ign.*72; φοῖνιξ Chaerem.39 (Sup.). **-καρτέρητος**, ον, *hard to endure*, Ph.2.73, Plu.*Phoc.*4, etc. Adv. **-τως** Porph.*Marc.*8, Herod.Med.ap.Aët.9.2. **-κατᾰγωγός**, όν, *making a landing difficult*, βράχη *Stad.*114. **-κατᾰγώνιστος**, ον, *hard to overcome*, Plb.15.15.8, D.H.3.7; *hard to refute*, Id.*Rh.*8.3; τὸ δ. *impregnability*, Corn.*ND*20. **-κατάθετος**, ον, *hard to bring*, πρὸς φιλίαν, f.l. for δυσσυγκάθετος, Iamb.*VP*31.194. **-κάτακτος**, ον, *hard to break*, Thphr.*HP*3.7.4, Dsc.3.22, Apollod.*Poliorc.*139. 8. **-κατάληπτος**, ον, *hard to comprehend*, D.S.1.3, Ph.2.216, M.Ant.5.10. **-κατάλλακτος**, ον, *hard to reconcile*, Plu.2.13d, Ath. 14.625b.

**δυσκατά-λῠτος**, ον, *hard to bring to an end*, πόλεμοι Str.14.1.28; *hard to overthrow*, δυναστεία J.*BJ*4.5.5. **-μάθητος** [μᾰ], ον, *hard to learn* or *understand*, Isoc.10.11, Pl.*Plt.*303d (Comp.), D.H.*Th.*9. Adv. μαθήτως, ἔχειν Isoc.2.33. **-μάχητος** [μᾰ], ον, *hard to overcome*, D.S.3.35; νόσος (sc. πενία) Lib.*Decl.*34.4. **-νόητος**, ον, *hard to understand*, διάλεκτος D.S.5.14, cf. Plu.2.47c. **-παυστος**, ον, *hard to check*, ἄλγος A.*Ch.*470 (lyr.); βοή Lxx 3*Ma.*5.7; of persons, Plu.*Alex.*31; *restless*, ψυχή E.*Med.*109 (anap.); τὸ -ότερον Thphr. *Vent.*35. **-πεπτος**, ον, *hard to digest*, Id.*CP*1.14.4. **-πληκτος**, ον, *hard to keep in awe*, Plb.1.67.4. **-πολέμητος**, ον, *hard to conquer*, D.S.2.48. **-πόνητος**, ον, *hard to execute*, M.Ant.6.19, Arr.*Epict.*3. 12.8; *hard to digest*, Sor.2.32. **-ποσία**, ἡ, *difficulty of swallowing*, Herod.Med. in *Rh.Mus.*58.86, Philum.ap.Aët.8.48. **-ποτέω**, *have difficulty in swallowing*, Herod.Med.ap.Orib.5.30.12. **-ποτος**, ον, *hard to swallow*, Arist.*Sens.*443ᵇ12, Archig.ap.Gal.12.976. **-πρακτος**, ον, *hard to effect*, X.*Cyr.*8.7.12 (Comp.).

**δυσκατάρτιστος**, ον, *hard to place rightly*, ἐν τῇ ἐπιβάσει, of stallions, *Hippiatr.*14.

**δυσκατά-σβεστος**, ον, *hard to extinguish*, D.S.4.54, Plu.2.417b. **-στᾰτος**, ον, *hard to restore* or *rally*, X.*Cyr.*5.3.43 (Comp.). **-φρόνητος**, ον, *not to be despised*, ib.8.1.42 (Comp.).

**δυσκατ-εργᾰσία**, ἡ, *indigestion*, Anon.Lond.6.10. **-έργαστος**, ον, *hard to work*, λίθος Str.17.1.33; καρποὶ -ότεροι *slower to mature*, Thphr.*CP*1.14.4; *hard of digestion*, Dsc.2.93, Ph.2.244. II. = δυσκατάπρακτος, X.*Mem.*4.2.7 (Comp.). III. *hard to tame*, γένος ταύρων Agatharch.76 (Sup.); *hard to overcome*, Luc.*Tyr.* 15. **-οπτος**· δυσθεώρητος, Hsch. **-όρθωτος**, ον, *hard to succeed in*, ἔργον Demetr.*Eloc.*127, Ph.2.83, Gal.*UP*15.7; τυραννίς Chio *Ep.*15 (Comp.). II. *hard to set right, remedy*, σπάνις τῶν ἀναγκαίων J.*AJ*2.5.6. **-ούλωτος**, ον, *hard to cicatrize*, Dsc.5.81; ἕλκη Apollon.*Mir.*42.

**δυσκάτοχος**, v. δυσκάθεκτος.

**δύσκαυστος**, ον, *hard to burn*, Apollod.*Poliorc.*139.8.

**δύσκε**, v. δύω.

❀ **δυσ-κέλᾰδος**, ον, *ill-sounding, shrieking*, φόβος Il.16.357; ζῆλος δ. envy *with its tongue of malice*, Hes.*Op.*196; δ. ὕμνος Ἐρινύος A.*Th.* 867 (anap.), cf. *Fr.*451 I; μοῦσα E.*Ion* 1098 (lyr.). **-κένωτος**, ον, *hard to excrete*, Gal.18(1).580 (Sup.). **-κέραστος**, ον, *hard to temper*, φύσις πρὸς τὸ πιθανὸν δ. Plu.*Dio*52; δύσμικτα καὶ δ. Id.2. 754c. **-κερδής**, ές, *with ill gains, ill-gotten*, Opp.*H.*2.417. **-κηδής**, ές, (κῆδος) *full of misery*, δυσκηδέα νύκτα φυλάσσω Od.5.466. II. (κήδομαι) δυσκηδέα· δυσφύλακτον, χαλεπόν, Hsch. **-κηλος**, ον, (κηλέω) *past remedy*, A.*Eu.*825 (cf. Sch. ad loc.): but perh. rather formed by analogy from εὔκηλος: hence, *spiteful*. **-κημον**· ἄφρονα, δυσοιώνιστον, Hsch.

**δυσκῑν-ησία**, Ion. **-ίη**, ἡ, *difficulty of moving*, Hp.*Aph.*3.17, Arist. *GA*780ᵃ25, *PA*685ᵃ8. **-ητέω**, *move with difficulty*, Herod.Med. in *Rh.Mus.*58.104. **-ητος**, ον, *hard to move*, Pl.*Ti.*56a, Ph.2.227 (Comp.), Thphr.*Vent.*35 (Sup.); πλοῖα Plb.1.22.3. Adv. **-τως**, ἔχειν πρὸς τοὺς ἀνέμους Arist.*Cael.*294ᵇ17. II. in mental relations, δ. πρὸς τοὺς φόβους Pl.*R.*503d; δ. ὑπὸ ὀργῆς Arist.*VV*1250ᵃ5; δ. ποιεῖν

τὴν διάνοιαν Id.*PA*686$^{a}$30; ἕξις -οτέρα διαθέσεως Id.*Cat.*9$^{a}$10; τὸ -ον *obstinacy*, Phld.*Lib.*p.55 O.; of language, *clumsiness*, τὸ ἄσχημον καὶ δ. Id.*Po.*994.35. Adv. -τως καὶ δυσμαθῶς ἔχειν Pl.*R.*503d. **2.** *firm, resolute*, Plu.*Thes.*36; *inexorable*, Ἅιδης *AP*7.221. **3.** *impervious to motion*, of the soul, Plot.1.4.8.

**δυσ-κλεής**, *ές*, *inglorious*, Il.9.22 (poet. acc. δυσκλέᾰ for δυσκλεέα); *infamous, shameful*, of persons and things, δ. θέα A.*Pr.*243; δυσκλεεστάτῳ μόρῳ Id.*Pers.*444; πρῶτον μὲν οὐκ οὖσ' ἄδικός εἰμι δυσκλεής E.*Hel.*270, cf. X.*Cyr.*3.3.53, Lxx 3*Ma.*3.23 (Sup.). Adv. -εῶς S.*El.*1006, E.*Hel.*993 codd., Plu.2.169a. **-κλεια**, ἡ, *ill-fame, infamy*, S.*Fr.*188, E.*Med.*218, Th.3.58, Pl.*Lg.*663a, etc.; ἐπὶ δυσκλείᾳ tending to *disgrace them*, S.*Aj.*143 (anap.). **II.** *ingloriousness*, D.60.24. **-κληδόνιστος**, *ον*, *of ill name, boding ill*, Luc.*Am.*39. **-κληρέω**, *to be unlucky in one's lot*, esp. in standing for an office, opp. λαγχάνω, Pl.*Lg.*690c. **-κλήρημα**, *ατος, τό, piece of ill luck*, Plb.30.20.9 (pl.); τῆς πατρίδος D.S.32.22 (pl.). **-κληρος**, *ον, unlucky*, Phryn.*PS*p.61 B. **-κλής**, poet. for δυσκλεής, Simm.*Secur.*6. **-κλητος**, *ον, in bad repute*, Heraclid.Tar.ap.Ath.3.120d. **-κλῐτος**, *ον, hard to inflect, irregular*, δ. ῥήματα, title of work by Eulogius, *EM*809.33. **-κλῠδώνιστον**· δυσέκβατον, Suid. **-κλῠτος**, *ον, ill-famed*, Hsch. **-κοίλιος**, *ον, bad for the bowels*, Dsc.1.105, Plu.2.137a. **2.** *costive*, Paul.Aeg.1.44. **-κοινώνητος**, *ον, unsocial*, Pl.*R.*486b; ἀρχή Plu.*Demetr.*3. **-κοιτέω**, *to have bad nights*, Hp.*VM*10, *Acut.*30. **-κοιτος**, *ον, making bed unpleasant*, Aristaenet.2.7. **-κολαίνω**, impf. ἐδυσκόλαινον Pl.*Phlb.*26d: fut. -κολᾰνῶ Isoc.15.149:—*to be peevish*, Ar.*Nu.*36; of a baby, Lys.1.11, cf. X.*Mem.*2.2.8; τινί D.37.15; *feel a difficulty*, δ. ὡς.. Pl. l.c.; in argument, *to be captious*, Arist.*Top.*160$^{b}$3, al. **2.** *cause trouble* or *annoyance*, οὔρησις δυσκολαίνουσα Hp.*Prorrh.*1.109. **-κολία**, ἡ, *discontent, peevishness*, Ar.*V.*106, Pl.*R.*411c. **II.** of things, *difficulty*, δ. ἔχειν D.5.1, Arist.*Pol.*1281$^{a}$14, etc.; πλείους παρέχειν δυσκολίας ib.1263$^{a}$11; δ. ὀνομάτων J.*AJ*2.7.4. **-κόλλητος**, *ον, hard to glue together*, Gal.11.124,133; *ill-glued* or *fastened, loose*, Luc.*Hist.Conscr.*11.

**δυσκολό-καμπτος**, *ον, hard to bend*: δ. καμπή an *intricate* flourish in singing, Ar.*Nu.*971. **-κοιτος**, *ον, making bed uneasy*, μέριμνα ib.420.

**δύσ-κολος**, *ον*, (κόλον): **I.** of persons, prop. *hard to satisfy with food* (cf. Ath.6.262a): but, generally, *hard to please, discontented, fretful, peevish*, Ar.*V.*942; γῆρας E.*Ba.*1251; δ. ψυχὴ καὶ ἀγρία Pl.*Lg.*649e, cf. Arist.*EN*1108$^{a}$30, etc.; τὸ δ. Pl.*Lg.*791c; of animals, *intractable*, Id.*Tht.*174d (Comp.): so in Adv. δυσκόλως, ἔχειν, διακεῖσθαι πρός τινα, D.19.132, Isoc.3.33; δυσκολώτερον διακεῖσθαι Pl.*Phd.*84e. **II.** of things, *troublesome, harassing*, δ. ἡ ἡνιόχησις Id.*Phdr.*246b; πυρετοί Hp.*Coac.*38: generally, *unpleasant*, ἄν τι δ. συμβῇ D.18.189, cf. Men.89; εἴ τι δ. πέπρακται Θηβαίοις πρὸς ἡμᾶς D.18.176; καιροὶ δ. *difficult* times, *IG*2$^{2}$.682.33. Adv. -λως, ὑπακούειν Hp.*Epid.*3.8. **2.** *difficult to explain*, Arist.*SE*180$^{b}$5, *Metaph.*1001$^{b}$1; δ. ἐστι it is *difficult*, *Ev.Marc.*10.24, cf. Onos.1.15 (Comp.); τὰ μὲν ῥᾴδια..τὰ δὲ δ. Phld.*Po.*994.24. Adv. -λως *hardly, with difficulty*, *Ev.Marc.*10.23, al. **-κολπος**, *ον, with luckless womb*, γαστήρ, of a woman whose child was dead before birth, *AP*7.583 (Agath.). **-κόμιστος**, *ον, hard to bear, intolerable*, πότμος S.*Ant.*1346 (lyr.); τέκνα E.*HF*1422. **-κοπάνιστος** [ᾰ], *ον, hard to bake*, ἄρτος *EM*150.35. **-κοπος**, *ον*, (κόπτω) *hard to bruise*, Democr.ap.Gal.13.636. **-κρᾱής**, *ές, intemperate*, Opp.*H.*2.517. **-κρανές**· αὐχμηρόν, Hsch.; cf. δυσχρανής. ⊛ **-κρᾱσία**, ἡ, *bad temperament*, of the air, Str.6.4.1, Plu.*Alex.*58 (pl.); σώματος *Stoic.*3.216; τῶν ἐν ἡμῖν δυνάμεων Ph.1.29. (δυσκρᾰσίη Man.4.543.) **-κρᾰτής**, *ές*, = sq., δυσκρατέστατον πάντων ὁ λόγος Stob.3.33.10. ⊛ **-κράτητος** [ᾰ], *ον, hard to control*, τὸ δ. τῆς ἐπιβολῆς D.S.3.3; *ungovernable, ill-disciplined*, J.*AJ*19.4.1; γηρῶντι ἤδη δ. εἶναι (sc. τὴν ἀρχήν) App.*Syr.*61. **-κρᾱτος**, *ον, of bad temperament*, ἀήρ Str.2.3.1, cf. Gal.9.912. Adv. -τως Id.10.518; διακεῖσθαι Ps.-Plu.*Vit.Hom.*202. **-κρῑνής**, *ές, hard to distinguish*, Plu.2.922a; = sq., Aët.5.10. **-κρίσιμος** [κρῐ], *ον*, = sq., Sch.Hp.2.272 D. **-κρῐτος**, *ον, hard to discern* or *interpret*, ἄστρων δύσεις A.*Pr.*458; κληδόνες ib.486; ὀνείρατα Id.*Ag.*981 (lyr.), cf. S.*Tr.*949 (lyr.); δ. νοῦσοι *hard to determine, doubtful*, Hp.*Aph.*3.8; but δύσκριτα ἐγένετο there was an *obscure crisis*, Id.*Epid.*3.12; δ. ἐστι πότερον .. ἢ .. *difficult of solution*, Id.*Aph.*1.12, Pl.*R.*433c. Adv. -τως *doubtfully, darkly*, A.*Pr.*662; δ. ἔχειν to be *in doubt*, Ar.*Ra.*1433. **-κροτος**, *ον, badly put together*: Adv. -τως, διακεῖσθαι to be in *bad* condition, Meno *Iatr.*13.20, cf. 9.16. **-κτητος**, *ον, hard to come by*, πραγματεία Plb.3.32.1; τἀγαθόν Phld.*Herc.*1251.4 (dub.). **-κῠβέω**, *to be unlucky at dice*, Ath.15.666d, Poll.9.94. **-κῠλίστως**, Adv. *rolling with difficulty*, δ. ἔχειν Philostr.Jun.*Im.*10. **-κύμαντος** [ῡ], *ον*, in A.*Ag.*653 δυσκύμαντα κακά evils *from the stormy sea*. **-κωφέω**, *to be hard of hearing*, Gal.12.653, *AP*7.731 (Leon.), Dsc.4.162. **-κωφία**, ἡ, *deafness*, Id.*Eup.*1.61. **-κωφος**, *ον, hard of hearing*, Hp.*Coac.*193, Arist.*Insomn.*459$^{b}$21, Lxx *Ex.*4.11, Str.14.2.21; τὸ τοῦ γήρως δ. Plu.2.13e. **-λέαντος**, (λεαίνω) *hard to pound* or *bray*, Archig.ap.Aët.3.184. **-λείωτος**, *ον*, = foreg., opp. εὐλείωτος, Asclep.ap.Gal.13.677. **-λεκτος**, *ον, hard to tell*, A.*Pers.*702 (anap.). **-λεκτρος**, *ον, ill-wedded*, Sch.S.*El.*492. **-λεπής**, *ές, rough-husked*, κάρυον Nic.*Al.*271. **-λεχής**, gloss on δυσηλεγής, Hsch. **-ληπτος**, *ον, hard to take hold of*, Sor.1.88; *hard to catch*, μοχθηρία Ph.2.366, cf. Luc.*Anach.*27; *hard to comprehend*, Str.13.4.12, A.D.*Synt.*225.28, Plu.2.17d. **-λίμενος** [λῐ], *ον*, gloss on δύσορμος, Sch.rec.A.*Pers.*448. **-λόγιστος**, *ον, hard to compute*, Anaximen.ap.Stob.2.8.17, Plu.2.981e, Gal.18(2).631, D.C.73.15. **II.** Act., *ill-calculating, misguided*, χείρ S.*Aj.*40. **-λοφος**, *ον, hard for the neck, hard to bear*, ζεύγλη, ζυγόν, Thgn.848,1024; χείρ B.12.46; δ. φρενί prob. l. in S.*Ichn.*4; δυσλοφωτέρους πόνους A.*Pr.*931. **II.** *impatient of the yoke*, ἡμίονοι Ael.*NA*16.9. Adv. -φως, φέρειν E.*Tr.*303. **-λῠτος**, *ον, indissoluble*, δυσλύτοις χαλκεύμασι A.*Pr.*19; ἄκος τῶν δ. πόνων E.*Andr.*121 (lyr.); ὦμοι *stiff*, Arist.*Phgn.*811$^{a}$4. Adv. -τως, ἔχειν X.*Oec.*8.13. **2.** *insoluble*, of a problem, Luc.*JTr.*12, Alex.Aphr. *in Metaph.*223.2; αἴνιγμα Plu.*Fr.*25.3; *hard to refute*, Alex.Aphr. *in Top.*558.25. **-λώσσων**· δυσχερῶν, Hsch.

**δυσμᾰθ-έω**, *to be slow at recognizing*, A.*Ch.*225. **-ής**, *ές, hard to learn*, Id.*Ag.*1255; δ. ἰδεῖν *hard to know* at sight, E.*Med.*1196; τὸ δ. *difficulty of knowing*, Id.*IT*478. **II.** Act., *slow at learning, dull*, Pl.*R.*358a, etc.: Comp., Plu.2.992d: Sup., Ph.2.175, Jul.*Or.*7.225b. Adv. δυσμαθῶς, ἔχειν Pl.*R.*503d. **-ία**, ἡ, *slowness at learning*, ib.618d (pl.), *Lg.*812e, etc.:—written **-μάθεια**, Id.*Ep.*315c, Iamb.*VP*20.95.

**Δύσμαιναι** (perh. f. l. for Δύμ-), = βάκχαι, at Sparta, Hsch.; title of play by Pratinas, Ath.9.392f.

**δυσ-μάλακτος** [μᾰ], *ον, hard to soften*, Ruf.ap.Orib.8.24.22. **-μᾱνής**, *ές, thick*, ὕδατα Thphr.*HP*7.5.2. **-μάραντος** [μᾰ], *ον, unfading*, *Trag.Adesp.*339. **-μᾰρής**, *ές, difficult*, opp. εὐμαρής, ἀποτέλεσμα Phld.*Rh.*2.119S. **-μάσητος** [μᾰ], *ον, hard to chew*, Gal.16.760. **-μάτωρ**, Dor. for δυσμήτωρ.

**δυσμᾰχ-έω**, *fight in vain against* or *fight an unholy fight with*, θεοῖσι δυσμαχοῦντες S.*Tr.*492; πρὸς τὴν βελτίονα [δύναμιν] Plu.2.371a: abs., *fight desperately*, ib.661c. **-ητέον**, *one must fight a losing battle with*, ἀνάγκῃ δ' οὐχὶ δ. S.*Ant.*1106. **-ητος**, *ον, keenly contested*, δῶρα Μοισᾶν *Lyr.Adesp.*86 B (cf. B.*Fr.*32). ⊛ **-ος**, *ον, hard to fight with, unconquerable*, X.*HG*4.2.10 (Comp.), E.*Hec.*1055 (Sup.); πάντων -ώτατον γυνή Id.*Fr.*544; of things, A.*Pr.*921, Pl.*Lg.*863b, D.1.4, etc. **2.** generally, *difficult*, δ. κρῖναι A.*Ag.*1561 (lyr.).

⊛ **δυσ-μεικτος** or **-μικτος**, *ον, hard to mix*: *without affinity*, Pl.*Ti.*35a, etc. **II.** *unsocial*: Adv. -τως, ἔχειν Plu.2.640d. **-μείλικτος**, *ον, hard to appease*, Id.*Art.*19; πικρία Id.2.553a. **-μελῴδητος**, *ον, hard to employ in melody*, of enharmonic intervals, Theo Sm.p.56 H. (Sup.).

⊛ **δυσμεν-αίνω**, *bear ill-will*, τινί *against* another, E.*Med.*874; δ. τοῖς κοινοῖς ἀγαθοῖς D.18.217; δ. τῆς ποτὲ βίας App.*Pun.*60: abs., Ph.1.145. **-εια**, Ion. **-ίη**, ἡ, *ill-will, enmity*, ἡ ἐκ σοῦ δ. S.*El.*619; ἐν δ. εἶναι ib.1124; δ. ἄρασθαί τινι E.*Heracl.*991: in Prose, Democr.191, Antipho 4.1.3, etc.; φθόνος καὶ δ. Isoc.5.68, Pl.*R.*500c; φθόνοι καὶ ἄλλαι δ. Id.*Prt.*316d. **-έων**, participial form, only masc., *bearing ill-will, hostile*, Od.2.72; δυσμενέοντες ib.73, 20.314. ⊛ **-ής**, *ές*, (μένος) *hostile*, ἄνδρες δ. Il.5.488; δυσμενέες *enemies*, 16.521, cf. *Schwyzer* 84.12; δυσμενέων ὄχλος A.*Th.*234 (lyr.), cf. 366 (lyr.), Hdt.3.82, S.*Aj.*662 (Sup.), etc.; οἱ ὑμέτεροι δ. X.*HG*5.2.33: c. dat., τῷ πατοῦντι δυσμενεῖς A.*Ag.*1193, cf. S.*Ph.*585; οὐδὲν τυράννου -έστερον πόλει E.*Supp.*429: less freq. c. gen., ἄνδρα δ. χθονός *an enemy of* the land, S.*Ant.*187, cf. Ph.2.136. Adv. -νῶς Pl.*Tht.*168b; δ. ἔχειν τινί Isoc.3.5; πρὸς τὴν πόλιν Id.14.6:—poet. **δυσμενέως**, Nonn.*D.*21.85 (v.l.). **II.** rarely of things, δ. χοαί S.*El.*440; δυσμενὲς ὁ τοῦ πλεονεκτεῖν ἔρως X.*Mem.*2.6.21, cf. E.*Alc.*617 (v.l.). **-ίδης**, *ου, ὁ*, = foreg., Ael.*VH*3.7. **-ικός**, *ή, όν, like an enemy, hostile*, Plb.6.7.8, etc. Adv. -κῶς Id.8.8.1.

**δυσμέριστος**, *ον, hard to chew up*, τραγήματα Philum.ap.Aët.9.23.

**δυσμετα-βλησία**, ἡ, *difficulty of alteration*, Sor.1.61. **-βλητος**, *ον, hard to alter*, Hp.*Alim.*51, Plu.2.952c. **-βολος**, *ον*, = foreg., Democr.ap.Gal.13.1003. Adv. -λως ib.1004. **-δοτος**, *ον, not imparting freely*, Str.17.1.29: c. gen., *reluctant to part with*, τῶν ἀναγκαίων Phld.*Herc.*1251.20. **-θετος**, *ον, hard to alter*, of persons, *opinionated*, Plb.12.26$^{d}$.5; προαίρεσις Plu.2.799b; *hard to remove*, Gal.11.215. **-κίνητος** [ῑ], *ον, hard to shift*, ψυχὴ δ. ἀπὸ τῶν χειρόνων J.*AJ*16.11.8; γυνή Plu.2.288d, Eust.1733.32. Adv. -τως, ἔχειν Alex.Trall.1.16. **-κλαστος**, *ον, hard to break* or *move*, Sch.S.*OT*12. **-κλητος**, *ον, hard to cure of a habit*, *Gp.*19.2.13. **-στρεπτος**, *ον, hard to divert*, Gal.19.489. Adv. -τως, gloss on ἀσκελέως, Apollon.*Lex.* **-τρεπτος**, *ον*, = foreg., Eust.1461.43. **-χείριστος**, *ον, hard to manage*, παῖς Pl.*Lg.*808d (Sup.), cf. Plu.*Mar.*37, al., Aen.Tact.39.7; ζῷα Ael.*NA*4.44; δίκτυα X.*Cyn.*2.6. **2.** *hard to attack*, στρατός Hdt.7.236, J.*BJ*1.7.1; of the tortoise's shell, Hierocl.p.13 A.

**δυσμέτρητος**, *ον, hard to measure*, Antipho Soph.106. **2.** *hard to traverse*, πέλαγος Philostr.*VA*4.15.

⊛ **δυσμή**, ἡ, (δύω) = δύσις, *setting*, mostly in pl., ἀελίου δ. S.*OC*1245, cf. A.*Fr.*69, Hp.*Epid.*7.5, Pl.*Phd.*61e; ἐπὶ δυσμῇσιν ἐών at the point of *setting*, Hdt.3.104; περὶ ἡλίου δυσμάς Lys.1.39; ἥλιος ἦν ἤδη περὶ δυσμάς *Hell.Oxy.*15.5: metaph., τὸ γῆρας δυσμαὶ βίου Arist.*Po.*1457$^{b}$25, cf. D.H.4.79, Ph.1.678, S.E.*M.*9.90, Diog.Oen.2, etc. **II.** *the quarter of sunset, west*, ἀπὸ ἑσπέρης τε καὶ [ἡλίου] δυσμέων Hdt.2.31; πρὸς ἡλίου δυσμέων Id.7.115, cf. 2.33; πρὸς δυσμαῖς A.*Pers.*232; opp. ἀνατολαί, *BGU*1049.8 (iv A. D.):—also **δυθμή**, Call.*Cer.*10 (pl.), *Fr.*539 (sg.).

**δύσ-μηνις**, *ι, wrathful*, θεός Poll.1.39; χόλος *AP*9.69 (Parmenion). ⊛ **-μήνῑτος**, *ον*, = foreg., δένδρεα *AP*7.141 (Antiphil.); ψυχαί Ptol.*Tetr.*159 (-ίτας). **-μήτηρ**, *ερος, ἡ*, in Od.23.97 μῆτερ ἐμὴ δύσμητερ my mother *yet no mother*, cf. Lyc.1174, Nonn.*D.*46.194. **-μητις**, *ι, contriving ill*, Suid., Hsch. (cod. -ήτης). **-μήτωρ**,

Dor. -μάτωρ, ορος, ὁ, ἡ, in A.*Supp.*67 (lyr.) δ. κότος *an ill mother's wrath.* -μηχᾰνέω, *to be at loss how* to do, c. inf., A.*Ag.* 1360. -μήχᾰνος, ον, *hard to effect*, Epimen.ap.D.L.1.113; *difficult*, Ἀρχύτεω δυσμήχανα ἔργα κυλίνδρων Eratosth.*Fr.*35.7; prob. f.l. for δύσμαχον, J.*BJ*4.1.2. II. Act., *at a loss*, πρός τι Them.*Or.* 10.137b. III. *devising ill*, Nonn.*D.*44.210; δόλος ib.35.273; also, *ill-devised, wicked*, ἔργον Opp.*H.*3.404.

**δυσμικός**, ή, όν, (δυσμή) = δυτικός, *western*, Str.2.5.11, Hld.8.15: Comp., Str.2.1.34, Ptol.*Alm.*2.13, Theo Sm.p.137 H.: Sup., Str. 2.1.32, Ptol.*Geog.*2.3.18.

**δύσ-μικτος**, v. δύσμεικτος. -μίμητος [ῑ], ον, *hard to imitate*, D.S.1.61, Luc.*Alex.*20, *CIG*3187 (Smyrna); τὸ δ. Plu.*Cat.Mi.*8: Sup., Anon.*Oxy.*1012ii34. -μίσητος [ῑ], ον, *much hated*, Lyc. 841. -μνημόνευτος, ον, *hard to remember*, Arist.*Rh.*1416$^b$22, Aen.Tact.24.2, Epicur.*Ep.*2p.35 U., D.S.1.3. II. Act., *remembering ill, unmindful*, Pl.*Ti.*74e (Comp.). ⊕ -μοιρος, ον, (μοῖρα) = δύσμορος, S.*OC*327. ⊕ -μορία, ἡ, *a hard fate*, *AP*9.351 (Leon.). -μορος, ον, *ill-fated*, Il.22.60, etc.; δυσμόρου γε δύσμορα (sc. σκῆπτρα) S. *OC*1109, cf. Men.*Sam.*40, Lyc.897, Opp.*C.*3.217: in Prose, Antipho 3.2.11. Adv. -ρως *with ill fortune*, prob. in A.*Th.*867 (lyr., cod. M -φόρως). -μορφία, ἡ, *misshapenness, ugliness*, Hdt.6.61, Phld. *Mort.*29, etc. -μορφος, ον, *misshapen, ill-favoured*, ἐσθής E.*Hel.* 1204, Lyc.692, Plu.2.670a. -μουσος, ον, = ἄμουσος, *unmusical*, αὐλός *AP*9.216 (Honestus). -μόχλευτος, ον, *hard to dislodge*, Aët.3.34, Simp.*in Cat.*236.27. -νίκητος [ῑ], ον, *hard to conquer*, ἔρως J.*AJ*18.1.6, cf. Plu.*Comp.Pel.Marc.*2, D.C.43.28. -νιπτος, ον, *hard to wash out*, δ. ἐκ δέλτου γραφή S.*Tr.*683. -νῐφος, ον, (νίψ) *snowed upon*, Nonn.*D.*2.685. 2. *chilly, wintry*, ὕδωρ ib.3. 210; οἶδμα ib.13.533. -νοέω, *to be ill-affected*, τινί Lxx 3*Ma.*3.24, Plu.*Cic.*38. -νόητος, ον, *hard to be understood*, Dariusap.D.L. 9.13, 2*Ep.Pet.*3.16; χρησμοί Luc.*Alex.*54. II. Act., *slow of understanding*, Vett.Val.345.26. -νοια, ἡ, *disaffection, ill-will, malevolence*, S.*El.*654, E.*Hec.*973, Pl.*Tht.*151d, Plu.*Demetr.*3, Phld. *Lib.*p.29 O., etc. -νομία, Ep. and Ion. -ίη, ἡ, *lawlessness, bad constitution*, Sol.4.32: personified in Hes.*Th.*230. -νομος, ον, *lawless, unrighteous*, *AP*6.316 (Nicodem.). -νοος, ον, contr. -νους, ουν, *ill-affected, disaffected*, τινί S.*Ant.*212; τῇ πόλει Th.2.60; πρὸς τὰ πράγματα X.*HG*2.1.2: abs., E.*IT*350, Plu.2.176b. Adv. δύσνως Poll.2.230. -νοστος νόστος a return *that is no return*, E. *Tr.*75. II. *from which no traveller returns*, ῥόος *App.Anth.*4. 54. -νουθέτητος, ον, *hard to be corrected*, θηρίον (sc. πενία) Men. *Georg.*78. -νύμφευτος, ον, *ill-wedded*, *AP*7.401 (Crin.). -νυμφος, ον, *ill-wedded* or *ill-betrothed*, E.*IT*216 (lyr.), *Tr.*144 (lyr.). -ξενος, ον, *inhospitable*, Poll.9.22. -ξήραντος, ον, *hard to dry*, Thphr.*CP* 1.4.3, Plu.2.627d, etc. -ξύμβλητος, ον, *hard to understand*, Corn.*ND*28, D.C.56.29. -ξύμβολος, ον, *hard to deal with, driving a hard bargain*, Pl.*R.*486b, X.*Mem.*2.6.3, Plu.*Phoc.*5. II. = foreg., Poll.5.150. III. *ill to meet*, ζῷα Artem.4.56 (v.l. δυσσυμβούλευτα). -ξύνετος, ον, *hard to understand*, δυσξύνετον ξυνετὸς μέλος ἔγνω E.*Ph.*1506 (lyr.); διαγράμματα X.*Mem.*4.7.3; τὸ δ., τὰ δ., Plu.2.975f (δυσξύνθετον codd.), Iamb.*VP*35.252. -ογκος, ον, *overheavy, burdensome*, πλοῦτος Plu.*Aem.*12.

**δῠσόδ-ευτος**, ον, *hardly passable*, App.*Syr.*21. -έω, *make bad way, get on slowly*, Plu.*Pyrrh.*32; of difficult breathing or childbirth, Ph.2.563, Sor.2.59: metaph., Arr.*Epict.*3.19.3. -ία, ἡ, *badness of roads*, App.*Syr.*21: pl., in concrete sense, Ptol.*Tetr.*197: metaph., *difficulty*, -ίαν παρέχειν τῷ λόγῳ Plu.2.418a, cf. Ph.2.67; δυσοδίᾳ ἐντροχάζειν δοκεῖ Demetr.Lac.1012.50 F.; δ. σκυβάλων Sor. 2.20.

**δυσ-οδμία, δύσοδμος**, v. sub δυσοσμ-. -οδοπαίπᾰλος, ον, *difficult and rugged*, prop. of a mountain road: metaph., A.*Eu.*387 (lyr.). -οδος, ον, *hard to pass, scarce passable*, Th.1.107, Poll.3. 96. -οίζω (aor. ἐδύσοιξα Hsch.), *to be distressed*, E.*Rh.*724 (lyr.); *fear, tremble at*, οὔτοι δυσοίζω θάμνον ὡς ὄρνις φόβῳ A.*Ag.*1316:— Med., *fear*, E.*Rh.*805. (Lacon. acc. to Hsch.) -οίκητος, ον, *bad to dwell in*, Hp.*Aër.*19, X.*Cyr.*8.6.21. -οικονόμητος, ον, *hard to digest*, Diph.Siph.ap.Ath.2.70a, Xenocr.73. II. *difficult to manage*, τὸ δ. Artem.2.58. -οικος, ον, gloss on ἄοικος, Sch.S. *Ph.*534. -οικτος· δυσθρήνητος, Hsch. -οιμος, ον, acc. to Sch. and Hsch., = δύσοδος, τύχα δ. A.*Ch.*945 (lyr.); or perh. (οἴμη), *a sad theme*, cf. δύσοιμος· ἐπὶ κακῷ ἤκουσα, Hsch. -οινος, ον, *yielding bad wine*, Poll.6.21. -οιστος, ον, (οἴσω) *hard to bear, insufferable*, ὀδμή Hp.*Mul.*2.181; πήματα, ἄλγη, πόνοι, A.*Pr.*690 (lyr.), *Ch.*745, S.*Ph.*508 (lyr.); βίου δύσοιστον ἕξομεν τροφάν Id.*OC* 1688 (lyr.); δ. ἀήρ Str.12.3.40; ὀργή Jul.*Gal.*161b.

**δῠσοιων-έω**, (οἰωνός) *augur ill of* a thing, Phryn.*PS*p.62 B. -ισμός, ὁ, *an ill omen*, Hsch. s.v. ἀπήχεια. -ιστικός, ή, όν, *ill-omened*, Suid. s.v. ἐς κόρακας. -ιστος, ον, = foreg., Ph.2.542, Hermog. *Stat.*3, Luc.*Eun.*6, D.C.41.49.

**δύσ-οκνος** [ῠ], ον, *very lazy*: Adv. -κνως, ἐξεγείρεσθαι M.Ant.5.1; *unwillingly*, καταλείπειν τέκνα Hdn.6.7.1. -όλισθος, ον, *not slipping easily*, Paul.Aeg.3.76.

**δύσομαι**, v. δύω.

**δύσομβρος** [ῠ], ον, *stormy*: metaph., βέλη S.*Ant.*358 (lyr.).

**δῠσομίλ-ητος** [ῑ], ον, *hard to live with*, σκαιὸς καὶ δ. Hierocl.p.59 A.; δ. παροικοῦσα πόλις ἐχθρά D.Chr.40.27. -ία, ἡ, *unsociableness*, Satyr.*Vit.Eur.Fr.*39 x 5. -ος, ον, *hard to live with*, Plu. *Demetr.*42. II. *bringing evil in one's company*, Ἐρινύς A.*Ag.*746 (lyr.).

**δῠσ-όμμᾰτος**, ον, *scarce-seeing, purblind*, A.*Eu.*388 (lyr.). -όμοιος, ον, *unlike*, Stratt.75, Hsch. -οναρ, *infaustus*, *Gloss.* -όνειρος, ον, *full of ill dreams*, ὕπνος Plu.2.15b. II. *bringing ill dreams*, βρώματα ib.734f, cf. Dsc.2.105. -οπαίοντα· δυστυχοῦντα, Hsch. -οπον· δύσφωνον, Id. -οπτος, ον, (ὄψομαι) *hard to detect*, Gal.*Anim.Pass.*2.3; τὸ δ. τῆς ἡμέρας *gloominess*, Plb.18.21. 2. -ορᾰσία, ἡ, *dim sight*, Ruf.ap.Orib.7.26.15 (pl.). -όρᾱτος, ον, *hard to see*, X.*Cyr.*1.6.40, Ph.1.570; δι' ὑπερβολὴν λαμπρότατος δ. Ecphant.ap.Stob.4.7.64; τὰ δυσόρατα *dark corners*, X.*Eq.Mag.*4. 18. II. *ill to look on, horrible*, App.*Hisp.*97.

**δῠσοργ-ησία**, ἡ, = *passionateness*, Hp.*Hum.*9 (pl.). -ητος, ον, = δύσοργος, Arist.*Phgn.*811$^a$31, [Babr.]11.12; θεός Poll.1.39. Adv. -τως D.H.6.47. -ία, ἡ, = δυσοργησία, v.l. in Hp.*VM* 10. -ος, ον, *quick to anger*, S.*Aj.*1017, *Ph.*377, *Tr.*1118 (wrongly expld. by κακοεργός, Hsch.).

**δῠσ-ορεξία**, ἡ, *lack of appetite*, Gal.7.128. -όριστος, ον, *difficult to adapt to a limit*, Arist.*Mete.*378$^b$24, *GC*329$^b$32. II. *difficult to define*, χαρακτήρ D.H.*Din.*5. -ορκέω, (ὅρκος) *swear falsely*, Phryn.*PS*p.65 B. -όρμιστος, ον, (ὁρμίζω) = sq., Poll.1. 101. ⊕ -ορμος, ον, *with bad anchorage*, νῆσος..δ. ναυσί A.*Pers.* 448; also τὰ δ. *rough* ground, *where one can scarce get footing*, X.*Cyn.* 10.7. II. Act., πνοαὶ δ. *that detained* the fleet *in harbour* or *that kept* it *from reaching harbour, foul* winds, A.*Ag.*193 (lyr.). -ορνις, ῑθος, ὁ, ἡ, = δυσοιώνιστος, *boding ill*, Id.*Th.*838 (lyr.), E.*Hipp.*757 (lyr.); *with ill auspices*, Plu.*Marc.*4. -όρφναιος, α, ον, *dusky*, τρύχη E.*Ph.*325 (lyr.). -οσμία, ἡ, *an ill smell*, S.*Ph.*876, *Fr.*538, Luc.*Tox.*29; -ίη Man.4.270. -οσμος, Ion. -οδμος, ον, (ὀσμή) *ill-smelling*, ἐν δυσοδμοτάτῳ [τόπῳ] γινόμενον εὐωδέστατόν ἐστι Hdt. 3.112; ὀσμή Arist.*Pr.*908$^b$29 (Comp.). II. *bad for scent*, in hunting, οἱ ὄμβροι τὴν γῆν ποιοῦσι δύσοσμον X.*Cyn.*5.3. III. Act., *having a bad nose*, Arist.*Insomn.*459$^b$22. IV. δύσοσμον, τό, = σκόρδιον, Ps.-Dsc.3.111.

**δῠσούλωτος**, ον, *hard to scar over*, Alex.Trall.4.1, Poll.4.196.

**δῠσουρ-έω**, *to have difficulty in micturition*, Diocl.*Fr.*141, Ruf.ap. Orib.8.24.6, Dsc.1.6, *POxy.*468.1, Aret.*SD*2.4:—Med., Hp.*Vict.*2. 54. -ητικός, ή, όν, *suffering from* δυσουρία, *Gloss.* -ία, Ion. -ίη, ἡ, *difficult micturition*, Hp.*Aph.*3.31 (pl.), Arist.*Fr.*486; ἐν -ίᾳ γενέσθαι Plu.2.733c. -ίασις, εως, ἡ, = foreg., Ar.Byz.*Epit.*146. 5, Suid. s.v. τέτανος. -ιάω, = δυσουρέω, Dsc.1.33, *Hippiatr.* 31. -ικός, ή, όν: πάθος δ., = δυσουρία, f.l. in Cic.*Fam.*7.26.

**δῠσ-ούριστος**, ον, (οὐρίζω) *driven by a too favourable wind, fatally favourable*, S.*OT*1315 (lyr.). -ουρον· δυσφύλακτον, Hsch. -οφθαλμος, ον, *offensive to the sight*, αἶσχος Telest.1.3.

**δῠσπάθ-εια** [πᾰ], or -ία (Hsch.), ἡ, *deep affliction*, Plu.2.112b. II. *firmness in resisting*, Plu.*Demetr.*21: in pl., *capabilities of endurance*, Id.2.666b; *insensitivity*, Alex.Aphr.*Pr.*1.39. -έω, *suffer a hard fate*, Mosch.4.84; of sickness, *suffer severely*, ῥινῷ δ. Nic.*Th.*381; *to be in a bad way*, Plb.29.7.4. II. *to be impatient*, ἐπί τινι, πρός τι, Plu.*Aem.*36, *Per.*33; ἔν τινι Id.2.77e. -ής, ές, (παθεῖν) *feeling to excess*, opp. ἀπαθής, ib.102d. II. *not easily affected*, τὸ ὅμοιον ὑπὸ τοῦ ὁμοίου -έστερον ib.651c: abs., *impassive*, ib.454c, Luc.*Anach.* 24, Plot.1.4.8.

⊕ **δυσ-παίπᾰλος**, ον, *rough and steep*, βῆσσαι Archil.115; κύματα B. 5.26; Ὄθρυς Nic.*Th.*145; *rough*, λάχνη Opp.*H.*2.369, cf. *C.*2.381, al. -παις, *unhappy child*, Sch.rec.S.*OT*1243. -πάλαιστος [πᾰ], ον, *hard to wrestle with*, [Epich.]254; ἀρά A.*Ch.*692; πράγματα Id.*Supp.*468; γῆρας E.*Supp.*1108; δύναμις X.*HG*5.2.18; cf. δυσπέλαστος. 2. *unskilled at wrestling*, Philostr.*Gym.*40. -πάλᾰμος [πᾰ], ον, *hard to struggle with*, δόλοι θεῶν A.*Eu.*847 (lyr.); *hard to beat*, περὶ τὴν τέχνην Tz.ap.Suid. s.v. Λυκόφρων. II. *helpless*: Adv. δυσπαλάμως, ὀλέσθαι *to perish helplessly*, A.*Supp.*867 (lyr.). -πᾰλής, ές, *hard to wrestle with*, δῖνα Id.*Eu.*559 (lyr.); *difficult*, c. inf., διακρίνειν..δυσπαλές [ἐστι] Pi.*O.*8.25, cf. *P.*4.273, Cerc.*Fr.Oxy.*26. 2. *dangerous, noxious*, ῥίζαι A.R.4.52. 3. *stubborn*, Nicom.*Harm.* 3. -πάμφαλος· δυστάραχος, δυσκίνητος, Hsch.; cf. δυσπέμφελος.

**δυσπαρά-βᾰτος**, gloss on δυσοδοπαίπαλος, Sch.A.*Eu.*387. -βλητος, ον, *incomparable*, Plu.*Ant.*27. -βοήθητος, ον, *hard to assist*, Plb.5.22.7. -βουλος, ον, *hard to persuade*, A.*Supp.*108 (lyr.).

**δυσπαράγγελτος**, ον, *hardly to be reduced to rule* or *formulated*, Plb.12.25$^i$.7.

**δυσπαράγρᾰφος**, ον, *hard to define*, ποσότης Plb.16.12.10; *hard to state precisely*, Id.18.15.1; *hard to terminate*, of life, Phld.*Herc.* 1251.16.

**δυσπαράγωγος** [ᾰγ], ον, *hard to mislead*, Poll.8.10.

**δυσπαρά-δεκτος**, ον, *hard to admit* or *believe*, S.E.*M.*9.42, Alex. Aphr.*in Sens.*18.18. II. Act., *hardly admitting*, Sor.2.62. Adv., metaph., δυσπαραδέκτως ἔχειν *to be sceptical*, Plb.12.4.7. -θελκτος, ον, *hard to assuage*, A.*Supp.*386 (lyr.).

**δυσπαραίτητος**, ον, *hard to move by prayer, inexorable*, φρένες A. *Pr.*34; ὀργή Plb.30.31.13; of a person, Plu.*Cat.Mi.*1. 2. *difficult to refuse*, Id.2.531d, 602f.

**δυσπαράκλητος**, ον, *inexorable*, Sch.S.*OT*334; τὸ δ. τοῦ τρόπου J.*AJ*16.5.4 (v.l. δυσπαραιτ-).

**δυσπαρᾰκολούθητος**, ον, *hard to follow*, i.e. *hard to understand*, Men.490, D.H.*Pomp.*5, Corn.*ND*7, J.*AJ*1.3.10, Arr.*Epict.*2.12. 10. II. Act., *hard of understanding, dull*, M.Ant.5.5 (Comp.).

**δυσπαρα-κόμιστος**, ον, *hard to carry along*, Plu.*Demetr.*19; πλοῦς δ. a *difficult* voyage, Plb.3.61.2. -μύθητος [μῡ], ον, *hard to appease*, Pl.*Ti.*69d, Plu.*Mar.*45. II. *admitting no consolation*, συμ-

φορά, πάθος, J.*AJ*2.9.2, Poll.3.101. **-πειστος**, ον, *hard to dissuade*, prob. in Arist.*Phgn.*809ᵃ35 (Comp.). **-πλευστος**, ον, *hard to sail along*, Str.16.4.18. **-πλους**, ουν, = foreg., D.S.3.44. **-ποίητος**, ον, *hard to alter* or *forge*, Gal.14.52, Ammon.*Diff.*74. **-τήρητος**, ον, *hard to observe*, Antig.*Mir.*126, Porph.*Abst.*3.4. **-τρεπτος**, ον, *hard to seduce* or *bribe*, Poll.8.10.

**δυσπάρευνος**, ον, *ill-mated*, λέκτρον S.*Tr.*791.

⊛ **δυσπαρηγόρητος**, ον, = sq., ἐπιθυμία J.*AJ*16.7.4. II. *inconsolable*, Plu.2.74e; *admitting no consolation*, συμφορά Phalar.*Ep.*144.1; *hard to soothe*, ἄλγημα Herod.Med.ap.Aët.9.2.

**δυσπαρήγορος**, ον, *hard to appease*, A.*Eu.*384 (lyr.).

**δυσπάρθενος**, ον, *a virgin to her cost*, Ἠχώ Nonn.*D.*16.324; Αὔρη ib.48.421.

**Δύσπᾰρις**, ιδος, ὁ, *unhappy Paris, Paris of ill omen*, Il.3.39, 13.769, Luc.*DMort.*19.1.

**δυσπάρ-ῑτος**, ον, *hard to pass*, X.*An.*4.1.25. **-οδος**, ον, *hard to enter*, Apollod.Hist.ap.Ath.15.682d. **-οξύνομαι**, Pass., *have a severe attack*, of fever, Alex.Trall.*Febr.*2.

**δυσ-πάτητος** [ᾰ], ον, *hard to the feet*, ὁδός Luc.*Trag.*227. **-παυστος**, ον, *hard to stop* or *appease*, Gal.1.334.

**δυσπειθ-εια**, ἡ, *indiscipline, disobedience*, App.*BC* .48. **-έω**, *to be refractory*, *POxy.*44.6 (i A.D.). **-ής**, ές, *hard to persuade, not easily talked over*, Pl.*Phdr.*271d. 2. *self-willed, disobedient*, Id.*Lg.*880a, Hierocl.p.63A.; κύνες X.*Mem.*4.1.3 (Sup.). 3. *hard to believe*, Phld.*D.*3.12. 4. Adv. -θῶς, ἔχειν πρός τι Plu.*Galb.*25; δ. φέρειν Id.*Lys.*15; *with difficulty*, κάμπτεσθαι Hero *Bel.*75.9.

**δυσ-πειρία**, Ion. -ίη, ἡ, *difficulty of learning by experiment*, Hp.*Hum.*1. **-πειστέω**, *disbelieve*, Tz.*H.*7.34. **-πειστος**, ον, *hard to persuade, opinionated*, Arist.*EN*1151ᵇ6; ὄμματα ἀκοῆς D.Chr.12.71 (Comp.). Adv. -τως, ἔχειν *to be incredulous*, Isoc.4.18. II. *disobedient*, X.*Eq.Mag.*1.23. **-πέλαστος**, ον, *dangerous to come near*, δ. ἀμαθία κακόν (Nauck δυσπάλαιστον) S.*Fr.*924. **-πεμπτος**, ον, *hard to banish*, A.*Ag.*1190. ⊛ **-πέμφελος**, ον, *rough and stormy*, εἰ καὶ δυσπέμφελος εἴη (sc. πόντος) Il.16.748: as a general epith. of the sea, οἳ γλαυκὴν δυσπέμφελον ἐργάζονται Hes.*Th.*440; ναυτιλίη δ. *stormy* passage, Id.*Op.*618; αὔρη Nonn.*D.*2.550: metaph., *rude, uncourteous*, Hes.*Op.*722; δ. εὐνή, of a wife, Max.88. **-πένθερος**, ον, *of an evil father-in-law*, θεσμά Nonn.*D.*3.309.

**δυσπενθ-έω**, *to be sore afflicted*, Plu.2.106a (v.l.). **-ής**, ές, *bringing sore affliction, direful*, κάματος Pi.*P.*12.10; δόλος ib.11.18; θαλάμοιο.. δυσπενθέα κόσμον *Epigr.Gr.*431 (Antioch); Ἀΐδας *IPE*2.286.5 (Panticapaeum). 2. *bitterly lamented*, of the dead, Opp.*H.*4.261.

**δυσ-πέπαντος**, ον, *hard to soften*, Sch.S.*Aj.*205. **-πεπτέω**, *digest with difficulty*, Dsc.5.6:—Pass., Id.4.82. **-πεπτος**, ον, *hard to digest*, Arist.*GA*776ᵃ12, al., Nicom.Com.1.31, Dsc.1.125; *refusing to be assimilated*, Pl.*Ti.*83a. 2. *unripe*, v.l. ap.Sch. in Nic.*Al.*297. **-περαίωτος**, ον, = sq., ποταμός Ps.-Callisth.3.10. **-πέρᾱτος**, ον, *hard to pass* or *cross*, ὑπερβολαὶ ὄρους Str.4.6.6, cf. 15.1.26 (Comp.): metaph., ἀμηχανίας δ. αἰών E.*Med.*646 (lyr.).

**δυσπερι-άγωγος** [ᾰγ], ον, *hard to wheel about*, Arr.*Tact.*16.8. **-αίρετος**, ον, *hard to strip off, peel*, φλοιός prob. in Thphr.*HP* 5.1.1. **-γένητος**, ον, *hard to overcome*, Ph.1.621. **-γράφος**, ον, *hard to treat comprehensively*, πραγματεία Sor.1.78. **-κάθαρτος** [κᾰ], ον, *hard to peel, clean off*, φλοιός Thphr.*HP*5.1.1 codd. (leg. -αίρετος). **-κτητος**, ον, *not successful in acquiring property*, Paul.Al.*N.*3. **-ληπτος**, ον, *hard to encompass*, γαστήρ Posidon.6 J.; πόλις τοῖς ἐναντίοις δ. Arist.*Pol.*1330ᵇ3; στελέχη δ. πέντε ἀνθρώποις Str.15.1.21. II. *hard to embrace in one view, treat synoptically*, D.S.1.3. III. *hard to get*, φιλήματα *AP*12.200 (Strat.). **-νόητος**, ον, *hard to conceive*, Ph.1.570. **-τρεπτος**, ον, *hard to overturn*, ἕδρα Gal.*UP*3.9. Adv. -τως Id.18(1).591. **-ψυκτος**, ον, *hard to chill*, Dsc.1.30, Sor.1.100.

**δυσπετ-έω**, *fall out ill*, Suid. **-ημα**, ατος, τό, *misfortune*, Lxx 2*Ma.*5.20. **-ής**, ές, *falling out ill, most difficult*, μαθεῖν δ. S.*Aj.*1046. Adv. -τῶς, Ion. -έως Hdt.3.107; δ. φέρειν Hp.*Prog.*15, A.*Pr.*752: Comp. -εστέρως Hp.*Morb.*1.22.

**δυσ-πεψία**, ἡ, *indigestion*, Machoap.Ath.8.341b, Ph.2.352, Dsc.5.45, Gal.7.66. **-πήμαντος**, ον, *full of grievous evil, disastrous*, A.*Eu.*481 (as Scaliger for δυσπήμαντ'; cf. δυσκύμαντος). **-πινής**, ές, *squalid*, στολαί S.*OC*1597, cf. Ar.*Ach.*426. **-πιστέω**, *mistrust*, τινί Plu.2.593a. ⊛ **-πιστία**, ἡ, *disbelief*, Aët.7.118. **-πιστος**, ον, *hard of belief, distrustful*: Adv. -τως, ἔχειν πρός τι *to be incredulous* about a thing, Pl.*Erx.*405b. II. Pass., *hard to be believed*, Vett.Val.108.13, Palaeph.30: Comp., D.Chr.32.64. III. *superstitious*, Hsch. **-πλάνος**, ον, *wandering in misery*, A.*Pr.*608 (lyr.); δ. ἀλατεία ib.900 (lyr.). **-πληκτος**, ον, *not easily terrified*, ὑπὸ φόβων Ph.2.665, cf. Andronic.Rhod.p.575M. II. *hard to hit*, Simp.*in Cat.*247.7. **-πλήρωτος**, ον, *hard to fill* or *fulfil*, Poll.9.21. **-πλῆτις**, f.l. for δασ-, Lyc.1452, Suid. **-πλοΐα**, Ion. -πλοΐη, ἡ, *difficulty of sailing*, *AP*7.630 (Antiphil.), Str.1.2.31: pl., Ph.1.601:—written -πλωΐα, *Cat.Cod.Astr.*2.178. **-πλοος**, ον, contr. -πλους, ουν, *dangerous for ships*, Κρῆτα *AP*7.275 (Gaet.). **-πλῦτος**, ον, *hard to wash clean*, Hp.*Mul.*2.122. **-πλωτος**, ον, = δύσπλοος, *AP*7.699. **-πνευστος**, ον, gloss on δυσαής, Hsch. **-πνοέω**, Ion. **-πνοιέω**, *breathe with difficulty*, Aret.*SD*1.11, Gal.19.423. **-πνόητος**, ον, dub. in Hp.*Judic.*15. **-πνοια**, ἡ, *difficulty of breathing, shortness of breath*, Id.*Aph.*3.31, X.*Cyn.*9.20, Nymphis 16, Aret.*SA*1.9, etc. II. *contrary winds*, Sch.A.R.4.1. **-πνοϊκός**, ή, όν, *short of breath*, Dsc.4.134 (v.l.), Asclep.ap.Gal.13.108, *Hippiatr.*27. **-πνοος**, ον, contr. **-πνους**, ουν, *scant of breath*, Hp.*Prog.*17 (Comp.), S.*Ant.*224. II. *unfit to breathe*, ἀήρ Thphr.*Ign.*24. III. δ. πνοαί *contrary* winds, S.*Ant.*588 (lyr.).

**δυσ-πολέμητος**, ον, *hard to war with*, A.*Supp.*648 (lyr., s.v.l.), Isoc.4.138; εἰ δέ τις.. δ. οἴεται τὸν Φίλιππον εἶναι D.4.4; δ. ὅπλον, of friendship, Luc.*Tox.*36. **-πόλεμος**, ον, *unlucky in war*, A.*Pers.*1013 (lyr.). II. = foreg., Γαλάται *IG*11(4).1105 (Delos, iii B.C.), Lxx 2*Ma.*12.21. **-πολιόρκητος**, ον, *hard to take by siege*, X.*HG*4.8.5 (Comp.), Plb.5.3.4, J.*AJ*2.10.2; τὸ δ. Corn.*ND*20. **-πολίτευτος** [ῑ], ον, *unfit for public business*, τὸ δ Plu.*Dio* 32.

**δυσπον-ής**, ές, *toilsome*, δυσπονέος καμάτοιο Od.5.493. Adv. -έως Max.194. **-ητος**, ον, *bringing toil and trouble*, δαίμων A.*Pers.*515; δυσπόνητον ἔξετ' ἀμφ' ἐμοὶ τροφήν *laborious*, S.*OC*1614. **-ία**, ἡ, *toil and trouble*, Man.4.260. **-ος**, ον, *toilsome*, S.*Ant.*1276 (lyr.).

**δυσπόρ-ευτος**, ον, *hard to pass*, πηλὸς τοῖς ἁμάξαις δ. X.*An.*1.5.7; ἀνοδίαι Ph.2.14; ὁδοί D.C.53.22. **-έω**, *have a toilsome march*, J.*BJ* 3.6.2.

**δυσπόρθητος**, ον, *hard to sack*, Sch.rec.A.*Pr.*166.

**δυσπορία**, ἡ, *difficulty of passing*, τοῦ ποταμοῦ X.*An.*4.3.7.

**δυσπόριστος**, ον, *hard to come by* or *procure*, opp. εὐπ., Epicur.*Ep.*3 p.63 U., cf. Phld.*Herc.*1251.12, D.H.1.37, D.Chr.7.152, Muson.*Fr.*18A p.94H., Plu.2.156f; σχήματα Alex.*Fig.*1.1; δ. ἡ ἀρετὴ τοῦ σωφρονεῖν J.*AJ*19.2.5; τὸ δ. *difficulty of getting*, τῶν ἀναγκαίων Ph.1.19, cf. Plu.*Sol.*23.

**δύσπορος**, ον, *scarcely passable*, Pl.*Cra.*420e, X.*An.*6.5.12. 2. *difficult to get*, τροφή Corn.*ND*28, Poll.5.105.

**δυσποτμ-έω**, *despair of oneself*, ἐν ἀρρωστίαις Plb.33.17.1. **-ία**, ἡ, *ill luck, ill success*, D.H.9.28, Them.*Or.*13.170a. ⊛ **-ος**, ον, *unlucky, ill-starred*, of persons and things, δ. θεός, of Prometheus, A.*Pr.*119; δ. βοῦς, of Io, Id.*Supp.*306; δ. εὐχαί, i.e. *curses*, Id.*Th.*820; χλιδά S.*OT*888 (lyr.); θήρα E.*Ba.*1144, cf. Ar.*Ach.*419; τύχαι D.H.1.17: Comp. -ώτερος E.*Ph.*1348: Sup. -ότατος Plu.*Comp.Per.Fab.*1. Adv. -μως A.*Pers.*272 (lyr.): Sup. -ότατα Plu.*Fab.*18.

**δύσποτος**, ον, *unpalatable*, πῶμα A.*Eu.*266.

**δύσπους**, ποδος, ὁ, ἡ, *slow of foot*, Call.*Fr.*1.63P.

**δυσπρᾱγ-έω**, *to be unlucky*, A.*Ag.*790 (anap.), Plu.*Ant.*63, Al.*Jb.*5.24. **-ής**, ές, *faring ill*, Vett.Val.16.21. ⊛ **-ία**, *ill luck, ill success*, Gorg.*Hel.*9 (pl.), Antipho 2.49, Ph.2.75, Jul.*ad Them.*257b.

**δυσ-πραγμάτευτος** [μᾰ], ον, *hard to manage*, λαός Plu.2.348f. **-πρακτος**, ον, *hard to do*, Poll.3.131, 5.105. **-πραξία**, ἡ, *ill success, ill luck*, A.*Pr.*966, S.*OC*1399, And.2.5, Men.707: pl., A.*Eu.*769, S.*Aj.*759, Isoc.6.102. **-πρᾱτος**, ον, *hard to sell*: name of a play by Antiphanes, Ath.6.262c. **-πράϋντος** [ᾰ], ον, *hard to tame*, Hsch. s.v. δυσγάργαλις. **-πρέπεια**, ἡ, *indecency*, J.*AJ*3.7.4. **-πρεπής**, ές, *base, undignified*, E.*Hel.*300. **-πριστος**, ον, *hard to saw through*, Thphr.*HP*5.6.3. **-πρόκοπος**, ον, *making progress with difficulty*, Vett.Val.76.24.

**δυσπρόσ-βᾰτος**, ον, *hard to approach*, Th.4.129, D.C.56.12. **-δεκτος**, ον, *hardly admitted, disagreeable*, Plu.2.39d. II. Act., *disinclined to entertain*, διαβολῆς M.Ant.1.5. **-ήγορος**, ον, *hard to speak with, repulsive*, D.C.*Fr.*11.6, Poll.1.42. Adv. -ρως Id.5.139. **-ῐτος**, ον, *difficult of access or attack*, πόλις D.H.4.54, cf. D.S.15.42, Onos.11.6; λιμὴν δ. ναυσί J.*BJ*4.10.5; τεῖχος D.C.40.34; of a man, E.*IA*345. **-μᾰχος**, ον, *hard to attack*, Plu.*Tim.*21. **-μεικτος**, ον, *hard to get into*, λιμήν Poll.1.101. **-οδος**, ον, *difficult of access*, χωρίον Th.5.65, cf. Aen.Tact.28.1 (Sup.); δ. τοῖς ἐναντίοις πόλις Arist.*Pol.*1330ᵇ3; *hard to assault*, τάξις, παρεμβολή, Plb.1.26.10, 2.65.12. 2. of men, *unsocial*, δ. αὑτὸν παρέχειν Th.1.130, cf. X.*Ages.*9.2, Luc.*Scyth.*6, Plu.*Demetr.*42, D.C.*Fr.*11.6. **-οιστος**, ον, *hard to approach*, S.*OC*1277. **-οπτος**, ον, *hard to look on, horrid to behold*, κάρα τὸ δ. ib.286; ὀνείρατα Id.*El.*460; ὄψις καὶ κίνησις Plu.*Aem.*12. Adv. -τως Agatharch.26. **-όρμιστος**, ον, *hard to land on, having few ports*, Plb.1.37.4; δ. ἀπόβασις a *difficult* landing, D.S.1.31. **ορμος**, ον, = foreg., Scymn.726. **-πέλαστος**, ον, *hard to get at*, Plu.*Pomp.*28; gloss on δ. σπλῆτις, Sch.Od.15.234. **-πόριστος**, ον, *bad for foraging in*, χώρα Aen.Tact.8.1. **-πτωτος**, ον, *hard to apply*, of stiff ointment, Gal.11.134 (ap. Orib.44.15.21). **-ρητος**, ον, *hard to speak with*, condemned by Poll.5.138.

**δυσ-πρόσωπος**, ον, *of ill aspect, sour looks*, Artem.3.47, f.l. in Plu.*Mar.*15, cf. Men.Rh.p.416S. **-προφορος**, ον, *hard to pronounce*, Mart.Cap.5.514. **-ρᾰγής**, ές, *hard to break*, Luc.*Anach.*24 (Comp.). **-ρᾰχῖτις**, ιδος, ἡ, name of a *plaster*, Crito ap.Gal.13.797. **-ρευστος**, ον, *hardly flowing*, of thick water, S.E.*M.*5.75 (Comp.). **-ρηκτος**, ον, *hard to break through*, Gal.*UP*15.5, D.C.62.8. **-ρητος**, ον, *that should not be spoken*, Demetr.*Eloc.*302. II. *hard to give a name to*, Gal.12.501. ⊛ **-ρῑγος**, ον, *impatient of cold, sensitive to cold*, ζῷα Hdt.5.10, cf. Arist.*HA*605ᵃ20 (Sup.), Men.1007, J.*AJ*14.3, Plu.2.916a; of plants, Thphr.*HP*6.7.3. Adv. -γως Ruf.ap.Orib.8.24.61, Agathin.ib.10.7.17: Comp. -οτέρως, διάγειν Arist.*Pr.*863ᵃ2.

**δυσ-ροέω**, *flow ill*, i.e. *to be unlucky*, Arr.*Epict.*1.28.30, al. **-ροητικός**, ή, όν, *leading to ill luck*, ib.4.1.58. **-ροια**, ἡ, *bad circulation*, Anon.Lond.4.17: metaph., *ill luck, misfortune*, Arr.*Epict.*2.17.18. **-ροος**, ον, contr. **-ρους**, -ρουν, *sluggish*, γαστήρ Orib.8.35.6, cf. Gal.8.358. **-σάρκωτος**, ον, *healing with difficulty*, of ulcers, Id.12.188, Aët.2.187.

**δυσσέβ-εια**, ἡ, *impiety, ungodliness*, πρὸς δυσσεβείας ἦν it verged on *impiety*, A.*Ch.*704; παντὸς ἔργου δ. S.*Ant.*301; *a charge of impiety*, τὴν δ. εὐσεβοῦσ' ἐκτησάμην ib.924.—In Lyrics also **-ία**, A.*Eu.*

533; -ίη Nonn.*D*.20.404. -έω, *to be ungodly*, S.*Tr*.1245; οἱ δυσσεβοῦντες A.*Eu*.910, E.*Med*.755. -ημα, ατος, τό, *impious act*, Lxx 2*Ma*.12.3, D.H.7.44, Scymn.684, etc. -ής, ές, *ungodly, impious, profane*, of persons, A.*Th*.598 (Comp. or Sup.), and their acts, δ. χάρις S.*Ant*.514; τὰ τῶν κακίστων δυσσεβέστατα Id.*OC*1190; δ. μέλαθρα E.*IT*694. Adv. -βῶς Id.*Fr*.825.—This family of words is chiefly found in Trag. (δυσσεβής occurs in Men.540, Diph.105, and later Prose as Jul.*Or*.5.174b (Sup.)); εὐσεβής, etc., are freq. also in Prose. -ία, ἡ, v. δυσσέβεια.

**δύσ-σειστος**, ον, *hard to shake*, Hsch. -σηπτος, ον, *not easily rotting*, κρέα Plu.2.725b; δένδρα Id.*in Hes*.7, cf. Gal.10.942, al. ※ -σοος, ον, *hard to save, ruined*, Theoc.3.24; τὰ δ. *the rogues*, Id.4.45, cf. *Riv. Indogr*.8.266 (Camarina, v B.C.).

**δυσσυγκάθετος**, ον, *condescending with difficulty*, πρὸς τὰς ἐξωτερικὰς φιλίας prob. cj. in Iamb.*VP*31.194.

**δυσσύλληπτος**, ον, *hard to conceive*, σπέρματα Sor.1.41.

**δυσσυλλόγιστος**, ον, *hard to reason out*, Gal.8.882.

**δυσσύμ-βᾰτος**, ον, *ill-agreeing*, πρὸς τὸ ἀλλόφυλον Plu.2.661c. -βλητος, -βολος, v. δυσξύμβ-. -βούλευτος, v. δυσξύμβολος. -πτωσία, ἡ, *difficulty in coalescing*, Gal.19.401. -πτωτος, ον, *not coalescing easily*, Id.8.873. -φῠτος, ον, *hardly growing together*, Id.10.336; τραύματα Sor.1.38.

**δυσσυν-αίσθητος**, ον, *hard to grasp as a whole*, of an argument, Simp.*in Ph*.1272.13. -ακτος, ον, *hard to bring together*, πλῆθος J.*BJ*4.4.6. -άλλακτος, ον, *hard to deal with*, Vett.Val.115.9. -είδητος, ον, *with a bad conscience*, Id.37.29, al. -εσία, ἡ, *lack of understanding*, Simp.*in Ph*.1147.9. -οπτος, ον, *hard to get a view of*, Plb.3.84.2, etc.: metaph., Iamb.*VP*30.182.

**δυσ-σώστως**, Adv. *with small chance of survival*, ἔχειν *Hippiatr*.71. -τακτος, ον, *ill-regulated, disordered*, Pl.*Lg*.781a. II. (for δύσ-στακτον) = κακοδάκρυτον, Hsch. -τάλᾶς, αινα, ἄν, *most miserable*, S.*Aj*.410, etc.: freq. in E. in fem., *Med*.1028, al., masc. twice in E., δ. σὺ τῆσδε συμφορᾶς *Hipp*.1407, cf. *Supp*.1034. ※-ταλτος, ον, (στέλλω) *hard to check*, *Hippiatr*.9. -τᾰμίευτος [ῐ], ον, *hard to manage*, πνεῦμα Arist.*Aud*.800$^b$31. -τάρᾰχος [τᾰ], ον, *very stormy*, Hsch. s. v. δυσήνεμον.

**δυστᾰτέω**, *to be unstable*, αἰσθήσεις Plu.2.1124b.

**δυσ-τέκμαρτος**, ον, *hard to make out from signs, hard to trace*, ἴχνος S.*OT*109; δ. τέχνη, of the art of interpreting auspices, A.*Pr*.497; ποικίλον τι καὶ δ. E.*Hel*.712; τέλος D.H.4.29; γνώμη Plu.*Cat. Mi*.72; δ. πατὴρ τῶν ὅλων Ph.1.467; *hard to estimate*, Aret.*CA*1.4. -τεκνία, ἡ, *ill luck in the matter of children*, Man.2.179. -τεκνος, ον, *unfortunate in one's children*, S.*OT*1248, Vett.Val.18.5, *Cat. Cod.Astr*.1.149. -τέρματον· δυσχερὲς τέλος ἔχον, ἢ μὴ ἔχον τέλος, Hsch. ※ -τερπής, ές, *ill-pleasing*, A.*Ch*.277. -τευκτος, ον, *unsuccessful*, Doroth.in *Cat.Cod.Astr*.2.174. -τευξία, ἡ, *difficulty in securing*, πραγμάτων Heph.Astr.2.28. -τηκτος, ον, (τήκω) *hard to melt*, Hp.*Alim*.51, Plu.2.701b.

**δυστηνία**, ἡ, = μοχθηρία, Hsch.

※ **δύστηνος**, Dor. **δύστᾱνος**, ον, *wretched, unhappy, unfortunate, disastrous*, poet. Adj.: 1. mostly of persons, as always in Hom. and mostly Trag., A.*Pers*.909 (anap.), etc.; δυστήνων δέ τε παῖδες ἐμῷ μένει ἀντιόωσιν *unhappy are they* whose sons.., Il.6.127. 2. of sufferings and the like, μόχθος δ. Pi.*P*.4.268; θέρος A.*Ag*.1655; αἰκίαι S.*El*.511 (lyr.); ὄνειδος Id.*Aj*.1191 (lyr.); ὄνειρος Ar.*Ra*.1333 (lyr.); πάθος D.H.6.20. Adv., Sup. δυστανοτάτως γηράσκω E.*Supp*.967 (lyr.). II. after Hom., in moral sense, *wretched*, S.*El*.121 (Sup., lyr.), *Ph*.1016; λόγοι E.*HF*1346.—Rare in Prose, though D.19.255 has δ. λογάρια, in latter sense: Sup. (v. supr. 1); no Comp. is found. (Cf. ἄστηνος.)

**δυστήρητος**, ον, *hard to keep*, κάλλος Ps.-Phoc.217; θηρίον Plu. *Cleom*.36.

**δυστίβευτος** [ῐ], ον, *bad for scent*, Plu.2.917e, 918a.

**δυσ-τῐθάσευτος** [ᾰ], ον, *hard to tame*, Str.15.1.42, Plu.2.529b; τὸ δ. Artem.3.12. ※ -τλήμων, ον, gen. ονος, *suffering hard things*, *h.Ap*.532, Orph.*Fr*.49 vi 95. -τλητος, ον, *hard to bear*, Ἀνάγκη Emp.116, A.*Ag*.1571 (anap.); δύστλητα τολυπεύειν *IG*14.2123.

**δυστόκ-εια**, ἡ, *one who has borne a child to misery*, dub. in Hsch. -εύς, έως, ὁ, ἡ, *suffering in child-birth*, δυστοκέες ὠλετρίδες Call.*Del*.242; *unhappy parent*, δ. τοκέες *IG*14.2125. -έω, *suffer in child-birth*, Hp.*Aph*.5.35, Pl.*Tht*.149d, Arist.*HA*587$^a$4: metaph., ἡ πόλις δυστοκεῖ Ar.*Ra*.1423, cf. Aristid.*Or*.31(11).11. ※-ία, ἡ, *painful delivery*, Arist.*HA*587$^a$10 (pl.), Thphr.*HP*9.16.1 (pl.). II. = δυστεκνία, Man.1.46. -ος, ον, *born for mischief*, δάκος E.*Fr*.863.

**δυστομέω**, (στόμα) *speak evil of*, τινά τι S.*OC*986.

**δυστομία**, ἡ, (στόμα) *difficulty in pronunciation*, Phld.*Po*.2.24.

**δύστομος** (A), ον, (στόμα) *hard-mouthed*, of a horse, ἱππεῖ *APl*.4.361, *Hippiatr.Praef*. II. *hard to pronounce*, συλλαβή Phld.*Po*.2.15.

**δύστομος** (B), ον, (τέμνω) *hard to cut*, Thphr.*HP*3.14.1.

**δύστονος**, ον, (στένω) *lamentable, grievous*, A.*Th*.989 (lyr., codd.), *Ch*.469 (lyr.).

**δυστοπ-άζοντες**· δυσχερῶς ὑπονοήσαντες, Hsch. -αστος, ον, *hard to guess*, ὅστις ποτ' εἶ σύ, δυστόπαστος εἰδέναι E.*Tr*.885; Φοίβου δυστόπαστ' αἰνίγματα Id.*Supp*.138, cf. Phld.*Mort*.37; αἰτία Plu.*Rom*.21; κοσμοποιός Ph.1.570.

**δύστος**, = δύστηνος, Hdn.Gr.1.217.

**δυστόχαστος**, ον, *hard to hit upon*, καιρός Plu.*Ant*.28, cf. Dsc.*Ther. Praef*.

**δυσ-τράπεζος** [ᾰ], ον, *fed on horrid food*, E.*HF*385 (lyr.). -τρᾰπελία or -εία, ἡ, *difficulty of managing*, D.S.4.11, 5.15; ἐν τοῖς καταγείοις Id.17.82; *unhealthiness*, τόπου Iamb.*VP*19.92. -τράπελος [ᾰ], ον, *difficult to deal with*, φλέψ Hp.*Oss*.16; πρᾶγμα Henioch.4.4, cf. Plu.2.419a; ὀφθαλμία Sor.2.15. 2. of persons, *intractable, stubborn*, S.*Aj*.914 (lyr.), Arist.*EE*1234$^a$5. Adv. -λως *awkwardly, clumsily*, X.*Oec*.8.16; *with difficulty*, Gal.14.114.

※ **δυστρᾰτοπέδευτος**, ον, *ill-suited for encamping*, Aen.Tact.8.1.

**δυσ-τρᾰχηλέω**, *to be stiff-necked, stubborn*, Tz.*H*.1.427. -τρητος, ον, *hard to pierce* or *bore*, of inferior pearls, Suid. -τριπτος, ον, *hard to bruise* or *grind*, Artem.1.70, *Hippiatr*.1. -τροπία, ἡ, *peevishness*, Poll.5.119, Jul.*Mis*.365b, Alex.Trall.7.9. -τροπικός, ή, όν, *peevish*, Sch.Ar.*Ra*.848. -τροπος, ον, (τρόπος) *ill-conditioned, surly, peevish*, δ. γυναικῶν ἁρμονία E.*Hipp*.161; δύσκολος καὶ δ. D.6.30, Ph.1.621; δ. καὶ σκυθρωπαὶ φύσεις Plu.2.361b. Adv. -πως, λογιστεύειν Philostr.*VS*1.19.2.

※ **Δύστρος** μήν, ὁ, name of a Macedonian month, *OGI*55 (iii B.C.), *AP*11.243 (Nicarch.), etc.

**δύσ-τροφος**, ον, *hard to rear*, Thphr.*CP*1.8.4. -τρύπητος [ῠ], ον, *hard to bore through*, Id.*HP*5.6.3 (Comp.). -τρωτος, ον, *hard to injure*, σιδήρῳ καὶ λίθῳ Plu.2.983d, cf. Apollod.*Poliorc*.139.8: Comp., Gal.*UP*1.2. -τύπωτος [τῠ], ον, *not easily taking an impress*, Id.1.322.

**δυστῠχ-έω**, Ion. impf. ἐδυστύχεον Hdt.8.105: aor. ἐδυστύχησα Pl.*Mx*.243a: pf. δεδυστύχηκα Id.*La*.183c, Isoc.4.55, Lyc.Trag.5:—Pass., v. infr.:—*to be unlucky, unfortunate*, Hdt. l. c., etc.; ἐπεύχομαι τῷδε μὲν εὐτυχεῖν.. τοῖσι δὲ δ. A.*Th*.482 (lyr.), cf. S.*Ant*.1159; γάμοις E.*Ph*.424; παίδων πέρι Id.*Andr*.713; ἔν τινι Ar.*Ra*.1449; εἴς τι Pl.*La*.183c; κατὰ γῆν καὶ κατὰ θάλατταν Id.*Alc*.2.148d; περί τι Plu.*Cam*.11: c. acc., πάντα δυστυχῶ E.*Hec*.429; δυστυχεῖν ἄμορφον γυναῖκα *to be curst with*.., *AP*11.287 (Pall.); μανίαν Ach.Tat.4.17; τῆς ἀλλοδαπῆς βαρυτέραν τὴν πατρίδα δυστυχήσασα Hld.10.16:—Pass. in same sense, ὅταν τις δυστυχηθῇ *is made unfortunate*, Pl.*Lg*.877e; τὰ ὑφ' ἑτέρων δυστυχηθέντα Lys.2.70, cf. Plu.*Pyrrh*.4. -ημα, ατος, τό, *piece of ill luck, failure, misfortune*, And.2.9, Lys.24.3 (pl.), Pl.*Cra*.395d (pl.), Onos.36.4 (pl.); esp. of *defeat* in war, X.*HG*4.5.18, etc. -ής, ές, *unlucky, unfortunate*, of persons and things, Th.7.87, Pl.*Lg*.832a, etc.; freq. in Trag., δυστυχῆ πράσσειν A.*Th*.339 (lyr.); δ. βίος S.*El*.602; δ. εἴς τι E.*Ph*.1642; τά τ' ἔνδον τά τε θύραζε δ. Id.*Or*.604; τὸ δυστυχές A.*Ch*.913. Adv. -χῶς Id.*Ag*.1660, Pl.*Lg*.687e, etc. 2. of the Erinyes, δ. κόραι *ill-starred, harbingers of ill*, A.*Eu*.791 (lyr.). ※ -ία, ἡ, *ill luck, ill fortune*, E.*Ba*.388 (lyr.), al.; τοῦ πάθους ἡ δ. Th.6.55, etc.

**δύσ-υδρος** [δῠ], ον, *scant of water*, J.*AJ*2.11.2, Ph.2.516. -υπέρβᾰτος, ον, *hard to pass over*, Ph.*Bel*.82.35.

**δυσυπν-έω**, *sleep ill*, Pl.*Lg*.790d. ※-ήτως, Adv. ἔχειν suffer from *insomnia*, Agathin.ap.Orib.10.7.27. -ος, ον, *sleeping badly*, ib.10.

**δῠσυποβίβαστος** [ῐ], ον, *hard to carry off by purging*, etc., Diph. Siph.ap.Ath.3.74c, Gal.6.535.

※ **δῠσύποιστος**, ον, *hard to endure*, *AP*5.162 (Mel.), J.*AJ*15.7.1; *hard to carry*, βάρος Archig.ap.Aët.13.120.

**δῠσυπο-μένητος**, ον, = sq., S.E.*M*.9.154. -μόνητος, ον, *hard to abide*, Ph.2.287, 432, Sor.1.80. -νόητος, ον, *hard to detect the nature of*, of a person, Ph.2.268; μῖσος ib.201. -στᾰτος, ον, *hard to withstand*, βία D.S.17.11; of a person, Plu.*Cor*.8. -χώρητος, gloss on δυσύποιστος, Suid.

**δυσ-φᾰής**, ές, *scarce visible*, ἥλιος Plu.2.431f. -φᾰνής, ές, *dark, obscure*, νύξ Id.*Luc*.9: metaph., σώματος ψυχὴ -έστερόν τι χρῆμα Them.*Or*.1.2c.

※ **δύσφαλτον**· δύσμαχον, Hsch.

**δυσ-φάντασστος**, ον, *hard to imagine*, Plu.2.432c. -φᾰτος, ον, *hard to speak, unutterable*, A.*Ag*.1152 (lyr.). II. *hard to explain*, Lyc.10. -φεγγής, ές, *shining ill, gloomy*, Poll.5.109. -φερής, ές, *intolerable*, Hsch. -φευκτος, ον, *hard to be avoided*, κακόν Men. *Georg*.12, cf. Ph.2.268.

※ **δυσφημ-έω**, *use ill words*, esp. *words of ill omen*, A.*Ag*.1078, S.*El*.905, Plu.*Cic*.22. II. trans., *speak ill of*, S.*El*.1183, E.*Heracl*.600, *Hec*.181 (lyr.), Phld.*Rh*.1.215 S., Them.*Or*.13.178a:—Pass., Phld. *Mort*.36. -ημα, ατος, τό, *word of ill omen*, Plu.2.1065e. -ία, ἡ, *ill language*, esp. *words of ill omen*, κατεῖχε.. πᾶν στρατόπεδον δυσφημίαις S.*Ph*.10, dub. in J.*AJ*16.4.1: pl., *curses*, Plu.2.587f, cf. *Pel*.8; but, *unsavoury details*, Demetr.*Eloc*.302. II. *blasphemy, slander*, D.H.6.48, etc. III. *ill fame, obloquy*, S.*Fr*.178 (pl.), Them.*Or*.7.99c. -ιστος, ον, = sq., Suid. s. v. δυσκληδόνιστος. -ος, Dor. -φᾶμος, ον, *of ill omen, boding*, Hes.*Op*.735; opp. εὔφημος, E.*Andr*.1144, Pl.*Hp.Ma*.293a. Adv. -μως, ἱερουργεῖν Zen.4.95. II. *slanderous, shameful*, ἔπη Thgn.307; λόγος Men.715; *abusive*, Plu.*Luc*.18. Adv. -μως Phryn.*PS* p.62 B. III. *of ill fame, evil*, κλέος Pi.*N*.8.37. -οσύνη, ἡ, *evil talk*, Phld.*Sto*.339.20.

※ **δύσ-φθαρτος**, ον, *hard to destroy*, S.E.*M*.9.19; *not easily spoilt*, Diph.Siph.ap.Ath.3.121c, Hices.ib.87d, Xenocr.73 (Comp.), Dsc.2.9. -φθεγκτος, ον, *unfit to be uttered*, Poll.3.129, 5.123. -φθογγος, ον, *hard-sounding*, Demetr.*Eloc*.246. -φῐλής, ές, *hateful*, δάκος A.*Ag*.1232; γαμήλευμα Id.*Ch*.624; γέρων S.*OC*1258, etc.

**δυσφορ-έω**, impf. ἐδυσφόρουν Hp.*Epid*.3.1.γ', X.*Cyr*.2.2.8:—*to be impatient, angry, vexed*, Hdt.5.19, A.*Supp*.513, S.*El*.255, Pherecr.22 D., Ar.*Th*.73, Men.543.7, etc.; κακοῖς E.*Andr*.1234; ἐπί τινι A.*Th*.780 (lyr.), J.*AJ*1.10.4, Hdn.3.9.7; περὶ τὰς ἀναστάσεις *to feel*

*ill* on getting up, Hp. l.c.; διά τι D.S.4.61 :—Med., X.*Cyr.*2.2.8, Procop.*Arc.*10,12 :—Pass., S.*Ichn.*329, v. l. in X.*Cyr.*2.2.5. **-ητος,** ον, *hard to be borne*, Hsch.; f. l. for διαφόρητος, E.*Cyc.*344. **-ία,** ἡ, *malaise, discomfort*, Hp.*Acut.*54, *Epid.*1.26.η′, *Coac.*260; classed as εἶδος λύπης, *Stoic.*3.100. 2. *vexation, distress*, Epicur.*Fr.*445 (pl.), Simp.*in Epict.*p.117 D. **-ικός,** ή, όν, *indicative of vexation*, Eust. 1581.22.

**δυσ-φόρμιγξ,** ιγγος, ὁ, ἡ, *unlike the lyre, mournful*, E.*IT*225 (lyr.). ❋ **-φορος,** ον, *hard to bear, heavy*, θώρακες X.*Mem.*3.10.13. 2. mostly of sufferings, *hard to bear, grievous*, θάμβος, μέριμνα, Pi.*N.*1.55, *Fr.* 248; ἄτα, βίος, A.*Eu.*372 (lyr., codd.), *Ag.*859, etc.; δ. γνῶμαι *false, blinding* fancies, S.*Aj.*51; τὰ δ. our *troubles, sorrows*, Id.*OT*87, cf. *El.*144 (lyr.); δύσφορόν [ἐστι] X.*Cyr.*1.6.17. Adv. δυσφόρως, διάγειν τὴν νύκτα Hp.*Epid.*5.95; δ. φέρειν Id.*Aph.*1.18 (Sup.), Hdn.1.8.4; δ. ἔχειν S.*OT*770; *impatiently*, τοὔνειδος ἦγον ib.783. 3. of food, *oppressive*, X.*Cyr.*1.6.17. 4. *bearing bad crops*, χώρα Men.Rh. p.345 S. II. (from Pass.) *moving with difficulty, slow of motion*, σώματα Pl.*Ti.*74e; ἵππος X.*Eq.*1.12 (Comp.). **-φορτος,** ον, *hard to be borne* or *carried*, *CIG*3127 (Teos). **-φράδεια** [φρᾰ], ἡ, *difficulty of pronunciation*, Eust.852.58. **-φρακτος,** ον, *cohesive*, Steph.*in Hp.*1.298 D. **-φραστος,** ον, *hard to tell* or *explain, mysterious*, Pl.*Ti.*50c: generally, *difficult*, κέλευθα Opp.*H.*2.60. II. Act., *speaking with difficulty*, γλῶσσα Ezek.*Exag.*114. Adv. -τως Lyc.1466. ❋ **-φρόνη,** ἡ, = -φροσύνη, in pl., *anxieties, troubles*, δυσφρονέων ἐπιλήθεται Hes.*Th.*102; in Pi.*O.*2.52, παραλύει δυσφρονᾶν should be read (metri gr.) for δυσφροσύναν παραλύει, cf. ἀφρόνη, εὐφρόνη. **-φροντις,** = δυσκηδής, Eust.1546.41. **-φρόντιστος,** gloss on δυσαρεής, Hsch. ❋ **-φροσύνη,** ἡ, *anxiety, care*, Hes. *Th.*528, Simon.86 (both times in Ep. gen. pl. δυσφροσυνάων): pl., E.*Tr.*597 (lyr.), Ph.2.75. **-φρων,** ον, gen. ονος, *sad at heart, sorrowful*, τὸ δ. στύγος A.*Ag.*547; ἄτα S.*OC*202 (lyr.); λῦπαι E. *Andr.*1043 (lyr.). II. *ill-disposed, malignant*, δράκοντες A.*Supp.* 511; ἰός Id.*Ag.*834; οἱ δ. ib.608; λόγοι E.*Andr.*288 (lyr.). III. = ἄφρων, *senseless, insensate*, A.*Th.*875 (lyr.); φρενῶν δυσφρόνων ἁμαρτήματα S.*Ant.*1261 (lyr.). Adv. -όνως *foolishly, rashly*, A.*Pers.* 552 (lyr.). **-φυής,** ές, *germinating tardily*, Thphr.*HP*7.1.3: Sup., ibid. **-φυΐα,** ἡ, *tardy germination*, opp. ταχυβλαστία, Id.*CP* 4.8.2. **-φυλακτέω,** = δυσωρέομαι, Eust.797.28. **-φύλακτος** [ῠ], ον, *hard to guard*, δυσφύλακτον οὐδὲν ὡς γυνή Alex.339; of a city, Plb.2.55.2; πλοῦτος Str.9.3.8; ἀρχή D.C.56.33. II. *hard to keep off* or *prevent*, κακά E.*Ph.*924, cf. *Andr.*728; *hard to guard against* or *avoid*, τενάγη Str.11.4.2; τὸ οἶδεῖν -ότατον Longin.3. 3. **-φυσις·** κακὴ φύσις, Hsch. **-φωνία,** ἡ, *roughness of sound*, Demetr.*Eloc.*48, Poll.2.112, *Cat.Cod.Astr.*2.167. **-φωνος,** ον, *ill-sounding, harsh*, Demetr.*Eloc.*69 (Comp.), 105; κολοιοί Babr.33. 4. **-φώρατος,** ον, *hard to detect*, Plu.2.51d. **-χαλέες·** βλάσφημοι, χαλεποί, Hsch. **-χαλίνωτος** [ῑ], ον, *hard to rein, unbridled*, Gal.19.94 (s.v. δυσήνιος). **-χάριστος** [ᾰ], ον, *thankless*, τῶν πυκνῶν φιλημάτων A.*Fr.*135. **-χειμερινός,** ή, όν, = sq., τὰ δ. *wintry climates*, Thphr.*HP*8.8.1. **-χείμερος,** ον, *wintry* or *stormy*, Hom. (only in Il.) epith. of Dodona, 2.750, al.; χώρη Hdt.4.28, cf. Arist. *HA*606$^{b}$5; φάραγξ A.*Pr.*15: metaph., δ. πέλαγος δύης ib.746; δ. ἆται Id.*Ch.*271. II. *bearing winter ill*, Arist.*HA*596$^{b}$5, *Gp.*19.2. 8. **-χείμων,** ον, gen. ονος, = foreg. 1, A.R.4.635. **-χείρωμα,** ατος, τό, *a hard conquest*, incorrect formation in S.*Ant.*126. **-χείρωτος,** ον, *hard to subdue*, Hdt.7.9.β′ (Sup.), D.61.37, Plu.*Alc.*4, D.C. 53.25 (Comp.): Sup. δυσχειρότατον is prob. f. l. in D.S.5.34.

**δυσχερ-αινόντως,** Adv. part. pres., *with disgust*, v.l. in Arist.*Rh.* 1408$^{a}$17. **-αίνω,** impf. ἐδυσχέραινον Pl.*Tht.*169d: aor. ἐδυσχέρᾱνα S.*OC*1282, Isoc.12.201: aor. Pass. ἐδυσχεράνθην Plu.2.820f: (δυσχερής):—*to be unable to endure* or *put up with, to be disgusted at*, c. acc., Isoc.14.46, Pl.*Tht.*195c, D.19.116, etc.; θεούς Pl.*Lg.*900a; δ. τὸ γενέσθαι τι X.*HG*7.4.2; τὸ ἀδικεῖν Pl.*R.*362b: c. acc. et part., *to be annoyed at* his doing, Aeschin.1.158. 2. mostly intr., *feel dislike, disgust* or *annoyance, to be displeased*, περί τινος And.3.35; τινί *at* a thing, D.55.11; ἐπί τινι Isoc.1.26; πρός τι D.H.*Th.*34, Plu. *Pyrrh.*21; κατά τινος Luc.*Nav.*10; also δ. ἑαυτῷ *to have misgivings*, Arist.*Metaph.*984$^{a}$29:—Pass., *to be hateful*, ὄνομα δυσχεραινόμενον Plu.*Publ.*1; δ. ὑπὸ πολλῶν Id.*Cic.*24. 3. c. inf., *scorn* to do a thing, Pl.*R.*388a: c. acc., δ. τι τῶν λεχθέντων *feel qualms about*, Id. *Plt.*294a; ταῦτ' οὐκ ἐδυσχέραινεν *felt* no *scruple about*, Aeschin.1. 54; *to be fastidious*, περὶ τὰ μαθήματα Pl.*R.*475b. II. causal, *cause annoyance*, ῥήματ' ἢ τέρψαντά τι ἢ δυσχεράναντ' S.*OC*1282; δ. τὴν ὁδόν *make* it *difficult*, App.*Ill.*18:—Pass., *to be disagreeable*, τοῖς ἀκούουσι Arist.*Rh.Al.*1432$^{b}$19: abs., ib.1437$^{a}$33. III. δ. ἐν τοῖς λόγοις *to make difficulties* in argument, *to be captious*, Pl.*Grg.* 450e. **-ανσις,** εως, ἡ, *disgust*, Andronic.Rhod.p.570 M., Plot. 1.9, Simp.*in Epict.*p.45 D. **-αντέον,** *one must boggle at*, θεόν Pl. *Lg.*828d, al. **-αντικός,** ή, όν, *peevish*, M.Ant.1.8, Hierocl.*in CA*11 p.444 M. Adv. -κῶς, ζῆν Simp.*in Epict.*p.35 D. **-ασμα,** ατος, τό, in pl., *harsh judgements*, Pl.*Phlb.*44d; *inconveniences*, Dam.*Isid.*66:—condemned by Poll.3.133. **-εια,** ἡ, opp. εὐχέρεια, I. of things, *annoyance, disgust* caused by a thing, τοῦ φορήματος, τοῦ νοσήματος, S.*Ph.*473,900, cf. Pl.*Plt.*286b; *unpleasantness*, of food, D.C.68.31: pl., Plu.2.654b. b. *odium, unpopularity*, Pl.*Lg.*967c (pl.). 2. *difficulty, troublesome question*, Id.*R.* 502d, Isoc.5.12 (pl.), etc.; δ. παρέχειν Plb.1.20.10; εἰς δ. ἐμπεσεῖν Id.8.7.1; κατὰ τὴν προφοράν, opp. εὐχέρεια, Phld.*Po.*994.8. 3. in argument, *difficulties*, δ. λογικαί Arist.*Metaph.*1005$^{b}$22, cf. 995$^{a}$ 33. II. of persons, *harshness*, Pl.*Phlb.*44c; *offensiveness*, Thphr. *Char.*19. 2. *loathing, nausea*, Pl.*Prt.*334c. ❋ **-ής,** ές, (χείρ) *hard to take in hand* or *manage*, opp. εὐχερής: I. of things, *annoying, vexatious*, θεωρία A.*Pr.*802; πᾶσι θαῦμα δ. S.*Ant.*254; Ἁρπάλου ἄφιξις Din.2.5; of actions, *odious, unpopular*, Isoc.12.63 (Sup.); *disagreeable*, Pl.*Lg.*779e (Comp.); τὸ δ., = δυσχέρεια, E.*Ph.* 390; δυσχερὲς εἰπεῖν D.18.3; δυσχερὲς ποιεῖσθαι to raise *difficulties*, Th.4.85. 2. *difficult*, Pl.*Hp.Mi.*369b (Sup.), etc.; τύχη Lys.24.6 (Sup.); βίος D.60.24; τὰ δυσχερῆ *difficulties*, Id.10.58, al.; καιροὶ δ. *difficult* times, *Inscr.Prien.*37.132. 3. of arguments, *contradictory, captious*, Pl.*Prt.*333d, D.20.113; τὰ δυσχερῆ *difficulties* in an argument or discussion, Arist.*EN*1145$^{b}$6, *Metaph.*1067$^{b}$35. II. of persons, *ill-tempered, unfriendly*, τινί to one, S.*El.*929; πρός τινα E. *Ion*398; ἄτοποι καὶ δ. D.19.308; δ. περὶ τὰ σιτία *fastidious*, Pl.*R.*475c, cf. Arist.*EE*1221$^{b}$3. 2. *unpleasant, offensive*, Thphr.*Char.*19.1; ὕδωρ D.C.68.31. III. Adv. δυσχερῶς, φέρειν, Lat. *aegre ferre*, Hp. *Aph.*1.25; ἀποδέχεσθαι Pl.*Euthphr.*6a; δ. ἔχειν to be *annoyed*, πρός τι Id.*Prt.*332a; ἐπί τινι Amphis 34.

**δυσχιδώτερον·** κακοτροπώτερον (Tarent.), Hsch.

**δύσχῑμος,** ον, *troublesome, dangerous, fearful*, δράκων A.*Th.*503; πλημμυρίς Id.*Ch.*186; κέλευθοι Id.*Pers.*567 (lyr.); ὄρη Id.*Fr.*342; χθών, πνεύματα, E.*Ba.*15, *Supp.*962 (lyr.). (It is doubtful whether -χῑμος (required by the metre in A.) is cognate with χεῖμα, *hiems*, cf. μελάγ-χῑμος: the form δύσχειμος is corrupt in A.*Fr.*342, E. ll. cc.)

**δύσχιστος,** ον, *hard to split*, Thphr.*CP*5.16.4.

**δυσχλαινία,** ἡ, *mean* or *shabby clothing*, E.*Hec.*240: in pl., τὰς ἐμὰς δυσχλαινίας Id.*Hel.*416.

**δυσχορήγητος,** ον, *difficult to stage*, Plu.2.712e.

**δύσχορτος,** ον, *with little grass* or *food*, δ. οἶκοι *inhospitable* dwellings, E.*IT*219 (lyr.).

**δυσχραής·** δυσχερής, and **δυσχρανής·** αὐχμηρός, Hsch.

**δυσχρηστ-έω,** *to be intractable*, Plb.27.7.10. II. *to be in difficulties* or *distress*, Id.4.60.8; ταῖς εἰρεσίαις Id.16.4.10; διά τι Id.1.51. 6; περὶ τὴν ἔξοδον ib.75.7:—also in Med., δ. ἐν τοῖς κινδύνοις ib.87.7; πράγμασι, λόγοις, Id.1.18.7, 3.11.4; of things, *to be useless*, Id.16.3.5:—Pass., *to be brought into distress*, ἐπὶ τοῖς ἀπαντωμένοις ὑπ' Ἀρχιμήδους Id.8.6.5; *to be annoyed*, D.S.18.39; ἐπί τινι Id.19.77. **-ημα,** ατος, τό, *inconvenience*, *Stoic.*3.23. **-ία,** ἡ, *difficult position, awkward circumstances*, εἰς δ. ἥκειν Plb.11.25.1, cf. 5.26.2, al.; *distress*, Phld.*Ir.*p.52 W., *Mort.*26 (pl.); of things, *inconvenience, disadvantage*, Plb.5.46.5: pl., Id.1.53.13; χρείας καὶ δ. Str.2.5.17; opp. πλεονέκτημα, Corn.*ND*18, cf. Plu.2.600a. II. (χράω) *difficulty in obtaining loans, 'tightness' of money*, Cic.*Att.*16.7.6. ❋ **-ος,** ον, (χράομαι) *hard to use, inconvenient*, opp. εὔχρηστος, Hp.*Aph.*2.54, cf. Sch.Il.*Oxy.*221 vii 14; ἱππικὸν στράτευμα ἐν νυκτὶ . . δ. X.*Cyr.*3.3. 26; *intractable*, κύνες Id.*Cyn.*3.11; of troops, Plb.4.11.8 (Sup.); δ. ἐξουσία *hard to use well*, Isoc.8.103; δύσχρηστα *inconveniences*, Cic. *Att.*7.5.3, cf. D.S.4.8. Adv. -τως, διακεῖσθαι to be *in difficulties, unmanageable*, of ships, Plb.1.61.4; of troops, ἀπαλλάττειν Id.4.64.7; δ. ἔχειν Plu.*Aem.*19:—synon. for οὐ χρησίμως, Str.17.2.4.

**δύσ-χροια,** ἡ, *bad colour*, Dsc.*Ther.*6, Gal.17(2).215, Asp.*in EN* 44.6. **-χροος,** ον, contr. **-χρους,** ουν, = sq., Hp.*Aph.*5.42. **-χρως,** ωτος, ὁ, ἡ, *of a bad colour, discoloured*, Id.*Coac.*136.

**δύσχῡλος,** ον, *with bad juices, ill-savoured*, Xenocr.12.

**δυσχῡμ-ία,** ἡ, *an ill taste*, Thphr.*CP*6.12.12. **-ος,** ον, *ill-savoured*, Arist.*GA*776$^{a}$30, Thphr.*CP*6.12.4.

**δυσχώρ-ητος,** ον, *hard to traverse*: *inextricable*, ἀκρισία Plb.23.1. 13 (s.v.l.). II. *difficult to digest*, τροφή Aët.9.30. **-ία,** ἡ, *rough ground*, X.*Cyr.*1.6.35; τῶν Ἰταλῶν Jul.*Or.*1.38c: in pl., X. *Cyr.*1.4.7, Isoc.6.80, Onos.11.3, Gal.*UP*2.1, etc. II. *want of room*, Ph.2.563, Ath.4.129c. III. *difficulty*, Alex.Aphr.*Fat.*200. 23.

**δυσχώριστος,** ον, *hard to separate*, Gal.2.700 (Comp.); *hard to distinguish*, ἡ κολακεία τῆς φιλίας δ. Plu.2.51a.

**δυσχῶται·** δυσχωρῇ, διακωλύεται, Hsch.

**δύσψυκτος,** ον, *not easily affected by cold*, Gal.1.346.

**δῠσωδέω,** *to be ill-smelling*, Ph.2.563.

**δῠσώδ-ης,** ες, (ὄζω) *ill-smelling, stinking, foul*, χωλός, δ. S.*Ph.* 1032; δ. πῦον Hp.*Prog.*7; καρπός Hdt.2.94; πνεῦμα Th.2.49; ὀσμαί Arist.*HA*626$^{a}$27: Comp., κόπρος Plu.*Fr.inc.*149. **-ία,** ἡ, *foul smell*, Arist.*Pol.*1311$^{b}$34, *HA*626$^{b}$20, Ph.2.96, Plu.2.90b, Phld. *Herc.*19.27, etc.

**δῠσώδῑνος,** ον, *causing grievous pangs*, *AP*6.272 (Pers.).

**δῠσώλεθρος,** ον, *hard to kill, tenacious of life*, Thphr.*HP*3.12.5.

**δῠσώμοτος,** ον, *hardly*, i. e. *reluctantly, swearing*, Poll.1.39.

**δῠσων-έω,** impf. ἐδυσώνουν *AP*11.169 (Nicarch.):—*beat down the price, cheapen*, Pl.Com.224:—Med., Arist.*Fr.*558. ❋ **-ης,** ου, ὁ, *one who beats down the price, hard bargainer*, Lync.ap.Ath.6.228c; οὐδεὶς δ. χρηστὸν ὀψωνεῖ κρέας *Com.Adesp.*277. **-ος,** ον, *hard to buy*, Hdn. *Epim.*213.

**δῠσωνῠμ-έω,** *have a bad name*, Hdn.*Epim.*203. **-ος,** ον, *bearing an ill name, hateful*, υἷες Ἀχαιῶν Il.6.255; ἠώς Od.19.571; μοῖρα Il.12.116; λέκτρα S.*OC*528 (lyr.); φθόνος E.*Fr.*403; κήρ A.R.2.258; esp. *bearing a name of ill omen*, such as Αἴας, S.*Aj.*914 (lyr.): Comp., Ph.1.680:—in S.*Fr.*88.9 (lyr.) perh. δ. γλώσσῃ *whose* tongue *earned him an ill name* (of Thersites).

❋ **δῠσωπ-έω,** aor. ἐδυσώπησα Luc.*Asin.*38: (ὄψ):—*put out of countenance, abash*, τινά Ph.1.291, Plu.2.418e, Luc. l.c., S.E.*P.*3.66, etc.; οὐδὲν αὐτὴν ἐδυσώπει X.Eph.4.5: c. acc. inf., *shame* a person with

doing a thing, J.*BJ*1.6.5, al.: esp. of importunate persons, δ. τινὰ δεήσει ib.3.8.6; so, *entreat*, ἥκειν ὑμᾶς καὶ παρακαλῶ καὶ δ. Hld.10.2: abs., *to be importunate*, αἰσχυνόμενοι ἀντιλέγειν τοῖς ἀγνωμόνως δυσωποῦσιν ὕστερον δυσωποῦνται τοὺς δικαίως ἐγκαλοῦντας Plu.2.532d:—Pass., θεὸν εἶναι τὴν ἠχὼ δυσωποῦμαι I *am constrained to believe* that, Jul.*Ep.*189, cf. Marcellin.*Puls.*23; *to be susceptible to importunity*, τὴν ὑπὸ τῶν ἀναισχύντως λιπαρούντων ἧτταν, ἣν ἔνιοι δυσωπεῖσθαι καλοῦσιν Plu.*Brut.*6; δυσωπεῖν τὴν ὄψιν *to disgust*, Id.*Lyc.*9; *alarm*, πάθος δ. τινά Procop.*Arc.*2. II. in early writers only Pass., impf. ἐδυσωπούμην Pl.*Phdr.*242c:—*to be put out of countenance*, abs., Id.*Plt.*285b, etc.; πρὸς ἀλλήλους Id.*Lg.*933a; δ. μή.. Id.*Phdr.* l.c.; τινί Plb.20.12.6; ἐπί τινι Ph.1.639; εἰ.. Id.2.423; περί τινος Phld.*Rh.*1.297 S.; of animals, *to be shy, timid*, X.*Mem.*2.1.4. 2. c. acc., *to be put to shame by*, τὴν ἀρετήν τινος Plu.*Cor.*15; τὴν χάριν Lib.*Decl.*37.19: but more freq. *fight shy of*, ὄνομα D.H.*Comp.*12 (so in Act., *look askance at*, δ. καὶ ὑποπτεύω μήποτ' οὐ Λυσίου ὁ λόγος Id.*Lys.*11), cf. Phryn.166; ὑφορᾶν καὶ δ. Them.*Or.*26.330b; διὰ τοὔνομα τὴν μοναρχίαν Plu.*Sol.*14; *regard with aversion*, ὄψα Ael.*Fr.*182; *disapprove of*, Phld.*Hom.*p.55 O.: c. inf., *to be ashamed to do*, ..εἰπεῖν D.Chr.32.7, cf. 36.54; also τὴν ἀντίδοσιν δ. *feel ashamed to reply*, Jul.*Ep.*184. III. intr. in Act., *to see with difficulty*, Luc.*Lex.*4. **-ημα**, ατος, τό, *a means of making* one *ashamed*, and so, *a corrective*, τῶν ἡμαρτημένων J.*BJ*1.25.5, cf. D.Chr.*Fr.*8. **-ητέον**, *one must be shy of using*, τὴν ταυτολογίαν Eust.173.12. **-ητικός**, ή, όν, *importunate*, Id.105.15 (Comp.), etc. Adv. **-κῶς** Sch.Ar.*Pl.*21 (v.l. -ωπικῶς). **-ία**, ἡ, *confusion of face, shamefacedness*, Phld.*Lib.* p.24 O., Ph.2.603 (pl.), Plu.2.95b; *false modesty*, ib.528e, al.; *cause for shame*, ib.707e, Cic.*Att.*13.33.2; δυσωπίαν *habere*, to have *an ugly look*, ib.16.15.2; τὰς δ. (v.l. δυστροπίας) τὰς ἐν τοῖς διαπορηθεῖσι dub. in Ph.1.330.

**δῠσωρέομαι**, (ὥρα) *keep painful watch*, ὡς δὲ κύνες περὶ μῆλα δυσωρήσονται ἐν αὐλῇ Il.10.183; but Apollon.*Lex.* read δυσωρήσωσιν, cf. Hsch., *EM*292.49.

**δύσωρος**, ον, (ὥρα) *unseasonable*, Poll.5.109.

**δυσωχεῖν**· δυσχεραίνειν, Hsch.

⊛ **δύτη**, Dor. **δύτα**, ἡ, *shrine* (?), *IG*4.823.42 (Troezen), 7.2477 (Cabireum).

**δύτης** [ῠ], ου, ὁ, (δύω) *diver*, Hdt.8.8; δ. βύθιος Poll.1.97.

**δῠτικός**, ή, όν, *able to dive*, ζῷον Arist.*Fr.*496; ἡ -κή (sc. τέχνη) Poll.7.139. II. (δύσις) later form for δυσμικός, *setting*, Euc. *Phaen.*p.10 M. 2. *western*, στοά J.*AJ*20.8.11; opp. ἀνατολικός, Ptol.*Alm.*2.11: Comp. -ώτερος *farther west*, ib.2.13; δ. ὠκεανός Nonn. *D.*12.1; -κόν, τό, *closing at sunset*, = κλύμενον, Ps.-Dsc.4.13; = φοῖνιξ, ib.43.

**δυτῖνος**, ὁ, unknown *water-bird*, Dionys.*Av.*2.13, 3.24.

**δύω**, v. δύο.

**δύω** (v. infr.), **δύνω**: A. causal Tenses, *cause to sink, sink, plunge in*; pres. only in Thphr.*HP*5.4.8 οὐκ ἐν ἴσῳ βάθει πάντα δύοντες τῆς θαλάσσης: aor. 1 ἔδῡσα (ἐξ-) Od.14.341; cf. the compds. ἀπο-, ἐκ-, ἐν-, κατα-δύω.

B. non-causal, *get* or *go into*, c. acc.: pres. δύω (v. I. 4); more freq. δύνω Il.17.202, Hes.*Op.*616, S.*Ph.*1331, etc.; Ep. impf. δῦνον Il.11.268: aor. ἔδῡνα Batr.245, part. δύνας Plb.9.15.9, Paus.2.11.7, Ael.*VH*4.1, but ἔδῡσα *Ev.Marc.*1.32, etc.: more freq. Med. δύομαι Il. 5.140, E.*Rh.*529 (lyr.), etc. (also in Att. Inscrr., as *IG*2².1241): impf. ἐδυόμην Pl.*Plt.*269a; Ep. δύοντο Il.15.345: fut. δύσομαι [ῡ] 7.298, E.*El.*1271: aor. ἐδῡσάμην A.R.4.865, (ἀπό) Nic.*Al.*302; Ep. 3 pl. δύσαντο Il.23.739, opt. δυσαίατο prob. in 18.376 (Prose and Com. in Compds.); Hom. mostly uses the Ep. forms ἐδύσεο, ἐδύσετο, imper. δύσεο 19.36, Hes.*Sc.*108, part. δυσόμενος (in pres. sense) Od.1.24, Hes.*Op.*384: more freq. aor. ἔδυν (as if from *δῦμι) Il.11.63, etc.; 3 dual ἐδύτην [ῡ] 10.254; 1 pl. ἔδυμεν S.*Fr.*367; ἔδυτε Od.24.106; ἔδυσαν, Ep. ἔδυν Il.11.263; Ion. 3 sg. δύσκεν 8.271; imper. δῦθι, δῦτε, 16.64, 18.140; subj. δύω [ῡ] 6.340, 22.99, but δύῃ [ῠ] Hes.*Op.*728; Ep. opt. δύη [ῡ] (for δυίη) Od.18.348; inf. δῦναι Il.10.221, Att., Ep. δύμεναι [ῡ] 14.63, ἐκ-δῦμεν 16.99; part. δύς, δῦσα, Hdt.8.8: pf. δέδῡκα Il.5.811, Sapph.52, Pl.*Phd.*116e; Dor. inf. δεδυκεῖν [ῡ] Theoc.1.102:—Pass., fut. and aor. δῠθήσομαι, ἐδύθην [ῠ], and a pf. δέδῠμαι only in compds., v. ἀπο-, ἐκ-, ἐν-δύω. [ῠ in δύω in pres. and impf. Act. and Med., Hom.; but A.R. has δῡομαι, δῡετο 1.581, part. δῡόμενος ib.925, Call. *Ep.*22; δῡεται Nonn.*D.*7.286; ἐκ-δέδῠκας *AP*5.72 (Rufin.).] I. of Places or Countries, *enter, make one's way into*, in Hom. the most freq. use, εἰ..κε πύλας καὶ τείχεα δύω (aor. 2) Il.22.99; πόλιν δύσεσθαι Od.7.18; ἔδυ νέφεα *plunged into* the clouds, of a star, Il.11.63; δῦτε θαλάσσης εὐρέα κόλπον *plunge into* the lap of Ocean, 18.140; γαῖαν ἐδύτην *went beneath* the earth, i.e. died, 6.19, cf. 411, etc.; πόλεμον δύμεναι *plunge into*.., 14.63; θεῖον δύσονται ἀγῶνα 7.298; ἐδύσετο οὐλαμὸν ἀνδρῶν 20.379; δύσεο δὲ μνηστῆρας *go in to* them, Od. 17.276; rarely in Trag., αἰθέρα δ. S.*Aj.*1192 (lyr.), cf. E.*El.*1271. 2. in Ep. less freq. with Preps., ἔδυν δόμον Ἄϊδος εἴσω Il.11.263; δύσομαι εἰς Ἀΐδαο Od.12.383; ἐς πόντον ἐδύσετο 5.352; δέρτρον ἔσω δύνοντες 11.579; δύσεθ' ἁλὸς κατὰ κῦμα Il.6.136; ὑπὸ κῦμα θαλάσσης αὐτίκ' ἔδυσαν 18.145; κατὰ σταθμοὺς δύεται *slinks* into the fold, 5.140; καθ' ὅμιλον ἔδυ Τρώων 3.36 (rarely c. gen., κατὰ σπείους κοίλοιο δέδυκεν Od.12.93); παῖς ὣς ὑπὸ μητέρα δύσκεν εἰς Αἴαντα *he got himself unto* Ajax, i.e. *got behind* his shield, Il.8.271; βέλος δ' εἰς ἐγκέφαλον δῦ ib. 85; ἀκίδες δεδυκυῖαι διὰ φλεβῶν Plu.*Crass.*25; in Prose and Trag. mostly with a Prep. (but δυόμενοι abs., *diving*, Th.7.25), δῦναι ἐς θάλασσαν Hdt.8.8; ἐς ἄντρον A.*Fr.*261; ἁρμὸν..πρὸς αὐτὸ στόμιον S.*Ant.*1217; κατὰ βάθος Pl.*Lg.*905a; κατὰ τῆς γῆς Id.*Phd.*113c, etc. 3. abs., εἴσω ἔδυ ξίφος the sword *entered his body*, Il.16.340; δύνει ἀλοιφή *sinks in* (where however βοείην may be supplied), 17.392:—Med., δύου πάλιν Ar.*V.*148. 4. of Sun and Stars, *sink into* [the sea], *set*, ἠέλιος μὲν ἔδυ Il.18.241, cf. Od.3.329, etc.; ἔδυ φάος ἠελίοιο 13.35; δύσετό τ' ἠέλιος 2.388, cf. Il.7.465, etc.; ἀελίω δύντος Sapph.*Supp.*25.8; so Βοώτης ὀψὲ δύων *late-setting* Boötes, Od. 5.272; δείελος ὀψὲ δύων Il.21.232; [σεληναία] δύεν Bion *Fr.*8.6; πρὸ δύντος ἡλίου Hdt.7.149; πρὸ ἡλίου δύντος D.15.22; δυσόμενος Ὑπερίων (to mark the West) Od.1.24; ἐδύετο εἰς τόπον [ὁ ἥλιος] Pl.*Plt.*269a; πρὸς δύνοντος ἡλίου towards the West, A.*Supp.*255: metaph., βίου δύντος αὐγαί Id.*Ag.*1123 (lyr.); ἔδυ πρόπας δόμος ib.1011 (lyr.); δεδυκὼς ζῆν live *in retirement*, Pl.*Lg.*781c. II. of clothes and armour, *get into*, Ἀρήϊα τεύχεα δ. Il.6.340, etc.; κυνέην δ. *put on* one's helmet, 5.845; δῦ δὲ χιτῶν' 18.416: metaph., εἰ μὴ σύ γε δύσεαι ἀλκήν if thou wilt not *put on* strength, 9.231; so ἀνάγκας ἔδυ λέπαδνον A.*Ag.*218 (lyr.): hence, 2. trans., *put on*, ἀμφ' ὤμοισιν ἐδύσετο τεύχεα Il. 3.328, etc.; ὤμοιϊν..τεύχεα δῦθι 16.64; χιτῶνα περὶ χροΐ..δῦνεν Od. 15.61; χρυσὸν..ἔδυνε περὶ χροΐ Il.8.43. 3. rarely abs. with a Prep., ὅπλοισιν ἔνι δεινοῖσιν ἐδύτην 10.272, cf. A.R.1.638; ἐς τεύχεα δύντε Od.22.201. III. of sufferings, passions, and the like, *enter, come over* or *upon*, κάματος..γυῖα δέδυκεν Il.5.811; ὄφρ' ἔτι μᾶλλον δύῃ ἄχος κραδίην Od.18.348; ἦτορ δῦν' ἄχος Il.19.367; ὀδύναι δῦνον μένος 11.272; κρατερὴ δέ ἑ λύσσα δέδυκε madness *is come over* him, 9. 239; δῦ μιν Ἄρης Ares, i.e. the spirit of war, *filled* him, 17.210; μιν ἔδυ χόλος 19.16.

**δῠωβολιαῖος**, α, ον, *weighing two obols*, Gal.13.92, al.

⊛ **δυώδεκα**, Ion., Ep., Lyr.; Att. **δώδεκα**, *twelve*, in all genders, Il. 2.637, Hdt.1.16, Pi.*N.*4.28, etc.; οἱ δώδεκα θεοί Aeschin.Socr.5, *Com.Adesp.*39.9 D.:—also **δυόδεκο**, *IG*5(2).3 (Tegea, iv B.C.).

⊛ **δυωδεκάβοιος** [ᾰ], ον, *worth twelve oxen*, Il.23.703.

**δυωδεκᾰδικός**, ή, όν, *belonging to the* δυωδεκάς I, Dam.*Pr.*276.

**δυωδεκά-δρομος**, ον, *running the course twelve times*, τέθριππα Pi. *O.*2.50. **-εθλος**, v. δωδ-.

**δυωδεκᾰϝέτης**, = δωδεκέτης, *Leg.Gort.*12.34.

⊛ **δυωδεκαΐς**, ίδος, Att.; Ion. **δωδεκηΐς**, ίδος, and **-ηΐς**, -ῆδος, ἡ, *sacrifice of twelve victims*, *SIG*²438 *D*37 (Delph.), *SIG*³604.9 (Delph., ii B.C.), Porph.*Abst.*1.22, etc.: as Adj., θυσίαι Eust.1386.48: hence name of a sacred mission to Delphi, *SIG*773.2 (i B.C.).

**δυωδεκά-μηνος**, **δυωδεκαταῖος**, **δυωδέκατος**, v. δωδ-. **-μοιρος**, ον, *divided into twelve parts*, *AP*7.641 (Antiphil.). **-πηχυς**, υ, *of twelve cubits*, εὖρος Opp.*H.*2.143. **-πλους**, ουν, *twelvefold*, *IG* 14.644 (Brutt.). **-πολις**, ιος, *formed of twelve united states*, Ἴωνες Hdt.7.95.

**δυωδεκάς**, άδος, ἡ, *the number twelve*, Procl. *in Euc.*p.174 F.; *group of twelve* divinities, Dam.*Pr.*348. II. *twelfth part*, of the signs of the zodiac, Arat.555 (pl.), 703; of an hour, *AP*9.779, 782 (Paul. Sil.).

**δυωδεκᾰτειχής**, ές, *having twelve walled cities*, λαός Tim.*Pers.*247.

**δυωδεκᾰτεύς** (sc. μήν), έος, ὁ, *twelfth month*, *IG*14.425 iv, 427 ii (Tauromenium).

**δυωκαιεικοσί-μετρος** [σῐ], ον, *holding twenty-two measures*, τρίπους Il.23.264. **-πηχυς**, υ, *twenty-two cubits long*, 15.678.

⊛ **δῶ**, τό, shortd. Ep. form for δῶμα, *house, dwelling*, Hom. only in nom. as Od.1.392, and acc. as Il.1.426.—As pl. for δώματα, only in Hes.*Th.*933.

**δωαί**· δικαίως, ὁσίως, Hsch.

**δώδεκα**, v. δυώδεκα.

**δωδεκᾰ-ακτῖονίκης** [νῑ], ου, ὁ, *twelve times victorious in the Actian games*, *BGU*1074.23 (iii A.D.). ⊛ **-βοιος**, ον, *of twelve oxen*, θυσία *IGRom.*4.555 (Ancyra). **-βωμος**, ον, *with twelve altars*, ναός Lyd. *Mens.*4.2. **-γναμπτος**, ον, *bent twelve times*, τέρμα the post (in the race-course) *that has been doubled twelve times*, Pi.*O.*3.33. **-γωνον**, τό, *dodecagon*, Plu.2.363a. **-δάκτῠλος**, ον, *twelve fingers long* or *broad*, Apollod.*Poliorc.*178.3; *of twelve digits*, of the apparent diameter of sun and moon, Cleom.2.3; δ. ἔκφυσις *the duodenum*, Herophil.ap.Gal.2.572, Ruf.*Anat.*42.

**δωδεκάδαρχος** [κᾰ], ὁ, *leader of twelve*, X.*Cyr.*3.3.11; codd. have -δεκάρχας, -δεκαδάρχας in ib.2.4.4.

**δωδεκά-δραχμος**, ον, *sold at twelve drachmae*, οἶνος D.42.20. II. *privileged to pay as poll-tax only twelve dr.*, *POxy.*258.8 (i A.D.), al. **-δωρος**, ον, *twelve palms long*, κέρα *AP*6.96 (Eryc.). **-εδρος**, ον, (ἕδρα) *with twelve surfaces*: δωδεκάεδρον, τό, *dodecahedron*, Euc.11 *Def.*28, 13.17, Arist.*Cael.*307ᵃ16.

**δωδεκάεθλος** [ᾰ], ον, *conqueror in twelve contests*, *Sammelb.*2134.4, *APl.*4.99 (also δυω- Nonn.*D.*35.335).

**δωδεκᾰ-ετηρίς**, ίδος, ἡ, *cycle of twelve years*, τοῦ Διός *Gp.*1.12 tit.: pl., title of Orphic work, Suid. **-ετής**, ές, or **-έτης**, ες, (ἔτος) *lasting twelve years*, χρόνος J.*AJ*15.9.6. II. *twelve years old*, Plu. *Comp.Lyc.Num.*4, 2.198c. **-ετία**, ἡ, *space of twelve years*, Ptol. *Tetr.*206; ὑπὲρ τῆς δ., title of a speech of Demades. II. *age of twelve years*, *BGU*592 i 3 (ii A.D.). **-ζῴδιος**, ον, *having twelve signs*, οὐρανός Lyd.*Mens.*4.67.

**δωδεκᾰ-ήμερος**, ον, *of twelve days*, Eust.128.13. ⊛ **-θεος**, ον, *of twelve Gods*, *cena*, Suet.*Aug.*70. II. Subst. **-θεον**, τό, *temple of the twelve Gods*, *Inscr.Cos*43. 2. *medicine compounded of twelve ingredients*, Paul.Aeg.7.11. 3. *primrose*, *Primula acaulis*, Plin. *HN*25.28.

**δωδεκάκις**, Adv. *twelve times*, Ar.*Pl.*852, Arist.*Fr.*347, D.C.60.7, etc.

**δωδεκά-κλῖνος,** *ον, holding twelve* κλῖναι, Anaxandr.41.11. **-κρουνος,** *ον, with twelve springs,* Cratin.186, Philostr.*VS*1.22.4. **-κυκλος,** *ον,* dub. sens., *Sammelb.*1958. **-κωλος,** *ον, of twelve clauses,* Sch.Ar.*Eq.*821. **-λῖνος,** *ον, of twelve threads,* X.*Cyn.*2.5. ⊛ **-μηνος,** *ον, of twelve months,* τέλος Pi.*N.*11.10 (but δυω- codd.): *-μηνον, τό, year,* Thd.*Da.*4.26, *POxy.*506.15 (ii A.D.):—poet. **δυωδεκάμ-,** *twelve months old,* Hes.*Op.*752. **-μήχᾰνος,** *ον,* (μηχανή) *knowing twelve arts* or *tricks,* ἄστρον E.*Fr.*755 (lyr.); of a courtesan, Ar.*Ra.*1327 (et Sch.), cf. Pl.Com.134. **-μν⟨α⟩ιαῖος,** *α, ον, weighing twelve minae,* Hsch. s. v. πέλεκυς. **-μορφος,** *ον, of twelve forms,* Olymp. *in Phd.*p.199 N. **-μοχθος,** *ον, of twelve labours,* epith. of Heracles, Lyd.*Mens.*4.67. **όργυιος,** *ον, of twelve fathoms,* Hero *Geom.*4.12. **-παις,** *παιδος, ὁ, ἡ, with twelve children,* λοχείη *APl.*4.132 (Theodorid.). **-πᾰλαι,** Adv. *twelve times* πάλαι, *ever so long ago,* Ar.*Eq.*1154; cf. δεκάπαλαι, μυριόπαλαι. **-πηχυς,** *υ, twelve cubits high,* κολοσσοί Hdt.2.153 (δυω-); σιρός Anaxandr.41.28, cf. *BCH*3⁻.243 (Delos, ii B.C.), Philostr.*VA*4.16. **-πλᾰσιάζω,** *multiply by twelve,* Heph.Astr.2.2. **-πλᾰσιασμός,** *ὁ, multiplication by twelve,* *Cat.Cod.Astr.*4.44. **-πλάσιος,** *ον, twelvefold,* Plu.2.1028c; also **-πλᾰσίων,** *ον,* gen. *ονος,* Orib.*Fr.*102. **-πλευρον,** *τό, twelve-sided figure,* v.l. in Gal.*Anim.Pass.*2.3. **-πλους,** *ουν,* = δωδεκαπλάσιος, Papp.609. ⊛ **-πους,** *ὁ, ἡ, πουν, τό,* gen. *ποδος, twelve feet long,* Men.364, Gal.10.33.

**δωδεκάρχης,** *ου, ὁ,* v. δωδεκάδαρχος:—also **-αρχος,** Hsch. s. v. δεκαδάρχαι.

**δωδεκάς,** *άδος, ἡ, group of twelve,* Pl.*Lg.*756b. **II.** = δυωδεκαΐς, Hsch. (pl.).

**δωδεκά-σεληνος** [ᾰ], *ον, having twelve moons,* ἐνιαυτός Sch.E.*Tr.*1075. ⊛ **-σημος,** *ον, of twelve times,* in music, Aristid.Quint.1.14, Sch.Ar.*Nu.*456 cod. Ven. **-σκαλμος,** *ον, twelve-oared,* Plu.*Caes.*38. **-σκῠτος,** *ον, of twelve strips of leather,* σφαῖρα Pl.*Phd.*110b, Plu.2.1003d. **-στάδιος** [στᾰ], *ον, twelve stades long,* etc., Posidon.18 J., Str.13.1.36. **-στάσιος** [στᾰ], *ον,* (ἵστημι) *weighing twelve times as much,* Pl.*Hipparch.*231d. **-στεγος,** *ον, with twelve stories,* πύργος Ps.-Callisth.2.18. **-στῦλος** (sc. οἶκος), *ὁ, colonnade of twelve columns,* *Milet.*7.59 (Didyma). **-σύλλᾰβος,** *ον, of twelve syllables,* Ἀλκαϊκὸν **δ.** (sc. μέτρον) Heph.10.3, 14.4. **-σχοινος,** *ἡ,* name of a district in Egypt, *OGI*210.5, 670.5, Ptol.*Geog.*4.5.74.

**δωδεκᾰταῖος,** *α, ον, on the twelfth day, in twelve days,* **δ.** ἀνεβίω Pl.*R.*614b, cf. Thphr.*HP*7.1.3; δυωδεκαταῖος ἀφ' ὧτέ νιν οὐδὲ ποτεῖδον Theoc.2.157. **II.** *twelve days old,* Hes.*Op.*751 (in poet. form δυωδ-), Arist.*HA*567$^{a}$5.

**δωδεκᾰτημόριον,** *τό, twelfth part,* [χώρας] Pl.*Lg.*848c, cf. *IG*12(7).237.56 (Amorgos, ii/i B.C.), Ph.1.673; *sign of the zodiac,* Hipparch.2.1.7, Ptol.*Tetr.*93, etc.

**δωδεκᾰτημόριος,** *ον,* = δυωδεκάμοιρος, Man.4.167:—also **-τήμορος,** *ον,* *PHib.*1.27.122 (iv/iii B.C.).

⊛ **δωδέκᾰτος,** *η, ον, twelfth,* Il.24.781, etc.; **δ.** τόκοι, 8$\frac{1}{3}$%, *SIG*364.74 (Ephesus, iii B.C.), etc.:—Ep. **δυωδ-,** Il.1.493, etc. **II.** δωδεκάτη, ἡ, = Χόες, Hsch.

**δωδεκά-τροπος,** *ἡ, fixed circle of twelve divisions* through which the zodiac is supposed to revolve, Vett.Val.179.33, *Cat.Cod.Astr.*5(3).89, al. **-φόρος,** *ον, bearing twelve times a year,* Luc.*VH*2.13. **-φυλλος,** *ον, with twelve petals,* ῥόδα **δ.** Thphr.*HP*6.6.4. **II.** *with twelve leaves,* κλάδος *PMag.Berol.*2.67. **-φῡλος,** *ον, of twelve tribes,* τὸ **δ.** *the twelve tribes* of Israel, *Act.Ap.*26.7. **-χορδος,** *ον, with twelve strings,* ὄργανον *EM*813.43.

**δωδεκᾰχῶς,** Adv. *in twelve ways,* *An.Ox.*2.3 (Theognost.).

**δωδεκά-χους** [ᾰ], *χουν, holding twelve* χόες, *PRev.Laws*40.11 (iii B.C.), al. **-ωρος,** *ον, of twelve hours,* Secund.*Sent.*4, S.E.*M.*10.182. **II.** δωδεκάωρος, *ἡ, circle of twelve animal figures* typifying the *double hours* of the Chaldaean νυχθήμερον, Teucer in *Cat.Cod.Astr.*7.195, al.

**δωδεκέμβριος,** *ὁ,* = *Dodecember,* month invented by Licinus, D.C.54.21.

⊛ **δωδεκ-έτης,** *ου,* or **-ετής,** *οῦ, ὁ, twelve years old,* Call.*Ep.*21 (δωδεκένη Meineke), Plu.*Aem.*35:—in form **δωδεχέτης,** *IG*4.51 (Aegina), *Annuario* 4/5.467 (Halic., iv B.C.):—fem. **-έτις,** *ιδος,* *AP*11.70 (Leon.). **-εύς,** *έως, ὁ,* = χοεύς *which held twelve cotylae,* Hsch. **-ήμερος,** *ἡ, period of twelve days,* *IG*1$^{2}$.374.89. **-ήρης,** *ους, ἡ, a ship with twelve banks of oars,* Callix.1.

**δωδεκῄς,** *ῇδος, ἡ,* v. δυωδεκαΐς.

**δωδεκόμφᾰλος,** *ον, with twelve knobs,* πόπανον *IG*2$^{2}$.1367.

⊛ **Δωδώνη,** *ἡ, Dodona,* in Epirus, the seat of the most ancient oracle of Zeus, Il.16.234, Od.14.327, Hes.*Fr.*134, 212, A.*Pr.*830, etc.: heterocl. forms Δωδῶνος, -ῶνι (as if from Δωδών), S.*Fr.*460, *Tr.*172: Δωδώνᾱθεν Pi.*N.*4.53; Δωδώνηθε Call.*Del.*284: a nom. Δωδώ, Simm. ap.Str.8.5.3:—Adj. ⊛ **Δωδωναῖος,** *α, ον,* Il.16.233, A.*Supp.*258, Cratin.5: prov., Δωδωναῖον χαλκεῖον *chatterbox,* Eust.335.45:—fem. **Δωδωνίς,** *ίδος,* S.*Fr.*456, Hdt.2.53, Pherecyd.90 J.

**δωΐα·** ὁμοία, Hsch.

⊛ **δωλέννετος·** ὑπόβλητος, Hsch.; cf. sq.

⊛ **δωλοδομεῖς·** οἰκογενεῖς, Hsch. (cf. δοῦλος and ἐβάθη· ἐγεννήθη, Id.: Lith. *gim̃ti* 'to be born').

**δῶλος,** Dor., = δοῦλος, *Leg.Gort.*1.1, al.; voc. δῶλε Theoc.5.5: but δῶλα· ὦτα (Cret.), Hsch.

**δῶμα,** *ατος, τό,* (δέμω) *house,* πατρώϊον ἵκετο **δ.** Il.21.44, etc.; mainly poet., but once in Hdt., 2.62 (pl.), and in late Prose (v. infr.), but never in Att. Prose: also, *chief room, hall,* θάλαμον καὶ δ. καὶ αὐλήν Il.6.316, cf. Od.17.329, al.: hence, pl. for *a single house,* 2.259, freq. in Trag., A.*Ag.*607, S.*Tr.*332, E.*Or.*301, etc. **2.** of the gods, ἀθάνατοι Ὀλύμπια δώματ' ἔχοντες Il.2.13, etc.; κλυτὰ δ. βένθεσι λίμνης, of Poseidon, 13.21; freq. of Pluto, **δῶμ' Ἀΐδαο** the nether world, Od.12.21; ὦ δῶμ' Ἀΐδου καὶ Περσεφόνης S.*El.*110; Πλούτωνος **δ.** E.*HF*808 (lyr.); of a temple, Pi.*P.*4.53, A.*Eu.*242, etc.: pl., Hdt.2.62, S.*OT*71. **3.** δῶμα Καδμεῖον, i.e. Thebes, ib.29. **4.** *housetop,* Lxx *De.*22.8, *Ev.Matt.*24.17, Babr.5.5, *POxy.*475.22 (ii A.D.), etc. **II.** *household, family,* A.*Ag.*1468 (lyr.), S.*OT*1226, etc.; cf. **δῶ.**

⊛ **δωμάτ-ιον** [ᾰ], *τό,* Dim. of **δῶμα,** Ar.*Ra.*100, *IG*12(8).442.8 (Thasos), Jul.*ad Them.*263a. **II.** *chamber, bedchamber,* Ar.*Lys.*160, Lys.1.17, 24, Pl.*R.*390c, and so prob. in X.Eph.2.1, Procop.*Arc.*23. **III.** *housetop* (cf. foreg. 1.4), J.*BJ*2.21.5, Hdn.1.12.8. **-ίτης** [ῑ], *ου, ὁ, of, belonging to the house,* Ποσειδῶν Paus.3.14.7, *IG*5(1).497, al. (Sparta); Ἀπόλλων Sch.Pi.*N.*5.81: fem., δωματῖτις ἑστία A.*Ag.*968. **-όομαι,** Pass., *have a house built for one, to be housed,* δεδωμάτωμαι οὐ σμικρᾷ χερί Id.*Supp.*958.

**δωμᾰτοφθορέω,** *ruin the house,* cj. for σωματοφθ-, A.*Ag.*948.

**δωμ-άω,** *build,* A.R.2.531, *IG*14.1868, *AP*7.142:—more freq. in Med., ib.11.400 (Luc.), Coluth.287, Orph.*A.*570: metaph., *build up, restore to life,* τινά Lyc.48:—Pass., **δ.** ἐκ λίθων Antyll.ap.Orib.9.13.6; of a statue, *to be set up,* *App.Anth.*2.534 (Halic.). ⊛ **-ημα,** *ατος, τό, chamber,* δω[μ]ήματι τύμβου Benndorf-Niemann *Reisen in Lykien* p.80 No.59 (Sidyma). **-ησις,** *εως, ἡ,* and **-ητύς,** *ύος, ἡ, building,* Hsch. ⊛ **-ήτωρ,** *ορος, ὁ, builder,* Man.6.415.

**δωμός,** Dor. for ζωμός, Epil.3 (prob. l.), *EM*316.56.

**δώνακος, δώνακι,** v. δόναξ.

**δωός,** v. ζωός.

⊛ **δωράκινον** (sc. μῆλον), *τό,* = Lat. *duracinum,* a kind of peach, *clingstone,* *Gp.*3.1.4, 10.13.1.

**δώραξ·** σπλήν (Maced.), Hsch.

⊛ **δωρ-εά,** Ion. **-εή,** *ἡ:* δωρειά in earlier Attic Inscrr., *IG*1$^{2}$.77, al., δωρεά first in ib.2$^{2}$.1.68:—*gift, present,* esp. *bounty* (= δόσις ἀναπόδοτος Arist.*Top.*125$^{a}$18), Hdt.2.140; δωρεὰν διδόναι Id.6.130, A.*Pr.*340; πορεῖν ib.616; δωρεῖσθαι Pl.*Plt.*290c; **δ.** δέχεσθαι, λαμβάνειν, Isoc.6.31, 15.40; ironically, θάνατόν τινι δωρεὰν ἀποδοῦναι Antipho 5.34; **δ.** ἔχειν S.*Aj.*1032, D.18.312; ἐν χάριτος μέρει καὶ δωρειᾶς D.21.165; δωρειὰν καὶ χάριν ib.172, cf. Pl.*Lg.*844d; of a *legacy,* D.27.41, 65; δωρεαί *privileges* and *immunities,* opp. δῶρα, *gifts in cash* or *kind,* Philostr.*VS*2.10.4. **2.** *estate granted* by a king, *fief,* Phoenicid.4.7, *PSI*5.511.4, 518.2 (iii B.C.). **II.** acc. δωρεάν as Adv., *as a free gift, freely,* Hdt.5.23, prob. in And.1.4; μηδὲν **δ.** πράττειν Plb.18.34.7, cf. Lxx *Jb.*1.9; **δ.** λειτουργεῖν *Test.Epict.*4.27, cf. *Inscr.Prien.*4.17 (iv B.C.); so κατὰ δωρεάν *IG*7.2711.13, al. (Acraeph., i A.D.); ἐν δωρεᾷ προσνεῖμαι Plb.22.5.4; but γῆν (ἀμπελῶνα, etc.) ἐν δωρεᾷ ἔχειν to hold land by a royal *grant,* *PRev.Laws*36.15 (iii B.C.), cf. 43.11, 44.3. **2.** *to no purpose, for naught,* *Ep.Gal.*2.21. **-εαῖος,** *α, ον, held by royal grant,* γῆ *Sammelb.*1178a, b, cf. 3937, 3938 (iii B.C.); v. foreg. II. ⊛ **-εαστικός,** *ή, όν, concerning grants,* γράμμα *PMasp.*13.26 (vi A.D.). **-ετικός,** *ή, όν,* = foreg., ὁμολογία *Sammelb.*4678.13 (vi A.D.). ⊛ **-έω,** fut. -ήσω Hom.*Fr.*17: aor. ἐδώρησα Hes.*Op.*82, Pi.*O.*6.78:—*give, present,* δῶρον Hes. l.c.; *present* one *with,* θυσίαις Ἑρμᾶν Pi. l.c.:—Pass., aor. δωρηθῆναι *to be given* or *presented,* Hdt.1.87, Isoc.4.26: in pf. Pass., παρὰ θεῶν δῶρα ὑμῖν δεδώρηται Pl.*Plt.*274c; and of persons, *to be presented with* a thing, χώρῃ Hdt.8.85, cf. S.*Aj.*1029. **II.** more freq. Med. **δωρέομαι,** ῥεῖα θεὸς .. ἵππους δωρήσαιτ' Il.10.557; δωρέεσθαί τί τινι *present* a thing *to* one, Hdt.2.126, 5.37, A.*Pr.*253, X.*An.*7.3.20, etc.; σπέρμα εἰς Πελοπόννησον δωρήσασθε Id.*HG*6.3.6; also **δ.** τινά τινι *present* one *with* a thing, Hdt.1.54, 3.130, A.*Pr.*778; **δ.** τινά *to make* him *presents,* Hdt.1.55: pf., δεδώρηται Pl.*Ti.*46e, *Lg.*672b, X.*Cyr.*[5.2.8]. **2.** in pres. and impf. also, *offer,* E.*Supp.*875. **-ημα,** *ατος, τό, gift, present,* Hdt.7.38, etc.: c. dat. pers., A.*Pers.*523, *Eu.*402, S.*Tr.*668: pl., E.*Or.*123, etc.—Rare in Prose, X.*Hier.*8.4, Arist.*EN*1099$^{b}$11, and later, Ph.2.9, *Ep.Jac.*1.17. **-ημᾰτικός,** *ή, όν,* = δωρητικός, D.H.8.60, Vett.Val.41.3. **-ητήρ,** *ῆρος, ὁ, giver,* *AP*6.305 (Leon.). **-ητής,** *οῦ, ὁ, benefactor,* *IG*12(2).645$^{b}$64 (Nesus, iv B.C.). **-ητικός,** *ή, όν, concerned with giving,* Pl.*Sph.*223c. **II.** *munificent,* Ph.1.254. **-ητός,** *όν,* of persons, *open to gifts* or *presents,* Il.9.526. **II.** of things, *freely given,* **δ.,** οὐκ αἰτητόν S.*OT*384, cf. Plu.*Cor.*16.

⊛ **Δωρι-άζω,** *dress like a Dorian girl,* i.e. in a single garment open at the side, Anacr.59. **II.** = Δωρίζω, *Anacreont.*10.6, Philostr.*VS*1.24.2. **-ᾰκός,** *ή, όν,* poet. for Δωρικός, πόλεμος Orac.ap.Th.2.54. **-αρχέω,** *to be archon of the Dorians,* *SIG*668.12 (Delph., ii B.C.), 770$^{B}$2 (Delph., i B.C.). **-εια,** *τά, festival at Cnidus,* *GDI*4271 (Cedreae):—also **Δώρεια,** ib.3660 (Cos). **-εύς,** *έως, ὁ, Dorian, descendant of Dorus* son of Hellen, *IG*12(5).225 (Paros): pl., Δωριεῖς, Ion. -ιέες, Att. -ιῆς, οἱ, *the Dorians,* Od.19.177, etc. **II.** as Adj., = Δωρικός, Pi.*P.*8.20.

**Δωρ-ίζω,** Dor. **-ίσδω,** *imitate the Dorians in life, dialect,* etc., *speak Doric Greek,* Theoc.15.93, Str.8.1.2, Plu.2.421b:—Pass., *to be written in the Doric dialect,* **δ.** τὰ Ἀλκμᾶνος A.D.*Synt.*279.25. ⊛ **-ικός,** *ή, όν, Doric,* Hdt.8.43, Th.3.95, etc.: Comp. -ώτερος A.D.*Adv.*159.27. Adv. -κῶς Id.*Pron.*48.27, S.E.*M.*1.78: Comp. -ώτερον A.D.*Synt.*159.16. ⊛ **-ιος,** *α, ον,* also *ος, ον* Pratin.Lyr.1.17, Arist.*Pol.*1276$^{b}$9:—*Dorian,* Pi.*O.*3.5; ἁπλοῦν τε καὶ **Δ.** Plu.*Lys.*5, etc.; esp. of the *Dorian* mode in music, Arist.*Pol.* l.c., 1290$^{a}$22. **-ίς,** *ίδος, ἡ.*

fem. Adj. *Dorian*, ἐσθής Hdt.5.88; φωνή Th.6.5, etc.: hence, 1. Δ. νᾶσος the *Dorian* island, of Aegina and Peloponnesus, Pi.*N*.3.3, S.*OC*696 (lyr.), etc. 2. (with or without γῆ) *Doris*, in Northern Greece, Hdt.8.31, Plu.*Them*.9, etc. 3. Δ. κόρα a *Dorian* damsel, E.*Hec*.934 (lyr.). 4. (sc. κοπίς) *Dorian knife* used at sacrifices, Id. *El*.819. 5. Δωρίς, = ἔχιον, Dsc.4.27. b. = λεοντοπέταλον, Ps.-Dsc.3.96 (also δωριπτερίς ibid.). **-ίσδω**, Dor. for Δωρίζω. **-ισμός**, ὁ, *speaking in the Doric dialect*, Demetr.*Eloc*.177. **-ιστί** [ῑ], Adv. *in Dorian fashion*, Δ. ζῆν Pl.*Ep*.336c. 2. *in the Dorian dialect*, λαλοῦσι Δ. Call.*Iamb*.1.354. II. ἡ Δ. ἁρμονία the *Dorian* mode or measure in music, Arist.*Pol*.1340$^b$4; so Δ. alone, Pl.*R*.399a; in Ar.*Eq*.989 (lyr.) with a play on δῶρον.

⊛ **δωρίτης** [ῑ] ἀγών, ὁ, game *in which the conqueror received a present*, Plu.2.820d.

⊛ **δωρο-γρᾰφία**, ἡ, dub. sens. in *Ostr.Strassb*.277.11, al. (ii A.D.). **-δειπνος**, ον, *giving dinner*, παῖς δ., i.e. a waiter, Ath.15.701b. **-δέκτης**, ου, ὁ, *one that takes bribes*, Lxx *Jb*.15.34. **-δοκέω**, *accept as a present*, esp. *take as a bribe*, ἀργύριον πολλόν Hdt.6.72; χρυσόν Pl. *R*.590a; κατὰ πεντήκοντα τάλαντα Ar.*V*.669. 2. abs., *take bribes*, Hdt.6.82, D.18.45, etc.; ἐπί τινι Lys.21.22, D.18.49. II. c. acc. pers. (only in later Gr., for δωροδοκοῦσιν is f.l. in Ar.*V*.675 and δωροδοκοῦντας (abs.) is interpol. in D.9.45), *corrupt by bribes*, D.S.13.64, Arr.*Epict*.4.1.148, Luc.*Pisc*.9, etc. 2. simply, *bestow gifts*, *AP*9.335 (Leon.): c. acc., ib.12.204 (Strat.). III. Pass., of persons, *to have a bribe given one*, Cratin.128, cf. Plb.6.56.2, D.H.4.55 (as v.l.); also ταῦθ' ἁπλῶς δεδωροδόκηται this *has been accomplished by bribery*, D.19.329 (v.l. -ηνται); τὰ περὶ τὴν Εὔβοιαν δωροδοκηθέντα *the bribery* in the matter of Euboea, Aeschin.3.221; τὸ δεδωροδοκημένον χρυσίον Din.1.66. **-δόκημα**, ατος, τό, *acceptance of a bribe*, *corruption*, D.18.20,31. 2. *bribe*, καταλαβεῖν Pl.Com.119. **-δοκία**, ἡ, *taking of bribes*, freq. in Oratt., as And.4.30; δωροδοκίαν καταγνῶναί τινος Lys.21.21; -ίας κατηγορεῖν Aeschin.2.3: pl., ibid.; also, *giving of bribes*, *corruption*, in pl., D.C.39.55, 50.7. **-δοκιστί**, Adv. *in bribe-fashion*, Ar.*Eq*.996, with a play on Δωριστί. **-δόκος**, ον, *taking presents* or *bribes*, *corrupt*, Pl.*R*.390d, D.18.61; Com., δωροδόκοισιν ἐπ' ἄνθεσιν ἵζων Ar.*Eq*.403. II. Act., *bribing*, Sch.Pl.*Alc*.2.149a, cf. *AB*242. 2. *munificent*, Aret.*SD*2.12. **-δοτέω**, *give presents*, Aq.*Ez*.16.33. **-δότης**, ου, ὁ, *giver of presents*, λάθας δ. *AP*12.49 (Mel.). **-δοχεῖον**, τό, *receptacle for offerings*, *alms-box*, Zonar. s.v. Κορβωνᾶς. **-κοπέω**, *bribe*, Lxx *Si*.32(35).12:—Pass., ib.3 *Ma*.4.19. **-κοπία**, ἡ, *bribery*, Aq.*De*.10.17, Sm.*Ps*.25(26).10. **-κόπος**, *one who bribes*, *Gloss*. **-ληπτέω**, *take presents*, Eust.91.17. **-λήπτης**, ου, ὁ, *greedy of gain*, Lxx *Pr*.15.27. **-ληψία**, ἡ, *taking of presents*, *Com.Adesp*.987, D.C.39.55.

⊛ **δῶρον**, τό, (δίδωμι) *gift*, *present*, *gift of honour*, ἀγλαὰ δ. Il.1.213, etc.; *votive gift* or *offering* to a god, φέρε δῶρον Ἀθήνῃ 6.293, cf. Lxx *Ge*.4.4, *Ev.Marc*.7.11; βωμοὶ δώροισι φλέγονται A.*Ag*.91; ποῦ μοι τὰ ..δ. κἀκροθίνια; Id.*Fr*.184; δῶρά τινος *the gifts of*, i.e. *given by*, him, θεῶν ἐρικυδέα δ. Il.20.265, cf. Od.18.142; δῶρ' Ἀφροδίτης, i.e. personal charms, Il.3.54,64; δ. Κύπριδος E.*Hel*.363 (lyr.); δ. τῶν Μουσῶν καὶ Ἀπόλλωνος, of μουσική, Pl.*Lg*.796e: c. gen. rei, ὕπνου δ. *the blessing* of sleep, Il.7.482; δῶρα *presents* given as tribute, 17.225; δῶρον τοῦ ποταμοῦ, of the land of Egypt, Hdt.2.5. 2. δῶρα *presents*, as retaining fees or bribes, D.18.109, Jusj.ib.24.150, Arist.*Ath*.55.5, *SIG*953.7 (Calymna), etc. (the usual sense of the word in Att. Oratt.): hence in Att. law, δώρων γραφή an indictment *for being bribed*, Aeschin.3.232, etc., cf. Harp.; δώρων κριθῆναι to be tried *for taking bribes*, Lys.27.3; δώρων ἑλεῖν τινα to convict him *of taking bribes*, Ar.*Nu*.591; δ. ὀφλεῖν to be found guilty *of taking bribes*, And.1.74; δώρων δίωξις Plu.*Per*.32. 3. in pl., *good qualities*, *talents*, τὰ βασιλέως δ. Lib.*Ep*.19. II. *front part of palm*, Poll.2.144. 2. *hand's breadth*, *palm*, as a measure of length, Nic.*Th*.398, Vitr.2.3.3, *Milet*.7.57 (Didyma); cf. δεκάδωρος.

**δωρο-ξενίας** γραφή, ἡ, *indictment of a* ξένος *for bribing the judges to declare him an Athenian*, Lys.*Fr*.196 S., Hyp.*Fr*.20, Arist.*Ath*.59.3. ⊛ **-τελέω**, *bring presents*, Orac.ap.D.43.66. **-φάγος** [ᾰ], ον, *devouring gifts*, *greedy of presents*, Hes.*Op*.221, 264, Plb.6.9.7. **-φορέω**, *bring presents*, τινί Pl.*Phdr*.266c, cf. *Euthphr*.14e, prob. in Epigr. ap.Ath.5.209e (Archimelos); *give as presents* or *bribes*, τί τινι Ar.*V*.675, cf. D.C.40.53. II. δ. τινά *present* him *with gifts*, Ael.*VH*1.32. **-φορία**, ἡ, *bringing of presents*, v.l. in *Ep.Rom*.15.31, Alciphr.1.6 (pl.), Poll.4.47. **-φορικός**, ή, όν, = sq., Pl.*Sph*.222d. II. *given as a present*, στολή Ael.*VH*1.22. ⊛ **-φόρος**, ον, *bringing presents*, Pi.*P*.5.86, f.l. in Epigr.ap.Ath.5.209e (Archimelos); *tributary*, Euph.78.

**δωρύττομαι**, Dor. for δωρέομαι, Theoc.7.43.

**δωρώνιον**, = σίον, corrupt in Ps.-Dsc.2.127.

⊛ **δώς**, ἡ, = δόσις, only in nom., Hes.*Op*.356.

**δωσί-άραις**· κακὰ διδούσαις, Hsch. ⊛ **-βῐος**, ον, *life-giving*, *Mus. Belg*.16.70. **-δῐκία**, ἡ, *administration of justice*, *IGRom*.3.563 (Tlos). **-δῐκος**, ον, *referring disputes to a court*, Hdt.6.42. 2. *subject to jurisdiction*, δ. παρασχεῖν τοὺς ἠδικηκότας Plb.4.4.3, cf. *UPZ*121.14. ⊛ **-πῡγος** or **δοσίπῡγος**, ον, = κίναιδος, Suid. s.v. ἀφέλεια.

**δώσων**, οντος, ὁ, fut. part. of δίδωμι, *always going to give*, *always promising*: hence Δώσων as a name of Antigonus II, Plu.*Cor*.11.

**δώτειρα**, ἡ, fem. of sq., Linus ap.Stob.3.1.70, Arat.113, Man.2.447, Nonn.*D*.19.45.

⊛ **δωτήρ**, ῆρος, ὁ, *giver*, δωτῆρες ἑάων *givers* of good, i.e. the gods, Od.8.325, Hes.*Th*.46, etc.: voc. δῶτερ ὑγείης *Rev.Arch*.1911.439 (Thrace).

**δώτης**, ου, ὁ, = foreg., Hes.*Op*.355.

⊛ **δωτῑνάζω**, *receive* or *collect presents*, Hdt.2.180.

⊛ **δωτίνη** [ῑ], ἡ, *gift*, *present*, Il.9.155, Od.9.268, Hdt.1.61; δωτίνην δοῦναι give *as a free gift*, ib.69, cf. Them.*Or*.21.260d. II. *rent in kind*, *IG*4.841.8,11 (Calauria, iii B.C.).

**δῶττις**· δώς, φέρνη, Hsch.

**δωτύς**, ύος, ἡ, Ion., = τροφή, Suid. (leg. ἐδητύς).

**Δωτώ**, οῦς, ἡ, *Giver*, name of a Nereid, Il.18.43, Hes.*Th*.248.

⊛ **δώτωρ**, ορος, ὁ, = δωτήρ, δῶτορ ἑάων *giver* of goods, addressed to Hermes, Od.8.335, *h.Hom*.18.12, cf. Luc.*Sat*.14; to Zeus, Call.*Jov*.91; θεοὶ τούτων δώτορες ἀμφοτέρων Thgn.134, cf. E.*Hyps.Fr*.7.5.

# E

**E ε, ἒ ψιλόν**, fifth letter of the Gr. alphabet: as numeral ε' = πέντε and πέμπτος, but ͵ε = 5,000:—its name was εἶ, q.v., later ἒ ψιλόν; cf. ψιλός.

**ἒ ἔ**, or repeated **ἒ ἒ ἒ ἔ**, an exclamation of pain or grief; *woe! woe!* A.*Ag*.1114, etc.; always doubled either once or twice and better written ἐέ (as in cod. Med. of A. and S.), or (where the metre requires an iambus) ἐή S.*OC*149; but ἠέ cod. Med. in A.*Th*.966.

**ἕ**, v. οὗ.

**ἔᾱ**, exclam. of surprise or displeasure, *ha! oho!* esp. before a question, ἔα, τί χρῆμα; A.*Pr*.300, E.*Or*.1573; ἔα, τίς οὗτος..; Id. *Hec*.501, cf. 733, al.; ἔα, τίς ἔσθ'; Ar.*Pl*.824; sts. extra versum, E. *Hec*.1116, *Med*.1005, al.; sts. doubled, ἔ. ἔα, ἄπεχε A.*Pr*.688 (lyr.); ἔα [ἕα], ἰδού S.*OC*1477 (lyr.).—Rare in Prose, ἔα, ἔφη, σοφισταί τινες Pl.*Prt*.314d; ἔα, τί ἡμῖν καὶ σοί; *Ev.Luc*.4.34.

**ἔᾱ**, Ep. and Ion. for ἦν, impf. of εἰμί. **ἔᾱγα, ἐάγην** [ᾰ], v. ἄγνυμι. **ἔακεν**· ἀλγεῖ, Hsch. **ἑᾱδα**, part. ἑαδώς, v. ἁνδάνω. **ἐάλη**, v. εἴλω. **ἐαλόν**· λυπηρόν, λυτήριον, Hsch. **ἑάλωκα, ἑαλώκειν**, v. ἁλίσκομαι.

⊛ **ἐάν** (so early Attic Inscrr., as *IG*1$^2$.3.20, εἰάν sts. after B.C. 400, ib.2$^2$.28.17, cf. *PEleph*.1.8,10 (iv B.C.)), also contr. ἤν and ἄν, v. ἤν, ἄν (B) [ᾱ], which by crasis with καί become κἄν:—*if haply*, *if*, regularly folld. by subj.: for its use and for examples, v. εἰ B. II, and ἄν (A) B. I. 1. II. in Hellenistic and late Greek, = ἄν after relative Pronouns and Conjunctions, as ὃς ἐάν whosoever, Lxx *Ge*.15.14, *PTeb*.107.8 (ii B.C.), *Ev.Matt*.5.19, al.; ὅσος ἐάν *PPetr*.3p.120 (iii B.C.), *Ev.Matt*.18.18; ὅστις ἐάν Ph.1.220, M.Ant.9.23; ὅπου ἐάν *Ev.Matt*.8.19, etc.; ὅθεν ἐάν *Gp*.1.3.3: folld. by ind., Lxx 1*Ki*.2.14. [The second syll. of ἐάν is long, S.*OC*1407, Ar.*V*.228, Sopat.6.9.]

**ἑάνδανε**, v. ἁνδάνω.

**ἑᾱνηφόρος**, ον, (ἑανός, ὁ) *wearing a thin robe*, Ἠώς Antim.84.

⊛ **ἑᾱνός**, ή, όν, Ep. Adj. (never in Od.):—*fine*, of fabrics and materials for wearing, ἑανῷ λιτί with *fine* linen, Il.18.352, 23.254; πέπλος ἑανός 5.734, 8.385; ἑανοῦ κασσιτέροιο tin *beaten out fine*, 18.613; ἱμάτιον Sapph.(?)122. II. as Subst., **ἑᾰνός**, ὁ, *fine robe*, once in nom., ἀμφὶ δ' ἄρ' ἀμβρόσιος ἑανὸς τρέμε Il.21.507; νεκταρέου ἑανοῦ 3.385; ἑανῷ ἀργῆτι φαεινῷ ib.419; ἀμβρόσιον ἑανόν (acc.) 14.178; ἑανῶν πτύχας ἱμεροέντων *h.Cer*.176; λεπταλέῳ ἑανῷ A.R.4.169; ἑανοῖς χρυσεϊδέσι *Hymn.Is*.109; also with the first syll. long, εἱανοῦ ἁπτομένη Il.16.9; cf. ἴανον. 2. *sail*, λῦε ἑανοῦ πτέρυγας *Lyr.Alex.Adesp*.20.9. [Hom. always makes ᾱ in the Adj., ᾰ in the Subst.; but later poets use ᾱ or ᾰ, as suits the metre, as Orph.*A*.877,1223.] (Cf. ἕννυμι (q.v.); the Subst. has the digamma, Il.14.178, 21.507, whereas the Adj. has not, 18.352, 613, 23.254.)

**ἐάνπερ**, v. εἰ B. II. **ἔαντο**· ἦσαν, Hsch.

**ἔαξα**, v. ἄγνυμι.

⊛ **ἔᾰρ** (A), τό, Hom. (only gen. ἔαρος), etc.; contr. ἦρ Alcm.76: gen., dat., ἦρος, ἦρι, Lyr. (Alc.45), Att., and prob. Ion., cf. Hdt.1.77, Hp. *Epid*.1.1 (but ἔαρος is found in codd. of Hdt.5.31, 7.162, al., Hp.l.c.): poet. gen., dat., εἴαρος, εἴαρι (metri gr.), Alcm.26, *h.Cer*.174 (nisi leg. ἤαρος), and later Poets (whence was formed late nom. εἶαρ Numen. ap.Ath.9.371e, Ter.Maur.653); cf. Hdn.Gr.1.408 (Hes. used ἔαρ as a monos., and ἔαρι as a trochee, *Op*.492, 462):—*spring*, ἔαρος δ' ἐπιγίγνεται ὥρη Il.6.148; ἔαρος νέον ἱσταμένοιο early *spring*, Od.19.519; ἔαρι πολεῖν Hes.*Op*.462; ἅμα τῷ ἔαρι at the beginning of *spring*, Hdt.5.31, cf. Th.4.117, 6.8; πρὸς ἔαρ Id.5.56, etc.; πρὸς τὸ ἔ. ib.17; περὶ τὸ ἔ. Id.3.116; ἐξ ἦρος εἰς Ἀρκτοῦρον S.*OT*1137: prov., μία χελιδὼν ἔαρ οὐ ποιεῖ Cratin.33; also of the *prime*, *flower* of anything, ἔφηβοι.. ἔ. τοῦ δήμου Demad.*Fr*.4 S., cf. Hdt.7.162, Arist.*Rh*.1411$^a$3; ἔ. δρόωσα looking *fresh and bright*, Theoc.13.45; γενύων ἔ. *the first down* on a youth's face, *AP*6.242 (Crin.); ὕμνων ἔ. *the freshest*, *brightest* of their kind, ib.7.12; τὸ ἔ. τῶν πτερῶν, of a peacock, Luc. *Dom*.11. (Ϝεσῄ-, cf. γέαρ, γίαρ[ες], Lat. *vēr*, Skt. *vasantas*, Lith. *vasara* 'summer'.)

**ἔᾱρ** (B) or **εἶαρ** (Hsch. ἦαρ, ἴαρα), τό, in Alex. Poets, *blood*, λύθρῳ τε καὶ εἴαρι πεπλήθασι Call.*Fr.anon*.20; Αἰακίδαο ἔαρος Euph.39.3; τὸ δ' ἐκ μέλαν εἶαρ ἔλαπτεν Call.*Fr*.247, cf. Nic.*Al*.314, Opp.*H*.2.618; cf. εἰαροπότης, εἰαροπῶτις. 2. *juice*, εἶαρ ἐλαίης Nic.*Al*.87; ἐκ λύχνου πῖον ἔλειξαν ἔαρ Call.*Fr*.201. (Cypr. acc. to Hsch.; identified with ἔαρ *spring*, by *EM*307.44, Suid.; cf. Skt. *ásṛk*, gen. *asnás*, Lett. *asinis* 'blood'.)

**ἐαρδάλη·** ἐπλησίασεν, Hsch. **ἐαρίδας·** τὰς κανθαρίδας, Id.

**ἐᾰρίδρεπτος** (–δροπος Bgk.), ον, *plucked in spring*, Pi.*Fr.*75.6.

**ἐᾰρίζω,** *pass the spring*, X.*An.*3.5.15. II. *bloom as in spring*, Ph.2.99:—Med., λειμῶνες ἄνθεσιν ἐαριζόμενοι Pl.*Ax.*371c. III. *to be like spring*, μετοπώρου ἐαρίζοντος Ph.1.13, cf. 2.643.

✻ **ἐᾰρῑνός,** ή, όν, Ep. **εἰαρινός** (also **ἠαρινός** *h.Cer.*401, *PPetr.*3 p.152 (iii B.C.)); in other Poets, **ἠρινός**:—*of spring*, εἰαρινὴ ὥρη *spring-time*, Il.16.643, cf. Plb.3.34.6; εἰαρινὰ ἄνθεα Il.2.89; πλόος εἰαρινός Hes.*Op.*678; θάλπος ἐαρινόν the heat *of spring*, X.*Cyr.*8.6.22; ἄνεμος ἠρινός Sol.13.19; ἠρινὰ φύλλα Pi.*P.*9.46; λειμῶνος ἠρινοῦ στάχυν E.*Supp.*448; ἐ. πυλαία *IG*9(1).111 (Elatea); τροπαί Ph.2.163; μῆλα ἐ. *apricots*, *PCair.Zen.*33.13 (iii B.C.):—neut. as Adv., *in spring-time*, μέλισσα λειμῶν' ἠρινὸν διέρχεται E.*Hipp.*77 (s.v.l., ἐαρινή Sch.); γῆ ἠρινὸν θάλλουσα Id.*Fr.*316.3: ἠρινὰ κελαδεῖν, of the swallow, Ar.*Pax* 800 (lyr.). Adv. ἐαρινῶς Hsch. s.v. ἦρις ὡς.

**ἐάριον·** ῥόδον, Hsch.

**ἔαρον,** τό, *ewer*, *IG*12(3).450$^{a}$1 (Thera, pl.); ἐαρόν, Hsch.

**ἐᾰρο-τρεφής,** ές, *flourishing in spring*, λειμῶνες Mosch.2.67. **–χροος,** ον, *spring-coloured, fresh green*, ἴασπις Orph.*L.*267.

**ἐάρτερος,** α, ον, poet. for ἐαρινός, Nic.*Th.*380.

**ἔᾱσι,** Ep. 3 pl. of εἰμί. **ἔασκον,** Ion. and Ep. impf. of ἐάω. **ἔασσα,** Dor. part. fem. of εἰμί.

**ἐασφόρος·** ἑωσφόρος, Hsch. **ἕᾰται, ἕατο,** Ion. 3 pl. pres. and impf. of ἧμαι.

**ἐᾱτέος,** α, ον, (ἐάω) *to be suffered*, E.*Ph.*1210: c. inf., ἐατέος ἐστὶ φεύγειν Hdt.8.108, cf. Pl.*R.*401b. 2. ἐατέον *one must suffer*, E.*HF* 173, etc. II. *to be let alone* or *given up*, ἐ. ὁ πλοῦτος Id.*Hel.*905, cf. Ph.1.564. 2. τὴν πόλιν ἐατέον τῆς κατοικίσεως we *must let* it *alone* as to foundation, Pl.*Lg.*969c; *one must dismiss* from one's mind, Id.*Grg.*512e; *one must omit*, Str.2.5.18.

**ἑαυτάδελφος** [ᾰ], ὁ, incorrect form for αὐτ–, *CPR*1.155.

**ἑαυτότης,** ητος, ἡ, *self-hood*, Procl.*Theol.Plat.*5.37.

✻ **ἑαυτοῦ,** ῆς, οῦ, ἑαυτῷ, ῇ, ῷ, ἑαυτόν, ήν, ό, pl. ἑαυτῶν, ἑαυτοῖς, ἑαυτούς άς, ά: Ion. **ἑωυτοῦ** *SIG*57.44 (Milet., v B.C.), etc.; also ὡὐτῆς Herod. 6.84, ὡὐτέου Aret.*SA*1.7 (Ion. ἑωυ– by contraction of ἕο αὐ–, from which also Att. ἑᾱυ–, freq. written ἑατοῦ in Pap. and Inscrr., as *SIG* 774.2 (Delph., i B.C.): Att. contr. **αὑτοῦ,** etc., which is the usual form in Trag., though ἑαυτοῦ, etc., are used (though rarely) when the metre requires, A.*Pr.*188 (anap.), al.; in Att. Inscrr. αὑτοῦ prevails after B.C. 300; Cret. **ϝιαυτοῦ** Kohler-Ziebarth *Stadtrecht von Gortyn* p.34; Dor. **αὑταυτοῦ, αὑσαυτοῦ** (q.v.); Thess. **εὑτοῦ** (dat.), *IG*9(2).517.16: gen. pl. **ηὑτῶν** *Schwyzer* 251 *A* 44 (Cos):—reflex. Pron. of 3rd pers., *of himself, herself, itself*, etc.; first in Alc.78, Hdt., and Att. (Hom. has ἕο αὐτοῦ, οἷ αὐτῷ, ἓ αὐτόν): αὐτὸ ἐφ' ἑαυτό (v.l. –τοῦ) itself by *itself, absolutely*, Pl.*Tht.*152b; αὐτὸ ἐφ' αὑτοῦ ib.160b; ὅταν τὸ ἐφ' ἑαυτὸν ἕκαστος σπεύδῃ Th.1.141; αὐτὸ καθ' αὑτό Pl.*Tht.*157a; αὐτὰ πρὸς αὑτά ib.154e; ἀφ' ἑαυτῶν, ἑαυτοῦ, of *themselves, himself*, Th. 5.60, X.*Mem.*2.10.3; ἐφ' ἑαυτοῦ, v. ἐπί; ἐν ἑαυτῷ γίγνεσθαι, ἐντὸς ἑαυτοῦ γ., v. ἐν, ἐντός; παρ' ἑαυτῷ at *his own* house, ib.3.13.3, etc.: esp. with Comp. and Sup., ἐγένοντο ἀμείνονες αὐτοὶ ἑωυτῶν they surpassed *themselves*, Hdt.8.86; πλουσιώτεροι ἑαυτῶν continually richer, Th.1.8; θαρραλεώτεροι αὐτοὶ ἑαυτῶν Pl.*Prt.*350a, cf. d; τῇ αὐτὸ ἑωυτοῦ ἐστι μακρότατον at its very greatest length, Hdt.2.8, cf. 149, 4.85, 198. II. in Att., Trag., and later, αὑτοῦ, etc., is used for the 1st or 2nd pers., as for ἐμαυτοῦ, αὐτὸς καθ' αὑτοῦ τᾆρα μηχανορραφῶ A.*Ch.*221, cf. S.*OT*138, etc.; for σεαυτοῦ, μόρον τὸν αὑτῆς οἶσθα A.*Ag.*1297, cf. 1141, Pl.*Phd.*101c (v.l.), Ph.*Bel.*59.16, etc.: so in pl., τὰ αὑτῶν (= ἡμῶν αὐτῶν) ἐκποριζώμεθα Th.1.82; δώσομεν ἑαυτούς Epicur.*Sent.Vat.*47; ἐφ' ἑαυτοῖς by *ourselves*, Lxx 1*Ki.*14.9, cf. *PPar.*47.26 (ii B.C.), 2*Ep.Cor.*7.1, etc.; ἑαυτῶν, = ὑμῶν αὐτῶν, *PPar.* 63.128 (ii B.C.). III. pl., ἑαυτῶν, ἑαυτοῖς, etc., is sts. used for ἀλλήλων, ἀλλήλοις, *one another*, διάφοροι ἑωυτοῖσι Hdt.3.49; παρακελευόμενοι ἐν ἑαυτοῖς Th.4.25, etc.; καθ' αὑτοῖν *one* against *the other*, S.*Ant.*144 (anap.); πρὸς αὑτούς D.18.19; περιιόντες αὑτῶν πυνθάνονται Id.4.10, cf. Pl.*Ly.*215b.

**ἑάφθη,** found only in Il.13.543 ἐπὶ δ' ἀσπὶς ἑάφθη καὶ κόρυς and 14.419 ἐπ' αὐτῷ ἀσπὶς ἑάφθη. (Acc. to Tyrannio ap.Sch.A, = ἥφθη, upon him *was fastened*, i.e. to him *clung*, his shield; acc. to Aristarch., connected with ἕπομαι, shield and helmet *followed after*: ἑ– Aristarch., ἐ– most Mss.; possibly connected with ἰάπτω (q.v.), *was hurled* over him; glossed by ἐκάμφθη, ἐβλάβη, Hsch.)

✻ **ἐάω,** contr. **ἐῶ** Il.8.428, etc.; Ep. **εἰῶ** 4.55; Ep. 2 and 3 sg. ἐάᾳς, ἐάᾳ, Od.12.137, Il.8.414; inf. ἐάαν Od.8.509: impf. εἴων, ας, α, Il.18.448, Od.19.25, Th.1.28, etc.; Ion. and Ep. ἔων Hdt.9.2, ἔα Il.5.517, 16.731; also ἔασκον or εἴασκον, 2.832, 5.802, etc.: fut. ἐάσω [ᾱ] 18.296, etc.: aor. εἴᾱσα (εἴᾰσεν is v.l. for εἴᾱσ' in 10.299) 24.684, etc.; Ep. ἔᾱσα 11.437: pf. εἴᾱκα D.8.37, 43.78, Cerc.17.35:—**Pass.,** fut. ἐάσομαι in pass. sense, E.*IA*331, Th.1.142: aor. εἰάθην Isoc.4.97: pf. Pass. εἴᾱμαι D.45.22.—Hdt. never uses the augm. in this Verb. [ᾰ in pres. and impf., ᾱ in fut. and aor. even in Ion. (so prob. in Anacr.56, 57; forms with –ασσ– occur as vv.ll. in Hom. and Parm. 8.7). Synizesis occurs in 3 sg. ἐᾷ Il.5.256, in 1 subj. ἐῶμεν 10.344, and prob. in ἐάσουσιν Od.21.233; also in Trag., in imper. ἔα S.*OT* 1451, *Ant.*95, Ar.*Nu.*932; ind. ἐῶ Id.*Lys.*734: Hsch. has the form ἧσεν· εἴασεν, cf. ἧσαι· παῦσαι]:—*suffer, permit*, c. acc. pers. et inf., τούσδε δ' ἔα φθινύθειν *leave* them *alone* to perish, Il.2.346; αἴ κεν ἐᾷ με ..ζώειν Od.13.359, etc.; ἐᾶν οἰκεῖν Th.3.48, cf. *IG*1$^{2}$.1; ἐ. τοὺς Ἕλληνας αὐτονόμους ib.2.17.9; ἐᾶν ἄκλαυτον, ἄταφον S.*Ant.*29, cf. *Tr.* 1083; ἐᾶν τί τινι Plu.2.233d:—so in Pass., Κρέοντί γε θρόνους ἐᾶσθαι *should be given up*, S.*OC*368. b. *concede, allow* in argument, c. acc. et inf., Pl.*Prm.*135b. 2. with neg., οὐκ ἐᾶν not *to suffer*: hence, *forbid, prevent*, τρεῖν μ' οὐκ ἐᾷ Παλλὰς Ἀθήνη Il.5.256; εἴπερ γὰρ φθονέω τε καὶ οὐκ εἰῶ διαπέρσαι 4.55; esp. of the law, Aeschin.3.21; δμωὰς δ' οὐκ εἴας προβλωσκέμεν Od.19.25, etc.: used elliptically with ἀλλά following, οὐκ ἐῶν φεύγειν, ἀλλὰ [κελεύων] μένοντας ἐπικρατέειν Hdt.7.104, cf. Th.2.21; also, *persuade* or *advise* not to do.., Id.1.133: an inf. may freq. be supplied, οὐκ ἐάσει σε τοῦτο will not *allow* thee [to do] this, S.*Ant.*538; κἂν μηδεὶς ἐᾷ even if all men *forbid*, Id.*Aj.* 1184, cf. *Ph.*444:—so in Pass., οὐκ ἐᾶσθαι, c. inf., *to be hindered*, E.*IT*1344, Th.1.142, D.2.16. II. *let alone, let be*, c. acc., ἔα χόλον Il.9.260; μνηστήρων μὲν ἔα βουλὴν *heed not* the suitors' plan, Od. 2.281; ἐπεί με πρῶτον ἐάσας as soon as thou *hast dismissed* me, Il. 24.557, cf. 569, 684; ἤ κέν μιν ἐρύσσεαι, ἤ κεν ἐάσῃς or *wilt leave* him *alone*, 20.311, cf. Hdt.6.108, etc.; ἐάσωμεν ἔκηλον αὐτόν S.*Ph.*825; [πρᾶγμα] ἀκάθαρτον ἐᾶν Id.*OT*256; τὰ παθήματα..παρεῖσ' ἐάσω Id. *OC*363, cf. Th.2.36; ἐᾶν φιλοσοφίαν Pl.*Grg.*484c: c. inf., ἐπὶ Σκύθας ἰέναι..ἔασον *let* it *alone*, Hdt.3.134; κλέψαι μὲν ἐάσομεν Ἕκτορα we *will have done with* stealing Hector, Il.24.71; ἐᾶν περί τινος Pl.*Prt.* 347c, etc.; ἐῶ γὰρ εἰ φίλον D.21.122: abs., ἀλλ' ἄγε δὴ καὶ ἔασον *have done, let be*, Il.21.221, cf. A.*Pr.*334; οὐ χρὴ μάχεσθαι πρὸς τὸ θεῖον, ἀλλ' ἐᾶν E.*Fr.*491.5; θεὸς τὸ μὲν δώσει, τὸ δ' ἐάσει he will give one thing, the other he will *let alone*, Od.14.444:—Pass., ἡ δ' οὖν ἐάσθω S.*Tr.*329, etc. 2. for ἐᾶν χαίρειν, v. χαίρω sub fin. (ἐϝάω, cf. ἔβασον· ἔασον, and εὔα· ἔα, Hsch. who also has ἔησον· ἔασον.)

✻ **ἑάων,** v. ἐΰς.

**ἐβαδίαστον·** μελανόβροχον, Hsch. **ἐβάθη·** ἐγεννήθη, Id.; cf. Lith. *gimti*. **ἐβάμωσεν·** ἡττήθη, Id.

**ἑβδεμαῖος,** Dor., = ἑβδομαῖος, *IG*4.952.26 (Epid.).

✻ **ἑβδεμήκοντα,** Dor. for ἑβδομ–, *GDI*2562.18 (Delph.), *Tab.Heracl.* 1.23:—also ✻**ἑβδέματος,** ον, = ἕβδομος, *Philol.*71.6 (Argos, iv B.C.).

**ἑβδομᾱ-γενής,** ές, *born on the seventh day* [of the month], epith. of Apollo, Plu.2.717e.

✻ **ἑβδομ-ᾱγέτης,** ου, ὁ, (ἡγέομαι) epith. of Apollo, to whom the Spartans *offered sacrifices on the seventh of every month*, A.*Th.*800, cf. Hdt.6.57. **–ᾰδικός,** ή, όν, *weekly*, ἀριθμός Antyll.ap.Orib. 9.3.1; περίοδος Gal.9.914, *Theol.Ar.*45. Adv. –κῶς Steph.*in Hp.*1.198 D. II. *septenary*, Procl.*in Ti.*3.108 D., Dam.*Pr.*264, 265. Adv. –κῶς ib.263. **–άζω,** *keep the Sabbath*, Lxx *Ez.*21.23(28), Tz.*H.*10.675. ✻ **–αῖος,** α, ον, *on the seventh day*, ἱδρώς Hp.*Aph.*4.36; ἑ. πυρετός a fever *recurring every seven days*, Id.*Epid.*1.24: ἑ. τραγῳδοί Luc.*Hist.Conscr.*1: with a Verb, διεφθείροντο ἑβδομαῖοι Th.2.49, cf. X.*HG*5.3.19, Plu.*Galb.*7; ἑ. ἡμέρα *PSI*6.690 (i/ii A.D.). 2. *seven days old*, τράγος Horap.1.48. II. **–αῖον,** τό, monthly festival of Apollo, *IG*2$^{2}$.1357 (iv B.C.), cf. ἑβδομαγέτης: pl., *Schwyzer* 687 *B*4 (Chios, vii/vi B.C.), 726.6 (Milet., v B.C.). **–άκις,** Adv. *seven times*, Call.*Del.*251. **–άς,** άδος, ἡ, *the number seven*, Ph.1.21, Dam.*Pr.*264, etc. II. *a number of seven*, *APl.*4.131 (Antip.(?)). 2. *period of seven days, week*, Hp.*Aph.*2.24, Lxx *Ex.*34.22, etc. b. *period of seven years*, Sol.27.7, Arist.*Pol.*1336$^{b}$40, *Placit.*4.11.4; ἐτῶν ἑ. J.*AJ*3.12.3.

**ἑβδομ-ᾰτικός,** = –αδικός, Ph.2.206, J.*AJ*11.8.6. ✻ **–ᾰτος,** ον, = ἕβδομος, *seventh*, Il.7.248, al. **–ειος,** *worshipped on the seventh day*, epith. of Apollo, *IG*2.1653. **–εύομαι,** Pass., of children, *receive a name at seven days of age*, as was customary, Lys.*Fr.*95 S.

**ἑβδομηκονθ-εβδόμᾰδος,** ον, *of seventy weeks*, χρόνος Tz.*H.*8.54. **–εκτος,** ον, *seventy-sixth*, ἡμέρας –ον (sc. μέρος) Gem.8.59.

✻ **ἑβδομήκοντα,** οἱ, αἱ, τά, indecl., *seventy*, Hdt.1.32, X.*An.*4.7.8, etc.

**ἑβδομηκοντάβιβλος** (sc. πραγματεία), ἡ, *work in seventy books*, Paul.Aeg.*Praef.*

**ἑβδομηκοντακαιεκᾰτονταπλᾰσίων,** ον, gen. ονος, *170 times as great*, Procl.*Hyp.*4.104.

**ἑβδομηκοντάκις,** Adv. *seventy times*, Lxx *Ge.*4.24, *Ev.Matt.*18.22.

**ἑβδομηκοντάπηχυς,** υ, *seventy cubits high*, Ph.Byz.*Mir.*4.3.

**ἑβδομηκοντάρουρος** [ᾰ], ον, *possessing seventy* ἄρουραι, *PCair.Zen.* 1.23 (iii B.C.), *PTeb.*62.30 (ii B.C.).

**ἑβδομηκοντάς,** άδος, ἡ, *group of seventy*, Tz.*H.*1.974.

**ἑβδομηκονταστάδιος** [στᾰ], ον, *seventy stades broad*, πορθμός Str. 9.5.13.

✻ **ἑβδομηκοντούτης,** ου, ὁ, *seventy years old*, Luc.*Alex.*34: fem. –οῦτις Id.*Rh.Pr.*24, D.C.46.18.

**ἑβδομηκοστό-δῠος,** ον, *seventy-second*, μόριον Plu.2.932a. **–μονος,** ον, *seventy-first*: τὸ ἑ. *one seventy-first part*, Archim.*Circ.*3. **–πεμπτος,** η, ον, *seventy-fifth*, Tz.*H.*12.908. **–τρῐτος,** ον, *seventy-third*, ib.13.439.

**ἑβδομηκοστός,** ή, όν, *seventieth*, Hp.*Epid.*7.7, Lxx *Za.*1.12.

✻ **ἕβδομος,** η, ον, (ἑπτά) *seventh*, Il.19.117, etc.; ἡ ἑβδόμη *the seventh day*, Hdt.6.57 (pl.), Arist.*HA*588$^{a}$8; *sabbath*, Ph.1.675, *Ep.Hebr.*4.4. 2. = ἑπτά, ἑβδόμαις πύλαις A.*Th.*125 (lyr., s.v.l.), cf. Thom.Mag.p.133 R.; ἐν κύκλοισιν ἑβδόμοις *Milet.*6.46. 3. ἕβδομα, τά, *seven years' work*, Lxx *Ge.*29.27.

**ἐβέβλις·** θήκη ἀργυρίου, καὶ κίστη, Hsch.

**ἐβένη,** v. ἔβενος.

**ἐβένινος,** η, ον, *of ebony*, δίφρος *CIG*3071 (Teos), cf. Str.15.1.54, *Peripl.M.Rubr.*36, *PMag.Berol.*1.279.

**ἐβενῖτις,** ιδος, ἡ, = πόλιον τὸ ὀρεινόν, Ps.-Dsc.3.110.

**ἔβενος,** ἡ (ὁ in *BCH*35.286 (Delos, ii B.C.)), *ebony*, Hdt.3.97, Theoc. 15.123:—being the black heart-wood of various species of Diospy-

rus, ἐ. Αἰθιοπική, = *D. mespiliformis*, ἐ. Ἰνδική, = *D. Ebenum*, Dsc. 1.98, cf. Arist.*Mete.*384$^{b}$17, Thphr.*HP*1.5.4 (but ἐβένη, ἡ, ib.4.4.6). (Prob. an Egyptian word.)

**ἐβενότρῐχον**, = ἀδίαντον, Ps.-Dsc.4.134; = καλλίτριχον, ibid.

**ἔβην, ἐβησάμην, ἐβήσετο**, v. βαίνω.

**ἐβῆνοι**· ἀλωπεκίδες, Hsch.; cf. εἴβηνος.

**ἐβίσκος**, ἡ, = ἀλθαία, Gal.11.867, Aët.1.96.

**ἔβλητο**, v. βάλλω. **ἐβλόν**· ἀπόπληκτον, Hsch.

**Ἑβραῖος**, α, ον, *Hebrew*: and as Subst., *a Hebrew*, 2*Ep.Cor.*11.22, Paus.1.5.5, App.*BC*2.71; Ἑ. ἐξ Ἑβραίων *Ep.Phil.*3.5, etc.; opp. Ἑλληνιστής, a Jew who used the Hebrew (Aramaic) language, *Act. Ap.*6.1:—Adj. **Ἑβραϊκός**, ή, όν, *Hebrew*, γράμματα *Ev.Luc.*23.38 (s.v.l.):—fem. **Ἑβραΐς**, ΐδος, διάλεκτος *Act.Ap.*21.40; γυναῖκες J. *AJ*2.9.5:—Verb **Ἑβραΐζω**, *speak Hebrew*, Id.*BJ*6.2.1:—Adv. **Ἑβραϊστί**, *in the Hebrew tongue*, Lxx *Si.prol.*, *Ev.Jo.*19.20, etc.

**ἐβρατάγησεν**· ἐψόφησεν, Hsch.; cf. ῥαθαγέω.

**ἔβρᾰχε**, v. βραχεῖν.

**ἔβρος**, ὁ, *he-goat*, Hsch.

**ἐγ**, for ἐν in compos. before γ κ χ ξ; also for ἐκ in Inscrr. and Pap. before δ λ μ.

**ἔγαν**· ἐγένετο, Hsch.

**ἐγγᾱγίς**· πέτρα, = γαγάτης, Nic.*Th.*37.

**ἐγγᾱέω**, = ἐνοικέω, ἐν τᾷ πόλι *IG*4.853.26 (Methana).

**ἔγγαιος**, α, ον, more commonly **ἔγγειος**, ον, (γαῖα, γῆ) *in* or *of the land, native*, ἧβα A.*Pers.*922 (anap.); τις..οἰωνοπόλων ἔγγαιος Id. *Supp.*59 (lyr.). 2. *within the land*, opp. ὑπερόριος, X.*Smp.*4. 31. II. of property, *in land, consisting of land*, οὐσία Lys.*Fr.*91, D.36.5; κτήσεις ἔγγειοι καὶ οἰκίαι *IG*9(2).338.9 (Thess.), cf. *CIG* 2056 (Odessus), Plb.6.45.3; τὰ ἔγγεια *the fixtures* of a farm, D.30. 30; συμβόλαιον ἔγγειον Id.33.3; στατῆρας δανεισάμενος ἐγγείων τόκων *on mortgage*, Id.34.23 (ἑκατὸν μνᾶς ἐγγείους (v.l. ἐγγύους) ἐπὶ τόκῳ δεδανεισμένας is read by codd. in Lys.32.15); ἔγγεια καὶ ναυτικά *PEleph.*1.13 (iv B.C.). III. *in* or *of the earth*, [φυτὰ] ἔγγεια *plants*, Pl.*R.*491d; φυτὸν οὐκ ἔγγειον, ἀλλὰ οὐράνιον Id.*Ti.*90a; λίθων τὰ ἔγγαια μέρη Plu.2.701c. IV. *in* or *below the earth*, = χθόνιος, Ἀϊδωνεύς *AP*7.480 (Leon.); χθόνιον καὶ ἔ. σκότος Plu.2.953a; opp. ἐναέριος, Them.*Or.*13.168b.

**ἐγγᾰληνίζω** τῷ βίῳ, *spend* life *calmly*, Epicur.*Ep.*1 p.4 U.

**ἔγγᾰλος**, ον, (γάλα) *giving milk, in milk*, of a ewe, Hsch.

**ἐγγᾰμ-έω**, *marry into a family*, Aesop.21c, Hsch. **-ίζω**, *give in marriage*, Eust.758.54, *Gloss.* **-ιος**, ον, *nuptial*, *PSI*2.220 (iii A.D.).

**ἐγγανᾶται**· διέφθαρται, Hsch.

**ἐγγᾰρ-εύω**, = ἀγγαρεύω, *PTeb.*5.182 (ii B.C.). ❊ **-έω**, dub. sens. in *Inscr.Olymp.*335.

**ἐγγαστρί-μαντις** [ρῐ], ὁ, ἡ, *one that prophesies from the belly*, Poll. 2.168, Suid. s.v. ἐγγαστρίμυθος. **-μάχαιρα** [μᾰ], ἡ, comic name of a glutton in Hippon.85, *one who makes havoc with his belly*. ❊ **-μῦθος**, ον, *ventriloquist*, mostly of women who delivered oracles by this means: hence, = ἐγγαστρίμαντις, Hp.*Epid.*5.63, Philoch.192, Lxx *Le.*19.31, Ph.1.654, Plu.2.414e, Luc.*Lex.*20; also, *the familiar spirit* of such a person, Lxx 1*Ki.*28.8.

❊ **ἐγγάστριος**, ον, *in the womb*, Man.1.189.

**ἐγγαστρίτης** [ῑ], ου, ὁ, = ἐγγαστρίμυθος, in Sch.Ar.*V.*1014.

**ἐγγαστρόχειρ**, χειρος, ὁ, = ἐγχειρογάστωρ, Sch.Par.A.R.1.989.

**ἔγγαυρον**· νοτερόν, ὑγρόν; also ἄωρον, πρόσφατον, Hsch. **ἔγγαυσον**· ἔνσκαμβον, Id.; cf. γαυσός. ❊ **ἐγγέαβλος**· νεωκόρος, Id.

**ἐγγέγαα**, Ep. pf. of ἐγγίγνομαι. **ἐγγεγωνώς**· βοήσας, Hsch.

**ἐγγείνωνται**, 3 pl. aor. 1 subj. in causal sense (no pres. ἐγ-γείνομαι being found), μὴ μυῖαι εὐλὰς ἐγγείνωνται lest the flies *breed* maggots *in* [the wounds], Il.19.26.

**ἔγγειος**, v. ἔγγαιος.

**ἐγγειό-τοκος** or **ἐγγεό-**, ον, *growing in the earth*, of truffles, Thphr. *HP*1.6.9, cf. *Fr.*167. **-φυλλος**, ον, *having leaves close to the ground*, Id.*HP*6.6.7.

**ἐγγείσωμα**, ατος, τό, (γεῖσον) *fracture of the skull*, such that one piece slips under the bone *like a cornice*, Heliod.ap.Orib.46.15.1, Sor. *Fract.*5, Gal.14.782.

**ἐγγελ-αστής**, οῦ, ὁ, *mocker, scorner*, E.*Hipp.*1000. **-άω**, fut. -άσομαι [ᾰ], *laugh at, mock*, τοῖς ποιουμένοις S.*El.*277, cf. E.*Med.* 1355; in tmesi, γέλωτ' ἐν σοὶ γελῶ S.*Ant.*551 codd.; κατά τινος Id. *OC*1339: without dat. expressed, Id.*El.*807, E.*Med.*1362; εἴς τινα Herod.1.77:—Pass., Luc.*Ind.*15. II. *laugh in* or *among*, αὔρα ἐγγελῶσα κύμασιν Sosicr.2.

**ἐγγεν-έτης**, ου, ὁ, *inborn, native*, δαίμονες A.R.4.1549. **-ής**, ές, *native*, Αἰγύπτιοι Hdt.2.47; opp. μέτοικος, ἐ. Θηβαῖος S.*OT*452; θεοὺς τοὺς ἐ. gods *of the race* or *country*, A.*Th.*582, S.*Ant.*199, cf. *El.*428; νόμος J.*AJ*15.7.10. 2. *born of the same race, kindred*, S.*OT*1168,1506, *Inscr.Cos* 124; ἐ. κηδεία connexion *with a kinsman*, E.*Supp.*134. Adv. **-νῶς** *like kinsmen*, S.*OT*1225. II. of qualities, *inborn, innate*, νοῦς Id.*El.*1328; σφίσιν ἐγγενὲς ἔμμεν ἀεθληταῖς ἀγαθοῖσιν '*tis in their race* to be good athletes, Pi.*N.*10.51; πόνος ἐ. *in the family*, A.*Ch.*466 (lyr.); τἀγγενῆ κακά S.*OT*1430. III. = Lat. *ingenuus*, *PGnom.*29. **-ικός**, ή, όν, *hereditary*, ἱερεύς *OGI*583.5 (Cyprus, i A.D.).

**ἐγγενν-άω**, *generate* or *produce in*, τινί Plu.2.132e: abs., Them.*Or.* 13.166d. **-ησις**, εως, ἡ, *place of generation*, νεοττῶν Pl.*Lg.*776a.

**ἔγγεον**· ἰοῦγον, Hsch.; cf. Lat. *jugum* 'taxable unit of land, etc.'

**ἐγγεότοκος**, ον, v. ἐγγειότοκος.

❊ **ἐγγεύομαι**, Pass., *taste of*, αἵματος Plb.7.13.7.

**ἐγγηῖσταί**, οἱ, *residents in a country*, *Supp.Epigr.*1.325 (Thrace).

**ἐγγήναλοι**· ὑπογράμματοι, Hsch.

❊ **ἐγγήρ-ᾱμα**, ατος, τό, *employment for old age*, Cic.*Att.*12.25.2, Plu. *Cat.Ma.*24. **-άσκω**, Lib.*Or.*61.9 (-άω Anon. *in EN*237.2), fut. -άσομαι [ᾱ] (v. infr.):—*grow old with* or *in*, μεγέθει σώματος Hp.*Aph.* 2.54; ταῖς βασιλείαις Plb.6.7.4, cf. D.S.11.23, Plu.*Tim.*15. 2. abs., *grow old in one, decay*, τὴν ἐπιστήμην ἐγγηράσεσθαι Th.6.18; πρὶν ἐγγηρᾶσαι τὴν ἀκμὴν τῆς ἐλπίδος Plu.*Nic.*14.

**ἐγγηροτροφέω**, = γηροτροφέω, Poll.2.13 (Pass.).

**ἐγγῆρυς**· ἡ γῆ, παρὰ Ἀττικοῖς, Hsch.

**ἐγγιάω**, *to be near akin*, Lxx *Ne.*13.4 (s.v.l.).

**ἐγγίγνομαι**, Ion. and later **ἐγγίνομαι** [ῑ], fut. ἐγγενήσομαι: 3 pl. Ep. pf. ἐγγεγάᾱσι (the only tense used by Hom.):—*to be born in*, τοὶ Ἰλίῳ ἐγγεγάασιν Il.6.493, cf. Od.13.233; of vermin, *to be bred in* the skin, Hdt.2.37; of stones, ἐν τῷ καρπῷ ἐ. ib.92. 2. of things, qualities, etc., *spring up, appear in* or *among*, ὅσα ἐν ἀνθρώπου φύσει ..ἐ. Id.8.83, cf. Pl.*R.*351d; αἴσθημά τι κἀν νηπίοις γε..ἐ. E.*IA*1244: c. dat., ἃ παρθένοις ἐγγίγνεται νοσήμαθ' Id.*Ion*1524, cf. Th.2.49, X. *Mem.*1.2.21, etc.; of persons, Pl.*Grg.*526a. 3. of events and the like, *take place* or *happen in* or *among*, τισί Hdt.5.3, cf. 3.1; χεῖμα σφοδρὸν ἐ. Pl.*Ax.*371d. II. *come in, intervene*, λόγους ἐγγίνεσθαι Hdt.2.121.δ'; χρόνου ἐγγινομένου, ἐγγενομένου, Id.1.190, Th.1. 113, etc.; ἵνα μοι χρόνος ἐγγένηται τῇ σκέψει Pl.*Prt.*339e, cf. *Smp.* 184a. III. ἐγγίγνεται, impers., *it is allowed* or *possible*, c. inf., Hdt.1.132, 6.38, And.1.141, Pl.*Phd.*66c; ὥστε μὴ ἐγγενέσθαι μοι ποιῆσαι Antipho5.17; ἐγγενόμενον ἡμῖν *when it was in* our *power*, Is.5.19. IV. for aor. ἐγγείνασθαι, v. ἐγγείνωνται.

**ἐγγιγνώσκω**, Ion. **ἐγγῑν-**, *acknowledge*, ἔρωτα Aret.*SD*1.5.

❊ **ἐγγίζω**, aor. ἤγγισα Arist. (v. infr.): pf. ἤγγικα Lxx *Ez.*7.4(7), *Ev. Matt.*3.2: (ἐγγύς):—*bring near, bring up to*, τῇ γῇ τὰς ναῦς Plb.8.4.7; τὰ φιλήματα τοῖς χείλεσι Ach.Tat.2.37; τινὰ πρός τινα Lxx *Ge.*48. 10. II. mostly intr., *approach*, Arist.*Mir.*845$^{a}$20; τινί Plb.18.4.1: c. gen., τῆς Αἰτωλίας Id.4.62.5, etc.; πρὸς τὸν θεόν Lxx *Ex.*19.21; εἰς θάνατον ib.*Jb.*33.22; ἕως ib.*Si.*37.30(33); μέχρι θανάτου *Ep.Phil.*2.30; *to be imminent*, ἤγγικεν ἡ παρουσία τοῦ Κυρίου *Ep.Jac.*5.8: also, c. gen., *approximate to*, Phld.*Herc.*1457.4. 2. *to be next of kin*, Lxx *Le.* 21.3. III. c. inf., *to be on the point of* doing, ναοῦ -οντος συμπεσεῖν *IG*12(1).1270.8 (Syme).

**ἐγγίων**, ον, **ἔγγιστος**, η, ον, Comp. and Sup. Adj., formed from Adv. ἐγγύς:—*nearer, nearest*, οὐδὲν ἡμῖν ἐστιν ἔγγιον ἡμῶν αὐτῶν Procl. *in Alc.*p.6 C.; ἔτη δέκα τὰ ἔγγιστα *IG*7.2225.24 (Thisbe): neut. ἔγγιον, ἔγγιστα, as Adv., Hp.*Vict.*1.35 (also -υτάτω ibid.), 2.44, etc.; ἐξ ἐγγίονος App.*BC*4.108; τοὺς ἔγγιστα τῆς Ἀττικῆς τόπους Decr.ap. D.18.165; οἱ ἔγγιστα the *next of kin*, Antipho4.4.1; ἔγγιστα *approximately*, of numbers, Autol.1.6, Vett.Val.153.21, etc.; αἱ ἔγγιστα τᾶς τοῦ ἀμβλυγώνου κώνου τομᾶς *asymptotes* of the hyperbola, Archim. *Con.Sph.Praef.*; of Time, *next, forthcoming*, ἡ ἔγγιστα ἀρίθμησις *POxy.*1258.7 (i A.D.).

**ἔγγλαυκ-ος**, ον, *blueish*, D.S.1.12. **-ῶσαι**· ἐμβλέψαι, Hsch.

❊ **ἐγγλοψούμενα**· ἔνωχρα, ἄχροα, Hsch.

**ἐγγλῠκ-άζω**, gloss on ἐγγλύσσει, Hsch. **-υς**, υ, *sweetish*, Dsc. 5.6.

**ἔγγλυμμα**, ατος, τό, in pl., *ornamental carvings*, *IG*4.1485.91,96 (Epid.). 2. *intaglio*, Them.*Or.*4.62b.

**ἐγγλύσσω**, *to have a sweet taste*, Hdt.2.92.

**ἐγγλῠφ-ή**, ἡ, *carving, engraving*, Phld.*Po.*1676.5. **-ος**, ον, *carved*, *TAM*2.210 (Sidyma), Prisc.p.311 D. **-ω**, *carve*, ζῷα ἐν λίθοισι Hdt.2.4; ζῷα ἐγγεγλυμμένα ib.124; αἱμασιὴ ἐγγεγλυμμένη τύποισι ib.138; λίθος εἰκόνα -γεγλυμμένος J.*AJ*19.2.3; *hollow out*, [γογγύλην] Dsc.2.110, al.:—Pass., ὀστοῦ -γλυφέντος *having a groove*, Gal.2.255.

**ἐγγλωττογάστωρ**, ορος, ὁ, ἡ, = γλωσσογάστωρ, Ar.*Av.*1695, cf. *EM* 309.51, etc.

**ἔγγλωττος**, gloss on κατεγλωττισμένος, Suid., cf. Sch.Ar.*Th.*138.

**ἐγγλωττοτῠπέω**, *talk loudly of*, Ar.*Eq.*782.

**ἐγγνάμπτω**, *bend in*, ἐν δὲ γόνυ γνάμψεν, i.e. caught the back of the knee with his foot so as to trip him up and throw him, Il.23.731.

**ἐγγοητεύω**, *bring on by charms*, ὕπνον ἐ. τινί Philostr.*VA*3.8.

**ἔγγομος**, ον, *laden*, κάμηλοι *OGI*629.166 (Palmyra, ii A.D.), *Gloss.*

❊ **ἐγγομφ-όω**, *nail, fix in*, Gal.2.336:—Pass., of the teeth, ib.754 (ap.Orib.25.6.4). **-ωσις**, εως, ἡ, *fixing in of teeth*, Gal.12.851.

**Ἐγγόνασιν** (= ἐν γόνασιν), ὁ, indecl., *kneeling figure*, name of the constellation Hercules, Arat.66,669, Gal.9.936, etc.

**ἐγγονεῖν**, written for ἐγκονεῖν in Hsch.

❊ **ἔγγονος**, ὁ, properly, *grandson*, D.H.6.37, etc.: **ἐγγόνη**, ἡ, *granddaughter*, *IGRom.*4.882 (Themisonium), Artem.4.69, Lyd.*Mag.*2. 1; also ἔγγονος, ἡ, Plu.*Per.*3. 2. simply, = ἔκγονος, *descendant*, Pl.*R.*364e, D.19.48,54, etc.; ἔκγ- is v.l. in ll.cc., and may be right in Arist.*Pol.*1335$^{a}$13, cf. ib.$^{b}$30; τὰ ἔγγονα *issue*, *Inscr.Cos* 36$^{a}$4, *PFreib.*10.8, etc.; of animals, Ph.2.396, al.; Ἔρως πυρὸς ἔγγονε *APl.*4.212 (Alph.). 3. *productive*, κακίας, μνήμης, Callistr.*Stat.* 10. [ἔγγ- may represent ἔκγ- (q.v.), both forms are found in Att. Inscrr. up to ca. 300 B.C.; ἐγγ- is rare in Hellenistic Greek, *OGI*49. 12 (iii B.C.), *PTeb.*124.25,33 (ii B.C.); but more freq. later; ἐνγ- is written in *SIG*333.25 (Samos, iv B.C.), dub. in *CIG*3185 (Smyrna).]

**ἐγγοργῶν**· φοβερῶς βλέψας, Hsch.:—also aor. Med. **ἐ(γ)γοργώψατο**, Id.; cf. γοργώψατο.

**ἐγγράμμᾰτος**, ον, *written*, λόγος φωνὴ ἐ. Pl.*Def.*414d, cf. Ph.1.321, Arr.*Epict.*1.20.4, S.E.*M.*1.100. II. *containing letters, descriptive of letters*, ῥῆσις Ath.10.454b. III. *literate*, *POxy.*1467.13 (iii A.D.).

**ἔγγραπτος**, ον, = ἔγγραφος, συνθῆκαι Plb.12.9.3, al.; νόμοι Str.6.1.8, D.S.1.94; πρᾶγμα ἔ. καὶ ἄγραφον *PAmh.*2.110 (i A.D.), etc.: ἔγγραπτον, τό, *written document*, *PMagd.*18.5 (iii B.C.).

⊛ **ἐγγραυλίς**, ίδος, ἡ, a fish, = ἐγκρασίχολος, Ael.*NA*8.18: pl., ἐγγραύλεις Opp.*H.*4.470.

**ἐγγρᾰφ-εύς**, έως, ὁ, *registrar*, *Gloss.* **-ή**, ἡ, Dor. **ἐγγροφά** *IG* 4.1485.126 (Epid.), *registration*, πολιτῶν Arist.*Ath.*43.1, cf. Ph.2.51; of persons on the list of their deme, D.39.5 (pl.), *IG*2².1028.6 (pl.); of ἄτιμοι, D.25.28; of public debtors, Id.37.6; of those subject to penalties, Arist.*Pol.*1322ᵃ1 (pl.). II. *engraving of an inscription*, Ἀρχ.Ἐφ.1911.141 (Gonni). 2. Geom., *inscribing* of a figure, Papp. 150.8, al.; cf. ἐκγραφή. **-ής**, ές, = ἔγγραφος, Anon. *in EN*245.30. ⊛ **-ος**, ον, Dor. **ἔγγροφος** *SIG*712.35 (Crete), *written*, Plb.3.21.4, Luc.*Herm.*24, etc.; ἔγγραφα, τά, *documents*, *OGI*335.137 (Pergam.). Adv. -φως *Inscr.Prien.*113.37 (i B.C.), J.*BJ*1.27.1, *SIG*880.68 (Pizus), Porph.*Chr.*27. II. *enrolled*, *IG*1².949. III. ἔγγραφοι πατέρες, = *patres conscripti*, D.H.2.12. ⊛ **-ω**, *make incisions into*, τὸ στέλεχος Thphr.*HP*5.1.2. 2. *mark in or on, paint on*, ζῷα ἐς τὴν ἐσθῆτα ἐ. Hdt.1.203; opp. ἐξαλείφω, Pl.*R.*501b. 3. *engrave, inscribe*, ἐν τῇσι στήλῃσι Hdt.2.102, cf. 4.91; νόμους Lys.30.2 (of codifiers, opp. ἐξαλείφω):—Med., ἣν ἐγγράφου σὺ μνήμοσιν δέλτοις φρενῶν A.*Pr.*789:—Pass., *to be written in*, ἐνεγέγραπτο δὲ τάδε ἐν αὐτῇ (sc. τῇ ἐπιστολῇ) Th.1.128; αὐτὸν εὗρεν ἐγγεγραμμένον κτείνειν found his name *entered in the letter* for execution, ib.132; δέλτον ἐγγεγραμμένην συνθήμαθ' S.*Tr.*157. 4. metaph., εἰ μέλλουσι τοιαῦται διάνοιαι ἐγγραφήσεσθαι ἀνθρώποις X.*Cyr.*3.3.52. 5. Geom., *inscribe* a figure in another, εἰς.. Euc.4.4, al.; ἐν.. Archim.*Sph.Cyl.*1.13, al. (Pass.). 6. Medic., *include in a prescription*, οἶνος ἐγγεγράφθω Aret.*CD*1.2. II. *enter in the public register*, esp. of one's deme or phratria, ἐς τὰ κοινὰ γραμματεῖα Is.7.1; ἐγγράψαι τὸν υἱὸν εἰς ἄνδρας D.19.230; εἰς τοὺς φράτερας Id.39.4; ἐ. εἰς τοὺς ἀτίμους Plu.*Them.*6; also ἱερὰν ἐ. τὴν οὐσίαν Alex.276:—Pass., εἰς τοὺς δημότας ἐγγραφῆναι D.18.261; Μαντίθεος ἐνεγεγράμμην by the name of M., Id.39.4; τοὺς μήπω δι' ἡλικίαν ἐγγεγραμμένους Arist.*Pol.*1275ᵃ15; πρὶν ἐγγραφῆναι καὶ λαβεῖν τὸ χλαμύδιον Antid.2; εἰς τοὺς ἐφήβους Pl.*Ax.*366e. (A.*Ch.*699 is corrupt.) 2. *indict*, Ar.*Pax*1180, D.37.24:—Pass., ἐγγράφεσθαι λιποταξίου *to be indicted* for desertion, Aeschin.2.148. 3. of state-debtors, *enter their names*, ἐγγραφόντων οἱ ἄρχοντες τοῖς πράκτορσιν Lex ap.D.43.71; ἐγγεγραμμένος [ἐν ἀκροπόλει] *registered* among the state-debtors, D.25.4, cf. Arist.*Ath.*48.1; also of ἄτιμοι, Pl.*Lg.* 784d. (Perh. written ἐκγρ–, *SIG*742.29.)

**ἐγγριμᾶσθαι**· ἐναγίσαι, Hsch. **ἐγγρισμός**· παροξυσμός, Id.; cf. ἀγγρίζειν. **ἐγγυάζων**· ἀντιφωνῶν, Id.

**ἐγγῠᾰλίζω**, Ep. and Lyr. Verb, (γύαλον) prop. *put into the palm of the hand, put into the hand*, ἔεδνα ὅσσα οἱ ἐγγυάλιξα Od.8.319; ἐγὼ δέ τοι ἐγγυαλίξω I *will put* him *into* your *hands*, 16.66; ὁ δ' αὖτ' ἐμοὶ ἐγγυάλιξεν (sc. τοὺς ἵππους) Il.23.278; freq. of the gods, καί τοι Ζεὺς ἐγγυάλιξε σκῆπτρόν τ' ἠδὲ θέμιστας 9.98; τιμήν.. ὄφελλεν Ὀλύμπιος ἐγγυαλίξαι 1.353; τότε οἱ κράτος ἐγγυαλίξω 11.192; ὁτέοισιν κῦδος.. ἐγγυαλίξῃ 15.491, cf. A.R.2.55, etc.; ἐ. ὄλβον Pi.*Pae.*6.133, cf. *I.*8 (7).46, Hegem.ap.Ath.15.698d.

**ἐγγύαλον**, = κοῖλον, Orion 51.2.

**ἐγγύαν**· ὀψωνίαν (Lacon.), Hsch.

⊛ **ἐγγῠάω**, impf. ἠγγύων (παρ–) S.*OC*94, E.*Supp.*700, X.*An.*4.1.17, etc.: aor. ἠγγύησα E.*IA*703, D.29.47, etc.: pf. ἠγγύηκα D.C.38.9: plpf. ἠγγυήκει Is.3.58:—Med., fut. -ήσομαι D.24.46: aor. ἠγγυησάμην And.1.44,73, D.22.53:—Pass., aor. ἠγγυήθην (ἐξ–, κατ–) Lys.23.11, D.59.49: pf. ἠγγύημαι (δι–) Th.3.70:—also treated as a compd., ἐνεγυησάμεθα *PEleph.*27.9 (iii B.C.), and freq. in codd.: impf. ἐνεγύων Is.3.45, D.41.16; ἐνεγύησα Is.3.36,70: pf. ἐγγεγύηκα ib.40, D. 59.53: impf. Pass. ἐνεγυᾶτο Is.3.70: pf. ἐγγεγύημαι D.33.24, *POxy.* 259.7 (i A.D.): plpf. ἐνεγεγύητο Is.3.55: but these forms are incorrect: (ἐγγύη):—*give or hand over as a pledge*:—Med., *have a thing pledged* to one, *accept as a surety*, δειλαί τοι δειλῶν γε καὶ ἐγγύαι ἐγγυάασθαι Od.8.351 (nowhere else in Hom.). 2. esp. of a father, *plight, betroth*, θυγατέρα ἐγγυᾶν τινι Hdt.6.57 (v. infr.); Ζεὺς ἠγγύησε καὶ δίδωσ' E.*IA*703:—Med., *have a woman plighted or betrothed to one*, c. acc., D.57.41:—Act. and Med. opposed, Hdt.6.130:—Pass., of the man, *to be betrothed*, θυγατρί τινος Pl.*Lg.*923d. II. Med., *pledge oneself, give security*, ἐγγύας ἐγγυησάμενοι πρὸς τὸ δημόσιον And.1.73, cf. Pl.*Lg.*953e; ἐπί τισι Lys.23.9; ἐ. τινὶ ὅτι.. Pl.*Euthd.*274b. 2. c. acc. et inf. fut., *promise or engage that*.., Pi.*O.*11(10).16, Ar.*Pl.* 1202, X.*An.*7.4.13, Pl.*Prt.*336d, etc.; ἐγγυᾶσθαί [τινα] καὶ ὁμολογεῖν παρέξειν Lys.13.23; ἐγγυωμένη δώσειν Babr.58.10. 3. c. acc. rei, *answer for*, ἐγγυᾶσθαι τὰ μέλλοντ' ἔσεσθαι D.18.191: c. acc. pers., Pl.*Lg.*855b; ἐγγυᾶσθαί τινά τινι *give surety for* him to another, D.33.28; ἐγγύην ἐγγυᾶσθαί τινα πρός τινα Pl.*Phd.*115d; ἐ. τὰ μετέωρα *give guarantees* without security, *SIG*364.46 (Ephesus, iii B.C.).

**ἐγγῠβᾰθής**, ές, = ἀγχιβαθής, Dion.Byz.1:—written **-βαθος** in Suid.

**ἐγγύδιον**· ἔγγιον, Hsch.

⊛ **ἐγγῠεύω**, = ἐγγυάομαι, *GDI*1804.3 (Delph.).

⊛ **ἐγγύ-η** (rarely **ἐγγύα**; but τὴν ἐγγύαν *IG*11(2).226 *A* 29 (Delph., iii B.C.), cf. Epich. (v. infr.), *PSI*4.346 (iii B.C.)), ἡ: (ἐν, γύαλον, cf. ἐγγυαλίζω):—*pledge put into one's hand*: generally, *surety, security*, whether received or given, Od.8.351; ἐ. τιθέναι τινί A.*Eu.*898; ἐγγύας ἀποτίνειν ὑπέρ τινος Antipho 2.2.12; ἐ. ἐγγυᾶσθαι (v. ἐγγυάω II); ἀποδιδόναι D.53.27; ἐ. ὁμολογεῖν, = Lat. *vadimonium facere*, D.H.11.32, *OGI*455.3 (Epist. M. Antonii); τῆς ἐ. τῆς ἐπὶ τὴν τράπεζαν D. 33.10; ἐγγύας ἄτα 'στι θυγάτηρ, ἐγγύα δὲ ζαμίας Epich.268: prov., ἐγγύη, πάρα δ' ἄτη Pl.*Chrm.*165a, etc. 2. *betrothal*, Pl.*Lg.*774e; ἐ. ποιεῖσθαί τινος Is.3.28. 3. ἐ.· σημεῖον ἐν θυτικῇ, Hsch. [ῠ; ῡ only in *AP*9.366.] **-ημα**, ατος, τό, *security*, *PMasp.*169.14 (vi A.D.). **-ησις**, εως, ἡ, *security*, *CIG*2953*b*38 (Delos(?)), *BGU*981. 36 (i A.D.), v.l. in D.24.73; *right of giving security*, *IG*2².10. II. *betrothal*, Is.3.53; κατ' ἐγγύησιν Alciphr.3.1. ⊛ **-ητής**, οῦ, ὁ, *one who gives security, surety, guarantor*, ἐγγυητὴν καθιστάναι Hdt.1.196, Antipho 5.17, Lys.23.12, *IG*2².1172.22, etc.; ἄξιος ἐ. τινος Thphr.*Char.* 18.6; παρέχειν Pl.*Lg.*871e; λαμβάνειν τινὰ ἐ. D.33.7; διδόναι Plb. 12.16.3, etc.; ἐπ' ἐγγυητῶν ἐκμισθοῦν under *securities*, X.*Vect.*3.14; ἐ. τοῦ ἀργυρίου ἀξιόχρεως for the money, Pl.*Ap.*38c; οἱ ἐ. τῆς τραπέζης *those who had given security* for the bank (and were liable in case of its failure), D.33.10; ὁ νόμος ἐ. ἀλλήλοις τῶν δικαίων Arist.*Pol.* 1280ᵇ11; τὸ νόμισμα οἷον ἐ. ὑπὲρ τῆς ἀλλαγῆς Id.*EN*1133ᵇ12; εἰ μή τις θεῶν ἐστιν ἐ., ὡς.. D.H.11.41. ⊛ **-ητικός**, ή, όν, *connected with suretyship*, πράγματα, πρόσωπα, Heph.Astr.2.28,30. ⊛ **-ητός**, ή, όν, always of a wife, *plighted, wedded*, ἐγγυητὴ γυνή, opp. to an ἑταίρα, Is.3.77, D.59.60. ⊛ **-ήτρια**, ἡ, fem. of ἐγγυητής, *Stud.Pal.*20.139 (vi A.D.).

⊛ **ἐγγύθεν** [ῠ], Adv., (ἐγγύς) *from nigh at hand*, ἐ. ἐλθεῖν to *approach*, Il.5.72; ἐ. σκοπεῖν S.*Ph.*467, cf. Th.3.13, Pl.*Plt.*289d, etc. 2. with Verbs of rest, *hard by*, ἐ. ἱσταμένη Il.10.508; ἐ. εἰσίν Od.6. 279. 3. c. dat., ἐ. τινί *hard by* him, Il.17.554, etc.; ἐπεὶ φόνος ἐ. αὐτῷ 18.133, cf. 19.409: c. gen., ἐ. Ἀρήνης 11.723; θνήσκοντος ἐ. παρών A.*Ch.*852. 4. of kinship, Od.7.205.

⊛ **ἐγγῠθήκη**, ἡ, *stand for vessels, tripods*, etc., Lys.*Fr.*34, Hegesand. 45; cf. ἐγγυοθήκη.

**ἐγγύθι** [ῠ], Adv. *hard by, near*, in Ep. mostly c. gen., Il.6.317, Hes.*Op.*343; αὐτοῖν Theoc.21.8: less freq. c. dat., Il.22.300: abs., 7.341, Hes.*Op.*288. II. of Time, *nigh at hand*, ἐγγύθι δ' ἠώς Il. 10.251.

**ἐγγυιόω**, *stretch the limbs upon*, v.l. for συνέκαμψεν, Lxx 4*Ki.*4.35; cf. ἐγγυιώσεται· συμπλακήσεται, ἐναγκαλισθήσεται, Hsch.

⊛ **ἐγγυμν-άζω**, *exercise in*, τὴν ψυχὴν θεάμασιν ἐ. Luc.*Salt.*6; τὴν γνώμην ἐνθυμήμασιν Polyaen.3*Praef.*:—more freq. in Med., ἐν σοὶ ἐγγυμνασόμενος *to practise* upon you, Pl.*Phdr.*228e; *practise oneself in*.., πολέμοις Plu.*Caes.*28, cf. Ph.1.551, Luc.*Lex.*22, Jul.*Or.*1.37c; ἐν ταῖς πράξεσιν D.C.36.32, cf. *BKT*3 p.25:—Pass., Hp.*Vict.*2.63; ἐγγυμνασθέντες περί τι Vett.Val.353.5; λόγοις Luc.*Hipp.*2. **-αστέον**, *one must practise oneself in*, Them.*Or.*4.51b.

**ἐγγῠοθήκη**, ἡ, = ἐγγυθήκη, Luc.*Lex.*2.

⊛ **ἔγγυος**, ον, (ἐγγύη, cf. ἀμφίγυος) *secured, under good security*, μνᾶς.. ἐγγύους ἐπὶ τόκῳ δεδανεισμένας Lys.32.15 (but v. ἔγγαιος II). 2. *reliable*, in Comp., ὅπλα -ώτερα Them.*Or.*15.197c (nisi leg. ἐχεγγ–). II. Subst., = ἐγγυητής, ἔγγυον παρέχειν Thgn.286, cf. X.*Vect.*4.20, Arist.*Oec.*1350ᵃ19, *SIG*364.41 (Ephesus), 976.13 (Samos), *PEleph.* 8.19, *Ep.Hebr.*7.22, etc.; ἔ. τῆς προξενίας *giving security* for.., *IG*9(2). 4 (Hypata), etc.: fem. in Aeschin.*Ep.*11.12, *BGU*1051.10 (i B.C./ i A.D.).

⊛ **ἐγγύς** [ῠ], Adv., Comp. ἐγγυτέρω (-τέρῳ *Hell.Oxy.*6.3), also -ύτερον Pl.*Lg.*704e: Sup. ἐγγυτάτω or -ύτατα (first in Hp., and Att.); also ἔγγιον, ἔγγιστα (v. ἐγγίων). I. of Place, *near, nigh, at hand*: freq. in Hom., ἐ. γὰρ νυκτός τε καὶ ἤματός εἰσι κέλευθοι Od.10.86: c. gen., *hard by, near to*; so λύπας ἐγγυτέρω *nearer to* grief, S.*OC*1217: c. dat., Il.11.340, E.*Heracl.*37; ἐγγὺς ὁδῷ dub. in *IG*1².974: mostly with Verbs of rest, ἐ. ἑστάναι, παρεστάναι, A.*Pers.*686, *Eu.*65; but ἐ. χωρεῖν Id.*Th.*59: c. gen., οἱ ἐγγυτάτω τῆς ἀγορᾶς κατεσκευασμένοι Lys.24.20, etc. II. of Time, *nigh at hand*, Il.22.453; ἐ. ἡμῖν ὁ ἀγών X.*Cyr.*2.3.2. III. of Numbers, etc., *nearly*, ἔτεσι ἐ. εἴκοσι Th.6.5; μισθὸς ἐ. ἐνιαυτοῦ X.*HG*3.1.28: generally, *nearly, almost*, ἐ. ἔγνως S.*Ichn.*301; οὐδ' ἐ. τινος not *nearly*, i.e. not *by a great deal*, nothing *like* it, Pl.*Smp.*198b; ἔχει οὐχ οὕτω ταῦτα οὐδ' ἐ. not so.. nor yet *nearly so*, D.21.30; οὐκ ἐποίουν τοῦτο, οὐδ' ἐ. Id. 18.96; *mostly*, Hp.*Mochl.*34. IV. of Qualities, *coming near*, ἐ. τι καὶ παραπλήσιον Pl.*Grg.*520a; ἐγγύτατα τοῦ νῦν τρόπου, τῆς ξυμπάσης γνώμης, Th.1.13,22; ὅτι ἐγγύτατα τούτων Id.7.86; κοινῇ δὲ πᾶσιν οὐδεὶς ἐγγυτέρω D.18.288; δοκεῖς δηλῶσαι ἐγγύτατα τὴν ῥητορικήν Pl.*Grg.*452e; ἐ. εἶναι, c. gen., Id.*Phd.*116b; ἐ. τυφλῶν Id.*R.* 508c; ἐ. τι τείνειν τοῦ τεθνάναι *very near* death, Id.*Phd.*65a; κακῶς παθεῖν ἐγγύτατα D.21.123. V. of Relationship, *akin to*, οἱ Ζηνὸς ἐ. A.*Fr.*162; ἐγγυτέρω γένει or γένους, Pl.*Ap.*30a, Is.3.72; ἐγγύτατα γένους A.*Supp.*388, Lys.*Fr.*41, Pl.*Hp.Ma.*304d; ἐγγυτάτω γένους *IG*1².77, Ar.*Av.*1666.

**ἐγγύτερος** [ῠ], α, ον, Comp. Adj., (ἐγγύς) *nearer*, Procop.Gaz.*Ep.* 62: Sup. **ἐγγύτατος**, η, ον, *nearest*, Aen.Tact.28.3 (s.v.l.), Lxx *Jb.* 6.15; δι' ἐγγυτάτου, = ἐγγυτάτω, Th.8.96.

**ἐγγύτης** [ῠ], ητος, ἡ, *nearness*, Str.8.6.19, A.D.*Pron.*24.4, Alex. Aphr.*Pr.*2.35, Them.*Or.*14.182b, etc.

⊛ **ἐγγώνιος**, ον, (γωνία) *forming an angle*, esp. *right angle*, σχῆμα Hp.*Art.*22; λίθοι ἐντομῇ ἐγγώνιοι cut *square*, Th.1.93; πύργοι J.*BJ* 7.8.3. Adv. -ίως Paul.Aeg.6.115. II. *cut into angles*, of ivy-leaves, Thphr.*HP*3.15.4 (Comp.).

**ἐγγωνοειδής**, ές, = foreg. II, Thphr.*HP*3.12.5.

**ἔγγωνον**, τό, *angular piece of land*, *Tab.Heracl.*2.107.

**ἐγδ–**, freq. for ἐκδ– in Inscrr. and Papyri:—also ⊛ **ἐγδάκτυλος**, = ἐξαδ–, *IG*2.809ᵇ195.

**ἐγδούπησαν**, v. γδουπέω.
**ἐγειρόφρων**, ον, gen. ονος, (φρήν) gloss on ἀερσίφρων, *EM*20.47.
⊛ **ἐγείλασαν**· συνήλωσαν, Hsch. (Perh. ἐϝ-, cf. γάλλοι.)
⊛ **ἐγείρω**, Aeol. inf. ἐγέρρην Alc.*Supp.*16.12, cf. *Et.Gud.*157.48: Ep. impf. ἔγειρον Il.15.594: fut. ἐγερῶ Pl.*Epigr.*28 (cf. ἐξ-, ἐπ-): aor. ἤγειρα, Ep. ἔγ- Od.15.44: pf. ἐγήγερκα Philostr.*Ep.*16: plpf. -κειν J.*AJ*17.7.4, D.C.42.48:—Pass., Pl.*R.*330e, etc.: fut. ἐγερθήσομαι Babr.49.3 (also fut. Med. ἐγεροῦμαι dub. in Polyaen.1.30.5): aor. ἠγέρθην Hdt.4.9, etc.; Ep. 3 pl. ἔγερθεν v.l. for ἄγ. in Il.23.287: pf. ἐγήγερμαι v.l. in Th.7.51: plpf. ἐγήγερτο Luc.*Alex.*19: also, in pass. sense, poet. aor. ἠγρόμην (ἐξ-) Ar.*Ra.*51; 3 sg. ἔγρετο, imper. ἔγρεο, Il.2.41, Od.23.5; 2 sg. subj. ἔγρῃ Ar.*V.*774; opt. ἔγροιτο Od.6.113; inf. ἐγρέσθαι (freq. written ἔγρεσθαι, as if from a pres. ἔγρομαι, cf. ἔγρω) ib.13.124; part. ἐγρόμενος 10.50 (and late Prose, Iamb.*Myst.*1.15): intr. pf. ἐγρήγορα (as pres.) Ar.*Lys.*306, Pl.*Prt.*310b, etc.: plpf. ἠγρηγόρη (as impf.) Ar.*Ec.*32; 3 pl. ἐγρηγόρεσαν Id.*Pl.*744; 3 sg. ἐγρηγόρει X.*Cyr.*1.4.20: Ep. pf. 3 pl. ἐγρηγόρθασι Il.10.419; imper. ἐγρήγορθε (v. infr. II); inf. ἐγρήγορθαι ib.67. I. Act., *awaken, rouse*, ἐ. τινὰ ἐξ ὕπνου 5.413, etc.; τοὺς δ᾽.. ὑπνώοντας ἐγείρει 24.344; ἐ. τινὰ εὐνῆς E.*HF*1050 (lyr.); simply, ἐ. τινά A.*Eu.*140, etc.: metaph., τὰς τέχνας Theoc.21.1. 2. *rouse, stir up*, Il.5.208; ἐπεί μιν ἔγειρε Διὸς νόος 15.242; ἐγείρειν Ἄρηα *stir* the fight, 2.440, etc.; ἐ. μάχην, φύλοπιν, etc., 13.778, 5.496, etc.; Τρωσὶν θυμὸν ἐ. (v.l. ἀγεῖραι) ib.510; ἐ. τινὰ ἐπὶ ἔργον Hes.*Op.*20; ἔγειρε νῆα *h.Ap.*408; ἐκδοχὴν πομποῦ πυρὸς ἐ. *wake up* the bale-fire, A.*Ag.*299; λαμπάδας ἐ. Ar.*Ra.*340: freq. metaph., ἐ. ἀοιδάν, λύραν, μέλος, θρῆνον, Pi.*P.*9.104, *N.*10.21, Cratin.222, S.*OC*1778 (anap.); μῦθον Pl.*Plt.*272d; τὸ οὖς ἐ. '*prick up*' the ears, Plot.5.1.12. 3. *raise from the dead*, νεκροὺς *Ev.Matt.*10.8, cf. 1*Ep.Cor.*15.42 (Pass.); or from a sick-bed, *Ep.Jac.*5.15. 4. *raise, erect* a building, Hyp.*Fr.*103, Call.*Ap.*64, *OGI*677.3 (ii A.D.); ναόν *Ev.Jo.*2.19, cf. Luc.*Alex.*10:—Pass., στῦλος ἐγηγερμένος Bito 66.5, cf. Plu.*Alex.*19, Jul.*Caes.*320c. II. Pass., with pf. Act. ἐγρήγορα, *wake*, ἐγειρομένων ἀνθρώπων Od.20.100, cf. Hdt.4.9, etc.; ἔγρετο δ᾽ ἐξ ὕπνου Il.2.41: metaph., ἐγειρόμενος εἰς ἐμαυτὸν ἐκ τοῦ σώματος Plot.4.8.1: in pf., *to be awake*, ἐγρηγόρθασι Il.10.419; ἐγρήγορθε *stay awake!* 7.371, 18.299 (whereas ἔγρεο is *wake up!* Od.15.46); ἐγρήγορας ἢ καθεύδεις; Pl.*Prt.*310b; πόλις ζῶσα καὶ ἐγρηγορυῖα Id.*Lg.*809d; καὶ ἐφρόνει καὶ ἐγρηγόρει X.*Cyr.*1.4.20, etc.; of things, ἐγειρομένου χειμῶνος *arising*, Hdt.7.49: so metaph., τὰ ἐκ τοῦ βαρβάρου ἐγειρόμενα ib.148; ἐγρηγορὸς φρούρημα A.*Eu.*706; ἐ. τὸ πῆμα Id.*Ag.*346, etc. 2. *rouse* or *stir oneself, be excited* by passion, etc., Hes.*Sc.*176, D.19.305: c. inf., ἐγηγερμένοι ἦσαν μὴ ἀνιέναι τὰ τῶν Ἀθηναίων *they were encouraged* to prevent the departure of the Athenians, v.l. in Th.7.51. III. intr. in Act., *arouse oneself*, Aesop.16b. IV. in ἀμφὶ πυρὴν.. ἔγρετο λαὸς Il.7.434, 24.789, ἔγρ. is for ἠγρ- (ἀγείρω); so in Maiist.52.
**ἐγέλα**· χαλινοί, Hsch. **ἐγέλωτοι**· ἀστέρες, Id. **ἔγεντο**, v. γίγνομαι. ⊛ **ἐγεργεῖ**· γρηγορεῖ, Id.
**ἐγερσι-βόης**, ου, ὁ, *raising the cry, loud-voiced*, *IG*3.82. **-βροτος**, ον, *awakening men*, Procl.*H.*7.18. **-γελως**, ωτος, ὁ, ἡ, *laughter-stirring*, *AP*11.60 (Paul. Sil.); Ἀφροδίτη Orph.*Fr.*183. **-θέατρος**, ον, *exciting the theatre*, *APl.*4.361. **-μάχας** [μᾰ], ου, ὁ, *battle-stirring*, *AP*7.424 (Antip. Sid.):—fem. **-χη**, ib.6.122 (Nicias). **-μαχέω**, *arouse strife*, Tz.*H.*12.654. **-μοθος**, ον, = ἐγερσιμάχας, Opp.*C.*1.207, Nonn.*D.*3.39.
⊛ **ἐγέρσῐμος**, ον, *from which one wakes*, ὕπνος, opp. the sleep of death, Theoc.24.7.
**ἐγερσίνοος** [ῐ], ον, *soul-stirring*, μέθη Nonn.*D.*12.376; φωνή ib.37.673; βίβλοι Procl.*H.*3.4.
**ἔγερσις**, εως, ἡ, *awaking*, Hp.*Coac.*82; personified in Emp.123.1: pl., Phld.*Rh.*2.206 S., Polyaen.2.2.6: metaph., ἡ τοῦ θυμοῦ ἔ. Pl.*Ti.*70c, Arist.*EN*1116$^{b}$30. b. *awaking* from death, *Ev.Matt.*27.53; *recovery*, ἐκ τοῦ πάθεος Aret.*SA*2.11. 2. *raising, erection*, τειχίων Hdn.8.5.4 (pl.), cf. Men.Eph.ap.J.*AJ*8.5.3.
**ἐγερσι-φαής**, ές, *light-stirring*, ἐ. πέτρος the flint, *AP*6.5 (Phil.). **-χορος**, ον, *leading the dance*, Opp.*C.*4.236.
**ἐγερ-τέον**, *one must raise*, E.*Rh.*690. **-τήριον**, τό, *excitement*, Ael.*VH*2.44: pl., -τήρια δρόμου, of the ears of a hare, Id.*NA*13.14. **-τί** [ῑ], Adv. *eagerly, busily*, κινεῖν τινα S.*Ant.*413; *wakefully*, Heraclit.63, E.*Rh.*524. **-τικός**, ή, όν, *waking, stirring*, νοήσεως Pl.*R.*523e, 524d. II. in Gramm., *enclitic*, because changing the grave accent of the preceding word into the acute, ἐ. ἐπίρρημα *AB*1147. **-τός**, ή, όν, = ἐγέρσιμος, ὕπνος Arist.*Somn.Vig.*454$^{b}$14.
⊛ **ἐγϝηληθίωντι**, v. ἐξειλέω. **ἐγήγαρτος**· ἐπίχαρτος, ἐπιχαρής, Hsch. (leg. ἔγχαρτος). **ἐγήρα**, v. γηράσκω.
**ἐγκαθαιρέω**, aor. inf. ἐγκαθελεῖν· καταβαλεῖν, Hsch.
⊛ **ἐγκαθ-αρμόζω**, *fit in*, Ar.*Lys.*682. **-εδρος**, ὁ, *assessor*, *Gloss.* **-έζομαι**, fut. -εδοῦμαι, *sit* or *settle oneself in*, Ar.*Ec.*23; εἰς θᾶκον Id.*Ra.*1523; εἰς ἐνέδραν Arr.*Tact.*15.5; *encamp in* a place, Th.3.1, 4.2; τῶν δαιμονίων -καθεζομένων J.*AJ*6.11.2. **-είργω** and **-γνῦμι**, *shut up, enclose*, ib.5.1.2; φορβειᾷ τὸ ῥαγδαῖον Plu.2.456c:—Pass., ib.951b, Jul.*Or.*7.206b:—also **ἐγκατείργω**, Agath.1.11, al.:—Pass., Aret.*SA*1.5, Herm.ap.Stob.1.49.44. **-ειρκτος**, ον, *shut in, enclosed*, Aesop.40. **-ετος**, ον, (ἐγκαθίημι) *put in secretly, suborned*, προέδρους ἐ. ὑφέντες Pl.*Ax.*368e, cf. D.*Ep.*3.34, Plb.13.5.1, *Ev.Luc.*20.20, J.*BJ*6.5.2. Adv. -τως, δημηγορεῖν D.S.16.68. II. of a child, = εἰσποιητός, Hyp.*Fr.*56. **-εύδω**, fut. -ευδήσω, *sleep among*, Arist.*HA*610$^{b}$31; *sleep upon*, ποδήρη ὦτα ὡς ἐγκαθεύδειν Str.15.1.57; στιβάδα ἐγκαθεύδειν τινὶ παρασκευάσαι Ael.*NA*6.42. 2. generally, *lie abed*, Ar.*Lys.*614. 3. *sleep in a temple* to effect a cure, *IG*4.951.25 (Epid.), 7.235 (Orop.), etc. **-έψω**, *boil in* anything, Hp.*Mul.*2.133. **-ηβάω**, *pass one's youth in*, E.*Hipp.*1096. **-ηλόω**, *fix in*, Heliod.ap.Orib.49.4.25 (Pass.). **-ημα**, ατος, τό, *that which settles in* a place, of foreign bodies in the eye, Orib.*Eup.*4.31. **-ημαι**, *sit in* or *on*, X.*Eq.*1.11; *lie in ambush*, ἐν τοῖς τρίβωσιν Ar.*Ach.*343, cf. *Th.*600; ἐ. καὶ ἐνεδρεύειν Aeschin.3.206; of garrisons, *lie in* a place, Plb.18.11.6, J.*BJ*5.1.2; *lie couched in*, as the men in the Trojan horse, Pl.*Tht.*184d: metaph., ἐ. μεταξύ.. Id.*Prm.*156d; ἐγκαθημένου ταῖς ψυχαῖς τοῦ φόβου Plb.2.23.7; ἐμπόδιον ἐγκαθήμενον Plot.6.9.7; *take one's stand upon*, τῷ ῥητῷ Mich. *in EN*68.31. **-ιδρύω** [ῠ], *erect* or *set up in*, ἄγαλμα ἐ. χθονί E.*IT*978, cf. Ath.11.473b, J.*BJ*2.13.7:—Pass., Philox.3.5 codd. Ath., Arist.*Mu.*397$^{b}$27, Hld.5.13. ⊛ **-ίζω**, Ion. **-κατίζω**, *seat in* or *upon*, εἰς θρόνον Pl.*R.*553c; ἐ. στρατιὰν ἐν τοῖς τόποις *station* a force *in* a place, Plb.16.37.4: aor. 1 Med., ναὸν ἐγκαθείσατο (vulg. ἐγκαθίσατο, cf. ἐγκαθισάμενοι τὰ ὅπλα v.l. in J.*BJ*5.1.2) *founded* a temple *there*, E.*Hipp.*31. 2. *administer a sitz-bath to* one, Sor.1.64, Herod.Med. ap.Orib.6.20.18, etc.:—Pass., Hp.*Mul.*1.35; also, *to be used for such*, Dsc.5.13, 30. 3. *cause to subside upon*, τοῖς κοιλώμασι τὴν ὑπερκειμένην γῆν Lyd.*Ost.*53. II. intr., *sit in* or *upon*, [θρόνῳ] Pi.*P.*4.153:—Med., ἐγκατίζεσθαι εἰς θρόνον *take one's seat* on.., Hdt.5.26. **-ίημι**, *let down*, ἐς τὴν χύτραν Ar.*Lys.*308. 2. *send in* as agents, Plu.*Pyrrh.*11:—Pass., of a catheter, *to be passed*, Ruf.*Ren.Ves.*7.11. II. *commit, entrust*, Ζεὺς ἐγκαθίει (for -ίησι) Λοξίᾳ θεσπίσματα A.*Fr.*86. **-ίννῦμαι**, = ἐγκαθίζω 2, Hp.*Mul.*2.210. **-ισμα**, ατος, τό, *sitz-bath*, Dsc.3.113, *Gp.*12.23.5, Sor.1.56, etc. II. *dwelling on a syllable in pronunciation*, D.H.*Comp.*20, 22 fin. **-ισμός**, ὁ, = foreg. II, Id.*Dem.*43 (pl.). **-ιστέον**, *one must administer a sitz-bath*, Sor.2.11, Herod.Med. in *Rh.Mus.*58.109. ⊛ **-ίστημι**, *place* or *establish in*, as king or chief, σὲ.. Μυκήναις ἐγκαταστήσω πάλιν E.*IT*982; ἐ. τινὰς ἡγεμόνας Th.1.4; τινὰ τύραννον D.17.10; also, *place as a garrison in* a place, v.l. in Id.9.15; φρουράν Plu.*Alc.*30; of institutions, ἐ. δημοκρατίας Arr.*An.*1.18.2:—Med., *establish for oneself*, βασιλείην Hellanic.79(a) J. II. Pass., with aor. 2, pf. and plpf. Act., *to be established* as ruler *in* a place, Lys.2.59, Th.1.122; also αὐλητῶν νόμῳ ἐγκαθεστώτων Id.5.70. **-οράω**, *look closely into*, τινὸς τῷ προσώπῳ Plu.*Demetr.*38; εἰς τὸ ὕδωρ *IG*4.951.66 (Epid.): abs., Pl.*Epin.*990e. II. *remark* something *in* a person or thing, Plu.*Brut.*16. **-ορμίζομαι**, Med., *run into harbour, come to anchor*, αὐτόσε Th.4.1, cf. D.C.48.49: aor. Pass., Arr.*An.*2.20.8. **-όρμισις**, εως, ἡ, *putting into harbour*, ib.1.18.5. **-υβρίζω**, *riot* or *revel in*, τρυφαῖς E.*Tr.*997. **-υφαίνω**, v.l. for καθ-, Lxx *Ex.*28.17.
**ἐγκαίν-ια**, τά, (καινός) *feast of renovation* or *consecration*, Thd.*Da.*3.2, Lxx 2*Es.*6.16; esp. that established by Judas Maccabaeus *at the reconsecration* of the Temple, *Ev.Jo.*10.22. **-ίζω**, *restore*, τεῖχος Lxx *Is.*16.11; βασιλείαν 1*Ki.*11.14; *make afresh*, ὁδόν *Ep.Hebr.*10.20; *consecrate, inaugurate*, οἶκον Κυρίου Lxx 3*Ki.*8.63:—Pass. *Ep.Hebr.*9.18, *IG*12(5).712.58 (Syros); χύτρα -ισμένα Archig.ap.Orib.8.46.4. II. *innovate*, prob. in *PPar.*16.24 (ii B.C.). **-ίς**, ίδος, ἡ, dub. sens. in Agath.5.21. (Perh. ἐγκενίς, = ἐπηγκενίς.) **-ισις**, εως, ἡ, *consecration*, Lxx *Nu.*7.88 (v.l. -ωσις). **-ισμός**, ὁ, = foreg., ib.1*Ma.*4.56 (v.l. -ιασμός), *Nu.*7.10, al.
**ἐγκαιρ-ία**, ἡ, *seasonableness*, opp. ἀκαιρία, Pl.*Plt.*305d; τροφῆς Aret.*CA*1.1. ⊛ **-ιος**, ον, = ἔγκαιρος, Pl.*Ti.*51d (Sup.), *PGrenf.*1.64. **-ιότης**, ητος, ἡ, = ἐγκαιρία, Sch.E.*Ph.*471. **-ος**, ον, *timely, seasonable*, Pl.*Plt.*282e, *Lg.*928a, Them.*Or.*26.331a: Sup., Pl.*Lg.*717a. Adv. -ρως Aristaenet.1.15: Sup. -ότατα Them.*Or.*9.120c.
⊛ **ἐγκαίω**, aor. 1 part. ἐγκέας *IG*1$^{2}$.374.96, but -καύσας *SIG*$^{2}$587.186:—*burn* or *heat in*, ὀβελοὶ ἐγκεκαυμένοι πυρί E.*Cyc.*393. 2. *brand*, Luc.*Pisc.*46:—Pass., βοῦς ἐγκεκαυμένας ῥόπαλον Arr.*An.*5.3.4. 3. *scorch*, of the sun, *Gp.*18.17.1. 4. *paint in encaustic*, i.e. *with colours mixed with wax*, *IG* l.c., 11(2).199*A*80 (Delos, iii B.C.), Lxx 2*Ma.*2.29, Plin.35.122. 5. Medic. in Pass., *to be overheated*, Gal.2.870, Aret.*CD*1.5. II. *make a fire in*, πῦρ Plu.*Alex.*24; οἶκοι ἐγκαιόμενοι *heated* chambers, Luc.*VH*2.11. III. metaph. of passion, Sm.*Ps.*38.4. IV. abs., *offer sacrifice*, Ἀπόλλωνι Paus.1.42.6.
**ἐγκᾰκέω**, *behave remissly in* a thing, ἐνεκάκησαν τὸ πέμπειν they *culpably omitted* to send, Plb.4.19.10, cf. Thd.*Pr.*3.11, Sm.*Ge.*27.46: c. part., τὸ καλὸν ποιοῦντες μὴ ἐγκακῶμεν *Ep.Gal.*6.9: abs., *Ev.Luc.*18.1, al., cf. *BGU*1043.3 (iii A.D.); cf. ἐκκακέω. II. ἐγκακοῦμεν· ὑψοῦμεν, Hsch.
⊛ **ἐγκᾰλέω**, *call in* a debt, Isoc.17.44, X.*An.*7.7.33, D.31.6, 36.14: generally, *demand* as one's due, ἀργύριον Lys.3.26. 2. *invoke*, τὴν τῶν θεῶν ἰατρείαν Str.14.1.44. II. *bring a charge* or *accusation against* a person:—Constr.: c. dat. pers. et acc. rei, *charge* something *against* one, φόνους ἐ. τινί S.*El.*778, cf. Pl.*Ap.*26c, etc.; ἐ. ἔγκλημά τινι Hyp.*Lyc.*18, cf. *Eux.*24; χόλον κατ᾽ αὐτῶν ἐ. S.*Ph.*328: folld. by a relat. clause, ἐ. τινὶ ὅτι.. X.*An.*7.5.7: c. inf., ἔστιν ἃ ἐνεκάλει τοῖς Ἀθηναίοις παραβαίνειν τὰς σπονδάς Th.4.123: c. part., ἐ. αὐτοῖς ἀμελοῦσιν Pl.*Prt.*346a: freq. c. dat. pers. only, *accuse*, Antipho 4.2.2, etc.; ἐ. περί τινων *Inscr.Prien.*28.8 (ii B.C.); ἐπὶ τοῖς διῳκημένοις ib.37.128 (ii B.C.): c. acc. rei only, *bring as a charge*, εἴ τι ἄλλο ἐνεκάλουν Th.5.46, cf. 6.53; τὸ νεῖκος ἐγκαλεῖν *throw the blame* of quarrel on another, S.*OT*702: abs., οἱ ἐγκαλέσαντες Arist.

Rh.Al.1437$^a$17: rarely c. gen. rei, τῆς βραδύτητος αὐτοῖς ἐνεκάλει Plu. Arist.10:—Pass., ἐγκαλεῖται τῇ τύχῃ *a charge is brought against*.., Arist.EN1120$^b$17; ἐνίων ἐγκληθέντων ἐπὶ τῷ βίῳ Phld.Piet.p.93 G.; τὰ ἐγκεκλημένα *charges*, OGI90.14 (ii B.C.): also with person. constr., ἐγκαλεῖσθαι ὑπέρ τινος D.H.7.46; τινός D.C.58.4:—Locr. part. ἐγκαλείμενος may be either Med. or Pass., IG9(1).334.41. 2. as law-term, *prosecute, take proceedings against*, οὔτ' ἐγκαλοῦντες οὔτ' ἐγκαλούμενοι D.34.1; ἐ. δίκην τινί Id.40.19; ἐ. τινὶ περί τινος Isoc.4.40: abs., Ar.Av.1455. 3. *object*, c. acc. et inf., Phld.Sign.29.

**ἐγκᾰλινδέομαι**, *roll about in*, τῇσι ψάμμοισι Aret.CD1.2: metaph., πολλῇσι συμφορῇσι Hp.Ep.17; ταραχαῖς καὶ κινδύνοις Agath.4.27; *wallow in*, ταῖς λιχνείαις Ath.6.262b, cf. Them.Or.29.346b.

**ἐγκαλλωπ-ίζομαι**, *take pride in*, τοῖς αἰσχροῖς Plu.Ant.36; βωμολοχίαις Agath.1.13, cf. Arr.Epict.3.22.59, Ael.VH9.35; *boast of*, ταῖς φίλαις τῇ ἀξιώσει J.AJ18.3.4: abs., Ph.2.28. **-ισμα**, ατος, τό, *ornament, decoration*, Th.2.62, Plot.3.5.9, Them.Or.6.83c; of a person, γένους Agath.Praef.p.135 D.

**ἐγκᾰλοσκελής**, οῦς, ὁ, *having his legs in the stocks*, Com.Adesp.988.

**ἐγκᾰλ-υμμός**, ὁ, *covering, wrapping up*, cj. in Ar.Av.1496. **-υπτέος**, α, ον, *fit to be veiled, hidden*, Ap.Ty.Ep.18. **-υπτήρια**, τά, *veiling-feast*, opp. ἀνακαλυπτήρια, Philostr.VS2.25.4. ⊕ **-ύπτω**, *veil, wrap up*, Ar.Ra.911:—Pass., *to be veiled* or *enwrapped*, Id.Pl.714, Pl.Phdr.243b; *to be wrapped up* (as for sleep), X.An.4.5.19, Pl.Prt. 315d; ἐγκεκαλυμμένος λόγος, a noted fallacy, Stoic.2.8,90, etc. II. Med., *hide oneself, hide one's face*, Ar.Pl.707, etc.; ἐγκαλυπτόμενος καθεύδειν And.1.17; of persons at the point of death, X.Cyr.8.7.26, Pl.Phd.118a, etc.: metaph., *conceal one's feelings*, c. part., νεμεσῶν ἐνεκαλύπτετο App.BC2.69. 2. as a mark of shame, Pl.Phd.117c, D.Ep.3.42, Aeschin.2.107: c. acc. pers., *feel shame before* a person, θεοὺς ἐγκαλυπτόμενος ὧν ἔμελλε δρᾶσειν App.BC1.16: c. inf., *to be ashamed to*.., PMasp.295.12 (VI A.D.). 3. -καλυπτόμενος σφυγμός, term invented by Archig., Gal.8.662. **-υψις**, εως, ἡ, *concealment*, Str.10.2.12 (pl.); τῆς ψυχῆς ὑπὸ τοῦ σώματος Plu.2.266e; ἐν ἐγκαλύψει εἶναι to be *wrapped in obscurity*, M.Ant.5.10.

**ἐγκάμνω**, *grow weary* or *slack in* or *at* a thing, τινί J.AJ2.15.5; *become slack*, ταῖς εὐτυχίαις Id.BJ3.10.2; ἐς ἔργον Aret.SD1.15.

**ἐγκάμπτω**, *bend in, bend*, X.Eq.1.8, Gal.18(2).353.

⊕ **ἐγκᾰνάσσω**, *pour in* wine, ἐγκάναξον E.Cyc.152, Ar.Eq.105; κύλικα Alciphr.3.36.

**ἐγκᾰνᾰχάομαι**, *make a sound on* a thing, ἐ. κόχλῳ *blow on* a conch, Theoc.9.27.

**ἐγκάνθιος**, α, ον, *in* or *of the inner angle of the eye*, Dsc.Eup.1.8, Gal.19.437.

**ἐγκανθίς**, ίδος, ἡ, *tumour in the inner angle of the eye*, Cels.7.7.5, Gal.UP10.11, etc.

**ἐγκαπῆ**· ἐπικαρπία, Hsch. **ἐγκάπνισμα**, ατος, τό, *fumigation*, Gloss.

⊕ **ἐγκάπτω**, pf. ἐγκέκᾰφα AP9.316.6 (Leon.):—*gulp down greedily, snap up*, Ar.Pax7, V.791, Stratt.25, Hermipp.26, Alex.128.7; ἐ. αἰθέρα γνάθοις *hold* one's breath, E.Cyc.629. II. ἐγκάπτει· ἐκπνεῖ, Hsch.

**ἔγκᾰρ**, ἄρος, ὁ, = φθείρ, Eust.757.27.

**ἐγκαρδι-αῖος**, α, ον, = sq., φῶς Iamb.Myst.2.7. ⊕ **-ος**, ον, *in the heart*, ἐγκάρδιόν ἐστί (or γίγνεται) τί τινι it goes *to* his *heart*, Democr. 262, D.S.1.45; τἀγκ. τις ἐρεῖ *what is in* his *heart*, Phld.Lib.p.14 O. Adv., ὅταν γεννηθῇς ἐγκαρδίως PMag.Par.1.1785. 2. *in close proximity*, of planets, Antioch.Astr. in Cat.Cod.Astr.8(3).105. II. ἐγκάρδιον, τό (ἐγκάρδιος, ὁ, S.E.M.9.119), *heart-wood, core*, Thphr. HP3.8.5, 5.3.2; *pith*, Dsc.1.109.5, Gp.12.25.3. 2. generally, *core*, Roussel Cultes Égyptiens 236 (Delos, ii B.C.).

**ἔγκᾰρος**, ὁ, (κάρ, κάρα) *the brain*, AP9.519.3 (Alc.), Lyc.1104.

**ἐγκαρπ-ασθέντας**· ἐγκριθέντας, ἐντυχόντας, Hsch. **-ία**, ἡ, perh. f.l. for εὐκ-, EM797.27. **-ιος**, ον, of fruit, *containing seed*: hence, *ripe*, Hp.Vict.2.55. II. ἐγκάρπια, τά, *unreaped crops*, SIG633.87 (Milet., ii B.C.). ⊕ **-ος**, ον, *containing fruit*, κάλυξιν ἐγκάρποις χθονός S.OT25; *fruitful*, σπέρματα Pl.Phdr.276b; of soil, Thphr.CP2.4.2; γᾶν ἔγκαρπον φέρειν may the earth bear *produce*, SIG526.41 (Crete); δένδρα Plu.2.2e; τέλη ἔγκαρπα *tithe of produce*, S.Tr.238: metaph., χρήσιμον καὶ ἔ. *fruitful*, Plu.2.776b, cf. Luc.Merc.Cond.39 (Sup.). Adv. -πως, διακεῖσθαι Aen.Tact.7.1. II. ἔγκαρπα, τά, *festoons of fruit* on friezes or the capitals of columns, Lat. *encarpa*, Vitr.4.1. 7. 2. ἔγκαρπα or ἔγκαρτα, = τοὺς κεκουρευμένους πυρούς, Phryn. Trag.4 (ap.Hsch.). **-ωσις**, εως, ἡ, *being in seed*, Gal.13.570.

**ἐγκάρσιος**, α, ον (ος, ον Gal.UP5.12 codd.), *athwart, oblique*, Th. 2.76, 6.99, Ach.Tat.3.2, Hld.3.2; of the ecliptic, Arist.Mu.392$^a$12 (v.l. -ίως).

**ἐγκαρτερέω**, *persevere* or *persist in* a thing, τινί v.l. in X.Mem.2.6. 22; ἐγκαρτερεῖν [τούτοις] ἃ ἔγνωτε Th.2.61; πρὸς δίψαν Plu.2.987e: c. inf., μὴ φιληθῆναι Id.Ages.11. 2. c. acc., *await stedfastly*, θάνατον E.HF1351, Andr.262. 3. abs., *hold out, remain firm under*, c. dat., ταῖς πληγαῖς Plu.Pomp.79; τοῖς δεινοῖς Luc.Anach.38: abs., Plu.Lyc.18, PAmh.2.78 (ii A.D.).

**ἐγκάς**, Adv. *deep in*, prob. in Hp.VC5, cf. Gal.19.94.

**ἔγκᾰτα**, τά, *inwards, entrails*, Hom., always in acc., as Od.9.293, exc. dat. ἔγκασι in Il.11.438; ἐν ἔγκασιν ᾅδου AP15.40.42 (Comet.): later, nom. sg. ἔγκατον Lxx 3Ki.17.22, Luc.Lex.3.

**ἐγκατα-βαίνω**, *go down into, put oneself in*, c. acc., κροκωτὸν σπάργανον ἐγκατέβα Pi.N.1.38: c. dat., dub. l. in D.S.14.28; εἰς.. Gal. UP2.15: abs., Id.8.686. **-βάλλω**, *throw down into*, μέσῃ δ' ἐνικάββαλε δίνῃ A.R.1.1239 (but written divisim, μέσῳ δ' ἐνὶ κ. ὁμίλῳ Il. 12.206); εἰς.. Alex.Aphr.Pr.2.67 (Pass.). **-βιόω**, *pass one's life in*, Plu.2.783d, Longin.44.11. **-βρέχω**, *wet* or *soak with*, Gp.13.1. 7. **-βυσσόομαι**, *penetrate deeply*, Democr.A.77 D. **-γηράσκω**, = ἐγγηράσκω, *grow old in*, τῇ ἀρχῇ Arist.Ath.17.1; ἐν πενίᾳ Plu.Phoc. 30; *become inveterate in*, Din.2.3:—also **-γηράω**, ταῖς μοναρχίαις Them.Or.19.232c.

**ἐγκατάγομαι** [ᾰγ], *put up at* a place, Nic.Dam.p.138 D., Poll. 1.73.

⊕ **ἐγκατα-γράφω** [γρᾰ], *write down among*, Ael.Fr.67; *portray*, Aen. Gaz.Ep.12. **-δᾰμάζω**, *overpower*:—Pass., ὑπὸ κωνώπων ἐγκαταδαμασθεὶς dub. in Hp.Epid.7.79 (sed leg. ἐν καταδήγμασιν). ⊕ **-δαρθάνω**, *sleep in*, Plu.2.647f. II. *go to sleep over* a thing, τῷ δίψῃ ib. 688f. **-δέω**, *bind fast in*, τινί Pl.Phd.84a, Them.Or.23.297a (Pass.), Opp.H.3.201. **-δύνω** [ῡ], aor. -κατέδυν, of the sun, *set upon* a place, Hp.Aër.6; *sink beneath*, ὕδασιν AP7.532 (Isid.); μυχόν Opp. H.1.153: abs., *sink, be absorbed in*, Archig.ap.Aët.3.167, Gal.7.217: metaph., *to be immersed in*, c. dat., Dam.Pr.10:—Med., τοῖς οἰκείοις ἐπιτηδεύμασι Procop.Arc.1. **-ζεύγνῡμι**, *associate with, adapt to*, νέας βουλὰς νέοισιν ἐγκαταζεύξας τρόποις S.Aj.736. **-θνῄσκω**, Ep. aor. ἐνικάτθανε, *die in*, A.R.2.834. **-κειμαι**, *lie in*, c. dat., κλισμῷ Thgn.1191. 2. *lie in bed, sleep*, παρά τινι Ar.Pl.742. **-κενόω**, *empty out into*, Hippiatr.74. **-κλεισις**, εως, ἡ, *enclosing*, Herod. Med. in Rh.Mus.49.553. **-κλειστος**, ον, *shut up in* a place, E.Fr. 1132.39. **-κλείω**, *shut up in, enclose*, τινὰ τῷ νεῷ Alex.40.3, cf. Arist.Pr.937$^a$29; τὸ θερμὸν Thphr.CP5.13.2:—Pass., Hp.Acut.16, Arist.Mete.378$^a$29. **-κλίνω** [ῑ], *put to bed in* a place, Ar.Pl. 621:—Pass., *lie down in*, σισύραν ἐγκατακλῖνῆναι μαλθακήν Id.Av. 122; ἐγκατακλιθῆναι εἰς τὸ ἱερόν Hyp.Eux.14. **-κλώθω**, *interweave*, Hsch. **-κνᾰκομῑγής**, ές, *compounded of* ἔγκατα *and* κνάκων, Philox.3.11. **-κοιμάομαι**, = ἐγκοιμάομαι, Hdt.8.134, IG4.952.9 (Epid.). **-κρούω**, χορείαν τοῖς μύσταις *tread* a measure *among* them, Ar.Ra.330. **-κρύπτω**, *hide in*, τί τινι Lyc.1231, cf. Gal. 2.305, al.; ὄνομα βυθοῖς in religious mysteries, IG3.900. ⊕ **-λαμβάνω**, *catch in* a place, *hem in*, Th.4.116; ἐ. τινὰ ὅρκοις *trammel* by oaths, ib.19; ἐὰν λογισμὸς ἐγκαταλαμβάνῃ αὐτόν Aeschin.3.60:—Pass., Th.3.33, Arist.Pr.926$^b$31. II. *follow in immediate succession*, παννυχὶς ἐ. ἑορτήν Aristid.Or.47(23).6, cf. 26(14).84; *attack immediately after*, ἡ ἐπὶ τῷ ἐμέτῳ ἀσιτία [τινὰ] ἐ. Id.47(23).60. ⊕ **-λέγω**, *build in*, πολλαὶ στῆλαι ἐγκατελέγησαν *were built into* the wall, Th. 1.93. 2. *count* or *reckon among*, Luc.Par.3; τινὰς εἰς τοὺς Εὐπατρίδας, = Lat. *adlegere inter patricios*, D.C.43.47; *enlist soldiers*, AP 11.265 (Lucill.). II. Pass., *lie in* or *on*, Ep. aor. ἐγκατέλεκτο A.R. 4.431. ⊕ **-λειμμα**, ατος, τό, *remnant, residue, trace*, Arist.Fr.13, cf. Lxx Je.11.23, al. 2. *residual trace*, εἰδώλου Epicur.Ep.1 p.12 U. 3. *kneading trough*, Lxx De.28.5,17. 4. *sediment*: hence, *silting-up*, PPetr.2 p.14 (iii B.C.). **-λείπω**, *leave behind*, παῖδα Hes.Op.378; ἐ. φρουρὰν ἐν τῇ νήσῳ Th.3.51; πλεῖον ἐ. ἐξιόντες ἐκ τῆς ὠνῆς PRev.Laws53.12; ἐ. τὸ κέντρον, of a bee, Pl.Phd.91c: hence of Pericles, τὸ κέντρον ἐγκατέλιπε τοῖς ἀκροωμένοις Eup.94.7; ἐ. τὴν μάχαιραν ἐν τῇ σφαγῇ Antipho5.69. 2. *leave in the lurch*, Pl.Smp. 179a, Lycurg.2, D.57.58, Ev.Matt.27.46, Lyr.Alex.Adesp.4.22, etc.; *abandon*, νεκροὺς Th.4.44; ἀκρόπολιν X.HG5.4.13. 3. *leave out, omit*, Hdt.3.119. 4. *leave traces behind*, Epicur.Nat.Herc. 1420. II. Pass., *to be left behind* in a race, Hdt.8.59. 2. *leave residual symptoms* or *sequelae*, Hp.Epid.6.2.6, 6.7.7.

**ἐγκατᾰλείφω**, *mix in an ointment*, λίπος Hp.Acut.(Sp.)33.

⊕ **ἐγκατά-λειψις**, εως, ἡ, *residual symptom* (v. -ληψις). **-λεκτέος**, α, ον, *to be reckoned among*, [πόλεσιν] εὖ πραττούσαις Philostr.VS2. 24.1. **-ληπτικός**, ή, όν, *inclusive*, Gal.19.235. **-ληψις**, εως, ἡ, *catching* or *being caught in* a place, *being hemmed in*, Th.5.72; *suppression* of urine, Hp.Epid.6.2.7 (codd. sed leg. ἐγκατάλειψις). 2. *concept* (= κατάληψις), Gal.14.685, cf. 19.350. **-λιμπάνω**, = ἐγκαταλείπω, Hp.Aph.2.12 (Pass.), Arist.Rh.1368$^b$19. **-λογίζομαι**, *reckon in*, Is.11.45. ⊕ **-λοχίζω**, *divide into relays* or *courses*, Lxx 2Ch.31.18. **-μείγνυμι** (-ύω Luc.Lex.25), *mix with*, τί τινι Timo 33, Luc.Hist.Conscr.13, etc.; φάρμακον πότῳ Ach.Tat.4.15; τινὰς λόχοις D.H.6.2; ἑαυτοὺς τοῖς στρατιώταις Hdn.7.12.7: metaph., κέντρον τωθασμοῖς Ph.2.570; θεὸν ἀνθρωπίναις χρείαις Plu.2.414f; of a sculptor, μανίην λίθῳ APl.4.57 (Paul. Sil.), cf. AP9.593:—Pass., *to be mixed in* or *with*, ἐγκαταμειγνύμενος ὕδατι Hp.Aër.6; ἐγκαταμεμιγμένα τοῖς λεγομένοις Isoc.15.10; ὀνόματα -μιγέντα τῇ λέξει D.H. Comp.25. **-μεμιγμένως**, Adv. *in a mixed manner*, Sch.rec.S.OT 95. **-μένω**, *remain in*, Thphr.HP1.3.4, Hld.1.33, etc.; *continue the use of*, τισί Antyll.ap.Aët.9.42. **-μιξις**, εως, ἡ, *intermingling, infusion*, Alex.Aphr. in Sens.74.26, Olymp. in Mete.157.29. **-μίσγω**, = -μείγνυμι, τῇ διηγήσει τὰς θεατρικὰς γοητείας D.H.Th.7:—Pass., Id.Dem.22, cf. EM770.52, Et.Gud.533.49. **-μυκτηρίζω**, gloss on ἐγκατιλλῶψαι, Hsch.

**ἐγκατάνα**· κατὰ γνώμην, κατὰ νοῦν, Hsch.

⊕ **ἐγκατα-ναίω**, aor. 1 -ένασσα, *make to dwell in*, οὐρανῷ τινὰ A.R.3. 116, Moero 1. **-νέμω**, *bestow upon*, τί τινι Jul.Or.5.179b.

**ἐγκαταντλ-έω**, *wash over with* a thing, Hippiatr.26. **-ησις**, εως, ἡ, *washing over*, Hp.Decent.8.

**ἐγκατα-νωτίζομαι**, *to be backed*, μέρεσι ἱππείοις Tz.H.6.965. **-ξηρος**, ον, *dry*, opp. κάθυγρος, Gp.2.13 tit. **-παίζω**, *mock at*, τινί Lxx Jb.40.14(19). ⊕ **-πήγνῡμι**, *thrust firmly in*, ξίφος.. κουλεῷ ἐγκατέπηξ' Od.11.98; ἐν δὲ σκόλοπας κατέπηξεν *planted* or *fixed* them *in*, Il.9.350; τὴν κεφαλὴν δόρατι ἐ. *having fixed* it *on*, Hdn.1.13.4. 2.

*sheathe*, ξίφος Plu.2.313e. **-πίμπρημι**, *burn in*, τινά τινι Phalar. *Ep.*122.4. **-πίνομαι** [ῐ], pf. -πέπομαι: aor. -επόθην, *to be swallowed up*, of a ship, Ph.1.670: metaph. of persons, Id.2.300, al.; *to be absorbed, immersed*, Dam.*Pr.*67. **-πίπτω**, poet. aor. ἐνικάππεσον, *fall* or *throw oneself upon*, λέκτροισιν A.R.3.655; ὅρμῳ *AP* 9.82 (Antip. Thess.). ❋ **-πλέκω**, *interweave, entwine*, ἀκάνθας δι' ἀλλήλων Plu.2.494a:—Pass., X.*Cyn.*9.12. **-πνίγω** [ῑ], *suffocate in*, Gal.7.673:—Pass., aor. inf. -πνῐγῆναι Diocl.*Fr.*55. **-ποσις**, εως, ἡ, *swallowing up*, Ph.1.116.

**ἐγκατᾰριθμέω**, *count, number, reckon in* or *among*, τὴν ἔκφρασιν τοῖς γυμνάσμασιν Hermog.*Prog.*10, cf. Alex.Aphr.*in Metaph.*46.9:—Pass., *to be counted in* or *among*, Arist.*SE*167ᵇ24.

**ἐγκατα-ρράπτω** (poet. aor. -ἔραψα Orph.*H.*48.3), *sew in*, Aen. Tact.31.4:—Pass., X.*Cyn.*6.1. **-σβέννῡμι** or -ύω, *quench in* a thing, τὸ λογικὸν ἐγκατέσβεσται τῆς ψυχῆς Plu.2.975c, cf.987d. **-σήπομαι**, *grow rotten* or *corrupt in*, Hp.*Mul.*1.63, E.ap.Stob.3.41.6. **-σκάπτω**, *demolish*, Tz.*H.*1.787. **-σκευάζω**, *prepare in* a place, ἐν ταῖς πόλεσι προδότας D.S.16.54; but the Prep. ἐν freq. has little force, Id.2.24 (s.v.l.), 14.91. **-σκευος**, ον, *elaborate, ornate*, of style, opp. ἁπλοῦς, D.H.*Comp.*18, al., cf. Phld.*Rh.*1.164S., Demetr.*Eloc.*15. Adv. -ως S.E.*M.*2.56. ❋ **-σκήπτω**, *fall upon*, of lightning, εἴς τινα D.C.49.15; of epidemics, πολλαχόσε ἐ. Th.2.47, cf. Gal.10.880: metaph., Ph.2.471, Ael.*Fr.*348. II. trans., *hurl down among* or *upon*, of lightning, ἐγκατάσκηψον βέλος S.*Tr.*1087; κακῶν ἃ Πέρσαις ἐγκατέσκηψεν θεός A.*Pers.*514. **-σκηψις**, εως, ἡ, *sudden attack*, Philum.*Ven.*4.5. **-σκιρόομαι**, Pass., *to be engrained*, κηλῖδας ἐγκατεσκιρωμένας Hipparch.ap.Stob.4.44.81. ❋ **-σπείρω**, *scatter, sow, implant in* or *among*, ἐλπίδα τῷ γένει τῶν ἀνθρώπων Ph.2.673; τι τῇ ὕλῃ Plu.2.1001b; φήμην Hdn.2.1.3:—Pass., Plu. *Cic.*14, Aen.Gaz.*Thphr.*p.69B. **-στηρίζω**, *fix firmly in*, Corn. *ND*6 (Pass.). **-στοιχειόομαι**, *to be implanted as a principle in*, τινί Plu.*Lyc.*13, 2.353e. **-στρέφω**, *return* a ball in a game, Antiph.234.6. **-συφράζω**· ἐνυβρίζω, Hsch. **-σφάττω**, *slaughter in*, τὸν υἱὸν τῷ κόλπῳ Plu.*Dem.*31:—also **-σφάζω**, γονέων ἐν ὄμμασι καὶ κόλποις τέκνα D.S.35.12. **-σχάζω**, *scarify*, Dsc.*Ther.*19 (Pass.). ❋ **-τᾰράσσω**, *throw into confusion*, Plu.2.592a (Pass.). **-τάσσω**, Att. -ττω, *arrange* or *place in*, Longin.10.7, Marcellin.*Puls.*474:—Pass., Onos.10.3; ῥυθμοὶ -τεταγμένοι ἀδήλως rhythms *introduced* unobtrusively, D.H.*Comp.*25 (cf. ἐγκαταχωρίζω). **-τέμνω**, *cut up* the foetus *in* the womb, Hp.*Foet.Exsect.*1. II. *cut up among* a number, Pl.*R.*565d. ❋ **-τίθημι**, *lay* or *put in*, ⟨ἔν⟩ τινι τι Orph.*H.*25.9; Ἐριχθόνιον..νηῷ ἐγκατέθηκε *IG*14.1389ii31. II. Hom. only in Med., ἱμάντα τεῷ ἐγκάτθεο κόλπῳ *put* the band *upon* or *round* thy waist, Il.14.219, cf. 223; ἄτην ἐῷ ἐγκάτθετο θυμῷ *stored up, devised* mischief *in* his heart, Od.23.223; τελαμῶνα ἐῇ ἐγκάτθετο τέχνῃ *stored up* the belt in his art, *designed* it by his art, Od.11.614; σὺ ταῦτα τεῷ ἐνικάτθεο θυμῷ *store it* up *in* thy heart, Hes.*Op.*27; στέρνοις ἐγκατέθεντο Simon.85.5; ὅκα φρεσὶν ἐγκατάθοιτο βουλάν Theoc.17.14; γλυφίδας ..ἐνικάτθετο νευρῇ A.R.3.282. **-τίλλω**, *shred in* lint, Hp.*Mul.* 2.205. **-τομή**, ἡ, *cutting up* of the foetus *in* the womb, Id. *Foet.Exsect.*tit. **-φλέγω**, *burn in*, βόθροις *Gp.*9.6.3. **-φῡσάω**, *spray*, οἴνῳ καὶ ἐλαίῳ *Hippiatr.*26. **-φύω**, gloss on ἠγκυροβόληται, Gal.19.102. **-χέω**, *pour out besides*, φόνον Epigr.ap.Plu.*Marc.* 30. **-χρίω** [ῑ], *smear over*, Dsc.*Eup.*1.118. **-χώννῡμι**, *overwhelm*, τινὰ τῷ πλήθει τῶν βελῶν D.H.9.21; *bury*, τὸ δεύτερον τοῦ κλήματος μέρος *Gp.*4.3.3:—Pass., μνήμη -χώννυται τῷ αἰῶνι M.Ant. 7.10. **-χωρίζω**, *place in*:—Pass., ῥυθμοὶ -κεχωρισμένοι ἀδήλως D.H.*Dem.*50 (cf. ἐγκατατάσσω).

**ἐγκατ-ειλέομαι**, *to be cooped up in*, Arist.*Mu.*395ᵇ33, dub. in Ph. 2.504. **-είργω**, v. ἐγκαθείργω. **-ερείδω**, *support heavily on*, τὸ ἰσχίον τῇ βάσει Philostr.*Gym.*31. **-εφάλλομαι**, Ep. aor. 2 ἐγκατέπαλτο, *leap down into*, Opp.*H.*4.661. ❋ **-έχω**, *contain within*, σῶμα κόρης..τύμβος ὅδ' ἐ. *IG*12(8).609.2; *retain*, Sor.1.46, Ruf.ap. Orib.8.24.8:—Pass., *to be contained*, Plu.2.691f; esp. *to be confined* in a temple, *UPZ*6.8 (ii B.C.). II. Pass., *to be owned* or *possessed*, *PFlor.*97.3 (ii A.D.). **-ίλλω**, f.l. for ἐγκατατίλλω (q.v.), Hp.*Mul.* 2.205. **-ιλλώπτω**, *scoff at*, ὑμῖν ἐγκατιλλώψας μέγα A.*Eu.*113, cf. *Fr.*226 (dub.).

**ἐγκᾰτόεις**, εσσα, εν, (ἔγκατα) *containing* or *enclosing intestines*, κεκρύφαλος Nic.*Th.*580.

**ἐγκατοικ-έω**, *dwell in*, Hdt.4.204; δόμοις E.*Fr.*188; *dwell among*, αὐτοῖς 2*Ep.Pet.*2.8. **-ίζω**, Att. fut. -ιῶ Lyc.1261:—*settle* or *place in* or *on*, Luc.*Asin.*25: metaph., τῇδε τῇ τάξει τὸ φρουρητικόν Dam. *Pr.*257; *implant*, Plu.2.779f (Pass.). ❋ **-οδομέω**, *to build in* a place, Th.3.18 (Pass.). II. *build in, immure*, εἰς ἔρημον οἰκίαν Aeschin. 1.182:—metaph. in Pass., ὁ [ἀὴρ] ἐν τοῖς ὠσὶν ἐγκατῳκοδόμηται Arist. *de An.*420ᵃ9, cf. Porph.*Abst.*4.3. **-ος**, ον, *indwelling*, Sch.Il.2.125.

**ἔγκατον**, v. ἔγκατα.

**ἐγκατ-οπτρίζομαι**, Med., aor. -ίξασθαι *IG*4.951.64 (Epid.):—*look at oneself as in a mirror*, ἐς τὸ ὕδωρ l.c.; λεκάνῃ Artem.3.30. II. *contemplate as in a mirror*, τὸ τῆς τέχνης ἔργον Ph.Byz.*Mir.Praef.* 2. **-ορύσσω**, Att. -ττω, *bury in*:—Pass., ἐγκατωρύχθαι τὴν ψυχὴν ἐν τῷ σώματι D.H.*Rh.*6.5, cf. Jul.*Or.*6.189c. **-οχέω**, (κάτοχος) *to be a recluse* (cf. sq.), τῷ κυρίῳ Σαράπιδι *IGRom.*4.1403 (Smyrna, iii A.D.). **-οχος**, ὁ, *recluse*, ἱερῶν Ptol.*Tetr.*163; ἐν ἱεροῖς Vett.Val.63.29, cf. *Sammelb.*1066. II. Adj., *fixing*, τὸ ἐ. Olymp.Alch.p.74B.

**ἐγκαττύω**, *stitch into the shoe-sole*, Alex.98.8 (Pass.).

**ἐγκᾰτώδης**, ες, *like the entrails*, Sch.Ar.*Eq.*1176.

**ἐγκαυλέω**, *to be in stalk*, Arist.*Pr.*926ᵃ26, Thphr.*HP*1.2.2.

❋ **ἔγ-καυμα**, ατος, τό, (ἐγκαίω) *mark burnt in, sore from burning*, Luc.*DDeor.*13.2, al. II. *encaustic picture*, Pl.*Ti.*26c, *JHS*41.195 (Delos, ii B.C.), Dicaearch.1.8, Plu.2.759c. III. *ulcer in the eye*, Aët.7.27. ❋ **-καυσις**, εως, ἡ, *encaustic painting*, *IG*2.808ᵈ.52, 4. 1484.266 (Epid., iv B.C.), *SIG*977ᵃ.7 (Delos), *IG*7.3073.11 (Lebad.), etc. II. *heat-stroke*, Dsc.5.13 (pl.), Gal.12.504: pl., Plu.2. 127b. ❋ **-καυστήρια**, τά, *instruments used by encaustic painters*, *IG* 11(2).287*A*44 (Delos, iii B.C.). **-καυστής**, οῦ, ὁ, *encaustic painter*, Plu.2.348f; ἀγαλματοποιὸς ἐ. *IG*14.1494:—also **-καυτής**, ib.1².374, *CIG*4958c. **-καυστικός**, ή, όν, *of* or *for burning in*: ἡ ἐ. (sc. τέχνη) *the art of encaustic painting*, Plin.*HN*35.122. 2. *inflammatory*, πυρετός Herod.Med.ap.Aët.5.129. ❋ **-καυστος**, ον, *burnt in, painted in encaustic*, Mart.4.47: *encausto pingere*, Plin *HN*35.149; *encausta pictura*, ib.122.

❋ **ἐγκαυχάομαι**, *pride oneself on*, ἔν τινι Lxx *Ps.*73(74).4; τινί Aesop. 230, Eustr. *in EN*272.14.

**ἔγκᾰφος**, (ἐγκάπτω) *mouthful, morsel*, Eup.330.

❋ **ἐγκαψικίδαλος**, ον, (κίδαλον) *onion-eating*, Luc.*Lex.*10 (prob. f. l. for ἐγκαψιπήδαλος, cf. καψιπήδαλος).

❋ **ἔγκειμαι**, fut. -κείσομαι: used as Pass. of ἐντίθημι: I. *lie in, be wrapped in*, ἐπεὶ οὐκ ἐγκείσεαι αὐτοῖς [τοῖς εἵμασι] Il.22.513; so, Hdt.2.73 (v.l. ἐσκειμένου); simply, *to be in*, ὀφθαλμὸς εἷς ἐνέκειτο μετώπῳ Hes.*Th.*145: in mal. part., Herod.5.3. 2. ἐγκεῖσθαί τινι *to be involved in*, πόθῳ Archil.84; βλάβαις S.*Ph.*1318; μόχθοις E.*Ion* 181 (anap.); πολλαῖς ξυμφοραῖς Id.*Hel.*269; κακοπαθείαις Plb.14.9.5 codd.: c. acc., μελεδῶνας ἔγκειμαι I *have* cares *laid on me*, A.R.2.627. b. *to be implied, involved in*, ἐ. τὸ αἰσθητικὸν εἶναι ἐν τῷ εἴδει Plot.6.7. 3. 3. abs., *to be inserted*, Pl.*Cra.*402e, *R.*616d. II. *press hard*, esp. of troops *pressing upon* a defeated or retreating enemy, Th.1. 49, 144, etc.; of opponents in politics or argument, ἐνέκειντο τῷ Περικλεῖ Id.2.59, cf. 5.43, etc.: freq. with Adj. or Adv., πολλὸς ἐνέκειτο λέγων *was* very *urgent*, Hdt.7.158, cf. Th.4.22; πολὺς τοῖς συμβεβηκόσι ἔγκειται he *insists* much upon.., D.18.199; ἄγαν ἐ. τινί *to be vehement against* one, Ar.*Ach.*309; ἰσχυρῶς ἐ. Th.1.69; βαρὺς ἐγκεῖσθαι D.H.6.62; ὅλος ἐγκεῖσθαί τινι *to be devoted to* one, Theoc. 3.33; ἐ. ἐπὶ τὰ πονηρά Lxx *Ge.*8.21. III. *to be upon*, ὁ δέ οἱ περὶ ποσσὶ..ἐνέκειτο, of a sandal, *IG*14.1389i27. IV. *to be a burden, annoyance*, Herod.4.47 (prob.).

**ἐγκείρω**, in pf. part. Pass., ἐγκεκαρμένῳ κάρᾳ with *shorn* head, E. *El.*108 (v.l. ἐν κεκ.).

❋ **ἐγκεκαροῦται**· ἐγκαταβλέπει, Hsch.

**ἐγκεκλῐμένως**, Adv. *with the accent thrown back*, Sch.Il.1.277, 6. 289.

**ἐγκέλᾰδος**, ὁ, *a buzzing insect*, like βομβύλιος, Sch.Ar.*Nu.*158.

❋ **ἐγκέλ-ευμα** or -ευσμα, ατος, τό, *encouragement*, X.*Cyn.*6.24, Cic. *Att.*6.1.8. **-ευσις**, εως, ἡ, = foreg., Str.13.1.35, *Sammelb.*4284.8 (iii A.D.), Them.*Or* 19.232b: pl., A.D.*Synt.*258.20; ἐξ ἐ. by *command*, *IG*14.926 (Portus, dub.), Zucker *Les temples immergés de la Nubie* p.3 (ii A.D.). **-ευσμᾰτικός**, ή, όν, = ἐγκελευστικός, ἐπίρρημα *EM*115.27. **-ευσμός**, ὁ, = -ευσις, ἐς ἀλλήλους Arr.*An.*2.21. 9. **-ευστικός**, ή, όν, *encouraging*, Max.Tyr.23.5; *hortatory*, ἐπίρρημα A.D.*Synt.*258.11. **-ευστος**, ον, *urged on*, ὑπό τινος X.*An.* 1.3.13. **-εύω**, *urge on, cheer on*, A.*Pr.*72; ἐ. κυσί X.*Cyn.*9.7:—Med., D.H.3.20, etc.; τὸ πολεμικὸν ἐγκελεύεσθαι *sound* a charge, Plu.*Arist.*21, cf. *Pomp.*70. 2. in Med. also, *command*, Arist. *Fr.*11; τοῖς στραταγοῖς *IPE*1².79.23 (Olbia), cf. Asp.*in EN*135.13: c. acc., *enjoin*, Ti.Locr.104a.

**ἐγκέλλω**, aor. 1 ἐνέκελσα, *fit into*, as a socket, Hp.*Fract.*30.

❋ **ἐγκεντ-έω**, *puncture*, *Gloss.* II. = ἐγκεντρίζω, Eust.1308. 62. **-ρια**, τά, *spurs*, Hsch. II. ἐγκέντριον, τό, *graft*, Mich. *in PN*105.9. ❋ **-ρίζω**, *goad, spur on*, Lxx *Wi.*16.11 (Pass.). II. of plants, *graft*, Thphr.*HP*2.2.5, Porph.*Gaur.*10.1 (Pass.), etc.: metaph., *Ep.Rom.*11.17, Plot.2.9.7; of a Centaur, ὃν φύσις ἐνεκέντρισεν ἵππῳ *APl.*4.116 (Euodus). III. (κέντρον) *concentrate*, Dam.*Pr.*74:—Pass., ib.263. **-ρίς**, ίδος, ἡ, *sting*, Ar.*V.*427. 2. *goad*, X.*Cyn.*6.1, Pl.Com.40; also, *spur*, Pherecr.48. 3. *pointed stile* for writing, Poll.8.16, Aristaenet.1.20. 4. *spike worn on the leg* for climbing, περιθέμενον..ἐγκεντρίδας ἀναδραμεῖν εἰς τοὺς τοίχους Arist.*Fr.*84. **-ρισις**, εως, ἡ, *inoculation* or *grafting of trees*, Colum. 3.9.6, Jul.*Ep.*180 (pl.). **-ρισμα**, ατος, τό, = foreg., *Gloss.* **-ρισμός**, ὁ, = foreg., *Gp.*4.12.2, *PSI*6.624.20. **-ριστής**, οῦ, ὁ, *agitator, instigator*, *Gloss.* **-ρος**, ον, *furnished with a sting*, [σφῆκες] Arist. *HA*627ᵇ27. II. of stars, *occupying a cardinal point*, Vett.Val.57. 30, Sch.Ptol.*Tetr.*148. 2. ἐ. κύκλος, opp. ἔκκεντρος, Theo Sm. p.162H., al. **-ρόω**, *thrust in a sting*: *fix firmly in*, Hsch. (Pass.):—Pass., *to be furnished with a sting*, Sch.Ar.*V.*1069.

**ἐγκεράννῡμι** or -ύω, *mix*, esp. wine, οἶνόν τ' ἐγκεράσασα πιεῖν Il.8. 189; τρεῖς μόνους κρατῆρας ἐγκεραννύω Eub.94.1 (cf. ἐγκίρνημι); ἐ. τι εἰς ὄνομα Pl.*Cra.*427c:—Med., *mix for oneself*: metaph., *concoct*, πρήγματα μεγάλα Hdt.5.124; ἐγκεράσασθαι παιδιάν *mix in* a little amusement, Pl.*Plt.*268d, cf. Luc.*Am.*19. II. Pass., *to be multiplied together*, of numbers, *Theol.Ar.*45.

**ἐγκέραστος**, ον, *mixed, blended*, Plu.2.660c.

❋ **ἐγκεραυλ-έω**, *play* on the Phrygian flute, Hsch.:—hence **-ης**, ου, ὁ, Id.

**ἐγκερτομέω**, *abuse, mock at*, E.*IA*1006.

**ἐγκέρχνω**, *make hoarse*, Hp.*Acut.*58.

**ἐγκεφᾰλ-αίωμα**, ατος, τό, = κεφαλαίωμα, *PLond.*2.38. ❋ **-ιον**, τό,

Dim. of ἐγκέφαλος I, *BGU*348.33. **-ίς,** ίδος, ἡ, *cerebellum*, f.l. for παρεγκεφαλίς, Gal.*UP*8.6. **-ίτης** [ῑ], ου, ὁ, *of the brain*, μυελός ib. 4. **-ος,** ον, (κεφαλή) *within the head*: as Subst., ἐγκέφαλος (sc. μυελός), ὁ, I. *brain*, Il.3.300, Od.9.458, etc.; τὸν ἐ. σεσεῖσθαι Ar. *Nu.*1276; ὁ ἐ. ἐστιν ὁ τὰς αἰσθήσεις παρέχων τοῦ ἀκούειν κτλ. Pl.*Phd.* 96b, cf. Arist.*Sens.*438b25 (but cf. *Metaph.*1013a6). II. *the heart* or '*cabbage*' of the date-palm, X.*An.*2.3.16, Thphr.*HP*2.6.2. III. Διὸς ἐ., prov. of rare and costly food, 'morsel for a king', Ephipp. 13.7, Clearch.5.

**ἐγκέχοδα,** v. ἐγχέζω. **ἐγκεχρημένος,** v. ἐγχράω.

⊛ **ἐγκηδεύω,** *bury in* a place, Lxx 4*Ma.*17.9 (Pass.), J.*AJ*9.5.3, *JHS* 6.359.

**ἐγκηρίς,** ίδος, ἡ, *lump of wax*, Androm.ap.Gal.13.693, al.

**ἔγκηροι** (κήρ)· θνητοί, Hsch.

**ἐγκηρόω,** *wax over, rub with wax*, *Gp.*10.21.5.

**ἐγκηρύσσω,** *invite tenders* for a contract, *PPetr.*3 p.101 (iii B.C.).

**ἐγκῐθᾰρίζω,** *play the harp in the midst*, *h.Ap.*201; μέσῳ ἤματι *at* midday, *h.Merc.*17.

**ἐγκίκρημι,** = ἐγκεράννυμι, Dor. imper. ἐγκίκρα Sophr.48.

**ἐγκῐλῐκ-εύομαι,** = sq., Suid. s. v. Κιλίκιος τράγος. ⊛ **-ίζω,** (Κίλιξ) *play the Cilician* to one, τινί, i. e. *cheat*, Pherecr.166. **-ίστρια·** περιαγνίστρια, Hsch.

**ἐγκίλλαφον** and **ἔγκιλλον,** = οὐρά, Hsch.

⊛ **ἐγκινδῡνεύω,** *take a risk*, *Cod.Just.*1.3.39.

**ἐγκῑνέομαι,** Med., *disturb, trouble*, τινί Ar.*Fr.*69.

**ἐγκίνῠμαι** [ῐ], *to be moved*, Q.S.13.245.

**ἐγκίρνημι,** poet. for ἐγκεράννυμι, *mix by pouring in*, [κρητῆρα] Pi.*N.* 9.50; ἐν δὲ κέρναις οἶνον (Aeol. for ἐγκιρνάς) Alc.34.4: metaph., ἤθεσι θεωρήματα Lysis ap.Iamb.*VP*17.77; τῇ μεταβολῇ τὸ ἀμετάβλητον Dam.*Pr.*412:—Pass., ἐν δ' ἐκίρνατο οἶνος *Com.Adesp.*1203.3, cf. Iamb. *in Nic.*p.81 P.

**ἔγκιρρος,** ον, *pale-yellow*, Dsc.1.13.

⊛ **ἐγκισσάω,** *have yearnings like one pregnant*, Lxx *Ge.*30.38.

**ἐγκισσεύομαι,** Pass., *twine like ivy*: metaph., *form a plexus*, φλεβίοις ἐς τὸν μυελόν Hp.*Oss.*14.

**ἐγκίσσησις,** εως, ἡ, *impregnation*, Zonar. (vulg. ἐγκίσσωσις).

⊛ **ἐγκλαστρίδια,** ων, τά, *ear-rings*, Poll.5.97.

⊛ **ἐγκλάω,** Ep. **ἐνικλάω,** aor. ἐνέκλασα, *thwart, frustrate*, μοι ἔωθεν ἐνικλᾶν ὅττι κεν εἴπω Il.8.408; ἦέ τίς ἄτη σωομένους.. ἐνέκλασεν; A.R. 3.307; later lit., *break in*, σιλφίον ἐ. Hp.*Mul.*2.133:—Pass., φωνὴ ἐγκεκλασμένη *weak* voice, Phld.*Mus.*p.80 K. II. Pass., *to be bent, inclined*, Apollod.*Poliorc.*187.16; of the eyes of swine, Plu.2.671a (s. v. l.); of a diadem, Heraclit.*Ep.*8.1.

**ἐγ-κλεισμός,** ὁ, *shutting up*, λόγου Eust.1391.63; ἐν ἐγκλεισμῷ under *lock and key*, *POxy.*1734.6. **-κλειστέον,** *one must shut up*, *Gp.*14.7.18. **-κλείω,** Ion. **-κληΐω,** Att. **-κλῄω,** Ep. **ἐνικλείω** A.R. 2.1029:—*shut in, close*, ὅκως τὰς πύλας ἐγκληΐσειε Hdt.4.78; θύρα ἐγκεκλῃμένη Pl.*Prt.*314d. II. *shut* or *confine within*, ἑρκέων ἐγκεκλῃμένος (for ἐντὸς ἑρκέων κεκλῃμένος) S.*Aj.*1274; δόμοις ἐγκεκλῃμένος Id.*Tr.*579: generally, *shut up, confine*, γλῶσσαν ἐγκλῄσας ἔχει Id.*Ant.*180; εἰ μὴ γλῶσσαν ἐγκλῄοι φόβος ib.505; στόμα ἐ. E.*Hec.* 1284. III. Med., *shut oneself up in*, X.*HG*6.5.9. 2. *shut up with oneself*, Luc.*Alex.*41.

**ἐγκλεπίς·** ἐπιθυμία, and **ἐγκλεφές·** ἐπιθυμητικόν, Hsch. ⊛ **ἐγκλέφωνος,** = ἐρεθιστής, διεφθαρμένος, Id.

⊛ **ἔγ-κλημα,** ατος, τό, (ἐγκαλέω) *accusation, charge*, ἔ. τινι ἔχειν S.*Ph.* 323, cf. *Tr.*361, Antipho 3.2.9, etc.; ἐγκλήματα ἔχειν τινός, = ἐγκαλεῖν τι, Th.1.26; ἔ. ποιεῖν τι make a thing *matter of complaint*, Id.3.53; ἐγκλήματα ποιεῖσθαι bring *accusations*, Id.1.126; τὰ ἐ. τὰ ἔς τινας *complaints* respecting.., ib.79; ἐν ἐγκλήματι γίγνεσθαι D.18.251; γίγνεταί or ἐστί ἔγκλημά μοι πρός τινα I have *ground of complaint* respecting him, X.*Cyr.*1.2.6, Lys.10.23; λύειν ἔ. *clear away* a charge, Plb.2.52.4; λόγοις τὰ ἐ. διαλύεσθαι Th.1.140. II. in Law, *written complaint*: generally, of *complaints* which were to lead to private suits, ἔ. λαγχάνειν τινί file *a complaint* against.., D.34.16, al., cf. *PTeb.*616 (ii A.D.). III. concrete, *a standing reproach*, τῆς τύχης καὶ τῶν θεῶν Plu.*Dio* 58. 2. *defect*, Gal.14.20. **-κλημᾰτίζω,** = ἐγκαλέω, *PFlor.*58.16 (iii A.D.), *Gloss.* **-κλημᾰτικός,** ή, όν, *liable to cause disputes*, Arist.*EN*1162b16, *Pol.*1335a4. Adv. **-κῶς** Vett.Val.293.35. II. ἐ. δίκη *criminal* suit, *Cod.Just.*4.20.16; αἰτία ἐ. *PMonac.*7.62 (vi A.D.). **-κλημάτιον,** τό, Dim. of ἔγκλημα, *PFlor.*332.26 (ii A.D.). **-κλημᾰτογρᾰφέω,** *draw up an indictment against*, ἐμέ *UPZ*124. **-κλημᾰτόομαι,** Pass., *shoot into twigs*; v. ἐκκλημ-. **-κλήμων,** ον, gen. ονος, *liable to a charge*, *AP*5.187 (Leon.).

**ἐγκληρ-όομαι,** Pass., *to be assigned* or *planted by lot*, Ael.*VH*8. 1. **-ος,** ον, *having a lot* or *share in*.., c. gen., οὐθ' ὑμεναίων ἔ. S. *Ant.*814 (lyr.); λαχεῖν ἔγκληρά τινι to have *an equal share with*.., ib.837 (lyr., dub.). 2. *having a share of an inheritance, heir* or *heiress*, E.*IT*682; ἔ. εὐνή a marriage *which brings wealth*, Id.*Hipp.* 1011; ἔ. πεδία land *possessed as an inheritance*, Id.*HF*468. 3. Astrol., *occupying a* κλῆρος, Serapio in *Cat.Cod.Astr.*8(4).225.

**ἐγκλησία,** ἡ, *blame, adverse criticism*, Anon.*Vit.Arist.*p.14 W.

**ἔγ-κλησις,** εως, ἡ, *accusation*, *PRyl.*65.16 (i B.C.), Man.1.221 (pl.), etc. **-κλητέος,** α, ον, *to be blamed*, ἀμέλειαι Plu.2.1051c. II. ἐγκλητέον *one must blame*, τινί Plb.4.60.9; τῇ προνοίᾳ M.Ant.12. 24. **-κλητος,** ον, *liable to a charge*, *PTeb.*27.42 (ii B.C.), Plu.2. 1051b, *PMasp.*97 ii 50 (vi A.D.). 2. written for ἔκκλ-, Hsch.

**ἐγκλῄω,** Att. for ἐγκλείω.

⊛ **ἐγ-κλῐδόν,** Adv. *leaning, bent down*, *h.Hom.*23.3; ἐ. ὄσσε βαλοῦσα *aslant* or *askance*, A.R.3.1008; ἐ. ὤμῳ κεφαλὴν ἐρεισαμένη *AP*5.249 (Paul. Sil.). ⊛ **-κλιζε·** τὰ ἑτέρων ἑτέροις ἐδίδου, Hsch. **-κλῐμα,** ατος, τό, *slope*, Plb.5.59.9 (pl.). 2. *inclination, tilt*, τοῦ κόσμου Hipparch.1.3.5, Gem.6.24; of an engine, Bito 55.10 (pl.). 3. *latitude*, Vett.Val.316.32. II. *turning*, i. e. *rout*, of an army, Plb.1.19.11; cj. for ἔκκλημα in D.S.20.12. III. Gramm., *inflected form*, A.D. *Synt.*83.2. 2. *form pronounced with grave accent*, Id.*Pron.*90.12.

**ἐγκλῐμᾰτικός,** = ἐγκλιτικός, *AB*1144.

⊛ **ἐγκλίνω** [ῑ], fut. -κλῐνῶ: pf. ἐγκέκλῐκα Plu.*Sull.*1: pf. Pass. ἐγκέκλῐμαι (v. infr.):—*bend in* or *inwards*, τὴν κνήμην Arist.*Mech.*857b 36; *bend*, τινά A.R.1.62 (v. l. ἀγκλῖναι):—Pass., σκέλη ἐγκεκλιμένα μικρόν X.*Cyn.*5.30; τὰ ἐγκλιθέντα v. l. for ἐκκλ- in Hp.*Art.*38. 2. *cause to incline*, τι εἰς δεξιά Pl.*R.*436e; τὰ πράγματά τισι Arist.*Oec.* 1348b3:—Med., ἐ. εἰς τὰ δεξιὰ *lean* to the right, Id.*Phgn.*813a17. 3. Pass., *lean on*, X.*Smp.*3.13: metaph., πόνος ὔμμι ἐγκέκλιται labour *lies upon* you, Il.6.78. 4. ἐ. νῶτόν τινι *turn* one's back *towards* another, E.*Hec.*739. 5. Pass., *give way*, ὑπείκει καὶ θέλων ἐγκλίνεται Id.*Fr.*431.5. 6. Gramm., *pronounce as an enclitic*, A.D.*Synt.* 120.10; *pronounce with the grave accent*, Trypho ap.eund.*Conj.*255. 16:—Pass., A.D.*Pron.*35.26. b. ἐγκλινόμενα, τά, *inflected forms*, opp. ὀρθά, D.H.*Comp.*5, cf. A.D.*Synt.*30.11 (s. v. l.). 7. ἐ. φωνήν *lower* the voice, Luc.*Philops.*6. II. intr., *incline towards*, [ἡ καρδία] μικρὸν ἐ. εἰς τὸν ἀριστερὸν μαστόν Arist.*HA*496a16, cf. *PPetr.*2 p.126 (iii B.C.); [ἡ πολιτεία] ἐγκλίνειν βούλεται πρὸς τὴν ὀλιγαρχίαν Arist. *Pol.*1266a7, cf. 1307a21. 2. abs., *give way, flee*, X.*HG*7.2.14, *Cyr.* 3.3.65, Plb.1.57.8, Plu.*Fab.*12, etc.; also ἐ. τινί *give way to* him, D.H.5.54: c. acc., *give way to*, Plb.14.8.8. 3. *decline, become worse*, Plu.*Sull.*1, etc. 4. in Tactics, *wheel*, ἐπὶ δόρυ ἢ ἐπὶ ἀσπίδα Arr.*Tact.*21.3.

**ἐγκλίς·** ἡ καγκελλωτὴ θύρα, *EM*518.22.

⊛ **ἔγ-κλῐσις,** εως, ἡ, *inclination*, ἔ. λαβεῖν, of the earth, D.L.2.9, cf. Pl.*Amat.*132b; of the ecliptic (ὁ λοξὸς κύκλος), Arist.*GC*336b4; of ground, ἔ. ἔχειν πρὸς ἕω Id.*Pol.*1330a39; εἰς νότον Porph.*Antr.* 26; ἐγκλίσεις τῆς κεφαλῆς εἰς τὰ δεξιά Arist.*Phgn.*808a13; ἐ. σχημάτων τριγώνων Onos.10.28 (pl.); ἐ. δορατίου, in signalling, Id.26.1. 2. *the inclination* or *slope*, as of a wave, κατὰ τὴν ἔ. σκιασθῆναι Arist.*Col.* 792a22. 3. Medic., *displacement*, Hp.*Fract.*39 (pl.): generally, ὄγκων cj. in Epicur.*Ep.*1 p.14 U. 4. *modulation* of a singer's voice, D.Chr.32.49. 5. *failure, defeat*, *PMag.Par.*1.2445. II. in Gramm., 1. *mood of a verb*, D.H.*Comp.*6, D.T.638.7, A.D. *Synt.*248.14, etc. 2. *throwing back* of the accent, Id.*Pron.*8. 7, al.; *change of acute to grave accent*, Id.*Adv.*169.23. 3. *inflexion*, Simp.*in Cat.*65.8, Dexipp.*in Cat.*33.8: generally, of *derivative forms*, Simp.*in Cat.*37.11. **-κλῐτέον,** *one must use as enclitic*, Sch.Il.12.204, Sch.Th.*Oxy.*853 vi 25. **-κλῐτικός,** ή, όν, of a word *which leans* (ἐγκλίνει) *its accent upon the one before* (cf. A.D.*Synt.*98. 2), *enclitic*, Trypho ap.eund.*Conj.*255.11, etc. Adv. **-κῶς,** ἀναγιγνώσκειν *EM*124.9, A.D.*Synt.*222.22, Hdn.Gr.2.70: Comp. **-ώτερον** A.D.*Synt.*140.28.

**ἐγκλοιόω,** *enclose in a collar*, Lxx *Pr.*6.21 (Med.).

**ἐγκλονέομαι,** Pass., *gurgle in*, Hp.*Mul.*1.2.

**ἐγκλῠδ-άζομαι,** Pass., *make a splash*, Hp.*Morb.*1.15. **-αξις,** εως, ἡ, *splashing*, Diocl.*Fr.*43. **-αστικός,** ή, όν, *gurgling*, '*splashy*', Hp.*Acut.*62.

**ἐγ-κλύζω,** fut. -ύσω, *rinse the inside of* a thing, οἴνῳ with wine, D.S. 1.91. 2. *soak*, Dsc.5.75. 3. *treat by clysters*, τινά Id.4.154:—Pass., *to be administered as a clyster* or *injection*, Id.1.73, *Eup.*1.197, etc. **-κλυσμα,** ατος, τό, *injection, clyster*, Id.4.3, al. ⊛ **-κλυστέον,** *one must give a douche*, Paul.Aeg.3.66.

**ἐγκλώθω,** *spin* or *fasten to*, Sch.rec.S.*OT*1264.

**ἐγκνήθω,** *grate in*, in Med., Nic.*Th.*911 (ἐνικν-), *Al.*368.

**ἔγκνισμα,** ατος, τό, *a piece of meat*, Argive word in Plu.2.296f.

**ἐγκνώσσω,** *sleep in*, Mosch.2.6 (in poet. form ἐνικν-).

**ἐγκοακίσαι·** ἐγχέαι λάθρα, Hsch.

**ἐγκοιλ-αίνω,** *hollow, scoop out*, f.l. in Hdt.2.73:—Pass., Thphr. *HP*5.2.4. **-ιος,** ον, (κοιλία) *in the belly*:—as Subst., ἐγκοίλια, τά (sg. -ιον D.S.1.35). 1. *intestines*, Id.1.91, *SIG*958.13 (Ceos), Lxx *Le.*1.9. 2. *ribs of a ship, belly-timbers*, Thphr.*HP*4.2.8, Moschio ap.Ath.5.206f. II. *flat-bellied*, *Cat.Cod.Astr.*7.202. **-ος,** ον, *hollow, sunken*, ὀφθαλμοί Hp.*Prog.*2; ἔγκοιλόν τι a *sinking in* of the lip, Arist.*HA*604a28; τὰ ἔ. τῆς γῆς Pl.*Phd.*111c: Comp. **-ότερος** *deeper*, Lxx *Le.*13.30. II. *concave*, Thphr.*HP*7.13.1.

⊛ **ἐγκοιμ-άομαι,** Pass. with fut. Med., *sleep in* a place, [ἐν σπηλαίῳ] Arist.*Mir.*839a3; esp. *sleep in* a temple, to seek prophetic dreams or to obtain cure for a disease, Str.11.7.1, 16.2.35, Plu.2.109c; ὑπὲρ ἐνεργείας Arr.*Epict.*2.16.17. 2. *sleep upon* or *after* a meal, Hp.*Acut.* 29. ⊛ **-ησις,** εως, ἡ, *a sleeping in a temple* (v. foreg.), D.S.1. 53. ⊛ **-ητήριος,** α, ον, *for sleeping on*, ψίαθοι Poll.6.11: **-τήριον,** τό, *grave*, *BSA*18.145 (Beroea, ii B.C.). ⊛ **-ήτριον,** τό, = sq., in form -ητριν, *UPZ*85.8 (ii B.C.). ⊛ **-ητρον,** τό, *counterpane*, *PCair.Zen.* 48.4 (iii B.C.), Ammon.p.140 V.; expld. by *dormitorium*, *Gloss.* (also -ηθρον, -ητρα, ib.). **-ήτωρ** χιτών *night-gown*, Poll.10.123. **-ίζω,** *lull to sleep in*.., *AP*7.260 (Carph.): metaph., Hero *Aut.*16.2:—Pass., *IG*4.951.90 (Epid.).

**ἐγκοισῡρόομαι,** Pass., *to be luxurious as Coesyra* (a female name in the Alcmaeonid family), ἐγκεκοισυρωμένη Ar.*Nu.*48.

**ἐγκοιτ-άζομαι,** = ἐγκοιμάομαι, *IG*4.951.95 (Epid.). II. *to be embedded*, μέχρι τοῦ ἡμίσους Apollod.*Poliorc.*161.4; *to be soaked*,

*PLeid.X.*98. **-άς**, άδος, ἡ, *serving for a bed*, ἀκρῶρειαι *AP*7.626. **-έω**, *sleep in* or *on*, τῷ Καπιτωλίῳ D.C.65.8. **-ιος**, ον, *belonging to a bed*, στρώματα *EM*255.44: ἐγκοίτιον, τό, = ἐγκοιμητρον, Hsch. s. v. ἐνευναίου.

**ἐγκοιωτός**, ά, όν, (κοῖον) *given as security*, *Leg.Gort.*9.35.

**ἐγκόλ-αμμα**, ατος, τό, *anything engraven*, Lxx *Ex.*36.13(39.6); *engraved inscription*, *Inscr.Prien.*42.9 (pl.). **-απτός**, όν, *engraven, sculptured*, ἱστορία Ath.11.781e, cf. *Inscr.Prien.*37.168 (ii B.C.), Lxx 3*Ki.*6.28(29). **-άπτω**, *cut* or *carve upon* stone, ἐ. γράμματα ἐς τὸν τάφον Hdt.1.187, cf. *IG*1².313.166; ἐν τᾷ στάλᾳ ib.12(1).694.9 (Camirus); τύποι ἐν πέτρῃσι ἐγκεκολαμμένοι, γράμματα ἐν λίθῳ ἐγκ., Hdt.2.106, 136, al., cf. Lxx 3*Ki.*6.33(35); ἐπὶ τρίποσι Hdt.5.59; ἐπὶ πίνακος Suid. s. v. βοῦς ἕβδομος; εἰς τὸ μέτωπον Plu.*Per.*21: metaph., [νόμους] ἡ φύσις κατὰ μέσης ἐνεκόλαψε τῆς ψυχῆς Lib.*Decl.*43.49. ⊛ **-αψις**, εως, ἡ, *engraving, inscribing*, *IG*4.1484.265 (Epid.), 7.3073.11 (Lebad.).

**ἐγκολεήσατο**, *sheathed his sword*, Hsch., Suid.

⊛ **ἐγκοληβάζω**, in Ar.*Eq.*263, *gulp down, swallow up*, v. Sch. ad loc., Hsch.; also expld. by ἐπὶ κόλοις βαίνειν, Suid. s. v. ἐκολαβήσας.

⊛ **ἐγκολλ-άω**, *glue on* or *to*, *IG*1².373.208, Lxx *Za.*14.5 (Pass.), Hero *Aut.*24.2. **-ησις**, εως, Dor. **ἐγκόλλᾱσις**, ιος, ἡ, *fastening, soldering*, *IG*4.1485.167 (Epid.). **-ος**, ον, (κόλλα) *adhering, fitting*, Ph.1.610, al.

**ἐγκόλλουρα**, *torunda*, a kind of *bread*, *Gloss.*

⊛ **ἐγκολπ-ίας** ἄνεμος, a local wind *blowing from a bay*, Arist.*Mu.*394$^b$15. **-ίζω**, *form a bay*, ἠϊὼν ἐγκολπίζουσα Str.5.4.5. **2.** *go into* or *follow the bay*, Id.9.5.22. **3.** *inject into the vagina*, Aët.1.126. **II.** Med., with pf. Pass., *take in one's bosom*, ὥσπερ ἑρπετὰ τοὺς ἀπορρήτους λόγους Plu.2.508d, cf. Plot.1.4.6; *embrace*, θεὸς ἐγκεκόλπισται τὰ ὅλα Ph.1.425; περίοδος πολλοὺς ἀγκῶνας ἐγκολπιζομένη a period *embracing* many turns of expression, D.H.*Dem.*4 (vulg. ἐγκαλλωπιζομένη); [ἰχθῦς] ἐ. τῇ σαγήνῃ *to catch* fish *in the belly* of the net, Alciphr.1.18. **2.** *conceive*, Porph.*Gaur.*5.4. **3.** *embrace in a bay*, ἄκρα πολὺν -ομένη λιμένα Dion.Byz.53. **-ιος**, ον, *in* or *on the bosom*, διδόναι τι ἐ. τῷ ἀέρι Heraclit.*All.*39. **-ισμός**, ὁ, *vaginal douche* or *clyster*, Aët.3.153. ⊛ **-όω**, *make full and round, like the folds of a robe*, Orph.*A.*1183 (tm.):—Pass., ἐγκεκολπῶσθαι *to be curved into a bay* or *bays*, Arist.*Mu.*393$^a$23:—Med., *put in the fold of one's robe*: hence metaph., 'have in one's pocket', τὴν τοῦ Καίσαρος ἰσχύν D.C.48.52:—Pass., *to have folded round one*, χιτῶνα ἐνεκεκόλπωτο Id.62.2: metaph., ἀρετήν Mich.*in EN*603.24.

**ἐγκομβ-όομαι**, Med., (κόμβος) *bind* a thing *on oneself, wear* it *constantly*, Apollod.Car.4, 1*Ep.Pet.*5.5. **II.** Pass., = δέομαι, ἐνειλοῦμαι (Hsch.), Epich.7. ⊛ **-ωμα**, ατος, τό, a sort of *frock* or *apron*, worn esp. by slaves to keep the ἐξωμίς clean, Longus 2.33, Poll.4.119, Thd.*Is.*3.20, cf. Varro ap.Non.p.870 L.

**ἔγκομμα**, ατος, τό, *obstacle, hindrance*, *PSI*5.500 (iii B.C.), Al.*Ex.*34.12, Hsch.

⊛ **ἐγκον-έω**, *to be quick and active*, esp. *in service*, Hom., only part. pres., with another Verb, ἐπεὶ στόρεσαν λέχος ἐγκονέουσαι *in haste*, Od.7.340, Il.24.648, cf. Critias *Fr.*16 D.: later also in imper., ἐγκόνει *make haste!* S.*Aj.*988, Ar.*Ach.*1088; also ἐγκονῶμεν S.*Aj.*811; ἐγκονεῖτε Id.*Tr.*1255, E.*HF*521; οὐ θᾶττον ἐγκονήσεις; Ar.*Av.*1324: c. acc. cogn., κέλευθον ἥνπερ ἦλθες ἐγκόνει πάλιν *hasten* back the way by which thou camest, A.*Pr.*962: c. inf., Opp.*H.*4.103, Q.S.1.157.—Rare in Prose, Luc.*Anach.*4. **2.** *urge on, incite*, κυσίν *AP*6.268 (Mnasalc., s. v. l.). **-ητί**, Adv. *actively, vigorously, by perseverance*, Pi.*N.*3.36. ⊛ **-ῑμα**, ατος, τό, *room for sprinkling sand* (cf. sq.), *IG* 9(2).31 (Hypata, prob.). **-ίομαι**, Med., (κονίω) *sprinkle sand over oneself* after anointing, and before wrestling, X.*Smp.*3.8:—Pass., Luc.*Am.*45; *to be in the dust*, prob. l. in Hp.*Vict.*3.76. **-ίς**, ίδος, ἡ, *maid-servant*, Suid. **-ιστής**, Boeot. **-άς**, οῦ, ὁ, *sprinkler*, χρούσιος ἐ. *IG*7.2420 (votive offering to Cabiri). **-ως**, Adv. *eagerly*, Hsch.

**ἐγκοπ-εύς**, έως, ὁ, *tool for cutting stone, chisel*, Luc.*Somn.*3. **-ή**, ἡ, *incision*, Gal.7.38; *fracture* of skull, Sor.*Fract.*3, cf. Heliod.ap.Orib.46.12.1. **2.** *steps* cut in the wall of wells, etc., Ael.Dion.*Fr.*90. **II.** *hindrance*, οἴησις προκοπῆς ἐ. Heraclit.131, cf. Phld.*D.*3.6, 1*Ep.Cor.*9.12, Vett.Val.2.7 (pl.); material *obstacle*, D.S.1.32; *interruption, check*, τῆς ἁρμονίας D.H.*Comp.*22; τοῦ λόγου Aristid.*Rh.*2 p.514 S., cf. Iamb.*Protr.*21; κατ' ἐγκοπάς *disjointedly*, Longin.41.3.

**ἐγ-κοπιάω**, *labour without ceasing*, ἔργων ἐπιμελείαις καὶ κατασκευαῖς *IPE*1².40.21 (Olbia). **-κοπος**, ον, *wearied*, *AP*6.33 (Maec.), Lxx *Jb.*19.2, *Is.*43.23. **II.** *wearisome*, ib.*Ec.*1.8. **III.** *interrupted, checked*, πρᾶξις *Cat.Cod.Astr.*2.161. Adv. **-πως** Phld.*Rh.*1.23 S.

**ἔγκοπρος**, ον, *full of manure*, Hsch.

**ἐγκοπτικός**, ή, όν, *checking, hindering*, Ath.Med.ap.Orib.*inc.*21.8, Vett.Val.182.12, al., Eust.1216.52.

**ἐγκόπτω**, *knock in*, πάτταλον Thphr.*HP*2.7.6; χιλίας (i. e. πληγὰς) ἐς τὸ νῶτον ἐγκόψαι Herod.5.33. **2.** *engrave*, τὸ ψήφισμα ἐς στήλην *SIG*279.33 (Zelea):—Med., *IG*12(3).536 (Thera). **3.** *incise*, Dsc.*Eup.*1.141 (Pass.). **II.** *oppose*, Hp.*Praec.*13; λόγον λόγῳ Olymp.*in Mete.*125.9. **III.** *check, hold* the breath, Sor.1.69: generally, *hinder, thwart*, τισί *Sammelb.*4305; τῇ δικαιοδοσίᾳ f.l. in Plb.23.1.12; *delay*, *Act.Ap.*24.4:—Pass., ἐνεκοπτόμην τοῦ ἐλθεῖν *Ep.Rom.*15.22, cf. Porph.*Antr.*19. **IV.** intr., *come to a stop*, Vett.Val.260.24.

**ἐγκορδῠλέω**, *wrap up in coverlets*, Ar.*Nu* 10.

**ἐγκορύπτω**, fut. ἐγκορύψομαι, *butt at*, ἐ. ἐπί τινι πληγήν Lyc.558.

**ἐγκοσμέω**, *arrange in*, ἐγκοσμεῖτε τὰ τεύχε' . . νηΐ Od.15.218:—Pass., εἰς ἑτέραν σύγκρισιν Simp.*in Ph.*28.21 (ἐκκ- codd.). **II.** Pass., *to be adorned*, v.l. in Aristid.*Or.*26(14).99; εὐσχημοσύνῃ Lxx 4*Ma.*6.2 (v. l. ἐκκ-).

**ἐγκόσμιος**, ον, *mundane*, δυνάμεις Porph.*Antr.*9, cf. Sall.6, Procl.*Inst.*165, Dam.*Pr.*24; αἴτια Iamb.*Myst.*5.3; θεοί Procl.*in Alc.*p.68 C.; νοῦ Id.*in Prm.*p.588 S.

**ἐγκοσμογενεῖς**· τοὺς ἅμα τῷ κόσμῳ ἐγκριθέντας, Hsch.

**ἐγκοτ-έω**, *to be indignant at*, τινί A.*Ch.*41 (lyr.), S.*Fr.*1042, Lxx *Ge.*27.41. ⊛ **-ημα**, ατος, τό, = sq., ib.*Je.*31(48).39, Hsch. **-ησις**, εως, ἡ, *anger at one, hatred*, Aq.*Ho.*9.7. **-ητικός**, gloss on ζάκοτος, Apollon.*Lex.* **-ος**, ον, *bearing a grudge, spiteful, malignant*, στύγος A.*Ch.*392 (lyr.); of the Erinyes, ib.924, 1054; φθόνος *AP*7.40 (Diod.). Adv. **-τως**, ἔχειν Ph.2.520. **II.** Subst. ἔγκοτος, ὁ, *grudge*, ἔγκοτον ἔχειν τινί Hdt.3.59, 9.110; τινός *for* a thing, Id.8.29; διά τι Id.6.73, cf. 133; also ἔγκοτον, τό, D.H.9.7.

**ἐγκοτύλη** [ῠ], ἡ, *a game of pick-a-back*, in which a boy was carried about kneeling *on the hollow* of another's folded hands (κοτύλαι) (cf. Poll.9.122), Ath.11.479a, Paus.Gr.*Fr.*143.

**ἐγκουράς**, άδος, ἡ, *painting on the ceiling*, A.*Fr.*142; also pl., = τὰ ἐν τῷ προσώπῳ στίγματα, Hsch.

**ἐγκραγγάνω**, = ἐμβοάω, Hsch.

**ἐγκράζω**, aor. ἐνέκρᾰγον: pf. -κέκραγα:—*to cry aloud at* one, esp. *in anger*, τινί v. l. in Ar.*Pl.*428; ἐπί τινα v. l. in Th.8.84; φωνεῖν ὀξὺ καὶ ἐγκεκραγὸς Arist.*Phgn.*813$^b$5.

**ἐγκραιπᾰλ-άω**, *to be drunk at* or *with*, τρυφῇ Hdn.2.10.6:—also **-ίζω**, dub. in Phld.*Rh.*1.173 S.

**ἐγ-κράνῐον** [ᾰ], τό, *cerebellum*, Gal.*UP*8.6:—also **-κρᾱνίς**, ίδος, ἡ, ib.11.

**ἔγκρᾱσις**, εως, ἡ, *blending* of sounds, Nicom.*Harm.*2: metaph., *multiplication* of numbers, κατ' ἔγκρασιν, opp. κατὰ σύνθεσιν (addition), *Theol.Ar.*9, 37.

**ἐγκρᾱσίχολος** [ῐ], a small fish, *anchovy*, Arist.*HA*569$^b$27, Call.*Fr.*38, Ael.*NA*8.18.

**ἐγκρατ-εια** [ᾰ], ἡ, *mastery over*, ἐ. ἑαυτοῦ *self-control*, Pl.*R.*390b; ἐ. ἡδονῶν καὶ ἐπιθυμιῶν *control over* them, ib.430e, cf. X.*Mem.*2.1.1, Isoc.1.21; περί τι Arist.*EN*1149$^a$21, al. **II.** abs., *self-control*, X.*Mem.*1.5.1, Isoc.3.44, Arist.*EN*1145$^b$8, al., Lxx *Si.*18.30, *Act.Ap.*24.25, etc. **-ευμα**, ατος, τό, *instance of self-control*, Iamb.*VP*17.72 (pl.). ⊛ **-εύομαι**, *exercise self-control*, Arist.*EE*1223$^b$12, Lxx *Ge.*43.31, 1*Ep.Cor.*7.9; *force oneself* to do a thing, Lxx 1*Ki.*13.12; *starve oneself*, Vett.Val.127.20 (cf. ἀποκαρτερεῖν). **II.** *to be a member of the Encratite sect*, *Anatolian Studies* 87 (Phrygia). **-ευτής**, οῦ, ὁ, *ascetic*, esp. *faster*, Eust.554.8. **-έω**, *to be master of, exercise control over*, τῷ ἀλόγῳ Metop.ap.Stob.3.1.115, cf. Lxx *Ex.*9.2. ⊛ **-ής**, ές, (κράτος) *in possession of power*, S.*OT*941. **II.** *holding fast*, χεὶρ -εστάτη a hand *with the firmest hold*, X.*Eq.*7.8. **2.** *stout, strong*, ἐ. σθένει A.*Pr.*55; τὸν -έστατον σίδηρον S.*Ant.*474; ἐ. σῶμα X.*HG*7.1.23. **III.** c. gen. rei, *having possession of*, χωρέων Hdt.8.49, cf. 6.106, S.*Ph.*75, *SIG*58.7 (Milet., v B.C.), etc.; ναὸς ἐγκρατῆ πόδα the sheet *that controls* the ship, S.*Ant.*715; ἐ. αὐτῶν *masters of* themselves, Pl.*Phdr.*256b, al.; ἐ. ἀφροδισίων καὶ γαστρός X.*Mem.*1.2.1, cf. 2.1.7, *Oec.*12.16. **2.** abs., *master of oneself, self-controlled*, Pl.*Def.*415d; *self-disciplined*, Arist.*EN*1145$^b$13, al. **IV.** Adv. **-τῶς**, Ion. **-τέως** Hp.*Foet.Exsect.*4, etc.; *with a strong hand, by force*, ἄρχειν Th.1.76; ἐ. ἔχειν τὴν ἀρχήν Arist.*Pol.*1284$^a$40; **-τέως** *forcibly*, Theoc.25.266. **2.** *with self-control, temperately*, ἐ. ἔχειν Pl.*Lg.*710a; φέρειν τι D.Chr.2.53; **-τέως** Archestr.*Fr.*23.20. **-ησις**, εως, ἡ, *holding in* the breath, D.L.6.77. **-ίτης**, ου, ὁ, *member of the Encratite sect*, *Cod.Theod.*16.5.9. **-ούντως**, Adv. = ἐγκρατῶς, Phld.*Rh.*2.62 S.

**ἐγκραυγάζω**, *shout at* a person, Phld.*Lib.*p.5 O. (Pass.).

**ἐγκρέκων** σφυγμός, term coined by Archig.ap.Gal.8.662.

**ἐγκρεμαννῠμαι**, Pass., *to be hung up in*, *Gp.*2.4.2, al.

**ἐγκρέμᾰσις**, εως, ἡ, *suspension*, Hp.*Art.*76 (v. l. ἐκκρ-).

**ἐγκρί**· κοίλῳ καὶ κενῷ, Hsch.

**ἐγκρῐδοπώλης**, ου, ὁ, *dealer in* ἐγκρίδες, Ar.*Fr.*256, Nicopho 19.

**ἐγκρῐκάδεια**, = ἐγκοτύλη, Hsch., Theognost.*Can.*164.27.

**ἐγκρίκια**· ξύλα κεκαμμένα, Hsch.

**ἐγκρῐκόω**, *enclose as in a ring, bind as in a hoop*, Hp.*Oss.*18.

**ἐγκρίμνᾰμαι**, *to be suspended*, Hp.*Art.*76 (v. l. ἐκκρ-).

⊛ **ἐγκρίνω** [ῑ], *reckon in* or *among*: *reckon as*, τίν' ἄνδρ' ἄριστον ἐγκρίνειεν ἄν; E.*HF*183. **2.** of persons, *select, admit*, ἐ. ἢ συγκρ. 2*Ep.Cor.*10.12:—Pass., εἰς τὴν αἵρεσιν Pl.*Lg.*755d; εἰς τὴν γερουσίαν D.20.107; ⟨εἰς⟩ τὸ στάδιον X.*HG*4.1.40; of ἔφηβοι, *IG*7.29 (iii/ii B.C.); of athletes, Artem.1.59; ἐγκρινόμενος, ὁ, subject of statue by Alcamenes, Plin.*HN*34.72. **3.** *admit, accept*, opp. ἀποκρίνω, Pl.*Lg.*936a; ἐν τοῖς φιλοσόφοις Id.*R.*486d, cf. *Lg.*952a, al.; τρία γένη σημείων Phld.*Sign.*32; παλιγγενεσίαν Sch.Pi.*O.*2.104; *regard as genuine*, νομίσματα Phld.*Rh.*1.256 S.; *admit, sanction*, e. g. an author as classical, Suid. s. v. Δείναρχος. **4.** *approve*, Plb.9.2.4 (Pass.), Plu.2.11f; ἀριθμὸς ἐγκρίνεται *is adopted*, Ael.*Tact.*8.3.

⊛ **ἐγκρίς**, ίδος, ἡ, *a cake made with oil and honey*, Stesich.2, Pherecr.83, Antiph.275, Lxx *Ex.*16.31, Ph.1.214; also expld. as, = ἀμανίτης, Hsch.

**ἔγ-κρισις**, εως, ἡ, (ἐγκρίνω) *approval, judgement*, *IG*9(2).338.17 (Epist. Flaminini). **2.** *examination* of athletes before admitting them to a contest, Luc.*Pr.Im.*11, Artem.1.59, Aristid.*Or.*29(40).18 (pl.). **II.** *junction, meeting*, ἡ ἐπὶ τοὺς μηροὺς ἔ. Alciphr.1.

39. **-κρῐτέον**, *one must admit*, εἰς ἀριθμόν τινα, opp. ἀποκρ-, Pl.*R.*537a, cf. 413d; διορισμὸν ἐ. ὡς πιθανώτατον Dam.*Pr.*436, cf. Jul. *Or.*7.219a; *one must approve, recommend*, αἰώρας Herod.Med. in *Rh.Mus.*58.86: also pl. ἐγκριτέα ib.112. **-κρῐτήριος**, α, ον, *of* or *for admission*: ἐ. οἶκοι rooms *where* the athletes *were examined before they were admitted* as candidates, *IG*4.203.12 (Corinth, ii A.D.). **-κρῐτος**, ον, *admitted, accepted*, Pl.*Lg.*966d, *IG*12(9).189.9 (Eretria, iv B.C.); ἔ. θεά Herod.Med. in *Rh.Mus.*58.106.

**ἐγκροαίνω**, *spread oneself in*, διηγήσεσιν Eust.1050.31.

⊕ **ἐγκροστόω**, = Lat. *incrustare, veneer* with marble, *Supp.Epigr.*2.698 (Attalia).

**ἐγκρότᾰφος**· ὁ ἀντικέφαλος, *Et.Gud.*

**ἐγκροτέω**, *strike on* the ground, ἐς ἓν μέλος ἐγκροτέοισαι ποσσίν *beating time* with the feet to one tune, Theoc.18.7:—Med., πυγμαὶ δ' ἦσαν ἐγκροτούμεναι the fists were *dashing one against the other*, E.*IT* 1368. II. Pass., *to be fastened by nails*, τοίχῳ Philostr.*VA*2.20.

**ἐγκρούω**, *knock* or *hammer in*, παττάλους εἰς τὸν τοῖχον Ar.*V.*130; ἥλους εἰς τὰ ὑποδήματα Thphr.*Char.*4.13; *strike*, ἐγκρούουσα ποσσὶ λάλους πτέρυγας, of the locust, *AP*7.195.4 (Mel.). II. *dance*, Ar.*Ra.*374.

**ἐγ-κρύβω** [ῠ], late form of ἐγκρύπτω, D.S.1.80 (Pass.), Apollod.3.13.6, Gal.6.620, *PHolm.*5.7. **-κρυμμα**, ατος, τό, *anything concealed, an ambuscade*, Eust.932.17. **-κρυπτέον**, *one must bury, cover up*, Herod.Med.ap.Orib.10.8.10. **-κρυπτος**, = ἐγκρυφίας, Hsch. ⊕ **-κρύπτω**, *hide* or *conceal in*, δαλὸν σποδιῇ ἐνέκρυψε μελαίνῃ Od.5.488, cf. Sotad.Com.1.29; [ᾠὰ] ἐν δέρματι λαγωοῦ Arist.*HA* 619b15; τι εἴς τι *Ev.Matt.*13.33, Apollod.1.5.1 (Pass.), etc. 2. πῦρ ἐ. *bank* it *up*, Ar.*Av.*841. 3. Med., *hide oneself*, μελάθροις Nonn.*D.*32.285. **-κρῠφιάζω**, intr., *keep oneself hidden, act underhand*, Ar.*Eq.*822. 2. *hide, conceal*, πάθος Procop.*Arc.*1: abs., Id.*Vand.*1.25. **-κρῠφίας** ἄρτος loaf *baked in the ashes*, Hp.*Vict.*2.42, Nicostr.Com.14, Luc.*DMort.*20.4, Ath.3.110b. **-κρύφιος**, ον, = sq., πῦρ *AP*5.123 (Phld.). **-κρῠφος**, ον, *hidden*, ἥβη Nonn.*D.*28.295. **-κρύφω** [ῠ], = ἐγκρύπτω, impf. ἐνέκρυφεν Q.S.14.556, Nonn.*D.*6.135. ⊕ **-κρυψις**, εως, ἡ, *banking up* of a fire, Arist.*Juv.* 470a12.

⊕ **ἐγκτάομαι**, *acquire possessions in* a foreign country, πόλιν ἐν Θρηΐκῃ (v.l. for ἐγκτισ-) Hdt.5.23; οἱ ἐγκεκτημένοι citizens *who possess property in* a deme not their own, opp. δημόται, D.50.8, cf. X.*Vect.*2.4, *PGnom.*243.

**ἐγκτερεΐζω**, *bury in*, τύμβῳ A.R.1.1060, cf. Tryph.179.

**ἔγ-κτημα**, ατος, τό, *land held in a country* by a person not belonging to it, And.3.15, D.7.42, *IG*2².43.27, App.*Mith.*47. ⊕ **-κτησις**, Dor. **-κτᾱσις**, εως, ἡ, *tenure of land in a country* or *district* by a person not belonging to it, X.*HG*5.2.19 (pl.); *the right of holding such property*, freq. granted as a privilege or reward to foreigners, ἔγκτασιν γᾶς καὶ οἰκίας Decr.Byz.ap.D.18.91, cf. *IG*5(1).4.12 (Sparta), etc.; εἶναι δὲ αὐτῷ οἰκίας ἔγκτησιν ib.2².53. 2. *estate, property*, Lxx *Le.*25.13, etc.; βιβλιοθήκη ἐγκτήσεων register *of properties*, *BGU*76 (ii A.D.), etc. 3. *acquisition of territory*, Plb.28.20.8 (prob. l.). **-κτητικόν**, τό, *a land-tax paid for the right of holding* ἐγκτήματα, *IG*2².1214. **-κτητος**, η, ον, *possessed in* a foreign country, Lxx *Le.*14.34, al. **-κτήτωρ**, ορος, ὁ, *landowner*, Keil-Premerstein *Dritter Bericht*86.

**ἐγκτίζω**, *found, build among*, πόλεις ἔθνεσιν Plu.2.328e:—Med., πόλιν ἐν Θρηΐκῃ v.l. in Hdt.5.23 (cf. ἐγκτάομαι).

**ἐγκῠαρ**, ἄρος, ἡ, *pregnant*, ὄϊς *Schwyzer*725.6 (Milet., vi B.C.).

**ἐγκῠβιστάω**, *plunge headlong into*, πράγμασιν Suid. s.v. κύβος.

⊕ **ἔγκῡδον**· ἔνδοξον, Hsch.

⊕ **ἐγκῠ-έομαι**, *to be borne in the womb*, Theon *Prog.*2. **-ησις**, εως, ἡ, *germination*, in plants, Thphr.*CP*1.6.3. **-ητήριον**, τό, *drug which promotes conception*, Hp.*Steril.*231.

**ἐγκῠκάω**, *mix up in*, Ar.*Ach.*939 (Med.):—Act., Dsc.*Ther.*2, Lyc.674.

⊕ **ἐγκυκλ-έομαι**, Pass., *roll* or *rotate in* the sockets, of the joints, Hp.*de Arte*10. II. in com. sense, *to be cooped up*, οὐκ οἶδ' ὅπῃ ἐγκεκύκλησαι Ar.*V.*699. III. Med., *surround*, Plu.*TG*5; τοὺς ἀμφὶ πλουσίαν τράπεζαν -κυκλουμένους Id.2.50d. **-ηθρον**, τό, Eust.976.15, is prob. f.l. for ἐκκύκληθρον, = ἐκκύκλημα. **-ημα**, ατος, τό (v. ἐκκύκλημα); but, II. ἐγκυκλήματα, τά, *movable property*, Arist.*Oec.*1346a13. **-ίζω**, *revolve*, τὰ ὀπίσθια *Hippiatr.*30. ⊕ **-ιος**, ον, also α, ον Orph.*A.*981: (κύκλος):—*circular, round*, χοροί E.*IT*429 (lyr.), Aeschin.1.10; τὸ ἐ. σῶμα Arist.*Cael.*286a11; ἐ. κίνησις, φορά, motion *in a circle*, ib.293a11, 296a35; δρόμημα θεῶν *Corp.Herm.*3.3. Adv. -ίως *in a circle*, φέρεσθαι Arist.*Mete.*339a12, cf. Euc.*Phaen.*p.2 M., Hero *Aut.*11.8, Plu.2.1004c; καθῆσθαι Asp.*in EN*10.31. II. *revolving in a cycle, recurrent*: hence, at Athens, λῃτουργίαι ἐ. public services *required regularly* every year, opp. to those required at uncertain times, D.20.21; ἐ. δίκαια rights *common to all citizens*, Id.25.74. III. *ordinary, everyday*, ἐν τοῖς ἐ. καὶ τοῖς καθ' ἡμέραν γιγνομένοις Isoc.3.22, cf. 8.87, Arist.*Pol.*1269b35; ἐ. διακονίαι *everyday* duties, ib.1263a21; τὰ ἐ. καὶ πολιτικά Epicur.*Sent.Vat.*58; ἡ ἐ. διοίκησις *IG*12(5).653.56 (Syros, i B.C.); ἐ. ἀναλώματα ib.1.329; ἐ. [τέλη] taxes *farmed out annually*, ib.11(2).161 A 36, 203 A 29 (Delos, iii B.C.); ταμίαι τῶν ἐ. *SIG*577.11 (Milet., iii/ii B.C.). b. μεγάλοις ἐ. συμπτώμασιν (sc. πάθος) *commonly liable to*, Phld.*Ir.*p.29 W. 2. Arist., τὰ ἐ. φιλοσοφήματα or τὰ ἐ., = τὰ ἐξωτερικά, *Cael.*279a30; ἐν τοῖς ἐ. εἴρηται *EN*1096a3. 3. ἐ. παιδεία *general* education, prior to professional studies, D.H.*Comp.*25, Plu.2.1135d; οἱ περὶ τὰ ἐ. παιδευταί Id.*Alex.*7; τὰ ἐ. παιδεύματα Id.2.7c, cf. Vitr.6 *Praef.*4, Quint.*Inst.*1.10.1, Ath.4.184b, Luc.*Am.*45; also ἐ. ἀγωγή instruction *in general knowledge*, Str.1.1.22; ἐ. τέχνη Olymp.Alch.p.91 B. IV. ἐγκύκλιον, τό, *tax on sales*, *PLond.*3.1200 (ii B.C.), *PAmh.*2.53 (ii B.C.), etc.

**ἐγκυκλοπαιδεία**, f.l. for ἐγκύκλιος παιδεία, Quint.*Inst.*1.10.1, cf. Plin.*HN Praef.*

⊕ **ἔγκυκλ-ος**, ον, *circular*, δίνη Epicur.*Ep.*2 p.52 U.; *round*, Matro *Conv.*116, Ezek.*Exag.*77. Adv. -ως Gal.18(2).439. II. ἔγκυκλον, τό, *woman's upper garment*, Ar.*Th.*261, *Lys.*113; ἐ. ποικίλον *IG*2.754.48. III. ἔγκυκλα· τὰ ἐγκυκλούμενα τῷ βίῳ καὶ συνήθη, Hsch. **-όω**, *move round in a circle*, ὀφθαλμόν E.*IT*76. II. *surround*, Str.2.5.24:—more freq. in Med. with pf. part. Pass., *encompass, encircle*, τοῦ χθόν' ἐγκυκλουμένου αἰθέρος E.*Ba.*292, cf. Ar.*V.*699; φωνή μέ τις ἐγκεκύκλωται a voice *has echoed around* me, ib.395; *surround, hem in*, Plu.*Marc.*6, etc.; of rivers or mountains, Str.2.1.36, D.C.49.37:—Pass., *to be surrounded*, Id.56.12 (s.v.l.). 2. in late Prose, *wander, roam about*, ἐγκυκλωθῆναι Σικελίαν D.S.4.23, etc. **-ωσις**, εως, ἡ, *surrounding, encompassing*, Str.2.1.36.

**ἐγκῠλίδωτος** (leg. ἐγκυλίωτος), ον, *rolled up*, ἔριον Hp.*Mul.*1.75.

**ἐγκῠλίνδ-ησις**, εως, ἡ, *rolling among*, ἐν πόρναις Plu.*Oth.*2. **-ω** (ἐγκυλίω Hp.*Mul.*1.75, Arist.*Pr.*914a22, Vett.Val.118.15, etc.), fut. -κυλίσω [ῑ]:—*roll* or *wrap up in*, πολλοῖς ἐμαυτὸν ἐγκυλίσαι πράγμασιν Pherecr.146.2; τι ἐς ἔριον Hp. l.c. II. metaph. in Pass., *to be involved in*, εἰς ἔρωτας ἐγκυλισθείς X.*Mem.*1.2.22, cf. Vett.Val. l.c.; εἰς τὰς πολιτικὰς πράξεις D.H.11.36; ἐν κακοῖς Porph.*Chr.*26; πράγμασι *Cat.Cod.Astr.*7.208:—in aor. Med., ἐγκυλίσασθαι Luc.*Hipp.*6.

**ἐγκύλ-ισμα** [ῠ], ατος, τό, = ἀλινδήθρα, Sch.Ar.*Nu.*32. **-ισμός**, ὁ, = ἐγκυλίνδησις, in mal. part., Vett.Val.118.17 (pl.).

**ἐγκύμᾰτος** [ῡ], ον, *on the waves*, ὁδοιπορία Secund.*Sent.*17.

⊕ **ἐγκῠμ-ονέω**, *become pregnant*, *Gp.*14.26.2; τὸν Δία *conceive*, Apollod.1.1.5. **-ων**, ον, gen. ονος, (κῦμα B) *pregnant*, X.*Cyn.*7.2, Arist.*HA*546b10, etc.; ἐ. γενέσθαι ὑπό τινος Id.*Fr.*76; ἵππος ἐ. τευχέων *big with* arms, of the Trojan horse, E.*Tr.*11; ἐ. ἄμυλος Pl.Com.174.8; πόα ἐ. σπέρματος Dsc.3.7: metaph., of the mind, Pl.*Smp.*209b, *Ph.*651, etc.; καμάτων ἐγκύμονα βίβλον *AP*9.210.

**ἐγκῠοποιέω**, *impregnate*: metaph. of a chemical reaction, Zos. Alch.p.211 B.

**ἔγκῠος**, ον, (κύω) = ἐγκύμων, Hdt.1.5, 6.131, Hp.*Aph.*5.42, etc.; πῶλος ἡσυχίης ἔγκυος, of the Trojan horse, *AP*9.156 (Antiphil.); γαστρὸς ἀπωσαμέναν μόρον ἔγκυον, of one dying in child-birth, *Epigr.Gr.* 238 (Smyrna), cf. *IG*12(7).301 (Amorgos). 2. of plants, Arist.*HA*595b27.

⊕ **ἐγκύπτω**, *stoop down and peep in*, ἐ. εἴς τι *look closely* into, Hdt.7.152; κατὰ [τὰς θυρίδας] Pl.*R.*359d: abs., ἐγκεκυφότες *stooping to the ground*, Ar.*Nu.*191, Th.4.4; δάκτυλοι ἐγκύπτοντες *retracted*, Hp.*Hebd.*51.

**ἐγκῠρ-έω**, v. ἐγκύρω. **-ησις**, εως, ἡ, *meeting with* or *happening*, Phld.*Rh.*1.71 S., S.E.*P.*1.37. 2. in Medicine, *definite phenomenon*, *BKT*3 p.30.

**ἐγκυρσεύω**, = ἐγκυρέω, Heraclit.17 (s.v.l.).

**ἐγκύρτ-ια**, τά, (κύρτος) *passages into the* κύρτος or *creel* or *fish-trap*, to which Pl. compares the throat, *Ti.*78b-d, cf. Gal. ad loc.p.20 D. **-ος**, ον, *curved* or *crooked*, Hp.*Mochl.*1, Arist.*Pr.*908b29. **-ωσις**, εως, ἡ, *curvature*, Cass.*Pr.*38.

**ἐγκύρω** [ῠ], impf. ἐνέκῡρον: fut. ἐγκύρσω: aor. ἐνέκυρσα:—**Pass.**, ἐγκύρομαι: **ἐγκυρέω**, aor. 1 ἐνεκύρησα, less freq. in early writers, Heraclit.72, freq. in Phld. as *Sign.*21, al., cf. Plb. and D.H. (v. infr.), Ael.*Tact.*1.2:—*fall in with, light upon, meet with*, c. dat., ἐνέκυρσε φάλαγξι Il.13.145; ἐγκύρσας ἀάτῃσιν Hes.*Op.*216; ὁκοίοις ἐγκυρέωσιν ἔργμασι Archil.70; ἐγκύρσαις (Aeol. aor. 1 part.) ἑκατονταετεῖ βιοτᾷ Pi.*P.*4.282, cf. 1.100; δύᾳ B.*Fr.*21; τμητοῖς ὁλκοῖς ἐγκῦρσαι S.*El.*863 (lyr.); στρατῷ ἐνέκυρσε ἀμφοτέρῃσι τῇσι μοίρῃσι Hdt.4.125; ἐνεκύρησαν στρατῷ Id.7.218, cf. Plb.8.35.5, etc.; δυσχωρίαις ἐγκυρήσαντες D.H.3.59; τυράννοις Phld.*Ir.*p.30 W.: in Hdt.7.208, c. gen., ἀλογίης ἐνέκυρσε πολλῆς (here Valck. proposed ἐκύρησε, which has been received by edd.): c. acc., Ἀΐδαν ἐγκύρσαντες ἀλάμπετον *Epigr.Gr.*241 (Smyrna).—Not in Att. Prose, once in Com., ἐγκυρῆσαι Cratin.35.

⊕ **ἐγκῠσίκωλος** [ῑ] or **ἐγκῠσόχωλος**, = ἄνωθεν ἀπὸ τοῦ κυσοῦ χωλός, *Com.Adesp.*6 D.

**ἔγκῠτα**, τά, Lacon., = ἔγκατα, Hsch.

**ἐγκῠτί**, Adv., (κύτος) *to the skin*, ἐγκυτὶ κεκαρμένος *close* shaven, Archil.27, cf. Call.*Fr.*311. [ῑ Archil., ῐ Call.]

**ἐγκύφωσις** [ῡ], εως, ἡ, *curvature*, Gal.8.246.

**ἐγκώλεος**, *trunculus*, *Gloss.*

**ἐγκωλύω**, aor. ἐνεκώλυσα, f.l. for ἐνεκόλλησα, Hero *Aut.*24.2.

**ἐγκωμάζω**, *take part in a* κῶμος, *revel*, *Gloss.*

**ἐγκωμι-άζω**, impf. ἐνεκωμίαζον Aeschin.3.86: fut. -άσω Pl.*Grg.*518e, 519a, Isoc.12.111, but -άσομαι Pl.*Smp.*198d, Aeschin.1.33: aor. ἐνεκωμίασα Pl.*La.*191b: pf. ἐγκεκωμίακα Id.*Lg.*629c, Isoc.7.71:—**Pass.**, aor. ἐγκωμιασθείς Hdt.5.5: pf. ἐγκεκωμίασμαι Pl.*Smp.*177c (the tenses being formed as if the Verb were a compound of ἐν and *κωμιάζω, and not derived directly from ἐγκώμιος):—*praise, laud, extol*, c. dupl. acc., ταῦτα τὴν δικαιοσύνην Id.*R.*363d; τινὰ ἐπὶ σοφίᾳ Id.*Euthphr.*9b; κατὰ τοῦτο Id.*La.*191b; περὶ τὴν μάχην Id.*Tht.*142b; τὴν τέχνην τινός Id.*Grg.*448e: abs., Phld.*Herc.*1457.8:—Pass., *to be praised*, Hdt.5.5, Pl.*Smp.*181a; *to be said in panegyric*, Phld.*Herc.*

1457 *Fr.*14, etc. -αστέον, *one must eulogize*, Id.*Rh.*1.219 S., S.E. *M.*2.101; θεούς Hermog.*Prog.*7. ⊛ -αστής, οῦ, ὁ, *praiser, panegyrist*, Str.15.1.68, Plu.2.605a. -αστικός, ή, όν, *panegyrical*, Arist.*Rh.Al.*1421ᵇ9, Plb.8.11.2, Ph.2.31; -ικόν, τό, Plu.2.743d, Longin.8.3, Demetr.*Eloc.*120. Adv. -κῶς Poll.4.26. -αστός, ή, όν, *to be praised*, Ph.1.453.

⊛ ἐγκωμικός, ή, όν, = ἐγκωμιαστικός, λόγοι *IG*12(9).95ᵃ (Tamynae).

ἐγκωμιο-γράφος [ἄ], ὁ, *panegyric-writer*, Artem.1.56 (pl.); εἰς τὸν αὐτοκράτορα *IG*7.1773.11 (Thebes). -λογικόν (sc. μέτρον), τό, *metre used in* ἐγκώμια, Heph.15.10. -λόγος, ὁ, *one who delivers panegyrics*, *IG*12(9).94 (Tamynae, i B.C.).

ἐγκώμιον, τό, v. sq. II.2.

⊛ ἐγκώμιος, ον, (κώμη) *in the village*: hence, *native, common*, v.l. for ἐγχώριος, Hes.*Op.*344. II. (κῶμος) *belonging to a* κῶμος, esp. that which escorted a victor in the games: hence, *belonging to the praise of a conqueror*, ἐ. μέλη, ὕμνοι, Pi.*O.*2.47, *P.*10.53; ἐ. ἀμφὶ τρόπον Id. *O.*10(11).77; στεφάνων ἐγκώμιος τεθμός the law *of praise* for prizes won, ib.13.29. 2. Subst. ἐγκώμιον, τό, *laudatory ode*, D.S.11.11, Ath.13.573f; generally, *eulogy, panegyric*, Ar.*Nu.*1205, D.18.207 (pl.), Thphr.*Char.*3.2, etc.; ἐγκώμια παλαιῶν ἀνδρῶν Pl.*Prt.*326a; ἐ. εἴς τινα, κατά τινος, Pl.*Min.*319c, D.6.9; ἐ. λογικόν in prose, *IG*7.2727 (Acraephia); ἐ. ἐπικόν ib.419 (Oropus); ὁ ἔπαινος τῆς ἀρετῆς, opp. τὰ ἐ. τῶν ἔργων, Arist.*EN*1101ᵇ33, cf. *Rh.*1367ᵇ28.

ἔγκων, coined as etym. of ἀγκών, Chrysipp.*Stoic.*2.47.

ἐγκώπαια· περιδέραια, Suid.

ἔγκωπον, τό, *part* of the ship *between the foremost and hindmost oars*, Callix.1.

ἔγμα· ὀχύρωμα, στῦλος, Hsch. ἔγμεν· ἔχειν, Id. ἐγνωδώς· σὺν θεῷ, Id.

ἐγξέω, *scratch, scrape*, E.*Fr.*298 (cj. Heath for ἐγξῦσαι).

ἐγξηραίνω, *dry in*, Hp.*Mul.*1.104.

ἔγξῦλος, ον, *wooden*, δέλτος f.l. in Aen.Tact.31.14; πυραί Tz.*H.*10.502.

ἐγξύρω [ῡ], *shave*, κεφαλήν Tz.*H.*3.512.

ἐγξύω [ῡ], = ἐγξέω, Hp.*Int.*42; *shred in*, ἐς μέλι Thphr.*HP*9.13.3.

ἐγρε-κύδοιμος [ῠ], ον, *rousing the din of war, strife-stirring*, epith. of Pallas, Hes.*Th.*925, Lamprocl.1. -μάχης [ᾰ], ου, ὁ, *exciting, rousing the fight*, S.*OC*1054 (lyr.): fem. ἐγρεμάχη, epith. of Pallas, *h.Cer.*424, *IG*1².573. -μοθος, ον, *stirring strife*, Nonn.*D.*20.291, al.

ἔγρεο, ἔγρετο, v. ἐγείρω and ἔγρω.

ἐγρεσί-κωμος [ῐ], ον, *stirring up to revelry*, epith. of Dionysus, *AP* 9.524.6. -οικος, ον, *building houses*, prob. in Man.4.325.

ἐγρήγορα, ἐγρήγορθε, -θαι, -θασι, v. ἐγείρω.

⊛ ἐγρηγορ-έω, f.l. in X.*Cyn.*5.11, Arist.*Pr.*877ᵃ9, etc. -ικός, ή, όν, *waking*, πράξεις, κινήσεις, Arist.*Somn.Vig.*456ᵃ28, *Div.Somn.*463ᵃ9. -ος, ον, *wakeful*, Adam.*Phgn.*2.28, Poll.3.120. Adv. -ρως Mich. *in PN*70.2, al., Sch.Il.10.182. -ότως, Adv. part. of ἐγρήγορα, *waking*, Plu.2.32a, Luc.*Herm.*1 (v.l.), Porph.*Plot.*9. -όων, Ep. part., *watching, awake*, Od.20.6. -σιος, ον, *keeping awake*, Pherecr.208. -σις, εως, ἡ, *waking, wakefulness*, Hp.*Hum.*9, Arist.*HA*536ᵇ24, Ph.1.71, al., Onos.10.11, D.Chr.3.85, Plot.6.8.16; περὶ ὕπνου καὶ ἐγρηγόρσεως, title of work by Arist. -τέον, *one must keep awake*, Antyll.ap.Orib.6.6.3. -τί [ῐ], Adv. *awake, watching*, Il.10.182.

⊛ ἔγρηνται· ἤρηνται, Hsch. ἐγρήσασα· μαθοῦσα, Id.

⊛ ἐγρήσσω, (ἐγείρω) *watch, awake*, Il.11.551, Od.20.33, 53, A.R.2.308, Aret.*CA*1.1, etc.

ἐγρῆτα· παρακαταβολὴν ἢ δίκης ἢ κρίσεως, Hsch. ἐγρυπνεῖ· ἀγρυπνεῖ, Id. ἔγρυσις, v. ἔκρ-.

⊛ ἔγρω, later form of ἐγείρω, imper. ἐγρέτω cj. in Sopat.10; ἔγρει Call.*Hec.*1.4.13:—Pass., ἔγρεσθε E.*Rh.*532; ἔγρεται Opp.*H.*5.241; ἔγρονται E.*Fr.*773.29 (lyr.); ἔγρετο Opp.*C.*3.421.

⊛ ἐγχαδές (prob. ἐγχαλές, cf. χάλις)· νέον ἄκρατον, Hsch.

*ἐγχαίνω, v. ἐγχάσκω.

ἐγχᾰλάω, *relax*, in Pass., Plu.2.690a, Antyll.ap.Orib.44.8.4.

ἐγχαλεῖν· καταχασμᾶσθαι (Lacon.), Hsch. ἐγχαλίδες· διαπεπαρμένοι ἧλοι, Id.

⊛ ἐγχᾰλῑνόω, *put a bit in the mouth of*, ἵππον Babr.76.14:—Pass., τὰ στόματα ἐγκεχαλινωμένους *having the bit in* their mouths, Hdt.3.14, cf. X.*An.*7.2.21. 2. metaph., Ph.1.117:—Pass., τὸν δῆμον ἐγκεχαλινωμένον τῇ ὀλιγαρχίᾳ *held in check* by the oligarchy, Plu.*Lys.*21; ὀργὴ -ωμένη τῷ λόγῳ Them.*Or.*17.214d. 3. metaph. of reins, *to be in the form of a bit*, Hp.*Oss.*19.

ἐγχαλκ-εύω, *to impress* or *design on brass*, Sch.B.Il.18.468. ⊛ -ος, ον, *in* or *with brass*: *moneyed, rich*, *AP*11.425. II. *for sale*, Ath. 13.584e. III. *with a flavour of copper*, Dsc.5.103.

ἐγχανδής, v. εὐχανδής.

ἐγχᾰρ-ακτέον, *one must scarify*, Paul.Aeg.3.27. ⊛ -αξις, εως, ἡ, *scarification*, Apollon.ap.Orib.7.19 tit., Aret.*CD*1.2. II. *furrow*, gloss on ὁλκός, Sch.A.R.3.413. ⊛ -άσσω, Att. -ττω, *engrave*, τινί *upon* a thing, D.H.2.55; ἐς στάλλαν *IG*12(2).67 (Mytilene); εἰς τὸ ἱερόν *GDI*2322.16 (Delph.), cf. Plu.*Per.*21, etc.; κατά τινος Id.*Them.*9; *insert* in a document, *CPR*19.18 (iv A.D.): metaph., *imitate*, ἐ. τὸν Ἀντισθένειον τύπον Jul.*Or.*7.217a:—Pass., τὰ ἐγκεχαραγμένα ἀγαθά *OGI*666.17 (i A.D.); μεγάλως ἐγκεχαραγμένος *with a great record*, Charito 2.6; of coins, Luc.*Alex.*58; δραχμαὶ ἐγκεχαραγμέναι γράμμασιν Ἑλληνικοῖς ἐπίσημα *Peripl.M.Rubr.*47; of soldiers, *to be entered on a muster-roll*, Agath.5.15. II. *to make an incision into* a thing, *Gp.*5.38.2; *scarify*, Antyll.ap.Orib.7.16.3.

⊛ ἐγχᾰρίζομαι, = χαρίζομαι, *AP*9.114 (Parmen., dub.).

⊛ ἐγχάσκω, fut. ἐγχανοῦμαι: aor. ἐγχανεῖν:—lit., *gape*, πρὸς τὴν σελήνην Luc.*Icar.*13; ἐ. τῷ πλακοῦντι *to gape for* it, Alciphr.1.22. II. *grin* or *scoff at* one, ἐγχάσκειν σοι Ar.*V.*721; προσέχειν διαλεγομένῳ καὶ ἐ. Phld.*Vit.*p.41 J., cf. Luc.*Merc.Cond.*14; τῇ 'μῇ μωρίᾳ S.*Ichn.*343; ἐγχανεῖται ταῖς ἐμαῖς τύχαισι Ar.*Ach.*1197; ἐγχανεῖται τῇ πόλει Id.*Eq.*1313: c. part., μὴ γὰρ ἐγχάνῃ ποτὲ.. ἐκφυγών *let* him not *taunt* [us] *with* his having escaped, Id.*Ach.*221.

ἐγχέζω, fut. -χέσω or -χεσοῦμαι: pf. ἐγκέχοδα, = Lat. *incacare*, Ar.*Ra.*479: c. acc., *to be in a horrid fright at* one, Id.*V.*627.

ἐγχει-βρόμος, ον, *thundering with the spear*, κόρα Pi.*O.*7.43. -γάστωρ· ὁ διὰ τοῦ δόρατος ζῶν, Zonar.

ἐγχεῖδαι· τηρηταὶ δανείων, Hsch.

⊛ ἐγχείη, ἡ, Ep. form of ἔγχος, *spear, lance*, Hom., esp. in Il.: gen. pl., ἐγχειάων 5.167; ἐγχείῃ ἐκέκαστο he excelled all *in the spear*, 2.530.

ἐγχείῃ, Ep. 3 sg. pres. subj. of ἐγχέω, Od.9.10.

ἐγχεικέραυνος, ον, *hurling the thunderbolt*, Ζῆνα Pi.*P.*4.194, *O.*13.77, Eust.839.10, etc.

ἐγχειμάζω, *pass the winter in*, Jul.*Ep.*185, Poll.1.62; πόλις ἐγχειμάσαι οἵα χειρίστη Dicaearch.1.21.

ἐγχεί-μαργος, ον, = ἐγχεσίμαργος, *EM*313.14. -μορος, ον, *dealing death with the spear*, ib.630.24.

⊛ ἐγχειρ-έω, Arc. ἰγχηρέω *IG*5(2).6.12 (Tegea, iv B.C.): (χείρ):—*take* a thing *in hand, undertake, attempt*, c. dat. rei, E.*Med.*377, X.*Vect.*6.1, etc.: later, c. acc. rei, ἔργον *PPetr.*2 p.37 (iii B.C.): c. inf., Pl. *Prt.*310c, X.*Mem.*2.3.12, etc.; τὸν ἐγχειρήσαντα συκοφαντεῖν Hyp. *Eux.*34: abs., *to make an attempt* or *beginning*, S.*El.*1026, Th.4.4, etc. 2. *lay hands on, attack*, πόλεσι ib.122: abs., X.*HG*4.5.16; πρὸς τὰ κατὰ τοὺς πολεμίους Plb.2.22.11. 3. *put hand to* a case requiring medical treatment, τινί Hp.*de Arte*3; τῇσι νούσοισιν ib. 13. 4. *try one's hand* in argument, εἰς ἑκάτερον Plu.*Cic.*21:—Pass., *to be discussed*, Id.2.687e codd. II. in late Poets, *take in hand*, c. acc., ἔργον *Epigr.Gr.*1038.36.—ἐπιχειρέω is more common in Att. -ημα, ατος, τό, *undertaking, attempt*, S.*OT*540, Pl. *Plt.*290d, Antiph.29, D.27.34, Aen.Tact.24.15, Plu.*Cleom.*25, etc.; *essay in argument*, Epicur.*Dial.*1413.7 (pl.). -ησις, εως, ἡ, *taking in hand, undertaking*, Th.6.83, Plu.*Caes.*66, etc. II. ἀνατομικαὶ ἐ., *Practical* Anatomy, title of work by Gal. -ητέον, *one must undertake*, X.*Ages.*1.1, Pl.*Plt.*304a, D.Chr.18.5: pl., -ητέα τῷ ἔργῳ Agath. *Praef.*p.133 D. -ητής, οῦ, ὁ, *one who undertakes*, καινῶν ἔργων Ar. *Av.*257; πράξεως Ph.2.27: abs., Adam.*Phgn.*2.39. -ητικός, ή, όν, *enterprising, adventurous*, X.*HG*4.8.22. Adv. -κῶς Archyt.ap.Stob.4.50.2. -ία, ἡ, *manipulation*, v.l. for εὐχ-, Hp.*Art.*35, cf. Phld.*Hom.* p.45 O.: pl., Hsch. -ίδιος, ον, (χείρ) *in the hand*, ἱκετῶν κλάδοι A.*Supp.*21 (anap.). II. as Subst. ⊛ -ίδιον, τό, *hand-knife, dagger*, Hdt.1.12, 214, Th.3.70, etc.; ἐγχειριδίῳ πλήττειν Lys.4.6, etc. 2. *handle*, Thphr.*HP*4.3.4, Callix.1. 3. *manual, handbook*, title of works by Epict. and others, cf. Demetr.Lac.*Herc.*1013.12 F., Philostr. *VS*2.1.14, Longin.*Proll.Heph.*p.86 C. 4. *tool, implement*, Lxx *Ex.*20.25. [-ῐδιον Hermipp.46.] -ίζω, Att. fut. -ιῶ X.*Oec.*8.10: pf. ἐγκεχείρικα Plu.*Phoc.*34:—*put into one's hands, entrust*, τί τινι or τινά τινι, Hdt.5.92.γ', Th.2.67, etc.; τὰς ἀρχὰς ἐ. τινί Hdt.5.72, cf. Arist.*Pol.*1305ᵃ16, prob. in Thphr.*Char.*30.15; ἐ. τινὶ τὴν φυλακήν Arist.*Pol.*1306ᵃ22; ἐ. ἐμαυτὸν τῇ ἀτυχίᾳ Antipho 2.4.1, etc.:—Pass., *to be entrusted*, τινί to one, Plb.5.44.1; τὴν ἐγχειρισθεῖσαν ἑαυτῷ πίστιν *IG*2².1028.72; ἡ -ισθεῖσά τινι χρεία *PFlor.*2.9 (iii A.D.); but ἐγχειρίζεσθαί τι *to be entrusted with* a thing, Luc. *Prom.*3, *Am.*39, Hdn.1.12.3, etc.: c. inf., διοικεῖν τὰ τῆς ἀρχῆς ἐγκεχειρίσμεθα we *have been entrusted with* the administration of the government, Id.8.7.5:—Med., *take in hand, encounter*, κινδύνους Th. 5.108, D.C.*Fr.*29.6, v.l. in S.E.*P.*1.91. II. *treat surgically*, *Hippiatr.*18.

ἐγχειρίθετος [ρῐ], ον, *put into one's hands*, ἐ. τινα παραδιδόναι Hdt. 5.106: Aeol. ἐγχερρίθετος prob. in Sapph.*Oxy.*1787 *Fr.*9.

ἐγχειριστέον, *one must undertake*, Aët.6.22.

⊛ ἐγχειρο-γάστωρ, ορος, ὁ, = γαστρόχειρ, Cleanth.ap.Clearch.16, Zonar. -τονέω, *elect*, Poll.2.150.

ἐγχελέω, Ep. for ἐγχέω, Hom.

ἐγχέλ-ειον, τό, Dim. of ἔγχελυς, in sg., Ar.*Fr.*318.7, Antiph.222.4: mostly in pl., Pherecr.108.12, Callias Com.3, Posidipp.14; ὀπτᾶτε τἀγχέλεια Ar.*Ach.*1043: but in ll.cc. prob. neut. pl. of ἐγχέλειος (sc. κρέα or τεμάχη); so τέμαχος ἐγχέλειον Pherecr.45, cf. Eust. 1231.36. -εών or -υών, ῶνος, ὁ, *eel-trap*, Arist.*HA*592ᵃ4, 16. -ις, = ἔγχελυς, Id.*Fr.*311. -ύδιον [ῠ], τό, Dim. of ἔγχελυς, Amphis 35, Ephipp.15.6.

ἐγχελυοτρόφος, ον, *keeping eels*, Arist.*HA*592ᵃ2, *Fr.*311.

⊛ ἔγχελυς Matro *Conv.*39, acc. -υν Archestr.*Fr.*8 (the accent ἐγχέλυς, etc., is sts. found as v.l.), ἡ (ὁ, is f.l. in Luc.*Anach.*1), Att. gen. εως, nom. pl. εις, cf. Ael.Dion.*Fr.*145; gen. pl. ἐγγέλεων acc. to Choerob. *in Theod.*1.331; but the Ion. forms -υος, -υες or -υς, -ύων, -υσι are freq. found as v.l. in Arist.*HA*; dat. sg. -υϊ Hp.*Mul.*2.115; acc. pl. ἐγχέλυας Archil.101:—*eel*, ἐγχέλυές τε καὶ ἰχθύες Il.21.203, cf. Epich.73, Arist.*HA*538ᵃ3, al., etc.; ἐ. Κωπαΐδας Ar.*Ach.*880; ἐ. Βοιώτιαι Antiph.236: prov., ἐγχέλεις θηρᾶσθαι, i.e. to 'fish in troubled waters', Ar.*Eq.*864, cf. *Nu.*559, Arist.*HA*592ᵃ6.

ἐγχελυών, v. ἐγχελεών.

**ἐγχελῠωπός**, όν, *eel-faced*, Luc.*VH*1.35.

⊛ **ἔγχερα**, τά, = ἐπίχειρα, *IG*$2^2$.1126.4 (Decr. Amphict.).

**ἔγχερσος**, = χερσός, ἄρουρα *POxy*.1912.138 (vi A.D.).

**ἐγχεσί-μαργος** [ῐ], ον, *raging with the spear*, *EM*313.7, Hsch. **-μωρος**, ον, *fighting with the spear*, Il.2.692, al., Od.3.188, Cerc.6.9: Comp., with play on μῶρος, *AP*11.16. (-μωρος is perh. cogn. with μάρναμαι.) **-παλοι**, οἱ, *wielders of the spear*, Hsch. **-χειρ**, χειρος, ὁ, *living by war*, Orph.*Fr*.285.18.

**ἐγχέσ-πᾰλος**, ον, (πάλλω) *wielding the spear*, Il.2.131, B.5.69, etc. **-φόρος**, ον, *spear-bearing*, Pi.*N*.3.61.

**ἐγχέω**, Ep. subj. ἐγχείῃ (v. infr.): fut. -χέω, late ἐγχύσω f.l. in Hero *Spir*.1.33: aor. ἐνέχεα, Ep. ἐνέχευα, but 3 pl. ἐνέχεαν in tmesi Od.8.436; imper. ἔγχεον E.*Cyc*.568: pf. Pass. ἐγκέχῠμαι:—*pour in*, ἐν δ' οἶνον ἔχευεν Od.3.40, 6.77; μέθυ.. ἐγχείῃ δεπάεσσι 9.10; ἔγχεε κέρναις ἕνα καὶ δύο Alc.41.4; οἶνον ἐς κύλικα Hdt.4.70; ὄξος τ' ἄλειφά τ' ἐγχέας ταὐτῷ κύτει A.*Ag*.322; φάρμακα X.*Cyr*.1.3.9; κἂν οἰνόν μοι μὴ 'γχῇς σὺ πιεῖν Ar.*V*.616; ἐγχεῖν alone, *fill the cup*, τοῖς νεανίσκοις ἐγχεῖν ἐκέλευε X.*An*.4.3.13, cf. Pl.*Smp*.214a: c. gen., *in honour of*, τινός Call.*Epigr*.31, *AP*5.135,136 (Mel.): also c. dat., ἔγχει καὶ Κήδωνι *Scol*.27; ἐγχεῖν σπονδήν *pour in* wine for a libation, Ar.*Pax* 1102, Antipho 1.19:—Med., ὕδωρ δ' ἐνεχεύατο πουλύ (with no med. sense) Od.19.387; but in strict sense of Med., *pour in wine for oneself, fill one's cup*, Ar.*V*.617; εἰς τὴν χεῖρα ἐγχέασθαι *pour* [wine] into *one's own* hand, X.*Cyr*.1.3.9; ποτὸν ἐγχεῖσθαι Id. *Smp*.2.26. **2.** of dry things, *pour in, shoot in*, ἐν δέ μοι ἄλφιτα χεῦον.. δοροῖσιν Od.2.354. **b.** ἐ. ἐς τὰς ῥῖνας πτερά *thrust* in, Ar.*Av*.1081. **3.** metaph., *infuse, instil*, in Pass., πᾶσιν ἡμῖν θανάσιμον -κέχυται τὸ τῆς γενέσεως φάρμακον Metrod.53; τὸ δ' αὖ τῆς ἡδονῆς πολὺ πλέον ἐγκεχυμένον Pl.*Phlb*.47a. **II.** sts. with acc. of the cup, *fill by pouring in*, κρατῆρα S.*Fr*.563; φιάλην X.*Smp*.2.23; ἔγχεον.. Διός γε τήνδε σωτῆρος Alex.232; ἐγχέασα.. ἀγαθοῦ δαίμονος (sc. κύλικα) Nicostr.20. **III.** ἐγχεῖν ὕδωρ τινί (v. κλεψύδρα) D.19.213, cf. 43.8:—Pass., ἐγχεῖται τὸ πρῶτον ὕδωρ Aeschin.3.197.

**ἔγχηλος**, ὁ, *bandage*, Hsch. **ἐγχημώμενοι**· ἐγχάσκοντες, Id. (leg. ἐγχασμ-). ⊛ **ἐγχηρωτύλει**· ἐπιχαίρουσιν, Id.

**ἐγχθόνιος**, ον, *in the earth*, σποδιὴ κειμένη ἐ. *Epigr.Gr*.298, prob. in *AP*7.740 (Leon.). **II.** *of the country*, κύλιξ *APl*.4.235 (Apollonid.).

**ἐγχίδιον**· ἔγγιον, Hsch.

**ἐγχίκτῠπος**, ον, *making a noise with the spear*, *EM*630.26.

**ἐγχλαινόομαι**, Pass., *to be clothed in*, ἐσθῆτα Lyc.974, cf. 1347.

**ἐγχλᾰμῠδόομαι**, *to be wrapped in a cloak*, Hsch. s.v. ἐντεθετταλίσθαι.

**ἐγχλῐαίνω**, *warm*, in Pass., Dsc.*Eup*.1.228.

**ἐγχλίαμα**· μαῦρον ὄνομα, Hsch.

⊛ **ἐγχλίω** [ι], *to deal wantonly with, insult*, Ἕλλησιν A.*Supp*.914.

**ἐγχλοάω**, *to be of a greenish hue*, Nic.*Th*.154. **II.** ἐγχλοᾶσθαι· ἐμφῦναι, Hsch.

**ἔγχλοος**, ον, = ἔγχλωρος, Nic.*Th*.506, al.; metapl. acc. ἔγχλοα ib. 676.

**ἐγχλωρίζω**, = ἐγχλοάω, Sch.Nic.*Th*.154.

**ἔγχλωρος**, ον, *greenish*, Thphr.*HP*3.12.5 (Comp.), Dsc.3.37.

⊛ **ἔγχνοος**, ον, contr. **-χνους**, ουν, *downy*, Nic.*Th*.762, Dsc.3.146.

**ἐγχόδια**· ἀθρόα, Hsch.

**ἐγχοιριλόω**, pf. part. Pass. ἐγκεχοιριλωμένην, = λεπράν, Hsch.

**ἐγχονδρ-ίζω**, *form into grains*, Archig.ap.Gal.12.661. **-ος**, ον, *in grains*, of manna, Dsc.1.68.6.

**ἔγχορδος**, ον, (χορδή) *stringed*, Poll.4.58.

**ἐγχορεύω**, *dance in*, ἐν Ἰνδίᾳ Plu.2.332b: generally, *disport oneself, take pleasure in*, παιδεύμασι, etc., Ph.1.252, al.; of birds, *sport in* the air, c. acc., Vett.Val.344.22 (s.v.l.).

**ἔγχορτος**, ον, *grass-grown*, *POxy*.1911.103 (vi A.D.), 1912.134 (vi A.D.).

⊛ **ἔγχος**, εος, τό, *spear, lance*, Il.6.319, etc.; ἔ. λογχωτά B.*Fr*.3. **II.** *weapon* in general: *sword*, S.*Aj*.287, al., E.*El*.696, etc.: pl., *weapons*, ἄτερ ἐγχέων Pi.*P*.9.28; πτερωτὰ ἔγχη *arrows*, E.*HF*1098; πῦρ.. Ἑκάτης ἔγχος S.*Fr*.535 (anap.); of Nausicaa's *ball*, τὸ δ' ἔ. ἐν ποσὶν κυλίνδεται ib.782: metaph., φροντίδος ἔ. Id.*OT*170 (lyr.). **III.** meton., *armed force*, Ἰηπύγων ἔγχος ἀπωσάμενοι Call.*Fr*.444.

⊛ **ἐγχοῦν**· τὸν στεάτινον (Lacon.), Hsch.

⊛ **ἔγχουσα**, ἡ, Att. for ἄγχουσα (q.v.), Ar.*Lys*.48, X.*Oec*.10.2.

**ἐγχουσίζομαι**, *rouge*, τὸ πρόσωπον, *EM*313.37; cf. ἀγχουσίζομαι.

**ἐγχόω**, = ἐγχώννυμι, impf. ἐνέχουν Str.7.4.7:—Pass., ἐγχούμενοι πόροι Id.9.2.18.

**ἐγχράω** and **ἐγχραύω**, Ep. **ἐνιχραύω** Nic.*Th*.277:—like ἐγχρίμπτω, *dash against*, ἐνέχραυεν ἐς τὸ πρόσωπον τὸ σκῆπτρον Hdt.6.75; κυνόδοντά τισι Nic. l.c. **II.** Pass., ἦσαν δὲ πρός τινας καὶ ἄλλους ἐγκεχρημένοι (sc. πόλεμοι) *there were* wars *undertaken*.., Hdt.7.145 (prob. f.l. for ἐγκεκρημένοι).

**ἐγχρεμετίζω**, fut. -ίσω, *to neigh in*, Poll.10.56.

**ἔγχρεμμα**, ατος, τό, *spitting*, in pl., Plu.2.82b (dub. l.).

**ἐγχρέμπτομαι**, *expectorate*, Luc.*Gall*.10.

**ἐγχρῄζω**, fut. -χρήσω Phld.*Rh*.1.147 S.:—*want, have need of*, c. gen., ib.1.3 S., *POxy*.1766.10 (iii A.D.). **II.** intr., *to be needful* or *useful*, εἰς ὕδωρ *Gp*.20.19 tit.; ἰατροῖς ἐγχρῄζει τὸ ψέγειν prob. in Phld.*Ir*.p.21 W., cf. *BGU*226.9 (i A.D.), Apollon.*Mir*.36; τὰ ἐγχρῄζοντα *necessaries*, condemned by Luc.*Hist.Conscr*.22.

**ἐγχρημᾰτίζω**, *execute* a deed, *PPetr*.2 p.43.

⊛ **ἐγχρίμπτω** or **-χρίπτω**, Philostr.*VA*8.19 (also -χριπτᾶται· ἐγγίζει, Hsch.): aor. ἐνέχριμψα Il.23.334, Hdt.2.60 (v.l. -χρίψαντες):—Med., fut. -χρίμψομαι A.R.4.939:—Pass., aor. ἐνεχρίμφθην Il.23.338:—*bring near to*, with collat. notion of force, *strike* or *dash against*, τῷ [τέρματι] σὺ μάλ' ἐγχρίμψας ἐλάαν σχεδὸν ἅρμα drive the chariot close *so as almost to touch* the post, ib.334 (so ἐν νύσσῃ δέ τοι ἵππος.. ἐγχριμφθήτω *let* him *almost touch* the post, ib.338); ἐ. τὴν βᾶριν τῇ γῇ *to bring* the boat *close to* land, Hdt.2.60; ἐ. (sc. τὴν ναῦν) τῷ αἰγιαλῷ Id.9.98; ἐ. τὸν ἵππον τῇ θηλέῃ Id.3.85; ἐ. ἐς τὴν γῆν App.*BC* 5.81. **II.** intr., *approach*, τινί S.*El*.898:—more freq. in Pass. in this sense, ἐγχριμφθείς *having come near to assault* one, Il.13.146; ἐνιχριμφθέντα πύλῃσιν 17.405; αἰχμὴ ὀστέῳ ἐγχριμφθεῖσα the point *driven to* the very bone, 5.662; ἀσπίδ' (i.e. ἀσπίδι) ἐνιχριμφθείς *dashed against* his shield, 7.272; νωλεμὲς ἐγχρίμπτοντο they *pressed* unceasing *on*, 17.413; later, *keep close to*, ἐ. (sc. τῇ γῇ), of fish, Hdt. 2.93; ἐν οὔδει Maiist.24; ἐ. γυναικί, = πλησιάζω, Hdt.4.113; κύνες ἐλάφοις ἐγχριμπτόμεναι *pursuing* them, E.*Hipp*.218 (anap.); of serpents, *attack*, τινί v.l. for -σκίμψῃ in Nic.*Th*.336, cf. A.R.4.1512, Philostr. l.c.; of elephants, Opp.*C*.2.535; of disease, *attack* a particular part, ἐς τοὺς βουβῶνας Hp.*Mul*.2.137; ἀρθρῖτις ἐ. ἐς ἄρθρα Aret. *SD*2.12.—Poet., Ion. and late Prose.

⊛ **ἔγ-χρῖσις**, εως, ἡ, (ἐγχρίω) *anointing, rubbing in*, Hp.*Decent*. 8. **II.** *slight wound, scratch*, Ael.*NA*3.22. **-χρισμα**, ατος, τό, *liniment, embrocation*, Hp.*Hum*.5. **-χριστέον**, *one must anoint*, Sor.2.16, *Gp*.16.6.1. **-χριστος**, ον, *rubbed in as an ointment*, Theoc.11.2; εἰς τοὺς ὀφθαλμούς Arist.*GA*$747^a9$.

**ἐγχρίω** [ῑ], *anoint*, ἀλείμμασιν ἑαυτόν Duris 10 J., cf. *AP*11.117 (Strat.); τοὺς ὀφθαλμούς *Apoc*.3.18: metaph., ψευδηγόροις φήμαις ἐγχρίειν ἔπη Lyc.1455:—Med., *anoint oneself*, ἰξοῦ Str.15.1.29; ἐ. τὸ πρόσωπον Nic.Dam.p.2 D.: abs., Arr.*Epict*.2.21.20, etc.:—Pass., Ph. 1.526. **II.** *sting, prick*, τινί Pl.*Phdr*.251d:—Pass., ἰὸς ἐγχρισθείς poison *injected by a sting*, Ael.*NA*1.54. **2.** *stick in*, τὸ κέντρον ib. 6.20.

**ἐγχρον-ία**, Ion. **-ίη**, ἡ, *chronic character*, νούσου dub. in Hp.*Praec*. 14. ⊛ **-ίζω**, *to be long about* a thing, *delay*, Th.3.27; περὶ ὑποχόνδριον Hp.*Acut*.50; ἐγχρονίσας *after long delay*, *Epigr.Gr*.815.7; ἐ. πρὸς τὸν γάμον Arist.*Rh*.$1411^a19$; εἰς καιρόν Phld.*Lib*.p.13 O.; τινί *in* a thing, Plb.15.36.6; ἐν τόπῳ D.C.44.46:—Pass., Pl.*Ep*.362a. **II.** *become chronic*, ἐγχρονίζει τὰ ἐμπυήματα Hp.*Prog*.17; ἐγχρονίζον ἔθος Ph.2.203; *continue in*, τῷ καταστήματι Procl.*Par.Ptol*.51:—Pass., ἐγχρονισθὲν τὸ νόσημα Pl.*Grg*.480b, cf. Arist.*HA*$586^a18$. **III.** Act., c. acc. pers., *waste* a person's *time*, Vett.Val.150.10. **-ιος**, ον, *temporal*, φύσεις Procl.*in Prm*.p.638 S. **-ισμός**, ὁ, *prolonged use*, Sor.1.46, Antyll.ap.Orib.9.23.10. **-ος**, ον, *lasting a short time*, App.*Fr*.3 (expld. by Suid. as *recent*). **2.** *in time, temporal*, opp. αἰώνιος, Ocell.1.2, Ascl.*in Metaph*.424.7, Procl.*Inst*.53, al., Dam. *Pr*.90, al., Simp. *in Ph*.461.12.

**ἐγ-χρύσεος** [ῡ], ον, = sq., *IG*14.268 (Selinus). **-χρῡσος**, ον, *golden*, ὅπλον *Schwyzer* 647.35 (Cyme, i A.D.); στολή Philostr.*Im*.1. 22; πρόσοψις D.S.3.39. **-χρῡσόω**, *gild*, Tz.*H*.3.975 (Pass.).

**ἐγχρῴζομαι**, Pass., *to be engrained*, ἐν ἅπασι τοῖς μέρεσιν ἐγκέχρωσται ἡ λευκότης Arist.*Xen*.$978^a11$: metaph., *to be amalgamated with*, πάθος ἐγκεχρωσμένον τῷ βίῳ Id.*EN*$1105^a3$; νόμον ἐν τοῖς ἤθεσι καὶ τοῖς ἐπιταδεύμασι τῶν πολιτᾶν ἐγχρῴζεσθαι δεῖ Archyt.ap.Stob. 4.1.138:—Act. only ἐγχρώσας· χρίσας, Hsch.

**ἐγχρωκουρίας**, ου, ὁ, = ἐν χρῷ κεκαρμένος, Orus ap.*Et.Gen*. s.v. ἐν χρῷ.

**ἐγχρώμᾰτος**, ον, *parti-coloured*, Sch.Ar.*Pl*.530.

**ἐγχῡλ-ης**, a kind of *fish*, Hsch. **-ίζω**, *convert into juice* (by pressing), Thphr.*CP*6.11.14. **-όομαι**, *to be converted into chyle*, τὰ ἐγκεχυλωμένα Gal.8.369. **-ος**, ον, *juicy, succulent*, Hp.*Aff*.59, Thphr.*CP*6.11.15 (Comp.); ἰχθύς Agatharch.40; *savoury*, Alex.124. 12; *soft-boiled*, of eggs, Gal.6.707. Adv. -λως dub. in Archig.ap. Gal.8.931. **-ωσις**, εως, ἡ, = ἔγχυμα II, Paul.Aeg.2.11, Aret.*CD* 2.13.

**ἔγχῠμα**, ατος, τό, *instillation*, Gal.12.649. **II.** *filling, content*, of a vessel, Hp.*Cord*.8, Gal.11.260, 7.524. **III.** = ἔγχυτος II, Hsch.

**ἐγχῠμᾰτ-ίζω**, *make an infusion* of, τι Dsc.1.45 (Pass.), *Gp*.4.7.3, Aesop.18. **II.** ἐ. τινά *treat by injections*, *Hippiatr*.129. **III.** *instil, inject*, Sor.1.64, Archig.ap.Gal.12.621, etc. **-ισμός**, ὁ, *injection, instillation*, Antyll.ap.Orib.10.26.1, Sor.1.56, *Hippiatr*. 68. **-ιστά**, τά, *injections*, Dsc.*Eup*.1.55. **-ιστέον**, *one must inject*, Sor.1.69, Orib.46.25.4. **II.** *one must make an infusion*, *Gp*.18.17.1.

**ἔγχῡμος**, ον, *moistened*, ἔγχυμα χυμῷ Hp.*Off*.11; *juicy, succulent*, σάρξ Pl.*Ti*.74d, cf. Thphr.*CP*5.4.3; *sapid*, Arist.*Sens*.$442^b29$.

**ἐγχύμωσις** [ῡ], εως, ἡ, *stirring up, enlivening*, in pl., Hp.*Epid*.2.4.4.

**ἐγχύνω**, late form of ἐγχέω, Luc.*Pr.Im*.29, etc.

**ἔγχῠσις**, εως, ἡ, (ἐγχέω) *pouring in*, Plu.2.38f, Hero *Spir*.1. 12. **II.** *pouring* of wine *into* casks, *PPetr*.2 p.136 (iii B.C.).

**ἐγχῠτέον**, *one must pour in*, *Gp*.6.7.4, al.

**ἐγχυτλόω**, *pour libations*, τοῖς καμοῦσι Herod.5.84.

**ἔγχῠτος**, ον, *poured in, infused*, Aret.*CD*2.3; ἔγχυτον, τό, *injection*, Hp.*Mul*.1.34, Apollon.ap.Gal.12.582. **II.** ἔγχυτος (sc. πλακοῦς), ὁ, *cake cast into a shape*, Hippon.37, Men.518.9, Euang.1.7:—also **ἐγχῠτοῦς**, ὁ, *Gloss*. **2.** ἔγχυτον, τό, = ἔγχυμα, *infusion*, Aret.*CA* 2.10.

**ἐγχύτρ-ιαι**· αἱ τὰς χόας τοῖς τετελευτηκόσιν ἐπιφέρουσαι, Sch.rec. Ar.*V*.289. **-ίζω**, *expose children in an earthenware vessel*, Hsch.: hence, *make away with*, Ar.*V*.289. ⊛ **-ίστρια**, ἡ, *woman who*

*gathered the bones* from a funeral pile *into an urn*, Pl.*Min*.315c (v.l. ἐγχυτίστρια), cf. *EM*313.41. II. *woman who exposed children*, acc. to Sch.Ar.*V*.289 (but cf. ἐγχύτριαι).

**ἔγχωμα**, ατος, τό, *bar of a river*, Plb.4.39.9.

**ἐγχώννῡμι** or -ύω, *fill up by depositing earth*, of rivers, Plb.4.40.4 (Pass.); ἐ. τάφρον App.*BC*5.36. II. *throw in earth*, εἰς τάφρον ἐνεχώννυον ib.2.75, cf. D.S.17.42.

⊛ **ἐγχωρ-έω**, *give room* to do a thing, *allow*, ὁ χρόνος οὐκ ἐγχωρεῖ, c. inf., Lys.26.6, X.*Eq*.12.13: abs., ὅσον ἐνεχώρεε ἡ δεκάτη so far as the money *allowed* her to go, Hdt.2.135; ἂν ἐγχωρῇ τὸ ὕδωρ (i.e. the water-clock), D.44.45. b. c. acc., *admit of*, κλίσιν Arr.*Tact*. 11.4. 2. ἐγχωρεῖ, impers., *there is time, it is possible* or *allowable*, c. dat. pers. et inf., ἐ. αὐτῷ εἰδέναι Antipho 1.7, cf. 5.90, Pl. *Prt*.321d, X.*HG*2.3.16, etc.; οἷς ἐ. ὑβρισταῖς εἶναι Lys.24.15: also abs., ἔτι ἐ. *there is yet time*, Pl.*Phd*.116e; οὐκέτ' ἐγχωρεῖ D.4.41;=ἐνδέχεται, Arist.*APr*.25$^b$10, al.; ἐφ' ὁπόσον ἂν ἐγχωρῇ D.H.*Comp*.6; ἐγχωροῦν ἐστί Paus.3.24.11; κατὰ τὸ ἐγχωροῦν as far as *possible*, Paul. Aeg.6.99. II. *pass*, εἰς ἑτέραν ὑποθήκην *BGU*907.15 (iii A.D.).⊛ -ιος, ον, also η or α, ον Hdt.6.35, Pi.*O*.5.11: (χώρα):—*in* or *of the country*, ἐσθὴς ἐγχωρίη Hdt. l. c.; ἐγχωρία λίμνα Pi. l. c.; βασιλῆες ib.9.56; ἐ. θεοί A.*Th*.14, S.*Tr*.183, *Sammelb*.5680 (iii B.C.); θεοὶ καὶ ἥρωες Th. 2.74; Ἑλληνικοῖς καὶ ἐ. γράμμασι *OGI*194.30 (i B.C.); κάρτα δ' ἔστ' ἐ. *a true-born* Theban, A.*Th*.413; ἐ. [πυροί], opp. ἐπείσακτοι, Arist.*Mir*. 836$^b$22; of winds, *local*, Thphr.*CP*5.12.11. 2. Subst., *dweller in* the land, ἐ. τῆσδε γῆς *inhabitants*, S.*OC*871, cf. E.*Ion* 1167; οἱ ἐ. Arist.*PA*673$^a$18, Wilcken *Chr*.1.2 (iii B.C.), etc. 3. τὸ ἐ. as Adv., *according to the custom of the country*, Th.4.78. Adv. -ίως Sch.E. *Ph*.134. II. *of* or *for the country, rustic*, Hes.*Op*.344 (v.l. ἐγκώμιον). III. ἐγχώριον· τόκος, δάνειον, Hsch. -ος, ον, (χώρα) = foreg., S.*Ph*.692 (lyr.), *OC*125 (lyr.), Lyc.509, etc.; φάσματα S.*Ichn*. 322 (lyr.).

**ἔγχωσις**, εως, ἡ, *silting up* of a channel, Arist.*Mete*.352$^b$34, Plb.4. 39.10, etc.: pl., Str.5.3.8. II. *bank, dyke*, αἱ ἐ. τῶν τάφρων Ph. *Bel*.100.24, cf. *Ostr.Strassb*.777.

**ἐγχωστήριος**, ον, *useful for filling up*, ὄργανα App.*BC*5.36.

**ἐγώ**, *I*: Pron. of the first person:—Ep. mostly ἐγών before vowels (so in Dor., before consonants, Epich.85, Sophr.81, Ar.*Ach*.748,754), rarely in Trag., A.*Pers*.932 (lyr.); Boeot. ἰών A.D.*Pron*.51.4:—strengthd. ἔγωγε, *I at least, for my part, indeed, for myself* (more freq. in Att. than in Hom.): Dor. ἐγώνγα Alcm.51, Ar.*Ach*.736, *Lys*.986, dat. ἐμίνγα *IG*2$^2$.1126.7 (Amphict. Delph.): Boeot. ἰώνγα Corinn.21; ἰώνει Ead.10; ἰώγα Ar.*Ach*.898: Lacon. and Tarent. ἐγώνη, Hsch., A.D.*Conj*.255.29. II. oblique cases from a difft. root, gen. ἐμοῦ, enclit. μου; Ion. and Ep. ἐμέο, ἐμεῦ, μευ, also ἐμέθεν Il.1.525, E.*Hel*. 177 (lyr.); Aeol. ἔμεθεν Sapph.*Supp*.23.7; ἐμεῖο *IG*3.1337; μεθέν Sophr.20; Dor. ἐμέος, ἐμεῦς, Epich.144; Boeot. ἐμοῦς Corinn.37; also ἐμῶς, ἐμίο, ἐμίω, ἐμίως A.D.*Pron*.74.17:—dat. ἐμοί, enclit. μοι (which may be compared with Skt. gen. *me* in κλῦθί μοι Il.5.115, al.); ὅ μοι πόσις *Schwyzer*683 (Cypr.); Dor. ἐμίν Epich.99, *AJA*29.461 (Rhodian, v B.C.), Ar.*Ach*.733, Theoc.4.30; Tarent. ἐμίνη Rhinth.13: acc. ἐμέ, enclit. με; Cypr. μι *Inscr.Cypr*.59,60H. III. dual, nom. and acc., νῶι, *we two*, Il.5.34, etc.; acc. νῶιν Zenod.ad Il.8.377; Att. νώ Pl.*Phdr*.278b (also Il.5.219, Od.15.475); νῶε Antim.39, Corinn.5: gen., dat. νῶιν; νῷν S.*Ant*.3; νῶι dat., Orph.*L*.773; νῶιν, = ἡμῖν, Q.S.1.213, etc. IV. pl., nom. ἡμεῖς (ἡμέες f.l. in Hdt.2.6, al., rejected by A.D.*Pron*.93.1); Aeol. ἄμμες Od.9.303, Alc.18.3, Pi.*P*. 4.144; Dor. ἁμές Alcm.65, Epich.42, Ar.*Lys*.168:—gen. ἡμῶν (also ἧμων A.D.*Synt*.130.23); Ion. ἡμέων Hdt.1.112, etc.; ἡμείων Od.24. 170, Herod.1.46; Aeol. ἀμμέων Alc.88, *Milet*.3 No.152.29; ἄμμων ib.74, A.D.*Pron*.95.3; Dor. ἁμέων Alcm.66; ἁμῶν [Epich.]266, Ar. *Lys*.168, Theoc.2.158; Cret., Boeot. ἁμίων *SIG*528.5, A.D.*Pron*.95. 21:—dat. ἡμῖν, in S. also ἥμιν (ῐ) (or ἧμιν Aristarch.ad Il.1.214, A.D. *Pron*.95.3); also rarely in Com., Phryn.Com.37, Ar.*Av*.386 (dub.); Aeol. ἄμμιν, ἄμμι, Il.1.384, Alc.80, al., Pi.*P*.4.155, A.*Th*.156 (lyr.), *Milet*.3 No.152; ἄμμεσιν Alc.100; Dor. also ἁμίν or ἅμιν, Alcm.77,78, A.*Eu*.347 (lyr.), Ar.*Lys*.1081; with ῑ, Id.*Ach*.821, Theoc.7.145:—acc. ἡμᾶς (also ἥμας Od.16.372); Ion. ἡμέας Il.8.211, *SIG*273.25 (Milet., iv B.C.); ἥμεας Od.4.294 (cf. Hdn.Gr.2.140); Aeol. ἄμμε Il.1.59, Sapph.115, Theocr.8.25; Dor. ἁμέ *SIG*1 (Abu Simbel, vi B.C.), Epich.173, Ar.*Ach*.759 codd., *Lys*.95.—On these dialectic varieties, v. A.D.*Pron*.50 sqq. (Cf. Skt. *ahám* (ἐγών), acc. pl. *asmā́n*; for νώ cf. Skt. *nau*):—freq. in answers, as an affirmative, esp. in form ἔγωγε, S.*Tr*.1248, Pl.*Tht*.149b, etc.; οὗτος ἐ. here am *I*, Pi.*O*. 4.26; ὅδ' ἐκεῖνος ἐ. S.*OC*138 (lyr.); rarely with Art., τὸν ἐμὲ *myself*, Pl.*Tht*.166a, *Sph*.239b (but ὁ ἐ. *the Self, the Ego*, Dam.*Pr*.444); τίς ὢν οὗτος ὁ ἐγὼ τυγχάνω; Plu.2.1119a; τί ἐστι φίλος; ἄλλος ἐ. Pythag. ap.Herm.*in Phdr*.p.166 A.; τί τοῦτ' ἐμοί; ἡμῖν τί τοῦτ' ἔστ'; Lat. *quid mea hoc refert?* Ar.*Th*.498, etc.; ἐγώ; in a question, Ar.*Eq*. 1336, al.; ἡμεῖς *the self*, ἔνθα δὴ ἡμεῖς μάλιστα Plot.1.1.7.

**ἐγώγυος** or -ιος, = ὠγύγιος, Hsch., Suid.

**ἐγῷδα, ἐγῷμαι**, Att. crasis for ἐγὼ οἶδα, ἐγὼ οἶμαι. **ἐγών, ἐγώνγα, ἐγώνη**, dialectic forms of ἐγώ, ἔγωγε (q. v.). **ἐδααία**· ἐρημία, Hsch. **ἐδάην**, ης, η, aor. 2 of *δάω. ⊛ **ἐδαλάχθη**· ἐδήχθη, Id. **ἐδάμην**, ης, η, Ep. aor. 2 Pass. of δαμάω. **ἐδάνη**· εἶδος ἀμπέλου, Id.

**ἐδᾰνός**, ή, όν, *eatable*: ἐδανόν, τό, *food*, A.*Ag*.1407.

⊛ **ἑδᾰνός**, ή, όν, as epith. of oil, Il.14.172, cj. in *h.Ven*.63; expld. by Gramm. as cogn. with ἡδύς, ἥδομαι, ἁνδάνω (q. v.), *sweet*, cf. Hdn.Gr. 2.89, Apollon.*Lex*. s. v.

**ἔδαρ**· βρῶμα, Hsch. (i. e. ἔδϝαρ, cf. εἶδαρ).

**ἐδᾰφ-εινός**, etym. of ταπεινός, *EM*745.54. -**ιαῖος**, α, ον, *belonging to a floor*, Tz.*H*.3.211; gloss on γουνπετής, Sch.E.*Ph*. 293. -**ίζω**, *beat level and firm like a floor* or *pavement*, Plb.6.33. 6, Thphr.*HP*9.3.1:—Pass., Id.*CP*4.8.2, Arist.*Pr*.934$^b$10. II. *provide with a floor*, οἶκον *IG*11(2).158*A*66 (iii B.C.), cf. *BCH*29. 475. III. *dash to the ground*, Lxx*Ps*.136(137).9, *Ev.Luc*.19. 44. -**ικός**, ή, όν, *pertaining to land*, ἔργα *PLond*.2.163.19 (i A.D.); ἐλάσσωμα *BGU*20.8 (ii A.D.). ⊛ -**ιον**, τό, Dim. of ἔδαφος 4, Alex. Aphr.*in Metaph*.738.17; τῶν κατηγοριῶν τὰ ἐ. Dexipp.*in Cat*.5.14, cf. Eust.1532.63, Tz.*H*.4.202, Sch.Pi.*O*.5.1. -**ιστήριον**, τό, = λίστρον, Hsch. s.h.v. -**ίτης** [ῑ], ου, ὁ, = ἐδαφιαῖος, Tz.*H*.1.906.

**ἐδᾰφοποιέω**, *raze to the ground*, J.*Vit*.19.

⊛ **ἔδᾰφος**, εος, τό, *bottom, foundation, base* of anything, τῆς κατασκευῆς τὰ ἐ. Th.1.10; ἐ. νηός *bottom* of a ship, Od.5.249; ἐ. πλοίου D.32.5, cf. Pherecr.12; ἐ. ποταμοῦ, τῆς θαλάττης, X.*Cyr*.7.5.18, Arist.*HA*534$^a$11; [ποτηρίου] Pherecr.143.2. 2. *ground-floor, pavement*, οἴκου Hdt.8.137; καθελεῖν ἐς ἐ. raze to the *ground*, Th. 3.68; τὸ ἐ. ὁμαλίσασι *IG*11(2).161*A*57 (Delos, iii B.C.); ἔπεσον εἰς τὸ ἐ. *Act.Ap*.22.7; ἀπὸ ἐδάφους μέχρι παντὸς ὕψους *CPR*95.17 (iii A.D.), etc. 3. *ground, soil*, περὶ τοῦ τῆς πατρίδος ἐδάφους ἀγωνίζεσθαι for our country's *soil*, Aeschin.3.134, cf. D.26.11 (pl.); ἐχθρὸς τῷ τῆς πόλεως ἐδάφει, of a mortal foe, Id.8.39, 10.11; ὀκρυόειν ἐ. *Eleg.Alex. Adesp*.1.7; *soil*, viewed in regard to its quality, Thphr.*CP*2.4.1 (pl.), 4.11.8: pl., ἐδάφη *lands and tenements* (incl. houses), Is.11.42, *IG* 2.780, *PTeb*.302.10 (i A.D.); also, *masses of earth*, Epicur.*Ep*.2 p.48 U. 4. *text* of a manuscript, opp. margin (μέτωπον), Gal.16.837, 18(2).864. b. *manuscript*, Id.16.468 (s.v.l.). 5. *background* of puppet-theatre, Hero *Aut*.30.1, al.

**ἐδᾰφόω**, pf. Pass. ἠδάφωται, *establish*, Hsch.

⊛ **ἐδέατρος**, ὁ, among the Persians, *one who tasted first, and named the order of dishes*, = θαλίαρχος, *seneschal*, Phylarch.*Fr*.44 J., cf. *EM* 315.37, Suid.; *steward*, *PCair.Zen*.31.18; cf. ἐλέατρος.

**ἐδέγμην**, v. δέχομαι. **ἐδεδέατο**, v. δέω *bind*. **ἐδεδμήατο**, v. δέμω. **ἐδέζετο**· ἐπολεμεῖτο, Hsch.

**ἐδέθλιον**, τό, = sq., Call.*Ap*.62, A.R.4.630, Nonn.*D*.3.258, al.

**ἔδεθλον**, τό, = ἔδαφος, Antim.28, Call.*Ap*.73, Lyc.987, A.R.4.331; τὰ χρυσόπαστα δ' ἔδεθλα should be read (with Auratus) in A.*Ag*.776 for ἐσθλά. II. *precinct, shrine*, *SIG*364.21 (Ephesus, iii B.C.); τόδε νάσω ἐ. *Epigr.Gr*.978.9 (Philae).

**ἐδείδῑμεν**, -ῑσαν, v. δείδω. **ἔδεκτο**, v. δέχομαι.

**ἐδελώνη**· ἄνθος, Hsch. ⊛ **ἔδεος**· Θεσσαλικὸς θρόνος, Id.

**ἔδεσμα**, ατος, τό, (ἔδω) *meat, food*, Pl.*Ti*.73a, Antiph.26.10: pl., *eatables, meats*, Batr.31, X.*Hier*.1.23, Pl.*R*.559b, Antiph.82.1, Porph. *Abst*.1.55: metaph., οὐ γὰρ ἡδύσματι χρῆται ἀλλ' ὡς ἐδέσματι τοῖς ἐπιθέτοις Arist.*Rh*.1406$^a$19:—Dim. **ἐδεσμάτιον**, τό, Procl.ad Hes.*Op*.41.

**ἐδεσμᾰτοθήκη**, ἡ, *food-hamper*, Sch.Od.6.76.

**ἐδεσ-τέον**, *one must eat*, Pl.*Cri*.47b, *Prt*.314a. -**τής**, οῦ, ὁ, *eater*, Hdt.3.99, Antiph.26.15. -**τός**, ή, όν, *eatable, good for food*, ζῷον Arist.*Pol*.1324$^b$41; ἐδεστά *eatables, meats*, E.*Fr*.472.19, Pl.*Ti*. 72e: sg., Call.*Fr*.128. II. *eaten*, S.*Ant*.206; *consumed*, ἐξ αὑτοῦ Id.*Tr*.677.

**ἐδήδοκα, ἐδήδεσμαι, ἐδήδοται, ἐδηδώς**, v. ἔδω, ἐσθίω.

**ἐδηδών**, όνος, ἡ, = φαγέδαινα, Hsch.

**ἐδητύς**, ύος, ἡ, *meat, food*, in Hom. always in phrase, πόσιος καὶ ἐδητύος ἐξ ἔρον ἕντο Il.1.469, etc.; exc. Od.6.250 δηρὸν γὰρ ἐδητύος ἦεν ἄπαστος.

**ἔδμεναι**, v. ἔδω.

**ἔδν-άς**· ἡ ἀπὸ τῶν ἕδνων ἐδητύς, Hsch. -**εύειν**· ἐνεχυράζειν, Id. -**ιος**, α, ον, *bridal*, χιτών Id.

⊛ **ἕδνον**, τό, Pi.*O*.9.10, Call.*Fr*.193, Theoc.25.114, 27.33, Orph.*A*. 873, Nonn.*D*.42.28, al.; elsewh. only pl. ἕδνα, ἔεδνα:—*bride-price* or *wedding-gifts* (φερνή being the bride's *portion*), ὅπυιε πορὼν ἀπερείσια ἕ. Il.16.178; ἠγάγετο.. ἐπεὶ πόρε μυρία ἕ. ib.190, cf. 22.472; μνάσθω ἐέδνοισιν διζήμενος Od.16.391; εἰς ὅ κέ μοι.. πατὴρ ἀποδῷσιν ἔεδνα 8.318; rare in Trag., ἕδνοις ἄγαγες Ἡσιόναν πιθὼν δάμαρτα A. *Pr*.559 (lyr.): later Prose, Parth.20.1. II. *wedding-gifts* made to the bride *by those of her own household*, Od.1.277, 2.196, E.*Andr*. 2, Pi.*O*.9.10; but, III. in Id.*P*.3.94, Orph. l. c., D.C.79.12, *wedding-presents* to a wedded pair *by their guests*. IV. generally, *gift*, Theoc.25.114.

**ἑδνοφορέω**, *bring wedding-presents*, Eust.1414.49.

⊛ **ἑδν-όω**, Ep. ἐεδν-, (ἕδνον) *promise for wedding-presents, betroth*, ἡμῖν ἕδνωσε θύγατρας Theoc.22.147:—Med. in Hom., of a father, ὥς κ' αὐτὸς ἐεδνώσαιτο θύγατρα Od.2.53; ἑδνώσομαί τε θυγατέρ' (Herm. for ἐδώσομαι) E.*Hel*.933. II. Med., of a husband, *dower* a wife, Hes. *Fr*.94.47; simply, *marry*, γυναῖκα *AP*7.648 (Leon.); *woo*, Nonn.*D*. 6.3. -**ωτή**, ἡ, *bride betrothed for* ἕδνα, Hsch. -**ωτής**, Ep. ἐεδν-, οῦ, ὁ, *father who portions a bride*, οὔ τοι ἐεδνωταὶ κακοί εἰμεν Il.13.382.

**ἔδομαι**, fut. of ἐσθίω, ἔδω. **ἔδον**, Ep. and Dor. 3 pl. aor. 2 of δίδωμι. II. impf. of ἔδω.

**ἐδοξοεῖ**· ἀγαλματοποιεῖ, Hsch. **ἐδοργύπευσεν**· ἔσφαξεν ἢ ἐπέρανεν, Id.

⊛ **ἕδος**, εος, τό, Ep. dat. pl. ἑδέεσσιν *IG*14.1389 ii 19:—*sitting-place*: 1. *seat, stool*, Il.1.534 (pl.), 581 (pl.), 9.194, etc.; ἕ. Θεσσαλικόν *straight-backed chair*, Hp.*Art*.7. 2. *seat, abode, dwelling-place*, esp. of the gods, ἐς Οὔλυμπον.. ἵν' ἀθανάτων ἕ. ἐστί Il.5.360; ἵκοντο θεῶν ἕ. αἰπὺν Ὄλυμπον ib.367, cf. Theoc.7.116; periphr., ἕ. Οὐλύμποιο, = Ὄλυμπος, Il.24.144, cf. Pi.*O*.2.12; of the abodes of men,

Θήβης ἕ. Il.4.406; Ἰθάκης ἕ. Od.13.344; ἕ. Μάκαρος *the abode* of Macar, Il.24.544: periphr., Τροίας ἕ. B.8.46; ἔποικον ἕ., = ἐποικίαι, A.*Pr.*412. 3. *seated statue* of a god, S.*OT*886 (lyr.), *El.*1374, *IG* 2.754, al., Isoc.15.2, X.*HG*1.4.12, Porph.*Abst.*2.18, Polem.Hist.90, Plu.*Per.*13, Paus.8.46.2; τὰ ἕ. τῶν θεῶν, i.e. the Lat. *Penates*, D.H. 1.47; also of a man worshipped as a hero, *IG*14.2133; τὰ τῶν θεῶν ἕδη καὶ τοὺς νεὼς Isoc.4.155; τοὺς νεὼς καὶ τὰ ἕδη καὶ τὰ τεμένη Lycurg.143; θεῶν ἕδη (v.l. ἄλση) καὶ ἱερά Pl.*Phd.*111b, cf. Tim.*Lex.* ἕδος· τὸ ἄγαλμα, καὶ ὁ τόπος ἐν ᾧ ἵδρυται, but this latter use is doubtful in early Prose; later, *temple*, Ph.2.314; ἕ. ὑπαίθριον D.C.51.1. 4. *foundation, base*, Hes.*Th.*117, Epigr.ap.Vitr.8.3.23. II. *act of sitting*, οὐχ ἕδος ἐστί 'tis no *time to sit idle*, Il.11.648, 23.205; cf. ἕδρα II. (Cf. Skt. *sádas* 'seat'.)

**ἕδρ-α**, Ep. and Ion. **ἕδρη**, ἡ: (ἕδος): I. *sitting-place*: 1. *seat, chair, stool, bench*, Il.19.77, Od.3.7; ἀγοραί τε καὶ ἕδραι 8.16, cf. 3.31; *seat of honour*, περὶ μέν σε τίον.. ἕδρῃ τε κρέασίν τε Il.8.162, 12.311; ἕδραις γεραίρειν τινά X.*Cyr.*8.1.39; τιμίαν ἕ. ἔχειν A.*Eu.*855; *throne*, ἐκβαλεῖν ἕδρας Κρόνον Id.*Pr.*203; θακεῖν παγκρατεῖς ἕ. to sit on an almighty *throne*, ib.391, cf. *Pers.*466. 2. *seat, abode*, freq. in pl., Pi.*O.*7.76, *P.*11.63, etc.; esp. of the gods, *sanctuary, temple*, Id. *I.*7(6).44, A.*Ag.*596, etc.; also νέοικος ἕ. *station* for ships, Pi.*O.*5.8; ναύλοχοι ἕδραι S.*Aj.*460: periphr., ἕδραισι Θεράπνας Pi.*P.*11.63; Παρνησοῦ ἕδραι A.*Eu.*11, cf. E.*Tr.*557 (lyr.); βλεφάρων ἕ. the eye, Id.*Rh.* 8 (anap.); ὄμματος ἕ. ib.554 (lyr.). 3. *seat* or *place* of anything, ἐξ ἕδρας out of its *right place*, Id.*Ba.*928, cf. Plu.*Fab.*3; καταναγκάσαι ἐς ἕδρην Hp.*Mochl.*38; ὁ ἥλιος ἐκλιπὼν τὴν ἕ. Hdt.7.37; τὴν τοῦ ἥπατος ἕ., σπλάγχνου, etc., Pl.*Ti.*67b, 72c, etc.; ἐκ τῆς ἕ. ὠθεῖν ib.79b; ἔχειν ἕδραν to keep its *place*, Arist.*Mete.*356ᵃ4; μεταθέσεις ἐξ ἕδρας ἀτόμων Epicur.*Fr.*61; ἕδραν στρέφειν to *wriggle*, Thphr.*Char.*27.14; στοὰν εἰς τὴν ἀρχαίαν ἕ. ἐπαναγαγεῖν D.C.57.21; *base*, Plu.*Demetr.*21: metaph. in Rhet., D.H.*Dem.*31, etc.; of a plant, *Gp.*5.9.9. 4. ἡ ἕ. τοῦ ἵππου *the back* of the horse, *on which the rider sits*, X.*Eq.*5.5, 12.9, *Eq. Mag.*4.1. 5. in pl., *quarters* of the sky in which omens appear, A.*Ag.*118 (lyr.), E.*HF*596. 6. *seat* of a physiological process, ἕ. ἀναθρέψεως Gal.18(2).105. II. *sitting*, esp. of suppliants, ἕδραν ἔχειν προστρόπαιον A.*Eu.*41, cf. S.*OT*13, *OC*112. 2. *sitting still*, Hp.*Aër.*20: hence, *inactivity, delay*, περιημέκτεε τῇ ἕδρῃ Hdt.9.41; ἀχθομένων τῇ ἕ. Th.5.7; οὐχ ἕδρας ἀκμή S.*Aj.*811; οὐχ ἕδρας ἀγών E.*Or.*1291; οὐχ ἕδρας ἔργον B.*Fr.*11; also οἰκίης ἕδρη *sitting* at home, Herod.4.92. 3. *position*, γονυπετεῖς ἕδραι kneeling, E.*Ph.*293 (lyr.); βέλεος ἕδρη *place occupied by* a weapon which fixes itself in the skull, Hp.*VC*7. 4. *sitting, session* of a council, etc., εὐθὺς ἐξ ἕδρας when he rose from *the sitting*, S.*Aj.*780 (but ἐξ ἕδρας ἀνίσταται ib.788, means from *quietude*); ἕδραν ποιεῖν to hold a *sitting*, And.1.111, cf. *IG*1².110.41. III. *seat, breech, fundament*, Hdt.2.87, Hp. *Aph.*5.22, Ar.*Th.*133, etc.; of birds and animals, *rump*, Arist.*HA* 633ᵇ8, Simon*Eq.*9, etc. IV. Geom., *face* of a regular solid, *Theol. Ar.*37. **-άζω**, *cause to sit, place*, ἐπὶ πλευρὰς D.H.*Comp.*6; ἄλλυδις *AP*15.24 (Simm.); *settle, establish*, Jul.*Or.*5.165a, Procl. *Inst.*64, Simp.*in Ph.*528.21, Sch.A.R.4.947:—Med. or Pass., *to be seated* or *fixed*, Callix.1, Haussoullier *Milet* p.163, Porph.*Marc.*19, Dam.*Pr.*138; ἡδρασμένος *secure*, θρόνος D.Chr.1.78, cf. Sor.2.22.

**ἕδρᾰθον**, ες, ε, poet. aor. 2 of δαρθάνω.

**ἑδραῖος**, α, ον, also ος, ον Pl.*R.*407b, Plu.2.288d:—*sitting, sedentary*, of persons or their occupations, ἔργον Hp.*Art.*53; οἱ πολλοὶ τῶν τὰς τέχνας ἐχόντων ἑδραῖοί εἰσι X.*Lac.*1.3; ἑ. ἀρχαί, opp. στρατεῖαι, Pl. *R.*407b; ἑ. βίος *AP*11.42 (Crin.). 2. ἑδραία ῥάχις the horse's back *on which the rider sits*, E.*Rh.*783. II. *steady, steadfast*, κάθησ' ἑδραία Id.*Andr.*266; δεῖ τὴν γυναῖκα ὥσπερ κύβον ἑδραῖον εἶναι Plu.2.288d, cf. 952d; κύβος -ότατον σῶμα Ti.Locr.98c; ἑ. βάσεις Pl.*Ti.*59d; ἑδραιότατον στοιχεῖον εἶναι τὴν γῆν Heraclit.*All.*41; ὃν τὸ πάντων -ότατον Plot.6.2.8; ἑ. ὕπνος *sound* sleep, Hp.*Epid.*6.4.15; of a cup, Ath.11.496a: metaph. in Rhet., *firmly based*, κατάληξις Demetr.*Eloc.*19, cf. Longin.40.4. Adv. -αίως *firmly*, Ath.Mech.36.10, Hdn.3.14.5; *steadily*, Procl.*Hyp.*3.21. 2. *permanently appointed*, *PStrassb.*40.11 (vi A.D.).

**ἑδραι-ότης**, ητος, ἡ, *stability*, Corn.*ND*14, Procl.*in Prm.*p.794S., *in Ti.*2.49D. II. *sedentary occupation*, D.Chr.7.110. **-όω**, *make stable*, Hdn.Gr.1.453:—Pass., *become* or *be stable*, Ps.-Luc. *Philopatr.*16. **-ωμα**, ατος, τό, *stay, support*, τῆς ἀληθείας 1*Ep.Ti.*3.15. **-ωσις**, εως, ἡ, *establishing*, Tz.*Il.*120.11.

**ἔδρᾰκον**, aor. 2 of δέρκομαι.

**ἕδρᾱμα**, ατος, τό, = ἕδρα I, *IG*4.951.115 (Epid.).

**ἔδρᾰμον**, aor. 2 of τρέχω.

**ἕδρᾰνον**, τό, poet. form of ἕδρα, *seat, abode, dwelling*, Πελασγῶν Hes. *Fr.*212, cf. Orph.*H.*18.7; ἑ. κόσμου ib.26.4: mostly in pl., A.*Pers.*4, *Supp.*103, S.*OC*176, 233, *Pae.Delph.*5, Maiist.36; ἀλλ' ἄνα ἐξ ἑδράνων rise from thy *rest* or *idleness*, S.*Aj.*192; Trag. only in lyr. exc. Id. *Fr.*1128.7 γῆ ἑδράνων ἔρημος, which is Stoic. 2. *chair*, Hsch. II. *stay, support*, said of an anchor, in sg., *AP*6.28 (Jul.).

**ἑδρᾰνῶς**, = στερεῶς, Eust.769.23, 29.

**ἕδρ-ασμα**, ατος, τό, = ἕδρα, E.*Fr.*305, Ph.1.336, *PMag.Par.*1.1153 (pl.). II. Pythag. name for *eight*, *Theol.Ar.*55. **-ασμός**, ὁ, *placing in position*, πίθων *Gp.*6.2 tit. **-αστέον**, (ἑδράζω) *one must place*, ib.6.2.2. II. (ἑδράζομαι) *one must sit*, Sch.Il.23.205. **-αστικός**, ή, όν, *establishing, making stable*, δυνάμεις Procl. *in Ti.*3.138D., cf. Dam.*Pr.*138; τοῦ δημιουργοῦ ἀγαθότης Simp.*in Ph.*1355.6. II. = ἑδρικός, φάρμακα Orib.*Eup.*4.12.

**ἑδρήεις**, εσσα, εν, = ἑδραῖος, Hsch. **ἔδρησα**, Ion. aor. 1 of δράω.

**ἑδρ-ίας**, ου, *blowing steadily*, of wind, Hsch. **-ιάω**, *seat* or *set*:—Pass., *sit*, only in Ep. forms ἑδριόωνται Hes.*Th.*388; ἑδριόωντο Il.10.198, Od.7.98; ἑδριάασθαι 3.35. II. intr. in Act., *sit*, Theoc.17.19, A.R.3.170. **-ικός**, ή, όν, *belonging to the anus*, Heliod.ap.Orib.48.58.7, Crito ap.Gal.13.306, Aët.14.3, etc. **-ιον**, τό, Dim. of ἕδρα II. 4, Hsch. 2. Dim. of ἕδρα I. 3, Id. s.v. ἑδώλια. **-ίς**· ἑδραῖος, Id. **-ισο**· καθῆσο, Id. **-ίτης** [ῑ], ου, ὁ, *suppliant sitting* on the hearth, Suid., *EM*316.53 (-ηστής Zonar.).

**ἑδρο-διαστολεύς**, έως, ὁ, *instrument for widening the passage of the anus*, Heliod.ap.Orib.44.23.66, Leonidas ap.Paul.Aeg.6.78, Gal.19.110. **-στρόφος**, ὁ, *wrestler who throws his adversary*, Argive fashion, *by a cross-buttock*, Theoc.24.111.

**ἐδύνη**, = ὀδύνη, Greg.Cor.p.597S.

**ἔδω**, old Ep. pres. (also Hp.*VM*4 (v.l.), Theoc.5.128), for which in Att. ἐσθίω is used, Ep. inf. ἔδμεναι, ἐέδμεναι Emp.128.10 (s.v.l.): impf. ἔδον, Ion. 3 sg. ἔδεσκε Il.22.501: fut. ἔδομαι 18.271, Od.9.369, Theoc.3.53: pf. part. ἐδηδώς Il.17.542, *h.Merc.*560:—Pass., pf. ἐδήδοται Od.22.56: aor. 1 subj. ἐδεσθῇ dub. l. in Hp.*Vict.*2.54:—for the Att. forms, v. sub ἐσθίω; cf. also ἔσθω:—*eat*, εἰωθότες ἔδμεναι ἄδην Il. 5.203; ὅσσα τοι ἐκπέποται καὶ ἐδήδοται Od.22.56; of worms, Il.22.509, cf. Od.21.395; κύτισόν τε καὶ αἴγιλον αἶγες ἔδοντι Theoc.5.128.—Rare in Com., Alc.Com.36, Eub.28; also E.*Cyc.*245. II. *eat up, devour*, esp. in phrases, βίοτον καὶ κτήματα, οἶκον, χρήματα ἔ., Od.2.123, 16.431, 389; ἡμέτερον κάματον νήποινον ἔδουσι 14.417. III. metaph., καμάτῳ τε καὶ ἄλγεσι θυμὸν ἔδοντες 9.75, cf. 10.379, Il.24.129, Semon.1.24 (s.v.l.).

**ἐδωγαθή**· ἡ τροφή, Hsch.

**ἐδωδή**, ἡ, *food, meat, victuals*, Il.19.167, Od.3.70, Hp.*Acut.*47, X. *Hier.*1.19, etc.; ἐ. καὶ πόσις Pl.*Lg.*782e, cf. *R.*350a, al.: pl., τῶν.. περὶ ἐδωδὰς ἡδονῶν ib.389e, cf. 519b. 2. *forage, fodder* for cattle, Il.8.504. 3. *bait* for fish, Theoc.21.43. II. *act of eating*, ὀδόντας ἔχει.. ἐδωδῆς χάριν Arist.*PA*683ᵃ4; τῇ ἐ. τοῦ βοὸς [χαίρει] ὁ λέων Id.*EN*1118ᵃ20; πουλύποδος Jul.*Or.*6.181a, al. 2. *meal*, ἐπὶ μιᾶς ἐ. Arist.*HA*596ᵃ4. 3. [ἀετὸς] ἀχθόμενος τῇ ἐ. wearied with *feeding* the young birds, ib.563ᵃ22.

**ἐδώδιμος**, ον, Thphr.*CP*6.11.10, 6.12.12; η, ον Hdt.2.92:—*eatable*, Hdt. l.c., 3.108, etc.; ἐδώδιμα *eatables, provisions*, Th.7.39, Arist.*Rh.*1373ᵃ30, Porph.*Abst.*1.12, etc. II. *prepared for eating, cooked*, Orib.15.1.8.

**ἐδωδός**, όν, *given to eating* (rather than drinking), Hp.*Aër.*7.

**ἑδωλι-άζω**, *furnish with seats*, *IG*11(2).287*A*81 (Delos, iii B.C.), Lycurg.*Fr.*2, Poll.4.121; ἡδωλιασμένη θέα *IG*2².1176.12. II. *lay a floor*, Suid. **-ον**, τό, *seat*, mostly pl., *abodes*, πωλικά, νυμφικά, A.*Th.*455 (lyr.), *Ch.*71 (lyr.); ἀρχαιόπλουτα S.*El.*1393 (lyr.), cf. *Fr.*566: Com. phrase, κριβάνων ἑ. Ar.*Fr.*155. II. ἑδώλια, τά, in a ship, *a raised quarter-deck* at the stern, Hdt.1.24, S.*Aj.*1277, E.*Cyc.*238, *Hel.*1571, Lyc.296; expld. as *rowers' benches* by Hsch., Suid., Eust.153.35. 2. sg., *step of the mast*, Arist.*Mech.*851ᵃ40. III. in a theatre, *semicircle of benches*, Poll.4.132 (on the breathing, cf. *EM*317.9; ἐδ- in codd. of A.*Th.* l.c., E. ll. cc.).

**ἐδώλιος** or **ἐδωλιός**, ὁ, a *bird* in Sch.Ar.*Av.*884, Hsch.

**ἔδωλον**, τό, = ἑδώλιον II, Lyc.1320.

**ἐδωλός**, name of a λόχος at Sparta, Hsch.

**ἕε**, poet. for ἕ, *him*, acc. of οὗ. **ἔεδνα, ἐεδνόω, ἐεδνωτής**, Ep. for ἐδν-. **ἐεικοσάβοιος, ἐείκοσι, -κόσορος, -κοστός**, Ep. for εἰκοσ-. **ἐεικώς**, v. εἴκω. **ἐείλεον**, v. εἴλω. **ἔειπα, ἔειπον**, Ep. for εἶπα, εἶπον.

**ἔεις**, Ep. for εἷς, Hes.*Th.*145, *IGRom.*1.1299.

**ἐεισάμην, ἐείσαο**, part. **ἐεισάμενος**, Ep. aor. of εἴδομαι, v. *εἴδω:—but **ἐείσατο, ἐεισάσθην**, v. εἶσομαι II.

**ἐέλδομαι, ἐέλδωρ**, Ep. for ἐλδ-. **ἐέλμεθα, ἐελμένος**, v. εἴλω. **ἐέλπομαι**, Ep. for ἔλπομαι. **ἐέλσαι**, v. εἴλω. **ἐεργάθω, ἔεργε, ἐεργμένος, ἐέργνυμι, ἐέργω**, Ep. for εἰργ-. **ἐερμένος, ἔερτο**, v. εἴρω. **ἐέρση, ἐερσήεις**, Ep. for ἐρσ-. **ἐέρχατο**, v. εἴργω. **ἐέσσατο** (A), Ep. 3 sg. aor. 1 Med. of ἵζω; v. sub ἐφίζω I. **ἐέσσατο** (B), Ep. 3 sg. aor. Med. of ἕννυμι. **ἔεστο**, Ep. 3 sg. plpf. Pass. of ἕννυμι.

**ἑετῶς**, *easily*, Hsch., Suid. **ἐεχμένη**· συνεχομένη, Hsch. **ἐϝέρην**, v. εἴρω. **ἔζελεν**· ἔβαλεν, Id. (cf. ζέλλω). **ἔζινεν**· ἐπεσβέννυεν, Id.

**ἕζομαι**, imper. ἕζευ Il.24.522: impf. and aor. 2 ἑζόμην: aor. 1 Pass. ἕσθην, only ἧ 'σθῶ; S.*OC*195 (s.v.l.):—*seat oneself, sit*, in Hom. only pres. and impf., εἰνὶ θρόνῳ Il.15.150; ἐς θρόνους Od.4.51; ἐπὶ δίφρῳ Il.6.354; κατὰ κλισμούς Od.3.389; ποτὶ βωμόν 22.379; ἐπὶ βάθρον S.*OC*100, cf. Ar.*Ra.*682 (s.v.l.); ἕ. ἐς Κολοφῶνα Mimn.9; ἀμφὶ κλάδοις E.*Ph.*1516 (anap.): c. acc. only, τόδ' ἕζετο μαντεῖον A. *Eu.*3; εἰρεσίας ζυγὸν ἑζόμενον S.*Aj.*249 (lyr.); ἐπὶ χθονὶ.. ἑζέσθην they *sank* to the earth, of a pair of scales, Il.8.74; once in Hdt., ἐκ τοῦ μέσου ἡμῖν ἕζεσθε 8.22, and in late Prose, J.*AJ*18.6.6, Luc.*Syr. D.*31, *Astr.*10; in Att. Prose καθέζομαι was always used. 2. *crouch*, in a posture of defence, Il.22.275, Od.14.31. 3. *sink* to the ground, *collapse*, Il.13.653, 14.495. II. Act., ἕζω *set, place*, is not found: for εἷσα, εἰσάμην, εἴσομαι, εἷμαι, v. ἵζω. (Cf. ἕδος.)

**ἐή**, fem. of ἑός. **ἐή**, exclam., v. ἕ. **ἐήλακεν**· ἐλήφθη, Hsch. **ἔην**, Ep. 3 sg. impf. of εἰμί (*sum*), Hom.: 1st pers., only Il.11.762 vulg.; v. εἰμί. **ἑήνδᾰνε**, Ep. 3 sg. impf. Act. of ἁνδάνω. **ἑῆος**, gen. masc. of ἐΰς (q.v.); cf. ἑός. **ἑῆς**, Ep. gen. of ὅς, *who*, Il.16.208:—but **ἑῆς**, gen. fem. of ἑός, *his*. **ἔησθα**, Ep. 2 sg. impf. of εἰμί (*sum*). **ἔησι**, Ep. 3 sg. subj. pres. of εἰμί (*sum*). **ἐητύς**, ύος, ἡ, *goodness*, Hsch. **ἔθα**· πάλιν, Id.

**ἐθάς**, άδος, ὁ, ἡ, (ἔθος) *accustomed*, ἐ. γενέσθαι Hp.*Mul.*1.12; ἐ. γενέσθαι τινός Th.2.44; εἶναι Plu.*Oth.*5; of persons, *familiar*, Philostr. *VA*8.30: c. dat., τῇ νούσῳ Hp.*Morb.Sacr.*12, cf. Opp.*H.*5.499. II. of things, *customary, usual*, νοῦσοι ἐ. ἀπὸ νεότητος Hp.*Mul.*2.125; ἡδονή Ph.1.316. III. *tame*, Them.*Or.*22.273c.

**ἐθεῖν**· ἐξ ἔθους ἔρχεσθαι, Hsch.

⊛ **ἔθειρα**, ἡ, *hair*, poet. Noun, Hom. only in Il., and always in pl., either of *a horse's mane*, 8.42; or of the *horsehair crest* on helmets, 16.795, 19.382. II. later sg., *hair of the head*, Pi.*I.*5(4).9, A.*Pers.* 1062 (lyr.), E.*Hel.*1124 (lyr.), Theoc.5.91, etc.: also pl., *h.Ven.*228, A.*Ch.*175, E.*Hel.*632, Euph.23, *IG*3.1376, etc.; of a lion's *mane*, Theoc.25.244; porcupine's *quills*, Opp.*C.*3.395; a bird's *feathers*, ib. 123; κρόκου θυόεσσαν ἔθειραν, of the *filiform stigmas* of the saffron, Mosch.2.68.

**ἐθειράζω**, *have long hair*, Theoc.1.34.

⊛ **ἐθειράς**, άδος, ἡ, = ἔθειρα, an old reading in Od.16.176, for γενειάδες, cf. Sch.Theoc.1.34.

**ἐθειρολόγος**, ὁ, *tweezer*, *Hermes* 38.282 (s.v.l.).

**ἐθείρω**, *tend, till*, once in Hom., χαίρει δέ μιν (sc. ἀλωήν) ὅστις ἐθείρῃ Il.21.347:—but in Pass., χρυσέαις φολίδεσσιν ἐθείρεται he *is decked* with golden scales, Orph.*A.*929, cf. Hsch.

**ἐθελ-ακρίβεια** [ῐ], ἡ, *pretence of accuracy*, Sch.Luc.*Gall.*32. **-ακρῑβής**, ές, *making pretence of accuracy*, Sch.Luc.*Vit.Auct.*21. **-άστειος**, ον, *aiming at fashion, foppish*, Hld.7.10. **-εχθρέω**, *bear a grudge against*, ὁ ἐμφανισθεὶς ἂν ἐθελεχθρῇ τῷ μηνύσαντι Charond.ap.Stob. 4.2.24. **-εχθρος**, ον, *bearing one a grudge*, Cratin.407, Ph.2.269. Adv. -ρως, ἔχειν πρός τινα D.39.36, cf. Ph.2.120, Paus.4.4.4. **-ημός**, όν, *willing, voluntary*, Hes.*Op.*118, Call.*Dian.*31, A.R.2.656. Adv. -μῶς Hsch. **-ήμων**, ον, gen. ονος, = foreg., Pl.*Cra.*406a.

**ἐθελο-δουλεία** (-ία Suid.), ἡ, *voluntary subjection*, Pl.*Smp.*184c, D.C.*Fr.*17.2, Procl.*in Prm.*p.737S. **-δουλέω**, *be* or *become a slave willingly*, D.C.45.35. **-δουλος**, ον, *serving voluntarily*, Pl.*R.*562d, Ph.1.376, Aristaenet.2.2. Adv. -λως, ἔχειν Plu.*Arat.*25. **-θρησκεία**, ἡ, *will-worship, self-chosen service*, *Ep.Col.*2.23. **-κᾰκέω**, of soldiers who let themselves be beaten, *play the coward deliberately*, Hdt. 1.127, 5.78, 9.67, Plb.4.38.6, Luc.*Somn.*18, Paus.1.35.2, etc. II. *do wrong deliberately, act of malice prepense*, Ph.2.523, al., *PMasp.*151. 216 (vi A.D.); ἐ. ἐπὶ συμφοραῖς *exult wrongfully* over.., Ph.2.73, cf. 539. **-κάκησις** [ᾰ], εως, ἡ, *wilful neglect of duty*, Plb.3.68.10; εἰς ἐ. ἄγειν to refer a thing to *malice prepense*, Id.27.15.13. **-κακία**, ἡ, = foreg., Suid. **-κᾰκος**, ον, = κακὰ θέλων, Hsch. II. *guilty of wilful cowardice*, of soldiers, τὸ τῶν στρατιωτῶν ἐ. D.H.9.7. Adv. -κως App.*Ital.*7 *Fr.* **-κᾰλος**, ον, *showing goodwill*, Phld.*Herc.* 1457.11. **-κίνδῡνος**, ον, *courting danger, foolhardy*, Poll.3.134. Adv. -νως App.*Pun.*120. **-κωφέω**, *affect deafness*, ἐπεγεῖσθαι S.E.*M.*11.202, Str.1.2.30, Procop.*Goth.*4.12. **-κωφία**, ἡ, *pretended deafness*, Phld.*Rh.*2.118S. **-κωφος**, ον, *pretending deafness, unwilling to hear*, Suid.

**ἐθελοντ-ηδόν**, Adv. *voluntarily, spontaneously*, Th.8.98, D.C.53.8; f.l. for sq., Plb.6.31.2. **-ήν**, Adv. *voluntarily*, Hdt.1.5, X.*Mem.* 2.1.3, Plb.1.49.5, al. **-ήρ**, ῆρος, ὁ, *volunteer*, Od.2.292. **-ής**, οῦ, ὁ, Prose form of foreg. (used by S.*Aj.*24), Hdt.5.104, 110, *IG*1².97. 15, Th.1.60, And.1.3: as Adj., ἐ. φίλος X.*An.*1.6.9 (dub.); τῶν ἐ. τριηράρχων D.18.99. II. = δεικηλιστής, Eust.884.27. **-ί**, Adv. = ἐθελοντηδόν, Th.8.2, Plb.2.22.5, D.S.18.53, etc. **-ως**, = foreg., Sch.Il.19.79.

**ἐθελό-πονος**, ον, *willing to work*, X.*Cyr.*2.1.22, Ael.*NA*4.43. **-πορνος**, ον, *voluntary catamite*, Anacr.21.7. **-πρόξενος**, ον, *one who voluntarily charges himself with the office of* πρόξενος (q.v.) to a foreigner or foreign state, Th.3.70. **-ρήτωρ**, ορος, ὁ, *would-be orator*, *AB*95.18. **-σέβεια**, ἡ, gloss on ἐθελοθρησκεία, Hsch. **-συχνος**, ον, *fond of repetition, a bore*, Crates Com.48 (s.v.l.).

**ἐθελ-ουργέω**, *work freely, indefatigably*, Ael.*NA*7.13. **-ουργός**, όν, *willing to work, indefatigable*, X.*Eq.*10.17, Ael.*NA*4.43; τὸ ἐ. Ph. 2.448. Adv. -γῶς Poll.3.121. **-ούσιος**, α, ον, *voluntary*, X.*Cyr.* 4.2.11; ἀνάγκη ἐ. Id.*Smp.*8.13; *of one's free will*, Pherecyd.(?)98J.; ἐθελούσιον ἱκετεύσαντα D.C.43.12; ἐθελουσίᾳ [τῇ προνοίᾳ] καὶ κατὰ γνώμην Jul.*Or.*5.166b. II. of things, *optional*, [τὸ ἐρᾶν] ἐθελούσιόν ἐστι love is a *matter of free choice*, X.*Cyr.*5.1.10; γνώμη Ph.2. 482; ἐθελουσίᾳ (sc. γνώμῃ) *voluntarily*, Hierocl.p.33A.: regul. Adv. -ίως X.*Hier.*11.12.

**ἐθελοφῐλόσοφος**, ον, *would-be philosopher*, *EM*722.17.

⊛ **ἐθέλω** or **θέλω** (v. infr.), Ep. subj. ἐθέλωμι Il.1.549, 9.397: impf. ἤθελον 14.120, etc.; Ep. and Lyr. ἔθελον 6.336, Thgn.606, B.10.73; Ion. ἐθέλεσκον Il.13.106, Hdt.6.12: fut. ἐθελήσω Il.18.262, etc.; θελήσω Antipho 5.99: aor. 1 ἠθέλησα Hdt.2.2, etc.; Ep. ἐθέλησα Il.18. 396; imper. θέλησον A.*Pr.*783; subj. θελήσῃ ib.1028, X.*Cyr.*2.4.19, etc.; opt. θελήσαιμι S.*OC*1133; part. θελήσας Id.*OT*649 (lyr.): pf. ἠθέληκα X.*Cyr.*5.2.9, Aeschin.2.139, D.47.5; τεθέληκα (Alexandrian acc. to Phryn.307) Lxx *Ps.*40(41).12, Phld.*Rh.*2.76S., S.E.*M.*2.37: plpf. ἠθελήκει X.*HG*6.5.21; ἐτεθελήκεσαν D.C.44.26 codd. (elsewh. ἠθελήκεσαν as 46.47):—θέλω is never found in Hom. or Hes. exc. Il.1.277 (dub.), ὅττι θέλοιεν Od.15.317 as v.l. (ἅσσ' ἐθέλοιεν Aristarch.), nor in Aeol.; rarely in early Ep. and Eleg., θέλοι *h.Ap.*46, θέλει Sol.27.12; but is found in Ion. Inscr., *SIG*45.16 (Halic., v B.C.), 1037.7 (Milet., iv B.C.), and in Semon.7.13, Hippon.22B, Anacr.92:—both forms in codd. of Hdt. and Hp. and in Heraclit. and Democr., also in Pi. and B.: Trag. never use ἐθέλω exc. in augmented forms, ἤθελον, -ησα: Com. never use θέλω exc. in phrases such as ἢν θεὸς θέλῃ, εἰ θεὸς θέλοι, Ar.*Pl.*347, *Ra.*533, or parodies of Trag.: early Att. Inscrr. have ἐθέλω *IG*1².6.41, etc., till 250 B.C., when θέλω becomes common: Att. Prose writers rarely use θέλω exc. in phrases such as ἂν θεὸς θέλῃ Din.2.3 or after a long vowel, e.g. μὴ θελῆσαι Th.5.72, μὴ θελήσας Is. 8.11, μὴ θέλοντας And.1.22, τῷ θέλοντι Id.4.7, etc.; but θέλω Antipho 3.4.3, θελήσουσιν Id.5.99: in later Gr. θέλω is regular exc. in the augmented forms; ἐθέλω is not found in Lxx or NT:—*to be willing* (of consent rather than desire, v. βούλομαι I), but also generally, *wish*, Od.3.324:—Constr.: abs., esp. in part., ἐθέλων ἐθέλουσαν ἀνήγαγεν ib.272; εἰ σύ γε σῷ θυμῷ ἐθέλοις Il.23.894; ἀλλά μοι ἤθελε θυμός Od.11.566: freq. folld. by inf. pres. or aor., *wish to*.., Il.7.364, etc.: with inf. supplied, εἰ δ' ἐθέλεις πεζός (sc. ἰέναι) Od.3.324: c. acc. et inf., *wish that*.., Il.19.274, Hdt.1.3; rarely folld. by ὥστε, E.*Hipp.*1327: later c. ἵνα, *Ev.Matt.*7.12, etc.: not used c. acc. only, exc. when an inf. is easily supplied, εὔκηλος τὰ φράζεαι ἅσσ' ἐθέλησθα (sc. φράζεσθαι) Il.1.554, cf. 9.397, 7.182, Od.14.172; σιτέονται δὲ οὐκ ὅσα ἐθέλουσι (sc. σιτέεσθαι) Hdt.1.71, cf. Th.5.50; εἰ καὶ τῆς ἀξίας ἔλαττον ἐθελήσειέ τις (sc. φράσαι) Jul.*Or.*1.132a: also with neut. Pron. or Adj., τί δὴ θέλων; with what *intent?* A.*Pr.*118. 2. with neg., almost, = δύναμαι, as μίμνειν οὐκ ἐθέλεσκον ἐναντίον they *cared* not to make a stand, i.e. they *were unable*, Il.13.106; οὐδ'.. ἤθελε θυμὸς τειρομένοις ἑτάροισιν ἀμυνέμεν 17.702: metaph. of things, of a stream, οὐδ' ἔθελε προρέειν ἀλλ' ἴσχετο *would* not run on, but stopped, 21.366, cf. Od.8.223, 316, *h.Cer.*45; αὔλειοι δ' ἔτ' ἔχειν οὐκ ἐθέλουσι θύραι Sol.4.28; τὰ δένδρα οὐδέν μ' ἐθέλει διδάσκειν Pl.*Phdr.* 230d, cf. *R.*370b (said to be an Att. use, Greg.Cor.p.135S.). 3. part., ἐθέλων or θέλων *willingly, gladly*, Od.3.272, etc. (also πιθοῦ θελήσας S.*OT*649 (lyr.)); οὐκ ἐθέλων, = ἀέκων, Il.4.300; with Art. like ὁ βουλόμενος, *whoever will*, i.e. *any one*, S.*Ph.*619, *Aj.*1146, Pl. *Grg.*508c, etc. 4. θέλεις οὐ θέλεις *nolens volens*, Arr.*Epict.*3.9.16; θέλει οὐ θέλει ib.3.3, M.Ant.11.15. 5. μὴ ἔθελε, c. inf., *do* not, Il.1.277, 2.247, E.*Fr.*174. 6. εἰ θέλεις if you *please*, S.*OT*343. 7. folld. by subj., τί σοι θέλεις δῆτ' εἰκάθω; in what *wilt* thou that I give way to thee? ib.651 (lyr.); θέλεις μείνωμεν αὐτοῦ; Id.*El.*80. 8. *maintain, hold*, c. acc. et inf., Plu.2.883e, Paus.1.4.6. 9. *delight in, love*, ἔν τινι Lxx 1*Ki.*18.22; τινά ib.*Ps.*17(18).20; but οἱ κακῶς τινὰς θέλοντες their ill-*wishers*, *Cat.Cod.Astr.*7.234. 10. *ordain, decree*, ἠθέλησεν [ὁ ἡγεμὼν] τὸν κίνδυνον τῆς προβολῆς εἶναι πρός τινας *CPR* 20.17 (iii A.D.), etc. II. of inanimate things (cf. supr. I. 2), 1. to express a *future* event, like our *will* or *shall*, εἰ ἐθελήσει ἀναβῆναι ἡ τυραννίς Hdt.1.109; εἰ ἐθελήσει ἐκτρέψαι τὸ ῥέεθρον ὁ Νεῖλος Id.2.11; εἰ θέλει τοι μηδὲν ἀντίξοον καταστῆναι Id.7.49, cf. Pl.*R.*370b, etc.:—in this sense, very rarely of living things, οὐ δοῦναι θέλοι, = οὐκ ἂν δοίη, A.*Eu.*429; εἶπερ.. οὗτός ⟨σ'⟩ ἐθέλει κρατῆσαι Ar.*V.*536, cf. Pi.*N.*7.90, Pl.*R.*375a. 2. *to be naturally disposed, to be wont* or *accustomed*, c. inf., συμβάσιες ἰσχυραὶ οὐκ ἐ. συμμένειν Hdt.1.74; μεγάλα πρήγματα μεγάλοισι κινδύνοισι ἐ. καταιρέεσθαι Id.7.50; αἱ πλευραὶ οὐκ ἐθέλουσιν ἐς τὸ εὐρὺ αὔξεσθαι Hp.*Art.*41; οὐκ ἐ. αἱ γνῶμαι.. ὁμοῖαι εἶναι Th.2.89; τοῦτ' ἐνδελεχὲς ἐ. γίγνεσθαι Arist.*Mete.*347ᵃ5, cf. *Metaph.*1013ᵇ27, al.; οὐ θέλει ζῆν, of premature births, Id.*HA*575ᵃ 28. 3. in phrases expressive of meaning, τὸ θέλει σημαίνειν τὸ τέρας Hdt.1.78; τὸ θέλει τὸ ἔπος εἶπαι Id.6.37; τὸ θέλει τὰ δῶρα λέγειν Id.4.131; τὸ ἔπος τοῦτο ἐθέλει λέγειν ὡς.. Id.2.13. 4. τοῦ θέλοντος, = τοῦ θελήματος, S.*OC*1220 (lyr., s.v.l.).

**ἕθεν** (i.e. ϝέθεν, cf. A.D.*Pron.*77.4), Ep., Lyr., and Trag. gen. for ἕο, οὗ, masc. and fem., *his, her, of him, of her*, Hom., etc.; αὐτοῦ ἕθεν, = ἑαυτοῦ, *IG*4.952.106 (Epid.). II. = ἑκάς, Hsch.

⊛ **ἐθημο-λογέω**, *gather customarily*, *AP*9.551 (Antiphil.). **-σύνη**, ἡ, *custom*, Hsch., Suid.

⊛ **ἐθήμων**, ον, gen. ονος, *accustomed*, c. dat., ἐλπίδι Musae.312: c. gen., κυδοιμοῦ Nonn.*D.*36.464. 2. *customary*, ib.1.433, al.

**ἔθην**, aor. 1 Pass. of ἵημι: but **ἔθην**, aor. 2 Act. of τίθημι.

⊛ **ἐθ-ίζω**, poet. **εἰθ-** *Carm.Aur.*35: Att. fut. ἐθιῶ X.*Cyr.*3.3.53: aor. εἴθισα D.20.68: pf. εἴθικα Pl.*Men.*70b, X.*HG*6.1.15:—Pass., fut. ἐθισθήσομαι D.H.4.11: aor. εἰθίσθην Ar.*V.*512, Hp.*Art.*41, Pl.*Lg.*681b: pf. εἴθισμαι E.*Med.*122 (anap.), Th.1.77; 3 pl. εἰθίδαται Hp.*Acut.*36; late ἠθισμαι *IG*12(5).662.14 (Syros, ii A.D.): plpf. εἴθιστο X.*Ages.*11. 2: (ἔθος):—*accustom*, ἐ. αὐτὸν χαίρειν Pl.*Grg.*510d, cf. Isoc.3.57; τὸ προαιρεῖσθαι.. πότερον ἂν ἐθίζοιμεν X.*Mem.*2.1.2: c. inf., ἐθίσας ἀεί τι λήζεσθαι App.*Hann.*44: c. acc. cogn., ἔθη ἐ. πονηρά Pl.*Lg.*706d; ἐ. τινὰ ταὐτά X.*HG*6.1.15; ἐ. τινὰ πρός τι Luc.*Anach.*20:—Pass., *to be* or *become accustomed* or *used to* do, c. inf., Hp.*Art.*41, Ar.*V.*512, Lys. 14.31, Th.1.77, etc.; εἰθισμένος ἀναισχυντεῖν And.2.4: c. acc. cogn., ἐθίζεσθαι ἔθη Pl.*Lg.*681b; ἐθίζεσθαι σὺν ἔθει τινί X.*Cyr.*1.6.33 (s.v.l.); ἐθίζεσθαι πρός τι Arist.*EN*1119ᵃ25; τι ib.1121ᵃ23; τινί Thphr.*CP*5.9. 11: abs., καθότι εἴθισται as *is the custom*, *PPetr.*3 p.116 (iii B.C.); κατὰ τὰ εἰθισμένα *BGU*1073.12 (iii A.D.), etc.:—in Plu.*Lyc.*12, Bekk. restored εἰθίζοντο from Porph. for the intr. Act. εἴθιζον. II. intr. in Act., *become accustomed*, M.Ant.10.22: c. inf., Id.12.2: c. acc., ἔθιζε καὶ ὅσα ἀπογινώσκεις ib.6: with inf. supplied, ὅπως ἀναγραφῇ τὸ ψήφισμα οὗ καὶ τὰ ἄλλα ἐθίζουσιν (sc. ἀναγράφαι) *BCH*48.370 (Thaumaci, i B.C.). **-ικός**, ή, όν, *arising from habit*, ἀρεταί Plu.2.3a. ⊛ **-ιμος**, ον, *accustomed, usual*, ἔθιμόν [ἐστι] μοι D.S.29.32; τὰν ἐ. τοῖς ἐφήβοις θυσίαν *Supp.Epigr.*1.327.3 (Callatis); ὁ ἐ. Ῥωμαίων ὅρκος *BGU*581.5 (ii A.D.), etc.; τὸ ἐ. *usage*, A.D.*Synt.*77.27; τὰ ἐ. *customs*, Ath.4. 151e; κατὰ τὰ ἐ. *IG*12(7).237.26 (Amorgos, i B.C.). Adv. -μως A.D. *Pron.*78.25. **-ισμα**, ατος, τό, (ἐθίζω) *custom, habit*, Pl.*Lg.* 793d. **-ισμός**, ὁ, *accustoming, habituation*, Arist.*EN*1098ᵇ4, al.; τὰ κατ' ἐθισμόν τινος Lxx *Ge.*31.35; πρός τι Hierocl.*in CA*26 p.479M.

pl., *habits*, Arist.*Pol.*1331b6; *usages*, Posidipp.25, Plb.1.17.11; οἱ ἐξ ἀρχῆς ἐ. *PTeb.*40.20 (ii B.C.); οἱ νόμοι καὶ οἱ ἐ. Phld.*Piet.*102, cf. *IG*2².1043.30 (i B.C.); οἱ πολύτροποι ἐ. τῶν λέξεων *customary modes* of speech, Epicur.*Nat.*28.1, al. **-ιστέον**, *one must accustom*, τῇ γνώμῃ ὑπηρετεῖν ἐ. τὸ σῶμα X.*Mem.*2.1.28, cf. Pl.*R.*396a, etc. **-ιστός**, ή, όν, *to be acquired by habit*, ἀρετή, opp. μαθητόν, Arist.*EN*1099a9, al. 2. *acquired by habit*, τὸ ἐ. ἐν τοῖς ἡδέσιν Id.*Rh.*1369b16.

**ἐθμή**, ἡ, *vapour*, Hsch. ※ **ἐθμοί**· πολλοί, δεσμοί, πλόκαμοι, Id.

**ἐθν-άρχης**, ου, ὁ, *ruler of a tribe* or *nation*, Ἄσανδρος ἀντὶ ἐθνάρχου βασιλεὺς ἀναγορευθεὶς Βοσπόρου Luc.*Macr.*17; *sheikh*, *OGI*616.2 (Arabia); of Abraham, Ph.1.513. 2. title of Jewish official, LXX 1*Ma.*14.47, Str.17.1.13, Nic.Dam.p.143 D., 2*Ep.Cor.*11.32, J.*AJ* 13.6.7. II. Adj., *ruling over nations*, ἐ. θεοί Jul.*Gal.*115d, cf. 143a. **-αρχία**, ἡ, *office of ethnarch*, J.*AJ*17.13.1. **-ηδόν**, Adv. *by nations, as a whole nation*, LXX 4*Ma.*2.19. **-ικός**, ή, όν, *national*, συστάσεις Plb.30.13.6; διαστάσεις Id.4.21.2; χρεῖαι D.S.18.13; ἰδιότητες Phld.*Rh.*1.154 S.; διαφοραί Str.2.3.1. II. *foreign, gentile*, *Ev.Matt.*5.47; ἐθνικῇ.. ἐν σοφίᾳ *Epigr.Gr.*430.6. Adv. -κῶς, opp. Ἰουδαϊκῶς, *Ep.Gal.*2.14. b. in the Roman Empire, *provincial*, *Cod. Just.*12.63.2.6. III. Gramm., *indicating nationality*, Str.14.2.28, D.T.636.11, A.D.*Synt.*190.20. Adv. -κῶς, παραχθέν ib.5, cf. Str.4.1.1, D.L.7.56. 2. *dialectal*, ἔθος A.D.*Synt.*46.1. IV. ἐθνικός, ὁ, *tax-collector*, *POxy.*126.13 (vi A.D.). **-ίτης** [ῑ], ου, ὁ, *of the same nation*, Eust.901.9, Suid.; **ἐθνιστής**, Hsch.

※ **ἔθνος**, εος, τό: (ϝέθνος, cf. Il.2.87, 7.115, al.):—*number of people living together, company, body of men*, ἑτάρων ἔ., ἔ. ἑταίρων, *band* of comrades, Il.3.32, 7.115, etc.; ἔθνος λαῶν *host* of men, 13.495; of particular tribes, Λυκίων μέγα ἔ. 12.330; Ἀχαιῶν ἔ. 17.552: pl., ἔθνεα πεζῶν 11.724, cf. 2.91; ἔ. νεκρῶν Od.10.526; of animals, ἔ. μελισσάων, ὀρνίθων, μυιάων, *swarms, flocks*, etc., Il.2.87,459,469; ἔθνη θηρῶν S.*Ph.*1147 (lyr.), *Ant.*344; ἔ. ἀνέρων, γυναικῶν, Pi.*O.*1.66, *P.*4.252; ἔ. βρότεον, θνατόν, Id.*N.*3.74, 11.42; ἔ. τόδε, of the Erinyes, A.*Eu.*366 (lyr.). 2. after Hom., *nation, people*, τὸ Μηδικὸν ἔ. (γένος being a subdivision of ἔθνος) Hdt.1.101; ἔ. ἠπειρογενές, μαχαιροφόρον, A.*Pers.*43,56 (anap.), etc.; τῶν μηδισάντων ἐθνέων τῶν Ἑλληνικῶν Hdt.9.106. b. later, τὰ ἔ. *foreign, barbarous nations*, opp. Ἕλληνες, Arist.*Pol.*1324b10; ἔ. νομάδων, of Bedawin, *LW*2203 (Syria); at Athens, athletic *clubs of non-Athenians*, *IG*2². 444, al.; in LXX, *non-Jews*, *Ps.*2.1, al., cf. *Act.Ap.*7.45; *Gentiles*, τῶν ἐθνῶν τε καὶ Ἰουδαίων ib.14.5, etc.; used of *Gentile Christians*, *Ep. Rom.*15.27. c. at Rome, = *provinciae*, App.*BC*2.13, Hdn.1.2.1, *PStrassb.*22.19 (iii A.D.), D.C.36.41, etc.: so in sg., *province*, ὁ τυραννήσας τοῦ ἔθνους D.Chr.43.11; ὁ ἡγούμενος τοῦ ἔθνους the governor of the *province*, *POxy.*1020.5 (iii A.D.). 3. *class* of men, *caste, tribe*, τὸ Θετταλῶν.. πενεστικὸν ἔ. Pl.*Lg.*776d; ἔθνος κηρυκικόν Id. *Plt.*290b; οἶσθά τι ἔ. ἠλιθιώτερον ῥαψῳδῶν; X.*Smp.*3.6; δημιουργικὸν ἔ. Pl.*Grg.*455b, cf. Arist.*Ath.Fr.*3; ἔ. Βραχμάνων D.S.17.102; τὰ ἱερὰ ἔ. the *orders* of priests, *OGI*90.17 (ii B.C.); *trade-associations* or *guilds*, ἔθνη καὶ ἐργαστήρια *PPetr.*3 p.67 (iii B.C.), al.; *class* in respect to rank or station, οὐ πρὸς τοῦτο βλέποντες.. ὅπως.. ἕν τι ἔ. ἔσται διαφερόντως εὔδαιμον Pl.*R.*420b, cf. 421c, D.21.131. 4. *sex*, θῆλυ, ἄρρεν ἔ., X.*Oec.*7.26. 5. *part, member*, Hp.*Loc.Hom.*1. II. of a single person, *a relation*, Pi.*N.*5.43.

**ἐθνοφύλαξ**, *gentilicius*, Gloss.

※ **ἔθος**, εος, τό, (ἔθω) *custom, habit*, ἔ. τὸ πρόσθε τοκήων (but prob. f.l. for ἦθος) A.*Ag.*728 (lyr.); τὸ σύνηθες ἔ. S.*Ph.*894; εἰ τὸ ἔ. συνθήκη Pl.*Cra.*435a; πάτρια ἔ. Id.*Plt.*295a: prov., "ἔ.", φασί, "δευτέρη φύσις" Jul.*Mis.*353a; ἐν ἔθει τῇ πόλει εἶναι to be *the habit*, Th.2.64; ἔ. ἐστίν τινι, c. inf., Cratin.Jun.7.1, Alex.253; ἔθος ἔχειν, c. inf., Plu. *Them.*4; ἔθει *by habit, habitually*, opp. φύσει, Arist.*EN*1179b21; ἐν ἔθει Id.*Fr.*122; δι' ἔθος, opp. ἐκ γενετῆς, Id.*EN*1154a33; ἐξ ἔθους ib. 1103a17; κατὰ τὰ Ῥωμαίων ἔ. *PSI*3.182 (iii A.D.), etc. (σϝέθ-, cf. Lat. *suesco*; v. βεσόν.)

**ἐθρίς**· τομίας (ταλμ- cod.) κριός, Hsch.; cf. ἶθρις.

**ἔθρισεν**, v. θερίζω.

※ **ἔθω**, *to be accustomed, to be wont*: pres. only in part., κακὰ πόλλ' ἔρδεσκεν ἔθων much ill he wrought *after his wont*, Il.9.540; οὓς παῖδες ἐριδμαίνωσιν ἔθοντες 16.260 (in these passages some Gramm. expld. ἔθων as, = βλάπτων, φθείρων (and it was so used by Call.*Fr.*108), and (in 16.260) ἐρεθίζων, cf. ἔθει· φθείρει, ἐρεθίζει, Hsch., ἐθρίς, ἶθρις): pf. εἴωθα Il.5.766, etc., Ep. and Ion. ἔωθα 8.408, etc., is used as pres.; plpf. εἰώθειν, Ion. ἐώθεα, as impf.; part. εἰωθώς, Ion. ἐωθώς, also in Archipp.48, Araros19; Dor. 3 pl. pf. ἐθώκατι Hsch.: mostly c. inf., Il.5.766, Hdt.3.31, Th.1.99, etc.: impers., ὡς εἴωθε as *is the custom*, Ar.*Ec.*282; ὥσπερ εἰώθει Plu.*Sull.*0, etc.: freq. abs. in part., of persons, *accustomed, customary, usual*, ἡνιόχῳ εἰωθότι Il.5.231; ὑμῖν.. τοῖς εἰωθόσιν *who are used* [to hear me], S.*Ph.*939; οὐκ εἰωθὼς *praeter morem*, Hdt.1.111; of things, τὰ ἐωθότα νοήματα Id.3.80; ἐν τῷ εἰ. τρόπῳ Pl.*Ap.*27b, etc.: freq. in neut., παρὰ τὸ εἰ. contrary to *custom*, Th.4.17,55; τὰ εἰ. *ordinary things*, Ar.*Ra.*1, Th.2.51, etc.

**εἶ**, indecl., name of the letter ε, pronounced like the letter itself, Pl.*Cra.*393d, 437a, al., *Michel*832.46 (Samos, iv B.C.), etc.; later pronounced ῖ, Hdn.Gr.2.390; written ῖ, *BGU*427.15.

※ **εἰ**, Dor., = *where*, *IG*9(1).682 (Corc.), 14.352 ii 13 (Halaesa); but εἰ μήν, later Greek, = ἦ μήν, LXX *Ge.*22.17, al., *PTeb.*22.13 (ii B.C.), etc.; Dor. εἰ μάν *IG*5(1).1390.27 (Andania, i B.C.).

※ **εἰ**, Att.-Ion. and Arc. (for εἰκ, v. infr. II ad init.), = Dor. and Aeol. αἰ, αἰκ (q.v.), Cypr. ἤ *Inscr.Cypr.*135.10 H., both εἰ and αἰ in Ep.:—Particle used interjectionally with imper. and to express a wish, but usu. either in conditions, *if*, or in indirect questions, *whether*. In the former use its regular negative is μή; in the latter, οὐ.

A. INTERJECTIONALLY, in Hom., *come now!* c. imper., εἰ δὲ.. ἄκουσον Il.9.262; εἰ δὲ καὶ αὐτοὶ φευγόντων ib.46; most freq. with ἄγε (q.v.), 1.302, al. 2. in wishes, c. opt., ἀλλ' εἴ τις.. καλέσειεν 10.111, cf. 24.74; so later, εἴ μοι ξυνείη μοῖρα S.*OT*863 (lyr.); εἴ μοι γένοιτο φθόγγος ἐν βραχίοσιν E.*Hec.*836: more freq. folld. by γάρ, αἲ γὰρ δὴ οὕτως εἴη Il.4.189, al.; εἰ γὰρ γενοίμην ἀντὶ σοῦ νεκρός E.*Hipp.* 1410; εἰ γὰρ γένοιτο X.*Cyr.*6.1.38; εἰ γὰρ ἐν τούτῳ εἴη Pl.*Prt.*310d; of unattained wishes, in Hom. only c. opt., εἰ γὰρ ἐγών.. Διὸς πάϊς αἰγιόχοιο εἴην Il.13.825; Ζεῦ πάτερ, αἰ γὰρ ἐμὸς πόσις εἴη Alcm.29; later with past tenses of ind., εἰ γάρ μ' ὑπὸ γῆν.. ἧκεν A.*Pr.*152 (anap.); εἰ γὰρ τοσαύτην δύναμιν εἶχον ὥστε.. E.*Alc.*1072: twice in Od. c. inf. (cf. the use of inf. in commands), αἲ γὰρ τοῖος ἐών.. ἐμὸς γαμβρὸς καλέεσθαι 7.311, cf. 24.376. b. εἴθε, Ep. αἴθε, is freq. used in wishes in the above constructions, εἴθε οἱ αὐτῷ Ζεὺς ἀγαθὸν τελέσειεν 2.33; εἴθ' ὡς ἡβώοιμι Il.7.157; ἰὼ γᾶ, εἴθ' ἔμ' ἐδέξω A.*Ag.*1537 (lyr.); εἴθε σοι, ὦ Περίκλεις, τότε συνεγενόμην X.*Mem.*1.2.46: later c. inf., γαίης χθαμαλωτέρη εἴθε.. κεῖσθαι *AP*9.284 (Crin.). c. εἰ γάρ, εἴθε are also used with ὤφελον (Ep. ὤφελλον), of past unattained wishes, αἴθ' ὤφελλες στρατοῦ ἄλλου σημαίνειν Il.14.84; εἰ γὰρ ὤφελον [κατιδεῖν] Pl.*R.*432c. d. folld. by a clause expressing a consequence of the fulfilment of the wish, αἲ γὰρ τοῦτο.. ἔπος τετελεσμένον εἴη· τῷ κε τάχα γνοίης.. Od.15.536, cf. 17.496, al.; sts. hard to distinguish from εἰ in conditions (which may be derived from this use), εἴ μοί τι πίθοιο, τό κεν πολὺ κέρδιον εἴη Il.7.28.

B. IN CONDITIONS, *if*: I. with INDIC., 1. with all tenses (for fut., v. infr. 2), to state a condition, with nothing implied as to its fulfilment, εἰ δ' οὕτω τοῦτ' ἐστίν, ἐμοὶ μέλλει φίλον εἶναι but *if* this is so, it will be.., Il.1.564: any form of the Verb may stand in apodosi, εἰ θεοί τι δρῶσιν αἰσχρόν, οὐκ εἰσὶν θεοί E.*Fr.*292.7; εἰ δοκεῖ, πλέωμεν S.*Ph.* 526; εἰ Φαῖδρον ἀγνοῶ, καὶ ἐμαυτοῦ ἐπιλέλησμαι Pl.*Phdr.*228a; κάκιστ' ἀπολοίμην, Ξανθίαν εἰ μὴ φιλῶ Ar.*Ra.*579, cf. Od.17.475; εἰ θεοῦ ἦν, οὐκ ἦν αἰσχροκερδής· εἰ δ' αἰσχροκερδής, οὐκ ἦν θεοῦ Pl.*R.*408c; εἰ ταῦτα λέγων διαφθείρω τοὺς νέους, ταῦτ' ἂν εἴη βλαβερά Id.*Ap.*30b, cf. 25b; εἰ οὗτοι ὀρθῶς ἀπέστησαν, ὑμεῖς ἂν οὐ χρεὼν ἄρχοιτε *if* these were right in their revolt, (it would follow that) you rule when you have no right, Th.3.40. b. to express a general condition, *if ever, whenever*, sts. with pres., εἴ τις δύο ἢ καὶ πλείους τις ἡμέρας λογίζεται, μάταιός ἐστιν S.*Tr.*943: with impf., εἴ τίς τι ἠρώτα ἀπεκρίνοντο Th.7.10: rarely with aor., D.S.31.26.1, S.E.*P.*1.84; cf. III. 2. 2. with fut. (much less freq. than ἐάν c. subj.), either to express a future supposition emphatically, εἰ φθάσομεν τοὺς πολεμίους κατακαίνοντες οὐδεὶς ἡμῶν ἀποθανεῖται X.*Cyr.*7.1.19; εἰ μὴ βοηθήσετε οὐ περιέσται τἀκεῖ Th.6.91; εἰ αὕτη ἡ πόλις ληφθήσεται, ἔχεται ἡ πᾶσα Σικελία ibid.; in threats or warnings, εἰ μὴ καθέξεις γλῶσσαν ἔσται σοι κακά E.*Fr.*5; εἰ τιμωρήσεις Πατρόκλῳ, αὐτὸς ἀποθανῇ Pl.*Ap.*28c, cf. D.28.21: or, b. to express a present intention or expectation, αἶρε πλῆκτρον εἰ μαχεῖ *if* you mean to fight, Ar.*Av.*759; ἐγὼ μὲν οὐκ ἀνήρ.. εἰ ταῦτ' ἀνατεὶ τῇδε κείσεται κράτη S.*Ant.*485, cf. Il.1.61, E.*Hec.*863. 3. with historical tenses, implying that the condition is or was unfulfilled. a. with impf., referring to present time or to continued or repeated action in past time (in Hom. always the latter, Il.24.715, al.): ταῦτα οὐκ ἂν ἐδύναντο ποιεῖν, εἰ μὴ διαίτῃ μετρίᾳ ἐχρῶντο they would not be able to do this (as they do), *if* they did not live an abstemious life, X.*Cyr.*1.2.16, cf. Pl.*R.*489b; οὐκ ἂν νήσων ἐκράτει, εἰ μή τι καὶ ναυτικὸν εἶχεν he (Agamemnon) would not have been master of islands, *if* he had not had also some naval force, Th.1.9; αἰ δ' ἦχες ἔσλων ἵμερον ἢ κάλων.. αἴδως κεν.. ἦχεν Sapph.28; εἰ ἦσαν ἄνδρες ἀγαθοί.. οὐκ ἄν ποτε ταῦτα ἔπασχον *if* they had been good men, they would never have suffered as they did, Pl.*Grg.*516e, cf. X.*Mem.*1.1.5; εἰ γὰρ ἐγὼ τάδε ᾔδε'.. οὐκ ἂν ὑπεξέφυγε *if* I had known this.., Il.8. 366. b. with aor. referring to past time, εἰ μὴ ἔφυσε θεὸς μέλι.. ἔφασκον γλύσσονα σῦκα πέλεσθαι Xenoph.38; εἰ μὴ ὑμεῖς ἤλθετε, ἐπορευόμεθα ἂν ἐπὶ βασιλέα had you not come, we should be on our way.., X.*An.*2.1.4; καὶ ἴσως ἂν ἀπέθανον, εἰ μὴ ἡ ἀρχὴ διὰ ταχέων κατελύθη Pl.*Ap.*32d, cf. Il.5.680, Od.4.364, D.4.5, 27.63: with plpf. in apodosi, εἰ τριάκοντα μόναι μετέπεσον τῶν ψήφων, ἀπεπεφεύγη ἂν Pl. *Ap.*36a. c. rarely with plpf. referring to action finished in past or present time, λοιπὸν δ' ἂν ἦν ἡμῖν ἔτι περὶ τῆς πόλεως διαλεχθῆναι, εἰ μὴ προτέρα τῶν ἄλλων τὴν εἰρήνην ἐπεποίητο *if* she had not (as she has done) made peace before the rest, Isoc.5.56, cf. Pl.*Ti.*21c. II. with SUBJ., εἰ is regularly joined with ἄν (Ep. κε, κεν), cf. ἐάν: Arc. εἰκαν in Tegean Inscrr. of iv B.C. (*IG*5(2).3.16,31, 6.2, *SIG*306.34) should be understood as εἰκ ἄν (εἰ : εἰκ = οὐ : οὐκ), since εἰ δ' ἄν is also found in *IG*5(2).3.2, 6.45, and εἰκ alone, ib.3.21; but ἄν (κε, κεν) are freq. absent in Hom. as Od.5.221, 14.373 (and cf. infr. 2), and Lyr., Pi. (who never uses εἰ with ἄν or κε(ν)) *P.*4.266, al.; in dialects, αἰ δείλητ' ἀγχωρεῖν *IG*9(1).334.6 (Locr., v B.C.), cf. Foed.Dor.ap.Th.5. 79; rarely in Hdt., εἰ μὴ ἀναβῇ 2.13; occasionally in Trag., A.*Eu.* 234, S.*OT*198 (lyr.), etc.; very rarely in Att. Prose, εἰ ξυστῶσιν αἱ πόλεις Th.6.21; εἴ τι που ἄλσος ἢ τέμενος ἀφειμένον ᾖ Pl.*Lg.*761c: in later Prose, εἴ τις θελήσῃ *Apoc.*11.5; εἰ φονεύῃ Plot.2.9.9, cf. Procl. *Inst.*26. 1. when the apodosis is fut., to express a future condition more distinctly and vividly than εἰ c. opt., but less so than εἰ c. fut. ind. (supr. I. 2a); εἰ δέ κεν ὣς ἔρξῃς καί τοι πείθωνται Ἀχαιοί, γνώσῃ ἔπειθ'.. *if* thou do thus.., thou shalt know, Il.2.364, cf. 1.128, 3.281, Od.17.549; ἂν δέ τις ἀνθιστῆται, σὺν ὑμῖν πειρασόμεθα χειροῦσθαι X. *An.*7.3.11; ἂν μὴ νῦν ἐθέλωμεν ἐκεῖ πολεμεῖν αὐτῷ, ἐνθάδ' ἴσως ἀναγ-

καθησόμεθα τοῦτο ποιεῖν *if* we be not now willing, D.4.50, cf. X.*Cyr.* 5.3.27: folld. by imper., ἢν εἰρήνης δοκῆτε δεῖσθαι, ἄνευ ὅπλων ἥκετε ib.3.2.13, cf. 5.4.30. 2. when the apodosis is present, denoting customary or repeated action, to express a general condition, *if ever*, ἤν ποτε δασμὸς ἵκηται, σοὶ τὸ γέρας πολὺ μεῖζον (sc. ἐστί) *whenever* a division comes, your prize is (always) greater, Il.1.166; ἢν ἐγγὺς ἔλθῃ θάνατος, οὐδεὶς βούλεται θνῄσκειν *if* death come near, E.*Alc.* 671; with ἄν omitted, εἴ περ γάρ τε χόλον..καταπέψῃ ἀλλά..ἔχει κότον Il.1.81. b. with Rhet. present in apodosis, ἐὰν μὴ οἱ φιλόσοφοι βασιλεύσωσιν, οὐκ ἔστι κακῶν παῦλα there is (i.e. can be, will be) no rest .., Pl.*R.*473d. III. with OPTATIVE (never with ἄν in early Gr., later ἐάν c. opt., Dam.*Pr.*114, al.), 1. to express a future condition less definitely than ἐάν c. subj., usu. with opt. with ἄν in apod., ἦ κεν γηθήσαι Πρίαμος Πριάμοιό τε παῖδες..εἰ σφῶιν τάδε πάντα πυθοίατο μαρναμένοιιν surely they would exult, *if* they should hear.., Il.1.255, cf. 7.28, Od.3.223; εἴης φορητὸς οὐκ ἄν, εἰ πράσσοις καλῶς A.*Pr.*979; οὐδὲ γὰρ ἄν με ἐπαινοίη, εἰ ἐξελαύνοιμι τοὺς εὐεργέτας X.*An.*7.7.11; οἶκος δ' αὐτός, εἰ φθογγὴν λάβοι, σαφέστατ' ἂν λέξειεν A.*Ag.*37, etc.: fut. opt. is f.l. in Pl.*Tht.*164a: with pres. ind. in apod., Xenoph.34.3, Democr.253: with fut. ind., Meliss.5. b. in Hom. sts. with pres. opt., to express an unfulfilled present condition, εἰ μὲν νῦν ἐπὶ ἄλλῳ ἀεθλεύοιμεν, ἦ τ' ἂν ἐγὼ τὰ πρῶτα φεροίμην *if* we were now contending, etc., Il.23.274: rarely in Trag., εἰ μὴ κνίζοι (= εἰ μὴ ἔκνιζε) E.*Med.*568; also εἰ ἀναγκαῖον εἴη ἀδικεῖν ἢ ἀδικεῖσθαι, ἑλοίμην ἂν μᾶλλον ἀδικεῖσθαι Pl.*Grg.*469c. 2. when the apodosis is past, denoting customary or repeated action, to express a general condition in past time (corresponding to use of subj. in present time, supr. II. 2); once in Hom., εἴ τίς με..ἐνίπτοι, ἀλλὰ σὺ τόν γ'..κατέρυκες Il.24.768; εἰ δέ τινας θορυβουμένους αἴσθοιτο.., κατασβεννύναι τὴν ταραχὴν ἐπειρᾶτο *if* he should see (*whenever* he saw) any troops in confusion, he (always) tried, X.*Cyr.*5.3.55, cf. *An.*4.5.13, *Mem.*4.2.40; εἴ τις ἀντείποι, εὐθὺς ἐτεθνήκει *if* any one made objection, he was a dead man at once, Th. 8.66; ἀλλ' εἴ τι μὴ φέροιμεν, ὤτρυνεν φέρειν E.*Alc.*755. For εἰ c. ind. in this sense v. supr. I. 1: ind. and opt. are found in same sentence, ἐμίσει, οὐκ εἴ τις κακῶς πάσχων ἠμύνετο, ἀλλ' εἴ τις εὐεργετούμενος ἀχάριστος φαίνοιτο X.*Ages.*11.3. 3. in oratio obliqua after past tenses, representing ἐάν c. subj. or εἰ with a primary (never an historical) tense of the ind. in oratio recta, ἐλογίζοντο ὡς, εἰ μὴ μάχοιντο, ἀποστήσοιντο αἱ πόλεις (representing ἐὰν μὴ μαχώμεθα, ἀποστήσονται) X.*HG*6.4.6, cf. D.21.104, X.*HG*5.2.2; ἔλεγεν ὅτι, εἰ βλαβερὰ πεπραχὼς εἴη, δίκαιος εἴη ζημιοῦσθαι (representing εἰ βλαβερὰ πέπραχε, δίκαιός ἐστι) ib.32, cf. *An.*6.6.25; εἰ δέ τινα φεύγοντα λήψοιτο, προηγόρευεν ὅτι ὡς πολεμίῳ χρήσοιτο (representing εἴ τινα λήψομαι, χρήσομαι) Id.*Cyr.*3.1.3; also, where oratio obliqua is implied in the leading clause, οὐκ ἦν τοῦ πολέμου πέρας Φιλίππῳ, εἰ μὴ Θηβαίους ..ἐχθροὺς ποιήσειε τῇ πόλει, i.e. Philip thought there would be no end to the war, *un*less he should make.. (his thought having been ἐὰν μὴ ποιήσω), D.18.145; ἐβούλοντο γὰρ σφίσιν, εἴ τινα λάβοιεν, ὑπάρχειν ἀντὶ τῶν ἔνδον, ἢν ἄρα τύχωσί τινες ἐζωγρημένοι Th.2.5. 4. c. opt. with ἄν, only when the clause serves as apodosis as well as protasis, cf. Pl.*Prt.*329b, D.4.18, X.*Mem.*1.5.3 (v. ἄν A. III. d). IV. c. INF., in oratio obliqua, only in Hdt., εἰ γὰρ δὴ δεῖν πάντως περιθεῖναι ἄλλῳ τέῳ τὴν βασιληΐην, [ἔφη] δικαιότερον εἶναι κτλ. 1.129; εἰ εἶναι τοῦτο μὴ φίλον 2.64, cf. 172, 3.105,108. V. after Verbs denoting *wonder, delight, indignation, disappointment, contentment*, and similar emotions, εἰ c. ind. is used instead of ὅτι, to express the object of the feeling in a hypothetical form, θαυμάζω εἰ μηδεὶς ὑμῶν μήτ' ἐνθυμεῖται μήτ' ὀργίζεται, ὁρῶν.. I wonder *that* no one of you is either concerned or angry when he sees.., D.4.43; οὐκ ἀγαπᾷ εἰ μὴ δίκην δέδωκεν, ἀλλ' εἰ μὴ καὶ χρυσῷ στεφάνῳ στεφανωθήσεται ἀγανακτεῖ Aeschin.3.147: after past tenses, ἐθαύμασε δ' εἰ μὴ φανερόν ἐστιν X.*Mem.*1.1.13; δεινὸν εἰσῄει, εἰ μὴ..δόξει D.19.33; ἐθαύμαζον εἴ τι ἕξει τις χρήσασθαι τῷ λόγῳ Pl.*Phd.*95a; οὐδὲ ᾐσχύνθη εἰ..ἐπάγει D.21.105: in oratio obliqua (expressed or implied) c. opt., ἐπεῖπεν ὡς δεινὸν (sc. εἴη) εἰ..μεγαλόψυχος γένοιτο Aeschin.2.157; ᾤκτιρον εἰ ἁλώσοιντο X.*An.*1.4.7; ἐθαύμαζε δ' εἴ τις ἀρετὴν ἐπαγγελλόμενος ἀργύριον πράττοιτο he wondered *that* any one should demand money, Id.*Mem.*1.2.7; ἔχαιρον ἀγαπῶν εἴ τις ἐάσοι I rejoiced, being content *if* any one should let it pass, Pl.*R.*450a:—in this use the neg. οὐ is also found, ἀγανακτῶ εἰ ὁ Φίλιππος ἁρπάζων οὐ λυπεῖ D.8.55; δεινὸν ἂν εἴη εἰ οἱ ἐκείνων ξύμμαχοι οὐκ ἀπεροῦσιν Th.1.121; τέρας λέγεις, εἰ οὐκ ἂν δύναιντο λαθεῖν Pl.*Men.*91d, etc. VI. in citing a fact as a ground of argument or appeal, *as surely as, since*, εἴ ποτ' ἔην γε *if* there was [as there was], i.e. *as sure as* there was such an one, Il.3.180, al.; εἰ τότε κοῦρος ἔα, νῦν αὖτέ με γῆρας ὀπάζει 4.321; πολλοὺς γὰρ οἶκε εἶναι εὐπετέστερον διαβάλλειν ἢ ἕνα, εἰ Κλεομένεα μὲν μοῦνον οὐκ οἷός τε ἐγένετο διαβαλεῖν, τρεῖς δὲ μυριάδας Ἀθηναίων ἐποίησε τοῦτο it seems easier to deceive many than one, *if* (as was the fact, i.e. *since*) he was not able.., Hdt.5.97, cf. 1.60, al. VII. ELLIPTICAL CONSTRUCTIONS: 1. with apodosis implied in the context, εἰ having the force of *in case, supposing that*, πρὸς τὴν πόλιν, εἰ ἐπιβοηθοῖεν, ἐχώρουν they marched towards the city [so as to meet the citizens], *in case* they should rush out, Th.6.100; ἱκέται πρὸς σὲ δεῦρ' ἀφίγμεθα, εἴ τινα πόλιν φράσειας ἡμῖν εὔερον we have come hither to you, *in case* you should tell us of some fleecy city (i.e. that we might hear of it), Ar.*Av.*120; παρέζεο καὶ λαβὲ γούνων, αἴ κέν πως ἐθέλῃσιν ἐπὶ Τρώεσσιν ἀρῆξαι sit by him and grasp his knees [so as to persuade him], *in case* he be willing to help the Trojans, Il.1.408, cf. 66, Od.1.94, 3.92; ἄκουσον καὶ ἐμοῦ, ἐάν σοι ἔτι ταὐτὰ δοκῇ hear me also [that you may assent], *in case* the same opinion please you, Pl.*R.*358b; ἰδὲ δή, ἐάν σοι ὅπερ ἐμοὶ συνδοκῇ look now, *in case* you approve what I do, ib. 434a. 2. with apodosis suppressed for rhetorical reasons, εἴ περ γάρ κ' ἐθέλῃσιν Ὀλύμπιος..στυφελίξαι *if* he wish to thrust him away, [he will do so], Il.1.580; εἰ μὲν δώσουσι γέρας—· εἰ δέ κε μὴ δώωσιν, ἐγὼ δέ κεν αὐτὸς ἕλωμαι *if* they shall give me a prize, [well and good]; but *if* they give not, then I will take one for myself, 1.135, cf. 6.150, Ar.*Pl.*468; καὶ ἢν μὲν ξυμβῇ ἡ πεῖρα—· εἰ δὲ μή.. and *if* the attempt succeed, [well]; otherwise.., Th.3.3, cf. Pl.*Prt.*325d. 3. with the Verb of the protasis omitted, chiefly in the following expressions: a. εἰ μή *except*, οὐδὲν ἄλλο σιτέονται, εἰ μὴ ἰχθῦς μοῦνον Hdt. 1.200; μὰ τὼ θεώ, εἰ μὴ Κρίτυλλά γ' [εἰμί]—nay, *if* I'm not Critylla! i.e. I am, Ar.*Th.*898; εἰ μὴ ὅσον *except* only, ἐγὼ μέν μιν οὐκ εἶδον, εἰ μὴ ὅσον γραφῇ Hdt.2.73, cf. 1.45, 2.20; εἰ μὴ εἰ Th.1.17, Pl.*Grg.*480b, etc.; εἰ μή τι οὖν, ἀλλὰ σμικρόν γέ μοι τῆς ἀρχῆς χάλασον *if* nothing else, yet.., Id.*Men.*86e; ironical, εἰ μὴ ἄρα ἡ τῆς ἀρετῆς ἐπιμέλεια διαφθορά ἐστιν X.*Mem.*1.2.8; εἰ μή πέρ γε τὸν ὑοσκύαμον χρήματα εἶναι φήσομεν Id.*Oec.*1.13. b. εἰ δὲ μή but *if* not, i.e. *otherwise*, προηγόρευε τοῖς Λαμψακηνοῖσι μετιέναι Μιλτιάδεα, εἰ δὲ μή, σφέας πίτυος τρόπον ἀπείλεε ἐκτρίψειν Hdt.6.37, cf. 56; after μάλιστα μέν, Th.1.32,35, etc.:—after a preceding neg., μὴ τύπτ'· εἰ δὲ μή, σαυτόν ποτ' αἰτιάσει don't beat me; *otherwise*, you will have yourself to blame, Ar.*Nu.* 1433; ὦ Κῦρε, μὴ οὕτω λέγε· εἰ δὲ μή, οὐ θαρροῦντά με ἕξεις X.*Cyr.*3.1.35; οὔτ' ἐν τῷ ὕδατι τὰ ὅπλα ἦν ἔχειν· εἰ δὲ μή Id.*An.*4.3.6, cf. Th.1.28,131, Pl.*Phd.*91c. c. εἰ δέ sts. stands for εἰ δὲ μή, εἰ μὲν βούλεται, ἐψέτω· εἰ δ', ὅτι βούλεται, τοῦτο ποιείτω Pl.*Euthd.*285c, cf. *Smp.*212c; εἰ δ' οὖν S.*Ant.*722; εἰ δ' οὕτως Arist.*EN*1094a24; εἰ δὲ τοῦτο and *if* so, Str.2.1.29. d. εἰ γάρ for *if* so, Id.7.3.6. e. εἴ τις *if* any, i.e. *as much as* or *more than* any, τῶν γε νῦν αἴ τις ἐπιχθονίων, ὀρθῶς B.5.5; ὅτλον ἄλγιστον ἔσχον, εἴ τις Αἰτωλὶς γυνή S.*Tr.*8, cf. *OC*734; εἴ τις ἄλλος, *siquis alius*, E.*Andr.*6, etc.; εἴ τινες καὶ ἄλλοι Hdt.3.2, etc.; εἴπερ τις ἄλλος Pl.*R.*501d; also κατ' εἰ δέ τινα τρόπον in *any* way, *IG* 5(2).6.27 (Tegea). f. εἴ ποτε or εἴπερ ποτέ *now if* ever, ἡμῖν δὲ καλῶς, εἴπερ ποτέ, ἔχει..ἡ ξυναλλαγή Th.4.20, cf. Ar.*Eq.*594; αἴ ποτα κἄλλοτα Alc.*Supp.*7.11, cf. X.*An.*6.4.12, etc.; but in prayers, εἴ ποτέ τοι ἐπὶ νηὸν ἔρεψα..τόδε μοι κρήηνον ἐέλδωρ Il.1.39. g. εἴ ποθεν (sc. δυνατόν ἐστι) *if* from any quarter, i.e. from some quarter or other, S.*Ph.* 1204 (lyr.); so εἴ ποθι somewhere, anywhere, Id.*Aj.*885 (lyr.); εἴ που Od.4.193. h. εἴ πως ib.388, X.*An.*2.3.11: in an elliptical sentence (cf. VII. 1), πρέσβεις πέμψαντες, εἴ πως πείσειαν Th.1.58. VIII. with other PARTICLES: 1. for the distinction between καὶ εἰ (or καὶ ἐάν, or κἄν) even *if*, and εἰ καί (or ἐὰν καί) even *though*, v. καί:—the opposite of καὶ εἰ is οὐδ' εἰ, not even *if*; that of εἰ καί is εἰ μηδέ, *if* (*although*) not even. 2. for ὡς εἰ, ὡς εἴ τε, ὥσπερ εἰ, etc., v. ὡς and ὥσπερ. 3. for εἰ ἄρα, v. ἄρα; for εἰ δή, εἴπερ, v. εἰ δή, εἴπερ; for εἴ γε, v. γέ. IX. in neg. oaths, = Hebr. *im*, LXX *Ps.*94(95).11, *Ev.Marc.*8.12, al.

C. IN INDIRECT QUESTIONS, *whether*, folld. by the ind., subj., or opt., according to the principles of oratio obliqua: 1. with IND. after primary tenses, representing the same tense in the direct question, σάφα δ' οὐκ οἶδ' εἰ θεός ἐστιν *whether* he is a god, Il.5.183; εἰ ξυμπονήσεις..σκόπει S.*Ant.*41. 2. with SUBJ. after primary tenses, representing a dubitative subj. in the direct question, τὰ ἐκπώματα οὐκ οἶδ' εἰ Χρυσάντᾳ τουτῳῒ δῶ *whether* I should give them, X.*Cyr.*8.4.16: sts. elliptical, ἐς τὰ χρηστήρια ἔπεμπε, εἰ στρατεύηται ἐπὶ τοὺς Πέρσας Hdt.1.75. 3. OPT. after past tenses, representing either of the two previous constructions in the direct question, ἤρετο εἴ τις ἐμοῦ εἴη σοφώτερος he asked *whether* any one was wiser than I (direct ἔστι τις σοφώτερος;), Pl.*Ap.*21a; ἐπεκηρυκεύετο Πεισιστράτῳ, εἰ βούλοιτό οἱ τὴν θυγατέρα ἔχειν γυναῖκα Hdt.1.60: rarely aor. opt. for the aor. ind., ἠρώτων αὐτὸν εἰ ἀναπλεύσειεν I asked him *whether* he had set sail (direct ἀνέπλευσας;), D.50.55: but aor. opt. usually represents aor. subj., τὸν θεὸν ἐπήροντο εἰ παραδοῖεν Κορινθίοις τὴν πόλιν ..καὶ τιμωρίαν τινὰ πειρῷντ' ἀπ' αὐτῶν ποιεῖσθαι they asked *whether* they should deliver their city to the Corinthians, and should try.., Th.1.25:—in both constructions the ind. or subj. may be retained, ψῆφον ἐβούλοντο ἐπαγαγεῖν εἰ χρὴ πολεμεῖν ib.119; ἐβουλεύοντο εἴτε κατακαύσωσιν..εἴτε τι ἄλλο χρήσωνται *whether* they should burn them or should dispose of them in some other way, Id.2.4; ἀνακοινοῦσθαι αὐτὸν αὐτῷ εἰ δῷ ἐπιψηφίσαι τοῖς προέδροις [he said that] he consulted him *whether* he should give.., Aeschin.2.68. 4. with OPT. and ἄν when this was the form of the direct question, ἠρώτων εἰ δοῖεν ἂν τούτων τὰ πιστά they asked *whether* they would give (direct δοίητε ἄν;), X.*An.*4.8.7. 5. the NEG. used with εἰ in indirect questions is οὐ, when οὐ would be used in the direct question, ἐνετέλλετο ..εἰρωτᾶν εἰ οὔ τι ἐπαισχύνεται *whether* he is not ashamed, Hdt.1.90, etc.; but if μή would be required in the direct form, it is retained in the indirect, οὐ τοῦτο ἐρωτῶ, ἀλλ' εἰ τοῦ μὲν δικαίου μὴ ἀξιοῖ πλέον ἔχειν μηδὲ βούλεται ὁ δίκαιος, τοῦ δὲ ἀδίκου (the direct question would be μὴ ἀξιοῖ μηδὲ βούλεται; he does not see fit nor wish, does he?) Pl.*R.* 349b:—in double indirect questions, εἴτε..εἴτε..; εἰ..εἴτε..; εἴτε.. ἢ.., either οὐ or μή can be used in the second clause, ὅπως ἴδῃς εἴτ' ἔνδον εἴτ' οὐκ ἔνδον S.*Aj.*7; σκοπῶμεν εἰ ἡμῖν πρέπει ἢ οὔ Pl.*R.*451d; εἰ ἀληθὲς ἢ μή, πειράσομαι μαθεῖν ib.339a; πολλὰ ἂν περιεσκέψω, εἴτε ἐπιτρεπτέον εἴτε οὔ· .. οὐδένα λόγον οὐδὲ συμβουλὴν ποιῇ, εἴτε χρὴ ἐπιτρέπειν σαυτὸν αὐτῷ εἴτε μή Id.*Prt.*313a,b; ἀνάγκη τὴν ἐμὴν μητέρα, εἴτε θυγάτηρ ἦν Κίρωνος εἴτε μή, καὶ εἰ παρ' ἐκείνῳ διῃτᾶτο ἢ οὔ, καὶ γάμους εἰ διττοὺς ὑπὲρ ταύτης εἱστίασεν ἢ μή..πάντα ταῦτα εἰδέναι τοὺς οἰκέτας Is.8.9; τοὺς νόμους καταμανθάνειν εἰ καλῶς κεῖνται ἢ μή.. τοὺς λόγους εἰ ὀρθῶς ὑμᾶς διδάσκουσιν ἢ οὔ Antipho 5.14.

⊛ **εἶα**, an exclamation used to cheer or urge on, *on! up! away!* used with the imper. sg. or pl., cf. E.*Med.*820, etc.; εἶα δή *come then!* A. *Ag.*1650, Ar.*Th.*659; εἶά νυν *well now!* Id.*Pax* 467; ἄγ' εἶα Id.*Ra.* 396; ἀλλ' εἶα E.*HF* 622, Ar.*Pl.*760; ὦ εἶα Id.*Pax* 459; εἶα ὦ ib.468; ἀλλ' εἶα δὴ.. σκεψώμεθα Pl.*Sph.*239b:—with interrog. οὐ, where the question is equivalent to a command, οὐκ εἶα.. δραμεῖσθε; E.*IT* 1423, cf. *Hel.*1597. (εἶα S.*Ichn.*87, cf. Hdn.Gr.1.495.)

**εἰάζω**, *cry* εἶα, E.*Fr.*844; cf. **ειαγχοῦν** (fort. ἰαχον)· βοῶσαν, Hsch.

**εἰαί**· τῶν ὀσπρίων τὰ ἀποκαθάρματα, Hsch.; cf. εἶοι. **ειακέν**· ἀσθενεῖν, Id.

**εἰαμενή** or **εἰᾰμενή**, ἡ, *a river-side pasture, meadow*, ἐν εἰαμενῇ ἕλεος in a marshy *meadow*, Il.4.483; λειμῶνες ὑπόδροσοι εἰαμεναί τε Theoc. 25.16, cf. Call.*Dian.*193, A.R.3.1202, Euph.138; εἰαμενὴ δὲ καὶ οὐ βυθός ἐστι θαλάσσης, of a *shallow creek*, Dem.Bith.4.5 (prob. a participial form): cf. also **εἰαμένον**· νήνεμον, κοῖλον, βοτανώδη, Hsch.

**εἰᾱνός**, ή, όν, Ep. for ἑανός, Il.16.9.

**εἶαρ, εἰᾰρινός**, v. ἔαρ (A and B), ἐαρινός.

**εἰᾰρό-εις**, εσσα, εν, poet., = ἐαρινός, Man.4.275. **-μασθος**, ον, *with youthful breasts*, *AP* 5.75 (Rufin.). **-πότης**, ου, ὁ, = αἱμοπότης, Hsch. **-πῶτις**, v.l. for ἠεροφοῖτις in Il.19.87; cf. ἔαρ (B). **-τερπής**, ές, *joying in spring*, Orph.*H.*51.15.

**εἴασκον**, Ion. and Ep. impf. of ἐάω.

**εἴαται, εἴατο**, Ep. 3 pl. pres. and impf. of ἧμαι. II. εἴατο, Med. form for ἦσαν (impf. of εἰμί *sum*), read by Aristarch. in Od.20. 106. 2. εἴατο, 3 pl. plpf. Med. of ἕννυμι.

⊛ **εἰβάτας**, Thess., = ἡβητής, *IG* 9(2).234 (Pharsalus).

**εἴβηνος**, ὁ, name of a breed of horses: metaph., of a maiden, Alcm. 23.59; cf. ἐβῆνοι, ἴβηνος.

**εἴβιμος**, ον, *trickling*, Eust.1471.30: as pr. n., Id.1336.28.

**εἰβιοβοσκός**, v. ἰβιοβοσκός.

⊛ **εἴβω**, Ep. for λείβω, *drop, let fall in drops*, ὑπ' ὀφρύσι δάκρυον εἶβε Od.4.153:—Med., ἀπ' ὄσσων.. δ' εἰβομένα ῥέος (prob. for λειβ-) A.*Pr.* 401; δάκρυ' εἰβομένη (Triclin. for δάκρυα λειβ-) S.*Ant.*527 (anap.):—Pass., *trickle down*, Hes.*Th.*910, A.R.2.664.

**εἰ γάρ**, v. εἰ A. **εἴγε**, v. γε. **εἰ δ' ἄγε**, v. εἰ A.

**εἰδαίνομαι**, aor. 1 εἰδήνατο, = εἴδομαι, *to be like*, τινί Nic.*Al.*76,600.

**εἰδαλίζεται**· ἐναλίζεται, Hsch.

**εἰδάλιμος**, η, ον, (εἶδος) *shapely, comely*, Od.24.279. II. *like, looking like*, c. gen., *AP* 7.491 (Mnasalc.).

**εἰδαλίς**· ὄρνις ποιός, Hsch.

**εἰδάλλομαι**, = εἰδαίνομαι, ἰνδάλλομαι, Hsch.

**εἶδαρ**, ατος, τό, Ep. word, *food*, παρὰ δ' ἀμβρόσιον βάλεν εἶ., of the horses of the gods, Il.5.369, 13.35; εἴδατα πόλλ' ἐπιθεῖσα, on the table, Od.1.140, 4.56, etc.; ἄνθινον εἶ., of the Lotophagi, 9.84; μελίσσης ἄνθιμον εἶ., of honey-cakes, Orph.*L.*735, cf. Theoc.15.115. (ἔδϝαρ, cf. ἔδαρ, ἔδω.)

**εἶδας**· εἰς αὔριον, Hsch. (Fort. ἕνας (v. ἕνος); sed cf. ἔνς ἄς.)

**εἰδέα**, written for ἰδέα in codd., as Ar.*Th.*436 (lyr.), Lxx *Ge.*5.3, *Ev.Matt.*28.3.

**εἰδετικός**, = εἰδητικός, Olymp. *in Alc.*p.18 C.

**εἰδέχθ-εια**, ἡ, *odious, ugly look*, Lxx *Wi.*16.3, Ph.1.38. **-θής**, ές, *of hateful look, ugly*, εἰ. ἀπὸ τοῦ προσώπου Thphr.*Char.*28.4, cf. *Com.Adesp.*21 (Comp.), *Stoic.*2.307, Plb.36.15.1, D.S.3.29, Ph.2.56 (Sup.); εἰ. ὁρᾶν Porph.*Abst.*3.20. II. *putrid, fetid*, Hp.*Mul.*2. 115,125.

**εἰ δή**, *if indeed*, S.*Tr.*27; *if that is to say*, Pl.*Smp.*218e, Arist.*Rh.* 1370$^a$30; εἰ δὴ.. γε Pl.*Tht.*166c, etc.

**εἰδηθμός**· συστροφή, φυγή, Hsch. (leg. εἰλ-). **εἰδηλήγε**· ἀναμάρτητον, Id.

**εἴδ-ημα**, ατος, τό, *knowledge*, Oenom.ap.Eus.*PE* 5.21 (pl.). **-ημονικός**, ή, όν, *belonging to knowledge*, ἀρχά, opp. κοινανικά, Archyt.ap. Stob.2.31.120. Adv. -κῶς *with knowledge, skilfully*, Suid. ⊛ **-ήμων**, ον, gen. ονος, *acquainted with* or *expert in* a thing, τινός D.L.6.14, *AP* 9.505.4, *IG* 14.885 (Suessa), S.E.*M.*1.79. Adv. -νως Hermog.*Meth.* 13, Vett.Val.348.19, Hsch.

**εἴδ-ησις**, εως, ἡ, *knowledge*, τῶν πραγμάτων Nausiph.2; = γνῶσις, Arist.*de An.*402$^a$1; γραμμάτων S.E.*M.*1.44, cf. *SIG* 685.24 (Magn. Mae., ii B.C.), Lxx *Si.*42.18, Ph.1.335, Porph.*Sent.*32, Plot.4.4.12, al., Iamb.*Protr.*3, etc.: in pl., *forms of knowledge*, μαρτυροῦσι δὲ καὶ αἱ αἰσθήσεις, εἰδήσεις εἶναι θέλουσαι Plot.6.7.29. **-ητικός**, ή, όν, *constituting an* εἶδος III. 2, ἀριθμός, opp. μαθηματικός, Arist.*Metaph.* 1086$^a$5, 1088$^b$34 (but later εἰ. ἀριθμός *capable of being represented by a geometrical pattern, figurate*, Iamb.*Comm.Math.*19); *formal*, αἰτία Alex. Aphr. *in Metaph.*124.9, Procl.*Inst.*178; αἴτια Olymp. *in Mete.*302.28; opp. εἰδητός (q.v.), Dam.*Pr.*81. 2. *concerned with* εἴδη, νόησις ib.5; ἀποδείξεις ibid.; *specific*, Alex.Aphr. *in Metaph.*113.6. II. Adv. -κῶς Dam.*Pr.*284,321, Procl. *in Prm.*pp.625,649 S. **-ητός**, ή, όν, *knowable*, εἶδος γάρ, ὅτι εἰδητὸν καὶ εἰδητικόν Dam.*Pr.*81, cf. ib. 303. **-ικός**, ή, όν, (εἶδος) *specific*, opp. γενικός, ὄνομα D.T.636.14, A.D.*Synt.*230.11 (Sup.), cf. Porph.*Intr.*4.16 (Sup.), al.; ἀντίρρησις S.E.*M.*1.39 (Comp.); ἀρεταί Phld.*D.*3 *Fr.*82, cf. Ph.1.140; τὰς γενικὰς καὶ τὰς εἰ. τῶν σημείων παραλλαγάς Phld.*Sign.Fr.*2; αἰσθήσεις *Placit.*4.10.1; εἰδικώτατον, τό, = Lat. *infima species*, *Stoic.*3.214, cf. Dam.*Pr.*87. Adv. -κῶς *specifically*, *Stoic.*2.77, Dsc.5.75. II. *special*, opp. *general*, Phlp. *in Mete.*4.27 (Comp.). Adv. -κῶς *specially*, *CIG* 2222.15 (Chios). III. *formal*, opp. *material*, διαφοραί Plot.5.7.1.

**εἴδιον**· νενοτισμένον, ὑγρόν, Hsch. (Perh. for ἴδιον, cf. ἰδίω.)

⊛ **εἰδογράφος** [ᾰ], ὁ, *classifier of literary forms*, of the critic Apollonius, *POxy.*1241 ii 10, Sch.Pi.*P.*2.1, *EM* 295.51.

**εἰδοί** or **ἰδοί**, ῶν, αἱ, = Lat. *Idus*, D.H.6.89, Plu.*Rom.*23, *Tab.Defix. Aud.*242.49 (Carthage, i A.D.): gen. pl. εἰδυῶν *IG* 7.2225 (Thisbe); cf. εἴδυιοι.

⊛ **εἰδομᾰλίδας**, ὁ, *fair-cheeked* (?), Alc.150 (cf. Alc.Com.37).

**εἰδοποι-έω**, *endue with form*, εἰ. ἕκαστα καὶ σχηματίζειν Chrysipp. *Stoic.*2.148; τὸν βίον Plu.*Alex.*1; αὐτοὺς εἰς ἀνθρώπους, of the gods, Hld.3.13; ἰδέαι εἰ. ἕκαστα τῶν ὄντων Ph.2.219; *characterize*, αἵρεσιν Gal.1.161:—Pass., Ph.2.261, Corn.*ND* 6, Plot.1.8.5, al., Syrian. *in Metaph.*8.13, etc.: c. acc., ἀριθμὸς τὴν ἐπ' ἄπειρον προχώρησιν -ούμενος *fashioned into the pattern of* an infinite progression, *Theol.Ar.*34: c. dat., *to be characterized by*, Asp. *in EN* 87.5. II. *portray, describe*, τινά Callistr.*Stat.*8. 2. *add specific detail to*, γραφήν Str.15.1.14 (prob.). **-ημα**, ατος, τό, *copy of an* εἶδος or *pattern*, τινός *Theol.Ar.*9 (pl.). **-ησις**, εως, ἡ, *construction of a typical form*, ἀριθμοῦ ib.36, cf. 34, Iamb. *in Nic.*p.15 P. **-ητικός**, ή, όν, = εἰδοποιός, Plot.1.8.3, Olymp. *in Mete.*297.28. ⊛ **-ία**, ἡ, *formation, structure*, αἱ κατὰ μέρος εἰ., opp. οἰκοδομία, Ph.*Bel.*50.51: in sg., *specific form*, Str.1.1.18. 2. Rhet., *descriptive quality*, σχημάτων Longin.18.1. 3. Philos., *production of forms*, Iamb.*Comm.Math.*14, Procl.*Inst.*144,157, Syrian. *in Metaph.*86.1. **-ός**, όν, *constituting a species, specific*, διαφορά Arist.*Top.*143$^b$7, cf. *EN* 1174$^b$5, Plot.6.3.18, Dam.*Pr.*308. II. *creating forms*, Procl.*Inst.*157, Dam.*Pr.*310: c. gen., *creating a form* or *pattern*, ἀριθμός.. δικαιοσύνης εἰ. *Theol.Ar.*28, cf. 10.

⊛ **εἶδος**, εος, τό, (εἴδω A) *that which is seen*: *form, shape*, freq. in Hom., of the human *form* or *figure*, esp. abs. in acc. with Adjs., εἶδος ἄριστος, ἀγητός, κακός, Il.3.39, 5.787, 10.316; ἀλίγκιος ἀθανάτοισιν Od.8.174; opp. φρένες, 17.454; opp. βίη, Il.21.316; δευτέρα πεδ' Ἀγιδὼν τὸ εἶ. Alcm.23.58; τὸ εἶδος τῆς γυναικὸς ὑπερεπαινέων Hdt.1.8, etc.; *appearance*, of a dog, Od.17.308; ὄφιες ποικίλοι τὰ εἴδεα Hdt.3.107; εἴδεα [τῶν θεῶν] σημήναντες Id.2.53; γυνή τό γ' εἶδος Ar.*Th.*267: hence, periphr. for *person*, S.*El.*1177; τὸ ἐπ' εἴδει καλόν Pl.*Smp.*210b. b. esp. of *beauty of person, comeliness*, εἴδεος ἐπαμμένος Hdt.1.199; πλούτῳ καὶ εἴδει προφέρων Id.6.127. c. Medic., *physique, habit of body, constitution*, Hp.*Nat.Hom.*9, *Hum.*1: more freq. in pl., Id.*Aër.*3, al.; εἴδεα εὔχροά τε καὶ ἀνθηρά ib.5. 2. generally, *shape*, σχῆμα καὶ εἶδος Id.*Off.*3, cf. *Mochl.*6, etc.; *pattern*, of 'figurate' numbers, Arist. *Ph.*203$^a$15; ἡ μονὰς εἶδος εἰδῶν τυγχάνει *Theol.Ar.*4, cf. 17; *decorative pattern* or *figure*, Plu.*Them.*29 (pl.); of a musical scale, τοῦ διὰ τεσσάρων τρία εἴδη Aristox.*Harm.*p.74 M. (identified with σχῆμα, ibid.): in pl., *shapes*, i.e. *various kinds of atoms* (cf. ἰδέα), Democr.ap.Thphr. *Sens.*51. b. Geom., δύο εἴδη τῷ εἴδει δεδομένα *two figures* given *in species*, Euc.*Dat.*53, etc.; esp. in central conics, *rectangle formed by a transverse diameter and the corresponding parameter*, Apollon.Perg. *Con.*1.14,21, al.; also, *species* of numbers, of the terms in an algebraical expression involving different powers of the unknown quantity, Dioph.*Def.*11. II. *form, kind*, or *nature*, τῶν ἀλλέων παιγνιέων τὰ εἴδεα Hdt.1.94; τὸ εἶ. τῆς νόσου Th.2.50, etc.; ἐν ἁρμονίας εἴδει εἶναι, γενέσθαι, to be or become *like*.., Pl.*Phd.*91d, cf. *Cra.*394d; ὡς ἐν φαρμάκου εἴδει by *way* of medicine, Id.*R.*389b; νόμων ἔχει εἶδος is in *the province* of law, Arist.*Pol.*1286$^a$3; *situation, state* of things, σκέψασθε ἐν οἵῳ εἴδει.. τοῦτο ἔπραξαν Th.3.62; *plan of action, policy*, ἐπὶ εἶδος τρέπεσθαι Id.6.77, 8.56; ἐπ' ἄλλ' εἶδος τρέπεσθαι take up another *line*, Ar.*Pl.*317; *specific notion, meaning, idea*, ἂν παρέχῃ τὸ ἓν εἰ. δύο ὀνόματα.., περὶ ἑνὸς εἴδεος δύο ὀνόματα οὐ τὰ αὐτά Aen.Tact.24. 1; *department*, Hp.*VM* 12 (but also, *elementary nature* or *quality*, ib. 15); *type, sort*, πυρετῶν Id.*Epid.*3.12; αὐγῆς Id.*Off.*3, etc.: Rhet., *style* of writing, τὰ εἴδη τῶν λόγων Isoc.13.17, cf. Arist.*Rh.Al.* 1441$^b$9 (pl.); later, *definite literary form*, Men.Rh.init., Procl.*Chrest.* p.243 W., *EM* 295.52; also, *example of a style*, ὅλοις εἴδεσι Isoc.15.74; later, *single poem*, applied to Pindar's odes by Sch.; also, *written statement*, ἀναγνωσθέντος εἴδους *PAmh.*2.65.11 (ii A.D.), cf. *PTeb.*287. 12 (ii A.D.). III. *class, kind*, πᾶν τὸ τῶν πίστεων εἶδος Isoc.15. 280, cf. D.24.192: freq. in Pl., περὶ παντὸς τοῦ εἴδους.. ἐν ᾧ.. *Tht.* 178a; ἑνὶ εἴδει περιλαβεῖν ib.148d; εἰς ταὐτὸν ἐμπέπτωκεν εἶδος ib. 205d, etc.; *logical species*, *Sph.*235d; ἓν εἶδος ἀποχωρίζειν *Plt.*262e; τὰς διαφορὰς ὁπόσαιπερ ἐν εἴδεσι κεῖνται, ib.285b, al., cf. Arist.*Metaph.* 1057$^b$7, al., *Cat.*2$^b$7; as a subdivision of γένος, Id.*Rh.*1393$^a$27; ἐπὶ τοῦ αὐτοῦ γένους πεύκη, εἴδει διαφέρουσα, Dsc.1.69. 2. = ἰδέα II. 2, Pl.*Phd.*103e, *R.*596a, *Prm.*132a, al., Arist.*Metaph.*990$^b$9, al., etc. 3. *form*, opp. matter (ὕλη), Id.*Ph.*187$^a$18, al., *Metaph.*1029$^a$29: hence, *formal cause, essence*, ib.1032$^b$1, etc. IV. in later Gr., *wares* of different kinds, *goods*, *POxy.*109.1 (iii/iv A.D.), *PFay.*34.7 (ii A.D.): hence, *payments in kind*, opp. χρυσίον, Just.*Nov.*17.8, cf. *Cod.Just.*1. 4.18, al.; *spices*, Lyd.*Mag.*3.61; *groceries*, Anon.post Max.p.120 L.; εἰ. ἰατρικόν *drug*, Hsch. s.v. νίτρον, cf. *Hippiatr.*129.54 and v. ἑξάειδος, τετράειδος, τρίειδος; of a chemical *reagent*, Zos.Alch.p.205 B.

**εἰδότης**, ητος, ἡ, *the quality of an* εἶδος, *'formality'*, Dam.*Pr.*65.

**εἰδότως**, Adv. of εἰδώς, *knowingly*, Aeschin.1.111; *as one who knows, scientifically*, Arist.*Ph.*188$^a$5.

⊛ **εἰ δ' οὖν**, v. εἰ B. VII. 4 C.

**εἰδοφορ-έω**, *represent* or *express* (in dancing), D.H.7.72. ⊛ **-ος**, ὁ, *part of a tomb which bore the figure* of the deceased (cf. ζωφόρος), *CIG* 2840, al. (Aphrodisias).

**εἴδυιοι**, οἱ, = εἰδοί, *SIG* 664.18 (Delos, ii B.C.).

**εἰδύλλιον**, τό, Dim. of εἶδος II: *short, highly wrought descriptive poem*, mostly *on pastoral subjects*, as those of Theoc., Bion, Mosch., *idyll*, Sch.Theoc.*Proll.*, cf. Plin.*Ep.*4.14.

**εἰδύλλομαι**, = εἰδάλλομαι, Pempel.ap.Stob.4.25.52 (nisi leg. εἰδυλλέτω).

**εἰδύλος** [ῠ], ον, = εἰδήμων, *EM*295.30, etc.:—fem. **εἰδυλίς**, ίδος, Call.*Fr.*451.

⊛ ***εἴδω**, no Act. pres. in use, ὁράω being used:—**Med.**, v. infr. A. II: aor. 2 **εἶδον** always in sense of *see* (so in pres. and aor. 1 Med., *to be seen*, i.e. *seem*): but pf. **οἶδα**, in pres. sense, *know*. (With ἔ-ϝιδον, cf. (ϝ)είδομαι, (ϝ)εἶδος, Lat. *videre*; with (ϝ)οἶδα, cf. Skt. *véda*, Goth. *wait*, OE. *wát* 'know'.)

A. aor. 2 εἶδον (late εἶδα Orph.*A.*118), serving as aor. to ὁράω, Ep. ἴδον, iter. ἴδεσκε Il.3.217, late Aeol. ἐΰιδον *Epigr.Gr.*990.11 (Balbilla); imper. ἴδε (in Att. written as Adv. ἰδέ, *behold!* Hdn.Gr.2.23), ἴδετε; subj. ἴδω, Ep. ἴδωμι Il.18.63; opt. ἴδοιμι; inf. ἰδεῖν, Ep. ἰδέειν; part. ἰδών: hence, fut. ἰδησῶ Theoc.3.37:—**Med.**, aor. 2 εἰδόμην, Ep. ἰδόμην, in same sense, poet., Ion., and later Prose (c. gen., Arat.430) (so in compds., even in Att. Prose, v. ἐπ-, προ-, ὑπ-ειδόμην); imper. ἰδοῦ (freq. written as Adv. ἰδού, = ἰδέ); subj. ἴδωμαι; opt. ἰδοίμην; inf. ἰδέσθαι; part. ἰδόμενος Hdt.1.88, al.: **1.** *see, perceive, behold*, ὀφθαλμοῖσι or ἐν ὀφθαλμοῖσι ἰδέσθαι *see* before the eyes, Il.1.587, etc.; ἰδεῖν ἐν ὄμμασιν E.*Or.*1020; ἄγε, πειρήσομαι ἠδὲ ἴδωμαι well, I will try and *see*, Od.6.126, cf. 21.159; *mark, observe*, Il.4.476, Od.4.412, etc.: folld. by relat. clause, ἴδωμ' ὅτιν' ἔργα τέτυκται Il.22.450; ἀλλ' ἄγε θᾶσσον ἰδώμεθα ὅττι τάδ' ἐστίν Od.10.44: freq. in inf. after Subst. or Adj., θαῦμα ἰδέσθαι a marvel *to behold*, Il.5.725; οἰκτραῖσιν ἰδεῖν A.*Pr.*240; ἐλεινὸς ἰδεῖν Pl.*R.*620a. **b.** *see* a person, i.e. *meet* him, *speak with* him, Th.4.125, X.*An.*2.4.15, etc. **c.** *see*, i.e. *experience*, νόστιμον ἦμαρ ἰδέσθαι Od.3.233, etc.; δούλειον ἦμαρ ἰδεῖν E.*Hec.*56; ἀέλιον ἕτερον ἰδεῖν S.*Tr.*835; τὴν δίκην ἰδεῖν Id.*Ant.*1270 (lyr.); ἀλόχου κουριδίης.. οὔ τι χάριν ἴδε he *saw* (i.e. *enjoyed*) not the favour of his wedded wife, Il.11.243. **2.** *look*, ἰδεῖν ἐς.. *look* at or towards, 2.271, etc.; ἰδεῖν ἐπί.. 23.143; πρός.. Od.12.244; εἰς ὦπα ἰδέσθαι *look* him in the face, Il.9.373, etc.; κατ' ἐνῶπα ἰδών 15.320; ἄντα, ἐσάντα, or ἄντην ἰδεῖν, 13.184, 17.334, Od.5.78, etc.: qualified by Adv. or Adj., ὑπόδρα ἰδών *looking* askance, Il.1.148, al.; ἀχρεῖον ἰδών *looking* helpless, 2.269; κέρδος ἰδεῖν *look to* gain, A.*Eu.*541 (lyr.). **3.** *see mentally, perceive*, ἰδέσθαι ἐν φρεσίν 'to *see* in his mind's eye', Il.21.61, cf. 4.249; ἰδεῖν τῇ διανοίᾳ Pl.*R.*511a. **b.** *examine, investigate*, Id.*Phd.*70e, *Tht.*192e; *consider*, ἴδωμεν τί λέγομεν Id.*Grg.*455a. **II.** Med., pres. **εἴδομαι**, Ep. ἐείδεται Theoc.25.58, part. ἐειδόμενος Pi.*N.*10.15: aor. εἰσάμην, Ep. part. ἐεισάμενος Il.2.22, al.:—only Ep. and Lyr., *to be seen, appear*, εἴδεται ἄστρα they *are visible, appear*, 8.559; εἰ. ἦμαρ ὑπὸ Τρώεσσι δαμῆναι 13.98; εἴσατο δέ σφι δεξιός 24.319; ὅπῃ τὸ Ταρτάρειον εἴδεται βάθρον *Epigr.Gr.*1034.19 (Callipolis), cf. Od.5.283; perh. also οὔ πῃ χροὸς εἴσατο none of the skin *was visible*, Il.13.191. **2.** c. inf., *appear* or *seem* to be, τὸ δέ τοι κὴρ εἴδεται εἶναι 1.228; τοῦτό τί μοι κάλλιστον ἐνὶ φρεσὶν εἴδεται εἶναι Od.9.11, etc.: with inf. omitted, οἱ τό γε κέρδιον εἴσατο θυμῷ 19.283, etc.; οὐ μέν μοι κακὸς εἴδεται Il.14.472, cf. Theoc.25.58; also, *look like* or *make a show of*, εἴσατ' ἴμεν ἐς Λῆμνον he *made a show of* going to Lemnos, Od.8.283; εἴσατο δ' ὡς ὅτε ῥινόν it *had the look as of* a shield, 5.281. **3.** strictly middle, c. dat., εἴσατο φθογγὴν Πολίτῃ she *made herself like* Polites in voice, Il.2.791, cf. 20.81; αὐδὴν εἰσάμενός τινι Rhian.50: esp. in part., *like*, εἰδομένη κήρυκι Il.2.280, etc.; τῷ δ' ὄψιν ἐειδόμενος Pi.*N.*10.15; εἰδόμενος τοκεῦσιν A.*Ag.*771 (lyr.); φάσμα εἰδόμενόν τινι Hdt.6.69.

B. pf., οἶδα I *see with the mind's eye*, i.e. I *know*, used as pres.: plpf. ᾔδεα (v. infr.), I *knew*, used as impf.:—pf. οἶδα, Aeol. ὄϊδα Alc.145; 2 sg. οἶδας once in Hom., Od.1.337, cf. *h.Merc.*456, Thgn.491, Hippon.89, Hp.*Acut.*67, E.*Alc.*780, Philem.44.3 codd.; οἶσθα elsewh. in Hom., Att., etc.; in Com. also sts. οἶσθας Cratin.105, Alex.15.11, Men.348.5, cf. Herod.2.55; pl., ἴσμεν, Ep., Aeol., and Dor. ἴδμεν, also Ion., Hdt.1.6, al.; ἴστε, ἴσασι [ῐσ- Od.2.211, al., but ῑσ- ib.283, al.]; οἴδαμεν Hdt.2.17, οἴδατε *AP*12.81 (Mel.), οἴδᾱσι Hdt.2.43, X.*Oec.*20.14 codd.; dual, οἴδατον Socr.*Ep.*22.1: imper. ἴσθι, ἴστω, Boeot. ἴττω, late ἰδέτω Phalar.*Ep.*122 codd.: from 3 pl. ἴσασι (ἴσαντι Epich.53) were formed Dor. 1 sg. ἴσᾱμι Epich.254, Pi.*P.*4.248; 3 sg. ἴσατι *IG*14.644.4 (Bruttii); 1 pl. ἴσᾱμεν Pi.*N.*7.14, ἴσαμες prob. in *Dialex.*6.12; Cret. 3 pl. subj. ἴθθαντι *GDI*5024; inf. ϝισάμην Kohler-Ziebarth *Stadtrecht von Gortyn* 34 No.3.19; part. ἴσας A.D.*Adv.*175.19, dat. sg. ἴσαντι Pi.*P.*3.29, Cret. pl. ἴθθαντες *GDI*5024: subj. εἰδῶ (εἰδέω, ἰδέω, Il.14.235, Od.16.236), Ion. 3 pl. εἰδέωσι *SIG*45.21 (Halic., v B.C.); Ep. also εἰδῶ Od.1.174, al. (cf. Hdn.Gr.2.131), εἴδομεν Il.1.363, εἴδετε Od.9.17: opt. εἰδείην, 1 pl. εἰδεῖμεν Pl.*La.*190b, *R.*582a: inf. εἰδέναι, Ep. ἴδμεναι, ἴδμεν, also ἰδέμεν Pi.*N.*7.25: part. εἰδώς, εἰδυῖα, Ep. also ἰδυῖα, Elean ϝειζώς *Schwyzer* 409:—plpf. ᾔδεα Il.14.71, Hdt.2.150, contr. ᾔδη S.*Ant.*18, Ar.*Av.*511, Pl.*Smp.*119a, ᾔδησθα Od.19.93, Eup.416, etc. (but ᾔδεισθα freq. in codd., Ar.*Ec.*551, E.*Cyc.*108, Pl.*Men.*80d, al.), ᾔδεε(ν) Il.17.402, al., ᾔδη 1.70, al. (also later Att., acc. to Aristarch.ap.Choerob. *in Theod.*2.86), Att. contr. ᾔδει(ν) E.*Ion* 1187, Ar.*V.*558, etc.; Ep. 2 and 3 sg. ἠείδης, ἠείδη (v.l. -εις, -ει), Il.22.280, Od.9.206; Att. also 1 sg. ᾔδειν D.37.24, 2 sg. ᾔδεις Ar.*Th.*554, etc.; pl., ᾔδειμεν Aeschin.3.82, Arist.*APo.*87$^{b}$40, ᾔδεμεν Men.14D. (to be read in S.*OT*1232), ᾔδειτε D.55.9, etc. (ᾔδετε prob. in E.*Ba.*1345), Ion. ᾔδέατε Hdt.9.58 (συν-), ᾔδεισαν Lxx *Ge.*42.23, Str.15.3.23, ᾔδεσαν Hdt.7.175, Thgn.54, etc.; late Ep. ᾔδειν, ἠείδειν, A.R.2.65, 4.1700, also ᾖσμεν, ᾖστε, ᾖσαν, Ar.*Fr.*149.4 (prob.), S.*Fr.*340, E.*Cyc.*231, etc.; Ep. 3 pl. ἴσαν Il.18.405, Od.4.772:—fut., in this sense, εἴσομαι Il.1.548, Hp.*VM*20, Ar.*Ach.*332, etc.; also εἰδήσω Od.7.327, Hdt.7.234, Isoc.1.44, Aen.Tact.31.5, Arist.*Top.*108$^{a}$28, Herod.5.78, Apollon.Perg.*Con.*1 *Praef.*, etc.; inf. εἰδησέμεν Od.6.257.—The aor. and pf. are usu. supplied by γιγνώσκω; aor. 1 inf. εἰδῆσαι is found in Hp.*Acut.*(*Sp.*)22, *Epid.*6.8.25 (ἐξ-), Arist.*EN*1156$^{b}$27, Thphr.*Char.Prooem.*4; imper. εἴδησον *PCair.Zen.*36.2 (iii B.C.); 3 pl. subj. εἰδήσωσιν Herzog *Koische Forschungen* No.190 (ii/i B.C.):—*know, have knowledge of, be acquainted with*, Hom., etc.: c. acc. rei, ὃς ᾔδη τά τ' ἐόντα τά τ' ἐσσόμενα πρό τ' ἐόντα Il.1.70; νοήματα, μήδεα οἶδε, Od.2.122, Il.18.363, etc.: less freq. c. acc. pers., τούτους μὲν δὴ οἶδα Od.4.551, cf. Pl.*R.*365e, D.54.34, etc.; πρῶτος ὧν ἡμεῖς ἴδμεν the first we *know of*, Hdt.1.6, etc.; παλαίτατος ὧν ἀκοῇ ἴσμεν Th.1.4: strengthd. by εὖ or σάφα, εὖ τόδ' ἴσθι *know* well, *be assured* of this, E.*Med.*593; σάφ' οἶδ' ἐγώ A.*Supp.*740, etc.: freq. in Hom. with neut. Adj., to express character or disposition, ἄγρια οἶδε *has* fierceness *in his heart*, Il.24.41; ἀθεμίστια ᾔδη *had* lawlessness *in his heart*, Od.9.189; αἴσιμα, ἄρτια ᾔδη, 14.433, 19.248; εἴ μοι ἤπια εἰδείη if he *were* kindly *disposed* towards me, Il.16.73; φίλα εἰδότες ἀλλήλοισιν Od.3.277; κεχαρισμένα, πεπνυμένα εἰδώς, 8.584, 24.442: c. gen., ὃς σάφα θυμῷ εἰδείη τεράων Il.12.229; ὃς πάσης εἰδῇ σοφίης 15.412; τόξων ἐῢ εἰδώς *cunning with* the bow, 2.718; αἰχμῆς ἐῢ εἰ. 15.525; οἰωνῶν σάφα εἰδώς Od.1.202; ἐῢ εἰδὼς τεκτοσυνάων 5.250; μάχης ἐῢ εἰδότε πάσης Il.2.823; κύνε εἰδότε θήρης 10.360; παῖδ' ἔτ' ἐόντ' οὔ πω μάλα εἰδότε θουρίδος ἀλκῆς 11.710; εἰδὼς πυγμαχίης 23.665; θεοπροπίων ἐῢ εἰδώς 6.438; χάριν εἰδέναι τινί *acknowledge* a debt to another, *thank* him, 14.235, Hdt.3.21, etc.: imper., freq. in protestations, ἴστω νῦν Ζεὺς αὐτός be Zeus *my witness*, Il.10.329; ἴστω νῦν τόδε Γαῖα 15.36, etc.; Boeot. ἴττω Ἡρακλῆς, etc., Ar.*Ach.*860, etc.: part. εἰδώς, abs., *one who knows, one acquainted with the fact*, ἰδυίῃ πάντ' ἀγορεύω Il.1.365; μετ' εἰδόσιν ἀγορεύειν 10.250; μακρηγορεῖν ἐν εἰδόσιν Th.2.36, cf. 3.53; μαθεῖν παρὰ τοῦ εἰδότος Pl.*R.*337d, etc.; also ἰδυίῃσι πραπίδεσσι with *knowing* mind, Il.1.608, al. **2.** c. inf., *know how* to do, οἶδ' ἐπὶ δεξιά, οἶδ' ἐπ' ἀριστερὰ νωμῆσαι βῶν 7.238, cf. S.*Ph.*1010, Ar.*V.*376; also, *to be in a condition, be able, have the power*, E.*Med.*664, D.4.40; of drugs, ὅσα λεπτύνειν οἶδε Alex.Trall.*Febr.*6; of a festival, οἶδε ἐκπέμπουσα δάκνειν Chor.p.124B.; *learn*, ἵν' εἰδῇ μὴ 'πὶ τοῖς ἐμοῖς κακοῖς ὑψηλὸς εἶναι E.*Hipp.*729. **3.** c. part., *to know that* such and such *is* the fact, the part. being in nom. when it is a predicate of the Subject of the Verb, ἴσθι μοι δώσων *know that* thou wilt give, A.*Ag.*1670; ἴστω ὑπὸ τοῦ ἀδελφεοῦ ἀποθανών Hdt.4.76; οὐ γὰρ οἶδα δεσπότας κεκτημένος E.*Hec.*397: in acc. when it is predicate of the Object, τοὺς φιλτάτους γὰρ οἶδα νῷν ὄντας πικρούς A.*Ch.*234; τὸν Μῆδον ἴσμεν ἐκ περάτων γῆς ἐλθόντα Th.1.69: with part. omitted, γῆν αὐτὰ οἶδεν ἀμφότερα (sc. ὄντα) Jul.*Or.*7.226a. **4.** less freq. c. acc. et inf., πλήθους.. ἂν σάφ' ἴσθ' ἕκατι βάρβαρον ναυσὶν κρατῆσαι A.*Pers.*337, cf. S.*Ph.*1329; εὖ ἴσθι τοῦτον.. ἰσχυρῶς ἀνιᾶσθαι X.*Cyr.*8.3.44; also εὖ τόδ' ἴσθι, μηδάμ' ἡμέρᾳ μιᾷ πλῆθος τοσουτάριθμον ἀνθρώπων θανεῖν A.*Pers.*431; ἕν γ' ἀκούσασ' ἴσθι, μὴ ψευδῶς μ' ἐρεῖν E.*IA*1005. **5.** c. acc. folld. by ὡς, ὅτι, etc., οἶδα κάμαυτὴν ὅτι ἀλγῶ S.*El.*332; ἐάν τινα εἰδῶσιν ὅτι ἄδικός ἐστι Pl.*Prt.*323b, etc. **6.** οὐκ οἶδ' εἰ.. I *know* not whether, to express disbelief or doubt, sts. with ἄν transposed, οὐκ οἶδ' ἂν εἰ πείσαιμί σε E.*Alc.*48, cf. D.45.7: with Verb omitted after εἰ, as οὐκ οἶδ' εἴ τις ἄλλος *perhaps* no other, Isoc.6.1, 12.10. **7.** in similar ellipses with other Conjunctions, οὐκ οἶδ' ὅπως I *know* not how, Pl.*R.*400b; οὐκ οἶδ' ὁπόθεν Id.*Cra.*396d. **8.** οἶδα, ἴσθι are freq. parenthetic, οἶδ' ἐγώ E.*Med.*948; σάφ' οἶδα ib.94, 963; also οἶδ' ὅτι, οἶσθ' ὅτι, ἴσθ' ὅτι, πάρειμι δ' ἄκων οὐχ ἑκοῦσιν, οἶδ' ὅτι (sc. πάρειμι) I *know it well*, S.*Ant.*276; οἶδ' ὅτι, freq. in D., as 9.1, al.; σάφ' ἴσθ' ὅτι Ar.*Pl.*889:—οἶσθ' ὅ, οἶσθ' ὡς, with imper., are common in Trag. and Com., οἶσθ' οὖν ὃ δρᾶσον; do—thou *know'st* what, i.e. make haste and do, Ar.*Eq.*1158, cf. *Pax* 1051, etc.; οἶσθ' ὡς πόησον; S.*OT*543; also οἶσθ'.. ὡς νῦν μὴ σφαλῇς; Id.*OC*75; οἶσθα νῦν ἅ μοι γενέσθω; E.*IT*1203: rarely with the fut., οἶσθ' οὖν ὃ δράσεις (nisi leg. δρᾶσον); Id.*Cyc.*131, cf. *Med.*600 codd.

**εἰδώ**· φρόνησιν, ὄψιν, Hsch.

**εἰδωλ-εῖον** or **-ιον**, τό, *idol's temple*, Lxx 1 *Ma.*1.47, 1 *Ep.Cor.*8.10. **-ικός**, ή, όν, *symbolical*, Sch.Pl.*Grg.*452d. Adv. **-κῶς** Porph.*Sent.*10, Sch.Pl.*Grg.*456a. **2.** *imaginary*, Syrian. *in Metaph.*7.32, Dam.*Pr.*453. **3.** *phantasmal*, ἔμφασις Iamb.*Myst.*3.13.

**εἰδωλό-θῠσία**, ἡ, *sacrifice to idols*, Gloss. **-θῠτος**, ον, *sacrificed to idols*: Subst. εἰδωλόθυτα, τά, *meats offered to idols*, *Act.Ap.*15.29, 1 *Ep.Cor.*8.1, etc. **-λάτρης**, ου, ὁ, ἡ, *idol-worshipper, idolater*, ib.5.10, etc. ⊛ **-λατρία**, ἡ, *idolatry*, *Ep.Gal.*5.20, 1 *Ep.Cor.*10.14. **-μορφος**, ον, *formed after an image*, *Gp.*10.9.1. **2.** *like a phantom*, of comets, Sch.Ptol.*Tetr.*75.

⊛ **εἴδωλον**, τό, (εἶδος) *phantom*, Il.5.451, Od.4.796, Hdt.5.92.η', Pl.*Lg.*959b; βροτῶν εἴδωλα καμόντων, of ghosts, Od.11.476, etc.; ψυχῶν Procl.*Inst.*64. **2.** *any unsubstantial form*, εἴδωλον σκιᾶς A.*Ag.*839, S.*Fr.*659.6, Chaerem.14.15; οὐδὲν ἄλλο πλὴν εἴδωλα.. ἢ κούφην σκιάν S.*Aj.*126; εἰ. ἄλλως a mere *form*, Id.*Ph.*947; αἰῶνος εἰ. Pi.*Fr.*131.3. **3.** *image reflected* in a mirror or in water, Pl.*Sph.*266b, Arist.*Div.Somn.*464$^{b}$9. **4.** in the system of Epicurus, *film* given off by any object and conveying an impression to the eye, Epicur.*Ep.*1 p.10 U., *Nat.*2.1, al., Cic.*Fam.*15.16.1, etc. **II.** *image in the mind, idea*, X.*Smp.*4.21; *phantom of the mind, fancy*, Pl.*Phd.*66c; εἰ. καὶ ψεῦδος Id.*Tht.*150c. **III.** *image, likeness*, γυναικὸς εἰ. χρύσεον Hdt.1.51, cf. 6.58: metaph., λόγος εἰ. ψυχῆς Isoc.3.7. **IV.** later, *image of a god, idol*, Lxx 4 *Ki.*17.12, 1 *Ep.Cor.*12.2, *OGI*201.8 (Silco, vi A.D.), etc. **V.** εἰ. οὐράνια *constellations*, A.R.3.1004, cf. Max.56.

**εἰδωλο-πλαστέω**, *form, model*, Heraclit.*All.*66. ⊛ **-πλαστος**, ον, *modelled*: hence, *ideal*, Lyc.173. **-ποιέω**, *form an image*, esp. in the mind, εἴδωλα εἰ. Pl.*R.*605c, cf. Arist.*de An.*427$^{b}$20; ὅσα εἰ. ὁ τῦφος Ph.1.671. **II.** *represent by an art-type*, Diogenian.

Epicur.2.61, Theo Sm.p.133 H.(Pass.); *portray in a bust*, D.S.31.25.2 (Pass.). **b.** *depict in words*, ὄψιν Longin.15.7. **-ποίησις**, εως, ἡ, *formation of mental images*, S.E.*P*.2.222 (pl.). **-ποιητής**, οῦ, ὁ, *seer of phantoms*, θεῶν ἢ νεκρῶν Vett.Val.112.34. **-ποιητικός**, ή, όν, *calling up phantasms*, τέχνη Iamb.*Myst*.3.28. **-ποιία**, ἡ, *formation of images*, as in a mirror, Pl.*Ti*.46a; or by painters, Id.*Criti*. 107b. **2.** *image formed in the mind, imagination*, D.S.1.96: pl., Longin.15.1. **3.** *putting of words into the mouth of one dead*, Hermog.*Prog*.9, Aphth.*Prog*.11. **4.** *production of mental images*, Iamb.*Myst*.2.10. **5.** *manufacture of idols*, ib.3.28. **-ποιικός**, ή, όν, *of* or *for image-making*, ἡ εἰ. (with or without τέχνη) Pl.*Sph*. 235b, 236c, al. **II.** *producing* εἴδωλα (in the Epicurean sense), σώματα Diog.Oen.7. **-ποιός**, ὁ, *image-maker*, Pl.*Sph*.239d, Iamb. *Myst*.3.28. **II.** Adj., *producing phantasmal appearances*, δύναμις ib.10.2, cf. 2.10.

**εἰδωλουργικός**, ή, όν, = εἰδωλοποιικός: -κή, ἡ, Pl.*Sph*.266d.

**εἰδωλο-φᾰνής**, ές, *like an image*, *Placit*.5.19.5. **-χᾰρής**, ές, *delighting in images*, Dam.*Pr*.453.

**εἴελος**· ἴλιγγος, Hsch.

**εἶέν** (for the aspiration, found in cod. Rav. of Ar., etc., cf. A.D. *Synt*.319.26, *An.Bachm*.1.208), Particle used in dialogue and oratory, in passing to the next point, *well, quite so, very good*, Ar.*Nu*. 1075, Pl.*Ap*.19a, etc.; "εἶέν" ἐρῶ καὶ κατανεύσομαι καὶ ἀνανεύσομαι Id.*R*.350e: folld. by a question, Ar.*Nu*.176, etc.; εἶέν· τί δῆτα.. ; S.*Ph*.1308; εἶέν· καὶ δὴ τεθνᾶσι E.*Med*.386: folld. by imper., S.*El*. 534; in argument, *so far so good*: εἶέν, ἐρεῖ δέ.. Antipho 4.2.3; εἶέν, τοῦτο μὲν ἡμῖν κείσθω· ἔφαμεν δέ.. Pl.*R*.350d; εἶέν, ἀλλὰ νὴ Δία.. D.20.75, cf. D.Chr.17.19, etc.; εἶέν δή Pl.*Smp*.213e. [At the beginning of a trimeter, εἶέν, ἀκούω, A.*Ch*.657, Ar.*Pax* 663: extra versum in E. l. c.]

**εἴεω**, a battle-cry of young warriors, Hsch.

**εἵην**, aor. 2 opt. of ἵημι: but **εἴην**, pres. opt. of εἰμί (*sum*).

⊛ **εἶθαρ**, Adv. *at once, forthwith*, Il.5.337, Theoc.25.213, Antim.16.5, A.R.2.408, Nic.*Th*.547.

**εἶθε**, Ep. **αἶθε**, v. εἰ A. **εἰθεῖν**· μαθεῖν, Hsch.

**εἰθίζω**, poet. for ἐθίζω.

⊛ **εἰθισμένως**, Adv., (ἐθίζω) *in the accustomed manner*, Arcesil.ap. D.L.4.35.

**εἰκ**, v. εἰ. **εἶκα**, pf. of ἵημι.

**εἰκᾰδάρχης**, ου, ὁ, *commander of twenty*, Hsch.

**εἰκάδιος** [ᾰ], α, ον, *belonging to, celebrated on the* εἰκάς, *EM* 297.59, *Et.Gud*.164.22.

**εἰκᾰδισταί**, ῶν, οἱ, epith. of the Epicureans, because they commemorated their founder's death *on the twentieth* (εἰκάς) of Gamelion, Ath.7.298d.

⊛ **εἰκάζω**, Aeol. **εἰκάσδω** Sapph.104: impf. εἴκαζον Hdt.4.133, but Att. ᾔκαζον Ar.*Ec*.385: fut. -άσω A.*Eu*.49: aor. εἴκασα Hdt.2.104, Att. ᾔκασα Ar.*Nu*.350, etc.: pf. εἴκακα Sch.Ar.*V*.151:—Pass., fut. εἰκασθήσομαι Ar.*Ach*.783: aor. εἰκάσθην X.*HG*7.5.22: pf. εἴκασμαι Hdt.3.28, Att. ᾔκασμαι (ἐξ-) Ar.*Eq*.230 (but εἴκασται Pl.*Cra*.439a).—This is the only Verb that augments ει- by η-:—*represent by an image* or *likeness, portray*, γυναῖκα γραφῇ εἰκάσας X.*Oec*.10.1; εἰκὼν γραφῇ εἰκασμένη a figure *painted to the life*, Hdt.2.182; αἰετὸς εἰκασμένος *a figure like* an eagle, Id.3.28; χειρὶ τεκτόνων δέμας.. εἰκασθέν E.*Alc*.349; κενταύροις ᾔκασαν αὑτάς *made* themselves *like* Centaurs, Ar.*Nu*.350; τοῦ θεοῦ.. ᾧπερ εἰκάζεις σεαυτόν Id.*Ra*.594. **II.** *liken, compare*, ὄρπακι βραδίνῳ σε μάλιστ' εἰκάσδω Sapph. l. c., cf. A.*Ch*.633 (lyr.), *Eu*.49, etc.; *describe by a comparison*, εἰ. τι ὡς εἰ.. Hdt.7.162, cf. 4.31, Arist.*EN*1106$^b$30:—Pass., *to be like, resemble*, τινί E.*Ba*.942, 1253, etc.; πρός τινα Ar.*Ach*.783. **III.** *infer from comparison, form a conjecture*, Hdt.1.68, 7.49, S.*OC*1504, 1677 (lyr.), Isoc.3.26; freq. in phrase ὡς εἰκάσαι so far as *one can guess*, ὡς εἰκάσαι, βασιληΐην τε καὶ πολιτηΐην αἰτεομένους Hdt.9.34, cf. 1.34, etc.; rarely without ὡς, ἀλλ', εἰκάσαι μέν, ἡδύς S.*OT*82: c. acc. et inf., Hdt.4.132, Antipho Soph.53, Th.5.9, etc.: omisso inf., 'Αμαζόνας.. ἂν ᾔκασ' ὑμᾶς (sc. εἶναι) A.*Supp*.288; τί τοῦτ' ἂν εἰκάσειας (sc. εἶναι); S.*Ant*.1244; εἰ. τι ἔκ τινος A.*Th*.356 (lyr.), Th.3.20; ἀπό τινος Id.1.10; εἰ. τι *make a guess* about it, A.*Ch*.518, Antipho 5.64; τινί Th.1.9, Plu.*Publ*.14; *estimate*, τὴν κριθήν, τὰ τετρυγημένα εἰς.., at a given quantity, *PSI* 5.522 (iii B.C.), *PGurob* 8.14 (iii B.C.): abs., εἰ. τεκμαιρόμενος Lys. 6.20; εἰ. καλῶς Men.852.

⊛ **εἰκαθεῖν**, inf. of aor. εἴκαθον, from εἴκω *yield*; subj. εἰκάθω S.*OT*651 (lyr.), *Ph*.1352; inf. εἰκαθεῖν Id.*El*.396, *Ant*.1096; part. εἰκαθών Id. *Tr*.1177. Cf. παρ-, ὑπ-εικαθεῖν.

**εἰκαιο-βουλία**, ἡ, *rashness*, Hsch. **-λογέω**, *talk at random*, Dosith.p.431 K. **-λογία**, ἡ, *random talking*, Ph.1.674. **-λόγος**, ον, *talking at random*, Phld.*Rh*.1.191 S. (Comp.). **-μῡθέω**, = εἰκαιολογέω, Hsch., Suid. **-μῡθία**, ἡ, *random talking*, Id. **-ρρημονέω**, = εἰκαιομυθέω, Id. **-ρρημοσύνη**, ἡ, = εἰκαιομυθία, Id.

⊛ **εἰκαῖος**, α, ον, (εἰκῇ) *without aim* or *purpose*, **1.** of things, *random, purposeless*, τίκτει γὰρ οὐδὲν ἐσθλὸν εἰκαία σχολή S.*Fr*.308; ὡς εἰκαῖον ὄν as being *useless*, Luc.*JConf*.6; εἰ. διήγημα J.*BJProoem*. 1. Adv. -ως, δοξάζειν cj. in Epicur.*Ep*.1 p.30 U., cf. Diotog.ap. Stob.4.1.96, D.L.2.128, Procl.*in Cra*.p.26 P.: Comp. -ότερον S.E. *M*.1.276: neut. pl. as Adv., Lyc.748. **2.** of persons, *rash, hasty*, Plb.7.7.5, etc.; οἱ πολλοὶ καὶ εἰ. Cebes 12; τὸ εἰ. *PRyl*.235.12 (ii A.D.). **3.** *ordinary, casual*, J.*BJ*2.10.2, Luc.*Am*.33; *taken at random*, ξύλα Iamb.*Comm.Math*.4; *careless*, σφίξις Heliod.ap.Orib. 50.9.10.

**εἰκαιοσύνη**, ἡ, *thoughtlessness*, Timo 36.

**εἰκαιότης**, ητος, ἡ, = foreg., Phld.*Rh*.1.190 S., *Vit*.p.29 J., Ph.1. 193, D.L.7.48.

**εἰκαιόψογοι** ψόγοι *random censure*, Demetr.*Eloc*.291 (dub. l.).

⊛ **εἰκάς**, άδος, ἡ, Aeol. dat. pl. εἰκάδεσσι B.*Scol.Oxy*.1361 *Fr*.1.5: (εἴκοσι):—*twentieth day of the month* (sc. ἡμέρα), Hes.*Op*.792, 820, Plu.2.1089c, etc.: pl., B. l. c., Epicur.*Fr*.217; ἡ πρώτη, δευτέρα, etc., μετ' εἰκάδα, εἰκάδας, the 21st, 22nd, etc., Men.320.3, *IG*2$^2$. 890, etc.; τετάρτῃ ἐπὶ εἰκάδι *IG*9(1).694.2 (Corc.): hence **εἰκάδες**, αἱ, *the last ten days* of the month, And.1.121; σελήνην ἄγουσαν εἰκάδας Ar.*Nu*.17; τρίτῃ εἰκάδι, i.e. the 23rd, Pl.*Lg*.849b. **II.** name of the sixth day of the Eleusinian mysteries (= Boedromion 20), E.*Ion* 1076 (pl., lyr.), cf. Plu.*Phoc*.28. **III.** pl., divisions of a tribe, Hsch.

**εἰκάσδω**, v. εἰκάζω.

**εἰκ-ᾰσία**, ἡ, *likeness, representation*, X.*Mem*.3.10.1. **II.** *comparison*, Plu.*Them*.29; *estimate*, ἐξ εἰκασίας *PTeb*.61(*a*).186, al. (ii B.C.). **III.** *conjecture*, Hp.*Morb*.1.1, Pl.*Sis*.390c, Ph.2.91, Hierocl. p.37 A. (pl.), etc.; *doubt*, Phld.*Rh*.1.249 S. **IV.** *apprehension of* or *by means of images* or *shadows*, Pl.*R*.511e, 534a. **-άσιμος**, ον, *that can be estimated*, Gloss. ⊛ **-ασμα**, ατος, τό, *likeness*, A.*Th*.523 (lyr.), Porph.*Plot*.1, Iamb.*Comm.Math*.8; θεὸς πολύμορφον εἰ. Secund. *Sent*.3. **II.** *probability*, Max.Tyr.9.3 (pl.). ⊛ **-ασμός**, ὁ, *conjecturing, guessing*, D.H.6.71 (pl.); εἰκασμοῦ ἐπίρρημα *conjectural* adverb (ἴσως), D.T.642.8; ἐξ εἰκασμοῦ λέγειν Str.17.3.1, cf. Plu.*Mar*.11, Luc. *Herm*.16. **-αστέον**, *one must liken, compare*, τί τινι Plu.2.374a, Max.Tyr.33.6. **-αστής**, οῦ, ὁ, *one who conjectures, diviner*, τῶν μελλόντων Th.1.138, cf. J.*AJ*18.9.2. **II.** *one who portrays, represents*, ἀληθείας D.H.*Isoc*.11, cf. *Lys*.19. **-αστικός**, ή, όν, *able to represent*: ἡ -κὴ τέχνη the art of *copying* or *portraying*, Pl.*Sph*.235d, etc. **II.** *able* or *liable to conjecture*, ψευδῶν Ph.1.160; τὸ εἰ. *the faculty of conjecturing*, Luc.*Alex*.22. Adv. -κῶς *conjecturally*, Phld. *Rh*.2.91 S. (dub.), Procl.*in Alc*.p.23 C. **2.** τὸ εἰ. *matter of conjecture*, Vett.Val.312.32. **-αστός**, ή, όν, *comparable, similar*, S.*Tr*. 699. **2.** *apprehended through an image*, opp. αἰσθητός, Ascl.*in Metaph*.142.10, Iamb.*Comm.Math*.8, Sch.Pl.*R*.509d. **3.** *conjectural*, Procl.*in Alc*.p.23 C.

**εἰκᾰτι, εἰκατίδειος**, v. εἴκοσι, εἰκοσιδύω. **εἴ κε, εἴ κεν**, v. εἰ B. II.

**εἰκέλιος**, α, ον, = εἴκελος, Man.3.237, 6.346.

**εἰκελόνειρος**, ον, *dream-like*, ἀνέρες Ar.*Av*.687 (anap.).

**εἴκελος**, η, ον, (εἰκός) *like*, τινί Il.22.134; χελιδόνι εἰ. αὐδήν Od.21. 411, cf. Hdt.8.8 (v.l. for ἴκελος), S.*Fr*.574.4, Plu.2.410e.

**εἰκελόφωνος**, ον, *of like voice*, χελιδόσιν *AP*6.247 (Phil.).

**εἰκέναι**, Att. for ἐοικέναι, inf. of ἔοικα.

⊛ **εἰκῇ**, *without plan* or *purpose, at random, at a venture*, Xenoph. 2.13, Heraclit.47, Hp.*Epid*.7.9, A.*Pr*.450, 885, Ar.*Eq*.431, D.28.5; εἰ. ζῆν S.*OT*979; πράττειν Pl.*Prt*.326d; λέγεσθαι Id.*Ap*.17c, etc.; νήφων παρ' εἰ. λέγοντας Arist.*Metaph*.984$^b$17, etc.; ἅρμενα εἰ. ἀποκλασθέντα Theoc.22.14. **II.** *in vain*, *PLips*.104.29 (i B.C.), 1*Ep. Cor*.15.2, al. **III.** *slightly, moderately*, ἀγγεῖα εἰ. πεπυρωμένα Agatharch.61. (Prob. for ἐϝεκῇ 'at will', cf. ἑκών.)

**εἰκλεῖ**· δειπνεῖ, and **εἶκλον**· δεῖπνον, Hsch.; cf. αἶκλον. **εἰκνεῖται**· ἄλλος αὐτὸν εἰσφέρει, Id.

⊛ **εἰκο-βολέω**, *talk at random*, γλῶσσ' εἰκοβολεῖ περὶ τῶν ἀφανῶν E. *Fr*.913.4, cf. Ar.*Fr*.689, Phld.*Rh*.1.247 S., *EM*297.32. **II.** *discharge missiles at random*, Plb.*Fr*.35. ⊛ **-βολία**, ἡ, *talking at random*, Phld.*Rh*.2.98 S. (pl.).

**εἰκον-ίδιον**, τό, Dim. of εἰκών I. 1, *POxy*.1449.8 (iii A.D.). ⊛ **-ίζω**, *copy* from a pattern, *PPar*.65.12 (ii B.C.). **2.** *draw up an official description*, *PFay*.36.23 (ii A.D.), etc. **3.** *mould into form*, τὰς ἀμόρφους ὕλας *Placit*.1.10.1; εἰ. ἀλήθειαν *to give the semblance of* truth, Aphth.*Prog*.1:—Med., *picture to oneself*, θάνατον Vett.Val.226. 19. **-ικός**, ή, όν, *representing a figure, copied from it*, εἰ. ἄγαλμά τινος *a portrait* statue, Callix.1; πίνακες *IG*2$^2$.995.8, cf. Plu.*Lys*.1; ὅπλον εἰ. shield *with* embossed *portrait*, *IGRom*.4.144; of actor's masks, Poll.4.148. **II.** *counterfeited, pretended*, *AP*11.233 (Lucill.). **III.** *belonging to* or *employing images*, φαντασία Plot. 3.6.18; διάκοσμος Dam.*Pr*.284, cf. 423 (Comp.). Adv. -κῶς Procl. *Inst*.65, *in Euc*.p.16 F., Dam.*Pr*.330, Simp.*in Ph*.160.24. ⊛ **-ιον**, τό, Dim. of εἰκών, Polem.Hist.18, Plu.2.753b, *BGU*423.21 (ii A.D.). ⊛ **-ισμα**, ατος, τό, *image*, λιθουργές S.*Fr*.573, cf. *AP*13.6 (Phal.), Porph.*Sent*.42, Plot.1.4.10; *portrait*, Herod.4.38. ⊛ **-ισμός**, ὁ, *delineation, description*, Plu.2.54b. **II.** *registered description* of individuals for purposes of census, *PRyl*.161.15 (i A.D.), *PLond.ined*. 2196 (i A.D.), etc.; term used by *publicani*, Sen.*Ep*.95 (pl.). ⊛ **-ιστής**, οῦ, ὁ, *registrar*, *POxy*.1.34$^v$ i 12 (ii A.D.).

**εἰκονο-γρᾰφέω**, *depict*, Ph.2.588; *describe*, Longin.10.6, Heraclit. *Incred*.15. **2.** *make an image*, dub. in *PPetr*.3 p.9. **-γρᾰφία**, ἡ, *sketch, description*, Str.15.1.69. **-γράφος** [ᾰ], ὁ, *portrait-painter*, Arist.*Po*.1454$^b$9, Them.*Or*.24.309b; prob. in *IG*7.3064 (Lebad.). **-λογέω**, *speak figuratively*, prob. in Antig.*Mir*.127. **-λογία**, ἡ, *figurative speaking*, Pl.*Phdr*.267c, 269a (pl.). **-μορφος**, ὁ, *portrait-sculptor*, Man.4.343 (pl.). **-ποιία**, ἡ, *image-making*, Dam.*Pr*. 341. **-ποιός**, ὁ, *portrait-sculptor* or *-painter*, Arist.*Po*.1460$^b$ 9. **-στάσιον** [ᾰ], τό, *shrine*, Anon.*in Rh*.78.2.

**εἰκονώδης**, ες, *fantastic*, Gloss.

⊛ **εἰκός**, Ion. **οἰκός**, ότος, τό, neut. part. of ἔοικα, *like truth*, i.e. *likely, probable, reasonable*, εἰ. (with or without ἐστί), c. inf. pres., aor., or fut.,

S.*El.*1026, A.*Ag.*575, Is.4.18; οὐ γὰρ εἰ., c. inf., S.*Ph.*230; οἷς εἰ. (sc. δοῦναι) ib.973; ὥσπερ εἰ. ἦν Ar.*Fr.*621, etc.: also pl., ἐοικότα γὰρ.. τυχεῖν Pi.*P.*1.34. **2.** neut. Subst., εἰκός, τό, *likelihood, probability*, τὰ οἰκότα *likelihoods*, Hdt.1.155, etc.; τὸ οὐκ εἰ. Th.2.89; κατὰ τὸ εἰ. in all *likelihood*, Id.1.121; ἐκ τοῦ εἰκότος Id.4.17; τῷ εἰκότι Id.6.18; παντὶ τῷ οἰκότι Hdt.7.103; τοῦ εἰκότος πέρα S.*OT*74; τῷ εἰκότι χρῆσθαι, opp. ἀπόδειξιν λέγειν, Pl.*Tht.*162e: in Poets without Art., λέγεις μὲν εἰκότα S.*Ph.*1373; εἰκὸς πέπονθα E.*IA*501; ἦν γ' ἐρωτᾷς εἰκότ', εἰκότα κλύεις ib.1134. **b.** in Logic, *probable proposition*, opp. positive fact, Arist.*APr.*70ᵃ4, *Rh.*1357ᵃ34. **II.** *reasonable, fair, equitable*, Th.2.74, Isoc.3.53, etc.; τὰ εἰ. καὶ δίκαια Th.5.90; παρὰ τὸ εἰ. un*reasonably*, 2.62: Comp. εἰκότερον Antipho 2.2.3.

⊛ **εἰκοσά-βοιος**, poet. ἐεικ- [ᾰ], ον, *worth twenty oxen*, Od.1.431. **-γράμμᾰτος**, ον, *of twenty letters*, [ὄνομα] *PMag.Par.*1.2634. ⊛ **-γωνος**, ον, *having twenty angles*: τὸ εἰ. Iamb.*VP*34.247.

**εἰκοσά-εδρος** [ᾰ], ον, *of twenty surfaces*: εἰκοσάεδρον, τό, *body with twenty surfaces*, Plu.2.719e, Gal.5.668. **-ετηρίς**, ίδος, ἡ, *period of twenty years*, Ptol.*Tetr.*205. ⊛ **-ετής**, ές, or **-έτης**, ες, *of twenty years*, παῖς Hdt.1.136; χρόνος Plu.2.113d, Wilcken *Chr.*41 iii 21 (iii A.D.):—better **εἰκοσιετής**, fem. **-ετίς**, Pl.*R.*460e, D.C.55.9; ϝικατιϝέτιες *IG*7.3068 (Lebad.). ⊛ **-ετία**, ἡ, *period of twenty years*, Ph.2.224, J.*AJ*8.5.3, *PTeb.*287.7.

**εἰκοσάκις**, *twenty times*, Il.9.379, Pl.*Lg.*771b, etc.

**εἰκοσά-κλῖνος**, ον, = εἰκοσίκλινος, D.S.1.49, Ath.12.548a. **-κωλος**, ον, *of twenty members*, εἴσθεσις Sch.Ar.*Nu.*1153. **-κωπος**, ον, *with twenty oars*, Hsch. s. v. ἐεικοσόροιο, etc. ⊛ **-μηνος**, ον, *twenty months old*, *AP*7.662 (Leon.). **-μναῖος**, α, ον, *weighing twenty minae*, Ph.*Bel.*95.10. **-πηχυς**, υ, = εἰκοσιπ-, Chares ap.Ath.12.538d, Luc.*DMort.*27.4. **-πλάσιος** [πλᾰ], α, ον, = sq., Aristarch. Sam.7, Procl.*Hyp.*3.68. **-πλᾰσίων**, ον, gen. ονος, *twentyfold*, Plu.2.925c. **-πλοῦς**, οῦν, *twentyfold*, Sch.Il.22.349, Hsch. s. v. ἐεικοσαβοιέων. ⊛ **-πρωτοι**, οἱ, *municipal council of twenty*, *OGI*629.10 (Palmyra), *Rev.Ét.Gr.*6.120 (Iasos):—hence **-πρωτεία**, ἡ, *office of* εἰ., *Dig.*50.4.18.26, and **-πρωτεύω**, *hold such office*, *JHS*15.118 (Lycia), *Jahresh.*5.199 (Arneae).

**εἰκοσ-άριθμος** [ᾰ], ον, gloss on εἰκοσινήριτος, *EM*297.44, Suid. **-άρουρος** [ᾰ], ὁ, *holder of twenty* ἄρουραι of land, *PTeb.*61(a).65 (ii B.C.), al.

**εἰκοσάς**, άδος, ἡ, *score*, Orac.ap.Luc.*Alex.*11, Vett.Val.339.1, S.E.*M.*4.32, Hierocl.*in CA* 20 p.464 M.

**εἰκοσα-στάδιος** [στᾰ], ον, *of twenty stadia*, Str.9.4.4. **-στεγος**, ον, *having twenty stories*, Ath.Mech.12.4.

**εἰκοσ-ετηρίς**, ίδος, ἡ, = Lat. *Vicennalia*, D.C.58.24. ⊛ **-έτης**, ου, ὁ, = εἰκοσαετής, *BMus.Inscr.*2.390 (Cypr.):—fem. **-ετίς**, ίδος, ἡ, *AP*7.166 (Diosc. or Nicarch.). **-ήρης**, ες, *with twenty banks of oars*, Ath.5.203d.

⊛ **εἴκοσι** (for εἴκοσιν v. infr.), Att., Ion., also Arc., *IG*5(2).3.1 (Tegea), and Aeol., ib.12(2).6.21 (Lesbos):—indecl., *twenty*, Il.2.510, 748, etc.; in Hom. more freq. in Ep. form **ἐείκοσι**, before a vowel ἐείκοσιν, 1.309, 6.217, al.; Dor. ϝίκατι *Leg.Gort.*4.13, etc.; ϝείκατι *Tab.Heracl.*2.71; Lacon. **βείκατι** Hsch.; **εἴκατι** *IG*9(1).693.10 (Corc.), Theoc.4.10, 5.86. (Orig. ϝίκατι and *ἐ-ϝίκοσι, whence ἐείκοσι in Hom.; ϝείκατι and εἴκατι are late spellings of (ϝ)ίκατι; εἴκοσι is contr. from *ἔϝικοσι. Cf. Lat. *viginti*, Skt. *viṃśatis*. εἴκοσιν is the only form used by Ar., whether before vowels or consonants (εἴκοσ' ἀπολογίζεται is dub. in *Fr.*465); also (before consonants) Herod.3.91, Phld.*Piet.*3, etc., but not common in Inscrr. or Pap., e.g. (before consonants) *Schwyzer* 707 *B* 2 (Ephesus, vi B.C.), *IG*2.804.155 (iv B.C.), (before a vowel) *PGrenf.*2.75.7 (iv A.D.); εἴκοσι ἔτη, εἴκοσι ἡμερῶν, *IG*1².94, 49.)

**εἰκοσι-δύω** or **-δυο**, *two and twenty*, *PSI*4.390 (iii B.C.), Eust. 726.13. **-εδρος**, ον, = εἰκοσάεδρος, Ti.Locr.98d. **-είς**, ενός, *twenty-one*, *UPZ* 81 ii 14 (ii B.C.). **-εκταῖος**, α, ον, *on the twenty-sixth day*, Gal.7.501. **-εννέα**, *nine and twenty*, *BGU*339 (ii A.D.), Ath.13.608a: **-έξ**, *six and twenty*, *Vit.Eur.*: **-επτά**, *seven and twenty*, Hp.*Oss.*1. **-επτάετής**, ὁ, ἡ, *twenty-seven years old*, *Annales du Service* 22.16. **-ετής**, ές, v. εἰκοσαετής. **-καιτετραπλᾰσίων**, ον, gen. ονος, *twenty-four times as great*, Procl.*Hyp.*3.51. **-κλῖνος**, ον, *with twenty places at table*, Antig.Caryst.ap.Ath.12.548a, D.S.1.49. **-μετρος**, ον, *holding twenty measures*, τρίπος Nonn.*D.*37.548, 610. **-μνως**, ων, *of twenty minae*, ἔρανος Lys.*Fr.*19.

**εἰκοσινήρῖτος**, ον, (εἴκοσιν, ἀρι- 'count', cf. ἀριθμός), δεκάκις τε καὶ εἰ. ἄποινα a ten-, yea *twentyfold* ransom, Il.22.349.

**εἰκοσι-οκτώ**, *twenty-eight*, D.S.14.102, *BGU*458 (iii A.D.), etc. **-πεδος**, ον, *twenty feet wide* or *long*, in Dor. form **ϝικατίπεδος** *Tab. Heracl.*1.62, al. **-πενταέτης**, *twenty-five years old*, *IG*3.1376 (fem.). ⊛ **-πεντάρουρος** [ᾰ], *holding twenty-five* ἄρουραι, *PHib.*1.87 (iii B.C.). **-πέντε**, *twenty-five*, Syngr.ap.D.35.10. **-πηχυς**, υ, *of twenty cubits*, βάθος Hdt.3.60. **-στάδιος** [ᾰ], ον, *of twenty stadia*, μέτρον Th.6.1. **-τέσσᾰρες**, ρα, *twenty-four*, Hp.*Oss.*1, D.S.14.92. **-τρεῖς**, neut. **-τρία**, *twenty-three*, Ath.13.585b. **-φυλλος**, ον, *with twenty petals*, ῥόδον Thphr.*HP*6.6.4.

⊛ **εἰκόσορος**, poet. ἐεικ-, ον, (εἴκοσι, ἐρέσσω) *with twenty oars*, Od.9.322, Teles p.27 H., *AP*5.203.10 (Mel.), 6.222 (Theodorid.): as Subst., εἰ. (sc. ναῦς), ἡ, D.35.18.

**εἰκοσταῖος**, α, ον, *on the twentieth day*, Hp.*Prog.*15, Antipho 1.20; εἰκοσταῖοί ἐσμεν ἀφ' οὗ ἐγδημοῦμεν *PLond.ined.*2090 (iii B.C.).

**εἰκοστή**, ἡ, v. εἰκοστός II.

**εἰκοστόγδοον**, τό, *one twenty-eighth*, Nicom.*Ar.*1.16.

**εἰκοστο-έβδομος**, ον, *twenty-seventh*, Plu.2.1027f. **-εκταῖος**, α, ον, *on the twenty-sixth day*, Gal.7.501. **-λόγος**, ὁ, ἡ, *one who collects the twentieth, tax-* or *toll-collector*, Ar.*Ra.*363. **-πεμπτος**, ον, *twenty-fifth*, *Gp.*8.23.2, Nicom.*Ar.*1.12. **-πρωτος**, ον, *twenty-first*, ibid.

⊛ **εἰκοστός**, ή, όν, *twentieth*, Od.5.34, etc.; Ep. also ἐεικοστός Il.24.765. **II.** **εἰκοστή**, ἡ, *a tax of a twentieth*, εἰ. τῶν γιγνομένων, τῶν κατὰ θάλασσαν, Th.6.54, 7.28. **2.** εἰ. ἐλευθερίας or -ιῶν, = Lat. *vicesima manumissionum*, *IG*3.1446, *BGU*96.8, etc.

**εἰκοστο-τέταρτος**, ον, *twenty-fourth*, Plu.2.935e:—also **-τεταρταῖος**, α, ον, Gal.7.501.

**εἰκοστώνης**, ου, ὁ, *farmer of the vicesima*, Arr.*Epict.*4.1.33.

**εἰκοσώρῠγος**, ον, (ὀργυιά) *of twenty fathoms*, δίκτυα X.*Cyn.*2.5.

**εἰκοτο-λογέω**, *infer from probabilities*, Str.13.3.2. **-λογία**, ἡ, *probability* or *inference therefrom*, Archyt.ap.Stob.1.41.5, Phld.*Rh.*1.80S., Str.13.3.1, Iamb.*VP*18.86 (pl.), Herm. *in Phdr.*p.74 A. (pl.), Simp.*in Ph.*18.30.

⊛ **εἰκότως**, Adv. of εἰκώς, Att. pf. part. of ἔοικα, *suitably*, c. dat., A.*Ag.*915; *fairly, reasonably*, Id.*Supp.*403 (lyr.), S.*OC*432, 977, Isoc.12.101, etc.; εἰ. ἔχει *'tis reasonable*, E.*IT*911, cf. *Or.*737 (troch.); εἰ. δοκεῖ And.1.140, cf. 142; οὐκ εἰ. un*reasonably*, Th.1.37: folld. by γάρ, ib.77: freq. at the end of sentences, D.1.10, al., Pl.*La.*183b.

**εἰκτέον**, (εἴκω) *one must yield*, Ph.2.68.

**εἰκτικός**, ή, όν, (εἴκω) *readily yielding*, φύσις, of the void, Phld.*Sign.*18, cf. Max.Tyr.13.3 (Comp.), Heliod.ap.Orib.44.10.2, Them. *in de An.*92.36: metaph., *weak, easily refuted*, λόγος Phld.*Sign.*13.

**εἶκτον, εἴκτην, ἔϊκτο**, v. ἔοικα.

**εἰκτός**, ή, όν, (εἴκω) *yielding*, Alex.Aphr.*Quaest.*62.4, *EM*297.8. **II.** (ἔοικα) *like*, Theognost.*Can.*15.

***εἴκω**, *to be like, seem likely*, v. ἔοικα.

⊛ **εἴκω**, Il.12.48, etc.: impf. εἶκον 16.305 (ὑπό-), Hdt.8.3: fut. εἴξω Th.1.141, etc.: aor. 1 εἶξα Il.24.718, etc., poet. ἔειξα or ἔϝειξα Alcm.31, Ion. εἴξασκε Od.5.332: pf. part. ἐεικώς *Chron.Lind.*D.96:—*give way, retire*, ὀπίσσω εἴκετε Il.5.606; ὅππῃ τ' ἰθύσῃ τῇ τ' εἴκουσι στίχες ἀνδρῶν 12.48: c. dat., *make way for*, οὐρεῦσι 24.716; *yield* to pressure, Gal.18(1).97. **2.** c. dat. pers. et gen. loci, μηδ' εἴκετε χάρμης Ἀργείοις *shrink* not *from* the fight for them, 4.509; εἴκειν τινὶ τῆς ὁδοῦ Hdt.2.80; εἴξατέ μοι νίκης Coluth.171: c. gen. only, εἴκειν πολέμου καὶ δηϊοτῆτος *withdraw from* war and strife, Il.5.348; εἶκε, γέρον, προθύρου *retire from* the door, Od.18.10, cf. Jul.*Or.*2.67b. **3.** *give way*, as a mark of honour, Il.24.100, Od.2.14; τῇ πατρίδι Jul.*Or.*8.246a. **4.** *give way to* any passion or impulse, ᾧ θυμῷ εἴξας Il.9.598; ὄκνῳ καὶ ἀφραδίῃσι 10.122; ὕβρει Od.14.262; βίῃ καὶ κάρτεϊ εἴκειν *give full play to* one's might and strength, 13.143; ὀργῇ δ' εἶξα μᾶλλον ἤ μ' ἐχρῆν E.*Hel.*80; τῇ ἡλικίῃ εἴκειν Hdt.7.18; of circumstances, πενίῃ εἴκων Od.14.157; κακοῖς A.*Pr.*322; ἀνάγκῃ Id.*Ag.*1071; ξυμφοραῖς Th.1.84; ζημίαις *to the force of* punishment, X.*Cyr.*1.6.21:—in S.*Ant.*718 θυμοῦ shd. prob. be read for θυμῷ. **5.** εἴκειν τινί τι *yield to* another *in* a thing, τὸ δ' ἂν μένος οὐδενὶ εἴκων *inferior to* none *in*.., Il.22.459, Od.11.515: c. acc. cogn., εἴκοντας ἃ δεῖ *yielding* in.., S.*OC*172 (lyr.), cf. *Aj.*1243: also c. dupl. dat., ἔλεσκον ἀνδρῶν.. ὅ τέ μοι εἴξειε πόδεσσι whoever *was inferior to* me in swiftness of foot, Od.14.221. **6.** c. gen., *retire from*, ἱερατείας *Chron.Lind.* l. c. **II.** trans., *yield up, give up*, εἶξαί τέ οἱ ἡνία *give* [the horse] the rein, Il.23.337; Εὖρος Ζεφύρῳ εἴξασκε διώκειν *gave up* [the ship] to Zephyrus to chase, Od.5.332. **2.** *grant, allow*, ὁπηνίκ' ἂν θεὸς πλοῦν ἡμὶν εἴκῃ S.*Ph.*465. **III.** impers., *it is allowable* or *possible*, ὅπῃ εἴξειε μάλιστα Il.22.321: c. inf., ὅθι σφίσιν εἶκε λοχῆσαι 18.520; φώναισ' οὐδὲν ἔτ' εἴκει Sapph.2.8; φερόμενοι πρὸς τὸ εἶκον attacking on the *line of least resistance*, Plu.*Fab.*16.

⊛ **εἰκών**, ἡ, gen. όνος, acc. όνα, etc.: poet. and Ion. nom. **εἰκώ** is implied (though not found) in gen. εἰκοῦς E.*Hel.*77, acc. εἰκώ A.*Th.*559, E.*Med.*1162, Hdt.7.69 (but εἰκόνα 2.143, both εἰκόνα and εἰκώ in Pl.*Ti.*37d), Maiist.15: acc. pl. εἰκοὺς E.*Tr.*1178, Ar.*Nu.*559: (*εἴκω, ἔοικα, ϝεικ- *Inscr.Cypr.*151 H.):—*likeness, image*, whether picture or statue, Hdt.2.130, 143, A.*Th.*559, etc.; εἰ. γεγραμμένη Plu.2.1117c; εἰ. γραπτά *IG*4.940.23, cf. 3.1330; of needlework, E.*IT*223 (anap.); *bust*, Luc.*Alex.*18; εἰ. βασιλικαί, = Lat. *imagines imperatorum*, Lib.*Or.*56.13: generally, εἰ. τοῦ νοητοῦ θεὸς αἰσθητός Pl.*Ti.*92c. **2.** *image in a mirror*, E.*Med.*1162, Pl.*R.*402b. **3.** *personal description*, *PTeb.*32.21 (ii B.C.), etc. **4.** metaph., *living image, representation*, εἰ. ζῶσα τοῦ Διός *OGI*90.3 (Rosetta, ii B.C.); τοῦ θεοῦ 2*Ep.Cor.*4.4. **II.** *semblance, phantom*, E.*HF*1002; οὐ γὰρ ἐκεῖνος τέθνηκεν, ἀλλ' ἐγὼ ἡ εἰ. αὐτοῦ Luc.*DMort.*16.1; *imaginary form*, Pl.*R.*588b; *image in the mind*, εἰκοὺς πατρός E.*Tr.*1178; δοξῶν καὶ λόγων Pl.*Phlb.*39c, etc.; εἰκόνας σῆς ἀρετῆς thy virtue's *counterparts*, of children, *Epigr.Gr.*435.4; περίβολον ἔχειν δεσμωτηρίου εἰκόνα Pl.*Cra.*400c; ἐν εἰκόνι βασιλείας Hdn.7.9.10. **III.** *similitude, comparison*, Ar.*Nu.*559, *Ra.*906, Pl.*Phd.*87b, *Men.*80c, Men.536.1; δι' εἰκόνος λέγεσθαι Pl.*R.*487e, cf. Arist.*Rh.*1407ᵃ11, Lib.*Ep.*8.1. **IV.** *pattern, archetype*, ποτὶ τὰν εἰκόνα [κόσμος] ἀπειργασμένος Ti.Locr.99d.

**εἰκώς**, v. ἔοικ-. **εἶλα**· ὀσπρίων καλάμη, Hsch.; cf. εἴλη II.2.

**εἰλαμίδες**, αἱ, *membranes of the brain or spinal cord*, Poll.2.44.

**εἰλαδόν** or **ἰλαδόν**, Adv., (εἴλη) = ἰληδόν, Hdt.1.172, App.*BC*2.63.

**εἰλᾰπῖν-άζω**, used by Hom. only in pres., *revel in a large company*, Od.2.57, so Pi.*P.*10.40: impf., Q.S.6.179: trans., *feast on*, Nonn.*D.*12.49, al.; δαῖτα Opp.*H.*3.219. **-αστής**, οῦ, ὁ, *feaster, guest, boon-companion*, Il.17.577, Orph.*Fr.*207. **II.** name of Zeus at

Cyprus, Hegesand.30. -η, ἡ, *solemn feast* or *banquet* (Ath.8.362e), γάμοι τ' ἔσαν εἰλαπίναι τε Il.18.491; εἰλαπίνη ἠὲ γάμος, both opp. ἔρανος, Od.1.226, cf. E.*Med.*193 (lyr.), *Hel.*1337 (lyr.), Pl.*Ax.*371d (pl.), A.R.1.13, Plu.2.169d (pl.), Ant.Lib.4.4, *BGU*1080.10 (iii A.D.); cf. ἐλλαπίνα. -ουργός, ὁ, *maker of feasts*, Man.4.300.

**εἶλαρ**, τό, used only in nom. and acc. sg., *covering, shelter, defence*, εἶ. νηῶν τε καὶ αὐτῶν *shelter for* ship and crew, Il.7.338, etc.; κύματος εἶ. *fence against* the waves, Od.5.257. (ϝέλϝαρ, cf. ἔλαρ Hsch., εἴλω.)

**εἰλαρχέω, εἰλάρχης**, v. ἰλ-.

**εἰλάτινος**, Ep. for ἐλάτινος.

**εἶλεα**· ἄθλια, χαλινοί, δεσμοί, φιμοί, δέραια, Hsch.; v. εἶλος.

⊛ **Εἰλείθυια**, ἡ, (ἐλυθ- *she that comes* in need, a participial form) *Ilithyia*, the goddess of child-birth, pl. in Hom., Il.11.270, 19.119, sg. in Hes.*Th.*922, etc. II. *parturition*, in pl., Opp.*H.*1.477, al.; *offspring*, ib.4.505. 2. metaph., σταφυλὴ βότρυος εἰ. Nonn.*D.*16.203. (There are numerous varieties of spelling, e.g. Ἐλείθυια Pi.*P.*3.9, *N.*7.1, *SIG*602 (Delph.), *IG*3.1320, etc.: Ἐλεῖθυα ib.12(3).192 (Astypalaea): Εἰλήθυια (q.v.) *IG*12(5).197 (Paros, prob.), Call.*Del.*132, *AP*6.200 (Leon.), Paus.2.5.4, etc.: Ἐλευθία, Ion. -ίη, *GDI* 4584 (Hippola), *IG*12(5).187 (Paros): Lacon. Ἐλευσία ib.5(1).236: Cret. Ἐλεύθυια *GDI*5149, al.: Boeot. Εἰλείθεια, -ια, *IG*7.2228, 3410; cf. Εἰλιόνεια, Ἐλευθώ.) Εἰλειθυιαῖον or -υαῖον, τό, *temple of Ilithyia*, ib.11(2).161*B*114, 118 (Delos, iii B.C.), *Inscr.Delos*338*Ab*84:—also ⊛Εἰλείθυιον, τό, *Lex.Rhet.*ap.Eust.1053.61.

**εἰλεός** or **ἰλεός**, ὁ, (εἰλέω) *intestinal obstruction*, Hp.*Aph.*3.22, Aret.*SA*2.6, v.l. (-ειοῖο) in Nic.*Al.*597, etc.; distd. fr. χορδαψός, Diocl.*Fr.*73; of other diseases, as *nephritis*, Hp.*Int.*44; εἰ. ἰκτερώδης *jaundice*, ib.45; εἰ. αἱματίτης *scurvy*, ib.46, cf. Lyc.ap.Orib.8.28.1, etc.; *staggers*, Arist.*HA*604$^a$30. II. *lurking-place, den, hole*, εἰλεόν, οὐκ οἴκησιν Theoc.15.9. III. = ἐλεός, *butcher's block*, Eust.749.7. IV. a kind of *vine*, Hippys7.

**εἰλετίας** (sc. κάλαμος), ου, ὁ, a kind of *reed*, *Ammophila arundinacea*, Thphr.*HP*4.11.13; εἰλεσίας, Hsch.

**εἰλέτις**· βλάσφημος, Hsch.

**εἰλέω, εἱλέω**, v. εἴλω.

**εἱλέω**, Ion. εἰλ-, (εἵλη) *sun*, Eust.1573.45:—Pass., πρὸς τὸν ἥλιον εἰληθέντες Hp.*Int.*45.

**εἰλεώδης**, ες, *of the nature of* εἰλεός I, τὰ εἰ. the symptoms thereof, Hp.*Epid.*3.1.θ'; οἱ εἰ. *those who suffer therefrom*, Dsc.1.30; *causing this disease*, Aret.*SA*2.6 (dub.). Adv. -δῶς Sor.2.29, Herod.Med. in *Rh.Mus.*58.108.

**εἴλη**, = ἴλη (q.v.).

**εἵλη**, ἡ, *the sun's heat* or *warmth*, Ar.*V.*772 (dub.), *Fr.*627, Luc.*Lex.*2, Alciphr.1.2, 12; cf. γέλαν (i.e. ϝέλαν)· αὐγὴν ἡλίου, Hsch. II. *chaff*, Id. 2. τῶν ὀσπρίων ἡ καλάμη, Id.; cf. εἶλα.

⊛ **εἰληδόν, εἰληδά**, Adv., (εἴλη) = ἰληδόν, εἰληδὰ φέρονται Arat.917. II. (εἰλέω) *by twisting* or *coiling round*, εἰληδὸν ἔδησε πόδας *AP*9.14.6 (Antiphil.).

**εἰληθερ-έω**, *bask in the sun*, Hp.*Morb.*2.68, 70, Xenarch.4.5, Philostr.*Gym.*58:—Med., Luc.*Rh.Pr.*17. ⊛ -ής, ές, (εἵλη, θέρω) *warmed by the sun*: *warm*, Hp.*Morb.*2.30, Gal.11.389; cf. ἑλαθερής.

**εἴληθι**, v. ἱλάσκομαι.

**εἰληθμός** (εἰδ- cod.), ὁ, *coiling up*, Hsch.

**Εἰλήθυια**, v. Εἰλείθυια. II. name of a kind of *comet*, Heph.Astr.1.24.

**εἰλήϊον**· ἐν ἡλίῳ θερμανθέν, Hsch.

**εἰλήλουθα, εἰληλούθειν, εἰλήλουθμεν**, v. ἔρχομαι.

⊛ **εἴλημα**, ατος, τό, (εἰλέω) *veil, covering, wrapper*, [Hdt.] ap.Stob.3.28.18$^a$. II. = εἰλεός I, Hp.*Flat.*9 (pl., dub.). 2. *a coil*, σχοινίου S.E.*M.*7.187; *roll* of a bandage, Gal.18(1).809. III. Archit., *arch* spanning intercolumniation, *Arch.Anz.*19.8 (Milet.), *CIG*2782.31 (Aphrodisias). IV. *vault, cellar*, prob. in *PLond.ined.*1821.387.

**εἰλῆς εἶ**· ἵλεως εἶ, Hsch.

⊛ **εἴλησις**, Att. εἵλ-, εως, ἡ, (εἰλέω) *eddy, vortex* of wind, fire, etc., Plot.1.8.14, *EM*20.3, Sch.A.R.1.438, Phryn.374; *revolution* of heavenly bodies, Poll.4.156.

**εἵλησις**, εως, ἡ, (εἱλέω) *sun-heat*, Pl.*R.*380e (pl.), 404b (pl.), Arist.*Ph.*197$^a$23, Plu.2.688a (pl.).

**εἰλ-ητάριον**, τό, *wrapper, roll*, Aët.15.13. -ητικός, v.l. for ἰλυσπαστικός (q.v.) in Arist.*HA*487$^b$21. -ητός, Att. εἱλ-, ή, όν, (εἰλέω) *wound*, Sch.Ar.*Ra.*342; *rolled*, ἐπίδεσμος Gal.18(1).813, cf. Heliod.ap.Orib.48.20.1.

**εἰλιγγιάω, εἴλιγγος**, v. ἰλ-.

**εἰλίγδην**, Adv. *wriggling*, ἕρπων Orac. in *App.Anth.*6.140.10.

**εἴλιγμα**, ατος, τό, Horap.1.59, *EM*723.35: -μός, ὁ, Mnesith.ap.Orib.8.38.9, Orph.*H.*38.12; poet. and Ion. for ἑλιγ-.

**εἴλιγξ**, v. εἶλιξ.

**εἰλικο-ειδής**, ές, = ἑλικ-, Suid., Zonar. -εις, εσσα, εν, = ἕλιξ, ἀσπίδες Nic.*Th.*201; κτίλοι *with crooked horns*, Opp.*C.*1.388; βότρυς Nonn.*D.*12.343; δράκων ib.9.130. -μορφος, ον, (ἕλιξ) *of twisted* or *spiral form*, Opp.*C.*2.98.

**εἰλικρίν-εια** [ῐ], ἡ, *unmixedness, purity*, opp. μίξις, Arist.*Col.*793$^a$10; ἀέρος S.E.*M.*9.73, cf. Alex.Aphr. in *Sens.*137.1: metaph., λογισμοῦ Iamb.*VP*16.68 (pl.); in bad sense, *unrelievedness*, κακοῦ Phld.*Ir.*p.25 W. II. *sincerity, uprightness*, 1*Ep.Cor.*5.8, al., *POxy.*1252 vii 38 (iii A.D.). -έω, *purify*, Arist.*Mu.*397$^a$35 (Pass.). II. *separate, distinguish*, Buther.ap.Stob.1 *Prooem.*5 (Pass.). -ής, ές, *unmixed, without alloy, pure*, ἐκ πυρὸς τοῦ -εστάτου καὶ ὕδατος Hp.*Vict.*1.35; θέρμη, ψῦξις, Id.*VM*19; διὰ τὸ εἰλικρινῆ ἕκαστα εἶναι (sc. τὰ φῦλα) *distinct and separate*, X.*Cyr.*8.5.14; εἴ τῳ γένοιτο αὐτὸ τὸ καλὸν ἰδεῖν εἰ., καθαρόν, ἄμεικτον Pl.*Smp.*211e; τὸ ἧττον εἰ., opp. τὸ καθαρώτερον, Arist.*Mete.*340$^b$8; τῶν χρωμάτων οὐδὲν ὁρῶμεν εἰ. οἷόν ἐστιν, ἀλλὰ πάντα κεκραμένα Id.*Col.*793$^b$13; τὸ λευκὸν [μέλι] οὐκ ἐκ θύμου εἰλικρινοῦς Id.*HA*627$^a$3; εἰ. καὶ ἀμιγής Id.*de An.*426$^b$4; ἐν μεγάλῳ εἰ. καὶ κενῷ Epicur.*Ep.*2 p.37 U. (fort. καὶ εἰ.); τὸ ἓν εἰ. καὶ καθαρόν Plu.2.393c. 2. *pure, simple, absolute*, αὐτῇ καθ' αὑτὴν εἰλικρινεῖ τῇ διανοίᾳ χρώμενος the *pure and absolute* intellect, Pl.*Phd.*66a; ψυχὴν αὐτὴν καθ' αὑτὴν εἰ. ἀπαλλάξεσθαι ib.81c; γνωσόμεθα.. πᾶν τὸ εἰ. *the pure and absolute*, ib.67b; τὸ καθαρόν τε καὶ εἰ. Id.*Phlb.*52d; τὰς τέρψεις εἰ. ἀποδιδόναι Isoc.1.46; ἡδονὴ εἰ. Arist.*EN*1176$^b$20; εὐπορία -εστάτη Epicur.*Sent.*14; also of evil things, *sheer, absolute*, ἀδικία X.*Mem.*2.2.3. 3. *sincere*, ἀπόδεξις *OGI*227.12 (Didyma, iii B.C.); εὔνοια ib.763.41 (Milet., ii B.C.); of persons, *Ep.Phil.*1.10. Adv. -νῶς *OGI*441.5 (i B.C.). 4. *total*, ἐκλείψεις Cleom.2.5. II. Adv. -νῶς *without mixture, of itself, simply, absolutely*, διὰ τὸ εἰ. εἶναι Ἕλληνας καὶ ἀμιγεῖς βαρβάρων Pl.*Mx.*245d; τὸ εἰ. ὂν *absolute* being, Id.*R.*477a; εἰ. ὑπὸ τοῦ ἔρωτος ὡρμημένους Id.*Smp.*181c; εἰ. ὅλον λευκόν Arist.*Ph.*187$^b$4; *without qualification*, -νῶς Ταραντῖνοι Arr.*Tact.*4.6: Ion. -έως, κρίνεσθαι to have a *clear crisis*, Hp.*Epid.*4.7.—The word is confined to Prose.

**εἰλικρῐνότης**, ητος, ἡ, *sincerity*, Gloss.

**εἰλικτήρ**, ῆρος, ὁ, = ἑλ., *IG*2.660.52, 698 ii 23.

**εἰλικτός**, ή, όν, (εἰλίσσω) poet. and Ion. for ἑλικτός, f.l. E.*Ion*40; of flames, *enveloping*, Ps.-Democr.Alch.p.50B.

**εἰλίνδησις**, εως, ἡ, = ἀλινδ-, Aq.*Ps.*54(55).6:—so **εἰλινδούμενοι**, v.l. in Alciphr.1.26.

**εἶλιξ**, ικος, ἡ, poet. for ἕλιξ; cf. **εἴλιξ** (fort. εἴλιγξ)· σκότωσις (prob. for εἰλισκότ- cod.), στρόφος, Hsch.

**Εἰλιόνεια**, ἡ, = Εἰλείθυια, Plu.2.277b.

⊛ **εἰλίονες**, poet. pl., = *brothers-in-law*, whose wives are sisters, Pollux3.32. (Prob. metri gr. for *ἐλίονες, cf. ἀέλιοι, OIcel. *svilar* (same meaning), Skt. *syālás* 'wife's brother'?)

**εἰλῐπόδης**, ου, ὁ, later form for sq., Nonn.*D.*1.160; Ἥφαιστος ib.29.356; ὀρχηθμός ib.17.214: metaph. of the scazon, Aus.*Ep.*10.31.

**εἰλίπους** [ῐ], ὁ, ἡ, πουν, τό, gen. ποδος: (εἴλω, πούς):—*rolling in their gait*, in Hom. (only in dat. and acc. pl., Il.6.424, 9.466) as epith. of oxen, which *bring round their hind legs with a circling* or *rolling motion*, cf. Hp.*Art.*8; εἰλίποδες, abs., for *oxen* or *kine*, Theoc.25.131; also of women, *having a rolling gait*, Eup.161; also expld. sens. obsc., Anacr.164, cf. Paus.Gr.*Fr.*154; cf. ἀνειλλίπους.

**εἰλίσσω**, v. ἑλίσσω.

**εἰλῐτενής**, ές, epith. of the plant ἄγρωστις, Theoc.13.42, prob. (from ἕλος, τείνω) *spreading through marshes*.

**εἰλίχατο**, v. ἑλίσσω. **εἰλκτής**· αἴτιος, Hsch. **εἵλλω, εἴλλω**, v. εἴλω.

⊛ **εἰλόπεδον**, τό, v.l. for θειλόπεδον in Od.7.123, cf. *EM*449.29, Eust.43.38.

**εἶλος**, = δεσμός, Hsch.; cf. εἶλεα. **εἰλύ**· μέλαν, Id.

**εἰλυθμός**, ὁ, (εἰλύω) *lurking-place, den*, Nic.*Th.*285; glossed by ἕλκος, τρόμος, Hsch. **εἰλύϊος**, ὁ, *wood-worm*, Id.

⊛ **εἴλῡμα**, ατος, τό, *wrapper*, εἴ. σπείρων Od.6.179, cf. Anacr.21.6, A.R.2.1129, Gal.19.367. (Cf. ἔλυμα.)

**εἰλυός** or ἰλ- [ῐ], ὁ, = εἰλυθμός, X.*Cyn.*5.16, A.R.1.1144, Nic.*Th.*143.

**εἰλύς**, ύος, ἡ, = ἰλύς, *mire, morass*, Hsch.

**εἴλῡσις**, εως, ἡ, *crawling* or *wriggling along*, Sch.S.*Ph.*291, Simp. in *Ph.*1229.22.

**εἰλυσπ-άομαι**, freq. v.l. for ἰλυσπάομαι. -όα, perh., = ἄγρωστις, Porph.*Abst.*2.7. -ωμα, ατος, τό, *worm-like motion*, Eust.1413.43.

**εἰλύσσεται**· εἰλεῖται, Hsch.

**εἰλυστήριον**, *place for rolling*, Gloss.

⊛ **εἰλυτά** (sc. μᾶζα), cake offered to Trophonius, *IG*7.3055 (Lebad.). (Cf. ἐλλ-.)

**εἰλῡφάζω**, = εἰλύω, only pres. and impf., *roll along*, ἄνεμος φλόγα Il.20.492. II. intr., *roll* or *whirl about*, of a blazing torch, Hes.*Sc.*275.

**εἰλῡφάω**, = foreg., Ep. part. -όων Il.11.156, Hes.*Th.*692; intr., Nonn.*D.*30.81. (Perh. wrongly expanded, for εἰλύφων.)

**εἰλύω**, Arat.432: fut. εἰλύσω [ῡ] Il.21.319:—Med., part. εἰλυόμενος, impf. εἰλυόμην, S.*Ph.*702 (lyr.), 291:—Pass., pf. εἴλῡμαι, Ep. 3 pl. εἰλύαται, plpf. εἴλῡτο, Il.5.186, Od.20.352, Il.16.640. [ῡ always in Hom. exc. in εἰλῠαται, also in S.; ῠ in Metag. (v. infr.), and late Ep., Arat.432, Nic.*Al.*18 (but εἰλυμένα *Th.*754).]:—*enfold, enwrap*, Act. once in Hom., κὰδ δέ μιν αὐτὸν εἰλύσω ψαμάθοισι Il.21.319; εἰλύγη δέ μιν εἰλύει ἀχλὺς Arat. l.c.:—Pass., *to be wrapped, covered*, βοέῃς εἰλυμένω ὤμους Il.17.492; εἰλυμένοι αἴθοπι χαλκῷ 18.522; νεφέλῃ εἰλυμένος ὤμους 5.186; αἵματι καὶ κονίῃσιν εἴλυτο 16.640; εἴλυτο δὲ πάνθ' ἁλὸς ἄχνῃ Od.5.403; νυκτὶ μὲν ὑμέων εἰλύαται κεφαλαί 20.352, cf. Il.12.286. II. Pass., after Hom., = ἰλυσπάομαι, *crawl, wriggle along*, of a lame man, εἰλυόμην δύστηνον ἐξέλκων πόδα S.*Ph.*291; εἰλυόμενος, παῖς ἄτερ ὡς ..τιθήνας ib.702; of a shoal of fish, Metag.6.4. 2. in Theoc.25.246 εἰλυθείς is used like ἐλυσθείς in Hom., *rolled up, crouching*; but εἰλυμένος is part. of εἰλύω (q.v.) in A.R.3.296.

⊛ **εἴλω** (also εἰλέω, εἱλέω, εἴλλω, εἵλλω, ἴλλω; εἰλῶνται is f.l. in Aret.*SD*1.2), a word whose meanings are traceable to various roots

of similar form, v. infr. D.—From εἵλω (pres. in Hom. only Pass. part. εἰλόμενος (v. infr.)), we have Ep. aor. ἔλσα Il.11.413, inf. ἐέλσαι 21.295, Dor. part. ἔλσαις Pi.O.10(11).43:—Med., aor. ἠλσάμην Semon.17:—**Pass.**, aor. 2 ἐάλην [ᾰ] Il.13.408; inf. ἀλῆναι, ἀλήμεναι, 16.714, 18.76; part. ἀλείς, εἶσα, ἐν 22.308: pf. ἔελμαι, part. -μένος 13.524:—for ἐόλει, ἐόλητο, v. ἐόλει.—From **εἰλέω** Il.2.294: impf. εἴλεον Od.22.460; contr. εἴλει Il.8.215, Od.12.210; ἐείλεον Il.18.447: fut. εἰλήσω Lxx*Jb*.40.21(26), *AP*12.208 (Strat.): aor. εἴλησα Lxx 4*Ki*.2.8, Dsc.5.87 (ἐν-):—**Med.**, impf. εἰλεῦντο Il.21.8; part. εἰλεύμενος Hdt.2.76:—**Pass.**, aor. εἰλήθην Hp.*Morb*.4.52: pf. εἴλημαι Lxx1*Ki*.21.9(10) and *Is*.11.5 (s.v.l.), Lyc.1202: plpf. εἴλητο J.*AJ* 12.1.9.

A. *shut in* (less freq. *shut out*, εἰλέσθων τοῦ ἱαροῦ *let them be shut out* from the temple, *IG*2².1126.48 (iv B.C.)); [Ὀδυσῆα] ἔλσαν ἐν μέσσοισι μετὰ σφίσι, πῆμα δὲ ἔλσαν (Zenod., v.l. πῆμα τιθέντες) Il.11.413; ὅτε Κύκλωψ εἴλει ἐνὶ σπῆϊ Od.12.210, cf. 22.460; ἔνθα δυώδεκα μὲν μένον ἤματα δῖοι Ἀχαιοί· εἴλει γὰρ Βορέης ἄνεμος μέγας οὐδ' ἐπὶ γαίῃ εἴα ἵστασθαι Od.19.200; ὅν περ ἄελλαι χειμέριαι εἰλέωσιν Il.2.294; εἰλεῖσθαι ἐν τῷ τόπῳ, μὴ δυνάμενον ἐκπλεῦσαι Arist.*Mir*. 840ᵃ33, cf. *EM*298.29; εἰς ἄστυ ἄλεν (for ἄλησαν) Il.22.12; κατὰ ἄστυ ἐελμέθα 24.662; ἐελμένοι ἔνδοθι πύργων 18.287; νηυσὶν ἔπι γλαφυρῇσιν ἐελμένοι 12.38; χειμέριον ἀλὲν ὕδωρ *ponded* water, *prevented* from flowing away, Il.23.420; ὅσοι πικροὶ.. χυμοὶ κατὰ τὸ σῶμα πλανηθέντες ἔξω μὲν μὴ λάβωσιν ἀναπνοήν, ἐντὸς δὲ εἰλλόμενοι (v.l. εἰλόμενοι) τὴν ἀφ' αὑτῶν ἀτμίδα τῇ τῆς ψυχῆς φορᾷ συμμείξαντες ἀνακερασθῶσι, Pl.*Ti*.86e. 2. *hinder, hold in check, prevent*, ἧστο Διὸς βουλῇσιν ἐελμένος Il.13.524, cf. A.*Fr*.25: ἔλλοψ (as though ἴλλοψ) is derived from ἴλλεσθαι = εἴργεσθαι and ὄψ = φωνή by Ath.7. 308c. 3. *enclose, cover, protect*, ὑπ' ἀσπίδος ἄλκιμον ἦτορ ἔλσας Callin.1.11; τῇ ὕπο (sc. τῇ ἀσπίδι) πᾶς ἐάλη he *was* entirely *covered*, Il.13.408.

B. *press*, as olives and grapes, Paus.Gr.*Fr*.155; ἀμφὶ βίην Διομήδεος.. εἰλόμενοι *huddling* around him, Il.5.782; ἵππων φειδόμενος, μή μοι δευοίατο φορβῆς ἀνδρῶν εἰλομένων, εἰωθότες ἔδμεναι ἄδην here where men *throng*, ib.203; πλῆθεν.. ἵππων τε καὶ ἀνδρῶν εἰλομένων· εἴλει δὲ.. Ἕκτωρ 8.215, cf. 1.409, 18.447, 21.295; πόλις δ' ἔμπλητο ἀλέντων ib.607; ἐς ποταμὸν εἰλεῦντο they *were forced* into the river, ib.8; εἰλουμένης τῆς τροφῆς the nourishment being *concentrated*, Thphr.*CP*6.11.8; θῆρας ὁμοῦ εἰλεῦντα Od.11.573; [λέων] ἰλλόμενός περ ὁμίλῳ hard-*pressed*, A.R.2.27; ἀπωθουμένου ὑπὸ τοῦ περιεστῶτος ἔξωθεν πνεύματος πάλιν ἐντὸς ὑπὸ τὸ δέρμα εἰλλόμενον κατερριζοῦτο Pl.*Ti*.76b:—Pass., of crowds, *swarm, jostle one another*, ἐν ὀλίγῳ εἰλουμένους Plu.*Crass*.25; of ants, Luc.*Icar*.19. 2. in aor. Pass., of a man or animal, *contract* his body, *draw himself together*, Αἰνείας δ' ἐάλη καὶ ἀπὸ ἕθεν ἀσπίδ' ἀνέσχεν Il.20.278; ἐνὶ δίφρῳ ἧστο ἀλείς (*huddled up*), ἐκ γὰρ πλήγη φρένας 16.403; of a lion when struck, ἐάλη τε χανών 20.168; of a warrior, Ἀχιλῆα ἀλεὶς μένεν 21.571; οἴμησεν δὲ ἀλεὶς ὥς τ' αἰετὸς ὑψιπετήεις 22.308, Od. 24.538. II. without the idea of pressure, *collect*, ἐν Πίσᾳ ἔλσαις στρατὸν λείαν τε πᾶσαν Pi.O.10(11).43:—Pass., Ἀργείους ἐκέλευσα ἀλήμεναι ἐνθάδε πάντας *to assemble*, Il.5.823.

C. (found only in the forms εἰλέω (εἰλ-), ἴλλω) *wind, turn round*, σκολιήν τε καὶ οὐ μίαν ἀτραπὸν ἴλλων Nic.*Th*.478; ἀπὸ δὲ τῶ[ν πετρῶν] ἴλλει ἡ στεφάνη ἐπὶ τὸν λόφον *GDI* iv p.847 (iv B.C.); νῆα δ' ἔπειτα πέριξ εἴλει ῥόος A.R.2.571; *roll*, γλῶσσαν dub. in Call.*Iamb*.1.144:—Pass., *revolve, move to and fro*, ἰλλομένων ἀρότρων S.*Ant*.340 (lyr.); οἱ ἀστέρες ἐν τῷ οὐρανῷ εἰλέονται Luc.*Astr*.29; περὶ τὴν γῆν ἀεὶ εἰλεῖν ἰών, as etym. of ἥλιος (ἀέλιος), Pl.*Cra*.409a; εἰλέονται ἐπὶ τὸ ὑγιὲς σκέλος they *pivot* or *swing round* on the sound leg, Hp.*Art*.52, cf. *Mochl*.20; of a flame, περὶ δ' αὐτὸν εἰλεῖτο φλόξ Mosch.4.104; κατ' αὐτὸν (sc. τὸν κισσὸν) ἕλιξ εἰλεῖται *is twined* round, Theoc.1.31; δαίμων ἐν μέσῳ τοῦ παντὸς εἰλουμένη Herm.ap.Stob.1.3.52; also of hair on the crown, *to be whorled*, Ruf.*Onom*.13. II. *roll up tight*, [κῶας] εἴλει ἀφασσόμενος A.R.4.181; τὴν μηλωτὴν εἰλήσας Lxx4*Ki*. 2.8:—Pass., ἰλλομένοις ἐπὶ λαίφεσι *furled*, A.R.1.329. 2. *bind fast*, δεσμοῖς ἰλλόμενος A.R.1.129, cf. 2.1249 (Pass.), cf. S.*Fr*. 158. III. metaph. in Pass., ἐν ποσὶ εἰλεῖσθαι to be familiar, Hdt. 2.76; οἱ περὶ τὰς δίκας εἰλούμενοι Max.Tyr.28.3, cf. Alciphr.3.60, 64.

D. It seems impossible to derive all the above uses from an orig. sense *squeeze*, though most of those under A and B, as well as C. II, might be so explained; but A seems to imply a root meaning *bar*, cf. ἀποϝηλέω, ἐγϝηληθίωντι, ϝήλημα (βήλημα), ἔλαρ, and C is to be compared with εἰλύω, Lat. *volvo*: some passages are doubtful in meaning, μή νυν περὶ σαυτὸν εἶλλε τὴν γνώμην ἀεί do not *roll* or *wrap* your thought round you, or do not *confine* your thought within you, Ar.*Nu*.761; γῆν.. ἰλλομένην (v.l. εἰλλ-, εἱλλ-) τὴν περὶ τὸν διὰ παντὸς πόλον τεταμένον Pl.*Ti*.40b was taken to mean *revolving* by Arist.*Cael*.293ᵇ31 (cf. περὶ τὸ μέσον εἰλεῖσθαι *Mete*.356ᵃ5) but expld. (omitting τήν) as *packed tightly* about.. by Procl.*in Ti*.3.136 D.; ἐν δὲ τῇ ταραχῇ (in the churning) εὐρυχωρίης γινομένης, εἰλέεται (sc. τὸ ὑγρόν) ἀποκεκριμένον καὶ θερμαίνει τὸ σῶμα perh. *is squeezed out*, Hp. *Morb*.4.51; πρὶν δὲ ταραχθῆναι οὐκ ἐκχωρέειν τὸ πλεῖον τοῦ ὑγροῦ, ἀλλ' ἄνω καὶ κάτω εἰλέεται μεμιγμένον τῷ ἄλλῳ ὑγρῷ *is driven up and down*, ibid.:—νῆα κεραυνῷ Ζεὺς ἔλσας (ἐλάσας Zenod.) ἐκέασσε prob. *striking* the ship.., Od.5.132, cf. 7.250 (only here in this sense).

**Εἵλως**, ωτος, Th.4.80, etc., and **Εἱλώτης**, ου, ὁ, Hdt.6.58, etc.; fem. **Εἱλωτίς**, ίδος, ἡ, Plu.*Ages*.3:—*Helot*, name of the Spartan *serfs*, derived by Hellanic.188 J., Theopomp.Hist.14, etc., from Ἕλος, a town of Laconia, whose inhabitants were enslaved: by others from Pass. of *ἕλω, = αἱρέω, cf. *EM*332.53.

**Εἱλωτ-εία**, ἡ, *the system of serfdom* at Sparta, Pl.*Lg*.776c. II. *the body of Helots*, Arist.*Pol*.1269ᵇ12, cf. 1264ᵃ35 (pl.). **-εύω**, *to be a Helot* or *serf*, Isoc.4.131. **-ίζομαι**, Pass., *to be Helotized*, cj. in Hermipp.71. **-ικός**, ή, όν, *of Helots*, τὸ Εἱ. *the Helots* collectively, Paus.4.23.1; Εἱ. πλῆθος Plu.*Sol*.22.

⊛ **εἷμα**, ατος, τό, Aeol. **ἔμμα** Alc.*Supp*.4.21 (pl.), *Lyr.Alex.Adesp*.9 (pl.); Cret. **ϝῆμα** *Leg.Gort*.3.38 (but gen. fem. ϝήμας 5.40): (ἕννυμι):—*garment*, freq. in Hom., in pl., φᾶρός τε χιτῶνά τε εἵματ' ἔθηκαν Od.6.214; χλαῖνάν τε χιτῶνά τε εἵματα ἕσσεν 10.542: in Hdt. mostly, *over-garment*, like ἱμάτιον, 1.155, 2.81, cf. A.*Ch*.81 (lyr.), S. *OT*1268; ἀγῶνα γυμνικὸν ἐν εἵμασι *Inscr.Prien*.112.91 (i B.C.). II. *rug, carpet*, A.*Ag*.921, 963, S.*Aj*.1145.

**εἱμάδες**· ποιμένων οἰκίαι, Hsch.

**εἷμαι**, pf. Pass. of ἕννυμι. II. pf. Pass. of ἵημι.

**εἱμάρσην**, ενος, ἡ, *woman clad in man's dress*, Dosiad.*Ara* 1.

**εἵμαρται, εἵμαρτο, εἱμαρμένος, Εἱμαρμένη**, v. μείρομαι.

**εἱμαρτός**, ή, όν, *fixed by fate*, χρόνος Plu.*Alex*.30, cf. *Epigr.Gr*.339; τὸ ἐπὶ πάντων ἀνθρώπων εἱ. *IG*12(7).396.21 (Amorgos, ii A.D.).

**εἱμᾰτανωπερίβαλλος**, ὁ, *one who wraps his cloak about him*, com. word in Hegesand.2.

**εἱμάτ-ιον**, v. ἱμάτιον. **-ισμός**, ὁ, *clothing*, *PEleph*.1.4 (iv B.C.), *IG*4.1390.15 (Andania), *SIG*999.5 (Lycosura).

**εἱματο-πώλης, -φυλάκιον, -φύλαξ**, v. ἱματ-.

**εἱμένος**, pf. part. Pass. of ἕννυμι and ἵημι.

⊛ **εἰμί** (*sum*), Aeol. ἔμμι Sapph.2.15, Theoc.20.32; Cret. ἠμί *GDI* 4959a; 2 sg. εἶ, Ep. and Ion. εἶς Od.17.388, al., Aeol. ἔσσι, Ep. and Dor. ἐσσί Il.1.176, Pi.O.6.90, Sophr.134; ἐσί *GDI*4959a; 3 sg. ἐστί, Dor. ἐντί *IG*12(1).677 (Rhodes), Theoc.1.17, etc.; 3 dual ἐστόν Th.3. 112; 1 pl. ἐσμέν, Ep. and Ion. εἰμέν (also in Pi.P.3.60), ἐμέν Call.*Fr*. 294, Dor. εἰμές Theoc.15.73, but ἠμέν *GDI*5178.34; 3 pl. εἰσί (-ιν), Ep. and Ion. ἔασι (-ιν) Il.7.73, Xenoph.8.1, Antim.29, Herod.4.84, Dor. ἐντί Pi.*N*.1.24, Theoc.11.45, *IG*9(1).32.22 (Phocis), etc.: imper. ἴσθι (ἔσθι Hecat.361 J.), Ep. and Lyr. also in Med. form ἔσσο Od.3. 200, Sapph.1.28, Maced.*Pae*.31, late Prose ἔσο Plu.2.241d, M.Ant.3. 5, Hld.5.12, Porph.*Marc*.34; 3 sg. ἔστω (ἤτω Lxx*Ps*.103.31, and late Inscrr., *CIG*2664, al.; but in Pl.*R*.361c leg. ἴτω), Dor. εἴτω, ἤτω, Heraclid.ap.Eust.1411.21, Elean ἤστω *Schwyzer*424; 3 pl. ἔστωσαν, but ἔστων Hom., Pl.*R*.502a, ὄντων Id.*Lg*.879b, and early Att. Inscrr., *IG*1².22, etc. (ἔστωσαν first in ii B.C., ib.2².1328), Dor. ἐόντων ib.1126: subj. ὦ, ᾖς, ᾖ, Ep. ἔω Od.9.18; 3 sg. ἔῃ Il.12.300, al. (also ἔῃσι 2.366, al., ᾖσι(ν) 19.202, Hes.*Op*.294), also Boeot. ἔνθω *IG*7.3172.165, μετείω Il.23.47 and perh. εἴῃ 9.245, etc.; Dor. 3 pl. ὦντι *SIG*940.3 (Crete), ἔωντι *GDI*5040.14 (Hierapytna), Boeot. ἴωνθι *IG*7.3171.46 (iii B.C.): opt. εἴην, -ης (εἴησθα Thgn.715), -η, also ἔοις, ἔοι, Il.9.284, 142, al., cf. Hdt.7.6; 3 pl. εἴοισαν Ἀρχ.Ἐφ.1911.133 (Gonni); 3 dual εἴτην Pl. *Prm*.149e, *Sph*.243e; 1 pl. εἶμεν E.*Alc*.921 (lyr.), Pl.; 2 pl. εἶτε Od. 21.195; 3 pl. εἶεν Il.2.372, etc., εἴησαν Hdt.1.2, etc.; Elean ἔα, = εἴη, *SIG*9 (vi B.C.), and σύν-εαν, = συνεῖεν, *GDI*1149 (vi B.C.): inf. εἶναι, Arc. ἦναι *SIG*306.9 (Tegea, iv B.C.); Ep. ἔμμεναι (also Aeol. ἔμμεν' Sapph.34), ἔμμεν (also Pi.*P*.6.42, S.*Ant*.623 (lyr.)), ἔμεναι, ἔμεν, also ἔμειν *SIG*1166 (Dodona); Dor. εἶμεν Foed.ap.Th.5.77, 79, *IG*7.1.7 (Megara), ἦμεν *Test.Epict*.5.16, *Tab.Heracl*.1.75, Cret. ἦμεν or ἤμην *Leg.Gort*.1.15, al., *GDI*4998i2, al., Megar. εἶμεναι Ar.*Ach*. 775, εἶμειν *IG*12(1).155.100 (Rhodes), 14.952 (Agrigentum); εἶν ib. 12(9).211.10 (Eretria), *SIG*135.4 (Olynthus), etc.: part. ὤν, Ep. ἐών, ἐοῦσα, ἐόν, Cypr. ἰών *Inscr.Cypr*.135.23 H.; Boeot. fem. ἰῶσα *IG* 7.3172.15 (Orchom.), Aeol. and Dor. fem. ἔσσα Sapph.75.4, *IG*4. 952.2 (Epid.), Theoc.28.16, ἐοῖσα Pi.*P*.4.265, ἔασσα *Lyr.Alex.Adesp*. 9, Diotog.ap.Stob.4.7.62, εὖσα Erinn.5.5 (also Ion., Herod.5.16, εὔντων 2.85), ἔασα Ti.Locr.96d, *IG*5(1).1470.8 (Messene), ἴαττα *Leg. Gort*.8.47; acc. sg. εὖντα Theoc.2.3; nom. sg. εἷς in Heraclid.ap. Eust.1756.13, pl. ἔντες *Tab.Heracl*.1.117; dat. pl. ἔντασσι ib.104; gen. pl. παρ-έντων Alcm.64: impf. ἦν Il.2.77, etc., Ep. ἔον (also Aeol., Alc.127, Sapph.*Oxy*.1787 *Fr*.3 ii 21), in Att. ἦ (dub. in Aeol., Alc. *Supp*.14.9), Ar.*Pl*.77, Pl.*Phd*.61b, etc., but usu. altered to ἦν in codd. (and ἦν is required by metre in E.*Ion* 280), contr. from Ep. and Ion. ἦα (Il.5.808, al., *IG*12(8).449.2 (Thasos), whence Hom. and later Ion. ἔα Il.4.321, al., ἔας Hdt.1.187, ἔατε Id.4.119); Ep. 3 sg. ἦεν, always with ν in Hom.; ἦν as 1 sg., only Il.11.762 (s.v.l., al. ἔον), freq. as 3 sg. (generally before a consonant, so that ἔεν is possible), sts. also ἤην; 2 sg. ἦσθα, later ἦς (wh. is v.l. in Pi.*I*.1.26), sts. in Lxx (*Jd*. 11.35, *Ru*.3.2, al.), cf. Pl.*Ax*.365e, Erinn.4.4, *Ev.Matt*.25.21, al., ἦσθας Men.*Epit*.156, Ep. ἔησθα; 3 sg. ἦν, Ep. ἔην, ἤην, ἦεν (v. supr.), Dor. and Aeol. ἦς Alc.*Supp*.30.1, Epich.102, Sophr.59, Theoc.2.90, *SIG*241.145 (Delph.); 3 dual ἤστην Il.5.10, E.*Hipp*.387, Ar.*Eq*.982, Pl.*Euthd*.272a, al.; Dor. 1 pl. ἦμες Plu.*Lyc*.21; 2 pl. ἦτε Pl.*Euthd*. 276c, ἦστε Ar.*Pax*821, *Ec*.1086; 3 pl. ἦσαν, Ion. and Poet. ἔσαν (in Hes.*Th*.321, 825, ἦν is not pl. for ἦσαν, but is rather a peculiarity of syntax, v. infr. v, but is 3 pl. in Epich.46, al., *SIG*560.15 (Epidamnus, iii B.C.)); Aeol. ἔον *Schwyzer*644.12; later ἤμην *PSI*4.362.21 (iii B.C.), *SIG*527.46 (Crete, iii B.C.), *IGRom*.4.1740 (Cyme), always in Lxx as *Ba*.1.19, cf. *Ev.Matt*.23.30, Plu.2.174a, etc., and sts. in codd. of earlier writers, Lys.7.34, *Trag.Adesp*.124 (cited from E. *Hel*.931 by Choerob. and from Id.*Tr*.474 by Aps.), X.*Cyr*.6.1.9, Hyp.*Ath*.26, 2 sg. ἦσο *Epigr.Gr*.379 (Aezani), 3 sg. ἦστο *Supp.Epigr*. 1.455.7 (Phrygia), 1 pl. ἤμεθα *PPetr*.2 p.11 (iii B.C.), Lxx *Ba*.1.19, 1*Ki*.25.16, *Ep.Eph*.2.3; subj. ὦμαι *PBaden*48.12 (ii B.C.), ἦται *GDI*

1696, ἦνται prob. in *IG*5(1).1390.83 (Andania); Ion. and Ep. also ἔσκον, used by A.*Pers*.656 (lyr.): fut. ἔσομαι, ἔσται, Ep. and Aeol. also ἔσσομαι, ἔσεται, ἔσσεται; Aeol. 2 sg. ἔσσῃ prob. in Alc.67,87; Dor. 2 and 3 sg. ἐσσῇ, ἐσσεῖται, Il.2.393, 13.317, Theoc.10.5, 3 pl. ἐσσοῦνται Foed.ap.Th.5.77 codd. (but ἔσσονται *Tab.Heracl*.1.113), inf. ἐσσεῖσθαι Sophr.57.—All forms of the pres. ind. are enclitic (exc. 2 sg. εἶ and 3 pl. ἐασι); but 3 sg. is written ἔστι when it begins a sentence or verse, or when it immediately follows οὐκ, καί, εἰ, ὡς, ἀλλά, or τοῦτ', Hdn.Gr.1.553 (also μή acc. to *EM*301.3); later Gramm. wrote ἔστι as Subst. Verb, Phot., Eust.880.22. A. as the Subst. Verb, I. of persons, *exist*, οὐκ ἔσθ' οὗτος ἀνήρ, οὐδ' ἔσσεται Od.16.437; ἔτ' εἰσί they *are* still *in being*, 15.433, cf. S.*Ph*.445, etc.; τεθνηῶτος.. μηδ' ἔτ' ἐόντος Od.1.289; οὐκέτ' ἐστί he *is* no more, E.*Hipp*.1162; οὐδὲ δὴν ἦν he *was* not long-*lived*, Il.6.131; ὁ οὐκ ὤν, οἱ οὐκ ὄντες, of *those who are* no more, Th.2.45,44; οἱ ὄντες the *living*, Plb.9.29.2; ὁ ὤν the *Eternal*, Lxx*Ex*.3.14, al., Ph.1.289; θεοὶ αἰὲν ἐόντες Il.1.290; ἐσσόμενοι *posterity*, 2.119; κἀγὼ γὰρ ἦ ποτ', ἀλλὰ νῦν οὐκ εἴμ' ἔτι E.*Hec*.284; ὡς ἂν εἶεν ἄνθρωποι *might continue in being*, Pl.*Smp*.190c; ζώντων καὶ ὄντων Ἀθηναίων D.18.72, cf. Arist.*GC*318$^b$25; of things, εἰ ἔστι ἀληθέως [ἡ τράπεζα] Hdt.3.17, etc.; of cities, ὄλωλεν, οὐδ' ἔτ' ἐστὶ Τροία E.*Tr*.1292, cf. *Heracl*.491; δοκεῖ μοι Καρχηδόνα μὴ εἶναι *censeo Carthaginem esse delendam*, Plu.*Cat.Ma*.27; ἂν ᾖ τὸ στράτευμα *be in existence*, D.8.17; of money, *to be in hand*, τῶν ὄντων χρημάτων καὶ τῶν προσιόντων *IG*1$^2$.91.25; τὰ ὄντα *property*, Pl.*Grg*.511a, Plu.*Ant*.24, etc.; τὸ ἐσόμενον ἐκ.. *future revenue* from.., *BCH*46.420 (Olymos, i B.C.); of place, τὴν οὖσαν ἐκκλησίαν the *local* church, *Act.Ap*.13.1; of time, τοῦ ὄντος μηνός in the *current* month, *BGU*146.4, etc.; *in office*, ἱερέων τῶν ὄντων *PPar*.5.4 (ii B.C.); αἱ οὖσαι [ἐξουσίαι] the powers *that be*, *Ep.Rom*.13.1. II. of the *real* world, *be*, opp. become, γίγνεται πάντα ἃ δή φαμεν εἶναι Pl.*Tht*.152d, etc.; τὸ ὄν *Being*, Parm.8.35, Protag.2, Pl.*Ti*.27d, etc.; opp. τὸ μὴ ὄν, Gorg.*Fr*.3D., etc.; οὐδὲν γίνεται ἐκ τοῦ μὴ ὄντος Epicur.*Ep*.1p.5U.; ἐξ οὐκ ὄντων ἐποίησεν αὐτὰ ὁ θεός Lxx 2*Ma*.7.28; τὰ ὄντα the *world of things*, Heraclit.7, Emp.129.5, etc.; ὄν indecl., τῶν ὂν εἰδῶν species *of Being*, Plot.6.2.10. 2. of circumstances, events, etc., *to happen*, τά τ' ἐόντα, τά τ' ἐσσόμενα, πρό τ' ἐόντα Il.1.70; ἡ ἐσβολὴ ἔμελλεν ἔσεσθαι Th.2.13, etc.; τῆς προδοσίας οὔσης since treachery *was there*, Id.4.103; ἕως ἂν ὁ πόλεμος ᾖ so long as it *last*, Id.1.58; αἱ σπονδαὶ ἐνιαυτὸν ἔσονται Id.4.118; τί ἐστιν; what *is* it? what's the matter? Ar.*Th*.193; τί οὖν ἦν τοῦτο; how *came* it *to pass*? Pl.*Phd*.58a: repeated with a relat. to avoid a positive assertion, ἔστι δ' ὅπῃ νῦν ἔ. things *are* as they *are*, i.e. are ill, A.*Ag*.67. III. *be the fact* or *the case*, διπλασίαν ἂν τὴν δύναμιν εἰκάζεσθαι ἢ ἔστιν twice as large as it *really is*, Th.1.10; αὐτὸ ὃ ἔστι καλόν beauty *in its essence*, Pl.*Smp*.211c, cf. *Phd*.74b; freq. in part., τὸν ἐόντα λόγον λέγειν or φαίνειν the *true* story, Hdt.1.95,116; τῷ ἐόντι χρήσασθαι tell the *truth*, ib.30; τὰ ὄντα ἀπαγγέλλειν Th.7.8; σκῆψιν οὐκ οὖσαν, λόγον οὐκ ὄντα, S.*El*.584, Ar.*Ra*.1052; τῷ ὄντι *in reality*, *in fact*, Pl.*Prt*.328d, etc.; to apply a quotation to a case in point, τῷ ὄντι κλαυσίγελως *real* 'smiles through tears' (with allusion to Il.6.484), X.*HG*7.2.9, cf. Pl.*La*.196d; κατὰ τὸ ἐόν according to the *fact*, *rightly*, Hdt.1.97; πᾶν τὸ ἐόν the whole *truth*, Id.9.11; τοῦ ἐόντος ἀποτεύξεται Hp.*VM* 2. IV. folld. by the relat., οὐκ ἔστιν ὃς or ὅστις *no one*, οὐκ ἔσθ' ὃς.. ἀπαλάλκοι Il.22.348; οὐκ ἔ. οὐδεὶς ὅς E.*El*.903; οὐκ ἔ. ὅτῳ, = οὐδενί, A.*Pr*.293 (anap.), cf. 989: freq. in pl., εἰσὶν οἵ, = Lat. *sunt qui*, used exactly like ἔνιοι, Th.6.88, 7.44, Pl.*Men*.77d, *Grg*.503a, etc. (εἰσί τινες οἵ.. Th.3.24); ἔστιν ἃ χωρία, πολίσματα, Id.1.12,65; ἔστιν ἃ εἰπεῖν Id.2.67; ἦσαν οἵ X.*An*.5.2.14; the sg. Verb is used even with masc. and fem. pl., ἔστιν οἵ, αἵ, Hp.*Fract*.1, *VC*4, X.*Cyr*.2.3.16; more freq. in oblique cases, ποταμῶν ἐστὶ ὧν Hdt.7.187; ἔστιν ἀφ' ὧν Th.8.65; ἐστὶ παρ' οἷς, ἔστιν ἐν οἷς, Id.1.23, 5.25: in questions ὅστις is used, ἔστιν ἥντινα δόξαν.. ἀπεκρίνατο; Pl.*Men*.85b: with relat. Particles, ἔστιν ἔνθα, = Lat. *est ubi*, X.*Cyr*.7.4.15, etc.; ἔ. ὅπῃ, ἔσθ' ὅπου, *somehow*, *somewhere*, Pl.*Prt*.331d, A.*Eu*.517, S.*OT*448, etc.; in questions expecting a neg. answer, ἔ. ὁπόθεν, ὅπως; Pl.*Phlb*.35a, *R*.493e, etc.; οὐ γάρ ἐσθ' ὅπως Pi.*Fr*.61, cf. Hdt.7.102, A.*Ag*.620; οὐκ ἔ. ὅπως οὐ *in any case*, *necessarily*, Ar.*Pax* 188; οὐκ ἔ. ὡς Pl.*Men*.76e, etc.; ἔ. ὅτε, ἔσθ' ὅτε, *sometimes*, Pi.*Fr*.180.2, S.*Aj*.56, Th.7.21, etc. V. ἦν is sts. used with pl. masc. and fem., usu. at the beginning of a sentence, *there was*, τῆς δ' ἦν τρεῖς κεφαλαί Hes.*Th*.321; (but in ἦν δ' ἐρῳδιοί τε πολλοί Epich.46, cf. 59, al., it may be taken as Dor. 3 pl.); ἦν δ' ἀμφίπλεκτοι κλίμακες S.*Tr*.520 (lyr.); ἦν ἄρα κἀκεῖνοι ταλακάρδιοι Epigr.ap.Aeschin.3.184; less freq. ἔστι, ἔστι δὲ μεταξὺ.. ἑπτὰ στάδιοι Hdt.1.26, cf. 7.34; ἔστι.. ἄρχοντές τε καὶ δῆμος Pl.*R*.463a; before dual Nouns, Ar.*V*.58, Pl.*Grg*.500d. VI. ἔστι impers., c. inf., *it is possible*, ἔστι γὰρ ἀμφοτέροισιν ὀνείδεα μυθήσασθαι Il.20.246; ἔστι μὲν εὕδειν, ἔστι δὲ τερπομένοισιν ἀκούειν Od.15.392; εἴ τί πού ἐστι (sc. πιθέσθαι) 4.193; τοιάδε.. ἐστὶν ἀκοῦσαι A.*Pr*.1055 (anap.); ἔστι τεκμήρια δρᾶν X.*An*.3.2.13, cf. Ar.*Ra*.1163, Aeschin.3.105, D.18.272, Arist.*Ath*.53.6, etc.; so in imper., opt., and subj., ἔστω ἀποφέρεσθαι τῷ βουλομένῳ *IG*1$^2$.10.7; μυρία ἂν εἴη λέγειν Pl.*Plt*.271e; ὅπως ἂν ᾖ δρᾶν *IG*2.1054.91: more freq. in neg. clauses, Il.6.267, etc.; folld. by ὥστε c. inf., S.*Ph*.656: c. acc. et inf., ἀδόντα δ' εἴη με τοῖς ἀγαθοῖς ὁμιλεῖν Pi.*P*.2.96; ἔστιν ἐκπεσεῖν ἀρχῆς Δία A.*Pr*.757: sts. not impers. in this sense, θάλασσα δ' οὐκέτ' ἦν ἰδεῖν Id.*Pers*.419. b. ἔστω in argument, *let it be granted*, ἔστω τοῦτο ἀληθὲς εἶναι D.H.*Comp*.25; ἔστω σοι τοῦθ' οὕτως Plu.2.987b; ἔστω εἶναί τινα τοιοῦτον D.Chr.74.24.

B. most freq., *to be*, the Copula connecting the predicate with the Subject, both being in the same case: hence, *signify*, *import*, τὸ γὰρ εἴρειν λέγειν ἐστίν Pl.*Cra*.398d; esp. in the phrase τοῦτ' ἔστι, *hoc est*; Σκαιόλαν, ὅπερ ἐστὶ Λαιόν Plu.*Publ*.17: with numerals, τὰ δὶς πέντε δέκα ἐστίν twice five *are* ten, X.*Mem*.4.4.7; εἶναί τις or τι, *to be* somebody, something, *be* of some consequence, v. τις; οὐδὲν εἶναι Pl.*R*.562d, etc. 2. periphr. with the Participle to represent the finite Verb: with pf. part. once in Hom., τετληότες εἰμέν, for τετλήκαμεν, Il.5.873; so in Trag. and Att., ἦν τεθνηκώς, for ἐτεθνήκει, A.*Ag*.869; ἔσται δεδορκώς ib.1179; εἰμὶ γεγώς S.*Aj*.1299; πεφυκός ἐστι Ar.*Av*.1473; δεδρακότες εἰσίν Th.3.68; κατακεκονότες ἔσεσθε X.*An*.7.6.36: with aor. part., once in Hom., βλήμενος ἦν Il.4.211; so προδείσας εἰμί, οὐ σιωπήσας ἔσει; S.*OT*90, 1146, cf. A.*Supp*.460: with pres. part., ἦν προκείμενον Id.*Pers*.371; φεύγων Ὀρέστης ἐστίν Id.*Ch*.136; εἴην οὐκ ἂν εὖ φρονῶν S.*Aj*.1330; τί δ' ἐστί.. φέρον; Id.*OT*991, cf. 274,708; λέγων ἐστίν τις E.*Hec*.1179; ἦν τίς σ' ὑβρίζων Id.*HF*313; πόρρω ἤδη εἶ πορευόμενος Pl.*Ly*.204b; βαδίζων εἶ Ar.*Ra*.36; freq. in Hdt., ἦσαν ἰέντες 1.57, al.; even εἰσὶ διάφοροι ἐόντες 3.49 (s.v.l.):—if the Art. is joined with the Part., the noun is made emphatic, Κᾶρές εἰσι οἱ καταδέξαντες the persons who showed her *were* Carians, Id.1.171; αὐτὸς ἦν ὁ μαρτυρῶν A.*Eu*.798; δόλος ἦν ὁ φράσας S.*El*.197 (anap.).

C. εἶναι is freq. modified in sense by the addition of Advbs., or the cases of Nouns without or with Preps.: I. εἶναι with Advbs., where the Adv. often merely represents a Noun and stands as the predicate, ἅλις δέ οἱ ἦσαν ἄρουραι Il.14.122, etc.; ἀκέων, ἀκὴν εἶναι, *to be* silent, 4.22, Od.2.82; σῖγα πᾶς ἔστω λεώς E.*Hec*.532; διαγνῶναι χαλεπῶς ἦν ἄνδρα ἕκαστον Il.7.424; ἀσφαλέως ἡ κομιδὴ ἔσται *will go on* safely, Hdt.4.134; ἐγγύς, πόρρω εἶναι, Th.6.88, Pl.*Prt*.356e: freq. impers. with words implying good or ill fortune, Κουρήτεσσι κακῶς ἦν *it fared* ill with them, Il.9.551; εὖ γὰρ ἔσται E.*Med*.89, cf. Ar.*Pl*.1188, etc.; ἡδέως ἂν αὐτοῖς εἴη D.59.30. II. c. gen., to express descent or extraction, πατρὸς δ' εἴμ' ἀγαθοῖο Il.21.109; αἵματός εἰς ἀγαθοῖο Od.4.611, cf. Hdt.3.71, Th.2.71, etc.; πόλεως μεγίστης εἶ X.*An*.7.3.19. b. to express the material of which a thing is made, ἡ κρηπὶς ἔστι λίθων μεγάλων *consists of*.., Hdt.1.93; τῆς πόλιος ἐούσης δύο φαρσέων ib.186; τοιούτων ἔργων ἐστὶ ἡ τυραννίς *is made up of*.., Id.5.92.η', etc. c. to express the class to which a person or thing belongs, εἶ γὰρ τῶν φίλων *you are one of* them, Ar.*Pl*.345; ἐτύγχανε βουλῆς ὤν Th.3.70; ὅσοι ἦσαν τῶν προτέρων στρατιωτῶν Id.7.44; Κριτίας τῶν τριάκοντα ὤν X.*Mem*.1.2.31; ἔστι τῶν αἰσχρῶν *it is in the class of* disgraceful things, i.e. *it is* disgraceful, D.2.2. d. to express that a thing belongs to another, Τροίαν Ἀχαιῶν οὖσαν A.*Ag*.269; τὸ πεδίον ἦν μέν κοτε Χορασμίων Hdt.3.117, etc.: hence, *to be of the party of*, ἦσαν.. τινὲς μὲν Φιλίππου, τινὲς δὲ τοῦ βελτίστου D.9.56, cf. 37.53; *to be dependent upon*, S.*Ant*.737, etc.; *to be at the mercy of*, ἔστι τοῦ λέγοντος, ἢν φόβους λέγῃ Id.*OT*917. e. to express one's duty, business, custom, nature, and the like, οὔτοι γυναικός ἐστι 'tis not a woman's *part*, A.*Ag*.940; τὸ ἐπιτιμᾶν παντὸς εἶναι D.1.16; τὸ δὲ ναυτικὸν τέχνης ἐστὶν *is matter of* art, *requires* art, Th.1.142, cf. 83. f. in Lxx, *to be occupied about*, ἦσαν τοῦ θύειν 2*Ch*.30.17; ἔσεσθαι, c. gen., *to be about to*, ἐσόμεθα τοῦ σῶσαί σε 2*Ki*.10.11. III. with the dat., ἐστί μοι I *have*, freq. in Hom., etc. 2. with two dats., σφίσι τε καὶ Ἀθηναίοισι εἶναι οὐδὲν πρῆγμα that they and the Athenians *have* nothing *to do* one with another, Hdt.5.84; μηδὲν εἶναι σοὶ καὶ Φιλίππῳ πρᾶγμα D.18.283; more shortly, σοί τε καὶ τούτοισι πρήγμασι τί ἐστι; Hdt.5.33; τί τῷ νόμῳ καὶ τῇ βασάνῳ; D.29.36; τί ἐμοὶ καὶ σοί; Lat. *quid tecum est mihi?* *Ev.Marc*.5.7, etc.; also ἐμοὶ οὐδὲν πρὸς τοὺς τοιούτους (sc. ἐστίν) Isoc.4.12; ἐν οἷς πρὸς τοὺς ἐναντίους ἐστὶ τῷ δήμῳ D.18.278; ἔσται αὐτῷ πρὸς τὸν θεόν, in tomb inscriptions, *JHS*18.113, etc. 3. with ἀσμένος, βουλόμενος, etc., added, ἐμοὶ δέ κεν ἀσμένῳ εἴη *'twould be* to my delight, Il.14.108; οὐκ ἂν σφίσι βουλομένοις εἶναι Th.7.35; προσδεχομένῳ Id.6.46; θέλοντι S.*OT*1356 (lyr.); ἡδομένοις Pl.*La*.187c. IV. with Preps., εἶναι ἀπό τινος, = εἶναί τινος (supr. II.a), X.*Mem*.1.6.9; εἰσὶν ἀπ' ἐναντίων αὗται πραγμάτων Pl.*Phlb*.12d; but εἶναι ἀπ' οἴκου *to be* away from.., Th.1.99. 2. εἶναι ἔκ τινος *to be sprung* from, εἴμ' ἐκ Παιονίης, Μυρμιδόνων ἔξ εἰμι, Il.21.154, 24.397, etc.; ἔστιν ἐξ ἀνάγκης *it is* of necessity, i.e. necessary, Pl.*Sph*.256d. 3. εἶναι ἐν.. *to be* in a certain state, ἐν εὐπαθείῃσι Hdt.1.22; ἐν ἀθυμίᾳ, etc., Th.6.46, etc.; ἐν ταραχαῖς D.18.218; εἶναι ἐν ἀξιώματι *to be* in esteem, Th.1.130; οἱ ἐν τέλει ἐόντες those in office, Hdt.3.18, etc.; but εἶναι ἐν τέχνῃ, ἐν φιλοσοφίᾳ, *to be engaged* in.., S.*OT*562, Pl.*Phd*.59a. b. ἐν σοί ἐστι *it depends* on thee, Hdt.6.109, S.*Ph*.963; ἐν σοὶ γάρ ἐσμεν Id.*OT*314; so also ἐπί τινι Id.*Ph*.1003, X.*Cyr*.1.6.2, etc. 4. εἶναι διά.., much like εἶναι ἐν.., εἶναι διὰ φόβου, = φοβεῖσθαι, Th.6.34; εἶναι δι' ὄχλου, = ὀχληρὸν εἶναι, Id.1.73; εἶναι διὰ μόχθων X.*Cyr*.1.6.25; εἶναι δι' αἰτίας, = αἰτιᾶσθαι, D.H.1.70; Geom., *pass* through, διὰ τῆς ἑτέρας διαμέτρου ἐόντος τοῦ ἐπιπέδου Archim.*Con.Sph*.20. 5. εἶναι ἐφ' ἑαυτῆς *to be* by oneself, D.25.23; εἶναι ἐπὶ ὀνόματος *to bear* a name, Id.39.21; εἶναι ἐπὶ τοῖς πράγμασιν *to be engaged* in.., Id.2.12; εἶναι ἐπί τινα *to be* against him, Id.6.33; εἶναι ἐφ' ἑξήκοντα στάδια *to reach* sixty stadia, X.*An*.4.6.11; εἶναι ἐπὶ τὰς ἁφὰς *pass* through the points of contact, Apollon.Perg.*Con*.4.1; εἶναι ἐπί τινι, v. supr. 3 b. 6. εἶναι πρός τινος *to be* in one's favour, Th.4.10,29, etc.; *to suit*, X.*An*.1.2.11, etc.; εἶναι πρός τινι *engaged* in, Pl.*Phd*.84c, Philostr.*VA*5.31; πρὸς τοῖς ἰδίοις *mind* one's own affairs, Arist.*Pol*.1309$^a$6, *Ath*.16.3; εἶναι πρὸς τὸ κωλύειν Plb.1.26.3; πρὸς τὸ πονεῖν Telesp.46 H.; εἶναι περί τι X.*An*.3.5.7, etc. 7. εἶναι παρά τινι or τινα, = παρεῖναι, Id.*Cyr*.6.2.15, Hdt.8.140.α' (s.v.l.). 8. εἶναι ὑπό τινα or τινι *to be* sub-

ject to.., X.*HG*5.2.17 (s.v.l.), 6.2.4. 9. περὶ τούτων ἐστὶν that is the question, Men.*Epit.*30. 10. εἶναι ἀπό.., in Geom., *to be constructed* upon, Archim.*Sph.Cyl.*2.9, *Con.Sph.*7.

**D.** ἐστί is very freq. omitted, mostly in the pres. ind. before certain predicates, as ἀνάγκη, ἄξιον, δυνατόν, εἰκός, ἕτοιμον, οἷόν τε, ῥᾴδιον, χρεών, etc., and after the neut. of Verbals in -τέος, and such forms as θαυμαστὸν ὅσον: less freq. with other persons and moods, εἰμί omitted, S.*OT*92, *Aj.*813; εἶ, Od.4.206; ἐσμέν, S.*Ant.*634; ἐστέ, Od.10.463; εἰσί, S.*OT*499 (lyr.), *IG*2.778*B*; subj. ᾖ, Il.14. 376, E.*Hipp.*659, Antipho 5.32; opt. εἴη, *IG*2².1183.12; impf. ἦν, ib.2.778*B*; fut. ἔσονται, Od.14.394.

**E.** the Inf. freq. seems redundant, 1. in phrases implying power or will to do a thing, ἑκὼν εἶναι (v. ἑκών); κατὰ δύναμιν εἶναι Is.2.32; εἰς δύναμιν εἶναι Pl.*Plt.*300c; τὸ ἐπ' ἐκείνοις εἶναι, *quantum in illis esset*, Th.8.48, X.*HG*3.5.9, cf. Lys.13.58; τὸ ἐπὶ σφᾶς εἶναι Th.4.28; τὸ κατὰ τοῦτον εἶναι X.*An.*1.6.9; κατὰ τοῦτο εἶναι Pl.*Prt.* 317a; τὸ τήμερον, τὸ νῦν εἶναι, Id.*Cra.*396e, *La.*201c, Theopomp. Com.98, Decr.ap.Arist.*Ath.*31.2, etc. 2. after Verbs of naming or choosing, σοφιστὴν ὀνομάζουσι τὸν ἄνδρα εἶναι Pl.*Prt.*311e; σύμμαχόν μιν εἵλοντο εἶναι Hdt.8.134; of giving, δῶκε ξεινήϊον εἶναι Il. 11.20.

**F.** impf. ἦν is sts. used where other languages take the pres., 1. after ἄρα, to express a fact which *is and has always been* the same, δέρμα δὲ ἀνθρώπου.. ἦν ἄρα σχεδὸν δερμάτων πάντων λαμπρότατον human skin then *it appears is*.., Hdt.4.64; Κύπρις οὐκ ἄρ' ἦν θεὸς E. *Hipp.*359; ὡς ἄρ' ἦσθ' ἐμὸς πατὴρ ὀρθῶς ib.1169; ἢ πολύμοχθον ἄρ' ἦν γένος.. ἀμερίων Id.*IA*1330; ἦ στωμύλος ἦσθα Theoc.5.79; so also when there is reference to a past thought, τουτὶ τί ἦν; what *is* this? Ar.*Ach.*157, cf. Pl.*Cra.*387c: so in the Aristotelian formula τὸ τί ἦν εἶναι (*APo.*82ᵇ38, al.), used to express *the essential nature* of a thing, where τί ἦν (for ἐστί) takes the place of the dat. in such phrases as τὸ ἀγαθῷ εἶναι, τὸ μεγέθει εἶναι, *APr.*67ᵇ12, *de An.*429ᵇ10.

**G.** ἐγώ εἰμι, in Lxx, pleonastic for ἐγώ, ἐγώ εἰμι οὐχ ἥμαρτον *Jd.* 11.27, cf. 6.18; also ἔσται πᾶς ἀποκτενεῖ με *Ge.*4.14.

⊛ **εἶμι** (*ibo*), 2 sg. εἶ S.*Tr.*83, Ar.*Av.*990, Ep. and Ion. εἶς Hes.*Op.* 208, εἶσθα Il.10.450, Od.19.69; 3 sg. εἶσι; pl. ἴμεν, ἴτε, ἴᾱσι: imper. ἴθι (also εἶ in the compd. ἔξει Ar.*Nu.*633 acc. to Sch., but prob. indic.), 3 pl. ἴτωσαν E.*IT*1480, Pl.*Lg.*765a, also ἰτων A.*Eu.*32, ἰόντων Th.4.118, etc.: subj. ἴω (εἴω Sophr.48); Ep. 2 sg. ἴησθα Il.10.67; Ep. 3 sg. ἴησι 9.701; Ep. pl. ἴομεν (for -ωμεν) 2.440: opt. ἴοιμι, οις, οι, 14.21, etc.; ἰοίην Sapph.159, *IG*4.760 (Troezen), X.*Smp.*4.16, (διεξ-) Isoc.5.98; Ep. ἰείη Il.19.209, cf. περι-ιείεν *IG*2².1126.18 (Amphict. Delph.), εἴη Il.24.139, Od.14.496, εἴηι *GDI*4986.7 (Crete): inf. ἰέναι, Ep. ἴμεναι (ι in Il.20.365) or ἴμεν, also ἰέμεν Archyt.ap.Stob.3.1.106 (dub. l.), ἴναι [ῐ] Orac.ap.Str.9.2.23, (ἐξ-) Macho ap.Ath.13.580c, cf. *EM*467. 18 (προσ-εῖναι dub. in Hes.*Op.*353): part. ἰών, ἰοῦσα, ἰόν: impf. ᾔειν, ᾔεις (δι-ῄεισθα Pl.*Ti.*26c, ἐπεξ-ῄεισθα *Euthphr.*4b), ᾔει or -ειν Id.*Ti.* 38c, *Criti.*117e; Ep. and Ion. ἤϊα, 3 sg. ἤϊε (-εν), contr. ᾖε Od.18.257; dual ᾔτην Pl.*Euthd.*294d; 1 and 2 pl., ᾖμεν, ᾖτε; 3 pl., Ep. and Ion. ἤϊσαν, Ep. also ἴσαν, Att. ᾖσαν (μετ-) Ar.*Eq.*605, cf. *Fr.*161, (ἐπ-) Od.19.445, later ᾔεσαν (εἰσ-) Arist.*Ath.*32.1, etc.; also 3 sg. ἴε Il.2. 872, al.; Ep. 1 pl. ἤομεν Od.10.251, al., 3 dual ἴτην Il.1.347; 3 pl. ἤϊον Od.23.370:—Med. pres. and impf. ἵεμαι, ἱέμην are mere mistakes for ἵεμαι, ἱέμην (from ἵημι), cf. S.*OT*1242, E.*Supp.*698:—for fut. εἴσομαι and aor. Med. εἰσάμην, in 3 sg. εἴσατο, ἐείσατο, 3 dual ἐεισάσθην, v. εἴσομαι II.—The ind. εἶμι usu. has pres. sense in Hom. (fut., Il.1. 426, 18.280), but in Ion. Prose and Att. it serves as fut. to ἔρχομαι (q.v.), I *shall go, shall come*: the pres. sense is sts. found in Poetry, prov. αὐτόματοι δ' ἀγαθοὶ ἀγαθῶν ἐπὶ δαῖτας ἴασι (cf. Pl.*Smp.*174b), cf. Theoc.25.90, also in compds. (προσ-) A.*Eu.*242, (ἐπ-) Th.4.61, (συν-) Str.3.2.2. [ῐ- in all tenses, exc. in Ep. Subj. ἴομεν for ἴωμεν at the beginning of a verse]:—*come* or *go*, the special senses being given by the context, οἴκαδ' ἴμεν *go* home, Il.17.155; τάχ' εἶσθα θύραζε Od.19.69, etc.; *come*, οὐδέ μιν οἴω νῦν ἰέναι Il.17.710, etc.; *go, depart*, Od.2.367; ὑπὸ τεῖχος ἰόντας Il.12.264. **II.** c. acc., 1. c. acc. loci, *go to* or *into*, Od.1.176, 18.194, S.*OT*637. 2. c. acc. cogn., ὁδὸν ἰέναι *go* a road, Od.10.103; so τὴν ὀρεινήν (sc. ὁδόν) X.*Cyr.* 2.4.22: metaph., ἄδικον ὁδὸν ἰέναι Th.3.64. 3. *go through* or *over*, τὸ μέσον τοῦ οὐρανοῦ, of the sun, Hdt.2.25, cf. 26: in Hom., freq. c. gen., ἰὼν πεδίοιο *going across* the plain, Il.5.597. **III.** c. inf. aor., ἀλλά τις εἴη εἰπεῖν Ἀτρεΐδῃ Od.14.496.—On the Homeric βῆ δ' ἴμεν, etc., v. βαίνω. 2. c. part. fut., Ἑλένην καλέουσ' ἴε *went* to call her, Il.3.383, cf. 14.200, Od.15.213; ἤϊα λέξων I *was going* to tell, Hdt.4.82; ἴτω θύσων Pl.*Lg.*909d; εἴ τις ἱστορίαν γράψων ἴῃ Luc. *Hist.Conscr.*39. **IV.** also of other motions besides walking or running, as of *going in a ship*, esp. ἐπὶ νηὸς ἰέναι Od.2.332, etc.; of the *flight* of bees, Il.2.87. 2. of the *motion* of things, [πέλεκυς] εἶσιν διὰ δουρός the axe *goes* through the beam, 3.61; of clouds or vapour, 4.278; of the stars, 22.317; of time, ἔτος εἶσι the year *will pass*, Od. 2.89; φάτις εἶσι the report *goes*, 23.362; χρόνος.. ἰὼν πόρσω Pi.*O.*10 (11).55; ἴτω κλαγγά, βοά, S.*Tr.*208 (lyr.), Ar.*Av.*857 (lyr.); ἡ μοῖρ' ὅποιπερ εἶσ' ἴτω S.*OT*1458, cf. Pl.*Ap.*19a. **V.** metaph. usages, ἰέναι ἐς λόγους τινί *to enter* on a conference with.., Th.3.80, etc.; ἰέναι ἐς τοὺς πολέμους, ἐς τὴν ξυμμαχίαν, Id.1.78, 5.30; ἰέναι ἐς χεῖρας *to come* to blows, Id.2.3, 81; ἰέναι ἐς τὰ παραγγελλόμενα *to obey* orders, Id.1. 121; διὰ δίκης ἰὼν πατρὶ S.*Ant.*742; ἰέναι διὰ μάχης, διὰ φιλίας, etc., v. διά A.IV.b. **VI.** imper. ἴθι (with or without δή) *come now!* mostly folld. by 2 sg. imper., ἴ. ἐξήγεο Hdt.3.72; ἴθ' ἐγκόνει, ἴθ' ἐκκάλυψον, S.*Aj.*988, 1003; ἴ. πέραινε Ar.*Ra.*1170; in full, ἴ. καὶ πειρῶ *go* and try, Hdt.8.57: with 1 pl., ἴ. οὖν ἐπισκεψώμεθα X.*Mem.*1.6.4, cf. Pl. *Prt.*332d; ἴτε δὴ ἀκούσωμεν Id.*Lg.*797d: 2 dual, ἴθι δὴ παρίστασθον Ar.*Ra.*1378: also 2 pl., ἴτε νεύσατε S.*OC*248, cf. *OT*1413. 2. ἴτω *let it pass, well then*, Id.*Ph.*120, E.*Med.*798. **VII.** part. added to Verbs, φρονείτω μεῖζον ἢ κατ' ἄνδρ' ἰών let him *go and* think.., S.*Ant.*768, cf. *OC*1393, *Aj.*304; βακχεύσεις ἰὼν E.*Ba.*343.—Cf. ἴσκω.

**εἵμορος**· πεπρωμένος, Hsch.

**εἰν**, Ep. and Lyr. (metri gr.) for ἐν, *in*, Il.2.783, al.; Trag. in lyr., A.*Supp.*871 (dub.), E.*Alc.*436; exc. εἰν Ἅιδου v.l. in S.*Ant.*1241; cf. εἰνί; also *Schwyzer* 707 *A* 3 (Ephesus, vi B.C.), and in compds., εἰνάλιος, εἰνόδιος.

⊛ **ἐΐν**, = οἱ, Corinn.36; cf. ἐΐν· ἀντωνυμία, ἐκεῖνος, Hsch.

**εἶν**, v. εἰμί.

⊛ **εἰνᾰ-ετής**, ές, or -έτης, ες, *of nine years, nine years old*, Orph.*L.* 348: neut. εἰνάετες, as Adv., *nine years long*, Od.14.240: fem. εἰναέτις, ιδος, *AP*7.643 (Crin.). **-ετίζομαι**, poet. for ἐνναετίζομαι, Call. *Dian.*179.

**εἰνάκις, εἰνᾰκισχίλιοι, εἰνᾰκόσιοι**, αι, α, v. ἐνάκις, etc.

**εἰνᾰλίδῖνος** [λῐ], η, ον, = ἐν ἁλὶ δινεύων, αἴθυιαι Arat.918.

**εἰνάλιος**, η, ον, poet. for ἐνάλιος.

**εἰνᾰλίφοιτος** [ῐ], ον, *roaming the sea*, of nets, *AP*6.16 (Arch.).

**εἰνάνῠχες** [ᾰ], as Adv., *nine nights long*, Il.9.470; cf. εἰνάετες.

**εἶναξ**· κάλλος, Hsch.

**εἰνάπηχυς**, υ, poet. for ἐννεάπηχυς, Lyc.860.

**εἰνάς**, άδος, ἡ, poet. for ἐννεάς II, Hes.*Op.*810.

⊛ **εἰνάτερες** [ᾰ], αἱ, *wives of brothers* or *of husbands' brothers, sisters-in-law*, Il.6.378, al. (never in Od.). (Sg. ἐνάτηρ Keil-Premerstein *Zweiter Bericht* 138 (not εἰνάτηρ as stated by Hdn.Gr.1.48, al.); dat. ἐνατρὶ Buresch *Aus Lydien* 147; καίνετ[έ]ραν (acc. sg.) is dub. in *Jahresh.* 18 *Beibl.*33 (Cilicia)), voc. εἰνάτερ Hdn.Gr.1.419, gen. εἰνάτερος Id.2.747, al.: εἰν- metri gr. in Ep., with ἐνάτηρ cf. Skt. *yā́tar-*, Lith. *jéntė*, gen. *jentefs*, Lat. *janitrīces* 'sisters-in-law'.)

**εἰνάτιον**· λοξόν, Hsch. **εἴνᾰτος**, v. ἔνατος.

**εἰνᾰφώσσων**, ον, gen. ωνος, *with nine sails*, στόλος Lyc.101.

**εἵνεκα, εἵνεκεν**, v. ἕνεκα.

**εἰνεσίαι**· ἐπιστολαί, Hsch.; cf. ἐννεσίη.

**εἰνί**, Ep. (metri gr.) for ἐνί, = ἐν (q.v.).

**εἰνόδιος**, ον, Ep. and Lyr. for ἐνόδ-, Il.16.260, E.*Ion* 1048, etc.

**εἰνοσίγαιος**, = ἐννοσίγαιος (q.v.).

**εἴνοσις**, = ἔνοσις, Hsch.

**εἰνοσίφυλλος** [ῐ], ον, (ἔνοσις) *with quivering foliage*, of wooded mountains, Il.2.632, Od.9.22, etc.

**εἴνυμι** or -ύω, v. καταέννυμι. **εἴξασι**, v. ἔοικα: **εἴξασκε**, v. εἴκω.

**εἶξις**, εως, ἡ, *giving way, yielding*, Sor.2.31, Plu.2.1122c, S.E.*M.* 10.221, D.L.10.43: pl., Plu.2.447a.

**εἷο**, v. οὗ. **εἶοι**· ὀσπρίων τὰ καθάρσια, Hsch.; cf. εἰαί. **εἷος**, v. ἕως. **εἰπάδεον**· ἐπίπονον, Id. (Fort. εἰπαλέον, cf. εἶπος.)

⊛ **εἴπερ** or εἴ περ, strengthd. for εἰ, *if really, if indeed*, Il.3.25, etc.; esp. *even if, even though*, Il.7.117, Od.1.167, etc.; εἴ. καὶ 9.35; εἴ. τε Il.10.225; εἴ. γε A.*Ch.*198, Pl.*Prt.*312a, etc.; εἴ. γε δή Id.*Tht.*182c; with words between, εἴ. γάρ τε χόλον γε.. Il.1.81; εἴπερ ἔσται γε A.*Ag.*1249, cf. Pl.*Plt.*275e; καλῶς, εἴπερ ποτέ, ἔχει Th.4.20; εἴπερ ἄρα Jul.*Or.*7.216b. **II.** in Att. and Trag. to imply that the supposition agrees with the fact, *if as is the fact, since*, Th.6.14, etc.; but with impf. it implies that it is contrary to the fact, εἴπερ ἦν πέλας *if* I had been (but I was not), S.*El.*312, cf. 604; also εἴ. ἐκτελεῖς ἅπερ λέγεις *if only* you will keep your word, Id.*Ichn.*48. **III.** with an ellipse, *if you must*, Ar.*Nu.*227; ἀλλ' εἴ. but *if so*, Pl.*Prm.*150b, Arist.*EN*1101ᵃ12; cf. εἰ B. VII.

**εἶπερ**, Dor. Adv. *where*, *IG*2².1126.15.

**εἶπον** (pres. ἔπω is used by Nic.*Al.*429, 490, etc., but the pres. in use is φημί, λέγω, ἀγορεύω (v. infr. IV), the fut. ἐρέω, ἐρῶ, the pf. εἴρηκα), Ep. and Lyr. ἔειπον Il.1.552, al., Pi.*O.*4.25; subj. εἴπω (Ep. εἴπωμι Od.22.392, -ησθα 11.224, -ησι Il.7.87); opt. εἴποιμι; inf. εἰπεῖν, Ep. -έμεναι, -έμεν, 7.375, 9.688, Dor. εἴπην (v. infr.); part. εἰπών: also aor. 1 εἶπα (ἔειπα Emp.17.15, Theoc.22.153), ὅπερ εἶπα as I *said*, Satyr.*Vit.Eur.Fr.*39 xvii 14, mostly in Ion. Prose, also Men. *Pk.*128, Herod.3.26, *UPZ*62.14 (ii B.C.), and the 2nd persons ind. and imper. of this form are preferred in Att., 2 sg. ind. εἶπας Il.1.106, 108, etc.; imper. εἶπον (on the accent v. Hdn.Gr.1.460) Simon.154, Pl.*Men.*71d, Men.891, Theoc.14.11, εἰπάτω (ἀν-ειπάτω *IG*2².1186.19 (iv B.C.), but ἀν-ειπέτω ib.1247.13 (iii B.C.)), -ατον, -ατε; 3 pl. εἶπαν *SIG* 333.3 (Samos, iv B.C.), later εἴπασαν *IG*7.2225.51 (Thisbe); part. εἴπας Philem.42, Aeol. εἴπαις Pi.*O.*8.46, cf. Ael.Dion.*Fr.*156; in compds. Med. ἀπείπασθαι (q.v.), διείπασθαι (q.v.), but never in good Att.: (redupl. aor. 2 from ϝεπ- 'say'; ϝείπην only cj. in Alc.55, Sapph. 28.2; ϝεῖπαι *Leg.Gort.*8.15; with ἔ-(ϝ)ειπον cf. Skt. *avocam*, redupl. aor. of *vac-* 'say'; cf. ἔπος):—*speak, say*, ὡς εἰπὼν Il.1.68, etc.; τινί 17.692, etc.; εἰς ἅπαντας E.*Hec.*303; εἰπεῖν ἔν τισιν or μετά τισιν *speak* among a number, Il.10.445, 3.85, etc.: c. acc. cogn., ἔπος, μῦθον, θεοπρόπιον, οὐνόματα, etc., 3.204, 1.552, 85, 17.260, etc.; τινί τι Od.1.169, al.; τι Alc., Sapph. ll. cc., etc.; τι ἔς or πρός τινα, S.*Tr.*487, *Aj.*292; εἰπεῖν περί τινος, ἀμφί τινι, Od.15.347, 14.364: c. gen., πατρός τε καὶ υἱέος *of* them, 11.174; εἰπεῖν ὅτι or ὡς *to say* that.., Il.17.655, Od.22. 373, etc.: but also c. inf., Hdt.2.30, Th.7.35, Pl.*Grg.*473a, etc. b. *recite*, ἔπη Id.*Ion* 535b. 2. in parenthesis, ὡς ἔπος εἰπεῖν so *to say*, limiting a general statement, A.*Pers.*714, etc.; *speaking loosely*, opp.

ὄντως, Pl.*Lg*.656e; opp. ἀκριβεῖ λόγῳ, Id.*R*.341b; ὡς εἰπεῖν Th.3.38, al., Pl.*Phdr*.258e, al.; ὡς ἀξίως εἰπεῖν Arist.*PA*651ᵇ36: without ὡς, οὐ πολλῷ λόγῳ εἰπεῖν Hdt.1.61; ἐς τὸ ἀκριβὲς εἰπεῖν Th.6.82; σχεδὸν εἰπεῖν Pl.*Sph*.237c: καθόλου εἰπεῖν Arist.*Cat*.12ᵃ27; ἢ ἁπλῶς εἰπεῖν ἀπόδειξις Id.*APo*.75ᵇ23; τὸ ξύμπαν εἶπαι, εἰπεῖν, Hdt.7.143, Th.1.138. **3.** εἴποι τις *as* one *might say*, dub. l. in Plb.15.35.1; ὥσπερ εἴποι τις Ar.*Av*.180 (s. v. l.); ὡς εἴποι τις D.Chr.64.5 (s. v. l.). **II.** c. acc. pers., *address, accost* one, Il.12.210, etc. **2.** *name, mention*, ib.1.90, etc. **3.** *call* one so and so, πολλοί τέ μιν ἐσθλὸν ἔειπον Od.19.334, cf. S.*OC*43, E.*Med*.465, etc. **4.** c. dupl. acc. pers. et rei, *tell* or *proclaim* so *of* one, Il.6.479 (where ἀνιόντα depends on εἴποι); εἰπεῖν τινα ὅτι.. Pi.*O*.14.22; ἀτάσθαλόν τι εἰ. τινά Od.22.314; κακὰ εἰ. τινά Ar.*Ach*.649; μηδὲν φλαῦρον εἰ. τ. Id.*Nu*.834; εὖ εἰ. τινά Od.1.302; εἰ. τεθνεῶτ' Ὀρέστην *speak of* him *as* dead, A.*Ch*.682. **5.** *celebrate*, of poets, Αἴαντος βίαν *AP*7.2.6 (Antip. Sid.). **III.** c. dat. pers. et inf., *order* or *command* one to.., Od.15.76, 22.262, etc.; also εἰπεῖν πρός τινα, c. inf., 16.151: c. acc. et inf., εἶπον τὰς παῖδας δεῦρ' ἄγειν τινά S.*OC*932, cf. Pl.*Phd*.59e, Herod.6.26: folld. by ἵνα, freq. in *NT*, *Ev.Matt*.4.3, al. **IV.** *propose, move* a measure in the assembly, εἰπὼν τὰ βέλτιστα D.3.12; εἰπεῖν τὰ δέοντα ib.15; εἶπε ψήφισμα Id.24.11: freq. as a formal prefix to decrees and laws, Λάχης εἶπε Th.4.118, cf. *IG*1².24, al.; cf. ἀγορεύω. **V.** *plead*, δίκην Il.18.508; δικίδιον Ar.*Eq*.347. **VI.** *promise, offer*, χρυσὸν εἴφ' ὃς ἂν κτάνῃ E.*El*.33. **VII.** imper. εἰπέ sts. used in addressing several persons, Ar.*Ach*.328, *Av*.366, D.4.10.

⊛ **εἶπος**, ὁ, = ἶπος, Call.*Fr*.233.

**εἴποτε** or **εἴ ποτε**, *if ever*, Il.1.39; strengthd. εἴ ποτε δή ib.503: used in asking a favour of any one, to call something to his mind, for εἴποτ' ἔην γε, i.e. *as surely as* he was. **II.** indirect, *if* or *whether ever*, Il.2.97, etc.

**εἴπου** or **εἴ που**, *if anywhere, if at all*, Od.3.93, etc.; εἴ τί που ἔστι *if* it is *any way* possible, 4.193; πάσας ξυνήθροισεν εἴ πού τις ἦν X.*HG*2.1.10, etc. **II.** indirect, *whether anywhere*, πευσόμενος.. εἴ που ἔτ' εἴης Od.13.415, etc.

**εἶρ·** λαῖλαψ, Hsch.: **εἴρ**, Suid.

**Εἰρᾰφιών**, ῶνος, ὁ, name of month at Amorgos, *IG*12(7).62.28; cf. sq.

⊛ **Εἰρᾰφιώτης**, ου, ὁ (Aeol. Ἐρρᾰφεώτας Alc.90), epith. of Bacchus, *h.Hom*.1.2, al., Call.*Fr.anon*.89, D.P.576, *IGRom*.4.360.27 (Pergam.); for various etymologies cf. Corn.*ND*30, Porph.*Abst*.3.17, *EM*302.53, 372.1. **II.** = ἔριφος (Lacon.), Hsch.

**εἰργαθεῖν**, v. ἐργαθεῖν.

**εἰργμός**, later **εἱργμός**, ὁ, (εἴργω) *cage, prison*, Pl.*R*.495d, *Phd*.82e. **2.** *imprisonment*, J.*AJ*18.1.3, Plu.2.84f: pl., Mitteis *Chr*.71.10 (iv A. D.); εἱργμοὶ καὶ δεσμοί, of a snake's *coils*, Ael.*NA*17.37; εἱργμοῦ γραφή action *for malicious imprisonment*, Poll.6.154.

**εἱργμοφύλαξ** [ῠ], ἄκος, ὁ, ἡ, *gaoler*, X.*HG*5.4.8.

**εἴργνῡμι** (-ύω And.4.27), Ep. impf. ἐέργνυ:—*shut in* or *up*, Od.10.238.

**εἴργω** or **εἵργω**, v. ἔργω. **εἰρέα**, ἡ, v. sub εἴρη (A). **εἰρέαται**, Ion. 3 pl. pf. Pass. of ἐρῶ. **εἰρέβαδε**, = εἰς ἔρεβος, Hsch. **εἰρεθύρη·** ὀρσοθύρα, ὁ στροφεύς, Id.

**εἰρελάω**, Eretrian for εἰσ-, *IG*12(9).90.11 (Tamynae, iv B. C.).

**εἴρεμος** (ἦρ- cod.), etym. of Ἑρμῆς, Hsch. s. v. Ἀργειφόντης.

**εἴρερος**, ὁ, *bondage, slavery*, εἴρερον εἰσανάγουσι Od.8.529.

⊛ **εἰρεσία**, Ion. -ίη, ἡ, (ἐρέσσω) *rowing, oarage*, πρῶτα μὲν εἰρεσίη, μετέπειτα δὲ κάλλιμος οὖρος Od.11.640; εἰρεσίῃ χρᾶσθαι Hdt.1.203, 4.110; εἰρεσίας ζυγόν S.*Aj*.249 (lyr.); εἰ. τῶν τριήρων Arist.*Mete*.369ᵇ10: metaph., εἰ. πτερῶν Luc.*Tim*.40; παρὰ δ' εἰρεσίᾳ μαστῶν ἕπεται Ἀστυάναξ close to her *throbbing* breast, E.*Tr*.570 (anap.); εἰρεσίῃ γλώσσης Dionys.Eleg.4.3. **2.** *oar*, Ph.1.352, 385. **II.** in collective sense, *rowers, oarsmen*, E.*Hel*.1453 (lyr.), *AP*7.287 (Antip.(?)); ξυνέχειν τὴν εἰ. keep *the oars* together or make *the rowers* keep time, Th.7.14. **2.** *boat-song, to which the rowers kept time*, αὐλεῖν εἰρεσίαν Plu.*Alc*.32, cf. Luc.*VH*1.40. **III.** pl., *rowers' benches*, Plb.1.21.2. (The Ep. form, due to metrical lengthening, is retained in Prose.)

**εἰρεσιώνη**, ἡ, (εἶρος) *branch* of olive or laurel *wound round with wool and hung with fruits*, dedicated to Apollo and borne about by singing boys at the Πυανόψια and Θαργήλια, while offerings were made to Helios and the Hours, and afterwards hung up at the house-door, Eup.119, Ar.*Eq*.729, *V*.399, *Pl*.1054, cf. Paus.Gr.*Fr*.157, Sch.Ar. ll. cc. **2.** the song itself, Hom.*Epigr*.15, Plu.*Thes*.22. **II.** *crown* hung up in honour of the dead, *IG*3.1337, Alciphr.3.37. **2.** generally, *wreath*, J.*AJ*3.10.4; cf. εἰρυσιώνη.

**εἰρέω**, *say*, only in Ep. part. fem. εἰρεῦσαι Hes.*Th*.38; for εἰρήσομαι, εἴρημαι, v. ἐρῶ. **II.** εἰρεῦντα· ἐρωτῶντα, Hsch.

**εἴρη** (A), ἡ, (εἴρω 'speak') old Ion., = ἀγορά or ἐκκλησία, *a place of assembly*, εἰράων προπάροιθε καθήμενοι Il.18.531 (cf. Sch. ad loc. and *EM*483.3); ἐπιμίσγεται.. εἴρας ἐς ἀθανάτων Hes.*Th*.804 (Herm. for εἰρέας): expld. by Hsch. as = ἐρώτησις, φήμη, κληδών (also written ἱρά, ἰρά, by Gramm., cf. Apollon.*Lex*., *EM*475.12, Suid.).

**εἴρη** (B), ἡ, v. εἶρις: also, = ἶρις, *rainbow*, Hsch.

**εἰρήδεται·** ἐρίζεται, Hsch.

⊛ **εἴρην**, ενος, or **ἰρήν**, ένος, ὁ, *Lacedaemonian youth who had completed his twentieth year*, X.*Lac*.2.11, Plu.*Lyc*.17, *IG*5(1).279.

**εἰρηνάζει·** κρατεῖ, Hsch.

**εἰρηναῖος**, α, ον, *peaceful*, εἰρηναῖον εἶναί τινι to live *peaceably* with any one, Hdt.2.68; οὐδὲν εἰ. ἀπαγγέλλειν Th.1.29; τὰ εἰ. *matters of peace*, Hdt.6.57; εἰ. βίος Phld.*Oec*.p.20 J.; εἰ. καὶ βέβαιος πλοῦς Dion. Byz.24: Sup., Max.Tyr.30.5. Adv. -αίως Hdt.3.145, Phld.*Oec*.p.39 J. **II.** εἰρηναῖον, τό, = Lat. *Templum Pacis*, D.C.72.24.

**εἰρηναρχ-εῖον**, τό, *office of* εἰρηνάρχης, *POxy*.141.5 (vi A. D.). **-έω**, *hold office of* εἰρηνάρχης, *OGI*537.6 (Pessinus), *BSA*18.149 (Beroea, ii/iii A. D.), *IGRom*.4.1437 (Smyrna), 3.208 (Ancyra). **-ης**, ου, ὁ, *police magistrate*, ib.203 (Ancyra), *OGI*550 (Phrygia), *BGU*151.4, *Cod.Just*.10.77, etc.:—also **εἰρήναρχος**, ὁ, *Milet*.1(7) No.263, *IGRom*.4.1543 (Erythrae), *Cod.Just*.10.1.9. **-ικός**, ή, όν, *of* or *for such an officer*, τιμαί *BCH*9.347 (Caria), cf. Sch.Ar.*Ra*.1103.

**εἰρήν-ευσις**, εως, ἡ, *reconciliation*, ἐναντίων δυνάμεων Iamb.*VP*33.229. **-εύω**, *bring to peace, reconcile*, D.C.77.12, gloss on Babr.39.4. **II.** intr., *keep peace, live peaceably*, Pl.*Tht*.180b; πρός τινα D.S.21.16; μετὰ πάντων *Ep.Rom*.12.18:—Med., πρὸς τοὺς κρείττους εἰρηνεύεσθαι Arist.*Rh*.1359ᵇ39, cf. *OGI*199.1 (Adule); χώρα -ομένη ἐκ παλαιοῦ Plb.5.8.7. **-έω**, = εἰρηνεύω II, Arist.*HA*608ᵇ29, D.L.2.5, D.C.37.52.

⊛ **εἰρήν-η** (v. infr.), ἡ, *peace*, Od.24.486, etc.; ἐπ' εἰρήνης in *time of peace*, Il.2.797; ἔθηκε πᾶσιν εἰ. φίλοις A.*Pers*.769; εἰ. τἀκεῖθεν τέκνοις on that side they have *peace*, have naught to fear, E.*Med*.1004; εἰ. γίγνεται *peace* is made, Hdt.1.74: hence later, *a peace, treaty of peace*, ἡ βασιλέως εἰ. *IG*2².103.24, etc.; εἰ. ποιεῖν Ἀρμενίοις καὶ Χαλδαίοις make *peace* between.., X.*Cyr*.3.2.12; εἰ. ποιεῖσθαι And.3.8, Aeschin.2.77; εἰ. κατεργάζεσθαι, πράττειν, And.3.8, 17; διαπράξασθαι X.*HG*6.3.4; εἰρήνης δεῖσθαι ib.2.2.13; εἰρήνην δέχεσθαι to accept *it*, ib.22; λαβεῖν And.3.7; εἰ. ἄγειν keep *peace*, be at *peace*, Ar.*Av*.386, etc.; πρὸς ἀλλήλους Pl.*R*.465b; εἰ. ἄγειν (v. l. ἔχειν) enjoy *peace*, X.*An*.2.6.6; λύειν break *it*, D.18.71; πολλὴ εἰ. τινὸς γίγνεται profound *peace*, Pl.*R*.329c; ἐν εἰρήνῃ λέγειν, τὸν βίον διάγειν, Id.*Smp*.189b, *R*.372d; πόλεμον εἰρήνης χάριν [αἱρεῖσθαι] Arist.*Pol*.1333ᵃ35; εἰρήνης ἄρξας, = εἰρηναρχήσας, *IGRom*.3.784, cf. 452. **II.** *the goddess of peace*, daughter of Zeus and Themis, Hes.*Th*.902, cf. Pi.*O*.13.7, B.*Fr*.3.1, *IG*3.170, Plu.*Cim*.13, etc. **III.** Pythag. name for *three*, *Theol.Ar*.16; for *six*, ib.37. **IV.** Hebraism in Lxx, ἐρωτῆσαί τινα εἰς εἰρήνην *greet* a person, inquire after their health, *Jd*.18.15, 1*Ki*.17.22; ἐρ. τινὰ τὰ εἰς εἰ. ib.10.4; so ἐπερωτᾶν εἰς εἰ. τοῦ πολέμου 2*Ki*.11.7; in salutations, εἰ. σοι; 4*Ki*.4.26, cf. *Ev.Luc*.24.36, al.; εἰ. ἡ εἴσοδός σου 3*Ki*.2.13. (ϝειράνα *IG*5(1).1509 (Sparta, iv B. C., dub.); ἰράνα ib.4.917 (Epid.), 12(3).29.12 (Telos); cf. Boeot. πολέμω καιράνας ib.7.2407, but Cret. πολέμω χ[ΓΙ]ρήνας *GDI*5018.5; εἰρήνα Pi. l. c., B. l. c., *SIG*241.80 (Delph., iv B. C.), later εἰράνα *IG*5(1).935.14 (ii B. C.).) ⊛ **-ικός**, ή, όν, *of* or *for peace*, λόγων -ώτατος Isoc.5.3; χρεία Arist.*Pol*.1254ᵇ32; θυσίαι *peace* offerings, Lxx 1*Ki*.11.15, al.; ἄγγελοι καὶ δαίμονες Herm.ap.Stob.1.49.45. **2.** *of* or *in peace, peaceful*, βίος, πρᾶξις, etc., Pl.*Lg*.829a, *R*.399b, etc.; ἐπιστῆμαι X.*Oec*.1.17: Sup., Ph.2.634. Adv. -κῶς *peaceably*, opp. πολεμικῶς, Isoc.5.46, Phld.*Hom*.p.45 O., etc.: Comp. -ώτερον Luc.*Fug*.5. **3.** *peaceable*, of persons, Isoc.2.24.

**εἰρηνο-δίκαι** [ῐ], ῶν, οἱ, = Lat. *Fetiales*, D.H.2.72, al.: sg., ib.15.9, App.*Sam*.5. **-πάτριος**, ὁ, *Father of Peace*, title of Chosroes, Men. Prot.p.16 D. **-ποιέω**, *to make peace*, Lxx *Pr*.10.10, *Ep.Col*.1.20, *Cat.Cod.Astr*.2.203:—Med., *make peaceful*, [ψυχὴ] τὸν ἴδιον δρόμον -εῖται Herm.ap.Stob.1.49.45. **-ποιός**, ὁ, *peace-maker*, X.*HG*6.3.4, *Ev.Matt*.5.9, Corn.*ND*23, Plu.*Nic*.11. **II.** pl., = Lat. *Fetiales*, Id.2.279b. **-φῠλᾰκέω**, *to be a guardian of peace*, Ph.2.209. **-φύλαξ** [ῠ], ἄκος, ὁ, ἡ, *guardian of peace*, X.*Vect*.5.1, Aeschin.3.159; of Caesar, Ph.2.567; title of police magistrate, Lib.*Or*.48.9 (pl.), *Sammelb*.4636.32, 36 (Panopolis, iii A. D.). **II.** pl., = εἰρηνοδίκαι, Plu.*Num*.12.

**εἰρητής·** αἴτιος, Hsch. **εἰρίνεος, εἴριον**, v. ἐρίνεος, ἔριον.

**εἶρις**, ἡ, = ἶρις II. 3, *SIG*1171.15 (Crete, acc. sg. written εἴρην): **εἴρινος**, = ἴρινος, *Edict. Diocl.* in *BCH*22.403 (Delph.). **II.** v. Ἶρις.

**εἰρκτέον**, (εἴργω) *one must prevent*, S.*Aj*.1250.

**εἱρκτή** or **εἰρκ-**, Ion. **ἑρκτή**, ἡ, (εἴργω) *an inclosure, prison*, Hdt.4.146, 148, Th.1.131, *PTeb*.5.260 (ii B. C.), etc.; of the body as *prison* of the soul, J.*BJ*2.8.11 (pl.): pl., E.*Ba*.497, X.*Cyr*.3.1.19. **II.** *inner part of the house, women's apartments*, Id.*Mem*.2.1.5.

**εἱρκτικός**, ή, όν, *preventive*, *Gloss*.

**εἱρκτο-φῠλᾰκέω**, *to be a gaoler*, Ph.1.290. **-φύλαξ** [ῠ], ἄκος, ὁ, *gaoler*, Ph.1.289, 2.53, J.*AJ*17.7.1.

**εἱρμός**, ὁ, (εἴρω A) *train, series, sequence*, Arist.*Pr*.916ᵃ31, Ph.1.6, Plot.3.1.2, etc.; εἰ. αἰτιῶν *concatenation* of causes, *Placit*.1.28.4, cf. Iamb.ap.Stob.1.5.17; so εἱρμός alone, Chrysipp.*Stoic*.2.284, cf. Hierocl. *in CA* 11 p.442 M. **2.** *connexion*, εἰ. λόγου πρὸς βίον Ph.1.569.

**εἶρξις**, εως, ἡ, *fencing in*, *IG*1².94.8. **II.** gloss on μεσόδμη, Gal.19.122.

**εἰροκόμος**, ον, *working in wool*, Il.3.387: as Subst., *AP*6.160 (Antip. Sid.).

**εἴρομαι**, Ion. for ἔρομαι, *ask*; v. εἴρω (C).

**εἰρομένως**, Adv. *running on*: *in order*, *PSI*4.439 (iii B. C.); *in continuation*, Apollon.Cit.2.

**εἰρο-πόκος**, ον, *wool-fleeced, woolly*, εἰροπόκοις ὀΐεσσιν Il.5.137; εἰροπόκων ὀΐων Od.9.443, Theoc.8.9, cf. Hes.*Op*.234. **-πόνος**, ον, *working in wool*, Suid.

**εἶρος**, εος, τό, *wool*, Od.4.135, 9.426. **II.** = γναφάλλιον, Ps.-Dsc.3.117. **III.** a kind of *fever*, Hp.ap.Erot. (with other expll.).

**εἰροχᾰρής**, ές, *delighting in wool*, τάλαρος *AP*6.39 (Arch.).

**εἴροψ**, οπος, ὁ, Boeot., = μέροψ, Arist.*HA* 559ᵃ4.

**εἰρτός**, ή, όν, (εἴρω A) *that can be threaded* or *sewn*, *Gloss.*

**εἰρύαται, εἰρύμεναι** [ῠ], v. ἐρύω.

**εἰρύσῐμον** [ῠ], τό, Ep. for ἐρύσιμον, Nic.*Th.*894.

**εἰρῠσιώνη**, ἡ, = εἰρεσιώνη II. 2, *wreath* dedicated to Apollo, Roussel *Cultes Égyptiens* 172 (Delos, i B.C.).

**εἰρύω, εἰρύομαι**, poet. for ἐρύω, ἐρύομαι (q.v.).

⊛ **εἴρω** (A), aor. εἶρα (v. infr.), also ἔρσα (v. διείρω) :—**Pass.**, pf. part. ἐρμένος (ἐν-) Hdt.4.190; Ep. ἐερμένος (v. infr.) :—mostly in compds., ἀν-, δι-, ἐν-, ἐξ-, συν-είρω :—*fasten together in rows, string*, used by Hom. only in Ep. pf. Pass., ἠλέκτροισιν ἐερμένος [a necklace] *strung* with pieces of amber, Od.18.296, and plpf. Pass., μετὰ δ' ἠλέκτροισιν ἔερτο 15.460; περὶ στήθεσσιν ἔερτο [μίτρη] A.R.3.868; τὸ εὖ εἰρόμενον *a connected system*, Plot.2.3.7. II. after Hom. in Act., στεφάνους εἰ. Pi.*N.*7.77; εἰ. τὰ θεῖα Plu.2.1029c; *insert*, εἰς βρόχον εἴρας τὸν τράχηλον Zaleuc.ap.Stob.4.2.19 ad fin., cf. *PMag.Par.*1.259; esp. in speech, *string together*, ὁ εἴρας καὶ συνυφάνας ἕκαστα [λόγος] Ph.1.499; θρῆνον J.*BJ*6.5.3; πολλὰ ὀνόματα Philostr.*VA* 1.20, cf. 6.17; οἱ μηδὲ δύο σχεδὸν ῥήματα δεξιῶς εἴρειν δυνάμενοι S.E.*M.*1.98 :—Pass., εἰρομένη λέξις *continuous*, *running* style, i.e. not antithetic or with balanced periods, Arist.*Rh.*1409ᵃ29. 2. εἰρόμενον, τό, *'dossier'* of documents, Mitteis *Chr.*184.9 (iii A.D.); εἰ. τραπεζιτικόν *PLips.*9.22. (Etym. dub., cf. either Lat. *sero* or Lith. *vérti* 'thread'.)

⊛ **εἴρω** (B), *say, speak, tell* :—Act. is used by Hom. only in Od., and in 1 pers., μνηστῆρσιν δ' . . τάδε εἴρω 2.162, cf. 13.7; τὰ δέ τοι νημερτέα εἴρω 11.137 :—Med. in same sense, καὶ εἴρετο δεύτερον αὖτις Il.1.513; εἴροντο δὲ κήδε' ἑκάστη Od.11.542, cf. Nic.*Th.*359 :—Pass., 3 sg. εἴρεται *is said*, Arat.172, 261: for other forms v. ἐρῶ. (Ϝέρ-yω, fr. root of ἐρῶ, q.v.)

*εἴρω (C), *ask*: for Act. forms (stem ἐρε(Ϝ)-), v. ἐρέω (A): for Med. forms (stems ἐρε(Ϝ)- and ἐρ(Ϝ)-), v. ἔρομαι, ἐπείρομαι.

**εἴρων**, ωνος, ὁ, ἡ, *dissembler, one who says less than he thinks*, Ar.*Nu.* 449, etc.; opp. ἀληθευτικός, Arist.*EN*1124ᵇ30, Thphr.*Char.*1.1; opp. ἀλαζών, Arist.*EN*1108ᵃ23; ἀλώπηξ εἰ. τῇ φύσει Philem.89.6; ὁ εἰ. ὡς ἐπὶ τὸ πλεῖστον ἀλαζόνος εἶδος Phld.*Vit.*p.38 J.; εἰ. ἐν τοῖς λόγοις Luc.*Anach.*18, cf. Cic.*Off.*1.30.108, J.*BJ*1.26.2.

**εἰρων-εία**, ἡ, *dissimulation*, i.e. *ignorance purposely affected* to provoke or confound an antagonist, a mode of argument used by Socrates against the Sophists, Pl.*R.*337a, cf. Arist.*EN*1124ᵇ30, Cic.*Acad.Pr.* 2.5.15: generally, *mock-modesty*, opp. ἀλαζονεία, Arist.*EN*1108ᵃ22; *sarcasm*, Hermog.*Id.*2.8, al.; *understatement*, Phld.*Lib.*p.13 O. II. *pretence, assumption*, when a person at first appears willing, but then draws back, D.4.7; τὴν ἡμετέραν βραδυτῆτα καὶ εἰρωνείαν ib. 37. III. generally, *dissembling*, Ph.1.345 (pl.), al. 2. *pretext*, *PSI*5.452.23 (iv A.D.). **-ευμα**, ατος, τό, in pl., *ironies*, Max. Tyr.24.5, 38.4. **-εύομαι**, *feign ignorance*, so as to perplex, Arist. *Rh.*1379ᵇ31; πρός τινα Pl.*Cra.*384a; πρὸς ὑμᾶς αὐτούς Din.2.11; *banter*, Arist.*Pol.*1275ᵇ27: generally, *dissemble, shuffle*, Ar.*Av.*1211, Pl.*Ap.*38a, D.60.18. 2. *employ understatement*, Polystr.p.15 W. II. trans., *treat with sarcasm*, τινά Him.*Ecl.*1.13. **-ευτής**, οῦ, ὁ, = εἴρων, Timo 25.3. ⊛ **-ευτικός**, ή, όν, = foreg., Sch.A.R. 1.486. **-ίζω**, = εἰρωνεύομαι, Philostr.*VS*1.7.1 (v.l. for εἰρωνικόν). **-ικός**, ή, όν, *dissembling*: hence, *hollow, insincere*, Pl.*Sph.* 268a; τὸ εἰ. εἶδος Id.*Lg.*908e; εἰρωνικόν τι ὑπομειδιάσας Hld.10.14. Adv. **-κῶς** *mockingly*, Ar.*V.*174, Pl.*Smp.*218d, etc.

**εἰρωτάω**, Ep., and **εἰρωτέω**, Ion., for ἐρωτάω.

⊛ **εἰς** or **ἐς**, PREP. WITH ACC. ONLY :—both forms are found in Hom., Ion. poets, and early metrical Inscrr.; ἐς is best attested in Hdt. and Hp., and is found in nearly all early Ion. Inscrr. (exc. *IG*12(8).262.16 (Thasos, v B.C.), ib.7.235.1 (Oropus, iv B.C.)); εἰς in Att. Inscrr. from iv B.C., *IG*2.115, etc.; and usu. in Att. Prose (exc. Th.) and Com. (exc. in parody): Trag. apptly. prefer εἰς, but ἐς is used before vowels metri gr.; ἐς was retained in the phrases ἐς κόρακας (whence the Verb σκορακίζω), ἐς μακαρίαν. Aeol. poets have εἰς before vowels, ἐς before consonants, and this is given as the rule in Hom. by *An.Ox.* 1.172, cf. Hellad.ap.Phot.*Bibl.*p.533 B. (Orig. **ἐνς**, as in *IG*4.554.7 (Argos), *GDI*4986.11 (Crete); cf. ἐν, ἰν. The diphthong is genuine in Aeol. εἰς, but spurious in Att.-Ion.) Radical sense *into*, and then more loosely, *to*: I. OF PLACE, the oldest and commonest usage, εἰς ἅλα *into* or *to* the sea, Il.1.141, al.; εἰς ἅλαδε Od.10.351; ἐς ῥ' ἀσαμίνθους 4.48; ἐς οἶνον βάλε φάρμακον ib.220; freq. of places, *to*, εἰς Εὔβοιαν 3.174; ἐς Αἴγυπτον, etc., Hdt.1.5, etc.; ἐς Μίλητον *into the territory of* Miletus, ib.14; εἰς Ἑλλήσποντον εἰσέπλει X.*HG*1.1.2; ἀφίκετο εἰς Μήδους πρὸς Κυαξάρην Id.*Cyr.*2.1.2; εἰς ἅρματα βαίνειν to step *into* . ., Il.8.115; εἰς ἐλάτην ἀναβῆναι 14.287; opp. ἐκ, in such phrases as ἐς σφυρὸν ἐκ πτέρνης, ἐς πόδας ἐκ κεφαλῆς, from heel *to* ankle-joint, from head *to* foot, 22.397, 23.169; ἐκ πάτου ἐς σκοπιήν 20.137; ἐς μυχὸν ἐξ οὐδοῦ Od.7.87; κῆς ἔτος ἐξ ἔτεος from year *to* year, Theoc. 18.15: with Verbs implying motion or direction, as of looking, ἰδεῖν εἰς οὐρανόν Il.3.364; εἰς ὦπα ἰδέσθαι to look *in* the face, 9.373, etc.; εἰς ὦπα ἔοικεν he is like *in* face (sc. ἰδόντι), 3.158, etc.; ἐς ὀφθαλμούς τινος ἐλθεῖν to come *before* another's eyes, 24.204; ἐς ὄψιν ἀπικνέεσθαί τινος Hdt.1.136; καλέσαι τινὰ ἐς ὄψιν Id.5.106, etc.; ἐς ταὐτὸν ἥκειν come *to* the same point, E.*Hipp.*273: less freq. after a Subst., ὁδὸς ἐς λαύρην Od.22.128; τὸ ἐς Παλλήνην τεῖχος *facing* Pallene, Th.1.56; ξύνοδος ἐς τὴν Δῆλον Id.3.104, cf. Pl.*Tht.*173d. b. Ep. and Ion., also c. acc. pers. (Att. ὡς, πρός, παρά), Il.7.312, 15.402, Od.14.127, Hdt.4.147; also in Att. with collective Nouns, ἐς τὸν δῆμον παρελθόντες Th. 5.45, or plurals, εἰς ὑμᾶς εἰσῆλθον D.18.103; esp. of consulting an oracle, ἐς θεὸν ἐλθεῖν Pi.*O.*7.31; εἰς Ἄμμων' ἐλθόντες Ar.*Av.*619. 2. with Verbs expressing *rest in* a place, when a previous motion *into* or *to* it is implied, ἐς μέγαρον κατέθηκεν ἐπὶ θρόνου he put it *in* the house (i.e. he brought it *into* the house, and put it *there*), Od.20.96; ἐς θρόνους ἕζοντο they sat them down *upon* the seats, 4.51, cf. 1.130; ἐφάνη λὶς εἰς ὁδόν the lion appeared *in* the path, Il.15.276; ἀπόστολος ἐς τὴν Μίλητον ἦν Hdt.1.21 (s.v.l.); αὐτὸς ἐς Λακεδαίμονα ἀπόστολος ἐγίνετο Id.5.38; ἐς κώμην παραγίνονται Id.1.185; παρῆν ἐς Σάρδις Id.6.1; ἐς δόμους μένειν S.*Aj.*80 (cod. Laur.); ἐς τὴν νῆσον κατέκλησε Th.1.109, cf. Hdt.3.13; ἀπόβασιν ποιήσασθαι ἐς . . Th.2.33, etc.; later used like ἐν, τὴν γῆν εἰς ἣν ὑμεῖς κατοικεῖτε LXX *Nu.*35.34; τὸ χρυσίον ὃ εἰλήφεσαν εἰς Ῥώμην D.S.14.117; οἰκεῖν εἰς τὰ Ὕπατα Luc.*Asin.*1; εἰς Ἐκβάτανα ἀποθανεῖν Ael.*VH*7.8; εἰς ἅπασαν τὴν γῆν Suid. s.v. Καλλίμαχος: generally, τοὔνομα εἰς τὴν Ἑλλάδα, φασίν, Ἱππομιγὴς δύναται Ael.*VH*9.16. 3. with Verbs of saying or speaking, εἰς relates to the persons *to* or *before* whom one speaks, εἰπεῖν ἐς πάντας, ἐς πάντας αὐδᾶ, Hdt.8.26, S.*OT*93; λέγειν εἰς τὸ μέσον τῶν ταξιάρχων X.*Cyr.* 3.3.7; αἱ ἐς τὸ φανερὸν λεγόμεναι αἰτίαι Th.1.23: with other Verbs, εἰς τοὺς Ἕλληνας σαυτὸν σοφιστὴν παρέχων Pl.*Prt.*312a; καλὸν ἐς τοὺς Ἕλληνας τὸ ἀγώνισμα φανεῖσθαι Th.7.56; ἐπαχθὴς ἦν ἐς τοὺς πολλούς Id.6.54; στρατιὰν ἐπαγγέλλων ἐς τοὺς ξυμμάχους Id.7.17; διαβεβλῆσθαι εἴς τινα Pl.*R.*539c. 4. elliptical usages, a. after Verbs which have no sense of motion to or into a place, τὴν πόλιν ἐξέλιπον εἰς χωρίον ὀχυρόν they quitted the city *for* a strong position, i.e. to seek a strong position, X.*An.*1.2.24; γράμματα ἑάλωσαν εἰς Ἀθήνας letters were captured [and sent] *to* Athens, Id.*HG*1.1.23, cf. Pl.*R.* 468a; ἀνίστασθαι ἐς Ἄργος E.*Heracl.*59, cf. Pl.*Phd.*116a. b. participles signifying motion are freq. omitted with εἰς, τοῖς στρατηγοῖς τοῖς εἰς Σικελίαν (sc. ἀποδειχθεῖσιν) And.1.11, etc. c. c. gen., mostly of proper names, as εἰς Ἀΐδαο, Att. εἰς Ἅιδου [δόμους], Il.21.48; ἐς Ἀθηναίης [ἱερόν] *to* the temple of Athena, 6.379; ἐς Πριάμοιο [οἶκον] 24.160, cf. 309; εἰς Αἰγύπτοιο [ῥόον] Od.4.581; ἐς τοῦ Κλεομένεος Hdt.5.51; εἰς Ἀσκληπιοῦ Ar.*Pl.*411; ἐπὶ δεῖπνον [ἰέναι] εἰς Ἀγάθωνος Pl.*Smp.* 174a: with Appellatives, ἀνδρὸς ἐς ἀφνειοῦ *to* a rich man's house, Il.24.482; ἐς πατρὸς Od.2.195; πέμπειν εἰς διδασκάλων send *to* school, X.*Lac.*2.1; εἰς δ. φοιτᾶν Pl.*Prt.*326c; ἐς σεωυτοῦ, ἑωυτοῦ, Hdt.1.108, 9.108, etc. II. OF TIME, 1. to denote a certain point or limit of time, *up to, until*, ἐς ἠῶ Od.11.375; ἐς ἠέλιον καταδύντα *till* sunset, 9.161 (but also, *towards* or *near* sunset, 3.138); ἐκ νεότητος ἐς γῆρας Il.14.86; ἐκ παιδὸς ἐς γῆρας Aeschin.1.180; ἐς ἐμέ *up to* my time, Hdt.1.92, al.: with Advbs., εἰς ὅτε (cf. ἔς τε) *against* the time when . ., Od.2.99; εἰς πότε; *until* when? how long? S.*Aj.*1185 (lyr., cf. εἰσόκε); εἰς ὁπότε Aeschin.3.99; ἐς τί; = εἰς πότε; Il.5.465; ἐς ὃ *until*, Hdt.1.93, etc.; ἐς οὗ Id.1.67, 3.31, etc.; ἐς τόδε Id.7.29, etc. 2. to determine a period, εἰς ἐνιαυτόν *for* a year, i.e. a whole year, Il.19.32, Od.4.526; *within* the year, ib.86 (cf. ἐς ἐνίαυτον Alc.*Supp.*8.12); εἰς ὥρας Od.9.135; ἐς θέρος ἢ ἐς ὀπώρην *for* the summer, i.e. *throughout* it, 14.384; ἡ ἐς ἐνιαυτὸν κειμένη δαπάνη εἰς τὸν μῆνα δαπανᾶται the expenditure *for* a year is expended *in* the month, X.*Oec.*7.36; μισθοδοτεῖν τινὰς εἰς ἓξ μῆνας D.S.19.15; χοίνικα κριθῶν εἰς τέσσαρας ἡμέρας διεμέτρει Posidon.36 J.; εἰς ἑσπέραν ἥκειν to come *at* even, Ar.*Pl.*998; εἰς τρίτην ἡμέραν or εἰς τρίτην alone, on the third day, *in* two days, Pl.*Hp.Ma.*286b, X.*Cyr.*5.3.27; ἥκειν ἐς τὴν ὑστεραίαν Id.*An.*2.3.25; ἥκειν εἰς τὸ ἔαρ *Hell.Oxy.*17.4; ἐς τέλος *at* last, Hdt.3.40; ἐς καιρόν *in* season, Id.4.139; οὐκ ἐς ἀναβολάς, ἀμβολάς, *with* no delay, Id.8.21, E.*Heracl.*270, etc.; ἐς τότε *at* this time, v.l. in Od.7.317 (but ἐς τότε *at* that time (in the fut.)), D.14.24, Pl.*Lg.*830b); ἐς ὕστερον or τὸ ὕστερον, Od.12.126, Th.2.20: with Advbs., ἐς αὔριον Il.8.538, Pl. *Lg.*858b; ἔς περ ὀπίσσω Od.20.199; ἐς αὖθις Th.4.63 (v. εἰσαῦθις); ἐς αὐτίκα μάλ' Ar.*Pax*367; εἰς ἔπειτα (v. εἰσέπειτα); ἐς τὸ ἔ., Th.2.64; ἐς ὀψέ Id.8.23; εἰς ἅπαξ, v. εἰσάπαξ; εἰς ἔτι, v. εἰσέτι. III. to express MEASURE OR LIMIT, without reference to Time, ἐς δίσκουρα λέλειπτο was left behind *as far as* a quoit's throw, Il.23.523; ἐς δραχμὴν διέδωκε paid them *as much as* a drachma, Th.8.29; ἱματισμὸν ζητῆσαι εἰς δύο τάλαντα Thphr.*Char.*23.8; so ἐς τὰ μάλιστα *to* the greatest degree, Hdt.1.20, etc.; ἐς τοσοῦτο τύχης ἀπίκευ Id.1.124; εἰς τοσοῦτο ἥκειν Lys.27.10; εἰς τοῦτο θράσους καὶ ἀναιδείας ἀφίκετο D.21.194; ἐς ὃ ἐμέμνηντο *so far as* they remembered, Th.5.66; ἐς τὸ ἔσχατον Hdt.7.229, etc.; ἐς ἅλις Theoc.25.17. 2. freq. with Numerals, ἐς τριακάδας δέκα ναῶν A.*Pers.*339; ναῦς ἐς τὰς τετρακοσίας, διακοσίας, *to the number of* 400, etc., Th.1.74, 100, etc.; εἰς ἕνα, εἰς δύο, εἰς τέσσαρας, one, two, four *deep*, X.*Cyr.*2.3.21; but εἰς τέσσαρας four *abreast*, Aen.Tact.40.6: with Advbs., ἐς τρίς or ἐστρίς *thrice*, Pi.*O.*2.68, Hdt.1.86; of round numbers, *about*, X.*An.*1.1.10. 3. distributive, ἐς φυλὰς *by* tribes, LXX 1*Ki.*10.21, cf. 2*Ki.*18.4. IV. to express RELATION, *towards, in regard to*, ἐξαμαρτεῖν εἰς θεούς A.*Pr.*945, etc.; ἁμάρτημα εἴς τινα, αἰτίαι ἐς ἀλλήλους, Isoc.8.96, Th.1.66; ὄνειδος ὀνειδίζειν εἴς τινα S.*Ph.*522; ἔχθρη ἔς τινα Hdt.6.65; φιλία ἐς ἀμφοτέρους Th.2.9; λέγειν ἐς . . Hdt.1.86; γνώμη ἀποδεχθεῖσα ἐς τὴν γέφυραν Id.4.98; ἡ ἐς γῆν καὶ θάλασσαν ἀρχή Th.8.46. b. of the subject of a work, esp. in titles, e.g. τὰ ἐς Ἀπολλώνιον Philostr. *VA*; of the object of a dedication, as in titles of hymns, ἐπινίκια, etc. 2. *in regard to*, πρῶτος ἐς εὐψυχίαν A.*Pers.*326; σκώπτειν ἐς τὰ ῥάκια Ar.*Pax*740, cf. *Eq.*90; διαβάλλειν τινὰ ἔς τι Th.8.88; αἰτία ἐπιφερομένη ἐς μαλακίαν Id.5.75; μέμφεσθαι εἰς φιλίαν X.*An.*2.6.30; εἰς τὰ πολεμικὰ καταφρονεῖσθαι Id.*HG*7.4.30; πόλεως εὐδοκιμωτάτης εἰς σοφίαν Pl.*Ap.*29d; *in respect of*, εὐτυχεῖν ἐς τέκνα E.*Or.*542, cf. Pl.*Ap.*35b, etc.; εἰς χρήματα ζημιοῦσθαι Id.*Lg.*774b, cf. D.22.55;

ἐς τὰ ἄλλα Th.1.1; εἰς ἅπαντα S.*Tr.*489; ἐς τὰ πάνθ' ὁμῶς A.*Pr.*736; εἰς μὲν ταῦτα Pl.*Ly.*210a; τό γ' εἰς ἑαυτόν, τὸ εἰς ἐμέ, S.*OT*706, E.*IT*691, cf. S.*Ichn.*346; ἐς ὀλίγους μᾶλλον τὰς ἀρχὰς ποιεῖν Th.8.53; ἐς πλείονας οἰκεῖν Id.2.37; for τελεῖν ἐς Ἕλληνας, Βοιωτούς, ἄνδρας, etc., v. τελέω. **3.** of Manner, ἐς τὸν νῦν τρόπον Id.1.6; τίθεμεν τἄλλα εἰς τὸν αὐτὸν λόγον; Pl.*R.*353d; ἐς ἓν μέλος Theoc.18.7: freq. periphr. for Advbs., ἐς κοινὸν φράζειν, λέγειν, A.*Pr.*844, *Eu.*408; ἐς τὸ πᾶν, = πάντως, Id.*Ag.*682 (lyr.); ἐς τάχος, = ταχέως, Ar.*Ach.*686; ἐς εὐτέλειαν, = εὐτελῶς, Id.*Av.*805; ἐς τἀρχαῖον Id.*Nu.*593; εἰς καλόν S.*OT*78, cf. Pl.*Phd.*76e; ἐς δέον γεγονέναι Hdt.1.119, cf. S.*OT*1416, and v. δέον. **V.** of an end or limit, ἔρχεσθαι, τελευτᾶν, λήγειν ἐς.., to end *in*.., Hdt.1.120, 3.125, 4.39, etc.; ἐς ἑβδομήκοντα ἔτεα οὖρον ἀνθρώπῳ προτίθημι Id.1.32; καταξαίνειν ἐς φοινικίδα to cut *into* red rags, Ar.*Ach.*320 (troch.); στρέφειν τι εἰς αἷμα *Apoc.*11.6; εἰς ἄνδρας ἐκ μειρακίων τελευτᾶν, εἰς ἄνδρα γενειᾶν, Pl.*Tht.*173b, Theoc.14.28; ἐκτρέφειν τὸ σπέρμα εἰς καρπόν X.*Oec.*17.10: so with εἶναι or γίγνομαι to form a predicate, ἔσται εἰς ἔθνη Lxx *Ge.*17.16; ἐγενήθη εἰς γυναῖκα ib.20.12; πιστὸς (sc. ἦν) εἰς προφήτην ib.1*Ki.*3.20; ἐγένετο εἰς δένδρον *Ev.Luc.*13.19, al. **2.** of Purpose or Object, εἰπεῖν εἰς ἀγαθόν, πείσεται εἰς ἀγαθόν, *for* good, *for* his good, Il.9.102, 11.789; εἰς ἀγαθὰ μυθεῖσθαι 23.305; ἐς πόλεμον θωρήξομαι 8.376, cf. Hdt.7.29, etc.; ἐς φόβον *to cause* fear, Il.15.310; ἐς ὑποδήματα δεδόσθαι Hdt.2.98; κόσμος ὁ εἰς ἑορτάς X.*Oec.*9.6; ἐπιτηδεότατος, εὐπρεπής, ἔς τι Hdt.1.115, 2.116; εἰς κάλλος ζῆν to live *for* show, X.*Cyr.*8.1.33, cf. *Ages.*9.1; ἐς δαίτην ἐκάλεσσε Call.*Aet.*1.1.5; εἰς κέρδος τι δρᾶν S.*Ph.*111; πάσας φωνὰς ἱέντων εἰς ἀπόφυξιν Ar.*V.*562; εἰς γράμματα παιδὶ δεκετεῖ ἐνιαυτοὶ τρεῖς Pl.*Lg.*809e; εἰς τὸ πρᾶγμα εἶναι to be *pertinent, to the purpose*, D.36.54; freq. of expenditure *on* an object, *IG*2$^{2}$.102.11, 116.41, al.; ἐς τὸ δέον Ar.*Nu.*859, etc.; ἐς δᾷδα ib.612.

**B.** Position: εἰς is sts. parted from its acc. by several words, εἰς ἀμφοτέρω Διομήδεος ἅρματα βήτην Il.8.115; εἰς δὲ μονάρχου δῆμος ἀϊδρίῃ δουλοσύνην ἔπεσεν Sol.9: seldom (only in Poets) put after its case, Il.15.59, Od.3.137, 15.541, S.*OC*126 (lyr.): after an Adv., αὔριον ἔς· τῆμος δὲ.. Od.7.318.

⊛ **εἷς**, μία, ἕν (μίη only in late Ion. Prose): gen. ἑνός, μιᾶς, ἑνός:—Ep. **ἕεις** Hes.*Th.*145, *AP*7.341 (Procl.), cj. in Il.5.603:—Dor. **ἧς** Rhinth.12, *Tab.Heracl.*1.136:—Ep., Aeol., and Ion. fem. ἴα Il.13.354, prob. in Hp.*Morb.*4.37; acc. ἴαν Alc.33.6 (prob.), Sapph.69.1 (cf. μηδεΐα), Corinn.*Supp.*2.56, *IG*9(2).517.22 (Thess.); gen. ἰῆς Il.16.173, 24.496; dat. ἰῇ 9.319, 11.174, etc.: neut. dat. (ἰῷ κίον ἤματι) 6.422. (In Com. οὐδὲ (μηδὲ) εἷς, οὐδὲ (μηδὲ) ἕν, occur, mostly at the end of an iambic trimeter, without elision, Cratin.302, Ar.*Ra.*927, *Pl.*37, 138, al.) (Orig. **ἕνς**, assim. ἕν(δ) prob. in *Leg.Gort.*9.50, from *ἕμς, I.-Eur. *sem-* (cf. ὁμός); μία from *sm-ia*; ἴα is not related to μία, but prob. to pronom. stem *i-* (Lat. *is*), cf. ἰός.) **1.** as a Numeral, εἷς κοίρανος ἔστω Il.2.204, etc.; strengthd., εἷς οἶος, μία οἴη, a single *one, one* alone, 4.397, Od.7.65; μία μούνη 23.227; εἷς μοῦνος Hdt.1.119, Ar.*Pl.*1053, etc.; εἷς καὶ μόνος D.H.1.74; εἷς ὤν S.*OT*247, E.*Ph.*894, etc.; opp. πολύς, μία τὰς πολλὰς ψυχὰς ὀλέσασα A.*Ag.*1456, cf. 1465, *Ch.*299, etc. **b.** emphatically with a Sup., εἷς οἰωνὸς ἄριστος Il.12.243, etc.: freq. in Trag., εἷς ἀνὴρ πλεῖστον..πόνον παρασχών A.*Pers.*327; πλείστας ἀνὴρ εἷς.. ἔγημε S.*Tr.*460; κάλλιστ' ἀνὴρ εἷς Id.*OT*1380; ἕνα κριθέντ' ἄριστον Id.*Ph.*1344; also in Prose, ἐπὶ πλεῖστον δὴ χλιδῆς εἷς ἀνὴρ ἀπίκετο Hdt.6.127, cf. Th.8.68; Μυτιληναίους μάλιστα δὴ μίαν πόλιν Id.3.39; πάντων εἷς ἀνὴρ μεγίστων αἴτιος κακῶν D.18.143: without a Sup., Ἐτεοκλέης ἂν εἷς πολὺς κατὰ πτόλιν ὑμνοῖθ' A.*Th.*6. **c.** in oppos., made emphatic by the Art., ὁ εἷς, ἡ μία, Il.20.272, Od.20.110, Pl.*Cri.*48a; τοῦ ἑνὸς οἱ δύο ἀγαθοὶ βελτίους Arist.*Pol.*1287$^{b}$13, cf. Theoc.6.22. **d.** with a neg., εἷς οὐδείς no *single man*, Hdt.1.32; ἓν οὐδὲ ἓν ἴαμα Th.2.51; οὐκ ἐν ἄλλῳ ἑνί γε χωρίῳ in no other *single* country, Id.1.80; οὐχ εἷς, i.e. more than *one*, A.*Th.*103, E.*Andr.*96; εἷς οὐ.., εἷς μή.., emphatic for οὐδείς, μηδείς, Ar.*Th.*549, X.*An.*5.6.12; more emphatic, οὐδὲ εἷς, μηδὲ εἷς, v. οὐδείς, μηδείς. **e.** εἷς ἕκαστος each *one*, each *by himself*, Hdt.1.123, Pl.*Prt.*332c, etc.; αἴσθησις μία ἑνός (sc. γένους) *one* of *each*, Arist.*Metaph.*1003$^{b}$19: pl., ἑκάτεροι ἕνες *POxy.*276.8 (i A.D.). **f.** with κατά, καθ' ἓν ἕκαστον each *singly*, piece by piece, Hdt.1.9, etc.; καθ' ἕν *one* by *one*, Pl.*Sph.*217a, etc.; καθ' ἕν, τό, *list*, *PEleph.*20.7 (iii B.C.), etc.; καθ' ἕν' ἡμῶν ἕκαστον ἀποστερεῖν to deprive each of us *singly*, D.21.142, cf. Men.*Epit.*164, 186; εἷς κατὰ εἷς *one* by *one*, *Ev.Marc.*14.19; but καθ' ἓν γίγνεσθαι, εἶναι, to be *united*, Th.8.46, X.*HG*5.2.16. **g.** with other Preps., ἓν ἀνθ' ἑνός *above all*, Pl.*R.*331b, *Phlb.*63c; but μίαν ἀντὶ μιᾶς *alternately*, *PStrassb.*25.13, etc.; ἐπὶ μίαν ἑκάστην ῥάβδον τιθέντες θεσπίζουσι *one by one, separately*, Hdt.4.67; ἐπὶ ἑνός Pl.*Tht.*157a; ἓν ἐφ' ἑνί Id.*Sph.*229b, *Lg.*758b: ἓν πρὸς ἕν, with or without συμβάλλειν, in comparisons, Hdt.4.50, Pl.*Lg.*647b; πρὸς ἕν' εἷς D.21.131: παρ' ἕνα *alternately*, Luc.*Salt.*12; εἰς ἓν συναγαγεῖν E.*Or.*1640; ἰσχὺς τοσαύτη εἰς ἓν ξυστᾶσα Th.6.85; εἰς ἓν μοίρας συνέκυρσας E.*Andr.*1172; ἐς μίαν βουλεύειν Il.2.379; in full, ἐς μίαν βουλήν Th.5.111; εἰς μίαν νοεῖν Ael.*NA*5.9; ἓν ἐξ ἑνὸς ἐπισεσώρευκεν Arr.*Epict.*1.10.5, cf. Luc.*Asin.*54; ἀπὸ μιᾶς with *one accord*, *Ev.Luc.*14.18; ὑφ' ἓν *at once*, S.E.*M.*10.124; also ὑφ' ἓν θέσθαι τὸ ὂν τῷ μὴ ὄντι Plot.6.2.1; cf. ὑφέν. **h.** in compd. numerals, as an ordinal, τῷ ἑνὶ καὶ τριηκοστῷ [ἔτει] Hdt.5.89, cf. Th.8.109, etc.; so in Att. Inscrr., *IG*2.660.30, al.: later εἷς alone, = *first*, Lxx *Ge.*1.5; μιᾷ τοῦ μηνός ib.8.13. **i.** μίαν μίαν, = κατὰ μίαν, S.*Fr.*201; εἷς εἷς Lxx 1*Ch.*24.6. **2.** *one*, i.e. *the same*, τώ μοι μία γείνατο μήτηρ Il.3.238, etc.; εἷς καὶ ὁ αὐτός *one* and the same, ἓν καὶ ταὐτὸν ἀριθμῷ Arist.*Metaph.*1039$^{a}$28, etc.; ὑπὸ μίαν καὶ τὰν αὐτὰν ἀρχάν Perict.ap.Stob.3.1.121; ταὐτὸν καὶ ἕν Arist.*Ph.*201$^{b}$3; so ἓν καὶ ὅμοιον Pl.*Phdr.*271a; εἷς καὶ κοινός Plu.2.699f: c. dat., ἐμοὶ μιᾶς ἐγένετ' ἐκ ματρός E.*Ph.*156; ἐκ μιᾶς οἰνοχόης Ἐπικούρῳ πεπωκότες Plu.2.1089a. **b.** *possessing unity*, ἧττον μία ἡ μίμησις ἡ τῶν ἐποποιῶν Arist.*Po.*1462$^{b}$3; λίαν ἓν ποιεῖν τὴν πόλιν Id.*Pol.*1263$^{b}$7; τὰ κυρίως ἕνα Dam.*Pr.*437. **3.** *one*, opp. *another*, ἓν μὲν..ἓν δὲ.. Arist.*EN*1139$^{a}$6, *Pol.*1285$^{b}$38, etc.; ὁ μὲν..εἷς δὲ..εἷς δ' αὖ.. Od.3.421 sq., cf. Pl.*R.*369d; εἷς μὲν..ἕτερος δὲ.. X.*HG*1.7.23. **4.** indefinitely, εἷς τις some *one*, S.*OT*118, Pl.*Grg.*471e, etc.; ἐξ ἑνός γέ του τρόπου Th.6.34; rarely τις εἷς S.*Ant.*269, Pl.*Prm.*145d; εἷς γάρ τις ἦν ἕκαστος οὑξειργασμένος each *single* one was suspected, S.*Ant.*262; εἷς ὁστισοῦν Arist.*Pol.*1325$^{b}$28; εἷς ὁ πρῶτος, Germ. *der erste beste*, Is.8.33, D.1.9, cf. Luc.*Herm.*61: alone, like our indef. Art., *a, an*, Κάδμου θυγατέρων μιᾷ E.*Ba.*917; εἷς κάπηλος, στρατηγός, Ar.*Av.*1292, Th.4.50; εἷς Ἀθηναίων D.21.87, cf. Lxx *Ge.*21.15, *Ev.Matt.*21.19, etc.; εἷς ἀπό.. Lxx *Le.*6.3(22). **5.** οὐχ εἷς *many*, A.*Th.*103, Call.*Dian.*33; οὐχ εἷς οὐδὲ δύο not *one* or two only, D.29.12; οὐ μίαν οὐδὲ δύο not *once* nor twice, Lxx 4*Ki.*6.10; ἓν ἢ καὶ δύο ληφθὲν μαρτύριον Plb.2.38.10; εἷς ἢ δεύτερος Jul.*Or.*6.190d: prov., εἷς ἀνὴρ οὐδεὶς ἀνήρ *one* man's no man, D.Chr.48.10. **6.** Math., τὸ ἓν *unity*, opp. πλῆθος, Pythag.*Fr.*5, etc.: pl., ἕνα *units*, Arist.*Metaph.*1056$^{b}$21; ὁ ἀριθμός ἐστιν ἕνα πλείω Id.*Ph.*207$^{b}$7; τῶν προτέρων ἑνῶν Dam.*Pr.*460. **7.** Philos., ἕν, τό, *unity*, the *One*, ἐκ πάντων ἓν καὶ ἐξ ἑνὸς πάντα Heraclit.10, cf. Emp.17.1, etc.: later indecl., ἓν εἶναι τοῦ ἓν παρουσίᾳ Plot.6.6.14, cf. 5.5.5.

**εἷσα**, v. ἵζω I.

**εἰσάγᾱν**, Adv., strengthd. for ἄγαν, Tz.*H.*1.11, 210.

**εἰσαγγελ-εύς**, έως, ὁ, *one who announces, usher* at the Persian and Ptolemaic courts, Hdt.3.84, D.S.16.47, *Klio*12.365 (Alexandria, ii B.C.), *PTeb.*179 (ii B.C.), cf. Plu.*Alex.*46, Jul.*Mis.*365b, etc. **2.** metaph. of the senses, Them.*in de An.*87.8. **II.** *accuser*, Suid. ⊛ **-ία**, ἡ, *information, news*, Plb.9.9.7. **2.** *public announcement*, *IG*12(3).325.16 (Thera, ii B.C.). **3.** *application* to an authority, *PStrassb.*56.25 (iii A.D.). **II.** at Athens, *state prosecution, impeachment*, Σόλωνος θέντος νόμον εἰσαγγελίας Arist.*Ath.*8.4, cf. And.1.43, Lys.30.22, X.*HG*1.7.9, Isoc.8.130, etc.; εἰ. δέδωκας ὑπέρ τινος Hyp.*Lyc.*12; εἰ. ἐδόθη εἰς τὴν βουλὴν ὑπὲρ Ἀριστάρχου Test.ap.D.21.121; εἰ. εἰσαγγέλλειν Arist.*Ath.*59.2. **2.** *a process* brought before the chief Archon, *to punish* κάκωσις (q.v.) or *maltreatment of parents by children, of* ἐπίκληροι *by their husbands*, or *of wards by their guardians*, Is.3.47. **3.** *a procedure employed against unfair arbitrators*, Harp. ⊛ **-λω**, *go in and announce* a person, Hdt.3.118, Lys.1.20, etc.; πρός τινα X.*Cyr.*8.3.20. **b.** *submit* a person's name, *PCair.Preis.*18.7 (iv A.D.), etc. **2.** *take a message in*, E.*Ba.*173: generally, *announce, report* a thing, τὰ ἐσαγγελλόμενα Th.6.41; of the senses, εἰ. πολλὰς διαφοράς Arist.*Sens.*437$^{a}$2, cf. *Insomn.*461$^{b}$3:—Pass., ἐσαγγελθέντων ὅτι.. *information having been given that*.., Th.1.116, cf. 3.3, 6.52. **3.** *lay information*, = μηνύω, X.*HG*3.3.5, *OGI*669.39 (Egypt, i A.D.). **II.** in the technical sense of εἰσαγγελία, *lay an impeachment*, περί τινος εἰς τὴν βουλήν Antipho 6.35, cf. And.1.37: abs., D.18.13; τινὰ περί τινος Id.20.79; τινὰ τῇ βουλῇ And.2.21; ἐν τῷ δήμῳ περί τινος Delat.ap.eund.1.14; τινὰ πρὸς τοὺς ἄρχοντας Pl.*Lg.*763e; τοῖς νομοφύλαξιν ib.910c; τινὰ εἰς τὸν δῆμον ἐπὶ τυραννίδος αἰτίᾳ D.H.8.77: c. inf., εἰ. τινὰ δημηγορεῖν Lys.10.1:—Med., εἰσαγγειλαμένων τῶν στρατηγῶν *SIG*742.21 (Ephesus, i B.C.):—Pass., *to be impeached*, D.18.250, Hyp.*Eux.*3. **-σις**, εως, ἡ, *announcing*, Pl.*Def.*414c. **-τικός**, ή, όν, *of* or *for an impeachment*, νόμος Lex ap.D.24.63, Hyp.*Eux.*3; λόγος D.H.*Din.*10.

**εἰσᾰγείρω**, *collect into* a place, ἐς (ἐν Aristarch.) δ' ἐρέτας..ἀγείρομεν (sc. ἐς τὴν νῆα) Il.1.142, Od.16.349:—Med., νέον δ' ἐσαγείρετο (v.l. -ατο) θυμόν he *gathered* fresh courage, Il.15.240, cf. 21.417:—Pass., θοῶς δ' ἐσαγείρετο λαὸς [ἐς τὰς νῆας] Od.14.248.

⊛ **εἰσάγω** [ᾰ], Ion. impf. ἐσάγεσκον Hdt.1.196: pf. -αγήοχα Epist.Philipp.ap.D.18.39: pf. Pass. ἐσῆγμαι Hdt.2.49:—*lead in* or *into*, esp. *into one's dwelling, introduce*, c. dupl. acc., αὐτοὺς εἰσῆγον θεῖον δόμον Od.4.43; Κρήτην εἰσήγαγ' ἑταίρους *he led* his comrades *to* Crete, 3.191; ἐσ. τινὰ ἐς.. Hdt.1.196, etc.: c. dat., τινὰ δόμοις E.*Alc.*1112 codd.; εἰ. ψυχᾷ χάριν Id.*Hipp.*526 (lyr.); ὅταν σε καιρὸς εἰσάγῃ, = ὅταν καιρὸς ᾖ σὲ εἰσιέναι, S.*El.*39; νὺξ εἰ. πόνον Id.*Tr.*29:—Med., *admit* forces into a city, Th.8.16, 108; *take in with one, introduce into* a league or conspiracy, Ὀτάνης ἐσάγεται Ἰνταφρένεα Hdt.3.70:—Pass., τὴν θερμότητα εἰσάγεσθαι εἰς τοὺς πόρους Thphr.*Ign.*38. **2.** ἐσαγαγεῖν or ἐσαγαγέσθαι γυναῖκα *to lead* a wife *into one's house*, Hdt.5.40, 6.63. **3.** *bring in*, σῖτον Th.4.26; *import*, οἶνον Ἀθήναζε κατ' ἐμπορίαν D.35.35:—Med., εἰσάγεσθαι καὶ ἐξάγεσθαι X.*Ath.*2.3, cf. D.18.145; εἰ. ὧν ἐνδεεῖς Arist.*Pol.*1257$^{a}$32:—Pass., εἰσαγόμενα καὶ ἐξαγ. *imports* and exports, Id.*Rh.*1359$^{b}$22, cf. Hdt.3.6, *SIG*37 (Teos, v B.C.). **4.** εἰ. εἰς τοὺς φράτερας *introduce* a child to the members of one's φρατρία, Lys.30.2 (Pass.), Is.3.75, cf. D.57.54; εἰς Κήρυκας And.1.127; εἰ. τινὰς εἰς τὴν πολιτείαν Arist.*Pol.*1308$^{a}$8; τινὰς ἐς σπονδάς *secure* their *adhesion*, Th.5.35; ἰατρὸν εἰσάγειν τινί *call in* a physician *for* another, X.*Mem.*2.4.3, cf. D.47.67:—Med., of the physician himself when ill, εἰσάγεσθαι ἄλλους ἰατρούς Arist.*Pol.*1287$^{a}$41. **5.** *introduce new* customs, Hdt.2.49 (Pass.); τελετὰς πονηράς E.*Ba.*260; σόφισμα Id.*Ph.*1408; δεινότατον ἔθος εἰς τὴν πολιτείαν D.19.2; εἰ. τὰ εἴδη the doctrine of ideas, Arist.*EN*1096$^{a}$13; αὐλὸν καὶ ῥυθμὸν εἰς τὸν πόλεμον ἀντὶ σάλπιγγος Plb.4.20.6. **6.** δούλιον εἰσᾶγον αἶσαν, for δ. ἆγον εἰς αἶσαν, A.*Ch.*77 (lyr.). **II.** *bring in, bring forward*, esp. on the stage, χορόν Ar.*Ach.*11; Ἥραν ἠλλοιωμένην Pl.*R.*381d; δράματα Id.*Ap.*35b, cf. Luc.*Hist.Conscr.*58; of an orator, εἰ. σεαυτὸν ποιόν τινα Arist.*Rh.*1417$^{b}$7; *represent* in art, Corn.*ND*28, al.

(Pass.). **2.** εἰ. τινὰ εἰς τὴν βουλήν *bring* a culprit *before* the Council, X.*HG*7.3.5, etc. **3.** as law-term, εἰ. δίκην or γραφήν *to bring* a cause *into court, of the prosecutor*, A.*Eu.*580,582, cf. D.24.10, *PHal.*1.125, etc.; ὑπόθεσιν *OGI*669.41 (Egypt, i A.D.); also of the εἰσαγωγεύς II, Antipho6.42, *IG*12(7).3.40 (Arcesine), etc.; οἱ δὲ θεσμοθέται εἰσαγόντων εἰς τὴν Ἡλιαίαν Lex ap.D.21.47. **b.** εἰ. τινά *bring forward* the case of an officer at the εὔθυναι (q.v.), D.18.117: generally, *bring* a person *into court, prosecute*, Pl.*Ap.*25c, al.; in full, εἰ. εἰς δικαστήριον ib.29a, *Grg.*521c (Pass.), cf. *Lg.*910e, al. **4.** *pay in*, τὴν τιμὴν ἐπὶ τὴν δημοσίαν τράπεζαν *IG*2².1013.28; ἀργύριον *PHib.*46.18 (iii B.C.), etc. **5.** *enter, register*, *POxy.*1535.8 (Pass.), etc. **III.** *introduce to* a subject, *instruct*:—Pass., εἰσαγόμενοι, οἱ, *beginners*, Ph.1.175, Gal.*Libr.Propr.Prooem.*, etc. **IV.** intr., *enter*, Sch.T.Il.6.252.

⊛ **εἰσᾰγωγ-εύς**, έως, ὁ, *introducer*, *Schwyzer*784ª7 (Tenos); δικαιοσύνης Arr.*Epict.*3.26.32; *director* of choruses, Pl.*Lg.*765a, cf. *IG*3.1193, *BCH*27.297 (Larymna). **II.** at Athens and elsewhere, *magistrate who brought cases into court*, *IG*1².63.7, Arist.*Ath.*52.2, D.37.33, *SIG* 364.5 (Ephesus), *IG*12(7).3 (Amorgos), *PHal.*1.40, *PTeb.*29.1 (ii B.C.), etc. **III.** in pl., at Samos, *importers* of corn on account of the state, *Ath.Mitt.*37.216 (ii/i B.C.). **IV.** *conduit*, Horap.1.21. **-έω,** *guide*, Zonar. ⊛ **-ή,** ἡ, *bringing in*, ὑδάτων, ὕδατος, Str.5.3.8, *IGRom.* 3.804 (Aspendus); σίτου *PSI*5.500 (iii B.C.). **2.** *introduction*, as of heirs by adoption, Is.10.9 (pl.); of children to a φρατρία, *IG*2². 1237.108. **3.** *importation* of goods, etc., Pl.*Lg.*847d, Arist.*Rh.* 1360ª14, *SIG*278.11 (Priene). **4.** *raising* of taxes, *PAmh.*2.31.6 (ii B.C.), etc. **II.** as law-term, *bringing of causes into court*, Pl. *Lg.*855d (pl.); τῶν κλήρων Is.4.12 (pl.). **III.** *introduction* to a subject, *elementary teaching*, Ph.*Bel.*56.12, D.H.*Amm.*2.1 (pl.), Ph.1. 487, Arr.*Epict.*1.29.23, S.E.*M.*8.428 (pl.); *elementary treatise*, Εἰ. εἰς τὴν περὶ ἀγαθῶν καὶ κακῶν πραγματείαν, title of work by Chrysippus, cf. Plu.2.43f (pl.), Gal.*Libr.Propr.Prooem.* **IV.** *channel of entrance* to a harbour, Str.17.1.18, *Peripl.M.Rubr.*37. **V.** *office of* εἰσαγωγεύς II, Hsch. **-ικός,** ή, όν, *of* or *for importation*, τέλη *import* duties, opp. ἐξαγωγικά, Str.17.1.13. **II.** *introductory, elementary*, συλλογισμοί Chrysipp.*Stoic.*2.7, Ptol.*Tetr.*16, etc. Adv. -κῶς Papp. ad Apollon.Perg.*Con.Prooem.*5: Comp. -ώτερον Ph.*Fr.*8 H. ⊛ **-ιμος,** ον, *that can* or *may be imported*, opp. ἐξαγώγιμος, Arist.*Oec.*1345ª21; τὰ εἰ. *imports*, Id.*Pol.*1280ª39; τέχνη εἰ. *requiring to be imported, foreign*, Pl.*Lg.*847d; εἰ. λαβεῖν E.*Fr.*984; εἰ. πόλεις, of colonies, opp. the αὐτόχθονες of Athens, ib.360.10. **II.** as law-term, of a plea, *maintainable*, μὴ εἰσαγώγιμον εἶναι τὴν δίκην D.33.3, 35.45, cf. Lys.23.5, Din.1.46, *PHal.*1.37; εἰ. χρήματα, with play on sense I, D.32.23. ⊛ **-ιον,** τό, *entrance-fee*, *SIG*1106.51 (Cos). **-ός,** ὁ, = εἰσαγωγεύς I, *CIG*2932 (Tralles). **II.** epith. of Hermes, *watching over imports*, *Ath.Mitt.*37.216 (Samos, ii/i B.C.). **III.** *conduit*, *PTeb.*86.4 (ii B.C.), etc.

⊛ **εἰσᾰεί,** for εἰς ἀεί, *for ever*, A.*Pr.*732, S.*Aj.*570; ἐσαιεί A.*Eu.* 836.

**εἰσᾰείρομαι,** Med., *take to oneself*, Διωνύσου δῶρ' ἐσαειράμενος Thgn. 976 codd.

**εἰσαθρέω,** *look at, descry*, εἴ που ἐσαθρήσειεν Ἀλέξανδρον Il.3.450, cf. Theoc.25.215; εἰκόνα τήνδ' ἐσάθρει *Epigr.Gr.*906 (Gortyn); ἀστέρας εἰσαθρεῖς Pl.*Epigr.*14: metaph., ἱστορίην ἐσαθρήσας *IG*3.716.—Poet. Verb.

**εἰσαίρω,** *bring* or *carry in*, ἡ τράπεζ' εἰσῄρετο Ar.*Ra.*518, cf. Anaxandr.2 (prob.).

**εἰσᾰΐσσω,** contr. -ᾴσσω, Att. -ᾴττω, fut. -ᾴξω: aor. -ῇξα:—*to dart in* or *into*, Ar.*Nu.*543, Aristid.*Or.*49(25).16, prob. in D.C.37. 32; cf. εἰσήκω.

**εἴσαιτο,** aor. opt. Med. of *εἴδω, Il.2.215.

⊛ **εἰσᾰΐω,** poet., = εἰσακούω, *catch the sound of, hear*, Sapph.*Supp.*1. 13, *Oxy.*1787 *Fr.*3; *listen, hearken to*, c. gen., Theoc.7.88, A.R.1. 764: c. acc., ὕμνον *AP*9.189, cf. Call.*Jov.*54, Nic.*Al.*220, Orac.ap. Luc.*Alex.*50: abs., Rhian.19. **II.** *perceive, feel the effect of*, Hp. *Morb.*4.37; contr. fut. and aor. forms ἐσᾴσει, ἐσᾴσειεν are prob. in ib.35,38, al.

**εἰσᾰκοή,** ἡ, *listening, hearkening*, Ph.1.593.

⊛ **εἰσᾰκοντίζω,** *throw* or *hurl javelins at*, τινά Hdt.1.43, 9.49; ἐς τὰ γυμνά Th.3.23: c. acc., τὴν χίμαιραν εἰσηκοντικώς Epin.2.10:—Pass., *dart*, εἰ. μυῖα καθάπερ βέλος Ph.2.101. **2.** abs., *spout*, of blood, E.*Hel.*1588.

⊛ **εἰσᾰκούω,** *hearken* or *give ear to* one, ὣς ἔφατ'· οὐδ' ἐσάκουσε . . Ὀδυσσεύς Il.8.97, cf. Hdt.4.133, al.: c. acc., φωνὴν ἐσάκουσαν *h.Cer.*284, cf. E.*Hec.*559, etc.: c. gen. pers., S.*Aj.*789; τῶν ἐμῶν λόγων E.*IA* 1368: c. dat. pers., Hdt.1.214, etc.; τινί τι Id.9.60; *give way, yield* to a request, Th.1.126, 3.4; of God, τινός or τῆς προσευχῆς Lxx *Ps.* 4.2, etc.:—so in Pass., of the prayer, *Ev.Luc.*1.13; of the person, *Ev.Matt.*6.7. **2.** in Poets, simply, *hear*, τούτου λέγοντος εἰσήκουσ' ἐγώ, ὡς . . S.*Tr.*351; τίνος βροτῶν λόγον τόνδ' εἰ.; Id.*El.*884, cf. *Aj.* 318, Axiop.1.12; ζῶντ' εἰσακούσας παῖδα E.*El.*416. **3.** *perceive, feel effect of*, τοῦ ἐγκεφάλου ἐσακούσαντος τοῦ τρώματος Hp.*Prorrh.*2. 14. **II.** Pass. in strict sense, ἔξωθεν εἰς τὰς οἰκίας εἰσακούεται μᾶλλον ἢ ἔσωθεν ἔξω Arist.*Pr.*903ᵇ13 (v.l. εἴσω ἀκ.).

**εἰσακτέον,** *one must bring into court* (cf. εἰσάγω II.3), ἀδίκημα Ar. *V.*840; τινάς X.*Eq.Mag.*1.10. **II.** *one must introduce*, in speaking, Hermog.*Id.*2.9; in argument, S.E.*M.*6.36.

⊛ **εἰσάκτης,** ου, ὁ, *introducer*, *Gloss.*

⊛ **εἰσᾰλείφω,** *smear* or *rub in*, ἐς τὸ στόμα τῶν ὑστερέων Hp.*Nat.Mul.* 9; *anoint*, Aristid.2.292 J.

**εἰσᾰ́λλομαι,** Ep. 3 sg. aor. 2 ἐσᾶλτο:—*spring* or *rush into*, ἐσήλατο τεῖχος Ἀχαιῶν Il.12.438; πύλας καὶ τεῖχος ἐσᾶλτο 13.679, cf. 12.466; πύργον -όμενοι Pi.*O.*8.38; later ἐσ. ἐς τὸ πῦρ *leap into* it, Hdt.2.66; εἰ. εἰς τὰ τείχη v.l. in X.*Cyr.*7.4.4; ἀνακειμένῳ εἰς τὸν αὐχέν' εἰσαλοίμην S.*Fr.*756; [εἰς ἀσκόν] upon a bladder, Eub.8; ἐπὶ κρατί μοι πότμος εἰσήλατο S.*Ant.*1345 (lyr.).

⊛ **εἰσᾰμείβω,** *go into, enter*, τεῖχος A.*Th.*558.

⊛ **εἰσάμην,** v. εἴσομαι II. **II.** Ep. aor. Med. of *εἴδω. **III.** εἰσάμην, aor. Med. of ἵζω, *SIG*1041.8.

**εἶσαν·** ὑπῆ⟨ρ⟩χον, συνῆκαν, ἢ εἴδησαν, ἢ ἐπεγίνωσκον, Hsch.

⊛ **εἰσαναβαίνω,** *go up to* or *into*, Ἴλιον εἰσανέβησαν Il.6.74; εἰσαναβᾶσ' ὑπερῷα Od.16.449, cf. 19.602; so λέχος, ἀκτὴν εἰσαναβαίνειν, Il. 8.291, v.l. in 24.97; ἀκροτάταν εἰσαναβᾶσ' S.*OT*876 codd. (lyr.).

**εἰσᾰναγκάζω,** *force* one thing *into* another, Hp.*Art.*47 (Pass.). **2.** *constrain*, τινά A.*Pr.*292 (anap.): c. inf., Pl.*Ti.*49a.

**εἰσαν-άγω** [ᾰγ], *lead up into*, εἴρερον *into* slavery, Od.8.529; ψυχὴν οὐρανὸν εἰ. *APl.*4.201 (Marian.); ζωγρείᾳ πρός τινα εἰσαναχθῆναι Plb. 1.82.2. **-αίρω,** *carry off, plunder*, *PFay.*108.16 (ii A.D.). **-ᾰλίσκω,** *expend upon*, τι εἰς ἑαυτόν Antiph.204.10 (troch.), *PPetr.*2 p.6.

⊛ **εἰσανδρόω,** *fill with men*, Λῆμνον παισίν A.R.1.874.

**εἰσαν-εῖδον,** *look up to*, οὐρανὸν εἰσανιδών Il.16.232, 24.307. **-ειμι,** *go up into*, ἠέλιος . . οὐρανὸν εἰσανιών 7.423, Hes.*Th.*761; ἱερόν A.R.1. 1092. ⊛ **-έχω,** intr., *rise above*, c. gen., ib.1360, cf. 4.291: c. acc., γαῖαν εἰσανέχει πέλαγος ib.1578. **-ορούω,** *rush up to*, οὐρανόν Q.S.2.658, 14.2.

**εἰσάντᾰ,** Adv. *right opposite*: ἐσάντα ἰδών looking *in the face*, Il.17. 334; ἰδεῖν Od.11.143; εἰ. ἰδέσθαι 5.217:—also **εἰσάνταν** B.5.110.

**εἰσαντλέω,** *pour in*, κεχηνότι τὴν τροφήν Clearch.12.

**εἰσάπαν,** shd. be read divisim εἰς ἅπαν as in Epict.*Ench.*33.5, Ph. 1.125, etc.

**εἰσάπαξ** [σᾰ], = εἰς ἅπαξ, *at once, once for all*, Hdt.6.125, A.*Pr.*750, Th.5.85, etc.

**εἰσαπο-βαίνω,** *pass out to* . ., c. acc., A.R.4.650, etc. **-δίδωμι,** *repay, refund*, *BGU*190 ii 3. **-κλείω,** *shut up in*, v.l. for ἐν-, Sever. in Rh.1 p.546 W. **-στέλλω,** *send in* or *to*, *PPetr.*3 p.113 (dub.), Ant.Lib.41.2.

**εἰσαπωξεία,** ἡ, dub. sens. in *POxy.*2052.5 (vi A.D.).

⊛ **εἰσᾰράσσω,** Att. -ττω, *dash* or *force into*, τὴν ἵππον ἐσ. *drive* the enemy's horse *in upon* his foot, Hdt.4.128, cf. D.C.51.26; σφέας ἐς τὰς νέας Id.5.116.

**εἰσαρπάζω,** *seize and carry in*, Lys.1.27 (Pass.), 3.11.

**εἰσαρτίζω,** *join* or *fit into*, ἔς τι Hp.*Morb.*2.33 vulg.

**εἰσᾰρύομαι,** *drain, exhaust*, dub. in Hp.*Gland.*12.

**εἰσᾴττω,** Att. for εἰσαΐσσω (q.v.).

**εἰσαυγάζω,** *look at, view*, *AP*5.105 (Diotim.).

⊛ **εἰσαῦθις,** = αὖθις, Ar.*Ec.*983.

**εἰσάφ-ασμα** [ᾰφ], ατος, τό, *touch, grasp*, A.*Fr.*204 (pl.). **-άσσω,** *feel in*, ἐσαφάσσειν τὸν δάκτυλον *feel by putting in* the finger, Hp.*Nat. Mul.*11; but ἐ. τῷ δακτύλῳ ib.36, al.

**εἰσαφέτης,** ου, ὁ, *charioteer*, *Gloss.*

**εἰσαφ-ίημι,** *admit*, X.*Cyr.*4.5.14 codd., Str.15.1.42, J.*BJ*1.13.3: —Pass., Aen.Tact.32.9. **-ῑκάνω** [ᾰ], = sq., πατέρα Od.22.99; δόμον Hes.*Sc.*45; Βέβρυκας Theoc.22.29. **-ικνέομαι,** Ion. **ἐσαπικνέομαι,** 2 sg. aor. subj. εἰσαφίκηαι Hes.*Fr.*170:—*come into* or *to, arrive at*, c. acc., Ἴλιον εἰσαφικέσθαι Il.22.17; συβώτην εἰ. *go into* his house, Od.13.404; Σειρῆνας S.*Fr.*861; Ἑλλάδα E.*Andr.*13; ὥς τινα εἰ. Isoc.4.45: c. dat., τῇ τε ἄλλῃ (sc. χώρῃ) καὶ δὴ καὶ ἐς τὸ Ἄργος Hdt.1.1; φήμη ἐσ. τοῖσι Ἕλλησι Id.9.100: abs., *arrive*, ib.101; οἱ εἰσαφικνούμενοι *visitors* to a country, X.*Vect.*3.12, cf. Pl.*Men.*92b, *IG*2².1191.17: c. gen., σοφιστοῦ (nisi leg. ⟨ἐς⟩) D.Chr.19.3. **-ιξις,** εως, ἡ, *right of settlement*, ἐς Μίλητον *SIG*273.7 (Milet., iv B.C.); εἰς Κύζικον ib. 645.88 (Seleucia in Cilicia, ii B.C.).

**εἰσᾰφύσσω,** *draw into*, A.R.4.1692 (Med.).

⊛ **εἰσβαίνω,** *go on board* a ship, mostly abs., *embark*, Od.9.103, Th.7. 13, etc.; ἐς [πεντηκόντερον] Hdt.3.41: c. acc., σκάφος E.*Tr.*686. **2.** generally, *enter*, πρὸς κόρης νυμφεῖον εἰ. S.*Ant.*1205; δόμους E.*Med.* 380; εἰ. κακά *come into* miseries, S.*OC*997; ἄτης ἄβυσσον πέλαγος A. *Supp.*470; reversely, ἐμοὶ γὰρ οἶκτος . . εἰσέβη S.*Tr.*298; κἀμὲ γὰρ τὸ δυσχερὲς τοῦτ' εἰσβέβηκεν E.*Hyps.Fr.*5(3).20. **3.** *come in, be imported*, εἰσέβαινον ἰσχάδες Alex.117. **4.** *project into*, *PTeb.*86.24 (ii B.C.), etc. **II.** causal in aor. 1, *make to go into, put into*, ἐς δ' ἑκατόμβην βῆσε θεῷ (sc. ἐς νῆα) Il.1.310, cf. E.*Alc.*1055 (lyr.), *Ba.* 466; ληΐδα A.R.2.167.

⊛ **εἰσβάλλω,** *throw into*, ἄνδρα εἰς ἕρκη S.*Aj.*60; εἰς πῆμα A.*Pr.*1075; φάρμακα ἐς φρέατα Th.2.48; ἐσ. στρατιὴν ἐς Μίλητον *throw* an army *into* the Milesian territory, Hdt.1.14; ἐσ. ὗς ἐς [τὴν ἄρουραν] Id.2.14, cf. E.*El.*79; πρόβατα *IG*12(1).677.31 (Rhodes, iii B.C.): c. dupl. acc., βοῦς πόντον εἰσεβάλλομεν *were driving* them *to* the sea, E.*IT*261:—Med., *put on board one's ship*, ἐς τὴν νέα Hdt.1.1, cf. 6.95: abs., Th. 8.31. **II.** ἐσ. τὴν στρατιὴν ἐς . ., of an invasion, Hdt.1.18: but usually without στρατιάν, *throw oneself* into, *make an inroad* into, ἐς Μίλητον ib.15, cf. 16, Th.2.47, etc.; ἐσβάλλειν ἐς τοὺς ὁπλίτας *to fall upon* them, Id.6.70; πρὸς πόλιν ἐσβάλλειν *make an assault* upon it, Id. 4.25: abs., Ar.*Ach.*762; of disease, *come on*, Aret.*CD*1.1, al.: *enter* a country, εἰς τὸν τόπον Thphr.*HP*9.7.1: poet. c. acc., χῶρον εἰ. E. *Hipp.*1198; λέπας Id.*Ba.*1045; *come upon, fall in with*, Βρομίου πόλιν ἕοιγμεν εἰσβαλεῖν Id.*Cyc.*99: abs., ἤφριζον, εἰσέβαλλον ἱππικαὶ πνοαί the horse's breath was foaming, *was close upon them*, S.*El.*719. **2.** of rivers, *empty themselves into, fall into*, ἐς τὰ ἀρχαῖα (sc. ῥέεθρα) Hdt.

1.75, cf. 4.48, al., Arist.*Mete.*351$^{a}$10, Plb.4.41.1; εἰσ. ἐς τὸν Εὐφρήτην ποταμὸν τὸ ῥέεθρον Hdt.1.179. 3. of ships, *make entrance* (sc. εἰς Πόντον), Syngr.ap.D.35.13. 4. abs., *begin*, ἀπό τινος Sch.Pi.*N.*7.1; εἰς λόγον Olymp.*in Mete.*102.12; κατὰ τὸ ἔαρ εἰσβάλλον Gal. 18(1).470.

**εἴσ-βᾰσις**, εως, ἡ, *an entrance*, εἰσβάσεις μηχανώμενοι devising *ways of entrance*, E.*IT*101; *embarkation*, Th.7.30, D.C.41.42; *introductory process, first stage* of a magical operation, *PMag.Par.*1. 397. ⊛ **-βᾰτικόν**, τό, tax in Egypt, *PLond.*2.333. **-βᾰτός**, ή, όν, *accessible*, τῇ τόλμῃ Th.2.41.

**εἰσβδάλλω**, *suck in*, cj. in Gal.*UP*4.7.

⊛ **εἰσβῐάζομαι**, *force one's way into*, εἰς τὰ πρῶτα γένη Plu.*Num.*1; πρός τινα D.S.14.9; ἐς τὸν Βόσπορον D.C.42.47. 2. *force oneself in*, ὁ μὲν γὰρ ὢν οὐκ ἀστὸς ἐσβιάζεται Ar.*Av.*32; τῶν αὑτοὺς εἰσβιαζομένων..ποιεῖσθαι *who force* [others] to adopt them into a family, D. 39.33, cf. *CIG*2685 (Iasos), *OGI*736.6 (Fayûm), *PPetr.*3 p.39 (iii B.C.), etc.

**εἰσβῐβάζω**, causal of εἰσβαίνω, *put on board ship*, τὸν στρατὸν [ἐς τὰς νέας] Hdt.6.95, cf. Th.7.60, etc.; τοὺς ξένους καὶ τοὺς δούλους ναύτας εἰ. *impress* them, Isoc.8.48. 2. generally, *make to go into*, ἐς τὸ περιοικοδομημένον Hdt.7.60; ἐς ἅρμα Id.1.60.

**εἰσβλέπω**, *look at, look upon*, mostly with εἰς, Hdt.7.147, 8.77, X.*Cyn.*10.12: c. acc., E.*Or.*105: abs., X.*Smp.*4.3, Lxx*Is.*37.17.

**εἰσβλητέον**, *one must throw in*, Dsc.2.76.

⊛ **εἰσβολή**, ἡ, (εἰσβάλλω II) *inroad, invasion*, Hdt.6.92, E.*Ion*722 (lyr.), etc.; ποταμῶν Plb.4.40.9; διὰ τὴν ἐς Σάρδις ἐσβολὴν Hdt.7.1; ἐ. ποιεῖσθαι τῇ πόλει Th.8.31 codd.; *irruption* of false opinions, Polystr.p.19 W.; of an illness, *attack*, Aret.*SD*2.12, *CA*1.1. 2. *entrance, pass*, ἐ. ἐξ ὀρέων στεινῶν ἐς πεδίον Hdt.2.75; ἡ ἐ. ἡ Ὀλυμπική *the pass* of Mount Olympus, Id.7.172, cf. Th.3.112; Συμπληγάδων ἐ. E.*Med.*1264 (lyr.): pl., of Thermopylae, Hdt.7.176, cf. 1. 185, 2.141, Jul.*Or.*2.98b. b. pl., *mouth of a river*, v.l. for ἐκβ. in Hdt.7.182. 3. *entering upon a thing, beginning*, καινὰς ἐσβολὰς δρῶ λόγων E.*Supp.*92; ἐ. στεναγμάτων Id.*Ion*677 (lyr.); σοφισμάτων Ar.*Ra.*1104; κανόνων ib.956; *proem, preface*, of a play, Antiph.191. 20, cf. D.H.*Lys.*17 (pl.), Longin.38.2.

**εἰσγένεσις**, εως, ἡ, *produce* of live-stock, *PStrassb.*24.43.

**εἰσγίγνομαι**, *arrive*, *PGiss.*69.17; dub. in Aeschin.*Ep.*11.8. II. τὰ εἰσγενόμενα *incomings, revenue*, *PBaden* 47 (ii B.C.).

⊛ **εἰσγρᾰφή**, ἡ, *enrolment*, εἰς τοὺς ἐφήβους D.C.59.2.

**εἰσγράφω** [ᾰ], *inscribe*, στηλῶν ἐς ἃς οἱ νόμοι ἐσεγράφοντο D.C.37.9; *enrol*, τινὰ εἰς τοὺς φίλους Id.36.53; τινὰς ἐς τὸν κατάλογον Id.*Fr.*109. 5; also of painting, πορφυραῖ σκιαὶ τοὺς ὀφθαλμοὺς εἰς κάλλος -ουσιν Ael.*NA*12.25:—Med., ἐς τὰς σπονδὰς ἐσγράψασθαι ἑαυτούς *to have* themselves *enrolled* in the league, Th.1.31:—Pass., D.C.61.21. 2. simply, *write down*, μαντεῖα S.*Tr.*1167; *send in a report*, *BCH*46. 400 (Mylasa).

**εἰσδᾰνείζω**, *lend at interest as well*, Pl.*R.*555c.

**εἰσδεκτός**, ή, όν, *acceptable*, Lxx*Le.*22.29 (s.v.l.).

**εἰσδέρκομαι**, with aor. Act. εἰσέδρᾰκον: pf. εἰσδέδορκα:—*look at* or *upon*, νῆσον ἐσέδρακον ὀφθαλμοῖσιν Od.9.146; ἐσέδρακον ἄντην Il.24. 223; τί μ' εἰσδέδορκεν; E.*El.*558, cf. *Andr.*615.

**εἰσδέχομαι**, Ion. ἐσδέκ-, *take into, admit*, ἐς τὸ ἱρόν Hdt.1.144, cf. 206: c. acc. pers., S.*OT*238; εἰ. φρουράν *IG*2².43.22: c. acc. loc., οὐκ εἰσεδέξατ' οἶκον E.*Supp.*876: c. dat., ἄντροις εἰ. τινά *receive* him *in* the cave, Id.*Cyc.*35: rarely c. gen., τόνδ' εἰσεδέξω τειχέων, = τειχέων εἴσω ἐδέξω (cf. Sch. ad loc.), E.*Ph.*451: c. acc. dupl., ἐσδέξασθαί τινα συνοικιστῆρα *admit* him as a fellow-colonist, Pi.*Fr.*186; εἰ. τινὰ ὑπόστεγον S.*Tr.*376: aor. 1 εἰσδεχθῆναι in pass. sense, Luc.*Tox.*30, *Merc.Cond.*10. 2. c. acc. rei, σκῆψιν ἀγὼν οὗτος οὐκ ἐσδέξεται Ar.*Ach.*392; εἰ. εὐνομίαν διὰ τῆς μουσικῆς Pl.*R.*425a. 3. of certain animals, *take in* their young after birth, Arist.*HA*566$^{b}$17, *GA*754$^{a}$29.

**εἰσδίδωμι**, intr., of rivers, *flow into*, ἐς.. dub. l. in Hdt.4.49, 50. II. *hand in a report* or *memorandum*, εἰ. περί τινος Aristeas 28, prob. in J.*AJ*12.2.3:—Pass., τὸ εἰσδοθέν *PTeb.*72.462 (ii B.C.); also of a question, *to be brought up* for discussion, ἐν ἀγάρρει *IG*14. 759.12. 2. *send in* the name of a person liable to service or taxation, *BGU*619.8 (ii A.D.), 1198.16 (i A.D.), etc. b. *lay information against*, τινά *PSI*4.417 (ii B.C.), etc. 3. *pay in*, *PPetr.*2 p.31 (iii B.C.).

**εἴσδοσις**, εως, ἡ, *report, memorandum*, Aristeas 28, 33, *PLond.*1.23 iv 1 (ii B.C.), prob. in J.*AJ*12.2.3.

**εἰσδοχή**, ἡ, *reception*, Olymp.*in Mete.*5.6; τοῦ σπέρματος Alex. Aphr.*Pr.*2.64; εἰσδοχαὶ δόμων *a hospitable* house, E.*El.*396. 2. *receipt* of corn, etc., *PTeb.*123.4 (i B.C.).

**εἰσδρομή**, ἡ, *inroad, onslaught*, E.*Rh.*604; of one who throws himself into a besieged place, Th.2.25; into a house, J.*BJ*5.10.3.

**εἰσδύνω**, and Med. **εἰσδύομαι** (v. δύω): fut. -δύσομαι, with aor. 2 -έδῡν: pf. -δέδῡκα:—*get* or *crawl into*, ἐς τὸν θησαυρόν Hdt.2.121. β'; ψυχὴ ἐς ἄλλο ζῷον ἐσδύεται ib.123; εἰσεδύοντο εἰς τοὺς πόδας οἱ ἱμάντες the thongs *entered into* their feet, X.*An.*4.5.14; εἰς τὴν Ἀμφικτυονίαν εἰσδεδυκώς *having wormed his way into* the League, D.11.4. 2. c. acc., *go into, enter*, ἀκοντιστὺν ἐσδύσεαι Il.23.622; ὁ ψὴν τὴν βάλανον ἐσδύνων Hdt.1.193; ἄκακον..τρόπον εἰσδύς *having put on..*, Anaxil.33.3. 3. folld. by relat., οὐκ εἶδεν οὗ γῆς εἰσέδυ saw not into what part of the earth she *entered*, E.*IA*1583. II. of feelings, δεινόν τι ἐσέδυνέ σφι great fear *came upon* them, Hdt. 6.138; εἰσέδυ με..οἴστρημα καὶ μνήμη κακῶν S.*OT*1317; [ἡ ἀλήθεια] εἰς τὰς ψυχὰς εἰσδύεται Plb.13.5.5; λύπη εἰσδύνουσα Andronic.Rhod. p.571 M.

**εἴσδῠσις**, εως, ἡ, *entrance*, Arist.*HA*616$^{a}$28, Agath.2.5; *room for* or *means of entrance*, εἰ. οὐδ' ἀθέρι prob. in *Lyr.Adesp.*2 B, cf. *Gp.*15.2.26.

**εἰσεάω**, *let in*, *Gp.*15.2.27.

**εἰσεγγίζω**, *approach*, dub. l. in Plb.12.19.6 (prob. ἐγγίζοντα).

**εἰσεῖδον**, Ep. εἴσιδον and in Med. form εἰσϊδόμην, v. εἰσοράω.

⊛ **εἴσειμι**, inf. -ιέναι, serving as fut. to εἰσέρχομαι: impf. εἰσῄειν:—*enter, go into*, οὐδ' Ἀχιλῆος ὀφθαλμοὺς εἴσειμι I *will* not *come before* Achilles' eyes, Il.24.463: more freq. with Preps., οὐκ εἴσειμι μετ' ἀνέρας Od.18.184; παρὰ βασιλέα Hdt.1.99; mostly with εἰς, ἐς τὸ μέγαρον ib.65, etc.; πρός τινα S.*Ph.*953, X.*Cyr.*2.4.5; ἐσιέναι ἐς σπονδὰς *enter* into a treaty, Th.5.30: abs., τὸν εἰσιόντα μῆνα the *ensuing* month, And.1.42; τὸν εἰσιόντα ἐνιαυτόν Arist.*Ath.*31.2, cf. *POxy.*1278.17 (iii A.D.), etc. II. of the Chorus or actors, *come upon* the stage, *enter*, Pl.*Lg.*664c; τὸ τοὺς τυράννους..εἰσιέναι *take the part of* king, D.19.247, cf. Lib.*Or.*30.28. III. of public speakers, *come into the assembly*, εἰς ἀγοράν D.24.60; καθ' ὅτι ἂν ἐσίῃ ἡ πρεσβεία Th.4.118; of judges, *come into court*, εἰ. κρινοῦντες D.18. 210. 2. of the parties to a lawsuit, *come before the court*, εἰς ὑμᾶς Antipho 5.80, etc.; εἰ. περί τινος D.19.211; πρός τινα Id.54.32. 3. of the charges or actions, ἡ δίκη εἰσῄει Is.5.17; δίκας εἰσιέναι κατά τινος *enter upon* actions, D.28.17, cf. Is.8.44. 4. *enter on* an office, εἰς ἀρχήν D.59.72; ὁ ἐσιών the *new* king, Hdt.6.59. IV. metaph., *come into one's mind*, Ἀστυάγεα ἀνάγνωσις ἐσῄιε Id.1.116; καίτοι μ' ἐσῄει δεῖμα E.*Or.*1668; ἔλεος εἰσῄει με Pl.*Phd.*58e: c. dat., ἄλγος εἰσῄει φρενί E.*IA*1580, cf. Pl.*Phd.*59a; δέος τινὶ εἰσῄει περί τινος Id.*R.*330d. 2. impers., εἰσῄει αὐτοὺς ὅπως ἄν.. they *began to think* how they might.., X.*An.*5.9.17: c. inf., οὐδενὸς εἰσῄει μοι φθονεῖν D.23.188. V. rarely of things, τὰ εἰσιόντα *what enters into one, food*, X.*Cyr.*1.6.17.

**εἰσέλ-ᾰσις**, εως, ἡ, *charge*, of scythe-chariots, Plu.*Art.*7. ⊛ **-αστικός**, ή, όν, *celebrated by a triumphal entry*, ἀγῶνες εἰ. *CIG*2932 (Tralles), 3426 (Philadelphia), *IGRom.*3.370 (Adada), cf. Plin.*Ep.*10.118; ἱεροὶ εἰ. [ἀγῶνες] *Ath.Mitt.*26.239 (Tralles). ⊛ **-αύνω**, Ep. -ελάω: fut. -ελάσω [ᾰ], Att. -ελῶ:—*drive in*, ποιμὴν εἰσελάων [τὴν ποίμνην] Od. 10.83; ἵππους δ' εἰσελάσαντες Il.15.385; τὴν θήλειαν ὁ ἄρρην εἰ. πρὸς τὰ ᾠά Plu.2.962f; εἰσελαύνειν τινὰ εἰς τὸν τοῦ πράγματος δρόμον *to keep him to the point*, Aeschin.1.176, cf. 3.206. II. as if intr., ἔνθ' οἵ γ' εἰσέλασαν [τὴν νῆα] that way they *rowed in*, Od.13.113; ἐπεὶ εἰσήλασεν εἰς τὴν πόλιν [τὸν ἵππον] when he *marched into..*, X.*An.*1.2.26, etc.: c. acc. loci, εἰ. λιμένα A.R.2.672, cf. 1265; *enter in triumphal procession*, Plu.*Marc.*8; τεθρίππῳ Id.*Publ.*9; εἰς τὰς Ἀθήνας Ael.*VH*12.58: c. acc. cogn., εἰσελαύνειν θρίαμβον Plu.*Mar.*12, *Cat.Mi.*31.

**εἰσελεύσιον**, τό, worse form for εἰσηλύσιον, *Gloss.*

**εἰσέλευσις**, εως, ἡ, *entrance, arrival*, Vett.Val.226.22, Hsch. s.v. ἧξις (prob. l.), Thom.Mag.p.302 R.

**εἰσέλκω**, *draw, haul, in* or *into*, Xenarch.4.13: aor. -είλκῠσα Hdt. 2.175, Ar.*Ach.*379.

**εἰσεμ-βαίνω**, *go on board*, *AP*7.374 (Marc. Arg., nisi leg. εἰσανέβην). **-πλέκω**, aor. 2 Pass. εἰσενεπλάκη, gloss on ἐνεδιάσθη, Hsch. **-πορεύομαι**, Pass., *enter* a country *as a trader*, εἰς τὴν χώραν *IG*1².57.20: expld. by τὸ εἰς πολεμίους ἐμπορίας χάριν ἀπιέναι, Hsch.

**εἰσεντίθημι**, *place in*, εἰσενέθηκε *Epigr.Gr.*517.8 (Edessa).

**εἰσέπειτα**, Adv. *for hereafter*, τὰ..πάρος τά τ' εἰ. S.*Aj.*35, etc.

**εἰσεπιδημέω**, *visit a foreign state*, Pl.*Lg.*952d.

**εἰσέργνῡμι**, *shut up in* (a mummy-case), τὸν νεκρόν Hdt.2.86.

**εἰσέρπω**, aor. εἰσείρπῠσα, *to go into*, ἐσέρπει ἐς ἄνθρωπον ψυχή Hp. *Vict.*1.7, cf. Plu.*Cleom.*8; ἐς τὸ ἱερὸν μὴ ἐσέρπεν (Dor. inf.) *IG*12(3). 183 (Astypalaea, iv/iii B.C.); διὰ τοῦ στομίου Luc.*DMort.*3.2: c. dat., φθόνος βραχέσιν εἰσερπύσας χωρίοις Ph.2.553.

**εἰσέρρω**, *go into, get in*: pf. εἰσήρρηκα Ar.*Th.*1075: aor. εἰσήρρησεν Id.*Eq.*4, Agath.*Praef.*p.139 D.

**εἴσερσις**, εως, ἡ, (εἴρω A) *binding in* or *to*, Sch.Th.1.6.

**εἰσερύω**, *draw into*, [νῆα] κοῖλον σπέος εἰσερύσαντες Od.12.317.

⊛ **εἰσέρχομαι**, fut. -ελεύσομαι: aor. -ήλῠθον, -ῆλθον: in Att., fut. is supplied by εἴσειμι, and impf. by εἰσῄειν:—*go in* or *into, enter*, in Hom. and Poets mostly c. acc., Φρυγίην εἰσήλυθον Il.3.184; ἀλλ' εἰσέρχεο τεῖχος 22.56; αὐλάν Pi.*N.*10.16; ἄλσος, δόμους, S.*Tr.*1167, E.*Alc.*563; οἴκαδε X.*HG*5.4.28; οἴκαδε εἰς ἐμαυτοῦ Pl.*Hp.Ma.*304d; εἰσῆλθ' ἑκατόμβας *invaded* the hecatombs, Il.2.321: but in Prose mostly with Preps., ἐς οἴκημα Th.1.134, etc.; ἐσ. ἐς τὰς σπονδὰς *come into* the treaty, Id.5.36; εἰς τὸν πόλεμον v.l. in X.*An.*7.1.27; εἰ. εἰς τοὺς ἐφήβους *enter the ranks of* the Ephebi, Id.*Cyr.*1.5.1; also εἰ. πρός τινα *enter* his *house, visit* him, ib.3.3.13; of a doctor, *pay a visit*, Gal.18(2).36; εἰ. ἐπὶ τὸ δεῖπνον X.*An.*7.3.21: abs., of money, etc., *come in*, προσόδους εἰσελθούσας Id.*Vect.*5.12. II. of the Chorus, actors, etc., *come upon* the stage, *enter*, Pl.*R.*580b, X.*An.* 6.1.9, etc.; *enter the lists*, in a contest, S.*El.*700; πρός τινα in competition with.., D.18.319. III. as law-term, of the accuser, *come into court*, εἰς ὑμᾶς (sc. τοὺς δικαστάς) D.59.1; but also τοὺς ὑπὲρ τῶν κοινῶν -εληλυθότας δικαστάς Id.18.278. 2. of the parties, c. acc., εἰ. τὴν γραφήν *enter* the charge, Id.18.105; εἰ. δίκας Id.28.17 (so also εἰ. [τὴν καταχειροτονίαν] Id.21.6; εἰ. λόγον κατά τινος Arg. Isoc.11). 3. of the accused, *come before the court*, δεῦρο Pl.*Ap.*29c; εἰς δικαστήριον Id.*Grg.*522b; εἰς ὑμᾶς D.18.103, cf. 21.176; εἰσελθόντες δ' ὡς ὑμᾶς is prob. in Arist.*Rh.*1410$^{a}$18. 4. of the cause, *to be brought in*, ποῖ οὖν δεῖ ταύτην εἰσελθεῖν τὴν δίκην; D.35.49. IV.

*enter on an office*, Antipho 6.44; εἰσ. ἐς τὴν ὑπατείαν D.C.41.39; ἐπὶ τὴν ἀρχήν Id.64.7. V. *consult* a table, εἰ. εἰς ὄργανον Vett.Val.20.12. VI. metaph., [μένος] ἄνδρας ἐσέρχεται courage *enters into* the men, Il.17.157; πείνη δ' οὔ ποτε δῆμον ἐσέρχεται famine never *enters* the land, Od.15.407; Κροῖσον γέλως ἐσῆλθε Hdt.6.125; ὥς με πόλλ' εἰσέρχεται.. ἄλγη A.*Pers*.845; πόθος μ' εἰσέρχεται E.*IA* 1410; νιν εἰσῆλθεν τάδε ib.57: c. dat., εἰσῆλθε τοῖν τρὶς ἀθλίοιν ἔρις S. *OC*372; [Κύπρις] εἰσέρχεται μὲν ἰχθύων..γένει Id.*Fr*.941.9; δέος εἰ. τινὶ περί τινος Pl.*R*.330d; ὑποψία εἰ. μοι Id.*Ly*.218c. 2. *come into one's mind*, Κροίσῳ ἐσελθεῖν τὸ τοῦ Σόλωνος Hdt.1.86, cf. Pl.*Tht*. 147c; ἐσελθεῖν τισι ἡδονήν, οἶκτον, Hdt.1.24, 3.14. b. impers., c. inf., τὸν δὲ ἐσῆλθε θεῖον εἶναι τὸ πρῆγμα *it came into* his *head* that.., Id.3.42; ἐσῆλθέ με κατοικτῖραι Id.7.46; εἰσῆλθε δή με..φοβηθῆναι Pl. *Lg*.835d; τὸν δὲ ἐσῆλθε ὡς εἴη τέρας Hdt.8.137; εἰσελθέτω σε μήποθ' ὡς.. A.*Pr*.1002.

**εἰσέτι**, Adv. *still, yet*, Theoc.27.19, etc.

⊛ **εἰσευπορέω**, *procure in plenty*, τὸ πλεῖστον *Supp.Epigr*.1.366.40 (Samos, iii B.C.); χρήματα τῇ πόλει D.S.16.40; ποθόδους τοῖς ἐγχωρίοις *GDI*3069 (Selymbria): abs., *SIG*364.74 (Ephesus).

⊛ **εἰσέχω**, used intr. by Hdt., *stretch into*, κόλπος ἐκ τῆς βορηΐης θαλάσσης ἐσέχων ἐπὶ Αἰθιοπίης a bay *running in* from the north sea towards Ethiopia, Hdt.2.11; ἡ μεγίστη τῶν διωρύχων ἐσέχει ἐς ποταμόν Id.1.193; ἦν θάλαμος ἐσέχων ἐς τὸν ἀνδρεῶνα the chamber *opened into* the men's apartment, Id.3.78; ἐς τὸν οἶκον ἐσέχων ὁ ἥλιος the sun *shining* into the house, Id.8.137: abs., ἐκ τοῦ Νείλου διώρυχες ἐσέχουσι (sc. ἐς τὴν γῆν) Id.2.138. II. in pictures, τὸ ἐσέχον is *the retiring part, the shade*, opp. ἐξέχον (the high lights), Philostr.*VA* 2.20. b. στέρνα ἐσέχοντα *hollow* chests, Id.*Gym*.35.

**εἰσέω**· ἱκετεύω, Hsch.

⊛ **εἰσηγ-έομαι**, Dor. **εἰσᾱγ-**, fut. -ήσομαι, *lead in*, εἰσηγοῦ σὺ λαβὼν ἡμᾶς Ar.*Av*.647; *bring in, introduce*, ἀοιδάς Simon.174 (dub.); of religious rites, Hdt.2.49; δημαγωγίαν Plb.2.21.8; ἔθος D.H.11.50. 2. *introduce, propose*, τὴν πεῖραν Th.3.20; γῆς ἀναδασμούς Pl.*Lg*.684e; νόμον Diph.38, cf. D.18.148, etc.; δόγμα Ph.1.140, al.; εἰ. περί τινος *make a proposal* on a subject, Isoc.4.170: c. inf., *propose*, εἰ. τὴν αὐλητρίδα χαίρειν ἐᾶν to let her go, Pl.*Smp*.176e, cf. *Cri*.48a, cf. D.H. 6.51, Plu.*Publ*.16; τοῦτο τὸ μάθημα, ὅτι καλὸν εἴη Pl.*La*.179e; εἰ. ὅπως.. Plu.*Them*.20; εἰσηγουμένου τινός *at* his *proposal, on* his *motion*, Th.4.76, cf. *IG*5(1).1451.6 (Messene, ii A.D.), etc. 3. εἰσηγεῖσθαί τινι *represent* to a person, ἐσηγεῖται..τοῖς ἐν τέλει οὖσιν ὡς οὐ χρεών.. Th.7.73: hence, *advise, instruct*, τοιαῦτα μέντοὐγὼ φρονεῖν τούτοισιν εἰσηγησάμην Ar.*Ra*.972; τοῖς νεωτέροις Isoc.1.4; εἰ. τοῖς πολεμίοις ἃ χρὴ καταλαβεῖν τῶν χωρίων Lys.14.35. 4. *relate, narrate, explain*, τινί τι Pl.*Smp*.189d; λόγον τινί Id.*Ti*.20d. **-ημα**, ατος, τό, *motion, proposal*, Aeschin.1.82: pl., Isoc.*Ep*.1.2. 2. *precept*, Nic.Dam.p.26 D. **-ησις**, εως, ἡ, *proposing, advising*, Th.5.30, Ph.2.211, Plu.2.11d; *introduction*, ἐθῶν καὶ νομίμων Ph.1. 166 (pl.); δογμάτων ib.410. II. *a motion*, D.C.36.38. **-ητέον**, *one must move*, Th.6.90. **-ητήρια**, τά, = εἰσιτήρια (quod fort. leg.), Hsch. **-ητής**, οῦ, ὁ, *one who brings in, author*, τῶν κακῶν τῷ δήμῳ Th.8.48, cf. Hyp.*Epit*.3, Arist.*Ath*.27.4, Aeschin.1.172, Ph. 1.103, al., Luc.*Anach*.14, etc. **-ήτρια**, ἡ, fem. of foreg., *she that introduces*, καινοῦ θεοῦ Corn.*Rh*.p.390 H. **-ορία**, ἡ, *reproach*, Suid., Zonar.

**εἰσηθέω**, *inject by a syringe*, Hdt.2.87.

**εἰσήκω**, *to have come in*, v.l. in Ar.*V*.606; of revenues, *BCH*6.18 (Delos, ii B.C.): fut., *to be about to come in*, ἔοικεν..ἐσήξειν (nisi leg. ἐσάξειν) A.*Ag*.1181; εἰς τὴν οἰκίαν ἐσήξειν (nisi leg. -άξειν) D.C. 37.32.

**εἰσηλεῖν**· εἰσάγειν, εἰσελαύνειν, Hsch. (prob. = εἰσειλεῖν).

**εἰσηλ-ῠσία**, ἡ, *coming in, entrance*, *AP*9.625 (Maced.). **-ύσιον**, τό, *entrance-fee*, *IG*2².1368.37, *Ath.Mitt*.32.294 (Pergam., ii A.D.). **-ῠσις**, εως, ἡ, *entrance, right of entrance*, *CIG*3278 (Smyrna).

**εἶσθα**, Ep. 2 sg. of εἶμι (*ibo*), Il.10.450, Od.19.69.

**εἶσθαι**, pf. inf. Pass. of ἵημι (v. ἀφίημι).

**εἴσθεσις**, εως, ἡ, *putting in*, Ph.1.278; opp. ἀφαίρεσις, Dam.*Pr*. 102. II. *insetting* of short lines in lyric strophes, Sch.Ar.*Pl*.253, *Ach*.565.

**εἰσθέω**, *run into* or *in*, J.*BJ*6.4.6, Philostr.*VA*1.28, D.C.62.16, etc.; ἐσθεῖ πρὸς ἡμᾶς *runs up* to us, Ar.*Av*.1169.

**εἰσθεωρέω**, *investigate*, Heph.Astr.3.37.

**εἰσθλᾰσις**, **εἰσθλάω**, v. εἰσφλ-.

⊛ **εἰσ-θλίβω** [ῑ], prob. f.l. for ἐκθλ- in Plu.2.688b, Them.*Or*.14. 197a. **-θλιψις**, prob. f.l. for ἔκθλ. in Philagr.ap.Orib.5.17.10.

**εἰσθρῴσκω**, aor. -έθορον, *leap into* or *in*, ὁ δ' ἄρ' ἔσθορε φαίδιμος Ἕκτωρ Il.12.462, cf. 21.18; διά τινος Ael.*NA*14.24: c. acc., πρὶν ἐμὸν ἐσθορεῖν δόμον A.*Th*.454 (lyr.).

**εἰσί**, 3 pl. of εἰμί (*sum*). **εἶσι**, 3 sg. of εἶμι (*ibo*). **εἰσιδεῖν**, Ep. εἰσιδέειν, aor. inf. of εἰσεῖδον; v. εἰσοράω.

**εἰσιδρύω**, *build in*, ἐσίδρυνται σφι Ἄρηος ἱρόν v.l. in Hdt.4.62.

**εἰσίζομαι**, *take one's station in*, ἐσίζεσθαι λόχον ἀνδρῶν Il.13.285.

**εἰσίημι**, fut. -ήσω: aor. -ῆκα:—*send into*, ἐς τὴν [λίμνην] εἰ. τὸ ὕδωρ, of rivers, Hdt.7.109; εἰ. τοὺς Πέρσας ἐς τὸ τεῖχος *let* them *in*, Id.3. 158; τὴν [κεδρίην] (sc. ἐς τὴν κοιλίην) Id.2.87:—Med., τοὺς πολεμίους ἔφη εἰσέσθαι said he *had let* them *in*, X.*HG*1.3.19; χάριτας *Sammelb*. 4324.8:—Pass., *IG*1².115.18 (Lex Dracontis). II. Med., αὖλιν ἐσιέμεναι *betaking themselves into their own* roost, Od.22.470.

**εἰσίθμη**, ἡ, (εἴσειμι) *entrance*, Od.6.264, Opp.*H*.1.738.

**εἰσικνέομαι**, *go into*, c. acc. loci, Hermesian.7.23. II. *penetrate*, Hdt.3.108; εἰσικνουμένου βέλει *piercing* her with a shaft, A.*Supp*. 556 (lyr., s. v.l.).

**εἰσιππεύω**, *ride into* or *in*, εἰς τὴν πόλιν D.S.17.12: abs., D.C.44.10.

**εἰσίπτᾰμαι**, = εἰσπέτομαι (q.v.).

**εἰσῐτ-έον**, *one must go in*, Iamb.*VP*23.105, al. **-ημα**, ατος, τό, *revenue*, *BCH*6.26 (Delos, ii B.C.): pl., Dor. -ᾱματα *SIG*244 *A* 20 (Delph.). ⊛ **-ήριος**, ον, (εἴσειμι) *belonging to entrance*: εἰσιτήρια (sc. ἱερά), τά, *a sacrifice at the beginning* of a year or *entrance on* an office, D.19.190; εἰ. ὑπὲρ τῆς βουλῆς ἱεροποιῆσαι Id.21.114, cf. *SIG* 695.25 (Magn. Mae., ii B.C.), D.C.45.17; εἰσιτήριοι θυσίαι Hld.7.2: sg., εἰσιτήριον, τό, *entrance-deposit*, *PRyl*.77.37 (ii A.D., ἰσητ- Pap.):— Att. Inscrr. have **εἰσιτητήρια**, *IG*2².17, al. **-ητέον**, *one must go in*, Luc.*Herm*.73. **-ητός**, ή, όν, *accessible*, Alciphr.1.23; εἰσιτητὰ τῷ στόλῳ ποιεῖν Procop.*Vand*.1.20: also **εἰσιτός** J.*BJ*6.4.5, Zonar.

⊛ **Εἰσῐτύχη** [ῠ], ἡ, *Isis-Fortuna*, *CIL*4.4138, 14.2867.

**εἰσκαθίημι**, *dispatch to* a place, ἀργύριον εἰσκατιέναι (sic) Ἀθήναζε *IG*1².6.116.

**εἰσκαθοράω**, *look down upon*, πόλιν ἐσκατορᾷς (Ion. form), Bgk. for ἐγκ-, Anacr.1.6.

**εἰσκαιεικοστός**, όν, *twenty-first*, *IG*11(2).164 *A* 45 (Delos, iii B.C.).

**εἰσκᾰλᾰμάομαι**, (κάλαμος I. 2) *haul in*, as an angler the fish which he has hooked, Ar.*V*.381.

**εἰσκᾰλέω**, *call in*, μάρτυρας Ar.*V*.936, D.28.5; τινὰ πρὸς αὑτόν X. *Cyr*.8.3.1, cf. Theoc.2.132, *PPetr*.2 p.31 (iii B.C.), etc.:—Med., *invite to one's house*, *Act.Ap*.10.23; also, *call* or *have called in*, Plb.21.22.2; [ἰητρόν] Hp.*Prog*.1; *summon*, *PPetr*.3 p.62 (iii A.D.).

**εἰσκατα-βαίνω**, *go down into*, c. acc., ὄρχατον Od.24.222; δόμον Orac.ap.Hdt.5.92.έ. **-δύνω**, = foreg., Timo 34.1. **-ρρήγνῡμι**, *break inwards*:—Pass., ἐσκαταρραγῆναι ῥωγμῇσι Hp.*VC*17. **-τίθημι**, *put down into*:—Med., ἑὴν ἐσκάτθετο νηδύν Hes.*Th*.487, 890 (v.l. ἐγκάτθετο).

**εἴσκειμαι**, used as Pass. of εἰστίθημι, *to be put on board ship*, Th. 6.32.

**εἰσκέλλω**, intr., *put to land*, ποίαν δὲ χώραν εἰσεκέλσαμεν σκάφει; Ar.*Th*.877.

**εἰσκηρύσσω**, Att. -ττω, *proclaim by herald*, Ar.*Ach*.135 (Pass.), *Inscr.Prien*.5.9 (Pass., iv B.C.); *call into the lists for combat*, S.*El*. 690:—Pass., εἰ. εἰς τοὺς ἀγῶνας *SIG*286.11 (Milet., iv B.C.), cf. D.C. 61.20.

**εἰσκλάω**, in Pass., *grow in*, of eyelashes, Dsc.*Eup*.1.50.

**εἰσκλείω**, *place under lock and key*, ἐν θησαυρῷ *PThead*.28.8 (iv A.D.).

⊛ **εἴσκλησις**, εως, ἡ, *summons*, *Cat.Cod.Astr*.2.195.

**εἰσκλύζω**, f.l. for ἐκκλύζω (q.v.) in Str.5.1.7.

**εἰσκλύω**, poet. for εἰσακούω, τευ ἐσέκλυον αὐδήσαντος *IGRom*.1. 1195 (Memnon), cf. Q.S.1.509.

**εἰσκνάω**, in Pass., ἐσκνᾶσθαι· ξυρῆσαι, Hsch.

**εἰσκολάπτω**, *carve upon*, in Pass., Lxx 3*Ki*.6.33(35) (s.v.l.).

**εἰσκολυμβάω**, *swim into*, Sch.Th.4.26.

**εἰσκομ-ῐδή**, ἡ, *importation* of supplies, ἡ ἐσκομιδὴ τῶν ἐπιτηδείων Th.7.4: pl., ib.24; *bringing in*, Orib.*Eup*.3.7.5. ⊛ **-ίζω**, pf. -κεκόμικα Porph. (v. infr.):—*carry in*, χόρτον Hes.*Op*.606; *guide in*, A. *Ag*.951:—Med., *bring in for oneself*, τὰ ἐκ τῶν ἀγρῶν ἐσκομίζεσθαι Th.2.13, cf. 1.117:—Pass., ἐσκομίζεσθαι εἰς τὰ τείχη *take shelter in*.., Id.2.100; ἐπειδὰν εἰσκομισθῶσιν πόλει E.*HF*242; τὸν σῖτον ἐκ τῆς χώρας -κομισθῆναι *IG*2.331.36; τοῖς εἰς ταὐτὸ διὰ ταὐτοῦ -ομένοις Plu.2.699f. II. metaph., *import* into a discussion, *introduce*, δύο λύσεις Porph. *in Cat*.139.30. **-ισμα**, ατος, τό, *that which is brought in*, and **-ιστέον**, *one must bring in*, *Gloss*.

**εἰσκρεμάννῡμι**, fut. -κρεμάσω, *hang up in* a place, *PLond*.3.964.19 (ii/iii A.D.).

**εἰσ-κρίνω** [ρῑ], *enrol, admit*, εἰς τοὺς ἐφήβους *POxy*.477.10 (ii A.D.), etc. II. *cause to enter*, πνεῦμα Iamb.*Myst*.3.13, cf. *PMag.Lond*. 121.432; ὀνείρους μερόπεσσιν Orac. in *App.Anth*.6.197: but more freq., III. Pass., *enter into, penetrate*, D.L.1.7, Ph.2.604, *Gp*. 15.6.2, Iamb.*Myst*.1.8. 2. *to be adjudged*, σοφὸς *AP*9.578 (Leo Phil.). ⊛ **-κρῐσις**, εως, ἡ, *entering in, penetration*, τοῦ ψυχικοῦ θερμοῦ *Placit*.5.25.3, cf. Plot.4.3.9, Zos.Alch.p.205 B.: pl., κατακλίνονται ταῖς εἰ. ἀκολουθοῦντες *order of admission*, Ph.2.481. II. *enrolment, admission*, *PFlor*.79.9 (i A.D.), etc. ⊛ **-κρῐτικόν**, τό, *due paid on enrolment* by ἔφηβοι, *Ostr*.136.

**εἰσκρούω**, *knock in*, πύνδακα Pherecr.105, Thphr.*Char*.30.11 (cj.).

**εἰσκτάομαι**, *acquire*, εὔκλειαν E.*Fr*.238.

⊛ **εἰσκυκλ-έω**, *wheel in*, esp. in a theatre, *turn* a thing *inwards by machinery*, and so, *withdraw it from the eyes of the spectators*, Ar.*Th*. 265, cf. Luc.*Lex*.8: generally, ὄψων παρασκευὴν εἰσκυκλουμένην Ath. 6.270e: metaph., πράγματα δαίμων τις ἐσκεκύκληκεν ἐς τὴν οἰκίαν some spirit *has wheeled* ill luck into the house, Ar.*V*.1475:—Pass., *plunge into*, τοῖς τῆς ἱστορίας διηγήμασι Lxx 2*Ma*.2.24:—Med., c. acc., [ἠρῷ' ἔπη].. εἰσκυκλήσομαι Poet. in *BKT*5(1) p.84. II. εἰσκυκλήσας· περιελθών, Hsch. **-ημα**, ατος, τό, *the mechanism on which the* ἐκκύκλημα *turns*, Poll.4.128.

**εἰσκῠλίνδω**, fut. -κυλίσω [ῐ], *roll into*, [νήσους] ὤχλισσε καὶ εἰσεκύλισε θαλάσσῃ Call.*Del*.33: Com., εἰς οἷ' ἐμαυτὸν εἰσεκύλισα πράγματα what trouble I'*ve rolled* myself *into*, Ar.*Th*.651.

**εἰσκύπτω**, *pop in*, ὄμματα ἐκκύπτοντα..κεἰσκύπτοντα, of a snail, Teucer ap.Ath.10.455e. 2. of a road, *overhang*, ἐπὶ Γαΐ Lxx 1*Ki*. 13.18.

**εἰσκύρω** [ῡ], *enter*, aor. εἰσέκυρσα Ezek.*Exag*.231.

**ἐΐσκω**, poet. Verb, only pres. and impf. (exc. fut. εἴξω, τίνι [σε] εἴξομεν; Jul.*Or.*2.52d):—*make like* (cf. ἴσκω), αὐτὸν.. ἤϊσκεν δέκτῃ he *made* him *like* a beggar, Od.4.247, cf. 13.313:—Pass., δέμας ἶσον ἐΐσκετό τινι he *became like*, Nonn.*D.*4.72. **II.** *deem like, liken*, τάδε νυκτὶ ἐΐσκει Od.20.362, cf. Il.5.181; Ἀρτέμιδί σε.. ἐΐσκω I *compare* thee to her, Od.6.152, cf. Il.3.197, Sapph.*Supp.*13.5, Ibyc.*Oxy.* 1790.45; οὔ σε δαήμονι φωτὶ ἐΐσκω I *do* not *deem* thee *like*, i.e. *take* thee *for*, a wise man, Od.8.159. **2.** c. acc. et inf., *deem, suppose*, οὔ τί σ' ἐΐσκομεν.. ἠπεροπῆα ἔμεν 11.363, cf. Il.13.446; ἄντα σέθεν γὰρ Ξάνθον.. ἤϊσκομεν εἶναι 21.332, cf. Theoc.25.199. **3.** abs., ὡς σὺ ἐΐσκεις as thou *deemest*, Od.4.148. (*Ϝε-Ϝίκ-σκω, cf. (Ϝ)έ-(Ϝ)οικ-α, (Ϝ)ε-(Ϝ)ικ-υῖα.)

**εἰσκωμάζω**, (κῶμος) *burst in like a party of revellers*: generally, *burst in upon*, τινί Luc.*Lex.*9; εἰς τὴν πόλιν Aristid.*Or.*51(27).30: c. acc. loci, Lyc.1355: metaph., εἰσεκώμασεν ὁ ἄργυρος silver *came romping in*, Ath.6.231e.

**εἰσλάμπω**, *shine in*, Thphr.*CP*2.7.4, Plu.2.929c, Plot.5.1.2.

**εἰσλεύσσω**, *look upon*, οἰκεῖα πάθη S.*Aj.*260 (anap.), cf. Man.4.36.

**εἰσμαίομαι**, used by Hom. only in Ep. aor. 1, *touch to the quick, affect greatly*, μάλα γάρ με θανὼν ἐσεμάσσατο θυμόν Il.17.564; ὅς ἐμόν γε μάλιστ' ἐσεμάσσατο θυμόν 20.425.—The pres. εἰσμαίομαι is not found, cf. ἐπιμαίομαι, εἰσματέομαι.

**εἰσμαρτῠρέω**, *introduce evidence*, Sch.E.*Or.*812.

**εἰσμάσσομαι**, Med., Dor. aor. 1 ἐσεμαξάμαν, *wipe upon*, κόλπον ἐς εὐώδη.. ἐσεμάξατο χεῖρας, metaph., of Aphrodite *imparting* her charms, Theoc.17.37.

**εἰσμᾰτέομαι**, *put in the hand to feel*, Hp.*Art.*32; ἐσμασάμενος ἐς τὴν κοιλίην ib.46; in full, τὴν χεῖρα ἔσω ἐσμάσασθαι Aret.*SD*2.9.— The spelling ἐσματευόμενον Hp.*Art.*38, *Mul.*1.70 (v.l.), is corrupt for ἐσματεύμενον, while ἐσματτευόμενον Bacch.ap.Erot. and ἐσμάττεσθαι Gal.18(1).453 are Atticizing forms.

**εἰσμετρέω**, *deliver corn*, *PEleph.*10.3 (iii B.C.), *PPetr.*2p.132 (Pass.), etc.

**εἰσναίω**, aor. Med. ἐσενασσάμην, *dwell in*, Hermesian.7.31.

⊛ **εἰσνέομαι**, *go into*, ἐς δὲ νέονται οὐρανόν *AP*9.59 (Antip. [Thess.]).

**εἰσνέω**, fut. -νεύσομαι, *swim into*, Th.4.26, Ael.*NA*13.6.

**εἰσνήχομαι**, *swim into*, Ael.*NA*14.24.

**εἰσνοέω**, *perceive, remark*, Il.24.700, Od.11.572, A.R.1.1053, *AP* 5.266 (Agath.).

**εἰσόβδην**, v. ὄβδη.

**εἰσοδ-εύω**, = εἴσειμι, εἰ. καὶ ἐξοδεύειν *PRyl.*162.25 (ii A.D.), cf. *Sammelb.*6152.14. **-ιάζω**, *collect* money, Eust.1788.2, etc.:— Pass., *come in*, of revenue, Lxx 4*Ki.*12.4, Vett.Val.291.27; *to be paid*, ὅπως -οδιασθῇ τὰ ὀφειλόμενα *IG*5(1).1432.7 (Messene, i B.C./i A.D.). **-ιασμός**, ὁ, *ingathering of revenue*, Charis.p.577 K., *Gloss.*: generally, *receipts*, opp. ἐξοδιασμός, *Arch.Pap.*1.493. ⊛**-ιος**, ον (α, ον D.H.11.29), *going* or *coming in*, Suid., Zonar.: εἰσόδιοι, οἱ, *visitors*, Antip.ap.Stob.4.22.103 (s.v.l.), cf. D.H. l.c.: εἰσόδιον, τό, *income, revenue*, *PPetr.*2p.54 (iii B.C.): pl., *PHib.*1.116 (iii B.C., -εια Pap.), Thd.*Da.*11.13. **II.** εἰσόδιον, τό, *introduction* to a speech, Aristid. 2.321 J.

**εἰσοδοιπορέω**, *walk in*, ἐς τὸ τέμενος *IG*12(1).677.11 (Ialysus).

⊛ **εἴσοδος** or **ἔσοδος**, ἡ, *entrance*: **I.** *place of entrance, entry*, Od. 10.90, Hdt.1.9, etc.; ἐσόδους Φοίβου *the entrance* to his temple, E. *Ion* 104 (anap.); of a mountain-pass, ἡ διὰ Τρηχῖνος ἔ. ἐς τὴν Ἑλλάδα Hdt.7.176; in a theatre, *entrance* for the Chorus, Ar.*Nu.*326, *Av.* 296, v. Sch.; *entrance-door* of a court of justice, Arist.*Ath.*63.2, etc.: metaph., καλῶν ἔσοδοι *paths* to glory, Pi.*P.*5.116. **II.** *entering, entrance*, εἰ. παρασχεῖν X.*HG*4.4.7, etc.: pl., A.*Eu.*30. **2.** *entrance into the lists* to contend in the games, ἱππείαν ἔ. (cf. εἰσέρχομαι II) Pi.*P.*6.50; also ἡ εἰ. τῆς δίκης εἰς τὸ δικαστήριον *the introduction* of it, Pl.*Cri.*45e. **3.** *right* or *privilege of entrance*, ἔσοδον εἶναι παρὰ βασιλέα ἄνευ ἀγγέλου Hdt.3.118. **4.** *visit*, κακῶν γυναικῶν εἴσοδοι E.*Andr.*930, cf. 952, Lys.1.20; of a doctor, Gal.16.523. **5.** *study, investigation*, Vett.Val.259.7; ἀκροθιγεῖς τὰς εἰσόδους ποιήσασθαι ib. 222.11; also, *method*, ib.108.19. **III.** *that which comes in, revenue*, opp. ἔξοδος, Plb.6.13.1, cf. *IG*14.423 (Tauromenium), 5(1).1390.64 (Andania), *PPetr.*3p.151.

**εἰσοιδαίνω**, *cause to swell*, τὸ δέρμα Aret.*CD*1.2.

**εἰσοικ-ειόω**, *bring in as a friend*, τινὰ γάμοις Plu.*Alex.*10:—Pass., *become intimate with*, X.*HG*5.2.25. **-έω**, *settle in*, dub. in *AP*7.320 (Hegesipp., leg. ἐν-). **-ησις**, εως, ἡ, *place for dwelling in, home*, ἄοικος εἰ. S.*Ph.*534 (dub.). **-ίζω**, *bring in as a dweller* or *settler*, Plb.5.100.8:—Med. and Pass., *establish oneself* or *be established in*, ἐσοικισθέντων ἐς τοὺς Αἰθίοπας Hdt.2.30; ἐς τὴν Κρήτην Id.7.171; εἰς τὸ ἐργαστήριον Aeschin.1.124: c. acc., εἰσοικίσασθαι χώραν Plu.*Sol.* 7: abs., -σαμένου τοῦ ἐσμοῦ *Gp.*15.4.2; βίᾳ εἰσῳκισμένοι Aristid.*Or.* 26(14).29; οἱ ὑπὸ σοῦ εἰσοικισθησόμενοι τῷ οἴκῳ *POxy.*1641.4 (i A.D.): metaph., *make oneself at home*, ἡ παρανομία κατὰ σμικρὸν εἰσοικισαμένη Pl.*R.*424d; λιμὸς εἰσοικίζεται Men.841: c. acc., Κυδίππην κρυμὸς ἐσῳκίσατο Call.*Aet.*3.1.19: c. dat., ἐμὸς αἰὼν κύμασιν αἰθυίης μᾶλλον ἐσῳκίσατο Id.*Fr.*111; but, *take to oneself, give entrance to*, τὴν ψυχήν Porph.*Gaur.*3.5; γυναῖκα *take* to wife, Just.*Nov.*18.11; ψυχῆς εἰσοικισθείσης Plot.5.1.2. **-ισμός**, ὁ, *bringing in as settler*, Hld.8.1.

**εἰσοικοδομέω**, *build into*, πλίνθους ἐς τεῖχος Th.2.75.

**εἰσοιστέος**, α, ον, *to be brought in*, νόμος D.24.25.

⊛ **εἰσοιχνέω**, poet. Verb, *go into, enter*, c. acc., χορὸν εἰσοιχνεῦσαν Od.6.157; οὐδέ μιν (sc. πάτον) εἰσοιχνεῦσι κυνηγέται 9.120; ὁπόσοι τὴν Διὸς αὐλὴν εἰσοιχνεῦσιν A.*Pr.*122 (anap.).

**εἰσόκα**, Dor. for sq., Bion *Fr.*10.14.

⊛ **εἰσόκε**, before a vowel **-κεν**, (εἰς ὅ κε) *until*, mostly with subj., Il. 2.332, 10.62, al. (in 3.409 ποιήσεται is Ep. for ποιήσηται), Emp.26.7, al.: rarely with opt., Il.15.70; in later Ep. with past tenses of ind., A.R.1.820, etc. **II.** *so long as*, c. subj., Il.9.609.

**εἰσολισθάνω**, aor. -ώλισθον, *slip in*, Plu.2.972b.

⊛ **εἴσομαι**, fut. of οἶδα (*εἴδω). **II.** Ep. fut. of (Ϝ)ει- 'rush', 'hasten', δεῦρ' εἴσεται Od.15.213: 3 sg. aor. εἴσατο Il.5.538, etc.; ἐείσατο 15.415; but sts. simply *go*, as εἴσῃ Od.16.313; πάλιν εἴσομαι Il.24.462, al.: c. inf. fut., ἐεισάσθην συλήσειν 15.544.

**εἰσομῑλέω**, *flatter, toady*, in impf., Hsch.

**εἰσομόργνῡμι**, *impress upon*, in Med., Chaerem.14.15 (codd. Ath., sed leg. ἐξ-).

**εἶσον**, imper. of εἶσα (ἵζω).

**εἰσόπιν**, (ὄπις) Adv. *back*: c. gen., εἰσόπιν χρόνου *hereafter*, A.*Supp.* 617.

**εἰσοπίσω** [ῐ], Adv. *in time to come, hereafter*, *h.Ven.*104, S.*Ph.* 1104 (lyr.), Rhian.66. **II.** *backwards*, Opp.*C.*4.362, Q.S.1.243, al.

**εἴσοπτος**, ον, *visible*, βλεφάροις θνατῶν ἔσ. Simon.58.4, cf. Hdt.2. 138, Antipho Soph.6.

⊛ **εἰσοπτρ-ίζω**, *reflect like a glass*, Plu.2.696a:—Med., *look at oneself in a glass*, ib.141c, Iamb.*Protr.*21.κδ'; *see as in a glass*, ἀμυδρῶς τὴν πάλαι λαμπρότητα Lyd.*Mag.*3.1. **-ικός**, ή, όν, *seen in a mirror*, εἰκόνες Plu.2.920f. **-ίς**, ίδος, ἡ, = εἴσοπτρον, *AP*6.307 (Phanias). **-ισμα**, ατος, τό, = sq., Secund.*Sent.*4. **-ισμός**, ὁ, *reflection as in a mirror*, Plu.2.936e.

**εἰσοπτροειδής** (ἐσ-), ές, *like a mirror* or *reflection*, *Placit.*2.20.12.

**εἴσοπτρον** (so *CPR*21.20 (iii A.D.)), mostly in the form **ἔσοπτρον**, τό, (ὄψομαι) *looking-glass, mirror*, Pi.*N.*7.14, J.*AJ*12.2.9, Plu.2.85b, 139f, *Lyr.Alex.Adesp.*37.26, *Anacreont.*6.3.

**εἰσοράω**, Ep. part. εἰσορόων, inf. Med. εἰσοράασθαι: fut. εἰσόψομαι: aor. εἰσεῖδον, Ep. inf. -ιδέειν:—*look into, look upon, behold*, common in Poets, Od.4.142, al., Sapph.*Supp.*13.3, etc., but rare in Prose (as X.*Cyr.*5.1.16, Pl.*Grg.*526c); ἐσορᾶν καλός Pi.*O.*8.19; ἐλεινὸς εἰσορᾶν A.*Pr.*248; ἐσ. τὴν νέα Hdt.8.92:—Med. in same sense, freq. in Hom., εἰσοράασθε ἵππους Il.23.495: mostly in inf., οὐ.. ὀξύτατον.. φάος εἰσοράασθαι whose eye is quickest *to discern*, 14.345; ὥς τε.. ἀθάνατος ἰνδάλλεται εἰσοράασθαι he is like an immortal *to behold*, Od.3. 246; μείζονες εἰσοράασθαι 10.396, cf. 24.252: aor. εἰσειδόμην, imper. ἐσίδεσθ' A.*Pr.*141 (anap.); εἰσιδόμαν ib.427 (lyr.):—Pass., ὅσσον.. ἠελίοιο μεσσηγὺς δύσιές τε καὶ ἀντολαὶ εἰσορόωνται A.R.1.85. **b.** c. part., εἰσορῶ τινὰ στείχοντα E.*Hipp.*51; πόλιν.. μοι ξυνοῦσαν εὔνουν S.*OC*772: parenthetic, ὡς ἕρποντος (εἰσορᾷς) ἐμοῦ since I (thou *seest*) am coming, Id.*Tr.*394 (s.v.l.). **2.** *look upon with admiration*, πάντες δὲ θεοὺς ὣς εἰσορόωσι Il.12.312; μιν.. θεὸν ὣς εἰσορόωντες Od. 7.71; simply, σε μᾶλλον Ἀχαιοὶ εἰσορόωσιν.. 20.166: hence, *pay regard to, respect*, πλοῦτον ἢ εὐγένειαν E.*El.*1097: with a Prep., ἐσορῶντες ἐς τὴν μαντικήν Hdt.4.68: generally, *look at* or *gaze upon steadily*, A.*Pers.*111 (lyr.), E.*Med.*264. **3.** *look on with the mind's eye, perceive*, οὐκ εἰσορᾷς; S.*El.*997, cf. 611; εἰ. ὡς.. Id.*Ph.*501. **4.** of angry gods, *visit*, θεοὶ γὰρ εὖ μὲν ὀψὲ δ' εἰσορῶσι Id.*OC*1536, cf. 1370. **5.** folld. by μή, *take care lest*.., Id.*El.*584.

⊛ **εἰσορμάω**, *bring forcibly into*, ῥυθμὸν Μούσῃ *AP*7.707 (Diosc.):— Pass., *rush into*, c. acc., θάλαμον εἰσορμωμένην S.*Tr.*913:—intr. in Act., εἰσορμᾶν πρὸς Ἱππότας Plu.2.775a.

⊛ **εἰσορμίζω**, *bring into port*:—Pass., *run into port*, of seafaring men, εἰσορμισθέντας X.*Vect.*3.1: aor. Med., εἰς τὸν ποταμὸν εἰσωρμίσαντο Plu.*Cim.*12.

**εἰσορούω**, *rush in*, v.l. in Pi.*O.*8.40.

**ἐΐσος**, η, ον [ῑ], Ep. form of ἴσος, *alike, equal*, Hom., only fem. sg. and pl., always in set phrases (exc. [ἵππους].. σταφύλῃ ἐπὶ νῶτον ἐΐσας *equal in height*, Il.2.765): **1.** most freq. of a feast, *equal*, i.e. *equally shared, of which each partakes alike*, esp. of sacrificial feasts or of meals given to a stranger (for on other occasions the greatest men had the best portions), δαιτὸς ἐΐσης 1.468, al. **2.** of ships, *even* or *well-balanced*, νηὸς ἐΐσης 15.729; νῆες ἐΐσαι Od.5.175, al. **3.** of a shield, *evenly balanced*, ἀσπίδα πάντοσ' ἐΐσην Il.12.294, 13.157, 160, etc. **4.** of the mind, *even, well-balanced*, φρένας ἔνδον ἐΐσας Od. 11.337, 14.178.

**εἰσότε**, for εἰς ὅτε, *against the time when*, Od.2.99, al.

**εἰσοφάγος** or **εἰσωφάγος** [ᾰ], etym. of οἰσοφάγος, Gal.19.125, Pall. *inHp.*2.192 D.

**εἰσοχετεύω**, *conduct into*, Hld.9.3.

**εἰσοχή**, ἡ, (εἰσέχω) *hollow, recess*, opp. ἐξοχή, Str.2.5.22 (pl.), cf. 12.2.4 (pl.); of intaglios, κατ' εἰσοχήν, opp. κατ' ἐξοχήν, *Stoic.*1.108.

⊛ **εἴσοψις**, εως, ἡ, *spectacle*, E.*El.*1085 codd.

**εἰσόψομαι**, fut. of εἰσοράω, Ep. ἐσο- Il.5.212, 24.206.

**εἰσπαίω**, aor. εἰσέπαισα, *burst* or *rush in*, S.*OT*1252, Xenarch.1.3, J.*BJ*4.1.9: c. acc. loci, κρυπτὸν λόχον εἰσπαίσας E.*Rh.*560 (lyr.).

(**εἰσ**)**παραδέχομαι**, *receive* (?), Hierocl.p.29 A.

**εἰσπαραδύομαι**, *slide gently into*, Ph.2.432.

**εἰσπέμπω**, *send in*, σύ μ' ἐσπέμπεις δόμους E.*HF*850, cf. Th.4.16; γράμματα πρὸς βασιλέα Id.1.137; *suborn* agents, S.*OT*705, And.2.4; ῥήτορας *send* them *into court, instruct* them, Pl.*Euthd.*305b; τῷ μὴ καλῷ θάρρει τὸν κάλλιστον φόβον *pit* against.., Id.*Lg.*671d.

**εἰσπεράω**, fut. -άσω [ᾱ], Ion. -ήσω, *pass over into*, Χαλκίδα τ' εἰσεπέρησα Hes.*Op.*655: abs., Orph.*A.*442.

**εἰσπέτομαι**, fut. -πτήσομαι: aor. εἰσεπτόμην Ar. (v. infr.), but 3 sg. -έπτατο Il.21.494; part. ἐσπτόμενοι D.C.45.17: also in Act.

form -έπτην Ath.9.395a, Plu.2.461e, etc.: aor. Pass. in med. sense, -πετασθῆναι Arist.*HA*624$^{b}$6:—*fly into, fly in*, c. acc., κοίλην εἰσέπτατο πέτρην Il. l.c.; ἐς τὸν ἀέρα Ar.*Av.*1173; of weapons, ἐς τοὺς ὀφθαλμοὺς καὶ πρὸς τὰς χεῖρας D.C.40.22: metaph. of reports, Hdt.9.100, 101.

**εἰσπηδάω,** *leap in*, ἐς τὰς λίμνας Hdt.4.132; εἰς τὸν πηλόν X.*An.*1.5.8. 2. *burst in*, εἰσπηδήσας πρός με νύκτωρ Μειδίας Test.ap.D. 21.22; εἰς τὴν οἰκίαν ib.78, cf. *PHal.*1.169 (iii B.C.); εἰς τὰ συνέδρια *Hell.Oxy.*10.2: abs., *rush in*, Men.*Sam.*219, *Act.Ap.*16.29.

**εἰσπηδησιών,** ῶνος, ὁ, *house-breaker*, *Gloss.*

**εἰσπίπτω,** fut. -πεσοῦμαι: aor. -έπεσον:—*fall into*, generally with a notion of violence, *rush* or *burst in*, ἐς τὰς πόλιας Hdt.5.15; ἐς τὰς νέας Id.8.56; ἐς οἴκημα Th.2.4, etc.; of the sea, Id.4.24: poet. c. dat., ἐσπίπτει δόμοις E.*Ion*1196. 2. simply, *fall into*, ἐς χωρίον Th.1.106; ἐς χαράδρας Id.3.98, etc.; ἐσ. ἐς εἱρκτήν *to be thrown* into prison, Id.1.131: in Poets, c. acc., ἐσπεσοῦσα δικτύων βρόχους E.*Or.*1315; ὄχλον γὰρ ἐσπεσεῖν ᾐσχυνόμην *to go into* the crowd, Id.*Hel.*415; ἐσ. πέπλους *seek shelter within* my robes, Id.*Tr.*1181; πτέρυγας ἐσπίτνων ἐμάς ib.751; κτύπου κέλευθον ἐσπεσόντος a noise *having come into* the street, Id.*Or.*1312. 3. *fall into a certain condition*, δούλειον ἦμαρ εἰ. Id.*Andr.*99; ξυμφοράν ib.983; γῆρας Id.*Ion*700: in Th.4.4 ἐνέπεσε shd. be read. II. *make an onset, attack*, Hdt. 1.63, S.*Aj.*55; ἐ. ἐς τὸν πεζόν Hdt.4.128; ἐς τοὺς ἀγρούς Th.2.22; ἐπὶ τὰς θύρας 'besiege the door', Plu.*Oth.*17. III. *come in*, of payments, Meyer *Ostr.*82.4 (iv A.D.).

**εἰσπίτνω,** poet. form of εἰσπίπτω, E.*Tr.*751.

**εἰσπίφρημι,** inf. -πιφράναι, = εἰσφρέω (q.v.), Arist.*HA*541$^{b}$11: aor. εἰσέφρηκα; inf. -φρῆναι Hsch.

⊛ **εἰσπλέω,** fut. -πλεύσομαι, *sail into, enter*, ἐς τὰ στενά Th.2.86, cf. 89, etc.: poet. c. acc., E.*IT*1389: c. acc. et dat., ὑμέναιον δόμοις εἰσέπλευσας S.*OT*423. 2. abs., *sail in*, ἐπ' ἀριστερὰ ἐσπλέοντι *as one sails in*, Hdt.6.33; στόμα ναυσὶ ταῖς μεγίσταις ἱκανὸν εἰσπλεῖν Pl.*Criti.*115d; εἰσπλέοντας ἐκπλέοντάς τε Pl.Com.183; Μεγαρεῦσι μηδὲν ἐσπλεῖν Th.3.51, cf. X.*HG*2.4.29; of corn, *to be imported*, D. 20.31.

**εἰσπληρόω,** *fill full*, in Med., Epicur.*Sent.*10 codd. (ἐκπλ- Diog. Oen.). II. *pay in full*, *PLond.*5.1841.26 (vi A.D.).

**εἴσπλοια,** ἡ, = sq., *EM*89.36.

⊛ **εἴσπλοος,** contr. -**πλους,** ὁ, *sailing in* of ships, βιάσασθαι τὸν ἔσ. Th.7.22, cf. 24 (pl.), X.*HG*2.2.9. 2. *right of entry*, εἶναι αὐτῷ εἴ. καὶ ἔκπλουν αὐτοῖς εἶναι καὶ ἐν πολέμῳ καὶ ἐν εἰρήνῃ *IG*12(7).8 (Amorgos), etc. II. *entrance of a harbour*, Th.4.8 (pl.); λιμὴν στενόν τινα ἔχων εἴ. Pl.*Ti.*25a.

**εἴσ-πνευσις,** εως, ἡ, *inhalation*, opp. ἔκπνευσις, Arist.*Ph.*243$^{b}$26. -**πνευστέον,** *one must inhale*, Gal.6.359.

**εἰσπνέω,** fut. -πνεύσομαι, *inhale*, opp. ἀναπνέω, ἐκπνέω, Arist.*Resp.*472$^{b}$3, *Pr.*887$^{b}$17. 2. c. acc., *inhale*, ἀέρα Hld.2.35; εὐοσμίας Aristaenet.1.3. II. *breathe upon*, με αὔρα τις εἰσέπνευσε Ar.*Ra.*314 (Pass., ἀνέμῳ ἐσπνεῖσθαι Philostr.*VA*2.8); τινί Ael.*VH*3.12 (a Lacedaemonian phrase for *inspire with love*); ἐς τὴν ἀναπνοήν Aret. *SA*1.7.

**εἰσπνήλας** or **εἴσπνηλος,** ου, ὁ, *lover* (cf. foreg. II), Call.*Fr.*169, Theoc.12.13.

**εἰσπνοή,** ἡ, *inspiration, inhalation*, opp. ἐκπνοή, Arist.*Resp.*471$^{a}$8, cf. Str.3.5.7; μιᾷ ἐσπνοῇ θνήσκουσι Aret.*SA*1.7.

**εἴσπνοος,** ον, *inhaling*, Hp.*Epid.*6.6.1.

⊛ **εἰσποι-έω,** *give in adoption*, υἱόν τινι Pl.*Lg.*878a; τὸν παῖδα εἰς τὸν οἶκόν τινος D.43.15; τοὺς σφετέρους παῖδας εἰς ἑτέρους οἴκους εἰσποιοῦσιν Is.10.17 (but the same phrase is used of a father who *begets*, Id.6.22); εἰ. τινὰ εἰς τὰ χρήματά τινος *make* him *heir* to the property, Id.10.12, cf. 16, 17, etc.; εἰ. σαυτὸν Ἄμμωνι, of Alexander, Plu.*Alex.*50: metaph., [ἡ παντάρβη] πᾶν τὸ ἐγγὺς ἐσποιεῖ αὐτῇ *attracts*, Philostr. *VA*3.46:—Med., *adopt as one's son*, D.44.34, Ph.2.86, D.C.44.5:—Pass., εἰσποιηθῆναι πρός τινα *to be adopted* into his family, D.44.27; ἐπὶ τὸ ὄνομά τινος ib.36. 2. generally, εἰ. τινὰς εἰς λῃτουργίαν *bring new* persons *into* the public service, Id.20.19, 20; τῶν πραττομένων εἰσεποίει κοινωνὸν αὑτόν *forced* himself *in* as partaker, Din.1.32; εἰ. ἐγκώμιον εἰς τὴν ἱστορίαν *introduce* panegyric into history, Luc. *Hist.Conscr.*9; εἰ. ἑαυτὸν εἰς δύναμίν τινος *thrust* himself into another's authority, Plu.*Pomp.*16; εἰ. Ἡσιόδῳ Θεογονίαν *father* it on him, Paus.9.27.2. 3. τὸ τάχος [τὴν τίγριν] ἐσ. τοῖς ἀνέμοις *adopts into the family of* winds, i.e. *makes* it *as swift as* the winds, Philostr.*VA*3.48. II. Med., *intervene, meddle* in an affair, *CPHerm.*6.10 (iii A.D.). -**ησις,** εως, ἡ, *adoption*, Is.10.14, Plu.*Oth.*16, etc. -**ητός,** ή, όν, *adopted*, Lys.*Fr.*55, D.44.34, 60.4.

**εἰσπομπή,** ἡ, *introduction*, Suid.

⊛ **εἰσπορεύω,** *lead in*, οἴκαδε E.*El.*1285:—Pass., *go into, enter*, X. *Cyr.*2.3.21, *UPZ*6.30 (iii B.C.); εἰς τὸ ἄδυτον *OGI*56.4 (iii B.C.); πρός τινα *Act.Ap.*28.30. Used for εἰσέρχομαι in later Gr., cf. *AB*91.

**εἰσπορίζω,** *supply*, v.l. in Isoc.5.121.

**εἰσ-πράκτης,** ου, ὁ, *exactor, taskmaster*, Aq.*Ex.*5.13. -**πρακτος,** ον, *chargeable*, *BGU*486.13 (ii A.D.). -**πράκτωρ,** ορος, ὁ, = εἰσπράκτης, Hsch. ⊛ -**πραξις,** εως, ἡ, *getting in* or *collection* of taxes or dues, τοῦ θύματος Th.5.53; τῶν εἰσφορῶν D.24.8, cf. *SIG*364*A*50 (Ephesus), *IG*2$^{2}$.1273.24, etc.; βαρύνεσθαι.. ἀδίκοις εἰσπράξεσι *exactions*, *OGI*669.5, cf. Plu.*Demetr.*27. II. *levy* of recruits, Wilcken *Chr.*469.4 (iv A.D.).

**εἰσπράσσω,** Att. -ττω, *get in* or *exact*, φόρον *IG*1$^{2}$.65.16, cf. 2$^{2}$.1172.18, Pl.*Lg.*949d, Plb.13.7.3, Plu.2.1044a: c. acc. pers., τοὺς ὑπερημέρους D.21.11, cf. 24.13; οὐκ εἰσέπραξε τὸν δῆμον *did* not *charge* the people [with it], Decr.ap.D.18.115: c. dupl. acc., τοσοῦτον πλῆθος χρημάτων εἰ. τοὺς συμμάχους Isoc.5.146; προσήκει ὑμᾶς τοῦτον εἰσπρᾶξαί μοι τὰ ἀναλώματα Id.50.67:—Med., *exact for oneself, have paid one*, κακὸν δίκαιον εἰσεπράξατο E.*IT*559; Med. is freq. interchangeable with Act., D.21.155: so in pf. Pass., πικρῶς εἰσπράττειν με, ὥσπερ καὶ παρὰ τῶν ἄλλων εἰσπέπρακται Id.35.44; also εἰ. τιμωρίαν *exact* vengeance, Jul.*Or.*2.58a:—Pass., of the money, *to be exacted*, D.19.21, *IG*2.814$^{a}$*A*24; of persons, *have* money *exacted from one*, *have to pay* it, D.33.24.

**εἰσπτήματα,** gloss on εἰσαφάσματα, Hsch.

**εἰσπτύω,** *spit upon*, τινί Arist.*HA*613$^{a}$4.

**εἰσράπτω,** *sew on*, in Pass., Gal.18(2).578.

**εἰσρέω,** fut. -ρυήσομαι Isoc.8.140, Luc.*Alex.*42: aor. -ερρύην:—*stream in* or *into*, E.*IT*260; opp. ἐκρεῖν, Pl.*Phd.*112b: metaph., πλοῦτος εἰ. εἰς τὴν πόλιν Isoc. l.c.; εἰσερρύη νόμισμα εἰς τὴν Σπάρτην Plu.*Lyc.*30; τὸ πάθος εἰσερρύη *slipped in*, Pl.*Phdr.*262b; ἐπιστῆμαι εἰσρέουσι Id.*Phlb.*62c; ἁμάρτημα εἰσρεῖ D.H.*Rh.*10.17; πόθος εἰσερρύη πάντας εὐνομίας Plu.*Num.*20.

**εἰσρήσσω,** gloss on *irrumpo*, Dosith.p.434K.

**εἰσ-ροή,** ἡ, *influx*, Ael.*NA*1.53, Marcian.*Peripl.*1.1; τοῦ ἀέρος Porph.*Gaur.*3.3. -**ροια,** ἡ, = foreg., ὑδάτων *POxy.*1409.19 (iii A.D.). -**ροος,** contr. -**ρους,** = foreg., Arist.*Mu.*393$^{a}$19. -**ρυσις,** εως, ἡ, = foreg., *IG*11(2).199*A*55 (Delos, iii B.C.).

**εἰσσπάομαι,** *draw into oneself*, τινὰ εἰς τὸν οἶκον Lxx *Ge.*19.10.

**εἶστε,** Delph., = ἔστε, *SIG*241.69, 120.

**εἰστείχω** (for εἰσστ-), = εἰσέρχομαι, *Schwyzer* 633.1, al. (Lesbos).

**εἰστελέω,** *contribute*, *PFay.*20.2 (iii/iv A.D.). II. Pass., *to be received into* a class, εἰς γένος Pl.*Plt.*290e.

⊛ **εἰστίθημι,** *put into, place in*, τι ἔς τι Th.4.100, cf. Hdt.1.123; τινὰ ἐς τὰς χεῖράς τινι ib.208, etc.; νεκρὸν ἐς ἅμαξαν Id.9.25. 2. esp. *put on board* ship, πάντα ἐσθέντες (sc. ἐς τὰς πεντηκοντέρους) Id.1.164:—Med., ἐσθέμενοι τέκνα καὶ γυναῖκας ibid., cf. 4.179, E.*Hel.*1566, X.*HG*1.6.20; *to take*, ἐς φορεῖον App.*BC*4.19. 3. Pass., *to be entered*, of a judgement in court, *PPetr.*3p.39 (iii B.C.).

**εἰστιτρώσκω,** aor. ἐσέτρωσα, *perforate, pierce*, τῷ ὀστέῳ μέσφα μήνιγγος Aret.*CD*1.2.

**εἰστοξεύω,** *shoot arrows at*, Hdt.9.49. II. ἐσ. βιβλία ἐς τὸ στρατόπεδον *shoot* papers *attached to arrows into..*, D.C.48.25. III. metaph., τὰ δρώμενα τὰ πάθη ταῖς ψυχαῖς εἰστοξεύονται Hld.3.7.

**εἰστρέπομαι,** *turn in*, [τὰ ἐκτὸς] ἐντὸς εἰ. *turn* outside *in*, Arist. *HA*621$^{a}$8, cf. Heliod.ap.Orib.46.10.4:—Pass., fut. εἰστρᾰπήσομαι Antyll.ap.Aët.7.74.

**εἰστρέχω,** aor. 1 subj. εἰσθρέξωσιν Lyc.1163: aor. 2 -έδρᾰμον Th. 4.67, Theoc.13.24: pf. εἰσδεδράμηκα Men.*Sam.*146:—*run in*, Th. l.c.; εἰσέδραμε Φᾶσιν, of a ship, Theoc. l.c.; ἡ θεὸς (sc. ποδάγρα) διὰ ποδῶν εἰ. Luc.*Ocyp.Praef.*

**εἰστρῡπάω,** intr., *slip in through a hole*, Ael.Dion.*Fr.*161, Suid.; cf. ἐκτρυπάω II.

**εἰσφαίνω,** *inform*, f.l. in Philomnest.Hist.1.

⊛ **εἰσφέρω,** fut. εἰσοίσω E.*Ba.*367: aor. 1 εἰσήνεγκα Archil.78.2 (s.v.l.): pf. εἰσενήνοχα D.27.36: plpf. -όχειν Id.24.19:—*carry in*, εἴσω Od.7.6; ἐσ. ἀγγελίας Hdt.1.114; ἐς τὠυτὸ ἐσ. Id.9.70; τινὰ εἰς τὸ λογιστήριον *PAmh.*2.77.22 (ii A.D.). 2. *bring in, contribute*, τῖμον Archil. l.c.; χρήματα X.*Hier.*9.7, Plu.*Publ.*12; εἰ. τινὶ ἔρανον Pl.*Smp.*177c, cf. X.*Cyr.*7.1.12; at Athens, etc., *pay the property-tax* (v. εἰσφορά II), ἐσ. ἐσφοράν Th.3.19, etc.; εἰσφοράς Antipho 2.2.12, Lys.18.7: and abs., εἰ. εἰς τὴν πόλιν D.27.36; εἰ. ἀφ' ὑπαρχούσης οὐσίας Id.21.157. 3. *bring in* or *upon*, πένθος δόμοις E.*Ba.*367; νόσον καινὴν γυναιξί ib.353; πόλεμον Ἑλλήνων χθονί Id.*Hel.*38; δειλίαν ἐσφέρει τοῖς ἀλκίμοισι *brings* cowardice *into* the brave, Id.*Supp.*540. 4. *introduce*, καινὰ δαιμόνια X.*Mem.*1.1.2; ψεῦδος Plb.2.58.12; esp. of political measures, *bring forward, propose*, γνώμην Hdt.3.80; γνώμην ἐς τὸν δῆμον Th.8.67; εἰ. νόμον, = Lat. *legem rogare*, D.23.218, 24.19; ψηφίσματα *IG*2$^{2}$.1329.10; τιμάς ib.1343.29: abs., ἐσ. ἐς τὰς βουλὰς περί τινος Th.5.38; εἰς τοὺς νομοφύλακας Pl.*Lg.*772c; τὴν δὲ βουλὴν εἰσενεγκεῖν, ὅτῳ τρόπῳ.. X.*HG*1.7.7:—Pass., τὰ εἰσφερόμενα [ψηφίσματα] Arist.*Pol.*1298$^{b}$33. b. of persons, *propose, nominate*, Pl.*Lg.*961b:—Pass., ibid.; τοὺς -ομένους ὑπὸ τῶν ὑπάτων πρεσβευτάς Plb.35.4.5. II. Med., fut. ἐσοίσομαι E.*Hel.*664 (lyr.): Ion. aor. 1 ἐσενείκασθαι Hdt. (v. infr.): pf. Pass. εἰσενήνεγμαι (v. infr.):—*carry with one, sweep along*, of a river, Il.11.495. 2. *bring in for oneself*, τὰ ἐκ τῶν ἀγρῶν ἐς τὸ τεῖχος Hdt.5.34, cf. Th.5.115:—so in Pass., σῖτον ἐσενηνεῖχθαι or -έχθαι Hdt.9.41. 3. *bring in with one, introduce*, τοὔνομα ἐς τὴν ποίησιν Id.2.23; πῶμ' ηὗρε κεἰσηνέγκατο θνητοῖς E.*Ba.*279; [λόγον] ἐσφέρεσθαι *to utter* it, Id.*Hel.*664 (lyr.); ν' μνᾶς εἰς τὸν οἶκον εἰσενηνεγμένη *having brought* 50 minae *as a dowry* into the family, D.27.4, cf. 41.4; προῖκα εἰσενεγκαμένη Thphr.*Char.*22.10. 4. *contribute*, εἰσενήνεκται.. οὐκ ἔλαττον μ' μνῶν Lys.19.43, cf. *Michel* 473.9 (Mylasa, ii B.C.); *apply, employ*, πᾶσαν εἰ. σπουδὴν καὶ φιλοτιμίαν Plb.21.29.12, cf. Chrysipp.*Stoic.*2.293, *IG*2$^{2}$.1343.23, *Inscr.Prien.*111.126 (i B.C.), D.S.1.84; ἀνδρείαν Onos.4.2; θάρσος J.*AJ*18.8.5; ἰσχύν ib.17.5.6; φιλονεικίαν Ael.*VH*12.64. 5. like προσφέρεσθαι, *eat*, Hp.*VM*3, Ant.Lib.11.1; *drink* water, Arist.*GA*767$^{a}$32. 6. *draw breath*, Id.*Somn.Vig.*456$^{a}$17. III. Pass., *to be brought in, introduced*, ἐσενειχθέντος σιδηρίου Hdt.9.37. 2. *rush in*, ἐς τὴν ὕλην Th.3.98.

**εἰσφθείρομαι,** aor. -εφθάρην [ᾰ], *make entry to one's undoing*, εἰς τὴν βασιλείαν J.*BJ*1.26.1, cf. Poll.9.158, Suid. s.v. εἰσέρρησεν; as an

abusive term, οὐκ εἰσφθερεῖσθε θᾶττον.. ἐκποδών; Men.*Pk*.276; θᾶττον εἰσφθάρηθι σύ Id.*Sam*.229.

**εἴσφλᾰσις**, ιος, ἡ, Ion. for ἔσθλ–, *crushing inwards*, Hp.*VC*3.

**εἰσφλάω**, Ion. for ἐσθλ–, *crush in*, Hp.*VC*2 (Pass.).

**εἰσφοιτ-άω**, pf. –πεφοίτηκα, *go often into*, ἐς τοὐπτάνιον Ar.*Eq*. 1033; πρὸς τὴν ἄλοχον E.*Andr*.945: abs., Lys.*Fr*.58: c. acc., κλισίας Q.S.3.433; *to be imported*, of goods, D.C.43.24, 60.11. **–ησις**, εως, ἡ, *inroad, invasion*, τῶν Περσῶν Agath.4.19 (pl.).

* **εἰσ-φορά**, ἡ, (εἰσφέρω) *carrying* or *gathering in*, X.*Oec*.7.40. II. at Athens, etc., *property-tax* levied for purposes of war, εἰσφορὰς εἰσφέρειν Antipho 2.2.12, Lys.30.26, cf. Th.3.19, etc. b. in Egypt, *special tax*, *PTeb*.89.74, 124.35 (pl.), etc. 2. generally, *contribution*, χρημάτων Pl.*Lg*.955d; αἱ εἰ. τῶν τελῶν Arist.*Pol*.1313[b] 26. III. *introduction, proposal*, νόμων D.H.10.4, cf. D.C.37. 51. **–φορέω**, = εἰσφέρω, Od.6.91, 19.32, Th.2.75, Diph.60.9, A.R. 4.1145. 2. Med., = εἰσφέρω II. 5, Parth.9.5. **–φόριον**, τό, *tax-payment*, *PFlor*.151.6. **–φορος**, ὁ, *person liable to pay*, *POxy*. 1117.15 (ii A.D.).

**εἰσφράσσω**, aor. 2 Pass., εἰσφρᾰγέντων τῶν τρυπημάτων v.l. in Nicom.*Harm*.10.

**εἰσφρέω**, impf. εἰσέφρουν D.20.53: fut. –φρήσω Ar.*V*.892, –φρήσομαι (in same sense) D.8.15: aor. 1 –έφρησα Plb.21.27.7, *PLips*.39. 11 (iv A.D.): impf. Med. εἰσεφρούμην E.*Tr*.652; cf. εἰσπίφρημι:—*let in, admit*, Ar. l.c.; στράτευμα D.20.53:—Med., *bring in with one*, E. l.c.; also εἰσφρήσασθαι· καυχήσασθαι, μετὰ σπουδῆς εἰσενεγκεῖν, Hsch. 2. *swallow*, Arist.*Mir*.831[b]11. II. intr., *let oneself in, enter*, Plb. l.c., Alciphr.3.53, Jul.*Caes*.315a.

**εἰσφύρω** [ῡ], *to mix in*, ἀναμὶξ πάντα ἐν τοῖς λόγοις Max.Tyr.28.6 (Pass.).

**εἰσχειρίζω**, *put into one's hands, entrust*, [ἀρχὴν] ἐμοὶ πόλις δωρητὸν οὐκ αἰτητὸν εἰσεχείρισεν S.*OT*384.

* **εἰσχέω**, *pour in* or *into*, Hdt.4.2, E.*Cyc*.389 (s.v.l.):—Med., aor. εἰσεχεάμην Aristid.*Or*.39(18).4:—Pass. with Ep. aor. ἐσεχύμην [ῠ], *stream in*, ἐσσυμένως ἐσέχυντο ἐς πόλιν Il.21.610, cf. Hdt.9.70; ψυχὴν ἔξωθεν οἷον εἰσχυθεῖσαν Plot.5.1.2.

**εἰσχράομαι**, *use*, μέτροις *POxy*.717.2 (i B.C.).

**εἴσχῠσις**, εως, ἡ, *estuary*, Ptol.*Geog*.2.3.1, al.

**εἰσχωρέω**, *penetrate*, διὰ τοῦ στομίου Hero*Spir*.1.19.

**εἴσω, ἔσω**, used by Ep., Lyr., and Trag. Poets acc. as a spondee or iambus is required; ἔσω (as ἐς for εἰς) prevailed in Ion. and old Att. Prose; but in other Prose and in Com. εἴσω was the only form admitted, whereas ἔσωθεν with the Comp. and Sup. ἐσώτερος, ἐσώτατος, ἐσωτέρω, ἐσωτάτω, seem to have been the only forms in use:—Adv. of εἰς, ἐς, *to within, into*: abs., μή πού τις ἐπαγγείλῃσι καὶ εἴσω lest some one may carry the news *into the house*, Od.4.775, cf. Hdt.1. 111, al.; so εἴπατε δ' εἴσω Od.3.427; also εἴσω δ' ἀσπίδ' ἔαξε he brake it through *to the inside*, Il.7.270; so ὀστέα δ' εἴσω ἔθλασεν Od.18.96; εἴσω ἐπιγράψαι τέρενα χρόα Il.13.553; ἐσσύμενοι εἴσω Pi.*P*.4.135; εἴσω κομίζου A.*Ag*.1035; πέπληγμαι.. ἔσω ib.1343; εἴσω.. δεῦρ' εἴσιθ' Ar. *Pl*.231; ἡγεῖσθαι εἴσω, φεύγειν εἴσω, X.*Cyr*.2.3.21, 7.5.26; παρακαλέσαι εἴσω Id.*An*.1.6.5. b. when a case follows, Hom. prefers the acc., δῦναι δόμον Ἄϊδος εἴσω Il.3.322; πέρησε δ' ἄρ' ὀστέον εἴσω αἰχμή 6.10, etc.; ἡγήσατο.. Ἴλιον εἴσω 1.71, etc.; more rarely with gen., κατελθόντ' Ἄϊδος εἴσω 6.284, cf. 22.425; ἐβήσετο δώματος εἴσω Od.7.135, cf. 8.290; so in Prose and Trag., Κύκλωπος ἔσω βλεφάρων ὤσας E. *Cyc*.485; it generally follows its case, but precedes in Il.21.125, 24.155, Od.8.290. 2. with Verbs of Rest, = ἔνδον, *inside, within*, εἴσω δόρπον ἐκόσμει 7.13; ἄντρον ἔσω ναίουσα *h.Merc*.6; ἔσω καθῆσθαι A.*Ch*.919; θακεῖν S.*Aj*.105; οὔτε πύργος οὔτε ναῦς ἔρημος ἀνδρῶν μὴ ξυνοικούντων ἔσω Id.*OT*57; τὸ ἔσω μέτωπον the *inner* front, Th.3.21; τὰ εἴσω νενοσηκότα σώματα Pl.*R*.407d; εἴσω τὴν χεῖρα ἔχειν ἀναβεβλημένον D.19.251. b. c. gen., μένειν εἴσω δόμων A.*Th*.232; γλῶσσαν εἴσω πυλῶν ῥέουσαν ib.557; εἴσω στέγης S.*Tr*.202; εἴσω ξίφους *within reach* of sword, E.*Or*.1531; εἴσω τῶν ὅπλων *within* the heavy-armed troops, i.e. *encircled by* them, X.*An*.3.3.7, 3.4.26; εἴσω τῶν ὀρέων *within*, i.e. *on this side of*, the mountains, ib.1.2.21; ἔσω τούτων *inside of* these people, i.e. *farther inland*, Th.2.100; εἴσω βέλους *within* bow-shot, Arr.*An*.1.6.8; τὰ δένδρα τῆς ὁδοῦ ποιεῖν εἴσω, i.e. *inside*, i.e. *by the side of*, the road, D.55.22; εἴσω τῆς εἰρωνείας ἀφικνεῖσθαι Id.*Prooem*.14; πάντα εἴσω τῆς συμφορᾶς Lib.*Or*.61. 18. II. later of Time, *within*, εἴσω ἡμερῶν εἴκοσι *PGiss*.34.6 (iii A.D.), Hermog.*Stat*.8, Arg.2 Ar.*Eq*. III. for Comp. and Sup., v. ἔσω.

**εἰσωθ-έω**, *thrust into*, τι ἐς τὸ ἔσω μέρος Hp.*Art*.34; χεῖρα Aret.*SD* 2.1; ἔνδον τὰς στάλικας Lib.*Descr*.10.4:—Med., *force oneself into, press in*, X.*An*.5.2.18; εἰς τοὺς ὄχλους Porph.*Hist.Phil.Fr*.12. **–ίζομαι**, = foreg., App.*BC*4.78.

**εἰσωπή**, ἡ, *aspect*, Opp.*H*.4.358.

* **εἰσωπός**, όν, *within*, i.e. *between* (perh. connected with ὀπή), εἰσωποὶ δ' ἐγένοντο νεῶν Il.15.653: abs., *in harbour*, A.R.2.751. 2. (ὤψ) *visible*, Arat.79, 122.

**εἴσωσις**, εως, ἡ, *inward thrust*, of spinal curvature, Gal.14.796.

* **εἰσώστη**, ἡ, *tomb*, in pl., *CIG*2824 (Aphrodisias), *JHS*20.76 (Caria). (Prob. from ὠθέω, cf. ὑπώστη.)

* **εἶτα**, Ion. **εἶτεν** (q.v., cf. ἔπειτα, –εν), Adv., used to denote the Sequence of one act or state upon another: I. of Sequence in time, without any notion of Cause, *then, next*, πρῶτα μέν.., εἶτα.. S.*El*.262, cf. Pl.*Phdr*.251a, etc.; *soon, presently*, S.*OT*452; εἶτα τί τοῦτο; *well*, what *then?* Ar.*Nu*.347, Pl.*Prt*.309a; εἶτα.. τότε *then*.. after that, Ar.*Eq*.1036 codd. (fort. τόδε): freq. repeated, sts. alternating with ἔπειτα, *then.., next.., then.., after* that.., etc., Men.154, etc.; with πάλιν, *SIG*1171; εἶτ' οὖν *also*, Sch.Pi.*O*.7.68. 2. freq. with finite Verb after a part., expressing surprise or incongruity, *and then, and yet*, μή μοι προτείνων κέρδος εἶτ' ἀποστέρει A.*Pr*.777; ἆρα κλύουσα, μῆτερ, εἶτ' ἔρξεις κακῶς; E.*El*.1058, cf. S.*El*.53, *Aj*. 468, 1092, 1094, X.*An*.1.2.25, etc.; cf. ἔπειτα I.3. II. to denote Consequence, *and so, therefore, accordingly*; esp. in questions or exclamations to express surprise, indignation, contempt, sarcasm, and the like, *and then..? and so..?* κᾆτ' οὐ δέχονται λιτάς; S.*Ant*. 1019, cf. *OC*418; εἶτ' ἐγὼ μὲν οὐ φρονῶ; E.*Andr*.666; κᾆτα ποῦ 'στιν ἡ δίκη; Id.*Ph*.548; εἶτ' ἐσίγας, Πλοῦτος ὤν; Ar.*Pl*.79; εἶτ' ἄνδρα τῶν αὑτοῦ τι χρὴ προϊέναι; Id.*Nu*.1214; εἶτ' οὐκ αἰσχύνεσθε; D.1.24, cf. Pl.*Ap*.28b; οὐκ οἴεσθε δεῖν χρήματα εἰσφέρειν, εἶτα θαυμάζετε..; D. 21.203; εἶτ' οὐκ ἐπῳδούς φασιν ἰσχύειν τινές; Antiph.217.15; εἶτ' οὐ περίεργόν ἐστιν ἄνθρωπος φυτόν; Alex.141.1, etc.

**εἶται**, 3 sg. pf. Pass. of ἕννυμι, Od.11.191.

* **εἰτακεῖν**· ἐληλυθέναι, Hsch.

**εἴτε**, Dor. **αἴτε**, generally doubled, εἴτε.. εἴτε.., Lat. *sive.. sive..*, *either.. or.., whether.. or..*, so that two cases are put as equally possible or equivalent; thrice repeated, S.*El*.606; εἴτ' οὖν.., εἴτε.. Id.*OT*1049; εἴτ' οὖν.., εἴτε καί.. A.*Ag*.843; εἴτ' οὖν.., εἴτ' οὖν.. Id.*Ch*.683; εἴτε.., εἴτ' ἄρ' οὖν.. S.*Ph*.345; εἴτε.., εἴτ' αὖ.. Pl. *Phlb*.34b; εἴτε καί.., εἴτε καί.. Id.*R*.471d: with Substantives, τὴν εἴθ' ἡδονὴν εἴτε ἀπονίαν ἢ εὐστάθειαν Plu.2.1089d: the first εἴτε is sts. omitted in Poets, ξεῖνος, αἴτ' ὦν ἀστός Pi.*P*.4.78; αἰνεῖν, εἴτε με ψέγειν θέλεις A.*Ag*.1403; μύραινά γ', εἴτ' ἔχιδν' ἔφυ Id.*Ch*.1002; λόγοισιν, εἴτ' ἔργοισιν S.*OT*517, cf. *Tr*.236; and even in Prose, πόλις, εἴτε ἰδιῶται Pl.*Lg*.864a, cf. 907d, *Sph*.224e: the first εἴτε is sts. replaced by εἰ, as εἰ.. εἴτε.., Lat. *utrum.. an..*, v.l. in Hdt.3.35; εἰ.. εἴτε καί.. A.*Ch*.768; εἰ.. εἴτε μή Id.*Eu*.468; εἰ μὲν.., εἴτε καὶ μή.. X.*Cyr*.2.1.7; sts. ἤ (ἠὲ καί.. v.l. in Il.2.349) stands for the second εἴτε, E.*El*.896, Pl.*Phdr*.277d, *IG*1.40.5; or for the first, S.*Aj*.178 (lyr.), E.*Alc*.115 (lyr.); εἴτε.. εἴτε.., c. subj. (cf. εἰ), v.l. in Archyt. ap Stob.3.1.105. II. in indirect questions, Od.3.90, etc.; σκοπεῖτε εἴτ' ὀρθῶς λογίζομαι ταῦτ' εἴτε μή D.15.11.

**εἶτε**, = εἴητε, 2 pl. pres. opt. of εἰμί (*sum*), Od.21.195.

**εἰτέα**, v. ἰτέα.

**εἶτεν**, = εἶτα, *SIG*57.29 (Milet., V B.C.), Scymn.330, al., *Ev.Marc*.4. 28, *IG*5(1).1390.31 (Andania), 7.3073.150 (Lebad.): condemned by Phryn.101; Ion. acc. to Ael.Dion.ap.Eust.1158.38.

**εἰτισκαί**· πηγή, παρὰ τῷ Κλειτῷ (prob. τοῖς Κλειτορίοις), Hsch.

**εἴχεται**· οἴχεται, Hsch. **εἰχόμενος**· κατεχόμενος, Id.

**εἰωθάς**, άδος, ἡ, = ἐθάς, of the domestic pigeon, Hdn.*Philet*.p.446P.

**εἰωθότως**, Adv. of εἴωθα (v. ἔθω), *in customary wise*, S.*El*.1456, Aristid.*Or*.51(27).48, etc.; εἰ. ἔλεξεν in his *usual manner*, Pl.*Smp*. 218d.

**εἴως**, Ep. for ἕως. **εἴωσεν**· ἀπεώσατο, Hsch.

* **ἐκ**, before a vowel **ἐξ**, also ἐξ τῷ ϝοίκῳ *Inscr.Cypr*.135.5 H., in Att. Inscrr. before σ ξ ζ ρ and less freq. λ; ἐγ– in Inscrr. before β γ δ λ μ ν; Cret. and Boeot. **ἐς** *Leg.Gort*.2.49, Corinn.*Supp*.2.67; ἐχ freq. in Att. Inscrr. before χ φ θ (and in early Inscrr. before σ, *IG*1[2].304. 20); also ἐ Ναυπάκτω ib.9(1).334.8 (Locr.); (ἐτ is for ἐπὶ in ib 9(2). 517.14 (Thess.)):—Prep. governing GEN. only (exc. in Cypr. and Arc., c. dat., *Inscr.Cypr*.135.5 H. (Idalium), (in form ἐς) *IG*5(2).6.49 (Tegea, iv B.C.)):—radical sense, *from out of*, freq. also simply, *from*. I. OF PLACE, the most freq. usage, variously modified: 1. of Motion, *out of, forth from*, ἐκ Πύλου ἐλθὼν τηλόθεν ἐξ ἀπίης γαίης Il.1. 269, cf. Pl.*Prt*.321c, etc.; μάχης ἔκ Il.17.207; ἂψ ἐκ δυσμενέων ἀνδρῶν 24.288; ἐξ ὀχέων, ἐξ ἕδρης, 3.29, 19.77; φεύγειν ἐκ πολέμοιο 7.119; ἐκ τῶν πολεμίων ἐλθεῖν X.*Cyr*.6.2.9; ἐκ χειρῶν γέρας εἵλετο Il.9.344, cf. S.*Ph*.1287 (but ἐκ χειρὸς βάλλειν or παίειν to strike with a spear *in* the hand, opp. ἀντιτοξεύειν or ἀκοντίζειν, X.*An*.3.3.15, *Cyr*.4.3.16; ἐκ χειρὸς τὴν μάχην ποιεῖσθαι ib.6.2.16, cf. 6.3.24, etc.); ἐκ χρυσῶν φιαλῶν πίνειν ib.5.3.3; ἐξ ἀγορᾶς ὠνεῖσθαι Pl.Com.190. 2. ἐκ θυμοῦ φίλεον I loved her *from* my heart, *with all* my heart, Il.9.343; ἐκ τῆς ψυχῆς ἀσπάσασθαι X.*Oec*.10.4; μέγαν ἐκ θυμοῦ κλάζοντες Ἄρη A.*Ag*.48 (anap.); δακρυχέων ἐκ φρενός Id.*Th*.919 (anap.); οὐδὲν ἐκ σαυτῆς λέγεις S.*El*.344; ἐξ εὐμενῶν στέρνων δέχεσθαι receive *with* kindly heart, Id.*OC*486; ἐξ ὀμμάτων ὀρθῶν δὲ κἀξ ὀρθῆς φρενός Id.*OT*528; ὀρθὸς ἐξ ὀρθῶν δίφρων *with* chariot still upright, Id.*El*.742; ἐξ ἀκινήτου ποδός Id.*Tr*.875; ἐξ ἑνὸς ποδός Id.*Ph*.91. 3. to denote change or succession, freq. with an antithetic repetition of the same word, δέχεται κακὸν ἐκ κακοῦ one evil comes *from* (or *after*) another, Il.19.290; ἐκ φόβου φόβον τρέφω S.*Tr*.28; πόλιν ἐκ πόλεως ἀμείβειν, ἀλλάττειν, Pl. *Sph*.224b, *Plt*.289e; λόγον ἐκ λόγου λέγειν D.18.313; πόρους ἐκ πόρων ὑπισχνούμενοι Alciphr.1.8; ἀπαλλάττειν τινὰ ἐκ γόων S.*El*.291; ἐκ κακῶν πεφευγέναι Id.*Ant*.437: hence, *instead of*, τυφλὸς ἐκ δεδορκότος Id.*OT*454; λευκὴν.. ἐκ μελαίνης ἀμφιβάλλομαι τρίχα Id.*Ant*.1093; ἐλεύθερος ἐκ δούλου καὶ πλούσιος ἐκ πτωχοῦ γεγονώς D.18.131, cf. X. *An*.7.7.28, etc. 4. to express separation or distinction *from* a number, ἐκ πολέων πίσυρες four *out of* many, Il.15.680; μοῦνος ἐξ ἁπάντων σωθῆναι Hdt.5.87; εἶναι ἐκ τῶν δυναμένων to be *one of* the wealthy, Pl.*Grg*.525e; ἐμοὶ ἐκ πασέων Ζεὺς ἄλγε' ἔδωκεν to me *out of* (i.e. *above*) all, Il.18.431, cf. 432; ἐκ πάντων μάλιστα 4.96, cf. S.*Ant*. 1137 (lyr.), etc.; redundant, εἷς τῶν ἐκ τῶν φίλων σου LXX *Jd*.15. 2. 5. of Position, *outside of, beyond*, chiefly in early writers, ἐκ βελέων *out of* shot, Il.14.130, etc.; ἐκ καπνοῦ *out of* the smoke, Od.19.7; ἐκ πατρίδος *banished from* one's country, 15.272; ἐκ μέσου

κατῆστο sate down *apart from* the company, Hdt.3.83; ἐξ ἠθέων τὸν ἥλιον ἀνατεῖλαι *out of* its accustomed quarters, Id.2.142; ἐξ ὀφθαλμῶν *out of* sight, Id.5.24; ἐξ ὁδοῦ *out of* the road, S.*OC*113. **6.** with Verbs of Rest, where previous motion is implied, *on, in,* δαῖέ οἱ ἐκ κόρυθος..πῦρ lighted a fire *from* (i.e. *on*) his helmet, Il.5.4; ἐκ ποταμοῦ χρόα νίζετο washed his body *in* the river (*with water from* the river), Od.6.224: freq. with Verbs signifying hang or fasten, σειρὴν..ἐξ οὐρανόθεν κρεμάσαντες having hung a chain *from* heaven, Il.8.19; ἐκ πασσαλόφι κρέμασεν φόρμιγγα he hung his lyre *from* (i.e. *on*) the peg, Od.8.67; ἀνάπτεσθαι ἔκ τινος fasten *from* (i.e. *upon*) a thing, 12.51; μαχαίρας εἶχον ἐξ ἀργυρέων τελαμώνων Il.18.598; πρισθεὶς ἐξ ἀντύγων gripped *to* the chariot-rail, S.*Aj.*1030, etc.; ἐκ τοῦ βραχίονος ἵππον ἐπέλκουσα leading it [by a rein] *upon* her arm, Hdt.5.12: with Verbs signifying hold, lead, ἐξ ἐκείνων ἔχειν τὰς ἐλπίδας to have their hopes *dependent upon* them, Th.1.84; ἐκ χειρὸς ἄγειν lead *by* the hand, Bion *Fr.*7.2; ἐκ ποδὸς ἕπεσθαι ib.6.2; ἐκ τῆς οὐρᾶς λαμβάνεσθαι Luc.*Asin.*23: with the Art. indicating the place of origin, οἱ ἐκ τῶν νήσων κακοῦργοι the robbers *of* the islands, Th.1.8, cf. 2.5,13; τοὺς ἐκ τῆς ναυμαχίας those *in* the sea-fight, Pl.*Ap.*32b; τοὺς ἐκ τῶν σκηνῶν those *in* the tents, D.18.169; ἁρπασόμενοι τὰ ἐκ τῶν οἰκιῶν X.*Cyr.*7.2.5; οἱ ἐκ τοῦ πεδίου ἔθεον Id.*An.*4.6.25: even with Verbs of sitting or standing, εἰσεῖδε στᾶσ' ἐξ Οὐλύμποιο *from* Olympus where she stood, Il.14.154; καθῆσθαι ἐκ πάγων to sit *on* the heights and look *from* them, S.*Ant.*411; στὰς ἐξ ἐπάλξεων ἄκρων E.*Ph.*1009; ἐκ βυθοῦ *at* the bottom, Theoc.22.40: phrases, ἐκ δεξιᾶς, ἐξ ἀριστερᾶς, *on* the right, left, X.*Cyr.*8.3.10, etc.; οἱ ἐξ ἐναντίας, οἱ ἐκ πλαγίου, ib.7.1.20; ἐκ θαλάσσης, opp. ἐκ τῆς μεσογείας, D.18.301. **7.** νικᾶν ἔκ τινος win a victory *over*.., *Apoc.*15.2. **II.** OF TIME, elliptic with Pron. relat. and demonstr., ἐξ οὗ [χρόνου] *since*, Il.1.6, Od.2.27, etc.; in apod., ἐκ τοῦ *from* that time, Il.8.296; ἐκ τούτου X.*An.*5.8.15, etc. (but ἐκ τοῖο there*after*, Il.1.493, and ἐκ τούτων or ἐκ τῶνδε usu. *after* this, X.*Mem.*2.9.4, S.*OT*235); ἐξ ἐκείνου Th.2.15; ἐκ πολλοῦ (sc. χρόνου) *for* a long time, Id.1.68, etc.; ἐκ πλέονος χρόνου Id.8.45; ἐκ πλείστου ib.68; ἐξ ὀλίγου *at* short notice, Id.2.11 (but also a short time *since*, Plu.*Caes.*28); ἐκ παλαιοῦ X.*Mem.*3.5.8; ἐκ παλαιτάτου Th.1.18. **2.** of particular points of time, ἐκ νεότητος..ἐς γῆρας Il.14.86; ἐκ γενετῆς 24.535; ἐκ νέου, ἐκ παιδός, *from* boyhood, Pl.*Grg.*510d, *R.*374c, etc.; ἐκ μικροῦ παιδαρίου D.53.19; ἐξ ἀρχῆς A.*Eu.*284, etc.; καύματος ἐξ *after* hot weather, Il.5.865; νέφος ἔρχεται οὐρανὸν εἴσω αἰθέρος ἐκ δίης *after* clear weather, 16.365; ἐκ δὲ αἰθρίης καὶ νηνεμίης συνδραμεῖν ἐξαπίνης νέφεα Hdt.1.87; so (like ἀπό II) ἐκ τῆς θυσίης γενέσθαι to have *just finished* sacrifice, ib.50, etc.; ἐκ τοῦ ἀρίστου *after* breakfast, X.*An.*4.6.21; ἐξ εἰρήνης πολεμεῖν to go to war *after* peace, Th.1.120; γελάσαι ἐκ τῶν ἔμπροσθεν δακρύων X.*Cyr.*1.4.28; κάλλιστον ἦμαρ εἰσιδεῖν ἐκ χείματος A.*Ag.*900; τὴν θάλασσαν ἐκ Διονυσίων πλόϊμον εἶναι Thphr.*Char.*3.3; ἐκ χειμῶνος *at the end of* winter, Plu.*Nic.*20. **3.** *at, in,* ἐκ νυκτῶν Od.12.286; ἐκ νυκτός X.*Cyr.*1.4.2, etc.; ἐξ ἡμέρας S.*El.*780; ἐκ μέσω ἄματος Theoc.10.5; ἐκ τοῦ λοιποῦ or ἐκ τῶν λοιπῶν *for* the future, X.*Smp.*4.56, Pl.*Lg.*709e. **III.** OF ORIGIN, **1.** of Material, *out of* or *of* which things are made, γίγνεταί τι ἔκ τινος Parm.8.12; ποιέεσθαι ἐκ ξύλων τὰ πλοῖα Hdt.1.194; πίνοντας ἐκ κριθῶν μέθυ A.*Supp.*953; εἶναι ἐξ ἀδάμαντος Pl.*R.*616c; ἐκ λευκῶ ἐλέφαντος αἰετοί Theoc.15.123; στράτευμα ἀλκιμώτατον ἂν γένοιτο ἐκ παιδικῶν X.*Smp.*8.32; συνετάττετο ἐκ τῶν ἔτι προσιόντων formed line of battle *from* the troops as they marched up, Id.*An.*1.8.14. **2.** of Parentage, ἔκ τινος εἶναι, γενέσθαι, etc., Il.20.106, 6.206, etc.; ἐκ γὰρ ἐμεῦ γένος ἐσσί (where γένος is acc. abs.) 5.896; σῆς ἐξ αἵματός εἰσι γενέθλης 19.111; ὦ παῖ πατρὸς ἐξ Ἀχιλλέως S.*Ph.*260; πίρωμις ἐκ πιρώμιος Hdt.2.143; ἀγαθοὶ καὶ ἐξ ἀγαθῶν Pl.*Phdr.*246a; τὸν ἐξ ἐμῆς μητρός S.*Ant.*466, etc. **3.** of Place of Origin or Birth, ἐκ Σιδῶνος..εὔχομαι εἶναι Od.15.425, cf. Th.1.25, etc.; ἐκ τῶν ἄνω εἰμί *Ev.Jo.*8.23; ἡ ἐξ Ἀρείου πάγου βουλή the Areopagus, Arist.*Ath.*4.4, etc.; οἱ ἐκ τῆς διατριβῆς ταύτης Aeschin.1.54; οἱ ἐκ τοῦ Περιπάτου the Peripatetics, Luc.*Pisc.*43; ὁ ἐξ Ἀκαδημείας the Academic, Ath.1.34b; οἱ ἐκ πίστεως *Ep.Gal.*3.7; οἱ ἐξ ἐριθείας *Ep.Rom.*2.8. **4.** of the Author or Occasion of a thing, ὄναρ, τιμὴ ἐκ Διός ἐστιν, Il.1.63, 2.197, cf. Od.1.33, A.*Pers.*707, etc.; θάνατος ἐκ μνηστήρων death *by the hand of* the suitors, Od.16.447; τὰ ἐξ Ἑλλήνων τείχεα walls *built by* them, Hdt.2.148; κίνημα ἐξ αὐτοῦ *spontaneous* motion, Plot.6.1.21; ὕμνος ἐξ Ἐρινύων A.*Eu.*331 (lyr.); ἡ ἐξ ἐμοῦ δυσβουλία S.*Ant.*95; ὁ ἐξ ἐμοῦ πόθος Id.*Tr.*631. **5.** with the agent after Pass. Verbs, *by,* Poet. and early Prose, ἐφίληθεν ἐκ Διός they were beloved *of* (i.e. *by*) Zeus, Il.2.669; κήδε' ἐφῆπται ἐκ Διός ib.70; προδεδόσθαι ἐκ Πρηξάσπεος Hdt.3.62; τὰ λεχθέντα ἐξ Ἀλεξάνδρου Id.7.175, cf. S.*El.*124 (lyr.), *Ant.*93, Th.3.69, Pl.*Ti.*47b; ἐξ ἁπάντων ἀμφισβητήσεται Id.*Tht.*171b; ὁμολογουμένους ἐκ πάντων X.*An.*2.6.1; τὰς ἐκ θεῶν τύχας δοθείσας S.*Ph.*1316, cf. Pl.*Ly.*204c: with neut. Verbs, ἐκ..πατρὸς κακὰ πείσομαι Od.2.134, cf. A.*Pr.*759; τλῆναί τι ἔκ τινος Il.5.384; θνῄσκειν ἔκ τινος S.*El.*579, *OT*854, etc.; τὰ γενόμενα ἐξ ἀνθρώπων Hdt.1.1. **6.** of Cause, Instrument, or Means *by* which a thing is done, ἐκ πατέρων φιλότητος *in consequence* of our fathers' friendship, Od.15.197; μήνιος ἐξ ὀλοῆς 3.135; ἐξ ἔριδος Il.7.111; τελευτῆσαι ἐκ τοῦ τρώματος Hdt.3.29; ἐκ τίνος λόγου; E.*Andr.*548; ἐκ τοῦ; *wherefore?* Id.*Hel.*93; λέξον ἐκ τίνος ἐπλήγης X.*An.*5.8.4; ποιεῖτε ὑμῖν φίλους ἐκ τοῦ Μαμωνᾶ τῆς ἀδικίας make yourselves friends *of* (i.e. *by means of*).., *Ev.Luc.*16.9; ζῆν ἔκ τινος X.*HG*3.2.11 codd.; ἐκ τῶν ἰδίων τρέφειν ἐμαυτόν Isoc.15.152; ἐκ τόξων ἀνύσαι γαστρὶ φορβάν S.*Ph.*710 (lyr.). **7.** *in accordance with,* ἐκ τῶν λογίων Hdt.1.64; ὁ ἐκ τῶν νόμων χρόνος D.24.28; ἐκ κελεύματος A.*Pers.*397, cf. Sophr.25; ἐκ τῶν ξυγκειμένων Th.5.25; ἐκ τῶν παρόντων ib.40, etc.; ἐκ τῶν ἔργων κρινόμενοι X.*Cyr.*2.2.21, cf. A.*Pr.*485. **8.** freq. as periphr. for Adv., ἐκ προνοίας *IG*1².115.11; ἐκ βίας *by* force, S.*Ph.*563; ἐκ δόλου Id.*El.*279; ἐκ παντὸς τρόπου ζητεῖν Pl.*R.*499a: esp. with neut. Adjs., ἐξ ἀγχιμόλοιο, = ἀγχίμολον, Il.24.352; ἐκ τοῦ ἐμφανέος Hdt.3.150; ἐκ τοῦ φανεροῦ, ἐκ τοῦ προφανοῦς, Th.4.106, 6.73; ἐκ προδήλου S.*El.*1429; ἐξ ἴσου, ἐκ τοῦ ἴσου, Id.*Tr.*485, Th.2.3; ἐξ ἀέλπτου Hdt.1.111, etc.: with fem. Adj., ἐκ τῆς ἰθέης Id.3.127; ἐκ νέης Id.5.116; ἐξ ὑστέρης Id.6.85; ἐκ τῆς ἀντίης Id.8.6; ἐκ καινῆς Th.3.92; ἐξ ἑκουσίας S.*Tr.*727; ἐκ ταχείας ib.395. **9.** of Number or Measurement, with numerals, ἐκ τρίτων *in* the third *place,* E.*Or.*1178, Pl.*Grg.*500a, *Smp.*213b; distributively, *apiece,* Ath.15.671b. **b.** of Price, ἐξ ὀκτὼ ὀβολῶν *SIG*²587.206; ἐκ τριῶν δραχμῶν ib.283; συμφωνήσας ἐκ δηναρίου *Ev.Matt.*20.2. **c.** of Weight, ἐπιπέμματα ἐξ ἡμιχοινικίου *Inscr.Prien.*362 (iv B.C.). **d.** of Space, θινώδης ὢν ὁ τόπος ἐξ εἴκοσι σταδίων *by the space of* twenty stades, Str.8.3.19.

B. ἐκ is freq. separated from its CASE, Il.11.109, etc.—It takes an accent in anastrophe, 14.472, Od.17.518.—Ep. use it with Advbs. in -θεν, ἐξ οὐρανόθεν, ἐξ ἁλόθεν, ἐξ Αἰσύμηθεν, Il.17.548, 21.335, 8.304; ἐκ Διόθεν Hes.*Op.*765; ἐκ πρῴρηθεν Theoc.22.11.—It is combined with other Preps. to make the sense more definite, as διέκ, παρέκ, ὑπέκ.

C. IN COMPOS. the sense of *removal* prevails; *out, away, off.* **2.** to express *completion,* like our *utterly,* ἐκπέρθω, ἐξαλαπάζω, ἐκβαρβαρόω, ἐκδιδάσκω, ἐκδιψάω, ἐκδωριεύομαι, ἐξοπλίζω, ἐξομματόω, ἔκλευκος, ἔκπικρος.

D. As ADVERB, *therefrom,* Il.18.480.

**ἑκᾱβόλος,** ον, Dor. for ἑκηβόλος.

⊛ **Ἑκαδήμεια,** ἡ, old form for Ἀκαδήμεια, from the name of a hero Hecademos, D.L.3.8.

**Ἑκάεργος,** ὁ, expld. by Gramm. (*EM*319.51, etc.) as, = ὁ ἕκαθεν εἴργων or ἐργαζόμενος, Ep. epith. of Apollo, either Subst., Il.1.147, etc., or Adj., 5.439, Od.8.323, Call.*Ap.*11, etc.: fem., ὦ ἑκάεργε, of Artemis, Ar.*Th.*972 (lyr.):—also ⊛ **Ἑκαέργη,** a daughter of Boreas, Call.*Del.*292. **II.** Pythag. name for *nine,* ἀπὸ τοῦ εἴργειν τὴν ἑκὰς πρόβασιν τοῦ ἀριθμοῦ *Theol.Ar.*58. (This word and its cognates (e.g. ἑκατηβελέτης), although connected by Greek writers with ἑκάς, may have originally contained the stem ἑκητ- (cf. ἑκών) 'at will'; for the formation of ϝεκα(τ)-ϝεργός, cf. γυναι(κ)-μανής.)

**ἕκᾰθεν,** Adv., (ἑκάς) *from afar,* Il.2.456, Pi.*O.*10(11).7, A.*Supp.*421 (lyr.), and late Prose, Corn.*ND*32, D.C.50.33: c. gen., ἕκαθεν πόλιος Il.13.107 (al. ἑκάς). **II.** = ἑκάς, *far off, far away,* Od.17.25. **III.** = ἀνέκαθεν, *Schwyzer* 702 (Erythrae, iv B.C.).

**Ἑκάλειος Ζεύς** [ᾰ], from Ἑκάλη, a lady who entertained Theseus, and for this received at Athens the yearly honour of the **Ἑκαλήσια** [ἱερά]: hence the epith. was given to Zeus as worshipped on the same day, Plu.*Thes.*14.

**ἑκαλία·** πόρρωθεν, Hsch. ⊛ **ἑκάλλιθμος·** ἱερός, ἀφειμένος, Id.

**ἕκᾱλος,** Dor. for ἕκηλος, Pi.*O.*9.58, *I.*7(6).41.

**ἑκανόμος·** ἀγελαῖος φιμός, Hsch.

⊛ **ἑκάς,** Adv. *afar, far off,* Il.20.422, etc.; οὐχ ἑκάς που S.*Ph.*41; rare in Prose, Th.1.69,80 (and later, Nic.Dam.p.6 D.): c. gen., *far from, far away from,* ἑ. Ἄργεος Il.9.246, etc.: freq. following its case, 13.263, Od.14.496, al.; οὐ Χαρίτων ἑ. Pi.*P.*8.21, cf. E.*Ph.*907; ἑ. ἀπὸ τείχεος Il.18.256; ἀπὸ τῆς νήσου ἑ. Hdt.3.41. **2.** Comp. ἑκαστέρω *farther,* Od.7.321, *h.Bacch.*29, Alc.*Supp.*5.8 (ἐκ-), Hdt.6.108, E.*HF*1047 (lyr.), etc.: c. gen., Hdt.2.169, al.; also ἑκαστοτέρω dub. in Theoc.15.7: Sup. ἑκαστάτω *farthest,* Il.10.113, Hdt.4.33: c. gen., τοὺς ἑωυτῶν ἑ. οἰκημένους *farthest from*.., Id.1.134; τῆς Λιβύης ἑ. ἦλθε *to the farthest point* of Libya, Id.4.204, cf. 9.14. **II.** of Time, ἑ. ἐών *afar,* i.e. *long after,* Pi.*P.*2.54; οὐχ ἑ. χρόνου in no *long* time, Hdt.8.144; οὐχ ἑ. A.*Ag.*1650. [ᾰ; ᾱ only in Call.*Ap.*2, in arsi.] (Prob. from ἕ and -κάς as in ἀνδρακάς; lit. 'by himself'.)

**ἑκάς,** άδος, ἡ, a division of land (?), *Rev.Phil.*48.98 (Dura).

**ἑκαστ-άκις,** Adv., (ἕκαστος) *each* or *every time,* *IG*9(1).694.8 (Corc.); οἱ ἑκαστάκις ἐόντες, = οἱ ἀεὶ ἄ., ib.22: **-άκι** *GDI* 3051 (Chalcedon). **-άτω,** v. ἑκάς. **-άχῃ,** Adv. *everywhere,* Suid.; f.l. for ἕκαστα in X.*Cyr.*6.2.5. **-ᾰχόθεν,** Adv. *from every side,* Th.7.20,21, X.*HG*3.4.3. **-ᾰχόθι,** Adv. = ἑκάστοθι, *on each side,* Plu.*Lys.*19, *PLips.*119ʳ. **-ᾰχοῖ,** Adv. *to each side, every way,* Plu.*Mar.*20, Hdn.Gr.1.502. **-άχόσε,** Adv. *to each side,* Th.4.55, 8.5, Pl.*Criti.*116a. **-ᾰχοῦ,** Adv. *everywhere,* Th.3.82, Pl.*Phdr.*257e, al. **-έρω,** v. ἑκάς. **-οθεν,** Adv. = ἑκασταχόθεν, Cleobul. ap.D.L.1.93. **-οθι,** Adv. *for each* or *every one,* Od.3.8 (v.l. ἑκάστοθεν), Aen.Tact.11.11.

⊛ **ἕκαστος,** η, ον, *each,* opp. the whole body, Il.2.805, etc.: sg. with pl. Verb, ἔβαν οἰκόνδε ἕκαστος they went home *each* to his own house, 1.606; δεδμήμεσθα ἕκαστος 5.878, cf. Hdt.3.158; so in Att., Ar.*Pl.*785, Pl.*Prt.*327e, etc.; ὅτι ἕκαστος ἐπίστασθε ἀγαθόν X.*Smp.*3.3: sg. in apposition with pl. Noun or Pron., which expresses the whole, Τρῶας δὲ τρόμος αἰνὸς ὑπήλυθε γυῖα ἕκαστον Il.7.215; ὔμμι..ἑκάστῳ 15.109; αἱ δὲ γυναῖκες..θαύμαζον..ἑκάστη 18.496, etc.; Περσίδες δ'..ἑκάστα..λείπεται A.*Pers.*135 (lyr.); αἱ ἄλλαι πᾶσαι [τέχναι] τὸ αὑτῆς ἑκάστη ἔργον ἐργάζεται Pl.*R.*346d, cf. *Grg.*503e; ὅστις ἕκαστος *every one* which.. (nisi leg. ὥς τις), Hes.*Th.*459. **2.** the Art. is sts. added to the Subst. (so regularly in earlier Att. Inscrr., *IG*1².22.14, al., exc. ἑκάστου μηνός ib.6.125) with which ἕκαστος agrees, in which

case ἕκαστος is commonly put first, καθ' ἑ. τὴν ἡμέραν *every single* day, Isoc.12.211, etc.; περὶ ἑ. τῆς τέχνης Pl.*Phdr.*274e: also following the Subst., κατὰ τὸν ὁπλίτην ἕκαστον Th.5.49; κατὰ τὴν ἡμέραν ἑκάστην Id.6.63, al. II. in pl., *all and each severally*, Il.1.550, al., A. *Supp.*932, etc.; οἷστισιν ἑκάστοις to whichsoever *severally*, Pl.*Lg.* 799a. 2. *each* of two or more groups or parties, Od.9.164, Hdt. 1.169, A.*Pr.*491, Th.6.77, etc. III. strengthd. by the addition of other Prons., εἷς ἕ. (v. εἷς); εἷς τις ἕ. S.*Ant.*262; ἕκαστός τις *each* one, Pi.*N.*4.92, Th.3.45, etc.; ταῦτα ἕκαστα Hdt.5.13, etc.; αὔθ' ἕκαστα *all in exact detail*, A.*Pr.*950. 2. with Preps., esp. κατά, καθ' ἕκαστον *singly, by itself*, Pl.*Tht.*188a, al.; καθ' ἕ. καὶ σύμπαντα Id. *Sph.*259b; τὸ καθ' ἕ., τὰ καθ' ἕκαστα, *particulars*, Arist.*Ph.*189ᵃ6, *EN* 1143ᵇ4, al.; παρ' ἕκαστον, παρ' ἕκαστα, in *every case*, Plb.4.82.5, 3.57.4, etc.; παρ' ἕκαστον καὶ ἔργον καὶ λόγον διδάσκοντες Pl.*Prt.*325d; παρ' ἕκαστον λέγων *constantly* interjecting, Men.*Epit.*48. 3. ὡς ἕκαστοι *each by himself*, Hdt.6.79, Th.1.15, etc.: in sg., τῶν δὲ ὡς ἑκάστῳ θύειν θέλει Hdt.1.132, cf. Pi.*P.*9.98; οὐχ ὡς ἕ. ἀλλὰ πάντες Arist.*Pol.* 1292ᵃ12, cf. 1283ᵇ34. IV. later, = ἑκάτερος, D.H.3.2 codd. (ϝέκαστος *Leg.Gort.*1.9, al., *Schwyzer* 409.4 (Elis), *IG*9(1).334.9 (Locris). Apptly. connected with ἑκάς by Dam.*Pr.*423.)

※ ἑκάστοτε, Adv. *each time, on each occasion*, Parm.16.1, Hdt.1.90, Antipho 6.13, X.*An.*2.4.10, Pl.*R.*393b; ἀεὶ.. ἑ. Ar.*Nu.*1280; ἑ. πολλάκις Pl.*Phlb.*58a; ἵνα ἑ. wherever *on each occasion*, Hdt.8.115.

ἑκαστοτέρω, v. ἑκάς.

※ ἑκᾰτᾱβόλος, ον, Dor. for ἑκατηβ-, Terp.2, Tim.*Pers.*249.

※ Ἑκᾰταῖος, α, ον, *of Hecate*, μαγίδες S.*Fr.*734. II. Ἑκάταιον or Ἑκάτειον (cj. in Ar.*V.*804, cf. Suid.), τό, *statue* or *chapel of Hecate*, placed at the entrance of houses or where three roads meet (ἐν τριόδοις), Ar. l.c., *Ra.*366, cf. Hsch. 2. Ἑκαταῖα, τά, v. Ἑκάτη II.

ἑκᾰτερ-άκις, Adv., (ἑκάτερος) *at each time*, X.*Cyr.*4.6.4; *in both directions*, Gal.*UP*8.7. ※ -έω, in dancing, *kick the rump with one heel after another*, Hsch. (but cf. ἑκατερίς). -η, Cret. Adv. *on either side*, *Schwyzer* 197.4 (iii B.C.); ϝεκ- ib.186.18 (ii B.C.). -θε, before a vowel -θεν, poet. Adv. = ἑκατέρωθεν, *on each side, on either hand*, ἀμφίπολος οἱ.. ἑ. παρέστη Od.1.335; τρεῖς ἑ. Il.11.27, cf. A.R. 1.564: also in late Ion. Prose, Aret.*SD*2.3. 2. c. gen., ἑ. ὁμίλου Il.3.340, 23.813, cf. 329; ἑ. πόληος Od.6.263. -ίς, ίδος, ἡ, a dance with χειρῶν κίνησις, Poll.4.102 (but cf. ἑκατερέω). -ος (Dor. ϝεκ- *Leg.Gort.*1.18, *Michel* 995 *A* 49 (Delph.)), α, ον, *each of two, each singly*, opp. ἀμφότεροι, Lys.2.33; εἷς ἑ. Syngr.ap.D.35.12; αὐτὸ τὸ ἑ. καὶ τὸ ἀμφότερον Pl.*Hp.Ma.*303a, cf. Pi.*I.*8(7).31, Th.1.20, etc.; when joined with a Subst., the Subst. almost always takes the Art. (so in Att. Inscrr. exc. *IG*1².372.137), as ἐφ' ἑ. τῷ κέρᾳ Th.5.67; ἐπὶ τῷ κέρᾳ ἑ. Id.4.93; ἑ. τῇ πόλει Id.5.16: sts. with Noun or Pron. in gen., ἑκάτερος ἡμῶν Id.6.17; ἑκατέρᾳ τῶν χειρῶν D.S.4.10: as nom. to pl. Verb, sts. in pl., esp. when one or both parties are in pl., ἐδικαίευν ἑκάτεροι Hdt.9.26, Pl.*R.*348b, etc.: in sg. with Verb in pl., ταῦτα εἰπόντες ἀπῆλθον ἑκάτερος ἐπὶ τὰ προσήκοντα X.*Cyr.*5.2.22, cf. 6.1.19; repeated in ref. to each of two parties, ἐὰν ἑκάτεροι ἑκατέρων τέμνωσιν ἀγρούς Pl.*R.*470d: with Particles and Preps., ὡς ἑκάτεροι Th.3.74; ἐφ' ἑκάτερα *both* ways, Id.5.73; καθ' ἑκάτερα X.*An.*5.6.7; ἐξ ἑκατέρων Luc.*Am.*14. 2. = ἕκαστος, Id.*Alex.*49. -ω, Dor. Adv. *on either side*, τᾶς τραπέζας *Schwyzer* 251 *A* 10 (Cos). -ωθεν, Adv. *on each side, on either hand*, Hdt.3.102, Th.2.75: c. gen., ἑ. τῆς πόλεως Id.3.6; τὸ ἑ. μέρος Pl.*Phd.*112e; *at each end*, *Gp.*5.27.4. 2. *on both sides, by father and mother*, Poll.8.85. -ωθι, Adv. *on either side*, Pi.*O.*2.69, Hdt.2.19, 106, Arist.*Ath.*54.8, etc. -ως, Adv. *in either way*, Pl.*Lg.*895e, Ph.1.316; *in both languages*, i.e. Greek and Latin, *Inscr.Prien.*105.30 (i B.C.). -ωσε, Adv. *to either side, either way*, ἀποβλέπειν, φοιτᾶν, X.*An.*1.8.14, Pl.*Grg.* 523c. 2. *both ways*, καθιέναι Id.*Phd.*112e; τὰ ὑπερβάλλοντα ἑ. Id.*R.*619a.

※ Ἑκάτη [ᾰ], ἡ, (ἕκατος) *Hecate*, lit. *she who works her will*, Hes.*Th.* 411, *h.Cer.*25, 52, E.*Fr.*955, etc.; Ἑ. φωσφόρος Ar.*Fr.*594a, E.*Fr.* 968. b. v. ἕκατος. II. Ἑκάτης δεῖπνον *Hecate's* dinner, a meal set out by rich persons at the foot of her statue ἐν τριόδοις on the 30th day of each month, when it became a sort of dole for beggars and paupers, Ar.*Pl.*594 et Sch. adloc., cf. Plu.2.280c, 290d, *AB*247: hence, as it consisted of offal, Ἑκαταῖα κατεσθίειν, of a rapscallion, D.54.39, cf. Luc.*DMort.*1.1.

ἑκάτη, ἡ, *stake* to which criminals were bound for scourging, Hsch.

ἑκᾰτη-βελέτης, ου, ὁ, = sq., ἄναξ Il.1.75, Hes.*Sc.*100: Subst., *h.Ap.*157:—fem. -βελέτις, ιδος, ἡ, Pythag. name for *six*, *Theol.Ar.* 37.

ἑκᾰτηβόλος, ον, Dor. ἑκατᾱ- (q.v.), epith. of Apollo, Hom., Hes.: as Subst., Il.15.231; also of Artemis, *h.Hom.*9.6. (Expld. by the ancients as, = *far-darting*, Hsch., etc. (or, *shooting a hundred* βέλη, Id.); but perh. originally, *hitting the mark at will*, cf. ἑκάεργος.)

Ἑκᾰτήσιον, τό, = Ἑκάταιον, Plu.2.193f. II. Ἑκατήσια, τά, *festival of Hecate*, *SIG*1066.15 (Cos). III. Adj., Ἑκατήσιος, α, ον, *of Hecate*, Man.5.302, Poll.1.37.

ἕκᾱτι, Dor. and Trag. for ἕκητι (q.v.), Pi.*O.*4.10, E.*Or.*26, etc.

Ἑκᾰτικός, ή, όν, *of Hecate*, φάσματα Marin.*Procl.*28; λόγοι *Tab. Defix.Aud.*41 *A* 11 (written -ικίοις).

※ ἑκᾰτόγ-γυιος, ον, *with a hundred limbs* or *bodies*, κορᾶν ἀγέλα ἑκατόγγυιος a band of 100 maidens, Pi.*Fr.*122.15. -κάρᾱνος [κᾰ], ον, = sq., A.*Pr.*355. -κεφάλας [φᾰ], α, ὁ, *hundred-headed*, Pi. *O.*4.8, Ar.*Ra.*473, *Nu.*336. -κέφᾰλος, ον, = foreg., E.*HF*883 (anap.). -κρᾱνος, ον, = foreg., Pi.*P.*8.16. -χειρ, χειρος, ὁ, ἡ, = sq., Acus.8 J., Pi.*Pae.*8.31, Orph.*Fr.*57, al., Corn.*ND*17, etc. -χειρος, ον, *hundred-handed*, of Briareus, Il.1.402.

※ ἑκᾰτόμ-βαιος, α, ον, epith. of Apollo and Zeus, *to whom hecatombs were offered*, Hsch., *EM*321.7. 2. (sc. μήν) name of a month, *Hemerolog.Flor.* II. ἑκατόμβαια, τά, = ἑκατόμβοια, *CIG*1715 (Delph.). -βαιών, ῶνος, ὁ, *the month Hecatombaeon*, in which ἑκατόμβαι were offered at Athens and elsewhere, Antipho 6.44, Plu. *Thes.*12, *IG*11(2).203 *A* 31, al. (Delos, iii B.C.), etc.: μῆνα ἐμβάλλειν Ἑ. ib.1².76.53. -βεύς, έως, ὁ (sc. μήν), = foreg., at Sparta, Hsch. -βη, ἡ, (ἑκατόν, βοῦς) prop. *an offering of a hundred oxen*; but even in Hom., generally, *sacrifice*, Il.6.115 (apptly. of twelve oxen, cf. 93), Od.3.59; of bulls and goats, Il.1.315; of fifty rams, 23.146; of three victims, *Schwyzer* 726.19 (Milet.); Com., πουλυπόδων ἑ. Anaxandr.41. 29 (anap.); ᾠῶν ἑ. Ephipp.8.4: metaph., ὅστις στρατηγεῖ μὴ στρατιώτης γενόμενος οὗτος ἑ. ἐξάγει τοῖς πολεμίοις Men.640. II. name of an *eye-salve*, Alex.Trall.2. III. festival at Geronthrae, *IG*5(1). 1120. ※ -βιος, ὁ, epith. of Apollo, *SIG*1024.30 (Myconos). II. (sc. μήν) name of month at Halos, *IG*9(2).109*b*50. III. Ἑκατόμβιον, τό, *shrine of Apollo* Ἑκατόμβιος, ib.9(1).87.76 (Hyampolis). 2. Ἑκατόμβια, τά, = Ἑκατόμβοια, at Amorgos, *IG*12(7).388, al. -βοίδιον· ἑκατὸν βοῶν τιμή, Hsch. ※ -βοιος, ον, (βοῦς) *worth a hundred oxen*, Il.2.449, etc.: expld. as *worth* 100 *pieces of money*, the ancient coins being stamped with an ox, Eust.252.18, *EM*320.47. II. ἑκατόμβοια (sc. ἱερά), τά, *festival at which hecatombs were offered*, *SIG* 36.36 (Delph., v B.C.), 82.6 (Delph., v B.C.), *BCH*29.243 (Delos), *IG* 5(2).142 (Tegea), Str.8.4.11 codd.: dat. Ἑκατομβούοις (sic) *Schwyzer* 91.19 (Argos). -πεδος, ον, (πούς) *a hundred feet long*, πυρὴ ἑκατόμπεδος ἔνθα καὶ ἔνθα *a hundred feet* all ways, Il.23.164; νεώς Th. 3.68 (v.l. -ποδος), *IG*1².256, al., cf. Pi.*I.*6(5).22, *Tab.Heracl.*2.24, al.; ὁ ἑ. Παρθενών Plu.*Per.*13; ἡ ἑ. Id.*Dio*45; τὸ Ἑ. on the Acropolis of Athens, *IG*1².4.10, 18; at Dodona, Ptol.*Geog.*3.13.5. -πηχυς, υ, *of* 100 *cubits*, Hsch. and Apollon.*Lex.* s.v. ἑκατόγχειρον. -πολις, ι, *with a hundred cities*, Κρήτη Il.2.649; of Laconia, Str.8.4.11:—also ἑκᾰτοντάπολις [τᾰ], Κρήτη Id.10.4.15. -πους, ποδος, ὁ, ἡ, *hundred-footed*: in S.*OC*718 (lyr.), ἑκατόμποδες Νηρῇδες, some take it literally to mean *the* 50 *Nereids* (the number assigned to them by Hes.*Th.*264, Pi.*I.*6(5).6, A.*Fr.*174, E.*IT*427), others *the* 100 *Nereids* (Pl.*Criti.* 116e), others merely to express a notion of *multitude*. -πτολίεθρος, ον, = ἑκατόμπολις, E.*Fr.*472.3 (anap.). -πῠλος, ον, *hundred-gated*, Θῆβαι Il.9.383, D.P.249. -φόνια (sc. ἱερά), τά, *sacrifice for a hundred enemies slain*, Paus.4.19.3, Plu.2.159e, *Rom.*25, Polyaen.2. 31.2.

ἑκᾰτόν, Arc. ἑκοτόν *IG*5(2).3 (Tegea, iv B.C.), οἱ, αἱ, τά, indecl.:—*a hundred*, Il.2.510, etc.: in compds. freq. loosely for *very many*. (Dissim. from *sém kmtóm*, cf. εἷς and Lat. *centum*, Lith. *šim̃tas*, etc.)

ἑκᾰτον-δεκάρουρος [ᾰρ], ὁ, *holder of* 110 ἄρουραι, *PCair.Zen.*1.23 (iii B.C.). -ζυγος, = ἑκατόζυγος, Hsch. -σεμνον· πολύ, μέγα, Id.

ἑκᾰτονστάτηρον [στᾰ], τό, *sum of* 100 *staters*, *Leg.Gort.*9.47.

ἑκᾰτοντά-βιβλος [τᾰ], ον, *in a hundred books*, πραγματεῖαι Gal. 10.37. -γράμμᾰτος, ον, *having a hundred letters*, ὄνομα *PMag. Par.*1.1209, 1380. -δόχος, ον, *holding a hundred*, ἀνδρῶνες Jul. *Ep.*180. -δραχμος, ον, *weighing a hundred drachms*, Gal. 13.491. -εβδομήκονταπλᾰσίων, ον, gen. ονος, 170 *times as great*, Olymp.*in Mete.*118.21:—also ἑκατοντάκαιεβδ-, Ptol.*Alm.*5. 16. -ετηρίς, ίδος, ἡ, *period of* 100 *years*, Pl.*R.*615a. -έτηρος, ον, *of a hundred years*, Orph.*A.*1108. -έτης, ες, *of a hundred years*, βιοτά Pi.*P.*4.282; 100 *years old*, LXX *Ge.*17.17. -ετία, ἡ, *period of* 100 *years*, Ph.1.101. -θύσᾰνος [ῠ], ον, *with a hundred tassels*, αἰγίς Jul.*Ep.*180. -κάρηνος, Dor. -ᾱνος [κᾰ], ον, *hundred-headed*, Pi. *P.*1.16. -κέφᾰλος, ον, = foreg., γίγας Jul.*Ep.*180. -κικαιεικοσάκι, 120 *times*, Ptol.*Alm.*5.19. -κις, Adv. *hundred times*, Hero *Bel.*113.7, Orib.*Fr.*113. -κλῖνος, ον, *with* 100 *couches, with room for* 100 *couches*, of a room, Chares ap.Ath.12.538c, D.S.17.16, J.*BJ*5. 4.4. -κρήπις, ιδος, ὁ, ἡ, *with a hundred steps*, βωμοί Jul.*Ep.*180.

ἑκᾰτον-τᾰλαντία, ἡ, *sum of* 100 *talents*, Poll.9.52. -τάλαντος [τᾰ], ον, *worth* 100 *talents*, γραφὴ ἑ. an action *for damages laid at that sum*, Ar.*Eq.*442.

※ ἑκᾰτοντά-μᾰχος [τᾰ], ον, *able to fight* 100 *men*, J.*AJ*13.12.5. -μιγμα, ατος, τό, *a compound remedy*, Gal.14.152.

ἑκᾰτόντ-ανδρος, ον, *consisting of* 100 *men*, λοχαγία Jul.*Ep.*180.

ἑκᾰτοντά-πεδος [τᾰ], ον, = ἑκατόμπεδος, νεώς Jul.*Ep.*180. -πηχυς, υ, *of* 100 *cubits*, J.*BJ*2.10.2. -πλάσιος [πλᾰ], ον, = sq., Simp.*in Ph.*1115.33. Adv. -ίως LXX 1 *Ch.*21.3. -πλᾰσίων, ον, gen. ονος, *a hundred times as much* or *many*, c. gen., X.*Oec.*2.3: without gen., *a hundredfold*, LXX 2 *Ki.*24.3; καρπός *Ev.Luc.*8.8. -πλεθρος, ον, *of* 100 *plethra*, ἄρουραι Jul.*Ep.*180. -πολις, v. ἑκατόμπολις. -πῠλος, ον, = ἑκατόμπυλος, Θήβη *AP*7.7, cf. Jul.*Ep.*180; Ῥώμη *IG*14.1389 ii 3 (-οπυλ- lapis).

ἑκᾰτοντ-άρουρος [ᾰρ], ον, *holder of* 100 ἄρουραι, *PHal.*20.4, 5 (iii B.C.), *PGiss.*2.10 (ii B.C.), etc. -αρχέω, *to be a centurion*, D.C.52. 25. ※ -άρχης, ου, ὁ, *leader of a hundred*, Hdt.7.81, A.*Fr.*182; = ταξίαρχος (q.v.), Ascl.*Tact.*2.8, etc.; = Lat. *centurio*, D.H.2.13 (v.l. -χοι), *Act.Ap.*10.1, J.*AJ*9.7.2, Plu.*Pomp.*78, etc. -αρχία, ἡ, *post of a centurion*, Onos.34.2 (pl.), D.C.78.5. II. *centurion's command, century*, J.*BJ*3.6.2, Ph.2.33 (pl.). 2. *body of* 128 *light-armed troops*, Ascl.*Tact.*6.3, etc. -άρχιον, τό, name of an *eye-salve*,

Aët.7.11, al. ® **-αρχος,** ὁ, = ἑκατοντάρχης, X.*Cyr*.5.3.41, *Ev.Matt.* 8.5, Ph.2.131, Plu.*Luc*.35, Arr.*Tact*.10.3. **-άς,** άδος, ἡ, the number *a hundred*, Hdt.7.184: pl., Ph.2.423, Jul.*Ep*.180.

**ἑκᾰτοντά-στῦλος,** ον, *having* 100 *columns*, Aristeas 116, *BCH* 11. 100 (Thyatira). **-φυλλος,** ον, *with* 100 *petals*, ῥόδα Thphr.*HP* 6.6.4. **-χειρ,** χειρος, ὁ, ἡ, = ἑκατόγχειρ, Plu.2.478f (as v.l.), Jul. *Ep*.180: also **-χειρος,** ον, Hsch. s.v. Βριάρεῳ. **-χοος,** ον, contr. **-χους,** ουν, *of* 100 *measures*: *yielding fruit a hundredfold*, Thphr.*HP* 8.7.4; κριθή Str.15.3.11.

**ἑκᾰτοντ-ερῖφον,** τό, *sacrifice of* 100 *kids*, *IG*12(5).908 (Tenos). **-όργυιος,** ον, 100 *fathoms high*, ἀνδριάς Pi.*Fr*.282: in Ar.*Av*.1131 μῆκος ἑκατοντορόγυιον shd. be read. **-ορος,** ον, (ἐρέσσω) *hundred-oared*, Poll.1.82. **-ούτης,** ου, ὁ, contr. for ἑκατονταέτης, Luc.*Macr.* 14:—fem. **-οῦτις,** ιδος, Ath.15.697e.

® **ἕκᾰτος,** ὁ, shortd. fr. ἑκατη-βόλος (q.v.), epith. of Apollo, Il.7.83, 20.295:—as Subst., **ἕκατος,** ὁ, 1.385, 20.71 (connected with ἑκατόν (sc. βέλη) by Simon.26A):—fem. **ἑκάτη,** epith. of Artemis, A.*Supp.* 676 (lyr.), Corn.*ND*32.

**ἑκᾰτοστ-εύω,** *bear a hundredfold*, Lxx *Ge*.26.12. **-ήριος,** α, ον, *subject to a tax of one per cent.*, οἰκίη *GDI*5661.13 (Chios):—Subst. ® **-ηρία,** Ion. **-ίη,** ἡ, *tax of one per cent.*, ib.48, *PCair.Zen*.12.76, al. **-ιαῖος,** α, ον, = ἑκατοστός: ἑκατοστιαῖοι τόκοι interest *of* $\frac{1}{100}$ *monthly*, i.e. twelve per cent. per ann., $IG2^{2}$.1104.4, *PGrenf*.2.89 (vi A.D.).

**ἑκᾰτοστο-εικοστόγδοον,** τό, *a* 128*th part*, Nicom.*Ar*.1.8. **-εικοστός,** ή, όν, 120*th*, Paul.Aeg.2.6.

**ἑκᾰτόστομος,** ον, *hundred-mouthed*, E.*Ba*.406 (lyr.).

® **ἑκᾰτοστός,** ή, όν, *hundredth*, Hdt.1.47, etc.; ἐπ' ἑκατοστὰ ἐκφέρειν to bear *a hundredfold*, Id.4.198. **II.** ἑκατοστή, ἡ, *tax of one per cent.*, Ar.*V*.658, X.*Ath*.1.17, *PGnom*.85, etc.; ἐκ τῶν χρημάτων ἑ. *IG*2.721 *A*i12: also, = τόκοι ἑκατοστιαῖοι, Plu.*Luc*.20.

**ἑκᾰτόστῦλος,** ον, = ἑκατοντάστυλος, *having* 100 *columns* (sc. κρήνη), *Abh.Berl.Akad*.1904(2).13.

® **ἑκᾰτοστύς,** ύος, ἡ, = ἑκατοντάς, X.*Cyr*.6.3.34, Plu.*Rom*.8. **II.** a division of a community, *a hundred*, Aen.Tact.11.10a, $IPE1^{2}$.79. 30 (Olbia, i A.D.), *Milet*.3 No.153 (Byzantium), *SIG*645.61 (Seleucia Cilic., ii B.C.), *CIG*3641*b* (Lampsacus), etc.

**ἑκᾰτόφυλλον,** τό, *hundred-petalled rose*, *Gloss.*

**ἑκᾰτῶρυξ,** ὕγος, ὁ, dub. sens. in *IPE*4.80*B*6.

**ἔκαχεν·** ὑπήντησεν, Hsch. (leg. ἔκιχεν).

**ἐκβᾰβάζω** (or perh. **-βαβράζω**), glossed by ἐκσαλεύω, S.*Fr*.139 (ap.Hsch.).

**ἐκβάζω,** *speak out*, *declare*, A.*Ag*.498.

**ἐκβαίνω,** fut. -βήσομαι: aor. ἐξέβην: pf. ἐκβέβηκα:—*step out of* or *off from*, c. gen., πέτρης ἐκβαίνοντα Il.4.107; ἔκβαιν' ἀπήνης A.*Ag*. 906; ἐ. ἐκ τῆς νεώς Th.1.137 (so in tmesi, ἐκ δὲ Χρυσηῒς νηὸς βῆ Il.1. 439): abs., *step out of* a ship or chariot, *disembark*, *dismount*, ἐκ δ' ἔβαν αὐτοί 3.113, cf. 1.437, Hdt.4.196, etc.; *step out of* the sea, Od. 5.415, 7.278; *debouch from* a defile, X.*An*.4.2.3; καταστρατοπεδεύσασθαι ἐπὶ λόφον ἐκβάντες ib.6.3.20: rarely exc. of persons, but βοὴ ..ἐξέβη νάπους S.*Aj*.892. **2.** *go out of*, *depart from*, ψυχὴ ἐ. ἐκ τοῦ σώματος Pl.*Phd*.77d; ἐκ τοῦ πολέμου Plb.3.40.7: c. gen., ἐ. τύχης E.*IT*907; ἐ. τῆς ἑαυτοῦ ἰδέας Pl.*R*.380d; τῆς λεκτικῆς ἁρμονίας Arist.*Po*.$1449^{a}27$; τι τῆς εἰωθυίας διαίτης Pl.*R*.406b; ἔνθεν ἐ. Id. *Ti*.44e; *withdraw from*, ἐκ τῆς νομοθεσίας Id.*Lg*.744a; μισθώσεως, γεωργίας, *BGU*1120.52 (i B.C.), *PTeb*.309.14 (ii A.D.). **3.** c. acc., *leave*, τὴν πλατεῖαν Herod.6.53, cf. Phld.*D*.3.11: but, **b.** usu. with the sense, *outstep*, *overstep*, γαίας ὅρια E.*HF*82; τὴν ἡλικίαν τοῦ γεννᾶν Pl.*R*.461b; τριάκοντα ἔτη ib.537d; τὸν ὅρκον v.l. in Id.*Smp*. 183b; τὸ μέσον Arist.*Pol*.$1296^{a}26$. **4.** in Poets, the instrument of motion is added in acc., ἐκβὰς..ἁρμάτων πόδα E.*Heracl*.802. **5.** *to be produced*, of crops, οἱ ἐκβησόμενοι καρποί *PLips*.23.20 (iv A.D.), etc. **6.** *project*, of ground, *PTeb*.84.91 (ii B.C.). **II.** metaph., **1.** *come out*, *turn out*, Hdt.7.209; τῇ περ ὤρων ἐκβησόμενα πρήγματα ταῦτα ibid.; τὰ μέλλοντά σφι ἐκβαίνειν ib.221, cf. Th.7.14, etc.; of a total obtained by measurement, *PAmh*.2.31 (ii B.C.). **2.** *to be fulfilled*, of prophecies, etc., D.19.28; also τοιοῦτον ἐκβέβηκεν S.*Tr*.672; κάκιστος ἐ. *to prove* a villain, E.*Med*.229; κατὰ νοῦν ἐ. τινί Pl.*Mx*.247d; ἄν τι μὴ κατὰ γνώμην ἐκβῇ D.1.16; τὸ ἐκβάν, τὰ ἐκβαίνοντα, *the issue*, *event*, D.1.11, Plb.2.27.5. **3.** *go out of due bounds*, ἐς τοῦτ' ἐκβέβηκ' ἀλγηδόνος E.*Med*.56; ποῖ ποτ' ἐξέβης λόγῳ; S.*Ph*.896; ἐξέβην γὰρ ἄλλοσε I *wandered* elsewhere in thought, E. *IT*781; in writing, *digress*, ἐπάνειμι ἔνθεν ἐξέβην X.*HG*6.5.1, cf. 7.4.1, D.18.211, Pl.*Lg*.864c. **4.** *project*, *extend beyond* a limit, *POxy*. 918xi20 (ii A.D.): metaph., *transcend*, ἐ. ὑπὲρ τὸ μέγα ὂν καὶ ὑπὲρ τὸ μικρόν Porph.*Sent*.34. **5.** *lapse*, πρὶν ἐκβῆναί τινι τὴν στρατηγίαν App.*Syr*.23. **6.** ἐκβαίνοντος μηνός, = φθίνοντος μ., *IG*14.105 (Syracus.).

**B.** causal, in aor. 1 -έβησα:—*cause to go out*, esp. *put ashore*, *land from* a ship, ἐκ δ' ἑκατόμβην βῆσαν Il.1.438; οἱ δ' ἐκβήσαντές [σε] ἔβησαν (where ἔβησαν is aor. 2) Od.24.301; ἐς γαῖαν ἐξέβησέ [με] E. *Hel*.1616.

**ἐκβάκχ-ευσις,** εως, ἡ, *Bacchic enthusiasm*, Eun.*VS*p.470B. ® **-εύω,** *excite to Bacchic frenzy*, φρένας E.*Tr*.408, cf. Pl.*Phdr*.245a; τὰς σοφιστικὰς ὑποθέσεις Philostr.*VS*2.10.4; *cause to rage* with anger, Phld. *Ir*.p.63W.:—Pass., *to be filled with Bacchic frenzy*, πᾶσα δ' ἐξεβακχεύθη πόλις E.*Ba*.1295, cf. Pl.*R*.561a, Hdn.5.8.1, etc.; ἔρωτι Aristaenet. 1.16; ὑπὸ τοῦ ἔρωτος Max.Tyr.24.9:—Med., E.*Supp*.1001 (lyr.):—intr. in Act., Alex.141.13; of anger, Phld.*Ir*.p.35W.

® **ἐκβάλλω,** Arc. **ἐσδέλλω** *IG*5(2).6.49 (Tegea, iv B.C.), fut. -βᾰλῶ: aor. -έβαλον: pf. -βέβληκα:—**Pass.**, fut. -βεβλήσομαι E.*Ba*.1313:—*throw* or *cast out of*, c. gen., 'Οδίον μέγαν ἔκβαλε δίφρου Il.5.39, etc.: abs., *throw out*, ἐκ δ' εὐνὰς ἔβαλον 1.436, etc.; καὶ τὴν μὲν..ἰχθύσι κύρμα γενέσθαι ἔκβαλον *threw* her *overboard*, Od.15.481, cf. Hdt.1.24: then in various relations, ἐκπίπτω being freq. used as its Pass.: **1.** *throw ashore*, τὸν δ' ἄρ'..νεὸς ἔκβαλε κῦμ' ἐπὶ χέρσου Od.19.278; ἄνεμος..τρηχέως περιέσπε..πολλὰς τῶν νεῶν ἐκβάλλων πρὸς τὸν Ἄθων Hdt.6.44; ἐ. ἐς τὴν γῆν Id.7.170 (but in 2.113 ἄνεμοι..ἐκβάλλουσι ἐς τὸ πέλαγος *carry out* to sea; ἐξέβαλεν ἄνεμος ἡμᾶς *drove* us *out of* our *course*, E.*Cyc*.20):—Med., *put ashore*, ἵππους ἐξεβάλλοντο Hdt. 6.101; *jettison*, Syngr.ap.D.35.11. **2.** *cast out of* a place, Κιμμερίους ἐκβαλόντες ἐκ τῆς Εὐρώπης Hdt.1.103; ἐ. ἐκ τῆς χώρας, of an enemy, Lycurg.99, cf. D.60.8; esp. of banishment, ἐκ πόλεως ἐ. *drive out of* the country, Pl.*Grg*.468d, cf. Ar.*Pl*.430, etc.; of a corpse, ἔξω τῆς πόλεως, τῶν ὁρίων, Pl.*Lg*.873b, 909c: c. acc. only, *drive out*, *banish*, Heraclit.121, S.*OC*646, 770, etc.; *turn out*, νεοττούς Arist.*HA*$618^{b}$ 12; *cast out of* the synagogue, *Ev.Jo*.9.34; ἐκ τοῦ τάγματος J.*BJ*2.8. 8; *exorcize*, *cast out* evil spirits, *Ev.Marc*.1.34, al.; also in weakened sense, *cause to depart*, ib.43. **3.** *expose* on a desert island, S.*Ph*.257, 1034, 1390; *expose* a dead body, ταφῆς ἄτερ Id.*Aj*.1388; ἐ. τέκνα *expose* children, E.*Ion*964. **4.** ἐ. γυναῖκα ἐκ τῆς οἰκίας *divorce* her, D. 59.83: with simple acc., And.1.125, D.59.63, D.S.12.18, etc.:—Pass., Lxx *Le*.21.7. **5.** *cast out of* his seat, *depose* a king, ἐ. ἕδρας Κρόνον A.*Pr*.203; ἐκ τυραννίδος θρόνου τ' ib.910; ἐκ τῆς τιμῆς X.*Cyr*.1.3.9: without ἐκ, ἐ. τινὰ πλούτου S.*El*.649:—Pass., *to be ejected*, of an occupier, *PPetr*.2 p.143 (iii B.C.), *PMagd*.12.8 (iii B.C.), etc.; χάριτος ἐκβεβλημένη S.*Aj*.808; ἐκ τῆς φιλίας X.*An*.7.5.6; ἐκ τῆς ἀρχῆς ἐξεβλήθησαν Isoc.4.70. **6.** *throw decisively* in wrestling, τίν' οὐ παλαίουσ' ἐς τρὶς ἐ.; S.*Fr*.941.13. **7.** ἐ. φρέατα *dig* wells, Plu.*Pomp*.32. **8.** of drugs, *get rid of*, τοξεύματα Dsc.3.32. **9.** *expel* afterbirth, Hp. *Mul*.1.78. **10.** *publish*, σύνταξιν Plb.30.4.11; *issue*, δόγμα ib.19.6; ἀπόκρισιν Id.29.19.5. **II.** *strike out of*, χειρῶν δ' ἔκβαλλε κύπελλα Od.2.396, cf. Theoc.22.210; ἐκβάλλεθ'..τευχέων πάλους *throw* them *out of* the urns, A.*Eu*.742: abs., δοῦρα ἐ. *fell* trees (prop., *cut* them *out of* the forest), Od.5.244. **2.** *strike open*, *break in*, ἐ. θύρετρα, πύλας, θύρας, E.*Or*.1474, *Hec*.1044, Lys.3.23, D.47.53. **III.** *let fall*, *drop*, χειρὸς δ' ἔκβαλεν ἔγχος Il.14.419; σφῦραν B.17.28; ξίφος E. *Andr*.629, cf. Ar.*Lys*.156; οἰστούς X.*An*.2.1.6: metaph., ἦ ῥ' ἅλιον ἔπος ἔκβαλον *let fall* an idle word, Il.18.324; εἰ μὴ ὑπερφίαλον ἔπος ἔκβαλε Od.4.503, cf. Hdt.6.69, A.*Ag*.1662, etc.; ἐ. ῥῆμα Pl.*R*. 473e: abs., *utter*, *speak*, D.L.9.7; *shed*, δάκρυα δ' ἔκβαλε θερμά Od. 19.362; ἐ. ἕρκος ὀδόντων *cast*, *shed* one's teeth, Sol.27, cf. E.*Cyc*.644, etc.; *throw up* blood, S.*Ant*.1238; *spit out*, Thphr.*HP*4.8.4; ἐκβαλεῦσι τὰς κούρας their eyes *will drop out*, prov. of covetous persons, Herod.4.64. **IV.** *throw away*, *cast aside*, *reject*, εὐμένειαν, χάριν, S.*OC*631, 636, cf. Plb.1.14.4; προγόνων παλαιὰ θέσμια E.*Fr*.360.45; θεούς Ar.*Nu*.1477; *recall*, *repudiate*, ἐ. λόγους Pl.*Cri*.46b; *annul*, τοὔπος S.*OT*849; *remove* an official from his post, D.21.87; *drive* an actor from the stage, Id.19.337: metaph., of a politician, Pl.*Ax*.368d: —Pass., Ar.*Eq*.525; ἐκβάλλεσθαι ἄξια Antipho 4.3.1. **V.** *lose*, properly by one's own fault, φρένας, τἀγαθόν, S.*Ant*.649, *Aj*.965, cf. Ar.*Eq*.404, *Ec*.751. **VI.** *produce*, of women, Hp.*Epid*.4.25 (of premature birth), Plu.*Publ*.21; esp. in case of a miscarriage or abortion, Hp.*Mul*.1.60, Thphr.*HP*9.18.8; βρέφος ἐκ τῆς γαστρός Ant.Lib. 34; with play on 1.2, D.L.2.102, etc.; *hatch* chicks, Sch.Ar.*Av*. 251. **b.** of plants, ἐ. καρπὸν *put forth* fruit, Hp.*Nat.Puer*.22; ἐ. στάχυν E.*Ba*.750:—Pass., τὰ ἐκβαλλόμενα *BGU*197.12 (i A.D.). **VII.** *put out* a bone or joint, Hp.*Fract*.31, *Art*.67; χεῖρα Arr.*Epict*.3.15. 4. **VIII.** *upset*, *undo the effect of* a speech, Plb.11.10.6. **IX.** Math., *produce* a line, in Pass., Arist.*Cael*.$271^{b}29$, *Mech*.$850^{a}11$, Str. 2.1.29, etc.; ἐ. εἰς ἄπειρον *produce* to infinity, in metaph. sense, τὰ δεινά Phld.*D*.1.12, cf. 13. **2.** *start counting*, in astronomical calculations, Procl.*Par.Ptol*.252. **X.** intr., *go out*, *depart*, ἵν' ἐκβάλω ποδὶ ἄλλην ἐπ' αἶαν E.*El*.96; of the sea, *break out of its bed*, Arist. *Mete*.$367^{b}13$; of a river, *branch off*, Pl.*Phd*.113a: metaph., ἐπειδὰν ἐς μειράκια ἐκβάλωσιν D.C.52.26.

® **ἐκβαρβᾰρ-όω,** *make quite barbarous*, πόλιν Isoc.9.20:—Pass., *become so*, Pl.*Ep*.353a, Aristox.*Fr.Hist*.90, Plb.3.58.8. **-ωσις,** εως, ἡ, *barbarization*, Plu.*Tim*.17.

® **ἐκβᾰσᾰνίζω,** *put to the question*, in Pass., J.*AJ*15.8.4; *test thoroughly*, *BGU*1141.47 (i B.C.), Philostr.*VA*2.31 (Pass.).

**ἐκβᾰσῐλίζομαι,** *to be raised to royal rank*, *POxy*.471.54 (ii A.D.):—prob. to be read for **ἐκβολίζεται·** εἰς βασιλέως ἔθη τρέπεται, Hsch.

**ἐκβάσιος** [ᾰ], ον, epith. of Apollo, = ἐκβατήριος, A.R.1.966.

® **ἔκβᾰσις,** εως, ἡ, *way out of*, esp. *out of* the sea, Od.5.410; κατὰ τὴν ἔκβασιν τὴν εἰς τὰ..ὄρη X.*An*.4.3.20, cf. 4.1.20; περὶ τὰς ἐκβάσεις about the *landing-places*, Plb.3.14.6. **2.** *going out of*, esp. *out of* a ship, *disembarkation*, ἔ. στρατοῦ A.*Supp*.771, cf. A.R.2.1049, Plb.4.64.5: metaph., ἄτης ἔ. *escape from*.., E.*Med*.279, cf. Plu. *Pyrrh*.23. **3.** = μετάβασις, Arist *Cael*.$268^{b}3$. **4.** *end* of a person's life, Lxx *Wi*.2.17: generally, *termination*, *completion*, ἐλαιουργίας *PFay*.91.21 (i A.D.); *accomplishment*, τῶν ἔργων Ruf.*Anat*. 1. **5.** *deviation*, *declension*, *departure*, παρὰ [τοῦ ἀγαθοῦ] Plot.1.8.7, cf. 3.7.6. **II.** *issue*, *event*, Men.696, Arr.*Epict*.2.7.9 (pl.); *fulfilment* of divination, Zeno *Stoic*.1.44, Chrysipp.ib.2.342. **III.** *emanation*, *procession*, Porph.*Sent*.35, Dam.*Pr*.283. **IV.** *produce*, ἐδαφῶν *PRyl*.122.5 (ii A.D.). **V.** *digression*, Serv. ad Virg.*G*.2.209.

® **ἐκβασμίδωσις** [ῐδ], εως, ἡ, in pl., *steps for descending from* an altar,

*Epigr.Gr.*229 (Ephesus):—also ❀**ἐκβάσμωσις**, *IGRom.*4.514 (Pergam.), *BCH*4.381 (Aeolis).

❀ **ἐκ-βᾰτήριος**, α, ον, *of* or *for disembarkation*, μέλη Him.*Ecl.*13.38; ἐκβατήρια (sc. ἱερά) νόσου *a sacrifice offered for escape* from an illness, Philostr.*VS*2.1.12. II. Subst. ἐκβατηρία, ἡ, *landing-place*, *PPetr.*3 p.89 (iii B.C.), Lyc.516, *PTeb.*33.9 (ii B.C.). **-βάτης** [ᾰ], ου, ὁ, = ἡνίοχος ἐκβιβάζων, *IG*2.1316. **-βᾰτός**, ή, όν, *coming to pass*, Gal. 19.354.

**ἐκβάω**, Dor. for ἐκβαίνω, ἐκβῶντας Foed.Dor.ap.Th.5.77.

**ἐκβεβαι-όομαι**, *confirm*, *establish*, Plu.2.283a; νίκημα Id.*Pomp.*19, cf. *Ages.*19. **-ωσις**, εως, ἡ, *confirmation*, Id.2.85c.

**ἐκβεβηλόω**, *profane*, v.l. in Lxx*Le.*21.9 (Pass.).

**ἐκβήσσω**, *cough up*, Arist.*HA*495ᵇ19:—Pass., Hp.*Morb.*2.46.

**ἐκβῐ-άζω**, *to force out*, *dislodge*, *expel*, prob. f.l. for -βιβάζω in Plu. 2.243d, 662a; also χεῖρα κατά τινος *lay violent* hands on, Lib.*Decl.*40.1 (s.v.l.):—elsewh. in Med. (fut. -βιάσομαι Men.*Pk.*252), Thphr.*HP* 8.10.4, *PSI*4.340.16 (iii B.C.), Plb.18.23.4; δίψαν Plu.2.584e:—Pass., τόξον χειρῶν ἐκβεβιασμένον the bow *forced from* mine hands, S. *Ph.*1129 (lyr.); ἐκβιασθέντες *forced from their position*, Plb.1.28.6, cf. Plu.*Thes.*27, etc.: rare in pres., τοὺς ἐκβιαζομένους Id.*Alex.*60. 2. Med., *constrain*, Hdn.2.3.4: c. inf., ἐ. τινὰ ὑπακοῦσαι Id.2.2.5; ἐς τὸ γράφειν Eun.*Hist.*p.216 D.:—Pass., τούτους ἀνελεῖν -βιασθήσομαι Lib.*Decl.*40.14. II. Med., *project with force*, Arist.*Aud.*800ᵇ12: metaph., *exploit to the full*, τὴν τόλμαν Eun.*Hist.*p.258 D. 2. *press upon*, ὅταν ἐκβιάσηται τὰ σπλάγχνα [ἡ ὑστέρη] Aret.*SA*2.11. III. Pass., *to be expressed in a forced, elaborate way*, of works of art, Plu. *Tim.*36. IV. in argument, *insist*, c. acc. et inf., Phld.*Rh.*1.74 S. ❀ **-άομαι**, = foreg., Hp.*de Arte*12:—Act., aor. ἐκβιᾶσαι Lxx*Jd.* 14.15. **-ασμα**, ατος, τό, prob. f.l. for ἔκβρασμα II, Vett.Val.161.18 (pl.). **-αστής**, οῦ, ὁ, *exactor*, *oppressor*, Aq., Thd.*Pr.*6.7. ❀ **-αστικός**, ή, όν, *oppressive*, *tyrannical*, Ptol.*Tetr.*155 (s.v.l.); cf. ἐκβιβ-.

❀ **ἐκβῐβ-άζω**, Att. fut. -βιβῶ, causal of ἐκβαίνω, *make to go* or *come out*, ἐκβίβασον ἐκ τοῦ βουτόμου τοὐρνίθιον Ar.*Av.*662; ἐ. ποταμὸν ἐκ τοῦ αὐλῶνος *turn* a river *out* of its channel, Hdt.7.130; ἐ. τῶν ὁδῶν X.*Eq.Mag.*1.18; ἐ. τινὰ δικαίων λόγων *stop* one *from* discussing the question of justice, Th.5.98. b. in athletic contests, ἐ. κλήρους *eliminate*, i.e. *win* heats, *IGRom.*3.626 (Xanthus), al.; ἅρματι ἐγβιβάζων *SIG*728 *H* (Delph., i B.C.). c. *bring to a close*, μέτρον, κῶλον, Phld.*Po.Herc.*1676.12. 2. esp. *land* persons or goods *from* a ship, *disembark*, Th.7.39, Pl.*Grg.*512a, *PMeyer*21.8 (iii/iv A.D.):—Pass., Artem.Eph.ap.Porph.*Antr.*4. 3. = ἐμβιβάζω 3 (quod fort. leg.), εἰς τὸν πόλεμον Plb.27.7.8. II. *carry out* a measure, etc., εἵνεκεν τοῦ τὸ ἐπίταγμα ἐκβιβασθῆμεν *IG*5(1).1432.8 (Messene), cf. *POxy.*1195 (ii A.D.). III. *levy execution on*, τινά *Cod.Just.*3.2.4, 12.60.7.3 (Pass.). IV. *satisfy* a person's claim, *PTeb.*398.18 (ii A.D.). ❀ **-ασμός**, ὁ, *execution* of a sentence or judgement, Aq.1*Ki.*15.23, *Cod.Just.*12.60.7.1. **-αστής**, οῦ, ὁ, *one who executes* a sentence, Aq.*De.*16.18, Lyd.*Mag.*3.11, 12, *Cod.Just.*7. 2.4.2. ❀ **-αστικός**, ή, όν, *extortionate*, *oppressive*, Procl.*Par.Ptol.* 219 (s.v.l.), cf. ἐκβιαστικός; *efficacious*, *Gloss.*

**ἐκβιβρώσκω**, *devour*, ἐκ μὲν ἐσχάτας βέβρωκε σάρκας S.*Tr.*1054:—Pass., *Gp.*2.35.7: metaph., Corn.*ND*18.

❀ **ἔκβῐος**, ον, *deprived of life*, Artem.4.32.

**ἐκβιούζει** (i.e. ἐκϝιύζει)· θρηνεῖ μετὰ κραυγῆς, Hsch.

**ἐκβῐόω**, *live out*, *complete*, ἑξηκοστὸν ἔτος *IG*14.420 (Lipara).

**ἐκβλαστ-άνω**, aor. 1 ἐξεβλάστησα Hp.*Alim.*6, but inf. ἐκβλαστεῖν Thphr.*CP*3.23.1:—*shoot*, *sprout*, Id.*HP*7.2.3: metaph., τύραννος ἐκ προστατικῆς ῥίζης ἐ. Pl.*R.*565d, cf. Procl.*Inst.*36. 2. c. acc., *grow out of*, τὴν ἰδίην ἰδέην Hp. l.c. II. *cause to grow*, *produce*, ἔξοδον χλοῆς Lxx*Jb.*38.27; *cause to revive*, τὴν φυήν Aret.*CA*2.3. **-έω**, = foreg., Sm.*Ps.*103(104).14. **-ημα**, ατος, τό, *new shoot*, *sprout*, v.l. in Dsc.5.92, cf. Ph.1.48, Gal.12.349. **-ησις**, εως, ἡ, *shooting*, *budding*, φύλλων Dsc.1.81, cf. *Gp.*5.25.1. 2. esp. *later budding*, Thphr.*HP*3.5.3 (nisi leg. ἐπι-).

**ἐκβλέπω**, *look*, ἁπαλά (prob.) Philostr.Jun.*Im.*1, cf. Aristid.*Or.* 48(24).32 (dub.). II. *get the power of sight*, Ael.*NA*3.25.

**ἐκ-βλήσιμος**, ον, *to be rejected*, *PGiss.*40 ii 17 (iii A.D.). **-βλητέον**, (ἐκβάλλω) *one must reject*, μύθους Pl.*R.*377c; *one must get rid of*, Orib.*Fr.*130. 2. Medic., ἐ. διαιρέσεις *one must make* incisions, Antyll.ap.Aët.7.71. **-βλητικός**, ή, όν, *serviceable for expelling*, τοξευμάτων Arist.*HA*612ᵃ5; βελῶν Antig.*Mir.*30. **-βλητος**, ον, *cast overboard*, E.*Hec.*699. II. *to be thrown out*, νέκυες κοπρίων ἐκβλητότεροι Heraclit.96, cf. Ph.1.477 (Comp.).

**ἐκβλίσαι**· ἐκθλῖψαι, and **ἐκβλιστέος**· ἐκθλιπτέος, Hsch.

**ἐκ-βλύζω**, *gush out*, Orph.*L.*499; οἴνῳ Lxx*Pr.*3.10. II. trans., *cause to gush out*, ἄμπελος ἐκβλύσει τὸν οἶνον Orph.*Fr.*255; νεκρὸς ὑγρῶν πλῆθος ἐξέβλυσεν Plu.*TG*13. **-βλυσμα**, ατος, τό, *sluice*, *PLand.*52.14 (i A.D.). ❀ **-βλύω**, = ἐκβλύζω, A.R.4.1417 [where ἐκβλῦοντα].

❀ **ἐκβλώσκω**, *come forth*, only aor. imper. ἔκμολε Il.11.604.

**ἐκβοάω**, *call out*, *cry aloud*, X.*Cyn.*6.10, Pl.*R.*492b, A.R.3.631 (tm.), Ph.1.129, al., Polyaen.8.52: c. acc., *drive away* (nisi leg. ἐκσοβῆσαι), *Anacreont.*25.19:—Pass., κραυγαὶ ἐξεβοῶντο *POxy.*1242. 54 (ii A.D.); ἐκβεβοημένος *notorious*, Sch.Lib.*Or.*11.207.

**ἐκβοήθ-εια**, ἡ, *sally*, Th.3.18; *marching out*, Arist.*Pol.*1327ᵃ 6. **-έω**, *march out to aid*, πανδημεί Hdt.6.16; ἐς τὸν Ἰσθμόν Id.9. 26: abs., Polyaen.1.1.3, Plu.2.773f; *make a sally*, Th.1.105, Thphr. *Char.*25.3. **-ησις**, εως, ἡ, *protection*, ἐμπυρισμῶν against fire, Ath. Mech.12.6.

❀ **ἐκβόησις**, εως, ἡ, *crying out* or *aloud*, Ph.2.159, al., Hld.10.17; ἡ ἐπὶ τῷ ἥδεσθαι ἐ. S.E.*M.*1.143: pl., *Anatolian Studies* 154 (Ephesus, V A.D.), *Cod.Just.*1.12.8.1.

**ἐκβολάς**, άδος, ἡ, *anything thrown out*; = σκωρία, *dross*, Str.9.1. 23. 2. ἐ. μήτρα, Lat. *vulva ejectitia*, a Roman dish, Hipparch.ap. Ath.3.101a, Sopat.8. II. an Egyptian *grape*, causing abortion, Plin.*HN*14.117.

**ἐκβολβίζω**, *peel*, as one does an onion of its outer coats, ἐ. τινὰ τῶν κῳδίων Ar.*Pax*1123. II. metaph., *uproot*, *destroy*, *Com.Adesp.*992.

**ἐκβόλ-ειον** σύαγρον, τό, prob. = ἐκβολὰς μήτρα, Dionys.Trag. 1. ❀ **-εύς**, έως, ὁ, *inspector of dykes*, *PLond.*5.1648 (vi A.D.), al. ❀ **-ή**, ἡ, (ἐκβάλλω) *throwing out*, ψήφων ἐ. *casting* the votes *out of* the urn, A. *Eu.*748. 2. *jettisoning* of cargo, Id.*Th.*769 (lyr.), Arist.*EN*1110ᵃ 9, *Act.Ap.*27.18 (but simply, *unloading*, *Sammelb.*1207): metaph., ἐ. τῆς δόξης *casting out* of it, *getting rid* of it, Pl.*Sph.*230b, *R.*412e; ἐ. ἐλέου Aphth.*Prog.*7, cf. Diog.Oen.4. II. *expulsion*, *banishment*, A.*Supp.*421 (lyr., pl.); μετὰ τὴν τῶν τυράννων ἐ. Arist.*Pol.*1275ᵇ36; ἐκβολαὶ ἐκ τῆς πόλεως Pl.*Lg.*847b; *dislodgement*, *ejection*, Plb.4.8. 4. 2. *divorce*, *repudiation*, γυναικός Lib.*Decl.*26.45. III. *letting fall* or *drop*, δακρύων ἐκβολαί E.*HF*742 (lyr.); ἐ. [ὀδόντων] *casting* or *shedding* of teeth, Arist.*GA*789ᵃ15. IV. *expulsion* of a foetus, Hp. *Mul.*1.78. 2. ἐ. σίτου *the time when* the corn *comes into ear*, Th.4. 1. 3. *shoot*, καυλοῦ Dsc.3.114. V. *putting out* of a joint, *dislocation*, ἐκβολαὶ τῶν ἄρθρων Plu.2.164f. VI. *putting forth*, *exposing*, μαστῶν Plb.2.56.7. VII. *debouchure*, *outlet*, ἐ. Πηνειοῦ Hdt.7. 128; *mouth* of a river, in pl., Th.2.102; in sg., Id.7.35, Pl.*Phd.* 113a: *pass leading out* of a chain of mountains, αἱ ἐκβολαὶ τοῦ Κιθαιρῶνος Hdt.9.38. 2. *by-way*, ἐ. ἐκ τῆς ὁδοῦ τῆς εὐθείας Paus.3.10.7: metaph., ἐ. λόγου *digression*, Th.1.97, Philostr.*Her.*19.14 (pl.), etc. 3. *close* of a verse, Eust.900.24. 4. *projection*, στόματος a snout, Philostr.Jun.*Im.*12. VIII. (from Pass.), *that which is cast out*, δικέλλης ἐ. *earth thrown up* by a mattock, *upcast*, S.*Ant.* 250; οὐρεία ἐ. *children cast* or *exposed* on the mountains, E.*Hec.*1079 (anap.). 2. *cargo thrown overboard*, *jetsam*, πλὴν ἐκβολῆς, ἣν ἄν.. ἐκβάλωνται Syngr.ap.D.35.11; so ἐκβολαὶ νεώς *wrecked* seamen, E.*IT*1424. IX. in Music, *interval of five* διέσεις, Plu.2.1141b, Bacch.*Harm.*42, Aristid.Quint.1.10. X. = ἐκβολάς I, Str.14.5. 28. **-ίζεται**, v. ἐκβασιλίζομαι. **-ῐμαῖος**, α, ον, = sq., Heph. Astr.1.1. **-ιμος**, ον, *thrown out*, *ejected*: ἐκβόλιμον *abortion*, Arist. *HA*575ᵃ28; τὰ ἐ. τῶν ἐμβρύων Id.*PA*665ᵇ1; τῶν ᾠῶν Id.*GA*752ᵇ4, cf. *POxy.*464.21. 2. metaph., *abortive*, *futile*, [δόξα] Phld.*Po.*5. 29, cf. Plu.2.44d; *to be rejected*, ἄκυρον καὶ ἐ. *PGrenf.*2.71 ii 11 (iii A.D.). **-ιον**, τό, *drug* or *other means for expelling the foetus* or *placenta*, Hp.*Mul.*1.78, Sor.1.60, Plu.2.134f. II. = δίκταμνον, Ps.-Dsc.3.32. **-ος**, ον, *thrown out* or *away*, *exposed*, ἔκβολον οἴκων βρέφος E.*Ph.*804 (lyr.); *rejected*, σφόνδυλοι *Supp.Epigr.*2.569.22 (Didyma); ἔ. βροτῶν βίου Luc.*Trag.*215. 2. *frustrated*, Lxx*Ju.* 11.11. 3. *cast out*, [ἔφοδος] ὡσανεὶ κόσκινον [ἀριθμοὺς] ὥσπερ ἔ. ἀποχωρίσει Iamb.*in Nic.*p.29 P.; τὰ διὰ κοσκίνου ἔ. ib.p.30 P. II. Subst. ἔκβολον, τό, *outcast*, ἔ. κόρης E.*Ion*555; νηδύος ἔ. Id.*Ba.*91 (lyr.). 2. ναὸς ἔκβολα seem to be *rags cast out from* the ship, Id. *Hel.*422; but, 3. in Id.*IT*1042 πόντου ἔκβολον *an outbreak*, a place where the sea *has broken in upon* the land.

**ἐκβομβ-έω**, *thunder forth*, Poll.1.118. **-ησις**, εως, ἡ, *shouting in token of approbation*, Them.*Or.*23.282d.

**ἐκβόσκω**, aor. ἐξεβόσκησα, *consume*, τὰ ὑγρά Alex.Aphr.*Pr.*2.29:—Med., ἐκβόσκομαι *feed on*, τι Nic.*Th.*803; *absorb*, ἰκμάδα Gal.1.517: metaph. of grief, ὀδύνη ἐ. με Aristaenet.2.5.

**ἐκβοτανίζω**, *exherbo*, *Gloss.*

**ἐκβραγμός**, v.l. for ἐκβρασμός, Lxx*Na.*2.10(11).

❀ **ἐκ-βράζω** or **-βράσσω**, fut. -βράσω: aor. -έβρασα:—*throw out*, *cast on shore*, ἐ. ποταμὸς περὶ τὰ χείλη χρυσίον Arist.*Mir.*833ᵇ16; of the sea, D.S.14.68, etc.; ἑαυτὸν ἐκβράσαι, of a dolphin, Ael.*NA*6.15:—Pass., τὰ ἐκ τῆς θαλάσσης -βρασσόμενα βρυώδη *Gp.*2.22.2; of ships, *to be cast ashore*, ἐς Κασθαναίην ἐξεβράσσοντο Hdt.7.188, cf. 190, Ath. 6.259b; of persons, Plu.2.294f. II. *throw off* humours, Hp.*Mul.* 2.113:—Pass., *gush out*, Id.*Gland.*4:—Med., Id.*Int.*1. III. *expel*, *drive out*, Lxx*Ne.*13.28, 2*Ma.*1.12: metaph., ὁ θυμὸς ἐ. τῆς ψυχῆς ἀκόλαστα ῥήματα Plu.2.456c. IV. intr. in Act., *boil over*, of water, Apollod.1.6.3; *pullulate*, of shoots, ἐκ μιᾶς ῥίζης *Gp.*2.6. 28. ❀ **-βρᾰσις**, εως, ἡ, *pullulation*, φθειρῶν Suid. 2. αἱ κοῖλαι ἐ. *breakers*, *EM*494.14. **-βρασμα**, ατος, τό, *thing cast up*, πόντου *Com.Adesp.*1218; *excretion*, Dsc.5.92, *Hippiatr.*85. II. *cutaneous eruption*, Ruf.ap.Orib.8.24.30 (pl.), cf. Crito ap.Gal.12.448; *scab*, Sm. *Le.*13.6. **-βρασμός**, ὁ, = foreg. II, Suid. and Phot. s.v. πομφόλυξ. II. *trembling*, *shaking*, Lxx*Na.*2.10(11); *confusion*, Hsch.

**ἐκβράσσω**, v. ἐκβράζω:—Ion. **ἐκβρήσσω**, Gal.19.95.

**ἐκ-βρεκτέον**, *one must soak*, Herod.Med.ap.Aët.4.47. **-βρέχω**, *cause to rot*, of water, in Pass., τὰ ἐκβεβρεγμένα ὑπὸ τοῦ ποταμοῦ *PPetr.*3 p.120.

**ἐκβροντάω**, *to strike out by lightning*, ἐξεβροντήθη σθένος he had strength *struck out of him by lightning*, A.*Pr.*364. II. intr., *thunder loud*, Poll.1.118.

**ἐκβρῡχάομαι**, *bellow forth* or *aloud*, E.*Hel.*1557; στεναγμὸν ἡδὺν ἐ. Id.*IT.*1390.

**ἔκβρωμα**, ατος, τό, *anything eaten out*, πρίονος ἔ. saw-dust, S.*Tr.* 700 (pl.); *piece eaten away*, Arist.*HA*625ᵃ9.

**ἐκβῠθίζομαι**, Pass., *come forth from the deep*, v.l. in Callistr.*Stat.*14.

**ἐκβυρσεύω**, *flay*, Al.*Le.*11.40.

**ἐκβυρσ-όω**, *cause to project from the skin*, Gal.18(2).721. **-ωμα**, ατος, τό, *projecting of the bones out of the skin*, ib.714. **-ωσις**, εως, ἡ, = foreg., Orib.*Fr*.88.

**ἐκγᾰλακτόω**, *turn into sap*, Thphr.*CP*3.23.1 :—Pass., *to be turned into sap*, of the seeds of plants, Id.*HP*8.6.1 ; also, *become like milk*, Sch.Hes.*Th*.353.

**ἐκγᾰληνίζω**, fut. -ιῶ, *soothe*, φρένας prob. in E.*Hyps.Fr*.3(1).3.

**ἐκγᾰμ-έομαι**, Pass., *to be given in marriage*, *AB*259, Suid. **-ιστής**, οῦ, ὁ, *matchmaker*, *Cat.Cod.Astr*.8(4).212.

**ἐκγαυρόομαι**, Pass., *to be proud of, admire greatly*, τι E.*IA*101.

**ἐκγέγᾰα, ἐκγεγάονται**, v. ἐκγίγνομαι.

**ἐκγείνασθαι**, aor. inf. Med., with no pres., *bring forth*, Luc.*Trag*.4.

**ἐκγελάω**, Ep. aor. ἐξεγέλασσα *h.Merc*.389, Theoc.4.37 :—*laugh out, laugh loud*, ἡδὺ δ' ἄρ' ἐκγελάσας μετεφώνεε Od.16.354, 18.35, cf. X.*Cyr*.1.3.9, etc. ; γέλωτι ὥσπερ κῦμα ἐ. Pl.*R*.473c ; ἐάν τις κνήσῃ, ἐ. Arist.*Pr*.965ᵃ24 : metaph. of a liquid that rushes out with a *gurgling* sound, ἐκγελᾷ φόνος E.*Tr*.1176.

**ἐκγελιώσαιμι**· ἐ(κ)χλευάσαιμι, Hsch.

**ἔκγελως**, ωτος, ὁ, *loud laughter*, Poll.6.199.

**ἐκγενέτης**, ου, ὁ, = ἔκγονος, δεσπόταις . . Λακεδαίμονος ἐκγενέταισι E.*Andr*.128 codd. (lyr.), cf. *Ba*.1155 (lyr.).

**ἐκγενής**, ές, v. ἐγγενής.

**ἐκγενν-άω**, *beget*, v.l. in Lxx *Ps*.109(110).3 ; also, *bring forth*, Eup. 99 : Boeot. 3 pl. fut. ἐσγεννάσονθ' Corinn.*Supp*.2.62. ❀ **-ημα**, Dor. **-ᾶμα**, ατος, τό, *offspring, issue*, *Supp.Epigr*.2.310.12 (Delph.).

**ἐκγῐγαρτίζω**, *take out the stone from*, τὴν σταφίδα Dsc.1.25, cf. Androm.ap.Gal.13.23, Archig.ib.12.585 ; μῆλα *Gp*.8.27.1.

**ἐκγίγνομαι**, later and Ion. **ἐκγίν-** [ῑ], fut. -γενήσομαι : Ep. pf. ἐκγέγαα, 3 dual ἐκγεγάτην ; part. ἐκγεγαώς, Aeol. ἐκγεγόνων Alc. *Supp*.25.10 :—*to be born of* a father, c. gen , οἱ Διὸς ἐξεγένοντο Il.5.637, cf. 20.231, etc. ; ἐκγεγάτην . . Ἠελίοιο Od.10.138 ; Ἑλένη Διὸς ἐκγεγαυῖα Il.3.199, 418 ; τοίων πατέρων ἐξ αἵματος ἐκγεγάᾰτε Hom. *Epigr*.16.3 (ἐκγεγάασθε Suid.) ; οἱ πὰρ θεοῦ ἐκγεγάαντο *AP*15.40.20 (Comet.). 2. c. dat., *to be born to*, Πορθεῖ μὲν τρεῖς παῖδες . . ἐξεγένοντο Il.14.115, cf. Hdt.1.30, 4.155 : fut. perf., παῖδες παίδεσσι διαμπερὲς ἐκγεγάονται *h.Ven*.197. 3. simply, *come into being*, Emp. 59.3, *PMasp*.153.12 (vi A.D.), *PLond*.5.1708.207 (vi A.D.). II. aor., *to be gone away*, c. gen., ἐκγενέσθαι τοῦ ζῆν *to have departed* this life, X.*HG*6.4.23 (s.v.l.). III. impers., ἐκγίγνεται *it is allowed, it is granted*, c. dat. pers. et inf., mostly with neg., οὐκ ἐξεγένετό τινι ἀπαγγεῖλαι *it was* not *granted* him to . ., Hdt.1.78, cf. 5.51, Ar.*Eq*.851, Lys.7.37 ; δικαιοτάτῳ ἀνδρῶν βουλομένῳ γενέσθαι οὐκ ἐξεγένετο Hdt.3. 142 : without a neg., ἐκγενέσθαι μοι . . τείσασθαι [I pray] *that it may be allowed* me to . ., Id.5.105 ; εἰ . . τότ' ἐξεγένετο D.28.2 : abs. in part., ἐκγενόμενον Isoc.16.36 : rarely c. acc. et inf., εἰ γὰρ ἐκγένοιτ' ἰδεῖν ταύτην με τὴν ἡμέραν Ar.*Pax*346.

**ἐκγλευκίζομαι**, *cease fermenting*, ἐκγεγλευκισμένος οἶνος *newly fermented* wine, Hp.*Epid*.7.64.

**ἐκγλισχραίνω**, *make very sticky*, Aret.*CD*2.3.

**ἐκγλῠκαίνομαι**, *grow sweet*, Olymp. *in Mete*.110.26.

**ἐκγλῠφή**, ἡ, *hatching*, Ael.*NA*4.12.

**ἐκγλύφω** [ῠ], *scoop out*, τὸν χόνδρον Meges ap.Orib.44.24.1 : pf. Pass. ἐξέγλυμμαι Pl.*R*.616d ; part. ἐκγεγλυμμένη Gal.18(2). 618. II. *hatch*, τὰ νεόττια Ael.*NA*2.33 :—Med., ᾠὰ ἐξεγλύψαντο Plu.*TG*17 :—also intr. in Act., τὰ ᾠὰ διὰ κα' (sc. ἡμερῶν) ἐκγλύφει *Gp*. 14.7.28.

**ἐκγοητεύω**, strengthd. for γοητεύω, Gorg.*Hel*.14, J.*BJ*1.11.3.

❀ **ἔκγονος**, ον (η, ον E.*Hel*.1647 codd., *Milet*.7.71 (Didyma), *IGRom*. 4.912 (Cibyra)), Dor., Arc. etc. **ἔσγονος**, *Schwyzer* 191.32 (Crete), *SIG*306.53 (Tegea, iv B.C.), etc. :—*born of, sprung from*, esp. Subst., *child*, whether *son* or *daughter*, Il.5.813, Od.11.236, Hdt.1.35, etc. ; ὁ Διὸς ἔ. E.*HF*876 (anap.) : pl., ἔκγονοι *descendants*, Hdt.2.167, 4. 179, E.*Hipp*.450, etc. ; ἐκγόνων ἔκγονοι *children's children*, Pl.*Criti*. 112c : metaph., τῆς χώρας ἔκγονοι Id.*Mx*.239d ; ἀδικία ἔ. ὕβρεως Id. *Lg*.691c ; δειλίας ἔ. ἀργία ib.901e ; also of interest as *the child* of the principal, Id.*R*.555e, cf. 507a. b. *grandchild*, *Milet*.l. c., *SIG*900. 5, etc. 2. neut., ἔκγονά τινος one's *offspring*, A.*Pr*.137 (lyr.) ; ἔ. κλυτᾶς χθονός S.*OT*171 (lyr.) ; [ποιηταὶ] ἔ. ἑαυτῶν καταλείπουσιν Pl. *Smp*.209d ; τὰ [ζωγραφίας] ἔ. Id.*Phdr*.275d ; cf. ἔγγονος.

**ἐκγρᾰφή**, ἡ, *erasure* from a list, in pl., *SIG*742.31 (Ephesus, but perh. written for ἐγγραφή).

❀ **ἐκγράφω** [ᾰ], *write out, copy*, *IG*9(1).687.12 (Corc.), cf. *CIG*2266 (Delos) :—Med., *copy for oneself*, [χρησμὸν] παρὰ τἀπόλλωνος ἐξεγραψάμην Ar.*Av*.982 ; Μορσίμου ῥῆσιν ἐξεγράψατο Id.*Ra*.151, cf. D.48.48, etc. II. *strike out, expunge from* a list, *IG*1².84.28, Decr.ap. And.1.77 (Pass.) ; τινὰ τῆς βουλῆς D.H.19.18. (Written ἐγγρ- *IG* 5(2).357.14 (Stymphalus, iii B.C.).)

❀ **ἐκγρῡτεύω**, (γρύτη) *search out from old lumber*, aor. ἐξεγρύτευσα, Hsch.

**ἐκγυμν-άζω**, *exercise, train*, *Gloss*. **-όω**, *bare, expose*, Hsch. s.v. ἐξώργησα.

**ἐκδαβῇ** (i.e. ἐκδαϝῇ)· ἐκκαυθῇ (Lacon.), Hsch. ; cf. δαίω.

**ἐκδᾳδόομαι**, *become glutted with resin*, Thphr.*CP*6.11.9.

**ἐκδακρύω**, *burst into tears, weep aloud*, S.*Ph*.278, E.*Ph*.1344 ; of trees, *exude* drops of gum, J.*BJ*1.6.6, Plu.2.384b.

**ἐκδάκτῠλος**, ον, Att. for ἐξαδάκτυλος, *IG*2.1054*f*6.

❀ **ἐκδᾰν-είζω**, *lend out at interest*, χρήματα Arist.*Oec*.1350ᵃ14 : fut. part. ἐκδανεισοῦντας *IG*9(1).694 (Corc., iii B.C.) ; 3 pl. -οῦντι ib.4. 841.16 (Calauria, iii B.C.) ; fut. also ἐκδανιῶ Lxx *De*.28.12 : pf. ἐκδεδάνεικα *AP*11.173 (Phil.) :—Med., *borrow*, *SIG*1068.15 (Patmos) : —Pass., *IG*12(7).237.23 (Amorgos). **-εισις**, εως, ἡ, *lending at interest*, ib.9(1).694 (Corc.). ❀ **-εισμός**, ὁ, *lending at interest*, ib. 12(7).515 (Amorgos), *BGU*362 xiv 21 (iii A.D.) ; εἶναι ἐν ἐ. *OGI*509. 16 (Aphrodisias). **-ειστής**, οῦ, ὁ, *one who lends at interest*, *Test. Epict*.6.30, *BMus.Inscr*.481*.131. **-ειστικός**, ή, όν, *relating to loans*, ἔγγραφα ib.311.

**ἐκδᾰπᾰνάω**, *exhaust*, χορηγίας Plb.21.10.9 ; προσόδους Id.24.7.4, cf. *PBaden* 19.19 (ii A.D.) ; τὸ αἷμα, τὸ ὑγρόν, Gal.10.192, 15.86 : metaph., τὰς προθυμίας εἰς τοὺς ἐχθρούς J.*AJ*15.5.1 ; τὸν θυμὸν εἴς τινας Lib.*Decl*.37.30 :—Pass., ἐκδεδαπανῆσθαι ὑπὲρ τῶν ψυχῶν ὑμῶν 2*Ep.Cor*.12.15.

**ἔκδαρμα**, ατος, τό, *excoriation*, Crito ap.Gal.12.449 (pl.) ; *hide*, *Et. Gud*. s. v. δορά.

**ἐκδαρτικός**, ή, όν, *suitable for flaying*, Tz. ad Hes.*Op*.502.

**ἐκδᾰσύνομαι**, Pass., pf. inf. -δεδασύνθαι, *become hairy*, Hsch.

**ἐκδεδῃτημένως**, Adv. *luxuriously*, Poll.6.185.

**ἐκδεής**, ές, (δέω B) *wanting, imperfect*, Anon.ap.Suid.

**ἔκδεια**, ἡ, *falling short, being in arrear*, φόρων καὶ νεῶν in tribute and ships, Th.1.99 (pl.), cf. Hyp.*Fr*.136, *BGU*976.19 (ii A.D.), Lib. *Or*.36.10 (pl.), v. l. in D.32.30. 2. *deficit*, *PRev.Laws* 17.1, al. (iii B.C.). 3. *shortage, lack*, ὕδατος *PRyl*.81.12 (ii A.D.).

**ἐκδείκνῡμι**, *exhibit, display*, S.*El*.348, E.*Hipp*.1298 :—Med., ἔθος τόδ' εἰς Ἕλληνας ἐξεδειξάμην, prob. for -λεξάμην, Id.*Supp*.341. II. *point out*, S.*OC*1021.

**ἐκδειμαίνω**, strengthd. for δειμαίνω, Hld.9.8, Hierocl. *in CA*13 p.448 M.

**ἐκδειμᾰτόω**, strengthd. for δειματόω, Pl.*R*.381e, Porph.*Chr*.49, Aen Gaz.*Thphr*.p.68 B. :— Pass., Lxx *Wi*.17.6, D.H.*Dem*.54.

**ἐκδεινόω**, strengthd. for δεινόω, J.*AJ*17.5.5.

**ἐκδειπνέω**, *finish a meal*, Poll.6.112.

**ἐκδείρω**, v. ἐκδέρω.

**ἐκδεκᾰτεύω**, *pay tithe of*, Ἡρακλεῖ τὴν οὐσίαν D.S.4.21.

**ἐκδεκτέον**, *one must admit, include*, Ath.5.189d, Dam.*Pr*.437.

❀ **ἐκδέκτωρ**, ορος, ὁ, *one who takes from another*, πόνων *one who relieves another's* toil, A.*Fr*.194. 2. *successor*, τῆς βασιλείας Nic.Dam. p.45 D.

**ἐκδέννῡμι**, = ἐκδέω, Papp.1130.15, al.

**ἐκδεξιάζομαι**, *salute*, *PTeb*.43.11 (ii B.C.).

**ἔκδεξις**, εως, ἡ, *succession*, τῆς βασιληΐης Hdt.7.3.

**ἐκδέρκομαι**, *look out from*, Il.23.477 (sed leg. κεφαλῆς ἐκ δέρκεται) ; λεπτὸν ἐκδέδορκε Adam.1.5.

**ἐκδερμᾰτ-ίζω**, *flay, skin*, Hsch. s.v. ἔδειραν, Suid. s.v. ἀσκὸν δέρειν. **-όω**, = foreg., Sch.Ar.*Th*.765.

**ἐκδέρω**, Ion. -δείρω, fut. -δερῶ, *strip off the skin from* one, κριὸν Hdt.2.42, cf. 7.26 (Pass.) ; βῶν *Dialex*.2.11 ; also δῶκε δέ μ' ἐκδείρας ἀσκὸν βοὸς Od.10.19 ; βύρσαν ἐ. E.*El*.824. II. *cudgel soundly, 'hide'*, Ar.*V*.450, Pl.*R*.616a, Hyp.*Fr*.200, *PSI*4.403 (ii B.C.) :— Pass., Macho ap.Ath.13.580b (Pass.).

**ἐκδεσμεύω**, *make binding, secure*, τὴν ἑκατέρων πίστιν εἰς ἀλλήλους Plb.3.33.8.

**ἔκδετος**, ον, (ἐκδέω) *fastened to*, ἐξ ἵππων *AP*9.97 (Alph.).

❀ **ἐκδέχομαι**, Ion. **ἐκδέκ-**, Ep. 3 pl. ἐκδέχαται Tryph.197 : fut. -δέξομαι :—Pass. (v. infr. 1.6). I. mostly of persons, 1. *take* or *receive from* another, οἱ οἱ σάκος ἐξεδέχοντο Il.13.710 ; Ὀρέστην ἐξεδέξαμην πατρί A.*Ch*.762 ; of a beacon-fire, τρίτον Ἀθῷον αἶπος . . ἐξεδέξατο Id. *Ag*.285 ; ἐ. τὴν αἰτίαν *take it on oneself*, D.19.37. 2. of a successor, ἐ. τὴν βασιληΐην Hdt.1.26, etc. : freq. with acc. omitted, ἐξεδέξατο Σαδυάττης (sc. τὴν βασιληΐην) S. *succeeded*, ib.16, cf. 103, al. ; παῖς παρὰ πατρὸς ἐκδεκόμενος τὴν ἀρχήν, [τὴν τέχνην], Id.1.7, 2.166 ; so ἐκδεξάμενοι (sc. τὴν μάχην) Id.7.211. 3. *take up the argument*, ὥσπερ σφαῖραν ἐ. τὸν λόγον Pl.*Euthd*.277b ; ἐκδεξάμενος (sc. τὸν λόγον) εἰπεῖν Id. *Smp*.189a ; ὁ μὲν πρῶτος εἰπὼν . . ὁ δ' ἐκδεξάμενος D.18.21. 4. *wait for, expect*, κεῖνον ἐνθάδ' ἐ. S.*Ph*.123 ; ἐλέφαντας Plb.3.45.6 ; ἀλλήλους 1*Ep.Cor*.11.33 ; ἐ. μεθ' ἡσυχίας ἕως . . D.H.6.67 ; πότε . . Tryph. l. c. : abs., *wait*, ἕως . . *POxy*.1673.8 (ii A.D.). 5. *take* or *understand in a certain sense*, οὕτω δὴ τὴν ἀσωτίαν ἐκδεχόμεθα Arist.*EN*1120ᵃ3 ; τοὺς λόγους Plb.10.18.12 ; πρὸς τὸ συμφέρον D.S.14.56. 6. *entertain*, μεγαλοπρεπέστερον ἐγδεχθῆναι *PTeb*.33.7 (ii B.C.). 7. *to be surety for*, τινά *PSI*4.349 (iii B.C.), Lxx *Ge*.43.9. II. of events, *await*, τοὺς Σκύθας . . ἐξεδέξατο οὐκ ἐλάσσων πόνος Hdt.4.1 ; ἐ. [αὐτοὺς] περίοδος τῆς λίμνης μακρή Id.1.185. 2. of contiguous countries, *come next*, ἀπὸ ταύτης (sc. τῆς Περσικῆς) ἐ. Ἀσσυρίη Id 4.39, cf. 99, *Peripl.M. Rubr*.27. 3. in Archit., *support*, καμάραν D.S.18.26.

**ἐκδέψηται**· ἐκμαστιγώσηται, Hsch.

**ἐκδέω**, *bind so as to hang from, fasten to* or *on*, c. gen., πέτρης ἐκ πείσματα δήσας Od.10.96 ; [δρῦς] ἔκδεον ἡμιόνων they *bound* the oaks *to* the mules, i. e. they *yoked* the mules to them, Il.23.121 ; τοῦ τείχους Aen.Tact.11.6 : abs., σανίδας ἐκδῆσαι ὄπισθε *bind* planks behind, Od. 22.174 ; χέρας βρόχοισιν ἐκδήσαντες E.*Andr*.556 : metaph., *trace the dependence of* one thing *on* another, Plot.3.3.1 :—Med., *bind a thing to oneself, hang it round one*, ἐκδήσασθαι ἀγάλματα Hdt.4.76 ; also, *bind* or *fasten for oneself*, ἀκταῖσιν . . πεισμάτων ἀρχάς E.*Hipp*.761 (lyr.) ; τὸν νεκρὸν ἐκ τοῦ δίφρου *IG*14.1284 :—Pass., Luc.*Hist.Conscr*. 29, al.

**ἐκδηθύνω**, *to be protracted*, of disease, Aret.*CD*1.1.

**ἐκδηϊόω**, *destroy, ravage*, in aor. 1, Hsch. :—Med., Procop.*Arc*.19.

**ἔκδηλος**, ον, strengthd. for δῆλος, *conspicuous*, ἵν' ἔ. μετὰ πᾶσιν Ἀργείοισι γένοιτο Il.5.2 : hence, *considerable*, σίτου μοῖρα *CPHerm*.

6.4. II. *quite plain*, πάντ' ἐποίησεν ἔκδηλα D.2.21, cf. *OGI*665.13 (i A.D.), etc.: Sup., ἐκδηλοτάτη ἐνάργεια Phld.*Herc.*1251.13. III. Adv. -λως *openly, manifestly, plainly*, Id.*Vit.*p.40 J., Ph.1.111, Plu. *Oth.*17, etc.: Comp., Id.2.625d, Them.*Or.*15.192a: Sup., Philostr. *Her.*19.12, D.C.60.3.

**ἐκδηλόω**, *show plainly*, Thphr.*Vent.*35.

**ἐκδημᾰγωγέω**, *win by the arts of a demagogue*, τὸ πλῆθος D.H.7.4.

**ἐκδημ-έω**, *to be abroad, to be on one's travels*, Hdt.1.30, S.*OT*114, etc.; *to be in exile*, Pl.*Lg.*864e; εἰς πόλιν *PPetr.*3 p.76. II. c. acc., *travel through*, δύσιν καὶ ἀνατολήν *IG*14.905. **-ητικός**, ή, όν, *on foreign service*, ἔξοδος στρατιωτῶν *Gloss.*, cf. *Cat.Cod.Astr.*8 (3).99; (sc. λόγος) title of a satire, Varro *Sat.Men.*p.191 B. **-ία**, ἡ, *going* or *being abroad*, E.*Fr.*768: pl., Id.*Hyps.Fr.*5(3).15 (prob.); ἐ. πολιτικαί (opp. κατὰ πόλεμον καὶ στρατείας ἀποδημίαι) public *missions*, Pl.*Lg.*950e. 2. *exile*, ib.869e. 3. metaph., *departure from life*, *AP*3.5 (lemma).

**ἐκδημοκοπέω**, strengthd. for δημοκοπέω, τοὺς δουλωθέντας Chio *Ep.*15.2.

**ἔκδημος**, ον, *away from home, abroad*, X.*Cyr.*8.5.26: c. gen., ἔ. τῆσδε χθονός E.*Hipp.*281; ἔ. στρατεῖαι expeditions *abroad*, Th.1.15; ἔ. ἔξοδος, φυγή, Id.2.10, E.*Hipp.*37; ἔ. ἔρως ib.32.

**ἐκδημοσιεύω**, in Pass., *to be made known*, D.C.61.12, 52.31.

**ἐκδιαβαίνω**, *pass quite over*, τάφρον Il.10.198.

**ἐκδῐαιτ-άω**, *decide a case as* διαιτητής, Arist.*Ath.*53.5; also, = κακῶς διαιτάω, in aor. 1, Hsch. II. more freq. Med. or Pass., *regulate one's habits*, Hp.*Insomn.*89; *change one's mode of life*, εἴ τί που ἐξεδεδιῄτητο ἐκ τῶν καθεστώτων νομίμων Th.1.132, cf. D.H.5.74; εἰς τὰ ἀμείνω καὶ Ἑλληνικὰ ἐκδεδιῃτημένη Ath.13.556c: abs., ἐκδεδιῃτημένος *having gone astray*, Ph.2.48; βίος ἐκδεδιῃτημένος *undisciplined*, Men.Prot. p.2 D.: later c. acc., Ph.2.128; ἐκδεδιῃτημένος τὰς ὑπογαστρίους ἡδονάς Dam.*Isid.*266:—so in Act., ἐξεδιῄτησε τὴν πάτριον ἁγνείαν J.*BJ*7.8.1; causal, *make to change one's habits*, ἔθνος Lxx 4*Ma.*4.19. **-ησις**, εως, ἡ, *change of habits*, Ph.1.360, Plu.*Alex.*45: c. gen., τῶν πατρίων, τοῦ κατὰ φύσιν βίου, Ph.2.76, Plu.2.493c.

**ἐκδιᾶν**· σπᾶν, καὶ κέραμον συντετριμμένον, Hsch.

**ἐκδιαπρίζω**, *saw off*, App.*BC*4.20 (prob. f.l. for διαπρίζων).

**ἐκδῐάστρα**· κλῶσμα, ὁ στήμων, Hsch.; cf. δίασμα.

**ἐκδιαφορ-έω**, *draw out and dissipate*, τὸ θερμόν Phlp.*in GC*146.37, cf. Olymp.*in Mete.*278.18:—Pass., Pall.*in Hp.*2.121 D., Phlp.*in Ph.*625.25. **-ησις**, εως, ἡ, *dissipation*, ib.157.2.

**ἐκδίδαγμα** [ῐ], ατος, τό, *prentice-work*, κερκίδος E.*Ion* 1419.

**ἐκδιδάσκω**, poet. aor. -διδάσκησα Pi.*P.*4.217:—*teach thoroughly*, τινά Sapph.71, Th.6.80, Pl.*Prt.*328e, etc.; ἐ. πάνθ' ὁ γηράσκων χρόνος A.*Pr.*981; λέγ' ἐκδίδασκε ib.698, etc.; ἐ. τινά τι Pi. l. c., S.*OC*1539, Antipho 5.14, Theoc.6.40:—Med., *have another taught*, of the parents, Hdt.2.154, E.*Med.*295, Pl.*Ep.*360e:—Pass., c. inf., S.*Tr.*1110, etc.; αἰσχροῖς γὰρ αἰσχρὰ πράγματ' ἐκδιδάσκεται Id.*El.*621; ὀψ' ἐκδιδαχθεὶς τῶν κατ' οἶκον.. *having learnt* too late from those at home, Id.*Tr.*934. 2. c. acc. pers. et inf., *to teach* one *to be* so and so, εἶναι κακήν Id.*El.*395, cf. *Ant.*298; ἐπιθυμεῖν (sc. αὐτοὺς) ἐξεδίδαξα Ar.*Ra.*1026: with inf. omitted, γενναίους ἐ. ib.1019. 3. *explain, expound*, ἐ. ὡς.. Hdt.4.118, S.*OT*1370: abs., ἐ. σαφῶς *Com.Adesp.*14.9 D.

**ἐκδιδράσκω**, Ion. -διδρήσκω, fut. -δράσομαι [ᾱ]: aor. ἐξέδραν E.*Heracl.*14 (nowhere else in Trag.), D.C.37.47; part. ἐκδράς Hdt.4.148, Ar.*Ec.*55:—*run away, escape*, ἐξ Αἰγύπτου Hdt.3.4, cf. 9.88, etc.; διὰ τῶν ὑδρορροῶν Ar.*V.*126: abs., Id.*Ec.*55, Th.1.126.

❋ **ἐκδιδύσκω**, = ἐκδύω, *strip, despoil*, νεκρούς Lxx 1*Ki.*31.8; *plunder*, πόλεις ὅλας J.*BJ*2.14.2.

❋ **ἐκδίδωμι**, 3 sg. ἐκδιδοῖ Hdt.1.80, al.:—*give up*, esp. something seized and detained unlawfully, Ἑλένην καὶ κτήμαθ' ἅμ' αὐτῇ Il.3.459, cf. Hdt.1.3: generally, *surrender*, esp. of *giving up* refugees, ib.74, 158 sq.; τινὰ τοῖς ἐχθροῖς S.*Ph.*1386, cf. *OT*1040, etc.; ἐ. τινὰ τοῖς κατηγόροις D.21.30, cf. 29.38; ἐ. δοῦλον *give up* a slave to be examined by torture, Antipho 6.27, D.29.14; αὐτὸν ἐξέδωκεν μαστιγῶσαι Εὐριπίδῃ Arist.*Pol.*1311$^b$32; αὐτὸν ἐς τιμωρίαν τοῖς δικασταῖς Polyaen.6.7.1; *surrender* a city, Ἀμφίπολιν D.19.253, cf. 257:—Med., θυμὸν ἐκδόσθαι πρὸς ἥβαν *give up one's* heart to jollity, Pi.*P.*4.295. 2. *give out of one's house*, a. ἐ. θυγατέρα *give* one's daughter *in marriage*, τινί Hdt.1.196, E.*IA*132 (anap.), cf. Thphr.*Char.*22.4; θυγατέρας παρὰ σφῶν αὐτῶν ἐκδόντες *having provided for* their *marriage* at their own expense, D.27.69; Ἄλκηστιν ἐ. πρὸς γάμον D.S.4.53; freq. also without any acc., *give in marriage*, ἐ. εἰς οὓς ἂν ἐθέλωσι Pl.*R.*613d, cf. 362b, Th.8.21, etc.: metaph., of the elements, συνοικίζειν καὶ ἐ. Pl. *Sph.*242d:—less freq. in Med., ἐκδίδοσθαι θυγατέρα Hdt.2.47, Thphr. *Char.*30.19; ἐξέδου κόρην ὅτῳ σε θυμὸς ἦγεν E.*Med.*309:—Pass., Arc. ἐσδοθένσᾳ (= ἐκδοθείσῃ) *given in marriage*, *SIG*306.7 (Tegea, iv B.C.). b. *give* one's son *for adoption*, τοὺς μὲν (sc. υἱοὺς) εἰς ἑτέρας οἰκίας Plb.31.28.2, cf. *POxy.*1206.6 (iv A.D.); also ἐ. τὸν παῖδα ἐπὶ τέχνην *put* him *out* as an apprentice, X.*Eq.*2.2, cf. *BGU*1021.6, etc. 3. *farm out, let for hire*, τὴν αὐλήν Hdt.1.68, cf. *SIG*1044.29 (Halic., iv/iii B.C.), etc.; ἐ. ἀνδράποδα *to let out* slaves for work, X.*Vect.*4.15; πῶλον Id.*Eq.*2.2 (also in Med., ἐξέδοτο [ἀμπελῶνα] γεωργοῖς *Ev.Marc.*12.1): c. inf., χαλινὸν χαλκεῖ ἐ. σκευάσαι Pl.*Prm.*127a; ἐ. [θύλακον] τῷ σκυτοδέψῃ ἐπιρράψαι Thphr.*Char.*16.6; ὅταν ἐκδῷ θοιμάτιον ἐκπλῦναι ib.22.8; ἐκδόντος μοι Δημοσθένους.. στέφανον χρυσοῦν ὥστε κατασκευάσαι Test.ap.D.21.22; ὥσπερ ἀνδριάντ' ἐκδεδωκὼς κατὰ συγγραφήν like *one who has contracted for* the execution of a statue, D.18.122. 4. *give in charge* to another, πολλοὺς ἐξέδωκα Προδίκῳ (with play on signf. 2) Pl.*Tht.*151b; ἐκδιδοὺς νεικέων so as to be out of the way of quarrels, E.*Ba.*293 (s.v.l.): c. inf., Δὶ τοῦτ'.. ἐκδώσομεν πράσσειν Pi.*O.*13.106. 5. *bring out*, ἀλλ' ἐκδότω τις.. δᾷδας Ar.*Pl.*1194; ἐκδότω δέ τις.. δίφρω δύο Id.*Fr.*348. 6. *lend out money* on security, etc., Lex ap.D.35.51; ναυτικὰ ἐκδεδομένα Lys.32.6. b. simply, *pay out*, Arist.*Oec.*1349$^b$31, *PSI*3.204 (ii A.D.). 7. *put out, publish*, of books, etc., chiefly in Pass., λόγος ὁ πρότερον ἐκδοθείς Isoc.5.11, cf. Plb.2.37.6, Str.1.2.2; τοῖς ἐκδεδομένοις λόγοις Arist. *Po.*1454$^b$18:—in Act., Plu.*Rom.*8. 8. of a woman, *bring to the birth*, App.*BC*1.83. 9. of land, etc., *return, yield, produce*, μέταλλα.. μονολίθους ἐκδιδόντα πλάκας Str.5.2.5. 10. *hand over, deliver* a document, ἀποχήν *BGU*260.6 (i A.D.), etc.:—Med., *PFlor.*384.113 (v A.D.). 11. *betray*, Hsch. II. intr., of rivers, *empty themselves, disembogue*, ἐς θάλασσαν, ἐς τὴν Σύρτιν, ἐς τὸν Μαίανδρον, etc., Hdt.1.80, 2.150, 7.26, etc. 2. τῶν ἄλλων [ζῴων] τὰ μὲν εἰς ὀδόντας ἐκδίδωσι.. τὰ δὲ εἰς κέρατα.. *run to* teeth, etc., Arist.*Pr.*898$^a$22; *find an outlet*, εἰς κεφαλήν ib.29. 3. *emerge*, τὴν Ἀφροδίτην ἐκδοῦναι τῆς θαλάσσης Philostr.*Im.*2.1 (leg. -δῦναι).

**ἐκδιέρχομαι**, *pass through, endure*, βλάβη καὶ δαπανήματα *BGU*1105.39 (i A.D.).

**ἐκδιηγέομαι**, *tell in detail*, Hp.*Prog.*1, Arist.*Rh.Al.*1434$^b$4, Ph.2.118, Lxx *Jb.*12.8, etc.

**ἐκδιηθέω**, *filter out*, Hp.*Morb.*4.37 (Pass.).

**ἐκδιίστᾰμαι**, *to be distinct, separate*, Gal.18(2).994.

**ἐκδῐκ-άζω**, pf. ἐκδεδίκακα *OGI*7.3 (Cyme):—Med., fut. -δικῶμαι Lxx *Le.*19.18:—*decide*, μίαν (sc. δίκην) Ar.*Eq.*50, cf. Lys.17.5; δίκας καὶ γραφὰς καὶ εὐθύνας X.*Ath.*3.2:—Pass., of the suit, *to be settled*, Pl.*Lg.*958a:—Med., *prosecute one's right against another*, Is.*Fr.*77, *Delph.*3(2).205 (iii B.C.); περί τινος *CIG*4259, cf. *Tab.Heracl.*1.129:—also in Pass., *have right done to one*, *BGU*195.37 (ii A.D.). II. *avenge*, πατέρων.. ἐκδικάζοντες φόνον E.*Supp.*1215, cf. 154 (dub. l.). **-αιόομαι**, fut. -ώσομαι, = ἐκδικέω III, Keil-Premerstein *Dritter Bericht* 117 (Tire, i A.D.); *conduct legal proceedings*, *AJA*16.14 (Sardes). **-ασία**, ἡ, = ἐκδικία I, ib.17.29 (pl., Sardes, i B.C.). **-άσις**, ιος, ἁ, Dor. for foreg., *SIG*563.14 (Aetol., found at Teos). **-αστής**, οῦ, ὁ, *avenger*, πατρός E.*Supp.*1152 (lyr.).

**ἔκδικεν**· ἐξέβαλεν, Hsch.

❋ **ἐκδῐκ-έω**, *avenge, punish*, φόνον Ctes.*Fr.*37; παρακοήν 2*Ep.Cor.*10.6; τινάς *PGen.*47.17 (iv A.D.); *exact vengeance for*, τὰ αἵματα τῶν δούλων Lxx 2*Ki.*4.8; τὸ αἷμα τὸ ἀναίτιον *SIG*1181.12 (Jewish, circ. ii/i B.C.). 2. *decide* a case, δίκην, ἀγῶνα, Ph.2.432, *POxy.*1020.6 (ii A.D.). II. *avenge* or *vindicate* a person, by taking up his cause, Apollod.2.5.11, *PAmh.*2.134.10 (ii A.D.), Plu.*Comp.Ag.Gracch.*5; ἑαυτούς *Ep.Rom.*12.19, etc.; ἐ. τινὰ ἀπό τινος *avenge* one on another, *Ev.Luc.*18.3: c. dat., Sch.Ar.*Pl.*627:—Pass., Lxx *Ps.*36(37).28. 2. *act as* ἔκδικος II. 3, *AJA*18.325 (Sardes, i B.C.), cf. *CIG*2824 (Aphrodisias), *BCH*23.182 (Pisidia). III. *claim*, *CIG*3488 (Thyatira), *Inscr.Perg.*245; σιτία καὶ ποτά Hierocl.*in CA*8 p.431 M. IV. ἐ. τισί *make retribution for* them, Aesop.279b. **-ησία**, ἡ, = sq., Lxx *Jd.*16.28 (dub.). ❋ **-ησις**, εως, ἡ, *avenging*, ἐ. ποιεῖσθαι to give *satisfaction*, Plb.3.8.10; ἐ. ποιεῖσθαί τινος *obtain* it *from*.., *CIG*2826 (Aphrodisias); *legal remedy*, *PLond.*5.1674.102 (vi A.D.); ἐ. ποιεῖν τινι *avenge* him, *Act.Ap.*7.24; τινὸς *Ev.Luc.*18.7, 8. **-ητής**, οῦ, ὁ, *avenger, vindicator*, Lxx *Ps.*8.3; τοῦ θεοῦ καὶ τοῦ νόμου J.*AJ*17.9.6. **-ητικός**, ή, όν, *revengeful*, Tz. ad Lyc.406. ❋ **-ία**, ἡ, = ἐκδίκησις, J.*AJ*13.1.4; τοῦ πατρός Gal.14.239, Sch.Pi.*Pae.*6.119; ἡ ἀπὸ θεῶν ἐ. Herm.ap.Stob.1.49.44; ἐ. ποιεῖσθαι Onos.37.4; ἐ. γίγνοιτο *IG*2$^2$.1121.45 (iv A.D.). 2. *decision* of a case, D.C.38.7. II. *office of* ἔκδικος II. 3, *CIG*2719 (pl.), 2771 (Aphrodisias), *POxy.*901.3 (iv A.D.); ἔχειν τὴν περί τινος ἐ. *BMus.Inscr.*481*.219. ❋ **-ος**, ον, *lawless, unjust*, ἔκδικα πάσχω A.*Pr.*1093 (anap.); of persons, S.*OC*920, Ael.*NA*16.5 (Sup.). Adv. -κως A.*Pr.*976, etc. II. *maintaining the right, avenging*, ἔχει θεὸς ἔ. ὄμμα Batr.97; ἔ. χρόνος *AP*12.35 (Diocl.), cf. Lxx *Wi.*12.12. 2. Subst., *avenger*, Hdn.7.4.5; αἱ Ἰβύκου ἔ. Plu.2.509f. 3. *public advocate* or *prosecutor*, *IG*9(1).61, Cic.*Fam.*13.56.1, *Michel* 459 (Telmessus), *BMus.Inscr.*481*.315 (Ephesus, ii A.D.). 4. generally, *legal representative*, *POxy.*261.14 (i A.D.), Plin.*Ep.Traj.*110, etc.

**ἐκδικόφως**, *punishing mortals*, *PMag.Par.*1.1373.

❋ **ἐκδιοικ-έω**, *collect* dues, etc., *PTeb.*27.57 (ii B.C., Pass.), al. **-ήσιμος**, ον, *alienable*, of property, *PTheb.Bank* 1.9 (ii B.C.). ❋ **-ησις**, εως, ἡ, *collection of dues*, *PTeb.*27.37.

**ἐκδιορύσσω**, *break open*, τάφον Tz.*H.*3.978.

❋ **ἐκδιφάω**, *'ferret out'*, Herod.7.78: aor. 1, Hsch.

**ἐκδιφρεύω**, *throw from a chariot*, in Pass., Luc.*DDeor.*25.3, *Electr.*2.

**ἐκδιψάω**, *to be parched with drought*, of plants, Thphr.*CP*5.9.3; of a person, *to be very thirsty*, Plu.*Cleom.*29.

**ἔκδιψος**, ον, *very thirsty*, D.S.19.109.

**ἐκδῐ-ωκτέον**, *one must chase away*, Plu.2.13c. ❋ **-ώκω**, *chase away, banish*, Th.1.24; ἐκ τοῦ τόπου Arist.*HA*618$^b$12; τῆς οἰκίας Luc.*Tim.*10; *attack, persecute*, *PMasp.*2 iii 4 (vi A.D.), etc.:—Pass., Hyp.*Fr.*238. **-ωξις**, εως, ἡ, *pursuit*, Plu.2.293c. II. *repulse*, βαρβαρικῆς ἐπιδρομῆς *PLond.*5.1663 (vi A.D.).

**ἐκδοκῐμάζω**, *test thoroughly*, Aq., Sm.*Jb.*7.18.

**ἐκδονέω**, *shake utterly, confound*, in Pass., ἐκδεδόνηντο.. φρένες *AP*11.64 (Agath.).

**ἐκδορά**, ἡ, *stripping off, removing*, λειχήνων Gal.12.844.

**ἐκδόριος** or -ειος, ον, *of* or *for flaying*: τὰ ἐ. (sc. φάρμακα) *medica-*

*ments which take off the skin*, Dsc.3.62, Aët.2.174; ἐπιθέματα Crito ap.Gal.12.448.

**ἐκ-δόσιμος**, ον, *contracted for, let out*, Poll.7.200, Ath.15.680d. **2.** ἐκδόσιμον, τό, *certificate* of delivery of a document, service of summons, etc., *POxy*.34$^v$ ii 6 (ii A.D.), etc. ❀ **-δοσις**, εως, ἡ, Arc. **ἔσδοσις** *IG*5(2).6.16:—*giving up, surrendering*, ἱκετέων Hdt.1.159; δμηρειῶν ἐκδόσεις εἰς ἀλλήλους Pl.*Plt*.310e. **2.** *giving in marriage, dowering*, ἐ. ποιεῖσθαι τῶν θυγατέρων Id.*Lg*.924d, cf. Arist.*Pol*.1335$^a$ 22; τὰς ἐ. τῶν γυναικῶν D.44.66. **3.** *letting, hiring*, or *farming out*, *PPetr*.3 p.148 (iii B.C.); τὰς ἐ. ἀγοράζειν παρὰ τῶν τιμητῶν Plb. 6.17.4; τὰς ἐ. ποιεῖσθαι *IG*7.303.27 (Orop.); ἐ. ἱερῶν ἔργων Plu.*Cat. Ma*.19, cf. *IG*5(2).l.c. **4.** *lending money on ships* or *exported goods, bottomry*, D.27.11, 29.35. **5.** *publication* of a book, D.H. *Amm*.1.10, Ael.*Tact.Praef*.4: in concrete sense, *a 'publication', treatise*, A.D.*Synt*.3.4, 313.6, Iamb.*VP*23.104. **b.** *edition*, of an author's work, Ἀριστοφάνειος Heph.*Poëm*.p.74 C., cf. A.D.*Pron*.89. 22, etc. **c.** *translation*, J.*AJ*12.2.4 (dub.). **II.** *bursting forth*, πηγῶν Philostr.*Im*.2.17; *delivery*, ἐμβρύου Sor.1.71. **2.** *motions* of the bowels, Archig.ap.Aët.6.27. **-δοτέον**, *one must give up*, τοὺς αἰτίους Plb.3.21.7; Καίσαρα τοῖς βαρβάροις Plu.*Caes*.22, cf. Ph.2.314. **2.** *one must give in marriage*, Ar.*Av*.1635, Pl.*Ep*. 361d. **-δοτήρ**, Arc. **ἐσδοτήρ**, ῆρος, ὁ, = sq., *IG*5(2).6.6 (Tegea, iv B.C.); ἐγδ- *IG*4.1485.4 (Epid.). **-δότης**, ου, ὁ, *one who farms out contracts* or *taxes*, ib.12(5).653.63, etc. **II.** *one who gives his daughter in marriage*, *POxy*.497.15 (ii A.D.). **III.** *betrayer*, Hsch. **-δότις**, ιδος, ἡ, *bride's mother*, *POxy*.1273.26 (iii A.D.). **-δοτος**, ον, *given up, delivered*, esp. *betrayed*, ἔκδοτόν μιν ἐποίησε ἐς τοὺς Πέρσας Hdt.3.1, cf. Isoc.4.122; τὴν Βοιωτίαν Θηβαίοις Aeschin.3.142; ἱκέτην ἐ. διδόναι D.23.85, etc.; τοῖς πολεμίοις παραδιδόναι Lycurg.85; οὔτε σοὶ οὔτε ἄλλῃ οὐδεμιᾷ περιστάσει δώσομεν ἑαυτοὺς ἐ. Metrod.*Fr*.49; λαβόν τινα ἐ. ὑπὸ τοῦ ὕπνου J.*AJ*6.13.9; ἔκδοτος ἄγεσθαι Hdt.6.85; γίγνεσθαι ibid., E.*Ion* 1251; ἐ. διὰ χειρὸς ἀνόμων *Act.Ap*.2.23: metaph., παρέχειν ἑαυτὴν ἐ. τινι *to give* herself *entirely up* to him, Luc.*DDeor*.20.13; ἐ. σεαυτὴν τῷ ποταμῷ ἐᾶσαι Porph. *Marc*.5; [χώρα] ἐ. τῷ κακῷ Id.*Chr*.49; πρὸς ὕβριν ἐ. Iamb.*Protr*. 2. **II.** *given in marriage*, *PMasp*.5.10 (vi A.D.).

**ἔκδουλος**, ὁ, *child of a slave*, Suid. s.v. Ἕρμιππος. **ἐκδούπησαν**· ἐβρόντησαν, Hsch. (ἐκ- for ἐγ-).

❀ **ἐκδοχ-εῖον**, τό, *reservoir, tank*, J.*BJ*1.15.1, *Peripl.M.Rubr*.27. ❀ **-εύς**, έως, ὁ, *forwarding agent*, *PEdgar*5.11 (iii B.C.), *OGI*140.8 (Delos, ii B.C.), Ptol.*Tetr*.179, *POxy*.1669.2 (iii A.D.). **-ή**, ἡ, Arc. **ἐσδοκά** *IG*5(2).6.40:—*receiving from* or *at the hands of another, succession*, πομποῦ πυρὸς A.*Ag*.299; ἐκδοχαῖς ἐπιφέρει θεὸς κακόν E.*Hipp*. 866; ἐ. ποιεῖσθαι πολέμου *to continue* the war, Aeschin.2.30. **2.** *receiving, containing*, ὄμβρων J.*BJ*5.4.3, cf. Paul.Aeg.6.106. **II.** *taking* or *understanding in a certain sense, interpretation*, ἐ. ποιεῖσθαι Plb.3.29.4, cf. *UPZ*110.86 (ii B.C.); ἐξ ὧν ἦν λαμβάνειν ἐκδοχὴν ὅτι.. Plb.22.7.6, cf. *SIG*557.18 (Magn. Mae., iii B.C.), Sch.Pi.*O*.13. 100. **III.** = προσδοκία, κρίσεως *Ep.Hebr*.10.27. **IV.** = ἀποδοχή, *recognition* for services rendered, *IG*12(5).722.8 (Andros). **V.** *giving of security*, προειδὼς ἀσφαλῆ τὴν ἐ. οὖσαν *PSI*4.349 (iii B.C.). **VI.** *contract*, *IG*5(2).l.c. **-ιον**, τό, = ἐκδοχεῖον, ὕδατος *Inscr.Prien*.208 (i B.C.); ἰχθύων θήρας ἐ. Dion.Byz.28: metaph., Μουσάων μυστικὸν ἐ. *AP*14.60. **-ιος**, ον, *receptive*, κόλπος τῆς θεότητος Procl. *in Ti*.3.175 D., cf. *Theol.Plat*.5.11.

**ἐκδρᾰκοντόομαι**, Pass., *become a very serpent*, A.*Ch*.549.

**ἐκδρᾰμεῖν**, v. ἐκτρέχω.

**ἐκδρασκάζω**, = ἐκδιδράσκω, Tz.*H*.5.889.

❀ **ἔκδραχμος**, ον, *of six drachms*, Hsch.

**ἐκδρέπομαι**, *pluck off*, τούτων φύλλον Aristaenet.1.3 (Pass.).

❀ **ἐκδρομ-άς**, άδος, ὁ, *one who has outrun the age of youth*, Eub.11, cf. Eust.1915.20. **-ή**, ἡ, *running out, sally, charge*, X.*HG*3.2.4, Arr. *An*.1.2.5, al.; τῶν ἐτησίων Aristid.*Or*.36(48).8. **2.** abstr. for concrete, *party of skirmishers*, Th.4.127. **II.** *shooting, sprouting*, of trees, Thphr.*CP*2.1.3. **2.** *issue*, ὕδατος Hp.*Morb*.4.57, cf. Herod. Med. in *Rh.Mus*.58.77. **III.** *digression in speaking*, Aristid.1.92 J. (pl.); ἡ ἐ. τοῦ λόγου Agath.1.3, cf. 4.29. **IV.** *lapse* of time, ἐτῶν τετρακοσίων Tz.*H*.8.56. **-ος**, ὁ, *one that runs out*: ἔκδρομοι *skirmishers*, Th.4.125, X.*HG*4.5.16.

**ἐκδυάζομαι**, Pass., *to be conjoined*, ποικίλως σὺν ἀλλήλαις Phld. *Herc*.1003.

**ἐκδυάς**, άδος, ἡ, fanciful etym. of ὀγδοάς, *Theol.Ar*.55.

❀ **ἔκδυμα**, f.l. in *AP*5.198 (Hedyl.; leg. ἐνδ-).

**ἐκδῠνᾰμόω**, gloss on ἐξανεμόω, Sch.Vind.Hp.*Mul*.1.34 (Pass.).

**ἐκδῠναστεύω**, *overpower, prevail over*, τινός Sm.*Je*.50(27).17.

**ἐκδύνω**, v. ἐκδύω. **ἔκδυον**· καλόν, κομψόν, Hsch.

❀ **ἐκδύσια** [ῠ] (sc. ἱερά), τά, festival at Phaestus, in Crete, when Galatea *put off* her woman's *clothes*, Ant.Lib.17.6.

**ἔκδυσις**, εως, ἡ, *getting out, escape*, opp. ἔσοδος, Hdt.2.121.γ'; τὴν ἐ. ποιεῖσθαι to make their *way out*, Id.3.109; οὐκ ἔστι Ἕλλησι οὐδεμία ἐ. μὴ οὐκ εἶναι δούλους Id.8.100, cf. Pl.*Cra*.426a; πόθεν ἔκδυσιν εὕρες λατρείης δοξῶν; Timo 48 (v.l. ἔκλυσιν). **II.** *stripping, deprivation*, Man.4.331 (pl.).

**ἐκδυσωπέω**, *put to shame*, τινά Hld.8.3; τὴν πλεονεξίαν τινός J. *BJ*1.2.2; ἐ. τινὰ μὴ ἁμαρτάνειν Id.*AJ*15.4.1.

**ἐκδῠτ-ήριον**, τό, = ἀποδυτήριον, *Gloss*. **-ης**, ου, ὁ, *one who undresses*, Id.

**ἐκδύω** (ἐκδύνω Hdt.1.9, etc.): **I.** causal in pres. ἐκδύω: impf. ἐξέδυον· fut. ἐκδύσω: aor. 1 ἐξέδῡσα: late pf. ἐκδέδῠκα *AP*5.72 (Rufin.):—*take off, strip off*, c. dupl. acc. pers. et rei, ἐκ μέν με χλαῖναν ἔδυσαν they *stripped* me *of* my cloak, Od.14.341; ἐκδύων ἐμὲ.. ἐσθῆτα A.*Ag*.1269; ἐκδύσας αὐτὸν [τὸν χιτῶνα] X.*Cyr*.1.3.17: c. acc. only, *strip*, πάντας ἐ. D.24.204; ἐξέδυσαν [ἐκεῖνον] Id.54.8. **2.** Pass., ἐκδύομαι, aor. 1 ἐξεδύθην [ῠ]: pf. ἐκδέδῠμαι:—*to be stripped of* a thing, τὸν χιτωνίσκον ἐκδεδύσθαι Lys.10.10; [Μαρσύας] τὸ δέρμα ἐκδύεται Palaeph.47: abs., *to be stripped*, ἐκδυθῆναι Antipho 2.2.5, cf. Plb.15. 27.9. **3.** Med., ἐκδύομαι, Cret. ἐσδ- *GDI*5100, fut. -δύσομαι: aor. 1 ἐξεδυσάμην:—*strip oneself of* a thing, *put off*, τεύχεά τ' ἐξεδύοντο they *were putting off* their armour, Il.3.114; ἐκδύσασθαι (leg. -δύεσθαι) τὸν κιθῶνα Hdt.5.106; ἐκδεδύσθαι θοἰμάτιον D.54.35; θηρία ἐκδύεται τὸ ἄγριον Plu.*Pomp*.28: abs., *put off one's clothes, strip*, θᾶττον ἐκδυώμεθα Ar.*Lys*.686, cf. X.*HG*2.4.19; technically, of ephebi, *SIG*527.99 (Dreros, iii B.C.), *GDI*5100: metaph. of death, 2*Ep.Cor*. 5.4. **II.** Act. in med. sense, *put off*, μαλακὸν δ' ἔκδυνε χιτῶνα Od. 1.437; ἐκδὺς χλαῖναν Id.14.460; τῶν ἱματίων κατὰ ἓν ἕκαστον ἐκδύνουσα Hdt.1.9: metaph., τὸ γῆρας ἐκδύς Ar.*Pax*336, cf. Arist.*HA*600$^b$15; τὸ κέλυφος ib.549$^b$25:—Pass., of the clothes, *to be put off*, ἅμα κιθῶνι ἐκδυομένῳ Hdt.1.8. **III.** aor. 2 ἐξέδυν: pf. ἐκδέδῡκα:—*go* or *get out of*, c. gen., ἐκδὺς μεγάροιο Od.22.334; ἐκδὺς καὶ ἀνακύψας τῆς θαλάσσης *emerging from*.., Pl.*Phd*.109d: metaph., ἐξέδυ δίκης E.*Supp*.416; ἐκδῦναι κακῶν Id.*IT*602. **2.** pf. and aor. 2 c. acc., *escape, shun*, νῶϊν δ' ἐκδῦμεν ὄλεθρον [grant] us *to escape*.., Il.16.99; ἐκδεδυκέναι τὰς λῃτουργίας D.20.1; τὸν φθόνον ἐκδύς Plu.*Pomp*.30; τὴν ἀληθινὴν οὐσίαν ἐκδεδυκέναι ταῦτα Plot.6.6.8. **3.** abs., *escape*, Thgn.358; *escape one's memory*, Pl.*Alc*.2.147e.

**ἐκδωριεύομαι**, Pass., *become a thorough Dorian*, Hdt.8.73 (pf. ἐκδεδωρίευνται: ἐκδεδωρίωνται Valck., ἐκδεδωρίδαται Dind.).

❀ **ἐκεῖ** (not in Hom.), Aeol. **κῆ** Sapph.51: Dor. **τηνεῖ** (q.v.):—Adv. *there, in that place*, opp. ἐνθάδε, Th.6.83; οἱ ἐ. S.*El*.685, etc.; τἀκεῖ *what is* or *happens there, events there*, E.*Fr*.578.5, Th.1.90; redundant, οὗ ἦν ἐ. Lxx 1*Ki*.9.10. **2.** freq. as euphem. for ἐν Ἅιδου, *in another world*, κἀκεῖ δικάζει τἀμπλακήματα Ζεὺς ἄλλος A.*Supp*.230, cf. *Ch*.359 (lyr.), S.*Ant*.76; εὐδαιμονοίτην, ἀλλ' ἐ. E.*Med*.1073; εὔκολος μὲν ἐνθάδ', εὔκολος δ' ἐκεῖ Ar.*Ra*.82, cf. Pl.*Phd*.64a, al.; in full, ἐκεῖ δ' ἐν Ἅιδου E.*Hec*.418; οἱ ἐ. euphem. for *the dead*, A.*Ch*.355 (lyr.), S.*OT*776, Pl.*R*.427b, Isoc.14.61. **3.** Philos., *in the intelligible world*, Plot.1.2.7, 2.4.5, etc. **II.** with Verbs of motion, for ἐκεῖσε, *thither*, ἐ. πλέομεν Hdt.7.147; ἐ. ἀπικέσθαι v.l. in Id.9.108; ὁδοῦ τῆς ἐ. S.*OC*1019; οἱ ἐ. καταπεφευγότες Th.3.71, cf. Plb.5.101.10; βλέψον δὲ κἀκεῖ Men.*Epit*.103. **III.** rarely, of Time, *then*, S.*Ph*.395 (lyr.), D.22.38.

**ἔκελεν**· ἐκέντησεν, Hsch.

❀ **ἐκεῖθεν**, poet. **κεῖθεν** (the only form used by Hom., also in Trag. where metre requires): Aeol. **κήνοθεν** Alc.86: Dor. **τηνῶθεν** Ar.*Ach*. 754; **τηνῶθε** Theoc.3.10:—Adv. *from that place, thence*, opp. ἐκεῖσε, S.*Ph*.490, etc.; of a person, τἀκεῖθεν εἰ ποθούμεθα *on his part*, Id.*Tr*. 632; ὁ ἐ. ἄγγελος Pl.*R*.619b; τὸ σκῆπτρον ἐ. παραλαβόντες Jul.*Or*. 6.181b. **2.** = ἐκεῖ, οἱ ἐ. Th.1.62: c. gen., τοὐκεῖθεν ἄλσους *on yon side of* the grove, S.*OC*505; ἕζοντο τὸ κεῖθεν E.*Or*.1411 (lyr.). **3.** by attraction for ἐκεῖσε, βῆναι κεῖθεν ὅθεν περ ἥκει S.*OC*1227 codd. (lyr.). **II.** *thence, from that fact*, γνοίη δ' ἄν τις ἐ. Isoc.12.224, cf. D.45.48, etc. **III.** of Time, *thenceforward*, Il.15.234; ἐ. ἤδη D.C.54.25.

❀ **ἐκεῖθι** and **κεῖθι** (the only form used by Hom. exc. Od.17.10, also by Trag. where metre requires), Aeol. **κῆθι** Sapph.*Supp*.25.18 (prob.): Dor. **τηνόθι** Theoc.8.44: poet. for ἐκεῖ, Il.3.402, Od.17.10: in late Prose, οἱ ἐκεῖθι Ael.*NA*6.15; κεῖθι Alciphr.3.53, Them.*Or*.4. 57a. **II.** = ἐκεῖσε, κεῖθι μολών Hes.*Fr*.134.10, cf. Musae.23, Opp. *H*.4.274, dub. in A.*Th*.809.

**ἐκείνῃ**, v. ἐκεῖνος III.

**ἐκείνινος**, η, ον, (ἐκεῖνος) *made of that material*, Arist.*Metaph*.1033$^a$ 7, 1049$^a$21.

❀ **ἐκεῖνος**, ἐκείνη, ἐκεῖνο, also **κεῖνος** (regular in Ep., Ion. (as *SIG*37. 3 (Teos, v B.C.), though Hdt. prefers ἐκεῖνος), and Lyr., in Trag. κεῖνος only where the metre requires, cf. A.*Pers*.230, 792, S.*Aj*.220 (anap.), etc.; but not in Att. Prose, and in Com. only in mock Trag. passages): Aeol. **κῆνος** Sapph.2.1: Dor. **τῆνος** Theoc.1.4, etc.: in Com., strengthd. **ἐκεινοσί** Eup.277 (prob.), Ar.*Eq*.1196, etc.; **ἐκεινοσίν** A.D.*Pron*.59.24: (ἐκεῖ):—demonstr. Pron. *the person there, that person* or *thing*, Hom., etc.: generally with reference to what has gone immediately before, Pl.*Phd*.106c, X.*Cyr*.1.6.9, etc.; but when οὗτος and ἐκεῖνος refer to two things before mentioned, ἐκεῖνος, prop. belongs to *the more remote*, in time, place, or thought, οὗτος to *the nearer*, Pl.*Euthd*.271b, etc.: but ἐκεῖνος sts. = *the latter*, X.*Mem*. 1.3.13, D.8.72, Arist.*Pol*.1325$^a$7, etc.: ἐκεῖνος is freq. the predicate to οὗτος or ὅδε, οὗτος ἐκεῖνος τὸν σὺ ζητέεις Hdt.1.32; τοῦτ' ἔστ' ἐκεῖνο E.*Hel*.622; ἆρ' οὗτός ἐστ' ἐκεῖνος ὅν..; Ar.*Pax* 240, etc.: also joined as if one Pron., τοῦτ' ἐκεῖνο.. δέρκομαι S.*El*.1115, etc.; κατ' ἐκεῖνο καιροῦ at *that point* of time, Plu.*Alex*.32, etc.; ἐς ἐ. τοῦ χρόνου D.C. 46.49; ἀλλ' ἐκεῖνο, *à propos*, Luc.*Nigr*.8. **2.** to denote well-known persons, etc., κεῖνος μέγας θεός Il.24.90; ἐκεῖνος ἡνίκ' ἦν Θουκυδίδης Ar.*Ach*.708; καίτοι φασὶν Ἰφικράτην ποτ' ἐκεῖνον.. D.21. 62; ὦ παῖ 'κείνου τἀνδρὸς Pl.*Phlb*.36d. **b.** ἐκεῖνα *the ideal world*, Id.*Phdr*.250a. **3.** for things, of which one cannot remember or must not mention the name, = ὁ δεῖνα, *so-and-so*, Ar.*Nu*.195. **b.** in formulae, τεθνάτω καὶ οἱ παῖδες οἱ ἐξ ἐκείνου *IG*1$^2$.10.33. **4.** with simple demonstr. force, Ἶρος ἐκεῖνος ἧσται Irus sits *there*, Od.18.239; νῆες ἐκεῖναι ἐπιπλέουσιν *there* are ships sailing up, Th.1.51. **5.**

in orat. obliq. where prop. the reflex. Pron. αὐτοῦ would stand, X. *HG*1.6.14, Is.8.22, etc. **6.** after a Relat. in apodosi almost pleon., X.*Cyr*.1.4.19 (s. v. l.). **7.** in Aeol. and Att. the Subst. with ἐκεῖνος prop. has the Art. (κῆνος ὤνηρ Alc.*Supp*.25.6), and ἐκεῖνος may precede or follow the Subst., ἐκείνῃ τῇ ἡμέρᾳ Th.1.20, Pl.*Phd*.57a; τὴν στρατείαν ἐ., τὸν ἄνδρ' ἐ., Th.1.10, Ar.*Pax*649: in Poets the Art. is freq. omitted, ἤματι κείνῳ Il.2.37, etc.; but when this is the case in Prose, ἐκεῖνος follows the Subst., ἡμέρας ἐκείνης Th.3.59, etc. **II.** Adv. ἐκείνως *in that case*, Id.1.77, 3.46; *in that way*, Hp.*Fract*.27; ζῆν Pl.*R*.516d, etc.: Ion. **κείνως** Hdt.1.120. **III.** dat. fem. ἐκείνῃ as Adv., **1.** of Place, *at that place, in that neighbourhood*, Hdt.8.106, Th.4.77, etc.; κείνῃ (sc. ὁδῷ) Od.13.111. **2.** of Manner, *in that manner*, Pl.*R*.556a, etc. **IV.** with Preps., ἐξ ἐκείνου *from that time*, X.*Ages*.1.17; ἀπ' ἐκείνου Luc.*DMar*.2.2; κατ' ἐκεῖνα *in that region*, X.*HG*3.5.17, etc.; μετ' ἐκεῖνα *afterwards*, Th.5.81; cf. ἐπέκεινα.

❀ **ἐκεῖσε**, poet. **κεῖσε** (the only form in Hom., used by Trag. where the metre requires), Adv. *thither, to that place*, opp. ἐκεῖθεν or ἐνθένδε, Hdt.2.29, A.*Pers*.717, etc.; ἐκεῖσε κἀκεῖσε *hither and thither*, E.*Andr*.1131, *Hel*.533; δεῦρο καὶ αὖθις ἐ. ib.1141 (lyr.); κἀκεῖσε καὶ τὸ δεῦρο Id.*Ph*.266; τῇδε ἐ. Id.*Tr*.333 (anap.); τὸ κεῖσε δεῦρό τε S.*Tr*.929; τὸ τῇδε καὶ τὸ κεῖσε καὶ τὸ δεῦρο Ar.*Av*.425. **2.** *to the other world*, E.*Alc*.363; ἐνθένδε ἐ. from this world *to the other*, Pl.*Phd*.117c. **3.** c. gen., ἄνειμι δ' ἐ. τοῦ λόγου Hdt.7.239, cf. Pl.*Lg*.864c. **II.** = ἐκεῖ, Hp.*Vict*.2.38, Chrysipp.*Stoic*.2.244, Plb.5.51.3, Lxx *Jb*.39.29, J.*AJ* 3.2.1, Sch.Pi.*O*.9.108; τοὺς ἐ. ὄντας *Act.Ap*.22.5.

**ἐκέκαστο**, v. καίνυμαι. **ἐκεκήδει**· ὑπε(κε)χωρήκει, Hsch. **ἐκέκλετο**, v. κέλομαι.

**ἐκεχειρία**, ἡ, (ἔχω, χείρ) *cessation of hostilities, armistice, truce*, *IG* 1².96.22, etc.; ἐ. ποιεῖσθαι Th.4.117; ἄγειν, ἔχειν, Id.5.26, X.*HG*4.2.16; ἐ. γίγνεταί τισι πρὸς ἀλλήλους Th.4.58; ἀπειπεῖν τὴν ἐ. denounce the *truce*, Id.5.32; ἡ Ὀλυμπιακὴ ἐ. Arist.*Fr*.533; Dor. **ἐκεχηρία** *IG* 2².1126.49, cf. *SIG*559.32 (Megalop., found at Magn. Mae.). **2.** generally, *rest from work, holiday*, J.*AJ*1.1.1, Luc.*Herm*.11, *Sammelb*.4224.17; ἐ. πόνων Jul.*Or*.4.153c; *leisure, opportunity*, τοῦ διαμαρτάνειν, εἰς τὸ ἁμαρτάνειν, Ph.1.430, 2.76: c. inf., ib.444. **3.** in Ar.*Pax*908 ὑπέχοντα τὴν ἐκεχειρίαν is a pun—'alleging the *truce*', and 'presenting the *hand-for-holding*' (as a beggar does). **4.** *licence, leave*, to do a thing, ἐ. διδόναι τινί Ph.2.542; coupled with ἄδεια, ib.447, al.; *time of licence*, ib.529. **5.** *self-restraint, abstinence*, περὶ τὰς κλοπὰς Str.15.1.53.

**ἐκεχείριον**, τό, *travelling allowance for* θεωροί *who announce a sacred truce*, *Inscr.Magn*.33.18.

**ἐκέχειρον**, τό, = foreg., *IG*12(5).1341.53 (Paros), 629.26 (Pergam., ii B. C.); cf. ἐκέχειρον· τὸ ἀργύριον, Hsch.

**ἐκεχειροφόρος**, ὁ, *herald of truce*, Poll.4.94: metaph., ἔδωκεν αὐτοῖς ὥσπερ ἐ. τὸν ἀέρα *mediator* between fire and water, Max.Tyr.15.3.

**ἐκζᾰλόομαι**, *to be surf-tossed, wave-beaten*, Gloss.

**ἔκ-ζεμα**, ατος, τό, *a cutaneous eruption, eczema*, Dsc.1.43 (pl.), Erot. s. v. ἐκθύματα (pl.), *Gp*.1.12.19 (pl.). **-ζεσις**, εως, ἡ, *boiling out* or *over, breaking out*, ἑλκῶν Arist.*Pr*.954ᵃ25 (pl.). **II.** = foreg., Erot. s. v. αἰθόλικες (pl.). **-ζεσμα**, ατος, τό, = ἔκζεμα, Archig.ap.Gal.12.468 (pl.), Crito ap.eund.12.485 (pl.). **-ζεστός**, όν, *boiled*, τευτλίον Diph.Siph.ap.Ath.9.371a; θρῖδαξ Did.ap.Aët.9.42; *hard-boiled*, ᾠά Alex.Trall.2. **-ζέω**, *boil out* or *over*: *break out*, in disease, Arist.*Pr*.861ᵇ10; ὅταν ἐκζέῃ τὸ αἷμα Ant.Lib.19.2: metaph., ἐξέζεσεν γὰρ Οἰδίπου κατεύγματα A.*Th*.709. **2.** c. gen., ζῷα εὐλέων ἐξέζεσε *bred* worms, Hdt.4.205: c. dat., ἐκζεῖν φθειρσί D.L.4.4: c. acc., σκώληκας Lxx *Ex*.16.20; of a country, ἐ. μύας ib.1*Ki*.6.1. **3.** *ferment*, Dsc.5.7. **II.** Pass., *to be boiled to a decoction*, Aret.*CD*2.5.

❀ **ἐκζητ-έω**, *seek out*, Aristid.1.488 J., *PMag.Osl*.1.354; τινάς *POxy*.1465.11 (i B. C.); περί τινος 1*Ep.Pet*.1.10. **II.** *demand an account of*, τὸ αἷμα Lxx 2*Ki*.4.11, al., cf. *Ev.Luc*.11.50 (Pass.). ❀ **-ησις**, εως, ἡ, *research*, 1*Ep.Ti*.1.4 (pl.). **-ητής**, οῦ, ὁ, *searcher out*, Lxx *Ba*.3.23.

❀ **ἐκζωόομαι**, Pass., *become full of worms*, Thphr.*CP*4.8.4.

❀ **ἐκζωπῠρ-έω**, *rekindle*, πόλεμον Ar.*Pax*310; ἄνθρακας Plu.*Mar*.44; παλαιὰν συγγένειαν Id.*Rom*.29. **-ησις**, εως, ἡ, *rekindling*, ἀνθράκων Id.2.156b.

**ἔκηα**, v. καίω.

**ἐκηβελέτης**, ου, ὁ, = ἐκηβόλος, Orph.*Fr*.297.11.

**ἐκηβολ-έω**, *to be an archer*, Max.Tyr.7.3. **-ία**, Ep. **-ίη**, ἡ, *skill in archery*, Il.5.54 (pl.): later in sg., Call.*Ap*.99, Str.8.3.33, *AP*6.26 (Jul.).

❀ **ἑκηβόλος**, Dor. **ἑκᾱβόλος**, ον, (ἑκών, βάλλω) *attaining his aim*, epith. of Apollo, Il.1.14, al.; also Ἑκηβόλος alone, ib.96, *h.Ap*.45, Pi.*Pae*.9.38, al.; of Artemis, S.*Fr*.401; ἑκηβόλοι Διὸς χέρες E.*Ion* 213 (lyr.); τόξα A.*Pr*.711, *Eu*.628; σφενδόναι E.*Ph*.1142; ἔθνος ὀϊστῶν Opp.*H*.4.205; in later Prose, ἑ. βέλη Plb.13.3.4; μάχαι D.H.10.16; ἑ. ἄνδρες Plu.*Luc*.28; τὰ ἑ. Onos.20.1; τοξεύματα, ὅπλα, Ael.*Tact*.2.8, Arr.*Tact*.3.3; τοξόται καὶ ἑκηβόλοι Agath.3.17: Dor. Sup. ἑκαβολέστατος Archyt.ap.Iamb.*Protr*.4. Adv. **-λως**, τοξεύειν Ath.1.25d. (Understood by later writers as *far-shooting* (ἑκάς).)

**ἐκηλία**, ἡ, = εὐκηλία, *rest, peace*, Hsch.

**ἕκηλος**, Dor. **ἕκᾱλος**, ον, *at rest, at one's ease*, in Hom. esp. of persons feasting and enjoying themselves, οἱ δὲ ἕκηλοι τέρπονται Il.5.759; ἕκηλος πῖνε Od.21.309; ἕκηλοι νεκροὺς ἂμ πεδίον συλήσετε ye will plunder them *at your ease*, i. e. *without let* or *hindrance*, Il.6.70; ἕκηλος ἐρρέτω let him be off *in peace*, 9.376; of mere inaction, *quiet*, only twice in Hom., ἔσθι' ἕκηλος Od.17.478; ἕκηλοι κάτθετε 21.259, cf. Theoc.25.100; ἕκαλος ἔπειμι γῆρας Pi.*I*.7(6).41; ἕ. εὕδειν S.*Ph*.769; ἐὰν ἕκηλόν τινα ib.826: neut. as Adv., ἕκηλα ἡμερεύειν Id.*El*.786: metaph. of a field, *lying at rest* or *fallow*, *h.Cer*.451; of trees, *unmoved*, A.R.3.969.

**ἕκητι**, Dor. **ἕκᾱτι** (so always used by Trag., as E.*Or*.26, al.): prob. an old case-form, used adverbially, but always with a gen., which usually precedes, *by the will of, by means of, by virtue of*, Hom. only in Od. (in Il. he uses ἰότητι, but cf. ἀέκητι), and always of gods, Διός.. ἕκητι *by the grace* or *aid* of Zeus, Od.20.42; Ἑρμείαο ἕ. 15.319; Ἀπόλλωνός γε ἕ. 19.86; Διὸς ἕ. B.1.6; Παλλάδος καὶ Λοξίου ἕκατι A.*Eu*.759, cf. *Ch*.214; ἕ. μὲν δαιμόνων, ἕ. δ' ἁμᾶν χερῶν ib.436 (lyr.). **II.** in Lyr. and Trag. of things, **1.** *on account of, for the sake of*, ἕκατι ποδῶν Pi.*N*.8.47; κεδνῶν ἕκατι πραγμάτων A.*Ch*.701; ἀρετῆς ἕ. S.*Ph*.669, cf. *Tr*.274, 353; γάμων ἕ. E.*Med*.1235: in Com., ὧν ἕ. τοῦτ' ἔδωκε Telecl.41.4. **2.** *as to*, πλήθους ἕ. A.*Pers*.337; κελευμάτων δ' ἕ. E.*Cyc*.655; ἐμεῦ μὲν ἕκητι *so far as I am concerned*, *AP*11.361.7 (Autom.); ἕκητ' ἀλκῆς *as far as* strength *goes*, Herod.2.77: in later Prose, βιβλίων ἕ. Jul.*Or*.3.124a, cf. 119c. **III.** = χωρίς, Hsch. (Perh. cogn. with ἑκών.)

**ἐκθᾰλαττόομαι**, Pass., *become all sea*, Str.1.3.7.

**ἐκθαλίς**, = ἐρυσίβη, *EM*378.49 (s. v. l.).

**ἐκθάλλω**, *put forth blossoms*, Sm.*Ca*.2.13, Al.*Hb*.3.17. **2.** metaph., *become active*, of heat in the ground, Adam.ap.Aët.3.163.

**ἐκθάλπω**, *warm thoroughly*, metaph. in Pass., ἔρωτι Phryn.*PS* p.71 B., cj. in S.*Fr*.474.

**ἐκθαμβ-έω**, *to be amazed*, Orph.*A*.1218 (tm.). **II.** trans., *amaze, astonish*, Lxx *Si*.30.9:—Pass., *Ev.Marc*.9.15, Gal.16.493. **-ησις**, εως, ἡ, *amazement*, Aq.*Is*.52.12. **-ητικός**, ή, όν, *astonishing*, Eust.1420.5. ❀ **-ος**, ον, *amazed, astounded*, Plb.20.10.9, *Act.Ap*.3.11, *Tab.Defix*.5.20, Orph.*Fr*.49 vi 88. **II.** *terrible*, Thd.*Da*.7.7.

**ἐκθαμνίζω**, *root out, extirpate*, A.*Th*.72, Tz.*H*.1.780 (Pass.).

**ἐκθαμνόομαι**, Pass., *grow bushy*, Thphr.*HP*1.3.3.

**ἐκθάπτω**, *disinter*, *CIG*2826.4, al. (Aphrodisias).

**ἐκθαρρ-έω**, strengthd. for θαρρέω, *have full confidence*, ἐκτεθαρρηκὼς τοῖς πράγμασι Plu.*Rom*.26; *to be encouraged*, ὑπό τινος Id.*Galb*.7. **-ησις**, εως, ἡ, *full confidence*, Porph.*Abst*.1.50.

**ἐκθάρσημα**, ατος, τό, *ground for confidence*, Plu.2.1103a.

**ἐκθαυμάζω**, strengthd. for θαυμάζω, Aristeas 312, D.H.*Th*.34, Longin.44.8; ἐπί τινος Lxx *Si*.27.23; ἐπί τινι *Ev.Marc*.12.17.

**ἐκθεάομαι**, *see out, see to the end*, S.*OT*1253. **II.** Pass., *to be made visible*, prob. for ἐκθειασθῇ in Ph.1.96.

**ἐκθεᾰτρίζω**, *bring out on the stage*, metaph. in Pass., Ath.11.506f; in bad sense, *make a public show of*, τὴν αὐτῶν ἀκρισίαν Plb.11.8.7; *expose to public shame*, τοὺς πολεμίους Id.3.91.10, etc.

**ἐκθει-άζω**, *make a god of, deify*, Luc.*Tox*.2, S.E.*M*.9.35 (Pass.), Hdn.4.2.1: metaph., τοὺς Αἰγυπτίους ὡς ἀρχαίους Herm. *in Phdr*. p.199 A.; *worship as a god*, τὰ θνητά Plu.*Rom*.28, cf. Ptol.*Tetr*.123, Jul.*Gal*.155d; τὴν φύσιν Vett.Val.251.28; τὴν Ὁμήρου σοφίαν ἐκτεθείακεν αἰὼν ὁ σύμπας Heraclit.*All*.79. **II.** of things, *treat* or *regard as supernatural*, Plu.*Sert*.11, Hdn.1.14.6 (Pass.). **-ασμός**, ὁ, *inspiration*, Sch.Ar.*V*.8. **-όω** (A), *make a god of, worship as such*, Pass., ἐκτεθειῶσθαι *to be deified*, D.H.2.75; ταῖς τιμαῖς Plu.2.856e. **-όω** (B), *desulphurate*, Zos.Alch.p.147 B.

❀ **ἔκθεμα**, ατος, τό, *public notice, proclamation, edict*, *PRev.Laws* 33.10 (iii B. C.), Plb.31.6(10).1 (pl.); ἀπ' ἐκθέματος, = Lat. *ex edicto*, *IG* 7.2712.26, 73 (Acraephia), cf. *SIG*1023.61 (Cos).

**ἐκθεμᾰτίζω**, *give public notice*, *PTeb*.27.108 (Pass., ii B. C.).

❀ **ἐκθέμεναι** or **ἐκθέμεν**, v. ἐκτίθημι.

**ἐκθεολογέω**, *attribute to the Deity*, ἡ τοῦ παντὸς ἐκτεθεολόγηται γένεσις Heraclit.*All*.40.

❀ **ἐκθεόω**, = ἐκθειόω (A), Ael.*NA*10.23, Porph.*Marc*.17:—Pass., *to be made* or *become divine*, Herm. *in Phdr*. p.135 A., Dam.*Pr*.100, Procl.*Inst*.129, al. **II.** of temples or places, *consecrate*, βωμόν App.*BC* 3.3. **III.** *drawn for magical purposes* (cf. ἀποθεόω), *PMag.Par*.1.2456.

**ἐκθεραπεύω**, strengthd. for θεραπεύω: **1.** *cure perfectly*, Plb.3.88.1, Agath.1.15:—Med., *get oneself quite cured*, Hp.*Vict*.3.83. **2.** *gain over*, Aeschin.1.169, D.S.14.19, Plu.*Sol*.31, *PSI*6.614.5 (iii B. C.), Agath.*Praef*.p.137 D.; τινὰς φιλανθρωπίαις D.H.5.76:—Pass., παρὰ τῶν κληρονόμων *Cod.Just*.1.3.45.6. **3.** Pass., *to be complied with*, Agath.5.10.

❀ **ἐκθερίζω**, *reap* or *mow completely*, of a crop, θέρος D.53.21, cf. *PEdgar*27.5 (iii B. C.), Lxx *Le*.19.9, Alciphr.3.16: metaph. of men, τοὺς γηγενεῖς ἐξεθερίσατε Sch.A.R.4.1031, cf. E.*Fr*.373:—Pass., Thphr.*CP*4.6.1. **2.** *cut out*, τὴν γλῶσσαν ἐκθερίξω (aor. subj.) *Anacreont*.9.7.

**ἐκθερμ-αίνω**, strengthd. for θερμαίνω, *warm thoroughly*, Arist.*HA*580ᵃ9, *Pr*.878ᵃ38, Philostr.*Gym*.35; ποτῷ γυῖα Nic.*Al*.461:—Pass., *become hot*, Hp.*VM*16, Arist.*Pr*.863ᵇ27; with wine, Timae.114. **II.** *cause to evaporate by heat*, Arist.*Pr*.870ᵃ17 (Pass.): metaph., τὸν εὐρῶτα τῆς ψυχῆς οὐκ ἐκτεθέρμαγκε διὰ φιλοσοφίας Plu.2.48c. **-αντέον**, *one must heat*, Herod.Med. in *Rh.Mus*.58.101. **-ος**, ον, *very hot*, Vett.Val.162.23, Gal.4.490, Aspasia ap. Aët.16.22.

**ἐκ-θεσία**, Ep. **-ίη**, ἡ, *exposure*, βρεφέων Man.4.368: abs., ib.596. **-θέσιμος**, ον, *exposed*, Vett.Val.61.18, *Gloss*. ❀ **-θεσις**,

εως, ἡ, *exposure*, of a child, Hdt.1.116, E.*Ion*956; also of *the putting out* of Ulysses on the shore of Ithaca, Arist.*Po.*1460$^a$36. 2. *exhibition*, ἀργυρωμάτων D.S.34/5.2.35 (pl.). II. *setting forth, exposition*, τῶν ὅρων Arist.*APr.*48$^a$25, 49$^b$6. b. *exhibition* of a particular instance, ἀποδεῖξαι τῇ ἐκθέσει ib.28$^b$14; κατὰ τὴν ἔ. ἑκάστου Id. *Metaph.*1090$^a$17, cf. 992$^b$10, Epicur.*Nat.*15.23, Chrysipp.*Stoic.*2.7 (pl.). III. pl., *stakes*, at play, Alciphr.3.54. IV. *public notice*, ἔ. ποιεῖσθαι *SIG*685.37 (Crete), cf. *PHib.*1.29.10 (iii B.C.). V. Medic., *prescription*, Alex.Trall.1.11. VI. Math., *setting out* of terms in a series, *Theol.Ar.*51 (pl.); *series*, Moderat.ap.Stob.1 *Prooem.*9, Nicom.*Ar.*1.7. b. Geom., *particular enunciation*, Procl.*in Euc.* p.203 F., al. VII. *salient angle*, Ph.*Bel.*82.3 (pl.); *projection* of bastions, *GDI*5597 (Ephesus). 2. *writing* of lyric verses *to the left* of the previous line, opp. εἴσθεσις (q.v.), Sch.Ar.*Ra.*1548, al. VIII. *list, schedule*, *POxy.*291.3 (i A.D.), etc. IX. *table* of musical notes, Aristid.Quint.1.11. X. = ὀφειλὴ παλαιά, Hsch.

**ἔκθεσμος**, ον, *lawless, unlawful*, Ph.2.502, Phint.ap.Stob.4.23.61, *POxy.*129.4 (vi A.D.); *monstrous*, ὄναρ Plu.*Caes.*32; ὑποθέσεις Phld. *Sto.*339.18; εὑρήματα Ph.1.335 (Sup.).

**ἐκ-θετέον**, (ἐκτίθημι) *one must set forth*, Str.17.1.1; *one must arrange, tabulate*, ἐφ' ἑνὸς στίχου πάντας [ἀριθμούς] Plu.2.1027d, cf. Iamb.*in Nic.*p.44 P. ❀ **-θέτης**, ου, ὁ, *balcony*, Sm.3*Ki.*6.4. **-θετικός**, ή, όν, *expository*, λόγος ἐ. τινος Aphth.*Prog.*8, cf. Theo *Prog.*4. II. ἐ. τρόπος, = ἔκθεσις II.b, Alex.Aphr.*in APr.*34.7. Adv. -κῶς Simp. *in Ph.*948.25. III. *enunciatory*, *Stoic.*2.62. **-θετος**, ον, *sent out of the house, sent away*, E.*Andr.*70; *exposed*, of a child, *Act.Ap.* 7.19, Man.6.52; *cast away*, Hsch. II. *projecting, salient*, Sor.1. 68; opp. κρυπτός, Heliod.(?) ap.Orib.49.4.23. b. neut., ἔκθετον, τό, = ἐκθέτης, Al.*Ez.*42.3.

❀ **ἐκθέω**, *run out*: *make a sally*, Ar.*Lys.*456; ἐκ τοῦ τείχους X.*HG* 3.1.7; of javelins, *fly out*, Plu.*Marc.*16: *rush, hurry out*, Arist.*EN* 1149$^a$28.

**ἐκθέ-ωσις**, εως, ἡ, *deification, consecration*, *OGI*56.53 (Canopus, iii B.C.), Ph.2.594, al. **-ωτικός**, ή, όν, *divinizing*, Procl.*in Prm.* p.838 S., *in Ti.*3.205 D.

**ἐκθηλάζω**, *suck the breast*, Lxx *Is.*66.11:—Pass., Hp.*Mul.*1.73; *to be sucked out*, Arist.*HA*587$^b$27.

**ἐκθήλ-υνσις**, εως, ἡ, *becoming soft, relaxation*, σαρκῶν Hp.*Aph.*5. 16, cf. *Art.*52:—also -ῦσις Nic.*Fr.*135. ❀ **-ύνω**, aor. -εθήλυνα D.H. 7.9:—*soften, weaken*, τὸ σκέλος ἐκτεθηλυσμένον γίνεται Hp.*Art.*52, cf. 56; *make effeminate*, στρατιὰν ταῖς ἡδοναῖς Str.5.4.13; τὴν νεότητα ταῖς ἀγωγαῖς D.H. l. c.; ψυχάς Corn.*ND*20:—Pass., ἐκτεθηλυμμένος καὶ τῇ ψυχῇ καὶ τῷ σώματι Plb.36.15.2, cf. 28.21.3, D.C.50.27; of plants, *become enfeebled*, Thphr.*CP*3.1.3. II. Gramm., *make a feminine of*, *EM*473.35.

**ἐκθηρ-άομαι**, *hunt out, catch*, X.*Cyn.*5.25, Plu.*Pomp.*26; τῇ ἀκοῇ πότερον.. Max.Tyr.31.3. **-ατέον**, *one must hunt out*, Plu.*Comp. Nic.Crass.*4, Max.Tyr.34.4. **-εύω**, = ἐκθηράομαι, Hdt.6.31, Arist. *Mir.*832$^a$29, Plu.*Crass.*31.

**ἐκθηριόω**, *make savage*, τινάς Ph.*Fr.*98 H.; ἑαυτόν Longus 1.20:—Pass., *become quite wild* or *savage*, Ph.1.430, Iamb.*Protr.*5; also, *assume animal shape*, E.*Ba.*1331.

**ἐκθησαυρίζω**, *exhaust a treasure*, Phalar.*Ep.*12 (dub. l.).

**ἔκθιβος** and **ἔκθροιβος**· τὸ λῶμα τοῦ χιτῶνος, Hsch.; cf. ὄχθοιβος.

**ἐκ-θλῖβή**, ἡ, *oppression*, Lxx *Mi.*7.2. ❀ **-θλίβω** [ῑ], *squeeze out*, Arist.*HA*578$^b$4, 626$^a$20, Epicur.*Ep.*2 p.50 U., Nic.*Al.*626:—Pass., Arist.*HA*522$^a$20; *to be forced from* one's position, Plu.*Sull.*19. 2. Pass., *to be crowded, cramped*, of troops, X.*An.*3.4.19. 3. *squeeze, press*, σταφυλήν Lxx *Ge.*40.11:—Pass., aor. 2 part. ἐκθλῐβείς Dsc.1. 112. b. *squeeze out*, Arist.*Mete.*342$^a$9 (Pass.). 4. Gramm., *elide* a letter at the beginning or end of a word, οὐ γὰρ οἷόν τε εὑρέσθαι τὸ ῡ -όμενον A.D.*Conj.*228.17, cf. D.H.*Dem.*43. **-θλιμμα**, ατος, τό, *pressure, bruise*, Hp.ap.Gal.18(2).510, cf. 12.343. **-θλιπτέον**, *one must squeeze out*, *Gp.*18.17.1. II. Adj. -τέος, α, ον, gloss on ἐκβλιστέος, Hsch. **-θλιψις**, εως, ἡ, *squeezing out*, Hp.*Aph.*7.85, Arist.*Mete.*342$^a$15, Epicur.*Ep.*2 p.50 U.; τοῦ λοιποῦ (sc. οὔρου) Gal. *UP*5.16. II. *affliction, distress*, Lxx *Ez.*12.18. III. Gramm., *ecthlipsis, ejection* of a letter, as σκῆπτρον, σκᾶπτον, A.D.*Conj.*230.10, etc.; also, *elision*, Eust.984.15 (pl.).

❀ **ἐκθνῄσκω**, fut. -θᾰνοῦμαι: aor. ἐξέθᾰνον:—*die away, to be like to die*, γέλῳ (for γέλωτι) ἔκθανον *were like to die* with laughing, Od.18.100; δρῶντες ἐξέθνῃσκον ἐπὶ τῷ πράγματι Antiph.190.7; ὑπὸ γέλωτος ἐ. Plu. 2.54c; ὑπὸ τοῦ δέους Luc.*Icar.*23, etc. 2. *to be in a death-like swoon*, ἐξέθανε πεντάκις ὥστε τεθνάναι δοκέειν, Hp.*Epid.*5.42, cf. Philem.1. 6D.; ὁ ἐκτεθνεώς, opp. ὁ ὄντως τεθνηκώς, Pl.*Lg.*959a; opp. ἀποθνήσκειν, Arist.*HA*521$^a$11, cf. *Pr.*962$^b$4:—so in S.*Tr.*568 (though Nessus was really dying) ἐκθνῄσκων may retain its usual sense, *fainting away, at the point of death*. 3. *become mortified*, τὸ φλεγμαῖνον ἐκτέθνηκεν Hp.*VC*19. 4. c. acc., *to be terrified of*, τὰς νόσους ἐκτεθνήκασι Phld.*Herc.*1251.18. II. later, = ἀποθνῄσκω, Luc.*Hist.Conscr.* 27, Aret.*SD*2.13, D.C.48.37.

**ἐκθοινάομαι**, *feast on*, c. acc., A.*Pr.*1025.

**ἐκθολόω**, *make turbid*, Procl.*Par.Ptol.*183.

**ἐκθόοντας**· ἐξερχομένους, Hsch. (leg. -θέοντας). ❀ **ἐκθοράζει**· ἐκδιώξει, Id. (fort. ἐκθράξει, = ἐκταράξει).

**ἐκθορέω**, = ἐκθρῴσκω, aor. -εθόρησα, Plu.*Nob.*19.

**ἐκθόρνυμαι**, later (unless read for ἐξέσσυται Democr.32 ap.Gal.17 (2).28) collat. form for ἐκθρῴσκω, τῇ ψυχῇ M.Ant.8.51; *start up* from sleep, Aret.*SA*2.9.

**ἐκθορῠβέω**, *disturb, disquiet*, Poll.1.117:—Pass., ἐκ τῶν ὕπνων ἐκθορυβούμενοι Aret.*SD*1.5.

**ἔκθρεψις**, εως, ἡ, *bringing up, rearing*, Ael.*NA*3.8, Porph.ap.Eus. *PE*3.11.

**ἐκθρηνέω**, *lament aloud for*, Luc.*Ocyp.*113.

**ἐκθρῐαμβίζω**, *make public, noise abroad*, *BGU*1061.19 (Pass., i B.C.).

**ἐκθροέω**, *speak out loud*, Poll.6.207. II. Pass., *to be startled out of*, τῶν ὕπνων Gal.16.221. **ἔκθροιβος**, v. ἔκθιβος.

**ἐκθρομβ-όω**, *clear from clots*, σώματα Antyll.ap.Orib.45.2.10; ἕλκος Paul.Aeg.6.60. **-ωσις**, εως, ἡ, *coagulation*, αἵματος Dsc.1.128.7; *curdling* of milk, Gal.14.142.

**ἐκθρῠλέω**, *chatter out*, Poll.6.207:—Pass., ἐκτεθρυλημένος ib.206.

❀ **ἐκθρῴσκω**, fut. -θοροῦμαι: aor. -έθορον:—*leap out of*, c. gen., ἔκθορε δίφρου Il.16.427; ἐκ δ' ἔθορε κλῆρος κυνέης 7.182, cf. 23.353; ἐ. ναῶν A.*Pers.*457; κραδίη δέ μοι ἔξω στηθέων ἐκθρῴσκει, of the violent *beating* of the heart, Il.10.95: abs., *leap forth*, Ἀπόλλων ἀντίος ἐξέθορε 21.539, cf. Corn.*ND*19: rarely c. acc., δίκτυον ἐ. *AP*9.371; *start up*, ἀπὸ τοῦ ὕπνου Luc.*DMar.*2.3; *come from the womb, to be born*, *h.Ap.* 119.

**ἐκθῠελλόω**, *carry away as by a storm*, Moschio *Hyp.*1.

**ἔκθῦμα**, ατος, τό, (ἐκθύω II) *pustule*, Hp.*Epid.*3.7 (pl.), al. II. (ἐκθύω I) *expiatory sacrifice*, Arist.*Ath.*54.6 (pl.).

**ἐκθῠμαίνω**, strengthd. for θυμαίνω, aor. ἐξεθύμηνα (-θύμησαν codd.) Ant.Lib.7.4: fut. ἐκθυμᾰνῶ Phld.*Ir.*p.16 W.

**ἐκθύμενος**· ταχύς, Hsch.

**ἐκθῡμία**, ἡ, *ardour, eagerness*, Plb.3.115.6.

**ἐκθῡμι-άω**, *burn as incense*, E.*Ion*1174. 2. *turn into vapour*, Str.15.1.22, Heraclit.*Ep.*6.4:—Pass., *to pass off in fumes*, Arist. *Mete.*388$^a$8, v.l. in Dsc.1.98, Ph.1.500, M.Ant.6.4. **-ασις**, εως, ἡ, *evaporation, expansion*, θερμοῦ Marcellin.*Puls.*59.

**ἔκθῡμος**, ον, *spirited, ardent*, φίλων ὑπηρεσίαι Plu.*Aem.*12, cf. App. *BC*5.38 (Sup.). Adv. -μως *ardently*, Diog.Oen.15; ἐρίζειν Luc.*JTr.* 16; *vehemently, bravely*, ὥρμησε Plb.2.67.7, cf. 1.17.9 (Comp.); ἀγωνίζεσθαι D.H.2.54, etc.

**ἐκθῠρίζω**, *stray, play truant*, Eust.1020.13.

**ἐκ-θῠσία**, ἡ, = ἔκθυσις I, Vett.Val.183.26 (pl.), Zos.2.1.2 (pl.):—written ἐχθυσία, *IG*11(2).142.59 (Delos, iv B.C.). **-θύσιμος** [ῠ], ον, *needing atonement*, Plu.2.518b. **-θῠσις**, εως, ἡ, (ἐκθύω I) *atonement*, *expiatory rites*, Id *Marc.*28. 2. *averting by sacrifices*, τῶν εἱμαρμένων Iamb.*Myst.*9.3, cf. 1.13 (pl.) (leg. ἐκλ-). II. (ἐκθύω II) *breaking out, eruption*, Hp.*Coac.*168. **-θῠτέον**, *one must eradicate*, φιλαυτίαν τῆς διανοίας Ph.*Fr.*100 H. **-θῠτικός**, ή, όν, = ἐκθύσιμος, Hsch. s. v. ἐξιατρός. **-θύω** [ῡ], *sacrifice*, S.*El.*572, E.*Cyc.*371 (lyr.); *destroy utterly*, Id.*Or.*191 (lyr.):—Med., ἐχθυσεῦνται (Dor. fut.) τὰ ἱερά *SIG* 1106.65 (Cos). 2. Med., *atone for, expiate by offerings*, c. acc. rei, ἄγος Hdt.6.91; τὰ ἀναγκαῖα Iamb.*Myst.*9.3 (leg. ἐκλ-): c. acc. pers., *propitiate, appease*, τινὰ μακάρων E.*Fr.*912.12 (anap.): abs., *make atonement*, ὑπέρ τινος (thing or person) Thphr.*HP*5.9.8, Plu.*Alex.*50, D.C.41.14; τοῖς θεοῖς Str.6.2.11. 3. Med., *avert by sacrifices*, τὰ εἱμαρμένα Iamb.*Myst.*9.3. II. *break out as heat* or *humours*, Hp. *Liqu.*6.

**ἐκθωπεύω**, gloss on sq., Hsch.

**ἐκθώπτω**, aor. -έθωψα, *gain by flattery, wheedle over*, S.*Fr.*857.

**ἐκκαγχάζω**, *burst out into loud laughter*, X.*Smp.*1.16; ἀθρόον ἐ. Arist.*EN*1150$^b$11:—spelt **ἐκκακχάζω**, Phld.*Ir.*p.49 W.: **ἐκκαχάζω**, v.l. in Sch.Ar.*Nu.*1242.

**ἐκ-κᾰθαίρω**, Ion. aor. 1 -εκάθηρα Hdt.2.86, Att. -εκάθᾱρα Din.2.5:—*cleanse out*: 1. with acc. of the thing cleansed, *clear out*, οὐρούς τ' ἐξεκάθαιρον Il.2.153; τὴν κοιλίην Hdt. l. c.; μήτρας, ὀδόντας, Hp. *Mul.*1.88, Orib.*Syn.*5.25.3; χθόνα ἐκκαθαίρει κνωδάλων he *clears* this land of monsters, A.*Supp.*264; τὸν βίον (i.e. the world) Luc.*DDeor.* 13.1; ἐ. τινά, ὥσπερ ἀνδριάντα, εἰς τὴν κρίσιν *clear* him *of all roughness, polish* him *up*, metaph. from the finishing touches of a sculptor, Pl.*R.* 361d; ἑαυτὸν ἀπό τινος 2*Ep.Ti.*2.21; ἐ. λογισμόν *clear off* an account, Plu.2.64f:—Pass., *to be cleansed, purified*, ἐκκεκαθαρμένοι τὰς ψυχάς X.*Smp.*1.4, cf. Pl.*R.*527d; *to be cleared up, explained*, Epicur.*Ep.*2 p.36 U. 2. with acc. of the thing removed, *clear away*, Pl.*Euthphr.* 3a, cf. Arist.*HA*625$^b$34; τὸ τοιοῦτον ἐ. γένος Diph.32.17; τὴν δωροδοκίαν ἐκ τῆς πόλεως Din. l. c.; κόπρον *APl.*4.92.7. ❀ **-κᾰθᾰρίζω**, = foreg., Lxx *De.*32.43. **-κάθαρσις** [κᾰ], εως, ἡ, *complete cleansing, purification*, Muson.*Fr.*20 p.111 H. 2. *sweeping out*, Hierocl.*in CA*14 p.451 M. 3. *polishing up*, θυρᾶν *IG*4.1484.283 (Epid.).

**ἐκκαθεύδω**, *sleep out of one's quarters*, X.*HG*2.4.24.

❀ **ἐκκαίδεκα**, οἱ, αἱ, τά, indecl., *sixteen*, Hdt.2.13, etc.

**ἐκκαιδεκά-γωνος** [ᾰ], ον, *having sixteen angles*, Hero *Geep.*164, Simp.*in Ph.*55.3. **-δάκτῠλος**, ον, *sixteen fingers long, broad*, etc., Ath.Mech.35.1. **-δωρος**, ον, *sixteen palms long*, Il.4.109. **-εδρον**, τό, *solid with sixteen surfaces*, Ps.-Ptol.*Centil.*60. **-ετηρίς**, ίδος, ἡ, *period of sixteen years*, Gem.8.39. ❀ **-έτης**, ου, ὁ, *sixteen years old*, Plu.2.754e. II. *consisting of sixteen years*, χρόνος D.C.69. 8. **-κις**, *sixteen times*, Dioph.2.29. **-κωλος**, ον, *of sixteen members* (sc. περίοδος), Sch.Ar.*Pax*382. **-λῐνος**, ον, *consisting of sixteen threads*, δίκτυον X.*Cyn.*2.5. **-πάλαιστος** [πᾰ], ον, *of sixteen palms*, Poll.2.157. **-πηχυς**, Dor. -πᾱχυς, υ, gen. εος, contr. ους, *sixteen cubits long* or *high*, Decr.Byz.ap.D.18.91, *IG*11(2).161 D120 (Delos, iii B.C.), Plb.5.89.6. **-πλάσιος** [πλᾰ], ον, *sixteen times as great*, Androm.ap.Gal.13.913. **-πους**, ποδος, ὁ, ἡ, *sixteen feet long*, Anon. *in Tht.*34.31.

**ἐκκαιδεκάς**, άδος, ἡ, *the number sixteen*, Dam.*Pr.*382.

**ἐκκαιδεκά-σημος** [ᾰ], ον, *of sixteen times*, χρόνος Aristid.Quint.1.14. **-στάδιος** [στᾰ], ον, *sixteen stades long*, περίβολος Str.12.4.7. **-σύλλᾰβος**, ον, *of sixteen syllables*, Σαπφικὸν -ον (sc. -μετρον) Heph.10.6, Arg.Theoc.28.

⊕ **ἐκκαιδεκᾰταῖος**, α, ον, *sixteen days old*, [σελήνη] Sch.Ar.*Th.*86.

**ἐκκαιδεκᾰτάλαντος** [τᾰ], ον, *worth sixteen talents*, γύναιον ἐ. *with a dowry of sixteen talents*, cj. in Men.402.11.

⊕ **ἐκκαιδέκᾰτος**, η, ον, *sixteenth*, Hdt.2.143, etc.

**ἐκκαιδεκ-έτις**, ιδος, ἡ, *sixteen years old*, *AP*7.600 (Jul.). **-ήρης**, ους, ἡ, *ship of sixteen banks*, Plb.18.44.6.

**ἐκκαιεβδομηκοντᾰετηρίς**, ίδος, ἡ, *period of seventy-six years*, Gem. 8.59.

**ἐκκαιεικοσάεδρον** [ᾰ], τό, *solid with twenty-six surfaces*, Papp. in Archim.2 p.536 H.

**ἐκκαινόω**, *restore, repair*, *Ostr.Strassb.*736.

**ἐκκαιπεντηκοντάγωνον** [ᾰ], τό, *figure of fifty-six sides*, prob. in Plu. 2.363a (ὀκτωκαι- codd.).

**ἔκκαιρος**, ον, *out of date, antiquated*, *AP*11.417; *unseasonable*, *POxy.*729.18 (ii A.D.).

**ἐκκαίω**, Att. **ἐκκάω**, fut. -καύσω: aor. 1 ἐξέκαυσα Hdt.4.134, but part. ἐκκέαντες E.*Rh.*97:—*burn out*, τοὺς ὀφθαλμούς τινος Hdt.7.18; τὸ φῶς Κύκλωπος E.*Cyc.*633, cf. 657 (anap.):—Pass., ἐκκάεσθαι τοὺς ὀφθαλμούς *to have one's* eyes *burnt out*, Pl.*Grg.*473c. II. *light up, kindle*, τὰ πυρά Hdt.4.134, cf. E.*Rh.* l.c.; ἐκκέας τῶν ξύλων ἅττ' ἂν ᾖ δανότατα Ar.*Pax* 1133 (lyr.): metaph., ἐ. πόλεμον, ἐλπίδα, Plb.3.3.3, 5.108.5; τοὺς θυμούς D.H.7.35; τὴν πρὸς αὐτὸν ὀργήν Plu.*Fab.*7; *provoke* to anger, ἔκ με κάεις Herod.4.49; *inflame* with curiosity, *excite*, τινά Luc.*Alex.*30; ἴσῃ φιλοτιμίᾳ πρός τε τὸν δῆμον ἑαυτοὺς καὶ τὸν δῆμον πρὸς ἑαυτοὺς ἐκκαύσαντες Plu.*Agis* 2:—Pass., *to be kindled, burn up*, τὸ πῦρ ἐκκάεται Eup.340; ἐ. τὸ κακόν Pl.*R.*556a; ὀργὴν ἐκκαῆναι Lxx 2*Ki.*24.1; ὁ δῆμος ἐξεκάετο Plu.*TG* 13, cf. Luc.*Cal.*3, etc.; ἐ. εἰς ἔρωτα Alciphr.3.67, cf. Charito 1.1; ὑπὸ μέθης Parth.24.2. 2. *stimulate*, τὴν βλάστησιν Thphr.*CP*2.1.3. III. *scorch*, ἐκκαίων ὁ ἥλιος Arist.*Pr.*867ᵃ20; of thirst, *parch*, Luc.*Dips.*4.

**ἐκκᾰκέω**, *to be faint-hearted, lose heart, grow weary*, v.l. for ἐγκ-, *Ev.Luc.*18.1, 2*Ep.Cor.*4.1, 16, al., cf. Vett.Val.201.15, *Gloss.*

**ἐκκακή**· ὧδε, Hsch.

**ἐκκᾰλᾰμάομαι**, *pull out with a* καλάμη, *fish out*: hence metaph., *wheedle out*, Ar.*V.*609.

**ἐκκαλάξαι**· κλῖναι τὸ ἱστίον, Hsch. (i.e. ἐκχαλάσαι).

⊕ **ἐκκᾰλέω**, *call out* or *forth, summon forth*, Il.24.582, etc.; τινὰ δόμων E.*Ba.*170; ἔνδοθεν Lys.3.8; *crave speech of*, τινά S.*OT*597 codd. II. Med., *call out to oneself*, ψυχάς Od.24.1, cf. Hdt.8.79, S.*Ph.*1264. 2. *call forth, elicit*, χαρὰ δάκρυον ἐκκαλουμένη A.*Ag.*270; ὀργὴν Aeschin. 2.3; ἴσως ἂν ἐκκαλέσαιθ' ὑμᾶς D.4.42, cf. Pl.*Euthd.*288d; λιμὸν ἐ. Antiph.217.23; τοὺς ἱππεῖς *entice, provoke to battle*, Plb.1.19.2, cf. Ascl.*Tact.*7.1. 3. c. inf., *call on* one *to* do, S.*Tr.*1206; ἐ. [τινὰ] ποτὶ ἔργα Ti.Locr.104b: plpf. in med. sense, ἐξεκέκλητο πρὸς τὴν πρᾶξίν τινας Plb.4.57.4:—Pass., -κληθῆναι πρὸς τὰς ὠφελείας Id.3.51.11; *to be provoked*, εἴς, ἐπί τι, Phld.*Ir.*pp.52, 95 W.; ἐς ὀργήν, δάκρυα, Philostr.*VS*2.8.4, 2.10.1. 4. *demand, require*, ὡς τὰ φαινόμενα -εῖται Epicur.*Ep.*2 p.36 U., cf. 53 U. III. Pass., = Lat. *evocari*, of foreign *numina*, Plu.2.278f. IV. Med., *appeal against*, κρίσιν ἐπί τινα ib.178f; *refer*, προβλήματα ἐπὶ τὴν τῶν ἀλόγων φύσιν ὥσπερ ἀλλοδαπὴν πόλιν ib.493b.

**ἐκκαλλύνω**, *sweep clean*, ἔδαφος πτεροῖς Arr.*Peripl.M.Eux.*21, cf. Hsch. s.v. ἐκκοροῦσι:—Pass., *EM*322.18.

**ἐκκάλυμμα**, ατος, τό, *means of discovery, token*, Plu.2.463a (pl.).

**ἐκκαλυπτικός**, ή, όν, *suited for discovery, indicative of*, c. gen., *Stoic.* 2.36, 72. Adv. -κῶς S.E.*P.*2.141.

⊕ **ἐκκᾰλύπτω**, *uncover*, τὸ παιδίον Hdt.1.112; *disclose, reveal*, ὀργὴ νόον ἐξεκάλυψεν Even.5; πάντ' ἐκκάλυψον A.*Pr.*195, cf. S.*Aj.*1003; πάντ' ἐ. ὁ χρόνος Id.*Fr.*918; λέγ' ἐκκαλύψας κρᾶτα E.*Supp.*111; ἐ. μυστικοὺς λόγους Phld.*Ir.*p.46 W.: folld. by relat., ἐκκάλυπτε.. ἡμῖν οὕστινας λέγεις λόγους E.*IA*872:—Med., *uncover one's head, unveil oneself*, Od.10.179 (tm.): pf. fut. ἐκκεκαλύψομαι Ar.*Av.*1503; opp. ἐγκαλύπτομαι, Pl.*Phd.*118a. 2. *unmask*, τινά Aeschin.3.55.

**ἐκκάμνω**, *grow quite weary of* a thing, τὰς ὀλοφύρσεις Th.2.51: c. part., πολεμοῦντες ἐξέκαμον Plu.*Sol.*8, cf. *Pomp.*32, D.C.40.24; ἐξέκαμεν ὑπὸ γήρως πρὸς τὰ δημόσια *he became unfit* through age for.., Plu.*Cat.Ma.*24; σίδηρος ἐξέκαμε πληγαῖς *it is worn out* (gnomic) with blows, Id.*Caes.*37; ἐ. ἡ ἀρετή τισι Max.Tyr.29.2.

**ἐκκᾰνάσσω**, *drink off*, τήνδ'.. ἐκκανάξει (sc. κύλικα) Eup.272, cf. Ael.*Ep.*4.

**ἐκκᾰπηλεύω**, lit., *sell off*:—Pass., ἐκκαπηλεύεσθαι τῆς χώρας Philostr.*VA*1.15. II. *adulterate*, Hsch.

**ἐκκαπνίζομαι**, *evaporate in smoke*, Olymp.Alch.p.73 B.

**ἐκκαρδιόω**, *cut out the heart*, Alex.Trall.1.15.

**ἐκκαρπ-εύομαι**, = ἐκκαρπόομαι, *PPetr.*2 p.143 (iii B.C.). **-έω**, *grow to seed*, Hp.*Art.*8, Gal.6.537. **-ησις**, εως, ἡ, *growing to seed*, ib.665. **-ίζομαι**, Med., *yield as produce*, A.*Th.*601. II. *reap, enjoy*, τὰ ἐκ τῆς γῆς γενήματα *PTeb.*105.30 (ii B.C.). III. of land, *exhaust*, Thphr.*CP*4.8.3. **-όομαι**, Med., *gather* or *enjoy the fruit of*, ἄλλης γυναικὸς παῖδας ἐ. *to have* children *by another wife*, E.*Ion*815; ἐ. φιλίαν D.C.37.56. II. *enjoy the fruit of* a thing, c. part., ἀμφοτέροις ἔνσπονδοι ὄντες ἐκκαρπώσασθαι Th.5.28; ἐ. τινάς *exhaust* them, *drain* them *dry*, D.24.2.

**ἐκκᾰρῡκεύω**, *make into* καρύκη (q.v.), in Pass., Hsch., Suid.

**ἐκκατᾰράσσω**, *damage completely*, Alex.Aphr.*Pr.*1.96 (Pass.).

**ἐκκατεῖδον**, aor. with no pres. ἐκκαθοράω in use, *look down from*, Περγάμου ἐκκατιδών Il.4.508, cf. Q.S.8.430.

⊕ **ἐκκαυλ-έω**, *run to stalk*, Arist.*Pr.*924ᵇ27, Dsc.2.136, cf. ἐκκαυλῆσαι· ἐπιδοῦναι, Hsch.; *develop a stem*, Thphr.*HP*1.2.2, *CP*4.3.5. **-ημα**, ατος, τό, *stalk put forth*, Gal.19.153 (s.v. φύσιγγα). **-ησις**, εως, ἡ, *shooting into a stalk*, Thphr.*CP*4.3.5. **-ίζω**, *pull out the stalk*: metaph., καυλοὺς τῶν εὐθυνῶν ἐ. *pull off* the sprouts, i.e. the profits, Ar.*Eq.*825.

**ἔκ-καυμα**, ατος, τό, (ἐκκαίω) *wood for lighting fires*, in pl., S.*Fr.*225, D.S.2.49: sg., Thphr.*Ign.*73: metaph., ἔ. τόλμης E.*Fr.*1031; *source of heat*, Aret.*CA*2.11. **-καυσις**, εως, ἡ, *kindling, burning*, Arist.*Mete.*342ᵃ2, Anthem.p.154 W. 2. *heating* of the body, Aret.*SA*1.7 (pl.); of baths, *PFlor.*385.88 (V A.D.), *Cod.Just.*1.4.26 *Intr.* (pl.). II. *sunstroke*, Gal.2.884; ἡλίου Alex.Aphr.*Pr.*1.88. **-καυστικός**, ή, όν, *inflammatory*, Ael.*VH*11.12.

**ἐκκαυχάομαι**, strengthd. for καυχάομαι, E.*Ba.*31.

**ἐκκαχλάζω**, *break, plash*, of waves, Apollon.*Lex.* s.v. κωφόν.

**ἐκκαχρύζω**, '*pearl*' *barley*, Hsch.

**ἐκκάω**, Att. for ἐκκαίω.

**ἐκκεδάννυμι**, *scatter*, ἦτορ ἀπὸ μελέων Q.S.10.124 (tm.).

**ἔκκειμαι**, serving as Pass. of ἐκτίθημι, *to be cast out* or *exposed*, ἐπορᾶν ἐκκείμενον (sc. τὸν παῖδα) Hdt.1.110, cf. 122, Longus 1.3; ἁπλοῦν τὸ ἦθος καὶ παντὶ ἰδεῖν ἐκκείμενον D.H.*Rh.*10.1. 2. of public notices, decrees, etc., *to be set up in public, posted up*, ἵν' ἐκκέοιτο πρὸ τῶν ἐπωνύμων D.21.103, cf. 58.9; *to be set forth*, ἡ ἐμὴ προθυμία ἐκκείσθω *POxy.*220 vi 5; ἐκκειμένων οὖν τῶν βίων Plu.*Comp.Ages.Pomp.*1. 3. *to be proposed*, ὁ σκοπὸς ἐ. καλῶς Arist.*Pol.*1331ᵇ31; μισθοὶ παρὰ βασιλέως ἔκκεινται Str.15.1.46; ἔλασσον τοῦ ἐκκειμένου *SIG*577.66 (Milet., iii/ii B.C.). 4. c. dat., *to be exposed to, be at the mercy of*, Str.5.2.6, Alciphr.3.29; τύχαις Plot.6.8.15; τῷ μέλλοντι Id.3.6.18; also πρὸς τὸ πάσχειν Procl.*Inst.*80. 5. *to be set forth, expounded*, Arist.*Rh.* 1419ᵇ23; in logical sense, Id.*Top.*103ᵇ29, cf. *APr.*48ᵃ8, Epicur.*Nat.* 28.1, Phld.*Sign.*19, etc. 6. Geom., *to be set out*, '*taken*', ἐκκείσθω κύκλος, ὁ ἐκκείμενος κῶνος, Archim.*Sph.Cyl.*1.5, 28. II. c. gen., *fall from out, be left bare of*, μηροὶ.. ἐξέκειντο πιμελῆς S.*Ant.*1011. 2. *project*, ἐκκειμένη εἰς θάλατταν ἄκρα Str.5.4.8; πύργοι ἔξω ἐκκείμενοι D.C.74.10; στέρνα προέχοντα καὶ ἐκκείμενα Philostr.*Gym.*35; φλέβες ἐκκ. Gal.17(2).97; in painting, *stand out*, Philostr.*Im.*2.1.

**ἐκκειμένως**, Adv. *openly*, ἐ. τοῦ ἤθους ἔχειν to be *open, frank*, Philostr.*VS*2.17.

**ἐκκεινόω**, v. ἐκκενόω.

**ἐκκείρω**, *shear completely*, Σκυθιστὶ ἐκκεκαρμένος *shorn* in Scythian fashion, S.*Fr.*473. II. *cut off*, ἐκ θέρος ἀνδρῶν κείρατε A.R.4.1033.

**ἐκ(κε)κελλήρικεν**· ἐκκέκληκεν, Hsch.

**ἐκκεκλασμένως**, Adv., gloss on σκεπαρνηδόν, Gal.19.138.

**ἐκκέλευθος**, ον, *out of the road*, λαθραῖα κἀκκέλευθα Lyc.1162 (but Dind. κὰκ κέλευθα, i.e. κατὰ κέλευθα).

**ἐκκενόω**, poet. **ἐκκεινόω**, *empty out, leave desolate*, ἄστυ Σούσων ἐξεκείνωσεν A.*Pers.*761, cf. Lxx *Ps.*136(137).7; *clear out*, οἴκημα Pl.*Prt.*315d; στωμυλίαν ἣ 'ξεκένωσε τὰς παλαίστρας Ar.*Ra.*1070; ἐ. θυμὸν ἐς σχεδίαν γέροντος *pour out* one's spirit into Charon's boat, i.e. *give up* the ghost, Theoc.16.40; χολῆς περισσὸν.. ἐ. τῶν ἐγκάτων *App.Anth.*3.158; ἐ. ἰοὺς *to shoot all* one's arrows, *AP*6.326 (Leon.):—Pass., *to be left desolate*, στένει γαῖ' Ἀσὶς ἐκκενουμένα A.*Pers.*549 (lyr.), cf. *Th.*330 (lyr.); Ἀττικὴ τῆς τῶν ἀνθρώπων ἀγέλης ἐκκενωθεῖσα Philostr.*VS*1.16.1; Μοιράων.. μίτος ἐξεκενώθη *was exhausted, spun out*, *IG*14.2002. 2. *unsheath*, μάχαιραν Lxx *Ez.*5.2. 3. *clear away*, πέτρας *Sammelb.*4368.

**ἐκκεντέω**, *prick out, put out*, ὄμματα Arist.*HA*508ᵇ6. II. *pierce, stab*, Plb.5.56.12, Lxx *Nu.*22.29, Polyaen.5.3.8. 2. *massacre*, Lxx *Jo.*16.10. III. intr., of hair, *stand out, project*, Luc.*Sat.*24.

**ἐκκεντρεπίκυκλος**, ον, *requiring both eccentric and epicycle*, ὑπόθεσις Procl.*Hyp.*2.3.

**ἐκκεντρίζω**, prob. written for ἐγκ-, *Cat.Cod.Astr.*7.185; f.l. for ἐκκεντέω, Alex.Trall.5.6.

**ἔκκεντρος**, ον, Astron., κύκλος *not having the earth as centre, eccentric*, Cleom.1.6, Gem.1.39, Ptol.*Alm.*3.3, etc. II. *not occupying a cardinal point*, opp. ἔγκ., Vett.Val.97.11.

**ἐκκεντρότης**, ητος, ἡ, *eccentricity*, Eudem.ap.Theon.Sm.p.201 H., Gem.1.39, Ptol.*Alm.*3.3, Iamb.*VP*6.31 (pl.), etc.

**ἐκκενωτέον**, *one must empty*, of venesection, Gal.10.313.

**ἐκκερᾰΐζω**, *plunder, pillage, sack*, Call.*Cer.*50; *cut down*, πίτυν *AP* 9.312 (Zon.).

**ἐκκεράννυμι**, *pour out and mix*, Ath.2.38a codd. (εἰσ- Kaibel).

**ἐκκερδαίνω**, *make a profit*, Just.*Nov.*102 *Pr.*

**ἐκκεχῠμένως**, Adv. pf. part. Pass. of ἐκχέω, *profusely, extravagantly*, ἐ. ζῆν Isoc.15.207; ἐ. λέγειν *without reserve*, Pl.*Euthphr.*3d; ἀγαπᾶν Aristaenet.2.16; πράττειν τι Just.*Nov.*74.4.

**ἐκκηλέω**, *cast a spell upon*, in aor. ἐξεκήλησεν, Hsch.

**ἐκκηραίνω**, *enfeeble, exhaust*, A.*Eu.*128.

**ἐκκηριόω**, *amaze, confound*, Hsch., in pf. Pass.; cf. ἐξεκηριώσας· ἐξέστησας, Id.

**ἐκκηρ-υγμός**, ὁ, *banishment by proclamation*, Sch.BT Il.21.575. **-υκτος**, ον, *banished, cast away*, Lxx *Je.*22.30, Hsch. ⊕ **-ύσσω**, Att. -ττω, *proclaim by voice of herald*:—Pass., νέκυν ἀστοῖσί φασιν ἐκκεκηρῦχθαι τὸ μὴ τάφῳ καλύψαι S.*Ant.*27, cf. 203. II. *banish by proclamation*, Hdt.3.148, Plb.4.21.8, D.S.14.97; τῆς πόλεως, ἐκ τῆς πόλεως, Aeschin.3.258, Lys.12.3:—Pass., ἐκ τοῦ γένους ἐκκεκηρῦχθαι

Pl.*Lg.*929b; ἐξεκηρύχθην φυγάς S.*OC*430. **2.** *cashier, 'drum out'* of the army, prob. in Arist.*Ath.*61.2.

**ἐκκῐναιδίζομαι,** strengthd. for κιναιδίζομαι, D.C.50.27.

**ἐκκῑνέω,** *move out of* [his lair], *put up*, ἔλαφον S.*El.*567: metaph., ἐ. τὴν νόσον Id.*Tr.*979 (anap.); τόδε τὸ ῥῆμα Id.*OT*354; so σύ γάρ μ' ἀπ' εὐνασθέντος ἐ. κακοῦ Id.*Tr.*1242:—Pass., σκώμμασι μᾶλλον ἢ λοιδορίαις ἐκκινούμεθα Plu.2.631c.

**ἐκκιρρόω,** pf. ἐκκεκίρρωκα, *become hardened*, *Hippiatr.*104.

**ἐκκίω,** *go out*, Od.24.492 (tm.).

**ἐκκλάζω,** *cry aloud*, ἐκ δ' ἔκλαγξ' ὄπα E.*Ion*1204.

⊛ **ἐκκλαστρίδιον,** τό, *a woman's ornament*, *IG*11(2).219*B*23 (Delos, iii B.C.), etc.

**ἐκκλάω,** *break off*, Pl.*R.*611d (Pass.), Alciphr.2.4 (Pass.); δάκτυλον Paus.8.40.2. **II.** Pass., *grow weak, to be enfeebled*, Plu.2.671a (s.v.l.); τὸ θράσος ἐκκέκλασται ib.762f, cf. Max.Tyr.35.3.

⊛ **ἐκκλείω,** Ion. **ἐκκληΐω** or **-κλῄω**, old Att. **ἐκκλῄω**: Att. fut. -κλῄσω E.*Or.*1127: Dor. aor. 1 -κλᾳξα *Com.Adesp.*1203.7 (dub.): pf. ἐκκέκλεικα Men.*Sam.*201:—*shut out from*, c. gen., ἐ. ἄλλον ἄλλοσε στέγης E. l. c.:—Pass., *to be shut out*, Id.*HF*330. **2.** metaph., *shut out, exclude from*, πόλιν τῆς μετοχῆς Hdt.1.144; τῆς συμμαχίας, τῶν ὅρκων, Aeschin.2.85, 3.74: c. acc. et inf., ἐξέκλειον λόγον τυγχάνειν τοὺς ἄλλους D.19.26. **3.** *hinder, prevent*, τῷ καιρῷ τὴν κατηγορίαν Plb.18.8.2; τὴν θήραν D.S.3.16:—Pass., ἐκκληϊόμενοι τῇ ὥρῃ *being prevented* by [want of] time, Hdt.1.31; ἐκκλεισθεὶς ὑπὸ τῶν καιρῶν D.S.18.3: c. inf., ἐ. ποιεῖν τι Id.4.32, cf. Arist.*MM*1198[b]16. **4.** *shut off, cut off*, ζωῆς ὁδούς Opp.*C.*2.342.

**ἐκκλέπτω,** aor. 2 Pass. -εκλάπην X.*HG*5.4.12:—*steal and carry off*, of persons, [Ἑρμῆς] ἐξέκλεψεν Ἄρηα he *stole away* Ares *from* his chains, Il.5.390, cf. Hdt.2.115 (s.v.l.), A.*Ag.*662, *Eu.*153, X.*Ap.*23, Plu.*Pyrrh.*2; τοὺς ὁμήρους ἐ. ἐκ Λήμνου Th.1.115, cf. D.S.12.27; τοὺς ἀδικοῦντας οἱ κατήγοροι ἐκκλέπτουσιν Lys.20.7; ἐκ δόμων πόδα E.*Or.*1499: c. gen., τῆσδε.. ἐκκλέψαι χθονός Id.*Hel.*741; ἐ. φόνου Id.*El.*286; ἐ. μ' θανεῖν ib.540; ἐ. τι τοῦ λόγου *to steal* it *from* the story, Pl.*R.*449c:—Pass., ὑπὸ τῆς ἀμήτορος παρθένου ἐκκλαπεῖσα Jul.*Mis.*352b. **II.** ἐ. τινὰ λόγοις *to deceive* him, S.*Ph.*55, cf. 968; μὴ.. ἐκκλέψῃς λόγον *disguise* not the matter, *speak* not *falsely*, Id.*Tr.*437.

**ἐκκληΐω,** Ion. for ἐκκλείω.

⊛ **ἔκκλημα,** ατος, τό, *subject of appeal*, *Jahresh.*14.168 (Tolophon, iii B.C.), *Foed.Delph.Pell.*2*B*20 (pl., iii B.C.).

**ἐκκλημᾰτόομαι,** Pass., *put forth* κλήματα, *run to wood*, Thphr.*CP* 3.15.4, *Gp.*5.40.1.

**ἐκκληπεῖ·** ἐκπορεύεται, Hsch.

**ἔκκληρος,** ον, *without share* or *lot*, *Gloss.*

⊛ **ἐκκλησί-α,** ἡ, (ἔκκλητος) *assembly duly summoned*, less general than σύλλογος, Th.2.22, Pl.*Grg.*456b, etc.; applied to the Homeric Assemblies, Arist.*Pol.*1285[a]11; to the Samian Assembly, Hdt.3.142; to the Spartan, Th.1.87; to the meeting of the Amphictyons at Delphi, Aeschin.3.124; at Athens, ἐ. κύριαι, opp. σύγκλητοι, Arist.Ath.43.4; κυρία ἐ., at Amorgos, *IG*12(7).237.46; ἐ. συναγείρειν, συνάγειν, συλλέγειν, ἀθροίζειν, *call an assembly*, Hdt.3.142, Th.2.60, 8.97, X.*HG*1.6.8; ἐ. ποιεῖν Ar.*Eq.*746, Th.1.139, al.; ἐ. ποιεῖν τινί Ar.*Ach.*169; διδόναι τινί Plb.4.34.6; ἐ. γίγνεται *an assembly* is held, Th.6.8; καταστάσης ἐ. Id.1.31; ἦν ἐ. τοῖς στρατηγοῖς And.1.2; ἐ. διαλύειν, ἀναστῆσαι, dissolve *it*, Th.8.69 (Pass.), X.*HG*2.4.42; ἀφιέναι Plu.*TG* 6; ἐ. ἀνεβλήθη was adjourned, Th.5.45; ἐ. περί τινος Ar.*Av.*1030, etc. **2.** = Lat. *Comitia*, ἐ. λοχῖτις, φρατρική, = *Comitia Centuriata, Curiata*, D.H.4.20. **3.** = ψήφισμα, ἀναγιγνωσκομένης ἐ. Philostr.*VS*2.1.11. **II.** in Lxx, *the Jewish congregation*, *De.*31.30, al. **2.** in *NT*, *the Church*, as a body of Christians, *Ev.Matt.*16.18, 1*Ep.Cor.*11.22; ἡ κατ' οἶκόν τινος ἐ. *Ep.Rom.*16.5; as a building, *Cod.Just.*1.1.5 *Intr.*, etc. ⊛ **-άζω,** fut. -άσω Ar.*Ec.*161, Isoc.8.2: impf. ἠκκλησίαζον D.18.265, 19.60; also ἐκκλησίαζον Lys.12.73 codd., but usu. with irreg. augm., as if the Verb were a compd. of ἐκ and *κλησιάζω, impf. ἐξεκλησίαζον Lys.13.73,76: aor. ἐξεκλησίασα Th.8.93, D.21.193 (freq. with vv.ll. ἐξεκκλησίαζον, ἐξεκκλησίασα):—Med., ἐξεκκλησιάσατο, = ἀγορήσατο, Hsch.s.h.v.:—*hold an assembly, debate therein*, X.*Ath.*1.9, Ar.*Av.*1027, X.*An.*5.6.37; περί τινος Th.7.2, Isoc.8.2; περὶ μου ἐπ' ὀλέθρῳ Ar.*Th.*84; ὑπὲρ τῆς πόλεως Isoc.8.13; τοιαῦτα ἐκκλησιάσαντες *having* thus *deliberated*, Th.8.77; ἐ. τὰς ἀναγκαίας ἐκκλησίας Arist.*Pol.*1292[b]28. **2.** *to be a member of the Assembly*, ἐ. ἀπὸ τιμήματος οὐδενός ib.1294[b]3. **II.** trans., *summon to an assembly, convene*, τοὺς αὑτοῦ στρατιώτας Aen.Tact.9.1; λαόν D.S.21.16; συναγωγήν Lxx *Le.*8.3, al.:—Pass., *to be called together*, ib.*Je.*33(26).9, al. **2.** metaph., τινὰ πρὸς ἑαυτὸν ἐ. *summon* considerations before one's mind, Eun.*Hist.*p.210 D. **-ασμός,** ὁ, *the holding an* ἐκκλησία, Plb.15.26.9. **-αστήριον,** τό, *the hall of the* ἐκκλησία, *IPE*1[2].24.9 (Olbia, iv B.C.), *BCH*35.76 (Delos), *CIG*2270.4 (Delos); = Lat. *Comitium*, D.H.4.38. **-αστής,** οῦ, ὁ, *member of the* ἐκκλησία, Pl.*Grg.*452e, *Ap.*25a, Arist.*Pol.*1275[a]26, *Rh.*1354[b]7. **-αστικός,** ή, όν, *of* or *for the* ἐκκλησία, ἐ. πίναξ *register of voters*, D.44.35; αἱ ἐ. ψῆφοι Plu.*Cor.*14; τὸ ἐ. [ἀργύριον] *pay received for sitting in the* ἐκκλησία at Athens and elsewhere, Sch.Ar.*Eq.*51 (also μισθὸς ἐκκλησιαστικός Luc.*Dem.Enc.*25, etc.), cf. *Michel*466 (Iasos, iii B.C.); τὰ ἐ. *IG*2[2].1272. **II.** *clerical*, *Cat.Cod.Astr.*7.216, *Cod.Just.*1.2.17.4. Adv. -κῶς Just.*Nov.*83.1. **-έκδῐκος,** ὁ, = Lat. *defensor ecclesiae*, *Cod. Just.*1.3.41.23, al.

⊛ **ἔκ-κλησις,** εως, ἡ, *appeal*, *IGRom.*4.1044 (Cos), Hsch. s.v. ἔφεσις. **2.** *challenging*, Plb.*Fr.*131 (pl.). **3.** = Lat. *evocatio numinum*, Plu.2.278f (pl.). **-κλητεύσιμος,** ον, gloss on ἐφέσι(μ)ον, Hsch. (ἐγκλ- cod.). **-κλητεύω,** *summon a witness under subpoena*, Aeschin.2.68:—Pass., Id.1.46, cf. Harp. s.v. κλητῆρες. **-κλητής,** οῦ, ὁ, *appellant*, *Gloss.* **-κλητικός,** ή, όν, *provocative, stimulative*, ὀρέξεως Dsc.2.151. Adv. -κῶς Suid. ⊛ **-κλητος,** ον, (ἐκκαλέω) *selected to judge* or *arbitrate* on a point, ἐ. πόλις an *umpire* city, Aeschin.1.89, *IG*2[2].111.49, al., cf. Plu.2.215c; ἐν ἐκκλήτῳ δικάσασθαι *Michel*1335.30; δίκην ὠφληκὼς ἐν τῇ ἐ. *IG*12(7).67.63 (Amorgos); χρόνος ἐ. time-limit *for appeals*, *PRev.Laws*21.15 (iii B.C.). **2.** οἱ ἔκκλητοι, in Sparta and elsewhere, *a committee of citizens chosen to report* on certain questions, X.*HG*2.4.38; ἐ. Ἀργείων ὄχλος E.*Or.*612, cf. 949. **3.** *subject to appeal*, δίκας *IG*2[2].111.74, D.C.52.22; κρίσις *PHal.*1.68 (iii B.C.); τὰς ἐκκλήτους [δίκας].. ἐφ' αὐτὸν ποιούμενος, prob. for ἐγκ-, Arist.*Oec.*1348[b]14; ἔκκλητον δικάζειν exercise *appellate* jurisdiction, D.C.51.19.

**ἐκκλῄω,** old Att. for ἐκκλείω.

**ἔκκλῐμα,** ατος, τό, *movement to a flank*, D.S.20.12.

**ἐκκλῑμᾰκίζω,** *torture on the rack*, *EM*322.38; cf. κλῖμαξ.

**ἐκ-κλῐνής,** ές, *inclined outwards*, Arist.*Phgn.*809[b]23; ὁ ἥλιος -έστερον ἡμῖν ποιεῖ τὸν κύκλον Id.*Pr.*912[a]12. **-κλίνω** [ῑ], *bend out of the regular line, bend outwards* or *away*, opp. ἐγκλίνω, Hp.*Art.*38 (s.v.l.); *change the form of* a word, Pl.*Cra.*404d. **2.** *dislocate*, Hp.*Art.*7 (Pass.). **3.** *embezzle*, Dionys.Com.3.10. **4.** *pervert*, δικαιώματα Lxx 1*Ki.*8.3. **II.** intr., *turn away*, ἀπό τινος Th.5.73, Lxx *Nu.*22.32(33); ἐκ τῆς ὁδοῦ ib.23; ἐκ νόμου θεοῦ ib.*Jb.*34.27: abs., *give ground, retire*, X.*Cyr.*1.4.23; *give way, fall from its place*, Id.*Cyn.*6.10. **2.** c. acc., *avoid, shun*, ἐ. τι καὶ μὴ πράττειν Pl.*Lg.*746c; ἐπερχόμενον ἐ. νέφος Demad.15; τὴν τῶν θηρίων ἔφοδον Plb.1.34.4; στρατείαν Id.5.42.4, etc.:—Pass., Epict.*Ench.*2. **3.** with Prep., *turn away* or *aside towards*, κατά τι X.*Cyr.*7.1.30; ἐπὶ τὰς ἔξω οἰκίας *BGU*1215.9 (iii B.C.); ἐ. εἰς δῆμον, εἰς ὀλιγαρχίαν, *decline* into a democracy or oligarchy, Arist.*Pol.*1273[a]5; πρός τινα *visit* a person on one's journey, Lxx *Ge.*19.3. **-κλῐσις,** εως, ἡ, *turning out of one's course, deflexion*, τῆς σελήνης Plu.2.929c (pl.). **2.** *tendency*, Arist.*Pr.*863[b]24. **II.** *dislocation*, Hp.*Art.*62. **III.** *avoidance, refusal*, opp. αἵρεσις, Cleanth.*Stoic.*1.129 (pl.); opp. ἐκλογή, *Stoic.*3.190; opp. ὄρεξις, Epict.*Ench.*2; τῶν ὀχληρῶν S.E.*M.*1.51; τῆς βλάβης Gal.13.124, cf. Plot.1.4.6, etc. **IV.** *moral declension*, ib.8.15. **-κλῐτέον,** *one must avoid*, τὸν εὖ βάλλοντα τῶν πολεμίων Plu.2.584d; *one must shun*, τὰς ἀθρόας πόσεις Ath.3.12cd, cf. Menemach.ap.Orib.7.23.3. **-κλίτης** [ῐ], ου, ὁ, *shirker*, dub. word in D.L.2.130. **-κλῐτικός,** ή, όν, *disposed to decline* or *shirk*, opp. ὀρεκτικός, δύναμις Arr.*Epict.*1.1.12. Adv. -κῶς, ἔχειν πόνου ib.3.12.7. **-κλῐτός,** όν, *to be avoided*, opp. ὀρεκτός, Simp.*in Epict.*p.109 D., cf. Phot. s.v. παλιναίρετα.

**ἐκ-κλύζω,** fut. -ύσω M.Ant.8.51:—*wash out, wash away*, τὴν βαφήν Pl.*R.*430a; τὸν ῥύπον Luc.*Vit.Auct.*3:—in Pass., Hp.*Loc. Hom.*13; ἐ. τὰ λύματα εἰς τὸν Τίβεριν Str.5.3.8; restored in ib.1.7; *to be washed ashore*, εἰς τὸ ξηρόν Arist.*HA*525[a]23. **2.** *wash thoroughly*, σῶμα Plu.*Sull.*36:—Med., Diocl.*Fr.*141. **II.** intr., *stream out*, Apollod.1.6.3 (nisi leg. -έβλυσεν). **-κλυσμα,** ατος, τό, *that which is washed away*, τὸ τῆς ἡδονῆς ἐ. Plu.2.1089b; *that which is washed up, produce of the sea*, of purple dye, Zos.Alch.p.164 B. ⊛ **-κλυστέον,** *one must wash out*, Aët.16.89. **-κλυστος,** ον, *washed out*, prob. in Eup.147.

**ἐκκναίω,** *wear out*: metaph. of troublesome loquacity, Theoc.15.88 (in Dor. 3 pl. fut. ἐκκναισεῦντι).

**ἐκκνάω,** aor. -έκνησα, *scrape off*, τὸν κηρὸν τοῦ δελτίου Hdt.7.239, cf. Aen.Tact.31.14 (prob.).

**ἐκκνημόω,** *destroy*, Call.*Iamb.*1.199:—Pass., Hsch.; cf. κνημόω.

**ἐκκοβᾰλῑκεύομαι,** *cheat by juggling tricks, cajole*, dub. in Ar.*Eq.*270.

**ἐκκοδοάζω,** Dor. aor. 1 ἐξεκοδόαξα, *pour out*, Hsch.; cf. ἐγκοακίσαι. **ἐκκοδομεύω,** *bake in an oven*, Id.

**ἐκκοιλαίνω,** *hollow out*, Plb.10.48.7.

**ἐκκοιλίζω,** (κοιλία) *disembowel*, Mithaec.ap.Ath.7.325f.

**ἔκκοιλος,** ον, *sunken*, ὀφθαλμός Hp.*Int.*43 (fort. ἔγκοιλος).

**ἐκκοιμάομαι,** *sleep off* the effects of a potion, Pl.*Lg.*648a.

**ἐκκοιτ-έω,** *keep night-watch, bivouac*, J.*BJ*6.2.6. **-ησις,** εως, ἡ, = sq., *Gloss.* **-ία,** ἡ, (κοίτη) *night-watch, bivouac*, in pl., Aen.Tact.13.3, Ph.*Bel.*93.5, D.S.30.10. **-ίζω,** gloss on ἐκκοχύζω, Hsch. **-ισμός,** ὁ, = ἐκκοιτία, *Gloss.*

**ἐκκοκκίζω,** Att. fut. -ιῶ Ar.*Lys.*364:—*take out kernels* or *seeds*, e.g. from pomegranates, Apollon.ap.Gal.12.649: hence metaph., οὐσίδιον.. ἐξεκόκκισα Nicom.Com.3; ἐ. σφυρόν *put out* one's ankle, Ar.*Ach.*1179; ἐ. τὰς τρίχας *pluck out* the hair, Id.*Lys.*448; ἐ. τὸ γῆρας *drive away* old age, ib.364; ἐ. τὰς πόλεις *sack, gut* the cities, Id.*Pax*63.

**ἐκκοκκύζω,** = μέγα κοκκύζω, Hyp.*Fr.*239.

**ἐκκολ-άπτω,** *erase, obliterate*, τὸ ἐλεγεῖον Th.1.132; τὸ ψήφισμα D.57.64; τῆς ἐπιγραφῆς any part of.., *CIG*(add.)4224*d* (Anticragus), cf. Aristid.1.425 J. **II.** *peck* the chick *out of* the egg, *hatch*, Arist.*HA*618[a]13; ἐ. τοὺς ἀνθρώπους Luc.*VH*1.22; ἧπαρ Id.*Prom.*9:—Pass., Arist.*HA*562[a]14; ᾠὸν ἐκκεκολαμμένον *empty* egg-shell, Thphr.*HP*3.16.4; of a seam of ore, Gal.12.239. **-αψις,** εως, ἡ, *breaking the shell*, of a chick, Arist.*HA*561[b]29.

**ἐκκολλαβήσαντα·** ἐκλακέντα, ἐκφρονήσαντα, Hsch.

⊛ **ἐκκολυμβάω,** *plunge into the sea from..*, c. gen., ναός E.*Hel.*1609: abs., Ar.*Fr.*80, cf. D.S.20.86, *Act.Ap.*27.42; *swim ashore*, εἰς τὴν γῆν D.H.5.24, cf. App.*Syr.*6.

**ἐκκομ-ῐδή**, ἡ, *removal*, Hdt.8.44; σίτου *IG*2².655.12. b. *purgation*, τῶν περιττωμάτων Dsc.4.176, cf. 2.103. 2. of a corpse, *burial*, ἐ. πολυτελής D.H.4.8, cf. *AP*11.92 (Lucill.), *IG*12(7).395.27 (Amorgos), *IPE*1².34.5 (Olbia, i B.C.). ⊛**-ίζω**, *carry* or *bring out*, Hdt. 1.34, 3.24, E.*Tr*.294; esp. to a place of safety, Hdt.1.160, 3.122, Th. 2.6; ἐκκομίζειν τινὰ ἐκ τοῦ μέλλοντος γίνεσθαι πρήγματος *to keep* him *out* of trouble, Hdt.3.43:—Med., Id.8.20, Th.2.78; ἐσεκομίσαντο καὶ ἐξεκομίσαντο ἃ ἐβούλοντο, of those relieved from a state of siege, Id.1. 117: abs., *remove*, ἐς τοὺς Λοκρούς Hdt.8.32. 2. esp. *carry out* a corpse, *bury*, Plb.35.6.2 (Pass.), Plu.*Cic*.42 (Pass.), etc. 3. ἐ. σῖτον, of a horse, *throw* the provender *out of* the manger, X.*Eq*.4.2. 4. *carry home*, ἄνδρας Id.*An*.6.6.36. II. *endure to the end*, τὸ πεπρωμένον E.*Andr*.1269. III. Med., *receive* what is due, λόγους, ὀψώνια, *PLille* 3.79 (iii B.C.), *PSI*4.436 (iii B.C.). **-ισμός**, ὁ, *exportation*, Str.3.2.4. II. *funeral*, Phld.*D*.1.25. **-ιστής**, οῦ, ὁ, *one who brings out*, *Gloss*.

**ἐκκομπ-άζω**, *boast loudly*, κατά τι S.*El*.569. **-έω**, aor. 1 ἐξεκόμπησεν· ἐξέπληξεν, Hsch.

**ἐκκομψεύομαι**, Med., *set forth in fair terms*, E.*IA*333 (but prob. εὖ κεκόμψευσαι).

**ἐκκονεῖ**· ἐγχωρεῖ, Hsch.

**ἐκκονίομαι** [ῑ], Pass., *to be in the dust*, Hp.*Vict*.3.76 (nisi leg. ἐγκ-); cf. ἐκκεκονίσθαι· τὸ εἰς κονίαν ἀναλελύσθαι, Hsch.

**ἐκκοπ-εύς**, έως, ὁ, *a knife for excising*, Heliod.ap.Orib.44.11.6, Gal. 2.592, prob. in Paul.Aeg.6.88. **-ή**, ἡ, *cutting out*, ὀφθαλμῶν Phld. *Ir*.p.33 W.; *excision* of ribs, Heliod.ap.Orib.44.11 tit. 2. *mutilation*, ἐ. μελῶν Vett.Val.110.10 (pl.). 3. *chiselling out, erasure*, γραμμάτων *SIG*252.41 (Delph., iv B.C.); of an arrow-point from a bone, Plu.*Alex*.63. II. *cutting down, felling*, δένδρων Plb.2.65.6 (pl.), cf. *BGU*1121.27 (i B.C.), etc.; ἐκκοπαὶ λόφων *levelling* of hills, Str. 5.3.8; ἐ. πυλῶν Onos.42.17. III. *incision, notch, mortise*, Ph. *Bel*.65.20, Hero *Aut*.27.1, *Bel*.92.4, Ath.Mech.30.3, Sor.1.83.⊛ **-ος**, ον, *weary*, Thd.*Is*.43.24.

**ἐκκοπρ-ίζω**, *discharge excrement*, ἀθρόα πολλά Hp.*Epid*.3.17.δ', cf. *Hippiatr*.31. **-όω**, *empty of excrement*, τὴν κοιλίην Hp.*Acut*.(*Sp*.) 71, cf. Dieuch.ap.Orib.4.8.11:—Pass., Aret.*CA*1.4. **-ωσις**, εως, ἡ, *cleansing from excrement*: ἐ. τῆς κοιλίης *emptying* of the stomach *by purging*, Hp.*Prog*.15. **-ωτικός**, ή, όν, *promoting passage of faeces*, Herod.Med.ap.Aët.9.2, Suid. s. v. ἀλοή.

**ἐκκοπτ-έον**, *one must excise*, Antyll.ap.Aët.7.74; *one must remove*, τὴν αἰτίαν Gal.10.662, al. II. *one must cut to pieces*, i.e. *destroy*, Plu.*Luc*.24, *Comp.Nic.Crass*.4. **-ης**, ου, ὁ, *one who excises*, *Gloss*. **-ικός**, ή, όν, *suitable for eradicating* or *expelling*, τύλων, ὑγρῶν, Asclep.ap.Gal.13.850, Herod.Med. in *Rh.Mus*.49.553. ⊛ **-ω**, *cut out, knock out*, τοὺς γομφίους Phryn.Com.68; τῶν ἑρπετῶν ἐξέκοψε τὸ φθέγμα Call.*Iamb*.1.163:—Pass., ἦν.. τωφθαλμὼ 'κκοπῇς *have* your eyes *knocked out*, Ar.*Av*.342; τὸν ὀφθαλμὸν ἐκκεκομμένος D.18.67; ἐξεκέκοπτο τὴν φωνήν *had lost* his voice, Luc.*JTr*.16. 2. *cut* [trees] *out of* a wood, *fell*, Hdt.6.37 (Pass.), 9.97, Th.6.99, etc.; δένδρα ἐκκεκόφασι X.*HG*6.5.37; παράδεισον *laid waste* the park, Id.*An*.1.4.10; χωρία D.H.8.87; νήσους καὶ πόλεις Plu.*Pomp*.24: hence, b. metaph., *cut off, make an end of*, τοὺς ἄνδρας Hdt.4.110; ἐ. φενακισμόν, ἱεροσυλίαν, Din.2.4, Is.8.39; *eradicate* abuses, *OGI*669.64 (Egypt, i A.D.); τὴν αἰσθητικὴν ἐνέργειαν Arist.*PA*656ᵇ5; *extirpate*, [λύπας] Diog.Oen.2:—Pass., ἡ θρασύτης ἐξεκέκοπτο Pl.*Chrm*.155c. c. ἐ. πλοῖα *scuttle* ships, *IG*12(7).386.9 (Amorgos). 3. as military term, *beat off, repulse*, τὰς ἀκροβολίσεις X.*Cyr*.6.2.15; τοὺς ἐπὶ τῷ λόφῳ Id. *HG*7.4.26. 4. *win*, in throwing the dice, Alex.44, Menecr.1 D.:—Pass., *to be ruined at play*, Hsch. 5. ἐ. θύρας *break open*, Lys.3.6; οἰκίαν ἐ. Plb.4.3.10. 6. *cut out* or *erase* an inscription, *SIG*38.38 (Teos, v B.C.), Arist.*Rh*.1400ᵃ33; οὐδενὶ ἐξέσται.. γράμμα ἐκκόψαι *CIG*3028 (Ephesus), al.; ἐ. τὴν χεῖρα *Ev.Matt*.5.30; *cut out*, as a surgeon does, Luc.*Cat*.24. 7. *coin, stamp* money, D.S.11.26. b. metaph., φαντασίαν ἐ. ὡς.. Phld.*Lib*.p.56 O.; γένη οὐκ ἐκκοπτόμενα ἰδίοις τέλεσι genders not *marked* by different terminations, A.D. *Synt*.104.23; ἐ. ἀναφθέγματα *coin* expressions, Phld.*D*.3.14. 8. *hinder, bring to a stop*, *PAlex*.4.1 (iii B.C.), Vett.Val.268.6. II. intr., *pause, come to a stop*, Id.260.24.

**ἐκκορᾰκίζω**, in Suid., Zonar., perh. f.l. for ἐσκορακίζω or σκορακίζω.

⊛ **ἐκκορέω**, *sweep clean*, τὰς κλίνας Thphr.*Char*.22.12 (nisi leg. ἐκκορίσας): metaph., μὴ 'κκόρει τὴν Ἑλλάδα Ar.*Pax* 59; and (with a play on κόρη) τίς ἐξεκόρησέ σε; who *has robbed* you *of your daughter?* Id.*Th*.760: generally, *sweep away*, τὸν τῦφον, τὴν κραιπάλην, Alciphr.1.37; ἐκκορηθείης σύ γε *clear out! pack off!* Men. *Georg*.53: prov., ἐκκόρει, κόρη, κορώνην maiden, *drive away* the crow—the opening of a wedding song—the crow being a prognostic of widowhood, *Carm.Pop*.25, cf. Horap.1.8.

**ἐκκορίζω**, (κόρις) *to clear of bugs*, *AP*9.113 (Parmen.), cf. foreg. II. (κόρη) sens. obsc., Eup.233.

**ἐκκορῠφόω** λόγον *tell* a tale *summarily, state the main points*, Hes. *Op*.106:—Pass., ἐκκεκορύφωται ὁ λόγος Hp.*Morb*.4.48.

**ἐκκοσμ-έω**, *deck out, adorn*, in Pass., Lxx 4 *Ma*.6.2, Aristid.1.148 J. **-ησις**, εως, ἡ, *decoration*, v.l. for κόσμησις, Dsc.5.94.

**ἐκκοττίζω**, in pf. part. Pass. -κεκοττισμένος *ruined at play*, Hsch. s. v. ἐκκεκομμένος.

**ἐκκότῠλος**, ον, *having a dislocated hip*, *Gloss*.

**ἐκκουφίζω**, *raise up, exalt*, Plu.*Mar*.9. II. *relieve* pain, etc., Id. *Crass*.33 (v.l.), Ruf.*Fr*.117. III. *weigh anchor*, Ael.*Fr*.71.

**ἐκκοχύζω**· ἐκκοιτίζω, Hsch.

**ἐκκραγγάνω**, *shout*, ἤκουσα τῶν ἐκκραγγανομένων Men.22 D.

**ἐκκράζω**, *cry out*, κυνηδὸν ἐξέκραξαν cj. in S.*Fr*.722; ἐ. μέγα Plu. *Mar*.44; ἐ. πολλὰ κυνηδόν D.C.66.15.

**ἐκκραυγάζω**, = ἐκκράζω, Epicur.*Fr*.605.

⊛ **ἐκκρέμ-αμαι**, Pass., *hang, be suspended*, v.l. in Hp.*Art*.76; τὴν γυναῖκα ἐκκρεμαμένην ἀποσεισάμενος Luc.*Tox*.61: c. gen., *hang from*, Pl.*Ion* 536a. II. *depend upon*, ἐξ ἐπιθυμιῶν Id.*Lg*.732e; τῆς τοῦ ζῆν ἐπιθυμίας Plu.*Mar*.12; ἐλπίδος *AP*9.411 (Maec.). **-άννῡμι**, fut. -κρεμάσω, *hang from* or *upon* a thing, Hp.*Art*.22 (dub.); τι ἔκ τινος Ar.*Eq*.1363; λίθον τοῦ ποδός *AP*11.100 (Lucill.); τινὰ ἐξ Ὀλύμπου Apollod.1.3.5. II. Pass., like ἐκκρέμαμαι, *hang on by, cling to*, c. gen., τῶν τε ξυσκήνων ἤδη ἀπιόντων ἐκκρεμαννύμενοι Th.7.75, cf. Luc.*Tox*.6. 2. metaph., *to be devoted to*, Ἄρεος E. *El*.950. **-ασις**, εως, ἡ, *hanging from* or *upon*, v.l. in Hp.*Art*. 76. **-ασμός**, ὁ, = foreg., Cass.*Pr*.6. **-ής**, ές, *suspended*, πήρα Hdn.1.9.3; τὸ -ές the *lobe* of the ear, Ruf.*Onom*.43: c. gen., *hanging from* or *upon*, χείλεος *AP*5.246 (Maced.); ἐπί τινι ib.240.8 (Paul. Sil.); ἀπὸ τοῦ ὤμου Agath.3.17; ἐπὶ γαστέρα ἐ. προβάλλειν Aret.*CA*1.5, cf. Porph.*Gaur*.3.3. II. Adv. -μῶς, Gramm., *in dependent construction*, opp. ἀπολύτως, Eust.1752.47.

**ἐκκρήμναμαι** or -κριμν-, = ἐκκρέμαμαι, v.l. in Hp.*Art*.76: c. gen., E.*HF*520; ῥόπτρων χέρας ἐκκρημνάμεσθα we *hang on to* the door-knocker by the hands, Id.*Ion* 1612:—later in Act. part. ἐκκρημνάς or -κριμνάς *hanging up*, Iamb.*VP*33.238.

**ἐκκρῐδόν**, Adv. *apart, alone*, prob. l. in Tryph.224.

**ἐκκρῐθιάσας**, in gloss on ἀγοστήσας, *AB*213.

**ἔκ-κρῐμα**, ατος, τό, *secretion*, Thphr.*Ign*.76. **-κρίνω** [ῑ], *single out*, Th.6.96:—Pass., ἀρετῇ πρῶτος ἐκκριθείς S.*Ph*.1425, cf. Th.6. 31. 2. *separate*, Arist.*HA*578ᵃ11, 572ᵇ22 (Pass.); ἐκ τοῦ μείγματος ἐκκρίνουσι τἆλλα *hold that* the rest *are separated out* from.., Id.*Ph*.187ᵃ23. 3. *exclude, expel*, X.*Cyr*.1.2.14 (Act. and Pass.), Luc.*Salt*.3 (Pass.); *reject, condemn*, Gal.18(2).693. 4. *secrete*, of the animal functions, Arist.*GA*765ᵇ10, al.; τραῦμα ἐ. ἰχῶρας Zen.6. 46:—freq. in Pass., Arist.*GA*738ᵃ1, al.; ἐκ πυρὸς -κρινόμενον καπνόν *given off* by.., Phld.*Sign*.36: metaph., ὅταν.. καθαρὸς ὁ νοῦς ἐκκριθῇ X. *Cyr*.8.7.20. 5. Pass., also of *excretions*, Hp.*Aph*.4.47, 76, etc. 6. of drugs, *remove*, λίθους Dsc.2.127. **-κρῐσις**, εως, ἡ, *separation*, Arist. *Mete*.342ᵃ15, Onos.9.1 (pl.). II. *secretion*, of the animal functions, Arist.*PA*689ᵃ16, *GA*727ᵃ2; τῶν ὑγρῶν Eun.*Hist*.p.263 D. III. = ἔκκριμα, of excrement, Hp.*Aph*.2.15; of the menses, Arist.*HA*583ᵃ 2, etc. **-κρῐτέον**, *one must pick out*, Pl.*Plt*.303b. **-κρῐτικός**, ή, όν, *secretive*, Arist.*Ph*.243ᵇ14; τῆς θερμότητος Thphr.*CP*6.1.3. 2. *tending to remove*, φυσῶν Dsc.2.152. **-κρῐτος**, ον, *picked out, select*, ἐ. δεκάς *a chosen* ten, A.*Pers*.340; πλῆθος ἐ. στρατοῦ ib.803, cf. *Th*. 57; ἔ. δικασταί Pl.*Lg*.926d; ἔ. δώρημα, = ἐξαίρετον, S.*Aj*.1302; ἔ. ἄλλων A.R.4.1185; ἔ. νομίζεσθαι Philostr.*Gym*.23: neut. ἔκκριτον, as Adv., *above all, eminently*, E.*Tr*.1241. 2. *evacuated*, Arist.*Pr*. 861ᵃ36.

**ἐκκροτέω**, *beat* or *knock out*, ὅπλα τῆς χειρός J.*AJ*6.2.2. II. *hammer out, form, educate*, Phryn.*PS*p.68 B.

**ἐκκρουνίζω**, *gush forth*, Sch.Il.20.470.

⊛ **ἔκ-κρουσις**, εως, ἡ, *beating out, driving away*, X.*Cyn*.10.12. II. *deduction*, *PTeb*.121.133 (i B.C.). **-κρουσμός**, ὁ, *waning* of the moon, ἐ. καὶ μείωσις Paul.Al.*G*.4. **-κρουστικός**, ή, όν, *fitted for expelling*, τοῦ ἐλέου Arist.*Rh*.1386ᵃ22; τοῦ λόγου Arr.*Epict*.2.18. 29. **-κρουστος**, ον, *beaten out, embossed*, A.*Th*.542. ⊛ **-κρούω**, *knock out*, παττάλους Ar.*Fr*.402b; τι ἐκ τῶν χειρῶν X.*Cyn*.10.12; for Ar.*Fr*.270 (Med.), v. πύνδαξ:—Pass., *BGU*1007.16 (iii B.C.). b. metaph., ἡ μείζων κίνησις ἐ. τὴν ἐλάττω *expels*, Arist.*Sens*.447ᵃ15; [ἡ ἡδίων ἐνέργεια] ἐ. τὴν ἑτέραν Id.*EN*1175ᵇ8; ἐ. τὸν λογισμόν, τὴν λύπην, ib.1119ᵇ10, 1154ᵃ27. 2. *drive back, repulse*, Th.4.131, X.*HG* 7.4.16; ἀπὸ [λόφου] Th.4.128: metaph., ἐ. τινὰ ἐλπίδος *to frustrate, cheat* one *of*.., Pl.*Phdr*.228e; τῆς προαιρέσεως Plu.*Sol*.14; ἵνα μὴ.. τοῦ παρόντος ἐμαυτὸν ἐκκρούσω D.18.313:—Pass., τὸν λογισμὸν ἐκκρουσθείς Plu.*Pyrrh*.30. 3. *hiss* an actor *off* the stage, ἐβόων, ἐξέκρουόν με D.19.23. 4. *put off, adjourn by evasions*, εἰς ὑστεραίαν τὴν.. γνώμην ib.144; [τὴν δίκην] Id.36.2, cf. 54.30; τοσαύτας τέχνας.. εὑρίσκων ἐκκρούει Id.21.81; ἐ. τοὺς λόγους *elude*, Pl.*Prt*.336c; ἐ. πρᾶγμα τῷ χρόνῳ 'talk out', Plu.*Caes*.13:—Pass., γραφῆς ἐκκρουομένης D.45. 4. 5. *discharge*, βέλη ἐκ μηχανῶν D.C.75.11. 6. Math., *subtract*, κοινὸν ἐκκεκρούσθω τὸ ἀπὸ ΒΖ *let* the square on BZ *be subtracted* from both, Papp.946.16; *cast out* by division, Vett.Val.20.20, 174.2; *deduct*, in Pass., *PTeb*.189,241 (i B.C.), etc. II. Med., *get rid of*, βῆχα Plu.2.515a. III. intr., *break forth*, κέρατα τῶν κροτάφων ἐκκρούει Philostr.*VA*1.19.

**ἐκκτῠπέω**, *burst forth with noise*, of thunder, Poll.1.118.

**ἐκκῠβεύω**, *play at dice*: metaph., ἐ. τοῖς ὅλοις, ὑπὲρ τῶν ὅλων, *to stake* one's all, Phylarch.58 J., Plb.1.87.8, cf. 3.94.4: c. acc., τὴν ἄδηλον τύχην Onos.32.3. II. Pass., *to be gambled out of, lose at play*, χιλίους ἐκκυβευθεῖσα δαρεικούς Plu.*Art*.17.

**ἐκκῠβιστάω**, *tumble headlong out of*, δίφρων ἐς κρᾶτα πρὸς γῆν ἐκκυβιστώντων βίᾳ E.*Supp*.692; ἐ. ὑπέρ τινος *to throw a somersault* over a thing, of dancers, X.*Smp*.2.11, cf. *An*.6.1.9.

**ἐκκύεις**· ἐρεθίζεις, ἐπισείεις, Hsch.

⊛ **ἐκκῠέω**, *bring forth, put forth as leaves*, *AP*7.385 (Phil.).

**ἐκκυκλ-έω**, *wheel out*, esp. by means of the ἐκκύκλημα (q. v.), ἀλλ' ἐκκυκλήθητι come, *wheel yourself out!* i.e. *show yourself*, Ar.*Ach*. 408; Answ., ἀλλ' ἐκκυκλήσομαι ib.409; ποῖός ἐστιν; Answ., οὗτος οὑκκυκλούμενος Id.*Th*.96; ἐφ' ὑψηλῆς μηχανῆς ἐ. τὴν φιλοσοφίαν Phi-

lostr.*VA*6.11. 2. metaph., *publish, divulge*, τι εἰς ἀγοράν Plu.2.80a: f.l. for ἐκκλίνω in D.H.*Rh*.10.9. -ημα, ατος, τό, *theatrical machine*, used to display an interior, Poll.4.128. -ηθρον, v. ἐγκ-.

**ἐκκῠλ-ίνδω**, *roll out*, ἐφ' ἐκκυλίνδων Ar.*Pax* 134: mostly in aor. 1, σε καταιγίδες ἐξεκύλισαν..γυμνὸν ἐπ' ἠϊόνι *AP*7.501 (Pers.), cf. 582 (Jul.); *overthrow*, πίτυν..γαίης ἐξεκύλισε ib.9.131; ἐξεκύλισε βίην ib. 543 (Phil.):—Pass., S.*OT*812: elsewh. aor. 1, ἐκ δίφροιο..ἐξεκυλίσθη he *rolled headlong from* the chariot, Il.6.42, 23.394, cf. *AP*11.399 (Apollinar.); but ἐκκυλισθέντος τοῦ τροχοῦ Pherecyd.37(a) J.; *plunge headlong*, εἰς ἔρωτας love-intrigues, v.l. for ἐγκ-, X.*Mem*.1.2.22, cf. Opp.*H*.4.20; γένος εἰς κακίαν ἐσχάτην ἐκκεκυλισμένον Max.Tyr.30.3. 2. *extricate*, ὅστις δὴ τρόπος ἐξεκύλισέ νιν Pi.*Fr*.7, cf. *AP*7.176 (Antiphil.):—Pass., *to be extricated from*, ὅτῳ τρόπῳ τῆσδ' ἐκκυλισθήσει τύχης A.*Pr*.87; ἐκκυλισθῆναι ἐκ δικτύων X.*Cyn*.8.8, cf. Plu.*Galb*.27. 3. Pass., *to be published abroad*, εἰς ἀγοράν Id.2.507e. -ίομαι, *to be unrolled*, Arist.*Mech*.855ᵃ30, al., S.E.*M*.3.75, al. -ιστὸς στέφανος *a* garland *closely wreathed* or *rolled together*, Archipp.40, etc.

⊕ **ἐκκῡμ-αίνω**, *swerve, bulge from the straight line*, of a line of soldiers, X.*An*.1.8.18, cf. Demetr.*Eloc*.84. 2. *cause to burst from their sockets*, τὤμματα Herod.6.68. II. Pass., *to be cast up by the waves*, D.H.10.53; ὑπὸ τῆς θαλάσσης Plu.2.357a. -ανσις, εως, ἡ, *breaking of waves on a beach*, Eust.31.45.

**ἐκκύματα**· ἐξανθήματα, Hsch. (prob. ἐκθύματα, q. v.).

**ἐκκῡμᾰτίζομαι**, Pass., *to be cast up by the waves*, Str.6.3.9.

**ἐκκῠνέω**, (ἔκκυνος) of hounds, *keep questing about*, X.*Cyn*.3.10, Poll.5.65:—also **ἐκκῠνόω**, ibid.

⊕ **ἐκκῠνηγέσσω**, aor. 1 inf. -κυνηγέσαι, *track out*, S.*Ichn*.75.

⊕ **ἐκκῠνηγετ-έω**, *pursue in the chase, hunt down*, τινά E.*Ion* 1422, prob. in A.*Eu*.231. -ητέον, *one must chase*, ἀρχάς Dam.*Pr*.45.

**ἔκκῠνος**, ον, (κύων) of a hound, *questing about*, X.*Cyn*.7.10, Poll.5.65. II ἔκκυνοι· νόσημά τι κυνῶν, Hsch.

⊕ **ἐκκύπτω**, *peep out of*, αἰγείρου Babr.50.13; ἐκ τῶν οἴκων Ant.Lib.39.6; ἐκκύψασαν ἁλῶναι to be caught *peeping out* (Reiske for ἐγκ-), Ar.*Th*.790: generally, *pop out*, Id.*Ec*.1052; of a snail's eyes, Teucer ap.Ath.10.455e: metaph., *proceed forth*, τοῦ νοητοῦ εἰς οὐρανόν Plot.4.3.15; cf. ἐκκέκυφεν· ἀνωρθώθη (-ωσεν cod.), Hsch. II. trans., *put forth*, Ael.*NA*15.21.

**ἐκκυρτόω**, *make curved*, in Pass., Philostr.Jun.*Im*.12 (nisi leg. ἐγκ-).

**ἐκκωδωνίζω**, *proclaim by a bell, publish abroad*, Ath.5.219b.

**ἐκκωμάζω**, *rush wildly out*, εἰς ἄλλην χθόνα E.*Andr*.603.

**ἐκκωπέω**, *furnish with oars*, or generally, *equip, fit out*: ἐκκεκώπηται S.*Fr*.145 ap.Hsch.

**ἐκκωφ-έω**, *deafen, stun*, τὰς Ἀθήνας ἐκκεκώφηκας βοῶν Ar.*Eq*.312:—Pass., αἱ δέ μευ φρένες ἐκκεκωφέαται Anacr.81: metaph., ἐς τὸ κάλλος ἐκκεκώφηται ξίφη *are blunted* at the sight of.., E.*Or*.1288, cf. sq. -όω, *make quite deaf*, τὰ ὦτα Pl.*Ly*.204c:—Pass., *become* so, Luc.*Nav*.10, etc.; πρὸς τὸ κάλλος Ath.5.188c; ἐς κάλλος (v. foreg.) Ael.*NA*1.38, v.l. in E.*Or*.1288.

**ἐκλᾰβή**, ἡ, *amount contracted for*, *IG*12(5).647.19 (Ceos, ἐγλ-).

**ἐκλαγχάνω**, pf. ἐκλέλογχα condemned by Luc.*Sol*.5:—*obtain by lot* or *fate*, ὅπως πατρῴας τύμβον ἐκλάχῃ χθονός S.*El*.760; τὸν αὐτὸν δαίμον' ἐξειληχότες Id.*OC*1337; κακῶν μέρος ἐξέλαχον Ar.*Th*.1071.

**ἐκλακτ-ίζω**, *kick out, fling out behind*, σκέλος οὐράνιον Ar.*V*.1492; τὸ Φρυνίχειον ἐ. ib.1525: abs., Eup.411, Hp.*Art*.82. 2. metaph., *escape, run away*, Men.16; also εἰς κραιπάλην Procop.*Pers*.1.24. -ισμα, ατος, τό, *dance*, in which the legs are *thrown up behind, fling*, Poll.4.102. -ισμός, ὁ, = foreg., Hsch.

**ἐκλᾰλ-έω**, *blurt out, blab, divulge*, D.1.26, Ph.1.64, al., Aen.Gaz.*Ep*.7; τὸ ἐκλαλοῦν *talkativeness*, E.*Fr*.219:—Pass., Hp.*Jusj*.1, Lib.*Or*.18.213. -ησις, εως, ἡ, *uttering*, condemned by Poll.5.147. -ητικός, ή, όν, *capable of expressing*, Diocl.ap.D.L.7.49.

⊕ **ἐκλαμβάνω**, fut. -λήψομαι Isoc.12.194:—*receive from* others, ἀριστεῖ' ἐκλαβὼν στρατεύματος *having received* the meed of valour *from* them, S.*Ph*.1429; ἐ. νόμους *to accept* laws *from* another, Plb.2.39.6. II. *seize and carry off*, βίᾳ τοὺς παῖδας Isoc. l.c.; ἐ. μέρος τι [τῆς μητρός] Arist.*GA*753ᵇ34: generally, *remove*, καρπόν *PRev.Laws* 29.13 (iii B.C.), etc.: Medic., *evacuate*, πύον Heliod.ap.Orib.44.10.7; *dissect out*, Antyll.ap.Orib.7.14.5. III. *receive in full*, Isoc.*Ep*.6.13; ἐ. τι παρά τινος E.*Ion* 1335, Isoc.5.100, Pl.*Lg*.958d; τὸ τέλεον καὶ ἱκανόν τινων ib.807d. IV. ἔργα ἐ., = ἐργολαβέω, *contract to do* work, Hdt.9.95, cf. *PMagd*.10.1 (iii B.C.), *IG*12(5).647 (Ceos), etc.: c. inf., ἐ. παρὰ τῆς πόλεως πίνακα γράψαι Plu.*Pel*.25, cf. 2.396e. 2. *hire*, ὀρχήστριαν *PGrenf*.2.67.5 (iii A.D.). V. *take in a certain sense, understand*, ἐ. τοὺς νόμους οὕτω Lys.11.6; ἐ. τι ἐπὶ τὸ χεῖρον Arist.*Rh*.1416ᵇ11; διχῶς Id.*APr*.32ᵇ26. 2. *take note of*, σηκώματα Nicom.*Harm*.6; ἐ. ἀντίγραφον *take* a copy, *PGen*.74.8 (iii A.D.). VI. *select*, τὰς προτάσεις Arist.*APr*.43ᵇ1; τὰ κακεμφάτατα Longin.10.3. VII. Med., ἐκλαμβάνομαι, = ὑπολογίζομαι, Din.*Fr*.16.4. 2. *take hold of*, c. gen., Ph.1.134. VIII. Pass., *to be picked out, adorned*, φιάλαις λιθοκολλήτοις Agatharch.102.

**ἔκλαμπ-ρος**, ον, *very bright*, φλόγες Lxx *Wi*.17.5, cf. Sch.Arat.169: neut. as Adv., ἔκλαμπρον γελᾶν Ath.4.158d. Regul. Adv. -ρως *brilliantly*, *Annuario*3.151 (Pisidia, ἐγλ- lapis). -ρύνω, *polish up*, Herod.7.12 (tm.): *adorn*, τὸ ἱερὸν κατασκευῇ ἀναθημάτων J.*BJ*7.3.3, cf. Max.Tyr.22.2:—Pass., *to be adorned*, πόλιν τούτοις -υνθεῖσαν D.H.2.3. -ω, *shine* or *beam forth*, Hdt.6.82, A.*Pr*.1083 (anap.); ὅπλα ὥστε κάτοπτρον ἐξέλαμπεν X.*Cyr*.7.1.2, etc.; ὀμμάτων ἐ. πόθος *APl*.4.182 (Leon.); ὥσπερ ἀστραπήν Hp.*Epid*.7.88; πῦρ ἐκ λίθων ἐ. Arist.*HA*516ᵇ11: metaph., δίκας δ' ἐξέλαμψε θεῖον φάος *Trag.Adesp*.500; ὥσπερ ἐκ πυρείων ἐ. Pl.*R*.435a; ἐξ. ἡ δόξα Plb.31.23.2; of persons, Ph.1.326, al.; *burst forth violently*, of a fever, Hp.*VM*16; of sound, *to be clearly heard*, [ἐκ τῆς κραυγῆς] ἐξέλαμψε τὸ καλεῖν τὸν βασιλέα Plb.15.31.1. 2. *to be distinguished*, δι' εὐφυΐαν Plu.*Cic*.2; τῶν ἄλλων Lib.*Or*.62.37. II. c. acc. cogn., *flash forth*, πυρωπὸν γλῆνος ἐκλάμψαν φλόγα A.*Fr*.300.4; σέλας dub. l. in E.*Fr*.330, cf. Lyc.1091; πῦρ App.*Syr*.56, cf. Bias *Fr.Lyr*.: metaph., νοῦς ἐ. αἰσθήσεις Ph.1.72; ἀπὸ τοῦ ἑνὸς ὁ θεὸς ἑαυτὸν ἐξέλαμψε Iamb.*Myst*.8.2. III. Astrol., = διαυγάζω III, *PLond*.1.132.95 (i/ii A.D.).

⊕ **ἔκλαμψις**, εως, ἡ, *shining forth, brightness*, Lxx 2*Ma*.5.3; ἡλίου Olymp.*in Mete*.49.9. II. metaph., *sudden development*, at puberty, Hp.*Epid*.6.114 (ἐκλάμψιας (acc. pl.) ap.Gal. ad loc.).

⊕ **ἐκλανθάνω**, *escape notice utterly*:—Med., *forget utterly*, c. gen. rei, ἐκ χόλω τῶδε λαθοίμεθα Alc.*Supp*.23.9; τοῦδ' ἐκλανθάνει thou *forgettest* this *entirely*, S.*OC*1005; ἐγλαθόμενος τῆς εὐθύνης *POxy*.1203.8 (i A.D.), cf. Ph.1.247, al.; ἐ. ὅτι.. Pl.*Ax*.369e. II. causal in pres. **ἐκληθάνω**, with aor. 1 ἐξέλησα, Aeol. ἐξέλασα (v. infr.): Ep. redupl. aor. 2 ἐκλέλᾰθον: 1. Act., *make one quite forgetful of* a thing, c. gen. rei, ἐκ δέ με πάντων ληθάνει ὅσσ' ἔπαθον Od.7.220; ἔκ μ' ἔλασας ἀλγέων Alc.95; c. acc. rei, ἐκλέλαθον κιθαριστύν *made* him *quite forget* his harping, Il.2.600: abs., Ἀΐδας ὁ ἐκλελάθων (redupl. pres.) Theoc.1.63. 2. Med. and Pass., *forget utterly*, ὀϊζύος ἐκλελαθέσθαι Il.6.285; ἀλκῆς ἐξελάθοντο 16.602; ὡς ἐκλέλησμαί γ' ἃ πάρος εἴπομεν E.*Ba*.1272: c. inf., ἐκλάθετο..καταβῆναι Od.10.557; λελάθοντο.., οὐ μὰν ἐκλελάθοντ' Sapph.93.

**ἐκλᾰπάζω**, = ἐξαλαπάζω, *cast out from*, ἑδωλίων A.*Th*.456 (lyr.).

**ἐκλάπτω**, fut. -λάψομαι Ar.*Pax* 885:—*drink off*, Id.*Ach*.1229, etc.

**ἐκλᾱτομέω**, *hew in stone*, Lxx *Nu*.21.18; *hew* or *hollow out*, ib.*De*.6.11:—Pass., Str.7*Fr*.35. II. *quarry stones from*, τὴν γῆν Jul.*Gal*.135c.

**ἐκλᾰχαίνω**, *dig* or *hollow out*, A.R.1.374, Tryph.208.

**ἐκλᾰχᾰνίζομαι**, *cut vegetables*, Thphr.*HP*7.11.3.

**ἐκλε-αίνω**, *smooth out* or *away*, ῥυτίδας Pl.*Smp*.191a: hence, *abolish, cause to disappear*, Hp.*Prorrh*.2.20 (Pass.), Plu.2.567f. 2. *smooth* or *polish off*, [λίθον] Agatharch.82; ἐ. τὰ φαντάσματα *smooth* them *down*, Plu.2.83c. -ασμός, ὁ, *attrition*, ἐντέρων Orib.*Fr*.56, cf. Aët.9.43.

**ἐκλέγω**, fut. Pass. ἐκλεγήσεσθαι *IG*1².76.16: pf. Pass. ἐξείλεγμαι Pl.*Alc*.1.121e, and in med. sense, D.20.131, but ἐκλέλεγμαι Diph.44, Posidipp.27.9 (prob.):—*pick* or *single out*, Th.4.59, etc.; esp. of soldiers, rowers, etc., X.*HG*1.6.19, Pl.*R*.535a; ἐκ πάντων κεφάλαια Id.*Lg*.811a:—Pass., Id.*Alc*.1. c.; ἐκλελεγμένος *select, recondite*, Diog.Oen.23:—Med., *pick out for oneself, choose*, Hdt.1.199, 3.38, D. l. c.; τὰ κάλλιστα Pl.*Smp*.198d, al.; ἐξ ἁπάντων Isoc.9.58. 2. Lit. Crit., *select*, λέξεις καλάς D.H.*Comp*.3; cf. ἐκλογή. 3. Med., of God, *elect, choose*, Lxx *De*.4.37, *Ep.Eph*.1.4, etc. 4. ἐκλέγειν τὰς πολιάς (sc. τρίχας) *pull out* one's grey hairs, Ar.*Eq*.908, *Fr*.410. II. *levy taxes* or *tribute*, χρήματα παρά τινος Th.8.44; τὰς ἐπικαρπίας And.1.92, cf. *IG*1².76.8 (Pass., ib.16); ἔκ τινων D.49.49; *take toll of*, χαλκοῦς Thphr.*Char*.6.4: c. acc. pers., ἐ. τέλη τοὺς καταπλέοντας Aeschin.3.113: c. acc. et gen., τὴν δεκάτην τῶν πλοίων X.*HG*1.1.22. III. *declare*, Prisc.p.294 D., *Gloss*.

**ἐκλείανσις**, εως, ἡ, = ἐκλεασμός, *Gloss*.

⊕ **ἔκ-λειγμα**, ατος, τό, *medicine that melts in the mouth, lozenge* or *jujube*, Aret.*CA*1.5, Dsc.2.158 (pl.), Archig.ap.Orib.8.2.27, Sor.1.123. ⊕ -λειγμᾰτώδης, ες, *of the consistency required for a lozenge*, Aët.3.111, 12.67. ⊕ -λεικτικός, ή, όν, *made into a lozenge*, v.l. in Hp.*Acut*.(*Sp*.)30. -λεικτόν, τό, = ἔκλειγμα, Hp. l.c., Dsc.4.185.

**ἐκλειοτρῑβέω**, *to powder very fine*, Dsc.*Ther*.19 (Pass.).

⊕ **ἐκλειόω**, *rub down* or *to pieces*, Alex.Trall.7.5, Steph.*in Hp*.1.156 D.

**ἐκλειπ-ία**, ἡ, *failure, lack*, πίστεως J.*AJ*19.4.6. -τέον, *we must omit*, Aristid.*Or*.43(1).3. -τικός, ή, όν, *of* or *caused by an eclipse*, σελήνης χρόνοι Hipparch.1.9.1; πανσέληνοι Plu.2.145c; ἐπισκοτήσεις ib.932a; συγκρίσεις ἡλίου καὶ σελήνης Str.1.1.12; ἀριθμός dub. in Doroth.ap.Heph.Astr.3.20; ἐκλειπτικόν, τό, *part of moon's orbit in which eclipses take place*, Gem.11.6, cf. Paul.Al.*O*.2; ἐ. ζῴδιον, τόπος, Vett.Val.5.28, 7.10, al. II. ὁ ἐ. (sc. κύκλος) *ecliptic*, = ὁ ἡλιακός, so called because it is *the circle in the plane of which the sun and moon must be to produce eclipses*, interpol. in Cleom.2.5, Ach.Tat.*Intr.Arat*.23. III. Gramm., *elliptical*, Pall.*in Hp*.2.145 D. -ω, *leave out, pass over*, πολλὰ δ' ἐκλείπω λέγων A.*Pers*.513; ἐ. ὄχλον λόγων Id.*Pr*.827, cf. D.25.47; ἐ. Ἄνδρον *leave out, pass over* Andros, Hdt.4.33; ἐ. ὁτιοῦν τῆς παρασκευῆς Th.7.48; τὴν στρατιάν X.*HG*5.2.22; εἴ τι ἐξέλιπον, σὸν ἔργον ἀναπληρῶσαι Pl.*Smp*.188e:—Pass., ὄνειδος οὐκ ἐκλείπεται *fails* not *to appear*, A.*Eu*.97. 2. *forsake, desert, abandon*, τὰς πατρίδας, τὴν ξυμμαχίην, etc., Hdt.1.169, 6.13, etc.; θήρας μόχθον E.*Hipp*.52; τὸ ξυνώμοτον Th.2.74; τὸν ὅρκον E.*IT*750; *abandon, quit*, τὴν τάξιν Hdt.8.24, al.; τὴν χώρην Id.4.105, 118, al.; τὸν πλοῦν S.*Ph*.911, cf. 58; *give up*, τὴν τυραννίδα Hdt.6.123; τὰ ὑπάρχοντα Th.1.144; θρήνους E.*Ph*.1635; v. infr. II.2. 3. freq. in elliptic phrases, ἐκλείπειν τὴν πόλιν εἰς τὰ ἄκρα *abandon* the city *and go* to the heights, Hdt.6.100, cf. 8.50, X.*An*.7.4.2; ἐξέλειπον οἴκους πρὸς ἄλλον εὐνάτορα E.*Andr*.1040 (lyr.). 4. εἴ τις ἐξέλιπε τὸν ἀριθμόν (of the Persian immortals) if any one *left* the number *incomplete*, Hdt.7.83. 5. *fail* one, ἐκλελοίπασιν ὑμᾶς αἱ προφάσεις Lys.8.16, cf. Pl.*Lg*.657d. II. intr., of the Sun or Moon, *suffer eclipse*, Th.2.28; in full, ὁ ἥλιος ἐκλιπὼν τὴν ἐκ τοῦ οὐρανοῦ ἕδρην Hdt.7.37; ἐ. τὰς ὁδοὺς Ar.*Nu*.

584. 2. *die*, οἱ ἐκλιπόντες the *deceased*, Pl.*Lg*.856e; τῶν ἄλλων ἐκλελοιπότων Is.11.10, etc.; of trees, *BGU*1120.33 (i B.C.); more freq. in full, ἐ. βίον S.*El*.1131; ὑφ' ὧν ἥκιστα ἐχρῆν τὸν βίον ἐκλιπών (= ἀποθανών) Antipho 1.21; so ἐ. φάος E.*Ion* 1186, etc. 3. *faint*, Hp.*Prorrh*.1.71. 4. generally, *leave off, cease*, τῇ μοι [ὁ λόγος] ἐξέλιπε Hdt.7.239; ἐ. πυρετός Hp.*Aph*.4.56, cf. Th.3.87; ἐκλέλοιπεν εὐφρόνη, i.e. it is day, S.*El*.19; ὥστε μὴ 'κλιπεῖν κλέος ib.985, cf. 1149; [αἱ ἐργασίαι] ἐκλελοίπασιν Isoc.8.20: c. part., *leave off* doing, Pl.*Mx*.234b, cf. 249b: c. gen., θεραπείας Plu.*Marc*.17. 5. *fail, be wanting*, ῥώμη γὰρ ἐκλέλοιπεν ἣν πρὶν εἴχομεν E.*HF*230, cf. Pl.*R*.485d; τῶν ἐπιτηδείων ἐκλειπόντων D.S.16.75; ἡ φωνὴ ἐξέλιπε Luc.*Nigr*.35; περὶ ὧν ἐ. [ὁ νόμος] Arist.*Pol*.1286$^a$37: Gramm., of words in a sentence, A.D.*Synt*.11.17; of grammatical forms, ib. 168.21. 6. *remain, be left*, Lxx 4*Ki*.7.13. 7. *depart*, A.*Pers*. 128 (lyr.), *Th*.219. 8. ἐκλείπων σφυγμός *remittent* pulse, Gal. 9.66.

**ἐκλείχω**, *lick up*, of taking honey, Hp.*Acut*.56, cf. Ph.1.458,527:—Pass., *to be taken as an* ἐκλεικτόν, Dsc.1.72, 2.158.

⊛ **ἔκλειψις**, εως, ἡ, (ἐκλείπω) *abandonment*, νεῶν, πολίων, Hdt.6.25, 7.37; τῆς πατρίδος D.C.41.13. II. (from intr.) of Sun or Moon, *eclipse*, ἡλίου ἐκλείψεις Th.1.23, cf. Arist.*Metaph*.1044$^b$10, etc.; ἔ. τελεία, μερική, Cleom.2.6; εἰλικρινής ib.5: metaph. (with play on 1), βασιλέως Plb.29.16.1, cf. Plu.*Aem*.17. 2. *failing, cessation*, τῶν δυνάμεων Id.2.433f (pl.), cf. Aret.*SD*1.7; *extinction* of a race, Str.9.5.12. 3. *defect, omission*, Id.5.3.7. 4. in Law, *failing to appear in court*, *AB*259. 5. ἔκλειψις χορίου *retention* of the afterbirth, Paul.Aeg.6.75.

**ἐκλεκτ-έος**, α, ον, *to be picked out, selected*, Pl.*R*.456b, al. II. ἐκλεκτέον *one must select*, ib.412d, Arist.*APr*.43$^b$6, Sor.1.78. ⊛ **-ικός**, ή, όν, *capable of exercising moral choice*, Chrysipp.*Stoic*.3.46. 2. ἐ. ἀξία value *deserving such choice*, Antip.ib.3?, al. II. *picking out, selective*, δυνάμεις D.H.*Comp*.2 fin.; οἱ ἐ. *the Eclectics*, philosophers *who selected such doctrines as pleased them* in every school, Gal.14.684; ἐ. αἵρεσις D.L.*Prooem*.21, Gal.19.353. III. Adv. -κῶς Hierocl. p.41 A. **-ός**, ή, όν, *picked out, select*, Ibyc.22, Th.6.100; τὸ τῶν ἐ. δικαστήριον Pl.*Lg*.938b; ἐ. δικασταί, = Lat. *iudices selecti*, *OGI*499.3 (ii A.D.). Adv. -τῶς interpol. in Suid. s.v. ἐπίλεκτος. 2. *choice, pure*, σμύρνη Lxx *Ex*.30.23; βοήθημα Asclep.ap.Aët.9.12; ἀνδρῶν *PRein*.43.9 (ii A.D.); ἐκλεκτόν, = *corn*, Aq.*Ps*.64(65).14. II. *chosen of God, elect*, Lxx *Is*.43.20, *Ev.Marc*.13.20, etc. **-όω**, in Pass., *to be separated*, i.e. *purified*, Lxx *Is*.52.11.

**ἐκλελᾰθεῖν, -θέσθαι**, v. ἐκλανθάνω.

**ἐκλελαμμένον**· ἐξεστραμμένον, Hsch. **ἐκλελαπτημένον**· ἐκπεπονημένον, Id. **ἐκλελι⟨α⟩σμένος**· ἐξεστραμμένος, Id.

**ἐκλελῠμένως**, Adv. pf. part. Pass. of ἐκλύω, *loosely, carelessly*, Isoc. *Ep*.6.6; ἐ. καὶ ἀτόνως Plu.*Lyc*.18; *freely, licentiously*, Ath.12.519f.

**ἔκλεμμα**, ατος, τό, (ἐκλέπω) *peel, rind*, Hp.*Morb*.2.13.

**ἔκλεξις**, εως, ἡ, *selection, choice*, Pl.*Phdr*.231d

**ἐκλεπεῖ**· ἐκπορεύεται, Hsch.; cf. ἐκκλητεῖ.

**ἐκλεπ-ίζω**, = ἐκλέπω, Hp.*Nat.Puer*.29 (Pass.), Ph.1.345 (quoting *Ge*.30.37, where Lxx λεπίζω). **-ισις**, εως, ἡ, *taking off the shell*: *hatching*, Suid. s.v. νεοττεία.

**ἐκλεπρόω**, *make* λεπρός, in Pass., Sch.Theoc.1.40.

**ἔκλεπτος**, ον, *very thin*, οὖρον Hp.*Coac*.572.

**ἐκλεπτόω**, = sq., in Pass., *Gloss*.

**ἐκλεπτύνω**, *make very thin*, f.l. for -πλύνω, *Gp*.16.6.3; *reduce to a fine state*, τὰς οὐσίας Syn.Alch.p.58 B.

**ἐκλεπῠρόω**, *strip off the bark*: metaph., *strip*, Sophr.22.

⊛ **ἐκλέπω**, *free from shell* or *rind, peel*, κόκκους Hp.*Mul*.1.81,84; of crocodiles and birds, *hatch* their young, Hdt.2.68, Cratin.108, cf. Ar. *Av*.1108; of serpents, Hdt.3.109; of insects and tortoises, Arist. *HA*553$^a$8, 558$^a$10:—Pass., fut. ἐκλᾰπήσομαι v.l. (ap.Erot.) in Hp. *Nat.Puer*.29: aor. ἐκλᾰπῆναι Ar.*Fr*.164.

**ἐκλευκαίνω**, ῥόθια δ' ἐκλευκαίνετε *dash the white* spray *off* the oar, E.*IT*1387. II. Pass., *become quite white*, Thphr.*CP*5.9.9, Thd. *Da*.12.10.

**ἔκλευκος**, ον, *quite white*, Hp.*Prog*.2, Arist.*HA*617$^a$12, *PCair.Zen*. 129.18, Lxx *Le*.13.24: Comp., *inclining to white*, Arist.*HA*592$^b$7.

**ἐκλήγω**, *cease utterly*, δακρυρροοῦσα S.*El*.1312: abs., Herod.3.87.

**ἐκ-ληθάνω**, v. sub ἐκλανθάνω II. **-λήθομαι**, = ἐκλανθάνομαι, τῶν συγκειμένων App.*Mac*.11.5.

**ἐκληπτ-έον**, *one must select*, Arist.*APr*.43$^b$16. 2. *one must take in a certain sense*, Sch.Ar.*Nu*.298, etc. II. *one must evacuate*, κύστιν Orib.*Syn*.9.55.1. **-ωρ**, ορος, ὁ, later **-λήμπτωρ**, *contractor of works*, *PFay*.58.6 (ii A.D.), etc. 2. *tax-collector*, Just.*Nov*.130.3, al.

**ἐκληρέω**, *play antics, behave absurdly*, Plb.15.26.8.

**ἔκλησις**, εως, ἡ, *forgetting and forgiving*, Od.24.485.

**ἐκλητουργέω**, *undertake and complete a public burden*, Is.7.40.

⊛ **ἔκληψις**, εως, ἡ, *taking out, collecting*, Dsc.1.68.4; *removing*, Id.3.90. 2. *farming of taxes*, *BGU*897.1, Just.*Nov*.123.6; of any trade *enterprise*, *PTeb*.38.11 (ii B.C.). 3. *isolation, dissecting out*, of an aneurism, Antyll.ap.Orib.45.24.3; of a varicose vein, ib.4.36.7. 4. *taking of extract* from a document, Mitteis *Chr*.185 (ii A.D.), *Cod.Just*. 10.11.8.4a, etc.

**ἐκλῐθεύω**, *clear of stones*, τὰς πέτρας *IG*11(2).199*A*85 (Delos, iii B.C., ἐγλ–).

**ἐκλῐθολογέω**, *clear by picking off the stones*, Thphr.*CP*3.20.5.

**ἐκλῐθόω**, *turn into stone*, Tz.*H*.1.556.

**ἐκλικμάω**, *winnow, sift, empty*, Lxx *Ju*.2.27, *Wi*.5.23.

**ἐκλικνίζω**, = foreg., *Gloss*.

**ἐκλῑμία**, ἡ, (λιμός) *exceeding hunger, faintness*, Lxx *De*.28.20, Aq. *Jb*.41.14.

**ἐκλιμν-άζω**, *flood completely*, τὸ πεδίον ἐ. ὁ ποταμός App.*BC*4.107: pf. Pass. ἐκλελιμνάσθαι Sch.Th.*Oxy*.853 x 12:—also **-λιμνιάζω**, abs., of a river, *overflow its banks*, App.*Fr*.1.3. **-όομαι**, *become a complete swamp*, D.H.1.61.

**ἔκλῑμος**, ον, *emaciated*, Thphr.*CP*2.4.6.

**ἐκλῑμώσσω**, *faint with hunger*, Aq.*De*.28.65.

**ἐκλιμπάνω**, = ἐκλείπω, *abandon*, E.*Med*.800, *PHamb*.27.14 (iii B.C.), Ant.Lib.16.3. II. intr., *cease*, οὔποτ' ἐξελίμπανον θρυλοῦσα E.*El*.909. 2. *to be lacking*, Them. *in APo*.38.29. 3. *to be eclipsed*, Ascl. *in Metaph*.11.31.

**ἐκλῐνάω**, *escape out of the net*, Eust.574.30.

**ἐκλῐπαίνω**, in fut. -λιπανῶ, *make smooth as oil*, πέλαγος Posidipp. ap.Ath.7.318d:—Pass., *to be enriched, fertilized*, Plu.*Mar*.21.

**ἐκλῐπᾰρέω**, *entreat earnestly, move by entreaty*, Str.17.1.29: c. inf., Plu.*Them*.5, Jul.*Or*.7.220b: abs., Ph.2.521, J.*AJ*5.7.8, Apollon. *Mir*.3; πολλὰ ἐ. D.L.4.7:—Pass., D.H.7.10, Str.14.5.10, Memn. 7.2.

**ἐκλῐπής**, ές, (ἐκλείπω) *failing, deficient*, ἡλίου ἐκλιπές τι ἐγένετο, = ἔκλειψις, Th.4.52: c. gen., *deficient in..*, Arist.*Xen*.980$^a$6. II. *omitted, overlooked*, Th.1.97, Arr.*An*.1.12.2.

⊛ **ἐκλιστράω**, *slap*, Eust.1119.59.

**ἐκλιχάζει**· ἐξορμᾶν ποιεῖ, ἐκσοβεῖ, Hsch.

**ἐκλιχμάομαι**, *absorb, exhaust*, Ph.1.124, Ael.*Fr*.82.

⊛ **ἐκλογ-εύς**, έως, ὁ, *collector of firstfruits, taxes*, etc., καρπῶν *IG*1$^2$.76.14; φόρου Lys.*Fr*.9, *IG*12(5).1001.14 (Ios, iv B.C., ἐγλ–), Ph.2.33, al. **-εύω**, *collect*, τὰ διάφορα *IG*5(1).1390.47 (Andania). **-έω**, *select*, *CPHerm*.p.80 (iii B.C.). II. mostly in Med., *excuse oneself*, ὑπέρ τινος App.*BC*5.77; ἐ. τὴν ἀνάγκην *plead in excuse*, ib.13: c. acc. et inf., *to state by way of excuse that..*, ib.3.48; μικρὰ ὑπὲρ ἐμαυτοῦ Them.*Or*.8.103d. ⊛ **-ή**, ἡ, *choice, selection*, τῶν ἀρχόντων Pl.*R*.414a, 536c; ἐ. ποιεῖσθαι Id.*Lg*.802b; ἐ. [τῶν ἀρίστων νόμων] Arist.*EN*1181$^a$18; τῶν ἐναντίων Id.*Metaph*.1004$^a$2; ὀνομάτων Phld.*Rh*.1.162 S., D.H. *Comp*.1, etc.; ὀνόματος A.D.*Synt*.71.10; κατ' ἐκλογὴν ἀριστίνδην κεκριμένοι Plb.6.10.9; ἐπὶ ἐγλογῇ γεωργεῖν *PTeb*.5.166 (ii B.C.). 2. *levying of troops*, Plb.5.63.11. 3. *collection of tribute*, etc., κριθῶν Lex Attica ap.Ath.6.235c; χρημάτων D.C.42.6; σίτου Crates ap.Ath. 6.235b. 4. Theol., *election*, *Ep.Rom*.9.11, etc.; σκεῦος ἐκλογῆς *Act. Ap*.9.15. 5. *balancing* of accounts, *PRyl*.157.6 (ii A.D.). II. *extract, quotation from a book*, Apollon.Cit.3, Ath.14.663c, Antig. *Mir*.15. 2. *choice collection* of passages, such as *the Eclogae* or '*Elegant Extracts*' of Stobaeus: ἐκλογαὶ Ἀρχιγένους *select prescriptions* of A., Gal.14.343. 3. διὰ τὴν ἐ. τῶν ἀνθρώπων because they were *picked* men, Plb.1.47.9, cf. Ph.2.362. 4. ἐκλογήν· κάλαθον (Lacon.), Hsch. **-ημα**, ατος, τό, *schedule of payments*, *PStrassb*.103.2 (iii B.C.). **-ίζομαι**, *compute, reckon*, τὰς εὐθύνας Harp. s.v. λογισταί; τὸ ἀργύριον *IG*9(1).694.104 (Corc.), cf. 2$^2$.1263.12:—Pass., ἀριθμὸν..ἐκ τῶν ἀντιγράφων -λογισθέντα ib.7.3073.56 (Lebad.). 2. *consider, reflect on*, τι Hdt.3.1, E.*IA*1409, Th.4.10; περί τινος Id.2.40, And.1.57; ἐ. πρὸς οἵους..ὁ ἀγὼν ἔσται Th.1.70; ἐ. ὅτι.. D.21.123; τίς ὢν πρὸς οὕστινας ἐπολέμει Aeschin.1.64: aor. ἐκλογισθῆναι in pass. sense, *to be calculated*, Plu.*Publ*.15. 3. *reckon on*, οὐδεὶς ἔθ' αὑτοῦ θάνατον ἐκλογίζεται E.*Supp*.482. 4. *reckon up, relate in detail*, Plb.3.99.3, 10.9.3, D.H.11.40. II. = ἐκλογέομαι, τινὶ περί τινος App.*BC*3.43. **-ισις**, εως, ἡ, *computation, reckoning*, Epicur.*Sent*. 18. **-ισμός**, ὁ, *keeping of accounts*, in pl., *Inscr.Prien*.108.214 (ii B.C.), Phalar.*Ep*.24; *computation, calculation*, Haussoullier *Cinquantenaire* p.88 (Didyma, ii B.C.), Plu.*Cat.Mi*.36; *consideration, reckoning*, in pl., Plb.1.59.2, D.H.*Th*.3, Plu.*Oth*.9 (v.l.), etc.; *setting out* of grammatical paradigms, D.T.629.8; *conclusion* of an argument, Hp.*Nat.Puer*.12. **-ιστευω**, *to be* ἐκλογιστής, *CIG*3886 (Eumeneia), *PEdgar*44 (iii B.C.). **-ιστήριον**, τό, *office of* ἐκλογιστής, *PLond*.1.23.110. ⊛ **-ιστής**, οῦ, ὁ, *accountant*, Lxx *To*.1.22; as public official, *Milet*.7.60 (Didyma), *PTeb*.72.449 (ii B.C.), *AJA*18. 324 (Sardes, i B.C.), *CIG*4956.36 (Oasis Thebarum, i A.D.), etc. 2. = ἐκλογεύς, φόρων Ph.1.338. ⊛ **-ιστία**, ἡ, *reckoning*: *accounts*, Lxx *To*.1.21, *Sammelb*.4423. **-ιστικός**, ή, όν, *capable of estimating*, τῶν οἴκῳ συμφερόντων Muson.*Fr*.3 p.10 H.: abs., Phld.*Herc*.1003. ⊛ **-ος** (A), ὁ, *tale*, A.*Fr*.219. II. *balance of accounts*, *PLond*.1.131.6 (i A.D.), etc. **-ος** (B), ον, *picked out, choice*, Ph.2.479,539; ᾠδή Max. Tyr.17.1. 2. ἔκλογον ὄν· μεταξὺ λόγων, Hsch.

**ἐκλοιπάζω**, *adjourn*, in Pass., *Gloss*.

**ἐκλου-στρίς**, ίδος, ἡ, *bathing-costume*, *PCair.Zen*.60.8 (iii B.C.). **-τήριος**, ον, *for washing out* or *rinsing*, χαλκίον ἐ. *IG*4.39.18 (Aegina). **-τρον**, τό, *washing-vessel*, Poll.10.46. **-ω**, *wash out*, Hp.*Steril*.241. II. *wash thoroughly*, Plb.3.88.1:—Pass., λουτροῖς ἐκλελουμένος δέμας A.*Fr*.32; ἐγλοηθεὶς *PPetr*.2 pp.72,73 (iii B.C.).

**ἐκλοφίζω**, *quarry from a hill*, Anon.ap.Suid. s.v. ἐξελοφίζετο.

**ἐκλόχ-ευμα**, ατος, τό, *an offspring*, Suid. s.v. Πολύευκτος. ⊛ **-εύω**, *bring forth*, Orph.*A*.129, *AP*9.602 (Even.):—so in Med., E.*Hel*. [258]: metaph., λόγον Orph.*A*.43:—Pass., *to be born*, E.*Ion*1458 (anap.).

⊛ **ἐκλοχίζω**, *pick out of a cohort* or *troop*, Lxx *Ca*.5.10 (Pass.).

**ἐκλοχμόομαι**, Pass., *become bushy*, Thphr.*CP*3.19.1.

**ἐκλῠγίζω**, *twist exceedingly*, ἐκλελυγισμέναι ὀρχήσεις *mazy* dances, Porph.*Abst*.1.33.

**ἔκλυρον**· χλωρόν, δίυγρον, ἡ νοτερόν, ἔνικμον, ὑγρόν, Hsch.

**ἔκλῠσις**, εως, ἡ, *release, deliverance from* a thing, ἀφροσύνης Thgn. 590 (=Sol.13.70); ἄθλων A.*Pr.*264; τοῦδε τοῦ νοσήματος S.*OT*306; δεσμοῦ Theoc.24.33; Ἀΐδεω *AP*6.219.24 (Antip.(?)). 2. *weakening* of an opponent's case, Hdn.*Fig.*p.91 S., cf. Alex.*Fig.*1.2. II. *feebleness, faintness*, Hp.*Aph.*7.8, etc.; τῆς πόλεως ἔ. καὶ μαλακία D. 17.29; ψυχικῶν δυνάμεων Ph.1.154; φυσική Agatharch.55; ἐκλύσιες κοιλίης *relaxations*, Hp.*Coac.*625. 2. *laxity*, of style, [Longin.] *Rh.*12. III. *lowering of the voice through three quarter-tones* (διέσεις), Bacch.*Intr.*41, Aristid.Quint.1.10, Plu.2.1141b.

**ἐκλυσσάω**, Att. -ττάω, strengthd. for λυσσάω, Ph.1.430, J.*AJ*13. 16.3.

**ἐκλῠτ-ήριος**, ον, *bringing release*, S.*OT*392: -τήριον, τό, *expiatory offering*, E.*Ph.*969. -ικός, ή, όν, *calculated to weaken*, Arist.*GA* 726ᵇ13; ὥρα Aët.16.22: metaph., τῶν λόγων Herm.*in Phdr.*p.103 A. ⊛ -ος, ον, *easy to let go, light, buoyant*, of missiles, E.*Andr.* 1133. II. *let loose, unbridled*, ἵμεροι Ti.Locr.102e; *lascivious*, φιλήματα Lyd.*Mag.*3.65; *unlimited, extreme*, βουλιμία Timocl.13.3; ἔ. καὶ βαρύ Olymp.*in Mete.*198.12. III. *relaxed, unnerved*, E.*Tr.* 1179, dub. in Eup.147; *exhausted*, Nic.Dam.p.98 D.; *deprived of force*, of an engine, Ph.*Bel.*85.10; *weak*, κίνησις Olymp.*in Mete.*169. 2; τόνος τοῦ φθέγματος Luc.*Im.*13; *diluted, watery*, οἶνος *Gp.*7.1.4, cf. Gal.12.278; *loose*, of proof, Eudem.ap.Theon.Sm.p.200 H.; *mild* (opp. σφοδρόν), γυμνάσιον Gal.6.156. Adv. -τως *by being relaxed*, Plu.*Lyc.*17; *weakly*, Agathin.ap.Gal.8.938. IV. *curing by* λύσις (opp. κρίσις), ἡμέραι Gal.9.817.

**ἐκλυτρ-όομαι**, Med., *redeem by payment of ransom*, *SIG*588.70 (Milet., ii B.C.), Sch.Od.4.33.—Act. only in Hsch. -ωσις, εως, ἡ, *redemption*, Lxx *Nu.*3.49.

⊛ **ἐκλύω** [ῡ, v. λύω], *set free*, πόνων *from* labours, A.*Pr.*328; *release*, ὕδατα *PTeb.*49.6 (ii B.C.):—Pass., *to be set free*, ἐκλέλυμαι πόθου Thgn. 1339; ἐκ δεσμῶν Pl.*Phd.*67d:—Med., *get one set free, release*, ἀλλ' ἄγε δή σε κακῶν ἐκλύσομαι Od.10.286; τοῦ φόβου σ' ἐξελυσάμην S.*OT* 1003; θανάτου νιν ἐκλύσασθε E.*Andr.*818; ἐξελυσάμην βροτοὺς τὸ μὴ μολεῖν A.*Pr.*237: c. acc. pers. only, ἐξελύσαντο τοὺς Ἀργείους X.*HG* 7.1.25: abs., ἐξελυσάμην I *delivered* him *from danger*, S.*Aj.*531. II. *unloose*, ἐ. τόξα *unstring* a bow, Hdt.2.173; ἐ. ἁρμοὺς E.*Hipp.*825; σκαιὸν ἐκλύσων στόμα *likely to let loose* a foolish tongue, S.*Aj.*1225. 2. *make an end of*, ἐξέλυσας.. σκληρᾶς ἀοιδοῦ δασμόν *paid* it *off*, Id.*OT* 35; ἐπίπονον ἁμέραν Id.*Tr.*654; μόχθον E.*Ph.*695; ἔριν καὶ φιλονικίαν D.9.14; ἐξελύσατε (v.l. -λύσασθε) τὰς παρασκευάς Id.18.26. 3. *relax*, Arist.*HA*610ᵃ27; τῆς φροντίδος τὸ ἀκριβές Luc.*Dom.*17:—Pass., *to be faint, fail*, Hp.*Aph.*2.41, Isoc.15.59, D.19.224, Phld.*Ir.* p.69 W., etc.; πρὸς τὸν πόλεμον Isoc.4.150; ἐκλυθῆναι τοῖς σώμασι, τῇ ψυχῇ, Arist.*Fr.*144, Plb.29.17.4 (so intr. in Act., J.*BJ*1.33.5), etc.; of things, *to be unserviceable*, τὰ τῶν πλοίων ἐκλελυμένα Arist.*Pol.* 1320ᵇ37; ἐκλύεται ὁ βοῦς, τὰ ῥεύματα, *cease*, Plb.4.43.9, 4.41.5. 4. Medic., ἐ. κοιλίαν *relax* the bowels, Dsc.4.169. 5. *pay in full*, δάνειον Plu.*Caes.*12 (Pass.). b. *purchase*, Herod.6.91. 6. *resolve* a doubt, in Pass., A.D.*Synt.*176.24; also τὰ ὑπ' ἀμφιβολίαν πίπτοντα ἐκλύεται τοῦ ἀμφιβόλου ib.311.11. 7. *dissolve*, τι ὄξει Gal.11.106. III. intr., *to break up, depart*, Lxx 2 *Ma.*13.16.

**ἐκλωβάομαι**, Pass., *sustain grievous injuries*, ἄγωγ' ὑπ' αὐτῶν ἐξελωβήθην S.*Ph.*330.

**ἐκλωπίζω**, (λῶπος) *lay bare*, ἐκ δ' ἐλώπισε πλευρόν S.*Tr.*925. II. =λωποδυτέω, Hsch.

**ἐκλωτίζομαι**, = ἐξανθίζομαι, Achae.31:—Act. in aor. 1, Hsch. (prob.).

⊛ **ἐκμᾰγεῖον**, τό, (ἐκμάσσω) *napkin*, Pl.*Ti.*72c, Meyer *Ostr.*62.5 (ii B.C.). 2. *that which wipes off, gets rid of*, αἵματος μέλανος, of the spleen, Aret.*SD*1.15; *rough towel*, Archig.ap.Gal.12.621, Paul.Aeg. 1.57. II. *that on* or *in which an impression is made*, κήρινον ἐ. *lump* of wax, Pl.*Tht.*191c, cf. 196a; of *matter* (φύσις) *as a recipient of impressions*, Id.*Ti.*50c, Arist.*Metaph.*988ᵃ1; [σῶμα] ἐ. αὐτῆς τῆς γενέσεως Ocell.2.3. 2. *impress, mould*, Pl.*Tht.*194d,e, Ph.1.279: metaph., ἐκμαγεῖον πέτρης *impress* of the rocks, of a fisherman who is always wandering over them, *AP*6.193 (Flacc.). 3. *model*, Pl. *Lg.*800b, 801d; μηχανῆς Procop.*Aed.*2.3.

**ἐκμᾰγεύω**, *bewitch*, Iamb.*Bab.*9.

**ἔκμαγμα**, ατος, τό, *impression in wax*, etc., Poll.9.131. II. = κροκόμαγμα, Hp.*Steril.*235.

⊛ **ἐκμάθησις** [ᾰ], εως, ἡ, *thorough knowledge*, Phld.*Po.*5.2.

**ἐκμαιεύομαι**, *bring to the birth*, Simp.*in Ph.*786.21.

⊛ **ἐκμαίνω**, *drive mad* with passion, ἐκμήνας θυμὸν ἔρωτι Pl.*Epigr.* 7.6, cf. Theoc.5.91; ἐπί τινι *with love for* her, Ar.*Ec.*966; φόβῳ τέτροπον ἐκμαίνων ὄχον E.*Hipp.*1229; πόθον ἐκμῆναι *to kindle mad* desire, S.*Tr.*1142; ἐκμῆναί τινα δωμάτων *to drive* one *raving from* the house, E.*Ba.*36:—Pass., with pf. 2 Act. ἐκμέμηνα, *go mad* with passion, ταῦτα ἐκμαίνεσθαι ἔς τινα *rage* so against one, Hdt.3.33, cf. 37, Paus. 1.11.15; ἔρωτι οὐρανίῳ ἐκμεμηνυῖα [διάνοια] Ph.1.482; of mania, Aret. *SD*1.6; ὑπὸ τοῦ ἀκράτου Luc.*Nigr.*5; of sexual passion, εἰς γυναῖκας ἐκμανείς J.*AJ*8.7.5: also, c. acc., ἐκμανῆναί τινα *to be madly in love with*.., *Anacreont.*11.4; τινί Aristaenet.1.15 tit.; of persons in delirium, Hp.*Epid.*3.17.ιγ'.

⊛ **ἔκμακτος**, ον, (ἐκμάσσω) *express*, εἴδη Emp.22.7.

**ἔκμακτρον**, τό, *impress*, ποδῶν E.*El.*535.

⊛ **ἐκμᾰλάσσω**, Att. -ττω, *relax, weaken*, τὰ σώματα Plu.*Fr.*20.1; *soften, mollify*, τραχύτητας γλώσσης Dsc.*Eup.*2.17: metaph., ὀργήν τινος J.*AJ*2.6.8.

**ἐκμαλθᾰκόω**, = foreg., Men.Prot.p.5 D.

**ἐκμάλθαξις**, εως, ἡ, *softening, enervating*, Erot. s.v. ἐκθήλυνσις.

**ἐκμᾰνής**, ές, *quite mad*, πρὸς τὰ ἀφροδίσια Nicias ap.Ath.10.437e; λύτται Ph.1.408. Adv. -νῶς Ath.13.603a.

**ἐκμανθάνω**, *learn thoroughly*, and, in past tenses, *to have learnt thoroughly, know full well*, ἐ. τὴν [Ἑλλάδα] γλῶσσαν Hdt.2.154; ἀνδρὸς ψυχήν S.*Ant.*175; ἐ. τι ἀπό τινος A.*Pr.*256; ἔκ τινος Pl.*Ax.*371a; παρά τινος S.*OT*286; τοῦ θεοῦ τί πρακτέον ib.1439, cf. *OC*114, Ar.*Ec.* 244; ἐ. ὅτι.. Hdt.3.134. II. *examine closely, search out*, Id.7. 28, E.*IT*667, X.*Cyr.*1.6.40. III. *learn by heart*, ὅλους ποιητάς Pl. *Lg.*811a, cf. Aeschin.3.135; ᾄσματα Thphr.*Char.*27.7; Σαπφοῦς τὰρωτικά Epicr.4; Διονυσίου δράματα Ephipp.16; ἵνα πολλάκις ἀκούοντες τῶν ἐπῶν ἐκμανθάνωμεν τὴν ἔχθραν Isoc.4.159.

**ἔκμαξις**, εως, ἡ, *wiping*, Arist.*Insomn.*460ᵃ16.

**ἐκμᾰραίνω**, aor. -μάρανα *AP*12.234 (Strat.):—*make to fade* or *wither away*, Thphr.*Ign.*11, *APl.*c.:—Pass., *wither away*, Theoc.3.30.

**ἐκμαργόομαι**, *go raving mad*, ἐξεμαργώθης φρένας E.*Tr.*992.

⊛ **ἐκμαρτῠρ-έω**, *to bear witness to* a thing, c. acc., φόνον A.*Eu.*461; ἐκμαρτύρησον.. τό μ' εἰδέναι Id.*Ag.*1196; εἰς πολλούς before many persons, Aeschin.1.107:—Pass., Str.12.8.6. II. *make depositions out of court*, Is.3.21, Test.ap.D.35.20, Aeschin.2.19. -ησις, εως, ἡ, *deposition of absent witness*, *POxy.*1208.30 (iii A.D.). -ία, ἡ, *the deposition of a witness taken out of court*, -ίας ποιεῖσθαι Is.3.21 (pl.), D.46.7, Aeschin.2.19, *SIG*953.41 (Calymna, ii B.C., pl.). -ιον, τό, *evidence*, Anon.ap.Suid.; ἐν ἐκμαρτυρίοις Just.*Nov.*90.2. II. *official certificate*, *PMasp.*87.21 (vi A.D.), *BGU*1094.16 (vi A.D.).

**ἐκμαρτύρομαι** [ῠ], *prove by evidence*, τι Just.*Nov.*22.14. 2. abs., *give testimony*, ib.91.2.

**ἐκμᾰσάομαι**, *chew completely*, in aor. Pass. -μασήθην Ph.1.334.

**ἐκμάσσατο**, 3 sg. aor. 1, he *devised* or *invented*, τέχνην *h.Merc.* 511; cf. μαίομαι.

⊛ **ἐκμάσσω**, Att. -ττω, pf. ἐκμέμαχα (-κα codd.) cj. in D.H.*Dem.*4: aor. 2 Pass. -εμάγην [ᾰ] Pl.*Tht.*191d; also aor. 1 part. ἐκμαχθείς Hsch.:—*wipe off, wipe away*, κάρᾳ κηλῖδας ἐξέμαξεν S.*El.*446; ἔκμασσε [τὸ αἷμα] E.*HF*1400; ἀλωπεκίας ὀθονίῳ Archig.ap.Gal.12.406:—Med., *wipe away one's tears*, *AP*5.42 (Rufin.). 2. *wipe dry*, ὑπὸ σπόγγου Hp.*Acut.*65 (Pass.), cf. Herod.6.9; [τοὺς ἔμπροσθεν πόδας] ἐ. εἰς τοὺς μέσους, of bees, Arist.*HA*624ᵇ1. II. of an artist, *mould* or *model* in wax or plaster, αὑτὸν ἐκμάττειν τε καὶ ἐνιστάναι εἰς τοὺς τῶν κακιόνων τύπους *to mould* and adapt oneself to.., Pl.*R.*396d; of pessaries, Hp.*Steril.*230:—so in Med., Id.*Nat.Mul.*109; ὧν ἔτι θερμὰ κονία.. ἐκμάσσεται ἴχνη of whose yet warm footsteps the dust *receives the impress*, Theoc.17.122; *express, imitate*, ἵππου γενεήν Nic.*Th.*740; τὸν Λυσιακὸν χαρακτῆρα ἐκμέμακται D.H.*Dem.*13 (so in Act., ib.4 codd., dub.); ἐς τὸ ἀκριβέστατον ἐξεμάξατο τὸν διδάσκαλον he *was the image of* his master, Alciphr.3.64:—Pass., μάλθης ἄναγνα σώματ' ἐκμεμαγμένοι (v.l. -μένα) S.*Ichn.*140; ἐκεῖνος αὐτὸς ἐκμεμαγμένος his very *image*, Cratin.255; βασιλέως.. εἰκόν' ἐκμεμ. *IGRom.*1.1190 (Memnon); ὃ ἂν ἐκμαγῇ whatever *be impressed*, whatever *impression be made* (cf. ἐκμαγεῖον), Pl.*Tht.*191d; τὴν ἰδέαν τοῦ παιδὸς ἐκμεμάχθαι *had impressed upon him* the image of the boy, Plu.*Cic.*44; ποιότης ἀπὸ μένοντος ἐκμαγεῖσα θείου λόγου Ph.1.548.

**ἐκμαστεύω**, *track out*, ὡς κύων νεβρὸν πρὸς αἷμα ἐ. A.*Eu.*247, Ph. Bybl.ap.Eus.*PE*1.9.

**ἐκμαστῑγόω**, *scourge*, in Med., Hsch. s.v. ἐκδέψηται.

**ἐκμεθύσκω**, *make quite drunk*: metaph., τὰς ῥίζας.. λίαν ἐ. *overcharge* them *with moisture*, Thphr.*CP*5.15.3; λύχνον ἐλαιηρῆς ἐ. δρόσου *AP*5.3 (Phld.).

**ἐκμείλιξις**, εως, ἡ, *appeasing, taming*, κυνῶν Eust.1749.43.

**ἐκμειλίσσω**, *soften*, Gal.11.317. II. mostly Med., *appease*, Corn.*ND*21, App.*BC*1.97, Plu.2.380c, D.C.79.19, Conon 18.

**ἐκμείρομαι**, *obtain for one's lot*, aor. 2 ἐξέμμορον Nic.*Th.*791; θεῶν ἐξέμμορε τιμῆς Od.5.335.

**ἐκμελαίνομαι**, *to be darkened, grow dark*, Heraclit.*All.*39; ὑπὸ [νυκτὸς] ib.45.

**ἐκμελᾰνίζω**, *lose colour*, Olymp.Alch.p.91 B.

**ἐκμέλεια**, ἡ, (ἐκμελής) *false note*, D.H.*Comp.*11: metaph., Corn. *ND*32. II. *carelessness*, Zos.1.23, al.

**ἐκμελετάω**, *train* or *teach carefully*, τινά Pl.*Hp.Ma.*287a. 2. *learn perfectly, con over, practise*, Antipho 3.2.7, Pl.*Hp.Ma.*286d; τὴν εἰς τὸ θεῖον ἐ. βλασφημίαν Men.715.

**ἐκμελής**, ές, (μέλος) *out of tune, dissonant*, Ph.1.375, al., Ti.Locr. 101b, Plu.*Demetr.*1; *unbridled*, φιλοτιμία Id.*Lys.*23; of persons, Just.*Nov.*136.6. Adv. -λῶς Poll.4.57.

**ἐκμελίζω**, *dismember*, Lxx 4 *Ma.*10.5,8.

**ἔκμελος**· ἀδύναμος, Hsch. **ἐκμεταιωροῦνται**· μετεωρίζονται, Id.

**ἐκμεταλλεύω**, *empty of ore* or *metal*, Str.14.5.28 (Pass.).

**ἐκμέταλλος**, ον, *from a mine*, ἅλς Sch.Nic.*Al.*518 (s.v.l.).

**ἐκμετρ-έω**, *measure out, measure*, χρόνον E.*IA*816; κύκλος τις ὡς τόρνοισιν ἐκμετρούμενος Id.*Fr.*382; ἐ. τὸν βίον *to end* life, to die, Tz. *H.*3.800: abs., *measure a distance*, ἐπὶ τὰς πόλεις Lxx *De.*21.2:—freq. in Med., *measure for oneself, measure out*, ἄστροις.. ἐκμετρούμενος χθόνα *measuring, calculating its position* by the stars (for he was an exile), S.*OT*795; *take measure of*, τὰ ἐκείνου ὅπλα X.*Cyr.*6.4.2, cf. Plb.5.98.2:—Pass., *PTeb.*61(*b*).258 (ii B.C.), etc. -ησις, εως, ἡ, *measurement*, Plb.5.98.10, *BGU*432 ii 10 (ii A.D.). -ητής, οῦ, ὁ, *measurer, surveyor*, *PAmh.*2.79.16 (ii A.D.), etc. -ος, ον, *out of measure, measureless*, ὄλβος S.*Fr.*353, cf. Man.4.464,626; of a verse, *exceeding the due length*, Luc.*Pr.Im.*18.

**ἐκμηκύνω**, strengthd. for μηκύνω, D.H.1.56 (Pass.), 6.83, J.*BJ*7.8.3 (Pass.).

**ἐκμηνίω**, strengthd. for μηνίω, Hsch.

❋ **ἔκμηνος**, ον, *of six months, half-yearly*, ἐκμήνους χρόνους (Pors. for ἐμμήνους) S.*OT*1137; βίος Arist.*HA*558ᵃ17: Subst. ἔκμηνος, ὁ, *half-year*, ἐντὸς ἐκμήνου Pl.*Lg*.916b; ἐν ἐγμήνῳ *IG*12(9).207.52 (Eretria, iii B.C.), cf. D.C.59.6; ἔ. (sc. ἀρχή), ἡ, Plb.6.34.3. II. *six months old*, of an animal, Arist.*HA*562ᵇ27; μὴ πρεσβύτερον ἐνιαυσίου καὶ ἐγμήνου *IG*12(5).647.8 (Ceos).

**ἐκμηνύω**, *inform of, betray*, Plu.*Pel*.9 (Pass.), Poll.5.154.

**ἐκμηρύομαι**, *wind off like a ball of thread*, Jul.*Gal*.135c; of an army, *make* it *defile out*, τὴν δύναμιν ἐκ τῶν δυσχωριῶν Plb.*Fr*.132; διὰ στενῆς θυρίδος.. ἐκμηρυόμενος αὐτόν Plu.*Aem*.26. II. intr., of the army, *defile*, X.*An*.6.5.22; τῆς χαράδρας Plb.3.53.5 (but τὰς δυσχωρίας ib.51.2). III. metaph., *evolve itself, develop*, Dam.*Pr*. 65, cf. eund.ap.Simp.*in Ph*.780.30.

**ἐκμηχανάομαι**, aor. Pass. ἐξεμηχανήθην, *contrive*, J.*AJ*8.3.4, Hsch.

**ἐκμιαίνω**, *pollute thoroughly, defile*, Opp.*H*.4.663:—Pass., *ejaculate semen*, Hp.*Superf*.31, Ar.*Ra*.753, Lxx *Le*.18.20.

**ἐκμιμ-έομαι**, *imitate faithfully, represent exactly*, E.*HF*1298, Ar. *Av*.1285, X.*Mem*.3.10.1, Duris 89 J. **-ησις**, εως, ἡ, *imitation*, Arg.2 Ar.*Av*.

**ἐκμισέω**, *hate much*, Plu.*Phil*.12 (Pass.).

**ἔκμισθος**, ον, *receiving no pay*, Hsch.

**ἐκμισθόω**, *let out for hire*, ὁλκάδας X.*Vect*.3.14; χωρίον Lys.7.4; [τέμενος] *SIG*1044.30 (Halic.), etc.: c. inf., ἐ. τινὰ ἑταιρεῖν Aeschin. 1.13:—Med., *contract for*, ἔργον Them.*Or*.4.53a.

**ἐκμολεῖν**, inf. of aor. 2 ἐξέμολον, Ep. 3 sg. ἔκμολε, *go out, go forth*, Il.11.604; ἐξέμολεν A.R.1.845; cf. βλώσκω.

**ἐκμολύνω**, *pollute*, in Pass., Ar.*Ra*.753 cod.V.

**ἐκμορφόω**, *represent, express in form*, Plu.2.537d:—Pass., τὰς ἐκμεμορφωμένας διὰ τῶν αἰσθήσεων τέρψεις Phld.*D*.3.14. II. *bring into shape*, Ael.*NA*2.19.

**ἐκμουσόω**, strengthd. for μουσόω, *teach fully*, τινά τι E.*Ba*.825:—Pass., ἐκμουσωθῆναί τι Ael.*VH*14.34.

❋ **ἐκμοχθέω**, *work out with toil*, κερκίσιν πέπλους E.*El*.307. 2. *struggle through*, πόνους Id.*IT*1455, cf. A.*Pr*.825, Porph.ap.Eus.*PE* 3.11. 3. *win by labour, achieve*, Ἑλένην ἐ. δορί E.*Tr*.873; ἐκμοχθῶν βίᾳ εὔκλειαν Id.*HF*1369. 4. *struggle out of*, τὰς τῶν θεῶν τύχας ib.309. 5. Pass., *to be worn out*, ὅσοι δεσμοῖς ἐκμεμόχθηνται βροτῶν Id.*Fr*.332.5 (s.v.l.).

**ἐκμοχλ-εία**, ἡ, *dislodgement*, φλέγματος Aët.16.21. **-ευσις**, εως, ἡ, f.l. for ἐκχόλωσις, Paul.Aeg.3.13. **-εύω**, *lift out with a lever*, Hp.*Art*.72 (and in Med., ib.76); πύλας ἐ. *to force* them *open with crow-bars*, Ar.*Lys*.429: generally, *force, compel*, τὴν φύσιν Plu.2. 662c; *dislodge*, τὰ λυποῦντα Gal.7.195, cf. Archig.ap.Orib.8.1.22; τὴν κακοχυμίαν τῶν σωμάτων Olymp.*in Grg*.p.143 J.

**ἐκμυελίζω**, *suck the marrow out of, deprive of strength*, Lxx *Nu*.24.8.

**ἐκμυζ-άω**, *suck out*, αἷμ' ἐκμυζήσας Il.4.218, cf. Luc.*Tim*.8, Ael.*NA* 3.39, Gal.*UP*6.15, Q.S.4.398; *exhaust* air from a vessel, Hero *Spir*. 1 *Praef*.: metaph., *extort*, Lyd.*Mag*.3.67:—also in form **ἐκμύζω**, Dsc.*Eup*.1.62, Phlp.*in Mete*.115.18:—Pass., Antyll.ap.Orib.7.16. 16:—also **ἐκμυζέω**, Alex.Aphr.*Pr*.2.59: metaph., *drain, exhaust*, [στάσις] ἐ. τὰς δυνάμεις Aristid.*Or*.23(42).31. **-ηθμός**, ὁ, = sq., Alex.Trall.3.3. **-ησις**, εως, ἡ, *sucking out*, Sor.1.77, Philum.*Ven*. 7.3, Alex.Aphr.*Pr*.2.59. **-ησμός**, ὁ, = foreg., Archig.ap.Gal.12. 656, Aët.13.24.

**ἐκμυθόω**, *make into a* μῦθος *or fable*, Philostr.*Im*.1.3 (Pass.).

**ἐκμυκάομαι**, *bellow aloud*, τὰς ὀλοφύρσεις Phalar.*Ep*.122.2.

**ἐκμυκτηρ-ίζω**, *hold in derision, mock at*, Lxx *Ps*.2.4, *Ev.Luc*.16. 14. **-ισμός**, ὁ, *derision*, Hsch.

**ἐκμυσάττομαι**, *abominate*, Ph.2.303.

**ἐκμύσσομαι**, Med., *blow the nose*, read by Gal. for ἀπο- in Hp.*Nat. Hom*.7.

**ἐκναρκάω**, *become quite torpid* or *sluggish*, Plu.*Cor*.31.

**ἐκναυσθλόω**, *cast on shore*, Lyc.726 (Pass.).

**ἐκνε-άζω**, *grow up afresh*, σπόρος κατ' ἔτος ἐκνεάζων Luc.*Am*. 33. II. *replace from fresh crop*, *PAmh*.2.147.9 (iv/v A.D.). **-ασμός**, ὁ, *renewal*, Simp.*in Ph*.4.36, *in Epict*.p.37 D.

**ἐκνέμω**, *pasture*, ἀγέλας Ph.2.233:—more freq. in Med. with aor. ἐξενεμήθην, *feed off* or *on*, τι Thphr.*HP*9.16.1, Nic.*Th*.571; *inhabit*, χώρας Ph.2.524: metaph., λύπης τὴν διάνοιαν ἐκνεμομένης Luc.*Am*. 25. II. *go forth to feed*: metaph. in Med., οὐκ ἄψορρον ἐκνεμῇ πόδα; S.*Aj*.369 (lyr., s.v.l.). III. Medic., *-όμενον* ἕλκος *rodent* ulcer, Alex.Trall.9.3. IV. ἐκνενεμήκασι· παραδεδώκασιν, and ἐκνενέμηται· ἐξῆλθεν, ἐξῆκται, Hsch.

**ἐκνεοττεύω**, *hatch*, Arist.*Mir*.842ᵇ11, Antig.*Mir*.15.

**ἐκνεύμυκτεν**· κατέβαλλεν, Hsch.

**ἐκνευρ-ίζω**, (νεῦρον) *cut the sinews*, Plu.2.451d; ἐκνενευρισμένοι *broken down, enfeebled*, D.3.31; ἡ πόλις ἐκνενεύρισται Plu.2.755c, cf. Ph.1.258, al.; ἐκνευρισθεῖσα χώρα *exhausted* soil, Id.2.434. **-ισις**, εως, ἡ, *unnerving*, ψυχῆς Eustr.*in APo*.223.27. **-ος**, *enervus*, *Gloss*. **-όω**, = -ίζω, *Tab.Defix.Aud*.234.18 (Carthage, i A.D.).

**ἔκνευσις**, εως, ἡ, *turning the head aside to avoid*, βολῶν ἐκνεύσεσι Pl.*Lg*.815a. 2. ἐκνεύσεις τῶν ὁδῶν *deviations*, Sch.Ar.*Ra*.113; cf. ἔκνευσις ὁδοῦ, *diverticulum*, *Gloss*.

❋ **ἐκνεύω**, aor. ἐξένευσα, *turn the head out of* its natural position, of a horse, ἐ. ἄνω *to toss* the head, X.*Eq*.5.4; τῇ κεφαλῇ ἐκνεύσας *by a side-movement* with the head, of the wild boar, Id.*Cyn*.10.12, cf. Lxx 4 *Ki*.23.16. 2. c. acc., *shun, avoid*, Phld.*Sign*.27, Ph.1.146, Orph.*A*.458; ξίφος Hegesias ap.D.H.*Comp*.18; πληγήν D.S.17. 100. II. *fall headlong*, εἰς θάνατον E.*Ph*.1268; ἐ. πρός τι *to turn aside*, Ph.1.297: c. gen., τῶν παρόντων Plot.6.7.34. III. *motion away*, ἐξένευσ' ἀποστῆναι πρόσω E.*IT*1330.

**ἐκνέφ-ελος**, ον, *bursting forth from clouds*, ἥλιος Thphr.*HP*8.10. 3. **-ίας** (sc. ἄνεμος), ὁ, *a hurricane, caused by clouds meeting and bursting*, Alex.46.5, Arist.*Mete*.365ᵃ1; νότος ἐ. D.S.20.88. 2. ἐ. ὄμβρος rain *with sunshine*, Hp.ap.Gal.19.96; ἐ. ἥλιος *seen through clouds*, Herod.Med.ap.Orib.10.9.1, cf. Philostr.*Gym*.58. 3. ἐ. πυρετός, perh. fever with sweating, Hp.ap.Gal. l. c. **-όομαι**, *become a cloud*, Thphr.*Vent*.7.

**ἐκνέω**, fut. -νεύσομαι: aor. 1 ἐξένευσα: pf. ἐκνένευκα Men.*Epit*. 355:—*swim out, swim to land*, E.*Hipp*.823; *escape by swimming*, Th.2.90: generally, *escape, get safely through*, Pi.*O*.13.114, E.*Hipp*. 470, Men. l. c., E.*IT*1186.

**ἐκνῆναι**· ἐξαπατῆσαι, Hsch.

**ἐκνηπιόω**, *rear from childhood*, Philostr.*VS*2.1.11:—Pass., *to be reared*, ὑπὸ λόγων Id.*VA*5.14.

**ἐκνηστεύω**, *continue fasting*, Hp.*Morb*.2.55, Plu.2.686e.

**ἐκνήφω**, fut. -ψω Lxx *Ge*.9.24:—*sleep off a drunken fit, become sober again*, l.c., Hippoloch.ap.Ath.4.130b, *AP*5.134, Plu.*Dem*.20: metaph., 1 *Ep.Cor*.15.34: c. gen., *recover from*, χάρμῃ ἐ. τῆς δυσθυμίης Aret.*SD*1.5. II. trans., *carry off*, ἀρρώστημα ἐκνήψει ὕπνος Lxx *Si*.34(31).2 (dub.).

**ἐκνήχομαι**, aor. 1 ἐξενηξάμην Plb.38.16.12: pf. inf. ἐκνενῆχθαι Ath.7.315d:— = ἐκνέω, *swim out* or *away*, πρὸς τὴν γῆν Plb. l. c.; εἰς.. Arist.*Mu*.398ᵇ32, Luc.*DMar*.8.2; πρός τινα Apollod.1.9.25: abs., Luc.*Merc.Cond*.2.

**ἔκνηψις**, εως, ἡ, *becoming sober* or *calm*, Lxx *La*.2.18.

**ἐκνίζω**, *wash out, purge away*, φόνον φόνῳ E.*IT*1224; of crimes, Pl.*Ep*.352c:—Med., *wash off from oneself*, οὐδέποτε ἐκνίψει τὰ πεπραγμένα σαυτῷ D.18.140; τὰ τῆς γυναικῶν Ph.1.365; ἄγος φόνου Paus. 3.17.7; τὸ θνητόν Plu.2.499c. b. ἐκνενιμμένοι τόποι *washed away*, *POxy*.1469.6 (iii A.D.). II. *wash clean, purify*, ψυχήν *AP*14.74: metaph., *restore to clarity*, τὴν αἴσθησιν Aret.*CA*2.3:—Pass., ἐκνενιμμένη, of a cup, Eub.56.5; ἐκνιφθεὶς ὁ στόμαχος Philum.ap.Aët.9.3.

❋ **ἐκνικ-άω**, *achieve by force*, ὁ χρυσὸς -νικᾷ τάδε E.*Ion*629; *carry one's point that*.., c. acc. et inf., Plu.*Ant*.63. 2. c. acc., ἐξενίκησε τὸν δῆμον καὶ τὸν εἴργοντα νόμον τῆς θέας τὰς γυναῖκας Ael.*VH*10.1:—Pass., ἄνεμος εἰς γαλήνην ἐξενικήθη Hld.5.23, cf. Ruf.ap.Orib.5.3. 9. II. intr., *win a complete victory*, Plb.15.3.6. 2. metaph., *gain the upper hand, come into vogue, prevail*, ἅπασι among all, Th. 1.3; ἐπὶ τὸ μυθῶδες ἐκνενικηκέναι *to have won its way* to the fabulous, ib.21; κακὸν εἰς τοὐμφανὲς ἐξενίκησε Luc.*Abd*.6; εἰς παροιμίαν Suid. s.v. Μάρας; εἰς δύναμιν Ph.1.420. ❋ **-σις**, εως, ἡ, *eviction*, *Cod. Just*.1.3.38(39).

**ἐκνίπτω**, = ἐκνίζω, Hsch. s.v. ἐκλούηται (Pass.).

**ἐκνιτρ-όω**, *cleanse with* νίτρον, τἀκπώματ'.. ἐκνενιτρωμένα θεῖναι Alex.2.4, cf. *IG*7.3073.86 (Lebad.), Archig.ap.Gal.12.406. **-ωσις**, εως, ἡ, Orib.*Fr*.74.

**ἔκνιψις**, εως, ἡ, (ἐκνίζω) *washing*, Hsch.

**ἐκνοέω**, *think out, contrive*, D.C.*Fr*.73.3 codd.

**ἔκνοια**, ἡ, (ἔκνοος) *loss of one's senses*, Arist.*Somn*.455ᵇ6 (pl.), 456ᵇ 10.

**ἐκνόμιος**, ον (η, ον Orph.*Fr*.121), *unusual, marvellous*, Pi.*N*.1.56; *lawless*, Orph. l. c. Adv. -ίως Ar.*Pl*.981: Sup. ἐκνομιώτατα ib.992.

**ἔκνομος**, ον, *outlawed*, A.*Eu*.92. II. = foreg., Orph.*A*.60; *unlawful, monstrous*, τιμωρίαι D.S.14.112, cf. Ael.*Fr*.217, Ph.2.165, al.: Sup., ib.280. III. Adv. -μως *discordantly*, A.*Ag*.1473 (lyr.).

**ἔκνοος**, ον, contr. -νους, ουν, *senseless*, ὑπὸ γήρως Plu.*CG*19.

**ἐκνοσηλεύω**, *cure completely*, Ph.1.631, Gal.10.522:—Pass., -όμενοι *convalescents*, Gal.6.726, Orib.3.15.7.

**ἐκνοσφίζομαι**, *take for one's own*, *AP*15.24 (Simm.). II. ἐκνοσφίσαι· ἐκβαλεῖν, Hsch.

**ἐκνοτίζω**, *drip*, Hsch. s.v. ἀπολείβεσθαι.

**ἐκνυκτερεύομαι**, *stand overnight*, *PLeid.X*.8.12.

**ἐκνύσσω**, *expungo*, *Gloss*.

**ἐκξέω**, *wipe off, erase*, *App.Anth*.7.56, 71, Tz. ad Lyc.874.

**ἐκξιφίζομαι**, *unsheathe the sword*, Tz.*H*.3.134.

**ἐκξυλόομαι**, *become woody*, Thphr.*HP*1.2.7.

**ἐκξύω**, *scrape out*, Herod.3.18.

**ἐκοντ-ηδόν**, Adv. = ἑκοντί, A.D.*Adv*.197.22. ❋ **-ήν**, Adv. = foreg., Theognost.*Can*.161.24, Arr.ap.Suid., *SIG*880.48 (Pizus).—The remark of Phryn.1 (ἑκοντὴν οὐ χρὴ λέγειν, ἀλλ' ἐθελοντήν) refers not to this Adv., but to a Noun **ἑκοντής**, οῦ, ὁ, used by Epict.*Gnom*.67; ἑαυτὸν ἑκοντὴν παρέχων *IPE*1².40.21 (Olbia, ii/iii A.D.). **-ί**, Adv. *willingly*, Ps.-Phoc.16, Them.*Or*.16.209a; but ἑκόντι may generally be read, Arist.*Rh.Al*.1431ᵇ20, Plu.*Comp.Eum.Sert*.2.

**ἑκοτόν**, Arc. for ἑκατόν (q. v.).

**ἑκουσι-άζομαι**, *offer* or *be offered freely*, ἐν τῷ ἑκουσιασθῆναι λαόν Lxx *Jd*.5.2; ὁ -όμενος τῷ νόμῳ ib.1 *Ma*.2.42. **-ασμός**, ὁ, *free-will offering*, ib.2 *Es*.7.16, Aq.*Jd*.5.2, etc. **-ος**, α, ον S.*Tr*.727, 1123, etc.; also ος, ον Id.*Ph*.1318, E.*Supp*.151, Antipho 2.2.3, Th.6.44, etc.: (ἑκών):—of actions, *voluntary*, πόνοι Democr.240; βλάβαι S.*Ph*. l. c.; φυγή E. l. c.; ἁμάρτημα Antipho 5.92, etc.; συμβόλαια Pl.*R*.556b; πράξεις ib.603c, al.; ἀδικήματα Id.*Lg*.860e, al., etc.; γυμνασιαρχία *undertaken voluntarily*, *POxy*.473.3 (ii A.D.); τὰ ἑ. *voluntary acts*, opp. τὰ ἀκούσια, *IG*1.1, X.*Mem*.2.1.18, Arist.*EN*1109ᵇ31. 2. rarely of

persons, *willing, acting of free will*, ἥμαρτεν οὐχ ἑκουσία S.*Tr.*1123; ἑ. ἀποθανεῖν Th.1.138. II. Adv. -ίως E.*Tr.*1037, etc.; also ἑκουσίῳ τρόπῳ Id.*Med.*751; ἐξ ἑκουσίας (sc. γνώμης) S.*Tr.*727; καθ' ἑκουσίαν Th.8.27.

**ἑκουσιότης**, ητος, ἡ, *willingness*, Memn.32.1.

⊛ **ἐκπαγλ-έομαι**, *to be struck with amazement, to wonder greatly*, only used in part., καί μιν ἐπεδείκνυσαν ἐκπαγλεόμενοι Hdt.7.181, cf. 8.92; ἐκπαγλεομένων ὡς.. Id.9.48. II. *wonder at, admire exceedingly*, c. acc., A.*Ch.*217, E.*Or.*890, *Tr.*929; rare in Prose, D.H.1.40. **-ος**, ον, Ep. and Ion. word, *terrible, violent*: I. of persons, ὧδ' ἔ. ἐών, of Achilles, Il.21.589; πάντων ἐκπαγλότατ' ἀνδρῶν, also of Achilles, 1.146, 18.170; of other heroes, 20.389, 21.452. 2. sts. of things, χειμὼν ἔ. Od.14.522; ἐκπάγλοις ἐπέεσσιν Il.15.198, Od.8.77; ἔδεισεν γὰρ ἐμὴν ἔ. ἐνιπὴν 10.448, cf. 17.216. 3. mostly Adv. -λως *terribly, vehemently, exceedingly*, ἐ. ἀπόλεσσαν Il.1.268; κοτέοντο 2.223; ἐθέλει οἰκόνδε νέεσθαι ib.357; μαίνεται 9.238; ὠδύσατ' ἐ. Od.5.340; ἔχθαιρε 11.437; ὀδύρεται 15.355; αἴθεται Hp.*Mul.*2.171 (ἐκπατίως Erot.); ἐ. πονέει ib.1.3: neut. as Adv., ἔκπαγλον ἐπεύξατο Il.13.413, cf. Nic. *Th.*448, etc.; οὐ γὰρ ἐγώ σ' ἔ. ἀεικιῶ Il.22.256: neut. pl., ἔκπαγλα φιλεῖν to love *beyond all measure*, 3.415, 5.423; ἦν ἔ. χαλεφθῇ Nic. *Th.*445. II. in later Poets the word freq. signifies merely, *marvellous, wondrous*, ἀνὴρ ἔ. Pi.*P.*4.79; σθένει ἔ. Id.*I.*7(6).22; ἐν πόνοις ἔ. ib.6(5).54: not freq. in Trag., ἔ. κακόν, τέρας, A.*Ag.*862, *Ch.* 548; δείπνων ἀρρήτων ἔκπαγλ' ἄχθη S.*El.*204 (lyr.). Adv. ἔκπαγλα *marvellously*, Id.*OC*716 (lyr.): in early Prose only once, ὅπλα τὰ ἐκπαγλότατα X.*Hier.*11.3; in Com., Eup.8.14D.(Sup.). (Metath. for *ἔκπλαγος (ἐκπλήσσω) acc. to Eust.68.18; perh. dissim. from *ἔκπλαγλος.)

**ἐκπαγλότης**, ητος, ἡ, *enormity*, Hsch. (-πλαγ- cod.).

**ἐκπάθεια** [πᾰ], ἡ, *violent passion*, Longin.38.3.

⊛ **ἐκπᾰθής**, ές, (πάθος) *passionate, furious*, Plb.16.23.5, J.*AJ*15.3.4, etc.; ἐπί τινι Plb.1.7.8; ἐ. πρός τι *passionately eager* for a thing, Id. 1.1.6, etc. Adv. -θῶς Teles p.35 H., J.*BJ*2.18.4. II. *out of harm, unhurt*, Anon.ap.Suid.

**ἐκπαίδ-ευμα**, ατος, τό, *nursling, child*, E.*Cyc.*601. **-εύω**, *bring up from childhood*, ib.276; *train thoroughly*, ἐκθρέψαι καὶ ἐ. Pl.*Cri.* 45d, Luc.*Alex.*5. II. *teach* one a thing, τινά τι J.*Ap.*2.29, D.C. 45.2; but, III. ἐ. τινί τι *impress* on one *by education*, E.*Fr.*52.5 (lyr., s. v. l.).

**ἐκπαίζω**, *laugh to scorn, mock at*, Lxx 1*Es.*1.49(51), Phld.*Rh.*2. 216 S.

**ἐκπαιφάσσω**, *rush madly to the fray*, Il.5.803.

**ἐκπαίω**, *throw* or *cast out of* a thing, με δόξης ἐξέπαισαν ἐλπίδες they *have dashed* me *from* my expectations, E.*HF*460. II. intr., *dash out, escape*, Anaxil.22.17 (Casaubon for ἐξέπεσε):—Med., Plu. *Brut.*51. (Cf. ἐμπαίω.)

**ἔκπᾰλαι**, Adv. for ἐκ πάλαι, *for a long time*, Ph.1.323, 2*Ep.Pet.* 3.5, J.*AJ*16.8.4, Plu.2.548d, Plot.6.4.14, *POxy.*938.3 (iii/iv A. D.), etc.

**ἐκπάλαιστα** (ἐκ- Meineke)· δεινά, ὑπερήφανα, Hsch.: **ἐκπάλαιστος**· ἄνανδρος, Id.

**ἐκπᾰλαίω**, *transgress the laws of wrestling*, Philostr.*Im.*1.6.

**ἐκπᾰλ-εία**, ἡ, *dislocation*, *PMed.Lond.*155.3.11. **-έω**, of a joint, *start out of the socket*, Hp.*Fract.*42, *Art.*55. ⊛ **-ής**, ές, *out of joint*, ib.53, Hsch. **-ησις**, εως, ἡ, *dislocation*, Hp.*Fract.*42.

⊛ **ἐκπᾰλιγκοτεῖν** (prob.), = ἐναντιολογεῖν, Hsch. **ἐκπαλλακίδιοι**· οἱ νόθοι, Id.

**ἐκπάλλω**, *shake out*:—Pass., *spring* or *spurt out*, μυελὸς.. σφονδυλίων ἔκπαλθ' Il.20.483; also ἐκπάλη· ἐχωρίσθη, ἀπέστη, ἐξέπεσεν, Hsch.

**ἔκπαλτος**, ον, *excited*, dub. in Gal.19.543.

**ἔκπᾱμον** (-πάλιον cod.)· ἀκλήρωτον, Hsch.; cf. παμῶχος.

**ἐκπᾰνουργέω**, strengthd. for πανουργέω, Sch.Ar.*Eq.*270.

**ἐκπαππόομαι**, Pass., of seeds, *become plumous*, Thphr.*HP*3.16.6, 6.4.8, Dsc.3.118.

**ἔκπαππος**, ὁ, *great great-grandfather*, *IGRom.*3.474.

**ἐκπαραπίπτω**, Astrol., *fail to combine*, Vett.Val.93.30.

**ἐκπαρθενεύω**, (παρθένος) *deflower*, Sch.Luc.*DMar.*7.1.

**ἐκπᾰτᾰγέω**, *deafen*, τὰ ὦτα Them.*Or.*21.253c: but aor. 1 ἐξεπατάγησαν· ἐξεφώνησαν, Hsch.

**ἐκπᾰτάσσω**, *strike, afflict*, τινὰ κακοῖσι E.*HF*890 (-πετάσουσιν codd.): metaph., γρηῢν βροντῆς ἐξεπάταξε φόβος *AP*9.309 (Antip. ⟨Thess.⟩):—Pass., φρένας ἐκπεπαταγμένος *stricken* in mind, Od.18. 327; ἐξεπατάχθη· ἐξεπλάγη, Hsch.

**ἐκπᾰτ-έω**, *withdraw from society*, D.L.1.112. II. pf. part. -πεπᾰτηκώς *having finished his walk*, Id.4.19. III. Pass., *to be avoided*, Metrod.60. **-ιος**, ον, (πάτος) *out of the common path*: *excessive*, ἄλγεα A.*Ag.*49 (anap.); expld. by Sch. as *lonely*. Adv. -ίως v.l. for ἐκπάγλως (ap.Erot.) in Hp.*Mul.*2.171. **-ος**, ὁ, = ἀπόπατος, Theognost.*Can.*24; cf. ὑσπέλεθος.

**ἔκ-παυμα**, ατος, τό, *total rest*, Hsch. **-παύω**, strengthd. for παύω, *set quite at rest, put an end to*, μόχθους E.*Ion* 144 (lyr.):—Med., *take one's rest*, Th.5.75.

**ἐκπαφλ-άζω**, *boil* or *bubble over*, Arist.*Pr.*936ᵇ23. **-ασμός**, ὁ, *boiling over*, ib.29.

**ἐκπᾰχύνω**, *make over-fat*, Thphr.*CP*4.1.4 (Pass.).

**ἔκπεδος**, ον, = ἔκπους, *IG*7.3073.75 (Lebad.).

**ἐκπείθω**, *persuade completely, over-persuade*, S.*OT*1024, *Tr.*1141, E.*HF*469, *PHal.*7.6 (iii B. C.), etc.

**ἐκπειρ-άζω**, *tempt*, c. acc., Lxx *De.*6.16, al., 1*Ep.Cor.*10.9. **-άομαι**, aor. ἐξεπειράθην [ᾱ], *make trial of, prove, tempt*, c. gen. pers., Hdt.3. 135: c. inf., ἐκπειρᾷ λέγειν; *art* thou *tempting* me to speak? S.*OT* 360 codd.: folld. by a relat., κἀξεπειράθην.. οἷον στέρεσθαι γίγνεται E.*Supp.*1089; ἐ. εἴτε.. Pl.*Ep.*362e. 2. *inquire, ask of another*, τί τινος Ar.*Eq.*1234.—Late in Act., Hld.7.19.

**ἐκπεκτουμένη**· κτενιζομένη, Hsch.

**ἐκπέλει**, impers., = ἔξεστι, *it is permitted* or *allowed*, S.*Ant.*478:— Hsch. has ἐξέπηλεν (leg. ἐξέπελεν)· ἐξεγένετο.

**ἐκπελεκάω**, *hew, cut away with an axe*, *IG*2.1054b9, Thphr.*HP*9.2. 7, *IG*11(2).144A64 (Delos, iv B. C.).

**ἐκπελεύει**· ἐξωθεῖ, Hsch.

**ἐκπεμπτέος**, α, ον, *that must be sent out*, Plu.2.595c. 2. ἐκπεμπτέον *one must reject*, Porph.*Abst.*2.31.

⊛ **ἐκπέμπω**: I. of persons, *send out* or *forth from*, c. gen. loci, ὅπως Πρίαμον.. νηῶν ἐκπέμψειε Il.24.681; ὅς τίς σε.. δώματος ἐκπέμψῃσι Od.18.336, cf. S.*El.*1128; ἐ. ἐκ τῆς πόλεως Isoc.6.78:—Med., δόμου ἐκπέμψασθε θύραζε Od.20.361, cf. S.*Aj.*612 (lyr.), etc. 2. *bring out by calling, call* or *fetch out*, τινὰ ἐκτὸς πυλῶν Id.*Ant.*19:—so in Med., Id.*OT*951:—Pass., *go forth, depart*, Id.*OC*1664. 3. *send forth, dispatch*, πρέσβεις, στρατιάς, οἰκήτορας, Th.1.90, 141, 4.49; ἐ. συμπρεσβευτὰς τοὺς ἐχθρούς Arist.*Pol.*1271ᵃ24; ἐ. ἀποικίας οἷον σμῆνη μελιττῶν Pl.*Plt.*293d, cf. Arist.*Pol.*1273ᵇ19:—Pass., τῶν -ομένων καὶ εἰσαγομένων ἐπιστολῶν Aen.Tact.10.6. 4. *send away*, τινὰ ἐς.. Hdt.1.160; ἐ. τινὰ ἄτιμον S.*OT*789; καθάρμαθ' ὥς τις ἐκπέμψας A.*Ch.* 98: in Prose, *divorce* a wife, ἐ. γυναῖκα Hdt.1.59, Lys.14.28, cf. D.59. 55:—also in Med., γῆς φυγάδας ἐκπέμψασθαι S.*OT*309. 5. c. dupl. acc., *conduct across*, τινὰ τὸν Ἰορδάνην Lxx 2*Ki.*19.31. II. of things, *send out, send abroad*, κειμήλια πολλὰ καὶ ἐσθλά.. ἵνα περ τάδε τοι σόα μίμνῃ Il.24.381; δῶρά τινι Hdt.1.136; σῖτόν τινι Th.4.16 (nisi leg. ἐσ-). 2. *export*, ἐ. ὧν ἐπλεόναζον Arist.*Pol.*1257ᵃ32:—Med., τὰ πλεονάζοντα τῶν γιγνομένων ἐκπέμψασθαι *export* their surplus products, ib.1327ᵃ27. 3. *send forth, give out*, σέλας A.*Ag.*281; πνεῦμα, [ὑγρόν], Arist.*PA*664ᵃ18, *HA*589ᵇ18; δυσοσμίαν Alciphr.3.28. 4. *utter, pronounce*, A.D.*Pron.*35.1 (Pass.).

**ἔκπεμψις**, εως, ἡ, *sending out* or *forth*, στρατιᾶς Th.4.85, cf. *SIG* 285.8. 2. *emission, expulsion*, πνεύματος Gal.*UP*6.2.

**ἐκπεπαίνω**, *make quite ripe* or *mellow*, καρπόν, χυλούς, Thphr.*HP* 5.1.1, *CP*1.16.2:—Pass., Medic., *to be concocted*, Hp.*Epid.*4.56.

**ἐκπεπληγμένως**, Adv., διακεῖσθαι *to be in a state of panic*, D.*Prooem.* 39.1.

**ἐκπέποται**, 3 sg. pf. Pass. of ἐκπίνω, Od.22.56.

**ἐκπεπτᾰμένως**, Adv., (ἐκπετάννυμι) *extravagantly*, X.*Cyr.*8.7.7.

**ἐκπεραίνω**, *finish off*, A.*Fr.*78; βίοτον E.*HF*428 (lyr.):—Pass., of oracles, *to be fulfilled*, Id.*Ion* 785, *Cyc.*696; of works, *to be accomplished*, X.*An.*5.1.13.

**ἐκπεραιόω**, *cross over*, Tz.*H.*3.494.

**ἐκπέρᾱμα**, ατος, τό, *coming out of*, δωμάτων A.*Ch.*655.

**ἐκπερᾰτόομαι**, *find one's limit*, Him.*Or.*1.13 (s. v. l.).

⊛ **ἐκπεράω** (Arc. ἐσ-, v. infr. 1.4), Ep. impf. ἐκπεράασκε *AP*9.381:— *go out over, pass beyond*, λαῖτμα μέγ' ἐκπερόωσιν Od.7.35; ἥ τ' ἐκπερᾷ μέγα λαῖτμα 9.323; χθόνα A.*Pr.*713; αὐλῶνα ib.731; χέρσον καὶ θάλασσαν Id.*Eu.*240; ἐ. βίον *go through* life, E.*IA*18 (anap.); ὀγδώκοντ' ἔτεα *AP*6.226 (Leon.); κῦμα συμφορᾶς E.*Hipp.*824. 2. abs., of an arrow, *pass through, pierce*, ὀϊστὸς ἀντικρὺ.. ὑπ' ὀστέον ἐξεπέρησεν Il. 13.652, cf. 16.346, etc.; of persons, *go forth*, X.*Cyn.*6.18; Ἀθήνας to Athens, Eub.10.5. 3. c. gen., *go* or *come out of*, μελάθρων E. *Cyc.*512 (lyr.). 4. *transgress*, ἐσπερᾶσαι πὰρ ἂν λέγῃ ἱεροθύτας *IG* 5(2).6 (Tegea, iv B. C.). II. *carry out* or *away*, Lxx *Nu.*11.31.

**ἐκπερδῑκίζω**, *escape like a partridge*, Ar.*Av.*768.

**ἐκπέρθω**, fut. -πέρσω, *destroy utterly, sack*, of cities, Il.1.19, al. (never in Od.), A.*Th.*427, etc.; also τὴν Διὸς τυραννίδ' ἐ. βίᾳ Id.*Pr.* 359: metaph., μὴ ἡμῖν.. τὸν Σιμωνίδην ἐκπέρσῃ Pl.*Prt.*340a. II. *take as booty from*, τὰ μὲν πολίων ἐξεπράθομεν Il.1.125.

**ἐκπερι-άγω** [ᾰ], *lead out round*, Plb.3.83.3; τοὺς ἀγκῶνας *tie behind the back*, Lys.ap.Iamb.*VP*17.78:—Pass., *to be passed round*, Porph. *Hist.Phil.Fr.*4. **-ειμι**, *go out and round, go all round*, X.*Cyn.*6.10, dub. in Hld.7.19; τὰ ὄρη Luc.*Rh.Pr.*5; τὴν κύκλῳ [ὁδόν] Jul.*Or.*7. 225c. **-έρχομαι**, = foreg., Plb.10.31.3, Onos.22.4, Plu.2.614c, Luc. *Asin.*18: c. acc., *traverse, include in one's survey*, τὰ φανερὰ πάντα Phld.*Sign.*19, cf. *Rh.*1.154 S.; τὸν Πόντον Plu.*Caes.*58; πόλεις J.*AJ* 6.1.1. 2. *surround, envelop*, Hdn.3.3.8. II. *circumvent*, J. *AJ*5.1.14, al. **-οδεύω**, *go all round*, ib.3.6.8. II. metaph., *survey completely*, Phld.*Mort.*37, S.E.*M.*7.188. 2. *circumvent*, J. *AJ*17.2.4, Plu.2.705d. **-πλέω**, fut. -πλεύσομαι, *to sail out round*, so as to attack in flank, Plb.1.23.9; τὰς σχεδίας J.*BJ*3.10.9; *circumnavigate*, Λιβύην Arr.*An.*4.7.5: abs., ib.6.28.6; ταῖς ναυσί Plu.*Aem.* 15:—Ion. -πλώω, Arr.*Ind.*20.1. **-πορεύομαι**, *make a detour*, 'fetch a compass', of a boundary, Lxx *Jo.*15.3. II. *march round*, Ael.*Tact.*34.4. **-σπασμός**, ὁ, an evolution consisting of *a right-about face* (περισπασμός) *followed by a wheel to r.* or *l.*, Plb.10.23.3, Ascl.*Tact.*10.8, etc. **-σπάω**, *execute this manœuvre*, ib.12.7, Arr. *Tact.*32.1:—Pass., Ascl.*Tact.*10.11.

**ἐκπερισσεύω**, *to be superfluous*, *Cod.Just.*10.27.2.4.

**ἐκπερισσῶς**, Adv. *more exceedingly*, *Ev.Marc.*14.31.

**ἐκπεριτρέχω**, *run all about*, Aristaenet.1.27: metaph., Procl.*in Prm.*p.781 S.

**ἐκπερονάω**, *string together*, χρησμούς *Rev.Ét.Gr.*4.281 (Erythrae).

**ἐκπέρῠσι**, Adv. *more than a year ago*, Luc.*Sol.*7.

⊛ **ἐκπέσσω**, Att. -ττω, *cook thoroughly*: hence, 1. of animals, *digest* or *concoct* food *thoroughly*, Hp.*VM*22. 2. of plants, *ripen*, τὸν καρπόν Thphr.*HP*2.2.4:—Pass., of nourishment, *to be assimilated*, Arist.*Col.*799$^a$11. 3. of eggs, *hatch*, Id.*HA*562$^b$18 (Pass.), al. 4. *ripen, bring to a head*, of an abscess, Dsc.*Eup.*1.142.

**ἐκπετάζω**, = ἐκπετάννυμι, Lxx 2*Es.*9.5.

**ἐκπέτᾰλος**, ον, *outspread, flat*, ἀγγεῖον Mosch.ap.Ath.11.485e (Comp.), cf. Sch.Ar.*Ach.*1109.

**ἐκπετ-άννῡμι**, fut. -πετάσω, *spread out*, of a sail, E.*IT*1135 (lyr.); πώγωνα Luc.*Tim.*54; χεῖρας Lxx *Is.*65.2; of wings, *AP*5.178.10 (Mel.); τὰ ὦτα ἐξεπετάννυτο ὥσπερ σκιάδειον Ar.*Eq.*1348; of a net, τὸ δὲ δίκτυον ἐκπεπέτασται Orac.ap.Hdt.1.62; στέφος ἐξεπέτασσε *scattered* it *to the winds*, Bion 1.88. 2. metaph., ἐπὶ κῶμον ἐκπετασθεὶς *wholly given up to* the revel, E.*Cyc.*497 (lyr.): pf. part. Pass. ἐκπεπταμένος *wide open*, κοῖλα καὶ ἐ. Hp.*VM*22; of *gaping* wounds, Id.*Off.* 11; ἐ. τοῖς βλεφάροις Ael.*NA*2.12. -ᾰσις, εως, ἡ, *spreading out*, Plu.2.564c. -ασμα, ατος, τό, *that which is spread out* or *unfolded*: pl., title of a work by Democritus, D.L.9.47. II. *planisphere*, Ptol.*Geog.*7.7 tit.

**ἐκπετήσιμος**, ον, *ready to fly out of the nest, just fledged*, Ar.*Av.* 1355, Ael.*NA*2.43, Procop.*Vand.*1.4: metaph., of a *marriageable girl*, πρὸς ἄνδρας ἐ. Ar.*Fr.*582.

⊛ **ἐκπέτομαι** (-πέταμαι Arist.*HA*554$^b$1), fut. -πτήσομαι Ar.*V.*208: aor. ἐξεπτόμην, part. -πτόμενος Id.*Av.*788; also ἐξεπτάμην E.*El.*944, Pl.*Ti.*81e, ἐκπτάμενος Ἀθηνᾶ 20.249 (Chios): also in act. form ἐξέπτην Hes.*Op.*98, Batr.211, Ant.Lib.1.5, Palaeph.12: for aor. ἐξεπετάσθην, v. πέτομαι:—*fly out* or *away*, ll. cc.: metaph., ἔπαινοι Ἔρωσι μικροῖς ἐοικότες ἐκπετόμενοι Luc.*Rh.Pr.*6.

**ἐκπετρίδδειν**· παχύνειν ἱμάτιον (Lacon.), Hsch.

**ἐκπεύθομαι**, = ἐκπυνθάνομαι, A.*Pers.*955 (lyr.).

**ἐκπεφῠῖαι**, pf. part. of ἐκφύω.

**ἔκπεψις**, εως, ἡ, *cooking, baking*, *BGU*1.17 (iii A.D.), etc.

**ἐκπήγνῡμι** (-ύω Plu.2.978b), *make stiff* or *torpid*, l.c.; esp. of frost, *congeal, freeze*, Thphr.*CP*5.14.2:—Pass., *become stiff, congeal*, Str. 7.5.11; *to be frozen, frost-bitten*, Thphr.*HP*5.14.3.

⊛ **ἐκπηδ-άω**, fut. -πηδήσομαι Luc.*Zeux.*8, -ήσω App.*Hisp.*20: pf. -πεπήδηκα Men.*Pk.*277:—*leap out*, ἐς τὴν θάλασσαν Hdt.8.118 (v.l. ἐκπηδέειν, cf. 1.24); ἐπί τινα Lys.3.12. 2. *make a sally*, X.*An.* 7.4.16, App. l.c.; ἐκ τῆς ἐνέδρας *Hell.Oxy.*16.2; *escape*, ἐκ τῆς πόλεως Men.*Per.Fr.*3, cf. Wilcken *Chr.*1 ii 13 (iii B.C.), Plb.1.43.1: metaph., ἐ. ἐκ τῶν τεχνῶν εἰς τὴν φιλοσοφίαν Pl.*R.*495d. 3. *leap up, start*, εὕδουσαν ἐ. S.*Tr.*175; τοῦ ὕπνου Philostr.*VA*2.36; *throb*, of the heart, Aristaenet.2.5; λόγος ἐ. τοῦ στόματος ib.10. II. *start out of place*, σπόνδυλος ἐ. Hp.*Art.*46. -ημα, ατος, τό, *leap out*, ὕψος κρεῖσσον ἐκπηδήματος a height too great *for over-leap*, A.*Ag.*1376. -ησις, εως, ἡ, *leaping forth*, ἐν ὕψει Pl.*Lg.*815a (pl.). -ητικός, ή, όν, *bounding*, of the pulse, Gal.8.487.

**ἐκπηκτικός**, ή, όν, *freezing*, ἀήρ Thphr.*CP*5.14.7.

**ἐκπηνίζομαι**, fut. -ιοῦμαι, *spin a long thread*, [οἱ ἀράχναι] φερόμενοι ὑπὸ τοῦ πνεύματος πολὺ ἐ. Arist.*Pr.*947$^b$2: metaph., of an advocate, αὐτοῦ ἐκπηνιεῖται ταῦτα *will wind* these things *out of* him, Ar.*Ra.* 578.

**ἔκπηξις**, εως, ἡ, *stiffening, freezing*, Thphr.*CP*5.14.1 (pl.), al.

**ἐκπῐ-άζω**, = ἐκπιέζω, Lxx *Jd.*6.38, Str.16.2.43, *PHolm.*18.18. -ασμα, ατος, τό, = ἐκπίεσμα, Hsch. s. v. ἐπίτερα: -ασμός, ὁ, v. ἐκπιεσμός.

**ἐκπῑδύομαι** [ῠ], *gush forth*, A.*Pers.*815 (Schütz for ἐκπαιδεύεται).

**ἐκπῐ-έζω**, *squeeze out*, σπόγγος ἐξ ὕδατος ἐκπεπιεσμένος Hp.*Acut.* 21, cf. Dsc.1.50; *thrust* or *force out*, τοὺς προσβάλλοντας Plb.18.32. 3:—Pass., *to be squeezed out*, Arist.*Mu.*397$^a$23, Dsc.1.52; ἕλκος ἐκπεπιεσμένον a sore *that protrudes out of the skin*, dub. in Hp.*Fract.*25 (cf. ἐκπλίσσομαι). II. *oppress*, Lxx 1*Ki.*12.3: a form ἐκπιεζέω ib.*Ez.*22.29:—Pass., Plb.3.74.2. -εσμα, ατος, τό, *that which is squeezed out, juice*, Dsc.1.52, Archig.ap.Gal.12.551. II. false form for ἐμπίεσμα (q.v.), Gal.19.432, 14.782. -εσμός, ὁ, *squeezing out*, Hp.*Nat.Puer.*21, Arist.*Mu.*394$^a$28, Epicur.*Ep.*2p.45 U. (ἐκπιασμόν codd.). II. *exophthalmos*, Aët.7.2. -εστήριον (sc. ὄργανον), τό, *press*, Demioprat.ap.Poll.10.135. -εστός, ή, όν, *squeezed out*: ἐ. ξύλα logs *cleft by the wedge and mallet*, Arist.*Pr.* 915$^a$9.

**ἐκπικρ-άζομαι**, = ἐκπικρόομαι II, Hp.*Mul.*1.26. -αίνομαι, *to be embittered*, Nic.Dam.p.34 D.; πρὸς τὴν ἀπειλήν D.H.19.5; πρός τινα J.*AJ*5.7.1; ἐπί τινι D.H.4.38, Ath.8.351b, etc. 2. = sq. II, Hp. *Mul.*2.133. -όομαι, *become very bitter*, Arist.*Pr.*880$^a$29, Thphr. *CP*4.2.1. II. *have a bitter taste in the mouth*, Hp.*Aph.*4.17. -ος, ον, *very bitter*, Arist.*Pr.*880$^a$24. -ωσις, εως, ἡ, *making bitter*, Gal. 12.558.

**ἐκπίμπλημι**, *fill up*, κρατῆρα E.*Cyc.*388; ἐκ δ' ἐπίμπλαμεν δρόσου κρατῆρας *filled* them *full of*.., Id.*Ion*1194. 2. *satiate*, ὄμματ' ἐξεπίμπλαμεν Id.*Andr.*1087; ἐκπιμπλάναι τὴν αὐτίκα φιλονικίαν Th.3. 82; τὰς ἐπιθυμίας D.C.41.27:—Pass., ὡς ἐξεπλήσθη [τὸ νόσημα] S.*Ph.* 759. II. *fulfil*, ἐξέπλησε μοῖραν τὴν ἑωυτοῦ *fulfilled* his destiny, Hdt.3.142; ἐ. τοῦ ὀνείρου τὴν φήμην Id.1.43; ἐ. τὸν νόμον *to satisfy the requirements of* the law, Id.1.199, 4.117; πέμπτου γονέος ἁμαρτάδα ἐξέπλησε *paid the full penalty of* the sin of Gyges, Id.1.91. III. *accomplish*, ἐνιαυτὸν ἐξέπλησεν S.*Tr.*253; ἀρὰς.. ἔοικεν ἐκπλῆσαι θεός E.*Ph.*1426; ἱερά τ' ἐξεπίμπλασαν Id.*Supp.*722; ἐ. πλῆθος κακῶν *to narrate in full*, A.*Pers.*430; μοχθήματα, etc., E.*Hel.*735, etc.; πανταχοῦ γὰρ ἄστεως ζητῶν νιν ἐξέπλησα I *have finished* seeking her in every part, Id.*Ion*1108. IV. *fill up* or *complete* a number, ἐ. τὸ ἐλλεῖπον (as v.l. for ἐκπληρώσατε) X.*Cyr.*4.5.39; τὸ ἱππικόν ib.6. 1.26, cf. Arr.*Tact.*14.2.

**ἐκπίμπραμαι**, *to be kindled*, Arist.*Mete.*346$^b$12.

⊛ **ἐκπίνω** [ῑ], fut. -πίομαι Amips.22.2, -πιοῦμαι Arist.*Rh.*1393$^b$31:—*drink out* or *off*, *quaff* liquor, Hom. only in Od., in Ep. aor., [ποτὸν] ἔκπιεν 9.353; ἔκπιον [οἶνον] 10.237: pf. Pass., ὅσσα τοι ἐκπέποται 22. 56, cf. Hdt.4.199; ἐκπίνουσ' ἀεὶ ψυχῆς.. αἷμα S.*El.*785; δι' αἵματ' ἐκποθένθ' ὑπὸ χθονὸς A.*Ch.*66 (lyr.); ἐκπίνειν ὑστάτην πόσιν Antipho 1. 20; also of bugs, ticks, and the like, *drain*, τὴν ψυχὴν ἐ. Ar.*Nu.*712; τὸ αἷμα Arist.*Rh.*1393$^b$31:—Pass., σῶμα.. ἐξεπόθη *IG*14.2002. 2. *drain* a cup *dry*, πλῆρες ἐ. κέρας S.*Fr.*483; μὴ 'κπιεῖν ἀλλ' ἢ μίαν (sc. κύλικα) Pherecr.143.9; ὅλην μύσας ἔκπιε Antiph.3, etc.; also ὡς ἔχιδν' ὑφειμένη λήθουσά μ' ἐξέπινες S.*Ant.*532. 3. metaph., ἐ. ὄλβον E.*Hipp.*[626]; τὰ χρήματα Pl.Com.9; ἀγρόν Alciphr.*Fr.* 6.2. 4. Pass., *to be absorbed*, Diog.Apoll.6.

**ἐκπιπίζω** or -πινίζω, *suck out*, *Gloss.* (perh. ff. ll. for -πιτίζω).

⊛ **ἐκπιπράσκω**, *sell off*, pf. Pass. ἐκπέπρᾱται D.9.39, cf. Poll.7.9.

⊛ **ἐκπίπτω**, fut. -πεσοῦμαι: aor. ἐξέπεσον: pf. ἐκπέπτωκα:—*fall out of*, δίφρου Il.5.585; ἵππων 11.179; ἀντύγων ἄπο E.*Ph.*1193, etc.: c. dat. pers., τόξον δέ οἱ ἔκπεσε χειρός Il.15.465; θαλερὸν δέ οἱ ἔκπεσε δάκρυ *fell from* his eyes, 2.266: abs., *fall out*, 23.467; *fall down*, of trees, Thphr.*HP*9.2.7; οἱ λεγόμενοι ἀστέρες ἐκπίπτειν *meteors*, Epicur. *Ep.*2p.54 U.—After Hom., in various relations, freq. as Pass. of ἐκβάλλω: 1. of seafaring men, *to be cast ashore*, ἐκ δ' ἔπεσον θυμηγερέων Od.7.283; ἐ. τῇσι νηυσὶ ἐς Ἰηπυγίην Hdt.3.138; πρὸς τὰς πέτρας Id.8.13; πρὸς πέτραις E.*Hel.*1211; ναυαγὸν ἐ. ib.539; ἐ. πρὸς τὴν χώραν Pl.*Lg.*866d; of things, *suffer shipwreck*, X.*An.*7.5.13; of fish, *to be cast up*, Arist.*HA*601$^b$32. 2. *fall from* a thing, i.e. *be deprived of* it, ἐκ πολλῶν καὶ εὐδαιμόνων ἐς πτωχηΐην Hdt.3.14, cf. Lys.*Fr.*1.1; τυραννίδος, ἀρχῆς, A.*Pr.*756, 757; [ἀπὸ] τῶν ἐλπίδων Th.8.81; ἐκ τῆς δόξης Isoc.5.64; τῶν ὑπαρχόντων Phld.*Ir.*p.51 W. 3. *to be driven out*, [ἐκ τῆς ἀκροπόλιος] Hdt.5.72; *to be banished*, ἐ. ἐκ τῆς πατρίδος Id. 1.150, cf. 6.121; ἐ. χθονός S.*OC*766, cf. *Aj.*1177; ἐ. πολέμῳ ἢ στάσει Th.1.2; γυμνὸς θύραζ' ἐξέπεσον Ar.*Pl.*244; ὑπό τινος by a person, ἐκ Πελοποννήσου ὑπὸ Μήδων Hdt.8.141; ὑπὸ τοῦ πλήθους Th.4.66, cf. *Inscr.Prien.*37.71; πρός τινος A.*Pr.*948, S.*Ant.*679:—in Th.7.50 the prep. ἐς is corrupt. 4. of limbs, *to be dislocated*, Hp.*Art.*8, etc.; of flesh, *mortify and separate itself*, Id.*Fract.*27; so ἐ. ὀδόντες, πτερά, Arist.*GA*745$^b$6, *HA*519$^a$26, etc.; of atoms, ἐκπεσοῦσαι κατέψυξαν Epicur.*Fr.*60. 5. *go forth, sally out*, Hdt.9.74; ἐκ τοῦ σταυρώματος X.*HG*4.4.11: abs., Id.*An.*5.2.17; of rays, *issue forth*, Alex. Aphr. *de An.*127.31. 6. *come out*, of votes, X.*Smp.*5.10; *turn out, happen*, Vett.Val.70.27, al. 7. *escape*, Th.6.95. 8. of oracles, *issue*, χρησμὸς ἐκπίπτει Luc.*Alex.*43, etc.; ἐκπεσεῖν φωνὴν ἐξ ἄλσους Plu.*Publ.*9; *to be published, become known*, εἰς ἀνθρώπους ἀπαιδεύτους Pl.*Ep.*314a; φήμη ἐ. ἐς τοὺς Ἕλληνας Plu.*Cleom.*5: abs., ἀπόκρισις ἐ. Plb.30.32.10. 9. *depart*, ἐκ τῆς ὁδοῦ X.*An.*5.2.31; ἐκ τοῦ ἐπιτηδεύματος Pl.*R.*495a. b. *digress*, Isoc.12.88; ἐ. ἐκ τοῦ λόγου Aeschin. 2.34; but ἐ. τῆς διανοίας *miss* the sense, Olymp. *in Mete.*7.26; *fall outside of* a class, Alex.Aphr. *de An.*169.17. 10. of things, *escape* one *unawares*, φασὶν ἐκπεσεῖν αὐτούς Arist.*EN*1111$^a$9, cf. Plu.*Per.*8; ἐ. τὴν αἴσθησιν Alex.Aphr. *in Sens.*147.18; of reason, *fail, be lacking*, Arist.*MM*1202$^a$3. 11. *degenerate*, εἰς ἀλλότριον ἦθος Pl.*R.*497b; εἰς τὴν Φρυγιστὶ ἁρμονίαν *slip* into.., Arist.*Pol.*1342$^b$11: abs., *come to naught*, *Ep.Rom.*9.6; *to be dilapidated*, *IG*2$^2$.204.74. 12. of actors or dramatic pieces, *to be hissed off the stage*, D.18.265, Arist.*Po.*1456$^a$ 18, 1459$^b$31: so of orators, Pl.*Grg.*517a, cf. *Phlb.*13d. 13. ἐ. ἑαυτοῦ *lose* one's self-control, Philostr.*VA*3.36; ἐ. σκοποῦ *miss* the mark, ib.8.7. 14. of things, *arise from*, ἔκ τινος A.D.*Adv.*136.3. 15. of money, *cease to be current*, *IG*7.303.14 (Oropus, iii B.C.). 16. *run to excess*, δι' ἀοριστίαν Epicur.*Sent.Vat.*63; [ὁ πλοῦτος] εἰς ἄπειρον ἐ. Id.*Sent.*15, cf. Luc.*JConf.*7. b. Geom., as Pass. of ἐκβάλλω, *to be produced*, Archim.*Spir.*14. 17. *die*, χθὼν ἐκπιπτόντων *Not. Scav.*1923.35 (unless, = *rubbish* heap).

**ἐκπίτνω**, = ἐκπίπτω, θρόνων A.*Pr.*912.

**ἐκπῐτ-ύζω**, *eject* water *under pressure*, Hero *Spir.*1.28 (Pass.). -υσμός, ὁ, *jet* of water, ibid.

⊛ **ἐκπλᾰγής**, ές, (ἐκπλήσσω) *panic-stricken*, Plb.1.76.7, al.; ἐπί τινι Id.2.3.3; τῷ πράγματι Luc.*DMar.*15.2.

**ἐκπλᾰνάω**, *delude, cause to go astray*, Hsch. s. v. ἐξηπάτησεν.

**ἐκπλάσσω**, *model exactly*, Chaerem.1.6 (Pass.). 2. *make into a plaster*, *Hippiatr.*10.

**ἔκπλαστο**· ἐξεπήδησεν, Hsch. (leg. ἔκπαλτο).

**ἐκπλᾰτύνω**, *flatten out*, Sor.1.102; ἀγγεῖον -υσμένον *broad at the top*, Sch.Il.23.243.

⊛ **ἐκπλεθρίζω**, *run round and round, in a course which narrows every time*, Gal.6.133.

⊛ **ἔκπλεθρος**, ον, *six plethra long*, Phryn.387; in ἔ. ἀγών, = στάδιον, E.*El.*883, and κῶλον ἔ. δρόμου Id.*Med.*1181 (where Sch. expl. μέγα καὶ ὑπερβαῖνον πλέθρου μέτρον) ἔ. is the better reading, *narrowing*.

⊛ **ἐκπλέκω**, *unfold*, διάνοιαν Alex.*Fig.*2.1.

**ἐκπλεονάζω**, strengthd. for πλεονάζω, Arist.*Pr.*882$^a$25.

**ἔκπλεος**, ον, neut. pl. ἔκπλεα D.C.38.20: poet. **ἔκπλειος**, α, ον: Att. **ἔκπλεως**, ων:—*quite full* of a thing, c. gen., δαιτός, βορᾶς, E.*Cyc.*247, 416. 2. *complete*, εὖρος τριγύνου *Tab.Heracl.*2.31; of a number of soldiers, ἱππεῖς ἔκπλεῳ.. εἰς τοὺς μυρίους X.*Cyr.*6.2.7; *abundant, copious*, ἐπιτήδεια ib.1.6.7, cf. D.C. l.c.

**ἔκπλευρος**, ον, *six-sided*, Phryn.387.

**ἔκπλευσις**, εως, ἡ, = ἔκπλους, τῶν στόλων Procl.*Par.Ptol.*117 (pl.).

⊛ **ἐκπλέω**, fut. -πλεύσομαι: pf. -πέπλευκα *IG*2.793$^a$7: Ion. **ἐκπλώω**, aor. -έπλωσα: pf. πέπλωκα Lyc.1084:—*sail out* or *away*, τοῦ Πόντου Hdt.6.5; ἔξω τοῦ Ἑλλησπόντου Id.5.103; τῆσδ' ἐ. χθονὸς S.*Ph.*1375; ἐκ τῆσδε γῆς ib.577; ἐ. ἐς ἀποικίην Hdt.6.22; κατ' Εὐρώπης ζήτησιν, κατὰ ληΐην, Id.2.44,152; ἐπί τινα against.., Th.1.37; of fish, *swim out*, ἀγεληδὸν ἐ. ἐς θάλασσαν Hdt.2.93. 2. metaph., ἐκπλεῖν τῶν φρενῶν *go out of* one's mind, *lose* one's senses, Id.3.155, Ael.*Fr.* 240. II. rarely c. acc. loci, *sail out past*, τὸ ἔθνος τῶν Ἰχθυοφάγων Arr.*Ind.*29.7, cf. Lyc.1084, A.R.2.645. 2. c. acc. cogn., ἐ. τὸν ὕστερον ἔκπλουν D.49.6. III. trans., ἐ. ἐς τὴν εὐρυχωρίαν τὰς τῶν πολεμίων ναῦς *outsail* them into the open sea, Th.8.102 (s.v.l.).

**ἔκπλεως**, v. ἔκπλεος.

⊛ **ἐκπλήγδην**, Adv. *terribly*, Suid.

**ἐκπλήγνῡμι**, = ἐκπλήσσω, Th.4.125 (Pass.).

**ἐκπληκτ-ικός**, ή, όν, *striking with consternation, astounding*, θόρυβος Th.8.92; ἐ. τοῖς ἐχθροῖς X.*Eq.Mag.*8.18 (Comp.); ἐκπληκτικώτερον *more surprising* or *startling*, Arist.*Po.*1460$^b$25: Sup., Plb.3.4.5, Onos. 22.4. II. Adv. -κῶς *terribly*, D.S.14.25: Sup. -ώτατα Ael.*NA* 11.32. 2. *with enthusiasm*, ἀποδέξασθαί τινα Plb.10.5.2. -ος, ον, *terrifying*, Luc.*Herm.*18. II. *amazed, terror-stricken*, Orph. *H.*39.10, Man.4.81, Poll.5.72. III. Adv. -τως *rashly*, Ael.*NA*3. 22. IV. *astounding*, *Riv.Fil.*53.208 (Crete).

**ἐκπλημμῡρέω**, *gush out and overflow*, τοῦ γενείου Philostr.Jun.*Im.* 4:—also -πλημμύρω, ib.8.

**ἐκπληξ-ία**, ἡ, = sq., Callistr.*Stat.*14. -ις, εως, ἡ, *consternation*, ἐκπλήξιες τῆς γνώμης Hp.*Aër.*16, cf. Pl.*Phlb.*47a, etc.; ἐ. κακῶν *terror caused by* misfortunes, A.*Pers.*606; ἐ. παρέχειν Antipho 5.6, Th.4.55; ἐς ἐ. καθιστάναι, ἀγαγεῖν, Id.6.36, Philostr.Jun.*Im.*4; ἐ. ἐνέπεσεν ἀνθρώποις Th.4.34. II. *mental disturbance, passion*, Plb.3.81.6.

⊛ **ἐκπληρ-όω**, *fill up*, ἑκατὸν ἐχίδναις ἀσπίδ' ἐ. E.*Ph.*1135. 2. *make up* to a certain number, ἐκπληροῦσι τὰς ἴσας μυριάδας ἐκείνοισι Hdt.7.186; ἐξεπληροῦτο τὸ ναυτικὸν ἐς τὰς..τριηκοσίας ναῦς Id.8.82; δέκατον ἐκπληρῶν ὄχον *making up the number of* ten chariots, S.*El.* 708; ἐ. τοὺς ἱππέας εἰς δισχιλίους X.*Cyr.*5.3.24. 3. *man completely*, τριήρεις Arist.*Pol.*1327$^b$14. 4. *fulfil*, ἡ χάρις ἐκπεπλήρωται Hdt. 8.144; μοῖραν Hp.*Vict.*1.5; εὐαγγελίαν *Act.Ap.*13.33. 5. *pay off*, τὸ χρέος Pl.*Lg.*958b. II. ἐ. λιμένα πλάτῃ *make one's way over*, E. *Or.*54. -ωμα, ατος, τό, *filling up*, ἐ. ποιεῖν τοῦ κοίλου Hp.*Art.*9; *pad* or *cushion to fill up*, ἐνθεὶς μασχάλῃ ἐ. Id.*Mochl.*5 (pl.). -ωσις, εως, ἡ, *filling up*, Apollon.Cit.1; κλεψύδρας Marcellin.*Puls.*265; *completion*, Aesar.ap.Stob.1.49.27, Dsc.1.58; ἐνιαυτοῦ Str.17.1.46; *filling up the measure*, ἁμαρτιῶν Lxx 2*Ma.*6.14; *satisfaction*, τῶν ἐπιθυμιῶν D.H.6.86, cf. Ph.1.567. II. *fulfilment* of a cosmic cycle, *Cat. Cod.Astr.*1.163. -ωτής, οῦ, ὁ, *one who fulfils*, τοῦ τεταγμένου D.C.38.24. -ωτικός, ή, όν, *filling up, completing*, τοῦ πάθους Ph. 1.685.

⊛ **ἐκπλήσσω**, Att. -ττω, *strike out of, drive away from, expel*, ἐκ δ' ἔπληξέ μου τὴν αἰδῶ A.*Pr.*134; ὃς (sc. κεραυνὸς) αὐτὸν ἐξέπληξε τῶν.. κομπασμάτων ib.362, cf. E.*Ion*635: abs., *drive away*, ἡ τέρψις τὸ λυπηρὸν ἐκπλήσσει Th.2.38; φόβος μνήμην ἐ. ib.87. II. *drive out of one's senses by a sudden shock, amaze, astound*, Od.18.231 (tm.); κάλλει καὶ ὥρᾳ διενεγκόντες ἐ. τινάς Aeschin.1.134; ὁ φόβος ἐκπλήσσων.. Antipho 2.1.7; κακοὶ εὐτυχοῦντες ἐκπλήσσουσί με *Trag.Adesp.* 465; ὅ μ' ἐκπλήσσει λόγου *frightens* me in speaking, E.*Or.*549:— in this sense most freq. in aor. 2 Pass., Ep. ἐξεπλήγην (v. infr.), Att. ἐξεπλάγην [ᾰ] (also aor. 1 ἐξεπλήχθην Id.*Tr.*183: pf. part. ἐκπεπληγμένος A.*Pers.*290, S.*Tr.*386, etc.); *to be panic-struck, amazed*, esp. by fear, ἐκ γὰρ πλήγη φρένας Il.16.403, cf. 13.394; ἡνίοχοι ἔκπληγεν 18.225: c. part., ἐκπεπληγμένον κεῖνον βλέποντες S.*OT* 922, cf. *Ant.*433, etc.; ἐκπλαγῆναί τινι *to be astonished at* a thing, Hdt.1.116, etc.; ὑπό τινος Id.3.64; διά τι Th.7.21; ἐπί τινι X.*Cyr.* 1.4.27; πρός τι Plu.*Thes.*19, etc.: also c. acc., ἐκπλαγῆναί τινα *to be struck with panic fear of..*, S.*Ph.*226, *El.*1045; ἡμᾶς δ' ἂν..μάλιστα ἐκπεπληγμένοι εἶεν Th.6.11, cf. 3.82. 2. generally, of any sudden, overpowering passion, *to be struck with desire*, Ar.*Pl.*673; *with love*, E.*Hipp.*38, *Med.*8; χαρᾷ, ἡδονῇ, A.*Ch.*233, S.*Tr.*629; *with admiration*, Hdt.3.148, etc.: c. acc. rei, ἐκπλαγέντα τὰ προκείμενα ἀγαθά Id. 9.82. 3. εἰς ὁμολογίαν ἐκπλήττειν *frighten* one into.., f.l. in Plb. 23.4.11.

**ἐκπλήωρον**· ἐκπεπληρωκυῖαν ἑαυτήν, Hsch.

**ἐκπλινθεύω**, *take out bricks* or *tiles*, Is.*Fr.*19 S. II. *turn into bricks*, γῆν πᾶσαν Jul.*Gal.*135b.

**ἐκπλίσσομαι**, *gape*, of a wound, Hp.*Fract.*25; of the womb, Id. *Prorrh.*2.24.

**ἐκπλοκή**, ἡ, *unravelling*: metaph., *escape*, Artem.4.57 (pl.); τινός Vett.Val.183.32.

⊛ **ἔκπλοος**, contr. -πλους, ὁ, *sailing out, leaving port*, κρυφαῖον ἐ. καθίστατο A.*Pers.*385; ποιεῖσθαι ἐ., = ἐκπλεῖν, Th.1.65, etc.; βιάζεσθαι τὸν ἐ. to force one's *way out*, Id.7.70; εἴσπλους καὶ ἐ. the right of using a port, *IG*12(7).8.12 (Amorgos), *GDI*5687.8 (Chios). II. *entrance of a harbour*, A.*Pers.*367, X.*HG*1.6.18.

**ἐκ-πλύνω** [ῡ], fut. -πλῠνῶ *IG*7.3073.87 (Lebad.):—*wash out*, esp. *wash out colours from* cloths, ἵνα..μὴ αὐτῶν ἐκπλύναι τὴν βαφὴν Pl.*R.* 430a; ἐκπλύναντας τὴν οἰσύπην *having washed out* the grease and dirt, Ar.*Lys.*575:—Pass., τὰ δὲ ζῷα οὐκ ἐκπλύνεσθαι the pattern *is* not *washed out*, Hdt.1.203. II. *wash out*, i.e. *wash thoroughly*, ὄναιο μέντἂν εἴ τις ἐκπλύνειέ σε Ar.*Pl.*1062; τὸν σαπέρδην Id.*Fr.*686; ἔντερα *SIG*1025.35 (Cos); τὰ γράμματα *IG*l.c.:—Med., Hdt.4.73. III. Medic., in Pass., *to be evacuated*, Gal.16.158. -πλῠσις, εως, ἡ, *washing out*, Hsch. s.v. στρουθίον. -πλῠτος, ον, *to be washed out*, of colours, Pl.*R.*429e; χιτωνίσκον περιήγητον ἐκπλύτῳ ἀλουργεῖ *IG*2. 754.21: metaph., *washed out*, μίασμα δ' ἔ. πέλει A.*Eu.*281; ἔ. τὸ μιανθέν Pl.*Lg.*872e. II. a kind of νάρδος, Gal.14.74.

**ἔκπλωτος**, ον, *navigable*, ὁλκάσι καὶ κώπῃ Him.ap.Phot.*Bibl.* p.371 B.

**ἐκπλώω**, Ion. for ἐκπλέω. **ἐκπνείω**, Ep. for ἐκπνέω.

**ἐκπνευμᾰτ-όω**, *turn into vapour*, Arist.*Pr.*866$^a$3, Thphr.ap.Plu.2. 292d; *fan into wind*, prob. in Epicur.*Ep.*2 p.48 U.:—Pass., *to be so turned*, Arist.*Pr.*897$^b$1, al. II. *deflate*, metaph., οἴημα, τῦφον, Plu.2.39d. III. in Pass., *to be inflated*, Thphr.*CP*4.9.3: metaph., ὑπὸ κτήσεως Phld.*Vit.*p.27 J. -ωσις, εως, ἡ, *turning into wind*, Epicur.*Ep.*2 p.54 U. 2. *flatulence*, Aët.5.68.

**ἔκ-πνευσις**, εως, ἡ, *exhalation*, opp. ἀνάπν-, Arist.*HA*492$^b$9, al. -πνέω, Ep. -πνείω Q.S.1.349, impf. -είεσκον Id.13.148: fut. -πνεύσομαι or -οῦμαι:—*breathe out* or *forth*, κεραυνὸς ἐκπνέων φλόγα A.*Pr.* 361; ἐ. ἀράς τινι E.*Ph.*876; ἐ. θυμόν Id.*Ba.*620: abs., Emp.100.1, Pl.*Phd.*112b, Arist.*HA*492$^b$6. 2. βίον ἐ. *breathe one's last, expire*, A.*Ag.*1493 (lyr.), E.*Hel.*142; ἐ. ψυχήν Id.*Or.*1163; alone, ὑφ' οὗ φονέως ἄρ' ἐξέπνευσας S.*Aj.*1026; πρός τινος E.*HF*886 (anap.): abs., Id.*Hyps.Fr.*60i 38, Parth.4.6: metaph., *lose power*, *Gp.*15.1.28; *lose lustre*, of pearls, *PHolm.*10.18. 3. *lose breath*, of a runner, Arist.*Rh.*1409$^a$32. II. abs., *cease blowing, become calm*, [ὁ δῆμος] ἴσως ἂν ἐκπνεύσειε E.*Or.*700; τὰ κατὰ τὸν πόλεμον ἐκπέπνευκε καὶ λελώφηκεν Sch.Ar.*Pax*942. 2. *blow out* or *outwards*, of a wind, ἔσωθεν ἐ. Hdt.7.36; ἐκ τοῦ κόλπου Th.2.84, cf. 6.104; *burst out*, σμικροῦ νέφους..ἐκπνεύσας μέγας χειμὼν S.*Aj.*1148; but simply, *blow*, of wind, Arist.*Mete.*365$^a$4, *Pr.*947$^a$31. -πνοή, ἡ, *breathing out, exhalation*, opp. ἀναπνοή, Pl.*Ti.*78e, Arist.*Sens.*436$^a$15; opp. εἰσπνοή, Id.*Resp.*471$^a$8; θανάσιμοι ἐ. E.*Hipp.*1438. 2. *death*, J.*AJ*19.8. 3. 3. *vent, blow-hole*, *Placit.*2.25.1; Τυφῶνος ἐκπνοαί, name of a marsh, Plu.*Ant.*3. II. *vapour*, Arist.*Mu.*394$^b$13 (pl.). -πνοος, ον, contr. -πνους, ουν, *breathless, lifeless*, Str.14.1.44. II. *breathing out, exhaling*, Hp.*Epid.*6.6.1; ἔ. μύρων *smelling of..*, Posidipp. ap.Ath.13.596c.

**ἐκποδών**, Adv., (ἐκ ποδῶν) opp. ἐμποδών, *away from the feet*, i.e. *out of the way, away*, ἐ. ἀπαλλάσσεσθαι depart and get *away*, Hdt.8.76; ἐ. σταθῆναι stand *aside*, A.*Ch.*20; ἀποστῆναι E.*Hel.*1023, etc.; ἐ. εἶναι Hdt.6.35; γενέσθαι X.*HG*6.5.38; ἐ. σαυτὸν ἔχειν, ἄγειν τινά, A.*Pr.* 346, S.*Ant.*1321 (lyr.); ἐᾶν Ar.*Ach.*305; ἄναγε σεαυτὸν ἐ. Id.*Ra.*853: abs., ἐκποδὼν *out of the way!* Id.*Ach.*240, *V.*1341: c. dat., ἐ. χωρεῖν τινί to get *out of* his *way*, E.*Hec.*52, etc.; ἐ. στῆναι ἀμφοτέροις Th.1.40; ἐκποδὼν εἶναι νέοις E.*Supp.*1113, cf. And.1.135; ἐκποδὼν τὰ ὄντα, τὰς ἐπιβουλὰς ποιεῖσθαι, X.*Cyr.*3.1.3, Isoc.4.173, etc.; ἐ. λέγειν declare *away* or *removed*, A.*Eu.*453: c. gen., ἐ. χθονὸς *far from* it, E.*Ph.* 978; ἐ. εἶναί or ἔχειν τινός, to be or keep *free from* a thing, X.*Cyr.*5.4. 34, E.*IT*1226; τὸ μὲν σὸν ἐ. ἔστω λόγου be thou *banished from* my words, Id.*Med.*1222.

**ἔκποθεν**, Adv. *from some place or other*, ἐ. ἀφράστοιο A.R.2.224, 824; ἐ. ἀπροφάτοιο Q.S.3.437: ἔκποθε, Id.9.420, 14.74.

⊛ **ἐκποι-έω**, *put out*: 1. *put out* a child, i.e. *give him to be adopted* by another, opp. εἰσποιέω, D.C.60.33:—Pass., *to be adopted*, ἂν ἐκποιηθῇ Is.7.25, cf. D.C.38.12. 2. *alienate*, Pherecr.65, *Cod. Just.*1.5.17.1, al. 3. *withdraw*, ἐμαυτὸν τοῦ δικαστηρίου Philostr. *VA*8.7. II. in Med., *produce, bring forth*, γαλᾶς, βότρυς, Ar.*Ach.* 255, *Pax*708, Epicur.*Nat.*2.5. III. *make complete, finish off*, Sophr.76, Hdt.2.125 (Pass.); οἰκίας *IG*12(5).252 (Paros, vi/v B.C.); τὰς ὁδοὺς γεφύραις ἐ. *furnish* them with.., D.C.68.15; πρὸς τὰ μεγέθη τὰ γεγραμμένα *IG*7.3073.101 (Lebad.): c. gen. materiae, Παρίου λίθου τὰ ἔμπροσθε ἐξεποίησαν they *made all* the front of Parian marble, Hdt. 5.62; ἱερὰ βασιλείοις -πεποιημένα τέλεσι Philostr.*VA*8.31. 2. *procure*, ὅπλα τινί Id.*Her.*19.4. IV. *cause*, βλαστάνειν οὐκ ἐ. τὸ τῆς ὥρας Thphr.*CP*1.14.2. 2. *permit*, τινί, c. inf., Lxx *Si.*18.4: impers., ἐκποιεῖ *it is allowable*, Hp.*Prorrh.*2.3; of the weather, *it is favourable*, Telesp.53 H.: intr., *to be sufficient*, Lxx 2*Ch.*7.7; ἐφ' ὅσους ἂν ἐκποιῇ μῆνας *SIG*976.57 (Samos, ii B.C.): impers., ἐκποιεῖ *it suffices*, Lys.*Fr.*57 S., cf. Chrysipp.*Stoic.*3.21: fut., περὶ τούτων ἐν τοῖς ἑξῆς σαφέστερον ἐκποιήσει κατανοεῖν Plb.2.24.17, cf. Ceb.8. ⊛ -ησις, εως, ἡ, *putting forth*: *emissio seminis*, Hdt.3.109. II. *giving out a child in adoption*, Poll.6.178, D.C.37.51. III. *completion, erection*, ναοῦ Id.37.44, cf. 45.6. IV. *alienation*, *Cod.Just.*1.2.17.5, al. -ητος παῖς a child *given to be adopted by another*, ἐ. εἰς οἶκόν τινος Is.7.23, cf. Aeschin.3.21; cf. εἰσποίητος. 2. *alienated from*, μητρός, Is.7.25: metaph., κακίας Plu.2.562f.

**ἐκποικίλλω**, strengthd. for ποικίλλω, Max.Tyr.10.2 (Pass.).

**ἐκποινίζομαι**, fut. -ποινιοῦμαι, v.l. for ἐκπην- in Sch.Ar.*Ra.*586.

**ἐκποκίζω**, Att. fut. -ιῶ, *pull out wool* or *hair*, Ar.*Th.*567.

**ἐκπολεμ-έω**, *provoke to war*, ἵν' ἐκπολεμήσειε τοὺς Ἀθηναίους πρὸς τοὺς Λακεδαιμονίους X.*HG*5.4.20 (codd. and Harp.), cf. Th.6.91:— Pass., ἐκπεπολεμῆσθαι πρὸς τὸν ἑαυτοῦ οἶκον Philostr.*VA*5.35. II. *go to war with*, Lxx *De.*20.10, al. -ιστής, οῦ, ὁ, *warrior*, Hsch. s.v. εἰέω. -όω, *make hostile, involve in war*, Hdt.4.120, *Hell.Oxy.* 2.2, 13.1, D.1.7, 3.7, Plb.15.6.6; τινὰς πρὸς ἀλλήλους Th.6.77:— Pass., fut. Med. -ώσομαι (J.*BJ*7.10.2), *become an enemy to, be set at feud with*, τινί Hdt.3.66, 5.73: abs., Th.8.57. -ωσις, εως, ἡ, *making hostile*, Plu.*Aem.*13.

**ἐκπολίζω**, *make into a city*, in Pass., πεδίων νομοὺς ἐκπεπολισμένους Aristid.*Or.*26(14).6.

**ἐκπολιορκ-έω,** *force a besieged town to surrender, force to capitulate,* Th.1.94,134, X.*HG*2.4.3, etc.: metaph. of argument, ἐ. τινὰ λόγῳ Chio*Ep*.10 :—Pass., *to be forced to surrender,* Th.1.117; ἐκ Βυζαντίου ἐκπολιορκηθείς ib.131, cf. *Inscr.Prien.*37.112; ὑπὸ τῶν τυράννων Arist.*Ath.*19.3: metaph., ἐκπολιορκηθέντος τοῦ σώματος ὑπὸ μακρᾶς νόσου Diog.Oen.39. **-ησις,** εως, ἡ, *reduction by siege, Gloss.*

**ἐκπολῑτεύω,** *change the constitution of a state, cause it to degenerate,* Lxx 4*Ma*.4.19.

**ἔκπομα,** = ἔκπωμα, Hsch.

**ἐκπομπεύω,** *conduct,* τὴν ἐπικηδείαν πομπήν Lib.*Decl.*40.15.

⊛ **ἐκπομπή,** ἡ, *sending out* or *forth,* λῃστῶν Th.3.51 (pl.); ἀποικιῶν Pl.*Lg.*740e. II. *divorce,* Antipho Soph.49 (pl.).

⊛ **ἐκπονέω,** *work out, finish off,* Sapph.98, Pi.*P*.4.236; ἄκη A.*Supp.*367; τὸ εὐπρεπὲς τοῦ λόγου Th.3.38; δολιχὰν τρίβον *AP*7.212 (Mnasalc.), Ar.*Av.*379; also, *form by instruction,* as Chiron did Achilles, E.*IA*209 (lyr.); ἐ. τινὰ πέπλοισιν *to deck* him *out,* Id.*Hipp.*632:—Pass., *to be wrought out, brought to perfection,* τὸ ναυτικὸν μεγάλαις δαπάναις ἐκπονηθέν Th.6.31; τὰ σῖτα X.*Cyr.*8.2.5; ὅπλα ἐκπεπόνηται εἰς κόσμον Id.*HG*4.2.7, cf. Pl.*R.*529e. 2. *practise,* τὰ πρὸς τὸν πόλεμον X.*Cyr.*5.1.30; ὀρχήσεις Plb.4.20.12:—Med., Pl.*Lg.*834e:—Pass., of persons, ἐκπεπονῆσθαι τὰ σώματα *to be in good training* or *practice,* X.*Cyr.*3.3.57; ἐκπεπονημένοι, ὡς ἂν κράτιστοι εἶεν Id.*HG*6.4.28. 3. *work through, execute,* τἀντεταλμένα E.*Ph.*1648; ἐ. ἀέθλους *finish* hard tasks, Theoc.*Ep.*22.5; ἃ ἂν μάθωσιν, ἱκανώτεροι τῷ σώματι ἐ. X.*Cyr.*4.3.11:—Med., E.*Med.*241:—Pass., ταῦτα δυοῖν ἐν ἔτοιν.. μόλις ἐξεπονήθη Cratin.237. 4. *labour for, provide by labour, earn,* σωτηρίαν E.*Fr.*729; βίον Id.*Hipp.*467: c. acc. et inf., τοὺς θεοὺς ἐ. φράζειν *prevail on* the gods to tell, Id.*Ion*375. 5. abs., *work hard,* σοὶ παρ' ἀσπίδ' ἐκπονῶν ὅπως.. Id.*Or.*653, cf. *Supp.*319. 6. *work out by searching,* Id.*Ion*1355, *Andr.*1052; *search out,* Id.*Hel.*1514. 7. of food, *to digest,* X.*Mem.*1.2.4, *Cyr.*1.2.16: abs., Id.*Oec.*11.12. 8. *labour to shield off from,* τέκνων θάνατον E.*HF*581. 9. *work at, till,* γῆν *SIG*22.9; νειοὶ δ' ἐκπονέοιντο ποτὶ σπόρον Theoc.16.94, cf. Str.5.4.5; αἱ [τὴν ὕλην] ἐκπονοῦσαι τέχναι Plu.*Per.*12. 10. Pass., *to be worn out, brought low,* ὑπό τινος Str.5.4.11; φροντίσιν ἐκπονούμενος Plu.*Oth.*9; τὰς ὄψεις ἐ. Id.2.854b.

**ἐκπορ-ευτέον,** *one must march out,* Aen.Tact.23.6. ⊛ **-εύω,** *make to go out, fetch out,* E.*Ph.*1068, *HF*723:—Med., with fut. Med. (X.*An.*5.1.8) and aor. Pass., *go out* or *forth, march out,* X. l. c., etc.; ἐπὶ λείαν Aen.Tact.24.4; εἰς στρατείαν ἐ. *to march out* to a place.., Plb.11.9.4: c. acc. loci, ἐ. τὸ βουλευτήριον ib.8; but ἐκ τοῦ χάρακος Id.6.58.4; ἐκ τοῦ στόματος Lxx *Pr.*3.16, al.: more generally, ὅ θ' ὑγρὸς εἰς γῆν ὄμβρος ἐκπορεύεται Critias 25.36.

**ἐκπορθ-έω,** *pillage,* πόλεις E.*Tr.*95; οἰκίας Lys.12.83, cf. Herod.3.5 (tm.), Plb.2.32.4, etc.:—Pass., of a person, *to be undone,* ὑπ' ἄτης ἐκπεπόρθημαι τάλας S.*Tr.*1104; γραῦς.. κρᾶτ' ἐκπορθηθεῖσ' E.*Tr.*142 (lyr.). II. *carry off as plunder,* τὰ ἐνόντα Th.4.57. **-ησις,** εως, ἡ, *sacking, wasting,* Str.9.1.17, Ph.2.122, Onos.42.23. **-ητικῶς,** Adv. *with a view to plundering completely,* Eust.1490.65. **-ήτωρ,** ορος, ὁ, *waster, destroyer,* E.*Supp.*1223.

**ἐκπορθμεύω,** *carry away by sea*:—E. has pf. Pass. in pass. sense, [Ἑλένη] ἐκπεπόρθμευται χθονός *Hel.*1179; but in med. sense, Μενέλαος αὐτὴν ἐκπεπόρθμευται χθονός ib.1517.

**ἐκπορ-ίζω,** *invent, contrive,* ἄδικα E.*Ba.*1042 (anap.); φόνον εἴς τινα Id.*Ion*1114; μηχανήν Ar.*V.*365; ἐ. ὅπως.. Id.*Lys.*421. II. *provide, furnish,* στέγη.. πάντ' ἐ. S.*Ph.*299; ἀργύριον ὑμῖν And.2.17; ὅπλα τινί Th.6.72; χρήματα, μισθόν, X.*Cyr.*3.1.30, *An.*5.6.19; τὸ συμφέρον ἑκάστῳ Pl.*R.*341d, etc.; *procure,* βίον Ar.*V.*1113, cf. Pl.*Men.*78e:—so in Med., *provide for oneself,* τὰ αὑτῶν Th.1.82, cf. 125; ταῖς ἡδοναῖς πλήρωσιν Pl.*Grg.*492a; γράμματα παρά τινος Plb.22.3.2 (but Med., also, *supply* to others, *BCH*48.3 (Brusa)). III. *discharge* a cargo, *OGI*521.27,30 (Abydos, v A. D.). **-ιστέον,** *one must bring about,* Gal.10.389.

⊛ **ἐκπορνεύω,** *commit fornication,* Lxx *Ge.*38.24, *Ep.Jud.*7:—Pass., in same sense, Poll.6.126. 2. metaph., of idolatry, Lxx *Ex.*34.15. II. c. acc., *prostitute,* τὴν θυγατέρα ib.*Le.*19.29; *cause to commit fornication,* ib.2*Ch.*21.11.

**ἐκπόρπ-ῐσις,** εως, ἡ, (πόρπη) lit., *unfastening,* hence μετ' ἐκπορπίσεως, of a compound fracture, Sor.*Fract.*24. **-όομαι,** = ἐκφιβλόομαι, Suid.

**ἐκποτάομαι,** Ion. **-έομαι,** = ἐκπέτομαι, *fly out* or *forth,* of snowflakes, Διὸς ἐκποτέονται Il.19.357; of a ghost, πεδ' ἀμαύρων νεκύων ἐκπεποτāμένα Sapph.68.4: metaph., πᾷ τὰς φρένας ἐκπεπότασαι; Theoc.11.72, 2.19.

**ἐκποτέον,** *one must drink to the dregs,* τὴν τρύγα Pherecr.249.

**ἔκπους,** ποδος, ὁ, ἡ, = ἑξάπους, *IG*1².313.93, al.

⊛ **ἐκ-πράκτης,** ου, ὁ, *tax-gatherer,* Aq.*Jb.*39.7. **-πραξις,** εως, ἡ, *exacting,* *IG*1².6.30; δανείων D.S.1.79:—Dor. **ἔσπραξις** *Foed.Delph.Pell.*2 B 16. **-πράσσω,** Att. **-ττω,** *bring about, achieve,* τι A.*Ag.*582, etc.; τόδ' ἐξέπραξεν ὥστε.. Id.*Pers.*723; χρέος *perform* a service, Id.*Supp.*472; ὡς.. S.*Ant.*303; δόλιον εὐνὴν ἐξέπραξ' E.*Hel.*20; τὸν καλλίνικον.. ἐξεπράξατε ἐς γόον ye *have made* the hymn of triumph *end in* wailing, Id.*Ba.*1161; in later Prose, τὸ δέον Paul.Aeg.6.118. II. *make an end of, kill, destroy,* A.*Ag.*1275, S.*OC*1659, E.*Hec.*515. III. *exact, levy,* αἵματος δίκην Id.*HF*43; καταδίκας *SIG*554.19 (Thermon); τόκους ib.672.39 (Delph., ii B.C.): c. dupl. acc., χρήματα ἐ. τινά Th.8.108: abs., τοὺς ταμίας ἐ. Pl.*Lg.*774e, cf. *IG*1².79:—Pass., *to be made to pay,* χρήματα ὑπό τινος Paus.7.12.1. 2. *exact punishment for* a thing, *avenge,* S.*OT*377; μητρῷον φόνον E.*Med.*1305:—Med., τὸν Δωριέος πρὸς Ἐγεσταίων φόνον ἐκπρήξασθαι Hdt.7.158.

**ἐκπρᾱΰνω,** strengthd. for πραΰνω, Plu.2.74d.

⊛ **ἐκπρεμνίζω,** *root out,* D.43.69, Philostr.Jun.*Im.*4.

**ἐκπρέπ-εια,** ἡ, *excellence,* Iamb.*VP*5.23. **-ής,** ές, *distinguished out of all, pre-eminent, remarkable,* ἐν πολλοῖσι Il.2.483; μία ἐ. [νίκα] Pi.*P.*7.12; μεγέθει ἐκπρεπεστάτα A.*Pers.*184; εὐγένειαν ἐκπρεπεῖς ib.442; εἶδος ἐκπρεπεστάτη E.*Alc.*333; ῥόδα.. τιθήνημ' ἔαρος -έστατον Chaerem.13; ἐ. φύσιν Nausicr.2.6; κότταβος.. ἐκπρεπὲς ἔργον Critias 2.1; ἐ. [ἰδέα] Pl.*Phdr.*238a; -έστερα ζῷα Arist.*Phgn.*810ᵃ8. Adv. -πῶς *splendidly,* κεκόσμηται Plb.5.59.8: poet. -έως *IG*3.121: Comp. -έστερον *more conspicuously,* D.C.44.40. II. of things, = ἔξω τοῦ πρέποντος, *extraordinary,* οὐδὲν -έστερον παθεῖν Th.3.55. Adv. -πῶς *without reasonable grounds,* Id.1.38: Sup. -έστατα τιμωρῆσαι X.*Smp.*8.31. **-όντως,** Adv. = ἐκπρεπῶς, D.C.74.1. **-ω,** *to be excellent* in a thing, εὐψυχίᾳ E.*Heracl.*597.

**ἐκπρεπώσοτον,** dub. in *IGRom.*4.144 (Cyzicus: so the stone, perh. an error for ἐκπρεπῶς ἐτῶν).

**ἔκπρησις,** εως, ἡ, *setting on fire, inflaming,* Plu.*Lys.*12.

**ἐκπρησμός,** gloss on πάφλασμα, Sch.Ar.*Av.*1243 (pl.).

**ἐκπρήσσω,** Ion. for ἐκπράσσω.

**ἐκπρίασθαι,** aor. 2 (v. *πρίαμαι), *buy off,* χρήμασι.. κίνδυνον ἐ. Antipho 5.63, cf. Lys.27.6; ἐ. τοὺς κατηγόρους Id.20.15. 2. *buy,* ἐ. τι παρά τινος Isoc.3.22; μεγάλων χρημάτων τὴν σωτηρίαν D.C.62.28.

**ἐκ-πρίζω,** = ἐκπρίω, *Gp.*9.11.7, Heliod. ap. Orib.47.14.3, etc. **-πρῖσις,** εως, ἡ, *sawing out,* Paul.Aeg.6.84. **-πρισμα,** ατος, τό, *that which is sawn out,* Arist.*GC*316ᵃ34; *section sawn out of* cylinder, Hero *Deff.*97 (pl.). **-πριστέον,** *one must saw out, excise,* Antyll. ap.Orib.44.23.20. **-πρίω,** fut. -πρίσω [ῑ] Men.*Epit.*41:—*saw off,* Th.7.25, Men. l. c.; *excise,* τὸ ὀστέον Hp.*VC*21; of bonds, Herod.5.25.

**ἐκπροβάλλω,** *expel,* βρέφος ἠλιτόμηνον Max.241.

**ἔκπροθεν·** ἐκ παλαιοῦ, Hsch.

**ἐκπροθεσμ-έω,** *to be later than the appointed day,* Ulp. ad D.21.80. **-ος,** ον, *beyond the appointed day,* τοῦ ὀφλήματος *for* the debt, Luc.*Herm.*80; ἐ. τῶν ἑπτὰ ἡμερῶν *after* seven days have expired, Id.*Sat.*2; ἐ. τοῦ ἀγῶνος *past the time of,* i.e. *too old for,* the games, Id.*Anach.*39; ἐ. φιλοτιμήματα honours *deferred till too late,* Id.*Nav.*40; πένθος Ph.2.169.

**ἐκπροθρῴσκω,** *spring out* or *forth,* aor. part. -θορών Orph.*A.*346, Man.6.33; ὅτ' ἂν βρέφος ἐκπροθόρῃσι Max.226.

**ἐκπροθῡμέομαι,** strengthd. for προθυμέομαι, E.*Ph.*1678.

**ἐκπροΐημι,** *send forth,* παγὰν ἐκπροϊεῖσαι E.*Ion*119 codd. (lyr.).

**ἐκπροικίζω,** *portion off,* Phalar.*Ep.*131 (Pass.).

**ἐκπρο-κᾰλέομαι,** *call forth to oneself,* ἐκπροκαλεσσαμένη μεγάρων Od.2.400; ἀπὸ μεγάροιο *h.Ap.*111; νόσφιν A.R.4.353. 2. *invoke,* ἄστρων σέλας Orph.*H.*7.1. **-κρίνω** [ῑ], *choose out,* πόλεος ἐκπροκριθεῖσα E.*Ph.*214 (lyr.). **-λείπω,** *forsake,* κοῖλον λόχον ἐκπρολιπόντες Od.8.515, cf. Thgn.1136; βίον *IG*14.2123. II. *spare,* Ps.-Phoc.85. **-μολεῖν,** aor. 2 (v. βλώσκω), *go forth from,* λίμνης A.R.4.1587: abs., Orph.*L.*706. **-πίπτω,** *fall down from,* ὑψόθεν εἰς γαῖαν ib.324. **-πτωσις,** εως, ἡ, *prolapsus,* Sor.2.85 (pl.). **-ρέω,** *flow forth from,* c. gen., Orph.*L.*203, *AP*9.669 (Marian.).

**ἐκπρο-τῑμάω,** *honour above all,* S.*Ant.*913. **-φαίνω,** *show forth,* aor. 2 part. -φᾰνοῦσα Orph.*H.*71.7. ⊛ **-φέρω,** *bring forth,* dub. in Man.6.733. **-φεύγω,** *flee away from,* τινός Hld.8.11; *escape,* τι Orph.*L.*397; μόρον *AP*6.218 (Alc.). **-χέω,** *pour forth,* ἰαχάν *AP*7.201 (Pamph.); πλοκάμους ib.22 (Simm.); ὅσσων δάκρυον *IG*14.2123.

**ἐκπτερόομαι,** *to be furnished with wings,* Hp.*Vict.*1.25 (f.l. for ἐκπυρούμενα).

**ἐκπτήσσω,** *scare out of,* οἴκων με ἐξέπταξας (Dor.) E.*Hec.*179 (lyr.).

**ἐκπτίσσω,** *pound, bray,* f.l. in Ael.*NA*17.31 (Pass.).

**ἐκπτοέω,** = ἐκπτήσσω, Tz.*H.*5.484:—Pass., *to be struck with admiration,* E.*Cyc.*185; τὰς ψυχὰς ἐξεπτόηντο *were greatly excited,* Hdn.5.4.1. 2. *to be scared,* Plb.5.36.3, 14.5.7. **ἔκπτοιος,** ον, *scared,* Phryn.*PS* p.15 B.

**ἔκπτυξις,** εως, ἡ, *spreading, parting* of the legs in riding, Aët.3.7.

**ἔκπτῠσις,** εως, ἡ, *expectoration,* αἵματος Alex.Trall.5.5.

**ἐκπτύσσω,** *unfold, spread out,* pf. part. Pass. ἐξεπτυγμένος, prob. for ἐξεστιγμ-, Erot. s. v. ἐκπεπταμένα.

⊛ **ἐκπτύω,** fut. -ύσομαι [ῠ] *AP*5.196 (Mel.):—*spit out,* στόματος δ' ἐξέπτυσεν ἅλμην Od.5.322, cf. *AP* l. c.; of the sea, *cast up,* ib.6.224 (Theodorid.): metaph., ὥσπερ χαλινὸν τὸν λόγον Plu.2.328c; so, of a ligature, Antyll. ap.Orib.45.24.7 (Pass.); *spit* or *blab out,* ἀπόρρητα Ael.*NA*4.44; of an abortion, ib.12.17 (Pass.). II. *spit* in token of disgust, Ar.*V.*792. 2. *spit at, abominate, Ep.Gal.*4.14.

**ἔκπτωμα,** ατος, τό, *dislocation,* Hp.*Art.*28. II. *collapse* of a dam, *PTeb.*72.78 (ii B.C.).

⊛ **ἔκπτωσις,** εως, ἡ, *breaking forth, escape,* [τοῦ θερμοῦ] Arist.*Mete.*370ᵃ5; [ὑγροῦ] Id.*Resp.*480ᵃ1; ἡ τῶν ὄψεων ἔ. *projection* of rays from the sun, Id.*Pr.*911ᵇ5; *emission,* πυρός Epicur.*Ep.*2 pp.46, 54 U. 2. *banishment,* Plb.4.1.8, D.S.13.65, *PMag.Osl.*1.222. 3. *disappointment,* Ceb.7 (pl.); *falling off,* πρὸς τὸ χεῖρον Str.10.3.9; ἔ. ψυχῆς, *error,* Arr.*Epict.*2.17.21; *abandonment* of duty, *Stoic.*3.163; *missing,* τοῦ σκοποῦ Plot.6.1.10; *falling away from,* λόγου ib.3.7; [τοῦ ἀγαθοῦ] Simp. *in Epict.* p.74 D. 4. in argument, ἔ. εἰς ἄπειρον, *regressus ad infinitum,* Gal.5.79. 5. *shipwreck,* Hero *Aut.*22.6. 6. *loss,* χρημάτων *Cod.Just.*1.3.45.9. II. *dislocation of a joint,* Hp.

*Fract.*1 (pl.); ἐ. τῶν ὑστέρων *expulsion* of the afterbirth, Id.*Aph.*5.49; *decay* of flesh, sinews, etc., as result of erysipelas, Id.*Epid.*3.4; τῶν ἐσχαρέων ἐ. *detachment* of the eschars, Id.*Art.*11 (pl.); *prolapsus uteri*, Aret.*SD*2.11.

**ἐκπτώσσω**, *to be in fear of*, ἐχθρούς Man.5.237 (s. v. l.).

**ἔκπτωτος**, ον, *abject*, Paul.Al.*O.*1; *banished*, Vett.Val.86.14, al.

⊛ **ἐκπῡ-έω**, *suppurate*, Hp.*Epid.*1.20, *Prog.*15, *Epid.*2.1.7:—Med., Id.*Aph.*7.38, *Fract.*27:—Pass., Id.*Aph.*6.20. **-ημα**, ατος, τό, *sore that has suppurated*, Id.*VM*22, *Prog.*15, *Coac.*278. **-ησις**, εως, ἡ, *suppuration*, Id.*Aph.*7.20, etc. ⊛ **-ητικός**, ή, όν, *bringing to suppuration*, ib.5.22. **-ΐσκομαι**, Pass., = ἐκπυέω, Id.*Prog.*15, v.l. ib.22:—later in Act., Gal.11.728.

**ἐκπυκτεύω**, *box*, Poll.2.147.

**ἐκπυνθάνομαι**, *search out, make inquiry*, Il.10.320; ἔκ τε πυθέσθαι ἠέ.. ib.308; ἵν' ἐκπυθώμεθα πόθεν.. E.*Cyc.*94, etc. 2. c. acc., *hear of, learn*, S.*Aj.*215 (anap.); τινός *learn from*.., E.*HF*529; τὸ πρᾶγμ' ὅπως ἔχει Ar.*Ec.*752; ἐ. τινός *question* him, Id.*Pl.*60: c. part., ἐ. τινὰ ἀφιγμένον E.*Hel.*817.

**ἐκπῡόω**, *cause to suppurate*, δοθιῆνας Dsc.2.155:—Pass., Erot.*Fr.*9.

**ἐκπῡράκτωσις**, εως, ἡ, *burning*, Tz.*H.*11.596 (pl.), Suid. s. v. φλογμός.

**ἐκπῡρην-ίζω**, (πυρήν) *squeeze out the stone*: generally, *squeeze out*, τὰ ἐνόντα Arist.*Ph.*214a33, Steph. *in Hp.*1.82 D.:—Pass., Alex.Aphr.*Pr.*1.119, *de An.*132.29. **-ισις**, εως, ἡ, *squeezing out*, Olymp. *in Mete.*38.25, Mich. *in PN*117.15. **-ισμός**, ὁ, *squeezing out*, Steph. *in Hp.*1.82 D.

**ἐκπῡρ-ιάω**, *heat*, Hp.*Aph.*5.63 (Pass., v. l. for ἐκπυρόομαι), Aret.*CA*1.6. **-ος**, ον, *burning hot*, Str.15.1.26, v. l. in Hdt.4.73; σῶμα Sor.2.54: metaph., ἵππου βλέμμα Poll.1.192: neut. pl. as Adv., τί μ' ἔκπυρα λούεις; *AP*5.81 (v. l. for ἔμπ-). **-όω**, *burn to ashes, consume utterly*, E.*IA*1070 (lyr.); ὕδραν Id.*HF*421 (lyr.). 2. *set on fire*, Arist.*Mete.*341a18. II. Pass., *catch fire*, ib.342b2, Onos.19.3: a term used in the Stoic philos. to express *the tendency* of all things *to pass into fire*, Zeno *Stoic.*2.182, etc. 2. *to be burnt up*, λαμπάσιν κεραυνίαις E.*Ba.*244, cf. Corn.*ND*17. 3. *to be much heated*, prob. in Hp.*Vict.*1.25, f.l. in *Aph.*7.38; *to become red-hot*, Plb.12.25.2. III. *heat, warm*, βαλανεῖα Philostr.*VA*1.16.

**ἐκπυρσεύω**, *kindle, inflame*: metaph., in Pass., τὴν ἐπιθυμίαν ὑπὸ φιλοσοφίας S.E.*M.*11.179 (Pass.). II. *give signals by a beacon-light*, J.*BJ*4.10.5. III. *give out* flame, τεῖχος ἐ. φλόγα ib.7.8.5.

**ἐκπύρ-ωσις** [ῠ], εως, ἡ, *conflagration*, Str.12.8.18 (pl.), Luc.*Vit.Auct.*14. 2. Philos., *conversion into fire*, Zeno *Stoic.*1.32, Chrysipp.ib.2.131, etc.; ἐ. πνεύματος Epicur.*Ep.*2 p.45 U. 3. *calcination*, Dsc.5.87. 4. *excessive heat, pyrexia*, in disease, Ptol.*Tetr.*199. 5. *eruption*, τοῦ Βεσβίου ὄρους J.*AJ*20.7.2. 6. metaph., of anger, Phld.*Ir.*p.26 W. II. *catching fire*, Arist.*Mete.*342b2. III. a kind of *dance*, Menipp.ap.Ath.14.629f. **-ωτικός**, ή, όν, *heating*, χρίσματα Aët.12.35. **-ωτός**, όν, *heated*, βαλανεῖον *AP*11.411 tit.

**ἔκπυστος**, ον, *heard of, discovered*, πρὶν ἐκπύστους γενέσθαι Th.3.30, cf. 4.70, 8.42, J.*AJ*19.1.7, Plu.*Cam.*3, etc.; ἐ. τι ποιεῖν Hdn.2.7.7, cf. 3.12.6.

**ἐκπῡτίζω**, *spit out*, Alex.141.12.

**ἐκπωλεῖσθαι**· προγυμνάζεσθαι, Hsch.

**ἔκ-πωμα**, ατος, τό, *drinking-cup, beaker*, Hdt.9.41, 80, S.*Ph.*35, Th.6.32, *IG*2.649.13, etc.:—Dim. **-πωμάτιον**, τό, Diph.19, Str.16.2.25. ⊛ **-πωμᾰτοποιός**, ὁ, *cup-maker*, name of a play by Alexis, Ath.15.691d. **-πωτάομαι**, poet. for ἐκποτάομαι, aor. 1 ἐξεπωτήθη Babr.12.1.

**ἔκπωτις**, ιδος, ἡ, = ἄμπωτις, *Cat.Cod.Astr.*1.137 (pl.).

**ἐκράανθεν**, v. κραίνω.

**ἐκραβδίζω**, *flog out, drive out with a rod*, Ar.*Lys.*576.

**ἐκρᾰγή**, ἡ, gloss on ἔκρηξις, Suid. (prob. f. l. for κραυγή, as in Zonar.).

**ἐκράθην** [ᾰ], v. κεράννυμι.

**ἐκραίνω**, *scatter out of, make to fall in drops from*, κόμης μυελὸν ἐ. S.*Tr.*781; ἐγκέφαλον ἐξέρρᾱνε E.*Cyc.*402: metaph., τὴν χεῖρα καὶ τὴν ἄλυσιν ἐκ τῆς μηχανῆς dub. in Plb.8.6.3.

**ἐκραίω**, *destroy utterly*, Orph.*L.*604 (tm.).

**ἐκρᾱπίζω**, *expel, reject*, Phld.*Po.*5.1, 29.

**ἐκραστωνῆσαι**· εὐχερῆ ἀποφῆναι, Hsch. **ἐκρέμω**, v. κρέμαμαι.

**ἐκρευμᾰτιστέον**, *one must allow to discharge*, ἕλκη Ruf.ap.Aët.11.29.

**ἔκρευσις**, εως, ἡ, = ἐκροή I, Sch.Lyc.1012 (pl.), Hsch. s. v. ἔκκρισις.

**ἐκρέω**, pf. -ερρύηκα (v. infr.): aor. Pass. ἐξερρύην in act. sense, Hp.*Aph.*6.27, Pl.*R.*452d, Dor. 3 sg. -ερρύα *IG*4.952.3 (Epid.):—*flow out* or *forth*, ἐκ δ' αἷμα μέλαν ῥέε Il.21.119; ἔκ τινος Pl.*Phd.*112a; of streams, ἐ. ἐς θάλασσαν Hdt.2.20; ἐ. ἔξω ib.149. 2. of feathers, *fall off*, ἐξερρύηκε τὰ πτερά Ar.*Av.*104; of hair, Arist.*HA*518a32. b. *shed fruit*, ἐκρυήσεται ἡ ἐλαία Lxx *De.*28.40. 3. metaph., *melt* or *fall away, disappear*, Pl.*R.*452d, *Thg.*130e; ἐξερρύησαν οἱ τοῦ Θεμιστοκλέους λόγοι τῶν Ἑλλήνων they *faded from* their *memory*, Plu.*Them.*12. II. c. acc. cogn., *shed, let fall*, χάριν ἐξέρρευσας *AP*11.374 (Maced.).

**ἐκρηγιάριος**, *attonitus*, *Gloss.*

⊛ **ἔκρηγμα**, ατος, τό, *piece torn off*, ἐκρήγματα τρυχίων Hp.*Art.*78. 2. *broken bed of a torrent, ravine*, Plb.12.20.4. II. *breaking forth* of a stream, ὑδάτων Thphr.*CP*1.5.2. 2. *sluice*, *PEdgar*30.16 (ἔγρ-, iii B. C.), *PSI*5.488 (ἔχρ-, iii B. C.); cf. ἔκχρημα. 3. *eruption, bedsore*, Hp.*Epid.*7.7 (pl.).

**ἐκ-ρήγνῡμι**, fut. -ρήξω S.*Aj.*775:—*break off, snap asunder*, νευρὴν δ' ἐξέρρηξε νεόστροφον Il.15.469: c. gen., ὕδωρ ἐξέρρηξεν ὁδοῖο the water *broke off* a piece of the road, 23.421:—Pass., *break, snap asunder*, of bows, εἰ τὸν πάντα χρόνον ἐντεταμένα εἴη, ἐκραγείη ἂν [τὰ τόξα] Hdt.2.173; of clothes, *to be rent asunder*, cj. in Chaerem.14.9. II. c. acc. cogn., *let break forth, break out with*, νεφέλη ὄμβρον ἐκρήξει Plu.*Fab.*12; ἐ. ὀργήν Luc.*Cal.*23:—Pass., *break out*, of an ulcer, Hdt.3.133; *burst*, of an abscess, Hp.*Aph.*4.82; ἔνθεν ἐκραγήσονται.. ποταμοὶ πυρός A.*Pr.*369; of a quarrel, ἐξερράγη ἐς τὸ μέσον *broke out* in public, Hdt.8.74; of persons, *break out into passionate words*, ἐκραγῆναι ἔς τινα Id.6.129, cf. Th.8.84: pf. ἐξερρωγέναι *throw aside restraint, become dissolute*, Procop.*Arc.*1. III. sts. intr. in Act., οὔ ποτ' ἐκρήξει μάχη S. l. c.; ἐκρήξας ἄνεμος Arist.*Mete.*366b32: pf. part. ἐξερρωγὼς *precipitous*, ὄρη J.*AJ*14.15.5. **-ρηξις**, εως, ἡ, *breaking out, discharge*, Hp.*Steril.*213; *bursting* of an abscess, *Hippiatr.*20, al.; ἐ. τοῦ ὕδατος Sch.Theoc.7.5. II. *bursting asunder*, τοῦ νέφους Arist.*Mu.*395a15. ⊛ **-ρήσσω**, = ἐκρήγνυμι, Theano *Ep.*6.4 (Pass.); *cause* an abscess *to burst*, Paul.Aeg.7.1.

**ἔκρῐζ-ος**, ον, neut. as Adv., *by the roots*, *Et.Gud.* **-όω**, *root out*, Lxx *Je.*1.10, al., Aesop.179, *Ev.Matt.*13.29:—Pass., Lxx *Wi.*4.4, Babr.36.8, etc.; ἁρπασθεῖσα ὑπὸ τοῦ δαίμονος ἐξεριζώθη *IG*12(7).405.24 (Amorgos); in a form of execration, ἐκριζωθήσεται πανγενεί ib.3.1424. **-ωτής**, οῦ, ὁ, *rooter out, destroyer*, Lxx 4*Ma.*3.5.

**ἔκριν**, ῖνος, ὁ, ἡ, *with prominent nose*, Aret.*SD*2.13.

**ἐκρῑνέω**, (ῥίνη) *file away, consume*, τὴν καρδίαν Alciphr.3.33.

**ἐκρῑνίζω**, (ῥίς) *smell out*, Ps.-Luc.*Philopatr.*22.

**ἐκρῐπ-ίζω**, *fan the flame, light up*, Arist.*Mete.*346a9: metaph., *stir up, rouse*, θυμόν Theopomp.Hist.300, *Com.Adesp.*504; τὸ μάχιμον Plu.*Pomp.*8:—Pass., τοῖς θυμοῖς Id.*Pel.*15, cf. Lib.*Or.*51.125; εἰς πόλεμον J.*BJ*2.16.3. II. *blow away*, Aristid.*Or.*26(14).99. III. metaph., *fling away, cast out*, τινὰ ὥσπερ ἀπὸ σφενδόνης Ach.Tat.5.9. **-ισμός**, ὁ, *blowing forth*, Epicur.*Ep.*2 p.45 U.

**ἐκ-ριπτέω**, = sq., f.l. for ἐκριπίζω, Plu.2.654e:—Pass., Agatharch.48, Lib.*Decl.*31.33. ⊛ **-ρίπτω**, *cast forth*, ἔξω με [γῆς].. ἐκρίψατε S.*OT*1412; ἔπη A.*Pr.*932; *discharge*, γάλα Sor.1.88:—Pass., δίφρων ἐκριφθεὶς S.*El.*512; of an orator, *to be hissed off*, μεταξὺ λέγων ὑφ' ὑμῶν ἐξερρίφη Aeschin.2.153. 2. Pass., *to be spread abroad*, Lxx *Jd.*15.9. **-ριψις**, εως, ἡ, *throwing out* or *away*, *Gloss.*

**ἐκροή**, ἡ, (ἐκρέω) = ἔκροος I, Pherecyd.Syr.7, Pl.*Grg.*494b (pl.), Jul.*Or.*2.64d. II. = ἔκροος II, Hp.*Epid.*2.1.7 (pl.), Arist.*Mete.*356a10, Pl.*Phd.*112d, al.; περὶ τὰς ἐκροὰς *the places of efflux*, in the human body, Arist.*PA*688b28.

**ἔκροια**, Ion. ἐκροίη, ἡ, Hsch., = ἔκρυσις II, Sor.2.47; αἵματος Aret.*CD*2.3 (pl.).

**ἐκροιβδέω**, *empty by gulping down*, in Pass., κρατὴρ ἐξερροίβδητ' οἴνου Mnesim.4.17.

**ἐκροιζ-έω**, *pour forth*, ἰδέας Dam.*Pr.*311. **-ησις**, εως, ἡ, *rushing forth*, φωτός ib.283.

⊛ **ἐκρομβ-έω**, *displace* air, of a falling weight, Ph.*Bel.*69.19. **-ίζω**, *excise*, v.l. in Dsc.4.170.

⊛ **ἔκροος**, contr. -ρους, ὁ, *outflow, issue*, ἔκροον ἔχειν ἐς θάλασσαν, of rivers, Hdt.7.129, cf. Arr.*An.*4.3.2 (pl.). 2. κατ' ἔκροον *by excretion*, Hp.*Epid.*2.1.7. II. *outlet*, Arist.*Mete.*351a10; *means of escape*, Hp.*Virg.*

**ἐκροφέω**, *drink out, gulp down*, cj. in Ar.*Eq.*701, cf. Pl.Com.149, Arist.*HA*612a30; *swill*, Jul.*Caes.*318c: metaph., ἐ. τὸν μισθὸν Ar.*V.*1118.

**ἔκρυθμος**, ον, *out of tune*, S.E.*M.*11.186, Philostr.*VA*8.7. II. of the pulse, *irregular*, Gal.8.516.

**ἐκρύομαι** [ῡ], *deliver*, E.*Ba.*258, *Fr.*190, A.R.4.83 (tm.): c. gen., φασγάνων Lyc.190.

**ἐκρῠπᾰρόω**, perh. *reduce to ashes*, Theopomp.Hist.317.

**ἐκρύπτω**, *wash* or *rinse out*, Poll.1.44, 7.39:—Med., ἐκρύπτεσθαι τὸ ἀδικεῖν Ph.1.613.

**ἔκρῠσις**, εως, ἡ, = ἔκροος II, Arist.*Mete.*351a5, *IG*11(2).144*A*73 ((ἐγρ-) Delos, iv/iii B. C.), Plb.4.39.8. II. *efflux, flooding*, differing from τρωσμός (miscarriage), Hp.*Sept.*9, Arist.*GA*758b6 (pl.), *HA*583a25 (pl.). III. ἐ. τριχῶν *loss* of hair, Thphr.*HP*7.14.1.

**ἐκσᾰγηνεύω**, *entangle in the toils*, Plu.2.52c.

**ἐκσᾰλ-άσσω**, *shake violently*, *AP*5.234 (Maced.), v.l. in Theoc.2.85. **-εύω**, = foreg., *Sammelb.*4324.16, Hsch. s. v. ἐκβαβάξαι; *shake out*, Suid.

⊛ **ἐκσᾰόω**, Ep. for ἐκσῴζω, ἐξεσάωσεν ὀϊόμενον θανέεσθαι Il.4.12; ἐξεσάωσε θαλάσσης Od.4.501; ψυχὴν δ' ἐξ. v.l. in Archil.6; [πέδιλον] ὑπ' ἰλύος A.R.1.10.

**ἐκσαρκ-ίζομαι**, Pass., *have the flesh stripped off*, Lxx *Ez.*24.4. **-όω**, *make grow to flesh*:—Pass., *grow to flesh*: metaph., of olives, Thphr.*CP*1.19.5. II. intr., = Pass., Dsc.*Eup.*1.75:—hence **-ωμα**, ατος, τό, *fleshy excrescence*, Id.5.74. **-ωσις**, εως, ἡ, *formation of such an excrescence*, Gal.13.317.

**ἐκσᾰρόω**, *sweep out*, Eust.725.35 (Pass.), *Gloss.*

**ἐκσβέννῡμι**, in pf. part. intr. ἐξεσβηκώς, *run dry* at the source, ἐξ. τὸ γάλα Hsch. s. v. ἀμο⟨λ⟩γίδα.

**ἐκσείω**, *shake out* or *off*, τῆς κεφαλῆς ἐ. [τὸ δέρμα] Hdt.4.64; ἐ. τὴν ἐσθῆτα *shake out* one's clothes, Plu.*Ant.*79:—Pass., ἐκσέσειεται χαμάζ' (sc. ὁ τρίβων) Ar.*Ach.*344, cf. Gal.7.624. II. *drive out* or *forth*, τῶν λογισμῶν ἐ. τινά Plu.*Ant.*14; ἐ. τὴν ἀπολογίαν *reject* it, D.S.18.66.

**ἐκσεμνύνω**, strengthd. for σεμνύνω, Ath.14.661e.

**ἐκσεύομαι**, Pass., pf. ἐξέσσῠμαι: plpf. ἐξέσσῠτο with sense of impf. (Od.9.373), but usu. aor. (v. infr.): aor. 1 ἐξεσύθην [ῠ]:—*rush out* or *burst forth from*, πυλέων ἐξέσσυτο Il.7.1; φάρυγος δ' ἐξέσσυτο οἶνος Od.9.373; βλεφάρων ἐξέσσυτο νήδυμος ὕπνος sleep *fled away from* his eyelids, 12.366: abs., *rush out*, ἐκ δ' ἔσσυτο λαός Il.8.58; νομόνδ' ἐξέσσυτο..μῆλα Od.9.438; αἰχμὴ δ' ἐξεσύθη the point *burst out*, Il.5.293 (v.l.); ἐξέσσυται ἄνθρωπος ἐξ ἀνθρώπου Democr.32.

**ἐκσηκόω**, *weigh in the balance, assay*, in Pass., *Gloss*.

**ἐκσημαίνω**, *disclose, indicate*, S.*El*.1191.

**ἐκσήπομαι**, *to be* or *become quite rotten*, Hp.*Aff*.5, Thphr.*CP*5.16.2.

**ἐκσηπόω**, f.l. for ἐξιπόω, Aët.15.13 (bis: ἐξυποῖ, ἐξυπεῖ, ἐξιπεῖ codd.).

**ἐκσηπτόομαι**, *to be decomposed*, Ps.-Democr.Alch.p.44 B. (v.l. ἐξιπωθείσης, quod fort. leg.). **ἔκσηψις**, εως, ἡ, *putrefaction*, Gal.18(2).796.

**ἐκσῑγάομαι**, *to be put to silence*, *AP*7.182 (Mel., tm.).

**ἐκσῑφωνίζω**, *empty by a siphon*: metaph., *drain*, in Pass., ἐ. ἡ ἰσχύς Lxx *Jb*.5.5.

**ἐκσῐωπάω**, *put to silence*, in Pass., Plb.28.4.13. II. intr., *to be quite silent*, Arr.*An*.6.4.5.

**ἐκσκᾰλεύω**, *scoop out*, Ar.*Lys*.1028.

**ἐκ-σκάπτω**, *dig out*, *PTeb*.50.23 (ii B.C.); χοῦν *POxy*.1758.10 (ii A.D.):—Pass., *to be hollowed out*, ἐξεσκαμμέναι κοιλότητες Gal.18(2).618. **-σκᾰφή**, ἡ, *digging out*, *PTeb*.342.27 (iii A.D.).

**ἐκσκεδάννῡμι**, *scatter to the wind*, τὴν εἰρήνην ἐξεσκέδασας Ar.*Eq*.795.

**ἐκσκευάζω**, *disfurnish of tools and implements*, ἡ γεωργία ἐξεσκευάσθη D.30.30:—Med., *carry away with one*, χρήματα εἰς Σοῦσα Str.15.3.9; *plunder*, οἴκους J.*BJ*4.7.2:—Pass., ἐξεσκευασμένος f.l. for ἐν-, Plu.*Cleom*.37.

**ἔκσκευος**, ον, *without equipment, without mask*, Sch.Ar.*Av*.95. II. ἔ. πρόσωπα *special* masks, Poll.4.141; but ἔκσκευα· τὰ παρεπόμενα πρόσωπα ἐπὶ σκηνῆς, Hsch.

**ἔκσκηνος**, ον, (σκῆνος) *disembodied*, S.E.*M*.9.73 (ἡλίου is interpol.).

**ἐκσκορπισμός**, ὁ, *scattering abroad*, Plu.2.383d.

**ἐκσκυζάω**, = σκυζάω, Cratin.25 D.

**ἐκσμάω**, *wipe out*, τὰ ποτήρια Hdt.3.148.

**ἐκσμήχω**, = foreg., Ar.*Fr*.33a D. (Pass.).

**ἐκσοβέω**, *scare away*, ὄρνεις Men.168; πτῶκας *AP*6.167 (Agath.); νόον ἐκ στέρνων ib.5.259 (Paul. Sil.).

**ἔκσπᾰσις**, εως, ἡ, *plucking out*, τριχῶν Eust.1372.14.

**ἐκσπαστέον**, *one must draw out*, *Gp*.9.11.3.

**ἐκσπάω**, fut. -άσω, *draw out*, ἐξέσπασε μείλινον ἔγχος Il.6.65; σπάρτον Hero *Aut*.25.6; *pull up*, [χάρακα] Plb.18.18.14:—and so Med., ἐκσπασσαμένω δολίχ' ἔγχεα *having drawn out their* spears, Il.7.255:—Pass., [τρίχες] ἐκσπῶνται Arist.*Pr*.893$^a$20, cf. Hero *Aut*.16.2. II. *remove by force*, τοὺς ἐν τῷ ἱερῷ παστοφόρους *OGI*736.7 (Fayûm).

**ἐκσπένδω**, *pour out as a libation*, E.*Ion* 1193, Eub.71.

**ἐκσπερμᾰτ-ίζω**, *semen emitto*, ἐ. σπέρμα, of a woman, *conceive*, Lxx *Nu*.5.28. **-όω**, *convert into semen*, αἷμα Steph. *in Hp*.1.123 D. II. Pass., *run to seed*, Thphr.*HP*7.1.7.

⊛ **ἐκσπεύδω**, *hasten out* or *forth*, Ar.*Th*.277.

**ἐκσπογγίζω**, *wipe off with a sponge*, Eub.83, Aen.Tact.31.13.

**ἐκσποδιάζω**, *remove ashes*, Al.*Nu*.4.13.

**ἔκσπονδος**, ον, (σπονδαί) *out of the treaty, not a party thereto*, Th.3.68, X.*HG*5.1.32, D.19.44; ἔ. τῶν συνθηκῶν Plb.21.30.5. II. *contrary to a treaty, violating it*, ἔ. τι παθεῖν D.H.2.72.

**ἐκσπονδῠλίζω** or **ἐκσφονδ-**, *break the vertebrae*, Lxx 4 *Ma*.11.18: condemned by *EM*324.44.

**ἔκσπουδος**, *praeproperus*, *Gloss*.

⊛ **ἐκστάδιος** [ᾰ], ον, *six stades long*, Luc.*Nav*.39 (but prob. ἑκστ. shd. be read).

**ἐκστάζω**, *exude*, ὕδωρ Plot.2.7.2; *drain out*, αἷμα *PMag.Par*.1.1545.

**ἐκστᾰσιάζω**, *provoke sedition*, Poll.6.130:—Pass., Id.2.229.

**ἔκστᾰσις**, εως, ἡ, (ἐξίστημι) *displacement*, ἄρθρων Hp.*Art*.56; πᾶσα κίνησις ἔ. ἐστι τοῦ κινουμένου Arist.*de An*.406$^b$13: hence, *change*, εἰς ἀντικείμενα Id.*GA*768$^a$27; αἱ κακίαι ἐ. Id.*Ph*.247$^a$3; ἔ. ἐστιν ἐν τῇ γενέσει τὸ παρὰ φύσιν τοῦ κατὰ φύσιν Id.*Cael*.286$^a$19; ἔ. τῆς φύσεως *degeneracy*, Thphr.*CP*3.1.6; opp. στάσις, Plot.6.3.2; *movement outwards*, ἔ. ἀπὸ τοῦ παράγοντος Dam.*Pr*.97 bis; ἔ. εἰς τὸ ἔξω ib.401; [σῶμα] ἐν ἐκστάσει λαβὸν τὴν ὑπόστασιν Porph.*Sent*.36; *differentiation*, ἔ. καὶ πλῆθος Plot.6.7.17; αἱ εἰς πλῆθος ἐ. Procl. *in Ti*.2.203 D. II. *standing aside*, Arist.*Rh*.1361$^a$37 (pl.). b. = Lat. *cessio bonorum*, *CPR* 20 ii 9 (iii A.D.); ἔ. χρημάτων Porph.*Abst*.1.53; *a tax on cessions*, *BGU*914.6 (ii A.D.), *PLond*.2.305.2 (*PTeb*.ii p.184). 2. *distraction* of mind, from terror, astonishment, anger, etc., Hp.*Aph*.7.5, *Prorrh*.2.9; ἔ. σιγῶσα Id.*Coac*.65; ἔ. μανική Arist.*Cat*.10$^a$1; ἔ. τῶν λογισμῶν Plu.*Sol*.8; νοῦ Plot.5.3.7; τὰ μηδὲ προσδοκώμεν' ἔκστασιν φέρει Men.149, cf. *Epit*.472, Epicur.*Fr*.113; εἰς ἔ. ἄγειν Longin.1.4. 3. *entrancement, astonishment*, *Ev.Luc*.5.26, *Ev.Marc*.5.42. 4. *trance*, *Act.Ap*.10.10, 22.17; *ecstasy*, Plot.6.9.11; ἔ. καὶ μανία Herm. *in Phdr*.p.103 A. b. *drunken excitement*, Corn.*ND*30.

**ἐκστᾰτικός**, ή, όν, *inclined to depart from*, τοῦ λογισμοῦ Arist.*EN* 1145$^b$11; δόξης, opp. ἐμμενετικὸς δόξῃ, ib.1146$^a$18. 2. *excitable*, ἐ. διὰ τὸν θυμόν Id.*PA*650$^b$34; *out of one's senses*, of Ajax, Id.*Pr*.953$^a$22, cf. Plu.2.22a. Adv. -κῶς, ἔχειν Id.*Dio* 55. II. Act., *able to displace* or *remove*, τινός Id.2.951c: abs., ἡ ἀλλοίωσις ἐ. κίνησις Plot.6.3.21; *causing mental derangement*, Thphr.*HP*9.13.4.

**ἐκστέλλω**, *fit out, equip*, περόνας αἷσιν ἐξεστέλλετο S.*OT*1269. II. *send out*, πολίτας *SIG*730.16 (Olbia).

**ἐκστέφω**, *take off the crown*: *empty* a full cup, opp. ἐπιστέφω (q.v.), Paus.Gr.*Fr*.159. II. *deck with garlands*, E.*Alc*.171; esp. of suppliants, τέκνα στολμοῖσι κρᾶτας ἐξεστεμμένα Id.*HF*526; but ἱκτηρίοις κλάδοισιν ἐξεστεμμένοι *with garlands* on the suppliant olive-branches, S.*OT*3, cf. 19. III. ἐξέστεψε θάλασσαν *he poured* it all round *like a garland*, Opp.*H*.2.33, cf. Sch.; but better, *crowned*, ὀφρύσι καὶ ῥηγμῖσι. IV. ἐκστέψας· λόγον γυμνώσας, Hsch.

**ἐκστηθίζω**, = ἀποστηθίζω, Eust.974.10.

**ἐκστραγγίζω**, *squeeze* or *strain out*, v.l. in Lxx *Ez*.23.34, Dsc.4.150 (leg. ἐκσπογγίσας).

**ἐκστρᾰτ-εία**, ἡ, *going out on service*, Luc.*Gall*.25, Anon.ap.Suid. s.v. ἀξιόλογος, D.C.41.39. **-ευμα**, ατος, τό, *expeditionary force*, Memn.15: metaph. of Nature, Steph. *in Hp*.2.418 D. **-εύσιμος**, η, ον, *fit to take the field*, Sch.Th.6.30. **-ευσις**, εως, ἡ, *expedition*, Tz.*H*.9.380, *EM*729.19. ⊛ **-εύω**, *march out*, ἐς Λεῦκτρα Th.5.54; ὡς δουλωσόμενος.. X.*Ages*.7.7: trans., ἐ. τινά *march* him *out*, D.H.*Rh*.9.5,6. II. in Med., abs., *take the field*, Hdt.1.190; ἐς Ἴρασα Id.4.159: pf. Pass., *to be in the field*, Th.2.12; ἐπὶ τοῖς ὁρίοις And.1.45. 2. in pf., *to have ended the campaign*, Th.5.55. b. pf. part. Pass. ἐξεστρατευμένοι *veterans*, App.*BC*3.46.

**ἐκστρᾰτοπεδεύομαι**, *encamp outside*, Th.4.129, X.*Cyr*.6.3.1:—later in Act., J.*BJ*3.7.5.

⊛ **ἐκστρέφω**, *turn out of*, βόθρου τ' ἐξέστρεψε [δένδρον] *rooted up* a tree *from* the trench it stood in, Il.17.58. II. *turn inside out*, τὰ βλέφαρα Ar.*Pl*.721: metaph., *change* or *alter entirely*, τοὺς τρόπους Id.*Nu*.88; τοὺς ἡμετέρους Ἱππέας ib.554:—Pass., ποσὶν ἐξεστραμμένοις πορευόμενοι with feet *turned outwards*, Arist.*Phgn*.813$^a$14; *to be distorted*, Gal.7.27. 2. metaph. in pf. part. Pass., γενεὰ ἐξεστραμμένη *perverse* generation, Lxx *De*.32.20. 3. *transmute* base metal, Zos.Alch.p.195 B.

⊛ **ἐκστροφή**, ἡ, *dislocation*, τῶν δακτύλων Alciphr.3.54; ἐ. τοῦ σφιγκτῆρος, *eversio ani*, *Hippiatr*.41: metaph., τοῦ λόγου Plu.2.1072c. II. *transmutation* of base metal, Zos.Alch.p.195 B. III. *inversion* of uterus, Sor.1.73. IV. *projection* of the eyes, Archig.ap.Orib.46.26.2.

**ἐκστρόφια** (sc. φάρμακα), τά, *remedies for haemorrhoids*, Asclep. ap.Gal.13.313.

**ἐκστροφόω**, *force* a door *from its hinges*, Hsch. s.v. ἐξαγκυρῶσαι.

**ἐκστρώννῡμι**, *spread*:—Pass., κλῖναι ἐξέστρωντο Diog.*Ep*.37.3.

**ἐκσῡριγγόομαι**, Pass., of an abscess, *discharge itself by a fistulous opening*, Hp.*Coac*.389.

**ἐκσῡρίζω**, Att. -ττω, fut. ἐκσυριῶ Lxx *Si*.22.1: aor. 1 ἐξεσύρισα D.C.51.17:—*hiss off the stage*, τινά D.19.337, Luc.*Nigr*.9:—Pass., Antiph.191.21. 2. *hiss loudly*, D.C. l.c.

**ἐκσυρτικός**, ή, όν, *depilatory*, ἔμπλαστρον Hierocl.*Facet*.221.

⊛ **ἐκσύρω** [ῡ], *sweep away*, in aor. Pass. ἐξεσύρη [ῠ] *AP*9.56 (Phil.).

**ἐκσφενδονάω**, *throw as from a sling*, Hld.9.5, Mich. *in PN*93.32 (Pass.).

**ἐκσφονδῠλίζω**, v.s. ἐκσπονδ-.

**ἐκσφρᾱγ-ίζομαι**, Pass., *to be shut out from*, ἐκ γὰρ ἐσφραγισμένοι δόμων καθήμεθ' E.*HF*53. II. *to be sealed*, of a contract, *BCH*35.43 (Delos). **-ισμα**, ατος, τό, *official copy*, ταύτης τῆς ἐπιγραφῆς *CIG*3276 (Smyrna), cf. *IGRom*.4.513 (Pergam.), *POxy*.1882 (vi A.D.): generally, Mich. *in PN*20.10.

**ἐκσχίζω**, *cleave asunder*:—Pass., *to be divided*, Arist.*Mu*.400$^b$4, *Mir*.846$^a$14.

⊛ **ἐκσῴζω**, Ep. **ἐκσαόω** (q.v.):—*preserve from danger, keep safe*, Hdt.9.107, S.*Aj*.1128, etc.; ἐ. Αἰγίσθου χερός E.*El*.28; ἐ. τινὰ ἐς φάος νεκρῶν πάρα *to bring* him *safe*.., Id.*HF*1222; τινὰ ἐκ κινδύνων Pl.*Grg*.486b:—Med., *save oneself*, Hdt.2.107; also, *save for oneself*, ὡς.. βίοτον ἐκσωσοίατο A.*Pers*.360; κλῶνας ὡς ἐκσῴζεται [δένδρα] S.*Ant*.713:—Pass., ὅταν..νῆσον ἐκσῳζοίατο *when they fled for safety to* the island, A.*Pers*.451; πῶς ἐξεσώθης E.*Supp*.751.

**ἐκσωρεύω**, *heap, pile up*, E.*Ph*.1195 (Pass.).

**ἐκτᾰ, ἔκτᾰμεν, ἔκτᾰν**, v. κτείνω.

**ἐκτᾰγή**, ἡ, (ἐκτάσσω) *delegation of powers*, *Cod.Just*.10.16.13.1 (pl.). II. *assessment of taxes*, *PGiss*.54.9 (iv A.D.), etc.

**ἐκτᾰ-δά** [δᾰ], = sq., Nonn.*D*.37.596, cj. ib.46.153. **-δην**, Adv., (ἐκτείνω) *outstretched*, ἐ. κεῖσθαι lie *outstretched*, i.e. dead, E.*Ph*.1698, Luc.*DMort*.7.2. **-διος**, η, ον, also ος, ον Opp.*C*.3.276:—*outstretched*, χλαῖναν..διπλῆν ἐκταδίην double, *with ample folds*, Il.10.134; ἐ. ὅπλα Orph.*A*.359; οὐρέα D.P.643.

⊛ **ἐκτᾰδόν**, Adv. = ἐκτάδην, Lib.*Or*.11.215, Agath.5.12.

**ἔκτᾰθεν**, v. κτείνω. **ἐκτᾰθήσομαι**, v. ἐκτείνω.

**ἐκταῖος**, α, ον, (ἕξ) *on the sixth day*, ἐν τοῖσι πυρετοῖσι ἐκταίοισιν ἐοῦσι Hp.*Aph*.4.29, cf. *Coac*.15, X.*An*.6.6.38, D.S.17.65. II. = ἕκτος, μοῖρα *AP*14.119.10 (Metrod.). III. ἐκταῖον· αἱ δύο κοτύλαι, and ἐκταίους (sc. ἄρτους)· τοὺς ἐκ χοινίκων ἕξ, Hsch.

⊛ **ἔκτακτος**, ον, *detailed* for special duties, of soldiers, Ascl.*Tact*.6.3, Ael.*Tact*.9.4, 16.2,4. II. *special, reserved*, *POxy*.646 (ii A.D.); δι' ἐκτάκτου *on a separate sheet*, *PStrassb*.34.15.

**ἐκτᾰλαιπωρέω**, *endure*, ἄλλα Ant.Diog.6.

**ἐκτᾰλαντόομαι**, *to be stripped of money*, ἐκταλαντωθείς Sopat.19.

**ἔκταλος**· ἀκάνθης εἶδος, Hsch.

**ἔκτᾰμα**, ατος, τό, *extent, length*, Sch.Ar.*Nu.*2, Suid. s. v. πῆχυς. 2. gloss on ὄρεγμα, Sch.E.*Ph.*308.

⊛ **ἐκτᾰμιεύομαι**, *dispense*, Agatharch.102. II. *receive from store*, *PRein.*15.16, al. (ii B. C.).

**ἐκτάμνω**, Ion. for ἐκτέμνω.

⊛ **ἐκτανθαρύ⟨ζ⟩ω**· τρέμω, Hsch.

⊛ **ἐκτᾰνύω**, = ἐκτείνω, βραχίονας Theoc.25.270:—Hom. has this form only, in the sense *to stretch out* (on the ground), *lay low*, ἐξετάνυσσ' ἐπὶ γαίῃ Il.17.58:—Pass., *lie outstretched*, ὁ δ' ὕπτιος ἐξετανύσθη 7.271; ἐξετανύσθη ἄμπελος it *spread out all ways*, *h.Bacch.*38. 2. *stretch tight*, ἐκ δ' ἐτάνυσσ' ἱμάντα βοός (f.l. for ἐν δ') Od.23.201; [δέρμα] Pi. *P.*4.242. 3. *extend*, ἐξετάνυσσας ὁδόν *Epigr.Gr.*1078.4 (Cilicia).—For S.*OC*1562, v. ἐξανύω.—Poet. word, used by Hp.*Fract.*43. [ῠ usu., but ῡ *Anacreont.*35.5 (s. v. l.).]

**ἔκταξις**, εως, ἡ, *array of battle*, ἔ. ποιεῖσθαι Plb.2.33.7, cf. D.S.11.17. II. *expedition*, ἔ. κατ' Ἀλανῶν, title of work by Arr. III. *disposal, distribution*, σίτου J.*AJ*15.9.2.

**ἐκτᾰπεινόω**, strengthd. for ταπεινόω, Plu.2.165b, *Cor.*14.

**ἐκτᾰρ-ακτικός**, ή, όν, *calculated to disturb*, v.l. in Hp.*Acut.*(*Sp.*) 50. **-αξις**, εως, ἡ, *agitation*, κοιλίης Hp.*Judic.*20. **-άσσω**, Att. -ττω, *throw into confusion*, τοὺς ἵππους Ascl.*Tact.*7.4, etc.; *agitate*, τὸν δῆμον Plu.*Cor.*19, cf. Jul.*Or.*2.97d:—Pass., *to be greatly troubled, be confounded*, ὑπό τινος Isoc.15.5, Ath.12.552f; πρός τι Luc. *Somn.*16. II. in Pass. also, *to have a bowel-complaint*, κοιλίη ἐκταραχθεῖσα Hp.*Aph.*4.60, *Epid.*1.15.

**ἐκταρβέω**, strengthd. for ταρβέω, in Pass., Hsch.

⊛ **ἐκταρσόομαι**, = ταρσόομαι, Hp.*Oss.*12.

**ἔκτᾰσις**, εως, ἡ, (ἐκτείνω) *stretching out, extension*, Hp.*Art.*19; σκέλους, κώλων, Arist.*IA*711ᵃ30, *PA*688ᵃ16; καμπὴ καὶ ἔ. Pl.*Lg.*795e: metaph., ἔ. ἄρρητος τῆς ἑαυτοῦ ⟨οὐσίας⟩ Porph.*Sent.*28; ἡ εἰς πλῆθος ἔ. Procl.*Inst.*128. 2. *extent*, φιλίας Max.Tyr.6.2; παμπληθὴ θεωρίας ἔ. Iamb.*VP*29.162. 3. mental *tension*, v.l. for ἔκστασις in D.H.*Comp.*15. 4. *making explicit*, κατ' ἔκτασιν, opp. κατ' ἐπίνοιαν, *Theol.Ar.*5, cf. 12. 5. *impulse*, τοῦ ὀρεκτικοῦ ἐπί τι Plot.1.1.5. 6. Tact., *extension, deployment*, συναγωγαὶ καὶ ἐκτάσεις στρατιᾶς Pl.*R.*526d, cf. Onos.10.2. II. *lengthening of a short syllable*, D.H.*Comp.*25 (pl.); κατ' ἔκτασιν παραλαμβάνεσθαι D.T.632.32; ἔστιν ἐν ἐκτάσει τοῦ ῑ A.D.*Adv.*161.6.

⊛ **ἐκτάσσω**, Att. -ττω, *draw out in battle-order*, of the officers, Plb.3.112.1, D.S.17.53; πρὸς μάχην Onos.1.13:—Med., *draw themselves out*, of the soldiers, X.*An.*5.4.12, etc.:—Pass., Plb.5.83.1. II. *keep muster-roll of*, λαόν Lxx 4*Ki.*25.19. 2. ἐκτάσσοντα· χαράσσοντα, γράφοντα, Hsch.

**ἐκτᾰτέον**, *one must pronounce long*, Sch.Il.21.262.

**ἐκτᾰτικός**, ή, όν, *given to lengthening*, Ἀθηναῖοι ἐ. τῶν φωνηέντων A.D.*Adv.*187.21. II. *preserving tension*, αὐτῶν δι' εὐτονίαν Chrysipp.*Stoic.*2.146 (codd. Plu., ἐκτικά Arnim).

**ἐκτᾰτός**, ή, όν, *capable of extension*, κῶλα ἐ. καὶ καμπτά Pl.*Ti.*44e.

**ἐκταφρεύω**, *to dig trenches*, in Pass., J.*BJ*5.2.2, App.*BC*3.65, Hsch.

**ἐκτέατο**, Ion. 3 pl. plpf. of κτάομαι.

⊛ **ἐκτείνω**, fut. -τενῶ A.*Pr.*325, etc.:—*stretch out*, χεῖρ' ἐπ' ἐκφορᾷ νεκροῦ Id.*Ch.*9; τὴν χ. ὑπτίαν Ar.*Ec.*782; τὰς χεῖρας ἐπί τι for something, Plb.1.3.6; πρός τινα, in sign of friendship, Id.2.47.2; πρὸς κέντρα κῶλον A.*Pr.*325; παῖδας ἐπὶ τὴν πυρήν Hdt.2.107; ἐκεῖσε κἀκεῖσ' ἀσπίδ' ἐ. E.*Andr.*1131; εἰς ἧπαρ ξίφος ἐ. Id.*Ph.*1421: abs., *offer food*, Ath.5.186c; τὰ γόνατ' ἐ. *straighten* the knees, Ar.*V.*1212; ἐ. τὰ σκέλη X.*An.*5.8.14; νοῦ ἄπο μυρίον ὄμμα *IG*3.716; ἐ. νέκυν E.*Hipp.*786; ἐν γὰρ ἐκτενεῖ σ' ἔπος *will lay* thee *prostrate*, Id.*Med.*585:—Pass., *to be outstretched, lie at length*, of sleepers, etc., S.*Ph.*858 (lyr.); ἐκταθεὶς ὥσπερ Ὀδυσσεὺς ἀφικέσθαι εἰς τὴν Ἑλλάδα X.*An.*5.1.2, etc.; of countries, etc., *extend*, Id.*Vect.*4.3, D.P.40. 2. *stretch, spread out* a net, A.*Ch.*991; *extend the line of* an army, E.*Heracl.*801, Arr. *Tact.*5.6; λαὸν ἐκτείνοντ' ἄνω (sc. ἑαυτόν) E.*Supp.*654; στράτευμα X.*HG*6.5.19:—Pass., *to be unfolded, smoothed*, ὡς ἂν Διὸς μέτωπον ἐκταθῇ χαρᾷ S.*Fr.*902. II. *spin out, prolong*, πλεῦνα λόγον Hdt.7.51; φροίμιον θεοῖς A.*Ag.*829; μακρὰν ἐξέτεινας ib.916, cf. E.*Med.*1351; μῆκος λόγου A.*Eu.*201; μείζονα λόγον S.*Tr.*679, etc.; βίον E.*Supp.*1109; τοὺς περιπάτους X.*Mem.*3.13.5:—Pass., λόγος ἐκταθεὶς Pl.*Lg.*887a; of Time, πολὺς ἐκτέταται χρόνος S.*Aj.*1402 (anap.). III. *put to the full stretch*, ἵππον ἐ. X.*Cyr.*5.4.5; ἐ. πάντα κάλων Pl.*Prt.*338a; πᾶσαν προθυμίην ἐ. *put forth* all one's zeal, Hdt.7.10.η'; τὸν θυμόν And.3.31; ἅπασαν ἀγωνίαν D.60.30: metaph. in Pass., *to be on the rack*, ἐκτέταμαι S.*OT*153 (lyr.). IV. *lengthen* a short syllable, A.D.*Pron.*27.2 (Pass.), al., interpol. in D.H.2.58. V. intr., *draw along*, Lxx *Jd.*20.37.

**ἔκτεισις**, Arc. ἐσ-, εως, ἡ, later **ἔκτισις**, *payment in full*, *IG*5(2).6.37 (Tegea, iv B. C.), *SIG*279.17 (iv B. C.), *PCair.Zen.*1.18, 44 (iii B. C.), *PPetr.*3 p.160 (iii B. C.), etc.; ζημίας Pl.*Lg.*855a (pl.); ἐ. δεκαπλασία Din.2.17; ἡ ἔ. ἣν ἐπὶ τῆς ἐνάτης πρυτανείας And.1.73; προικός D.40.56; ἔ. ποιεῖσθαι, = ἐκτίνειν, Id.27.67; ἔγγυος εἰς ἔκτεισιν *PHib.*1.94 (iii B. C.), etc.; ἔ. δίκης, προστίμου, Iamb.*Myst.*4.5, *PLond.*1.113 (vi A. D.).

**ἔκτεισμα**, later **ἔκτισμα**, ατος, τό, *payment*, *IG*11(2).144*A*20 (Delos, iv B. C.), 162*A*41. II. *penalty*, Pl.*Lg.*868b, D.H.10.52 (pl.).

**ἐκτειχ-ίζω**, Att. fut. -ιῶ, *fortify completely*, Th.7.26, X.*HG*3.2.10, etc.:—Pass., τὸ τεῖχος ἐκτετείχισται ταχύ Ar.*Av.*1165. **-ισμός**, ὁ, *fortification*, Arr.*An.*6.20.1.

**ἐκτεκμαίρομαι**, aor. 1 part. Pass. ἐκτεκμαρθείς, *to be made out by guessing*, Orac.ap.Eus.*PE*5.23.

⊛ **ἐκτεκνόω**, *engender*, ἡ φύσις ἐ. πάθεα Hp.*Acut.*43:—Med., παῖδας ἐκτεκνούμενος λάθρᾳ E.*Ion* 438.

**ἐκτεκταίνομαι**, aor. 1 ἐξετεκτηνάμην, *construct*, τὰς φλιὰς τῶν ὀνίσκων Hp.*Art.*47.

**ἐκτελέθω**, *spring from*, τινός Emp.17.10.

**ἐκτελ-ειόω** or **-εόω**, *bring to perfection*, Thphr.*CP*4.1.5, etc.; βίον Plu.*Publ.*23. **-είωσις**, εως, ἡ, *completion*, Thphr.*CP*1.9.3.

**ἐκτελευτάω**, *bring to an end, accomplish*, Pi.*P.*12.29 (tm.), Semon.1.5: c. inf., ἐ. γενέσθαι *to bring* it *at last* to be, Pi.*P.*4.19; ἐ. μῆκος χρόνου A.*Pr.*1020:—Pass., *to be the end of*, πόνων S.*Tr.*170. II. intr. in Act., *turn out*, καλῶς A.*Supp.*411.

**ἐκτελ-έω**, Ep. impf. ἐξετέλειον Il.9.493, Od.4.7: Ep. fut. -τελέω Il.2.286, 10.105: aor. part. ἐκτελέσαντες Sapph.*Supp.*6.5: fut. Med. in pass. sense (v. infr.):—*bring to an end, accomplish, achieve*, ἐκτελέσας μέγα ἔργον Od.3.275; ὥς κεν.. ἐκτελέσειεν ἀέθλους 8.22; ὁδὸν ἐκτελέσαντες 10.41, etc.; *fulfil* a promise, etc., οὐδέ τοι ἐκτελέουσιν ὑπόσχεσιν Il.2.286; μή οἱ ἀπειλὰς ἐκτελέσωσι θεοί 9.245; οὔ θην Ἕκτορι πάντα νοήματα.. Ζεὺς ἐκτελέει 10.105, etc.; ἐπιθυμίην Hdt.1.32; ἔρωτα Pl.*Smp.*193c; τἀντεταλμένα E.*Ph.*1648 codd.; μυστήρια *PMag.Osl.*1.306: abs., Δαρείου ἐκτελέσας (sc. τὸ ἔργον) κατὰ νοῦν Epigr.ap. Hdt.4.88:—Pass., ὧδε γὰρ ἐκτελέεσθαι ὀΐομαι *will be accomplished*, Il.12.217, cf. 7.353; ἐκτελοῖτο δὴ τὰ χρηστά A.*Pers.*228. 2. of Time, Hes.*Op.*565, Hdt.6.69, Pi.*P.*4.104:—Pass., μῆνές τε καὶ ἡμέραι ἐξετελεῦντο Od.11.294. **-ής**, ές, (τέλος) *brought to an end, perfect*, ἀγάθ' ἐκτελῆ γενέσθαι A.*Pers.*218; of corn, *ripe*, Hes.*Op.*466; also of persons, ἤδη πεφυκότ' ἐκτελῆ νεανίαν E.*Ion*780, cf. A.*Ag.*105 (lyr., s. v. l.). Adv. -λῶς *in full, completely*, *BGU*1116.9 (i B. C.).

**ἐκτέμνω**, Ep. and Ion. **ἐκτάμνω** (as always in Hom.), fut. -τεμῶ: aor. 2 ἐξέταμον (v. infr.) or -έτεμον S.*Tr.*1196, Ar.*Ra.*575: fut. perf. ἐκτετμήσομαι Pl.*R.*564c, Ph.1.458:—*cut out*, μηροὺς ἐξέταμον Il.1.460, etc.; μηροῦ ἔκταμ' ὀϊστόν *cut* an arrow *from* the thigh, 11.829, cf. 515; ἐ. γλῶσσαν Hdt.9.112; ἐ. τὸν λάρυγγά τινος Ar.*Ra.*575; of a surgeon, *cut out* a diseased part, Pl.*R.*564c (Pass.); σχῆμα τῆς γῆς Arist.*Mete.*362ᵃ35. 2. *cut* trees *out of* a wood, *cut down*, Il.12.149, S.*Tr.*1196; also of planks, etc., *hew out, hew into shape*, ὅς ῥά τε τέχνῃ νήϊον ἐκτάμνῃσιν Il.3.62, cf. 4.486; ἐ. τὰ πρέμνα *to cut* the stumps *out of the ground*, Lys.7.19. 3. ἐ. ἶνας *cut away* the sinews, and so, *weaken*, Pi.*I.*8(7).57; ἐ. ὥσπερ νεῦρα ἐκ τῆς ψυχῆς Pl.*R.*411b; ῥόδον ἐ. ῥίζης *IG*14.2040: metaph., ἐλπίδας ἐξέταμες ib.1362; 'nip in the bud', πάθος Alex.Trall.1.17:—Pass., ἐκτέμνεσθαι νοῦν καὶ λόγον Ph.1.17. II. *castrate*, παῖδας Hdt.6.32, 8.105; ὄρχεις ἐ. S.*Fr.*620; οἱ ἐκτετμημένοι *eunuchs*, Arist.*HA*518ᵃ31; ἐ. τὰ θήλεα *circumcise* females, Str.17.2.5, cf. 16.4.9 (Pass.). III. = κείρειν, γῆς ἐκτεμνομένης D.H.9.57 (s. v. l.). IV. ἐκτέμνεσθαί τινας φιλανθρωπίᾳ *to disarm and deceive* by kindness, Plb.30.30.8.

**ἔκτεμπροι**· προσμένοντες, Hsch.

⊛ **ἐκτέν-εια**, ἡ, *zeal, assiduousness*, Molpis 3, *PPetr.*3 p.18 (iii B. C.), Phld.*D.*3.2, etc.; '*gush*', '*empressement*', Cic.*Att.*10.17.1; ἐ. καὶ φιλοτιμία *IG*2².1343.28, cf. Hierocl.p.62 A.; τὰν πᾶσαν ἐ. καὶ κακοπαθίαν παρεχόμενος *IG*12(1).1032.10 (Carpathos), cf. *Inscr.Prien.*107.20, al. (ii B. C.), *UPZ*110.12 (ii B. C.), etc.; ἐν ἐκτενείᾳ *eagerly*, *Act.Ap.*26.7, cf. Lxx *Ju.*4.9; μετὰ πάσης ἐ. ib.2*Ma.*14.38. II. *abundance*, ξύλων Hdn.7.2.4, cf. 8.2.6. III. *extension*, Dam.*Pr.*65. **-ής**, ές, *strained*: hence of persons, *warmly attached, friendly*, Plb.21.22.4 (Sup.), cf. D.S.34.2.39, Socr.ap.Stob.4.31.130; *assiduous*, περί τινα *Supp.Epigr.*2.277.5 (Delph., ii B. C.): Comp. -έστερος τῇ προθυμίᾳ *IGRom.*4.293ᵃii 38 (Pergam., ii B. C.): Sup. -εστάτη προθυμία Chrysipp.*Stoic.*2.293, cf. *Vit.Philonid.*p.9 C.; πρόνοια *UPZ*110.46 (ii B. C.). 2. *extended*, Dam.*Pr.*64; *capable of extension*, ἐ. ἐστι τὸ μεταδιδὸν τῶν ἑαυτοῦ καὶ τοῖς ἄλλοις Herm.*in Phdr.*p.121 A. 3. *abundant*, γάλα Sor.1.94. II. Adv. -νῶς (Elean ἐκτενέωρ *GDI*1172.12; Cret. ἐκτενίως ib.5138.13; Ion. -έως Ps.-Hdt.*Vit.Hom.*7) *earnestly, zealously*, ἀγαπᾶσθαι Macho ap.Ath.13.579e; ποιεῖν τι Arist. *MM*1210ᵃ27; συναγωνίζεσθαι *IG*2².945, cf. *SIG*538.17 (Delph., iii B. C.); εὐχὴ ἐ. γινομένη *Act.Ap.*12.5: Comp. -έστερον Cic.*Att.*13.9.1: Sup. -έστατα D.S.29.4. 2. in Adv. also, *eagerly, freely, splendidly* (condemned by Phryn.285), προσδέξασθαί τινα Plb.8.19.1, cf. D.S.2.24, etc.; of public duties, λαμπρῶς καὶ ἐ. τετελεκότα *CIG*2771 ii 14 (Aphrodisias): Comp., πολυτελῶς καὶ ἐκτενέστερον τῶν ἄλλων Agatharch.*Fr.Hist.*6 J.—Not in early writers, corrupt in A.*Supp.*983.

**ἔκτεξις**, εως, ἡ, *child-birth*, Arist.*Mir.*847ᵇ6, Anon.Lond.18.21, Sor.2.54, S.E.*M.*5.55.

⊛ **ἐκτέος**, α, ον, (ἔχω) *to be held*, Ar.*Ach.*259. II. **ἑκτέον**, *one must have*, χάριν τινί X.*Mem.*3.11.2; πρόνοιαν Aen.Tact.*Praef.*3; πλέον ἑ., = πλεονεκτητέον, Pl.*Grg.*490c. 2. *one must behave, comport oneself*, πρὸς τοὺς κινδύνους εὐρώστως Iamb.*VP*30.173.

**ἐκτετᾰμένως**, Adv., (ἐκτείνω) *lengthened*, of a short syllable, Ath.3.105e, *AB*383, etc. II. = ἡπλωμένως, Hsch.

**ἑκτεύς**, έως, ὁ, (ἕκτος) *the sixth part* (*sextarius*) *of the* μέδιμνος, πυρῶν, κριθέων, *Schwyzer* 725 (Milet., vi B. C.), cf. *IG*1².76.6, Ar.*Ec.*547, Men.91.

**ἐκτεύχω**, *work out, produce*, Hp.*Ep.*23 (Ps.-Democr.).

**ἐκτεφρ-όω**, *burn to ashes, calcine*, in Pass., Str.5.4.9, Dsc.1.68.4, 5.81, Plu.2.696b: metaph., of bile, Alex.Trall.*Febr.*7. **-ωσις**, εως, ἡ, *burning to ashes*, Str.5.4.8.

**ἐκτεχνάομαι**, *devise a plan*, τοιόνδε τι ἐξετεχνήσαντο Th.6.46.

**ἐκτεχνολογέω**, *set forth in technical language, reduce to system*, Phld.*Rh.*1.203 S. (Pass.).

⊛ **ἕκτη**, ἡ, a silver coin, *the sixth of a stater*, *IG*1².310, al. II. *tax*

*of one-sixth*, ἕ. παραδείσων *PTeb.*343.69 (ii A.D.), cf. *PHib.*1.109 (iii B.C.), *PRev.Laws* 36.9 (iii B.C.). III. *liquid measure*, ἕ. οἴνω *Schwyzer* 725 (Milet., vi B.C.).

⊛ **ἐκτήκω**, fut. -ξω E.*Or.*134:—*melt out*, Κύκλωπος ὄμματ' ἐ. πυρί Id.*Cyc.*459; τὰ γράμματ' ἐ. *melt out* the letters written on wax, Ar. *Nu.*772. 2. metaph., *let melt, pine* or *waste away*, ὄμμα δακρύοις E.*Or.*134, cf. 529; δάκρυσι χρόα Id.*Hel.*1419; τὸν θυμόν Pl.*R.*411b; λῆστις δ' ἐ. μνημοσύνην πραπίδων Critias 6.12 D.; τὴν ὑπάρχουσαν ἐ. κρᾶσιν Plu.*Lyc.*5; ἐ. τινὰ εἰς δάκρυα Id.*Brut.*23; λύπῃ καὶ λιμῷ ἑαυτόν Ael.*NA* 10.41. II. Pass., with pf. ἐκτέτηκα: aor. ἐξετάκην [ᾰ]:—*melt and ooze out*, Hp.*Coac.*629; τὸ ἐκτετηκός *flabby condition*, Id.*Aph.*2.35. 2. metaph., *pine, waste away*, ἐκτέτηκα καρδίαν E. *Hec.*433; ἐξετηκόμην γόοις Id.*Or.*860, etc.; τὰς ὁράσεις ἐκτετηκυῖα ὑπὸ τῶν δακρύων D.H.8.45, cf. Luc.*Gall.*29,31; μάλα μοι τόδ' ἐμμένοι καὶ μήποτ' ἐκτακείη *may it* never *melt from* my remembrance, A.*Pr.* 535 (lyr.), cf. Critias l.c.

⊛ **ἐκτημόρ-ιοι**, οἱ, = ἕκτα τῶν γινομένων τελοῦντες, those *who paid a sixth* (or *five-sixths*) *of the produce* as rent, Plu.*Sol.*13:—also **ἐκτήμοροι**, Arist.*Ath.*2.2. II. ἐκτημόριον, τό, *a sixth part*, S.E.*M.*10.140, Protag.Nicae.ap.Heph.Astr.3.30. III. ἐκτήμορος (sc. κύαθος), ὁ, a *liquid measure*, Herod.1.80. **-ίτης** [ῑ], ου, ὁ, = ἐκτημόριον, Gal.1.144.

**Ἔκτηνες**, οἱ, primitive inhabitants of Boeotia, Paus.9.5.1.

**ἔκτηξις**, εως, ἡ, *melting away*: hence, *attenuation*, φλεβῶν Hp. *Aër.*10 (v.l. ἔκτασιν). II. *cancelling* of contract, *BCH* 37.91 (Beroea).

**ἐκτῐθᾰσεύω**, strengthd. for τιθασεύω, Poll.4.28.

⊛ **ἐκτίθημι** (inf. -τιθεῖν *IG*7.235.41), fut. -θήσω: pf. -τέθεικα *UPZ* 62.4 (ii B.C.):—*set out, place outside*, πυκινὸν λέχος Od.23.179; *expose* on a desert island, S.*Ph.*5; *expose* a new-born child, Hdt.1.112, Ar.*Nu.*531, etc.; τὸν παῖδ'.. ἐξέθηκε δωμάτων E.*Ion* 344:—so in Pass., τέθνηκε.. θηρσὶν ἐκτεθείς ib.951; *expose*, ἑαυτὸν βέλεσι Polem.*Cyn.*7:—Med., ἐκτίθεσθαι λείαν εἰς Βιθυνούς *export* it thither, Plu.*Alc.*29. II. *set up, offer for a prize*, λέβητας ἐκτιθεὶς φέρειν S.*Fr.*378; ἆθλα Plb.15.9.4. b. *fix* or *grant* allowances, rates of pay, etc., *PSI*5.498 (iii B.C.), *PEdgar* 2.4 (Pass.), etc. 2. *exhibit publicly, post up*, νόμους πρὸς τοὺς ἐπωνύμους Decr.ap.And.1.83, cf. Lex ap.D.24.23; ἔκθεμα *PPetr.*2 p.44 (iii B.C.); ὀνόματα εἰς στοάν *SIG*577.28 (Milet., iii/ii B.C.):—Pass., ὅπως ἐκτεθῶσι [οἱ νόμοι] *IG*2$^2$.487.6, etc. 3. *expose for sale*, D.C.46.14 (Pass.). III. *set forth, expound*, τὴν πρόθεσιν Arist.*Rh.Al.*1437$^b$35; κατὰ γένος Thphr.*Char.Praef.*3:—also Med., λόγους καθόλου Arist.*Po.*1455$^b$1; τὴν ἑαυτῆς ἐρημίαν D.S.12.18, etc. 2. Philos., *predicate separate existence* of a thing, *explain by means of abstraction*, Arist.*Metaph.* 1086$^b$10. IV. Med., *set forth, select* particular instances of a rule, [ποιεῖν τὴν ἀπόδειξιν] τῷ ἐκθέσθαι Id.*An.Pr.*28$^a$23:—Pass., τὸ ἐκτεθέν ib.30$^a$11. 2. *set out* terms in syllogistic form, ib.48$^a$1, al. 3. *isolate* in thought, Id.*SE* 179$^a$3. 4. *pick out for separate treatment*, Id.*Ph.*235$^a$28. 5. ἐ. καθόλου *set out* in general form, Id. *Po.*1455$^b$1.

**ἐκτῐθηνέω**, *rear up, foster*, Plu.2.1070c (Med.).

**ἐκτῐκεύομαι**, *suffer from hectic fever*, Alex.Trall.*Febr.*4 (aor. part. -κωθέντας corrupt, ib.5).

**ἐκτικός**, ή, όν, (ἕξις) *formed by* or *forming habit*, τὸ βέβαιον καὶ ἐ. Chrysipp.*Stoic.*3.138; ἐ. δύναμις ib.2.149; ποιεῖν τι ἐκτικόν to do a thing *as a matter of habit, easily*, Arr.*Epict.*2.18.4; ἐ. πρὸς τὴν τέχνην Democr.ap.Gal.13.1001. Adv. -κῶς *from habit, easily, fluently*, γράμματα ἀναγινώσκειν Artem.1.53, cf. D.S.3.4, Plu.2.802f: Comp. -ώτερον Arr.*Epict.*3.24.78; but also ἐ. διαμένειν [λίθον] remain *fixed in its nature*, Porph.*Abst.*4.20. 2. ἐ. αἰτία *sustaining* causes, Chrysipp.*Stoic.*2.273 (s.v.l.). 3. *capable of*, φύσις τινὸς ἐ. Phld.*Ir.* p.14 W. II. *hectic, consumptive*, f.l. in Arist.*Pr.*920$^b$27; of fevers, Gal.7.315, Alex.Aphr.*Pr.*1.88; σφυγμός Gal.8.460. Adv. -κῶς Id. 10.603.

**ἐκτίκτω**, aor. 2 ἐξέτεκον Arist.*HA* 621$^b$20: pf. ἐκτέτοκα Pl.*Tht.* 210b:—*bring forth*, Arist.*HA* 571$^b$11, al.; of fish, *spawn*, ib.547$^a$2, 621$^b$20: metaph., Pl. l. c.

**ἐκτῑλάω**, *void* excrement, *Hippiatr.*90, Sch.Ar.*Av.*791.

⊛ **ἐκ-τίλλω**, fut. ἐκτῐλῶ Hsch. s. v. ἐκποκιῶ: aor. inf. ἐκτῖλαι· ἐκτινάξαι, Id.:—Pass., fut. ἐκτιλήσομαι Lxx *Si.*40.16: aor. 2 ἐξετίλην [ῐ] Dsc.*Eup.*1.52, Thd.*Da.*7.4:—*pluck out*, τρίχας Arist.*HA* 603$^b$22; πτερόν ib.519$^a$27 (Pass.); of a person, κόμην ἐκτετιλμένος Anacr.21.11. II. *pluck, strip bare*, τὴν τράμιν Hippon.84; τὴν ῥοδωνιάν D. 53.16. 2. *strip the leaves off*, ὀρίγανον, κρόμμυον, Arist.*Mir.*831$^a$30, *Pr.*924$^a$32. **-τιλτέον**, *one must pluck out*, τὰς τρίχας Aët.9.8.

⊛ **ἐκτῑμ-άω**, *honour highly*, S.*El.*64 (Pass.), Plb.30.19.3, etc.; *honour too highly*, πλοῦτον Longin.44.7; ἐκτετιμημένος *overpriced*, Arist. *Oec.*1352$^b$5. II. *estimate*, Pl.*Ep.*347b. **-ησις**, εως, ἡ, *high esteem*: *estimation*, Str.14.1.23, Porph.*Abst.*2.24. II. *valuation*, *PKlein.Form.*78 (v/vi A.D.). **-ητρα**, Dor. -ατρα, τά, *penalties*, *SIG* 1146 (possibly, = *reward for redemption from slavery*). **-ος**, ον, (τιμή) *without honour*, γονέων ἐκτίμους ἴσχουσα πτέρυγας.. γόων restraining them *so that they show not the honour due* to parents, S. *El.*242 (lyr.). II. *highly priced*, Hsch.

⊛ **ἐκτῐν-αγμός**, ὁ, *shaking out, violent shaking*, Lxx *Na.*2.10(11), Ph. 1.415; perh. *winnowing* or *threshing*, *PFay.*114.22 (i A.D.). ⊛ **-ακτρον**, τό, *winnowing-shovel*, *POxy.*1733.5 (iii A.D.). **-αξις**, εως, ἡ, = -αγμός, Heph.Astr.1.20, *EM* 281.18. ⊛ **-άσσω**, *shake out*, in cleaning, ἔρια, ἱμάτια, *BGU* 827.22; *expel*, ἕλμινθας Diph.Siph.ap. Ath.2.51f, cf. Dsc.1.126; ἔμβρυα ib.76:—Pass., ἐκ δ' ἐτίναχθεν ὀδόντες Il.16.348, cf. Plu.*Cat.Ma.*14; [ὁ Φαέθων] ἐκτινάσσεται *is thrown out*, Palaeph.52, cf. Agath.4.20. 2. *shake off*, τὸν κονιορτὸν τῶν ποδῶν *Ev.Matt.*10.14, etc.:—Med., *Act.Ap.*13.51. 3. *search thoroughly*, τοὺς βαδίζοντας Diog.*Ep.*37.5. II. intr., *make a disturbance*, Hp. *Epid.*6.2.19; *make a thorough search*, *UPZ* 5.12 (ii B.C.); *kick out*, of animals, εἰς τοὺς πλησίον ἵππους Ael.*Tact.*19.2.

**ἐκτίννυμι**, = sq., v.l. in D.S.16.29, J.*BJ* 3.8.5, Hermog.*Inv.*2.3, etc.: **ἐκτιννύω**, Cyr.

⊛ **ἐκτίνω** [ῐ], fut. -τείσω: aor. 1 ἐξέτεισα: pf. ἐκτέτεικα D.40.52:—*pay off, pay in full*, [ζημίην] χίλια τάλαντα Hdt.6.92; εὐεργεσίας Id. 3.47; Ἄργει δ' ἐκτίνων τροφάς *making a return for* bringing one up, A.*Th.*548; χάριτας πατρῴας E.*Or.*453, etc.; τροφεῖα Pl.*R.*520b; ἔκ τινα τῖσαι ἀμοιβήν Maiist.40; δίκην ἐ. *pay full* penalty, E.*El.*260, Lys. 23.14; τινός *for* a thing, Hdt.9.94; so τίσιν ἐ. τινί Id.6.72; ἄποινα ib.79; ἐ. βλάβην *to make* it *good*, Pl.*Lg.*936e, cf. A.*Ag.*1562 (lyr.), 1582; τὸ βλάβος D.21.43; δίκην ἐ. ὑπὲρ χρημάτων Is.10.15. II. Med., *exact full payment for* a thing, *avenge*, E.*HF* 547; *take vengeance on*, τινά Id.*Med.*267. 2. ἐ. ὕβριν *wreak* despite, S.*Aj.*304.

**ἔκτισις**, v. ἔκτεισις. **ἔκτισμα**, v. ἔκτεισμα.

⊛ **ἐκτιστής**· ἀποδότης, Hsch.

**ἐκτιτθεύω**, = ἐκτιθηνέω, *rear by suckling*, Arist.*HA* 522$^a$6.

**ἐκτιτράω**, fut. -τρήσω, *bore through*:—Pass., ἐκτιτρώμενος Orib. 46.20.10: pf. Pass. ἐκτετρῆσθαι Hero *Bel.*96.2, part. ἐκτετρημένος Poll.2.70.

**ἐκτιτρώσκω**, *bring forth untimely*, βρέφος D.S.3.64, 4.2, *PGoodsp. Cair.*15.15 (iv A.D.). 2. abs., *miscarry*, Hdt.3.32, Hp.*Aph.*3.12, Arist.*HA* 585$^a$22:—so in Med., Hp.*Aër.*10. 3. *attempt to procure abortion*, Id.*Mul.*1.78.—Ion. and later Prose for Att. ἐξαμβλόω, Phryn.184.

**ἐκτλάω**, *bear, sustain to the end*, aor. inf. ἐκτλῆναι Ph.2.464 (s.v.l.).

**ἔκ-τμημα**, ατος, τό, *section, segment*, τῆς γῆς ἐκτμήματα, of the zones, Arist.*Mete.*362$^b$5. **-τμησις**, εως, ἡ, *castration*, Id.*Pr.*895$^a$1; *excision*, *Gloss.* **-τμητέον**, *one must cut out*, Ph.2.212, Max.Tyr. 13.7, Philum.*Ven.*16.6.

**ἔκτοθεν**, Adv., (ἐκτός) Ep. for ἔξωθεν, = ἔκτοσθεν, *from without, outside*, c. gen., ἐ. ἄλλων μνηστήρων *outside* their circle, *apart from* them, Od.1.132; λίμνας ἐ. A.*Pers.*871 (lyr.); πύργων δ' ἐ. βαλών having struck them *from* the wall, Id.*Th.*629 (lyr.); ἐ. ἐρώτων *AP* 5.301.7 (Agath.). 2. abs., *outside, without*, οὐδ' ἀπ' ἄλλων ἐ. A.*Ch.*473 (lyr.); ἐ. βοᾶν S.*El.*802; ἐ. γαμεῖν marry *from an alien house*, E. *Andr.*975; τὰ ἐ. things *abroad*, Theoc.10.9:—ἔκτοθεν αὐλῆς is dub. in Od.9.239 (perh. *outside* in the court). 3. *without, unaccompanied by*, τινός Nonn.*D.*11.428.

**ἔκτοθι**, Ep. Adv., (ἐκτός) *out of, outside, far from*, νηῶν, πυλάων, Il.15.391, 22.439, cf. A.R.1.243. 2. simply, *from*, σέο δ' ἐ. μῆτις ὄρωρεν ib.1291. 3. abs., *outside*, Id.3.255. 4. *without*, i.e. *not having*, νίκης Nonn.*D.*22.252, al.

**ἐκτοιχωρῠχέω**, *break into a house and rob it*: generally, *pillage, plunder*, τοὺς βίους Plb.4.18.8; τὴν βασιλείαν Id.18.55.2.

**ἐκτοκ-εύω**, = sq., Aq.*Is.*66.9. ⊛ **-ίζω**, *lend at interest*, *BGU* 1246. 24 (iii B.C.); *exact interest*, Lxx *De.*23.19(20). II. *make to bring forth*, Sm.*Is.*66.9. **-ος**, ον, (τίκτω) = ἔκγονος, Ael.*NA* 10.14.

**ἔκτολμος**, ον, *audacious*, f.l. in Suid. s. v. λαῖμα. Adv. -μως Man. 3.331.

**ἐκτολογ-έομαι**, (ἕκτη) *to be subject to a tax of one-sixth* of the produce, ἀμπελὼν -λογούμενος *Arch.Pap.*5.392. **-ία**, ἡ, *tax of one-sixth*, *PRyl.*225.52 (ii/iii A.D.).

**ἐκτολῡπεύω**, *wind off* a ball of wool: metaph., *bring to an end*, χαλεπὸν πόνον ἐκτολυπεύσας Hes.*Sc.*44; οὐδὲν.. καίριον ἐκτολυπεύσειν A.*Ag.*1032 (lyr.).

**ἐκτομ-άζω**, *castrate*, *Gloss.* ⊛ **-άς**, άδος, ἡ, *wicket-gate*, Aen.Tact. 24.5, *Stud.Pal.*20.211.9. II. = περικεφαλαία, Hsch. III. a kind of *spear* (nisi leg. ἐκτομάδια), Id. **-εύς**, έως, ὁ, (ἐκτέμνω) *one that cuts out*, Id. ⊛ **-ή**, ἡ, (ἐκτέμνω) *cutting out, excision*, Plu.*Alc.*16 (pl.): metaph., ἡδονῶν, λόγου, Ph.1.450, 170; *cutting off*, καρπῶν Porph. ap.Eus.*PE* 3.11. 2. *castration*, Hdt.3.48,49, Pl.*Smp.*195c (pl.), etc. b. *circumcision* of women, Str.16.2.37. II. *segment*, Plu. *Num.*13; ἐ. γῆς *sod*, Id.*Pomp.*41 (pl.). 2. *cutting*, κρημνώδης Id. *Flam.*3. 3. *excision* in woodwork, Ph.*Bel.*64.27 (pl.). **-ιαῖος**, α, ον, = sq., σῦς *PMag.Par.*1.3118. **-ίας**, ου, ὁ, *one that is castrated, eunuch*, παῖδες ἐ. Hdt.3.92; ἐκτομίαν ποιεῖν τινα Id.6.9; βόες ἐ. Arist. *Pr.*897$^b$27; κάπρος Antiph.133.5. **-ίζω**, = ἐκτέμνω, ἐκδομίζοντος (sic) αὐτοῦ τὴν ὅλην ἀλήθειαν *PMag.Par.*1.2452. **-ίς**, ίδος, ἡ, pecul. fem. of ἐκτομεύς, *cutting down*, δρεπάνη καυλῶν *AP* 6.21.2. II. ἐ. (sc. μήτρα), = ἐκβολάς, Ath.3.101a. **-ον**, τό, *black hellebore*, Hp.*Mul.*1.78, Thphr.*HP* 9.10.4, Diocl.*Fr.*151; but, *white hellebore*, Ps.-Dsc.4.148. II. ἔκτομος (sc. λίθος), ὁ, *stone forming interior angle*, *Rev.Phil.*29.240 (Didyma), 49.6 (ibid.).

**ἐκτονίζομαι**, *lose force*, -ιζομένου πνεύματος Herod.Med. in *Rh.Mus.* 58.99.

**ἐκτοξεύω**, *shoot out, shoot away*, τὰ βέλη ἐξετετόξευντο Hdt.1.214, etc.; ἐ. γραφήν Hld.9.5: metaph., τὸ σῶφρον ἐξετόξευσεν *has shot away all its arrows*, i.e. has no resource left, E.*Andr.*365; πολλὴν ἐκτετοξεῦσθαι βίον Ar.*Pl.*34. 2. metaph., *reject, banish*, ἀλήθειαν Ph.1.528:—Pass., ὑπερόριος ἐ. ib.252. 3. abs., *shoot from* a place, *shoot arrows*, X.*An.*7.8.14, Arr.*An.*1.1.11. 4. Pass., of the pulse, Gal.8.486.

**ἐκτοπ-ίζω**, *remove from* a place, *PTeb.*38.18 (ii B.C., Pass.), etc.; ἐ.

ἑαυτούς *take* themselves *off*, Arist.*Mir*.842b12, Plb.1.74.7, Lxx 2*Ma*. 8.13; ἐκτετοπισμένα *remote regions*, Str.3.4.19; "Ομηρος ἐκτοπίζει τὸν Ἰάσονος πλοῦν Sch.Pi.*P*.4.370, cf. Max.Tyr.14.2; ἄνθρωποι -τετοπισμένοι τῆς καθ' ἡμᾶς οἰκουμένης *outside the bounds of* our world, Procl.*in Cra*.p.74 P. 2. metaph., ἐ. εἰς μῦθον *pervert* into a fable, Str.4.1.7. II. intr., *take oneself from a place, go abroad*, like ἀποδημέω, οἱ ἐκτοπίζοντες τύραννοι ἀπὸ τῆς οἰκείας Arist.*Pol*.1314b9, etc.; of birds of passage and fish, *to migrate*, Id.*HA*600a14. 2. metaph., of a speaker, *travel far*, Id.*Rh*.1414b28. III. *avoid, shun*, τὸν πολιτισμόν D.L.4.39. **-ιος**, α, ον, = ἔκτοπος, ἀπάγετ' ἐ. με S.*OT*1340 (lyr.); ἐ. συθείς Id.*OC*119 (lyr.); ἠνύσατ' ἐκτοπίαν φλόγα, = ἐξετοπίσατε (as the Sch.), ye have *put away* the fire, Id.*OT*166 (lyr.). II. *foreign*, Ath.14.659a; *outlandish*, ὁρμαί Orph.*H*.58.10. **-ισις**, εως, ἡ, *removal from a place, deportation, Gloss.* ⊛ **-ισμός**, ὁ, *migration*, τοὺς ἐ. ποιεῖσθαι Arist.*HA*599a4. II. *being away, distance*, Str.4.5.5, prob. in Cic.*Att*.12.12.1. **-ιστικός**, ή, όν, *migratory*, ἐ. ζῷα, opp. ἐπιδημητικά, Arist.*HA*488a14; βίος Id.*PA*694a5. ⊛ **-ος**, ον, *away from a place*, c. gen., τῶνδ' ἑδράνων πάλιν ἔ. ἔκθορε S.*OC*233 (lyr.); *distant*, ἄρουρα Id.*Tr*.32; ἔ. ἔστω let him *leave the place*, E.*Ba*. 69 (anap.). II. *foreign, strange*, [τέθνηκεν] αὐτὴ πρὸς αὑτῆς, οὐδενὸς πρὸς ἐκτόπου by no *strange* hand, S.*Tr*.1132. 2. *out of the way, strange, extraordinary*, δένδρον Ar.*Av*.1474 (lyr.); ὁτιοῦν τῶν ἐ. Pl. *Lg*.799c; χειμών Thphr.*CP*6.18.12; ἱστορία ἔ. Plu.2.977e; of persons, *eccentric*, Arist.*Pr*.954b2. Adv. -πως *extraordinarily*, Id.*Mir*. 833a14, *PPetr*.3 p.150, Plb.32.3.8: Comp. -ωτέρως Arist.*Metaph*.989b 30 codd. 3. ἔκτοπον· ἔξοδον, Hsch.

⊛**'Εκτόρειος, 'Εκτόρεος**, v. "Εκτωρ.

**ἐκτορεύω**, *chase*, Hld.2.11 (Pass.).

**ἐκτορέω**, *transfix*, αἰῶνα *h.Merc*.42.

**ἐκτορμέω**, (τόρμη) *turn from the way*, Paus.Gr.*Fr*.310.

**ἐκτορνεύω**, *carve*, Sm.*Ex*.25.35(36).

**ἔκτορνος**, ον, *rounded*, ἀξονίσκος Ph.*Bel*.76.25.

⊛ **ἕκτος**, η, ον, (ἕξ) *sixth*, Il.2.407, etc.; ἕκτος (sc. μήν), ὁ, Plu.2.268a; ἕκτη, ἡ, v. sub voc. (ϝέκτ- *Tab.Heracl*.2.106.)

**ἐκτός**, ή, όν, (ἔχω); ἐκτά, τά, the *qualities* of substances (opp. aggregates), *Stoic*.2.129,150; ἐκτά in Ath.10.420d appears to be corrupt.

⊛ **ἐκτός** (ἐχθός, *IG*9(1).333 (Locr., v B.C.), *Michel* 995 *C*35 (Delph., etc.), Adv., (ἐκ) *without, outside*, opp. ἐντός: 1. as Prep. with gen., which may either precede or follow, ἐ. κλισίης Il.14.13; τείχεος ἐ. 21.608; *out of, far from*, καπνοῦ καὶ κύματος ἐ. Od.12.219; esp. in prov. phrases (v. ἔξω I fin.), ἐ. κλαυμάτων ἔχειν πόδα S.*Ph*. 1260; ἐ. ἔχειν πόδα (sc. τῶν κακῶν) Pi.*P*.4.289; ἐ. τῶν ἐλαῶν *beyond* the olives, i.e. out of the course, Ar.*Ra*.995 (lyr.); Geom., *beyond*, τοῦ A σημείου Apollon.Perg.*Con*.1.8, al.; also ἐ. ἀτασθαλίης *outside of, free from*.., Thgn.754, cf. 744; ἐ. αἰτίης Hdt.4.133, A.*Pr*.332, etc.; ἐ. πημάτων S.*Ph*.504; ἄτας Id.*Ant*.614 (lyr.); τῶν κακῶν Id.*Fr*.724, cf. Pl.*Grg*.523b; ἐ. στρατειῶν *exempt from*.., Id.*R*.498c; ἐ. ἑωυτῆς *beside* herself, *out of* her wits, Hp.*Epid*.7.90, cf. S.*Aj*.640 (lyr.); ἐ. ἐλπίδος *beyond* hope, Id.*Ant*.330; ἡ ἐ. καὶ παρ' ἐλπίδας χαρά, i.e. ἡ ἐκτὸς ἐλπίδων καὶ παρ' ἐλπίδας, ib.392; δοκημάτων ἐ. E.*HF*771 (lyr.). 2. of Time, *beyond*, πέντε ἡμερέων Hdt.3.80. 3. *except*, *IG* l.c., etc.; ἐ. ὀλίγων X.*HG*1.2.3; *besides, apart from*, Pl.*Grg*. 474d, *PTeb*.19.7 (ii B.C.), etc.: abs., *besides, as well*, *GDI*1742.12; also ἐ. εἰ μή *unless*, 1*Ep.Cor*.15.2, Herod.Med.ap.Orib.7.8.1, Vett. Val.37.20, al., Luc.*Pisc*.6; ἐ. ἐὰν μή *Cat.Cod.Astr*.7.216; ἐ. ὅτι.. Hld.10.5. 4. *without the consent of*, τινός *PMag.Par*.1.356. II. abs., ἃ δ' ἐ. *external things*, E.*Ion* 231 (lyr.), cf. Plb.2.4.8, etc.; οἱ ἐ. *strangers, foreigners*, Pl.*Lg*.629d, Plb.2.47.10, etc.; also, *the vulgar, the common herd*: *the Gentiles*, Lxx *Si.prol*.4. III. with Verbs of motion, ῥίπτειν ἐ. to throw *out*, S.*Tr*.269; ἧξας Id.*El*.1402 (lyr.); ἐκπέμπειν Id.*Ant*.18; ἕλκειν Pl.*R*.616a; οὐκ ἐ. εἶ; = ἔξιθι, S.*OT*676; χώρει ἐ. E.*IA*1117; εἰ δ' ἐ. ἔλθοις if thou *transgressest*, S.*Tr*.1189.

**ἔκτοσε**, Adv. *outwards*: c. gen., *out of*, ἔκτοσε χειρός Od.14.277.

⊛ **ἔκτοσθε** and **-θεν** (not only before vowels, cf. Il.7.341, al.), Adv., = ἔκτοθεν, *outside*, c. gen., τείχεος ἔ. 9.552; αὐλῆς, δόμων, Od.7. 112, 23.148; θεῶν ἔκτοσθεν ἁπάντων *out of the number of* the gods, Hes.*Th*.813; ἔ. παλαίστρας Theoc.2.51. 2. abs., ἔ... πάγοι ὀξέες *outside* are.., Od.5.411; ἔ. γενέσθαι to be *delirious*, Hp.*Epid*.5.85.— Ion. and late Prose, as Luc.*Merc.Cond*.41.

⊛ **ἔκτοτε**, Adv. for ἐκ τότε, *thereafter*, Socr.Rhod.1, Arr.*An*.1.26. 4, Plu.*Caes*.48, *POxy*.486.9 (ii A.D.), Vett.Val.168.28, Sm.*Is*.16.13, Sch.D.T.p.427 H.: condemned by Luc.*Sol*.7.

**ἐκτότης**, ητος, ἡ, *being* ἐκτός, *absence*, νόσου Gal.10.54.

**ἐκτρᾰγῳδέω**, *deck out in tragic phrase, exaggerate*, Plb.6.15.7, Agath. 4.8:—Pass., Plb.6.56.8. 2. *declaim tragically*, Ps.-Luc.*Philopatr*. 18; simply, *declaim*, Ath.9.403d. 3. *describe impressively*, Luc. *Tox*.11. II. *unmask*, Id.*Pisc*.38, *Merc.Cond*.41.

**ἐκτρᾰνόω**, *signify clearly*, Astramps.*Onir*.57.

**ἐκτράπεζος** [ᾰ], ον, *banished from the table*, Luc.*Gall*.4.

⊛ **ἐκτρᾰπελόγαστρος**, ον, *with an enormous paunch*, ὄνοι Epich.67.

⊛ **ἐκτράπελος** [ᾰ], ον, *turning from the common course, perverse, strange*, νόμοι Thgn.290, cf. Pherecr.145.23, Ael.*NA*14.9; ζῷα (i.e. Κύκλωπες) Hermog.*Id*.2.10; *monstrous*, of huge children, Plin.*HN*7. 76. Adv. -λως, ἔσθων *AP*11.402 (Luc.). II. *odious*, κέρδεα, ἔπος, prob. in Pi.*P*.1.92, 4.105.

**ἐκτράπω**, Ion. for ἐκτρέπω.

**ἔκτρας**· ἐν ῥυμῷ πάσσαλος, Hsch. (leg. ἔκτρα· ὁ).

**ἐκτρᾰχηλ-ίζω**, Att. fut. -ιῶ, prop. of a horse, *throw the rider over its head*, X.*Cyr*.1.4.8, Plu.2.58f: generally, *break* a person's *neck*, Ar. *Lys*.705; *overturn*, τὰ ὄρη *Tab.Defix.Aud*.271.26 (Hadrumetum, iii A.D.); κλίμακας Ph.*Bel*.85.38:—Pass., *break one's neck*, Ar.*Nu*.1501, *Pl*.70, Luc.*Merc.Cond*.42. 2. metaph., *ruin, pervert*, D.9.51, Luc. *Rh.Pr*.10, Alciphr.3.40, Porph.*Abst*.1.42; εἰς ὑπερηφανίαν Mich.*in EN*523.20:—Pass., εἰς ἀτόπους πράξεις Ph.*Fr*.102 H. II. metaph., *cause to lose control of one's language*, ἐ. τινὰς αἱ τραγῳδίαι Hermog. *Id*.1.6. III. *behead, Gloss.* **-ισμός**, ὁ, *beheading*, Id.

**ἐκτρᾰχύνω** [ῡ], *make rough*, τὴν ἐπιφάνειαν ἐκτετραχυσμένος Luc. *Pisc*.51. II. metaph., *exasperate*, Plu.*Alc*.14; τὸ πλῆθος App. *BC*2.12:—Pass., ἐκτραχύνεσθαι πρός τινα Plu.*Arat*.49: abs., App.*BC* 1.10.

⊛ **ἐκτρέπω**, Ion. **-τράπω** [ᾰ], *turn out of the course, turn aside*, τοῦ ποταμοῦ τὸ ῥέεθρον Hdt.1.186, cf. 2.11, Th.5.65; μηδ' εἰς Ἑλένην κότον ἐκτρέψῃς A.*Ag*.1464 (lyr.), cf. *Th*.628 (lyr.); τὸ δυστυχὲς δὲ τοὔτ' ἐς ἄλλον ἐκτρέπει E.*Supp*.483; ἑαυτοῦ μιαρίαν εἴς τινα ἐ. Antipho 2. 3.9; ἐ. [τινὰ] πρὸς ποίμνας S.*Aj*.53:—Pass. and Med., *turn off* or *aside*, ἐκτραπέσθαι ὁδὸν μακροτέρην Hdt.1.104: abs., Id.2.80, X.*HG*7. 4.22, etc.: c. gen., *turn aside from*, τοῦ πρόσθεν λόγου S.*OT*851, also ἐ. ἐκ.. Hdt.1.75; ἀπὸ.. ἐπί.. Pl.*Sph*.222a; πόθεν δεῦρο ἐξετραπόμεθα Id.*R*.543c. 2. *turn* a person *off the road, order* him *out of the way*, S.*OT*806:—Pass. (fut. -τραπήσομαι Luc.*Herm*.86) and Med., ἐκτρέπεσθαί τινα *get out of* one's *way*, D.19.225, cf. Ar.*Pl*.837, Luc.*Tim*. 5; *avoid*, τὸν ἔλεγχον Plb.35.4.14; τὴν φιλοσοφίαν Jul.*Or*.7.223d: c. inf., ὀφθῆναι *AP*10.56.10 (Pall.): abs., cj. in S.*OC*1541. 3. τὴν δρῶσαν ἐ. *prevent* her *from* acting, Id.*El*.350. 4. ἀσπίδας θύρσοις ἐ. *turn* shields *and flee before* the thyrsus, E.*Ba*.799. II. Med., *turn away*, φίλους Democr.101; also ἐκτρέπεσθαι τὰ ἐντὸς ἐκτός *turns itself* inside out, Arist.*HA*621a7. III. Medic. in Pass., *to be diverted* or *everted*, Hp.*Steril*.213, *Off*.14, Dsc.2.15 (perh. *to be put out of joint*, *Ep.Hebr*.12.13, *Hippiatr*.26). IV. *turn* or *change*, εἰς ἄσπορον *PRyl*.133.22 (i A.D.), cf. Ael.*NA*14.28:—Pass., εἰς ὀλιγαρχίαν ἐκτραπῆναι Plb.6.4.9; ὑπ' ἀγεννείας εἰς μέμψεις Arr. *Epict*.1.6.42. V. Pass., *to be brought to birth*, Astrol. t.t., Vett. Val.50.27, al.

**ἐκτρέφω**, *bring up from childhood, rear up*, Hdt.1.122, A.*Ch*.750, etc.; ἐξέφυσε κἀξέθρεψέ με S.*OT*827; ἐκτεθραμμένοι σκύμνοι λεόντων *true-bred*.., E.*Supp*.1222; of plants, τὸ ἐκτρέφον τὴν ῥίζαν Hdt. 1.193; ἐκτρέφει ἡ γῆ τὸ σπέρμα X.*Oec*.17.10; ποταμοῦ πνεῦμα τραχύτερον ἐκθρέψαντος Plu.2.357d:—Med., *rear up for oneself*, τινά *h.Cer*. 166; ἤνεγκα κἀξέσωσα κἀξεθρεψάμην, says the παιδαγωγός, S.*El*.13, cf. *Fr*.387, Pl.*Lg*.929a:—Pass., εἴ σοί τις υἱός ἐστιν ἐκτεθραμμένος Ar.*Nu*.796; ἐγένου τε καὶ ἐξετράφης Pl.*Cri*.50e, cf. Lys.19.8. II. Med., of pregnant animals, *nourish*, [ζῷα] μεγάλα ἐντὸς ἐκθρέψωνται Pl.*Ti*.91d:—Act., *bring to birth*, τὰ κυήματα Arist.*GA*773a34.

⊛ **ἐκτρέχω**, fut. -δρᾰμοῦμαι Diph.19.3: pf. ἐκδεδράμηκα Arist.*Aud*. 802a21:—*run out* or *forth*, ἐκ δὲ θύραζε ἔδραμον ἀμφ' Ἀχιλῆα Il.18.30; τῆς συγκλήτου εἰς τὸν δῆμον Hdn.7.11.5; *make a sally*, ἐκ πόλεως Th. 4.25, etc.; ἐπὶ [σῦν] Arist.*Fr*.571, cf. *PGurob*8.11 (iii B.C.). 2. *run off* or *away*, Ar.*Av*.991. 3. of horns, *spring up, grow*, ταχέως Arist.*Aud*. l.c.; of plants, *run* or *shoot up*, Thphr.*CP*2.15.5: c. gen., ἐ. τῶν ἄλλων Id.*HP*6.8.1. 4. c. acc., *exceed*, τὸν καιρόν Lycon ap. D.L.5.65: abs., of anger, *exceed bounds*, S.*OC*438. 5. *digress, wander from the point*, *Corp.Herm*.1.16. 6. c. gen., *escape from the clutches of*, δανειστοῦ App.*Fr*.22. b. *to be born of*, τῆς μητρός Lib. *Ep*.1036.9. 7. of Time, *expire, come to an end*, *PSI*4.444 (iii B.C.).

**ἔκτρεψις**, εως, ἡ, *displacement, distortion*, Hp.*Off*.3.

**ἔκ-τρημα**, ατος, τό, *hole made in trepanning*, Heliod.ap.Orib.46.11. 16. **-τρησις**, εως, ἡ, *hole*, Hp.*Steril*.222 (pl.), Aret.*SD*2.13 (pl.), Heliod.ap.Orib.46.11.26.

**ἐκτρῐαινόω**, *shake with the trident*, Ἑλλάδα Ps.-Theopomp.Hist.ap. Luc.*Pseudol*.29.

**ἐκ-τρῐβή**, ἡ, = ἔκτριψις, *destruction*, Lxx *De*.4.26. ⊛ **-τρίβω** [ῑ], fut. -τρῐβήσομαι S.*OT*428:—*rub out*, i.e. *produce by rubbing*, πῦρ ἔκ τινος X.*Cyr*.2.2.15; φλόγα Poll.9.155 (but in S.*Ph*.296 ἐν πέτροισι πέτρον ἐκτρίβων.. ἔφην' ἄφαντον φῶς *rubbing hard*): metaph., λύπην Plu.2.610b:—Pass., τὰ ψυχικὰ προτερήματα διὰ τὰ ἐπαθλα οἷον ἐκτρίβεται Longin.44.3. II. *rub out*, i.e. *to destroy root and branch*, σφέας πίτυος τρόπον ἀπειλέε ἐκτρίψειν (cf. πίτυς) Hdt.6.37; ἐ. τινὰ πρόρριζον E.*Hipp*.684; τὴν ποίην ἐκ τῆς γῆς ἐκτρίβειν Hdt.4.120; αὕτη μ' ἡ γυνή ποτ' ἐκτρίψει Herod.6.27, dub. in E.*Cyc*.475; βίον ἐ. *bring* life *to a wretched end*, = Lat. *conterere vitam*, S.*OT*248, cf. 428:—Pass., πρόρριζος ἐκτέτριπται Hdt.6.86.δ'; ὁπλὰς ἐκτετριμμένος with the hoofs *worn off*, Luc.*Asin*.19. III. *rub constantly, wear out*, Ἄτλας.. νώτοις οὐρανὸν ἐκτρίβων E.*Ion* 2 (s.v.l.). IV. *rub, thresh out*, f.l. in Nic.*Fr*.68.3. V. *polish*, Thphr.*HP*4.11.6, Plb. 10.20.2; ἀργυρώματα *Class.Phil*.19.234 (iii B.C.); cf. ἐξετρίβετο· σφόδρα ἐκοσμεῖτο, Hsch. 2. *wipe out*, Herod.1.79. **-τριμμα**, ατος, τό, *sore caused by rubbing, excoriation*, Hp.*Fract*.29 (pl.); ἐκτρίμματα ὑποδημάτων Dsc.2.151. II. *rubber, towel*, Philox.2.41. **-τριψις**, εως, ἡ, *violent friction*, νεφῶν D.L.2.9; πνεύματος Ruf.*Onom*.228. II. *destruction*, Lxx *Nu*.15.31.

**ἔκτρομος**, ον, *trembling*, v.l. for ἔντρ., *Ep.Hebr*.12.21; τὸν ποιοῦντα ἔ. τὴν γῆν ἅπασαν *Tab.Defix.Aud*.271.26 (Hadrumetum, iii A.D.).

**ἐκτροπ-ή**, ἡ, (ἐκτρέπω) *turning off* or *aside*, ἐ. ὕδατος *diversion of* water from its channel, Th.5.65; διὰ τὰς ἐ. τὰς ἐπὶ τὴν χώραν on account of [the river] *being turned off* over the country, Plb.9.43. 5. II. (from Med.) *turning aside, escape*, μόχθων *from* labours, A.*Pr*.913; ἐ. (sc. λόγου) *a digression*, Pl.*Plt*.267a, Aeschin.3.206

(pl.), D.Chr.7.128 (pl.); ἐπὶ τὴν ἐ. ἐπάνιμεν *the point from which we digressed*, Plb.4.21.12; ἡ ἐπὶ ταύτας τὰς αἰτίας ἐ. Arist.*Metaph.* 1089ᵃ1. 2. *fork, branch* in a road, Ar.*Ra.*113, E.*Rh.*881, X. *HG*7.1.29, Aen.Tact.15.6 (pl.); *bypath*, σκολιαὶ ἐ. D.S.3.15,26, cf. Varro *Sat.Men.Fr.*418 B. b. *branch* of a canal, *PPetr.*2 p.40 (iii B.C.). 3. ἐ. ὀνόματος *a collateral form*, Ath.11.490e. 4. ἐκτροπαὶ ποταμῶν *overflowings*, Lyd.*Ost.*55. 5. metaph., *change of life*, Philostr.*VA*6.36. 6. Astrol. t.t., *moment of birth*, Vett.Val. 51.37, al., Ptol.*Tetr.*108. b. = ὡροσκόπος, Paul.Al.*R.*1. 7. Medic., *eversion* of the eyelid, Antyll.ap.Aët.7.74, Id.ap.Orib.10.23. 24. **-ιάζομαι**, *expel as accursed*, Eust.1070 fin. **-ίας** οἶνος *turned* (i.e. *sour*) wine, Alciphr.1.20, Poll.1.248. **-ιον, τό**, *everted eyelid*, a disease in which the lid is turned outward, opp. τριχίασις, Cels.7.7, Antyll.ap.Aët.7.74, Dem.Ophth.ib.73. **-ος, ον**, *turning out of the way*. Adv. -πως Erot. s. v. ἐκπατίως.

**ἐκτροφή**, ἡ, *bringing up, rearing, nurture*, E.*Fr.*317.5 (pl.), Sor.1. 81, Arist.*HA*542ᵃ30 (pl.), *GA*754ᵃ8, al.; ἐ. καρπῶν J.*AJ*5.1.21: metaph., *breeding*, κακοδαιμονίας Phld.*Ir.*p.27 W.

**ἔκτροφος**, ἡ, *nursing mother*, *Epigr.Gr.*872.6 (Patmos).

**ἐκτροφωλέων**· σποδοειδῶν, Hsch. (Cf. τροφιωδέων· σποδιωδῶν, Erot.; ἐκ στροφωδέων Hp.*Prorrh.*1.156 codd.)

**ἐκτροχάζω**, *rush out*, Apollod.2.7.3. II. *treat summarily*, Dsc. *Ther.*2.

**ἐκτρόχαλον**· ἔκτροχον, Hsch.

**ἐκτρῡγ-άω**, *gather in the vintage*, *PGurob*8.10 (iii B.C.), Lxx *Le.* 25.5. **-ίζω**, *clear from lees*, *Gp.*5.2.12 (Pass.); of molten silver, prob. in *PLeid.X.*20 (ἐκτροχιστῇ Pap.).

**ἐκτρῡπ-άω**, *bore* or *hollow out*, πρέμνον *Gp.*10.23.5, cf. Ph.*Bel.*92. 8. II. intr., *slip out through a hole*, Ar.*Ec.*337. **-ημα, ατος, τό**, *dust made by boring*, Thphr.*HP*5.6.3. II. pl., *holes* made in a wall, Ph.*Bel.*92.16. **-ησις, εως, ἡ**, *boring through*, Hp.*Ep.*22: pl., Ph.*Bel.*100.36.

**ἐκτρῡφάω**, *to be over-luxurious*, Clearch.39, Ath.12.519f.

❋ **ἐκτρῡχόω**, *wear out, grind down, exhaust*, Th.3.93, 7.48:—Pass., ὑπὸ πόνων Luc.*Merc.Cond.*39; ῥάκη ἐκτετρυχωμένα *worn-out* rags, Id.*Tox.*30.

**ἐκτρύχω** [ῡ], = foreg., D.C.77.9.

**ἐκτρύω**, aor. -έτρῡσα, *wear out*, τινὰ ταῖς ἀπορίαις App.*BC*2.66; cf. ἐκτρυωθείς (sic)· φθαρείς, Hsch.

**ἐκτρώγω**, *eat up, devour*, Ar.*V.*155, Lxx *Mi.*7.4:—Pass., of a letter in a Ms., Demetr.Lac.*Herc.*1012.26 F.

**ἔκ-τρωμα, ατος, τό**, = παιδίον νεκρὸν ἄωρον, Hsch.; *untimely birth*, Arist.*GA*773ᵇ18 (pl.), Lxx *Jb.*3.16, al., 1*Ep.Cor.*15.8, Ph.1.59; as a term of contempt, Tz.*H.*5.515. **-τρωμᾰτιαῖος**, *abortive*, *Gloss.*:— also **-τρωμᾰτικός**, Id. **-τρωμᾰτισμός, ὁ**, = ἐκτρωσμός, Id. **-τρωσις, εως, ἡ**, *miscarriage*, Arist.*Pr.*860ᵃ18 (pl.); ἐκτρώσει ἐν τόκῳ v.l. in Hp.*Mul.*2.122, cf. Sor.2.49. **-τρωσμός, ὁ**, = foreg., Arist.*HA*583ᵇ 12, Aret.*SD*2.11, *Sammelb.*3451.5; *attempted abortion*, Hp.*Mul.*1.78, Ptol.*Tetr.*116. **-τρωτικός, ή, όν**, *abortive*, δύναμις Plu.2.974d.

**ἐκτῠλίσσω**, *unfold, develop*, ἕλικα Ti.Locr.97c.

**ἐκτῠλ-όω**, *excise a callosity*, Antyll.ap.Orib.44.23.32, Crito ap. Gal.13.794. **-ωσις, εως, ἡ**, *removal of callosity*, Paul.Aeg.4. 49. **-ωτέον**, *one must excise a callosity*, Id.3.75. **-ωτικός, ή, όν**, *removing callosities*, Antyll.ap.Orib.44.23.29, cf. Paul.Aeg.4.49.

**ἐκτυμπάνωσις** [ᾰ], εως, ἡ, *swelling out like a drum*, τῆς γαστέρος Str.16.4.13.

**ἔκτῠπε**, 3 sg. aor. 2 of κτυπέω. **ἐκτυπέω**, f.l. for ἐκκτυπέω (q.v.).

❋ **ἔκτῠπ-ος, ον**, *worked in relief*, Ion Trag.42, Aristeas 58, D.S.18. 26, etc.; φιάλη.. ἐ. ζῷα ἔχουσα *IG*11(2).161*B*76 (Delos, iii B.C.); ἔκτυπα, τά, Plin.*HN*35.152. 2. *distinct*, φαντασία *Stoic.*2.21: Comp., Hsch. Adv. -πως *with a distinct impression* or *character*, opp. συγκεχυμένως, S.E.*M.*7.171. II. *formed in outline*: ἔκτυπον, τό, *rough sketch*, δι' ἐκτύπων γεγραμμένη [ἱστορία] Marcellin.*Vit.Thuc.* 44. **-όω**, *model* or *work in relief*, ἐν τῷ βάθρῳ τὰ ἑαυτοῦ ἔργα ἐξετύπωσεν X.*Eq.*1.1:—Pass., οἱ ἐν στήλαις ἐκτετυπωμένοι Pl.*Smp.*193a, cf. *Ti.*50d; οἱ ἐκτυπωθέντες *these who are formed on this model*, Isoc. 13.18; *to be shaped*, ἐν τῇ διεξόδῳ Hp.*Prorrh.*2.4; εἰς τὸν Πρίαπον Porph.ap.Eus.*PE*3.11; of the foetus, Agath.4.25. II. metaph. in Med., ἐκτυποῦσθαί τι εἰς ὕδωρ, etc., *form an image* of a thing in.., Pl.*Tht.*206d, cf. *Lg.*775d. **-ωμα, ατος, τό**, *figure in relief*, Id.*Ti.* 50d, Apion ap.J.*Ap.*2.2, Philostr.*VA*2.33; ἐκτυπωμάτων πρόσωπα Men.24.4. II. *reflection*, of light, Olymp.*in Mete.*33.1. ❋ **-ωσις, εως, ἡ**, *modelling in relief*, Aesar.ap.Stob.1.49.27. II. *figure*, J. *AJ*12.2.9. 2. metaph., *allegory*, Ph.1.163. **-ωτός, ή, όν**, = ἔκτυπος, *IG*11(2).199*B*7 (Delos, iii B.C.).

**ἐκτυφλ-όω**, *make quite blind*, τινά Batr.238, Hdt.4.2, 9.93, X.*Eq.* 10.2, Ar.*Pl.*301, etc.; ἐκτυφλοῦν τιν' ἀστραπή Antiph.195.4: abs., κονιορτὸς ἐκτυφλῶν Ar.*Fr.*569.2:—Pass., λαμπτῆρες ἐκτυφλωθέντες σκότῳ (expl. by σβεσθέντες in Sch.) A.*Ch.*536: metaph., Philostr. *VA*4.36; of buds destroyed by hail, Id.*Her.*2.11. **-ωσις, εως, ἡ**, *making blind*, Hdt.9.94.

❋ **ἔκτυφος** [prob. ῠ], ον, *deluding, empty*, μοῦσα Oenom.ap.Eus.*PE* 5.11.

**ἐκτῡφόω**, *delude, deceive*, τὰ πλήθη Ph.1.1. 2. *puff up*, ἑαυτόν Id.2.569, cf. 215:—Pass., Plb.16.21.12. II. Pass., *vanish into smoke*, εἰς καπνὸν ἐκτυφοῦται Dsc.1.68.2; but perh. ἐκτύφεται shd. be read; ἐκτύφονται is v.l. for -τυφοῦνται in Id.1.68.5.

❋ **ἐκτύφω** [ῡ], *burn in a slow fire*; cf. ἐξύθυψεν (sic, post ἐξήια)· ἐξέκαυσεν, Hsch.:—metaph. in Med., ἔρωτα ἐκτύφεσθαι *light a slow fire* of love, Alciphr.3.50:—Pass., aor. 2 ἐξετύφην [ῠ], ἐξ. κλαίουσα *my face swelled up* with weeping, Men.*Epit.Fr.*9.

❋ **ἕκτωρ, ορος, ὁ, ἡ**, (ἔχω, cf. Pl.*Cra.*393a) *holding fast*, v.l. for ἕστωρ, Il.24.272, cf. *EM*383.25; epith. of Zeus, Sapph.157; of anchors, ἕκτορες πλημμυρίδος Lyc.100, cf. Luc.*Lex.*15: as Subst., = κροκύφαντος, *hair-net*, Leon.ap.Hsch.; also pl., = πάσσαλοι ἐν ῥυμῷ, Id. II. Hom. only as pr. n. *Hector, the prop* or *stay* of Troy, οἶος γὰρ ἐρύετο Ἴλιον Ἕκτωρ Il.6.403:—Adj. **Ἑκτόρεος**, α or η, ον, also ος, ον E.*Rh.* 1 (anap.):—*of Hector*, Hom., B.12.154, etc.: also **Ἑκτόρειος, ον**, Anaxil.38; κόμαι Lyc.1133.

**ἔκυλος**· εἶδος βοτάνης, Suid.

❋ **ἑκῠρ-ά**, ἡ, Ep. for πενθερά, *mother-in-law*, Il.22.451, 24.770; also in Plu.2.143a, *CIG*(add.)3846*q* (Aezani). **-εύω**, Boeot. ἑκουρεύω, *to be a father-in-law*, Corinn.*Supp.*2.85. ❋ **-ός, ὁ**, Ep. for πενθερός, *father-in-law*, Il.3.172, 24.770, also *CIG*9136 (Cyrene), Jul.*Or.*3.127c. [ῠ only in *AP*14.9.] (I.-E. *swekuro-, cf. Skt. *śváśuras*, Lat. *socer*, etc.)

**ἔκῠσα**, aor. 1 of κυνέω; but **ἔκῡσα**, of κύω. **ἐκφᾰγεῖν**, v. ἐξεσθίω.

**ἐκφαιδρύνω**, strengthd. for φαιδρύνω, *make quite bright, clear away*, σταγόνα ἐκ παρῄδων E.*Ba.*768.

❋ **ἐκφαίνω**, fut. -φᾰνῶ, Ion. -φανέω in Luc.*Syr.D.*32: aor. ἐξέφηνα, Dor. -έφᾱνα Pi.*N.*4.68:—Pass., Ep. aor. 1 -εφαάνθην Il.13.278. I. of persons, *bring to light, reveal*, σήμερον ἄνδρα φόωσδε.. Εἰλείθυια ἐκφανεῖ 19.104; ἐ. τινά *produce* him, Hdt.3.36; εἰ μὴ τὸν αὐτόχειρα.. ἐκφανεῖτ' ἐς ὀφθαλμοὺς ἐμούς S.*Ant.*307, cf. *OT*329: c. part., ἐ. σεωυτὸν ἐόντα τοῦ πατρὸς οὐδὲν ἥσσω Hdt.3.71; κακοὺς θνητῶν ἐξέφηνε.. χρόνος E.*Hipp.*428:—Pass., οὕνεκ' Ἀχιλλεὺς ἐξεφάνη *showed himself, came forth to view*, Il.19.46, cf. Od.10.260, al.; Χαρύβδιος ἐξεφαάνθη he *came up from out* Charybdis, 12.441; ὅ τε δειλὸς ἀνὴρ ὅς τ' ἄλκιμος ἐξεφαάνθη *is revealed*, Il.13.278; δίκαιοι δ' αὖθις [ὄντες] ἐκφανούμεθα S.*Ph.*82; σὺ μὲν.. ἐκφανεῖ κακή Id.*OT*1063; ἔκτον ἦμαρ ἐκπεφασμένος Id.*Ichn.*273. 2. *inform against*, τινά *Cod.Just.*1.5.16.5. II. of things, *bring to light*, δῶρα καὶ κράτος ἐγγενὲς Pi.*N.*4.68; *disclose, reveal*, τινὶ ἄρρητα ἱρά Hdt.6.135, al. (so abs., ὡς τὸ μαντεῖον ἐξέφηνεν.. ἐμοί S.*OT*243); ἐ. ἑωυτοῦ γνώμην Hdt.5.36; τὴν αἰτίην Id.6.3; τὴν ἀληθείην Id.1.117; λόγον E.*Hipp.*881; ἐ. ἐς φάος κακά ib.368; δειλίαν Pl.*Mx.*246e:—Pass., with fut. Med., *shine out*, οἱ ὄσσε δεινὸν ὑπὸ βλεφάρων, ὡς εἰ σέλας, ἐξεφάανθεν Il.19.17; *appear plainly*, πλευρὰ παρ' ἀσπίδος ἐξεφαάνθη 4.468, cf. Diog.Apoll.6; ἀστέρων ἐκφανέντων Th.2.28, cf. Phld.*Sign.*10: metaph., ταὶ Διωνύσου πόθεν ἐξέφᾰνεν (for -ησαν) χάριτες; Pi.*O.*13.18; ἐκφανήσεται *it shall be disclosed*, E.*Hipp.* 42, cf. Pl.*Hp.Ma.*295a; ἕως ἂν ἡμῖν ἐκφανήτον ἐφ' ᾧ αὐτὼ σπουδάζετον Id.*Euthd.*288c. 2. *exhibit*, κακότητα ἔς τινα Hdt.5.92.η'. 3. ἐ. πόλεμον πρός τινα *to declare*.., X.*An.*3.1.16.

**ἐκφᾰλαγγίζω**, *swerve from line*, Demetr.*Eloc.*84.

**ἐκφάν-δην**, Adv., = ἐκφανῶς, *openly*, Philostr.*VA*7.20. **-εια** [φᾰ], ἡ, *emergence above horizon*, Epicur.*Ep.*2 p.40 U. **-ής, ές**, *showing itself*, κάρυον ἐκφανὲς ἐκ λεπίδων *AP*6.102.4 (Phil.); *bright-shining*, ἀστέρες Artem.2.36; less freq. of persons, ἐ. γιγνόμενος *disclosing oneself*, Pl.*Ion*535b; *plain, manifest*, τἀνδρὸς ἐκφανὲς τέκμαρ A.*Eu.*244, cf. Pl.*Phdr.*250d (Sup.); ἐκφανὴ γένοιτο ὅπῃ ἔχει Id.*R.* 528c; ἐ. ἰδεῖν A.*Pers.*398, etc. Adv. -νῶς Plb.5.1.3, Iamb.*Protr.*21. κς'. 2. *illustrious*, Artem.2.30. **-ίζω**, = ἐκφαίνω:—Pass., ἐκφανίζεται· μηνύεται, Hsch. **-όω**, pf. part. Pass. ἐκπεφανωμένος· ἀπόπληκτος, Id. ❋ **-σις, εως, ἡ**, *exhibition, manifestation*, Plot.3.5. 9, Jul.*Or.*7.220b, Olymp.*in Mete.*106.9, Dam.*Pr.*432, Procl.*Inst.*125.

**ἐκφαντ-άζομαι**, *form in imagination*, Alciphr.1.13. ❋ **-ικός, ή, όν**, = ἐκφαντορικός, Procl.*in Alc.Praef.* (s. v.l.). **-ορία, ἡ**, *revealing of secret things*, Suid. **-ορικός, ή, όν**, *revealing*, τῆς ἀληθείας Procl.*Theol.Plat.*6.12; τῆς οὐσίας Id.*in Cra.*p.16 P., al., cf. Dam.*Pr.* 367. **-ος, ον**, *shown forth, revealed*, Poll.5.147, Hsch. **-ωρ**, sine expl., Id.

**ἐκφάσθαι**, pres. inf. Med. of ἔκφημι.

**ἔκφᾰσις, εως**, Ion. ιος, ἡ, (ἔκφημι) *declaration*, Hdt.6.129. II. (ἐκφαίνω) *emergence, reappearance*, of an eclipsed body, Phld.*Sign.* 10 (pl.); *rising* of the sun, Agatharch.105; prob. f.l. for ἔκφανσις in Procl.*in Prm.*pp.480, 520 S.

**ἐκφατν-ίζω**, *throw out of the manger*: generally, *throw away*, Posidon.9(a) J. (Pass.); of teeth, Eust.1784.45 (Pass.). II. Med., *eat out of the manger*, Nic.Dam.p.3 D. **-ισμα, ατος, τό**, *that which is cleaned out of the manger*: mostly in pl., *scraps, remnants*, Philostr. *VA*1.19; ἄρτων Ath.6.270d. II. *a board of the manger taken out in cleaning it*, Poll.10.166. **-ώμα, ατος, τό**, = φατνώμα, Id.7.122.

**ἔκφᾰτος**, ον, *beyond power of speech*, Max.451. II. (ἔκφημι) Adv. -τως *with loud voice* or *ineffably, impiously*, A.*Ag.*706.

**ἐκφαυλ-ίζω**, *depreciate, disparage, pour contempt on*, J.*AJ*2.14.1, al., Arr.*An.*1.13.6, Luc.*Merc.Cond.*11, Hld.10.12; τινὰ τῆς ὀργῆς J. *AJ*5.8.6; *reject with scorn*, Ael.*VH*9.41, *NA*4.37 (Pass.): c. inf., *disdain to do*, ib.11.31. **-ισμός, ὁ**, *contemning*, τῶν θείων J.*AJ* 3.8.9. **-ως**, Adv., f.l. for -φύλως, Philostr.*VS*1.16.4.

**ἐκφερομῡθέω**, *reveal*, of secrets, Aen.Tact.22.5 (Pass.), *SIG*360.25 (Chersonesus, iii B.C.), Corn.*ND*30.

❋ **ἐκφέρω**, fut. ἐξοίσω Hdt.3.71: Ion. aor. ἐξήνεικα:—Pass., ἐξοισθήσομαι E.*Supp.*561: fut. Med. ἐξοίσομαι in pass. sense, Hdt.8.49, 76:— *carry out of*, τινὰ πολέμοιο Il.5.664, etc.; ὅπλα ἐκ μεγάρου ἐξενηνειγμένα Hdt.8.37, cf. E.*Ph.*779; ἐ. πεύκας Ar.*Fr.*599; γραμματεῖον Id.*Nu.* 19; ἐξένεγκέ μοι τὴν κοπίδ' ἔξω Men.*Pk.*332. 2. *carry out* a corpse for burial, ἐξέφερον θρασὺν Ἕκτορα δάκρυ χέοντες Il.24.786, cf. Hdt.7. 117, Antipho6.21 (Pass.), etc.; also, *cause death*, εἰ ὑπερβάλλουσιν

ἀλγηδόνες, ἐξοίσουσι Plot.1.4.8. 3. *carry away*, τρί' ἄλεισα Od.15.470, cf. *Test. Epict.* 2.22, etc.; *carry off* as prize or reward, ἄεθλον Il.23.785:—more freq. in Med., τὠυτὸ (of a victory) ἐξενείκασθαι Hdt.6.103; κλέος, δόξαν, S.*El.*60, D.14.1, etc.; *accomplish*, Aeschin.2.66. 4. *carry ashore*, ἐπὶ Ταίναρον Hdt.1.24, etc.; *cast ashore*, πόντου νιν ἐξήνεγκε.. κλύδων E.*Hec.*701:—Pass., with fut. Med., *come to land, be cast ashore*, ἐς τοὺς ἑωυτῶν ἐξοίσονται Hdt.8.49, cf. 76, 2.90. II. *bring forth*, in various senses: 1. of women, = φέρειν μέχρι τέλους, *bring to the birth*, Hp.*Nat.Mul.*19; εἰς φῶς κύημα Pl.*R.*461c, cf. Arist. *HA*577ᵇ23, al.; of plants, *bear* seed, Id.*GA*731ᵃ22; of the ground, *bear* fruit, Δήμητρος καρπὸν ἐ. Hdt.1.193, 4.198. 2. *bring about, accomplish*, μισθοῖο τέλος Il.21.451; τὸ μόρσιμον Pi.*N.*4.61; κακίας μεγάλας ὥσπερ ἀρετὰς αἱ μεγάλαι φύσεις ἐ. Plu.*Demetr.*1:—Pass., διὰ ἀνοήτων οὐδὲν ἂν καλῶς ἐξενεχθείη D.61.7. 3. *publish, deliver*, χρηστήριον Hdt.5.79; ἐ. λόγον S.*Tr.*741, Pl.*Mx.*236c, cf. Plu.*Them.*23; εἰς τοὺς Ἕλληνας τὰ τῆς πόλεως ἁμαρτήματα Isoc.8.14; of public measures, *refer*, ἐξενεῖκαι ἐς τὸν δῆμον Hdt.9.5; ἐς πολύφημον ἐξενείκαντας Id.5.79; ἐ. προβούλευμα εἰς τὸν δῆμον *bring* a project of law before the people, D.59.4 (so in Med., ἐκφέρεσθαι προβούλευμα εἰς τὴν ἐκκλησίαν Aeschin.3.125): abs., freq. in Att. Inscrr., ἡ δὲ βουλὴ ἐς τὸν δῆμον ἐξενεγκέτω ἐπάναγκες *IG*1².76.61, cf. 2².360.47; of authors, *publish* a work, Isoc.9.74, Arist.*Po.*1447ᵇ17, D.H.*Comp.*1, Plu.2.10c, etc.:—Med., ἐκφέρεσθαι γνώμην *declare one's* opinion, Isoc.5.36:—Pass., εἰς Ἕλληνας ἐξοισθήσεται E.*Supp.*561. 4. *produce, exhibit*, Lys.19.30; *display*, δείγματα εἰς φῶς Pl.*Lg.*788c, cf. D.19.12; φανερῶς τὸ μῖσος εἴς τινας Plb.15.27.3; ἐ. τὴν ἰατρικὴν ἐπιστήμην D.S.5.74. 5. *disclose*, τι πρὸς τὸν μάγον Hdt.3.71; τὴν ἀπάτην ib.74; τὴν ἐπιχείρησιν Id.8.132. 6. *put forth, exert*, δύναμιν E.*Ion*1012:—and in Med., μέγα τι σθένος ἁ Κύπρις ἐκφέρεται νίκας S.*Tr.*497 (lyr.). 7. ἐ. πόλεμον *begin* war, D.1.21; ἐπί τινα Hdt.6.56; πρός τινα X.*HG*3.5.1; τινί Plb.2.36.4, etc. 8. *show the marks of, betray, reproduce*, ἐκφέρουσι γὰρ μητρῷ' ὀνείδη E.*Andr.*621. 9. ὅρον ἐ. *produce* a definition, Arist.*Metaph.*1040ᵇ2; *express*, διάνοιαν Phld.*Po.*5.26, al.; '*word*' a sentence, D.H.*Comp.*3 (Pass.), 7; *utter*, Demetr.*Eloc.*94; *cite, adduce*, ib.142; πρὸς ἑαυτὸν ἐ. *soliloquize*, Sch.Pi.*O.*1.5. b. *pronounce*, Ath.3.94f; ὅταν μακρῶς ἐκφέρηται D.H.*Comp.*15, cf. Archyt.1, Str.9.5.17. 10. *pay as indemnity*, δισχίλια τάλαντα Plb.3.27.5, etc. b. Pass., of words, *to be formed*, κατὰ μίμησιν Demetr.*Eloc.*220; ἐπιρρηματικῶς A.D.*Adv.*175.28; διὰ τοῦ ε̄ ἐ. ib.193.5. 11. *exact*, ἀργύριον Lxx 4*Ki.*15.20. III. Pass., *to be carried beyond bounds*, ἔξω ὅρων ἐξενεχθὲν ἀκόντιον Antipho 3.2.4: mostly metaph., *to be carried away* by passion, ἀπαιδευσίᾳ ὀργῆς Th.3.84, cf. Chrysipp.*Stoic.*3.127; πρὸς ὀργὴν ἐκφέρει *givest way* to passion, S.*El.*628; ἐ. πρὸς αἰδῶ *is inclined* to feel respect, E.*Alc.*601 (lyr.); λέγων ἐξηνέχθην Pl.*Cra.*425a; ἐξενεχθεὶς ὥστε κωμῳδοποιὸς γενέσθαι Id.*R.*606c; πρὸς τὸ ἄγριοι πολῖται γενέσθαι X.*Cyr.*1.6.34; πάθος defined as ὁρμὴ ἐκφερομένη καὶ ἀπειθὴς λόγῳ *Stoic.*3.92:—later in Act., [θυμὸς] ἐ. τινὰ τοῦ λογισμοῦ Philostr. *Im.*2.21. IV. *bring to* one's end, *bring on* to the trail, εὖ δέ σ' ἐκφέρει.. βάσις S.*Aj.*7; κινδυνεύει ὥσπερ ἀτραπός [τις] ἐκφέρειν ἡμᾶς [ἐν τῇ σκέψει] Pl.*Phd.*66b, cf. *IG*1².94.37:—Pass., ἐξηνέχθην εἰς ἅπερ Πρωταγόρας λέγει Pl.*Cra.*386a. V. intr. (sc. ἑαυτόν) *shoot forth* (before the rest), ὦκα δ' ἔπειτα αἱ Φηρητιάδαο.. ἔκφερον ἵπποι· τὰς δὲ μέτ' ἐξέφερον Διομήδεος.. ἵπποι Il.23.376, cf. 759; also, *to run away*, X.*Eq.*3.4. 2. *come to fulfilment*, ὁρᾷς τὰ τοῦδε.. ὡς ἐς ὀρθὸν ἐκφέρει μαντεύματα S.*OC*1424; *come to an end*, Id.*Tr.*824 (lyr.).

* **ἐκ-φεύγω**, fut. -ξομαι Ar.*V.*157, Pl.*Smp.*189b, and -ξοῦμαι Id.*R.*432d:—*flee out* or *away, escape*: abs., ἐκφυγέειν μεμαώς Od.19.231, cf. A.*Pers.*510, etc.; φεύγων ἐκφεύγειν Hdt.5.95. b. of persons accused, *to be acquitted*, Ar.*V.* 157. 2. c. gen., *escape out of*, ἐξέφυγον πολιῆς ἁλὸς ἤπειρόνδε Od.23.236; νούσου *Epigr.Gr.*1041.9; of things, βέλος ἔκφυγε χειρός Il.5.18: with Prep., ματρὸς ἐκ κόλπων *APl.*4.182 (Leon.). 3. c. acc., *escape*, ἐξ αὖ νῦν ἔφυγες θάνατον Il.11.362; κῆρας Od.4.512; κακότητα 5.414; θανάτοιο τέλος Archil.6; νοῦσον Hdt.1.25; Σκύθας Id.6.40; τὴν πεπρωμένην A.*Pr.*518; τὰν θεῶν νέμεσιν S.*Ph.*518 (lyr.), etc. b. simply, *to have escaped, to be beyond*, οὐ πολλὰ ἐκφεύγεις παιδιὰς ἔτη Pl.*Plt.*268e. c. of things, ἐκπεφεύγασιν γάμοι με E.*Hel.*1622; ἐκφύγοι τὰ πράγματ' αὐτόν D.18.33, cf. 19.123; ἐ. τὰς αἰσθήσεις *escape* one's sense, Arist.*Fr.*208; also, *escape* one's lips, Pl.*Ly.*213d: abs., ἐκφεύγει ταμελούμενον S.*OT*111, cf. Arist.*Metaph.*1090ᵇ21. d. ἐκφεύγοντες τὴν χιόνα τόποι places *free from* snow, Plb.3.55.7. e. Astron., of stars, *emerge* from the Sun's rays, *become visible*, Autol.1.9, Gem.13.9, etc. f. *pass over, omit*, Apollon.Cit.1. 4. c. inf. (with or without Art.), Pl.*Sph.*235b; οὐκ ἐκφεύγει μὴ οὐκ εἶναι.. Id.*Phdr.*277e; τὸ μὴ ἕτερα εἶναι Id.*Prm.*147a; ἐ. τὸ ἀποθανεῖν Id.*Ap.*39a; μικρὸν ἐξέφυγε μὴ καταπετρωθῆναι X.*An.*1.3.2; ἐκφεύξεται τὰ δύο *will not admit of* duality, Plot.3.8.9. **-φευκτικός**, ή, όν, *of* or *for escape*, σύμβολον Sch.Ar.*Pl.*63:—also **-φεύξιμος**, ον, ὁδός Sch.A.R.1.246. **-φευκτος**, ον, *escapable*, cj. in Hsch. s. v. δυσάλωτος (cj. -υκτος). **-φευξις**, εως, ἡ, *escape*, Apollon.*Lex.* s. v. ἀλεωρή.

**ἔκφημι**, *speak out* or *forth, utter loudly*:—Ep. only in Med., ἐκφάσθαι ἔπος Od.10.246, cf. 13.308; νόον ἔκφατο A.R.1.439: later aor. 1 ἐξέφησε *EM*687.30.

**ἐκφθέγγομαι**, *utter*, *IGRom.*1.1192 (Memnon).

**ἐκφθείρω**, *destroy utterly*, Scymn.344, Str.17.1.44, etc.:—Pass., ἐκφθείρομαι *to be undone, ruined*, ἐξεφθαρμένη E.*Hec.*669: Com., 'go to the devil', ἐκφθαρεὶς οὐκ οἶδ' ὅποι Ar.*Pax*72; ἐκφθείρου Luc.*DMer.*15.2.

**ἐκφθίνω**, in Hom. only in 3 plpf. Pass., νηῶν ἐξέφθιτο οἶνος the wine *had all been consumed out of* the ships, Od.9.163; νηὸς ἐξέφθιτο ἤϊα πάντα 12.329; ἐξέφθινται they *have utterly perished*, A.*Pers.*679 (lyr.), 927 (anap.).

**ἐκφιβλοῦσθαι**, gloss on ἐκπορποῦσθαι, Suid.

**ἐκφιλέω**, *kiss heartily*, *AP*12.250 (Strat.). 2. *love dearly*, prob. in *Epigr.Gr.*522.6.

***ἐκφλαίνω**, = ἐκφλύω, only aor. inf. ἐκφλῆναι E.*Fr.*470.

* **ἐκφλαυρίζω**, *make light of*, πρᾶγμα f.l. in Plu.2.680c, cf. *Pomp.*57, prob. in Sch.Ar.*Pl.*885.

**ἐκφλεγμᾰτόομαι**, Pass., *to turn into phlegm*, Hp.*Acut.*61.

**ἐκφλέγω**, *to set on fire*: metaph., τὴν πόλιν Ar.*Pax*608, Lxx 4*Ma.*16.3:—Pass., metaph., ἐκφλέγεσθαι τὴν διάνοιαν *to be inflamed*.., Plu.2.766a. 2. *warm up*, Aret.*SA*2.1.

**ἐκφλίβω** [ῑ], Ion. for ἐκθλίβω, Hp.*Loc.Hom.*9.

**ἐκφλογ-ίζω**, = ἐκφλέγω, Cleanth.ap.Stob.1.17.3 (Pass.). **-όω**, *scorch*, Phlp. *in Mete.*44.33:—Pass., *blaze up*, Arist.*Mir.*833ᵃ9, Dsc.1.68.2. **-ωσις**, εως, ἡ, *upper part of a torch*, D.S.17.115.

**ἐκφλοΐζω**, *deprive of rind, peel*, *PHolm.*24.2 (Pass.).

**ἐκφλοίομαι**, f.l. for ἐκβδάλλομαι, Nic.*Al.*322.

**ἐκφλύζω** or **ἐκφλύσσω**, *spirt out*: c. acc. cogn., ἐκφλύξαι γόον *give vent to* a groan, A.R.1.275.

**ἐκφλυνδάνω**, *break out*, of sores, Hp.*Int.*13, 46 (-φινδάνω f.l. in Gal.19.96).

**ἐκφλύω** [ῠ], gloss on ἐκβράσσω, Gal.19.96.

**ἐκφοβ-έω**, *alarm*, φρένας A.*Pers.*606, cf. Pl.*Grg.*483c, etc.; τὸ ἐκφοβῆσαι so as *to cause alarm*, Th.2.87; ἐ. τινὰ ἐκ δεμνίων E.*Or.*312; ἐ. τινά τι *fright* one *with* a thing, Th.6.11:—Pass., *fear greatly*, c. acc., S.*El.*276; ὡς.. ib.1426; ὑπέρ τινος Id.*OT*989. **-ημα**, ατος, τό, *means of scaring*, Sch.A.*Th.*280. **-ησις**, εως, ἡ, *frightening*, Hdn.*Epim.*21, Sch.A.*Pr.*922, Hsch. s.v. ἔκπληξις. **-ητικός**, ή, όν, *terrifying*, Eust.1966.16. **-ητρον**, τό, *bogey*, Sch.Ar.*Pax*473. **-ος**, ον, *affrighted*, Arist.*Phgn.*812ᵇ29, Lxx *De.*9.19, *Ev.Marc.*9.6, Plu.*Fab.*6.

**ἐκφόδιος**, dub. sens. in *POxy.*387 (i A.D.).

**ἐκφοινίσσω**, *make all red* or *bloody*, E.*Ph.*42:—Pass., *to be bloodshot*, ἐ. τοὺς ὀφθαλμούς Arist.*Phgn.*812ᵃ37. II. ἐκφοινίξαι· ἀναγνῶσαι, Hsch.

* **ἐκφοιτ-άω**, Ion. -έω, *go out constantly, be in the habit of going out*, ἐπὶ θήρην Hdt.4.116; simply, *go out*, ἐκ τῆς ἀκροπόλιος Id.3.68, cf. E.*El.*320. 2. of things, *to be spread abroad*, λόγοι παρὰ τῆς γυναικὸς ἐξεφοίτων Plu.*Lyc.*3. 3. ἐ. εἰς μανίαν *to end* in madness, Ael.*NA* 11.32. 4. *issue*, κἂν μήπω τέλειον αὐτῆς ἐκφοιτήσῃ τὸ γέννημα, prob. for ἐμφ., Ph.1.105. **-ησις**, εως, ἡ, *becoming public*, J.*AJ*19.1.7.

* **ἐκφορ-ά**, ἡ, (ἐκφέρω) *carrying out*, esp. of a corpse to burial, A.*Th.*1029, *Ch.*9, 430 (lyr., pl.), Th.2.34; ἐπ' ἐκφορὰν βαδίζειν Ar.*Pl.*1008; ἐπ' ἐ. ἀκολουθεῖν τινί Lys.1.8; also of meats at a sacrifice, Theopomp. Com.70, Euphro 1.20, prob. in Ar.*Pl.*1138; τῶν κρεῶν μὴ εἶναι ἐ. ἔξω τοῦ τεμένεος *IG*7.235.32 (Orop.). 2. *blabbing, betrayal of secrets*, λόγων ἀπορρήτων ἐ. D.L.1.98. II. (from Pass.) of horses, *running away*, ἡ πρὸς οἶκον ἐ. X.*Eq.*3.5. 2. *passing out*, ἡ τοῦ πνεύματος ἐ. D.S.2.12. III. *projection in a building*, Vitr.3.5.1, 6.2.2 (pl.). IV. *utterance, pronunciation*, Phld.*Po.*994.24, Str.16.4.18, D.H.*Comp.*14. V. *expression, enunciation* of ideas, *Stoic.*2.58, al., D.H.*Comp.*8, Plu.2.1112e, Alex.Aphr. *in Metaph.*371.7; esp. *mode of expression, grammatical construction*, ἐ. προστακτική A.D. *Synt.*69.20; ἐνεργητική ib.150.19; ἐ. ἑνικαί, πληθυντικαί, Chrysipp. *Stoic.*2.6. VI. *digression*, εἰς ἐ. ἐκπίπτειν wander from the point, Gal.8.629. **-έω**, = ἐκφέρω, *carry out*, as a corpse for burial, Od.22.451, 24.417 (tm.). 2. generally, *carry out*, Hdt.1.197, 9.116, Is.6.42 (Pass., ib.41):—Med., *take out with one*, E.*Cyc.*234, etc.:—Pass., *move forth*, ὡς τότε ταρφειαὶ κόρυθες.. νηῶν ἐκφορέοντο Il.19.360. 3. *dig out*, of earth dug from a trench, Hdt.2.150 (Pass.), 7.23; of metal from mines, X.*Vect.*4.2 (Pass.). 4. *sack, plunder*, πόλιν D.S.17.13 (Pass.). 5. in Pass., *to be cast on shore*, Hdt.8.12. 6. *blab, blurt out*, dub. in Hermesian.7.98. 7. Med., *distrain upon goods*, D.47.53, 75. 8. *make away with*, *PSI*5.463 (ii A.D.), *POxy.*1642.22 (iii A.D.). 9. ἐκφορεῖ· σπανίζει ὑπάρχοντα, Hsch. **-ιαστής**, οῦ, ὁ, *collector of* ἐκφόριον II, *IGRom.*3.576 (Lycia, ii A.D.). **-ίζω**, *exhaust by parturition*, Sch.Orib.3 p.681 D. (Pass.). **-ικός**, ή, όν, *belonging to* or *producing expression*: τὸ ἐ. *the power of expressing oneself in words*, Plu.2.1113c; but, *capable of being expressed*, νοήματα *Stoic.*2.77. Adv. -κῶς Plu.2.1112d. * **-ιον**, τό, *that which the earth produces*, Hdt.4.198 (pl.), Lxx *Le.*25.19 (pl.), *Milet.*3.149 (ii B.C.), Poll.1.237. II. *payment assessed on produce*, = δεκάτη, Arist.*Oec.*1345ᵇ33; esp. *rent paid in kind*, ἐ. ἀπότακτον *PAmh.*2.87 (ii A.D.), cf. *PTeb.*377.23 (iii A.D.), *OGI*669.30, etc. **-όομαι**, Pass., *to be worn into holes*, τῇ καύσει Thphr.*Lap.*14, cf. 15. **-ος**, ον, *exportable*, f.l. for ἐκφορά, Ar.*Pl.*1138. 2. *to be made known* or *divulged*, εἰ δ' ἔ. σοι ξυμφορὰ πρὸς ἄρσενας E.*Hipp.*295; οὐδεὶς γὰρ ἔ. λόγος Pl.*La.*201a; cf. ἐκφορά I. 2. 3. *carried astray*, Plu.2.424a; ἵππος ἔ. a *runaway* horse, Gal.5.510. 4. ἔκφορα, τά, *produce* of the earth, Antipho Soph.60. II. Act., *carrying out*:—in A.*Eu.*910 τῶν δυσσεβούντων ἐκφορωτέρα is not, *more ready to carry* them *out to burial* (v. ἐκφορά I), but rather, *more ready to weed* them *out*, as a gardener does noxious plants (ἀνδρὸς φιτυποίμενος δίκην, in next line). 2. *blabbing, betraying* secrets, Ar.*Th.*472. 3. = εὐέκφορος (quod fort. leg.), γυναῖκες Arist.*Fr.*283. 4. *expressive*, κίνησις ἔ. τινος Chrysipp.*Stoic.*3.112. III. as Subst., ἔκφοροι, οἱ, *reefing-ropes*, = τέρθριοι, Sch.Ar.*Eq.*438, Phot. s. v. ἡνιόχους.

* **ἐκφορτίζομαι**, Pass., *to be sold for exportation*: metaph., *to be kidnapped, betrayed*, v.l. for ἐμφ-, S.*Ant.*1036.

**ἐκφόρτιον**, f.l. for ἐκφόριον I, Lxx *De*.28.33.

**ἐκφούγιν**, dub. in *Supp.Epigr*.2.727 (Pisidia, fort. = ἐκφύγιον, i.e. *place of refuge*).

**ἐκφράζω**, *tell over, recount*, A.*Pr*.950, dub. l. in E.*HF*1119; *denote*, δύναμιν τοῖς τῶν θεῶν ὀνόμασιν Plu.2.24a. II. *describe*, Hermog. *Prog*.10, *Id*.2.4, Men.Rh.p.373 S.:—Pass., Theon *Prog*.2. 2. *express ornately*, τὸ ἐ. τὰ γέλοια ὅμοιόν ἐστι καὶ καλλωπίζειν πίθηκον Demetr.*Eloc*.165.

**ἐκ-φρακτικός**, ή, όν, (ἐκφράσσω) *for clearing obstructions*, ἐ. τῶν πόρων Gal.11.743; τὰ ἐ. *opening medicines*, *Hippiatr*.2; τροχίσκος Paul.Aeg. 7.12. **-φραξις**, εως, ἡ, *removal of obstructions*, Gal.1.391, 10.775.

**ἐκφρᾰσείδιον**, τό, Dim. of sq., Eust.1065.20.

**ἔκφρᾰσις**, εως, ἡ, *description*, D.H.*Rh*.10.17 (pl.), Luc.*Hist.Conscr*. 20, Hermog.*Prog*.10, Aphth.*Prog*.12, etc.; title of works *descriptive of works of art*, as that of Callistratus. II. = ἐπιθυμία, Hsch.

**ἐκφράσσω**, Att. -ττω, aor. 1 Pass. ἐκφραχθῆναι D.S.18.35:—*remove obstacles, open*, Gal.11.730, D.S. l. c.

**ἐκφραστέον**, *one must describe*, Aphth.*Prog*.12.

**ἐκφραστικός**, ή, όν, *descriptive*: τὸ ἐ. *the faculty of describing*, D.L. 5.65.

**ἐκφρέω** (v. εἰσφρέω), poet. impf. ἐξεφρίομεν (fort. -φρίεμεν) Ar.*V*. 125: fut. ἐκφρήσω ib.156: aor. ἐξέφρησα (v. infr.), also ἐξέφρηκα Hsch.: imper. ἔκφρες prob. for ἔκφερε Ar.*V*.162:—*let out, bring out*, μή.. οὐκ ἐκφρῶσιν restored in E.*Ph*.264 (for οὐ μεθῶσιν) from the Sch. and Phot. (leg. Εὐριπίδης), cf. Ar. ll. cc.; ἐξέφρησα ἐμαυτόν Luc.*Lex*.9:—Med., ἔκφρηται· ἐκφέρεται, Hsch.:—Pass., *go out*, ἐκφρησθῆναι Ael.*Fr*.89.

**ἐκφρίττω**, *tremble at*, Orac. in *App.Anth*.6.128.

**ἐκφρονέω**, *to be demented*, D.C.55.13, *Fr*.9.2. II. c. gen., = καταφρονέω, *AB*141.

**ἐκφροντίζω**, *think out, discover*, E.*IT*1323, Ar.*Nu*.695, Th.3.45, etc.

**ἐκφροσύνη**, Dor. -σύνα, ἡ, (ἔκφρων) *madness, nonsense*, Ti.Locr. 102e.

**ἐκφρύγομαι** [ῡ], *to be dried up, parched*, c. acc. cogn., ἅπασαν ἐ. τοῦ στόματος τὴν ἰκμάδα Gal.*UP*11.10, cf. 17(1).181: aor. 2 subj. ἐκφρυγῇ Damocr.ap.eund.13.989. II. *to be consumed*, ἔρωτι Ael.*NA*14.18.

**ἐκφρύττω**, *dry, parch thoroughly*, Alex.Trall.12 (Pass.).

**ἔκφρων**, ον, gen. ονος, (φρήν) *out of one's mind, beside oneself*, Hp. *Mul*.2.117, Luc.*Nigr*.38, Plot.2.9.8; *senseless, stupid*, D.19.267; also, *frenzied, enthusiastic*, of poets, Pl.*Ion*534b; of Bacchantes, Luc. *Bacch*.1, *AP*6.220.2 (Diosc.), cf. Pl.*Lg*.790e. II. Adv. -φρόνως, ἥττων γίγνεσθαι τῶν προσπιπτόντων Hld.6.9.

**ἐκφυάς**, άδος, ἡ, = ἀποφυάς, Eratosth.26.

**ἐκφυγγάνω**, = ἐκφεύγω, A.*Pr*.525, Diph.7, Plb.18.15.11; *recover from* disease, Hp.*Morb*.2.26.

**ἔκφῠγε**, v. ἐκφεύγω.

**ἐκφῠγή**, ἡ, *escape*, Lxx 3*Ma*.4.19.

* **ἐκφῠής**, ές, *abnormally developed*, τοῖς ὀδοῦσιν ἢ τοῖς ὀφθαλμοῖς Vett. Val.110.15; *projecting*, Procl.*Hyp*.3.16. II. *eminent, extraordinary*. Adv. -ῶς App.*Ill*.25.

* **ἐκφυλάσαι**· ἐκσπάσαι, Hsch.

**ἐκφῠλάσσω**, *guard* or *watch carefully*, S.*OC*285, E.*Or*.1259; ἴχνος ἐκφύλασσ' ὅπου τίθης Id.*Ion*741.

* **ἐκφυλλοφορ-έω**, *expel* or *condemn by leaves*, used of the Athen. βουλή, which used olive-leaves as voting-papers, Aeschin.1.111, cf. *AB*248. **-ησις**, εως, ἡ, *sentence passed by leaves*, Tz.*H*.10.40. **-ία**, ἡ, = foreg., *EM*325.9.

**ἔκφῠλος**, ον, *foreign, alien*, Luc.*Lex*.24, *Sol*.11, Porph.*Abst*.1.4; ἔ. παρὰ τὴν γένεσιν *alien* to generation, Simp. *in Ph*.220.12: metaph., *strange, unnatural, horrible*, Str.4.4.5, Plu.*Brut*.36; ἀνὴρ ἔ. τὸ μέγεθος Id.*Caes*.69. Adv. -λως, ἀττικίζειν Philostr.*VS*1.16.4.

**ἔκφῡμα**, ατος, τό, *eruption of pimples*, v.l. in Hp.*Insomn*.89. 2. *outgrowth* of vine tendrils, *EM*330.29.

**ἐκφῦναι**, v. ἐκφύω.

**ἐκφύρω** [ῡ], strengthd. for φύρω, aor. 1 Pass. ἐξεφύρθην Lxx *Je*.3.2.

**ἐκφῡσ-άω**, *blow out*, ἔνθα ποταμὸς ἐκφυσᾷ μένος *pours forth* its strength, A.*Pr*.720; of elephants *spouting* water through their trunks, Plb.3.46.12: metaph., ἐ. πόλεμον *blow up* a war from a spark, Ar.*Pax*610; also ἐκπεφυσημένος *a puffed up, conceited* person, Plb. 3.103.7. 2. *blow away*, Lxx *Hg*.1.9:—Pass., Plb.1.48.8; *to be dissipated*, Aret.*SD*2.1. 3. *sublimate* volatile elements, Zos.Alch. p.148 B., al.:—Pass., Dsc.5.75. II. *breathe out*, βαρὺν ὕπνον ἐ., i.e. snore loudly, Theoc.24.47; αἷμα Herod.2.72. III. intr., *snort*, Lyc.743; *burst forth*, φλόγες ἐκφυσήσασαι Arist.*Mu*.400ᵃ32. **-ημα**, ατος, τό, *pustule*, Poll.4.190. 2. *volcanic eruption*, Sch.A.R.3.41; πυρὸς ἐ. D.S.3.53 (pl.): pl., = πέτραι ὑπερέχουσαι τῆς γῆς, Hsch. **-ησις**, εως, ἡ, *emission of breath*, Gal.8.251, prob. in *EM*98.20. II. gloss on ἀποφύσιας, Hsch. **-ιάω**, poet. for ἐκφυσάω, A.*Ag*.1389.

* **ἔκφῠσις**, εως, ἡ, (ἐκφύω) *growing out* or *forth*: *germination*, Thphr. *HP*8.1.5; *growth, increase*, Arist.*PA*658ᵇ5, Diog.Oen.28; ἐ. ἀρετῆς Pl.*Lg*.777e, cf. Hierocl. *in CA*24 p.471 M.; *manner of growth*, Thphr. *HP*1.14.2. II. *outgrowth*, A.*Fr*.252, Pl.*Phdr*.251b; γενύων Opp. *C*.2.497 (pl.). 2. *bony projection*, Hp.*Art*.45; *origin, attachment* of muscles, nerves, etc., Gal.8.61, al. 3. *shoot*, Thphr.*HP*1.10. 7: in pl., *suckers*, *Gp*.12.19.1; *seedlings*, Thphr.*HP*7.4.3 (so in sg., *crop of seedlings*, ib.3.3.7); *roots*, Plb.18.18.6.

**ἐκφῠτεύω**, *plant out*, πήγανον εἰς συκῆν Arist.*Pr*.924ᵇ36. II. *plant*, χώραν Heraclid.*Pol*.36; ἄλσος Philostr.*VS*1.23.2:—Pass., ib. 2.23 3.

**ἔκφῡτον**, τό, = ἔκφυσις II. 3, Alex.Aphr.*Pr*.2.16.

**ἐκφύω**, *generate*: mostly of the male, *beget*, S.*OT*437, 827, etc.; ὃς ἐξέφυσεν Ἀερόπης λέκτρων ἄπο Ἀγαμέμνον' E.*Hel*.391. 2. rarely of the female, *bear*, S.*OC*984. 3. generally, *produce*, ἡ γῆ κατὰ καιρὸν ἐκφύουσα πάντα Arist.*Mu*.397ᵃ26; ἐ. κέρατα Id.*HA*611ᵇ13: abs., of seed, *germinate*, D.24.154. II. Pass., with pf. and aor. 2 Act., *to be engendered, born from*, κεφαλαὶ τρεῖς ἑνὸς αὐχένος ἐκπεφυυῖαι (Ep. pf. part.) Il.11.40; πατρός, μητρὸς ἐκφῦναι, S.*Aj*.487, 1295, E. *Ion*542; λάλημα ἐκπεφυκός *a born* tattler, S.*Ant*.320. 2. *grow*, of hair, μέχρις ἂν [αἱ τρίχες] ἐκφυῶσι Archig.ap.Gal.12.407; *spring, take rise*, of muscles, ib.18(2).981. III. intr. in pres. Act., ἕλκεα ἐκφύουσιν Hp.*Epid*.6.5.15, cf. Arist.*Pr*.883ᵇ26.

**ἐκφων-έω**, *cry out*, Ph.2.49, Plu.*Caes*.66. II. *utter*, Id.2.1010a (Pass.), Demetr.*Eloc*.15; *pronounce*, D.H.*Comp*.14 (Pass.). 2. *publish, promulgate*, *POxy*.136.39 (vi A.D., Pass.), *Cod.Just*.10.16.13 (Pass.). **-ησις**, εως, ἡ, *pronunciation*, A.D.*Synt*.13 9, S.E.*M*.1. 102, al.; *exclamation*, Ph.1.618 (pl.), Plu.2.1111d (pl.), A.D.*Synt*.4. 26 (pl.). 2. *acclamation*, *Sammelb*.3924.36 (i A.D.). II. *meaning, signification*, Marin.*Procl*.28 (pl.).

**ἐκχᾰλάω**, *let go from*, τεγέων δέμας *AP*11.354.18 (Agath.). 2. *relax*, τὴν ὀργήν Chor. in *Rev.Phil*.1.68. II. intr., *become loose* or *slack*, Hp.*Sept*.1.

**ἐκχᾰλῑνόω**, *unbridle*, Plu.*Pel*.33.

**ἐκχαλκεύω**, *work from brass*, J.*AJ*3.7.6.

**ἐκχᾰραδρόω**, strengthd. for χαραδρόω, Plb.4.41.9:—Pass., τόποι ἐκχαραδρούμενοι χειμάρροις Str.11.3.4.

**ἐκχᾰράσσω**, Att. -ττω, *erase*, Plu.2.873d, D.Chr.31.71, al.

**ἐκχαρεών**· μαγειρείων, Hsch. (Lacon. for ἐσχ-).

**ἐκχᾰρυβδίζω**, *swallow like Charybdis*, Pherecr.95 (s. v. l.); cf. ἐξεχαρυβδαάνθη (sic)· ἀνεπόθη, Hsch.

**ἐκχάσκω**, in pf. ἐκκέχηνα, *gape, gaze*, εἴς τινα Lxx 1*Es*.4.19.

**ἔκχαυνος**, ον, *very loose*, Erot. s. v. πλάδος.

**ἐκχαυνόω**, *puff up, make vain and arrogant*, ἐκ δὲ παίδων χαύνοις φρένας Alc.51; [πόλιν] ἐκχαυνῶν λόγοις E.*Supp*.412, cf. Phld.*Lib*. p.32 O.; ἐ. τὸν πολὺν ὄχλον *to make* them *gape and stare*, Hp.*Art*.42.

* **ἐκχέζω**, = Lat. *ecacare*, πεδία ὅλα Anon.ap.Demetr.*Eloc*.126, v.l. in Arist.*HA*551ᵃ7.

**ἐκχερσεύω**, *dry up*, Hsch. s. v. ἐκκεχιλωμένη (Pass.).

**ἐκχεύω**, = sq, Nic.*Fr*.74.34.

* **ἐκχέω** (later -χύνω *Ev.Matt*.23.35 (Pass.), etc., condemned by Luc. *Pseudol*.29), fut. -χέω (v. χέω): aor. 1 ἐξέχεα (also imper. ἔκχυσον Hsch.); Ep. aor. Med. ἐκχευάμην Od.24.178: pf. ἐκκέχῠκα Men. 915:—*pour out*, prop. of liquids, οἶνον Il.3.296; αἷμ' ἐκχέας πέδοι A. *Eu*.653, cf. *Ev.Matt*.23.35 (Pass.); ἀναίτιον αἷμα *SIG*1181.5 (Jewish, ii B.C.); πηγάς E.*HF*941; δάκρυα Pl.*Smp*.215e (Pass.), Plu.*Alc*.6; ὁ οἶνος ἐκχεῖται *is spilt*, *Ev.Matt*.9.17: metaph., (in Med.) ταχέας δ' ἐκχεύατ' ὀϊστοὺς he *poured forth* his arrows, Od.22.3, 24.178; σοί.. δαίμονες.. ἐλπίδας ἐξέχεαν Pl.*Epigr*.7.4. b. *pour away*: hence, *spill*, a vessel, ποδάνιπτρον Ar.*Fr*.306; τὸν χόα Men. l. c.:—Pass., *to be drained*, εἰς [διώρυχα] *PRyl*.154.18 (i A.D.). 2. of words, *pour forth, utter*, Ar.*Th*.554; μολπάς E.*Supp*.773; πολλὴν γλῶσσαν ἐκχέας μάτην S.*Fr*.929, cf. A.*Ag*.1029 (lyr.). 3. *pour out like water, squander, waste*, ὄλβον Id.*Pers*.826; τὰ πάντα Id.*Ch*.520, cf. S.*El*. 1291; πλοῦτον ἐξέχεεν εἰς δαπάνας *AP*9.367 (Luc.); ἐ. τά τε αὑτοῦ καὶ ἑαυτόν Pl.*R*.553b; *spoil*, τὸ πᾶν σόφισμα S.*Ph*.13. 4. *spread out*, λίνα, ὀθόνας, A.R.2.902 (tm.), Luc.*Am*.6. 5. *throw down*, τινὰ κατὰ τοῦ κρημνοῦ D.H.13.8, cf. 4.7, 14.10. 6. ὕπνον ἐ. *shed*, i.e. *shake off* sleep, Herod.7.7. 7. = συγχέω, ὅρκια Hsch. s. v. ἐξέχεαν. II. Pass., used by Hom. mostly in plpf. ἐξεκέχυντο, as also in 3 sg. Ep. aor. ἐξέχυτο or ἔκχυτο, part. ἐκχύμενος [ῡ]: later fut. ἐκχυθήσομαι Hero *Aut*.4.1:—*pour out, stream out* or *forth*, prop. of liquids, Il.21.300, Od.19.504, etc.; ἐκ δ' ἄρα πᾶσαι χύντο χαμαὶ χολάδες Il.4.525; so ἐξεχύθη τὰ σπλάγχνα *Act.Ap*.1.18: metaph., of persons, σφήκεσσιν ἐοικότες ἐξεχέοντο Il.16.259; ἱππόθεν ἐκχύμενοι *pouring from* the [wooden] horse, Od.8.515; ἐκχυθέντες ἁλέες ἐκ τοῦ τείχεος Hdt.3.13: generally, *to be spread out*, πολλὰ δὲ [δέσματα].. μελαθρόφιν ἐξεκέχυντο Od.8.279; σάρκες εἰς ὑπέρογκον ἐκκεχυμέναι πιότητα Luc.*Am*.14. 2. metaph., ῥηθέντα ματαίως ἐκκέχυται *to* *be cast away, forgotten*, ἐκκέχυται φιλότης Thgn. 110; αἱ πρόσθεν ὁμολογίαι ἐκκεχυμέναι εἰσίν Pl.*Cri*.49a. 3. *give oneself up to any emotion, to be overjoyed*, Ar.*V*.1469 (lyr.); ἐ. εἰς ἑταίρας, εἰς τὸν κίνδυνον, *give oneself up to*.., Plb.31.25.4, 3.19.1; ἐπὶ τὰ εὐτρεπισθέντα, of a glutton, Ph.1.38; ἁβρὰ γελῶν ὄμμασιν ἐκκέχυσαι *AP*12.156. 4. *lie languidly*, ib.5.54.8 (Diosc.). 5. metaph., of Time, ἐ. κατὰ τὴν χρονικὴν παράτασιν Procl.*Inst*.55. 6. *extend*, of a piece of land, *CPR*1.8, al. (i A.D.).

**ἐκχῐλόω**, *cover all over with grass* (χιλός): γῆ ἐκκεχιλωμένη land *that bears nothing but grass*, Paus Gr.*Fr*.323.

**ἐκχλευάζω**, strengthd. for χλευάζω, τινά Sm.*Pr*.14.9, Lib.*Decl*.48.45.

* **ἐκχλοιόομαι**, Pass., *to be* or *grow sallow*, Hp.*Coac*.480.

* **ἐκχοΐζω**, *dig out*, *Ostr.Strassb*.677 (ii A.D.), Suid. II. Pass., *to be decanted into jars*, of wine, *PSI*5.517 (iii B.C.).

**ἐκχοίρηξις**· ἐκχοιρηλωμένος (Lacon.), Hsch.

**ἐκχοιρῐλόω**, only pf. part. Pass. ἐκκεχοιριλωμένη (sc. κωμῳδία) expld. by οὐ Χοιρίλου οὖσα, Hsch.

**ἐκχολ-άω**, *to be angry*, Lxx 3*Ma*.3.1. **-ίζω**, *purge of bile*, ὄρνεα *Gp*.14.19.3 (v.l. -χολῶσαι). **-όω**, *turn into bile*, Herod.Med. in *Rh.Mus*.49.555:—Pass., Gal.6.449, 626, Alex.Aphr.*Pr*.1.79. II. Pass., *to be charged with bile*, κοιλίαι ἐκχολοῦνται Dieuch.ap.Orib.4.7.

15. **-ωσις**, εως, ἡ, *turning into bile*, Alex.Trall.1.15, Steph.*in Hp.*1.130 D.

**ἐκχονδρίζω**, (χόνδρος) *cut away, remove cartilage*, Gal.14.791.

**ἐκχορδόομαι**, Pass., *to be deprived of strings*, Sopat.16.

**ἐκχορεύω**, *break out of the chorus*: generally, *break out*, ἐς ἄτην Opp.*H.*4.215; *exult*, Hld.10.38. II. Med., *drive out of the chorus*, ἄν τέ ποτ' Ἄρτεμις ἐξεχορεύσατο E.*Hel.*381 (anap.).

⊛ **ἐκχράω** (v. χράω c), *declare as an oracle, tell out*, τὰ πόλλ'.. ὅτ' ἐξέχρη κακά S.*OC*87. II. *suffice*, οὐκ ἐξέχρησέ σφι ἡ ἡμέρα Hdt.8.70: impers., c. inf., κῶς ταῦτα βασιλέϊ ἐκχρήσει περιυβρίσθαι; how *will it suffice* him, how *will he be content* to..? Id.3.137.

**ἐκχρέμπτομαι**, *cough up, bring up*, Hp.*Morb.*2.26.

**ἔκχρημα**, ατος, τό, misspelling of ἔκρηγμα, Wilcken *Chr.*11.10 (ii B.C.).

**ἐκχρηματίζομαι**, *squeeze money from, levy contributions on*, τινά Th.8.87, D.C.53.10.

**ἔκχρησις**, εως, ἡ, *loan*, *SIG*742.52 (pl., Ephesus, i B.C.).

**ἐκχρησμῳδέω**, *deliver an oracle*, Sch.Pi.*O.*7.168 (v.l. ἐχρησμ-).

**ἐκχρυσόομαι**, *turn to gold*, Tz.*H.*1.107.

**ἐκχρώννυμι**, *impart a colour*, ἥλιος σκοτεινὸν ἄνθος ἐξέχρωσε λιγνύος εἰς σῶματ' ἀνδρῶν Theodect.17.2.

**ἐκχυλ-ίζω**, *squeeze out, express juice* or *liquor*, Hp.*Mul.*1.44; *suck out*, Arist.*HA*596$^b$12. **-όω**, in Pass., *to be squeezed out*, Gal.12.14.

**ἐκχύμενος**, v. ἐκχέω.

**ἐκχυμ-ίζω**, = ἐκχυλίζω, Arist.*HA*594$^a$15. **-όω**, *extract juice from*, σίδια Hp.*Morb.*2.47. II. in Pass., of the small veins, *shed the blood and leave it extravasated under the skin*, Id.*Fract.*11. ⊛ **-ωμα**, ατος, τό, *ecchymosis*, ib.11 (pl.), *Art.*50:—also **-ωσις**, εως, ἡ, Id.*Liqu.*1, Gal.10.232, al.

**ἐκ-χύνω**, v. ἐκχέω. **-χυσιαῖος**, α, ον, *for a sluice*, ἧλοι *POxy.*1220.16 (iii A.D.). **-χυσις**, εως, ἡ, *outflow*, Arist.*Mete.*354$^a$26; *pouring out*, Thphr.*Vent.*50, Lxx *Le.*4.12; βαλανείου *PTeb.*86.9 (ii B.C.); *shedding*, αἵματος Porph.*Antr.*11. II. *effusion* of pus, Erasistr.ap. Gal.8.318. III. *sluice* or *drain*, *CPR*176.16 (iii A.D.), al. **-χυτήριον**, τό, *drain*, *Gloss.* **-χύτης** [ῠ], ου, ὁ, *spendthrift*, Luc.*Vit. Auct.*24. 2. *drain*, *Gloss.* **-χυτο**, v. ἐκχέω. **-χυτος**, ον, (ἐκχέω) *poured forth, unconfined*, κόμη *AP*9.669.8 (Marian.); *outstretched*, ἔκχυτος ὕπνῳ κεῖτο ib.5.274 (Paul. Sil.). 2. *immoderate*, γέλως Suid. s.v. καγχασμός. II. Subst., ἔκχυτον, τό, dub. sens. in *AP*9.395 (Pall.; ποτόν tit., εἶδος βρώματος Sch.); title of dialogue on ψοσκοπία by Hermagoras, *Stoic.*1.102.

**ἐκχυτρίζω**, *pour out of a pot*, Hsch.

**ἔκχωνεν**· ἔκκλινεν (Lacon.), Hsch.; cf. κωνάω.

**ἐκχωνεύω**, *melt down, coin anew*, D.C.68.15 codd.

**ἐκχώννυμι**, *raise a mound*, Aq.*Ez.*17.17:—usu. in Pass., *to be raised on a bank* or *mound*, τῆς πόλιος ἐκκεχωσμένης ὑψοῦ Hdt.2.138; μάλιστα ἡ ἐν Βουβάστι πόλις ἐξεχώσθη ib.137. II. of a bay, *to be filled up by the deposit* of a river, v.l. ib.11. III. *to be removed*, of rubbish, *PFay.*110.5 (i A.D.).

⊛ **ἐκχωρ-έω**, *depart*, ἐκ χώρας *SIG*679.53; *leave a country, emigrate*, Hdt.1.56, Hecat.30 J.; *withdraw*, ἐκ τῆς οἰκίας *PAmh.*2.30.44 (ii B.C.), etc.: metaph., ἐ. ἐκ τοῦ ζῆν Plb.2.21.2: so abs., Id.7.2.1. 2. *slip out of*, ἀστράγαλος ἐξεχώρησε ἐκ τῶν ἄρθρων Hdt.3.129. 3. *give way, retire*, E.*IA*367, D.41.5; τῶν ὑπαίθρων Plb.1.15.7; τῶν ὑπαρχόντων Id.31.28.3; χειμῶνες ἐκχωροῦσιν εὐκάρπῳ θέρει S.*Aj.*671; ἐ. τινί τινος *give way* to a person in a thing, Hp.*Jusj.*; τινὶ περί τινος Plb.21.20.1. 4. impers. of a *motion* of the bowels, Hp.*Epid.*5.33. II. trans., *give up, cede*, τινί τι *IG*12(3).324.15 (Thera), *PEleph.*15.2 (iii B.C.), *Sammelb.*4414.8, etc.; τῷ δαίμονί τι Vett.Val.156.4:—Pass., *CIG*4268 (Xanthus). ⊛ **-ησις**, εως, ἡ, *going out*, *Placit.*4.22.1. 2. *retirement, withdrawal from*, c. gen., τῶν πολλῶν Epicur.*Sent.*14; ἐκ τῶν οἰκητηρίων *BGU*1115.48 (i B.C.). II. *concession*, *CIG*3394 (Smyrna). 2. *deed of surrender*, *PSI*1.93 (iii A.D.). **-ητέον**, *one must retire*, πάντων τῶν τόπων Plb.18.45.9. **-ητικός**, ή, όν, *concessory*, *Gloss.*

⊛ **ἐκχωρίζω**, *cut off, separate*, *PRyl.*378.11 (ii A.D., Pass.). II. Pass., *to be voided*, of excrements, Arist.*HA*551$^a$7.

**ἔκψυξις**, εως, ἡ, *cooling*, v.l. in Aret.*SA*2.2.

**ἐκψύχω** [ῡ], fut. -ξω, *lose consciousness, swoon*, Hp.*Morb.*1.5, Lxx *Jd.*4.21; ἐκ τάχα ψύξειν Herod.4.29; *give up the ghost, expire*, Babr.115.11, *Act.Ap.*5.5, 12.23. II. *to be short of breath, gasp*, Arist.*Pr.*886$^b$14. III. Pass., *to be thoroughly cooled, chilled*, ib.882$^a$36, Plu.2.695d.

**ἐκψωμίζω**, of corn, *to be infested with grubs*, Hsch. s.v. ψώμηκες.

**ἔκω**, barbarism for ἔχω in Ar.*Th.*1197, 1220.

⊛ **ἑκών**, ἑκοῦσα, ἑκόν: (ϝεκ- *IG*9(1).334.12 (Locr.), *GDI*5131*b* (Crete), cf. γεκαθά; cf. Skt. *váśmi* 'wish'):—*readily*, Od.4.649, etc.; freq. contrasted with ἄκων, ἑ. ἀέκοντί γε θυμῷ Il.4.43; οὐ γάρ τίς με βίῃ γε ἑ. ἀέκοντα δίηται 7.197; ἑκόνθ' ἑκόντι Ζηνὶ συμπαρασταπεῖν A.*Pr.*220; πάρειμι δ' ἄκων οὐχ ἑκοῦσιν S.*Ant.*276; ἑκόντα μήτ' ἄκοντα Id.*Ph.*771; βίᾳ τε κοὐχ ἑκών Id.*OC*935; ἑ. παρ' ἑκόντος λαμβάνειν, i.e. by mutual consent, D.21.44; τὴν φύσιν ἑκοῦσαν καὶ οὐ παθοῦσαν τὰ δέοντα ποιεῖν Gal.19.171. 2. *wittingly, purposely*, ἑκὼν δ' ἡμάρτανε φωτὸς Il.10.372, etc.; σφόδρ' ἑκών.. ἀγνοεῖν προσποιούμενος D.29.13. 3. in Att. Prose (cf. Phryn.241), ἑ. εἶναι *as far as depends on one's will, as far as concerns one*, with a neg., Hdt.7.104, 8.116, Pl.*Ap.*37a, al.; also in oblique cases, ὑπὸ σοῦ ἑκόντος εἶναι Id.*Grg.*499c; or in a sentence implying a neg., θαυμάζοιμεν ἂν εἰ.. τις ἑκὼν εἶναι (fort. delendum).. ἀφικνεῖται; Id.*Lg.*646b: once affirm., ἑκὼν εἶναι.. οἴχετο Hdt.7.164. II. rarely of things, κακὰ ἑ. κοὐκ ἄκοντα S.*OT*1230. III. for Adv. see ἑκοντήν, ἑκοντί: regul. Adv. ἑκόντως is dub. in Aristid.2.187, 226 J.

⊛ **ἔλα**· ἥλιος, αὐγή, καῦμα (Lacon.), Hsch. (ϝελ-, cf. βέλα, γέλαν). II. imper. of ἐλάω, v. ἐλαύνω. **ἐλάα**, Att. for ἐλαία. **ἐλάαν**, Ep. inf. pres. of ἐλάω, ἐλαύνω, Hom.: but fut. in Il.17.496.

⊛ **ἐλάδιον**, τό, Dim. of ἐλάα, *young olive-tree*, Alciphr.3.13 (pl.). II. *a little oil*, Telesp.41 H., Sotad.Com.1.7, Arched.2.11, *PSI*4.418.11 (iii B.C.). (Written ἐλαδ- in codd., but ἐλαιδ- *PSI* l.c.)

**ἐλάεως**· ἀμπέλου εἶδος, Hsch. ⊛ **ἐλαθερής**, ές, = εἰληθερής, Id. **ἐλαθρά**· ἐλαφρά, ἢ ἐν ἐλαίῳ ἑφθά, Id.

⊛ **ἐλαία**, Att. **ἐλάα**, ἡ, *olive-tree*, Hom., esp. in Od., 11.590, al.; ἱερὴ ἐ. 13.372, cf. Pi.*O.*3.13, Hdt.8.55, S.*OC*701 (lyr.), etc.; ἡμέρη ἐλαίη Hdt.5.82 (opp. ἀγρία ἐ. or κότινος); φέρεσθαι ἐκτὸς τῶν ἐλαῶν to run beyond *the olives*, which stood at the end of the Athenian race-course, i.e. to go too far, Ar.*Ra.*995, ubi v. Sch.; of the Indian *Olea cuspidata*, Thphr.*HP*4.4.11. 2. variety of δάφνη III, ib.4.7.2, Str.16.3.6. II. *olive*, Ar.*Ach.*550, Pl.*R.*372c, D.18.262, Dsc.1.119, etc.—Acc. to Gramm. ἐλάα was the proper form in this sense, ἐλαία in the first; but ἐλάα is simply the Att. form, cf. *IG*1$^2$.94.33, 2.476.21, 1055.36 (also *PHal.*1.98 (iii B.C.), etc.). III. *naevus on the skin*, Melamp.p.508 F. IV. = δίφρου Κυρηναϊκοῦ μέρος, Hsch. [In ἐλάα, the penult. is long, E.*Fr.*360.46, Ar.*Ach.*550, *Pax* 578, *Av.*617, etc.; but ἐλᾰῶν in Alex.261.3 (where perh. ἐλῶν—ἐλᾶς is acknowledged by Ael.Dion.*Fr.*162, and found in *PRyl.*97.7 (ii A.D.), ἐλᾶν in 130.11 (i A.D.)—should be restored), and ᾰ in ἐλάη, *AP*4.2.12 (Phil.), 6.102 (Id.).]

**ἐλαί-αγνος** or **ἐλέ-αγνος** (Hsch.), ὁ, *goat's willow*, *Salix Caprea*, Thphr.*HP*4.10.1, 2. **-άεις** [ᾱ], Att. for ἐλαιήεις. **-ακόνη**, ἡ, *whetstone used with oil*, Paul.Aeg.7.3 (s.v. λίθοι).

**ἐλαιάω**, = διεγείρω, Suid., Zonar.

**Ἐλαιβάριος**, epith. of Apollo at Isinda, *Jahresh.*18 *Beibl.*6.

**ἐλαιεμπορία**, ἡ, = ἐλαιωνία, prob. in *Dig.*50.4.18.19.

**ἐλαιεύς**, έως, ὁ, = ἐλαιών, Ἐφ.Ἀρχ.1902.31 (Chalcis).

**ἐλαΐζω**, *cultivate olives*, Ar.*Fr.*119. II. *to be olive-green*, Hsch.

⊛ **ἐλαι-ήεις**, Att. **-άεις**, εσσα, εν, *of the olive-tree*, φλοιός Nic.*Th.*676, etc.; *planted with olives*, ἐλαιήεντες ἄρουραι *IG*14.1389 i 50. II. *oily*, νηδύς S.*Fr.*457; *full of oil*, Nonn.*D.*5.226. ⊛ **-ηρός**, ά, όν, *of* or *for oil*, κεράμια Hp.*Mul.*2.114; γόμος *OGI*629.48 (Palmyra, ii A.D.); *of oils*, εἶδος Pl.*Ti.*60a; ἐ. δρόσος, i.e. oil, *AP*5.3 (Phld.); κόλον ἐ. *PSI*5.535.46 (iii B.C.); ἐ. ἐν πεδίῳ *oil-producing*, *IG*14.933. 2. *oily*, λιβάς ib.12(2).129.6 (Mytil.), cf. Gal.6.547. 3. of bees, *honied*, dub. in Pi.*Fr.*123.8.

⊛ **ἐλᾰ-ϊκός**, ή, όν, *of olives* or *oil*, πλήθη Aristeas 117; καρπός *BGU* 603.10; εἴδη *PFay.*64.4 (ii A.D.); τόκος *IG*5(1).1208.22 (Gythium): **-κή**, ἡ, *oil monopoly*, *PPetr.*2 p.84 (iii B.C.), *PRev.Laws* 43.15 (iii B.C.), etc. Adv. **-κῶς** Arr.*Epict.*2.20.18. **-ϊνεος**, α, ον, = sq., ῥόπαλον Od.9.320; μοχλός ib.394. ⊛ **-ϊνος**, η, ον, *of olive-wood*, ἐλαΐνῳ ἀμφὶ πελέκκῳ Il.13.612; στειλειόν Od.5.236, cf. Thphr.*HP* 5.3.7, *PLond.*3.1177 (ii A.D.), etc. b. *of olive-branches*, στέφανος D.Chr.31.110. c. *of the olive-tree*, φυλλάς Str.16.4.13. 2. *of olive-oil*, Orph.*L.*717. 3. *of olives*, ἔλαιον Lxx *Le.*24.2, J.*AJ*3.8.3. (Also spelt ἐλαίινος *IG*2.678 *B*.)

**ἐλαιο-βαφής**, ές, *dipped in oil*, Hsch. s.v. ἐλαιωτῷ (-θεῖ cod.). **-βραχής**, ές, Antyll.ap.Orib.7.21.8, Sor.1.82:—and **-βρεχής**, ές, Gal.13.581, = sq. **-βρεκτος**, gloss on ἐλαιόδευτον, Zonar. **-βροχος**, ον, *soaked in oil*, Clearch.44. ⊛ **-γᾰρον**, τό, *fish preserved in oil*, Steph. *in Hp.*2.309 D. **-δευτος**, ον, = ἐλαιόβροχος, Suid., Zonar. **-δόκος** or **-δόχος**, ον, *holding oil*, Hdn.*Epim.*78, Suid. s.v. ληκύθιον. **-ειδής**, ές, = ἐλαιώδης, Aret.*SA*2.6; ἰχὼρ Aët.13.23. **-θεσία**, ἡ, *provision of oil*, *IGRom.*3.484 (Oenoanda, ii A.D.), *BCH*11.399 (Attalia). **-θέσιον**, τό, *oiling-room* in the palaestra, Vitr.5.11.2. II. = foreg., *SIG*900.18 (Zeus Panam.). **-θετέω**, *provide oil* at the baths, ib.12 (ibid.), *Ephes.*3 No.15 (iii A.D.). **-θέτης**, ου, ὁ, *official who supplied oil*, *IG*5(2).50 (Tegea, ii A.D.). **-θηλος**, ον, *nurturing olives*, νᾶμα ib.14.1374. **-θρεπτος**, ον, f.l. for ἐλεόθρεπτον, *Et.Gud.* s.v. Ἑλένη. **-κάπηλος** [ᾰ], ὁ, *oil-dealer*, *PLille*3.55 (iii B.C.), Lib. *Decl.*26.18. **-κομέω**, *cultivate olives*, Poll.7.141. **-κομία**, ἡ, *the cultivation of olives*, ib.140. **-κομικός**, ή, όν, *belonging to* ἐλαιοκομία: **-κή**, ἡ, ibid. **-κόμιον**, τό, *olive-yard*, *IG*14.352 i 69 (Halaesa). **-κόμος**, ον, *rearing olives*, *AB*248, perh. to be restored in Lys.*Fr.*28; but II. ἐλαιόκομος, ον, (κόμη) *olive-clad*, Μαραθών Nonn.*D.*13.184. ⊛ **-κονία**, ἡ, *plaster made from lime and oil*, Eust.382.37, Steph. *in Hp.*2.384 D.: **-κόνιον**, τό, = *malta*, *Gloss.* **-λογέω**, *pick olives*, Lxx *De.*24.20, Ph.2.390. **-λόγος**, Att. **ἐλαολόγος**, ον, (λέγω) *olive-gatherer*, Ar.*V.*712. **-μελι**, ιτος, τό, *sweet gum from the olive-tree*, Dsc.1.31, etc. **-μετρέω**, *provide oil for*, τοὺς βουλευτάς *IGRom.*4.216 (Ilium).

⊛ **ἔλαιον**, τό, (ἐλαία) *olive-oil*, in Hom. mostly *anointing-oil*, used after the bath, λοεσσαμένω καὶ ἀλειψαμένω λίπ' ἐλαίῳ Il.10.577, cf. 14.171, 18.350, etc.; before wrestling and other gymnastic exercises, πωλησεῦντι τὸ ἐ. εἰς τὸ γυμνάσιον *IG*12(1).3 (Rhodes); ἐ. θεῖναι to provide *oil* at the baths, ib.4.597, 606 (Argos): prov., πῦρ ἐλαίῳ κοιμίσαι *Lyr.Alex.Adesp.*8(a); ἐλαίῳ πῦρ κατασβεννύναι Luc.*Tim.*44; εὐῶδες ἐ. Od.2.339; ῥοδόεν (rose-scented) Il.23.186; ἐ. ῥόδινον Hp.*Mul.*2.135; ἐ. λευκόν ib.136; τοῦ λευκοτάτου πάντων ἐ. Σαμιακοῦ Antiph.331. II. *any oily substance*, ἐ. χήνειον Hp.*Mul.*2.194; κίκινον, ἀμυγδάλινον ἐ., etc., Dsc.1.32, 33, etc.; ῥαφάνινον ἔλαιον *PAmh.*2.93 (ii A.D.), etc.; ἐ. ἀπὸ σελαχῶν, like our 'cod-liver oil',

Arist.*HA*520$^{a}$18; ἔ. ἀπὸ γάλακτος *butter*, Hecat.154 J. III. at Athens, *oil-market*, ἀναμενῶ σε..πρὸς τοὔλαιον Men.896.

**ἐλαιο-πάροχος**, ὁ, *purveyor of oil*, *IG*5(2).47.5, al. (Tegea, i A.D.). **-πῐνής**, ές, *stained with* or *soaked in oil*, Hp.*Salubr*.3. **-πλήθης**, ες, *full of oil*, Phryn.*PS*p.70 B. **-ποιΐα**, ἡ, *making of oil*, *PRyl.* 393, Poll.7.140. **-πράτης** [ᾰ], ου, ὁ, *oil-dealer*, *PKlein.Form.* 699, al. **-πρῳρος**, ον, *like an olive at top*, Arist.*Ph*.199$^{b}$12. ⊛ **-πώλης**, ου, ὁ, *oil-merchant*, D.25.47, *PHib*.1.53.6 (iii B.C.), Lib.*Or*.58.5. **-πώλιον**, τό, *oil-shop*, *Gloss.* **-ροος**, ον, *flowing with oil*, παλαίστρη Man.1.100. **-ρῠτος**, ον, = foreg., Epic.*Oxy*.1015.11.

**ἔλαιος**, ὁ, = κότινος, *wild olive*, ἄγριος ἔ. Pi.*Fr*.46, S.*Tr*.1197, Paus. 2.32.10. II. a *bird*, prob. a kind of *warbler*, Alex.Mynd.ap.Ath. 2.65b, cj. in *AP*7.199 (Tymnes); cf. ἐλέα.

**ἐλαιο-σπάρᾰγος** [σπᾰ], ὁ, *olive-shoots* used as a vegetable, *POxy.* 1849, 1861 (vi A.D.). **-σπονδα** (sc. ἱερά), τά, *drink-offerings of oil*, Porph.*Abst*.2.20. **-στάφῠλος** [ᾰ], ὁ, *vine grafted on an olive*, *Gp.* 9.14 tit. **-τόκος**, = δίκταμνος, *Gloss.* ⊛ **-τρίβιον** (or **-τριβεῖον**), *oil-press*, *Gloss.* **-τροπικός**, ή, όν, *for pressing olives*, ἄρμενα *CIG* 2694*b* (Mylasa). **-τρόπιον**, τό, *olive-press*, *Gp*.6.1 tit., *BCH*26. 182 (Syria, iii A.D.). **-τρῠγον**, τό, *lees of oil*, = ἀμόργη, Hsch. (-τρωγ- cod.).

**ἐλαιουργ-έω**, *manufacture oil*, *PRev.Laws* 50.20, al. (iii B.C.), *PTeb*.314.21 (ii B.C.). **-ία**, ἡ, *manufacture of oil*, *PFay*.91.22 (i A.D.), etc. **-ιον** (-εῖον *Gloss.*), τό, *oil-press*, Arist.*Pol*.1259$^{a}$13, *PRev.Laws* 44.4, al., D.L.1.26, etc. **-ός**, ὁ, *manufacturer of oil*, *PRev.Laws* 44.8, etc.

**Ἐλαιοῦς**, epith. of Zeus in Cyprus, Hsch.

**ἐλαιο-φᾰνής**, ές, *resembling oil in appearance*, of urine, Gal.19.588. **-φῐλοφάγος** [ᾰ], ον, *fond of eating olives*, κιχῆλαι Epich.157. **-φόρος**, ον, *olive-bearing*, ὄχθος E.*HF*1178 (anap.); χώρα ἐ. land *fit for olives*, Thphr.*CP*2.4.4: **-φόρον**, τό, *oil-shop*, *Gloss.* **-φῠής**, ές, *olive-planted*, πάγος E.*Ion* 1480 (anap.). **-φυλλον**, τό, = φύλλον, *Dog's Mercury, Mercurialis perennis*, Ps.-Dsc.3.125. **-φυτεία**, ἡ, *planting of olives*, St.Byz.s.v. Φελλεύς. **-φῠτος**, ον, *olive-planted*, A.*Pers*.883 (lyr.), Str.12.7.1; ἐ. δένδρεσι *set with olive*-trees, Id.17.1.35. II. Subst. ἐλαιόφυτον, τό, *olive-yard*, Plu.2.524a. ⊛ **-χρίστης**, ου, ὁ, *municipal official responsible for supply of oil*, *POxy*.300 (i A.D.), *BGU* 576.14 (ii/iii A.D.). **-χριστία**, ἡ, *supply of oil* for anointing, D.L. 5.71 (codd. **ἐλαιοχρηστία**, *use of oil*):—also ⊛ **-χρ(ε)ίστιον**, *IG*12(9). 236.17 (Eretria), *Ath.Mitt*.33.382 (Pergam.), *JHS*9.231 (Paphos):—Boeot. **ἐληοχρίστιον**, *BCH*26.156 (Thespiae); *tax* levied for this purpose, *Ostr.Strassb*.178 (ii/i B.C.). **-χροος**, ον, contr. **-χρους**, ουν, *olive-coloured*, Hsch. s.v. ἐλαΐζων. 2. *of the colour of oil*, of urine, Gal.19.588. **-χῠτέω**, *anoint with oil*, Paul.Aeg.6.74, Sor.2. 60. **-χύτης** [ῠ], ου, Dor. **-τας**, ὁ, = φαρμακεύς (Rhod.), Hsch. II. *attendant who served out oil in the gymnasium*, *CPHerm*.57.9, 59. 7. **-χύτησις** [ῠ], εως, ἡ, *anointing with oil*, Sor.2.61 (pl.). **-χῠτος**, ον, *oil-distilling*, κοτύλαι Epic.*Oxy*.1015.14.

**ἐλαιόω**, *oil*:—only Pass., *to be oiled*, Arist.*HA*605$^{b}$20; σπόγγος ἠλαιωμένος Ph.1.433; ἐλαιοῦται θρίξ S.*Fr*.624, cf. Pi.*Fr*.305. 2. *bring to an oily consistency*, in Alchemy, Zos.Alch.p.163 B. II. *gather olives*, Poll.7.146.

**ἐλαιρόν**, τό, a kind of *vessel*, *IG*7.3498.52 (Orop., iii/ii B.C.). (Perh. for ἐλαιηρόν (sc. ἀγγεῖον).)

⊛ **ἐλαιρός**, ὁ, a *liquid measure*, Hero *Geom*.23.64.

**ἐλᾰ-ΐς**, ΐδος, ἡ, *olive-tree*, Att. pl. ἐλᾶδες Ar.*Ach*.998, cf. *IG*2.836$^{ab}$ 29. II. = αἰγίλωψ, Hsch. **-ϊστήρ**, ῆρος, and **-ιστής**, οῦ, ὁ, *olive-gatherer*, Poll.7.146, 10.130. **-ϊστήριον**, τό, *olive-press*, *CIG* 2694*b* (Mylasa).

**ἐλαι-ώδης**, ες, *oily*, Hp.*Epid*.3.17.α', Philum.*Ven*.17.1; *oleaginous*, λιπαρότης Arist.*HA*522$^{a}$22; τῇ γεύσει Dsc.1.39. ⊛ **-ών**, ῶνος, ὁ, *olive-yard*, *PCair.Zen*.57.2 (iii B.C.), Lxx *Ex*.23.11, al., Str.16.4. 14, Ph.2.289, *Gp*.3.11.1. II. *the Mount of Olives, Olivet*, *Act.Ap.* 1.12, al., J.*AJ*7.9.2. **-ωνέω**, *purchase oil for the state*, *Inscr.Cos* 113. **-ώνης**, ου, ὁ, *purchaser of oil for the state*, *IGRom*.3.739 xix 17 (Lycia), *IG*2$^{2}$.1100. **-ωνία**, ἡ, *purchase of oil for the state*, *Dig.* 27.1.6.8, *Cod.Just*.10.(56)55.1. **-ωνίδιον**, τό, Dim. of ἐλαιών, *PBaden*33.8 (ii A.D.). **-ωνικός**, ή, όν, *concerning* or *belonging to the* ἐλαιῶναι, *Sammelb*.5126 (iii A.D.). **-ώνιον**, τό, = ἐλαιωνία, *IG* 5(1).1176 (Gythium, ἐλε- lapis). ⊛ **-ωνοπαράδεισος**, ὁ, *garden and olive-yard*, *POxy*.639 (ii A.D.), etc. **-ωσις**, εως, ἡ, *treatment with oil* or *reduction to an oily consistency*, in Alchemy, Zos.Alch. p.215 B. **-ωτός**, ή, όν, *oiled*, Hsch. (-οτῷ cod.).

**ἕλανδρος**, ον, *man-destroying*, epith. of Helen, A.*Ag*.689 (lyr.).

**ἑλάνη** (ἑλένη Hsch.), ἡ, *torch of reeds*, Neanth.4 J.; also, *bundle of reeds*, Nic.*Fr*.89.

**ἔλανος**· ἰκτῖνος, Hsch. **ἐλαολόγος, ἐλαοφόρος**, v. ἐλαιο-. **ἐλάπεδον**· τέμενος, Id.

**ἐλαπρός**, όν, barbarism for ἐλαφρός, Ar.*Th*.1180.

**ἔλαρ** (i.e. ϝέλαρ)· βοήθεια Hsch. **ἔλαρα**, = ἄλαρα, *butt of spear-shaft*, Id.

**ἔλᾰσα, ἐλάσασκε, ἐλασαίατο**, v. ἐλαύνω.

**ἐλασᾶς**, ὁ, an unknown *bird*, Ar.*Av*.886.

**ἐλᾰσ-είω**, (ἐλαύνω) Desiderat., *wish to march*, Luc.*Cont*.9. **-ία**, ἡ, = ἔλασις, *riding*, X.*Eq.Mag*.4.4; *march*, J.*AJ*2.10.2. II. *striking* from a die, *Gloss.*

**ἐλᾰσίβροντος**, ον, *thunder-hurling*, Pi.*Fr*.144 (dub., prob. -βροντᾶ, voc. of -βρόντᾱς). II. *hurled like thunder*, ἔπη ἐ. Ar.*Eq*.626.

⊛ **ἐλάσιος** [ᾰ], α, ον, *driving away* epilepsy, Plu.2.296f.

**ἐλάσιππος** [ᾰ], ον, *horse-driving, horse-riding, knightly*, Pi.*P*.5.85; ἁμέρα *Lyr.Adesp*.97; of the sun, Orph.*H*.8.18.

⊛ **ἔλᾰσις**, εως, ἡ, *driving away, banishing*, τῶν ἐναγῶν Th.1.139, Ph.1. 140; ἔ. βοσκημάτων *driving* of them *away* as booty, Plu.*Rom*.7. 2. (sc. στρατοῦ) *march, expedition*, ἐπὶ Σκύθας Hdt.4.1, etc.; ἔλασιν ποιέεσθαι Id.7.37; also, *procession*, X.*Cyr*.8.3.34; ἡ ἅλαδε ἔ. *IG*2$^{2}$.847. 20. 3. (sc. ἵππου) *riding*, X.*Eq*.9.6, *Eq.Mag*.8.2, Aristaenet.1.8; *charge of horse*, D.H.6.12, Plu.*Sull*.19. b. *driving* a chariot, Luc. *DDeor*.25.2. 4. (ἐλαύνω II) *striking*. Apollon.*Lex*. s.v. ἐλαύνωσι.

**ἐλᾰσίχθων**, ονος, ὁ, *earth-striking*, Ποσειδῶν Pi.*Fr*.18.

**ἔλ-ασμα**, ατος, τό, *metal beaten out, metal-plate*, Ph.*Bel*.69.51, D.S.5.33, Dsc.5.81, Paus.10.16.1. 2. general name for *probes* and other surgical *instruments*, Gal.2.574; ἔ. ξύλινον ibid.: esp. *flat end* of a probe, Heliod.ap.Orib.44.11.3. II. = ἔλασις, Eust.1306. 55. ⊛ **-ασμάτιον** [μᾰ], τό, Dim. of foreg., Dsc.*Eup*.2.168, Heliod. ap.Orib.49.4.59, Gal.19.148. **-ασμίη**· κυρία, Hsch. **-ασμός**, ὁ, = ἔλασμα I, Aristeas 65, D.C.46.36. II. = ἔλασις, *Hippiatr*.1.

**ἔλασσα**, Ep. aor. 1 of ἐλαύνω.

⊛ **ἐλασσονέω**, *to be deficient, wanting*, *PMagd*.26.2 (iii B.C.), *BGU* 1195.19 (i B.C.).

**ἐλασσόνως**, Adv. of ἐλάσσων, *in a lesser degree*, Hp.*Vict*.1.35, etc.; ἐ. ἢ κατ' ἀξίαν Antipho 4.4.6.

⊛ **ἐλασσ-όω**, Att. **-ττόω**: aor. ἠλάττωσα Lys.13.9, Plb.16.21.5: pf. ἠλλάττωκα D.H.*Comp*.6, etc.:—Pass., fut. -ωθήσομαι Th.5.34, D. 21.66: fut. Med. in same sense, Hdt.6.11, Th.5.104: aor. ἠλασσώθην, -ττώθην, Id.1.77, D.10.33: pf. ἠλάττωμαι Apollod.Com.7.3, Plb. 18.4.3:—*make less* or *smaller, diminish, reduce in amount*, *PTeb*.19.11 (ii B.C.), *PLips*.105.28 (i A.D.):—Pass., *POxy*.918 xi 3 (ii A.D.). 2. in early writers, *lower, degrade*, τὴν πόλιν Lys.13.9, Isoc.8.17; ἠλάττωσας αὐτὸν βραχύ τι παρ' ἀγγέλους Lxx *Ps*.8.6; *cut down, shorten*, συναλοιφαῖς τὰ ῥήματα D.H.*Comp*.6: c. gen., *detract from*, μὴ προστιθέναι τιμήν, ἀλλὰ μὴ ἐλασσοῦν τῆς ὑπαρχούσης Th.3.42:—Med., *reduce the power of*, τινάς Plb.22.15.1. II. Pass., 1. abs., *to be lessened, suffer loss, be depreciated*, of things, Th.2.62; of persons, Id. 4.59, al., *OGI*139.10 (ii B.C.), *PTeb*.382.13 (i B.C.), Phld.*Lib*.p.32 O., al., *Ev.Jo*.3.30, etc.; μέγα τοῦθ' οἱ πατέρες ἠλαττώμεθα Apollod.Com. 7.3; also, *take less than one's due, waive one's rights* or *privileges*, Th. 1.77, D.56.14; but, *fall short of one's professions, act dishonestly*, Isoc.1.49. 2. c. dat. rei, *have the worst of it*, Hdt.6.11, Th.5.104, etc.; τῷ πολέμῳ Id.1.115; *to be inferior*, τῇ ἐμπειρίᾳ Id.5.72; πολλαῖς ναυσί X.*HG*1.5.15; πᾶσι τούτοις ib.6.2.28; ἠλαττωμένος τοῖς ὄμμασι, of a one-eyed man, Plb.18.4.3; πρός τινα *POxy*.215 ii 18: c. gen., *fall short of*, τῶν ἀρχετύπων Ph.1.606. 3. c. gen. pers., *to be at a disadvantage with* a person, πολλὰ μὲν οὖν ἔγωγ' ἐλαττοῦμαι κατὰ τουτονὶ τὸν ἀγῶν' Αἰσχίνου D.18.3; ἐλαττοῦσθαί τινός τινι Pl.*Alc*.1. 121b; μηδὲν τῶν δημιουργῶν Id.*Grg*.459c. 4. c. gen. rei, *suffer loss in respect of*, κεφαλαίου, τόκων, *BGU*155.10 (ii A.D.); *to be in want of*, Lxx 1*Ki*.21.15(16): also c. dat., ib.2*Ki*.3.29. **-ωμα**, ατος, τό, = ἐλάττωμα, D.L.9.68; *reduction in amount* or *number*, *BGU*20.8 (ii A.D.), etc. ⊛ **-ων**, Att. **-ττων**, ον, gen. ονος: Sup. ἐλάχιστος (q.v.):—*smaller, less*, formed from ἐλαχύς (q.v.), but serving as Comp. to μικρός, δουρηνεκὲς ἢ καὶ ἔλασσον Il.10.357; τοὔλασσον ἔχειν to have the *worse, be worse off*, πάντη Thgn.269; οὐδὲν ἔλασσον ἔχειν τῇ μάχῃ Hdt.9.102; ἐ. ἔχειν παρά τινι D.21.187; ἐλάττων γίγνεσθαι Ar.*Eq.* 441, D.3.29; οὐκ ἐλάσσονα πάσχειν A.*Pers*.813; ἐλάττω νομίσας τὴν ἀρχὴν ἢ κατὰ τὴν αὑτοῦ φύσιν εἶναι *too small* for.., Isoc.11.11: abs., *too small*, Thphr.*Char*.23.9; *below the average in height*, *PLips*.1.9, etc. 2. c. gen. pers., *worse than, inferior to*, Ar.*V*.599, etc.: but c. gen. rei, *giving way to, subservient to*, σιτίων X.*Lac*.5.8; πάθους Plu.*Cor*.34: abs., *worse, inferior*, τόποι *Gp*.2.48.1. 3. neut. with Preps., περὶ ἐλάσσονος ποιεῖσθαι to consider of *less account*, Hdt.6.6; ἐν ἐλάττονι θέσθαι Plb.4.6.12; παρ' ἔλαττον τοῦ δέοντος ἡγεῖσθαι Pl.*R.* 546d; ἐπ' ἔλαττον (sc. ἁρμοσθῆναι) Id.*Phd*.93b; δι' ἐλάσσονος at *less distance*, Th.7.4; πάντ' ἐν ἐλάττονι ποιεῖσθαι τῆς ἡδονῆς Heraclid.Pont. ap.Ath.12.537c. II. of Number, *fewer*, οἱ ἐλάσσονες *the minority*, Hdt.3.121; ἐλάσσονες ἀριθμόν Id.8.66; ἐ. πλῆθος Th.1.49. III. of Time, *shorter*, Pl.*Pol*.295c, etc. IV. of worth or rank, οἱ ἐ. the *meaner sort*, Isoc.2.13, Alex.116.12. V. neut. ἔλασσον, as Adv., ἐ. ἢ μηδέν A.*Pr*.938, cf. S.*El*.598, Pl.*R*.564d, etc.; ἐ. ἄπωθεν *less* far off, Th.4.67; πλείω ἔλαττον, with numbers, more or *less*, *PLips*.28. 10 (iv A.D.), etc.: neut. pl., as Adv., = ἐλαττονάκις, Pl.*Cri*.53a, al.: regul. Adv. ἐλασσόνως (q.v.). VI. with indecl. Numerals, the ἤ of Comparison is often omitted, οὐκ ἐλάττους ὀγδοήκοντα D.S.14.8; esp. in Adv. ἔλασσον, as μὴ ἔ. δέκα ἔτη Pl.*Lg*.856d, al. (Orig. ἐλάχγων, cf. ἐλάχ-ιστος, ἐλαχύς.) **-τέον**, *one must diminish*, Archig. ap.Aët.6.28.

**ἐλασ-τής**, οῦ, ὁ, = ἐλατήρ I, *EM*325.38. **-τός**, = ἐλατός, *PLeid. X*.36, 70 (iii/iv A.D.). **-τρέω**, Ep. and Ion. for ἐλαύνω, πολλοὶ δ' ἀροτῆρες..ζεύγεα δινεύοντες ἐλάστρεον they *drove* the teams, Il.18.543; κατ' ἁμαξιτὸν ἣν ἠλάστρεις Thgn.600; ἐ. τινά *to drive about*, of the Furies, E.*IT*971; in later Prose, δαιμονίοις χόλοις ἐλαστρηθέντες D.H.1.23; *row*, Ion. part. ἐλαστρεῦντας (-εύοντας codd.) Arr.*Ind.* 32.9:—Pass., of ships, *to be rowed*, Hdt.2.158, 7.24; cf. ἐλαστροῦται (sic)· ἐλαύνεται, Hsch.; **-ιῶν**· διαγινώσκων, Id. **-τρον**, τό, *that which drives*, *EM*325.34. **-τωρ**, ορος, ὁ, = ἐλατήρ, *App.Anth*.3.175.

**ἐλάσω** [ᾰ], fut. of ἐλαύνω. **ἐλᾶται**· ἠλιοῦται, Hsch.

**ἐλάτ-ειρα** [ᾰ], fem. of ἐλατήρ, ἵππων ἐ., of Artemis, Pi.*Fr*.89; βοῶν ἐ. Σελήνη Nonn.*D*.1.331. **-έον**, *one must ride*, X.*Eq.Mag*.2.7.

⊛ **ἐλάτη** [ᾰ], ἡ, *silver fir, Abies cephalonica*, ὑψηλή Il.5.560; περιμή-

κετος 14.287; οὐρανομήκης Od.5.239, cf. Thphr.*HP*3.9.6, etc.; also, *Abies pectinata*, ib.5.8.3. **II.** *oar*, as *made of pine-wood*, λευκαίνον ὕδωρ ξεστῇς ἐλάτῃσιν Od.12.172, cf. Il.7.5; later, *ship* or *boat*, E.*Ph.*208 (lyr.), *Alc.*444 (lyr.). **III.** *the spathe of the date inflorescence*, Dsc.1.109.4 (but, = βόρασσος (q. v.), ib.5), cf. Epich.160, Gal.12.151. **IV.** *sea-weed* supposed to resemble the fir, *Cystoseira Abies-marina*, Thphr.*HP*4.6.2.

**ἐλᾰτηΐς**, ΐδος, ἡ, *like the pine*, σμῖλος Nic.*Al.*611.

⊛ **ἐλᾰτ-ήρ**, ῆρος, ὁ, (ἐλαύνω) *driver*, esp. of horses, *charioteer*, Il.4.145, 11.702, Alc.*Supp.*8.14, etc.; ἵππων ἐ. A.*Pers.*32 (anap.); ἐ. βροντᾶς *hurler* of thunder, Pi.*O.*4.1; ἐ. λύρας *striker* of the lyre, *AP*7.18 (Antip. Thess.). **2.** *rower*, Luc.*Am.*6, Nonn.*D.*39.306. **II.** *one that drives away*, Call.*Jov.*3, Opp.*C.*1.119; [μυώψ] βοῶν ἐ. Coluth.43. **III.** *a broad, flat cake* (ἀπὸ τοῦ ἐληλάσθαι εἰς μέγεθος, Hsch.), Ar.*Ach.*246, *Eq.*1183, Callias Com.21, *IG*2.841 b 7, *SIG*1026.9 (Cos). **IV.** *hoop-stick*, Antyll.ap.Orib.6.26.4. **-ήριος**, ον, *driving, driving away*, c. gen., καθαρμοῖσιν ἀτᾶν ἐ. A.*Ch.*968 (lyr.). **II.** ἐλατήρια φάρμακα *purgatives*, Hp.*Acut.*2, cf. *Epid.*5.7, Erot. **b.** ἐ. ἀπόβαμμα *lustral water*, *IG*4.1607 (Cleonae). **2.** Subst. -τήριον, τό, *squirting cucumber, Ecballium Elaterium*, Hp.*Steril.*238, *Epid.*6.5.15, Dsc. 4.150, Thphr.*HP*4.5.1; *drug prepared therefrom*, ib.9.9.4, 9.14.1. **-ης**, ου, ὁ, = ἐλατήρ, ποίμνας E.*Fr.*773.28 (lyr.), *Ostr.Strassb.* 649.2 (iii A. D.), Glauc.ap.*POxy.*1802.37. **II.** epith. of Poseidon at Athens, Hsch. **-ικός**, ή, όν, *of* or *for rowing*, ἐπίφθεγμα, i. e. ὠόπ, Sch.Ar.*Ra.*180. **II.** ἐ. κύνες *hounds*, Hsch.

**ἐλατίνη**, ἡ, *cankerwort, Linaria spuria*, Dsc.4.40, Plin.*HN*27.74.

**ἐλάτινος** [ᾰ], η, ον, also ος, ον Anaxil.22.17: Ep. **εἰλάτινος**, η, ον, as also E.*Hel.*1461 (lyr.), *Hec.*632 (lyr.): —*of the fir*, ὄζοι εἰ. Il.14.289, cf. E.*Ba.*1070; ὕλα εἰ. Id.*Hec.*632; [ῥητίνη] Thphr.*HP*9.2.2; ξύλα *SIG*135.11 (Olynthus, iv B. C.). **2.** *made of fir* or *pine-wood*, ἱστὸς εἰ. Od.2.424; πλᾶται E.*Hel.*1461, cf. Anaxil. l. c. **II.** *of the date inflorescence*, ἔλαιον Dsc.1.44.

**ἐλᾰτός**, ή, όν, (ἐλαύνω) of metal, *ductile*, Arist.*Mete.*385$^{a}$16, etc. **II.** *beaten*, *POxy.*85 ii 16 (iv A. D.); χαλκός Hero *Bel.*96.10, Heliod.ap.Orib.49.3.8; *of beaten work*, σάλπιγγες Lxx *Nu.*10.2; θώρακες Jul.*Or.*2.57b.

**ἐλατρεύς**, έως, ὁ, *thrice-forged iron*, Hsch.

**ἔλατρον**, τό, = ἐλατήρ III, *SIG*57.36 (Milet., v B. C.), *Inscr.Prien.* 174.11 (ii B. C.), Hsch. **II.** a *garment*, Eucrat.ap.eund.

**ἐλαττον-άκις**, Adv. *fewer times, multiplied by a less number*, opp. πλεονάκις, Pl.*Tht.*148a. **2.** *less frequently*, Arist.*Mete.*368$^{b}$25. ⊛ **-έω**, *receive less*, Lxx *Ex.*16.18; but, *give less*, ib.30.15. **2.** *waste, be consumed*, ib.3*Ki.*17.16; *to be missing, defective*, *PMagd.*26.12 (iii A. D.). **3.** Med., *lack, want*, ib.11.22. **-ότης**, ητος, ἡ, *being less*, opp. μειζονότης, Iamb.*in Nic.*p.33 P. **-όω**, *diminish*, Lxx *Pr.* 14.34, al.:—Pass., ib.*Ge.*8.3, 18.28.

**ἐλαττ-όω**, v. ἐλασσόω. **-ωμα**, ατος, τό, *inferiority, disadvantage*, D.18.237, Phld.*Rh.*2.29 S.; ἐ. ποιεῖν Plb.6.16.3. **2.** *loss, defeat*, *IPE* $1^2$.32 *B* 15 (pl., Olbia, iii B. C.), Plb.1.32.2, Onos.32.8 (pl.), etc. **3.** *defect*, κατὰ τὴν ὄψιν D.H.5.23; περὶ τὴν λέξιν Id.*Th.*35; τὰ τῶν παιδικῶν ἐ. Chor. in *Rh.Mus.*49.510; σωματικὰ ἐ. Hierocl.p.49 A., cf. Phld.*Ir.*p.52 W., al., Iamb.*Protr.*20 (v. ἐλάσσωμα). **-ωμάτιον**, τό, Dim. of foreg. 3, *Gloss.* **-ων**, Att. for ἐλασσ-. **-ωσις**, εως, ἡ, *making smaller* or *less, lessening*, ἡ ἐπιείκεια ἐλάττωσις τῶν συμφερόντων καὶ δικαίων Arist.*Top.*141$^{a}$16, cf. Pl.*Def.*412b; τροφῆς Epicur. *Fr.*428a: abs., *loss, diminution*, Diog.Oen.64. **2.** *depreciation, disparagement*, Arist.*Rh.Al.*1436$^{b}$34 (pl.), *VV*1251$^{a}$5 (pl.). **II.** *defeat*, in peace or war, Antipho Soph.*Oxy.*1364.164, Plb.2.36.6, Onos.36.3. **III.** *fault, defect*, Phld.*Lib.*p.20 O. (pl.); τῆς φύσεως Plu.2.2c. **2.** *loss* of health or property, ἐ. σωματικαὶ καὶ αἱ τῶν ἐκτὸς Hierocl.p.49 A. **-ωτικός**, ή, όν, *reducing, diminishing*, Sor. 1.42. **II.** *inclined to take less, not insisting on his full rights*, opp. ἀκριβοδίκαιος, Arist.*EN*1138$^{a}$1, cf. 1136$^{b}$21; τῶν δικαίων Id.*MM*1198$^{b}$26; ἐ. ἑαυτοῦ M.Ant.5.15, Porph.*Abst.*3.26.

**ἐλαύνω**, Il.12.62, etc.: Ion. impf. ἐλαύνεσκον (ἀπ-) Hdt.7.119: fut. ἐλάσω [ᾰ], part. ἐλάσοντας X.*An.*7.7.55 codd., cf. D.H.2.36, (ἐξ-) Hp.*Loc.Hom.*46, *Nat.Mul.*32 (ἐλάσσω (παρ-) is f. l. in Il.23.427, and ξυνελάσσομεν is subj. in Od.18.39); ἐλάω A.R.3.411; Att. ἐλῶ, ᾷς, ᾷ, inf. ἐλᾶν, also Hdt.1.207, etc., and so Hom. in the resolved form ἐλόω Il.13.315, Od.7.319: inf. ἐλάαν (though this is also inf. pres., v. infr.) Il.17.496, Od.5.290: aor. 1 ἤλᾰσα, Ep. ἔλασα Il.5.80, ἔλασσα 18.564, Ion. 3 sg. ἐλάσασκεν 2.199: pf. ἐλήλᾰκα (ἀπ-, ἐξ-) X.*Cyr.*4.2.10, Ar.*Nu.*828: plpf. ἐληλάκειν (ἐξ-) Hdt.5.90:—Med. (v. infr. I. 2), fut. ἐλάσομαι (παρ-) dub. l. in Arr.*An.*3.30.3: aor. ἠλασάμην Il.11.682, rare in Att., as Pl.*Grg.*484b; 3 sg. ἠλάσατο Ibyc.55; Ep. ἐλάσαιο, -ασαίατο, -ασσάμενος, Od.20.51, Il.10.537, Od.4.637:—**Pass.**, fut. ἐλασθήσομαι (ἐξ-) D.H.4.9: aor. ἠλάθην [ᾰ] E.*Heracl.*430, Ar.*Ec.*4; later ἠλάσθην *AP*7.278 (Arch.), *Sammelb.*997 (iv A. D.), (ἐξ-, συν-) Plb.8.24.9, 18.22.6, etc. (in Hdt. the Mss. vary between the two forms, ἐξελαθείς 7.165, ἀπηλάσθησαν 3.54): pf. ἐλήλαμαι Od.7.113, Hdt.7.84 (ἐξ-), etc.; ἐλήλασμαι Hp.*Mul.* 2.133, Aen.Tact.31.4 (prob.), (ἐξ-) Plb.6.22.4, (συν-) A.D.*Conj.*233.30: plpf. ἠλήλατο Il.5.400; poet. also ἐλήλατο 4.135; 3 pl. ἠλήλαντο Hes.*Sc.*143, also ἐληλέδατ', ἐληλέατ', ἐληλάδατ' vv. ll. in Od.7.86.—The pres. **ἐλάω** is rare and mainly Poet., imper. ἔλα Pi.*I.*5(4).38, A.*Fr.* 332, E.*HF*819, *Fr.*779.1 (also non-thematic 3 pl. ἐλάντω *SIG*1025.8 (Cos)): inf. ἐλᾶν Canthar.4, X.*HG*2.4.32: inf. ἐλάαν as Ep. inf. pres. is freq. in Hom. (v. infr. I. 2): part. ἐλάουσα Emp.4.5: impf. 3 pl. ἔλων Od.4.2, 3 sg. ἔλαεν A.R.3.872; ἀπ-ἔλα X.*Cyr.*8.3.32; but ἀπ-ήλαον in Ar.*Lys.*1001 is prob. an error for -ήλα(ν, Dor. for -ήλασαν:—radic. sense, *drive, set in motion*, of driving flocks, εἰς εὐρὺ σπέος ἤλασε μῆλα Od.9.237; κακοὺς δ' ἐς μέσσον ἔλασσεν Il.4.299; aor. Med. ἠλασάμην in act. sense, 10.537, 11.682: freq. of horses, chariots, ships, *drive*, ἐλάαν (inf. pres.) ἅρμα καὶ ἵππους 23.334; ἐς τὴν ἀγορὴν τὸ ζεῦγος Hdt. 1.59; ἐ. ἵππον *ride* it, Id.4.64, al.; κέλητας καὶ ἅρματα ἐ. *ride* and *drive*, Id.7.86; ἐ. νῆα *row* it, Od.12.109, etc.; στρατὸν ἐ. Pi.*O.*10(11).66, Hdt. 1.176, 4.91, etc. **b.** with acc. omitted, intr., *go in a chariot, drive*, μάστιξεν δ' ἐλάαν (sc. ἵππους) he whipped them *on*, Il.5.366, al., cf. S.*El.*734,739; βῆ δ' ἐλάαν ἐπὶ κύματα he *drove on* over the waves, Il. 13.27; διὰ νύκτα ἐλάαν *travel* the night through, Od.15.50; ἐς τὸ ἄστυ ἐ. *drive* into the city, Hdt.1.60; ἐπὶ ζευγέων ἐ. ib.199; *ride*, Id. 7.88, X.*Eq.Mag.*3.9, etc.; ἐλῶν ἐς Θρηΐκην *marching*.., Hdt.9.89, etc.; *row*, μάλα σφοδρῶς ἐλάαν Od.12.124; ἐλαύνοντες *rowers*, 13.22, etc. **c.** in this intr. sense, it sts. took an acc. loci, γαλήνην ἐλαύνειν *to sail* the calm sea, i. e. over it, 7.319; so τὰ ἕσπερα νῶτ' ἐ. E.*El.* 731 (lyr.); also ἐλαύνειν δρόμον *run* a course, Ar.*Nu.*28; ὁδόν D.P. 586. **d.** Pass., [νηῦς] ἐλαυνομένη a ship *under way*, Od.13.155 (but πλοῖα ὑπὸ σκληρῶν ἀνέμων ἐλαυνόμενα *Ep.Jac.*3.4); τὰ κατάντη ἐλαύνεσθαι, of horses, *to be ridden* on steep ground, X.*Eq.Mag.*8.3. **2.** *drive away, carry off*, in Hom. of stolen cattle or horses, βοῶν ἀρίστας Od.12.353; ἵππους Il.5.236; ἐ. ὅ τι δύναιντο X.*HG*4.8.18:—Med., Od.4.637, 20.51; ῥύσι' ἐλαυνόμενος Il.11.674, etc. **3.** *drive away, expel*, ἐ. [τινὰ] ἐκ δήμου 6.158; ἄνδρας ἀπ' Οἰνώνας Pi.*N.*5.16: freq. in Trag., ἐ. τινὰ γῆς E.*Med.*70; μύσος, μίασμα ἐ., A.*Ch.*967 codd., *Eu.* 283 (Pass.), cf. S.*OT*98; ἄγος ἐ., = ἀγηλατέω, Th.1.126; ἐ. λῃστάς Ar.*Ach.*1188, etc.:—Pass., γῆν πρὸ γῆς ἐλαύνομαι A.*Pr.*682. **4.** *drive* (to extremities), *persecute, plague*, οἵ μιν ἄδην ἐλόωσι.. πολέμοιο who will *harass* him till he has had enough of war, Il.13.315; ἔτι μέν μίν φημι ἄδην ἐλάαν κακότητος I think I *shall persecute* him till he has had enough, Od.5.290; θεὸς ἐλαύνει πόλιν S.*OT*28; Ἰωνίαν ἤλασεν βίᾳ A.*Pers.*771; μή τι δαιμόνιον τὰ πράγματα ἐλαύνῃ D.9.54; σὺ δ' ἀπειλεῖς πᾶσιν, ἐλαύνεις πάντας Id.21.135, cf. 173:—Pass., ἐλαυνομένων καὶ ὑβριζομένων Id.18.48; λύπῃ πᾶς ἐλήλαται κακῇ S.*Aj.*275; κακοῖς πρός τινος E.*Andr.*31; ὑπ' ἀνάγκης καὶ οἴστρου Pl.*Phdr.*240d; τὴν ψυχὴν ἐρωτικῇ μανίᾳ Ael.*NA*14.18; ἐλαύνεσθαι τὴν γνώμην *to be out of one's* mind, Philostr.*VS*2.27.5. **5.** = βινέω, Ar.*Ec.*39, Pl. Com.3.4. **6.** intr. in expressions like ἐς τοσοῦτον ἤλασαν they *drove it* so far (where πρᾶγμα must be supplied), Hdt.5.50; ἐς πᾶσαν κακότητα Id.2.124; εἰς κόρον ἐλαύνειν *push matters* till disgust ensued, Tyrt.11.10; εἰς ἴσον (sc. τισί) Onos.*Praef.*4: hence, *push on, go on*, ἐγγὺς μανιῶν E.*Heracl.*904 (lyr.); ἔξω τοῦ φρονεῖν Id.*Ba.*853; πόρρω ἐ. σοφίας go far in.., Pl.*Euthphr.*4b, cf. *Grg.*486a, X.*Cyr.*1.6.39. **II.** *strike*, ἐλάτῃσιν πόντον ἐλαύνοντες Il.7.6; κιθάραν πλήκτρῳ E.*HF*351 (lyr.). **2.** *strike* with a weapon, but never with a missile, τὸν σκήπτρῳ ἐλάσασκεν Il.2.199; ξίφει ἤλασε κόρσην 5.584; κόρυθος φάλον ἤλασεν 13.614; ὀδόντας ἐ. *knock out*, A.R.2.785: **c.** dupl. acc., τὸν μὲν.. μεταδρομάδην ἔλασ' ὦμον him he *struck* on.., Il. 5.80; χθόνα δ' ἤλασε παντὶ μετώπῳ *struck* earth with his forehead, of a falling man, Od.22.94: **c.** acc. cogn., *inflict* a wound, οὐλὴν τήν ποτέ με σῦς ἤλασε 21.219:—Pass., c. acc. νῶτον ὄπισθ' αἰχμῇ δουρὸς ἐληλαμένος Tyrt.11.20; ἐλαύνεται εἰς τὸν μηρόν Luc.*Tox.*61. **3.** *strike* one thing against another, πρὸς γῆν ἐ. κάρη Od.17.237; of weapons, *drive through*, διαπρὸ χαλκὸν ἔλασσε 22.295; [δόρυ] διὰ στήθεσφιν ἔλασσε Il.5.57, cf. 20.269; ἤλασε Λυγκέος ἐν πλευραῖσι χαλκόν Pi.*N.*10.70:—Pass., *go through*, Il.4.135, 13.595; *to be fixed in*, ὀϊστὸς ὤμῳ ἐνὶ στιβαρῷ ἠλήλατο 5.400; διὰ [σφονδύλου] διαμπερὲς ἐληλάσθαι Pl.*R.*616e. **III.** metaph., **1.** *beat out* metal, *forge*, ἀσπίδα.. ἣν ἄρα χαλκεὺς ἤλασεν Il.12.296; πέντε πτύχας ἤλασε *beat out* five plates, 20.270; περὶ δ' ἕρκος ἔλασσε κασσιτέρου *make* a fence *of beaten* tin (with a play on signf. 2), 18.564; εὐνὴ Ἡφαίστου χερσὶν ἐληλαμένη χρυσοῦ a bed of *beaten* gold, Mimn.12.6; σίδηρος λεπτῶς ἐληλ. Plu.*Cam.*41. **2.** *draw a line of* wall, trench, etc., ἀμφὶ δὲ τάφρον ἤλασαν Il.7.450; ἀμφὶ δὲ τεῖχος ἔλασσε πόλει Od.6.9; σταυροὺς δ' ἐκτὸς ἔλασσε 14.11; τοῖχοι ἐληλέατ' 7.86; τεῖχος τοὺς ἀγκῶνας ἐς τὸν ποταμὸν ἐλήλαται the wall *has its* angles *carried down* to the river, Hdt.1.180, cf. 185,191; ἐληλαμέναι πέρι πύργον *having* a wall *built* round, A.*Pers.*872 (lyr.); ὄγμον ἐλαύνειν *work one's way* down a ridge or swathe in reaping or mowing, Il.11.68; ἐ. αὔλακα Hes. *Op.*443; ἀμπελίδος ὄρχον ἐ. *to draw* a line of vines, i. e. *plant* them *in line*, Ar.*Ach.*995: generally, *plant, produce*, ἐλᾷ τέσσαρας ἀρετὰς αἰών Pi.*N.*3.74. **3.** κολῳὸν ἐλαύνειν *prolong, keep up* the brawl, Il. 1.575. **4.** ἐξ ὅσσων ἐς γαῖαν ἐ. δάκρυ E.*Supp.*96.

**ἐλαύτατον**· δεινότατον, Hsch.

⊛ **ἐλάφειος** [ᾰ], ον, *of a stag* or *hart*, κέρας *hart*shorn, Arist.*HA*534$^{b}$23; ἐ. κρέα *venison*, X.*An.*1.5.2, *PSI*6.594.15 (iii A. D.). **b.** ἐ. δίκτυα *for catching stags*, Aen.Tact.16, 38.7. **2.** *deer-like, cowardly*, *EM*326.10. **3.** ἐλάφειον, τό, = ὠκιμοειδές, Ps.-Dsc.4.28.

**ἐλαφῆ**, ἡ, *deerskin*, Poll.7.90.

**ἐλᾰφη-βολία**, Ep. -ίη, ἡ, *shooting of deer*, Call.*Dian.*262: in pl., S.*Aj.*178 (lyr.). **-βόλια** (sc. ἱερά), τά, *festival of Artemis*, *IG*9(1).90 (Phocis), Plu.2.66cd. **-βολιών**, ῶνος, ὁ (sc. μήν), the ninth month of the Attic year, in which *the Elaphebolia* were held, Foed.ap.Th.4.118, etc.; also at Iasos, *CIG*2675; at Apollonia in Chalcidice, Hegesand.40. **-βόλος**, ον, *shooting deer*, Il.18.319; of Artemis, *h.Hom.* 27.2, Anacr.1.1: Dor. ἐλαφαβ- S.*Tr.*213 (lyr.).

**ἐλᾰφ-ίαι**· οἱ τῶν ἐλάφων ἀστράγαλοι, Hsch. **-ικόν**, τό, = ἐλαφόβοσκον, Ps.-Dsc.3.69. **-ίνης**, ου, ὁ, *young deer, fawn*, Aq. 1*Ki.*24.3, Hsch. **-ιον**, τό, Dim. of ἔλαφος, Sm., Th.*Pr.*5.19, *Gp.*2.

18.5. II. = κώνειον, Hsch. ✻ -ιος, ὁ (sc. μήν), = Ἐλαφηβολιών, at Elis, Paus.5.13.11. -ίς, ίδος, ἡ, a *bird*, perh. *heron* or *egret*, Dionys.*Av.*2.11.

**ἐλᾰφό-βοσκον**, τό, (-βοσκός, ὁ, Hsch.) *plant eaten by deer* as an antidote against the bite of snakes, *parsnip*, *Pastinaca sativa*, Dsc.3.69, Plin.*HN*22.79, Aët.13.21. II. = ἐλελίσφακον, Dsc.3.33; = σκόρδον, Ps.-Dsc.2.152. **-γενές**· τῆς ἐλάφου ὁ μυελός, Hsch. **-ειδής**, ές, *deer-like*, Plb.34.10.8. **-κρᾱνος**, ον, *deer-headed*, ἵπποι Str.15.1.56. **-κτόνος**, ον, *deer-killing*, θεά E.*IT*1113 (lyr.). **-πους**, ποδος, ὁ, ἡ, *deer-footed*, interpol. in *Hippiatr.*115.

✻ **ἔλᾰφος**, ὁ and ἡ, *deer*, *Cervus elaphus*, whether male, *hart* or *stag*, Il.3.24, etc.; or female, *hind*, 11.113, etc.; κεραός, ὑψίκερως, ib.475, Od.10.158; κεροῦσσα S.*Fr.*89; ἐ. βαλιαί E.*Hipp.*218 (anap.); ἐ. ἀντὶ παρθένου Lib.*Ep.*785.1; κραδίην ἐλάφοιο [ἔχων] with heart *of deer*, i.e. a coward, Il.1.225; φυζακινῇς ἐλάφοισιν ἐοίκεσαν 13.102, cf. Pl.*La.*196e. (Fem. as a generic term, in Trag. and X.*Cyn.*9.11, 10.22, cf. αἱ ἐ. τὰ κέρατα ἀποβάλλουσιν Arist.*HA*611ᵃ27.) II. κέρας ἐλάφου *hartshorn*, *Gp.*13.8.2. III. *deerskin*, ἐλάφου πήρα Longus 3.15. IV. a kind of *cake*, Ath.14.649e. V. *figure of a deer* used as a weight, *IG*5(2).125 (Tegea, ii A.D.). (-φος as in ἔρι-φος, etc., ἐλα- from ἐλη̥-, cf. ἐλλός (from *ἐλνός), Lith. *élnis* 'stag'.)

**ἐλᾰφό-σκορδον**, τό, a kind of *garlic*, Ps.-Dsc.2.152. II. = ἀπόκυνον, ib.4.80. **-σσοΐα**, Ep. -ίη, ἡ, (σεύω) *deer-hunting*, *AP*6.253.8 (Crin.). **-στικτος**, ον, *tattooed with figure of a deer*, Lys.13.19.

✻ **ἐλαφρ-ία**, ἡ, *lightness*: *levity*, 2*Ep.Cor.*1.17. II. *alleviation*, Aret.*CD*2.2. III. = ὀλιγότης, Suid. **-ίζω**, *make light*: hence, *lift up*, *carry*, Coluth.29,156; Ep. 3 sg. impf. -ίζεσκε, κούρην Mosch.2.130; ἐ. ἑαυτὸν ὑψοῦ Ael.*NA*9.52; πτεροῖς ἑαυτήν Plu.2.317e. 2. *make light of*, *scorn*, Archil.87, cf. Hsch. II. intr., *to be light and nimble*, E.*Fr.*530.8, Call.*Del.*115, Anyt.ap.Poll.5.48, Opp.*C.*1.85. III. Pass., *to be relieved* of forced contributions, *IG*5(1).1146.28 (Gythium, i B.C.). **-ιος**, ὁ (sc. μήν), month at Cnidus, *SIG*953.85.

**ἐλαφρό-γειος**, ον, (γῆ) *of light soil*, *Gp.*3.3.11. **-νοος**, ον, *light-minded*, Phoc.9, Nonn.*D.*10.247.

✻ **ἐλαφρ-ός**, ά, όν, and in Pi.*N.*5.20 ός, όν: (v. ἐλαχύς):—*light in weight*, τόν οἱ ἐ. ἔθηκε (sc. λᾶαν) Il.12.450; ξύλον ἐλαφρότερα Hdt.3.23; πῦρ Parm.8.57; opp. βαρύς, Pl.*Ti.*63c, etc.; in Epitaphs, γαῖαν ἔχοις ἐλαφράν '*sit tibi terra levis*', *Epigr.Gr.*195 (Vaxos), cf. *Sammelb.*315. Adv., τά (sc. δένδρεα) οἱ πλώοιεν ἐλαφρῶς Od.5.240. 2. *light to bear*, *easy*, καί κεν ἐλαφρότερος πόλεμος Τρώεσσι γένοιτο Il.22.287; συμφορὰν ἐλαφροτέραν καταστῆσαι Antipho 3.3.12; πόνος -ότερος ἑαυτοῦ συνηθείῃ γίνεται Democr.241: later, Comp. ἐλαφρώτερον ἄλγος Max.173; ἐλαφρόν [ἐστι] 'tis *light*, *easy*, Pi.*N.*7.77, A.*Pr.*265, etc.; *easy to understand*, [προβλήματα] ἐ. καὶ πιθανά Plu.2.133e, cf. D.Chr.18.11; ἐν ἐλαφρῷ ποιήσασθαί τι to make *light* of a thing, Hdt.3.154; οὐκ ἐν ἐ. ποιεῖσθαι Id.1.118; οὐκ ἐν ἐ. no *light matter*, Theoc.22.212. Adv. -ρῶς, φέρειν ζυγόν to bear it *lightly*, Pi.*P.*2.93. 3. *light of digestion*, Plu.2.137a. 4. *shallow*, διάπλους *Peripl.M.Rubr.*55; δῖναι ib.40. 5. Act., *ease-giving*, B.*Fr.*8, Theoc.2.92. II. *light in moving*, *nimble*, γυῖα δ' ἔθηκεν ἐ. Il.5.122; ἦ μάλ' ἐ. ἀνήρ 16.745; ἐλαφρότατος ποσσί 23.749; χεῖρες..ἐπαΐσσονται ἐ. ib.628; κίρκος..ἐλαφρότατος πετεηνῶν 22.139, Od.13.87; [ἵπποι] ἐλαφρότατοι θείειν 3.370; ἐλαφραῖς πτερύγων ῥιπαῖς A.*Pr.*125 (anap.); ἐ. ποδὶ ib.281 (anap.); γονάτων ἐλαφρὸν ὁρμάν Pi.*N.*5.20; ἐ. ποδῶν ἴχνι' ἀειράμεναι Call.*Fr.anon.*391; ἐλαφρὰ ἡλικία the age of *active* youth, X.*Mem.*3.5.27; ἐλαφροί, οἱ, *light troops*, Id.*An.*4.2.27 (restricted to cavalry who fight at close quarters, Ascl.*Tact.*1.3): metaph., πόλιας θῆκεν ἐλαφροτέρας made them *easier in condition*, *Epigr.Gr.*905 (Gortyn). Adv. -ρῶς *nimbly*, Ar.*Ach.*217; ὀρχεῖσθαι πυρρίχην X.*An.*6.1.12. III. metaph., *light-minded*, *unsteady*, *fickle*, πᾶν πλῆθός ἐστιν ἐ. Plb.6.56.11; ἐ. λύσσα *light-headed* madness, E.*Ba.*851. b. *gentle*, *mild*, σφᾶς αὐτοὺς -οτάτους τοῖς συνοῦσι παρέχοντας Isoc.12.31, cf. Pl.*Ep.*360c. 2. *small*, ποταμός Plb.16.17.7; *of small power* or *strength*, πόλεις Id.5.62.6. 3. *relieved* of a burden, ψυχὴ ἐ. καὶ δι' αὑτῆς Plot.4.3.32. IV. Ἐλαφρός· Ζεὺς ἐν Κρήτῃ, Hsch. **-ότης**, ητος, ἡ, = ἐλαφρία, *lightness*, *nimbleness*, Pl.*Lg.*795e, Plu.*Lyc.*17, al.

**ἐλαφροτοκία**, ἡ, *low rate of interest*, *IGRom.*4.292.4 (Pergam., ii B.C.).

✻ **ἐλαφρ-όω**, = sq., Hsch. s. v. ἀλεγύνεται. **-ύνω**, *make light*, *lighten*, πόλεμον Jul.*Or.*1.18c, cf. Babr.111.6 (Pass.), Aq.*Jb.*39.34 (40.4). 2. *relieve*, ἀνίας Eus.Mynd.1; κεφαλήν Ruf.ap.Orib.8.47(*b*).1:—Pass., ἐλαφρυνθήσεται τοῦ ὄγκου *Hippiatr.*126. b. *relieve* of fiscal burdens, ἑαυτὸν ἐ. τῆς συντελείας Just.*Nov.*43.1.2:—Pass., ibid.

**ἐλαχία**· ἐδάρη (Cret.), Hsch. **ἐλαχίζει**· πλανᾶται, Id.

**ἐλᾰχιστ-άκις**, Adv. *fewest times*, *least often*, Hp.*Fract.*42. **-ιαῖος**, α, ον, *minute*, *infinitesimal*, μέγεθος Diog.Oen.2. ✻ **-ος** [ᾰ], η, ον, Sup. of ἐλαχύς: Comp. ἐλάσσων (q.v.):—*smallest*, *least*, freq. with a neg., γέρας, δύναμις οὐκ ἐ., *h.Merc.*573, Hdt.7.168, etc.; λόγου ἐλαχίστου of *least* account, Id.1.143; ἐλαχίστου ἐδέησε διαφθεῖραι *narrowly* missed destroying them, Th.2.77; περὶ ἐλαχίστου ποιεῖσθαι Pl.*Ap.*30a; παρ' ἐλάχιστον ἐποίησεν αὐτοὺς ἀφαιρεθῆναι D.17.22. 2. of Time, *shortest*, δι' ἐλαχίστου (sc. χρόνου) Th.3.39; δι' ἐλαχίστης βουλῆς with *shortest* deliberation, Id.1.138. 3. of Number, *fewest*, Pl.*R.*378a; ἐ. τὸν ἀριθμόν Arist.*Pol.*1312ᵃ30; ἐν ἐλαχίστοις δυοῖν between two *at least*, Id.*EN*1131ᵃ15. 4. Math., ἐλάχιστα καὶ μέγιστα *minima* and maxima, Apollon.Perg.*Con.*1 *Praef.* II. τὸ ἐλάχιστον, τοὐλάχιστον, *at the least*, Hdt.2.13, X.*An.*5.7.8, D.4.21; ἐλάχιστα *least* of any one, Th.1.70; ὡς ἐ. as *little as possible*, Pl.*Phd.*63d. III. from ἐλάχιστος came a new Comp. ἐλαχιστότερος *less than the least*, ἐ. πάντων ἁγίων *Ep.Eph.*3.8: Sup. ἐλαχιστότατος *very least of all*, S.E.*M.*3.54, 9.406. **-ότης**, ητος, ἡ, = *exiguitas*, *Gloss.*

**ἔλαχος**, ον, = ἐλαχύς, Call.*Fr.*349.

**ἐλᾰχύ-νωτος** [ῠ], ον, *short-backed*, prob. in Pi.*Pae.*4.14. **-πτέρυξ**, υγος, ὁ, ἡ, *short-finned*, of the dolphin, Id.*P.*4.17.

✻ **ἐλαχύς**, ἐλάχεια (not -εῖα, Hdn.Gr.1.249), ἐλαχύ, *small*, *short*, *mean*, *little*: old Ep. Positive, whence ἐλάσσων, ἐλάχιστος are formed: in early Ep. only fem., *h.Ap.*197, v.l. in Od.9.116, 10.509 (v. λάχεια): in later Ep., Archyt.Amphiss.2, Euph.11, Nic.*Th.*324, Opp.*C.*3.480, Nonn.*D.*37.314: neut. ἐλαχὺ σκάφος *AP*7.498 (Antip.). (*legᵘh-* or *lengᵘh-*, cf. Lat. *levis*, Lith. *leñgvas* 'light'.)

**ἔλαψ**, = ἔλλοψ, *Gp.*20.7.1.

**ἐλάω**, Ion. ἐλόω, poet. pres. for ἐλαύνω; v. ἐλαύνω init.

✻ **ἐλαών**, = ἐλαιών, *PLond.*5.1769 (vi A.D.).

✻ **ἔλδομαι** and **ἐέλδομαι**, poet. Verb, only pres. and impf., *wish*, *long*, c. inf., Il.13.638, Od.4.162, Pi.*O.*1.4: c. gen., *long for*, σὴν ἄλοχον τῆς αἰὲν ἐέλδεαι Od.5.210; ἐλδόμεναι πεδίοιο (of mules) *eager to reach* it, Il.23.122: c. acc., *desire*, ἐὸν αὐτοῦ χρεῖος ἐελδόμενος Od.1.409, cf. Il.5.481: abs., νόστησαι ἐελδομένοισι μάλ' ἡμῖν Od.24.400:—Pass. only once, νῦν τοι ἐελδέσθω πόλεμος be war now *welcome* to thee, Il.16.494.

**ἔλδωρ**, Hdn.Gr.2.770 (ἐλδ- ib.938 cod.), Ep. **ἐέλδωρ**, τό, *wish*, *longing*, *desire*, Il.1.41, Hes.*Sc.*36, etc.: fem., Ibyc.18 (s. v.l.).

**ἐλεά**· κάνεα, πλέγματα, Hsch.

**ἐλέα**, ἡ, perh. *reed-warbler*, *Salicaria arundinacea*, Arist.*HA*616ᵇ12: ἔλεια, Call.*Fr.*100c.14; cf. ἐλεᾶς.

**ἐλέαγνος**, v. ἐλαίαγνος.

**ἐλεαίρω**, Ep. impf. ἐλεαίρεσκον Il.24.23: aor. 1 ἐλέηρα A.R.4.1308, *Sammelb.*2134:—lengthd. form of ἐλεέω, *take pity on*, τινά Il.6.407, Od.10.399, etc.—Ep. word, used by Ar.*Eq.*793 (anap.), Luc.*Trag.*305.

**ἐλεᾶς** (ἐλέας Hsch.), ὁ, an unknown *bird*, perh. = ἐλέα, Ar.*Av.*302.

✻ **ἐλέατρος**, ὁ, = ἐδέατρος, *seneschal* or *steward*, *PCair.Zen.*59.5, 71.1 (iii B.C.), dub. in Ath.4.171b: but, = μάγειρος, acc. to *Et.Gud.*, where it is distd. from ἐδέατρος (q. v.).

✻ **ἐλεάω**, later form of ἐλεέω, *EM*327.29, Lxx *Pr.*21.26.

✻ **ἐλεγαίνω**, *to be wrathful*, *wanton*, *violent*, *EM*152.50, 327.6.

✻ **ἐλεγ-εία**, = ἐλεγεῖον, Str.13.1.48, Plu.*Sol.*8, Heph.1.5, al. **-ειακός**, ή, όν, *elegiac*, πεντάμετρον D.H.*Comp.*25, cf. Heph.1.5; *written in distichs*, ἐπίνικον Ath.4.144e, etc. **-ειδάριον**, τό, Dim. of ἐλεγεῖον, Petron.109: also **-είδιον**, τό, Pers.1.51.

✻ **ἐλεγεινή**· χαλεπή, Hsch.

✻ **ἐλεγείνω**, = ἐλεγαίνω, Suid.

**ἐλεγειογράφος** [ᾰ], ὁ, *writer of elegies*, *AP*9.248 tit.

✻ **ἐλεγεῖον**, τό, *distich consisting of hexameter and pentameter*, Critias 4.3 D., Th.1.132, Arist.*Po.*1447ᵇ12. II. in pl., ἐλεγεῖα, τά, *elegiac poem* or *inscription*, merely in reference to the metre, not to the subject, Pl.*R.*368a, Arist.*Rh.*1375ᵇ32, Lycurg.142, D.59.98; even in two hexameters, Pherecr.153.7; sg., Ps.-Hdt.*Vit.Hom.*36. 2. later, *lament*, *elegy*, Paus.10.7.5, Luc.*Tim.*46; cf. ἐλεγεῖα· τὰ ἐπιτάφια ποιήματα, Hsch.: in sg., D.S.11.14, D.H.1.49, Plu.*Them.*8, etc. III. *a single line in an elegiac inscription*, prop. *the pentameter*, Id.2.1141a, Heph.15.14.

✻ **ἐλεγειοποιός**, ὁ, *elegiac poet*, Arist.*Po.*1447ᵇ14, Ath.14.632d.

**ἐλεγεῖος**, α, ον, *elegiac*, δίστιχον Ael.*VH*1.17.

**ἐλεγίαμβος**, ὁ, the verse – ◡◡ – ◡◡ – ◡ – ◡ – ◡, Mar.Vict.p.145 K.

**ἐλεγῖνος**, ὁ, a *fish*, Arist.*HA*610ᵇ6.

**ἐλεγκ-τέον**, (ἐλέγχω) *one must refute*, Pl.*Lg.*905d; *one must reject*, *disapprove*, Ath.Med.ap.Orib.*inc.*23.13. b. *one must test*, Onos.1.19. c. *one must convict*, τινά τινος Them.*Or.*21.253a. 2. ἐλεγκτέος, α, ον, *to be refuted*, Str.2.1.35. **-τήρ**, ῆρος, ὁ, *one who convicts* or *detects*, τῶν ἀποκτεινάντων Antipho 2.4.3. **-τικός**, ή, όν, *fond of cross-questioning* or *examining*, Pl.*Sph.*216b, etc.; ὁ ἐ. ἐκεῖνος that *cross-questioner*, Id.*Tht.*200a; *fond of reproving*, *critical*, τῶν ἁμαρτανομένων Arist.*Rh.*1381ᵃ31, cf. Longin.4.1 (Sup.); ἐ. βίος Jul.*Or.*6.191a. Adv. -κῶς X.*Smp.*4.2, etc.; Sup., Luc.*Demon.*55. 2. *refutative*, of indirect modes of proof such as the reductio ad absurdum, ἐνθυμήματα Arist.*Rh.*1396ᵇ25. Adv. -κῶς Alex.Aphr.*in Metaph.*272.32. 3. -κά, τά, *means of detecting*, πάθους Alex.Trall.1.15. **-τός**, ή, όν, *fit to be refuted* or *worthy of reproof*, Hsch.

**ἐλεγμός**, ὁ, = ἔλεγξις, Lxx *Ps.*149.7 (pl.), al., 2*Ep.Ti.*3.16.

**ἐλεγξίγᾰμος** [ῐ], ον, *testing a wife's fidelity*, ποταμός *AP*9.125.

**ἐλεγξῖνος**, ὁ, *wrangler*, pun on the name of the philosopher Alexinus, D.L.2.109.

**ἔλεγξις**, εως, ἡ, *refuting*, *reproving*, Lxx *Jb.*21.4, al.; πικρὸς πρὸς τὰς ἐ. Philostr.*VA*2.22 (pl.). 2. *conviction*, παρανομίας 2*Ep.Pet.*2.16.

✻ **ἔλεγος**, ὁ, *song*, *melody*, orig. accompanied by the flute, cf. ἄλυρος ἐ. E.*Hel.*185 (lyr.), *IT*146 (lyr.); Ἀσίας ἐ. ἰήιος Id.*Hyps.Fr.*3(1)iii 9; so Ἔλεγοι, title of a νόμος αὐλῳδικός, Plu.2.1132d; of the *song* of the nightingale, Ar.*Av.*218 (pl.); ἔλεγον οἶτον, of the halcyon, E.*IT*1091 (lyr.); later, *lament*, *song of mourning*, A.R.2.782. II. *poem in elegiac distichs*, Call.*Fr.*121; ἱλαροὶ ἐ. *AP*10.19 (Apollonid.). (Commonly derived from ἒ ἒ λέγειν, to cry woe! woe! *EM*326.49.)

**ἐλεγχ-είη**, ἡ, *reproach*, *disgrace*, Il.22.100, al., A.R.3.1114 (pl.),

Q.S.1.22. ⊛ **-ής**, *ές*, *worthy of reproof*; of men, *cowardly*, ἐλεγχέες Il.4.242, 24.239: irreg. Sup. ἐλέγχιστος 2.285, etc. II. *reproachful*, μῦθος Nonn.*D*.40.35. **-ιον**, *τό*, Dim. of ἔλεγχος (B) IV, *Gloss.*

**ἐλεγχοειδής**, *ές*, *like a refutation*, Arist.*SE*174$^{b}$18, 175$^{a}$40.

**ἔλεγχος** (A), *εος*, *τό*, *reproach*, *disgrace*, *dishonour*, δὴ γὰρ ἔλεγχος ἔσσεται εἴ κεν νῆας ἕλῃ κορυθαίολος Ἕκτωρ Il.11.314; ἡμῖν δ' ἂν ἐλέγχεα ταῦτα γένοιτο Od.21.329, cf. Pi.*N*.3.15; of men, the abstr. being put for the concrete, κάκ' ἐλέγχεα base *reproaches* to your name, Il.5.787, al., Hes.*Th*.26; ἐλέγχεα alone, Il.24.260.

⊛ **ἔλεγχος** (B), *ὁ*, *argument of disproof* or *refutation*, πολύδηρις ἔ. Parm.1.36, cf. Pl.*Phdr*.276a; ὁ ἔ. συναγωγὴ τῶν ἀντικειμένων ἐστίν Arist.*Rh*.1410$^{a}$22, cf. 1396$^{b}$26; ἔ. δὲ συλλογισμὸς μετ' ἀντιφάσεως τοῦ συμπεράσματος Id.*SE*165$^{a}$2, cf. *APr*.66$^{b}$11; ἐλέγχου ἄγνοια, *ignoratio elenchi*, Id.*SE*168$^{a}$18; ὅταν ὑπὸ τῶν ἐ. πιέζωνται Phld.*D*.3.8. II. generally, *cross-examining*, *testing*, *scrutiny*, esp. for purposes of *refutation*, οὐκ ἔχει ἔλεγχον does not admit of *disproof*, Hdt.2.23; τῶνδ' ἔλεγχον, abs., *as a test* of this, S.*OT*603; τὰ ψευδῆ ἔλεγχον ἔχει Th.3.53; ἔ. παραδοῦναί τινι to give him *an opportunity of refuting*, Pl.*Phdr*.273c; δόμεν τι βασάνῳ ἐς ἔ. to submit it to *scrutiny*, Pi.*N*.8.21; χρυσὸς νόθου ἀρετῆς ἔ. *Com.Adesp*.195; ἀρετῆς ἔ. δοῦναι *a proof* or *test* of it, And.1.150; ἔ. διδόναι τοῦ βίου to give *an account* of one's life, Pl.*Ap*.39c; οἱ ἔ. περὶ ὀρφανῶν Is.4.22; τὸ πρᾶγμα τὸν ἔ. δώσει D.4.15; ἔ. ποιεῖν τινός to *test* it, Ar.*Ra*.786; ἔ. ποιήσασθαι τῶν πεπραγμένων Antipho 1.7; ἔ. λαβεῖν τινός make *trial* of it, ib.12; ἐλέγχους ἀποδέχεσθαι to admit *tests*, Lys.19.6; ἐλέγχους προσφέρειν to allege them, Ar.*Lys*.484; διάπειρα βροτῶν ἔ. Pi.*O*.4.20; οὐδὲ ἔ. παρασχὼν οὐδὲ βάσανον Antipho 2.4.7; ἔ. διδόναι And.2.4; εἰς ἔ. πεσεῖν to be *convicted*, E.*Hipp*.1310, cf. *HF* 73; δεικνυμένων ἐ. Id.*Heracl*.905 (lyr.); οὔτ' εἰς ἔ. χειρὸς οὐδ' ἔργου μολών S.*OC*1297; εἰς ἔ. ἐξιέναι to proceed to the *proof*, put to the *test*, Id.*Ph*.98; or, to be put to the *proof*, Id.*Fr*.105; ἐξελθεῖν E.*Alc*.640; εἰς ἔ. ἰέναι περί τινος Pl.*Phdr*.278c; εἰς ἔ. ἔρχεσθαί τινος Philem.93.3; καταστῆναι εἰς ἔ. καὶ λόγον Isoc.12.150; ἔ. φεύγειν Antipho 5.38; οἱ περὶ Παυσανίαν ἔ. *the evidence on which* he *was convicted*, Th.1.135; πίστις πραγμάτων ἔ. οὐ βλεπομένων *Ep.Hebr*.11.1. III. Ἔλεγχος personified, Men.545, Luc.*Pseudol*.4. b. applied to *Conscience*, τὸ συνειδὸς ἔ. ἀδέκαστος Ph.1.236; ἔ. κατάλογον ποιεῖται τῶν ἁμαρτημάτων [τῆς ψυχῆς] ib.291. IV. *catalogue*, *inventory*, *Gloss.*, Suet.*Gramm*.8 (pl.). V. *drop-pearl*, Plin.*HN*9.113, Juv.6.459.

⊛ **ἐλέγχω**, Od.21.424, etc.: fut. ἐλέγξω Ar.*Nu*.1043, etc.: aor. ἤλεγξα Il.9.522, etc.:—Pass., fut. ἐλεγχθήσομαι Antipho 2.4.10, X.*Mem*.1.7.2: aor. ἠλέγχθην Antipho l.c., Pl.*Grg*.458a, etc.: pf. ἐλήλεγμαι Id.*Lg*.805c: 3 sg. ἐλήλεγκται Antipho l.c. (ἐξ-ηλεγμένοι is f.l. in Lys.6.44): plpf. ἐξ-ελήλεγκτο D.32.27:—*disgrace*, *put to shame*, μῦθον ἐ. *treat* a speech *with contempt*, Il.9.522; ἐ. τινά *put* one *to shame*, Od.21.424.—This usage is only Ep. II. *cross-examine*, *question*, Hdt.2.115, Pl.*Ap*.18d, etc.; μὴ 'λεγχε τὸν πονοῦντα A.*Ch*.919; φύλαξ ἐλέγχων φύλακα S.*Ant*.260; τί ταῦτ' ἄλλως ἐλέγχεις; Id.*OT*333, cf. 783; ἔλεγχ', ἐλέγχου Ar.*Ra*.857; ἐ. τινὰ περί τινος Id.*Pl*.574; ἕνεκά τινος Antiph.207.10; τὰς ἀρχὰς βασάνοις χρώμενοι ἐλεγχόντων Pl.*Lg*.946c: c. acc. et inf., *accuse* one of doing, E.*Alc*.1058:—Pass., *to be convicted*, Hdt.1.24, 117; ἐλεγχόμενοι εἴ τι περιγένοιτο τῶν χρημάτων D.35.36, cf. Pl.*Prt*.331c,d: with part., ἐλεγχθεὶς διαφθείρας Antipho 2.3.9, cf. 2.4.10; ἐλεγχθήσεται γελοῖος ὢν X.*Mem*.1.7.2. 2. *test*, *bring to the proof*, ἀνδρῶν ἀρετὰν παγκρατὴς ἐλέγχει ἀλάθεια B.*Fr*.10.2; πρᾶγμ' ἐ. A.*Ag*.1351 (Pass., τὸ πρᾶγμ' ἐλεγχθέν Ar.*Ec*.485); λόγον Pl.*Sph*.242b (Pass., Id.*Tht*.161e): with subject. clause, ἐ. τινά, εἰ.., A.*Ch*.851, Ar.*Eq*.1232. 3. *prove*, τοῦτο ἐ. ὡς.. Pl.*Phdr*.273b, cf. *Sph*.256c: abs., *bring convincing proof*, ὡς ἡ ἀνάγκη ἐ. Hdt.2.22; αὐτὸ τὸ ἔργον ἐ. Th.6.86; περί τινος D.21.5. 4. *refute*, *confute*, τινά or τι, Pl.*Grg*.470c, al., D.28.2, Luc.*Nigr*.4:—Pass., Pl.*Tht*.162a; χρυσὸς κληῖδας ἐλέγχει *proves that* they *avail not*, *AP*5.216 (Paul. Sil.). b. *put right*, *correct*, *prove by a reductio ad impossibile*, ὅσα ἔστιν ἀποδεῖξαι, ἔστι καὶ ἐλέγξαι τὸν θέμενον τὴν ἀντίφασιν τοῦ ἀληθοῦς Arist.*SE*170$^{a}$24; παράδοξα ἐ. Id.*EN*1146$^{a}$23. 5. *get the better of*, στρατιὰν ὠκύτατι ἐ. Pi.*P*.11.49, cf. D.P.750, Him.*Or*.1.16. 6. *expose*, τινὰ ληροῦντα Pl.*Tht*.171d, cf. X.*Mem*.1.7.2, M.Ant.1.17; *betray* a weakness, Democr.222. 7. *decide* a dispute, ἀνὰ μέσον τῶν δύο Lxx *Ge*.31.37.

**ἐλεδέμας**, corrupt in A.*Th*.83.

**ἐλεδώνη**, *ἡ*, a kind of *octopus*, Arist.*HA*525$^{a}$17, Henioch.3, Artem.2.14.

**ἐλεεινολογ-έομαι**, *speak piteously*, Hermog.*Stat*.3, *Id*.2.7, Herm. *in Phdr*.p.196 A. **-ία**, Att. **ἐλεινο-**, *ἡ*, *piteous appeal*, ἐ. καὶ δείνωσις Pl.*Phdr*.272a, cf. Hermog.*Id*.1.1; πρὸς -λογίαν λέγειν Agatharch.21.

**ἐλεεινός**, *ή*, *όν*, **ἐλεινός** *h.Cer*.284, Att. (Eup.25) and Trag. (v. infr.), but **ἐλεεινός** Men.*Sam*.156 Pap.: written **ἐλεηνός** in Lxx *Da*.9.23, 10.11: (ἔλεος):—*finding pity*, *pitied*, δός μ' ἐς Ἀχιλλῆος φίλον ἐλθεῖν ἠδ' ἐλεεινόν Il.24.309; *moving pity*, *piteous*, 23.110, etc.; ἐλεινὸς εἰσορᾶν *piteous* to behold, A.*Pr*.248; ἐλεινὸν ὁρᾷς thou lookest *piteous*, S.*Ph*.1130 (lyr.); ἐσθῆτ' ἐλεινήν Ar.*Ach*.413; ἵν' ἐλεινοὶ τοῖς ἀνθρώποις φαίνοιντ' εἶναι Id.*Ra*.1063; ἐλεινοὶ οἱ ἀδικοῦντες Lys.24.7; ποιῶν ἑαυτὸν ὡς ἐλεινότατον D.21.186; -ότερος ἀνθρώποις τε καὶ θεοῖς Pl.*Lg*.729e. b. *having received mercy*, Lxx ll. cc. 2. *showing pity*, ἐ. δάκρυον a tear *of pity*, Od.8.531, 16.219, Men. l.c.; οὐδὲν ἐλεινόν no *feeling of pity*, Pl.*Phd*.59a, cf. *R*.606b. II. Adv. ἐλεεινῶς, Att. ἐλεινῶς, *pitiably*, S.*Ph*.870, Ar.*Th*.1063; ἐλεινῶς διακεῖσθαι D.19.81: neut. pl. ἐλεεινά as Adv., Il.2.314.

**ἐλεεινότης**, *ητος*, *ἡ*, = ἔλεος, Sch.E.*Or*.960.

**ἐλε-έω**, impf. ἠλέουν Apollod.Com.4.1: aor. ἠλέησα, Ep. ἐλέησα (v. infr.):—Pass., pf. ἠλέημαι Men.595.2: (ἔλεος):—*to have pity on*, *show mercy to*, ὁ δ' ἐρύσατο καί μ' ἐλέησεν Od.14.279; σύ μ' ἐλέησον S.*Ph*.501, cf. Eub.1 D., etc.; ἐλέησον αὐτῶν τὴν ὄπα Ar.*Pax*400; ἐ. [τινα] ἐπὶ τοῖς ἀκουσίοις παθήμασι Antipho 1.27; τῆς τύχης τινά X.*Eph*.5.4:—Pass., Pl.*Ap*.34c, *R*.336e, *Ax*.368d; ἵνα.. ἧττον ὑφ' ὑμῶν ἐλεοίμην D.27.53; ἅμ' ἠλέηται καὶ τέθνηκεν ἡ χάρις Men.595.2, cf. 844. 2. abs., *feel pity*, Ar.*Ach*.706. **-ημοποιός**, *όν*, *giving alms*, Lxx *To*.9.6. **-ημοσύνη**, *ἡ*, *pity*, *mercy*, Call.*Del*.152. 2. *charity*, *alms*, Lxx *To*.4.7, *Ev.Matt*.6.2, D.L.5.17. **-ήμων**, *ον*, gen. *ονος*, *pitiful*, *merciful*, Od.5.191, D.21.101, Lxx *Ps*.111(112).4, *Ev.Matt*.5.7; of God, Lxx *Ex*.34.6, al.: c. gen., Ar.*Pax*425:—Comp. and Sup., ἐλεημονέστερος, -τατος, Arist.*HA*608$^{b}$8, Lys.24.7. Adv. -μόνως, condemned by Poll.8.11. **-ήσατο**, prob. corrupt for ἐληΐσατο, Hsch. **-ητικός**, *ή*, *όν*, *merciful*, *compassionate*, Arist.*Rh*.1389$^{b}$8. **-ητός**, *ή*, *όν*, *to be pitied*, Sch.A.*Pr*.355. **-ητύς**, *ύος*, *ἡ*, Ep. and Ion. = ἔλεος, *pity*, *mercy*, Od.17.451.

⊛ **ἐλεθαινομένη**· ἀκολασταίνουσα, Hsch. **ἔλεια**, v. ἐλέα.

**ἐλειήτης**, *ου*, *ὁ*, *dwelling in marshes*, λέων Call.*Fr.anon*.88.

**ἐλειθερεῖ**· εὐδίᾳ, and **ἐλειθερεῖς** (ἐλειτεθ- cod.)· ἐν ἡλίῳ τιθέμενοι ἢ θερμοί, Hsch.; cf. εἰληθερής.

**Ἐλείθυια**, *ἡ*, v. Εἰλείθυια. **ἑλεῖν**, v. αἱρέω. **ἐλεινός**, v. ἐλεεινός.

**ἐλειο-βάτης** [ᾰ], *ου*, *ὁ*, *walking the marsh*, *marsh-dwelling*, A.*Pers*.39 (anap.). **-γενής**, *ές*, *marsh-born*: τὸ ἐ., = ὄρυζα, Hsch. ⊛ **-δίακτος**, *ὁ*, *conduit for draining marshes*, *CIG*2782.40 (Aphrodisias). **-μᾰλάχη** [ᾰχ], or **-μολόχη**, *ἡ*, *marsh-mallow*, Apul.*Herb*.40,38 (*elaeo-* codd.). **-νόμος**, *ον*, *dwelling in the marsh* or *meadow*, Νύμφαι A.R.2.821; ποίη Orph.*A*.1054; *situate there*, ib.157. **-ρριζον**, *τό*, = κύπειρος, Hsch.

**ἕλειος**, *ον* (*α*, *ον* Ar.*Av*.244 (lyr.), Dsc.4.52): (ἕλος):—*of the marsh* or *meadow*, ἕ. ὕδωρ *marsh*-water, Hp.*Aër*.10; ἕ. δάπεδον the surface *of the meads*, Ar.*Ra*.352 (lyr.). 2. *growing* or *dwelling in the marsh*, δόναξ A.*Pers*.494; τῶν Αἰγυπτίων οἱ ἕ. Th.1.110; βίος ἕ. Arist.*PA*693$^{a}$15; [ζῷα] ἕ. ib.674$^{b}$31; σχοῖνος Dsc. l.c.; ἀκτή Ps.-Dsc.4.173; ἕλειον, *τό*, = *asparagus*, *Gloss.* II. Ἑλεία, *ἡ*, title of Artemis in Cos, *Schwyzer* 251 *B*5.

**ἐλειός** or **ἐλειός**, *ὁ*, a kind of *dormouse*, *Myoxus glis*, Arist.*HA*600$^{b}$12, Artem.3.65; μύες ἐ. *Edict.Diocl*.4.38. II. a kind of *hawk*, Hsch., prob. in Arist.*HA*620$^{a}$21. III. *wood-worm*, Aristarch. ap.Hsch.

**ἐλειο-σέλῑνον** or **ἐλεο-**, *τό*, *marsh-celery*, *Apium graveolens*, Thphr.*HP*7.6.3, Dsc.3.64. **-τροφος**, *ον*, *bred in the marsh*, Archestr.*Fr*.15.7. **-χρῡσος**, = ἑλίχρυσος, Thphr.*HP*6.8.1, 9.19.3.

**ἐλεϊσμός**, *ὁ*, = ἔλεος, Aq.*Je*.36(43).7, 38(45).26 (leg. -ησμός).

⊛ **ἐλείτης**, *ου*, *ὁ*, *marsh-growing*, κάλαμος Dion.Byz.23. II. Ἑλείτας, *ὁ*, title of Apollo in Cyprus, *Schwyzer* 682.15.

**ἔλεκτο**, v. λέγω.

**ἐλελεῦ**, doubled ἐλελεῦ ἐλελεῦ, *a cry* of pain, A.*Pr*.877 (anap.); also an exclamation used at the ceremony of the ὠσχοφόρια, Plu.*Thes*.22:—in form ἐλελελεῦ, a *war-cry*, Ar.*Av*.364, cf. Sch. ad loc.

⊛ **ἐλελίζω** (A), Ep. redupl. of ἑλίσσω (v. infr.), rare in pres., as Pi.*O*.9.13; impf. ἠλέλιζον Hsch., poet. ἐλέλιζον Maiist.42, Nonn.*D*.2.525: mostly in aor. (v. infr.):—Pass., impf. *h.Hom*.28.9: Ep. aor. ἐλέλικτο Il.13.558: pf. ἐλέλιγμαι Cerc.6.18:—*whirl round*, περὶ σχεδίην ἐλέλιξε [τὸ κῦμα] Od.5.314; ἡ δ' ἐλελίχθη [ἡ νηῦς] 12.416. 2. Med. and Pass., *move in coils* or *spires*, of a serpent, τὴν δ' ἐλελιξάμενος πτέρυγος λάβεν Il.2.316; ἐπ' αὐτοῦ (sc. τελαμῶνος) ἐλέλικτο δράκων 11.39, cf. A.R.4.143; σπείρας ὄφεων ἐλελιζομένη Ar.*Fr*.500. II. in Il. of an army, *cause* it *to turn* and face the enemy, *rally* it, σφεας ὦκ' ἐλέλιξεν Αἴας 17.278:—in Pass., οἱ δ' ἐλελίχθησαν 5.497, 6.106; cf. ἑλίσσω II. 1. III. *cause to vibrate*, μέγαν δ' ἐλέλιξεν Ὄλυμπον, of Zeus, ib.1.530, cf. 8.199; φόρμιγγα ἐ. *make* its strings *quiver*, Pi.*O*.9.13; ἀστεροπὰν ἐλελίξαις Id.*N*.9.19:—Med., ἵππον.. ἀγωνίῳ ἐλελιζόμενος ποδὶ μίμεο Simon.29:—Pass., *quake*, *tremble*, *quiver*, ἐλελίχθη γυῖα Il.22.448; ἐλέλικτο, of a *brandished* spear, 13.558; ἀμφὶ δὲ πέπλος ἐλελίζετο ποσσίν *h.Cer*.183; μέγας δ' ἐλελίζετ' Ὄλυμπος *h.Hom*. l.c.; φόρμιγξ ἐλελιζομένα Pi.*P*.1.4. (In Hom. ἐλελ- may have been substituted for ἐϝελ- (ϝεϝελ- in ἐλέλικτο); cf. ἑλίσσω.)

⊛ **ἐλελίζω** (B), aor. ἠλέλιξα X.*An*.5.2.14, Ep. ἐλ- Call.*Del*.137:—*cry* ἐλελεῦ, hence, *raise the battle-cry*, τῷ Ἐνυαλίῳ X.*An*.1.8.18: generally, *raise a loud cry*, E.*Ph*.1514 (lyr.); of a shield, *ring*, Call. l.c.:—Med., of the nightingale, *trill her lay of sorrow*, E.*Hel*.1111 (lyr.): c. acc., Ἴτυν ἐλελιζομένη *trilling her lament for* Itys, Ar.*Av*.213 (lyr., but punctuation is dub.).

**ἐλελίστροφε**· εὔστροφε, δλόστροφε, Hsch.

**ἐλελισφᾰκ-ίτης** [ῑ] οἶνος wine *flavoured with sage*, Dsc.5.61. **-ον**, *τό*, = sq., Id.3.33, 4.103. II. = ψευδοδίκταμνον, Ps.-Dsc.3.32. ⊛ **-ος**, *ὁ*, *salvia*, *Salvia triloba*, Thphr.*HP*6.1.4, 6.2.5.

**ἐλελίχθ-ημα**, *ατος*, *τό*, (ἐλελίζω A) *violent shaking*, Hsch. **-ων**, *ον*, gen. *ονος*, (ἐλελίζω A) *earth-shaking*, τετραορία Pi.*P*.2.4; Ἐλέλιχθον, i.e. Poseidon, ib.6.50:—in S.*Ant*.153 Dionysus is called ὁ Θήβας ἐ. because *the ground shook* beneath the feet of his dancing bands.

**ἐλελόγχειν**, v. λαγχάνω.

⊛ **ἐλελύζω**, Aeol., = ὀλολ-, Sapph.*Supp*.20c.3.

**ἕλεμα**, *ατος*, *τό*, (ἑλεῖν) gloss on ἕλωρ, Sch.Il.17.667.

⊛ **ἕλεμος**· σπέρμα ὅπερ ἕψοντες Λάκωνες ἐσθίουσιν, Hsch.

**ἐλέναυς**, *ἡ*, *ship-destroying*, epith. of Helen, prob. for ἑλέναυς, A.*Ag*.689 (lyr.).

**ἐλένη,** ἡ, *torch,* Hsch.; cf. ἑλάνη. 2. *corposant, St. Elmo's fire,* Lyd.*Ost.*5. II. *wicker-basket,* to carry the sacred utensils at the feast of the Brauronian Artemis, Poll.10.191:—hence **ἐλενηφόρια,** *the feast itself,* ibid.

**Ἑλένια** (sc. ἱερά), τά, *feast in honour of Helen* in Laconia, Hsch.

**ἑλένιον,** τό, *calamint, Calamintha incana,* Chaerem.14.12, Thphr.*HP*6.6.2, Dsc.1.29. 2. *elecampane, Inula Helenium,* ib.28. 3. = σύμφυτον, Ps.-Dsc.4.9.

**ἑλένιος·** ἀγγεῖον χωροῦν τέταρτον, Hsch. **ἑλενοί·** κλήματα τὰ τῶν ἀμπέλων, Id.; cf. ἕλινος.

**Ἑλενοφόντης,** ου, ὁ, *slayer of Helen,* Sch.E.*Or.*1140.

**ἐλεοδύτης** [ῠ], ου, ὁ, *sacrificial cook* at Delos, Ath.4.173a.

**ἑλεόθρεπτος,** ον, (ἕλος) *marsh-bred,* σέλινον Il.2.776, Nic.*Th.*597.

**ἐλεοκόπος,** ὁ, dub. sens. in Lys.*Fr.*28. (Expld. either fr. ἐλεός I or as, = οἱ τὰ ἕλη κόπτοντες.)

**ἐλεόν,** Adv. *piteously,* Hes.*Op.*205: Comp. -ώτερον Hsch.

**ἐλεός,** ὁ, *kitchen table, dresser,* in pl., Il.9.215, Od.14.432:—later **ἐλεόν,** τό, Ar.*Eq.*152,169. II. a kind of *owl,* Arist.*HA*592$^{b}$11.

**ἔλεος,** ὁ, *pity, mercy, compassion,* Il.24.44, etc.: also in pl., Pl.*R.*606c, D.25.83; μ' ἔ. τινος ἐσῆλθε *pity for..,* E.*IA*491; ἔλεον ποιήσασθαι ἐπί τινι D.24.111; ἐλέου τυχεῖν παρά τινος Antipho 1.27:—later ἔλεος, τό, Plb.1.88.2, Lxx *Ge.*19.19, etc.: pl., ἐλέη, τά, ib.*Ps.*16(17).7; ἐ. ποιεῖν μετά τινος ib.*Ge.*24.12, al. (but masc. is also found, ib.*Ps.*83(84).12, Plb.33.11.3, Agatharch.83, Phld.*Rh.*1.65 S., *Ep.Jac.*2.13, etc.). II. personified, worshipped at Athens, Sch.S.*OC*260; at Epidaurus, *IG*4.1282; Ἔ. ἐπιεικὴς θεός Timocl.31. III. *object of compassion, piteous thing,* E.*Or.*832.

**ἐλεπόδιον·** εἶδός τι βάνανσος (fort. βαλαυστίου), Hsch. **ἐλέποκες·** ἰχθὺς ὅμοιος φυκίδι, Id.

⊛ **ἑλέπολις,** poet. **ἑλέπτολις,** ι, εως, *city-destroying,* epith. of Helen, A.*Ag.*689 (lyr.); of Iphigenia, E.*IA*1476 (lyr.), 1511 (lyr.); of Lamia, *Com.Adesp.*303. II. fem. Subst., *engine for sieges,* invented by Demetrius Poliorcetes, D.S.20.48, Plu.*Demetr.*21, Ph.*Bel.*95.39, Vitr.10.16.4, etc.; ἄνευ μηχανῆς καὶ ἑ. Alciphr.3.45: pl., ἑ. μηχαναί D.H.9.68. 2. metaph., of a person, ἑ. τῆς Ἑλλάδος Hp.*Ep.*11; also ἡ τῶν ἀνοσίων ἑ. τοῦτο (sc. πένθος) Ph.2.191.

**ἑλεσπίς,** ίδος, ἡ, = ἕλος, *marsh-lands, meadow,* A.R.1.1266.

**ἑλετός,** ή, όν, (ἑλεῖν) *that can be taken* or *caught,* Il.9.409, Max.Tyr.18.3. 2. = αἱρετός, Procop.*Pers.*1.16.

⊛ **Ἐλευθεραί,** αἱ, *Eleutherae,* on frontier of Attica and Boeotia:—hence **Ἐλευθερεύς,** έως, ὁ, title of Dionysus, Paus.1.38.8, etc.

⊛ **ἐλευθ-ερία,** Ion. **-ίη,** ἡ, *freedom, liberty,* Pi.*P.*1.61, Hdt.1.62,95; ἐλευθερίας φῶς A.*Ch.*809 (lyr.), cf. 863 (anap.); δι' ἐλευθερίας μόλις ἐξῆλθες, i.e. μόλις ἠλευθερώθης, S.*El.*1509 (anap.); ὑπῆρξαν ἐλευθερίας τῇ Ἑλλάδι And.1.142; *freedom from* a thing, ἀπὸ πασῶν ἀρχῶν Pl.*Lg.*698a; τινός Id.*R.*329c, cf. *AP*6.228 (Adaeus). b. *manumission,* ἡ εἰκοστὴ τῶν ἐ., = Lat. *vicesima manumissionum, BGU*326ii11 (ii A.D.). 2. *licence,* ἀκολασία καὶ ἐ. Pl.*Grg.*492c; of Diogenes, Jul.*Or.*6.185c. 3. later, = ἐλευθεριότης, *UPZ*62.7. 4. name of a *dance,* S.E.*M.*1.293. **-έρια** (sc. ἱερά), τά, *festival of Liberty,* held every four years at Plataea, in memory of the battle there, Posidipp.29, D.S.11.29, Paus.9.2.6, etc.; at Syracuse, in memory of the restoration of the republic, D.S.11.72; at Samos, in honour of Eros, Erxias ap. Ath.13.562a: generally, ἐ. θύειν Henioch.5.10. II. *thanksgiving for liberty, IG*9(2).1034 (Thess.). **-εριάζω,** *speak* or *act like a freeman,* Pl.*Lg.*701e, Arist.*Pol.*1314$^{a}$8, Ph.1.380; ἐ. τοῖς λόγοις Plu.2.6e; πρός τινα Luc.*Cat.*1; ἐλευθεριάξαντας (Dor. aor.) Epimenid.ap.D.L.1.113; *to be free,* ἀπὸ τοῦ πλούτου Crat.*Ep.*8; esp. from public burdens, *PFlor.*382.7 (iii A.D.): c. gen., πολυτελείας Chaerem.ap.Porph.*Abst.*4.8. ⊛ **-ερικός,** ή, όν, *free,* πολιτεία Pl.*Lg.*701e (Sup.); τὸ ἐ. καὶ ἀνελεύθερον ib.919e. ⊛ **-έριος,** ον, also α, ον X.*Smp.*8.16:—*speaking* or *acting like a freeman, free-spirited,* ἐ. καὶ δημωφελής Democr.282, etc.; ἀνδρεῖοι καὶ ἐ. Pl.*Lg.*635d; opp. δουλοπρεπής, X.*Mem.*2.8.4 (Comp.); of certain animals, as the lion, ἐ. καὶ ἀνδρεῖα καὶ εὐγενῆ Arist.*HA*488$^{b}$16. b. esp. *freely giving, bountiful,* ἐ. εἰς χρήματα X.*Smp.*4.15 (Comp.), cf. Arist.*EN*1120$^{a}$8, etc. 2. of pursuits, etc., *fit for a freeman, liberal,* πτηνῶν θήρας.. ἔρως οὐ σφόδρα ἐ. Pl.*Lg.*823e, cf. *Grg.*485b; ἐπιστήμη Id.*Ax.*369b (Sup.); τέχναι Plu.2.122d; βίος Men.408 (dub.); διαγωγή Arist.*Pol.*1339$^{b}$5; παιδεία ib.1338$^{a}$32; πρᾶξις, ἔργα, ib.1263$^{b}$12, *Oec.*1344$^{a}$28; ἡδοναὶ -ώταται, κινήσεις -ώτεραι, Id.*EN*1118$^{b}$4, *Pol.*1340$^{b}$10; τὸ ἐ., = ἐλευθεριότης, X.*Mem.*3.10.5: prov., ὕδωρ πίοιμι ἐ., i.e. may I become *free,* because slaves set free at Argos were then first allowed to drink of the spring Κυνάδρα, Antiph.25. 3. of appearance, *frank, noble,* εὐπρεπής τε ἰδεῖν καὶ ἐ. X.*Mem.*2.1.22, cf. *Lac.*11.3 (Comp.); ἵππος Id.*Eq.*10.17. II. Adv. -ίως, ζῆν Arist.*Pol.*1326$^{b}$31; τεθραμμένους Isoc.4.49, 7.43 (prob.): Comp. -ιώτερον, ζῆν X.*Mem.*1.6.3: Sup. -ιώτατα ib.4.8.1. III. Ζεὺς Ἐ. Zeus *the Deliverer,* Pi.*O.*12.1, Simon.140.4, Hdt.3.142, etc. IV. Ἐ., ὁ (sc. μήν), = Ἐλευθεριών, *SIG*1044.26. **-εριότης,** ητος, ἡ, *the character of an* ἐλευθέριος, esp. *freeness in giving, liberality,* Pl.*R.*402c, Arist.*EN*1119$^{b}$22, etc.; ἡ τῶν χρημάτων ἐ. Pl.*Tht.*144d: generally, *generosity,* ἡ ἐ. τῆς ὑπουργίας Plu.*Pomp.*73. **-εριών,** ῶνος, ὁ (sc. μήν), name of month at Halicarnassus, *Inscr.Cos* 13. **-εριωτικός,** ή, όν, *claiming freedom,* λόγος Him.*Ecl.*7 tit.

**ἐλευθερό-γλωσσος,** ον, *free of speech,* Vett.Val.16.31. **-λάτομοι** [ᾱ], οἱ, *free quarrymen, PPetr.*3 p.105 (iii B.C.); δεκάταρχοι τῶν ἐ. ib.2 p.33 (iii B.C.). ⊛ **-παις,** ὁ, ἡ, gen. παιδος, *having free children,* Βενέτων δῆμος *APl.*5.359. **-ποιός,** όν, *making free,* θεός Ph.1.401; δόγμα Arr.*Epict.*4.1.176; *creating freedom,* Plot.6.8.12. **-πρᾱσίου** δίκη, ἡ, prosecution *for selling a freeman as a slave,* Poll.3.78. **-πρέπεια,** ἡ, *disposition of a freeman,* condemned by ib.119. **-πρεπής,** ές, *worthy of a freeman,* Pl.*Alc.*1.135c. Adv. -πῶς ibid.

⊛ **ἐλεύθερος,** α, ον (ος, ον A.*Ag.*328, E.*El.*868): later **ἐλαύθερος** *BCH*22.76 (Delph.); Elean **ἐλεύθαρος** *Schwyzer* 416.3:—*free,* Hom. has the word only in Il. in two phrases, ἐλεύθερον ἦμαρ the day *of freedom,* i.e. *freedom,* Il.6.455, 16.831, al.; and κρητὴρ ἐλεύθερος the cup drunk *to freedom,* 6.528; ἐ. πιοῦσαν οἶνον ἀποθανεῖν Xenarch.5 codd. Ath. (fort. -ριον, cf. ἐλευθέριος I. 2); of persons, Alc.*Supp.*25.11, Hdt.1.6, A.*Pr.*50, S.*Aj.*1020, Th.8.15, etc.: Comp., X.*Cyr.*8.3.21: Sup., Id.*Hier.*1.16; τὸ ἐ. *freedom,* Hdt 7.103, etc.; τοὐλεύθερον E.*Supp.*438: c. gen., *free* or *freed from* a thing, φόνου, πημάτων, φόβου, A.*Eu.*603 codd., *Ch.*1060, E.*Hec.*869; αἰτίας Men.*Sam.*272; ἔξω αἰτίας ἐ. S.*Ant.*445; ἐ. ἀπ' ἀλλήλων *independent,* X.*Cyr.*3.2.23, Pl.*Lg.*832d. b. ἐλευθέρα, ἡ, *married woman,* Ath.13.571d; *wife, POxy.*1872.8 (v/vi A.D.); but, *freedwoman, IG*14.2490 (Vienne). c. *free,* of cities, in Roman Law, *BGU*316.3 (iv A.D.). 2. of things, *free, open to all,* ἀγορά X.*Cyr.*1.2.3; ἐ. φυλακή, = Lat. *libera custodia,* D.S.4.46; περιωπή Ael.*NA*15.5; *unencumbered,* of property, D.35.21, *IG*9(1).32.10 (Stiris), *SIG*364.36 (Ephesus, iii B.C.). 3. ἐλεύθερον εἶναί τινι, c. inf., *legally permissible, open to..,* ib.45.42 (Halic., v B.C.). II. = ἐλευθέριος, *fit for a freeman, free, frank,* φρήν Pi.*P.*2.57; ἐλευθερωτέρη ὑπόκρισις Hdt.1.116; ἐλεύθερα βάζειν A.*Pers.*593 (lyr.); ὦ μηδὲν ὑγιὲς μηδ' ἐ. φρονῶν S.*Ph.*1006; δούλη μέν, εἴρηκεν δ' ἐ. λόγον Id.*Tr.*63, cf. *El.*1256; φρονήματα Pl.*R.*567a; βάσανοι ἐ. tortures *such as might be used to a freeman,* Id.*Lg.*946c (so φάσγανα E.*Fr.*495.38); τὸ ἐ. Pl.*Mx.*245c: freq. in Adv. -ρως, εἰπεῖν Hdt.5.93, al.; χαίρειν.. καὶ γελᾶν ἐ. S.*El.*1300; τεθραμμένους Isoc.7.43 codd. (fort. -ερίως); παιδευθεὶς ἐ. Aeschin.3.154 codd. (fort. -ερίως); ἐ. δούλευε, δοῦλος οὐκ ἔσει Men.857; ἐλεύθεροι ἐλευθέρως free and *like free men,* Pl.*Lg.*919e. (Cf. Lat. *līber,* fr. Ital. *loufero- (cf. Osc. *Luvfreis* 'Liberi'), I.-E. *(e)leudh-ero-*: the connexion with Slav. *liud,* OHG. *liut,* etc. 'people' is doubtful.)

**ἐλευθεροστομ-έω,** *to be free of speech,* A.*Pr.*182 (lyr.), E.*Andr.*153; in later Prose, Ph.1.474, al. **-ία,** ἡ, *freedom of speech,* D.H.6.72. **-ος,** ον, *free-spoken,* γλῶσσα A.*Supp.*948.

**ἐλευθερόψῡχος,** ον, *free-souled,* Tz.*H.*10.620.

⊛ **ἐλευθερ-όω,** *set free,* τὰς Ἀθήνας Hdt.5.62; Ἰωνίην Id.4.137; πατρίδα A.*Pers.*403; πόλιν Id.*Ch.*1046, D.21.144; δούλους Th.8.15, etc.; ἐ. τὸν ἔσπλουν *set* the entrance *free, clear* it, Id.3.51; *release* a debtor, Hdt.6.59; τό γ' εἰς ἑαυτὸν πᾶν ἐλευθεροῖ στόμα he *keeps* his tongue altogether *free,* i.e. does not commit himself by speech, S.*OT*706; *free from blame, acquit,* τινά X.*HG*1.7.26:—Pass., *to be set free,* Hdt.1.95,127, al.; τυράννων Id.5.62; *indulge in licence,* Pl.*R.*575a. 2. c. gen., *set free, release from,* φόνου E.*Hipp.*1449; χρεῶν Pl.*R.*566e; ἀρότρου βοῦν Hld.5.23; also ἐλευθεροῦντες ἐκ δρασμῶν πόδα, i.e. ceasing to flee, E.*HF*1010:—Pass., τῶνδε τῶν τόπων ἐ. Pl.*Phd.*114b; ἀπὸ τῶν πλουσίων Id.*R.*569a. **-ωμα,** ατος, τό, *release from,* κακῶν Procop.Gaz.p.141 B. **-ωσις,** εως, ἡ, *liberation,* Hdt.9.45; ἀπό τινος Th.3.10; δούλων ἐ. ποιεῖσθαι Arist.*Pol.*1315$^{a}$37, cf. *POxy.*48.2 (i A.D.), etc.: pl., Plu.*Galb.*5. II. *licence,* Pl.*R.*561a. **-ωτέον,** *one must set free,* Plb.18.45.9. ⊛ **-ωτής,** οῦ, ὁ, *liberator,* Max.Tyr.21.6, Luc.*Vit.Auct.*8, D.C.41.57.

⊛ **Ἐλευθία, Ἐλευθώ,** v. Εἰλείθυια.

⊛ **ἐλεύθω,** causal of stem ἐλυθ- (cf. ἔρχομαι), *bring,* Dor. fut. ἐλευσίω· οἴσω, Hsch., Dor. 3 pl. aor. ἐλεύσαν Ibyc.*Oxy.*1790.18; cf. ἐπελεύθω.

**ἐλευσέαν·** τὴν βρυωνίαν, Hsch. (ἐλεψέαν poscit ordo).

⊛ **Ἐλευσίνιος,** α, ον, *of Eleusis, h.Cer.*266, Hdt.9.57, etc.; epith. of Zeus in Ionia, Hsch.; of Artemis in Sicily and Antioch, Id., Lib.*Or.*11.109; but mostly of Demeter, Antim.63, etc.; Δηὼ Ἐ. S.*Ant.*1120 (lyr.); Ἐλευσείνιαι (sic) *Demeter and Cora, IG*4.955.14 (Epid.): hence, II. Ἐλευσίνιον, τό, *their temple at Eleusis,* And.1.110, *IG*$1^{2}$.6.129. III. Ἐλευσίνια, τά, *their festivals,* ib.$1^{2}$.5, $2^{2}$.847.24, Hyp.*Fr.*112, Paus.4.33.5, etc.: prov., Ἀττικοὶ τὰ Ἐ., of groups of persons confabulating, Duris 95 J.: Lacon. Ἐλευhύνια, τά, *IG*5(1).213.11 (v B.C.). IV. Ἐλευσίνιος, ὁ (sc. μήν), name of month in Crete, *GDI*5183: also spelt Ἐλευσύνιος *SIG*712.8 (Olus), and so in Thera, *Test.Epict.*2.7, 3.3. [σῑ, exc. in *h.Cer.* l. c., S.*Ant.*1120 (lyr.).]

⊛ **Ἐλευσίς,** ῖνος, ἡ, *Eleusis,* an old city of Attica, sacred to Demeter and Cora, first in *h.Cer.*97; late Ἐλευσίν Str.9.1.12 codd. (but Ἐλευσίς 9.1.20), Corn.*ND*28. II. Advs. **Ἐλευσῖνι** *at Eleusis, IG*$1^{2}$.76.10, al., And.1.111, Lys.6.4, etc.; later ἐν Ἐ. *IG*$2^{2}$.1028.11, al.: **Ἐλευσῖνάδε** *to Eleusis,* Lys.12.52, X.*HG*2.4.24: **Ἐλευσῖνόθεν** *from Eleusis,* And.1.111, Lys.6.45.

**ἔλευσις,** εως, ἡ, *coming, arrival,* εἰς βίον Corn.*ND*28, cf. Tz.*H.*7.572, Sch.A.R.4.887, Hsch. 2. *the Advent* of Christ, *Act.Ap.*7.52.

**ἐλευσίω,** v. ἐλεύθω.

**ἐλευστέον,** (ἔρχομαι) *one must come,* Lxx 2*Ma.*6.17.

**ἐλεφαίρομαι,** old Ep. Verb, perh. connected with ὀλοφώϊος (q.v.), *cheat with empty hopes,* said of the *false* dreams that come through the *ivory* gate (with play on ἐλέφας, cf. κραίνω), οἱ μέν κ' ἔλθωσι διὰ πριστοῦ ἐλέφαντος, οἵ ῥ' ἐλεφαίρονται Od.19.565: generally, *cheat, overreach,* ἐλεφηράμενος.. Τυδεΐδην Il.23.388. II. of the Nemean lion, ἐλεφαίρετο φῦλ' ἀνθρώπων he *used to destroy* them, Hes.*Th.*330. (Act. only in Hsch., who also has aor. 1 ἐλεφῆραι· ἀπατῆσαι.)

**ἐλεφαντ-ᾰγωγός,** ὁ, *elephant-driver,* Poll.1.140. ⊛ **-άρχης,** ου, ὁ, *commander of a squadron of sixteen elephants,* Ascl.*Tact.*9, Phylarch.31 J., Plu.*Demetr.*25, Lxx 2*Ma.*14.12. **-αρχία,** ἡ, *squadron of sixteen elephants,* Ael.*Tact.*23. **-ειος,** ον, *of an ele-*

*phant*, Dsc.2.76.17, Opp.*C*.2.500. **-εύς**, έως, ὁ, *ivory-worker*, *PPar.* 5 xliii. **-ηγός**, όν, *transporting elephants* (sc. νῆες), Agatharch. 83, cf. *PPetr.* 2 p.135 (iii B.C.). **-ῖασις**, εως, ἡ, the disease *elephantiasis*, Cels.3.25, Dsc.2.70.3, Plu.2.731a. **-ιασμός**, ὁ, = foreg., *EM*561.4. **-ιάω**, *suffer from elephantiasis*, Phld.*Rh*.2.120 S., Dsc. 1.77, Ptol.*Tetr*.151, Antyll.ap.Orib.6.27.2. **-ίνεος**, α, ον, *of elephants*, ὀδόντες *IG*3.1376. ⊛ **-ῖνος**, η, ον, *of ivory*, Alc.33.1, Ar. *Eq*.1169, *Pl*.815, al.; δίφρος ἐ., = Lat. *sella curulis*, Plb.6.53.9 (pl.), al.; οἶκοι ἐ. LXX *Am*.3.15; τὸ ἐ. the *substance of ivory*, Pl.*Hp.Ma.* 290c. 2. *white as ivory*, μέτωπον *Anacreont*.15.12; τάριχος Crates 29. **-ίσκιον**, τό, Dim. of ἐλέφας, *young elephant*, Ael.*NA*8. 27. **-ιστής**, οῦ, ὁ, *elephant-driver*, Arist.*HA*497b28 (cf. Demetr. *Eloc*.97), Porph.*Abst*.3.6. II. *shield of elephant-hide*, App.*Pun*.46.

**ἐλεφαντό-βοτος**, ον, *feeding elephants*, γαῖα Nonn.*D*.39.26. **-δετος**, ον, *inlaid with ivory*, δόμοι E.*IA*582 (lyr.); φόρμιγξ Ar.*Av*.219 (lyr.). **-θήρας**, ου, ὁ, *elephant-hunter*, Agatharch.54 (pl.), *Sammelb.* 4144, 4151. **-κομία**, ἡ, *care of elephants*, Ael.*NA*6.8. **-κωπος**, ον, *ivory-hilted*, ξιφομάχαιρα Theopomp.Com.25; ξίφη Luc.*Gall.* 26. **-μᾰχία**, ἡ, *battle of elephants*, Plu.*Pomp*.52. **-μάχος** [μᾰ], ον, *fighting against elephants*, ζῷον Str.16.4.15, cf. D.S.3.26. **-νωτος**, ον, *ivory-backed*, ἡνίαι Eust.583.44. **-πηχυς**, ὁ, ἡ, *ivory-armed*, Max.Tyr.14.6. **-πους**, ὁ, ἡ, gen. ποδος, *ivory-footed*, κλίνη Pl.Com. 208; τράπεζα Luc.*Gall*.14; ἐλεφαντόποδες τὰ ἐνήλατα καὶ κλιντῆρες Ph.1.666. **-τόμος**, ὁ, *ivory-cutter*, Opp.*C*.2.514.

**ἐλεφαντ-ουργική** (sc. τέχνη), ἡ, *the art of ivory-working*, Sch.Paul. Al.*P*.1. ⊛ **-ουργός**, όν, *working in ivory*, ὄργανα Philostr.*VA*5.20: -γός, ὁ, *ivory-worker*, A.D.*Pron*.31.19, Them.*Or*.18.224b: **-ουργία**, ἡ, *ivory-working*, Vett.Val.3.23.

**ἐλεφαντο-φάγος** [ᾰ], ὁ, *elephant-eater*, Agatharch.55, Str.16.4. 10. **-φανής**, ές, *like ivory*, ὀδόντες Eust.1877.42. **-χρως**, ὁ, ἡ, gen. -χρωτος, *ivory-coloured*, ὀδόντες ib.36.

**ἐλεφαντ-όω**, *inlay with ivory*, τράπεζα ἠλεφαντωμένη *IG*1².283. **-ώδης**, ες, *like an elephant*, ὦτα Aret.*SD*2.13. **-ωσις**, εως, ἡ, = *personacia* (i.e. ἄρκιον), *Gloss.* **-ωτός**, ή, όν, *inlaid with ivory*, *IG* 2.706 *A* b 14.

⊛ **ἐλέφας**, αντος, ὁ (θήλεια ἐ. Phylarch.36 J.): irreg. gen. ἐλεφάντου *BCH*35.286 (Delos, ii B.C.); dat. pl. -τοις LXX 1 *Ma*.1.17 (v.l.):—*elephant*, first mentioned by Hdt. as a native of Africa, 3.114, 4.191; ἐλέφαντος ὀδόντες Id.3.97; of the Indian *elephant*, first in Arist. *Cael*.298a13, *HA*610a15, cf. Paus.1.12.4. II. in Hom. only of *elephant's tusk*, *ivory*, Il.5.583, cf. Hes.*Sc*.141, Pi.*O*.1.27, Pl.*R*.373a, *GDI*5500, etc.: Aeol. **ἐλέφαις** Sapph.*Supp*.20a10. III. = ἐλεφαντίασις, Aret.*SD*2.13, *IG*3.1423, Gal.15.331. IV. a *precious stone*, Thphr.*Lap*.37. V. a kind of *cup*, Damox.1.1. VI. = ἐλεφάντωσις, Apul.*Herb*.36.

**ἐλεφιτίς**, ὁ, a *fish*, corrupt in Hp.*Vict*.2.48 (ἀλφηστὴς Coraes).

**ἐλέχει**· ψηλαφᾷ, Hsch. **ἐλεών**· θάμνος, Id. II. the *snake* called σκυτάλη, Id.

**ἐλέωτρις**, ιδος, ἡ, a *fish of the Nile*, Ath.7.312b.

**ἕλη**, ἡ, = εἵλη, ἀλέα (B), Ar.*V*.772 (Sch. Rav.), Eust.667.22, 1573.45.

**ἕλη, ἕλῃαι**, v. αἱρέω.

**ἐληγός**, ὁ, *oil-merchant*, *OGI*521.25 (v/vi A.D.).

**ἐληθερέω**, = εἱλ-, Gal.19.97 (Pass.).

**ἐλήλᾰκα, ἐλήλαμαι, ἐληλέδατο** or **-άδατο**, v. ἐλαύνω. **ἐλήλεγμαι**, v. ἐλέγχω. **ἐλήλιγμαι**, v. ἑλίσσω. **ἐλήλυθα, εἰλήλουθα, ἐλθεῖν, ἐλθέμεν, ἐλθέμεναι**, v. ἔρχομαι.

**ἐλθετέον**, = ἐλευστέον, Herod.Med.ap.Orib.10.4.1, Philum.ap.Aët. 9.12.

**ἐλθετῶς**· ἀντὶ τοῦ ἐλθέ, Σαλαμίνιοι, Hsch. **ἐλίβοτρυς**· ἄμπελός τις μέλαινα, Id.

**ἑλῐ́γ-δην**, Adv., (ἑλίσσω) *whirling, rolling*, A.*Pr*.882 (anap.); cf. εἰλίγδην. ⊛ **-μα**, ατος, τό, *fold, wrapping*, ἱμάντων ἑλίγμασι, of straps *bound round* the leg, Ephipp.14.9; στρουθωτὰ ἑ. Sophr.100. II. *bracelets*, in pl., Hsch., prob. in Sapph.*Supp*.20a.8. III. *curl, lock* of hair, *AP*6.211 (Leon.). IV. *depression of the skull without fracture*, = θλάσμα, Sor.*Fract*.1. V. *packet*, σμύρνης καὶ ἀλόης v.l. in *Ev.Jo*.19.39. **-μᾰτώδης**, ες, = ἑλικοειδής, *twisted*, *Lex. de Spir.* p.195 V. **-μός**, Ep. εἱλ-, ὁ, *winding, convolution*, of the Labyrinth, Hdt.2.148; πολλοὺς ἑ. ἄνω καὶ κάτω πλανᾶσθαι X.*Cyr*.1.3.4; of the gut, ἑ. ἔχει Arist.*HA*532b7; of the Fallopian tubes, ib.510b19; of the brain, Erasistr.ap.Gal.5.603; of a snake, Sch.Nic.*Th*.159; of dancers' feet, Orph.*H*.38.12: generally, *rotatory motion*, Plu.2. 404f; ὀφθαλμῶν ἑλιγμοί *rolling* of eyes, Procop.Gaz.p.151 B.; ἑ. καὶ ἀναστροφαὶ ὀργάνων Max.Tyr.19.4: pl., *the plies* of a knot, Plu.*Alex.* 18; ῥευμάτων ἑλιγμοί Id.*Caes*.19; ὀρῶν Lib.*Or*.61.8.

**ἔλιγξ**, v.l. for ὄλιγξ, Poll.2.67.

**Ἐλιεύς**, ὁ, title of Zeus at Thebes, Hsch.

**ἑλῐκ-άμπυξ**, ῠκος, ὁ, ἡ, *wreathed with a circlet*, Σεμέλα Pi.*Fr*.75.20; θεά Id.*Pae*.3.15. **-άστερος**, ον, *with circling orbit*, epith. of the moon, Man.4.224. **-αυγής**, ές, *with circling rays*, κύκλος, of the sun, Orph.*Fr*.236.1; of the moon, *Cat.Cod.Astr*.1.173. ⊛ **-η**, ἡ, (ἕλιξ) *winding*: hence, I. *the constellation of the Great Bear*, from its *revolving round* the pole, Arat.37, A.R.3.1195. II. *convolution* of a spiral shell, Arist.*HA*524b12, *PA*680a22, al.; of the bowels, ib.682a15; of the ear, Id.*GA*781b15. III. in Arcadia, *crack willow*, *Salix fragilis*, from its pliant nature, Thphr.*HP*3.13.7. **-ηδόν**, Adv. = ἑλίγδην, *spirally*, ib.1, Luc.*Hist.Conscr*.19. II. *revolving in a circle*, Nonn.*D*.1.195. **-ίας**, ου, ὁ, *forked lightning*, Arist.*Mu.* 395a27 (pl.).

⊛ **ἑλῐκο-βλέφᾰρος**, ον, *with ever-moving eyes, quick-glancing*, epith. of Aphrodite, *h.Hom*.6.19, Hes.*Th*.16, Pi.*Fr*.123.5; of Alcmene, Id.*P*.4.172. **-βόστρῡχος**, ον, *with curling hair*, Ar.*Fr*.334 (lyr.). **-γρᾰφέω**, *describe a curve*, of the Nile, Anon.*Geog.Comp.* 31. **-δρόμος**, ον, *running in curves, twisting*, Orph.*H*.9.10; *circular*, E.*Ba*.1067 (cj. for ἕλκει δρόμον). **-ειδής**, poet. εἱλικ-, ές, *of winding* or *spiral form*, [σαυνία] D.S.5.30; γραμμή Plu.*Num*.13; of planetary orbits, Cleom.1.4; ἔντερον Aret.*SD*2.3; τόποι S.E.*P*.1. 126; σελήνη D.L.7.144. Adv. -δῶς Cleom.1.4, Dsc.2.165, Olymp. in *Mete*.13.9. **-κέρατος**, ον, *with curled horns*, Hsch. s.v. ἕλικας. **-πέτᾰλος**, ον, *with twining leaves*, prob. in Sacerd.p.540.1 K. **-ρροος**, ον, *with winding stream*, Orac.ap.Paus.4.20.1.

⊛ **ἑλῐκός**, ή, όν, *eddying*, of water, Call.*Fr*.290 (Sup.); χορεία *Hymn. Is*.155.

**ἑλῐκοστέφᾰνος**, ον, *with twisted diadem*, κούρα B.8.62.

**ἑλικ-τήρ**, ῆρος, ὁ, *anything twisted*: *ear-ring*, Ar.*Fr*.320.14, Lys. 12.19, *IG*2.747.5. **-τήριον**, τό, = foreg., Apollon.*Lex.Hom.* s.v. ἕλικας. **-τικός**, ή, όν, *coiled*, τὸ ἑ. τῆς οὐρᾶς Doroth. in *Cat. Cod.Astr*.2.158. ⊛ **-τός** (or εἱλ-), ή, όν, *rolled, twisted, wreathed*, βοῦς κεράεσσιν ἑλικτάς *h.Merc*.192; δράκων S.*Tr*.12, cf. *Pae.Delph*.19; κισσός E.*Ph*.652 codd. (lyr.); στέφανος Chaerem.7; βόστρυχος Theodect.6.4; κλῖμαξ ἑ. *winding* staircase, Callix.1; ἑ. κύτος a *wheeled* ark, E.*Ion*40; εἱλικτὸν κρούειν πόδα, of dancers (cf. ἑλίσσω 1.3), Id.*El.* 180 (lyr.); σῦριγξ περὶ χεῖλος ἑλικτά Theoc.1.129; ἑλικτά, of insects *that can roll* or *double themselves up*, Arist.*PA*682b24, 692a2: Comp. ἑλικτότερος Hsch. II. metaph., *tortuous, not straightforward*, ἑλικτὰ κοὐδὲν ὑγιές E.*Andr*.448; *obscure*, Lyc.1466. **-ώδης**, ες, = ἑλικοειδής, Plu.2.648f, Nonn.*D*.1.370. **-ων**, ωνος, ὁ, *thread spun from the distaff to the spindle*, Hsch. II. a *nine-stringed instrument*, Aristid.Quint.3.3, Ptol.*Harm*.2.2.

⊛ **Ἑλῐκών**, ῶνος, ὁ (Ϝελ- Corinn.*Supp*.1.29), *Helicon*, a hill in Boeotia, the seat of the Muses, Hes.*Op*.639, etc.:—hence ⊛ **Ἑλῐκωνιάδες** (sc. παρθένοι), αἱ, *dwellers on Helicon*, i.e. *Muses*, Pi.*Pae.Fr*.16.14, *I*.2.34; Μοῦσαι Hes.*Op*.658, *Th*.1, *CIG*3067.10 (Teos):—also ⊛ **Ἑλῐκωνίδες** Νύμφαι S.*OT*1108 (lyr.); Μοῦσαι E.*HF*791 (lyr.), *IG*4.682. 13 (Hermione): sg., of a poet's *reed-pen*, *AP*9.162. II. Ἑλικωνιάς, άδος, ἡ, = ὑάκινθος, Ps.-Dsc.4.62.

⊛ **Ἑλῐκώνιος**, α, ον, *Heliconian, of Helicon*, παρθένοι Pi.*I*.8(7).63. II. title of Poseidon, Ἑ. ἄναξ Il.20.404: acc. to Sch., from Helice in Achaia, where he was especially honoured, 8.203 (but cf. Aristarch. ap.*EM*547.16, *h.Hom*.22.3).

**ἑλῐκ-ωπός**, όν, = ἑλικώψ, Orph.*H*.6.9. **-ωτός**, ή, όν, *threaded like a screw*, Orib.49.20.6. ⊛ **-ωψ**, ωπος, ὁ, ἡ, fem. **-ῶπις**, ιδος, *with rolling eyes, quick-glancing*, as a mark of youth and spirits (not in Od.), ἑλίκωπες Ἀχαιοί Il.1.389, al.; ἑλικῶπις κούρη ib.98; νύμφη Hes.*Th*.298, cf. Sapph.*Supp*.20a.5; παρθένοι, Ἀφροδίτη, Pi.*Pae*.2.99, *P*.6.1.

⊛ **ἔλῐνος**, ὁ, (ἑλίσσω) *vine-tendril*, Philet.ap.*EM*330.39. 2. fem., *the vine*, Nic.*Al*.181, Opp.*C*.4.262, D.P.1157. [Later ἔλινος prob. in Nonn.*D*.12.299.]

**ἐλῐνότροπος**, ον, *like vine-tendrils*, *Hymn.Is*.18.

⊛ **ἐλῐνοφόρος**, Ep. εἰλ-, ον, *bearing vine-tendrils*, κόρυμβος Nonn.*D*. 16.278; Διόνυσος ib.17.333.

⊛ **ἐλῐνύες**, αἱ, *days of rest, holidays*: ἐλινύας ἄγειν, of the Roman *supplicatio*, Plb.21.2.1.

**Ἐλινύμενος**, title of Zeus at Cyrene, Hsch.

⊛ **ἐλῐνύω**, Hdt.1.67, Hp.*Acut*.47, A.*Pr*.53: impf. ἐλίνυον Hdt.8.71, ἠλ- App.*Mith*.43; Ion. ἐλινύεσκον A.R.1.589: fut. -ύσω [ῡ] Pi.*N*.5.1, *I*.2.46: aor. ἐλίνῡσα Hdt.7.56, A.*Pr*.529 (lyr.), etc.:—Poet. and Ion. Verb, also used in Trag. and late Prose (as Plu.*Num*.14), *keep holiday, take rest, repose*, freq. in Hp., as *Acut*.47; μὴ ἐλινύειν Hdt.1.67; διέβη ὁ στρατὸς.. ἐλινύσας οὐδένα χρόνον without any *cessation*, Id.7. 56; ἐλινύσοντα.. ἀγάλματα *to stand unmoved* on their pedestals, Pi. *N*.5.1, cf. *I*.2.46; ὡς μή σ' ἐλινύοντα προσδερχθῇ πατήρ see thee *standing idle*, A.*Pr*.53; οὐκ ἐλινύειν ἐχρῆν Ar.*Th*.598; ἐ. μίαν ἡμέραν Orac. ap.D.21.53. 2. c. gen. rei, *rest from*, πλήθεος βρώμης Hp.*Acut.* 47 (v.l. (ἐκ)); ἔργων D.H.1.33. 3. c. part., *rest* or *cease from* doing, ἐλίνυον οὐδένα χρόνον.. ἐργαζόμενοι Hdt.8.71, cf. A.*Pr*.529 (lyr.), Call.*Cer*.48, *Fr*.248. [υ of the impf. short in A.R.1.862, long ib.589, indeterminate in Trag.] (Written ἐλιννύω in some codd.)

⊛ **ἕλιξ** (A), ῐκος, ὁ, ἡ, as Adj., *twisted, curved*: in Hom. and Hes., as in S.*Aj*.374 (lyr.), Theoc.25.127, epith. of oxen, commonly understood of their *twisted, crumpled horns*, cf. ἑλικτός 1; also expld. of the movement of their bodies as they walk, *rolling*: freq. coupled with εἰλίποῦς, cf. Il.12.293 and Sch. ad loc., etc.; ἕλιξ abs., = βοῦς, E.*Ba.* 1170 (lyr.): later of various objects, ποταμός Pi.ap.Sch.Il.*Oxy*.221 ix 15; ἕλικα ἀνὰ χλόαν on the *tangled* grass, E.*Hel*.180 (lyr., cf. sq. III); δρόμος Nonn.*D*.2.263; σειρή Tryph.322.

⊛ **ἕλιξ** (B), poet. **εἷλιξ**, ῐκος, ἡ, (ἑλίσσω) *anything which assumes a spiral shape*: once in Hom., γναμπτάς θ' ἕλικας, of *armlets* or *ear-rings*, Il.18.401 (cf. ἑλικτήρ), cf. *h.Ven*.87, Arist.*Mir*.840b20:—afterwards in various relations: II. *whirl, convolution*, ἕλικες στεροπῆς *flashes of forked* lightning, A.*Pr*.1083 (anap.); of *circular* or *spiral motion*, αἱ κινήσεις καὶ ἕλικες τοῦ οὐρανοῦ Arist.*Metaph*.998a5; ἕλικα ἐκτυλίσσειν Ti.Locr.97c; *wreath* of smoke, A.R.1.438. III. *tendril of the vine*, Thphr.*CP*2.18.2; βοσκὰς εὐφύλλων ἑλίκων E.*Hel*.1331 (lyr.); βότρυος ἕλικα πανσίπονον *the clustering* grape, Ar.*Ra*.1321 (lyr.). 2. *tendril* of ivy, Id.*Th*.1000; also, *ivy*, *Hedera Helix*, Thphr.*HP*3.18.6, 7. 8.1. 3. *curl* or *lock of hair*, *AP*10.19 (Apollonid.), 12.10 (Strat.), *Anacreont*.16.6. 4. *coil* of a serpent, E.*HF*399 (lyr.): pl., *feelers* of

the polypus, *AP*9.14 (Antiphil. Byz.). **5.** *volute* on the capital of a column, Callix.1, Vitr.4.1.12. **IV.** *convolution* of a spiral shell (cf. ἑλίκη II), Arist.*HA*547ᵇ11: pl., *convolutions* of the bowels, Id.*PA* 675ᵇ24: sg., *colon*, ib.675ᵇ20; also of the ear, Id. *de An.*420ᵃ13, Ruf. *Onom.*44. **V.** *spiral* running round a staff, Ael.*VH*9.11, Ath.12. 543f; on a child's ball, A.R.3.139; *spiral strip* folded round the scytale, Plu.*Lys.*19. **2.** Geom., *spiral*, Epicur.*Ep.*2 p.40 U., Hermesian.7.86; περὶ ἑλίκων, title of work by Archim.; also, = κύκλος, Hsch. **b.** of planets' *orbit*, Eudox.*Ars*5.3, Theo Sm.p.201 H.; but also of the sun's and moon's *orbits*, Eudox.*Ars*9.2. **3.** *helix, screw-windlass*, employed in launching ships, invented by Archimedes, Moschio ap.Ath.5.207b. **4.** *treadmill used to raise water*, Ph.1.410. **VI.** pl., *involved sentences*, D.H.*Th.*48. **VII.** Adj. *winding*, ὁ ῥοῦς φέρεται ἕλικα πορείαν Dion.Byz.3.

**ἕλιξις,** ιος, ἡ, *rolled bandage*, Hp.*Off.*10. **2.** *convolution* of the bowels, Aret.*SA*2.6.

**ἑλιξό-κερως,** ωτος, ὁ, ἡ, *with crumpled horns*, κριός *AP*9.240 (Phil.). **-πορος,** ον, *revolving*, ἄτρακτος Procl.*H.*1.48.

**ἕλις·** μόνος καὶ ὅλος, Hsch.

❀ **ἑλίσσω** or **ἑλίσσω** (the latter more freq. in codd. of Hom.), Att. **-ττω,** Ep. inf. -έμεν Il.23.309; Ion. **εἱλίσσω** or **εἰλίσσω** (εἰ. is found in codd. of Hdt. (v. infr.), but κατ-ειλίσσειν Hp.*Acut.(Sp.)*37, κατειλίξαι Id.*Morb.*2.18, al.): fut. ἑλίξω E.*Ph.*711: aor. εἵλιξα Pl.*Ti.*73a (εἵλ- codd., but κατ-ειλίξας *IG*2².204.32); part. ἑλίξας Il.23.466, Ion. εἱλίξας Hdt.4.34:—**Med.,** Il.23.320: fut. ἑλίξομαι 17.728: aor. ἑλιξάμην 12.467, 17.283:—**Pass.,** fut. ἑλιγήσομαι Lxx *Is.*34.4: aor. 1 εἱλίχθην E.*Or.*358; part. ἑλιχθείς Il.12.74: pf. εἵλιγμαι Hes.*Th.*791, ἐλήλιγμαι Paus.10.17.12: plpf. εἵλικτο E.*HF*927; Ion. 3 pl. εἱλίχατο Hdt.7.90. —The Ion. form is found in Trag. (v. infr., codd. usu. εἱλ-; but τ' εἰ. A.*Pr.*138 (lyr., cod. Med.), cf. Ar.*Ra.*1314, 1348 (cod. Rav.)), in *IG* l. c., and codd. of Pl. (as *Ti.* l. c., ἀν-ειλίττων *Phlb.*15e); ἐπειλίξας is f. l. in D.23.161. (ϝελ-, ἐϝελ-, cf. εἴλω, ἐλελίζω ad fin.):—*turn round* or *about*: Act. in Hom. always of *turning* a chariot *round the doubling-post*, οἶσθα γὰρ εὖ περὶ τέρμαθ' ἑλισσέμεν| ἵππους Il.23.309, cf. 466. **2.** generally, *roll*, ἑ. βίου πόρον *roll* life's stream *along*, Pi.*I.*8(7).15; of the chariot of Day, αἰθὴρ κοινὸν φάος εἱλίσσων A.*Pr.*1092 (anap.); ἥλιος.. εἱλίσσων φλόγα E.*Ph.*3; εἰ. κόνιν *roll the eddying* dust, A.*Pr.* 1085 (anap.); ἑ. δίνας, of the Euripus, E.*IT*7, cf. 1103 (lyr.); ἑ. κόρας, βλέφαρα, Id.*HF*868 (troch.), *Or.*1266 (lyr.). **3.** of any rapid motion, ἅλιον.. ἑ. πλάταν *ply* it *swiftly*, S.*Aj.*358 (lyr.); of the dance, ἑ. πόδα *move the swift* foot, cj. in E. *Or.*171 (lyr.), cf. *IA*215 (lyr.); εἰ. θιάσους *lead the dancing* bands, Id.*IT*1145 (lyr.); ἑ. χορούς Stratt.66.5: abs., *dance*, E.*Ph.*234 (lyr.), cf. *Or.*1292 (whence ἑ. τινά *dance in honour of* .., Id.*HF*690 (lyr.), *IA*1480 (lyr.)); ἑ. βωμόν *dance round* it, Call. *Del.*321. **4.** *roll* or *wind round*, πλόκαμον περὶ ἄτρακτον Hdt.4.34, cf. 2.38; λίνον ἠλακάτᾳ δακτύλοις ἑ. E.*Or.*1432 (lyr.); χεῖρας ἀμφὶ γόνυ ἑ. *clasp* them round.., Id.*Ph.*1622. **5.** metaph., *turn in one's mind, revolve*, τοιαῦθ' ἑ. S.*Ant.*231, cf. Pl.*Epin.*978d; μῆτιν A.R.1.463; ἑ. κακοὺς λόγους *speak wily* words, E.*Or.*892. **6.** κόλπους ἑ. *form winding* reaches, of rivers, D.P.630; ἀγκῶνας Id. 979. **II.** Med. and Pass., *turn oneself round* or *about* (but in Il. 12.49 εἱλίσσεθ' ἑταίρους (as read by Nicanor) *rallied his* comrades), ἑλιχθέντων ὑπ' Ἀχαιῶν *when* they *turned to face* the foe, ib.74, cf. 408; so of a wild boar, ἑλιξάμενος *having turned to bay*, 17.283; of a serpent, *coil himself*, ἑλισσόμενος περὶ χειῇ 22.95; ἡ δέ τ' ἑλισσομένη πέτεται (sc. καλαῦροψ) the shepherd's staff flies *spinning through the air*, 23.846; κνίση.. ἑλισσομένη περὶ καπνῷ *rolling* with the smoke, 1.317; ἑλισσόμενοι περὶ δίνας *whirled round* in the eddies, 21.11; of a river, δίνῃς ἀργυρέῃς εἱλιγμένος Hes.*Th.*791, cf. D.S.1.32; of the waves, τὸ ἑλισσόμενον αἰεὶ κυμάτων Pi.*N.*6.55; of ocean, ἑλίσσεσθαι περὶ πᾶσαν χθόνα A.*Pr.*138; ὧραι ἑλισσόμεναι the *circling* hours, Pi. *O.*4.3. **2.** *turn hither and thither, go about*, ἀν' ὅμιλον Il.12.49; καθ' ὅμιλον ib.467; ἑλίσσετο ἔνθα καὶ ἔνθα *turned himself* hither and thither, doubting what to do, Od.20.24. **3.** metaph., *to be constantly in* or *about* a thing, περὶ φύσας Il.18.372; ἔν τινι, εἴς τι, Pl.*Tht.* 194b, Porph.ap.Eus.*PE*3.4: c. gen., μέλιτός τε καὶ ἔργων εἱλίσσονται (sc. μέλισσαι) Arat.1030. **4.** *whirl in the dance*, E.*Ba.*569 (lyr.), *IA* 1055 (lyr.). **5.** Med. in act. sense, ἧκε δέ μιν σφαιρηδὸν ἑλιξάμενος he threw it *with a whirl* like a ball, Il.13.204. **6.** τὰς κεφαλὰς εἱλίχατο μίτρῃσι *have their* heads *rolled round* with turbans, Hdt.7.90.

**ἑλίτροχος,** ον, (ἑλίσσω) *whirling the wheel round*, σύριγγες ἑ. A.*Th.* 205 (lyr.).

**ἑλιχάζει·** πλανᾶται, Hsch.

❀ **ἑλίχρῡσος,** ὁ, *gold-flower, Helichrysum siculum*, Alcm.16, Ibyc.6, Cratin.98; ξανθοτέρα ἑλιχρύσοιο Theoc.2.78.

**ἑλιχώνη,** ἡ, *funnel* in an oil-press, *CPR*242 i 10 (i A. D.).

**ἑλκαίνω,** (ἕλκανον) *fester*, A.*Ch.*843.

**ἕλκᾰνον,** τό, = ἕλκος, *wound*, Hsch., who also has **ἑλκανῶσα,** = ἑλκαίνουσα.

**ἑλκείδιον,** τό, Dim. of ἕλκος, Plu.300a (s.v.l.).

**ἑλκεσί-πεπλος** [ῐ], ον, *trailing the robe, with long train*, Il.6.442, al., Mus.286, Nonn.*D.*1.103. **-χειρος,** ον, *drawing the hand after it*, τρύπανα *AP*6.103 (Phil.).

**ἑλκε-τρίβων** [ῑ], ωνος, ὁ, *cloak-trailer*, nickname of a Laconian, Pl. Com.124. **-χίτων** [ῐ], ωνος, ὁ, *trailing the tunic, with a long tunic*, epith. of the Ionians, Il.13.685, *h.Ap.*147.

**ἑλκ-έω,** = ἕλκω, *drag about, tear asunder*, in impf. νέκυν.. ἑλκέομεν ἀμφότεροι Il.17.395: also in fut. and aor. κύνες ἑλκήσουσιν ib.558; σὲ μὲν κύνες ἠδ' οἰωνοὶ ἑλκήσουσ' 22.336; Λητὼ γὰρ ἥλκησε he *did violence to* Leto, Od.11.580; ἑ. τινὰ πέπλοιο Arat.638:—Pass., ἑλκηθείσας τε θύγατρας Il.22.62. **-ηδόν,** Adv. *by dragging, pulling*, ἐμάχοντο πύξ τε καὶ ἑλκηδόν Hes.*Sc.*302. **-ήεις,** εσσα, εν, *full of ulcers*, Man.1.162. **-ηθμός,** ὁ, *being carried off, violence suffered*, σῆς τε βοῆς σοῦ θ' ἑλκηθμοῖο πυθέσθαι Il.6.465. **-ηθρον,** τό, *stock of the plough*, Thphr.*HP*5.7.6. **-ητς·** ἡ λιθάργυρος, Hsch. **-ημα,** ατος, τό, *that which is torn in pieces, prey*, κυνῶν ἕ. E.*HF*568. **-ησίσταχυς,** υ, *drawing the ears of corn*, νομῆες Orac.ap.Paus.8.42. 6. ❀ **-ητήρ,** ῆρος, ὁ, *one that drags*, κτένες ἑλκητῆρες, of a harrow, *AP*6.297 (Phan.).

**ἕλκιμος,** ον, = ἑλκύσιμος, Olymp. *in Mete.*320.37.

**ἑλκίνα,** = περδίκιον, Ps.-Dsc.4.85.

**ἑλκο-ποιέω,** *make wounds* or *sores*: metaph., *rip up old sores*, Aeschin.3.208. **II.** *make an incision in* a tree, πρέμνον *Gp.*5.38. 2. **-ποιός,** όν, *having power to wound*, A.*Th.*398; cf. ἑλκοποιόν· κανθαρίς, Hsch.

**ἕλκος,** εος, τό, *wound*, Il.4.190, al. (never in Od.), Pi.*P.*2.91, E.*Tr.* 1232 (pl.), etc. **2.** *festering wound, sore, ulcer*, ἕ. ὕδρου *the festering bite* of a serpent, Il.2.723; *plague-ulcer*, Th.2.49, X.*Eq.*5.1, etc. (Gal. 10.232 defines ἕ. as ἡ τῆς συνεχείας λύσις ἐν σαρκώδει μορίῳ, and both 1. 1 and 1. 2 are treated in Hp.*Ulc.*; ἕ. is applied to amputations in *Art.*68.) **II.** metaph., *wound, loss*, Sol.4.17, S.*Ant.*652, al.; ἕ. δήμιον A.*Ag.*640; ὑποκάρδιον ἕ. Theoc.11.15; γίγνεται ἕ. ἐφ' ἕλκει Lib.*Ep.*1063.6. (Orig. *ἕλκος, cf. Lat. *ulcus*, Skt. *árśas* (n.) 'haemorrhoid': ἕ- by influence of ἕλκω.)

❀ **ἑλκόω,** *wound, lacerate*, E.*Hec.*405; ἑ. ὄνυξιν Arist.*HA*630ᵃ5, etc. **2.** *ulcerate*, βλέφαρα Hp.*VM*19, al.:—Pass., of persons, *to suffer from wounds* or *sores*, *Com.Adesp.*106.8, *Ev.Luc.*16.20; of sores, *suppurate*, X.*Eq.*1.5. **3.** *make an incision in* a tree, Thphr. *HP*4.16.1 (Pass.), *CP*3.2.2 (Pass.). **II.** metaph., ἑ. φρένας, οἴκους, E.*Alc.*878 (lyr.), *Supp.*223:—Pass., τὴν διάνοιαν ἑλκοῦσθαι Ph.2.551.

**ἑλκ-τέον,** *one must drag*, Pl.*R.*365c. **-τικός,** ή, όν, *fit for drawing, attractive*, πρός τι ib.523a, cf. Thphr.*CP*3.17.3 (Comp.), Ael.*NA* 17.6. **-τός,** ή, όν, *that can be drawn, tensile*, Arist.*GA*743ᵇ5, *Mete.*385ᵃ16. **-ύδριον,** τό, Dim. of ἕλκος, *slight sore*, Hp.*Art.*63, Ar.*Eq.*907. **II.** = κάδος, Dionys.Trag.12. **-υθμός,** ὁ, later form of ἑλκηθμός, Tryph.21. **-ύσιμος** [ῠ], ον, *that may be drawn*, Phot. s.v. ἐρύσιμον. **-ῠσις,** εως, ἡ, *attraction*, πύου Aret.*SD*1.10. **2.** *drawing*, ἕ. τῆς σικύης, in cupping, Hp.*Loc.Hom.*22. **-υσμα,** ατος, τό, *that which is drawn*, i. e. *spun wool*, Hsch. s. v. ἀφρῖνον (pl.). **2.** pl., κυνῶν ἑ. *bodies torn* by dogs, Man.4.200. **3.** = σκωρία, *dross of silver*, because *drawn off with a hook*, Dsc.5.86, Gal.12.236, Orib.*Fr.* 90. **-υσμός,** ὁ, *attraction*; esp. of *idle fancy*, διάκενος ἑ. Chrysipp. *Stoic.*2.22, cf. Ph.1.151 (pl.). **II.** *dragging*, in pl., Anon.*Fig.*p.156 S. **-υστάζω,** Frequentat. of ἕλκω, *drag about*, ἵνα μή μιν ἀποδρύφοι ἑλκυστάζων Il.23.187, 24.21. **-υστέος,** α, ον, *to be dragged*, X.*Ag.*9. 4. **II.** ἑλκυστέον *one must draw*, αἷμα Gal.ap.Aët.8.50. **2.** *one must drink*, οὐκ ἀθρόον πόμα Herod.Med.ib.4.47. **-υστήρ,** ῆρος, ὁ, *instrument for drawing*: surgeon's *crochet*, Hp.*Mul.*1.70; *a rein*, Sch. Il.16.475, Hsch. s. v. ῥυτήρ. **II.** as Adj., ἑ. πόνος toil *of dragging*, Opp. *H.*5.20. **-υστήριος,** α, ον, *fit for drawing*, ζῷα *draught* animals, Men.Prot.p.17 D. **-υστικός,** ή, όν, *drawing*: *extracting*, c. gen., σκολόπων Dsc.2.84. **2.** *attractive*, ἑ. τι ἔχειν πρὸς φιλίαν Ath.5.185c; τὰ πιθανὰ καὶ ἑ. Arr.*Epict.*3.12.14. **-υστίνδα,** Adv. = διελκυστίνδα, Eust.1111.24. ❀ **-υστός,** ή, όν, *ductile*, Hsch. s. v. βύσιον, *Gloss.* **2.** *drawn*, ἑ. ἅμαξα *transport*-wagon, *PMasp.*303.7 (vi A. D., -ιστή Pap.). **II.** ἑ. ἔλαιον *refined, fine-drawn* oil, *CIG*2719.21 (Stratonicea); cf. ἑλκυστῷ· λείῳ, Hsch. ❀ **-υστρον,** τό, *handle* or *lever* for raising a swing-beam, Apollod.*Poliorc.*162.10. **2.** *halter*, Hsch. s.v. φορβεῖα.

❀ **ἕλκω** (ἑλκύω late, Tz.*H.*6.621), Il.24.52, etc., impf. εἷλκον A.*Fr.*39, etc., Ep. ἕλκον Il.4.213, al. (never εἵλκυον): fut. ἕλξω A.*Supp.*909, etc., rarely ἑλκύσω [ῠ] Hp.*Fract.*2, Philem.174: aor. εἵλκῠσα Batr.232, Pi.*N.*7.103, Trag. and Att., E.*Ph.*987, Ar.*Nu.*540, *SIG*³587.23, al., etc.; ἥλκυσα *IG*11(2).287 *B*61 (Delos, ii B. C.), *CIG*4993, 5006 (Egypt, iii A. D.); later εἷλξα, poet. ἕλξα *AP*9.370 (Tib. Ill.), Orph.*A.*258, Gal.*Nat.Fac.*1.12: pf. εἵλκῠκα D.22.59; pf. part. ἑολκώς prob. in Epich. 177:—Med., fut. -ύσομαι (ἐφ-) Antyll.ap.Orib.6.10.9: aor. εἱλκυσάμην (ἀφ-) v. l. in Hp.*Art.*11, subj. ἀφελκύσωμαι Ar.*Ach.*1120; rarely εἰλξάμην Gal.4.534:—Pass., fut. ἑλκυσθήσομαι A.*Th.*614 (ξυγκαθ-), Lyc.358, ἑλχθήσομαι Gal.*UP*7.7: aor. εἱλκύσθην Hp.*Epid.*4.14, (ἐξ-) Ar.*Ec.*688, ἑλκ- Hdt.1.140, ἡλκ- *IG*12(7).115.11 (Amorgos); later εἵλχθην Ph.2.11, Philostr.*VA*8.15, D.L.6.91: pf. εἵλκυσμαι Hp.*Superf.*16, E.*Rh.*576, Ph.1.316, (καθ-) Th.6.50, ἕλκυσμαι (ἀν-) Hdt.9.98, ἥλκυσμαι *BGU*1256.11 (ii B.C.): plpf. εἵλκυστο Hp.*Epid.*4.36.—In Att., ἕλκω, ἕλξω were alone used in pres. and fut., while the other tenses were formed from ἑλκυ-; cf. ἑλκέω (q. v.), ἑλκυστάζω. In Hom., Aristarch. rejected the augm. (Cf. Lat. *sulcus*, Lith. *velkù* 'drag'):—*draw, drag*, with collat. notion of force or exertion, ὡς εἰπὼν ποδὸς ἕλκε *began to drag* [the dead body] by the foot, Il.13.383; ἥν περ.. ποδῶν ἕλκωσι θύραζε Od.16.276; τινὰ τῆς ῥινός Luc.*Herm.*73; Ἕκτορα.. περὶ σῆμ' ἑτάροιο ἕλκει Il.24.52; *drag away* a prisoner, 22.65 (Pass.); *draw* ships down to the sea, 2.152, etc.; *draw along* a felled tree, 17.743; of mules, *draw* a chariot, 24.324; ἑλκέμεναι νειοῖο.. πηκτὸν ἄροτρον *draw* the plough *through* the field, 10.353, cf. 23.518; ἕ. τινὰ ἐπὶ κνάφου Hdt.1.92; περιβαλόντας σχοινία ἕ. *haul at* them, Id.5.85. **2.** *draw after one*, ἐν δ' ἔπεσ' Ὠκεανῷ.. φάος ἠελίοιο, ἕλκον νύκτα μέλαιναν Il.8. 486; πέδας ἕ. *trail* fetters *after one*, Hdt.3.129; ἕ. χλανίδα *let* one's cloak *trail behind*, Ephipp.19 (anap.); θοἰμάτιον Archipp.45. **3.** *tear*

*in pieces* (used by Hom. only in the form ἑλκέω), ὀνύχεσσι παρειάν E.*Tr.*280; *worry*, τὰς κύνας ὤλαφος ἕλκοι Theoc.1.135; ἑλκυσθῆναι ὑπὸ κυνὸς Hdt.1.140. b. metaph., *carp at*, Pi.*N.*7.103. 4. *draw* a bow, ἕλκε.. γλυφίδας τε λαβὼν καὶ νεῦρα βόεια Il.4.122, cf. Od.21.419, Hdt.3.21, X.*An.*4.2.28, etc. 5. *draw* a sword, S.*Ant.*1233, E.*Rh.*576 (Pass.):—Med., ἕλκετο δ' ἐκ κολεοῖο.. ξίφος Il.1.194. 6. ἕ. ἱστία *hoist* sails, Od.2.426:—also in Med., *h.Bacch.*32. 7. *lift up* scales, so as to poise them, ἕλκε δὲ μέσσα λαβών Il.8.72, 22.212. II. after Hom., 1. *pull* a barge-pole, Hdt.1.194. 2. *tow* a ship, Th.2.90, etc. 3. *drag into court*, ἕλκω σε κλητεύσοντα Ar.*Nu.*1218, cf. 1004 (Pass.); εἰς ἀγοράν *Act.Ap.*16.19; *drag about*, esp. with lewd violence, ἕλκει καὶ βιάζεται D.21.150; μηδένα ἕλξειν μηδ' ὑβρίειν ib. 221; ἕλκειν γυναῖκα Lys.1.12: metaph., ἄνω κάτω τοὺς λόγους ἕ. Pl.*Tht.*195c, cf. Arist.*SE*167ᵃ35; ἡμέας ὁ καιρὸς ἕλκει Herod.2.10; also ἥλκυσμαι λαμπαδάρχης *I have been compelled to serve as* λ., *BGU* l.c. 4. *draw* or *suck up*, [ἥλιος] ἕλκει τὸ ὕδωρ ἐπ' ἑωυτόν Hdt.2.25; ἕ. τὸν ἀέρα *draw* it *in*, *breathe* it, Hp.*Aër.*19, Ti.Locr.101d (Pass.), cf. Philyll.20: ζωὴν φύσιν Archel.ap.Antig.*Mir.*89; esp. of persons drinking, *drink in long draughts*, *quaff*, μέθυ E.*Ion* 1200; ἄμυστιν Id.*Cyc.*417; τὴν.. τοῦ Πραμνίου [σπονδήν] Ar.*Eq.*107; οἶνον ἐκ.. λεπαστῆς Teleclid.24 (lyr.); ἀπνευστί Antiph.74.14, etc.: with acc. of the cup, δέπας μεστόν.. ἕλκουσι γνάθοις ἀπαύστοις Id.237, cf. Eub.56.7, al.; so ἕ. μαστόν *suck* it, E.*Ph* 987; *inhale*, ὀσμήν Antig.*Mir.*89; of roots, *draw up* nourishment, Thphr.*HP*1.6.10: metaph., χανδὸν καὶ ἀμυστὶ τῶν μαθημάτων ἕ. Eun.*VS* p.474 D. 5. *draw* from a receptacle, ἐξ ἑκάστου κιβωτίου πινάκιον ἐν Arist.*Ath.*64.1. 6. ἕ. βίοτον, ζόαν, *drag out* a weary life, E.*Or.*207 (lyr.), *Ph.*1535 (lyr.); προφάσιας ἕ. *keep making* excuses, Hdt.6.86; πάσας τε προφάσεις.. ἕλκουσι Ar.*Lys.*727; ἕ. χρόνους *make long*, in prosody, Longin.*Proll. Heph.*p.83 C.: hence intr., ἐπὶ τοσοῦτο λέγεται ἑλκύσαι τὴν σύστασιν.. that the conflict *dragged on*, *lasted*, Hdt.7.167, cf. *PHib.*1.83.9 (iii B.C.):—Pass., τῶν ἐγκλημάτων εἰκλυσμένων πλείονα χρόνον *Supp. Epigr.*2.281 (Delph., ii B.C.); also of a person, ἑλκόμενος καὶ μόγις Pl. *R.*350d. 7. ἕ. κόρδακα *dance* in *long, measured* steps, Ar.*Nu.*540; ἐν τουτὶ (σχῆμα) Id.*Pax* 328. 8. *draw to oneself*, *attract*, of the magnet, E.*Fr.*567; by spells, τινὰ ποτὶ δῶμα Theoc.2.17, cf. X.*Mem.*3.11.18, Plot.4.4.40, etc.; πείθειν καὶ ἕ. Pl.*R.*458d; ἐχθροὺς ἐφ' ἑαυτόν D.22.59; *draw on*, ἐπὶ ἡδονάς Pl.*Phdr.*238a; εἰς τυραννίδας ἕ. τὰς πολιτείας Id.*R.*568c:—Pass., *to be drawn on* as by a spell, ἴυγγι δ' ἕλκομαι ἦτορ Pi.*N.*4.35; πρὸς φιλοσοφίαν Pl.*R.*494e. 9. of things weighed, ἕ. σταθμὸν τάλαντα δέκα *draw down* the balance, i.e. *weigh* ten talents, Hdt.1.50, cf. Eup.116: abs., τὸ δ' ἂν ἑλκύσῃ whatever it *weigh*, Hdt.2.65; πλεῖον ἕ. Pl.*Min.*316a. b. ἕ. τὰς ψήφους *cast up* the account, *PPetr.*2 p.37 (iii B.C.), *PHib.*1.17.25 (iii B.C.). 10. *draw* or *derive* from a source, ἐντεῦθεν εἵλκυσεν ἐπὶ τήν.. τέχνην τὸ πρόσφορον αὐτῇ Pl.*Phdr.*270a, cf. Jul.*Or.*7.207a; τὸ γένος ἀπό τινος Str.11.9.3; *assume*, μείζω φαντασίαν Plb.32.10.5; ὁ ἄρτος ἕλκει χρῶμα κάλλιστον Ath.3.113c. 11. ἑλκύσαι πλίνθους *make* bricks, Hdt.1.179, cf. *PPetr.*3 p.137; ἕ. λάγανον Chrysipp.Tyan.ap.Ath.14.647e. 12. αἱ θυρίδες ἕλκουσι the windows *draw in* air, Thphr.*Vent.*29. 13. ἕ. ἑαυτόν, expressing some kind of athletic exercise, Pl.*Prm.*135d.

B. Med., ἕ. χαίτας ἐκ κεφαλῆς *tear one's* hair, Il.10.15; ἀσσοτέρω πυρὸς ἕλκετο δίφρον *drew his* chair nearer to the fire, Od.19.506, cf. Semon.7.26. 2. *draw to oneself*, *scrape up*, *amass*, τιμάς, ἄφενος ἕλκεσθαι, Thgn.30. 3. ἕλκεσθαι στάθμας περισσᾶς in Pi.*P.*2.90, means lit., *to drag at* too great a line, i.e. *grasp* more than one's due—but whence the metaphor is taken remains unexplained.

C. Pass., *to be drawn* or *wrenched*, νῶτα.. ἑλκόμενα στερεῶς, of wrestlers, Il.23.715; of the nails, to be *curved*, Hp.*Morb.*2.48; *to close in* when the core is removed, of the timber of certain trees, Thphr.*HP*5.5.2. 2. *to be drawn* or *to flow at a place*, of streams, Lyc.702; πρὸς ἀντολίην ἕ. αἶα D.P.1086. 3. *to be drawn* or *contracted*, εἱλκύσθη ἐπὶ τὰ δεξιὰ τράχηλος Hp.*Epid.*4.14.

⊛ **ἑλκ-ώδης**, ες, *like a wound* or *sore*, *ulcerated*, στόματα Hp.*Epid.*3.7; χρώς E.*Hipp.*1359 (anap.); κνῆμαι Arist.*Pr.*895ᵃ31. 2. *causing* or *accompanied by soreness*, ἀφή S.E.*M.*7.179; κόπος Gal.7.179; πόνος Archig.ap.eund.8.106; κονιορτός Lyd.*Ost.*1. II. metaph., *irritable*, Plb.32.11.8; θυμός Plu.2.454b. **-ωμα**, ατος, τό, *sore*, *ulcer*, Hp.*Epid.*3.7, *POxy.*1088.2,9 (i A.D.). II. *part wounded*, Thphr.*HP*9.2.1. **-ωμᾰτικός**, ή, όν, *causing sores*, *ulcerating*, Dsc.5.91. **-ωσις**, εως, ἡ, *ulceration*, Hp.*Aph.*3.21, Th.2.49, Ph.2.100; of plants, Thphr.*CP*1.14.2, al. ⊛ **-ωτικός**, ή, όν, = ἑλκωματικός, Dsc.1.128.3: metaph., *exasperating*, δριμύτης Plu.2.854c.

**ἑλλά**, ἡ, Lacon. for καθέδρα, Hsch.:—also Ἕλλα· Διὸς ἱερὸν ἐν Δωδώνῃ, Id.

**Ἑλλᾰδαρχ-έω**, *hold office of* Ἑλλαδάρχης 3, *IGRom.*3.202 (Ancyra, ii A.D.). **-ης**, ου, ὁ, *president of the* κοινὸν τῶν Ἀχαιῶν, *IG*4.1600 (Corinth, ii A.D.), *SIG*846.5 (Delph., ii A.D.). 2. *official of the Delphic Amphictyony*, Ἑ. ἀμφικτυόνων *IG*4.590 (Argos, ii A.D.). 3. *official of the Greek community in the province of Galatia*, *IGRom.*3.211 (Ancyra, ii A.D.). 4. as an honorary title, *OGI*528.10 (Prusias).

**Ἑλλᾰδικός**, ή, όν, *Hellenic*, ἀοιδαί Xenoph.6; κλίμα Herm.ap.Stob.1.49.45; [ἵπποι] Str.11.13.7; οἱ Ἑ. Plu.2.676b. II. Ἑλλαδική, ἡ, name of a *plaster*, Alex.Trall.9.1; Ἑλλαδικὸν μάλαγμα Aet.15.11.

⊛ **ἔλλᾱθι**, = ἵληθι, B.10.8; Aeol. for ἵλαθι, *Et.Gud.* s.v. χίλιοι: pl., ἔλλατε Call.*Fr.*121.

**ἐλλᾰλέω**, *talk amongst*, μειρακίοις Pherecr.64 (prob.).

⊛ **ἐλλαμβάνω**, *receive*, *Supp.Epigr.*2.264.6 (Delph., ii B.C.). II. Med., aor. 2 ἐνελαβόμην *IG*12(5).1061.10 (Carthaea):—*seize hold of*, τῶν δένδρων ταῖς ἕλιξι Dsc.4.183, cf. Ph.1.21, al., J.*AJ*6.7.5, etc.

⊛ **ἐλλαμπρύνομαι**, Pass., *gain distinction*, ἰδίᾳ ἐ. τῷ τῆς πόλεως κινδύνῳ Th.6.12; *pride oneself*, Luc.*Dom.*1; ἔργῳ D.C.73.10; ἱππεῦσιν App.*BC*3.66; πρὸς τὰς φίλας ἐ. λόγοις J.*AJ*18.3.4.

**ἐλ-λάμπω**, *shine*, Σείριος.. ὀξὺς ἐ. Archil.61: c. dat., *shine upon*, *irradiate*, τῇ ψυχῇ Ph.1.273; πᾶσιν Procl.*Inst.*23; εἰς ψυχήν Hierocl. *in CA* 10p.433 M.; εἰς τὴν οἰκείαν ἕδραν Jul.*Or.*4.134b; *shine* or *be reflected in*, ἐν τοῖς ὄμμασι τῶν πλησίον Plu.2.40d: c. dat., Iamb.*Myst.*2.3, al. II. trans., *illuminate*, ἐλλάμπουσα ἀεὶ ἐλλάμπεται Plot.2.9.2, cf. Procl.*in Ti.*2.285 D., al.; ὅταν [ἡ ψυχὴ] οἷον ἐλλάμψῃ πρὸς ἑαυτήν Plot.6.4.16:—metaph. in Med., *distinguish oneself*, *gain glory in* or *with*, [τῷ ἱππικῷ] ἐπεῖχε ἐλλάμψεσθαι Hdt.1.80; τῇσι νησοί Id.8.74. 2. *cause to shine upon*, καλλονὴν ἑκάστῳ Them.*Or.*4.52b; *cause to shine*, ἡ τῶν θεῶν παρουσία τὸ φῶς ἐ. Iamb.*Myst.*2.6. **-λαμψις**, εως, ἡ, *shining*, *flashing*, *Placit.*3.3.12 (v.l.), Plu.*Fr.inc.*150: metaph., *illumination*, *irradiation*, Plot.6.4.15, 5.8, al., Dam.*Pr.*34; τῆς ἀληθείας Hierocl. *in CA* 20p.465 M. II. *radiation* of heat, Steph. *in Hp.*1.134 D., al.

**Ἑλλάνιος**, Dor. for Ἑλλήνιος.

⊛ **Ἑλλᾰνοδίκ-αι** [ῐ], ῶν, οἱ, *the chief judges at the Olympic games*, Pi.*O.*3.12 (sg.), Hellanic.113 J. (sg.), Paus.5.9.5 sq.; also, *at the Nemean games*, *IG*4.587 (Argos); at Epidaurus, ib.946 (iii B.C.). II. at Sparta, *court-martial to try cases arising among the allied troops*, X.*Lac.*13.11.—The Dor. form (Elean **Ἑλλανοζίκας** *Schwyzer* 409) is used in Att., but **Ἑλληνοδίκαι** is found in *SIG*1073.20, and is v.l. in Hdt.5.22, cf. Hsch. s.v. et s.v. Δίαρχοι. **-έω**, *to be a judge at the games*, Paus.6.1.5, 24.3. **-εών**, ῶνος, ὁ, *the place where the* Ἑλλανοδίκαι *held their meetings*, Id.6.24.1.

**ἐλλαπίνα**, Aeol., = εἰλ., *Et.Gud.*165.44.

**Ἑλλάς**, άδος, ἡ, *Hellas*, said to have been originally the name of the region round Dodona, Arist.*Mete.*352ᵃ34, Sch.Il.21.194. 2. a city of Thessaly, founded by Hellen, οἵ τ' εἶχον Φθίην ἠδ' Ἑλλάδα Il.2.683. 3. *part of Phthiotis*, inhabited by the Μυρμιδόνες, 9.395, al. 4. *Northern Greece*, opp. Peloponnesus, D.19.303, Ptol.*Geog.*3.14.1: sts. so expld. in the phrase καθ' Ἑλλάδα καὶ μέσον Ἄργος Od.1.344, 4.726, al. 5. *Greece*, from Peloponnesus to Epirus and Thessaly inclusively, Hes.*Op.*653, Hdt.8.44, 47, A.*Pers.*50 (anap.), 234 (troch.): used collectively for Ἕλληνες, E.*Or.*648, Th.1.6, etc. 6. as a general name for *all lands inhabited by Hellenes*, including Ionia, etc., Hdt.1.92, Th.1.3, X.*An.*6.5.23, etc.; οὔθ' Ἑ. οὔτ' ἄγλωσσος S.*Tr.*1060: hence ἡ ἀρχαία Ἑ. Old Greece, Plu.*Tim.*37; ἡ μεγάλη Ἑ. *Magna Graecia*, Plb.2.39.1, Ath.12.523e; including Sicily, Str.6.1.2. 7. Ἑλλάδος Ἑ., Ἀθῆναι *AP*7.45 (Thuc.): pl., τὴν Ἑ. Ἑλλάσι πολλαῖς παραυξήσας Ph.2.567. 8. (sc. φωνή) *the Greek language*, Ael.*VH*9.16. II. fem. Adj. *Greek*, γλῶσσα Hdt.6.98, al.; πόλις Id.5.93; χθών A.*Supp.*243; στολή S.*Ph.*223, etc.; masc., Id.*Fr.*17; τίς Ἑ. ἢ βάρβαρος ἢ τῶν προπάροιθ' εὐγενετᾶν ἕτερος..; E.*Ph.*1509.

**ἐλλάσαι**· συγκλεῖσαι, κωλῦσαι, Hsch.

**ἐλλεβορ-ιάω**, *need hellebore*, i.e. *to be mad*, Call.Com.28. **-ίζω**, Ion. ἐλλ-, fut. -ιῶ Hp.*Ep.*20:—*dose with hellebore*, Id.*Mochl.*30, Plu.*Alex.*41, Archig.ap.Orib.8.1.1 (Pass.), etc.; and so, *to bring one to his senses*, τί σαυτὸν οὐχ ἐλλεβορίζεις; D.18.121: -όμενοι, title of play by Diph., *AB*100. **-ίνη**, ἡ, *rupture-wort*, *Herniaria glabra*, Thphr. *HP*9.10.2, Dsc.4.108. **-ισμός**, ὁ, *treatment with hellebore*, Hp.*Ep.*21. **-ίτης** [ῑ] οἶνος wine *flavoured with hellebore*, Dsc.5.72. II. **-ίτης**, ου, ὁ, = κενταύρειον μικρόν, Ps.-Dsc.3.7.

**ἐλλεβορο-δότης** ἰατρός doctor *who prescribes hellebore*, Gal.*Thras.*24. **-ποσία**, ἡ, *drinking of hellebore*, Hp.*Epid.*5.83.

**ἐλλέβορος**, Ion. ἐλλ-, ὁ, *hellebore*, Hp.*Acut.*23, *Aph.*4.13, Thphr. *HP*9.10.1, etc. (ἐ. λευκός white *hellebore*, *Veratrum album*, Dsc.4.148; ἐ. μέλας *hellebore*, *Helleborus orientalis* (or *cyclophyllus*), ib.162); given to the insane, Hp.*Vict.*1.35: hence, πῖθ' ἐλλέβορον, i.e. you are mad, Ar.*V.*1489; ἐλλέβορον ἤδη πώποτ' ἔπιες; Men.69 (prob. l.); ἐλλέβορον πιεῖν Hp.*Fract.*11, cf. Str.9.3.3, etc.; πικρότερον ἐλλεβόρου *AP*5.28 (Cillactor). 2. = σησαμοειδὲς τὸ μέγα, Dsc.4.149. II. = ἐλλόβιον, of women, Ar.*Fr.*320.6, Nicostr.33, cf. Hsch.

**ἐλλεβοροσήματα**, = λειμώνιον, Ps.-Dsc.4.16.

**ἐλλεδᾰνός**, ὁ, *band for binding corn-sheaves*, in pl., Il.18.553, *h.Cer.*456, Hes.*Sc.*291: sg., in Suid.

⊛ **ἔλλειμμα**, ατος, τό, *defect*, *deficiency*, Hp.*Praec.*9, Phld.*D.*3.2 (pl.), etc.; τὰ καθ' ὑμᾶς ἐλλείμματα *shortcomings* dependent on yourselves, D.2.27; *arrears*, Id.22.44; τοῦ γεγραμμένου νόμου ἔ. Arist.*Rh.*1374ᵃ26; τὸ περὶ τὴν διάλεκτον ἐ. D.H.*Dem.*20. 2. *remnant*, v.l. in Lxx *2Ki.*21.2.

**ἔλλειν**· ἴλλειν, κατέχειν, Hsch.:—Pass., ἐλλόμενα· περικλειόμενα, Id.; cf. εἴλω.

**ἐλλειπ-ασμός**, f.l. for λοιπασμός (q.v.). **-ής**, freq. written for ἐλλιπής (q.v.). ⊛ **-όντως**, Adv. *incompletely*, Plot.1.3.6; opp. σφοδρῶς, Hsch. s.v. ἀκραῆ. **-τικός**, ή, όν, in Gramm., *elliptic*, *defective*, σχῆμα Eust.66.24, cf. A.D.*Conj.*226.20: c. gen., τῶν μορίων Id.*Synt.*141.14. Adv. -κῶς Phlp. *in APr.*316.30, Eust.1080.17. b. *summary*, *brief*, Gal.15.796. Adv. -κῶς Id.18(1).881. ⊛ **-ω**, *leave in*, μόνον.. ἐλλελειμμένον *left in* a race, S.*El.*736; *leave behind*, οὐδ' ἐλλέλοιπας ἐλπίδα E.*El.*609; τοῖόν σφιν ἐνέλλιπε θέλκτρον ἀοιδῆς A.R.1.515. 2. *leave out*, *leave undone*, freq. with neg. Pron. neut., μηδὲν ἐ. ὅσων χρὴ πονεῖν S.*Aj.*1379; οὐδὲν ἐλλείψουσι.. χειρουργίας Ar.*Lys.*673; λέγε μηδὲν ἐλλείπων Pl.*Plt.*269c, cf. *Ti.*17b, X.*Mem.*4.3.17; ἐ. τι τῶν νομίμων Id.*Cyr.*1.2.14; τοῦτ' αὐτὸ ἐ. Pl.*Plt.*267c, cf. *R.*362d;

ἔνια, σμικρά, Id.*Cra.*431c,d, etc.:—Pass., Id.*Phlb.*18d; τῆς προθυμίας οὐδὲν ἐλλέλειπται Lys.12.99; εὑρήσει οὐδὲν ἐλλειφθὲν D.18.303. b. *fail to pay, leave unpaid*, ἐλλελοιπότες εἰσφορὰν Id.24.172, cf. Arist. *Ath.*48.1; τινὰ τῶν ὀψωνίων τοῖς μισθοφόροις Plb.4.60.2. 3. intr., *fall short, fail*, οὐ μὴν Τρίοπός γ' ἐνέλειπεν *h.Ap.*213; ἄτας οὐδὲν ἐλλείπει S.*Ant.*584 (lyr.); ἥνπερ μὴ 'λλίπωσιν αἱ δίκαι Ar.*Pl.*859; ἐ. ἐν τῷ ἔργῳ Th.1.120; τοῖς ἱππικοῖς Plb.15.3.5; opp. περιγίγνεσθαι, Pl. *Lg.*740d; opp. πλεονάζειν, Isoc.2.33; opp. ὑπερβάλλειν, Pl.*Lg.*719d, Arist.*EN*1108b18; *fail in duty*, X.*HG*7.5.8, *Eq.*8.5; τὸ ἐλλεῖπον [τῆς ἐπιστήμης] *a deficiency* of.., Th.6.69; τὸ ἐ. ἐκπληρώσατε X.*Cyr.*4.5.39, etc.; *to be too small*, Id.*Cyn.*5.26; ἐλλείπων, ὁ, name of a *throw of the dice*, Eub.57.4. b. Geom., *fall short*, χωρίῳ *by* an area, Pl.*Men.* 87a, cf. Euc.6.27, al. 4. c. gen. rei, *to be in want of, fall short of, lack*, τὸν ἐλλείποντ' ἔτι ἥβης ἀκμαίας A.*Th.*10; ἐ. [χρημάτων] Th.1.80; τῆς δόξης Id.2.61; τὰ τῶν ἱκανῶν ἐλλείποντα X.*Hier.*4.8; τὸ τίμημα ἐνέλιπε τῶν ἑξακισχιλίων διακοσίοις ταλάντοις *fell short* of the 6000 by 200, Plb.2.62.7; τοσοῦτον ἐλλείπει τοῦ λυπεῖσθαι so far does he *fall short* of feeling pain, Arist.*EN*1108b5; πολλοῦ γε καὶ τοῦ παντὸς ἐλλείπω (sc. τοῦ ταρβεῖν) A.*Pr.*961: with a neg., προθυμίας γὰρ οὐδὲν ἐλλείπεις ib.341, cf. Pl.*Ti.*20c; οὔτε ἀνοίας οὐδὲν ἐλλείπει οὔτε ἀναισχυντίας Id.*R.*571d: impers., ἐλλείπει πωμάτων *there is lack* of drink, Id.*Lg.*844b; οἷς ἂν τῆς γενέσεως ἐλλείπῃ ib.740c; ὧν δ' ἐνέλειπε τῇ πόλει.. D.18.302. 5. c. gen. pers., *to be inferior to*, Pl.*Alc.*1.122c; ἐμπειρίᾳ μηδὲν ἐκείνων ἐ. Id.*R.*484d: also c. gen. rei, τἀνθάδε τῶν ἐκεῖ ἐ. Id.*Alc.*1.122d. 6. folld. by μή c. inf., τί γὰρ ἐ. μὴ παραπαίειν; in what *does* it *fall short* of madness? A.*Pr.*1056 (anap.); οὐδὲν ἐλλείψω τὸ μὴ.. πυθέσθαι S.*Tr.*90. 7. c. part., ὅτι ἄν τις ἐλλείπῃ λέγων Pl.*Phdr.*272b; οὐκ ἐλλείψει εὐχαριστῶν *will* not *fail* to give thanks, Decr.ap.D.18.92: abs., οἱ ἐλλείποντες *defaulters*, Id.22.44. 8. of things, *to be wanting* or *lacking to*.., c. dat., X.*Mem.*2.1.8. II. c. acc. pers., ἐλλείπει τινά τι something *fails* one, Plb.9.41.11; ἵνα μηδὲν αὐτὰς ἐλλείπῃ τῶν ἐπιτηδείων Id.10.18.11. III. Pass., *to be surpassed*, ἐλλείπεσθαι εὖ ποιῶν X.*Mem.*2.6.5. 2. *to be wanting, fail*, Id.*Cyr.*6.2.37, *Eq.*3.8, etc.; *to be inferior*, Pl.*R.*484d: c. gen., τινὸς εἰς σύνεσιν Id.*Amat.*136a.

⊛ ἐλλείχω, *lick in, take one's fill of*, τινός Com.*Adesp.*125 Meineke.

ἔλλειψις, εως, ἡ, *falling short, defect*, opp. ὑπερβολή, Democr. 102, Pl.*Prt.*356a; opp. ὑπεροχή, Arist.*Ph.*187a17, *Metaph.*1042b25; ὑπερβολὴ καὶ ἔ. καὶ τὸ μέσον Id.*EN*1106b17. 2. *the conic section ellipse*, Apollon.Perg.*Con.*1.13 (so called because the square on the ordinate is equal to a rectangle with height equal to the abscissa and applied to the parameter, but *falling short* of it). 3. ἐν ἐλλείψεσιν ἐνυπάρχειν to be present in *deficiency*, of the negative terms in an algebraical expression, Dioph.1*Praef.*p.14T. 4. Gramm., *ellipse*, Ath. 14.644a, A.D.*Synt.*117.19; *omission* of a letter, Id.*Pron.*56.28. 5. = ἔκλειψις, Olymp.*in Mete.*67.37 (s.v.l.). 6. Pythag. name for *two*, *Theol.Ar.*10.

ἔλλερος, dialectic for κακός, Call.*Fr.*434, cf. Eust.635.5, Hsch.

Ἐλλεσίη· ἡ Ἀθηνᾶ, Hsch.

ἔλλεσχος, ον, *talked of in the* λέσχαι, *commonly talked of*, Hdt.1. 153.

⊛ ἔλλετε, = ἔρρετε, Call.*Fr.*292; cf. ἔλλατε (v. ἔλλαθι).

ἔλλευκος, *albatus*, *Gloss.*

ἐλλήγω, *come to an end in*, *PLond.*1.98r31.

ἐλληκέω, in aor. 1 ἐνελήκησα, = ἔπλησα, ἐψόφησα, Hsch. (dub.).

⊛ Ἕλλην, ηνος, ὁ, *Hellen*, son of Deucalion, Hes.*Fr.*7.1. II. Ἕλληνες, οἱ, *the Thessalian tribe of which Hellen was the reputed chief*, Il.2.684. 2. of all *Greeks*, Epigr.ap.Paus.10.7.6, Hdt.1.56, Th.1.3, etc.; cf. Πανέλληνες. 3. *Gentiles*, whether heathens or Christians, opp. Jews, Lxx *Is.*9.12, *Ev.Jo.*7.35, etc. 4. *non-Egyptian* (incl. Persians, etc.), *PTeb.*5.169 (ii B.C.). 5. *pagan*, Jul.*Ep.*114, Eun. *VS* p.524B., Dam.*Isid.*204, *Cod.Just.*1.11.10. III. as Adj., = Ἑλληνικός, στρατός Pi.*N.*10.25, etc.: with fem. Subst., Ἕλλην' ἐπίσταμαι φάτιν A.*Ag.*1254; στολήν γ' Ἕλληνα E.*Heracl.*130; Ἕ. γυνή Philem.55; Ἕ. ἀληθῶς οὖσα, of fortune, Apollod.Car.5.10; Πυλῶν Ἑλλήνων D.18.304: with neut. Subst., ἐν χωρίῳ Ἕλληνι Them.*Or.*27. 332d. IV. *those who spoke* or *wrote Hellenistic Greek*, opp. Ἀττικοί, ἄρτι· οἱ μὲν Ἀ. τὸ πρὸ ὀλίγου, οἱ δὲ Ἕ. καὶ ἐπὶ τοῦ νῦν λέγουσι Moer. 68, al., cf. *POxy.*1012*Fr.*16; opp. οἱ παλαιοί, Moer.145.

⊛ Ἑλλην-άρχης, ου, ὁ, *chief of the Greek community*, title at Tanais, *IPE*2.423, al. -ίζω, impf. ἐλλήνιζον without augm., Charito4. 5 codd.: aor. Act. ἐλληνίσαι D.C.55.3: aor. Pass. without augm., Th.2.68 codd.: pf. Pass. ἡλλήνισται J.*AJ*1.6.1:—*speak Greek*, Ἕλλην μέν ἐστι καὶ ἑλληνίζει Pl.*Men.*82b, cf. *Chrm.*159a, *Prt.*328a, etc.; ἑ. τῇ φωνῇ, τὴν φωνήν, Aeschin.3.172, Charito l.c.; esp. *speak* or *write pure* or *correct Greek*, Arist.*Rh.*1407a19, D.H.*Pomp.*2.5; ἄκρως ἑ. S.E.*M.*1.186; opp. βαρβαρίζω, ib.246. b. οὐδὲ γὰρ ἂν ἑλληνίζοι οὕτως τὸ ἐρώτημα λεχθὲν *would* not *be Greek*, Arist.*SE* 182a34. c. *speak common Greek*, opp. the Attic dialect, σὺ μὲν ἀττικίζεις.. οἱ δ' Ἕλληνες ἑλληνίζομεν Posidipp.28. II. trans., *make Greek, Hellenize*, τὴν βάρβαρον Lib.*Or.*11.103; *translate into Greek*, D.C. l.c.:—Pass., ἑλληνισθῆναι τὴν γλῶσσαν ἀπό τινος *acquire the Greek language* from.., Th. l.c.; τὰ ὀνόματα.. ἡλλήνισται *have assumed an Hellenic form*, J.*AJ*1.6.1. ⊛ -ικός, ή, όν, *Hellenic, Greek*, Hdt.4.108, etc. 2. ἑλληνική (sc. γλῶσσα), ἡ, *the Greek language*, *Apoc.*9.11. 3. τὸ Ἑ. *the Greeks* collectively, Hdt.7.139, al.; *Greek soldiery*, X.*An.*1.4.13. b. *Greek culture*, D.H.1.89: pl., Hdt.4.78. 4. τὰ Ἑ. *the history of Greek affairs*, Th.1.97, etc.; title of works by X., Theopomp.Hist., etc.; *Greek literature*, App. *BC*4.67. II. *like the Greeks*, οὐ.. πατρῷον τόνδ' ἐδεξάμην νόμον, οὐδ' Ἑ. E.*Alc.*684, cf. Ar.*Ach.*115, Plu.*Luc.*41: Comp. -ώτερος Id. *Comp.Lyc.Num.*1; ἡ συγγνώμη τῆς τιμωρίας -ώτερον Lib.*Ep.*75.4: Sup. -ώτατος D.19.308, D.H.1.89. Adv. -κῶς *in Greek fashion*, Hdt.4. 108, E.*IT*660, Antiph.184. III. *pure Greek*, οὐχ Ἑ. λέξις Orusap. Eust.859.55, cf. Ael.Dion.*Fr.*207, S.E.*M.*1.187. Adv. -κῶς *in pure Greek*, opp. βαρβαρικῶς, Phld.*Lib.*p.13O., cf. S.E.*M.*1.243, Porph. *Abst.*3.3. 2. *in Hellenistic Greek*, opp. Ἀττικῶς, Moer.1, al.; but also, opp. κοινόν 'in common speech', Id.347, al. IV. *pagan*, Lxx 2*Ma.*4.10, al., Jul.*Ep.*84a, Suid. s.v. Διοκλητιανός. ⊛ -ιος, Dor. Ἑλλάνιος [ᾱ] (also in Ar.*Eq.*1253), α, ον, = foreg., Ζεὺς Ἑ., Ἀθανᾶ Ἑ., Rhetra ap.Plu.*Lyc.*6 (Συλλ- codd.); Ζεὺς Ἑ. Hdt.9.7.α', cf. Pi.*N.*5.10, *IG*12(5).910 (Tenos), etc.; Ἀθηνᾶ Ἑ. E.*Hipp.*1121 (lyr.); θεοὶ οἱ Ἑ. Hdt.5.49,92.η', Luc.*Herc.*2 codd., Hld.2.23. II. Ἑλλήνιον, τό, *Greek factory* (with temples of Θεοὶ Ἑλλήνιοι) at Naucratis, Hdt.2. 178; also of buildings at Arsinoe and Memphis, *BGU*133.6 (ii A.D.), Wilcken *Chr.*221 (iii B.C.). III. Ἑλλανία, ἡ, = Ἑλλάς, E.*Hel.* 1147 (lyr.), etc. ⊛ -ίς, Dor. Ἑλλᾱνίς, ίδος, ἡ, = fem. of Ἑλλήνιος, Pi.*P.*11.50; ἀρεταὶ ἀέθλων Id.*Pae.*4.23, cf. Cratin.293, Lys.30.18, Th. 1.35, D.18.304, etc.; Ἑ. διάλεκτος, γλῶττα, Phld.*D.*3.14. II. Ἑλληνίς (sc. γυνή), ἡ, *Grecian woman*, E.*El.*1076, Men.79. 2. *pagan woman*, Jul.*Ep.*112. -ισμός, ὁ, *imitation of the Greeks, Hellenism*, Lxx 2*Ma.*4.13. II. *use of a pure Greek style and idiom*, as an ἀρετὴ λόγου, Diog.Bab.*Stoic.*3.214, cf. Phld.*Po.*2.18, A.D.*Pron.*71.25, S.E.*M.*1.98; ἔνιοι λέγουσιν Ἑ. εἶναι τὸν ποιητήν (i.e. Homer), *Lex.Vind.*311; περὶ Ἑλληνισμοῦ, title of works by Seleucus, Ath.9.367a; by Ptolemy of Ascalon, Philoxenus and Tryphon, Suid.; κανόνες Ἑλληνισμοῦ, title of work by Irenaeus, Id. 2. *use of the* κοινή, opp. to strict Atticism, *POxy.*1012*Fr.*17. III. *paganism*, Jul.*Ep.*84a; ἡ τοῦ Ἑ. δυσσέβεια *Cod.Just.*1.11.9.1. -ιστής, οῦ, ὁ, *one who uses the Greek language*: *a Greek Jew*, *Act.Ap.*6.1, etc. II. *gentile, heathen*, Jul.*Ep.*84a. ⊛ -ιστί, Adv. *in the Greek language*, Pl.*Ti.*21e, *PTaur.*1v4 (ii B.C.), Ph.2.546, J.*AJ*14.10.2, etc.; Ἑ. ξυνιέναι to understand *Greek*, X.*An.*7.6.8; Ἑ. γινώσκεις; *Act.Ap.*21.37; *in Greek fashion*, Luc.*Scyth.*3.

Ἑλληνο-γαλάται [λᾰ], οἱ, = *Gallograeci*, D.S.5.32. -δίκαι, -δικέω, v. Ἑλλανο-. -κοπέω, *flatter the Greeks*, Plb.25.3.1; *affect Greek fashions*, Id.20.10.7. -μεμφῖται, οἱ, *Greeks resident at Memphis*, *PSI*5.531.6 (iii B.C.). -τᾰμίαι, ῶν, οἱ, *stewards of Greece*, i.e. *treasurers of the Confederacy of Delos*, *IG*1².191.1, al., Antipho 5. 69, And.3.38, Th.1.96, etc.:—hence -τᾰμιεία, ἡ, their *office*, X.*Vect.* 5.5 (-ταμία codd.). -τρωοφθόρος, ον, *destroying Greeks and Trojans*, μάχη Tz.*H.*5.772. -φρων, ονος, ὁ, ἡ, *with Greek tastes*, Dam.*Isid.*108.

Ἑλλησ-ποντιακός, ή, όν, *of the Hellespont*, X.*An.*1.1.9, etc.:—also -πόντιος, α, ον, Hdt.7.95, X.*HG*3.4.11. -ποντίας, Ion. -ίης (sc. ἄνεμος), ου, ὁ, *wind blowing from the Hellespont*, i.e. *from the NE.*, Hdt.7.188; = καικίας, Arist.*Mete.*364b19, cf. *Pr.*946b33, Thphr. *Vent.*62. -ποντιάς, άδος, ἡ, fem. Adj. *of the Hellespont*, θάλασσα Archestr.*Fr.*35.14B. -πόντιος, α, ον, *of the Hellespont*, Hdt.7. 95, X.*HG*3.4.11. II. Subst. -ποντία, ἡ, name of a *plaster*, Heras ap.Gal.13.914. -ποντίς, ίδος, fem. Adj., = -ποντιάς, πηλαμύς S. *Fr.*503. ⊛ -ποντος, ὁ, *Hellespont* or *sea of Helle* (daughter of Athamas, who was drowned therein), now *the Dardanelles*, Il.2.845, Hdt. 4.38, etc.:—sts. taken to include the Propontis, Id.1.57, etc.:—*the adjacent country*, Th.2.9, etc.: in this sense without Art. in Att. Inscrr., *IG*1².106.16, al.: said to be used of the Aegean, Str.7 *Fr.* 58. -ποντοφύλᾰκες [ῠ], οἱ, *customs officials* established by Athens to control the trade of the Hellespont, *IG*1².57.36.

ἐλλίζων· τίλλων, Hsch.

ἔλλιθος, ον, *containing a precious stone*, δακτυλίδιον *PLond.ined.* 2199 (iv A.D.).

⊛ ἐλλῐμεν-ίζω, *exact harbour-dues*, Ar.*Fr.*455. -ικός, ή, όν, only neut. pl. -ικά, τά (sc. τέλη), *harbour-dues*, Pl.*R.*425d. ⊛ -ιος, α, ον, *in the harbour*, [πύργοι] Str.1.3.20. II. Subst. -ιον, τό, *harbour-dues, customs*, Eup.48, *SIG*524.6 (Crete, iii B.C.), *Milet.*3 No.37 *d*68, Arist.*Oec.*1350a16, Plb.30.31.12: pl., *GDI*5018 (Cret.). -ισις, εως, ἡ, *coming into port*, Sch.rec.S.*OT*196. ⊛ -ιστής, οῦ, ὁ, *farmer of harbour-dues* or *customs*, Aen.Tact.29.5, D.34.34.

ἐλλῑπαίνω, aor. 1 ἐνελίπᾱνεν, glossed by ἔπλησεν, ἔπληξεν, Hsch.

⊛ ἐλλῐπής, ές, (ἐλλείπω) Act., *leaving out, omitting*, τινός Pl.*Lg.* 924b. II. Pass., *wanting, defective*, μνήμης Th.7.8; ἐ. κάλλους, ἀκριβείας, Pl.*Lg.*669a, *R.*504b, etc.: c. dat., προθυμίᾳ ἐλλιπεῖς Th.6. 69; δεῖπνον.. μηδενὶ ἐλλιπές Euang.1.3; ἐν τοῖς πεζικοῖς τῷ καθοπλισμῷ Plb.18.22.5. 2. abs., *failing*, ἐ. καὶ μὴ δυνατὸς ἐπιμελεῖσθαι *negligent*, Pl.*Lg.*901c; τὸ μὴ ἐπιχειρούμενον ἀεὶ ἐλλιπὲς ἦν τῆς δοκήσεως whatever was not attempted was *so much lost* of their reckoning, Th.4.55, cf. 5.1; τὸ ἐ. τῆς γνώμης ὑμ.. φήθημεν πράξειν the *failure* of judgement in respect of.., Id.4.63; τὸ ἐ. *defect*, Arist. *Rh.*1371b4; τὸ τῆς νομοθεσίας ἐ. Plb.6.49.6: Comp. -έστερος ib.11.3. Adv. -πῶς *inadequately, deficiently*, λέγειν Isoc.*Fr.*3.β'.5; πρός τι ἔχειν Aret.*CD*1.2; ἔχειν τινός *Cod.Just.*1.1.7.11; γεγραμμένα Gal. *Libr.Propr.*2; opp. περιττῶς, Philostr.*VS*1.11: Comp. -έστερον *OGI* 56.13 (iii B.C.); ἐ. τῆς ἀληθείας εἰρηκέναι Plb.5.32.2. III. of a number, *not equal to the sum of its factors*, opp. ὑπερτελής, Theo Sm. p.46H. Adv. -πῶς Iamb.*in Nic.*p.53P. IV. Gramm., *elliptical*, φωνή S.E.*P.*1.188, cf. Sch.S.*OT*324, etc. Adv. -πῶς Sch.A.R.1.252.

ἔλλιπος, ον, *greasy*, τῇ γεύσει Vett.Val.4.3 (Sup.), cf. *Cat.Cod. Astr.*7.220 (Sup.).

**ἐλλἴσάμην**, v. λίσσομαι. **ἐλλῖτάνευε**, v. λιτανεύω.

**ἐλλόβιον**, τό, (λοβός) *that which is in the lobe of the ear, ear-ring*, Nic. Dam.p.5 D., Luc.*Gall*.29, S.E.*P*.3.203, Them.*Or*.13.167d.

**ἐλλοβόκαρπος**, ον, *bearing fruit in a pod*, Thphr.*HP*6.5.3. **ἔλλοβος**, ον, *in a pod*, καρπός ib.3.14.4, 4.2.8. **ἐλλοβοσπέρμᾰτος**, ον, *with its seed in a pod*, opp. γυμνοσπ., ib.7.3.2.

**ἐλλοβώδης**, ες, *with pods*, Thphr.*HP*8.2.5.

**ἐλλογ-άω**, v.l. for sq. in *Ep.Rom*.5.13, *Ep.Philem*.18. **-έω**, (λόγος) = ἐν λόγῳ τιθέναι, *reckon, put to an account*, *Ep.Philem*.18; τινί *PRyl*.243.11 (ii A.D.), etc.:—Pass., *to be reckoned in*, *IG*9(1).61.37 (Daulis, ii A.D.), *PStrassb*.1.32.10 (iii A.D.), etc. 2. metaph., *impute*, *BGU*140.32 (ii A.D.):—Pass., *Ep.Rom*.5.13. ❊ **-ιμος**, ον, *held in account* or *regard* (ἐν λόγῳ), *in high repute*, Hdt.2.176, Pl.*Prt*. 327c, *Smp*.197a, al.; ἐ. ἐπὶ σοφίᾳ Id.*Prt*.361e: Sup., Plb.1.2.1, Philostr.*VS*1.9.1, al. Adv. -μως ib.2.11.1; ἔχειν τινός ib.33.2. II. *eloquent*, Men.Rh.p.354 S. (Sup.), Poll.2.125. Adv. -μως *Gloss*. III. = ἔλλογος, opp. ἄλογος, *Corp.Herm*.12.6. ❊ **-ιμότης**, ητος, ἡ, *capability of reasoning*, *Gloss*. **-ος**, ον, *endowed with reason*, opp. ἄλογος, Arist.*EN*1172ᵇ10, Plot.3.8.1.

**Ἐλλοί**· Ἕλληνες οἱ ἐν Δωδώνῃ, καὶ οἱ ἱερεῖς, Hsch.; cf. Σελλοί.

**ἔλλοιπος**, ον, = ἐλλιπής, *IG*1².373.48, 2².244.4.

**ἐλλοξοτέρως**, Adv. Comp. (λοξός) *rather obliquely*, Paul.Aeg.6.40.

**Ἐλλοπία**, Ep. -ίη, ἡ, (Ἔλλοψ, son of Ion) *the land of Dodona*, Hes.*Fr*.134.1. II. *a district in Euboea*, Hdt.8.23, etc.:—hence **Ἐλλοπιῆες**, its inhabitants, Hsch.

**ἐλλοπιεύω**, (ἔλλοψ) *fish*, Theoc.1.42: **ἐλλοπεύω** corrupt in *EM* 331.49.

❊ **ἐλλοπίης**, ου, ὁ, name of a *fish*, cj. for ἀλλ- in Numen.ap.Ath.7.326a.

**ἐλλόποδες** (so *EM*331.53, -ιδες Hsch.), *the young of birds* or *serpents*, Cratin.408.

**ἔλλοπος**, ὁ, v. ἔλλοψ I. **ἐλλοπῶ**· ἀγαθήν, Hsch.

**ἐλλός** or **ἐλλός** (A), ὁ, *a young deer, fawn*, ποικίλος Od.19.228, cf. Ant.Lib.28.3, Eust.1863.40. (Prob. from *ἐλνός, cf. ἔλαφος.)

**ἐλλός** (B), ἡ, όν, = ἔλλοψ (q.v.); also variously expld. (ἀγαθόν, γλαυκόν, χαροπόν..ταχύ..ὑγρόν) by Hsch.

**ἐλλοφόνος**, ον, *fawn-slaying*, of Britomartis, Call.*Dian*.190.

**ἐλλοχ-άω**, *lie in ambush* (λόχος), Pl.*Tht*.165d:—Med., Phalar.*Ep*.5. II. *lie in wait for*, τινά Pl.*Smp*.213b, Ael.*NA*6.4. III. Pass., ἐλλοχᾶσθαι κακοῖς *to be filled with lurking* mischiefs, Alciphr. 2.3. **-ησις**, εως, ἡ, *lying in ambush*, Anon.ap.Suid. s. v. δεξιός. **-ίζω**, *lie in ambush*, E.*Ba*.722. II. *place in ambush*, ὁπλίτας Polyaen.3.1.2, cf. Plu.*Phil*.14.

**ἔλλοψ**, οπος, ὁ, ἡ, epith. of fish (exc. ἔλλοπι κούρᾳ, of Echo, Theoc. *Syrinx*18), expld. as *dumb* by Hsch. (also by δασεῖς, τραχεῖς, ποικίλοι), but perh. rather, *scaly* (cf. λεπίς): ἔλλοπας ἰχθῦς Hes.*Sc*.212; ἔλλοπος μυνδοῦ δίκην Lyc.1375:—also **ἔλλοπος**, Emp.117: **ἐλλός**, ἰχθύες ἐλλοί Titanomach.*Fr*.4; ἐλλοῖς ἰχθύσιν S.*Aj*.1297. II. as Subst., *fish*, in general, Nic.*Al*.481, Lyc.600, Opp.*H*.2.658, 3.55,89; fem., Lyc.796. 2. an unknown *sea-fish*, Arist.*HA*505ᵃ15, etc.; also **ἔλοψ**, Epich.71, Archestr.*Fr*.11.1, Matro *Conv*.69, Apio ap.Ath. 7.294f, Plu.2.979c; identified with ἱερὸς ἰχθῦς by Ael.*NA*8.28. 3. *a serpent*, Nic.*Th*.490.

**ἔλλυες**· ζῷα ἐν τῷ Σμαράγδῳ ποταμῷ, Hsch.

**ἔλλῡπος**, ον, *in grief, mournful*, Plu.2.621a.

**ἔλλυσις**, Cret. for ἔκλυσις, Hsch. **ἐλλύτατον**· οἰκτρότατον, Id.

❊ **ἐλλύτης**, Dor. -ας, ὁ, a kind of *cake*, *Test.Epict*.5.35, al., Hsch.

**ἐλλυχᾶται**· πλανᾶται, διατρίβει, Hsch.

**ἐλλυχν-ιάζω**, *furnish* a lamp *with a wick*, *PMag.Par*.1.1099, *PMag.Lond*.121.376:—Pass., Dsc.1.72.4. ❊ **-ιον**, τό, *lamp-wick* (Att. θρυαλλίς), Hdt.2.62, Hp.*Nat.Mul*.26, *Mul*.2.203, Thphr.*Char*. 10.13, *Inscr.Délos* 316.76 (iii B.C.), Apollon.*Mir*.36, etc. 2. *surgical dressing*, Sor.2.11, Gal.10.954. **-ιωτός**, ή, όν, *made of wick-cotton*, μοτός Gal.14.795, Paul.Aeg.3.24.

**ἐλλωβάομαι**, *commit an outrage*, εἰς τὸν οἶκόν τινος Ant.Lib.11.7.

**Ἑλλωτία** or **Ἑλλωτίς**, ίδος, ἡ, epith. of Athena, Sch.Pi.*O*.13.56. 2. Ἑλλωτίς, ἡ, *wreath worn at the* Ἑλλωτία, Seleuc.ap.Ath. 15.678a, cf. Hsch. II. Ἑλλώτια (sc. ἱερά), τά, *festival* of Athena at Corinth, Pi.*O*.13.40; of Europa in Crete, Hsch.

**ἐλμακίνη** λειμῶνος· ἡ λεπτὴ σχοῖνος, Hsch. **ἔλματα**· ὁμιλήματα, ἐνειλήματα, σανιδώματα, Id.

**ἐλμινθ-ιάω**, (ἕλμινς) *suffer from worms*, Arist.*HA*612ᵃ31. **-ιον**, τό, Dim. of ἕλμινς, *little worm*, Hp.*Epid*.4.16, Arist.*HA*570ᵃ14.

**ἐλμινθοβότᾰνον**, τό, a *herb used as a specific for worms*, Alex.Trall. *Verm*.2 p.595 P.

**ἐλμινθώδης**, ες, *like a worm*, Arist.*HA*538ᵃ5.

❊ **ἕλμινς** (Hp.*Morb*.4.54), ινθος, ἡ, dat. pl. ἕλμινσι Choerob. *in Theod*. 1.299:—also nom. **ἕλμις**, Arist.*HA*602ᵇ26; acc. ἕλμιθα *IG*4.952.10, 18; nom. pl. ἕλμεις Dsc.*Eup*.2.67; dat. ἕλμῖσι Opp.*H*.3.180: also gen. ἕλμιγγος Hp.*Epid*.1.26.ιβ':—*worm*, I. *intestinal-worm*, either flat (πλατεῖα) or round (στρογγύλη), Id.*Morb*.4.54, cf. *Prog*.11, *Aph*. 3.26, Arist.*HA*551ᵃ8, Thphr.*HP*9.12.1. II. *parasitic worm* in sponges, Arist.*HA*548ᵇ15.

**ἑλξίνη** [ῑ], ἡ, (ἕλκω) *pellitory, Parietaria officinalis*, Dsc.4.85, Apollon.*Mir*.30. II. *bindweed, Convolvulus arvensis*, Dsc.4.39. III. = μῖλαξ τραχεῖα, Ps.-Dsc.4.142. IV. ἑ. μείζων, = περικλύμενον, ib.14.

**ἕλξις**, εως, ἡ, (ἕλκω) *dragging, trailing*, τὰς Ἕκτορος ἕλξεις Pl.*R*. 391b; ἱματίων ἕλξεις Id.*Alc*.1.122c. 2. *attraction, attractive power*, Id.*Ti*.80c, Hp.*Gland*.7; ἕλξει ἐκ γῆς ἀναδίδοται τὰ σπέρματα Porph. *Gaur*.3.3. 3. *drawing* of the bow, ἀπὸ τῆς χειρός Hero *Bel*.75.10, cf. Philostr.*Her*.11. 4. *retching*, Hp.*Coac*.55.

**ἑλξῖτις**, ιδος, ἡ, = ἑλξίνη, Ps.-Dsc.4.39.

**ἕλοιμι, ἑλοίμην, ἑλόμην, ἕλον**, v. αἱρέω.

**ἑλονόμος**, ον, *dwelling in marshes*, f.l. for ὑλο-, Hp.*Vict*.2.49.

❊ **ἕλος**, εος, τό, *marsh-meadow*, ἵπποι ἕλος κάτα βουκολέοντο Il.20.221, cf. 4.483: generally, *marshy ground*, ἂν δόνακας καὶ ἕλος Od.14.474, cf. Hdt.1.191, Th.1.110, *Inscr.Cypr*.135.9 H. (Idalium), X.*HG*1.2.7, etc. 2. *backwater*, δάσκιον ἕ. A.R.2.1283.

**ἔλοψ**, v. ἔλλοψ. **ἐλόωσι**, v. ἐλαύνω.

**ἐλπῐδο-δώτης**, ου, ὁ, *giver of hope*, *AP*9.525.6, cj. in Timo 65. ❊ **-κοπέω**, *lead by false hopes*, ἐπιθυμίας S.E.*M*.6.26, cf. Eust. 1063.60 (Pass.). **-ποιέω**, *raise hopes*, Sch.Od.18.160, Hsch. s. v. ἔλπει.

❊ **ἐλπίζω**, Att. fut. -ιῶ Lxx*Ps*.43(44).7, *Ep.Rom*.15.12; ἐλπίσω Gal.10.656 (ἐλπίσω in A.*Ch*.187 is aor. subj.): aor. ἤλπισα Hdt.8.24, S.*Ph*.1175 (lyr.), etc. (ἤλπιζα (sic) *IG*3.1350): pf. ἤλπικα *Ev.Jo*.5. 45, (προ-) Posidipp.27.8: plpf. ἠλπίκειν Plu.*Alc*.17, Luc.*Herm*.71, Hdn.8.5.1:—Med., App.*Pun*.115 (s. v.l.), *Supp.Epigr*.2.461 (Histria, i B.C.):—Pass., aor. ἠλπίσθην S.*OC*1105, *APl*.4.222 (Parmen.): pf. ἤλπισμαι D.H.5.40:—Att. form of ἔλπομαι, used also by Hdt., *hope for*, or rather (in earlier writers) *look for, expect*:—Constr.: c. acc., A.*Th*.589, *Ch*.539, etc., τι παρά τινος X.*Mem*.4.3.17, D.19. 102: freq. with a dependent clause in inf., *hope to* do, or *hope* or *expect that*..; c. fut. inf., ἐ. μιν ἀποθανέεσθαι Hdt.3.143, cf. Antipho 2. 3.6, Th.4.71, Lys.16.2; ἐ. τὴν Εὐρώπην δουλώσεσθαι (v.l. -ασθαι) Id. 2.21: c. aor. inf., ἐ. ποτὲ δεῖξαι S.*Ph*.629; ἤλπιζον ἑλεῖν X.*Ag*.7.6: also with ἄν, οὐδαμὰ ἐλπίζων ἂν ἡμίονον τεκέειν Hdt.3.151, Th.2.53; the inf. may be omitted, ἔκλυον ἄν..οὐδ' ἂν ἤλπισ' αὐδάν (sc. κλύειν) S. *El*.1281; also ἐ. ὅπως.., with fut., E.*Heracl*.1051, S.*El*.963:—Pass., τὸ μηδαμὰ ἐλπισθὲν ἥξειν Id.*OC*1105; ὁ ἐλπισθεὶς αὐτοκράτωρ *POxy*. 1021.6 (i A.D.). 2. of evils, *look for, fear*, in same constr., δύστανον ἐ. αἶσαν S.*Tr*.111 (lyr.); ἔξοδον ὀλεθρίαν Αἴαντος ἐλπίζει φέρειν Id. *Aj*.799, cf. Lys.12.70; τουτί..τὸ κακὸν οὐδέποτ' ἤλπισα Ar.*Av*.956; ἐ. πάγχυ ἀπολέεσθαι Hdt.8.12; θῆράς σφε τὸν δύστηνον ἐλπίζει κτανεῖν E.*Ion*348: with μή folld. by aor. subj., οὐδαμὰ ἐλπίσας μή κοτε ἐλάσῃ Hdt.1.77; οὐκ ἂν ἤλπισε μή κοτέ τις ἀναβαίη Id.8.53. 3. c. pres. inf., *deem, suppose that*.., Emp.11.2; ἐλπίζων εἶναι..ὀλβιώτατος Hdt. 1.30; ἐλπίζων σιτοδείην τε εἶναι ἰσχυρὴν..καὶ τὸν λεὼν τετρῦσθαι ib. 22; οἰκότα ἐλπίζων ib.27, cf. A.*Th*.76, *Ch*.187; βοῦν ἢ λέοντ' ἤλπιζες ἐντείνειν βρόχοις; E.*Andr*.720; ἐλπίζει δυνατὸς εἶναι ἄρχειν Pl.*R*. 573c; ὅστις ἐλπίζει θεοὺς..χαίρειν ἀπαρχαῖς *Trag.Adesp*.118.2: sts. of future events, τίς ἂν ἤλπισεν ἁμαρτήσεσθαί τινα τῶν πολιτῶν τοιαύτην ἁμαρτίαν; Lys.31.27; οὐδὲν..ποιήσειν ἐλπίζων D.4.7. 4. c. dat., *hope in*.., τῇ τύχῃ Th.3.97; ὀνόματι *Ev.Matt*.12.21: also with Preps., ἔν τισι Lxx4*Ki*.18.5; πρός τι ib.*Jd*.20.36; ἐ. εἴς τινα *Ev.Jo*.5.45, al.; ἐπί τινι *Ep.Rom*.15.12, al.; ἐπί τινα 1*Ep.Pet*.3.5.

❊ **ἐλπ-ίς**, ίδος, ἡ, (v. ἔλπω) *hope, expectation* (δόξα μελλόντων Pl.*Lg*. 644c), ἔτι γὰρ καὶ ἐλπίδος αἶσα Od.16.101, 19.84; personified, Hes. *Op*.96: pl., Pi.*P*.2.49, etc.; πολλῶν ῥαγεισῶν ἐλπίδων after the wreck of many *hopes*, A.*Ag*.505; ἔτι ἐν αὐτοῖς εἰσὶν ἐλπίδες, νέοι γάρ Pl.*Prt*. 328d; κεναῖσιν ἐλπίσιν θερμαίνεται S.*Aj*.478; *expectancy*, Id.*OT*771 (pl.), *OC*1749 (lyr., pl.), Pi.*N*.1.32 (pl.), etc.:—Constr., in Att., with gen. both of subject and object, as (where both are conjoined) Πελοποννησίων τὴν ἐλπίδα τοῦ ναυτικοῦ *the hope of* the P. *in* their navy, Th. 2.89; also αἱ τῶν Ἑλλήνων ἐς ὑμᾶς ἐλπίδες Id.3.14; ὑμέτεραι ἐλπίδες, = ἐς ὑμᾶς, Id.1.69; ἐλπίδ' ἔχω, = ἐλπίζω, with fut. inf., μὴ οὐ δώσειν δίκην Hdt.6.11, etc.: with aor. inf., κλέος εὑρέσθαι Pi.*P*.3.111: with ὡς and fut. inf., S.*OC*385; ὥστε μὴ θανεῖν E.*Or*.52; περὶ τῆς ἐμαυτοῦ ψυχῆς οὐ πολλὰς ἐλπίδας ἔχω D.H.5.27; ἐν ἐλπίδι εἰμί, c. fut. inf., Th.7.46; ἐν ἐλπίσι καλαῖς γενόμενος Plu.*Brut*.40; ἐλπίς [ἐστί] μοι with acc. and fut. inf. or aor.. ἐλπίς τις αὐτὸν ἥξειν A.*Ag*.679; τοσοῦτόν γ' ἐστί μοι τῆς ἐλπίδος, τὸν ἄνδρα..προσμεῖναι S.*OT*836; πλείων ἐλπὶς φιλίαν ἢ ἔχθραν γενέσθαι Pl.*Phdr*.232e: c. pres. inf., Id.*Sph*.250e: folld. by ὡς.., E.*Tr*.487; ἐς ἐλπίδα ἐλθεῖν τινος Th.2.56; ἐπ' ἐλπίδας ἀφανεῖς καθίστασθαι Id.5.103; ἐλπίδα λαβεῖν X.*Cyr*.4.6.7; ἐλπίδας μεγάλας ἔν τινι ἔχειν ib.1.4.25, cf. Isoc.4.121; τίν' ὑπάγεις μ' ἐς ἐλπίδ'; E.*Hel*. 826; ἐλπίδας ἐμποιεῖν ἀνθρώποις, ὑποθεῖναί τισι, X.*Cyr*.1.6.19, *HG*4. 8.28; ἐλπίδας μεγίστας παρέχεται ποιῆσαι Pl.*Smp*.193d; ἐλπίδα or ἐλπίδας ὑπογράφειν, Epicur.*Ep*.3 p.65 U., Plb.5.36.1; ἀποκεκομμένης τῆς ἐλπίδος Id.3.63.8, cf. A.R.4.1272; ἐκτὸς ἐλπίδος beyond *hope*, S.*Ant*.330; ἀπ' ἐλπίδος πεσεῖν A.*Ag*.999; παρ' ἐλπίδα ib.899, S.*Ph*. 882: prov., πεινῶμεν ἐπὶ ταῖς ἐλπίσιν Antiph.123.7; κάπτοντες αὔρας ἐλπίδας σιτούμενοι Eub.10.7; αἱ δ' ἐλπίδες βόσκουσι τοὺς κενοὺς Men. *Mon*.42. 2. *object of hope, a hope*, Ὀρέστης, ἐ. δόμων A.*Ch*.776; ὑμεῖς, ἡ μόνη ἐ. Th.3.57; Εὐτυχος, ἡ γονέων ἐ. *IG*3.1311. 3. *reason to expect* or *believe*, πολλὴ ἐ. κτήσασθαι, νοητὸν εἶναι, Pl.*Phd*. 67b, *Lg*.898d. II. *anxious thought on the future, boding*, A. *Ag*.1434, Hp.*Coac*.267, E.*Or*.859, Pl.*Lg*.644c. **-ισμα**, ατος, τό, *hope, confidence*, Epicur.*Fr*.68 (= Metrod.*Fr*.5): pl., D.Chr.20. 24. **-ισμός**, ὁ, *expectation*, Phld.*Rh*.1.288 S. **-ιστέον**, *one must expect*, Lyd.*Ost*.24. **-ιστικός**, ή, όν, *producing expectation*, Arist.*Mem*.449ᵇ12. II. οἱ ἐ. a sect *who made hope the only stay of life*, Plu.2.668e. **-ιστός**, ή, όν, *to be expected*, Pl.*Lg*.853d; τὸ μέλλον ἐστὶ δοξαστὸν καὶ ἐ. Arist.*Mem*.449ᵇ11.

**ἔλπος**· ἔλαιον, στέαρ, εὐθηνία, Hsch.; cf. ἔλφος. (Cf. Skt. *sarpiṣ* 'melted butter', OHG. *salba*.) **ἐλπτέοντες**· ἐλπίζοντες, Id.

**ἔλπω** (ἐέλπω only Hsch. s. v. ἐέλποιμεν), causal, only found in pres.

(exc. ἔλπεον· ἤλπιζον, Id.), *cause to hope*, πάντας μὲν ἔλπει she *feeds* all *with hope*, Od.2.91, 13.380; perh. also, *cause to expect*, Max.178 (but may, = *expect*). II. elsewh. in Med., **ἔλπομαι**, Ep. **ἐέλπομαι**, ἠλπόμην Od.9.419, Alc.*Supp.*22.8, Pi.*P.*4.243, etc.: Ep. 3 sg. impf. ἔλπετο and ἐέλπ–, Od.3.275, Il.12.407 (ἔλπετο also in Luc.*Syr.D.*22): pf. ἔολπα Il.22.216, Od.5.379, Hes.*Op.*[273], A.R.2.147, etc.: 3 sg. plpf. ἐώλπει Il.19.328, Od.20.328, A.R.3.370, Theoc.25.115:—*hope* or *expect*, Ep., Lyr., Ion. (not in Hp.) for Att. ἐλπίζω (q.v.):—Constr., like ἐλπίζω: c. acc. and fut. inf., Il.13.8, B.*Fr.*12: c. aor. inf., Il.7.199, Pi.*P.*4.243 codd., *N.*4.92: c. pf. inf., Il.15.110: sts. the inf. must be supplied, ἐκτελέσας μέγα ἔργον ὃ οὔ ποτε ἔλπετο θυμῷ (sc. ἐκτελέειν) Od.3.275: c. acc. rei, Il.13.609, 15.539; ἅσσα οὐκ ἔλπονται Heraclit.27: later, c. gen. rei, πολυληγαγέος ἐνιαυτοῦ Arat.1100: ὡς.., dub. l. in Orph.*A.*846: abs., Heraclit.18: Homeric phrases, ἔλπετο θυμῷ Il.17.404, al.; also μάλα δέ σφισιν ἔλπετο θυμός 17.495; ἔλπετο θυμὸς ἐνὶ στήθεσσιν ἑκάστου 15.701; ἤλπετ' ἐνὶ φρεσὶ Od.9.419. 2. *expect anxiously, fear*, ἐλπόμενός τί οἱ κακὸν εἶναι *having a foreboding that*.., Hdt.9.113. 3. generally, *deem, suppose*, οὐ ποθι ἔλπομαι οὕτως δεύεσθαι πολέμοιο..'Αχαιούς Il.13.309, cf. Theoc. 7.31; ἐπὴν ἡμέας ἔλπῃ ποτὶ δώματ' ἀφῖχθαι Od.6.297, cf. 23.345; ἔλπετο γὰρ κατὰ θυμὸν..ἑταίρους..ἰέναι (pres. inf.) Il.10.355; οὐ γὰρ ὅ γ' ἀθανάτων τιν' ἐέλπετο..Τρώεσσιν ἀρηξέμεν Il.13.8, cf. 7.199, 15.110, Orac.ap.Hdt.1.65, *AP*5.115 (Marc. Arg.); λάσην Alc. l.c. (ϝελπ–, ἐϝέλπομαι, ϝέϝολπα, cf. Lat. *volup.*)

❋ **ἐλπωρή**, ἡ, Ep. form of ἐλπίς, c. fut. inf. et aor., ἐλπωρή..κακῶν ὑπάλυξιν ἔσεσθαι Od.23.287; ἐ. φίλους ἰδέειν 6.314: pl., A.R.3.1255. (Dissim. from *ἐλπωλή, cf. φειδωλή, etc.)

**ἔλσαι**, inf. and **ἔλσας**, aor. 1 part. of εἴλω (q.v.).

**ἔλσῃ**, **ἔλσοιμι**, **ἐλσῶν**, Lacon. for ἐλθ–, Ar.*Lys.*105,118,1081.

**ἐλσούς**· τὰς μυίας, Hsch.

**ἐλύδριον**, τό, = χελιδόνιον, used to make yellow dye, *PHolm.*11.16, *PLeid.X.*68, Ps.-Democr.Alch.p.48B., v.l. in Paul.Aeg.3.2.

❋ **ἔλῠμα**, ατος, τό, (ἐλύω) *the stock of the plough*, Hes.*Op.*430,436: also expld. by νύσσα, καὶ τὸ ἱμάτιον, καὶ ἡ αἰών, Hsch.

❋ **ἐλύμνιαι**· δοκοὶ ὀροφῆναι, Hsch.

❋ **ἔλῠμος**, ὁ, (ἐλύω) *case, quiver*, Hsch. II. a kind of Phrygian *pipe*, made of box-wood, with a horn tip and bend in the left pipe, ἔλυμοι αὐλοί S.*Fr.*450,644, Call.Com.18; used by the Cyprians, Cratin.Jun.3. III. ἔλυμος, ἡ (masc. in pl., Procop.*Pers.*1.12), = μελίνη, *millet*, Hp.*Mul.*2.110, Ar.*Fr.*398, Plb.2.15.2, *CGI*55.16 (Telmessus, iii B.C.), Str.12.3.15, Dsc.2.98.

**ἐλύσσει**· εἰλεῖται, Hsch. **ἔλυστα**· ἄμπελος μέλαινα, Id.

❋ **ἐλυτροειδής** χιτών, *tunica vaginalis testiculi*, Cels.7.18, Antyll.ap. Orib.44.23.75, Ruf.*Onom.*197 (written ἐρυτρο– Gal.18(2).998).

❋ **ἔλυτρον**, τό, (ἐλύω) *covering*: 1. *bow-case*, S.*Fr.*1043 (pl.); *sheath* of a spear, Ar.*Ach.*1120; *mirror-case*, *IG*2.706*A*$^b$13; χοᾶ ἐν ἐ. ib.11(2).219*B*76 (Delos, iii B.C.); *case* of a shield, D.S.20.11 (pl.). 2. *sheath* of the spinal cord, Hp.*Art.*45: the *shard* of a beetle's wing, Arist.*HA*532$^a$23; *shell* of a crab, Ael.*NA*9.43; of the eye-*lids*, Arist. *de An.*421$^b$29; of the umbilical cord, Id.*HA*586$^b$23. 3. *husk* or *capsule* of seeds, J.*AJ*3.7.6; the flowering *glume* of ζέα δίκοκκος, Dsc. 2.89. 4. *the body*, as being *the case* or *shell* of the soul, Pl.*R.*588e, Poet.ap.Luc.*Demon.*44. 5. *reservoir for water*, Hdt.1.185, 4.173, Paus.2.27.7, al.; *tank* for fish, Palaeph.27. (Cf. Skt. *varūtram* 'cloak', *varūtár-* 'protector'.) [ῠ Ar. l.c.]

**ἐλυτρόω**, *cover, encase*, Hp.*Art.*45 (Pass.).

**ἐλύω**, *roll round* (cf. εἰλύω): only aor. 1 Pass., ῥυμὸς ἐπὶ γαῖαν ἐλύσθη the pole *rolled* to the ground, Il.23.393; προπάροιθε ποδῶν 'Αχιλῆος ἐλυσθείς *rolled up, crouching* before Achilles' feet, 24.510, cf. A.R.3.281, 1.1034; λασίην ὑπὸ γαστέρ' ἐλυσθείς *coiled* close *up*.., Od. 9.433; ἔρως ὑπὸ καρδίην ἐλυσθείς Archil.103. II. in later Ep., = εἰλύω, *wrap up, cover*, ἐνὶ κτερέεσσιν ἐλυσθείς *shrouded* in them, A.R. 1.254; ἐν πηλοῖσιν ἐλυσθείς Opp.*C.*3.418, cf. *H.*2.89; διὰ φλογὸς εἶθαρ ἐ. A.R.3.1313.

**ἔλφος**, εος, τό, Cypr., = βούτυρον, Hsch.; v. ἔλπος. **ἐλωγή**· ἔλεγον, Id.

❋ **ϝέλχανος**, epith. of Zeus in Crete, *GDI*5118, Hsch. (Γελ–):—hence **ϝελχάνια**, τά, *BCH*13.61 (Βελχ–): ❋ **'Ελχάνιος**, ὁ (sc. μήν), month at Cnossus, ib.29.204.

**ἐλώδης**, ες, *marshy, fenny*, ὕδατα Hp.*Aër.*1; χωρίον Th.7.47, cf. Arist.*HA*596$^b$3, Onos.8.2 (v.l.); τὰ ἐ. Arist.*Pr.*910$^a$4. II. *frequenting marshes*, of the elephant, Id.*PA*659$^a$2. III. *bred in marshes*, πυρετός Gal.17(1).889.

**ἔλωμα**, ατος, τό, = ἕλος, prob. in Python 1.2.

**'Ελωός**, epith. of Hephaestus among Dorians, Hsch.

**ἔλωρ**, τό, Ep. word (twice in Trag., v. infr.), only nom. and acc. sg. and pl.: (ἑλεῖν):—*spoil, prey*, in sg., of unburied corpses, ἀνδράσι δυσμενέεσσιν ἕ. καὶ κύρμα γενέσθαι Il.5.488, cf. 17.151; μὴ θήρεσσιν ἕ. κ. κ. γένωμαι Od.5.473, cf. 3.271, A.R.1.1251; of valuables, μή..ἕ. ἄλλοισι γένηται Od.13.208; κυσὶν πρόβλητος οἰωνοῖς θ' ἕ. S.*Aj.*830: pl., κυσὶν δ' ἕλωρα..πέλειν A.*Supp.*800 (lyr.). II. in pl. also, Πατρόκλοιο δ' ἕλωρα..ἀποτείσῃ may pay *penalty for the slaughter* of P., Il.18.93.

**ἐλώρη**· πελώρη, Hsch.

❋ **ἑλώριον**, τό, = ἕλωρ, A.R.2.264: pl., ἑλώρια τεῦχε κύνεσσι Il.1.4.

**ἐλώριος**, ὁ, a *water-bird*, Clearch.73 (nisi leg. ἐρῳδιός).

**ἐλώσθη**· ἐφοβεῖτο, ἐμαλακίσθη, Hsch.

**ἐμ**, = ἐν, before labials.

❋ **ἐμαυτοῦ**, **ἐμαυτῆς**, reflexive Pron. of first pers., *of me, of myself*: only gen., dat., and acc. sg., both masc. and fem.: not found in early Ep.; Aeol. ἔμ' αὔτῳ, ἔμ' αὔτᾳ, Alc.72, Sapph.*Supp.*15.11, cf. A.D. *Pron.*80.10; ἐμαυτόν is dub. in Xenoph. (*PLG*2 p.116 B.) and Anacr. 64; Ion. ἐμεωυτοῦ Hdt.4.97 (but ἐμωυτοῦ A.D.*Pron.*74.4), ἐμεωυτῷ Hdt.3.142, ἐμεωυτόν Heraclit.101; ἐμᾶτοῦ, ἐμᾶτόν, *Lyr.Alex.Adesp.*4.23, *SIG*741.12 (i B.C.): in pl. always separated, ἡμῶν αὐτῶν, etc.; ἐν ἐμαυτῷ συννοεῖσθαι in or with *oneself*, E.*Or.*634; πρὸς ἐμαυτόν Ar. *Ra.*53, etc.; strengthd., ἴσχυόν τ' αὐτὸς ἐμαυτοῦ Id.*V.*357, cf. *Lys.*1125; but ἐν ἐμαυτοῦ (sc. οἴκῳ) εἶναι, metaph., to be *master of oneself*, Pl.*Chrm.*155d: nom. ἐμαυτός, com. formation in Pl.Com.78.

**ἔμβᾱ**, Poet. aor. 2 imper. of ἐμβαίνω.

**ἐμβᾰβάζω**, *interrupt*, ἐμβαβάξαντες prob. l. for ἐμβιβ–, Hippon.53.

**ἐμ-βᾰδᾶς**, ᾶ, ὁ, *cobbler*, name given to Anytus, Theopomp.Com.57, cf. Archipp.30. **–βᾰδεία**, ἡ, = ἐμβατεία, *POxy.*485.33 (ii A.D.), *BGU*832.12, etc. **–βάδευσις** [ᾰ], εως, ἡ, = foreg., prob. in *POxy.* 274.24 (i A.D.). **–βᾰδεύω**, = ἐμβατεύω, ib.1118.7 (i/ii A.D.), *BGU* 101.16 (ii A.D.). **–βᾰδίζω**, *walk on*, ὄχθαις Ael.*NA*10.24; simply, *walk, march*, Ph.1.232, D.C.59.14. **–βᾰδικός**, όν, *square*, πήχεις *PTeb.*472 (ii A.D.), cf. Hero *Mens.*23.2, al. II. –κόν, τό, *tax paid by tenants of land*, *Ostr.*1024. **–βάδιον** [ᾰ], τό, Dim. of ἐμβάς, Ar.*V.*600, *Pl.*847,941. **–βᾰδομετρικός**, ή, όν, *belonging to the measuring of surfaces*, Hero *Deff.*133. **–βᾰδόν** (A), Adv. *by land*, = πεζῇ, Il.15.505; *wading*, Paus.10.20.8. **–βᾰδόν** (B), τό, *a surface, area* (opp. περίμετρος, Herm.*in Phdr.*p.108A.), Plb.6.27.2, Phld.*Sign.*15, al., Hero *Deff.*117, *POxy.*505.6 (ii A.D.), Theo Sm. p.126H., etc.: hence, in Arith., *product* of integers (opp. περίμετρος 'sum'), *Theol.Ar.*10. II. as Adj., δάκτυλος ἐμβαδὸς *square* inch, Hero *Mens.*23. **–βᾰδοποιός**, ὁ, *shoemaker*, *Gloss.*

❋ **ἔμβαθρα**, ων, τά, a kind of *shoes*, Poll.7.93.

**ἐμβαθρικὸν** χωρίον, dub. sens. in *Inscr.Magn.*122*b*6.

**ἐμβαθύνους**· σεσοφισμένους, σοφούς, Hsch.

**ἐμβᾰθύνω**, *make deep, hollow out*, βόθρια Alciphr.3.13; *cause to sink deep in*, κακίαν ἑαυτοῖς Plu.2.1128e. II. intr., *go deep into*, τοῖς νόμοις, ταῖς ἐπιστήμαις, Ph.1.18,341; *sink deep in*, εἰς κάθισιν Lxx *Je.*30.8(49.30).

❋ **ἐμβαίνω**, fut. –βήσομαι: pf. –βέβηκα; Ep. part. ἐμβεβαώς, –υῖα, Il. 5.199, Hes.*Th.*12, etc.: aor. 2 ἐνέβην; Ep. 3 sg. ἔμβη Od.4.656; dual imper. ἔμβητον Il.23.403:—*step in*, μή τις..ἐμβήῃ let none *step in* (so as to interfere), 16.94: c. dat., ποταμῷ οὐκ ἔστιν δὶς τῷ αὐτῷ ἐμβῆναι Heraclit.91; εἰς πηλόν Id.5; ἐμβέβακεν ἴχνεσιν πατρός Pi.*P.*10.12. 2. *go on, go quickly*, ἔμβητον, says Antilochus to his horses, Il.23.403; ἔμβα *advance!* E.*El.*113 (lyr.). 3. *embark* on a ship, ἐρέται δ' ἐν ἑκάστῃ πεντήκοντα ἐμβέβασαν Il.2.720; τότε δ' ἔμβη νηὶ Πύλονδε Od.4.656, cf. Il.1.311; ἐς ἕτερον πλοῖον ἐ. (v.l. for ἐσβ–) Hdt.2.29, cf. Th.1.18 (v.l.), Lys.2.40, Pl.*Mx.*243c: c. acc., λέμβον ἐ. Plb.30.9.11: abs., *embark*, E.*Tr.*455 (troch.), Ar.*Ra.*188, etc.: generally, *step into, mount*, εἰς τὸ φορεῖον Plu.*Galb.*26: pf., *to be mounted on*, ἵπποισι καὶ ἅρμασιν ἐμβεβαῶτα Il.5.199; ἐπ' ἀπήνης ἐμβεβώς S.*OT*803: also c. acc., Τροίαν 'Ιλιάδ' ἐμβεβαῶτα E.*Hec.*922 (lyr.); στέγην τήνδ' ἐμβεβῶτες Id.*Cyc.*92. 4. *step upon*, τῷ δ' ἐγὼ ἐμβαίνων Od.10.164; πεδίλοις ἐμβεβαυῖα Hes.*Th.*12; τοῖσδ' ἁλουργέσιν A.*Ag.*946; δαίμων ἐνέβη Περσῶν γενεᾷ *trampled upon* it, Id.*Pers.* 911 (anap.); μὴ 'μβαινε τῷ δυστυχοῦντι Men.*Mon.*356: abs., *tread on* one's *toes*, Thphr.*Char.*15.6; cf. βοῦς VIII. 5. *enter upon*, ἐς τόνδε χρησμόν dub. in A.*Ag.*1567; εἰς κίνδυνον X.*Cyr.*2.1.15: c. acc., ἐ. κέλευθον E.*Supp.*989 (lyr.). b. metaph., *enter upon, embark in*, μεγαλανορίαις Pi.*N.*11.44; τῷ ἐπιτηδεύματι Pl.*Phdr.*252e; ἐν αὐτοῖς τοῖς δεινοῖς ἐμβεβηκὼς *embarked, engaged in*.., D.18.248; *light upon*, εἰς ἀρχήν τε καὶ τύπον τῆς δικαιοσύνης Pl.*R.*443c: abs., *enter upon office*, *IG*5(1).1390.31 (Andania). 6. rarely c. gen., *step upon*, νάυς Alc.19; γῆς ὅρων S.*OC*400. 7. Poets, with acc. of the instrument of motion, ὄχοις..ἐμβεβὼς πόδα S.*Fr.*672; ἐς ἄντλον ἐμβήσει (2 sg.) πόδα E.*Heracl.*168. 8. *to be fixed* or *fastened*, κατά τι Il.24.81; *to be fixed in*, εἰς ἐμπυελίδας Hero *Aut.*2.3. 9. = ἐμβατεύω II, *SIG*364.75 (Ephesus, iii B.C.). II. causal in aor. 1 ἐνέβησα, *make to step in, put in*, ἐν δὲ τὰ μῆλα..ἐβήσαμεν Od.11.4; δίφρον ἐμβῆσαί τινα E.*Heracl.*845, cf. *Cyc.*467; ἐ. τὰν ἀρχάν *Schwyzer* 485.9 (Thespiae, iii B.C.): metaph., ἐμβῆσαί τινα ἐς φροντίδα *plunge* him into anxiety, Hdt.1.46. III. intr., *step, march* or *dance*, ὀρθῶς Pl. *Alc.*1.108c; πρὸς ῥυθμόν Luc.*Salt.*10.

**ἐμβακανίτης**· τὸ μετὰ τοῦ ταρίχους καὶ στέατος σκευαζόμενον βρῶμα, Hsch.

**ἐμβακχεύω**, *revel in*, τοῖς ἡμετέροις κακοῖς Hld.2.4.

❋ **ἐμβάλλω**, fut. –βαλῶ: pf. –βέβληκα: aor. 2 ἐνέβαλον (Pass. is mostly supplied by ἐμπίπτω):—*throw in*, τινὰ πόντῳ Il.14.258; μιν.. χερσὶν 'Αχιλλῆος θεὸς ἔμβαλεν *let* him *fall into* Achilles' hands, 21.47; ἐ. νιν βροτοῦ ἀνέρος εὐνῇ 18.85; ἐ. τινὰ εἰς τὸ βάραθρον Ar.*Ra.*574, *Nu.* 1450; εἰς τὸ δεσμωτήριον D.53.14; ἐ. τινὰ εἰς συμφοράς Antipho 3.4.10; εἰς ἀτυχίας Aeschin.3.79; εἰς αἰσχύνην καὶ ἀδικίαν Din.3.7; εἰς ὑποψίαν Plu.*Them.*23; ἐς γραφάς Ar.*Ach.*679, cf. Hdt.4.72, etc.; εἰς ἀπορίαν Pl.*Phlb.*2ca; εἰς ἔχθραν D.18.70. 2. of things, ἵπποις χαλινοὺς ἐ. Thgn.551, X.*Eq.*6.7 (Pass.), 9.9, cf. Il.19.394; πώλοις ἡνίας E.*IT*1424; ἐ. ψήφους εἰς τὸν καδίσκον D.57.13, cf. X.*Cyr.*2.2.21; ἐ. μοχλόν (sc. εἰς τὴν θύραν) Id.*An.*7.1.12; ἐ. σῖτον (sc. εἰς τὴν φάτνην) Id.*Cyr.*8.1.38; τοῖς ὑποζυγίοις ἐ. *throw* food *to*.., Thphr.*Char.*4.8; simply, *lay* or *put in*, [ἱμάντα] οἱ ἔμβαλε χερσὶν *put it into* his hands, Il.14.218; ἐνέβαλον τῶν χρημάτων [εἰς τὸ κανοῦν] Arist.*Pol.*1304$^a$3, cf. Ael.*VH*11.5; *hand in, submit* a petition, *PPetr.*3 p.39 (iii B.C.), etc.; ἐ. τὴν χεῖρά τινι *slide* one's hand *into* another's, Ar.*V.*554; ἔμβαλλε

χεῖρα δεξιάν as a pledge of good faith, S.*Tr.*1181, cf. Ar.*Ra.*754; ἔμβαλλε χειρὸς πίστιν, to which Neoptolemus answers—ἐμβάλλω μενεῖν *I give my pledge* to remain, S.*Ph.*813 (troch.). 3. freq. of the mind, ἐνὶ φρεσὶν ἐ. Od.19.10 (cf. infr. III. 2); εἰς νοῦν τινί Plu. *Tim.*3; ἐ. ἵμερον, μένος τινί, Il.3.139, 16.529; ἐ. νεῖκός τισι *to throw in* strife between them, 4.444; τισὶ λύσσαν ἐρισμοῦ Timo 28.3; ἐ. λόγον Pl.*R.*344d; βουλὴν ἐ. περί τινος X.*Cyr.*2.2.18 (and abs., ἐ. τινὶ περί τινος *to give* one *advice* on a thing, ib.5.5.43 (nisi addendum ⟨βουλήν⟩)); ἐ. πρᾶγμα εἰς γέλωτα καὶ λοιδορίαν D.10.75. 4. *throw upon* or *against*, νηῒ κεραυνόν Od.12.415; δαλὸν νήεσσι Il.13.320; πέτρον στέρνῳ Pi.*N.*10.68; [Ἀχαιοὺς] πέτραις E.*Hel.*1129 (lyr.); πῆχυν στέρνοις Id.*Or.*1466 (lyr.); λίθον τινὶ εἰς κεφαλήν Antipho 5.26; πληγάς τινι X.*An.*1.5.11, cf. Plu.*Caes.*66; so ἐμβαλέτω ἰσχυρότατα (sc. πληγάς) *let him lay on* . ., X.*Eq.*8.4; ἐ. ἕλκεα *to inflict* them, Pi.*Fr.*111; ἐ. πῦρ *set fire to*. ., Th.7.53; ἐ. ῥήγεα *lay on* blankets, Od.4.298: metaph., ἐ. φόβον τινί *strike* fear into him, Hdt.7.10.ε′; ἄταν A.*Th.*316 (lyr.); φροντίδας v.l. in Antipho 2.2.2; *impose*, ἔργα εἰς τὴν γῆν *PTeb.*37.7 (Pass., i B.C.); of a fine, *BCH*8.307 (Delos). 5. ἐ. ὦμον *put* one's shoulder *to* the work, in archery, Hp.*Fract.*2. 6. *put into* its place, *to set* a broken or dislocated limb, ib.24 (Pass.), *Art.*1, al., Arist.*PA*685b6. 7. Medic., *put in*, ἀμυχάς, διαίρεσιν, Philum.*Ven.*7.4, Antyll.ap.Orib.45.24.4. 8. *graft* a tree, D.53.15 (Pass.); but simply, *plant*, τὰ φυτά *IG*12(7).62.29. 9. ἐ. τινί (sc. μάρμαρον) *to throw at* another, Il.12.383. 10. *insert* a word or a letter, Pl.*Prt.*343d, *Cra.*414c, al.; εἰς κωμῳδίαν στίχον Plu.2.334f. 11. ἐ. οἰκίαν τινί *bring* it *down upon* him, Ar.*Ach.*511, cf. *Nu.*1489. 12. τάφρον ἐ. *make* a trench, Plu.*Pyrrh.*27, *Mar.*15. 13. *pay, contribute*, ἀργύριον *IG*7.235.13 (Oropus); τροφάν *GDI*1884.12 (Delph.). 14. *denounce* an offender, ἐς τὰν βωλάν *SIG*527.103 (Dreros, iii B.C.). 15. *intercalate* a month, *IG*1².76.53. II. intr. (sc. στρατόν), *make an inroad* or *invasion*, v.l. for ἐσβ. in Hdt.4.125, 5.15, 9.13, cf. X.*Ages.*1.29; in full, ἐ. στράτευμα A.*Th.*583, 1024: metaph., *attack*, Pl.*Tht.*165d. b. generally, *burst, rush in*, ἐμβάλλειν εἰς τὴν ἀγοράν Aeschin.2.164, Lycurg.5, etc.; *embark* upon, ἐμβάλωμεν εἰς ἄλλον λόγον E.*El.*962: c. dat., εἰκασίαις Hierocl.p.57A.; βίβλοις μακραῖς καὶ δυσελίκτοις Jul.*Or.*7.227b. 2. *strike* a ship *with the ram* (ἔμβολος I. 3), *charge* or *ram* it, νηΐ Hdt.8.84, al., cf. 7.10.β′; ἐ. ταῖς λοιπαῖς (sc. ναυσί) Th.4.14; ξυνετύγχανε. . διὰ τὴν στενοχωρίαν τὰ μὲν ἄλλοις ἐμβεβληκέναι τὰ δὲ αὐτοὺς ἐμβεβλῆσθαι on one side *had charged* others, on the other *had been charged* themselves, Id.7.70. b. of water, ἐ. τοῖς ὄρεσι *to dash against* them, Hdt.2.28: abs., τὸ ὕδωρ ἐμβαλὸν τὰ χωρία ἐλυμήνατο D.55.11. 3. κώπης ἐ. (sc. χεῖρας) *lay oneself* to the oars, Od.10.129, cf. Pi.*P.*4.201; ἐ. alone, *pull hard*, Ar.*Eq.*602, *Ra.*206, X.*HG*5.1.13. 4. of a river, *empty itself*, εἰς. . Pl.*Phd.*113c. III. Med., *throw in what is one's own*, ὅρκον εἰς τὸν ἐχῖνον D.49.65, cf. 27.51: abs., *draw lots*, *SIG*1006.3 (Cos, iii B.C.). 2. metaph., μή μοι φύξιν ἐμβάλλεο θυμῷ Il.10.447; μῆτιν ἐ. θ. 23.313; εἰς τὸν νοῦν ἐμβάλλεσθαί τι D.18.68 (later in Act., *PTaur.*4.9); τὸ καρτερὸν ἐμβαλόμενοι X.*Cyr.*4.2.21 (cf. supr. I. 3). 3. c. gen., ἐμβάλλεσθε τῶν λαγῴων *fall upon* the hare's flesh, Ar.*Pax* 1312. 4. *put on board ship*, *PHib.*1.152 (iii B.C.), *POxy.*1292.3 (i A.D.), Luc.*VH*1.5, etc. 5. *set to work upon*, τῇ γεωργίᾳ *PStrassb.*111.3 (iii B.C.). IV. Pass., *to be dashed against*: of ships, *charge* (v. supr. II. 2), Th.7.34, 70.

⊛ **ἔμβαμμα**, ατος, τό, *sauce, soup*, X.*Cyr.*1.3.4, Theopomp.Com.8, Ath.Med.ap.Orib.*inc.*23.4, Aret.*CD*1.3, etc.

**ἐμβαμμάτιον** [μᾰ], τό, Dim. of foreg., Anaxipp.1.35.

**ἐμβαπτίζω**, = sq., Nic.*Fr.*70.12:—Pass., τοῖς τέλμασιν Plu.*Sull.* 21.

⊛ **ἐμβάπτω**, *dip in*, τί τινι Hippon.36; τὴν χεῖρα ἐν τῷ τρυβλίῳ *Ev.Matt.*26.23; εἰς ἅλμην Cratin.143; ἐς τὸν κηρόν Ar.*Nu.*150:—Med., Id.*Fr.*151, Arched.2.10, Luc.*Asin.*6.

⊛ **ἔμ-βᾰρος**, ον, *of weighty sense*, Men.*Phasm.Fr.*3, Id.11 D. (where perh., = ἔμβαρος II), cf. Paus.Gr.*Fr.*163; but also, = ἠλίθιος, μωρός, Hsch. II. *pregnant, Gloss.* ⊛ **-βᾰρύθω** [ῠ], *to be heavy upon*, κράατι Nic.*Th.*324: abs., of disease, ib.468, v.l. in *Al.*541. II. of smell, *to be offensive*, Id.*Th.*512.

**ἐμβάς**, άδος, ἡ, (ἐμβαίνω) *felt-shoe* or *slipper*, used by the Boeotians, Hdt.1.195; at Athens by old men, Ar.*Eq.*870, *Nu.*858, *V.*103, 275, 447, al.; by poor persons, Is.5.11; ἐ. Σικυωνία a woman's *shoe of white felt*, Luc.*Rh.Pr.*15; ἐ. ὠμοβοεῖς *AP*6.21. 2. = κόθορνος, Callix.2, Plu.*Demetr.*41, v.l. in Luc.*Gall.*26; χρυσαῖ ἐ. Id.*Pseudol.* 19, etc. II. *part of the* χελώνη, Hsch.

**ἐμβᾰσᾰνίζω**, *test, examine*, dub. l. in Hero *Bel.*73.10.

**ἐμβᾰσῐ-κοίτας**, ου, ὁ, name of a *cup*, Ath.11.469a, Petron.24. **-κοιτος**, ον, epith. of shepherds, *sleeping on the ground* (?), Man.4.247.

**ἐμβᾰσῐλεύω**, *to be king in* or *among*, c. dat., πόλεσι Od.15.413; Μολοσσίᾳ Pi.*N.*7.38; ἀνδράσιν A.R.1.173; οὐρανῷ Hes.*Th.*71, etc.; τοῖς ἀνθρώποις Iamb.*Protr.*20; δθ' ἄρ' Ἄδρηστος πρῶτ' ἐμβασίλευεν Il.2.572: c. gen., πάντων Theoc.17.85.

**Ἐμβάσιος** [ᾰ], ον, *favouring embarkation*, epith. of Apollo, A.R.1.359, 404.

⊛ **ἔμβᾰσις**, εως, ἡ, *embarkation*, Plb.4.10.3; *place of entering*, ποταμοῦ Id.3.46.1; *entrance*, τῆς πλατείας *Ephes.*3 No.71. 2. *step*, εὔτακτος ἔ. τοῦ ποδός interpol. in Luc.*Salt.*10. 3. ἐμβάσεις θαλάσσης *sea-bathing*, Herod.Med.ap.Orib.10.8.11, cf. Alex.Aphr.*Pr.*1.112; *bathing-place*, ποταμὸς παρρρεῖ χωρίον ἔ. ἔχον παγκάλην καὶ εὐειδῆ Aristid.*Or.*51(27).53. 4. ἔ. Ὀσίριδος εἰς τὴν σελήνην Plu.2.368c; of planets, = ἐπέμβασις, Vett.Val.37.5 (pl.). 5. *entering into possession*, *SIG*364.77 (Ephesus, pl.). II. *that on which one goes* or *steps*, πρόδουλος ἔμβασις ποδός, i.e. *a shoe*, A.*Ag.*945. 2. *foot, hoof*, δίχηλος E.*Ba.*740. III. *bathing-tub, bath*, Arist.*Fr.*236, *AP*12.207 (Strat.), Ath.1.24c; εἰς τὴν ἔ. τοῦ ἐλαίου κατάβασις Dsc.*Eup.*1.223.

**ἐμβᾰσίχυτρος** [ῐ], ὁ, *pot-visitor*, name of a mouse in Batr.137.

**ἐμβαστάζω**, *bear in* or *on, carry*, Luc.*Ocyp.*14.

**ἐμβᾰτ-εία**, ἡ, *entering into possession*, *AB*249, *EM*334.35. **-έον**, *one must put into a bath*, Orib.*Fr.*131. ⊛ **-εύω**, *step in* or *on, frequent, haunt*: c. acc., of tutelary gods, νῆσος. . ἣν ὁ φιλόχορος Πὰν ἐμβατεύει A.*Pers.*449, cf. E.*El.*595; Πὰν Πελασγικὸν Ἄργος ἐμβατεύων Cratin.321; ἵνα Διόνυσος ἐμβατεύει S.*OC*679 (lyr.): c. dat., ὁ -εύων τῷ χωρίῳ δαίμων D.H.1.77: c. gen., in simple sense, *set foot upon*, μήτ' ἐμβατεύειν πατρίδος S.*OT*825: abs., *enter* a sacred cave, *OGI*530.15 (Iasus). II. ἐ. κλήρους χθονός *enter on, come into possession of*, E.*Heracl.*876, cf. Lxx *Jo.*19.49: more freq. ἐ. εἰς τὴν ναῦν *enter on possession of* the vessel, D.33.6; εἰς τὴν οὐσίαν Id.44.19; εἰς τὸ χωρίον Is.9.3: abs., *enter on an inheritance*, *PEleph.*2.14 (iii B.C.). 2. metaph., νέων ψυχάς Him.*Or.*4.5. III. *mount, cover*, of the male, Palaeph.39. IV. *to be initiated* into the mysteries, *Jahresh.*15.46 (Notium), cf. *Ep.Col.*2.18. ⊛ **-έω**, = foreg., Nic.*Th.*147:—Med., Lyc.642. II. prob. f.l. for ἐμβοτ–, *lead to pasture*, *AP*7.657 (Leon.). ⊛ **-ήρ**, ῆρος, ὁ, = βατήρ, prob. in *IG*4.481.2 (Nemea), cf. Hsch. ⊛ **-ήριος**, ον, *of* or *for marching*, ἐ. παιάν Plu.*Lyc.*22, cf. Ath.14.630f; κινήσεις ἐ. Phillis 3. II. Subst., ἐ. (sc. μέλος), τό, *marching tune*, Plb.4.20.12, Polyaen.1.10; of the anapaests of Tyrtaeus, D.Chr.2.59. 2. ἐ. (sc. ἱερά), τά, *offerings made on embarking, before weighing anchor*, ἐ. θύειν Philostr.*VA*5.43; ᾄδειν καὶ σπένδειν Hld.5.15: also ἐ. θυσία Id.4.16. ⊛ **-ης** [ᾰ], ου, ὁ, a kind of *half-boot of felt*, X.*Eq.*12.10, Duris 14 J. 2. = κόθορνος, Luc.*JTr.*41, Lib.*Or.*64.98, etc. II. *modulus* or *unit of measurement* in Greek architecture, Vitr.4.3.3. **-ικός**, = ἐμβαδικός, *PLond.*2.191.19 (ii A.D.). II. (ἔμβατός II) *for a bath*, θόλος *POxy.*896.11 (iv A.D.). ⊛ **-ός**, όν (-ή, όν Lib.*Decl.*18.35), *passable, accessible*, Plb.34.5.2 (nisi leg. ἐμβαδόν), D.S.1.57 (nisi leg. εὐβ.), D.H.1.79. II. ἐμβατή, ἡ, *bath*, Dsc.*Eup.*2.59, Sch.Ar.*Eq.*1057, Hsch. s.v. πύελος.

**ἐμβάφ-ιας**· λοπάδες βαθεῖαι, Hsch. ⊛ **-ιον**, τό, *flat vessel for sauces, saucer*, Hippon.112; τὰ δὲ λύχνα ἐστὶ ἐμβάφια ἔμπλεα. . ἐλαίου Hdt.2.62: as a measure, = ὀξύβαφον, Hp.*Loc.Hom.*13.

**ἔμβαχον**· ἔμβρυον, Hsch.

**ἐμβέβᾰα, ἐμβέβᾰσαν, ἐμβεβᾰώς**, v. ἐμβαίνω.

**ἐμβεβαιόομαι**, *confirm*, τὸ νίκημα τῇ φυγῇ τῶν πολεμίων Plu.*Lyc.* 22 codd.

**ἐμβεβρυττόμενος**· ἀναίσθητος, ἐμβρόντητος, Hsch. **ἐμβεκανεῖται**· ἐμπέπλεκται, Id.

**ἐμβελής**, ές, *within range of missiles*, διάστημα, τόπος, Plb.8.5.2, D.S.20.44.

**ἔμβη, ἔμβητον, ἐμβήῃ**, v. ἐμβαίνω.

**ἐμβῐβ-άζω**, Att. fut. -βιβῶ, causal of ἐμβαίνω, *set in* or *on*, τινὰ ὡς εἰς ὄχημα Pl.*Ti.*41e; ἐ. εἰς ἴχνος Id.*Tht.*193c:—Pass., *to be put into, take* a bath, Herod.Med.ap.Orib.10.37.16. 2. *put on board ship, cause to embark*, ἄνδρας ἐς κελήτιον (v.l. for ἐσ–) Th.1.53; εἰς πλοῖα X.*An.*5.3.1; ἐ. ναυσίν Plu.*Ant.*7, cf. Chariton 8.3: abs., *put on board*, X.*An.*5.7.8, etc.:—Med., ἐμβιβασάμενος αὐτοὺς εἰς τὰς ναῦς Id.*HG*5.1.19. 3. *lead, guide* to a thing, εἰς τὸ λῷστον E.*HF*856; εἰς τὴν δικαιοσύνην τοὺς οἰκέτας X.*Oec.*14.4; εἰς λόγους D.19.97; εἰς ἀπέχθειαν Plb.16.38.1; εἰς μέτρα ἐ. χρησμούς Philostr.*VA*6.11; τὴν ἀπᾴδουσαν εἰς τὸ μέλος Id.*Im.*2.1; τοῖς ἀνθρωπίνοις πάθεσιν τὸν θεὸν ἐ. Plu.2.416f. 4. *set* a dislocated joint, Hp.*Art.*7. 5. ἐ. τινὰ εἰς. . *put in possession of*. ., *PFlor.*55.31 (i A.D.), etc. 6. intr., οἱ τῆς σταδιαίας πάλης ἐμβιβάζοντες Philostr.*VS*1.22.4. **-άσκω**, = foreg., πρόβατα εἰς τὸ τέμενος *IG*12(7).62.36 (Amorgos). **-ασμός**, ὁ, *introduction, Gloss.* ⊛ **-αστέον**, *one must cause to enter* (a bath), Herod.Med.ap.Orib.10.38.2. II. *one must set to hatch eggs*, τὰς ὄρνις *Gp.*14.7.18. **-αστής**, οῦ, ὁ, *introducer, Gloss.*

**ἔμβῐ-ος**, ον, *having life*, [Ζηνὸς] ἐργαζομένου ἔμβια τὰ ὑπὸ τῷ αἰθέρι Philostr.*Her.*2.19; *tenacious of life, established*, of trees which will bear transplanting, Thphr.*CP*5.6.5; of cuttings, ib.3.5.3 (Comp.); but εἰ σπέρμα ἔ. γένοιτο if the seed should *germinate*, ib.5.4.5, cf. Antipho Soph.15; τὸ ἔ. their *living and growing*, of trees, Ael.*VH* 13.1. 2. ἡ ἔ. ὑγρότης the moisture *necessary to life*, Thphr.*CP*1.1.3; αἷμα ἔ. τῇ γῇ πινόμενον Philostr.*Im.*1.24. II. *lasting one's whole life*, ἔ. τιμωρία D.C.78.12. III. ἔ. γενέσθαι *recover consciousness* after a swoon, Longus 2.30. **-οτεύω**, of epilepsy, *flourish in* certain conditions, Aret.*CD*1.4. ⊛ **-όω**, fut. -ώσομαι Philostr.*Her.*2.3:—*live in*, ἐν νήσῳ D.S.5.19; ταῖς Ἀθήναις Lib.*Or.*18.31; ἐ. πέντε. . ἡγεμονίαις Plu.*Galb.*29, etc.; ἐ. πολιτικαῖς πράξεσιν Id.2.789a. II. of plants, *become established*, Thphr.*HP*3.6.4; simply, *take root*, ib.6.7.3; τῇ γῇ Philostr. l. c. **-ωσις**, εως, ἡ, *maintenance of life*, Lxx *Si.*38.14. 2. *way of living*, ib.3 *Ma.*3.23. II. *taking root*, Plu.2.64cd. **-ωτήριον**, τό, *place to live in, dwelling*, D.S.5.19.

**ἐμβλᾰκεύομαι**, gloss on ἐνδιαθρύπτομαι, Sch.Theoc.3.36.

**ἐμβλαστ-άνω**, *grow on* a plant, as mistletoe, Thphr.*CP*5.15.4. **-ημα**, ατος, τό, = ἐλάτη III, Aët.1.412. **-ησις**, εως, ἡ, *growing on* a plant, Thphr.*CP*5.4.5 (pl.).

**ἔμ-βλεμμα**, ατος, τό, *looking straight at*, X.*Cyn.*4.4. ⊛ **-βλέπω**, pf. ἐμβέβλοφα *PLond.*1.42.21 (ii B.C.):—*look in the face, look at*, τινί τοῖς ὀφθαλμοῖς Pl.*Chrm.*155c, cf. D.19.69; ἐ. εἰς τὸν ὀφθαλμόν Pl.*Alc.*

1.132e, etc.: c. acc., ἐμβλέπω σε, παῖ, *Com.Adesp.*17.7 D., cf. Herod. 2.68, *AP*11.3, *Ev.Marc.*8.25: abs., X.*Mem.*3.11.10, Arist.*EN*1175ᵃ 9. b. ἐ. εἰς *consider*, τὰ πετεινὰ τοῦ οὐρανοῦ *Ev.Matt.*6.26; *look into* a matter, *PTeb.*28.15 (ii B.C.). 2. simply, *look*, ποῖ ἐμβλέψασα ..; S.*El.*995; δεινὸν ἐ. Pl.*Ion* 535e, Plu.*Pyrrh.*34, etc.; πῦρ ἐ. Philostr.*Im.*1.28; ἱρὰ ἐς λῷον -οντα Herod.4.80. **-βλεψις**, εως, ἡ, *looking at*, Hp.*Epid.*7.7.

**ἐμ-βλήθρα**, ἡ, *place of lading*, *PPetr.*3 p.317. ⊕ **-βλημα**, ατος, τό, *insertion*, τὸ εἰς τὸν σίδηρον ἔ. τοῦ ξύλου *the shaft fitting into the* spear-head, Plu.*Mar.*25. 2. *chased* or *embossed* ornament used in decoration of plate, τὰ ἀργυρᾶ τὰ χρυσοῦν τι ἔ. ἔχοντα D.C.57.15, cf. Cic.*Verr.*4.17.37, etc. 3. *graft*, Poll.1.241. 4. Lat. *emblema*, *mosaic*, Lucil.85 Marx, Varro *RR*3.2.4. 5. *inner sole put into the shoe in winter*, etc., Ph.*Bel.*102.39. 6. *sluice-gate*, *PThead.* 24.8 (iv A.D.). 7. *payment*, *PCair.Zen.*22.22 (iii B.C.), *BGU*1040.24 (ii A.D.); *fine*, *BCH*8.307 (Delos). **-βλησις**, εως, ἡ, (ἐμβάλλω II) *impaction*, Hp.*Loc.Hom.*47. II. *reduction* of dislocations, Paul. Aeg.6.114. **-βλητέον**, *one must put in*, Pl.*Phlb.*62b, Antyll.ap. Orib.46.27.8. II. ἐμβλητέος, α, ον, *to be put in*, *set*, Hp *Mochl.*38.

**ἐμβο-άω**, *call upon*, *shout to*, τινί X.*Cyn.*6.17; ἑαυτοῖς D.H.11.38, etc.: abs., *shout aloud*, Th.2.92, 4.34; μέγα ἐμβοῶν Diog.Oen. 25. **-ησις**, εως, ἡ, *shouting*, Aret.*CA*1.2, Ruf.ap.Orib.*inc.*20.27, Antyll.ap.eund.6.6.5.

**ἐμβοθρ-εύω**, *make holes in* mud, Philostr.*VA*2.15. **-όομαι**, *to be embedded in* a cavity, Hp.*Cord.*5. **-ος**, ον, *like a pit* or *hole*, *sunken*, Thphr.*HP*9.3.1.

**ἐμβολ-άδην**, (ἐμβάλλω) *fitting in*, ἐ. ἐστραμμέναι ἀλλήλῃσι prob. in *h.Merc.*411 (ἀμβ- cod. Leid.). ⊕ **-άδιον**, τό, Dim. of sq., *grafted tree*, prob. in *JHS*18.308 (Mopsuestia: lapis -άδιν). **-άς**, άδος, ἡ, fem. Adj. *grafted*, ἄπιοι v.l. in Arist.*Fr.*274: Subst., μορεῶν ἐμβολάδες Plu.2.640b. **-εύς**, έως, ὁ, *anything put in*: *piston*, Hero *Spir.*1.28, cf. Hsch. s. v. κίουρος; *peg*, Anthem.pp.151,152 W.; *dibble* or *stick for setting plants*, *AP*6.21.6. II. *model* (usu. wooden) for metal fittings or stone-work, Ph.*Bel.*70.13, Hero *Bel.*96.5. ⊕ **-εύω**, *load a ship*, *POxy.*522.8 (ii A.D.), *BGU*14 iii 20. ⊕ **-ή**, ἡ, *putting in*, Thphr.*Od.*26 (pl.): esp. *putting into* its place, *setting* or *reduction* of a fracture or a dislocated limb, ἐμβολὴν ποιεῖσθαι Hp.*Fract.*13; *mode of setting*, Id.*Art.*2. 2. *insertion* of a letter, ἐ. ποιεῖσθαι Pl.*Cra.* 437a. 3. *lading* of a cargo, *PStrassb.*111.16 (iii B.C.), *POxy.*62. 11 (iii A.D.): esp. *shipment* of corn to Rome and Constantinople, *BGU*15 ii 3 (ii A.D.), etc.; αἰσία ἐ. Just.*Edict.*13.4.1. II. *inroad into an enemy's country*, *foray*, X.*An.*[4.1.4], *HG*4.3.10; ἡ Θηβαίων ἐ. Arist.*Pol.*1269ᵇ37. 2. *charge*, of a bull, E.*HF*869; of an army, X. *Cyr.*7.1.18, Arr.*Tact.*12.10. b. esp. *ramming of one ship by another*, A.*Pers.*279 (lyr.), 336; ἀντιπρῴροις χρῆσθαι ταῖς ἐ. Th.7.36, etc. (opp. προσβολή, *collision*, ib.70); ἐμβολὰς ἔχειν to receive *such charges*, X.*HG*4.3.12; δοῦναι to make *them*, Plb.1.51.6, etc.; in A.*Pers.*415 ἐμβολαῖς χαλκοστόμοις with *shocks* of brazen beaks (nisi leg. ἐμβόλοις). c. *shock* of battering-ram, Onos.42.5 (pl.). 3. *stroke* or *discharge* of a missile, E.*Andr.*1130, Plb.8.7.3, Luc.*Nigr.*36, etc. 4. *entrance*, *pass*, X.*HG*5.4.48; in Hdt.1.191 ἡ ἐμβολὴ τοῦ ποταμοῦ is explained by the words τῇ ἐς τὴν πόλιν ἐσβάλλει; also, *mouth* of a river, Thphr.*HP*4.11.8. 5. pl., *gusts* of wind, πνευμάτων σφοδρῶν ἐ. Ascl.*Tact.*12.10. III. *battering-ram*, τὸ προέχον τῆς ἐ. Th. 2.76.

**ἐμβολίδες**· αἱ περιθεταί (sc. κόμαι), Hsch.

**ἐμβολ-ιμαῖος**, α, ον, = sq., Aus.*Ecl.*16. ⊕ **-ιμος**, ον, *intercalated*, μὴν ἐ. *intercalary* month, Hdt.1.32 (without μήν, 2.4); ἐ. μῆνα ἄγειν *CIG*2693e (Mylasa); ἡμέρα *Inscr.Prien.*105.76, D.C.48.33. 2. τὰ ἐ. *choral interludes*, Arist.*Po.*1456ᵃ29. 3. ἐ. ἔπη *interpolated* lines, Hsch.; ἐ. παῖδες *supposititious* (nisi leg. ἐκβ-), Eup.103; ἐ. βασιλεύς *fictitious*, J.*Ap.*1.26. **-ίνη**, ἡ, = ἐπικακτίς, Plin.*HN*13.114. ⊕ **-ιον**, τό, *missile discharged*, *javelin*, D.S.1.35. II. *interlude*, *episode*, Cic.*QF*3.1.7. III. *small net* used to fill a gap, Poll.5.35, 10. 141. IV. = ἔμβλημα 2, *IPE*1².105 (Olbia), *IG*11(2).128.44 (iii/ii B.C.); ποτήριον ἐ. ἔχον Πανίσκον *SIG*²588.126 (Delos, ii B.C.). V. *insertion*, ἐ. ξύλινον Ph.*Bel.*74.19. VI. *shoot* for lading corn, *PLond.*3.1164h 10 (iii A.D.). **-ισμα**, ατος, τό, *patch*, Aq., Thd. *Ez.*16.16. **-ῖται**, οἱ, *members of guild* meeting in an ἔμβολον 8, *Ephes.*3 No.59.

**ἐμβολο-δέτης**, ου, ὁ, = ὁ τοῦ παραξονίου δεσμός, Poll.1.146. **-ειδής**, ές, *wedge-shaped*, σχῆμα Ascl.*Tact.*7.2; τάξις ib.3, Arr.*Tact.*16.6.

⊕ **ἔμβολος**, ὁ, or **ἔμβολον**, τό, *anything pointed so as to be easily thrust in*, *a peg*, *stopper*, *CIG*2855.27, Poll.1.145; *linch-pin* (masc.), Pherecyd.37(a) J.: Com. for πέος, Ar.*Fr.*317 (masc.). 2. τῆς χώρης ἔμβολον *tongue* of land, Hdt.4.53; Ἀσίας ἔμβολον prob. the *headland* of Κυνὸς σῆμα in Caria, Pi.*O.*7.19 (ἔμβολος Ἀσίας ἡ Λυκία Sch. ad loc.). 3. *brazen beak*, *ram*, masc. in Hdt.1.166, *Tab.Heracl.*1. 166,182; neut. in *AP*6.236 (Phil.), Paus.6.20.10; gender doubtful in Pi.*P.*4.191, Th.7.36. b. οἱ ἔ., = Lat. *rostra*, *tribune* of the Roman forum, Plb.6.53.1, Plu.*Cat Mi.*44. 4. *wedge-shaped order of battle*, neut. in X.*HG*7.5.22, Plb.1.26.16; of a march-formation, Ael.*Tact.*37.6, Arr.*Tact.*29.5; τὸ τρίγωνον σχῆμα ἔμβολόν τε καὶ σφηνοειδὲς ὀνομάζεται Ascl.*Tact.*7.6; ἡ ὅλη [τάξις] λέγεται ἔμβολος ib.11. 5. b. ἔμβολον, τό, *half a ῥόμβος* (q. v.) *of cavalry*, ib.7.3, Ael.*Tact.* 19.5. 5. *bolt*, *bar*, E.*Ph.*114 (neut., anap.). 6. λάϊνα κίοσιν ἔμβολα prob. = τὰ κίοσιν ἐμβεβλημένα, *architrave*, Id.*Ba.*591 (lyr.). 7. *graft*, *Gp*10.77.4. 8. *portico*, *IG*11(2).161 D118 (Delos, iii B.C.), *Ephes.*3 No.8, *CIG*4662b (Gerasa), interpol. in Hld.2.26; ἐ. τῆς κρατίστης βουλῆς *BCH*11.474 (Lydia). 9. ἔμβολος· εἶδος θηρίου ἐν λαχάνοις, Hsch.

**ἐμβομβέω**, *buzz in*, θεάτροις Him.*Or.*7.13.

⊕ **ἐμβόσκομαι**, *feed on* or *in*, Ph.2.289: metaph., τόποις ib.351.

**ἐμβοτέω**, v. ἐμβατέω.

**ἐμβουκολέω**, dub. sens. (perh. *deceive*) in *Com.Adesp.*25.35 D.

**ἐμβράγχια**, τά, = βράγχια, θύννου *Gp.*20.46.6.

**ἐμβρᾰδύνω**, *remain long in* or *on*, τῷ στόματι τῆς γαστρὸς Phlp.*in APo.*378.14: abs., Menemach.ap.Orib.10.14.2. 2. *dwell on*, τινί Luc.*Dom.*3,23, S.E.*M.*9.1, Herm.*in Phdr.*p.158 A. II. *go slowly* in winding-up a machine, Hero *Bel.*85.3.

**ἐμβραμένα**, ἡ, Sicil. for εἱμαρμένη, Sophr.119; cf. ἔμβραται· εἵμαρται, Hsch.

**ἐμβράσσω**, *cast up*, of the sea, in Pass., Aq., Sm., Thd.*Is.*57.20.

**ἔμβρᾰχυ**, Adv. *in brief*, *in fine*, in Att. with relat. such as ὅστις, ὅπου, etc.; in sense, *at all*, *soever*, παρέχειν ὅ τι τις εὔξαιτ' ἔ. Cratin. 254, cf. Ar.*V.*1120, *Th.*390, Hyp.*Fr.*41, prob. in Lys.13.92, Is.9.11; ἐρᾶτε ἔ. ὅτι βούλει Pl.*Hp.Mi.*365d, al.; later without relat., *in a word*, D.Chr.36.31. II. *slightly*, *somewhat*, ὑψηλότερον ἔ. Gal.18(2).410.

**ἔμ-βρεγμα**, ατος, τό, *lotion*, Dsc.2.124, Aret.*CA*1.1, Archig.ap. Gal.8.150. **-βρεκτέον**, *one must soak*, Herod.Med.ap.Aët.4.47, Id. in *Rh.Mus.*58.91. **-βρεκτός**, ή, όν, *soaked*, dub. in Hsch. s. v. ἔντριτον.

**ἐμβρέμομαι**, Med., *roar* or *bluster in*, ἀήτης ἱστίῳ ἐμβρέμεται Il.15. 627.

**ἐμβρενθυόμενος**, *infrendens*, *Gloss.*

**ἔμβρεος**· ἐνεός, μωρός, Hsch.

⊕ **ἔμβρεφος**, ον, *boy-like*, *AP*14.111.

**ἐμβρέχω**, *treat with embrocations*, Philum.ap.Aët.5.120, Plu.2. 74d. 2. *wet*, ἱμάτια J.*BJ*3.7.13:—Med., *soak*, Nic.*Al.*237:—Pass., *to be dipped*, *plunged*, Sotion p.183 W.; *to be soaked*, Dsc.*Eup.*1.1: aor. 2 part. Pass. ἐμβραχείς Paul.Aeg.3.43.

**ἔμβρημα**, ατος, τό, *abortion* (?), dub. in *PLond.*1821.

**ἐμβρίθ-εια** [ῐ], ἡ, *weight*, *dignity*, Suid., Zonar.; prob. in *Inscr. Prien.*108.65 (ii B.C.). II. *clumsiness of parts*, opp. λεπτομέρεια, Epicur.*Nat.*14.4. III. *severity*, μετὰ ἐμβριθείας κολαστέος Jul.*Ep.* 89a. **-ής**, ές, (βρίθω) *weighty*, of ropes, Hdt.7.36; ἐ. καὶ βαρύ Pl. *Phd.*81c; -εστέραν ποιεῖ τὴν πληγὴν Arist.*PA*69cᵃ19. 2. metaph., *weighty*, *grave*, *dignified*, ἦθος Pl.*Ep.*328b; φρόνημα δημαγωγίας -έστερον Plu.*Per.*4; φύσις Id.*Brut.*1; τὸ ἐ. *dignity*, D.H.*Amm.*2.2; ἐ. καὶ στερρὸς τὰ ἤθεα Hp.*Ep.*11; σεμνὸς καὶ ἐ. Jul.*Or.*2.88a; οἱ -έστεροι *the more sedate*, opp. οἱ ὀξεῖς, Pl.*Tht.*144b. 3. *weighty*, *cogent*, τεκμήριον Phld.*Rh.*1.46 S.; διάνοια ib.2.209 S. (Comp.). Adv. -θῶς, opp. εὐτελῶς καὶ ἐλαφρῶς, Id.*Po.*5.4. 4. in bad sense, *heavy*, *grievous*, Parm.8.59; κακόν A.*Pers.*693; τῆς ἀνάγκης οὐδὲν -έστερον S.*Fr.*757; *difficult*, Pl.*Cra.*407a (Comp.); *burdensome*, φυλακή *SIG*731.8 (Comp., Tomi, i B.C.); of persons, *vehement*, Hdn.3.11.1. II. Adv. -θῶς *with severity*, D.C.69.6; *violently*, Hdn.4.3.3: Comp. -έστερον φέρειν to bear *with greater constancy*, Pl.*Phdr.*252c. **-ω**, *press heavily*, *AP*7.532 (Isid.). 2. *to be heavy*, ἀνίῃς Nic.*Th.*867.

**ἐμβρῑμ-άομαι** (Act. only in Hsch., Suid.), c. aor. Med. et Pass., *snort in*, ἵππους ἐν ἀμπυκτῆρσιν ἐμβριμωμένας, of horses, A.*Th.*461, cf. Luc.*Nec.*20. 2. of persons, *to be deeply moved*, τῷ πνεύματι, ἐν ἑαυτῷ, *Ev.Jo.*11.33,38. II. *admonish urgently*, *rebuke*, E.*Fr.* 1099: c. dat. pers., Lxx *Da.*11.30, *Ev.Matt.*9.30, *Marc.*1.43. **-ημα**, ατος, τό, *indignation*, Lxx *La.*2.6. **-ησις**, εως, ἡ, = foreg., Aq., Sm.*Ps.*37(38).4, Thd.*Is.*30.27, Eustr. *in EN*119.21, Steph. *in Hp.*1. 76 D. (pl.).

**ἔμβριον**· θεῖον, Hsch. **ἐμβρόνιον**· μικρὸν καὶ ἀπόρφυρον ἱμάτιον Τιβερικόν (leg. Ἰβηρικόν), Id.

**ἐμβροντ-αῖος**, α, ον, *struck by lightning*: τὸ ἐ. *place struck by lightning*, Lat. *bidental*, D.S.8.9. **-άω**, *dumbfounder*, τίς ἐνεβρόντησέ μοι; Eup.17 D.; τὸ κακὸν ἐνεβρόντησέ με Ach.Tat.3.15. II. Pass., *to be struck by lightning*, distd. fr. κεραυνῷ πληγῆναι, X.*HG*4.7. 7. 2. metaph., ἐμβεβροντῆσθαι, = ἐμβρόντητον εἶναι, D.19.231, Men.*Georg.Fr.*5. **-ησία**, ἡ, *sheer stupidity*, Id.*Sam.*196, S.E.*M.* 9.40. 2. *madness*, Plu.2.1119b, Philostr.*VS*2.27.5. **-ητος**, ον, *thunderstruck*, *stupefied*, *stupid*, ἐ. ποιεῖν τινά v.l. in X.*An.*3.4.12; ὦμβρόντητε σύ thou *gaping fool*, Ar.*Ec.*793; ἐγένετ' ἐ. Antiph.233.4; ἠλιθίους καὶ ἐ. Pl.*Alc.*2.140c, cf. Men.*Pk.*273; ἐμβρόντητε, εἶτα νῦν λέγεις; D.18.243. II. later of ideas, *crack-brained*, *mad*, ἐ. καὶ πεπλανημένον σόφισμα Porph.*Chr.*35; ἐμβρόντητα δὲ πάντα Orph.*Fr.* 47.

**ἐμβροχ-άς**, άδος, ἡ, *layer of the vine*, *Gp.*4.3.7. **-ή**, ἡ, (ἐμβρέχω) *infusion*, Dsc.1.43; *embrocation*, Antyll.ap.Orib.9.22.1, Plu.2. 42c. II. (βρόχος) *noose*, *halter*, Luc.*Lex.*11. **-ημα**, ατος, τό, = foreg. 1, Herod.Med. in *Rh.Mus.*58.83.

**ἐμβρόχθιος**, ον, (βρόχθος) *in the throat*, λίθος Tz.*H.*No.413 tit.

**ἐμβροχίζω**, (βρόχος) *catch in a noose*, Apollod.2.5.4.

**ἔμβροχος** (sc. γῆ), ον, (βρέχω) *inundated*, *PTeb.*74.38 (ii B.C.), al., *PLond.*2.256ᶠ6 (i A.D.).

**ἐμβρύειον** [ῠ], τό, *flesh of embryos*, Ar.*Fr.*569.4.

⊕ **ἐμβρύκω** [ῡ], *bite*, v.l. in Nic.*Th.*824:—Pass., Id.*Al.*338.

**ἐμβρῠο-δόχος**, ον, *receiving the foetus*, Luc.*Lex.*6. **-θλάστης**, ου, ὁ, *instrument to extract a foetus*, Gal.19.104.

**ἐμβρύοικος** [ῠ], ον, (ἐν, βρύον, οἰκέω) *dwelling in sea-weed*, ἄγκυρα *AP*6.90 (Phil.).

**ἔμβρῠον**, τό, *young one*, ὑπ' ἔμβρυον ἧκεν ἑκάστῃ put *a young one* under each dam (to be suckled), Od.9.245, al., cf. Arist.*PA*676ᵃ

17. II. *embryo, foetus*, A.*Eu.*945 (lyr.), Hp.*Aph.*5.52, Arist.*GA* $746^{a}1$, al. (From βρύω; expld. as τὸ ἐντὸς τῆς γαστρὸς βρύον by Eust. ad Od.l.c.)

**ἔμβρῠος**, ον, (βρύω) *growing in*, βρέφος ἔ., = ἔμβρυον, Ps.-Phoc. 184. II. (βρύον) *grown with sea-weed*, Nonn.*D.*41.29.

**ἐμβρῠο-σφάκτης**, ου, ὁ, = -θλάστης, Herophil.ap.Tertull.*de An.* 25. **-τομέω**, *cut up the foetus in the womb*, c. acc., Olymp.*in Grg.*p.257 J., Aspasia ap.Aët.16.22 :—Pass., of the foetus, *to be cut up in the womb*, Vett.Val.53.27, Procl.*Par.Ptol.*214. **-τομία**, ἡ, *cutting up of the foetus*, Gal.19.107, Philum.ap.Aët.16.23, Olymp.*in Grg.*p.258 J., *PTeb.*676, Ptol.*Tetr.*149, etc. **-τόμος**, ὁ, *instrument for cutting up the foetus*, Sor.2.63.

**ἐμβρῠουλκ-έω**, *extract the foetus*, Colum.7.3.16 :—Pass., Sor.2. 55. **-ία**, ἡ, *extraction of the foetus*, Id.1.68 (pl.), Archig.ap.Aët.16. 91, Gal.19.107. **-ός**, ὁ, (ἕλκω) *crochet, hook*, Sor.2.61, Gal.19.97.

**ἔμβρωμ-α**, ατος, τό, *that which is eaten away*, ἔ. ὀδόντος *cavity in* a tooth, Dsc.1.77. II. *meal, snack*, ἔ. πρωϊνόν Ath.1.11c, cf. Sor.1. 40. **-ᾰτίζω**, = ψίχω, ψίω, *EM*819.6, Suid. :—aor. Pass. in med. sense, *take a meal* or *snack*, Apollon.*Lex.* s.v. δειελιήσας. **-άτιον**, τό, Dim. of ἔμβρωμα, Sor.1.40.

**ἔμβρωμος**, ον, = βρωμώδης, Dsc.3.33, Aët.9.30.

**ἐμβῠθίζω**, *cause to sink to the bottom*, Plu.2.981a (Pass.).

⊛ **ἐμβύθιος** [ῠ], ον (η, ον *AP*9.227 (Bianor), 423 (Id.)), *at the bottom* of the sea, πέτρα ib.7.504 (Leon.); ἄγρη ib.9.227; κρηνίδες D.H.1. 32; πίννα Isid.Char.20.

**ἐμβῠκᾰνάω**, *blow with the trumpet*, κέρασι D.H.2.8.

**ἐμβυρσόω**, *sew up in skins*, Ps.-Plu.*Fluv.*5.2 (Pass.).

**ἐμβύω** [ῡ], *stuff in, stop with* a thing, Ar.*V.*128; ἔμβυσον τιμὴν εἰς τὴν χεῖρά τινι Herod.2.82.

**ἐμβώμιος**, ον, *on the altar*, σῦκον θυσίας ἁπάσης ἐ. Jul.*Ep.*180.

**ἐμέθεν, ἐμεῖο, ἐμείω**, etc., v. ἐγώ. **ἐμειάς**· διαχρήματα, ἑαυτούς, Hsch. **ἐμέμηκον**, v. μηκάομαι. **ἔμεν, ἔμεναι**, Ep. for εἶναι, v. εἰμί. **ἐμέν**, = ἐμέ, v. ἐγώ. **ἕμεν, ἕμεναι**, Ep. for εἶναι, v. ἵημι. **ἐμέο**, v. ἐγώ.

**ἐμέρα**, coined as etym. of ἡμέρα, Pl.*Cra.*418c.

**ἐμ-εσία**, ἡ, (ἐμέω) *disposition to vomit*, Hp.*Morb.*2.40,43 (pl.). **-εσις**, εως, ἡ, *vomiting, being sick*, ib.74. **-εσμα**, ατος, τό, *vomit*, Id.*Prog.*13 (pl.).

**ἐμετ-ηρίζω**, *give an emetic*, Hp.*Loc.Hom.*33. ⊛ **-ήριος**, ον, = ἐμετικός 1: ἐ. φάρμακον *an emetic*, ibid.: pl. -τήρια, τά, Aret.*CD*1. 3. **-ιάω**, *feel sick*, Arist.*Pr.*$873^{b}24$. **-ικός**, ή, όν, *provoking sickness*, ib.36. Adv. -κῶς, σπαραττόμενος Gal.13.155. II. *inclined to vomit*, Hp.*Acut.*67; of certain animals, Arist.*HA*$632^{b}$ 11. 2. *one who uses emetics*, like the Roman gourmands, Plu. *Pomp.*51. b. ἐμετικὴν (sc. δίαιταν) *agebat*, he was taking *a course of emetics*, Cic.*Att.*13.52.1.

⊛ **ἐμετο-ποιέομαι**, Med., *purge by vomiting*, τὴν ἄνω κοιλίην Hp.*Int.* 38. **-ποιΐα**, ἡ, *causing to vomit*, Dionys.Aeg.ap.Phot.*Bibl.* p.130 B. **-ποιός**, όν, Dsc.2.9.

**ἔμετ-ος**, ὁ, *vomiting*, Hp.*Aph.*1.2 (pl.); ἐμέτοισι θηρώμενοι τὴν ὑγιείην Hdt.2.77; ἔ. ποιεῖσθαι Arist.*HA*$612^{a}6$; *disposition to vomit, sickness*, ναυτίαι καὶ ἔμετοι ib.$584^{a}7$. **-ός**, ή, όν, *vomited*, Suid. **-ώδης**, ες, *accompanied by sickness*, ὑποστροφαί Hp.*Coac.* 560. Adv. Ion. -δέως *as in vomiting*, ἑλκόμενα Id.*Prorrh.*1.117.

**ἐμεῦ, ἐμεῦς**, v. ἐγώ.

**ἐμέω** Il.15.11, impf. ἤμουν Ar.*Fr.*351, X.*An.*4.8.20, Ion. ἤμεον Hdt.7.88: fut. ἐμέσω Hp.*Morb.*2.15, Att. ἐμῶ (ἐνεξ-) Polyzel.4: fut. Med. ἐμέομαι Hp.*Nat.Hom.*5, ἐμοῦμαι A.*Eu.*730: aor. ἤμεσα Hp. *Epid.*1.26.ε', etc., (ἐξ-) Ar.*Ach.*6, inf. ἐμέσαι Hdt.1.133; Ep. ἔμεσσα (ἀπ-) Il.14.437 (prob. ἐξήμεσσα should be restored for -ήμησα in Hes. *Th.*497; ὑπερ-έμησα occurs in the Mss. of Hp.*Morb.*2.17): pf. ἐμήμεκα Luc.*Lex.*21, Ael.*NA*17.37: plpf. ἐμημέκεε Hp.*Epid.*5.42, ἐμημέκει D.L.6.7 :—**Pass.**, fut. ἐμεθήσομαι (ἐξ-) Lxx *Jb.*20.15: aor. inf. ἐμεθῆναι Gal.7.219: pf. ἐμήμεσμαι Ael.*VH*13.22 :—*vomit, throw up*, αἷμ' ἐμέων Il.15.11, cf. Hdt.7.88; ἐμοῦσα θρόμβους A.*Eu.*184; ἰόν ib. 730: abs., *vomit, be sick*, Hdt.1.133, X.*An.*4.8.20; ἐμέειν ἀπὸ συρμαϊσμοῦ Hp.*Art.*40; ἐ. πτίλῳ *to make oneself sick* with a feather, Ar. *Ach.*587. 2. metaph., *throw up a flood of words*, Eun.*VS*p.488 B. (ϝεμε-, cf. Skt. *vámiti* 'vomit', Lat. *vomo, vomitus*, Lith. *vémti*, etc.)

**ἐμεωυτοῦ**, Ion. for ἐμαυτοῦ. **ἔμηνα**, v. μαίνομαι II.

**ἐμίας**, ου, ὁ, *one who is inclined to vomit*, Eup.412.

**ἐμίν, ἐμίνγα, ἐμίνη**, v. ἐγώ.

**ἔμμα**, ατος, τό, Aeol. for εἶμα, Alc.*Supp.*4.21, Sapph.*Supp.*20a.8, *Lyr.Alex.Adesp.*9.

**ἐμμᾰγεῖον**, τό, *mould, matrix* (nisi leg. ἐκμ-), Procl.*in Cra.*p.104 P.

**ἐμμαίνομαι**, *to be mad at*, τινί *Act.Ap.*26.11, J.*AJ*17.6.5.

**ἐμμᾰκεδονίζω**, *play the Macedonian*, *Com.Adesp.*324.

**ἐμμαλάξαι**· ἐμμεῖναι, τῇ χειρὶ ἐπιλαβέσθαι, Hsch.

**ἔμμαλλος**, ον, *woolly, fleecy*, Luc.*Cyn.*5.

⊛ **ἐμμᾰνής**, ές, *frantic, raving*, Hdt.3.25, S.*Ichn.*15, etc.; ἐμμανεῖ σκιρτήματι A.*Pr.*675; ἀοίνοις ἐμμανεῖς θυμώμασιν *maddened by* .., Id. *Eu.*860; θεοῦ πνοαῖσιν ἐ. E.*Ba.*1094; ἐ. Ἥρας ὕπο Id.*Cyc.*3; ὥσπερ ἐ. ἐπεισπεσών Men.*Sam.*200; of elephants in the rutting season, Arist. *HA*$571^{b}34$; κῶμαι Lxx *Wi.*14.23: Comp. -έστερος Luc.*Am.*14: Sup. -έστατος, ἔρωτες Pl.*Lg.*734a, cf. Plu.*Arat.*17. Adv. -νῶς D.C.65.16; ἐρᾶν Eun.*VS*p.455 B.: Sup. -έστατα, ἐρῶν Men.336.

**ἔμμᾱνις**, v. ἔμμηνις.

**ἐμμᾰπέως**, Adv., (μαπέειν) *quickly, hastily*, ἐ. ἀπόρουσε Il.5.836; ὑπάκουσε Od.14.485, *h.Ven.*180; ὑπέδεκτο Hes.*Sc.*442.

**ἐμμάρτῠρος**, ον, *on testimony*, Them.*Or.*11.144b. Adv. -ρως Eust. 64.33.

**ἐμμάσαι**· ἐνερεῖσαι, Hsch.

**ἐμμάσσομαι**, Att. **-ττομαι**, aor. 1 ἐνεμαξάμην (v. infr.), *knead bread in*, ἐν θυείᾳ στρογγύλῃ 'νεμάττετο Ar.*Nu.*676 (cj. Dobr. for γ' ἀνεμάττετο). II. *press upon, inflict*, αὐχένι κέντρον Nic.*Th.*767; κῆρά τινι Opp.*H.*2.502; ὀργήν τινι Call.*Dian.*124; ἰδμοσύνην στέρνοις ἐνεμάξατο *APl.*4.273 (Crin.) :—late in Act., *smear*, ζωγραφίαν μέλανι *PMag.Lond.*121.230.

**ἐμμᾰταιάζω**, *talk idly*, Hsch. (leg. -ματᾴζω).

**ἐμμᾰτέω**, *put the finger down the throat to cause sickness*, Nic.*Al.* 138 (perh. f.l. for ἐμμαπέως, but cf. ἐμματέων· ψηλαφῶν, Hsch.). 2. *implant* a sting, of a bee, Nic.*Th.*809. 3. ἐμματούμενος, = μασώμενος, v.l. for ἐνδατούμενος in Sch.S.*Tr.*791.

**ἐμμάχομαι** [ᾰ], *fight a battle in*, πεδίον ἐπιτήδειον ἐ. Hdt.9.7.β', cf. D.C.50.12.

**ἐμμέθοδος**, ον, *according to rule* or *system*, S.E.*P.*2.21; τὸ ἐ. *systematic arrangement*, Ph.2.512. Adv. -δως *systematically*, Cleom.2.1, Hero *Deff.*138.5, A.D.*Synt.*155.21, S.E.*M.*1.188, etc.: Comp. -ώτερον Procl.*Hyp.*6.2.

**ἐμμεθύσκομαι**, Pass., *to be drunk in*, τοῖς ἁγίοις J.*BJ*4.4.3.

**ἐμμείγνῡμι**, *mingle*, ἄκρατον πρὸς τὸ κώνειον Plu.2.61b: metaph., τῇ σαρκὶ τὴν ψυχὴν ὁ θεὸς οἷον ἅλας ἐνέμιξεν Porph.*Abst.*3.20; ἐ. ἑαυτόν, ἑαυτούς τινι, *meddle* with .., Plu.2.805e, Just.*Nov.*124.4; εἴς τινα ib.117.15.1 :—more freq. in Pass., *to be mixed* or *mingled in*, ἐν δὲ γαίᾳ ζόα .. μέμεικται A.*Th.*937, cf. Plu.*Per.*4 (dub.); μικροῦ ἐμμειγνυμένου Arist.*GC*$315^{b}13$, cf. *Mete.*$357^{a}16$. II. of persons, *encounter*, ἔν τ' Ὠκεανοῦ πελάγεσσι μίγεν πόντῳ τ' ἐρυθρῷ Λαμνιᾶν τ' ἔθνει γυναικῶν Pi. *P.*4.251. 2. intr. in Act., ἔνθ' οἶμαι Θησέα καὶ τὰς .. ἀδελφὰς .. τάχ' ἐμμείξειν (sc. ἀλλήλοις) S.*OC*1057 (lyr.).

**ἐμμειδιάω**, *smile in*, ὀφθαλμοῖς καὶ παρειαῖς Philostr.*Ep.*51; *to be glad at*, πρὸς τὰ ἴχνη, of hounds, X.*Cyn.*4.3.

**ἐμμέλεια**, ἡ, (ἐμμελής) *harmony in music* or *the fit modulation of spoken words*, D.H.*Dem.*50: generally, *harmony, gracefulness*, ἀνασῴζειν τὴν ἐ. Plu.2.747b; ἐ. ἀγριοφανῆ καὶ αὐστηράν, of Pan, Corn. *ND*27; οὐ παρέργως, ἀλλὰ μετά τινος ἐ. Jul.*Or.*7.217a. II. *a tragic dance*, opp. πυρρίχη, Pl.*Lg.*816b; opp. σίκιννις and κόρδαξ, Ath.1. 20e, 14.631d, Luc.*Salt.*26; *the tune of this dance*, Hdt.6.129. II. Com., ἐ. κονδύλου knuckle-*dance*, Ar.*V.*1503.

**ἐμμελετ-άω**, *exercise* or *train in* a thing, τινὰ ἀγῶσι Plu.*Cim.*18, etc.; ἐμαυτόν σοι ἐμμελετᾶν παρέχειν *to practise upon*, Pl.*Phdr.*228e; *give a lecture*, τισί Plu.2.932d. **-ημα**, ατος, τό, *that on which an art is practised*, χρυσὸν καὶ ἄργυρον, τέχνης ἐ. Lxx *Wi.*13.10; *instrument for practice*, τῆς πάρος ἁρμονίης *AP*6.83 (Maced.). **-ητέον**, *one must practise oneself in*, τινί Plu.2.531f.

⊛ **ἐμμελής**, ές, (μέλος) *in tune, harmonious*, opp. πλημμελής, ἐ. φωνή Ti.Locr.101b, Plu.2.1014c, etc.; προσόδιον *SIG*662.9 (Delos, ii B.C.); ἁρμονιῶν -εστάτη κρᾶσις Plu.*Phoc.*2; λέξις ἐ. D.H.*Comp.*25; also of a poet, *tuneful*, Theoc.*Ep.*21, cf. Philostr.*Im.*2.12. II. metaph., 1. of persons, *harmonious, orderly*, τὸν πλημμελοῦντα ἐμμελῆ ποιεῖν Pl. *Criti.*106b; ἵνα γένοιντο -έστεροι ib.121b; also -εστάτη καὶ κοσμιωτάτη πολιτεία Plu.*Pel.*19. b. *suitable, fit, proper*, κριτής Pl.*Lg.*876d; πρός τι Plu.*Demetr.*2 (Sup.). c. *witty*, ἐ. καὶ χαρίεσσα θεραπαινίς Pl.*Tht.*174a. 2. of things, *in good taste*, ἐμμελέστερόν [ἐστι], c. inf., Ar.*Ec.*807; ἐ. ὁμιλία Arist.*EN*$1128^{a}1$. 3. *well-proportioned*, κτήματα .. ποῖα ἄν τις κεκτημένος ἐμμελεστάτην οὐσίαν κεκτῇτο; Pl.*Lg.* 776b; *reasonable*, οὐκ ἐ. Id.*Sph.*259e: hence, *modest, small*, opp. μέγιστος, Id.*Lg.*760a (Sup.); πόλις μεγέθει ἐμμελεστέρα Arist.*Pol.* $1327^{b}15$. b. *suitable*, λόγος ἐ. ἐπὶ τὴν χρείαν Plu.*Luc.*1. III. Adv. -λῶς, Aeol. and Ion. -λέως, *harmoniously*, opp. πλημμελῶς, Pl. *Lg.*816a; *in time*, πόδεσσιν ὠρχεῦντ' Sapph.54. 2. *elegantly*, ἐ. καὶ μουσικῶς Arist.*Cael.*$290^{b}30$; *in good taste*, παίζειν Id.*EN*$1128^{a}9$; δαπανῆσαι μεγάλα ἐ. ib.$1122^{a}35$. 3. *suitably, rightly*, οὐδέ μοι ἐμμελέως τὸ Πιττάκειον νέμεται Simon.5.8; ἐ. πάντων ἔχειν to be *suitably* provided with .., Pl.*Prt.*321c; ἐ. φέρειν τὰς τύχας Arist.*EN*$1100^{b}21$; ἐ. εἰρῆσθαι ib.$1170^{b}21$, etc.: Comp. -εστέρως, ἔχειν Pl.*Phdr.*278d; -έστερον Id.*R.*474a: Sup. -έστατα ib.581b. 4. *at a reasonable price*, διδάσκειν Id.*Ap.*20c.

**ἐμμεμᾰώς**, υῖα, ός, *in eager haste, eager*, of persons, Il.5.142, al., Plu.2.619e, etc.; of things, ἠχή (or πέτρη) Hes.*Sc.*439: later c. dat., ἐμμεμαὼς Βέβρυξι A.R.2.121. (Cf. *μάω, μέμονα.)

**ἐμμέμονα**, *to be lost in passion*, ἐμμέμονε φρήν S.*Tr.*982 (lyr.).

**ἐμμεμφής**, ές, Arc. **ἰνμενφής**, *liable to censure*, *IG*5(2).262 (Mantinea, v B.C.).

**ἔμμεν, ἔμμεναι**, Ep. for εἶναι, v. εἰμί.

**ἐμμεν-ετέον**, *one must abide by* or *endure*, D.L.7.93. II. ἐμμενετέος, α, ον, *to be endured*, Cleanth.*Stoic.*1.128; *to be maintained, held fast*, ὠφελήματα *Stoic.*3.22, cf. Chrysipp.ib.72. **-ετικός** or **-ητικός**, ή, όν, *disposed to abide by*, τῷ λογισμῷ, τῇ δόξῃ, Arist.*EN*$1145^{b}$ 11, $1151^{b}5$; τοῖς ὀρθῶς κριθεῖσι *Stoic.*ap.Stob.2.7.$5^{b2}$: c. gen., ἕξις -ητικὴ νόμου Pl.*Def.*412b. Adv. -ητικῶς Chrysipp.*Stoic.*3.73. **-ετός**, ή, όν, *maintainable*, ἀγαθά *Stoic.*3.22. ⊛ **-ής**, ές, *abiding in*: τὸ ἐ. *steadfastness*, Timo 58.1 (s.v.l.).—Hom. has only neut. ἐμμενές as Adv., always in phrase, ἐ. αἰεί *unceasing* ever, Il.10.361, Od.9.386, etc. (without αἰεί in later Ep., as Arat.83; ἐ. ἤματα πάντα Id.339): also Adv. -νέως, ἐμάχοντο Hes.*Th.*712.

⊛ **ἐμμενύτρωτος**· μέτριος, Hsch.

**ἐμμένω**, fut. -μενῶ S.*OC*648, etc.: pf. ἐμμεμένηκα Th.1.5 :—*abide in* a place, πολὺν χρόνον μελάθροις ἐμμένειν E.*Fr.*362.12; ἐν τῇ κεφαλῇ

Ar.Ec.1120; ἐν τῇ Ἀττικῇ Th.2.23, cf. X.An.4.7.17, Epist.Phil.ap. D.12.22: abs., Th.8.31. 2. abide by, stand by, cleave to, be true to, c. dat., τοῖς ὁρκίοις Hdt.9.106; πιστώμασι A.Ch.977, etc.; τῷ κηρύγματι S.OT351; ὀρθῷ νόμῳ Id.Aj.350; ἐ. ταῖς συνθήκαις καὶ ταῖς σπονδαῖς Th.5.18, cf. Isoc.7.81; τοῖς νόμοις X.Mem.4.4.16; τῷ τιμήματι Pl.Ap.39b; τῇ ὁμολογίᾳ Id.Tht.145c, etc.; ἐ. τοῖς Καρχηδονίοις remain constant to them, App.Hisp.24; ἐ. ἐν ταῖς σπονδαῖς τὸν ἐνιαυτόν Indut.ap.Th.4.118; ἐν τῇ τάξει Pl.Lg.844c; ἐν τῇ φιλοσοφίᾳ Isoc.9.89: abs., stand fast. be faithful, E.Ph.1241, PTeb.382.22 (i B.C.). 3. of things, remain fixed, stand fast, hold good, εἴ σοί γ' ἅπερ φῂς ἐμμενεῖ S.OC648; μάλα μοι τοῦτ' ἐμμένοι may it remain fixed in my mind, A.Pr.534 (lyr.); εἴ σφι ἔτι ἐμμένει [ἡ φιλίη] Hdt.7.151; τέσσαρα καὶ δέκα ἔτη ἐνέμειναν αἱ σπονδαί Th.2.2; ἐ. ὁ νόμος Pl.Lg.839c; ἐὰν.. [ὁ λόγος] ἐμμένῃ Id.Phdr.258b; τὸ σιδηροφορεῖσθαι τοῖς ἠπειρώταις ἐμμεμένηκεν continued as a custom, Th.1.5.

**ἐμμερίζομαι**, to be divided, distributed, J.BJ5.7.3.

**ἐμμέριμνος**, ον, in anxiety, Cat.Cod.Astr.2.210, Sch.E.Or.93. Adv. -νως Eust. ad D.P.Praef.

**ἔμμεσος**, ον, intermediate, [ψυχὴ] δεσμὸς ἔ. τυγχάνει τῶν ἄκρων Alex.Aphr.Pr.2.67; having a mean, ἔ. ἐναντία having an intermediate term, Simp.in Cael.340.33; ἔφη Πλάτων πάντα ἔ. Olymp.in Mete.242.28. II. inserted, μεταξυλογία ib.41.23. III. mediate, γνῶσις Eustr.in EN331.2. Adv. -σως mediately, Them.in APo.31.6.

**ἐμμεστόομαι**, Pass., to be filled quite full, S.Ant.420 (tm.), El.713 (tm.), unless in both passages ἐν be adverbial, v. ἐν B.3.

**ἔμμεστος**, ον, filled full of a thing, τινός S.Ichn.282, Pl.Ep.338d.

**ἐμμετάβολος**, ον, admitting of modulation, σύστημα Cleonid.Harm.8,11.

**ἔμμεται**· ὀρχεῖται, Hsch.

**ἐμμετεωρίζομαι**, Pass., to be carried aloft, τῷ αἰθέρι Philostr.VA1.5.

**ἐμμετρ-έω**, measure by or according to, τῇ προθυμίᾳ τὰ σιτία AP4.3.18 (Agath.), v.l. for συμμ- in Luc.Gall.27. 2. simply, measure out, provide, PMasp.138iv 1 (vi A.D.). -ία, ἡ, fit measure, opp. ἀμετρία, Pl.R.486d, Phlb.52c. -ος, ον, in measure, proportioned, opp. ἄμετρος, Id.R.486d, Lg.716c, al.; τὸ ἔ. due measure, proportion, Id.Phlb.26a, cf. 52d; πολιτεῖαι ἔ. well-balanced, title of work by Critias, Phlp.in de An.89.12. Adv. -τρως, πρός τι proportionably to.., Pl.Plt.282e. 2. fitting, suitable, ἔπαινος Id.Lg.823d; θεοῖσι ἀναθήματα χρεὼν ἔμμετρα τὸν μέτριον ἄνδρα.. δωρεῖσθαι ib.955e. Adv. -τρως Id.Cra.395c, M.Ant.1.16: Sup. ἐμμετρώτατα Pl.R.474d; also -ότατα Lg.674c, prob. in Aristaenet.1.18. 3. of persons, ἐμμετρότατος (v.l. -ώτατος) reasonable, moderate, Pl.Lg.926a; -ότερος (v.l. -ώτερος) Id.Ti.90e; ἔ. οἰνοχόος Aristaenet.1.3. II. measuring, containing, δέπας ἔ. ὡς τριλάγυνον Stesich.7. III. in metre, metrical, Pl.Smp.197c, Phdr.252b, Arist.Rh.1408$^{b}$21; ἔμμετρα λέγειν ἢ ἄμετρα Id.Po.1451$^{b}$1, cf. 1450$^{b}$14; φθόγγος ἔ. Phld.D.3.13; ἔ. ποιηταί poets who use regular metres, i.e. epic and tragic, opp. οἱ τῶν ᾀδομένων, D.60.9. Adv. -τρως, χρησμῳδεῖν Plu.2.623c.

**ἐμμηλάδας** αἶγας· τὰς μετὰ τῶν προβάτων νεμομένας, Hsch.

**ἐμμηναῖος**, α, ον, epith. of the moon, Gloss.

**ἐμμήνιος**, ον, monthly: τὰ ἐ. the menses of women, Hp.Nat.Mul.7; ἐ. αἷμα γυναικῶν J.BJ4.8.4.

**ἔμμηνις**, ιος, ὁ, ἡ, Cret. -ᾱνις, wroth, θεός SIG527.78 (iii B.C.), cf. GDI5041.18, etc.

⊛ **ἔμμηνος**, ον, (μήν) lasting a month, ἔμμηνον τὰν περίοδον ἀποδίδωτι, of the moon, Ti.Locr.96d; περίοδος, of women, Plu.2.495e; ἔργον Pl.Lg.956a. II. done or paid every month, monthly, ἱερά S.El.281, Pl.Lg.828c; σιτηρέσιον Plu.Caes.8; ἁρμαλιή Theoc.16.35. 2. in Law, ἐ. δίκαι suits in which judgement must be given within thirty days, D.37.2, Arist.Ath.52.2; εἰσάγειν ἔμμηνα ib.3. 3. ἔ., τά, the menses of women, Dsc.3.36, al.: sg., Sor.1.19. III. neut. ἔμμηνα as Adv., in the course of a month, IG1$^{2}$.65.47.

**ἔμμηρος**, ὁ, poet. for ἐνόμηρος, as a hostage, Demetr.Com.Vet.2.

**ἔμμητρος**, ον, (μήτρα) containing core, ξύλον Antiph.220, Thphr.HP1.6.5, Theoc.25.209.

**ἔμμι**, Aeol. for εἰμί.

**ἐμμιαίνω**, pollute, Tz.H.1.665.

**ἔμμιλτος**, ον, tinged with red, Dsc.5.112.

**ἐμμίμνω**, poet. for ἐμμένω, Emp.35.11, Q.S.6.497.

**ἐμμίσγω**, = ἐμμείγνυμι, Ep. part. ἐνιμίσγων Opp.H.3.408.

**ἔμμισθος**, ον, in receipt of pay, hired, Th.6.22; ξένοι Pl.Lg.816e, al.; ἔ. τινος paid for a thing, Luc.Merc.Cond.13; ἔ. τινα ποιεῖν to make him pensionary, παῖδας ὀρφανούς Plu.Alex.71; ὅλην τὴν πόλιν Id.Per.12. 2. of work, paid, ὀργάνων καὶ ἔργων γένεσις ἔ. Pl.Lg.920e. 3. metaph., mercenary, εἰ ἔ. ἡ θεραπεία Ph.2.19.

**ἐμμογέω**, toil in, ἄθλοις Sch.Pi.Pae.2.57.

**ἔμμοιρος**, ον, partaking, sharing, φύσεως ἀγαθοῦ Plot.4.8.6, cf. Porph.Gaur.6.2.

**ἐμμολύνω**, pollute in or with, in Pass., LxxPr.24.9(10).

**ἐμμον-εύω**, = ἐμμένω, ἐν τῷ γυμνασίῳ δι' ἐνιαυτοῦ IG12(9).235 (Eretria). -ή, ἡ, continuance, opp. ἀπαλλαγή, τοῦ κακοῦ Pl.Grg.479d. -ίαι· συνθῆκαι, Hsch. ⊛-ος, ον, abiding, lasting, ψυχῇ βίαιον οὐδὲν ἔ. μάθημα Pl.R.536e; διάνοιαι X.Cyr.3.3.52; παρρησία Phld.Lib.p.34O.; λύπη Them.Or.32.359c (Comp.); τῆς κακίας τὸ ἔ. Plot.1.5.6; of persons, steadfast, X.Cyr.3.3.55: c. dat., abiding by, Andronic.Rhod.p.578M. Adv. -νως, ὑπομεῖναι βασάνους Plu.2.208c. II. of disease, chronic, λέπρα LxxLe.13.51; ἀρρώστημα ib.Si.30.17.

**ἔμμορε, ἐμμόρμενος, ἔμμορον**, v. μείρομαι.

**ἔμμορος**, ον, (μείρομαι) partaking in, endued with, τιμῆς.. ἔμμοροί εἰσι καὶ αἰδοῦς Od.8.480. II. ἔμμορον· εἱμαρμένον, Hsch.

**ἔμμορφος**, ον, endued with form, ἀρχαί Thphr.Metaph.14; ἄγαλμα Plu.Num.8, cf. 2.362d; ὕλην ἔ. ἀποτελεῖσθαι Plot.5.9.4.

**ἐμμοτέω**, plug, stop, σωλῆνας Steph.in Hp.2.384D.

**ἔμμοτος**, ον, treated with tents (μοτοί), Hp.Aph.5.47, Art.49, Mochl.36. II. used with such tents, Dsc.1.68; ἔ. φάρμακα Gal.11.125; ἔ. σύστασις Id.13.500; ἔ. ἀγωγή treatment by tents, Paul.Aeg.6.3. 2. metaph., ἔμμοτον τῶνδ' ἄκος (Schütz for ἑκάς) a salve or plaster to heal these wounds, A.Ch.471 (lyr.).

**ἔμμουσος**, ον, = μουσικός, πράγματα Heph.Astr.2.32: Sup. -ότατον, θεώρημα Nicom.Ar.2.2; ἐμμούσοις γράμμασιν in literature, IG9(1).235 (Larymna). Adv. -σως, παίζειν Plu.2.1119d.

**ἔμμοχθος**, ον, toilsome, βίοτος E.Supp.1004 (lyr.); δάχμα Nic.Th.756.

**ἐμμυέω**, initiate in: μῶν ἐνεμυήθης δῆτ' ἐν αὐτῷ τὰ μεγάλα; what, were you initiated at the great mysteries in that shabby coat? Ar.Pl.845 cod. R.

**ἐμμῡθόω**, form a myth, ὡς.. Tz.H.3.248.

**ἐμμῠχᾰτεύειν**, = ἐγκεκλεῖσθαι, dub. cj. for ἐνμαχ-, Rhinth.p.189 K.

**ἐμμύχιος**, v. ἐννύχιος III.

**ἔμμωμος**, ον, blemished. Sm., Thd.Ma.1.14.

**ἐμνιωβέλιον**, v. ἡμιωβέλιον. **ἔμολον**, aor. 2 of βλώσκω.

**ἔμος**, εος, τό, = εἶμα, Supp.Epigr.2.710 (Pednelissus).

⊛ **ἐμός**, ή, όν, possess. Pron. of 1st pers.: (ἐγώ, ἐμοῦ):—mine; contr. with the Art., οὑμός, τοὐμόν, τοὐμοῦ, τὠμῷ, τἀμά, Trag. (not Com., τἀμὰ γὰρ διοίχεται is paratrag. in Ar.Ec.393), rarely in Prose, οὑμός Pl.Ep.354c; τἀμά Id.Plt.258b; οὑμός even in Il.8.360; and (acc. to some Gramm.) τὠμῷ 11.608, Od.4.71; τῆμῇ Il.9.654:—poet. ἀμός (q.v.): I. with a Subst.: 1. subjectively, mine, of me, ἐμὰ δάκρυα Il.1.42; χεῖρες ἐμαί ib.166; ἐμός τε πατὴρ καὶ σός Hes.Op.633: with the Art., τὸν ἐμὸν χόλον Il.4.42, etc.: in Poets sts. joined with gen., to strengthen the possessive notion, ἐμὸν αὐτοῦ mine own, 6.446, Od.2.45; δαὴρ.. ἐμὸς ἔσκε κυνώπιδος Il.3.180; θρῆνον ἐμὸν τὸν αὐτῆς A.Ag.1323; τἀμὰ δυστήνου κακά S.OC344, cf. El.252; τὸν ἐμὸν αὐτοῦ.. βίον Ar.Pl.33. b. mine, i.e. favourable to me, τεκμήρια ἐμά, οὐ τούτων Antipho 2.4.10. 2. objectively, relating to me, against me, ἐμῇ ἀγγελίῃ Il.19.336; τὸν ἐμὸν γάμον Od.2.97; τὴν ἐμὴν αἰδῶ respect for me, A.Pers.699 (troch.); τἀμὰ νουθετήματα warnings to me, S.El.343; τὠμῷ πόθῳ by love for me, Id.OT969; αἱ ἐμαὶ διαβολαί slanders against me, Th.6.90; δωρεὰ ἐμή a gift to me, X.Cyr.8.3.32; sts. with another gen. added, τὰς ἐμὰς Λαΐου διαφθοράς murder of L. by me, S.OT572; τοὐμὸν αἷμα πατρός his blood shed by me, ib.1400; τὰ ἐμὰ δῶρα Κύπριδος (Dind. for Κύπρις) her gifts to me, E.Hel.364 (anap.). II. without a Subst., mine, οὐ γὰρ ἐμὸν παλινάγρετον my word, Il.1.526; τὸ μὲν ἐμόν [ἐστι] 'tis my counsel, Pi.I.8(7).42: in Trag. and Prose, it is my duty, my business, E.Ion 1020, Pl.Lg.664b. 2. ἐμοί my friends, Il.20.205; οἱ ἐμοί X.Cyr.3.2.28, etc.; ὁ ἐμὸς Ἡράκλειτος my dear Heraclitus, Arr.Epict.2.2.17. 3. τὰ ἐμά my property, Pl.Prt.310e, etc.: of children, S.El.538, OC922; τὸ τύπτειν καὶ ἐμὲ καὶ τὰ ἐμὰ ἀδίκως Pl.Grg.508e; of servants. PEdgar 4.6 (iii B.C.), etc.; but also τὰ ἐμά or τὸ ἐμόν, my part, my affairs, my interest, οὕτω τὸ ἐμὸν ἔχει things stand thus with me, Hdt.4.127; τὰ τούτου μᾶλλον ἢ τοὐμόν S.Aj.124; ἔρρει τἀμὰ παντελῶς X.Cyr.6.1.3; τὸ ἐμὸν εὖ πράττει Pl.R.463e, etc.; in full, τοὐμὸν μέρος S.Tr.1215: hence in Trag. and Att., my conduct (almost periphr. for ἐγώ), Id.El.1302, Tr.1068, Ar.Th.105; τὸ μὲν οὖν ἐμὸν οὐκ ἐμποδὼν ὑμῖν ἔσται Lys.8.19, cf. Pl.Grg.452c, etc.: abs., τό γε ἐμόν for my part, as far as concerns me, Hdt.1.108, Pl.Prt.338c, Sph.237b. 4. ἡ ἐ. (sc. γῆ) my country, Th.6.78; also (sc. γνώμη) my opinion, ἐὰν ἡ ἐ. νικᾷ Pl.R.397d; κατά γε τὴν ἐ. Ar.Ec.153, Pl.Plt.277a.

**ἐμοῦς**, v. ἐγώ. **ἐμπᾶ**, v. ἐμπᾶς. ⊛ **ἐμπᾰγή**, ἡ, suretyship, Sm.Pr.11.15.

**ἐμπάζομαι**, used only in pres. (and later impf., Bion Fr.7.9, Coluth.113, Nonn.D.15.214), busy oneself about, take heed of, care for, c. gen., ἐμῶν ἐμπάζεο μύθων Od.1.271, al.; οὔτε θεοπροπίης ἐμπάζομαι Il.16.50, cf. Od.2.201; οὔτε ξείνων ἐμπάζομαι οὐθ' ἱκετάων 19.134; οὐκ ἐμπαζόμενον δόξης Timo 59: once c. acc. pers., οὐχ ἱκέτας ἐμπάζεαι Od.16.422; also Ἔριν δ' ἀγέραστον ἐάσας οὐ Χείρων ἀλέγιζε καὶ οὐκ ἐμπάζετο Πηλεύς Coluth.38:—Ep. word, used in late Prose, οὐκ ἀλέγων Ἀδράστειαν οὐδὲ Νέμεσιν ἐμπαζόμενος Ael.Fr.325.

⊛ **ἐμπάθ-εια** [ᾰ], ἡ, physical affection, τῆς σαρκός Gal.18(1).447. II. passion, φυσικαὶ ἐ. Ptol.Tetr.92, cf. Hierocl.in CA24p.470M. III. partiality, Mich.in EN61.28. -ής, ές, in a state of emotion, Arist.Insomn.460$^{b}$7 (Comp.); ἐ. τινι much affected by or at a thing, Plu.Alex.21; πρὸς τὰ θεῖα Id.2.1125d; ἐ. φιλία passionate affection, Alciphr.2.4.12; τὸ ἐ. sentiment, emotion, Plu.2.25d. Adv. -θῶς, with deep emotion, [τὴν δεξιὰν] πιέσας Plb.31.24.9; passionately, αἰτιάσασθαί τινα J.AJ16.4.2: Comp. -έστερον ἔχειν πρός τι Plu.Cic.6; -εστέρως dub. in Phld.Oec.p.42 J.: Sup. -έστατα Plu.2.668c; -έστατα παρεστηκότες τῇ φιλοσοφίᾳ Vit.Philonid.p.9C. II. opp. ἀπαθής, subject to passivity, Plot.4.7.13, 5.9.4; opp. ἐνδρανής, Procl.Inst.80. III. Rhet., pathetic, D.H.Dem.21. Adv. -θῶς, εἰρηκέναι Demetr.Eloc.28. IV. Gramm., modified, inflected, A.D.Synt.47.16.

⊛ **ἐμπαιγ-μα**, ατος, τό, jest, mocking, delusion, LxxIs.66.4; μαγικῆς ἐμπαίγματα τέχνης ib.Wi.17.7. -μονή, ἡ, mockery, 2Ep.Pet.3.3. -μός, ὁ, mockery, mocking, LxxSi.27.28, al., Ep.Hebr.11.36 (pl.).

**ἐμπαιδεύω**, *lecture amongst*, τισί Philostr.*VS*1.21.3 :—Pass., *to be brought up in*, ἐλευθέροισι τρόποις E.*Fr.*413.

**ἐμπαιδο-τρῐβέομαι**, *to be brought up* or *educated in*, ὀρχήστρᾳ D.C. 77.21 ; βίβλοις J.*BJ*2.8.12. **-τροφέομαι**, Med., ἐ. τῇ τινὸς οὐσίᾳ *bring up one's children on* another person's property, D.44.23.

⊛ **ἐμπαίζω**, fut. -ξομαι Lxx*Hb.*1.10 : pf. ἐμπέπαιχα ib.*Nu.*22.29 :—*mock at, mock*, τινί Hdt.4.134 ; τινά *PCair.Preis.*3.10 (iv A.D.) : abs., S.*Ant.*799 :—Pass., ψυχὴ ὑπό.. σωμάτων καὶ πραγμάτων ἐμπαιζομένη Ph.1.568, cf. Luc.*Trag.*333. 2. euphem. in mal. part., Lxx*Jd.* 19.25. 3. Pass., *to be deluded*, *Ev.Matt.*2.16, *AP*10.56.2 (Pall.), Vett.Val.16.14 ; *to be defrauded*, of the revenues, *Cod.Just.*1.34. 2. II. *sport in* or *on*, ὡς νεβρὸς χλοεραῖς ἐ. λείμακος ἡδοναῖς E.*Ba.* 866 (lyr.) ; τοῖς χοροῖσιν ἐ. *to sport in* the dance, Ar.*Th.*975 ; τῷ γυμνασίῳ Luc.*Lex.*5.

**ἐμπαίκτης**, ου, ὁ, *mocker, deceiver*, Lxx*Is.*3.4, 2*Ep.Pet.*3.3, *Ep.Jud.* 18.

**ἔμπαιος** (A), ον, *knowing, practised in*, c. gen., οὐδέ τι ἔργων ἔμπαιον οὐδὲ βίης [penult. short] Od.20.379 ; κακῶν ἔμπαιος ἀλήτης 21. 400 ; ἐ. δρόμων Lyc.1321.

**ἔμπαιος** (B), ον, (παίω) *bursting in, sudden*, τύχαι A.*Ag.*187 (lyr.) ; πολλὰ δὲ δείλ' ἔμπαια prob. in Emp.2.2.

⊛ **ἔμπαις**, παιδος, ἡ, *with child*, ἡ παῖς ἔμπαις Cratin.287 (Kock cj. ἔκπαις *no longer a child*), cf. Hsch.

⊛ **ἔμπαισ-μα**, ατος, τό, *embossed work*, Eust.883.54 (pl.). **-τική** τέχνη the art *of embossing*, Ath.11.488b. **-τός**, όν, *embossed*, Eust.1357.40.

**ἐμπαίτονται**· ἐμπαίζουσιν, Hsch. (Fort. -παίττ-, Lacon. for -παίζ-.)

⊛ **ἐμπαίω**, *strike in, stamp, emboss*, σκίπων χρυσᾶς ἕλικας ἐμπεπαισμένος Ath.12.543f. II. intr., ἐμπαίει τί μοι ψυχῇ *bursts in upon* my soul, S.*El.*902.

**ἐμπακτόω**, *close by stuffing in* or *caulking*, τὰς ἁρμονίας ἐν ὦν ἐπάκτωσαν τῇ βύβλῳ Hdt.2.96.

**ἐμπάλ-αγμα** [πᾰ], ατος, τό, = ἐμπλοκή, *embrace*, A.*Supp.*296 (pl., cf. Sch. ad loc., Hsch., παλλαγμάτων codd.). **-άσσομαι**, Pass., *to be entangled in*, ἐν ἕρκεσι Hdt.7.85 ; τῷ ἀγκίστρῳ, of fish, Ael.*NA*15. 1 : abs., οἱ δὲ ἐμπαλασσόμενοι κατέρρεον *entangled one with another*, Th.7.84.—Act. ἐμπαλάξαι· ἐμπλέξαι, Hsch. (Cf. ἐμπελάζω III.)

**ἔμπᾰλῐ**, poet. for sq., Orph.*H.*73.5, *AP*7.421.5 (Mel.), 12.5 (Strat.), etc.

⊛ **ἔμπᾰλιν**, Adv., in Trag. and Prose freq. with Art., **τὸ ἔμπαλιν** or **τοὔμπαλιν, τὰ ἔμπαλιν** (as always in Hdt.) or **τἄμπαλιν** :—*backwards, back*, κατὰ δ' ἐ. αὐτὸς ἔβαινε *h.Merc.*78 ; δεδορκὼς Hes.*Sc.*145 ; ἐς τοὔ. δέδορκεν S.*Ichn.*113 ; πρόσωπον ἐ. στρέφοντα E.*Hec.*343 ; τοὔ. ὑποστρέψαντας X.*An.*6.6.38 ; τὰ ἐ. ἀπαλλάσσεσθαι Hdt.9.26 ; ἄπιμεν ἅπαντες τοὔ. X.*An.*1.4.15, etc. b. τὸ ἐ. καὶ ἀνάπαλιν *as before* and vice versa, Nech.ap.Vett.Val.154.28. II. *contrariwise, the opposite way*, τοὔ. σπεύδειν, κραίνειν, A.*Pr.*204, *Ag.*1424 ; λέγειν S.*Tr.* 358 ; ἀνατρέπειν ἐ. turn *upside down*, E.*Ba.*348 ; ἐ. ὑποδεῖσθαι to put on one's shoes *contrariwise* (i.e. on the wrong feet), Pl.*Tht.*193c ; ἐκ τοὔ. ἤ.. from *the opposite side* to.., Th.3.22. 2. c. gen., *contrary to*, τέρψιος, γνώμας ἐ., Pi.*O.*12.11, *P.*12.32 ; τὰ ἐ. πρήσσων τοῦ πεζοῦ doing the *opposite* thing to the army, Hdt.7.58 ; τὰ. τῶνδε *the reverse* of these things, A.*Pers.*223 ; τοὔ. πεσεῖν φρενῶν to be brought to *the opposite opinion*, E.*Hipp.*390 ; τοὔ. οὗ βούλονται X.*Cyr.*8.4.32 ; folld. by ἤ, Emp.100.20 ; γνώμην ἔχω τὰ ἐ. ἢ οὗτοι Hdt.1.207 ; ᾔσαν τὰ ἐ. ἢ Λακεδαιμόνιοι Id.9.56. 3. *on the contrary*, Nic.*Th.*288, Ph. 1.264, Porph.*Abst.*1.44 ; f.l. for ἔμπολιν in S.*OC*637 ; τοὔ. *on the other hand*, Epicur.*Ep.*3 p.63 U.

**ἐμπάλλομαι**, poet. ἐνιπ-, *shake* or *quiver in*, δόμοις ἐνιπάλλεται αἴγλη A.R.3.756. (Act. ἐμπάλλομεν apptly. occurs in Tyrt.1.64 Diehl.)

⊛ **ἔμπᾱμα**, ατος, τό, *property*, Boeot. ἔππ-, *IG*7.3172.163 (Orchom., iii B.C.).

**ἐμπάμων**, ον, gen. ονος, (πέπᾱμαι) = ἐπίκληρος, Hsch.

**ἐμπᾰνηγῠρίζω**, *hold festal assemblies in*, Plu.*Comp.Per.Fab.*1 ; *make a display in*, Id.2.532b.

**ἐμπαρα-βάλλομαι**, *throw oneself into*, τιμωρίαις into punishment, Phalar.*Ep.*132 ; ἐ. τῇ ψυχῇ *to venture to believe* in one's heart, ib. 130. **-γίγνομαι**, *come in upon*, τινί Lxx*Pr.*6.11. **-θετος**, ον, *laid in* or *on*, Suid., cf. eund. s.v. Σέλευκος Ἐμεσηνός. **-λιμπάνω**, *pass over*, c. acc., Them.*in Ph.*11.29. **-σκευάζω**, *to prepare*, φόβον τοῖς ἀνδράσι Clin.ap.Stob.3.1.76, cf. Aen.Tact.9.3. **-σκευος**, ον, *prepared*, Sm.*Ps.*26(27).3 ; ἐμπαράσκευον, τό, a kind of *wind-screen* for engines, Ath.Mech.33.1. Adv. -ως Suid. s.v. ἑτοίμως.

⊛ **ἐμπαρ-έχω**, *hand over* to another, *put into* his *power*, τὴν πόλιν ἐμπαρασχόντες προκινδυνεῦσαι Th.7.56 ; μηδὲ τούτῳ ἐμπαράσχητε.. ἐλλαμπρύνεσθαι *put into* his *power, allow* him to gain distinction, Id. 6.12 ; ἐ. ἑαυτόν τινι *give* oneself *up* as his tool, App.*BC*5.68 ; but ἐμπαρασχεῖν ἑαυτὸν τοιούτῳ τινί (sc. δείπνῳ) *accept an invitation*, Luc. *Symp.*28 :—Med., ποτὶ τὸν θίασον.. εὔνουν ἑαυτὸν -εχόμενος *Rev. Arch.*22(1925).64 (Callatis), cf. Ph.2.127. II. *supply, furnish*, ψυχῇ τέρψιν, δυνάμεις τισί, Id.1.12, 2.383, al. ; ὄνομά τινι Plu.*Galb.* 29. ⊛ **-ίσταμαι**, Pass. with aor. 2 Act., *stand by*, Hld.7.19.

**ἐμπαροιν-έω**, aor. ἐνεπαροίνησα J.*Ap.*1.8 :—*behave like one drunken*, Luc.*Tim.*14 ; *act offensively*, τινί to another, Ph.2.403, Luc.*DDeor.* 5.4 ; τοῖς πράγμασι J.*AJ*6.12.7 ; ἐ. ψεύσμασιν *indulge recklessly in* slanders, ib.20.8.3. **-ημα**, ατος, τό, *object of drunken treatment*, Longus 4.18.

**ἔμπαρος**· ἔμπληκτος, Hsch. [Prob. ᾰ, cf. ἔμπηρος.]

**ἐμπαρρησιάζομαι**, *speak freely against*, τινί Plb.38.12.7. II. τῇ προαιρέσει τῆς ἐπιβουλῆς -σάμενοι *drawing courage* from their purpose *to speak openly* of the plot, J.*AJ*15.8.4. III. abs., ἐ. ἔναντι Κυρίου Lxx*Jb.*22.26.

**ἔμπαρσις**, εως, ἡ, = διάπαρσις, Aët.8.50.

⊛ **ἔμπᾱς** (A), Pi.*P.*4.86, etc. (so always in Trag., exc. ἔμπᾰ S.*Aj.* 563) : Ep. **ἔμπης** also in late Ion. prose, Aret.*SA*2.8, *SD*2.11 : Dor. also **ἔμπᾱν**, Pi.*P.*5.55, *N.*6.4, 11.44 ; and **ἔμπᾰ** (v. supr.), Id.*N.*4.36, Call.*Ep.*14 :—poet. Adv. 1. = ὁμοίως, *alike*, Ζεὺς δ' ἐ. πάντ' ἰθύνει Il.17.632 ; ἐ. ἐς γαῖάν τε καὶ οὐρανὸν ἵκετ' ἀϋτμή 14.174 ; ἐ. τὰ καὶ τὰ νέμων Pi.*P.*5.55. 2. *in any case*, νῦν δ' ἐ. γὰρ κῆρες ἐφεστᾶσιν θανάτοιο, ἴομεν Il.12.326 ; οὐκ ἐφάμην ῥιγωσέμεν ἐ. Od.14.481 ; *anyhow, as things are*, σὺ δὲ χαῖρε καὶ ἐ. 5.205, cf. Il.19.308, v.l. for αὔτως in Od.16.143 ; ὄφρ' ἔτι μᾶλλον Τρωσὶ μὲν εὐκτὰ γένηται ἐπικρατέουσί περ ἐ. though they are victorious *as it is*, Il.14.98. 3. *in the same way, so*, ἐ. μοι τοῖχοι.. φαίνοντ' ὀφθαλμοῖς ὡς εἰ πυρὸς αἰθομένοιο Od.19.37, cf. 18.354. II. = ὅμως, *all the same, nevertheless*, ἐ. δ' οὐκ ἐδάμασσα Il.5.191 ; πρῆξαι δ' ἐ. οὔ τι δυνήσεαι 1.562, cf. Od.19. 302, 2.199 ; after ἀλλά, ἀλλὰ καί, ἀλλ' ἐ. μιν ἐάσομεν 16.147, cf. Il. 8.33, Od.4.100, al. ; ἀλλὰ καὶ ἐ. αἰσχρόν but *even so*.., Il.2.297, cf. 19.422 ; ἐγὼ δ' αἰσχύνομαι ἐ. Od.18.12, cf. 15.214 ; following part. with περ, = καίπερ, Νέστορα δ' οὐκ ἔλαθεν πίνοντά περ ἐ. Il.14.1, cf. Od. 15.361, 18.165 ; rarely before the part., ἄλγεα δ' ἐ. ἐν θυμῷ κατακεῖσθαι ἐάσομεν ἀχνύμενοί περ Il.24.522. (Signff. I and II were distd. by Aristarch., cf. Sch.T Il.14.1.) III. in later Poets sts. in a milder sense, *at any rate, yet*, A.*Pr.*48, *Eu.*229, S.*Ant.*845, E.*Cyc.*535 (lyr.) ; after δέ, Pi.*P.*4.86 ; ἀλλ' ἔμπας A.*Pr.*189 (lyr.), E.*Alc.*906 (lyr.) ; ἀλλ' ἔμπαν Pi.*N.*6.4, 11.44 ; ἔμπα, καίπερ ἔχει.. ib.4.36, cf. S.*Aj.*563 : with a part., ib.1338 ; δύστηνον ἔμπας, καίπερ ὄντα δυσμενῆ ib.122 ; also with Adj., ἀφωνήτῳ περ ἔμπας ἄχει Pi.*P.*4.237.

**ἔμπας** (B), πασα, παν, *all*, dub. in *IG*7.2712.69 (Acraeph., i A.D.).

**ἐμπασένταs**· ἀρχεῖόν τι ἐν Λακεδαίμονι, Hsch.

⊛ **ἔμπᾱσις**, εως, ἡ, (πέπᾱμαι) = ἔγκτησις, *IG*5(2).11 (Tegea), 7.8.9 (Megara, iii B.C.), Hsch. (pl.) ; Boeot. **ἔππασις** *IG*7.3166 (Orchom., iii B.C.) ; also **ἔπασις** ib.3167, al. ; Arc. **ἴμπασις** ib.5(2).17 (Tegea), 394 (Lusi).

**ἔμ-πᾰσις**, εως, ἡ, *sprinkling, dusting*, εἰς ἔμπασιν *BKT*3 p.32. **-πασμα**, ατος, τό, *dusting-powder*, Antyll.ap.Orib.10.31.1, cf. 8.6. 7. **-πάσσω**, Att. -ττω, fut. -πάσω [ᾰ] :—*sprinkle in* or *on*, τι ἔς τι Thphr.*Lap.*67 ; τῆς τέφρας some *powder*, Pl.*Ly.*210a ; τί τινι Gal. 11.134 : in Hom. only metaph., *weave* rich patterns *in* a web of cloth, πολέας δ' ἐνέπασσεν ἀέθλους Il.3.126, cf. 22.441. **-παστέον**, *one must sprinkle*, Archig.ap.Aët.9.28.

⊛ **ἐμπαστῆρας**· μύθων· πιστωτάς, μάρτυρας, Hsch. ; cf. ἔμπαιος (A).

**ἐμπαστήρια**· μελίπη(κ)τα, Id.

**ἐμπᾰτᾰγέω**, *make a noise with*, μάστιξιν Them.*Or.*4.50b.

**ἐμπάτακτος** [πᾰ], ον, = ἐμβρόντητος, Ptol.*Tetr.*165.

**ἐμπᾰτέω**, *walk in* or *into*, c. acc., μέλαθρον A.*Ag.*1434. II. c. acc., *trample on*, νεκρούς J.*BJ*6.9.4 : metaph., τὰ κοινὰ τῶν ἀνθρώπων νόμιμα Agath.4.15 :—Med. or Pass., *tread* the wine-press, Poll. 7.151.

⊛ **ἔμπατον**· καταθύμιον, Hsch.

**ἔμπεδα**, v. ἔμπεδος.

**ἐμπεδ-έω**, = ἐμπεδόω, *Schwyzer* 414.3 (Elis). **-ής**, ές, = ἔμπεδος, *Trag.Adesp.*208. Adv. Ion. ἐμπεδέως *Scol.*25.

⊛ **ἐμπέδιος**, ον, *deep-rooted*, cj. in Numen.ap.Ath.9.371c.

**ἐμπεδό-καρπος**, ον, *ever-fruiting*, Emp.77. **-λώβης**, ου, ὁ, *ever-hurting*, Man.4.196. **-μοχθος**, ον, *ever-painful*, βίος Pi.*O.*1. 59. **-μῡθος**, ον, *steadfast to one's word*, Ἄτροπος, Πειθώ, Nonn.*D.* 12.141, 38.43.

**ἐμπεδορκέω**, *abide by one's oath*, Hdt.4.201, X.*Lac.*15.7 ; ταῦτα *IG*2².1.111.79 :—with a play on πέδη, Ar.*Fr.*772.

**ἔμπεδος** (A), ον, (πέδον) *in the ground, firm-set*, τεῖχος Il.12.12 ; λέχος Od.23.203. 2. mostly of qualities, etc., *steadfast*, μένος, ἴς, Il.5.254, Od.11.393 ; φρένες, ἦτορ, νόος, Il.6.352, 10.94, 11.813 ; χρὼς ἐ. 19.33 ; of a person, ἐ. οὐδ' ἀεσίφρων (of Priam) 20.183 ; λίσσεται ἔμπεδον εἶναι [τὴν πομπήν] prays that it may be *sure and certain*, Od.8. 30, cf. Pi.*N.*7.57 ; δίκη δέ τοι ἐ. ἔστω καὶ θέμις A.R.4.372, etc. ; once in A., ἐ. σίνος a *cleaving* or *clinging* mischief, *Ag.*561 ; ἐ. φρονήματα S.*Ant.*169 ; συντρόφοις ὀργαῖς ἐ. *continuing steadfast in*.., Id.*Aj.*640 (lyr.) ; ἔμπεδα φωνεῖν Nic.*Th.*4 : Comp. -ώτερος, νόος Luc.*Salt.* 85. 3. of Time, *lasting, continual*, φυλακή Il.8.521 ; κομιδή Od.8. 453 ; αἰών Emp.17.11 ; δουλοσύνα Pi.*P.*12.14 ; χρῆμα Simon.85.1 (s.v.l.) ; πόνος S.*OC*1674 (lyr.). II. neut. ἔμπεδον as Adv. (freq. in Hom.), στήλη μένει ἐ. stands *fast*, Il.17.434 ; Δαναοὶ Τρῶας μένον ἐ. *firmly*, 5.527 ; θέειν ἐ. run *on and on*, run *without resting*, 13.141 ; ἐ. βρύουσα B.12.178 ; strengthd., ἐ. αἰέν Il.16.107 ; ἐ. ἀσφαλὲς αἰεί 15.683 ; μάλ' ἀσφαλέως θέεν ἐ. Od.13.86 : pl., τίκτη δ' ἔμπεδα μῆλα the flocks bring forth *without fail*, 19.113 ; δρύες ἔμπεδα ῥίζαις ἑστᾶσιν *firmly*, *AP*9.291 (Crin.) : in Trag., ἴσθι τόδ' ἔμπεδον *of a surety*, S. *Ph.*1197 (anap.) ; more freq. regul. Adv. ἐμπέδως *continually*, Semon. 7.20 (nisi leg. -πεδῶς, cf. ἐμπεδής) : so in Trag., *constantly, firmly*, A.*Ag.*854, 975, *Eu.*335 (lyr.), S.*Tr.*487 ; also in later Prose, ἐ. οἶδα *of a surety*, Pl.*Ax.*372a ; ἔτη τριάκοντα μείναντες ἐ. Plb.2.19.1, Porph. *Abst.*2.41. III. = χθόνιος, Hippon.113A.

**ἔμπεδος** (B), ον, (πέδη) *fettered*, Luc.*Lex.*10.

**ἐμπεδο-σθενής**, ές, *with force unshaken*, βίοτος *a settled, unruffled* life, Pi.*N.*7.98. **-φρων**, ον, gen. ονος, (φρήν) *steadfast of mind*, Phalar.*Ep.*37.2. **-φυλλος**, ον, *ever-green*, Emp.77.

**ἐμπεδ-όω**, impf. ἠμπέδουν X.*Cyr.*8.8.2: aor. ἐνεπέδωσα D.C.60.28: (ἔμπεδος):—*confirm, ratify*, σὺ δ' ἐμπέδου δόσιν S.*Ichn.*50; ὅρκον E.*IT*790, cf. Ar.*Lys.*211,233, Polem.Hist.83; σπονδάς X.*HG*3.4.6; τὰ.. ὀρκωμόσιά τε καὶ ὑποσχέσεις Pl.*Phdr.*241b; ὅρκους καὶ δεξιάς τινι X.*Cyr.*5.1.22; συνθήκας Plb.29.24.4; ὁμολογίας D.H.4.79; ἀποδείξεσι δόγμα Gal.5.315; *uphold*, νόμους Plu.*Sol.*25:—Med., σπονδήν, ἀσφάλειαν ἐμπεδώσασθαι, Ph.1.439, Luc.*Hipp.*4. **-ωσις**, εως, ἡ, *making good*, ὅρκων D.H.5.10.

**ἐμπειρ-άζω**, *to make an attempt on*, c. gen. rei, v.l. for ἀπο-, Plb.15.35.5. **-ᾱμος**, ον, poet. for ἐμπέραμος (q.v.). **-άομαι**, Dep., *make trial of*, τινός Hp.*Nat.Mul.*99. **-έω**, *to be experienced in, have knowledge of*, c. gen. rei, τῆς χώρας Plb.3.78.6, etc.; τῆς ὁδοῦ Lxx *To.*5.6. **-ία**, ἡ, *experience*, E.*Ph.*529, Th.4.10; opp. ἀνεπιστημοσύνη, Id.5.7; ἡ ἐκ πολλοῦ ἐ., opp. ἡ δι' ὀλίγου μελέτη, Id.2.85; ἡ μὴ 'μπειρία want of *experience*, Ar.*Ec.*115; δι' ἐμπειρίαν Pl.*Prm.*137a; ἐπιστήμῃ, οὐκ ἐμπειρίᾳ οἰκείᾳ κεχρημένον Id.*R.*409b: pl., D.*Prooem.*45. 2. c. gen. rei, *experience in, acquaintance with*, τῶν πραγμάτων Antipho 5.1; μάχης ἐμπειρίᾳ τῆς ἐκείνων Th.3.95; ἀμφοτέρων τῶν ἡδονῶν Pl.*R.*582b; also ἐ. περί τι X.*HG*7.1.4; ἐ. ἡ κατὰ τὴν πόλιν Th.2.3; ἐ. ἡγεμονική Plb.10.24.4, etc. II. *practice*, without knowledge of principles, esp. in Medicine, *empiricism*, ἰατρὸς τῶν ταῖς ἐμπειρίαις ἄνευ λόγου τὴν ἰατρικὴν μεταχειριζομένων Pl.*Lg.*857c (hence οἱ ἀπὸ τῆς ἐ. ἰατροί S.E.*M.*8.191, Gal.*Sect.Intr.*1); κατ' ἐμπειρίαν τὴν τέχνην κτᾶσθαι *empirically*, Pl.*Lg.*720b; οὐκ ἔστιν τέχνη, ἀλλ' ἐ. καὶ τριβή Id.*Grg.*463b, cf. 465a, *Lg.*938a (whereas Plb. opposes ἐ. to ἀπειρία καὶ τριβὴ ἄλογος 1.84.6): but also, 2. *craft*, τοῖς περὶ τὰς ἐ. γεγυμνασμένοις Isoc.13.14; πραγμάτων ἐ., including τέχνη and ἐπιστήμη Metrod.61; αἱ ἄλλαι ἐ. καὶ τέχναι the other *crafts* and arts, Arist.*Pol.*1282a1; αἱ περὶ τῶν τοιούτων ἐ. ib.1297b20; also, *experiments*, πολλαὶ τέχναι ἐκ τῶν ἐ. ηὑρημέναι Pl.*Grg.*448c. **-ικός**, ή, όν, *experienced*, ἁλιεῖς Arist.*HA*532b20. Adv. -κῶς, ἔχειν τινός Id.*GA*742a17, cf. Alex.243, etc. 2. οἱ ἐμπειρικοί *the Empiric school of physicians*, Cels.1 *Praef.*, Gal.*Sect.Intr.*1, al., S.E.*M.*8.327, al.; ἡ -κή their doctrine, = Lat. *empirice*, Plin.*HN*29.5; in full, ἐ. αἵρεσις Gal.l.c.; so ἐ. ἱστορία Phld.*Rh.*1.93 S. Adv. -κῶς *empirically*, ἰατρεύειν S.E.*M.*8.204, cf. Gal.15.8.

**ἐμπειρο-θάλασσος** [θᾰ], ον, = sq., Phot.ap.Sch.Aristid.p.185 F. **-πλους**, ουν, *experienced in navigation*, Tz. ad Hes.*Op.*687. **-πόλεμος**, ον, *experienced in war*, D.H.6.14, Ph.1.426: Sup., App.*BC*3.97. Adv. -μως ib.2.36. **-πράγμων**, ον, gen. ονος, *versed in affairs*, Suid. s. v. νόμος.

**ἔμπειρος**, ον, (πεῖρα) *experienced* or *practised in* a thing, *acquainted with* it, c. gen., τῆς θυσίης Hdt.2.49; τῶν χώρων Id.8.132; Βοιωτῶν Id.9.46; τῆς ἐκείνου διανοίης Id.8.97; κακῶν A.*Pers.*598; γάμων S.*OC*752; θαλάσσης Th.1.80 (Sup.); τοῦ ἀγωνίζεσθαι Antipho 5.7; ὁ περὶ τῶν νόμων ἔ. Pl.*Lg.*632d; οἱ μάλιστα περὶ ταῦτα τῶν ἱερέων ἔ. Id.*Ti.*22a: abs., οἱ ἔ. the *experienced*, S.*OT*44, *OC*1135; *experts*, Pl.*Lg.*765b; ναυσὶν ἐμπείροις for ships *skilfully handled*, Th.2.89; τὸ ἐμπειρότερον αὐτῶν their *greater experience*, ib.87. II. Adv. -ρως, τινὸς ἔχειν to *know* a person or thing *by experience, by its issue*, X.*An.*2.6.1, Antiph.3, etc.; παιδεῦσαι D.59.18; διώκειν Aen.Tact.2.6; πόλεμον διενεγκεῖν Jul.*Or.*2.95a: Comp. -οτέρως Aeschin.1.82.

**ἐμπειρότοκος**, ον, *having borne a child*, Hp.*Mul.*1.4.

**ἐμπείρω**, *fix on* or *in*, ἥλους ἐκπώματι Ath.11.488d (Pass.); [δόρατος] ἐμπαρέντος ταῖς πύλαις Plu.2.298a; of fish bones in the throat, Aët.8.53 (Pass.); ἐμπεπαρμένος πόνος *fixed* pain, Archig.ap.Gal.8.91. 2. *impale*, ὡς ἐμπαρείη ταῖς ἑαυτοῦ λόγχαις J.*AJ*16.10.3; ἥλοις ἐμπεπαρμένη βακτηρία *studded*, Alciphr.3.55. II. metaph., ψυχὴ τοῖς ἀλόγοις πάθεσιν ἑαυτὴν ἐ. Simp. *in Epict.*p.125 D.:—Pass., ibid.

**ἐμπελαγίζω**, *to be in* or *on the sea*, *IPE*1².35 (Olbia, i B.C.), Ach.Tat.5.9.

⊛ **ἐμπελ-άδην** [ᾰ], Adv. = sq., Nic.*Al.*215. **-ᾰδόν**, Adv. *near, hard by*, ἱστίῃ Hes.*Op.*734. **-άζω**, *bring near*, δίφρους ἐμπελάσαντες *having brought up* the chariots, Id.*Sc.*109:—Pass., *come near, approach*, κοίτης S.*Tr.*17. II. intr. in Act., *approach*, c. dat., ἐμπελάσειν πυκινῷ δόμῳ *h.Merc.*523; εἴδωλα ἐ. τοῖς ἀνθρώποις Democr.166; ποῦ δ' ἐμπελάζεις τἀνδρί..; S.*Tr.*748; τῇ ἀκοῇ Arist.*Mu.*395a19: abs., ib.b28, Porph.*Abst.*2.22; κρήνης μηδὲ σχεδὸν ἐμπελάσειας Orph.*Fr.*32a. III. in Pass., wrongly used for ἐμπαλάσσομαι, τοῖσι αὐτοῖσι Hp.*Ep.*17; ἀλλήλοις D.C.36.49, 62.16; αὐτοῖς Id.72.19.

⊛ **ἐμπελάνα**· πόπανα, Hsch.

**ἐμπέλ-ᾰσις**, εως, ἡ, *approaching*, S.E.*M.*9.393, 11.98. **-αστικῶς**, gloss on ἐμπελάδην, Sch.Nic.*Al.*215. **-άτειρα** [λᾰ], ἡ, = πελάτις, πλᾶτις, Call.*Fr.*170, Euph.9.11. ⊛ **-άω**, imper. ἐμπέλα, *IG*14.271 (Selinus), Hsch.:— = ἐμπελάζω, Nic.*Al.*498:—Med., ib.356.

**ἐμπέλιος**, ον, *livid*, Nic.*Th.*782.

**ἐμπέλωρος**, ὁ, title of Laconian official, = ἀγορανόμος, Hsch.

**ἐμπέπτας**, ου, ὁ, *hollow wheaten cake*, Seleuc.ap.Ath.14.645d; Rhodian, acc. to Hsch.

⊛ **ἐμπέρᾰμος**, ον, = ἔμπειρος, *skilled in the use of*, νηῶν Call.*Jov.*71; πάσης ἐ. σοφίης *IG*14.1957, cf. 888 (Suessa), *Arch.Anz.*1904.8 (Milet.): abs., ἐμπέραμος φώς Androm.ap.Gal.14.37:—also **ἐμπειρᾰμος**, Lyc.1196, Man.4.536, *AP*10.14 (Agath.), Nonn.*D.*39.181. Adv. ἐμπεράμως Call.*Lav.Pall.*25.

**ἐμπερδολεκᾰνᾰρύταινα** [ῠ], ἡ, dub. sens. in *Com.Adesp.*55 D.

**ἐμπερής**, ές, poet. for ἔμπειρος, S.*Fr.*464.

**ἐμπερι-άγω** [ᾰ], *bring round*, τὸν θεὸν κατὰ ἔθνος -άγοντα τὴν ἀρχὴν J.*BJ*5.9.3. **-βάλλω**, *embrace, comprehend*, dub. in Phld.*Herc.*1251.8. **-βολος**, ον, (περιβολή) *ornate, expanded*, Aristid.*Rh.*2 p.533 S.; λόγος Hermog.*Id.*1.11; προοίμια Men.Rh.p.400 S. **-γράφω** [ᾰ], *comprehend in a thing*, v.l. for συμπ-, S.E.*P.*1.206 (Pass.); *describe around*, κύκλον τηλίᾳ Poll.9.108. **-εκτικός**, ή, όν, *comprehending, inclusive*, c. gen., A.D.*Pron.*4.7, al.: abs., Id.*Synt.*231.3. **-έρχομαι**, *pass round*, prob. in Gal.2.826: metaph., μηδὲν ἐ. ἀκριβείᾳ λογισμοῦ Ph.2.61. **-έχω**, *encompass, surround, enclose*, Arist.*MM*1187a3, *Mu.*395b18, Thphr.*HP*1.11.1; *include*, A.D.*Adv.*124.22; *garrison*, τὸ βασίλειον τῷ μαχιμωτάτῳ J.*AJ*17.10.3:—Pass., *to be embraced, encompassed*, Arist.*Mu.*392a9, Ph.1.385; *to be contained, included in*, λόφος -εχόμενος τῇ πόλει D.H.10.31; τῷ κόσμῳ Ocell.1.8: abs., Id.3.2: metaph., *to be contained* or *involved in*, ἔν τινι Plb.9.32.4, Corn.*ND*26; καθ' ἑκάστην ἰδέαν Longin.8.1. 2. Astrol., *blockade*, Vett.Val.268.20. **-ισχάνω**, = foreg., Nech.ap.eund.280.3 (Pass.). **-κλείω**, *enclose on all sides*, Eust.105.22. **-λαμβάνω**, *encompass, enclose*, Hp.*Ep.*23, Thphr.*CP*5.3.4; ὕδωρ ἐρύμασι Plu.*Ant.*63; τῇ αὐτοῦ οἰκίᾳ ψιλοὺς τόπους *Sammelb.*5233.7 (i A.D.); ὅρος J.*BJ*3.7.7; *comprehend*, ἑνὶ ὀνόματι [ἄμφω] Arist.*PA*644a12; ψήφισμα πάσας ἐ. τὰς ἀρετάς τινος *Inscr.Prien.*105.27 (i B.C.):—Pass., Arist.*Mete.*388b21; ἐμπερειείληπται ὁ διαβάλλων *is involved* in the charge, Id.*Rh.*1416a20; τύποις -ειλημμένα Epicur.*Ep.*1 p.22 U.; ὑπὸ τοῦ κόσμου ib.2 p.38 U. **-ληπτικός**, ή, όν, *comprehending, inclusive*, τινός A.D.*Synt.*36.1, al.: abs., ἐ. τρόπος Epicur.*Nat.*28.2. **-ληψις**, εως, ἡ, *encompassment*, τοῦ πυρός Arist.*Mete.*369b19; τοῦ φωτός Epicur.*Ep.*2 p.45 U.; *embracing*, χρόνων ἀξιολόγων D.H.*Dem.*38. **-νοέω**, *include in the thought of*, συνάψαι φάσμα τούτοις ἐμπερινενοημένον Epicur.*Nat.*11.9. **-οδος**, ον, *in periods, periodic*, of style, D.H.*Comp.*9. Adv. -δως Corn.*ND*27. **-οχή**, ἡ, *encompassing*, Cleom.1.3. **-πᾰτέω**, *walk about in*, [ἐμβάταις] Luc.*Ind.*6; μέσοις τοῖς ἁγίοις J.*BJ*4.3.10: metaph., ταῖς διανοίαις Ph.1.643, cf. 274; ἐ. ἐν ὑμῖν *tarry among* you, Lxx *Le.*26.12, cf. *2Ep.Cor.*6.16: abs., *walk about*, ἅμα τῷ συμποσίῳ Luc.*Symp.*13: c. acc. cogn., ἐ. διαύλους τινάς *walk* several times to and fro, Ach.Tat.1.6. II. *walk about upon*, τὴν ὑπ' οὐρανόν (sc. γῆν) Lxx *Jb.*1.7, al.; *trample on*, *PHolm.*18.30: metaph., *insult*, τινί Plu.2.57a. **-πείρω**, *impale upon*:—Pass., ἐμπεριπαρεὶς ταῖς σαρίσσαις Str.17.1.8 (prob. f.l. for περιπ-). **-πίπτω**, *fall upon*, ἔθνει ἐ. νοῦσοι Hp.*Flat.*6 (s.v.l.). **-πλέω**, prob. f.l. for ἐκπεριπλέω in J.*BJ*3.10.9. **-ποιέω**, *produce in*, δυνάμεις τισί Ptol.*Tetr.*50. **-ρρήγνῡμι**, *break all round*, v.l. in Arist.*HA*557b26. **-σπούδαστος**, ον, *zealously frequented*, of temples, interpol. in J.*Ap.*2.35. **-στέγω**, *encase*, Sor.1.57. **-σχεσις**, εως, ἡ, Astrol., *hemming in* of a planet by two others, Vett.Val.5.15, Porph. *in Ptol.*188, *Cat.Cod.Astr.*8(3).114.23, Heph.Astr.1.15.

**ἐμπερκάζω**, = περκάζω, Hsch.; cf. ἐμπερ⟨καίν⟩ονται· ἐμποικίλλονται, Id.

**ἐμπερον-ατρίς**, ίδος, ἡ, = ἐμπερόνημα 1, Hsch. ⊛ **-άω**, *fasten with a clasp, buckle on*, in Med., θώρακα.. ἐμπερονᾶται Hermipp.47, J.*BJ*7.2.2. II. Pass., of nails, *to be fixed in*, Ath.11.488b. **-ημα**, Dor. -ᾱμα, ατος, τό, *a garment fastened with a brooch* on the shoulder, Theoc.15.34. II. *clasp, brooch*, Agath.3.15.

**ἐμπερπερεύομαι**, = περπερεύομαι, Cic.*Att.*1.14.4, Arr.*Epict.*2.1.34.

**ἔμπεσον**, Ep. aor. 2 of ἐμπίπτω.

**ἐμπετᾰλίς**, ίδος, ἡ, *dish consisting of cheese wrapped in a leaf* (ἐν πετάλῳ), Hsch.

**ἐμπετ-άννῡμι** or -ύω, fut. -πετάσω (v. infr.), *to unfold and spread in* or *on*, X.*Cyr.*1.6.40, J.*BJ*3.7.10: metaph., σφιν ἐμπετάσει λάθαν *will spread* oblivion, *Hymn.Is.*22:—Pass., *to be spread*, ἐπί τινος Callix.1. II. in Pass., ἐ. ὕφεσι *to be hung about with* cloths, Socr.Rhod.1. **-ασμα**, ατος, τό, *curtain*, *Inscr.Perg.*236, J.*AJ*15.11.3.

**ἔμπετες**, Dor. for ἐνέπεσες, aor. 2 of ἐμπίπτω, Pi.*P.*8.81.

**ἐμπέτομαι**, *fly into*, aor. inf. ἐμπτῆναι, εἰς τὸ στόμα Arcesil.ap.D.L.4.32.

**ἔμπετρος**, ον, (πέτρα) *growing on rocks*: τὸ ἔ. *sea-heath, Frankinia pulverulenta*, Dsc.4.179, Gal.11.875.

**ἐμπευκής**, ές, (πεύκη) *bitterish*, ὀπός Nic.*Al.*202.

**ἐμπεφῡκότως**, Adv. *clinging firmly*, gloss on ἀπρίξ, Sch.Theoc.15.68, cf. Hsch. s.v. φῦ χειρί.

**ἐμπεφυρμένως**, Adv. *confusedly*, Tz.*Trag.Poes.*150.

**ἔμπη**, Dor. for πῇ, *AP*13.5 (Phal.).

⊛ **ἐμπήγνῡμι**, *fix* or *plant in*, c. dat., μεταφρένῳ ἐν δόρυ πῆξε Il.5.40; ἐνέπαξαν ἕλκος ἑᾷ καρδίᾳ Pi.*P.*2.91; ἐ. τι εἴς τι Hp.*Art.*72, Arist.*Pr.*889b1; ὀδόντα εἴς τινα *AP*5.265 (Paul. Sil.), cf. 11.374 (Maced.):—Pass., with pf. and plpf. Act., *to be fixed* or *stuck in, stick in*, λόγχη τις ἐμπέπηγέ μοι δι' ὀστέων Ar.*Ach.*1226; ἔν τί σοι παγήσεται Id.*V.*437: abs., Thphr.*HP*1.8.3: metaph., ἐμπέπηγα τῷ διακονεῖν Diph.43.25; ταῖς ἑαυτῶν περιουσίαις ἐμπηγνύμενοι Just.*Nov.*98 *Pr.* II. *congeal, freeze*, Thphr.*CP*5.12.2 (v.l. for ἐκ-):—Pass., *to be congealed*, ib.1.22.7 (v.l. for ἐκ-); *freeze to death*, Arist.*HA*603a27.

**ἐμπηδ-άω**, *jump upon*, αὐτῇ ἐχούσῃ ἐν γαστρί Hdt.3.32: metaph. of sense-impressions, Archig.ap.Orib.8.2.5. 2. ἐ. εἰς.. *leap* or *spring into*, ἐς τὴν ναῦν Hermipp.54, cf. Plb.12.8.4. 3. abs., *beat*, of the heart, Ph.1.67: aor. part. ἐμπηδήσας *eagerly, greedily*, Luc.*Hist.Conscr.*20. **-ησις**, εως, ἡ, *leaping in* or *upon*, Hp.*Epid.*2.1.9.

**ἐμπηκτέον**, *one must stick in*, Gp.18.2.2.

⊛ **ἐμπήκτης**, ου, ὁ, *one who sticks up judicial notices*, Arist.*Ath.*64.2, al.

**ἔμπηλος**, ον, *muddy*, Gp.2.5.7, *Hippiatr.*22.

⊛ **ἐμπηνός**· ἧλος, Hsch.

**ἔμπηξις**, εως, ἡ, *impaction*, Gal.2.738. II. *solidification*, Meno

*Iatr.*15.33. 2. in concrete sense, ἔ. ὑμενώδης, of the χόριον, Porph.*Gaur.*10.3.

**ἔμπηρος**, ον, *crippled, maimed*, Hdt.1.167,196, Hp.*Morb.*1.1, etc.

**ἔμπης**, Adv., Ep. for ἔμπας.

⊛ **ἐμπήσσομαι**, = ἐμπήγνυμαι, Apollod.*Poliorc.*142.1, Sch.Il.4.535, *EM*709.9.

**ἐμπῑ-έζω**, *press, squeeze*, in Pass., Hp.*Gland.*13, Plu.2.1005a. **-εσις**, εως, ἡ, *pressure*, of massage, Sor.1.102 (pl.). **-εσμα**, ατος, τό, *depressed cranial fracture*, Id.*Fract.*6, Heliod.ap.Orib.46.14.1, Paul.Aeg.6.90.

**ἐμπικραίνομαι**, Med. or Pass., *to be bitter against*, τινί Hdt.5.62, D.C.47.8: abs., Eus.Mynd.54; of disease, *become virulent*, J.*AJ* 17.6.5.

**ἔμπικρος**, ον, *rather bitter*, Dsc.1.4, 2.122.

**ἐμπῑλέομαι**, Pass., *to be compressed*, Pl.*Ti.*74e, D.S.2.52.

⊛ **ἐμπίλια** [πῐ], τά, (πῖλος) *felt shoes*, Charis.p.552 K.; *bandage for horses' legs*, Hsch. s. v. νακτά.

**ἐμπίμελος** [ῐ], ον, *of a fatty substance*, Dsc.2.61, Xenocr.63.

**ἐμπίμπλημι**, Ion. 2 sg. pres. ἐμπιπλεῖς Hp.*Morb.*2.14, part. -πιπλῶν ib.12; 3 sg. ἐμπιπλέει Hdt.7.39 (with vv. ll. -πιπλεῖ, -πιπλᾷ): 1 sg. impf. ἐνεπίμπλων D.C.68.31: fut. -πλήσω Pl.*Lg.*875c: aor. ἐνέπλησα, Ep. subj. ἐνιπλήσῃς Od.19.117: pf. ἐμπέπληκα (v. infr.):—*fill quite full*, ἐν ὧν ἔπλησαν τοῦ νεκροῦ τὴν κοιλίην Hdt.2.87; τὸ πεδίον, τὴν ὁδόν, X.*HG*7.1.20, 2.4.11. 2. c. gen., *fill full of* a thing, ἐμπίπληθι ῥέεθρα ὕδατος Il.21.311, etc.; δέπας ὕδατος Od.9.209; [ἵππον] ἀνδρῶν ἐμπλήσας 8.495; μὴ.. θυμὸν ἐνιπλήσῃς ὀδυνάων 19.117; ἐ. [τὰ θυλάκια] τῆς ψάμμου Hdt.3.105, cf. 4.72, 5.114; τοὺς κοφίνους.. ἐμπίμπλη (imper.) πτερῶν Ar.*Av.*1310; ἐ. ἵππων τὸν ἱππόδρομον X.*Eq.Mag.*3.10: metaph., τὴν ψυχὴν ἔρωτος Pl.*Phdr.*255d; τινὰ ἐλπίδων κενῶν Aeschin. 1.171. 3. *fill* a hungry man *with food*, Od.17.503. b. metaph., ἐ. τινὰ μύθων E.*Hel.*769; τοῦ πολεμεῖν Isoc.9.63; ἐκκεκώφωκε τὰ ὦτα καὶ ἐμπέπληκε Λύσιδος Pl.*Ly.*204c; ἐρώτων.. ἐμπίμπλησιν ἡμᾶς Id. *Phd.*66c; ἐμπιμπλὰς ἁπάντων τὴν γνώμην X.*An.*1.7.8. 4. *satiate*, τὴν ἀναιδῆ γνώμην αὐτοῦ D.21.91; ἵμερον A.R.4.429; ἕως νυκτὸς ἀλλήλους Longus 2.38. 5. *fulfil, accomplish*, τὴν αὐτοῦ μοῖραν Pl.*Lg.* 959c. II. Med. (with aor. Pass.), ἐμπίμπλαμαι E.*Ion*925; ἐμπιμπλάμενος Cratin.142, Pherecr.80, Epicur.*Nat.*117G.: impf. ἐνεπιμπλάμην X.*An.*7.7.46, Aeschin.3.230, etc.: later 3 pl. ἐνεπιμπλῶντο D.S.34/5.2.29:—*fill for oneself* or *what is one's own*, ἐμπλήσατο νηδὺν Od.9.296; μένεος ἐμπλήσατο θυμόν *he filled his* heart *with* rage, Il.22. 312; θαλέων ἐμπλησάμενος κῆρ ib.504; τὸ ἄγγος τοῦ ὕδατος ἐ. Hdt.5. 12. 2. abs., *eat oneself full, eat one's fill*, ἐνιπλησθῆναι ἀνώγει Od.7. 221, cf. Hdt.8.117, Ar.*V.*911, X.*Mem.*1.3.6, etc.: metaph., ἐπειδὴ τάχιστα ἐνέπληντο (ἐνεπέπληντο codd.)Lys.28.6. III. **Pass.**, aor. 1 ἐνεπλήσθην (v. infr.): aor. 2 ἐνεπλήμην Ar.*V.*911,1304, prob. in Lys. 28.6; opt. ἐμπλήμην (v. infr.): plpf. ἐνεπεπλήμην f.l. in Lys. l.c., late ἐμπέπληστο Max.Tyr.18.7; ἐνέπλησθεν δέ οἱ.. αἵματος ὀφθαλμοὶ Il.16.348; δακρύων τὰ ὄμματα X.*Cyr.*5.5.10; ἔμπληντο βροτῶν ἀγοραὶ Od.8.16; πόλις δ' ἔμπλητο ἀλέντων Il.21.607; ἐνέπλητο πολλῶν κἀγαθῶν Ar.*V.*1304; φακῆς ἐμπλήμενος ib.984, cf. *Ec.*56: metaph., υἷος ἐνιπλησθῆναι.. ὀφθαλμοῖσιν *to take my fill of* my son with my eyes, i.e. *to sate myself with* looking on him, Od.11.452; ὀργῆς καὶ μένους ἐμπλήμενος Ar.*V.*424; πλεονεξίας ἐμπίμπλασθαι Pl.*Criti.*121b. 2. c. dat., ἀμπελίνῳ καρπῷ ἐ. *to be filled with*.., Hdt.1.212; ἐμπιπλάμενοι πυριάτῃ Cratin.142; ἐμπίπλαται.. αἵματι ὁ βωμός Paus.3.16.10. 3. c. part., μισῶν οὔποτ' ἐμπλησθήσομαι γυναῖκας E.*Hipp.*664, cf.*Ion*925; βάλλων.. οὐκ ἂν ἐμπλήμην Ar.*Ach.*236; οὐκ ἐνεπίμπλασο ὑπισχνούμενος X.*An.*7.7.46; ἔμπλησο λέγων speak thy *fill*, Ar.*V.*603.—The two last constructions are post-Homeric. (Freq. written -πίπλ-, but the evidence of the best codd. of Att. writers is in favour of -πίμπλ-.)

**ἐμπίμπρημι** (pres. not in Hom. who has impf. ἐνέπρηθον, v. ἐμπρήθω), 3 pl. impf. ἐνεπίμπρασαν Th.6.94; also (as if from **ἐμπιπράω**) inf. ἐμπιπρᾶν Plu.*Cor.*26; part. ἐμπιπρῶν Plb.1.53.4: impf. ἐνεπίμπρων X.*HG*6.5.22: fut. ἐνιπρήσω Il.15.702, ἐμπρήσω Ar.*Th.*749, 3 pl. -πρήσοντι *Tab.Heracl.*1.145: aor. 1 ἐνέπρησα Hom., etc.: aor. 1 Med. ἐνεπρησάμην *PTeb.*61(*b*).289 (ii B. C.), Q.S.5.485:—**Pass.**, part. ἐμπιπράμενος Hdt.1.19: fut. ἐμπεπρήσομαι (v.l. ἐμπρήσομαι, as in Id.6.9), Paus.4.7.10; Ep. inf. ἐνιπρήσεσθαι Q.S.1.494: aor. ἐνεπρήσθην Hdt. 5.102, 6.25, Th.4.29, etc.: pf. ἐμπέπρησμαι Hdt.8.144 (v.l. -πέπρημαι), Ph.1.391:—*kindle, set on fire*, πυρὶ νῆας Il.8.182, al.; τῷ Λημνίῳ.. πυρὶ ἔμπρησον S.*Ph.*801; τὸν [νηὸν] ἐνέπρησαν Hdt.1.19, cf. 5.101, al.: c. gen., πυρὸς αἰθομένοιο νῆας ἐνιπρήσωσι *burn* them by force of fire, Il.16.82; ἐμπιμπράναι οἰκίαν Ar.*Nu.*1484, cf. Pl.*R.*471c:—Pass., *to be set on fire*, Hdt.1.19, etc.; ῥίζαι -πεπρησμέναι Ph.1.c.; *to be inflamed*, Aret.*SA*2.10: metaph. of anger, Luc.*Cat.*12. (Freq. written ἐμπίπρ- in codd., but cf. ἐμπιμπράντων Phld.*Ir.*p.53 W.)

**ἐμπινής**, ές, *soiled, dirty*, Antig.ap.D.L.5.67. II. = ἐξηρτισμένος, *Gloss.*

**ἐμπίνω** [ῑ], fut. -πίομαι: pf. -πέπωκα:—*drink*, πολλὰ καταφαγών, πόλλ' ἐμπιών Epich.35.7, cf. E.*Cyc.*336, X.*Cyr.*7.1.1: c. gen., ἐ. τοῦ αἵματος *to drink of* the blood, Hdt.3.11, 4.64, cf. Ph.1.324. 2. abs., *drink one's fill*, f.l. in Thgn.1129, cf. Ar.*Pax*1143,1156; ἐμπεπωκότες *drunken*, Id.*Ec.*142.

**ἐμπῑπάσκομαι**, = ἐμπάομαι, *acquire*, χρήματα *SIG*56.22 (Argos, v B. C.).

⊛ **ἐμπῑπίσκω**, aor. ἐνέπισα Pi.*Fr.*111.1:—**Pass.**, aor. 1 ἐνεπίσθην:—causal of ἐμπίνω, *give to drink*, Pi. l.c., Nic.*Al.*519:—Med., *fill oneself*, ἐμπίσασθαι ὕδατι, ὄξει, Id.*Th.*573, *Al.*320:—Pass., of liquor, *to be drunk*, Νύμφαις ἐμπισθὲν Id.*Th.*624.

⊛ **ἐμπιπράσκω**, *sell in*, Poll.7.9 (Pass.), Hsch. (Pass.).

⊛ **ἐμπίπτω**, fut. -πεσοῦμαι: aor. ἐνέπεσον, Ep. ἔμπεσον (v. infr.): lyr. aor. ἔμπετες Pi.*P.*8.81:—*fall in* or *on*, c. dat., τρύφος ἔμπεσε πόντῳ Od.4.508; ὁ δ' ὕπτιος ἔμπεσε πέτρῃ Il.4.108; ἐν δ' ἔπεσ' ὠκεανῷ, of the Sun, 8.485; πῦρ ἔμπεσε νηυσίν fire *fell upon* them, 16.113; αὐχένι.. ἔμπεσεν ἰός 15.451, cf. 624; with ἐν, ὡς δ' ὅτε πῦρ.. ἐν ἀξύλῳ ἐμπέσῃ ὕλῃ 11.155; κεραυνοὶ αὐτοῖσι ἐνέπιπτον Hdt.8.37; ἐμπέσοι γέ σοι (sc. ὁ πύργος) Ar.*Pl.*180, etc.: abs., ῥύμῃ ἐ. Th.2.76, cf. Hdt.1. 34: c. gen., ὠκεανοῖο Arat.635. b. Geom., *meet*, of a line *meeting* another, Euc.1 *Post.*5, etc.; *to be placed*, ἐὰν εἰς τὸν κύκλον εὐθεῖα ἐμπέσῃ Archim.*Sph.Cyl.*1.9; ἡ ἐμπεσοῦσα ibid. c. of a dislocated limb, *fall into place*, Hp.*Art.*8. 2. *fall upon, attack*, ἐν δ' ἔπεσον προμάχοις Od.24.526, cf. Il.16.81; στρατῷ E.*Rh.*127; τοῖς πολεμίοις X.*Eq.Mag.*8.25, etc.; ἐμπεσόντες *having fallen on* them, Hdt. 3.146, cf. 7.16.α': metaph., *insult*, ἄλλοισι δ' ἐμπίπτων γελᾷ Pi.*I.*1. 68; so, 3. of evils, diseases, etc., *fall on* one, *attack*, κακὸν ἔμπεσε οἴκῳ Od.2.45; λὺγξ τοῖς πλέοσιν ἐνέπιπτε κενή Th.2.49; νόσημα ἐμπέπτωκεν εἰς τὴν Ἑλλάδα D.19.259; πρὶν ἐμπεσεῖν σπαραγμόν S. *Tr.*1253; ὕπνος ἐ. Pl.*Ti.*45e: of passions, of frames of mind, χόλος, δέος ἔμπεσε θυμῷ, Il.9.436, 17.625; ἔρως μή τις ἐμπίπτῃ στρατῷ A.*Ag.* 341; Ἔρως, ὃς ἐν κτήμασι πίπτεις S.*Ant.*782 (lyr.); ἐμοὶ.. οἶκτος Id. *Ph.*965; τοῖς Ἀθηναίοις ἐνέπεσέ τι γέλωτος Th.4.28; μὴ λύσσα τις ἡμῖν ἐμπεπτώκοι X.*An.*5.7.26; ἔλεος ἐμπέπτωκέ τίς μοι Philippid.9.1; ἐ. εἰς.., Hdt.7.43, E.*IA*443, Th.2.48 codd., Lys.1.18, etc.: rarely c. acc., οὐδείς ποτ' αὐτοὺς.. ἂν ἐμπέσοι ζῆλος S.*OC*942; ἐμπέπτωκ' ἔρως .. Ἑλλάδα E.*IA*808. b. of words, καί μοι ἔπος ἔμπεσε θυμῷ *came into* my mind, Od.12.266; λόγος ἐμπέπτωκεν ἀρτίως ἐμοὶ *came to* my ears, S.*OC*1150; κἂν περὶ ἀνδρῶν γ' ἐμπέσῃ λόγος τις a report *arose*, Ar.*Lys.*858, cf. Pl.*R.*354b, *Lg.*799d, Thphr.*Char.*2.2; so τόποι ἐμπίπτοντες *available, suitable* topics, Hermog.*Prog.*7, etc., cf. Ph.1. 179. 4. *light* or *fall upon*, πρὶν ἁλίῳ γυῖον ἐμπεσεῖν before his body *was exposed* to the sun, Pi.*N.*7.73; [θηρία] ἐμπίπτοντα ταῖς ὄψεσι Hdn.3.9.5; also εἰς τὴν ὄψιν, εἰς τὴν αἴσθησιν, Pl.*Ti.*67d, *R.* 524d. b. *fall into*, ἐ. ἐν ἀπορίᾳ Id.*Euthd.*293a; ἐπὶ συμφορὴν Hdt. 7.88; more freq. ἐ. εἰς.., ἐ. εἰς ἄτας S.*El.*216 (lyr.); εἰς βάρβαρα φάσγανα E.*Hel.*864; εἰς ἐνέδραν X.*Cyr.*8.5.14; εἰς ἔρωτα Antiph.235. 3; εἰς νόσον Antipho1.20; εἰς ὑποψίας Id.2.2.3; εἰς φαῦλον σκέμμα Pl.*R.*435c; εἴς τινα βυθὸν φλυαρίας Id.*Prm.*130d; εἰς πράγματα D. 18.292; ἐ. εἰς τὰ πεπραγμένα, in speaking, *come upon* the exploits, ib.211; εἰς λόγους ib.42, cf. 59. 5. τῷ ἀκοντίῳ ἐ. τῷ ὤμῳ *throw oneself on* the javelin with one's shoulder, i.e. to give all one's force to the throw, Hp.*Aër.*20. **6.** *break in, burst in*, στέγῃ S.*OT*1262; πύλαις E.*Ph.*1146; εἰς τὴν θύραν κριηδὸν Ar.*Lys.*309; *intrude*, εἰς τὸ ἀρχεῖον Arist.*Pol.*1270$^b$9: abs., A.*Ag.*1350; ἐμπεσὼν *violently, rashly*, Hdt.3.81. 7. εἴς τι *fall within* the province of, Pl.*Tht.* 205d; εἰς τὰς εἰρημένας αἰτίας Arist.*Metaph.*986$^a$15, cf. *Rh.*1401$^b$29, *Ph.*196$^b$9; εἰς ἄλλο πρόβλημα Id.*Pol.*1268$^b$25. b. of income, εἰς τὸν λόγον τινός ἐ. *PLille* 16.5 (iii B. C.), cf. *POxy.*494.21 (ii A. D.). c. of suits, *come before*, εἰς δικαστῶν πλῆθος Arist.*Pol.*1300$^b$35, cf. Plu. *Sol.*18. **8.** ἐ. εἰς δεσμωτήριον *to be thrown* into prison, Din.2.9, cf. D.25.60 (abs., *get into prison*, Luc.*Tox.*28); εἰς ζήτρειον Eup.19D.; so ἐ. εἰς τὸν Τάρταρον Pl.*Phd.*114a: Com., εἰς τὸν οὐρανὸν *Com.Adesp.* 9D. **9.** of circumstances, *happen, occur*, Paus.7.8.4. **10.** *desert*, πρός τινα Lxx 4*Ki.*25.11.

**ἐμπίς**, ίδος, ἡ, *mosquito, gnat*, Ar.*Nu.*157; ἐμπίδες ὀξύστομοι Id.*Av.* 245, cf. Arist.*HA*490$^a$21, Porph.*Abst.*3.20; the gnat *Chironomus*, Arist.*HA*551$^b$27; prob. *may-fly*, ib.601$^a$4. 2. *larva of the* οἶστρος, ib.487$^b$5 (v.l.).

**ἐμπῖσαι, ἐμπισθῆναι**, v. ἐμπιπίσκω.

⊛ **ἐμπίσιον**· καὶ τὸ βραχὺ καὶ τὸ δαψιλῶς πιεῖν, Hsch. (Fort. ἐμπιεῖν.)

**ἐμπίστ-ευσις**, εως, ἡ, *trusteeship*, *Cat.Cod.Astr.*2.161. ⊛ **-εύω**, *entrust*, τινί τι D.S.1.67, Plu.*Phoc.*32; Ἔρως ταῖς βολαῖς τῶν ὀμμάτων ἐ. τὴν τόξευσιν Lib.*Descr.*30.8:—Pass., τινί *PStrassb.*5.10; but also, *to be entrusted with*, τι Luc.*Demon.*51, *Gp.*2.44.1; ὁ ἐγκέφαλος.. ἀσφάλειαν ἐμπεπιστευμένος Hp.*Ep.*23. II. *trust in, give credence to*, τινί Lxx *De.*1.32, al., Nic.Dam.*Fr.*130.19J.; ἔν τινι Lxx 2*Ch.*20. 20; ἐπί τινι ib.3*Ma.*2.7.

**ἐμπίτνω**, poet. for ἐμπίπτω, *fall upon*, εἰς ὅμιλον B.9.24; τινί A. *Ag.*1468 (lyr.), *Supp.*120 (lyr.), cf. S.*Aj.*58.

**ἐμπῑτυάζομαι**, *to be curdled*, of milk, Paul.Aeg.5.57.

**ἐμπλάζω** (A), *drive about in*:—hence in Pass., *wander about in* or *among*, ὕλῃ ἐνιπλαγχθεὶς Orph.*A.*645; πολλὴν ἀταξίαν τὰ σκευοφόρα τοῖς μαχομένοις -όμενα παρεῖχε Plu.*Oth.*12. 2. metaph., τεχνῖται -ονται μᾶλλον χρῆσθαι συνετωτέροις κριταῖς Phld.*Rh.*1.376S. II. intr., *wander in*, ἀγυιαῖς Nic.*Al.*189.

**ἐμπλάζω** (B), poet. for ἐμπελάζω, Nic.*Th.*779.

⊛ **ἐμπλᾰνάομαι**, *wander in*, πολλοῖς τόποις Hld.2.29: abs., αἵματος περίττωμα ἐ. Plu.2.495e: metaph., δύναμις -πλανωμένη *erratic*, ib. 336f.

**ἔμ-πλασμα**, ατος, τό, *plaster*, Phld.*Po.*2.66. ⊛ **-πλάσσω**, Att. -ττω, *plaster up*, τὸν πατέρα ἐν σμύρνῃ ἐ. Hdt.2.73; ἀσφάλτῳ ἐμπλασθεὶς Str.16.1.15. 2. *stuff in*, κηρὸν εἴς τι Arist.*Pr.*919$^b$9. 3. *stop up*, τὰ φλέβια, Thphr.*Sens.*66; *clog* the teeth of a saw, Id.*HP*5.6. 3:—Pass., -πλασσομένων τῶν πόρων Id.*Sens.*14. 4. *form in*, κηρία ἔν τινι D.C.78.25. 5. *cause to adhere*, τῇ γαστρὶ χυμόν Gal.6.428:—Pass., Id.15.204. b. abs., *to be viscous*, Id.6.495. II. Pass., *have an impression left* or *made*, Hp.*Mul.*2.116, al. **-πλαστέον**, f.l. for ἐμπαστέον, Archig.ap.Aët.9.28. **-πλαστικός**, ή, όν, *causing to adhere*, δύναμις Dsc.1.102. **-πλαστός**, ή, όν, *daubed on* or *over*:

ἔμπλαστον (with or without φάρμακον), τό, *plaster, salve*, Hp.*Hum.* 5:—also **ἔμπλαστος**, ἡ, Alex.Aphr.*de An.*25.1. **-πλάστριον**, τό, Dim. of ἔμπλαστρος, Paul.Aeg.4.48, 6.16. **-πλαστροποιΐα**, ἡ, *making of plasters*, Gal.13.898. **-πλαστρος**, ἡ, *salve* or *plaster*, Dsc.1.32; said to be later form of ἔμπλαστος, Gal.13.372; also ® **ἔμπλαστρον**, τό, Hierocl.*Facet.*221, *PSI*3.297 (v A.D.).

**ἐμπλαστρώδης**, ες, *like a plaster*, Dsc.*Eup.*1.196, Gal.12.512, 13.396; **-τώδης**, Antyll.ap.Orib.*Syn.*2.60.36.

**ἐμπλᾰτ(ε)ιάσασα·** ἐν πλατείαις τύπτουσα ταῖς χερσὶν ἢ τρυφερ(ευ)ομένη, Hsch.

**ἐμπλᾰτής**, ές, *square*, πούς Anon.*in Tht.*30.1.

**ἐμπλατία**, Arc. **ἰμπ-**, ἡ, a kind of *cake*, *IG*5(2).4 (iv B.C.).

**ἐμπλᾰτύνω**, *widen* or *extend*, τὰ ὅρια LxxEx.23.18: metaph., δόμα ἀνθρώπου ἐ. αὐτόν ib.*Pr.*18.16:—Pass., λόγοις ἐμπλατύνεσθαι *to expatiate*, Str.8.7.3.

**ἔμπλᾰτυς**, υ, in Comp., *broader, more general*, εἴδη Plot.5.3.9.

**ἐμπλέγ-δην**, Adv. *by interlocking*: hence in Math. of proportion, *alternando*, Nicom.*Ar.*2.29. **-μα**, ατος, τό, *plait*: ἐ. γυναικεῖα Artem.4.83.

**ἔμπλειος**, v. ἔμπλεος.

**ἐμπλέκ-της**, ου, ὁ, *one who plaits hair*, *Gloss.*:—fem. **-πλέκτρια**, ib., *EM*528.5. **-τος**, ον, *inwoven*: ἔμπλεκτον, τό, *ashlar filled up with rubble*, Vitr.2.8.7. **-ω**, Ep. **ἐνιπλέκω**, pf. ἐμπέπλεχα Hp.*Oss.* 17, ἐμπέπλεκα Call.*Iamb.*1.352, v.l. in Hp. l.c.: fut. Pass. ἐμπλᾰκήσομαι Lxx*Pr.*28.18:—*plait* or *weave in, entwine*, χεῖρα ἐ. *entwine* one's hand *in* another's clothes, so as to hold him, E.*Or.*262; εἰς ἀρκυστάταν μηχανὰν ἐμπλέκειν παῖδα ib.1421 (lyr.); τῇ καλλίστῃ τέχνῃ τοὔνομα ἐ. *connect* the name *with*.., Pl.*Phdr.*244c; ποιηταὶ τοιαῦτα ἐμπλέκοντες καὶ συγκυκῶντες Id.*Lg.*669d; ἐ. τὴν ἡδονὴν εἰς τὴν εὐδαιμονίαν Arist.*EN*1153b15; ποίῃ ἐνιπλέξω σε (sc. ἀοιδῇ); Call.*Del.*29; ἐ. τινὰ εἰς φιλίαν τινός Plb.27.7.11:—Pass., *to be entangled in* a thing, πλεκταῖσιν αἰώραισιν ἐμπεπλεγμένην S.*OT*1264; ἡνίαισιν ἐμπλακείς E.*Hipp.*1236; ἐν δεσμοῖσιν ἐμπεπλεγμένη Ar.*Th.*1032; εἰς δίκτυον ἄτης ἐμπλεχθήσεσθε A.*Pr.*1079: metaph., *to be involved*, ἐν πόνοις, ἐν κακοῖς ἐμπλακῆναι, Pl.*Lg.*814e, Isoc.8.112; εἰς ἀσχολίας βαθυτέρας τῶν ἐγκυκλίων Epicur.*Ep.*1 p.35 U.; εἰς τὰ κατὰ τὴν Σικελίαν Plb.1.17.3; *form a connexion with*, ἔθνει Id.24.6.1; γυναικὶ ἐμπλακείς D.S.19.2; εἴς τινα Vett.Val.118.4; of troops, *to be incorporated with* hoplites, Ascl.*Tact.*6.1; but also ἐμπλεκέντες τινὶ *having had a scuffle with*.., *PTeb.*39.17 (ii B.C.). **2.** metaph., *weave by subtle art*, ἐ. αἰνίγματα A.*Pr.*610; ἐ. πλοκάς E.*IA*936.

**ἔμπλεξις**, εως, ἡ, *interweaving, entwining*, στήμονος Pl.*Plt.*282e.

**ἐμπλεονάζω**, *to be profuse in*, αἵματι Heraclit.*Ep.*7.6; ταῖς πυρίαις Sor.1.77.

**ἔμπλεος**, α, ον, Att. **-πλεως**, ων, Ep. **ἔμπλειος**, **ἐνίπλειος**, η, ον, Od. (v. infr.); later **ἐνίπλεος** A.R.3.119, Orph.*L.*192: heterocl. acc. ἔμπλεα (fem.) Nic.*Al.*164:—*quite full of* a thing, γαστέρα.. ἐμπλείην κνίσης τε καὶ αἵματος Od.18.118; φαρέτρην ἰῶν ἐμπλείην 22.3; σκύφος.. οἴνου ἐνίπλειον 14.113; δῶμα.. ἐνίπλειον βιότοιο 19.580; κύων ..ἐνίπλειος κυνοραιστέων 17.300; λέβητες κρεῶν.. ἔμπλεοι Hdt.1.59, cf. 2.62, Hp.*Epid.*6.4.8; γῆς ἢ κόπρου ἔμπλεων Pl.*Tht.*194e. **2.** of persons, δυσκολίας ἔ. Id.*R.*411c; πάσης πονηρίας Plb.27.15.6, etc. **3.** *in full measure, complete*, ἔμπλεα καὶ ὁλόκληρα καὶ τέλεα προσάγοντες Ph.1.185; f.l. for ἔμπεδος in Orph.*Fr.*261.

**ἐμπλευρία**, τά, *pleural cavities*, *Hippiatr.*26.

**ἐμπλευρόομαι**, *dash against* one's *ribs, charge* him, S.*Fr.*53.

**ἔμπλευρος**, ον, *with large sides*, ἀθλητής Ph.1.70 (v.l. εὔπ-); τράγοι *Gp.*18.9.6.

**ἐμπλέω**, *sail in*, [πλοίοις] Hdt.7.184: abs., οἱ ἐμπλέοντες Th.3.77, X.*Oec.*8.8. **2.** in Ion. form **-πλώω**, *float in* or *upon*, Nic.*Al.*426, Opp.*H.*1.260 (ἐνιπ-), Aret.*SD*1.9, 2.1: part. ἐμπλέων *loose*, πῶρος Heliod.ap.Orib.45.6.8. **3.** Pass., of the sea, πελάγη ναυσὶν ἐμπλεόμενα Ph.1.28, cf. 2.514.

**ἐμπλήγ-δην**, Adv., (ἐμπλήσσω) *madly, rashly* (or *mightily*, or *capriciously*), Od.20.132. **-ής**, ές, = ἔμπληκτος, *mad, rash*, ἀφροσύνη Nic.*Al.*159.

® **ἐμ-πλήδην**, Adv. *fully, as a whole*, Nic.*Al.*129. **-πληθής**, ές, = ἔμπλεος, Id.*Th.*948. ® **-πλήθομαι**, Ep. **ἐνιπλ-**, *to be filled*, Q.S.2.472. **-πληθύνομαι**, *to be filled with*, ἀλογιστίας Lxx3*Ma.*5.42.

**ἐμπληκτᾰδοῦς**, ὁ, = ἔμπληκτος, coined by Eust.971.43.

**ἐμπληκτικός**, ή, όν, (ἐμπλήσσω) *stupid*, θέατρα Plu.2.748d (sed leg. ἐμπλήκτων):—in Id.*Sull.*34 f.l. for ἐμπληκτότατον. Adv. **-κῶς** Apollon.*Lex.* s.v. ἐμπλήγδην.

**ἔμπληκτος**, ον, (ἐμπλήσσω) *stunned, amazed*, ὑπὸ τῶν κυνῶν γενέσθαι X.*Cyn.*5.9: hence, *stupid, senseless*, ἔ. καὶ μανικός Plu.*Rom.*28, Agath.3.24, etc.; ἔμπληκτα ληρεῖν Gal.8.693. **2.** in Att., *impulsive*: hence, *unstable, capricious*, S.*Aj.*1358, Arist.*EE*1240b17; αἱ τύχαι, ἔ. ὡς ἄνθρωπος, ἄλλοτ' ἄλλοσε πηδῶσι E.*Tr.*1205; [ἡ φιλοσοφία] τῶν ἑτέρων παιδικῶν πολὺ ἧττον ἔ. Pl.*Grg.*482a; ἔ. τε καὶ ἀσταθμήτους Id.*Ly.*214d; ἔ. ταῖς ἐπιθυμίαις Plu.*Dio* 18. **II.** Adv. **-τως** *rashly, madly*, Isoc.7.30, etc.; τὸ ἐ. ὀξὺ *frantic* vehemence, Th.3.82; *foolishly*, Gal.1.535.

**ἐμπλημμῡρέω**, *welter in*, πηγαῖς αἵματος Philostr.*Im.*1.29; ἐμπλημμυροῦντος αὐτοῖς (sc. τοῖς νηπίοις) τοῦ γάλακτος ib.2.3.

**ἔμπλην** (A), Adv. *near, next, close by*, c. gen., Βοιωτῶν ἔ. Il.2.526; before its case, Lyc.1029: abs., Hes.*Sc.*372 (cf. πλη-σίος).

**ἔμπλην** (B), Adv. strengtnd. for πλήν, *besides, except*, c. gen., Archil.111, Call.*Del.*73, Nic.*Th.*322.

**ἔμπληντο**, Ep. 3 pl. aor. 2 Pass. of ἐμπίμπλημι.

**ἐμπληξία**, ἡ, *amazement*: hence, *stupidity*, Aeschin.3.214, Aristid.1.413, 427 J., Gal.8.690; ἐ. ἡ ἄλογος φιλανθρωπία App.*Sam.*4.4. **2.** πολιτείας ἐ. *capriciousness* of policy, Aeschin.2.164. **3.** *frantic energy*, Plu.2.56c.

**ἔμπληξις**, εως, ἡ, = foreg., Ael.*VH*2.19.

**ἐμπλήρ-ωμα**, ατος, τό, *space filled up*, dub. l. in Gal.18(1).376. **-ωσις**, εως, ἡ, *quenching*, δίψους Herod.Med.ap.Orib.5.30.25.

**ἔμπλησις**, εως, ἡ, f.l. for ἔκ-, Epict.*Gnom.*17.

**ἐμπλήσσω**, Att. **-ττω**, in Hom. **ἐνιπλ-**: **I.** intr., *strike against, fall upon* or *into*, c. dat., ὡς δτ' ἂν ἢ κίχλαι.. ἠὲ πέλειαι ἕρκει ἐνιπλήξωσι Od.22.469; τάφρῳ Il.12.72; νηῒ ἐ. *fall upon* it, of a storm, Arat.423: abs., *dash*, A.R.1.1203, 2.602. **II.** c. acc. pers., *attack*, Id.3.1297. **2.** ἐ. φόβον τινὶ *strike* terror *into*.., Opp.*H.*3.480. **3.** pf. part. Pass. ἐμπεπληγμένος, = ἄνεως, Gal.*Lex.Hipp.* s.h.v.; cf. ἔμπληκτος.

**ἐμπληστέος**, α, ον, (ἐμπίμπλημι) *to be filled with*, ὄγκου Pl.*R.*373b.

**ἐμπλητο**, v. ἐμπίμπλημι.

**ἐμ-πλοκή**, ἡ, *braiding*, κόμης Str.17.3.7, cf. Nic.Dam.p.2 D., 1*Ep.Pet.*3.3. **2.** *scuffle*, *PRyl.*124.28 (i A.D.), 150.12 (i A.D.). **II.** *interweaving*, Epicur.*Nat.*1420 (dub.); *entanglement*, Plu.2.916d (pl.); of the *matted* roots of trees, Ph.Byz.*Mir.*1.5 (pl.); τόποις ἐμπλοκὰς ἔχειν, of districts, *to run into one another*, Str.13.4.12. **III.** Math., κατ' ἐμπλοκήν, = ἐμπλέγδην, Iamb.*in Nic.*p.124 P., al. **-πλόκια**, τά, festival at Athens, Hsch. ® **-πλόκιον**, τό, *a fashion of plaiting women's hair*, Machoap.Ath.13.579d. **2.** *hair-clasp*, *BGU*1300.24 (iii/ii B.C.), Lxx*Ex.*35.22, *Nu.*31.50.

® **ἔμπλουμος**, ον, (Lat. *pluma*) = *plumatus, embroidered*, *PMasp.*6 ii 88 (vi A.D.), etc.

**ἐμπνείω**, poet. for ἐμπνέω.

**ἐμπνευμᾰτοποιέομαι**, *suffer from flatulence*, Alex.Aphr.*Pr.*2.43. **II.** *become gaseous*, ib.76.

**ἐμπνευμᾰτ-όω**, *inflate*, in Pass., Thphr.*Ign.*17, Anon.Lond.27.13, Sor.2.31, etc.; *to be filled by the wind*, of sails, Luc.*Lex.*15. **II.** *cause flatulence*, Diph.Siph.ap.Ath.2.54d, Dsc.2.173:—Pass., *suffer from flatulence*, Gal.16.833. **III.** Pass., *to be asthmatic*, Id.7.959. **IV.** *fill with the breath of life*, σῶμα *PMag.Leid.W.*7.15; ἐ. τινὰ θείου πνεύματος *PMag.Par.*1.966. **V.** intr., *to be inspired, show genius*, Apollon.Cit.3. ® **-ωσις**, εως, ἡ, *blowing up, inflation*, μήτρας *Placit.*5.6.1, cf. Sor.2.31, Ath.2.53c. **2.** Medic., *flatulence*, Dsc.2.58 (pl.), Gal.*UP*4.9. **-ωτικός**, ή, όν, *causing flatulence*, Dsc.5.6.

® **ἔμ-πνευσις**, εως, ἡ, *on-breathing*, Lxx*Ps.*17(18).16. **-πνευστικὰ** ὄργανα *wind*-instruments, Luc.Tarrh.ap.Sch.D.T.p.111 H. **-πνευστός**, ή, όν, *blown into*: ἐ. ὄργανα *wind*-instruments, Aristocl.ap.Ath.4.174c, Ps.-Plu.*Vit.Hom.*148, Nicom.*Harm.*2; τὰ ἐ. alone, Theo Sm.p.57 H., Iamb.*in Nic.*p.122 P. **II.** = ἄφρων, Hsch.

® **ἐμπνέω**, poet. **-πνείω**, fut. **-πνεύσομαι** E.*Andr.*555; later **-πνεύσω** Aen.Gaz.*Ep.*11:—*blow* or *breathe upon*, c. dat., πόντῳ Hes.*Op.*508; ἐμπνείοντε μεταφρένῳ, of horses so close behind as *to breathe upon* one's back, Il.17.502; of a lover, Hsch.; κατ' οὖρον, ὥσπερ ἱστίοις, ἐμπνεύσομαι τῇδε E.l.c.; ἄνεμος ἐμπνεύσας δορί Id.*Cyc.*19; [αὐλοῖς] ἐμπνεῖν *breathe into, play* the flute, *AP*9.266 (Antip.): c. acc. cogn., χείλεσι μοῦσαν ἐ., of Pan, *APl.*4.226 (Alc.):—Pass., ἐμπνεόμενα ὄργανα Poll.4.67; πνεῦμα **-πνεόμενον** τῷ αὐλῷ S.E.*P.*1.54. **2.** abs., *breathe in, inhale*, Hp.*Flat.*4; but usu., **b.** *breathe, live, be alive*, A.*Ag.*671, Ar.*Th.*926, Pl.*Ap.*29d, etc.; τὰ ἐμπνέοντα, = ἔμψυχα, Call.*Iamb.*1.127; ἐ. τᾷ τέχνᾳ *AP*9.777 (Phil.); of one expiring, βλέποντα κἀμπνέοντ' ἔτι S.*Ph.*883; σμικρὸν ἐμπνέουσ' ἔτι E.*Alc.*205; βραχὺν δὴ βίοτον ἐμπνέων ἔτι Id.*Hipp.*1246. **3.** c. gen., *breathe of, be laden with*, Ἀραβίης ὀδμῆς Perict.ap.Stob.4.28.19; ἐ. ἀπειλῆς καὶ φόνου *Act.Ap.*9.1. **II.** trans., *blow into*, ἄνεμος μέσον ἱστίον ἐ. *swell* the sail, *h.Bacch.*33, cf. Pi.*I.*2.40. **2.** *breathe into, infuse into*, μένος, θάρσος τινί, Il.20.110, Od.9.381, al.; [Μοῦσαι] ἐνέπνευσαν δέ μοι αὐδήν Hes.*Th.*31; πατρί.. πατρὸς ἐνέπνευσεν μένος Pi.*O.*8.70: also c. inf. pro acc., φᾶρος ἐνέπνευσε φρεσὶν ὑφαίνειν *breathed into* my mind (i.e. *inspired* me *with the thought*) to weave it, Od.19.138:—Pass., *to be inspired*, ὑπὸ θεοῦ Longin.16.2; εἰς μαντικὴν Plu.2.421b. **-πνοή**, ἡ, *force* of wind, Str.4.1.7. **-πνοια**, ἡ, *inbreathing, inhalation*, Luc.*Hes.*9. **2.** *breath of life*, *Sammelb.*4127.16. **-πνοίησις**, εως, ἡ, *inspiration*, θεόμοιρος Ecphant.ap.Stob.4.6.22. ® **-πνοος**, ον, contr. **-πνους**, ουν, (πνοή) *with the breath in one, alive*, οὐκ ἀπέθανε, ἀλλ' ἦν ἔμπνοος Hdt.7.181; ἔτ' ἔμπνους E.*Ph.*1442; ἔμπνους ἔτι ἀρθείς Antipho 2.1.9; ἔτι ἔμπνουν ὄντα Th.1.134; ἔ. ἐγένετο *revived*, Pl.*Lg.*944a; μορφᾶς τύπος ἔμπνουν, of a statue, *Epigr.Gr.*860.3; of pictures, τὸ ἔ. Philostr.*VA*2.20; also ἔ. νεκρός, of old age, Secund.*Sent.*12; θάλαττα πλωτὴ καὶ οἷον ἔ., of a sea which is *not a dead* calm, Philostr.*Im.*2.17. **II.** ἔ. μοῦσα, of a flute, Sopat.10. **2.** *blown upon*, κόμη ὑπ. ἀνέμου ἔ. Philostr.*Im.*1.23: metaph., *inspired*, σεμνολογία ἔ., ὥσπερ ἐκ τρίποδος Id.*VS*1.25.10.

**ἔμπνῡτο**, read by Aristarch.Il.22.475, Od.5.458, al. for ἄμπνυτο; also ἐμπνύνθη for ἀμ- Il.5.697.

**ἐμποδ-εία**, ἡ, *impediment, hindrance*, Epicur.*Nat.*11.6 (pl.). **-έω**, = **-ίζω**, dub. in A.D.*Adv.*172.2, 185.16 codd. (leg. **-ποδών**). **-ιζομένως**, Adv. pres. part. Pass., *as if fettered*, Pl.*Cra.*415c. ® **-ίζω**, Att. fut. **-ιῶ** Id.*Ly.*210b, later **-ίσω** *Gp.*2.49.1:—**Med.** (v. infr. II.2):—Pass., fut. **-ποδισθήσομαι** Porph.*Abst.*1.17, Gal.ap.Orib.7.23.28, or (in med. form) **-ίσομαι** Antip.*Stoic.*3.256: pf. **-πεπόδισμαι** (v. infr.): (ἐν, πούς):—*put the feet in bonds*: hence, *put in bonds, fetter*, τοὺς

μάντιας Hdt.4.69:—Pass., ἐμπεποδισμένος τοὺς πόδας ib.60; [ὀλιγοδρανίᾳ] ἐμπεπ. A.*Pr.*550 (lyr.). II. generally, *hinder, thwart*, τὸ θεῖον ἐνεπόδιζέ με Ar.*Av.*965, cf. *Lys.*359, X.*Cyr.*2.3.10; τοὺς τῆς πόλεως καιροὺς Aeschin.3.223; ἐ. τοῦ ἰέναι *to hinder* from.., Pl.*Cra.*419c; πρός τι *in* a thing, Isoc.*Ep.*4.11, Arist.*Pol.*1341$^a$6, al., Ph.1.466:—Pass., χαὶ σοφαὶ γνῶμαι..ἐμποδίζονται θαμά S.*Ph.*432; ἐμποδίζοιτο ἂν μὴ πράττειν *would be hindered from* doing, Pl.*Smp.*183a; τῆς εἰς τοὔμπροσθε πορείας D.S.14.28. 2. c. dat. rei, *to be a hindrance to, interfere with*, πολλαῖς ἐνεργείαις Arist.*EN*1100$^b$29; ἀλλήλαις Id.*Pol.*1299$^b$8; ταῖς χορηγίαις Plb.5.111.4: c. dat. pers., τοῖς γεωργοῖς *Gp.*2.49.1; τοῖς εἰς ἀρετὴν ἀφικνουμένοις Porph.*Ep.Aneb.*26: rarely c. acc. rei, ἐ. τὸ κοινὸν ἔργον Arist. *Top.*161$^a$37:—so in Med., ἐμποδίζεται δόσιν Philem.164. 3. abs., *to be a check* or *hindrance*, Arist.*Pol.*1288$^b$24. III. dub. in κέχηνεν ὥσπερ ἐμποδίζων ἰσχάδας Ar.*Eq.*755; prob. *playing bob-fig*, i.e. catching figs dangled by the stalk (πούς); Sch. and Lexx. also expl. as *stringing, chewing*, or *trampling* figs. -ιος, ον, *at one's feet*, Pl.*Tht.*201a; *coming in the way, meeting*, Eleg.ap.Plu.*Rom.*21. 2. commonly, *in the way, presenting an obstacle, impeding*, c. dat. pers. et rei, ἡ Βαβυλὼν οἱ ἦν ἐ. Hdt.1.153, cf. 2.158, 5.90; ἐ. κώλυμα E.*Ion*862 (lyr.); εἰ τοῦτ' ἐ. σοι Ar.*Lys.*531, etc.; ἐ. ταῖς ἐνεργείαις Arist.*EN*1175$^b$2; ἐ. τινὶ πρός τι Id.*Mu.*399$^b$12. 3. c. gen. rei, εἰρήνης Th.1.139; ἐ. γίγνεσθαι τοῦ μὴ ἀσκεῖν Pl.*Lg.*832b: c. inf., μή..ἐ. γένηται θέσθαι τι Th.1.31. 4. ὅπῃ ταύτῃ ἀρετὴ ἀσκεῖται πάντῃ ἐ. Pl.*R.*407c. 5. ἐ. πρός τι Arist.*EN*1170$^b$27, *Pol.*1311$^a$18, Plb.4.81.4, Hierocl.*in CA*11p.441M. -ισις, εως, ἡ, = sq., *IG*3.49.14 (Epist. Plotinae). ⊛ -ισμα, ατος, τό, *impediment, hindrance*, Pl.*Plt.*295b, D.3.4. -ισμός, ὁ, *hindering, impeding*, ταῖς βουλήσεσι Arist.*Rh.*1378$^b$18; τῶν συμπερασμάτων Id.*Top.*161$^a$15; ἡδονῶν Secund.*Sent.*10. -ιστής, οῦ, ὁ, *hinderer*, J.*AJ*17.10.3. -ιστικός, ή, όν, *trammelling*, Arist.*EN*1153$^b$2, *Ph.*215$^b$11, Plb.5.16.6, Phld.*D.*3.9, Lxx 4*Ma.*1.4, M.Ant.8.41. -όομαι, = ἐμπεδόομαι, Hsch. -ος, ον, = ἐμπόδιος, dub. in Ascl.*Tact.*2.1.

⊛ **ἐμποδοστᾰτ-έω**, *to be in the way*, Epicur.*Ep.*1p.9U., *PTeb.*24.54 (ii B.C.), Ph.1.186:—also **ἐμποδιοστᾰτέω**, v.l. Lxx *Jd.*11.35. -ης, ου, ὁ, (στῆναι) *in the way*, ib.1*Ch.*2.7.

**ἐμποδών**, Adv. perh. formed by anal. to ἐκποδών:—*before the feet, in the way, in one's path*, κτείνειν πάντα τὸν ἐ. γενόμενον every one that came *in the way*, Hdt.1.80; πᾶν ἔθνος τὸ ἐ. Id.2.102; τοὺς αἰεὶ ἐ. γινομένους Id.4.118, cf. 7.108; τὸ μὴ ἐ. those who are absent, Th.2.45; μή που λαθών τις ἐ. (sc. γενόμενος) Ar.*V.*247. 2. *in one's way*, i.e. *presenting an hindrance*, ὁ θεὸς..[οἱ] ἐ. ἕστηκε Hdt.6.82; ὥς σφι τὸ ἐ. ἐγεγόνεε καθαρόν when *all impediments* had been cleared away, Id.7.183; τί τοὐμπ.; Ar.*Lys.*1161; οὐδὲν ἐ. [ἐστι] A.*Pr.*13; ἐ. ἕστη δορί Id.*Th.*1021; παρεῖναι S.*OT*445; οὐδεὶς ἐ. κεῖται νόμος E.*Ion*1047; καθῆσθαι Ar.*Pax*473; σὺ δ' ἡμῖν μηδὲν ἐ. γένῃ E.*Hec.*372; ἐ. τινι φῦναι Id.*Or.*605: c. inf., ἐ. εἶναι τῷ ποιεῖν X.*HG*2.3.23; ἐ. γενέσθαι, εἶναί τινι μὴ πράττειν, *prevent* a person's doing, Ar.*Pax*315, Th.6.28, etc.; τί ἐ. μοι μὴ οὐ..; what *prevents* my doing? X.*Eq.*11.13, cf. *An.*3.1.13; so ἐ. τὸ μὴ εἶναι ib.4.8.14; ἐ. γίγνεσθαι τοῦ μὴ δρᾶν Id.*Cyr.*2.4.23; ἐ. εἶναι ἀλλήλοις τινός to *hinder* each other from a thing, ib.8.5.24, cf. Plu.*Them.*4, etc.; λόγων τίς ἐ.ὅδ' ἔρχεται; E.*Supp.*395; ποιεῖσθαι ἐ. τι to regard it as *a hindrance*, suffer it to *hinder*, Lys.13.88, X.*Cyr.*4.2.46, D.21.104. 3. *in one's way, before one's eyes, manifest*, πόθεν ἄρξομαι, ἐ. ἁπάντων ὄντων; And.4.10; Χαρίτων ἱερὸν ἐ. ποιοῦνται Arist.*EN*1133$^a$3; ἃ δ' ἐ. μάλιστα ταῦθ' ἥκω φράσων E.*Ph.*706; ἡ ἐ. παιδεία *everyday* education, Arist.*Pol.*1337$^a$39; πολλοῖς ἐ. εἶναι καὶ γνωρίζεσθαι Plb.2.17.1. 4. of Time, *immediately*, Polem.Hist.83.

⊛ **ἐμποι-έω**, *make in*, ἐν δ' αὐτοῖσι (sc. πύργοις) πύλας ἐνεποίεον Il.7.438, cf. Ar.*Ec.*154:—Med., Ἑλικῶνι χοροὺς ἐνεποιήσαντο Hes.*Th.*7, cf. *PFlor.*212.10 (iii A.D.):—Pass., χελιδὼν ἦν τις ἐμπεποιημένη *introduced by the poet's art*, Ar.*Av.*1301, v. Sch. 2. *put in*, ἐ. ἴχνεσιν ἴχνη, i.e. *put* their feet *in* the same tracks, X.*Cyn.*5.20. 3. *foist in*, ἐς τὰ Μουσαίου ἐ. χρησμόν Hdt.7.6; χρησμοὶ ἐμπεποιημένοι τοῖς Σιβυλλείοις D.H.4.62; simply, *insert*, opp. ἐξαγρέω, *Schwyzer*412.3 (Elis). II. *produce* or *create in*, ἡ χρεία καπήλων..γένεσιν ἐ. τῇ πόλει Pl.*R.*371d; οἱ χρηματισταὶ..πολὺν τὸν κηφῆνα καὶ πτωχὸν ἐ. τῇ πόλει ib.556a, etc.; δύναμιν (sc. τῇ πόλει) Isoc.9.47. 2. of states of mind, ἐπιθυμίαν ἐ. τοῖς Ἀθηναίων ξυμμάχοις ἐς τοὺς Λακεδαιμονίους Th.4.81; κακόν τι ἐ. ταῖς ψυχαῖς Pl.*Phd.*115e; ἐν αὐτῷ δειλίαν ἐ. Id.*R.*590b; ἐλπίδας ἐ. ἀνθρώποις X.*Cyr.*1.6.19; ψυχῇ ἐπιστήμην Id.*Mem.*2.1.20; ταραχήν τισι Men.*Sam.*9: without a dat., *produce, create*, μῖσος, λήθην, Pl.*R.*351d, *Phlb.*63e, D.19.3; ἡδονήν Arist.*EN*1126$^a$22; χρόνους [ψηφίσμασι] D.23.93; χαρὰν X.*Hier.*8.4; ὀργὰς καὶ λύπας ib.1.28: c. inf. pro acc., ἐ. τινὶ ἀκολουθητέον εἶναι *produce in* one's *mind the persuasion* that he must follow, Id.*Oec.*21.7; folld. by ὡς.., Id.*An.*2.6.8. 3. of conditions, *produce, cause*, ὀδύνην, σηπεδόνας, Hp.*Acut.*16, Aret.*SD*1.9; φθόρον Th.2.51; στάσεις Id.1.2; πολέμους καὶ στάσεις ἡμῖν αὐτοῖς ἐ. Isoc.4.168; χρόνου διατριβὴν ἐ. Th.3.38; κίνησιν Arist.*Ph.*250$^b$26. III. Med., ἐμποιεῖσθαι, = ἀντιποιεῖσθαι, *lay claim to*, ἱερωσύνης Lxx 1*Es.*5.38, cf. *AJA*16.13 (Sardes, iv/iii B.C.), *BGU*13.13 (iii A.D.), etc.; τοῦ λαοῦ μου Lxx *Ex.*9.17. ⊛ -ησις, εως, ἡ, *production*, δογμάτων Arr.*Epict.*4.11.8: f.l. for πτόησιν, D.C.37.16. II. (ἐμποιεῖσθαι) *laying claim to*, *BGU*94.14 (iii A.D.), etc. -ητέον, *one must create by means of* or *in*, τι ἐν τοῖς πράγμασιν Arist.*Po.*1453$^b$14; ἐλπίδα τοῖς ὑπηκόοις Them.*Or.*7.96a. -ητικός, ή, όν, *productive of* a thing *in*, ἄλλοις τῶν τοιούτων λόγων Arist.*Metaph.*1025$^a$4; πάθους S.E.*M.*7.191; δασείας A.D.*Pron.*78.11, cf. Andronic.Rhod.p.572M., Antyll.ap.Orib.6.7.1.

**ἐμποικίλλω**, *embroider upon*, νῖκαι ἐμπεποικιλμέναι Plu.*Tim.*8; γίγαντας ἐμπεποίκιλται [πέπλος] Sch.E.*Hec.*468, cf. 471.

**ἐμποίνιμος**, ον, (ποινή) *liable to punishment*, ὅρκος οὐκ ἐ. *that may be violated with impunity*, *Trag.Adesp.*525, cf. Corn.*ND*24. Adv. -μως Eust.1243.3.

**ἐμποίνιος**, ον, = foreg., Suid. **ἔμποιον**· τὸ γαλακτῶδες ὑγροῦν (leg. ὑγρόν), Hsch. (leg. ἔμπυον).

**ἔμποκος**, ον, *unshorn*, of sheep, *PThead.*8.6 (iv A.D.).

**ἐμπολ-αῖος**, α, ον, *of* or *concerned in traffic*, epith. of Hermes as god of commerce, etc., Ar.*Ach.*816, *Pl.*1155, Corn.*ND*16. ⊛ -άω, impf. ἠμπόλων Ar.*V.*444, (ἀπ-) E.*Tr.*973: fut. -ήσω S.*Ant.*1063: aor. ἠμπόλησα, but in Is.11.43 ἐνεπόλησα (Scaliger for ἐνέπωλ-): pf. ἠμπόληκα S.*Aj.*978, Ar.*Pax*367; late ἐμπεπόληκα Luc.*Cat.*1:—**Med.** (v. infr.):—Pass., aor. ἠμπολήθην S.*Tr.*250: pf. ἠμπόλημαι, Ion. ἐμπ- (ἐξ-) Hdt.1.1, S.*Ant.*1036:—*get by barter* or *traffic*, once in Hom., in Med., βίοτον πολλὸν ἐμπολόωντο they *were getting* much substance *by traffic*, Od.15.456:—Act., *get by sale*, ἐξ ὧν [προβάτων etc.] ἐνεπόλησαν τετρακισχιλίας [δραχμάς] Is. l.c., cf. X.*An.*7.5.4: hence, *earn, procure*, τό γ' εὖ πράσσειν..κέρδος ἐμπολᾷ S.*Tr.*93. 2. *deal* or *traffic in*, ἐμπολᾶτε τἀπὸ Σάρδεων ἤλεκτρον Id.*Ant.*1037; *purchase, buy*, Id.*OT*1025, Ar.*V.*444, *Pax*367, 563, etc.; οὐκ ἐλεύθερος ἀλλ' ἐμποληθεὶς S.*Tr.*250:—Med., λαθραίαν ἐμπολωμένη Κύπριν E.*Cret.*7. 3. ἐ. τὴν ἐμὴν φρένα *make profit of* my mind *by dealing* with me, S.*Ant.*1063. II. abs., *traffic*, ἵν' ἐμπολᾷ βέλτιον Ar.*Pax*448; νυνὶ δὲ πεντήκοντα δραχμῶν ἐμπολῶ to the amount of 50 drachmae, ib.1201; οὐκέτ' ἐμπολῶμεν οὐδ' εἰς ἥμισυ Id.*Th.*452. 2. metaph., *deal* or *fare* in any way, ἠμποληκότα τὰ πλεῖστ' ἀμείνονα *having dealt in* most things with success, A.*Eu.*631; κάλλιον ἐμπολήσει *will fare* better *in health*, Hp.*Morb.*4.49; ἆρ' ἠμπόληκας ὥσπερ ἡ φάτις κρατεῖ; S.*Aj.*978. III. ἐμπολῶντο· ἐνεβάλλοντο, Hsch.

**ἐμπολεμ-έω**, *wage war in*, τὴν χώραν οὐ παρέχουσιν ἐ. And.3.27, cf. Plu.2.252a. ⊛ -ιος, ον, *pertaining to war*, ταῦτα τὰ ἐ. Hdt.6.57; θεοὶ D.C.42.48. 2. *belonging to the forces*, ὅσον ἐ. Pl.*Lg.*755e; τὰ ἐ. *branches of the service*, ib.756a. 3. *warlike*, ἔθνη D.C.56.40. -ος, ον, = foreg., Hsch. -όω, *make enemies*, *EM*336.24, Suid.

**ἐμπολ-εύς**, έως, ὁ, *merchant, trafficker*, *AP*6.304 (Phan.). -έω, Ion. and late form for ἐμπολάω, Herod.6.63, Tz.*H.*1.820: Ion. part. Pass., δάπεδον ἐμπολεύμενον or -ευμένον dub. sens. in Keil-Premerstein *Erster Bericht* p.9 (Claros). -ή, ἡ, Arc. ἰνπολά *IG*5(2).3.27 (pl., Tegea, iv B.C.):—*merchandise*, Pi.*P.*2.67, Ar.*Ach.*930 (lyr.); ὁλκάδας γεμούσας..ἐμπολῆς X.*HG*5.1.23: metaph., μέλεον ἐ. E.*Hyps* *Fr.*41(64).87 (lyr.): pl., *wares*, *IG* l.c. II. *traffic, purchase*, E.*IT*1111 (lyr.), X.*Cyr.*6.2.39: pl., *ventures*, S.*Fr.*555.4. III. *gain made by traffic, profit*, ἀναθέμεν τῷ Ἀσκλαπιῷ τὰς ἐ. τῶν ἰχθύων Ἀρχ.Ἐφ.1918.168 (Epid., iv B.C.), cf. Palaeph.45; esp. *harlot's hire*, Artem.1.78 (pl.), D.C.79.13 (pl.). ⊛ -ημα, ατος, τό, *matter of traffic, freight* or *cargo of a ship*, κόρην παρεισδέδεγμαι λωβητὸν ἐ. (metaph.) S.*Tr.*538: pl., *wares, merchandise*, E.*Cyc.*137. II. *gain made by traffic*, Thphr.*Char.*6.9. -ησις, εως, ἡ, *buying, trafficking*, Poll.3.124. -ητός, ή, όν, *bought*, οὑμπολητὸς Σισύφου Λαερτίῳ the son of Sisyphus *bought by* or *palmed off upon* L., S.*Ph.*417. -ίζω, *inclose within the city*, λόφον D.H.2.1 (Pass.). II. (πόλος) *insert at the pole*, Ptol.*Alm.*8.3, Procl.*Hyp.*6.7, al. ⊛ -ιον, τό, *casing for a dowel*, ἐ. χαλκᾶ *IG*2.1054*f*4, 1054*g*A6.

**ἐμπολῐορκέω**, *besiege in* a place, in Pass., Str.6.2.6; ὑπό τινος Id.16.2.9:—Act., ἐνισχύσας πόλιν -ῆσαι Lxx *Si.*50.4.

**ἔμπολ-ις**, εως, ὁ, ἡ, *belonging to the city* or *state*, = ἀστός, Eup.137; ὁ ἔ. τινι one's *fellow-citizen*, S.*OC*1156, prob. for ἔμπαλιν in ib.637. -ῐσις, εως, ἡ, *fixing of the pole*, Ptol.*Alm.*8.3.

**ἐμπολῑτεύω**, *to be a citizen, hold civil rights* in a place, Th.4.106; ἐ. ἐκεῖ ib.103:—Pass., οἱ ἐμπολιτευθέντες Isoc.5.5; τῇ πόλει καὶ τοῖς ἐμπολιτευομένοις Plb.5.9.9. 2. metaph., ἀφροσύνη ἐνεπολίτευσε τῷ ἔθνει J.*AJ*17.10.6; τὰς -ομένας ἡδονὰς ἐν Ῥώμῃ Philostr.*VA*5.36:—Med., ἐ. τῷ βίῳ Jul.*Or.*4.157b. 3. ἐμπολιτεύεσθαί τινι *to talk politics with* one, Cic.*Att.*7.7.7 codd. II. trans., *introduce into a state, naturalize*, ἐ. ἀκολασίαν οὐρανῷ Heraclit.*All.*69.

**ἐμπολόωντο**, v. ἐμπολάω I. 1.

⊛ **ἐμπομπεύω**, *walk in procession*: hence metaph., c. dat., *plume oneself upon*, Plu.2.527f; τῇ κιθάρᾳ Luc.*Ind.*10, cf. Arg.2 D.20; ἐν πολλαῖς ῥάβδοις D.C.77.5; τῷ λόγῳ Procop.Gaz.*Ep.*69; γῇ ἐ. ἄνθεσιν Id.p.141B.; τοσούτοις δήμοις Hld.3.7.

⊛ **ἐμπον-έω**, *work on*, [τῇ γῇ] Alciphr.3.25, cf. *JHS*33.338 (Macedonia, ii A.D.). II. c. acc., *elaborate*, θεωρίαν Gal.4.760. -ημα, ατος, τό, in pl., *agricultural improvements*, Just.*Nov.*64.1, al.

⊛ **ἔμπονος**, ον, *patient of labour*, Hp.*Aër.*12; ἀρετῆς ἔργα φέρει ἔμπονος ἥβη Poet.ap.Sch.Heph.p.286C.; ἔμπονοι κόπῳ Ezek.*Exag.*208. II. *toilsome, painful*, τὰ ἔμπονα Aret.*SA*1.9; ἐ. κραυγή *vehement* outcry, Lxx 3*Ma.*1.28.

**ἐμπορ-εῖον**, τό, later form of ἐμπόριον, Arist.*Oec.*1348$^b$21. -ευμα, ατος, τό, *merchandise*, in pl., X.*Vect.*3.4, *Hier.*9.11. II. *traffic*, Hsch. -εύομαι, fut. -πορεύσομαι: aor. I ἐνεπορεύθην:—**Med.**, aor. I -ευσάμην Pl.*Ep.*313d:—*travel*, ξένην ἐπι..γαῖαν S.*OT*456; ὡς τύραννον Id.*Fr.*873; ποῖ δ' ἐμπορεύῃ; Id.*El.*405; τηνῶθεν Ar.*Ach.*754. 2. abs., *walk*, Epich.53, Metag.10. II. *travel for traffic* or *business*, χρηματισμοῦ χάριν Pl.*Lg.*952e; εἰς Πόντον Chion *Ep.*7, 8, cf. *SIG*1166 (Dodona): metaph., ἐ. εἰς ἰατρικὴν *inveigh against* the art of healing, Hp. *de Arte* 1. 2. *to be a merchant, traffic*, Th.7.13, X.*Vect.*3.3, etc.; λόγοισιν *Com.Adesp.*269: c. acc., *trade in*, γῆν Lxx *Ge.*34.21. 3. c. acc. rei, *import*, Pl.*Ep.*313e; πολλὰς διὰ θαλάσσης

ὠφελείας D.H.6.86; πορφύραν ἀπὸ Φοινίκης D.L.7.2; γλαῦκας Luc. *Nigr.Prooem.* b. metaph., δίαιταν ἥντιν' ἐμπορεύεται what manner of life he *leads*, E.*Fr.*812.6; ἐ. τὴν φιλοσοφίαν *to make a trade of* it, Ph.2.486, Them.*Or.*23.298d, cf. J.*AJ*4.6.8; πλήθη καλῶν γυναικῶν Ath.13.569f; in bad sense, *trade on*, τὴν λήθην τῶν δικαστῶν Ph.2.536. 4. c. acc. pers., *make gain of, overreach, cheat*, πλαστοῖς λόγοις ὑμᾶς 2*Ep.Pet.*2.3:—also in Act., Plb.38.12.10. **-ευτέα**, *one must tramp*, Ar.*Ach.*480. **-ευτικός**, ή, όν, *commercial, mercantile*, Pl.*Plt.*290a, Max.Tyr.36.2.

⊛ **ἐμπορ-ία**, Ion. -ίη, ἡ, (ἔμπορος) *commerce* (acc. to Arist.*Pol.*1258ᵇ22, of three kinds, ναυκληρία, φορτηγία, παράστασις (qq.vv.)), mostly used of *commerce* or *trade by sea* (cf. ἔμπορος III), Hes.*Op.*646, Thgn.1166, Simon.127, etc.; ἐμπορίαν ποιεῖσθαι Isoc.2.1; ἐμπορίας οὐκ οὔσης Th.1.2; ἐὰν κατὰ θάλατταν ἡ ἐ. γένηται Pl.*R.*371a; κατ' ἐμπορίην, Att. -ίαν, for *trade-purposes*, Hdt.3.139, Simon. l.c., Isoc.17.4, etc.; ἐμπορίας ἕνεκα or -κεν, Th.1.7, 6.2; πρὸς ἐμπορίαν Ar.*Av.*718: pl., τὰς ἐ. τὰς κερδαλέας ib.594 (anap.); περὶ τὰς ἐ. διατρίβειν Arist.*Pol.*1291ᵃ5, cf. D.56.8. 2. *a trade* or *business*, *AP*6.63.8 (Damoch.), *Ev.Matt.*22.5. 3. *errand, business*, E.*Hyps.Fr.*5.11 (anap.), Luc.*Scyth.*4; *journeying*, πενία ἀζήμιωτος ἐ. Secund.*Sent.*10. II. *merchandise*, X.*Vect.*3.2, *AP*7.500 (Asclep.); αὐτοῦ τὴν ἐ. ἔφασκεν εἶναι Lys.32.25; ἐπὶ τῇ ἐμπορίᾳ ἣν ἦγεν ἐν τῇ..νηΐ Test.ap.D.35.23. ⊛ **-ιάρχης**, ου, ὁ, *supervisor of trade*, *IGRom.*4.796 (Apamea). **-ίζομαι**, Pass., *to be provided*, Men.714. II. *acquire*, πολιτείας Procop.*Aed.*1 *Praef.* **-ικός**, ή, όν, *of* or *for commerce, mercantile*, οἶκος Stesich.80; ἐ. τέχνη or ἐ. alone, = ἐμπορία I. 1, Pl.*Euthphr.*14e, *Sph.*223d, al.; ἐ., τά, Id.*Lg.*842d; ἐ. δίκαι Arist.*Ath.*59.5, D.7.12; κατὰ τοὺς ἐ. νόμους Id.35.3: ἐ. συμβολαῖα ib.47; τὰ ἐ. χρήματα money *to be used in trade*, ib.49; ἡ μνᾶ ἡ ἐ. the mina *of commerce*, *IG*2².1013.34 (ii B.C.); ἐμπορικόν, τό, *the class of merchant-seamen*, Arist.*Pol.*1291ᵇ24; *with an aptitude for trade*, παῖς Lib.*Decl.*33.7: Comp. -ώτερος Ptol.*Tetr.*66: -κοί, οἱ, *camp-traders, sutlers*, Arr.*Tact.*2.1. 2. *imported, foreign*, ἐ. χρήματα διεμπολᾶν Ar.*Ach.*974; φόρτος Plu.*Lyc.*9. 3. διήγημα ἐ. *a traveller's* tale, i.e. *a romance*, Plb.4.39.11. II. Adv. -κῶς *in mercantile fashion*, Str.8.6.16. ⊛ **-ιον**, τό, *trading-station, mart, factory*, Hdt.1.165, al., Th.1.100, Ar.*Av.*1523, *IPE*1².47.9 (Olbia, i A.D.), etc.; προστάται τοῦ ἐ. Hdt.2.178; ἐ. παρέχειν, of Corinth, Th.1.13. b. *market-centre* for a district which had no πόλις, *SIG*880.22 (Macedonia, iii A.D.). 2. τὸ ἐ., at Athens, *the Exchange*, where the merchants resorted, δανείσασθαι χρήματα ἐν τῷ ἐμπορίῳ D.35.1, cf. 18.309; ἐκ τοὐμπορίου τινές foreign *merchants*, Diph.17.3, cf. 43.9. II. ἐμπόρια, τά, *merchandise*, X.*Vect.*1.7. **-ιος**, ὁ, = μέτοικος, Hsch. **-ῖται**· μέτοικοι, Id. (-ίσαι cod.). **-ιωνήτας** (-ιδον- cod.)· ἐνοικίου πρακτῆρας, i.e. those who *farm the tax paid by* ἔμποροι, Id. **-ος**, ον, *one who goes on ship board as a passenger*, Od.2.319, 24.300. II. = ὁ ἐν πόρῳ ὤν, *wayfarer, traveller*, B.17.36, A.*Ch.*661, S.*OC*25,303, E.*Alc.*999 (lyr.). III. *merchant, trader*, Semon.16, Hdt.2.39, Th.6.31, etc.; distd. from *the retail-dealer* (κάπηλος) by his making voyages and importing goods himself, Pl.*Prt.*313d, *R.*371a, Arist.*Pol.*1291ᵃ16, Sch.Ar.*Pl.*1156: metaph., ἐ. κακῶν A.*Pers.*598; ἐ. βίου *a trafficker* in life, E.*Hipp.*964; ἐ. περὶ τὰ τῆς ψυχῆς μαθήματα Pl.*Sph.*231d; ὥρης ἐ. *a dealer in* beauty, *AP*9.416 (Phil.); ἐ. γυναικῶν *IG*14.2000. 2. as Adj., = ἐμπορικός, ναῦς ἐ. D.S.5.12.

**ἐμπορπ-άω**, *fasten with a brooch* or *pin*:—Pass., εἵματα ἐνεπορπέατο (Ion. for -ηντο) they *wore* garments *fastened with a brooch upon the shoulder*, Hdt.7.77; ἐμπεπορπημένος διπλᾶ τὰ ἱμάτια Lycurg.40, cf. D.H.2.70, Plu.*Mar.*17: metaph., ἐμπεπορπημένοι ὠμότητα Lxx 3*Ma.*7.5. **-ημα**, ατος, τό, *garment secured by a brooch*, Hsch. **-όομαι**, Pass., = ἐμπορπάομαι, Lxx 1*Ma.*14.44, Hsch. (Act. only *EM*336.6.)

**ἐμπόρφῠρος**, ον, *inclining to purple*, Dsc.3.100, Orib.*Syn.*2.56.17, *Cat.Cod.Astr.*8(4).251.

**ἔμποτος**, ον, (ἐμπίνω) *drinkable*, Aret.*CD*1.13.

**Ἔμπουσα**, ἡ, *Empusa, a hobgoblin*, assuming various shapes, said to be sent by Hecate, Ar.*Ra.*293, *Ec.*1056, D.18.130; sts. identified with *Hecate*, Ar.*Fr.*500.

**ἐμπρακτ-ικός**, ή, όν, *efficacious*, Dsc.1.39 (Comp.), 2.78 (Sup.). ⊛ **-ος**, ον, *within one's power to do, practicable*, μαχανά Pi.*P.*3.62: Comp. -ότερος, κένωσις Philum.ap.Orib.45.29.5, cf. Sor.2.9; χρόνος ἔ. εἰς πάντα *propitious*, Heph.Astr.2.30, cf. Vett.Val.205.32, al.; ἐ. ῥητορικὴ *working* rhetoric, Phld.*Rh.*1.10S., al.; also of persons, *active*, ἀνὴρ τὰ περὶ τὸν πόλεμον ἔ. D.S.13.102; τόλμαν ἔχειν ἔμπρακτον πρός τι *ready for*.., ib.70; τὸ ἔ. *vigour*, of oratory, Longin.11.2. Adv. -τως *actively*, Plu.*Sert.*4; *effectively*, Phld.*Lib.*p.38O., Archig.ap.Aët.12.1. b. *holding office*, ἄρχοντες *Cod.Just.*1.2.24.1. 2. ἔ. ἡμέρα day *on which legal business may be transacted*, *POxy.*1882.14 (vi A.D.). II. *under bond* to pay, = εἴσπρακτος, *IG*7.3171.54 (Orchom. Boeot.).

**ἔμπραξις**, εως, ἡ, *claim under a bond*, *IG*7.3172.156 (pl., Orchom. Boeot.).

**ἔμπρεον**· ἔμπειρον, Hsch.

**ἐμπρεπής**, ές, *conspicuous among* or *above* others, θύννος..πᾶσιν ἰχθύεσσιν ἐ. ἐν μυττωτῷ Anan.5.8. II. *conspicuous for*, ἠλέμοισιν ἐ. A.*Supp.*115 (lyr.); cf. sq. III. *suitable, fitting*, Ph.1.501; ἐμπρεπές ἐστι, c. inf., it is *fitting*, ib.435, al.: Comp., ib.617: Sup., ib.695.

⊛ **ἐμπρέπω**, *to be conspicuous in*, πενταέθλοισιν B.8.27; αἰθέρι, of the stars, A.*Ag.*6; ἐπ' ὀμμάτων ἐ. (εὖ πρ. cod. Med.) *to be conspicuous* on the face, ib.1428 (lyr.); Βάκχαις ἐ. *among* them, Ar.*Nu.*605:—Med., Λύδαισιν ἐμπρέπεται γυναίκεσσιν Sapph.*Supp.*25.6. 2. *to be conspicuous* or *famous*, A.*Ch.*356 (lyr.), E.*Heracl.*407; ἀνδράσι *for* men, Pi.*P.*8.28; ἄλγεσι S.*El.*1187; ἐσθήμασι Id.*Fr.*769; ἐν ὅπλοις δεινῶς ἐ. D.C.40.41; ἐνέπρεπον ἔχοντες.. Hdt.7.67,83. 3. *suit*, τῇ φωνῇ καὶ τὴν τραυλότητα ἐμπρέψαι λέγουσι Plu.*Alc.*1: impers., *it is fitting* or *suitable*, c. inf., Hld.5.8.

**ἐμπρήζω**, = ἐμπρήθω II, *Gloss.*

**ἐμ-πρήθω**, *blow up, inflate*, of the wind, ἐν δ' ἄνεμος πρῆσεν μέσον ἱστίον Il.1.481:—Pass., *to be bloated* or *swollen*, ἐμπεπρησμένης ὑός Ar.*V.*36 (-πρημ- cod. R), cf. Gal.ap.Orib.8.19.7. II. *burn*, ἐνέπρηθον μέγα ἄστυ Il.9.589:—Pass., Ath.Med.ap.Orib.1.2.4; cf. ἐμπίμπρημι. **-πρησις**, εως, Ion. -ιος, ἡ, *burning*, Hdt.8.55, D.H.4.40; οἰκιῶν Pl.*R.*470a: pl., ἐμπρήσεις οἰκιῶν Aeschin.3.157. II. *inflammation*, Gal.12.693. **-πρησμός**, ὁ, = foreg., *SIG*679.85 (Magn. Mae., ii B.C.), Plu.2.824e, Gal.9.824, *BGU*163.6 (ii A.D.); opp. κατακλυσμός, prob. in Ph.2.515. **-πρηστής**, οῦ, ὁ, *one that burns*, Aq.*De.*8.15; *incendiary*, Ptol.*Tetr.*165.

**ἐμπρίζω**, = ἐμπρίω, Meges ap.Orib.44.24.19 (Pass.).

**ἐμπρῖόεις**, εντος, *pungent*, v.l. in Nic.*Al.*533, cf. Hsch. (-προιέντα cod.).

**ἐμ-πριστικός**, ή, όν, *like a saw*, of the pulse, Gal.8.478. **-πρίω** [ῑ], Ep. ἐνιπ-, *saw into*, ὀστέον, vulg. for ἐκ-, Hp.*VC*21; τὸ οὖς ἐνέπρισε τοῖς ὀδοῦσι *bit deep into* it, D.S.10.17. II. *gnash together*, ὀδόντας ἐμπεπρικώς *having* the teeth *fixed in a bite*, Id.17.92, v.l. in Luc.*Somn.*14; ἐ. γένυν χαλινοῖς Opp.*H.*5.186, cf. *C.*2.261. III. intr., *bite, be pungent*, σίνηπυν, ὀνόγυρον, etc., Nic.*Al.*533 (dub. l.), *Th.*71, al. 2. ἐμπρίων σφυγμός *saw-like, hard* pulse, Gal.8.474, Alex.Trall.6.1.

**ἐμπρόθεσμος**, ον, *within* or *before the stated time*, opp. ἐκπρόθ., πένθος Ph.2.170; χρόνος Sor.1.33; ἀγῶνες Plu.2.502a; ἐμπρόθεσμόν (v.l. -μως) τινα πέμπειν Luc.*VH*2.27. Adv. -μως Ph.2.532, Sch.Ar.*Eq.*392, *POxy.*61.12 (iii A.D.).

**ἐμπροίκιος**, ον, (προίξ) *given by way of dower*, ἐ. δοθῆναι, δεδόσθαι, App.*Mith.*75, *BC*1.10; δισμύρια τάλαντα ἐ. Anon.Hist. in *Rev.Ét.Gr.*5.321:—also **-ροικος**, ον, *Gloss.*

**ἐμπρό-κειμαι**, *to be impending, imminent*, Carneisc.*Herc.*1027.9. **-μελετάω**, *train oneself in beforehand*, θήραις Ph.2.90, cf. 1.521.

**ἔμπροσθ-α**, Adv., Aeol. and Dor. for sq., *Tab.Heracl.*1.57,101, A.D.*Adv.*153.17. ⊛ **-εν**, sts. also **ἔμπροσθε** Hdt.5.62, 7.144, al., Isoc.*Ep.*4.10, in Poets metri gr., Hegesipp.Com.1.20, Nicom.Com.1.14, A.R.4.590: neither form in Hom. or Trag., τοὔμπροσθεν dub. in E.*Hipp.*1228. I. Adv., 1. of Place, *before, in front*, Hdt.7.126, X.*Cyr.*4.2.23; τὸ and τὰ ἔ. *the front, the foreside*, Id.*HG*2.3.55, Hdt.5.62, etc.; εἰς τὸ ἔ. *forwards*, Id.4.61; στὰς ἐκ τοῦ ἔ. *in front, opposite*, X.*Cyr.*2.2.6: metaph., εἰς τοὔμπ. προελθεῖν Isoc. l.c. 2. of Time, *before, of old*, Pl.*Phdr.*277d, etc.; τὰ ἔ. Id.*Grg.*448e; τὰ ἔ. τούτων ῥηθέντα Id.*Lg.*773e; οἱ ἔ. our *ancestors*, Id.*Plt.*296a, Hegesipp. l.c.; οἱ ἔ. χρόνοι *PPetr.*2 p.19 (iii B.C.), etc. II. as Prep. c. gen., *before, in front of*, 1. of Place, ἐ. αὐτῆς (sc. τῆς νηός) Hdt.8.87, cf. 2.110, etc. 2. of Time, ἔ. ταύτης (sc. τῆς γνώμης) Id.7.144; ἔ. εἶναι τῶν πραγμάτων to be *beforehand with* events, D.4.39. 3. of Degree, ἔ. τοῦ δικαίου *preferred before* justice, Id.56.50. **-ίδιος**, α, ον, = sq., A.D.*Adv.*157.2, *PMag.Berol.*2.46. **-ιος**, ον, *fore*, like πρόσθιος, of the feet of a quadruped, opp. ὀπίσθιοι, ἐ. πόδες Hdt.4.60; σκέλη X.*Eq.*11.2, Arist.*PA*688ᵃ12, *BCH*35.286 (Delos); κῶλα Arist.*PA*687ᵇ28; οἱ ἐ. ὀδόντες Id.*Ph.*198ᵇ25; ἐ. τραύματα wounds *in front*, D.H.10.37. II. Astron., *preceding* in the daily motion of the heavens, Cleom.1.1.

**ἐμπροσθό-κεντρος**, ον, *with a sting in front*, of dipterous insects, Arist.*HA*490ᵃ18. **-τονία**, ἡ, *tetanic procurvation*, opp. ὀπισθοτονία, Cael.Aur.*CP*3.6. **-τονικός**, ή, όν, *suffering from* ἐμπροσθοτονία, ibid. **-τονος**, ον, *drawn forwards and stiffened*, opp. ὀπισθότονος, Aret.*SA*1.6.

**ἐμπροσθουρητικός**, ή, όν, (οὐρέω) *making water forwards*, opp. ὀπισθουρητικός, Arist.*HA*509ᵇ2.

**ἐμπροσθοφᾰνής**, ές, *showing on the front*, Gal.18(1).820.

**ἐμπρόσοδος**, ον, *furnishing revenue*, μέταλλον dub. in Str.6.2.10.

**ἐμπρόσωπος**, ον, *before the face of, in the presence of*, c. dat., Phalar.*Ep.*147.

**ἔμπρωρος**, ον, *depressed towards the prow*, ἔ. τὰ σκάφη ποιεῖν Plb.16.4.12.

**ἐμπταίω**, *fall into*, ἐς ἄρκυν Lyc.105.

**ἐμπτίσσω**, *pound in*, in Pass., Aq., Thd.*Pr.*27.22.

**ἐμπτοέω**, in Pass., *to be stirred by passion*, πρός τινα Procop.Gaz.p.156B.

**ἐμ-πτύσις**, εως, ἡ, *spitting*, of blood, Aret.*SA*2.2. **-πτυσμα**, ατος, τό, *spitting on*, Lxx *Is.*50.6. **-πτύω**, *spit into*, ἐς ποταμόν Hdt.1.138; εἰς στόμα ἑρπετοῦ Dsc.4.25. II. *spit upon*, εἴς τι Ath.8.345c; εἰς τὸ πρόσωπον *PMagd.*24.7 (iii B.C.), Plu.2.189a; ἐς τὸ πρόσωπόν τινος Herod.5.76, Lxx *Nu.*12.14, *Ev.Matt.*26.67; εἴς τινα *Ev.Matt.*27.30: c. dat., Arist.*Fr.*347, *Ev.Marc.*10.24, etc.:—Med., Lxx *De.*25.9:—Pass., *to be spat upon*, Muson.*Fr.*10 p.52 H.

**ἔμ-πτωσις**, εως, ἡ, *falling into*, Corn.*ND*22: generally, *falling*, [καρπῶν] *Cat.Cod.Astr.*7.186. 2. *falling upon, pressure*, D.H.9.23. 3. *incidence, impact*, εἰδώλων Epicur.*Sent.Vat.*24, Cic.*Att.*2.3.2 (pl.); τοῦ ἡλίου εἰς τὰ νέφη *Placit.*3.2.10. 4. *propensity*, διανοίας Onos.1.11. 5. *reduction* of dislocation, Gal.18(1).325. 6. *inundation* of the Nile, Heph.Astr.1.21. **-πτωτος**, ον, *falling into, inclined*, εἰς τὸ κακόν M.Ant.10.7; τῷ πάθει Aët.7.54.

**ἐμπύγια** [ῠ], τά, *region of the anus*, *PTeb.*1.18.

**ἐμπυέλ-ίδιον**, τό, Dim. of sq., Hero *Aut.*10.1. **-ίς**, ίδος, ἡ, (πύελος) *socket* or *bearing* to receive a κνώδαξ, ib.2.3.

**ἐμπυ-έω,** *suppurate,* Hp.*Prog.*18, Aret.*SD*1.8, etc. **-ημα,** ατος, τό, *gathering, abscess,* esp. internal, Hp.*Prog.*18, *Epid.*3.1.α', Arist. *HA*624$^a$17; of the kidneys, Ruf.*Ren.Ves.*1.5; of the chest, Archig. ap.Aët.8.73, Gal.17(2).793. **-ημᾰτικός,** ή, όν, *suppurating,* Hp. *Art.*41. **-ησις,** εως, ἡ, *suppuration,* Id.*Aph.*5.65, Aret.*CA*1.7, etc. **-ητικός,** ή, όν, *causing suppuration,* Hp.*Acut.*22. **-ῐκός,** ή, όν, = ἐμπυηματικός, Aret.*SD*.1.9. 2. *suffering from* ἐμπύημα, ἐ. καὶ φθισικοί Dsc.1.72, cf. Archig.ap.Aët.8.73, Alex.Aphr.*Pr.*2.34. **-ίσκω,** *cause suppuration*: —Pass., *suppurate internally,* Hp. *VC*2, *Morb.*3.16:—also intr. in Act., Aret.*SD*1.14.

**ἐμπῠκάζω,** *wrap up in*:—Pass., νόος οἱ ἐμπεπύκασται his mind *is shrouded, hard to make out,* v.l. for εὖ πεπ. in Mosch.1.15.

⊛ **ἐμπύλαι·** αἱ νύμφαι, Hsch.; cf. τιτύπαι.

**ἐμπύλιος** [ῠ], α, ον, *at the gate,* epith. of Artemis Hecate, Orph.*A.*902: Boeot. **ἐμπύληος** (= -λαιος), epith. of Poseidon at Thebes, *IG*7.2465 (iv/iii B.C.).

**ἐμπυ-όομαι,** Pass., *suppurate,* Hp.*Morb.*1.27. **-ος,** ον, (πύον) *suffering from an abscess* or *suppurating wound,* Id.*Prog.*18, *Aph.*5.10, D.54.12, Isoc.19.26, Men.1009, *IG*4.952.57 (Epid.); τῷ ἐ. βέλτιον τὸ καίεσθαι τοῦ διαμένειν Iamb.*Protr.*2; ἵπποι Arist.*HA*604$^b$6. II. *festering, suppurating,* βάσις S.*Ph.*1378; στέρνων ἀπολύσεται ἔμπυον ἰλύν Androm.ap.Gal.14.35; ἐ. μοτός *tents,* Gal.19.97.

**ἐμπῡ́ρ-ετος** [ῠ], ον, *in fever heat,* Alex.Trall.5.4. **-ευμα,** ατος, τό, *a live coal covered with ashes,* so as to allow of the fire being re-kindled (λείψανον, Hsch.; ἔναυσμα, Suid.), Arist.*Fr.*225, 226, Gal.11.629: metaph., Ph.2.59, al., Longus 1.29; ἀρετῆς Jul.*ad Ath.*269d: pl., ζωῆς ἐ. *embers, hidden sparks,* Simp.*in Cael.*677.11. **-εύω,** *set on fire,* Ar.*Lys.*372:—Med., *catch fire,* Thphr.*HP*5.9.6; *light a fire,* Philostr.*Im.*2.24:—Pass., Arist.*PA*649$^a$26. 2. *set aglow,* τὴν ψυχὴν ἐμπεπύρευκεν Id.*Resp.*474$^b$13, cf. *Juv.*469$^b$16 (Pass.). II. *kindle in* the body, θερμότητα Id.*GA*739$^b$10. III. *roast in* or *on the fire,* φηγόν Ar.*Pax*1137. **-ία** (leg. **-εία**), ἡ, *divination by fire,* in Boeotia, Hsch.; also, = ὅρκος δημόσιος, i.e. *ordeal by fire,* Id.

**ἐμπῡρῐβήτης,** ου, ὁ, (ἐν, πῦρ, βαίνω) *made for standing on the fire,* μέγαν τρίποδ' ἐμπυριβήτην Il.23.702.

⊛ **ἐμπῡρ-ίζω,** = ἐμπυρεύω, Lxx *Jo.*8.28, D.S.2.36, 12.43:—Pass., *Chron.Lind.*D.41, *PTeb.*5.135 (ii B.C.), Diog.Oen.8, Alex.Trall. *Febr.*2; [ψυχὴ] τοῖς πάθεσιν -ομένη Simp.*in Epict.*p.126 D. (In Thd. *Ge.*4.4,5 ἐ. is a mistranslation due to confusion of Hebr. *yiša'* and *'išeh.*) **-ιος** [ῠ], ον, *belonging to the empyrean,* θεός (opp. αἰθέριος, ὑλαῖος) Procl.*Theol.Plat.*4.39, cf. Iamb.*Myst.*7.2, Lyd.*Mens.*4.22. ⊛ **-ισμός,** ὁ, = ἐμπρησμός (less Att., acc. to Phryn.313), Hyp. *Lyc.Fr.*4, Plb.9.41.5, Lxx *Le.*10.6, *Mon.Anc.Gr.*19.8, Ath.Mech.12.6; *burning* of weeds, *PSI*4.338.7, al. (iii B.C.). ⊛ **-ιστής,** οῦ, ὁ, *one who sets on fire,* ὁ ἐ. Ἕκτωρ Eust.1023.26.

**ἐμπῡρισχησίφως** [σῐ], ὁ, *deriving light from the empyrean,* *PMag. Par.*1.601.

⊛ **ἐμπῡρίφοιτος** [ῐ], ον, *dwelling in fire,* δαίμονες Orph.*H.*1.33 (prob.).

⊛ **ἔμπῡρος,** ον, (πῦρ) *in, on* or *by the fire,* σκεύη ἔ. implements *used at the fire,* opp. ἄπυρα, Pl.*Lg.*679a; ἡ ἔ. τέχνη the work *of the forge, smith's* art, Id.*Prt.*321e (but in E.*Ph.*954, *the art of divining by fire, soothsaying* trade (v. infr. III)); χειρώνακτες Ael.*NA*2.31. II. *exposed to fire* or *sun, burnt, scathed,* νεκρός E.*Ph.*1186; *roasted,* σάρξ *AP*6.89 (Maec.); *fiery hot, torrid,* χώρα Str.16.1.10; ἀήρ Thphr. *CP*1.13.5; [ἡ ὥρα] -ωτάτη ib.4; *feverish,* Hp.*Morb.*2.40 (v.l. ἐμπύρετος); λοιμοί Lxx *Am.*4.2; *inflammatory,* of a bite, Arist.*Mir.*846$^b$16; *heated,* of a cautery iron, *PMed.Lond.*155.3.2. 2. *burning, scorching,* ἥλιος *AP*9.24 (Leon.): metaph. of persons, *fiery,* Plu.*Num.*5. Adv. -ως, ἐρᾶν Poll.3.68. 3. *lighted,* λαμπάς *AP*6.100 (Crin.); βωμός ib.10.7 (Arch.). III. *of* or *for a burnt-offering,* ὀρθοστάται E.*Hel.*547. 2. as Subst., ἔμπυρα (sc. ἱερά), τά, *burnt sacrifices,* opp. ἄπυρα, Pi.*O.*8.3, cf. A.*Ch.*485 (prob.); δι' ἐμπύρων σπονδὰς καθεῖναι to make libations at *the burnt-offerings,* E. *IA*59 (hence ἔμπυρα are improperly used for σπονδαί, S.*El.*405); κατάρας ἐπὶ ἐμπύρων ποιεῖσθαι swear upon *the sacrifice,* Plb.16.31.7, cf. App.*Hisp.*9; esp. of *burnt-offerings* as used *for purposes of divination* (v. supr. I), S.*Ant.*1005; εἰς ἔμπυρ' ἦλθε E.*IT*16; also ἐμπύρους ἀκμάς Id.*Ph.*1255; ἔμπυρα σήματ' ἰδέσθαι A.R.1.145: rarely sg., ἔμπυρον, τό, *PMag.Osl.*1.69, dub. sens. in *PCair.Zen.*14.17.

**ἐμπῡρο-σκόπος,** ὁ, *one who divines by* ἔμπυρα, Sch.Il.**24**.221, Eust.1346.39. **-τέχνης,** ου, ὁ, *smith,* Arg.Man. (post Max.p.101 L.).

⊛ **ἐμπῡρόω,** = ἐμπυρεύω, *Inscr.Prien.*17.13 (iii B.C.), v.l. in Dsc.5.114 (Pass.), cj. in Hsch. s.v. πυρέας.

**ἔμπυρρος,** ον, *ruddy,* Arist.*Col.*797$^b$13.

**ἐμπυρσεύω,** gloss on πυρακτῶ, Suid.

**ἐμπύρωσις** [ῠ], εως, ἡ, *kindling, heating,* Arist.*Resp.*478$^a$30.

**ἐμπῡτιάζω,** *curdle with rennet,* γάλα Dsc.*Alex.*26 (Pass.); cf. ἐμπιτυάζομαι.

**ἐμπῡτίζω,** *spit into,* Gp.20.33.

**ἐμπύωμα,** ατος, τό, = ἐμπύημα, *Gloss.*

**ἐμπωλέω,** *dwell amongst,* [φθιμένοις] *Epigr.Gr.*316 (dub.).

**ἔμσκεψις,** εως, ἡ, *investigation, PSI*3.168.31 (ii B.C.).

⊛ **ἐμύς** or **ἑμύς,** ύδος, ἡ, *fresh-water tortoise,* esp. *Emys lutaria,* Arist. *HA*558$^a$8, al.; also ὁ, ib.600$^b$22.

**ἐμφάατον** (post ἔμφατον)· πλακοῦντα τετυρωμένον, Hsch.

**ἐμφᾰγεῖν,** inf. of aor. 2 ἐνέφαγον (no pres. ἐνεσθίω being in use), *eat,* Eub.89, J.*AJ*9.4.5, Plu.*Tim.*12, Ael.*NA*5.29, Luc.*Nigr.*22; esp. in X., *eat hastily,* 'snatch a bite', ἐμφαγόντες ὅ τι δύναιντο *HG*4.5.8; ἐκέλευον αὐτοὺς ἐμφαγόντας πορεύεσθαι *An.*4.2.1, cf. *Cyr.*7.1.1, 8.1.44. II. *eat in* or *upon,* χρυσὸς κοῖλος ἡμῖν ἐμφαγεῖν Luc. *Nav.*20.

⊛ **ἐμφαίνω,** *exhibit, display in,* οἷον ἐν κατόπτρῳ χρώματα Pl.*Ti.*71b:—Pass., τὸ -όμενον μέλαν (in the moon) *Stoic.*2.199. 2. *exhibit, display,* φαντασίαν μήκους Arist.*Mu.*395$^b$6; τὴν ἰδέαν τοῦ σώματος Plu.*Alex.*4; εὐοδμίαν Thphr.*CP*6.5.2, cf. 6.3.4 (Pass.); αἱρέσεις καὶ διαλήψεις Plb.3.31.8; δυσχερασμόν Phld.*Lib.*p.8 O.; οὐδὲν τοιοῦτον ἐμφαίνει *presents* no such *appearance,* Luc.*DDeor.*26.1; ἡ φροντὶς ἐ. τινὰ ψυχρότητα ἤθους Demetr.*Eloc.*171. 3. *indicate,* ψυχρίαν Chrysipp.*Stoic.*3.50; εὔνοιαν Plb.22.7.9; ἐ. ὅτι.. D.S.1.87, Plu.2.112f, al.; περί τινος ὡς περὶ ἰδίας Plb.3.23.5. 4. *lay information, IG*9(1).267 (Opus). II. Med. or Pass., with fut. ἐμφανήσομαι Phld.*Lib.*p.23 O.: 1. *to be seen in* a mirror, *reflected,* ἐν ὕδασι ἢ ἐν κατόπτροις Pl.*R.*402b, al., cf. Arist.*Mete.*345$^b$26, *APo.*98$^a$27 (where ἠχεῖ and ἐμφαίνεται are quasi-impersonal), Thphr.*Sens.*27; ἐν χαλκείῳ X.*Smp.*7.4; τῷ εἴδει Plu.*Alc.*4. 2. *become visible, to be manifested,* X.*Cyr.*1.4.3; τὰ ἤθη τὰ ἐπὶ τοῦ προσώπου -όμενα Arist. *Phgn.*806$^a$30, cf. Lxx *Ps.*79(80).2, etc.; ἐν ἅπασιν ἐμφαίνεται τὸ ἄρχον καὶ τὸ ἀρχόμενον Arist.*Pol.*1254$^a$30; ἐμφαίνεται impers., *it is manifest,* Plu.2.953e:—also in Act., ἐμφαίνει οὕτως Ceb.21. 3. *to be exemplified* or *implied in..,* ἐν τῇ κατηγορίᾳ τῇ τοιαύτῃ Arist.*Metaph.*1028$^a$28; ἐνυπάρχειν καὶ ἐ. Id.*de An.*413$^a$15, *EN*1096$^b$22. 4. *to be indicated,* τῆς ἡδονῆς -ομένης τέλους Chrysipp.*Stoic.*3.8, cf. Gal.10.126.

**ἐμφαλκόομαι,** dub. in Plb.*Fr.*136 (ap.Suid.).

**ἐμφάν-εια** [ᾰ], ἡ, *manifestation,* εἰς ἐ. ἄγειν bring to *light,* Thphr. *Ign.*2; τοῦ θεοῦ J.*AJ*15.11.7 (pl.); τὴν ἐ. τινων ποιεῖσθαι produce for *inspection, PLips.*52.9 (iv A.D.), etc. **-ερος,** ον, *designated, Gloss.* ⊛ **-ής,** ές, *showing in* itself, *reflecting,* of mirrors, Pl.*Ti.*46a. II. *visible to the eye, manifest,* a. of persons, S.*Tr.*199, etc.; esp. of the gods *appearing bodily* among men, E.*Ba.*22, Ar.*V.*733, Pl.*Alc.*2.141a; so ὄψις ἐ. ὑπνίων A.*Pers.*518; τέκμαρ *Ch.*667; ἐ. τινὰ ἰδεῖν see him *bodily,* S.*Aj.*538, cf. Ar.*Th.*682; μαθεῖν S.*El.*1454; πῶς ἂν ὑμὶν ἐμφανὴς.. γενοίμην; how could I make it *manifest?* Id.*Ph.*531; ἐμφανὴς τιμαῖσιν, = ἐμφανῶς τιμώμενος, Id.*OT*909 (lyr.); ἐ. ζῷα *familiar* animals, Epicur.*Ep.*2 p.43 U. b. as legal term, ἐμφανῆ παρέχειν τινά to produce a person or thing *in open court,* Antipho 5.36, cf. D.56.38; so ἐμφανῆ καταστῆσαι produce *in court,* either the property or the vouchers, Id.52.10; ἐμφανῶν κατάστασις, *actio ad exhibendum,* Is.6.31, D.53.14. c. of things, οὐ γάρ ἐστι τἀμφανῆ κρύπτειν S.*OC*755; ἐ. τεκμήρια *visible* proofs, Id.*El.*1109; ἄλγος ἐ. Pi.*Fr.*210; κλαυθμός Hdt.1.111; μεῖξις ib.203; χυμοί Thphr. *CP*6.3.4 (Sup.); ἐ. κόσμος *visible* sky, Vett.Val.8.12; τὰ ἐ. κτήματα the *actual* property, X.*HG*5.2.10; τοῦ μέλλοντος καὶ μὴ -οῦς Th.3.42; εἰς τοὐμφανὲς ἰέναι to come into *light,* come *forward,* X. *Mem.*4.3.13; εἰς τοὐ. ᾠοτοκεῖν, ζῳοτοκεῖν, Arist.*HA*510$^b$20, 511$^a$23; ἀεὶ ἐ. εἶναι to be constantly *in evidence,* X.*Ages.*9.1. 2. *manifest, palpable,* τυραννίς Ar.*V.*417; βία Th.4.86; ἐ. λόγος *a plain* speech, A.*Eu.*420; τῷ ἐμφανεῖ λόγῳ *openly,* Th.7.48; τὴν διάνοιαν ἐ. ποιεῖν διὰ φωνῆς Pl.*Tht.*206d; ἐμφανές ἐστιν ὅτι.. X.*Hier.*9.10. 3. *well-known,* τὰ ἐ. Hdt.2.33; ἐμφανὴ γὰρ ἦν S.*Ant.*448; *conspicuous, notable,* ἀνήρ D.S.1.68. III. Adv. -νῶς, Ion. -νέως, *visibly, openly,* Hdt.1.140, A.*Ag.*626, Th.7.48, etc.; λέγειν Ar.*Ach.*312; ἐ. ἐλευθεροῦν *without doubt,* Hdt.6.123; ἐ. ἠμύνατο *openly,* i.e. *not secretly* or *treacherously,* S.*Tr.*278; οὐ λόγοις, ἀλλ' ἐ. but *really,* Ar.*Nu.*611: Comp. -έστερον Pl.*Phlb.*31e. 2. neut. Adj., ἐκ τοῦ ἐ. Hdt.3.150, 4.120, al.; ἐν τῷ ἐ. Th.2.21, X.*An.*2.5.25. **-ία,** ἡ, *information laid, IG*9(1).267.10 (Opus). ⊛ **-ίζω,** Att. fut. -ιῶ E.*Fr.*797: pf. ἐμπεφάνικα *PSI*4.400.2 (iii B.C.): *show forth, manifest, exhibit,* αὐτὸς αὐτόν E.l.c., cf. Philoch.20, Plb.30.17.2, etc.; ἐ. τινὰ ἐπίορκον, ἐχθρόν, *exhibit* or *represent* him as.., X.*Ages.*1.12, D.14.36; ἐ. οὐκ οὖσαν ἀγαθὸν τὴν ἡδονήν Arist.*EN*1173$^b$31; πᾶν σύμπτωμα Metrod.10:—Med., *exhibit in court, PMasp.*32.33 (vi A.D.):—Pass., *to become visible, be manifested,* τινί Lxx *Wi.*1.2, *Ev.Matt.*27.53, Ph.1.107, J.*AJ*1.13.1, D.L.1.7. 2. *make clear* or *plain,* Pl.*Sph.*244a, Men.*Sam.*140, etc.; ἄστρα ἡμῖν τῆς νυκτὸς τὰς ὥρας ἐ. X.*Mem.*4.3.4: with a relat., τὰ παθήματα δι' ἃς αἰτίας γέγονε ἐ. Pl.*Ti.*61c; ἐ. τοῦτο ὅτι.. X. *Cyr.*8.1.26. 3. *declare, explain,* Arist.*APr.*46$^a$24; *give orders,* τινὶ ποιεῖν τι Plb.6.35.8; *report,* περί τινος *SIG*412.4 (Delph., iii B.C.), cf. *UPZ*42.18 (ii B.C.), *IG*9(2).517.5 (Larissa), *Michel*431.6 (Iasus), etc.:—Pass., *GDI*2502*B*41 (Delph., iv B.C.). 4. *lay an information against,* τινά Arg.Ar.*Lys.*:—Pass., ὁ -ισθείς Charond.ap.Stob.4.2.24. **-ισιμα,** τά, *fees paid at installation* in a benefice, Just.*Nov.*56.1 (but -ιστικά, τά, ib.*Praef.*). ⊛ **-ισις,** εως, ἡ, *exposure,* ψευδοῦς συλλογισμοῦ Arist.*SE*176$^b$29; πράξεων ἢ λόγων πρὸς ἄλληλα ἐναντιουμένων Id.*Rh.Al.*1427$^b$14. 2. *indication,* A.D.*Synt.*67.27. 3. *exhibition, production* in court, Just.*Nov.*15.3 (pl.). 4. *proof, demonstration, PMasp.*89.5 (vi A.D.). **-ίσκω,** = ἐμφανίζω, Iamb.*VP*35.260. ⊛ **-ισμός,** ὁ, *manifestation,* Pl.*Def.*413e; *information, disclosure, PAmh.*2.30.2, al. (ii B.C.), Lxx 2*Ma.*3.9, *BCH*48.369 (Thessaly, i A.D.); *indication,* τινός A.D.*Synt.*50.27, al.; *explanation,* Ptol.*Tetr.*22. **-ιστέον,** *one must set forth, declare,* Pl. *Ti.*65c, Str.2.5.17. **-ιστής,** οῦ, ὁ, *informer,* Aristeas 167, *PTaur.*1.8 (ii B.C.). **-ιστικός,** ή, όν, *declaratory,* λόγος Pl.*Def.*414e; *expressive,* Longin.31.1 (Comp.): c. gen., Porph.ap.Eus.*PE*3.11, Dam.*Pr.*350; τὸ -κὸν αὐτόθεν ἔχειν, of names which carry their own *meaning,* Ptol.*Tetr.*34. II. v. ἐμφανίσιμα. 2. -κόν, τό, *deposit paid on laying an information, PMasp.*89.5 (vi A.D.).

**ἐμφανόν,** *moechulus, Gloss.*

⊛ **ἐμφαντ-άζομαι,** Pass., *to be associated in idea with,* [τῷ ἀποθανεῖν]

M.Ant.2.12. 2. *to be imagined*, Dam.*Pr*.7. II. *to be mirrored in*, Plot.3.6.17; *take visible shape*, εἰς τὴν ὕλην Id.1.8.8, cf. Iamb. *Comm.Math*.14, al. III. *have visions*, Zos.Alch.p.110B. **-ᾰσις,** εως, ἡ, *imagination*, Plot.3.6.17. **-ικός,** ή, όν, *expressive, indicative*, τινός of a thing, Ph.1.149, Plu.2.747e, 1010c, Demetr.*Eloc*.283, A.D.*Pron*.8.9, etc.; τῆς δικαιοσύνης -ωτάτη ἡ πεντάς *Theol.Ar*.27: abs., *expressive, vivid*, παράκλησις Plb.18.23.2, cf. Plu.2.1009e (Comp.), Ph.1.302 (Sup.). Adv. -κῶς *vividly, forcibly*, of a painter, Plu.*Arat*.32; ἐ. γράφεσθαι Plb.12.25g.2; τρανοῦν Ph.2.140: Comp. -ώτερον Plb.12.27.10: Sup. -ώτατα Ph.1.50: also -κῶς τοῦ κινδύνου *setting forth* the danger *clearly*, Plb.11.12.1.—ἐμφατικός (q.v.) is a common v.l.

**ἐμφαρμάσσω,** *smear upon*, in Pass., τοὺς ἐμπεφαρμαγμένους τοῖς βέλεσιν [ἰούς] Gal.*Nat.Fac*.1.14.

**ἐμφᾰρύγγομαι,** aor. 1 part. -υξάμενος, *gulp down*, *Com.Adesp*.996, Dsc.*Ther*.19.

⊛ **ἔμφᾰσις,** εως, ἡ, (ἐμφαίνομαι) *appearing in* a smooth surface, *reflection*, as in a mirror or in water, Arist.*Mete*.373b24, 377b17; κατ' ἔμφασιν by *reflection*, Id.*Mu*.395a29; ἔμφασιν ποιεῖν Thphr.*Lap*.30; ἀμυδραὶ ἐ. τῆς ἀληθείας faint *reflections* or *images*, Plu.2.354c: generally, ἔ. προσώπου (in the moon) Epicur.*Ep*.2 p.41 U., *Stoic*.2.198, cf. Plot.4.3.18; τοῦ ὄντος Dam.*Pr*.69; τῶν πρώτων ἐν τοῖς ἐσχάτοις Procl.*in Alc*.p.69C.; στερεοῦ πρώτη ἔ. ἐν τῇ τετράδι εὑρίσκεται Hierocl *in CA* 20 p.465 M. 2. *outward appearance, impression, presentation*, τὰς ἔ. κρίνειν Arist.*Div.Somn*.464b12; φαντασιῶν *Stoic*.2.24 (pl.); κατὰ τὴν ἔ. Plb.5.63.2; ποιεῖν ἔμφασίν τινος give *the appearance of*.., *suggest*, Chrysipp.*Stoic*.2.257; ποιεῖν ἔ. ὡς.. make as if.., Plb.5.110.6; ποιεῖν, c. fut. inf., Str.8.3.30; ἔ. λαβεῖν τινος Phld.*Ir*. p.95 W., al.; ἔ. ἔχειν τινός D.H.*Th*.16; ἔ. ἔχειν ὡς.. D.S.11.89; ἔ. γίγνεταί τινος Id.1.38; of taste, ἔ. ἁλυκότητος Dsc.5.87. II. (ἐμφαίνω) *setting forth, exposition, narration*, Plb.6.5.3, etc.; ποιεῖν ἐμφάσεις κατά τινος to make *statements* against, Id.28.4.8; συμβόλων -σεις *explanations*, Iamb.*VP*23.103. III. *meaning, significance*, Agatharch.21, Corn.*ND*15; esp. in Rhet., *significance, emphasis*, Quint.8.3.83, 9.2.3, Trypho *Trop*.p.199 S., Tib.*Fig*.14: coupled with δείνωσις, Demetr.*Eloc*.130. 2. *suggestion, hint*, ib.57, 171. IV. *moral* of a fable, Babr.116.15.

**ἐμφᾰτικός,** ή, όν, *forcible, expressive*, Phld.*Rh*.1.326 S.: Comp., Demetr.*Eloc*.51. Adv. -κῶς Phld.*Po*.5.1425.29, Gal.17(1).826: Comp. -ώτερον Hsch. (Freq. f.l. for ἐμφαντικός, as A.D.*Adv*.131.23: so in Adv. -κῶς S.E.*M*.1.194.)

**ἔμφατον·** αἰνιγματοειδῶς εἰρημένον, Hsch.

**ἐμφέρβομαι,** poet. **ἐνιφ-,** Pass., *feed in*, σταθμοῖς Mosch.2.80.

**ἐμφέρ-εια,** ἡ, *likeness*, Ps.-Dsc.1.1, Ph.1.15, Corn.*ND*9, Plu.*Num*.13; πρός τι Ph.1.433, al., Plu.*TG*2: pl., τὰς ἀριθμοῦ ἐ. καὶ ἀφομοιώσεις *Theol.Ar*.58. **-ής,** ές, *answering to, resembling*, ἀνθέμοισι Sapph.85, freq. in Hdt., as 2.76, al.: Sup., 3.37, al.; also in Trag. and Ar., as A.*Ch*.206, *Supp*.279 (Comp.), S.*Aj*.1152, Ar.*Nu*.502; ἐ. τινι τοὺς τρόπους Id.*V*.1103 (Sup.); also in Prose, X.*Cyr*.5.5.31, Arist.*HA*626a6, Thphr.*HP*7.6.3, Phld.*D*.3 *Fr*.66, Ph.1.316 (Sup.), etc.; καὶ τὰ ἐ. 'and the *like*', Sor.1.2. Adv. -ρῶς *similarly*, D.L.6.103; ἐ. ἔχειν τινί Ath.1.27a: Sup. -έστατα Ar.*Fr*.68.

⊛ **ἐμφέρω,** *bear* or *bring in* (v. infr. II):—Pass., *to be borne* or *carried in*, ἔν τινι Hp.*Epid*.7.40 (vulg. ἐκφ.); δίναις A.R.4.613; βένθεσι πόντου Opp.*H*.1.81:—Med., *carry with oneself*, τι Arat.701. II. *enter in* an account, ἐν λήμματι *PEleph*.15.4 (iii B.C.):—Pass., ἐνεφέρετο *an account was given*, Gloss. ad Plb.14.12. III. Pass., *to be contained* in, εἶδος ἐ. γένει Ph.1.460, al.: abs., Id.2.1, al.; τὰ ἐμφερόμενα τῷ πράγματι *matters appertaining to* the subject, Longin.12.2, prob. in Id.10.1. 2. ἐμφέρεσθαι τῇ αἰτίᾳ, = ἐνέχεσθαι, *IG*12(3).174.12 (Astypalaea, Epist. Aug.); ὁ ἐμφερόμενος the party *concerned*, *CPHerm*.53.12 (pl., iii A.D.), etc. IV. ἐμφέρω, Thess., = εἰσφέρω, *IG*9(2).205.20 (Melitaea); also, = εἰσφέρω I.4, *Berl.Sitzb*.1927.8 (Locr., v B.C.).

**ἐμφεύγω,** *fly in* or *into*, εἰς.. Luc.*Pseudol*.27 (s.v.l.).

**ἐμφθέγγομαι,** = φθέγγομαι ἐν, *speak then* or *there*, Luc.*Eun*.7 (s.v.l.).

**ἐμφθορής,** ές, (φθορά) *lost* or *destroyed in*.., Nic.*Al*.176.

**ἐμφῐληδέω,** *delight in*, τινί Porph.*Abst*.2.47, M.Ant.5.5 (ἐμφιληδονοῦντι Casaub.).

**ἐμφῐλο-δοξέω,** *seek fame in*, πράγματι Phld.*Rh*.2.140 S. **-κᾰλέω,** *pursue honourable studies in*.., Plu.2.122e; ἐ. τινί *to be engaged in* such a pursuit, Id.*Phil*.4. **-νεικος,** ον, = φιλόνεικος, λόγοι Sch.E.*Med*.637. Adv. -κως Sch.E.*Andr*.289. **-σοφέω,** *study philosophy in*, τῇ Σικελίᾳ Philostr.*VA*5.18, cf. 1.7: abs., Porph.*Abst*.4.6, Lib.*Or*.18.187. ⊛ **-σοφος,** *philosophical*, αἰσθήσεις Ph.2.22, cf. Ptol.*Tetr*.158, D.L.2.40; τέχνη Olymp.Alch.p.70 B. **-τεχνέω,** *bestow pains on*, τῇ παρούσῃ φαντασίᾳ M.Ant.7.54. **-χωρέω,** *to be fond of dwelling in, haunt*, τῇ μνήμῃ Luc.*Hist.Conscr*.1; τοῖς ἀγροῖς Alciphr.3.15; τῇ οἰκήσει J.*AJ*2.7.2; ἐν δόμῳ Agath.5.7: abs., Archemach.1; of things, Gal.16.556. ⊛ **-χώρως,** Adv., metaph., *dwelling upon*, φωνὴ ἀναστρέφεται ἐ. περὶ τὰς μέσας μελῳδίας Ptol.*Harm*.3.11.

**ἔμφῑμος,** ον, *closed*, opp. ἄπωμος, Zos.Alch.p.113 B.

**ἐμφλάω,** Ion. for ἐνθλάω, Hp.*Prorrh*.2.14.

**ἐμφλεβοτομέω,** *split up veins into branches*, Hp.*Oss*.18.

**ἐμφλέγω,** *kindle in*, ἐν φρεσὶ πυρσόν *APl*.4.198 (Maec.):—Pass., *to be inflamed*, Nic.*Th*.338.

**ἔμφλοιος,** ον, *with a bark*, Thphr.*HP*5.1.2.

**ἐμφλοιοσπέρμᾰτος,** ον, *with the seed covered by an integument*, Thphr.*HP*7.3.2.

**ἔμφλοξ,** ογος, ὁ, ἡ, *with fire in it*, πέτρος *AP*6.5 (Phil.).

⊛ **ἐμφοβ-έω,** *terrify, intimidate*, *BGU*613.18 (ii A.D.):—Pass., *to be alarmed*, Ezek.*Exag*.82. ⊛ **-ος,** ον, *terrible*, θεαί S.*OC*39. II. Pass., *in fear, timorous*, ὕπειξις τῆς ψυχῆς Thphr.*Char*.25.1; *terrified, frightened*, Lxx *Si*.19.24, *Ev.Luc*.24.5, al., *Bull.Soc.Alex*.6.45. Adv. -βως Hsch. s.v. ὀρρωδέως.

**ἐμφοιτάω,** *invade*: metaph., κόλλυβός τις ἐμπεφοίτηκεν εἰς [τὴν ἀγοράν] *OGI*515.50 (Mylasa).

**ἐμφονεύω,** *kill in*.., τι ἔν τινι *Gp*.16.19.

**ἐμφορβιόομαι,** Pass., *to have the mouth-band on* (cf. φορβειά II), Ar.*Av*.861.

⊛ **ἐμφόρβιος,** ον, *eating away, consuming*, τινός Nic.*Th*.629. II. ἐμφόρβιον, τό, *pasture-money*, Hsch.

⊛ **ἐμφορβ-ίω,** Arc. **ἰμφ-,** *muzzle* (or *impose a pasture-tax*), *IG*5(2).3 (Tegea, iv B.C.):—also ⊛ **-ισμός,** ὁ, *muzzling* (or *imposition of a pasture-tax*), ibid.

**ἐμφορ-έω,** = ἐμφέρω:—Pass., *to be borne about in* or *on*, c. dat., κύμασιν ἐμφορέοντο Od.12.419; ὕδασι A.R.4.626. II. *pour in*, ἄκρατον D.S.16.93; *fill*, πολέμων καὶ ταραχῶν ἅπαντα Agath.1.1:—Med. and Pass., *fill oneself with* a thing, *take one's fill* or *make much use of* it, ἐνεφορέετο τοῦ μαντηΐου Hdt.1.55; *to be filled full of*, Duris 27 J.; οἴνου, ἀκράτου, Hdn.4.11.3, Plu.2.1067e; κακίας, ἀμαθίας, Ph.1.204, 97; ἀγαθῶν *PLips*.119 ii 6 (iii A.D.); ἐξουσίας, ὕβρεως, Plu.*Cic*.19, *Sert*.5, etc.; τοῦ τέλους Dam.*Pr*.288: c. acc. rei, ἄκρατον D.S.4.4, Ph.2.403, cf. Alciphr.1.35, Thrasym.4, Porph.*Abst*.1.23, Gal.6.243: abs., Alciphr.1.1:—Act. in this sense is dub. in Democr. 1a. III. metaph., *put upon, inflict on*, πληγάς τινι D.S.19.70, Plu.*Pomp*.3; ἐ. ὕβρεις εἴς τινα Alciphr.1.9:—Med., App.*BC*3.28. 2. *cast in one's teeth*, φόνους ἐ. τινί S.*OC*989. **-ησις,** εως, ἡ, *greedy eating and drinking*, Ath.1.10b; σαρκῶν -σεις Plu.2.472b; τῶν ἀλλοτρίων σωμάτων Porph.*Abst*.1.34; *repletion*, Paul.Aeg.6.96.

⊛ **ἔμφορος,** ον, *productive, profitable*, γῆ *PLond*.3.882.13 (ii B.C.); περιστερεών *PEdgar*49.3 (iii B.C.). II. ἔμφορα προσβεβλημένα· ἀγέλη προβάτων (ad ἐμφόρβιον pertinens), Hsch.

**ἐμφορτ-ίζομαι,** Med., = sq., metaph., πολὺν τῇ γαστρὶ κόρον Onos.12.2. II. Pass., *to be laden*, ἱκανῶς ἐμπεφορτισμένος Timae.Astr. in *Cat.Cod.Astr*.1.98. **-όομαι,** Med., *load with a cargo, freight*, ναῦν Aesop.37cb. **-ος,** ον, *laden with*, ἐδωδῆς Opp.*H*.2.212: abs., *laden*, πλοῖον D.L.1.31; σαγήνη Iamb.*VP*8.36.

**ἔμ-φραγμα,** ατος, τό, (ἐμφράσσω) *barrier, obstacle*, Isoc.7.40, Plu.2.745f (pl.). 2. *wooden framework, casing*, in pl., Ph.*Bel*.66.47. 3. pl., *impacted faeces*, Archig.ap.Aët.6.27. 4. *impaction* of foetus, Hp.*Oct*.10. **-φραγμός,** ὁ, = ἔμφραξις, Lxx *Si*.27.14. **-φρακτικός,** ή, όν, *likely to obstruct, stop*, Hp.*Acut*.(*Sp*.)9, Aët.1 p.5v 20. **-φραξις,** εως, ἡ, *stoppage*, [τῶν πόρων] Arist.*Pr*.870b19; τοῦ φάρυγγος ib.901a1, cf. Str.16.1.10, Porph.*Antr*.19 (pl.); as a morbid condition, Diocl.*Fr*.40; ἔ. λίθων *impaction*, Aret.*CA*2.9. **-φράσσω,** Att. **-ττω,** pf. ἐμπέφρᾰκα Sch.Ar.*Nu*.1240: fut. Pass. -φραχθήσομαι Lxx *Mi*.5.1(4.14): aor. 2 part. Pass. ἐμφρᾰγείς Ph.*Fr*.41 H.:—*bar a passage, stop up, block up*, τὸ μεταξύ Th.7.34; τοὺς ἔσπλους Id.4.8; ἐ. συγκλείουσά τε Pl.*Ti*.71c; ἐ. τὸ στόμα D.19.208; ἐ. τὰς ὁδοὺς τῶν ἀδικημάτων Lycurg.124. 2. *bar the passage of, stop*, τὰς κατὰ σοῦ τιμωρίας Aeschin.3.223; πᾶσαν παρείσδυσιν Epicur.*Sent.Vat*.47 (= Metrod.49); τὰς βοηθείας D.S.14.56; τὴν περὶ τὰ αἰσθητήρια ἀκρίβειαν Ph.1.246; τὴν φωνήν Plu.2.606d. 3. Med. in act. sense, Nic.*Al*.191. II. *stuff in*, φύλλα εἰς τὰς ὀπάς (v.l. φύλλοις τὰς ὀ.) *Gp*.13.5.3; τινί τι v.l. in Nic.*Th*.79 (Med.).

**ἐμφρονέω,** *come to one's senses*, Hp.*Epid*.5.22.

**ἔμφροντις,** ιδος, ὁ, ἡ, *anxious*, Them.*Or*.18.219b, Sch.Od.13.421.

**ἐμφρονώδης,** ες, *showing intelligence*, Hp.*Epid*.7.7.

**ἐμφρουρ-έω,** *keep guard in* a place, Th.4.110, 8.60: c. acc. loci, D.C.47.30, 50.12:—Pass., *to be imprisoned*, τέχναις Phalar.*Ep*.122.4. **-ος,** ον, *on guard at a post*, X.*HG*1.6.13. 2. *liable to military duty* (cf. φρουρά), opp. ἄφρουρος, Id.*Lac*.5.7. II. Pass., *held by garrisons*, πόλεις ἐμφρούρους ποιεῖ Decr.ap.D.18.182, cf. Plb.2.41.10, etc. III. *shut up in*, τῷ ταύρῳ Phalar.*Ep*.147.3; οἷον ἔ. *kept* as it were *in prison*, Longin.44.4, cf. Jul.*ad Ath*.272d.

**ἐμφρύγω,** = φρύγω ἐν, Ael.*NA*14.18:—also **ἐμφρύττω,** Poll.6.64.

⊛ **ἔμφρων,** ον, gen. ονος, (φρήν) *in one's mind* or *senses, sensible*: opp., 1. to one mad, σε Ζεὺς τίθησιν ἔμφρονα brings thee *to thy senses*, A.*Pr*.848; ἔ. εἰμί Id.*Ch*.1026; ἔ. καθίσταμαι I come *to myself*, S.*Aj*.306; ποιητὴς..οὐκ ἔ. ἐστίν Pl.*Lg*.719c; ἀντὶ μανικῶν.. ἕξεις ἔμφρονας ἔχειν ib.791b. 2. to one dead, ἔτ' ἔ. S.*Ant*.1237, cf. Antipho 2.3.2; ἔ. γίγνεσθαι to *recover from* a swoon or lethargy, Hp.*Coac*.136. 3. to one asleep, S.E.*M*.7.129. II. *rational, intelligent*, ζῷα ἔ., opp. εἴδωλα ἄφρ., X.*Mem*.1.4.4; also ζωή, βίος ἔ., Pl.*R*.521a, *Ti*.36e; ἡ πρεσβυτῶν ἔ. παιδιά Id.*Lg*.769a; τέχνη -εστέρα Arist.*Rh*.1359b6; ὅταν ἐς ἥβην ἐξικώμεθ' ἔμφρονες when we come to years *of discretion*, prob. in S.*Fr*.583.6. 2. *sensible, prudent*, Thgn.1126, Pi.*O*.9.74, S.*OT*436; ἔ. σωφροσύνη Th.1.84; ἔ. περί τι *wise* about or in a thing, Pl.*Lg*.809d; τῶν δημιουργῶν ἢ τῶν ἄλλων τῶν ἐ. ἀνδρῶν *experts*, Id.*Hipparch*.226c. Adv. -όνως *sensibly, wisely*, Id.*R*.396d, al., Antiph.104: Comp. -έστερον Phalar.*Ep*.67.3: Sup. -έστατα Plu.*Ant*.14.

**ἐμφῠής,** ές, *inborn*, ἦθος Pi.*O*.11(10).20; *engrafted*, Jul.*Ep*.180.

**ἐμφύλιος,** ον, = ἔμφῡλος (q.v.).

**ἐμφυλλ-ίζω,** *engraft*, *Gp*.10.37.1 (Pass.). **-ιον,** τό, *graft*, Eust.1423.38. **-ισμός,** ὁ, *engrafting, side-graft*, *Gp*.10.75.1. **-ος,** ον, *leafy*, ib.4.15.4.

⊛ **ἔμφῡλος** and **ἐμφύλιος**, ον, the latter being preferred in Trag.: (φῦλον):—*in the tribe*, i.e. *of the same tribe* or *race*, ἀνὴρ ἔμφυλος Od. 15.273; ἐμφύλιοι *kinsfolk*, S.*Ant.*1264 (lyr.), Pl.*Lg.*871a; ἐμφύλιον αἷμα the guilt of *kindred* blood, i.e. the murder *of a kinsman*, Pi. *P.*2.32, Pl.*R.*565e, cf. S.*OT*1406; τοὔμφυλον αἷμα Id.*OC*407; στάσιές τε καὶ ἔμφυλοι φόνοι ἀνδρῶν Thgn.51; ἔμφυλοι παρ' ἑκατέροις *registered in a tribe*, *GDI*5040.15 (Hierapytna). 2. γῆ ἐμφύλιος *one's native* land, S.*OC*1385. II. *in* or *among one's people* or *family*, μάχα Alc.*Supp.*23.11; ἔμφυλος στάσις *intestine* discord, Sol. 4.19, Hdt.8.3, Democr.249; Ἄρης ἐμφύλιος A.*Eu.*863; μάχη Theoc. 22.200; πόλεμος Plb.1.65.2, cf. Plu.*Pomp.*24.

**ἐμφῠρᾱμᾰτοπώλης**, ου, ὁ, *seller of confectionery*, *Gloss.*

**ἐμφύρω** and **-άω** [ῠ], *mix up, confuse*, ἵπποι δ' ἐφ' ἵπποις ἐμπεφυρμένοι A.*Fr.*38, cf. Lyc.1380; Ep. aor. 1 ἐνιφυρήσαντες Opp.*H.*3.498: aor. Med. ἐνεφύραντο v.l. in Lxx *Ez.*22.6: also fr. ἐμφυράω, pf. part. Pass. ἐμπεφυραμένος Archig.ap.Orib.8.2.18.

**ἐμφῡσ-άω**, *blow in*, ἐς τὰς ῥῖνας Aret.*CA*1.2, cf. *POxy.*1088.37; αὐλητρὶς ἐνεφύσησε *breathed into* the flute, Ar.*V.*1219; οἴνῳ ἐ. Hippiatr.11. II. *breathe upon*, τινί, εἴς τινα, Lxx *Jb.*4.21, *Ez.*37.9, cf. *Ev.Jo.*20.22. III. *blow up, inflate*, τὸ μὲν [τῆς τροφῆς] ἐμφυσᾶν, τὸ δὲ σαρκοῦν Arist.*HA*603$^{b}$30; ἐ. τὰς φλέβας Id.*Pr.*881$^{b}$14:—Pass., *to be inflated* or, generally, *swollen*, Hp.*Coac.*154, Arist.*HA*524$^{a}$17, al.: metaph., τῇ κολακείᾳ ἐμφυσώμενος Clearch.25. **-ημα**, ατος, τό, *an inflation* of the stomach, peritoneum, or cellular tissue, mostly of the stomach, Hp.*Epid.*3.17.ιγ', Gal.19.132; *swelling* of the eye, Dem.Ophth.ap.Aët.7.14; of the knee, Gal.12.203. **-ημᾰτώδης**, ες, *like an* ἐμφύσημα, Id.7.609. **-ησις**, εως, ἡ, *inflation*, Plu.2.1077b; *flatulence*, Ath.1.32e (pl.). **-ητέον**, *one must blow in*, *Gp.*16.6.2; εἰς τὰς ῥῖνας ὄξος Herod.Med. in *Rh.Mus.*58.79. **-ητής**, οῦ, ὁ, *one who inflates*, *Gloss.* **-ητικός**, ή, όν, *inflating*, Gal.19.132 (Sup.).

⊛ **ἐμφῡσιόω**, (φύσις) *inspire, infuse life into*, τὴν ἀνάγνωσιν Lxx 1 *Es.* 9.48:—Pass., *to be inspired*, τοῖς ῥήμασιν ib.55. II. *implant, instil into*, τὸ αἰδεῖσθαι ἐμφυσιῶσαί τινι X.*Lac.*3.4; ἐνεφυσίωσαν τοῖς γινομένοις ἐξ ἑαυτῶν τὴν βούλησιν τοῦ θεοῦ *Michel*855.9 (Magn. Mae.):—Pass., μάθησις δεξιῶς ἐμφυσιωθεῖσα Hp.*Lex* 2; ἵνα ἐμφυσιῶται ἑκάστῳ τὸ κάλλιστον Charond.ap.Stob.4.2.24; ἐμπεφυσιωμένη κακία Diog. *Ep.*28.1.

**ἔμφῠσις**, εως, ἡ, *insertion* of a muscle, Gal.*UP*1.21, Orib.25.31.6.

⊛ **ἐμφῠτ-εία**, ἡ, *grafting*, in pl., Arist.*Juv.*468$^{b}$23, Thphr.*HP*1.6. 1, 2.1.4, al. **-ευμα**, ατος, τό, in Roman law, *hereditary leasehold held on cultivating tenure*, Just.*Nov.*7.3.2; *quitrent* paid on such property, *Cod.Just.*1.4.32, *PMasp.*298.40 (vi A.D.). ⊛ **-ευσις**, εως, ἡ, *tenure of such a holding*, Just.*Nov.*7 *Pr.*1, al.; κατ' ἐμφύτευσιν ἔχειν *PMasp.*257.5 (vi A.D.). ⊛ **-ευτής**, οῦ, ὁ, *holder of such an estate*, *PKlein.Form.*314 (v/vi A.D.), Just.*Nov.*7 *Pr.*1. ⊛ **-ευτικός**, ή, όν, *concerning* ἐμφύτευσις or ἐμφυτεύματα, κανών, συγγραφή, ib.7.3.2; δίκαιον *PMasp.*298.39 (vi A.D.). ⊛ **-εύω**, *implant, engraft*, Pl.*Ti.* 70c, *IG*12(7).62.34 (Amorgos):—Pass., Thphr.*CP*1.6.1, etc.; ἐλαίας ἐμπεφυτευμένας ἐν τοῖς κοτίνοις D.S.5.16: metaph., of souls, σώμασιν ἐμφυτευθῆναι Pl.*Ti.*42a. 2. metaph., ἐμφυτεύειν μονάρχους τοῖς Ἕλλησι Plb.2.41.10, cf. 9.29.6; ἐν τῇ ψυχῇ παράδεισον ἀρετῶν Ph. 1.335. II. Pass., of land, *to be granted on terms of* ἐμφύτευσις, *PMasp.*298.17 (vi A.D.), Just.*Nov.*7.3.3.

**ἔμφῠτος**, ον, *inborn, natural*, ἐ. μαντικὴν εἶχε Hdt.9.94; πατρὸς αἷμα S.*OC*1671 (lyr.); τοῖς πλουτοῦσι τοῦτο δ' ἔ. E.*Fr.*776.1, cf. Men. 15.1 D.; ἔρως ἔ. τοῖς ἀνθρώποις Pl.*Smp.*191d; ἡ μὲν [ἰδέα] ἔ. οὖσα, ἐπιθυμία ἡδονῶν Id.*Phdr.*237d, cf. D.60.1; αἰσχροκέρδεια, πονηρία, Din. 1.108; κακία Lxx *Wi.*12.10; ἔ. ἡ ἀρετή, opp. διδακτός, Pl.*Erx.*398c, cf. Lys.33.7; τὸ ἔ. θερμόν Hp.*Aph.*1.14; ἔ. θερμότης Arist.*Mete.*355$^{b}$ 9; οὐκ ἦν ταῦτα τοῖς Ἀθηναίοις πάτρια.. οὐδ' ἔ. D.18.203; τὰν ἔ. αὐτοῖς ἀθεσίαν *IPE*1.185 (Chersonesus). Adv. **-τως** Ph.*Fr.*70H. II. *planted*, χωρίον *PHamb.*23.16 (vi A.D.); ἐλαῖαι *BGU*241.28 (ii A.D.). 2. *implanted*, λόγος *Ep.Jac.*1.21.

**ἐμφύω**, *implant*, θεὸς δέ μοι ἐν φρεσὶν οἴμας παντοίας ἐνέφυσεν *planted* them *in* my soul, Od.22.348; ἐμφῦσαι ἔρωτά τινι X.*Mem.*1.4.7; νόον τινί Eleg.ap.Ath.7.337f, cf. Ph.1.631, al. II. Pass., with pf. ἐμπέφυκα and aor. 2 ἐνέφυν: pf. subj. ἐμπεφύῃ Thgn.396: 1. *grow in* or *on*, τινί, ὅθι τε τρίχες ἵππων κρανίῳ ἐμπεφύασι (Ep. for ἐμπεφύκασι) Il.8.84; τὰ ἐμφυόμενα Hp.*Aër.*5; ἐμφύεσθαι ἐν [νήσῳ] Hdt.2.156: hence of qualities, φθόνος ἀρχῆθεν ἐμφύεται ἀνθρώπῳ *is implanted* in him, Id.3.80; ᾧ (sc. μάντει) τἀληθὲς ἐμπέφυκεν S.*OT*299; τὸ πιστὸν ἐμφῦναι φρενί Id.*OC*1488; πάντ' ἐμπέφυκε τῷ γήρᾳ κακά Id.*Fr.*949; τὸ μῶρον γυναιξὶν ἐμπέφυκε E.*Hipp.*967; οὐδεὶς χαρακτὴρ ἐμπέφυκε σώματι *is set by nature on* the body, Id.*Med.*519; κακία τῇ πόλει ἐμφύεται, X.*Mem.*3.5.17, etc.: the pf. part. abs., *innate*, νόσημα πόλεως ἐ. Pl. *Lg.*736a, cf. 863b. 2. *to be rooted in, cling closely*, ὡς ἔχετ' ἐμπεφυυῖα (Ep. part.) she hung on *clinging*, Il.1.513; ἔν τ' ἄρα οἱ φῦ χειρί *clung fast* to his hand, *clasped* his hand *tight*, as a warm greeting, 6.253, etc.; ἔφυν ἐν χερσί Od.10.397; ἐν χείρεσσι φύοντο 24.410; so χεῖρες.. ἐμπεφυκυῖαι ἦσαν τοῖσι ἐπισπαστῆρσι *stuck fast* to the handles, Hdt.6.91; ἐμφύντε τῷ φύσαντι S.*OC*1113, cf. E.*Ion*891 (anap.); ὀδὰξ ἐν χείλεσι φύντες *biting* the lips *hard*, in suppressed anger, Od.1.381, 18.410, 20.268 (so ἐμφῦσαι ὀδόντας *to fix* the teeth *in*, Ael.*NA*14.8); ἀμὺξ ἐμφῦναι Nic.*Th.*131: c. gen., D.H.11.31 (s.v.l.): abs., ἐμφὺς Hdt.3.109; ἐμφὺς ὡς βδέλλα Theoc.2.56; ἐμπεφυκὼς πόνος *fixed* pain, Archig.ap.Gal.8.110. 3. metaph., *cling to*, ταῖς ἐλπίσι καὶ ταῖς παρασκευαῖς Plu.2.342c; τοῖς ἠθικοῖς καὶ πολιτικοῖς δόγμασι Id.*Cat.Mi.* 4; τοῖς πολεμίοις Id.*Nic.*14; τὴν πόλιν ἀφέντας -φῦναι ταῖς ναυσίν Id. *Them.*9.

**ἐμφωλεύω**, *lurk in*.., Ph.1.315, al., Plu.2.314e, Dam.*Isid.*296, Just. *Nov.*80.9; ἡ κακηγορία -ευε τοῖς ὠσί Men.Prot.p.70 D.; esp. of disease, Aret.*SD*2.13, Gal.17(1).165. II. *dwell in caves* or *lairs*, *OGI*424.5 (Qanawât). III. Act., *hide, conceal*, Horap.2.90.

**ἐμφωνέομαι**, Pass., *to be expressed* in certain terms, *PMasp.*6 ii 118 (vi A.D.).

**ἔμφωνος**, ον, *vocal*, Ael.*NA*15.27.

**ἔμφωτον**, τό, *hollow* of a cone, Hero *Stereom.*1.55.

⊛ **ἐμψάω**, poet. **ἐνιψ-**, *wipe in* or *upon*, Call.*Fr.*121 (Med.).

**ἐμψηφίζω**, *enter* a debt in one's books, Hsch.; cf. ἐνιψηφίζομαι.

**ἔμψηφος**, ον, *adorned with gems*, φιάλη *IPE*1$^{2}$.107 (Olbia).

**ἐμψίω**, *feed with pap*, prob. in A.*Fr.*51, cf. Bgk. ad Hippon.33.

**ἐμψοφ-έω**, *make a noise in*, Hp.*Loc.Hom.*16. **-ος**, ον, *sounding*, *AP*5.243 (Paul. Sil.).

**ἐμψυκτικός**, ή, όν, *cooling*, Gal.11.419; ἀγωγή Id.10.555; ἔμπλαστρος Orib.*Fr.*76. Adv. Comp. **-ώτερον** Aët.15.33.

**ἔμψυξις**, εως, ἡ, *cooling, refreshing*, Aret.*SA*1.9, Ruf.ap.Orib.*inc.* 9.1, Gal.6.626.

**ἐμψῡχ-ήτος**, v.l. for ἔμψυχος in Luc.*Vit.Auct.*6. **-ία**, ἡ, *having life in one, animation*, Epicur.*Fr.*310, Plu.2.1053b, S.E.*P.*2.25, Theo Sm.p.187 H., Dam.*Pr.*18, Simp.*in Ph.*638.2. ⊛ **-ος**, ον, *having life in one, animate*, opp. ἄψυχος, Hdt.1.140, al., Simon.106.4, S.*OC* 1486, E.*Alc.*139, Pl.*Phdr.*245e, al.; ἔ. νεκρός '*a breathing* corpse', S. *Ant.*1167; γῦπες ἔ. τάφοι Gorg.*Fr.*5a D.; μὴ κτείνειν τὸ ἔ., of Empedocles, Arist.*Rh.*1373$^{b}$14, cf. E.*Fr.*472.18 (anap.); ἔμψυχον οὐδὲν ἐσθίει Alex.27.2, cf. 220.3; δοῦλος ἔ. ὄργανον Arist.*EN*1161$^{b}$4; εἶναι τὸν βασιλέα ἔ. νόμον Ph.2.135, cf. Diotog.ap.Stob.4.7.61; ἔμψυχα, τά, *animals*, Th.7.29, *PGiss.*40 ii 22 (iii A.D.): Sup., ὅσα ἐμψυχότατα.. ἦν *most full of vital fluid*, Pl.*Ti.*74e. 2. of diction, *animated, vivid*, λέξεις Arist.*Fr.*129 Bonitz, cf. Luc.*Dem.Enc.*14; so ἔ. ἄγαλμα *AP*12.56 (Mel.); πάθη Longin.34.4: Comp., ἡ ἀληθὴς εὐφημία -οτέρα τῶν Δαιδάλου ἔργων Them.*Or.*28.342d. Adv. **-ως** Plu.2.790f: Sup. **-ότατα** Herm.*in Phdr.*p.61 A. ⊛ **-όω**, *animate*, ἐνεψύχωσε δ' ὁ γλύπτας τὸν λίθον *AP*9.774 (Glauc.):—Pass., *Gp.*15.2.28, Porph. *Gaur.*tit. **-ρία**, ἡ, *cold*, *Placit.*2.4.5. ⊛ **-ρος**, ον, *cold*, Hp.*Epid.* 6.6.2: Comp., Thphr.*Sens.*53. **-ω**, *cool, refresh*, Philonid.ap.Ath. 15.676c, Antyll.ap.Orib.6.4.1, Aret.*CA*2.3, Gal.11.387: aor. 2 part. Pass. ἐμψῠγέντες S.E.*P.*1.51. **-ωσις**, εως, ἡ, *animating*, Gal.4. 763, Plot.4.3.9, Porph.*Gaur.*2.4, al.

⊛ **ἐν**, poet. **ἐνί**, **εἰν**, **εἰνί** (Il.8.199, etc.), forms used by Ep. and Lyric Poets as the metre requires, but only as f.l. in Trag., εἰν S.*Ant.* 1241; εἰνί E.*Heracl.*893: Arc. and Cypr. ἰν *IG*5(2).3.5, al., *Inscr. Cypr.*135.9 H., al.

PREP. WITH DAT. AND ACC. Radical sense, *in, into.*

A. WITH DAT.

I. OF PLACE, 1. *in*, νήσῳ ἐν ἀμφιρύτῃ Od.1.50; ἐν δώμασ' ἐμοῖσιν Il.6.221; ἐνὶ προθύροισιν 11.777; κοίλῃσ' ἐνὶ νηυσί Od.2.27; with names of cities or islands, as ἐν Ἀθήνῃς, ἐν Τροίῃ, Il.2.549, 162; ἡ ἐν Κερκύρᾳ ναυμαχία Th.1.57; ἡ ἐν Σαλαμῖνι μάχη Isoc.5.147 (but in Att. the Prep. is sts. omitted, as with Ἐλευσῖνι, Μαραθῶνι; where ἐν is used, it = *in the district of*.., ἐν Ἐλευσῖνι *IG*2$^{2}$.1028.11, ἐμ Μαραθῶνι ib.1243. 21): ἐν χερσὶν ἐμῇσι *in* my arms, Il.22.426; ἐνὶ θυμῷ Od.16.331, etc.; ἐν αὑτῷ εἶναι to be *in* one's senses, be oneself, ἔτ' ἐν σαυτῷ (v.l. -τοῦ) γενοῦ S.*Ph.*950; also ἐν αὑτοῦ, cf. signf. 2. b. ἐν τοῖς ἰχθύσιν *in* the fish-market, Antiph.125; ἐν τῷ μύρῳ Ar.*Eq.*1375; so ἐν τοῖν δυοῖν ὀβολοῖν ἐθεῶρουν ἄν *in* the two-obol seats, D.18.28. 2. elliptic, in such phrases as ἐν Ἀλκινόοιο Od.7.132, cf. *Leg.Gort.*2.21, etc.; εἰν Ἀΐδαο Il.22.389, Att. ἐν Ἅιδου (v. Ἅιδης): later ἐν τοῖς τινός *PRev. Laws*38.1 (iii B.C.), *Ev.Luc.*2.49; ἐν ἡμετέρου Hdt.1.35, 7.8.δ'; ἐμ Πανδίονος *IG*2$^{2}$.1138.8; ἐν Δημοτιωνιδῶν ib.2.841$^{b}$21; ἐν τῶν πόλεων ib. 1$^{2}$.56.14: mostly with pr.n., but sts. with Appellatives, as, ἐν ἀφνειοῦ πατρός Il.6.47; ἐν ἀνδρὸς εὐσεβεστάτου E.*IA*926; ἐν παιδοτρίβου, ἐν κιθαριστοῦ, *at the school of*.., Ar.*Nu.*973, Pl.*Tht.*206a; ἐν γειτόνων (v. γείτων); ἐν αὑτοῦ (αὑτῷ cod. Rav.) Ar.*V.*642, cf. Men.*Sam.*125; οὐκέτ' ἐν ἐμαυτοῦ ἦν Pl.*Chrm.*155d; ἐν ὑμῶν αὐτῶν γένεσθε Lib.*Or.* 35.15. 3. *in, within, surrounded by*, οὐρανὸς ἐν αἰθέρι καὶ νεφέλῃσι Il.15.192; after Hom., of clothing, armour, etc., ἐν ἐσθῆτι Hdt.2.159; ἐν πεπλώματι S.*Tr.*613; ἐν ἔντεσι Pi.*O.*4.24; ἐν ὅπλοισι *in* or *under* arms, Hdt.1.13, etc.; also of particular kinds of arms, ἐν τόξοις, ἀκοντίοις, etc., *equipped with* them, dub. in X.*Mem.*3.9.2; ἐν μαχαίρῃ *PTeb.* 16.14 (ii B.C.); ἐν μεγάλοις φορτίοις βαδίζειν καὶ τρέχειν X.*Cyr.*2.3. 14; ἐν βαθεῖ πώγωνι Luc.*Salt.*5. 4. *on, at* or *by*, ἐν ποταμῷ Il. 18.521, Od.5.466; ἐν ὄρεσσιν 19.205; οὔρεος ἐν κορυφῇς Il.2.456; ἐν θρόνοις Od.8.422; νευρὴ ἐν τόξῳ the string *on* the bow, Il.15.463; ἐν [ξίφει] ἧλοι 11.29; κατεκλάσθη ἐνὶ καυλῷ ἔγχος was broken off *at* or *by* the shaft, 13.608; ἐν πέτροισι πέτρον ἐκτρίβων S.*Ph.*296; ἐν οἴνῳ *at* wine, prob. in Call.*Ep.*23, Luc.*Dem.Enc.*15. 5. *in the number of, amongst*, freq. in Hom., ἐν Δαναοῖσι, προμάχοισι, μέσσοισιν, νεκύεσσι, Il.1.109, 3.31, 7.384, Od.12.383, al.; οἵη ἐν ἀθανάτοισιν Il. 1.398; and with Verbs of ruling, ἐν δ' ἄρα τοῖσιν ἦρχ' 13.689; ἀνδράσιν ἐν πολλοῖσι.. ἀνάσσων Od.19.110; φῦλον ἐν ἀνθρώποισι ματαιότατον Pi.*P.*3.21; ἐν τοῖς οἰκείοισιν ἀνὴρ χρηστός S.*Ant.*661; ἐν γυναιξὶν ἄλκιμος E.*Or.*754:—for ἐν τοῖς c. Sup., v. ὁ. b. *in the presence of*, ἐν πᾶσι Od.2.194; πτωχὸς ὢν ἐν ἐσθλοῖσιν λέγειν E.*Fr.* 703; λέγοντες ἐν τῷ δήμῳ Pl.*R.*565b; μακρηγορεῖν ἐν εἰδόσι Th.2.36; ἔλεγον ἐν τοῖς τριάκοντα Lys.12.6; ἐν τοῖς ὄχλοις εἰπεῖν Isoc.3.21; λέγειν ἐν ἀνδράσιν (of a woman) Lys.32.11; of a trial, διαγωνίζεσθαι, διαδικάζεσθαι ἔν τισι, Pl.*Grg.*464d, *Lg.*916b; προὐκαλούμην ἐν τοῖς αὐτοῖς δικασταῖς Antipho 6.23. 6. *in one's hands, within one's reach* or

power, νίκης πείρατ' ἔχονται ἐν ἀθανάτοισι θεοῖσι Il.7.102; δύναμις γὰρ ἐν ὑμῖν Od.10.69 (comp. the Homeric phrases θεῶν ἐν γούνασι κεῖται Il.17.514; ἐν γὰρ χερσὶ τέλος πολέμου 16.630); freq. in Hdt. and Att., ἔστιν ἔν τινι, c. inf., it depends *on* him to.., rests *with* him to.., ἔστιν ἐν σοὶ ἤ.. ἤ.. Hdt.6.109, cf. 3.85, etc.; ταῦτα δ' ἐν τῷ δαίμονι καὶ τῇδε φῦναι χἀτέρᾳ S.*OC*1443; ἐν σοὶ γάρ ἐσμεν Id.*OT*314; ἐν σοὶ δ' ἐσμὲν καὶ ζῆν καὶ μή E.*Alc.*278; ἐν ταῖς ναυσὶ τῶν Ἑλλήνων τὰ πράγματα ἐγένετο Th.1.74; ἐν τῷ θεῷ τὸ τέλος ἦν, οὐκ ἐμοί D.18.193; also ἐν τούτῳ εἰσὶν πᾶσαι αἱ ἀποδείξεις depend *on* this, Pl.*Prt.*354e; ἐν τούτῳ λύεται ἡ ἀπορία ἢ ἄλλοθι οὐδαμοῦ ib.321e; ἔν γ' ἐμοί so far as rests *with* me, S.*OC*153 (lyr.); ἐν δὲ σοὶ λελείψομαι E.*Hipp.*324; also ἐν ἐμοί *in* my judgement, S.*OC*1214 (lyr.); ἐν θεοῖς καλά *in the eyes of* the gods, Id.*Ant.*925. **7.** *in respect of*, ἐν πάντεσσ' ἔργοισι δαήμονα φῶτα Il.23.671; ἐν γήρᾳ σύμμετρός τινι *in point of* age.., S.*OT*1112; ἐν ἐμοὶ θρασύς *in* my case, *towards* me, Id.*Aj.*1315; ἐν θανοῦσιν ὑβριστής ib.1092; ἡ ἐν τοῖς ὅπλοις μάθησις Pl.*La.*190d; also οὐδὲν δεινὸν μὴ ἐν ἐμοὶ στῇ stop *with* me, Id.*Ap.*28b. **8.** in a pregnant construction with Verbs of motion, *into*; implying both *motion to* and subsequent *position in* a place, ἐν κονίῃσι χαμαὶ πέσεν *fell* [to the dust and lay] *in* it, Il.4.482, etc.; βάλον ἐν κονίῃσι 5.588; νηῒ δ' ἐνὶ πρύμνῃ ἔνχρα θῆκ' 10.570; ἐν χερσὶ τιθέναι 1.441, etc.; ἐν χερσὶ βαλεῖν 5.574; ἐν στήθεσσι μένος βαλεῖν ib.513; ἐν Τρωσὶν ὅρουσαν 16.258; ἐν χερσὶ πεσέειν 6.81; λέων ἐν βουσὶ θορών 5.161; ἐν δ' οἶνον ἔχευεν ἐν δέπαϊ χρυσέῳ Od.20.261; ἐν τεύχεσσιν ἔδυνον Il.23.131: in Trag. and Att., ἐν ποίμναις πίτνων S.*Aj.*184 (lyr.), cf. 374 (lyr.); ἐν χωρίῳ ἐμπεπτωκώς Th.7.87; ἡ ἐν τῷ Σπειραίῳ τῶν νεῶν καταφυγή Id.8.11; ἐν τόπῳ καταπεφευγέναι Pl.*Sph.*260c; ἐν ᾅδου διαπορευθεὶς Id.*Lg.*905b; ῥιπτοῦντες σφᾶς ἐν τῇ θαλάσσῃ Arr.*An.*1.19.4; later, with Verbs of *coming* and *going*, διαβάντες ἐν τῇ Σάμῳ Paus.7.4.3, cf. Lxx *To.*5.5, Arr.*Epict.*1.11.32, etc.: τὸν ἐν Σικελίᾳ πλοῦν is f.l. in Lys.19.43 codd. **9.** πίνειν ἐν ποτηρίῳ to drink *from* a cup, Luc.*DDeor.*6.2; ἐν ἀργύρῳ πίνειν Id.*Merc.Cond.*26; ἐν μικροῖς D.L.1.104. **10.** ἄργυρος ἐν ἐκπώμασι silver *in the form of* plate, Plu.2.260a; ἐμ φέρνῃ, ἐν θέματι, *as* a dowry, pledge, *PPetr.*1 p.37, *PTeb.*120.125 (i B.C.). **11.** in citations, ἐν τοῦ σκήπτρου τῇ παραδόσει *in* the passage of the Il. describing this, Th.1.9, cf. Pl.*Tht.*147c, *Phlb.*33b.

**II.** Of State, Condition or Position: **1.** of outward circumstances, ἐν πολέμῳ Od.10.553; ἐν δαιτί Il.4.259; ἐν καρὸς αἴσῃ 9.378; ἐν μοίρῃ Od.22.54; οὐμὸς ἐν φάει βίος E.*Ph.*1281; ἐν γένει εἶναί τινι to be related to.., S.*OT*1016; of occupations, pursuits, ἐν φιλοσοφίᾳ εἶναι to be engaged *in* philosophy, Pl.*Phd.*59a, cf. *R.*489b; οἱ ἐν ποιήσι γενόμενοι poets, Hdt.2.82; οἱ ἐν τοῖς πράγμασι ministers of state, Th.3.28; οἱ ἐν τέλει the magistrates, Id.7.73, etc.; τοὺς ἐν ταῖς μοναρχίαις ὄντας Isoc.2.5; ὁ ἐν ταῖς προσόδοις *PPetr.*1 p.62; ὁ μάντις ἦν ἐν τῇ τέχνῃ *in the practice of* it, S.*OT*562. **2.** of inward states, of feeling, etc., ἐν φιλότητι, ἐν δοίῃ, Il.7.302, 9.230; ἐν φόβῳ γενέσθαι Pl.*R.*578e; οὐκ ἐν αἰσχύνῃ τὰ σά E.*Ph.*1276; ἐν σιωπῇ τἀμά Id.*Ion* 1397; ἐν ὀργῇ ἔχειν τινά to make him the object of one's anger, Th.2.21; ἐν ἔριδι εἶναι ibid.; ἐν αἰτίᾳ σχεῖν τινά to blame him, Hdt.5.106; ἐν αἰτίᾳ βαλεῖν S.*OT*656 (lyr.); ἐν αἰτίᾳ εἶναι to have the blame, X.*Mem.*2.8.9, etc.; οἱ ἐν ταῖς αἰτίαις D.*Ep.*2.14. **3.** freq. with neut. Adj., ἐν βραχεῖ, = βραχέως, S.*El.*673; ἐν τάχει, = ταχέως, Id.*OT*765, etc.; ἐν καλῷ ἐστί, = καλῶς ἔχει, E.*Heracl.*971; ἐν ἀσφαλεῖ [ἐστί] Id.*IT* 762; ἐν εὐμαρεῖ [ἐστί] Id.*Hel.*1227; ἐν ἐλαφρῷ ποιήσασθαι Hdt.3.154; ἐν ἴσῳ, = ἴσως, ἐν ὁμοίῳ, = ὁμοίως, Th.2.53: less freq. in pl., ἐν ἀργοῖς, = ἀργῶς, S.*OT*287; ἐν κενοῖς, = κενῶς, Id.*Aj.*971: with a Subst., ἐν δίκᾳ, = δικαίως, opp. παρὰ δίκαν, Pi.*O.*2.16, cf. S.*Tr.*1069, Ar.*Eq.*258, Pl.*R.*475c, al.; ἦσαν οὐκέτι ὁμοίως ἐν ἡδονῇ ἄρχοντες Th.1.99, cf. Pl.*Epin.*977b.

**III.** Of the Instrument, Means or Manner, ἐν πυρὶ πρήσαντες Il.7.429; δῆσαι ἐνὶ δεσμῷ 5.386, cf. Od.12.54, etc.; but in most cases the orig. sense may be traced, to put *in* the fire and burn, *in* fetters and bind, etc.; so ἐν πόνοις δαμέντα A.*Pr.*425 (lyr.); ἔζευξα πρῶτος ἐν ζυγοῖσι κνώδαλα ib.462; ἔργον ἐν κύβοις Ἄρης κρινεῖ Id.*Th.*414; also ἐν ὀφθαλμοῖσιν or ἐν ὄμμασιν ὁρᾶσθαι, ἰδέσθαι, to see *with* or *before* one's eyes, i.e. have the object *in* one's eye, Il.3.306, Od.10.385, etc.; ἔν τε τῇ ὄψει διαγιγνώσκειν καὶ ἐν τῇ ἀκοῇ Pl.*Tht.*206a; also ἐν ὠσὶ νωμῶν ὄρνιθας A.*Th.*25; also ἐν λιταῖς *by* prayers, S.*Ph.*60; ἐν δόλῳ *by* deceit, ib.102; ἐν λόγοις *by* words, A.*Ch.*613 (lyr.); ἀπέκτειναν ἐν τῇ προφάσει ταύτῃ Lys.13.12, cf. Antipho 5.59; ψαύειν ἐν κερτομίοις γλώσσαις S.*Ant.*961 (lyr.); ἐν τοῖς ὁμοίοις νόμοις ποιήσαντες τὰς κρίσεις Th.1.77; esp. with Verbs of showing, σημαίνειν ἐν ἱεροῖς καὶ οἰωνοῖς X.*Cyr.*8.7.3; τὰ πραχθέντα.. ἐν.. ἐπιστολαῖς ἴστε ye know *by* letters, Th.7.11; ἐν τῇδε ῥάβδῳ πάντα ποιήσεις Ezek.*Exag.*132, cf. *PMag.Osl.*1.108. **2.** of a personal instrument, ἐν τῷ ἄρχοντι τῶν δαιμονίων ἐκβάλλει τὰ δαιμόνια *Ev.Matt.*9.34.

**IV.** Of Time, ὥρῃ ἐν εἰαρινῇ Il.16.643; ἐν νυκτί Hdt.6.69, X.*Smp.*1.9; ἐν χρόνῳ μακρῷ S.*Ph.*235, *OC*88; ἐν τούτῳ (sc. τῷ χρόνῳ) *in* this space of time, Hdt.1.126, etc.; ἐν ᾧ (sc. χρόνῳ) *during the time* that, S.*Tr.*929, etc. (also ἐν οἷς Arist.*Mu.*391a2); ἐν ὅσῳ Th.3.28; ἐν ταῖς σπονδαῖς *in the time of* the truce, X.*An.*3.1.1; ἐν τῇ ἑορτῇ Th.7.73 (but in some phrases the ἐν is omitted, as μυστηρίοις *in the course of* the mysteries, Ar.*Pl.*1013; τραγῳδοῖς *at the performance of*.., Aeschin.3.36). **b.** ἐν ἄρχοντι Μητροδώρῳ *during* the archonship of M., *IG*7.1773 (Thebes, ii A.D.); ἐν ἄρχοντι Σύλλᾳ ib.3.113. **2.** *in, within*, ἐν ἡμέρῃ Hdt.1.126; ἐν ἔτεσι πεντήκοντα Th.1.118; ἐν τρισὶ μησὶ X.*HG*1.1.37, etc.; μυρίαις ἐν ἁμέραις *in*, i.e. *after*, countless days, E.*Ph.*305 (lyr.); ἐν ἡμέραις πολλαῖς νοσῆσαι Procop.*Arc.*9.35.

**V.** Of Numbers generally, ἐν δυσὶ σταδίοις *within* two stadia, D.S.20.74, cf. 19.39, dub. in Th.6.1. **2.** with gen. of price, ἐν δύο ταλάντων Lxx 3*Ki.*16.24. **3.** *amounting to*, προῖκα ἐν δραχμαῖς ἐννακοσίαις *BGU*970.14 (ii A.D.), etc.

**B.** With Acc., *into, on, for*, Arc. ἰν, νόμος ἰν ἄματα πάντα *IG*5(2).5; γράψαι ἐν χάλκωμα ib.511; ἐν πελτοφόρας ἀπεγράψατο ib.7.210 (Aegosthenae), etc.; also poet., ἐν πάντα νόμον Pi.*P.*2.86.

**C.** Without Case, as Adverb, in the phrase ἐν δέ.., **1.** *and therein*, Il.9.361; ἐν μέν.. ἐν δέ Od.13.244. **2.** *and among them*, Il.2.588, etc.; in Hdt., mostly ἐν δὲ δή.. 3.39, 5.95; or ἐν δὲ καί.. 2.43, 172, 176. **3.** *and besides, moreover* (not in Att. Prose), S.*Aj.*675, *OT*181 (lyr.), al.; ἐν δ' ὑπέρας τε κάλους τε πόδας τ' ἐνέδησεν ἐν αὐτῇ Od.5.260. **4.** ἔνι, = ἔνεστι, ἔνεισι, Il.20.248, etc.

**D.** Position: ἐν freq. stands between its Subst. and the Adj. agreeing therewith, Il.22.61, B.5.41, etc.: without an Adj., τῷ δ' ἐν ἐρινεὸς ἐστι μέγας Od.12.103: most freq. in Hom. in the form ἐνί, which is then written by anastrophe ἔνι, Il.7.221, Od.5.57; in Pi. between Subst. and gen., χόρτοις ἐν λέοντος *O.*13.44, al.—One or more independent words sts. come between the Prep. and its dat., as in Od.11.115; also in Prose, Hdt.6.69.

**E.** In Compos., **I.** with Verbs, the Prep. mostly retains its sense of being *in* or *at* a place, etc., c. dat., or folld. by εἰς.., or ἐν..: in such forms as ἐνορᾶν τινί τι, in translating, we resolve the compd., to remark a thing *in* one. **b.** also, *at* a person, ἐγγελᾶν, ἐνυβρίζειν τινί. **2.** with Adjs., it expresses **a.** a modified degree, as in ἔμπηλος, ἔμπικρος, ἔνσιμος, *rather*... **b.** the possession of a quality, as in ἔναιμος *with* blood *in it*, ἐνάκανθος thorny: ἔμφωνος *with* a voice: ἔννομος *in accordance with* law, etc. **II.** ἐν becomes ἐμ- before the labials β μ π φ ψ; ἐγ- before the gutturals γ κ ξ χ; ἐλ- before λ; ἐρ- before ρ; rarely ἐσ- before σ; but Inscrr. and Papyri often preserve ἐν in all these cases.

**ἐναβρύνομαι**, fut. -αβρῠνοῦμαι App.*BC*4.68:—*pride oneself on*, c. dat., D.H.*Dem.*5, App. l.c., etc.; χώρα ἐ. ὕδασιν Procop.*Goth.*4.20. **2.** *to be effeminate* in dress, Luc.*Salt.*2, D.C.43.43.

**ἐνάγᾰμαι** [ᾰγ], *admire in*, v.l. for ἐναυγάζομαι (q.v.), Ph.1.449.

**ἐναγγειόσπερμος**, ον, *having the seed in a capsule*, Thphr.*HP*1.11.3, *CP*4.7.5.

**ἐνᾰγείρω**, *gather together in* or *with*, Nic.*Th.*945 (tm.):—Med., A.R.3.347: Ep. aor. part. Pass. ἐναγρόμενος Opp.*H.*2.351.

**ἐνᾰγελάζομαι**, Pass., *assemble like a flock in*, πειρῶ φίλων ἀγέλας ἐ. σου τῇ οἰκίᾳ Epict.*Gnom.*41.

⊛ **ἐνᾰγ-ής**, ές, = ἐν ἄγει ὤν, *under a curse* or *pollution* because of bloodshed, of the Alcmeonidae, Hdt.1.61, 5.70 sq.; ἀπὸ τούτου ἐναγεῖς καὶ ἀλιτήριοι τῆς θεοῦ ἐκαλοῦντο Th.1.126; ἐναγὴς τοῦ Ἀπόλλωνος Aeschin.3.110: Sup., Hermog.*Inv.*1.4. **II.** in S.*OT*656 (lyr.), τὸν ἐναγῆ φίλον one *who has invoked a curse upon his head* (in case of treachery). **-ίζω**, fut. -ιῶ Is.6.51, 7.30:—*offer sacrifice to the dead*, opp. θύω (to the gods), τινί Hdt.1.167; ἐ. τινὶ ὡς ἥρωϊ, opp. θύειν τινὶ ὡς ἀθανάτῳ, Id.2.44, cf. Is.6.51, al., Plb.23.10.17; τοῖς κατὰ πόλεμον τελευτήσασιν *IG*2².1006.26 (ii B.C.): c. acc. rei, ἐ. ἀποπυρίδας τινί Clearch.16; κριόν Plu.*Thes.*4, etc. **-ικός**, ή, όν, *of an* ἐναγής, χρήματα Id.2.825c. **-ιος**, α, ον, *under a curse*, χρόνοι *PMag.Par.*1.844. **-ισμα**, ατος, τό, *an offering to the dead*, Ar.*Fr.*488.12, Arist.*Ath.*58.1, Epicur.*Fr.*217, Luc.*Merc.Cond.*28, D.C.67.9. ⊛ **-ισμός**, ὁ, *offering to the dead*, *CIG*1976 (Thessalonica), 3645 (Lampsacus), J.*AJ*19.4.6 (pl.), Plu.*Pyrrh.*31, D.C.77.12. **II.** generally, *sacrifice*, in pl., J.*BJ*1.1.1, al. **-ιστήριον**, τό, *place for offering to the dead*, *IG*4.203.9 (Corinth).

**ἐναγκᾰλ-ίζομαι**, Med., *take in one's arms*, *AP*7.476.10 (Mel.), Lxx *Pr.*24.48; τέκνα Plu.*Cam.*5, *IG*12(7).395.25 (Amorgos): metaph., Νεῖλος [πόλιν] ἐ. Procop.Gaz.*Ep.*133; of a science, Apollon.Cit.3. **II.** Pass., *to be taken in the arms*, D.S.3.58. **-ισμα**, ατος, τό, *that which embraces*, ὠκεανὸς κόσμου ἐ. Secund.*Sent.*2.

**ἐναγκοινέομαι**, (ἄγκοινα) *hurl like a javelin*, κεραυνόν Eust.839.11.

**ἐναγκῠλ-άω** and -όω, *fit thongs* (ἀγκύλαι II. 2) *to* javelins, for the purpose of throwing them by, ἐναγκυλῶντες X.*An.*4.2.28 (D.S.14.27 has -οῦντες):—Med., Ach.Tat.2.34, Plu.2.18cd (-ούμενον):—Pass., ἀκόντιον ἐνηγκύληται *has a dart ready to throw*, Ael.*NA*5.3. ⊛ **-ίζω**, *fit as it were into a thong* (ἀγκύλη), εἴς τι Plb.27.11.5 (Pass.).

**ἐναγκωνίζω**, Att. fut. -ιῶ, *lean on the elbow*, Hsch.

⊛ **ἐναγλᾰΐζομαι**, Med., = ἐναβρύνομαι, Agath.3.28, Eust.9.43.

**ἔναγμος**, ον, *of a fracture*, περιφέρεια Sor.*Fract.*10.

**ἐναγοράζειν**· ἐναθροίζεσθαι, Hsch.

**ἐναγρόμενος**, v. ἐναγείρω.

**ἔναγρος**· ἔπαγρος, Hsch. **II.** epith. of Apollo at Siphnos, Id.

**ἐναγρυπνέω**, = ἐπαγρυπνέω, c. dat., Lyd.*Mag.*3.58, al.

⊛ **ἔναγχος**, Adv. *just now, lately*, Ar.*Nu.*639, Eup.181.2, Lys.19.50, Pl.*Grg.*462c, D.21.36; τὸ ἔ. Ar.*Ec.*823; opp. πάλαι, Isoc.19.43; τὸ ἔ. πάθος the *recent* misfortune, App.*BC*1.9: c. gen., ἔ. τοῦ χρόνου D.H.7.45.

**ἐνάγω** [ᾰ], *lead in*, Ti.Locr.99e; *bring in*, Anon.*in EN*225.3 (Pass.). **II.** *lead on, urge, persuade*, ἐνῆγόν σφεας οἱ χρησμοὶ Hdt.5.90; ἐνῆγε τῇ συμβουλῇ κελεύων.. Id.3.1, cf. 5.104, Th.4.21, etc.: mostly c. inf., μαίνεσθαι ἐνάγει ἀνθρώπους (sc. Bacchus) Hdt.4.79; ἐνάγει προθυμίη τινὰ ἀποθνήσκειν Id.5.49; ἐνῆγέ σφεας ὥστε ποιέειν Id.4.145; ἐ. τινὰ εἴς τι Plu.*Brut.*46, etc.:—Med., App.*Pun.*65. **2.** c. acc. rei, *urge on, promote*, τὸν πόλεμον Th.1.67, cf. 4.24; τὴν ἔξοδον Id.2.21; τὴν στρατείαν Id.6.15; περί τινος ib.61. **III.** *bring into court, accuse*, κλοπῆς of theft, J.*AJ*2.6.7 (Pass.); ἐ. πρὸς

τινας δίκην *CPR*232.24 (ii/iii A. D.); ὁ ἐνάγων *the prosecutor*, Heph. Astr.3.34; ἐναγόμενος *defendant*, ibid., *Cod.Just.*4.21.16.

**ἐνᾰγωγή**, ἡ, *prosecution, suit, claim*, *Sammelb.*5357.13 (v A. D.), *Cod.Just.*3.10.2, etc.

**ἐνᾰγων-ίζομαι**, Ion. fut. -ιεῦμαι Hdt.3.83:—*compete* in a contest *with*, τινί Id.2.160, 3.83. 2. *take part in*, ἡ τύχη ἐ. τοῖς τῶν ἀνθρώπων βίοις Plb.1.4.5, cf. 5.85.7. II. ἐναγωνίσασθαι εὐμενῆ τοῖς Ἕλλησιν favourable for them *to fight in*, Th.2.74; πεδιὰς ἱππεῦσιν ἐ. ἐπιτήδειος Jul.*Or.*2.6ʹd. ⊕ -ιος, ον, *of* or *for a contest, contending in the games*, παῖς Pi.*N.*6.13; freq. in later Prose, αἱ νῖκαι αἱ ἐ. Arist.*VV* 1250ᵇ37; ἐ. κόσμος Duris70J.; ὄρχησις D.H.7.72, Luc.*Salt.*32. 2. ἐ. θεοί gods *who presided over the games*, esp. Hermes, Pi.*P.*2.10, Simon.18.1, A.*Fr.*384, cf. Ar.*Pl.*1161, *IG*2.1181; Ἀφροδίτη ib.3. 189. II. *of, in* or *for battle*, πυκνώσεις ἐ. closing of the ranks *in battle*, Plb.18.29.2; παρακελευσμός Id.10.12.5; ἐνέργεια D.S.20.95; σχῆμα D.H.6.13; ἀρετή Onos.1.13 (v.l.). III. Rhet., *suited for forensic oratory* or *debate*, λόγος, πνεῦμα, λέξις, D.H.*Is.*20, *Th.*23, *Dem.*18, cf. Demetr.*Eloc.*193; *vehement*, κίνησις D.S.18.67; πάθος Longin.22.1. 2. of style, *energetic, vivid*, opp. διηγηματικός (as epith. of Il. compared with the Od.), Id.9.13, cf. Arg. Od. Adv. -ίως *incisively, vehemently*, Plu.2.771a, Longin.18.2. -ισις, εως, ἡ, *struggle*, Procop.*Goth.*4.32 (s.v.l.).

**ἐνᾰδημονέω**, *to be greatly afflicted in*, ἐρημίαις J.*AJ*15.7.7.

**ἐνᾰδιαφορέω**, *submit to*, τῇ αἰκίᾳ τοῦ Πατρόκλου Sch.Il.17.168.

**ἐνᾰδικός**, ή, όν, *pertaining to unity*, Dam.ap.*AB*1369. Adv. -κῶς Procl. *in Prm.*p.625S.

**ἐνᾰδολεσχέω**, *prate about*, Ph.2.59.

**ἐνάδοντες**· ἐμπεσόντες, Hsch.

**ἐνάδω**, *sing among others*, Arist.*Pr.*918ᵇ22.

⊕ **ἐνᾰείρομαι**, *lift up in*, κῶας χερσίν A.R.4.171.

**ἐνάενος** [ᾰ], ον, *of a year old*, Thphr.*HP*8.11.5, *Stud.Pal.*1.62.33, al. (i A. D.).

**ἐνᾰέξω**, aor. ἐνηέξησα, *produce in*, ἀρούραις Nic.*Al.*102; ἐν μὲν ἀέξειν ποίην, ἐν δὲ νομούς D.P.998.

**ἐνᾰερίζω**, *lift in air*, Hsch.

⊕ **ἐνᾰέριος**, ον, *in the air*, ζῷα Ti.Locr.101c, Gal.*Thras.*40; μεῖξις Luc.*Musc.Enc.*6; opp. ἔγγειος, Them.*Or.*13.168b, cf. Porph.*Gaur.* 10.6.

**ἐνάερος** [ᾰ], ον, *tinted like the air*, χρῶμα Plu.2.915c.

**ἐνᾰετία**, ἡ, *period of nine years*, *PSI*4.281.40 (ii A. D.); cf. ἐνναετία.

**ἐνᾰθλέω**, = ἀθλέω ἐν, τοῖς πολέμοις, ταῖς τοξείαις, D.S.1.54, 3.8; ἐν γυμνασίοις καὶ πόνοις Id.16.44; μαθήμασι Luc.*Am.*45; [ὑπολήψεσι] Arr.*Epict.*3.16.13:—Med., ἐνηθλήσω προνοίᾳ *AP*7.117 (⟨Zenod.⟩). 2. *bear up bravely under*, ταῖς βασάνοις Ael.*VH*2.4; πρὸς τοὺς πόνους Iamb.*Protr.*20.

**ἔναθλος**, ον, *laborious*, πόνοι Ph.1.646. II. ἔναθλον, τό, *contest*, in pl., dub. in *IG*7.2532.

**ἐναθρέω**, = ἀθρέω ἐν, *to look searchingly on* or *in*, Hsch.

**ἐν⟨α⟩θροίζομαι**, gloss on ἐναγοράζειν, Hsch.

**ἐναθύρω** [ῡ], = ἀθύρω ἐν, χοροῖς καὶ μέλεσι Him.*Or.*21.8, cf. 4.9.

**ἐναΐδιος**, ον, (αἶα) *underground*, οἶκος *Epigr.Gr.*321.9; cf. ὑπαΐδιος.

**ἐναιέτια**, τά, (ἀετός III) *pediment-sculptures*, *BSA*16.193 (Parthenon), *IG*1².348.76, 4.1484.112 (Epid.).

⊕ **ἐναιθέριος**, ον, *in upper air*, M.Ant.12.24; θεοί Poll.1.23.

⊕ **ἐναίθομαι**, Pass., *burn in*, Q.S.11.94.

**ἐναίθριος**, ον, *fully exposed*, τόποι Thphr.*CP*5.14.2.

**ἐναικίζω**, *scourge*, *Et.Gud.*188.8, Suid.

**ἐναιλέω**, v. ἐναιρέω.

**ἐναιμάσσω**, = sq., Sch.S.*Ph.*1002.

**ἐναιμ-ἀτόω**, *supply with blood*, Hp.*Oss.*18. -ήεις, εσσα, εν, = sq., κέντρα μύωπος *AP*6.233 (Maec.). ⊕ -ος, ον, *with blood in one*, θεοὶ ἔ. καὶ σαρκώδεις *of* flesh and *blood*, Hdt.3.29; *charged with blood*, opp. ἄναιμος, ἔναιμον καὶ πυκνόν, οἷον ἧπαρ Hp.*VM*22; πλεύμων Arist. *PA*669ᵃ25, al.; ἔναιμα *particles of blood*, Pl.*Ti.*81a; ἐναίμων κολλητικά *bleeding wounds*, Dsc.1.110; τὰ ἔ., of sacrifices, Ph.2.250. 2. τὰ ἔ. *red-blooded animals*, Arist.*HA*489ᵃ30, *PA*665ᵇ11, al. 3. χρῶμα ἔ. *blood*-colour, Pl.*Ti.*68b. 4. metaph., *full of blood, vigorous*, χλωρὰ καὶ ἔ. τὰ πράγματα Gorg.ap.Arist.*Rh.*1406ᵇ9 (nisi leg. ἄναιμα). II. ἔναιμα (sc. φάρμακα) medicaments *for stanching blood*, Hp.*Art.*63: sg., *Fract.*24; φάρμακον ἔ. Thphr.*HP*4.7.2. 2. ἔ. ἀγωγή treatment *of bleeding wounds*, Orib.46.8.15, cf. 45.18.31. Adv. -μως ibid., Antyll.ib.44.23.46. -ότης, ητος, ἡ, *having blood in one*, Hp.*VM*22. -ώδης, ες, *bloody, like blood*, Antipho Soph. 35. -ων, ον, gen. ονος, = ἔναιμος, Hp.*Oss.*19.

**ἐναιονάω**, *foment*, Gal.18(2).838.

**ἐναιρέω**, *capture in* a place, Cret. aor. part. Pass. ἐναιλεθέντος *Leg. Gort.*2.30.

⊕ **ἐναίρω**, also ἐνναίρω v.l. in Batr.274: aor. 2 ἤνᾰρον Pi.*Pae.*6.114, E.*Andr.*1182 (lyr.), (κατ-) S.*Ant.*871 (lyr.); poet. ἔναρον Pi.*N.*10.15, E.*Supp.*821 (hex.); inf. ἐναρεῖν (ἐξ-) Hes.*Sc.*329: later, aor. 1 ἔνηρα (κατ-) Orph.*A.*666:—Med., Il.16.92: 3 sg. aor. 1 ἐνήρατο 5.43, Hes.*Th.*316:—Pass. (v. infr.):—poet. Verb (used by Trag. mostly in lyr. passages), *slay* in battle, freq. in Il.; ῥηΐτεροι ἐναιρέμεν easier *to kill*, 24.244; but also κατ' οὔρεα θῆρας ἐ. 21.485; θῆρα.. τόξοις ἐ. S.*Ph.*956; τοὺς εὐγενεῖς γὰρ κἀγαθοὺς.. φιλεῖ Ἄρης ἐναίρειν Id.*Fr.*724; of a hunter, κάπρους ἔναιρε Pi.*N.*3.47 (cf. ἔναρα):—Med., much like Act., Ἰδομενεὺς δ' ἄρα Φαῖστον ἐνήρατο Il.5.43, cf. 59, 6.32, Od.24.424, Hes.*Th.*316; Τρῶας ἐναιρόμενος Il.16.92; once in the Od., of things, *to make away with, destroy*, μηκέτι νῦν χρόα καλὸν ἐναίρεο *destroy, disfigure* it not, 19.263:—Pass., ἀδελφαῖς χερσὶν ἠναίρονθ' ἅμα A.*Th.* 811; πόλις ἐναίρεται σθένει S.*OC*842 (lyr.).

**ἐναίσαρι**· στερεοῦ· οἱ δὲ ἐνάσαρι, Hsch. **ἐναίσασθαι**· φθαρῆναι, γηράσαι, Id. **ἐναισιμία**· διοσημία, Id.

**ἐναίσ-ιμος**, ον, (αἶσα) Ep. Adj. (rare in Trag.) *ominous, fateful*, οὐδ' ἦλθον ἐναίσιμον (as Adv.) Il.6.519; ὄρνιθας γνῶναι καὶ ἐναίσιμα μυθήσασθαι Od.2.159; οὐδέ τε πάντες ἐναίσιμοι [ὄρνιθες] ib.182; esp. in good sense, *seasonable*, of omens, ἐ. σήματα φαίνων Il.2. 353: generally, *favourable, boding good*, λιγνὺν ἐναίσιμον ἀΐσσουσαν A.R.1.438. II. of persons, their thoughts, etc., *righteous*, ἀνὴρ ὃς ἐ. εἴη Od.10.383; οἵ τινές εἰσιν ἐ. οἵ τ' ἀθέμιστοι 17.363; ᾧ οὔτ' ἂρ φρένες εἰσὶν ἐ. (of Achilles) Il.24.40, cf. Od.18.220; ἐμοὶ νόος ἐστὶν ἐ. 5.190; so τοῦτό γ' ἐναίσιμον οὐκ ἐνόησεν 2.123, 7.299; ἐ. τίει [βίον] A.*Ag.*775 (lyr.); γῆρας γὰρ ἐ. ἄνδρα τίθησι makes him *honoured*, Opp.*H.*1.683. 2. of things, *fit, proper*, ἐ. δῶρα δ. δοῦναι ἀθανάτοις Il.24.425, cf. *h.Cer.*369. Adv. -μως *fitly, becomingly*, αἰνεῖν A.*Ag.* 916; μή νυν ὑπέρβαλλ', ἀλλ' ἐ. φέρε E.*Alc.*1077. ⊕ -ιος, ον, = foreg. I, opp. ἐξαίσιος, D.C.38.13. II. = foreg. II. 1, S.*OC*1482 (lyr.). 2. = foreg. II. 2, ὑβρισμοὺς οὐκ ἐ. A.*Fr.*179.

**ἐναΐσσω**, *rush in*, aor. part. ἐνάξας v.l. (*1 Oxy.*2093) in S.*Aj.*305.

**ἐναισχύνομαι**, *to be ashamed*, c. inf., Sch.S.*Tr.*803, f.l. in D.C.38. 38. (Act. is f.l. in Hsch. s.v. κυπτάζειν.)

**ἐναιτέω**, *claim* a penalty, = Lat. *petere*, prob. in *Supp.Epigr.*1. 161.56.

**ἐναιχμάζω**, *fight in*, Lyc.546, *AP*12.147 (Mel.).

**ἐναιωρ-έομαι**, *float* or *drift about in*, θαλάσσῃ E.*Cyc.*700: abs., *to be always in motion*, ὀφθαλμοὶ ἐναιωρεύμενοι Hp.*Prog.*2. 2. οὖρα ἐνῃωρημένα *containing suspended matter*, Id.*Prorrh.*1.4. 3. -ούμεναι συστάσεις *movable* concretions, Sor.1.88. -ημα, ατος, τό, *suspended matter* in urine, Hp.*Epid.*1.26.ζ, Orib.*Syn.*6.4.7. II. *outer part of an extension apparatus for broken limbs*, Gal.18(2).581.

**ἐνάκανθος** [ᾰκ], ον, *spinous*, Thphr.*HP*3.10.1.

**ἐνᾰκέομαι**, *repair*, τοῖχον *IG*11(2).203*A*55 (iii B. C.).

**ἐνᾰκηδέκᾰτος**, ον, Boeot., *nineteenth*, *IG*7.3172.96, *Schwyzer*485. 41 (Thespiae, iii B. C.).

⊕ **ἐνάκις**, Ep. **εἰνάκις** [ᾰ], Adv. *nine times*, Od.14.230:—usu. written **ἐννάκις** in codd.: **ἐννεάκις** is v.l. in Nicom.*Harm.*8: also **ἐννάκι** δ' ἐννέα Μοῦσαι *AP*14.120.8; **ἐνάκι** Iamb. *in Nic.*p.17P.

**ἐνᾰκισχίλιοι** [χῑ], αι, α, *nine thousand*, Pl.*Ti.*23e (v.l. ἐνν-), *OGI* 214.57 (Milet., iii B. C.); Ion. **εἰνακισχίλιοι** Hdt.3.95, al. (Generally written ἐνν- in codd.)

**ἐνακμάζω**, = εἶναι ἐν ἀκμῇ, τὰ ἐνακμάζοντα ἄνθη Ael.*VH*3.1; of fire, *rage*, Id.*NA*2.8; of cold, ib.16.26: metaph., τῆς ἐπιθυμίας -ούσης αὐτῷ Chor. in *Hermes*17.216: abs., Agath.5.18. II. *flourish in*, πάθος ἐ. τῇ Ἑλλάδι Max.Tyr.25.1; βασιλείοις ὅροις Him.*Or.*7.16; ταῖς Ἑλληνικαῖς Procop.Gaz.*Pan.*501.5.

**ἔνακμος**, ον, = ἐν ἀκμῇ, *in full bloom* or *strength*, Poll.2.10.

**ἐνακολασταίνω**, *indulge one's lust in* or *upon*, τινί Clearch.10.

**ἐνᾰκοντίζω**, *discharge a missile*, *Gloss.*

⊕ **ἐνᾰκόσι-οι**, αι, α, *nine hundred*, Th.5.12, *SIG*495.88 (Olbia, iii B. C.), *IG*5(1).1146.10 (Gytheion, i B. C.), ib.11(2).165.53 (Delos, iii B. C.); Ion. **εἰνακόσιοι** Hdt.2.13, 145. ⊕ -οστός, v. ἐνναк-.

**ἐνᾰκούω**, *hear*, Lxx *Na.*1.12 (Pass.); *obey*, 1*Es.*4.10, Vett.Val 42. 7 (Pass.), *POxy.*120.4 (iv A. D.); *listen to*, c. gen. rei, S.*El.*81. II. *take in* sounds, *be sensitive to*, ἰαχῆς Hp.*Cord.*8, cf. *Liqu.*2: metaph., ἐ. τῆς ξυμφορῆς *to be affected* by it, Id.*Art.*53; ἐνακούει ἐμβαλλόμενα, of dislocations, they *obey* the surgeon's hand, i.e. *are set*, Id.*Fract.*40; ἐ. ἰητρείης *yield to* treatment, Id.*Art.*62.

**ἐνάκρα**, ἡ, *promontory*, Dion.Byz.20.

**ἐναλγής**, ές, *painful*, Paul.Aeg.3.75.

**ἐναλδαίνω**, *cause to grow up on*, aor. 1 ἐνάλδηνα Nic.*Al.*409 (vv. ll. ἐναλδήσασα, ἐνανθήσασα): aor. Med. ἐναλδόμενος *growing in*, πρασιῇσι ib.532.

**ἐνάλ-ειμμα** [ᾰ], ατος, τό, *eyesalve*, Arist.*Pr.*876ᵇ13. ⊕ -ειπτος, ον, *anointed with*, Hp.*Acut.*(*Sp.*)65. -είφω, *anoint with*, τί τινι Id.*Morb.*2.36; ὀφθαλμοὶ ὀστρείῳ ἐναληλιμμένοι Pl.*R.*420c:—Med., *anoint onself*, *AP*11.112 (Nicarch.); ἐ. τὰς ῥῖνας *one's* nose, Alex. 190; τὴν κόμην φαρμάκῳ Plu.2.771b; τὼ ὀφθαλμὼ Hld.7.14. II. *paint within* outlines, ὑπογράψαντες ταῖς γραμμαῖς οὕτως ἐναλείφουσι τοῖς χρώμασι τὸ ζῷον Arist.*GA*743ᵇ24: generally, χύδην ἐ. Id.*Po.* 1450ᵇ1:—Pass., τὸ ἐναλειφθὲν *coat of stucco*, interpol. in Id.*GA*726ᵇ27.

**ἐνᾰλήθης**, ες, *accordant with truth*, Longin.15.8. Adv. -θως *probably*, Luc.*VH*1.2.

**ἐνᾰλίγκιος**, ον, also η, ον A.R.3.857:—*like, resembling*, c. dat., Il. 5.5, al., Parm.8.43, Theoc.22.94, etc.: c. acc. rei, θεοῖς ἐναλίγκιος αὐδήν Od.1.371; χεῖρας Ἄρεϊ Pi.*I.*8(7).41: neut. as Adv., Man.6. 443.—Poet. word.

**ἐνᾰλινδέομαι**, Pass., *to be involved in*, συμφορῇσι v.l. in Hp.*Ep.*17; *wallow in*, ὥσπερ πορνείῳ τῇ πόλει J.*BJ*4.9.10. (Act. only Hsch. ἐναλῖσαι· ἐγκυλῖσαι.)

⊕ **ἐνᾰλίνω**, Cypr. **ιναλίνω**, *engrave, inscribe*, pf. part. Pass ἰναλαλισμένα *Inscr.Cypr.*135.26 H.

⊕ **ἐνάλιος** [ᾰ], α, ον, and ος, ον E.*Andr.*855 (nisi leg. ἐνάλου), Plu. *Luc.*39: Ep. and Lyr. also **εἰνάλιος**, α, ον (ος, ον E.*Hel.*526, lyr.): (ἅλς B):—*in, on, of the sea*, κῆτος, κορῶναι, Od.4.443, 5.67, etc.; νομός Archil.74.8; εἰνάλιον πόνον ἐχοίσας βαθὺν σκευᾶς ἑτέρας while the rest of the tackle is at work fishing deep *in the sea*, Pi.*P.*2.79, cf. Theoc.21.39; ἐ. πόροι A.*Pers.*453; ἐ. θεός, of Poseidon, S.*OC*888 (troch.), 1493 (lyr.); ἐ. λεώς *seamen*, Id.*Aj.*565; πόντου εἰναλία

φύσις, i.e. the fish, Id.*Ant.*345 (lyr.); of islands, ἐ. Εὐβοῦς αἶα Id.*Fr.*255; ἐ. χθών, of Tyre, E.*Ph.*6.—Poet. word, used in later Prose, ἐ. νῆσοι Arist.*Mu.*392$^{b}$19; δίαιται Plu.*Luc.*39; ὄργανα Porph.*Antr.*35.

**ἐνᾰλίσκομαι,** *to be convicted in,* ᾠκοδόμηται τὰ δικαστήρια τοῖς πονηροῖς -ίσκεσθαι Lib.*Decl.*16.28; ἐναλόντα· συλληφθέντα, κρατηθέντα, Hsch.

**ἐνᾰλῐταίνω,** = ἀλιταίνω ἐν, aor. 2 ἐνήλῐτον Q.S.13.400, 14.436.

**ἐναλλ-άγδην,** Adv. = ἐναλλάξ, *AP*5.301.16 (Agath.), Man.4.181, Doroth.ap.Heph.Astr.3.30, Agath.1.12, al. ⊛ **-ᾰγή,** ἡ, *interchange,* κατ' ἐναλλαγὰν *alternando,* of proportion, Ti.Locr.99b. **2.** Gramm., *interchange,* στοιχείων S.E.*M.*9.278; πτώσεως A.D.*Pron.*54.13; χρόνων D.H.*Th.*24; ἡμερῶν *POxy.*1413.22 (iii A.D.); κεφαλαίων Hermog.*Stat.*11: abs., *enallage,* A.D.*Synt.*157.12. **II.** *variation,* τῶν ὑποκειμένων Plot.2.6.3; τῶν ζῳδίων Ptol.*Tetr.*152 (pl.); *change,* Lyd. *Mag.*2.16. **-αγμα,** ατος, τό, *change*: in pl., *perverse actions,* Aq. *Is.*66.4. **-άκτης,** ου, ὁ, *perverse person,* ib.3.4. **-ακτικός,** ή, όν, *altering.* προαιρέσεως ἐ. σχέσις *Placit.*1.29.1: hence, *perverse, wanton,* Aq.*De.*22.14. **-άξ,** Adv. *crosswise,* οὐδ' ἴσχειν τὼ πόδ' ἐ. Ar.*Nu.*983, cf. Hp.*Mul.*2.144, *IG*2$^{2}$.463.80. **2.** Math., *alternando,* Arist.*EN*1131$^{b}$6, *APo.*74$^{a}$18, 99$^{a}$8; *permutando,* Euc.5*Def.*12. **3.** *alternately,* Pi.*N.*10.55, Pl.*Criti.*113d, 119d; [γέρανοι] καθεύδουσιν ἐπὶ ἑνὸς ποδὸς ἐ. Arist.*HA*614$^{b}$25; ἐ. ἐναντίως *alternately* contrariwise, Id. *IA*712$^{a}$13; of the teeth of carnivorous animals, ἐ. ἐμπίπτουσιν Id.*PA*661$^{b}$21; πρήσσειν ἐ. to have *alternations* of fortune, Hdt.3.40: c. dat., ἤν τε μὴ ἐ. αἱ εὐτυχίαι τοι τῇσι πάθῃσι προσπίπτωσι *alternately with* misfortunes, ibid.; ἐ. ἀλλήλοις Aen.Tact.26.1: c. gen., D.S.5.7. **4.** *in inverted order, upside down,* Lib.*Descr.*13.8. **-αξις,** εως, ἡ, *crossing, interlacing,* φλεβῶν Arist.*PA*668$^{b}$26, cf. Olymp.*in Mete.*31.20. **II.** Gramm., = ἐναλλαγή, Longin.23.1 (pl.). **-ασσομένως,** Adv. *by enallage,* A.D.*Synt.*260.15. **-άσσω,** Att. **-ττω,** pf. ἐνήλλαχα Plb.6.43.2, Phld.*Mus.*p.73K.:—*exchange,* φόνον θανάτῳ ἐ., i.e. *pay for* murder by death, E.*Andr.*1028 (lyr.); μεταβολὰς ἐ. *undergo* changes, Plb. l.c.; παντοίας μορφὰς ἐ. *to assume..,* Apollod.2.5.11: c. inf., ἐνήλλαξεν θεὸς τὴν τοῦδ' ὕβριν πρὸς μῆλα..πεσεῖν *turned aside, diverted* his fury so as to fall upon the sheep, S.*Aj.*1060. **2.** *cross,* τὼ πόδε Philostr.*Im.*2.7; also intr., *cross one another,* of veins and arteries, Arist.*PA*668$^{b}$21. **3.** Astrol., *exchange domicile,* of planets, Vett.Val.73.15. **4.** ἐχρῆν ἐνηλλαχέναι one should *have reversed* the statement, Phld. l.c. **II.** *give in exchange,* τι ἀντί τινος App.*BC*3.27, 5.12:—Med., *receive in exchange,* τί δ' ἐνήλλακται τῆς ἡμερίας νὺξ ἥδε βάρος; what heavy *change* from the day *hath* this night *received?* S.*Aj.*208, cf. Ph.2.638. **III.** Pass., *to be interarticulated,* ἄρθρα ἐνηλλαγμένα Hp.*Art.*46; also τὸ μέτρον τοῖς δισυλλάβοις ἐναλλάσσεται the metre *employs* the various disyllabic feet *interchangeably,* Anon.Metr.*Oxy.*220 iii 13. **2.** *have commercial relations with,* ὅσοι Ἀθηναίοις ἤδη ἐνηλλάγησαν Th.1.120.

**ἐναλλοι-όω,** *alter, PSI*5.483 (iii B.C.):—Pass., Ph.2.659, Herm. ap.Stob.3.11.31. ⊛ **-ωσις,** εως, ἡ, *alteration,* Ptol.*Tetr.*93.

⊛ **ἐνάλλομαι,** fut. -ᾰλοῦμαι Plu.2.1087b: aor. 1 -ηλάμην S.*OT*263, etc.: aor. 2 -ηλόμην (v. infr.):—*leap in* or *on,* ὡς ἄγαν βαρὺς ποδοῖν ἐνήλου..γένει A.*Pers.*516, cf. X.*HG*2.4.16, D.54.8; τινὶ τῷ σκέλει Philem.1.5D.; εἰς τὸ κείνου κρᾶτ' ἐνήλαθ' ἡ τύχη S.*OT*263; εἰς τὸν ποταμόν Wilcken *Chr.*11*A*42; εἰς τὸν ἀσκόν Corn.*ND*30; εἰς τὴν γαστέρα Plu.*Luc.*11. **2.** *rush at* or *against,* πύλαις ἐνήλατο S.*OT*1261, cf. Ar.*Ra.*39. **3.** abs., *jump about, dance,* Id.*V.*1305.

⊛ **ἔναλλος,** ον, *changed, contrary,* Theoc.1.134, *AP*5.298 (Agath.). Adv. -λως Plu.2.1045e.

**ἔνᾰλος,** ον, = ἐνάλιος, πόλις *h.Ap.*180, Critias *Fr.*2.7D.; ἀκταί E. *Hel.*1130 (lyr.), Tim.*Pers.*100; πρῷραι E.*El.*1348 (anap.); ἐ. θρέμματα Arion 1.9; in later Prose, κώπη, opp. ἔξαλος, S.E.*M.*7.414.

**ἐνᾰλύω,** = ἀλύω ἐν, *revel in, exult over,* c. dat., ἐ. καὶ ἐνυβρίζειν Ph.2.369, cf. 372; simply, *dwell upon,* ὅταν ἐναλύῃ αὐτοῖς ὁ λόγος Philostr. *Im.*2.8; θεραπείᾳ τῇ περὶ τὴν θεὸν ἐ. Hld.7.9; κόμη ἐναλύουσα τῷ μετώπῳ hair *hanging wildly over* the face, Philostr.*Im.*1.10.

**ἐνᾰμάομαι,** Med., *heap upon,* Sch.S.*Ant.*255 (nisi leg. ἐπ-).

⊛ **ἐνάμαρτος** [ᾰμ], ον, *faulty,* and Adv. -τως, *Gloss.*

**ἐναμβλύνω,** *deaden* or *discourage besides,* τοὺς συνάρχοντας Plu.*Nic.*14.

⊛ **ἐνᾰμείβω,** *change, alter,* Lyd.*Mag.*3.39.

**ἐνᾰμέλγω,** *milk into,* γαυλοῖς Od.9.223.

**ἐνᾰμιλλ-άομαι,** = ἁμιλλάομαι, πρός τι Them.*Or.*21.254c. **-ος** [ᾰ], ον, (ἅμιλλα) *engaged in equal contest with, a match for,* τὴν φύσιν ἐ. τοῖς ἡλικιώταις Pl.*Prt.*316b, cf. Isoc.5.68; ἐ. τινὶ πρός τι Pl.*R.*433d, *Criti.*110e, cf. Arist.*Pol.*1283$^{a}$5; τοῖς πολίταις ἐ. παρασκευάζων ἑαυτόν *IG*2$^{2}$.835.12, cf. Plu.*Comp.Ag.Gracch.*3; τὰ λοίπ' ἐ. τούτοις *on a par with,* D.25.54; τοῖς κρατίστοις ἐ. τὸν κυνισμὸν εἶναι Jul.*Or.*6.182c. Adv. -λως, τινί *equally with,* Isoc.12.7.

**ἔναμμα,** ατος, τό, (ἐνάπτω) *thing bound* or *tied on, thong,* ἔ. ἀγκύλης Plu.*Phil.*6. **2.** *garment, covering,* ἔ. νεβρίδος a deerskin *cloak,* D.S.1.11.

⊛ **ἐνᾰμοιβᾰδίς,** Adv. = ἀμοιβαδίς, *alternately* or *one after another,* A.R.1.380, 4.1030.

**ἐναμπέχομαι,** Pass., *to be clad in,* τι Ph.1.635.

**ἐναμπῠκίσαι·** ἐγχαλινῶσαι, Hsch.

**ἐνανάπτω,** *tie,* dub. in Gal.18(1).750.

⊛ **ἐναναστρέφομαι,** Pass., *to be conversant with,* τινί Aristox.ap.Stob.3.1.49, Hsch. s.v. ἐγκαλινδεῖται.

**ἔνανδρον·** κενὸν ἀνδρῶν, Hsch. (leg. ἄν- vel κέν-).

**ἐνανειλέω,** *roll back,* in Pass., dub. in Gal.6.177.

**ἐνανθέω,** f.l. for ἐναλδαίνω, Nic.*Al.*409.

⊛ **ἐνανθρωπέω,** *put on man's nature,* ψυχὴ -ήσασα Hld.2.31.

**ἔναντα** (ἐνάντᾳ Tim.*Pers.*11), Adv. *opposite, over against,* c. gen., ἔ. Ποσειδάωνος ἄνακτος ἵστατ' Ἀπόλλων Il.20.67; τοὶ δ' ἔ. στάθεν Pi. *N.*10.66; τὸν δ' ἔ. προσβλέπειν νεκρόν S.*Ant.*1299 (lyr.); ἔ. ἐλθεῖν E. *Or.*1478 (lyr.).

**ἔναντι,** Adv. *in the presence of,* c. gen., Lxx *Ge.*12.19, al., *IG*7.2225.52 (Thisbe, ii B.C.), *Ev.Luc.*1.8, *GDI*2072.26 (Delph.); cf. ἔναντι.

**ἐναντῐ-αῖος,** α, ον, *of contrary nature,* Hp.*Liqu.*2. ⊛ **-βῐος,** ον, *set against, hostile,* αἰθυίαις οὔποτ' ἐναντίβιος *AP*10.8 (Arch., Herm. for οὔποτε ἀντιβίας): elsewh. neut. as Adv., *face to face, against,* μαχέσασθαι, πολεμίζειν, Il.8.168, 10.451, etc.; ἐλθεῖν 20.130; στῆναι 21.266: c. gen., Ἀχιλῆος ἐ. πολεμίξειν 20.85.—Only poet.

⊛ **ἐναντῐο-βουλία,** ἡ, *contrary purpose,* Vett.Val.201.13. ⊛ **-βουλος,** ον, *of contrary purpose,* Polem.*Phgn.*66, Vett.Val.61.28, al. **-γνώμων,** ον, gen. ονος, (γνώμη) *of contrary opinion,* ib.29: gloss on ἀγνώμων, Sch.S.*OC*86. **-δρομέω,** *run opposite ways*: hence, *go the opposite way,* Thphr.*Vent.*28; ἐ. ἀλλήλοις Str.16.1.5. **-δρομία,** ἡ, *running contrary ways, Placit.*1.7.22: prob. for ἐναντιοτροπή, D.L.9.7. **-δύνᾰμος** [ῠ], ον, *of opposite function* (as odd and even), Nicom.*Ar.*1.9. **2.** gloss on ἀντίβιος, Eust.108.3. **-ζύγως** [ῠ], Adv. *in an opposite series, Theol.Ar.*11. **-θετος,** ον, Astrol., *in opposition, Cat.Cod.Astr.*8(4).148. ⊛ **-λογέω,** *contradict,* αὐτὸν αὑτῷ Pl.*Sph.*268b: abs., Str.15.1.3. **-λογία,** ἡ, *contradiction,* -ίᾳ συνέχεσθαι Pl.*Sph.*236e, cf. Arist.*GC*323$^{b}$17. **-λογικός,** ή, όν, *given to contradicting,* Gal.*Anim.Pass.*1.3.

**ἐναντίον,** Adv., v. ἐναντίος.

**ἐναντῐό-ομαι,** Ion. part. ἐναντιεύμενος Hdt.7.49: impf. ἠναντιούμην Th.1.127, etc.:—Med., fut. -ώσομαι A.*Pr.*786, Ar.*Pax*1049, etc.:—Pass., fut. ἐναντιωθήσομαι Lxx 4*Ma.*5.26, D.H.4.51: aor. ἠναντιώθην And.1.67, Pl.*Ap.*32b, etc.: pf. ἠναντίωμαι Th.2.40 codd., etc., but in Ar.*Av.*385 the metre requires ἐνηντίωμαι:—*set oneself against, oppose, withstand,* τινί And.1.67, cf. Hdt.7.49, Th.1.127, Ar.*Av.*385, *Pax*1049; also ἐ. ὑπὲρ τῆς ἐλευθερίας Lys.13.17; ὑπὲρ ὑμῶν Id.20.8; τινί τινος Th.1.136, X.*An.*7.6.5: abs., Th.4.21: c. inf., οὐκ ἐναντιώσομαι τὸ μὴ οὐ γεγωνεῖν I *will* not *refuse* to speak, A.*Pr.*786; τοὺς χορευτὰς ἐναντιούμενος ἡμῖν ἀφεθῆναι τῆς στρατείας D.21.15. **2.** *contradict, gainsay,* E.*Alc.*152; πρός τι Pl.*Cra.*390e, etc.: c. inf., τοῦτο..μοι ἐ. τὰ πολιτικὰ πράττειν Id.*Ap.*31d: with a neg., τίς ἐναντιώσεται μὴ οὐχὶ..εἶναι; Id.*Smp.*197a. **3.** of the wind, *to be adverse,* οὐκ ἔστι λῃσταῖς πνεῦμ' ἐναντιούμενον S.*Ph.*643; of circumstances, Th.8.23; ἄνεμοι ἐ. ἀλλήλοις Hp.*Aër.*8. **4.** τὰ ἐς ἀρετὴν ἐνηντιώμεθα τοῖς πολλοῖς in respect of goodness we *are the opposite of* most men, Th.2.40; *behave in the opposite way,* Meno *Iatr.*15.41. **5.** Astrol., *to be in diametrical aspect,* Vett.Val.126.5. (Act. only in doubtful form ἐναντιόωντα Man.4.473.) **-πᾰθέω,** *have contrary properties,* Nicom.*Harm.*4, *Theol.Ar.*10. **-πᾰθής,** ές, *of contrary properties.* Adv. -θῶς Nicom.*Harm.*10. **-πετής,** gloss on παλιμπετής, Hsch. **-ποιολογικός,** ή, όν, *of* or *for making contradictions,* -κή (sc. τέχνη), ἡ, Pl. *Sph.*268c. **-πρᾱγέω,** *oppose,* D.S.3.65, 4.49, al.

**ἐναντίος,** α, ον, *opposite,* = ἀντίος (which is rare in Prose): **1.** of place, *on the opposite side, opposite,* c. dat., ἀκταὶ ἐναντίαι ἀλλήλῃσιν Od.10.89; Πάτροκλος δέ οἱ..ἐ. ἧστο Il.9.190, cf. Od.23.89: hence, *fronting, face to face,* αὐτῳ οὔ πω φαίνετ' ἐναντίη 6.329; ὄττις ἐ. τοι ἰσδάνει Sapph.2.2; δεῖξον..τὸ σὸν πρόσωπον δεῦρ' ἐ. πατρί *before* him, E.*Hipp.*947; τἀναντία τινί *things open to* one's *sight,* X.*Cyr.*3.3.45: abs., ἐ. στάνθ' E.*Hipp.*1078 (but ἐ. κεῖσθαι look *opposite* ways, Pl.*Smp.*190a). **b.** with Verbs of motion, *in the opposite direction,* ἔνθα οἱ..ἐναντίη ἤλυθε μήτηρ came *to meet* him, Il.6.251; ἐναντίοι ἀλλήλοισιν ὄγμον ἐλαύνωσιν 11.67; δύο ἅμαξαι ἐ. ἀλλήλαις Th.1.93; ἄνεμος ἐ. ἔπνει X.*An.*4.5.3. **c.** Astrol., *in diametrical aspect,* Vett.Val.70.16, Man.3.360. **2.** in hostile sense, *opposing, facing* in fight, c. gen., ἐναντίοι ἔσταν Ἀχαιῶν Il.5.497, cf. S.*Aj.*1284, X.*An.*4.3.28, etc.: c. dat., Il.5.12, E.*Supp.*856, *IT*1415; οἱ ἐ. *one's adversaries,* A. *Th.*375, Gorg.*Fr.*12D., etc.; *the enemy,* Hdt.7.225, Th.4.64, etc. **b.** generally, *opposed to,* τινί X.*An.*3.2.10; τὸ ἐ. *the opposite party,* Id. *Ath.*1.4; *presenting obstacles, hindering,* τινί S.*Ph.*642. **c.** ὁ δι' ἐναντίας the *opponent* in a lawsuit, *PFlor.*1.58.15 (iii A.D.), etc. **3.** of qualities, acts, etc., *opposite, contrary, reverse,* τἀναντί' εἰπεῖν A.*Ag.*1373; δίκαια καὶ τἀναντία S.*Ant.*667: mostly c. gen., τὰ ἐ. τούτων the *very reverse* of these things, Hdt.1.82, cf. Th.7.75, etc.; δείξας..ἄστρων τὴν ἐ. ὁδόν, i.e. τὴν τοῦ ἡλίου ὁδὸν ἐ. οὖσαν τοῖς ἄστροις E.*Fr.*861: also c. dat., Ὀρφεῖ δὲ γλῶσσαν τὴν ἐναντίαν ἔχεις A.*Ag.*1629; τἀναντία πρήσσειν [τῇ ὑγιείῃ] Democr.234; δύο τὰ -ώτατα εὐβουλίᾳ Th.3.42; ἀγαθῷ κακὸν -ώτερον ἢ τῷ μὴ ἀγαθῷ Pl.*R.*491d; ἐναντία λέγει αὐτὸς αὑτῷ Id.*Prt.*339b, cf. Ar.*Ach.*493; τἀναντία τούτοις Pl.*Prt.*323d; ἐναντία γνῶναι ταῖς πλείσταις [πόλεσιν] X.*Lac.*1.2; τὴν ἐ. τινὶ ψῆφον θέσθαι D.19.65; simply τὴν ἐ. θέσθαι τινί Pl.*La.*184d: folld. by ἤ, τοὺς ἐ. λόγους ἢ ὡς αὐτὸς κατεδόκεε Hdt.1.22; τοὐ. δρῶν ἢ προσῆκ' αὐτῷ ποιεῖν Ar.*Pl.*14; τοὐ. ἔπαθεν ἢ τὸ προσδοκώμενον Pl.*Lg.*966e, cf. *R.*567c, etc.: freq. strengthd., πᾶν τοὐ., πάντα τἀ., quite *the contrary, Lg.*967a, X.*Mem.*3.12.4; πολὺ τοὐ. Stratt.57; τὸ δὲ πολὺ ἐναντίον ἀποβήσεται Pl.*Ap.*39c. **b.** τὰ ἐ. *opposites* in Philos., Pherecyd.Syr.3, Arist.*Metaph.*986$^{b}$3, etc. **4.** in the Philos. of Arist., τἀναντία (dist. fr. other ἀντικείμενα, *Metaph.*1018$^{a}$25) are *contraries,* esp. the two attributes within the same genus which differ most widely from each other (as hot and cold), *Cat.*6$^{a}$18, al. **b.** ἐ. ἀποφάνσεις, προτάσεις, *contrary* propositions (All *B* is *A*, No *B* is *A*), opp. *contradictory* (v. ἀντιφατικῶς), Id.*Int.*17$^{b}$4, *APr.*63$^{b}$28. **II.** freq. in Adv.

usages: 1. from Hom. downwds., neut. ἐναντίον as Adv., *opposite, facing*, ἐ. ὧδε κάλεσσον here *to my face*, Od.17.544; εἰς ὦπα ἰδέσθαι ἐ. to look one *in the face*, 23.107; ἐ. προσβλέπειν τινά E.*Hec*.968, etc.; γυναῖκας ἀνδρῶν μὴ βλέπειν ἐ. ib.975: abs., D.4.40, etc.: hence, like a Prep. c. gen., *in the presence of*, τῆς βουλῆς *IG*1².91; τῶνδ' ἐ. S.*OC*1002; μαρτύρων ἐ. Ar.*Ec*.448; ἐ. τοῦ παιδίου Id.*Lys*.907; ἐ. ἁπάντων λέγειν Th.6.25; ἐ. Διός Plb.7.9.2; also neut. pl., *IG*7.1779 (Thespiae). b. in hostile sense, *against*, c. gen., ἀνέσταν.. σφοῦ πατρὸς ἐ. Il.1.534; ἐ. ἰέναι τινός 21.574; ἐ. μάχεσθαί τινος 20.97; ἐ. ἵστασ' ἐμεῖο 13.448: abs., ἐ. μίμνειν stand one's ground *against*, ib. 106: c. dat., νεικεῖν ἀλλήλοισιν ἐ. 20.252; ἐ. θεοῖς E.*Or*.624; ἐ. τῷ ὅρκῳ πράττειν *IG*2².1258.2. c. *contrariwise*, in Att. also with the Art., τοὐναντίον *on the other hand*, τοὺ. δέ.. Antiph.80.4; ἢ πάλιν τοὐ. Men.460.5; *conversely*, Pl.*Men*.89e. d. neut. pl. ἐναντία as Adv., c. dat., Hdt.6.32, Th.1.29, etc. 2. with Preps., ἐκ τοῦ ἐ. *over against, opposite*, opp. ἐκ πλαγίου, X.*HG*4.5.15, etc.; ἐξ ἐναντίας, Ion. -ίης, Hdt.7.225, Th.4.33; οἱ ἐξ ἐ. the *opposing parties*, prob. in *PGrenf*. 2.78.26 (iv A. D.); ἐκ τῶν ἐ. *on the contrary*, Plb.5.9.9; ἀπ' ἐναντίας Ascl.*Tact*.1.2; ἀπ' ἐ. χωρεῖν Procop.*Arc*.4; κατὰ τὰ ἐ. Pl.*Ti*.39a: Geom., αἱ κατ' ἐναντίον τοῦ παραλληλογράμμου πλευραί the *opposite* sides of the parallelogram, Archim.*Aequil*.1.9; αἱ κατ' ἐ. τομαί *opposite* sections (i.e. branches) of the hyperbola, Apollon.Perg.*Con*. 3.23. 3. regul. Adv. -ίως *contrariwise*, c. dat., τούτοις οὐκ ἐ. λέγεις A.*Eu*.642; ἐ. διακεῖσθαί τινι Pl.*R*.361c; ἐ. ἀντικεῖσθαι Arist.*Int*.17ᵇ 20; πικρῶς καὶ ἐ. *like an enemy*, D.19.339; ἐ. ἢ ὡς ἀνδραπόδοις τραφεῖσι Pl.*Tht*.175d; ἐ. ἔχειν to be *exactly opposed*, Id.*Euthd*.278a; πρός τι to be *contrary* in respect of.., D.1.4; in the Logic of Arist., *Metaph*.1057ᵇ11, al., cf. Procl.*in Alc*.p.268C.

**ἐναντιότης**, ητος, ἡ, *contrariety, opposition*, Pl.*Phd*.105a, A.D.*Conj*. 253.16, Ph.1.7, etc.; πρὸς ἀλλήλω Pl.*Tht*.186b, etc.: pl., Ocell.2. 4. II. in the Philos. of Arist., *contrariety*, *Int*.21ᵃ29, *EN*1108ᵇ 27; v. ἐναντίος I. 4.

**ἐναντῐο-τροπία**, ἡ, *contrariety of character*, τῶν ἐθνῶν Aristid.Quint. 2.13. **-φᾰνής**, ές, *containing an apparent contradiction*, Sch.E.*Or*. 424. **-φημος**, ον, *contradicting oneself*, gloss on παλίγγλωσσος, Sch.Pi.*N*.1.88. **-φρων**, ον, gen. ονος, = ἐναντιογνώμων, *Cat.Cod. Astr*.8(4).194. **-φωνος**, ον, *contradicting*, Hsch. s. v. ἀντίφωνα.

**ἐναντῐ-όω**, v. ἐναντιόομαι. **-πέρᾱ**, Adv. *on the opposite side*, *Epigr. Gr*.981.6 (Philae). **-ωμα**, ατος, τό, *anything opposite* or *opposed, obstacle, hindrance*, Th.4.69, D.18.308, Plu.*Lys*.23; ἐχθροῖς ἐναντιώματα *opposition offered* to them, D.18.309. 2. *incompatibility*, Pl. *R*.524e: pl., *conflicting impulses*, ib.603d; *differences, discrepancies*, πρός τι Arist.*PA*695ᵃ18. **-ωμᾰτικός**, ή, όν, *marking opposition*, σύνδεσμος D.T.643.14, A.D.*Conj*.251.3. Adv. -κῶς Eust.809. 36. **-ωνῠμέω**, *have an opposite name*, Nicom.*Ar*.1.10. **-ώνῠμος**, ον, *having an opposite name*, ib.9. **-ωσις**, εως, ἡ, *opposition*, Th. 8.50, Pl.*R*.454a; in social intercourse, Arist.*EN*1126ᵇ34; *opposition*, *Sammelb*.5356.25 (iv A. D.). 2. *disagreement, discrepancy*, Isoc.12.203 (pl.), Pl.*R*.607c, etc.: pl., *contrarieties*, Arist.*Metaph*.986ᵇ 1, al. **-ωτέον**, *one must answer, oppose*, τινί Id.*Top*.160ᵇ16. **-ωτικός**, ή, όν, *opposing*, τινί Stob.2.7.11ᵏ. Adv. -κῶς Thessal.ap.Gal.18 (1).288.

**ἐναντλέω**, *draw in*: metaph. in Pass., ἀκοὴ φωναῖς ἁπάσαις -ουμένη Ph.1.574 (v. l. ἐπ-).

**ἔναξε**, v. νάσσω.

**ἐναξονίζω**, *fit with an axle*, in Pass., γῆ τροχοῦ δίκην -ισμένη *Placit*. 3.13.3.

**ἐνάολλής**, ές, = ἀολλής, dub. l., Nic.*Th*.573, *Al*.236.

**ἐνάπᾰλος** [ᾰπ], ον, *somewhat soft*, Dsc.1.64.

**ἐναπ-άρχομαι**, Med., *make a beginning*, Aesop.291b. **-ασχολέω**, *to be wholly occupied in*, Steph.*in Hp*.1.134D. **-ειλέω**, *threaten*, prob. f. l. for ἐπ-, τιμωρίας D.H.5.54.

**ἐναπειροκᾰλέω**, *show bad taste in*, διαλεκτικῇ S.E.*P*.2.245 (s. v. l.).

**ἐναπ-ενῐαυτίζω**, *dwell for a year in a strange place*, Parmenisc.ap. Sch.E.*Med*.273 (s.v.l.). **-εργάζομαι**, *produce in*, τινί τι Pl.*Plt*.273c, *Sph*.236a, v. l. in Isoc.7.38, etc. ⊕ **-ερείδω**, *support* or *rest upon*, ὁ φωνῶν ἐ. αὐτὸν ἐν φθόγγῳ Plot.5.5.5:—Pass., *depend upon*, dub. in Phld.*Lib*.p.63O. II. Med., ἐναπερείδεσθαι τὸ κέντρον ἐν νεύρῳ *fix it in*, Gal.8.196; ἐ. τὴν ὀργήν εἴς τινα *vent it upon*.., Plb.22.13.2; τὸν ἀγῶνα τοῦ λόγου τινί J.*BJ*2.2.5; χρήματα ἐν ὑμῖν Phalar.*Ep*.69.2. 2. *fix attention upon*, τῇ τῶν νεῶν φροντίδι Plot.4.3.17:—Pass., *to be so fixed*, -ομένης ταύτῃ τῆς δυνάμεως ib.23. 3. *struggle with, resist*, τῇ μνήμῃ Plu.2.126e (s. v. l.). **-έρεισις**, εως, ἡ, *fixing of attention*, Plot.4.4.1. **-ερεύγω**, *vomit forth upon*, metaph. of lust, τὸ πάθος τινί Ph.2.393, cf. 202.

**ἐναπεσφρᾱγισμένως**, Adv., (ἐναποσφραγίζω, q. v.) *expressly, distinctly*, *Stoic*.2.31.

**ἐναπῆκε**, Ion. for ἐναφῆκε, 3 sg. aor. 1 of ἐναφίημι.

**ἐναπῆπτε**, Ion. for ἐναφῆπτε, 3 sg. impf. of ἐναφάπτω.

**ἐναπηχέω**, in Pass., *to be a faint echo* or *resonance*, τὸ οἷον -ηθὲν τοῖς σώμασιν Plot.4.4.22.

**ἐνάπιγμα**, ατος, τό, dub. in *Annuario* 4/5.483 (Tymnos, v/iv B. C.).

**ἐναπιλλημένους**· διακρατηθέντας, Hsch.

**ἐνάπλωσις**, εως, ἡ, *resolution into the elements*, Simp.*in Epict*. p.43D.

**ἐναπο-βάπτω**, *dip quite in*, πρίονα ὕδατι Hp.*VC*21. **-βλέπω**, *look in and see*, *PHolm*.3.14. **-βρέχω**, *steep, soak in*, τινί τι Hp. *Haem*.4, *Gp*.12.19.2:—Pass., Heraclid.Tar.ap.Gal.14.187, Dsc.5. 35. **-γεννάω**, *beget in*, σώμασιν Plu.2.767d. **-γράφομαι** [γρᾰ], *inscribe for oneself*, [τὸ ἡγεμονικὸν] εἰς τοῦτο ἑκάστην τῶν ἐννοιῶν ἐναπογράφεται *Placit*.4.11.1. ⊕ **-γρᾰφος**, ον, *registered*, esp. of cultivators or serfs, *POxy*.135.15, 137.12 (vi A. D.), *PAmh*.2.149.6 (vi A. D.), Just.*Nov*.54*Pr*., al. **-δείκνῠμαι**, Med., *exhibit*, πίστιν τινί *to show one's* loyalty to a person, Plb.1.82.9; ἐ. εὔνοιαν, ἔχθραν εἴς τινα, Id.10.34.10, 3.12.4; ἡδονὴ ἐ. ἀλγηδόνας Diog.*Ep*.28.5:—Pass., εὔνοιαν ἴσην πᾶσιν ἐναποδεδεῖχθαι *IG*2².1042*b*18. II. ἐναπεδεικνύατο (Ion. impf. Pass.) *approved themselves, gained distinction among* others, Hdt.9.58. **-δείκτως**, Adv. *demonstrably*, *PMasp*.151. 180 (vi A. D.). **-δέω**, *bind up in* a thing, ἄχνην λόπῳ Hp.*Mochl*.2:— Pass., Pl.*Erx*.400a. II. ἐ. τὴν χεῖρα *fasten to* a bag, Hp.*Liqu*. 6. **-δύομαι**, Pass. with pf. Act., *strip in* a place, Him.*Or*.17.2, Men.Prot.p.1D., Agath.*Praef*.p.132D. **-ζέννῡμι**, *boil in* a thing, Gal.13.118: aor. 1 part. -ζέσας Dsc.4.176. **-θεσις**, εως, ἡ, *depositing*, καταλήψεων S.E.*P*.3.188. **-θησαυρίζω**, *store up in* a place, Iamb.*VP*29.162:—Pass., ὅσα δι' ὁράσεως -ίζεται Ph.1.278. **-θλίβω** [ῑ], *squeeze in*, ib.541 (s.v.l.), Archig.(?)ap.Gal.12.858:—Pass., Harp.Astr. in *Cat.Cod.Astr*.8(3).148. **-θνῄσκω**, *die in* a place, ἐν τῇ νήσῳ Th.3.104, cf. 2.52, Hdt.9.65; ἐν [λάροις] *among* the gulls, Phryn.Com.69: abs., *Schwyzer* 182.20 (Gortyn); *die in* or *during*, ἐναποθανεῖν ἐν τοῖς καλλίστοις ἔργοις Plb.18.41.9; ταῖς ὑπεροχαῖς Id. 15.35.5; τοῦτο εἴ τις φάγοι, ἐ. if he were to eat, he *dies of it*, Thphr. *HP*4.4.12; ἐ. βασάνοις *die under* torture, Ath.13.596f; ἀτυχίαις Ph. 2.192; ἱμάτιον ἐ. ἐπιτήδειον D.L.2.35. **-θραύω**, *break off in*, οἰστοὺς τοῖς τραύμασι Plu.*Crass*.25.

**ἐναποικοδομέω**, *enclose by a wall*, τινά Polyaen.8.51.

**ἐναπο-κάμνω**, *to be exhausted in*, ταῖς φυγαῖς J.*BJ*3.6.1. **-κειμαι**, Pass., *to be stored up in*, τόποις Plu.*Aem*.14, *CPHerm*.6.14 (iii A. D.): metaph., ψυχῇ, μνήμῃ, Ph.1.293, Porph.*Plot*.1, cf. Plot.3.6.2. **-κινδῡνεύω**, *run a hazard in* or *with*, στόλῳ D.C.49.2, cf. J.*AJ*2.9. 4. **-κίχραμαι**, Med., *contract a loan*, *PSI*4.317.21 (i A. D.). **-κλάω**, *break off short in*, τὰ δοράτια ἐναπεκέκλαστο Th.4.34. **-κλείω**, *enclose in*, Olymp.*in Mete*.315.20, Alex.Trall.2:—Pass., Alex.Aphr. *Pr*.1.53, Artem.2.2, Philum.ap.Aët.5.78. **-κλίνω** [ῑ], *lay down in*, ἑαυτὸν στιβάδι Philostr.Jun.*Im*.3. **-κλύζω**, in Pass., *to be stirred about in*, τινί Dsc.3.34. **-κρύπτω**, *conceal*, τὰς δυνάμεις Jul.*Or*.1.38c:—Pass., τῷ δάσει τῶν δένδρων Str.15.3.7, cf. Sch.Luc. *Cat*.14. **-κῠβεύω**, = ἐναποκινδυνεύω, ταῖς τῶν μισθοφόρων ψυχαῖς D.S.16.78. ⊕ **-λαμβάνω**, *cut off and enclose, intercept*, [τὸν ἀέρα] ἐν ταῖς κλεψύδραις Arist.*Ph*.213ᵃ27, cf. Onos.21.5; ἐξ ζῴδια Ph.2.153:— Pass., εἰς τὸ μέσον ἐ. Pl.*Ti*.84e; [μῦς] ἐναποληφθεῖσα ἐν ἀγγείῳ Arist. *HA*580ᵇ11; [ἀήρ] ἐ. Id.*Cael*.294ᵇ27, cf. *Pr*.868ᵇ25, Epicur.*Nat*.2.993. 1; ἐ. τῇ δίνῃ *to be involved in it*, D.S.1.7. II. Astrol., *annul by adverse influence*, Vett.Val.112.14 (Pass.). ⊕ **-λαύω**, *enjoy*, *PLond*. 1727.26 (vi A. D.); προνομίῳ Just.*Nov*.111.1. **-λείπω**, *leave behind in* or *on*, ταῖς χερσὶ ποιότητα Xenocr.58; τι Plu.2.91b:—Pass., Arist. *Mete*.352ᵇ35, Ph.1.8. **-λειψις**, εως, ἡ, *leaving* of empty spaces *within*, κενῶν Thphr.*Sens*.62. **-ληψις**, εως, ἡ, *intercepting, catching, retention*, Arist.*Mete*.370ᵃ1, *Spir*.482ᵇ31, Thphr.*CP*2.9.3, Dsc.*Eup*. 1.62. 2. *being caught up, involved in*, τὰς ἐ. τῶν συστροφῶν ἐν τῇ τοῦ κόσμου γενέσει Epicur.*Ep*.1 p.28U.

**ἐναπόλλῡμαι**, *perish in* a place, X.*HG*3.1.4.

**ἐναπο-λογέομαι**, *defend oneself in*, τῇ πόλει Aeschin.1.122. **-λογίζομαι**, *account for before*, [τῷ κοινῷ] *IG*12(9).909 (Chalcis, iv/iii B. C.). **-λούομαι**, *wash oneself* or *bathe in*, Ath.2.43a. **-λύω**, *acquit*, *PLond*.2.354.25 (i B. C.). **-μαγμα**, ατος, τό, *impression, image*, Herm.*in Phdr*.p.68A. **-μᾰραίνομαι**, *wither on*, τοὺς καρποὺς -ανθῆναι τοῖς φυτοῖς Lyd.*Ost*.23: metaph., οὐ γὰρ χρόνῳ ἡ τοῦ δημιουργοῦ δύναμις -μαραίνεται Aen.Gaz.*Thphr*.p.44B. II. *shrivel up in*, ἐλαίῳ Orib.8.27.4. ⊕ **-μάσσω**, *wipe off upon*, e. g. pigments, Plu. 2.99b:—Med., *receive an impression*, λογισμοὶ ἐ. τύπους φρονήσεως Ph.1.59, al.:—Pass., *to be stamped on*, κηροῖς Plu.2.3e, cf. D.L.7.46; *to be imaged in*, τῷ κατόπτρῳ Ach.Tat.5.13; also φαντασία κατ' αὐτὸ τὸ ὑπάρχον -μεμαγμένη Zeno *Stoic*.1.18. 2. Med., ἐναπομάξασθαι χεῖράς τινι *wipe one's* hands *on*, cj. in Alciphr.3.44; of a snake, λυσσᾶν τοῦ ἐναπομάξεται τὸν ἰόν Sch.Gen.Il.22.95. II. *rub, dry*, Alex. Trall.*Febr*.1. **-μειξις**, εως, ἡ, *intermixture*, Thphr.*CP*6.1.1, 6.3. 1. **-μεμαγμένως**, Adv. *by a distinct impression*, *Stoic*.2.31. **-μένω**, *remain in*, καρποὶ ἐ. τῇ χάρᾳ Lyd.*Mag*.3.61; τῷ αἰσθητῷ καὶ φαινομένῳ κάλλει Herm.*in Phdr*.p.100A., cf. Aen.Gaz.*Thphr*.p.67B.: abs., Hld.1.15.

**ἐναπομόργνῡμι**, *wipe off upon, impart*, e.g. colour *to* one, Iamb. ap.Stob.3.3.26:—Pass., ἐ. τύπος τῆς φαντασίας εἰς τὸ πνεῦμα Porph. *Sent*.29.

**ἐναπόμορξις**, εως, ἡ, *imbuing*, v. l. for -μειξις in Thphr.*CP*6.1.1.

**ἐναπο-μύττομαι**, *blow the nose upon*, ταῖς παροψίσιν Plu.2.1128b. **-νέμω**, *allot, assess*, Lyd.*Mens*.3.23. ⊕ **νίζω**, *wash clean in* a thing, τινί Polyzel.4:—Med., ἐναπονίζεσθαι τοὺς πόδας ἐν τῷ ποδανιπτῆρι *wash one's* feet in it, Hdt.2.172; χεῖρας Id.1.138. II. Med., *wash off from oneself in*, τῷ ποταμῷ τὸ αἷμα Paus.9.30.8. **-πᾰτέω**, *ventrem exonerare in*.., Ar.*Pax*1228, Polyzel.4. **-πλύνω** [ῡ], *wash away in*, τὰ χρώματα ἐν τῷ ὑγρῷ Arist.*Sens*.441ᵇ15; ἐσθῆτα Paus.3. 25.8. **-πνέω**, *expire in*, ταῖς πατρῴαις οἰκίαις D.S.13.89, cf. M.Ant. 5.4; ἱκεσίαις *expire in the act of*.., Plu.*Cor*.33; τῳ αὐλῷ Luc.*Harm*. 2. **-πνίγω** [ῑ], *suffocate, drown in*, aor. 2 Pass. ἐναποπνιγῆναι ἐν οἴνῳ Terpsicl.ap.Ath.7.325d, cf. Jul.*Ep*.82; καπνῷ Luc.*Peregr*. 24. **-πτύω**, *spit into*, Dsc.4.24.

**ἐναπορέω**, dub. l. for ἐπαπορέω, *to be in doubt*, Plb.29.27.6; πῶς.. Id.12.25ᶜ.1.

**ἐναπο-ρρίπτω**, *throw aside*, Dsc.*Eup.*1.68 (dub.). **-σβέννῡμι**, aor. -έσβεσα, *quench in* a thing, Hp.*Mul.*1.78; τὴν θερμότητα Arist. *Pr.*937ᵇ13; τι ὕδατι Gal.14.377; δᾷδας γλεύκει *Gp.*7.12.8:—Pass., Arist.*Mete.*369ᵇ16, Cass.*Pr.*31, Hld.1.15. **-σημαίνω**, *indicate* or *point out in*, ἱστορίᾳ Plu.*Cim.*2:—Med., *impress* or *stamp on* a thing, σεισμοὶ τὴν ἁρμονίαν τῶν ὀρῶν ἐναπεσημήναντο τοῖς τμήμασι Philostr. *Im.*2.17, cf. Ph.1.291. **-σκηπτικός**, ή, όν, *supervening*, [πυρετός] Cass.*Pr.*15. **-σκήπτω**, *cause to descend*, θεὸς ἐ. νόσον τισί J.*AJ* 2.14.6. II. intr., *supervene, attack*, -σκηπτούσης τῆς φλεγμονῆς Cass.*Pr.*30, cf. Phlp. *in de An.*339.5. **-σκηψις**, εως, ἡ, *supervening*, *AB*435. ❋ **-σπάω**, *tear off*, βίᾳ τὸ χόριον Aët.16.20. **-στάζω**, *drip with*, λύθρου Lib.*Decl.*40*Intr.*1. **-στέγω**, *keep in*, Gal.7.709, 15.180. **-στηρίζομαι**, Med., *fix oneself in* or *on*, ἐς τὴν γλῶσσαν Hp.*Acut.*(*Sp.*)9, cf. *Placit.*2.20.10. **-σφάττομαι**, Pass., *to be slain among*, J.*BJ*4.6.3. **-σφρᾱγίζω**, *impress in* or *on*, ψυχῆς ὁμοιότητα εἰς παιδὸς χαρακτῆρα Lxx4*Ma.*15.4: abs., D.L.7.46:—Med., οὐ γὰρ ἂν -σφραγίσαιτο τὰ ἔξω τὴν ἑαυτῶν φύσιν Epicur.*Ep.*1 p.11 U.:—Pass., Zeno*Stoic.*1.18. ❋**-τελέω**, in Pass., *to be produced*, Alex.Aphr.*Pr.*1.124. **-τέμνω**, in Pass., *to be cut off in*, Str.2.5.27. **-τήκω**, *dissolve in*, ἐλαίῳ στέαρ Gal.11.489. ❋ **-τίθεμαι**, *lay aside* or *store up in*, Id.*Nat.Fac.*3.12; ἐναποθέσθαι τὰ ξίφη εἰς τοὺς κολεούς D.C.73.10; τὸ γεγονὸς τῇ διανοίᾳ Ph.2.42; *deposit*, Gal.*Nat. Fac.*3.7; κηλῖδας τῇ ψυχῇ Jul.*Or.*1.15d; *include*, τι τοῖς γράμμασι Procop.Gaz.p.169B.; but ἐναποτίθεσθαι τὴν ὀργήν εἴς τι *vent one's* anger upon.., D.S.26.16; *produce in*, ψύξιν τῷ σπλάγχνῳ Alex.Trall. 10:—Pass., Phld.*Herc.*862.14. **-τίκτω**, *produce in*, γνώμην τινί Procop.Gaz.*Ep.*31. **-τῑμάω**, *take in payment at a valuation*, τί τινι D.53.20:—Pass., D.C.41.37. **-τίνω**, *pay* or *spend in litigation in* a place, πόλις κοινὴ ἐναποτεῖσαι χρήματα Ar.*Av.*38. **-τῠπόομαι**, Pass., *receive impressions*, Thphr.*Sens.*53, Zeno*Stoic.*1.18; *to be impressed upon*, παιδίων ψυχαῖς Plu.2.3e. II. *express*, ὁ λόγος ἐ. τὴν τελειότητά τινος Hierocl. *in CA*26 p.480 M. **-φέρω**, in Med., *receive by heredity*, τι τῶν τεκόντων Lib.*Decl.*43.56. **-χράομαι**, *abuse*, τινί D.17.23. II. later in Act., *peculate*, *PAmh.*2.79 (ii A. D.). **-χρησις**, εως, ἡ, *peculation*, ibid. **-ψάω**, *wipe in* or *on*, Sch.Ar.*Ach.*843. **-ψύχω** [ῡ], *ease oneself in*, euphem. for ἐναποπατέω, Hes.*Op.*759. 2. *cool off*, *PHolm.*6.12 (Pass.). II. *give up the ghost*, *AP*9.1 tit., Hsch.

❋ **ἐνάπτω**, *bind on* or *to*, σπάργανά τινι E.*Ion* 1490 (anap.); τι εἴς τι X. *Cyn.*6.8, cf. Aeschin.Socr.41 (Pass.):—Pass., θώρηκος κύτει ἐνημμένῳ κάλλιστα *fitted on, fitting* beautifully, Ar.*Pax* 1225. 2. Pass., of persons, *to be fitted with, clad in*, c. acc., λεοντέας ἐναμμένοι (Ion. for ἐνημμ-) Hdt.7.69; διφθέραν ἐνημμένος Ar.*Nu.*72; παρδαλᾶς ἐνημμένους Id.*Av.*1250, cf. Str.15.1.71 (v.l.), Luc.*Herc.*1:—also in Med., ὁ χορὸς.. ἐναψάμενος δέρματα Ar.*Fr.*253, cf. Luc.*Tim.*6. II. *kindle, set on fire*, Ar.*Pax* 1032 (Pass.):—Med., *get oneself a light*, Lys.1.14. III. *lay hands on*, *GDI*1760.11, al. (Delph.).

**ἔναρ**, Lacon., = ἔνας, Hsch.; v. ἔνος (B).

**ἔνᾰρα**, ων, τά, (ἐναίρω) only pl., *arms and trappings of a slain foe, spoils*, φέρειν ἔ. βροτόεντα Il.6.480; φέρομαι 8.534; πόλλ' ἔ. Τρώων *taken from* them, 13.268; so ἔ. βροτόεντα Δόλωνος 10.570: generally, *spoil, booty*, τὴν [φόρμιγγα] ἄρετ' ἐξ ἐνάρων 9.188, cf. 6.68, Hes.*Sc.* 367.—Ep. word (used by S.*Aj.*177 (lyr.)) for Trag. σκῦλα, λάφυρα.

**ἐνάραι**· ὑγιᾶναι, Hsch. **ἐναράνει**· ἐντρυφᾷ, Id.

**ἐνάραξις** [ᾰρ], εως, ἡ, *beating*, τυμπάνων prob. in Plu.2.56e (pl.).

**ἐνᾰράομαι**, = ἐνεύχομαι, *adjure by*, ἐ. σοι τὴν ὑγίειαν τοῦ πατρὸς *PSI* 4.416.7 (iii B. C.).

**ἐνᾰρᾰρίσκω**, aor. 1 ἐνῆρσα, *fit* or *fasten in*, ἐν δὲ σταθμοὺς ἄρσε Od. 21.45. II. pf. ἐνάρηρα, intr., *to be fitted in*, εὖ ἐναρηρός 5.236; οὐρανῷ εὖ ἐνάρηρεν ἀγάλματα Arat.453.

**ἐνᾰράσσω**, *dash against*, κριοὶ ἐ. βίᾳ τὰ κέρατα Paus.4.13.1, cf. Dexipp.Hist.p.184 D.:—Pass., *to be dashed against*, ἐς τὰς πέτρας App.*BC*5.98.

**ἐναράτιον**, τό, = ἐνηρόσιον, *IG*12(1).924.20 (Rhodes, iii B. C.), dub. in ib.9(2).1229.10 (Phalanna, ii B. C.).

❋ **ἐνάργ-εια**, ἡ, *clearness, distinctness, vividness*, Pl.*Plt.*277c. 2. Philos., *clear and distinct perception*, Epicur.*Ep.*1 p.11 U., al. 3. Rhet., *vivid description*, D.H.*Lys.*7; joined with συντομία, Phld. *Po.*5.3. II. *clear view*, Ἰταλίας Plb.3.54.2, etc. III. *self-evidence*, Phld.*Sign.*15, al.; ἡ ἐ. δείκνυσιν Diogenian.Epicur.4.10; παρὰ τὴν ἐ. contrary to *manifest facts*, Olymp. *in Mete.*215.12. **-ημα**, ατος, τό, *clearly perceived phenomenon, datum of experience*, Epicur. *Ep.*1 p.24 U., al.: pl., *evident facts*, opp. τὰ μὴ δῆλα, Phld.*Sign.*36, cf. *Po.*2.54. ❋**-ής**, ές, *visible, palpable, in bodily shape*, esp. of the gods appearing in their own forms, χαλεποὶ δὲ θεοὶ φαίνεσθαι ἐναργεῖς Il.20.131; οὐ γάρ πως πάντεσσι θεοὶ φαίνονται ἐναργεῖς Od.16.161, cf. 3.420, 7.201; freq. of a dream or vision, ἐναργὲς ὄνειρον ἐπέσσυτο 4. 841; [ὄναρ] A.*Pers.*179, etc.; ὄψιν ἐνυπνίου τῷ ἑωυτοῦ πάθεϊ ἐναργεστάτην *most clearly relating to..*, Hdt.5.55, cf. 7.47; ἐνύπνια Hp. *Prorrh.*1.5; ἐ. ταῦρος *in visible form* a bull, a *very* bull, S.*Tr.*11; ἐ. τινὰ στῆσαι to set him *bodily before one*, Id.*OC*910; ἐ. βλεφάρων ἵμερος desire *beaming* from the eyes, Id.*Ant.*795 (lyr.). b. *prominent*, ἄρθρα Aret.*SD*1.8. 2. *manifest to the mind's eye*, τάδ' ἀντίπρῳρα δή σοι βλέπειν πάρεστ' ἐ. S.*Tr.*224; λῃστὴς ἐ. the *manifest* robber, Id.*OT*535, cf. *Ant.*263; τοῖς δρῶσιν ἐ. ἡ ὕβρις φαίνεται D.21.72. Adv. -γῶς *visibly, manifestly*, A.*Th.*136, S.*El.*878; ἐ. ἡ θεός σ' ἐπισκοπεῖ Ar. *Eq.*1173. 3. of words, etc., *clear, distinct*, ἐ. βάξις ἦλθεν A.*Pr.*663; freq. in Prose, ἐ. τεκμήριον, σημεῖον, ἀπόδειξις, etc., Pl.*Ion* 535c, *Ti.*72b (Comp.), D.18.300, etc.; -εστέρα γνῶσις Pl.*Tht.*206b, cf. Epicur.*Ep.*3 p.60 U.; -εστάτη αἴσθησις Arist.*Pr.*886ᵇ35; ἐ. τοῦ πράγματος ἐπίνοια Epicur.*Fr.*255; καὶ τοῦτο ἐ. ὅτι.. (for δῆλον ὅτι) Pl.*Tht.*150d; ἐναργὲς τοῦτο συμβαλεῖν Ar.*V.*50. Adv. -γῶς, Ion. -γέως, λέγειν Hdt.8.77; παραστῆσαι Ael.*Tact.*1.5: Comp. -έστερον, εἰπεῖν, διόψεται, Pl.*Ti.*49a, *R.*611c: Sup. -έστατα, γνῶναι Id.*Alc.*1.132c. II. *brilliant, splendid*, βωμός Pi.*O.*7.42. **-ότης**, ητος, ἡ, = ἐνάργεια, Poll.4.97.

**ἐναργῠρ-ίζω**, *to be of silvery appearance*, Heph.Astr.1.24. **-όω**, in Pass., *to be silver-plated*, ἀργυρούμενα ἢ ἐνηργυρώμενα σκεύη Timae. Astr. in *Cat.Cod.Astr.*1.97.

**ἐναργώδης**, ες, = ἐναργής I, ὄνειροι Aret.*SD*1.5.

**ἐναρδ-εύω**, *irrigate*, and **-ευτής**, οῦ, ὁ, *one who irrigates*, *Gloss.*

**Ἐνάρεες** ('Ενάριες v.l. in Hdt.4.67, **'Αναριεῖς** prob. in Hp.*Aër.*22), οἱ, prob. a Scythian word, = ἀνδρόγυνοι, Hdt.1.105, 4.67; cf. Hp. l. c.

❋ **ἐνάρετος** [ᾰρ], ον, *virtuous*, Chrysipp.*Stoic.*3.72, Plot.1.2.7: interpol. in Epict.*Ench.*24.3; *valiant*, J.*BJ*6.1.8. Adv. -τως Aristo*Stoic.* 1.86, *IG*5(2).463 (Megalop.), *CIG*2771 i 7 (Aphrodisias), Alex.Aphr *in Top.*331.11. II. *productive*, [γῆ] *PFlor.*50.4 (iii A. D.).

**ἐνᾰρηρώς**, v. ἐναραρίσκω. **ἐνάρης**· ἐνηρμοσμένος, Hsch.

❋ **ἐνᾰρηφόρος** (Dor. -ᾱφορος Hsch.), ον, *wearing the spoils*, *APl.*4.72.

**ἐνάρθμιος**, ον, *having an affinity with*, οἴνῳ Emp.91 (prob.).

**ἐναρθρ-όομαι**, *to be articulated by* ἐνάρθρωσις, Gal.2.735. **-ος**, ον, *jointed*: of speech, *articulate*, φωνὴ ἔ. Diog.Bab.*Stoic.*3.212, D.H. *Comp.*14, Babr.*Prooem.*1.7: Comp., Diog.Oen.18. Adv. -ρως, λέγειν Artem.4.19. II. *strong in limb*, Aret.*SD*2.5. **-ωσις**, εως, ἡ, a kind of *articulation*, when the ball is *deep set in* the socket, Gal.2.736.

**ἐνᾰρίζω** Il.1.191, etc.: impf. ἠνάριζον A.*Ag.*1644; Ep. ἐνάριζον (v. infr.): fut. -ίξω (ἐξ-) Il.20.339: aor. Ep. and Lyr. ἐνάριξα 22.323, Pi.*N.*6.52, later ἠνάριξα Lyc.486, ἠνάρισα *AP*7.226 (Anacr.):—Med., aor. ἐναρίξατο Opp.*C.*2.20:—Pass., S.*Tr.*94 (lyr.): aor. ἠναρίσθην: pf. ἠνάρισμαι (v. κατ-):—*strip a slain foe of his arms* (ἔναρα), c. dupl. acc., ἔντεα.. τὰ Πατρόκλοιο βίην ἐνάριξα Il.17.187; ἀλλήλους ἐνάριζον ib.413: hence, *slay in fight*, Hes.*Sc.*194: generally, *slay*, Il.1.191, A. l. c.:—in Pass., νὺξ ἐναριζομένα *when dying*, i.e. *when yielding* to day, S. l. c.; cf. ἐναίρω.

**ἐνᾰριθμ-έω**, *reckon in* or *among*, in Pass., Arist.*SE*170ᵃ8, *MM* 1204ᵃ23, Luc.*Eun.*8. II. *account*, ἴσα καὶ τὸ μηδέν as nothing, S. *OT*1188 (lyr.):—Med., = ἐν ἀριθμῷ ποιεῖσθαι, *make account of, value*, E.*Or.*623. **-ησις**, εως, ἡ, *reckoning in*, v.l. for ἐξ- in Sch.Nic.*Th.* 156. **-ητέος**, α, ον, *to be reckoned in*, Plu.*Nob.*1. 2. **-ητέον**, *one must reckon in*, Eust.1719.7. **-ιος**, ον, (ἀριθμός) *in the number, making up the number*, ἄλλην ἐνίησι πατὴρ ἐναρίθμιον εἶναι Od.12.65; *counted among*, i. e. *among*, ζῴοις Theoc.7.86; ὑποχθονίοις A.R.1.647; ἐ. *among men, in the world*, *IG*7.2543.6 (Thebes, iii/iv A. D.); δήμου ἐ. f.l. in Epigr.ap.D.L.7.27; cf. ἀρίθμιος. II. *taken into account, valued*, οὔτε ποτ' ἐν πολέμῳ ἐ. οὔτ' ἐνὶ βουλῇ Il.2.202; ἐναρίθμια· φίλα, συνήθη, Hsch. **-ος**, ον, = foreg. I, Pl.*Sph.*258c, Orph.*A.*109; τὰ ἐ., = αἱ μονάδες, Arist.*Metaph.*991ᵇ22 (s. v. l.). II. *taken into account, esteemed*, οὐκ ἐλλόγιμον οὐδ' ἐ. Pl.*Phlb.*17e (with play on signf. 1).

**ἐνᾰρῐκύμων** [ῡ], ονος, ὁ, ἡ, f.l. for ἀρικύμων, Hp.*Aër.*5.

**ἐνᾰρίμβροτος**, ον, *man-slaying*, Μέμνων Pi.*P.*6.30; μάχα Id.*I.* 8(7).57.

**ἐνᾰριστάω**, *take breakfast in..*, Eup.25c, Suid. s. v. Νικόλαος. II. *take a snack for breakfast* (cf. ἐμφαγεῖν I), Hp.*Vict.*3.68, 80.

**ἐναρκέω**, *suffice, be able*, c. inf., Sch.Pi.*N.*6.97: ἐναρκεῖ· ἐνδέχεται. Hsch.

**ἐναρκτεύει**· φονεύει, κρίνει, Hsch.

**ἐναρκτικός**, ή, όν, *inchoative*, *Gloss.*

**ἐναρμογή**, ἡ, *fitting* of a surgical tube, Antyll.ap.Orib.10.19.4.

**ἐναρμ-όζω** and **-ττω**, Dor. aor. inf. -μόξαι Pi.*O.*3.5, *IG*4.952.68 (Epid.):—*fit* or *fix in*, ἔγχος σφονδύλοις E.*Ph.*1413; πλευροῖς βέλη Id. *HF*179, cf. Ar.*Lys.*413; ξύλα ἀλλήλοις Thphr.*HP*5.3.5; πήχεις Luc. *DDeor.*7.4:—Pass., *SIG*694.37 (Elaea, ii B. C.). b. Math., *insert* a mean term, Nicom.*Ar.*2.27:—Pass., Geom., *to be inserted*, Archim. *Fluit.*2.10. 2. metaph., *fit, adapt*, Δωρίῳ φωνὰν ἐ. πεδίλῳ Pi. l. c., cf. *I.*1.16; τι εἴς τι Pl.*Lg.*819c, D.H.*Isoc.*3; ἐ. αὑτόν *make* himself *popular*, Plu.*Alex.*52:—Pass., *to be fitted, adapted*, Plot.6.7.34:—Med., τὴν Δωριστὶ (sc. ἁρμονίαν) ἐναρμόττεσθαι.. τὴν λύραν *tune* it to the Dorian mode, v.l. in Ar.*Eq.*989 (lyr.). II. intr., *fit into*, ἐς τὸ κοῖλον τῆς ἀγκύλης Hp.*Art.*6; εἰς [γωνίαν] Archim.*Aren.*1c, al.: metaph., *suit, be convenient*, εἰς τὴν πρόληψιν Epicur.*Sent.*37; ἔν τινι Ar.*Ra.*1202; τινί Pl.*Lg.*894c: abs., τὸ ἐναρμόττον μέγεθος Epicur.*Ep.* 1 p.12 U. 2. c. dat. pers., *please*, Plu.*Them.*5. **-όνιος**, ον, of *musical sound, musical*, ἔνρυθμος καὶ ἐ. αἴσθησις Pl.*Lg.*654a; ἐ. ἡ φωνὴ φερομένων κύκλῳ τῶν ἄστρων Arist.*Cael.*290ᵇ22; ἐναρμόνιον μελῳδεῖν Luc.*DDeor.*7.4; νέκταρ, of music, *AP*7.29 (Antip. Sid.): metaph., *in harmony with*, ταῖς τῶν βίων ὑποθέσεσι Ti.Locr.103c. Adv. -ίως Ph.1.107, Corn.*ND*32, Eustr.*inEN*9.2, Eust.1422.19. 2. in Lit. Crit., *harmonious*, περίοδος D.H.*Dem.*24; μεταβολαὶ ἐ. changes *of harmony*, Id.*Comp.*19, cf. ib.6 (Comp.). II. in Music, *enharmonic*, συστήματα Aristox.*Harm.*p.17 M.; δίεσις ib.p.47 M.; ἐ. μέλη Arist.*Pr.*918ᵇ22 (s. v. l.), cf. *POxy.*667.1, etc. **-οσις**, εως, ἡ, *fitting in*, Archim.*Stom.*1 (pl.), Procl.*Hyp.*6.9. **-οστος**, ον, *harmonious*, συμφωνίας Lxx4*Ma.*14.3; *concordant*, πρὸς ἄλλα Iamb. *Myst.*3.18. **-όττω**, v. ἐναρμόζω.

**ἔναρξις**, εως, ἡ, = καταρχή, Procl.*Par.Ptol.*131. II. *introduction*, τῶν λεχθησομένων Sch.E.*Hec.*313.

**ἐνᾰροκτάντας**, Dor. for -της, ου, ὁ, *spoiler and slayer*, of death, A. *Fr.*151 (lyr.).

⊕ **ἔνᾰρος**, ον, (ἀρά) *subject to a curse*, *Rev.Ét.Gr.*24.415 (Itanos, ii B.C.), Hsch.

**ἐνᾰρόω**, *plough in*, τῇ γῇ σπέρμα Antipho Soph.60.

⊕ **ἐναρσφόρος**, ον, = ἐναρηφόρος, Hes.*Sc.*192, prob. in Alcm.23.3.

**ἐναρτάω**, *fasten on*, σπάρτους Hero *Aut.*26.5:—Pass., Sch.Arat.441.

⊕ **ἐνάρχομαι**, fut. -ξομαι prob. in E. (v. infr.):—in sacrifices, *begin the offering*, by taking the barley from the basket, κανᾶ δ' ἐναρχέσθω τις E.*IA* 1470, cf. Men.*Sam.*7; προχύτας χέρνιβάς τ' ἐνάρξεται E.*IA* 955: pf. in pass. sense, κανοῦν δ' ἐνῆρκται Id.*El.*1142; ἐνῆρκται τὰ κανᾶ Aeschin.3.120. 2. generally, *begin*, *Sammelb.*4369(b).23 (iii B.C.), etc.; τῆς θερείας ἐναρχομένης Plb.5.30.7: c. inf., πολεμεῖν ib.1.5; γενειᾶν D.H.6.13: ἐ. τινός *make a beginning of*, τῆς ἐπιβολῆς Plb.5.1.3; τοῦ λόγου Plu.*Cic.*35; ὁμιλιῶν *engage in*, Ath.Med.ap.Orib.*inc.*21.9; ἐνῆρκται folld. by a quotation, Apollon.Cit.1: abs., *begin to speak*, Plu.*Cam.*32. II. later, in Act., *hold office*, *IG*12(5).526.5 (Ceos).

**ἔναρχος**, ον, (ἀρχή) *in office, in authority*, App.*BC*1.14, Wilcken *Chr.*41 iii 10 (iii A.D.); οἱ ἔ. ὄντες ἀεί *GDI*2520.12 (Delph.); συνέδρους ἀεὶ τοὺς ἔ. *those who were in office* at the time, *CIG*3046.13 (Teos); ἔ. ἀρχιερεύς *IGRom.*1.1060.4 (Alexandria); ὑπομνηματογράφος *OGI* 715 (ibid.), etc. 2. *under authority*, Stob.2.7.3[a].

**ἑνάς**, άδος, ἡ, (ἕν) = μονάς, *unit*, Pl.*Phlb.*15a: pl., of an order of existences, Dam.*Pr.*40,99, al.; οἱ νόες πλείους τῶν θείων ἑ. Procl.*Inst.*62, cf. 6.

**ἕνας**, v. ἕνος (B).

**ἐνασεβέω**, = ἀσεβέω ἐν, Diog.*Ep.*28.4; τῇ Ἀρτέμιδι Sch.Gen.Il.21.401:—Pass., ὑπό τινων Themist.*Ep.*8.

**ἐνᾰσελγ-αίνω**, *behave lewdly*, εἰς τὰς γυναῖκας D.S.34/5.2.12:—Pass., *to be treated with insult in* a thing, cj. in Ar.*V.*61 (ἀνασελγ- codd.). -έω, = foreg., Aq.*Jd.*19.25.

**ἐνᾶσθαι**· φθαρῆναι, γηράσαι, Hsch.; cf. ἐναίσασθαι.

**ἐνασθενέω**, prob. f.l. for ἐξ-, γήρᾳ Ph.2.493.

**ἐνασκέω**, *train* or *practise in* a thing, αὐτόν Plu.*Alex.*17:—Pass. with fut. Med. (Luc.*Vit.Auct.*3), *to be trained*, c. dat., Ph.1.448, al., Luc.l.c.: c. acc., ἀτρεκίην *AP*11.354.10 (Agath.):—Act. intr., like Pass., Plb.1.63.9. II. Pass., τῷ ὕφει ἐνησκῆσθαι *to be wrought in* it, J.*AJ*3.7.5.

**ἐνασμενίζω**, *take pleasure in*, τινί Ph.1.36.

**ἐνασπάζομαι**, *welcome*, Plu.2.987d.

**ἐνασπίδ-ιος** [πῐ], ον, = Lat. *clipeatus*, [εἰκόνες] *JRS*16.250 (Ancyra, ii A.D.). -όομαι, *fit oneself with a shield*, Ar.*Ach.*368.

**ἔνασσα**, v. ναίω II.

**ἐναστεΐζομαι**, = ἐνοικῶ, Hsch.

**ἐναστράπτω**, *flash in* or *on*, metaph., δικαιοσύνῃ ἐ. Them.*Or.*4.51d, cf. Iamb.*Myst.*3.11; πρὸς τὴν οὐσίαν Jul.*Or.*4.137b: c. acc. cogn., ἐ. φέγγος τινί Ph.1.448.

**ἔναστρος**, ον, *among the stars*, Achae.16; *starry*, ἰδέαι *Corp.Herm.*3.2 (s.v.l.).

**ἐνασχημονέω**, *behave oneself unseemly in*, βαθεῖ πώγωνι καὶ ἀρετῇ Luc.*Icar.*21; ἀρχαῖς Plu.2.336b, cf. Id.*Sert.*27.

**ἐνασχολέομαι**, *to be engrossed with*, μαθήμασιν Phlp.*in GC*26.23; περί τινος Id.*in Mete.*18.1, cf. Men.Prot.p.80D.

**ἐνᾰταῖος**, α, ον, (ἔνατος) *on the ninth day*, Hp.*Aph.*4.36, Th.2.49, *PSI*4.286 (iii/iv A.D.); of recurring fevers, Hp.*Epid.*1.24.

**ἐνᾰτεν-ίζω**, fut. -ιῶ Crates *Ep.*15:—*fix steadfastly on*, τὰς ἀκοάς τινι Iamb.*VP*15.65; τὸ πρόσωπον εἰς.. Ser.1.70. II. intr., *look fixedly on* one, Lxx 3*Ma.*5.30, Hld.7.7, *PMag.Leid.W.*5.44; ἐ. δριμὺ καὶ τιτανῶδες Lib.*Decl.*51.10: c. dat., [ἡδοναῖς] Crates l.c.; ἡλίῳ S.E.*P.*1.45, cf. Syrian.*in Metaph.*45.16; διαγράμματι Iamb.*in Nic.*p.88 P. -ισις, εως, ἡ, *gazing intently*, πρὸς τὸ πρᾶγμα Procl.*in Prm.*p.598S.

⊕ **ἐνᾰτεύω**, in Pass., *have the ninth part removed for sacrifice*, *SIG* 1024.23 (Myconos), *Supp.Epigr.*2.505 (Thasos, v B.C.).

⊕ **ἐνάτηρ**, v. εἰνάτερες.

**ἐνᾰτισταί**, οἱ, members of a religious guild at Delos, *IG*11(4).1228, 1229.

**ἔνατμος**, ον, *full of vapour*, D.S.2.49.

⊕ **ἔνᾰτος**, η, ον, (ἐννέα) *ninth*, Il.2.313, Hes.*Op.*772, *IG*1².304.15, *PGrenf.*2.24.1 (ii B.C.), etc.; Ep. **εἴνατος** Il.2.295, 8.266; Aeol. **ἔνοτος** *BCH*37.166 (Cyme, iii B.C.); τὰ ἔνατα (sc. ἱερά), *sacra novendialia*, Is.8.39, Aeschin.3.225. (Freq. written ἔννατος in codd.)

**ἐνατρεμέω**, *to be at rest*, Them.*Or.*4.51d.

**ἐναττικίζω**· ἐναττικίζουσι τῷ χωρίῳ αἱ ἀηδόνες the nightingales *sing in* this place *just as in Attica*, Philostr.*Her.Prooem.*

**ἐναυγ-άζω**, *illuminate*, τὴν ἀχλὺν τῆς ψυχῆς Ph.1.52:—Pass., Id.2.300. 2. intr., *shine, be seen*, ἐναυγάζοντος λύχνου Ael.*NA*1.58. II. *behold*, Lyc.71:—so in Med., Ph.1.449,471:—Pass., ib.422. -ασμα, ατος, τό, *illumination*, ἐ. θεῖον ib.88.

⊕ **ἐναυγής**, perh. f.l. for εὐαυγής, Pi.*Pae.Fr.*19.25.

**ἔναυδος**, ον, *speaking, living*, Hsch.

**ἐναυλᾰκοφοῖτις**, ιδος, ἡ, *wandering in the fields*, Ὧραι *AP*6.98 (Zon.).

**ἐναύλ-ειον**, τό, f.l. for ἔναυλος (A). II, E.*Hel.*1107 (lyr.). -ήματα, τά, *barley meal soaked in wine and oil*, *EM*338.8, *AB*259, Suid. (cf. θυλήματα). -ίζω, intr., *dwell* or *abide in* a place, S.*Ph.*33; νύκτ' ἐναυλίσαι μίαν prob. in E.*Hyps.Fr.*3(i).18. II. Med., *take up one's quarters* during the night, νύκτα οὐδεὶς ἐναυλίζεται [ἐν τῷ νηῷ] Hdt.1.181; ἐν Τανάγρῃ νύκτα ἐναυλισάμενος Id.9.15; esp. of soldiers, *take up night-quarters, bivouac*, Th.3.91, 4.54, 8.33, X.*An.*7.7.8, etc.; ἐν τῇ γῇ *GDI*5597.14 (Ephesus, iii B.C.). III. metaph., of diseases, *lodge*, ἐν τῷ στήθει Hp.*Nat.Hom.*12. ⊕-ιος, α, ον, (αὐλή) *inside the court*: ἐναύλιος (sc. θύρα), ἡ, *the door leading into the house*, τὴν ἐναύλιον ὠθῶν pushing it open, *Com.Adesp.*1203.6. 2. ἐναυλίαν (sc. ζωήν) ἄγοντες the *inner life*, Zos.Alch.p.229B. 3. ἐναύλιον, τό, *haunt, abode*, Ἀστεροπῖοιο Euph.51.11; Ἰοχεαίρης Nonn.*D.*41.147. -ισμα, ατος, τό, *dwelling-place, abode*, Artem.4.47. ⊕ -ιστήριος, ον, *habitable*, ἄντρον *AP*6.219.13 (Antip.(?)). -ον, τό, = sq. II, κατ' ἔναυλ' ὀρέων E.*Fr.*740, cf. *AP*9.102 (Anton. Arg.).

⊕ **ἔναυλος** (A), ὁ, Subst.: I. (αὐλός) *bed of a stream*, τάχα κεν.. ἐναύλους πλήσειαν νεκύων Il.16.71; *torrent, mountain-stream*, ὅν ῥά τ' ἔναυλος ἀποέρσῃ 21.283, cf. 312. II. (αὐλή) *dwelling, shelter*: pl., *haunts* of the country-gods, οὔρεα μακρὰ θεῶν χαρίεντας ἐναύλους Νυμφέων Hes.*Th.*129, cf. *h.Ven.*74,124, E.*Ba.*122 (lyr.), *HF*371 (lyr.); also ἁλὸς ἐναύλους, of the sea, Opp.*H.*1.305; Ποσειδάωνος ἐ. ib.3.5.—Ep. word, used by E. in lyr. III. Adv. -ως *by means of pipes*, διάγειν *AB*464.

⊕ **ἔναυλος** (B), ον, Adj.: I. (αὐλός) *on* or *to the flute, accompanied by it*, κιθάρισις Philoch.66; θροῦς Philostr.*Im.*1.2. 2. mostly metaph., λόγος, φθόγγος ἔ., words, voice *ringing in one's ears, still heard* or *remembered*, Pl.*Mx.*235c, Luc.*Somn.*5; ἔ. φόβος *fresh* fear, Pl.*Lg.*678c; ἔναυλον ἦν πᾶσιν ὅτι.. all had it *fresh in memory* that.., Aeschin.3.191; ἔναυλα καὶ πρὸ ὀμμάτων D.H.9.7; ἔ. δύναμις Arist.*Pr.*928[b]7; ἔ. ἔχειν ὅτι to have it *fresh in one's mind*, that.., Plu.2.17d; τὰ ὦτα ἔναυλος ὢν διαμέμνηται τοῦ μέλους Max.Tyr.7.7. II. (αὐλή) = ἐναύλιος, *dwelling in dens*, λέοντες E.*Ph.*1573 (anap.); *in one's den, at home*, opp. θυραῖος, S.*Ph.*158 (lyr.).

**ἐναυλοστᾰτέω**, *make a fold in*, *SIG*685.82 (Itanos).

**ἐναυξάνω**, aor. 1 ἐνηύξησα, *increase*, ἐπιθυμίαν ἀρετῆς X.*Cyn.*12.9:—Pass., c. dat., *grow in*.., τρυφῇ Hdn.2.10.6; **ἐναύξομαι**, v.l. for ἀέξομαι, Emp.106.

**ἔναυρος**, ον, (αὔρα) *exposed to the air*, Thphr.*HP*8.11.6. II. Ἔναυρος, epith. of Apollo, Hsch. **ἐναύρω**· πρωΐ (Cret.), Id.

⊕ **ἔναυσις**, εως, ἡ, *taking* from a neighbour, ὑδάτων τε πηγαίων καὶ πυρός Plu.*Cim.*10.

**ἔναυσμα**, ατος, τό, (ἐναύω A) *spark*: metaph., Max.Tyr.11.8; ζῴοισιν ἐ. *that which gives life* to animals, Orph.*H.*11.16; ἡ φύσις τοῖς σώμασιν ἐντίθησιν τῆς οἰκείας ἰδιότητος ἐ. Procl.*in Cra.*p.30P., cf. Iamb.*Protr.*21.ιζ'. 2. metaph., *spark, glimmer*, Plb.9.28.8, Plu.*Flam.*11 (pl.); ἐναύσματα εὐγενείας Ph.2.437: pl., *slight indications* of a testator's wishes, Just.*Nov.*107 *Pr.* 3. *stimulus, incentive*, τῶν ἀρετῶν ἐ. D.S.10*Fr.*11.2 (pl.); τοιαῦτα ἔχων ἐ. ἐς βασιλείας ἐπιθυμίαν Hdn.2.15.2.

**ἐναυχένιος**, ον, *in* or *on the neck*, βρόχος *AP*7.493 (Antip. Thess.).

**ἐναυχέω**, *boast*, Ph.1.422, Hsch.

⊕ **ἐναύω** (A), impf. ἐνηυον Hdt.7.231: aor. 1 opt. ἐναύσειε Diph.62, inf. ἐναῦσαι Plu.*Phoc.*37:—Med., Cratin.409: fut. -σομαι *Com.Adesp.*25.23D., Longus 3.6: aor. ἐναύσασθαι Pl.*Ax.*371e, etc.:—*kindle*, ἐ. πῦρ τινί *light* one a fire, *give* him *a light*, as was the duty of a neighbour, X.*Mem.*2.2.12, cf. Hdt.l.c., Diph.l.c., Call.*Iamb.*1.191; τοῦτον μήτε πόλει δέχεσθαι μήτε πῦρ ἐ. Plb.9.40.5, cf. Din.2.9:—Med., πῦρ ἐναύεσθαι *light oneself* a fire, *get* a light, ἐκ τῆς Αἴτνης Luc.*Tim.*6; ἀπὸ ἑτέρου πυρός Plu.*Num.*9: metaph., ἐ. τὸ θάρσος *borrow* courage, Pl.l.c.; τῆς ἐλευθερίας v.l. in Plb.18.11.7; of Poets, *draw* inspiration, Ἔφεσον ὅθεν πῦρ οἱ τὰ μέτρα μέλλοντες τὰ χωλὰ τίκτειν μὴ 'μαθῶς ἐναύονται Call.*Iamb.*1.335; ἐντεῦθεν ἐ. τὸν λόγον Ael.*Fr.*246; ἐξ αὐτοῦ διδασκαλίαν ἐ. ib.89. 2. *apply fire* to smoke out a swarm of bees, Hsch. (Cf. αὔω, ἐπαύω; the gloss ἔνανον (i.e. ἔναυον for ἔναυσον)· ἔνθες (Cypr.), Id., belongs to this word.)

**ἐναύω** (B), *cry aloud in*, Sch.Il.5.333.

**ἐναύω** (C), = ἱκετεύω πρὸς τοῖς ναοῖς, Suid., Zonar.

**ἐναφᾰνίζω**, *cause to disappear, hide*, τῶν ἡδονῶν τὰς σωματικὰς αἱ πρακτικαὶ τῷ χαίροντι τῆς ψυχῆς ἐ. Plu.2.1099d:—more freq. in Pass., *to be lost in*, ἔν τινι Str.1.3.3; τινί Ph.2.118, Longin.17.2, Plu.2.489a, M.Ant.7.10, al.: abs., of the pulse, *die away, disappear in*, ταῖς ἀντιβάσεσιν Agathin.ap.Gal.8.936.

**ἐναφάπτω**, Ion. ἐναπ-, *tie up* or *hang in* a thing, ἐναπῆπτε τὴν κεφαλὴν ἐς τὸν ἀσκόν f.l. in Hdt.1.214 (cf. ἐναφίημι); *attach*, Arist.*Cael.*301[b]26.

**ἐναφέσιος**, ὁ, *holder of land* ἐν ἀφέσει (cf. ἄφεσις I.1a), *PTeb.*352.6 (ii A.D.), etc.

**ἐναφέψημα**, ατος, τό, *decoction*, Aret.*CA*1.1.

**ἐναφέψω**, *boil down in*, Gal.6.291: pf. Pass. εναφέψημαι Hp.*Mul.*2.167, Orib.8.6.5: aor. 1 part. ἐναφεψηθείς Dsc.1.7, 2.129.

⊕ **ἐναφίημι**, *let drop into, put in*, in aor. 1 ἐναπῆκε Hdt.1.214 (cf. ἐναφάπτω); *insert*, Arist.*GA*723[b]23. II. *discharge in* or *into*, γόνον Id.*HA*553[b]24; τῇ κοίτῃ (sc. κόπρον) Artem.2.26. III. of land in Egypt, *release*, i.e. *transfer to private tenure*, in Pass., *POxy.*918 xiii 9 (ii A.D.), etc. 2. *leave*, ἐναφῆκέν μου τὰ κτήματα ἀγεώργητα *PMasp.*5.20 (vi A.D.). IV. *permit*, διατρέχειν τὸ πνεῦμα ἐν αὐτοῖς (sc. τοῖς νεύροις) ἐ. Orib.*Fr.*37.

**ἐναφροδισιάζω**, *venerem exerceo in*.., κόρῃ Aristaenet.1.15, 2.1.

**ἐνᾰχῶς**, *in nine ways*, Syrian.*in Metaph.*171.4.

**ἑνᾰχῶς**, *in one way*, prob. in Simp.*in Ph.*399.24.

**ἔναψις**, εως, ἡ, *attachment*, Ph.*Bel.*82.39 (pl.); ἐνάψεις ἀγκυρῶν ib.98.33.

⊕ **ἔνβενος**· ὑελοειδής, Hsch.

**ἐνγεταυθί**, in Ar.*Th.*646, com. tmesis for ἐνταυθί γε. **ἔνγλαυσιν**· ἐν γλαύκεσιν, Hsch. ⊕ **ἐνδαγεῖ**· ἐμμανεῖ, Id.

**ἐνδᾱδ-όομαι**, Pass., of a pine, *suffer from resin-glut*, Thphr.*HP*9.2.7. -ος, ον, (δᾴς) *resinous, full of resin*, ib.3.9.3.

**ἔνδαες**· ἐν διανοίᾳ ἑκάστου, Hsch.

⊛ **ἐνδαίνῠμαι**, Med., *feast on*, τι f.l. in Ath.7.277a.

**ἔνδαις**, αιδος, or **ἔνδᾳς**, ᾳδος, ὁ, ἡ, *with lighted torch*, σπονδαί A.*Eu.* 1044 (prob.).

**ἐνδαίω** (A), *light* or *kindle in*: metaph., ἐ. πόθον τινί Pi.*P.*4.184:—Med., *burn* or *glow in*, ἐν δέ οἱ ὄσσε δαίεται Od.6.131; βέλος δ' ἐνεδαίετο κούρῃ A.R.3.286.

⊛ **ἐνδαίω** (B), *distribute*, in Pass., ἐνδεδασμέναι ἡλικίαι Pyth.ap.Iamb. *VP*31.201; cf. ἔνδασαι· μέρισον, Hsch.

**ἐνδάκνω**, *bite into, seize with the teeth*, ἔχιδνα δ' ὥς μέ τις πόδ' ἐνδακοῦσ' ἔχει A.*Supp.*897 (dub.); ἐ. στόμια γνάθοις *take* the bit *between the teeth*, of runaway horses, E.*Hipp.*1223; ἐ. χαλινόν Pl.*Phdr.*254d; τὸ χεῖλος Luc.*Cal.*24: abs., Aret.*SA*1.7. 2. metaph., of sharp things, *fix themselves firm in*, τῇ γῇ Apollod.*Poliorc.*145.9; of mustard, *to be pungent*, Nic.*Fr.*70.16.

⊛ **ἔνδακρυς**, υ, gen. υος, *in tears, weeping*, J.*AJ*1.19.4, Luc.*Somn.*4.

**ἐνδακρύω**, *weep in* or *with*, ἐ. ὄμμασι *suffuse* them *with tears*, A.*Ag.* 541.

**ἐνδᾰμάζω**, *subdue*, σιδήρῳ Steph.*in Hp.*2.332 D. (Pass.).

**ἐνδᾱμέω**, **ἐνδᾱμία**, Dor. for ἐνδημ-.

**ἐνδανδαίνει**· ἀτενίζει, κατατολμᾷ, Hsch.

⊛ **ἐνδάπιος** [ᾰ], α, ον, *native of the country*, Mosch.2.11, Coluth.238, *AP*9.153 (Agath.); Ἕλλησι καὶ ἐνδαπίοισιν ἀμοιβήν *Bull.Inst.Egypt.* 1912.91; ἐ. Παλλάς Nonn.*D.*4.423: also in late Prose, Agath.2.15; cf. ἀλλοδαπός.

**ἔνδᾰσυς**, υ, *somewhat rough, hairy*, Dsc.2.142.

⊛ **ἐνδατέομαι**, *divide*, δὶς . . τοὔνομ' ἐνδατούμενος *dividing* the name of Polynices (into πολὺ νεῖκος), A.*Th.*578 (v. Sch.); ἐ. λόγους ὀνειδιστῆρας *distribute* or *fling about* reproaches, E.*HF*218. 2. c. acc. objecti, a. *speak of in detail*, i.e., in bad sense, *reproach, revile*, τὸ δυσπάρευνον λέκτρον ἐ. S.*Tr.*791; in good sense, *dwell on, celebrate*, εὐπαιδίας A.*Fr.*350.1; βέλεα θέλοιμ' ἂν . . ἐ. S.*OT*205 (lyr.) (perh. *scatter* or *shower* them *abroad*). b. *tear in pieces, devour*, Lyc. 155. II. Pass., *to be ground small*, Nic.*Th.*509, acc. to Sch.

**ἔνδαυλον**· λοχ(μ)ῶδες, δασύ, Hsch.

**ἐνδαύω**, *sleep in*, Lyc.1354.

⊛ **ἐνδαψῐλεύομαι**, *to be liberal in*, Hld.8.14. II. ὀλίγης πρὸς τὸ πέρας [τῶν ξυνθηκῶν] αὐτῷ -ομένης παραδρομῆς ἡμερῶν when the lapse of a few days was all that it would have *cost* to complete the agreement, Men.Prot.p.102 D.

**ἐνδέ-ημα**, ατος, τό, *deficiency*, *PRyl.*214.23 (ii A.D.), *POxy.*71ii5 (pl., iv A.D.). ⊛ **-ής**, ές, neut. pl. ἐνδεᾶ: (ἐνδέω B): *wanting* or *lacking in, in need of*, c. gen., ἐ. εἶναι or γεγενῆσθαί τινος, Hdt.1.32, Antipho 5.77; ἐνός μοι μῦθος ἐ. ἔτι E.*Hec.*835; πολλῶν ἐ., opp. αὐτάρκης, Pl.*R.*369b; ποιητοῦ δ' ἐστὶν ἐ. . . πρὸς τὸ ἐπιδεῖξαι, *caret vate sacro*, Id.*Smp.*195d, cf. *Lg.*697e; σμικροῦ τινος ἐ. εἰμι πάντ' ἔχειν Id.*Prt.* 329b. 2. abs., *in want, in need*, X.*HG*6.1.3 codd., etc. b. *lacking, deficient*, freq. in Comp., ἐνδεέστερα πρήγματα Hdt.7.48; φαίνεται ἐνδεεστέρα [ἡ στρατεία] Th.1.10; -εστέρα παρασκευή Id.4.65; ἐνδεέστεροι ταῖς οὐσίαις Isoc.4.105; also in Posit., οὐδὲν ἐνδεὲς ποιεῖσθαι leave nothing *unsaid*, S.*Ph.*375; τοῦτο πολλ ᾧ τοῦ παρόντος ἐνδεὲς E.*Heracl.* 170; μηδὲν ἐνδεὲς λίπῃς Id.*Ph.*385; ἐνδεὲς φαίνεταί τι Th.5.9; ἐνδεές τι ἐν τῷ σώματι ἔχειν X.*Cyr.*8.1.40; ἐ. τὸν βίον Men.592; τὴν ὄψιν Luc.*DMar.*1.2; τὸ ἐ. *lack, want, defect*, = ἔνδεια, Th.1.77; τὸ αὐτῶν ἐ. their *deficiency*, Id.3.83. 3. *inferior*, τὰ κρείσσω μηδὲ τἀνδεᾶ λέγειν *the worse*, S.*OC*1430; γένει οὐδενὸς ἐνδεής X.*HG*7.1.23; τῆς δυνάμεως ἐνδεᾶ πρᾶξαι to act *short of* your real power, Th.1.70; τούτου ἐνδεᾶ ἐφαίνετο (sc. τὰ πράγματα) their power was *unequal to* the purpose, ib.102: Comp. ἐνδεέστερός τινος S.*Ph.*524; τῆς δόξης Th.2.11; αὐτοῦ Plu.*Cic.*35. 4. *inadequate, insufficient*, πρός τι Pl.*Prt.*322b; ἐ. ξυνθῆκαι Th.8.36. 5. Gramm., *defective*, A.D.*Synt.*239.18. 6. Adv. ἐνδεῶς *defectively, insufficiently*, opp. ἱκανῶς, Pl.*Phd.*88e, *R.*523e; ἐ. ἔχειν τινός to be *in want of*, E.*Fr.*898.8; τῶν ἀναγκαίων Plu.*Nic.*27; μὴ ἐνδεῶς γνῶναι judge not *insufficiently*, Th.2.40: Comp. ἐνδεεστέρως παρεῖχεν ἢ πρὸς τὴν ἐξουσίαν *less* than, Id.4.39; ἐ. πρὸς ἃ βούλεται δηλοῦσθαι Id.2.35; ἐ. ἔχειν Pl.*Phd.*74e; ἐ. ἢ προσῆκεν τιμωρήσασθαι Epist. Philipp.ap.D.12.12: rarely -έστερον A.D.*Synt.*209.21. **-ητικός**, ή, όν, *deficient*, περὶ τὸ τέλος Vett.Val.15.20.

**ἔνδεια**, ἡ, *want, lack*, δυνάμεως Th.4.18; τῆς ἀναγκαιοτάτης διαίτης Id.7.82; χρημάτων X.*Ath.*1.5, Pl.*Hp.Ma.*283d, etc. II. abs., *deficiency, defect*, opp. ὑπερβολή, Id.*Prt.*357b, Arist.*EN*1109a4: pl., opp. ὑπερβολαί, Isoc.2.33, cf. 8.90. 2. *want, need*, coupled with ἐπιθυμία, Pl.*Grg.*496d,e: pl., αἱ ἔνδειαι τῶν φίλων, τοῦ σώματος, X.*Cyr.* 8.2.22, Pl.*Erx.*401e, al. 3. *want of means, poverty*, ἀεὶ ἐνδείᾳ σύνοικος Id.*Smp.*203d; αἰσχρόν τι ποιεῖν δι' ἔνδειαν D.18.257; *famine*, Jul. *Or.*2.66c. 4. Gramm., *defect*, opp. πλεόνασμα, A.D.*Synt.*133.15.

**ἔνδειγμα**, ατος, τό, (ἐνδείκνυμι) *evidence*, ὅτι . . Pl.*Criti.*110b, cf. Iamb.*Myst.*1.11; *token*, εὐνοίας D.19.256, cf. Dam.*Pr.*46.

**ἐνδείκ-νῡμι** or -ύω, fut. -δείξω, *mark, point out*, τι Pi.*O.*7.58; πρίν γ' ἂν ἐνδείξω τί δρῶ S.*OC*48; ἐ. τῷ δικαστηρίῳ τἀδικήματα Antipho 6. 37, etc.; *indicate*, τοὺς καιρούς Gal.1.204: c. part., *show that* a thing is, Pl.*Plt.*278b; also ἑκάστοις ἐ. τὰ ἔργα ἀποτελεῖν ib.308e. 2. law-term, *inform against*, τινά Id.*Ap.*32b: abs., Isoc.18.20; ἐ. ταῖς ἀρχαῖς Pl.*Lg.*856c, cf. And.1.8, etc.; τῷ φήναντι ἢ ἐνδείξαντι *IG*2². 1128.18; ἐ. πρὸς τοὺς μαστῆρας ib.12(7).62.53 (Amorgos, iv B.C.):—Med., Plu.*Sol.*24:—freq. in Pass., κακοῦργος ἐνδεδειγμένος Antipho 5. 9; ἐνδειχθείς Lys.6.15, *OGI*669.45 (Egypt, i A.D.); ἐνδειχθέντα δικάζειν ὀφείλοντα τῷ δημοσίῳ D.21.182. 3. *exhibit, display*, ὑπερήφανον αἰχμάν A.*Pr.*406 (lyr.). 4. Med., *declare* the possession of goods to fiscal authorities, *PRev.Laws* 54.10 (iii B.C.). II. Med., *show forth oneself* or *what is one's own*, once in Hom., Πηλεΐδῃ ἐνδείξομαι I *will declare myself* to Achilles, Il.19.83; ἐνδεικνύμενοι τὴν ἑαυτῶν γνώμην Hdt.8.141; ἐ. περί τινος Plb.4.28.4; τι μετ' ἀποδείξεως Id.5. 16.7. 2. *show, make plain*, c. part., πῶς δ' ἂν . . μᾶλλον ἐνδείξαιτό τις πόσιν προτιμῶσ' . . ; E.*Alc.*154, cf. *Ba.*47, X.*Cyr.*1.6.10; τὴν δύναμιν κρείττω οὖσαν ἐ. D.21.66; also ἐ. ὅτι . . Th.8.82, Pl.*Ap.*23b, X. *Cyr.*8.3.21; ἐ. ὁποῖα τούτων ἀληθῆ Pl.*Tht.*158e:—Pass., ἐνδεδεῖχθαι τὸ βούλεσθαι D.8.12. b. *prove, demonstrate*, *PMagd.*3.10 (iii B.C.), Phld.*Sign.*11, al. 3. c. acc. rei, *display, exhibit*, τὸ εὔψυχον Th.4. 126; εὔνοιάν τινα Ar.*Pl.*785; τῷ σώματι τὴν εὔνοιαν, οὐ χρήμασιν οὐδὲ λόγοις, ἐνεδείξατο τῇ πατρίδι D.21.145; τύπῳ τἀληθὲς ἐ. Arist.*EN* 1094b20; of a name, *denote*, Pl.*Cra.*394e. 4. ἐνδείκνυσθαί τινι *display oneself to* one, *make a set at* him, *court* him, D.19.113, Aeschin. 3.217, etc.; ἐνδεικνύμενοι καὶ ὑπερκολακεύοντές τινα D.19.160; *make a show, show off*, τινί Pl.*Prt.*317c, Arist.*Oec.*1352b13. **-της**, ου, ὁ, *informer, complainant*, *UPZ*69.4 (ii B.C.), Lxx 2*Ma.*4.1, Philostr. *VS*2.29. **-τικός**, ή, όν, *probative*, as the Protag. of Plato, D.L.3. 51. II. *indicative*, Gal.*Phil.Hist.*9, S.E.*P.*2.100, etc. Adv. -κῶς Id.*M.*8.155,289, Gal.10.928, al. **-τός**, ή, όν, *liable to prosecution*, ποτὶ δραχμὰς ἑκατόν *IG*5(2).266.44 (Mantinea, i B.C.).

**ἐνδείμᾰτος**, ον, *accompanied by fear*, ὑποδοχή Iamb.*Protr.*20.

**ἐνδεινῶς**, Adv. *terribly*: Comp. -ότερον dub. in Them.*Or.*4.56a.

**ἔνδειξις**, εως, ἡ, *indication*, ἔνδειξιν τῷ λόγῳ ἐνδείκνυσθαι, opp. ἐννοεῖν, Pl.*Lg.*966b, cf. Plb.3.38.5, *Ep.Rom.*3.25, A.D.*Synt.*14.18, Ptol. *Phas.*p.10 H., D.C.62.23, etc.; esp. in disease, Gal.10.126, al., S.E. *P.*1.240. 2. as law-term, *laying of information against* one who discharged public functions for which he was legally disqualified, *writ of indictment* in such a case, And.1.10, D.20.156 (pl.), Arist.*Ath.* 52.1 (pl.), cf. Decr.ib.29.4, *IG*2².1128.35. II. *demonstration, display of one's good will* (cf. ἐνδείκνυμι II.4), ἡ εἰς Ἀλέξανδρον ἔ. Aeschin. 3.219. III. *proof, demonstration*, Phlp.*in Mete.*123.34.

⊛ **ἕνδεκα**, οἱ, αἱ, τά, indecl., *eleven*, Il.2.713, etc. II. at Athens, οἱ ἕ. *the Eleven, the Police-Commissioners*, Ar.*V.*1108, Antipho 5.70, Lys.14.17, Pl.*Phd.*59e, Arist.*Ath.*7.3, etc. 2. certain officers at Delos, *Hermes* 17.5.

**ἑνδεκα-γράμμᾰτος**, ον, *of eleven letters*, πούς prob. in Ath.10.455b. **-γωνος**, ον, *having eleven angles*, Hero *Metr.*1.24, al. **-ετής**, ές, *of eleven years*, χρόνος *IG*12(5).860.42 (Tenos).

**ἑνδεκάζω**, *celebrate the tenth* of the month, cited by Harp. fr. D.58. [40].

**ἑνδεκᾰ-ήμερος**, ον, *lasting eleven days*, Gal.7.510. **-κις** [ᾰ, parox.], Adv. *eleven times*, Arist.*HA*562b25, TheoSm.p.126 H. **-κλῑνος**, ον, *with eleven couches*: κεφαλὴ ἑ. *big enough to hold eleven couches*, Telecl.44. **-κρούμᾰτος**, ον, *employing eleven notes*, μέτροις ῥυθμοῖς τε Tim.*Pers.*242. **-μετρον** μέτρον measure *of eleven* μέτρα, *PFay.*90.14. **-μηνος**, ον, *of eleven months*, Hp.*Oct.*13, Arist.*Fr.* 283. **-ούγκιον**, τό, *eleven ounces*, Gloss. **-πηχυς**, υ, gen. εος, *eleven cubits long*, ἔγχος Il.6.319; δοκός *IG*11(2).161 *D* 125 (iii B.C.); διάστημα S.E.*M.*10.160. **-πους**, ὁ, ἡ, πουν, τό, gen. ποδος, *eleven feet long* or *broad*, λίθος *Milet.*7.58 (Didyma), cf. Poll.1.72.

**ἑνδεκάς**, άδος, ἡ, *the number Eleven*, Pl.*Lg.*771c, Arist.*Metaph.* 1084a26.

**ἑνδεκᾰσύλλᾰβος**, ον, *eleven-syllabled*, ἑ. Πινδαρικόν (sc. μέτρον) Heph.14.2.

**ἑνδεκᾰταῖος**, α, ον, *on the eleventh day*, Hp.*Aph.*4.36, Th.2.97; ἔραμαι σχεδὸν ἑνδεκαταῖος *for* nearly *eleven days*, Theoc.10.12.

⊛ **ἑνδέκᾰτος**, η, ον, *eleventh*, Od.3.391, etc.; ἑνδεκάτη (sc. ἡμέρη), ἡ, *eleventh day*, 2.374.

**ἑνδεκάχορδος** [ᾰ], ον, *eleven-stringed*, λύρα Ion Eleg.3.1.

**ἑνδεκᾰχῶς**, *in eleven ways*, Simp.*in Ph.*553.2.

**ἑνδεκ-έτης**, ες, = ἑνδεκαετής, prob. in *CIG*(add.)3846 *z* 61 (Aezani):—fem. -έτις, ιδος, *AP*7.164.6 (Antip. Sid.). **-ήρης**, ες, *with eleven banks of oars*, Thphr.*HP*5.8.1, Callix.2.

**ἐνδέκομαι**, Ion. for ἐνδέχ-.

**ἐνδεκτόν**· ἐστι, = ἐνδέχεται, A.D.*Synt.*148.4, al.

**ἐνδελέχ-εια**, ἡ, *continuity, persistency*, πέτρην κοιλαίνει ῥανὶς ὕδατος ἐνδελεχείῃ Choeril.10; πάντα γὰρ ταῖς ἐνδελεχείαις καταπονεῖται πράγματα Men.744.—Freq. confused with ἐντελέχεια (q.v.). **-έω**, *continue*, c. acc., μάστιγάς τινι Lxx *Si.*30.1:—Pass., *to be persistently afflicted* with a malady, Steph.*in Hp.*1.136 D. **-ής**, ές, (v. δολιχός) *continuous, perpetual*, μνήμη Pl.*Lg.*718a; λειτουργία Isoc.15.156 (Sup.); πῦρ Lxx 1*Es.*6.24; θυσίαι Ph.2.569,587; πόλεμος Plu.*Per.*19; of persons, *plodding, persevering*, φροντισταὶ σύντονοι καὶ ἐ. Phld. *Oec.*p.52 J., cf. Plu.*Mar.*13; τὸ περὶ τοὺς πόνους ἐ. *perseverance*, ib.6. Adv. -χῶς Critias 19.5, Pl.*R.*539d, al., Diod.Com.1, Men.521, *IG*2². 1028.33, Lxx *Ex.*29.38, Plu.*Fab.*19, etc.—Freq. confused with ἐντελεχής in codd., as Ph. l.c. **-ίζω**, = ἐνδελεχέω, *persevere*, ἐν φιλοσοφίᾳ Epicur.*Fr.*195, cf. Lxx *Si.*9.4:—Pass., fut. -ισθήσομαι Hsch. **-ισμός**, ὁ, = ἐνδελέχεια, *persistence*, Philum.ap.Orib.45. 29.21; θυμίαμα -ισμοῦ *perpetual* incense, Lxx *Ex.*30.8; esp. of daily sacrifices, ib.29.38, al. (-ιστόν is f.l. in Thd.*Da.*11.31), cf. J.*AJ*11. 4.1 (pl.).

**ἐνδελιπές**· παντελές, Hsch.: **ἐνδελιστές**, sine expl. (Syrac.), Theognost.*Can.*162: **ἐνδελῖτες** Epich.183.

**ἔνδεμα**, ατος, τό, (ἐνδέω A) *thing bound on*, *Gloss.*: pl., *amulets*, Dsc. *Eup.*2.136.

**ἐνδέμω**, *wall up*, τὰς διασφάγας Hdt.3.117. II. *build in* a place, τρεῖς μέν οἱ πολίων ἑκατοντάδες ἐνδέδμηνται Theoc.17.82:—Med., *build* or *make for oneself in*, κοῖτον θάμνῳ Nic.*Th.*419.

**ἐνδενδίλλειν**· ἐμβλέπειν, Hsch. ⊛ **ἔνδενδρος**, epith. of Zeus in Paros, *IG*12(5).1027 (prob.); of Zeus at Rhodes, and of Dionysus in Boeotia, Hsch.

**ἐνδεξιόομαι**, *go round from left to right*, βωμόν E.*IA*1473.

⊛ **ἐνδέξιος**, α, ον, Hom. only neut. pl. ἐνδέξια, *towards the right hand, from left to right*, mostly as Adv., θεοῖς ἐνδέξια πᾶσιν οἰνοχόει he filled for all the gods *from left to right*, Il.1.597; δεῖξ' ἐνδέξια πᾶσιν 7.184; βῆ δ' ἴμεν αἰτήσων ἐνδέξια φῶτα ἕκαστον Od.17.365; τὴν ἐπὶ πυρκαϊῆς ἐ. φασὶ κέλευθον Ἑρμῆν τοὺς ἀγαθοὺς.. ἄγειν *AP*7.545 (Hegesipp.): regarded as lucky, hence ἐνδέξια σήματα *propitious* omens, Il.9.236, cf. *SIG* 1025.25 (Cos). 2. after Hom. without any sense of motion, *on the right*, v.l. in E.*Hipp.*1360 (anap.); ἐνδέξιος σῷ ποδὶ παρασπιστής *on thy right*, Id.*Cyc.*6; εἰσιόντων ἐνδέξια *on the right* as one enters, *PPetr.*3 p.203; ἡ παραστὰς ἡ ἐνδεξία *Inscr.Prien.*19.46 (iii B.C.): c. gen., ἐνδέξια τῆς εἰκόνος ib.53.74 (ii B.C.). II. *clever*, ἔργα *h.Merc.*454. Adv. -ίως Sch.Th.2.41.

**ἐνδεόντως**, Adv. *deficiently*, κατά τι ἐ. ἔχειν Gal.6.839.

**ἐνδέρω**, *wrap in skin*, of sacrificial offerings, in Pass., *SIG*1025.48 (Cos), 1026.8 (ibid.), cf. Hsch. s.v. ἔνδρατα.

**ἐνδέρως**, Adv. *after wrapping in skin* (cf. foreg.), θύεται Ἐφ.Ἀρχ. 1902.3 (Chalcis).

**ἔν-δεσις**, εως, ἡ, (ἐνδέω A) *binding on*, of the point of the *pilum*, Plb. 6.23.11: pl., *fastenings*, Ph.*Bel.*99.47; *junction*, τοῦ ποδός Hp.*Oss.* 16. 2. *swaddling*, Sor.1.84. II. *entanglement*, M.Ant.10. 28. 2. *cohesion* of superstructure and foundation, Ph.*Bel.*84. 20 (pl.). **-δεσμα**, ατος, τό, *amulet*, Dsc.2.114. **-δεσμεύω**, *bind to* or *in*, τινὰς εἰς καταπέλτας D.S.20.71:—Pass., Dsc.*Eup.*1.146; τῇ χέρσῳ D.S.3.40. **-δεσμέω**, = foreg., Aq.*Ex.*23.22, al., v.l. in Dsc.4.43 (Pass.): metaph., πρὸς ἃ -εῖται ἡ ψυχή Procl.*in Alc.* p.108 C. II. *tie up in*, τινί *Gp.*8.1.3. **-δεσμίς**, ίδος, ἡ, *fillet-band*, *IG*11(2).161 *B*116 (pl., Delos, ii B.C.). ⊛ **-δεσμος**, ὁ, *bundle, bag*, Dsc.3.83, Lxx 3*Ki.*6.10, al., Luc.*Lex.*10; ἐ. ἀργυρίου *purse*, Lxx *Pr.*7.20. II. Archit., *bonding*, τείχους *SIG*²587.308 (pl., written ἐνδέσζμων); ἐ. ποιεῖσθαι τοῦ ἔργου Procop.*Pers.*2.26.

**ἔνδετος**, ον, *bound to, entangled in*, πάγαις *AP*9.372.

**ἐνδευκής**, ές, *like, similar*, Hsch.

**ἐνδεύω** (A), Aeol. for ἐνδέω (B), *to be wanting*, *IG*12(2).6 (Mytilene).

⊛ **ἐνδεύω** (B), *soak* or *dye in*, βάμματι Nic.*Al.*414 (Med.).

**ἐνδεχ[έτηρος]**, ον, = ἐνδεκέτης, *IG*9(1).882.13 (Corc., ii A.D.).

⊛ **ἐνδέχομαι**, Ion. -δέκομαι, fut. -ξομαι, *take upon oneself*, ταλαιπωρίας Hdt.6.11. II. *accept, admit, approve*, τὸν λόγον Id.1.60; τοὺς λόγους Id.5.92.α', 96, al., Ar.*Eq.*632; τὰ λεγόμενα Th.3.82; τὴν συμβουλίην Hdt.7.51; διαβολάς Id.3.80; ἀπόστασιν, = τὸν περὶ ἀποστάσιος λόγον, ib.128; so ἐ. [τὴν τοῦ Ἀλκιβιάδου κάθοδον] Th.8.50. 2. in Hdt. freq. *give ear to, believe*, mostly with a neg., ἀρχὴν.. οὐδὲ ἐ. τὸν λόγον 5.106; τοῦτο δὲ οὐκ ἐ. ἀρχήν 4.25, cf. 3.73, 7.237: c. inf., *believe* that.., οὐ γὰρ ἔγωγε ἐ. Ἠριδανόν τινα καλέεσθαι ποταμόν 3.115. 3. abs., *give ear, attend*, σὺ δ' ἐνδέχου E.*Andr.*1238, cf. Pl.*Cra.*428b; περί τινος οὐδ' ὁπωσοῦν ἐ. refuse *to hear a word* about it, Th.7.49. III. of things, *admit, allow of*, τὸ προμηθὲς λογισμὸν οὐκ ἐνδέχεται περί τινος Id.4.92; μεταβολήν, ἀλλοίωσιν ἐ., Pl.*Phd.*78d; καθ' ὅσον φύσις ἐνδέχεται, *quantum recipit humana condicio*, Id.*Ti.*69a, cf. *Sph.*254c: c. inf., τὸ ναυτικὸν.. οὐκ ἐνδέχεται ἐκ παρέργου μελετᾶσθαι *does* not *admit of* being practised, Th.1.142, cf. Pl.*Ti.*90c, *Lg.*834d; ὅσων αἱ ἀρχαὶ μὴ ἐνδέχονται ἄλλως ἔχειν Arist.*EN*1139ᵃ7. 2. abs., *to be possible*, ἃ πολλὰ ἐνδέχεται Th.4.18; ἐὰν ἐνδεχόμενον ᾖ if it be *possible*, *PGrenf.*2.14.4 (iii B.C.); freq. in Arist., *APr.*25ᵃ38, al.; ἐνδέχεσθαι ἢ εἶναι οὐδὲν διαφέρει ἐν τοῖς ἀϊδίοις *Ph.*203ᵇ30; ἐ. μέν, οὐ μὴν ἀναγκαῖον *Pol.*1275ᵇ6: esp. in part. ἐνδεχόμενος, η, ον, *possible*, ἐκ τῶν ἐνδεχομένων *by all possible means*, X.*Mem.*3.9.4, D.S.1.54; αἱ ἐ. τιμωρίαι Lycurg.119; τὴν ἐ. ἀϊδιότητα Jul.*Or.*4.157b; εἰς τὸ ἐ. *so far as possible*, Hyp.*Epit.*41; and freq. in Arist., τὸ ἐ. ἀληθές *Metaph.*1009ᵇ 34; τῆς ἐ. αὐτοῖς εὐδαιμονίας μετέχειν *Pol.*1325ᵃ10; ζωῆς τῆς ἐ. ἀρίστης ib.1328ᵃ36, al.: freq. c. inf., τὰ ἐ. καὶ εἶναι καὶ μὴ εἶναι *contingent* events, *GA*731ᵇ25, cf. *Metaph.*1050ᵇ11; τὰ ἐ. ἄλλως ἔχειν *EN*1134ᵇ 31, al.; τὰ μὴ ἐ. αὐτῷ πρᾶξαι ib.1140ᵃ32, al. 3. ἐνδέχεται impers., *it admits of* being, *it is possible that..*, c. acc. et inf., Th.1.124, 140, etc.; εἴπερ ἐνεδέχετο (sc. γράφειν) D.18.239; καθ' ὅσον ἐνδέχεται Pl. *Phdr.*271c; εἰς ὅσον ἐ. Id.*R.*501c; ὅσα ἐ. Arist.*Rh.*1354ᵃ32; μέχρι οὗ ἐ. ib.1355ᵇ13; ὡς ἐ. μάλιστα Plb.3.49.1: acc. abs., ὥσπερ ἐνδεχόμενον εἶναι, = ὥσπερ εἰ ἐνδέχοιτο, Arist.*GA*765ᵇ23: gen. abs., ἐνδεχομένου *where possible*, Id.*PA*683ᵃ20. b. c. dat. pers., *it is allowed*, X.*Hier.*4.9, D.29.50.

**ἐνδεχομένως**, Adv. of foreg., = ὅσον ἐνδέχεται, Decr.ap.D.18.165, Plb.1.20.4, al., D.S.20.26, Lxx 2*Ma.*13.26, etc.; ὡς ἐ. *PPetr.*2 p.53; ἀντέγραψεν ἐ. *to the best of his ability*, Aristeas 41.

⊛ **ἐνδέω** (A), fut. -δήσω (v. infr.), *bind in, on* or *to*, τι ἔν τινι Od.5. 260; εἰς σῶμα Pl.*Ti.*43a, cf. Dsc.3.83; more freq. τί τινι Ar.*Ach.* 929, etc.; ὅσα κατέρρωγεν τοῦ τείχους ἐνδήσει θράνοις *IG*2².463:—Med., ἐνεδήσατο δεσμῷ *bound* them *fast*, Theoc.24.27; ὥσπερ κέραμον ἐνδησάμενος *having packed* it *up*, Ar.*Ach.*905; πλίνθους εἰς ἄσφαλτον ἐνδησαμένη D.S.2.7:—Pass., ἱρὰ ἐνδεδεμένα ἐν καλάμῃ Hdt.4.33; ἐνδεθῆναι εἰς σῶμα, ἐν τῷ σώματι, Pl.*Phd.*81e, 92a; ἄστρα ἐνδεδεμένα τοῖς κύκλοις *fixed* stars, Arist.*Cael.*289ᵇ33; also οὐρανὸς [ἀστράσιν] ἐνδέδεται *AP*9.25 (Leon.); Αἰγαῖον ὕδωρ Κυκλάδας ἐνδέδεται *App. Anth.*3.82.6 (Archim.). II. metaph., Ζεύς με.. ἄτῃ ἐνέδησε βαρείῃ *entangled* me *in* it, Il.2.111, cf. S.*OC*526 (lyr.); ἀναγκαίῃ ἐνδέειν τινά Hdt.1.11:—Pass., ἐνδεδέσθαι ὁρκίοισι Id.3.19; ἀναγκαίῃ Id.9.16; ἐνδεδεμένος εἰς τὴν πίστιν τῆς συγκλήτου Plb.6.17.8; τῇ χάριτι Id.20. 11.10; ἐ. κατὰ τὰς οὐσίας, i.e. in debt, Id.13.1.3; ἐνδεδέσθαι τὴν ἀρχήν *to have* the government *secured*, Id.9.23.2:—Med., *bind to oneself*, ὅρκοις τὸν πόσιν E.*Med.*162; τινὰ εἰς τὴν τῶν Ῥωμαίων φιλίαν Plb. 10.34.1. III. Pass., *to be possessed by an evil spirit*, J.*AJ*8.2.5.

⊛ **ἐνδέω** (B), fut. -δεήσω Hdt.7.18, etc.:—*fall short*, c. inf., τίνος ἐνδέομεν μὴ οὐ χωρεῖν; what *do we lack* of going? E.*Tr.*797, cf. *IA*41 (anap.); ὅσον ἐνδέουσιν.. τὰ αὐτὰ ἔχειν how much they *fall short* of being indentical, Pl.*Cra.*432d; ἕως γ' ἂν μηδὲν ἐνδέῃ τοῦ ποιμενικὴ εἶναι Id.*R.*345d, cf. 529d, *Phd.*74d:—also in Med., *to be in want of, lack*, δριμύτητος ἐνδεῖται Id.*Plt.*311a, cf. X.*Cyr.*2.2.26, etc.:—so in aor. Pass., στρωμάτων ἐνδεηθέντες ib.6.2.30. 2. *to be wanting* or *lacking*, ποίεε.. ὅκως τῶν σῶν ἐνδεήσει μηδέν that nothing *may be wanting* on your part, Hdt.l.c.; ὁ σταθμὸς ἐνδεῖ App.*Mith.*47: c. dat., ἐνδεῖ τι τῷ ἔργῳ Luc.*Tyr.*10; οὐδὲν ὑμῖν ἐνδεήσει Hdn.2.5.8; ἐ. ταῖς παραγγελίαις *to be deficient* for.., App.*BC*1.21; ἐς βάθος τῷ ἀριθμῷ ἐνδέον Arr.*Tact.*16.12; τὸ ἐνδέον the *deficiency*, *POxy.*1117.8 (ii A.D.). 3. impers., ἐνδεῖ *there is need* or *want*, c. gen. rei, τοῦ ἴσου ἡμῖν ἐνδεῖ πρὸς τὸ εἰδέναι Pl.*Euthd.*292e; πολλῶν ἐνέδει αὐτῷ ὥστε.. he *had need of, was wanting in* much, X.*An.*7.1.41; ἅπαντος ἐνδεῖ τοῦ πόρου *there is a deficiency* of all revenue, D.1.19; ἐνδεῖ κωπῶν *IG* 2.789ᵃ6.

**ἐνδηΐδες**· αἱ Νύμφαι ἐν Κύπρῳ, Hsch.

**ἔνδηλος**, ον, *visible, manifest, clear*, ἔνδηλα καὶ σαφῆ λέγειν S.*Ant.* 405; ἔ. τι ποιεῖν Th.4.132. 2. *manifest, discovered, known*, mostly of persons, Ar.*Eq.*1277, Th.6.36; τινί Id.4.41: with a part., ἔνδηλοι ἔστε.. βαρυνόμενοι Id.2.64, cf. Pl.*Phd.*88e, *Tht.*174d, D.21.198; of things, τί τὸ ὑποκείμενον, οὐκ ἔστιν ἔνδηλον Arist.*de An.*422ᵇ34. II. Adv. -λως: Sup. -ότατα, προλέγειν Th.1.139.

**ἐνδημ-έω**, Dor. ἐνδᾱμέω, *live at* or *in* a place, Lys.9.5, *IG*12(5). 534.6 (Ceos, ii B.C.); simply, *stay, remain in* a place, μέχρις ἂν ἐνδημῶσιν οἱ πρέσβεις Aen.Tact.10.11; ἐνδημῶν καὶ ἀποδημῶν Mitteis *Chr.*284.3 (ii B.C.), etc.: metaph., ὁ θεὸς ἐνδεδήμηκεν εἰς τὴν ἐμὴν ψυχήν Chariton 6.3; ἐ. ἐν τῷ σώματι, πρὸς τὸν Κύριον, 2*Ep.Cor.*5.6, 8. ⊛ **-ία**, Dor. ἐνδᾱμία, ἡ, *dwelling in* a place, *lodging, sojourning*, τὴν ἐ. ποιεῖσθαι *IG*12(5).533.5 (Ceos, ii B.C.), cf. 4.679.18 (Hermione), 5(1).7 (Sparta), Hsch. **-ιος**, ον, = ἔνδημος, Opp.*H.*4.264. **-ιουργέω**, *manufacture, produce*, φάσματα Plu.2.17b; τι ἔν τινι ib.664f:—Pass., ib.636c. **-ος**, ον, *dwelling in* a place, *native*, Hes.*Op.*225, Thgn. 794, etc.; ἔ. παρών being here *at home*, A.*Ch.*570; ἐνδημότατοι *the greatest 'stay-at-homes'*, opp. ἀποδημηταί, Th.1.70. 2. of things, βοὴ ἔ. *intestine* war, A.*Supp.*683 (lyr.); πόλεμοι D.H.8.83; τὰ ἔ. *home-affairs*, opp. τὰ ὑπερόρια, Arist.*Pol.*1285ᵇ14; ἀρχαί (opp. ὑπερόριοι) Id.*Ath.*24.3, cf. Aeschin.1.45, Foed.ap.Th.5.47; *endemic*, νοσήματα Gal.15.429, 17(1).11; also τὰ ἔ. βιβλία applied to the surgical treatises of Hippocrates, Pall.*in Hp.Fract.*12.271 C.

**ἔνδια**· ὀδύνη, λεῖψις πράγματος, ἡ μεσημβρία, διατριβή, Hsch.

⊛ **ἐνδιαβάλλω**, *calumniate*, Ctes.*Fr.*29.10, Lxx *Ps.*108(109).4, Luc. *Cal.*24 (Act. and Pass.). 2. *stand in the way as an adversary*, Lxx *Nu.*22.22.

**ἐνδιάβολος**, ον, *containing a slander*, *PMag.Par.*1.2572.

**Ἐνδιάγρος**, epith. of Artemis, Hsch.

**ἐνδιάγω** [ᾰ], *pass one's life in*, ἐν τοῖς στρατιωτικοῖς καταλόγοις Heph.Astr.1.1; f.l. for ἐνδιάω in *AP*5.291 (Agath.).

**ἐνδῐᾰερῐαυερῐ(-αυρι- Dind., prob.)νήχετος**, ον, *floating in midday airy breezes*, dithyrambic parody in Ar.*Pax*831.

**ἐνδιάζω**, (ἔνδιος I. 1) *pass the noon, take a siesta*, Plu.*Rom.*4, 2. 726f. II. *weave in*, in Pass., Hsch.

**ἐνδιά-θεσις**, εως, ἡ, only in phrase ὁ κατὰ-θεσιν λόγος, = λ. ἐνδιάθετος, *Placit.*4.11 tit. **-θετος**, ον, *residing in the mind* (ἐν τῇ διαθέσει, opp. ἐν τῇ προφορᾷ, Porph.*Abst.*3.3), ἐ. λόγος *conception, thought*, opp. προφορικὸς λ. (expression), *Stoic.*2.43, etc.; of the *immanent* reason of the world, Ph.1.598; ἕξις ib.36, Plu.2.48d; ὁ ἐ. ἄνθρωπος the *inner* man, *Corp.Herm.*13.7 (s.v.l.). 2. *innate*, περιαυτολογία Plu.2.44a: hence, *unaffected, spontaneous*, Hermog.*Id.*2. 7; τὸ ἐ. ib.1.11, al. 3. τὸ σὸν εἰς ἡμᾶς ἐ. your *disposition* towards us, *PAmh.*2.145.12 (iv/v A.D.). Adv. **-τως** λέγειν speak *from the heart*, Hermog.*Id.*2.7; βοᾶν Sch.Arat.968; εὔχεσθαι Eust. ad D.P. 739. II. *deep-seated*, opp. ἐπιπόλαιον, ἄλγημα Gal.14.739. 2. Adv. *fixedly*, opp. προσκαίρως, Sor.1.92. **-θηκος**, ον, *committed to writing*, λόγος Hsch. **-θρύπτομαι**, *play the prude towards*, τινί Theoc.3.36.

**ἐνδῐαιτ-άομαι**, Ion. -έομαι, *live* or *dwell in* a place, ἐν τῷ ἱρῷ Hdt. 8.41; μνήμη παρ' ἑκάστῳ ἐ. Th.2.43; οἰκία ἡδίστη ἐνδιαιτᾶσθαι X.*Mem.* 3.8.8, cf. Crates Theb.15; ἐπίνοια ἐ. ἡμῖν Plu.2.608e; ἡδονὴ ἐ. τῇ γνώμῃ Lib.*Or.*64.116. ⊛ **-ημα**, ατος, τό, *dwelling-place*, D.H.1.37, Ph.1.52, al., Plu.2.968b, Phalar.*Ep.*34 (pl.), Agath.3.23; ἐ. δαιμόνων τὴν ψυχὴν κατασκευάσας Porph.*Marc.*11. **-ησις**, εως, ἡ, *dwelling in* a place, Ph.1.334 (pl.), 2.234, Them.*Or.*27.334a.

**ἐνδιά-κειμαι**, Pass., *to be set in*, λίθοι σχοινίοισιν ἐ. J.*AJ*12.2. 9. **-κειμένως**, Adv. = ἐνδιαθέτως, λέγειν τι Hermog.*Id.*2.7. **-κοσμέω**, = διακοσμέω ἐν.., Ocell.3.1. **-λαμβάνω**, in pf. part. Pass. ἐνδιειλημμένος *divided at intervals*, γόνασιν Dsc.2.94.

⊛ **ἐνδιαλλάσσω**, Att. -ττω, *alter*, Arist.*Phgn.*806ᵃ13:—Pass. -αγμένος, ὁ, *sodomite*, Lxx 3*Ki.*22.47, Aq.*Ge.*38.21.

**ἐνδιαλύω**, *loosen, disperse* a clot of blood, Sor.2.32.

**ἐνδιάλῳ**· μεσημβρίας ὥρᾳ, Hsch. (Fort. ἐν δειέλῳ, vel ἐν διάλῳ, = δεάλῳ, δήλῳ.)

**ἐνδια-μένω**, *remain in* (sc. the body), dub.l. in D.H.8.62. **-περονάω**, *transfix with a pin*, *Gloss.* (Pass.). **-πράττω**, f.l. for δια-,

Pl.*Phdr.*253c (Med.). **-πρέπω**, *to be distinguished in*, γυμνασίαις πολεμικαῖς D.S.36.4.5.

**ἐνδιαρκής**, ές, *sufficient, adequate*, *PStrassb.*40.32 (vi A.D.).

**ἐνδια-σκευάζω**, *work up*, in literary composition, Sch.Ar.*Ra.*1488 (Pass.), Sch.Il.3.393. **-σκευος** διήγησις, in Rhet., *elaborate, highly wrought* statement, Hermog.*Inv.*2.7. Adv. **-ως** ib.3.15, Eust. 177.31. **-σπείρω**, *sprinkle*, *Gp.*6.8.1 :—Pass., *to be dispersed in*, τινί Arist.*Fr.*217 : abs., ἔθνος -εσπαρμένον Lxx *Es.*3.8 (v.l.); *to be distributed*, of nerves, Gal.2.370. II. [σπέρματα] πᾶσι χυμοῖς καὶ ὀσμαῖς -εσπαρμένα *impregnated* with, Epicur.*Fr.*250. **-στέλλομαι**, *distinguish clearly*, Stob.2.7.$4^{a}$. **-στροφος**, ον, *perverted*, Phlp. *in de An.*21.24. **-τάσσω**, *draw up in*, χῶρος ἐπιτήδειος ἐνδιατάξαι (sc. τὸν στρατόν) Hdt.7.59. **-τίθεμαι**, Med., *dispose* : hence, *set forth in*, οἷς -θήσονται τὸ εὐχάριστον Ph.2.524. II. = ἐν διαθέσει εἶναι, ἐνδιάθετος εἶναι, ἀεὶ -θέμενος Plot.5.3.11. **-τρίβω** [ῐ], pf. -τέτρῐφα Arist.*Mete.*$357^{a}4$ :—*spend* or *consume in* doing, χρόνον Ar.*Ra.*714, Th.2.18,85. II. abs. (sc. χρόνον or βίον), *spend time in* a place, αὐτόθι D.33.5; τῇ χώρᾳ Plb.3.88.1, etc.; ἐν τόπῳ D.S. 5.44; ἀνθρωπίσκοις *among* them, Luc.*Alex.*33. 2. *waste time by staying in* a place, *linger* there, Th.5.12, 7.81, etc. 3. *continue in* the practice of a thing, τοῖς ἤθεσι..τοῖς ἀρχαίοις Ar.*Ec.*585, cf. Pl. *Grg.*484c, *R.*487d; ἐὰν ἐνδιατρίβειν τὴν ὄψιν ἔν τινι let one's eyes *linger on* it, X.*Cyr.*5.1.16; ἐ. λόγοις καὶ ἔργοις *linger fondly on* them, Luc.*Nigr.*7; τῇ περὶ τοὺς βίους ἀναγραφῇ Plu.*Per.*2; κατὰ φιλοσοφίαν Epicur.*Fr.*217; περὶ μουσικήν Ath.14.623e; ἐ. ὅθεν ἡσυχεῖ Epicur. *Nat.*27 G.; esp. *dwell upon a point* (in speaking), Aeschin.3.201, cf. Arist.*Pol.*$1258^{b}35$, Jul.*Or.*1.45b; περί τινος Arist.*Metaph.*$989^{b}27$; τῷ χρησίμῳ Hermog.*Prog.*7, etc. **-τριπτέον**, *one must dwell upon*, τινί Luc.*Hist.Conscr.*6; *one must stay in* a place, Ath.Med.ap. Orib.*inc.*23.13; ἐ. τούτοις *one must continue the treatment*, Sor.1. 46. **-τριπτικός**, ή, όν, *fondly dwelling in*, τόποις καὶ πράγμασι τοῖς αὐτοῖς M.Ant.1.16.7. **-τριπτος**, ον, *spent, consumed* in a process, ἐνιαυτός, ὁ ἐ. χρόνος *EM*342.34, cf. *Et.Gud.* s. v. ἐνιαυτός.

**ἐνδιαυγέω**, *shine through*, Pass., νέφη -εῖσθαι Sch.Arat.858.

**ἐνδια-φθείρω**, fut. -ερῶ, *to destroy in*, dub. in Plu.2.658c; *destroy* a child *in* the womb, Hp.*Carn.*19. **-φορος**, ον, *differing, varying*, στηριγμοί Paul.Al.*G.*1; περὶ τὸ γένος Vett.Val.105.33. 2. *containing differences*, νοῦς *Corp.Herm.*12.6. **-χειμάζω**, *winter in*, νήσῳ Str.2.3.4.

**ἐνδιάω**, (ἔνδιος) *stay in the open air*: generally, *linger in* or *haunt* a place, c. dat., βάτοις *AP*5.291.6 (Agath.); ἔνθα δ' ἀνὴρ..ἐνδιάασκε Theoc.22.44: also c. acc., πάγους καὶ πρῶνας Opp.*C.*3.315: abs., περὶ σπήλυγγας ib.4.81: metaph., [ὄμμασιν] ἐλπὶς ἐνδιάει *AP*5.269.10 (Paul. Sil.); ἐ. εἰς κενεὰς εἰκόνας ib.4.4.10 (Agath.) :—abs. in Med., ἀκτῖνες ἐνδιάονται *are bright as day* (of the moon), *h.Hom.*32.6; but ἐνδιῶνται· μεσημβριάζουσι, Hsch. II. trans., ποιμένες μῆλα ἐνδιάασκον shepherds *drove* their sheep *afield*, Theoc.16.38 (s. v.l.).

**ἐνδιδομένως**, Adv., (ἐνδίδωμι) *remissly*, Phot., Suid. s. v. ὑφειμένως.

**ἐνδιδύσκω**, *put on*, τινά τι Lxx 2*Ki.*1.24, *Ev.Marc.*15.17 :—Med., *put on oneself*, *Ev.Luc.*8.27, J.*BJ*7.2.2 (Act. is v.l.): written ἐνδυδισκόμενος *SIG*²857.13 (Delph.). II. *clothe*, τινὰ ἱματίῳ *Gp.*16.21.9.

❋ **ἐνδίδωμι**, *give in*: hence, I. *give into* one's *hands, give up to*, ἀσκὸν ἔνδος μοι E.*Cyc.*510 (lyr.), etc.; ἑαυτόν τινι Pl.*R.*561b, cf. Ar.*Pl.*781 (v.l.); τινὰ τοῖς πολεμίοις Pl.*R.*567a; ἐ. πόλιν *surrender* a city, esp. by treachery, Th.4.66, cf. X.*HG*7.4.14, etc.; τοῖς Ἀθηναίοις τὰ πράγματα ἐ. Th.7.48, cf. 2.65 :—Pass., τῷ Ἱπποκράτει τὰ ἐν τοῖς Βοιωτοῖς ἐνεδίδοτο Id.4.89: impers., οὐδὲν ἐνεδίδοτο ἀπὸ τῶν ἔνδον no *sign of surrender was made*, Arr.*An.*1.20.6. 2. *put in, apply to*, ἅρμασι κέντρον E.*HF*881 (lyr.). 3. *hand in* a report, ἐ. ἀναφοράν Mitteis *Chr.*68.2 (i A.D.). 4. Pass., *to be interposed*, ἐνδοθεισῶν ὀλίγων ἡμερῶν Aët.13.121. II. *lend, afford*, ἐνδιδόναι τινὶ χερὸς στηρίγματα *lend* him a supporting hand, E.*IA*617; ἐ. ἀφορμὰς *give* an occasion, Id. *Hec.*1239; λαβὴν Ar.*Eq.*847; πρόφασίν τινι κακῷ γενέσθαι Th.2.87, cf. D.18.158; καιρὸν Id.4.18; ἐ. ὑποψίαν ὡς.. *give ground for suspicion that*.., Pl.*Lg.*887e; ἐλπίδας τινί τινος Plu.*Alc.*14 :—*cause, excite*, λὺγξ σπασμὸν ἐνδιδοῦσα Th.2.49; ποθήν, δίψαν, Aret.*SA*2.1, *CA* 1.10; τάδε τῆς ψυχῆς τοῦ στομάχου -όντος εἶναι δεῖ τὴν πάθην Id.*SD* 2.6. III. *show, exhibit*, δικαιοσύνην καὶ πιστότητα ἐνέδωκαν, ἄχαρι δὲ οὐδέν Hdt.7.52; μαλακὸν ἐνδιδόναι οὐδὲν *show* no *sign* of flagging, Id.3.51,105, Ar.*Pl.*488; ἢν δ' ἐνδιδῷ τι μαλθακόν E.*Hel.*508; ἵνα σοὶ μηδὲν ἐνδοίην πικρὸν Id.*Andr.*225. IV. *grant, concede*, εἰ δ' ἐνδιδοίης, ὥσπερ ἐνδίδως, λόγον ib.965; ἐ. οὐδέν *make* no *concession*, Th. 2.12; ἐ. τι *make a concession*, ib.18; ἐ. ὁποσονοῦν Id.4.37; κἂν παίζων τίς σοι ἐνδῷ ὁτιοῦν Pl.*Grg.*499b. V. intr., *allow, permit*, ὅσον ἐνέδωκαν αἱ μοῖραι Hdt.1.91; *give in, give way*, οὐ πρότερον ἐνέδοσαν ἤ.. Th.2.65; ὡς εἶδον αὐτοὺς ἐνδόντας ib.81; *flag, fail*, ἐνδόντες τύχῃ παρεῖσαν αὐτούς E.*Tr.*692; τὸ ἐνδιδὸν *the weak spot*, Luc.*Anach.*26; ἐ. τινὶ *yield to*.., οἴκτῳ Th.3.37; ἀλλήλοις Id.4.44; τῇ τῶν πλειόνων γνώμῃ D.*Prooem.*34; τῇ διακρίσει Dam.*Pr.*303; πρὸς ὕπνον Plu.*Sull.* 28; ἐ. πρὸς τὰς διαλύσεις *show an inclination* towards.., Id.*Flam.* 9. 2. of ailments, *abate*, Aret.*SA*1.10; but ἢν τὸ οὖρον μὴ ἐνδῷ does not *pass*, Hp.*Prog.*19:—in S.*OC*1076, Elmsl. restored ἐνδώσειν from Sch. 3. of elastic substances, *give way, yield*, οἰσοφάγος ἐ. Arist.*PA*$664^{a}34$; of the air, Id.*Pr.*$937^{b}34$; of trees, *be flexible*, Thphr. *HP*5.6.1; of the flanks and eyes, *fall in*, Arist.*Pr.*$876^{a}37$, cf. *GA*$747^{a}$16; of a corpse, *decompose*, Parth.31.2; of a funeral-pile, Thphr. *HP*9.3.3; ἐρείσματα ἐ. the props *give way*, Plb.5.100.5. 4. εἴσω ἐνδιδοῖ τὸ ἄλγος *penetrates* inwardly, Aret.*CA*1.10. 5. of a river, *disembogue, empty itself*, Hdt.3.117 codd., but prob. ἐσδ-; cf. ἐκδίδωμι. VI. *give the key-note* of a tune, *strike up*, τοῖς ἵπποις τὸ ὀρχηστικὸν μέλος Arist.*Fr.*583: abs., ἡγεῖτο.. εἷς ἀνήρ, ὃς ἐνεδίδου τοῖς ἄλλοις τὰ τῆς ὀρχήσεως σχήματα D.H.7.72, cf. Luc.*Rh.Pr.*13; τὰ ἐνδιδόμενα *orders, words of command*, Arr.*Tact.*31.6: metaph., *give the key-note*, of a speech, Arist.*Rh.*$1414^{b}26$; cf. ἐνδόσιμος (but ἐ. φωνήν *cry aloud*, Lxx *Nu.*14.1): τοῖς μεθ' ἑαυτὸ τὴν γόνιμον ἐ. πρόοδον Procl.*Inst.*152.

**ἐνδιές**· ἔνυδρον, Hsch. **ἐνδίες** ἵπποι, f.l. for Ἐνετίδες, Id.

**ἐνδι-εσπαρμένως**, Adv., (σπείρω) *in scattered passages*, τὸν βίον ἀναγράφειν τοῖς βιβλίοις Eun.*VSp.*454 B. **-ηθέω**, *strain*, οἶνον Plu.2.692b tit. **-ήκω**, *pervade*, as the essence pervades the individuals of a class, αἱ ἐνδιήκουσαι ἐν τοῖς κατὰ μέρος κοινότητες S.E. *M.*8.41. **-ημερεύω**, *pass the day in*, cj. in Thphr.*Char.*8.14.

**ἐνδίημι**, *chase, pursue*, only 3 pl. impf. ἐνδίεσαν Il.18.584.

**ἐνδῐκ-άζομαι**, *to be a litigant, sue*, *IG*5(2).6.34 (Tegea). **-ία**, ἡ, = ἐκδ-, *Michel*459.14 (Telmessus). **-ος**, Arc. **ἴνδικος**, ον, (δίκη): I. of things, *according to right, just, legitimate*, Pi.*P.*5.103; γόος ἔ. A.*Ch.* 330 (lyr.); ὀνείδη Id.*Eu.*135; λέκτρα *IG*12(5).675.4 (Syros); κρίμα *Ep.Rom.*3.8: τὸ μὴ 'νδικον, = τὸ ἄδικον, S.*OT*682 (lyr.); τὰ πάντων ἐνδικώτατα Id.*OC*925; μὴ λέγων γε τοὔνδικον not speaking *truth*, Id. *OT*1158. 2. *legal*, ἔ. ἡμέρα *a court-day*, Poll.8.25. b. *having a locus standi*, μὴ οἱ ἔστω ἴνδικον μηδέποθι ἀλλ' ἤ.. he shall not have *the right to sue*, *IG*5(2).6.33 (Tegea, iv B.C.), cf. *Foed.Delph.Pell.*2 A 16, Pl.*Lg.*915d, *IG*2².46c56. c. = ἔνοχος δίκᾳ, *Leg.Gort.*3.23, 11. 22. d. ἔ. πόλις a city *in which justice is done*, Pl.*Hp.Ma.*292b; *in which sales may be publicly registered*, *Milet.*3.140. II. of persons, *upright, just*, A.*Eu.*699, S.*Ant.*208; πρὸς ἐνδίκοις φρεσίν A.*Ag.*996 (lyr.); δῆμος ἐνδικώτατος Id.*Fr.*196: c. dat., ἔ. γάμοις *favourable* to them, Id.*Supp.*82 (lyr.). 2. *possessed of right*, τίς μᾶλλον ἐνδικώτερος; who *has a better right?* Id.*Th.*673. III. Adv. **-κως** *right, with justice, fairly*, Id.*Pr.*63, *Ch.*462 (lyr.), etc.; ὀρθῶς ἐ. τ' ἐπώνυμος Id.*Th.*405: Sup. -ώτατα Pl.*Ti.*85b. 2. *justly, naturally, as one has a right to expect*, S.*OT*135, E.*Andr.*920.

**ἐνδῖνα**, τά, *entrails*, ὁππότερός κε φθῇσιν.., ψαύσῃ δ' ἐνδίνων Il.23. 806.

**ἐνδῑν-ευτής**, οῦ, ὁ, *one who evades*, '*shuffler*', *Gloss.* ❋ **-εύω**, = sq., Longus 1.23. **-έω**, *roll*, ἐνδεδινημένα ὄμματα Hp.*Epid.*5.99, cf. Gal.16.610. II. *revolve, go about*, ἐνδινεῦντι, Dor. for ἐνδινοῦσι, Theoc.15.82.

**ἐνδίολκος**, ον, (ἕλκω) *attractive*, Ph.1.517 (v.l.).

**ἐνδῖον**, τό, *place of sojourn in the open air*, ἔνδια πέτρης, of a grotto, Opp.*H.*4.371; ἔνδιον εὐφροσύνης *seat* of joyousness, epith. of a wine-cask, *AP*11.63 (Maced.); ἐ. Ἀμαδρυάδων ib.9.668 (Marian.); σοὶ δὲ ..ἔνδιον ᾗ Πιτάνη *IG*5(1).730.14 (Sparta, ii A.D.).—Poet. word.

**ἐνδιορθόομαι**, *correct*, κακίαν τῆς φύσεως Porph.*Marc.*35.

❋ **ἔνδιος**, ον, *at midday, at noon* (but ἔνδιον τὸ δειλινόν Plu.2.726e), ἔνδιος δ' ὁ γέρων ἦλθ' Od.4.450; ἔνδιοι ἱκόμεσθα Il.11.726; ποιμένας ἐνδίους πεφυλαγμένος Theoc.16.95; ἔνδῖον Κυνὸς ἄσθμα *AP*10.12; ἄλκαρ ἵδεος ἐνδίοιο Call.*Fr.*124; ἔνδῖον ἦμαρ ἔην A.R.4.1312; but also ἐνδίοις· ὀρθρίνοις (ὀρθηνίοις cod.), Hsch. 2. *in the daytime*, Arat.498; ἐ. οἰνοπότης *AP*7.703 (Myrin.). 3. *from the sky*, ὕδωρ Arat.954; *hanging in mid-air*, ἀκρεμόνες *AP*9.71 (Antiphil.). II. Subst. ἔνδιον, τό, *noon*, ποτὶ τὤνδιον Call.*Cer.*39 (also in masc., δείελος ἀλλ' ἢ νὺξ ἢ ἔνδιος ἢ ἔσετ' ἠώς Id.*Hec.*1.4.1). 2. *evening*, ἐς ἔνδῖον A.R. 1.603, cf. Plu. l.c. [ῑ Hom.; ῑ and ῐ later (v. supr.).] (From ἐν δῐϜί, cf. Skt. *div*- '*daylight, sky*', Lat. *diu* '*by day*'.)

**ἐνδιόω**, Dor., pf. part. ἐνδεδιωκότα: πεφυτευμένα καὶ ἐ., perh. *established*, of plants, *Tab.Heracl.*1.121; perh. cf. ἐμβιόω.

**ἐνδιπλ-ἀσιάζω**, = sq., Hp.*Epid.*2.2.22 (Pass.). II. Gramm., *reduplicate*, *EM*499.11 (Pass.). **-όω**, *fold in two*, Gal.*UP*14.6, 7. 12 (Pass.), Sor.1.14; *fold in* at the edge, Paul.Aeg.6.65 :—hence **-ωμα**, ατος, τό, and **-ωσις**, εως, ἡ, *folding*, Gal.11.508.

**ἐνδίσματα**· ἐναλίσματα, Hsch.

❋ **ἐνδίφριος**, ον, (δίφρος) *sitting on the same seat*, ἐκαθεζόμην ἐνδίφριος αὐτῷ X.*An.*7.2.33, cf. 38.

**ἐνδογεν-ής**, ές, *born in the house*, = οἰκογενής, *SIG*²854.5, al. (Delph.), Lxx *Le.*18.9. **-ικός**, ή, όν, = foreg., *PFlor.*294.52 (vi A.D.).

❋ **ἔνδοθεν**, Adv. *from within*, Od.20.101, Ar.*Nu.*1164 (lyr.), etc.; ὑπό τινων ἔνδοθεν πρασσόντων Th.2.79: c. gen., ἔ. στέγης *from inside* the tent, S.*Aj.*741. 2. *of oneself, by one's own doing*, A.*Th.*194; οὔτ' ἔ. οὔτε θύραθεν neither *of oneself* nor by help of others, S.*Tr.* 1021 (lyr.). II. *within*, c. gen., αὐλῆς Il.6.247; οἴκου v.l. in Hes. *Op.*523. 2. abs., θυμὸν τέρπεται ἔ. Pi.*P.*2.74, cf. Hdt.2.68, *Com. Adesp.*21.31 D., etc.; εἴ οἱ φρένες..νοήμονες ἔ. ἦσαν Theoc.25.80; οἱ ἔ. the *domestics*, Ar.*Pl.*228,964; also, the *citizens*, Pl.*Ti.*17d; ὁ ἔ. θόρυβος Th.8.71; τἄνδοθεν ibid. (but, *the inner man*, Pl.*Phdr.*279b); ὁ καρπὸς ὁ ἔ. the produce *of* her *own property*, *Leg.Gort.*3.27.

❋ **ἔνδοθι**, Adv. *within, at home*, Od.5.58; τά τ' ἔ. καὶ τὰ θύρηφι 22. 220; σὺ δ' ἔ. θυμὸν ἀμύξεις Il.1.243, etc.; rare in Att., ἔ. μέν ἐστι Πρωταγόρας Eup.146a codd., cf. Posidipp.24. 2. c. gen., ἐελμένοι ἔ. πύργων Il.18.287; ἔ. νήσου Hes.*Fr.*76.4; οἴκου Id.*Op.*523.

❋ **ἐνδοθίδιος**, α, ον, *belonging to the house*, *Leg.Gort.*2.11.

**ἔνδοι** (not ἐνδοῖ, A.D.*Adv.*197.10, Hdn.Gr.1.502), Dor. for ἔνδοθι, Theoc.15.1,77, Call.*Cer.*77, *IG*4.1484.66 (Epid.).

**ἐνδοι-άζω**, aor. ἐνεδοίασα Hermog.*Id.*2.6, App.*Mith.*33, Luc.*Gall.* 11: (ἐν δοιῇ):—*to be in doubt, at a loss*, c. inf., ὅταν.. ἐνδοιάζῃ χωρίον προσλαβεῖν Th.1.36: abs., οἱ ἐνδοιάζοντες *the waverers*, Id.6.91; μηδὲν ἐνδοιάσας Luc.*Herm.*25; ἐ. τῇ γνώμῃ Plu.*Sull.*9; ὑπέρ τινος Id.*Cat. Mi.*17; περί τινος Luc.*Phal.*2.2; ἐ. εἰ.. D.H.4.58:—Pass., of things,

*to be matter of doubt*, λόγῳ ἐνδοιασθῆναι Th.1.122; ἐνδοιαζόμενον D.H. 7.59, cf. Ph.1.622; ἐνεδοιάζετο δὲ πότερον.. Luc.*VH*2.21: aor. 1 also in act. sense, Parth.9.6. **-άσιμος** [ᾰ], ον, *doubtful*, J.*AJ*16. 11.7, Luc.*Scyth.*11. Adv. -μως, ἔχειν περί τινος J.*AJ*16.10.4. **-ασις**, εως, ἡ, *doubt, uncertainty*, Hermog.*Id.*1.6. **-ασμός**, ὁ, = foreg., ibid., Ph.2.67, al., Eust.146.18. **-αστής**, οῦ, ὁ, *doubter*, Ph.1.459, 2.582. **-αστικός**, ή, όν, *expressing doubt* or *ambiguous*, ὀνόματα Id.*Fr.*15 H.; ἐπίκρισις Hermog.*Id.*2.7,8: Gramm., *dubitative*, σύνδεσμος Ammon.*in APr.*68.10. Adv. -κῶς Eust.1080.69. **-αστός**, ή, όν, *doubtful*, Hp.*Prorrh.*2.15, J.*AJ*19.1.4. Adv. -τῶς *doubtfully*, προθύμως, οὐδ' ἔτι ἐ. Hdt.7.174, cf. Th.8.87; ἐ. ἀκροᾶσθαι Id.6.10.

**ἐνδοιΐτιναι**, οἱ, *those who can trace citizen-ancestry through seven generations*, Hsch. **ἐνδοκία**· ἡ μήτηρ, παρὰ Ἀθηναίοις, Id. **ἔνδοκος**· ἐνέδρα, Id.

**ἔνδομα**, ατος, τό, (ἐνδίδωμι) *diminution* of fever, Gal.19.398.

**ἐνδομαρία**· ἡ κτῆσις, ἡ παροικία (κτίσις ἡ παροιμία cod.), Hsch.

**ἐνδομᾰτικά**, τά, *court-fees*, *Cod.Just.*10.19.9.6, Lyd.*Mag.*3.70, *PLips.*28.15 (iv A.D.). 2. *douceurs, gratuities*, Just.*Edict.*13.7.

**ἐνδομάχας** [μᾰ], α, ὁ, *fighting* or *bold at home*, epith. of a dunghill-cock, Pi.*O.*12.14.

**ἐνδομεν-ία** (-εία Corn.*ND*14, *POxy.*[v. infr.]) or **ἐνδυμενία** (Phryn.312, *PAmh.*2.152.16 (v/vi A.D.)), ἡ, *household goods*, Plb.4. 72.1, Olympias ap.Poll.10.12, Paul.Al.*L.*4; freq. in wills, as *POxy.* 493.17 (ii A.D.); *furniture supplied to public guests*, *Gloss.* **-ικός**, ή, όν, *belonging to household stock*, *PGiss.*35.2 (iii A.D.), *PLips.*28.15 (iv A.D.).

**ἐνδομ-έω**, *build in*, ἐνδεδόμηται Hp.*Cord.*6; κίονες ἐνδεδομημένοι J. *AJ*15.11.5. **-ησις**, εως, ἡ, *thing built in, structure*, τοῦ τείχους *Apoc.*21.18; esp. *mole* or *breakwater*, J.*AJ*15.9.6; cf. ἐνδώμησις.

**ἐνδο-μῠχέω**, *lurk in the recesses* of a house, Sch.Ar.*V.*964; *lie hidden*, φλὸξ -οῦσα *Gp.*2.3.9; *to be latent*, of περιττώματα, Steph. *in Hp.*1.164 D. **-μῠχί**, Adv. *in secret*, Hsch. ⊛ **-μῠχος**, ον, *in the inmost part of a dwelling, lurking within*, S.*Ph.*1457 (anap.), Call. *Cer.*88, Nonn.*D.*8.329. 2. *insidious*, νόσημα Gal.9.837. II. of persons, *treacherous*, Ptol.*Tetr.*158. 2. *stay-at-home*, Paul.Al. *M.*4, Vett.Val.18.20.

⊛ **ἔνδον**, Adv. *within*, Il.11.98, etc.; ἦσαν ἡμῖν ἔ. ἑπτὰ μναῖ Lys.19. 22, cf. D.27.10; φρένες ἔ. εἶσαι Od.11.337, al.; κραδίη ἔ. ὑλάκτει 20. 13; τἄνδον οὐχ οὕτω φρονῶν *in one's heart*, E.*Or.*1514 (troch.; but lit. τᾰ. ἀνακάλλυνον Phryn.Com.2 D.); *at home*, Pl.*Prt.*310e, etc.; οἱ ἔ. those *of the house*, the *family*, esp. the *domestics*, S.*El.*155 (lyr.), *Tr.* 677, Pl.*Smp.*213c; τἄνδον *family matters, household affairs*, S.*Tr.* 334, etc.; also, = οἱ ἔ., E.*Hec.*1017; οἱ ἔ. καθήμενοι the βουλή, And.1. 43. 2. c. gen., Διὸς ἔ., Ζεφύροιο ἔ., *in the house* of Zeus, of Zephyrus, Il.20.13, 23.200; μὴ κεύθετ' ἔ. καρδίας A.*Ch.*102; σκηνῆς ἔ. S.*Aj.* 218 (anap.); γῆς ἔ. Pl.*Prt.*320d. b. ἔ. ὢν αὑτοῦ *master of* oneself, self-possessed, Antipho 5.45; so σῶν φρενῶν οὐκ ἔ. ὤν E.*Heracl.*709: abs., ἔ. γενοῦ A.*Ch.*233 (οὐκ ἔ. ἔ. ἐστίν with a play on signf. 1, Ar. *Ach.*396). 3. Pi. uses it c. dat. as strengthd. for ἐν, *N.*3.54, 7.44, cf. E.*Fr.*203. 4. *below*, in a book, ἔ. γέγραπται D.L.5.4. 5. with Verbs of motion, = εἴσω, D.Chr.7.56, Ael.*NA*9.61. II. Comp. and Sup., v. ἐνδοτέρω.

⊛ **ἐνδοξ-άζομαι**, Pass., *to be glorified*, ἔν τινι Lxx *Ex.*14.4, al., 2*Ep. Thess.*1.10, *PMag.Leid.W.*4.17. **-ασμός**, ὁ, *glorifying*, Sm.*Ps.* 45(46).4, Al.*Is.*24.14.

**ἐνδοξο-κοπέω**, *covet fame for*, θαυμαστὸν ἔργον Vett.Val.4.20. **-λογέω**, *speak for fame*, D.L.6.47. **-πωλος**, gloss on κλυτόπωλος, Hsch.

⊛ **ἔνδοξ-ος**, ον, (δόξα) *held in esteem* or *honour*, *of high repute*, πρός τινος by one, X.*Oec.*6.10 codd. (Sup.); -ότατοι ποιηταί Id.*Mem.*1.2. 56; πόλις -οτέρα εἰς τὰ πολεμικά ib.3.5.1; νέοι πλούσιοι καὶ ἔ. Pl.*Sph.* 223b; μὴ πλουσιώτερος ἀλλ' -ότερος Isoc.1.37; ὀλίγοι καὶ ἔ. ἄνδρες Arist.*EN*1098$^{b}$28, cf. Epicur.*Sent.*7, etc. 2. of things, *notable*, πράγματα Aeschin.3.231, cf. Diod.Com.2.21; *generally approved*, τὸ καλόν, = τὸ ἔ., Epicur.*Fr.*513; *glorious*, ταφαί Plu.*Per.*28; ἡδὺ καὶ ἔ. καὶ ὠφέλιμον Id.2.99f. Adv. -ξως, freq. in Inscrr., *SIG*442.7 (Erythrae, iii B.C.), etc., cf. *Vit.Philonid.*p.12 C., Plu.*Alc.*1, etc.: Comp. -οτέρως, τὰ ἔνδοξα ἐ. λέγειν Hermog.*Id.*1.9; also στῆλαι ἔχουσαι ἐπιγραφὰς -ξως *conspicuously* placed, *Sammelb.*6152.22 (i B.C.): Sup. -ότατα, ἐβουλεύσασθε D.18.65. II. *resting on opinion, probable, generally admitted*, ἔ. τὰ δοκοῦντα πᾶσιν ἢ τοῖς πλείστοις ἢ τοῖς σοφοῖς, opp. to what is necessarily true (τὰ πρῶτα καὶ ἀληθῆ), Arist.*Top.*100$^{b}$21, cf. *EN*1145$^{b}$5, *Rh.*1355$^{a}$17, al.; ἡ ἔ. διδασκαλία *popular* teaching, Gal.2.247. 2. Adv. -ξως, συλλογίζεσθαι *plausibly*, opp. ἀληθῶς, Arist.*SE*175$^{a}$31. III. *conceited*, οὐκ ἔνδοξοι πρὸς τὸ μαθεῖν ἃ μὴ ἴσμεν not *too proud* to learn, Erot.*Fr.*60. **-ότης**, ητος, ἡ, *distinction, glory*, Hsch. s.v. εὔκλεια, Eust.1279.44. II. as a honorific address, Just.*Nov.*41 *Pr.*, *Sammelb.*4736.1, etc.

**ἐνδόπυος**, ὁ, ἡ, *having an internal abscess*, Theognost.*Can.*162 (misprinted -πυρος by Cramer).

**ἔνδορα**, τά, (ἐνδέρω) *offerings wrapped in hide*, *SIG*1025.48 (Cos), 1026.8 (ibid.).

**ἔνδορχις**, ὁ, *with concealed testicles*, Theognost.*Can.*162.

⊛ **ἐνδόρωμα**, ατος, τό, perh. *ornament in plaster* of a sarcophagus, Μουσ.Σμυρν.1884/5 p.24 No.241; cf. δόρωσις.

⊛ **ἔνδος**, Dor., = ἔνδον, *GDI*1752.4 (Delph.), Theognost.*Can.*162. 9. **ἔνδοσε**, = εἴσω, *IG*12(5).593$^{A}$14 (Iulis, v B.C.).

**ἐνδόσ-θια**, τά, (ἔνδον) = ἐντόσθια, Lxx *Ex.*12.9, al. ⊛ **-θίδια**, τά, = foreg., *IG*4.914.15 (Epid.), and prob. for -ιαῖα, v.l. in Lxx *Le.*6.33 (7.3).

⊛ **ἐνδόσιμος**, ον, *serving as a prelude*, ᾆσμα Artem.2.66; ψαλμὸς ἐ. τῇ ᾠδῇ, Suid.: but usu. neut. ἐνδόσιμον, τό (τὸ πρὸ τῆς ᾠδῆς κιθάρισμα, Hsch.); *that which gives the key to the tune*, in music, Arist.*Rh.*1414$^{b}$24, *Mu.*399$^{a}$19, Hld.3.2, Ael.*NA*11.1, Poll.1.210: metaph., *key-note* of a speech, Arist.*Rh.*1415$^{a}$7, *Pol.*1339$^{a}$13, cf. Max.Tyr.7.7, Jul.*Ep.* 186: generally, *signal* for a race, Hld.4.3; [πρόβατα] πρὸς τὰ ἐ. τῆς σύριγγος ποιμαινόμενα Id.5.14: metaph., τὸ τοῦ καιροῦ καὶ τῆς ὥρας ἐ. Id.4.16; τοῦ φιλοσοφεῖν ἐ. ἔδωκαν Phld.*Acad.Ind.*p.5 M.; ὥσπερ ἐ. ἕξει πρός τι Plu.2.73b; τοῦ λογισμοῦ τὸ ἐ. παρεσχηκότος Porph.*Sent.* 32, cf. Luc.*Symp.*30 (also ἐ. παρασχέσθαι Dam.*Pr.*415); λαβεῖν Luc. *Alex.*19; μέχρις ἂν τὸ ἐ. τῆς διαλύσεως σημήνῃ M.Ant.11.20; ἐ. τοῖς στρατιώταις ἔργῳ διδούς Hdn.3.6.10 (so prob. as Adj., [σιτία] ἐ. τῇ πέψει *giving the signal* for digestion, Plu.2.131c). II. *yielding*, τὸ ἐ. καὶ πειθήνιον ib.442c, cf. Max.Tyr.1.2, Hld.9.4; of arguments, *easily refuted*, κατηγόρησεν ἐνδόσιμα Hyp.*Fr.*241; ἐνδόσιμα προτείνειν D.H.*Rh.*8.15.

**ἔνδοσις**, εως, ἡ, *striking of the key-note* (cf. foreg. 1), Arist.*Mu.*398$^{b}$26, Anon.ap.Suid. s.v. ἐνδόσιμον. 2. *imparting*, τῆς ὑγρότητος Thphr. *CP*1.15.3; τοῦ εἴδους Simp.*in Ph.*440.8; τὰς πολλὰς οὐσίας ἐνδόσεις εἶναι κατὰ ἔλλαμψιν ἀπὸ τῆς μιᾶς οὐσίας προϊούσας εἰς πάντα ὄντα Dam. *Pr.*100. II. *giving in, alleviation, remission*, Hp.*Ep.*1. 2. *relaxation*, τόνου Plu.*Lys.*12. 3. *yielding, giving way*, of pillars, Str.15.3.10; of sand, D.S.1.30, cf. Ph.*Bel.*78.3: metaph., Plu.*Per.*31; πρός τι Id.2.457a; *way out* of a difficulty, Simp.*in Ph.*137.21; *retirement*, of troops, Plb.5.100.2.

**ἐνδοτάτω**, v. sq.

⊛ **ἐνδοτέρω**, Adv. Comp. of ἔνδον, *more within, quite within*, ἐ. συστέλλειν ἑαυτόν to draw himself *within* his means, Plu.*Cat.Ma.*5; ἐ. τῆς χρείας προσαγαγέσθαι to unite into greater intimacy, Id.*Arat.*43; *within*, *Placit.*5.21.2; (sc. κόσμου) ib.1.18.4; ἐ. τείχους J.*AJ*15.11.3; *farther on, below*, in a book, D.L.10.43, etc. 2. of Time, *within* a certain limit, *sooner*, Hp.*Fract.*33. 3. Sup. ἐνδοτάτω *quite within*, Luc.*Am.*16; *innermost*, Procl.*Hyp.*6.12; οἱ ἐνδοτάτω Θρᾷκες Hdn.6.8.1: c. gen., *very far in*, Plu.2.918f. II. Adj. ἐνδότερος, ον, *inner*, *PLond.*4.1768.2 (vi A.D.): Sup. ἐνδότατος *inmost*, Ἀρμενία Just.*Nov.*31.1 *Intr.*; τόποι Hsch. s.v. μυχοί.

**ἐνδοτικός**, ή, όν, *yielding, soft*, Alex.Aphr.*in Mete.*201.14: metaph., ὀφθαλμοί Aristaenet.1.4 (s.v.l.). Adv. -κῶς Chrysipp.*Stoic.* 3.124. II. Subst. -κόν, τό, *suppository*, Ruf.ap.Orib.8.39.9.

**ἐνδουπέω**, *fall in with a heavy sound*, μέσσῳ ἐνδούπησα Od.12.443; ἄντλῳ δ' ἐνδούπησε πεσοῦσα 15.479.

**ἐνδουχία**, ἡ, (ἔχω) = ἐνδομενία, Plb.18.35.6.

**ἐνδοχεῖον**, τό, = δοχεῖον, Hp.*Ep.*23.

**ἐνδράν-εια** [ρᾰ], ἡ, (δραίνω) *activity*, *Gloss.* **-ής**, ές, *active*, opp. ἐμπαθής, Procl.*Inst.*80, Suid.

**ἐνδράσσομαι**, pf. part. Pass. ἐνδεδραγμένος, *grasp*, *PMag.Par.*1. 2137.

**ἔνδρατα**· τὰ ἐνδερόμενα σὺν τῇ κεφαλῇ καὶ τοῖς ποσί, Hsch.; cf. ἔνδορα. **ἐνδριώνας**· δρόμος παρθένων ἐν Λακεδαίμονι, Id. (ἐν δριῶνας Mein.). **ἔνδροια**, written for ἔνδρυα II, Id.

**ἐνδρομ-έω**, *run into*, τινί Max.282 (v.l. ἐπι-). II. *run through*, Λιβυκῶν πόρων *AP*7.395 (Marc. Arg.). **-ή**, ἡ, *air played during the pentathlon*, Plu.2.1140d. ⊛ **-ίς**, ίδος, ἡ, a sort of *high shoe*, worn by Artemis in the chase, Call.*Dian.*16, *Del.*238, *APl.*4.253; soldier's *high boot*, Ph.*Bel.*100.8. II. Adj., *used in the foot-race*, ἀσπίδες *GDI*2517.11 (Delph.). 2. Subst., *bath-wrapper* or *draw-sheet*, Herod.Med.ap.Orib.10.37.5, 38.1; also, *thick wrapper worn by runners*, after exercise, for fear of cold, Mart.4.19, Juv.3.103, 6. 246. **-ος**, ον, *running on, hastening*, εἰς Ἀΐδαν *IPE*2.197 (Panticapaeum, ii A.D.).

**Ἐνδρομώ**, ἡ, epith. of Demeter at Halicarnassus, Hsch.

**ἔνδροσος**, ον, *bedewed, dewy*, εὐνή A.*Ag.*12, cf. Str.6.1.9, Dion. Byz.29, Alciphr.*Fr.*6.6· αὖραι Ph.2.292, cf. Dsc.5.53; λειμῶνες Jul. *Or.*7.236a.

**ἔνδρῠον**, τό, (δρῦς) *oaken peg* or *pin* by which the yoke is fixed to the pole, Hes.*Op.*469. II. *heart-wood* of trees, Hsch.

**ἐνδυ-άζω, -ασμός**, written for ἐνδοι-, Hsch.

**ἔνδυδαν**· ἔωθεν, Hsch. (Fort. ἐνδύλαν· ἔσωθεν, cf. ἐνδύλω.)

**ἐνδῠκέως**, Adv. *sedulously, kindly*, freq. in Hom. (esp. in Od.), with Verbs expressing friendly actions, as πέμψαι Od.14.337; ὁμαρτεῖν Il.24.438; φιλέειν καὶ τιέμεν Od.15.543; παρέχειν βρῶσίν τε πόσιν τε ib.491; so ἐ. δέκεσθαι θυσίαισιν Pi.*P.*5.85; ῥύεσθαι Theoc.25.25, etc.; ἔχραεν A.R.2.454. II. *steadfastly*, μαρνάμεθ' ἐ. B.5.125, cf. 112. 2. *greedily, ravenously*, ἐσθίειν Od.14.109; ἐ. ῥινὸν σχίσας, of a lion tearing his prey, Hes.*Sc.*427.—No Adj. ἐνδυκής occurs: but neut. ἐνδυκές, as Adv., is prob. l. in A.R.1.883; used for συνεχές, Nic.*Th.*263; expld. by συνεχές, συνετόν, ἀφελές, ἀσφαλές, γλυκύ, κτλ., Hsch. (Etym. dub.: for sense 1 perh. cf. ἀ-δευκής.)

**ἐνδύκιον**· πιστόν, φίλον, κτλ., Hsch. **ἐνδύλω**· ἔνδοθεν, Id.

⊛ **ἔνδῡμα**, ατος, τό, (ἐνδύω) *garment*, *IG*12(5).593$^{A}$4 (Iulis, v B.C.), Men.*Pk.*269, Lxx 4*Ki.*10.22, al., *BCH*6.25 (Delos, ii B.C.), *PFay.*12. 20 (ii B.C.), Str.3.3.7, *Ev.Matt.*7.15, Plu.*Sol.*8, Porph.*Abst.*1.31, etc.; *covering*, τῶν ἀστῶν Gal.19.367, prob. in Hp.*Cord.*8.

**ἐνδῡμάτια**, τά, name of a musical festival at Argos, Plu.2.1134c.

**ἐνδυμενία**, v. ἐνδομενία.

**ἐνδύμιος**, v.l. for ἐνθύμιος, Thd.*Pr.*26.22.

**ἐνδύνᾰμ-ος** [ῠ], ον, *mighty*, Ps.-Ptol.*Centil.*38, Them.*Or.*34 p.446 Dind. Adv. -ως *Gloss.* **-όω**, *strengthen, confirm*, Lxx *Jd.*6.34, 1*Ep.Ti.*1.12, al.:—Pass., ἐπὶ τῇ ματαιότητι Lxx *Ps.*51(52).9; τῇ πίστει

*Ep.Rom.*4.20, al. **II.** *endow with vitality*, in Pass., metaph. of scientific theorems, Plot.4.9.5.

⊛ **ἐνδῠναστεύω**, *to have power* or *exercise dominion in* or *among*, τισί A.*Pers.*691; παρά τισι Pl.*R.*516d; ἐ. ἐν τῷ σώματι Hp.*VM*20, cf. Iamb.*Myst.*3.28: abs., Eus.Mynd.39. **II.** *procure by one's authority* or *influence*, ἐνδυναστεύει Ἐπαμεινώνδας ὥστε μὴ φυγαδεῦσαι τοὺς κρατίστους X.*HG*7.1.42. **ἐνδυνέω, ἐνδύνω,** v. ἐνδύω.

**ἔνδῠο,** Adv. *one-two*, i.e. *quickly*, Men.198.

**ἔνδῠσις,** εως, ἡ, (ἐνδύω) *entry*, coined by Pl.*Cra.*419c; [σελήνη] ἐν Κρόνου ἐνδύσει Alex.Trall.12. **2.** = κατάδυσις, Hsch. **II.** *putting on*, ἱματίων 1*Ep.Pet.*3.3; *dressing, dress*, Lxx *Es.*5.1, Aristeas 96, Agatharch.57.

**Ἐνδυσποιτρόπιος,** ὁ (sc. μήν), name of tenth month at Delphi, *SIG*672.40 (ii B.C.).

**ἐνδυστῠχέω,** *to be unlucky in* or *with*.., ἐνδυστυχῆσαι τοὔνομ' ἐπιτήδειος εἶ in name thou art fit *to be luckless*, E.*Ba.*508, cf. *Ph.*727; τῇ πόλει Plu.*Comp.Per.Fab.*3.

**ἐνδύτας·** αὐλωτὸς στάμνος, Hsch.

**ἐνδῠτ-έον,** *one must put on*, χιτῶνάς τισι Herod.Med. in *Rh.Mus.* 58.103. **-ήρ,** ῆρος, ὁ, *for putting on*, πέπλος S.*Tr.*674. **-ήριος,** α, ον, = foreg., χιτὼν ἄπειρος ἐ. κακῶν Id.*Fr.*526. **-ης,** ου, ὁ, *garment*, Aq.1*Ki.*17.38. ⊛ **-ός,** όν, *put on*, ἐσθήματα A.*Eu.*1028 codd.; στέφη E.*Tr.*257 (anap.); στολαί Antiph.36. **2.** ἐνδυτόν (sc. ἔσθημα), τό, *garment, dress*, Simon.179.10, Call.*Ap.*32, dub. in Herod.8.65; ἐ. νεβρίδων *a dress* of fawn-skin, E.*Ba.*111 (lyr.), cf. 138 (lyr.); ὅπλων ἐνδυτά Id.*IA* 1073 (lyr.): metaph., ἐ. σαρκός the skin, Id.*Ba.*746; τοὔνδυτον τῆς κοιλίας Alex.98.14. **II.** *clad in, covered*, στέμμασιν E.*Ion* 224 (lyr.).

⊛ **ἐνδύω** or **ἐνδύνω** (ἐνδυνέω v.l. in Hdt.3.98), with Med. **ἐνδύομαι,** fut. -δύσομαι: aor. 1 -εδυσάμην; Ep. aor. or impf. -εδυσόμην: aor. 2 Act. -έδυν: pf. -δέδῡκα: **I.** c. acc. rei vel loci, *go into*, **1.** of clothes, *put on*, ἔνδυνε χιτῶνα Il.2.42; ἔνδυνε περὶ στήθεσσι χιτῶνα 10.21; χιτῶν' ἐνδῦσα 5.736; τι ὡς θώρηκα ἐνδύνουσι Hdt.3.98; ἐνδύντες τὰ ὅπλα Id.1.172; τὴν σκευὴν ib.24; πέπλον ἐνδὺς S.*Tr.*759, etc.: pf. ἐνδέδυκα, *wear*, κιθῶνας λινέους Hdt.2.81, cf. 7.64, 9.22; λεοντῆν ἐνδέδυκε Pl. *Cra.*411a:—Med., ἐν δ' αὐτὸς ἐδύσετο χαλκόν Il.2.578, 11.16; ἐνδύεσθαι ὅπλα v.l. in Hdt.7.218; σκευάς Th.1.130; ἐνδύσεται στολήν E.*Ba.* 853: metaph., ἐνδυόμενοι τόλμημα Ar.*Ec.*288; also τὸν Ταρκύνιον ἐνδύεσθαι *assume* the person of T., D.H.11.5; τὸν καινὸν ἄνθρωπον *Ep.Eph.* 4.24:—Pass., *to be clothed in, have on*, ἐσθῆτα ἐνδεδύσθαι Hp.*Insomn.* 91, cf. Men.432. **2.** *enter, press into*, c. acc., ἐν δέ οἱ ἦτορ δῦν' ἄχος ἄτλητον Il.19.367; ἀκοντιστὺν ἐνδύσεαι thou *wilt enter* the contest (Aristarch. ἐσδύσεαι), 23.622; τὴν τοῦ Θερσίτου [ψυχὴν] πίθηκον ἐνδυομένην Pl.*R.*620c; εὔνοια ἐνδύεταί τινα Id.*Lg.*642b; ἔρως δεινὸς ἐνδέδυκέ τινος Id.*Tht.*169c; also ἐ. εἰς.. Ar.*V.*1020, Arist.*HA*609$^b$21; εἰς τὴν ἐπιμέλειαν ἐνδῦναι *enter upon* it, *undertake* it, X.*Cyr.*8.1.12: abs., *enter*, Pl.*Phd.*89d: c. dat., ἐ. ταῖς ψυχαῖς τῶν ἀκουόντων *insinuate oneself into* their minds, X.*Cyr.*2.1.13; τοῖς ταύροις τὸν οἶστρον ἐνδύεσθαι Plu.2.55e, etc.; ἐνὶ χροΐ δύετο ῥινὸς ἐντυπάς Epic. in *Arch.Pap.*7. 3: pf. Pass., φυσικαῖς ἐνδεδυμένος αἰτίαις dub. in Plu.2.435f (leg. -δεδεμένος): abs., *creep in*, v.l. for ἐσ-, Hdt.2.121.β'; ἐ. διά τινος *slip through*, Plu.2.38a, etc. **3.** *sink in*, hence τρίβος ἐνδεδυκὼς *sunken* path, Id.*Arat.*22; ῥίς *sunken* nose, Id.*Publ.*16. **II.** causal in pres. ἐνδύω, fut. -δύσω: aor. 1 -έδυσα:—*put on* another, *clothe in*, c. dupl. acc., τὴν ἐξωμίδ' ἐνδύσω σε Ar.*Lys.*1021; ὃς ἐμὲ κροκόεντ' ἐνέδυσεν Id. *Th.*1044, cf. X.*Cyr.*1.3.3. **2.** *clothe*, ἐνδύουσι τὤγαλμα Hdt.2.42; ἐὰν.. πένητα γυμνὸν ἐνδύσῃς Philem.176; σύ με ἐνδέδυκας [prob. ῠ] *PGiss.*77.8 (ii A.D.).

**ἔνδω,** = ἔνδον, *GDI*1767 (Delph.), *Michel*995*D*31 (ibid.).

**ἐνδώμησις,** εως, ἡ, *enclosing with a wall*, τεμένους *SIG*996.30 (Smyrna), cf. *BCH*28.78 (Tralles), J.*AJ*15.9.6 (v.l.), *Apoc.*21.18 (v.l.).

**ἐνδωσείω,** *to be inclined to yield*, D.C.46.37 (cj.), Agath.1.9.

**ἐνεάζω,** (ἐνεός) *strike dumb, astonish*, *AB*251, *EM*340.50.

**ἐνεᾰρίζω,** = ἐαρίζω ἐν.., c. dat., Plu.2.77cb.

**ἔνεγγυς,** f.l. for ἐγγύς, Q.S.4.326.

**ἐνέγκαι, ἐνεγκεῖν,** v. φέρω. **ἐνεγλαύκως·** φοβερὸς ἰδεῖν, Hsch. **ἐνεγύησα,** irreg. aor. of ἐγγυάω.

⊛ **ἐνέδρ-α,** ἡ, *sitting in*: hence, *lying in wait, ambush*, Th.5.56 (pl.), etc.; ἐ. ποιεῖσθαι Id.3.90; ἐνέδραι κατασκευάζονται X.*Eq.Mag.*4.10; ἐνέδραν τιθέναι D.S.19.108; θέσθαι Plu.*Rom.*23; εἰς ἐ. ἐμπίπτειν X. *Cyr.*8.5.14; ἐκ τῆς ἐ. ἀνίστασθαι ib.5.4.4; θέειν ἐκ τῆς ἐ. Th.4.67. **b.** *men laid in ambush*, τὴν ἐ. ἐξανιστάναι X.*HG*4.8.37. **2.** metaph., *trickery, treachery*, δόλου καὶ ἐνέδρας πλήρης Pl.*Lg.*908d, cf. D.19.77; ἐνέδρας ἕνεκα Antiph.124.7; ἐξ ἐνέδρας, opp. φανερῶς, Ph.2.422; μετ' ἐνέδρας App.*BC*1.30, cf. Archig.ap.Orib.8.2.20. **II.** *position*, ναρθήκων Hp.*Fract.*16,27. **III.** *delay*, περί τι *POxy.*62.10 (iii A.D.), etc. **-άζω,** *to be firmly established*, pf. part. ἐνηδρακὼς Gal. *UP*3.8. ⊛ **-εία,** ἡ, = ἐνέδρα, Epich.103. **II.** *creation of difficulties, obstruction*, *POxy.*900.19 (iv A.D.). **-ευτής,** οῦ, ὁ, *ensnarer, plotter*, Sm.1*Ki.*22.8, Ptol.*Tetr.*159. **-ευτικός,** ή, όν, *fit for ambush*, χωρία Aen.Tact.1.2, cf. Str.3.3.6; *tricky, deceitful*, Ph.2.269, Gal.9.217, 19.138. **-ευτος,** ον, f.l. for -ευτής, Timae.Astr. in *Cat. Cod.Astr.*1.98. **-εύω,** impf. ἐνήδρευον X.*Cyr.*1.6.39: fut. ἐνεδρεύσω Plu.*Ant.*63: aor. ἐνήδρευσα Th.4.67, X.*An.*4.1.22, etc.:—Med., fut. -σομαι (in pass. sense) Id.*HG*7.2.18:—Pass., aor. ἐνηδρεύθην D.28.2: pf. ἐνήδρευμαι Luc.*Cal.*23: (ἐνέδρα):—*lie in wait for, lay snares for*, τινά D.40.10, Men.*Kol.*44:—Pass., *to be caught in an ambush, to be ensnared*, of animals, X.*Mem.*2.1.5; μέλιτι Porph. *Antr.*16; of persons to whom poison has been given, Phylarch.10J.: metaph., ὑπὸ νόμων τοὺς πολίτας ἐνεδρεύεσθαι Lys.1.49; εἰ.. μὴ τῷ χρόνῳ ἐνηδρεύθημεν if we *had* not *been deceived* by time, D.28.2. **2.** abs., *lay* or *set an ambush*, ἐς τὸ Ἐνυάλιον Th.4.67, cf. X.*An.*1.6.2, 4. 1.22, etc. **II.** *place in ambush*, πεζοὺς App.*BC*2.76, v.l. in J.*AJ*5. 8.11:—Med., abs., *set an ambush*, X.*HG*4.4.15:—Pass., metaph., οἱ ἐνηδρευμένοι τῇ δημηγορίᾳ λόγοι Hld.10.17. **III.** *hinder, obstruct*, τινάς *POxy.*1773.33 (iii A.D.); διάπρασιν *PGiss.*105.24 (v A.D.):—Pass., *PAmh.*2.143.9 (iv A.D.). **-ιον,** τό, *row of reserved seats* in a theatre, *IGRom.*4.1414 (Smyrna). **-ον,** τό, = ἐνέδρα I, Lxx *Jo.* 8.2, 12, al. **II.** *hindrance, obstruction*, *POxy.*892.11 (iv A.D.). ⊛ **-ος,** ὁ, *inmate, inhabitant*, S.*Ph.*153 (lyr.). **II.** ἔνεδρος, α, ον, *anal*, σύριγγες Meges ap. Orib.44.24.1, 11.

**ἐνεείσατο,** v. ἐνίζω.

**ἐνέζομαι,** *sit in* or *upon*, Arist.*Pr.*881$^b$36. **II.** *have one's seat* or *abode in*, c. acc. loci, τόδ' ἐ. στέγος A.*Pers.*140 (lyr.).

**ἐνεθίζω,** *accustom to* a thing, τινὰ φιλοσοφίᾳ Socr.*Ep.*27.2:—Pass., ἐνειθίσθαι ταῖς παρατηρήσεσι Ptol.*Tetr.*5, cf. D.L.3.23; ἀέρι Hdn.6. 6.2.

**ἐνειδέσσιν·** ἐν διαφοραῖς, Hsch. **ἐνειδημένους·** πορθήσαντας, Id.

**ἐνεῖδον,** aor. 2 with no pres. in use, ἐνοράω being used instead, *see* or *observe in*, τι ἔν τινι Th.1.95; τί τινι X.*An.*7.7.45: c. acc., *observe, remark*, S.*Ph.*854 (lyr.): c. part., πλέον ἐνεῖδον σχήσοντες Th. 7.36: c. inf., ἃ ἀρωγὰ ἐνείδομεν.. ἔσεσθαι ib.62: c. dat., *gaze at*, ἀτενὲς ἐ. αὐγῇ Orib.*Eup.*4.13.1.

**ἐνειδοφορέω,** of a sculptor, *work into shape*, πέτρον ἐνειδοφορῶν *AP* 12.57 (Mel.).

**ἐνεῖκαι, ἔνεικας, ἔνεικε, ἔνεικαν,** v. φέρω.

**ἐνεικονίζω,** *impart form to*, τὰς ἀμόρφους ὕλας *Placit.*1.10.1:—Med., *have portrayed in* a thing, τοὺς ἑαυτοῦ [λόγους] τοῖς ἑτέρων ἐνεικονίζεσθαι Plu.2.40d; *represent as by an image*, Simp. in *Ph.*1355.11; τὸ θεῶν κάλλος δι' ἐγκοσμίων εἰδῶν Hierocl. in *CA*23 p.468 M., cf. Procl.*Inst.*152:—Pass., *find a place in a metaphor* or *piece of symbolism*, Id. in *Prm.*pp.480, 503 S.

**ἐνειλάσιμος,** dub. in *Sammelb.*4116 (fort. εὐιλάσιμος, = εὐίλαστος).

**ἐνειλ-έω,** *wrap in*, τι ὀθονίῳ Dsc.5.72:—Med., τινὰ κακοῖσι Q.S. 14.294:—Pass., *to be enwrapped*, ἐν [τῇ γῇ] Arist.*Mu.*396$^a$14; ἐν τῷ ἱματίῳ Lxx 1*Ki.*21.9(10); τῃ λεοντῇ Philostr.*Her.*12$^a$.1; ῥάκεσι Artem.1.13; ἱστίοις δοράτια ἐνειλημένα Aen.Tact.29.6, cf. 31.7; φύλλοις Dsc.2.80. **II.** metaph., *engage*, ἐνίων αὐτοὺς ἐνειληκότων οἰκονομίαις *PTeb.*24.62 (ii B.C.):—Pass., *to be engaged, entangled in* or *with*, τοῖς πολεμίοις Plu.*Art.*11; ὅπλοις Id.*Brut.*45; ὥσπερ θηρίον ταῖς πάντων χερσίν Id.*Caes.*66; ὥσπερ ἄρκυσιν ἐνειλημένους prob. for -λημμ-, J.*BJ*6.2.8; βρέφη -ημένα τὰς χεῖρας Artem.1.c.; *come to blows with*, *PRyl.*144.18 (i A.D.). **-ημα,** ατος, τό, *wrapper, cover*, J.*AJ*12.2. 11, Artem.1.74 (pl.). **-ησις,** εως, ἡ, *wrapping, bandaging*, Herod. Med.ap.Orib.10.18.7. **II.** *confinement* of intestinal gases, Ruf. ap.eund.8.24.9. **-ητέον,** *one must enwrap*, Herod.Med. in *Rh. Mus.*58.85.

**ἐνειλινδέομαι,** v.l. for ἐναλ- (q.v.), J.*BJ*4.9.10.

**ἐνειλίσσω,** Ion. for ἐνελίσσω.

⊛ **ἐνείλλω,** *wrap up in*, πηλὸν ἐν ταρσοῖς καλάμου Th.2.76 (ἐνιλλ- codd.).

**ἐνειματιῶν·** ὁ τὰ ἐνπάσματα τοῖς ἀνδράσιν ἐκτιθείς, Hsch.

**ἔνειμεν,** Ep. 1 pl. of ἔνειμι, Il.5.477:—but **ἔνειμεν,** 3 sg. aor. 1 of νέμω.

**ἐνειμένος,** η, ον, pf. part. Pass. of *ἐν-έννυμι (which is not found), *clad*, c. acc., θώρακας Agath.2.8; χλαμύδα Id.4.1.

⊛ **ἔνειμι** (εἰμί, *sum*), 3 sg. and pl. ἔνι freq. for ἔνεστι, ἔνεισι (v. infr.): inf. ἐνεῖμεν *IG*2$^2$.1126.24 (Amphict. Delph.): 3 sg. ἔνι freq. for fut. ἐνέσομαι:—*to be in*, ἄργυρος ἀσκῷ ἔνεστι Od.10.45; ἔνι (for ἔνεστι) κήδεα θυμῷ Il.18.53; ἔνι τοι φρένες οὐδ' ἠβαιαί Od.21.288; εἰ.. χάλκεον.. μοι ἦτορ ἐνείη Il.2.490; εἴ τι ἐνέοι (sc. τοῖς χρησμοῖσι) Hdt.7.6; νοῦς ἔνεστιν ὑμῖν ἐγγενὴς S.*El.*1328; τοῖς λόγοις ἔ. κέρδος ib.370; πόλλ' ἔ. τῷ γήρᾳ κακά Ar.*V.*441; πλήθη, ἐν οἷς τὸ ἓν οὐκ ἔνι Pl.*Prm.*158c; στάσιν ἐνέσεσθαι τῇ γνώμῃ Th.2.20; εἴ σοι πυκνότης ἔνεστ' ἐν τῷ τρόπῳ Ar.*Eq.*1132; ἐνῆν ἄρ'.. κἀν οἴνῳ λόγος Amphis 41; ἀγαθὸς βαφεὺς ἔνεστιν ἐν τῷ παιδίῳ Diph.72: ἔνι τις καὶ ἐν ἡμῖν παῖς Pl.*Phd.*77e; also ἐν τοῖσιν οὔρεσι δένδρεα ἔνι ἄγρια Hecat.292J.; ἐν [ὄρει] ἔνι μέταλλα Hdt.7.112; ἐν τῷ προθυμεῖσθαι ἐνοῦσαν ζημίαν A.*Pr.*383, etc. **b.** c. dat. pl., *to be among*, Thgn.1135, Hdt.3.81, al.; οὐκ ἔνι ἐν ὑμῖν οὐδεὶς σοφὸς 1*Ep.Cor.*6.5. **c.** c. Adv. loci, οἴκοι ἔνεστι γόος Il.24.240; ἔνεστιν αὐτόθι is in this very place, Ar.*Eq.*119; ἐνταῦθα Id.*Nu.*211, etc. **2.** abs., *to be present in* a place, οἶνος ἐνέην Od.9.164; οὐδ' ἄνδρες νηῶν ἔνι τέκτονες ib.126; οὐδ' ἔνι στάσις A.*Pers.*738 (troch.); Ἄρης οὐκ ἔνι χώρᾳ Id.*Ag.*78 (anap.); σίτου οὐκ ἐνόντος as *there was* no corn *there*, Th.4.8; τὰ ἐνόντα ἀγαθά the good *that is therein*, ib.20; ἱερῶν τῶν ἐνόντων the temples *that were in the place*, ib.97; ἀμέλειά τις ἐνῆν καὶ διατριβή Id.5.38; πόλεμος οὐκ ἐνῆν Pl.*Plt.*271e; μηδὲ μύλαν ἐνεῖμεν μηδὲ ὅλμον *IG*2$^2$. l. c.; also, *to be mentioned in* a treaty, Th.8.43, cf. Ar.*Av.*974; χρόνος ἐνέσται time *will be necessary*, Th.1.80; ἡ βὴξ ἔνι the cough *is persistent*, Hp.*Epid.*7.12. **II.** *to be possible*, ἄρνησις οὐκ ἔ. ὧν ἀνιστορεῖς S.*OT*578; τῶνδ' ἄρνησις οὐκ ἔ. μοι Id.*El.*527; τίς δ' ἔνεστί μοι λόγος; what plea *is possible* for me [to make]? E.*IT*998; οὐκ ἐνῆν πρόφασις X.*Cyr.*2.1.25; οὐκ ἐνεστι αὐτῷ λόγος οὐδὲ εἷς D.21.41; εἴ τι ἄλλο ἐνῆν Id.18.190; ἐνούσης οὐδεμιᾶς ἔτ' ἀποστροφῆς Id.24.9. **2.** impers., c. dat. pers. et inf., *it is in one's power*, S.*Tr.*296, *Ant.*213, etc.: c. inf. only, οὔκουν ἔ. καὶ μεταγνῶναι; Id.*Ph.*1270; οὐ γὰρ δὴ τοῦτό γ' ἔνεστιν εἰπεῖν D.29.14; πῶς ἔ. ἢ πῶς δυνατόν; Id.57.24, etc.;

οὐκ ἔνεστι *it is* not *possible*, Anaxil.22.7; ὃ μὴ νεώς γε τῆς ἐμῆς ἔνι which *it is* not *possible* [to get] from my ship, S.*Ph.*648 (sed leg. ἔπι): ἔνι is freq. in this sense, ἃ δὲ ἔνι [λέγειν] D.2.4; δι' ὀργήν γ' ἔνι φῆσαι πεποιηκέναι Id.21.41; ὡς ἔνι ἥδιστα in the pleasantest way *possible*, X. *Mem.*4.5.9, cf. 3.8.4; ὡς ἔνι μάλιστα Plb.21.4.14, Ph.1.465, Luc. *Prom.*6, Jul.*Or.*7.218c: impf., ὡς ἐνῆν ἄριστα Luc.*Tyr.*17. b. ἔνεστιν ὑμᾶς εἰδέναι *it is relevant, pertinent, BGU*486.12 (ii A.D.). 3. part. ἐνόν, abs., ἐνὸν αὐτοῖς σῴζεσθαι *since it was in* them, *was possible for* them, Hdn.8.3.2, cf. Luc.*Anach.*9. 4. τὰ ἐνόντα *all things possible*: τὸ πλῆθος τῶν ἐ. εἰπεῖν the *possible materials* for a speech, Isoc. 5.110, cf. 11.44; τῶν ἐ.. ἐν τῷ πράγματι Pl.*Phdr.*235b; τῶν φαινομένων καὶ ἐ. τὰ κράτιστα ἑλέσθαι D.18.190; ἐκ τῶν ἐ. *as well as one can under the circumstances*, ib.256; τὰ ἐ. καὶ τὰ ἁρμόττοντα Arist.*Po.* 1450ᵇ5: in sg., πᾶν τὸ ἐνὸν ἐκλέγων Th.4.59. b. τὰ ἐνόντα *cargo* or *stores* in a ship, Pl.*R.*488c; *contents* of a basket, *PTeb.*414.20 (ii A.D.).

**ἐνείργω**, aor. ἐνεῖρξα, *shut up in*, εἰς κιβωτόν Sch.Pi.*P.*10.72; τῷ ταύρῳ Phalar.*Ep.*136.1:—Pass., χοῖρος ἐνειρχθεὶς σιρῷ Tz.*H.*6.250.

**ἐνείρω**, aor. 1 ἐνεῖρα (v. infr.), *entwine, enwreath*, τέττιγας ταῖς θριξὶ Ael.*VH*4.22:—Pass., ἀνθερίκων ἐνειρμένων περὶ σχοίνους Hdt.4. 190. 2. *thread, pass through*, Ael.Tact.31.18; also καρίδα ἀγκίστρῳ Ael.*NA*1.15; ὀστέοις καὶ νεύροις τινά Lxx *Jb.*10.11; ῥίζαν λίνῳ Dsc.2.166. 3. *string together*, Thphr.*HP*9.9.1, 9.12.1 (Pass.). II. *insert*, πῆχυν μεταξὺ τῶν μηρίων Hp.*Art.*70; χεῖρας εἰς σφαίρας Dionys. Eleg.3.3; ἐνεῖραν [πεύκη] σφῆνας Babr.38.2.

**ἐνειρωνεύομαι**, *employ irony in* a matter, Procl.*in Prm.*p.728 S.

⊛ **ἕνεκα**, Il.1.110, etc., or **ἕνεκεν** (twice in Hom., Od.17.288, 310, rare in Trag., as E.*Med.*999 (lyr.), and early Prose, Th.6.2, X.*HG*2.1.14, Pl.*Smp.*210e; in Com., Men.*Epit.*330; twice in fourth-cent. Att. Inscrr., *IG*2.987A2, 611b13, but prevalent in later Inscrr., cf. *SIG* 577.7 (Milet., iii/ii B.C.); in late Prose, Sch.Pi.*O.*7.10), Ep., Ion., and poet. **εἵνεκα** (also in Pl., *Lg.*778d, al.), or **εἵνεκεν** (both forms in Hdt. and Hp. and not uncommon in codd. of later writers; εἵνεκεν B.12.136, Pi.*I.*8(7).35 codd.; **εἵνεκε** Aret.*CA*1.2, f.l. in Hdt.7.133): **ἕνεκε** *SIG*333.14 (Samos, iv B.C.), *Supp.Epigr.*1.351.10 (ibid.), *CIG* 3655.18 (Cyzicus, iii/ii B.C.): Aeol. **ἔννεκα** Alc.*Supp.*9.1, *IG*12(2). 258.8 (Lesbos, i A.D.), but **ἕνεκα** ib.11(4).1064b32 (Delos), 12(1). 645a38 (Nesus): late **ἕνεκον** *JHS*37.108 (Lydia), etc.:—Prep. with gen., usu. after its case; also before, Il.1.94, B.12.136, Hdt.3.122, etc. When it follows its case, it is sometimes separated from it by several words, as in Hdt.1.30, D.20.88, etc. 1. *on account of*, Τρώων πόλιν.. ἧς εἵνεκ' ὀϊζύομεν κακὰ πολλὰ Il.14.89, etc.; ὕβριος εἵνεκα τῆσδε 1.214; τοῦδ' ἕνεκα *for* this, ib.110; ὧν ἕ. *wherefore*, 20. 21; τίνος ἕ. βλάβης; A.*Fr.*181; παῖσαι ἄνδρας ἕνεκεν ἀταξίας X.*An.* 5.8.13; στεφανοῦσθαι ἀρετῆς ἕνεκα Aeschin.3.10; *for the sake of*, τοῦ ἕ.; Pl.*Prt.*310b; τῶν δὲ εἵνεκα, ὅκως.., or ἵνα.., Hdt.8.35,40; κολακεύειν ἕ. μισθοῦ X.*HG*5.1.17; διὰ νόσον ἕ. ὑγιείας by reason of sickness *for the sake of* health, Pl.*Ly.*218e, cf. *Smp.*185b; τὸ οὗ ἕ. the *final cause*, Arist.*Ph.*194ᵃ27, *Metaph.*983ᵃ31; τὸ οὗ ἕνεκεν Id.*Ph.*243ᵃ 3, *Metaph.*1059ᵃ35. 2. *as far as regards*, ἐμοῦ γ' ἕνεκα *as far as depends on* me, Ar.*Ach.*386, D.20.14; τοῦ φυλάσσοντος εἵνεκεν Hdt. 1.42; εἵνεκεν χρημάτων *as for* money, Id.3.122, etc.; ἕνεκά γε φιλονικίας Pl.*R.*548d, cf. 329b; ἐμπειρίας μὲν ἄρα ἕ. ib.582d; ὅμοιοι τοῖς τυφλοῖς ἂν ἦμεν ἕνεκά γε τῶν ἡμετέρων ὀφθαλμῶν X.*Mem.*4.3.3. 3. *in consequence of*, εἵνεκα τέχνας *by force of* art, *AP*9.729. 4. pleon., ἀμφὶ σοὔνεκα S.*Ph.*554 codd.; ὅσον ἀπὸ βοῆς ἕ. *as far as* shouting *went*, Th.8.92, X.*HG*2.4.31; τίνος χάριν ἕ.; Pl.*Lg.*701d, cf. *Plt.*302b. II. Conj., for οὕνεκα (q.v.), *because*, *h.Ven.*199, Call.*Aet.*3.1.6, *Fr.*287. 2. εἵνεκεν, = ὁθούνεκα, *that*, Pi.*I.*8(7).35 codd.

**ἐνεκέχειρον**, τό, = ἐκέχειρον, *travelling allowance for* θεωροί, *Inscr. Magn.*38 (Megalopolis): pl., ib.40 (Argos), 41 (Sicyon):—also **-χηρον**, ib.35 (Same), 42 (Corinth).

**ἐνεκπλύνω** [ῡ], *wash off* (dirt) *in* a thing, Polyzel.4.

**ἐνελαύνω**, *drive in* or *into*, c. dat., ἐν δεινῷ σάκει ἤλασεν ἔγχος Il.20. 259, cf. Pi.*N.*10.70: metaph., καρδίᾳ κότον Id.*P.*8.9:—Med., *drive in* or *on*, D.C.49.30.

⊛ **ἐνελίσσω** or **-ειλ-**, *roll up in*, σίλφιον μέλιτι Aret.*CA*1.6; τι εἰς ὀθόνην Gal.15.713:—Med., *wrap oneself in*, ἐν ἱματίῳ Hdt.2.95:—Pass., *to be wrapped in*, ὀλίγῳ ὄγμῳ Nic.*Al.*287; ἐπιστολῇ *POxy.* 1153.23 (i A.D.); ἐνειλιγμένος τοὺς πόδας εἰς πίλους *having* one's feet *wrapped in*.., Pl.*Smp.*220b. 2. *wrap round*, λήνεα ἠλακάτῃ Nonn. *D.*6.147.

**ἐνέλκω**, in Pass., *to be charged, imposed upon* an estate, τοῦ ἐνελκομένου σοι φόρου ἢ ἐνελκυσθησομένου τὸ ἥμισυ *PFlor.*370.14 (ii A.D.), cf. *PLond.*5.1695.12 (vi A.D.), etc.; of land, *to be assigned for forced cultivation*, *PFlor.*50.75 (iii A.D.).

**ἔνελος**· νεβρός, Hsch.

**Ἐνελυσκίς**, title of Demeter at Samos, Hsch.

**ἔνεμα**, ατος, τό, (ἐνίημι) *injection, clyster*, Dsc.2.118 (pl.), Gal.13. 295, Orib.*Fr.*60, etc.

⊛ **ἐνεμᾰτίζω**, *treat with a clyster*, τινά Hierocl.*Facet.*176.

**ἐνεμέω**, *vomit in*, ἔς τι Hdt.2.172: metaph., Πιερίδεσσιν ἀπλυσίην ἐλέγων *AP*7.377 (Eryc.).

**ἐνεμπορεύομαι**, *trade with one in*, σοι ἐν ψυχαῖς Lxx *Ez.*27.13.

**ἐνενήκοντα**, οἱ, αἱ, τά, indecl., *ninety*, Il.2.602, etc.; cf. ἐνήκοντα, ἐννήκοντα. (ἐννεν- freq. in codd., but Inscrr. have ἐνεν- *IG*1².324. 109, *Hermes* 17.5 (Delos), etc.:—also gen. pl. ἐνενηκόντων *GDI*5653c 26 (Chios).)

**ἐνενηκοντᾰ-εννέα**, *ninety-nine*, Lxx *Ge.*17.1. **-έξ**, *ninety-six*, ib. 1*Es.*8.63(66). **-ετής**, ές, *ninety years old*, ib.2*Ma.*6.24, Ph.1.606 (dub. l.):—contr. **-ούτης**, ου, Luc.*DMort.*27.7, App.*Pun.*106, D.C. 69.17. **-μερίς**, ίδος, ἡ, *ninetieth degree* from the ὡροσκόπος, Firm. 8.2.1. **-μοιρία**, ἡ, *arc of ninety degrees*, Pancharius ap.Heph. Astr.2.11. **-πέντε**, *ninety-five*, Hero *Geom.*17.5. **-πηχυς**, ὁ, ἡ, *ninety cubits long*, θύρσος Callix.2. **-πλάσιος** [πλᾰ], ον, *ninety times as large*, c. gen., Gem.6.38.

**ἐνενη-κοστός**, ή, όν, *ninetieth*, interpol. in X.*HG*1.2.1, cf. Aët.1. 112: **-κοστογδαῖος**, α, ον, *on the ninety-eighth day*, Gal.7.501: **-κοστόπρωτος**, η, ον, *ninety-first*, Tz.*H.*13.530: **-κοστοτέταρτος**, η, ον, *ninety-fourth*, ib.10.479: **-κοστότρῐτος**, η, ον, *ninety-third*, ib.11.838.

**ἐνενίαυτα** [ῐ], Adv., (ἐνιαυτός) *in the course of the year*, *BGU*920. 18 (ii A.D.).

**ἐνένῑπε**, v. ἐνίπτω.

**ἐνένωτο, -νωκασι**, Ion. for ἐνενόητο, -νοήκασι, v. νοέω.

**ἐνεξεμέω**, *vomit in*, λεκανίῳ Polyzel.4.

⊛ **ἐνεξουσιάζω**, *show independence in*, τοῖς ῥυθμοῖς D.H.*Comp.*19; τῇ γραφῇ Id.*Th.*8; ἐν τοῖς συνθετικοῖς μορίοις ib.24. 2. *exert authority, be supreme in*, ἔστι τούτων τῶν θεῶν -άζειν τοῖς ὅλοις Procl.*Theol. Plat.*6.15, cf. ib.2, Id.*in Cra.*p.98 P.; περὶ τὸν κόσμον Iamb.*Myst.*2.3: abs., ib.3.18. II. Med., *usurp authority*, Lxx *Si.*20.8. III. Pass., *to be brought into subjection*, ἐν τῷ σώματι ib.47.19.

**ἐνεορτ-άδια** [ᾰδ], τά, *dues paid at festivals*, *OGI*484.30 (Pergam.). **-άζω**, *keep holiday in*, τόπῳ Str.12.3.36, cf. Plu.*Comp.Per.Fab.*1, *OGI*383.98 (Antioch. Commag.).

⊛ **ἐνεός** (in codd. sts. ἐννεός *Act.Ap.*9.7, etc.), ά, όν, *dumb, speechless*, freq. joined with κωφός, as Pl.*Tht.*206d, Arist.*HA*536ᵇ4, *Pr.* 961ᵇ14, *Sens.*437ᵃ16; without κωφός, ἐνεοῖς ἀνθρώποις ὁμοίους Epicur. *Fr.*356, cf. Lxx *Is.*56.10, Plu.*Num.*8, D.C.62.16: acc. to Hsch., ὃς οὔτε ἀκούει οὔτε λαλεῖ *deaf and dumb*, as in X.*An.*4.5.33. Adv. **-εῶς** dub.l. in Orac.ap.Polyaen.6.53. 2. *senseless, stupid*, ἀπείρους καὶ ἐ. Pl.*Alc.*2.140d. 3. of things, *useless*, Hp.*Off.*8; ἐς τὸ ἐ. κεῖσθαι ibid. 4. *dumbfounded, astonished*, εἱστήκεισαν ἐ. *Act.Ap.* l.c.

⊛ **ἐνεοστᾰσία**, Ep. -ίη, ἡ, *standing dumb*, A.R.3.76.

**ἐνεότης**, ητος, ἡ, *dumbness*, Arist.*Pr.*895ᵃ16. 2. *stupidity*, dub. in Cratin.188.

**ἐνεόφρων**, ον, gen. ονος, *stupid*, prob. in Panyas.12.11.

**ἐνεπαγγελία**, ἡ, *token, sign*, ἡ ῥὶς ἐ. θυμοῦ Hld.2.35.

**ἐνεπάγομαι** [ᾰ], Med., *attack*, Aesop.234.

**ἐνέπαλτο**, v. ἐνεφάλλομαι.

**ἐνεπηρεάζω**, = ἐπηρεάζω, Poll.8.30:—Pass., ὑπό τινος Phld.*Ir.* p.9 W.

**ἐνεπι-δείκνῡμαι**, Med., *display in*, τὴν εὔνοιαν ἔν τισι Isoc.19.24; σύνεσιν πράγμασι Ph.1.398, cf. Plu.2.90e. II. abs., *show off, make a display*, Ph.2.28, Lib.*Decl.*16.28. **-δημέω**, *sojourn in*, Ael.*VH* 12.52, Ath.6.233a; opp. κατοικέω, Id.8.361f, D.C.51.17. **-μένω**, *remain in* or *about*, ἐπί τινα τόπον *Peripl.M.Rubr.*65. **-ορκέω**, *forswear oneself by*, [Ἀθηνᾷ] Aeschin.3.150. II. Pass., *have false witness given against one*, ὑπό τινων Themist.*Ep.*8. **-πεδος**, ον, *flat*, ὀροφή Gal.18(1).518. **-σημος**, gloss on ἀριφραδής, Sch.Il. 23.206. ⊛ **-σκημμα**, ατος, τό, *claiming of property alleged to belong to the state* (cf. ἀπογράφω III.2), Harp. ⊛ **-σκήπτομαι**, Med., *claim property alleged to belong to the state*, ἐνεπισκήψασθαι ἐν τῇ οὐσίᾳ τῇ ἐκείνου ἐνοφειλόμενον αὐτῷ ἀργύριον D.49.45, cf. Harp., Poll.8.61. 2. generally, *take proceedings to enforce a claim*, *PGurob* 2.28 (iii B.C.). **-τρέπω**, *impose* a contribution *upon*, τινί *PLond.*5.1677.15 (Pass.).

⊛ **ἐνέπω**, lengthd. **ἐννέπω**, both forms in Hom. and Pi. (ἐνν- *P.*9. 96, ἐν- *N.*6.59), ἐνν- Sapph.*Supp.*4.2; in Trag. only ἐνν-, exc. E. in lyr., as *Hipp.*572, 580 (anap.), *Heracl.*95 (lyr.), al.: pres. is used by Hom. only in imper. ἔννεπε, opt. ἐνέποιμι Od.17.561, part. ἐνέπων, also 3 sg. impf. ἔννεπε; pres. ind. not before Pi. ll.cc.; inf. Boeot. ἐνέπιν Corinn.*Supp.*2.73: impf. ἤνεπον Pi.*N.*10.79, Call.*Fr.* 1.58 P.: aor. 2 ἔνισπον, ἔνισπες Il.24.388, ἔνισπε 2.80; imper. ἐνίσπες Il.11.186, 14.470, Od.3.101, A.R.1.487, ἔνισπε Od.4.642, A.R.3.1; subj. ἐνίσπω Il.11.839; opt. ἐνίσποις, -οι, Od.4.317, Il.14.107; inf. ἐνισπεῖν Od.4.323: fut. ἐνισπήσω 5.98, ἐνίψω 2.137, al. Pres. ἐνίσπω in later Poets, as Nic.*Th.*522, D.P.391:—*tell* or *tell of*, Διὸς δέ σφ' ἔννεπε μῦθον Il.8.412; τὸν Ἕκτορι μῦθον ἐνίσπες 11.186; νημερτέα πάντ' ἐνέποντα Od.17.549; εἴ τινά μοι κληηδόνα πατρὸς ἐνίσποις if thou *couldst tell* me any tidings of my father, 4.317; ἄνδρα μοι ἔννεπε *tell* me *the tale of*.., 1.1; τίς.. ἄριστος ἔην, σύ μοι ἔννεπε, Μοῦσα Il.2.761; μνηστήρων.. θάνατον καὶ κῆρ' ἐνέπουσα Od.24.414: abs., *tell news* or *tales*, πρὸς ἀλλήλους ἐνέποντε 23.301, cf. S.*El.*1439 (lyr.): freq. in Tragg., who use ἐννέπω as a pres. to the aor. εἰπεῖν (aor. ἔνισπον only in imper. ἔνισπε A.*Supp.*603, inf. ἐνισπεῖν E.*Supp.*435); ἐνν. τινὶ ὅτι .. S.*El.*1367. 2. simply, *speak*, μύθοισι σκολιοῖς ἐνέπων Hes.*Op.* 194, cf. A.*Ch.*550; πρὸς τίν' ἐννέπειν δοκεῖς; S.*Tr.*402. 3. c. acc. et inf., *bid* one *do* so and so, Pi.*P.*9.96, S.*OT*350, *OC*932. 4. *call, name*, ἀγώνων, τοὺς ἐνέποισιν ἱερούς Pi.*N.*6.59; ἐνν. τινὰ δοῦλον E.*HF*270. 5. *address, accost*, τινά S.*Aj.*764. (In Hom. ἐνέπω, ἐννέπω, ἐνισπεῖν (Subst. ἐνοπή), = *tell, relate*; ἐνίπτω and ἐνίσσω (qq. vv., cf. ἐνιπή), *reprove, upbraid*; Pi. and later Ep. used ἐνίπτω, = ἐνέπω.) (For the root, v. ἕσπον.)

**ἐνεραδνούμιον**, τό, dub. sens. in *PMasp.*151.168 (vi A.D.).

**ἐνεργ-άζομαι**, *make* or *produce in*, ἡ φορὰ τῆς τοξίτιδος ἐ. τῷ βέλει κίνησιν Ph.*Bel.*68.41; τι ἐν τῷ σώματι v.l. for ἀπ- in Hp. *VM*22; τι τοῖς ἀνδριᾶσιν X.*Mem.*3.10.6; τὸ πείθεσθαι τοῖς νόμοις [τῇ Σπάρτῃ] ib.4.4.15; πολλοῖς ἔρωτα Gorg.*Hel.*18; [δόξαν] ib.13;

ἔκπληξιν Pl.*Phlb.*47a; ἐπιστήμην Chrysipp.*Stoic.*2.39; δέος τοῖς πολίταις D.60.25; μοχθηρὰς συνηθείας τινί Id.61.3; εὔνοιαν ἐν πᾶσι Plb. 6.11$^{a}$.7, cf. Ph.2.80, etc.: aor. 1 ἐνειργάσθην in pass. sense, *to be made* or *placed in..*, X.*Mem.*1.4.5. **2.** *work for hire in*, of harlots, αἱ ἐνεργαζόμεναι παιδίσκαι Hdt.1.93; ἐ. τῇ οὐσίᾳ *trade* with the property, D.44.23; ἁλιεῖς ἐνειργασμένοι τοῖς τόποις Plb.10.8.7. **-εια**, ἡ, *activity, operation*, opp. ἕξις (disposition), Arist.*EN*1098$^{b}$33, al.; ζῴου Plb.1.4.7; ἡ χαρὰ καὶ ἡ εὐφροσύνη κατὰ κίνησιν ἐνεργείᾳ βλέπονται Epicur.*Fr.*2; opp. ἀογία, Hierocl. *in CA*19 p.461 M.: pl., παντοδαπαὶ ἐ. Polystr.p.30 W.; ἐ. καὶ σπουδή *PTeb.*616 (ii A.D.); physiological *function*, Gal.6.21; *performance*, τῶν καθηκόντων Ph.1.91; *activity*, of drugs, Gal.6.467; *force*, of an engine, D.S.20.95 (but, *mechanism, 'action'*, Hero *Aut.*1.7). **b.** *workmanship*, Aristeas 59. **2.** esp. of divine or supernatural *action*, *Ep.Eph.*1.19, al., Aristeas 266; ἐ. θεοῦ Διὸς Βαιτοκαίκης *OGI*262.4 (Syria, iii A.D.); magical *operation*, ἱερὰ ἐ. *PMag.Par.*1.159. **3.** pl., ἐνέργειαι *cosmic forces*, Herm.ap.Stob.1.41.6. **4.** Gramm., *active force*, opp. πάθος, D.T.637.29, A.D.*Synt.*9.9 (pl.), al.; ἐνέργειαι καὶ πάθη *active* and passive *forms*, Alex.*Fig.*2.14. **5.** Rhet., *vigour of style*, Arist. *Rh.*1411$^{b}$28. **II.** in the philos. of Arist., opp. δύναμις, *actuality*, *Metaph.*1048$^{a}$26, al.; opp. ὕλη, ib.1043$^{a}$20; ἡ ὡς ἐ. οὐσία, substance in the sense of *actuality*, ib.1042$^{b}$10; opp. ἐντελέχεια, as *actuality* to *full reality*, ib.1050$^{a}$22, 1047$^{a}$30; ἐνεργείᾳ *actually*, opp. δυνάμει, ib.1045$^{b}$19, al., etc. **-είς·** ἡ εἰς γλουτοὺς κάθεσις τῶν χειρῶν, Hsch. **-έω**, *to be in action* or *activity, operate*, Arist.*Rh.*1411$^{b}$26; εὐδαίμων ὁ κατ' ἀρετὴν τελείαν -ῶν Id.*EN*1101$^{a}$15: c. acc., ἐνεργεῖς ποσὸν καὶ δυάδα Plot.6.6.16; esp. of divine or supernatural *action*, freq. in *NT.*, τινί, ἔν τινι, *Ep.Gal.*2.8, *Ev.Matt.*14.2:—Med., *Ep. Rom.*7.5, al. **2.** *to be efficacious*, of drugs, Diocl.*Fr.*147, Dsc.1.98, al.; ἐοικότα ἐ. ib.106; ἐνήργησε τὸ φάρμακον Plot.6.1.22; *to be effective*, of troops, ταῖς σαρίσαις Ael.*Tact.*14.6:—Pass., *to be the object of action*, Arist.*de An.*427$^{a}$7, *Ph.*195$^{b}$28; ὁ ἐνεργούμενος λίθος *IG*7.3073.108 (Lebad.); also, *to be actualized*, Plot.3.7.11. **II.** trans., *effect, execute*, πάντα κατὰ δύναμιν Plb.18.14.8; τὰ τοῦ πολέμου Id.7.5.8; χρείαν Ath.Mech.14.2, cf. Aristid.Quint.2.9:—Pass., *to be actively carried on*, ὁ πόλεμος ἐνηργεῖτο Plb.1.13.5, cf. D.S.20.95; τὰ κατὰ πρόθεσιν ἐνεργούμενα *things executed*, Plb.9.12.7; μηδὲν ἐνέργημα.. ἐνεργείσθω M.Ant.4.2. **III.** Medic., of sexual intercourse, τὴν τοιαύτην πρᾶξιν -οῦσι μετρίως Diocl.*Fr.*141, cf. *Cat.Cod.Astr.*8(4).176: euphem. for βινεῖν, *in opere esse*, Theoc.4.61; ἐ. τινά Alciphr. 3.55; ἐρωτικόν τι Id.1.39. **IV.** *operate*, in surgery, Orib.45.18.5, Paul.Aeg.6.73; ὁ ἐνεργῶν, ὁ ἐνεργούμενος, the *surgeon*, the *patient*, Gal.18(2).626,683. **-ημα**, ατος, τό, *action, activity, operation*, Plb. 4.8.7, D.S.4.51 (of the labours of Heracles), Ph.1.213, M.Ant.4.2, Procl.*Inst.*158, al.: pl., φύσεων Iamb.*Myst.*4.13; opp. πάθος, *Stoic.* 2.59, cf. 3.134, Chrysipp.ib.2.295. **2.** *realized object*, [νοῦς] αὐτοῦ ἐ. Plot.6.8.16, cf. 6.9.2. **3.** dub. for ἐνάργημα, Epicur.*Ep.*1 p.4 U.; τὸ κατὰ φιλοσοφίαν ἐ. Metrod.*Herc.*831.8, cf. Phld.*Po.*2.68. **-ής**, ές, later form of ἐνεργός, *active, effective*, μηχανὰς ἐνεργεῖς ποιοῦντες D.S. 17.44, etc.; of medicines, *strong*, *POxy.*1088.56 (i A.D.), Dsc.5.88, etc.: Comp. -έστερος *more effective*, πρός τινα Arist.*Top.*105$^{a}$19: Sup. -έστατος, πρός τι D.S.1.88, cf. Dsc.1.19, A.D.*Synt.*291.9. **-ητέος**, α, ον, *to be done*, dub. l. in Zeno *Stoic.*1.49. **-ητικός**, ή, όν, *able to act upon, acting upon*, τοῦ κινητοῦ Arist.*Ph.*202$^{a}$17. **2.** *productive*, τινός *Gp.*12.35.1. **II.** *active*, Arist.*EE*1220$^{b}$3; αὐτοπάθεια Plb. 12.28.6. Adv. -κῶς *actively*, S.E.*M.*7.223,293. **2.** Gramm., ἐ. ῥῆμα an *active* verb, D.H.*Amm.*2.7; of Nouns, A.D.*Adv.*161.18; ἐκφορά, διάθεσις, Id.*Synt.*150.19, 210.19. Adv. -κῶς ib.276.20, Phryn. *PS* p.9 B. **III.** *efficacious, stimulating*, *Gp.*2.33.4 (Sup.). **-ήτρια**, ἡ, *effectrix*, *Gloss.* **-ίς**, epith. of Demeter, Hsch. **-μός**, ὁ, *a way of playing on the lyre*, Phryn.Com.6. **2.** *peg* on the κιθάρα for tuning the strings, Euphron.ap.*EM*340.3.

**ἐνεργο-βᾰτέω**, *step vehemently, pass wonderfully* from one thing to another, εἴς τι Ps.-Luc.*Philopatr.*3. **-λᾰβέω**, *exploit*, Aeschin.3. 150, Procop.*Arc.*20,25; τοὺς ἑτέρων βίους Just.*Nov.*17.13.

**ἐνεργός**, όν, *at work, active, busy*, Hdt.8.26, etc.; ζῷα ἐ., opp. εἴδωλα ἀκίνητα, X.*Mem.*1.4.4; δικασταί, κυβερνῆται, ἐ. ὄντες *on duty*, Pl.*Lg.*674b; ὅπως ἂν ἐ. ὦσι that they may *begin business*, D.35.7; ἐ. περί τι γίγνεσθαι Plb.3.17.4; *effective, fit for service*, νῆες, στράτευμα, Th.3.17, X.*Cyr.*2.2.23; πεζὸν σὺν ἵπποις -ότατον Id.*Eq.Mag.*9.7; ἐ. προσβολή *vigorous* attack, Plb.4.63.8; ἐ. ὑσσοί *effective* javelins, Id.1.40.12; πελέκεις D.S.5.39; ἐ. ποιεῖσθαι τὴν πορείαν march *with rapidity*, Plb.5.8.3; τὸ τῆς ὥρας πρὸς τὰς νόσους -ότατον D.S.14. 70; τόποι (in logical sense) -ότατοι *most effective*, Arist.*Top.*154$^{a}$16; ἡ γεωργία ἐ. ποιεῖ τὴν τροφήν calls *into action* the nutritive properties (of the soil), Id.*Pr.*924$^{a}$17. **2.** *actual*, opp. *potential*, *Theol.Ar.*6, 12. **II.** of land, *productive*, opp. ἀργός, X.*Cyr.*3.2.19, cf. 5.4.25, *HG*4.4.1, Plu.*Sol.*31 (Comp.); simply, *tilled*, *SIG*685.72 (Itanos); πεδίον πολλαῖς ἐνεργὸν μυριάσι *producing enough* for multitudes, Plu. *Caes.*58; μυλαῖον ἐ. *in working order*, *PRyl.*167.10 (i A.D.); also of mines, X.*Vect.*4.2; ἐνεργά (sc. χρήματα) *employed capital, which brings in a return*, D.27.7,10, cf. X.*Hier.*11.4; θησαυρὸς ἐ. *PLond.*2.216 (i A.D.); τὸ δάνειον ἐ. ποιεῖν to put out *to interest*, D.56.29. **III.** Adv. -γῶς *with activity*, μαχεῖται X.*Mem.*3.4.11; γυμνάζειν Plb.1.9.7, al.: Comp., Id.4.59.3.

**ἐνερείδω**, *thrust in*, μοχλὸν.. ὀφθαλμῷ ἐνέρεισαν Od.9.383; δακτύλους Hp.*Art.*34; βέλος ἐνερεισθὲν τοῖς ὀστέοις Plu.2.344c; *apply*, ἐν δὲ πλατὺν ὦμον ἔρεισεν A.R.1.1198: metaph., μὴ ἐνέρειδε μηθένα *Sammelb.*5905; *fix upon*, τὴν ὄψιν τινί Plu.2.586d; τοὺς ἄκμονας τῷ τραχήλῳ Ant.Lib.28.4; τὸν θυμόν τισι Oenom.ap.Eus.*PE*5.34; τὴν ψυχήν Luc.*Nigr.*7:—Med., ἐνερεισάμενος πέτρᾳ γόνυ *his own* knee, Theoc.7.7, cf. Orph.*A.*1090. **II.** intr., *lie in* or *on*, τὰ ἐνηρεικότα στομάχῳ *adherent to..*, Dsc.3.23:—Med., πεσὼν ἐνερείσατο γαίῃ A.R. 1.428.

**ἐνέρεισις**, εως, ἡ, *pressure*, Hp.*Off.*12: pl., Arr.*Tact.*16.13.

**ἐνερεύγομαι**, *belch on*, γυίοις ἰόν Nic.*Th.*185: also aor. 2 Act., ἔμοιγε ..τυροῦ κάκιστον.. ἐνήρῠγεν Ar.*V.*913.

**ἐνερευθ-ής**, ές, *somewhat red*, ἄστρον Str.3.1.5; ἀφρός Dsc.1.100: Comp., Sor.1.13; of the countenance, *flushed*, Phld.*Ir.*p.5 W., Cic. *Att.*12.4.1; τῷ χρώματι γενόμενος ἐ. *blushing*, Plb.31.23.8; παρειῶν τὸ ἐ. Luc.*Im.*7, cf. Antyll.ap.Orib.7.16.3. **-ομαι**, *to be somewhat ruddy*, Nic.*Th.*511,871.

**ἔνερθε** and **-θεν**; Dor. **ἔνερθα** A.D.*Adv.*153.17; also **νέρθε** and **-θεν**: **I.** Adv. *from beneath, up from below*, αὐτὰρ νέρθε Ποσειδάων ἐτίναξε Il.20.57; πέμψατ' ἔνερθεν ψυχὴν εἰς φῶς A.*Pers.*630; τήνδ' ἔπεμψας νέρθεν ἐς φάος E.*Alc.*1139, cf. 985 (lyr.); ν. ἀνακαλούμενον Id.*Hel.*966. **2.** without sense of motion, *beneath, below*, ἔ. πόδες καὶ χεῖρες ὕπερθε Il.13.75, cf. 78; ῥαίνοντο δὲ νέρθε κονίῃ [ἵπποι] 11.282, cf. 535, etc.; πρόσωπά τε ν. τε γοῦνα Od.20.352; esp. of the nether world, οἱ ἔ. θεοί the gods *below*, Il.14.274; τοῖς ἔ. νεκροῖς S.*Ant.*25 (lyr.), cf. *El.*1068; κοίταν ἔχει ν. Id.*OC*1707 (lyr.); ἔνερθ' ὑπὸ γῆς, ὑπὸ γᾶν, Hes.*Th.*720, Pi.*P.*9.81; τοῖς.. ν. κἀπὶ γῆς ἄνω S.*OT*416; *below*, i.e. in the vale, E.*Ba.*752; βαιὸν δ' ἔ. S.*Ph.*20. **II.** as Prep. with gen., before or after its case, *beneath, below*, ἀγκῶνος ἔ. Il.11.252, cf. 234; γαίης ν. καὶ.. θαλάσσης 14.204; ν. γῆς Od.11.302; ἔνερθ' Ἀΐδεω Il.8.16; γῆς ἔνερθ' ὤχου θανών S.*Fr.*686, cf. E.*Ph.* 505. **b.** *from below*, γῆς ἔνερθεν ἐς φάος A.*Pers.*222 (troch.). **2.** *subject to, in the power of*, ἐχθρῶν ἔ. ὄντα S.*Ph.*666.—Never in Att. Prose; used by Hdt., ἔ. τῆς λίμνης 2.13 (abs. in metaph. sense, *inferior*, τοῖς ἅπασι 1.91); also in *IG*4.1485.57 (Epid.), Aret.*CD*1.3, Luc.*Rh.Pr.*4; in form νέρθε, *IG*12(2).74*b*21 (Mytil., iii B.C.).

**ἔνερμα**, ατος, τό, = ὅρμος, Sch.Pi.*O.*2.135.

**ἔνερξις**, εως, ἡ, = ἐνεργμός, *EM*340.2, Hsch.

**ἔνεροι**, οἱ, *those below, those beneath the earth*, of the dead and the gods below, ἐνέροισιν ἀνάσσων Il.15.188, Hes.*Th.*850; ἄναξ ἐνέρων Il.20.61, etc.; βασιλεῦ ἐνέρων A.*Pers.*629 (anap.); ἐνέρων ἀρωγός, i.e. of the murdered Agamemnon, S.*El.*1391 (lyr.); οἱ ἔνεροι Pl.*R.* 387c, cf. *Tab.Defix.*99.9. (Perh. fr. ἔρα.)

**ἐνερόχρως**, ωτος, ὁ, ἡ, *cadaverous*, Alciphr.1.3, Agath.2.23, *EM* 340.10.

**ἔνερσις**, εως, ἡ, (ἐνείρω) *fitting in, fastening*, ἐνέρσει χρυσῶν τεττίγων, used by old men at Athens to fasten up their hair, Th.1.6.

**ἐνέρτερος**, α, ον, Comp. of ἔνεροι, *lower, of the nether world*, οἵ περ ἐ. εἰσι θεοί Il.15.225; οἱ ἐ., = ἔνεροι, A.*Ch.*285; ἱστός *Lyr.Adesp.*132: c. gen., ἦσθα ἐ. Οὐρανιώνων *below* them, Il.5.898. **2.** simply, *lower*, Nonn.*D.*44.164.—After Hom. usu. in form νέρτερος (q.v.). **II.** Sup., ἐνέρτατον βένθος *lowest*, Emp.35.3; cf. νέρτατος.

**ἐνέρυθρος**, ον, = ἐνερευθής, *reddish*, ὀφθαλμοί Aret.*SD*1.6.

**ἐνεσία**, ἡ, (ἐνίημι) *suggestion*, used only in Ep. form **ἐννεσίη**: dat. pl., with gen. pers., once in Hom., κείνης ἐννεσίῃσι *at* her *suggestion*, Il.5.894; Γαίης, Διός, Ἥρης ἐνν., Hes.*Th.*494, *h.Cer.*30, Call.*Dian.* 108; ὑπ' ἐννεσίῃσι A.R.1.7, prob. in Q.S.3.475: gen. pl., ἐννεσιάων A.R.3.1364.

**ἔνεσις**, εως, ἡ, (ἐνίημι) *injection*, φύσης ἐνιεμένης ἐς τὴν κοιλίην Hp. *Art.*48, cf. Hero *Spir.*2.18, Orib.*Syn.*9.14.1.

⊛ **ἐνεστιάομαι**, *give an entertainment in*, Luc.*Am.*12.

**ἐνέστιος**, ον, *offered at the public hearth*, τὸ ἐ. θῦμα οἶν *Inscr.Magn.*36. 20 (Ithaca):—also **ἐνίστιος**, ον, ib.72.40 (Syrac.):—Subst. **ἐνέστιον** (sc. θῦμα), τό, ib.42.12 (Corinth):—Arc. **ἰνίστιον** ib.38.41 (Megalop.).

**ἐν-ετέον**, (ἐνίημι) *one must treat with injections* or *clysters*, Sor.2.44, Orib.*Fr.*60, Herod.Med. in *Rh.Mus.*58.85. **-ετή**, ἡ, (ἐνετός) = περόνη, *pin, brooch*, Il.14.180, Call.*Fr.*149, *Mus.Belg.*16.71 (Attica, ii A.D.). **-ετήρ**, ῆρος, ὁ, *clyster-syringe*, Cass.Fel.48, Alex.Trall. 8.2; περὶ ἐνετήρων on *clysters*, Sever.*Clyst.*tit., cf. Steph. *in Gal.*1.331 D. **II.** *siege-engine of war for hurling projectiles*, Ph.*Bel.*91.45, 100.18. **-ετήρια**, τά, *taxes on admission* to citizenship, *IG*9(1). 334.9 (Locr., v B.C.). **-ετός**, ή, όν, *inserted*, σκυταλίδες J.*AJ*3. 6.5; *for injection*, τροχίσκοι Paul.Aeg.7.12 (v.l. ἐνετικῶν). **II.** *suborned*, X.*Cyr.*1.6.19, *An.*7.6.41, App.*BC*1.22, *Mith.*59.

**ἐνευδαιμονέω**, *to be happy in*, Th.2.44, D.S.34.3; τῷ καιρῷ Lib.*Or.* 14.43.

**ἐνευδιάω**, *float in the clear sky*, ἐνευδιόων πτερύγεσσι A.R.2.935.

**ἐνευδοκῐμέω**, *gain glory in*, ὅτῳ τὰ τῶν Ἑλλήνων ἀτυχήματ' ἐνευδοκιμεῖν ἀπέκειτο D.18.198, cf. D.S.34.2.18, J.*Ap.*1.5, Plu.2.71a; περί τι *Cod.Just.*1.2.25.1. **2.** *enjoy repute with* another, Ael.*VH*8.12.

**ἐνεύδω**, *sleep in* or *on*, χλαῖναν.. καὶ κώεα, τοῖσιν ἐνεῦδεν Od.20.95, cf. 3.350, al., Theoc.5.10; τρίβωνι D.L.6.22.

**ἐνευεργετέω**, in Pass., ἐνευεργετημένος *well-treated*, dub. in *PLond.* 2.177.26 (i A.D.).

**ἐνευημερέω**, *to be lucky in*, τοῖς θεάτροις, τοῖς ὕδνοις, Plu.2.289d, 665d.

**ἐνευθηνέομαι**, *abound in*, Sch.Ar.*Pl.*586.

**ἐνευκαιρέω**, *pass one's time in*, διαβολαῖς Ph.2.522, cf. 1.387.

**ἐνευλογέομαι**, Pass., *to be blessed in*, τῷ σπέρματί σου *Act.Ap.*3.25, ἐν σοί Lxx *Ge.*12.3, *Ep.Gal.*3.8:—Med., *take a blessing to oneself*, ἀπαρχῆς Lxx 1 *Ki.*2.29.

**ἐνευν-άζομαι**, Med., aor. 1 ἐνευνάσσαντο, *sleep in*, Nic.*Fr.*19. **-αιος**, ον, *on which one sleeps*, ἐστόρεσεν δ' ἐπὶ δέρμα.. ἐνεύναιον a skin *to*

*sleep on*, Od.14.51; χήτει ἐνευναίων for want *of bed-furniture*, 16.35; τὰ ἐ. *bed-clothes*, Hierocl.p.25 A. **-οι·** ἐπιτήδειοι τόποι εἰς Κύπριοι, Hsch.

**ἐνευπᾰθέω,** = εὐπαθέω ἐν.., Lib.*Or.*11.257,268.

**ἐνευρίσκω,** *discover in*, J.*BJ*5.13.5 (Pass.), cf. Aristid.*Or.*28(49).13 (dub. l.).

**ἐνευστομέω,** *sing sweetly in*, τοῖς ἄλσεσι Philostr.Jun.*Im.*6.

**ἐνευσχημονέω,** = εὐσχημονέω ἐν.., Hierocl.*in CA*5 p.427 M.

**ἐνευσχολέω,** *have leisure for*, λογισμοῖς Luc.*Am.*35.

**ἐνευτῠχέω,** = εὐτυχέω ἐν.., Aristid.1.111 J.

**ἐνευφραίνομαι,** = εὐφραίνομαι ἐν.., Lxx *Pr.*8.31, Ph.1.232, al.

⊛ **ἐνεύχομαι,** *adjure, implore*, *Test.Epict.*1.12, Herod.6.46; ἐνεύχομαι ὑμῖν θεοὺς καὶ θεὰς *IG*5(1).1208.50 (Gythium): c. dat., of god invoked, *PMag.Par.*1.2258; also ἐνεύχομαί σοι τὴν Ἀφροδίτην μὴ ἀποτινήσῃς I *adjure* you by A. not to.., *PBaden* 51 (ii A.D.).

**ἐνευωχέομαι,** = εὐωχέομαι ἐν.., abs., Str.17.1.15.

**ἐνεφάλλομαι,** aor. 2 ἐνέπαλτο, *leap upon*, Q.S.10.467.

**ἐνέφει·** ἐρείδει, Hsch.

**ἐνεχθήσομαι, ἐνέχθητι, ἐνεχθείην, ἐνεχθῶ, ἐνεχθῆναι,** v. φέρω.

**ἐνεχῠρ-άζω,** fut. -άσω D.47.79 (but -χυρῶ Lxx *De.*24.17):—*take a pledge from* one, τινός Lexap.D.21.10: metaph., ἡ φύσις ἐ. τοῦ μὲν ὄψιν, τοῦ δὲ ἀκοήν Pl.*Ax.*367b. 2. c. acc. rei, *take in pledge*, D.24.197; ἐ. ὁ νόμος τὰς οὐσίας τῶν ὑπευθύνων Aeschin.3.21, cf. Lxx *De.*24.6, al., D.H.6.29, *PPetr.*3 pp.56,69: abs., Plb.6.37.8 (ἐνεχυριάζων codd.):—Pass., τὰ χρήματα ἐνεχυράζομαι I *have my goods seized for debt*, Ar.*Nu.*241:—Med., *have security given one, take it for oneself*, τόκου *for* interest, ib.35; *seize as a pledge*, Id.*Ec.*567. **-ἀσία,** ἡ, *taking* property *in pledge, security* taken, *pledge*, Pl.*Lg.*949d, *IG* 2.1055.7 (iv B.C.), *POxy.*1.288 (ii A.D.), etc.; ἐ. ποιήσασθαι D.47.76, 80. **-ασμα,** ατος, τό, *pledge, thing pawned*, Lxx *Ex.*22.26(25), al., *PHamb.*10.42 (ii A.D.). ⊛ **-ασμός,** ὁ, = ἐνεχυρασία, Lxx *Ez.*18.7, Plu.*Cor.*5 (pl.). **-αστής,** οῦ, ὁ, *one who distrains*, *Schwyzer* 177.8 (Crete, v B.C.), Hsch. s. v. δήμαρχιν. **-αστός,** ή, όν, *seizable for debt*, *Test.Epict.*5.19. ⊛ **-ιάζω, -ιασμός,** later forms for ἐνεχυράζω, -ασμός, Just.*Nov.*134.7, 52.1, *Gloss.*:—also **-ιασία, -ίασις, -ιαστής,** ib. **-ιμαῖον,** = ἐνέχυρον, censured by Phryn.342. **-ιος,** ον, *pledged*, Socr.*Ep.*9.1 (Aristippus). II. Subst. ἐνεχύριον, τό, = sq., *BGU*907.11 (ii A.D.). ⊛ **-ον,** τό, (ἐχυρός) *pledge, security*, ἐ. ἀποδεικνύναι and ὑποτιθέναι to offer *a pledge*, Hdt.2.136; ἐνέχυρα ἀποδιδόναι And.1.39; λαμβάνειν ibid., X.*An.*7.6.23; ἐνέχυρα βίᾳ φέρειν Antipho 6.11; ἐνέχυρον φέρειν τῶν γειτόνων Hermipp.29; τὰ ἐ. τινων *PHib.*1.46 (iii B.C.), etc.; ἐ. τιθέναι τι make a thing *a pledge*, put it *in pawn*, Ar.*Pl.*451, cf. *Ec.*755; ἐ. κεῖται Pl.*Lg.*820e; ἐπ' ἐνεχύρῳ δοῦναι give on *security*, D.49.2; ἐπ' ἐνεχύροις δανείζειν Ph.1.634; ἐκ τῶν ἐ. τῶν ὠφληκότων τὴν δίκην from the forfeited *pledges*, *IG*2.814ᵃ*A* 26 (iv B.C.): metaph. in pl., *hostages*, of wives and children, Aen.Tact.5.1, cf. Ph.1.323 (sg.). **-όω,** *pledge*, *POxy.*729.44 (Pass., ii A.D.). **-ωμα,** ατος, τό, = -ασμα, *EM*706.41 (pl.). **-ως,** Adv. *safely*, *Peripl.M.Rubr.*43.

**ἐνέχω,** *hold* or *keep fast within*, χόλον ἐνέχειν τινί *harbour* a grudge against one, Hdt.1.118, 6.119 (v. II. 2). II. Pass., with fut. and aor. Med. (v. infr.), *to be held, caught, entangled in*, c. dat., τῇ πάγῃ Id.2.121.β'; ἐνεχομένων τῶν πελτῶν τοῖς σταυροῖς X.*An.*7.4.17; ἐν τοῖς τῆς νεὼς σκεύεσι Pl.*La.*183e. 2. metaph., ἐ. ἀπορίῃσι Hdt.1.190; φιλοτιμίᾳ E.*IA*527; ὀργαῖς πολυχρονίοις Phld.*Ir.*p.63 W.; ἐν ἄγεϊ Hdt.6.56; ἐν ταῖς αὐταῖς δυσχερείαις Arist.*Cael.*309ᵃ29; ἐν θώματι ἐνέσχετο *was seized with* wonder, Hdt.7.128. 3. *to be liable* or *subject to*, οὐ δικαίοις Ζεὺς ἐνέξεται λόγοις A.*Supp.*169 (Pors. for ἐνεύξεται, lyr.), cf. And.1.44; πράγμασιν, λειτουργίαις, *BGU*473.7 (ii A.D.), *PFlor.*382.31 (iii A.D.), etc. b. in legal formulae, ἐν ἐπιάρῳ κ' ἐνέχοιτο *SIG*9.9 (Elis, vi B.C.); ἐ. ἀρᾷ Διός Pl.*Lg.*881d (in tmesi, ἐν τῆπαρῇ ἔχεσθαι *SIG*38.34 (Teos, v B.C.)); ζημίᾳ, αἰτίᾳ, Pl.*Lg.*935c, *Cri.*52a; τοῖς ἐσχάτοις ἐπιτιμίοις D.51.11; ἐν τοῖς αὐτοῖς ἐπιτιμίοις Aeschin.3.175; νόμῳ *Schwyzer*634*B*49 (Nesus, iv B.C., prob.), Plu.*TG*10; ἐν τοῖς αὐτοῖς νόμοις Pl.*Lg.*762d; νοθείᾳ *in an imputation of* bastardy, Plu.*Them.*1; ἱεροσυλίαις *PTeb.*5.5 (ii B.C.): abs., ἐὰν ἐνσχεθῶσι *PSI*3.168 (ii B.C.). 4. in good sense, ἐνέχεσθαι ἀγγελίᾳ *meet with* a message, Pi.*P.*8.49. 5. in aor., *come to a standstill*, ἔν τινι Pl.*Tht.*147d. III. intr., *enter in, pierce*, εἴς τι X.*Cyn.*10.7. 2. *to be urgent against*, τινί Lxx *Ge.*49.23, *Ev.Marc.*6.19, *Ev.Luc.*11.53.

**ἐνέψ-ημα,** ατος, τό, *a thing boiled* or *infused*, Aret.*CA*1.1. **-ητέον,** *one must boil in, infuse*, ibid.

**ἐνεψίημα,** ατος, τό, *plaything*, Nic.*Al.*233. [ῑ metri gr.]

**ἐνέψω,** *boil in* or *among*, Aret.*CA*1.1: pf. Pass., ἐνήψηται ib.6: aor. 1 Pass., ἐνεψηθέντα..καμάτοισι μελίσσης Nic.*Al.*71.

**ἐνέωρα,** Adv. *up* (cf. μετέωρος), *Philol.*65.637 (Milet.).

**ἐνέωσα,** aor. 1 of ἐνωθέω, A.R.4.1243.

**ἐνϝοικέω,** = ἐνοικέω, *Leg.Gort.*4.34.

**ἐνζάω,** *live in*, f.l. in Ph.1.65: metaph., ἐν τῇ τινῶν μνήμῃ prob. in *IGRom.*4.146 (Cyzicus, i A.D.).

**ἐνζεύγνῡμι,** *yoke*, ἐνιζευχθέντες βόες A.R.1.686; *bind fast*, ἄρθρα ποδοῖν S.*OT*718. II. metaph., *involve in*, ἀνάγκαις ταῖσδ' ἐνέζευγμαι A.*Pr.*108; τί ποτέ μ'..ἐνέζευξας..ἐν πημοσύναις; ib.578 (lyr.).

**ἐνζέω,** *boil in*, πήγανον ἐνεζέσθη Aret.*CA*1.2.

**ἐνζύμιον,** = κώνειον, Ps.-Dsc.4.78.

**ἐνζωγρᾰφέω,** *paint in* or *on*, Pl.*Phlb.*40a (Pass.), Tz.*H.*12.560.

**ἐνζώννῡμι,** aor. 1 -έζωσα, *gird*, ἑαυτόν Plu.*Sull.*28:—Med., ἐνζωσάμενοι κῴδια Dicaearch.2.8.

**ἔνζῳος,** ον, *full of beasts*, ἄλση dub. in Nic.*Fr.*31.2.

**ἔνη,** v. ἕνος (B). **ἕνη καὶ νέα,** v. ἕνος 2.

**ἐνηβ-άω,** *spend one's youth in*, Longus 3.13. II. of plants, *flourish in*, νάπαισι δ' ἀνθέρικος ἐνηβᾷ Cratin.325, cf. Nic.*Fr.*85. 2. III. intr., ἐνηβώαις ἵπποις mares *in the prime of youth*, *IG* 5(1).213.15, al. (Sparta, v B.C.). **-ητήριον,** τό, *place of amusement*, Hdt.2.133, Ael.*NA*11.10. **-ος,** ον, *in the prime of youth*, from fifteen upwards, Sch.Theoc.8.3.

**ἐνήδ-ομαι,** Pass., *rejoice in*, τινί Mich.*in EN*532.4, Sch.Il.8.51, Hsch.: abs., Gal.16.566. **-ονος,** ον, *full of joy, delightful*, Sch.E.*Hec.*828; ἐ. ὀφθαλμός '*glad eye*', Heph.Astr.1.1. **-ύνω,** *cheer, gratify*, τὰς ἀκοάς Ps.-Luc.*Philopatr.*3. **-ῠπᾰθέω,** = ἡδυπαθέω ἐν.., Ph.2.326.

**ἐνη-είη,** ἡ, *kindness, gentleness*, νῦν τις ἐνηείης Πατροκλῆος..μνησάσθω Il.17.670, cf. Opp.*H.*5.519. **-ής,** ές, Ep. Adj. *kind, gentle*, ἑταῖρον..ἐνηέα τε κρατερόν τε Il.17.204; ἑτάροιο ἐνηέος ὀστέα λευκά 23.252; ἑταῖρον ἐ., of Athena, Od.8.200; μευ ἀεὶ μέμνησαι ἐνηέος Il.23.648; φιλότητος ἐνηέος Hes.*Th.*651: later in nom. ἐνηής *IG*14.1648.8; etym. of Ἐνυώ, Corn.*ND*21: pl., ἐνηέες Opp.*C.*2.89; ἐνηέες Id.*H.*2.644; of stars, *propitious*, Max.262, al. (ἐν and -ηής, cf. Skt. *ávas* 'help', 'favour', *ávati* 'he helps'.)

**ἐνήκοντα,** indecl. *ninety*, *IG*11(2).199*B*32 (Delos, iii B.C.).

**ἐνήκω,** *appertain, belong*, *PMasp.*124.10 (vi A.D.).

**ἐνηλάσιον** [ᾰ], τό, *rent*, *GDI*5661.5, al. (Chios, iv B.C.).

⊛ **ἐνήλᾰτον,** τό, (ἐνελαύνω) *anything driven in*: as Subst. mostly pl., ἐνήλατα (sc. ξύλα), τά, I. *the four rails*, which make the frame *of a bedstead*, ἐ. ξύλα S.*Fr.*315, cf. Ph.1.666 (Att. κραστήρια, acc. to Phryn.155): later in sg., ἐνήλατον, τό, *bedstead*, Sor.2.61; τὸ τῆς κλίνης ἐ. *PSI*6.616.17 (iii A.D.). II. *rungs* of a ladder, which are *fixed in* the poles or sides, κλίμακος ξέστ' ἐνηλάτων βάθρα E.*Ph.*1179; ἄκρα κλιμάκων ἐνήλατα Id.*Supp.*729. III. ἀξόνων ἐνήλατα *the pins driven into the axle, linchpins*, Id.*Hipp.*1235. IV. ἐνήλατον· μέρος νεώς, Hsch.

**ἐνηλεγής** (-είς cod.)· ἐν ἐπιθυμίᾳ ὤν, Hsch. **ἐνηλεῦσαι·** δογματίσαι, Id. **ἐνηλίαζ·** ἑορτὴ τοῦ Ἐνυαλίου, Id.

**ἐνήλῐκος,** ον, = sq., *Sammelb.*4638.11 (ii B.C.), *IG*7.2712.70 (Acraeph.), Plu.*Cat.Ma.*24, etc.

⊛ **ἐνῆλιξ,** ῐκος, ὁ, ἡ, *of age, in the prime of manhood*, *OGI*338.21 (Pergam., ii B.C.), Lxx 4*Ma.*18.9, *POxy.*646 (ii A.D.), etc.

**ἐνηλῐόομαι,** *to be exposed to the sun*, Aët.8.16; ἐνηλιωμένα *sunlit* objects, Gal.17(2).396.

**ἐνηλλαγμένως,** Adv. pf. part. Pass. of ἐναλλάσσω, *reversely, in reverse order*, Meno *Iatr.*17.42; *inverting the true order*, Plot.3.7.13. 2. *crosswise*, = ἐναλλάξ, τοῖς ποσὶν ἵστασθαι Procop.Gaz.p.163 B.

**ἔνηλος,** ον, *clavatus*, *Gloss.*

**ἐνηλόω,** *nail to*, in Pass., Cels.ap.Orig.*Cels.*6.34,36.

**ἐνηλύσιος** [ῠ], ον, (ἠλύσιον II) *struck by lightning*: ἐνηλύσια, τά, *places set apart from worldly uses*, because a thunderbolt has fallen there, A.*Fr.*17, cf. *EM*341.5, Hsch.

**ἐνήλωσις,** εως, ἡ, *ornamental nail*, Callix.1.

⊛ **ἐνῆμαι,** used as pf. of ἐνέζομαι, *to be seated in*, ἵν' ἐνήμεθα πάντες Od.4.272, cf. Theoc.22.44; θάκοις..ἐνήμενοι E.*Fr.*795.

**ἐνημερεύω,** *spend the day in*, ἁρπαγαῖς D.S.17.70; μελέταις Id.32.16, cj. in Thphr.*Char.*8.14.

**ἐνημμένος,** η, ον, pf. part. Pass. from ἐνάπτω.

⊛ **ἐνήνοθε,** only found in compds.: v. ἐπ-, κατ-, παρ-ενήνοθε.

**ἐνήνοχα, ἐνήνεγμαι,** v. φέρω.

**ἐνηρεμέω,** = ἠρεμέω ἐν.., Ph.2.140, Hld.1.18.

**ἐνήρης,** ες, *with a single bank of oars*, ναῦς Plu.*Brut.*28, *Sull.*24, etc.

**ἐνηρόσιον,** τό, *rent for corn-land*, ἐ. τῶν ἱερῶν χωρίων *Inscr.Délos* 354.168 (iii B.C.): also in pl., ἐνηρόσια, τά, *IG*11(2).142.20, 144*A*9, al. (Delos, iv B.C.); cf. ἐναράτιον. II. *right of tillage*, *SIG*1044.18 (Halic., iv/iii B.C.). III. gloss on γαλάσιον, Hsch.

**ἐνηρυθμοί,** v. ἐνιαυθμός.

**ἐνησῠχάζω,** = ἡσυχάζω ἐν.., *to be quiet in*, Chio *Ep.*16.7, Ph.2.140.

**ἐνήφαιστος,** ον, *volcanic*, Tz.*H.*10.502.

**ἐνήχ-έω,** *to be resonant*, Aret.*SA*1.6: c. dat., *ring in the ears of*, Plu.2.589d; in full, τοῖς ὠσί τισιν Id.*Lib.*4; ἐ. ἀκοαῖς σάλπιγξ Onos.1.13. 2. *teach by voice, word of mouth*, Eustr.*in EN*112.19 (Pass.). **-ημα,** ατος, τό, *a sound in* one's ears, Iamb.*VP*15.65 codd. **-ησις,** εως, ἡ, *musical accompaniment* of a song, *Et.Gud.*576.34. **-ος,** ον, *sounding within*, of wind-instruments, opp. ἔγχορδος, Phillis ap.Ath.14.636c: generally, *sounding, noisy*, ἀναπνοή Herod.Med. in *Rh.Mus.*58.77; ἐ. ὕδατα Philostr.*VA*6.26. II. c. gen., *acquainted, conversant with*, Lxx *Si.prol.*9 (s. v. l.).

⊛ **ἔνθᾰ,** Adv.: I. Demonstr., 1. of Place, *there*, Il.14.216, etc.: also with Verbs of motion, *thither*, 13.23, 14.340, Od.3.297, 6.47, 12.5; ἔ. καὶ ἔ. *hither* and *thither*, 2.213, etc.; διῃρέθη τὸ ὕδωρ ἔ. καὶ ἔ. Lxx 4*Ki.*2.8; also ἢ ἔ. ἢ ἔ. Od.10.574: rare in Trag. and Com., A.*Supp.*33 (anap.); ἔ. καὶ Πείσανδρος ἦλθε Ar.*Av.*1556: in Prose in such phrases as ἔ. μὲν..ἔ. δὲ.. *in one place.. in another..*, Pl.*Smp.*211a; later γενόμενοι ἔ. *POxy.*896.32 (iv A.D.). 2. of Time, *thereupon, then*, Il.5.1, etc.; ἔ. δ' ἔπειτα and *thereupon*, Od.7.196, 10.516; ἔ. δή *hereupon*, *and so*, Hdt.1.59, X.*HG*2.4.39. II. Relat., 1. of Place, *where*, Il.1.610, 9.194, Alc.*Supp.*25.5, etc.; repeated, Hes.*Sc.*334, Theoc.8.45; also ἔνθα τε Il.2.594, 5.305; in later Prose, Ph.2.580, Wilcken *Chr.*41 iii 11 (iii A.D.); ἔνθα περ, v. ἔνθαπερ: c. gen., γαίας ἔ.. *in that spot* of earth *in which..*, S.*Aj.*659; ἔ. πημάτων κυρῶ *at what point* of misery I am, E.*Tr.*685, cf. A.R.3.771: with Verbs of motion, *whither*, Od.1.210; ὁδοιποροῦμεν ἔ. χρῄζομεν S.*El.*

1099, cf. *Ph.*1466 (anap.), Th.4.42,75; *to the place where*, S.*OT*796; *at the place whence*.., Id.*El.*436, X.*Oec.*18.1: rarely in indirect questions, Αἴγισθον ἔνθ' ᾤκηκεν ἱστορῶ S.*El.*1101. 2. of Time, *when*, interpol. in X.*An.*5.1.1; ἔστιν ἔ. *sometimes*, S.*El.*1042, cf. X.*Cyr.* 7.4.15; ἔ. τοῦ χρόνου *at which point* of time, Ael.*VH*10.18.

⊕ **ἐνθάδε** [ᾰ], Adv.: I. of Place, *thither, hither*, Od.15.492, S.*Ph.*304, Th.6.36, etc. 2. after Hom. more freq., = ἔνθα, *here* or *there*, ἐνθάδε αὐτοῦ μένων Ar.*V.*765; *in this world*, opp. the nether-world, Pi.*O.*2. 57, Pl.*Grg.*525b; ὁ δ' εὔκολος μὲν ἐνθάδ' εὔκολος δ' ἐκεῖ Ar.*Ra.*82; οἱ ἐ., opp. οἱ κάτω, A.*Supp.*923, S.*Ant.*75; also, the people *of this country*, Id.*OC*42; τοῖς ἐνθάδ' αὐτοῦ ib.78; τις τῶν ἐνθάδ' αὐτοῦ Eup.357; τὰ ἐνθάδε, opp. τὰ ἐκεῖ, Th.6.17. II. of circumstances, *in this case* or *state*, X.*Cyr.*2.4.17; ἐνθάδ' ἥκων having come *to this point*, S. *Ph.*377: c. gen., ἐ. τοῦ πάθους *at this stage* of my suffering, ib. 899. 2. of Time, *here, now*, οὔτ' ἐνθάδ' ὁρῶν οὔτ' ὀπίσω neither *the present* nor the future, Id.*OT*488 (lyr.); αὐτίκ' ἐ. Id *OC*992.

**ἐνθαδί** [ῑ], Att. strengthd. for foreg., Ar.*Pl.*54, *Lys.*1010, Eup.2, etc.

**ἐνθάδιος** [ᾰ], α, ον, = ἐντόπιος, Hsch.: σεῦτλον ἐ. *Gp.*12.1.3.

**ἐνθακ-έω**, *sit in* or *on*, θρόνοις τοῖσιν πατρῴοις S.*El.*267, cf. *OC* 1293. **-η**, ἡ, = ἐνέδρα, *LW*1471 (Pompeiopolis). **-ησις**, εως, ἡ, *sitting in*, ἡλίου διπλῆ πάρεστιν ἐ. a twofold *seat in* the sun, i.e. both at morn and evening, S.*Ph.*18.

**ἐνθαλάμια**· πλάσματα ἐκ μήκωνος καὶ σησάμης, Hsch.

**ἐνθᾰλασσ-εύω**, Att. **-ττεύω**, *live at sea*, Ael.*NA*9.63; *to be at sea*, Longus 2.12; πρὸς ἐναντία πνεύματα νῆες -εύουσαι Ph.1.287. **-ιος**, ον, = sq., νεῶν ποιμαντῆρσιν ἐνθαλασσίοις S.*Fr.*432.10. **-ος**, Att. **-ττος**, ον, *in the sea*, σπιλάδες D.S.3.44; *by the sea*, πόλις Ath.Mech.32.3.

**ἔνθαλλος**, ον, *sprouting*, κριθή *PAmh.*2.133.4 (ii A.D.).

**ἐνθάλλω**, pf. part. ἐντεθηλώς, = θάλλω, Hsch., Suid.

**ἐνθάλπω**, *warm in*, D.S.2.52.

**ἐνθαλύξας**· σφοδρῶς πατάξας, Hsch.

**ἐνθᾰνᾰτόω**, *condemn to death*, ψήφῳ Philoch.144.

**ἔνθᾰπερ**, Adv. *there where, where*, stronger form of ἔνθα, Il.13.524, Hdt.1.14, Th.6.32, X.*Lac.*5.7, al.; *to the place where*, S.*El.*1495, *Ph.* 515 (lyr.).

**ἐνθάπτω**, *bury in* a place, *CIG*2839.10 (Aphrodisias), al.:—Pass., aor. 2 ἐνετάφην Aeschin.1.99, D.S.1.66, *IG*12(8).114 (Imbros), *CIG* 2824 (Aphrodisias); part. ἐνθαφείς (sic) ib.2839.11 (ibid.): fut. 2 ἐνταφήσομαι ib.2826 (ibid.), Ph.2.108, Plu.*Dio*43.

**ἐνθαυθοῖ**, = ἐνταυθοῖ (q.v.). **ἐνθαῦτα**, v. ἐνταῦθα.

**ἐνθεάζω**, *to be inspired*, Hdt.1.63, Luc.*DDeor.*18.1:—Med., Id. *Alex.*13, Plu.2.623c, etc.

**ἐνθέακτος**, gloss on ἐνθρίακτος, Hsch. (fort. -θέαστος).

**ἐνθεάομαι**, *behold*, *Sammelb.*4127.9.

⊕ **ἐνθεαστικός**, ή, όν, *inspired*, Pl.*Lg.*682a; ψυχαί, μέλη, Procl.*in Prm.*p.742 S., *in Ti.*1.355 D. Adv. -κῶς Luc.*Am.*14, Procl.*in Prm.* p.530 S., Syrian.*in Metaph.*42.14: Sup. -ώτατα Procl.*in R.*1.133 K. II. *neurotic*, ἴλιγγος Ruf.ap.Orib.7.26.177; πνιγμός Mnesith. Cyz.ib.*inc.*15.3; πάθος Praxag. ap. Herod.Med. in *Rh.Mus.*49.549 (-ατικόν codd.).

**ἐνθεάτης** (leg. -αστής), ου, ὁ, *seer, prophet*, *Gloss.*

**ἔνθεμα**, ατος, τό, *thing put in, graft*, Thphr.*CP*1.6.8. II. *deposit*, of money in a bank, *CIG*3599.15 (Ilium). III. *ornament*, ἐ. τῶν τραχήλων Lxx *Ca.*4.9. IV. *reservoir*, *POxy.*1830.9, al. (vi A.D.). (Cf. ἔνθημα.)

**ἐνθεμᾰτίζω**, *engraft*, *Gp.*10.23.4.

⊕ **ἐνθεμέλιοι** θεοί gods *who make foundations secure*, prob. in *Milet.* 1(7).298 (ii A.D.).

**ἐνθέμεν**, poet. aor. 2 inf. of ἐντίθημι.

**ἐνθέμιον**, τό, *cabin on the poop of a ship*, Poll.1.90. II. *socket* of a lampstand, Lxx *Ex.*38.16(37.19).

**ἔνθεν**, Adv.: I. Demonstr., *thence*, 1. of Place, Il.10.179, etc.: also in tracing pedigrees, γένος δέ μοι ἔ. ὅθεν σοί 4.58; ἔ. μὲν .. ἑτέρωθι δὲ.. *on the one side* and on the other, Od.12.235, cf. 59; αἱ μὲν ἐξ ἀριστερᾶς, αἱ δ' ἔ. E.*Hec.*1152; ἔ. καὶ ἔ. *on this side* and *on that*, Hdt.4.175, Th.7.81, Pl.*Prt.*315b, etc.; ἔ. μὲν.., ἔ. δὲ.., *on one side* .. *on the other*.. X.*An.*3.5.7; ἔ. μὲν.., ἐξ εὐωνύμου δὲ.., Hdt.1. 72; ἔ. μὲν.., ἑτέρωσε δὲ.., Pl.*Sph.*224a: c. gen., ἔ. καὶ ἔ. τῶν τροχῶν *on both sides of*.., X.*Cyr.*6.1.30, cf. *An.*4.3.28. 2. of Time, *thereupon, thereafter*, Il.13.741; τὰ δ' ἔ. *what follows*, A.*Ag.*248 (lyr.); τὸ δ' ἔ. S.*OC*476. 3. of occasion, *thence, from that point*, ἔ. ἑλών [τὴν ἀοιδήν], Lat. *inde exorsus*, Od.8.500, cf. D.L.1.102; *from that cause* or *circumstance*, E.*Tr.*951. II. Relat., for ὅθεν, 1. of Place, *whence*, δέπα ἔ. ἔπινον *from which*.., Od.19.62, cf. 4.220; freq. answering to ἔνθα, ὁ μὲν ἔνθα καθέζετ' ἐπὶ θρόνου ἔ. ἀνέστη Ἑρμείας *from which*.., 5.195, etc.; of origin, τὸ κέρδος ἔ. οἰστέον S.*Ant.*310; ἔ. ἦν γεγώς Id.*OT*1393, cf. 1485; *to the place whence*, ἄξουσιν ἔ. ἕξουσι τὰ ἐπιτήδεια X.*An.*2.3.6; in speaking, ἐπάνειμι ἔ... ἐξέβην Id.*HG*6. 5.1, cf. *Oec.*6.1. 2. of occasion, *whence*, Ἄρει.. ἔ. ἔστ' ἐπώνυμος πέτρα πάγος τ' Ἄρειος A.*Eu.*689, cf. E.*El.*38, etc.

**ἐνθενᾰρίζω**, (θέναρ) = ἐγχειρέω, Hsch.

⊕ **ἐνθένδε**, Adv. *hence*, Il.8.527, Od.11.69, etc.; *from this quarter*, i.e. *from people here*, S.*OT*125; ἐ. τὰ δίκαια ἀρξόμεθα λαμβάνειν, i.e. *from you*, X.*An.*7.7.17; καλῶς τά γ' ἐ. all's well *on this side*, E.*Or.* 1278; opp. κάτωθεν, Pl.*Phdr.*229b; ὡς ἐ. ἰδεῖν Id.*Plt.*289d: ἤρξατο ἐ. ποθέν Id.*Euthd.*275d, cf. *Smp.*178a; ἐνθένδ' αὐτόθεν *from this* very *city*, Ar.*Ach.*116: with Verbs of motion, τοὺς ἐ. ἐκεῖσε πορεῦσαι carry those *here*, i.e. *in this world*, thither, Pl.*Phd.*107e, cf. *Ap.*40c; ὁ ἐ. στρατός the army *from this place*, i.e. the Athen. army, E.*Supp.*695; οἱ ἐ. ἑταῖροι X.*Cyr.*2.4.16. 2. of Time or Consequence, *from that time*, Th.2.1; τὸ ἐ. or τοὐνθ. *thereafter*, S.*Ph.*895, E.*IT*91; τοὐνθ. or τἀνθ. *what followed*, the *event*, τοὐνθ. δεινὸν ἦν θέαμ' ἰδεῖν Id.*Med.*1167, cf. S.*OT*1267, *El.*1307. 3. ἐ. *from the following point of view*, Pl. *Tht.*178a; ἐ. ἂν γίγνοιτο γνώριμον Jul.*Or.*4.136c.

**ἐνθενδί**, Att. strengthd. for foreg., Ar.*Lys.*429.

**ἔνθενπερ**, *from the point whence*, Arr.*An.*1.2.3.

**ἐνθεόομαι**, *to be inspired*, Sch.D.T.p.61 H.

**ἔνθεος**, ον, in later Prose contr. **ἔνθους** Ph.2.542, App.*Hisp.*18, Aen.Gaz.*Thphr.*p.12 B.:—*full of the god, inspired, possessed*, ἔ. γυναῖκες, of the Bacchantes, S.*Ant.*964 (lyr.); ἔ. Ἄρει *possessed* by him, A.*Th.*497; ἐκ Πανὸς E.*Hipp.*141; ὑπὸ τοῦ ἔρωτος X.*Smp.*1.10: c. gen. rei, τέχνης νιν Ζεὺς ἔνθεον κτίσας φρένα A.*Eu.*17; also ἔ. πρὸς ἀρετὴν *inspired with a love for* it, Pl.*Smp.*179a: Sup. -ώτατη, φύσις, of Homer, Max.Tyr.32.4. II. of divine frenzy, *inspired by the god*, τέχναι A.*Ag.*1209; μαντική Pl.*Phdr.*244b; μαντεῖαι Id.*Ti.*72b; ἔνθεον ἡ ποίησις Arist.*Rh.*1408b19; ἔ. φιλία Plu.2.752c; τὰ ἔ. *frenzied rites*, prob. in Herod.8.70. Adv. ἐνθέως Men.*Mon.*229, App.*Hisp.*26, Jul.*Or.*7.215b, Iamb.*VP*32.216.

**ἐνθερίζω**, *spend summer in* a place, Poll.1.62; πόλις ἐνθερίσαι οἷα βελτίστη Dicaearch.1.21.

⊕ **ἐνθερμαίνω**, *heat*, in Pass., ἐντεθέρμανται πόθῳ *is heated by* passion, S.*Tr.*368.

**ἔνθερμος**, ον, *hot*, φύσις Hp.*Epid.*6.4.13; αἷμα Arist.*Pr.*898a6; πνεῦμα Zeno *Stoic.*1.38, Antip.ib.3.251; Λιβύη Plu.2.951f. 2. metaph., *passionate*, μειράκιον prob. in *Com.Adesp.*24.10 D.; *hot, fervid*, διάνοια Arist.*Phgn.*806b26, cf. Ph.1.605, al.

**ἐνθεσίδουλος** [ῐ], ὁ, = ψωμόδουλος, *Com.Adesp.*999.

**ἔνθεσις**, εως, ἡ, (ἐντίθημι) *putting in, insertion*, τοῦ νῦ Pl.*Cra.*426c; εἴδους Plot.5.9.3, cf. Porph.*Abst.*4.20; *putting into the mouth*, τῆς τροφῆς Aret.*CA*1.4. II. *that which is put in the mouth, mouthful*, Ar.*Eq.*404 (troch.), Pherecr.108.6, Telecl.1.10, Hermipp.41, etc. 2. *grafting, graft*, Ph.1.301, *Gp.*10.37.1.

**ἔνθεσμος**, ον, *lawful*, λιτανεία Lxx *3Ma.*2.21, cf. Plu.*Nic.*6; βασιλεὺς *Peripl.M.Rubr.*23; *authorized*, τράπεζα *BGU*1127.30 (i B.C.); *valid*, συγχωρήσεις *POxy.*271.21 (i A.D.). Adv. -μως, βασιλεύειν Gal.14.216.

**ἐνθετ-έον**, (ἐντίθημι) *one must insert*, Plot.1.3.1, *Gp.*6.1.4, Antyll. ap.Orib.44.23.42; *one must dip* in water, Archig.ap.Aët.9.6. **-ικός**, ή, όν, *fit for implanting*, τινός Stob.2.7.2. 2. ἡ -κὴ τῶν σιτίων προθυμία the *swallowing* impulse, Orib.*Fr.*74. **-ος**, ον, *capable of being put in*, εἰ.. ἦν ἔ. ἀνδρὶ νόημα Thgn.435; ἐξαίρετα καὶ ἔ. Orib. 49.4.80. 2. *grafted*, τὰ ἔ. τῶν δένδρων Hp.*Nat.Puer.*26.

**ἐνθετταλίζομαι**, *become a Thessalian*, i.e. *wear the large Thessalian cloak* (Θετταλικὰ πτερά), Eup.201.

**ἐνθεῦτεν**, Ion. for ἐντεῦθεν, Hdt.

**ἐνθεωρέω**, *observe in*, in Pass., τὰ -ούμενα τοῖς ἀριθμοῖς Nicom.*Ar.* 1.16, cf. Eust.1722.62; ἔν τινι Eustr.*in EN*281.25.

⊕ **ἐνθηκάριος**, ὁ, *factor, broker*, *Gloss.*

⊕ **ἐνθήκη**, ἡ, *store*, Ph.2.525 (pl.), Sm.*Ge.*41.36, Artem.2.37, *Cod. Just.*9.49.7.1 (pl.), Just.*Nov.*128.8 (pl.). II. *capital*; late word for ἀφορμή, Phryn.199, Arg.D.36. III. *insertion*, λίθων Procop.*Aed.* 2.1. IV. *enclosure*, *BGU*890.11 (ii A.D.).

**ἐνθηλῠπᾰθέω**, *to be effeminate*, J.*BJ*4.9.10.

**ἔνθημα**, ατος, τό, = ἔνθεμα II, *IG*12(1).937.11 (Rhodes). II. f.l. for σύνθ., Iamb.*Myst.*1.21 (pl.).

⊕ **ἔνθηρος**, ον, (θήρ) *full of wild beasts, haunted, infested by them*, δρυμός E.*Rh.*289; πάγος S.*Ichn.*216; [ὗλαι] [Arr.]*Peripl.M.Eux.*12. II. metaph., *wild, rough*, τιθέντες ἔ. τρίχα A.*Ag.*562; ἔ. πούς '*angry*', of the ulcerated foot of Philoctetes, S.*Ph.*698 (not = θηρόδηκτος, as Sch.); τὸ ἔ. *savagery*, Ael.*NA*6.63.

**ἔνθῑνος**, ον, Cret., = θεῖος (in the sense of εὐσεβής), ἔνορκον τε ἔστω καὶ ἔ. *GDI*5039.11 (Hierapytna), cf. 5041.7 (ibid.); cf. θῖνος.

**ἐνθῖνος**, = ἐνθάδιος, prob. in *GDI*3087.33 (Cherson.).

**ἔν-θλᾰσις**, εως, ἡ, *dint* or *injury caused by pressure*, Ael.*NA*16.22, Gal.7.39. **-θλασμα**, ατος, τό, = foreg., Id.14.81. **-θλάω**, Ion. **ἐμφλάω**, *indent by pressure*, Hp.*Int.*44, Aristid.*Or.*47(23).13; *impress* (on coin), σημεῖον Ael.*NA*6.15.

**ἐν-θλίβω** [ῑ], *press in*, Nic.*Al.*454, Aret.*SA*1.9, Gal.*UP*5.15, S.E. *P.*3.68:—Pass., Arist.*HA*599b20, *Pr.*927a25; ἄνθρωποι ἐντεθλιμμένοι τὴν ῥῖνα *Peripl.M.Rubr.*62. **-θλιπτικός**, ή, όν, *pressing*. Adv. -κῶς *by pressure*, S.E.*P.*3.69. **-θλιψις**, εως, ἡ, *pressing in*, Archig.ap.Gal.8.110, Aret.*SA*1.6, etc.; *pressure*, Apollon.Cit.2.

**ἐνθνήσκω**, *die in*, χθονὸς.. τοσοῦτον, [ὥστε] ἐνθανεῖν μόνον S.*OC* 790, cf. E.*Rh.*869; σῇ χερί Id.*Heracl.*560. 2. of the hand, *grow rigid* or *torpid in*, τινί Id.*Hec.*246.—Dub. in Prose, Lys.16.15 (ἐναπο- Markland), Plu.2.357d (ἐκθ- Reiske).

**ἐνθολή**· ἰσόρροπον, Hsch. (Fort. ἀνθολκή.) **ἐνθοργάζει**· πονεῖ, Id. **ἐνθορίσκει**· ἐνθρύπτει, Id.

**ἔνθορος**, ον, (ἐνθορεῖν) *impregnated*, of animals, v.l. in Nic.*Th.*99.

**ἐνθορῠβέω**, *disturb*, Tz.*H.*13.494 (Pass.).

**ἔνθους**, ουν, contr. for ἔνθεος (q.v.).

**ἐνθουσί-α**, ἡ, = ἐνθουσιασμός, Procl.*in Alc.*p.198 C., Hsch., Zonar. **-άζω**, in Trag. always **ἐνθουσιάω** (also in Ph., 1.148, al.); in Pl. both forms occur (v. infr.):—*to be inspired* or *possessed by a god, to be in ecstasy*, ἐνθουσιᾷ δὴ δῶμα A.*Fr.*58; ὥσπερ ἐνθουσιῶν X.*Cyr.*1.4.8; ἡ ψυχὴ.. ἐνθουσιάζουσα Pl.*Ion* 535c, cf. 536b; ἐνθουσιάζοντες Id.*Ap.* 22c; ἐνθουσιῶντες Id.*Phdr.*253a; ἐνθουσιάσας Id.*Tht.*180c; ὑπὸ τῶν

Νυμφῶν.. ἐνθουσιάσω Id.*Phdr.*241e; ὑφ' ἡδονῆς ἐνθουσιᾷ Id.*Phlb.*15e; ἐνθουσιάσαι ποιεῖν τοὺς ἀκροατάς Arist.*Rh.*1408$^{b}$14: c. dat., ἐνθουσιᾷς τοῖς σαυτοῦ κακοῖς E.*Tr.*1284; ταῖς φωναῖς -άζοντες Phld.*Lib.*p.4 O.; περὶ φιλοσοφίαν Plu.*Cat.Ma.*22; εἴς τι Ael.*NA*4.31; πρὸς τὴν ἀλήθειαν Jul.*Or.*4.136b. II. c. acc., *inspire*, ἔρωτας ἐνεθουσίασε θεοῖς Herm.ap.Stob.1.49.44 codd. **-ασις,** εως, ἡ, = sq., Pl.*Phdr.*249e (pl.), Ph.2.344 (pl.), Iamb.*Myst.*3.6. **-ασμός,** ὁ, *inspiration, enthusiasm, frenzy*, Democr.18, Pl.*Ti.*71e, Ph.1.535 (pl.), S.E.*M.*9.20 (pl.); ἄλογος ἐ. Phld.*Ir.*p.67 W.; produced by certain kinds of music, Arist.*Pol.*1340$^{a}$11, 1342$^{a}$7. **-αστής,** οῦ, ὁ, *person inspired, possessed*, Ptol.*Tetr.*180, Eust.47 fin. **-αστικός,** ή, όν, *inspired*, φύσις Pl.*Ti.*71e; esp. by music, Arist.*Pol.*1340$^{a}$11; ἡ ἐ. σοφία *divination*, Plu.*Sol.*12; ἐ. ἔκστασις Iamb.*Myst.*3.8; τὸ ἐ. *excitement*, Pl.*Phdr.*263d: Sup. -ώτατος Sch.Iamb.*Protr.*p.129 P. Adv. -κῶς, διατιθέναι τινά Plu.2.433c: Comp. -ώτερον Marin.*Procl.*6. II. Act., *inspiring, exciting*, of certain kinds of music, Arist.*Pol.*1341$^{b}$34; νοσήματα μανικὰ καὶ ἐ. Id.*Pr.*954$^{a}$36: Comp. -ώτερα, ἀκούσματα Pl.*Ep.*314a. **-άω,** v. ἐνθουσιάζω. **-ώδης,** ες, *ecstatic*, ὁρμαί D.H.*Comp.*1, cf. Plu.*Lyc.*21; φοραί Id.*Pyrrh.*22, etc.; τὸ ἐ. Ph.1.689. Adv. -δῶς Hp.*Ep.*17, Sch.Il.*Oxy.*1086.41.

**ἐνθραδές·** ἐμμανές, Hsch.

**ἐνθράσσω,** *prick*, τὰ ὀστέα τὰ κατεηγότα ἐ. τὸν χρῶτα Hp.*Art.*46 (= ἐγκείμενον νύττει, Gal.19.98); = ὑποκινεῖν, ταράττειν, Tim.*Lex.* post ἕδος.

**ἐνθρεῖν·** φυλάσσειν, Hsch.

**ἐνθρην-έω,** = θρηνέω ἐν.., Aristid.*Or.*18(20).9. **-ος,** ον, *mournful*, ἀνθυπήχησις Schubart *Papyruskunde* p.42.

**ἔνθρι-α·** ζῴδια, Hsch. **-άζειν·** παρακινεῖν, ἀπὸ τῶν μαντικῶν θριῶν, Id. **-ακτος** [ῐ], ον, (θριάζω) *inspired*, S.*Fr.*544.

⊛ **ἐνθρίζειν·** ἐνατενίζειν, νύσσειν, and **ἐνέθριξε·** προσωρμίσθη, Hsch.

**ἐνθριμματίς,** a spelling of ἐνθρυμματίς, Id.

**ἐνθρῑόω,** (θρῖον) *wrap in a fig-leaf*: *muffle up*, in pf. Pass., ἐντεθριῶσθαι Ar.*Lys.*664. II. metaph., *deceive, cozen*, Men.*Sam.*241; cf. ἐντεθρίωκεν· ἐνείληκεν, ἐσκεύακεν, Hsch.

**ἐνθρίτης,** = ἐνθρύπτης, and ἐνθρίτας· *intritas*, *Gloss.*

**ἐνθρομβ-όομαι,** *become clotted*, of blood, Aspasia ap.Aët.16.72; *become full of clotted blood*, Gal.8.409. **-ωσις,** εως, ἡ, = θρόμβωσις, Antyll.ap.Orib.7.11.2.

**ἐνθρον-ιαστικά,** τά, *fees* paid by bishops *on enthronization*, Just.*Nov.*123.3. **-ίζω,** *place on a throne*, metaph., τὸν ἡγεμόνα νοῦν Lxx 4*Ma.*2.22:—in lit. sense only Pass., ib.*Es.*1.2; τοῖς βασιλείοις D.S.33.13. **-ισμα,** ατος, τό, *consecrated seat*, θεῶν *OGI*383.46 (Nemrud Dagh). **-ιος,** ον, *enthroned*, Poll.10.52. **-ισμός,** ὁ, *enthroning*, title of προσόδια by Pindar, Suid.

**ἐνθρύβω,** = ἐνθρύπτω, Harp. s. v. ἔνθρυπτα.

**ἐνθρυμμᾰτίς,** ίδος, ἡ, *sop*, Anaxandr.41.42 (anap.).

**ἔνθρῠος,** ον, *reedy*, *CPHerm.*7 ii 16, *PRyl.*207 *a* 7.

**ἐνθρύπ-της,** = *intritio* (fort. *intritor*), *Gloss.* ⊛ **-τος,** ον, *crumbled and put into liquid*: τὰ ἔ. *sops* or perh. a kind of cake, D.18.260, cf. *SIG*1016.4 (Iasos), Poll.6.77, Hsch. s.v. ἀττανίδες, *AB*250. II. Ἔνθρυπτος, title of Apollo at Athens, Hsch. **-τω,** poet. **ἐνιθρ-,** *crumble into liquid, make sop*, ἄρτος ἐν οἴνῳ ἐντεθρυμμένος Hp.*Salubr.*7, cf. Lxx, Thd.*Bel* 33; κεδρίδας ἐς ὄλπην Nic.*Th.*81; βάρος οἴνης ib.655:—Med., ἕλικας νύμφαις Id.*Al.*266:—Pass., Lynceus ap.Ath.3.109e.

**ἔνθρυσκον,** τό, = ἄνθρυσκον (q.v.).

⊛ **ἐνθρῴσκω,** aor. 2 ἐνέθορον, Ep. ἔνθορον:—*leap in, on*, or *among*, c. dat., ἔνθορε μέσσῳ [ποταμῷ] Il.21.233; ἔνθορ' ὁμίλῳ 15.623; ὡς δὲ λέων ἐν βουσὶ θορών 5.161, cf. 20.381; ὄρει πῦρ ἐνθορόν Pi.*P.*3.37; ἐνθρῴσκει τάφῳ E.*El.*327; λὰξ ἔνθορεν ἰσχίῳ *kicked* him on the hip, Od.17.233; λὰξ ἐ. τινί D.C.74.14: metaph., κόσμοις Orac.Chald.ap.Dam.*Pr.*182.

**ἐνθυίων·** ἐρωτικόν, Hsch. **ἐνθυλήματα,** cj. for ἐναυλήματα (q.v.).

**ἐνθῡμ-άζω·** ἐμπίπτω, καὶ ἐνορμῶ, Hsch. **-έομαι,** fut. -ήσομαι Lys.12.45, later -ηθήσομαι Philostr.*VS*2.26.3, Epict.*Ench.*21, etc.: aor. ἐνεθυμήθην Ar.*Ra.*40, Th.2.62, Lys.31.27, etc.: pf. ἐντεθύμημαι Th.1.120: plpf. ἐνετεθύμητο Lys.12.70:—*lay to heart, ponder*, ἤτοι κρίνομέν γε ἢ ἐνθυμούμεθα ὀρθῶς τὰ πράγματα Th.2.40; ἄξιον ἐνθυμηθῆναι Antipho 6.20; πρὸς ἐμαυτόν And.1.50; ἐ. καὶ λογίζεσθαι freq. joined in D., as 1.21, al. b. c. gen., ἐνθυμεῖσθαί τινος *think much* or *deeply of*, τοῦ θανόντος Semon.2; τούτων οὐδὲν ἐ. Hermipp.41; τῶν λεγομένων Antipho 5.6; ὧν ἐνθυμηθέντες Th.1.42, cf. Pl.*Mx.*249c, X.*Mem.*1.1.17; τῶν προγόνων ἐ. ὅτι.. Lys.16.20; also περί τινος Pl.*R.*595a. c. folld. by a relat., ἐ. ὅτι.. *notice* or *consider* that .., Ar.*Nu.*820, Th.5.111, etc.; ὡς.. how.., Ar.*Ra.*40, X.*Mem.*4.3.3, etc.; εἰ.. Isoc.15.60; μή.. Pl.*Euthd.*279c, *Hp.Ma.*300d. d. c. part., οὐκ ἐντεθύμηται ἐπαιρόμενος *is* not *conscious* that he is becoming excited, Th.1.120, cf. 6.78, X.*HG*4.4.19. 2. *take to heart, be concerned* or *angry at*, τι A.*Eu.*222; ξυμφοράν Th.7.18, cf. 5.32 (v. ἐνθυμίζομαι); εἰ μηδεὶς ὑμῶν μήτ' ἐνθυμεῖται μήτ' ὀργίζεται D.4.43: abs., *to be concerned*, Hp.*Aër.*22; = ἐνθύμιον ποιεῖσθαι, D.C.57.4. 3. *form a plan*, κράτιστος ἐνθυμηθῆναι Th.8.68, cf. 2.60; *take care, see to it*, ἐ. ἵνα μηθεὶς ἀδικῇ *PSI*4.436.9 (iii B.C.). 4. *infer, conclude*, τί οὖν ἐκ τούτων.. ἐνθυμεῖσθαι δεῖ; D.21.54. II. Act., ἐνθυμέω Epich.99.4, Aen.Tact.37.6 (s. v. l.); ἐνθυμέομαι, in pass. sense, *to be in a person's thoughts, to be desired*, κρατεῖν τῶν ἐνθυμουμένων App.*BC*5.133: pf. (cf. 1.3), ταυτὶ μὲν ἡμῖν ἐντεθύμηται καλῶς Ar.*Ec.*262; εὖ ἐντεθυμημένον Pl.*Cra.*404a (nisi leg. φιλοσόφου.. καὶ εὖ ἐντεθυμημένου). ⊛ **-ημα,** ατος, τό, *thought, piece of reasoning, argument*, S.*OC*292, 1199, Isoc.9.10 (pl.), Aeschin.2.110. 2. *meaning, sense*, opp. λέξις, Olymp.*in Mete.*4.23. 3. in Aristotle's Logic, *enthymeme, rhetorical syllogism drawn from probable premises* (ἐξ εἰκότων ἢ σημείων), opp. ἀποδεικτικὸς συλλογισμός, *APr.*70$^{a}$10, cf. *Rh.*1355$^{a}$6, etc.; ἐ. δεικτικά, ἐλεγκτικά, ib.1396$^{b}$24. II. *invention, device*, X.*HG*4.5.4, 5.4.52, *An.*3.5.12, *Cyn.*13.13 (pl.), Men.*Epit.*295. **-ημᾰτικός,** ή, όν, *determined, resolute*, πρός τι Hp.*Decent.*3. 2. *skilled in the use of enthymemes*, Arist.*Rh.*1354$^{b}$22. II. *consisting of* or *in the form of enthymemes*, ῥητορεῖαι ib.1356$^{b}$21; θόρυβοι Epicur.*Nat.*14.9: Comp. -ώτερον, [σχῆμα] Corn.*Rh.*p.397 H. Adv. -κῶς Arist.*Rh.*1418$^{b}$36, Theon *Prog.*5, etc. **-ημᾰτίζομαι,** *form an enthymeme*, Steph. *in Rh.*265.29. **-ημάτιον,** τό, Dim. of ἐνθύμημα, v.l. in Gell.7(6).13.4. **-ημᾰτώδης,** ες, *enthymematic*, Arist.*Rh.Al.*1439$^{a}$5. **-ησις,** εως, ἡ, *consideration, esteem*, E.*Fr.*246. II. *consideration, reflection*, Th.1.132, *Ev.Matt.*9.4 (pl.), Sm.*Jb.*21.27, Vett.Val.301.8, etc. 2. *idea, conception*, εἰς ἐ. ἐσθήτων ἦλθον Diog.Oen.10; τὰς ἐ. ὀξύς Luc.*Salt.*81. III. *anxiety, worry*, Hp.*Praec.*4. IV. *resolution*, *BGU*1024 iv 12 (iv A.D.). **-ητέον,** *one must reflect*, νυκτός Epich.270; τόδε, ὅτι.. And.1.7; ἐ. [ὑμῖν].. παρ' ἄλλων ἀκούουσι D.4.3. ⊛ **-ία,** ἡ, *cause of misgiving*, ἐς ἐνθυμίαν τινὶ προβάλλεσθαι Th.5.16. **-ιάζομαι,** = sq., Nic.Dam.*Fr.*130.30 J., *EM*341.22 (*Et.Gen.*):—Act., ἐνεθυμίαζον Hsch. **-ίζομαι,** later form of ἐνθυμέομαι, D.C.*Fr.*57.80b, Poll.2.231 (citing Th.5.32), Hsch. II. = ἐπιθυμέω, τι App.*Mith.*120.—Act. **-ίζω** only in Hsch. **-ιος,** ον, (θυμός) *taken to heart, weighing upon the mind*, μὴ δή τοι κεῖνός γε λίην ἐνθύμιος ἔστω let him not lie too *heavy on* thy *soul*, take not too *much thought for* him, Od.13.421; ἐνθύμιόν οἱ ἐγένετο ἐμπρήσαντι τὸ ἱρόν he had *pricks of conscience* for having done it, Hdt 8.54; ἐνθύμιόν τί τινι προσθεῖναι Antipho 3.1.2; τί δ' ἐστί σοι τοῦτ'.. ἐ.; what is't *that weighs upon* thy *heart?* S.*OT*739; ἐπειδή σοι τόδ' ἐστ' ἐ. if this matter *causes* thee *any scruple*, E.*HF*722; ἐ. γίγνεταί τινί τις Antipho 2.3.10, cf. App.*BC*5.133; ἐνθύμιον ποιεῖσθαί τι, = ἐνθυμεῖσθαι, to take *to heart*, to have a *scruple about* it, Th.7.50; ἐ. ποιεῖσθαί τινος D.C.58.6; ἐ. τιθέναι τί τινι to make him have *scruples about* it, E.*Ion* 1347; ἐ. ἔχειν ὡς, c. part., *Inscr.Cos* 319.10; ἐ. ὑπολείπεσθαί τι Antipho 3.4.9; ἐ. εὐναί a couch *full of care*, S.*Tr.*110 (lyr.); ἐνθύμιον ἔστω Δάματρος, formula in a curse, *GDI*3541.7 (Cnidos): ἐνθύμιον, τό, *wrath*, Lxx *Ps.*75(76).10. II. ἐνθύμια, τά, *meaning*, Ph.2.484; *ideas*, Iamb.*VP*5.20; ἐνθύμιον ποιεῖσθαι *reflect*, c. acc. et inf., Alciphr.3.10; λαμβάνω τὸ ἐ. I take the *hint*, Ach.Tat.2.7. ⊛ **-ιστός,** ή, όν, *taken to heart*, ἐ. ποιεῖσθαι make *a scruple of* a thing, Hdt.2.175 (nisi leg. -ητόν). **-ος,** ον, *spirited*, Arist.*Pol.*1327$^{b}$30.

**ἐνθύριον·** μέρος τι τῆς νεώς, Hsch.

**ἐνθῠσιάζω,** *sacrifice in..*, Lxx *Si.*34(31).7.

**ἐνθύσκει·** ἐντυγχάνει, Hsch. **ἐνθύσκος·** ὁ ἀσφαλός, τὸ ὄρνεον, Id. **ἐνθύω,** = θύω, τῇ Ἀρτέμιδι χοῖρον *IG*11.153.11. **ἔνθω, ἔνθοι, ἐνθών,** Dor. for ἔλθω, etc.; v. ἔρχομαι. **ἐνθωκεῦσαι·** ἐμφωλεῦσαι, ἐγκρύπτεσθαι, Hsch.

**ἐνθωρᾱκίζω,** *arm*: pf. part. Pass. ἐντεθωρακισμένος *mailed*, X.*An.*7.4.16.

**ἐνί,** poet. for ἐν, both Ep. and Att., also in Ion. prose.

**ἑνί,** dat. from εἷς.

**ἔνι,** for ἔνεστι, ἔνεισι, ἐνέσται; v. ἔνειμι.

**ἑνιαῖος,** α, ον, (ἕν) *single, unitary*, λόγος Aristid.Quint.1.3; αἰτία Iamb.*Myst.*8.3; οὐσία ἑ. καὶ ἀμέριστος Procl. *in Prm.*p.564 S., etc.: pl., ἑνιαῖα *individual elements*, Iamb. *in Nic.*p.81 P.; *concerned with unity*, γνῶσις Dam.*Pr.*25 bis. Adv. -αίως Ptol.*Tetr.*1, Iamb.*Comm.Math.*10, Procl. *in Prm.*p.589 S., Dam.*Pr.*1, etc.

**ἑνιάκις,** *sometimes*, Sor.*Fract.*2.

**ἐνιαυθμός,** ὁ, (ἐνιαύω) *abode*, *EM*342.35, prob. in Call.*Fr.*127 (ἐνηρυθμοί [-μοῖ] codd. Stob.). [ῑ metri gr.]

**ἐνῐ-αυσιαῖος,** α, ον, = sq. III, Arist.*Cat.*5$^{b}$5, D.S.11.69 (s. v. l.); κύκλος Jul.*Or.*4.155b; χρόνος *PMasp.*159.20 (vi A.D.); ζῴδιον, = ἐνιαυτοῦ κύριον, Balbillus in *Cat.Cod.Astr.*8(4).240. II. = sq. I, ἄρνες J.*AJ*3.10.1; ἄμπελοι *Gp.*3.2.1. III. = sq. II, J.*BJ*2.16.4, *Gp.*[illegible].44.2. ⊛ **-αύσιος,** α, ον, Hdt.4.180, E.*Hipp.*37, X.*Ages.*2.1, *SIG*167 (Mylasa, iv B.C.), etc.; also ος, ον Th.4.117, 5.[illegible], Arist.*Mu.*400$^{b}$21 (v.l.): (ἐνιαυτός):—*of a year, one year old*, σῦς Od.16.454, cf. D.27.63, etc.; τίκτει ἡ θήλεια [ὗς] ἐ. Arist.*HA*545$^{a}$29. II. *annual*, Hom.*Epigr.*15.11; ὁρτή Hdt.4.180, etc.; τῇ τρίτῃ ἐπὶ τοῖς ἐνιαυσίοις *IG*12(5).593 *B* 5 (Ceos, v B.C.): neut. pl. as Adv., Hes.*Op.*449. Regul. Adv. -ίως Sch.Arat.462, *PLond.*1.113(4).11 (vi A.D.). III. *lasting a year*, Hp.*Aph.*6.45; ἐ. φυγή *a year's* exile, E.*Hipp.*37; χρόνος Id.*Hel.*775 (dub.); ἐκεχειρία Th.4.117, 5.15; ὁδός X. l. c.; κἀνιαύσιος βεβώς gone, absent *for a year*, S.*Tr.*165. **-αυτίζομαι,** *spend a year*, Pl.Com.113: late in Act., Sch.E.*Or.*1645, Suid. **-αύτιος,** α, ον, = ἐνιαύσιος, *IG*2$^{2}$.1126.44 (Amphict. Delph.), *SIG*1025.37 (Cos). ⊛ **-αυτοκράτωρ** [ρᾰ], ορος, ὁ, zodiacal sign *presiding over the year according to the Chaldean dodekaeteris*, Serapio in *Cat.Cod.Astr.*8(4).231. ⊛ **-αυτός,** ὁ, (ἐνί, αὐτός) prop. *anniversary*, μηδὲ τᾷ ὑστεραίᾳ μηδ' ἐν ταῖς δεκάταις μηδ' ἐν τοῖς ἐνιαυτοῖς *Michel* 995 *C* 49 (pl., Delph.): hence πρὸ τῶ ἐ. before the *lapse of a year*, *Leg.Gort.*9.29; ἐνιαυτῷ *on the expiry of a year*, ib.1.35; and so, *any long period of time, cycle, period*, ἔτος ἦλθε περιπλομένων ἐνιαυτῶν as *times* rolled on the year came, Od.1.16; ἐπιπλομένων ἐ. Hes.*Th.*493, *Sc.*87; χρονίους ἐτῶν παλαιῶν ἐνιαυτούς Ar.*Ra.*347; πόλιν ἐνιαυτόν τινα ἔδοσαν ἐνοικεῖν Th.3.68; ὁ μέγας ἐ., of a Pythagorean *cycle*, Eudem.ap.Theon.Sm.p.198 H.; also of *the Metonic Cycle* of nineteen years, D.S.12.36; of a period of 600 years, J.*AJ*1.3.9:—ἀΐδιος ἐ. Apollod.3.4.2. 2. = ἔτος, *a year*, εἰνατός ἐστι περιτροπέων ἐ. Il.2.295; δεκάτους περιτελλομένους ἐ. 8.404; Διὸς ἐνιαυτοί 2.134; μῆνές τε καὶ ἐνιαυτῶν περίοδοι

Pl.*Ti.*47a; ἐ. ἡμερῶν LXX *Le.*25.29; ἐνιαυτόν *during a year*, Od.1.288; αἱ σπονδαὶ ἐνιαυτὸν ἔσονται Indut.ap.Th.4.118; ἐπεί κε ὠνίαυτος ἐξέλθῃ *IG*12(2).1.12 (Mytil., iv B.C.); τὸν πρῶτον ἐ. Lys.32.8; ὁπηνίκα..τοὐνιαυτοῦ at what time *in the year*, Ar.*Fr.*569.7; δὶς τοῦ ἐ. twice *a year*, Pl.*Criti.*118e; τοῦ ἐ. *every year*, X.*Vect.*4.23; ἑκάστου ἐ. Id.*Ath.*3.4; but ἕκαστον τὸν ἐ. *IG*2.1055.4: with Preps., δι' ἐνιαυτοῦ Antipho *Fr.*28; δι' ἐ. πέμπτου *every five years*, Pl.*Criti.*119d; θητεύσαμεν εἰς ἐ. for *a year*, Il.21.444; τελεσφόρον εἰς ἐ. 19.32; κατ' ἐνιαυτὸν ἄρξαι for *a year*, Th.1.93; or, *every year*, Isoc.3.17, Diph.38.5; καθ' ἕκαστον ἐ. Id.89; ἐπ' ἐ. for *a year*, Pl.*Lg.*945b, etc.; μετὰ τὸν ἐ. at the end of *the year*, Th.1.138; παρ' ἐνιαυτὸν ἄρχειν in alternate *years*, D.S.4.65; πρὸ ἐνιαυτοῦ *a year* before, Plu.2.147e; ἐς τὸν σᾶτες ἐ. for the current *year*, *IG*14.256 (Phintias); ἐν τῷ καθ' ἔτος ἐ. in the current *year*, *CIG*3641*b*5 (Lampsacus). 3. Ἐνιαυτός, personified, Ael.*Fr.*19, Orph.*Fr.*127.3 (s. v.l.), Procl.*in Ti.*3.41 D. II. name for a *Cornucopiae*, Callix.2, cf. Ath.11.783c.

**ἐνιαυτο-φᾰνής**, ές, *yearly seen*, Ptol.*Phas.*p.9 H. **-φορέω**, *bear fruit a year* before it ripens, Thphr.*HP*3.4.1.

**ἐνιαύω**, *sleep among*, [ταῖς ὑσί] Od.15.557, cf. 9.187; *sleep in*, [φάρεσι] Bion 1.72.

**ἐνιᾰχ-ῇ**, Adv., (ἔνιοι) *in some places*, c. gen., τοῦ Λιβυκοῦ χωρίου Hdt.2.19; τῆς Κύπρου Id.1.199. II. *sometimes*, Plu.2.427f, Ath.11.478b. **-οῦ**, Adv., (ἔνιοι) *in some places*, Arist.*HA*545$^a$32, D.H.*Rh.*5.7, etc.; *in some cases*, Pl.*Phd.*71b, Jul.*Gal.*152d; *sometimes*, *BGU*747ii9 (ii A.D.).

**ἐνιβάλλω, ἐνιβλάπτω**, poet. for ἐμβ–.

**ἔνιγμα**, ατος, τό, (ἐνίσσω) *rebuke*, *Et.Gud.*

**ἐνίγυιος** [ῐ], ον, *joined in one body*, Ibyc.16.3. II. *lame of one foot*, Suid. (ἐνίγυος codd.).

**ἐνιδεῖν**, v. ἐνεῖδον.

**ἐνιδρόω**, *sweat in, labour hard in*, X.*Smp.*2.18.

**ἐνίδρ-ῡσις**, εως, ἡ, *settling, establishment*, ἐν τοῖς αἰτίοις Herm.*in Phdr.*p.145 A. **-ύω**, *set in* a place, Plu.2.745c; *establish in*, ἕνωσις τὸ πᾶν κῦρος ἐνιδρύουσα τοῖς θεοῖς Iamb.*Myst.*5.26:—Med., *found, establish*, ἐνιδρύσασθαι πόλιας, βωμοὺς καὶ τεμένεα, Hdt.1.94, 2.178:—Pass., *to be established in*, ἐν.. Id.4.53: c. dat. loci, Συρακούσσαις Theoc.*Epigr.*18.5, cf. 17.102, *AP*10.9; κόρσῃ (v.l. κόρσην)..ἐνιδρυθεῖσα ἀλώπηξ Call.*Dian.*79; ταῖς ψυχαῖς, τοῖς θεοῖς, Iamb.*Myst.*1.5, 15; *frequent*, ταῖς ὁμιλίαις αὐτῆς Σειρῆνες ἐνίδρυντο Alciphr.1.38: abs., prob. cj. in E.*Hipp.*33. II. Act. intr., *settle in*, Plot.1.3.4; ταῖς μακάρων ἐνιδρῦσαι νήσοις Hierocl.*in CA*27p.483 M.

**ἐνιζάνω**, *sit* or *settle in* or *on*, αἰδοίῃσιν Il.20.11; of food, τοῖς ὀδοῦσιν Alciphr.1.22, cf. Lib.*Or.*60.11: metaph. of ψυχή and its object, Plot.4.6.3.

**ἐνιζεύγνῡμι** or **-ύω**, poet. for ἐνζ–.

**ἐνίζ-ησις**, εως, ἡ, *sitting in*, ἔς τι Aret.*CA*1.4. **-ω**, *to set in*, Ep. aor. 1 Med. ἐνεείσατο he *placed upon*, πρύμνῃ κούρην A.R.4.188. II. intr., = ἐνιζάνω, pf. ἐνίζηκα, *sit in* or *on*, c. acc., θάκους ἐνίζουσαν E.*Hel.*1108 (lyr.), prob. in A.*Ch.*801 (lyr.): c. dat., σώματι καὶ ψυχῇ..ἐνίζει Ἔρως Pl.*Smp.*196b; νεῦρα τοῖς μυσὶν -ηκότα Gal.2.691; ἡ -ηκυῖα τοῖς μορίοις ποιότης τοῦ φαρμάκου Id.11.354:—Med., ἐς ἕψημα τῶν βοτανῶν Aret.*CA*2.8.

**ἑνίζω**, *to be a partisan of the One*, i.e. *teach a monistic doctrine*, Arist.*Metaph.*986$^b$21, Procl.*in Prm.*p.597 S. II. *treat as a unity*, τι τῇ διανοίᾳ Plot.6.9.6:—Pass., ὡς μονὰς καὶ σημεῖον -ίζεται ibid. III. *unite*, ἑαυτὸν τῷ ἐραστῷ Procl.*in Alc.*p.33 C.; *unify*, τὰς ἐμφύτους ἐννοίας Porph.*Marc.*10; τὰ ὄντα Procl.*Inst.*13:—Pass., Porph.*Sent.*11; πλῆθος -ιζόμενον *reduced to unity*, ib.36; τὸ -ιζόμενον, opp. τὸ ἑνίζον, Dam.*Pr.*13. IV. Med., *concentrate*, Hero *Deff.*136.25.

**ἐνῆλαι**· κωλῦσαι, Hsch.; cf. εἴλω. **ἐνιηλίζειν**· τὴν Ἐνυάλιον ἑορτὴν ἄγειν, Id. **ἐνίηλος**· ἀνόητος, Id.

⊛ **ἐνίημι**, fut. -ήσω Th.4.115: aor. -ῆκα, Ep. -έηκα: [mostly ἐνῑημι in Ep., always ἐνῐημι in Trag.; but ἐνῐετε Il.12.441]:—*send in* or *into*, ἄλλους δ' ὀτρύνοντες ἐνήσομεν *will send into the battle*, ib.14.131; ἄλλην ἐνίησι πατὴρ ἐναρίθμιον εἶναι Od.12.65. 2. *implant, inspire*, c. acc. rei et dat. pers., ἐνῆκε δέ οἱ μένος ἠΰ Il.20.80; καί οἱ μυίης θάρσος ἐνὶ στήθεσσιν ἐνῆκε 17.570; τοῖσιν κότον αἰνὸν ἐνήσεις 16.449; ἐνεὶς ἐλαφρὴν λύσσαν E.*Ba.*851; ἐ. τισὶ δαπάνην *involve* them *in* expense, *PAmh.*2.133.9 (ii A.D.):—Pass., κίνησις παρ' ἄλλου ἐνιεμένη *introduced from* without, Plot.6.3.23. 3. reversely, c. acc. pers. et dat. rei, *plunge into*, τὸν..Ζεὺς ἐνέηκε πόνοισι Il.10.89; νῦν μιν μᾶλλον ἀγηνορίῃσιν ἐνῆκας *plunged* him *in*, *inspired* him *with* pride of soul, 9.700; so ἥδε δ' ὁδὸς καὶ μᾶλλον ὁμοφροσύνῃσιν ἐνήσει (sc. ἡμᾶς) *shall bring us* yet more *to* harmony, Od.15.198. 4. generally, *throw in*, ἐπεί ῥ' ἐνέηκε (sc. φάρμακον οἴνῳ) ib.4.233; τάμισον [πυρῷ] Theoc.11.66; νηυσὶν ἐνίετε θεσπιδαὲς πῦρ Il.12.441, cf. E.*Tr.*1262 (so in Pass., πῦρ ἐνίετο ταῖς ἀσπίσιν Jul.*Or.*1.27d); also ἐς τὰς πόλις ἐ. πῦρ Hdt.8.32, cf. Th.4.115; of ships, *launch* them *into* the deep, ἐνήσομεν εὐρέϊ πόντῳ (sc. νῆα) Od.2.295, 12.293. 5. *send into* the assembly, *employ*, ἄλλους ῥήτορας Th.6.29; ἐ. διαβολάς Plb.28.4.10. 6. *inject* poison, of spiders, X.*Mem.*1.3.12; ἰὸν ἐ. τινί A.R.4.1508; also of clysters, Nic.*Al.*197, Aret.*CA*1.6, Dsc.1.30, etc. b. *infuse*, in Pass., ἐνείσθω ἐν αὐτέῳ ἄνηθον Aret.*CA*1.1; κάνναβις ἐνεσμένη (ἐνεεσμένη Geronthr.) ἰς χόλη *soaked* (?), *Edict.Diocl.*32.17. 7. *urge on, incite*, πόθος μ' ἐνέηκε v.l. for ἀν- in Mosch.2.157. 8. Med., of trumpets, *begin to sound*, D.S.17.106. II. intr., *press on*, X.*Cyr.*7.1.29, *HG*2.4.32:—Med., *plunge into*, ὑδάτεσσι Arat.943.

**ἐνιθνήσκω, ἐνιθρύπτω**, Ep. for ἐνθ–.

**ἐνῑθύνω**, *direct by*, [δόγμασι] οἴακα βιοτῆς *App.Anth.*4.48.2.

**ἐνι-κάββαλε, -κάππεσε**, Ep. aor. 2 of ἐγκαταβάλλω, -πίπτω. **-κάτθανε**, Ep. 3 sg. aor. 2 of ἐγκαταθνήσκω. **-κάτθεο, -κάτθετο**, Ep. aor. 2 of ἐγκατατίθημι.

**ἐνικλάω**, poet. for ἐγκ- (q.v.), *break off*: metaph., ἔωθεν ἐνικλᾶν ὅττι κεν εἴπω is wont *to frustrate* what I devise, Il.8.408, cf. 422; ἐνέκλασσας (Ep. aor. 1) δὲ μενοινήν Call.*Jov.*90; γάμον βαρὺς ὅρκος ἐνικλᾷ Id.*Aet.*3.1.22; τίς ἄτη σωομένους μεσσηγὺς ἐνέκλασε; A.R.3.307.

**ἐνικλείω**, Ep. for ἐγκ-, A.R.2.1029.

**ἔνικμος**, ον, (ἰκμάς) *with wet in it, humid*, γῆ Arist.*HA*570$^a$17, Thphr.*CP*1.2.1; διαφύσεις Ph.1.8; δένδρα *Gp.*10.75.2, cf. Dsc.2.101; τὸ ἔ. τῶν ἄντρων Porph.*Antr.*5; of young pigs, Ar.Byz.ap.Ath.9.375a; of perspiring patients, Orib.*Fr.*116.

⊛ **ἐνικνέομαι**, *arrive at*, τοὺς ἐνικομένους ταῖς ἡλικίαις *IG*9(1).32.16 (Phocis).

**ἐνικνήθω, ἐνικνώσσω**, poet. for ἐγκ-, Nic.*Th.*911 (Med.): divisim, Mosch.2.6.

**ἑνῐκός**, ή, όν, (ἕν) *single*: Gramm., ἀριθμὸς ἑ. the *singular* number, opp. δυϊκός, πληθυντικός, Chrysipp.*Stoic.*2.99, D.T.635.30, A.D.*Pron.*12.11, al.; τὰ -κά Longin.24.1. Adv. -κῶς D.H.*Comp.*6, A.D.*Synt.*258.24, St.Byz. s.v. Ἄγρα. II. *exhibiting unity, individual*, in Comp., Plot.6.9.6, Syrian.*in Metaph.*34.17, Procl.*in Prm.*p.58 S.: Sup., ib.p.820 S., *in Alc.*p.255 C. Adv. -κῶς Theo Sm.p.21 H., Plot.2.4.13.

**ἐνικρίνω**, Ep. for ἐγκ-, A.R.1.48 (Pass.).

**ἑνῑλάσιμος** [ᾰ], ον, *propitious*, *Sammelb.*4116.5 (-ειλ- lapis).

**ἐνίλλω**, *look askance*, Paus.Gr.*Fr.*209:—also ⊛ **ἐνιλλώπτω**, Ael.Dion.ibid.

**ἐνῑοβολέω**, *cast venom upon*, βοτάναις Hp.*Ep.*16.

**ἔνιοι**, αι, α, *some*; never in Ep., Lyr., or Att. Poets before Men., exc. Ar.*Pl.*867 (cf. however ἐνίοτε); first used in Ion. Prose, as Hdt.1.120, 8.56, Hp.*Praec.*6; πολλοὶ μὲν.. ἔνιοι δὲ.. Lys.25.19; ἔνιοι μὲν.. ἔνιοι δὲ.. Pl.*Tht.*151a, X.*Mem.*4.2.38; ἔνιοι μὲν..οἱ δὲ.. Pl.*Mx.*238e; ἐνίοι τινες Isoc.15.258: later in sg., οὐ πᾶσα κίνησις θερμαίνει, ἀλλ' ἐνία ψύχει Arist.*Pr.*884$^b$13, cf. Thphr.*Vert.*1; περὶ ψυχῆς ἐνίας θεωρῆσαι Arist.*Metaph.*1026$^a$5: neut. pl. as Adv., συμμανῆναι ἔνια δεῖ Men.421; ἔστι καὶ ταὐτόματον ἔνια χρήσιμον Id.486.

**ἐνίοκα**, Dor. for sq., Archyt.ap.Stob.[illegible].114.

**ἐνίοτε**, Adv. *at times, sometimes*, E.*Hel.*1213, Ar.*Pl.*1125, Hp.*Praec.*14, etc.; ἐ. μὲν.., ἐ. δὲ.. Pl.*Grg.*467e; ἐ. μὲν..ἔστι δ' ὅτε.. Id.*Tht.*150a; ἐ...τότε δὲ.. Id.*Phlb.*46e; ἐ. μὲν..ὅτε δὲ.. Arist.*Mete.*360$^b$2.

**ἐνιπάζων**· τύπτων, Hsch.:—also **ἐνιπῆσαι** (as if from ἐνιπάω)· ἀπειλῆσαι, βοῆσαι, Id.

**ἐνῑπή**, ἡ, (ἐνίπτω, v. ἐνέπω fin.) poet. Noun, *rebuke, reproof*, Il.4.402, etc.; κρατερὴν δ' ἀποθέσθαι ἐνιπὴν 5.492; ἐνιπῇ ἀργαλέῃ 14.104; ἔδδεισεν γὰρ ἐμὴν ἔκπαγλον ἐ. Od.10.448; *abuse, contumely*, ἐπίσχετε θυμὸν ἐνιπῆς 20.266: pl., *angry threats*, φεύγων..Ποσειδάωνος ἐνιπάς 5.446, cf. *h.Merc.*165; ψευδέων ἐνιπά *reproach* of lying, Pi.*O.*10(11).6. 2. later, of any *violent attack*, as of the sun's rays or thirst, Opp.*C.*1.133, 299.

**ἐνί-πλειος**, ον, Ep. for ἔμπλεος. **-πλήσασθαι, -σθῆναι, -σωσι**, v. ἐμπίπλημι. **-πλήσσω**, Ep. for ἐμπλήσσω. **-πλώω**, v. ἐμπλέω.

**ἐνιππ-άζομαι**, = sq., Arr.*An.*2.6.3, Plu.*Mar.*25. **-εύω**, *ride in*, χωρίον ἐπιτήδεον ἐνιππεῦσαι Hdt.6.102. **-ομᾰχέω**, *fight a cavalry action in*, ἐπιτήδειον πεδίον -ῆσαι D.H.2.13.

**ἐνιπρῆσαι**, Ep. for ἐμπρ-, v. ἐμπίμπρημι.

**ἐνιπρίω** [ρῑ], Ep. for ἐμπρίω, Opp.*C.*2.261.

**ἐνιπτάζω**, lengthd. for ἐνίπτω, A.R.1.492, 864.

**ἐνιπτύω**, Ep. for ἐμπτύω.

**ἐνίπτω**, fut. ἐνίψω Il.7.447: aor. ἠνίπᾰπε [ῐ] 2.245, al., also ἐνένιπε 15.546, al. (with vv. ll. ἐνένισπεν, ἐνένιπτεν, Od.18.321, Il.23.473):—Ep. Verb (once in A. (v. infr.)), *reprove, upbraid*, freq. with words added to strengthen the sense, χαλεπῷ ἠνίπαπε μύθῳ Il.2.245; χαλεποῖσιν ὀνείδεσι θυμὸν ἔνιπτε 3.438; ἐνένιπεν ὀνειδείοις ἐπέεσσιν Od.18.326; τὸν δ' αἰσχρῶς ἐνένιπε ib.321, Il.23.473; or simply πόσιν δ' ἠνίπαπε μύθῳ 3.427; κραδίην ἠνίπαπε μύθῳ *reproved* his soul with words, Od.20.17: without a modal word, εἴ τίς με καὶ ἄλλος ἐνίπτοι were another *to attack* me, Il.24.768; τόν ῥ' Ἕκτωρ ἐνένιπεν 15.552, cf. 546; καί τίς μ' ἐνίπτων εἶπε A.*Ag.*590: without acc., Od.18.78, cf. 24.161. II. after Hom., = ἐνέπω, *tell, announce*, ἀδείας ἐνίπτων ἐλπίδας Pi.*P.*4.201, cf. Nonn.*D.*27.59. Cf. ἐνίσσω.

**ἐνισκέλλω, ἐνισκήπτω, ἐνισκίμπτω**, Ep. for ἐνσ–.

**ἐνίσον**, Adv. *equally*, dub. l. in Iamb.*Comm.Math.*25.

**ἐνισόω**, *mix in equal proportions*, *Gp.*6.6.1 (Pass.).

**ἐνισπεῖν**, v. ἐνέπω. **ἐνισπείρω**, Ep. for ἐνσπ–. **ἐνισπέσθαι**· ὁ νῦν μὴ καταπίνων, Hsch. **ἐνισπήσω, ἐνίσπω**, v. ἐνέπω.

**ἐνίσσω**, Ep. collat. form of ἐνίπτω, *attack, reproach*, ἐκπάγλοις ἐπέεσσιν ἐνισσέμεν Il.15.198; ὀνειδείοισιν ἐνίσσων 22.497; ἔπεσσ' αἰσχροῖσιν ἐνίσσων 24.238: also generally, *maltreat*, ἔπεσίν τε κακοῖσιν ἐνίσσομεν ἠδὲ βολῇσιν Od.24.161:—Pass., βαλλόμενος καὶ ἐνισσόμενος ib.163.

⊛ **ἐνίστημι**, causal in pres., fut. and aor. 1 Act., and aor. 1 Med.:—*put, place in*, ἵππον ἐν λίθοις ἐνιστάναι X.*Eq.Mag.*1.16; στήλας ἐνίστη ἐς τὰς χώρας Hdt.2.102; εἰς αὐτὴν (sc. τὴν πόλιν) ἡνίοχον ἐνστῆσαι Pl.*Plt.*266e; τοὺς ἱπποκόμους εἰς (i.e. amongst) τοὺς ἱππέας ἐ. X.*Eq.Mag.*5.6: c. dat., ἱστὸν ἐνεστήσαντο μεσόδμῃ A.R.1.563. 2. in Law, *institute* an heir, ἐ. κληρονόμους τοὺς υἱούς *PMasp.*151.75 (vi A.D.). 3. aor. 1 Med., also, *begin*, ὅσαι τὸ πρᾶγμα τοῦτ' ἐνεστήσαντο Ar.*Lys.*268; οὐδὲν πώποτε τῶν πραγμάτων ἐνεστήσασθ' ὀρθῶς D.10.21; ὁ τοιοῦτον

ἀγῶν' ἐνστησάμενος Id.18.4; ἐ. τὸ πρᾶγμα, Lat. *rem instituere*, Arist.*Pr*.951$^{a}$28; ἀρχὰς τῆς γενέσεως Thphr.*HP*7.10.4; ὀργὴν καὶ μῖσος πρός τινα ἐνστήσασθαι *to begin to show*.., Plb.1.82.9; πρᾶξιν Plu.*Arat*.16: c. inf., D.S.14.53. **4.** ἐνστήσασθαι τὸ μέγεθος *determine* the size, Ph.*Bel*.50.29.

**B.** Pass., with aor. 2, pf., and plpf. Act.:—*to be set in, stand in*, λόχοις E.*Supp*.896; ἐν τῷ νηῷ Hdt.2.91: abs., πύλαι ἐνεστᾶσι ἑκατόν Id.1.179, cf. Pl.*Ti*.50d, etc. **2.** *enter upon, take possession of*, ὁ νικάσας ἐν τὰν οὐσίαν ἐνίσταται τὰν τοῦ ἁλόντος *Foed.Delph.Pell*.2B 14. **II.** *to be appointed*, σοῦ ἐνεστεῶτος βασιλέος Hdt.1.120, cf. 6.59; ἐς ἀρχήν Id.3.68; ἐς τυραννίδας Id.2.147. **III.** *to be upon, threaten*, c. dat. pers., τοιούτων τοῖσι Σπαρτιήτῃσι ἐνεστεώτων πρηγμάτων Id.1.83; τὸν πόλεμον τὸν ἐνστάντα σοὶ καὶ τῇ πόλει Isoc.5.2; in war, *press hard*, τινί Plb.3.97.1: abs., *begin*, τοῦ θέρους] ἐνισταμένου Thphr.*HP*9.8.2; ἐνισταμένου τοῦ ἐνιαυτοῦ Lxx 3*Ki*.12.24; *to be at hand, arise*, ὁ τότ' ἐνστὰς πόλεμος D.18.89, cf. 139, Plb.1.71.4; τοῦ πολέμου πρὸς Φίλιππον ὑμῖν ἐνεστηκότος Aeschin.2.58: esp. in pf. part., *pending, present*, μιᾶς ἐνεστώσης δίκης Ar.*Nu*.779, cf. Is.11.45, D.33.14; ὁ νῦν ἐνεστηκὼς ἀγών Lycurg.7; so οὐδενὸς ἡμῖν ἐνεστῶτος πρὸς αὐτούς *PStrassb*.91.21 (i B.C.); of Time, *instant, present*, τοῦ ἐνεστῶτος μηνός Philipp.ap.D.18.157; ἡ ἐνεστῶσα κακία, ἀνάγκη, *PPetr*.2 p.60, 1*Ep.Cor*.7.26; κατὰ τὸν ἐ. καιρόν Arist.*Rh*.1366$^{b}$23; ἀγαθὸν ἐνεστὼς ἢ μέλλον *Stoic*.3.94; cf. ἐνεστηκέναι τὸν πάντα χρόνον ὡς τὸν ἐνιαυτὸν ἐνεστηκέναι λέγομεν Apollod.*Stoic*.3.260. **2.** esp. Gramm., ὁ ἐνεστὼς (sc. χρόνος) the *present tense*, *Stoic*.2.48, D.T.638.22, A.D.*Pron*.58.7, al.; also ἐνεστῶσα συντέλεια *the state of completion expressed by the perfect tense*, Id.*Synt*.205.15: also in aor., τοῦ ποτὲ ἐνστάντος *when* the moment *has arrived*, Plot.4.3.13; τὰ ἐνεστηκότα πράγματα *present* circumstances, X.*HG*2.1.6; so τὰ ἐνεστῶτα Plb.2.26.3. **IV.** *stand in the way, resist, block*, τοῖς ποιουμένοις Th.8.69; τῇ φυγῇ Plu.*Luc*.13; τῇ αὐξήσει Id.*Rom*.25; πρὸς πᾶσάν τινι πολιτείαν Id.*Arist*.3, cf. *Marc*.22: abs., *stand in the way*, Th.3.23; in argument, ἐνέστηκεν ὃ νυνδὴ Κέβης ἔλεγε Pl.*Phd*.77b; ὁ ἐνεστηκώς *the opponent* in a lawsuit, *SIG*45.28 (Halic., v B.C.). **2.** in Logic, *object*, τῷ καθόλου Arist.*Top*.157$^{b}$3; πρὸς τὸν ἔξω λόγον Id.*APo*.76$^{b}$26: abs., Id.*Rh*.1402$^{b}$24, al.; ἐ. ὅτι.. Id.*APr*.69$^{b}$6; ὡς.. Id.*EN*1172$^{b}$35, A.D.*Synt*.176.22. **3.** of the Roman tribunes, *exercise the right of intercessio, veto*, Plb.6.16.4, Plu.*TG*10, al. **V.** of fluids, *congeal, freeze*, ὕδωρ ἐνεστηκός Thphr.*CP*5.13.1; *become impacted in*, ἐνιστάμενον ἐπὶ τὰ τοῦ στομάχου στενά (sc. γάλα) Dsc.*Alex*.26.

**ἐνίστιος**, v. ἐνέστιος.

**ἔνισχνος**, ον, *somewhat thin, slight*, Nic.*Al*.147, *Cat.Cod.Astr*.7.196.

**ἐνισχῡρίζομαι**, *rely upon*, τινί D.44.8.

**ἐνισχύω**, *strengthen, confirm*, ὁ χρόνος ταῦτα -ύσει πάντα Hp.*Lex* 3; ἄγγελος ἐνισχύων αὐτόν *Ev.Luc*.22.43:—Pass., Jul.*Gal.Fr*.7. **II.** intr., *prevail in* or *among*, ἐν ταῖς πόλεσι ἐνισχύει τὰ νόμιμα Arist.*EN* 1180$^{b}$4: abs., Id.*PA*653$^{a}$31 al.; τοῦτ' ἐνισχύειν ἑκάστῳ Thphr.*Sens*.63, cf. 67; παρά τισιν ἐ. ἐν παροιμίας μέρει D.S.20.58; ἐνίσχυσεν ὡς.. *the opinion prevailed* that.., Id.5.57.

**ἐνίσχω**, = ἐνέχω:—Med., ἐνίσχεσθαι τὴν φωνήν *to keep in one's* voice, Plu.*Cic*.35:—Pass., *to be held fast*, Hdt.4.43; προχοῇσιν A.R.1.11; ἔν τινι v.l. for ἐνεχ- in X.*An*.7.4.17; of phlegm, etc., *to be impacted*, χυμοὶ ἐνισχόμενοι Gal.15.221.

**ἐντελέω**, *complete*, τὰ κατάλοιπα τῶν ἔργων *BCH*20.323 (Lebad.).

**ἐνιτρέφω, -τρίβω**, Ep. for ἐντ-. **ἐνιφέρβομαι, -φύρω**, Ep. for ἐμφ-.

**ἐνίχνιον**, τό, *footprint* (?), Prisc.*Inst*.14.36, *Gloss*.

**ἐνιχραύω, -χρίμπτω**, Ep. for ἐγχ-. **ἐνιψάω**, poet. for ἐμψάω.

**ἐνιψηφίζομαι**, *put to the vote*, Maiuri *Nuova Silloge* 443.

**ἐνίψω**, v. ἐνίπτω. **ἔνκομον**· ἐν τῷ μαρίῳ ἴσον θείας κελεύσεως, Hsch.

**ἐνλαξεύω**, *carve in* or *on*, pf. Pass. ἐνλελάξευνται *AP*3.9 Arg.

**ἐνλᾰπῐθάζεσθαι**· μαχέσασθαι Λαπίθαις, ἢ ἐνθυμηθῆναι, Hsch.

**ἔνλῐθος**, ον, *adorned with jewels*, μασχαλιστήρ *CPR*22.5 (ii A.D.).

⊛ **ἐνλῑμενίζειν**, *exact harbour-dues*, Hsch.

**ἐνμαχατεύειν**, v. ἐμμυχατεύειν.

**ἐνμεντευθενί**, Com. tmesis for ἐντευθενὶ μέν, Metag.6.5.

**ἐννάγωνον** [ᾰ], τό, *nonagon*, Hero *Metr*.1.22.

**ἐννᾰετήρ**, ῆρος, ὁ, (ἐνναίω) *inmate, inhabitant*, *AP*9.495 (Arch.), v.l. in Mosch.2.123:—fem. **ἐννᾰέτειρα**, *APl*.4.94 (Arch.).

**ἐννᾰ-ετηρίς**, v. ἐννεετηρίς. **-έτηρος**, ον, = sq., *nine years old*, Hes.*Op*.436. ⊛ **-έτης** (A), ες, *nine years old*, Theoc.26.29: Ep. neut. εἰνάετες, as Adv., *for nine years*, Hes.*Th*.801:—fem. **-έτις**, poet. εἰν-, ιδος, *AP*7.643 (Crin.). ⊛ **-έτης** (B), ου, ὁ, = ἐνναετήρ, Isyll.38, A.R.2.517, *APl*.4.331 (Agath.), etc.:—fem. **-έτις**, ιδος, A.R.1.1126. **-ετία**, ἡ, *period of nine years*, Sch.Il.1.1; cf. ἐναετία. **-ετίζομαι**, v. εἰνα-.

**ἔνναιον**, τό, f.l. for ναιον (= ναόν, cf. Hsch.), Cliniasap.Sch.A.R.2.1085, cf. Suid., Zonar.

**ἐνναίω**, *dwell in*, τοισίδ' ἐνναίει δόμοις E.*Hel*.488; ὅσοισι [κακοῖσι] ..δρᾷς ἐνναίοντά με S.*Ph*.472, cf. *Lyr.Alex.Adesp*.35.22; ἐκεῖ S.*OC* 788: c. acc. loci, *inhabit*, Mosch.4.36, A.R.1.1076: in later Prose, [Κόρινθον] ἐ. ἐν μέσοις τοῖς ἀγαθοῖς Aristid.*Or*.46(3).27: 3 pl. fut. Med. ἐννάσσονται A.R.4.1751: 3 pl. aor. 1 Med. ἐννάσσαντο ib.1213, Call.*Del*.15: 3 sg. aor. 1 Pass. ἐννάσθη A.R.3.1181.

**ἐννάκις** [ᾰ], **ἐννᾰκόσιοι, ἐννᾰταῖος, ἔννᾰτος**, v. ἐνακ-, ἐνατ-.

**ἐννάσσω**, *bung up*, πίθον *Gp*.6.6.1.

**ἐνναυλοχέομαι**, Dep., = ναυλοχέω ἐν.., D.C.50.12.

**ἐνναυμᾰχέω**, = ναυμαχέω ἐν.., Plu.2.1078d.

**ἐνναυπηγέομαι**, Pass., *have ships built in it*, of a place, v.l. in Th.1.13.

⊛ **ἐννέᾰ**, Dor. also ἐννῆ (q.v.), indecl., *nine*, Il.6.174, Od.8.258, etc.; Μοῦσαι ἐννέα Hes.*Th*.917, Od.24.60; τρὶς ἐννέα κλῶνας, in a religious ceremony, S.*OC*483; τρὶς ἐ. ἔτη Orac.ap.Th.5.26. **2.** as a round number for, *many*, τρὶς ἐννέα φῶτας ἔπεφνεν Il.16.785, cf. Od.11.577, Sch.Nic.*Th*.781. (Cf. Lat. *novem*, Skt. *náva*, etc.)

**ἐννεά-βοιος** [ᾰ], ον, *worth nine beeves*, Il.6.236, *Eleg.Alex.Adesp*.1.3:—but also glossed by **ἐνν⟨ε⟩άβυρσος**, Hsch. **-γηρα** κορώνη *nine times (as) old (as a man)*, Arat.1022 (ἐννεάνειρα cj. Lobeck). **-γράμμᾰτον**, τό, *word of nine letters* (λιθάργυρα), Olymp.Alch.p.71 B. (-γραμμον codd.). **-γωνος**, ον, of a class of figurate numbers, *enneagonal*, Theo Sm.p.40 H. **-δάκτῠλος**, ον, *with nine fingers*, Ptol.Heph.ap.Phot.*Bibl*.p.147 B. **-δεσμος**, ον, *with nine joints, many-jointed*, Nic.*Th*.781. **-δικός**, ή, όν, *based on* or *calculated by division by nine*, ἀγωγή, [κλιμακτήρ], Vett.Val.147.31, 148.14. **-ετηρικός**, ή, όν, *nine-yearly*, ἀγών *BSA*16.117 (Pisidia, ii/iii A.D.). **-έτης**, ου, ὁ, *nine years old*, *IG*9(2).639 (Larissa), *Annales du Service* 19.223. **-ετία**, ἡ, *period of nine years*, *EM*343.28.

**ἐννεάζω**, *spend one's youth in*, μεγέθει σώματος ἐννεάσαι *to be of* great stature *in one's youth*, Hp.*Aph*.2.54; τῇ τῶν πραγμάτων ἀκριβεστέρᾳ καταλήψει Ph.1.622; ἐ. [τῇ βασιλείᾳ] καὶ ἐγγηράσκει, of one crowned in his mother's womb, Agath.4.25; ῥόδον ἐννεάσαν τῷ ἦρι *having bloomed* in spring, Philostr.*Ep*.51.

**ἐννεᾰκαίδεκα**, indecl., *nineteen*, Il.24.496, etc.

**ἐννεᾰκαιδεκα-ετηρίς**, ίδος, ἡ, *cycle of nineteen years*, D.S.12.36, *Placit*.2.32.2, Ptol.*Tetr*.205. **-έτης**, ου, ὁ, *of nineteen years*, χρόνος D.S.2.47. **-μηνος**, ον, *nineteen months old*, *IG*14.1970. **-πλάσιος** [πλᾰ], α, ον, = sq., Procl.*Hyp*.4.110. **-πλᾰσίων**, ον, gen. ονος, *nineteen times as large as*, τῆς γῆς *Placit*.2.25.1, cf. Ach.Tat.*Intr.Arat*.20.

**ἐννεᾰκαιδεκ-άς**, άδος, ἡ, = sq., Vett.Val.339.2, Tz.*H*.2.885. ⊛ **-ατος**, η, ον, *nineteenth*, Hp.*Epid*.3.1.γ', *CIG*2220 (Chios), *IG*2.677.6 (ii A.D.). ⊛ **-έτης**, ες, = ἐννεακαιδεκαέτης, poet. gen. -τευς *AP*7.11 (Asclep.), 9.190:—fem. **-έτις**, *IG*3.1370: written -δεχέτις *Epigr.Gr*.205.

**ἐννεᾰκαιεικοσῐ-καιεπτᾰκοσιοπλᾰσιάκις**, Adv. *seven-hundred-and-twenty-nine times*, Pl.*R*.587e. **-χοίνῐκος**, ον, *containing twenty-nine* χοίνικες, *PHib*.1.85.18 (iii B.C.).

**ἐννεᾰκέφᾰλος**, ον, *nine-headed*, Sch.Hes.*Th*.313, Tz.*H*.2.237.

⊛ **ἐννεάκις**, Adv. = ἐνάκις, v.l. in Nicom.*Harm*.8.

**ἐννεᾰκισχίλιοι** [χῐ], αι, α, *nine thousand*, D.S.17.66, Ael.*VH*6.12.

**ἐννεά-κλῑνος**, ον, *with nine dining-couches*, Phryn.Com.66, D.S.31.9, Them.*Or*.18.223a. **-κότῠλος** [ᾰ], ον, *containing nine* κοτύλαι, *PCair.Zen*.61.3 (-κυτ- Pap.). **-κροσσον**· πολλοὺς κροσσοὺς ἔχον, Hsch. **-κρουνος**, ον, *with nine spouts*, name of a well at Athens, in earlier times (as at this day) called Καλλιρρόη, Hdt.6.137, Th.2.15, Polyzel.2: metaph. of an orator, *copious*, Lib.*Ep*.1493.4. **-κυκλος**, ον, *in nine circles*, Coluth.214, Nonn.*D*.4.317. **-λῐνος**, ον, *of nine threads*, ἄρκυς X.*Cyn*.2.4. **-μηνιαῖος**, α, ον, = sq., *Theol.Ar*.47. **-μηνος**, ον, *of* or *in nine months*, τίκτειν Hdt.6.69, cf. Hp.*Septim*.8; χρόνος Gal.*Nat.Fac*.3.3; λόγος *BGU*977.13 (ii A.D.). **-μορφος**, ον, *of nine forms*, *PMag.Leid.W*.10.1, 21. **-μυκλος**, ον, (μύκλος) *having nine stripes* or *folds*, hence, *nine years old*, ὄνος Call.*Fr*.180, cf. Hsch.

**ἐννεάνειρα**, v. ἐννεάγηρα.

⊛ **ἐννεά-πηχυς** [ᾰ], υ, *nine cubits broad* or *long*, ζυγόδεσμον Il.24.270, al.; cf. εἰνάπηχυς. **-πλάσιος** [πλᾰ], α, ον, *ninefold*, dub. in Ibyc.33. **-πνεύμων**, ον, gen. ονος, '*nine winds strong*', ζάλη Secund.*Sent*.8 (prob.). **-πολις**, *having nine cities*, Πύλος Sch.Od.3.7. **-πον**· λοξόν, Hsch. **-πους**, ποδος, ὁ, ἡ, *nine feet long*, λίθος *Milet*.7.57 (Didyma).

**ἐννεάρμενος**, ον, *having nine sails*, Tz. ad Lyc.101.

**ἐννεάς**, άδος, ἡ, *body of nine*, Theoc.17.84 (pl.), *AP*7.17 (Tull. Laur.); ἡ ὑμνουμένη ἐ. ἐν τῷ νοητῷ Dam.*Pr*.117: Porph. divided the works of his master Plotinus into six enneads, *Plot*.24. **II.** *the number nine*, Plu.2.726d, 744a, Nicom.*Ar*.1.19, etc. **III.** *the ninth day of the month*, v. εἰνάς.

**ἐννεάστεγος**, ον, *of nine stories*, κατασκεύασμα D.S.20.91.

**ἐνν⟨ε⟩άστερος**, ον, *containing nine stars*, δορά Sch.Arat.322.

**ἐννεᾰ-σύλλᾰβος**, ον, *nine-syllabled*, Steph.*in Rh*.321.16, *AP*13.19 tit.: -σύλλαβον (sc. μέτρον), τό, Σαπφικόν Heph.10.2. **-σφαιρος**, ον, *having nine spheres*, Phlp.*in Mete*.110.23.

**ἐννεατηρίς**, v. ἐννεετηρίς.

**ἐννεᾰ-φάρμᾰκος**, ον, *consisting of nine ingredients*, of remedies, Heraclid.Tar.ap.Gal.14.186, Cels.5.19.1, Androm.ap.Gal.13.310, Orib.*Fr*.142. **-φθογγος**, ον, *of nine notes*, μέλος *Trag.Adesp*.546.11. **-φωνος**, ον, = foreg., σῦριγξ Theoc.8.18. **-χειλος** (A), ον, *with nine lips*, Nicom.*Ar*.1.14. **-χειλος** (B), ον, Ion. for sq., read by Aristarch. in Il.5.860, and mistranslated as, = ἐννεάχειλος (A). **-χῑλοι**, αι, α, Ep. for ἐνάκις χίλιοι, *nine thousand*, Il.5.860 (v. foreg.); ἄνδρες Ps.-Luc.*Philopatr*.6: sg., κτύπος -χιλος noise *as of* 9,000, Nonn.*D*.8.45. **-χορδος**, ον, *of nine strings*: Subst. ἐννεάχορδον (sc. ὄργανον), τό, Phillisap.Ath.14.636b. **-χρονος**, gloss on ἐννέωρος, Sch.Od.11.311. **-χωρος**, ον, *containing nine terms* or *places*, στίχος *Theol.Ar*.28. **-χῶς**, *in nine ways*, Procl.*in Prm*.p.961 S. **-ψῡχος**, ον, *with nine lives*: prov., ἐ. ὁ κύων (as we say of the cat) Hsch.

**ἔννεεν**· ἐξέτεινεν, Hsch.

**ἐννεετηρίς**, ίδος, ἡ, *nine-year period*, Pl.*Min*.319e, *IG*2.985$^{A}$2, *Delph*.

3(2).48.8; written ἐννεατηρίς in Vett.Val.337.17; ἐνναετ- Plu.2.293b; ἐννετ- (v.l. ἐννεατ-) Thphr.*HP*4.11.2: v. ἐννεαετ-.

**ἔννεκα**, Aeol., = ἕνεκα (q.v.).

**ἐννεκρόομαι**, Pass., *die in*, ταῖς γαλήναις Plu.2.792b.

**ἐννεμέθομαι**, Pass., *feed in*, Opp.*H.*1.611, 3.546.

**ἐννεμέσιμος**, ον, *just, righteous*, Cyr.

**ἐννέμω**, *feed* cattle *in* a place, *SIG*685.82 (Itanos), D.C.72.3:—Med., of the cattle, Ph.2.118 (prob.); of fish, Opp.*H.*1.5; also, *live amongst*, Lxx 3*Ma.*3.25.

**ἐννενή-κοντα, -κοστός, -κονταετής**, ff.ll. for ἐνεν-.

**ἐννενώκασι**, Ion. for ἐννενοήκασι, 3 pl. pf. of ἐννοέω.

❋ **ἐννεόβολον**, τό, *sum of nine obols*, *IG*7.235.22 (Orop.).

**ἔννεον**, Ep. for ἔνεον, impf. of νέω *swim*, Il.21.11 (v.l. νῆχοντ').

**ἐννεόργυιος**, ον, *nine fathoms long*, Od.11.312, Matro *Conv.*45.

**ἐννεοσσεύω**, Att. -ττεύω, later ἐννοσσεύω Lxx *Je.*22.23, *Gp.*5.48.1:—*make a nest in* a place, ἔν τινι Ar.*Av.*1108: metaph., Pl.*Lg.*949c; as etym. of νόσος, Anon.Lond.3.22:—Med., D.S.5.43. II. c. acc., *hatch as in a nest*, ἔρωτα Pl.*Alc.*1.135e; παιδείας ψυχαῖς Them.*Or.*24.307d:—Pass., *to be hatched*, ἐπιθυμίαι ἐννενεοττευμέναι Pl.*R.*573e.

**ἐννεόω**, *break up* land, *Gp.*3.1.9.

**ἐννέπω**, v. ἐνέπω. **ἐννεσία**, ἡ, v. ἐνεσία.

**ἔννευμα**, ατος, τό, *signal, wave of the hand*, δακτύλων ἐννεύμασι Lxx *Pr.*6.13.

**ἐννευρόκαυλος**, ον, *with fibrous stalk*, Thphr.*HP*6.1.4.

**ἐννεύω**, *nod* or *make signs to*, ἐννεύει με φεύγειν Ar.*Fr.*75, cf. Luc. *DMeretr.*12.1; ἐ. τινὶ τὸ τί ἂν θέλοι.. *ask* him *by signs* what.., *Ev. Luc.*1.62.

**ἐννέω**, *swim in*, Aristid.*Or.*48(24).21.

**ἐννέωρος** (cf. ὥρος), Ep. Adj. *in the ninth season*: hence, 1. Μίνως ἐννέωρος βασίλευε Διὸς.. ὀαριστής perh. *at nine years old* or *after nine years*, Od.19.179, cf. Apollon.*Lex.*; Pl.*Min.*319b couples ἐ. ὀαριστής taking counsel with Zeus *every ninth year*. 2. *nine years old*, of the Aloidae, Od.11.311; βοῦς 10.19 (unless, = πενταέτηρος, ὥρος meaning a *season*, i.e. half-year, cf. Arist.*HA*575b6); σίαλοι Od.10.390; ἄλειφαρ Il.18.351. (Perh. = *of full age*, ἐννέα being taken as a round number, cf. Sch.Il.l.c.) 3. (ὥρα) *nine hours long*, νύκτες Herod.8.5.

❋ **ἐννῆ**, = ἐννέα, *SIG*240*E*43 (Delph., iv B.C.); also at Cyrene, Hsch.

**ἐνν-ήκοντα**, Ep. for ἐνενήκοντα, Od.19.174. **-ῆμαρ**, Ep. Adv. *for nine days*, Il.1.53, al. **-ήρης**, ες, *of nine banks of oars*, ναῦς Plb. 16.7.1, Ath.5.203d.

**ἐννησιάδες** Νύμφαι *island*-Nymphs (Lesb.), Hsch.

**ἐννήυσκλοι**· ὑποδήματα Λακωνικῶν ἐφήβων, Hsch. (ἐννήϊσκλοι cod.): fr. ἐννῆ and ὕσκλος.

**ἔννηφιν**, v. ἔνος (B).

**ἐννήφω**, *to be sober in*, ἑκατέρῳ (sc. good and evil fortune), M.Ant. 1.16.10.

**ἐννήχομαι**, *swim* or *float in*.., τινί Ph.1.385, Plu.2.994b, Antyll. ap.Orib.6.27.5: metaph., νοήματα ἐ. ὡς ἐν ποταμῷ τῷ λόγῳ Ph.1.693: —later in Act., Gal.*UP*15.5, prob. in Lib.*Decl.*32.20: metaph., Gal. 2.461.

**ἔννιον**, τό, *handle of an oar*, Hsch.

**ἐννιτρόγεως**, ων, *with soil impregnated with nitre*, Hero *Geom.*23.68.

**Ἐννοδία**, v. ἐνόδιος.

**ἐννο-έω**, Ion. aor. 1 part. ἐννώσας Hdt.1.68,86: pf. ἐννένωκα Id.3.6:—Att. also Dep. **ἐννοοῦμαι**, with aor. 1 Pass. ἐνενοήθην:—*have in one's thoughts, consider, reflect*, ἐ. ὅτι.. Id.1.86, etc.; ἐ. ὡς.. Pl.*Ap.* 40c; εἴτε.. Id.*Phd.*74a; ἐ. μή.. *take thought, be anxious* lest.., X. *An.*4.2.13, etc.; ἐννοούμενοι μὴ οὐκ ἔχοιεν ib.3.5.3; ἐννοούμενοι (v.l. -οῦντες) οἷα πεπονθὼς ἦ Lys.9.7: abs., ὧδε γὰρ ἐννόησον Pl.*Prt.*324d; also τέκνων ἐννοουμένη πέρι E.*Med.*925. 2. c. acc., *reflect upon, consider*, τὰ λεγόμενα Hdt.1.68, cf. 3.6; τοῦτ' ἐννοοῦμαί πως ἐγὼ Eup. 11.6 D.; ἐ. τὸ γιγνόμενον, ὅτι.. Pl.*Tht.*161b, cf. S.*Ant.*61; τοῦτ' ἐννοεῖσθ', ὅταν πορθῆτε γαῖαν, εὐσεβεῖν Id.*Ph.*1440; ταῦτ' ἐννοήσασ' (v.l. ἐννοηθεῖσ') E.*Med.*882, cf. 900; γένος ἐπιεικὲς ἀθλίως διατιθέμενον Pl.*Criti.*121b. 3. c. gen., *take thought for*, μητρὸς οὐδὲν ἐννοούμενοι κακῶν E.*Med.*47; ἐνενόησεν αὐτῶν καὶ ὡς.. he *took note of* them that.., X.*Cyr.*5.2.18; *notice*, ἐννενόηκας τῶν λεγομένων πονηρῶν, σοφῶν δέ, ὡς.. Pl.*R.*519a; ἐννενόηκά σου λέγοντος ὅτι.. Id.*Hp.Mi.* 369e, cf. *Tht.*168c; ἔκ τινος ἐννοεῖσθαι *draw conclusions* from.., Id. *Hp.Ma.*295c. II. *understand*, εἰ σὺ μὴ τόδ' ἐννοεῖς, ἐγὼ λέγω σοι A.*Ag.*1088 (lyr.); οὐ γὰρ ἐννοῶ S.*OT*559, *Ph.*28: c. part., ἐννοοῦμαι φαῦλος οὖσα E.*Hipp.*435. III. *intend* to do, c. inf., ἐννοεῖς ἡμᾶς προδοῦναι S.*OT*330, cf. Lxx *Ju.*9.5, Aristeas 133: c. acc. rei, S.*Aj.* 115. IV. *think of, invent*, Id.*Tr.*578; ὁδόν X.*An.*2.2.10; μηχανήν Pl.*Lg.*798b. V. *form a notion of*, τι Id.*Phd.*73c sq.; *suppose*, ὃ δ' ὑμεῖς ἐννοεῖτε, ὅτι.. X.*An.*6.1.29. VI. of words, *mean, signify*, τί σοι ἄλλο ἐννοεῖ.. τὸ ῥῆμα; Pl.*Euthd.*287c codd. **-ημα**, ατος, τό, *notion, concept*, Arist.*Metaph.*981a6, Epicur.*Ep.*1 p.5 U., Lxx *Si.*21.11, Aristeas 189, D.H.*Comp.*25, Plot.6.6.12, etc.; *object of thought*, Zeno *Stoic.*1.19, etc. **-ημᾰτικός**, ή, όν, *notional*, *Stoic.* 2.75; *subjective*, Ascl.*in Metaph.*106.26; opp. οὐσιώδης, Gal.1.306. Adv. -κῶς Ascl.*in Metaph.*106.27, Procl.*in Prm.*p.632 S.; gloss on ἐμφαντικῶς, *EM*331.53. II. *inventive*, Vett.Val.42.33. Adv. -κῶς Id.166.7. **-ησις**, εως, ἡ, *consideration*, Pl.*R.*407c. **-ητέον**, *one must consider*, Id.*Lg.*636c. **-ητικός**, ή, όν, *thoughtful*, Arist.*Phgn.* 813a29.

**ἔννοια**, ἡ, (νοῦς) *act of thinking, reflection, cogitation* (συντονία διανοίας Pl.*Def.*414a): ἄξιον ἐννοίας Id.*Lg.*657a, al. 2. *notion, conception*, χρόνου ἔννοια Id.*Ti.*47a; ἐν ταῖς περὶ τὸ ὂν.. ἐννοίαις Id.*Phlb.* 59d; ἐ. λαβεῖν to form *an idea*, opp. αἴσθησιν λαβεῖν, Id.*Phd.*73c; τοῦ καλοῦ ἐ. ἔχειν Arist.*EN*1179b15; ἐννοίας χάριν λέγειν Id.*Metaph.* 1073b12; ἔννοιαι, opp. φαντασίαι, αἰσθήσεις, Id.*MA*701b17; κατὰ ἀθρόαν ἐ. Epicur.*Ep.*1 p.23 U. (but κατὰ πᾶσαν ἐ. θυμοῦ every *kind, variety* of anger, Phld.*Ir.*p.90 W.); δοξαστικαὶ ἐ. Epicur.*Sent.*24; εἰς ἐ. ἔρχεσθαί τινος Plb.1.57.4; εἰς ἐ. τινὸς ἄγειν τινά ib.49.10; ἡ κοινὴ ἐ. the common *notion*, Id.10.27.8; κοιναὶ ἐ. *axioms*, heading in Euc.; general *ideas*, Chrysipp.*Stoic.*2.154, etc.; ψιλὴ ἐ. mere, i.e. vague, *notion*, Simp.*in Ph.*18.1. 3. *intent*, E.*Hel.*1026; ἔννοιαν λαβεῖν form *a design*, Id.*Hipp.*1027; *intention* of a testator, Is.1.13; ἐ. ἔχειν περί τι Pl.*Lg.*769e; ἐ. ἐμποιεῖν put an *idea* into one's head, Isoc.5.150; ἐ. ἐμπίπτει τινί X.*An.*3.1.13. 4. *good sense, better judgement*, παρὰ τὴν ἔννοιαν Plu.2.1077d. II. *sense* of a word, D.C.69.21. III. Rhet., *thought*, opp. *diction* (λέξις), Hermog.*Id.*2.4, cf. *Prog.*6.

**ἐννοιάδες** αἶγες, αἱ μὴ κορύπτουσιν, Hsch. (post ἐνοί).

**ἐννόμιος**, ον, *of* or *for pasturage*, ὅσ' ἄλλα ἐ. (sc. χωρία) *IG*2.1059.13 (iv B.C.), cf. *OGI*55.14 (Telmessus, iii B.C.); τὸ ἐ. *dues paid for pasturage*, *IG*2.584c7, 7.3171.49 (Orchom. Boeot.), *Inscr.Délos* 353*A* 34 (iii B.C.), *PSI*4.368.4 (iii B.C.), *OGI*629.173 (Palmyra, ii A.D.), etc.

**ἐννομολέσχης**, ου, ὁ, *prater about laws*, Timo 25.

**ἔννομος**, ον, *ordained by law, lawful, legal*, Pi.*O.*7.84; [χθονὸς αἶσα] Id.*P.*9.57; δίκα A.*Supp.*384 (lyr.), cf. E.*Ph.*1651, etc.; ἔννομα πείσονται they will suffer *lawful punishment*, Th.3.67; ἐ. ὁμολογία, πολιτεία, Pl.*Lg.*921c, Aeschin.1.5; σὺμ ψάφοις ταῖς ἐ. *Supp.Epigr.*2. 277 (Delph., ii B.C.); ἐκκλησία *IG*9(1).3 (Locr.), *Act.Ap.*19.39; ἡλικία, χρόνοι, *POxy.*247.12 (i A.D.), *Michel*468.20 (ii B.C.). Adv. -μως, ζημιοῦσθαι, διοικεῖσθαι, Lys.9.12, 30.35, cf. D.C.56.7: Comp. -ώτερον *POxy.*1204.24 (iii A.D.). 2. of persons, *keeping within the law, upright, just*, A.*Supp.*404 (lyr.), Pl.*R.*424e; also, *subject to the law*, μὴ ὢν ἄνομος Θεοῦ, ἀλλ' ἐ. Χριστοῦ 1*Ep.Cor.*9.21. II. (νέμομαι) *feeding in*, i.e. *inhabiting*, οἳ γᾶς τότ' ἦσαν ἔννομοι A.*Supp.*565 (lyr.).

**ἔννοος**, ον, always contr. **ἔννους**, ουν, *thoughtful, shrewd, sensible*, νηπίους ὄντας τὸ πρὶν ἔννους ἔθηκα A.*Pr.*444, cf. S.*OT*916; οὐδεὶς ἔ. ἐφάπτεται μαντικῆς ἐνθέου Pl.*Ti.*71e; ἔ. γίγνομαι I come *to my senses*, E.*Ba.*1270, D.31.2; ἔ. γεγονέναι ὅτι.. to be *aware* that.., Lys.10.20: Sup. ἐννούστατος Hsch. II. *intellectual*, ζωή Plot.6.2.21.

**ἔννος**, v. ἔνος (B).

**ἐννοσία**· ἀλογία, ἀργία, Hsch.

**Ἐννοσίγαιος** [σῐ], ὁ, Ep. for Ἐνοσίγ-, *Earth-shaker*, as a name of Poseidon, Il.13.43, al., Mosch.2.149, Nonn.*D.*36.126, etc.: **ἐνοσί-**, Luc.*JTr.*9.

**Ἐννοσίδᾱς** [ῑ], α, ὁ, Dor. for Ἐννοσίγαιος, Pi.*P.*4.33, *Pae.*4.41.

**ἔννοσις**, v. ἔνοσις.

**ἐννοσίφυλλος** [ῐ], ον, = εἰνοσίφυλλος, Ep. for ἐνοσιφ-: ἀήτα Simon. 41.

**ἐννοσσεύω**, v. ἐννεοσσεύω.

**ἐννοσσοποιέομαι**, Med., *make oneself a nest on*, Lxx 4*Ma.*14.16.

**ἐννότιος**, α, ον, *wet, moist*, Call.*Fr.*350.

**ἐννοχλέω**, poet. for ἐνοχλέω, Theoc.29.36.

**ἔννυθεν**· ἐκέχυντο, Hsch.

**ἐννυκτερεύω**, *pass the night in*, ἐν τῇ χώρᾳ Plb.3.22.13: abs., Hld. 3.4. 2. *stand for a night*, of preparations, Dsc.2.76.9, Philum.ap. Orib.45.29.7, Gal.13.1046.

❋ **ἕννυμι** or **ἐννύω** (Hsch., cf. ἀμφι-, καθ-), Ion. **εἵνυμι, εἱνύω** (cf. ἐπι-, κατα-): fut. ἕσω (ἀμφι-) Od.5.167, Ep. ἕσσω 16.79, etc.: Ep. aor. ἕσσα Il.5.905 (the common form only in compd. ἀμφι-έσαιμι, ἀμφι-έσασα):—**Med.**, ἐννύμαι Od.6.28: impf. ἕννυτο 5.230: Ep. fut. ἕσσομαι (ἐπιϕ-, ἐφ-) Pi.*N.*11.16, A.R.1.691: aor. (ἀμφι)..ἕσατο Il. 14.178, Ep. (ἐπί)..ἕσσαντο ib.350: Ep. 3 sg. (ἀμφὶ)..ἑέσσατο 10.23, Od.14.529:—**Pass.**, pf. εἷμαι, εἷται, 19.72, 11.191, but 2 sg. ἕσσαι 24. 250, 3 sg. ἕσται (ἐπι-) Orac.ap.Hdt.1.47: plpf. 2 sg. ἕσσο Il.3.57, Od. 16.199, 3 sg. ἕστο Il.23.67, Ep. ἕεστο 12.464, 3 dual ἕσθην 18.517, 3 pl. εἵατο ib.596; part. εἱμένος (v. infr.). (*ves-*, cf. Lat. *vestis*, Skt. *váste* 'clothes himself': ϝεσ- in βέστον, γεστία, γέστρα (qq. vv.), cf. ϝῆμα *Leg.Gort.*3.38.):—*put clothes on* another, c. dupl. acc., κεῖνός σε χλαῖνάν τε χιτῶνά τε ἕσσει he *will clothe* thee in cloak and frock, Od. 15.338, cf. 16.79; χαρίεντα δὲ εἵματα ἕσσε Il.5.905. II. Med. and Pass., c. acc. rei only, *clothe oneself in, put on, wear*, κακὰ δὲ χροΐ εἵματα εἷμαι Od.23.115; χλαίνας εὖ εἱμένοι 15.331; freq. of armour, ἕσσαντο περὶ χροΐ νώροπα χαλκόν Il.14.383, etc.; [ἀσπίδας] ἑσσάμενοι, of tall shields which *covered* the whole person, ib.372; [ξυστὰ] κατὰ στόμα εἱμένα χαλκῷ shafts *clad* with brass at their point, 15.389; of any covering, *wrap, shroud oneself in*, χλαίνας.. καθύπερθεν ἕσασθαι, of bed-clothes, Od.4.299; ἐπὶ δὲ νεφέλην ἕσσαντο Il.14.350; ἠέρα ἑσσαμένω ib.282; εἱμένος ὤμοιιν νεφέλην 15.308: metaph., λάϊνον ἕσσο χιτῶνα thou *hadst been clad* in coat of stone, i.e. stoned, 3.57; τὸν ἀεὶ κατὰ γᾶς σκότον εἱμένος S.*OC*1701; τρυχηρὰ περὶ τρυχηρὸν εἱμένην χρόα λακίσματ' E.*Tr.*496: metaph. also, φρεσὶν εἱμένος ἀλκήν Il.20.381.—Twice in Trag., elsewh. in Compds., as always in Prose.

**ἐννῠχ-εύω**, *to sleep in* or *on*, τῷ σηκῷ Plu.2.434e: metaph., Ἔρως, ὃς ἐν μαλακαῖς παρειαῖς νεάνιδος ἐννυχεύεις S.*Ant.*784 (lyr.). II. *sink*, of a star, Babr.124.16. **-ιος** [ῠ], α, ον Hes.*Th.*10, etc.; ος, ον S.*Aj.*180 (lyr.): (νύξ):—*by night, at night*, ἐ. προμολών Il.21.37; [νῆες] ἐννύχιαι κατάγοντο Od.3.178; ἐννύχιαι στεῖχον Hes. l.c.; ἐ. μέλπεσθαι Pi.*P.*3.79; ἐ. τέρψις S.*Aj.*1203 (lyr.); Ῥιπαὶ *gloom-encompassed*, Id.*OC*1248 (lyr.); φροντίδες Ar.*Eq.*1290, etc.: neut. as Adv., dub. in Parrhas.3. II. ἐννυχίων ἄναξ Ἀϊδωνεῦ king *of those who dwell in the realms of Night*, S.*OC*1558 (lyr.); cf. sq. II. III.

ἐννύχιον κρύπτεις· σκοτεινῶς καὶ δολίως, τινὲς δὲ ἐμμύχιον ἐν τῷ μυχῷ Hsch., cf. Call.*Aet.*3.1.21. **-ος**, ον, = foreg., ἄγγελος ἦλθε.. ἐννυχος Il.11.716, cf. Maiist.16; ἐ. κοῖται Pi.*P.*11.25; ὄψεις A.*Pr.*645: neut. pl. as Adv., ἔννυχα λίαν ἀναστάς *Ev.Marc.*1.35: Comp. -ώτερον Aesop.110. II. epith. of Hades, S.*Tr.*501 (lyr.).

**ἔννωθρος**, ον, *dazed*, Dsc.1.31.

**ἐννῶσαι, -νώσας**, Ion. aor. 1 inf. and part. of ἐννοέω (q. v.).

**ἐννωτίζομαι**, *carry on one's back*, Tz.*H.*4.5.

⊛ **ἐνό, ἔνο**, Dor. and Aeol., = ἐνί, Axiop.1.5, cf. *An.Ox.*1.176.

**ἐνόβρυζος**, ον, *pure, assayed*, χρυσός dub. in *POxy.*1430.16 (iv A.D.).

**ἔνογκος**, ον, *swollen*, φλέβες Steph. *in Hp.*1.206 D. II. *possessing bulk, corporeal*, Porph.*Sent.*27; τὸ ἐ. καὶ διαστατόν Iamb.*Comm. Math.*8.

⊛ **ἐνόδιος**, α, ον, Ep. **εἰνόδιος**, η, ον Il.16.260, and so Trag. in lyr., in fem. εἰνοδία: Thess. Ἐννοδία *IG*9(2).358, 1286; later ος, ον Paus. 3.14.9:—*in* or *on the way*, σφήκεσσιν ἐοικότες.. εἰνοδίοις like wasps *that have their nests by the way-side*, Il.16.260; ἐ. σύμβολοι omens *seen on the way*, portending good or ill success, A.*Pr.*487; πόλεις Plu.*Aem.*8; στάσεις σκηνῶν Id.*Ant.*9; ὅπλα *for use by the way*, D.H. 4.48. 2. Subst. ἐνόδια, τά, *nets for stopping the pathways*, X.*Cyn.* 6.9. b. *blisters caused by walking*, Thphr.*Sud.*15. II. epith. of divinities, who had their statues *by the way-side* or *at cross-roads*, most freq. of Hecate, εἰνοδίας Ἑκάτης S.*Fr.*535.2; also of Persephone, ἐνοδία θεός Id.*Ant.*1199; εἰνοδία θυγάτηρ Δάματρος E.*Ion* 1048; δαίμων ἐνοδία *IG*14.1390; and Ἐνοδία alone, Hp.*Morb.Sacr.*1, E.*Hel.*570, *AP*6.199 (Antiphil.), *IG* ll. cc.; ἡ Ἐνόδιος Paus. l.c., v.l. in Hp. l.c.; also of Hermes, Theoc.25.4, etc.

**ἐνοδῖτις**, εως, ἡ, = ἐνοδία, Orph.*H.*72.2.

⊛ **ἔνοδμος**, ον, (ὀδμή) *sweet-smelling, fresh*, Nic.*Th.*41.

⊛ **ἔνοδος**, ἡ, *visit*, *PLond.*3.1159.4 (ii A.D.).

**ἑνο-είδεια**, ἡ, *singleness*, Steph. *in Rh.*318.28. **-ειδής**, ές, *single, simple*, φωνή Nicom.*Harm.*12. II. *resembling, having the form of unity*, Plot.6.9.5, Jul.*Or.*4.139b, al., Procl. *in Prm.*p.540 S., etc.; opp. πληθοειδής, Dam.*Pr.*45: Comp., ib.38, Procl.*Inst.*62: Sup., Id. *in R.*1.177. Adv. -δῶς Jul.*Or.*4.143b, Nicom.*Ar.*1.6, Iamb.*Myst.* 1.3, Dam.*Pr.*237. ⊛ **-ζυγος**, ον, *of single pairs* of gladiators matched with beasts, κοντοκυνηγέσιον *IGRom.*4.1632.

**ἐνοιδ-έω**, *swell up in*, Hp.*Hum.*8 vulg., Antyll.ap.Orib.7.16.6: metaph. of the wounds of love, Plu.*Fr.*25.4. **-ής**, ές, *swollen*, Nic.*Al.*422. **-ίσκομαι**, = ἐνοιδέω, of vine-buds, Gal.12.187.

**ἐνοικ-άδιος**, ον, = ἐνοικίδιος, γαλεοί Aret.*CD*1.4. **-ειος**, ον, *contained in a house*: τὰ ἐ. *furniture, contents of a house*, *Rev.Ét.Gr.* 32.171 (Delos, iv/iii B.C.). **-ειόω**, *introduce among*, τὴν ἐπιείκειαν.. τοῖς ἀνθρώποις D.S.1.93:—Pass., *creep in*, τὰ κατὰ μικρὸν -ούμενα πάθη Plu.2.960a. II. *to be related*, τινί Lxx *Es.*8. 1. **-έτις**, ιδος, ἡ, *she who inhabits*, ἐ. τῶν νήσων ἡ Ἀφροδίτη Suid. **-έω**, *dwell in*, c. dat. loci, Θήβαις E.*HF*1282, etc.; χώρα καλὴ ὥστε ἐ. X.*An.*5.6.25; κατὰ στέγην E.*Alc.*1051; ἐνταῦθα Ar.*Nu.* 95: abs., οὔ τι γὰρ κεκτήμεθ'.. αὐτὸ (sc. τὸ σῶμα), πλὴν ἐνοικῆσαι βίον.. we possess it not, save *to dwell in* during life, E.*Supp.*535, cf. *Leg.Gort.*4.34, *IG*12(5).568, 1100 (Ceos, v B.C.); [Θυρέαν] ἔδοσαν ἐνοικεῖν *dwell in*, Th.4.56, cf. Hdt.2.178. 2. *to be present at*, συνελεύσει *PMasp.*3.10 (vi A.D.). 3. metaph., *dwell upon*, '*be at home in*', ἐν τοῖς φυσικοῖς Arist.*GC*316$^a$6; τοῖς συγγράμμασιν Clearch. 45. II. c. acc., *inhabit*, Th.1.18, S.*OC*1533, etc.: abs., οἱ ἐνοικοῦντες *the inhabitants*, Hdt.2.66, cf. 1.4, Th.1.91, Arist.*Pol.*1330$^b$ 8. **-ήσιμος**, ον, *habitable*, Sch.S.*OC*27. **-ησις**, εως, ἡ, *dwelling in* a place, Th.2.17, D.H.2.1. II. *right of occupation*, οἴκου *BGU*1115.39 (i B.C.), etc. **-ητήριον**, τό, *abode*, Poll.1. 73. **-ήτωρ**, ορος, ὁ, *inhabitant*, St.Byz. s. v. Πικεντία. **-ί**, Adv. *in the house, at home*, Hdn.*Epim.*255. **-ίδιος**, ον, or α, ον, *domestic*, ὄρνιθες Poll.10.156. **-ίζω**, *settle in* a place, *plant, fix in*, A.*Fr.*252; παρά τισί τι ἐ. Pl.*Epin.*978c:—Med., ἀλλοεθνεῖς -ισάμενοι γυναῖκας J.*AJ*11.5.4:—Pass., *take up one's abode in* a place, Hdt.1. 68 (so in aor. Med., Th.6.2); also, = ἐνοικέω 1. 3, ἐπιτηδεύμασι Pl. *Ax.*371c. 2. *introduce* a tenant into premises, ἐ. καὶ ἐξοικίζειν *BGU* 1116.18 (i B.C.). **-ιολόγος**, ὁ, *rent-collector*, Artem.3.41, *BGU*3, etc. **-ιος**, ον, *in the house, keeping at home*, ἐ. ὄρνις *dunghill* cock, A.*Eu.*866. II. as Subst., 1. ἐνοίκιον, τό, *house-rent*, Lys.*Fr.* 27, Is.6.21, D.48.45, *AP*11.251 (Nicarch.), Plu.*Sull.*1: pl., *BCH*6. 10 (Delos, ii B.C.), Ps.-Luc.*Philopatr.*20, *POxy.*104.15 (i A.D.): metaph., τῷ σώματι τελεῖ ἐ. ἡ ψυχή Thphr.ap.Plu.2.135e; *rent* in general, ἀποθήκης, θησαυροῦ, *BGU*32.3, *PTeb.*520. b. *allowance in lieu of quarters*, *IG*11(2).144.27 (Delos, iv B.C.). 2. ἐνοίκιον, τό, *dwelling*, D.P.668. ⊛ **-ισμα**, ατος, τό, *dwelling*, Suid. s. v. ἐναύλισμα. **-ισμός**, ὁ, *right of occupation*, οἰκίας *POxy.*104.21 (i A.D.), cf. 1641.7 (i A.D.).

**ἐνοικο-δομέω**, *build in* a place, [τῇ νήσῳ] πύργον Th.3.51; [ἐν τῇ Λακωνικῇ] τείχισμα Id.8.4; θύρετρον *BCH*6.24 (Delos, ii B.C.):—Pass., ἐν τῇ Μιλήτῳ φρούριον Th.8.84:—Med., ἐ. τεῖχος *build oneself* a fort *there*, Id.3.85. II. *build up, block up*, τὰς θύρας τῶν οἰκιῶν *PPetr.*2 p.28; θυρίδα Arr.*An.*6.29.10; εἴσοδον D.S.11.45; πυλίδα τινὰ ἐνῳκοδομημένην Th.6.51 (or perh. *built into* the wall), cf. Polyaen. 1.40.4; φάραγξ -ημένη D.S.3.37. **-δομία**, ἡ, *walling*, φρέατος *Jahresh.*11.63 (Theangela). **-λογέω**, *receive rent*, *PFlor.*1.7 (ii A.D.): c. acc., *receive rent for*, οἰκίας *PLond.*5.1708.39 (vi A.D.). **-λόγος**, ὁ, *rent-collector*, *POxy.*2008.1, *PKlein.Form.*87.2. **-νομέω**, *supply, furnish*, τῆς φύσεως τὸ γάλα ἐ. Sor.1.87.

⊛ **ἔνοικος**, ον, *inhabitant*, A.*Supp.*611, etc.; ἐ. θεός Hierocl. *in CA*11 p.441 M.: mostly c. gen. loci, *inhabitant of* a place, A.*Pr.*415 (lyr.), S.*Tr.*1092, Th.4.61, etc.: c. dat., *dweller in* a place, Pl.*Criti.*113c; ἑσμὸς τεχνιτῶν ἔνοικος πόλει Limen.20. 2. Pass., *dwelt in*, Παλλάδος ἔνοικα μέλαθρα E.*Ion* 235 (lyr.) (nisi leg. Παλλάδι συν-)

**ἐνοικουρέω**, *keep house*, of a garrison, ἐν.. D.H.6.3: metaph., ἡ μνήμη ἐνοικουροῦσα Luc.*Philops.*39.

**ἔνοινος**, ον, *full of wine*, Longus 2.1.

**ἐνοινο-φλύω**, *prate in one's cups*, Luc.*Lex.*14 (dub. l.). **-χοέω**, *pour in wine*, c. acc. cogn., οἶνον ἐνοινοχοεῦντες v.l. in Od.3.472; νέκταρ ἐνῳνοχόει v.l. ant. in Il.4.3.

**ἐνοκλάζω**, *squat upon*, τοῖς ὀπισθίοις, of a dog, Philostr.Jun.*Im.*3.

**ἔνολβος**, ον, *prosperous, wealthy*, Man.4.85.

**ἐνολισθάνω**, later **-αίνω**, aor. 2 ἐνώλισθον, *fall in*, of the ground, χάσμασι πολλοῖς Plu.*Cim.*16; *slip and fall*, of birds, Id.*Pomp.*25.

**ἔνολμος**, ον, (ὅλμος) *sitting on the tripod*, epith. of Apollo, S.*Fr.* 1044 (ἐνολμίς *Et. Gen.*).

**ἐνομήρης**, ες, = ὁμήρης ἐν.., *joined*, Nic.*Al.*238; cf. Hsch. s. v. ἐμπήρους.

**ἐνομῑλέω**, = ὁμιλέω ἐν.., D.C.43.15; τοῖς ἀνθρωπείοις καὶ φθαρτοῖς Ph.1.363, al. II. *to be well acquainted with*, πολλὰ τοῖς Πάρθων ἤθεσιν ἐνωμιληκώς Plu.*Ant.*41. III. Pass., *to be made familiar*, εὐθὺς ἐκ παιδίων -ημέναι δέξαι Polystr.p.32 W.

**ἐνομμᾰτόω**, *to furnish with eyes*, Ph.1.586, al.:—Pass., ib.540, al.

**ἐνόμνῠμαι**, Med., *make an affidavit*, ὑπέρ τινων *PHal.*1.71 (iii B.C.):—Pass., μαρτυρίαι ἐνομωμοσμέναι *sworn* depositions, ib.77. (Act. dub. in *Schwyzer* 167$^a$(3).)

**ἐνομόργνῡμι**, *wipe on*:—Med., *impress*, τῷ ἐπιπέδῳ γραμμήν Plu. 2.1081b; ἐνομόρξασθαι [τῇ ψυχῇ] τὰ τῶν πολλῶν πάθη *impress* the feelings of the vulgar *upon* it, Id.*Cic.*32.

**ἐνονυχίζει**· ἀποδέχεται *EM*344.41, *AB*258.

**ἐνόπη**, ἡ, *ear-ring*, S.*Fr.*54.

⊛ **ἐνοπή**, ἡ, (ἐνέπω) *crying, shouting*, as of birds, Τρῶες μὲν κλαγγῇ τ' ἐνοπῇ τ' ἴσαν, ὄρνιθες ὥς Il.3.2; esp. *war-cry, battle-shout*, μάχη ἐνοπή τε 12.35, 16.246, etc. (hence, *battle*, *AP*6.163 (Mel.)); also, *cry* of sorrow, ἐνοπήν τε γόον τε Il.24.160; *wild cry*, ἐν Φρυγίαισι βοαῖς ἐνοπαῖσί τε E.*Ba.*159 (lyr.). 2. generally, *voice*, ἐνοπήν τε πυθοίμην Od.10. 147; Φοίβου.. γλώσσης ἐνοπαί E.*El.*1302 (anap.), cf. *Hyps.Fr.*11(9). 13 (lyr.); νύχιοι ἐ. Id.*IT*1277 (lyr.); ταύρων ἐ. Nic.*Th.*171. 3. of things, *sound*, αὐλῶν συρίγγων τ' ἐνοπήν Il.10.13; ἰαχήν τ' ἐνοπήν τε, of thunder, Hes.*Th.*708; κιθάρας ἐ. E.*Ion*882 (anap.); σαρκῶν ἐ. ἠδ' ὀστέων *crushing*, Pi.*Fr.*168.—Ep. and Lyr. word, used by E. in lyr.

**ἐνόπιος**, v. ἐνώπιος.

**ἐνοπλ-ίζω**, *adapt to..*, ὠλέναις πλάτην Lyc.205. II. Med., *arm oneself*, Ath.1.16a:—Pass., pf. part. -ωπλισμένος *armed*, Aq.*Ex.* 13.18. ⊛ **-ιος**, ον, (ὅπλον) = ἔνοπλος, ἔρις Gorg.*Fr.*6; πρύλις Call. *Dian.*241; ἐπιστήμη D.H.20.2; πυρρίχη Anon.Vat.64: neut. as Adv., ἐλέλιξεν ἐνόπλιον Call.*Del.*137. II. ἐνόπλιος (with or without ῥυθμός), ὁ, '*martial*' *rhythm*, X.*An.*6.1.11, etc.; ῥυθμὸς κατ' ἐνόπλιον Ar.*Nu.*651; ἐ. σύνθετος Pl.*R.*400b; also νόμος Epich.75; ἀγωνία Phld.*Hom.*p.28 O.; ἐ. μέλη Ath.14.630f; Κουρήτων ἐ. παίγνια Pl. *Lg.*796b; θεῖν τὸν ἐ. Him.*Or.*2.20: hence ἐνόπλια παίζειν Pi.*O.*13. 86.—On the ῥυθμὸς κατ' ἐνόπλιον, v. Sch.Pi.*P.*2.127, Sch.Ar.*Nu.* 651. III. ἐνόπλιον, τό, *contest in arms*, of a race of war-chariots, *SIG*802 A 10 (i A.D.). **-ισμός**, ὁ, mistranslation of Hebr. *ḥōmeš* 'belly' (*ḥāmuš* = 'in battle-array'), Aq.2*Ki.*2.23, 3.27. ⊛ **-ος**, ον, *in arms, armed*, Tyrt.16, S.*OT*469 (lyr.), E.*HF*1164, *PGurob*1.7 (iii B.C.), D.H.5.28, Heraclit.*Incred.*19, etc.; κινήσεις τῶν ἐ. δραματικῶν Phld.*Mus.*p.15 K. II. *containing arms* or *armed men*, of the Trojan horse, E.*Tr.*520 (lyr.). III. εἰκὼν ἔ., = Lat. *imago clipeata*, portrait-statue *in armour*, *IPE*1.185 (Cherson., ii B.C.). IV. Adv. -ως Hsch. s. v. περιχορίζειν.

**ἐνοποι-έω**, *combine in one, unite*, Arist. *de An.*410$^b$11:—Pass., Plb. 8.4.11. II. *unify*, τὸ διακεκριμένον Dam.*Pr.*391:—Pass., ὑπό τινος Procl. *in Prm.*p.541 S. **-ός**, όν, *combining in one, uniting*, λόγος Arist.*Metaph.*1045$^b$17, cf. Porph.*Intr.*6.23. II. *creating unity*, Procl.*Inst.*13, Dam.*Pr.*33, cf. 298. Adv. -ῶς Ascl. *in Metaph.*439.25.

**ἐνοπτιλίζειν**· ἐμβλέπειν, Hsch.

**ἔνοπτος**, ον, *visible in* a thing, Arist.*Pr.*865$^b$17.

**ἐνοπτρ-ίζω**, *reflect*, Damian.*Opt.*10:—Pass., *to be seen as in a mirror*, Porph.*Marc.*13, Olymp. *in Mete.*230.17:—Med., *see as in a mirror*, ἑαυτούς Ph.1.451, cf. Plu.2.696a; τὸ τῆς ἀληθείας κάλλος Hierocl. *in CA Praef.*p.416 M. ⊛ **-ικοί**, οἱ, *optical geometers*, Olymp. *in Mete.* 69.18. II. neut. pl. ἐνοπτ(ρ)ικά, τά, title of work by Philip of Opus, Suid. s. v. φιλόσοφος. **-ισις**, εως, ἡ, *representation as in a mirror, reflection*, Plot.3.6.17. **-ον**, τό, *mirror*, E.*Hec.*925 (lyr.), *Or.*1112, *Not.Scav.*1920.328: generally, *reflecting surface*, ἐν ὕδατι καὶ τοῖς τοιούτοις ἐ. Arist.*Mete.*345$^b$26, cf. 372$^a$33.

**ἐνόρ-ᾱσις**, εως, ἡ, *beholding*, θεοῦ Porph.*Marc.*13. **-άω**, fut. ἐνόψομαι Iamb. *in Nic.*p.38 P.: aor. ἐνεῖδον (q. v.): aor. 1 Pass. ἐνώφθην *Theol.Ar.*30:—*see, remark, observe* something *in* a person or thing, τί τινι Th.3.30, X.*Cyr.*1.4.27, etc.; τι ἔν τινι Hdt.1.89, Th.1.95, Lys. 33.9 codd.; ἐν γὰρ τῷ οὐκ ἐνεώρα (sc. τὸ τυραννικόν) Hdt.3.53; ἐν τῷ χαλκίῳ ἐνορῶ γέροντα δειλίας φευξούμενον Ar.*Ach.*1129: c. acc. et fut. part., ἐνεώρα τιμωρίην ἐσομένην he *saw* that vengeance would come, Hdt.1.123, al.: c. dat. pers. et part., ἐνορῶ ὑμῖν οὐκ οἵοισί τε ἐσομένοισι πολεμεῖν Id.8.140.β':—Pass., Iamb. *in Nic.*p.43 P. II. *look at, behold*, Arist.*Fr.*153; δεινὸν ἐ. τοῖς παισί Plu.*Publ.*6; ἐνορῶντες ἐς ἀλλήλους δεινόν Paus.4.8.2.

⊛ **ἐνοργείας**· τὰς νεοσσείας (Cret.), Hsch.

**ἐνόρειος**, ον, (ὄρος) *in the mountains*, prob. for ἐνόριον, Scymn.832.

**ἐνορθιάζω**, *raise up*, πλέον τῆς φύσεως ἑαυτήν Ph.2.265 (dub.).

**ἐνόριος**, ον, (ὅρος) *within the boundaries*, Poll.9.8; *on the boundaries*, θεοί Hld.10.1: Subst. ἐνορία, ἡ, *territory* of a city, πόλις καὶ ἐ. *POxy.*1101.5 (iv A.D.), cf. *Cod.Just.*1.2.25.1, etc.

**ἐνορκ-ίζομαι**, Med., *make* one *swear*, ἐ. τινὶ ποιεῖν τι *IG*12(5).697.4 (Syros); ἐ. τινὶ ὅρκον ib.9(1).643 (Cephallenia), cf. J.*AJ*8.15.4 (v.l. ἐνωρκήσατο):—later in Act., ἐνορκίζω ὑμᾶς τὸν κύριον ἀναγνωσθῆναι τὴν ἐπιστολήν 1*Ep.Thess.*5.27; ἐ. ὑμῖν τὸν βασιλέα τῶν δαιμόνων *Tab. Defix.Aud.*26.15 (Cyprus, iii A.D.). ❀ -ιος, ον, = ἔνορκος, λόγος Pi. *O.*2.92. 2. Subst. ἐνόρκιον, τό, *oath*, Lxx *Nu.*5.21. II. = ἔνσπονδος, *GDI*3045 (Olympia). ❀ -ος, ον, *having sworn, bound by oath*, ἔνορκόν τινα θέσθαι to bind one *by oath*, S.*Ph.*811; ἔ. λαμβάνειν τὸν Ἀθηναίων δῆμον Aeschin.3.90, cf. 2.116, Arist.*Rh.*1396ᵇ19: c. dat. pers., ἔ. οὐδενί S.*Ph.*72. 2. = ἔνσπονδος, *included in a treaty*, Th.2.72. II. *that whereto one is sworn*, θεῶν ἔ. δίκη S.*Ant.*369 (lyr.); ἔνορκον [εἶμεν] τοῖς ἐπιοίκοις μὴ ποσταμεν *IG* 1².334.11 (v B.C.); παρακαταθήκην ἔνορκον εἰληφὼς παρὰ τῶν νόμων, of the jurors, D.25.11; ἔ. προσφώνησις *Stud.Pal.*22.184.88 (ii A.D.); ἔνορκόν τι καταστῆσαι Aeschin.2.176; τῷ μὴ βουλομένῳ μὴ εἶναι ἔνορκον συμμαχεῖν X.*HG*6.5.18; of a decree, *Rev.Ét.Gr.*24.415 (Itanos, ii B.C.); ἔνορκον ποιεῖσθαι to bind oneself *by oath*, Pl.*Phd.*89c; ἔνορκον ἐποίσει τὴν ψῆφον, Lat. *juratus feret sententiam*, D.H.7.45. Adv. -κως Lxx *To.*8.20, Ath.6.274e, Poll.1.39. b. *consecrated by oath*, λίθος Pl. *Lg.*843a. -όω, *adjure*, *BGU*836.9 (vi A.D.), etc.; ἐνορκῶ σε κατὰ τοῦ πατρός Sch. Luc.*Cat.*23.

❀ **ἐνορμ-άω**, *rush in*, εἴς τι Plb.16.28.8 (prob. for ἐνήρμοσεν); ἐνορμῶντα, τά, = πνεύματα (viz. φυσικόν and ψυχικόν), Hp.ap.Gal.7.597 and Pall. *in Hp.*2.200 D. (v.l. in Hp.*Epid.*6.8.7). -έω, *ride at anchor in* a harbour, Plb.16.29.13: metaph., Ph.1.523:—Med., J.*AJ*15.9.6. -ίζω, *bring* a ship *to land*: hence metaph., κύρτον ῥοθίοισι Opp.*H.*3.409:—Med., *enter harbour*, Str.5.4.6, D.H.1.56, Ph.2.8, etc.: metaph., λιμέσιν ἀρετῆς Id.1.658, al.:—also in Pass., ἐκ θυελλῶν ἐνωρμίσθην Thgn.1274. ❀ -ιον (ἐνόρμιν ostr.), τό, *harbour-dues*, *Ostr.*263,304, Hsch. s.v. ἀγκυροβόλῳ δείπνῳ. -ισμα, ατος, τό, *anchorage, roadstead*, App.*BC*4.106. -ίτης [ῑ], ου, poet. -τας, αο, ὁ, *in harbour*, *AP*10.2 (Antip. Sid.), 10.14.9 (Agath.). -ος· ἡ ὥρα παρὰ Θετταλοῖς, Hsch.

**ἐνόρνυμι**, aor. 1 ἐνῶρσα: Ep. aor. 2 Pass. ἐνῶρτο:—the only two tenses used by Hom.:—*arouse, stir up in* a person, τῇσιν γόον ἐνῶρσεν Il.6.499; [Ἀχαιοῖς] ἀνάλκιδα φύζαν ἐνόρσας 15.62; ἐν δὲ σθένος ὦρσεν ἑκάστῳ 2.451; φόβον τινί 11.544; [μάχαν] (sc. ἄμμιν) Alc.*Supp.*23.12; θάρσος δ' ἐνῶρτε.. στρατῷ E.*Supp.*713:—Pass., *arise in* or *among*, ἐνῶρτο γέλως θεοῖσιν Il.1.599.

**ἐνορούω**, *leap in* or *upon*, usu. of an assault, c. dat., Τρωσὶ.. ἐνόρουσεν Il.16.783; ὡς δὲ λέων.. αἴγεσιν ἢ ὀΐεσσι.. ἐνορούσῃ 10.486: abs., ἐν δ' Ἀγαμέμνων πρῶτος ὄρουσε 11.217; ὕδωρ ἀνέδην ἐνοροῦον prob. in Hp.*Cord.*2; of fish, νήεσσιν ἐ. Opp.*H.*2.516.

**ἐνορύσσω**, *dig*, plpf. Pass. ἐνωρώρυκτο, κολυμβήθρα Philostr.*VA*2.27.

**ἐνορχέομαι**, = ὀρχέομαι ἐν.., Alciphr.3.65.

**ἐνόρχ-ης**, ου, ὁ, = ἔνορχος, Ar.*Eq.*1385, al., Arist.*HA*632ᵃ20; **ἐνορχής**, ές, *SIG*57.20 (Milet., vi B.C.). 2. Dor. τὸν ἐνόρχαν (acc.), *he goat*, Theoc.3.4 (ἐνόρχαν v.l. ap.Sch.). 3. title of Dionysus at Phigalia, Lyc.212; at Samos, Hsch. ❀ -ις, ιος, ὁ, ἡ, Ion. for foreg., Hdt.6.32, 8.105, Luc.*DDeor.*4.1. -ος, ον, (ὄρχις) *with the testicles in, uncastrated, entire*, ἔνορχα.. μῆλ' ἱερεύσειν, i.e. rams, Il.23.147; τὰ ἔ. *entire animals*, Hp.*Vict.*2.49; also of palm-trees, Arist.*Fr.*267 codd. Ath.

**ἔνος** (A), ὁ, *year*, Lyd.*Mens.*4.1, Hsch.

**ἔνος** (B), η, ον, found only in oblique cases of fem., gen. ἔνης, Ep. ἔνηφι, dat. ἔνῃ, acc. ἔνην, in the sense of εἰς τρίτην, *the day after tomorrow*: ἔς τ' αὔριον ἔς τε ἔνηφιν Hes.*Op.*410 (v.l. ἔς τ' ἔννηφι); gen. ἔνης Ar.*Ec.*796, Dor. ἔνας Theoc.18.14; εἰς ἔνην Ar.*Ach.*172; αὔριον ⟨καὶ⟩ τῇ ἔνῃ Antipho6.21; ἐς ἔνης ἡ prob. l. (for ἐς ἓν ἡ σή) in D.C.47.41; cf. ἔναρ· ἐς τρίτην (Lacon.), Hsch., and v. ἐπέναρ. (Demonstr. stem *eno-* (*ono-*), cf. Umbr. *enom* 'tum', Slav. *onŭ* 'he'.)

❀ **ἕνος** (C), η, ον (so Att. Inscrr., Ar.*Nu.*1134, Pl.*Cra.*409b; in codd. freq. written ἔνος, as Hes.*Op.*770, etc.), *belonging to the former of two periods* (τὸ ἕνον..· τὸ πρότερον καὶ παρεληλυθὸς δηλοῖ, Harp.; ἕνην· τὴν παλαιάν, Suid.), ὁ νόμος ἐπὶ Κρόνου ἕνος (opp. νεωστί) Dam. *Pr.*348: hence, *last year's*, ἕναι ἀρχαὶ *last year's* magistrates, D.25.20, prob. in Arist.*Pol.*1322ᵃ12; στρατηγοὶ ἕνοι Id.*Ath.*4.2; Ἑλληνοταμίαι ἕνοι *IG*1².324.26; ἕνης ἐπιφορᾶς ib.218138; ἕνος [καρπός] *last year's* fruit, Thphr.*HP*3.4.6; also ἕνος ὄνος *a year old*, *BGU*806: generally, *old, by-gone*, νέον δέ που καὶ ἕνον ἀεί ἐστι περὶ τὴν σελήνην τοῦτο τὸ φῶς Pl.*Cra.*409b:—in Ar.*Ach.*610 ἤδη πεπρέσβευκας σὺ πολιὸς ὢν ἕνη, the Sch. takes ἕνη as an Adv. = ἐκ πολλοῦ, *long ago*; but the passage is prob. corrupt. 2. ἕνη καὶ νέα (sc. ἡμέρα) *the old and new day*, i.e. *the last day of the month*, *IG*1².374.276, Ar.*Nu.*1134sq., Lys.23.6: first used by Solon, acc. to D.L.1.57; Σκιροφοριῶνος ἕνῃ καὶ νέᾳ *IG*2².916.10, cf. Decr.ap.D.18.29; ἕνη alone, Hes. *Op.*770. (Cf. Lith. *sěnas* 'old', Lat. *senex*, etc.)

**ἐνοσίζεται**· τρέμει, σείεται, Cyr.

**ἔνοσις**, εως, ἡ, *shaking, quake*, Hes.*Th.*681, 849; αἰθερίαι ἐ. E.*Hel.*1363 (lyr.), cf. Orph.*Fr.*285.24; ἔννοσις· κίνησις, Hsch. II. personified in poet. form Ἔννοσις, prob. in E.*Ba.*585 (lyr.).

**Ἐνοσίχθων**, ονος, ὁ, *Earth-shaker*, epith. of Poseidon, Il.7.445, al.; Ἐ. alone, 13.89, al. II. later, as Adj., *earth-stirring*, ἄροτρον Euph.152; σίδηρος Nonn.*D.*2.67.

**ἑνότης**, ητος, ἡ, (εἷς) *unity*, Arist.*Metaph.*1018ᵃ7, *Ph.*222ᵃ19, Plot.6.6.16, etc.; ἡ ἐ. ἐν ἑτερότητι Porph.*Sent.*36; τοῦ αἵματος Arist.*PA* 667ᵇ30. II. *union*, συμπάθεια πρὸς ἀλλήλους καὶ ἐ. ἰδιότροπος Epicur.*Ep.*1 p.13 U.; τοῦ πνεύματος τῆς πίστεως *Ep.Eph.*4.3, 13; ἑνότητα ποιεῖν Plu.2.769f. III. in concrete sense, ἀπογεγεννημένη ἐ. Epicur.*Nat.Herc.*1634.1; τῶν αἰσθητῶν ἐ. Demetr.Lac.1055.7 F., cf. Phld.*Piet.*80 (pl.).

**ἔνοτος**, Aeol., = ἔνατος (q.v.).

**ἔνουλα**, τά, (οὖλον) *gums inside the teeth*, Poll.2.94.

❀ **ἐνουλίζομαι**, Pass., *to be curly*, of hair, Aristaenet.1.1, Alciphr.*Fr.*5.4.

**ἔνουλον**, τό, *wound*, Phld.*D.*1.24.

**ἔνουλος**, ον, *curled, curly*, πλόκαμοι ἔ. Callistr.*Stat.*3.

**ἐνουράνιος** [ᾰ], ον, *in heaven, heavenly*, *AP*9.223 (Bianor), Poll.1.23; ἀνάγκη *Sammelb.*5620.9.

**ἐνουρ-έω**, aor. 1 ἐνεούρησα Eup.45:—*make water in*, ἔς τι Hdt.1.138, 2.172; εἰς τὰ ὦτα Porph.*Abst.*3.3; ἔν τινι Hermipp.82.1: abs., ὥσπερ ἐνεουρηκότες like *piss-a-beds*, Ar.*Lys.*402, cf. Arist.*Pr.*876ᵃ15, Dsc.*Eup.*2.106, Paul.Aeg.3.45. -ήθρα, ἡ, or -ηθρον, τό, *chamber-pot*, S.*Fr.*485. -ητής, οῦ, ὁ, = *subulciolus*, *Gloss.*, Sch.Ar.*Eq.*399.

**ἐνουσι-ακῶς**, Adv. dub. sens. in *BGU*277 ii 10 (ii A.D., fort. ἐν οὐσιακοῖς). -όομαι, *acquire substance*, τῇ φύσει τῆς γῆς Dam.*Pr.*74, cf. 81; ὁ τοῦ χρόνου λόγος ἀΐδιος [φύσει] ἐνουσιωμένος Id.ap.Simp.*in Ph.*780.5. II. *subsist in*, ὁ τοῖς λογικοῖς γένεσιν ἐνουσιωμένος ὅρκος Hierocl.*in CA*20 p.422 M. ❀ -ος, ον, = συμφυής, Hsch. 2. = πολυκτήμων, Id. 3. Adv. -ίως *on the security of one's property*, *CPR*4.15 (iv A.D.).

**ἐνοφείλω**, *owe on security*, *IG*14.956ᴮ16 (iv A.D.): generally, *owe*, *POxy.*986:—Pass., *to be due upon a security*, τινί to one, D.50.10; ἐν οὐσίᾳ *secured on property*, Id.49.45: generally, *to be due, owing*, ὅ τι ἐνοφείλεται *Rev.Laws*18.17, al. (iii B.C.), cf. *IG*2.1134, *PTeb.*17.6 (ii B.C.), etc.

**ἐνοφθαλμ-ιάζομαι**, Pass., *admit of being inoculated*, Plu.2.640b tit. -ιάω, *cast longing eyes upon*, v.l. for ἐπ-, Poll.2.62. -ίζω, *inoculate, bud*, δένδρον ἐν ἀπὸ πλειόνων Thphr.*CP*5.5.4, cf. *Gp.*10.77.1:—Pass., *Inscr.Délos*366 B 20, Procl.*in Cra.*p.39 P. -ισμός, ὁ, *budding*, *Gp.*10.77.1: pl., Thphr.*CP*1.6.1, 2, Plu.2.640b.

**ἔνοφρυς**, υ, *with bushy eyebrows*, *Gloss.* (dub.).

❀ **ἐνοχή**, ἡ, *liability, obligation*, *PLand.*48.11 (vi A.D.), etc.; ἀγωγὴ καὶ ἐ. conduct and *responsibility* of a transaction, *POxy.*133.7 (vi A.D.).

❀ **ἐνοχία**, ἡ, dub. in *PTeb.*112.10 (ii B.C.).

❀ **ἐνοχλ-έω**, Aeol. and poet. 2 sg. ἐννοχλεῖς Theoc.29.36: impf. with double augm. ἠνώχλουν X.*Cyr.*5.3.56, Isoc.5.53, etc.: fut. ἐνοχλήσω Id.15.153: aor. ἠνώχλησα D.19.206: pf. ἠνώχληκα Id.21.4:—Pass., fut. -ηθήσομαι D.H.10.3, Polystr.p.8 W.; also -ήσομαι (in pass. sense) Id.p.6 W., App.*BC*1.36, Gal.*UP*11.19 (as v.l.): aor. part. ἐνοχληθείς Hp.*Coac.*510: pf. ἠνώχλημαι (παρ-) D.18.50:—*trouble, annoy*, τινά Pl.*Alc.*1.104d, Diod.Com.2.18, X.*Mem.*3.8.2, etc.; *simply, address*, *PMag.Leid.W.*3.34:—Pass., *to be troubled* or *annoyed*, X.*Cyr.*5.4.34, D.19.20; ἡ ἐκκλησία ἠνωχλεῖτο Aeschin.2.43; *to be unwell*, Lxx *Ge.*48.1, al.; of a horse, *PPetr.*3 p.73 (iii B.C.); *to be overburdened with work*, *PHamb.*27.18 (iii B.C.), etc. 2. c. dat., *give trouble* or *annoyance to*, Lys.24.21; τοῖς ἀκούουσιν Isoc.4.7; τῇ ὑμετέρᾳ εὐδαιμονίᾳ X.*An.*2.5.13, cf. Amphis 15, Epicur.*Nat.*11.10; ἠνώχλει ἡμῖν D.3.5, etc. 3. abs., *to be a trouble, a nuisance*, Hp.*Aph.*2.50, Ar.*Ra.*708, Epicur.*Ep.*3 p.61 U., etc.: with neut. Adj., ὅσα.. ἠνώχλησεν all *the trouble* he *has given*, D.21.15: c. part., τὸ δὲ μὴ οὐκ ἠνώχλει λέγων X.*Cyr.*5.3.56. II. *worry about, fuss over*, τὰς ἀρετὰς τὰς ὑπὸ τούτων ἐνοχλουμένας Diog.Oen.25.—Prose word, sts. used in Com., never in Trag. -ημα, ατος, τό, *trouble, worry*, Epicur.*Fr.*154. II. Medic., *distress, malaise*, Apollon.ap.Orib.7.2.3. -ησις, εως, ἡ, *annoyance*, Philem.92.3 (pl.), *PLond.*3.971.4 (iv A.D.); ἐ. σοφιστικαί Arist.*Int.*17ᵃ7, cf. D.L.7.14, 112, Procl.*in Alc.*p.333 C. -ητέον, *one must annoy*, οὐκ ἐ. τῷ θεῷ Max.Tyr.11.4.

**ἐνοχο-ποιέω**, *convict*, τινα ἐπί τινι Anon.*in Rh.*237.25. -ποιός, όν, *creating obligations*, *Gloss.*

❀ **ἔνοχος**, ον, = ἐνεχόμενος, *held in, bound by*, τοιαύταις δόξαις Arist. *Metaph.*1009ᵇ17; ταῖς εἰρημέναις βλάβαις Id.*Pol.*1337ᵇ17; [ἔθεσι γεροντικοῖς] Apollod.Com.7.. 2. c. gen., *connected with*, κοιλίης Hp.*Ep.*23. II. as law-term, *liable to, subject to*, νόμοις, δίκαις, Pl.*Lg.*869b; τῇ γραφῇ X.*Mem.*1.2.64; τῇ κρίσει *Ev.Matt.*5.22; τῷ ὅρκῳ *PRyl.*82.14 (ii A.D.), etc.; τοῖς ἐπιτιμίοις τοῦ φόνου Antipho4.1.6; ζημίαις Lys.14.9; ταῖς ἀραῖς D.19.201; δεσμῷ Id.51.4; ὅρκῳ *PHib.*1.65.22 (iii B.C.), etc.; ἐ. ἀνοίαις *liable to the imputation of* it, Isoc.8.7; ἁμαρτήμασι Aeschin.2.146; τοῖς αἰσχίστοις ἐπιτηδεύμασιν Id.1.185. 2. ἔνοχος ψευδομαρτυρίοις *liable to action for*.., Pl.*Tht.*148b: c. gen., ἐ. τοῦ φόνου Antipho6.46; βιαίων, λιποταξίου (sc. δίκῃ, γραφῇ), Pl.*Lg.*914e, Lys.14.5; ἱεροσυλίας Lxx 2*Ma.*13.6; μοιχείας Vett.Val.117.10; ἐ. θανάτου *liable to the penalty of* death, D.S.27.4, *Ev.Matt.*26.66 (but θανάτῳ Wilcken *Chr.*13.11 (i A.D.)): c. inf., ἔ. ἔστω ἀποτῖσαι *CIG*2832.8 (Aphrodisias). 3. less freq. with Preps., ἐ. ἐν τοῖς αὐτοῖς Decr.ap.And.1.79; περὶ ταῦτα Arist.*Rh.*1384ᵇ2; ἔνοχοι ἔντω ἐνς Ἀθαναίαν *IG*4.554 (Argos, vi/v B.C.). 4. *guilty, liable to the penalty for*, ἐ. τῷ φόνῳ Antipho1.11, Arist.*Pol.*1269ᵃ3, cf. *Rh.*1380ᵃ3: abs., Antipho4.1.1, 6.17, Pl.*Sph.*261a, etc. b. of property, *subject to liability*, *PMasp.*312.86 (vi A.D.).

**ἔνοψις**, εως, ἡ, (ὄψομαι) = ἔποψις, Them.*Or.*13.177d.

❀ **ἑνόω**, (εἷς) *make one, unite*, λίαν τὴν πόλιν Arist.*Pol.*1261ᵇ10: τὰ

ἐναντιώτατα Archyt.ap.Stob.1.41.2; τὰ πολυμιγῆ Herm.ap.eund.1.49.3; τὸ ἀκούειν τῷ πράττειν Ph.1.609: ἐνοῦν τινὰ τῇ γῇ to bury him, Philostr.*Im.*2.29; of *mixing* drugs, ἀκριβῶς ἕνωσον Dsc.*Eup.* 1.13, cf. 1.31 (Pass.):—Pass., Ph.1.471, al., Cleom.2.1, etc.; ἡνῶσθαι τὰ πάντα Arr.*Epict.*1.14.2; λίμνη.. ἡνωμένη τῇ θαλάσσῃ Ath.7.311d; τὰ φύσει ἡνωμένα *things united* by nature, Longin.22.3; τὰ ἡ. *propositions couched in the singular number*, Id.24.1; ἡνωμένοι, opp. ἀσύντακτοι, of troops, J.*BJ*3.2.2; esp. in Philos., *unified*, τὸ μὲν ὂν ἀριθμὸς ἡνωμένος Plot.6.6.9; τὸ ἡ., = τὸ ὄν, Dam.*Pr.*20, cf. 68, al.

ἐνρ-, see also ἐρρ-.

* **ἐνραβῶς**· ἐγγράψας, Hsch.

**ἐνράπτω**, *sew up in*, βυβλίον εἰς ἡνίαν χαλινοῦ Aen.Tact.31.9, Plu. *Arat.*25:—Med., Διόνυσον ἐνερράψατο ἐς τὸν μηρόν into *his* thigh, Hdt. 2.146, cf. *IG*14.1285,1292:—Pass., *to be sewed up in*, ἐνερράφη Διὸς μηρῷ E.*Ba.*286; ἱμάντα ἐν ᾧ ἐπιστολὴ ἐνέρραπτο Aen.Tact.31.32; λίθοι ἐνερραμμένοι τῷ ἐσθῆνι J.*AJ*3.8.9.

**ἐνράσσω**, *dash against*, ταῖς πύλαις J.*AJ*5.8.10.

**ἔνρειθρον**, *endoriginum*, *Gloss.*

**ἐνρήγνῦμι**, *break into*:—Pass., *discharge itself into*, ἐς ἔντερον Aret. *SA*1.10. II. intr. in pf. part. Act. ἐνερρωγώς, υῖα, ός, *broken*, κλῖναι *IG*11(2).199*B*90 (iii B.C.).

**ἔνρηξις**, εως, ἡ, *impact*, *Gloss.* **ἐνρήσσω**, = ἐνρήγνυμι, Apollod. *Poliorc.*141.2.

**ἐνρητορεύω**, *show eloquence in*, πατρῴοις λόγοις Heraclit.*All.*63.

**ἐνρῑγισκάνω**, *shiver in*, τριβώνιον πονηρὸν οἷον -ειν *Com.Adesp.*10 D.

**ἐνρῑγόω**, = ῥιγόω ἐν, *shiver* or *freeze in*, Ar.*Pl.*846.

**ἔνριζ-ος**, ον, *with a root*, *Gp.*3.4.6. **-όω**, *implant*, τῷ ἐγκεφάλῳ Hp.*Oss.*12; -οῦσα τὸ νεῦρον ὡς εἰς γῆν τὰ μόρια Gal.*UP*7.15; Εὔβοιαν θαλάσσῃ Nonn.*D.*42.411: Pass., Gal.*UP*11.14: so metaph., *to be rooted*, *grounded in*, τῇ οἰκείᾳ ἀκρότητι Dam.*Pr.*258; τῇ σφῶν αἰτίᾳ ib.34; of conditions, *become firmly established*, ἡ διάθεσις ἐνερριζῶσθαι φαίνεται Orib.*Syn.*9.12.1. **-ωσις**, εως, ἡ, *rooting in*, Simp.*in Ph.* 637.1.

**ἐνρίπτω**, *throw in*, αὐτὸν ἐς τὴν πόλιν Arr.*An.*6.10.4; λίθον D.C. 74.14.

* **ἔνρυθμος**, ον, *of rhythm*, αἴσθησις Pl.*Lg.*654a; *possessing rhythm* (opp. εὔρυθμος), D.H.*Comp.*11; διάλεκτος Ephor.6 J.; opp. ἔκρυθμος, S.E.*M.*11.186. Adv. -μως Ath.5.179f, 14.631b (prob.).

**ἐνρῡσόομαι**, *become wrinkled*, ἐνερρυσωμένος *rugose*, Meges ap.Orib. 44.24.2.

**ἐνς ἅς**· αὔριον, Hsch. (ἔνσας cod.: Cretan or Argive form); cf. εἰς, ἅας.

**ἐνσαλπίζω**, *sound a trumpet in*, τοῖς ὠσί Gal.12.656.

**ἔνσαρκος**, ον, *of flesh*, ἐ. βορά *flesh* meat, Porph.*Abst.*1.1, cf. *Gaur.* 3.2.

**ἐνσᾰρόομαι**, Pass., *to be swept about in*.., πόντου.. ἐνσαρούμενος μυχοῖς Lyc.753.

**ἐνσάττω**, *stuff in*, of one eating sausages, Alciphr.3.7.

**ἐνσᾰφῶς**, Adv. *clearly*, *BGU*713.

**ἐνσβέννῠμαι**, Pass., *to be quenched in*, ὕδατι Dsc.5.80.2.

* **ἔνσειμι**, Cret. for εἴσειμι, *enter*, 3 sg. pres. subj. ἐνσείῃ *Leg.Gort.* 5.36.

* **ἐν-σεισμός**, ὁ, *attack*, of engines of war. Thd.*Ez.*26.9. * **-σείω**, pf. ἐνσέσεικα *BGU*136.11 (ii A.D.):—*brandish* or *hurl at*, c. acc. rei, ἐ. βέλος κεραυνοῦ S.*Tr.*1087; ὀξὺν δι' ὤτων κέλαδον ἐ. πώλοις *drive* a shrill sound into their ears, Id.*El.*737; ἐνέσεισε.. μεταντιπτρίδα Philetaer.1. 2. c. acc. pers., *plunge in*, *drive into*, ἐ. τινὰ ἀγρίαις ὁδοῖς S.*Ant.*1274; ἑαυτοὺς τῇ ἐπιτροπῇ *BGU* l.c.; ἑαυτὸν τῇ ἑστίᾳ Luc.*Asin.*31; σπινθῆρας πυρὸς ὑγιαίνοντι σώματι Gal.7.182; οἱ κακῶν αὐτὴν ἐνέσεισας Alciphr.3.27; τὸν Ἀρχίαν εἰς τὸν πότον Plu.2.588b; εἰς βάραθρον ἐ. τινά Luc.*Merc.Cond.*30; ἐ. τὴν πόλιν εἰς πόλεμον Plu. *Phoc.*23; ἐ. χιόνα εἰς τὸν ἄκρατον Macho ap.Ath.13.579f:—Pass., εἰς ὠνήν *to be jockeyed* into a purchase, Hyp.*Ath.*26. b. c. acc. rei, *loosen*, *damage*, μέρος τοῦ χάρακος *BGU*1215.15 (iii B.C.). 3. Pass., *to be interpolated*, Sch.Il.23.104. 4. *shake*, *jar*, Hp.*Off.*25 (Pass.); ἐ. βάσιν *jar* one's foot, Luc.*Ocyp.*9. 5. *dash to the ground*, νήπια Lxx 4*Ki.*8.12. 6. Pass., ἐνσεσεισμένη *broken by age*, *Com. Adesp.*1001. 7. metaph., *shake thoroughly*, Pass., ἐνσείσθητι Arr. *Epict.*3.14.3. II. intr., *rush upon*, *attack*, (sc. ναυσί) πλαγίαις D.S. 13.40; εἰς τὰς ναῦς Id.14.60; τοῖς πολεμίοις κατὰ τὸ δεξιὸν κέρας D.H. 9.16, cf. Plu.*Alex.*60; πόνοι ἐ. εἰς ὀσφὺν *shoot*, Ruf.*Ren.Ves.*1.3:—Med., *jostle*, Arr.*Epict.*4.4.24, v.l. in Epict.*Ench.*4:—Pass., τοῖς κιόσιν ἐνσεισθεὶς J.*AJ*5.8.12.

**ἐνσεμνύνομαι**, Pass., *glory in*, προγόνοις Onos.1.24.

**ἐνσήθω**, *sift in*, Aret.*CA*1.1.

**ἐνσημαίνω**, *contain a signification*, *imply*, ὅτι ἀγαστὸς.. ἐνσημαίνει τὸ ὄνομα Ἀγαμέμνων Pl.*Cra.*395b. 2. *report*, *signal*, τὴν αἴσθησιν Arist.*de An.*423ᵃ4:—Pass., *to be indicated or expressed*, ἐ. ἡ ἀναίδεια ἐν τοῖς ὀφθαλμοῖς Longin.4.4. 3. *show in*, Philostr.*VA*6.22. II. Med., *give notice of*, *intimate*, τινὶ τὴν ὀργήν Isoc.20.22, cf. Arist.*Ath.* 18.2; τοῦτο, ὅτι.. X.*Cyr.*8.2.3:—Pass., *POxy.*396 (i A.D.). 2. *give signs one to another*, X.*Cyn.*6.22. 3. *impress* or *stamp upon*, σημεῖα Pl.*Tht.*191d, cf. 209c; τύπον ἐ. ἑκάστῳ Id.*R.*377b: Pass., *to be imprinted*, εἴς τι Id.*Tht.*194c, cf. Ph.1.242; ὑπὸ τῶν ἐννοιῶν ἐνσεσημασμένον.. λόγον Diog.Bab.*Stoic.*3.216.

* **ἔνσημος**, ον, *significant*, *important*, Hp.*Superf.*17: f.l. for ἐπίσημος, κώμη *Peripl.M.Rubr.*54. II. *coined*, νόμισμα Tz.*H.*1.928.

**ἐνσήπομαι**, Pass., *putrefy within*, Hp.*Morb.*1.18, Lyd.*Mag.*3.61.

**ἔνσηστρον**, τό, *sieve*, *Gloss.* (prob.).

**ἔνσῑμος**, ον, *somewhat snub nosed*, *PPetr.*3p.21 (iii B.C.), etc.: f.l. for ἔνσημος, Hp.*Superf.*17:—written ἔσσιμος, *PCair.Zen.*76.11. II. *concave*, of surfaces, Ruf.*Anat.*40,52.

**ἐνσῑνής**, ές, (σίνος) *injured*, Man.2.445; *in ill-health*, *BGU*560.22 (iv A.D.).

**ἐνσῑτ-έομαι**, Med., *feed upon*, Lxx *Jb.*40.25(30). **-ος**, ον, *public guest*, a title of honour at Sparta, *IG*5(1).53.35, al. II. *fed*, *replete*, *Hippiatr.*111.

**ἐνσκέλλω**, Ep. ἐνισκ-, *dry* or *wither up*, μή τοι ἐνισκήλῃ.. Nic.*Th.* 694:—Pass., with pf. Act. ἐνέσκληκα, *to be dry*, *withered*, Hp.*Morb.* 1.28; ἐνεσκληκὼς γὰρ ἀνίαις *AP*12.166 (Asclep.): also of timber, *to be dry*, *seasoned*, A.R.3.1251.

**ἐνσκέπαρνος**, ον, *oblique*, of bandages, Heliod.ap.Orib.48.64.2.

**ἐνσκευ-άζω**, *get ready*, *prepare*, δεῖπνον Ar.*Ach.*1096; *harness*, ἵππους Polyaen.7.21.6:—Med., *contrive*, διαβολάς J.*BJ*1.3.2. 2. *dress in*, ἱματίῳ τινά Plu.*Lyc.*15, cf. Luc.*Nec.*8; ὅτι ἤ σε.. Ἡρακλέα 'νεσκεύασα *dressed* you *up* as Hercules, prob. l. in Ar.*Ra.*523:—Med., *dress oneself up*, Id.*Ach.*384, Pl.*Cri.*53d; δουλικῶς Phryn.Com.2 D.; *arm oneself*, X.*Cyr.*8.5.11; ἱππεῖς -σάμενοι τοὺς ἵππους *having put trappings on their* horses, Jul.*Or.*2.76d:—but Med. just like Act., Luc.*Asin.*37:—Pass., *to be equipped*, ἐνεσκεύαστο γὰρ οὕτως Hdt.9. 22; ἀναξυρίσι καὶ χειρῖσιν ἐ. Plu.*Oth.*6; εἰς εἰκόνα τοῦ δημιουργοῦ, τοῦ ἡλίου, Porph.ap Eus.*PE*3.12: metaph., σωφροσύνην ἐνεσκευασμένος Ph.1.682. **-ος**, ον, *with a mask on*, v.l. for ἔκσκευος, Poll.4.141.

**ἔνσκεψις**, in form ἔμσκεψις, q. v.

**ἐνσκηνοβᾰτέομαι**, Pass., *to be brought on the stage*, Alciphr.2.4.6.

**ἐνσκην-ος**, ον, *furnished with an awning*, *PLond.*5.1714.32 (vi A.D.). * **-όω**, *encamp*, dub. in Lxx *Ge.*13.12.

**ἐνσκήπτω**, Ep. ἐνισκ-, *hurl*, *dart in* or *upon*, ὁ θεὸς ἐνέσκηψε βέλος [ἐς οἰκίην] the god *darted* his lightning *on* it, Hdt.4.79; τούτων ἐκγόνοισι ἐνέσκηψε ἡ θεὸς.. νοῦσον Id.1.105; ἐνισκ. ἰόν v.l. in Nic.*Th.* 140, cf. 336 (v. ἐνσκίμπτω). II. intr., *fall in* or *on*, ἐνέσκηψαν οἱ λίθοι ἐς τὸ τέμενος Hdt.8.39; ἐν οἷς ἂν [δένδροις] ἐνσκήψῃ ἡ ἶρις Arist.*Pr.*906ᵇ24; κεραυνὸς ἐνσκήψας εἰς τὸν βωμόν Plu.*Aem.*24; τινὶ Ael.*NA*14.27; ὁκόσα κύστι καὶ νεφροῖσι ἐνσκήπτει Aret.*SD*2.2; εἰς κεφαλήν D.C.53.29: abs., Ruf.*Fr.*118; of love, εἴς τινα Alciphr.1.13.

**ἔνσκηψις**, εως, ἡ, *falling*, κεραυνῶν Lyd.*Ost.*41 (pl.).

**ἐνσκῐᾱτροφέομαι**, Pass., (σκιά, τρέφω) *to live in the shade*, ἐ. ἐλπίσι *to feed* on *sickly* hopes, Plu.2.476e.

**ἐνσκιμβέω**, in pf. ἐνεσκίμβηκα, = ἐνσκιρρόομαι, Hsch.

**ἐνσκίμπτω**, poet. ἐνισκ-, Ep. and Lyr. form of ἐνσκήπτω, *lean upon*, οὔδει ἐνισκίμψαντε καρήατα, of horses *hanging* their heads *in grief* for their master's loss, Il.17.437; *fix*, *plant in*, βέλος ἐνισκ. τινὶ A.R.3.153; ἐ. βολῇσι *smite* with its beams, of dawn, Id.4.113:—Pass., *stick in*, δόρυ οὔδει ἐνεσκίμφθη Il.16.612. II. *hurl upon* one, κεραυνὸς ἐνέσκιμψε μόρον Pi.*P.*3.58 (v.l. ἐνέσκηψε); ὁππότ' ἀνίας.. πραπίδεσσιν ἐνισκίμψωσιν Ἔρωτες A.R.3.765; of a snake, ἐνισκ. ἰόν Nic.*Th.*140; βλοσυρὸν δάκος ib.336.

**ἔνσκῐος**, ον, (σκιά) *tarnished*, Ps.-Democr.Alch.p.55 B.

**ἐνσκιρρόω**, *harden*:—Pass., *become callous*, *inveterate*, of diseases, X.*Eq.*4.2, Thd.*Is.*27.1, Sch.Ar.*V.*920.

* **ἐνσκολιεύομαι**, *catch in a snare*, Lxx *Jb.*40.19(24).

* **ἐνσκοπέομαι**, *consider the while*, Hld.8.10 (perh. f.l. for ἐπισκ-).

**ἐνσοβέω**, *step proudly in*, πεδίῳ Philostr.*VA*6.10. II. *agitate*:—Pass., τὸ ἐνσεσοβημένον *agitation*, Chrysipp.*Stoic.*3.127.

**ἔνσομφος**, ον, *spongy*, οἴδημα [Gal.]14.384.

* **ἐνσόριον**, τό, (σορός) *place for a sarcophagus*, *IGRom.*4.1452 (Smyrna), *AJA*18.68 (Sardes, iii A.D.), etc.

**ἐνσοφιστεύω**, = σοφιστεύω ἐν.., ἀκακωτάτοις ἤθεσι Ph.1.315: abs., Id.2.59.

**ἔνσοφος**, ον, *wise in* a thing, Man.4.549: abs., ἔ. ἄνδρες *IG*14.1020.

**ἐνσπᾰθάω**, = σπαθάω ἐν.., ταῖς τοῦ θεοῦ δωρεαῖς Ph.2.372.

**ἐνσπᾰθίζω**, *stir* boiling liquid, Orib.*Fr.*133.

**ἐνσπαργᾰνόω**, *wrap as in swathing bands*, in Pass., ἔθεσι καὶ ἐπιτηδεύμασι Longin.44.3; ἔπεσι Heraclit.*All.*1.

**ἐνσπειράομαι**, Pass., *to be coiled up in*, φωλεῷ S.E.*M.*7.410: metaph., *to be involved*, *wrapped up in*, ἔπεσιν Heraclit.*All.*2.

**ἐνσπείρω**, Ep. ἐνισπ-, *sow in*, ἐνισπείρας [ὀδόντας] πεδίοισιν A.R.3. 1185:—Pass., ἡμῖν οὐδέν τι παραπλήσια ψυχὴ τοῖς ἄλλοις ἐ. ζῴοις Jul. *Or.*6.194c; ὑπὸ φύσεως Iamb.*Myst.*3.27.

**ἐνσπέρμᾰτος**, ον, *possessing seed*, Phan.Hist.31.

**ἔνσπερμος**, ον, *prolific*, of a plant, Dsc.3.23.

**ἔνσποδος**, ον, *ashen*, τῇ χροᾷ Dsc.5.88.

**ἔνσπονδος**, ον, (σπονδή) *included in a truce* or *treaty*, opp. ἔκσπονδος, ἐ. ποιεῖσθαι Th.3.10; ἔ. τινι *in alliance with* one, E.*Ba.*924, Th. 1.40, 3.65, al.: as Subst., *ally*, οὐδενὸς Ἑλλήνων ἔ. Id.1.31; οἱ ἔ. *the allies*, ib.35. 2. of animals, *gently disposed*, πρός τινα Ael.*NA*1.3; ἔνσπονδα εἶναί τινι πρός τινα ib.57. II. *under truce* or *safe-conduct*, E.*Ph.*171.

**ἔνσπορος**, ον, = ἔνσπερμος, *Corp.Herm.*3.3.

**ἐνσπουδάζω**, *employ oneself actively in*, τῇ Σμύρνῃ Philostr.*VS*1.25. 2, al.; πόλις ἐνσπουδάσαι ἀγαθή Lib.*Or.*11.268.

**ἐνστάζω**, fut. -ξω, *drop in* or *into*, τινί τι Ar.*V.*702, Pi.*P.*9.63 (tm.); [χάριν] φρασίν B.12.229; ἁπαλὰς τροφάς Ph.2.470:—Pass., εἰ δή τοι σοῦ πατρὸς ἐνέστακται μένος ἠΰ *is instilled into* thee, Od.2.271; ἀλλά οἱ δεινὸς τις ἐνέστακτο ἵμερος Hdt.9.3, cf. Dsc.*Eup.*1.35, Plu.*Ages.*11, Paus.4.32.4.

**ἐνστακτέον**, *one must instil*, Philum.ap.Aët.5.120, Paul.Aeg.3.23.

**ἔνστακτον**, τό, *instillation* for the eyes, Gal.12.782.

**ἐνστᾰλάζω**, = ἐνστάζω, τι εἴς τι Ar.*Ach.*1034, Luc.*Tox.*37 : aor. 2 part. Pass. ἐνσταλαγεῖσα v.l. for ἐνσταγεῖσα in Dsc.1.77.

**ἐνστᾱλόω**, Dor. for ἐνστηλόω, *set upon a pillar*, *IGRom.*1.1295 (Philae).

**ἐν-στᾰσία**, ἡ, = sq., Hp.*Ep.*23. ※ **-στᾰσις**, εως, ἡ, (ἐνίσταμαι) *origin, beginning*, τῶν ὅλων πραγμάτων Aeschin.2.20 ; τοῦ πολέμου Plb.4.62.3; πραγμάτων Ph.2.75 ; *institution* of legal proceedings, τὴν ὅλην ἔ. τοῦ ἀγῶνος Aeschin.1.132. 2. ἔ. βίου *a way* of life, D.L.6. 103, cf. Jul.*Or.*6.201a. 3. *institution* of an heir, *Cod.Just.*1.2.25 *Intr.*, *PMasp.*151.274 (vi A.D.) ; *inheritance*, ib.312.55 (vi A.D.). II. in Medic., *lodgement*, λίθων Aret.*CD*2.3. 2. *impaction, obstruction*, ὄγκων Asclep.ap.Gal.10.101, Herod.Med.ap.Orib.5.30.5, etc. : generally, *interference*, ὀνύχων Iamb.*Protr.*21.ιθ'. III. in Logic, *objection* to an argument, ἔ. πρότασις προτάσει ἐναντία Arist.*APr.*69ᵃ 37, cf. *Top.*157ᵃ35, *Rh.*1402ᵃ31, Hermog.*Inv.*3.6, etc. 2. generally, *opposition*, Plb.6.17.8 (pl.), Ph.2.60. 3. *prosecution*, ἐν μολποῖς *SIG* 633.66 (Milet., ii B.C.). 4. χαλεπὴ ἔ. difficult *situation*, *IG*12(5). 509.4 (Seriphos, iii/ii B.C.). IV. (ἐνίστημι) *winding up* an engine, Ph.*Bel.*61.21, 57.41 (nisi leg. ἔντασις). V. *impact, interference* of an object of vision, *Placit.*4.13.2, Plot.4.5.2. **-στᾰτέον**, *one must oppose, resist*, ταῖς ἐπιθυμίαις Sor.1.53. **-στάτης** [ᾰ], ου, ὁ, *adversary*, S.*Aj.*104, Ael.*Fr.*248. **-στᾰτικός**, ή, όν, *setting oneself in the way, stubborn, savage*, of beasts, Arist.*HA*488ᵇ13. II. *opposing, checking*, Plu.2.975a ; ἐ. ταύτης τῆς ὁδοῦ *hindering from* this course, M.Ant.5.20. Adv. -κῶς, gloss on διασταδόν, Sch.Opp.*H.*1.502. III. *able to find objections*, Arist.*Top.*164ᵇ3, *Cael.*294ᵇ11 ; *controversial*, ἐνέργεια Procl. *in Prm.*p.502S. ; *addicted to controversy*, Id.*in Alc.*p.23C. ; οἱ ἐνστατικοί Grammarians *who started difficulties* in Homer, opp. λυτικοί or ἐπιλυτικοί, Eust.1166fin. : -κόν, τό, Hermog.*Inv.*3.6. Adv. -κῶς ibid.

**ἐνστείνω**, *straiten, coop up in*, Q.S.9.179 (Pass.).

**ἐνστέλλω**, *dress in* :—Pass., ἱππάδα στολὴν ἐνεσταλμένος *clad in* a horseman's dress, Hdt.1.80. II. νομίσματα -στελλόμενά τινι *paid over*, *PMasp.*6ii 32 (vi A.D.).

**ἐνστερνισάμενος**· περιπτυξάμενος, Hsch.

**ἐνστερνομαντίαις**· ἐγγαστριμύθοις, f.l. in Hsch., cf. S.*Fr.*59.

**ἐνστηλῑτόω**, *record*, in Pass., ἱεροῖς γράμμασιν *OGI*666.21.

**ἐνστηλόω**, v. ἐνσταλόω.

**ἔνστημα**, ατος, τό, *objection*, εἴς τι Epicur.*Ep.*2p.39U. II. *check, obstacle*, Chrysipp.*Stoic.*2.268, M.Ant.8.41, S.E.*M.*7.253, al.

**ἐνστηρίζω**, *fix* or *press in*, πρίονα ἔς τι Hp.*VC*21 : metaph., τινὶ τὸ δρᾶμα Plot.3.5.2 :—Pass., γαίῃ ἐνεστήρικτο it *stuck fast in* earth, Il. 21.168 ; πόντῳ, of Delos, Call.*Del.*13 : the Med. in A.R.4.1518.

**ἐνστίζομαι**, Pass., *to be embroidered in* a web, D.C.63.6.

**ἐνστοιβάζω**, *pack, stuff in*, *Gloss.*

**ἐνστομ-ίζω**, *put into one's mouth*, *PMag.Par.*1.2144, cf. Suid. **-ιος**, ον, *in the mouth*, ἕλκος Dsc.1.06 ; τραύματα Antyll.ap.Orib.45.16.4 ; χυλός Ph.1.373 ; θερμασία *PMed.Lond.*155.2.5. **-ισμα**, ατος, τό, *bit, curb*, metaph., J.*AJ*18.9.3 (s.v.l.).

**ἐνστόρνῡμι**, *lay*, τραπέζας Ἐφ.Ἀρχ.1902.29 (Chalcis) :—Pass., ἐνεστρωμένοι ὑμένες *spread over*, Antyll.ap.Orib.45.2.5.

**ἐνστρᾰτοπεδεύω**, *encamp in*, Th.2.20 ; ἐν τῇ πόλει Plu.*Thes.*27 :—Med., χῶρος ἐπιτηδεότερος ἐνστρατοπεδεύεσθαι Hdt.9.2, D.C.50.12.

※ **ἐνστρέφω**, *turn in* :—Med., ἄρθρα ἐνστρέφεσθαι *turn* or *move one's* limbs, Hp.*Dieb.Judic.*8 :—Pass., *turn* or *move in*, μηροῦ ἰσχίῳ ἐνστρέφεται Il.5.306. 2. c. acc. loci, σηκοὺς ἐνστρέφειν *visit* them, f.l. in E.*Ion* 300.

※ **ἐνστρηνές**· ἰσχυρόν, ἢ σαφές, Hsch.

**ἐνστροβῑλίσας** (or -ήσας)· συνστρέψας, Hsch., Suid.

**ἐνστροφή**, ἡ, in pl., *haunts*, Aristid.*Or.*27(16).15.

**ἔνστροφος**, ὁ, a kind of *ear-ring*, Poll.5.97.

**ἐνστρωφάομαι**, Frequentat. of ἐνστρέφομαι, Hp.*Art.*58, Q.S.1.308.

**ἐνστύφω** [ῡ], *to be bitter, astringent*, πόμα, ποτόν, Nic.*Al.*299,321.

**ἐνσυγκαταζέω**, *make to boil together*, Mnesith.ap.Orib.4.4.4.

**ἐνσύζῠγος**, ον, in choric lyrics, *assigned to* συζυγίαι, Sch.Ar.*Ra.* 357.

**ἐνσύνθηκος**, ον, *ratified by treaty*, φιλία App.*Mith.*14.

**ἐνσφαιρόω**, *spread all round*, Nonn.*D.*32.77.

**ἐνσφηκόομαι**, v. sq.

**ἐνσφηνόομαι**, Pass., *to be wedged in, fit close*, Dsc.5.21, Paul.Aeg. 3.77, Procl. ad Hes.*Op.*425 ; πιθάκνη ἐνεσφηνωμένη καλάμῳ *stoppered* with a reed, Dsc.5.31 (v.l. -σφηκ-).

**ἐνσφίγγω**, *bind tight to* a thing, τινί J.*AJ*12.2.9.

**ἐνσφονδύλια** [ῠ], τά, *bones of the* ὀσφύς, Poll.2.179.

**ἐνσφρᾱγ-ίζω**, Ion. **ἐνσφρηγ-**, *stamp, impress as with a seal*, Ph.1. 661 ; ἐνεσφρήγισσεν Ἔρως εἰκόνα βένθεϊ σῆς κραδίης *AP*5.273 (Paul. Sil.) :—Med. freq. in Ph., as τύπον ψυχῇ 2.353 :—Pass., *to be impressed upon*, τινί Luc.*Am.*5,14 ; ἕν τι -ιζόμενον ἐν πολλοῖς Plot.6.5. 6. II. Pass., *to be kept under seal*, *CPR*18.37 (ii A.D.). **-ισις**, εως, ἡ, *imprint*, in pl., Plot.4.3.26, 4.6.1.

**ἐνσχέδιος**, ον, *superficial, perfunctory*, κάθαρσις f.l. in Aret.*SD*2.10.

**ἐνσχερώ**, Adv. *in a row*, A.R.1.912, prob. in Antim.16.5.

**ἐνσχημᾰτίζω**, *arrange* or *set* a fracture, Gal.18(2).333.

※ **ἐν-σχίζω**, *split* or *rend asunder*, λεοντῆν Tz.*H.*7.63. **-σχισμός**, ὁ, *incision*, *Gloss.* (pl.). **-σχιστος**, ον, *split, cleft*, Thphr.*CP*5.17.2.

**ἐνσχολάζω**, *spend one's leisure in* a place, Arist.*Pol.*1331ᵇ12 : metaph., *reside in*, φρόνησις ἐ. ψυχῇ Ph.1.358. 2. *spend time upon*, θεωρήμασι Id.2.428, cf. Them.*Or.*2.39b : abs., *theorize*, *in his molestiis* Cic.*Att.*7.11.2.

**ἐνσωμᾰτ-ίζω**, = -όω, Herm.ap.Stob.1.49.69 (Pass.). **-ος**, ον, *corporeal*, opp. ἀσώματος, Ph.1.43. ※ **-όω**, *embody*, ψυχήν Porph. *Abst.*4.20 :—Pass., ibid., Herm.*in Phdr.*p.167A., Anon.*in Tht.*53. 7. **-ωσις**, εως, ἡ, *incarnation, embodiment*, τῶν ψυχῶν Iamb.ap. Stob.1.49.40, cf. Anon.*in Tht.*57.30, Herm.ap.Stob.1.49.44.

**ἔνσωμος**, ον, = ἐνσώματος, ἐ. φράσις *materialistic* language, Zos. Alch.p.228B.

**ἐνσων**· ἕλκων, Hsch.

**ἐνσωρεύω**, *heap on* or *in*, τῷ κολπώματι χρυσόν Sch.Pi.*P.*7 *Intr.* :—Pass., σῖτος εἰς τὰ δώματ' -εύεται Emp.*Sphaer.*12.

**ἐντᾰγ-ής**, ές, *duly authorized*, κουφισμός *PLond.*5.1646.47 (vi A.D.). **-ιον**, τό, *order for delivery*, esp. *requisition* by the state, τὰ ἐ. τῶν ἀννωνῶν, τῆς ἐσθῆτος, *PGiss.*54.15 (iv A.D.), *PLips.*58.13 (iv A.D.) ; private *order for payment* or *delivery*, *PKlein.Form.*988, 1065 (v A.D.). 2. *receipt*, *PSI*1.36 (iv A.D.), etc. II. *entrance-fee*, *PLond.*3.1178 (ii A.D.), *BGU*1074.15 (iii A.D.).

**ἐντάδε**, = ἐνθάδε, *Schwyzer* 105 (Methana, vi B.C.).

**ἐντακτ-έον**, *one must introduce, place next in order*, Dam.*Pr.* 44. **-ος**, ον, *ordered, rhythmical*, κίνησις Herod.Med. in *Rh.Mus.* 58.70.

**ἐντᾰλαιπωρέομαι**, *persevere*, ταῖς ζητήσεσιν Olymp. *in Alc.*p.64C.

**ἔνταλμα**, ατος, τό, = ἐντολή, Lxx *Is.*29.13, *Ev.Matt.*15.9, al.

**ἐντᾰμιευόμενον**· ἐνθησαυριζόμενον, Hsch.

**ἐντᾰμίευτος** [ῐ], ον, *fitted for* a purpose, πρός τι Gal.18(1).224.

**ἐντάμνω**, Ion. for ἐντέμνω.

**ἐντάν-ῠσις** [ᾰ], εως, ἡ, *stretching*, Eust.1913.37. **-υσμός**, ὁ, gloss on τανυστύς, Sch.Od.21.112. **-ύω**, poet. and Ion. for ἐντείνω, *stretch tight*, of the bow-string, νευρὴν ἐντανύσαι Od.19.587, al. ; also, *stretch* a bow *tight*, i.e. *bend* or *string* it, 21.306, al. ; τὰ τόξα ἐντανύουσι *string* their bows, opp. ἐκλύουσι, Hdt.2.173, cf. Theoc.24. 107 :—Med., δυνήσεται ἐντανύσασθαι *string* the bow, Od.21.403 :—Pass., fut. inf. ἐντανύεσθαι ib.92. 2. *stretch* or *strain tight* with cords or straps, ἐντανύσας [τὸν θρόνον ἱμᾶσιν] *cover* it *with stretched* straps, Hdt.5.25. 3. ἐ. αὔλακας *draw long* furrows, Pi.*P.*4.227.

**ἐντάξιμος**· *insertícius*, *Gloss.*

**ἔνταξις**, εως, ἡ, *putting in, insertion*, Ptol.*Geog.*2.1.7. II. *placing of light-armed soldiers alternately with hoplites in the phalanx*, Ael. *Tact.*31.3, Arr.*Tact.*26.6, Suid.

**ἐντᾰράσσω**, Att. -ττω, Ion. **ἐνθράσσω** (q. v.), *toss about*, τὴν στρωμνήν Aristaenet.2.22 :—Med., *cause confusion in*, τῷ ὁμίλῳ Philostr. *VA*3.20 :—Pass., -τεταραγμένοι ὀφθαλμοί Arist.*Phgn.*812ᵇ8.

**ἐντᾰρῑχεύω**, *pickle in the sun*, Paul.Aeg.3.18 (Pass.).

※ **ἔντᾰσις**, εως, ἡ, (ἐντείνω) *inscribing*, εἰς τὸν κύκλον Pl.*Men.*87b. II. *tension, straining*, τοῦ ὑποχονδρίου Hp.*Epid.*3.1.β' ; τοῦ σώματος Id. *Aër.*4 ; τῶν ῥάβδων Id.*Fract.*30 ; ὀφθαλμῶν *fixed stare*, prob. in Aret. *CD*1.3 (pl.) ; *distension*, αἰδοίων Gal.7.728. 2. *exertion*, Plu.2. 948b, Aret.*SA*2.2 ; pl., *retchings*, Id.*CD*2.13. 3. ἡ τοῦ προσώπου ἔ. *the assumption of a serious* face, Luc.*Symp.*28 ; *earnestness*, περὶ ἑκάστου Porph.*Abst.*1.54 ; *strictness*, νόμων *PSorb.*675.14 (iii A.D.). 4. Arch., *swelling* in the outline of a column, Vitr.3.3.13.

**ἔντᾰσις**, ιος, ἡ, Thess. for ἔγκτησις, *IG*9(2).511 (iii B.C.), al.

**ἐντάσσω**, Att. -ττω, *insert* or *register in*, ἐν τοῖς δημοσίοις γράμμασι *CIG*2737 a50 (Aphrodisias, M. Antonius), cf. *PFay.*91.46 (i A.D., Pass.), etc. ; ἐ. τινὰ τῇ ἀρχαίᾳ κωμῳδίᾳ Ath.1.5b :—Pass., τῷ σφενδονᾶν ἐντεταγμένῳ *who takes post* to use the sling, X.*An.*3.3.18 (as v.l.) : in lit. sense, *insert*, πυρὴν -έσθω μήλης Paul.Aeg.6.66. 2. *arrange light-armed troops and hoplites alternately*, Ael.*Tact.*31.3, Arr.*Tact.* 26.6 : generally, *insert* men *alternately*, ib.25.4 (Pass.). II. = ἀντιτάσσω, τινὶ δόρυ E.*Rh.*492. III. *issue orders*, ἐντεταχέναι τὸν στρατηγόν *PCair.Preis.*32.3 (ii A.D.).

**ἐντᾰτ-ικός**, ή, όν, *stimulating, aphrodisiac*, Xenocr.16, cf. Gal.12. 341, Aët.11.35. 2. *sexually vigorous*, [ζῷον] -άτερον πρὸς τὴν μεῖξιν *Gp.*19.5.4. II. ἐντατικόν, τό, = σατύριον, Ps.-Dsc.3.128. ※ **-ός**, ή, όν, (ἐντείνω) *stretched* : ἐ. ὄργανα *stringed* instruments, Str.7.5.7, Ps.-Plu.*Vit.Hom.*148, Ath.4.182e, Nicom.*Harm.*2.

**ἐνταῦθα**, Ion. **ἐνθαῦτα** (also **ἐντοῦθα**, q. v.), Elean **ἐνταῦτα** *SIG*9 (Olympia, vi B.C.) : Adv., formed from ἔνθα, but more common in Prose : I. of Place, *here, there*, Hdt.1.76, A.*Pr.*82, etc. ; ἐνταυθά που *hereabouts*, Ar.*Av.*1184 : folld. by ἵνα, ὅπου, etc., S.*Ph.*429, *Tr.* 800, etc. b. *in this material world*, opp. ἐκεῖ (in the ideal world), Arist.*Metaph.*990ᵇ34, etc. 2. *hither, thither*, Il.9.601 ; παριέναι ἐνθαῦτα Hdt.5.72 ; ἐνταῦθα πέμπειν A.*Pers.*450, etc. ; ἐ. πέμψειν ἔνθα μήποθ' ἡλίου φέγγος προσόψῃ S.*El.*380 ; ὅθεν δ' ἕκαστον ἐς τὸ φῶς ἀφίκετο, ἐνταῦθ' ἀπελθεῖν E.*Supp.*533 ; φέρε δεῦρο.. ἐ. Ar.*Ec.*739 ; ἐ. προελήλυθας Pl.*Tht.*187b ; μέχρι ἐ. Id.*Cra.*412e. 3. freq. c. gen., ἐ. τοῦ οὐρανοῦ X.*Mem.*4.3.8 ; ἐ. τῆς ἠπείρου Th.1.46 ; ἐ. τοῦδ' ἀφικόμην κακοῦ A.*Ch.*891 ; ἐ. που ἤμεν τοῦ λόγου Pl.*Tht.*177c ; ἐνταῦθ' ἑαυτὸν τάξας τῆς πολιτείας *in that department of*.., D.18.62. II. of Time, *at the very time, then*, A.*Pr.*206 ; in apodosi, ἡνίκα.., ἐνταῦθα δὴ μάλιστα.. S.*Tr.*37 ; after ὅτε, Id.*OT*802 ; after ἐπειδή, ἐπεί, Th.1.11, X. *An.*3.4.25 ; ἐ. δή Id.*Cyr.*4.5.9, etc. 2. c. gen., ἐ. ἤδη εἶ τῆς ἡλικίας Pl.*R.*328e. III. of Sequence, *thereupon*, Hdt.1.61,62. IV. generally, *herein*, S.*OT*582, *Fr.*77, Pl.*Ap.*29b, etc. ; *in this position*, ἐ. ἕστηκε τὸ πρᾶγμα D.21.102 ; ἐνταῦθ' ἔνι depends upon *that circumstance*, S.*OT*598.—In Att. also strengthd. **ἐνταυθί** [ῑ], Pl.Com.173.8 (prob.), Pl.*Prt.*310a, D.15.22, al.

**ἐνταυθοῖ** (ἐνθαυθοῖ *IG*1².76.13), Adv. *hither*, ἐ. νῦν κεῖσο *come* and lie down *here*, Il.21.122 ; ἐ. νῦν ἧσο Od.18.105, 20.262 ; *here*, ἡ ἐ. μονή Arist.*Phys.*229ᵇ28, cf. D.27.54 : freq. with or without v.l. ἐνταυθί in

Com. and Prose, Cratin.37, Ar.*Ra*.273, *Lys*.568, al., Pl.*Ap*.18d, 33d, al., Antipho 5.2, 10.—Once in Trag., E.*IT* 1010 (s. v. l.).

⊛ **ἐντᾰφ-ή**, Dor. -ά, *burial*, *IGRom*.4.1302.10 (Cyme), *GDI* 3502.9 (Cnidos), *SIG* 1234.5 (Lycia). **-ήϊα**, v. ἐντοφήϊα. **-ιάζω**, *prepare for burial*, *lay out*, Lxx *Ge*.50.2, *Ev.Matt*.26.12, Plu.2.995c, *AP* 11.125: metaph., τὴν τυραννίδα τῇ πόλει Plu.*Dio* 44:—Med., τὸ λοιπὸν ἐντεταφιασμένος περιπατεῖ Phld.*Mort*.38. **-ιασις**, εως, ἡ, = sq., Suid. **-ιασμός**, ὁ, *laying out for burial*, *Ev.Marc*.14.8, Sch.Ar.*Pl*. 1009, etc. ⊛ **-ιαστής**, οῦ, ὁ, *undertaker*, *embalmer*, Lxx *Ge*.50.2, *POxy*. 476.8 (ii A.D.), *PPar*.7.6 (i B.C.), Ptol.*Tetr*.180, *AP* 11.125, etc.; of the Bactrian dogs, Str.11.11.3. **-ιαστικός**, ή, όν, *of an* ἐνταφιαστής, τάξις *PSorb*.675.14 (iii A.D.). **-ιεύω**, = -ιάζω, Charis.p.566 K.

**ἐντᾰφιοπώλης**, ου, ὁ, *undertaker*, *Dialex*.1.?, Artem.4.56.

**ἐντάφιος** [ᾰ], ον, *of, belonging to* or *used in burial*, κόσμοι D.H.2.67. II. as Subst., 1. ἐντάφιον, τό, *shroud*, *winding-sheet*, *AP* 11.125; ἐ. δὲ τοιοῦτον οὔτ' εὐρὼς οὔτε.. ἀμαυρώσει χρόνος Simon.4.4; καλὸν ἐ. ἡ τυραννίς Isoc.6.45; κάλλιστον ἐ. ἔξουσι τὸν ὑπὲρ τῆς πατρίδος θάνατον Plb.15.10.3; ὁ πλοῦτος δ' οὐκ ἐμὸν ἐ. *AP* 9.294 (Antiphil.). b. μηδ' ἐντάφια καταλιπόντι *money for funeral expenses*, Plu.*Arist*.27: later in sg., *funeral expenses*, *PLond*.5.1708.205 (vi A.D.). 2. ἐ. (sc. ἱερά), τά, *offerings to the dead*, *obsequies*, S.*El*.326, Is.8.38, *Epigr. Gr*.313.13 (Smyrna): Cyren. ἐντόφιον *Notiz.Arch*.4.96.

**ἐντᾰχύ**, *quickly*, *presently*, *Sammelb*.365: Comp. ἐντάχιον *as soon as possible*, *BGU* 326 (ii/iii A.D.), etc.

**ἔντε**, = ἔστε, *until*, *GDI* 2561 *B* 44, *C* 18 (Delph.); ἔντε ib.1707.7 (ibid.); ἔντε κ' ἀποτείσῃ *IG* 9(1).334.15 (Locr., v B.C.); of numbers, *up to*, τὰς ὑπὲρ πέντε μνᾶς ἔντε δέκα *Foed.Delph.Pell*.1 *A* 4.

⊛ **ἔντεα**, τά, *fighting gear*, *arms*, *armour*, ἔ. ἀρήϊα Il.10.407, Od. 23.368; ἔ. πατρός 19.17; esp. *coat of mail*, *corslet*, Il.10.34; ἔντε' ἔδυνεν 3.339, etc. II. *furniture*, *appliances*, *tackle*, ἔ. δαιτός Od. 7.232; ἔ. νηός *rigging*, *h.Ap*.489, Pi.*N*.4.70; ἔ. ἵππεια *trappings*, *harness*, ib.9.22, cf. *P*.4.235; ἔντη δίφρου *harness*, A.*Pers*.194 (but ἔντεα alone for *chariots*, Pi.*O*.4.24); ἔντεα αὐλῶν periphr. for αὐλοί, ib.7.12; also ἔντεα alone, *musical instruments*, Id.*P*.12.21; of the *instruments* of the Γάλλαι, *Lyr.Adesp*.121; ἔντεα Φοίβου Call.*Ap*. 19.—Ep. and Lyr. word, once in Trag. (v. supr.):—sg. ἔντος only in Archil.6.

⊛ **ἐντείνω**, *stretch* or *strain tight*, esp. of any operation performed with straps or cords, 1. ἐνέτεινε τὸν θρόνον [ἱμᾶσι] Hdt.5.25 (cf. ἐντανύω):—more freq. (as always in Hom.) Pass., δίφρος.. ἱμᾶσιν ἐντέταται *is hung on tight-stretched* straps, Il.5.728; [κυνέη] ἔντοσθεν ἱμᾶσιν ἐντέτατο στερεῶς *was* strongly *lined* inside *with tight-stretched* straps, 10.263; so [τὰς γεφύρας] ἐδόκεον ἐντεταμένας εὑρήσειν expected to find the bridge *with the mooring-cables taut*, Hdt.9.106; σχεδίαι ἐντετ. Id.8.117; κλίνη ἐντετ. Polyaen.7.14.1; εἰ ἡ ἔντασις τῶν ῥάβδων χρηστῶς ἐνταθείη Hp.*Fract*.30; τράχηλος ἐντετ. *with sinews taut*, Phld.*Ir*.p.5 W.: metaph., ἐντεταμένου τοῦ σώματος *being toned*, *tempered*, Pl.*Phd*.86b, cf. 92a. 2. *stretch* a bow *tight*, *bend* it for shooting, A.*Fr*.83, cf. E.*Supp*.886: metaph., καιροῦ πέρα τὸ τόξον ἐ. ib.745:—Med., *bend one's* bow, Id.*IA* 549 (lyr.), X.*Cyr*.4.1.3:—Pass., τόξα ἐντεταμένα bows *ready strung*, Hdt.2.173, Luc.*Scyth*.2: hence, com., κέντρον ἐντέταται *is ready for action*, Ar.*V*.407. b. of the strings of the lyre, τῆς νεάτης ἐντεταμένης Arist.*Pr*.921b27. 3. ἐ. ναῦν ποδί *keep* a ship's sail *taut* by the sheet, ναῦς ἐνταθεῖσα ποδὶ ἔβαψεν E.*Or*.706. 4. ἐ. ἵππον τῷ ἀγωγεῖ *hold* a horse *with tight* rein, X. *Eq*.8.3. 5. *tie tight*, βοῦν.. ἐ. βρόχοις E.*Andr*.720. II. metaph., *strain*, *exert*, τὰς ἀκοάς Polyaen.1.21.2; ἑαυτόν Plu.2.795f:—Med., φωνὴν ἐντεινάμενος Aeschin.2.157; ἐντεινάμενοι τὴν ἁρμονίαν *pitching* the tune *high*, Ar.*Nu*.968:—Pass., πρόθυμοι καὶ ἐντεταμένοι εἰς τὸ ἔργον *braced up* for action, X.*Oec*.21.9; τῇ διανοίᾳ περί τι Plb.10.3.1; ἐνταθῆναι περί τινος *PSI* 4.340 (iii B.C.); ἐντεινόμενος *on the stretch*, *eager*, opp. ἀνιέμενος, X.*Mem*.3.10.7, cf. *Cyn*.7.8; μᾶλλον ἐντεινάμενος εἶπον Pl.*R*.536c; πρόσωπον ἐντεταμένον a *serious* face, Luc.*Vit. Auct*.10. 2. *intensify*, *carry on vigorously*, τὴν πολιορκίαν Plu. *Luc*.14; *excite*, θυμὸν ἀνόητον Plu.2.61e, cf. 464b. III. intr. in Act., *exert oneself*, *be vehement*, E.*Or*.698, *Fr*.340. 2. intr. in Act., *penem erigere*, Arist.*Pr*.879a11:—Pass., εἰκόνες ἐντεταμέναι D.S.1. 88. IV. *stretch out at* or *against*, πληγήν *lay* a blow *on* him, X.*An*.2.4.11, cf. Lys.*Fr*.75.4; without πληγήν, *attack*, Pl.*Min*. 321a; πύξ τινι D.C.57.22. V. *place exactly in*, ἐς κύκλον χωρίον τρίγωνον *inscribe* an area as a triangle in a circle, Pl.*Men*.87a (Pass.). 2. esp. *put into verse*, ἐ. τοὺς Αἰσώπου λόγους Id.*Phd*. 60d; ἐ. εἰς ἐλεγεῖον Id.*Hipparch*.228d; τοὺς νόμους εἰς ἔπος Plu.*Sol*. 3; ἔπεσιν ἐ. τὴν παραίνεσιν Jul.*Or*.6.188b; *set to music*, ποιήματα εἰς τὰ κιθαρίσματα Pl.*Prt*.326b:—Med., Ἰθάκην ἐνετείνατο.. Ὅμηρος ᾠδῇσιν Hermesian.7.29.

**ἐντείρω**, = τείρω ἐν.., Q.S.1.671 (Pass.).

**ἐντειχ-ίδιος**, ον, = ἐντείχιος, Luc.*Par*.42, Onos.42.12. **-ίζω**, *build* or *fortify in* a place, ἀκροπόλεις ἐν ταῖς πόλεσιν Isoc.4.137, cf. X.*HG* 4.8.1; φρούρια Id.*Cyr*.3.1.27; πόλιν ἐν τῷ ἀγκῶνι D.H.3.44; φρουροὺς τοῖς χωρίοις J.*AJ* 9.10.3:—Pass., τὰ τείχη ἃ ἐνετετείχιστο X.*Ages*.2.19. II. Med., *wall in*, i.e. *blockade*, Th.6.90; but also, *fortify*, Nic.Dam.*Fr*.66.32 J., Plu.*Pomp*.28: plpf. ἐνετετείχιστο D.C. 42.38. **-ιος**, ον, *enclosed by walls*, οἰκήσεις D.H.1.26.

**ἐντεκμαίρομαι**, *infer*, τοῖς ἄλλοις σημείοις f.l. in Hp.*Superf*.10.

**ἐντεκν-όομαι**, *beget children in*, Plu.*Cat.Mi*.25. **-ος**, ον, *having children*, opp. ἄτεκνος, Luc.*DMort*.6.3.

**ἐντεκταίνομαι**, *build* or *fix in*, v.l. for ἐκ-, Hp.*Art*.47, cf. Apollon. Cit. ad loc.

**ἐντελέθω**, = τελέθω ἐν.., Nic.*Th*.660.

⊛ **ἐντέλεια**, ἡ, (ἐντελής) *completeness*, τοῦ λόγου A.D.*Synt*.186. 15. II. *full rights*, *GDI* 1339.11 (Dodona).

**ἐντελετέω**, *to be inspired*, *frenzied*, Hsch. s. v. κορυβαντιᾷ.

**ἐντελευτάω**, *end one's life in*.., Th.2.44, Lib.*Or*.18.31.

**ἐντελέχ-εια**, ἡ, (ἐντελής, ἔχειν) *full, complete reality*, opp. δύναμις, ψυχή ἐστιν ἐ. ἡ πρώτη σώματος φυσικοῦ δυνάμει ζωὴν ἔχοντος Arist. *de An*.412a27; ὑπὸ τοῦ ἐντελεχείᾳ ὄντος τὸ δυνάμει ὂν γίνεται Id.*GA* 734a 30; distd. fr. ἐνέργεια, *actuality*, opp. *activity*, Id.*Metaph*.1050a23, *Ph*.257b8, cf. Ph.1.625 (ἐνδ- codd.), Plot.4.7.8; later, τὸ ᾠὸν κατὰ δύναμιν μέν ἐστι νεοσσός, κατ' ἐντελέχειαν δὲ οὐκ ἔστιν S.E.*M*.10.340, cf. Theo Sm.p.37 H.: confused with ἐνδέλεχεια (q. v.) by Cic.*Tusc*. 1.10.22, Luc.*Jud.Voc*.10. **-ής**, ές, only as f.l. for ἐνδ-, e.g. Thphr. *CP* 5.1.10, Ph.2.587; and so Adv. -ῶς Pl.*Lg*.905e.

⊛ **ἐντελ-έω**, dub. in Phld.*Ir*.p.12 W. **-ής**, ές, (τέλος) *complete*, *full*, τὸν μισθὸν ἀποδώσω 'ντελῆ Ar.*Eq*.1367, cf. Th.8.45; δώσειν ἐ. τὴν δραχμήν ib.29; τροφὴν ἐ. δοῦναι ib.78; δεῖπνον ἐ. καὶ μηδὲν ἐλλιπές Euang.1.2 (but τὸ ἐ. ὀνομαζόμενον δεῖπνον the *last* course, Luc.*Symp*. 38); ἵν' ἐ. ὦσι [οἱ λόγοι] Phld.*Herc*.1251.13; opp. ἐλλιπής, A.D. *Synt*.38.9, al.: Sup. -έστατος, βάσανος Ael.*Tact*.21.3; ἐντελὲς τρίγωνον ⸫ Luc.*Vit.Auct*.4. 2. of victims, *perfect*, *unblemished*, δώδεκ' ἐντελεῖς ἔχων βοῦς S.*Tr*.760, cf. Luc.*Sacr*.12. 3. of military equipment, *in good condition*, Th.6.45; τριήρεις Aeschin.2.175. 4. of men, οὐ γὰρ ἐντελῆς.. προσφέρειν *full-grown* so as to offer, A.*Ch*. 250; ἐ. τὴν ἡλικίαν Ael.*NA* 3.40; *finished*, *accomplished*, ἐ. καὶ ἔνδοξοι Artem.2.35, cf. Sch.Hes.*Th*.242; also ἐντελῆ τὴν ἀνδρείαν εἰσφέρονται Onos.4.2: Comp. -έστερος Hsch.: Sup., Id. 5. Adv. -λῶς, Ion. -λέως, *entirely*, *completely*, Arist.*Rh.Al*.1436a12, Herod.4. 79, Plb.10.30.3, etc.; *perfectly*, J.*AJ* 19.6.2: Comp. -έστερον Marin. *Procl*.15. II. *possessing full rights*, ἱππεῖς ἐ. Ῥωμαίων D.S.34.2. 31; *qualified to hold public office*, opp. ἀτελής, *SIG* 286.10 (Milet., iv B.C.):—dub. cj. in A.*Ag*.105. **-ικός**, ή, όν, f.l. for ἐντολικός, A.D.*Synt*.112.27.

⊛ **ἐντέλλω**, *enjoin*, *command*, Act. only in Pi.*O*.7.40, S.*Fr*.269:—mostly in Med., τινί τι Hdt.1.47, etc.; in a will, φίλοις ταῦτα ἐντέλλομαι Diog.Oen.66: c. dat. pers. et inf., Hdt.1.53, Pl.*R*.393e, etc.; ἐντείλασθαι ἀπὸ γλώσσης *command* by word of mouth, Hdt.1.123: so in pf., ἐντέταλται Lxx 3*Ki*.13.17; ἐντεταλμένοι εἴησαν Plb.18.2.1, cf. Hdn.1.9.9:—Pass., τὰ ἐντεταλμένα *commands*, Hdt.1.60, 5.73, S. *Fr*.462, X.*Cyr*.5.5.3. II. *invest with legal powers*, *authorize to act*, ἐ. σοι καὶ ἐπιτρέπω *PLips*.38.5 (iv A.D.), cf. *PMasp*.124.6 (vi A.D.).

**ἐντελόμισθος**, ον, *receiving full pay*, D.50.18.

**ἐντεμεν-ίζω**, *place within a precinct*, Poll.1.11. **-ιος**, ον, *having statues in the* τέμενος, θεοί *SIG* 1037.4 (Milet.), *Inscr.Prien*.123.10 (i B.C.).

⊛ **ἐντέμνω**, Ion. -τάμνω, *cut in*, *engrave upon*, ἐν τοῖσι λίθοισι γράμματα Hdt.8.22; of a map, χάλκεον πίνακα, ἐν τῷ γῆς.. περίοδος ἐνετέτμητο Id.5.49: *cut* or *scoop* a hollow in a thing, in Pass., ἐντετμέαται Hp.*Art*.72; ἐντετμημένου τοῦ σπληνίου Orib.46.25.4. II. *cut up* a victim, *sacrifice*, ἥρωϊ to a hero, Th.5.11, cf. Luc.*Scyth*.1; ἐ. σφάγιά τινι Plu.*Sol*.9:—Med., εἰ.. ἵππον τόμιον ἐντεμοίμεθα *should get it cut up*, Ar.*Lys*.192:—Pass., ἐντέμνεται σφάγια Dion.Byz.14. 2. *cut in*, *shred in*, of herbs in a remedy, metaph., A.*Ag*.16. 3. *cut*, ναῦς ἐ. κύματα Ph.1.352, cf. Luc.*Tim*.22 (Pass.), *Tox*.37, *Hist.Conscr*.25.

⊛ **ἐντενής**, ές, *on the stretch*, *intent*: only neut. ἐντενές as Adv., A.R. 2.933.

**ἐντεομήστωρ**, v. ἐντεσιμήστωρ.

**ἐντερ-επιπλοκήλη**, ἡ, *intestinal and omental hernia*, Gal.19.448. **-εύω**, *gut* fish, Archipp.25. **-ίδια**, τά, Dim. of ἔντερα, Alex. 84. **-ικός**, ή, όν, *intestinal*, ἀποφυάδες Arist.*PA* 675a17. **-ινος**, η, ον, *made of gut*, Sch.Ar.*Ra*.232. ⊛ **-ιον**, τό, *privy parts*, M.Ant. 6.13. **-ιώνη**, ἡ, *inmost part*, *pith* or *heart-wood* of plants, Hp.*Mul*. 1.78, Thphr.*HP* 3.17.5, 1.2.6, Porph.*Gaur*.3.3, Luc.*VH* 2.37.

⊛ **ἐντερο-ειδής**, ές, *like intestines*, Arist.*HA* 508b11. **-κήλη**, ἡ, *intestinal hernia*, *rupture*, Dsc.1.74 (pl.), Gal.7.36, Cels.7.18. **-κηλήτης**, ου, ὁ, *one who suffers from rupture*, Gloss.:—hence **-κηλικός**, ή, όν, *suffering from intestinal hernia*, Dsc.1.110.2, Gal.14.789.

**ἐντερόμφᾰλον**, τό, *umbilical hernia*, Gal.14.786. II. **-όμφαλος**, ὁ, *patient suffering therefrom*, Id.19.444.

⊛ **ἔντερον**, τό, *piece of the guts* or *intestines*, ἐϋστρεφὲς ἔντερον οἰός a string of sheep's *gut*, Od.21.408: elsewh. in Hom. always pl., ἔντερα *guts*, *bowels*, Il.13.507, al., cf. A.*Ag*.1221, Ar.*Eq*.1184, *Ra*. 476, Pl.*Ti*.73a: in sg., *gut*, *bowel*, Arist.*HA* 524b13; τοὔντερον τῆς ἐμπίδος Ar.*Nu*.160; collectively, *bowels*, Arist.*HA* 514b13, al.; *womb*, *belly*, Archil.142, cf. Luc.*Lex*.6; ἐπὶ μετρίῳ ἐντέρῳ for moderation *in eating*, Lxx *Si*.34.20, cf. *AP* 9.170 (Pall.): metaph., *inside* of fruit, ib.14.57. II. ἔντερα γῆς *earth-worms*, Arist.*IA* 705b28, 709a28, Arat.959, Numen.ap.Ath.7.305a; but *worm-casts*, Arist.*HA* 570a16, Thphr.*Sign*.42, Nic.*Th*.388. III. *bag made of gut*, Hp.*Morb*.3. 1. (I.-E. *en-tero-, Comp. of *en 'in'.)

⊛ **ἐντερόνεια**, ἡ, = ἐντεριώνη, Hsch., Suid.; ἐ. εἰς τριήρεις *timber for the ribs* of a ship, *belly-timber*, Ar.*Eq*.1185 (with a pun on τοῖς ἐντέροις), v. Sch.

**ἐντερο-πράτης** [ᾱ], ου, ὁ, = sq., Sch.Ar.*Eq*.155. **-πώλης**, ου, ὁ, *tripe-seller*, *AB* 379. **-φύλαξ** [ῠ], ακος, ὁ, name of a *surgical instrument*, *Hermes* 38.282.

**ἔντεσα**· ἔσωθεν, Hsch. (cf. ἔξεσα).

⊛ **ἐντεσῐ-εργός**, όν, *working in harness*, ἡμίονοι ἐ. *draught*-mules, Il. 24.277. **-μήστωρ**, ορος, ὁ, *skilled in arms*, Hsch. (also ἐντεομ-).

**ἐντέταμαι, ἐντεταμένος,** pf. Pass. from ἐντείνω.

**ἐντετᾰμένως,** Adv., (ἐντείνω) *vehemently, vigorously*, Hdt.1.18, 4.14, J.*AJ*11.4.5.

**ἐντετριμμένως,** Adv., (ἐντρίβω) *adroitly, 'like an old hand'*, Poll. 5.144.

**ἐντετῠπωμένως,** gloss on ἐντυπάς, Eust.1343.55.

**ἔντευγμα,** ατος, τό, = ἔντευξις, D.S.39.9.

⊛ **ἐντεῦθεν,** Ion. **ἐνθεῦτεν,** Adv., (related to ἔνθεν, as ἐνταῦθα to ἔνθα): I. of Place, *hence* or *thence*, Od.19.568, Hdt.1.2, al., A.*Pr.* 836, *Pers.*488, Th.8.42, etc.; τὸ γένος ἐ. ποθεν ἐκ Χίου Pl.*Euthd.*271c; τἀντεῦθεν *matters there*, i.e. in the house, S.*El.*1339; ἐ. καὶ ἐ. Lxx *Nu.*22.24, *Ev.Jo.*19.18; ἐ. κἀκεῖθεν Sch.D.T.p.29H.; ἐντεῦθεν εἰς τυχόν *'go to Jericho'*, Men.*Pk.*184. II. of Time, *henceforth, thereupon*, S.*El.*728, *Ph.*384 (lyr., dub. l.), etc.; also τὸ ἐ. Hdt.1.9,27, al., Pl.*Tht.*198b; Att. also τοὐντεῦθεν E.*Med.*792, al.; τἀντεῦθεν A.*Eu.* 60; τὸ ἐ. ἐπὶ τούτοις Ael.*NA*8.17. III. causal, *thence, from that source*, τὸν βίον ἐ. ἐποιοῦντο Th.1.5; ἐ. αἱ μάχαι Arist.*EN*1131ᵃ23; ἐ. ποθεν Id.*Pol.*1286ᵇ15; *therefore, in consequence*, E.*Andr.*949, Pl.*Cra.* 399c.—Att. strengthd. **ἐντευθενί** [ῑ], Ar.*Av.*10, *Lys.*92, etc.; cf. ἐμμεντευθενί.

⊛ **ἐντευκτικός,** ή, όν, *affable*, Plu.*Alc.*13, 2.9f.

**ἐντευξίδιον,** τό, Dim. of sq. 4, *little petition*, Arr.*Epict.*1.10.10.

**ἔντευξις,** εως, ἡ, (ἐντυγχάνω) *lighting upon, meeting with*, c. dat., αἱ τοῖς λῃσταῖς ἐντεύξεις Pl.*Plt.*298d. 2. *converse, intercourse*, πρὸς τοὺς πολλούς Arist.*Rh.*1355ᵃ29: c. gen., *Vit.Philonid.*p.7C.; ἐντεύξεις ποιεῖσθαί τισι *hold converse with*.., Isoc.1.20; [ἡ πραγματεία] χρήσιμος πρὸς τὰς ἐ. Arist.*Top.*101ᵃ27, cf. *Metaph.*1009ᵃ17, etc.; τὴν ἡλικίαν τῇ ἐντεύξει γνωρίζομεν Sor.2.8. b. *manners, behaviour*, Aeschin.2.47, Thphr.*Char.*5.1, 20.1. c. esp. *sexual intercourse*, Epicur.*Sent.Vat.*51, *Fr.*61. 3. ἐντεύξεις ὀχλικαί *speeches* to the mob, D.H.*Th.*50. 4. *petition*, *PSI*4.383.6 (iii B.C.), *PFlor.*55.18 (i A.D.), Plu.*TG*11, etc.; *intercession* for a person, D.S.16.55, Nic. Dam.*Fr.*130.7 J., 1*Ep.Ti.*2.1 (pl.). 5. *reading, study*, ἡ ἐ. τῆς πραγματείας Plb.1.1.4, etc.

**ἐντευτενί,** for ἐντευθενί, barbarism in Ar.*Th.*1212.

⊛ **ἐντευτλᾰνόομαι,** Pass., *to be stewed in beet* (v. τεῦτλον), of eels, Ar. *Ach.*894 (prob. ἐντετευτλιωμένης), Aret.*CA*1.2.

⊛ **ἐντεύχω,** *produce*, ἐρυθήματα Archig.ap.Orib.8.1.1 (Pass.).

**ἔντεφρος,** ον, (τέφρα) *ash-coloured*, Dsc.5.74, Ath.9.395e.

**ἐντεχν-άζω** λόγον *introduce an elaborate* argument, Lib.*Eth.*6. 5. **-ής,** ές, f.l. for ἔντεχνος, Sch.Pi.*N.*8.24. **-ος,** ον, *within the range* or *province of art*, αἱ πίστεις ἔντεχνόν ἐστι μόνον Arist.*Rh.* 1354ᵃ13. 2. *furnished* or *invented by art, artificial, artistic*, Pl. *Prt.*321d, al.; opp. ἄτεχνος, πίστεις Arist.*Rh.*1355ᵇ36; ἡ ἐ. μέθοδος the *regular* method, ib.ᵃ4. Adv. -ως Id.*SE*172ᵃ35 (condemned by Phryn.327 (who however cites Adv. -ῶς from Lys.*Fr.*314 S.)). II. of persons, *skilled*, ἐ. δημιουργός a *cunning* workman, Pl.*Lg.*903c, cf. *Plt.*300e.

**ἔντηκτος,** ον, *liquefied*, αἷμα Aret.*CD*2.13.

**ἐντήκω,** *pour in while molten*, μόλιβδον D.S.2.8; ἐ. μόλιβδον [τῇ κεφαλῇ] Plu.*CG*17: metaph., ἐ. τέτανον τερπνόν v.l. in Ar.*Lys.* 553. II. Pass., with pf. Act. ἐντέτηκα, *to be dissolved in*, ὕδατι Aët.9.42. 2. *to be cast*, ἀνδριάντα χαλκῷ ἐντετηκότα D.Chr.64.4: but usu., 3. metaph., of feelings, *sink deep in*, μῖσος ἐντέτηκέ μοι S.*El.*1311, cf. Pl.*Mx.*245d; τὸ δέος ἐντετηκὸς ταῖς ψυχαῖς D.H.6.72; ἐν ταῖς ψυχαῖς ἐντέτηκεν ἡ δεισιδαιμονία D.S.1.83; ἐντήκεται γὰρ πλευμόνων ὅσοις ἔνι ψυχή (sc. Κύπρις) *sinks in*..as the breath of life, S.*Fr.* 941.7. 4. of persons, οὐδ' ἂν εἰ κάρτ' ἐντακείη τῷ φιλεῖν *should be absorbed by* love, Id.*Tr.*463; θρήνοισιν ἐντακεῖσα Lyc.498.

⊛ **ἐντηρέω,** *guard*, Procop.*Arc.*4, *PGrenf.*1.61.13 (vi A.D.).

**ἐντί,** v. εἰμί.

⊛ **ἐντίθημι,** fut. ἐνθήσω: poet. aor. 1 inf. ἐνθέμεν Thgn.430:—*put in* (esp. *put on board* a ship), οἶνον ἐρυθρὸν ἐνθήσω Od.5.166; ἐνθείς τινα εἰς τὸ πλοῖον Antipho 5.39:—freq. in this sense in Med., κτήματά τ' ἐντιθέμεσθα Od.3.154, cf. X.*An.*1.4.7, *Oec.*20.28; ἐν δ' ἱστὸν τιθέμεσθα..νηΐ Od.11.3; ἐνθέσθαι εἰς τὴν ναῦν φορτία D.34.6. 2. generally, *put in* or *into*, ἐνέθηκε δὲ χερσὶν ἅρπην Hes.*Th.*174; χειρὶ δ' ἔνθες ὀξύην E.*Heracl.*727; σε μήτηρ ἐνθεμένη λεχέεσσι Il.21.123; ἐντιθέναι αὐχένα ζυγῷ E.*Hec.*376. cf. 1045; also ἐς τι Hdt.2.73, Ar. *Ach.*920; ἐς τὼ κοθόρνω τὼ πόδ' ἐνθεὶς Id.*Ec.*346, cf. *V.*1161:—Med., ἐνθεμένης τὸ κυμβίον εἰς τὸν κόλπον D.47.58. b. metaph., ἐνθέμεν φρένας ἐσθλάς Thgn.430; ἄρτι μοι τὸ γῆρας ἐντίθησι νοῦν Pherecr. 146.6; ἐ. ἀθυμίαν Pl.*Lg.*800c; ἰσχὺν D.3.33; ἐνθεῖναι φόβον *inspire* fear, X.*An.*7.4.1, etc.; ἐ. ταῖς χορδαῖς τὴν ἁρμονίαν Plot.4.7.8:—so in Med., χόλον ἔνθεο θυμῷ thou *hast stored up* wrath *in thy* heart, Il.6.326; κότον ἔνθετο θυμῷ Od.11.102; opp. ἵλαον ἔνθεο θυμόν Il. 9.639; τὴν εἴς τινα εὔνοιαν *PMag.Lond.*125.26; μῦθον πεπνυμένον ἔνθετο θυμῷ *laid it to his* heart, Od.21.355; μή μοι πατέρας..ὁμοίῃ ἔνθεο τιμῇ *put* not *our* fathers *in* like honour, Il.4.410. 3. *put in the mouth*, τινί τι Ar.*Eq.*717; ψώμισμα (sc. τῶν νηπίων στόματι) Plu. 2.320d:—Med., ἐνθοῦ *put in*, i.e. *eat*, Ar.*Eq.*51; cf. ἔνθεσις II. 4. *insert*, δέλτα ἀντὶ τοῦ νῦ Pl.*Cra.*417b. 5. *put on*, χλαίνας Il.24.646; κόσμον τάφῳ E.*IT*632:—Med., σάκος ἔνθετο νώτῳ A.R.3.1320. 6. *engraft, bud*, ἀφ' ἑτέρων δενδρέων ὀφθαλμοὶ ἐνετέθησαν Hp.*Nat.Puer.* 26. 7. of cautery, ἐνθεῖναι ἐσχάρας Id.*Art.*11, cf. Paul.Aeg.6.44.

**ἐντίκτω** (for ἐντέξῃ v. infr. I. 2), *bear* or *produce in*, δόμοις τοῖσδ' ἄρσεν' ἐντίκτω κόρον E.*Andr.*24; ᾠὰ ἐ. ἐς τὴν ἰλὺν *drop* eggs into the mud, Hdt.2.93: abs., *bear children in* a place, Th.3.104; ἐντίκτουσιν ἐνταῦθα Arist.*HA*552ᵇ29; ἐν τῇ τῶν ἐλαττόνων ὀρνίθων νεοττιᾷ ἐ., of the cuckoo, ib.563ᵇ31. 2. *create* or *cause in*, τὸ κακοῦργον.. ἐντίκτει Κύπρις ἐν ταῖς σοφαῖσιν E.*Hipp.*642; ἐ. ἔρωτας, ἔχθρας ὄγκον, φθόνους, ἀνελευθερίαν, εὐχέρειαν τοῖς νέοις πονηρίας, σωφροσύνην, Pl.*Lg.*870a, 843b, 870c, *Phdr.*256e, *R.*392a, 410a; τοῖς νέοις ζῆλον Plb.12.26ᶜ.4; ἐντέξῃ is dub. in Ar.*Lys.*553. II. pf. part. ἐντετοκώς, intr., *inborn, innate*, νόσον..ἐν τῇ πόλει ἐντετοκυῖαν Id.*V.*651.

**ἐντῑλάω,** *void excrement upon*, τινί τι Ar.*Ach.*351.

**ἔντιλτος** πλακοῦς, ὁ, prob. a cake *seasoned with* τιλτόν (q.v.), Clearch.65 (s.v.l.).

**ἐντῑμ-άω,** *value in* or *among*, ἐν ταῖς μ' μναῖς ἐνετιμᾶτο τὰ χρυσία καὶ τὰ ἱμάτια τῶν χιλίων [δραχμῶν] D.41.27; ἐς τὰς προῖκας ἐντετιμῆσθαι D.C.48.8; ἐντετιμημένος *highly valued, valuable*, Sophr.100 codd. Ath. (ἐντεταμένα Meineke):—Med., *value* in giving a dowry, Poll. 8.142. **-όομαι,** Pass., *to be held in honour*, Lxx 4*Ki.*1.13. ⊛ **-ος,** ον, (τιμή), 1. of persons, *in honour, honoured*, opp. ἄτιμος, Pl. *Euthd.*281c, etc.; τινί by another, S.*El.*239 (lyr.), *Ant.*25, etc.; παρά τινι Pl.*Ti.*21e: c. dat. rei, *honoured with*, σπονδαῖς E.*Or.*1688 (anap.); *in office*, Pl.*R.*564d; of *men of high rank* in Persia, X.*Cyr.*2.1.8, al.; opp. ἄδοξοι, D.3.29; = ἐπίτιμος, Decr.ap.eund.59.104. 2. of things, τὰ θεῶν ἐ. *what is honoured in* their sight, their *ordinances* or *attributes*, S.*Ant.*77; ἐ. ποιῆσαι τὴν τέχνην hold it *in honour*, Isoc.4.159; ἐ. ποιεῖν τι Arist.*Pol.*1286ᵇ15; ἔργα -ότερα (opp. ἀναγκαιότερα) ib. 1255ᵇ28; δαπανήματα -ότατα Id.*EN*1122ᵇ35; χώρα ἐ. place *of honour*, Pl.*Epin.*985e; ἐ. ἀπόλυσις, = Lat. *honesta missio*, *PHamb.*1.31.19 (ii A.D.). 3. Adv. -μως, ἄγειν τι Pl.*R.*528c, cf. Satyr.*Vit.Eur.Fr.* 39 xviii 27 (Pass.); ἔχειν τι Pl.*R.*528b; also ἐ. ἔχειν to be *in honour*, X.*An.*2.1.7: Sup. -ότατα D.C.63.17; -μως ἀπολελυμένος, = Lat. *missus honesta missione*, *POxy.*1471.6 (i A.D.), al. II. *doing honour, honourable* (to a person), λόγος Pl.*Lg.*855a. III. *valuable, highly valued*, [χώρα] Arist.*Mete.*352ᵃ12 (Comp.), cf. *PLond.*5. 1708.33 (vi A.D.); of currency, *accepted* in exchange, opp. ἀδόκιμον, νόμισμα Pl.*Lg.*742a. **-ότης,** ητος, ἡ, *honour, rank*, Arist.*Rh.* 1390ᵇ19.

**ἐντῐν-αγμός,** ὁ, *shaking*, Lxx *Si* 22.15 (v.l. ἐντίναγμα, as in Sch. Od.17.231). **-άσσω,** *hurl against*, δοκόν τινι D.L.6.41, cf. Lxx 1*Ma.*2.36, 2*Ma.*4.41, Aesop.357:—Pass., *to be shaken*, aor. 2 ἐνετινάγη *PFlor.*163.3 (iii A.D.). II. intr., *collide with* (nisi leg. ἐκτ- (q.v.)), εἰς τοὺς πλησίον ἵππους Ael.*Tact.*19.2.

**ἐντῑτός,** όν, *liable to be sued*, αὐτῷ ἐντιτὸν ἔστω ἐπὶ τᾷ δόσει *GDI* 5087ᵃ6 (Crete); cf. ἐντιτόν· ἔνδικ[τ]ον, Hsch.

**ἐν-τμήγω,** Ep. for ἐντέμνω, Nic.*Fr.*82. **-τμημα,** ατος, τό, *cut in* a thing, *incision, notch*, X.*Cyn.*2.7. **-τμησις,** εως, ἡ, = foreg., Apollon.*Lex.* s.v. ἁρματροχιή.

**ἔντο,** 3 pl. aor. 2 Med. of ἵημι, Hom.

**ἔντοθεν,** v. ἔντοσθεν.

**ἐντοίχιος,** ον, *on the walls*, γραφαί D.H.16.3; τὰ ἐ. γράφειν prob. cj. in X.*An.*7.8.1; ἐ. ὄρυγμα Ruf.ap.Orib.49.32.5.

**ἔντοκος,** ον, *with young*, Lyc.185, *PTeb.*53.20 (ii B.C.). 2. *bearing interest*, *PStrassb.*92.8 (iii B.C.), etc.

**ἐντολ-εύς,** έως, ὁ, = ἐντολικάριος, *agent, representative*, *Cod.Just.*4. 20.16.1, *PGrenf.*1.62.8 (vi A.D.). ⊛ **-ή,** ἡ, *injunction, order, command*, freq. in pl., *orders, commands*, Pi.*Fr.*177, Hdt.1.22, 3.147, A.*Pr.*12, etc.; ἐντολαὶ θεοῦ 1*Ep.Cor.*7.19; ἐντολὰς δοῦναι Decr.ap.D.18.75; ἐντολὴν ἐπιτελέειν Hdt.1.157; royal *ordinance*, *PTeb.*6.10 (ii B.C.); θεῖαι ἐ., of Imperial *ordinances*, *SIG*888.51 (iii A.D.); ἀπ' ἐντολῆς by *proxy*, Luc.*Pr.Im.*16.—Rare in Trag. and Att. Prose. **-ίδιον,** τό, Dim. of foreg., *POxy.*1767.17 (iii A.D.). ⊛ **-ικάριος,** ὁ, *mandatory*, *IG*14.956*B*15 (iv A.D.), Mitteis *Chr.*78.8 (iv A.D.), etc. **-ικός,** ή, όν, *of* or *for a command*, νόμος prob. in *CIG*2712.8 (Mylasa, v A.D.); ἐπιστολίδιον *POxy.*1677.5 (iii A.D.). II. Subst. -κόν, τό, *authorisation, power of attorney*, *PFlor.*142.2 (iii A.D.), etc. 2. *prescription, recipe*, *BGU*953.1 (iii/iv A.D.), dub. sens. in *POxy.*1775.13 (iv A.D.). **-ῐμαῖον** γράμμα power *of attorney*, *PMasp.*161.14, al. (vi A.D.). ⊛ **-ιος,** ὁ, dub. sens. in *CRAcad.Inscr.*1905.158 (Egypt).

**ἐντολμάομαι,** Dep., = τολμάω ἐν.., Ael.*Fr.*212.

**ἐντομ-ή,** ἡ, *slit, groove*, Hp.*Art.*33, 47; in insects, *notch, incision*, Arist.*HA*487ᵃ33 (pl.), 523ᵇ14 (pl.); ἐντομαὶ κτενός Luc.*Am.*44. 2. *hewing* of masonry, λίθοι ἐντομῇ (v.l. ἐν τομῇ) ἐγγώνιοι Th.1.93. 3. *narrow gorge, cleft*, D.S.1.32. **-ίας,** ου, ὁ, *eunuch*, Hsch.; *castrated animal*, Sch.Il.9.539. **-ιος,** ον, dub. sens. in *PLond.*5.1656 (iv A.D.). ⊛ **-ίς,** ίδος, ἡ, *incision, gash*, Lxx *Le.*19.28, 21.5. II. *grave, burial-vault*, *Ath.Mitt.*16.368 (Thessalonica). III. ἐντομίδας· μαμιλάρι (leg. σμιλάρια), ψαλίδια, Hsch. ⊛ **-ος,** ον, *cut in pieces*, esp. in neut. pl. ἔντομα *victims* offered to the dead, ἱερεῖα being prop. used in reference to gods (Eust.1671 fin., cf. ἐναγίζω), ἔ. ποιεῖν offer *as victims*, Hdt.2.119, cf. 7.191; ἔ. μήλων A.R.1.587, cf. Call. ap.Sch.*Th.Oxy.*853 x 38. II. ἔντομα (sc. ζῷα), τά, *insects*, καλῶ δὲ ἔντομα ὅσα ἔχει κατὰ τὸ σῶμα ἐντομάς Arist.*HA*487ᵃ33, cf. 523ᵇ13, Ant.Lib.4.7. III. ἔντομοι· ἔνορκοι, Hsch.

**ἐντον-ία,** ἡ, = Lat. *distentio penis*, Horap.1.46 (v.l. εὐτ-). **-ιον,** τό, *apparatus for stretching the* τόνοι *of a torsion-engine*, Ph.*Bel.*57.46, 61.12, Hero *Bel.*107.1. ⊛ **-ος,** ον, (ἐντείνω) of persons, *sinewy*, v.l. for εὐ-, Hp.*Aër.*4; τὰ μέλη ἐντόνοις ὅμοια Zeno *Stoic.*1.58. 2. *violent*, of wind, etc., νότος Olymp.*in Mete.*195.39; ἀκτῖνες -ώτεραι ib.259. 23: metaph., *intense, eager, vehement*, γνώμη Hdt.4.11; σπλάγχνον E.*Hipp.*118; Μοῦσα..ἔ. Ἀχαρνική Ar.*Ach.*666; ἔ. καὶ δριμεῖς Pl.*Tht.* 173a; -ώτατος πρός τι S.*Fr.*842; δρᾶν ἔ. χέρες E.*Fr.*291 (s.v.l.). Adv. -νως *eagerly*, χωρεῖν Th.5.70; ἀπαιτεῖν X.*An.*7.5.7; ζητεῖσθαι Pl.*R.*528c: Comp. -ώτερον *PPetr.*3 p.111 (prob.). II. Subst.

ἔντονος, ὁ, dub. l. for τόνος, Pl.*Lg.*945c.—Freq. confounded with εὔτονος.

**ἐντοπ-ίζω**, sine expl., Suid. **-ιος**, ον, *local*, θεοὶ ἐ., = ἐγχώριοι, Pl.*Phdr.*262d; νόμισμα, πλοιάρια, *Peripl.M.Rubr.*49,36; πόλεμοι ἐ. *civil* wars, D.H.8.83; ἡ ἐ. ἱστορία D.L.7.35; ἐντόπιοι *local residents*, opp. ξένοι, *IG*5(2).491 (Megalopolis, ii/iii A.D.); opp. Ἀλεξανδρεῖς, *PLond.*2.192.94 (i A.D.). 2. Medic., *local*, βάρος Antyll.ap.Aët.9.40. **-ος**, ον, *in* or *of a place*, S.*Ph.*212 (lyr.), 1171 (lyr.), *OC*1457, Pl.*Lg.*848d, prob. in Nausicr.1; ἔλαιον prob. in *OGI*629.70 (Palmyra, ii A.D.).

**ἐντορεύω**, *carve in relief on . .*, Plu.*Cic.*1:—Pass., Id.2.164a, 399f, Luc.*Ind.*8.

**ἐντορν-εύω**, *turn by the lathe*, in pf. Pass. ἐντετορνεύσθω Hero *Aut.*16.2. **-ία**, ἡ, *raised rim* or *flange*, Id.*Bel.*97.5. **-ος**, ον, *turned with the lathe*, Pl.*Lg.*898a; [ὁ κόσμος] κατ' ἀκρίβειαν ἔ. perfectly *rounded*, Arist.*Cael.*287ᵇ15, cf. *IG*2.1054*f* 24; πρὸς τὴν ἔ. (sc. γραμμήν) στρογγύλα *IG*2².244.101 (Piraeus). Adv. -νως Hero *Aut.*23.3.

**ἔντος**, τό, v. ἔντεα, τά.

⊛ **ἐντός**, (ἐν) *within, inside*, opp. ἐκτός: I. Prep. c. gen., which mostly follows, but may precede, τείχεος ἐ. Il.12.380, al., cf. Ἀρχ. Ἐφ. 1920.33 (Boeot., v B.C.); ἐ. Ὀλύμπου Hes.*Th.*37; στέρνων ἐ. A.*Ag.*77 (anap.); σ' ἔθρεψεν ἐ. . ζώνης Id.*Eu.*607; ἐ. ἐμεωυτοῦ *in* my *senses, under* my own *control*, Hdt.7.47; ἐ. ἑωυτοῦ γίνεσθαι Id.1.119, cf. Hp.*Epid.*7.1; ἐ. ὢν εἰπεῖν αὐτοῦ D.34.20; ἐ. τῶν λογισμῶν Plu.*Alex.*32; ἐ. ὑμῶν *in* your *hearts*, *Ev.Luc.*17.21; τῶν μαθημάτων ἐ. Dicaearch.1.30; γραμμάτων ἐ. Sor.1.3; ἐ. εἶναι τῶν συμβαινόντων παθῶν *acquainted with*, Chrysipp.*Stoic.*3.120; ἐ. τοξεύματος *within* shot, E.*HF*991, X.*Cyr.*1.4.23; οὐδ' ἐντὸς πολλοῦ πλησιάζειν not *within* a great distance, Pl.*Smp.*195b, cf. Th.2.77; ἐ. ποιεῖν put *within*, τῶν τειχῶν Id.7.5; ἐ. ποιεῖσθαι τῶν ἐπιτάκτων Id.6.67; ἐ. πλαισίου ποιησάμενοι X.*An.*7.8.16; of troops, ἐ. αὐτῶν *within* their own *lines*, ib.1.10.3: also with Verbs of motion, τείχεος ἐ. ἰόντες Il.12.374; πύργων ἔπεμψεν ἐντός E.*Tr.*12. 2. *within*, i.e. *on this side*, ἐ. Ἅλυος ποταμοῦ Hdt.1.6, cf. 8.47, Th.1.16; ἡ ἐ. Ἱσπανία, = Lat. *Hispania Citerior*, Plu.*Cat.Ma.*10; ἐ. τοῦ Πόντου Hdt.4.46; ἐ. ὅρων Ἡρακλείων Pl.*Ti.*25c; ἐ. τῶν μέτρων τετμημένον μέταλλον *within* the bounds of the adjacent property, an encroachment, Hyp.*Eux.*35; τῶν μέτρων ἐ. D.37.36; also ἐ. τῶν πρῳρέων . . καὶ τοῦ αἰγιαλοῦ *between . .*, Hdt.7.100. 3. of Time, *within*, ἐ. οὐ πολλοῦ χρόνου Antipho 5.69; ἐ. εἴκοσιν ἡμερῶν Th.4.39, cf. *IG*1².114.40, etc.; ἐ. ἑξήκοντ' ἐτῶν Amphis 20.2; ἐ. ἑσπέρας *short of*, i.e. *before*, evening, X.*Cyn.*4.11; ἐ. ἑβδόμης *before* the seventh of the month, Hsch.; οἱ τῆς ἡλικίας ἐ. γεγονότες *short of* manhood, Lys.2.50; τῆς πρεπούσης ἐ. ἡλικίας *within* the fitting limits of age, Pl.*Ti.*18d. 4. with Numbers, ἐ. εἴκοσιν [ἐτῶν] *under* twenty, Ar.*Ec.*984; ἐ. δραχμῶν πεντήκοντα *within*, i.e. *under . .*, Pl.*Lg.*953b. 5. of Degrees of relationship, ἐ. ἀνεψιότητος *within* the relationship of cousins, *nearer than* cousins, ib.871b, Lexap.D.43.57. II. Adv. *within*, ἐ. ἐέργειν Il.2.845, Od.7.88; χώρην ἐ. ἀπέργειν Hdt.3.116; ἐ. ἔχειν τινάς Th.7.78; ἐ. ποιῆσαι or ποιήσασθαι, Id.5.2, 6.75: freq. with the Art., ἐκ τοῦ ἐ., = ἔντοσθε, Id.2.76; τὰ ἐ. the *inner parts* of the body (of ἥ τε φάρυγξ καὶ ἡ γλῶσσα), ib.49, cf. Pl.*Prt.*334c, etc.; τοὐντός, opp. τοὔξω, S.*Ichn.*302; ἐ. *in the Mediterranean*, Arist.*Mu.*393ᵃ12.

**ἐντόσαρκες**· ἐντὸς τοῦ σώματος, Hsch.

**ἔντοσθε** and **ἔντοσθεν** (the latter both before vowels, as Il.12.455, al., and before consonants, as ib.296, al.), Adv. *from within*, Od.2.424; also, = ἐντός, abs., Il.22.237: c. gen., ἔντοσθε χαράδρης 4.454, etc.; after its case, δόμων ἔ. Od.1.380: never in Att. or Trag., unless read metri gr. for ἔνδοθεν in A.*Pers.*991 (lyr.): rare in Prose, Hp.*Medic.*11, D.S.1.35, Luc.*VH*1.24.—The form **ἔντοθεν**, mentioned in Sch.D.T.p.278 H., *An.Ox.*1.178, is sts. found in codd., as Luc.*Vit. Auct.*26, and is conjectured in Od.9.239,338.

**ἐντοσθίδια**, τά, = ἐντόσθια, Hp.*Steril.*230, Arist.*PA*684ᵇ32; cf. ἐνδοσθίδια. II. as Adj., ἐντοσθίδιον πάθος *intestinal* complaint, Androm.ap.Gal.14.42.

**ἐντόσθιος**, ον, *intestinal*, ἕλμιθες Lyd.*Ost.*32: but mostly, II. Subst. **ἐντόσθια**, τά, *inwards, entrails*, Arist.*PA*685ᵃ3, Ti.Locr.100b:—also **ἐνδόσθια**, Lxx *Ex.*12.9, al., Hsch., *EM*345.21.

**ἐντότερος**, α, ον, *inner*, τὴν αὐλὴν τὴν ἐ. Lxx *Es.*4.11.

**ἐντοῦθα**, = ἐνταῦθα, *Schwyzer* 792 (Cumae), 811.17 (Oropus).

**ἐντουρίων**, ωνος, ὁ, dub. sens. in *OGI*262.7 (Syria).

**ἐντοφήϊα**, τά, Delph., = ἐνταφ–, *offerings buried in tombs*, *Michel* 995 *C*20. **ἐντόφιον**, v. ἐντάφιος.

**ἐντρᾰγεῖν**, prop. aor. 2 inf. of ἐντρώγω, used in Att. as regul. aor. of τρώγω (q.v.), *eat dessert*, ἔντραγε τουτί Ar.*V.*612, cf. *Eq.*51, Phryn. Com.25, Alciphr.1.22, etc.: c. gen., ἰσχάδων, μήλου, καρύων, Luc.*Merc.Cond.*24, Plu.2.279f, Hld.2.23.

**ἐντραγεῖ**· ἐντρυφᾷ, Hsch. **ἐντραγούμενοι**· μασώμενοι, Id.

**ἐντρᾰγῳδέω**, *come the hero over*, τισί Luc.*Sat.*19.

**ἐντρᾱν-ής**, ές, *clear, manifest*, *PMasp.*32.54 (vi A.D.). II. ἐντρανῆ τόνον· ἰσχυρόν, Hsch. (ἐντραγήτονον cod.). **-ίζω**, *look keenly at*, Eust.259.8, Sch.Theoc.10.18; τῷ ἀγαθῷ Eustr. *in EN* 312.1.

**ἐντρᾰπεζίτης** [ῐ], ου, ὁ: fem. **-ῖτις**, ιδος, *parasite*, Suid., Zonar.

⊛ **ἐντράπελος** [ᾰ], ον, (ἐντρέπω II.4) *shameful*, dub. l. in Pi.*P.*4.105, Thgn.400 cod. A.

**ἔντρᾱχυς**, εια, υ, *somewhat rough*, Dsc.5.159. II. of music, *somewhat harsh*, S.E.*M.*6.50.

**ἐντρεπ-τικός**, ή, όν, *fit to put one to shame*, Ael.*NA*3.1; τὸ ἐ. the *sense of shame*, Arr.*Epict.*1.5.3,9. II. *commanding respect*, Herm. *in Phdr.*p.72 A. III. Adv. -κῶς· ἐλεγκτικῶς, Hsch. **-ω**, *turn about*, τὰ νῶτα Hdt.7.211; ἐξεστραμμένην ἕδραν ἐ. *reduce* prolapsed anus, Gal.12.365; of a muscle, *turn* the eye *in*, Id.*UP*10.9 (Pass.). 2. mostly metaph., *make one turn, put him to shame*, 1*Ep.Cor.*4.14, Ael.*VH*3.17, S.E.*P.*3.135, D.L.2.29. 3. *alter*, Luc.*Hist.Conscr.*15; τὴν φωνὴν εἰς μέλος Id.*Pseudol.*7. 4. Med., ἐντρέψασθαι· τὸ εἴσω τρέψαι τὸ ἱμάτιον, Hsch. II. Med. or Pass., fut. ἐντραπήσομαι Lxx *Le.*26.41, al.: *turn about, hesitate*, esp. *feel misgiving* or *compunction*, στείχωμεν ἤδη μηδ' ἔτ' ἐντρεπώμεθα (where Sch. compares ἐντροπαλιζόμενος) S.*OC*1541; ἐνετρέποντο . . ἐν ἑαυτοῖς Plb.31.2.6 (prob. cj.). 2. c. gen. pers., *turn towards, give heed* or *regard to, respect, reverence*, οὐδέ νυ σοί περ ἐντρέπεται φίλον ἦτορ ἀνεψιοῦ κταμένοιο; Il.15.554, cf. Od.1.60; συμμάχου S.*Aj.*90; δωμάτων Id.*OT*1226; νόμων Pl.*Cri.*52c, etc.; ὧν ἐντρέπου σὺ μηδέν S.*OT*724: c. inf., *take heed to . .*, φεύγειν ὀλεσήνορας ὅρκους ἐντρέπευ cj. in Thgn.400: aor. 2 Pass., (οὐκ) ἐντρεπέντος τοῦ Ἀμώσιος since A. *paid* no *attention*, *UPZ*5.24 (ii B.C.). 3. later c. acc., *reverence, feel regard for*, τὴν πολιάν Alex.71, cf. Plb.3.10.3, al., *Ev.Marc.*12.6. b. *feel shame on account of*, Plb.2.49.7. 4. abs., *feel shame* or *fear*, *UPZ* 62.29 (ii B.C.), 2*Ep.Thess.*3.14, *Ep.Tit.*2.8.

⊛ **ἐντρέφω**, poet. ἐνιτ–, = τρέφω ἐν, *bring up* or *train in*, τέκνα E.*Ion* 1428; ἐνιθρέψασ' ὀροδάμνοις βότρυας *AP*9.231 (Antip.):—Med., φυτὰ ἐνθρέψασθαι Hes.*Op.*781, cf. Hp.*Aër.*12 (Pass.):—Pass., *to be raised* or *bred in*, γυμνάσια οἷσιν ἐνετράφην E.*Ph.*368, cf. Call.*Iamb.*1.184; νόμοις Pl.*Lg.*798a; ποιήμασι, ἤθει, Plu.2.32e, 38b; διαλογισμοῖς Arr.*Epict.*4.4.48; τοῖς λόγοις τῆς πίστεως 1*Ep.Ti.*4.6.

⊛ **ἐντρέχ-εια**, ἡ, *skill, aptitude*, Corn.*ND*18, M.Ant.1.8, Vett.Val.61.15, S.E.*M.*1.141, etc.; ἐ. φυσική Gal.14.213, cf. 306: in pl., ἐ. τῶν ζῴων *instincts*, Antig.*Mir.*26, cf. 60: so generally, *instinct*, Anon.Lond.1.24. b. concrete, *an industry*, Str.17.1.15. **-ής**, ές, *skilful, ready*, ἐν πόνοις καὶ μαθήμασι καὶ φόβοις ἐντρεχέστατος Pl.*R.*537a: abs., Longin.44.1, M.Ant.6.14, etc.; τὸ ἐ. Perseusap.Philetaer.Gramm. in *Rh. Mus.*43.416. Adv. -χῶς Iamb.*Protr.*5: Comp. -έστερον M.Ant.7.66; -εστέρως *An.Ox.*3.188. II. ἐντρεχέστερον· γοργότερον, Hsch. **-ω**, aor. -έδραμον, *run in, be active in*: hence, *fit, suit*, once in Hom., εἰ ἐντρέχοι ἀγλαὰ γυῖα if his limbs *moved freely in* [the armour], Il.19.385. 2. *to be current among*, λόγος ἀνθρώποις Arat.100. II. *slip in, enter*, Luc.*Am.*24; πόντῳ *AP*9.370.3 (Tib. Illustr.). III. *come in the way, intervene*, Phld.*D.*3.8, *Ir.*p.75 W.; εἴ τις ἐ. νῆσος Str.17.1.4; *occur*, τὰ ἐντρέχοντα Philostr.*VA*2.36; ἐ. τοῖς Τυρρηνοῖς ἰδέαι δελφίνων Id.*Im.*1.19; ἄχρι ἂν μηδὲν ἐντρέχῃ μολυβδῶδες *is met with*, Dsc.5.81; κεφαλαιώματα τοῦ ἐντρέχοντος κοινοῦ τοῖς πολλοῖς Procl. *in Prm.*p.564 S. IV. c. dat. pers., *apply to*, *BGU*1197.11 (i A.D.).

**ἐν-τριβάσαι**· ἐναντίαν τύψαι, Hsch. ⊛ **-τρῑβής**, ές, metaph. from the touchstone, *proved by rubbing, versed* or *practised in*, ἀρχαῖς τε καὶ νόμοισιν ἐ. S.*Ant.*177; τέχνῃ Pl.*Lg.*769b; περί τι Isoc.15.187; πληγῶν Sch.Il.11.559. 2. ἐ. ὁδός *beaten* track, App.*Hann.*4. **-τρίβω** [ῑ], *rub in*, esp. unguents or cosmetics, ψιμύθιον τῷ προσώπῳ Luc.*Hist.Conscr.*8; οἴνῳ λίθον ἐ. *crumble* a stone *into* wine, Orph.*L.*344. 2. metaph., ἐ. κόνδυλόν τινι *give* him *a drubbing*, Plu.*Alc.*8, Luc.*Prom.*10:—Med., ἐντρίβεσθαί τινι πληγάς *cause* them *to be given* him, D.H.7.45; ἐ. κακόν τινι Luc.*DDeor.*20.2. II. c. acc. pers., *rub* one *with* cosmetics, ὑποχρίουσι καὶ ἐντρίβουσιν αὐτούς X.*Cyr.*8.8.20:—Med., ἐ. τὰ πρόσωπα Ath.12.523a:—Pass., *have* cosmetics *rubbed in, to be anointed, painted*, Ar.*Lys.*149, *Ec.*732, X.*Cyr.*8.1.41; ἐντετριμμένη ψιμυθίῳ Id.*Oec.*10.2; ἀλφίτοισιν Hermipp.26: also c. acc. rei, ἐντετρ. χρῶμα Luc.*DDeor.*20.10: metaph., παιδέρωτ' ἐ. Alex.98.18. III. *rub away, wear by rubbing*, Ar.*Ra.*1070. IV. Pass., *to be familiar with*, γυναικῶν ἐντριβεῖσα παθήμασιν Procop.Gaz. p.163 B., cf. *Cod.Just.*10.27.3 *Intr.* **-τριμμα**, ατος, τό, *cosmetic*, Plu.*Crass.*24 (pl.), Them.*Or.*13.167c (pl.).

**ἔντριτον**· τὸ διονίου ἔμβρωμα, ὃ Γαλάται ἔμβρεκτόν φασιν, Hsch. (Fort. ἔντριπτον.)

**ἔντρῐτος**, ον, *of three strands, threefold*, σπαρτίον Lxx *Ec.*4.12. II. = Lat. *sequester*, Gloss.

**ἐντρῐτωνίζω**, Com. word in Ar.*Eq.*1189, *to third* with water, i.e. *to mix three* parts of water with two of wine, with a pun on Τριτογενής.

**ἔντρῐχ-ος**, ον, *hairy*, *AP*14.62, Sm.*Ps.*67(68).22; *with the hair on*, δέρμα Tz. ad Lyc.634. II. Subst., τὸ ἔ. *wig*, Poll.2.30. III. ἔντριχον· ἀσθενές, Hsch. **-ωμα**, ατος, τό, *edges of the eyelids, eyelashes*, Poll.2.69. II. *hair-sieve*, also ἠθμός, Plu.2.912e. **-ώσεις**· αἱ βλεφαρίδες τῶν ὀφθαλμῶν, Hsch.

**ἔντριψις**, εως, ἡ, *rubbing in*, of cosmetics, X.*Cyr.*1.3.2; ἀσβόλου Hld.6.11. II. *cosmetic*, Ael.*VH*12.1.

**ἔντρομος**, ον, *trembling*, Plu.*Fab.*3, *AP*5.203 (Mel.); γῆ Lxx *Ps.*17(18).8, *Act.Ap.*7.32, Sor.1.89, *PMag.Par.*1.3076.

**ἐντροπάδην**· ἐναλλὰξ μεταβολῇ χειρῶν, Hsch.

**ἐντροπᾰλ-ίζομαι**, Pass., Frequentat. of ἐντρέπω, only pres. part., *often turning round*, ἄλοχος δὲ φίλη οἰκόνδε βεβήκει ἐντροπαλιζομένη Il.6.496; esp. of men retreating with their face to the enemy, θηρὶ ἐοικώς, ἐντροπαλιζόμενος 11.547, cf. 17.109, 21.492, Q.S.12.583. **-ισμός**, ὁ, *turning round*, Sch.Aristid.3 p.213 D.

**ἐντροπ-ή**, ἡ, *turning towards*: only metaph. (cf. ἐντρέπω II.2), ἐντροπήν τινος ἔχειν *respect for* one, S.*OC*299, cf. Plb.4.52.2, *OGI*323.7 (Pergam., ii B.C.), etc.: abs., *modesty*, Hp.*Decent.*5, 1*Ep.Cor.*6.5, etc.; ἐ. καὶ αἰδώς Iamb.*VP*2.10. 2. *humiliation*, Lxx *Ps.*34(35).26,

al. —**ημᾰτικός**, ή, όν, gloss on δεινός, Apollon.*Lex.* —**ία**, Ion. -ίη, ἡ, = ἐντροπή, Hp.*Decent.*2. II. δόλιαι ἐντροπίαι subtle *twists, tricks, dodges, h.Merc.*245. —**ίας** οἶνος, ὁ, = τροπίας, Hsch., Suid.; cf. ἐκτροπίας. —**ίδες**· ὑποδήματα, Hsch. (before ἐντροπάδην: fort. leg. ἐνδρομίδες). —**ικός**, ή, όν, = αἰδήμων, Hdn.*Epim.*28. —**ον**, τό, an *ornament*, Poll.5.96. —**όω**, *fasten* the oars *with thongs*, Hsch.:—Med., Agath.5.22; cf. τροπωτήρ.

**ἔντροφος**, ον, (ἐντρέφω) *living in* or *acquainted with*, σὺ γάρ με μόχθῳ τῷδ' ἔθηκας ἔ. S.*OC*1362; παλαιᾷ μὲν ἔ. ἁμέρᾳ, λευκῷ δὲ γήρᾳ Id.*Aj.* 622 codd.; ἔ. ὕλῃ *reared in..*, A.R.1.1117. 2. as Subst., ἔ. τινος *nursling* of.., E.*IA*289 (lyr.), cf. Arist.*Fr.*675, *AP*9.242 (Antiphil.).—Poet. word.

⊛ **ἐντροχ-άζω**, = ἐντρέχω, *intervene, occur*, κοινότητος ἐντροχαζούσης φωνῶν Demetr.Lac.*Herc.*1014.48, cf. 57,62 F., al. II. *exercise* a horse *in a ring, Hippiatr.*33. —**ος**, ον, = ἐντρεχής, *EM*762.29.

⊛ **ἐντρῠγ-άω**, *gather grapes in*, Moeris s. v. ἄρριχος. —**ηφάνιον**· ὁ δεύτερος οἶνος, Hsch. —**ος**, ον, *containing sediment* or *lees, Hippiatr.*34.

**ἐντρυλλίζω** or -τρῡλίζω, *whisper in one's ear*, Ar.*Th.*341; term used in quail-baiting, Poll.9.109.

**ἐντρῠφ-άω**, *revel in, delight in*, c. dat., ἐξουσίᾳ E.*Fr.*362.24; γαμηλίῳ λέχει Men.535.8; ἡδοναῖς D.S.19.71, cf. Luc.*JTr.*21; in good sense, δικαιοσύνῃ Ph.2.258; of persons, Πελοπίδᾳ Plu.*Pel.*30; ἔν τινι D.C.65.20; in bad sense, ἐν ταῖς ἀγάπαις 2*Ep.Pet.*2.13; κόμαι ἀνέμοις ἐνετρύφων it was *playing in* the wind, Chaerem.1.7: abs., X.*HG*4.1. 30, Ph.1.666. II. *treat haughtily* or *contemptuously*, τινί E.*Cyc.* 588, Plu.*Them.*18, Alciphr.1.35; *exult over*, τινὸς συμφοραῖς Jul.*ad Ath.*279c; ἔν τινι Lxx *Hb.*1.10: abs., Plu.*Alc.*23:—Pass., *to be made a mock of*, Id.*Lys.*6, *Caes.*64. III. *use* or *abuse at pleasure*, τοῖς νόμοις, τοῖς συνοῦσι, Luc.*Abd.*10, *Merc.Cond.*35, al. —**ημα**, ατος, τό, *thing to take pleasure in, a delight*, Lxx *Ec.*2.8 (pl.), Ph.1.690. —**ής**, ές, *luxurious, wanton*, Man.4.85.

⊛ **ἐντρύχομαι** [ῡ], Pass. or Med., *waste away*, D.C.38.46 codd.

**ἐντρώγω**, v. ἐντραγεῖν.

**ἔντῠβον**, τό, *endive, Gp.*12.1.7.

**ἐντυγχάνω**, fut. -τεύξομαι: aor. 2 ἐνέτῠχον: pf. ἐντετύχηκα Ph. 1.395, also ἐντέτευχα *Klio* 15.35 (Delph., i B. C.): aor. 1 Pass. ἐνετεύχθην Ph.2.170, Plu.*Cat.Ma.*9:—*light upon, fall in with, meet with*, c. dat. pers., Hdt.1.134, al., Ar.*Nu.*689, etc.; ὀλίγοι τινὲς ὧν ἐντετύχηκα (i. e. τούτων οἷς..) Pl.*R.*531e, cf. *Grg.*509a, *Prt.*361e; κατ' ὄψιν ἐ. τινί Plu.*Lyc.*1. 2. c. dat. rei, κακοῖς ἐ., = τυγχάνω ὢν ἐν κακοῖς, S.*Aj.*433; οὐντυγχάνων (sc. τοῖς πράγμασιν) cj. Valck. in E.*Fr.*287; ἐ. τῷ νώτῳ, of the crocodile, Hdt.2.70; ὁ ἐ. τοῖς.. τοξεύμασι *he who fell in* their *way*, Th.4.40; of obstacles, ἐ. τάφροις X.*An.*2.3.10; λόφῳ ib.4.2.10. 3. abs., E.*Alc.*1032, Ar.*Ach.*848, Thphr.*Char.*24.8; οἱ ἐντυχόντες *chance persons*, Th.4.132; οἱ ἐντυγχάνοντες Isoc.18.36; τὴν ὠμότητα, ᾗ καθ' ἁπάντων χρῆται τῶν ἐντυγχανόντων D.21.88, cf. 183: sg., ὁ ἐντυχών Isoc.3.61, Pl.*Alc.*2.144b. b. ἐν δὲ μηνὸς πρῶτον τύχεν ἆμαρ it *chanced to be..*, Pi.*Pae.*2.75. 4. *obtain an audience* or *interview*, S.*Fr.*88.8, Thphr.*Char.*1.3:—Pass., *to be appealed to, consulted*, περί τινων Ph.2.170. 5. of thunder, *strike*, κεραυνὸς οἷς ἂν ἐντύχῃ X.*Mem.*4.3.14; but hardly so in S.*Ph.*1329, παῦλαν ἴσθι.. μήποτ' ἐντυχεῖν νόσου (ἂν τυχεῖν Pors.). 6. rarely c. gen., λελυμένης τῆς γεφύρης ἐντυχόντες *having found* the bridge broken up, Hdt.4.140; τῶν παρ' ἡμῖν ἐντυχὼν Ἀσκληπιδῶν *having falling in with* them, S.*Ph.* 1333. II. *converse with, talk to*, τινί Pl.*Ap.*41b, *Phd.*61c, etc.; οὐκ ἄχαρις ἐντυχεῖν Id.*Ep.*360c; οὐκ ἀηδὴς ἐ. Men.*Pk.*112. 2. *have sexual intercourse with*, τινί Plu.*Sol.*20. 3. *petition, appeal to*, τινί περί τινος (masc.) *Act.Ap.*25.24; τῷ βασιλεῖ περὶ τούτων Plb.4.76.9; ὁ ἐντυγχάνων *the petitioner, OGI*669.5; ἐ. κατά τινος *plead* against, *PGiss.*1.36.15 (ii B. C.), Lxx 1*Ma.*8.32, *Ep.Rom.*11.2; τῷ βασιλεῖ τὴν ἀπόλυσιν Lxx 3*Ma.*6.37; τῷ διοικητῇ *PTeb.*58.43 (ii B. C.): c. inf., *entreat* one *to* do, Nic.Dam.*Fr.*47 J., Plu.*Pomp.*55; ἐ. ὅπως.. Id.*Ages.* 25:—Pass., ὑπὲρ φυγάδων ἐντευχθεὶς Id.*Cat.Ma.*9. III. of books, *meet with*, βιβλίῳ ἀνδρὸς σοφοῦ Pl.*Smp.*177b, cf. *Ly.*214b; οἱ ἐντετυχηκότες ταῖς ἱερωτάταις βίβλοις Ph.1.395: hence, *read*, Luc. *Dem.Enc.*27, Plu.*Rom.*12, Jul.*Or.*7.210d, etc.; οἱ ἐντυγχάνοντες *readers*, Plb.1.3.10, Longin.1.1; ἐντυχὼν ὑμῶν τῷ ψηφίσματι *IG*12(3). 176 (Epist. Hadriani), cf. 5(1).1361.7 (Epist. Commodi).

⊛ **ἐντύλ-η** [ῠ], ἡ, *rug* (or *cushion*), *PLond.*2.402ᵛ15 (ii B. C.). —**ίσσω**, *wrap up*, Ar.*Pl.*692, *Nu.*987 (Pass.), Diocl.Com.13, Gal.10.541; σῶμα σινδόνι *Ev.Matt.*27.59. —**όομαι**, Pass., *grow hard*, of callous lumps, dub. l. for -τυπ-, Dsc.2.43.

**ἐντυμβεύω**, *entomb*, in Pass., ψυχὴ ἐ. ὡς ἂν ἐν σήματι τῷ σώματι Ph.1.65, cf. 2.367.

⊛ **ἐντύνω** [ῡ], fut. ἐντῠνῶ Lyc.734: aor. 1 ἔντῡνα Il.14.162, E.*Hipp.* 1183; imper. ἔντῡνον Il.9.203:—also **ἐντύω** [ῡ], Thgn.196; imper. ἔντυε *AP*10.118; impf. ἔντυον Il.5.720:—Med., Call.*Ap.*8: aor. ἐντῡνάμην Hom. (v. infr.):—**Pass.**, A.R.1.235: (ἔντεα):—*equip, deck out, get ready*, ἔντυεν ἵππους *was harnessing* them, Il.5.720 (so once in Trag., ἐντύναθ' ἵππους ἅρμασιν E.*Hipp.*1183); ἔντυον εὐνήν *were getting* it *ready*, Od.23.289; δέπας δ' ἔντυνον (aor. 1 imper.) ἑκάστῳ *prepare* the cup, i. e. mix the wine, for each, Il.9.203; λιγυρὴν δ' ἔντυνον ἀοιδήν *raise* the loud strain, Od.12.183; εὖ ἐντύνασαν ἓ αὐτήν *having decked* herself well *out*, Il.14.162; θοίνας ἔντῡνε B.*Fr.*18; ἐ. ὑπόσχεσιν *make* it *good, implement* it, A.R.3.737; ὑποσχεσίην ib. 510:—Med., ὄφρα τάχιστα ἐντύνεαι (trisyll.) *may'st get thee ready*, Od.6.33; ἦλθ' ἐντυναμένη 12.18; μολπήν τε καὶ ἐς χορὸν ἐντύνεσθε Call.*Ap.*8, cf. Mosch.2.30: more freq. in Hom. c. acc., *prepare for oneself*, only in the phrases ἐντύνεσθαι ἄριστον, δαῖτα, δεῖπνον, Il.24. 124, Od.3.33, 15.500, al.; ἄρμενον ἐντύνασθαι *provide one* what is needful, Hes.*Op.*632; ἀγλαΐην A.R.4.1191:—Pass., *to be furnished with*, τι Id.1.235. II. c. acc., *make* one *ready, urge* him *on*, κρατερή μιν ἀνάγκη ἐντύει Thgn.196, cf. Pi.*O.*3.28: also c. inf., *urge to* do a thing, Id.*P.*9.66, *N.*9.36.

**ἔντυος**· κόσμος, Hsch.

**ἐντῠπ-άδεια** (-δία cod.)· ὅταν τῷ ἱματίῳ τὴν χεῖρα πρὸς πρόσωπα κατειλημμένος στήσῃ, Hsch. ⊛ —**άζω**, pf. Pass. ἐντετύπασται, *enwrap, shroud, BSA*16.107 (Pisidia). —**άς**, Adv., once in Hom., Il.24.163 ἐντυπὰς ἐν χλαίνῃ κεκαλυμμένος (of Priam in his grief) lying wrapt up in his mantle so closely *as to show the contour of his limbs* (τύπος), cf. Sch. ad loc., Hsch.; ἐ. ἐν λεχέεσσι καλυψάμενος A.R.1.264, cf. 2.861, Q.S.5.530, Epic.in *Arch.Pap.*7 p.3. —**ές**· πύκτην, ἔμπληκτον, Hsch. —**ή**, ἡ, *plan, scheme, PSI*5.502.20 (iii B. C.). II. *pattern, PGiss.*12.6 (ii A. D.). —**ος**, ον, *coined*, ἀργύριον Poll.3.86. II. *receiving impressions, impressible*, Plot. 4.6.3 (Sup.). —**όω**, *carve* or *mould in* or *upon*, τῷ νομίσματι ἐνετύπωσεν ἀπήνην Arist.*Fr.*568; ἐς τὰ νομίσματα ξιφίδια δύο D.C.47.25; ἄγαλμα Plot.5.8.6; also of a painter, *APl.*4.282 (Pall.): metaph., σχῆμα τῇ ψυχῇ ἐντετύπωκεν ὁ θεός Ph.1.106:—Med., Φειδίαν ἐν μέσῃ τῇ ἀσπίδι τὸ ἑαυτοῦ πρόσωπον ἐντυπώσασθαι Arist.*Mu.*399ᵇ35:—Pass., Aristeas 67; τύλοι ἐντετυπωμένοι Dsc.2.43; *to be imprinted*, of a birth-mark, Jul.*Or.*2.81c; also, *to be flattened* by pressure, Gal.*UP* 4.7, *Hippiatr.*38: metaph., ἐντετύπωται ταῖς θύραις *is like a piece of carving on* the doors, Philostr.*VA*8.7.11. II. metaph., τὸ ἰδίωμα τῇ λέξει ἐ. Longin.10.6. —**ωδῶς**, gloss on ἐντυπάς, Eust.1343. 56. —**ωμα**, ατος, τό, *that which is graved*, χηλῆς ἐ., of a pier, Agatharch.92. —**ωσις**, εως, ἡ, *impression, dint, pit*, Thphr.*Sens.* 51, Antyll.ap.Orib.45.2.1: metaph., Gal.10.74.

**ἐντυραννέομαι**, Pass., *live under a tyranny*, Cic.*Att.*2.14.1.

**ἐντῡρ-εύω**, = ἐνταράσσω, *Com.Adesp.*998. —**ίτης** (sc. ἄρτος), ὁ, *cheese-cake, Gloss.* —**όω**, in Pass., *to be turned into cheese*, prob. in Nic.*Al.*364.

**ἐντυφλόω**, *blind*, Al.*Le.*26.16.

**ἐντύφω** [ῡ], fut. -θύψω, *smoke* as one does wasps, Ar.*V.*459:—Pass., *smoulder, be on fire*, Ph.1.455, al. II. ἐντεθυμμέναι ἄμπελοι *frost-bitten, EM*458.42.

**ἐντύχ-αλός**· ἐντευκτική, Hsch. —**ημα**, ατος, τό, = sq., in pl. prob. for εὐτ., Plu.*Phoc.*5, cf. Him.*Ecl.*32.4. —**ία**, ἡ, = *conversation, intercourse*, Plu.2.67c, 582e. 2. *meeting*, Plb.6.11ᵃ.4; *interview*, πρός τινα Aristeas 1. II. *petition, PTeb.*61(*b*).26 (ii B. C.), Lxx 3*Ma.*6.40, J.*AJ*16.9.4, Heph.Astr.3.20, Seren.ap.Stob.3.13.48; *prayer*, ἐ. πρὸς ἥλιον *PMag.Par.*1.1930, cf. *PMag.Leid.W.*4.10. III. pl., *records* of verdicts, etc., Lyd.*Mag.*3.8. —**ικά**, τά, *petitions*, Heph.Astr.3.20.

**ἐντυψίω**· ἐντινάξω, Hsch.

**ἐντύω**, v. ἐντύνω.

⊛ **ἐναίνειν**· τρυφᾶν, Hsch.

**Ἐνυαλία**, ἡ, name of a tribe at Mantinea (fr. sq.), *IG*5(2).271.

⊛ **Ἐνυάλιος** [ᾰ], ὁ, *the Warlike*, in Il. as epith. of the War-god, Ἄρης δεινὸς Ἐνυάλιος 17.211, 20.69: written Ἐνοιάλιος *IG*4.717 (Hermione), Ἐνυιάλιος *JRS*15.254 (Antioch. Pisid.): abs., as his name, ἀτάλαντος Ἐνυαλίῳ ἀνδρειφόντῃ Il.2.651, 7.166, cf. Archil.1, S.*Aj.* 179 (lyr.), E.*Andr.*1015 (lyr.), Aen.Tact.24.2; ξυνὸς Ἐ. Il.18.309: in later authors, distinct from Ares, Ar.*Pax*457, cf. Alcm.104; object of a special cult, *SIG*1014.34 (Erythrae), cf. Plu.*Sol.*9, etc.; Ἐνυαλίῳ ἐλελίζειν, ἀλαλάζειν, X.*An.*1.8.18, 5.2.14: Ἐνυάλιον, τό, *temple of* Ἐνυάλιος, Th.4.67. 2. *battle*, κοινὸν Ἐ. μαρναμένους E.*Ph.*1572 (anap.); ὁ Ἐ. *the battle-cry*, Hld.4.17; also τὸν Ἐ. παιᾶνα τῶν στρατοπέδων ἐπαλαλαζόντων Jul.*Or.*1.36b. 3. = Lat. *Quirinus*, Plb.3.25. 6, D.H.2.48: hence ὁ Ἐ. λόφος, = *Collis Quirinalis*, Id.9.60. II. after Hom. generally (in Opp.*C.*2.58, ιη, ιον), *warlike, furious*, ἰωχμός Theoc.25.279; ἀϋταί Opp. l. c.; epith. of Dionysus, *Lyr.Adesp.*108. [ῠ *Lyr.Adesp.* l. c.; elsewh. ῡ, prob. metri gr.]

**ἐνυβρ-ίζω**, *insult* or *mock* one *in* a thing, τινά τινι S.*Ph.*342; τινὰ ἐν κακοῖς E.*El.*68; μή μου ἐνυβρίξῃς ἁγνὸν τάφον *Epigr.Gr.*195 (Vaxos). 2. c. dat. pers., *insult*, γυναιξίν Plb.10.26.3, cf. *POxy.*237 vi 17 (ii A. D.); εἴς τινα D.S.34.2. 3. abs., Ar.*Th.*720. 4. in Pass., Medic., of ulcers, *to be irritated*, Sor.1.120. —**ισμα**, ατος, τό, *victim of outrage*, J.*Vit.*42, Plu.2.350c.

**ἐνυγρ-αίνω**, *moisten*, Gal.12.692, Alex.Trall.7.4. —**αντέον**, *one must moisten*, Aët.7.20.

**ἐνυγρό-βιος**, ον, = ἐνυδρόβιος, *EM*232.45. —**θηρευτής**, οῦ, ὁ, *one who seeks his prey in the water, fisherman*, Pl.*Lg.*824b. —**θηρικός**, ή, όν, *of* or *for fishing*, Id.*Sph.*220a, 221b.

⊛ **ἔνυγρος**, ον, *in the water, aquatic*, of animals, Arist.*Spir.*482ᵃ21: = ἔνυδρος, of plants, Thphr.*CP*1.21.6, 6.11.13, v.l. in Ps.-Dsc.4. 134. II. *wet, damp*, τόποι Arist.*Mete.*351ᵃ19; ἔτος Id.*HA*569ᵇ 21. III. *watery*, καρπός D.S.12.58. IV. Astrol., *involved in* loss at *sea*, πραγμάτων φθορεὺς καὶ ἔνυλός τε καὶ ἔνυγρος Rhetor. in *Cat.Cod.Astr.*1.151 (cf. ἕξει.. χρημάτων ἀποβολὴν καὶ ἐμπρήσεις καὶ ναυαγίας Heph.Astr.1.1).

**ἐνυδρ-ένται**· καθυγραίνονται, Erot. (not found in text of Hp.). —**ίας** ἄνεμος *rainy* wind, Call.*Fr.*39. —**ιος**, ον, = ἔνυδρος, Orac.ap. Lyd.*Mens.*3.5; [θεοί] Iamb.*Myst.*1.9. Adv. -ίως ibid.

⊛ **ἔνυδρις**, ἡ, gen. ιος, Hdt.: **ἐνυδρίς**, ίδος, Arist.*HA*594ᵇ31:—*otter, Lutra vulgaris*, Hdt.2.72, 4.109, Arist. l. c. II. *water-snake, Enhydris*, Plin.*HN*32.82.

**ἐνυδρόβῐος**, ον, *living in the water*, χῆνες *AP*6.231 (Phil.).

⊛ **ἔνυδρος**, ον, (ὕδωρ) *with water in it, holding water*, ἔ. τεῦχος, i.e. a bath, A.*Ag*.1128 (lyr.); of countries, *well-watered*, Ἄργος ἔ. Hes. *Fr*.24; Αἴγυπτος ἐοῦσα..ὑπτίη τε καὶ ἔ. Hdt.2.7 (ἄνυδρος codd.), cf. X.*Cyr*.3.2.11; opp. χερσαῖος, *PMasp*.188.5 (vi A.D.); τὸ ἔ. *abundance of water*, Hdn.6.6.4. 2. *of water, watery*, νάματα, λίμνη, E.*Ph*.659 (lyr.), *Ion*872 (anap.). 3. *living in* or *by water*, νύμφαι ἔ. λειμωνιάδες who haunt the *watery* meads, S.*Ph*.1454 (anap.); of plants, *growing in water*, δόναξ Ar.*Ra*.234, cf. Thphr.*HP*1.14.3, 5.3.4; of animals, Pl.*Sph*.220b, *Plt*.264d; of fish, Arist.*IA*713ᵃ10, Ti. Locr.104e; of birds, Arist.*HA*559ᵃ21; τὰ ἔ. (sc. ζῷα) ib.487ᵃ26. 4. of land, *in the water, submerged*, Id.*Mete*.352ᵃ22.

**ἐνυδρώθη**· ὑδρωπικὸς ἐγένετο, Hsch.

**ἐνύει**· ἔνδον (Lacon.), Hsch.

**Ἐνύειον** [ῡ], τό, *the temple of Bellona* (Ἐνυώ) at Rome, D.C.42.26, 50.4.

**ἐνῡλισμένον**· κεκαθαρμένον, Hsch.

**ἔνῡλος**, ον, (ὕλη) *involved* or *implicated in matter*, τὰ πάθη λόγοι ἔ. εἰσιν Arist.*deAn*.403ᵃ25, cf. Procl.*Inst*.195, etc.; ἡ ἔ. καὶ γεννητικὴ ψυχή Plot.2.3.17, cf. Dam.*Pr*.126 bis: Comp., ib.414. Adv. -λως Iamb.*Myst*.6.3, Syrian. *in Metaph*.50.5. II. *wooded*, f.l. for ἔναυλος in Ar.Did.*Epit*.11. III. Astrol., *involved in* loss by *wood*, i.e. by *fire*, v. ἔνυγρος IV.

**ἐνῠμενόσπερμος**, ον, *with seeds enclosed in a membrane*, i.e. *husk*, Thphr.*HP*8.3.4.

**ἔνυον**· ἔφορον, Hsch.

**ἐνυπάλλαγμα**, ατος, τό, *pledge*, *PLond*.3.1166.17 (i A.D.).

**ἐνυπάρχω**, *exist* or *be present in*, τὸ ἔμβρυον τὸ ἐνυπάρχον Arist.*HA* 577ᵃ14; -άρχουσα ψυχή Epicur.*Ep*.1 p.21 U. 2. *to be immanent* or *inherent*, τὸ πρῶτον ἐ., = ὕλη, Arist.*Ph*.193ᵃ10, cf. 194ᵇ24; ἐν ἅπαντι χρόνῳ τὸ [νῦν] ἐ. ib.233ᵇ35; ἐξ ὧν (sc. στοιχείων) ἔστι τὰ ὄντα ἐνυπαρχόντων *the inherence* whereof is the cause of existences, Id.*Metaph*. 998ᵃ31, cf. 1014ᵃ26, Plot.5.3.11, Jul.*Or*.4.140c, etc. 3. in Logic, *to be contained in, inhere*, ἐνυπάρχειν τοῖς κατηγορουμένοις ἢ ἐνυπάρχεσθαι, of the predicates, *to be contained in* the subjects or *to have* them *inhering*, Arist.*APo*.73ᵇ17; ἐ. ἐν τῷ τί ἐστι ib.84ᵃ25; ἐν τῷ λόγῳ Id. *Metaph*.1022ᵃ29; τοῖς ὅροις Id.*APr*.28ᵃ6.

**ἐνυπνι-άζω**, *dream*, Arist.*Insomn*.459ᵃ21, *Somn.Vig*.453ᵇ19, *HA* 537ᵇ13, al.:—in Med. and Pass. c. acc., ἐνυπνιάζεσθαι θορυβώδεα Hp. *VM*10, cf. Arist.*HA*587ᵇ10, Ph.1.672, Plu.*Cat.Ma*.23: so in fut. Pass. -ασθήσομαι Lxx *Jl*.3.1, Lyd.*Ost*.33: aor. Med. -ασάμην Lxx *Jd*. 7.13, Pass. -άσθην ib.*Ge*.37.5,6,10. **-αστής**, οῦ, ὁ, *dreamer*, ib.37.19, Ph.1.664. **-άστρια**, ἡ, *she who dreams*, title of book, prob. in *IG*2.992 ii 6.

**ἐνυπνίδιος**, ον, = ἐνύπνιος, φαντασία S.E.*M*.9.43.

**ἐνυπνιο-κρίτης** [κρῐ], ου, ὁ, *interpreter of dreams*, *UPZ*84.79.

⊛ **-μαντις**, εως, ὁ, *one who divines by dreams*, Hsch. s.v. βριζόμαντις.

**ἐνύπν-ιον**, τό, (ὕπνος) *thing seen in sleep*, in appos. with ὄνειρος, θεῖός μοι ἐνύπνιον ἦλθεν ὄνειρος a dream from the gods, *a vision in sleep*, came to me, Od.14.495, Il.2.56; ἐ. τὰ ἐς ἀνθρώπους πεπλανημένα Hdt.7.16.β'; ἐ. παιδὸς *the vision* of a boy, *AP*12.125 (Mel.): used adverbially, ἐ. ἑστιᾶσθαι 'to feast with the Barmecide', Ar.*V*.1218; κακοδαίμον' οὕτω δεσπότην οὐδ' ἐ. ἰδών Men.*Pk*.169; later κατ' ἐνύπνιον *AP*11.150 (Ammian.); cf. sq. 2. after Hom., = ὄνειρος, *dream*, ὄψις ἐνυπνίου the vision *of a dream*, Hdt.8.54; ὄψις ἐμφανὴς ἐνυπνίων A. *Pers*.518, cf. 226, Pl.*R*.572b; ἐνυπνίῳ πιθέσθαι Pi.*O*.13.79; ἐ. ἰδεῖν Ar.*V*.25, Pl.*Plt*.290b; τέλεον τὸ ἐ. ἀποτετέλεσται Id.*R*.443b; ἐνύπνια κρίνειν Theoc.21.29, *Sammelb*.685 (ii B.C.):—Artem. (1.1b) distinguishes ἐνύπνιον *a mere dream*, and ὄνειρος *a significant, prophetic one*; but the distn. is not generally observed, exc. by Philo. **-ιος**, ον, *in sleep, in dreams appearing*, φαντάσματα A.*Th*.710; ἐνύπνιος ἦλθε *AP*12.124 (inc. or Artemon). **-ιώδης**, ες, *dreamlike*, ὑπολήψεις Str.15.1.59; κινήσεις Plu.2.1024b; ἀσήμαντα καὶ ἐ. Artem. 1.10. **-ος**, ον, = ἐνύπνιος, φάντασμα *Trag.Adesp*.375 (anap.); ὄψις (prob. for ἐνύπνιον) E.*Hec*.703 Herm. **-όω**, *sleep on*, ἄντλῳ ἐνυπνώοντα (Ep. part.) Nic.*Th*.546.

**ἐνυπο-γρᾰφή**, ἡ, *description*, Dexipp. *in Cat*.2.13. **-γρᾰφος**, ον, *executed and signed*, ὁμολογία *PFlor*.323.9 (vi A.D.). **-δύομαι**, *slip into*, λόγοις S.E.*M*.2.49. **-κειμαι**, *subsist in*, ἐ. καὶ τᾷ ὕψι καὶ τῷ ἀέρι τὸ δυνάμι διαφανές Aristombr.ap.Stob.1.52.21, cf. Hierocl. *in CA*11 p.438 M. **-κρῑνομαι** [ῑ], *play the hypocrite*, τῷ νόμῳ Lxx *Si*.36(33).2. **-κρῐτος** ὑποστιγμή a stop *put after the protasis*, Sch.D.T.p.24 H.; cf. ἀνυπόκριτος.

**ἐνύποπτος**, ον, *suspicious*, Sor.1.79. 2. Act., *suspecting*: Adv. -τως Ps.-Callisth.1.9.

**ἐνυπό-σαπρος**, ον, *partly putrid*, Hp.*Coac*.437 (ἦν ὑποσ. Littré). **-στᾰτος**, ον, *substantial*, Phlp. *in Ph*.4.20, Eustr. *in EN*40.23. **-τάσσω**, fut. Pass. ἐνυποταγήσομαι, *to be made subject*, τισί Lxx *To*.14.9 cod. Alex.

**ἐνυπτιάζω**, *throw back upon*, ἑαυτὸν τῇ γῇ Philostr.*Im*.2.16; ἐ. τῇ σεμνότητι *glorying in* his pomposity, Id.*VS*1.10.

**ἔνυρεν**· ἔτρισεν, Hsch. **ἐνυρήσεις**· θρηνήσεις, Id.

**ἔνυστρον**, τό, = ἤνυστρον, Lxx *De*.18.3, *Ma*.2.3, J.*AJ*4.4.4.

**ἐνῠφ-αίνω**, *weave in as a pattern*, [πιλήματι] χρυσοῦ ποικιλίαν Duris 14 J.; τῆς σκιᾶς τὴν πορφύραν Men.561; ἐν τοῖς ἑπομένοις ἐνυφήνας τὰ Τρωικὰ πάθη Jul.*Or*.8.240c:—Pass., *to be inwoven*, ζῷα ἐνυφασμένα θώρηκι Hdt.3.47, cf. 1.203; γράμματα *IG*2.754.9, cf. Arist.*Mir*.838ᵃ22; αὐλαία ἔχουσα Πέρσας -ασμένους Thphr.*Char*.5.9; [χιτῶνα] ἀρετῶν ποικίλμασιν ἐνυφασμένον Ph.1.654: metaph., ἅπαν καλὸν ὄνομα ἐνυφανται τῇ ποιήσει [τῆς Σαπφοῦς] Demetr.*Eloc*.166. II. *weave in* a place, *Leg.Gort*.2.51. **-άντης**, ου, ὁ, *embroiderer*, prob. in *PAmh*.2.131. 12 (ii A.D.). **-αντός**, όν, *inwoven*, Theoc.15.83. **-ασμα**, ατος, τό, *pattern woven in*, D.S.17.70, Antyll.ap.Orib.9.14.7.

**ἐνυφ-ίζω**, aor. 1 ἐνυφίζησα, *settle down in*, *Gp*.6.5.7. **-ίσταμαι**, *subsist in*, M.Ant.4.14; ἐν τῷ ἑνί Id.6.25. II. *withstand*, τὸν πόλεμον J.*BJ*4.1.5.

**ἐνυψόω**, *exalt, excite*, in Pass., -ούμενος ὑπὸ τοῦ οἴνου Lxx *Da*.5.1.

**Ἐνῡώ**, οῦς, ἡ, *Enyo*, goddess of war, Il.5.333; companion of Ares, ib.592, A.*Th*.45, etc.; daughter of Phorcys and Ceto, Hes.*Th*. 273. II. = Lat. *Bellona*, Plu.*Sull*.9.

**ἐνφέρνιοι** θεοί, dub. sens. in *Tab.Defix.Aud*.155 *B* 3 (Rome, iv/v A.D.; perh. for Lat. *inferni*).

⊛ **ἐνῳδάς**· ἐν ᾧ ὁ ἴουλος ἐπιγίνεται, Hsch.

⊛ **ἐνώδιον**, τό, = ἐνώτιον, *IG*2.652ᵃ17, 11(2).199 *B* 46 (Delos, iii B.C.), *PPetr*.3 p.37 (iii B.C.), *PRyl*.124.30 (i A.D.).

**ἔνῳδος**, ον, *musical*, Nicom.*Harm*.2, al. Adv. -δως ibid.

**ἐνωθέω**, aor. 1 ἐνέωσα A.R.4.1243:—*thrust in* or *upon*, τινὰ ἠϊόνι l.c.; τοὺς ἵππους εἰς τὰ ὅπλα Plu.*Luc*.28.

**ἕνωμα**, ατος, τό, *concrete unity*, Dam.*Pr*.53, 107 (pl.).

**ἐνωμένως**, Adv., f.l. for ἡν-, Hero *Geom*.12.8.

**ἔνωμος**, ον, *rather raw*, κρέας Archestr.*Fr*.57.5 (Comp.); μόρα Diph.Siph.ap.Ath.2.51f; of bread, *under-baked*, Hp.*VM*14; *not too much cooked*, Id.*Mul*.2.211 (Comp.); of fruit, *rather crude, unripe*, Dsc.1.115, cf. *Gp*.8.20 (Comp.), Ruf.ap.Orib.45.11.2; of swellings, *hardish*, opp. χαῦνος, Hp.*Aph*.5.67.

⊛ **ἐνωμοτ-άρχης**, ου, ὁ, *leader of an* ἐνωμοτία (q.v.), Th.5.66 codd., X.*Lac*.11.4, Ascl.*Tact*.2.2:—also **-αρχος**, X.*An*.3.4.21 (v.l.), Arr. *Tact*.6.2. **-ία**, ἡ, (ἐνώμοτος) prop. *band of sworn soldiers*: hence, *division of the Spartan army*, Hdt.1.65, Th.5.68, X.*HG*6.4.12, *Lac*.11. 4, etc. II. later, = λόχος, cj. in Ascl. *Tact*.2.2; also, *a quarter of a* λόχος, Arr.*Tact*.6.2. **-ίς**, ίδος, ἡ, = foreg., *EM*345.10. **-ος**, ον, (ὄμνυμι) *bound by oath*, ὅρκων οἷσιν ἦν ἐνώμοτος S.*Aj*.1113; μάρτυρες Luc.*Deor.Conc*.15. Adv. -τως *on oath*, Plu.*Caes*.47. 2. *confirmed by oaths*, συνθῆκαι *PLond*.1.113.1 (vi A.D.). Adv. -τως *POxy*.904.3 (v A.D.). II. Subst., *conspirator*, Plu.*Sert*.26.

⊛ **ἐνωνά**, ᾶ, *right of purchase in* a state, γᾶς κὴ ϝυκίας (Boeot., = γῆς καὶ οἰκίας) *IG*7.3287 (Chaeronea).

**ἐνωπ-ᾰδίς**, Adv. = sq., A.R.4.354. **-ᾰδίως**, Adv., (ἐνωπή) *in one's face, to one's face*, Od.23.94 (v.l. ἐνωπιδίως). **-ᾰδόν**, Adv. = foreg., Q.S.2.84.

**ἐνωπάλιζεν**· ἐνέτεινεν, ἐνεδίδου, Hsch.

**ἐνωπ-ή**, ἡ, (ὤψ) *face, countenance*, used by Hom. only in dat. ἐνωπῇ, as Adv., *before the face, openly*, Il.5.374, [21.510]; later ἐνωπῆς γλήνεα Nic.*Th*.227. **-ια**, τά, perh. *face* of a wall, ἐ. παμφανόωντα Il.8. 435, Od.22.121, al.; perh. *façade*, A.*Supp*.146 (lyr.): later in sg., ἑκατέρῳ ἐνωπίῳ τῶν στοῶν *SIG*²588.245 (Delos, ii B.C.). **-ίδες**, αἱ, = θεράπαιναι, Did.ap.*EM*345.3. **-ιδίως**, v. ἐνωπαδίως. ⊛ **-ιος**, ον, (ὤψ) *facing, to the front*, πρό τ' ἐνώπια Alc.*Supp*.4.17; ἐνώπιος ἐνωπίῳ λαλεῖν *face to face*, Lxx *Ex*.33.11; ἄρτοι ἐ. *shewbread*, ib.25.29(30); διαστολῶν γεγονυιῶν ὑμῖν καὶ ἐνοπίοις (sic) καὶ διὰ γραμμάτων *in person*, *UPZ*110.36 (ii B.C.), cf. *Sammelb*.3925.6 (ii B.C.). II. neut. ἐνώπιον as Adv., *face to face*, Theoc.22.152; *in person*, *IG*12(5). 1061.10 (Carthaea), *PTeb*.14.13 (ii B.C.): as Prep. c. gen., Aeschin. 3.43 codd., *PCair.Zen*.73.14 (iii B.C.), *PGrenf*.1.38.11 (ii/i B.C.), *Ep. Rom*.12.17, *Ep.Gal*.1.20, Hermog.*Inv*.1.1; ἐ. θεῶν *SIG*²843.7 (Delph., ii A.D.). Regul. Adv. -ίως Suid. **-ῶς**· ἐμφανῶς, Hsch.

**ἐνωραΐζομαι**, *beautify oneself for the benefit of*, τοῖς γυναίοις Luc.*Am*. 9. II. *give oneself airs in*, τῷ βασιλείῳ θάκῳ Agath.2.26.

**ἔνωρος**, ον, *early*, in Adv. Comp. -ότερον, Epist.Hadrian. in *Gloss*. iii p.37, Gem.12.5, 13.9: irreg. Comp. **ἐνωρίστερος**, *earlier*: Adv. -τερον, τοῦ κατειθισμένου καιροῦ Phylarch.44 J.

**ἐνῶρσε, ἐνῶρτο**, v. ἐνόρνυμι. **ἐνῶσα**, Ion. contr. from ἐνόησα.

**ἕνωσις**, εως, ἡ, (ἑνόω) *combination into one, union*, Philol.10, Archyt. ap.Stob.1.41.2, Arist.*Ph*.222ᵃ20, *GC*328ᵇ22, Phld.*Po*.2.17, Ph.1.45, al.; τοῦ συμφραζομένου A.D.*Synt*.175.16, cf. Hermog.*Id*.2.11: pl., Procl.*Inst*.63. II. *compression*, Heliod.ap.Orib.46.11.20.

**ἐνωτ-άριον**, τό, *ear-ring*, Hsch. s.v. βοτρύδια. **-ίδιον**, τό, = foreg., *IG*11(2).287 *B* 19 (Delos, iii B.C.), *Rev.Ét.Gr*.12.71 (Tanagra).

**ἐνωτίζομαι**, (οὖς) *give ear, hearken to*, λόγους Lxx *Ge*.4.23; ῥήματα *Act.Ap*.2.14: c. dat., ἐντολαῖς Lxx *Ex*.15.26.

**ἑνωτικός**, ή, όν, (ἑνόω) *serving to unite* or *unify*, δύναμις Ph.1.31; εὔνοια Id.2.210, cf. Plu.2.428a; τινῶν Procl.*Inst*.13, al., Dam.*Pr*.47. Adv. -κῶς *EM*54.10.

**ἐνώτιον**, τό, (οὖς) *ear-ring*, A.*Fr*.102, Testamentum Platonis ap. D.L.3.42, Aen.Tact.31.7, *IG*11(2).161 *B* 26 (Delos, iii B.C.), Hedyl. ap.Ath.8.345b, etc.; cf. ἐνώδιον.

**ἐνώτισις**, εως, ἡ, = σύνεσις, ἡ σύνοψις τῶν ῥημάτων, Zonar.

**ἐνωτοκοίτης**, ου, ὁ, *with ears large enough to sleep in*, Str.2.1.9, 15. 1.57.

**ἔνωχρος**, ον, *yellowish*, Arist.*PA*673ᵇ29, *Phgn*.812ᵇ10, Dsc.3.2.

**ἐξ**, v. ἐκ.

⊛ **ἕξ**, οἱ, αἱ, τά, indecl., *six*, Il.5.270, al.: dat. pl. ἑξάσιν *OGI*200.28 (Axum); ϝέξ *Tab.Heracl*.2.34, al., *GDI*1267.27 (Pamphyl.), 4968 (Gortyn): ἐκ ποδῶν is written in *IG*1².372.175; cf. ἕκπους. 2. ἕξ, τό, *the six* in ἀστράγαλοι used as dice, = Κῷον, Ruf.*Oss*.38. (Cf. Skt. *ṣáṭ*, Avest. *xšvaš*, Lat. *sex*, Welsh *chwech*, etc.)

**ἑξά-βιβλος** [ᾰ], ον, *in six books*, πραγματεία Erot.*Praef*. **-βρᾰχυς** πούς foot *of six short syllables*, Sch.Ar.*Av*.738, etc.

**ἐξαβρύνω**, *make delicate*, νασμοῖς δέμας Aristonous 1.43.

**ἐξᾰγᾰνακτέω**, *to be very wroth*, πρός τινα J.*AJ*4.2.1.

**ἐξάγαστον**· ἄξιον θαύματος, Hsch.

**ἐξαγγ-ελία**, ἡ, *secret information sent out* to the enemy, X.*Cyr*.2.4.23 (pl.). II. *expression*, of style, Longin.*Rh*.p.186 H. **-έλλω**, *tell out, proclaim, make known*, freq. with collat. sense of *betraying* a secret, εἰ μὴ μητρυιῇ..Ἑρμέᾳ ἐξήγγειλεν Il.5.390; εἰσὶ γάρ, εἰσὶν οἱ πάντ' ἐξαγγέλλοντες ἐκείνῳ D.4.18, cf. Th.4.27, Lys.20.9, v.l. in X.*An*.1.6.5; ἐ. τινὶ ὅτι.. Hdt.5.33; ἐ. τινὶ προσιὸν τὸ στράτευμα X.*HG*7.5.10; τινὶ οὕνεκα.. S.*OC*1393; τινὶ περί τινος Pl.*R*.601d; τινὶ τὰ περί τι ib.359e; ἐ. κατά τινος Arist.*Pol*.1313$^{b}$34; of traitors and deserters, X.*Cyr*.6.1.42, etc.; cf. sq.:—Med., *cause to be proclaimed*, Hdt.5.95, 6.10, S.*OT*148: c. inf., *promise to* do, E.*Heracl*.531:—Pass., *to be reported*, Hdt.5.92.β', al.; ἐξηγγέλθη βασιλεὺς ἀθροίζων the king *was reported to be* collecting, X.*Ages*.1.6: impers., ἐξαγγέλλεται *it is reported*, c. acc. et inf., Id.*HG*3.2.18; πολιορκεῖσθαι τοὺς..στρατιώτας ἐξηγγέλλετο D.21.162. II. *express*, ἔννοιαν Hermog.*Id*.2.5:—Pass., ἐ. λέξει *to be expressed*, Arist.*Po*.1460$^{b}$11; ὀνόμασι Ti.Locr.102e. III. *narrate*, Them.*Or*.15.184b. ⊛ **-ελος**, ὁ, ἡ, *messenger who brings out news* from within: hence, *one who betrays a secret, informer*, ἐ. γίγνεται ὡς.. Th.8.51; ἐ. γίγνεσθαί τινος Pl.*Lg*.964e, etc. II. on the Greek stage, *messenger* who told what was doing *in the house* or *behind the scenes* (opp. ἄγγελος, who told news from a distance); first used by Aeschylus, Philostr.*VS*1.9. **-ελσις**, εως, ἡ, *statement*, Arist.*Rh.Al*.1426$^{b}$26. **-ελτέον**, *one must report*, τί τινι Agatharch. 21. **-ελτικός**, ή, όν, *conveying information*, Arist.*Pr*.903$^{a}$24. 2. *expressive*, c. gen., ὀνόματα τῶν θείων διακόσμων Procl.*in Cra*.p.72 P. 3. *apt to tell tales, gossiping*, Arist.*Rh*.1384$^{b}$5. **-ελτος**, ον, *told of*, τοῦ μὴ ἐξάγγελτοι γενέσθαι Th.8.14.

**ἐξαγγίζω**, (ἄγγος) *pour out of a vessel*, Hp.*VM*22; cf. ἐξαλίζω.

**ἐξαγέτης**· καλαμίνθη, Hsch.

**ἐξᾰγιάζω**, *assay*, *Gloss*.:—Pass., of measures, *to be fixed*, Hero *Stereom*.2.54.3.

**ἐξᾰγίζω**, (ἄγος) *drive out as accursed*, ἐξαγισθέντας δόμων..διπλῇ μάστιγι A.*Ag*.641: or perh. fr. ἁγίζω, *taken as victims from* many homes.

**ἐξᾰγῑνέω**, Ion. for ἐξάγω, *lead forth*, τινὰ ἐς γυμνάσια Hdt.6.128.

⊛ **ἐξάγιον**, τό, *assaying, testing*, ποιεῖσθαί τινος *Gp*.2.32 tit.

⊛ **ἐξάγιον**, τό, weight of 1½ dr., Orib.*Fr*.1,67.

⊛ **ἐξάγιστος** [ᾰ], ον, (ἐξαγίζω) *devoted to evil, accursed, abominable*, usu. of persons, D.25.93, D.H.6.89, Ph.1.265, etc.; of things, λιμήν Aeschin.3.113; βουλεύματα Jul.*Or*.2.99b. II. in S.*OC*1526 ἃ δ' ἐξάγιστα μηδὲ κινεῖται λόγῳ what things are *matters of religion*: cf. Hsch.

**ἐξαγκῡλόω**, *fasten by an* ἀγκύλη, Poll.5.56 (Pass.):—Med., *take* a spear *by the* ἀγκύλη, Sch.Nic.*Th*.170.

**ἐξαγκυρῶσαι** θύραν· ἐκστροφῶσαι, Hsch. (ἐξανκιρῶσαι cod.).

**ἐξαγκωνίζω**, *nudge with the elbow*, Ar.*Ec*.259. II. *bind* one's *hands behind his back*, D.S.34.2, Ph.2.564; ἐξηγκωνισμένος D.S.13.27: metaph., ἐξηγκωνισμένος τὸν λογισμόν Ph.2.128.

**ἐξαγμός**, ὁ, *selected portion*, *POxy*.1917.124,127 (vi A.D.).

**ἐξάγνῡμι**, *break and tear away, rend*, ὡς δὲ λέων..ἐξ αὐχένα ἄξῃ πόρτιος Il.5.161; ἐξ αὐχέν' ἔαξε 17.63: aor. 2 part. Pass. ἐξεάγεῖσα A.R.4.1686 (nisi leg. ἐξᾰγεῖσα).

**ἐξᾰγορ-άζω**, *buy from*, τι παρά τινος Plb.3.42.2; *buy up*, Plu.*Crass*.2; *buy off*, μικροῦ διαφόρου τὸν ἀδικηθέντα Dicaearch.1.22; *redeem*, D.S.36.2; ἐκ τῆς κατάρας τοῦ νόμου *Ep.Gal*.3.13:—Med., ἐξαγοράζεσθαι τὸν καιρόν *Ep.Col*.4.5, cf. *Ep.Eph*.5.16 (but -άζειν τὸν κ. LXX *Da*.2.8). **-ασία**, ἡ, *ransom, redemption*, *Gloss*. ⊛ **-εία** or **-ία**, ἡ, *excantation* of disease, *cure by confession*, Ptol.*Tetr*.170. ⊛ **-ευσις**, εως, ἡ, *telling out, betrayal*, D.H.*Rh*.8.14. II. = ἐξαγορεία, Ptol.*Tetr*.154. ⊛ **-ευτής**, οῦ, ὁ, *one who confesses* his sins, ib.158. ⊛ **-ευτικός**, ή, όν, *fit to tell* or *explain*, τινός Luc.*Salt*.36. **-εύω**, fut. ἐξαγορεύσω *Epic.Alex.Adesp*.2.55: aor. supplied by ἐξειπεῖν, fut. and pf. (exc. in late authors) by ἐξερῶ, ἐξείρηκα:—*tell out, make known, declare*, ἑκάστη ὃν γόνον ἐξαγόρευεν Od.11.234; *betray* a secret or mystery, Hdt.2.170; τι πρός τινα Id.9.89; ἐ. ἀπόρρητα Luc.*Pisc*.33; *confess*, τὰς ἁμαρτίας LXX *Le*.5.5, Plu.2.168d: abs., Rhetor.in *Cat.Cod.Astr*.8(4).148:—Pass., -εύεσθαι τὸ πάθος Sch.Ptol.*Tetr*.142.

**ἐξαγρέω**, = ἐξαιρέω, *Schwyzer*412.3 (Elis), cf. Hsch.

**ἐξαγρι-αίνω**, *make savage*, Pl.*Ly*.206b; λέοντα Ph.1.670; τινὰ πρός τινα Plu.*Dio*7; τινὰ ἐπί τινι J.*AJ*17.6.5:—Pass., *to be made* or *become savage*, Pl.*R*.336d, Arist.*HA*571$^{b}$31; πρός τινα Thd.*Da*.8.7. II. intr. in Act., = Pass., App.*Ill*.23. **-όω**, *make wild* or *waste*, χώραν, opp. ἐξημερόω, D.S.20.69:—Pass., *to be made so*, Isoc.9.67; ὑπό τινος Aeschin.1.98, cf. Porph.*Abst*.4.21. II. = foreg., *make savage*, Hdt.6.123, E.*Ph*.876:—Pass., *to be brutalized*, ὑπὸ πόθων Pl.*Lg*.870a, cf. Ph.1.584, al. III. intr., *become* or *be savage*, J.*AJ*17.6.1; ἐπί τινι, κατά τινος, ib.19.1.15, 17.6.4.

**ἐξαγροικίζω**, *barbarize*, Eust. ad D.P.875 (Pass.).

⊛ **ἐξάγω**, pf. -ῆχα D.42.19, -αγήγοχα *PHib*.1.34.10 (iii B.C.):—*lead out, lead away*: I. of persons, mostly c. gen. loci, μεγάροιο, πόληος, ὁμίλου, Od.22.458, 23.372, Il.5.353; μάχης ib.35: with ἐκ.., Od.8.106, 20.21; ἐ. ἐκ τῆς χώρης Hdt.4.148, al.; Ἄργεος ἐξαγαγόντες *having brought* her *out from* Argos, Il.13.379; *bring out of* prison, *release*, *PHib*.1.34.4, al. (iii B.C.), *Act.Ap*.16.39; *bring forth into the world*, τόν γε..Ἐλείθυια ἐξάγαγε πρὸ φόωσδε Il.16.188; νεοττοὺς *lead out of the nest*, Arist.*HA*613$^{b}$12; ἐ. Λυδοὺς ἐς μάχην Hdt.1.79, etc.; ἐπὶ θήραν τινά Ar.*Fr*.2 D., cf. X.*Cyr*.1.4.14; *lead out* to execution, Hdt.5.38, X.*An*.1.6.10, etc.: c. acc. cogn., με τήνδε τὴν ὁδὸν..ἐξήγαγε S.*OC*98. b. seemingly intr., *march out* (sc. στρατόν), X.*HG*4.5.14, 5.4.38, etc.: generally, *go out*, ὡς εἰς θήραν Id.*Cyr*.2.4.18; εἰς προνομάς ib.6.1.24: once in Hom., τύμβον..ἕνα χεύομεν ἐξαγαγόντες let us *go out* and pile one tomb for all, Il.7.336 (Aristarch.); also, *come to an end*, οἱ μεγάλοι πόνοι συντόμως ἐ. soon *pass away*, Epicur.*Fr*.447, cf. M.Ant.7.33. 2. *draw out from, release from*, ἀχέων τινά Pi.*P*.3.51; ἐ. τινὰ ἐκ τοῦ ζῆν, i.e. put him to death, Plb.23.16.13; ἑαυτὸν ἐκ τοῦ ζῆν commit suicide, Id.38.16.5; τοῦ ζῆν Plu.2.1076b; τοῦ σώματος Id.*Comp.Demetr.Ant*.6; simply ἐ. ἑαυτόν Chrysipp.*Stoic*.3.188, cf. Paul.Aeg.5.29; ὅταν ἡμᾶς τὸ χρεὼν ἐξάγῃ Metrod.49. 3. *eject* a claimant from property (cf. ἐξαγωγή II), D.30.4, 32.17, 44.32, etc.:—Pass., *to be turned out*, ὑπὸ τοῦ παιδοτρίβου Aeschin.Socr.37. II. of merchandise, etc., *carry out, export*, ῥῶπον χθονός A.*Fr*.263, cf. Ar.*Eq*.278,282, etc.; εἴ τις ἐξαγαγὼν παῖδα ληφθείη *exporting* him as a slave, Lys.10.10, cf. 13.67:—Pass., And.2.11, Th.6.31, X.*Vect*.3.2, etc.; τὰ -όμενα *exports*, Arist.*Rh*.1359$^{b}$22; οὔτε γὰρ ἐξήγετο..οὐδὲν οὔτ' εἰσήγετο D.18.145:—Med., X.*Ath*.2.3. 2. *draw off* water, Id.*Oec*.20.12 (Pass.), D.55.17; *draw out*, of perspiration, ὑπὸ τοῦ ἡλίου Hp.*Aër*.8 (Pass.); so, *carry off* by purgative medicines, ἕλμινθας *Gp*.12.26.1, cf. Dsc.2.152.2, Plu.2.134c, Aret.*CA*2.5: generally, *get rid of*, Thphr.*HP*5.6.3. 3. of building, *draw* or *carry farther out*, αἱμασιάν D.55.22:—Pass., ὁ περίβολος πανταχῇ ἐξήχθη τῆς πόλεως Th.1.93. 4. of expenses, ἐπὶ πλεῖστον ἐξάγεσθαι D.C.43.25. III. *bring forth, produce*, οὐκ ἐξάγουσι καρπὸν οἱ ψευδεῖς λόγοι S.*Fr*.834; ᾠά *hatch*, Arist.*HA*564$^{b}$8; *call forth, excite*, δάκρυ τινί E.*Supp*.770:—Med., γέλωτα ἐξαγαγέσθαι X.*Cyr*.2.2.15; μικρὰ ἆθλα πολλοὺς πόνους ἐξάγεται *elicit, induce*, Id.*Hier*.9.11. IV. *lead on, carry away, excite*, τινά E.*Alc*.1080, *Supp*.79; τινὰ ἐπ' οἶκτον Id.*Ion*361, cf. *HF*1212 (anap.); ἐς τοὺς κινδύνους Th.3.45; in bad sense, *lead on, tempt*, οὐδέ με οἶνος ἐ. ὥστε εἰπεῖν Thgn.414; ἐ. ἐπὶ τὰ πονηρότερα τὸν ὄχλον Th.6.89:—Med., E.*HF*775 (lyr.); εἰς τὸ διδόναι λόγον Plu.2.922f:—Pass., *to be led on to* do a thing, c. inf., ἐξήχθην ὀλοφύρασθαι Lys.2.61; ταῦτα..ἐξήχθημεν εἰπεῖν Pl.*R*.572b, cf. X.*An*.1.8.21; ἃ μὲν ἄν τις ἐξαχθῇ πρᾶξαι D.21.41, cf. 74; εἰς ἅμιλλαν Plu.*Sol*.29: abs., *to be carried away* by passion, Din.1.15; ὑπὸ τοῦ θυμοῦ Paus.5.17.8, etc.; ἐξάγουσα ὀδύνη *distracting* pain, Herod. Med.ap.Orib.7.8.1. 2. *lead away*, [λόγον] εἰς ἄλλας ὑποθέσεις Plu.2.42e; προβλήματα ἐ. εἰς ὀργανικὰς κατασκευάς *reduce*, Id.*Marc*.14 (also εἰς ἔργον πρόβλημα ibid.); ἐ. εἰς τὸ ἀνώτερον, Lat. *altius repetere*, Id.2.639e; πρὸς τὴν Ἑλληνικὴν διάλεκτον ἐξάγειν τοὔνομα *express* in Greek, Id.*Num*.13. V. *exercise*, τὴν ἀρχὴν οὐκέτι βασιλικῶς, ἀλλὰ τυραννικώτερον D.H.2.56, cf. *IG*2$^{2}$.1304.4,14; *carry out* instructions, *Michel*409.18 (Naxos, iii B.C.). VI. *give directions* in a will, ἐμαυτὸν οὕτως ἐξάγω Lycon ap.D.L.5.72. VII. intr., *pass one's life*, D.S.3.43.

⊛ **ἐξαγωγ-εύς**, έως, ὁ, *one who leads out* troops, D.S.15.38, also of the queen-bee, Arist.*HA*625$^{a}$22. II. = ἐξαγωγίς, *Gloss*. ⊛ **-ή**, ἡ, *leading out* of troops, X.*Eq.Mag*.4.9 (pl.), Plb.5.24.4 (pl.). 2. *drawing out* of a ship from shallows, Hdt.4.179. 3. *carrying out, exportation*, πωλεῖν ἐπ' ἐξαγωγῇ Id.5.6, cf. 7.156; ἐξαγωγὴν δοῦναι, παρέχεσθαι, grant *a right of exporting*, Isoc.17.57, Pl.*Lg*.705b; ἐ. λαβεῖν τοῦ σίτου *receive an export licence*, D.34.36, cf. *PCair.Zen*.93.13 (iii B.C.); ἐπ' ἐξαγωγῇ *for removal from the country*, for *deportation*, ἀδελφὴν ἐπ' ἐ. πέπρακε D.24.203, cf. 25.55; ἐ. σίτου, σιτική, Plb.28.2.2, 28.16.8. 4. *evacuation*, Arist.*Pr*.869$^{b}$28; αἱ κατὰ φύσιν ἐ. Plu.2.134c. 5. intr., *going out*: hence, *ending* of a thing, τῶν παρόντων κακῶν Plb.2.39.4, etc.; ἐ. ἐκ τοῦ ζῆν, ἐ. βίου, *departure from* life, Epicur.*Sent*.20, *Sent.Vat*.38; ἐ. alone, *suicide*, Chrysipp.*Stoic*.3.188, Varro *Sat.Men*.p.227 B., etc. 6. *the Exodus*, Ph.1.438, al.; title of poem by Ezekiel. II. as law-term, *ejectment*, Is.3.22, D.44.34. **-ικός**, ή, όν, *of* or *for exports*, τέλη ἐ. *export* duties, opp. εἰσαγωγικά, Str.17.1.13. **-ιμος**, ον, *exportable*, ἐξαγώγιμον ποιεῖν τι Lycurg.26; τὰ ἐξαγώγιμα *exports*, Arist.*Oec*.1345$^{b}$21. 2. *unsettled, migratory*, of people, v.l. for εἰσ-, E.*Fr*.360.10. II. *for drawing off* water, αἱ ἐ. τῶν ὑδάτων τάφροι D.H.4.44. **-ιον**, τό, *duty on exports*, *Inscr.Prien*.3.28 (iv B.C.), Decr.ap.J.*AJ*14.10.6, Just.*Edict*.13.15. ⊛ **-ίς**, ίδος, ἡ, *drain*, *IG*11(2).287 *A* 50 (Delos, iii B.C.), Ph.*Bel*.100.32 (pl.). **-ός**, ὁ, *waste-pipe* for letting off water, Timarch. ap.Ath.11.501f, *PLond*.3.1177.315 (ii A.D.). II. *overflow drain*, *PPetr*.2 p.14 (iii B.C.), etc.

**ἐξᾰγωνίζομαι**, *fight, struggle hard*, E.*HF*155; περί τινος D.S.13.73 codd.

**ἐξάγων-ίζω**, (ἑξάγωνος) *to be in sextile aspect*, Ptol.*Tetr*.115. **-ικός**, ή, όν, *hexagonal*, Procl.*Hyp*.1.16, Simp.*in Ph*.419.14; *of a hexagon*, πλευραί ib.57.16; ἐ. ἀριθμοί, of a kind of figurate numbers, Iamb.*in Nic*.p.60 P.: Astrol., *sextile*, Paul.Al.*R*.3; also of the moon's phase, Gal.9.902.

**ἐξᾰγώνιος**, ον, (ἀγών) *beside the mark, irrelevant*, Aeschin.ap.*AB*260; ἐ. καὶ πόρρω τοῦ σκοποῦ Luc.*Anach*.19; cf. ἀγών I.2. II. *excluded from competition*, Ph.2.60; = ἔξω τοῦ ἀγῶνος ὤν, Hsch.

⊛ **ἑξάγωνος** [ᾰ], ον, *hexagonal*, Arist.*Cael*.306$^{b}$7, *HA*554$^{b}$25; δακτύλιος *SIG*$^{2}$588.189: Math., ἀριθμός Nicom.*Ar*.2.11. II. Astrol., *in sextile aspect*, Vett.Val.20.2.

**ἑξαδακτῠλ-ία**, ἡ, *possession of six fingers*, Phlp.*in GA*.194.4. **-ιαῖος**, α, ον, *six inches long*, Heliod.ap.Orib.49.4.41. ⊛ **-ος**, ον, = foreg., *six inches long*, Hp.*Nat.Mul*.32,109, Dsc.4.43, Orib.8.6.15, D.L.4.34, Ammon.*in APr*.46.1. II. *having six fingers*, Gal.19.454, Eustr.*in EN*376.1, Tz.*H*.7.902.

**ἐξάδαρχος** [ᾰδ], ὁ, (ἑξάς) *leader of a body of six*, X.*Cyr*.3.3.11.

※ **ἐξάδελφος** [ᾰ], ὁ, ἡ, *cousin-german*, *TAM*2.224 (Sidyma): fem. also ἐξαδέλφη *CIG*3891 (Eumenia). II. *nephew*, Lxx *To*.1.22(25), J.*AJ*20.10.3.

**ἐξαδιαφορ-έω**, *to be utterly indifferent to*, Ph.1.214, 2.279. **-ησις**, εως, ἡ, *utter indifference to*, τῶν ἀδιαφόρων Id.1.509.

**ἑξᾰδικός**, ή, όν, (ἑξάς) *consisting of six* or *sixes*, εἰδοποίησις *Theol. Ar*.34. 2. *sixfold*, Dam.*Pr*.264.

**ἑξαδραχμ-ία**, ἡ, *tax of six drachmae*, *POxy*.1457.2 (i B.C.), 1438.19 (ii A.D.). ※ **-ον**, τό, *sum of six drachmae*, Arist.*Oec*.1347ᵃ34, 1353ᵃ18.

**ἐξαδρ-όομαι**, = sq., f.l. in *Gp*.4.8.5. **-ύνομαι**, Pass., *come to maturity*, Hp.*Septim*.1.

※ **ἐξαδῠνᾰτέω**, *to be quite unable* or *incapable*, c. inf., Arist.*Pol*.1282ᵇ4, Plu.*Alc*.23; πρός τι Arist.*GA*785ᵃ10: abs., Id.*HA*575ᵃ21, Plb.1.58.5; τῷ σώματι Plu.*Mar*.33; ἐ. τὸ γεννᾶν generation *becomes impossible*, Thphr.*CP*1.16.3.

※ **ἐξᾴδω**, *sing out*, *sing one's last song*, of the swan, Pl.*Phd*.85a; of Arion, Plu.2.161c; ἐξᾴσας τὸ κύκνειον Plb.31.12.1. 2. *sing the* ἔξοδος, of a chorus, Plot.6.9.8. II. trans., *sing away by means of a spell*, Luc.*Philops*.16; *disenchant*, Id.*Trag*.173:—Pass., ὑπό τινος J.*AJ*6.8.2. 2. *sing of*, *laud*, E.*Tr*.472.

**ἑξά-εδρος** [ᾰ], ον, *with six surfaces*, *Theol.Ar*.25. II. Subst. ἑξάεδρον, τό, *hexahedron*, Gal.5.669. **-ειδος**, ον, (εἶδος IV) *composed of six ingredients*, Phlp.*in GC*192.29, 269.34; cf. τετράειδος, τρίειδος.

**ἐξαείρω**, v. ἐξαίρω.

**ἐξᾱερ-ίζω**, = sq., Simp.*in Cael*.571.8 (Pass.). **-όω**, Ion. -ηερ-, *make into air*, *volatilize*, τι Arist.*Pr*.938ᵇ34, Luc.*Peregr*.30:—Pass., *evaporate*, Hp.*Nat.Puer*.25, Arist.*Pr*.933ᵃ36; *to be dissipated in perspiration*, Aret.*SD*2.1. **-ωσις**, εως, ἡ, *evaporation*, Id.*CD*2.2.

**ἑξᾰ-έτηρος**, ον, = sq. 1, Nonn.*D*.38.14. **-ετής**, ές, or **-έτης**, ες, (ἔτος) *six years old*, *IG*3.1336, *BGU*983.18, J.*AJ*19.9.1, etc.:—fem. **-έτις**, ιδος, Theoc.14.33 (v.l.). II. *of six years*, χρόνος Plu.*Pyrrh*.26. Adv. ἑξάετες *for six years*, Od.3.115; cf. ἑξέτης. **-ετία**, ἡ, *term of six years*, Ph.2.371, J.*AJ*16.1.1, *POxy*.101.17 (ii A.D.), etc. **-ήμερος**, ον, *of* or *in six days*, ἡ ἑξαήμερος (sc. περίοδος) *the six days* of creation, Ph.1.69: also -ον, τό, Id.2.197.

**ἐξαηρμένον**· ἐξῃρημένον, Hsch.

**ἐξᾰθέλγω**, *draw* or *drain off*, in Pass., Hp.*Oss*.19, Hsch.

**ἐξᾰθερ-ίζω**, *scorn*, Eust.1046.58. **-ισις**, εως, ἡ, *scorning*, Id.1910.2.

**ἔξαθλος**, ον, *past athletic exercise*, Luc.*Lex*.11. II. *disqualified*, in an athletic competition, Sch.Od.21.76.

**ἐξαθρέω**, *look at carefully*, dub. in Thesp.(*Fr*.2)ap.Chrysipp.*Stoic*.2.55.

**ἐξαθροίζομαι**, Med., *seek out and collect*, E.*Ph*.1169.

**ἐξαθῡμέω**, strengthd. for ἀθυμέω, *PSI*4.418.25 (iii B.C.), Plb.11.17.6, Plu.*Cic*.6.

**ἑξάθῠρος** [ᾰ], ον, *having six sluices*, *PLond*.2.139*b*,166*b* (i A.D.), *PFay*.365 (ii A.D.).

**ἐξαιάζω**, strengthd. for αἰάζω, E.*Tr*.198 (lyr.).

**ἐξαιγειρόομαι**, Pass., of the white poplar (λεύκη), *degenerate into a black poplar* (αἴγειρος), Thphr.*CP*2.16.2.

**ἐξαιθᾰλόω**, *turn into soot*, Zos.Alch.p.168B. (Pass.).

**ἐξαιθερόω**, *change into ether*, Chrysipp.*Stoic*.2.184 (Pass.).

※ **ἐξαιθραπεύω**, *to be a satrap*, *SIG*167.2 (Mylasa, iv B.C.); cf. ἐξαιτραπεύω.

※ **ἐξαιθριάζω**, *expose to sun and air*, Hp.*Int*.35, Dsc.5.16, Apollon. ap.Gal.12.478:—Pass., *Com.Adesp*. in *PLond.ined*.2294 (iii/ii B.C.).

**ἐξαιμάσσω**, Att. -ττω, *make quite bloody*, τοὺς πόδας *IG*4.952.134 (Epid.); τὸν ἵππον τῷ κέντρῳ X.*Cyr*.7.1.29:—Pass., τῇ μάστιγι Philostr.Jun.*Im*.11, prob. in Paul.Aeg.6.110. 2. metaph., ἐ. τὰς λύπας *open* one's griefs *afresh*, D.H.6.81.

**ἐξαιμᾰτ-ίζω**, *take blood from*, φλέβας *Hippiatr*.1. **-όω**, *change into blood*, Gal.8.359:—Pass., Arist.*Somn.Vig*.456ᵇ4, Ph.2.244. ※ **-ωσις**, εως, ἡ, *conversion into blood*, of food, ibid., Alex.Aphr.*Pr*.2.63, Gal.11.139. **-ωτικός**, ή, όν, *blood-producing*, δύναμις Alex.Aphr.*Pr*.2.63.

**ἔξαιμ-ος**, ον, (αἷμα) *bloodless*, *drained of blood*, Hp.*VC*16, *Epid*.5.6, D.S.3.35, etc. **-ων**, ον, gen. ονος, = foreg., Poll.4.186, 8.79.

**ἐξαίνῠμαι**, *take out* or *away*, νηῒ δ' ἐνὶ πρύμνῃ ἐξαίνυτο κάλλιμα δῶρα *took out* (*and placed*), Od.15.206: in Il. always in phrase ἐξαίνυτο θυμόν, *animam eripuit*, 5.155, al.; νάρθηκος νηδὺν ἐ. Nic.*Al*.272.

**ἐξαιονάω**, *spray*, *douche*, *EM*348.24 (Pass.).

**ἑξάϊππος** [ᾰ], ον, *with six horses*, Sch.A.*Pers*.48.

**ἐξαιρ-έσιμος**, ον, (ἐξαιρέω) *that can be taken out*, ἡμέραι ἐ. days *taken out of the calendar*, Arist.*Oec*.1351ᵇ15, cf. Cic.*Verr*.2.2.52.129. ※ **-εσις**, εως, ἡ, *taking out* the entrails of victims, Hdt.2.40: pl., *the entrails* themselves, *offal*, Dionys.Com.3.12; *extraction* of teeth, Arist.*Mech*.854ᵃ25, Paul.Aeg.6.28; of weapons, Gal.2.283; *taking out* of patients from a bath, Philum.*Ven*.15.8. b. *removal*, *purgation*, τῶν παθῶν Porph.*Abst*.2.43. 2. *way of taking out*, τὴν ἐ. τοῦ λίθου Hdt.2.121.α'. 3. Rhet., *taking exception*, *questioning of* an adversary's arguments, Ulp. ad D.24.66. b. in Law, = Lat. *exceptio*, Just.*Nov*.136.2. 4. *transcendence*, τοῦ ἑνδεοῦς Dam.*Pr*.13. II. *place where cargoes are landed*, *wharf*, Hyp.*Fr*.186, *PTeb*.5.26 (ii B.C.). III. as law-term, ἐξαιρέσεως δίκη action against one who has asserted the free birth of a slave, Is.*Fr*.70. IV. *killing*, ὑός Str.8.6.22. **-ετέος**, α, ον, *to be taken out* or *removed*, ἐκ τῆς στρατιᾶς X.*Cyr*.2.2.23. II. ἐξαιρετέον *one must take out*, *remove*, τὴν ἀναρχίαν ἐκ παντὸς τοῦ βίου Pl.*Lg*.942c, cf. *Tht*.157b. 2. *one must pick out*, *select*, X.*Cyr*.4.5.52. **-έτης**, Lacon. **-έταρ**· ἁρπάγη, ἡ ἅρπαξ ὁ πρὸς τὰ ἀντλήματα, Hsch.; cf. ἐξαι(ρέ)της· ἀφαιρέτης, Suid. ※ **-ετός**, ή, όν, *removable*, Hdt.2.121.α'; βάλανοι Aen.Tact.20.3; στελεοί J.*AJ*3.6.6; ἐξαίρετα, τά, *removable parts* of a machine, Orib.49.5.81. II. **ἐξαίρετος**, ον, *taken out*, and so, 1. *picked out*, *chosen*, *choice*, κοῦροι Ἰθάκης ἐξαίρετοι Od.4.643; γυναῖκες Il.2.227; ἕνα ἐ. ἀποκρίνειν Hdt.6.130; esp. of booty and things *given as a special honour*, *not assigned by lot*, χρημάτων ἐ. ἄνθος A.*Ag*.954; δώρημα Id.*Eu*.402, etc.; ἐ. τι ἐκτῆσθαι Hdt.8.140.β'; ἐ. οἰκόπεδον *SIG*141.5 (Issa, iv B.C.); διδόναι X.*Cyr*.8.4.29; δίδοσθαι Hdt.2.98, 3.84. 2. *excepted*, ἐ. τίθημι τὴν ἀκουσίαν S.*Fr*.746; ποιεῖσθαι Th.3.68, cf. D.40.14; ἐ. μοι δὸς τόδ' E.*IT*755; οὐδ' ἔστιν ἐ. ὥρα τις ἣν διαλείπει D.9.50, cf. D.H.6.50; τριήρεις ἑκατὸν ἐξαιρέτους ἐψηφισάμεθα εἶναι to be *set apart for special service*, And.3.7; χίλια τάλαντα ἐ. ποιήσασθαι Th.2.24. 3. *special*, *singular*, *remarkable*, ἐ. μόχθος Pi.*P*.2.30; οὐδὲν ἐ. οὐδ' ἴδιον πεποίημαι D.18.281; ἐ. αὐτῷ τυραννίδα περιποιεῖσθαι Aeschin.3.89; βασιλείαν ἐ. αὐτοῖς παρ' ἐκείνων ἔλαβον Isoc.6.20; στρατηγία ἐ. *extraordinary* praetorship, Plu.*Cat.Mi*.39; τούτῳ μόνῳ ἐξαίρετόν ἐστι ποιεῖν ὅτι ἂν βούληται he alone has *the special privilege*.., Lys.10.3, cf. D.19.247; κατ' ἐξαίρετον *specially*, *POxy*.907.10 (iii A.D.), etc.; *par excellence*, Eustr.*in EN*348.1; ἐ. τινος *peculiar to*, Jul.*Or*.1.5c; ἰδιότητος Procl.*Inst*.21. III. ἐξαίρετα, τά, = ἀναλώματα, *Ath.Mitt*.13.249 (*CR*40.18), Heberdey-Wilhelm *Reisen in Kilikien* p.161. IV. Adv. **-τως** *specially*, φίλανδρος *IG*12(7).395.14 (Amorgos), cf. Plu.2.667f, *POxy*.1675.6, etc.; *in a special degree*, Arr.*Epict*.1.6.12; ὃν ἐ. τῶν φίλων στέργω *BMus.Inscr*.481*.393 (Ephesus, ii A.D.); *exclusively*, *characteristically*, A.D.*Synt*.194.1; *for choice*, *for preference*, *PMag.Lond*.121.652. ※ **-έω**, fut. -ήσω, later ἐξελῶ D.H.7.56, etc.: aor. 2 ἐξεῖλον, Ep. and Lyr. ἔξελον Il.16.56, Pi.*O*.1.26; inf. ἐξελεῖν:—Med., fut. ἐξαιρήσομαι A.*Supp*.924; later ἐξελοῦμαι Alciphr.1.9: aor. 2 ἐξειλόμην, rarely 1 ἐξῃρησάμην Ar.*Th*.761 (perh. interpol.):—Pass., pf. -ῄρημαι, Ion. -αραίρημαι Hdt.:—*take out*, ἔνθεν.. ἔξελε πέπλους Il.24.229; ἐπεί νιν καθαροῦ λέβητος ἔξελε Κλωθώ Pi.l.c.; τὸ δέλτα τοῦ ὀνόματος Pl.*Cra*.413e; simply, *take out*, τὴν κοιλίην, τὴν νηδύν, Hdt.2.40 (tm.), 87; πρὶν ἀνταράξας πῖαρ ἐξέλῃ γάλα Sol.36.21:—Pass., εἰ τὸ ἔαρ ἐκ τοῦ ἐνιαυτοῦ ἐξαραιρημένον εἴη Hdt.7.162, cf. Pericl.ap.Arist.*Rh*.1365ᵃ33. 2. Med., *take out for oneself*, φαρέτρης ἐξείλετο πικρὸν ὀϊστόν from *his* quiver, Il.8.323; ἐξελέσθαι τὰ μεγάλα ἱστία *their* large sails, X.*HG*1.1.13; ἐ. τὰ φορτία *discharge their* cargoes, Hdt.4.196; τὰ ἀγώγιμα X.*An*.5.1.16; τὸν σῖτον ἐς [τὴν στοὰν] ἐξαιρεῖσθαι Th.8.90: abs., Syngr.ap.D.35.13, etc.:—Pass., *to be discharged*, of a cargo, Hdt.3.6, D.34.8. II. *take from* a common stock, *reserve*, κούρην, ἣν ἄρα μοι γέρας ἔξελον υἷες Ἀχαιῶν Il.16.56; Ἀλκινόῳ δ' αὐτὴν γέρας ἔξελον Od.7.10, cf. Il.11.627; βασιλέϊ τεμένεα ἐξελῶν καὶ ἱερωσύνας Hdt.4.161; Νίσῳ ἐ. χθόνα S.*Fr*.24.5; θεοῖσιν ἀκροθίνια E.*Rh*.470; κλήρους τοῖς θεοῖς Th.3.50:—Med., *choose for oneself*, *carry off as booty*, τὴν ἐκ Λυρνησσοῦ ἐξείλετο Il.2.690, cf. 9.130; *choose*, μενοεικέα Od.14.232; μίαν ἕκαστος σιτοποιὸν ἐ. Hdt.3.150, cf. X.*An*.2.5.20; ταύτας ἐξείλεθ' αὑτῷ κτῆμα S.*Tr*.245; δῶρον.. πόλεος ἐξελέσθαι *to have accepted* as a gift, Id.*OC*541 (lyr.):—Pass., *to be given as a special honour*, τινί to one, Th.3.114; ἐξαραιρημένος Ποσειδέωνι *dedicated* to him, Hdt.1.148; γέρεα.. σφι ἦν τάδε ἐξαραιρημένα Id.2.168; ἐ. αὐτοῖς *set apart* for them, Pl.*Criti*.117c; τὰ τεμένη τὰ ἐξῃρημένα *IG*1².45.10; of funds, to be *set apart*, *ear-marked*, *SIG*577.64 (Milet., iii/ii B.C.); but τοῦ ἀργυρίου τοῦ ἐκ τοῦ λιθοτομείου ἐξαιρουμένου moneys *received* from.., *IG*2².47. 2. *take out of* a number, *except*, μητέρας ἐξελόντες Hdt.3.150; Σιμμίαν ἐξαιρῶ λόγου Pl.*Phdr*.242b, cf. X.*Mem*.1.4.15. III. *remove* people from their country, Hdt.2.30; τοὺς ἐν τῇ λίμνῃ κατοικημένους Id.5.16; στρουθοὺς (sc. ἐκ τοῦ νηοῦ) Id.1.159: generally, *remove*, τὸν λίθον Id.2.125; ἐκ τοῦ λυχνούχου τὸν λύχνον Alex.102; πατρὸς φόβον E.*Ph*.991, cf. Isoc.2.23; ὀδυρμούς, ἀγνοιαν, ἔρωτα, Pl.*R*.387d, *Lg*.771e, *Smp*.186d; ἀλλήλων τὴν ἀπιστίαν X.*An*.2.5.4:—Med., νεῖκος E.*Med*.904; ὑμῶν ἐ. τὴν διαβολὴν.. ταύτην *remove* this prejudice from your minds, Pl.*Ap*.19a, cf. 24a. 2. *get rid of*, [ὗν] ἐκ τῆς χώρας Hdt.1.36; θῆρας χθονὸς E.*Hipp*.18; *make away with*, παῖδας, θῆρα, Id.*HF*39, 154; Ἀθηναίους X.*HG*2.2.19. b. *destroy*, πόλιν Hdt.1.103, al., cf. Th.3.113, 4.69, D.18.30; χωρία Id.23.115; οἰκίδιον Men.*Pk*.199, cf. 278; φρούριον D.H.8.86. c. *annul*, *bring to naught*, θέσφατα S.*OT*908 (lyr.), cf. D.23.36. 3. Med., ψυχήν, θυμόν, φρένας ἐξελέσθαι, either c. acc. pers., *bereave* a person *of* life, etc., as μιν ἐξείλετο θυμὸν Il.15.460, 17.678 (so in Trag., E.*Alc*.69, *IA*972): or c. gen. pers., as μευ φρένας ἐξέλετο Ζεύς Il.19.137, cf. Hes.*Sc*.89; σεῦ ψυχὴν χαλκῷ Il.24.754; μου τέρψιν ἐξεῖλου βίου E.*Alc*.347, etc.: rarely, c. dat. pers., Γλαύκῳ φρένας ἐξέλετο Ζεύς Il.6.234; [οἰωνοῖς] τέκνα Od.16.218: in tmesi, ἐκ δέος εἵλετο γυίων 6.140; ἐκ θυμὸν ἕλοιο 20.62, cf. Il.11.381:—Med., *take away from one*, τὰ φίλτατα S.*El*.1208:—Pass., ἐξαιρεθέντες τὸν Δημοκήδεα *having had* him *taken out of their hands*, Hdt.3.137; τὸ ἐπιθυμοῦν τοῦ πλοῦ οὐκ ἐξῃρέθησαν Th.6.24, cf. Pl.*Grg*.519d, etc. 4. Pass., *to be removed from*, i.e. *transcend*, τοῦ τῶν ὄντων πλήθους Procl.*in Prm*.p.546S.; ἑνάδες ἐξῃρημέναι *transcendent*, ib.p.547S., cf. Dam.*Pr*.7; τὸ μᾶλλον -μένον μᾶλλον καὶ χωρεῖ διὰ τῶν ἄλλων ib.325. Adv. ἐξῃρημένως *transcendently*, ib.270; *ultimately*, opp. προσεχῶς, Phlp.*in de An*.270.14. IV. Med., *set free*, *deliver*, τινά A.*Supp*.924, Ar.*Pax*316; ἐκ τῶν κινδύνων τινά Decr.ap.D.18.90; ἐκ τῆς ἀνάγκης *PPetr*.3p.74; ἐκ τῶν θλίψεων *Act.Ap*.7.10; ἐξαιρεῖσθαι εἰς ἐλευθερίαν *claim* as a freeman, Lys.23.9, D.8.42, 10.14. 2. *bring to an end*, *accomplish*, πᾶν γὰρ ἐξαιρεῖ

λόγος E.*Ph.*516.— Freq. confounded with ἐξαίρω. **–ημα,** ατος, τό, *sum deducted*, *SIG*1106.78 (Cos, iv/iii B.C., pl.). II. *reserved portion* of an estate, *AJA*16.13 (iv/iii B.C.). **–ῖτις,** ιδος, ἡ, *ladder*, Ath.Mech.36.7.

**ἐξαιρόομαι,** Pass., (αἶρα) *turn into darnel*, Thphr.*CP*2.16.2.

❀ **ἐξαίρω,** Ep. **ἐξᾰείρω** Hom. (v. infr.), also in Ion. Prose, Hp.*Fract.* 21, cf. ἀείρω, αἴρω: aor. 1 ἐξῆρα S.*OC*358, etc.:—*lift up, lift off the earth*, ἐκ μὲν ἅμαξαν ἄειραν Il.24.266; ἐκ δὲ κτήματ' ἄειραν Od.13.120 (elsewh. Hom. uses only Med., v. infr.); ἐξάρας [αὐτὸν] παίει ἐς τὴν γῆν Hdt.9.107; ἐ. χεῖρας in prayer, Plb.3.62.8; κοῦφον ἐξάρας πόδα S.*Ant.*224; βάθρων ἐκ τῶνδέ μ' ἐξάραντες *having bidden* me *rise* (from suppliant posture), Id.*OC*264, cf. *Tr.*1193; τίς σ' ἐξῆρεν οἴκοθεν στόλος; *made* thee *start*, Id.*OC*358; ἡδοναῖς ἄμοχθον ἐ. βίον Id.*Tr.*147; ἐ. θώρακα *take* it *out* (of its case), Ar.*Ach.*1133; πυρσόν Hero *Aut.*22.5:—Pass., ib.22.6. b. seemingly intr., *rise from the ground*, of a bird, D.S.2.50; ἐ. τῷ στρατεύματι *start*, Plb.2.23.4, cf. Lxx *Nu.*2.9. 2. *raise in dignity, exalt, magnify*, Κλεισθένης [τὴν οἰκίην] ἐξῆρε (v.l. -ήγειρε) Hdt.6.126; ἐξάρας με ὑψοῦ καὶ τὴν πάτρην Id.9.79; ἄνω τὸ πρᾶγμα ἐ. *exaggerate* it, Aeschin.2.10; ἐπὶ μεῖζον ἐ. τὰ γενόμενα D.H.8.4; ὑψηλὸν ἐ. αὐτὸν ἐπί τινι Pl.*R.*494d; ἐ. ὑπόθεσιν Procl.*in Prm.*p.522S.; Rhet., *treat in elevated style*, Hermog.*Id.*2.3; τὸν τῆς ἑρμηνείας τύπον ἐ. παρὰ τὸ εἰωθός Procl.*in Prm.*p.484S.; ἐπιστολαὶ μικρὸν ἐξηρμέναι Demetr.*Eloc.*234; of music, ἐξηρμένον καὶ τεθαρρηκός Heraclid.Pont.ap.Ath.14.624d 3. *arouse, stir up*, θυμὸν ἐς ἀμπλακίην Thgn.630; μηδὲν δεινὸν ἐξάρῃς μένος S.*Aj.*1066; ἐ. σε θανεῖν *excites* thy *wish* to die, E.*Hipp.*322; ἐ. φρένα λακεῖν Id.*Alc.*346; ἐ. χάριν χορείας Ar.*Th.*981. 4. *pervert*, λόγους δικαίων Lxx *De.*16.19. 5. *remove*, ἔπιπλα *PLond.*1.177.21 (i A.D.); *make away with, get rid of*, ἐξάρατε τὸν πονηρὸν ἐξ ὑμῶν αὐτῶν 1*Ep.Cor.*5.13:—Pass., *to be carried away*, of a dam, *PRyl.*133.19 (i A.D.). II. Med. (Hom. only in 3 sg. aor. ἐξήρατο), *carry off for oneself, earn*, δοιοὺς μισθοὺς Od.10.84; ὅσ' ἂν οὐδέ ποτε ἐκ Τροίης ἐξήρατ' Ὀδυσσεύς 5.39; ἐξάρατο ἕδνον *won* it as a dower, Pi.*O.*9.10; θοῶν ἐξήρατ' ἀγώνων, . .κειμήλια Theoc.24.122. (In Hom. ἐξήρατο may have displaced ἐξήρετο, aor. of ἐξάρνυμαι, v. ἀείρω.) 2. ἐξαίρεσθαι νόσον *take* a disease *on oneself, catch* it, S.*Tr.*491. 3. *carry off*, Pl.*Prt.*319c. III. Pass., *to be raised*, [τὸ τεῖχος] ἐξήρετο διπλήσιον τοῦ ἀρχαίου Hdt.6.133; *rise up, rise*, ἐξαιρόμενον νέφος οἰμωγῆς E.*Med.*106; φλόξ Plb.14.5.1; κονιορτός Id.3.65.4. 2. *swell*, dub. in Hp. *VC*15; ἐξαειρόμενα (-εύμενα codd.) ὑπὸ τῆς πιέξιος *swellings* caused by compression, Id.*Fract.*21. 3. *to be excited, agitated*, ἐλπίδι S.*El.*1461; ἐξαρθεὶς ὑπὸ μεγαλαυχίας *puffed up*, Pl.*Lg.*716a: c. part., ἐξήρθης κλύων E.*Rh.*109. 4. ἐξηρμένος prob. f.l. in Plb.4.4.5.

**ἐξαίσι-ος,** ον, also α, ον X.*HG*4.3.8:—*beyond what is ordained* or *fated*, opp. ἐναίσιος: hence, 1. *outstepping right, lawless*, ῥέξας ἐξαίσιον having done some *lawless act*, Od.4.690; ἤ τινά που δείσας ἐ. . . fearing some *lawless man*, 17.577; Θέτιδος . . ἐ. ἀρήν Il.15.598; ἀφροσύναι B.14.58. 2. of omens, *portentous*, opp. ἐναίσιος, D.C.38.13: Sup., Id.45.17. 3. of things, *extraordinary*, ἐ. τὸ θερμόν Hp.*Epid.*7.94; *violent*, of a wind, Hdt.3.26, X.*HG*5.4.17; χειμών, σεισμοί, Pl.*Ti.*22e, 25c; ὄμβροι X.*Oec.*5.18; ἐ. δεῖμα A.*Supp.*514; γέλωτες καὶ δάκρυα Pl.*Lg.*732c: ἐ. φυγή *headlong* flight, X.*HG*4.3.8; ἐ. βρονταί Plb.18.20.7, cf. *BJ*4.4.5; ὑπουργία *Vit.Philonid.*p.5 C.; κάλλος Ph.2.166; χελῶναι ἐ. τοῖς μεγέθεσιν D.S.3.21; ἐ. τὸ μέγεθος καὶ τὸ ὕψος Id.13.82. Adv. -ίως Them.*Or.*26.312d. **–ότης,** gloss on ἐκπαγλότης, Hsch.

**ἐξαΐσσω,** contr. -ᾴσσω, Att. -ᾄττω, *rush forth, start out*, ἐκ δὲ τὼ ἀΐξαντε πυλάων Il.12.145; ἐξηξάτην οὖν δύο δράκοντ' ἐκ τοῦ νεώ Ar.*Pl.*733; ὁ δ' ᾤχετ' ἐξᾴξας γε Id.*Ra.*567; ἐ. ἐν τοῖς ὕπνοις *start*, Arist.*Pr.*957ᵃ32; ἐξαττούσης [τῆς ψυχῆς] καὶ φερομένης πρός τι Phld.*Mus.*p.12 K., cf. Max.Tyr.37.5; τὸ ἐξᾶττον αὐτῶν *the violence* of these passions, Plu.2.83e:—Pass., ἐκ δέ μοι ἔγχος ἠΐχθη παλάμηφιν Il.3.368.

**ἐξαϊστόω,** *bring to naught, destroy*, A.*Pr.*668.

**ἐξαισχύνομαι** [ῡ], *to be ashamed*, c. inf., Procl.*in Prm.*p.648S.

**ἐξαιτ-έω,** *demand* or *ask for from* another, c. dupl. acc., τήνδε μ' ἐξαιτεῖ χάριν S.*OC*586, cf. E.*Or.*1657, *Supp.*120; ἐ. τινὰ πατρός *ask* her *in marriage* from . ., S.*Tr.*10; ἐ. τινά *demand the surrender of* a person, esp. a criminal, Hdt.1.74, cf. D.18.41 (Pass.), *IG*2².457b17 (iv B.C.); *demand* a slave for torture, Antipho 6.27, Lys.7.36; τὸν ἐλεύθερον ἐ. D.29.14 (also ἐ. τὴν βάσανον ib.13); ἐ. [τινὰ] βασανίζειν Id.37.51; σμικρὸν ἐ. *ask* or *beg for* little, S.*OC*5; ἐ. τινὰ ποιεῖν τι Id.*OT*1255, E.*Rh.*175. II. Med., *ask for oneself, demand*, Act., Hdt.1.159, 9.87, S.*El.*656, etc.; χάριν παρά τινος Lys.20.31; τινά *Ev.Luc.*22.31; πέμψον τὸν δαίμονα ὃν ἐξῃτησάμην *for* whose *aid* I *prayed*, *PMag.Par.*1.434, cf. 1290. 2. in Med. also, = παραιτοῦμαι, *beg off, gain* his *pardon* or *release*, A.*Ag.*662, X.*An.*1.1.3, Lys.20.15 (Pass.), Plu.*Per.*32, etc.; αὐτὸν ἐξαιτήσεται D.21.99; also ἐ. ὑπέρ τινος *make intercession for* . ., E.*Ba.*360: c. inf., τοὺς κάτω . . ἐξῃτησάμην τύμβου κυρῆσαι I *begged* of them *to allow* me to obtain, Id.*Hec.*49, cf. *Med.*971. 3. c. acc. rei, *avert by begging*, τὰ πρόσθεν σφάλματα Id.*Andr.*54; τὰς γραφὰς παρανόμων Aeschin.3.196. **–ησις,** εως, ἡ, *demanding* one *for punishment* or *torture*, D.49.55, *IG*2².457b19 (iv B.C.), *Inscr.Prien.*121.26 (i B.C.). II. *intercession*, ἡ τῶν φίλων ἐ. D.59.117. III. *demand for satisfaction*, D.S.8*Fr.*25. IV. *petition, prayer*, *PMag.Par.*1.434. **–ητέον,** *one must beg off*, τινὰ παρά τινος Lycurg.135.

**ἐξαιτιολογέω,** *explain fully*, τὸ ὅθεν ὁ φόβος ἐγίνετο ἐ. Epicur.*Ep.*1 p.31 U.

**ἔξαιτος,** ον, (ἐξαίνυμαι) *picked, choice, excellent*, οἶνόν τ' ἔ. μελιηδέα Il.12.320; νῆα καὶ ἐ. ἐρέτας Od.2.307; ἐ. ἑκατόμβας 5.102: in later Poets like ἐξαίρετος, A.R.4.1004, *AP*6.332.5 (Hadr.), Man.2.226, 3.354, *Mus.Belg.*16.71 (Attica, ii A.D.).

**ἐξαιτρᾰπ-εύω,** = ἐξαιθραπεύω, *to be a satrap*, prob. in *SIG*134.3 (Milet., iv B.C.). **–ης,** ου, ὁ, *satrap*, Ἰωνίης ib.30.

**ἐξαίφν-ης,** Adv. *on a sudden*, Il.17.738, 21.14, Pi.*O.*9.52, A.*Pr.*1077 (anap.), S.*OC*1610, etc.: c. part., ψυχὴν θεωρεῖν ἐ. ἀποθανόντος ἑκάστου *the moment that* he is dead, Pl.*Grg.*523e; ἀκούσαντι ἐ. *at first* hearing, Id.*Cra.*396b: c. Art., τό γ' ἐ. D.18.153; but τὸ ἐ. *the instantaneous*, that which is between motion and rest, and not in the time-series, Pl.*Prm.*156d; but, = τὸ ἐν ἀναισθήτῳ χρόνῳ διὰ μικρότητα ἐκστάν, Arist.*Ph.*222ᵇ15. **–ίδιος,** ον, also α, ον Pl.*Cra.*414a, Gal.6.185:—*sudden*, αὔξη Pl. l.c.; μεταβολή Gal. l.c.; ἐπιδρομαὶ τῆς τύχης Hierocl.p.60 A.

**ἐξαιχμᾰλωτεύω,** *make captive*, Hsch. s.v. ἐλεήσατο.

❀ **ἐξαΐω,** *hear*, εὐχῆς ἐξάϊων *Klio* 15.46 (Delph., iii B.C.).

**ἐξαιωρέομαι,** Pass., *to be suspended from* a thing, Hp.*Art.*70.

❀ **ἐξᾰκανθ-ίζω,** *pick out thorns*: metaph., '*pick holes in*', Cic.*Att.*6.6.1. ❀ **–όομαι,** Pass., *become prickly*, prob. in Thphr.*HP*6.4.2 (ἐξανθ- codd.).

**ϝεξακάτιοι,** v. ἑξακόσιοι.

**ἐξᾰκ-έομαι,** *heal completely*, Hp.*Vict.*3.67: hence, *make amends*, αἱ δ' ἐξακέονται ὀπίσσω (sc. Λιταί) Il.9.507, cf. Pl.*Lg.*885d. II. c. acc., *appease*, τότε κεν χόλον ἐξακέσαιο Il.4.36, cf. Od.3.145; *quench*, δίψος D.C.60.9; *make up for*, τὰς ἐνδείας φίλων X.*Cyr.*8.2.22; τὰ δεινά Iamb.*Myst.*1.11. 2. in common language, *mend*, ἱμάτια Pl.*Men.*91d; δίκτυον Men.863.—Late in aor. Act. ἐξακέσας, *Carm.Aur.*66. **–εσις,** εως, ἡ, *thorough cure*, νόσων Ar.*Ra.*1033 (pl.). ❀ **–εστήριος,** α, ον, *remedying evil*, Ζεύς Lex Solonis ap.Poll.8.142; epith. of Hera, Hsch.; θεοί D.H.10.2. 2. *expiatory*, θυσία Id.5.54.

**ἑξάκῐς** [ᾰ], Adv., (ἕξ) *six times*, Pi.*O.*7.86, Pl.*R.*337b, etc.:—also **ἑξάκι,** cj. in Simon.156, Call.*Fr.*120, *AP*14.129 (Metrod.), 141 (Id.), *CIG*2834.4 (Aphrodisias).

**ἑξᾰκισ-μύριοι** [ῠ], αι, α, *sixty thousand*, Hdt.4.86, X.*Cyr.*2.1.6. **–μῡριοτετρᾰκισχῑλιοστός,** ή, όν, 64,000th, Theo Sm.p.126 H. **–χίλιοι** [χῑ], αι, α, *six thousand*, Hdt.1.192, al., Th.2.13, etc.: also **ἑξάκῑχήλιοι,** *Abh.Berl.Akad.*1925 No.5 p.25 (Cyrene).

**ἑξάκλῑνος,** ον, *with six couches*, also **ἕξκλινος,** *EM*346.14:—as Subst. **ἑξάκλινον,** τό, *couch to hold six*, Mart.9.59.9.

**ἐξακμάζω,** *to be gone by*, of an opportunity, Sch.S.*Aj.*594.

**ἑξάκνημος,** ον, of a wheel, *six-spoked*, Sch.Pi.*P.*2.73.

❀ **ἐξᾰκολουθέω,** *follow*, of persons, τοῖς φίλοις Plb.18.10.7, cf. Lxx *Jb.*31.9; μύθοις 2*Ep.Pet.*1.16, J.*AJProoem.*4. 2. of things, *follow, result from*, c. dat., Epicur.*Fr.*181; *attend*, c. dat., εὔνοια, φήμη ἐ. τινί, Plb.4.5.6, 5.78.4; ἔπαινοί τισι κατορθουμένοις D.H.*Comp.*24; esp. of penalties, ἐ. πρόστιμά τισι *UPZ*112v10 (ii B.C.), *PTeb.*5.132 (ii B.C.); also of obligations, *fall on* one, *CPR*5.15, etc. 3. abs., *follow, result*, Ph.*Bel.*58.5, Antyll.ap.Orib.45.15.4; also of logical consequences, πάντα ταῦτα ἐ. Arr.*Epict.*1.22.16, cf. Polystr.p.5 W.

**ἐξακολουθοῦσθαι·** ἐκθρυλεῖσθαι, Hsch.

**ἐξακονάω,** strengthd. for ἀκονάω, Lxx *Ez.*21.11(16).

**ἑξᾰκοντᾰμοιρία,** ἡ, *arc of sixty degrees*, Heph.Astr.2.11 cod.

**ἐξᾰκοντ-ίζω,** *dart* or *hurl forth, launch*, ἐ. τὰ δόρατα X.*HG*5.4.40; φάσγανον πρὸς ἧπαρ ἐ. *strike* it home, E.*HF*1149: c. dat., ἐ. τοῖς δόρασι, τοῖς παλτοῖς, X.*HG*4.6.11, *An.*5.4.25; ἐ. ἐπί τινα Plu.*Art.*9; κατὰ συός D.S.9*Fr.*29; -ίζεται τὸ αἷμα Gal.4.708. b. intr., *dart away*, [ὁ κάραβος] μακρὰν -ίζει Arist.*HA*590ᵇ29. 2. metaph., freq. in E., ἐ. κῶλον τῆσδε γῆς, i.e. *flee precipitately*, *Ba.*665; ἐ. χεῖρας γενείου γονάτων τε *dart out* the hands *towards* his chin and knees [in supplication], *IT*362; τοὺς Ὀδυσσέως πόνους ἐ. *shoot forth*, i.e. *proclaim loudly*, *Tr.*444 (troch.); ταῦτα πρὸς τὰ σὰ *Supp.*456; so γλῶσσαν ματαίους ἐ. λόγους Men.1091; τοσαύτην ἐ. πνοήν Antiph.217.7. **–ισις,** εως, ἡ, *ejaculation, emission*, σπέρματος Gal.19.168. **–ισμα,** ατος, τό, *jet*, αἵματος Sch.Od.22.19. **–ισμός,** ὁ, = foreg., Gal.4.523, Antyll.ap.Orib.7.10.2; *shooting* of a shooting star, Arist.*Mu.*395ᵇ5.

**ἑξᾰκοσί-αρχος** [ῐ], ὁ, *captain of six hundred men*, Polyaen.*Prooem.*2. ❀ **–οι,** αι, α, *six hundred*, Hdt.1.51, etc.: Dor. **ϝεξακάτιοι** *Tab.Heracl.*2.41. **–οστός,** ή, όν, *six hundredth*, Lxx *Ge.*7.11.

**ἑξᾰκοτῠλιαῖος,** α, ον, *of six cotylae*, πλῆθος S.E.*P.*3.95.

**ἐξᾰκου-στέον,** Gramm., *one must understand* (a word), Sch.Pi.*O.*1.157 (v.l.), Sch.Str.7.3.2. ❀ **–στος,** ον, *heard, audible*, Ph.*Bel.*93.51; κραυγή D.S.20.67; λόγος D.H.10.41; ἦχος, ψόφος, Ath.8.361e, Porph.*Abst.*3.3; of persons, J.*AJ*4.8.12. 2. *famous*, Sch.D.P.13, Hsch. **–ω,** *hear* or *catch a sound*, esp. *from a distance, give ear to*, c. acc. rei, κληδόνος βοήν A.*Eu.*397; σοῦ τάδ' ἐξήκουσ' ὕπο S.*El.*553: c. part., ὅσοισι [κακοῖς] . . ἐξήκουσας ἐναίοντά με Id.*Ph.*472: abs., λόγῳ μὲν ἐξήκουσ', ὄπωπα δ' οὐ μάλα ib.676: c. gen., τῶν ῥητόρων ἵν' ἐξακούω Ar.*Th.*293, cf. X.*Cyr.*4.3.3 (v.l.): c. gen. rei, Plu.*Fab.*6:—Pass., *to be audible*, Arist.*Pr.*901ᵃ7, D.L.8.82. II. *understand* in a certain sense, Id.7.89.

**ἐξακρῑβ-άζω,** *know accurately*, τὰ νόμιμα J.*AJ*19.7.4:—Med., Lxx *Nu.*23.10, al. **–ολογέομαι,** = sq., Sch.D.T.p.109 H. (Pass.). **–όω,** *make exact, precise*, or *accurate*, ἐ. λόγον *make a distinct* or *precise* statement, S.*Tr.*426; τὸ τρανὸν τῆς κλήσεως J.*BJ*4.1.1; ἐ. τι ἐπὶ πλεῖον *labour after* too great *exactness*, Arist.*EN*1102ᵃ25, cf. 1101ᵇ34; ἕκαστα . . ἐξακριβοῦσιν οἱ μεθ' ἡδονῆς ἐνεργοῦντες *achieve* each activity *more completely*, ib.1175ᵃ31; κατὰ μέρος ἐ. *work out* in detail, Epicur.*Ep.*1 p.31 U.:—Med., ἐξακριβώσομαί σοι λόγῳ *shall describe* it *exactly*, Philostr.Jun.*Im.*10:—Pass., Arist.*EN*1180ᵇ11, Thphr.*HP*9.16.6,

Epicur.*Ep.*1 p.4 U.,al. II. intr., *speak accurately*, ὑπέρ τινος Arist. *EN*$1096^b30$; περί τινος Plb.2.56.4, cf. Porph.*Abst.*1.39. 2. *observe the exact interval*, Arist.*HA*$583^a30$. **-ωσις**, εως, ἡ, *strict observance*, τοῦ νόμου J.*AJ*17.2.4. II. *exact statement*, Eustr.*in EN* 108.6.

**ἐξακρίζω** αἰθέρα *skim the upper* air, E.*Or.*275; cf. ὑπεξακρίζω.

**ἔξακρος** Μενεκρίτου (physician of Tiberius), name of a *bandage for the wrist and hand*, Heliod.ap.Orib.48.53.

**ἐξακ-τέον**, (ἐξάγω I. 2) *one must put out of the way, kill*, αὐτόν M. Ant.3.1. 2. *one must lead out*, Aët.9.8. II. (ἐξάγω I. 1 b) *one must march out*, X.*HG*6.5.18. **-τέω**, *collect revenue*, Hsch. **-της**, ου, ὁ, title of an official, *BGU*849.2 (iv A.D.).

**ἐξάκτ-ωρ**, ορος, ὁ, = Lat. *exactor*, *BGU*21 ii 17, Tz.*H.*5.607:—hence **-ορία**, ἡ, *his office*, *PLond.*2.378.8, *PGen.*56.32.

**ἐξάκυκλος** [ᾰ], ον, *six-wheeled*, ἅμαξαι Hp.*Aër.*18.

**ἐξάκωλος** [ᾰ], ον, *of six members*, περίοδος Sch.Ar.*Ach.*836.

**ἐξᾰλάομαι**, *migrate*, πανοικεσίᾳ Antipho Soph.108.

**ἐξᾰλᾰόω**, *blind utterly*, υἱὸν φίλον Od.11.103; ὀφθαλμὸν..τὸν ἀνὴρ κακὸς ἐξαλάωσεν *put* it *quite out*.., 9.453, cf. 504. 2. *make blind and useless*, ὅλον δέμας Opp.*C.*3.228.

❀ **ἐξᾰλᾰπ-άζω**, *sack, storm*, πόλιν Il.4.40, 1.129, etc.; also, *empty* a city *of its inhabitants, clear* it *out*, so as to plant new settlers in it, μίαν πόλιν ἐξαλαπάξας Od.4.176: generally, *destroy utterly*, νῆας, τεῖχος, Il.13.813, 20.30: metaph., ἀλλά με νόσος ἐξαλάπαξεν Theoc. 2.85.—Ep. word, used by X.*An.*7.1.29. **-ίζω**, (Lat. *alapa*) *slap in the face*, *Gloss.*

**ἐξαλγέω**, c. acc., *suffer pain in*, τοὺς πόδας Ps.-Callisth.3.27.

**ἐξαλδαίνει**· ἐκβλαστάνει, Hsch.

**ἐξᾰλεείνω**, = ἐξαλέομαι, Opp.*H.*5.398.

**ἐξᾰλειπ-τέον**, *one must wipe out, erase*, τοὺς νόμους Lys.6.8. **-της**, ου, ὁ, = κονιάτης, Gal.19.98. **-τικός**, ή, όν, *obliterating*, τύπος ἐ. τοῦ προτέρου S.E.*M.*7.373. ❀ **-τρον**, τό, *unguent-box*, Ar.*Ach.* 1063, Antiph.208, Lxx *Jb.*41.22(23), *IG*2.751 *B* ii *d* 4, 11(2).161 *B* 125 (Delos, iii B.C.), etc.

**ἐξᾰλείφω**, pf. Pass. ἐξαλήλιμμαι (v. infr.): subj. aor. 2 Pass. ἐξαλῐφῇ v.l. in Pl.*Phdr.*258b:—*plaster* or *wash over*, τοῦ σώματος τὸ ἥμισυ ἐξηλείφοντο γύψῳ Hdt.7.69; ᾗ ἔτυχε..οὐκ ἐξαληλιμμένον τὸ τεῖχος where it was not *whitewashed*, Th.3.20; τοὺς βωμοὺς ἐξαλείψαντι *IG*11.161 *A* 103 (Delos, iii B.C.):—Med., *anoint*, μύρῳ βρενθείῳ ἐξαλείψαο Sapph.*Supp.*23.20. II. *wipe out, obliterate*, ἐξαλειφθεῖσ' ὡς ἄγαλμα E.*Hel.*262: metaph., *wipe out of one's mind*, πάντα τὰ πρόσθεν Pl.*Tht.*187b; τὸ γιγνώσκειν D.37.34; [ὑπόνοιαν] Men.*Pk.*310(prob.); *cancel*, ἐ. ψηφίσματα And.1.76; νόμους Lys.1.48; αἰτίας Arist.*Ath.*40. 3; ἐξαλειφόντων (sc. τὸ ὀφείλημα) *IG*$1^2$.91.10; esp. at Athens, ἐ. τινὰ ἐκ τοῦ καταλόγου *strike* his *name off* the roll, X.*HG*2.3.51, cf. Arist. *Ath.*36.2; so ἐ. τινά Ar.*Eq.*877, cf. D.39.39; opp. ἐγγράφω, Ar.*Pax* 1181, Lys.30.2, etc.; ὑμᾶς ἐκ παντὸς τοῦ Ἑλληνικοῦ Th.3.57:—Med., ἐξαλείψασθαι τὰς ἀπογραφάς *to get* one's inventory *cancelled*, Pl.*Lg.* 850d: metaph., ἐ. πάθος φρενός *blot* it *out from* one's mind, E.*Hec.* 590. 2. metaph., *wipe out, destroy*, μὴ 'ξαλείψῃς σπέρμα Πελοπιδῶν A.*Ch.*503, cf. E.*Hipp.*1241:—Pass., ἡ Σπάρτης εὐδαιμονίη οὐκ ἐξηλείφετο Hdt.7.220; τιμὰς μὴ 'ξαλειφθῆναι A.*Th.*15; οὐδ' ἄπαις δόμος.. ἐξαλειφθείη ποτ' ἄν E.*IT*698.

**ἐξάλειψις** [ᾰ], εως, ἡ, *whitewashing*, τοῦ ἀποδυτηρίου *BCH*23.566 (Delph., iii B.C.). II. *blotting out, destruction*, Lxx *Mi.*7.11, al.

**ἐξᾰλέομαι**, *beware of, avoid, escape*, ἔκ τ' ἀλέοντο Il.18.586; mostly in Ep. aor. 1 inf., Διὸς νόον ἐξαλέασθαι Hes.*Op.*105, cf. 758, 802, Orac. ap.Ar.*Eq.*1080: abs., τάων οὔτινά φημι διαμπερὲς ἐ. A.R.2.319, cf. 3.466: pres. ἐξαλέονται Q.S.2.385.—Ep. word, cf. sq.

**ἐξᾰλεύομαι**, = foreg., ὡς ἂν..μῆνιν..ἐξαλεύσωμαι θεᾶς S.*Aj.*656 codd., but ἐξαλύξ- (Hsch.) is prob. l.

**ἐξᾰληθίζομαι**, *to be truly recorded*, *EM*327.44.

**ἐξαλίζω**, *evacuate*, in Pass., Hp.*VM*22 ap.Gal.19.98 (v.l. ἐξαγγ-). II. ἐξαλίζεται· συναθροίζεται, Hsch. [ᾱ.]

**ἐξᾰλίνδω**, only aor. part. ἐξαλίσας [ῐ], pf. ἐξήλῑκα:—*roll out* or *thoroughly*, ἄπαγε τὸν ἵππον ἐξαλίσας οἴκαδε take him away *when you have given* him *a good roll on the* ἀλινδήθρα, Ar.*Nu.*32 (cf. X.*Oec.*11. 18); to which Strepsiades retorts, ἐξήλικας ἐμέ γ' ἐκ τῶν ἐμῶν you *have rolled* me *out of* house and home, Ar.*Nu.*33.

**ἐξᾰλίπτης**, f.l. for ἐξαλείπτης (q.v.).

**ἐξᾰλίστρα**, ἡ, = ἀλινδήθρα, Poll.1.183.

❀ **ἐξαλλ-ᾰγή**, ἡ, *complete change, alteration*, τῶν εἰωθότων νομίμων Pl. *Phdr.*265a; ἐ. εἰς ἕτερον γένος Thphr.*CP*4.4.5; τῶν κρεῶν ἐ. *variety*, Ath.1.25e; ποικίλων μαθημάτων Iamb.*Protr.*21.κα'. 2. ἐξαλλαγαὶ τῶν ὀνομάτων *variations in the forms* of nouns, Arist.*Po.*$1458^b2$: generally, *variation*, Procl.*Inst.*162, 175 (pl.). **-αγμα**, ατος, τό, *recreation, amusement*, in pl., Anaxandr.20, Parth.24.1 (dub.). **-ακτέον**, *one must change*, Sor.2.24. ❀ **-άκτης**, ου, ὁ, = ἀλαζών, Hsch. s.v. διαμέσταν, cf. *PSI*4.392.7 (iii B.C.). **-αξις**, εως, ἡ, = ἐξαλλαγή, Str.2.3.1, Gal.7.52, al., Longin.*Fr.*3; λόγου Alex.*Fig.*1.2. **-άσσω**, Att. **-ττω**, *change utterly* or *quite*, strengthd. for ἀλλάσσω, ἐσθῆτα E.*Hel.*1297; τινὰς κοσμήσεσι Plu.*Thes.*23; αἰὼν..ἄλλ' ἄλλοτ' ἐξάλλαξεν Pi.*I.*3.18. b. intr., of evolution, τὰ δὲ..ἐξαλλάσσει ἐς τὴν μέζω τάξιν Hp.*Vict.*1.6; ἐ. γένος εἰς ἕτερον *degenerate*, Thphr.*HP*8. 8.3:—Pass., ἐξηλλαγμένος πρός τι ib.4.4.14. c. Med., κακοῖσιν ὅστις μηδὲν ἐξαλλάσσεται who *sees no change take place* in his miseries, S.*Aj.*474:—Pass., ἰδιωτικῆς ἑστίας ἐξηλλαγμένη ἡγεμονία D.S.10*Fr.* 20. 2. Rhet., *vary* common words and phrases, ἐ. τὸ εἰωθός Arist. *Rh.*$1406^a15$, cf. $1404^b8$; ἐ. τὸ ἰδιωτικόν *vary* the common idiom, Id. *Po.*$1458^a21$; ἐξηλλαγμένον [ὄνομα] *altered* form, ib.$1458^a5$: c. gen., ἐξηλλαγμένος τινός *different from*, Isoc.8.63. b. pf. part. Pass. ἐξηλλαγμένος *extraordinary, strange*, Plb.2.37.6, D.S.1.94, Ant.Lib. 41.8, etc.; *varied*, ὄφεις ταῖς ποικιλίαις ἐ. D.S.17.90. 3. c. acc. loci, *withdraw from, leave*, Εὐρώπαν E.*IT*135 (lyr.). II. ἐ. τί τινος *withdraw* or *remove from*, τὴν ἑαυτοῦ γύμνωσιν ἐ. τῶν ἐναντίων Th.5.71. 2. intr., *change from*, τῆς ἀρχαίας μορφῆς Arist.*GA* $766^a26$; μικρὸν ἐ. *exceed the limit* by a little, Id.*Po.*$1449^b13$; ἐ. ἀπὸ τῆς νεώς Philostr.*Her.Prooem.*3; ἐς ἄνδρας Id.*VA*3.28: abs., ἐξαλλάσσουσα χάρις *unusual, rare* grace, E.*IA*564 (lyr.); *to be different from*, πάντων τῶν παρ' ἡμῖν Phld.*Sign.*9. b. ἐξαλλάσσουσαι στολαί *changes of* raiment, v.l. in Lxx *Ge.*45.22. 3. *turn another way, move back and forward*, κερκίδα E.*Tr.*200 (lyr.); ἐ. δρόμον *change* one's course, X.*Cyn.*10.7; ποίαν (sc. ὁδόν) ἐξαλλάξω; which *other* way *shall* I *take?* E.*Hec.*1060 (lyr.). 4. *divert, amuse*, Men.747, Philippid.35; *coax, win over*, ὀψαρίοις *POxy.*531.18 (ii A.D.).

**ἐξαλλοι-όω**, *change, alter*, Lxx 3 *Ma.*3.21:—Pass., *change utterly*, πρὸς τὸ χεῖρον Thphr.*CP*2.15.2, cf. Ph.1.674. **-ωσις**, εως, ἡ, *metabolism*, of food, prob. for -αλλάττωσις, Gal.15.250.

**ἐξάλλομαι**, fut. -ᾰλοῦμαι Lxx *Mi.*2.12: aor. -ηλόμην S.*OT*1311 (lyr.), -ηλάμην Luc.*Asin.*53, Dor. -άλατο Theoc. (v. infr.); Ep. aor. part. -άλμενος (v. infr.):—*leap out of* or *forth from*, ἐξάλλεται αὐλῆς, of a lion, Il.5.142: elsewh. used by Hom. only in aor. part. ἐξάλμενος, abs., 15.571: c. gen., προμάχων ἐξάλμενος, τῶν ἄλλων ἐ. *springing out from the midst* of.., 17.342, 23.399 (not in Od.); ἐξάλατο ναός Theoc.17.100; ἐ. κατὰ τοῦ τείχους *leap* down *off*.., X. *HG*7.2.6: abs., *jump, hop off*, Ar.*V.*130, *Act.Ap.*3.8; ὦ δαῖμον, ἵν' ἐξήλου; *to* what point *didst thou leap forth*, i.e. to what misery hast thou come? S.*OT*1311 (lyr.); of fish, *leap out of* the water, Arist. *HA*$602^a29$, cf. $528^a32$. 2. *start from its socket, be dislocated*, of a limb, ἐ. ἔξαλσιν Hp.*Art.*46; of a broken bone, Plu.2.341b; of wheels, *start from the axle*, X.*Cyr.*7.1.32. II. *leap up*, Id.*An.* 7.3.33; μήκιστα ἐ. Ph.1.318; of horses, *rear*, X.*Cyr.*7.1.27. 2. ἐξάλλετο γαστήρ *swelled, became distended*, Call.*Cer.*88 (s.v.l.). 3. metaph., ἐ. πρός τι *fly off* to, *have recourse* to, Plu.2.382e.

**ἔξαλλος**, ον, *special, distinguishing*, ἐσθῆτες Plb.6.7.7, cf. Lxx 2 *Ki.* 6.14; στέφανος *OGI*737.19 (ii B.C.); στολαί Ph.1.468; τὰ ἔ. τοῦ βαρβαρικοῦ κόσμου Plu.2.330a. Adv. -ως *strangely*, of superstitious veneration, Plb.32.15.7.

**ἐξαλλοτρι-όω**, *export*, Str.5.1.9. II. *divert, alienate*, πόρον εἰς ἑτέρας χρείας *BSA*17.229 (Pamphyl.), cf. *PGiss.*2.24 (ii B.C.). 2. *alienate, estrange*, τὸν πολιτικὸν ὄχλον D.H.11.39; τοὺς πολλοὺς πρὸς τοὺς ἀρίστους S.E.*M.*2.42:—Pass., *to be estranged*, Lxx 1 *Ma.*12. 10. **-ωσις**, εως, ἡ, *alienation*, *POxy.*94.7 (i A.D.), etc.

**ἔξαλμα**, ατος, τό, (ἐξάλλομαι) = πήδημα, Hsch. II. *distance, interval*, τὸ μέγιστον ἔ. οὐρανὸς καὶ γῆ A.D.*Adv.*209.2 (s.v.l.), cf. Sch. D.P.30 (nisi leg. ἔξαρμα); ἐ. ἀπὸ ζῳδίου ἐπὶ ζῴδιον, of the sun or moon, Paul.Al.*S.*1, cf. Barbill. in *Cat.Cod.Astr.*8(3).104 (pl.).

**ἐξαλμίζω**, *deprive of saltness*, Bilabel Ὀψαρτ. p.11.

**ἐξαλμός**, ὁ, = ἔξαλσις, opp. ἄφαλσις, Antyll.ap.Orib.6.31.1.

**ἐξαλμῠρ-όομαι**, *become salt*, *PTeb.*72.11 (ii B.C.). **-ος**, ον, *having lost its saltness*, of earth, Thunell *Sitologenpapyri* $1^v$ iii 11.

**ἐξᾰλογόομαι**, *become irrational*, Eustr.*in EN*276.6.

❀ **ἔξᾰλος**, ον, (ἅλς B) *out of the sea*, ἔ. ἰχθύς *leaping out of the sea*, Emp. 117; ἔ. τὸ σκάφος ἀνασπᾶν Luc.*Am.*8; ἔ. ἀΐσσειν Opp.*H.*2.593; πληγὴ ἔ. a blow on a ship's hull *above water*, Plb.16.3.8; τὰ ἔ. τῆς νεώς Luc.*JTr.*47; *rising high out of the water*, of islands, Str.17.1.52.

**ἔξαλσις**, εως, ἡ, *leaping with the legs held together* (κομιδῇ σκελῶν συνεχής) for exercise, Aret.*CD*1.2. II. *dislocation, displacement*, Hp.*Art.*46.

**ἐξάλυξις** [ᾰ], εως, ἡ, *escape*, Eustr.*in APo.*221.22.

**ἐξᾰλύσκω**, aor. ἐξήλυξα, *flee from*, c. acc., E.*El.*219, *Hipp.*673 (lyr.): abs., *escape*, A.*Eu.*111, E.*Hec.*1194: c. gen., Opp.*H.*3.104; cf. ἐξαλεύομαι.

**ἐξᾰλύω**, = ἐξαλέομαι, μόρον *h.Bacch.*51.

**ἐξάλφεις**· εὑρίσκεις, Hsch.; ἐξαλφήσεις· ἐκτ⟨ι⟩μηθήσῃ μεγάλως,.. τινὲς δὲ ἐκλάμψεις, Id.

❀ **ἐξᾰμαρτ-άνω**, fut. -ήσομαι (-ήσω Hp.*Acut.*(*Sp.*)13):—*miss the mark, fail*, c. part., ἐ. παίοντες X.*Cyr.*2.1.16: abs., *miss one's aim*, S.*Ph.*95; opp. κατορθοῦν, Isoc.7.72. 2. *err, do wrong*, abs., A. *Pr.*1039, etc.; τοῖς πᾶσι κοινόν ἐστι τοὐξ. S.*Ant.*1024, cf. Men.15.1 D.; opp. εὖ ποιεῖν, Lys.25.16; ἔς τινα Hdt.1.108, Lys.12.20; εἰς τοὺς οἰκέτας Isoc.2.5; εἰς θεούς A.*Pr.*945; περί τινα Isoc.4.110, 9.24; ἔν τινι in a thing, Pl.*R.*336e; περὶ τὰ μέγιστα X.*An.*5.7.33: c. part., ἐ. διατρίβων Id.*Cyr.*3.3.56: c. acc. cogn., ἐ. τι *commit* a *fault*, Hdt. 3.145, S.*Ph.*1012, etc. II. Pass., *to be mismanaged, to be a failure*, ἡ ἐξαμαρτανομένη πρᾶξις Pl.*Prt.*357d; ἐξημαρτήθη τὰ νοσήματα X.*Eq.* 4.2; πολιτεῖαι ἐξημαρτημέναι Arist.*Pol.*$1289^b9$. III. trans., *cause to sin*, Lxx 3 *Ki.*15.26, al. **-ία**, ἡ, *error, transgression*, S.*Ant.*558, Them.*Or.*32.362c.

**ἐξᾰμάρτῠρος**, ον, *attested by six witnesses*, συγγραφή *UPZ*124.11; δάνεια *BGU*813.10 (ii A.D.); ἀποχή *PHaw.*303.20 (ii A.D.), *BGU*260. 7 (*Arch.Pap.*5.205, i A.D.): neut. as Subst., *BGU*1239.20 (ii B.C.).

**ἐξᾰμαυρ-όω**, *obscure utterly*, E.*Fr.*781.64 (lyr., Pass.):—Pass., of a plant, *lose its natural character*, Thphr.*CP*2.16.4: metaph., ἐ. ὅσον ἐν τῷ γένει λαμπρόν Ph.2.438; τὰ χείρονα τοῖς βελτίοσι Plu.2.469a; τὰ σοφίσματα ἐ. τὸ μέγεθος Longin.17.2, dub. l. in Hp.*Alim.*6. **-ωσις**, εως, ἡ, *disappearing*, μετάλλων Plu.2.434a (pl.).

**ἐξαμάχανα**· ἐξαίφνης, Hsch. (before ἐξαμαρτάνει).

**ἐξᾰμάω** (A), *mow* or *reap out, finish mowing* or *reaping*, ἐξαμᾷ θέρος A.*Pers.*822, cf. *Ag.*1655 (troch.), E.*Ba.*1315; σπείρων..κἀξαμῶν ἅπαξ sowing and *reaping*, S.*Tr.*33; χρυσοῦν θέρος ἐξαμησάμενος Plu.*Demetr.* 4:—Pass., γένους ἅπαντος ῥίζαν ἐξημημένος (pf. part.) *having* all the race *cut off* root and branch, S.*Aj.*1178, cf. Paus.8.7.7.—Poet. and later Prose. [On the quantity, v. ἀμάω.] (ἐξαμοῦν· ἐκθερίζειν is corrupt in Hsch.)

⊕ **ἐξᾰμάω** (B), = ἐξαφύσσω (cf. ἀμάω B), τἄντερ' ἐξαμήσω Ar.*Lys.* 367:—Med., τὰ σπλάγχν' ἔφασκον ἐξαμήσεσθαι E.*Cyc.*236; ἐξαμησάμενος τὴν λατύπην *IG*2².244.81 (iv B.C.)

**ἐξαμβλ-έομαι**, Pass., *miscarry*, Hp.*Mul.*1.25 (s.v.l.); cf. ἐξαμβλέβει· διαφθείρει, ἐγκυμονεῖ, Hsch. **-ίσκω**, = sq., Ael.*Fr.*49, Hsch. (-ύσκω Procop.*Arc.*9 is f.l.). ⊕ **-όω** (ἐξαναβλ- is dub. in Hsch.), aor. 2 inf. -αμβλῶναι prob. f.l. for -ῶσαι in Them.*Or.*2.33b:—*make to miscarry*, νηδὺν ἐξαμβλοῦμεν E.*Andr.*356:—Pass., of the foetus, *miscarry*, βρέφος ἐξαμβλωθέν Apollod.3.4.3: metaph., αὕτη ἡ ἐλπὶς ἐξήμβλωτο αὐτῇ Ael.*Fr.*57. 2. *make abortive*: metaph., φροντίδ' ἐξήμβλωκας you *have made* a notion *miscarry*, Ar.*Nu.*137; to which Strepsiades retorts, εἰπέ μοι τὸ πρᾶγμα τοὐξημβλωμένον your *abortive thought*, ib.139, cf. Pl.*Tht.*150e; ἐ. θείας γονάς Ph.1.219:—Pass., ὁ πυρὸς ἐξαμβλούμενος Thphr.*CP*4.5.3; σώματος ἰσχὺς ἐξαμβλοῦται Plu. 2.2e. II. intr., *prove abortive*, Ael.*NA*2.25: impers., ἐξαμβλοῖ *a miscarriage follows*, Arist.*HA*577ᵇ6. ⊕ **-ύνω**, *blunt, weaken*, τὰς τῶν ὑγρῶν διαφθοράς Dsc.1.88:—Pass., Plu.*Fab.*23. **-ωμα**, ατος, τό, *abortion*, Artem.1.51 (pl.). **-ωσις**, εως, ἡ, *miscarriage*, Hp.*Nat.Puer.*18 (pl.), Thphr.*HP*9.9.2, Gal.19.178. **-ώσκω** (v.l. -ώττω), = ἐξαμβλόω, Dsc.2.164.

**ἐξαμβρακοῦται**· ἐκλύεται, Hsch.

**ἐξαμ-βρόσαι** and **-βρῦσαι**, v. ἐξαναβρύω.

**ἐξᾰμείβω**, *exchange, alter*, σαρκὸς ἐξαμείψασαι τρόμον *having put away* fear *from* one, E.*Ba.*607 (troch.); ἄλλην ἄλλοτε χρόαν Plu.2. 590c:—Med., *exchange places with*, i.e. *take the place of*, ἔργου δ' ἔργον ἐξημείβετο one labour *came hard upon* another, E.*Hel.*1533. 2. intr. in Act., φόνῳ φόνος ἐξαμείβων Id.*Or.*816 (lyr.). II. of Place, *change one for another, pass over*, c. acc., A.*Pers.*130 (lyr.), E.*Ph.* 131; so ἐξαμείψας Μακεδονίαν εἰς Θετταλίαν ἀφίκετο X.*Ages.*2.2: abs., *withdraw, depart*, E.*Or.*272:—so in Med., *pass*, διά τινος Id.*Fr.*781. 45; τηνεῖ πρὸς τὴν σχοῖνον ἐξαμείβεο *APl.*4.255. III. Med., *requite, repay*, τινὰ ποιναῖς A.*Pr.*225 (v.l. ἀντημείψατο).

**ἐξᾰμειψις** [ᾰ], εως, ἡ, *alternation*, Plu.2.426d (pl.).

**ἐξᾰμέλγω**, *milk out, suck out*, γάλα A.*Ch.*898:—Pass., f.l. for ἐξαθελγ-, Erot. II. *press out*, πλήρωμα τυρῶν ἐξημελγμένον E.*Cyc.*209.

**ἐξᾰμελέω**, *to be utterly careless of*, τινός Hdt.1.97: abs., *show no care, be negligent*, ἐπὶ τῶν γυναικῶν Arist.*Pol.*1269ᵇ22:—Pass. impers., ἐξημέληται περὶ τῶν τοιούτων *no care is taken*.., Id.*EN*1180ᵃ27; ἐξημέλητο τὰ τῶν θεῶν αὐτοῖς Plu.*Cam.*18; ἐξαμελουμένων [τῶν παίδων] *being uncared for*, Arist.*EN*1180ᵃ30; -ούμενον ἅπαν χεῖρον γίγνεται Thphr.*HP*3.2.2.

**ἐξᾰμέρ-εια**, ἡ, *division into six parts*, Stob.2.7.2. **-ής**, ές, *in six parts*, of the hexameter, Orph.*Fr.*356.

⊕ **ἐξάμετρος** [ᾰ], ον, *of six metres*, ἐν ἑ. τόνῳ in *hexameter* measure, Hdt.1.47; ἐν ἔπεσι ἑ. Id.7.220, cf. Pl.*Lg.*810d; ἑξάμετρα (sc. ἔπη) Arist.*Rh.*1404ᵃ34, *Po.*1449ᵃ27, Demetr.*Eloc.*1, etc.

**ἐξαμεύω**, in pf. Pass. ἐξήμευσαι· ἀπο(κε)κίνησαι, Hsch.

**ἐξᾰμηνιαῖος**, α, ον, = ἑξάμηνος, Apollod.3.4.3; ἡμέρα Gem.6.15. II. = ἑξάμηνος II, πῶλος *Hippiatr.*20.

**ἐξᾰμηνόβῐος**, ον, *living six months*, σαῦρος v.l. in Arist.*HA*558ᵃ17.

⊕ **ἐξᾰμηνος**, ον, *of, lasting six months*, ἀρχαί Arist.*Pol.*1299ᵃ6, 1308ᵃ 15; ἀνοχαί Plb.21.5.11. 2. Subst. ἑ. (sc. χρόνος), ὁ, *half-year*, X. *HG*[2.3.9]; ἑξαμήνου σῖτος a *half-year's* supply, ib.3.4.3; ἑξάμηνον διαλείπειν Arist.*HA*573ᵃ13; ἐν -μήνῳ Thphr.*HP*8.2.7 also ἡ ἑ. (sc. ὥρη) Hdt.4.25. II. *six months old*, ὗες Arist.*HA*545ᵇ2.

**ἐξαμηχᾰνέω**, *get out of a difficulty*, εἰ μή τι τούτων -ήσομεν E. *Heracl.*495.

**ἐξᾰμιλλάομαι**, aor. 1 part. ἐξαμιλλησάμενος and -ηθείς, E.*Hel.*1471 (lyr.), 387: imper. ἐξαμίλλησαι Id.*Hyps.Fr.*2:—*struggle vehemently*: c. acc. cogn., τὰς τεθρίππους Οἰνομάῳ..ἁμίλλας ἐξαμιλληθείς *having contested* the chariot-race with him, Id.*Hel.*387: abs., ib.1471; διαφόροις ὁδοῖς πρὸς ἓν καὶ ταὐτὸν ἄκρον Constantius in Them.*Or.*p.22 D. II. *drive out of*, ἐξαμιλλῶνταί σε γῆς E.*Or.*431; *drive out of his wits*, τινὰ φόβῳ ib.38. III. aor. 1 in pass. sense, *to be rooted out*, of the Cyclops' eye, πυρί Id.*Cyc.*628.

**ἐξάμῑτος** [ᾰ], η, ον, *of six strands*, θρίξ prob. in *AP*7.702 (Apollonid.).

**ἔξαμμα**, ατος, τό, (ἐξάπτω) *handle*, Them.*Or.*13.166a. II. ἔξαμμα πυρός, = ἄναμμα (q.v.), *Stoic.*2.196,199.

**ἐξαμμᾰτίζω**, gloss on ἐπαλλάξαντες, Apollon.*Lex.*

**ἑξα-μν⟨α⟩ιαῖος**, = ἑξάμνους, Hsch. s.v. πέλεκυς. ⊕ **-μναῖος**, α, ον, *owning six minae*, *SIG*363.9 (Ephesus, iii B.C.). **-μνους**, ουν, *worth* or *weighing six minae*, Eust.1878.57.

**ἐξαμοιβάς**· ἑτέροις καὶ ἑτέραις, Hsch.

**ἑξᾰμοιρία**, ἡ, *arc of six degrees*, Vett.Val.356.30.

**ἑξάμορος** [ᾰ], ον, for *ἑξάμοιρος, *one-sixth*, Nic.*Th.*594.

**ἐξαμοῦν**· ἐκθερίζειν, Hsch.; cf. ἐξαμάω (A).

**ἐξαμπρεύω**, *haul out*, Ar.*Lys.*289.

**ἐξάμπρον**, τό, *team of oxen*, *Gloss.*

**ἐξᾰμυγδᾰλίζω**, *make like an almond*, Aq.*Ex.*25.32(33):—also -όω, ib.35(36).

**ἐξᾰμύνομαι** [ῡ], Med., *ward off from oneself, drive away*, νόσους A. *Pr.*483; αἶθρον θεοῦ E.*Supp.*208; τινά Id.*Or.*269:—Act. is dub. l. in Them.*Or.*23.284b.

**ἐξᾰμυστίζω**, *drink off at a draught*, Pl.Com.189.

**ἐξᾰμφοτερίζω**, *make ambiguous*, ἐξημφοτέρικεν τὸν λόγον has *led* the argument *into a contradiction* (by answering 'neither and both'), Pl.*Euthd.*300d; ἐξαμφοτερίσας· τὸ ἀμφίβολον ποιῆσαι, καὶ τὸ δύο πραγμάτων ἐκπεσεῖν, Hsch., cf. *EM*347.7.

**ἐξάμφω**, *both*, *PMasp.*311.14 (vi A.D.). **ἔξαν**, v. ἐξῆς.

⊕ **ἐξανα-βαίνω**, *get to the top of*, Artem.2.28; ἀτραπὸν ἐξανάβα *Epigr.* *Gr.*782 (Halic.). **-βλύζω**, *gush forth*, *PMag.Par.*1.942 (Pap. -βλύδω). **-βρύω**, causal of foreg., τύχας ὀνησίμους γαίας ἐξαμβρῦσαι (Pauw for ἐξαμβρόσαι) *cause* happiness *to spring forth from* the earth, A.*Eu.*925 (lyr.). **-γεννάομαι**, Pass., *to be born again*, Jul.*Ep.*61c. **-γιγνώσκω**, *read through*, Plu.*Cat.Mi.*68, *Cic.*27, etc.

**ἐξᾰναγκάζω**, fut. -άσω S.*Ichn.*212:—*force* or *compel utterly*, τινὰ δρᾶν τι Id.*El.*620, cf. E.*Or.*1665, etc.: with the inf. omitted, S.*OC* 603, Ar.*Av.*377:—Pass., ὑπὸ τοῦ λόγου Hdt.2.3. 2. *force out*, ἔδρηνHp.*Haem.*2. 3. *enforce*, τὸν ταγὸν..ἐξξανακάδην *IG*9(2).257 (Thess., v B.C.). II. *drive away*, τὴν ἀργίαν πληγαῖς X.*Mem.*2.1.16.

**ἐξαναγνωρίζω**, gloss on ἐπαναγνῶναι, Hsch.

**ἐξανάγω** [ᾰγ], *bring out of* or *up from*, ἐ. τινὰ Ἅιδου μυχῶν E. *Heracl.*218:—Pass., *put out to sea, set sail*, of persons, Hdt.6.98, al., S.*Ph.*571, Th.2.25, etc.; of ships, Hdt.7.194: metaph., τῆς τῶν ψευσμάτων καὶ σοφισμάτων χώρας -αναχθησόμεθα Ph.1.517.

**ἐξανα-δείκνῡμι**, *show forth, declare*, ἀρετὴν κρήνης..ἐξανέδειξεν *IPE* 2.37 (Panticapaeum). **-δοσις**, εως, ἡ, *eruption, scab*, Aq.*Le.*13.6, 18. **-δύομαι**, aor. 2 Act. ἐξανέδυν, *rise out of, emerge from*, as a diver from the water, c. gen., ἁλός, κύματος ἐξαναδύς, Od.4.405, 5.438; ἰλύος Them.*Or.*20.240c; ἀφ' ὕδατος Batr.133; γενέσεως ἐ. *arise from, emerge from*, Pl.*R.*525b. 2. *escape from*, c. gen., ἐξαναδύεσθαι φανερᾶς μάχης Plu.*Sert.*12: c. acc., Ἀΐδεω μέγα δῶμ' Thgn.1124; λόχον Orac.ap.Paus.4.12.4. **-ζέω**, *boil up with*: c. acc. cogn., metaph., τοιόνδε..ἐξαναζέσει χόλον *will let* such fury *boil forth*, A.*Pr.*372. **-θλίβω** [ῑ], *squeeze out, express*, *Placit.*2.13.2.

**ἐξαν-αιρέω**, *take out of*, πυρός *h.Cer.*254, cf. A.R.3.867:—Med., ἦ καί σφ' Ἀθάνα γῆθεν ἐξανείλετο; E.*Ion* 269. **-αισθητέω**, *to be utterly without feeling*, Porph.*Abst.*1.39 codd.

**ἐξανα-κᾰλύπτομαι**, Med., *uncover oneself*, Sch.Ar.*Nu.*3. **-κολυμβάω**, *rise again after diving*, Arist.*HA*591ᵃ27. **-κρούομαι**, Med., *retreat from* a place *by backing water*, τῇσι λοιπῇσι [νηυσί]..ἐξανακρουσάμενοι Hdt.6.115. **-κτίζω**, *rebuild*, πόλιν Tz.*H.*13.7. **-λαμβάνω**, cited in error from Th. by *AB*93.

**ἐξανᾱλίσκω**, pf. Pass. ἐξανήλωμαι Hp.*Nat.Puer.*30, but -ανάλωμαι Pl.Com.175:—*spend entirely*, τὰ πλεῖστα τῶν ἰδίων ἐ. Plu.*Pomp.*20:—Pass., τὰ ἀλλότρι'..ἐξανάλωται Pl.Com. l.c.; τὰ παρ' ἐμοῦ ἐξανηλωμένα D.50.15. 2. *exhaust*, ἐξανήλωσεν ὁ ἥλιος [τὸ ὑγρόν] Thphr. *Vent.*15, etc.; ἐ. δύναμιν ἔν τινι Plu.*Cat.Mi.*20:—Pass., *to be used up, exhausted*, Arist.*GA*750ᵃ34; εἴς τι Hp.*Nat.Puer.* l.c.; διὰ τῆς καθάρσεως Sor.1.31; πόνος ἐξανηλώθη Babr.95.44. 3. *destroy utterly*, ἐξαναλῶσαι γένος A.*Ag.*678:—Pass., ἐξανήλωνται δ' οἵ τ' ἴδιοι πάντες οἶκοι καὶ τὰ κοινὰ τῇ πόλει D.13.27, Aeschin.3.103.

**ἐξανᾱλόω**, = foreg., Max.Tyr.13.3:—Pass., Ph.2.511.

**ἐξαναλύω**, *set quite free*, ἄνδρα..θανάτοιο δυσηχέος ἐξαναλῦσαι Il. 16.442; Μοιρᾶν μίτον ἐ. *IG*14.1449. II. *resolve into its elements*, *PMag.Par.*1.439.

**ἐξανάλωσις** [ᾰλ], εως, ἡ, *entire consumption*, τῆς δυνάμεως Plu.*Marc.* 24.

**ἐξανα-νεόομαι**, Med., *renew*, συγγένειαν Str.9.4.2. **-πείθω**, *win over*, θεούς Hermesian.7.8. **-πληρόω**, *supply, replace*, D.51.6:—Pass., *be renewed*, of the bark of trees, Thphr.*HP*3.17.1. **-πνέω**, *recover breath*, Pl.*Phdr.*254c, *Sph.*231c. **-πτύσσω**, *unfold, explain*, Tz.*Il.*6.41.

**ἐξαν-άπτω**, *hang from* or *by*, τί τινος E.*IT*1351, cf. 1408:—Med., *attach to oneself*, δύσκλειαν Id.*Or.*829 (lyr.). II. *kindle*, πυρσὸν τοῖς νέοις *AP*5 *Prooem.* (Cephalas); σβεννυμένην φύσιν Plu.2. 752a. ⊕ **-ᾰριθμέω**, *reckon, number*, *IGRom.*4.661.34 (Pass., Acmonia). **-αρπάζω**, *snatch away*, E.*Hel.*1565, *IA*75.

**ἐξανα-σπάω**, *tear away from*, ἐκ τῶν βάθρων Hdt.5.85; βάθρων E. *Ph.*1132: *tear up from*, [ἐλάτην] χθονός Id.*Ba.*1110. **-στάσις**, εως, ἡ, *removal, expulsion*, Plb.2.21.9, al. II. intr., *emigration*, τινῶν ἐκ τῆς οἰκείας Str.2.3.6. 2. *rising from bed to go to stool*, Hp. *Prog.*11; later simply, *going to stool*, Aret.*SD*2.9 (pl.), Sever.*Clyst.* pp.3,34 D., etc. b. *rising from bed in the morning*, Porph.*VP*40; ἐ. ὕπνου Gal.7.96. 3. ἡ ἐ. ἡ ἐκ νεκρῶν *resurrection* from the dead, *Ep. Phil.*3.11. 4. woman's *ornament*, *BGU*717.11 (ii A.D.). **-στᾰτόομαι**, = ἐξανίσταμαι, *PTeb.*2(*d*).16 (Poet. Alex.). **-στέφω**, strengthd. for ἀναστέφω, E.*Ba.*1055. **-στημα**, ατος, τό, *erection*, Eust.1719.39 (pl.).

**ἐξαναστράπτω**, *lighten*, [Emp.]*Sphaer.*66.

**ἐξανα-στρέφω**, *turn upside down*, μακέλλῃ Ζηνὸς ἐξαναστραφῇ S. *Fr.*727: c. gen. loci, *hurl headlong from*.., δαιμόνων ἱδρύματα.. ἐξανέστραπται βάθρων A.*Pers.*812. ⊕ **-τέλλω**, *cause to spring up from*, ποίην χθονὸς A.R.4.1423: metaph., θόρυβον ἐκ κεφαλῆς Telecl. 44. 2. intr., *spring up from*, χθονός Emp.62.4; ἀφ' αἵματος Mosch. 2.58. ⊕ **-φαίνω**, *bring up and show*, Orph.*A.*1357 (tm.), Man.2. 153. **-φανδόν**, Adv. *openly*, ἐρέω δέ τοι ἐ. Od.20.48. **-φέρω**, *bear up*, of buoyant sea-water, Arist.*Fr.*217. 2. ἐ. λόγχης τύπον *exhibit* the form of a spear, Plu.2.563a. II. intr., *weather the storm*, Id.*Pyrrh.*15: metaph., ἐν νοσήματι κατειλημμένος ἐ. Id.2.

147c; πρὸς τὴν ἀδηλότητα Id.*Oth.*9: abs., ἐ. καὶ διωθεῖσθαι τὸ πάθος Id.2.446b, cf. 541a, 550c. 2. *rise in the scale*, ἐπὶ ζυγοῦ πρὸς τὰ βελτίονα ib.469b. **-φορά**, ἡ, *recovery*, Phld.*D.*3 *Fr.*43. **-φύομαι**, aor. 2 ἐξανέφυν, *grow up from*, γαίης Orph.*Fr.*285.36. **-χωρέω**, *go out of the way, withdraw, retreat*, ἐπὶ τὸν ποταμόν, πρὸς τὸ ὄρος, Hdt.1.207, 5.101, cf. Ph.1.229, al.; ἀπὸ τῶν φορτίων Hdt.4.196; of a plant, [γῆς] συνημερουμένης ἐ. Thphr.*HP*6.3.3. II. c. acc., ἐξανεχώρει τὰ εἰρημένα *sought to back out of* his words, Th.4.28. **-ψήχω**, *corrode*, interpol. in Stob.*Flor.*38.53 Meineke.

**ἐξανδήρισον**· ἐκπέρασον, Hsch.

**ἐξανδρᾰποδ-ίζω**, *reduce to utter slavery*, Ἀθήνας Hdt.6.94, cf. X.*HG*2.1.15:—mostly in Med. **-ίζομαι**, τοὺς Τεγεήτας Hdt.1.66, cf. And.4.22, X.*HG*2.2.16, etc.; τῶν τεθνεώτων ἐ. τοὺς βίους *confiscate* the substance of the deceased, Plb.32.5.11.—The Att. fut. ἐξανδραποδιοῦμαι, Ion. -ιεῦμαι, which is mostly trans. (as in Hdt.1.66), takes a pass. sense in Id.6.9: so aor. 1 ἐξηνδραποδίσθην ib.108, D.50.4: pf. part. ἐξηνδραποδισμένος Plu.*Ant.*3, Luc.*Cal.*19. **-ισις**, εως, ἡ, *selling into slavery*, Hdt.3.140. **-ισμός**, ὁ, = foreg., Plb.6.49.1. **-ιστής**, οῦ, ὁ, *enslaver, kidnapper*, *Gloss.*

**ἐξανδρόομαι**, *come to man's years*, ἐξανδρωμένος Hdt.2.63, cf. Antipho Soph.61; ἐξανδρούμενος E.*Ph.*32, Ar.*Eq.*1241. II. λόχος δ' ὀδόντων ὄφεος ἐξηνδρωμένος the host *having grown to men* from teeth, E.*Supp.*703. III. ἐξηνδρωμένον· ὀρθιάζοντα, Hsch.

**ἐξαν-εγείρω**, *raise* a cry, Aq.*Is.*15.5. **-ειμι**, *go forth from*, Ἑλλάδος A.R.2.459; αἴγλη ὕδατος ἐξανιοῦσα *being reflected from*.., Id.3.757; ἐ. οὐρανοῦ *go up* the sky, of stars, Theoc.22.8 codd. II. *come back from*, ἄγρης *h.Pan.*15.

**ἐξᾰνεμ-ίζω**, strengthd. for ἀνεμίζω, Sch.Il.20.440. **-όω**, *blow out with wind, inflate*:—Pass., *to be inflated*, Hp.*Mul.*1.34; *to be impregnated by the wind*, of mares, Arist.*HA*572ᵃ13, cf. Ael.*NA*4.6: metaph., Ἥρα ἐξηνέμωσε τἀμ' Ἀλεξάνδρῳ λέχη E.*Hel.*32:—Pass., ἐξηνεμώθην μωρίᾳ *I was puffed up*, Id.*Andr.*938, cf. Ph.1.698. II. Pass., of corn, *to be parched by wind*, '*wind-bitten*', Thphr.*HP*8.10.3. 2. of hair, *float in the wind*, Apollod.1.6.3. III. metaph., *excite*, εἰς δρόμον ἐ. τινά Ael.*NA*13.11:—Pass., τὴν διάνοιαν ἐξηνεμώθη ib.15.29.

**ἐξαν-ερευνάω**, *search*, τὴν πήραν Tz.*H.*5.83. **-έρχομαι**, *come forth from*, γῆς ἐξανελθὼν E.*Tr.*753. **-ερωτάω**, *inquire*, Tz.*H.*6.596. **-έσασα**· ἐπιστρέψασα, Hsch. **-ευρίσκω**, *invent*, S.*Ph.*991; *discover*, Plu.*Sol.*20, *Arat.*22. ※ **-έχω**, *hold up from*: mostly intr., *jut out from, stand up upon*, ἀγκὼν ἐ. γαίης A.R.2.370; στήλη ἐ. τύμβου Theoc.22.207. II. Med. (impf. and aor. 2 with double augm. ἐξηνειχόμην, ἐξηνεσχόμην, cf. ἀνέχω), *bear up against, endure, suffer*, with part., οὗ λόγων ἄλγιστ' ἂν ἐξανασχοίμην κλύων S.*OC*1174, cf. *Ph.*1355, E.*Alc.*952; οὐ γὰρ ἐξηνέσχετο ἰδὼν Ar.*Pax*702; ταῦτα παῖδας ἐξανέξεται πάσχοντας; E.*Med.*74, cf. *Andr.*201; ταῦτα δόξανθ'.. ἐξηνέσχετο that these things should be decreed, Id.*Heracl.*967.

**ἐξᾰνέψιοι**, οἱ, *children of* ἀνεψιοί, *second cousins*, Plb.6.11ᵃ.4, Ar. Byz. post Hdn.*Epim.*286, Hsch.: fem., ἐξανέψιαι Men.1010 (*children of* ἀνεψιαδοῖ (-δαῖ) Poll.3.29, wrongly): sg., ἐξανέψιος *Inscr.Mus. Alex.*72.16, *POxy.*270.4 (i A.D.), 502.14 (ii A.D.): proparox., Trypho ap.Ammon.*Diff.*p.53 V.

**ἐξανηλ-ίσκω**, **-ωσις**, later forms for ἐξαναλ-, *PSI*4.400 (iii B.C.), 6.604 (iii B.C.).

**ἐξανήσας**· ἐξαντήσας, Hsch. (leg. ἐξαμήσας· ἐξαντλήσας).

※ **ἐξανθ-έω**, *put out flowers*, γῆ ἐξανθοῦσα X.*Cyn.*5.5; *bloom*, of flowers, Thphr.*HP*4.7.2; of the growth of hair, ἐ. ἡ τῆς ἥβης τρίχωσις Arist.*GA*728ᵇ27: c. acc. cogn., ἐ. ποικίλα *put forth* varied *flowers*, Luc.*Pisc.*6; ἐ. φλόγα, σφῆκας, Plu.*Alex.*35, *Cleom.*9; μέλι Alciphr.3.23. 2. metaph., *burst forth from* the surface, like an efflorescence, ὡς αἱματηρὸν πέλαγος (v.l. πέλανον) ἐξανθεῖν ἁλὸς E.*IT*300; ὕβρις γὰρ ἐξανθοῦσ' ἐκάρπωσε στάχυν ἄτης *bursting into flower, breaking out*, A.*Pers.*821; ἐκ ταύτης τῆς ὑπολήψεως ἐξήνθησεν ἡ δόξα Arist.*Metaph.*1010ᵃ10; κακίαι Plu.*Thes.*6. 3. of ulcers, etc., *break out*, Hp.*de Arte*9; ἐ. λεύκη Arist.*Col.*797ᵇ15; ὡς φλυκταίνας -ῆσαι *IG*4.955.25 (Epid.); also of the skin, τὸ ἔξωθεν σῶμα.. φλυκταίναις καὶ ἕλκεσιν ἐξηνθηκὸς *breaking out* with boils and ulcers, Th.2.49, cf. Luc.*DMort.*20.4; τὸ ἔδαφος σκόλοψι ἐξηνθήκει Luc.*VH*2.30; also πλῆθος μυῶν ἐξανθῆσαν Str.13.1.48. II. *to be past its bloom, lose its bloom*, of colour, Plu.2.287d; of wine, ib.692c; ἐξηνθηκυῖα ἐλαία, i.e. when the flower has dropped and the fruit is forming, Dsc.3.125. 2. metaph., *degenerate, run wild*, πέφυκεν ἀνδρεία.. κατὰ μὲν ἀρχὰς ἀκμάζειν ῥώμῃ, τελευτῶσα δὲ ἐξανθεῖν.. μανίαις Pl.*Plt.*310d; τὸν ἐγγύτατα χρόνον ἀεὶ τῆς ἀφέσεως κάλλιστα πάντα διάγει.. τελευτῶντος δὲ ἐξανθεῖ τοῦ χρόνου (sc. ὁ κόσμος) ib.273d. ※ **-ημα**, ατος, τό, *efflorescence, eruption, pustule*, Hp.*Aph.*6.9, *Epid.*1.9, cf. Arist.*HA*518ᵃ12, Ph.2.225: metaph., [πάθη] χρηστῆς φύσεως οἷον ἐ. Plu.2.528d. **-ησις**, εως, ἡ, = foreg., Hp.*Aph.*3.20, Ph.2.101, Archig. ap.Gal.12.468; *growth of young hair*, Sch.A.R.1.972, etc. II. *fading*, ὥσπερ ἐ. τις τῆς προϋπαρχούσης ὀσμῆς Thphr.*CP*6.15.2 codd. **-ίζω**, *deck as with flowers, paint in various colours*, γυναῖκες.. αἱ καθήμεθ' ἐξηνθισμέναι Ar.*Lys.*43; ἄνωθεν ἐξηνθισμένον, of a fish, Philem.79.6; παντοίᾳ κομμωτικῇ.. ἐξηνθισμένη Hld.7.19; ἐλέφας φοίνικι -ισμένος Max.Tyr.40.2. II. Med., *gather flowers*, Plu.2.661f. **-ισμα**, ατος, τό, f.l. for ἐξάνθημα, Hp.*Coac.*435. **-ισμός**, ὁ, = ἐξάνθημα, v.l. in Dsc.2.82.3.

**ἐξανθρᾰκόω**, *burn to ashes*, Ion *Trag.*28.

**ἐξανθρωπ-ίζω**, *humanize, bring down to men*, τὰ θεῖα Plu.2.360a; φιλοσοφίαν, of Socrates, ib.582b. II. [πνεύμασι καὶ χυμοῖσι] χρῆται (sc. the new-born child) ἧσσον -ισμένοισι less *humanized* (than those enjoyed by the foetus), Hp.*Oct.*1-2. **-ος**, ον, *unsociable*, of epileptics, Aret.*SD*1.4. II. ἐ. ἡ συμφορή it (epilepsy) is an *inhuman* calamity, Id.*SA*1.6.

※ **ἐξαν-ίημι**, poet. impf. ἐξανίεσκον A.R.4.622: fut. ἐξανήσω, also -ήσομαι E.*Andr.*718: pf. part. Pass. -ειμένος Orib.46.19.20:—*send forth, let loose*, εὔπρηστον ἀϋτμὴν ἐξανιεῖσαι Il.18.471; [ὀδμὴν] A.R.l.c.; ἐξανῆκε γᾶ ὕψιν E.*Ph.*670 (lyr.); κρήνην ἐξανῆκ' οἴνου θεός Id.*Ba.*707; ἐ. αἷμα *make* it *spout forth*, Id.*IT*1460; [ῥόον] Call.*Del.*207; ἀρὰς σφῷν ἐξανῆκα I *have sent forth* curses against you, S.*OC*1375. b. c. gen., *send forth from*, τίς σε πολιᾶς ἐξανῆκεν γαστρός; Pi.*P.*4.99; θύρσους ἐξανιεῖσαι χερῶν E.*Ba.*762; νάματ' ὅσσων μηκέτ' ἐξανίετε Id.*HF*625. 2. *let go*, Id.*IA*372; τὴν ἀρετὴν ἐ. *relax, slacken*, Plu.*Cat. Ma.*11:—Pass., *to be set free from*, πόνων Hp.*Nat.Hom.*12: abs., Ph.2.371. 3. *loosen, undo*, στροφίδας E.*Andr.*718:—Pass., Plu.2.788b. 4. *dilute*, Herasap.Gal.13.795:—Pass., pf. part. -ειμένος Orib.l.c. II. intr., *slacken, relax*, Hp.*Nat.Hom.*7; ἀνίκ' ἐξανείη.. ἄτα (Herm. for ἐξανίησι) S.*Ph.*705: c. gen., ὀργῆς ἐξανεὶς κακῆς E.*Hipp.*900. 2. *burst forth from*, γῆς, of a river, A.R.4.293: abs., of seed, *spring up*, Arist.*Mir.*833ᵇ2. **-ῑμάω**, *draw up*, ποτὸν Ph.1.296. **-ιστάνω**, = sq., *drive out of one's senses*, Dsc.4.73. **-ίστημι**: I. causal in pres., impf., fut., and aor. 1: 1. *raise up*, τοὺς θανόντας S.*El.*940; *make* one *rise from his seat*, Pl.*Prt.*310a; *bid* one *rise* from suppliant posture, ἐγώ σ' ἕδρας ἐκ τῆσδε.. ἐξαναστήσω E.*Andr.*263, cf. 267; ἐ. τὴν ἐνέδραν *order* the men in ambush *to rise*, X.*HG*4.8.37. 2. *make* a tribe *emigrate, remove* or *expel*, ἐ. τινὰς ἐκ τῶν νήσων, ἐξ ἠθέων, etc., Hdt.1.171, 5.14, etc.; ἄνδρας δόμων S.*Ant.*297; ἐ. πόλεως *bid* one *depart from*.., Id.*OC*47; simply ἐ. τινάς Hdt.6.127, Th.4.98, etc. (v. infr. II. 2). b. *challenge* a juror, *PHal.*9.5 (iii B.C.), *PGurob*2.10 (iii B.C.), etc. 3. *depopulate, destroy*, πόλιν Hdt.1.155, al.; Ἰλίου ποτ' ἐξαναστήσας βάθρα E.*Supp.*1198; Ἑλλάδα Id.*Tr.*926. 4. ἐ. θηρία *rouse* them *from their lair*, X.*Cyr.*2.4.20. 5. τουτὶ ἐ., *erigere penem*, E.*Cyc.*169. II. intr. in Pass., with aor. 2, pf. and plpf. Act.: 1. *stand up from one's seat*, Hdt.3.142; ἐκ τοῦ θρόνου Id.5.72, cf. Pl.*Ly.*211a; θάκων X.*Hier.*7.7; ὁδῶν τινί, in courtesy, Id.*Smp.*4.31; *rise* to speak, S.*Ph.*367; *rise* from ambush, λόχου E.*El.*217: without λόχου, Th.3.107; *rise* after dinner, Pl.*R.*328a, etc.; πρὸ μέθης Isoc.1.32; from bed, λέχους E.*El.*786; ἐξ εὐνῆς X.*Oec.*10.8; ἐξαναστῶμεν εἰς τὴν αὐλὴν *let us rise and go* into.., Pl.*Prt.*311a; εἰς περίπατον X.*Smp.*9.1. 2. c. gen., *arise and depart from, emigrate from*, Λακεδαίμονος Pi.*P.*4.49, cf. E.*Andr.*380; ἐκ τῆς γῆς τῆσδε Hdt.4.115: abs., *break up, depart*, Th.7.49, etc. 3. *to be driven out* from one's home, *to be forced to emigrate*, ἐξ ἠθέων ὑπό τινος Hdt.1.15, cf. 56, al.; πρὸς δάμαρτος ἐξανίσταται θρόνων A.*Pr.*767. 4. of places, *to be depopulated*, ἐξαναστάσης πάσης Πελοποννήσου ὑπὸ Δωριέων Hdt.2.171; Τροίης ἐξανεστάθη βάθρα E.*Hel.*1652, cf. D.16.25. 5. *rise to go to stool*, Hp.*Epid.*1.26.δ', etc. 6 *rise from the plain*, of a mountain, Plb.1.56.4. b. so of ulcers, *rise*, Aret.*SD*2.13; of an excrescence, κέρχνος ἐ. S.*Fr.*279. **-ίσχω**, = ἐξανέχω, *rise*, of the sun, Eust.419.17. **-οίγω**, *lay open*, μηχανὰς Σισύφου Ar.*Ach.*391; διάφραγμα D.S.1.33:—Pass., Str.16.1.10, Ath.Mech.36.9: pf. inf. ἐξανεῷχθαι *to be exposed*, of high ground, Ath.Med.ap.Orib.9.12.1. **-οιδέω**, *swell up*, Arist.*Mete.*367ᵃ3. **-οιξις**, εως, ἡ, *opening*, Str.16.1.10.

**ἐξανόμεναι**· ἐκκενούμεναι, Hsch.

**ἐξαντάω**, v. ἐξαντῶν.

**ἐξάντες**· ἐξεναντίας, ὅτε δὲ τὸ ὑγιές, Hsch.

**ἐξάντης**, ες, of patients, *out of danger, healthy*, ἐ. γίνεται Hp.*Morb.*3.3, *Mul.*1.41; ἐξάντη ποιεῖν τινα Pl.*Phdr.*244e. b. *harmless*, ἐξάντη φάσκοντες ποιήσειν (sc. μῆνιν Ἑκάτης) D.Chr.4.90. 2. c. gen., *free from*, κακοῦ Ael.*NA*3.5; νούσου Hp.*Morb.*1.14, cf. *Com.Adesp.*1279 (= *Trag.Adesp.*151); δειλίας Jul.*Or.*6.192b. 3. = ἐξεστηκώς, μαινόμενος, *EM*346.42.

**ἐξαντίαι**, Adv. = *opposite*, *SIG*306.12 (Tegea, iv B.C.).

**ἐξάντιον**, τό, Dim. of ἐξᾶς, Epich.10.

**ἐξαντλ-έω**, *drain* or *draw off*, Pl.*Lg.*736b, *PTeb.*123.6 (i B.C.), Aret.*SA*2.4:—Pass., Arist.*HA*570ᵃ8. 2. metaph., *endure to the end, see out*, ἐκείνων μείζον' ἐ. πόνον E.*Cyc.*10; τὸν αὐτὸν δαίμον' ἐ. ἐμοί ib.110; τὸν αὐτὸν ἐ. βίον Id.*Fr.*454; βίον οἰκτρὸν ἐ. Men.74; στρατῷ γόους E.*Supp.*838. 3. *empty out*, Hld.1.3; *squander*, [πλοῦτον] Luc.*Tim.*18, cf. 17 (Pass.); δύναμιν πόνοις Id.*Anach.*35, cf. Alciphr.1.21. **-ημα**, ατος, τό, *douche*, Aret.*CD*2.12 codd. ※ **-ησις**, εως, ἡ, *douching*, Sor.1.99, Antyll.ap.Orib.10.30.6. **-ητέον**, *one must douche*, ib.13.19.

**ἐξαντῶν**· ἀντιάζων τῆς κόρρης καὶ τοῦ πώγωνος, οἷον ὑπογεν⟨ε⟩ιάζων, Hsch. (with a second and less prob. expl.).

**ἐξάν-ῠσις** [ᾰ], εως, ἡ, *exaction in full*, *PMon.*7.26 (vi A.D.); *exaction*, τῶν δημοσίων Just.*Nov.App.*4.1, cf. *Cod.Just.*10.19.9 *Intr.* **-ύω**, Att. -ύτω [ῡ], fut. -ύσω [ῡ] (v. infr.), but Ep. fut. -ύω Il.11.365: pf. inf. ἐξηνυκέναι Critias 16.14:—*accomplish, make effectual*, Θέτιδος δ' ἐξήνυσε βουλὰς Il.8.370; θεῶν θέσμι' ἐξήνυσε S.*Aj.*712 (lyr.); ἔμελλες ἐξανύσειν κακὰν μοῖραν ib.926 (lyr., -ύσσειν cod. Med.); τί μοι ἐξανύσεις χρέος; Id.*OT*156 (lyr.); πάθεα E.*Ion*1066 (lyr.); λειτουργίαν *POxy.*904.8 (v A.D.):—Med., *accomplish* or *finish for oneself*, κακῶν μῆχος E.*Andr.*536 (lyr.); τέκνοις τάφον Id.*Supp.*285 (dact.). 2. *finish, dispatch*, i.e. *kill*, ἤ θήν σ' ἐξανύω (fut.) Il.11.365; κενταυροπληθῆ πόλεμον E.*HF*1273. b. *conquer*, ἔθνη App.*Ill.*15. 3. of Time and Distance, *bring to an end, finish, accomplish*, βίοτον S.*Tr.*1022 (dact.); ἁμέραν τάνδε E.*Med.*649 (lyr.); δρόμον, ἴχνος, πόρον, Id.*Ph.*163 (lyr.), *Tr.*232 (lyr.), *IT*897 (anap.): abs. (like ἀνύω I. 6), *finish*

*one's way to* a place, *arrive at* it, ἐς or ἐπί.., Hdt.6.139,7.183: also c. acc. loci, ἐξανύσαι τὰν νεκρῶν πλάκα (Vauvill. for ἐκτανύσαι) S.*OC* 1562; πόλον ἐξανύσας E.*Or.*1685 (anap.). **4.** c. inf., *manage* to do, ἐ. κρατεῖν Id.*Hipp.*400. **5.** Med., *obtain, borrow,* τι παρά τινος Id.*Ba.*131 (lyr.).

**ἐξάνω·** ἄνωθεν ἐξάγει, ἐξενέγκει, Hsch.

® **ἐξά-ξεστος,** ον, *containing six* ξέσται, μέτρον Hero *Geom.*23.66, cf. *Gloss.* **-ούγκιον,** τό, *six ounces,* ib.

**ἐξαπ-ᾰείρω,** *carry away,* Philox.2.39. **-αιολεῖσθαι·** παραλογίζεσθαι, prob. in Hsch. (ἐξαποίνασθαι cod.). **-αιτέω,** strengthd. for ἀπαιτέω, dub. in Jul.*Mis.*349b (ἐξαπατῶσι codd.).

**ἐξᾰπάλαστος** [πᾰ], ον, *of six hands-breadth,* Hdt.1.50, 2.149 (v.l. -αιστος).

**ἐξαπ-αλλάσσω,** Att. **-ττω,** *set free from, remove from,* τινὰ κακῶν E.*IA*1004; (sc. ἑαυτόν) ταλαίνης ζόης Id.*Hec.*1108:—Pass., *get rid of, escape from,* κακῶν ἐξαπαλλαχθείς Hdt.5.4; ἄλυπος ἄτης ἐξαπαλλαχθήσεται S.*El.*1002; τῶν εἰρημένων ἐξαπαλλαγῆναι *escape from* his own words, Th.4.28. **-αντάω,** *meet,* v.l. in X.*Cyr.*3.3.24.

**ἐξᾰπᾰτάω,** Ep. iter. ἐξαπάτασκον Ar.*Pax*1070 (hexam.):—Pass., fut. -απατηθήσομαι Pl.*Grg.*499c; but -απατήσομαι in pass. sense, X. *An.*7.3.3:—*deceive* or *beguile, deceive thoroughly,* εἴ τινά που..ἔτι ἔλπεται ἐξαπατήσειν Il.9.371, cf. Od.9.414, Pi.*O.*1.29, Hdt.1.153, Ar. *V.*901, etc.; ἐ. τινὰ φρένας Id.*Pax*1099 (hexam.); ἐ. καὶ φενακίζειν D.21.204; *seduce* a woman, Hdt.2.114: c. dupl. acc., ἐ. τινά τι *in* a thing, X.*Cyr.*3.1.19; also ἐ. ἐπὶ τοῖς ἰδίοις συμβολαίοις Isoc.10.7; περὶ σαυτὸν ποιεῖσθαι..ἐφ' οἷς ἐξαπατᾷς ἔλεον surround yourself with compassion for your *swindling tricks,* D.21.196; ἐ. τινὰ ὡς.. *cheat* him *into believing* that.., X.*An.*5.7.6, cf. Pl.*Cra.*413d; ἐ. νόσον *beguile* or *assuage* it, Luc.*Nigr.*7:—Pass., ὡς ἐξαπατηθείς Hdt.9.94; ἐνόμιζον ἐξηπατῆσθαι Th.5.42; ᾔδει ὑπὸ τῆς μητρυιᾶς ἐξαπατωμένη Antipho 1.19; τὸ δεῖπνον ἐξαπατώμενος Ar.*V.*60; ἐ. ἀπάτην Plot.2.9.6:—Med. like Act., f.l. in Pl.*Cra.*439c.

**ἐξαπάτερθεν·** ἐκ τοῦ ἑτέρου, Hsch.

® **ἐξᾰπάτ-η** [πᾰ], ἡ, *deceit,* Hes.*Th.*205 (pl.), Thgn.390 (pl.), X.*An.*7.1.25, App.*BC*5.22. **-ημα,** ατος, τό, gloss on φήλωμα, *EM*791.32. **-ησις,** εως, ἡ, strengthd. for ἀπάτησις, Ath.9.387e. **-ητέον,** *one must deceive,* Pl.*Cri.*49e. **-ητήρ,** ῆρος, ὁ, *deceiver,* Hom. *Cercop.* **-ητής,** οῦ, ὁ, = foreg., Ptol.*Tetr.*165. **-ητικός,** ή, όν, *calculated to deceive,* τῶν πολεμίων X.*Eq.Mag.*4.12, S.E.*M.*2.93. Adv. -κῶς Poll.4.24. **-ύλλω,** Com. Dim. of ἐξαπατάω, *cheat a little, humbug,* Ar.*Ach.*657, *Eq.*1144.

**ἐξᾰπᾰφίσκω,** Ep., = ἐξαπατάω, Hes.*Th.*537: aor. ἐξήπᾰφον Od.14.379; subj. ἐξαπάφω 23.79; part. ἐξαπαφών, -οῦσα, *h.Ap.*379, *h.Ven.*38, E.*Ion*704 (lyr.), Alex.Aet.3.19, etc.: Hom. also has 3 sg. aor. opt. Med. ἐξαπάφοιτο in act. sense, Il.9.376, 14.160: later aor. 1 ἐξαπάφησε *h.Ap.*376, Q.S.1.137, Opp.*H.*3.94.

**ἐξά-πεδος** [ᾰ], ον, *six feet* long, Hdt.2.149, *IG*14.352.1.62 (Halaesa). **-πεζος,** ον, *six-footed,* Lyc.176.

**ἐξαπ-εῖδον,** inf. ἐξαπιδεῖν: aor. without any pres. ἐξαφοράω in use, *observe from afar,* only in S.*OC*1648 (lyr.). **-ειλέω,** *menace,* dub. in Chor. in *Rev.Phil.*1.71. **-ελαύνω,** *drive away out of,* δόμων μ' ἐμῶν ἐ. *IG*12(5).564.3 (Carthaea).

**ἐξᾰπέλεκυς,** εως, ὁ, ἡ, *with six axes,* ἐ. ἀρχή, = Lat. *sexfascalis, of the praetor,* Plb.3.40.9; ἐ. ἡγεμών or simply ἐ. *a praetor,* Id.2.24.6, 3.40.11; στρατηγός ib.106.6, D.S.31.42: pl., App.*Syr.*15.

**ἐξαπ-ελευθερόω,** *manumit,* *POxy.*722.13, al. (Pass., i A.D.). **-εύχομαι,** strengthd. for ἀπεύχομαι, Tz.*H.*13.606. **-ηλιωτικός,** ή, όν, *easterly,* *PFlor.*50.105 (iii A.D.).

**ἐξάπηχυς** [ᾰ], υ, *six cubits long,* Hdt.2.138, Hp.*Art.*72, X.*An.*5.4.12 codd.; ξύλα ἐξαπήχη *PCair.Zen.*112.6; cf. ἕξπηχυς.

**ἐξάπῑν-ᾰ** [ᾰπ], later form of ἐξαπίνης, Lxx *Nu.*4.20, *Ev.Marc.*9.8, *PGiss.*1.68.6 (ii A.D.), Procop.*Aed.*2.11. **-αιος,** proparox., or **-αῖος,** α, ον, or ος, ον, = ἐξαιφνίδιος, Hp.*Acut.*28, X.*Hier.*10.6, Plb.25.2.1, Call.*Jov.*50, Ruf.ap.Orib.6.38.25. Adv. -ως Hp.*Art.*43, Th.3.3, al. **-ης,** Dor. and Aeol. **-ας,** = ἐξαίφνης, Il.15.325, Alc.27, Pi. *P.*4.273, Hdt.1.74,87, Hp.*Acut.*28, Epicur.*Nat.*14.8; never in Trag., sts. in Att., as Ar.*Pl.*336, 339, 815, Th.1.50, Nicol.Com.1.6:—with a Subst., ἔαρ ἐξαπίνας *sudden* spring, Theoc.9.34. **-ον,** dub. l. in Hp.*Aff.*4, for ἄπνουν or ἐξαίφνης.

**ἐξαπλᾰσι-άζω,** *multiply by six,* in Pass., *Theol.Ar.*48, *EM*595.15. **-επίτρῐτος,** ον, *six and one-third times as much,* Procl.*Hyp.*4.109. **-ος,** α, ον, Ion. **-πλήσιος,** η, ον, *six times as large as,* τινός Hdt.4.81: abs., Plu.2.1020a, 1028f: neut. -πλάσιον κηροῦ *six times as much* wax, Orib.*Fr.*99. **-ων,** ον, gen. ονος, = foreg., χρόνος Arist.*Mu.*399$^{a}$10.

**ἐξά-πλεθρος,** ον, *of six* πλέθρα, *six* πλέθρα *long,* Hdt.2.149. **-πλευρος,** ον, *with six sides,* Plot.6.3.14. **-πλήσιος,** v. ἐξαπλάσιος. **-πλόος,** όη, όον, *sixfold,* *GDI*5075.38 (Crete). **-πλόω,** = ἐξαπλασιάζω, *multiply by six,* Paul.Al.*E.*1.

**ἐξαπλ-όω,** *unfold, roll out,* οὐρανὸν ὡς δέρριν ἐξαπλῶσαι Ps.-Luc. *Philopatr.*17; ἐ. τὴν χεῖρα S.E.*M.*2.7: metaph., πᾶσαν τὴν ἔννοιαν εἰς τὰ πάντα Dam.*Pr.*1:—Pass., *to be unfolded, spread out,* ὕπτιος ἐξήπλωτο νεκρὸν δέμας Batr.106; ἀϊδιότης -ωθεῖσα κατὰ τὴν χρονικὴν παράτασιν *unrolled* successively, Procl.*Inst.*55. **2.** *unfold, explain,* ἀμφιβόλους λέξεις Ph.1.302:—Pass., Demetr.*Eloc.*254, S.E. *M.*7.233. **3.** Medic., *open out* a fistula, Heliod.ap.Orib.44.23.50 (Pass.). **-ωσις,** εως, ἡ, *unfolding,* δακτύλων S.E.*M.*2.7; τῶν ὑμένων εἰς πλάτος Aret.*SA*1.8; opp. πίλησις, Ph.1.385 (pl.). **2.** *opening out,* of roots, Archig.ap.Orib.8.2.12. **II.** *explanation,* Erot. *Prooem.* **III.** *expansion* or *paraphrase* of an expression, S.E.*M.*7.51. **b.** Math., *expansion,* εἰς μονάδας Nicom.*Ar.*2.10. **-ωτέον,** *one must explain,* Gal.18(2).669.

**ἐξαποβαίνω,** *step out of,* νηός Od.12.306; νηὸς χέρσονδε A.R.3.199, etc.

**ἐξᾰποδία,** ἡ, *hexapody, hexameter,* Anon.*in Rh.*190.31.

**ἐξαποδύνω,** *put off,* εἵματα Od.5.372. **ἐξαποίνασθαι,** v. ἐξαπαιολεῖσθαι.

® **Ἑξάπολις** [ᾰ], εως, ἡ, *league of six cities,* of the Asiatic Dorians, Hdt.1.144, Sch.Ar.*Pl.*385.

® **ἐξαπόλλῡμι** (-ύων prob. cj. in A.*Ch.*837 (lyr.)), *destroy utterly,* A. l.c., S.*El.*588, E.*Heracl.*950, Thphr.*HP*8.7.2, etc. **II.** Pass., with pf. 2 ἐξαπόλωλα: aor. 2 ἐξαπωλόμην:—*perish utterly out of,* c. gen., Ἰλίου ἐξαπολοίατ' Il.6.60; ἐξαπόλωλε δόμων κειμήλια 18.290; ἠέλιος δὲ οὐρανοῦ ἐξαπόλωλε Od.20.357; σπέρμα πάσης ἐξαπόλλυται χθονός A.*Ag.*528: abs., *perish utterly,* Hdt.4.173, S.*Fr.*236.

**ἐξαπο-λογία,** ἡ, title of three speeches of Antipho, *second defence, rejoinder* (nisi scribendum ἐξ ἀπολογίας: cf. ἐκκατηγορία). **-νέομαι,** *return out of,* Il.16.252, 20.212 (or ἐξ ἀ.). **-νίζω,** *wash thoroughly,* πόδας Od.19.387.

**ἐξαποξύνω,** *sharpen well,* E.*Cyc.*456 (s.v.l.).

**ἐξαπο-πᾰτέω,** strengthd. for ἀποπατέω, Hp.*Morb.*4.43. **-πειρῆσθαι·** πειρᾶσθαι, Hsch. (ἐξαπειρῆσθαι cod.). **-πέμπω,** *send quite away,* Tz.*H.*3.887. **-πνέω,** *breathe quite away,* τὸν βίον ib.364, 6.185. **-πτύω,** *spit quite out,* ib.7.

**ἐξαπορέω,** strengthd. for ἀπορέω, to be in *great doubt* or *difficulty,* Plb.4.34.1; τοῖς πράγμασι Arist.*Ath.*23.1:—Med., ἀπορούμενοι, ἀλλ' οὐκ ἐ. 2*Ep.Cor.*4.8: so in aor. Pass. ἐξηπορήθην Lxx *Ps.*87(88).15, D.S.24.1, Plu.*Alc.*5; ἐξαπορηθῆναι ἀργυρίου *to be without* money, D.H.7.18; τῶν κοινῶν ἐξηπορημένων *SIG*495.12 (Olbia, iii B.C.), cf. *PEleph.*2.10 (iii B.C.).

**ἐξαπο-σταλτέος,** α, ον, *to be dispatched,* *Gloss.* **-στέλλω,** fut. -στελῶ Lxx 4*Ki.*8.12: pf. ἐξαπέσταλκα Attal. (v. infr.):—*dispatch,* πρεσβευτάς Plb.3.11.1; στρατηγόν D.S.19.102; θεωρούς *SIG*629.8 (Delph., ii B.C.); βιβλίον τινί Attal.ap.Hipparch.1.3.3:—Pass., *to be dispatched,* Philipp.ap.D.18.77, *OGI*90.20 (Rosetta, ii B.C.); ὑπό τινων *Vit.Philonid.*p.7 C.; ἐξαπεσταλμένοι μάχεσθαι Aristeas 13; also ἡμῶν ὁ λόγος -εστάλη *Act.Ap.*13.26. **2.** *send forth,* [δαίμων] -στέλλων ὕδατα καὶ ἀνέμους *Sammelb.*4324.16. **3.** of prisoners, *send* before a tribunal, ἐ. τινὰ δέσμιον πρός τινας *PTeb.*22.18 (ii B.C.), etc.:—Pass., *PTaur.*1 iii 13 (ii B.C.). **II.** *send away, dismiss,* e.g. a prisoner, Plb.4.84.3; ἐ. τινὰ κενόν *send away* empty-handed, *Ev.Luc.*1.53; *divorce* a wife, Lxx *De.*24.4; *expel,* ἐκ τοῦ παραδείσου ib.*Ge.*3.23. **III.** *discharge* a projectile, Hero *Bel.*81.4 (Pass.). **IV.** *destroy,* ὀχυρώματα ἐν πυρί Lxx 4*Ki.*8.12. **V.** *emit, display,* φαντασίαν Procl.*Hyp.*5.72. **-στολή,** ἡ, *sending away,* *IG*2.985 *A* 1 (ii B.C.), Plb.1.66.2, Lxx 3*Ma.*4.4; ἐ. θανάτου Ph.1.233: pl., Plb.9.5.5. **II.** *discharge* of an engine or projectile, Ph.*Bel.*53.46, Hero *Bel.*79.4, 110.10. **-στολος,** ὁ, = πρεσβευτής, *PAmh.*2.138.10 (iv A.D.). **-τίνω** [ῑ], *satisfy in full,* Ἐρινύας ἐξαποτίνοις Il.21.412.

**ἑξάπους** [ᾰ], ὁ, ἡ, πουν, τό, gen. ποδος, *six-footed,* Arist.*PA*683$^{b}$2. **II.** = ἑξάπεδος, Luc.*Sat.*17; κολοσσός Plu.*Luc.*37; λίθος *Milet.*7.57 (Didyma). **2.** of metre, *of six feet,* D.H.*Comp.*4. Cf. ἕξπους.

**ἐξαπο-φαίνω,** strengthd. for ἀποφαίνω, Luc.*Hes.*1. **-φθείρω,** *destroy utterly,* A.*Pers.*464, S.*Tr.*713. **-χέω,** in Pass., *pour forth from,* Tz.*H.*3.327.

® **ἑξά-πρυμνος,** ον, *with six stems,* i.e. *ships,* Lyc.1347. ® **-πτέρῠγος,** ον, *six-winged,* *Gloss.*

**ἐξαπτίς,** ἡ, *cloak,* *Gloss.*

**ἑξάπτῠχος,** ον, *with six folds,* Sch.Il.12.295, Hsch. s.v. ἐξήλατον.

**ἐξάπτω,** *fasten from* or (as we say) *to,* πεῖσμα νεὸς..κίονος ἐξάψας μεγάλης *having fastened* it *to* a pillar, Od.22.466, cf. Il.24.51; ἐ. τι χροός E.*Tr.*1220; τὴν πόλιν τοῦ Πειραιῶς Plu.*Them.*19; ἐ. τι ἔκ τινος Hdt.4.64; ἀπό τινος X.*Cyn.*10.7; also ἐ. ἐκ τοῦ νηοῦ σχοινίον ἐς τὸ τεῖχος Hdt.1.26; ἐξάψας διὰ τῆς θυρίδος τὸ καλῴδιον Ar.*V.*379:—Pass., περὶ τὴν κεφαλὴν ἐξῆμμαι πηνίκην τινά I *have* a wig *fastened* on my head, Id.*Fr.*898 (s.v.l.). **2.** metaph., ἐ. στόματος λιτάς *let* prayers *fall from* one's mouth, E.*Or.*383; τῆς τύχης ἐ. τὰ πραττόμενα *consider* actions *as dependent upon* chance, Plu.*Sull.*6; ἐ. τὴν διαδοχὴν τῶν ἀξίων λόγου *continue* the narrative, D.L.8.50; ἐξαμμένος ἐκ σώματος *dependent on* it, Ti.Locr.102e. **3.** ἐ. τινί τι *place upon,* ἱκετηρίαν γόνασιν E.*IA*1216; κόσμον νεκρῷ Id.*Tr.*1208; ἐ. βρόχον ἀμφὶ δειρήν Id.*Ion*1065 (lyr.). **II.** Med., *hang by, cling to,* πάντες ἐξάπτεσθε all *hang on,* Il.8.20; ἐ. τῆς οὐραγίας, τῆς πορείας, *hang on* the enemy's rear, *on* his line of march, Plb.4.11.6, 3.51.2; τῶν πολεμίων, τῆς μάχης, D.S.11.17, 13.10; τῶν Ἑλληνικῶν ἐ. *attend to..,* Plu.*Them.*31; τοῦ πολέμου D.H.6.25; *cling to* an authority, Plu.2.1111f. **2.** *hang* a thing *to oneself, carry* it *suspended about one, wear,* κώδωνας D.25.90; πέπλους χροός E.*Hel.*1186; σφραγίδια Ar.*Th.*428; also ἐ. ναῦς *fasten* them *to one's own ship, take in tow,* D.S.14.74; ἐ. τοὺς ἐραστάς *have* them *hanging about one,* Philostr.*VA*8.7.6, cf. Luc.*Am.*11.

**B.** Act. also, *set fire to,* [ὕλαν] Ti.Locr.97e, cf. Thphr.*HP*9.8.6, App.*Hisp.*5. **II.** *kindle, inflame,* πόλεμον Ael.*NA*12.35; πυρετόν Gal.6.240; of love, Chor. in *Rh.Mus.*49.495; νόσημα *aggravate,* Id. in *Hermes* 17.234:—Pass., πῦρ ἐ. ἐκ λίθων Arist.*PA*655$^{a}$15; ὑπὸ φιλοσοφίας ὥσπερ πυρός *to be inflamed* by.., Pl.*Ep.*340b; αὖθις οὐκ -ονται they *are* not *rekindled* (like Heraclitus' sun), Id.*R.*498b; ὑπ' ὀργῆς ἐξαφθέντες D.H.5.38; πόλεμος ἐξήφθη Str.9.3.8; ψυχαὶ -ονται *are turned to flame,* M.Ant.4.21.

**ἐξά-πτωτος**, ον, (πτῶσις) *with six cases*, Prisc.*Inst.*5.77. **-πῦλα**, τά, a gate at Syracuse, Plb.8.3.6, D.S.14.18, Plu.*Marc.*18.

**ἐξαπωθέω**, *thrust away*, E.*Rh.*811.

**ἐξάπωλος** [ᾰ], ον, *with six colts* or *horses*, ἅρμα Hdn.5.6.7.

**ἐξάραγμα** [ᾰρ], ατος, τό, = σύντριμμα, Hp.ap.Gal.19.98.

**ἐξαραι-όω, -ωσις**, strengthd. for ἀραι-όω, -ωσις, Aret.*CA*2.6, *SA* 2.2.

**ἐξαραιρημένος, ἐξαραίρηται**, v. ἐξαιρέω.

⊛ **ἐξαράομαι**, *utter curses*, ἐκ δ' ἀρὰς ἠρᾶτο S.*Ant.*427. II. *dedicate with solemn prayers*, νεών Aeschin.3.116.

**ἐξᾰράσσω**, Att. -ττω, *dash out*, ἐκ δέ οἱ ἱστὸν ἔραξε Od.12.422; ἐ. λίθῳ ὀδόντας Semon.7.17; ἐ. αὐθαδίαν τινός *knock* his self-will *out of* him, Ar.*Th.*704; *shatter*, τὴν ῥῖνα Hippon.60; τὴν κιγκλίδα Ar.*Eq.* 641; πεφραγμένην ἔξοδον Ael.*NA*15.16; in cookery, *beat up*, Ruf.ap. Orib.4.2.6. II. c. acc. pers., ἐ. τινὰ κακοῖς καἰσχροῖσι *assail* him *furiously* with abuse, Ar.*Nu.*1373.

**ἐξαργέω**, *to be quite torpid*, ἐξηργηκώς Arist.*EN*1099$^a$2; τὴν δύναμιν ἐξηργηκέναι Id.*Pol.*1312$^a$13. II. Pass., *to be quite neglected*, ἔργα δρῶμεν', οὐκέτ' ἐξαργούμενα S.*Ph.*556; [γῆ] ἐξαργηθεῖσα Plu.2.2e.

**ἐξάργματα**, τά, (ἐξάρχομαι) *the first pieces cut from the victim's flesh*, = μασχαλίσματα, A.R.4.477.

**ἐξαργῠρ-ίζω**, *turn into money*, v.l. for ἐξαργυρόω in Th.8.81; ἐ. τὴν οὐσίαν D.5.8, cf. Mitteis*Chr.*88iv23 (ii A.D.):—Med., ἐξαργυρίσασθαι τὸν οἶκον Is.5.43, cf. D.S.22.1, Plu.2.850d. II. ἐξαργυρίζεσθαί τινα *plunder* him, Plb.32.6.1. **-ισμός**, ὁ, = Lat. *adaeratio*, *conversion of payment in kind into money payment*, *PFlor.*95.9, *Cod. Just.*12.37.19.3, etc. **-όω**, *turn into money*, τὰ ἡμίσεα πάσης τῆς οὐσίης Hdt.6.86.α', cf. Th.8.81.

**ἐξάρδω**, *water*, πεδία E.*Antiop.*B58p.21A.

**ἐξάρεν**· ἐκτός ἐστιν, Hsch. **ἐξαρέσασθαι**· διῶξαι, Id. (cf. eund. s.v. ἀραχθείς).

**ἐξάρεσκ-εύομαι**, v.l. for sq. (q.v.). ⊛ **-ομαι**, *make oneself acceptable*, *make offerings*, τοῖς θεοῖς X.*Oec.*5.3,19 (with v.l. -ευομένους, nisi leg. θεούς). 2. c. acc. pers., ἐξαρέσασθαί τινα δώροις *win* him *over* by gifts, D.60.25, cf. 26.

**ἐξαρῆξαι**· ἐκφορῆσαι, Hsch.

**ἐξαρθρ-έω**, *dislocate the joints of*, οἱ Ἀμαζόνες ἐ. τὸ ἄρσεν γένος τὸ ἑωυτῶν Hp.*Art.*53:—Pass., ἐξαρθρέεται τὰ τοιαῦτα ib.58, cf. Gal.6. 876. II. intr., *to be dislocated*, ἐξαρθρήσαντα ὀστέα Hp.*Art.*29; *suffer from dislocations*, ib.8,53. **-ημα**, ατος, τό, *dislocation*, ib.58, Gal.6.876. **-ησις**, εως, ἡ, = foreg., Hp.*Art.*53, Gal.6.876. **-ος**, ον, (ἄρθρον) *dislocated*, Lxx 4*Ma.*9.13, Gal.6.10; τοῦ σκέλους ἔξαρθρος γενέσθαι J.*AJ*3.11.6. II. *with distorted*, *clumsy joints*, Hp.*Art.* 10; *loose-jointed*, Gal.1.178. **-όω**, *dislocate*, Lxx 4*Ma.*10.5. II. ἐξηρθρωμένος, = foreg. II, ἐπωμίδες Arist.*Phgn.*810$^b$35. **-ωμα**, ατος, τό, **-ωσις**, εως, ἡ, = ἐξάρθρημα, -ησις, Gal.18(2).323.

**ἐξαριθμ-έω**, *enumerate*, *count*, τὸν στρατόν Hdt.7.59,60, etc.; *reckon up*, πᾶν τὸ λυποῦν Phld.*Ir.*p.25 W.:—Pass., μυριάδες ἐξηριθμήθησαν Hdt.4.87. II. *count out*, ἐ. χρήματα *pay in ready* money, D.27.58. III. *recount*, κινδύνους Isoc.4.66:—later in Med., τὰ κατὰ μέρος D.H.5.72, cf. D.C.44.48: pf. Pass. in med. sense, Plb.9. 2.1:—Pass., Arist.*Rh.*1410$^b$2. **-ησις**, εως, ἡ, *numbering*, *enumeration*, J.*AJ*7.13.1, App.*BC*2.82, D.C.43.46, A.D.*Conj.*244.21, Plot.6.3.19, etc.; προβάτων *PLond.*2.376.7 (ii A.D.). II. *reckoning up*, *recounting*, τῶν πεπραγμένων Plb.16.26.5.

**ἐξάριθμος** [ᾰ], ον, *supernumerary*, τῆς τάξεως Ascl.*Tact.*2.9.

**ἐξάριθμος** [ᾰ], ον, *sixfold*, Pi.*O.*10(11).25, cf. Sch.

**ἐξαρκ-έω**, I. of objects, *to be quite enough for*, *suffice for*, τινί Heraclit.114, S.*OC*6, 1116, *Ph.*459, etc.; ἔμοιγ' ἐ. ὡς ἂν μὴ κακὸς ᾖ Pl.*Prt.*346c; ὁ βίος μοι δοκεῖ τῷ μήκει τοῦ λόγου οὐκ ἐξαρκεῖν Id.*Phd.* 108d; ἐ. εἴς τι Lys.19.55, 30.20; πρός τι Pl.*R.*526d, X.*Mem.*4.1.5: c. inf., μία μεσότης ἂν ἐξήρκει.. συνδεῖν Pl. *Ti.*32a: abs., *suffice*, μέτρια δ' ἐξαρκεῖν ἔφη E.*Supp.*866, cf. And.4.15; βραχὺς.. ἐξήρκει λόγος D. 18.196. 2. impers., ἐξαρκεῖ *it is enough for*, *suffices for*, c. dat. pers., Pl.*Prt.*336c, al.: with inf. added, ἐ. ἡμῖν ἡσυχίην ἄγειν Hdt.7.161; ἐ. σώματι εἶναι σώματι Pl.*R.*341e; also ἐξαρκέσει σοι τύραννον γενέσθαι Id.*Alc.*2.141a; ἐξαρκέσει εἰπεῖν D.27.12; οὐκ ἐξαρκεῖ περὶ τούτου μόνον αὐτῷ ψεύσασθαι Lys.3.25, cf. Isoc.19.47: c. dat. pers. et part., ταῦτα ἔχουσιν οὐκ ἐξήρκεσεν αὐτοῖς D.47.52: abs., οὐκ ἂν ἐξαρκέσειεν Id.21. 129; ἐξαρκεῖ *enough!* Pl.*Grg.*503a, *Hp.Ma.*302b; ὡς ἐξαρκέσαν, εἰ.. Is.6.13. II. of the subject, *to be satisfied* or *content with*, κτεάτεσσι Pi.*O.*5.24; ἐ. διαίτῃ *to be strong enough* for it, Hp.*Aph.*1.9; πᾶσιν ἐ. *to be a match* for all, E.*Supp.*574: abs., ἐξαρκέσας ἦν Ζεύς Zeus was *strong enough*, ib.511: c. part., τὸν νοῦν διδάσκαλον ἔχουσα ἐξήρκουν ἐμοί I *contented myself*, *was satisfied* with having, Id.*Tr.*653, cf. Ar.*Eq.*524; πῶς ἂν.. ἐξαρκέσειε.. ἐκτίνων; how *could* he pay *enough?* X.*Hier.*7.12:—Pass., οὐκ ἐξηρκεῖτο φυγαδεύειν dub.l.in Plb. 13.6.6. III. *assist*, *succour*, φίλοις Pi.*N.*1.32: c. acc., ταῦτα ὁ φίλος πρὸ τοῦ φίλου ἐξήρκεσεν X.*Mem.*2.4.7. **-ής**, ές, *enough*, *sufficient*, πλοῦτος ἐ. δόμοις A.*Pers.*237 (troch.); τἄνδον ἐξαρκῆ τιθέναι put *in order*, S.*Tr.*334. **-ούντως**, Adv. pres. part. of ἐξαρκέω, *enough*, *sufficiently*, Ar.*Ra.*377 Isoc.12.8; -ως ἔχει is *content with*.., Pl.*Grg.*493c.

**ἔξαρμα**, ατος, τό, (ἐξαίρω) *rising*, *swelling*, Hp.*Epid.*4.31; of the *tragus* of the ear, Ruf.*Onom.*44. II. *meridian height* or *elevation* of the heavenly bodies, τοῦ ἡλίου Str.2.1.18, cf. 1.1.21; τοῦ πόλου Hipparch.1.3.6, Gem.6.24, Plu.*Mar.*11, Ptol.*Alm.*2.3,6, *Tetr.*76; opp. ἀντέξαρμα, *Theol.Ar.*25; τοῦ ἐξάρματος ὁ ἐξῆρται Plu.2.410f.

**ἐξαρμόζω**, in Pass., *to be displaced*, *wrenched out*, τὰ πλευρὰ ἐξηρμοσμένοι τῶν σπονδύλων Philostr.*Her.*1.3; ἐξηρμοσμέναι πέτραι Id.*Im.* 2.17; ἐξήρμοσται τὰς κνήμας ib.4.

**ἐξαρμόνιος**, ον, *out of harmony*, *discordant*, καμπαί Pherecr.145.9, cf. ib.26.

**ἔξαρμος**, ον, *with dislocated limbs*, v.l. in Lyd.*Mag.*3.57.

**ἐξαρν-έομαι**, aor. 1 ἐξηρνησάμην Hdt.3.74, Att. ἐξηρνήθην Pl.*Smp.* 192e, *Lg.*949a, Cret. aor. subj. ἐξαννήσεται *Leg.Gort.*3.6:—*deny utterly*, τὸν φόνον Hdt. l. c.; οὔ τοι τοῦτό γ' ἐξαρνήσομαι E.*Hel.*579, etc.; ἤν τις ὀφείλων ἐξαρνῆται *should deny a debt*, Ar.*Ec.*660; μὴ λαβεῖν ἐξαρνούμενος D.27.16; οὐκ ἐ. πράττειν Aeschin.3.250. **-ησις**, εως, ἡ, *denial*, Pl.*R.*531b. **-ητικός**, ή, όν, *apt at denying*, Ar.*Nu.* 1172. ⊛ **-ος**, ον, *denying*: ἐ. εἰμι or γίγνομαι, = ἐξαρνέομαι, abs., Ar. *Nu.*1230, Antipho5.51, And.1.12, etc.; οὐ πώποτε ἐ. ἐγενόμην Pl. *Hp.Mi.*372c; ἐ. γίγνεσθαι περί τινος D.23.176; ὑπέρ τινος D.H.7.34; also ἐ. εἶναί τι Lys.3.27, cf. Pl.*Chrm.*158c; ἐ. ἦν τοῦ φόνου J.*AJ*14. 11.4: freq. folld. by μή c. inf., ἐ. ἦν μή.. ἀποκτεῖναι Σμέρδιν Hdt.3.67, cf. Ar.*Pl.*241; ἐ. γεγονέναι τὸ παράπαν μηδ' εἶναι ψεῦδος Pl.*Sph.*260d; τὸ καλὸν μὴ καλὸν εἶναι Id.*Hp.Ma.*288c; by μὴ οὐ.., Luc.*DMort.*14.1; also ἐ. ἦ μὴν οὐκ ἐγερεῖσθαι τὸ τεῖχος Polyaen.1.30.5; ἐ. ἐγένετο ὡς οὐ.. D.34.49.

**ἐξάρνυμαι**, v. ἐξαίρω II. 1.

**ἐξαροτριάω**, *plough up*, Gloss.

⊛ **ἐξαρπάζω**, fut. -άσομαι Ar.*Eq.*708: aor. 1 ἐξήρπαξα Hom. (v. infr.), ἐξήρπασα Hdt.8.135, Plu.*Comp.Per.Fab.*2:—*snatch away from*, φῶτ' ἐξαρπάξασα νεός Od.12.100; ἐ. τι παρά τινος Hdt. l. c.; τι ἐκ χερῶν τινος E.*IA*315; *rescue*, τὸν δ' ἐξήρπαξ' Ἀφροδίτη Il.3.380, cf. 20.443, 21.597; τῆς πολιορκίας Μάριον Plu.*Sull.*29:—Pass., *to be carried off*, οἱ μὲν ἐξηρπασμένοι σπεύδουσιν *the captured ones* are speeding on their way, S.*OC*1016 (s.v.l.): c. acc., ἐξαρπάζεσθαι τὸ νοτερόν *to have* the moisture *forcibly drawn out*, Pl.*Ti.*60d. II. *tear out*, ἐ. σου.. τἄντερα Ar.*Eq.*708; *tear off*, Asclep.ap.Gal.12.418.

**ἔξαρσις**, εως, ἡ, (ἐξαίρω) *removal*, κακῶν ἁπάντων Ἀρχ.Ἐφ.1919.52 (Pharsalus, v/iv B.C.); *destruction*, Lxx *Je.*12.17. II. (from Pass.) *setting out*, ib.*Nu.*10.6. 2. *rising*, *height* of water in a vessel, Cleom.1.1.

**ἐξαρτ-άω**, *hang upon*, τι ἔκ τινος Plb.18.18.4; ἀπό τινος Arr.*An.* 2.19.2; τί τινος Longus1.32: metaph., *make dependent upon*, ἐπαίνων ἐ. τὴν δόξαν Plu.*Arat.*1; πρᾶξιν τῆς προδοσίας Id.*Fab.*22; τὴν ποίησιν μέθης Ath.10.429b, cf. Plot.6.7.42:—Med., E.*Tr.*129, cf. Gal.*Anim.Pass.*1.9 (prob. l.). 2. *stretch out*, Ael.*NA*4.21. II. Pass., mostly in pf. ἐξηρτῆσθαι: fut. Med. in pass. sense, ἐξαρτήσομαι X.*Cyr.*5.4.20:—*to be hung upon*, *hang upon*, χειρός E.*Hipp.* 325; περὶ σὸν γένειον Id.*IA*1226: abs., Ar.*Pax*470; *to be attached to*.., ἔκ τινος Arist.*HA*495$^b$33; ἐ. τινί ib.496$^a$26. 2. *depend upon*, *be attached to*, σοῦ γὰρ ἐξηρτήμεθα E.*Supp.*735, etc.; τῆς ἰσχύος X. *Cyr.*5.4.20; ἑνός Plu.*Galb.*8; ἔκ τινος Pl.*Ion*536a, *Lg.*732e, etc.; τῶν ἐλπίδων Isoc.8.7. 3. of countries, *be adjacent to*, πεδία τῶν λόφων ἐ. Plu.*Ant.*46. 4. abs., *to be elevated*, ἐξήρτηται τὸ χωρίον Th.6.96; ἐξήρτηται ἡ χώρα πρὸς Νότον (Casaub. ἐξῆρται) Str.7.1.3. 5. *hang upon oneself*, πήραν ἐξαρτήσασθαι Luc.*Fug.*15 (s.v.l.): esp. in pf. part. Pass., c. acc. rei, *having* a thing *hung on one*, ἐπιστολὰς.. ἐξηρτημένος ἐκ τῶν δακτύλων Aeschin.3.164; παιδίον ἐξηρτημένη τοῦ τραχήλου Plu. *Brut.*31: hence, *equipped* or *furnished with*, πώγωνας ἐξηρτημέναι Ar. *Ec.*494; τοιοῦτον ἐξηρτῆσθαι στρατόπεδον D.9.49. **-ηδόν** (ἐξαρτιδὼν cod.)· μετὰ τοῦ ἐκκρεμάσθαι, Hsch. **-ημα**, ατος, τό, *that which is suspended from*, τῶν νεῶν Sch.Ar.*Eq.*759; *weight*, Theo Sm.p.65 H., Iamb.*VP*26.117, Nicom.*Harm.*6; of the ligaments of the uterus, Sor.2.84. II. *that which is attached* or *dependent*, Dam.*Pr.*130 (pl.). **-ησις**, εως, ἡ, *attachment of parts* of the body *one to another*, νεύρων Hp.*Fract.*37; ἡ τῶν ἐμβρύων ἐ. Arist.*HA*511$^a$33; τὴν ἐ. ἔχειν ἔκ τινος ib.519$^b$9; τινί ib.497$^a$19. II. *suspension* of a weight, μολύβδου Sor.1.72. **-ία**, ἡ, *equipment*, *PFlor.*241.6 (iii A.D.), etc.: pl., σὺν πάσαις ἐ. ib.285.13 (vi A.D.). ⊛ **-ίζω**, *complete*, *finish*, τὰς ἡμέρας *Act.Ap.*21.5; *finish* a building, *IG*12(2).538 (Mytilene); [βιβλία] *POxy.*296.7 (i A.D.):—Pass., πόδες (sc. τραπέζης) ἕως τῶν κάτω τελέως -ισμένοι J.*AJ*3.6.6. II. *equip and dispatch*, σκάφας εἰς.. *Peripl.M.Rubr.*33:—Pass., πλοῖα, γένη, ib. 9, 14; simply, *equip*, ναῦς -ισμένας D.S.19.77; *furnish*, Wilcken*Chr.*176.10 (i A.D.):—Pass., ἐξηρτισμένον ἅπασι *completely furnished*, *PAmh.*2.93.8 (ii A.D.); πρὸς πᾶν ἔργον ἀγαθὸν ἐξηρτισμένος 2*Ep.Ti.*3.17: c. acc., *provide oneself with*, τὰ ἄλλα ἐξήρτιστο Luc.*VH*1.33. **-ιος**, ον, *for suspension*, σχοινία *Et.Gud.* II. Subst. ἐξάρτιον, τό, = ἐξαρτία, *PLond.*3.994. 12 (vi A.D.). **-ιόω**, = ἐξαρτύω, πτέ]ρυγη.. σ]φην[ισκ]οις ἐξηρτίωται Herod.7.23. **-ισις**, εως, ἡ, of an engine, *preparation* for discharge, *'gun-laying'*, Ph.*Bel.*56.45, 57.40 (-τυσις codd. in both passages), Hero*Bel.*74.2 (-ήσεως v.l.). **-ισμός**, ὁ, *equipment* of a ship, *Peripl.M.Rubr.*21 (pl.): pl., *fittings*, *PRyl.*233.13 (ii A.D.): metaph., τρόπων Aristeas 144. ⊛ **-ιστήριον**, τό, *place of equipment*, *Gloss.* **-ῦσις**, εως, ἡ, *equipment*, esp. of *musical arrangement*, Callicrat.ap.Stob.4.28.16, Eurypham.ib.39.27; of the soul, Iamb. *VP*15.64 (pl.), 25.114. **-ύω** [ῡ], *get ready*, τἄνδον ἐξάρτυε E.*El.* 422; *equip thoroughly*, *fit out*, ἐπίπλουν Th.2.17:—more freq. in Med., *get ready for oneself*, *fit out*, ναυτικόν Id.1.13, al.; τὰ ἡμέτερα ib.82; φόνον γε μητρὸς ἐξαρτύσομαι *will set about* it, E.*El.*647: c. inf., οἷον ἐξαρτύεται γάμον γαμεῖν A.*Pr.*908:—Pass., *to be got ready*, πάντα σφι ἐξήρτυτο ἐς τὴν κάτοδον Hdt.1.61; πόλεμος ἐξαρτύεται *is preparing*, E.*Heracl.*419: esp. in pf. part. Pass., *equipped*, *harnessed*, Id.*Hipp.* 1186: c. dat. rei, *furnished* or *provided with*, ἐξηρτυμένος νεηνίῃσι καὶ κυσί Hdt.1.43; ὕδατι καὶ σιτίοισι εὖ ἐ. Id.2.32; τόξοισιν ἐξηρτυμένοι

(ἐξηρτημένοι cod. Med.) A.*Pr.*711; ναυτικὰ πλοίοις μακροῖς ἐ. Th.1.14; τοῖς ἄλλοις ἅπασιν ἄριστα ἐ. ib.80; καὶ ναυσὶ καὶ πεζῷ ἅμα ἐξαρτυθεὶς Id.6.31; τὰ πρὸς τὴν χρείαν D.S.20.4. II. Med., *train musically*, Plu.2.973d. III. ἐξαρτύειν· παιδεραστεῖν, Hsch.

**ἐξάρῠσις**, εως, ἡ, = ἀπάντλησις, Gal.19.98.

**ἐξᾰρύω** [ῡ], *draw* or *drain off*, Hp.*Fract.*48 (vulg.), Plu.2.637f:— ἐξαρ(υ)όμεναι· ἐξ ἀγκῶνος φλεβοτομούμεναι, Hsch. (ἐξαρώμεναι cod.).

**ἐξαρχῆς**, Adv., more correctly ἐξ ἀρχῆς, *from the beginning*, v. ἀρχή.

**ἐξαρχ-ίδιος**, ον, = ἐξ ἀρχῆς γενόμενος, ἐπιτροπά *SIG*712.3 (Delos, ii B. C.), dub. in *CIG*5235, Ps.-Philol.21. ⊕ **-ος**, ὁ, ἡ, (ἄρχω) *leader, beginner*, c. gen., ἀοιδοὶ θρήνων ἔξαρχοι Il.24.721. 2. *leader of a chorus*, D.18.260: generally, *leader, chief*, τῶν ἱερέων (= *pontifex maximus*) Plu.*Num.*10; τῆς ἀποστάσεως, τῆς στάσεως, Polyaen.4.6.6 (pl.), 2.1.14 (pl.): *military commander*, Ael.*Tact.*9.2, Arr.*Tact.*10.1: ἐ. Παλμυρηνῶν, title of Odaenathus, *OGI*643; Συβαριτῶν Iamb.*VP* 17.74: metaph., δικαιοσύνην τὴν ἐ. καὶ ἡγεμονίδα τῶν ἀρετῶν Ph.1. 347. ⊕ **-ω**, *begin, take the lead in, initiate*, c. gen., Θέτις δ' ἐξῆρχε γόοιο Il.18.51; μολπῆς ἐξάρχοντες Od.4.19, Il.18.606; ἐξῆρχον ἀοιδῆς Μοῦσαι Hes.*Sc.*205; ἐξάρχετε φωνᾷ (sc. τῆς μολπῆς) Pi.*N.*2.25; πτολέμω Corinn.26; ἐ. πετροβολίας X.*An.*6.6.15; παιᾶνος Plu.*Lyc.*22; δόγματος Id.*Galb.*8, etc.:—Med., κακῆς ἐξάρχετο βουλῆς Od.12.339. 2. c. acc., βουλὰς ἐξάρχων ἀγαθάς Il.2.273; χορούς *h.Hom.*27.18; ἐ. παιήονα Archil.76; ᾠδάν Theoc.8.62; παιᾶνα X.*Cyr.*3.3.58 (so in Med., 4.1.6):—Med., ἐξάρχου κανᾶ (cf. ἐνάρχομαι) E.*IA*435: c. dupl. acc., εἰ δὴ μ' ὧδ' ἀεὶ λόγους (v.l. λόγοις) ἐξῆρχες S.*El.*557; μολπὰν.. οἵαν ἐξῆρχον θεούς E.*Tr.*152 (lyr.). 3. *teach*, οἱ λόγων ἀπτόμενοι ἀσεβῶν ἄλλοις τε ἐξάρχοντες Pl.*Lg.*891d; ἐ. ὅρκον *dictate*.., E.*IT*743: also, = διδάσκω III, οἱ -οντες τὸν διθύραμβον Arist.*Po.*1449ᵃ11. 4. *hold office*, Polem.*Cyn.*18; *rule*, c. gen., Eustr *in EN*2.32. 5. c. part., ἐξάρχεσθαι ἀεθλεύων A.R.1.362. **-ων**, οντος, ὁ, *ruler, president*, τῶν Ἑβραίων Müller-Bees *Inschriften der jüdischen Katakombe am Monteverde* No.14 (ii/iii A. D.).

**ἐξᾶς**, ᾶντος, ὁ, a coin, Lat. *sextans*, as adopted by the Sicil. Greeks, Arist.*Fr.*510, cf. Hsch.; cf. ἐξάντιον.

⊕ **ἑξάς**, άδος, ἡ, (ἕξ) *the number six*, Ph.1.3, Luc.*Sat.*4, Plu.*Lyc.*5, etc.: pl., ἑξάδες ἄρτων, υἱῶν, Ph.2.239,418.

⊕ **ἐξασελλάνωμεν**· ἀναπληρώσωμεν, Hsch.

**ἑξάσημος** [ᾰ], ον, *of six times*, συζυγία Heph.14.1; ῥυθμοί Aristid. Quint.1.14.

**ἐξασθεν-έω**, *to be utterly weak*, Hp.*Morb.*4.43, Arist.*MM*1203ᵇ11; of plants, *to be exhausted*, Thphr.*CP*5.9.11: metaph., τοῖς λογισμοῖς Agatharch.*Fr.Hist.*20(a) J., cf. D.S.20.78; *to be in financial straits*, *PTeb.*50.33 (ii B. C.), etc.: c. inf., *to be too weak to*.., ὁσάκις ἂν ὁ λόγος -ήσῃ ἐναργῶς παραστῆσαι Ael.*Tact.*1.5. **-ής**, ές, *financially weak*, *PMasp.*151.12 (vi A. D.).

**ἐξασθμαίνω**, *exhale, pant*, Gloss.

**ἑξασκελής**, ές, *six-tailed*, of a bandage, Heliod.ap.Orib.48.22 tit., Gal.18(1).774, Paul.Aeg.6.60.

**ἐξασκ-έω**, *adorn, deck out, equip*, ἐσθῆτί τινα S.*OC*1603: c. dupl. acc., ἁγώ νιν ἐξήσκησα in which.., E.*Hel.*1383 codd.; πλόκαμον ἐ. κόμης *arrange* or *dress* it, Id.*El.*1071:—Pass., *to be adorned* or *furnished with*, ὀργάνοισιν ἐξησκημένος Id.*Rh.*922; φυτοῖσιν Lyc.858; παισίν Luc.*Am.*10: abs., [ἡ χώρα] ὑπὸ τῶν Ἀθηναίων ἐξήσκητο καὶ διεπεπόνητο *Hell.Oxy.*12.5; πώλους.. ἐξησκημένας *decked out, ready*, Eub.84; μνῆμα εἰς κάλλος ἐξησκημένον beautifully *wrought*, Luc.*DMort.*24. 1. II. *train thoroughly*, τινά Pl.*Clit.*407b; τὸ ναυτικόν D.C.48. 49:—Pass., *to be trained* or *practised in*, τι X.*Eq.Mag.*2.1; περί τι ὑπό τινος Plu.*Nic.*5. 2. *practise*, ἕξιν Id.*Per.*4; τέχνην Them.*Or.* 18.217c. **-ητέον**, *one must practise*, σωφροσύνην Nicostr.ap.Stob. 4.23.65.

**ἑξασσός**, ή, όν, *in six copies*, *POxy.*908.38 (ii A. D.), *PStrassb.*29.46; cf. δισσός, τρισσός, τετρασσός.

**ἑξαστάδιος** [στᾰ], ον, *of six stades*, χῶμα Str.5.3.7.

**ἑξάστερον**, τό, *the six stars*, i.e. the Pleiades, Sch.Hes.*Op.*383, Eust.870.26.

**ἔξαστις**, ιος, ἡ, *selvage* of linen or cloth, Hp.*Off.*11, Heliod.ap. Orib.46.19.2 (pl.): **ἔξεστις** in Gal.18(2).791. II. *fringe*, Michel 832.15 (Samos, iv B. C.).

**ἑξά-στῐχος**, ον, *of six lines*, σχῆμα Sch.D.T.p.191 H. **-στοιχος** κριθή barley *with six rows of grain on the ear*, Thphr.*HP*8.4.2: **-στῐχος** in Colum.2.9.14.

**ἐξαστράπτω**, *flash as with lightning*, Lxx *Na.*3.3, *Ev.Luc.*9.29; of the sun's light, Zos.Alch.p.111 B.; φόβῳ καὶ κάλλει Tryph.103.

**ἑξά-στῡλος**, ον, *with six columns in front*, of temples, Vitr.3.3. 7. **-σύλλᾰβος**, ον, *of six syllables*, πόδες Aristid.Quint.1.22; χορίαμβος Sch.Ar.*Av.*738.

**ἐξασφᾰλίζω**, *make secure*, Cic.*Att.*6.4.3, Archig.ap.Aët.6.50, Gal. 14.298: more freq. in Med., τὰ καθ' αὑτόν Phld.*Rh.*2.141 S.; τὸν τόπον Str.17.1.54; τὰ κύκλου σάνισιν *Ath.Mitt.*32.259 (Pergam.); *secure the allegiance of* persons, ὅρκοις τινάς J.*BJ*2.8.7.

**ἐξατῑμ-άζω**, *dishonour utterly*, S.*OC*1378, v.l. in Lxx 1*Ki.*17.42:— also **-ατῑμάω** (s. v.l.) Phld.*Rh.*2.174 S. **-όομαι**, Pass., *to be utterly dishonoured*, Lxx *Ez.*16.61.

**ἐξατμ-ιάω**, = sq., Hp.*Morb.*4.49:—also **-ῐδόω**, ibid., Olymp. *in Phd.*p.240 N. **-ίζω**, *turn into vapour, draw up as vapour*, ἐκ τῆς γῆς τὸ ὑγρόν Arist.*Mete.*347ᵇ27, cf. 355ᵃ18, Aret.*SD*1.16:—Pass., *evaporate*, Arist.*Mete.*388ᵃ29, Ph.2.508, Gal.6.536. II. intr. in Act., = Pass., Arist.*Mete.*383ᵃ16, al., *GA*782ᵃ29. **-ισμός**, ὁ, *evaporation*, Epicur.*Nat.Herc.*908.6.

**ἐξατον-έω**, *to be tired out*, Arist.*HA*630ᵇ8; *to be weakened*, ἐκ νηστείας Ph.2.672. **-ίζομαι**, *become relaxed*, Sor.1.46.

**ἑξάτονος** [ᾰ], ον, *in* or *of six tones*, Plu.2.1028e, Aristid.Quint.1.9, Alex.Eph.ap.Theon.Sm.p.141 H.

**ἐξατράπης**, v. σατράπης. ***ἐξαττάομαι**, v. ἐξηττημένη.

**ἐξαττῐκίζω**, *express in Attic form, Atticize*, Phryn.*PS*p.19 B.

**ἐξάττω**, Att. for ἐξαΐσσω.

**ἐξαυ-άζω**, (αὖος), = sq., Thphr.*Fr.*172.2. **-αίνω**, *dry up*, ὁ νότος.. τὰ ἔλυτρα τῶν ὑδάτων ἐξηύηνε (aor. 1) Hdt.4.173:—Pass., τὰ δένδρεα.. ἐξαυανθῇ ib.151, cf. Hp.*Carn.*11, Ar.*Fr.*612, Arist.*GA* 750ᵃ22, Hsch. s. v. ἐξευασμένον.

**ἐξαυγ-ής**, ές, (αὐγή) *dazzling white*, in Comp., χιόνος E.*Rh.*304. **-ος**, ον, *not* ὕπαυγος, i.e. more than fifteen degrees from the sun, Olymp. *in Mete.*56.2, Porph.ap.Heph.Astr.2.18, Steph. *in Hp.*2.363 D.

**ἐξαυδάω**, *speak out*, ἐξαύδα, μὴ κεῦθε νόῳ Il.1.363; τόδ' ἐξαύδασ' ἔπος Pi.*N.*10.80, cf. S.*Fr.*210.71; οὐδὲν ἐξαυδᾷς σοφόν Id.*Ph.*1244:— Med., A.*Ch.*151, 272. (Com. only paratrag., Ar.*Ach.*1183.)

**ἐξαυθᾰδίζομαι**, strengthd. for αὐθαδίζομαι, J.*AJ*15.10.4.

**ἐξαῦθις**, Adv., v. ἐξαῦτις.

**ἐξαυλᾰκίζω**, *pour forth*, πλοῦτον Lyd.*Mag.*2.8; ἑστίαν ib.3.65.

⊕ **ἐξαυλέω**, *pipe away, wear out*, of the mouthpieces of clarionets, Poll.4.67.

**ἐξαυλίζομαι**, *leave one's quarters*, ἐ. εἰς κώμας *go out of camp* into villages, X.*An.*7.8.21; -ισάμενοι ἀνεμένομεν v.l. in Luc.*VH*1.37.

**ἔξαυλος**, ον, *piped away, worn out*, of a flute, Poll.4.73.

**ἐξαυξω**, *increase*, Thphr.*CP*1.22.1:—Pass., *grow too fast*, Id.*HP* 6.6.6.

**ἔξαυος**, ον, *dry, parched, thirsty*, Alc.*Supp.*4.11 (dub. l.).

⊕ **ἐξαυσ-τήρ**, ῆρος, ὁ, *flesh-hook for taking meat out of a pot*, A.*Fr.* 2, Poll.6.88, *EM*346.56, Hsch.; [ἐξ]αυστήρ *IG*2.818.27; ἐξ[αυστήρ] ib.689. **-τριον**, τό, Dim. of foreg., ib.11(2).161 C70 (Delos, iii B. C.).

⊕ **ἐξαυτῆς**, Adv., for ἐξ αὐτῆς [τῆς ὁδοῦ], *at once*, Thgn.231, Cratin. 34, Aen.Tact.22.29, Arat.641, Plb.2.7.7, *Ev.Marc.*6.25, *POxy.*64.3 (iii/iv A. D.), etc.

⊕ **ἐξαῦτις**, Ep. Adv. *once more, anew*, Il.1.223, etc., Archil.6, *PLips.* 27.25 (ii A. D.). II. of place, *back again, backwards*, Il.16.654, A.R.3.482. III. = ἔπειτα, Rhian.25.

**ἐξαυτομολέω**, *desert from* a place, πρός τινα Ar.*Nu.*1104. II. Pass., *to be betrayed by deserters*, τὸ σύνθημα Aen.Tact.24.16.

**ἐξαυχενισμός**, ὁ, *rebellion*, Aq.*Na.*3.1.

**ἐξαυχέω**, *boast loudly, profess*, c. part., ἐξηύχει λαβών A.*Ag.*872 codd.: c. inf. fut., S.*Ant.*390; c. inf. pres., E.*Supp.*504: c. acc. rei, τοῦτ' ἂν ἐξηύχησ' ἐγώ S.*Ph.*869.

**ἐξαυχμέω** or **-άω**, *suffer from drought*, ὅταν -ῶσι Thphr.*CP*5.9. 8. II. **ἐξαυχμόω**, in Pass., *to be dried up*, ἐξαυχμοῦται D.L.7.141.

**ἐξαύω** (A), *take out*, esp. *dressed meat* (cf. ἐξαυστήρ), τὸν ἐγκέφαλον.. ἐξαύσας καταπίνει Pl.Com.38, cf. Hsch. ἐξαῦσαι· ἐξελεῖν.

**ἐξαύω** (B), *heat*, aor. 1 Med., ἐξαύσατο βαυνόν Eratosth.24.

**ἐξαύω** (C), *cry out*, ἐκ δ' ἤϋσ' ἐγώ S.*Tr.*565.

**ἐξαφάζων**· ἐξ ἑαυτοῦ γιγνόμενος, καὶ περιβλέπων, Hsch.

**ἐξαφαιρέω**, *take away*:—Med., εἰσόκε πασέων ψυχὰς ἐξαφέλησθε Od. 22.444, cf. S.*El.*1157; ἐ. φρενῶν τὸν νοῦν τὸν ἐσθλόν *Trag.Adesp.*296; f.l. in D.8.42.

**ἐξαφανίζω**, *destroy utterly*, παίδων ἀγόνων γόνον ἐ. Eub.107.11; γένος J.*AJ*3.15.1; τι τῆς μνήμης ἐκκάθαιρε καὶ ἐ. Iamb.*Protr.*21.κθ':—Pass., *disappear utterly*, Pl.*Plt.*270e, Sor.1.34.

**ἑξᾰφάρμᾰκον**, τό, *remedy containing six ingredients*, Orib.*Fr.*89.

**ἐξαφεδρόομαι**, Pass., *to be excreted*, νοστίμου αἵματος -ουμένου dub. in Herm.ap.Stob.1.42.7 codd.; v. **ἐξαφρόομαι**.

**ἐξαφή**, ἡ, *contact*, Gloss.

**ἐξαφ-ίημι**, *send forth, discharge*, [παλτόν] X.*Eq.*12.12; *dispatch*, γροσφομάχους Plb.10.39.1; *let go* an elastic board, Aët.6.87. II. *set free from*, ἐξαφεῖται τοῦδε (sc. τοῦ πονεῖν) S.*Tr.*72, cf. J.*AJ*18.1. 1; *set free*, ἐ. σῶον Lxx 2*Ma.*12.24; *let loose*, ἀγέλας εἰς καρποὺς *PLips.* 35.8 (iv A. D.):—Pass., *to be allowed to escape*, J.*BJ*4.6.3. III. *squander*, πλοῦτον S.*Ichn.*156. **-ινα**, = ἐξαίφνης, Bell *Jews and Christians in Egypt*, No.1914.3 (iv A. D.). **-ίστημι**, *remove*, αἱ ἁμαρτίαι.. ἐξαπέστησαν τὰ ἀγαθὰ ἀφ' ὑμῶν v.l. in Lxx *Je.*5.25. 2. *dispatch*, ἐφ' οὓς καθήκει *BGU*1253.16 (ii B. C.). II. Pass., with aor. 2, pf., and plpf. Act., *depart* or *withdraw from*, τινός S.*OC*561, E.*IA*479; *grow out of*, ἡλικίας *PLond.*5.1708.263 (vi A. D.).

**ἐξαφολέκτης**, sine expl., Hsch. **ἐξαφορήσωσιν**· εὐπορίσωσιν, Id.

**ἑξάφορον** [ᾰ], τό, at Rome, *litter borne by six men*, Mart.2.81. 1. II. **ἑξάφοροι**, οἱ, *bearers of such a litter*, Vitr.10.3.7.

**ἐξαφρ-ίζω**, *remove the froth* by boiling, τὸ ἐξηφρισμένον [μέλι] *despumated*, Dsc.2.82.3:—Med., metaph. from a horse, αἱματηρὸν ἐξαφρίζεσθαι μένος *exhaust by foaming*, A.*Ag.*1067. **-όομαι**, Pass., *turn into foam*, cj. in Herm.ap.Stob.1.42.7 (-αφεδρ- codd.).

**ἐξᾰφύω** [ῠ], *draw forth*, οἶνον.. ἐξαφύοντες Od.14.95: poet. aor., ἰὸν ἐξήφυσσεν ὀδόντων Opp.*H.*1.573: Ep. fut. 3 pl., ἐξαφύουσιν· ἐξαντλήσουσιν, Hsch.

⊕ **ἑξά-χαλκος** [ᾰ], ὁ, *coin of the value of six* χαλκοῖ, *IG*5(1).1433.29 (Messene). ⊕ **-χειρ**, χειρος, ὁ, ἡ, *six-handed*, Luc.*Herm.*74, *Tox.*62:— also **-χειρος**, ον, Ps.-Callisth.3.28. **-χῆ**, Adv. *in six parts*, σχίσας Pl.*Ti.*36d; *in six ways*, κινεῖσθαι Ph.1.44:—also **ἕξαχα**, Hdn.Gr.1. 496. ⊕ **-χοίνῐκος**, ον, *containing six choenices*, Ar.*Fr.*640. **-χοος**, οον, contr. **-χους**, ουν, *holding six* χόες, Arist.*Ath.*67.2, Plu.*Sol.*

23. **-χρονος**, ον, *of six times*, [πούς] Heph.3.2, cf. Procl. *in Prm.* p.990S.

⊕ **ἐξᾰχῠρόω**, *clear of husks*, Hsch. s. v. λεπυριῶσαι.

⊕ **ἐξᾰχῶς**, Adv. *in six ways*, Arist. *Top.* 112ᵇ27, Gal.9.702.

**ἔξαψις**, εως, ἡ, *fastening*, Theo Sm.p.72H. (pl.), Iamb. *in Nic.*p.112 P. (pl.). II. *heating*, σιτίων ἔξαψιν ποιεῖν Hp. *Acut.(Sp.)*46 (v.l. ἔφ-). 2. *lighting, kindling*, Arist. *Mu.*395ᵇ3, Ph.2.256, Plot.3.6.15, Anthem.p.152W.: pl., *Placit.*3.3.9: metaph., θερμασίης καὶ τόλμης Aret. *CA*2.11.

**ἑξάωρος** [ᾰ], ον, *of six* equinoctial *hours*, *Theol.Ar.*52; **ἑξάωρον**, τό, *period of six* such *hours*, Balbill.(?) in *Cat.Cod.Astr.*8(4).243.

**Ἑξ-γῦον**, said to be a town in Sicily with six streets (ἓξ ἀγυιαί), Eust.450.48. **-δάκτῠλος**, ον, *six digits long*, *IG*2.807*a*117; cf. ἑκ-, ἑγ-δάκτυλος.

**ἐξεᾱγείς**, v. ἐξάγνυμι.

**ἐξεγγῠ-άω**, *give up* a slave *on security* to be examined, Antipho 5.47; *free* one *by giving bail for* him, D.24.73:—Pass., *to be bailed*, ἐξεγγυηθέντες κριθῆναι And.1.44, cf. D.19.169; ἐφ' οἷς ἐξηγγυήθη [to fulfil the conditions] on which *security was given*, Lys.23.10. ⊕ **-η**, ἡ, f. l. for ἐγγύη, Is.5.3. **-ησις**, εως, ἡ, *giving of bail* or *surety*, esp. to take one out of prison, -ησιν ποιεῖν D.24.77.

⊕ **ἐξεγ-είρω**, *awaken*, S. *OT*65, *Tr.*978:—Pass., *to be awaked*, ὑπαὶ κώνωπος A. *Ag.*892; *wake up*, Hdt.1.34, E. *Or.*1530: aor. 2 Med. ἐξηγρόμην Ar. *Ra.*51; Ep. 3 pl. ἐξέγροντο Theoc.24.21; 3 sg. ἐξέγρετο Hsch.; inf. ἐξεγρέσθαι Pl. *Smp.*223c; ἐξεγρόμενος ibid.: so also pf. Act. ἐξεγρήγορα Ar. *Av.*1413: 2 sg. aor. 2 Pass. ἐξέγρης· ἐξηγέρθης, Hsch. 2. *raise from the dead*, 1*Ep.Cor.*6.14:—Pass., A. *Ch.* 495. 3. metaph., *awake, arouse*, εὕδοντα φόνον E. *El.*41; ἄνθρακα Ar. *Lys.*315; τὸν ἵππον X. *Eq.*11.12; πόλεμον D.S.14.44; ὁ ἄνεμος τὸ πῦρ ἐ. Arist. *Pr.*866ᵃ18. **-ερσις**, εως, ἡ, *awakening*, Plb.9.15.4 (pl.). 2. *waking up*, D.H.3.70, Plu.2.909d. **-έρτης**, ου, ὁ, *one who arouses*, *PMag.Leid.V.*7.13.

**ἐξεγκᾰτίζω**, *disembowel*, *Gloss.*

**ἐξεγκεφᾰλίζω**, *remove the brains*, *Gloss.*

**ἐξεδᾰφισθέν**, *desolatum*, *Gloss.*

**ἐξέδοντα**, τά, *erosion*, dub. in Gal.18(2).573.

**ἐξεδούαζεν**· ἐξήνεγκεν, Hsch. post ἐξεκοδόαξεν.

⊕ **ἐξ-έδρα**, ἡ, *hall* or *arcade furnished with recesses and seats*, in the gymnasia, E. *Or.*1449 (anap.), Men. *Kon.*10, *IPE*1².182 (Olbia), *IG* 12(3).1091 (Melos), *BGU*931.26 (i A. D.), etc.; in the schools of Philosophers, Phld. *Acad.Ind.*p.100M., Str.17.1.8, Cic. *Fin.*5.2.4, Vitr.5.11.2; in a private house, Gal.14.18. 2. *bench, seat*, in front of a house, D.L.4.19; any *public bench*, Str.13.4.5, D.Chr.28.2; *belvedere*, Nic.Dam. *Fr.*1 J. 3. *parlour* or *saloon*, Lxx *Ez.*40.44, Cic. *de Orat.*3.5.17, *ND*1.6.15, Vitr.6.7.3, 7.3.4, *POxy.*912.13 (iii A. D.); *the hall in Pompey's theatre at Rome*, where the Senate met, Plu. *Brut.*14, 17. **-έδριον**, τό, Dim. of foreg., *IG*12(9).907.27 (Chalcis, iv A. D.), *GDI*5075.58 (Latos), Roussel *Cultes Égyptiens* 224 (Delos, ii B. C.), Cic. *Fam.*7.23.3. **-εδροποιός**, όν, *driving out of*, φρενῶν, gloss on ἔξεδροι φρενῶν, Sch.E. *Hipp.*934. ⊕ **-εδρος**, ον, (ἕδρα) *away from home*, opp. ἔντοπος, S. *Ph.*212 (lyr.); πνεῦμα ἔ. γενόμενον ἐκ τῶν οἰκείων τόπων Arist. *Mu.*395ᵇ32: metaph., *strange, extravagant*, Id. *Rh.*1406ᵃ31. 2. c. gen., *out of, away from*, χθονὸς E. *IT*80: metaph., ἔξεδροι φρενῶν λόγοι insensate words, Id. *Hipp.*935. II. of birds of omen, ἔ. χώραν ἔχειν to be *out of a good* (i.e. *in an unlucky*) quarter, Ar. *Av.*275 (nisi leg. χρόαν cum Sch.); ἔ. ὄρνιθες D.C. 37.25.

**ἐξεζητημένως**, Adv., (ἐκζητέω) *exquisitely, in a recherché manner*, *Gloss.*

**ἐξεθίαζε**· χορείας ἐπετέλει, and **ἐξεθιασθέν**· λαμπρυνθέν, Hsch.

**ἐξεθ-ίζομαι**, Pass., *to be habituated, accustomed*, c. inf., Ph.2.363, 391. **-ισμός**, ὁ, *change of habit*, Ath.Med.ap.Orib. *inc.*1.7.

**ἐξεῖ**· ἔξω (Lacon.), Hsch. **ἐξεῖα**· τὰ ἑξῆς, Id.

**ἐξείδιον**, τό, Dim. of ἕξις, *EM*347.54, *Et.Gud.*

**ἐξείη**· ἔξοδος, κέλσος, Hsch. (fort. ἐξεσίη et ⟨πλεον⟩εξίη).

**ἐξεῖδον**, inf. ἐξιδεῖν, aor. in use of pres. ἐξοράω:—*look out, see far*, μέγ' ἔξιδεν ὀφθαλμοῖσιν he saw far, saw well, Il.20.342: also aor. imper. Med. ἐξιδοῦ *see well to* it! S. *Ph.*851 (lyr.).

**ἐξείης**, Adv., poet. for ἑξῆς (q. v.).

**ἐξεικάδιοι**· οἱ ἐκτὸς ⟨τῆς⟩ αὐτῆς εἰκάδος, καὶ τάγματος τοῦ αὐτοῦ, Hsch.

⊕ **ἐξεικ-άζω**, *make like, adapt*, αὐτὸν ταῖς τῶν φιλούντων ὑπουργίαις X. *Hier.*1.38:—Pass., ἐξείκαστό τινι *was like* it, Id. *Cyr.*1.6.39: mostly in pf. part., οὐδὲν ἐξῃκασμένα not *mere semblances*, but the things themselves, A. *Ag.*1244; κεραυνὸν οὐδὲν ἐξῃκασμένον.. θάλπεσιν τοῖς ἡλίου Id. *Th.*445; στέρνα τ' ἐξῃκασμένα *portrayed*, E. *Ph.*162; οὐ γὰρ ἔστιν ἐξῃκασμένος he is not *represented by a portrait-mask*, Ar. *Eq.* 230. **-ασμα**, ατος, τό, *representation, copy*, dub. l. in Jul. *Or.*8.247d.

⊕ **ἐξεικάττιοι**, Thess., = ἑξακόσιοι, *Supp.Epigr.*2.264.4 (ii B. C.).

**ἐξεικονίζω**, *explain by a simile*, Plu.2.445c. II. Pass., *to be fully shapen* or *formed*, Lxx *Ex.*21.22sq., Hsch. 2. *to be exactly like*, τῷ φύσαντι Aristaenet.1.19; μητρῴῳ γένει.. -ισθέν *formed in the image of*.., Ph.1.661.

**ἐξειλεγμένως**, Adv., (ἐκλέγω) *elegantly*, *Gloss.*

**ἐξειλ-έω**, *slip out* from its cover, ἣν ἐξειλήσῃς [βιβλίον] Luc. *Merc. Cond.*41; τὸ ψυχάριον ἀπὸ τοῦ σώματος ἐξειλεῖται the soul *slips out* of [its envelope], M.Ant.10.36. II. intr., *escape*, aor. ἐξείλησα *PAmh.*2.142.9 (iv A. D.), cf. *EM*348.12. ⊕ **-ησις**, εως, ἡ, *release, escape* from, αὐχένων καὶ χειρῶν καὶ πλευρῶν, in wrestling, Pl. *Lg.*796a.

⊕ **ἐξείλλω**, = ἐξειλέω, *disentangle*, τὰ ἴχνη, of hounds at a check, X. *Cyn.*6.15. 2. *keep forcibly from, debar from*, ἐάν τις ἐξείλλῃ τινὰ τῆς ἐργασίας D.37.35, cf. Sol. *Oxy.*221 xiv 13; αἰ δέ χ' ὑπὸ πολέμω ἐγϝηληθίωντι (= ἐξειληθῶσι) *Tab.Heracl.*1.152. 3. *force* a stone *from* the urethra, prob. in Gal.19.659 (ἐξιλεῶσαι '*relieve the patient*', Kühn).—ἐξίλλω is a v.l.

**ἐξειλύω**, *unfold*:—Pass., ἐξειλυσθέντες ἐπὶ χθονὶ γαστέρας, of serpents *gliding* along the ground, Theoc.24.17.

**ἔξειμι** (A), (εἶμι *ibo*) Ep. 2 sg. ἔξεισθα (v. infr.); ἔξει wrongly expld. as imper. by Sch.Ar. *Nu.*633; Dor. 3 sg. ἔξειτι Hsch.; inf. ἐξιέναι, also ἐξῖναι Macho ap.Ath.13.580c: serving as Att. fut. of ἐξέρχομαι, but with impf. ἐξῄειν, Ion. ἐξήϊα Hdt.2.139:—*go out, come out*, esp. out of the house, Hom. mostly in Od., ἔξεισθα θύραζε 20.179: c. gen. loci, ἐξιέναι μεγάρων 1.374; τῆς χώρας S. *OC*909; so ἐκ τῆς χώρης Hdt.1.94; but ἐ. ἐκ τῶν ἱππέων *leave* the knights, *quit service* as one, ib.67; ἐκ τῆς ἀρχῆς ἐ. D.C.60.10. 2. εἰς ἔλεγχον ἐξιέναι *come forth* to apply the test, S. *Ph.*98; but, *submit* to the test, Id. *Fr.*105; λόγων.. εἰς ἅμιλλαν ἐξιών E. *Fr.*334. 3. abs., ἔξει Ar. *Nu.*633; esp. *march out with an army*, Th.5.13, X. *Cyr.*3.3.20, etc.; οἱ ἐξιόντες Th.1.95: c. acc. cogn., ἐκδήμους στρατείας οὐκ ἐξῇσαν ib.15; πολλοὺς ἀγῶνας ἐ. S. *Tr.*159; ἐξόδους ἐ. *go out* in procession, D.48.55; ἐ. ὑστάτην ὁδόν E. *Alc.*610; ἐ. τὴν ἀμφίαλον (sc. ὁδόν) X. *HG*4.2.13; τὰς πύλας Ath.8.351d. 4. *come forward on the stage*, οὐξιὼν πρώτιστα Ar. *Ra.*946. II. of Time or incidents, *come to an end, expire*, Hdt.2.139; ὅταν περ τὸ κακὸν ἐξίῃ S. *Ph.*767; ἐξιούσης τῆς ἀρχῆς Lys.9.6; ὅποι ἔξεισι τὰ ἴχνη where they *cease*, X. *Cyn.*8.3.

⊕ **ἔξειμι** (B), (εἰμί *sum*), only used in impers. forms (v. ἔξεστι), exc. in αἱ ἐλεύθεροι μὴ ἐξεῖεν if [a woman] shall leave no free-born *issue*, *Leg.Gort.*7.9.

**ἔξειον**· ἐπιζήμιον τὸ καταδικάζειν τοῖς ἑκουσίοις, οἱ δὲ ἀπόλυσιν ἐγκλήματος, Hsch.

**ἐξεῖπον**, inf. ἐξειπεῖν, aor. 2 in use of ἐξαγορεύω; ἐξερῶ (q. v.) being the fut.: also aor. 1 ἐξεῖπας S. *El.*521:—*tell out, declare*, ἐξείπω καὶ πάντα διίξομαι Il.9.61; αὐτίκ' ἂν ἐξείποι Ἀγαμέμνονι 24.654, cf. Od.15.443; ἐ. ὅτι μοι παρορᾷς Ar. *Av.*454 (lyr.); ἀκριβείᾳ χαλεπὸν ἐ. Th.7.87. 2. c. dupl. acc., κακὰ ἐ. τινά *tell* evil *tales of* a person, D.21.79; τίν' ἀρχὴν σ' ἐξείπω κακῶν; E. *El.*907; πολλὰ πρὸς πολλούς με δὴ ἐξεῖπας, ὡς.. S. *El.*521, cf. 984.

**ἔξειρα**· σκορπίος, ὁ ἰχθύς, Hsch.

**ἐξειργασμένως**, Adv. pf. part. Pass. of ἐξεργάζομαι, *carefully, accurately*, Plu. *Alex.*1.

**ἐξείργω**, Att. for ἐξέργω (q. v.).

**ἔξειρξις**, εως, ἡ, *exclusion, expulsion*, Eust.1769.35.

**ἐξείρομαι**, Ion. for ἐξέρομαι. **ἐξειρύω**, v. ἐξερύω.

⊕ **ἐξείρω**, *put forth*, τὴν χεῖρα Hdt.3.87; τὴν γλῶσσαν Hp. *Int.*7 codd.; τὸ κέντρον Ar. *V.*423. II. *pull out*, τὴν γλῶσσαν Id. *Eq.*378 (lyr.), Hermipp.Hist.43.

**ἐξειρωνεύομαι**, *turn into jest, ridicule*, τοὺς λόγους J. *AJ*15.3.6; τοῦτ' ἐκεῖνος -όμενος ἔφερεν ἐγκρατῶς ib.15.7.4.

**ἔξεισθα**, v. ἔξειμι (A). **ἐξεκᾰτέρωθεν**, Adv. *on either side*, Procl. *Par.Ptol.*188.

**ἐξεκελέμησεν**, sine expl., Hsch. **ἐξεκηρύωσας**· ἐξέστησας, Id. (fort. ἐξεκηρίωσας· ἐξέσμησας).

**ἐξεκκλησιάζω**, = ἐκκλησιάζω, Arist. *Oec.*1348ᵃ11.

**ἐξεκοδόαξεν**· ἐξέχεεν, Hsch.

**ἐξελάαν**, Ep. pres. inf. of ἐξελαύνω: **ἐξελᾶν**, Att. fut. inf.

**ἐξελαιόω**, *make into oil*, Thphr. *CP*6.8.1:—Pass., *become oily*, ib.6.7.4.

**ἐξελ-ᾰσία**, ἡ, *driving out* cattle, Plb.12.4.10. II. intr., *expedition*, Ps.-Hdt. *Vit.Hom.*9. **-ᾰσις**, εως, ἡ, *driving out, expulsion*, τῶν Πεισιστρατιδέων Hdt.5.76; τινὸς ἐκ τῆς νήσου Id.6.88. II. intr., *marching out, expedition*, βασιλέος ἐκ Θέρμης Id.7.183, cf. X. *Cyr.*8.3.1, etc.; *charge of cavalry*, Plu. *Art.*16 (pl.). **-ᾰτέος**, α, ον, *to be driven out*, Jul. *Ep.*89b. II. ἐξελατέον *one must expel*, Epicur. *Ep.*1 p.24U.; ψεῦδος ψυχῆς Them. *Or.*21.259a. **-αύνω**, fut. -ελῶ Hdt.4.148, 5.63, *IG*1².39.4: pf. -ελήλᾰκα:—Ep. pres. part. **ἐξελάων** Od.10.83; inf. ἐξελάαν Il.8.527, Od.11.292, Hes. *Th.*491 (v.l. -άειν): Arc. 1 sg. pres. opt. ἐξελαύνοια *IG*5(2).343.65 (iv B. C.):—*drive out*, ἄντρου ἐξήλασε μῆλα Od.9.312, cf. 227, 11.292: abs., *drive afield*, of a shepherd, 10.83. 2. esp. *drive out, expel from* a place, μήτι.. ἡμέας ἐξελάσωσιν γαίης ἡμετέρης 16.381; ἐξήλασέν με κἀπέκλῃσε δωμάτων A. *Pr.*670; πάτρας, χθονός, S. *OC*376, 823; γῆς ἐκ πατρῴας ἐξελήλαμαι ib.1292; ἐκ τῆς πατρίδος Hdt.5.91; ἐκ τῆς οἰκίας Ar. *Nu.*123; ἐκ τῶν πόλεων Pl. *Grg.*466d; Τιτῆνας ἀπ' οὐρανοῦ Hes. *Th.*820; τὸ βάρβαρον ἐκ τῆς θαλάττης Pl. *Mx.*241d; ἐξεληλαμένος τῆς βουλῆς Plu. *Cic.*17; ἐ. τινά *banish*, Hdt.1.60, Ar. *Ach.*717, Pl. *Ap.*30d:—Med., Th.4.35, 7.5. 3. *drive out* horses, etc., ἵππους ἐξέλασε Τρώων *out of* the ranks of the Trojans, Il.5.324, cf. 10.499; ἁρμάτων ὄχους E. *Ph.*1190:—Med., *drive out one's* horses, ἵππους ἐξελάσασθαι ὑφ' ἅρματι Theoc.24.119 (but, *drive off* captured cattle, Plb.4.75.7); ἐ. στρατόν, στρατιήν, *lead out* an army, Hdt.1.76, 7.38; ἐ. νῆα ὅρμου A.R.1.987; *lead out* a procession, ἐ. τὸν Ἴακχον Plu. *Alc.*34; θρίαμβον Id. *Marc.*22: hence, b. freq. with the acc. omitted, as if intr., ἐς δίφρον ὀρούσας ἐξέλασ' ἐς πληθύν he *drove out*, Il.11.360, etc.; *ride out*, Th.7.27, X. *Cyr.*1.3.3, etc.; ἐ. ἐκ τῶν ἄλλων ἱππέων Lys.20.28; *march out*, Hdt.4.80, 8.113, etc.; *go out*, X. *Cyr.*8.3.1. 4. *expel, banish, get rid of* a thing, τῶν ὀμμάτων τὸ αἰδούμενον Plu.2.654d; by washing, κόνιν λαγόνων Call. *Lav.Pall.*6. 5. metaph., *reject*, Jul. *Caes.*306c. II. *knock out*, χαμαὶ δέ κε πάντας ὀδόντας γναθμῶν ἐξελάσαιμι Od.18.29. III. *beat out* metals, ἐ. ἡμιπλίνθια ἐκ χρυσοῦ Hdt.1.50; ἐθηεῖτο σίδηρον

ἐξελαυνόμενον ib.68, cf. 7.84; κέντρον ἐπὶ λεπτὸν ἐξεληλασμένον Plb. 6.22.4.

**ἐξελ-εγκτέος**, α, ον, *to be refuted*, Pl.*Grg*.508a. **-έγχω**, strengthd. for ἐλέγχω, *convict, confute, refute*, Simon.75, S.*OT*297, *Ant*.399, Ar.*Nu*.1062; τοῖς ἔργοις τοὺς λόγους ἐ. Antipho 6.47; ἐν τῷ δήμῳ ἐ. [τινά] D.21.16:—Pass., ἐπ' αἰσχραῖς αἰτίαις ἐξελήλεγκται Lys.6.44; ὑπὸ τῶν εἰκότων Antipho 2.1.9; ἔκ τινος Ar.*Ra*.960; ἐξελεγχόμενος περί τινος Pl.*Hp.Ma*.304d; ὑπ' ἐμοῦ ἐξελεγχθήσονται ἔργῳ Id.*Ap*.17b. 2. c. dupl. acc. pers. et rei, *refute* one in a point, ib.23a, *Ly*.222d:—Pass., τοσοῦτον.. ἡλίκον οὗτος νῦν ἐξελήλεγκται *has been convicted of* .., D.21.147; οὐ τοῦτό γ' ἐξελέγχομαι I am not *to blame* in this, E.*El*.36. 3. with predicate added in part., *convict* one *of* being .., ἐ. τινὰ ἀδύνατον ὄντα Pl.*Grg*.522d; ἐ. τινὰ τεχνάζοντα D.29.19; ἐ. τινὰ ὡς οὐ.. Pl.*Grg*.482b:—Pass., ἵν' ἐξελέγχοισθε πονηρευόμενοι Heraclit.125a; κἀξελέγχεται.. κάκιστος ὢν E.*Hipp*.944; ἐξελέγχεται συμβεβουλευκώς D.19.5, etc. II. *put to the proof, bring to the test*, ὁ ἐξελέγχων.. ἀλάθειαν χρόνος Pi.*O*.10(11).53; in a court of justice, A.*Eu*.433; τὴν ποίησιν Ar.*Ra*.1366; ἐ. τὴν τύχην, τὰς ἐλπίδας, Plb. 21.14.4, 1.62.4; ἐ. τοὺς Θηβαίους εἰ διαμαχοῦνται Plu.*Ages*.19:—Pass., πάντες ἦσαν ἐξεληλεγμένοι all had *had their sentiments well ascertained*, D.18.23; ἃ δ' ἡ φύσις ἀεὶ ἐβούλετο, ἐξηλέγχθη ἐς τὸ ἀληθές *was fully proved* to be true, Th.3.64; χρυσὸς μὲν οἶδεν ἐξελέγχεσθαι πυρί Men.691. 2. Medic., *find out one's weak points*, Gal.15.902:—Pass., Id.6.323. III. *compute*, χαλκὸν μυρίον Pi.*N*.10.46. IV. *establish a claim to*, ὀγδοήκοντα τάλαντα D.38.20.

**ἐξελευθερ-ικός**, ή, όν, *of the class of freedmen* or *their offspring*, φῦλον D.H.4.22; οἱ ἐ. Plu.*Ant*.58. II. νόμοι ἐ. laws *concerning freedmen*, D.ap.Poll.3.83; καθάρματα ἐ. the refuse *of the freedmen*, Plu.*Sull*.33; φιάλαι ἐ. *presented by freedmen* on manumission, *IG*2. 720*A*i5,15. ❀ **-ος**, ὁ, *freedman*, Hyp.*Fr*.197, Cic.*Att*.6.5.1: fem. -έρα *IG*14.1907.—The special application of ἐ. to a *released* debtor (cf. Ammon.p.23 V., Eust.1751.2) is not confirmed by usage; ἐξ- and ἀπελεύθερος are used of the same person by D.C.39.38. **-οστομέω**, strengthd. for ἐλευθ-, S.*Aj*.1258. **-όω**, *set at liberty*, D.C.36.42, Hsch.

**ἐξέλευσις**, εως, ἡ, later word for ἔξοδος, Lxx 2*Ki*.15.20.

**ἐξελεύσομαι, ἐξελθεῖν**, fut. and aor. inf. of ἐξέρχομαι.

**ἐξελθεῖν·** ἐξωθεῖν, Hsch.

**ἐξελ-ιγμός**, ὁ, *countermarching*, ἐ. Μακεδονικός, Λακωνικός, Κρητικός, Ascl.*Tact*.10.13,14,15, cf. Arr.*Tact*.23.2,3,4; οἱ ἐπὶ τῶν ἵππων ἐ. Them.*Or*.1.2b. II. *doubling*, of the hare, Arr.*Cyn*.16.3 (pl.); so of *turning* movements in walking or driving a hoop, Antyll.ap.Orib. 6.21.18, 26.1. III. *revolution* of the heavenly bodies, Nicom.*Ar*.1. 6. 2. esp. of the *shortest period containing a whole number of synodic months, days, and* ἀποκαταστάσεις of the moon, Gem.18.1, Ptol.*Alm*. 4.2. **-ίκτρα**, ἡ, *roller, cylinder*, of a windlass, Hero *Aut*.5.3: ❀ **-ικτρον**, τό, *bobbin*, Ph.*Bel*.67.38. **-ιξις**, εως, ἡ, *evolution*, λόγων Plot.5.7.3; of troops, ἐξελίξεις ἐπ' ἀσπίδα, ἐπὶ δόρυ, Aristid.Quint.2.6.

**ἐξέλιπον·** ἐξώλισθον, Hsch.

❀ **ἐξελίσσω**, Att. -ττω, *unroll, unfold*, περιβολὰς σφραγισμάτων E.*Hipp*.864; ταρσούς Aen.Tact.29.8; χάρτην Hero *Aut*.26.8: metaph., *unfold*, θεσπίσματα, λόγον, E.*Supp*.141, *Ion* 397; θεῖον νόμον Porph. *Marc*.26; οὐδ' ἄρα [τὸν αἰῶνα] ἐξελίξεις Plot.3.7.6; προσελθοῦσα ἡ πηλικότης ἐξελίττει εἰς μέγεθος τὴν ὕλην; Id.2.4.9:—Pass., ὁ.. κύκλος .. ἴσην ἐξελίττεται γραμμὴν *is unrolled so as to form* a line, Arist.*Mech*. 855ᵃ29, cf. *Pr*.914ᵃ30, Hero *Aut*.25.3. 2. of any rapid motion, ἴχνος ἐ. ποδὸς *evolve the mazy* dance, E.*Tr*.3; χορείαν Aristid.1.97 J.; ἐ. τινὰ κύκλῳ *hunt* one round and round, E.*HF*977; ἐ. κύκλους περί τινα *wheel* in circles round him, Hld.5.14; ἐ. τὸν αὐτῆς κύκλον [ἡ σελήνη] Plu.2.368a; of the hare, δρόμον ἐ. *double*, Arr.*Cyn*.17.3:—Pass., -ιχθῆναι τοὺς ἑλιγμοὺς ib.21.3; *wheel about*, ἐπὶ δεξιὰ Plu.*Cam*. 5, cf. *Tim*.27: c. acc. loci, τοὺς κόλπους ἐ. *follow the windings of* the bays, App.*BC*5.84; ἐ. τὴν τάφρον Plu.*Pyrrh*.28. b. intr. in Act., Arr.*Cyn*.25.2; ἐξελίττει τῇ καὶ τῇ Ael.*NA*13.14 (also ἐ. ἑαυτὸν *escape*, ib.3.16); of ships, παρὰ τὴν γῆν -ξασαι διέφυγον Plb.1.28.12, cf. 1.51. 11. 3. *evolve*, in Pass., ζωὴ ἐξελιττομένη εἰς τέλος Plot.1.4.1; ὅσα τὰ πολλά, τοσαῦτα τὸ ἕν, ἀφ' οὗ ἐξελίττεται Dam.*Pr*.4. II. as military term, = ἀναπτύσσειν, *extend* the front by bringing up the rear men, *deploy*, τὴν φάλαγγα X.*Cyr*.8.5.15, *HG*4.3.18; ἐξελίττεται ὁ στίχος Id.*Lac*.11.8. b. *countermarch*, Ascl.*Tact*.10.13, etc. c. generally, *manœuvre*, Arr.*Tact*.25.6:—Med. or Pass., ib.16.8. 2. *extricate*, τὴν δύναμιν τῶν στενῶν Plu.*Alex*.20.

**ἐξελκόω**, *cause sores in*, [τὴν σάρκα] Arist.*Pr*.883ᵇ31; τὸ πρόσωπον D.S.14.88:—Pass., *break out into sores*, ἐξελκοῦται τὸ χωρίον Hp.*VM* 18; ἐξηλκοῦτο τὰ σώματα J.*AJ*2.14.4.

**ἐξελκ-τέον**, *one must drag along*, γόνυ πρός τι E.*El*.491. **-υσμός**, ὁ, *pulling out, removal*, Ruf.ap.Orib.8.39.13. II. *extension*, Heliod. ap.Orib.49.10.6. **-ω**, fut. -έλξω Ar.*Eq*.365 (Pors.): aor. 1 -είλκυσα; inf. -ελκύσαι Id.*Pax* 315, 506:—Pass., -ελκυσθῇ Hdt.2.70:—*draw, drag out*, Il.23.762: c. gen. loci, Od.5.432 (Pass.); φάσγανον .. ἐ. κολεοῦ E.*Hec*.544; Ἑλλάδ' ἐ. δουλίας *rescue from* slavery, Pi. *P*.1.75; δύστηνον ἐ. πόδα, of a lame man, S.*Ph*.291: abs., without πόδα, of one wounded, E.*Andr*.1121; ἐξέλξω σε τῆς πυγῆς θύραζε Ar. *Eq*.365 (Pors. for ἐξελῶ); ἐξελκύσαι τὴν πᾶσιν Εἰρήνην φίλην *drag* her *out of the* cave, Id.*Pax* 294, cf. 315, 506; rare in Prose, as Pl.*R*. 515e; ἐξελκυσθεὶς Arist.*Pol*.1311ᵇ30; τέχναι τινὰ ἐ. τῆς πενίας Lib. *Or*.39.14.

**ἐξέλκωσις**, εως, ἡ, *causing of sores in* or *on*, τῶν χειρῶν D.S.3.29 (pl.).

**ἐξελληνίζω**, *turn into Greek*: ἐ. ὄνομα *trace* it *to a Greek origin*, Plu. *Num*.13; *put* it *in a Greek form*, J.*AJ*1.6.1. II. intr., *to be good Greek*, Anon.*in SE*63.37.

**ἐξελυτρόω**, (ἔλυτρον) in aor. ἐξελύτρωσας· ἐγύμνωσας, Hsch.

**ἐξέμεν**, Ep. aor. 2 inf. of ἐξίημι, Il.11.141.

**ἐξέμεν**, Ep. fut. inf. of ἔχω, Il.5.473.

**ἐξεμέω**, pf. ἐξεμήμεκα Aristid.*Or*.50(26).5 (v.l. ἐξημεκώς), Hsch.:—*vomit forth, disgorge*, of Charybdis, ὅτ' ἐξεμέσειε.. Od.12.237; ὄφρ' ἐξεμέσειεν ὀπίσσω.. ib.437: aor. 1 ἐξήμησε Hes.*Th*.497 codd.; ἐ. τὸ νόσημα Pl.*R*.406d; πάντα ἐ. ἀκριβῶς Diocl.*Fr*.139; λώπιον μεστὸν ὢν ἐξήμεσε κακῶν *IG*4.952.128 (Epid.): metaph., *disgorge* ill-gotten gains, τὰ τάλαντα Ar.*Ach*.6; ἅττ' ἂν κεκλόφωσί μου Id.*Eq*.1148: abs., Lib.*Or*.63.22; also νειόθεν ἐξεμέσαι Cerc.4.55; also of *rejecting* an opinion, Gal.5.325. 2. abs., *vomit, be sick*, Ar.*Ra*.11.

**ἐξέμμορον**, v. ἐκμείρομαι.

**ἐξέμπαλιν·** ἐπαριστέρως, Hsch.

**ἐξεμπεδόω**, *keep firm, observe strictly*, τὰς συνθήκας X.*Cyr*.3.1.21 codd. II. *unfetter*, Hsch.

**ἐξεμπολάω**, Ion. (and later Prose, J.*AJ*8.7.2) -έω, *gain by trading*, κέρδος ἐ. *drive* a gainful *trade*, S.*Ph*.303:—Pass., pf. ἐξημπόλημαι I *am bought and sold, betrayed*, Id.*Ant*.1036. II. *sell off*, τὸν φόρτον D.H.3.46:—Pass., ἐξεμπολημένων σφι σχεδὸν πάντων Hdt.1.1.

**ἐξεναίρω**, strengthd. for ἐναίρω, aor. inf. ἐξεναρεῖν Hes.*Sc*.329.

**ἐξέναντι**, Adv. *right opposite*, τοῦ μνημείου *BMus.Inscr*.918 (Halic.), cf. *TAM*2.210 (Sidyma).

**ἐξενᾰρίζω**, *strip* or *spoil* a foe slain in fight, τινά Il.4.488, etc.; also τεύχεα ἐ. *strip off* his arms, 13.619, etc. 2. *kill, slay*, Od.11.273; ἔγχεϊ Il.6.30, cf. Hes.*Th*.289, B.5.146, Lyc.50, etc.—In Hom. more freq. than the simple Verb.

**ἐξενεῖκαι, -νειχθῆναι**, Ion. aor. 1 Act. and Med. of ἐκφέρω.

**ἐξενέπω**, *speak out, proclaim*, τι Pi.*N*.4.33; ἐξένεπεν Αἴγιναν πάτραν *declared* Aeg. [to be] his country, Id.*O*.8.20:—Pass., Nic.*Fr*.73. 2. abs., *speak*, A.R.1.764.

**ἐξενεχυριάζω**, strengthd. for ἐνεχυριάζω, D.L.6.99.

**ἐξενιαυτ-ίζω**, *spend a year in exile*, Sch.E.*Or*.1645. **-ος**, ον, *in arrears, carried over from one year to the next*, *PLond*.1.17.19 (ii B.C.), *UPZ*21.12 (ii B.C.). II. Adv. -ίαυτα *yearly*, *PAmh*.2.85.14 (i A.D.).

**ἐξεντερίζομαι**, Pass., *have the entrails taken out*, Dsc.2.62; of plants, *have the pith taken out*, Id.4.162:—also -όομαι, *Gloss*.

**ἐξεντισμέναι·** κεκοσμημέναι, Hsch. (Cf. ἐντεσμέναι Id., and Ar. *Lys*.43.) **ἐξεόω**, v. ἐξωθέω.

**ἐξεπ-ᾴδω**, *charm away*, Pl.*Phd*.77e, Plu.2.384a:—Pass., ἐξεπᾴδεσθαι φύσιν *to be charmed out of* their nature, S.*OC*1194. **-αίρω**, *stir up, excite* one to do, c. inf., Ar.*Lys*.623; ὅ σ' ἐξεπαρεῖ (fut.) μεῖζον ἢ χρεὼν φρονεῖν E.*Fr*.963.

**ἐξεπείγω**, *to be urgent, pressing*, *PPetr*.3 p.143.

**ἐξέπερεν·** ἐξεῖλεν, ἐπόρθησεν (-σαν cod.), Hsch. (fort. ἐξέπερσεν).

**ἐξεπερώτησις**, εως, ἡ, *formal question* put to a contracting party, *PMasp*.243.22 (vi A.D.).

**ἐξεπεύχομαι**, *boast loudly that*.., c. inf., S.*Ph*.668.

**ἐξέπηλεν·** ἐξεγένετο, Hsch. (fort. ἐξέπελεν).

**ἐξεπικαιδέκᾰτος**, η, ον, = ἑκκαιδέκατος, *AP*12.4 (Strat.).

**ἐξεπιπολῆς**, v. ἐπιπολή.

**ἐξεπίσταμαι**, *know thoroughly*, τι Hdt.2.43, 5.93: c. part., *know well that*.., ἐ. τὸν Κῦρον οὐκ ἀτρεμίζοντα Id.1.190, cf. S.*OC*1584; τὸν θεὸν τοιοῦτον (sc. ὄντα) ἐ. Id.*Fr*.771: c. inf., *know well how* to do, Id. *Ant*.480: with εὖ, Hdt.3.146, A.*Ag*.838; καλῶς S.*OC*417, etc.: c. acc. et inf., *know that*, Id.*Ant*.293. II. *know by heart*, τὸν λόγον Pl.*Phdr*.228b.

**ἐξεπισφρᾱγίζομαι**, Pass., *to be stamped deep on* a thing, Chaerem. 14.10.

**ἐξεπιτάξ·** ἐξεπίτηδες, Hsch. (ἐξεπίταξεν cod.).

**ἐξεπίτηδες**, Adv. = ἐπίτηδες, *on purpose*, Hp.*Art*.47, Ar.*Pl*.916, Pl.*Grg*.461c, al., Men.*Epit*.328. 2. *with malice prepense*, D.21.56, 187, Phld.*Lib*.p.62 O.

❀ **ἐξεπομβρέω**, *rain on*, S.*Fr*.524.4: c. acc., τὰς δρόσους Tz.*H*.3.59.

**ἐξέπτη**, 3 sg. aor. 2 Act. of ἐκπέτομαι, Hes.*Op*.98.

❀ **ἐξέρ-ᾰμα**, ατος, τό, *vomit, thing vomited*, 2*Ep.Pet*.2.22. **-ᾰσις**, εως, ἡ, *vomiting*, Eust.1856.5. II. *dye-extract*, *PHolm*.15.39.

**ἐξεραυνάω**, v. ἐξερευνάω.

❀ **ἐξεράω**, aor. ἐξήρᾱσα (v. infr.):—Pass., aor. 1 part. ἐξεραθείς Hp. *Mul*.2.121:—*evacuate*, esp. by *purge* or *vomit*, Id.*Morb*.4.49; *draw off* a patient's water from the chest, ib.2.61:—Pass., *to be vomited*, Dsc. *Eup*.2.160; ὡς μὴ.. ἐξερῆται that (the wound) *may not keep on discharging*, Hp.*VC*15 (prob. cj.). II. *disgorge*, τὴν χύτραν χρὴν ἐξερᾶν τὰ τεῦτλα Crates Com.14.8; μαλάχας ἐ., = ἐξερυγγάνειν, Pherecr. 131.1. 2. *pour out, let fall*, τοὺς λίθους.. χαμᾶζε πρῶτον ἐξεράσατε Ar.*Ach*.341; φέρ' ἐξεράσω [τὰς ψήφους] *let me pour out* the ballots *from* the urn (in order to count them), Id.*V*.993; ἐξέρα τὸ ὕδωρ *pour* it *out*, D.36.62, cf. Aen.Tact.31.13, D.H.2.69; ὥσπερ ἐ. [τὸν ἀέρα] *drive forth* air from the lungs, Arist.*Pr*.960ᵇ26, cf. *Placit*.4.22.3. III. *give out* a dye, *PHolm*.15.37, al.; ὅταν δόξῃ ἐξερακέναι τὰ φάρμακα ib. 18.16.—Cf. συνεράω: the simple ἐράω is not found.

❀ **ἐξεργ-άζομαι**, fut. -άσομαι: aor. -ηργασάμην, Dor. -ηργάξατο *IG* 1.423: pf. -είργασμαι, Ion. -έργασμαι, both in act. and pass. sense (v. infr.): aor. -ειργάσθην always Pass., Isoc.5.7, Plu.*Num*.9: so fut. -εργασθήσομαι Isoc.*Ep*.6.8:—*work out, bring to completion*, Hdt.1.93, 4.179 (Pass.), etc.; τίς βλέποντα σώματ' ἐξεργάζεται; E. *Hel*.583; οὐδὲ.. μελετῶντες αὐτὸ (i.e. seamanship) ἐξείργασθέ πω Th.1.142; τὰ ἐπιμαχώτατα ἐ. *finish* [fortifying] the most assail-

able points, Id.4.4, cf. 5.75, 6.101 (Pass.); τέχνην ἐ. X.*Smp*.4.61, cf. *Cyr*.8.2.5 (Pass.); τοιούτους ἐ. τινάς *make* them *exactly* such, Id.*Smp*.4.60. 2. *accomplish, achieve*, ἥδ' ἔστ' ἐκείνη τοὔργον ἠξειργασμένη S.*Ant*.384, cf. Men.*Epit*.474; ἐ. τάραχον *work utter* confusion, X.*Eq*.9.4; πήματα E.*Heracl*.960; ἐ. συμμαχίαν *bring* it *about*, Aeschin.3.239; πραγματικῶς ἐ. τὴν ὑπόθεσιν Plb.5.26.6: c. dupl. acc., κακὸν ἐ. τινά *work* him mischief, Hdt.6.3, cf. Pl.*Ep*. 352d, etc.:—Pass., σφιν ἔργον ἐστὶν ἐξειργασμένον A.*Pers*.759, cf. Hdt.9.75; ἐπ' ἐξεργασμένοισι after *the deed had been done*, usu. of crimes or acts of violence, Id.4.164, 8.94, cf. A.*Ag*.1379, S.*Aj*.377; ἐπ' ἐ. κακοῖσι E.*Ba*.1039; τοὐξειργασμένον S.*Aj*.315. 3. *contrive* or *manage that..*, ἐξειργάσατο βασιλεὺς προσαγορευθῆναι Plb.31.33.3, cf. Luc.*Tox*.32, Plu.*Cat.Ma*.3. 4. *work at*, esp. in Pass., ἀγροὶ εὖ ἐξεργασμένοι well-*cultivated* lands, Hdt.5.29, cf. 6.137; [ἡ γῆ] ὅσῳ ἄμεινον ἐξείργασται Th.1.82; of plants, *train*, Thphr.*CP*5.3.5. 5. of an author, *work out*, D.H.*Th*.15: abs., *treat fully*, ἐ. κατὰ μέρος περί τινος Plb.3.26.5:—Pass., τὰ κατ' ἐπιτομ]ν ἐξειργασμένα Phld.*Lib*. p.1 O. II. *undo, destroy*, esp. of men, *ruin*, Hdt.4.134, 5.19, E. *Hel*.1098, etc.; in Trag., also ἐ. αἷμα μητρός Id.*Or*.1624:—Pass., ἐξειργάσμεθα we *are undone*. Id.*Hipp*.565; ὡς μή τι ἐξεργάσωνται that they may *do no harm*, Hp.*Morb*.3.16 as cited by Gal.19.182, cf. 212 (ἐξ- [or κατ-]εργάσηταί τι κακόν codd. Hp.). **-ασία**, ἡ, *working out, completion*, Plb.10.45.6. II. *labour at a thing*, ἡ πεπονημένη ἐ. [τῆς γῆς] high *state of cultivation*, App.*BC*1.11: abs., ἀκριβὴς καὶ πολλὴ ἐ. Thphr.*CP*3.1.6: *treatment, discussion* of a subject by an author, D.H.*Isoc*.4, Gal.5.664, etc.; ἡ καθ' ἕκαστον ἐ. Plu.2.1004e, cf. Phld.*Rh*.1.121 S.; ποιητικὴ ἐ. Id.*Po*.5.1: pl., ib.2.47; ἐ. λογικὴ Iamb.*Comm.Math*.24. **-ασμός**, ὁ, = ἐξεργασία I, Simp.*in Cat*.240. 26. **-αστέον**, *one must treat, discuss*, Gal.15.467, al. **-αστικός**, ή, όν, *able to accomplish*, τινός X.*Mem*.4.1.4 (in Sup.), Plb.15.37.1; τὸ ἐ. τοῦ λόγου *diligent inquiry*, A.D.*Synt*.312.9. II. Adv. **-κῶς** *elaborately, in detail*, Phld.*Rh*.1.156S., *Piet*.19: Comp. **-ώτερον** Corn. *ND*35, A.D.*Synt*.282.10. ⊛**-άτης** [ᾰ], ου, ὁ, *workman*, *PBasel*19.6 (vi A.D.).

**ἐξέργω**, Att. **ἐξείργω**, fut. -είρξω Ar.*Ach*.825:—*shut out from* a place, *debar*, ἐξέργειν τινά Hdt.3.51, etc.; ἐξείργειν τινὰ χθονός, γῆς, E.*Heracl*.20, 25; ἐξ ἀγορᾶς, ἐκ τοῦ ἄστεος, Pl.*Lg*.936c; ἀπὸ τοῦ βήματος Aeschin.1.32; ἐκ τῶν ἱερῶν Lys.6.16; ἐκ τοῦ θεάτρου D.21.178; ἐ. θύραζε *drive away and shut* him out of doors, Ar.*Ach*.825, cf. D.18. 169:—Pass., ἐξείργεσθαι πάντων Th.2.13; ἐξειργόμενοι δίκης Plu.*Rom*. 23. 2. *prevent, preclude*, καιρὸν ἐ. λόγος S.*El*.1292; τῶνδ' οὐδὲν ἐξείργει νόμος E.*Andr*.176; ἐ. δέει τὸ δίκην λαμβάνειν D.21.124: abs., ὅταν μὴ ἡ ὥρα τοῦ ἔτους ἐξείργῃ X.*Oec*.4.13:—Pass., πολέμοις ἐξειργόμενοι Th.1.118; ἐὰν μὴ χρόνῳ ἐξείργηται Arist.*Cat*.13ᵃ31: c. inf., *to be hindered from* doing, D.H.*Th*.15. 3. *constrain, compel*, τινὰ πληγαῖς Pl.*Lg*.935c:—Pass., ἀναγκαίῃ ἐξέργεσθαι ἔς τι *to be constrained* by necessity to undertake a thing, Hdt.7.96: c. inf., ἀναγκαίῃ ἐ. γνώμην ἀποδέξασθαι ib.139; ὑπὸ τοῦ νόμου ἐξεργόμενος Id.9.111; νόμῳ Th.3.70.

**ἐξερεείνω**, Ep. Verb, 1. c. acc. rei, *inquire into*, ἐξερέεινεν ἕκαστα Od.10.14. 2. c. acc. pers., *inquire after*, ἠ.. φίλον πόσιν ἐξερεείνοι 23.86; *inquire of*, ἄλλος ἄλλον ἐ. A.R.4.1250: abs., *make inquiry*, Il. 9.672, etc.:—Med., ἐξερεείνετο μύθῳ 10.81. II. *search thoroughly*, πόρους ἁλὸς ἐξερεείνων Od.12.259; μυχούς *h.Merc*.252: metaph. of a harp, *try* its *tones, tune* it, ib.483.

**ἐξερεθ-ίζω**, strengthd. for ἐρεθίζω, Pi.*P*.8.13, Ph.2.359, Plu.*Aem*. 30, etc.; of a plaster, *stimulate*, Crateuas*Fr*.8. **-ιστής**, οῦ, ὁ, *one who provokes*, *AB*251. **-ω**, strengthd. for ἐρέθω, *AP*5.243 (Paul. Sil.).

**ἐξερείδω**, *prop firmly*, ταῖς ἀντηρίσι Plb.8.4.6; *support*, ἐ. μου βάσιν τρέμουσαν Luc.*Trag*.55; ἐ. ἀτονίαν σώματος Dsc.1.69.4:—Pass., *to be underpinned*, Plb.16.11.5, Sor.1.47.

**ἐξερείπω**, *strike off*, ὄζους δρυὸς πελέκει Pi.*P*.4.264. II. more freq. intr. in aor. 2 ἐξήρῐπον, inf. ἐξερῐπεῖν:—*fall to earth*, ὡς δ' ὅθ' ὑπὸ ῥιπῆς πατρὸς Διὸς ἐξερίπῃ δρῦς Il.14.414; χαίτη ζεύγλης ἐξεριποῦσα the mane *streaming downwards from* the yoke-cushion, 17.440; [κάπροι] αὐχένας ἐξεριπόντες *letting* their necks *fall on the ground*, Hes.*Sc*. 174; *fall down*, Id.*Th*.704.—Mostly Ep., but ᾗ ἐξήριπε τὸ κάτηγμα where the fractured part *projects*, Hp.*Off*.12.

**ἐξέρ-εισις**, εως, ἡ, *fixing firmly*, αἱ πρὸς τὴν γῆν ἐ. Plb.6.23.4. ⊛**-εισμα**, ατος, τό, *prop, support*, metaph., Longin.40.4 (pl.). **-ειστικός**, ή, όν, *resistent, tense*, of the pulse, πληγή Archig.ap.Gal.8. 651, cf. 938; dub. l. in Epicur.*Sent*.14.

**ἐξέρεκτα**· ἐκπέσῃ, Hsch.

⊛**ἐξερεύγομαι**, *vomit forth*, πλῆθος βατράχων Lxx *Wi*.19.10, al.; ἀφρόν, of honey when boiled, Gal.6.273: metaph., λόγον ἀγαθόν Lxx *Ps*.44(45).1. II. of a tumour, *break out*, Hp.*Prorrh*.1. 168. III. Med. or Pass., of rivers, *empty themselves*, Hdt.1.202, Arist.*HA*603ᵃ14, D.H.1.9, etc.; of veins, *discharge*, Hp.*Oss*.14. (Cf. ἐξερυγγάνω.)

**ἐξερευν-άω** (later -εραυν- Lxx *Ps*.118(119).2, al.), *search out, examine*, S.*OT*258, *El*.1100; τὰ περὶ τὴν πόλιν Aen.Tact.28.4; λογισμὸς τὰς αἰτίας ἐ. Epicur.*Ep*.3 p.64 U.; τὰς προσόδους Plb.14.1.13, cf. Lxx l. c., al.; τὰ πρόσφορ' ἤν πως ἐξερευνήσας λάβω E.*Hel*.429:—Med., D.C.52.6; τόπους Plb.9.5.8, cf. 18.21.1. **-ησις**, εως, ἡ, *inquiry, investigation*, Lxx *Ps*.63(64).7 (in form -εραυν-), cj. in Lyd.*Ost*. 16. **-ητικός**, ή, όν, *good as a spy* or *scout*, Str.3.3.6.

**ἐξέρευξις**, εως, ἡ, *belching*, Aret.*SA*2.2 (pl.).

**ἐξερευνάω**, = ἐξερευνάω, Hsch.

**ἐξερέω** (A), Att. contr. ἐξερῶ, fut. of ἐξεῖπον (q. v.):—I *will speak out, tell out, utter aloud*, Hom. always abs. in sg., ἐξερέω Il.8.286, 12. 215, Od.9.365, al.; in tmesi, ἔκ τοι ἐρέω Il.1.204, 233, al.: c. acc. in Trag., τἀληθὲς ἐξερῶ S.*OT*800, cf. 219, etc.: c. dupl. acc., τοιαῦτά τοι νῷ πᾶς τις ἐ. Id.*El*.984; ἐ. ὅτι.. Id.*Ant*.325:—after Hom., also pf. Act. ἐξείρηκα Id.*Tr*.350, 374: 3 sg. plpf. Pass. ἐξείρητο Id.*OT*984: 3 sg. fut. Pass. ἐξειρήσεται Id.*Tr*.1186.

⊛**ἐξερέω** (B), Ep. pres., = ἐξέρομαι (of which it is an Ep. form) and ἐξερεείνω: 1. c. acc. rei, *inquire into* a thing, Od.3.116, 14.375:—Med., πάντα.. ἐξερέεσθαι 13.411, cf. 4.119. 2. c. acc. pers., *inquire of* a person, 10.249, etc.:—Med., 3.24, 19.99. II. *search through*, κνημοὺς ἐξερέησι 4.337. 2. *search for*, ὕδωρ A.R.4.1443.

**ἐξέρημα**, sine expl., Hsch.

**ἐξερημόω**, *make quite desolate*, ἐ. οἶκον *leave* it *destitute of heirs*, D. 43.76, cf. Lxx *Le*.26.31, al.; ἐξερημῶσαι γένος S.*El*.1010 (but ἐ. δόμους *abandon* them, E.*Andr*.597, 991); πόλεις -ωμένας Pl.*Ep*.332e; ἐ. τὰ ἑαυτῶν *leaving* their own places *destitute* (of troops), X.*Vect*.4. 47; δράκοντος γένυν ἐ. *making* it *destitute* of teeth, E.*HF*253:—Pass., *to be left destitute*, Ἑλλὰς ἐξερημωθεῖσα Ar.*Pax*647; εἰς τὸν ἐξηρημωμένον.. οἶκον Pl.*Lg*.925c.

**ἐξερίζω**, *to be contumacious*, Plu.*Pomp*.56, App.*BC*2.151.

**ἐξερῑθεύομαι**, *bind to oneself by party ties*, τοὺς νέους διὰ [τῆς στρατηγίας] Plb.10.22.9.

**ἐξερῑνάζω**, strengthd. for ἐρινάζω: metaph., *fertilize*, ἐρινὸς.. ἀχρεῖος ὢν ἐς βρῶσιν ἄλλους ἐξερινάζει λόγῳ S.*Fr*.181.

**ἐξέρ-ισμα**, ατος, τό, f.l. for ἐξορισμός, Porph.*Abst*.1.10. **-ιστής**, οῦ, ὁ, *stubborn disputant*, τῶν λόγων E.*Supp*.894. **-ιστικός**, ή, όν, *captious, disputatious*, dub. l. in Epicur.*Sent*.14; cf. ἐξερειστικός.

**ἐξερμηνεύω**, *interpret, translate*, εἰς τὴν Ἑλλάδα γλῶσσαν τοὔνομα D.H.1.67, cf. Jul.*Or*.2.77d:—Pass., Plb.2.15.9, D.H.4.67, Plu.2. 383d, etc. II. *describe accurately*, Luc.*Hist.Conscr*.19.

**ἐξέρομαι**, Ion. -είρομαι, fut. -ερήσομαι: aor. 2 -ηρόμην, inf. -ερέσθαι: 1. c. acc. rei, *inquire into* a thing, Διὸς ἐξείρετο βουλήν Od. 13.127; so also ἀναξίου μὲν φωτὸς ἐξερήσομαι.. τί νῦν κυρεῖ *will inquire concerning* him, what he is now about, S.*Ph*.439. 2. c. acc. pers., *inquire of*, Ζῆν' ὕπατον.. ἐξείρετο Il.5.756; ἢ τοὐπίτριπτον κίναδος ἐξήρου μ' ὅπου; S.*Aj*.103; ἐ. καὶ προσέειπε Il.24.361.—Ion. pres. ἐξείρομαι A.R.3.19: in Hom. more freq. ἐξερέω, ἐξερεείνω, ἐξερέομαι.

⊛**ἐξέρπω**, aor. ἐξείρπῠσα Arist.*HA*599ᵃ26, Aret.*SD*2.13:—*creep out of*, ἔκ τινος Ar.*Nu*.710. 2. abs., *creep out* or *forth*, of a lame man, S.*Ph*.294; εἴ τις ἐξέρποι θύραζε Ar.*Eq*.607; of insects, Arist.*HA* 550ᵃ5, 599ᵃ26. II. generally, *go out*, Hp.*Vict*.1.24; *go forth*, of an army or general, οὐ ταχὺ ἐξέρπει X.*An*.7.1.8, cf. Chilo ap.D.L.1. 73. 2. *go away*, ὑγιὴς ἐξῆρπε *IG*4.951.97 (Epid.). III. trans., *make to come forth, produce*, βατράχους Lxx *Ps*.104(105).30.

**ἐξέρρω**, in imper., ἔξερρε γαίας *away out of* the land! E.*Hipp*.973; impf. ἐξέρρον· ἐξεπορεύοντο, Hsch. (ἐξέρον cod.).

**ἐξέρρωσας**· ἐπ' ἐμὲ ἀφῖξαι, ἤτοι ἐπὶ τῶν νεύρων, Hsch.

**ἐξερσις**, εως, ἡ, *unthreading*, [λίνου] prob. cj. in Aen.Tact.31.19.

**ἐξερυγγάνω**, *utter*, aor. 2 (in tmesi) ἐξ ἂν ἔπει καὶ τῶν ἤρυγες ἱστορίην Call.*Aet*.3.1.7; cf. ἐξερεύγομαι.

**ἐξερυθρ-ιάω**, *to be very red*, Hp.*Nat.Mul*.9. **-ος**, ον, *very red*, κατακαύματα Id.*Coac*.154; χρῶμα Thphr.*HP*4.6.10; τὸ πρόσωπον *red* in the face, Arist.*Pr*.869ᵃ8, cf. 903ᵃ3.

**ἐξερυθρώδης**, ες, *very red*, Hp.*Prorrh*.1.127.

**ἐξερύκω** [ῡ], *ward off, repel*, τὰ κακά S.*Ph*.423.

**ἐξερύω**, Ion. ἐξειρύω, aor. 1 ἐξείρυσα, Ep. ἐξέρῠσα and ἐξείρυσσα; also ἐξερύσασκον (v. infr.):—*draw out of*, βέλος.. ἐξέρυσ' ὤμου Il.5.112; ἰχθύας, οὕς θ' ἁλιῆες.. πολιῆς ἔκτοσθε θαλάσσης δικτύῳ ἐξέρυσαν Od.22. 386, cf. Hdt.1.141; τοῖο δ' ἅμα ψυχήν τε καὶ ἔγχεος ἐξέρυσ' αἰχμήν Il. 16.505; *snatch out of*, ἐξείρυσε χειρὸς τόξον 23.870; but τὸν.. λαβὼν ποδὸς ἐξερύσασκε *by* the foot, 10.490; *draw out*, τοὺς δ' ἐξείρυσσαν Ἀχαιοὶ 13.194; *tear out*, μήδεά τ' ἐξερύσας Od.18.87; τὴν γλῶσσαν ἐξειρύσας Hdt.2.38. (Pres. supplied by ἐξέλκω.)

⊛**ἐξέρχομαι**, fut. -ελεύσομαι (but in Att. ἔξειμι (A) supplies the fut., also impf. ἐξῄειν): aor. 2 ἐξῆλθον, the only tense used in Hom.:—*go* or *come out of*, c. gen. loci, τείχεος, πυλάων, πόληος, Il.22.237, 413, 417; ἐκ δ' ἦλθε κλισίης 10.140; ἐ. δωμάτων, χθονός, etc., A.*Ch*.663, S.*El*. 778, etc.; ἐ. ἐκ.. Hdt.8.75, 9.12, S.*OC*37, etc.; ἔξω τῆσδ'.. χθονός E.*Ph*.476; of an actor, *come out* on the stage, Ar.*Ach*.240, *Av*.512: abs., *come forth*, ἐ. καὶ ἀμῦναι Il.9.576. b. rarely c. acc., ἐξῆλθον τὴν Περσίδα χώραν Hdt.7.29; ἐ. τὸ ἄστυ Id.5.104, cf. Arist.*Pol*.1285ᵃ5, Lxx *Ge*.44.4. c. abs., *march out, go forth*, Th.2.11, etc.; ἐπί τινα Hdt.1.36. d. of an accused person, *withdraw from the country* to avoid trial, opp. φεύγω, D.23.45. e. ἐ. ὑπηρέτης to be commissioned to carry out an order of the court, Mitteis *Chr*.89.36 (ii A.D.), etc. f. c. acc. cogn., *go out on* an expedition, etc., ἐ. ἐξόδους X.*HG*1.2.17; στρατείαν Aeschin.2.168; so παγκόνιτ' ἐ. ἄεθλ' ἀγώνων *went through* them, S.*Tr*.506 (lyr.); νίκης ἔχων ἐξῆλθε.. γέρας Id.*El*.687. g. with Preps., ἐ. ἐπὶ θήραν, ἐπὶ θεωρίαν, etc., X.*Cyr*.1.2.11, Pl.*Cri*.52b, etc.; ἐπὶ πλεῖστον ἐ. *pursue their advantages* to the utmost, Th.1.70; εἰς τόδ' ἐ. ἀνόσιον στόμα *allow oneself to use* these impious words, S. *OC*981; also ἐ. εἴς τινας *come out of* one class into another, as εἰς τοὺς τελείους ἄνδρας, opp. ἔφηβοι, X.*Cyr*.1.2.12. h. of disease, *pass off*, ἣν ἐκ τοῦ ἄλλου σώματος ἡ νοῦσος ἐξεληλύθῃ Hp.*Morb*.2.13. i. of offspring, *issue from* the womb, τὰ μὲν τετελειωμένα, τὰ δὲ ἀτελῆ ἐ. Arist.*Pr*.896ᵃ18; ἐκ τῆς γαστρὸς M.Ant.9.3. 2. ἐ. εἰς ἔλεγχον *stand forth and come* to the trial, E.*Alc*.640; ἐς χερῶν ἅμιλλαν ἐ. τινί Id.*Hec*.226: abs., *stand forth, be proved to be*, ἄλλος S.*OT*1084; *come forth* (from the war), Th.5.31. 3. c. acc. rei, *execute*, ἃ ἂν.. μὴ

ἐξέλθωσιν (v.l. for ἐπεξ–) Id.1.70; τὸ πολὺ τοῦ ἔργου ἐξῆλθον (v.l. for ἐπεξ–) Id.3.108. 4. abs., *exceed all bounds*, Pl.*Lg*.644b; so ἐ. τὰ νόμιμα Nymphis 15. 5. with acc. of the instrument of motion, ἐ. οὐδὲ τὸν ἕτερον πόδα Din.1.82. II. of Time, *come to an end, expire*, Hdt.2.139, S.*OT*735, *PRev.Laws* 48.9 (iii B.C.), etc.; τοῦ ἐξελθόντος μηνός Hyp.*Eux*.35; ἐπειδὰν.. ὁ ἐνιαυτὸς ἐξέλθῃ Pl.*Plt*.298e; ἐλέγοντο αἱ σπονδαὶ ἐξεληλυθέναι X.*HG*5.2.2. 2. of magistrates, etc., *go out of office*, ἡ ἐξελθοῦσα βουλή Decr.ap.And.1.77, cf. Arist.*Pol*.1273ᵃ 16. III. of prophecies, dreams, events, etc., *to be accomplished, come true*, ἐς τέλος ἐ. Hes.*Op*.218: abs., τὴν ὄψιν συνεβάλετο ἐξεληλυθέναι Hdt.6.108, cf. 82; ἐξῆλθε (sc. ἡ μῆνις) *was satisfied*, Id.7.137; ἰσόψηφος δίκη ἐξῆλθ' ἀληθῶς A.*Eu*.796; κατ' ὀρθὸν ἐ. *come out* right, S.*OT*88; ἀριθμὸς οὐκ ἐλάττων ἐ. X.*HG*6.1.5; of persons, μὴ ..Φοῖβος ἐξέλθῃ σαφής *turn out* a true prophet, S.*OT*1011. 2. of words, *proceed*, παρά τινος Pl.*Tht*.161b; of goods, *to be exported*, Id.*Alc*.1.122e.

**ἐξερῶ**, v. ἐξερέω (A).

**ἐξερωέω**, *swerve from the course*, of shy horses, αἱ δ' ἐξηρώησαν Il.23.468; ἐξηρώησε κελεύθου Theoc.25.189.

**ἐξερωτάω**, *search out, inquire*, Pi.*P*.9.44. 2. c. acc. pers., *question*, E.*Fr*.579, *BGU*1141.34 (i B.C.).

**ἔξεσα**· ἔξωθεν (Lacon.), Hsch. (ἐξέσας cod.; cf. ἔντεσα).

**ἐξεσθίω**, fut. ἐξέδομαι: pf. ἐξεδήδοκα: aor. ἐξέφαγον:—*eat away, eat up*, ἐξέδεταί σου τοὔψον Ar.*Eq*.1032, cf. Epimenid.10; ἐκ τῶν πόλεων τὸ σκῖρον ἐξεδήδοκεν Id.*V*.925; ἐὰν μή σ' ἐκφάγω ἐκ τῆσδε τῆς γῆς Id.*Eq*.698; ἐξεσθίουσι αὐτὰ (the grubs) αἱ μέλιτται Arist.*HA*554ᵇ 4, cf. Dsc.*Eup*.1.150.

**ἐξέσθω**, = foreg., A.*Ch*.281.

***ἐξεσία**, ἡ, (ἐξίημι) *sending forth, mission, embassy*, Hom. only in phrase, ἐξεσίην ἐλθόντι Il.24.235, cf. Od.21.20: acc. pl. in Hsch.

**ἔξεσις**, εως, ἡ, *dismissal, divorce*, γυναικός Hdt.5.40.

**ἐξέσσυτο**, v. ἐκσεύω.

***ἔξεστι**, imper. ἐξέστω, subj. ἐξῇ, inf. ἐξεῖναι, part. ἐξόν: impf. ἐξῆν: fut. ἐξέσται, opt. ἐξέσοιτο X.*Ages*.1.24, part. ἐξεσόμενον (v. infr.): impers. (v. ἔξειμι B):—*it is allowed, is possible*, c. inf., Hdt.1.183, etc.: c. dat. pers. et inf., ib.138, A.*Eu*.899, etc.; ἔ. σοι ἀνδρὶ γενέσθαι X.*An*.7.1.21; ἔ. εὐδαίμοσι γενέσθαι '*licet esse beatis*', D.3.23: with acc. instead of second dat., ἔ. ὑμῖν φίλους γενέσθαι Th.4.20: c. acc. pers. et inf., Ar.*Ach*.1079, Pl.*Plt*.290d: neut. part. abs., ἐξόν τοι.. ἕτερα ποιέειν *since it was possible* for thee to.., Hdt.4.126; ἐξόν σοι γάμου τυχεῖν A.*Pr*.648; ἐξὸν κεκλῆσθαι S.*El*.365; ὡς οὐκ ἐξεσόμενον τῇ πόλει δίκην.. λαμβάνειν Lys.14.10.

**ἔξεστις**, ιος, ἡ, v. ἔξαστις.

***ἐξετ-άζω**, fut. ἐξετάσω, rarely ἐξετῶ Isoc.9.34, cf. *AB*251: aor. ἐξήτασα Ar.*Th*.438, S.*OC*211 (lyr.), etc., Dor. ἐξήταξα Theoc.14.28: pf. ἐξήτακα Pl.*Tht*.154d, etc.:—Pass., fut. –ετασθήσομαι D.2.20: aor. –ητάσθην (v. infr.): pf. –ήτασμαι (v. sub fin.):—*examine well* or *closely, scrutinize, review*, ἐ. φίλους, ὅντιν' ἔχουσι νόον Thgn.1016, cf. Ar. l. c., etc.; τὴν ὑπάρχουσαν ξυμμαχίαν ἐ. Th.2.7; βίον αὐτοῦ πάντα ἐξετάσω D.21.21; ἐκ τοῦ εἰκότος ἐξετασθῆναι δεῖ τὸ πρᾶγμα Antipho 5.37; ἐ., opp. ὑπέχειν λόγον, Arist.*Rh*.1354ᵃ5; τὸ δι' ἀκριβείας –αζόμενον exactly *weighed* words, Pl.*Tht*.184c; ἐ. τι ⟨διὰ⟩ τῶν εἰδότων *make inquiries into* a thing *from*.., Plb.10.8.1: folld. by Relat., ἐ. ὅστις ἦν D.45.82; ἐ. τί καὶ πῶς λέγουσι Pl.*Phdr*.261a; ἐ. τινά, τίνος ἐστὶ γένους Epicr.11.17. 2. of troops, *inspect, review*, Th.7.33,35, etc.; στρατιώτας σὺν τοῖς ὅπλοις *Hell.Oxy*.10.1:—Pass., στρατὸς δὲ θάσσει κἀξετάζεται E.*Supp*.391, cf. Th.6.97. 3. ἐ. τὴν βουλήν, τὸ βουλευτικόν, = Lat. *legere senatum, revise the roll of* the Senate, D.C.52.42, 54.13. 4. *examine, approve, PRev.Laws* 40.19 (Pass., iii B.C.), etc. 5. *pass in review, enumerate*, ἁμαρτήματα ἀκριβῶς ἐ. Isoc.7.63, cf. D.20.52,58. II. *examine* or *question* a person *closely*, Hdt.3.62, S.*Aj*.586, *OC*211; τινὰ περί τινος Pl.*Phdr*.258d; τινά τι Id.*Grg*.515b, X.*Cyr*.6.2.35; δικαίως αὐτὸν ἐξετάσω D.21.154, cf. 18.20; τὸν δεσπότην ὁ δοῦλος ἐξετάζει Id.45.76:—Pass., Men.*Epit*.65. III. *estimate*, τι πρός τι one thing with reference to another, D.6.7; πρὸς ἐκείνους ἐ. καὶ παραβάλλειν ἐμέ Id.18.314; ἰσοστάσιος ἦν ἡ πορφύρα πρὸς ἄργυρον ἐξεταζομένη Theopomp.Hist.114, cf. Jul.*Or*.3.119a; ἐ. τινὰ παρ' ἄλληλα D.18.265, cf. Isoc.8.11; *compare*, πρὸς Ἀριστογείτονα ἐμαυτόν D.*Ep*.3.43. IV. *prove by scrutiny* or *test*, of gold, Chilo 1 (Pass.); ἐ. τοὺς κακούς τε κἀγαθοὺς X.*Oec*.20.14; τοὺς χρησίμους D.34.38: c. part., ἐξητακὼς στερεοὺς ὑπάρχοντας τοὺς τόπους Plb.3.79.1:—more freq. in Pass., ἐὰν μὴ παρὼν ἐ. unless he is *proved* to have been present, Pl.*Lg*.764a; καὶ λέγων καὶ γράφων ἐξηταζόμην τὰ δέοντα D.18.173; ἐξήτασαι πεποιηκὼς ib.197; ἐξετάζεσθαι φίλος (sc. ὤν) E.*Alc*.1011; ἐχθρὸς ἐξεταζόμενος D.21.65; κατήγορος Id.22.66; μέτριοι ἐν τοῖς ἀνηκέστοις Plu.2.74b; of things, τὰ φοβερὰ ἐξετασθήσεται μέχρι λόγου τοιαῦτα ὄντα D.H.6.63. V. Pass., *to be numbered, counted*, c. gen., ὧν εἷς ἐγὼ βουληθεὶς ἐξετάζεσθαι And.4.2; τῶν ἐχθρῶν εἷς ἐξετάζεσθαι *to be found in the number of*.., D.19.291; μετὰ τῶν ἄλλων ἐξητάζετο he *appeared among*.., Id.18.217; ἔν τισι D.H.6.59; *to be placed on a roll*, ἐν τοῖς ἱππικοῖς among the *Equites* at Rome, Plu.*Pomp*.14; of the census, ἐξητάσθησαν αἱ πᾶσαι πεντεκαίδεκα [μυριάδες] Id.*Caes*.55. 2. Pass., *present oneself, appear*, D.21.161; πρὸς τὸν ἄρχοντα.. οὐδέπω.. ἐξήτασται Id.37.46, cf. 18.277. **–ἀσία**, ἡ, = sq., τῶν δούλων *IG*12(3).174.29 (Astypalaea, Epist. Aug.). ***–ἄσις**, εως, ἡ, *close examination, scrutiny, test*, Pl.*Ap*.22e, *Tht*.210c; ἡδονῆς ἐ. πᾶσαν ποιήσασθαι Id.*Phlb*.55c; ἐ. ποιεῖσθαι περί τινος Lycurg.28; ἐ. λαμβάνειν undertake *an inquiry*, D.18.246; ἐ. τινος ἔχειν Th.6.41; ἔσχον τὸ ἴσον εἰς ἐ. I received the copy for *examination, PLond*.2.338.24 (ii A.D.), etc.; ἐ. γίγνεται πρός τι *comparison* is made with.., Luc.*Prom*.12. 2. *a military inspection* or *review*, ἐ. ὅπλων, ἵππων ποιεῖσθαι, hold *a review of*.., Th.4.74, 6.45,96; τῶν Ἑλλήνων καὶ τῶν βαρβάρων ποιεῖσθαι X.*An*.1.2.14; ἐ. σὺν τοῖς ὅπλοις ἐγίγνετο ib.5.3.3. b. at Rome, ἐ. ἱππέων, = Lat. *transvectio equitum*, Plu.*Aem*.38, D.C.55.31; ἐ. ἐτησία Id.63.13. c. ἐ. τῶν βουλευτῶν, = Lat. *lectio Senatus, revision* of the Senatorial roll, Id.54.26. d. ἐ. βίων, of the Roman *Census*, Plu.*Aem*.38, cf. J.*AJ*3.12.4. e. *inspection* of articles, *IG*2².333.11. 3. *arrangement, order*, Nicom.*Harm*.6. **–ασμός**, ὁ, = foreg., ἐ. ποιεῖσθαι D.18.16, cf. *Hell.Oxy*.10.1,2, *IG*2².500.12 (pl.), Plu.2.106cb; ψυχῶν ἐν Ἅιδου D.H.*Pomp*.6. II. *visitation*, Lxx *Wi*.4.6. **–αστέον**, *one must scrutinize*, Pl.*R*.599a, Gal.1.357; *one must examine carefully*, ὅπως.. Jul.*Or*.7.226d. **–αστήριον**, τό, *office of public auditor*, *SIG*976.61 (Samos, ii B.C.). **–αστής**, οῦ, ὁ, *examiner, inquirer into*, τινός D.H.2.67, Plu.*Ages*.11. 2. *auditor of public accounts*, Arist.*Pol*.1322ᵇ11, *SIG*284.10 (Erythrae), 976.77 (Samos), 1015.32 (Halic.). 3. at Athens, *officer who checked payments to* ξένοι, etc., Aeschin.1.113, *IG* 2².641 (iii B.C.). **–αστικός**, ή, όν, *capable of examining into*, τῶν ἔργων X.*Mem*.1.1.7; ἐ. καὶ κριτικός Luc.*Herm*.64; ἐ. πρὸς ἀκρίβειαν *exacting*, Hierocl. *in CA*7 p.429 M.: abs., *fitted for inquiry*, of Dialectic, Arist.*Top*.101ᵇ3 (in *Po*.1455ᵃ34 ἐκστατικοί is prob. l.). Adv. –κῶς D.17.13. II. ἐ. (sc. ἀργύριον), τό, *salary of an* ἐξεταστής, Id.13.4.

**ἐξέτειον**· ἐκ τούτου τοῦ ἔτους, οἷον ἐπέτειον, Hsch.

***ἐξέτεροι**, αι, α, later form of μετεξέτεροι, Nic.*Th*.412,744.

**ἑξέτης**, ες, *six years old*, ἵππον.. ἑξέτε' ἀδμήτην Il.23.266, cf. 655, Pi.*N*.3.49, Ar.*Nu*.862:—fem. **ἑξέτις**, μετὰ τὸν ἑξέτη καὶ τὴν ἑξέτιν Pl.*Lg*.794c. II. *lasting six years*, ἀρχή Lys.30.2.

***ἐξέτι**, Prep. with gen., ἐξέτι τοῦ ὅτε.. *ever since* the time when.., Il.9.106; ἐ. πατρῶν *from* our fathers' time, Od.8.245; ἐ. νηπυτίης A.R.4.791; ἐ. κεῖθεν Call.*Ap*.104; ἐ. παίδων *IG*14.1549: also in late Prose, ἐ. νέου, νεαροῦ, App.*BC*2.86, Ael.*NA*5.39; ἐ. σπαργάνων Ph.2.94.

**ἐξευασμένου**· τεθνεῶτος, γενομένου, Hsch. (v. ἐξαναίνω).

**ἐξευγεν-ίζω**, = ἐλευθεροποιέω, Hsch.; τινάς *produce noble offspring*, Vett.Val.119.26; *make noble*, Sophon. *in de An*.145.14:—but **–ισμός**, ὁ, apptly., = *degeneration*, *Gloss*. (pl.).

**ἐξευδιάζω**, *calm utterly*, τοὺς χειμῶνας τῶν πραγμάτων Ph.2.345, cf. Hsch.

**ἐξευθετίζω**, *set in order*, prob. in S.*Ichn*.270.

**ἐξευθύνω** [ῡ], *straighten*, δακτύλους *IG*4.951.29 (Epid.), cf. Gal.*UP* 14.3 (Pass.). II. *examine*, τοὺς ἄρχοντας Pl.*Lg*.945d.

**ἐξευ-κρῑνέω**, *handle with discrimination*, Hp.*Fract*.15; ἐ. τὰς διαφορὰς *treat* them *systematically*, Plb.35.2.6. ***–λᾰβέομαι**, *guard carefully against*, τι Pl.*La*.199d, al.; ἐ. τοῦτο μή.. E.*Andr*.644; ἐ. μή.. A.*Fr*.205. **–λῡτέω**, *discharge* a debt, *POxy*.271.22 (Pass., i A.D.). **–μᾰρίζω**, *make light* or *easy*, συμφορὰς E.*HF*18; ᾠδῇ ἐ. τὴν ἔνδειαν Ph.2.477; θεὸς ἐ. πάντα ib.83, cf. 426 (Pass.), Babr.[46a], Simp. *in Cael*.667.25. II. Med., *prepare*, E.*HF*81:—Pass., ἐξευμαρίσθη· παρεσκευάσθη, Hsch.

**ἐξευμεν-ίζω**, *propitiate*, θεόν J.*AJ*8.13.8:—Med., ib.12.2.14, Lxx 4*Ma*.4.11, Plu.*Fab*.4, Ph.2.2, al., Herm. *in Phdr*.p.89 A.:—Pass., ὑπό τινος, περί τινος, Ph.2.520,533, cf. Porph.*Abst*.2.37. **–ισις**, εως, ἡ, *propitiation*, *Gloss*. **–ιστέον**, *one must propitiate*, Eust.676.16. **–ισμός**, ὁ, '*friendship's offering*', Nicom.*Harm*.12. **–ιστήριον**, τό, *propitiatory offering*, *Gloss*.

**ἐξευνουχίζω**, strengthd. for εὐνουχίζω, metaph., τὸν ἄκρατον Plu.2.692c:—Pass., Ph.1.224; –ισμένῃ ψυχῇ ib.389.

**ἐξευπορέω**, *supply abundantly*, ἐπικουρίαν ταῖς χρείαις Pl.*Lg*.918c. II. abs., *find a way out*, περί τι ib.861b.—The form ἐξευπορίζω, in X.*An*.5.6.19, is prob. f. l. for ἐκπορίζω.

**ἐξεύρ-εσις**, εως, ἡ, *searching out, search*, Hdt.1.67. 2. *finding out, invention*, ib.94. 3. *discovery*, τοῦ ὄντος Pl.*Min*.315a. **–ετέος**, α, ον, *to be discovered*, νοῦς Ar.*Nu*.728 (v.l. for εὑρητέος). II. ἐξευρετέον αὐτοῖς they *must find out*, Pl.*R*.380a. **–ετικός**, ή, όν, *inventive, ingenious*, M.Ant.1.9:—written **–ητικός**, Sch.E.*Med*.408. **–ημα**, ατος, τό, *thing found out, invention*, Hdt.1.53,94,171, A.*Th*.649, Metrod.*Fr*.7 (pl.); ἐ. σοφόν Ar.*Ec*.578 (lyr.); Παλαμηδικὸν.. τοὐξεύρημα Eup.351.6; τὰ καλὰ τῆς ψυχῆς ἐ. Metrod.*Fr*.6; *stratagem*, Phryn.Com.22 (pl.). **–ίσκω**, fut. –ευρήσω: aor. 2 ἐξηῦρον, Med. –ηυρόμην or –ηυράμην (Men.161.4 codd. Stob.):—*find out, discover*, Il.18.322, Th.8.66, Pl.*R*.566b, etc.; ἐ. ὁπόθεν *find out* from what source.., Ar.*Eq*.800; *invent*, Hdt.1.8, etc.; βωμολόχον τι Ar.*Eq*.1194; ἀριθμόν, μηχανήματ' ἐ., A.*Pr*.460, 469; ἐ. ἐπ' ἐμοὶ δεσμόν ib.97; simply, *find*, [πόλεώς] σε σωτῆρ' ἐ. (sc. ὄντα) S.*OT*304; αὐτὸν ἐ. ἐχθίω Φρυγῶν Id.*Aj*.1054; ποῦ τὸν ἄνδρα.. ἐξευρήσομεν; Ar.*Eq*.145: c. inf., ἄλλο τι ἐξευρήκασι.. γενέσθαι Hdt.1.196; οὐκ ἐξευρίσκω τι ἄλλο ποιεῖν *POxy*.1588.10 (iv A.D.); ἐν γὰρ πόλλ' ἂν ἐξεύροι μαθεῖν *would lead* one *on* to learn, S.*OT*120:—Pass., Hdt.1.94, al.: impers., ὧδέ σφι ἐς τὴν ἕψησιν τῶν κρεῶν ἐξεύρηται this *invention has been made*.., Id.4.61. 2. *seek out, search after*, Id.7.119, 5.33. 3. *win, get, procure*, ἀέθλων κράτος Pi.*I*.8(7).4; τὸ κάλλος ἄλγος ἐ. S.*Tr*.25; γαστρὶ μὲν τὰ σύμφορα τόξον τόδ' ἐ. Id.*Ph*.288; νόμους σεαυτῷ Antipho 5.12; ἄνδρα ἐ., of a girl, Phoen.2.11:—Med., τὴν τέχνην Men. l. c.; παλαίσματα Theoc.24.114. II. *search* a place, ἄλσος θέναρ Pi.*I*.4(3).56.

**ἐξευτελ-ίζω**, strengthd. for εὐτελίζω, Acus.28 J., J.*AJ*6.5.3, Plu.*Alex*.28, Ath.11.494d. II. ἐ. τὴν δίαιταν *reduce* one's standard of living, J.*AJ*18.1.3. **–ισμός**, ὁ, *disparagement*, D.H.*Th*.3, Sm.*Ps*.122(123).3. **–ιστής**, οῦ, ὁ, *disparager*, τῶν ἄλλων ἀνθρώπων Phld.*Vit*.p.14 J., cf. p.42 J.

**ἐξευ-τονέω**, strengthd. for εὐτονέω, Arr.*Epict.*4.1.147. **-τρεπίζω**, strengthd. for εὐτρεπίζω, E.*El.*75. **-φραίνομαι**, *to be delighted*, *Corp.Herm.*1.30. II. *show rejoicing*, Lxx*Ez.*23.41 (v.l.).

**ἐξεύχομαι**, *boast aloud, proclaim*, ἐ. τι [εἶναι] *boast* that.., Pi.*O.*13.61, A.*Ag.*533; Ἀργεῖαι γένος ἐξευχόμεσθα we *boast to be* Argives by race, Id.*Supp.*275; also ἐ. γένος *boast of* it, ib.272. II. *pray earnestly for*, ἐς ὄψιν ἥκεις ὧνπερ ἐξηύχου Id.*Ch.*215: c. acc. et inf., E. *Med.*930. III. ἐξεύχομαι· ἀφίξομαι, Hsch.

**ἐξευωνίζω**, *cheapen*, *Dacia* 2.127 (Callatis).

**ἐξεφάλλομαι**, only in Hsch., ἐξέπαλτο (-τον cod.)· ἐξεπήδησεν (-σαν cod.), but cf. ἐκπάλλομαι.

**ἐξέφᾰνεν**, poet. for -φάνησαν, Pi.*O.*13.18.

⊛ **ἐξέφηβος**, ὁ, *one who is beyond the age of an* ἔφηβος, *a youth of seventeen*, Censorin.*Nat.*14.8.

**ἐξεφίημι**, = ἐφίημι:—only Med. ἐξεφίεμαι, *enjoin, command*, c. inf., ἐκεῖνον εἴργειν Τεῦκρος ἐξεφίεται S.*Aj.*795, cf. E.*IT*1468.

**ἐξεχαρυβδαάνθη**· ἀνεπόθη, Hsch.; cf. ἐκχαρυβδίζω.

**ἐξεχέ-βρογχος**, *having the thyroid cartilage* (*Adam's apple*) *prominent*, Hp.*Art.*41, Aret.*SD*1.8. **-γλουτος**, ον, *with prominent buttocks*, Hp.*Art.*56.

**ἐξεχέμεναι**· χωρὶς ἐμοῦ (Lacon.), Hsch.

**ἐξεχής**, ές, *gradual*: neut. as Adv., dub. l. in Aret.*CD*1.8.

⊛ **ἐξέχω**, *stand out* or *project from*, τινός Ar.*V.*1377; πέτρα ἐξέχουσα ὑπὲρ κοιλάδος *SIG*827 iii 11 (ii A.D.). 2. abs., *stand out, be prominent*, Hp.*VC*1; ἐξέχοντα ὦτα Corn.*ND*27; ἐξέχοντα *convexities*, opp. κοῖλα, Pl.*R.*602c; τὸ ἐξέχον in painting, Philostr.*VA*2.20:—Pass., τὰ ἐξεχόμενα *projecting* panels, Lxx 3*Ki.*7.16(29). b. of the sun, *shine out, appear*, ἢν ἐξέχῃ ἕλη κατ' ὄρθρον Ar.*V.*771; ἔξεχ', ὦ φίλ' ἥλιε *shine out*, fair sun, Id.*Fr.*389; πρὶν ἥλιον ἐ. before sun*rise*, Lex ap. D.43.62. c. metaph., *to be prominent, distinguished*, ἀρετῇ Ascl. *Tact.*7.2; ὁ ἐξέχων ἀνήρ Demetr.*Eloc.*146; οἱ τῶν στρατιωτῶν ἐξέχοντες Hdn.2.7.7; ἐξέχει ἐν ἑκάστῳ ἄλλο each *has* its own *distinction*, Plot.5.8.4. II. *to be attached to, depend on, cling to*, τοῦ θείου Porph. *Marc.*11:—but usu. Med., τινός D.H.1.79, *POxy.*1027.6 (i A.D.), D.Chr.45.5; σώματα ψυχῶν ἐξέχεται Dam.*Pr.*99, cf. Procl.*Inst.*100 (but prob. corrupt in sense *give up, withdraw from*, J.*AJ*3.12.3).

**ἐξεψάμενος**· κατασχών, περιπλακείς, Hsch. (leg. ἐξαψ-).

**ἐξέψω**, *boil thoroughly*, Hdt.4.61:—Pass., *to be boiled out*, v.l. in Arist.*Mete.*384ᵃ2.

**ἕξζευξις**, εως, ἡ, *team of six*, Gloss.

**ἔξηβος**, ον, (ἥβη) *past one's youth* (acc. to Hsch., thirty-five years old), A.*Th.*11.

**ἐξηγ-έομαι**, *to be leader of*, c. gen. pers., τῶν δ' ἐξηγείσθω Il.2.806 (for And.1.116, v. II.3). 2. c. acc. pers., *lead, govern*, in Th., τὰς πόλεις 1.76; τὴν Πελοπόννησον ib.71. b. abs., Hdt.1.151, 9.11. 3. c. dat. pers. et acc. rei, *show* one *the way to*, τοῖσι ἐχθροῖσι τῆς πατρίδος ἅλωσιν Hdt.6.135; ἃ δ' ἐξηγεῖσθε τοῖς ξυμμάχοις Th.3.55: c. dat. pers. only, *go before, lead*, ἡμῖν S.*OC*1589, etc.: c. acc. loci only, *lead the way to*, χῶρον ib.1520. 4. c. gen. rei, ἐ. τῆς πράξεως X.*Cyr.*2.1.29; with dat. pers. added, πᾶσι κάλλους τε καὶ τελειότητος Jul.*Or.*4.132d. 5. ἐ. εἰς τὴν Ἑλλάδα *lead an army* into Greece, X.*An.*6.6.34. II. *dictate* a form of words, ἐ. τὸν νόμον τῷ κήρυκι D.19.70; ἐξηγοῦ θεούς *dictate, name* them, E.*Med.*745. 2. generally, *prescribe, order*, ποιήσουσι τοῦτο τὸ ἂν κεῖνος ἐξηγέηται Hdt. 5.23; ὅ τι χρὴ ποιέειν ἐξηγέο σύ Id.4.9, cf. 7.234; ᾗ ὁ νόμος ἐξηγεῖται Pl.*R.*604b: of a diviner, c. inf., *order* one to do, A.*Eu.*595; τἄλλα δ' ἐξηγοῦ φίλοις Id.*Ch.*552; esp. freq. of religious forms and ceremonies, οἷς τῶν ἄλλων θεῶν οἱ Μάγοι ἐξηγοῦντο, = τοῖς ἄλλοις θεοῖς οὓς .. X.*Cyr.*8.3.11, cf. 4.5.51, 7.3.1; τί φῶ; δίδασκ' ἄπειρον ἐξηγουμένη A.*Ch.*118, cf. S.*OC*1284, etc.; οὗτος ὁ θεὸς περὶ τὰ τοιαῦτα.. ἐ. Pl.*R.*427c, cf. 469a. 3. *expound, interpret*, ἐ. τὸ οὔνομα καὶ τὴν θυσίην Hdt.2.49; τὸν ποιητήν Pl.*Cra.*407a; ἃ Ὅμηρος λέγει Id.*Ion* 531a; ὁ τὸν Ἡράκλειτον.. ἐξηγούμενος Antiph.113.3; τὰ νόμιμα D.47.69: abs., ἄγραφοι νόμοι καθ' οὓς Εὐμολπίδαι ἐξηγοῦνται according to which they *expound* things, Lys.6.10, cf. And.1.116 (leg. κηρύκων ὧν); cf. ἐξηγητής II. III. *tell at length, relate in full*, Hdt.2.3, A.*Pr.*216, 702, Th.5.26; *set forth, explain*, τὴν ἔλασιν the line of march, Hdt. 3.4, 7.6; ἃ μετὰ χεῖρας ἔχοι καὶ -ήσασθαι οἷός τε Th.1.138; τὰ τοῦ νομοθέτου βουλήματα Pl.*Lg.*802c, cf. *R.*474c: c. acc. et inf., *explain* that.., S.*Aj.*320: folld. by relat., ἐ. ὀτέῳ τρόπῳ.. Hdt.3.72, etc.; ἐ. περί τινος X.*Lac.*2.1. **-ημα**, ατος, τό, *explanation*, D.H.*Rh.* 9.8. **-ηματικός**, ή, όν, = ἐξηγητικός, ὕμνοι Men.Rh.p.337 S. 2. *having a gift for exposition*, Olymp.*Proll.*10.25. 3. Adv. Comp. -ώτερον, λέγειν τῆς λέξεως Id. *in Alc.*p.205 C. **-ησις**, εως, ἡ, *statement, narrative*, ἐ. ποιήσασθαι Th.1.72; ὑπέρ τινος Plb.6.3.1. II. *explanation, interpretation*, περὶ τοὺς νόμους Pl.*Lg.*631a; ἐνυπνίων D.S. 2.29; Ἐ. τῶν Ἐμπεδοκλέους, title of a work by Zeno Eleaticus; so in Gramm., Sch.Il.8.296. ⊛ **-ητεία**, ἡ, *office of* ἐξηγητής, *PRyl.*77.35, al. (ii A.D.). **-ητέον**, *one must relate, set forth*, Plb.3.4.6. **-ητεύω**, *hold the office* of ἐξηγητής, *PLond.*2.153.14 (ii B.C.), *Sammelb.*176 (ii A.D.), *PFay.*85.1 (iii A.D.). ⊛ **-ητής**, οῦ, ὁ, *one who leads on, adviser*, πρηγμάτων ἀγαθῶν Hdt.5.31 codd.; οὑτοσὶ δὲ.. ἁπάντων ἦν τούτων ὁ ἐ. D.35.17. II. *expounder, interpreter*, esp. of oracles, dreams, or omens, Hdt.1.78; at Athens, of sacred rites or customs, modes of burial, expiation, etc., *spiritual director*, Pl.*Euthphr.*4d, 9a, *Lg.*759c, e, 775a, D.47.68, Is.8.39, Thphr.*Char.*16.6: as an official title, ἐ. Πυθόχρηστος *IG*3.241; ἐ. ἐξ Εὐπατριδῶν ib.267; ἐ. ἐξ Εὐμολπιδῶν Lys.6.10, etc., cf. Suid. s.v.; πάτριος ἐ., of Apollo, Pl.*R.*427c. b. at Rome, of the *pontifices*, D.H.2.73. 2. *guide, cicerone*, to temples, etc., Paus.5.15.10, *SIG*1021.20 (Olympia). 3. *commentator*, Gal. 15.518, Mich. *in EN*50.8. ⊛**-ητικός**, ή, όν, *of* or *for narrative*, Diom. p.428 K.: Comp. Adv. -ώτερον Antig.*Mir.*60. 2. *explanatory*, Hermog.*Id.*1.6, Alex. Aphr. *in Metaph.*358.13, S.E.*M.*9.132, etc. Adv. -κῶς ib.7.28. II. ἐξηγητικά (sc. βιβλία), τά, title of work on religious rites by Anticlides, Plu.*Nic.*23: -κόν, τό, work by Timosthenes, Sch.A.R.3.847. **-ορέω**, = ἐξειπεῖν, in pf. part., Hsch. **-ορία**, ἡ, *utterance*, Lxx *Jb.*33.26. 2. *confession*, ib. 22.22.

**ἐξηέρωσις**, v. ἐξαέρωσις.

**ἐξηθέω**, *filter out, purify*, in Pass., Arist.*Pr.*967ᵃ15, Thphr.*CP*6. 13.1.

**ἐξήια**· θυμιάματα, Hsch.

**Ἐξηκεστῐδαλκίδαι**, = κιθαρῳδοί, called after Ἐξηκεστίδης and Ἀλκίδας, Hsch.

**Ἐξήκεστος**· ἡταιρηκώς, ὅθεν καὶ τοὺς πρωκτοὺς ὁμωνύμως ἐξηκέστους ἔλεγον, Hsch.

⊛ **ἐξηκονθ-ημερισία**, ἡ, *sixty days' crop*, *PCair.Zen.*54(c).5 (iii B.C.). **-ήμερος**, ον, *on the sixtieth day*, ἀπόφθαρμα Hp.*Epid.*2.2. 13.

⊛ **ἐξήκοντα** (ϝεξ- *SIG*56.30 (Argos, v B.C.)), οἱ, αἱ, τά, indecl., *sixty*, Il.2.587, etc.; οἱ ἐ., a college of γελωτοποιοί at Athens, Telephan. ap. Ath.14.614d.

**ἐξηκοντά-βιβλος** [ᾰ], ον, *consisting of sixty books*, Suid. s.v. Ἱπποκράτης. **-δύο, -τέσσᾰρες, -πέντε, -έξ, -επτά, -οκτώ, -εννέα**, 62, 64, 65, 66, 67, 68, 69, Thd.*Da.*5.31, Ph.1.21, Lxx*Nu.*3.50, *Ge.*46.26, 1*Es.* 5.15, *Ne.*11.6, 1*Es.*2.14. **-έτης**, ες, *sixty years old*, Mimn.6, Hp. *Epid.*5.25; also -ετῶν λυκαβάντων *IG*12(7).290 (Amorgos). **-ετία**, ἡ, *the age of sixty*, Ph.2.276, Plu.*Cic.*25. **-κις**, poet. **-κι**, Adv. *sixty times*, Pi.*O.*13.99. **-κλῖνος**, ον, *with sixty couches*, οἶκος D.S. 16.83. **-λῐθος**, ὁ, *precious stone of many colours*, Plin.*HN*37. 167. **-μοιρία**, ἡ, *arc of sixty degrees*, Heph.Astr.2.11 (ἐξακ- cod.). **-μοιρος**, ον, *consisting of sixty degrees*, Sch.Arat. 644. **-πηχυς**, υ, *sixty cubits long*, Callix.2. **-πους**, ὁ, ἡ, -πουν, τό, gen. ποδος, *sixty feet square*, Gal.10.33.

**ἐξηκοντάρουρος** [ᾰ], ον, *possessing sixty* ἄρουραι, *PCair.Zen.*1.24, 57 (iii B.C.).

**ἐξηκοντάρχιον**, τό, name of an *eyesalve*, Aët.7.103.

⊛ **ἐξηκοντάς**, άδος, ἡ, *the number sixty*, Vett.Val.300.17, al., Iamb. *Myst.*5.8. II. *sixtieth part*, Str.2.5.7.

**ἐξηκοντα-στάδιος** [στᾰ], ον, *of sixty stades*, δίαρμα Str.6.2.3. **-τᾰλαντία**, ἡ, *sum of sixty talents*, D.14.19.

**ἐξηκοντ-όργυιος**, ον, *sixty fathoms high*, Tz.*H.*9.587. **-ούτης**, ες, = ἐξηκονταέτης, Pl.*Lg.*755a, 812b, Luc.*Alex.*35, *Philops.*5.

**ἐξηκοσταῖος**, α, ον, *on the sixtieth day*, Hp.*Art.*69.

**ἐξηκοστός** (Aeol. **ἐξήκοιστος** *IG*11(4).1064*b*15), ή, όν, *sixtieth*, Hdt.6.126, etc. II. ἐξηκοστή, ἡ, *customs duty* or *tax of* $\frac{1}{60}$, *IG*12 (2).3 (Mytil.), *PEleph.*14.11 (iii B.C.). III. ἐξηκοστόν, τό, $\frac{1}{60}$ *of a degree, second*, Gem.18.7; but, $\frac{1}{60}$ *of a grand circle*, Id.16.6, al. IV. τόκοι ἐ. ἐφ' ἔτη δέκα interest *at the rate of* $\frac{1}{60}$, *OGI*444.14 (Ilium).

**ἐξηκοστοτέταρτος**, ον, *sixty-fourth*, Nicom.*Ar.*1.8, Hero *Geom.*12. 68, al.

**ἐξήκω**, *to have reached* a certain point, ἐξήκεις ἵνα φανεῖς *hast reached* a point at which thou wilt show, S.*Tr.*1157; ἅλις ἵν' ἐξήκεις δακρύων Id.*OT*1515 (troch.); ἀτελές τι καὶ οὐκ ἐξῆκον ἐκεῖσε οἷ πάντα δεῖ ἀφήκειν Pl.*R.*530e; δεῦρ' ἐ. Id.*Epin.*987a; ἐπειδὰν αἱ κλήσεις ἐξήκωσιν εἰς τὸ δικαστήριον Plu.2.833f, etc.: c. acc. cogn., ἐ. ὁδόν S.*El.* 1318. II. of Time, *to have run out* or *expired*, Hdt.2.111, S.*Ph.* 199, Lys.7.11, X.*An.*6.3.26, *IG*2².682.69, etc.; πρίν μοι μοῖραν ἐξήκειν βίου S.*Ant.*896; ἐξήκει ἡ ἀρχή, ἡ προθεσμία, Pl.*Lg.*766c, Lex ap. D. 43.16. 2. of prophecies, dreams, etc., *to have come to an accomplishment, turn out true*, Hdt.1.120, 6.80; τὰ πάντ' ἂν ἐξήκοι σαφῆ S. *OT*1182; of magical operations, *succeed*, *PMag.Par.*1.1273.

**ἐξήλᾰσα**, Ep. **ἐξήλασσα**, v. ἐξελαύνω.

**ἐξήλᾰτος**, ον, *beaten out*, ἀσπίδα χαλκείην ἐξήλατον Il.12.295.

**ἐξηλέκατα**· φανερῶς γενόμενα, Hsch. (leg. ἐξέλεγκτα). **ἐξῆλθον**, v. sub ἐξέρχομαι.

**ἐξηλῐάζω**, *hang in the sun*, as a form of torture, Lxx 2*Ki.*21.6, 13:—Pass., *to be burnt by the sun*, Hsch.

**ἐξηλίμβωρ**· ἔβλεπε (Lacon.), Hsch.

**ἐξηλῐόομαι**, Pass., *to be sunny, light*, Plu.2.929d.

**ἐξηλίφαμεν**· ἐξεκαθάραμεν, Hsch.

**ἐξηλλαγμένως**, Adv., (ἐξαλλάσσω) *strangely, unusually*, D.S.2.42, Plu.2.745f, S.E.*M.*8.187, Iamb.*Protr.*5, etc.

**ἐξηλόω**, *remove nails from, unfasten*, θύρας *PTeb.*332.15 (ii A.D.), cf. *PFlor.*69.21 (iii A.D.):—Pass., -ωμένος *unfastened*, *POxy.*1272.8 (ii A.D.).

**ἐξήλῠσις**, εως, ἡ, *way out, outlet*, τοῦ πυρὸς οὐκ ἔχοντος (nisi leg. -τες) ἐξήλυσιν ἐκ τοῦ ἄστεος Hdt.5.101; of a river, ἔχοντος οὐδαμῇ ἐ. Id.3.117; ἐ. ἐς θάλασσαν κατήκουσα Id.7.130.

**ἐξῆμαρ**, Adv. *for six days, six days long*, Od.10.80, 14.249.

⊛ **ἐξήμαρε**· ἐπέρασεν, Hsch.

**ἐξημαρτημένως**, Adv., (ἐξαμαρτάνω) *wrongly, to no purpose*, Pl.*Lg.* 891d.

**ἐξήμερος**, ἡ, *space of six days*, Vett.Val.369.24, Procl.*Hyp.*3.56.

**ἐξημερ-όω**, *tame* or *reclaim entirely*, χῶρον [ἀκανθώδη] Hdt.1.126; ἐ. γαῖαν *free* the land *from wild beasts*, etc., E.*HF*20, 852; *reclaim* wild plants, κοτίνους εἰς συκᾶς ἐ. Plu.*Fab.*20, cf. Thphr.*HP*2.2.12 (Pass.), al.: metaph., *soften, humanize*, τὸ τῆς ψυχῆς ἀτέραμνον Pl.*R.* 4.

21.4; διανοίας Ph.2.402; τὰς τῶν ἠθῶν καὶ παθῶν ὕλας Lxx 4Ma.1.29; αὐτὸν διὰ παιδείας Plu.*Num.*3; τὴν νῆσον ἐξηγριωμένην ὑπὸ κακῶν.. ἐξημέρωσε Id.*Tim.*35, cf. Parth.20.1; ἡ ἐξημερωμένη ἐν τοῖς νῦν χρόνοις ἀναστροφή our present *civilized* life, Phld.*Sto.*339.19. **-ωσις,** εως, ἡ, strengthd. for ἡμέρωσις, Plu.*Num.*14, Porph.*Abst.*3.18, etc.

**ἐξήμευσαι,** v. ἐξαμεύω. **ἐξήμησε,** v. ἐξεμέω.

**ἐξημμένως,** Adv., (ἐξάπτω B) *angrily*, Sch.Il.9.512.

**ἐξημοιβός,** όν, (ἐξαμείβω) *serving for change,* εἵματα δ' ἐξημοιβὰ *changes of* raiment, Od.8.249; τεύχεα Q.S.7.437; ἐξημοιβαί· ἕτεραι, Hsch. **ἐξήνεγκα, ἐξήνεγκον,** v. ἐκφέρω.

**ἐξηνθισμένως,** *carptim, Gloss.*

**ἐξήνιος,** ον, (ἡνία) *unbridled, uncontrollable,* Plu.2.510e.

**ἐξήπᾰφον,** v. ἐξαπαφίσκω.

**ἐξηπειρόω,** *join to the mainland,* of rivers which form deposits at their mouths, πόρον, νήσους, Str.1.3.7, 10.2.19:—Pass., νησῖδες Id. 11.4.2.

**ἐξηπεροπεύω,** *cheat utterly,* Ar.*Lys.*840.

**ἐξηπέτριπται·** δεδαπάνηται (Lacon.), Hsch.

**ἐξηπῐάλόομαι,** Pass., *change into an* ἠπίαλος, Hp.*Judic.*11.

**ἐξηπλωμένως,** Adv., (ἐξαπλόω) *fully, diffusely,* Sch.Opp.*H.*2.113.

**ἐξήρᾰτο,** v. ἐξαίρω II. 1.

**ἐξήρετμος,** ον, *of six banks of oars,* ἐξηρέτμοις πτέρυξιν ἠγλαϊσμένος, i.e. in command of a ἑξήρης, *Epigr.Gr.*337 (Cyzicus).

**ἐξῃρημένως,** Adv. *transcendentally,* v. ἐξαιρέω.

**ἑξ-ήρης,** ες, *with six banks of oars,* ναῦς Plu.*Cat.Mi.*39. II. Subst. **ἑξήρης** (sc. ναῦς), ἡ, Plb.1.26.11, etc. **-ηρικὸν πλοῖον,** = foreg. II, Id.*Fr.*39.

**ἐξηρώτησα,** aor. 1 of ἐξερωέω (q.v.).

✱ **ἑξῆς,** Ep. **ἑξείης,** Adv., Dor. **ἑξαν** (accent unknown), *IG*12(1). 155.108 (Rhodes, ii B.C.), *SIG*1023.80 (Cos, iii/ii B.C.), al.:—*one after another, in order, in a row,* ἑξῆς εὐνάζοντο Od.4.449; ἑξῆς δ' ἑζόμενοι ib.580 (elsewh. Hom. uses the form ἑξείης, Il.6.241, Od.4.408); πάντας ἑ. .. κτείνοντες Th.7.29, cf. E.*Fr.*657.2; τὰ ἑ. v.l. in Arist. *Cael.*310ᵇ12. b. Math., ἑ. ἀνάλογον in *continued* proportion, Euc. 8.1, al.; οἱ ἑ. ἀριθμοί *successive* numbers, Archim.*Spir.Praef.*; γραμμαὶ ἑ. κείμεναι placed *in order,* ib.11; τούτου ἑ. γινομένου if this be done *continually,* Id.*Sph.Cyl.*1.11. 2. ἑ. διεξελθεῖν, λέγειν, *in a regular, consequential manner,* Pl.*Plt.*257b, 286c; τοῦ ἑ. ἕνεκα περαίνεσθαι τὸν λόγον Id.*Grg.*454c; ὁ ἑ. λόγος the *following* argument, Id.*Ti.*20b; ἐν ἅπασι τούτοις ἑ. Longin.9.14, cf. 4.4. 3. Gramm., τὸ ἑ. *grammatical sequence,* opp. ὑπερβατόν, A.D.*Pron.*41.3, al.; καὶ τὰ ἑ., Lat. *et cetera, PTeb.*319.34 (iii A.D.), etc. 4. of Time, *thereafter, next,* A.*Fr.*475, Ar.*Ec.*638; τὸν ἑ. χρόνον Pl.*Plt.*271b; ἡ ἑ. ἡμέρα *Ev.Luc.* 9.37; ἐν τῷ (v.l. τῇ) ἑ. *next day,* ib.7.11; εἰς τὸ ἑ. for the *future, POxy.*474.28 (ii A.D.), etc. b. of Place, *next,* E.*IA*249, Arist. *Mu.*392ᵃ26. II. c. gen., *next to,* τινός Ar.*Ra.*765; τὰ τούτων ἑ. Pl.*R.*390a; τούτων ἑ. *next after..,* D.18.102; of logical connexion, Pl.*Phlb.*42c: c. dat., *next to,* Λάχητι..τὴν ἑ. θύραν Ephipp.16; τούτοις ἑ. *next in order to,* Pl.*Cra.*399d, al.; τὸ ἑ. τῇ γεωμετρίᾳ *what comes next to..,* Id.*R.*528a; τὸ ἑ. ἔργον τοῖς Μαραθῶνι *next after,* Id. *Mx.*241a; ἑ. Ἀριστογείτονι *beside* A., Ar.*Lys.*633; παρὰ τὸ ἑ. τῷ νοερῷ ζῴῳ *that which befits..,* M.Ant.4.5; ἐπεχορήγησα αὐτῇ τὰ ἑ. made *suitable* provision for her, *POxy.*282.7 (i A.D.).

**ἐξητασμένως,** Adv., (ἐξετάζω) *after full investigation, deliberately,* M.Ant.1.16, Them.*Or.*16.203c; *with deliberate precision* (in the choice of words), Ph.1.605, al., Aristid.*Or.*45(8).4.

**ἐξητρῐάζω,** *filter*: pf. Pass. ἐξητρίασμαι Hp.ap.Gal.19.98.

**ἐξηττάομαι,** strengthd. for ἡττάομαι, τῆς σπουδῆς Plu.*Alex.*14; διαβολῶν Arr.*An.*7.12.5; ὑπὸ κακοῦ ib.4.9.1; ὑπὸ λόγου Ph.1.179.

**ἐξηττημένη,** pf. part. Pass., *sifted,* Antiph.34.5: pres. not found, cf. διαττάω: fort. ἐξεττημένη.

✱ **ἐξηχ-ευη,** *stupes, Gloss.* (leg. -εύη). **-έω,** *sound forth,* Lxx *Jl.* 3(4).14, Nech.ap.Vett.Val.241.17: c. acc. cogn., τὸ κύκνειον ἐξηχεῖν *sound forth* the swan's song, i.e. *give vent to* dying prayers, Plb.30. 4.7, cf. Ph.2.24:—Pass., Id.2.107, 1*Ep.Thess.*1.8, Hsch., etc. II. *utter senseless sounds,* of idiots, Polem.*Phgn.*51. **-ησις,** εως, ἡ, *unpleasant sound,* Ael.Dion.*Fr.*298. 2. *mode of utterance, PMag. Par.*1.923. **-ία,** ἡ, *stupidity, nonsense,* Porph.*Chr.*35, Hsch. s.v. ἀφραδίῃσι. **-ος,** ον, *rudely sounding*: hence, *absurd, stupid,* Porph.*Chr.*35, *EM*696.39.

**ἐξῐάλλω,** = ἐκβάλλω, Suid.

**ἐξῐ-άομαι,** fut. -άσομαι, Ion. -ήσομαι:—*cure thoroughly,* Hdt.3. 132, 134, E.*Rh.*872, Ph.1.541; φόβους Pl.*Lg.*933c; πείνην ἢ δίψαν Id.*Phlb.*54e; *make full amends for,* τὴν βλάβην Id.*Lg.*879a; πόλεως ἄλωσιν E.*El.*1024. **-ᾱτέον,** *one must heal,* τὴν ἕλκωσιν Aët.16. 36. **-ατρός·** ἐκθυτικός, Hsch.

✱ **ἐξῐδῐ-άζομαι,** Med., *appropriate to oneself,* Diph.42, *SIG*1106.46 (Cos), *Klio*16.163 (Delph.), *Sammelb.*4638.10, D.S.1.23, etc. 2. *win over,* Plb.8.25.7, al. 3. *receive for one's own use,* παρά τινος *PRein.*14.18 (ii B.C.). **-ασμός,** ὁ, *winning over,* τῶν πόλεων Plb. 22.6.1; *appropriation,* Str.17.1.8. ✱ **-όομαι,** = ἐξιδιάζομαι I, Isoc. 12.43, X.*HG*2.4.8.

**ἐξῐδῐοποι-έομαι,** = ἐξιδιάζομαι, D.S.5.57, Ath.2.50f, Aesop.12, A.D.*Synt.*199.6. **-ησις,** εως, ἡ, *appropriation, Gloss.*

**ἐξῐδίω** [δῐ], *exude*: in Ar.*Av.*791 euphem. for τιλάω.

**ἐξιδρόω,** *perspire,* Hp.*Vict.*4.89, D.S.4.78, Dsc.*Eup.*1.97: c. acc. cogn., ὕδωρ ἐ. Alex.Aphr.*Pr.*1.119.

**ἐξιδρύω,** fut. -ύσω [ῡ], *make to sit down,* S.*OC*11:—Med., βίοτον ἐξιδρυσάμην *I have settled,* E.*Fr.*884.

**ἐξίδρωσις,** εως, ἡ, *violent sweat,* Plu.2.949e (pl.), Sor.1.46.

**ἐξιερ-ιστεύω** (fort. -ιερατ-), *vacate a priesthood, IG*12(1).701 (Rhodes, i B.C.). **-όω,** *consecrate,* Hsch.

✱ **ἐξίημι** (v. ἵημι), *send out, let one go out,* ἱππόθεν ἐξέμεναι (Ep. aor. 2 inf. for ἐξεῖναι) Od.11.531; μηδ' ἐξέμεν ἂψ ἐς Ἀχαιούς Il.11.141; ἐπὴν γόου ἐξ ἔρον εἴην *had dismissed, satisfied* it, 24.227; πόθον prob. in Sapph.*Supp.*23.23; [τοὺς ἐπικούρους] ἐξῆκε ἐπὶ τοὺς Πέρσας Hdt.3. 146; ἐ. ἱστίον *let out* the sail, Pi.*P.*1.91; ἐξιέναι πάντα κάλων (v. sub κάλως); ἐ. ἀφρὸν *throw out* or *forth,* E.*Ba.*1122; ἐ. ἐκ τῆς κοιλίης τὴν κεδρίην *take* it *out,* Hdt.2.87; ἐ. τι εἴς τι *discharge* it into.., Pl.*Ti.* 82e. 2. intr., of rivers, *discharge themselves,* ἐς θάλασσαν Hdt. 1.6 (in 3 sg. ἐξίει, cf. ib.180), al., Th.4.103. II. Med., *put off from oneself, get rid of,* freq. in Hom. in the phrase πόσιος καὶ ἐδητύος ἐ. ἔρον ἕντο Il.1.469, al.; ἱμερτῶν ἔργων ἐξ ἔρον ἱέμενος Thgn.1064. 2. *send from oneself, divorce,* τὴν ἔχεις γυναῖκα ἔξεο Hdt.5.39 (ἐκσέο codd.).

**ἐξίθμη** (-ίθνη cod.)· ἔξοδος, Hsch. **ἐξιθυίω·** ἔξω καθίσω, Id.

**ἐξῐθύνω,** *make straight,* στάθμη δόρυ νήϊον Il.15.410; εἰ ἱκανῶς ἐξιθύνεται Hp.*Fract.*3, cf. *Art.*42. 2. *direct aright,* πηδάλιον A.R.1.562.

**ἐξῐκᾰνόω,** *suffice,* τῇ χώρᾳ Procop.*Aed.*4.2.

**ἐξῐκάνω** [ᾱ], *arrive at,* impf. ἐξίκανε [ῑ] Orph.*A.*194; cf. ἐξίκω.

**ἐξῐκετεύω,** *entreat successfully, persuade by entreaty,* S.*OT*760, Parth.17.5, J.*AJ*3.11.3, Polyaen.6.16.5.

**ἐξικμ-άζω,** (ἰκμάς) *send forth moisture, cause to exude,* ἡ θερμότης ἐ. τὸ ὑγρὸν ἐκ τοῦ γεώδους Arist.*GA*718ᵇ19; τὸ σπέρμα ib.727ᵇ24, cf. *HA*583ᵃ11:—Pass., *to be exuded* or *evaporated,* Id.*Mete.*385ᵇ8, *Sens.* 443ᵃ14. 2. intr. in Act., = Pass., Id.*Mete.*384ᵇ9, *Pr.*930ᵇ34. II. *deprive of moisture, suck dry,* Id.*HA*594ᵃ13; ἐ. τὴν ὑγρότητα Thphr. *CP*4.8.4 (cod. Urb.):—Pass., ἐξικμασμένη τροφή *digested,* Pl.*Ti.*33c, Arist.*PA*675ᵇ31; τὰ παλαιὰ σπέρματα ἐξίκμασται τὴν δύναμιν Id.*Pr.* 924ᵇ30; *lose all moisture,* Thphr.*HP*5.7.4, 7.5.1; of athletes, τοῦ περιττοῦ -άζεσθαι Philostr.*Gym.*58. III. in E.*Andr.*398, ἐξικμάζω seems to be corrupt (perh. for ἐξιχμάζω). **-ᾰσις,** εως, ἡ, *drying,* Gal.17(2).496. **-αστέος,** α, ον, *that must have moisture removed,* c. acc., -τέοι τοὺς ἱδρῶτας Philostr.*Gym.*52. **-αστικός,** ή, όν, = ἀναποτικός, *sucking up,* τῶν ὑγρῶν Procl.*Par.Ptol.*27.

✱ **ἐξικνέομαι,** poet. aor. ἐξικόμην Il.9.479, augm. ἐξίκοντο [ῑ] Sapph. 1.13:—*reach, arrive at* a place, Hom. always in aor. and mostly c. acc. loci, ἄλλων ἐξίκετο δῆμον Il.24.481, etc.; Φθίην δ' ἐξικόμην ἐριβώλακα .. ἐς Πηλῆα ἄνακτα 9.479; δεῦρο Simon.171, cf. Pi.*P.*3.76, A.*Pr.*810: abs., Sapph. l.c.: with Preps., ἐ. ἐς βυσσὸν Hdt.2.28; ἐς ἥβην S. *Fr.*583.6; ἐπ' ὄρος A.*Ag.*303; πρὸς πεδία Id.*Pr.*792; μέχρι γάμου καὶ γενεᾶς Plu.2.149d. II. *come to* as a suppliant, c. acc. pers., Od. 13.206, 20.223, Pi.*P.*11.35; πρός τινα Ant.Lib.38.2. 2. c. acc. rei, *arrive at, reach* an object, σοφίας ἄωτον ἄκρον Pi.*I.*7(6).19; ἔργῳ οὐδὲ τἀναγκαῖα ἐ. *complete, accomplish,* Th.1.70; τεθνηκόσιν γὰρ ἔλεγεν, οἷς οὐδὲ τρὶς λέγοντες ἐξικνούμεθα (by attract. for οὓς) Ar.*Ra.*1176, cf. Plu.2.347e: c. gen., E.*El.*612; ἀλλήλων X.*HG*7.5.17; also πρός τι Plb.1.3.10, etc. 3. abs., *reach* to a distance, of an arrow, ὅσον τόξευμα ἐξικνέεται Hdt.4.139; of sight, ἐπὶ πολλὰ στάδια ἐ. X.*Mem.* 1.4.17, cf. 2.3.19, E.*Ba.*1060; of mental operations, ὅσον δυνατός εἰμι ⟨ἐπὶ⟩ μακρότατον ἐξικέσθαι ἀκοῇ so far as I can *get* by inquiry, Hdt. 1.171; ἐπ' ὅσον μακρότατον ἱστορεῦντα ἦν ἐξικέσθαι Id.2.34, cf. 4.16, 192; ἐ. φρονήσει ἐπ' ἀμφότερα Pl.*Hp.Ma.*281d; περαιτέρω τῆς χρείας ἐ. τῇ θεωρίᾳ Plu.*Sol.*3. b. *suffice,* of persons, πρὸς τὸν προκείμενον ἄεθλον Hdt.4.10; ἐπί τι Plu.*Pomp.*39; of things, ἂν ἐξικνῆται τὰ ἡμέτερα χρήματα Pl.*Prt.*311d: prov., ἂν μὴ λεοντῇ γ' ἐξίκητ', ἀλωπεκῆν πρόσαψον *Com.Adesp.*49 D.

**ἐξικόρ·** ἐκτικός, Hsch.

**ἐξίκω** [ῑ], = ἐξικάνω, Orph.*A.*392.

**ἐξῐλᾰρόω,** *cheer,* Ath.10.420e.

**ἐξῐλ-ᾰσις** [ῐ], εως, ἡ, *propitiation, atonement,* Lxx *Nu.*29.11, D.L. 1.110, Iamb.*Myst.*1.13 (pl.). **-άσκομαι,** fut. -άσομαι [ᾰ], *propitiate,* Δία Orac.ap.Hdt.7.141; Ἀπόλλωνα X.*Cyr.*7.2.19; τὴν θεὸν Men.544.6, cf. J.*AJ*12.2.14; τὴν ὀργήν τινος Plb.1.68.4; τὸ μήνιμα Plu.2.149d. 2. *atone for,* ἁμαρτίαν *IG*2².1365, 1366:—Pass., τὸ ἀπολύσεις ἐξιλασθὲν *that which is atoned for* by.., Pl.*Lg.*862c. 3. abs., *make atonement,* περὶ τῶν ψυχῶν, περὶ τῆς ἁμαρτίας, Lxx *Ex.*30. 15, 32.30; ὑπὲρ τοῦ οἴκου Ἰσραήλ ib.*Ez.*45.17. [ῑ in Orac.ap.Hdt. l.c.] **-ασμα,** ατος, τό, *ransom, propitiatory offering,* Lxx 1*Ki.*12. 3, *Ps.*48(49).8. **-ασμός,** ὁ, = ἐξίλασις, ib.*Le.*23.27, al., Procl.*Par. Ptol.*24. **-αστήριος,** ον, *propitiatory,* in neut. pl., Sch.A.R.2. 485. **-αστικός,** ή, όν, = foreg., Corn.*ND*32 (v.l. -κῶς), Sch.A. *Th.*268. **-εόω,** *appease,* Hld.4.15, 1.8 (Pass.):—Med., Str.4.4. 6 (s.v.l.), Onos.5 tit., Hermog.*Stat.*3, Zen.4.93, Jul.*Or.*2.68b. – Cf. ἐξείλλω 3. **-έωμα,** ατος, τό, = ἐξίλασμα, Hsch. s.v. ἀποτροπίασμα (ἐξιλέωσμα cod.). **-έωσις,** εως, ἡ, = ἐξίλασις, Sch.A.*Pers.*229, *Gloss.* **-εωτός,** ή, όν, *appeasable,* ib.

**ἐξίλλω,** v. ἐξείλλω. **ἐξίμεναι,** poet. inf. of ἔξειμι (A).

**ἐξῐν-ιάζω,** (ἶνες) *take out the fibres from,* καλάμους *Peripl.M.Rubr.* 65:—Pass., Ath.9.406a. **-ίζω,** = foreg. (wh. shd. perh. be restored), Ruf.ap.Orib.8.47.4, Gal.12.672, al. **-όω,** *strip of fibre and sinew, destroy,* Lyc.841 (Pass.); but ἐξινώμενος (from ἐξινάω), = ἐκκενούμενος.., Hsch.; = κεκαθαρμένος, dub. in *Com.Adesp.*1004.

**ἐξιονθίζω,** (ἴονθος), τρίχα *shoot out* hair, S.*Fr.*729.

**ἐξῐόω,** (ἰός) *clean from rust,* Arr.*Epict.*4.11.13, *PLeid.X.*6:—Pass., *to be freed from rust,* ib.10; *from poison,* Aët.8.16. II. *make poisonous,* τοὺς χυμοὺς Herod.Med. in *Rh.Mus.*58.104.

**ἐξιπόω,** *press* or *squeeze out,* Hp.*Art.*50 (Pass.); ἰὸν Aët.15.14. 2.

*dry thoroughly*, ἥλιος ὄρος ἐ. Aristid.*Or.*36(48).69 :—Pass., prob. l. in Ps.-Democr.Alch.p.44 B. II. *press heavily upon*, Ar.*Lys.*291.

**ἐξιππ-άζομαι**, *ride out* or *away*, Lxx *Hb.*1.8, J.*AJ*9.3.2. **-εύω**, = foreg., Plu.*Arat.*42 ; πρός τινας D.S.17.78 ; ἔς τινας App.*Hann.* 35.

**ἔξιππον**, τό, *six-horsed chariot*, *Com.Adesp.*1281 (pl.), Plb.30.25.11 (pl.), *Gloss.*

**ἐξίπταμαι**, later form of ἐκπέτομαι, Arist.*Fr.*346, Lxx *Pr.*7.10, Plu.2.90c, Jul.*Or.*2.101a.

**ἐξῑπωτικός**, ή, όν, *fit for squeezing out, expressive*, φάρμακα Gal.13. 993, cf. Act.12.31.

**ἕξις**, εως, ἡ, (ἔχω) : I. (ἔχω trans.) *having, being in possession of, possession*, ἐπιστήμης ἕ., opp. κτῆσις, Pl.*Tht.*197b ; νοῦ Id.*Cra.* 414b ; ἡ τῶν ὅπλων Id.*Lg.*625c, cf. *R.*433e, *Sph.*247a, al., Arist. *Metaph.*1022$^b$4 ; opp. στέρησις, ib.1055$^b$13, S.E.*P.*3.49. 2. in surgery, *posture*, Hp.*Off.*3 ; ἕ. ἢ θέσις ib.15. II. (ἔχω intr.) *a being in a certain state, a permanent condition* as produced by practice (πρᾶξις), diff. from σχέσις (which is alterable) (v. infr.): 1. *state* or *habit* of body, Id.*Aph.*2.34, cf. Pl.*Tht.*153b ; ἕ. ὑγιεινή (so also X.*Mem.*1.2.4), opp. διάθεσις ἀθλητική, Hp.*Alim.*34 ; σχέσις καὶ ἕ. καὶ ἡλικίη Id.*Mochl.*41 ; ἡ φύσις καὶ ἡ ἕ. Id.*Acut.*43 : pl., Thphr. *Sens.*69 : generally, *condition*, ἐν ἕξει τοῦ δρᾶν D.H.*Comp.*25 ; ἕ. λεπτὴ κατὰ τοῦτο τὸ μέρος Hp.*Art.*12 ; τῷ θερμὴν ἕ. ἔχοντι Polystr. p.26 W. ; *outward appearance*, ἡ ἕ. τοῦ σώματος κρείσσων Lxx *Da.* 1.15, cf. 1*Ki.*16.7, Sm.*La.*4.7 ; *habit* of a vine, Thphr.*CP*3.14.5 ; of material objects, ὑπὸ μιᾶς ἕξεως συνέχεσθαι S.E.*M.*7.102, cf. Ph.2. 511, *Stoic.*2.124, al. b. Medic., *the system*, Ath.2.45e, Mnesith. ib.54b, Paul.Aeg.3.59. 2. *state* or *habit of mind*, ἕ. κακίης Democr. 184 ; τὰς φύσεις τε καὶ ἕξεις τῶν ψυχῶν Pl.*Lg.*650b, etc. ; ἡ ἐν τῇ ψυχῇ ἕ., opp. ἡ τῶν σωμάτων ἕ., Id.*Tht.* l. c. ; πονηρᾶς ψυχῆς ἕξει ib.167b ; λαμβάνειν ἕξιν τιμιωτέραν Id.*R.*591b. b. esp. *acquired habit*, opp. ἐνέργεια, Arist.*EN*1098$^b$33, al. 3. *trained habit, skill*, Pl.*Phdr.* 268e, Arist.*Pr.*955$^b$1, Plb.10.47.7, D.S.2.29 ; τέχνη defined as ἕ. ἢ διάθεσις ἀπὸ παρατηρήσεως Phld.*Rh.*1.69 S. ; ἄκρα ἕ. D.H.*Comp.*11 : c. gen., τὴν τῶν Ἰουδαϊκῶν γραμμάτων ἕξιν Aristeas 121 ; ἕ. πολιτικῶν λόγων Phld.*Rh.*2.35 S. (Almost confined to Prose, but cf. Orph.*A.* 391.)

**ἐξῐσ-άζω**, *make equal*, τοῖς ἐνθυμήμασι τὴν λέξιν Steph. *in Hp.*1.57 D. ; σεαυτὸν τῷ θεῷ *Corp.Herm.*11.20, cf. Sch.Il.13.745 :—Med., *make oneself equal*, Lxx *Si.*35(32).9(13).—Pass., *to be equal*, τῇ Ἰνδικῇ Str.2.1.31. II. Act. intr., *to be equal*, Id.17.3.1, Hermog.*Stat.*1, Olymp. *in Mete.*158.15. 2. *to be coextensive*, Ascl. *in Metaph.*381. 31, Procl. *in Prm.*p.857 S., Dam.*Pr.*144 ; ταῦτα ἀλλήλοις ἐξισάζει Procl. *in R.*1.29 K. **-ασμός**, ὁ, *equalization*, Simp. *in Epict.*p.8 D., *in Cael.*162.28. ⊛ **-όω**, *make equal* or *even, bring to a level with*, τινί τινα S.*OT*425 ; μηδ' ἐξισώσῃς τάσδε τοῖς ἐμοῖς κακοῖς ib.1507 ; ἐ. τοῖς μεγίστοις ἐγκλήμασι τὸ πρᾶγμα Antipho 4.2.1 ; ἐ. ζυγά *bring* the teams *abreast*, S.*El.*738 :—Med., *make oneself equal*, δράκοντι μῆκος ἐξισουμένην σαύραν Babr.41.2 :—Pass., *to be* or *become equal*, c. dat., Hdt. 2.34, 6.111, Pl.*R.*563a, etc. ; *to be reduced to a level with*, τινί Hdt.8. 13 ; *to be a match for, rival*, Th.2.97, D.S.2.52 ; πρός τινα Plu.*Agis* 7. 2. *put on a level*, τοὺς πολίτας Ar.*Ra.*688, cf. Isoc.4.91, Arist. *Mu.*397$^a$8 (Pass.). 3. Pass., φύλοπις οὐκέτ' ἐξισοῦται is *levelled, equalized*, i. e. *resolved in harmony*, S.*El.*1072 (lyr.) ; lit., ἐξισωθέντος τοῦ μέχρι τῶν τειχῶν διαστήματος *levelled*, J.*BJ*5.3.5. II. intr., *to be equal* or *like*, μητρὶ δ' οὐδὲν ἐξισοῖ *acts* in no way *like* a mother, S. *El.*1194 ; ἐ. τοῖς ἄλλοις Th.6.87 ; τισί *make* a line of battle *equal* to the enemy's, Id.5.71.

**ἐξιστάνω**, later form of ἐξίστημι, Lxx 3*Ma.*1.25, Dsc.4.73 :—also **ἐξιστάω**, *Act.Ap.*8.9.

⊛ **ἐξίστημι**, A. causal in pres., impf., fut., aor. 1 :—*displace* : hence, *change, alter utterly*, τὰν φύσιν Ti.Locr.100c, Arist.*EN*1119$^a$ 23, cf. Plot.6.2.7 ; τὴν πολιτείαν Plu.*Cic.*10 ; ἐ. τῆς ποιότητος τὸν οἶνον Id.2.702a. 2. metaph., ἐξιστάναι τινὰ φρενῶν *drive* one *out of* his senses, E.*Ba.*850 ; νοῦ οἶνος ἐξέστησέ με E.*Fr.*265 ; τοῦ φρονεῖν X.*Mem.*1.3.12 ; ταῦτα κινεῖ, ταῦτα ἐξίστησιν ἀνθρώπους αὐτῶν D. 21.72 ; simply ἐ. τινά *drive* one *out of his senses, confound, amaze*, Hp.*Coac.*429 ; ἐξιστάντα καὶ φοβοῦντα τοὺς ἀνθρώπους Muson.*Fr.*8 p.35 H. ; ἐξίστησι *diverts the attention*, Arist.*Rh.*1408$^b$23 ; *excite*, ib. 36, *Ev.Luc.*24.22 ; τὸν λογισμόν, τὴν διάνοιαν, Plu.*Sol.*21, *Crass.*23 ; also ἐ. τινὰ τῶν λογισμῶν Id.*Fab.*5 ; εἰς ἀπάθειαν ἐ. τὴν ψυχήν Id.*Publ.* 6. 3. *get rid of, dispose of the claims* of a person, *Sammelb.*5246. 14 (i B. C.), etc. 4. ἐξεστᾰκότα (ἐξεστηκότα cod.)· εἰς δίκην κεκλη-κότα, Hsch.

B. intr. in Pass. and Med., with aor. 2, pf., and plpf. Act. : 1. of Place, *arise out of, become separated*, ἐξ.. ἵστατο Νεῖκος Emp.36, cf. 35.10 ; *stand aside from*, ἐκστάντες τῆς ὁδοῦ *out of* the way, Hdt.3.76 ; ἐκ τοῦ μέσου X.*An.*1.5.14 ; θάκων καὶ ὁδῶν ἐ. [τινί] *stand out of* the way *for* him, *make way for* him, Id.*Smp.*4.31 ; ἐκστῆναί τινι S.*Ph.*1053, *Aj.* 672, Ar.*Ra.*354, etc. : abs., in same sense, E.*IT*1229 (troch.), Ar. *Ach.*617, etc. : metaph., ἐξ ἕδρας σοι πλόκαμος ἐξέστηχ' *is displaced, disordered*, E.*Ba.*928 ; οὐδὲ μένει νοῦς.. ἀλλ' ἐξίσταται S.*Ant.*564. 2. c. acc., *shrink from, shun*, νιν οὐκ ἂν ἐξέστην ὄκνῳ Id.*Aj.*82 ; οὐδέν' ἐξίσταμαι D.18.319 ; οὐδένα πώποτε κίνδυνον ἐξέστησαν Id.20.10. 3. *go out of joint*, ἐ. ἰσχίον Hp.*Aph.*6.59, cf. *Fract.*14, 6. II. c. gen. rei, *retire from, give up possession of*, τῆς ἀρχῆς Th.2.63, 4.28 ; ἐκστῆναι τῆς οὐσίας, ἁπάντων τῶν ὄντων, become bankrupt, Antipho 2.2.9, D.36.50 ; τῶν ὑπαρχόντων *BGU*473.11 (ii A. D.). 2. *cease from, abandon*, τῆς φιλίας, τῶν μαθημάτων, Lys.8.18, X.*Cyr.*3.3.54 ; τῶν σπουδασμάτων Pl.*Phdr.*249c, etc. ; οἱ τῶν πολιτικῶν ἐξεστηκότες Isoc. 4.171 ; τῆς ὑποθέσεως D.10.46 ; τῶν πεπραγμένων, i. e. *disown* them, Id.19.72 ; ἐ. τινὸς εἴς τι Pl.*Lg.*907d ; also ἐ. ἄθλου τινί, στρατηγίας τινί, *abandon* it in his favour, Nic.Dam.73 J., Plu.*Nic.*7 ; τῆς Σικελίας τινι Id.*Pomp.*10. 3. ἐκστῆναι πατρός *lose* one's father, *give* him *up*, Ar.*V.*477 ; καρδίας ἐξίσταμαι τὸ δρᾶν I *depart from* my heart's purpose, S.*Ant.*1105 ; esp. φρενῶν ἐκστῆναι *lose* one's senses, E.*Or.* 1021, etc. ; διὰ τὸ γῆρας τοῦ φρονεῖν Isoc.5.18 ; ἐμαυτοῦ Aeschin.2.4, Men.*Sam.*276 ; ψυχὴ ἐξεστηκυῖα τῶν λογισμῶν Plb.32.15.8 : abs., *to be out of one's wits, be distraught*, ἐ. μελαγχολικῶς Hp.*Prorrh.*1.18, cf. Men.*Sam.*64, etc. ; ἐξέστην ἰδών Philippid.27 ; ἐ. ὑπὸ γήρως *Com. Adesp.*860 ; ταῖς διανοίαις Vett.Val.70.25 ; ἐξίστασθαι καὶ μαίνεσθαι πρὸς τὴν ὀσμήν Arist.*HA*577$^a$12 ; of anger, εὐθέως ἐξεστησόμενος Phld. *Ir.*p.78 W. ; *to be astonished, amazed*, *Ev.Matt.*12.23, *Ev.Marc.*2.12, etc. ; *lose consciousness*, of Sisera, Lxx *Jd.*4.21. 4. ἐξίστασθαι τῆς αὑτοῦ ἰδέας *depart from, degenerate from* one's own nature, Pl.*R.*380d ; ἐκ τῆς αὑτοῦ φύσεως Arist.*HA*488$^b$19 ; [δημοκρατία] ἐξεστηκυῖα τῆς βελτίστης τάξεως Id.*Pol.*1309$^b$32 ; αἱ δημοκρατίαι ἐ. εἰς τὰς ἐναντίας πολιτείας *degenerate* into.., ib.1306$^b$18, cf. *Rh.*1390$^b$28 : abs., ἐ. μὴ μεταφυτευόμενον Thphr.*HP*6.7.6, etc., cf. Plu.2.649e ; χυμὸς ἐξιστάμενος *changing its properties, turning*, Hp.*VM*24 ; οἶνος ἐξεστηκώς or ἐξιστάμενος *changed, sour* wine, D.35.32, Thphr.*CP*6.7.5 ; πρόσωπα ἐξεστηκότα *disfigured* faces, X.*Cyr.*5.2.34. 5. abs., *change one's position, one's opinion*, ἐγὼ μὲν ὁ αὐτός εἰμι καὶ οὐκ ἐξίσταμαι Th.2.61 : opp. ἐμμένειν τῇ δόξῃ, Arist.*EN*1151$^b$4. 6. of language, *to be removed from common usage*, Id.*Rh.*1404$^b$13. III. *stand out, project*, ἐξεστηκός *convex*, opp. κοῖλον, Id.*HA*493$^b$4.

**ἐξίστιον**· ἔχθιστον, Hsch. **ἔξιστον**· ἱερεῖον, Id.

**ἐξιστορέω**, *search out, inquire into*, τι A.*Th.*506, *Ch.*678, E.*Hec.* 744, J.*AJ*3.14.2, Porph.*Abst.*2.49. 2. *inquire of*, τινά τι Hdt.7. 195, E.*Hec.*236 ; ἐ. τινὰ εἰ.. Id.*Or.*289. 3. *roam about*, πόλιν X. Eph.1.12. II. *explain, set forth*, τὴν τοῦ πράγματος διάθεσιν *POxy.* 486.12 (ii A. D.).

**ἐξίστως**, ων, *fringed*, χιτωνίσκος *IG*2$^2$.1514.30, 1516.9 ; cf. ἔξαστις.

**ἐξίσχιος**, ον, *projecting at the hip*, σκέλος Hp.*Art.*58.

**ἐξισχν-αίνω**, strengthd. for ἰσχναίνω, βόας Them.*Or.*1.10a :—Pass., ἐξισχνάνθη τὸ σῶμα D.C.*Fr.*17.11. **-όομαι**, Pass., *dry up*, Hp.*Mul.*1.27 codd. **-ωσις**, εως, ἡ, *thinning, refining*, χαλκοῦ Zos. Alch.p.169 B.

⊛ **ἐξισχύω** [ῡ], *have strength enough, be able*, ὥστε ποιεῖν Str.17.1.3 : c. inf. only, Lxx *Si.*7.6, *Ep.Eph.*3.18, J.*BJ*1.23.2 ; ἐξίσχυσεν τὰ βιβλείδια ἀθετηθῆναι *procured* the rejection of the petition, *POxy.*1120. 7 (iii A. D.) : abs., *prevail*, Str.16.1.15, Jul.*Or.*5.160c ; ἐξισχῦσαι καὶ κρατῆσαι τῶν πολλῶν Plu.2.801e. II. c. gen., τὸ δαιμόνιον παίδων ἐξισχῦον fate *prevailing over* the children, Ael.*VH*6.13, cf. Steph. *in Hp.*1.71 D. III. Med., of flames, *gather force*, Thphr.*Ign.*71.

**ἐξίσχω**, = ἐξέχω, once in Hom., ἐξίσχει κεφαλὰς δεινοῖο βερέθρου *puts forth* her heads *from*.., Od.12.94. II. intr., *stand out, project*, Paus.5.12.1 ; ἐξίσχοντες ὀφθαλμοί *prominent* eyes, Hp.*Prog.*2, cf. Ruf.ap.Orib.45.30.27 ; of bones, Aret.*SA*2.8.

**ἐξίσ-ωσις** [ῐ], εως, ἡ, *equalization*, *CIG*3546.18 (Pergam.) ; κτημάτων Plu.*Cleom.*18 ; πρός τι Id.2.1078a, cf. Aq.*Za.*4.7. 2. = Lat. *peraequatio*, *Cod.Just.*10.16.13 *Intr.* II. *filling up, levelling* of hollow ulcers, Sor.1.122. **-ωτέον**, *one must claim an equal right*, S.*OT*408. **-ωτής**, οῦ, ὁ, *officer* (of the empire) *who apportioned and equalized the taxes* among the payers, Lat. *peraequator*, ἐπόπτης ἢ ἐ. *Cod.Just.*10.16.13 *Intr.* (v A. D.), cf. Ps.-Luc.*Philopatr.*19 ; ἐξισωτής· ἐπόπτης, Suid.

⊛ **ἐξίταλα**· ἀναλώματα, Hsch. ; cf. ἐσσίταλα.

**ἐξιτέον**, *one must go forth*, Artem.3.34.

**ἐξιτηλία**· μωρία, Hsch.

⊛ **ἐξίτηλος** [ῑ], ον, (ἐξιέναι) *going out* : hence, *losing colour, fading, evanescent*, πορφυρίδες ἐξίτηλοι X.*Oec.*10.3 ; of paintings, *faded*, ἐ. ὑπὸ τοῦ χρόνου Paus.10.38.9, cf. Poll.1.44 ; γράμματα Id.5.150. 2. metaph., ἐ. τροφή food *that has lost its properties during assimilation*, Hp.*Alim.*4 ; so of seed sown in alien soil, Pl.*R.*497b ; of a drug or wine *that has lost its power*, Phylarch.10 J., Dsc.5.6 ; ἐ. γενέσθαι, of a family, to become *extinct*, Hdt.5.39 ; οὔπω σφιν ἐ. αἷμα δαιμόνων is not yet *extinct*, A.*Fr.*162.4, cf. Pl.*Criti.*121a ; ἐξιτήλου ἐόντος where *attenuation* takes place, Hp.*Praec.*9 ; of acts, *extinct, obsolete*, τῷ χρόνῳ ἐ. Hdt.*Prooem.*, cf. Isoc.5.60, 7.47, Plu.2.68b, Max.Tyr.16.2, etc. ; τρίχας ἐ. ποιεῖν *eradicate*, Dsc.2.76.19.

**ἐξιτήριος**, ον, *of* or *for departure*, ἐξιτήρια εὐωχεῖσθαι *IG*3.1184.21 (iii A. D.) : **-τήρια**, τά, *day of leaving office*, at Athens, Hsch.

⊛ **ἐξίτης** [ῑ], ου, ὁ, (ἕξ) *the throw of six* on the dice, = Κῷος, *Epigr. Gr.*1038.2 (pl., Attalia), Poll.9.100.

**ἐξῐτ-ητέον**, (ἔξ-ειμι *ibo*) *one must go forth*, X.*Mem.*1.1.14. ⊛ **-τήρια**, τά, = ἐξιτήρια, *IG*2$^2$.1039.57. **-ητός**, όν, = ἐξιτός, οὐδενὶ -τόν Alciphr.3.30 ; ἐξιτητὰ εἶναι ἐπὶ τοὺς πολεμίους Procop.*Goth.*1. 19. **-ός**, ή, όν, *to be come out of*, τοῖς οὐκ ἐξιτόν ἐστι for whom there is no *coming out*, Hes.*Th.*732.

**ἐξίχν-ευσις**, εως, ἡ, *tracking out*, *Gp.*2.6.22, Vett.Val.242.1. II. *reduction* of copper ore, Syn.Alch.p.66 B. **-ευτέον**, *one must track out*, Luc.*Fug.*26, Vett.Val.276.12. II. Adj. **-τέος**, α, ον, Iamb.*Protr.*21.ιζ'. **-ευτής**, οῦ, ὁ, *one who tracks out*, *Gloss.* **-εύω**, *track out*, τινά E.*Ba.*352, 817 ; τὰς βοῦς ὅπῃ βεβᾶσι S.*Ichn.*160 ; τοὺς λανθάνοντας Plu.*Pomp.*27 ; [κύνες] ἐ. τοὺς πολεμίους Polyaen.4.2.16 : metaph., τι A.*Ag.*368 (lyr.) ; τὴν ἀλήθειαν Arg.Men.*Oxy.*1235.49 ; ἐ. Ἑλλάδα γλῶσσαν *'feel for', try to talk* Greek, Tim.*Pers.*161. **-ιάζω**,

= ἐξιχνεύω, Lxx *Jd.*18.2, *Jb.*5.27, 10.6, al. **-ιασμός**, ὁ, = ἐξίχνευσις, ib.*Jd.*5.16 (v.l.), Aq.*Jb.*11.7.

**ἐξιχνοσκοπέω**, *seek by tracking*, ἵππους S.*Tr.*271:—so in Med., τὸν σὸν μόρον διώκων κἀξιχνοσκοπούμενος Id.*Aj.*997.

**ἐξιχωρίζω**, (ἰχώρ) *cleanse from humours*, Suid. (Pass.), prob. in Aët.6.50.

**ἐξίωσις** [ῑ], εως, ἡ, (ἰός) *reduction to metallic state*, χαλκοῦ Syn. Alch.p.66 B., cf. Maria ap.Zos.Alch.p.148 B.

**ἑξκαί-δεκα**, *sixteen*, Hp.*Acut.*(*Sp.*)8, Plu.2.367f: **-δέκᾰτος**, *sixteenth*, Hp.*Epid.*1.26.ε′.

**ἑξκαιδεκά-εδρος** [ᾰ], ον, *with sixteen surfaces*, Ps.-Ptol.*Centil.*222. **-κροτος**, ον, *with sixteen oars*, ναῦς Ael.*Tact.*[4]. **-σύλλᾰβον**, v.l. for ἑκκ., Heph.10.6.

**ἑξκαιπεντηκονταπλάσιος** [πλᾰ], ον, *fifty-six fold*, Plu.2.925c.

**ἑξκαιτεσσᾰρᾰκοντάμετρος** [τᾰ], ον, *of forty-six measures*, περίοδος Sch.Ar.*Pax*974.

**ἕξκλῑνος**, ον, = ἑξάκλινος, *EM*346.14.

**ἑξμέδιμνος**, ον, *holding six medimni*, Ar.*Pax*631.

**ἕξμετρα**· ἑξάμετρα, Hsch.

**ἐξό**, Dor., = ἔξεστι, *An.Ox.*1.160.20.

**ἐξογκ-έω**, (ὄγκος) *form a prominence*, Hp.*Art.*11; *swell*, Aret.*CA* 1.7 bis. **-ος**, ον, *prominent*, ὀφθαλμοί Plu.*Fr.inc.*149, cf. Steph.*in Hp.*1.187 D. **-όω**, *heap up*, σπλῆνας (compresses), Hp.*Art.*14: metaph., μητέρα τάφῳ ἐξογκοῦν *honour* her *by raising* a tomb, E.*Or.* 402, cf. ἐξόγκωμα:—Pass., *to be swelled out*, πάντα ἐξώγκωτο, of Alcmeon with his garments stuffed with gold-dust, Hdt.6.125, cf. Arr. *Tact.*35.4; τραπέζαις ἐξογκοῦσθαι *to be a luxurious liver*, E.*Supp.*864: metaph., *to be puffed up, elated, proud*, πάτρῃ ἐξωγκωμένοι Hdt.6.126; σὺ σός τ' ἀδελφὸς ἐξωγκωμένοι E.*Andr.*703; τὰ ἐξωγκωμένα *full-sailed* prosperity, Id.*IA*921; ὑπὸ φθόνου καὶ λύττης πρὸς τὸν ἐμφύλιον ἐξώγκωτο πόλεμον Eun.*Hist.*p.222 D.:—Med., fut., E.*Hipp.*938: aor., ἐξωγκώσατο Ath.7.290a. **-ῠλόω**, = -ογκόω, Tz.*H.*11.731. **-ωμα**, ατος, τό, *anything raised* or *swollen*, ἐ. λάϊνα cairns, E.*HF*1332; *swelling*, Hp.*Epid.*2.2.24. **-ωσις**, εως, ἡ, *raising, elevation*, Eust. ad D.P.285. **II.** *swelling*, Antyll.ap.Orib.6.1.6, Aret.*CA*1.7; σώματος *corpulence*, Ruf.*Fr.*62: metaph., τῶν μετρίων Phld.*Rh.*1.219 S. (pl.).

**ἐξοδ-άω**, *sell*, E.*Cyc.*267. **II.** ἐξοδῆσαι· ἐξοδεῦσαι, Hsch. ⊛ **-εία**, ἡ, prob. for ἐξοδία, *expedition*, Plb.4.54.3, Str.5.4.11. **II.** ἐ. τῶν ναῶν *procession from* the shrines, *OGI*90.42 (pl., Rosetta, ii B.C.). ⊛ **-εύω**, *march out*, Plb.5.94.7, Lxx 1*Es.*4.23, D.S.19.63, Nic.Dam.92 J., etc.; simply, *depart*, εἰς Τεβτῦνιν *PTeb.*55.3 (ii B.C.); εἰσοδεύειν καὶ ἐ. ingress and *egress*, *CPR*187.13 (ii A.D.). **II.** *depart this life*, Lxx *Jd.*5.27 (Pass.). **-ία**, Ion. -ίη, ἡ, *marching out, expedition*, Hdt.6.56, Lxx *De.*16.3, *Sammelb.*293. **2.** *journey*, *PSI*4.406.27 (iii B.C.). **-ιάζω**, *scatter*, [ὀστᾶ] πρὸς τὸν ἄνεμον Nic.Dam.118 J. **2.** *pay in full, defray, discharge*, τὸ ἀνάλωμα *IG*5(1).1167 (Gythium); τινὶ τὸ διάφορον ib.1390.52 (Andania); τὰ γεγραμμένα τισί *Test.Epict.*7.8, cf. *IG*12(3). 168.7 (Astypalaea):—Pass., Lxx 4*Ki.*12.12(13): metaph. in Act., Gal.*Anim.Pass.*1.2 (dub.). **-ιάριος**, ὁ, at Rome, *actor in the Atellana* (cf. ἐξόδιος II.2), Lyd.*Mag.*1.40. ⊛ **-ιασμός**, ὁ, = ἐξοδία, f.l. for ἐξιδιασμός, Plb.22.6.1. **II.** *payment*, *Sammelb.*4425 vi 1 (ii A.D.), Artem.1.57, etc. **-ιαστής**, οῦ, ὁ, *spendthrift*, Anon.*in Rh.*119. 6. **-ικός**, ή, όν, *belonging to departure*: τὰ ἐ., = ἐξόδιος II.1, Sch. Ar.*V.*270. **II.** = διεξοδικός, θεωρίαι Syrian.*in Metaph.*24.15. Adv. -κῶς *from beginning to end*, D.L.9.64. ⊛ **-ιος**, ον, *of* or *belonging to an exit*, ἐ. νόμοι *finale* of a play, Cratin.276. **II.** as Subst., ἐξόδιον (sc. μέλος), τό, *finale of a tragedy*, Philist.42, Plu.*Alex.*75: metaph., *catastrophe, tragical conclusion*, Id.*Crass.*33; also ἦν ὁ χειμὼν ἐπ' ἐξοδίοις ἤδη Jul.*Or.*1.26b. **2.** Lat. *exodium, after-piece*, Liv.7.2 (pl.), Juv.3.175, Suet.*Tib.*45 (pl.). **3.** among the Jews, *a feast to commemorate the Exodus*, Lxx *Le.*23.36, *De.*16.8. **4.** *gateway*, *POxy.* 243.16 (i A.D., -ωδ- Pap.).

**ἐξοδοιπορέω**, *go out of*, στέγης S.*El.*20.

**ἐξοδοντίζομαι**, *have one's tusks removed*, Sch.Od.18.29.

⊛ **ἔξοδος** (A), ἡ, *going out*, opp. εἴσοδος, S.*Aj.*798, 806, etc.; ἐκ τῆς χώρης Hdt.1.94; ἔστι.. λήθη μνήμης ἔ. Pl.*Phlb.*33e; λήθη ἐπιστήμης ἔ. Id.*Smp.*208a; ἔ. τοῦ βίου *PLond.*1.77.57 (vi A.D.). **2.** *marching out, military expedition*, Hdt.9.19; κοινὰὶ ἔ. ib.26; ἔ. ποιεῖσθαι Th. 3.5, etc., cf. Ar.*Nu.*579; τὴν ἐπὶ θανάτῳ ἔ. ποιεῖσθαι, of Leonidas, Hdt.7.223; ἔ. ἐξελθεῖν X.*HG*1.2.17; ἐξόδους ἕρπειν κενάς S.*Aj.*287; τὴν ἐπ' Ὠρεὸν ἔ. D.18.79; ἔ. πεζαί ib.100 (s.v.l.). **3.** *procession*, Hdt.3.14; esp. of women of rank with their suite, ἔ. γυναικεῖαι Pl. *Lg.*784d, cf. Thphr.*Char.*22.10; ἐξόδους λαμπρὰς ἐξιοῦσαν D.48.55, cf. Lex Solonis ap.Plu.*Sol.*21. **4.** *divorce*, *BGU*1105.24 (i B.C.). **II.** *way out, outlet*, διὰ τῶν στεγέων Hdt.2.148 (pl.), cf. Th.1.106, 2.4 (sg.); πυλῶν ἐπ' ἐξόδοις A.*Th.*33, cf. 58, 285; πρὸς θυρῶνος ἐξόδοις S.*El.*328; εἴσοδοι καὶ ἔ. entrances and *exits*, *POxy.*241.20 (i A.D.); of a river, ἔ. ἐς θάλασσαν Hdt.7.130; ἡ Ἀρκαδία οὐκ ἔχει ἐξόδους τοῖς ὕδασιν εἰς θάλατταν Arist.*Pr.*947ᵃ19. **b.** esp. of the Jewish *Exodus*, Lxx *Ex.* tit., etc. **2.** *way out* of a difficulty, Pl.*R.*453e. **3.** of *orifices* in the body, ἡ ἔ. τοῦ περιττώματος, of the vent or anus, Arist.*PA* 675ᵇ9; τῆς τροφῆς Id.*HA*507ᵃ32, cf. 532ᵇ6; so of other *orifices* in the body, ib.511ᵃ27, etc. **4.** *delivery*, ἡ τοῦ ἐμβρύου ἔ. Id.*GA*777ᵃ 27, cf. 752ᵇ12; πρὸς ἔξοδον ἔχειν Lyd.*Ost.*44. **5.** *emission* of semen, Arist.*HA*586ᵃ15, al.; κοιλίης ἔξοδοι *discharges* from the bowel, Aret. *SD*2.3. **III.** *end, close*, ἐπ' ἐξόδῳ εἶναι (of a truce) Th.5.14; ἐπ' ἐ. τῆς ἀρχῆς X.*HG*5.4.4; ἐπ' ἐ. (-ου vulg.) τοῦ ζῆν J.*AJ*4.8.2; ἔ. τοῦ βίου *PLond.*1.77.57: abs., *departure, death*, *Ev.Luc.*9.31, 2*Ep.Pet.* 1.15, Arr.*Epict.*4.4.38. **2.** *end, issue* of an argument, Pl.*Prt.* 361a. **b.** *decision* of a court, *BGU*168.15 (ii A.D.). **3.** *end of a tragedy*, i.e. all that follows the last choral ode, Arist.*Po.*1452ᵇ21; ἔξοδον αὐλεῖν play the chorus *off the stage* (their exit being led by an αὐλητής), Ar.*V.*582, cf. Sch. **IV.** *outgoing, payment of money*, *IG*14.422 (Tauromenium), 5(1).1390.50 (Andania, i B.C.), Plb.6.13. 2; opp. εἴσοδος, *Test.Epict.*6.34: pl., D.H.10.30. **V.** *street*, Lxx 2*Ki.*22.43.

**ἔξοδος** (B), ον, *promoting the passage*, λίθων Aret.*CD*2.3.

**ἐξοδῡνάω**, strengthd. for ὀδυνάω, E.*Cyc.*661 (Pass.).

**ἐξόζω**, intr., *smell*, κακὸν ἐξόσδειν (Dor.) *smell* foully, Theoc.20.10, cf. Gal.7.76, al., Artem.5.33. **II.** c. gen., *smell* of a thing, σησάμου Thphr.*Od.*20. **2.** ἐ. τῶν ἄλλων *smells stronger than*.., ib.47.

⊛ **ἐξόθεν**, Adv. for ἐξ οὗ (sc. χρόνου), *since when*, Nic.*Th.*318.

⊛ **ἔξοθεν**, = ἔξωθεν (cf. ἔνδοθεν), Stesich.81, Ibyc.30 Diehl, *Foed.Delph. Pell.*2 A 14, *PCair.Zen.*21.28, 42 (iii B.C.).

**ἔξοι**, Dor. for ἔξω (cf. ἔνδοι), τᾶς πόλεως *SIG*527.67 (Crete, iii B.C.), cf. *Schwyzer* 176 (ibid.), Eust.140.15.

**ἐξοίγνῡμι**, *open, cut open*, Hermipp.30 (Pass.):—also **-οίγω** Hp. *Loc.Hom.*25 (Act. and Pass.).

**ἔξοιδα**, pf. in pres. sense, plpf. ἐξῄδη as impf., S.*Ant.*460, dub. in *Tr.*988 (lyr.): Ep. inf. ἐξίδμεναι A.R.3.332:—*know thoroughly, know well*, S.*OT*129, E.*Ph.*95, etc.: with part. agreeing with the subject, ἔξοιδ' ἔχουσα S.*Tr.*5; ἐ. ἀνὴρ ὢν Id.*OC*567; with the object, ἐ. σε οὐ ψιλὸν ἥκοντα ib.1028, cf. *Ph.*79, 407; ὑφ' ἡμῶν οὐδὲν ἐξειδὼς *having learnt*, Id.*OT*37: c. gen., ὧν γ' ἂν ἐξειδὼς κυρῶ, as if it were an Adj., Id.*Tr.*399: abs., Id.*El.*222 (lyr.), etc.

**ἐξοιδ-αίνω**, = sq., Aret.*CA*1.1: metaph., Porph.*Marc.*7. **-έω**, *swell* or *be swollen up*, πληγαῖς πρόσωπον.. ἐξῳδηκότα E.*Cyc.*227; νεκρὸς ἐξῳδηκώς Luc.*DMort.*14.5, cf. Aristid.*Or.*24(44).44: metaph., *swell beyond its proper size*, of a body in the state, Plb.6.18.7. **-ησις**, εως, ἡ, *swelling*, Herod.Med. in *Rh.Mus.*58.86, Gal.12.875. ⊛ **-ίσκομαι**, Pass., = ἐξοιδέω, Hp.*Morb.*2.57, Gal.6.790.

**ἐξοικ-ειόω**, *appropriate, assimilate*, μένε μέχρι -ειώσῃς σεαυτῷ καὶ ταῦτα, ὡς ὁ ἐρρωμένος στόμαχος πάντα -εἰοῖ M.Ant.10.31, cf. Sor.1.46 (Pass.):—Med., *appropriate*, χώραν Str.4.1.8; *conciliate, win over*, Id.5.4.12; ἀνθρώπους μεταδόσει Id.2.3.4, cf. J.*BJ*1.8.9; ὄχλον εἴς τι Ph.2.529. **2.** Pass., ἐξοικειοῦσθαί τινι *adapt oneself to* one, Plu. 2.649e. **II.** *reduce to its proper nature*, Gal.14.298. **-είωσις**, εως, ἡ, = Lat. *emancipatio*, *Gloss.* **-έω**, *emigrate, remove*, εἰς τὴν ὑπερορίαν Lys.31.9, cf. Hyp.*Ath.*29; Μέγαράδε D.29.3, cf. *PLond.*2. 391.17 (v A.D.): abs., Arist.*Ath.*39.1. **II.** Pass., *to be completely inhabited*, Th.2.17. **-ήσιμος**, ον, *habitable, inhabited*, S. *OC*27. **-ησις**, εως, ἡ, *emigration, deportation*, Pl.*Lg.*704c, 850b, Arist.*Ath.*39.4, 40.4. **-ίζω**, *remove* one *from his home, eject, banish*, Th.1.114, 6.76; ἐξῴκισέν [με] γάμος οἴκων E.*Hec.*948 (lyr.); τινὰς εἰς Ῥώμην Plu.*Rom.*24; *give notice to quit*, *BGU*1116.18 (i B.C.); ἐ. χρυσὸν τῆς Σπάρτης Plu.*Comp.Arist.Cat.*3:—Pass. and Med., *go from home, emigrate*, φροῦδοι.. εἰσιν ἐξῳκισμένοι Ar.*Pax*197; ἐξῳκίσαντο ib.203; *quit a house* or *shop*, opp. εἰσοικ-, Aeschin.1.124; *to be deported*, εἰς ἄλλην χώραν Pl.*Lg.*929a; τὸν πόλεμον τῆς Ἑλλάδος -ισάμενον Plu.*Ages.*15: metaph., ἡ ἀλήθεια τοῦ νόμου διὰ τὸν φόβον ἐξῳκίσθη *was banished*, cj. in Gorg.*Hel.*16. **II.** *dispeople, empty*, Λῆμνον ἀρσένων ἐξῴκισαν E.*Hec.*887; *lay waste*, πόλεις D.H.5.77:—Med., Plu.*Comp.Ages.Pomp.*3. **-ισμός**, ὁ, *expulsion of inhabitants*, Sm.*Ez.*3.11, dub. l. in Ph.2.526. **-ιστής**, οῦ, ὁ, *one who expels*, δαίμονες Charond.ap.Stob.4.2.24. **-ιστος**, ον, *expelled from home*, Ps.-Callisth.2.21.

**ἐξοικοδομ-έω**, *build*, Hdt.2.176, 5.62; *make a building good*, *IG* 2².463.48: metaph., τέχνην μεγάλην ἐ. Pherecr.94:—Med., Plb.1. 48.11:—Pass., ἐξῳκοδόμηταί σοι τὸ τεῖχος *is finished*, Ar.*Av.*1124. **2.** ἐ. κρημνὸν *build up a road along* it, Plb.3.55.6. **II.** *unbuild, lay open*, τὰς πύλας D.S.11.21, cf. Plu.*Dio*50. **-ησις**, εως, ἡ, *building up*, τειχῶν J.*AJ*19.7.2. **-ητον**, τό, *tomb-chamber*, *IGRom.*4. 798 (Apamea).

**ἐξοικονομ-έω**, *eliminate*, Sor.1.107, Philum.ap.Orib.45.29.48 (Pass.). **II.** *alienate, dispose of*, *BGU*184.21 (i A.D.), *PFay.*31.14 (ii A.D.). **III.** *handle, treat* a subject, Phld.*Lib.*p.47 O. **-ησις**, εως, ἡ, *alienation*, *CPR*220.6 (i A.D.), *PHamb.*14.24 (iii A.D.).

**ἔξοικος**, ον, *houseless*, Lxx *Jb.*6.18.

**ἐξοιμώζω**, *wail aloud*, οἰμωγὰς S.*Aj.*317; γόοισιν Id.*Ant.*427.

**ἐξοιν-έω**, (οἶνος) *to be tipsy*, Hegesand.21, Poll.6.21. **II.** *get sober*, Paul.Aeg.1.33. **-ία**, ἡ, *drunkenness*, Antig.Car.ap.Ath.12. 547f. **-ίζω**, *become sober*, Orib.*Syn.*5.34.2. **-όομαι**, Pass., *to be drunk*, ἐξῳνωμένος (Elmsl. for ἐξοιν-) *drunken*, E.*Ba.*814, Ath.2. 38e. **-ος**, ον, *drunken*, Alex.63, Plb.*Fr.*40, Macho ap.Ath.8.349a, Alciphr.1.39; λογισμὸς ὥσπερ ἔ. ὢν Ph.1.382. Adv. -νως, censured by Poll.6.21.

**ἔξοισις**, εως, ἡ, *bringing out, divulging*, λόγων J.*AJ*17.4.1 (pl.).

**ἐξοιστ-έος**, α, ον, (ἐξοίσω, fut. of ἐκφέρω) *to be brought out*, Ar.*Lys.* 921. **II.** ἐξοιστέον, *one must bring out*, E.*Ph.*712, Pl.*Prm.*128e, Aen.Tact.2.7. **-ικός**, ή, όν, *extravagant*, χαρά Ptol.*Tetr.*11, cf. Heph.Astr.1.1. **-ός**, ή, όν, *to be uttered*, S.E.*M.*7.122.

**ἐξοιστρ-άω** or **-έω**, *make wild, madden*, -εῖν Luc.*DMar.*10.2:—Pass., -ᾶται Ael.*NA*15.19; ἐξοιστρημένοι Vett.Val.356.6. **II.** intr., *rave*, -ᾶν (v.l. -εῖν) Ph.1.380; *go mad*, -εῖν Sch.Od.22.299: aor. -ήσασα v.l. in Palaeph.42.1. **-ηλᾰτέομαι**, Pass., *to be driven to madness*, ὑπό τινος Ps.-Plu.*Fluv.*18.1.

**ἐξοίσω**, fut. of ἐκφέρω.

**ἐξοιχ-νέω**, *go out* or *forth*, ἐξοιχνεῦσι (Ion.) Il.9.384. **-ομαι**, *to have gone out*, *to be quite gone*, Il.6.379,384, S.*OC*867; ἐ. θύραζε Pl.Com.69.11: metaph., ἐκ τῆς γνώμης ἐ. Antipho Soph.49; τὸ βέβαιον αὐτῶν ἐξοίχεται Pl.*R*.503c.

**ἐξοιωνίζομαι**, *avoid as ill-omened*, τὸν ἴδιον δαίμονα Plu.*Dem*.21; τὸ γαμεῖν Id.2.289b.

⊛ **ἐξοκέλλω**, intr., of a ship, *run aground*, ἐς τὰς ἐκβολὰς τοῦ Πηνειοῦ Hdt.7.182; πρὸς κραταίλεων χθόνα A.*Ag*.666; also [δελφῖνες] ἐ. εἰς τὴν γῆν Arist.*HA*631b2. 2. metaph., *drift into*, ἐ. εἰς τραχύτερα πράγματα Isoc.7.18; εἰς λόγου μῆκος Id.*Ep*.2.13; εἰς ἀσέλγειαν Plb.18.55.7; πρὸς ἀπληστίαν Ph.1.686; ἐς ἐπιθυμίας ἀνοήτους Paus.8.24.9; εἰς κύβους Plu.2.5b; εἰς ὕβριν Phylarch.45 J.; εἰς τρυφὴν ibid., Plb.7.1.1, Ath.12.523c (= Arist.*Fr*.584); μέχρι τῶν ἐσχάτων Phld.*Ir*. p.35 W.: abs., *to be ruined*, Plb.4.48.11. II. trans., *run* (a ship) *aground*: metaph., *drive headlong*, τινὰ εἰς ἄτην E.*Tr*.137 (lyr.); ὁ πλοῦτος ἐξώκειλε τὸν κεκτημένον εἰς ἕτερον ἦθος Men.587:—Pass., metaph., δεῦρο δ' ἐξοκέλλεται things *are coming* to this *pass*, A.*Supp*.438.

**ἐξολεθρ-ευμα**, ατος, τό, *destruction*, Lxx 1*Ki*.15.21. **-ευσις**, εως, ἡ, *destruction*, ib.*Jd*.1.17, al., interpol. in J.*AJ*11.6.6. **-ευτικός**, ή, όν, *destructive*, Sch.Ar.*Pl*.443 (Comp.). ⊛ **-εύω**, *destroy utterly*, Lxx *Ge*.17.14, al., *Act.Ap*.3.23, v.l. in J.*AJ*8.11.1. (The spelling -ολοθρ- in this group of words is freq. in later codd. and Pap., as *PMasp*. 2 iii 28 (vi A.D.).)

**ἐξολιγωρέω**, *hold of slight account*, τύφῳ τὰ θεῖα -ώρηται Ph.2.181.

⊛ **ἐξολισθάνω**, later **-αίνω** Epicur.*Ep*.2 p.45 U., Sm.*Ps*.35(36).3: aor. 2 -ώλισθον:—*glide off*, *slip away*, ἐκ δὲ οἱ ἧπαρ ὄλισθεν Il.20.470; *glance off*, as a spear-point from a hard substance, E.*Ph*.1383; αὐτῶν *away from* them, Arist.*HA*590b17; of leaves, *drop off*, Ael.*NA*12.18; *slip out*, *escape*, Hippon.37, Ar.*Pax*141; of things, Epicur. l.c., *Fr*.383 bis; of a bandage, Diocl.*Fr*.188; ἐ. εἰς ἡδονὰς *slip imperceptibly* into.., Hdn.1.3.1: c. acc., *slip out of*, διαβολὰς Ar.*Eq*.491; ὡς μήποτ' ἐξολίσθῃ ἡμᾶς *slip from* our *memory*, Id.*Ec*.286.

**ἐξολκή**, ἡ, *extraction*, Sor.1.69, Antyll.(?) ap.Orib.45.18.21, Paul. Aeg.3.72.

**ἐξόλλῡμι** and **-ύω**, fut. -ολῶ: aor. 1 ἐξώλεσα: pf. ἐξολώλεκα:—*destroy utterly*, τοὺς Ζεὺς ἐξολέσειε Od.17.597, cf. E.*Hipp*.725, Pl.*Euthd*.285a, Men.*Pk*.230, etc. II. Med., with pf. 2 ἐξόλωλα, *perish utterly*, Emp.11.3, S.*Tr*.84, Ar.*Pax*366, Pl. l. c., etc.; ὑπὸ τοῦ γε λιμοῦ.. ἐξολωλότες Ar.*Pax*483: opt. in imprecations, ἐξολοίμην Id.*Fr*.105; ἐξόλοιο Alex.120.

**ἐξολοθρ-**, v. ἐξολεθρ-.

**ἐξολολύζω**, *howl aloud*, Batr.101, Hld.10.19.

**ἐξομᾰλίζω**, *make quite smooth*, πρὸς τὸν κανόνα τὸν λίθινον *IG*1².373.209; τὴν ῥάχιν Sor.1.102, cf. Herod.Med.ap.Orib.10.37.9 (Pass.) (also in Med., τὰ σώματα Str.15.1.54); *level*, τὸν τῆς πόλεως περίβολον J.*BJ*7.1.1:—Pass., ἔδαφος -ισμένον D.S.2.10. 2. *render homogeneous*, Hp.*Medic*.10. 3. *smooth away*, κακὰ Babr.60 ad calcem. II. *form according to rule*, A.D.*Synt*.310.5 (Pass.), al.

**ἐξομβρ-έω**, *pour out like rain*, γνῶσιν, βδέλυγμα, Lxx *Si*.1.19, 10.13. **-ιστήριον**, τό, perh. *overflow-tank*, *Gloss*.

**ἐξόμειννος**, Thess., = ἐξάμηνος, *IG*9(2).506.4 (Larissa, ii B.C.).

**ἐξομήρ-ευσις**, εως, ἡ, *demand for hostages*, Plu.*Rom*.29, *Cam*.33. **-εύω**, *bind by taking hostages*, [τοὺς δούλους] ταῖς τεκνοποιΐαις ἐ. *bind* slaves *to one's service by the pledges* of wives and children, Arist.*Oec*.1344b17, cf. Phld.*Oec*.p.33 J.:—Med., νήπιοι ψυχῆς φίλτρα -εύσασθαι δυνάμενα στρατηγὸν πρὸς πατρίδα Onos.1.12; also, *produce by hostages*, φιλίαν Str.6.4.2; *bind to oneself*, D.S.27.7; *win over*, *SIG*656.21 (Abdera, ii B.C., found at Teos).

**ἐξομῑλ-έω**, *have intercourse*, *live with*, τινί X.*Ages*.11.4: metaph., *bear one company*, στεφάνων οὐ μία χροιά.. τάχ' ἐξομιλήσει E.*Cyc*.518 (lyr.); φιλανθρώπως ἐ. Plu.*Cim*.6. II. c. acc., *win over*, *conciliate*, τινά Plb.7.4.6, Plu.2.824d, etc. III. Med., *to be away from one's friends*, *be alone in the crowd*, E.*IA*735. **-ος**, ον, *out of one's society*, *alien*, S.*Tr*.964 (lyr.).

**ἐξόμμᾰτ-ος**, ον, = ἐξόφθαλμος, Poll.5.69. **-όω**, *open the eyes of*, τὰ τέως μεμυκότα καὶ τυφλὰ Ph.1.455:—Pass., *to be restored to sight*, ἀντὶ τυφλοῦ ἐξωμμάτωται S.*Fr*.710, cf. Ph.1.109, Ael.*NA*17.20. 2. metaph., *make clear* or *plain*, φλογωπὰ σήματα ἐξωμμάτωσα A.*Pr*.499. II. *bereave of eyes*, E.*Fr*.541. **-ωσις**, εως, ἡ, *clearing* or *cleansing of the eyes*, interpol. in Poll.2.48.

⊛ **ἐξόμνῡμι** and **-ύω**, fut. ἐξομοῦμαι: aor. ἐξώμοσα:—*swear in excuse*, ἐξώμοσεν ἀρρωστεῖν τουτονί D.19.124. II. mostly, *swear in the negative*, ἐξομῇ τὸ μὴ εἰδέναι; S.*Ant*.535; μαρτυρεῖν ἢ ἐξομνύειν D.29.20:—mostly in Med., aor. ἐξωμοσάμην, *deny* or *disown upon oath*, *swear formally that one does not know* a thing, *abjure*, τὰς διαβολὰς Id.57.36; ἃ μὲν οἶδεν ἐξόμνυσθαι Is.9.19: abs., ib.18, Pl.*Lg*.949a, etc.; οὐκ ἂν ἐξομόσαιτο μὴ οὐκ εἰδέναι D.57.59, cf. *PHal*.1.230 (iii B.C.); *forswear*, *renounce*, συγγένειαν ἐξόμνυσθαι Lxx 4*Ma*.4.26, 10.3. 2. *decline* or *refuse* an office *by an oath* that one has not means or health to perform it, ἐξομόσασθαι τὴν πρεσβείαν Aeschin.2.94, cf. D.19.124; [τὴν ἀρχήν] Arist.*Pol*.1297a20, Plu.*Marc*.6, 12, cf. Thphr.*Char*.24.5. 3. *forswear*, *renounce*, τὴν ἐλευθερίαν Luc.*Apol*.6; τὴν ἐπικουρίαν Jul.*Or*.2.60d. III. later, simply, *swear*, *make affidavit*, *PFlor*.32 *A* 12 (iii A.D.).

**ἐξομοι-άζω**, = sq., Callicrat.ap.Stob.4.22.101. **-όω**, *make quite like*, *assimilate*, τὸ εἶδος Hdt.3.24; αὑτὸν τῇ πολιτείᾳ Pl.*Grg*.512e; ἐ. τοὺς καρποὺς *produce* fruit *exactly like*, Thphr.*HP*2.2.4; *adapt*, τοῖς ἤθεσι τῶν λεγόντων καὶ τῶν ἀκουόντων τοὺς λόγους Anon.*Oxy*.1012 i 28; *compare*, *liken*, τί τινι Str.2.5.22, Ph.2.11, al.:—Pass., *become* or *be like*, ἄνδρας γυναιξὶν ἐξομοιοῦσθαι φύσιν E.*Andr*.354, cf. S.*Aj*.549, X.*Oec*.7.32; ὁ Ἄψος σχῆμα ἐ. πρὸς τὸν Πηνειόν Plu.*Flam*.3. **-ωσις**, εως, ἡ, *assimilation*, Thphr.*CP*4.3.1, Gal.7.225. II. *becoming like*, Ph.1.35, Plu.*Per*.2, Dam.*Pr*.341, Procl. *in Ti*.3.200D. **-ωτικός**, ή, όν, *causing similitude*, παρουσία οὐ τοπική, ἐ. δέ Porph.*Sent*.35.

**ἐξομολογ-έομαι**, *confess*, τὰς ἁμαρτίας Lxx *Da*.9.20, *Ev.Matt*.3.6, al., J.*AJ*8.4.6; *admit*, *acknowledge*, μυθογραφίαν Str.1.2.35; ἧτταν Plu.*Eum*.17; πίστεις *PGnom*.18; ὅτι.. *Ep.Phil*.2.11, Luc.*Herm*.75; διότι.. Lxx 2*Ma*.7.37; esp. in legal formulae, ἐ. εἰληφέναι *PAvrom*.1.7 (i B.C.); *acknowledge*, υἱόν *POxy*.1473.9 (iii A.D.): abs., *acknowledge a liability*, *PHib*.1.30.18 (iii B.C.). 2. *make grateful acknowledgements*, *give thanks*, *sing praises*, Lxx 2*Ki*.22.50, al., Ph.1.59, al., *Ev.Matt*.11.25: c. acc., τοῦτο τῷ Κυρίῳ Lxx *Ge*.29.35. II. later in Act., *agree*, *consent*, *Ev.Luc*.22.6:—Pass., ἐξωμολογημέναι ἀποδείξεις *agreed*, *admitted* proofs, *SIG*685.95 (Magn. Mae., ii B.C.). **-ησις**, εως, ἡ, *admission*, *confession*, ἥττης Plu.2.987d; ἄρτου, i.e. of the possession of a loaf, J.*BJ*5.10.3; *confession of gratitude*, Ph.1.60, al. **-ητικός**, ή, όν, *giving thanks*, *thankful*, ibid.; τρόπος ib.84.

⊛ **ἐξομόρ-γνῡμι**, fut. ἐξομόρξω, *wipe off from*, ἐκ δ' ὄμορξον στόματος πέλανον E.*Or*.219:—Med., *wipe off from*, *purge away a pollution*, νασμοῖσι with water, Id.*Hipp*.653; αἷμα ἐξομόρξασθαι πέπλοις *wipe off* blood *on your* garments, Id.*HF*1399, cf. *El*.502. II. metaph., ἐξομόρξασθαί τινι μωρίαν *wipe off* one's folly *on* another, i.e. give him part of it, Id.*Ba*.344, parodied by Ar.*Ach*.843. 2. = ἀπομάττομαι, *stamp* or *imprint upon*, ἃ ἑκάστη ἡ πρᾶξις αὐτοῦ ἐξωμόρξατο εἰς τὴν ψυχήν Pl.*Grg*.525a, cf. *Lg*.775d, prob. in Chaerem.14.15. **-ξις**, εως, ἡ, *wiping off*: metaph., *impression*, Pl.*Ti*.80e.

**ἐξομπλάριον**, τό, in form ἐξονπλάριν, *sample*, *POxy*.1066.7 (iii A.D.).

**ἔξομπλον**· ἴσον, Hsch. (Lat. *exemplum* 'copy'.)

**ἐξόμφᾰλος**, ον, *with prominent navel*, as in umbilical hernia, Gal.7.730. II. as Subst., ἐξόμφαλος, ὁ, *prominent navel*, Dsc.4.69, Gal.19.444, Paul.Aeg.6.51.

**ἐξονειδ-ίζω**, strengthd. for ὀνειδίζω: 1. c. acc. rei, *cast in one's teeth*, κακά, ὄνειδος, S.*El*.288, E.*IA*305; τισὶ τὸν φόβον J.*AJ*5.1.18; ἐξονειδισθεὶς κακὰ *having* foul *reproaches cast upon* one, S.*Ph*.382. b. simply, *bring forward*, Lat. *objicere*, τὸ τόλμημ' οἷον ἐξωνείδισεν E.*Ph*.1676. 2. c. acc. pers., *reproach*, abs., S.*OC*990; τινά D.S.5.29. **-ισμός**, ὁ, *reproach*, ἁμαρτημάτων J.*BJ*2.16.4 (pl.). **-ιστικός**, ή, όν, *throwing reproach on*, τοῖς ἄλλοις M.Ant.1.16.5.

**ἐξονειρ-ιασμός**, ὁ, = ἐξονειρωγμός, Diocl.*Fr*.141 (pl.). **-όω**, = ἐξονειρώττω, Hp.*Mul*.2.175. **-ωγμός**, ὁ, = ὀνειρωγμός, Arist.*Pr*.877a9 (pl.), Thphr.*Lass*.16. **-ωκτικός**, ή, όν, *subject to* ὀνειρωγμοί, Arist.*Pr*.884a7, Thphr.*Lass*.16. **-ωξις**, εως, ἡ, = ἐξονειρωγμός, Phlp. *in GA*96.29. **-ώσσω**, Att. **-ττω**, = ὀνειρώττω, Hp.*Genit*.1, Arist.*GA*739a23, *IG*4.951.105 (Epid.).

⊛ **ἐξονομ-άζω**, *utter aloud*, *announce*, γενεήν *h.Merc*.59; freq. in Hom. in the phrase ἔπος τ' ἔφατ' ἔκ τ' ὀνόμαζε he spoke the word and *uttered* it *aloud*, Il.1.361, al.; cf. E.*IA*1066 (lyr.). II. *call by name*, Plu.*Cic*.40:—Pass., *to be referred to by name*, *PTeb*.28.17 (ii B.C.), etc. **-αίνω**, *name*, *speak of by name*, ἄνδρα Il.3.166; αἴδετο.. γάμον ἐξονομῆναι *name*, *tell* it, Od.6.66, cf. *h.Ven*.252; τὸ πλῆθος τοῦ ἀργυρίου *SIG*527.122 (Crete, iii B.C.). **-ακλήδην**, Adv. *by name*, ἐ. ὀνομάζων Il.22.415; ἐκ δ' ὀ. Od.4.278; ἐμὲ δὲ φθέγγοντο καλεῦντες ἐ. 12.250; προκαλεῖσθαι Critias 68 D.

**ἐξονῠχίζω**, *try* a thing's smoothness *by drawing the nail over* it: hence, *scrutinize closely*, Ath.3.97d, Artem.1.16, Jul.Laod. in *Cat. Cod.Astr*.4.103; μὴ λίαν ἐξακριβοῦν ταῦτα μηδ' ἐ. τὰ τοιαῦτα Jul.*Or*.7.216a, cf. Phryn.256. II. *deprive of the base of the petal*, ῥόδα Orib.5.33.1; of lilies, in Pass., Aët.1.115. 2. *trim the hoof*, *Hippiatr*.123.

**ἐξοξύνομαι**, Pass., *turn sour*, Thphr.*CP*6.7.7.

**ἐξοπάζω**· ἐκπέμπω, Hsch.

**ἐξοπίζω**, *squeeze out the juice*, ὀπὸς εἰς ἔριον ἐξοπισθεὶς Arist.*HA*522b3.

**ἐξόπ-ῐθεν** and **-ῐθε**, Adv., Ep. for ἐξόπισθεν, *behind*, *in rear*, Il.4.298, al., Hes.*Sc*.130. II. Prep. with gen., *behind*, ἐ. κεράων Il.17.521. **-ιν**, Adv., = foreg. 1, A.*Ag*.115 (lyr.). **-ισθεν**, poet. **-ισθε**, Adv., Att. for ἐξόπιθεν, Ar.*Eq*.22, Pl.*Lg*.947d, Lxx 1*Ch*.19.10, etc.; εἰς τὸ ἐ. *backwards*, Pl.*Ti*.84e, etc.; τὸ ἐ. τῆς κεφαλῆς Arist.*HA*512b14. II. Prep. with gen., Ar.*Ach*.868, Lxx 3*Ki*.19.21; τὰ ἐ. χειρὸς ἐς τὰ δεξιὰ S.*Fr*.598. **-ισθίως**, Adv. *backwards*, Tz.*H*.5.104. **-ιστο** (-θο cod. Rav.), barbarism for -ισθεν, Ar.*Th*.1124. **-ίσω**, Adv., I. of Place (as always in Il.), *backwards*, *back again*, Il.11.461, 13.436; ἀποπέμπειν ἐ. Hes.*Op*.88. II. as Prep. with gen., *behind*, ἐ. νεκροῦ χάζεσθαι Il.17.357; ἐ. χερὸς ὄμμα τρέπουσ' S.*Fr*.534. III. of Time (as always in Od.), *hereafter*, Od.4.35, al., Hes.*Th*.500, Tyrt.12.30, Pi.*O*.7.68, *Pae*.2.27.

**ἐξοπλ-ᾰσία**, ἡ, = -ισία, Arist.*Ath*.15.4, *IG*12(5).647.39 (Ceos), *SIG*410.10 (pl., Erythrae, iii B.C.), v.l. in D.S.16.3, 19.3. **-ίζω**, *arm completely*, Hdt.7.100, X.*Cyr*.4.5.22, al.; poet., ἐ. Ἄρη A.*Supp*.683, 702, cf. 99 (all lyr.):—Med. and Pass., *arm oneself*, στολὴν.. λέοντος, ἧπερ.. ἐξωπλίζετο, of Hercules, E.*HF*466; *get under arms*, *stand in armed array*, Id.*IT*302; ὄπισθεν τῶν ἁρμαμαξῶν ἐξοπλίσθητε X.*Cyr*.6.3.32; ἐξωπλισμένος *fully armed*, Ar.*Lys*.454, Pl.*R*.555d, etc. 2. generally, ἐξωπλισμένος *fully prepared*, *ready*, Ar.*Pax*566; μᾶζα.. πρὸς εὐτέλειαν ἐξωπλισμένη Antiph.226.2, cf. 217.19. II. *disarm*,

*deprive*, Καίσαρα τῆς στρατιᾶς App.*BC*2.28, cf. Max.Tyr.29.3, 40.5. -ῐσία, ἡ, *muster of troops under arms, review*, Aen.Tact.10.13 (pl.); ἐν τῇ ἐξοπλισίᾳ *under arms*, X.*An*.1.7.10, Plb.11.9.4, Str.15.3.18, etc. 2. *field-day, manœuvres*, Ael.*Tact*.24.1 (pl.); ταῖς ἐ. γυμνάζειν Man.Hist.42. -ισις, εως, ἡ, *getting under arms*, πολλοῦ χρόνου δέονται εἰς ἐξόπλισιν X.*Cyr*.8.5.9, cf. Arist.*Pr*.922b14. -ος, ον, *unarmed*, Plb.3.81.2.

**ἐξοπτ-άω**, *bake thoroughly*, ἐν τῇ καμίνῳ τοὺς ἀμφορέας Hdt.4.164; σάρκας πυρί E.*Cyc*.403, cf. Ar.*Ach*.1005:—Pass., τεμάχη ἐξωπτημένα Pherecr.108.10, cf. Eub.15.8; ἐ. τὴν κάμινον *heat* it *violently*, Hdt.4.163. II. metaph., of love, ἐξοπτᾷ δ' ἐμέ S.*Fr*.474.3. ⊛-ος, ον, *well-baked*, Hp.*VM*14; of bricks, *PGrenf*.1.21.8 (ii B.C.).

**ἐξοράω**, *see from afar*:—Pass., ὥστ' ἐξορᾶσθαι E.*Heracl*.675, *Hel*.1269; cf. ἐξεῖδον. II. *have the appearance*, ὡς ἀγχόμενος Hp.*Morb*.2.68.

**ἐξοργ-άω**, strengthd. for ὀργάω, Plu.2.652d:—hence -ησις, εως, ἡ, Herm.*in Phdr*.p.62 A. (pl.).

**ἐξοργιάζω**, *excite to mystic frenzy*, χρῆσθαι τοῖς ἐξοργιάζουσι τὴν ψυχὴν μέλεσι Arist.*Pol*.1342a9; *stir to frenzy*, Phld.*Mus*.p.49 K. II. intr., *become frenzied*, ib.p.26 K.

**ἐξοργίζω**, *enrage*, ἵππον X.*Eq*.9.2; τινάς Aeschin.1.192; τὰς ψυχὰς πρὸς τοὺς πολεμίους X.*Mem*.3.3.7:—Pass., *to be enraged, furious*, Batr.[184a], Satyr.*Vit.Eur.Fr*.39 x 33 (prob.), Plb.6.57.8, al., Phld.*Mus*.p.78 K., Aristaenet.2.20.

**ἐξορθιάζω**, *lift up the voice, cry aloud*, A.*Ch*.271. II. intr., *stand erect*, Plu.2.371f.

**ἐξόρθ-ιος**, ον, = sq., Sch.Arat.161. -ος, ον, *upright*, Ath.11.496d. -όω, *set upright*, τὸ πεσόν Pl.*Lg*.862c. 2. metaph., *set right, correct*, τὸν σὺν ἐξόρθου πότμον S.*Ant*.83; διεφθαρμένας περιόδους Pl.*Ti*.90d; ἤν τι μὴ καλῶς ἔχῃ, γνώμαισιν ὑστέραισιν ἐξορθούμεθα E.*Supp*.1083, cf. 1086.

⊛ **ἐξορθρίζω**, in pf. part. Pass., μήτρα -ισμένη womb *of the morning*, Aq.*Ps*.109(110).3.

⊛ **ἐξορία**, ἡ, v. ἐξόριος.

⊛ **ἐξορίζω** (A), (ὅρος) (3 sg. aor. subj. ἐξορύξη [from *ἐξορϝίξ-] *Inscr.Cypr*.135.11 H.):—*send beyond the frontier, banish*, E.*Heracl*.257, Pl.*Lg*.874a, etc.; γαθέν τινα E.*Tr*.1106 (lyr.); τὸ σῶμά τινος ἐ. (cf. ἐξόριστος) Plu.*Phoc*.37:—Pass., ἐξορισθῆναι καὶ ἀποθανόντα, μηδὲ ἐν τῇ πατρίδι ταφῆναι Hyp.*Lyc*.20. 2. *expose* a child, E.*Ion* 504 (lyr.). 3. *banish, get rid of*, ἀγριότητα Pl.*Smp*.197d; αἰσχρολογίαν ἐκ τῆς πόλεως Arist.*Pol*.1336b5; τοὺς ἀνιάτους Id.*EN*1180a10: c. gen., τι τῆς ἀκοῆς Jul.*Or*.6.186b. II. c. acc. loci only, ἄλλην ἀπ' ἄλλης ἐ. πόλιν *pass* from one to another, E.*Heracl*.16. III. Pass., *come forth from*, τινός Id.*Hipp*.1380 (lyr.).

**ἐξορίζω** (B), (ὀρός) *press out the whey from cheese*, *EM*349.29, Hsch.

**ἐξορίνω** [ῑ], *exasperate*, τινὰ ὑλάγμασιν A.*Ag*.1631.

**ἐξόρ-ιος**, α, ον, (ὅρος) *out of the bounds of one's country*, Poll.6.198. II. Subst., **ἐξορία** (sc. ζωή), ἡ, *exile*, Marcellin.*Vit.Thuc*.47, Eust.1161.35. -ισιμαῖος, gloss on δηπορτᾶτος (*deportatus*), Hsch. -ισμός, ὁ, *sending beyond the frontier*, ἐ. καὶ φυγή D.H.5.12; νεκρῶν Plu.2.549a; ζῴων prob. cj. in Porph.*Abst*.1.10. -ιστέον, *one must expel*, Id.*Sent*.32, Them.*Or*.23.300a. -ιστος, ον, *expelled, banished*, ἐξόριστος ἀνῃρῆσθαι to be ruined *by banishment*, D.21.105: c. gen., τῆς Ἰταλίας Plb.2.7.10; οἰκείων Porph.*Abst*.1.30. 2. *put beyond the borders*, of the dead body of a criminal, τὸν ..ἀλιτήριον ἀποκτείναντες ἐ. ἐκ τῆς πόλεως ποιῆσαι Din.1.77.

⊛ **ἐξορκ-ίζω**, = ἐξορκόω, D.54.26 (codd., -οῦντες Harp.), *PRev.Laws* 56.12 (iii B.C.), Plb.3.61.10, *GDI*5075.25 (Crete, i B.C.), etc.: c. dupl. acc., *SIG*524.29 (Crete, iii B.C.):—Pass., ib.46.6 (Halic., v B.C.), Plb.6.26.4, *IG*2².1346. 2. *conjure*, ἐ. σε κύριον τὸν θεόν Lxx *Ge*.24.3, cf. *PMag.Lond*.121.269; ἐ. [τινὰ] τοῖς μεγάλοις ὀνόμασιν ib.892; ἐ. σε κατὰ τοῦ θεοῦ *Ev.Matt*.26.63; also τινὰ κατά τινος *PMag.Par*.1.356. II. *exorcise* an evil spirit, *Tab.Defix*. in *Rh.Mus*.55.248. -ισμός, ὁ, *administration of an oath*, Plb.6.21.6. -ιστής, οῦ, ὁ, *exorcist*, *Act.Ap*.19.3, Luc.*Epigr*.23, Ptol.*Tetr*.182. -ος, ον, *bound by oath*, Pi.*O*.13.99. -όω, earlier form of ἐξορκίζω, *administer an oath to* one, c. acc. pers., or abs., ἐξορκούντων οἱ πρυτάνεις Foed.ap.Th.5.47, cf. D.21.65, *IG*2².1174.15: c. fut. inf., ib.2.841*b*35: folld. by ἦ μήν (Ion. ἦ μέν) Hdt.3.133, 4.154: later, c. pres. inf., J.*AJ*9.7.4: c. acc. pers. et rei, *make one swear by*, ἐ. τινὰ τὸ Στυγὸς ὕδωρ Hdt.6.74. -ωσις, εως, ἡ, *binding by oath*, Id.4.154. II. *exorcism*, J.*AJ*8.2.5 (pl.).

**ἐξορμάω**, *send forth, send to war*, A.*Pers*.46, E.*IT*1437; πάλιν ἐ. *bring quickly* back, Id.*IA*151 codd. (anap.); ἐ. τὴν ναῦν *start* the ship, *set* it *agoing*, Th.7.14; κοῦφον ἐ. πόδα Ar.*Th*.659:—Pass., *set out, start*, Hdt.9.51, etc.; πρὸς ἔργον E.*Or*.1240; ἐπ' ἔργον Men.*Epit*.162; of arrows, *dart from* the bow, γλυφίδες τόξων ἐξορμώμεναι E.*Or*.274, cf. A.*Eu*.182; *move rapidly, rush*, S.*OC*30; τὸ κεῖσε δεῦρό τ' ἐ. Id.*Tr*.929. 2. *excite to action, urge on*, E.*Rh*.788, Th.6.6, 88; ἐ. τινὰ ἐπὶ τὴν ἀρετήν X.*An*.3.1.24. II. intr., like Pass., *set out, start*, esp. in haste, μή σε λάθησιν κεῖσ' ἐξορμήσασα (sc. νηῦς) Od.12.221; δεῦρο ἐξορμῶμεν πεζῇ X.*An*.5.7.17: c. gen., *set out from*, χθονός E.*Tr*.1131, etc.: metaph., *break out*, ἤνθηκεν, ἐξώρμηκεν [ἡ νόσος] S.*Tr*.1089.

**ἐξορμενίζω**, (ὅρμενος) *shoot forth, sprout*, S.*Ichn*.275: metaph., ῥήτορες ἐξωρμενικότες Nicostr.Com.34. 2. *run to seed*, Poll.6.54.

⊛ **ἐξορμ-έω**, *to be out of harbour, run to sea*, Lycurg.17, And.1.11, Is.6.27: metaph., ἐ. ἐκ τῆς πόλεως Aeschin.3.209; ἐ. ἐκ τοῦ νοῦ *to be out of* one's senses, Paus.3.4.1. -ή, ἡ, *going out, expedition*, ἐπὶ στρατείαν Pl.*Thg*.129d. -ησις, εως, ἡ, *urging on*, ἐς τὰ καλά Arr.*An*.3.9.7, cf. J.*AJ*19.1.10. II. *rushing forth*, κύματος ἐπὶ τὴν γῆν Sch.Th.3.89; *vehement attack*, ἡ δι' ὀλίγου ἐ. D.C.75.6; *setting out, start*, οἴκοθεν Arr.*An*.1.11.5. III. *cutaneous eruption*, Gal.17(1).366 (= 9.138 Chart.). -ητικός, ή, όν, *stimulating*, εἰς πόλεμον Sch.Pl.*R*.400b. -ίζω, *bring out of harbour*, τὴν ναῦν ἐξορμίσαι ἐκ τοῦ λιμένος D.33.9:—Pass., *put out to sea*, Sophr.52, Ph.1.670. 2. *let down*, ἐς πόντον E.*Hel*.1247: pf. Pass. in med. sense, ἐξώρμισαι σὸν πόδα thou *hast come forth*, Id.*Ph*.846. -ιστόν, τό, a *fish* similar to the μύραινα, Cassiod.*Var*.12.4, 14. ⊛ -ος, ον, *sailing from a harbour*, c. gen., Κρήτας E.*Hipp*.156 (lyr.), prob. in Id.*IA*149 (anap.). II. (ὁρμή) *issuing forth*, dub. l. in Arist.*PA*694a23.

⊛ **ἐξόρνυμι**, in Med., *rush out*, aor. ἐξῶρτο (or ἐξ ὦρτο), A.R.1.306.

**ἐξοροθύνω**, *excite greatly*, Cypr.*Fr*.7.9, Q.S.2.431.

**ἔξορος**, ον, (ὅρος) = ἐξόριος, Poll.6.198.

**ἐξορούω**, *leap forth*, Πάριος δὲ θοῶς ἐκ κλῆρος ὄρουσεν Il.3.325; ἄνεμοι δ' ἐκ πάντες ὄρουσαν Od.10.47.

**ἐξορύξη**, v. ἐξορίζω.

⊛ **ἐξορύσσω**, Att. -ττω, *dig out* the earth from a trench, τὸν ἀεὶ ἐξορυσσόμενον χοῦν Hdt.7.23; τόποι ἐξορυσσόμενοι Arist.*Mir*.833b4:—Med., ἐξορύξασθαι χάρακας *make oneself* a vallum, D.H.9.55. II. *dig out* of the ground, *dig up*, τοὺς νεκρούς Hdt.1.64, cf. *BGU*1024 iv 4 (iv/v A.D.); ἄγλιθας Ar.*Ach*.763; [μορίαν] Lys.7.26:—Pass., τοῦ χοὸς τοῦ -ομένου *PHal*.1.109 (iii B.C.); φυτά X.*Oec*.19.4. 2. *gouge out*, ἐ. αὐτῶν τοὺς ὀφθαλμούς Hdt.8.116, cf. Lxx *Jd*.16.21, Plu.*Art*.14. 3. metaph., τὸν ἐξορύσσοντα λόγον τὰ κεκρυμμένα τῶν πραγμάτων Ph.1.72.

**ἐξορχέομαι**, *dance away, hop off*, αὐταῖς πέδαις D.22.68. II. c. acc. cogn., ἐ. ῥυθμόν *dance out* a figure, *go through* it, Philostr.*Im*.2.12; ἀσελγήματα Suid. s. v. Ἀστυάνασσα. III. c. acc. rei, *dance out*, i.e. *let out, betray*, ἐ. τὰ ἀπόρρητα, prob. of some dance which burlesqued those ceremonies, Luc.*Salt*.15; τὰ μυστήρια Id.*Pisc*.33, Alciphr.3.72, Ach.Tat.4.8, Anon.*Oxy*.411.25; ἐξαγγέλλεις αὐτὰ καὶ ἐ. παρὰ καιρόν Arr.*Epict*.3.21.16. 2. ἐ. τινά *disgrace* him *by one's conduct*, Plu.*Art*.22; πολιτείαν Id.2.1127b; and ἐ. τὴν ἀλήθειαν *scorn* it, ib.867b; ἐ. τοὺς Σαλαμινίους 'dance out of their graves', Philostr.*VA*4.21. 3. πόλεμον *dance away*, i.e. *lose*, Ael.*NA*16.23. 4. *celebrate with dances*, ἱερωσύνην Hdn.5.5.3.

⊛ **ἔξος**, Delph., = ἔξω, *SIG*244 ii 43 (iv B.C.), cf. *An.Ox*.2.164.

**ἐξόσδω**, Dor. for ἐξόζω (q. v.).

**ἐξοσιόω**, *dedicate, devote*, Plu.*Cam*.20, prob. in E.*Ba*.70:—Med., Plu.*Arat*.53. II. Med., *avert by expiation*, D.S.15.9 (nisi leg. -ιάσατο), Plu.2.586f. III. ἐξοσιοῦν· δικαιοῦν, Hsch.

⊛ **ἐξοστεΐζω**, *take out the bones*, prob. l. in Horap.2.38, cf. Suid. s. v. ἔξαρθρος; *take out of the bone*, μυελόν Dsc.2.77: metaph., of fruits, *remove the seeds* or *kernels*, μῆλα.. ἐξωστεϊσμένα Id.5.75; ἐλαιῶν -ισμένων Ruf.ap.Orib.47.7.

**ἐξοστρᾰκ-ίζω**, *banish by ostracism*, Hdt.8.79, And.4.32, Lys.14.39, Pl.*Grg*.516d; ἐκ τοῦ οὐρανοῦ Luc.*Sacr*.4:—Pass., Themist.*Ep*.2; also (with a play on *broken pots*, ὄστρακα) ἀμφορεὺς ἐξοστρακισθεὶς Ar.*Fr*.593; ἐξωστράκισται πᾶν τὸ χρήσιμον ἐκ τῶν πραγμάτων Demad.53; ἐξωστρακίσθησαν τῆς ἀληθείας Anon.Alch. in *Gött.Nachr*.1919.14. -ισμός, ὁ, *banishment by ostracism*, ἐ. ποιεῖσθαι κατά τινος Plu.*Them*.22, cf. Themist.*Ep*.1. II. ἐ. τῆς γῆς *formation of any external shell*, interpol. in Corn.*ND*17 (nisi leg. ἐξοστεϊσμόν).

**ἐξόστωσις**, εως, ἡ, (ὀστέον) *diseased excrescence on the bone, node*, esp. on the temples, Gal.7.728, 10.1013.

⊛ **ἐξότε**, Adv., (ἐξ ὅτε) = ἐξ οὗ, Ar.*Av*.334, Call.*Ap*.48, *AP*11.383 (Pall.), *IG*3.171.

**ἐξότολον**· φανερόν, Hsch.

**ἐξοτρύνω**, *stir up, urge on, excite*, σ' ἵμερος ἐ. τελεῖν A.*Th*.692 (lyr.), cf. E.*Supp*.24; τινὰ ἐπί τι Th.1.84, etc.:—Pass., Ph.2.564.

**ἐξουδεν-έω**, = sq., Lxx 4*Ki*.19.21, al., *BGU*1117.31 (i B.C.). -ίζω, = ἐξουδενόω, Plu.2.308e, 310c. -ισμός, ὁ, *scorn, contempt*, Aq.*Ps*.122(123).4. -όω, *set at naught*, Lxx *Jd*.9.38. -ωμα, ατος, τό, *contempt*, ib.*Ps*.89(90).5, Hsch. s. v. προπηλακισμός. -ωσις, εως, ἡ, *contempt*, Lxx *Ps*.30(31).19. -ωτής, οῦ, ὁ, *one who sets at naught*, Phld.*Vit*.p.42 J.

**ἔξουθα**, dialectic form for ἔξωθε(ν), Hsch.

**ἐξουθεν-έω**, = ἐξουδενόω (cf. οὐ σὲ ἐξουθενήκασιν, ἀλλ' ἢ ἐμὲ ἐξουδενώκασιν Lxx 1*Ki*.8.7), ib.*Wi*.4.18, al., *Ev.Luc*.23.11, *Ep.Rom*.14.10, J.*BJ*6.5.4. ⊛ -ημα, ατος, τό, *object of contempt*, ἐ. λαοῦ Lxx *Ps*.21(22).6. -ητικός, ή, όν, *inclined to set at naught*, τοῦ θείου D.L.7.119. -ία, ἡ, *scornfulness*, Gloss. -ίζω, = ἐξουδενόω, Decr.ap.J.*AJ*19.5.3, Sch.Ar.*Ach*.443; τὰ μυστήρια Ps.-Plu.*Fluv*.12.1. -ισμός, = ἐξουδενισμός, Gloss. -όω, = ἐξουδενόω, v.l. in *Ev.Marc*.9.12 (Pass.), *Ev.Luc*.23.11 (Act.). -ωσις, εως, ἡ, *extinction*, Phld.*Rh*.2.63 S. (s.v.l.).

**ἐξούλης** δίκη, ἡ, (ἐξείλλω) action *of ejectment*, brought by a plaintiff alleged to have been unlawfully ejected from or dispossessed of property, Phryn.Com.42, *Com.Adesp*.652, D.30 and 31 tit., cf. Harp. ap.Suid. s. v. II. action *of ejectment* brought by one who claims property in consequence of a judgement of court and is excluded (ejected) from it by the former defendant or his agent, against a defendant who has seized or refused to surrender property, D.21.81, 91, 52.16. III. metaph., of an action brought to *expel* or *eject* an interloper or trespasser, νόμων [? νόμῳ] ἐξούλης λαχεῖν Aristid.*Or*.

54 p.688 D.; also ἐξούλης ὑμῖν οὐδ' ἂν εἷς λάχοι τῆς γῆς Id.1.103 J. (Mostly found in gen., but τὴν ἐξούλην D.21.44 (codd. opt.); ἐξούλας ἢ γραφὰς ὦφλον And.1.73.)

**ἐξουρ-έω**, *pass with the urine*, Arist.*HA* 577ᵃ22; (λίθον) Dsc.*Eup.*2.118:—Pass., Mnesith.ap.Orib.*inc.*15.12. II. abs., *make water*, Ael.*NA* 11.18; *finish making water*, Hierocl.*Facet.*118. **-ησις**, εως, ἡ, *passing with the urine*, αἵματος Aët.ap.Phot.p.179 B. **-ικός**, ή, όν, *cleared of whey*, γάλα Ps.-Democr.Alch.p.54 B. (cf. ἐξορίζω (B)). **-ισμός**, ὁ, *drawing forth of urine*, Dsc.*Eup.*2.113.

**ἔξουρος**, ον, (οὐρά) *conical*, πρόσθετα Hp.*Mul.*2.133; *contracted*, αἰδοῖα v.l. ib.148.

**ἐξουσ-ία**, ἡ, (ἔξεστι) *power, authority* to do a thing, c. inf., χαίρειν καὶ νοσεῖν ἐ. πάρεστι S.*Fr.*88.11 codd.; αὐτῷ ἐ. ἦν σαφῶς εἰδέναι Antipho 1.6, cf. Th.7.12; ἐξουσίαν ὁ νόμος δέδωκε *permission* to do.., Pl.*Smp.*182e; ἐ. ποιεῖν Id.*Cri.*51d, etc.; ἐ. λαβεῖν And.2.28, X.*Mem.*2.6.24, etc.; λαβὼν ἐ. ὥστε.. Isoc.3.45; ἐπὶ τῇ τῆς εἰρήνης ἐ. with the *freedom permitted* by peace, D.18.44: c. gen. objecti, ἐ. ἔχειν θανάτου *power* of life and death, Poll.8.86; πρᾶγμα οὗ τὴν ἐ. ἔχουσιν ἄλλοι *control* over.., Diog.Oen.57; ἐ. τινός *power over, licence in* a thing, τοῦ λέγειν Pl.*Grg.*461e; ἐν μεγάλῃ ἐ. τοῦ ἀδικεῖν ib.526a, cf. *R.*554c; κατὰ τὴν οὐκ ἐ. τῆς ἀγωνίσεως from want of *qualification for*.., Th.5.50: abs., *power, authority*, E.*Fr.*784. 2. *abuse of authority, licence, arrogance*, ὕβρις καὶ ἐ. Th.1.38, cf. 3.45, D.19.200; ἡ ἄγαν ἐ. ib.272; ἄμετρος ἐ. *OGI* 669.51 (i A.D.). 3. Lit. Crit., ἐ. ποιητική poetic *licence*, Str.1.2.17, Jul.*Or.*1.10b. II. *office, magistracy*, ἀρχαὶ καὶ ἐ. Pl.*Alc.*1.135b; οἱ ἐν ταῖς ἐ. Arist.*EN* 1095ᵇ21; οἱ ἐν ἐ. ὄντες Id.*Rh.*1384ᵃ1; οἱ ἐπ' ἐξουσιῶν Lxx *Da.*3.2; ἡ ὑπατικὴ ἐ. the *consulate*, D.S.14.113, etc.; also ἡ ὕπατος ἐ. D.H.7.1; ἡ ταμιευτικὴ ἐ. the *quaestorship*, Id.8.77; δημαρχικὴ ἐ., v. δημαρχικός; ἡ τοῦ θαλάμου ἐ., in the Roman empire, *lordship* of the bedchamber, Hdn.1.12.3. 2. concrete, *body of magistrates*, D.H.11.32; αἱ ἐ. (as we say) the *authorities*, *Ev.Luc.*12.11, al., Plu.*Phil.*17. b. ἡ ἐ. as an honorary title, *POxy.*1103 (iv A.D.), etc. III. *abundance of means, resources*, ἐξουσίας ἐπίδειξις Th.6.31; πλοῦτος καὶ ἐ. Id.1.123, cf. D.21.138; ἐνδεεστέρως ἢ πρὸς τὴν ἐ. Th.4.39; τῶν ἀναγκαίων ἐ. Pl.*Lg.*828d; *excessive wealth*, opp. οὐσία, *Com.Adesp.*25a.5 D. IV. *pomp*, Plu.*Aem.*34. ⊕**-ιάζω**, fut. -άσω Phld. (v. infr.):—*exercise authority*, Lxx *Ec.*8.4: c. inf., *have power*, Phld.*Rh.*1.6 S., D.H.9.44. 2. *exercise authority over*, τοῦ μνήματος *CIG* 4584 (Palestine); τινῶν *Ev.Luc.*22.25, cf. 1 *Ep.Cor.*7.4; τῶν ἑαυτῆς ἐδνων *PMasp.*15.170 (vi A.D.):—Med., ἐπὶ τὸν λαόν Lxx *Ne.*5.15; ἔν τινι ib.*Ec.*8.9:—Pass., *to be held under authority*, 1 *Ep.Cor.*6.12. 3. *enjoy licence*, Arist.*EE* 1216ᵃ2. **-ιαστής**, οῦ, ὁ, *mighty one, person in authority*, Lxx *Is.*9.6(5), *Cat.Cod.Astr.*5(3).86, *PGen.*53.2 (iv A.D.). **-ιαστικός**, ή, όν, *authoritative, powerful*, Vett.Val.6.3, al., Sm.*Ec.*8.4, Eustr. *in EN* 119.21; πράξεις Heph.Astr.3.4; [θεάματα], ἐνεργήματα, Iamb.*Myst.*2.4. Adv. -κῶς Id.*VP* 32.217: Comp. -ώτερον Plb.5.26.3. II. *free, self-determining*, δύναμις Diogenian.Epicur.3.65. **-ιος**, ον, (οὐσία) *stripped of property*, Ph.2.528, *EM* 323.45.

**ἐξοφέλλω**, *increase exceedingly*, ἐξώφελλεν ἔεδνα *offered higher and higher* dowry, Od.15.18.

**ἐξοφθαλμ-ιάζω**, *have no eye for, disregard*, τοῖς ἐμοῖς καμάτοις *PGoodsp.Cair.*15.22 (iv A.D.). **-ίσας**, *occaecatus*, *Gloss.* **-ος**, ον, *with prominent eyes*, opp. κοιλόφθαλμος, X.*Eq.*1.9, Pl.*Tht.*209c. II. *manifest*, Plb.1.10.3. Adv. -μως Diog.Oen.36. III. *having a keen eye for*, [ὑποθήκης] *PRyl.*119.21 (i A.D.).

**ἐξοφρυόω**, in pf. part. Pass. ἐξωφρυωμένος *supercilious*, Hsch., *EM* 350.22.

**ἔξοχα**, v. ἔξοχος.

**ἐξοχάδες**, ων, αἱ, (ἔξοχος) *external piles, haemorrhoids* (the internal being called ἐσοχάδες), Paul.Aeg.3.59.

**ἐξοχετ-εία**, ἡ, *drawing into channels* or *sluices*, Str.4.6.7. **-ευσις**, εως, ἡ, *drawing off*, αἵματος Paul.Aeg.6.79. **-ευτέον**, *one must draw off*, τὸ οὖρον *Gp.*18.2.1. **-εύω**, *draw off*, ποταμοὶ ἐ. τὸ ὕδωρ ἐκ τῶν πεδίων Hp.*Aër.*18; εἰς τὸ στόμα τὸ σίαλον ἐ. οἱ ἀδένες Gal.*UP* 10.11: metaph., λόγου λόγον -εύων Emp.35.2; ὑψόθεν ἁρμονίης ῥύμα Procl.*H.*1.4.

**ἐξοχ-ή**, ἡ, (ἐξέχω) *prominence*, ἐ. κεράτων *elevated nature*, Arist.*PA* 663ᵃ8; πέτρας Lxx *Jb.*39.28; ζῴων ἐξοχαὶ *embossed figures* on shields, D.S.5.30; εἰσοχαὶ καὶ ἐ. S.E.*P.*1.120, cf. Simp. *in Cael.*409.13; *wart*, Dsc.2.104; ἐ. ἀκανθώδεις Id.3.16; also, = ἐξοχάδες, ib.80; *extremities* of animals, J.*AJ* 3.10.3. II. metaph., *pre-eminence*, ἐ. *in nullo est*, Cic.*Att.*4.15.7; ἀπεργάσασθαι τὴν ἐ. Longin.10.3; δι' ἐξοχὴν μορφῆς Hierocl.p.55 A.; κατ' ἐξοχήν *par excellence*, Str.1.2.10, Ph.1.65, A.D.*Synt.*26.15, *OGI* 764.52 (ii B.C.), etc.; οἱ κατ' ἐξοχὴν τῆς πόλεως *leading* men, *Act.Ap.*25.23. **-ία**, ἡ, *eminence*, *EM* 384.28. ⊕**-ος**, ον, *standing out, jutting*, πρῶνες Pi.*N.*4.52; ἀφαί Sch.E.*Hipp.*530: c. gen., ἔξοχος Ἀργείων κεφαλὴν *prominent above* them, Il.3.227. II. more freq. metaph., *eminent, excellent*, ἔξοχον ἄνδρα Il.2.188; αἶσα Pi.*N.*6.47: Comp. -ώτερος ib.3.71: Sup. -ώτατος ib.2.18, A.*Ag.*1622, E.*Supp.*889; τῶν φίλων τὸν -ώτατον Phld.*Lib.*p.20 O.; ἐξοχώτατος, = Lat. *eminentissimus*, ἔπαρχος *OGI* 640.16 (iii A.D.), *POxy.*1469.1 (iii A.D.), cf. *IG* 14.2433 (Massilia, iii A.D.); οἱ -ώτατοι τῆς βουλῆς Hdn.2.12.6. b. c. gen., *standing out from, raised above*, freq. used like a Sup., *most eminent, mightiest*, ἔξοχος ἡρώων Il.18.56; τέμενος τάμον ἔ. ἄλλων 6.194, etc.; βοῦς ἀγέληφι μέγ' ἔ. ἔπλετο πάντων 2.480; ἀριθμὸν ἔ. σοφισμάτων A.*Pr.*459; οὐδεὶς ἔ. ἄλλος ἔβλαστεν ἄλλου S.*Fr.*591; ἁπάσης νοῦν τε καὶ ἀνορέαν ἔξοχος ἡλικίας *beyond* all his contemporaries, *IG* 1².1021. c. c. dat., αἶγας.. αἳ πᾶσι μέγ' ἔξοχοι αἰπολίοισιν Od.21.266, cf. 15.227; also ἐκπρεπέ' ἐν πολλοῖσι καὶ ἔξοχον ἡρώεσσιν Il.2.483. 2. freq. in Hom. in pl., ἔξοχα as Adv. (cf. ὄχα), *especially, above others*, ὅς κ' ἔ. μὲν φιλέῃσιν, ἔ. δ' ἐχθαίρῃσιν Od.15.70, cf. Il.5.61; ἔ. λυγρὰ ἰδυῖα Od.11.432; ἐμοὶ δόσαν ἔ. gave me *as a high honour*, 9.551: with Sup., ἔξοχ' ἄριστοι *beyond compare* the best, Il.9.638, Od.4.629, al. b. c. gen., ἔ. πάντων *far above* all, Il.14.257, etc.; ἔξοχ' ἑταίρων Pi.*P.*5.26; ἔ. πλούτου *above all* wealth, Id.*O.*1.2.—Regul. Adv. -χως ib.9.69, E.*Ba.*1235, Lyc.1195, Arist.*Mu.*400ᵇ1, Lxx 3 *Ma.*5.31: Comp. -ώτερον Sor.1.99: Sup. -ώτατα Pi.*N.*4.92. **-ότης**, *eminentia*, *Gloss.*

**ἐξοχυρόω**, strengthd. for ὀχυρόω, J.*AJ* 13.5.11, Plu.*Cam.*10 (Pass.).

⊕**ἐξπελευστής**, οῦ, ὁ, = *compulsor*, *Cod.Just.*10.19.9.1, al.

**ἔξπηχυς**, = ἐκπηχυς, prob. in S.*Fr.*1045 (ἐξπηχυστὶ codd. *EM*).

**ἐξποδιαῖος**, α, ον, *six feet high* or *broad*, *CIG* 2860ᵢ9 (Didyma).

**ἔξπους**, ὁ, ἡ, = ἑξάπους, Pl.Com.242.

⊕**ἐξυβρίζω**, *break out into insolence, wax wanton*, Pherecyd.Syr.5, Hdt.4.146, 7.5; εὐπραγίαις Th.1.84; ὑπὸ πλούτου X.*Cyr.*8.6.1; ἐ. ἐς τόδε *come* to this pitch *of insolence*, Th.3.39: with neut. Adj. or Pron., παντοῖα ἐ. *commit* all kinds of *violence* or *extravagance*, Hdt.3.126; τάδ' ἐ. S.*El.*293; ἐ. πλείω περὶ τοὺς θεούς Lys.2.9; τι εἴς τινα Luc.*Fug.*18; εἴς τινα Plu.*Phoc.*2, Eus.Mynd.54, Ant.Lib.21.3. 2. c. acc. pers., *treat with insolence* or *violence*, Id.12.2; also ἐ. τοὺς ἔρωτας Conon 24.2:—Pass., ἡ πόλις ὑφ' ὑμῶν -ίζετο Hyp.*Phil.*9; τὰ -ισμένα *despised* things, Longin.43.5. II. of the body, *break out* from high feeding, Pl.*Lg.*691c; of plants, *to be over-luxuriant*, Arist.*GA* 725ᵇ35, Thphr.*CP* 2.16.8; ὥσπερ ἐξυβρίσαντα τὸν δῆμον ἀναφῦσαι πλῆθος συκοφαντῶν Plu.*Arist.*26.

**ἐξυγι-άζω**, *heal thoroughly*, Plb.3.88.2:—Pass., αὐτὰ ὑφ' ἑωυτοῦ ἐ. Hp.*de Arte* 8. **-αίνω**, *recover health*, Id.*Fract.*9:—Pass., Id.*de Arte* 4.

**ἐξυγρ-αίνω**, *saturate*, Arist.*Pr.*877ᵃ33, al.:—Pass., *to be full of moisture*, τοῦ ἀέρος -ομένου ib.944ᵃ21, etc. 2. *make watery*, of the blood, Id.*HA* 521ᵃ12 (Pass.), cf. Plu.2.97b (Pass.): metaph., ἐ. τὰ σώματα ταῖς ἡδοναῖς ib.136b:—Pass., *to be so*, of plants, Thphr.*CP* 6.6.4. II. Pass., *to be deprived of moisture*, Id.*Lap.*10. III. Pass., of liquid purgations, τὰ τῆς κοιλίης ἐξυγρασμένα ἦν ἰσχυρῶς Hp.*Prog.*2; so -αίνεσθαι τὴν κοιλίαν Plu.*Arat.*29, cf. 2.914e. **-ος**, ον, *watery, liquid*, Hp.*Acut.*(*Sp.*)1.

**ἐξυδαρόω**, *make watery*, Aët.4.10 (unless = *wash off*): metaph., ἐ. τὴν τῶν γινομένων δύναμιν ἡ τοῦ ποιοῦντος ῥαθυμία Simp. *in Epict.* p.94 D.:—Pass., *become water*, Arist.ap.Ath.10.434f, Alex.Aphr.*Pr.*1.81.

**ἐξυδατ-ίζω**, = sq., Hsch. **-όω**, *make into water* or *make watery*, τὸ ἁλμυρόν Hp.*Fist.*7; ὥσπερ ἐ. τὰς ὀσμάς Thphr.*Od.*66; τὸ γάλα Sor.1.93:—Pass., Corn.*ND* 17, Archig.ap.Orib.44.26.6, etc.; *become dropsical*, Hp.*Epid.*4.49. **-ωσις**, εως, ἡ, *changing into water*, Herod.Med. in *Rh.Mus.*49.556 (= Diocl.*Fr.*46), Zos.Alch. p.202 B. **-ωτικός**, ή, όν, *tending to make watery*, Sor.1.98.

**ἐξυδραργυρ-όω**, *cleanse of mercury*, Zos.Alch.p.123 B. (Pass.). **-ωσις**, εως, ἡ, *expulsion of mercury*, Id.pp.122, 123 B.

⊕**ἐξυδρίας** ἄνεμος *rainy* wind, Arist.*Mu.*394ᵇ19, Ach.Tat.*Intr.*p.68 M.

**ἐξυδρωπιάω**, *become dropsical*, ὄμματα Arist.*HA* 553ᵃ16.

**ἐξυθλέω**, in Pass., *to be foolishly spoken*, Phld.*Rh.*1.249 S.

**ἐξυλακτέω**, *bark out*: *burst out in rage*, Plu.*Arat.*50; πρός τινα Aeschin.Socr.38: c. acc. cogn., ἐ. γόον *yell it out*, Lyc.764.

**ἐξυλίζω**, *filter out* or *through*, Gal.19.673.

**ἐξυμεν-ίζω**, (ὑμήν) *strip off the skin* or *membrane*, Dsc.2.76.1; τὸ στέαρ Archig.ap.Aët.16.48. **-ιστέον**, *one must strip off the coat* or *membrane*, Dsc.2.76.5. **-ιστήρ**, ῆρος, ὁ, *flaying* or *dissecting knife*, Paul.Aeg.6.5.

**ἐξυμνέω**, strengthd. for ὑμνέω, Plb.6.47.7, Phld.*Rh.*1.219, 2.148 S., D.S.9 *Fr.*26, Procl. *in Alc.*p.84 C.:—Pass., Lyc.1195.

**ἐξυνῆκα**, ἐσύνηκα, = ξυνῆκα, poet. aor. c. dupl. augm. of συνίημι, Anacr.146 (ἐξ-), Alc.131 (ἐσ-).

**ἐξυπ-άγω** [ᾰ], *go over thoroughly, coat*, [λίθους] πηλῷ ἠχυρωμένῳ *IG* 2².463.42. **-ακουστέον**, *one must supply, understand* a word, Sch.Pi.*O.*9.131. **-άλυξις** [ᾰ], εως, ἡ, *escape*, Orph.*A.*684 codd. **-αλύσκω**, *escape from*, τι or τινά, Q.S.12.502, Orph.*L.*584. **-ανίστημι**, only in intr. aor. 2, σμῶδιξ μεταφρένου ἐξυπανέστη a weal *started up from under* the skin of the back, Il.2.267, cf. Pythag.ap.Porph.*VP* 40. **-ειπεῖν**, = ὑπειπεῖν, *advise*, E.*Ba.*1265.

**ἐξυπερ-ζέω**, aor. part. -ζέσας, *boil over*, τῷ θυμῷ Tz.*H.*3.267. **-θε**, Adv., = ὕπερθε, *above*, S.*Ph.*29. **-οπτάω**, *bake* or *dry extremely*, Gal.19.626, 649. **-όπτησις**, εως, ἡ, *over-heating*, ξανθῆς χολῆς Pall. *in Hp.*1.139 D.

**ἐξυπέρχομαι**, aor. ἐξυπῆλθον, *withdraw*, S.*Ichn.*205.

**ἐξυπηρετ-έω**, *assist to the utmost*, S.*Tr.*1156; τῇ ἑαυτοῦ παρανομίᾳ Lys.12.23, cf. Chrysipp.*Stoic.*3.123; ταῖς σαῖς χρείαις J.*AJ* 13.3.1: abs., Phld.*Sto.*339.9:—later in Med., ἀρχὰς καὶ λιτουργίας τῇ πατρίδι ἐ. *IG* 12(7).406 (Amorgos):—Pass., οὕτω πᾶσα περίστασις -ηθήσεται every emergency *will be provided for*, Ael.*Tact.*35.1. **-ησις**, εως, ἡ, *service, provision*, ἔργων *BGU* 1159.7 (i A.D.), cf. Vett.Val.355.17 (pl.). **-ητέον**, *one must supply*, Theano *Ep.*6.3.

**ἐξύπισθα**, Aeol. for ἐξόπισθεν, *Lyr.Adesp.*67.

**ἐξυπν-ίζω**, (ὕπνος) *awaken from sleep*, οἱ κόρεις εὐχρήστως -ίζουσιν ἡμᾶς Chrysipp.*Stoic.*2.334, cf. *Ev.Jo.*11.11:—Pass., *wake up*, Lxx *Jd.*16.14, Plu.*Ant.*30, M.Ant.6.31. (Condemned by Phryn.200,

etc., dub. in *Com.Adesp.*43.) **-ος**, ον, *awakened out of sleep*, ἐ. γενέσθαι Lxx 1*Es.*3.3, *Act.Ap.*16.27, J.*AJ*11.3.2, Zos.Alch.p.118B. Adv. -νως *PGiss.*1.19.4 (ii A.D.). **-όω**, *wake out of sleep*, τινά Sm., Al.*Ps.*138(139).18: also intr. metaph., ἀπὸ φιλοσοφίας Lxx 4*Ma.* 5.10.

**ἐξυπονοέω**, *suspect*, J.*AJ*15.7.7 (s.v.l.).

**ἐξυπτιάζω**, *turn* a person *quite on the back*, ὄμμα (ὄνομα codd.) *throw* his eyes *upwards* or *backwards*, A.*Th.*577; ἐ. ἑαυτόν *throwing back* his head haughtily, Luc.*Cat.*16: abs., Id.*Gall.*12, *Herc.*3, *Ind.*21:—Med., ἐξυπτιάζεσθαι τὴν κεφαλήν *throw* it *back*, Arist.*Fr.*106. II. intr., *lie back*, of the horns of wild cattle, Id.*HA*499$^{a}$7.

⊛ **ἐξῠφ-αίνω**, *weave*, φᾶρος Hdt.2.122, 9.109, cf. *PCair.Zen.*44.3 (iii B.C.); [πέπλον] Batr.182; of bees, ἐ. κηρία X.*Oec.*7.34 (Pass.); σάγους ἀπ' ἐρέας Str.4.4.3:—Med., Nicopho 5, Them.*Or.*21.250d:—Pass., ἐξύφανται ὑμέσι *are tissues of* membranes, Aret.*SA*2.7; -ασμένη πάπυρος, of rolls, Porph.ap.Eus.*PE*3.7. 2. *finish weaving*, ἱστὸν ἐξυφαγκέναι Artem.4.40; πρὶν ἐξυφῆναι (sc. τὰ κηρία) *Gp.*15.5.2. II. metaph., *finish*, ἐ. μέλος Pi.*N.*4.44; τὶν χάριτες ἐξυφαίνονται Id.*P.*4.275; of speech or writing, βύβλους τεσσαράκοντα καθαπερανεὶ κατὰ μίτον ἐξυφασμένας Plb.3.32.2, etc.; τὸ συνεχὲς τῆς ἐπιβολῆς ἐ. Id.18.10.3. **-ασμα**, ατος, τό, *finished web*, κερκίδος ἐ. σῆς E.*El.*539.

**ἐξυφηγέομαι**, = ὑφηγέομαι, S.*OC*1025.

⊛ **ἐξυψόω**, *exalt*, σεαυτόν Lxx *Si.*1.30; τὸν θεόν ib.*Da.*3.(51); *elevate*, παίγνια καὶ κώμους Αἰσχύλος -ωσεν *AP*7.411 (Diosc.).

⊛ **ἔξω**, Adv. of ἐξ, as εἴσω of εἰς: I. of Place, 1. with Verbs of motion, *out* or *out of*, ἔ. ἰών Od.14.526; χωρεῖν ἔ. Hdt.1.10; πορεύεσθαι Pl.*Phdr.*247b; βλέπειν D.18.323; ἔ. τοὺς Χριστιανούς (sc. φέρε) Luc.*Alex.*38, etc. b. as Prep., c. gen., ἔ. χροὸς ἕλκε Il.11.457; ἔ. βήτην μεγάροιο κιόντε Od.22.378; ἔ. or γῆς ἔ. βαλεῖν, A.*Th.*1019, S.*OT*622, etc.: pleon. with ἐκ, κραδίη δέ τοι ἔ. στηθέων ἐκθρῴσκει Il.10.94; ἐκ τῆς ταφῆς ἐκφέρειν ἔ. Hdt.3.16, cf. E.*Hipp.*650: ἐκπλώσαντες ἔ. τὸν Ἑλλήσποντον sailing *outside* the H., Hdt.5.103; ἔ. τὸν Ἑλλ. πλέων 7.58. 2. without any sense of motion, *outside*, Od.10.95, etc.; τὸ ἔ. the *outside*, Th.7.69; τὸ ἔ. τῶν ὀμμάτων their *prominency*, Pl.*Tht.*143e; τὰ ἔ. *things outside* the walls or house, Th.2.5, X.*Oec.*7.30; *external things*, Pl.*Tht.*198c; τὰ ἔ. πράγματα *foreign* affairs, Th.1.68; οἱ ἔ. those *outside*, Id.5.14; of exiles, Id.4.66, cf. S.*OC*444 (but in *NT*, the *heathen*, 1*Ep.Cor.*5.12); ἡ ἔ. στηλέων θάλασσα ἡ Ἀτλαντὶς καλεομένη Hdt.1.202, cf. Pl.*Criti.*108e; ἡ ἔ. θάλασσα, opp. ἡ εἴσω, Aristid.*Or.*40(5).9; ἔ. τὴν χεῖρα ἔχειν keep one's arm *outside* one's cloak, Aeschin.1.25. b. as Prep., c. gen., οἱ ἔ. γένους, opp. τὰ ἐγγενῆ, S.*Ant.*660; ἔ. τῶν κακῶν οἰκεῖν Id.*OT*1390; ἔ. τοξεύματος *out of range of* arrows, Th.7.30; ἔ. βελῶν, τῶν β., X.*Cyr.*3.3.69, *An.*5.2.26; ἔ. τοῦ πολέμου *unconcerned with* the war, Th.2.65; τοῦ πάσχειν κακῶς ἔ. γενήσεσθε D.4.34; τῶν ἔ. τοῦ πράγματος ὄντων persons *unconcerned in* the matter, Id.21.45, cf. ib.15; πράξεις ἔ. τῆς ὑποθέσεως λεγομένας *away from* the subject, Isoc.12.74; ἔ. τοῦ πράγματος Arist.*Rh.*1354$^{a}$22; ἔ. τοῦ δικαστηρίου [ἔπαινοι] Luc.*Hist.Conscr.*59; ἔ. λόγου τίθεσθαι, θέσθαι, Plu.2.671a, *Tim.*36; ἔ. πάτου ὀνόματα *out-of*-the-way words, Luc.*Hist.Conscr.*44; ἔ. πίστεως *beyond* belief, Id.*DMar.*4.1; ἔ. φρενῶν *out of* one's senses, Pi.*O.*7.47; ἔ. ἐλαύνειν τοῦ φρονεῖν E.*Ba.*853; ἔ. σαυτοῦ γίγνῃ Pl.*Ion* 535b; ἔ. γνώμης E.*Ion* 926; οὐδὲν ἔ. τοῦ φυτεύσαντος δρᾷς *unlike* thy sire, S.*Ph.*904; ἔ. τῆς ἀνθρωπείας..νομίσεως *alien to* human belief, Th.5.105: prov., αἴρειν ἔ. πόδα πηλοῦ keep *clear* of difficulties, Suid.; so ἔ. κομίζων πηλοῦ πόδα A.*Ch.*697; πημάτων ἔ. πόδα ἔχειν Id.*Pr.*265; ἔ. πραγμάτων ἔχειν πόδα E.*Heracl.*109. II. of Time, *beyond, over*, ἔ. μέσου ἡμέρας X.*Cyr.*4.4.1; ἔ. τῆς ἡλικίας D.3.34; ἔ. πέντ' ἐτῶν Id.38.18. III. *without, except*, c. gen., ἔ. σεῦ Hdt.7.29, cf. 4.46; ἔ. ἤ.. Id.2.3, 7.228; ἔ. τοῦ πλεόνων ἄρξαι *besides*.., Th.5.97, cf. 26; ἔ. τοῦ ἐφθακέναι ἀδικοῦντες *except* the being first to do wrong, Epist. Philipp.ap.D.18.39, cf. *PSI*6.577.17, *PCair.Zen.*225.4. IV. τὰ κατὰ τὸν Φίλιππον ἔ. τελέως ἐστί, Philip is 'played out', Plb.5.28.4.—Cf. ἐξωτέρω, -τάτω.

**ἕξω**, fut. of ἔχω.

**ἐξω-βάδια**· ἐνώτια (Lacon.), Hsch. **-βλητος**, ον, *outcast*, Id.

**ἐξώγλουτοι**, gloss on ῥοικοὶ μηροί, Bacchius ap.Erot.*Fr.*43.

**ἐξώδων**, οντος, ὁ, ἡ, *with prominent teeth*, *Hippiatr.*115.

⊛ **ἔξωθεν**, rarely **ἔξωθε** Diog.Oen.18, Adv., (ἔξω) *from without* or *abroad*, ἔ. εἴσω A.*Th.*560, cf. Pl.*Plt.*293d, etc.; ἔ. εἰστρέχειν Men.*Sam.*37. II. = ἔξω, Hdt.1.70, Pl.*Ti.*33c, etc.; οἱ ἔ. those *outside*, Hdt.9.5, etc. (but *heathen* in 1*Ep.Ti.*3.7); οἱ ἔ. περιεστηκότες Aeschin.2.5; τὰ ἔ. *matters outside the house*, opp. τἄνδον, A.*Th.*201, cf. E.*El.*74, etc.; αἱ ἔ. πόλεις *foreign* states, Pl.*Plt.*307e; οἱ ἔ. λόγοι *foreign to the subject*, D.18.9; ἀκαταξέστους ἐκ τοῦ ἔ. *IG*1$^{2}$.372.61. b. c. gen., ἐντὸς ἢ ἔ. δόμων; E.*Med.*1312; ἔ. ὅπλων συγκαθήμενοι X.*An.*5.7.24; *free from*, ξυμφορᾶς S.*El.*1449; δειμάτων E.*HF*723. c. c. gen., *besides, apart from*, Gal.6.409, 16.502. III. Gramm., ἔ. προσλαμβάνειν *supply* or *understand* a word, A.D.*Synt.*107.3; προσνεῖμαι ib.92.1; ὑπακούεσθαι ib.22.21. 2. *initially*, Id.*Pron.*58.5, al.; *finally*, ib.60.6, al.

⊛ **ἐξωθ-έω**, aor. 1 ἐξέωσα (v. infr. II), *thrust out, force out*, ἐκ δ' ὦσε γλήνην Il.14.494, cf. 17.618; even by pulling, *wrench out*, ἐκ δ' ἄρα οἱ μηροῦ δόρυ μείλινον ὦσε θύραζε 5.694; *displace*, Hp.*Art.*46 (Pass.); *expel, eject, banish*, γῆς τινά S.*OC*1296; πάτρας ib.1330; *put away* a wife, *PSI*1.41.16 (iv A.D.); *thrust back*, τοὺς δίκῃ νικῶντας S.*Aj.*1248; *drive*, τοὺς Λακεδαιμονίους ἐς τὰς ἁμάξας Th.5.72; πλοῖον εἰς αἰγιαλόν *Act.Ap.*27.39, cf. Jul.*Or.*2.60c; τὴν πόλιν εἰς χαλεπόν Plu.*Nic.*12; ἐ. εἰς ἅπαν ἀπὸ τῆς ὄχθης Arr.*An.*1.15.4; ἐ. νόμον Plu.*Comp.Ag.Gracch.*5:—Pass., ἐξωθέεσθαι ἐκ τῆς χώρης Hdt.4.13, cf. 5.124; μάχῃ Id.6.83; πατρίδος ἐξωθούμενος S.*OC*428; ἐξωσθήσομαι εἰπεῖν *shall be debarred* from.., D.24.61. 2. ἐ. γλώσσας ὀδύναν *put forth* painful words, *break forth into* cruel words, S.*Ph.*1142 (lyr.). II. *drive out of the sea, drive on shore*, τὰς ἄλλας [ναῦς] ἐξέωσαν πρὸς τὴν γῆν Th.2.90, cf. 8.104; ἐς τὴν γῆν Id.7.52:—Pass., πνεύμασιν ἐξωσθέντες E.*Cyc.*279 (cf. ἐξώστης II): metaph., ἐξωσθῆναι τῇ ὥρᾳ ἐς χειμῶνα Th.6.34. (Late inf. ἐξεοῦν Just.*Nov.*59.4 *Intr.*, pres. ind. Pass. ἐξεοῦται *Cod.Just.*1.2.24.6, formed fr. ἐξέωσα.) **-ησις**, εως, ἡ, *expulsion*, Alex.Aphr.*Pr.*1.90, Aët.8.53. 2. Gramm., *expulsion* of a letter, Eust.378.3, 1542.32.

**ἐξώκαρπος** πάλη a form of wrestling, Eust.1572.39.

**ἐξωκεᾰν-ίζω**, Geog., *represent as placed out in the ocean*, Str.1.2.17, 7.3.6:—Pass., Eust.1050.64. **-ισμός**, ὁ, *a placing out in the ocean*, Κίρκης, Μηδείας, Str.1.2.10.

**ἐξωκέλης**, ητος, ὁ, *barebacked horse*, Suid. II. *piratical craft*, Id.

**ἐξώκοιτος**, ον, *sleeping out*, Hsch.:—as Subst., **ἐξώκοιτος**, ὁ, *a fish which comes upon the beach to sleep*, = ἄδωνις, Clearch.73, Thphr.*Fr.*171.1, Ael.*NA*9.36, Opp.*H.*1.158.

**ἐξωλαίμας**· οὐκ αἰσίους, Hsch.

⊛ **ἐξώλ-εια**, ἡ, (ὄλλυμι) *utter destruction*, ἐπαρώμενον ἐξώλειαν ἑαυτῷ ἐπιορκοῦντι *IG*1$^{2}$.10.15, cf. Antipho 5.11, Lys.12.10, Jusj.ap.D.24.151; κατ' ἐξωλείας ὀμόσαι, ἐπιορκεῖν, D.21.119, 57.22; ὑπόχον ἐξωλείας αὑτὸν ποιεῖν ib.53. ⊛ **-ης**, ες, *utterly destroyed, ruined*, ἐ. γίνεσθαι Hdt.7.9.β′; ἐξώλεις καὶ προώλεις ποιεῖν τινας ἐν γῇ καὶ ἐν θαλάσσῃ D.18.324, cf. 19.71; freq. in imprecations, ἐ. ἀπόλοιο Ar.*Pax* 1072, Men.*Sam.*152; ἐξώλη αὐτὸν εἶναι καὶ γένος Lex ap.And.1.98, cf. 126; ἐξώλη γίνεσθαι καὶ αὐτὸν καὶ τοὺς ἐκείνου πάντας *SIG*167.15 (Mylasa, iv B.C.); ἐ. ἀπολοίμην καὶ προώλης D.19.172. II. metaph., of persons, *pernicious, abominable*, Αἰγύπτου γένος A.*Supp.*741; γέρων Eup.45; οὐδὲν πέφυκε ζῷον -έστερον Ar.*Pl.*443, cf. *Ec.*1053, 1070, D.58.63, Antiph.159.12, etc.

**ἐξώμαλλος**, ον, *with the nap outside*, Sch.D.Chr.72.1 p.789 Emp.

**ἐξωμ-εύς**, έως, ὁ, *one who wears an* ἐξωμίς, Diog.*Ep.*29.2. **-ίας**, ου, ὁ, *one with arms bare to the shoulder*, Luc.*Vit.Auct.*7.

**ἐξωμῐδοποι-ΐα**, ἡ, *manufacture of* ἐξωμίδες, X.*Mem.*2.7.6. **-ός**, ὁ, *maker of* ἐξωμίδες, Poll.7.159.

**ἐξωμ-ίζω** τὸν ἕτερον βραχίονα *bare* one arm *up to the shoulder, as when wearing an* ἐξωμίς, Ar.*Ec.*267. ⊛ **-ίς**, ίδος, ἡ, (ὦμος) = χιτὼν ἑτερομάσχαλος, *tunic with one sleeve*, leaving one shoulder bare, worn by slaves and the poor, Id.*V.*444 (cf. Sch. ad loc.), *Lys.*662, X.*Mem.*2.7.5, etc.; by Laconizers, Ael.*VH*9.34; by Cynics, S.E.*P.*1.153; by the rich when not on ceremony, Suid. s.v.; by women, Ar.*Fr.*8; at Rome, *sleeveless tunic*, Plu.*Cat.Ma.*3, Gell.6(7).12.3.

**ἔξωμος** χιτών, = foreg., Hsch., cf. Aq.*Is.*15.4.

⊛ **ἐξωμοσία**, ἡ, *denial on oath that one knows anything* of a matter, Ar.*Ec.*1026, *PEleph.*34.1 (iii B.C.). II. *declining an office*, D.19.129. III. *vow*, Al.*Le.*22.18.

**ἐξωνέομαι**, *buy off, redeem*, c. gen. vel dat. pretii, χρημάτων τινὰς ἐ. Arist.*Oec.*1352$^{a}$13; χρήμασι τοὺς κινδύνους Lys.24.17; ἀτιμίας μείζοσι τιμαῖς Arist.*Pol.*1315$^{a}$24, cf. *PFay.*21.20 (ii A.D.); τρισχιλίων ἐ. παρὰ τῶν γονέων..μὴ ἀπαχθῆναι Luc.*Peregr.*9, cf. J.*BJ*1.18.4; *redeem*, ἅπαντα τὰ σφάλματα ἑνὶ ὕψει καὶ κατορθώματι Longin.36.2. 2. generally, *buy* (in impf., *bid for*, Hdt.1.196), ὁ ἐξωνούμενος the *purchaser*, Aeschin.3.66; *bribe*, Paus.4.17.3.

**ἐξώνῠχον**, τό, = λιθόσπερμον, Dsc.3.141, Id.*Eup.*2.118.

**ἐξώπιος**, ον, (ὤψ) *out of sight of*, hence, *out of*, freq. in E., δόμων ἐ. βέβηκε *Supp.*1038; δωμάτων *Med.*624, *Alc.*546; used in parody by Ar.*Th.*881.

**ἐξώπροικα**, τά, = ἕδνα, *EM*316.40, Sch.Od.2.195.

⊛ **ἐξωπῠλ-ῖται**, οἱ, *dwellers outside the gates*, as an organized body, *BGU*34 ii 21 (ii A.D.), etc. **-ος**, ον, *out of doors*, Sch.A.R.1.1174.

**ἐξωραϊσμένον**· κεκοσμημένον, κεκαλλωπισμένον, Hsch.

**ἐξωριάζω**, (ὥρα) *leave out of thought, neglect*, f.l. for εὐωριάζω, A.*Pr.*17.

⊛ **ἔξωρος**, ον, (ὥρα) *untimely, out of season, unfitting*, ἔξωρα πράσσω S.*El.*618. 2. *too late, too old, superannuated*, Aeschin.1.95, Plu.*Sull.*36, Luc.*Herm.*78, al. (also glossed by ἑξαέτης as though ἕξωρος, *EM*350.2): c. gen., *too old for*.., τοῦ ἐρᾶν Luc.*Merc.Cond.*7. Adv. -ρως, ἔχειν τοῦ ἀποδημεῖν Philostr.*VS*1.21.8.

**ἐξώροφος**, ον, (ὄροφος) *with* or *of six stories*, πύργοι D.S.14.51.

**ἐξῶρτο**, v. ἐξόρνυμι.

**ἔξ-ωσις**, εως, ἡ, *putting out, displacement*, Hp.*Art.*46, Gal.14.778. 2. *thrust*, ἡ κατὰ τὴν ἔ. βία Marcellin.*Puls.*99. II. *purgation, evacuation*, Sever.*Clyst.*25 D. **-ωσμα**, ατος, τό, *banishment*, Lxx *La.*2.14 (pl.). ⊛ **-ώστης**, ου, ὁ, *one who drives out*, Ἄρης E.*Rh.*322. 2. ἐ. ἄνεμοι violent winds *which drive ships ashore* (cf. ἐξωθέω II), Hdt.2.113, Hp.*VM*9, Aeschin.*Ep.*1.3. 3. ὁ ἐ. (sc. σφυγμός), term coined by Archig.ap.Gal.8.662. 4. = ἐξώστρα III, *Cod.Just.*8.10.12.5b (pl.), *Gloss.* **-ωστικός**, ή, όν, *expulsive*, τρόπος Epicur.*Nat.*2.5. **-ώστρα**, ἡ, *stage-machine* identified with the ἐκκύκλημα (q.v.) by Hsch. and Poll.4.127, but distd. from it, ib.129: metaph., τῆς τύχης ἐπὶ τὴν ἐ. ἀναβιβαζούσης τὴν ὑμετέραν ἄγνοιαν Plb.11.5.8:—also **-ωστρον**, τό, *IG*11(2).199*A*95 (pl., Delos, iii B.C.). II. *bridge thrust out* from the besiegers' tower against the walls of the besieged place, Lat. *exostra*, Veget. *de Re Milit.*4.21. III. *balcony*, Sm.4*Ki.*1.2; = Lat. *maenianum*, *Gloss.*

**ἐξωστῷον**, τό, *outer porch*, Hdn.*Epim.*267.

**ἐξω-τάτω**, Adv., Sup. of ἔξω, *outermost*, Pl.*Phd.*112e, Arist.*Cael.*

279$^a$20, Ph.2.331, etc. :—later, Adj. ⊛**ἐξώτατος**, Lxx 3*Ki*.6.30 ; τὸ ἐ. Ph.1.95. **-τεριαῖος**, α, ον, *external*, *superficial*, λίθοι *POxy*.498.18 (ii A.D.). **-τερικός**, ή, όν, opp. ἐσωτερικός, *external*, *belonging to the outside*, τὰ ἐ. *the exterior members*, such as hands and feet, Arist. *GA*786$^a$26 ; ἐ. ἀρχή *foreign* dominion, Id.*Pol*.1272$^b$19 ; ἐ. πράξεις *external* activities, ib.1325$^b$22 ; ἐ. ἀγαθά ib.1323$^b$25 ; οἱ ἐ. *persons outside* the Pythagorean school, Iamb.*VP*32.226. **II.** οἱ ἐ. λόγοι *popular* arguments or treatises, opp. οἱ κατὰ φιλοσοφίαν, Arist.*EE* 1217$^b$22, *Pol*.1278$^b$31, *Metaph*.1076$^a$28, *EN*1102$^a$26, al. ; ταῦτα -κωτέρας σκέψεως Id.*Pol*.1254$^a$33 ; ἐ. λόγοι, opp. ἀκροαματικοί or ἐσωτερικοί (q. v.), Gell.20.5.2 ; ἐ. διάλογοι, opp. τὰ ἠθικά, τὰ φυσικὰ ὑπομνήματα, Plu.2.1115b ; cf. ἐσωτερικός. **-τέρω**, Adv., Comp. of ἔξω, *more outside*, δρόμου ἐ. A.*Ch*.1023, cf. Arist.*Metaph*.1055$^a$25, Lxx*Jb*.18.17, etc. :—hence later, Adj. **ἐξώτερος**, *outer*, Lxx*Ex*.26.4, etc., *Ev.Matt*.8.12 ; ξυστός *POxy*.896.14 (iv A.D.). ⊛ **-τικός**, ή, όν, *foreign*, οἰκονομίαι Iamb.*VP*21.97 ; of a plant, *PHolm*.17.31 ; *outlying*, κτήματα *PMasp*.21 ii 1 (vi A.D.) ; *alien*, opp. συγγενής, *CIG* 2686 (Iasos) ; of heirs, Just.*Nov*.22.20.2 ; ὑμνῳδοί *IGRom*.4.353c11 (Pergam.) ; ἐ. ἑστιάσεις banquets *in other men's houses*, opp. ἰδιωτικαί, Epict.*Ench*.33.6 (v.l.). **2.** *uninitiated*, c. gen., τῆς θρησκείας Porph.*Abst*.4.6. **3.** Adv. -κῶς f.l. in Democr.179. **-φᾰνής**, ές, *convex*, of mirrors, Phlp. *in Mete*.28.17. **-φορος**, ον, *brought out*, *published*, ἐ. ποιήσασθαι Iamb.*VP*34.247, cf. Stob.2.7.11$^k$. **II.** *tending outwards*, πνεῦμα Marcellin.*Puls*.65. **-χείριον ποιῶ**, = Lat. *emancipare*, *Gloss*. **-χειριότης**, = Lat. *emancipatio*, ibid.

**ἔξωχρος**, ον, *very pale*, Arist.*HA*631$^b$28, Thphr.*HP*4.6.3, Aret.*SD* 2.6.

**εὀ-**, written for εὐ- in Ion. Inscrr., *SIG*168.5, etc.

**ἕο**, Ep. for οὗ : **ἑοῖ**, Ep. for οἷ. **ἔοι**, Ep. for εἴη, 3 sg. pres. opt. of εἰμί.

**ἔοικα**, ας, ε, etc., pf. with pres. sense, *to be like* : rarely in other tenses, 3 sg. impf. εἶκε *it was opportune*, Il.18.520 (unless fr. εἴκω III) : fut. εἴξω *will be like*, Ar.*Nu*.1001 ; pf. 3 dual ἔϊκτον Od.4.27 ; 1 pl. ἔοιγμεν S.*Aj*.1239, *Ichn*.95, E.*Cyc*.99 ; ἐοίκαμεν Pl.*La*.193d ; 3 pl. εἴξασι E.*Hel*.497, Ar.*Av*.96, Pl.*Plt*.291a, *Sph*.230a, Pl.Com.22, 153, Eub.98.8 ; ἐοίκασι Pl.*R*.584d ; inf. εἰκέναι E.*Fr*.167, Ar.*Nu*.185 (cf. προσέοικα) ; part. εἰκώς (also ἐϊκώς Il.21.254, v. sub εἰκός) ; εἰοικυῖαι 18.418 : Ion. (not Ep.) οἶκα, ας, ε, Hdt.4.82, 5.20, 106, part. οἰκώς Id. 6.125 ; but ἔοικα, ἐοικώς are found in other Ionic writers, as Semon. 7.41, Anacr.84, Heraclit.1, Hp.*Aër*.6, Democr.266, and codd. of Hdt. vary ; 2 sg. εἶκας (v.l. οἶκας) Alcm.80 : plpf. ἐῴκειν, εις, ει, Od. 1.411, etc. ; 3 pl. ἐῴκεσαν Th.7.75, etc., Ep. ἐοίκεσαν Il.13.102 ; Ep. 3 dual ἐΐκτην 1.104, Od.4.662, Hes.*Sc*.390 codd. : Att. plpf. ᾔκειν Ar. *Av*.1298 (Dawes from Sch.) :—**Pass.**, 3 sg. pf. ἤϊκται Nic.*Th*.658 : plpf. ἤϊκτο Od.20.31, al., ἔϊκτο Il.23.107. **I.** *to be like*, *look like*, c. dat., Il.14.474, etc. ; Μαχάονι πάντα ἔοικε 11.613 ; κεφαλήν τε καὶ ὄμματα καλὰ ἔοικας κείνῳ Od.1.208 ; so εἶδός τε μέγεθός τε, δέμας, etc., Il.2.58, 21.285, etc. ; εἰς ὦπα ἔοικεν, ἄντα ἐῴκει, 3.158, 24.630, al. ; μελαίνῃ κηρὶ ἔοικε *is considered like*, i.e. *hated like*, death, Od.17.500 : c. part., αἰεὶ γὰρ δίφρου ἐπιβησομένοισιν ἐΐκτην *seemed* always just about to set foot upon the chariot, Il.23.379 ; ἔοικε σημαίνοντι *seems* to indicate, Pl.*Cra*.437a ; τοὐναντίον ἔοικεν σπεύδοντι *seems* to urge the opposite, Id.*Prt*.361b, cf. X.*Mem*.1.6.10, 4.3.8, Arist.*Sens*.437$^b$24 ; ἔοικεν τοῦτο ἀτόπῳ this *is like* an absurdity, *seems* absurd, Pl.*Phd*. 62d ; δαιμονίᾳ ἔοικεν εὐεργεσίᾳ D.2.1 : used by A. in this sense only in part. εἰκώς *like*, c. dat., *Ag*.760 (lyr.), *Ch*.560 (cf. IV. 1). **2.** ἐοικέναι κατά τι *to be analogous to*, Plot.4.4.39. **II.** *seem*, c. inf. (where we make the Verb impersonal) : c. inf. pres., *methinks*, ἔοικα δέ τοι παραείδειν ὥς τε θεῷ I *seem* to sing (i.e. *methinks* I sing) to thee, as to a god, Od.22.348 ; χλιδᾶν ἔοικας *methinks* thou art delicate, A.*Pr*.971 ; ἔοικα θρηνεῖν μάτην Id.*Ch*.926, cf. 730 ; ἔοικα..οὐκ εἰδέναι S.*OT*744 ; ἔοικα..ἐποικτίρειν σε Id.*Ph*.317 : c. fut. inf., θέλξειν μ' ἔοικας *it seems likely* that thou wilt.., A.*Eu*.900 ; ἐρεῖν ἔοικας Id.*Pr*.984 ; ἔοικα θεσπιῳδήσειν Id.*Ag*.1161 ; κτενεῖν ἔοικας Id.*Ch*.922 ; τὸν ἄνδρ' ἔοικεν ὕπνος ἕξειν S.*Ph*.821 ; ἔοικα πράξειν οὐδέν E.*Hec*.813, cf. *Cyc*.99 : c. aor. inf., πικροὺς ἔοιγμεν..ἀγῶνας κηρῦξαι *methinks* we proclaimed, S.*Aj*.1239 : c. pf. inf., ἔοικεν ἐπωνομάσθαι Pl.*Cra*.419c : c. part., ἔοικε κεκλημένη *seems* to be called, ibid. ; ἐοίκατε ἡδόμενοι X.*HG*6.3.8 ; κατακεκομμένη ἔοικεν ἡ σύνθεσις καὶ εὐκαταφρόνητος Demetr.*Eloc*.4. **2.** impers., ἔοικε *it seems* : ὡς ἔοικε as *it seems*, S.*Ant*.576, 740, *El*.772, 1341, E.*Andr*.551, etc., used by Pl. merely to modify a statement, *probably*, *I believe*, *Phd*.61c, *R*.332b, al. ; ἔοικεν in answers, *so it seems*, ib.334a, 346c, al. **3.** personal in the same sense, ὡς ἔοικας S.*El*.516, *Tr*.1241 ; ὡς εἴξασιν E.*Hel*.497. **III.** *beseem*, *befit*, c. dat. pers., τὸ μὲν ἀπιέναι..οὐδενὶ καλῷ ἔοικε X.*An*.6.5.17 (unless οὐδενὶ κ. is neut.) ; ἀνδράσι ἔοικεν τὰ τῆς γεωργίας *POxy*. 899.18 (200 A.D.) : c. dat. et inf., τὰ μὲν οὔ τι καταθνητοῖσιν ἔοικεν ἄνδρεσσιν φορέειν Il.10.440 ; cf. III. 2 fin. **2.** most freq. impers., ἔοικε *it is fitting*, *reasonable*, mostly with neg. and folld. by inf., οὐκ ἔστ' οὐδὲ ἔοικε τεὸν ἔπος ἀρνήσασθαι Il.14.212 ; οὐ γὰρ ἔοικ' ὀτρυνέμεν 4.286 : freq. c. acc. et inf., 12.212, al. ; in Od.22.196 an inf. must be supplied, εὐνῇ ἔνι μαλακῇ καταλέγμενος, ὥς σε ἔοικεν (sc. καταλέξασθαι) ; ἐπεὶ οὐδὲ ἔοικε (sc. εἶναι) Il.1.119 :—rare in Att., ἔοικεν νέῳ.. ὀργὴν ὑποφέρειν Pl.*Lg*.879c. **IV.** part. ἐοικώς, εἰκώς, Ion. οἰκώς, υῖα, ός, **1.** *seeming like*, *like*, Il.3.449, etc. :—the longer form is found in Att. Prose, φόβος οὐδενὶ ἐοικώς Th.7.71 ; εἰκώς A.*Ag*.760 (lyr.), *Ch*.560, E.*Cyc*.376, Ar.*V*.1321. **2.** *fitting*, *seemly*, μῦθοί γε ἐοικότες.., ὧδε ἐοικότα μυθήσασθαι, Od.3.124, 125, cf. 4.239 ; ἐοικότι κεῖται ὀλέθρῳ 1.46 ; ἐϊκυῖαν ἄκοιτιν *a suitable* wife, 'a help *meet for him*', Il.9.399. **3.** *likely*, *probable*, εἰκός ἐστι, = ἔοικε, S.*El*.659, 1488, etc. ; esp. ὡς εἰκός, Ion. ὡς οἰκός, = ὡς ἔοικε, Hdt.1.45 (sc. ἦν), S.*Ph*.498, etc. ; οἷον εἰκός Pl.*R*.406c ; καθάπερ εἰκός Id.*Ti*.24d ; also ὡς τὸ εἰκός Id.*Phd*.67a, *R*.407d, etc. ; οἱ εἰκότες λόγοι, μῦθοι, Id.*Ti*. 48d, 59c ; ἀδύνατα εἰκότα *plausible* miracles, opp. δυνατὰ ἀπίθανα, Arist.*Po*.1460$^a$27. **4.** καὶ τὰ ἐοικότα and *the like*, αἶγες, αἴλουροι, καὶ τὰ ἐ. S.E.*P*.1.47, cf. 3.180 ; ἄρτιον, περιττόν, τέλειον, τὰ ἐ. Nicom. *Ar*.1.3. **5.** neut. Subst. εἰκός (q. v.).

⊛**ἐοικότως**, Att. **εἰκότως**, Ion. **οἰκότως**, Adv. of part. ἐοικώς, *similarly*, *like*, τινί A.*Ag*.915. **2.** *reasonably*, *fairly*, *naturally*, *as was to be expected*, Hdt.2.25, A.*Supp*.403 (lyr.) ; οὐκ εἰ. un*fairly*, Th.1.37 ; freq. emphat. at the close of a sentence or clause, ib.77, 2.93, Isoc. 1.48, etc.

**ἑοῖο**, Ep. gen. of ἑός. **ἔοις**, Ep. 2 sg. opt. of εἰμί. **ἐοῖσα**, Aeol. for ἐοῦσα, οὖσα, part. fem. of εἰμί.

**ἐόλει**, *caused to waver*, πῦρ δέ νιν οὐκ ἐόλει (3 sg. impf.), as Böckh for αἰόλλει in Pi.*P*.4.233 :—Pass., ἐόλητο (3 sg. plpf.) *was troubled*, ἐόλητο νόον μελεδήμασι A.R.3.471 ; ἐόλητο θυμὸν..ὑποδμηθεὶς βελέεσσι Κύπριδος Mosch.2.74 ; cf. ἐόληται· τετάρακται, ἐπτόηται, ὠδύνηται, Hsch. (Perh. cf. εἴλω.)

**ἔολον**· πρόσφορον, χρηματιστόν, Hsch. (fort. ἐσλόν).

**ἔολπα**, ας, ε, poet. pf. with pres. sense of ἔλπομαι (q. v.).

**ἔον**, Ep. (Il.23.643) and Aeol. for ἦν, 1 sg. impf. of εἰμί (q. v.) :— but **ἐόν**, Ion. for ὄν, part. neut. of εἰμί.

**ἔορ**· θυγάτηρ, ἀνεψιός, and ἔορες· προσήκοντες, συγγενεῖς, Hsch. (Cogn. with Skt. *svasar*–, Lith. *seser*– 'sister', etc.)

**ἔοργα**, ας, ε, poet. pf. of ἔρδω, Il.3.57, al., Hecat.6 J., Hdt.3.127 ; 3 pl. ἔοργαν for ἐόργασιν, Batr.179 ; part. ἐοργώς Il.9.320, Od.22.318 : Ion. 3 sg. plpf. ἐόργεε Hdt.1.127.

**ἐόργη**, ἡ, = τορύνη, Poll.6.88 (cf. εὐέργη). **ἐοργῆσαι**· τορυνῆσαι, ibid.

**ἑορτάζω**, in Ion. Prose **ὁρτάζω** : impf. ἑώρταζον (with irreg. augm.) Isoc.19.40, Paus.4.19.4 : fut. -άσω Luc.*Merc.Cond*.16, Alciphr.3.18, etc. : aor. ἑώρτασα D.C.48.34, etc. ; inf. ἑορτάσαι Ar.*Ach*.1079, Pl. *R*.458a ; cf. διεορτάζω : (ἑορτή) :—*keep festival* or *holiday*, Hdt.2.60, 122, E.*IT*1458, etc. ; ἑορτὰς ἑ. *celebrate* festivals, X.*Ath*.3.2 ; ἡμέρας τέτταρας Plu.*Cam*.42 ; τὴν γενέθλιόν τινος *OGI*493.26 (Ephesus, ii A.D.) ; ἑ. τῷ θεῷ Luc.*Anach*.23. **II.** *celebrate as a festival*, νίκην ἑ. *celebrate* it *by a festival*, Plu.2.349f, cf. *Ant*.56 ; at Rome, *celebrate by a triumph*, D.C.51.21.

**ἔορται**· ἔδοξε, Hsch. **II.** = κρεμνᾶται (cf. αἰωρέω), Id. **III.** ἐόρτας· ἀρεσκούσας, καλάς, Id.

**ἑορτ-αῖος**, α, ον, *festal*, καιροί D.H.4.74. **-άσιμος** [ᾰ], ον, *of a festival*, ἡμέρα J.*AJ*11.6.13, cf. Plu.2.270a, *OGI*524.8 (Thyatira) ; ἐμαυτῷ οὐχ ἑορτάσιμα ὄντα though I was *in* no *holiday mood*, Luc.*Sat*. 11. **-άσιος** [ᾰ], ον, perh. = Lat. *sollemnis*, *Arch.Anz*.38/39.154 (Antioch). **-ᾰσις**, εως, ἡ, *holiday-keeping*, Pl.*Lg*.657d. **-ασμα**, ατος, τό, *festival*, *holiday*, Lxx *Wi*.19.16. **-ασμός**, ὁ, = ἑόρτασις, Plu. 2.1101e (nisi leg. -ασίμων), *Gloss*. **-αστής**, οῦ, ὁ, *reveller*, Poll.1. 34, Max.Tyr.6.8 (pl.), Procop.*Aed*.1.10. ⊛ **-αστικός**, ή, όν, *fit for a festival*, μάχαι (i.e. tourneys) Pl.*Lg*.829b ; ἡμέρα Luc.*Am*.1, Alciphr. 3.57 ; θυσία Ael.*VH*3.37. **-ή**, in Ion. Prose **ὁρτή** (so *Schwyzer* 726.21 (Milet., v B.C.), prob. in Ion Trag.21, but ἑορτή *Schwyzer* 725.12 (Milet., vi B.C.)), ἡ, *feast*, *festival*, *holiday*, ἐπεὶ καὶ πᾶσιν ἑ. Od.20.156 ; ἑ. τοῖο θεοῖο 21.258 ; ἐούσης ὁρτῆς τῇ Ἥρῃ τοῖσι Ἀργείοισι Hdt.1.31 ; ὁρτὴν ἄγειν keep *a feast*, ib.147, cf. Th.4.5, etc. ; ἄξεις τότ' ἀμελιτῖτιν ὀρτὴν ἐξ ὀρτῆς Herod.5.85 ; ὁρτὴν ποιευμένους Hdt.1.150 ; ὁρτὴν ἀνάγειν Id.2.40, 48, al. ; ἑορτὰς ἑορτάσαι X.*Ath*.3.2 ; ἑορτὴν τῇ θεῷ ποιεῖν Th.2.15 ; ἡ τῶν Παναθηναίων ἑ. D.4.35 : metaph., οἵας ἑορτῆς ἔστ' ἀπόπτυστοι θεοῖς στέργηθρ' ἔχουσαι, of the Eumenides, A.*Eu*. 191 ; ἑορτὴ ὄψεως Ael.*VH*13.1. **2.** generally, *holiday-making*, *amusement*, *pastime*, παιδιᾶς καὶ ἑορτῆς χάριν Pl.*Phdr*.276b, etc. ; so ἑορτὴν ἡγεῖσθαι τὸ τὰ δέοντα πρᾶξαι Th.1.70. **3.** prov., κατόπιν ἑορτῆς ἥκειν to have come the day after *the fair*, Pl.*Grg*.447a ; ἀεργοῖς αἰὲν ἑορτά every day's *a holiday* to those who don't work, Theoc. 15.26, cf. Herod.6.17 ; ἄγουσιν ἑ. οἱ κλέπται Suid. **4.** *assembled multitude at a festival*, ὄχλος καὶ ἑ. καὶ στρατὸς καὶ πλῆθος Plot.6.6. 12. **-ικός**, ή, όν, = ἑορταῖος, *PStrassb*.40.49 (vi A.D.) : ἑορτικά, τά, *presents given at festivals*, *POxy*.724.6 (ii A.D.). **-ίς**, ίδος, ἡ, = ἑορτή, Sch.Il.5.299 ; coined to expl. ἔροτις. **-ολόγιον**, τό, *calendar of holidays*, Suid. **-ώδης**, ες, *festal*, *solemn*, J.*AJ*16.2.1, Ph.1.450, al., Sch.Th.5.54. **-ών**, μὴν Ἀττικός Eust.1698.35 (misunderstanding Hdn.Gr.ap.Choerob. *in Theod*.1.280 : ἡμερὼν καὶ ἑ., εἰ τύχοι, ὤφειλον λέγεσθαι).

⊛**ἑός**, ἑή, ἑόν, dat. written εἱῷ [⏑ –] Maiist.10 ; Boeot. **ἱός** Corinn. *Supp*.2.73 ; possess. Adj. of 3 pers. sg., *his*, *her own*, Hom., Pi., Dor., Thess. (*IG*9(2).250) ; not in Att. Prose (unless in A.*Fr*.350 the word is Plato's), dub. in Trag., E.*El*.1206 (lyr.) :—τὸν ἑόν τε Πόδαργον *his own* Podargus, Il.23.295 ; strengthd., ἑῷ αὐτοῦ θυμῷ in *his own inmost* soul, 10.204 ; ἑοὶ αὐτοῦ θῆτες *his own* labourers, Od.4. 643. **II.** after Hom. (also v.l. Il.1.393, al.), of other persons, **1.** as Adj. 3 pers. pl., *their*, Hes.*Op*.58, Pi.*P*.2.91, freq. in later Ep., as Batr.103, A.R.1.1113, etc. **2.** in Alex. Poets, = ἐμός, A.R.2. 226. **3.** also, = σός, Batr.23, A.R.2.634, 3.140, Theoc.17.50. **4.** = ἡμέτερος, A.R.4.203. **5.** = ὑμέτερος, Id.2.332, 3.267, *AP*7.730 (Pers.), Q.S.1.468. (I.-E. *sewo*-, Lat. *suus* ; cf. ὅς.)

**ϝέος**, Locr. gen. sg., = οὗ (ἕο), *IG*9(1).334.32.

**ἐοσσητήρ**· ἐπίκουρος, τιμωρός, ἀντὶ τοῦ ἀοσσητήρ, Hsch.

**ἑοῦ**, = ἕο, read by Zenod. in Il.2.239, cf. A.R.4.803. **ἑοῦς**.

Boeot. for ἕο, οὗ, gen. of pers. Pron. 3 pers., Corinn.2. **ἐοῦσα,** Ion. and Ep. for οὖσα, pres. part. fem. of εἰμί.

**ἐπᾰβελτερόω,** *make a yet greater ass of,* ἐπαβελτερώσας τόν ποτ' ὄντ' ἀβέλτερον Men.*Per.Fr.*1.

**ἐπάγᾰθος** [ᾰγ], ον, = χρηστός, used in προσκυνήματα, *CIG*4991, 5020 (Nubia); also τὸ ἐ. γόνιμον νέον ὕδωρ, of the Nile, *Sammelb.* 991.4 (iii A.D.).

**ἐπᾰγαίομαι,** Pass., *exult in,* κάρτεϊ A.R.3.1262; *feel a malignant joy in,* ἄτῃ ib.470: Ep. aor. ἐπαγάσσατο Epic.ap.Parth.21; ἐπαγασσαμένη· ἐκπλαγεῖσα, Hsch. (ἐπατασσομένη cod.).

**ἐπαγαλλιάζων,** v. ἐπαγγαλιάζων.

**ἐπᾰγάλλομαι,** Pass., *glory in, exult in,* c. dat., πολέμῳ καὶ δηϊοτῆτι Il.16.91, cf. Q.S.7.327, Tryph.671; πόρνησ' ἐπαγαλλόμενος πυγῇσιν Crates Theb.4; ἁμίλλῃ Them.*Or.*11.151c; εἰκόσιν Artem.3.31; ἐπί τινι X.*Oec.*4.17.

**ἐπᾰγᾰνακτέω,** *to be indignant,* abs., J.*BJ*2.13.3, Plu.*Alc.*14, *Ages.* 19.

**ἐπᾰγάνωσις** [γᾰ], εως, ἡ, *polishing* (with oil or wax), ἀγαλμάτων *IG*7.4149.18 (Ptoön); cf. γάνωσις, ἐπιγανόω.

**ἐπαγγαλιάζων·** ἐπιχαίρων, Hsch. (leg. ἐπαγαλλιάζων).

⊛ **ἐπαγγ-ελία,** ἡ, *command, summons,* Plb.9.38.2. b. *announcement, notice,* *IG*2$^{2}$.1235.7 (iii B.C.); τοῦ ἀγῶνος *SIG*561.9 (Chalcis), prob. in Lxx 1*Ma.*10.15; v.l. in 1*Ep.Jo.*1.5. 2. as law-term, ἐ. (sc. δοκιμασίας) *summons to attend* a δοκιμασία τῶν ῥητόρων (v. ἐπαγγέλλω 3), ἐ. τινὶ ἐπαγγέλλειν Aeschin.1.64, cf. 81; πρὸς τοὺς θεσμοθέτας ἔσθ' ἡμῖν ἐ. D.22.29: generally, *notification, summons, Sammelb.* 4434 (ii A.D.). 3. *offer, promise, profession, undertaking,* D.21.14; τὰς ὑπερβολὰς τῶν ἐ. Arist.*EN*1164$^{a}$29, cf. Phld.*Herc.*1251.20; ἐπαγγελίας ποιεῖσθαί τινι Plb.1.72.6; ἐν ἐπαγγελίᾳ καταλιπών having left it as *a promise,* Id.18.28.1; τὴν ἐ. ἐπὶ τέλος ἀγαγεῖν ibid., cf. *SIG*577.11 (Milet., iii/ii B.C.); ὤμων ἐπαγγελίᾳ *the promise* of his shoulders, Philostr.*Im.*1.4; ἐξ ἐ., = ἐπαγγειλάμενος, *BCH*11.12 (Lagina); ἐ. ποιησάμενος ἐκ τῶν ἰδίων *Michel*473.10 (Mylasa); ἐβεβαίωσεν τὴν ἐ. *Inscr.Prien.*123.9, cf. *GDI*3624*a*34 (Cos). 4. *indication,* τοῦ ἐσομένου A.D.*Synt.*205.13. 5. pl., *canvassing,* = Lat. *ambitus,* prob. f.l. for παρ-, Plu.2.276d. 6. = ἐπάγγελμα 2, *subject* of a treatise, Gal.*Libr.Propr.Prooem.* 7. the *curative property claimed* for prescriptions or drugs, ταῖς τῶν φαρμάκων ἐ. their *advertised properties,* Herod.Med.ap.Orib.10.5.1, cf. Gal.13.504, al.; ἐ. ἐπιτηδεύματος *public exercise* of a profession, Men.Prot.p.1 D. ⊛ **-έλλω,** aor. Pass. -ηγγέλθην *IG*1$^{2}$.188.25, -ηγγέλην ib.1$^{2}$.76.19:—*tell, proclaim, announce,* Od.4.775, Ar.*Lys.*1049 (lyr.); τινὶ ὡς.. Hdt.3.36; τῷ δήμῳ ὑπέρ τινος ὅτι.. *Inscr.Prien.*5.17 (iv B.C.); esp. *proclaim by authority, notify publicly,* ἐ. [τὴν ἐκεχειρίαν] Th.5.49; ἐ. πόλεμον Pl.*Lg.*702d:—Pass., *to be proclaimed, IG* ll. cc., etc.; μὴ ἐπηγγέλθαι πω τὰς σπονδάς Th.5.49, cf. 8.10; βουλῆς -θείσης a meeting *having been summoned,* D.C.56.29:—Med., *cause proclamation to be made,* Hdt.2.121.ζ΄. 2. *give orders, command,* abs., Id.1.70: c. acc. et inf., *give orders that..,* ἐπαγγείλας τοὺς Λακεδαιμονίους παρεῖναι ib.77, cf. Th.6.56: c. dat. et inf., *order* one to do, D.42.7, etc.: c. acc. rei, στρατιὰν ἐς τοὺς ξυμμάχους ἐ. *send* them *orders* to furnish their contingents, Th.7.17; κατὰ πόλεις τεσσαράκοντα νεῶν πλῆθος ἐ. Id.3.16: abs., βοηθεῖν.. καθ' ὅ τι ἂν -ωσιν αἱ πόλεις Foed.ap.Th.5.47:—Med., ἐπαγγέλλεσθαί τινι ἑτοιμάζειν στρατιήν Hdt.7.1, cf. 4.200; ἐ. τινί E.*HF*1185 (lyr.); ἐ. τισί ὅκως ἂν ἀπέλθοιεν Hdt.5.98:—Pass., τὸ ἐπαγγελλόμενον Id. 2.55. 3. as law-term, prop. δοκιμασίαν ἐ. *denounce and summon to* a δοκιμασία τῶν ῥητόρων one who, having incurred ἀτιμία, yet takes part in public affairs (v. ἐπαγγελία 2), ἐπήγγειλα αὐτῷ τὴν δοκιμασίαν ταυτηνί Aeschin.1.2, cf. ib.32; πρὸς τοὺς θεσμοθέτας D.22.23 (but ἐπηγγέλθη αὐτοῖς ὅτι ἐπεξίοιμι is f.l. for ἀπ- in Antipho 1.11). 4. *promise, offer,* ξείνοις δεῖπνα Pi.*P.*4.31; θεοῖς εὐχάς A.*Ch.*213:—more freq. in Med., *promise unasked* (opp. ὑπισχνέομαι) or *offer of one's free will,* ἐ. τι ἐς τὴν δωρεὴν τοῖσι ἀδελφεοῖσι Hdt.3.135; ἐ. καταγωγὴν καὶ ξείνιά τινι Id.6.35; παίδων.. ἐ. γονάς E.*Med.*721; ἀπηγγελλόμην what I *was proposing,* S.*El.*1018, cf. D.4.15; ἐ. τάδε, ὡς.. Hdt.6.9: c. inf., *promise* or *offer,* ξυμπολεμεῖν Th.6.88; διαθήκας ἀποφαίνειν (-φανεῖν Dobree) Is.1.15; ἐ. τῇ βουλῇ μηνύσειν And.1.15; τισὶν τριήρεις ἔχων ἐκπλεύσεσθαι Lys.28.4, cf. D.18.132, etc.; τινὶ ὥστε βοηθεῖν Th.8.86; ἐ. ὅ τι χρὴ δρᾶν *offering* (to do) what in justice he ought to do, Pl.*Lg.*915a. 5. Med., *profess, make profession of,* c. acc., ἀρετήν X.*Mem.*1.2.7; θεοσέβειαν 1*Ep.Ti.*2.10; esp. of Sophists, as in Pl.*Euthd.*273e; τί ἐστιν ὃ ἐ. τε καὶ διδάσκει Id.*Grg.*447c; τοῦτό ἐστι τὸ ἐπάγγελμα ὃ ἐπαγγέλλομαι Id.*Prt.*319a; ἐπαγγελλόμενος πάντα ..οὐδὲν ἐπιτελεῖ Arist.*EN*1164$^{a}$5; [γνῶσιν] 1*Ep.Ti.*6.21: c. inf., ἐ. ἀποκρίνεσθαι ὅ τι ἄν τίς σε ἐρωτᾷ Pl.*Grg.*447d; ἐ. οἷός τε εἶναι ποιῆσαί τι Id.*La.*186c, *Thg.*127e; ταῦτα ἐπαγγέλλεται δεινὸς εἶναι D.35.41; οἱ σοφισταὶ ἐ. διδάσκειν τινά Arist.*EN*1180$^{b}$35; παιδεύειν D.35.41: and abs., *profess* an art, Pl.*R.*518b, Arist.*SE*172$^{a}$32. 6. *demand, require,* cj. in D.H.5.65:—Med., D.19.193; but, *ask a favour,* ib. 41. ⊛ **-ελμα,** ατος, τό, *promise, profession,* D.19.178 (pl.); τὸ Πρωταγόρου ἐ. Arist.*Rh.*1402$^{a}$25, cf. Pl.*Prt.*319a; ὑπὸ τοῦ μεγέθους τοῦ ἐ. οὐδὲν θαυμαστὸν ἀπιστεῖν Id.*Euthd.*274a: pl., Metrod.ap.Phld. *Rh.*1.88 S.; ἐπαγγέλματι, opp. κατ' ἀλήθειαν, S.E.*M.*1.182. 2. *subject* of a treatise, that which it *purports* to contain, τὸ ἐ. τοῦ λόγου D.H.*Dem.*33; τὸ ἐ. τοῦ συγγράμματος Ael.*Tact.Praef.*7. 3. = ἐπαγγελία 7, Crito ap.Gal.13.878, Id.ap.Aët.15.16. 4. *art, profession,* τὸ ἐ. τῆς ἀρτοποιΐας M.Ant.3.2. **-ελτήρ,** ῆρος, ὁ, *envoy who announces a festival,* etc., *SIG*558.5 (Ithaca). **-ελτής,** *promissor, sponsor,* Gloss. **-ελτικός,** ή, όν, *given to promising,* ἐπεκλήθη Δώσων ὡς ἐ. Plu.*Aem.*8; also [λόγος] πρὸς τοὺς πολλοὺς ἐ. Phld.*Rh.*2.2 S., cf. Iamb.*Myst.*3.30. Adv. -κῶς Ath.Mech.15.9: Comp. -κώτερον, εἰπεῖν *too professorially,* Arist.*Rh.*1398$^{b}$30. 2. *promised,* οὐ δύνασθαι τελεῖν τὸ ἐ. ἀργύριον *SIG*832.7 (Epist. Hadr.). **-ελτος,** η, ον, *voluntary,* παραγενηθεὶς ἐπάγγελτος coming forward *voluntarily,* ib. 708.21 (Istropolis, ii B.C.).

**ἐπᾰγ-είρω,** *gather together, collect,* of things, Il.1.126:—Pass., of men, *assemble,* πρὶν ἐπὶ ἔθνε' ἀγείρετο Od.11.632, cf. Pi.*P.*9.54 (Act.). **-ερσις,** εως, ἡ, *mustering* of forces *against* an enemy, Ξέρξης τοῦ στρατοῦ ἐ. ποιέεται Hdt.7.19.

**ἐπάγην** [ᾰ], v. πήγνυμι.

**ἐπᾰγῑνέω,** Ion. for ἐπάγω, *bring to,* Hdt.2.2, Q.S.6.235.

**ἐπαγκᾰλίζομαι,** *embrace,* Pall. *in Hp.Fract.*12.278 C.

**ἐπαγκρούω,** v. ἐπανα-.

**ἐπαγκῠλ-έω,** *furnish with a thong,* ἐπηγκυλημένα ξύλα Suid. (Pass.). **-ίζομαι,** Pass., *to be fitted with an* ἀγκύλη, Sch.E.*Or.* 1476. **-ωτός,** όν, *fitted with a thong,* βρόχος Heraclas ap.Orib. 48.14.1.

**ἐπαγκων-ίδιον,** τό, *cushion,* Aët.16.108(98). **-ισμός,** ὁ, a kind of *dance,* Ath.14.630a.

⊛ **ἐπαγλᾰΐζω,** *honour, grace,* δῆμον ὠφελίαισι βίου Ar.*Ec.*575, cf. *Fr.*682; ὃν σοφίας μῦθος ἐ. *IG*12(9).954.7 (Chalcis), cf. 7.2532 (Thebes). II. Med., *pride oneself on* a thing, *glory* or *exult in* it, οὐδέ ἕ φημι δηρὸν ἐπαγλαϊεῖσθαι (fut. inf.) Il.18.133. 2. Pass., ἐπηγλαϊσμέναι..τράπεζαι *dressed out,* Cratin.301.

**ἐπάγνῡμι,** *break,* οὗ τ' ἐπὶ νῶτα ἔᾱγε (intr. perf.) Hes.*Op.*534.

**ἐπᾰγορ-άζω,** *purchase a title to the next vacancy* of a priesthood, *SIG*1014.17 (Erythrae, iii B.C.). **-ευσις,** εως, ἡ, *funeral oration,* Them.*Or.*20 p.285 D. **-εύω,** = ἀν-, *proclaim,* στεφάνους *IG*7.21.33 (Megara, iii/ii B.C.).

**ἐπᾱγορία,** v. ἐπηγ-.

⊛ **ἔπαγρ-ος,** ον, (ἄγρα) *in quest of prey,* Arist.*HA*616$^{b}$34; οὐκέτι χεῖρες ἔπαγροι φιλητέων Call.*Hec.*1.4.10. **-οσύνη,** ἡ, *good luck in hunting, fishing,* etc., Theoc.*Beren.*1.

**ἐπαγρυπν-έω,** *keep awake and think over, keep a watchful eye on,* τινί Luc.*Tim.*14; πράξεσι Onos.1.4: abs., Luc.*Gall.*31, Plu.*Brut.*37; ὡς.. *PTeb.*27.75 (ii B.C.). 2. *watch for,* ἀπωλείᾳ τινὸς -ηκώς D.S. 14.68: abs., Aristaenet.1.27. **-ησις,** εως, ἡ, *watching for,* ibid.; εἴς τι Aristeas 167; *watchfulness,* Phld.*Lib.*p.7 O. **-ία,** f.l. for εὐαύγεια, Iamb.*VP*3.13. ⊛ **-ος,** ον, *wakeful, sleepless,* κηδεμονία Mitteis *Chr.*77.11 (Sup., iv A.D.), cf. Vett.Val.11.16, Aristaenet.1.27.

**ἐπαγχάζομαι,** in aor. ἐπαγχάσασθε· ἐπαναχωρήσατε, Hsch.

**ἐπαγχάλιξον·** ἄκρατον ἐπίχεον, prob. in Hsch. (ἐπαγλαΐζον cod.).

**ἐπάγχιστος,** ον, *next of kin,* *IG*9(1).334.17; neut. pl. as Adv., οἱ ἐπάγχιστα πεπαμένοι *GDI*4986 (Gortyn).

**ἐπαγχωνίζω,** dub. sens. in *Tab.Defix.Aud.*155 *B*11 (Rome, iv/v A.D.).

⊛ **ἐπάγω** [ᾰ], *bring on,* οἷον ἐπ' ἦμαρ ἄγῃσι πατήρ Od.18.137; ἐ. πῆμά τινι Hes.*Op.*242; νύκτ' Id.*Th.*176; ἐλεύθερον ἦμαρ Bacis ap.Hdt.8. 77; ἄτην ἐπ' ἄτῃ A.*Ch.*404 (lyr.), cf. S.*Aj.*1189 (lyr.); κινδύνους τινί Is.8.3; πόλεμον ἐπὶ τὰς Θήβας Aeschin.3.140; νόσους γῆράς τε ἐ. Pl. *Ti.*33a; πάθος ἐ. Hp.*Morb.Sacr.*3. 2. *set on, urge on,* as hunters do dogs, ἐπάγοντες ἐπῆσαν (sc. κύνας) Od.19.445, cf. X.*Cyn.*10.19:—in Med., ib.6.25. b. *lead on* an army *against* the enemy, Ἄρη τινί A.*Pers.*85 (lyr.); τὴν στρατιήν Hdt.1.63, cf. 7.165; τὸ δεξιὸν κέρας Ar. *Av.*353; στρατόπεδον Th.6.69; τινὰ ἐπί τινα Id.8.46: intr., *march against,* τισί Plb.2.29.2: abs., dub. in Luc.*Hist.Conscr.*21: metaph., Diph.44 (nisi leg. ἐπῇττε). c. *quicken* the pace, Ar.*Eq.*25, *Nu.*390, Pl.*Cra.*420d; θάττονα ῥυθμὸν ἐ. X.*Smp.*2.22. 3. *lead on by persuasion, influence,* Od.14.392, Th.1.107; ἐλπὶς ἥ σ' ἐπήγαγεν E.*Hec.* 1032: c. inf., *induce* one to do, ib.260, Isoc.14.63:—Pass., οἷς ἐπαχθέντες ὑμεῖς D.5.10 (cod. S). 4. *bring in, invite* as aiders or allies, τὸν Πέρσην Hdt.9.1, cf. 8.112; τὸν Π. ἐπὶ τοὺς Ἕλληνας Epist. Phil.ap.D.12.7; Μήδους Ar.*Th.*365 (v. infr. II. 2). 5. *bring to* a place, *bring in,* S.*Tr.*378, E.*Ph.*905; ἅμαξαι..τοὺς λίθους ἐπῆγον Th. 1.93:—Med., *draw in* nourishment, of roots, Thphr.*HP*1.1.9:—Pass., τροφὰ ἐπάγεται τῷ σώματι Ti.Locr.102b. 6. *bring in, supply,* ἐπιτήδεια Th.7.60; τὰ ἐκ τῶν διωρύχων ἐ. νάματα Pl.*Criti.*118e; λίμνην..εἰς τὴν ἅλμην Ephipp.5.12: metaph., ἐπάγει ἡ ψυχὴ τὸ ἓν ἄλλῳ Plot.6.9.1. 7. *lay on* or *apply* to one, ἐ. κέντρον πώλοις, of a charioteer, E.*Hipp.*1194; ἐ. πληγὴν ἐπί τινα Lxx *Is.*10.24; ἐ. ζημίαν, = ἐπιτιθέναι, Luc.*Anach.*11; ἔπαγε τὴν γνάθον *lay* your jaws *to it,* Ar. *V.*370; ἐ. τὴν διάνοιάν τινι *apply* it, Plu.*Per.*1. 8. *bring forward,* ἐ. ψῆφον τοῖς ξυμμάχοις *propose* a vote to them, like ἐπιψηφίζειν ἐς.. Th.1.125, cf. 87; ψῆφος ἐπῆκτό τινι περὶ φυγῆς *against* him, X.*An.*7. 7.57, cf. D.47.28; ἐ. ὅρκον τισί Paus.4.14.4, cf. *IG*9(1).334.13 (Locr.); also ἐ. δίκην, γραφήν τινι, *bring* a suit *against* one, Pl.*Lg.*881e, D.18. 150; γραφάς, εὐθύνας, εἰσαγγελίας ib.249; λεγέτω πρότερος ὁ ἐπάγων τὰν δίκαν *Foed.Delph.Pell.*1 *A*10; ἐ. αἰτίαν τινί D.18.141; αἰτίαν ἐπήγαγέ μοι φόνου ψευδῆ Id.21.110, cf. 114. b. *introduce* a person before the assembly, *IG*12(7).389.5, *BCH*50.251, etc. 9. *bring in over and above,* παροψώνημα A.*Ag.*1446; τῷ λόγῳ τὸ ἔργον Plu.*Lyc.*8:—Pass., τὸ ἐπαγόμενον φωνῆεν the vowel *which follows, EM*176.55; ὁ ἐ. ἀγών *extraordinary, CIG*3491 (Thyatira). b. *intercalate* days in the year, Hdt.2.4, D.S.1.50; αἱ ἐπαγόμεναι, with or without ἡμέραι, *intercalated* days, ib.13, Plu.2.355e, *Inscr.Cypr.*134 H., *PStrassb.*91. 6, Vett.Val.20.26, 36.9, etc. 10. in instruction or argument, *lead on,* τινὰς ἐπὶ τὰ μήπω γιγνωσκόμενα Pl.*Plt.*278a:—Pass., ἐπαχθέντων αὐτῶν Aristox.*Harm.*p.23 M. b. esp. in the Logic of

Aristotle, *teach* or *convince by induction*, ἐπάγοντα ἀπὸ τῶν καθ' ἕκαστον ἐπὶ τὸ καθόλου καὶ τῶν γνωρίμων ἐπὶ τὰ ἄγνωστα *Top.*156$^{a}$4:—Pass., ἐπαχθῆναι μὴ ἔχοντας αἴσθησιν ἀδύνατον *APo.*81$^{b}$5, cf. 71$^{a}$21,24: abs., συλλογιζόμενον ἢ ἐπάγοντα by syllogism or *by induction*, *Rh.*1356$^{b}$8, cf. *Top.*157$^{a}$21, al.; οὐδ' ὁ ἐπάγων ἀποδείκνυσιν *APo.*91$^{b}$15. **c.** also ἐ. τὸ καθόλου *bring forward, advance*: hence, *infer* the general principle, τῇ καθ' ἕκαστα ἐπὶ τῶν ὁμοίων ἐπαγωγῇ ἐ. τὸ καθόλου *Top.*108$^{b}$11, cf. *SE* 174$^{a}$34; so later, *adduce the argument*, ὅτι.. Alex.Aphr.*in SE*6.2; *conclude, infer*, Arr.*Epict.*4.8.9. **11.** ἐ. τὴν κοιλίαν *move* the bowels, v.l. for ὑπ–, Dsc.4.157. **II.** Med., *bring to oneself, procure* or *provide for oneself*, ἐκ θαλάσσης ὧν δέονται ἐπάξονται Th.1.81, cf. 6.99: metaph., Ἅιδα φεῦξιν ἐ. *devise, invent* a means of shunning death, S.*Ant.*362 (lyr.); τὴν τῶν ξυμμάχων δούλωσιν Th.3.10; τῶν..κακῶν ἐ. λήθην Men.467. **2.** of persons, *bring into* one's country, *bring in* or *introduce* as allies (v. supr. I.4), Hdt.2.108, Th.1.3, 2.68, 4.64, al.; οἰκιστὴν ἐ. Hdt.6.34, cf. 5.67; ἐπιϝοίκους ἐ. *Berl.Sitzb.*1927.8 (Locr., v B.C.). **3.** μάρτυρας ποιητὰς ἐ. *call* them *in* as witnesses, Pl.*R.*364c, cf. *Lg.*823a, Arist.*Metaph.*995$^{a}$8; ἐ. ποιητὰς ἐν τοῖς λόγοις *introduce* by way of quotation, Pl.*Prt.*347e; τὸν Ἡσίοδον μάρτυρα Id.*Ly.*215c; ἐ. μαρτύρια *adduce* testimonies, X.*Smp.*8.34; εἰκόνας ἐ. Id.*Oec.*17.15; ὅρκον ἐ. πάντα τὰ ζῷα Porph.*Abst.*3.16. **4.** *bring upon oneself*, νύκτα ἐν μεσημβρίᾳ Pl.*Lg.*897d; φθόνον X.*Ap.*32; συμφορὰν ἐμαυτῷ Lys.4.19; αὐθαίρετον αὑτοῖς δουλείαν D.19.259; πράγματα Id.54.1; ἑαυτοῖς δεσπότην ἐ. τὸν νόμον Pl.*Grg.*492b; μητρυιὰν ἐ. κατὰ τῶν ἰδίων τέκνων D.S.12.12. **5.** *bring with one*, προῖκα πολλήν Nicostr.ap.Stob.4.22.102. **6.** *bring over to oneself, win over*, τὸ πλῆθος Th.5.45; τινὰ εἰς εὔνοιαν Plb.7.14.4: c. acc. et inf., ἐ. τινὰς ξυγχωρῆσαι *induce* them to concede, Th.5.41. **7.** *put in place*, λίθον *Princeton Exp.Inscr.*1175 (iii A.D.).

**ἐπαγωγ-εύς**, έως, ὁ, *coat of clay* on a wall, *IG*2$^{2}$.1672.61 (fort. pro ὑπ– legendum, Ar.*Av.*1149, sed cf. ἐξυπάγω). ⊛ **–ή**, ἡ, *bringing on* or *to*, τῶν ἐπιτηδείων Th.5.82, 7.24. **2.** *bringing in to one's aid, introduction*, τὴν τῶν Ἀθηναίων ἐ. Id.3.100, cf. 82 (pl.); *introduction* of food through the gullet, Arist.*Spir.*483$^{a}$9. **3.** *invasion, attack*, ἐπὶ τοὺς ἐναντίους Plb.10.23.7: abs., Id.11.15.7. **4.** *allurement, enticement*, ταῖς ἐλπίσι καὶ ταῖς ἐ. D.19.322. **b.** *incantation, spell*, in pl., Pl.*R.*364c, *Lg.*933d; Ἑκάτης φάσκων ἐπαγωγὴν γεγονέναι saying that Hecate had put it under a *spell*, Thphr.*Char.*16.7. **5.** *process of reasoning*, Aristox.*Harm.*pp.4,53 M. **b.** esp. in the Logic of Aristotle, *argument by induction* (cf. ἐπάγω I.10b), ἐ. ἡ ἀπὸ τῶν καθ' ἕκαστον ἐπὶ τὰ καθόλου ἔφοδος *Top.*105$^{a}$13; μανθάνομεν ἢ ἐπαγωγῇ ἢ ἀποδείξει *APo.*81$^{a}$40; διδασκαλία..ἡ μὲν δι' ἐπαγωγῆς ἡ δὲ συλλογισμῷ *EN*1139$^{b}$27; ἔστι τὸ μὲν παράδειγμα ἐ., τὸ δ' ἐνθύμημα συλλογισμός *Rh.*1356$^{b}$3; so later συλλογισμοὺς ἢ ἐπαγωγὰς περαίνοντας Polystr.p.11 W., cf. Plot.2.4.6, etc.; also of *dialectical argument* which leads an opponent into a trap, Gell.6(7).3.34, D.L.3.53. **6.** in Tactics, *sequence formation*, one wing following the other, opp. παραγωγή, Ascl.*Tact.*10.1, 11.2,4. **7.** *leading away into captivity, captivity*, Lxx *Is.*14.17: generally, *distress, misery*, ib.*Si.*23.14 (pl.), cf. Hsch. **8.** ἡ τῆς τριχὸς ἐ. *direction of growth*, D.S.3.35. **–ικός**, ή, όν, *inductive*, τρόπος S.E.*P.*2.196, cf. Asp.*in EN*2.25. Adv. –κῶς S.E.*P.*2.195, Sch.Pi.*O.*1.20. **II.** (from Med.) *attractive*, v.l. for ὑπαγωγικός in D.H.*Comp.*4. **–ιμος**, ον, *imported*, Plu.*Lys.*17, *IG* 14.422 iii 46,60 (Tauromenium). **–ιον**, τό, *foreskin, prepuce*, Dsc. 3.22. **–ίς**, *femella*, *Gloss.* ⊛ **–ός**, όν, *bringing on*, μανίας A.*Fr.*57.5 (anap.); ἡδονῆς Gorg.*Hel.*10; ὕπνου Pl.*Ti.*45d; κίνησις ἐ. δράσεως Ph.2.359. **II.** *attractive, alluring*, τὰ ἐπαγωγότατα λέγειν Hdt.3.53, cf. Th.4.88; ἀκούσαντες..ἐπαγωγὰ καὶ οὐκ ἀληθῆ, of ex-parte statements, Id.6.8, cf. 5.85; ὀνόματος ἐπαγωγοῦ δυνάμει ἐπισπάσασθαι ib. 111; ἐ. πρός τι X.*Oec.*13.9; λόγοι ἐ. D.59.70; of *dainty* dishes, ὄψον ..ἐ. πάνυ Antiph.242: Sup., δελέατα καὶ φίλτρα –ότατα Ph.1.396: c. gen., ἐ. ἡδονῇ τῶν ἀκροωμένων D.H.*Isoc.*3; τοῦ δήμου Plu.*Publ.*2; also ἔμφασιν κάλλους ἐπαγωγὸν εἶναι τοῦ ἔρωτος Chrysipp.*Stoic.*3.181; ἐπαγωγόν ἐστι, c. inf., it is a *temptation* to.., X.*Mem.*2.5.5; τὸ ἐ. *seductiveness*, Pl.*Phlb.*44c: neut. as Adv., ἐπαγωγὸν μειδιᾶν Luc.*DMeretr.*1.2, 6.3. Adv. –γῶς Poll.4.24: Sup. –ότατα Paus.9.12.5.

⊛ **ἐπάγων**· ἠαφνήδιος, κασάνδρα, Hsch.

**ἐπᾰγωνίζομαι**, *contend with*, τινί Plu.*Fab.*23; *continue to attack*, Aeschin.*Ep.*2.2. **2.** c. dat. rei, *contend in*, εὐνοίᾳ *IG*12(5).860.19 (Tenos); *contend for*, τῇ πίστει *Ep.Jud.*3: *lay stress on*, ἐ. τῷ λόγῳ Gal.14.246; τεκμηρίοις ἐ. Plu.*Num.*8; ἐ. τῇ λέξει τὰ ἰσοδυναμοῦντα παρατιθείς Aristid.*Rh.*1p.500 S.: abs., S.E.*M.*3.93; *exert oneself*, *IG*2$^{2}$.1343.16. **3.** *contend again*, in games, D.H.*Rh.*7.6. **b.** *speak after* a person, *follow* him, Philostr.*VS*1.25.7; ἐ. τῷ λόγῳ Lib.*Arg.D.*22.

**ἐπάει**· ἐπαίρει ἀρᾶ, Hsch.

⊛ **ἐπᾰείδω**, contr. Att. **ἐπᾴδω**, fut. –ᾴσομαι Ar.*Ec.*1153, etc.; –ᾴσω Ach.Tat.2.7:—*sing to* or *in accompaniment*, μάγος ἀνὴρ..ἐ. θεογονίην Hdt.1.132; ᾠδὰν χορῷ E.*El.*864 (lyr.):—Pass., Arr.*An.*2.16.3. **2.** *sing as an incantation*, ἃ αἱ Σειρῆνες ἐπῇδον τῷ Ὀδυσσεῖ X.*Mem.*2.6.11; χρὴ τὰ τοιαῦτα ὥσπερ ἐπᾴδειν ἑαυτῷ Pl.*Phd.*114d, cf. 77e; ἐ. ἡμῖν αὐτοῖς τοῦτον τὸν λόγον Id.*R.*608a; ἐ. τινί *sing to* one *so as to charm* or *soothe* him, Id.*Phdr.*267d, *Lg.*812c, al.:—Pass., Porph.*Chr.*35: abs., *use charms* or *incantations*, Pl.*Tht.*157c; ἐπαείδων *by means of charms*, A.*Ag.*1021 (lyr.), cf. Pl.*Lg.*773d, *Tht.*149d.

**ἐπᾰείρω**, poet. for ἐπαίρω (q.v.).

**ἐπᾰέξω**, *make to grow, prosper*, θεὸς δ' ἐπὶ ἔργον ἀέξῃ Od.14.65:—Pass., *increase, grow*, Semon.7.85 (κἀπ– may be for καὶ ἀπ–), Nic.*Th.*449.

**ἐπαεσσούριον**· κατήγορον, Hsch.

**ἐπαθλοκομέω**, *train for contest*, φῶτας *IG*7.3226 (Orchom. Boeot., i B.C.).

⊛ **ἔπαθλον**, τό, *prize of a contest*, mostly in pl., E.*Ph.*52, etc.; τὰ ἔ. τοῦ πολέμου Plu.*Flam.*15; *rewards*, ἀρετῆς D.S.28.4, cf. *OGI*455.3 (Aphrodisias, M.Antonius), Hdn.1.17.11; οὐδ' ἐπὶ σαφέσι τοῖς ἐ. not even if the *advantages* (of taking an emetic) were obvious, Archig. ap.Orib.8.23.2: also in sg., δοὺς ἑκάστῳ τὸ ὑπὲρ τῆς φιλοπονίας ἔ. *Inscr.Prien.*113.31 (i B.C.); προτιθεμένου ἐ. τῷ λύσαντι γαμεῖν τὴν Ἰοκάστην D.S.4.64; ἔ. πόνων Plu.*Cor.*23.

**ἔπᾰθον**, v. πάσχω.

**ἐπαθρέω**, = εἰσαθρέω, *look with favour on*, B.12.227, prob. l. in Id. 5.8; simply, *behold*, v.l. in Q.S.1.111.

**ἐπαθροίζομαι**, Pass., *assemble besides*, *Ev.Luc.*11.29, Plu.*Ant.*44.

**ἐπαιάζω**, *cry* αἰαῖ *over, mourn over*, τῷ νεκρῷ Luc.*DDeor.*14.2; *bewail*, μόρον Nic.*Al.*303. **II.** *join in the wail*, Bion 1.2, etc.; ἐ. πρὸς τὸ μέλος Luc.*Luct.*20.

**ἐπᾱΐγδην**, Adv. *impetuously*, Opp.*H.*2.616.

**ἐπαιγῐᾰλῖτις**, ιδος, ἡ, *on the beach*, χηλή *AP*10.8 (Arch.).

**ἐπαιγίζω**, (αἰγίς II) *rush upon*, twice in Hom. of a stormy wind, Ζέφυρος..λάβρος ἐπαιγίζων Il.2.148; οὖρον..λάβρον ἐπαιγίζοντα δι' αἰθέρος Od.15.293; λάβρως ἐ. ὁ βορρᾶς Alciphr.3.42: metaph., Ἔρως λάβρον ἐπαιγίζων *AP*5.285 (Paul. Sil.): c. dat., *rush over*, ἐπαιγίζει πεδίοισι, of a stream that has burst its banks, Opp.*C.*2.125: c. acc., πόντον ἐπαιγίζει, of the dolphin, Id.*H.*2.583.

**ἐπαιδέομαι**, fut. –αιδεσθήσομαι E.*IA*900 (troch.): aor. –ῃδέσθην Pl.*Lg.*921a:—*to be ashamed*, c. inf., E. l.c.; σὺ δ' οὐκ ἐπαιδῇ..εἰ..; *te non pudet si..?* S.*Ant.*510: c. dat., *to be ashamed of*, Babr.43.14: abs., *feel compunction*, E.*Hyps.Fr.*60.21. **II.** c. acc., *reverence*, A.*Fr.*135, Antipho Soph.*Oxy.*1364.270, Pl. l.c., Herod.2.39.

**ἐπαιθύσσω**, *flash at*, σπινθῆρας Ὀλύμπῳ Nonn.*D.*2.322, etc.:—Pass., *to be blown over*, πλόκαμοι..ἐ. προσώπῳ ib.11.247. **2.** intr., *rush violently on*, Opp.*C.*4.176.

⊛ **ἐπάϊκλα**, τά, *additions to the ordinary meal* (αἶκλον), Dor. for ἐπιδείπνια, ἐπιδόρπια, Pers.*Stoic.*1.101, Sphaer.ib.142: sg., Molpis 3:—also **ἐπαΐκλεια**, ibid., Apion ap.Ath.14.642e.

**ἐπαίμονες**· ἀπόγονοι, Hsch.

**ἐπαίν-εσις**, εως, ἡ, *praise*, E.*Tr.*418 (pl.). **–ετέον**, *one must praise*, Pl.*R.*390e, Luc.*Hist.Conscr.*9. **2.** Adj. **–ετέος**, έα, έον, Philostr.*VS*1.15.1: –τέοι οἱ θεοὶ τῆς διανοίας Id.*VA*2.33, cf. S.E.*M.*2.104. **–ετέω**, = ἐπαινέω, Phld.*Rh.*1.83 S. (s.v.l.). ⊛ **–έτης**, ου, ὁ, *praiser, commender*, Hp.*Acut.*6, Th.2.41, Pl.*R.*366e, Timocl. 8.9, etc.:—fem. **–έτις**, ιδος, φιλοσοφία –έτις παμβασιλείας Them.*Or.*18.219d. **II.** *rhapsodist*, Pl.*Ion* 536d; cf. ἐπαινέω IV. **–ετικός**, ή, όν, *given to praising, laudatory*, Arist.*EN*1125$^{a}$7; λόγος ἐ. Luc.*Pr.Im.*19. Adv. –κῶς Eust.102.37. **–ετός**, ή, όν, *to be praised, praiseworthy, laudable*, Pl.*Cra.*416c, *Lg.*660a, etc.; τὸ ἐ. *the object of praise*, Arist.*EN*1101$^{b}$13: Comp., Theon *Prog.*12. Adv. –τῶς Phld.*Po.*2.26, Ph.1.682, al.

⊛ **ἐπαιν-έω**, Aeol. **ἐπαίνημι** Simon.5.19; Lacon. **ἐπαινίω** Ar.*Lys.*198: impf. ἐπῄνεον Il.3.461 (tm.): fut. –έσω Semon.7.29, S.*El.*1057, E.*Andr.*465 (lyr.), *Heracl.*[300], Pl.*Smp.*214e (dub. l.), X.*An.*1.4.16, 5.5.8: but more freq. –έσομαι E.*Ba.*1195 (lyr.), Pl.*Smp.*199a, *R.*379e, 383a, X.*HG*3.2.6, D.2.31, etc.; poet. –ήσω Thgn.93 codd., Pi.*P.*10.69: aor. 1 ἐπῄνεσα S.*Aj.*536, Th.1.86, etc. (v. infr.); poet. (not Trag.) ἐπῄνησα Il.2.335, 18.312, Thgn.876, Pi.*P.*4.168,189: also Aeol. prose, *Schwyzer* 622.21, 623.31, 636.17 (but –έσαι 623.34): pf. ἐπῄνεκα Isoc.12.207,261, Pl.*Plt.*307a, etc.:—Med., aor. ἐπῃνησάμην Them.*Or.*16.200c; –εσάμην Phalar.*Ep.*147:—Pass., fut. ἐπαινεθήσομαι And.2.13, Pl.*R.*474d; later ἐπαινηθήσομαι Longus 4.4 codd.: aor. ἐπῃνέθην Th.2.25, Isoc.12.146, etc.; but ἐπῃνήθην *SIG*708.20 (Istropolis, ii B.C.): pf. ἐπῄνημαι Hp.*Acut.*51, Isoc.12.233:= αἰνέω (for which it is regularly used in Att.):—*approve, applaud, commend*, in Hom. mostly abs., ἐπὶ δ' ᾔνεον ἄλλοι Ἀχαιοί Il.3.461, etc.: c. acc. rei, μῦθον ἐπαινήσαντες Ὀδυσσῆος 2.335; μῦθον ἐ. πρεσβυτέροισι *h.Merc.*457; σύνθεσιν Pi.*P.*4.168: c. dat. pers., *agree with, side with*, Ἕκτορι μὲν γὰρ ἐπῄνησαν Il.18.312: abs., *assent, agree*, Ar.*Av.*1616; ἐπαινεσάντων δ' αὐτῶν on their *assent*, Th.4.65. **2.** *praise, commend* in any way (the usu. sense in Att. and Trag.), τινά or τι, Alc. 37A, Hdt.3.34, 6.130; τὸ λίαν ἧσσον ἐ. τοῦ μηδὲν ἄγαν E.*Hipp.*264; ἐ. τινά τι *commend* one *for* a thing, but in this case the thing is always a neut. Pron. or Adj., τὰ μέν σ' ἐπαινῶ A.*Pr.*342 (cf. III); πάντ' ἔχω σ' ἐπαινέσαι S.*Aj.*1381, cf. Pl.*Smp.*222a; in Din.3.22 ἐπαινεῖσθαι ταῖς ζητήσεσιν, ⟨ἐπί⟩ shd. be read; ἐπί τινι..καὶ διότι *Inscr.Prien.*44.17 (ii B.C.); εἴς τι Pl.*Alc.*1.111a; κατά τι D.S.1.37; πρός τι Pl.*Tht.*145b; also ἐ. τινά τινος Plu.2.1c, Luc.*Herm.*42 (but ἐ. τί τινος *praise* something in some one, Pl.*Prt.*361d): c. acc. cogn., ἔπαινον ἐ. Id.*La.*181b: c. part., ἐπαινέσεσθαί τινα ἀνασχόμενον D.21.73; ἐ. τινὰ ὅτι.. Pl.*Grg.*471d; ἐ. τινὰ πρός τινα *praise* one man to another, Id.*R.*501c; esp. *compliment publicly*, [Βρασίδας] πρῶτος τῶν κατὰ τὸν πόλεμον ἐπῃνέθη ἐν Σπάρτῃ Th.2.25; freq. in honorary Inscrr., cf. *IG*2$^{2}$.102, *Inscr.Prien.* l.c., etc.: c. dat. pers., τῷ δήμῳ τῷ Σαμίων *IG*1$^{2}$.101.2, cf. *SIG*604.11 (Delph., ii B.C.). **3.** of things, [πολιτεία] ὑπὸ πάντων –ουμένη Isoc.12.118, cf. Arist.*Pol.*1289$^{a}$1; νόμοι –ούμενοι Id.*Rh.*1375$^{b}$24; *approve*, πόλις ἄλλως ἄλλοτ' ἐ. τὰ δίκαια A.*Th.*1077. **4.** *agree to* or *undertake to do*, ῥώμην μ' ἐπαινῶ λαμβάνειν E.*Andr.*553; ἐ. εἰς τὸ λοιπόν *PTeb.*8.18 (iii B.C.). **5.** aor. ἐπῄνεσα in Att. in pres. sense, ἐπῄνεσ' ἔργον I *commend* it, S.*Aj.*536: abs., *well done!* Id.*Fr.*282, Ar.*Ach.*485, cf. E.*Alc.*1095, *Med.*707. **II.** = παραινέω, *recommend, advise*, τοιούσδ' ἐπαινεῖς δῆτα σὺ κτᾶσθαι φίλους; S.*Aj.*1360, cf.

A.*Th.*596, *Supp.*996: c. dat. et inf., ὑμῖν δ' ἐπαινῶ γλῶσσαν εὔφημον φέρειν Id.*Ch.*581; σιγᾶν ἐπῄνεσ' (cf. I. 5) S.*El.*1322, cf. *OC*665. **III.** as a civil form of declining an offer or invitation, I *thank you*, I *am much obliged*, κάλλιστ', ἐπαινῶ Ar.*Ra.*508 (ubi v. Sch.), cf. A.*Pr.*342; so ἐ. τὴν κλῆσιν *decline* it, X.*Smp.*1.7, cf. *An.*7.7.52. **IV.** of Rhapsodists, *recite, declaim publicly*, Pl.*Ion* 536d, 541e. ⊛ **-ος,** ὁ, *approval, praise, commendation*, Simon.4.3, Pi.*Fr.*181; ἔ. ἔχειν πρός τινος Hdt.1.96; πολλῷ ἐχρᾶτο τῷ ἐ. Id.3.3: freq. in Trag. and Att., ἐπαίνου τυχεῖν ἔκ τινος S.*Ant.*665, etc.; κλεινὴ καὶ ἔπαινον ἔχουσα meriting *praise*, ib. 817; ἔπαινον ἐπαινεῖν Pl.*La.*181b: pl., *praises*, S.*OC*720, *El.*976, X.*Mem.*2.1.33; τιμαὶ..καὶ ἔ. Pl.*R.*516c, etc. **2.** *complimentary address, panegyric* (but distd. fr. ἐγκώμιον, as the general from the particular, Arist.*EE*1219b15, *Rh.*1367b27); ἔ. ποιεῖσθαι περί τινος Pl.*Phdr.*260c; λόγον εἰπεῖν ἔπαινον Ἔρωτος Id.*Smp.*177d; συντιθεὶς λόγον ἔ. κατά τινος Id.*Phdr.*260b; οἱ κατὰ Δημοσθένους ἔ. Aeschin.3.50; εἴς τινα Pl.*Lg.*947c; ὑπέρ τινος Plb.1.1.1, D.S.13.22, D.H.10.57.

**ἐπαινός,** ή, όν, only in fem. ἐπαινή, *awesome*, epith. of Περσεφόνεια in Il.9.457, Od.10.491, al., Hes.*Th.*[768]; of Hecate, Luc.*Nec.*9; of Demeter, prob. in *AP*11.42 (Crin.).

⊛ **ἐπαινουμένως,** Adv. pres. part. Pass., *praiseworthily*, D.S.16.88.

⊛ **ἐπαιονάω,** *bathe, foment* (trans.), Ath.2.41c:—Med., *bathe* (intr.), λοετροῖς Nic.*Al.*463:—also **-έω,** τῷ ἐλαίῳ Philostr.*Gym.*42.

⊛ **ἐπαίρω,** Ion. and poet. **ἐπᾰείρω** Hdt.1.204 and always in Hom.: fut. ἐπᾱρῶ (contr. from ἀερ-) E.*IA*125 (anap.), *Supp.*581 (prob. l.), X.*Mem.*3.6.2: aor. ἐπῆρα, part. ἐπάρας Hdt.1.87, etc.: pf. ἐπῆρκα Amphis 13, Them.*Or.*8.114b:—Pass., aor. ἐπήρθην, part. ἐπαρθείς: *lift up and set on*, [αὐτὸν] ἀμαξάων ἐπάειραν *lifted and set* him *upon*.., Il.7.426; ὀβελοὺς..κρατευτάων ἐπάειρας 9.214. **2.** *lift, raise*, κεφαλὴν ἐπαείρας 10.80; καί μ' ἔπαιρε S.*Ph.*889; ἐπαίρων βλέφαρα Id.*OT*1276 codd.; ἐπάειρε δέρην E.*Tr.*99 (anap.); ἔπαιρε σαυτόν Ar.*V.*996; σεμνῶς ἐπηρκὼς τὰς ὀφρῦς Amphis l.c.; πάντες ἐπῆραν (sc. τὴν χεῖρα) *SIG*1109.24; οὐδεὶς ἐπῆρε *IG*3.1132; ἐπάρας τὴν φωνήν D.18.291; ἐπαιρόμενα ἱστία, opp. ὑφιέμενα, Plu.*Luc.*3:—Med., με τεῷ ἐπαείραο μαζῷ *didst lift and put* me *to* thy breast, A.R.3.734; [λόγχην] E.*IT* 1484; ὅπλ' ἐπαίρεσθαι θεῷ Id.*Ba.*789; ἱστούς Plb.1.61.7; βακτηρίαν Plu.2.185b: metaph., τί..στάσιν γλώσσης ἐπήρασθε; S.*OT*635; πολλοὺς καὶ θρασεῖς τῇ πόλει λόγους ἐπαιρόμενος D.18.222; κοινὸν ἡ πόλις ἐπήρατο πένθος D.S.34.17. **3.** *exalt, magnify*, ἐπαείρειν Λοκρῶν ματέρ' Pi.*O.*9.20; ἐπαρεῖς τὸν πατρῷον οἶκον X.*Mem.*3.6.2. **4.** intr., *lift up one's leg* or *rise up*, Hdt.2.162; *rise from table*, Euang.1.10. **5.** Pass., *swell up*, Hp.*Liqu.*2, Gal.6.264, 18(2).119; ἐπῆρται τοῦτό γε, in mal. part., Ar.*Lys.*937; ὁ καυλὸς ἐπαίρεται *Hippiatr.*54. **6.** Gramm., ἐ. τὴν προσῳδίαν *make* the accent *acute*, Sch.Il.11.636. **II.** *stir up, excite*, πολλά τέ μιν καὶ μεγάλα τὰ ἐπαείροντα..ἦν Hdt.1.204; τίς σ' ἐπῆρε δαιμόνων; S.*OT*1328; πέρα τοῦ καιροῦ τοὺς ἑτέρους ἐ. D.16.23; ἐ. θυμόν τινι E.*IA*125; τοῦτό σε ψυχὴν ἐπαίρει Id.*Heracl.*173; ἑαυτὸν ἐπί τινι Diog.Oen.64; ἵππον *urge on*, Them.*Or.*1.13c; *induce, persuade* to do, c. inf., εἰρωτᾶν εἰ οὔτι ἐπαισχύνεται ἐπάρας Κροῖσον στρατεύεσθαι Hdt.1.90, cf. Isoc.4.108, Aeschin.1.192; ἥτις με γῆμ' ἐπῆρε Ar.*Nu.*42, cf. *Ra.*1041; ἐ. τινὰ ὥστε.. E.*Supp.*581; ὅστις μ' ἐπάρας ἔργον (sc. πρᾶξαι) Id.*Or.*286:—Pass., *to be roused, led on, excited*, τῷ μαντηΐῳ Hdt.1.90, cf. 5.91; τοῖσι δωρήμασι Id.7.38; τοῖς τῆς πόλεως κακοῖς And.1.37; ὑπὸ τῆς τύχης Lys.2.10; πλούτῳ, τιμῇ, Pl.*R.*434b, 608b; ὑπὸ λόγων Ar.*Av.*1448; τῇ ἐλπίδι ὡς.. Th.1.81, cf. Lys.9.21; τοῖς λόγοις Th.4.121; δεινότητι καὶ ξυνέσεως ἀγῶνι Id.3.37 (so τὸ ἐπαιρόμενον τοῦ λόγου τῇ δεινότητι Plu.*Cic.*25); ὑπὸ μεγάλου μισθοῦ Th.7.13; ἐ. ἐς τὸ νεωτερίζειν Id.4.108; ἐπὶ τὴν βασιλείαν Lxx 3*Ki.*12.[24]: c. inf., ἐπήρθην γράψαι Isoc.5.10; τῷ or τὸ λέγειν (dub. l.) Pl.*Phdr.*232a (but ναυτικῷ προύχειν -όμενοι *flattering themselves* that they were superior.., Th.1.25): abs., *to be excited, on tiptoe*, Ar.*Nu.*810; and so Ἑλλὰς τῇ ὁρμῇ ἐπῆρται Th.2.11. **2.** Pass., also, *to be elated at* a thing, εὐδαιμονίῃ μεγάλῃ Hdt.5.81; ψυχρῇ νίκῃ Id.9.49, cf. 1.212, 4.130; ἐπὶ πλούτῳ X.*Mem.*1.2.25; πρός τι Th.6.11, 8.2; ἐκ τοῦ γεγονότος προτερήματος Plb.1.29.4: abs., Th.4.18.

⊛ **ἐπαισθ-άνομαι,** *have a perception* or *feeling of*, c. gen. objecti, μῶν Ὀδυσσέως ἐπῃσθόμην; S.*Ph.*1296; ὀμφῆς τῆς ἐμῆς Id.*OC*1351, cf. *Ant.*1183; διαφορᾶς Epicur.*Nat.*14.10; esp. of symptoms of disease, τῶν καθ' ἕκαστα σαθρῶν D.11.14: hence abs., ἐ. τι τῷ σώματι *to be indisposed*, D.C.52.24. **2.** c. acc., *perceive*, τι A.*Ag.*85 (anap.); οὐδέν S.*Aj.*553, D.2.21; τὸν σὸν μόρον ἐ. *hear of* it, S.*Aj.*996: c. part., ἐπῄσθετ' ἐκ θεοῦ καλούμενος Id.*OC*1629; ᾐσθέντα δ' αὐτὸν ὡς ἐπῃσθόμην E.*Cyc.*420. **3.** abs., *become sensible, recover one's senses*, Hp.*Morb.*3.8. **-ημα,** ατος, τό, *perception*, Epicur.*Fr.*36, *Placit.*4.8.2, Phld.*Mus.*p.66 K. **-ησις,** εως, ἡ, *perception*, τὴν ἐ. τὴν ἐπί τινος ποιεῖν Epicur.*Ep.*1 p.13 U., cf. Phld.*Mus.*p.42 K., al., Sor.2.19; τινός Epicur.*Nat.*125 G., Porph.*Abst.*1.57, 3.15.

**ἔπαισοι·** καθήκοντες, ἐπιβάλλοντες, Hsch. (cf. ἐπάσιοι: fort. ἐπάσιστοι, v. ἆσσον I, ἐπάγχιστος).

**ἐπαΐσσω,** Ep. aor. ἐπήϊξα Od.10.322, Iterat. ἐπαΐξασκε Il.17.462: contr. **ἐπᾴσσω,** Att. **-ττω,** fut. -ᾴξω:—*rush at* or *upon*: c. gen. (never in Od.), ἵππων ἐπαΐξαι *rush at* them, Il.5.263; νεῶν 13.687. **2.** c. dat. pers., Κίρκῃ ἐπαΐξαι *rush upon* her, Od.10.295: in Il. only c. dat. instrum., ξίφει, δουρὶ ἐ., 5.584, 10.369, etc.; so μοι..ἐπήϊσσον μελίῃσιν Od.14.281. **3.** c. acc., *assail, assault*, Ἕκτορα Il.23.64; τεῖχος 12.308 (never so in Od.):—Med., ἐπαΐξασθαι ἄεθλον *rush at* (i.e. *seize upon*) the prize, Il.23.773. **4.** abs. (so usu. in Hom.), of a hawk, ταρφέ' ἐπαΐσσει *makes* frequent *swoops*, 22.142; of the wind, ἐπαΐξας..ἐκ νεφελάων 2.146, etc.; σῦς ἐπαΐσσων βίᾳ B.5.116, cf. Ar.*Ach.*1171 (lyr.); ἐπᾴξας ἐς δόμους S.*Aj.*305; rare in Prose, as Pl.*Tht.*190a (metaph.), Arist.*HA*629b25:—also Med., χειμῶνος μέλλοντος ἐπαΐσσεσθαι ὁδοῖο Arat.1139. **5.** τὰ νεῦρα ἐπαΐσσεται ἀμφὶ τὰς φύσιας τῶν ἄρθρων (in the development of the embryo), dub. in Hp.*Nat.Puer.*17. **II.** later, with acc. of the Instrument of motion, ἐ. πόδα *move with hasty* step, E.*Hec.*1071 (lyr.); ἐ. ξίφος A.R.1.1254:—Pass. even in Hom., χεῖρες ὤμων ἀμφοτέρωθεν ἐπαΐσσονται ἐλαφραί they *move lightly*, Il.23.628 (v. l. ἀπ-). [ᾱ- Ep., ᾰ- Att.]

**ἐπάϊστος,** ον, (ἐπαΐω) *heard of, detected*, usu. c. part., ἐ. ἐγένετο ἐργασμένος Hdt.2.119; ἐ. ἐγένετο προδιδούς Id.8.128, cf. 6.74; ἐ. ἐγένετο ὑπὸ Καμβύσεω Id.3.15, cf. 7.146; *perceived*, Ant.Lib.34.4. Adv. **-τως** Onat.ap.Stob.1.1.39 (dub.).

**ἐπαισχ-ής,** ές, (αἶσχος) *shameful*, Nic.Dam.5 J., D.C.56.13. **-ρος,** ον, = foreg., Antioch.Astr.in *Cat.Cod.Astr.*7.115, Vett.Val.11.17, al. **2.** in physical sense, *ugly*, Id.110.23. **-ύνομαι,** fut. -αισχυνθήσομαι, *to be ashamed at* or *of*, τῷ οὐνόματι Hdt.1.143; τινά or τι, X.*HG*4.1.34, Pl.*Sph.*247c: c. inf., *to be ashamed* to do, A.*Ag.*1373: c. part., *to be ashamed of* doing or having done a thing, Hdt.1.90, S.*Aj.*1307, *Ph.*929, etc.: abs., *feel shame, show a sense of shame*, Pl.*R.*573b, Men.625. **II.** late in Act., *make ugly, mar*, Nonn.*D.*20.61, 42.421.

**ἐπαιτ-έω,** *ask besides*, εἰ καί νύ κεν..ἄλλο μεῖζον ἐπαιτήσειας Il.23.593; ὧν ἐπαιτεῖς S.*OT*1416: abs., *ask for more*, φαγὼν ἔτ' ἐπῄτεον Posidipp.ap.Ath.10.412e:—so in Med., S.*El.*1124. **2.** *beg as a mendicant*, ἄλλους ἐ. τὸν καθ' ἡμέραν βίον Id.*OC*1364, cf. E.*Rh.*715: abs., Vett.Val.68.30, Luc.*Asin.*35. **3.** simply, *demand*, *PTeb.*26.13 (ii B.C., Pass.), etc. **-ης,** ου, ὁ, *beggar*, Teles p.14 H., Nech.ap.Vett.Val.290.2, Ath.5.192f, D.C.66.8 codd. **-ησις,** εως, ἡ, *begging*, Lxx *Si.*40.28, 30. **-ητάριον,** τό, *little beggar*, name of an amulet, *PMag.Par.*1.2378.

⊛ **ἐπαιτιάομαι,** fut. -άσομαι [ᾱ], Ion. -ήσομαι, *bring a charge against, accuse*, τινά Hdt.2.121.β', etc.; θεὸν ἐ. Hp.*Aër.*22; ἐ. τινά τινος *accuse* one of a thing, Th.6.28, D.21.114; ἢ κἀμὲ γάρ τι ξυμφοραῖς ἐπαιτιᾷ; for your mishaps, A.*Pr.*974; also κείνην ἐπαιτιῶμαι τοῦδε βουλεῦσαι τάφου I *accuse* her of this burial, that she planned it, S.*Ant.*490: c. inf., ὧν ἐπαιτιᾷ με δρᾶν Id.*OT*645; ὃν..με..τρέφειν μιάστορα ἐπῃτιάσω Id.*El.*604; Αἴσωπον..φιάλην ἐπῃτιῶντο κλέψαι Ar.*V.*1447, etc.; τὴν πρόμαντιν ἐ. αὐτὸν πεῖσαι Th.5.16; so ἐ. τινὰ ὅτι.. Hdt.6.30, Th.2.70: c. acc. rei, *lay the blame upon*, τὴν ξυμφορὰν τῆς φυγῆς Id.8.81; τὸ μῆκος τῆς πορείας Pl.*Ep.*329a: also c. acc. cogn., μέζονα ἐπαιτιώμενος *bringing* heavier *accusations*, Hdt.1.26; τοῦτο ἐπαιτιῶμαι, c. acc. inf., I *complain of* this, viz. that.., Pl.*R.*497b: also c. dupl. acc., ἃ ἐπαιτιῶμαι τὴν γυναῖκα ταύτην the charges which I *bring against* her, Antipho 1.10; τῷ μὲν νῷ οὐδὲν χρώμενον οὐδέ τινας αἰτίας ἐπαιτιώμενον nor *ascribing* any *causes* to it, Pl.*Phd.*98b.

**ἐπαιτίνδα** παίζειν play *at beggars*, Hdn.Gr.1.495.

**ἐπαίτιος,** ον, (αἰτία) *blamed for* a thing, *blameable, blameworthy*: **1.** of persons, οὔ τί μοι ὔμμες ἐπαίτιοι Il.1.335; τινός *for* a thing, A.*Eu.*465, E.*Hipp.*1383 (lyr.); *accused of* a thing, Th.6.61; ἐ. τινὰ ποιεῖν πρός τινας Plu.*Comp.Dion.Brut.*2. **2.** of things, ἀναχώρησις Th.5.65; ἐπαιτιώτατοι τῶν κινδύνων Lys.7.39. **II.** ἐπαίτια, τά, *legal punishments*, = προστιμήματα, Solon ap.Poll.8.22, Lex ap.D.24.105.

⊛ **ἔπαιτον,** τό, dub. sens. in *PFay.*81.13 (ii A.D.), *BGU*792.12, etc.

**ἐπαιτοσύνη,** ἡ, = ἐπαίτησις, Charis.p.554 K.

**ἐπᾱΐω,** contr. **ἐπᾴω** E.*HF*773 (lyr.): aor. 1 ἐπήϊσα Hdt.9.93, A.R. ll. cc.: (v. ἀΐω, εἰσαΐω):—*give ear to*, θεῶν οὐδὲν ἐπαΐοντες A.*Supp.*759 (lyr.), cf. E. l. c.; *hear*, τῆς φωνῆς Plu.*Brut.*16. **2.** *perceive, feel*, τι Pi.*Fr.*75.15 (v. l. ἐπάγοισιν); θεοὶ ἔναιμοί τε καὶ σαρκώδεες καὶ ἐπαΐοντες σιδηρίων Hdt.3.29; δηγμάτων Ael.*NA*1.5; τῶν ὄντως ἀγαθῶν Hierocl. *in CA*24 p.472 M.: c. part., καταγελώμενος οὐκ ἐπαΐεις Ar.*V.*516; ὥστε μηδὲ θιγγανόμενος ἐπαΐειν Hp.*Prorrh.*2.16; ἂψ ἀνιόντας, αὐτοὺς παριόντας, A.R.1.1023, 2.195: abs., ὡς ἐπήϊσε when *he perceived it*, Hdt.9.93. **3.** *understand*, c. acc., τὴν βάρβαρον γὰρ γλῶσσαν οὐκ ἐπαΐω S.*Aj.*1263; esp. of persons under instruction, ἐπαΐονθ' ὁποῖός ἐστι τῶν ῥυθμῶν κατ' ἐνόπλιον κτλ., Ar.*Nu.*650; ἐ. τό τε καλὸν καὶ μή Pl.*Lg.*701a; ἐ. τίς πολιτεία συμφέρει Arist.*Rh.*1360a31; ἐ. τι τῆς Ῥωμαίων γλώσσης Luc.*Laps.*13, etc. **4.** *to have knowledge of* any subject, *to be an expert in* such subjects, οὓς ἂν οἴωμαί τι τούτων ἐπαΐειν Pl.*Tht.*145d; τοὺς μηδὲν αὐλήσεως ἐπαΐοντας Id.*Prt.*327c; ὁ ἐπαΐων περὶ τῶν δικαίων καὶ ἀδίκων, i.e. a moral philosopher, Id.*Cri.*48a; ἐπαΐεις οὐδὲν περὶ γυμναστικῆς Id.*Grg.*518c, cf. *Ap.*19c, *R.*598c, *Hp.Ma.*289e: abs., ὁ ἐπαΐων Id.*Prt.*314a, *Phdr.*275e; τὸ εἰδέναι καὶ τὸ ἐ. Arist.*Metaph.*981a24.

**ἐπαιώνιος,** ον, *ruling over the* αἰῶνες, θεός *Tab.Defix.Aud.*271.9 (Hadrumetum, iii A.D.).

⊛ **ἐπαιωρέω,** *keep hovering over* another, στέφανον καρήνῳ, πέτρον καρήνων, Nonn.*D.*5.132, 4.456; *keep floating in*, ἐ. πτερὸν ἠέρι πολλῷ *Epigr.Gr.*312.5 (Smyrna): metaph., ἐ. [εὐτυχίαις] βίον *AP*7.645 (Crin.). **II.** Pass., *hover over* or *on the surface, float upon*, ἐπανθισμὸς ἐ. χαλκείοις Dsc.5.92, cf. 75; ἐλπίσιν ἐπαιωρούμενοι *buoyed up* by.., Luc.*Alex.*16; ἐπαιωρεῖσθαι πολέμῳ *hang over* it, *conduct* it *remissly*, Plu.*Pel.*29; in Hp.*Art.*75, of one who *throws his whole weight upon* another, during a surgical operation. **2.** *overhang, threaten*, σφιν ἐπὶ δέος ᾐωρεῖτο A.R.1.639; Σκύθαι τοῖς μέσοις ἐπαιωροῦντο Them.*Or.*8.119c; ξίφος αὐχένι ἐ. Hdn.5.2.1: c. gen., τῶν πολεμίων Plu.*Fab.*5: abs., τὰ ἐκτὸς ἐπῃωρημένα Ph.1.650. **3.** *rise, swell*, ὄγκος -εύμενος ἔξω Aret.*CA*1.7.

**ἐπᾰκανθίζω,** in pres. part., *pointed*, Thphr.*HP*3.10.1, al.; *thorny, set with thorns*, ib.4.8.8, 6.4.1, al.

**ἐπᾰκέομαι**, Delph. ἐφακ-, *repair*, τὸν δρόμον, τὰς γεφύρας, *IG* 2². 1126.37,41 (Amphict. Delph.).

⊛ **ἐπακμ-άζω**, *to be in one's prime*, Ph.1.33; also of things, Id.2.434, Aristaenet.2.1, Hld.7.8: metaph., *come to its height*, Luc.*Abd.*17, Ath.1.18e; ἐπήκμασαν οἱ ἐτησίαι *were blowing hard*, Str.15.1.17. **II.** of persons, *flourish in succession to*, τινί D.H.*Pomp.*4; οἱ ἐπακμάσαντες ib.1; also νέα ἐ. παλαιοῖς, of animals and crops, Ph.1.28, 2.424. **-αστικός**, ή, όν, *coming to a height* or *crisis*, opp. παρακμαστικός, πυρετός Gal.10.615.

**Ἐπακμόνιος**, epith. of Poseidon in Boeotia, Hsch.

**ἔπακμος**, ον, (ἀκμή) *in the bloom of age*, κόραι D.H.4.28 (v.l.). **II.** *pointed*, ἄκανθα Dsc.1.90; ὀδούς Plu.2.966c; *sharp-edged*, Sor.1.80; σμιλίον Gal.ap.Orib.*inc.*12.1.

**ἐπᾰκολουθ-έω**, *follow close upon, follow after, pursue*, τινί Ar.*V.* 1328, Pl.*Ap.*23c, al.; *move with*, τῷ ἄλλῳ σώματι Hp.*Fract.*16; ἐ. ἡ χεὶρ τοῦ νεκροῦ X.*Cyr.*7.3.8. **2.** *pursue* as an enemy, Th.4.128, 5.65, X.*An.*[4.1.1], etc. **3.** *attend to, follow* mentally, *understand*, τῷ λόγῳ Pl.*Phd.*107b; τοῖς λεγομένοις Id.*Lg.*861c; αὐτοῖς λέγουσι Id.*Sph.*243a; κάλλιστ' ἐπακολουθεῖς Id.*Lg.*963a, etc. **4.** *attend to, follow*, i.e. *obey* or *comply with*, ταῖς τῶν συμμάχων γνώμαις Isoc.6.90; τοῖς πάθεσι D.26.18; αὐτῶν τῇ προαιρέσει Philipp.ap.D.18.167; ταῖς τῶν ποιητῶν βλασφημίαις ἐ. *follow* them (as authorities), Isoc.11.38: c. dat. pers., Arist.*EN*1096ᵇ7. **5.** *attend to*, i.e. *execute*, a task, τῷ πραττομένῳ Pl.*R.*370c; *wait upon*, of bees, τοῖς βασιλεῦσι Arist.*GA* 760ᵇ15. **6.** *supervise, attend to*, τῇ ἐγχύσει τοῦ γλεύκους *PPetr.*2 p.136 (iii B.C.), cf. *PAmh.*2.40.24 (ii B.C.), etc.: abs., *POxy.*1024.33 (ii A.D.), etc. **7.** *concur*, *PFay.*24.19 (ii A.D.). **8.** *verify, check*, *PEleph.*10.8 (iii B.C.), *PGen.*22.1 (i A.D.), etc. **II.** *accompany, result, accrue*, τινί Phld.*Ir.*p.59 W., al.; βλάβος, ζημία ἐ., *PRyl.*126.19 (i A.D.), *BGU*3.14 (iii A.D.). **2.** τὰ ἐπακολουθοῦντα σημεῖα *confirmatory, authenticating* signs (cf. I.7), *Ev.Marc.*16.20. **3.** of the offspring of cattle, πρόβατα σὺν τοῖς -οῦσι ἄρνασι *POxy.*245.11 (i A.D.), cf. 244.9 (i A.D.). **-ημα**, ατος, τό, *consequence*, τινός Plu.*Nic.*4, Plot.6.2.9, Iamb.*in Nic.*p.38 P. (pl.); κατ' ἐπακολούθημα *consequentially*, Alex.Aphr.*Fat.*178.13, S.E.*M.*7.34; τὰ κατ' ἐ. πάθη Anon.Lond.1.29. **II.** *secondary consideration*, Him.*Ecl.* 3.19. **-ησις**, εως, ἡ, *cognizance, concurrence*, *PRyl.*233.14 (ii A.D.), etc.; γράμματα ἐπακολουθήσεως documents in proof of *compliance*, i.e. *settlement* of debts, *POxy.*1473.8 (iii A.D.). **2.** *consequence*, κατ' ἐ. *consequentially*, opp. προηγουμένως, *Stoic.*2.333, Stoic. ap.Plu.2.1015c, M.Ant.6.44, S.E.*M.*1.194; *result*, εὐεξία κατ' ἐ. τῆς ὑγιείας συνισταμένη Gal.19.382. **-ητέον**, *one must follow*, τινί D.61.4. **-ητικός**, ή, όν, *capable of following*, δύναμις Plu.*in Hes.* 21. **-ήτρια**, ἡ, *concurring party*, *PLips.*9.6 (iii A.D.), etc. **-ος**, ον, *following*, τὸ ἐ. τῆς ἐπαγγελίας Aristid.*Rh.*2 p.522 S.: Comp., *PMag.Par.*1.1536. Adv. -θως *agreeably to*, τῷ ἑαυτῶν τρόπῳ Antip. ap.Stob.4.22.103, cf. *PMasp.*97 ii 68 (vi A.D.).

**ἐπᾰκονάω**, *whet*, in Pass., *IG*7.3073.104,119 (Lebadea). **II.** *whet against*, δημίου ξίφος ἑαυτῷ Lib.*Decl.*40.35.

**ἐπᾰκοντ-ίζω**, *dart* a thing *at* a person; Socr.*Ep.*30.13 codd. **-ισμός**, ὁ, *casting of dice* (βόλου ὄνομα), Hsch. **-ιστής**, οῦ, ὁ, *dicer*, Poll.7.204.

**ἐπάκοος**, Dor. for ἐπήκοος (q.v.).

**ἐπᾰκου-ός**, όν, *attentive to*, c. gen., ἀγορῆς ἐπακουὸν ἐόντα Hes.*Op.* 29, cf. Call.*Fr.*236; cf. ἐπήκοος. **-σις**, εως, ἡ, *hearing*, μαρτυριῶν *GDI*3591.43 (Cnidus). **-στός**, όν, *to be listened to*, Emp.2.7. **II.** *to be obeyed*, Lxx 1 *Es.*4.12. **-ω**, fut. ἐπακούσομαι ib. *Ge.*30.33, later ἐπακούσω *Psalm.Solom.*18.3:—*hear*, c. acc. rei, ὃς πάντ' ἐφορᾷς καὶ πάντ' ἐπακούεις, of the Sun, Il.3.277, cf. Od.11.109; prov., ὁπποῖόν κ' εἴπησθα ἔπος, τοῖόν κ' ἐπακούσαις as thou speakest, so *wilt* thou *be answered*, Il.20.250; φωνὴν ἐ. *Ilc* 3.*Op.*448; χρησμόν Ar.*Eq.*1080: c. acc. rei et gen. pers., ἔπος ἐμέθεν Od.19.98: c. gen. rei, εὐχῆς Ar.*Nu.*263; τῆς φωνῆς Hdt.2.70: abs., Th.1.53, Hdt.9.98, etc. **2.** *overhear*, μή τις τῶν ἀμυήτων ἐπακούσῃ Pl.*Tht.*155e, cf. Ar.*Th.*628. **3.** *hear about, hear tell of*, μόχθων E.*Tr.*165 (lyr.); c. part., οἷον γᾶς Ἀσίας οὐκ ἐπακούω.. βλαστὸν φύτευμα S.*OC*695 (lyr.); τινά τι δρῶντα Pl.*Lg.*729b. **4.** *give ear, listen*, A.*Ch.*725 (anap.): c. gen. pers., ἐμοῦ 'πάκουσον S.*OT*708, cf. Pl.*Prt.*317d; ἐ. μοι 'pray *attend*', Id.*Sph.*227c: esp. of *giving ear* to one who prays, of God, Lxx *Is.*49.8, *UPZ*78.24 (ii B.C.); or to advice, commands, etc., i.e. *obey*, βουλῆς Il.2.143; δίκης Hes.*Op.*275; ἐμῶν μύθων S.*Ph.*1417 (anap.): c. dat. rei, τῷ κελεύσματι Hdt.4.141; ταῖς εὐχαῖς D.H.13.6, cf. Lxx *Ho.*2.21(23). **5.** later, like ἐπαΐω, *perceive, understand*, τῶν ᾀδομένων Luc.*Salt.*64, cf. Plu.*Flam.*10 (or, *hear distinctly*). **6.** ἐπακούσεταί μοι ἡ δικαιοσύνη μου *shall answer for* me, Lxx *Ge.*30.33.

**ἐπακρῑβ-ής**, ές, *accurate*: neut. as Adv., -ὲς πάντα ἐπεξιέναι Aps. *Rh.*p.316 H. **-όω**, *develop in detail*, Epicur.*Ep.*1 p.27 U.:—Med., D.S.37.8.

**ἐπακρ-ίδες** πόλεις, (ἄκρα) cities *on the hills*, *EM*353.1. **-ίζω**, *reach the top of* a thing, πολλῶν αἱμάτων ἐπήκρισε (= ἐπ' ἄκρον ἦλθε, Sch., τέλος ἐπέθηκεν, Hsch.) he *reached the farthest point* in deeds of blood, of Orestes, A.*Ch.*932. ⊛ **-ιος**, α, ον, *on the heights*, epith. of Zeus, Polyzel.7. **II.** ἡ ἐπακρία (sc. χώρα), a district in Attica, Str.9.1.20.

⊛ **ἐπακρο-άομαι**, = ἐπακούω, abs., Pl.Com.16, Nic.Dam.*Vit.Caes.*29: c. gen. pers., *Act.Ap.*16.25, Luc.*Icar.*1: c. gen. rei, Hld.2.17: c. acc. rei, πάντ' ἐπακροάσει Men.*Epit.Oxy.*1236ᵛ16; τὸν λόγον Ant. Lib.11.6 **-ᾱσις**, εως, ἡ, *hearkening, obedience*, Lxx 1 *Ki.*15.22. **-ᾱτής**, οῦ, ὁ, *hearer, listener*, Gloss.

**ἔπακρος**, ον, (ἄκρα) *pointed at the end*, Hp.*Morb.*2.61.

**ἐπακταῖος**, α, ον, = ἐπάκτιος, Opp.*H.*2.127, 4.273. **II.** epith. of Poseidon at Samos, Hsch.

**ἐπακ-τέον**, *one must bring upon*, πόλεμον τῇ χώρᾳ Cic.*Att.*9.4.2. **2.** *one must apply*, μέτρον τινί Luc.*Hist.Conscr.*9, cf. D.H.*Rh.* 2.6; τοῦτο ἐ., ὅτι.. S.E.*P.*3.135. ⊛ **-τήρ**, ῆρος, ὁ, Ep. word, = ὁ κύνας ἐπάγων, *hunter, huntsman*, ἐς βῆσσαν ἵκανον ἐπακτῆρες Od.19.435; ἄνδρες ἐ. Il.17.135; later, *fisherman*, A.R.1.625. **-τήρεσιν·** ἀλλεπαλλήλοις, συνεχέσιν, Hsch. (Leg. ἐπασσυτέροισιν.) **-τικός**, ή, όν, *leading on*: **1.** in Logic, *inductive*, πρότασις, λόγοι, Arist. *APo.*77ᵇ35, *Top.*108ᵇ7, *Metaph.*1078ᵇ28, Phld.*Rh.*1.11 S. Adv. -κῶς, σκοπεῖν Arist.*Ph.*210ᵇ8. **2.** *conducive*, εἰς εὔνοιαν Hld.4.3; *stimulating*, πρὸς πότον Ath.2.52d (Sup.). **3.** *attractive*, ἐν τῇ ὀσμῇ Dsc. 1.26; διὰ τὴν ἡδονήν Id.4.83; ἀκρόασις Vett.Val.260.26; of persons, Id.250.22.

**ἐπάκτιος**, ον, E.*Fr.*670.2, and ία, ιον S.*Tr.*1151, *Fr.*549, E.*Andr.* 853 (lyr.): (ἀκτή):—*on the strand* or *shore*, ll.cc., S.*Aj.*413 (lyr.); epith. of Apollo, A.R.1.403 codd.; of Hermes at Sicyon, Hsch.

⊛ **ἐπακ-τός**, όν, or ή, όν (cf. III infr.), (ἐπάγω) *brought in*, ὕδατα Hp. *Aër.*9; esp. *brought in from abroad, imported*, ἐ. σῖτος Th.6.20; πάντων ἐπακτῶν δεῖσθαι Id.7.28; *acquired*, τῇ Ἑλλάδι πενίη μὲν.. σύντροφός ἐστι, ἀρετὴ δὲ ἐ. Hdt.7.102; ὕδωρ εἴτ' ἐ. εἴτε συμφυὲς Arist.*Mete.*382ᵇ 11, cf. *GA*750ᵃ9; ἐ. πημονή E.*Hipp.*318; κακόν Philem.93.5; ἐ. παρ' ἄλλων δίκαιον Pl.*R.*405b; ὅρκος ἐ. an oath *imposed* by the other party, Lys.*Fr.*251 S., Isoc.1.23; *adventitious*, ἐ. χρώμασι κοσμεῖσθαι Socr. *Ep.*6.3, cf. Plot.1.4.3. **2.** of persons, ἐ. ποιμήν an *alien* lord, Pi. *O.*10(11).89; ἐ. δικασταί dub. in *IG*11(4).1065*b*20 (Delos); ἱκέσιος ἐ. *Notiz.Arch.*4 p.98 (Cyrene); esp. of *foreign* allies or mercenaries, ἐ. στράτευμα, στρατός, A.*Th.*583, S.*Tr.*259; δόρυ Id.*OC*1525; ἐπακτῷ δυνάμει with an *alien, mercenary* force, Isoc.10.37, cf. Pl.*R.*573b; also λαβὼν ἐπακτὸν ἄνδρα, i.e. an adulterer, S.*Aj.*1296; ἐ. πατήρ a *false* father, E.*Ion*592: metaph., ὄμβρος ἐ. ἐλθών rain coming *as an invader*, Pi.*P.*6.10. **II.** like αὐθαίρετος, *brought upon oneself*, νόσος S.*Tr.*491; γάμων ἐ. ἄταν E.*Ph.*343 (lyr.). **III.** ἐπακταί (sc. ἡμέραι), αἱ, *intercalary days*, Isid.*Etym.*6.17.29, Zonar. **IV.** ἐπακτόν, τό, *charm, spell*, *GDI*3545 (Cnidus). **V.** ἐ. ὅρκος oath *administered*, *PMon.*6.8 (vi A.D.). **-τρεύς**, έως, ὁ, = ἐπακτήρ, Hsch., Eust.1539.25. **-τρίς**, ίδος, ἡ, *light vessel, skiff*, X.*HG*1.1.11, Aul.Gell.10.25.5. **-τροκέλης**, ητος, ὁ, *light piratical skiff*, Aeschin.1.191, Arist.*Int.*16ᵃ26. **-τρον**, τό, = ἐπακτρίς, Nic.*Th.*824.

**ἐπᾰλαζονεύομαι**, *boast over*, τινί J.*BJ*2.18.4.

**ἐπᾰλαλάζω**, *raise the war-cry*, A.*Th.*497,951 (lyr.), D.S.19.30; τῷ Ἐνυαλίῳ X.*Cyr.*7.1.26; τὸν ἐνυάλιον παιᾶνα Jul.*Or.*1.36b.

**ἐπᾰλαλκέμεν**, v. ἐπαλέξω.

**ἐπᾰλάομαι**, *wander about* or *over*, πόλλ' ἐπαληθείς Od.4.81; Αἰγυπτίους ib.83: subj. aor. ἐπαληθῇ 15.401.

**ἐπᾰλαστέω**, *to be full of wrath at* a thing, τὸν δ' ἐπαλαστήσασα προσηύδα Od.1.252, cf. A.R.3.369,557.

**ἐπαλγ-έω**, *grieve over*, φθιμένων E.*Supp.*58 (lyr.); δουλώσει πατρίδος J.*AJ*19.1.9. **-ής**, ές, *painful*, Aristeas 167, Str.11.13.2, Philum. ap.Aët.5.127, Aët.15.13, Opp.*H.*4.508: Comp., Lxx 4 *Ma.*14.10, Onos.42.19, Aret.*SD*2.3. Adv. -γῶς Poll.3.99. **-ύνω**, *give pain*, Nic.*Al.*335; *afflict*, τινά Q.S.4.416:—Med., *feel pain at*, ταῖς συμφοραῖς Tz.*H.*4.398.

**ἐπάλ-ειμμα** [ᾰλ], ατος, τό, *unguent*, ἐκζεμάτων Dsc.1.43.4, cf. *Inscr.Prien.*112.90, al. (i B.C.), *Michel* 544.20 (Themisonium, ii B.C.). ⊛ **-ειπτέον**, *one must anoint*, Orib.*Syn.*5.53.17, Paul.Aeg. 2.46. ⊛ **-είφω**, *smear over*, ἐπὶ δ' οὔατ' ἀλεῖψαι ἑταίροισ Od.12.47; ἐπ' οὔατα πᾶσιν ἄλειψα ib.177; κηρὸν.. ὅν σφιν ἐπ' ὠσὶν ἄλειψ' ib. 200; ὁπόταν.. λεαίνῃ ἐπαλείφουσα τὰ τραχυνθέντα Pl.*Ti.*66c; ἐ. χρόαν ἑτέραν ἐφ' ἑτέραν Arist.*Sens.*440ᵃ9: prov., τοὺς τοίχους τοὺς δύο ἐ. 'run with the hare and hunt with the hounds', Paus.6.3.15:—Pass., τὸ ἐπαλειφθέν Pl.*Ly.*217c; ἐπαλήλιπται ὁ κύτταρος Arist.*HA*555ᵃ6; χρυσὸς ἐπαληλιμμένος J.*AJ*17.10.2. **2.** metaph., from anointing athletes, *prepare for contest, stir up, irritate*, τινὰ ἐπί τινα Plb.2.51.2; ἐ. τινάς τινι *set* them *upon* him, D.L.2.38; μέθυσμα ἐ. θυμούς Ph.1. 680; so perh. in physical sense, *irritate*, Hp.*Mul.*1.99, *Epid.*5. 20. **-ειψις**, εως, ἡ, *painting over* of colours, Alex.Aphr.*in Sens.* 63.5. **2.** *smearing over, anointing*, *EM*69.41 (pl.).

**ἐπᾰλέξ-ησις**, εως, ἡ, etym. of ἔπαλξις, *EM*353.22. **-ω**, Ep. Verb, *defend, succour*, τινί Il.8.365, 11.428, v.l. in Batr.174; κακῇ ἐπαλαλκέμεν ἄτῃ (Ep.aor.2 inf.) *lend aid against*.., Nic.*Th.*352. **II.** *ward off, keep off*, ἐπὶ Τρώεσσιν ἀλεξήσειν κακὸν ἦμαρ Il.20.315.

**ἐπᾰλετρεύω**, *grind at*, μύλης πελάνους A.R.1.1077.

**ἐπαληθείς**, v. ἐπαλάομαι.

**ἐπαληθ-εύω**, *prove true, substantiate, verify*, τὴν αἰτίαν, τὸν λόγον, Th.4.85, 8.52; ἔργοις τὴν προσηγορίαν J.*BJ*7.8.1:—Pass., D.H.1. 58. **2.** *prove one's right to*, τοὔνομα, τὴν πρόσρησιν, Ph.2.6, 263. **II.** intr., *to be true, genuine*, ἐπαληθεῦον καὶ παγίως ἐνιδρυμένον ib.311, cf. Dam.*Pr.*31 bis, Sch.Pi.*O.*10.17. **2.** ἐ. τῷ ὀνόματι *use* the name *correctly*, Plot.5.9.5; *assert truly*, Dexipp.*in Cat.*50.24 (Pass.); but οὐ γὰρ -εύει τῷ ἐξῃρημένῳ τὸ οἰκεῖον ὄνομα κατ' ἀκρίβειαν the transcendent *is* not strictly *entitled* to its own name, Dam.*Pr.* 7. **-ίζω**, = foreg., Hsch.

⊛ **ἐπαλής**, ές, (ἀλέα B) *open to the sun, sunny*, λέσχη Hes.*Op.*493 (nisi leg. ἐπ' ἀλέα, cf. ἀλής).

**ἐπαλθ-έω**, *heal, cure*, fut. ἐπαλθήσουσιν Nic.*Al.*395: aor. ἐπαλθήσειε ib.614:—Med., aor. ἐπαλθήσαιο Id.*Th.*654. **-ής**, ές, *healing*, ib.500 **II.** *healed*, Id.*Al.*156.

**ἐπᾰλινδέομαι**, Pass., lit., *roll on*: hence ἴχνια ἐπηλίνδητ' ἀνέμοισιν *had been effaced*, A.R.4.1463:—also **ἐπᾰλίνδομαι**, Nic.*Th.*266.

**ἐπαλίνω** [ῐ], = ἐπαλείφω, aor. 1 inf. ἐπαλ[ε]ῖναι, Hsch.

**ἐπαλκής**, ές, *strong*, dub. in A.*Ch.*415 (lyr.).

**ἐπαλλ-αγή**, ἡ, = ἐπάλλαξις, γάμων ἐπαλλαγή, = ἐπιγαμία, Hdt.1.74; τὰς ἐ. τῶν σωμάτων their *fitting into one another*, Democr.ap.Arist.*Fr.*208; *crossing*, νεύρων Aret.*SD*1.7. II. *premium on exchange* of currency, *PCair.Zen.*22.2 (iii B.C.). **-ακτικῶς**, gloss on ἐπαμοιβαδίς, Sch.Od.5.481. **-άξ**, Adv., = ἐναλλάξ, *crosswise*, Hp.*Nat. Mul.*5, X.*Eq.*1.7; *alternately*, D.S.19.30. ⊕ **-αξις**, εως, ἡ, *interweaving* or *dovetailing*, AntiphoSoph.20 (pl.); αἱ ἐ. τοῦ χάρακος Plb. 18.18.11; ἡ ἐ. τῶν δακτύλων *crossing* of two fingers so as to feel double, Arist.*Metaph.*1011ᵃ33, *Insomn.*460ᵇ20, *Pr.*958ᵇ14; *linking together*, Id.*Mete.*387ᵃ12. 2. *overlapping* of species, Id.*GA*732ᵇ15; *confusion* of different things, Str.12.8.2. b. *alternation*, Pl. *Sph.*240c. 3. *change*, θέσεως Hierocl.*in CA*1 p.419 M.; διαιτημάτων Gal.6.59 (pl.); *varieties* of abnormal constitutions, ib.385 (pl.). **-άσσω**, Att. **-ττω**, *change over*: once in Hom., τὼ..ὁμοιΐου πτολέμοιο πεῖραρ ἐπαλλάξαντες ἐπ' ἀμφοτέροισι τάνυσσαν *crossing*, i.e. *tying*, the rope-end of balanced war, Il.13.359 (vv.ll. τοί, ἀλλήλοισι, in which case the metaph. is from a tug of war, *pulling alternately this way and that*); ἐ. ἅλματα ἐμποιοῦντες ἴχνεσιν ἴχνη *interchange* leaps, i.e. one to leap into the other's steps, X.*Cyn.*5.20 (cf. ἐπηλλαγμένα [ἴχνη] 8.3); of καρχαρόδοντα, ἐ. τοὺς ὀδόντας *have* their teeth *fitting in* like two saws, Arist.*HA*501ᵃ18:—Med., [νεῦρα] ἀλλήλοισι ἐπαλλαξάμενα ἐς χιασμὸν σχήματος Aret.*SD*1.7:—Pass., *cross one another*, δόρατα..ὡς ἥκιστα ἂν ἀλλήλοις ἐπαλλάττοιτο X.*Eq.Mag.*3.3; ἐπηλλαγμέναις δι' ἀλλήλων ταῖς χερσίν with the arms *crossed*, Plu. *Luc.*21; θώρακες ἁλύσεσι λεπταῖς σιδηραῖς ἐπηλλαγμένοι Arr.*Tact.*3. 5; ποὺς ἐπαλλαχθεὶς ποδί *closely joined*, E.*Heracl.*836: metaph., μή πῃ ὁ λόγος ἐπαλλαχθῇ that it *be* not *entangled*, X.*Mem.*3.8.1; of permutations and combinations, -όμεναι συζυγίας ἀποτελοῦσιν ἐννέα Gal.6.112. II. intr., *alternate*, ὀδόντες ἐπαλλάσσοντες *interlocking* teeth, Arist.*PA*661ᵇ18; of leaves, dub. in Thphr.*HP*4.6.10. 2. *overlap*, of classes or species, ib.1.3.2; ἀλλήλοις Arist.*GA*733ᵃ27; τοῦτο μόνον ἐ. *overlaps* both classes, ib.774ᵇ17; ἡ φώκη ἐ. τῷ γένει τῶν ἰχθύων *forms a link with*.., Id.*HA*501ᵃ22; ταῦτα συνδυαζόμενα ποιεῖ τὰς πολιτείας ἐπαλλάττειν causes them to *overlap*, Id.*Pol.*1317ᵃ2; so διὰ τὸ τὴν δύναμιν ἐπαλλάττειν αὐτῶν (sc. two species of τυραννίς) καὶ πρὸς τὴν βασιλείαν ib.1295ᵃ9; ὃ ποιεῖ τοὺς λόγους ἐ. makes the arguments *confused*, ib.1255ᵃ13, cf. 1257ᵇ35. b. *become confused* or *intermixed*, ἐ. τὰ μόρια Id.*GA*769ᵇ34; *to be interchangeable with*, τὰ νοσώδη ἐ. τοῖς βραχυβίοις Id.*Long.*464ᵇ28. 3. ἐ. τοῦτο τὸ σύμπτωμα τοῖς τοιούτοις this accident *invades, makes its way into* this class, Id.*GA*770ᵇ6. ⊕ **-ηλία**, ἡ, *sequence, unbroken series*, φωνηέντων Eust.11.32 (pl.), cf. *EM*576.2; ἐ. τῶν φαρμάκων *taking one* drug *after another*, '*mixing* medicines', Gal.19. 679. ⊕ **-ηλος**, ον, also η, ον D.C.74.10, al.:—*one close after another, in close order*, φάλαγξ, τάξεις, Plb.2.69.9, 11.11.7; ἄρτοι κατὰ ἓξ ἐ. J.*AJ*3.6.6; θυρίδας πέριξ ἐ. D.C.74.10; γυμνασίαι, φθοραί, κτλ., Ph.2.288,175, al.; *continuous*, βοή Hdn.2.7.6; δαπάναι *IG*7.2712. 54 (Acraephia); ἐ. πληγαί *given in quick succession*, Alciphr.3. 6. b. Gramm., τὸ ἐ. τῶν δύο εὐθειῶν *succession, sequence* of two nominatives, A.D.*Synt.*79.13, al. II. ἐπαλλήλοιν χεροῖν by *one another's* hands (Hermann for ἐπ' ἀλλ-), S.*Ant.*57. 2. γόμφοι ἐ. *mortised into one another*, Longin.41.3. III. Adv. **-λως** *again and again*, δι' ὅλου τοῦ ἔτους Dsc.1.115.5; Rhet., ἐ. ῥῆμα ἐπιτιθέναι *repeat* (e.g. μικρὸν μικρόν), Alex.*Fig.*2.2. 2. ἐ. ἔχειν τὰ ἔμπροσθεν *lean against one another*, Ath.10.456e. 3. *in alternate succession*, Ph.1.397. **-ηλότης**, ητος, ἡ, *repetition, duplication*, ἐν -τητι ἔχει ἕνα σύνδεσμον τὸν δή A.D.*Conj.*257.5.

**ἐπαλλόκαυλος**, ον, *clinging to another plant, quasi-parasitic*, prob. cj. in Thphr.*HP*3.18.9, 11.

**ἐπάλμενος**, v. ἐφάλλομαι.

**ἐπάλξ-ιον**, τό, *parapet*, *IG*2².463.56; cf. sq. **-ις**, εως, ἡ, (ἐπαλέξω) *means of defence*: mostly in pl., *battlements*, Il.12.263, Hdt.9.7, A.*Th.*30,158 (lyr.), E.*Ph.*1158, etc.; τὰς ἐ. ἀπώσαντες Th.3.23; αἱ οἰκίαι..ἐπάλξεις λαμβάνουσι Id.4.69, cf. 115. b. in sg., mostly, *line of battlements, parapet*, Il.12.381, al. (never in Od.); οἱ παρ' ἔπαλξιν the defenders of the wall, Th.2.13, cf. 7.28, Ar.*Ach.*72: pl., of individual *crenellations*, Th.3.21. 2. generally, *defence, protection*, πλούτου A.*Ag.*381 (lyr.); σωτηρίας E.*Or.*1203, etc. 3. court for trial of homicide, *EM*353.26, *AB*243. **-ίτης** [ῑ] λίθος *coping-stone*, *EM*353.28.

**ἔπαλπνος**, ον, (v. ἄλπνιστος) *cheerful, happy*, Pi.*P.*8.84 codd.; expld. by ἡδύς, προσηνής, Sch.

**ἐπαλφῐτόω**, *add meal* to wine, prob. in Ath.10.432b.

**ἐπᾰλωστής**, οῦ, ὁ, (ἀλοάω) *one who threshes with oxen*, X.*Oec.*18.5.

**ἐπαμ-**, before labials poet. or dial. for ἐπανα- (q.v.).

**ἐπᾰμαξεύω**, = ἐφαμ-, *traverse with cars*, γῆ..ἐπημαξευμένη τροχοῖσι *marked with the tracks* of wheels, S.*Ant.*251.

**ἐπᾰμάομαι**, *scrape together for oneself*, εὐνὴν ἐπαμήσατο χερσί *heaped him up* a bed (of leaves), Od.5.482; γῆν ἐπαμησάμενον Thgn. 428, cf. Thphr.*HP*4.13.5, *AP*7.446 (Hegesipp., tm.); γῆν ἐπαμησάμενος *having heaped up* a grave or barrow, Hdt.8.24; so ἐ. κόνιν Polyaen.2.1.23; ἐ. τινί τι Plu.2.982b; γῆν εἰς τοὺς ὀφθαλμούς Porph. *Abst.*4.9:—later in Act., κόνιν ἐπαμῆσαι D.L.6.79, cf. Iamb.*VP*31. 192: written ἐφαμᾶν in Hld.2.20.

**ἐπαμ-βαίνω**, poet. for ἐπαναβαίνω, Opp.*H.*3.638. **-βᾰτήρ**, ῆρος, ὁ, poet. for *ἐπαναβάτης, *one who mounts upon, assailant*: metaph., νόσοι σαρκῶν ἐπαμβατῆρες, of leprous eruptions, A.*Ch.*280. **-βλήδην**· ἀναβαλλόμενος, ἀνακρουόμενος, Hsch.; cf. ἐπαναβληδόν.

**ἐπαμβλύνω**, v.l. for ἀμβλύνω in Artem.3.38.

**ἐπᾰμείβω**, *exchange, barter*, τεύχεα δ' ἀλλήλοις ἐπαμείψομεν Il.6. 230; φύσεις ἐ. Orph.*A.*422:—Med., *come one after another, come in turn to*, νίκη δ' ἐπαμείβεται ἄνδρας Il.6.339; ἐξαῦτις δ' ἑτέρους ἐπαμείψεται (sc. κήδεα) Archil.9.9.

**ἐπᾱμέριος**, = sq., Pi.*Fr.*182.

⊕ **ἐπάμερος** [ᾱ], ον, Dor. and Aeol. for ἐφήμερος, Pi.*P.*8.95, Theoc. 30.31: neut. ἐπάμερον, as Adv., = αὐθημερόν, *IG*4.800 (Troezen).

**ἐπαμέτραιον**· μέτρον τι παρὰ Κνιδίοις, Hsch.

**ἐπαμμένος**, Ion. for ἐφημμένος, pf. part. Pass. of ἐφάπτω.

**ἐπαμμένω**, poet. for ἐπαναμένω, A.*Pr.*605 (lyr.).

**ἐπᾰμοιβ-άδίς**, Adv., (ἐπαμείβω) *interchangeably*: hence ὡς ἄρα πυκνοὶ ἀλλήλοισιν ἔφυν ἐ. so thick they grew *with interwoven boughs*, Od.5.481, cf. A.R.4.1030 (v.l.):—in Hsch. also **-ᾰδόν**. **-ή**, ἡ, *dovetailing*, *BCH*35.43 (pl.). **-ῐμος**, ον, = sq.; ἐ. ἔργα *barter*, *h.Merc.* 516 (ἐπ' ἀμοίβημα cod. M, ἐπαμοίβια cett.). **-ός**, όν, *one upon another, continuously*, of tiles, A.R.2.1075; cf. ἐπημοιβός.

**ἐπαμπέχω** and **-ίσχω** (v. infr., cf. ἐπαμφίσκω), *put on over, overwrap*, ἐπαμπίσχοντες γῆν τινι E.*Tr.*1148; *enwrap*, αἴσχιστα ἔργα εὐπρεπέσι κλήσεσιν Ph.2.379; ὕβρει καὶ κόμπῳ ἐπαμπέχειν τι Plu.*Oth.* 5:—Med., Ph.1.358, al., D.Chr.6.26; διὰ φόβον δόξας Plu.2.1102d:—Pass., φύσις λογισμῷ -ομένη Id.*Sert.*10.

**ἐπαμπήγνῡμι**, poet. for ἐπαναπ- (q.v.).

⊕ **ἐπᾰμύν-τωρ**, ορος, ὁ, *helper, defender*, Od.16.263; as fem., Orph.*L.* 587. **-ω**, *come to aid, succour*, τινί Il.6.361, 18.99, al., Th.3.14, al., Lys.12.99, etc. 2. abs., Il.16.540, al. (never in Od.), Hdt.1.82, Th.1.25,101, Lys.3.16, etc.; τῶν ἐπαμυνούντων λόγων ὡς εἰσὶ θεοί *apologetic* arguments *to prove* that.., Pl.*Lg.*891b. 3. *ward off*, δολίην v.l. for ἀπ- in *AP*5.6 (Asclep.).

**ἐπαμφέρω**, poet. for ἐπαναφέρω (q.v.).

**ἐπαμφι-βάλλω**, *use ambiguous terms*, Gal.17(2).24. **-έννῡμι**, *cloak* or *veil*, ἐπαμφιέσαι [τὴν ἀτυχίαν] χρήμασιν prob. l. in Men.404.5; in later form ἐπαμφιασαμένη Aristid.*Or.*30(10).18:—Pass., ἐπημφιεσμένος πτίλον [S.]*Fr.*1127.2. **-λλογος**, ον, *disputed*, *SIG*683.51 (ii B.C.).

**ἐπαμφισβητέω**, *dispute a claim*, *CPR*188.21 (ii A.D.).

**ἐπαμφίσκω**, = ἐπαμπίσχω, Hsch.

⊕ **ἐπαμφόδιος**, ἡ, (ἄμφοδος) *street-walker*, prob. in Luc.*Rh.Pr.*24.

**ἐπάμφορος** δίκα, (ἐπ-ανα-φέρω) suit *sent for retrial* after conviction of witnesses for perjury, *Foed.Delph.Pell.*i A 14, ii B 5.

**ἐπαμφοτερ-ής**, ές, *double-dealing*, διχόνους καὶ ἐ. Ph.*Fr.*20 H. (sed leg. **-ιστής**). **-ιζόντως**, Adv. *ambiguously*, Sch.Ar.*Pax* 854. **-ίζω**, *to be double*: hence, *play a double game*, '*run with the hare and hunt with the hounds*', Pherecr.19, Th.8.85; *halt between two opinions*, Pl.*Phdr.*257b, Arr.*Epict.*4.2.4; ἐ. τὴν γνώμην Ph.2.170; τοῖς λογισμοῖς Plu.*Mar.*40; τὸ -ίζον τῆς διανοίας Ph.1. 346. 2. of statements or arguments, *to be ambiguous, susceptible of two interpretations*, λόγους ἀμφιβόλους καὶ -ίζειν δυναμένους Isoc.12. 240, cf. Pl.*R.*479b; λοξὰ καὶ -ίζοντα..ἀποκρινόμενος Luc.*DDeor.*16. 1. b. of fevers, *partake of both kinds*, Gal.10.749. 3. of vowels, *to be doubtful* in quantity, Aristid.Quint.1.20. II. *lie half-way between*, of *intermediate* species, e.g. seals and bats, Arist. *PA*697ᵇ1, *HA*589ᵃ21; of apes, ἐ. ἀνθρώπῳ καὶ τετράποσι *share the properties of*.., ib.502ᵃ16; ἐ. τὴν μορφὴν *to be intermediate* in shape, Id.*PA*689ᵇ32; ὁ ἄνθρωπος ἐ. πᾶσι τοῖς γένεσι Id.*GA*772ᵇ1; of amphibious animals, Thphr.*Fr.*171.1. III. abs., *suffice for both*, Arist. *GA*777ᵃ16. **-ισμός**, ὁ, *inclination both ways, wavering*, ἐνδοιασμὸς καὶ ἐ. Ph.1.409, cf. Arr.*Epict.*4.2.5. II. *uncertainty* of parentage, τῶν τέκνων Ph.2.202. **-ιστής**, οῦ, ὁ, *waverer*, ἐνδοιασταὶ καὶ ἐ. Id.1.459, cf. 176. **-ος**, ον, *ambiguous*, τὸ ἐ. Philostr.*VS*1.25.10. Adv. **-ρως**, εἰπεῖν ib.21.5.

⊕ **ἐπάμων**, ονος, ὁ, (ἕπομαι) = ὀπάων, *attendant*, restored in Clitarch. Gloss.ap.Ath.6.267c, cf. Hsch. (pl.).

**ἐπάν**, Conj., later form of ἐπήν (v. ἐπεί A. II), Arist.*Ath.*42.2, Thphr.*Char.*24.10, *IG*2².1298.18 (iii B.C.), Plb.2.2.9, Agatharch.32, Str.10.4.20, etc.: c. ind. in late Greek, ἐπὰν ἑάλω Sch.Luc.*Peregr.* 9. [ᾱ Men.223.2, Alex.269.]

**ἐπανα-βαθμός** (v.l. **-βασμός**), ὁ, *step of a stair*, Pl.*Smp.*211c (pl.). ⊕ **-βαίνω**, poet. **ἐπαμβ-**, Opp.*H.*3.638:—*get up on, mount*, ἐπί τι Ar.*Nu.*1487, *Eq.*169; ἐπαναβεβηκότες *mounted* (on horseback), Hdt.3.85; of a star, *rise above the horizon*, Arist.*Mete.*342ᵇ34. 2. of animals, *cover*, Id.*HA*540ᵃ22, Clearch.36. 3. *come upon*, τὸ γῆρας ἐπαναβάν *Com.Adesp.*612. II. *go up* inland, Th. 7.29. III. *to be promoted*, εἰς τὰς τῶν ταξιάρχων χώρας X.*Cyr.*2.1. 23. 2. of αἰτίαι and ἀρχαί, *mount upwards*, ἐπὶ τὰ ἀνωτέρω Arist. *Metaph.*990ᵃ6, cf. *Ph.*257ᵃ22; τὸ ἐπαναβεβηκός *higher* or *more ultimate principle*, S.E.*P.*1.174; the *genus*, Sor.2.6; [ἀρχῆς] οὐδεὶς ἂν εὕροι ἁπλουστέραν οὐδὲ ἐπαναβεβηκυῖαν ἡντινοῦν Plot.2.9.1; *search for higher principles*, ἐ. ἀεὶ εἰς ἄπειρον Id.3.6.1; ἐπαναβεβηκότα τῇ ψυχῇ [νοῦν] Id.6.9.5. b. *transcend*, c. gen., Anon.*in Prm.* in *Rh. Mus.*47.617; also c. dat., ἐνέργεια -βεβηκυῖα πάσαις καὶ χρωμένη αὐταῖς ὡς ὀργάνοις ibid. ⊕ **-βάλλω**, *throw on* or *over*:—Med., ἐπαναβάλλεσθαι θαἰμάτια (cf. ἐπαναβληδόν) Ar.*Ec.*276. II. *lift up*, τὰ λευκὰ τῶν ὀφθαλμῶν Ath.12.529a. III. Med., *put off, defer*, τρία ἔτεα ἐ. τὴν Σαρδίων ἅλωσιν Hdt.1.91, cf. Phalar.*Ep.*95 (prob.). **-βάσις**, εως, ἡ, *search for higher principles*, Plot.6.7.27. II. *rise, diastole*

of the pulse, Gal.7.430. -βασμός, v. -βαθμός. -βιβάζω, causal of ἐπαναβαίνω, *make to mount upon*, ἄνδρας (sc. τοῖς πύργοις) Th.3.23, cf. D.C.50.23. -βιβασμός, ὁ, in pl., *ascending steps* in argument, Herm. *in Phdr.* p.64 A. -βλαστάνω, *grow upon*, Choerob. in *An.Ox.*2.198.30, Sch.Dsc.p.362 Matth. -βληδόν, Adv. *thrown over*, ἐπὶ [τοῖς κιθῶσι] εἰρίνεα εἵματα.. ἐ. φορέουσι Hdt.2.81; cf. ἐπαμβλήδην. -βοάω, *cry out*, Ar.*Pl.*292 (lyr.). -γιγνώσκω, *read over, read out*, f.l. in Lys.10.18, cf. Plb.31.13.10; ἐ. τινὶ ἔντευξιν *PPetr.*2 p.3 (iii B.C.); of a teacher, S.E.*M.*10.19, Porph.*Chr.*58:—Pass., D.7.19.

⊕ἐπᾰναγκ-άζω, *compel by force, constrain*, c. acc. et inf., A.*Pr.*671, Ar.*Av.*1083, *PHib.*1.34.3 (iii B.C.), etc.: —Pass., ἀροῦν ἐπαναγκασθεὶς Ar.*Pl.*525, etc.: freq. with inf. omitted, οὐδ' ἐπηνάγκαζε οὐδὲ εἷς (sc. αὐτοὺς προϊέναι) Hdt.8.130, cf. Ar.*Pl.*533, Th.5.31. -αστέον, *one must constrain*, Dam.*Pr.*74. -αστής, οῦ, ὁ, *taskmaster*, Sm.*Jb.*3.18. -αστικός, ή, όν, *coercive, potent*, *PMag.Par.*1.2567. ⊕ -ης, used only in neut.: 1. ἐπάναγκές [ἐστι] *it is compulsory, necessary*, c. inf., And.1.12, Pl.*Lg.*878e, etc.; μηδὲν ἐ. ἔστω let there be no *compulsion*, ib.765a, cf. *Smp.*176e. 2. as Adv., *on compulsion*, ἐ. κομῶντες wearing long hair *by fixed custom*, Hdt.1.82; ἐ. λέγειν, ἐντίθεσθαι, Aeschin.1.24, D.34.7; ἐ. λαβεῖν Men.576; ἐ. βουλὴν ἀθροισάτω *IG*2[2].1100.50, etc.; τὰ ἐπάναγκες *Act.Ap.*15.28. ⊕ -ος, ον, = foreg., *Leg.Gort.*4.28, *SIG*1219.17 (Gambreum, iii B.C.), *PGen.*20.17 (ii B.C.), *POxy.*270.38 (i A.D.). II. = ἐπαναγκαστικός, *PMag.Par.*1.2574, etc.

ἐπανᾰγορεύω, *proclaim publicly*:—impers. in Pass., ἐπαναγορεύεται *proclamation is made*, Ar.*Av.*1071.

⊕ ἐπαν-άγω [ᾰγ], *bring up*: hence, 1. *stir up, excite*, τὸν θυμόν Hdt.7.160. 2. *exalt, elevate*, εἰς ἡρωϊκὴν ἐπανῆκται τάξιν D.60.9. II. *bring up*, πρὸς τὸ φῶς Pl.*Lg.*724a. 2. *lead* or *draw back*, τὸ στρατόπεδον ἐς τὴν εὐρυχωρίαν Th.7.3; ἐ. τὰ δεξιὰ X.*Eq.*12.13; τὸν ἄνθρωπον ἐπανήγαγεν ὡς ὑμᾶς D.18.133; σύαγρον εἰς τὴν οἰκίαν Antiph.42 (s.v.l.). 3. *bring back*, τινὰ εἰς τὸν περὶ τοῦ πράγματος λόγον Pl.*Lg.*949b; τὸν λόγον ἐπὶ τὴν ὑπόθεσιν X.*Mem.*4.6.13; ἐ. ἐμαυτὸν ἀπὸ τῶν κακῶν Pl.*Ep.*325a; εἰς ἐλευθερίαν τὰ πράγματα v.l. in D.15.19; *restore*, τὰς αἱρέσεις τῶν ἱερέων εἰς τὸν δῆμον D.C.37.37; τὸν οἶκον Philostr.*VA*1.28; τὰ ἱερά ib.2 (Pass.); τὰ ἀδικήματα εἰς τὰ κοινὰ δικαστήρια ἐ. *refer* them to.., Pl.*Lg.*846b, cf. Epicur.*Ep.*3 p.62 U.; ἐ. τὸ διασταζόμενον εἰς τὸν κανόνα *UPZ*110.57 (ii B.C.); but τῷ Δὶ ἐ. *make acknowledgements* to Zeus, ib.6:—Pass., *to be referred back*, ἐπαναγέσθω πάλιν ἐπὶ τοὺς ἄρχοντας Arist.*Pol.*1298[b]37; *to be restored*, ἐπὶ ἀρχὰς καὶ στρατηγίας App.*BC*4.15. 4. ἐ. ἐπί τι *lead to, entail*, ἐπ' ἀλγοῦν Epicur.*Sent.*26,30. III. intr., *withdraw, retreat*, X.*Cyr.*4.1.3; *revert*, ἐπὶ τὴν ἀρχήν Plb.3.5.9, etc.; *recur*, in argument, ὅθεν ἐξέβην Jul.*Or.*7.226c; *return*, ἐπὶ ὕψιστον Lxx *Si.*17.26; *turn back*, ἀπὸ δικαιοσύνης εἰς ἁμαρτίαν ib.26.28. 2. ἐ. τῷ σώματι *recover one's health*, Apollon.Perg.*Con.*1 *Praef.* IV. *put out to sea*, τὸ κέρας ἀπὸ τῆς γῆς X.*HG*6.2.28: abs., *Ev.Luc.*5.3:—Pass., *put to sea against*, τινί Hdt.9.98; ἐπανάγεσθαι ταῖς ναυσί with one's ships, Th.8.42: abs., Hdt.7.194, X.*HG*2.1.24; ἐπὶ τὴν Χίον ib.1.6.38; *sail up* the Nile, *PStrassb.*102.19 (iii B.C.). V. Pass., also, *to be carried to* a place, ἐπαναχθέντας Hdt.4.103, where however the v.l. ἐπαναχθέντες (in signf. IV) is to be preferred. -ᾰγωγή, ἡ, *sailing against, naval attack*, Th.7.34; ἐπανήγαγεν τὰς ἐ. καθ' ἕκαστον μῆνα ποιούμενος perh. held the monthly naval *manœuvres*, *IG*2[2].1227.12 (Salamis, ii B.C.). II. *leading up, exalting*, τοῦ βελτίστου πρὸς τὴν τοῦ ἀρίστου θέαν Pl.*R.*532c. 2. Rhet., *return to the point*, Corn.*Rh.*p.397 H. (pl.). -ἀγωγὸς Τύχη, = Lat. *Fortuna Redux*, D.C.54.10.

ἐπαναδέρω, *strip off the scalp*, Hp.*Vid.Ac.*8.

ἐπανα-δίδωμι, intr., *increase more and more*, πυρετὸς ἐ. καθ' ἡμέρην ἑκάστην Hp.*Epid.*1.25. -διπλάζω, poet. ἐπανδ-, *reiterate questions*, A.*Pr.*817. -διπλᾰσιασμός, ὁ, *doubling*, τοῦ αὐτοῦ συμφώνου *EM*605.17; *repetition*, Elias *in Porph.*20.22. -διπλόω, *repeat yet again*, Arist.*Pr.*910[b]25, Gal.15.879:—Pass., *to be repeated*, Arist.*APr.*49[a]11, *Metaph.*1003[b]28. -δίπλωμα, ατος, τό, *fold, double*, Id.*HA*506[b]14. -δίπλωσις, εως, ἡ, *doubling, folding*, of the intestines, ib.507[b]30 (pl.); of the spermatic glands, Id.*GA*717[a]33; τοῦ δέρματος Leonid.ap.Aët.15.5. II. *repetition*, Arist.*APr.*49[a]26. 2. Rhet., = ἀναστροφή (q.v.), Tib.*Fig.*25. III. Medic., '*reduplication*', i.e. *combination* of two kinds of fevers, Gal.7.433. -δοσις, εως, ἡ, *restitution*, Just.*Nov.*97.5. -ζεῦξαι· ἐπανελθεῖν, Hsch. -ζευξις, εως, ἡ, *return*, Ascl. *in Metaph.*399.19. -ζώννῦμαι, Med., *gird on one's clothes*, Ph.2.479. -θαρρέω, = ἀναθαρρέω, ἐπί τινι Onos.14.4: abs., Id.33.5. -θεάομαι, *contemplate again*, X.*Cyr.*5.4.11. -θερμαίνομαι, *receive warmth again*, v.l. in Hp.*Epid.*1.26.α'. -θέω, *run up against*, τινί Onos.18: abs., Id.6.1.

ἐπαν-αίρεσις, εως, ἡ, *slaughter, destruction*, Plb.2.37.8: pl., μεγάλαι ἀνθρώπων ἐ. Nech. in *Cat.Cod.Astr.*7.140. -αιρέω, *make away with, destroy*, D.S.19.51; *remove*, τὰ γεῖσα *IG*2[2].463.54:—Med., Plb.2.19.9, etc.; ἐπαναιρεῖσθαί τινα φαρμάκῳ Id.8.12.2; ἐ. τὰς Συρακούσας Id.1.10.8:—Pass., ἐπανῄρηται φαρμάκῳ *PTeb.*43.19 (ii B.C.). 2. *kill after* or *together with*, App.*BC*4.15, al.; μετά τινα ἑαυτόν ib.4.26. II. Med. (pf. Pass., f.l. in Pl.*Ly.*219a, cf. Plu.*Comp.Alc.Cor.*2), *take upon one, enter into*, φιλίαν Pl.l.c.; esp. into a profession, τέχνην, λατρείαν, Luc.*BisAcc.*1, *Apol.*4; [βίον] Men.Rh.p.376 S., Just.*Nov.*149.2; ἐ. πόλεμον *enter upon* a war, Plb.9.29.8:—Pass., of cures, *to be employed*, Aret.*SD*2.12. b. *gain*, δόξαν Vett.Val.173.24; in bad sense, *incur*, ἔχθραν Jul.*Mis.*355a. c. *receive* as one's share in a division of property, *BGU*234.7 (ii A.D.), etc. 2. *withdraw*, τὸν φιλάνθρωπον νόμον Plu.*TG*10, cf. *CG*4. -αίρω, *lift up, raise high*, τὰς κεφαλάς X.*Cyn.*6.23:—Med., κἀπαναίρονται δόρυ (Herm. for κἀπαναιροῦνται) *raise* the spear *one against the other*, S.*OC*424; but ἐπανήρατο τὴν βακτηρίαν *raised his* staff *against* him, Th.8.84, cf. Hsch. s.v. ἐπανήραντο:—Pass., *rise up*, ἀλλ' ἐπαναίρου Ar.*Eq.*784. -αίσθητος, f.l. for ἀνεπ-, Aret.*SD*1.14. -αιτέω, *demand*, dub. in *BGU*330.6 (ii A.D.). -αιώρημα, ατος, τό, f.l. for ἐναιώρημα (q.v.) ap.Erot.

ἐπανα-καινίζω, *renew, revive*, Lxx *Jb.*10.17, Phld.*Acad.Ind.*p.4 M.: also -καινόω, Herod.Med. in *Rh.Mus.*49.549. ⊕ -κᾰλέω, *invoke besides*, A.*Ag.*145. II. *recall*, Aret.*SD*2.13 (Pass.):—Med., τινὰς ὡς ἐπὶ τὸ στρατόπεδον Arr.*An.*4.27.1, cf. Dam.*Pr.*245, Procl. *in Alc.*p.182 C.:—Pass., πρὸς τὸ δέον Hierocl. *in CA*7 p.429 M. -κάμπτω, intr., *come back again*, ἐπὶ τὴν ἀρχήν Arist.*Pr.*916[a]32: abs., *bend back*, of ducts or veins, Id.*HA*510[a]21, 514[a]11; *return*, Aq., Sm., Thd.*Is.*35.10. -καμψις, εως, ἡ, *return*, ἐπὶ τὴν πρώτην ἡλικίαν Ocell.1.14. -κειμαι, *to be imposed upon* as punishment, τινί X.*Cyr.*3.3.52. II. *to be superadded*, κακὸν κακῷ -κείμενον Numen. ap.Eus.*PE*14.8. 2. *to be entered as well* in a register, *Stud.Pal.*1.62.33 (i A.D.). -κεφᾰλαιόομαι, = ἀνακεφαλαιόω, Hermog.*Stat.*3, Olymp. *in Mete.*319.25. -κεφαλαίωσις, εως, ἡ, *recapitulation*, ib.30. -κλαγγάνω, *give tongue again and again*, X.*Cyn.*4.5, 6.23. -κλησις, εως, ἡ, *recall, reaction*, ἐπανάκλησιν θέρμης ποιέεσθαι Hp.*Aph.*5.21, Aret.*CA*2.3: metaph., ἡ ἐ. τῶν ἀπορρεόντων μερῶν ἀπὸ τοῦ ὅλου εἰς αὐτὸ τὸ ὅλον Dam.*Pr.*241; *call to repentance*, Hierocl. *in CA*7 p.429 M. II. *double inspiration*, Hp.*Epid.*2.3.7, Gal.7.899. -κλίνω [ῑ], *make to lie down*, τινά Hp.*Acut.*(*Sp.*)37, cf. Sm.*Ca.*2.5; *incline* one valve of the heart *towards* the other, Hp.*Cord.*10. -κοινόω, *communicate*, τινί τι Pl.*Lg.*918a. -κομίζω, *bring back*:—Pass., *return*, D.C.40.44. -κράζω, *call out to*, in aor. imper. ἐπανακραγέτω, Poll.5.85. -κρεμάννῦμαι, *to be dependent*, Arist.*Pol.*1318[b]38. -κρουσις, εως, ἡ, *putting back*, Sch.Ar.*Av.*649. -κρούω, poet. ἐπαγκρ-, *put* a ship *back* (v. ἀνακρούω), Hsch.: metaph., πάλιν ἐπαγκρούων Isyll.6:—Med., *put back*, Ar.*Av.*648. -κτάομαι, *recover*, *SIG*799.10 (Cyzicus, i A.D.).

ἐπανακτ-έον, *one must recall*, τὸν λόγον ἐπί τι Him.*Ecl.*36.7, cf. Jul.*Or.*6.192a. -ικός, ή, όν, *indicating return*, πρός τινας Phld.*D.*3 *Fr.*75.

ἐπανα-κτῠπέω, dub. l. in Arr.*Tact.*41.2. -κυκλέω, *recur*, of intermittent fevers, Gal.7.412. II. Pass., *make a counter revolution*, Pl.*R.*617b; but simply, *revolve*, ἀπὸ τοῦ αὐτοῦ πρὸς ταὐτόν Dam.*Pr.*23. -κύκλησις, εως, ἡ, *return* of a circle *into itself*, Pl.*Ti.*40c. -κύπτω, *have an upward slope*, X.*Eq.*12.13. II. *rise up to thwart*, ταῖς ἐλπίσιν τινός J.*BJ*1.31.1. 2. ἐπανέκυψε λόγος *a new* argument *rose up*, Plu.2.725c. -λαμβάνω, *take up again, resume, repeat*, πῶς, ὡς.., Pl.*Grg.*488b, X.*Lac.*13.2; εἴπωμεν ἐπαναλαβόντες Arist.*Metaph.*1035[b]4, cf. Pl.*Tht.*169e: the part. may be best rendered by an Adv., πολλάκις ἐπαναλαμβάνων ἐκέλευέν οἱ λέγειν he ordered him *repeatedly*, Id.*Phdr.*228a. II. *revise, correct*, Id.*Lg.*781b; τῇ τροφῇ τὴν κακοπάθειαν Thphr.*CP*3.7.8. III. *undertake*, *PMasp.*151.136 (vi A.D.). -λέγω, *repeat*, Alex.*Fig.*1.13 (Pass.).

ἐπανᾰλείφω, *plaster on*, Gal.6.577 (f.l. for ἐπαλ-).

ἐπανα-ληπτέον, *one must resume*, Jul.*Gal.*351a. -ληπτικῶς, Adv. *by repetition*, Eust.624.46. ⊕ -ληψις, εως, ἡ, in Rhet., *resumption, repetition*, Demetr.*Eloc.*196, Hermog.*Id.*1.4 (pl.), *Meth.*9, Alex.*Fig.*1.13, etc. II. = ἐπαναδίπλωσις III, Gal.7.433.

ἐπανᾰλίσκω, *consume still more*, [χρόνον] D.50.42: aor. 1 ἐπανάλωσα Hadr.Rh.p.45 H. II. *spend in addition*, τὸ ἐπαναλωθὲν *IG*12(7).24 (Amorgos); but ἐπανηλωθέντος *PCorn.*1.88.

ἐπανά-λῡσις, εως, ἡ, = ἀναποδισμός, *retracing one's steps*, Hsch. -λύτης, = Lat. *remeabilis*, *Gloss.* λύω, *return*, *POxy.*942.3 (vi (?) A.D.).

ἐπανᾱλωτής, οῦ, ὁ, *spendthrift*, Lat. *sumptuarius*, *Gloss.*

ἐπανα-μένω, poet. ἐπαμμένω, *wait longer*, Hdt.8.141, Ar.*Ec.*790. II. *wait for* one, τινά Id.*Nu.*803; ἐ. τινὰ ἐλθεῖν Id.*Lys.*74: impers., ὅ τι μ' ἐπαμμένει παθεῖν what *there is in store* for me to suffer, A.*Pr.*605 (lyr.); οὗ σφιν κακῶν ὕψιστ' ἐπαμμένει παθεῖν Id.*Pers.*807; τίς ἄρα με πότμος.. ἐπαμμένει; (Herm. for ἐπιμένει) S.*OC*1718. -μιμνήσκω, *remind* one *of, mention again* to one, τινά τι Pl.*Lg.*688a, cf. Arist.*Mem.*451[a]12, Porph.*Abst.*1.30; ἕκαστον ὑμῶν, τίς.. D.6.35. -μνησις, εως, ἡ, *mentioning again*, τῶν προαποδεδειγμένων πραγμάτων D.H.*Rh.*10.18, cf. Corn.*Rh.*p.370 H. -νεάζω, *to be recrudescent*, Gal.19.210. ⊕ -νεόομαι, Med., *revive*, τὸν λόγον Pl.*R.*358b; *renew*, τὰ διαστρώματα *POxy.*237 viii 41 (ii A.D.). -νέωσις, εως, ἡ, *renewal*, Just.*Const.*Δέδωκεν init. -παυσις, εως, ἡ, *lighting down, descent*, Sm.*Is.*30.30 (Auct.p.30 F.). -παύω, *rest upon*, τῇ λαβῇ τοῦ ξίφους τὴν χεῖρα Procop.Gaz.p.170 B., cf. Ael.*NA*5.56:—Med. (fut. -παύσομαι, later -παήσομαι v.l. in *Ev.Luc.*10.6), *rest upon*, ταῖς χερσί J.*AJ*8.3.6, Hdn.2.1.2; *rest in* or *upon*, τινί Lxx 1 *Ma.*8.12; *rest one's hopes on*, νόμῳ *Ep.Rom.*2.17; *rest content with, rely on*, ταῖς παλαιαῖς ἀποδόσεσιν Artem.4.65; τῇ ἐφημέρῳ τροφῇ Trypho *Trop.*p.194 S.; ταῖς διωρισμέναις ἐννοίαις Dam.*Pr.*37: in Logic, *to be based on*, ὁ δεύτερος συλλογισμὸς ἐ. τῇ ἐννοίᾳ τοῦ ἑνός ib.321. II. Med., *come to rest*, of a machine, Hero *Aut.*24.4: metaph., ἐ. ἔν τινι *come to rest in*, Iamb.*Comm.Math.*8; ἐπαναπαύσεται ἐπ' αὐτὸν (sc. τὸν οἶκον) ἡ εἰρήνη ὑμῶν *Ev.Luc.*10.6; ἐπανεπαύσατο ἐπ' αὐτοῖς πνεῦμα Lxx *Nu.*11.26. -πέμπω, *send back to* a point, Hp.*Mul.*2.133, prob. in *PPetr.*2 p.64 (iii B.C.). -περάω, *cross over again*, Nic.Dam.

*Vit.Caes.*6 codd. **-πέτομαι**, aor. 2 inf. -πτῆναι *fly up*, Hsch. s.v. ἐπαναπτήσιμον. **-πήγνῡμι**, *fix in* or *on* :—Med., δούρατ' ἐπαμπήξασθαι *fix their* spears *in the ground*, Orph.*A*.319. **-πηδάω**, *leap upon*, Ar.*Nu*.1375. **-πιπράσκω**, *put up to sale again* :—Pass., aor. part. -πραθέν *PPetr*.3p.120 (iii B.C.): fut. -πραθήσομαι *PTheb. Bank* 1.24 (ii B.C.), cf. *UPZ*112iii12 (ii B.C.). **-πίπτω**, *lie down on*, φύλλοις ῥόδων Ael.*VH*9.24. **-πλάσσω**, Att. -ττω, = ἀναπλάσσω, Axionic.8. **-πλέω**, *put to sea against*, ἐπί τινα Hdt.8.9, cf. 16; ἐπ' ἀργυρολογίαν X.*HG*4.8.35. 2. *sail back again*, ib.24, D. 56.29, Plb.1.28.10. II. *rise to the surface*: metaph., ἐπαναπλέει ὑμῖν ἔπεα κακά ill language *rises to* your *tongue*, Hdt.1.212, cf. Ph.2. 174. **-πληρόω**, *fill up, supply*, Thphr.*Sens*.8 (Pass.). **-πνέω**, *have a double inspiration* (cf. ἐπανάκλησις II), ἐ. διπλόον Hp.*Epid*.7. 92. ⊛ **-ποδίζω**, *retrace one's steps* in argument, Alex.Aphr.*in Metaph*.813.20. **-ποδιστέον**, *one must re-examine*, Arist.*GC*317ᵇ19. **-πολέω**, *repeat yet again*, Pl.*Phlb*.60a, *Lg*.723e. **-πόλησις**, εως, ἡ, *repetition*, Ph.1.254. **-πορεύομαι**, *return*, *PSI*4.353.3 (iii B.C.). **-πρίασθαι**, aor., *buy at a re-sale*, ὁ ἐπαναπριάμενος τὰ παλίμπωλα *IG*7.3073.26 (Lebad.). **-πτήσιμος**, ον, *ready to fly*, *Com.Adesp*.1006. **-πωλέω**, = -πιπράσκω, *PPetr*.3p.120 (iii B.C.):—Pass., *UPZ*112v22 (ii B.C.). **-ρρήγνῡμι**, *tear open again*, τὸ τραῦμα Plu.*Cat.Mi*.70 :—Pass., *burst open afresh*, Hp.*Loc.Hom*. 14. **-ρριπίζω**, = ἀναρριπίζω, J.*AJ*19.2.2. **-ρρίπτω** or -έω, *throw up in the air*: seemingly intr. (sc. ἑαυτόν), *spring high in the air*, X.*Cyn*. 5.4. **-ρρύεται**· μετὰ κρίσιν θύει, κρέα δίδωσιν, Hsch. **-ρρυμα**, ατος, τό, = τὸ ἐν Ἀρείῳ πάγῳ ἐπίθυμα, *AB*417, cf. Phot. s.v. κρέας. **-ρρῠσις**, εως, ἡ, = foreg., Suid. s.v. ἀναρύει. **-σεισις**, εως, ἡ, *brandishing against*, τῶν ὅπλων Th.4.126. **-σείω**, *lift up and shake*, Hp.*Foet.Exsect*.4: metaph., ἐ. τὴν δημαρχικὴν ἐξουσίαν *threaten* one *with it*, D.H.11.6; κατηγορίαν Procop.*Arc*.23 :—Pass., of soldiers, -όμενοι τοῖς κρατίστοις *being used to overawe*.., J.*AJ*19. 1.16, cf. 17. **-σκοπέω**, *consider yet again*, Pl.*Cra*.428d, *Hp.Mi*. 369d; πάλιν ἐπανασκεψόμεθα Id.*Tht*.154e. **-σπείρω**, *sow again*; and **-σπορά**, ἡ, *second sowing*, Tz.ad Hes.*Op*.444. ⊛ **-στάσις**, εως, ἡ, *rising up* to go to stool: hence in pl., concrete, *stools*, Hp.*Prorrh*. 1.146. 2. *rising up again*, D.S.18.31. 3. *rising up against, insurrection*, Hdt.3.44,118, Th.2.27, etc.; ἐγένετο ἡ ἐν Σάμῳ ἐ. ὑπὸ τοῦ δήμου τοῖς δυνατοῖς Id.8.21; ἐ. μέρους τινὸς τῷ ὅλῳ τῆς ψυχῆς Pl.*R*.444b; παθῶν Hierocl.*in CA* 1p.418M.; opp. ἀπόστασις, D.H. 3.8, Sch.Th.3.39. b. concrete, ἐπαναστάσεις θρόνων *rebellions* (i.e. *rebels*) *against* the throne, S.*Ant*.533. II. *rising up, swelling*, Hp.*Coac*.216; *prominent growth*, Thphr.*HP*3.7.4; *prominence* on the head, Arist.*HA*500ᵃ5; φλυκταινῶν Dsc.*Ther*.9, cf. Sor.2.18, Antyll.ap.Orib.8.17.2. III. metaph., *rise* in rhetorical *tone*, Demetr.*Eloc*.278. **-στέλλω**, *check, resist*, αἱ γενέσεις ἐ. τὰς φθορὰς Arist.*Mu*.397ᵇ3 (v. ἀνασηκόω). **-στημα**, ατος, τό, *rising, blister*, Sch.Ar.*Ra*.238. 2. *eminence, hill*, ἐ. γῆς Phlp.*in de An*.311. 24. 3. *crest* of a helmet, Hsch. s. vv. λόφος, χαλκόλοφον, *EM*570. 4. ⊛ **-στρέφω**, intr., *turn back upon* one, *wheel round and return to the charge*, Ar.*Ra*.1102, Th.4.130, 8.105, X.*HG*6.2.21 :—Pass., Ar. *Eq*.244, X.*Eq.Mag*.8.25; εἴς τι Porph.*Marc*.13. II. Pass., *return to the surface*, Arist.*Fr*.335. III. Pass., *to be charged upon*, τῇ ἐμῇ περιουσίᾳ *PMasp*.151.136 (vi A.D.). **-στροφή**, ἡ, = ἀναστροφή, *return*, of the chorus, Sch.Ar.*Nu*.596. 2. Rhet., *repetition* of the last word or words of a sentence at the beginning of the next, Hermog.*Id*.1.12; of the syllables -μια in Σαμία μία ναῦς Eust.1751. 40. **-σχίζω**, *split open*, Philum.*Ven*.7.12 (Pass.). **-σωστικός**, ή, όν, *bringing safely home*, Τύχη Ἐ., = Lat. *Fortuna Redux*, Inscr.ap. Lyd.*Mens*.4.132. **-τάσις**, εως, ἡ, *stretching upwards, holding up*, τοῦ σκήπτρου Arist.*Pol*.1285ᵇ12; μάστιγος S.E.*M*.8.271. II. metaph., *threatening*, Ph.1.282 (pl.), al., *POxy*.237 viii 10 (ii A.D.), Iamb.*Myst*. 6.6; *brandishing*, σιδήρου *PHal*.1.186 (iii B.C; misspelt ἐπάντασις). **-τείνω**, poet. ἐπαντ-, Orph.*A*.61, 332 :—*stretch out and hold up*, τὸν τράχηλον, f.l. for ἐπέρανα-, X.*An*.7.4.9; ἐ. τὰς χεῖρας, as in prayer, D.S.32.6, cf. Orph.*A*. ll.cc.; ἐ. ἐλπίδας τινί *hold out* hopes, X.*Cyr*.2.1.23 (Pass.). II. freq. in Med., ἐπανατείνεσθαι σίδηρόν τινι *brandish threatingly*, *PHal*.1.186 (iii B.C.); βάκτρον τινί Luc.*Cat*. 13, cf. Jul.*Or*.6.196b; ἐ. φόβους τινί Plb.2.44.3: c. inf., ἦ τι πράξειν *threaten* to do, Id.15.29.14 :—Pass., *POxy*.1408.17 (iii A.D.). 2. *speak with prolixity*, D.H.*Rh*.8.14. 3. *set oneself up, rebel*, Philostr. *VA*7.14. ⊛ **-τέλλω**, poet. **ἐπαντέλλω**, *raise*, ποδὸς ἴχνος E.*Ph*.105 (anap.); ἐ. κέρας ἐκ μετώπου *send forth*, Opp.*C*.2.97. II. intr., *rise*, [τὸν ἥλιον] ἐπανατεῖλαι Hdt.2.142; ἡλίου ἐπανατείλαντος Id.3. 84; ὡς ἐπανέτελλε ὁ ἥλιος Id.7.54; ἐπαντέλλων ἀστράσιν ἠέλιος *AP*12. 178 (Strat.); ἐπανατεταλκέτω τὸ Η Arist.*Mete*.376ᵇ29; of a star, *Sammelb*.2134.7; *rise again*, Gem.6.10; εὐνῆς ἐπαντείλασαν *having risen* from bed, A.*Ag*.27; ἐκ τοῦ χάρακος Plu.*Aem*.18; *show oneself, appear*, λευκὰς δὲ κόρσας τῇδ' ἐπαντέλλειν νόσῳ A.*Ch*.282; φόνος -τέλλει E.*HF*1053 (anap.); ὁ ἐπαντέλλων χρόνος the time *coming to light, the future*, Pi.*O*.8.28. **-τέμνω**, Ion. -τάμνω, *cut open further*, Hp.*VC* 13; *cut open again*, Aret.*CA*1.4. ⊛ **-τίθημι**, *lay upon*, ἐπαναθῶ σοι καὶ ξύλον Ar.*V*.148: metaph., *shift* a burden, *PSI*4.286.7 (iii/iv A.D.): —Pass., μείζων δύναμις ἐ. τινί *is entrusted* to him, Pl.*Lg*.926d. II. Med., *shift one's position*, of patients under operation, Gal.18(2). 425. III. Med., *bequeath*, *PLips*.29.7 (iii A.D.). IV. *shut*, σανίδας Il.21.535 (Aristarch.). **-τολή**, ἡ, invisible *rising* of stars just *after* sunrise or sunset, Ptol.*Alm*.8.4. **-τρέπω**, *overturn, upset*, Hdn.3.8.5. II. intr., *return*, εἰς τὸν λόγον Cratin.181 (dub.). **-τρέφω**, *feed up, recruit, nourish*, Hp.*Aph*.2.7, Aret.*CD* 1.5. **-τρέχω**, aor. 2 ἐπανέδραμον, *return, recur*, Phld.*Ir*.p.63 W., *return to*, τὴν ἀρετὴν J.*AJ*18.9.6; ἐπὶ τοὺς κυρίους D.S.36.8. II. of property rights, *pass*, ἐπί, εἴς τινα, *PLond*.3.1044.14 (vi A.D.), 5. 1727.46 (vi A.D.). **-τρίβω** [ῐ], *scrub again*, Asclep.ap.Gal.12. 412. **-τροπιάζω**, *relapse* (Lat. *recidit*), *Gloss*. **-τρῠγάω**, *glean after the vintage*, c. acc., Lxx *De*.24.21, *Le*.19.10. ⊛ **-φέρω**, poet. **ἐπαμφέρω**, fut. ἐπανοίσω Epicur.*Sent*.25: aor. 1 -ήνεγκα :—*throw back upon*: hence, *ascribe, refer*, μή τι θεοῖς τούτων μοῖραν ἐπαμφέρετε Sol.11.2; τι εἴς τινα or εἴς τι, Ar.*Nu*.1080, Pl.*R*.434e, D.5.11, 27. 49; ἐπί τι Pl.*Lg*.680d; ἐπί τι αἴτιον Arist.*Ph*.196ᵃ13; ἐπὶ τὸ τέλος Epicur.*Sent*.25; πρός τι Hp.*VM*1 (v.l.); ἐπί τινα, of an analogous case, ib.10: abs., πάλιν ἐ. And.3.33; ἐ. τινὶ ὑπέρ τινος, Lat. *referre alicui de re*, Plb.21.4.14 :—Pass., ἐπανενεχθεισῶν τῶν συνθηκῶν εἰς τὴν Ῥώμην Id.1.17.1. b. intr. in Act., *rise* or *be referred* to a cause, ἐπί τι Pl.*Ly*.219c. 2. *put into the account*, D.41.20, cf. *IG*2².1607*a* 7. 3. *bring back a message*, X.*HG*2.2.21 (Act. with Med. as v.l.); ὥς τινα Plu.*Art*.29. 4. *vomit*, Aret.*SA*2.2. II. intr., *recover consciousness*, ἐπανενέγκαντες θνήσκουσι Hp.*Coac*.1 (unless = *sigh*, cf. ἀναφέρω 1.2). 2. of disease, *abate*, Aret.*SA*2.1. III. Pass., *rise*, as an exhalation, X.*Cyn*.5.2; as stars or the sun, Gem.7.11, Plu.2.19e, cf. 735a; esp. in Astrol., *occupy the position following a* κέντρον, Ptol.*Tetr*.115. 2. *move in counter revolution*, Ti.Locr. 96d. IV. Rhet., *repeat* a word (cf. sq.), Demetr.*Eloc*.59 :—Pass., ib.268, D.H.*Dem*.40. **-φορά**, ἡ, *referring, reference*, ἐπί τι Arist. *EN*1130ᵃ29; πρός τι Thphr.*HP*1.2.4. 2. *reference* of a question to an assembly, And.3.33; to the people, Harp. II. Rhet., *repetition* of a word at the beginning of several clauses, Longin.20.2 (pl.), Demetr.*Eloc*.61, Hermog.*Id*.1.12, Ps.-Plu.*Vit.Hom*.33. III. *rising*, ἀτμῶν Aret.*CA*1.6. IV. Astrol., τόπος *which follows a* κέντρον (q.v.), Ptol.*Tetr*.112, S.E.*M*.5.14, Paul.Al.*L*.2. **-φορικός**, ή, όν, *of* or *for* ἐπαναφορά, σχῆμα Sch.Ar.*Pl*.545, cf. Eust.67.35. **-φορος**, v. ἐπάμφ-. **-φῡσάω**, *play on the flute in accompaniment*, Ar.*Th*. 1175. **-φύω**, *put forth again*, Ael.*NA*10.13. **-φωνέω**, *pronounce in addition* or *after*, opp. προαναφωνέω, S.E.*M*.1.130 (Pass.). **-χάζομαι**, v. ἐπαγχ-. ⊛ **-χέω**, *pour out upon*, *EM*329.17 (Pass.). **-χρεμπτήριος**, ον, *promoting expectoration*, Hp.*Loc.Hom*.17. **-χρέμπτομαι**, *expectorate*, ib.14. **-χρεμψις**, εως, ἡ, *expectoration*, ib.17, 18. **-χωρέω**, *retreat, return*, Charon *Fr*.2, Ar.*Lys*.461, Th.6.49; δεῦρο Pherecr.59; ἐς τὰς Θήβας Hdt.9.13; ἐς τὸ τεῖχος Th.1.63, cf. 3.96; πρὸς τὰ μετέωρα Id.4.44; ἐπὶ τὰ πρῶτα λεχθέντα Pl.*Lg*.781e; εἰς θεοὺς ἐ. τῆς τῶν πράξεων ἀρχῆς *return from*.., Plu.2.580a; ἐ. τῶν πραγμάτων *withdraw from*, *PLond*.5.1727.16 (vi A.D.). **-χώρησις**, εως, ἡ, *return*, κύματος Th.3.89; *retreat*, D.S.25.6.

**ἐπανδιπλάζω**, poet. for ἐπαναδιπλάζω (q.v.).

⊛ **ἔπανδρ-ος**, ον, (ἀνήρ) *manly*, Demad.37, Phld.*Ir*.p.65 W., Vett. Val.14.24, al.; πρᾶξις D.S.4.50; ἐργασία *IG*14.951 (i B.C.); τὸ ἔ. *masculine spirit*, Corn.*ND*20; ἔργα Hierocl.p.63 A. (Comp.). Adv. -δρως S.E.*M*.11.107; ἀγωνίσασθαι *CIG*4239 (Tlos), cf. *SIG*709.6 (Cherson., ii B.C.). ⊛ **-όω**, *make manly*, ψυχὰς νέων Lxx 2*Ma*.15.17.

**ἐπαν-εγείρω**, = ἀνεγείρω, Hp.*Prorrh*.2.4, Plu.2.101a. **-έγερσις**, εως, ἡ, gloss on ἐπανάστασις, Hsch. **-ειλέω**, *unroll*, Gal.19. 91. **-ειμι**, (εἶμι *ibo*) used as fut. of ἐπανέρχομαι, *go back, return*, Th.6.102, etc.; αὐλὸς.. ἐπάνεισιν the music of the flute *will rise again*, S.*Tr*.642 (lyr.); in writing or speaking, *go back* or *return* to a point, ἐπὶ τὸν πρότερον λόγον Hdt.7.138; ἐγὼ δ' ἔνθεν ἐξέβην ἐπάνειμι X.*HG*7. 4.1; μικρὸν ἐ. Id.*Cyr*.1.2.15; ἐ. δὴ πάλιν ἐπὶ τὰς ἀποδείξεις D.18.42, cf. 21.196; περὶ φύσεως πάσης ἐπανιόντα τῆς τῶν σώματων *recurring* to first principles of physiology, Pl.*Lg*.857d. 2. c. acc. rei, *return to, recapitulate*, τοὺς λόγους ib.693c; τὰ ὑποτεθέντα ἐ. αὖθις Id.*Ti*. 61d. II. *rise*, [ὕδωρ] κάτωθεν ἐ. πέφυκεν ib.22e; *go up*, Ὀλυμπίαζε Id.*Hp.Mi*.363d; *ascend*, ἀπὸ.. Id.*Smp*.211b,c; ἡ νόησις ἐπὶ τὸ εἶναι ἐ. Dam.*Pr*.81; *rise up*, Hp.*VC*17. **-ειπεῖν**, *offer publicly besides*, ἀργύριον τῷ ἀποκτείναντι Th.6.60. **-είρομαι** or **-έρομαι** (Hp.*Prog*.7), *question again and again*, Hdt.1.91, 3.32: Trag. and Att. only in aor. 2 ἐπανηρόμην, τάδε σ' ἐπανερόμαν A.*Pers*.973 (lyr.); μηδ' αὖθις ἐπανέρῃ με Ar.*Ra*.439; *inquire further*, Hp. l.c. 2. *ask again*, εἰ ἐπανέροιτό τινά τι Pl.*Prt*.329a, cf. *Grg*.451b; ὅντινα.. J.*AJ*18.6. 6. **-έλευσις**, εως, ἡ, (ἐπανέρχομαι) *return*, Eust.1393.8. **-ελευστέον**, *one must return, recur*, ἐπί τι Apollon.Cit.3. **-ελίττω**, *roll up again*, Eust.1688.40. **-έλκω**, *draw up* on shore, τὴν ναῦν Arr. *An*.2.19.3. **-εμέω**, *vomit thereafter*, ἰώδεα Hp.*Epid*.1.12. II. of ruminants, *bring back into the mouth*, Gal.2.545.

**ἐπάνεμος** [ᾰ], ον, *windy*, ὥρη Hp.*Epid*.6.8.13.

**ἐπαν-ερεύγομαι**, = ἀνερεύγομαι, Hp.*Acut*.67; ἅλμαν Tim.*Pers*.95. **-έρχομαι**, *go back, return*, ἐκ ποταμοῦ Anacr.23; ἐκ Πειραιέως And. 1.81, cf. Th.4.16; ἐς τὴν Κόρινθον ib.74; θάλασσα -ελθοῦσα ἀπὸ τῆς γῆς Id.3.89; in writing or speaking, *go back* or *return* to a point, ἐκεῖσε δὴ 'πάνελθε, πῶς.. E.*IT*256; ἐπί τι X.*HG*1.7.29; ἐπανελθεῖν ὁπόθεν.. ἐξέβην βούλομαι D.18.211; ἀλλ' ἐκεῖσε ἐπανέρχομαι ib.66; εἰς τὰ γράμματα ταῦτα ἐπανελθεῖν *refer to*.., Id.28.5. b. *recur*, of intermittent fevers, etc., Gal.7.412, 16.711. 2. c. acc. rei, *return to, recapitulate*, Pl.*Ti*.17b, X.*Oec*.6.2, *Ages*.11.1. II. *go up, ascend*, εἰς ὄρη Id.*HG*4.8.35; δοκέει.. ἐνθεῦτεν γεωμετρίη.. ἐς τὴν Ἑλλάδα ἐπανελθεῖν *to have gone up, passed over*, Hdt.2.109. 2. *rise up* (cf. ἐπάνειμι II), Hp.*VC*17. **-έρομαι**, v. ἐπανείρομαι. ⊛ **-ερωτάω**, of persons, *question again*, v.l. in Id.*Prog*.7; τινά Pl.*Cra*.413a, X.*Mem*. 3.1.11 :—Pass., Pl.*Clit*.409d. 2. of things, *ask over again*, Id.*Grg*. 454c, *Lg*.645d. ⊛ **-εσις**, εως, ἡ, (ἐπανίημι) *abatement*, of fevers, Aret.*CA*1.1 (pl.). II. name of a *bandage*, Heliod.ap.Orib.48.43.

I. -έχω, *hold up, support*, τὰ οἰκεῖα πάθη τοῖς δημοσίοις ἐπανέχων Plu.*Dem.*22:—Med., *take upon oneself*, τὸν πρὸς Γέτας πόλεμον Anon. ap.Suid. s.v. ἐπανέσχετο. 2. *hold*, χώραν D.S.17.115. II. seemingly intr. (sc. ἑαυτόν), *rest upon*, ἐπὶ ταῖς ἐλπίσιν v.l. in D.19.51; *to be contented with*, τινί Alciphr.1.38; *rely on, rest contented with*, τοῖς βιβλίοις Artem.1.12; cf. ἐπαναπαύομαι. 2. c. dat., *attend to*, *POxy.*1033.6 (iv A.D.). ® -ήκω, pf. ἐπάνηκα *PAmh.*2.50.5 (ii B.C.):—*to have come back, return*, E.*IA* 1628 (anap.), Pl.Com.68 (cj.), Ph.2.117; ὥς τινα D.47.55; πρός τινα Plb.6.58.3; ἐκ νόσου πρὸς εὐδαιμονίαν Paus.3.9.2; εἰς τὸν οἶκον Lxx*Pr.*7.20. -ηλογέω, f.l. in Hdt.1.90 ἐπανηλόγησε πᾶσαν τὴν ἑωυτοῦ διάνοιαν (leg. ἐπαλιλλόγησε from Poll. 2.120, cf. Hdt.1.118). -ήλωμα, ατος, τό, *additional expense*, *PPetr.* 2 p.113 (iii B.C.).

**ἐπάνθεμα**, ατος, τό, in pl., *additional offerings*, *IG*4.526 (Heraeum).

**ἐπανθεμίζω**, metaph., *flit* like a bee from flower to flower, S.*Ichn.* 323 (lyr.).

**ἐπανθερεών**, ῶνος, ὁ, *chin*, dub. (fort. ἀνθερεών) in Gal.18(1).831.

**ἐπάνθετα**, τά, things *dedicated in addition*, *IG*7.3498.29, al. (Oropus), *Schwyzer* 462 *B*28 (Tanagra, iii B.C.).

® **ἐπανθ-έω**, *bloom, be in flower*, Theoc.5.131, Lxx *Jb.*14.7. II. metaph., of any thing that *forms on the surface*, ἅλμην ἐπανθέουσαν [τοῖσι ὄρεσι] Hdt.2.12, cf. Str.11.13.2; χνοῦς ὥσπερ μήλοισιν ἐπήνθει Ar.*Nu.*978; τὸ τρυφερὸν.. ἐπὶ τοῖς μήλοις ἐπανθεῖ Id.*Ec.*903; τὴν ἐπανθοῦσαν τρίχα ib.13; also of hair turning grey, κύκνου..πολιώτεραι δὴ αἵδ' ἐπανθοῦσιν τρίχες Id.*V.*1065, cf. X.*Cyn.*4.8. 2. generally, *to be upon the surface*, τρηχύτης ἐπήνθει Hp.*Epid.*7.43; ἐμοὶ.. ἐπάνθεεν ἁδύ τι κάλλος Theoc.20.21; ἐπὶ σμικρῷ ἰκτέρῳ ἡ χροιὴ μέζων ἐπανθέει Aret.*SD*1.15. b. abs., *show itself, appear plainly*, τοὐπιχώριον ἐπανθεῖ Ar.*Nu.*1174; ὅπερ.. παισὶ καὶ θηρίοις.. σύμφυτον ἐπανθεῖ Pl.*Lg.*710a; τῷ Ἰσοκράτει πολλαὶ χάριτες ἐπήνθουν D.H.*Comp.*19; πᾶσιν ἐπανθεῖ.. ἡ χάρις Luc.*Im.*9, cf. *Hist.Conscr.*55; τῷ προσώπῳ τὸ θηριῶδες ἐ. Callistr.*Stat.*12; τὰ -οῦντα τῇ αἰσθήσει τῶν ζῴων θελκτήρια ib.7. III. *to be bright*, πτερίσκοις πορφυροῖς ἐπανθούντων Babr. 118.5. -ημα, ατος, τό, *efflorescence*, [γέλως] ὥσπερ τι ἐ. ὑπάρχων Iamb.*Protr.*21.κϛ'; *fine flower*, Id.*in Nic.*p.39 P., al.; ἀριθμῶν ἑκάστου ἐπανθήματα *special virtues*, ib.p.118 P. -ησις, εως, ἡ, *flowering, bloom*, Plot.4.3.13 (pl.). -ιάω, poet. for ἐπανθέω, Ep. part. ἐπανθιόωντας ἰούλους A.R.3.519. -ίζω, *deck as with flowers, make bright-coloured*, ἐ. τινὶ ἐρύθημα *give* one a red *tint*, Luc.*Hist. Conscr.*13; ἐλέφαντα ἐ. τῷ χρυσῷ ib.51; *brighten, give lustre to* a dye, *PHolm.*17.9, al.:—Pass., χρώμασιν ἐπηνθισμένος D.S.1.49. 2. metaph., *deck as with flowers, decorate, adorn*, κωκυτοῖς ἐ. παιᾶνα A.*Ch.*150; πολλοῖς ἐ. πόνοισι γενεάν Id.*Th.*949:—Pass., ἀπαγγελία ἐπηνθισμένη ὀνόμασι ποιητικοῖς Philostr.*VS*1.15.4.—The aor. Med. ἐπηνθίσω is prob. corrupt in A.*Ag.*1459 (lyr.). ® -ισμα, ατος, τό, lit. *efflorescence*: hence ἀφρῶδες ἐ. *coloured froth*, Hp.*Prorrh.*1.21, cf. Aret.*SD*1.11. -ισμός, ὁ, *efflorescence, scum*, πορφύρας Dsc.5.92. II. name for a *vein*, Dionys.ap.Ruf.*Onom.*205.

**ἐπανθοπλοκέω**, *plait of flowers*, κόρυμβον *AP*12.8 (Strat.).

**ἐπανθρακ-ίδες**, ων, αἱ, (ἀνθρακίς) *small fish for frying, small fry*, Ar.*Ach.*670, *V.*1127. -ίζω, *broil on the coals*, Cratin.143 (cod. A Ath.). II. *blacken with charcoal*, ὦπας *AP*11.66 (Antiphil.). -όομαι, Pass., *to be broiled on the coals*, Poll.6.55.

**ἐπᾰνιάομαι**, *to be annoyed at* a thing, X.Eph.1.15, Poll.5.129.

**ἐπαν-ίημι**, *let loose at*, σοὶ δ' ἐπὶ τοῦτον ἀνῆκε Il.5.405. II. *let go, give up*, c. acc., ταῦτ' ἐπανέντας D.2.30; *dismiss*, τὸν παρόντ' ἐπανεῖναι φόβον Id.18.177; *remit*, τοῖς νέοις τὰ σκληρότατα τῆς ἀγωγῆς Plu.*Lyc.*22; *release from*, τὰς κύνας ἐ. τῶν πόνων X.*Cyn.*7.1; *relax*, τῆς ὀργῆς Ruf.ap.Orib.6.38.5. 2. *relax*, τὸν δακτύλιον (v. δακτύλιος II. 2) Dsc.*Eup.*2.56: more freq. intr., *relax, leave off*, τέμνων οὐκ ἐπανῆκεν πρὶν.. Pl.*Phdr.*266a: abs., of spasms, σιηγὼν ἐπανῆκε Hp.*Epid.*3.17.β'; μὴ ἐπανιεὶς without *slackening speed*, X.*Cyn.*4.5; ἐπανῆκεν ὁ σῖτος corn *became easier* in price, D.32.25; ἐπανέντα *lukewarm*, opp. θερμά, Sosip.1.53. -ίπταμαι, = ἐπαναπέτομαι, Man. 5.220. -ῐσόω, *make equal, balance evenly*, τινὰς πρὸς ἀλλήλους Th.8.57; ἐ. τὰ μέτρα *IG*2².1013.15; τοῖς ἀδελφοῖς τὸ διαφέρον Just. *Nov.*92.1 *Intr.*; τὰς τῆς κράσεως πλεονεξίας Ruf.(?)ap.Orib.*inc.*4.2; τὸ ἐλαττούμενον Polyaen.7.16.2; *reduce*, εἰς τὸ μέτριον τὴν ὑπερβολὴν Arist.*Resp.*478a3; τἆλλα οὕτως ἐπανισῶν ἔνεμε the others likewise he *made equal* to one another, distributing to them their faculties, Pl.*Prt.*321a:—Pass., *to be made equal*, τινὶ Id.*Lg.*745d. -ίστημι, *set up again*, τὰ τείχη ib.778d. 2. *make to rise against*, ἄνδρας ἐκ χαράδρας ἐ. τινί Plu.*Sert.*13; *raise in revolt against*, Ἰβηρίαν Ῥωμαίοις App.*Hisp.*101. 3. *cause to arise*, Plu.2.654f. II. Pass., with fut. Med. (Hdt.3.62, 1.89), aor. 2 and pf. Act., *stand up after* another or *at* his *word*, once in Hom., οἱ δ' ἐπανέστησαν Il.2.85. b. *rise from bed, rise*, Ar.*Pl.*539; ἐπὶ τοῦ καταστρώματος X.*HG*1.4.18; *rise* to speak, Id.*Smp.*4.2, D.19.46; of buildings, in pf., *to be raised* or *built*, ἣν τοῦτ' ἐπανεστήκῃ Ar.*Av.*554: c. gen., *rise above*, ἱερῷ -στηκότι τῆς ἀγορᾶς D.H.2.50; ταῖς -ισταμέναις (ἐκ add. cod. unus) τῶν ὑδάτων πομφόλυξιν Dsc.5.75. 2. *rise up against, rise in insurrection against*, τινί Hdt.1.89,130, 3.62; τῷ δήμῳ Th.1.115, etc.; τοῖς πράγμασι Din.1.19: abs., *rise in insurrection*, opp. ἀφίσταμαι, Th.3.39, al.; οἱ ἐπανεστεῶτες *the insurgents*, Hdt.3.63: c. inf., ἐάν τις τυραννεῖν ἐπαναστῇ if any one *aim at* tyranny, Lexap.And.1.97; in mal. part., ἐ. ἀλλήλοις πώγωνας ἔχουσι Theopomp.Hist.217c; παρθένοις Ael.*Ep.*15. 3. Medic., of tumours, etc., *rise, swell*, Hp.*Prorrh.* 1.165; [ὦτα] ἐπανεστηκότα *projecting, prominent*, Arist.*PA*691a13; λόφος αὐτῶν τῶν πτερῶν ἐ. crest *which sticks up* and is composed of feathers, Id.*HA*504b10. -ίσωσις [ῐσ], εως, ἡ, *making equal, equalizing*, Ph.2.479. -ῑτάω, pf. part. ἐπανιτακώρ, = ἐπανεληλυθώς, *Schwyzer* 425.8 (Elis). -ῑτέον, *one must return* to a point, Pl.*R.*532d, Arist.*PA*682a31, etc. -οδευτέον, gloss on ἐπανιτέον, Hsch. -ŏδος, ἡ, *rising up*, ἐκ τοῦ καταγείου εἰς τὸν ἥλιον Pl.*R.* 532b, cf. 521c; of phlegm from the lungs, Hp.*Acut.*17. II. *return*, Lxx*Si.*17.24, etc.; εἰς τὴν Ἑλλάδα Plu.*Tim.*38; ὡς ἐπί τινα νόσσαν Iamb.*in Nic.*p.76 P.; *to one's country*, ταχυτέραν ποιήσασθαι τὴν ἐ. E.*Ep.*2.2, cf. Hdn.8.7.7: metaph., *ascent* of the soul, Dam.*Pr.*75; simply, *journey*, *PLips.*45.17 (iv A.D.). 2. in speaking, *recapitulation*, Pl.*Phdr.*267d, Arist.*Rh.*1414b2. b. *fuller statement* of a point, Alex.*Fig.*2.7, Tib.*Fig.*45, etc. ® -οίγω, *open*, τὸ ἡρῷον *CIG*4259 (Pinara): in aor. Med., *cause to be opened*, *Epigr.Gr.*340. -οιδέω, *swell up, rise on the surface*, Hp.*Nat.Mul.* 2, Arist.*HA*531b3:—Pass., -οιδίσκομαι in same sense, Hp.*VC* 13. -οίκτης, ου, ὁ, = sq., Arg.Man.post Max.p.102 L., *EM*459.5. -οίκτωρ, ορος, ὁ, *one who bursts open*, θυρέτρων Man.1.310. -οιξις, εως, ἡ, *breaking into, forcible entry*, τοῦ ταμιείου *PHib.*1.31.12,23 (iii B.C.). -οιστέον, (ἐπαναφέρω) *one must refer*, Plb.1.37.3.

® **ἐπανορθ-όω**, impf. with double augm., ἐπηνώρθουν Isoc.12.200: aor. ἐπηνώρθωσα Lys.1.70: pf. ἐπηνώρθωκα Iamb.*Comm.Math.*23:—Med., fut. ἐπανορθώσομαι Pl.*La.*200b, D.15.34 (but in pass. sense, D.C.73.1): impf. ἐπηνωρθούμην Pl.*Tht.*143a: aor. ἐπηνωρθωσάμην Isoc.4.165, D.7.18:—Pass., fut. ἐπανορθωθήσομαι Aeschin.3.177: aor. ἐπηνωρθώθην D.9.76: pf. ἐπηνώρθωμαι Id.18.311:—*set up again, restore*, τὴν δύναμιν.. καίπερ πεπτωκυῖαν Th.7.77; τὰ δυστυχηθέντα Lys. l.c.; τὴν πολιτείαν Isoc.7.15; τὸ ἱππικόν Din.1.96, etc. 2. *correct, amend, revise*, νόμους Pl.*Lg.*769e; τὰς διαθήκας Is.1.18; τὸ ἁμάρτημα Pl.*Prt.*340d; ἐ. τινά *correct* one, *teach* him *better*, Ar.*Lys.* 528, cf. Isoc.1.3, Iamb. l.c.; εἰς τὸ ψήφισμα τὸ πρότερον *IG*1².108.49:—Med. in proper sense, *correct oneself*, Pl.*R.*361a: but more freq. trans., *correct, amend*, Id.*Euthphr.*9d, *Tht.*143a, Isoc.4.165, D. 1.11, etc. 3. *supply*, χρείας Jul.*Ep.*89b. -ωμα, ατος, τό, *correction*, Pl.*Prt.*340a,d, *Tht.*183a, D.25.16, Arist.*EN*1135a13, 1137b12. ® -ωσις, εως, ἡ, *setting right, correcting*, τᾶς ψυχᾶς Ti.Locr. 104b; κόλασις εἰς -σιν φέρουσα Jul.*Or.*2.80c; ἐδεσμάτων Diocl.*Fr.* 138; *revision*, νόμων Lexap.D.24.22; ἐ. ἔχειν to be capable of *improvement*, opp. ἀνίατον εἶναι, Arist.*EN*1165b18; of circumstances, *amendment*, Plb.1.66.12, 1.11.2, etc. -ωτέος, α, ον, *to be corrected*, Pl.*Lg.*809b. II. ἐπανορθωτέον *one must correct*, Plu.2.24a, Gal.6.226. ® -ωτής, οῦ, ὁ, *corrector, restorer*, τοῦ κάμνοντος D.H.8.67; of writings, Gal.7.894; τῶν τρόπων, = Lat. *corrector morum*, D.C.54.30; also, = Lat. *corrector civitatis*, *IG*4.1417 (Epid.), 5(1).541 (Sparta), 7.91 (Megara). -ωτικός, ή, όν, *corrective, restorative*, τῶν ἠθῶν Str.1.2.3; τὸ ἐ. δίκαιον Arist.*EN*1132a18; τέχνη Gal. 1.303. Adv. -κῶς Sch.D.3.33.

**ἐπαντέλλω**, poet. and Ion. for ἐπανατέλλω.

**ἐπάντης**, ες, rare form for ἀνάντης, *steep*, Th.7.79.

**ἐπαντιάζω**, *to be present*, prob. in *h.Ap.*152.

**ἐπαντίθετος**, ον, *reversed*, ἐπείλησις Sor.*Fasc.*12.515 C.

**ἐπαντλ-αῖος**, ον, = ἱμαῖος, Hsch. s.h.v. (ἐπανταῖος cod.). -έω, *pump over* or *upon, pour over*, Pl.*Phd.*112c (Pass., ib.d.); ἐπί τι Id.*Phdr.*253a; λόγους τινὶ ἐ. *pour a flood* of words *over*, E.*Fr.*899.4, cf. Ael.*NA*6.51; κακά Diph.107; *irrigate*, ἐ. καὶ ἄρδειν τὰ φυτά Plu. 2.688e: metaph., μυριάδας χιλιάδας τῇ Σμύρνῃ Philostr.*VS*1.25.2; ἑσμὸν ἡδονῶν Id.*VA*6.11: abs., Luc.*Tim.*18:—Pass., *to be irrigated*, D.S.1.33, *Stud.Pal.*17 p.13 (ii A.D.), etc.; νάμασι λόγων Ph.2.345; *overflowed*, φροντίσιν ἐπηντλημένος Plu.2.107a. -ημα, ατος, τό, *fomentation*, γαγγραίνης Dsc.2.109. -ησις, εως, ἡ, *pouring over*, as of water over a person bathing, Hp.*Acut.*65 (pl.), D.S.2.10 (v.l. ὑπ-, pl.). 2. *pumping*, ὑδάτων *Stud.Pal.*10.259.15 (v A.D.). ® -ησμός, ὁ, = foreg., *PLond.ined.*2179 (iii A.D.). -ητέον, *one must douche*, Dem.Ophth.ap.Aët.7.75. -ητός, ή, όν, *artificially irrigated*, *PRev. Laws* 24.8 (iii B.C.), *PCair.Zen.*176.230 (iii B.C.).

**ἐπᾰνύω**, fut. -ύσω [ῠ], *complete, accomplish*, οὐδέ ποτέ σφιν νίκη ἐπηνύσθη, ἀλλ' ἄκριτον εἶχον ἄεθλον Hes.*Sc.*311:—Med., *procure*, οἵαν .. ἐπί μοι μελέῳ χάριν ἠνύσω codd. in S.*Tr.*995 (lyr.); *carry into effect*, Ph.1.77.

® **ἐπάνω** [ᾰ], Adv., (ἄνω) *above, on the upper side* or *part*, Ar.*Lys.* 773, Pl.*R.*514b, etc.; with Art., ὁ ἐ. πύργος the *upper* tower, Hdt. 3.54, etc. 2. as Prep., c. gen., Id.1.179 (in tmesi, ἐπὶ τοῦ σήματος ἄνω ib.93), Pl.*Phd.*109d; ἐ. τῆς χώρας *IG*12(5).872.32 (Tenos, iii B.C.); ἐ. γεγονότες κακίας having risen *superior to*.., Plu.2.1063c; γίγνεται ἐ. τῆς πληγῆς J.*BJ*1.4.2; ἐ. χρημάτων εἶναι D.L.6.28 (but ἐ. χρημάτων τεταγμένος set *over*, Vett.Val.48.5). 3. *before, in front of*, c. gen., Lxx*Ge.*18.2, *2Ki.*24.20; *in the presence of*, τινός *POxy.* 903.14,20 (iv A.D.). II. *above*, in a book, ἐν τοῖς ἐ. εἴρηται X.*An.* 6.3.1 (interpol.), cf. Arist.*Metaph.*1012b6; τὰ ἐ. λεχθέντα Str.2.5.8; καθὼς ἐ. γέγραπται *IG*9(1).694.131 (Corc.), cf. *CIG*3059.3 (Teos), Polystr.p.22 W. III. of Time, ἐν τοῖς ἐ. χρόνοις in *former* times, D.S.16.42, 18.49; ἐν τῷ ἐ. μηνί *OGI*764.40 (Pergam.). IV. of Relationship, πατέρες καὶ τούτων ἐ. D.60.7; οἱ ἐ. πρόγονοι J.*Ap.*1.7; ἐ. ὄντες Εὐρωπαῖοι citizens of Europus *in unbroken descent*, Cumont *Fouilles de Doura-Europos* p.300. V. in Logic, τὸ ἐ. γένος the genus or species *above*, opp. τὰ ὑποκάτω, Arist.*Top.*122a4, 143a21; τὰ ἐ. τοῦ γένους ib.122a34. VI. of Number, *above, more*, ἀπὸ εἰκοσαετοῦς καὶ ἐ. Lxx*Ex.*30.14, al.; *above, more than*, ἐ. τριακοσίων δηναρίων *Ev.Marc.*14.5; ὤφθη ἐ. πεντακοσίοις 1*Ep.Cor.*15.6.

**ἐπάνωθεν** or **-ωθε**, Adv. *above, on top*, κοῦφα σοι χθὼν ἐπάνωθε πέσοι E.*Alc*.463: c. gen., Pl.*Ti*.45a, Luc.*Epigr*.39. 2. *up country, inland*, Th.2.99. II. of Time, *of old*, χαῶν τῶν ἐ. prob. in Theoc.7.5; τῶν ἐπάνωθε μουσοποιῶν Id.*Ep*.22.3; ἐν τοῖς ἐ. in *former times*, *CPR*188.19 (ii A.D.).

**ἐπαξῐ-έραστος**, ον, *amiable*, Ph.2.166. **-ος**, α, ον, *worthy, deserving* of.., πάντων Pi.*N*.7.89; τῆς δίκης ἐπάξια A.*Eu*.272 (lyr.), cf. *Ch*.95; θαυμάτων ἐπάξια E.*Ba*.716; σπουδῆς οὐ..πολλῆς τινος ἐ. Pl.*Sph*.218e: c. inf., ἐ. [εἶ] κατοικτίσαι *deserving* of pity, S.*OC*461: abs., ἐ. φύσει καὶ τροφῇ *worthy, qualified* by birth and breeding, Pl.*Lg*.961b. 2. *deserved*, στεφάνωμα Pi.*I*.4(3).44; *worthy, meet*, ἄλγος A.*Th*.865 (lyr.); γάμοι S.*El*.971, etc.; κυρεῖν τῶν ἐπαξίων meet with *one's deserts*, A.*Pr*.70. Adv. -ίως S.*OT*133, Iamb.*Myst*.3.20. 3. *worth mentioning, notable*, Hdt.2.79, 7.96 (sed v. ἀπαξιοί); *worth while* to do a thing, Hp.*Art*.72. **-όω**, *think right, deem it right*, c. inf., τοῦτ' ἐπηξίωσα δρᾶν S.*Ph*.803, cf. *El*.1274 (lyr.). 2. *expect, believe*, c. acc. et inf., τὰ δ' ἄλλα..ἐπαξιῶ σε..ἐξειδέναι ib.658; but ὁ γὰρ ξένος σε..ἐπαξιοῖ δικαίαν χάριν παρασχεῖν *deems* thee *worthy of honour*, so as to render thee a due return, Id.*OC*1497 (lyr.). **-ωσις**, εως, ἡ, *valuing, estimation*, D.H.19.15 (v.l. ἀπ-).

**ἐπαξον-έω**, (ἄξων I) *place on axles*, Orph.*Fr*.49.39. 2. (ἄξων II) *enroll in tablets, register*, Lxx *Nu*.1.18. **-ιος**, ον, (ἄξων I) *upon an axle*, δίφρῳ Theoc.25.249 (v.l. ἐν ἀξ-).

**ἐπαοιδ-έω**, = ἐπᾴδω, Steph.*in Hp*.2.458 D. **-ή**, ἡ, Ion. and poet. for ἐπῳδή (q.v.). **-ία**, ἡ, later form of foreg., Ps.-Luc.*Philopatr*.9, Hsch. **-ός**, ὁ, = ἐπῳδός, Lxx *Ex*.7.11, 22, al., Ph.1.449 (pl.), Arr. *Epict*.3.24.10, Man.5.183 (pl.). Adv. **-ῶς** *by way of a charm*, Steph. *in Hp*.2.458 D.

**ἐπᾰπειλέω**, *hold out as a threat to* one, λῆγ' ἔριδος, τὴν πρῶτον ἐπηπείλησ' Ἀχιλῆϊ Il.1.319; ἀπειλάων τὰς -ησε Od.13.127, cf. Hdt.6.32; δεῖν' ἐ. ἔπη S.*Aj*.312, etc. 2. c. dat. only, *threaten*, ἐπαπειλήσας Ἑλένῳ Il.13.582. 3. c. fut. inf., *threaten* to do, Hdt.1.189, S.*El*.779, Ar.*Av*.630: but the inf. is freq. omitted, ὥς ποτ' ἐπηπείλησεν as he *threatened*, Il.14.45, cf. S.*Ant*.752, Antim.24. 4. ἐ. εἰ μή.. X.*An*.6.2.7. 5. Pass., πρὸς σοῦ τὰ δεῖν'..ἐπηπειλημένοι *threatened*, S.*Ant*.408.

**ἐπαπερείδομαι**, Pass., *lean upon*, δυσίν Posidon.26 J.:—Med., τὸν ἀγῶνα τοῦ λόγου ἐ. τινί *rest* the weight of the argument *on*.., J.*BJ* 2.2.5. II. *support*, τοῖς βάρεσι τῶν μελλόντων Ph.Byz.*Mir*.6.2.

**ἐπαπηχεῖαι** (sic)· ἀπηχῆσαι, καὶ ἐπὶ πολὺ ἐξικέσθαι, ἔνιοι δὲ καὶ ἐπὶ ἀπεχθείᾳ καὶ ἔχθρᾳ ἀπέδοσαν, *AB*253.

**ἐπαπογᾰμέω**, *marry again*, dub. in *Cat.Cod.Astr*.8(3).188.

**ἐπαπο-δίδωμι**, *make good*, τοῦ πλείονος χρόνου *GDI*1832.24 (Delph.). **-δρόμιον**· ἡ ἱέρεια παρὰ Κρησίν, Hsch. **-δύω**, *strip* one *for combat against* another, *set* him *up as a rival to*, τινά τινι Plu.2.788d:—Med., *strip and set to work at* a thing, τῷ πράγματι Ar.*Lys*.615; πολυοινίᾳ Ph.1.360; *set upon, attack*, τοῖς νενικηκόσιν Plu.*Marc*.3. ⊛ **-θνήσκω**, *die after* another, τινί Pl.*Smp*.180a, 208d, J.*BJ*5.12.3; ἐ. λόγοις *die while* yet speaking, Id.*AJ*13.11.3: abs., Plu.*Aem*.35.

**ἐπαποικίζω**, *colonize anew*, Καρχηδόνα D.C.52.43.

**ἐπαπο-κτείνω**, *kill besides*, D.C.49.23:—also **-κτιννύω**, Aristid.*Or*.25(43).23. **-λαύω**, *revel in*, ἡδοναῖς D.S.37.3: c. gen., ἡλίου σελασμάτων Tz.*H*.9.315; *profit by*, τινός Anon.*in Rh*.111.28.

**ἐπαπόλλῡμι** or **-ύω**, *kill in addition*, Ael.*NA*10.48, Luc.*Merc.Cond*.42:—Med., *die after*, τινί D.C.60.34: abs., Aristid.*Or*.25(43).22.

**ἐπαπο-λογέομαι**, = ἀπολογέομαι, v.l. in Plu.*Marc*.27. **-λογος**, ον, in Arc. form ἐπαπύ-, *requiring defence*, *SIG*306.34 (iv B.C.).

**ἐπαπολύω**, *discharge against*, Hsch. s. v. ἐπαφῆκεν.

**ἐπαπονίνᾰμαι**, Pass., *enjoy besides*, Ph.1.327.

**ἐπαποπνίγω** [ῑ], *choke besides*:—Pass., aor. 2 ἐπαποπνῐγείης *may you be choked besides*, Ar.*Eq*.940 (Elmsl. for ἀποπν-).

⊛ **ἐπαπορ-έω**, *raise a new doubt* or *question*, πότερον.. Plb.6.3.6; δύο ταῦτα, εἰ.., τί.. Ph.2.216, cf. S.E.*P*.1.225, Ph.Byz.*Mir*.4.2, Procl. *in Prm*.p.529 S.:—Pass., ἐπαπορεῖταί τι *a new doubt is raised*, Thphr.*Vert*.9; τὰ ἐπαπορηθέντα Plb.6.5.3. II. c. dat., *criticize*, Diog. Oen.18. **-ησις**, εως, ἡ, = ἀπορία, Hsch. **-ητικός**, ή, όν, *dubitative*: -κόν, τό, a kind of rhetorical question, *Stoic*.2.61, cf. D.L.7.68; σύνδεσμος Gal.16.722. Adv. -κῶς Phlp.*in APo*.359.15, Eust.1114.30.

⊛ **ἐπαπο-στέλλω**, *send after*, γράμματα ἐπαπεστάλη αὐτοῖς Plb.31.2.14; ἐ. στρατηγὸν ἕτερον *send* another general *after him* (to supersede him), Id.6.15.6. II. *send to attack*, Id.32.5.11; τινάς τισι Id.2.8.12; συκοφάντην ἐπί τινα D.S.12.24, cf. Lxx *Jb*.20.23. **-στολή**, ἡ, *sending against*, Sm.*Ps*.77(78).49; δαιμόνων Heph.Astr.1.23. **-σφάζω**, aor. 2 Pass. -εσφάγην [ᾰ], *slay afterwards*, D.C.57.2. **-τίνω**, *repay*, Thd.*Is*.59.18.

**ἐπάπτω**, Ion. for ἐφάπτω.

**ἐπαρά**, Ion. **ἐπαρή**, ἡ, *solemn curse, imprecation*, θεοὶ δ' ἐτέλειον ἐπαράς Il.9.456, cf. Thebaïs *Fr*.2.7; ἐπαρὴν ποιῆσαι *SIG*38.30 (Teos); ἐπαρὰς ἐποιήσαντο ib.167.28 (Mylasa). [ἐπᾰρ- in Hom.]

**ἐπαράμενοι**· οἱ παρὰ μοῖραν ἀπολλύμενοι, Hsch.

⊛ **ἐπᾰράομαι**, Cret. part. ἐπαριόμενον *Leg.Gort*., Cyren. ἐπαρεώμενοι *Abh.Berl.Akad*. (v. infr.):—*imprecate curses upon*, Πέρσησι πολλὰ ἐπαρησάμενος Hdt.3.75; ἐ. ἐξώλειαν (q.v.) ἑαυτῷ *IG*1².10.15, Antipho 5.11, Lys.12.10; τῶν ἱερῶν *by* the temples, Isoc.4.156. 2. c. dat. only, *curse solemnly*, Pl.*Lg*.931b, Jul.*Or*.2.50b, *Leg.Gort*.2.40, etc. 3. c. acc. rei only, τίνα..τόνδ' ἐπηράσω λόγον; what *imprecation* is this *that thou didst utter*? S.*El*.388; τί ταῦτ' ἐπήραμαι; D.18.142: c. acc. et inf., *Abh.Berl.Akad*.1925(5).23 (Cyrene). 4. with κατά τινος, *Schwyzer*688 C7 (Chios, v B.C.). 5. c. acc. pers., Pl.*Lg*.684d. 6. c. fut. inf., *swear, vow*, ἐ. τάδε.., τούτῳ ξυναμυνεῖν E.*IA*60; *vow in addition*, βοῦν προσάξειν, εἰ.. Babr.23.7.

⊛ **ἐπᾰρᾰρίσκω**, aor. 1 -ῆρσα: aor. 2 -ήρᾰρον:—*fit to* or *upon, fasten*, θύρας σταθμοῖσιν ἐπῆρσεν *on* or *to* the posts, Il.14.167; ἐπὶ δὲ ζυγὸν ἤραρεν ἀμφοῖν *h.Merc*.50. II. intr. in Ion. pf. ἐπάρηρα [ᾰρ], plpf. ἐπᾰρήρειν:—*fit tight* or *exactly*, μία δὲ κληῒς ἐπαρήρει a cross-bolt *was fitted therein*, Il.12.456; part. ἐπαρηρώς, υῖα, ός, *close-fitting, well fixed*, εὖ ἐπαρηρὼς ποσσὶν *firm on* his feet, Arat.83: also ἐπάρμενος, η, ον, Ep. aor. part. Pass., *well-fitted, prepared, ready*, βίον, ὅπλα, Hes.*Op*.601, 627:—also in form ἐφάρμ-, *suited*, c. dat., Nonn.*D*.12.35.

**ἐπαράσαι**· κουφίσαι, ἐπαράσσασθαι, Hsch.

**ἐπᾰράσιμος** [ρᾱ], ον, *abominable*, Ps.-Phoc.18.

**ἐπᾰράσσω**, Att. -ττω, *dash* or *clap to*, τὴν θύραν Pl.*Prt*.314d, cf. Plu.*Art*.29; τὸν πῆχυν τῷ αὐχένι ὥσπερ μοχλόν Hld.10.31; ναρθήκια κατὰ τῶν ἰσχνῶν μορίων ἐ. *strike* rods *against* the thin parts, Gal.10.998.

**ἐπάρᾰτος** [ᾰρ], ον, (ἐπαράομαι) *accursed, laid under a curse*, ἐ. ποιεῖσθαι Th.8.97; ὃ ἐπάρατον ἦν μὴ οἰκεῖν which it was *accursed* to inhabit, Id.2.17; τῷ δὲ ἐπάρατον τύχην [γενέσθαι] Pl.*Lg*.877a; of persons, Arist.(?)*Fr*.148, *Ev.Jo*.7.49, J.*AJ*6.6.3: Sup., γενεά Ph.1.516; used in imprecations on those who violated graves, *CIG*2824 (Aphrodisias), etc.

**ἐπάργεμος**, ον, *having a film over the eye*, Arist.*HA*609b16, 620a1. II. metaph., *dim, obscure*, σήματα, θέσφατα, λόγοι, A.*Pr*.499, *Ag*.1113, *Ch*.665.

**ἐπάργματα**, τά, = ἀπαρχαί, *IG*1²(3).436.14 (Thera).

**ἐπαργῠρ-όομαι**, *to be overlaid with silver*, *IG*2².1485.48: metaph., of costly dinners, μὴ πόλλ' ἄγαν..μηδ' ἐπηργυρωμένα Mnesim.3.2. **-ος**, ον, *overlaid with silver*, κλῖναι Hdt.1.50, 9.80, cf. *IG*1².276, *BMus.Inscr*.4.481*.472; πανοπλίαι Onos.1.20.

**ἐπάρδ-ευσις**, εως, ἡ, *watering*: hence, *shower*, of rain, Epicur.*Ep*.2 p.44 U.: metaph., in pl., *influx*, ib.p.38 U. 2. *irrigation*, *POxy*.1631.14 (iii A.D.), al. **-ευτής**, οῦ, ὁ, *irrigator*, *PTeb*.120.137 (i B.C.), al. **-εύω**, = -ω, Nonn.*D*.11.166; γῇ ἐ. τοῖς φυτοῖς τροφὴν Gal.4.625. ⊛ **-ια**, τά, *irrigated land*, *PAmh*.2.36.11 (ii B.C.). **-ω**, *irrigate*, Arr.*An*.4.6.5: metaph., ἐ. ἀρεταῖς τὴν ψυχὴν Luc.*Am*.45, cf. Lxx 4*Ma*.1.29, Plot.6.7.33; ὁ δικαστὴς τὰ δίκαια ἐ. τοῖς ἐντευξομένοις Ph.2.345; Ἀττικὰ ἐ. τὰ νάματα [τῇ ψυχῇ] Him.*Ecl*.32.6:—Pass., J.*BJ*4.8.3; of the body by nourishment, Ti.Locr.102b.

**ἐπᾰρέσκομαι**, *to be satisfied*, ὡς.. Eustr.*in EN*270.16: aor. Med., ἐπηρέσσατο· εὐαρέστους ἐποίησεν, Hsch.

**ἐπᾰρ-ήγω**, *come to aid, help*, τινί Il.23.783, Od.13.391, E.*El*.1350 (anap.), Ar.*V*.402: abs., νῦν ἐπάρηξον A.*Ch*.725 (anap.); οὐπαρήξων S.*El*.1197; also in Prose, X.*Cyr*.6.4.18, Lxx 2*Ma*.13.17. **-ηγών**, όνος, ὁ, ἡ, *helper*, A.R.1.1039, *Milet*.1(7).205a (pl., ii A.D.): c. gen., ἄθλων, νίκης, Orph.*A*.348, *L*.677. **-ηξις**, εως, ἡ, *help, aid*, Eust.52.38.

**ἐπάρην** [ᾰ], v. πείρω.

**ἐπᾰρήρει, ἐπᾰρηρώς**, v. ἐπαραρίσκω.

**ἐπᾰριθμέω**, *count in addition*, Paus.10.5.8; ἐ. ταῖς ἡμέραις τὰς πόλεις *count* the cities by the days, i. e. visit a city a day, Aristid.*Or*.26(14).93.

**ἐπάρισμα**· ἀφανῆ, ἄσημα, Hsch. (fort. ἐπάργεμα).

**ἐπᾰριστερ-εύομαι**, *to be awkward, clumsy*, Hsch. s. v. σκανεύεσθαι. **-ος**, ον, *towards the left, on the left hand*, τὰ ἐπαρίστερα (nisi scrib. ἐπ' ἀρ-) Hdt.2.36, 93, 4.191; but ἐπὶ τὰ ἀριστερά Id.2.36. 2. *written from right to left*, *Tab.Defix*.67 a 8 (iii B.C.). II. *left-handed*, D.C.72.19: usu. metaph., '*gauche*', Ephipp.23; ἐ. ἔμαθες γράμματα *at the wrong end*, Theognet.1.7; βουλεύματα D.S.8 *Fr*.5; ἐ. Κάτωνες *awkward* imitators of Cato, Plu.*Cat.Ma*.19. Adv. -ρως, λαμβάνειν τι Men.325.2; τὴν τύχην δεξιὰν παρισταμένην ἐ. λαμβάνειν Plu.2.467c. **-ότης**, ητος, ἡ, *awkwardness*, Arist.*VV*1251a2.

**Ἐπάριτοι**, οἱ, the soldiers of the Arcadian Federation (371 B.C.), X.*HG*7.4.33-6, Ephor.215 J., Androt.54. (Arc. ἐπάριτοι 'picked', 'selected' (= ἐπίλεκτοι, D.S.15.62), cf. pr. nn. Ἐπήριτος, Πεδάριτος: fr. root of ἀριθμός.) ('Ἐπαρῖται is a misquotation of Ephor. l.c. by St.Byz., Ἐπαρόητοι f. l. in Hsch.)

⊛ **ἐπάρκ-εια**, ἡ, *help, support*, Plb.1.48.5, al.: pl., αἱ τῶν συμμάχων ἐ. Id.6.52.5; ἐ. καὶ χορηγίαι ib.49.7. **-εσις**, εως, ἡ, *aid, succour*, γένους S.*OC*447, cf. E.*Hec*.758. **-έω**, fut. -έσω (v. infr.): Ep. aor. inf. ἐπαρκέσσαι A.R.2.1161, cf. *IG*5(1).730.18:—*to be strong enough for* a thing, in Hom. always of cases of danger or injury: 1. c. acc. rei et dat. pers., *ward off* something from one, οὐδέ τί οἱ τό γ' ἐπήρκεσε λυγρὸν ὄλεθρον Il.2.873; οὔτε τι Τηλέμαχος τό γ' ἐπήρκεσεν Od.17.568; οὐδὲν γὰρ αὐτῷ ταῦτ' ἐπαρκέσει τὸ μὴ οὐ πεσεῖν *prohibebit quominus*.., A.*Pr*.918. 2. c. acc. rei, *ward off, prevent*, ἐπαρκέσσαι κακότητα A.R.2.1161; σέ τοι μόνον δέδορκα πημονᾶν (Reiske for ποιμένων) ἐ. S.*Aj*.360 (lyr.). 3. c. dat. pers. only, *help, assist*, Thgn.871, Hdt.1.91, Lys.13.93, 1*Ep.Ti*.5.10, etc.: rarely c. acc. pers., E.*Or*.803 (troch.): abs., τίς ἄρ' ἐπαρκέσει; *who will aid?* A.*Th*.91 (anap.), cf. S.*OC*777. II. *supply, furnish*, ἄκος δ' οὐδὲν ἐπήρκεσαν, τὸ μὴ πόλιν..παθεῖν A.*Ag*.1170 (lyr.); ἐ. τινί τι Pl.*Prt*.321a, cf. Ar.*Pl*.830, Lxx 1*Ma*.11.35, etc.; also ἐ. τινὶ τῶν ἑαυτοῦ *impart* to him *a share of*.., X.*Mem*.1.2.60: c. dat. rei, *supply with*, πέπλοις E.*Cyc*.301. III. abs., *to be sufficient, enough*, ὅσσον ἐπαρκεῖ Sol.5.1 (v.l. ἀπαρκεῖ); ἐπαρκέσει νόμος ὅδ' this law *shall prevail*, S.*Ant*.612 (lyr.). 2. *stand to the credit of*, c. dat., γενεᾷ Pi.*N*.6.60. ⊛ **-ής**, ές, *helpful*, κρᾶσις Emp.22.4; of remedies, *effective*, Nic.

*Al.*564. II. *sufficient*, οὐσία ταῖς δαπάναις ἐ. Plu.*Cic.*7, cf. D.P. 1101. Adv. -κῶς *IG*4.491 (Cleonae). -ιος, ον, *sufficient*, Opp. *H.*4.377, *AP*10.76 (Paul. Sil.); [ἀγαθῶν] χρῆσιν ἐπάρκιον ἡμερίοισιν *Inscr.Perg.*324.8. -ούντως, Adv. pres. part., *sufficiently*, S.*El.* 354.

⊛ **ἔπαρμα**, ατος, τό, (ἐπαίρω) *something raised, a swelling*, Hp.*Epid.* 1.1; τῶν ἀγγείων Sor.1.48; τὰ τῶν φολίδων ἐ. Ach.Tat.3.7. II. metaph., *elation, vanity*, ἔ. τύχης Sotad.9.4. b. in good sense, *elevation*, πόσον ἔ. ψυχὴ λαμβάνει Ath.Med.ap.Orib.*inc.*21.21. 2. *height*, Lxx 2*Es.*6.3.

**ἐπάρμενος**, v. ἐπαραρίσκω.

**ἔπαρμον**· σῶμα κάθυγρον, Hsch.

**ἐπαρνέομαι**, *deny*, Phld.*Rh.Supp.*p.13S.

**ἔπαρξις**, εως, ἡ, f.l. for ἔπαρσις, Lxx*Za.*12.7.

**ἐπαρότης**, ου, ὁ, = ἀροτήρ, *PLond.*1.131r262 (i A.D.).

**ἐπᾰρούρ-ιον** (sc. τέλος), (ἄρουρα) *land-tax*, *Ostr.*332, al. (ii B.C.), *BGU*1422 (ii A.D.). -ος, ον, *attached to the soil* as a serf, βουλοίμην κ' ἐ. ἐὼν θητευέμεν ἄλλῳ Od.11.489.

**ἔπαρσις**, εως, ἡ, (ἐπαίρω) *rising, swelling*, κοιλίης Hp.*Coac.*85; τῶν μαστῶν Arist.*HA*581a27; ἐ. ἰονθώδεις *eruptions* accompanying the sprouting of the beard, Thphr.*Sud.*16. 2. *lifting up*, χειρῶν Lxx *Ps.*140(141).2. 3. *devastation*, ib.*La.*3.47; in concrete, *heap of ruins*, ib.4*Ki.*19.25 (pl.). 4. *raising, erection* (?), τοῦ θυρέτρου *IG* 11(2).287*A*116, *B*153 (Delos, iii B.C.). b. αἰδοίων Arist.*HA*572b 2. 5. *elevation, projection*, of a machine, Hero*Aut.*28.2. II. *elation*, ψυχῆς Zeno*Stoic.*1.51 (pl.), cf. Chrysipp.ib.3.116; ἡδονή, = ἄλογος ἔ. *Stoic.*3.95, al., Andronic.Rhod.p.570M., cf. Lxx*Za.*12. 7. 2. *elevation* of style, τοῦ λόγου Thom.Mag.p.175R.

**ἐπαρτ-άω**, *hang on* or *over*, φόβους τοῖς ἀκροωμένοις Aeschin.1.175, cf. Porph.*Abst.*1.2; τισὶν ὀχλήσεις Polystr.p.30W.; τιμωρίαν τινί Ael.*VH*7.15:—Med., lit., *hang upon*, τινί τι Orph.*A.*1337:—Pass., *hang over, impend*, τοσοῦτος ἐπήρτηται φόβος D.23.140; ἀπαλλαγὴν τῶν ἐπηρτημένων φόβων Id.18.324; ἀγών τινι -ημένος Hdn.2.3.7; κίνδυνος *IGRom.*4.151 (Cyzicus), *BGU*1027.23 (iv A.D.). II. τὸ ἐπηρτημένον [τοῦ ζυγοῦ] *the elevated part* of the beam, Arist.*Mech.* 850a23. -είνη· εὐπρεπίνη, Hsch. (fort. ἐπαρτεῖ νηΐ· εὐτρεπεῖ νηΐ). -ηίαν· παρασκευήν, Id. (fort. ἀπαρτίην). ⊛ -ής, ές, (cf. sq.) *ready-equipped*, ἐπαρτέες εἰσὶν ἑταῖροι Od.8.151, cf. 14.332; νῆες, ἐδωδή, A.R.1.235, 3.299. II. (ἐπαρτάω) *depending*, ἐπαρτέες ἐκ νεφελάων..πηγυλίδες Orph.*Fr.*270.1 (s.v.l.). -ίζω, *get ready*, in Ep. aor. ἐπαρτίσσειεν A.R.1.1210:—Med., c. inf., ib.877. II. intr., *fit in*, ἐς τὸν μυκτῆρα Hp.*Morb.*2.33. -ικός, ή, όν, (ἐπαίρω) *making to rise* or *swell*, τοῦ στομάχου Aret.*CD*1.2. -ύω and -ύνω [ῡν], *fit* or *fix on*, αὐτίκ' ἐπήρτυε πῶμα Od.8.447. II. *prepare*, ἐπὶ γὰρ Ζεὺς ἤρτυε πῆμα Od.3.152; ὄλεθρόν τινι Opp.*C.*2.443:—Med., δεῖπνον ἐπηρτύνοντο they *prepared them* a meal, *h.Cer.*128.

**ἐπᾰρ-υστήρ**, ῆρος, ὁ, (ἀρύω) *vessel for pouring* oil into a lamp, Lxx *Ex.*25.37(38). -υστρίς, ίδος, ἡ, = foreg., ib.*Nu.*4.9, al. -ύτω [ῠ], *draw* a liquid from one vessel *into* another, metaph. in Med., ἐκ τῶν ἀγαθῶν τοῖς κακοῖς Plu.2.600d:—Act., dub. in D.Chr.12.70.

⊛ **ἐπαρχ-εία**, ἡ, *office of praefectus*, *IG*12(3).336.22 (Thera). II. = ἐπαρχία I. *SIG*683.65 (ii B.C.), *IG*14.951 (i B.C.), etc. ⊛ -εῖον, τό, = ἐπαρχία I, ἄρξαντι -είου Νουμιδίας *IG*14.911:—also -ειος (sc. χώρα), ἡ, *IPE*1².54 (Olbia), *IG*14.1078a, *IGRom.*1.580 (Nicopolis ad Istrum), *Ath.Mitt.*48.113 (ibid.). -έω, *to be an* ἔπαρχος, *CIG*2047 (Philippopolis). ⊛ -ή, ἡ, = ἀπαρχή, *IG*2².1672.182, 263, 2².1215.13, 7.235. 20 (Oropus), *Delph.*3(2).88. ⊛ -ία, ἡ, *the government of an* ἔπαρχος, or *the district governed by him*, = Lat. *provincia*, Plb.2.19.2, *SIG*888. 45 (Scaptopara, iii A.D.), Str.3.4.20, 17.3.25 (pl.), D.S.37.10, 38. 8, al., *Act.Ap.*23.34, Plu.*Caes.*4; of Carthage, *empire*, Phleg.*Mir.* 18. II. military '*command*', *force occupying a district*, Ph.*Bel.* 96.49 (pl.). ⊛ -ικός, ή, όν, *of* or *for an* ἔπαρχος, ἐ. ἐξουσία the office of *praefectus urbi*, D.C.75.14. II. ἐπαρχικοί, οἱ, *provincials*, Plu.*Cic.*36, *IG*2².1121.33 (iv A.D.). -ιώτης, ου, ὁ, *a provincial*, Hadrian.Epist.ap.Justin.M.*Apol.*1.68, Jul.*Ep.*14, *BGU*1024vi 24 (iv A.D.):—also written -εώτης, Just.*Nov.*128.21, al., *Cod.Just.*1.33. 4. ⊛ -ος, ον, *commander*, Κιλίκων A.*Pers.*327; νεῶν Id.*Ag.*1227 (Canter for ἄπαρχος); *governor of a country*, Plb.5.46.7. 2. = Lat. *praefectus* (in all senses), Id.11.27.2, Plu.*Flam.*1, etc.; ἔ. τεκτόνων or τεχνιτῶν, *praef. fabrum*, Id.*Cic.*38, *Brut.*51; ἔ. τῆς πόλεως, *praef. urbi*, D.H.4.82, etc.; ἐ. παρεμβολῶν, *praef. castrorum*, *Gloss.*; ἔ. Αἰγύπτου *PFay.*21 (ii A.D.); ἔ. τῆς αὐλῆς, *praef. praetorio*, Plu.*Galb.*2, cf. ib.8, 13; ἔ. Ἑῴας *prefect* of the East, *Epigr.Gr.* 919.4 (Sidyma); ἀπὸ ἐπάρχων, *ex praefecto*, *CIG*2593 (Gortyn, iv A.D.). II. as Adj., ἀρχὴν ἔπαρχον στόλου the office of admiral, *IG*14.873 (Misenum, iii A.D.). -ότης, ητος, ἡ, = ἐπαρχία, Lyd. *Mag.*1.15, al., Just.*Nov.*38*Pr.*3.

**ἐπάρχω**, *rule over*, χώρας πολλῆς X.*Cyr.*4.6.2; τῶν ὁμόρων Isoc.4. 140; τῶν ἔξωθεν Pl.*Criti.*116e; [νήσων] prob. in Thphr.*HP*9.4.10; *to be governor, commandant of* a place, *Hell.Oxy.*16.6: c. dat., Epigr. ap.Paus.6.19.6: abs., ὁ ἐπάρχων, = ἔπαρχος, Hdn.4.12.1; of consular authority, Plu.*Sull.*8. 2. *rule besides* one's hereditary dominions, X.*Cyr.*1.1.4. II. Med., ἐπάρξασθαι δεπάεσσιν *pour the first drops* before a libation, freq. in Hom.:—οἰνοχόος μὲν ἐπαρξάσθω δεπάεσσιν, ὄφρα σπείσαντες κατακείομεν *let* him *begin by pouring* wine into the cups, Od.18.418, cf. 7.183; κοῦροι..κρητῆρας ἐπεστέψαντο ποτοῖο, νώμησαν δ' ἄρα πᾶσιν ἐπαρξάμενοι δεπάεσσιν Il.1.471, al. 2. generally, *serve, offer*, νέκταρ τε καὶ ἀμβροσίην χερσὶν ἐπήρξατο *h.Ap.*125; ἐπάρχεσθαι δὲ τοὺς χοροὺς [χορ]είας (dub.) τῷ Διονύσῳ *IG*12(9).192.10 (Eretria, iv B.C.). 3. = ἀπάρχομαι, τῇ ἐπαρχῇ ἣν ἐπάρχονται οἱ δημόται ib. 2².1215.13. 4. *begin*, c. inf., *PTeb.*27.34 (ii B.C.).

**ἐπᾰρωγ-ή**, ἡ, (ἐπαρήγω) *help, aid*, A.R.1.302; ἐπαρωγὴν ποιεῖσθαί τινι Charond.ap.Stob.4.2.24. II. ἐ. τινος *aid against* a thing, Orac.ap.Luc.*Alex.*28: hence, *opposition*, *IG*14.2012*A*5. -ής, ές, *efficacious*, of remedies, Nic.*Al.*110. -ός, ὁ, *helper, aider*, Od.11. 498, E.*Hec.*164 (lyr.), etc.: also fem., A.R.4.196: neut., τὸ ζωᾶς ἐπαρωγόν *AP*6.219.21 (Antip., v.l. τὸν).

**ἐπασθμαίνω**, *breathe hard, pant in working*, Lxx 4*Ma.*6.11; μαντικὸν ἐ. Philostr.Jun.*Im.*5.

**ἐπάσιοι**, v. ἔπαισοι. **ἔπᾱσις**, ά, v. ἔμπᾱσις.

**ἐπασκ-έω**, *labour* or *toil at, prepare* or *finish carefully*, ἐπήσκηται δέ οἱ αὐλὴ τοίχῳ καὶ θριγκοῖσι Od.17.266. II. *adorn, exalt*, τινὰ τιμαῖς Pi.*N.*9.10, cf. *Fr.*194.4; τινὰ μήδεσι Id.*Parth.*2.71. III. *practise, cultivate*, τέχνην, τὰ ἐς πόλεμον, Hdt.2.166; πεντάεθλον, μουνομαχίην, Id.6.92; τὰ ἄλλα κατὰ ταὐτὰ Σκύθῃσι ἐ. Id.4.17; ἀρετὴν Id. 3.82; δι' ἐμπύρων τέχνην E.*Hyps.Fr.*34(60).59; σοφίαν Ar.*Nu.*517; παγκράτιον Aeschin.3.179; μνήμην ἐ. *cultivate* memory, Hdt.2.77; δύναμίν τινος ἐ. *increase* his strength, Aeschin.2.136: abs., *to be in training as an athlete*, Achae.3:—Pass., ταῦτα Ῥωμαίοις ἐκ παλαιοῦ ἐπήσκηται Arr.*An.*5.8.1. 2. *set on* one *against* another, τινὶ τοὺς ἐχθροὺς D.C.46.40. 3. *train for* the contest, ἀέθλοισιν..ἐφήβους *IG*3.121.4: also c. inf., τινὰς τάξει χρῆσθαι Arr.*Tact.*16.6. -ημα, ατος, τό, *method of fighting*, ib.22.6 (pl., v.l.). -ητέον, *one must practise*, ib.9.3. -ητής, οῦ, ὁ, *athlete*, Hsch.

**ἐπάσκιον**, τό, = χώνη (Sicilian), Hsch.

**ἔπασμα**, ατος, τό, (ἐπᾴδω) *enchantment*, Elias*in Porph.*31.14, Zonar., Tz.*H.*13.262.

**ἐπασπαίρω**, *pant over* or *at*, μόχθῳ Opp.*H.*5.407.

**ἐπασπῐδόομαι**, Pass., *take as a shield*, εὐλάβειαν cj. in Ph.1.669 (ἐπασπιδήσεται cod. unicus); cf. ἐνασπιδόομαι.

⊛ **ἐπασσύτερος** [ῠ], α, ον, Ep. Adj. *one upon another, one after another*, mostly in pl., ἐπασσύτεραι κίνυντο φάλαγγες Il.4.427; πάντας ἐπασσυτέρους πέλασε χθονὶ 8.[277]; σκοποὶ ἷζον αἰὲν ἐπασσύτεροι watchers sat *one after another*, i.e. at short distances, Od.16.366; τρηκοσίας πέτρας πέμπον ἐ. Hes.*Th.*716; ἐ. ποσὶν ἕρπον Nic.*Th.*717: and in sg., κῦμα..ὄρνυτ' ἐπασσύτερον wave *upon* wave, Il.4.423. II. *frequent, repeated*, λυγμοί Nic.*Th.*246: with sg. word, ἐ. οὖρος, perh. *following* breeze or *ever-freshening*, A.R.1.579; and so ἐ. βιότοιο χρησμοσύνη *ever-growing* penury, Id.2.472. (Perh. from ἐπ-αν(α)-σ(ε)υ-.)

**ἐπασσῠτεροτρῖβής**, ές, *following close one upon another*, τὰ χερὸς ὀρέγματα A.*Ch.*426 (lyr.).

**ἐπαστέον**, *one must recite a charm*, Pl.*Chrm.*158c, Plot.5.3.17.

**ἐπαστράπτω**, *lighten upon*, ἐνίοις ἐπήστραψε δεξιόν Plu.2.594e: metaph., βασίλειον ἐ. τῷ κόλπῳ Lib.*Or.*61.10: abs., *AP*7.49 (Bianor): c. acc. cogn., ἐ. πῦρ *flash* fire, *APl.*4.141 (Phil.); σπινθῆρας Nonn.*D.* 18.74.

**ἐπασφᾰλίζω**, *shore up*, *PLond.*1.131r44 (i A.D.). 2. *close up* a wound, -ισάμενος ῥαφαῖς Paul.Aeg.6.67.

**ἐπασχάλλω**, *to be indignant at*, ἐφ' ὕβρει Man.3.86.

**ἐπᾰτενίζω**, *gaze steadfastly at*, εἴς τι Thphr.*Vert.*9.

**ἐπατρεμέω**, *remain quiet after* a thing, Hp.*Art.*34.

**ἐπάττω**, Att. for ἐπαΐσσω.

**ἐπαυγάζω**, *illumine on the surface*, Max.26. 2. Med., *look at by the light, examine carefully*, ἕκαστον ἀκριβέστερον Ph.2.412; simply, *behold*, *AP*9.58.8 (Antip.): Ep. aor., ἐπηυγάσσασθε ib.12.91 (Polystr.). II. intr., *shine*, Them.*Or.*4.52b; f.l. for ὑπ-, Polyaen. 1.39.1.

**ἐπαυδάω**, *call to* or *say in addition*, Hsch., Suid.:—Med., *call upon, invoke*, τινά S.*Ph.*395 (lyr.).

⊛ **ἐπαυλ-έω**, *accompany on the flute*, τῇ θυσίᾳ Luc.*Sacr.*12: abs., Id. *Salt.*10. 2. c. acc. cogn., ἐ. τινὶ τὸν ἐνόπλιον Epich.75:—Pass., μέλος ἐπαυλεῖται *is played on the flute*, E.*HF*897 (lyr.). -ημα, ατος, τό, *musical phrase played on the flute*, *EM*757.32.

**ἐπαυλ-ία**, Ion. -ίη, epith. of Artemis, *IG*12(8).359 (Thasos, v B.C.). -ίζομαι, Dep. with aor. Med., *encamp on the field*, Th. 3.5, 4.134; cf. αὐλίζομαι. 2. *encamp near*, τῇ πόλει Plu.*Sull.* 29. 3. *pass the night*, Hsch. 4. of birds, *roost in*, [αἰγείρῳ] A.R.3.929. ⊛ -ιον, τό, Dim. of sq. 2, *SIG*344.98 (Teos, iv B.C.), *OGI*765.13 (Priene), Call.*Fr.*131.4, Plb.4.4.1, Plu.2.508d, Alciphr. *Fr.*6.4. II. τὰ ἐπαύλια or ἡ ἐπαυλία (sc. ἡμέρα) *the day after the wedding*, Id.3.49, Poll.3.30, Hsch., Suid.; also, *presents given to the bride*, Poll. l.c. III. ἐπαύλιος· ἡ τῆς αὐλῆς ὁδός, Suid., Zonar. -ις, εως, ἡ, *steading*, Hdt.1.111; οὐκ ἀσφαλὲς λέοντι καὶ προβάτοις ὁμοῦ ποιεῖσθαι τὴν ἔπαυλιν Plb.5.35.13, cf. *IG*14.1284, etc. 2. *farm-building, country house*, D.S.12.43, Plu.*Pomp.*24, Alciphr.*Fr.* 6.1, etc. 3. in military language, *quarters*, ἐ. ποιεῖσθαι encamp, Pl.*Alc.*2.149c; ἐπὶ στρατοπεδείᾳ Plb.16.15.5. 4. *unwalled village*, Lxx*Le.*25.31, al. -ισμα, ατος, τό, gloss on ἔπαυλα, Sch.A.*Pers.* 870. -ισμός, ὁ, *passing the night*, Sch.S.*Ant.*356. ⊛ -ος, ὁ, (αὐλή) mostly in pl., ἔπαυλοι Od.23.358, A.R.1.800; ἔπαυλα S.*OT* 1138, *OC*669 (lyr.):—*fold* for cattle at night, Od. l.c., S.*OT* l.c. 2. generally, *dwelling, home*, A.*Pers.*870 (lyr.), S.*OC* l.c.

**ἐπαυλόσυνος**, f.l. for ἀπ-, *AP*6.221.8 (Leon.).

**ἐπαυξ-άνω** (Pl.*Ti.*19a (Pass.), D.3.33, etc.) or **-αύξω** (X.*Oec.*7.43 (Pass.), *OGI*90.38 (Rosetta, ii B.C.)): fut. -αυξήσω:—*increase, enlarge*, Emp.17.32; τὴν πατρίδα νικήσαντας ἐπαυξῆσαι Th.7.70, cf. 2.36, D. l.c.; τὰμ βασιλείαν *SIG*629.5 (Delph., ii B.C.); τὸν ἔρανον *IG*12 (1).155iii84 (Rhodes); τὴν φιλαγαθίαν ib.12(7).232.6 (Amorgos):—

Pass., *grow, increase*, X. l. c., Pl. l. c., etc. II. intr., *grow, increase*, Aristaenet.1.16. -η, ἡ, = ἐπαύξησις, Pl.*Lg.*815e. -ημα, ατος, τό, = foreg., Dosith.p.381 K., *PMasp.*26*B*8 (pl., vi A.D.). -ής, ές, *increasing, growing*, νόσοι Hp.*Epid.*6.5.15 (but perh. = diseases *of adolescence*, cf. Gal.17(2).288); πάθεα Aret.*SA*2.7. -ησις, εως, ἡ, *increase, increment*, τῶν δικαίων Pl.*Lg.*957d; τῆς φορολογίας *PTeb.* 27.47 (ii B.C.); τῶν μέτρων Plu.*Sol.*15; εἰς τὴν ἐ. τῶν πολιτῶν to their *profit*, Plb.5.88.6. -ω, v. ἐπαυξάνω.

**ἐπαύρ-εσις**, εως, ἡ, *enjoyment of the fruit* of a thing, *fruition*, μεγάλαι.. ἐπαυρέσιες Hdt.7.158; ταχείας τὰς ἐ. ποιεῖσθαι Th.2.53; ἐ. γίγνεται ἀπό τινος Democr.278. ⊛-έω and -ίσκω, ἐπαυρεῖ Hes.*Op.*419, ἐπαυρίσκουσι Thgn.111: aor. ἐπαῦρον Pi.*P.*3.36, subj. ἐπαύρω, ῃς, ῃ (v. infr.), inf. ἐπαυρεῖν, -έμεν, Hom. (v. infr.):—Med., ἐπαυρίσκομαι Il.13.733, Democr.172, Hp.*Nat.Puer.*12, *Morb.*4.39: fut. ἐπαυρήσομαι Il.6.353: 2 sg. aor. 1 ἐπηύρω (ἐπηύρου Elmsl.) A.*Pr.*28, inf. ἐπαύρασθαι Hp.*Jusj.*fin., *Ep.*27, Plb.18.11.7: aor. 2 ἐπηυρόμην E.*Hel.* 469, poet. 2 sg. ἐπαύρεο Pi.*N.*5.49, 3 sg. ἐπηύρετο prob. in Arist.*EN* 1163$^a$20; Ep. 2 sg. subj. ἐπαύρηαι Il.15.17, -ῃ (cf. II. 3), 3 pl. -ωνται 1.410; inf. ἐπαυρέσθαι E.*IT*529, And.2.2 (v. infr. II):—Pass., aor. ἐπαυρεθέντα· ἐπιβάλλοντα, Hsch. I. Act., *partake of, share*, c. gen. rei, τῶν.. βέλτερόν ἐστιν ἐπαυρέμεν Il.18.302; αὐτὸν.. σε βούλομ' ἐπαυρέμεν (gen. omitted) Od.17.81; πλεῖον νυκτὸς ἐπαυρεῖ *enjoys* a greater *share* of night, of Sirius, Hes.*Op.*419; γειτόνων πολλοὶ ἐπαῦρον many *have had enjoyment of* (i.e. *suffered loss from*) neighbours, Pi.*P.*3.36; τὸ μέγιστον ἐπαυρίσκουσι *have enjoyment* in the highest degree, Thgn.111; *obtain, meet with*, εἴ κε.. κυβερνητῆρος ἐπαύρῃ A.R.2.174. 2. of physical contact, *touch, graze*, esp. of slight wounds, c. acc., παρος χρόα λευκὸν ἐπαυρεῖν (sc. τὰ δοῦρα) Il.11.573; μή τις χρόα χαλκῷ ἐπαύρῃ 13.649: c. gen., λίθου δ' ἀλέασθαι ἐπαυρεῖν take care not *to touch*, 23.340: abs., καὶ εἴ κ' ὀλίγον περ ἐπαύρῃ if the spear *touch* ever so little, 11.391, cf. Nic.*Th.*763. II. Med., *reap the fruits, enjoy the benefit of* a thing, whether good or bad: 1. c. gen., in good sense, τοῦ πολλοὶ ἐπαυρίσκονται Il.13.733; μόχθων ἀμοιβὰν ἐπαύρεο Pi.*N.*5.49; τοῦδ' ἐπαυρέσθαι θέλω E.*IT*529, cf. A.R. 1.677, 4.964; μικροῦ δὲ βιότου ζῶντ' ἐπαυρέσθαι χρεών *Trag.Adesp.* 95.4 (= *Com.Adesp.*1207.4); τῆς ζόης ἐ. Herod.3.2, cf. 7.26; τῆς ἐλευθερίας Plb.18.11.7; οὐδὲ φάους.. πολλὸν ἐπαυράμενον *IG*12(7). 302.5 (Amorgos), cf. *Epigr.Gr.*839 (Lebena): rare in Prose, εἰ.. χρὴ ἀγαθὸν ἐμοῦ ἐπαυρέσθαι And.2.2; ἀποδοτέον.. ὅσον ἐπηύρετο Arist.*EN* 1163$^a$20; τάχα δ' ἄν τι καὶ τοῦ οὐνόματος ἐπαύροιτο *may have got* his fate from his name, Hdt.7.180; τίν' αἰτίαν σχὼν ἧς ἐπηυρόμην ἐγώ; E. *Hel.*469. b. more freq. in bad, though not ironical, sense, ἵνα πάντες ἐπαύρωνται βασιλῆος that all *may enjoy their* king, i.e. feel what it is to have such a king, Il.1.410; οὐ μὰν οἶδ' εἰ αὖτε κακορραφίης.. ἐπαύρηαι 15.17: c. acc. et gen., τοιαῦτ' ἐπηύρω τοῦ φιλανθρώπου τρόπου such *profit didst* thou *gain from*.., A.*Pr.*28: abs., τῶ καί μιν ἐπαυρήσεσθαι ὀΐω I doubt not he *will feel* the consequences, Il.6.353; ἀπό τινος κακὰ ἐ. Democr.172. 2. ἐ. ἀπό τινος *get nourishment from*.., Hp.*Morb.*4.39. 3. c. acc. rei, *bring upon oneself*, μή πού τι κακὸν καὶ μεῖζον ἐπαύρῃ Od.18.107 (v.l. ἐπαύρῃς, but perh. better taken as 3 sg. aor. Act., lest a greater evil *reach* thee).—Mainly poet. and Ion.

**ἐπαυρίζω**, (αὔρα) *breathe* or *blow gently*, J.*BJ*1.21.5.

**ἔπαυριν**· ἀπολέσαι, Hsch. (Leg. ἐπαυρεῖν· ἀπολαῦσαι.)

**ἐπαύριον**, Adv. *on the morrow*, τῇ ἐ. ἡμέρᾳ *PLille*1.15 (iii B.C.); ἡμέρᾳ ἡ ἐ. LXX *Nu.*11.32; usu. τῇ ἐ. *on the morrow*, Plb.3.53.6, al., *Ev. Matt.*27.62, al.; εἰς τὴν ἐ. Plb.8.13.6, al. (Sts. written ἐφ–, *PHamb.* 1.27.4 (iii B.C.), *PTeb.*119.17 (ii B.C.).)

**ἐπαΰσας, ἐπᾰ́ϋσον** [ῡ], v. ἐπαΰω.

**ἐπᾰϋτέω** [ῡ], *make a noise* or *creak besides*, ἐπὶ δὲ πλῆμναι μέγ' ἀΰτευν Hes.*Sc.*309. II. = ἐπευφημέω, ἐπηΰτησε δὲ λαὸς Call.*Ap.*102, Q.S.4.262; Βέβρυκες δ' ἐπαΰτεον Theoc.22.91; of horses, Q.S.11. 327: c. acc. cogn., ἐ. βοήν Call.*Dian.*58.

**ἐπαυτίκᾰ** [ῐ], Adv. *immediately*, Orph.*L.*334.

**ἐπαυτομολέω**, *pass over*, πρὸς τὸ ἥμερον Ael.*NA*2.11.

**ἐπαυτοφάδες**· ἐπ' αὐτοφώρῳ, Hsch.

**ἐπαυτόφωρος**, ον, = αὐτόφωρος, *palpable*, Sch.Il.24.556.

**ἐπαυχένιος**, ον, (αὐχήν) *on* or *for the neck*, ζυγόν Pi.*P.*2.93; κύναγχα *AP*6.34 (Rhian.).

**ἐπαυχέω**, aor. -ηύχησα Ar.*Av.*629:—*exult in* or *at*, c. dat. rei, S. *Ant.*483, Ar. l. c. 2. c. acc. et inf., *to be confident that*.., S.*El.*65.

⊛**ἐπαυχμέω**, *send drought upon*, τυραννίδι Ζεὺς ἐπαυχμήσας S.*Fr.* 524.4.

**ἐπαΰω**, *shout over*, ἐπαΰσας πατρὸς ἔργῳ A.*Ch.*828 codd. (lyr.); in Theoc.23.44 τρὶς ἐπᾰ́ϋσον [ῡ], ὦ φίλε, κεῖσαι is dub.

**ἐπαφαίρ-εσις**, εως, ἡ, *a fresh taking away* of blood, Aret.*CA*1.1, Archig.ap.Gal.8.150, Philum.ap.Orib.45.29.1; of a beard, Mart.8. 52. -ετέον, *one must let blood again*, Herod.Med. in *Rh.Mus.*58. 81. -έω, *take away again*, esp. blood, Aret.*CA*2.10, Gal.6.299.

**ἐπαφᾰνίζω**, *make to disappear besides*, Lysis ap.Iamb.*VP*17.77.

**ἐπαφαυαίνομαι**, Pass., *to be withered*: hence ἐπαφαυάνθην γελῶν I *was quite spent* with laughing, Ar.*Ra.*1089 (anap.).

⊛**ἐπᾰφάω** (v. ἀφάω), *touch on the surface, touch lightly*, Hecat.22 J., A.*Pr.*849, *Trag.Adesp.*458.7, Pl.*Cra.*404d:—also in Med., abs., τῷ δακτύλῳ Hp.*Mul.*2.165: c. gen., ἐ. χερσί τινος Mosch.2.50; κιθάρης *AP*5.221.1 (Agath.); μουσικῆς Alciphr.3.12: c. acc., παλάμῃ κρᾶτ' ἐπαφησάμενος *IG*14.2123.

**ἐπαφετέον**, *one must admit*, [τοὺς κριοὺς] ταῖς θηλείαις *Gp.*18.3.1, cf. *Hippiatr.*14.

**ἐπαφ-ή**, ἡ, (ἐπαφάω) *touch, touching, handling*, A.*Supp.*17, Pl.*Ti.* 46b, al.; σφυγμοῦ Marcellin.*Puls.*114, al.; ἐ. μωσικὰ [τῆς λύρας] Euryph.ap.Stob.4.39.27: pl., ἐπαφαὶ χειρῶν Plu.2.2d. 2. *severe handling, punishment*, ἐ. καὶ νουθεσία ib.46d; esp. of Pythagorean *treatment*, Iamb.*VP*15.64 (pl.), 25.114. 3. *touch, contact*, ἡδεῖα ἐ. *IGRom.*4.503.11 (Pergam.). b. metaph., of *apprehension*, Epicur.*Fr.*250; ἡ τοῦ ἀγαθοῦ εἴτε γνῶσις εἴτε ἐ. Plot.6.7.36, cf. Iamb. *Comm.Math.*8; τοῦ μέλλοντος Id.*Myst.*3.26. 4. Geom., *point of contact*, Euc.*Phaen.*p.68 M., Procl.*Hyp.*2.7; περὶ ἐπαφῶν, on the theory of *tangents*, title of work by Apollonius of Perga, Papp.636. 21, al. II. *the sense of touch*, Pl.*Tht.*186b. III. in phrases such as ἐκτὸς ἱερᾶς νόσου καὶ ἐ. *PLips.*4.20 (iii A.D.), πλὴν ἐ. καὶ ἱ. ν. *POxy.*94.11 (i A.D.), etc., prob. *external claim*, cf. *PStrassb.*79.7 (i B.C.). -ημα, ατος, τό, *a touch*, Diog.*Ep.*10.1 (pl.). -ητός, όν, *capable of being touched*; χερσὶ μὲν οὐδαμῶς ἐ., διανοίᾳ δὲ μόνῃ κρατητός Porph.*Marc.*8.

⊛**ἐπαφίημι**, *throw at, discharge at*, τὰ παλτὰ X.*Cyr.*4.1.3; κεραμίδα τινί Plu.2.241b; *let loose upon*, πρόβατα *allow* them *to graze*, Thphr. *HP*8.7.4, cf. *BGU*1251.11 (iii/ii B.C.), etc.; τοὺς ἱππεῖς τοῖς ἱππεῦσι Plb.11.22.8; τοὺς εὐζώνους Id.10.39.3; ἐλέφαντας ἐ. τινί Paus.1.12. 3, etc.; ἐμαυτόν τισι Alciphr.1.22:—Pass., εὐθὺ τὸν λίθον ἐπαφίεσθαι Aen.Tact.32.6. 2. *let in upon*, ὕδωρ τῷ σίτῳ Thphr.*CP*2.5.5:— Pass., Jul.*Or.*1.30a. 3. *discharge, emit*, ἐ. ὑγρότητα Arist.*HA* 550$^a$13; ἐ. φωνὴν *utter*, Id.*Mir.*847$^b$2.

⊛**Ἐπάφιος**, epith. of Dionysus, Orph.*H.*50.7, 52.9.

**Ἔπαφος**, ὁ, a son of Zeus and Io, A.*Pr.*851 (v. ἀφή); the Hellenic representative of the Egyptian god Apis, Hdt.2.153, 3.27, 28.

**ἐπαφρ-ιάω**, *foam against*, Ep. part. -όωσα Nonn.*D.*43.318 (v.l. ὑπ–). -ίζω, *foam up* or *on the surface*, Mosch.*Fr.*1, Nic.*Al.* 32. 2. c. acc., *foam out*, αἰσχύνας *Ep.Jud.*13.

**ἐπαφροδ-ῑσία**, ἡ, *loveliness, elegance*, Lync.ap.Ath.6.242c, Ptol. *Tetr.*86, Vett.Val.160.13; περὶ τοὺς λόγους D.Chr.37.33; ἐν τοῖς πρασσομένοις Artem.2.20; *charm*, *PSI*4.328.6 (iii B.C.), *UPZ*33.9 (ii B.C.), *PMag.Osl.*1.224, *PMag.Lond.*122.5, etc. -ῖτος, ον, (Ἀφροδίτη) *lovely, fascinating, charming*, of persons, Hdt.2.135, Aeschin.2.42; of things, ἔπη καὶ ἔργα X.*Smp.*8.15 (Comp., codd.); ποίησις Isoc.10. 65: Sup. -ότατος X.*Hier.*1.35. Adv. -τως, γράφειν D.H.*Lys.*11, cf. Alciphr.2.1, Philostr.*VA*6.3. II. used to translate Sulla's epithet *Felix*, *favoured by Venus*, i.e. *fortune's favourite* (metaph. from the dice), Plu.*Sull.*34, App.*BC*1.97. III. *gracious*, ἡγεμονία *PRyl.*77.36 (ii A.D.).

**ἔπαφρος**, ον, *frothy*, Hp.*Epid.*1.26.β', Aret.*SA*2.1.

**ἐπᾰφύσσω**, *pour over*, θερμὸν ἐπήφυσεν Od.19.388.

⊛**ἐπάχθ-εια**, ἡ, *trouble, annoyance*, Just.*Nov.*115.3.14, al.: pl., *onerous charges*, *Cod.Just.*1.3.38.2. -έω, *load, burden with*, τινί Tryph. 690:—Pass., *to be overloaded* (?), Sor.1.84. -ής, ές, (ἄχθος) *heavy, ponderous*, ῥήματα Ar.*Ra.*940. II. metaph., *burdensome, grievous*, ἅπαντ' ἐπαχθῆ (so Stanley for ἐπράχθη) A.*Pr.*49; εἰ μὴ ἐπαχθές ἐστιν εἰπεῖν Pl.*Phd.*87a; ἐπαινεῖν ἐπαχθέστερόν [ἐστι] Id.*Lg.*688d; ἵνα μηδὲν ἐπαχθὲς λέγω not to say anything *offensive*, D.18.10; ἐπαχθεῖς αἱ ὑπερβολαί Arist.*EN*1127$^b$8: Sup. -έστατος, θάνατος Phalar. *Ep.*1; κακά Ph.2.402; τὸ ἐ. τῶν λόγων *invidiousness, offence*, Pl. *Euthd.*303e; τὸ ἐ. [τῆς σοφιστικῆς τέχνης] Id.*Prt.*316d. Adv. -θῶς, ἐνέγκαι, = Lat. *aegre ferre*, D.H.*Th.*41. 2. of persons, ἐ. ἦν ἐς τοὺς πολλούς Th.6.54, cf. Pl.*Men.*90a; κινδυνεύει τὸ λίαν εὐτυχεῖν.. ἐπαχθεῖς ποιεῖν D.21.205. Adv. Comp. -έστερον, τισὶ βιῶναι Pl.*Ep.* 327b. -ίζομαι, *to be burdened with*.., λείαν, ἀγγεῖα, Ph.2.103, 113; βάρος πραγματειῶν ib.288: abs., ἐπηχθισμένοι ib.450. -ομαι, *to be annoyed at*.., κακοῖς E.*Hipp.*1260.

**ἐπαχλύω**, *to be obscured* or *dim*, A.R.4.1480, Q.S.14.462, Ant. Lib.9.2. II. trans., *darken*, Them.*Or.*11.144c:—Pass., -ύεται ὁ λογισμὸς ὑπὸ πάθους ib.19.232d. [ῡ even in pres., A.R. l. c.; in Arat.906 Schneider restored ἐπαχλύων (signf. I) for -ύῶν.]

**ἐπαχνίδιος**, α, ον, (ἄχνη) *lying like down upon*, κόνις *AP*9.556 (Zon.).

**ἐπάχνῠμαι**, Pass., *grieve over*, τινί Tryph.424.

**ἐπὰψ** θέμεναι· πάλιν ἐπικλεῖσαι καὶ ἐπιθεῖναι *EM*354.25 (leg. ἐπ' ἂψ θ., v.l. in Il.21.535).

**ἐπεάν**, v. ἐπεί A.II. **ἐπέβρᾰχε**, v. ἐπιβραχεῖν.

**ἐπεγ-γελάω**, fut. -άσομαι, Ep. iterative ἐπεγγελάασκε Q.S.14.397: —*laugh at, exult over*, τινί S.*Aj.*989, X.*An.*2.4.27; κατά τινος S.*Aj.* 969; ταῖς συμφοραῖς τινῶν J.*AJ*11.6.10: abs., S.*Aj.*454, Aeschin.2. 182, Phld.*Mort.*20; ἐπεγγελόωσα Opp.*H.*2.303: c. acc. cogn., ὑβριστήν τινα γέλωτα Aristaenet.2.6. -γρᾰφος, ον, *added to the list*: of non-citizens who were *admitted* to contend for prizes, *IG*3.1092 (i/ii A.D.), al.

**ἐπεγγῠάω**, = ἐγγυάω, Lex ap.Lys.10.17; 3 pl. impf. ἐπενεγύων *SIG* 705.43 (ii B.C.):—Pass., Dor. pres. part. ἐπεγγυάμενοι Sophr.60.

**ἐπεγ-είρω**, *awaken, rouse up*, τινά Od.22.431, Thgn.469, Ar.*Av.* 83:—Pass., *to be roused from sleep, wake up*, Hom., only in aor. forms ἐπέγρετο, ἐπεγρόμενος, Il.10.124, 14.256, Od.20.57; μέχρι ἐπέγρωνται Hp.*Morb.Sacr.*1; φεύγετε.. ἀνδρ' ἐπεγειρόμενον E.*HF*1083 (anap.); δόξαι, αἳ ἐρωτήσει ἐπεγερθεῖσαι ἐπιστῆμαι γίγνονται Pl.*Men.* 86a: pf. ἐπήγερται is dub.l. in Luc.*Zeux.*4. II. metaph., *awaken, excite*, πόλεμον εὕδοντ' Sol.4.19; διωγμόν *Act.Ap.*13.50; τὸ πάλαι κείμενον κακόν S.*OC*510 (lyr.); ἐπὶ.. θρῆνον ἐ. ib.1778 (anap.); ὅσον ἐσμὸν λόγων ἐπεγείρετε Pl.*R.*450b; *stir up*, τὸ Ἑλληνικόν Hdt.7.139; τὰς ψυχὰς *Act.Ap.*14.2; ἡμᾶς εἰς τὴν νεότητα μνήμῃ ἐ. Pl.*Lg.*657d; τοῦ ἐπεγείροντος ὥσπερ μύωπος δεήσει Socr.*Ep.*1.6:—Pass., ἐπηγέρθη [ἡ Ταλθυβίου μῆνις] Hdt.7.137; ἐπηγείροντο ταῖς ψυχαῖς D.S.

14.52. III. *erect, raise*, τὰς ἀκάνθας -ων *erecting* his prickles, like certain fish when irritated, *Com.Adesp.*1338 ( = [S.]*Fr.*1121); ὅταν ἐπεγερθῶσιν φλύκταιναι Philum.*Ven.*17.5. **-ερσις,** εως, ἡ, *being roused, awaking*, Hp.*Prorrh.*1.112, Max.Tyr.16.6. **-ερτικός,** ή, όν, *awakening*, Arist.*Pr.*886$^{a}$9. II. *stimulating*, ἐ. ὁρμῆς Plu.2.138b; ἐ. εἰς τὰ ἀφροδίσια *Cat.Cod.Astr.*2.197.

**ἐπεγ-κᾰλέω,** *bring a charge against*, τινί Lys.8.1; τυραννίδα τινί Procop.*Arc.*18; τινὶ ὡς ψευσαμένῳ Gal.18(2).295; τισί c. inf., Hierocl.*in CA*25 p.477 M.:—Med., πολιτείαν Olymp. *in Alc.*p.155 C. **-κᾰνάσσω,** *drink* or *pour in besides*, Hsch. (-κενάξαι cod.). **-κάπτω,** *eat up besides, gulp down*, Ar.*Eq.*493. **-κᾰχάζω,** *laugh at*, τινί Lyc.285. **-κειμαι,** *press hard*, Sch.Il.24.657. **-κέλευμα,** ατος, τό, gloss on ἐπίσιγμα, Hsch. **-κελεύω,** *give an order* or *signal to* others, E.*Cyc.*652; *exhort, encourage*, τινί prob. in Id.*El.*1224 (lyr.). **-κεράννῠμαι,** Med., *mix in with*, Pl.*Plt.*273d, Nic.*Al.*166, etc.; τινί τι Plu.2.1025b. **-κλάω,** *turn towards*, τὰ βλέφαρα εἴς τινα D.C.51.12; τοὺς ὀφθαλμούς Id.79.16. **-κλημα,** ατος, τό, *accusation*, Sopat. in Rh.5.209 W. ⊛ **-κλίνω** [ῑ], *incline, turn towards* either side, v.l. in Gal.*UP*12.9. **-κολάπτω,** *engrave upon* or *besides*, Lyc.782. **-κρᾱνίς,** ίδος, ἡ, *cerebellum*, Erasistr. ap.Gal.*UP*8.13. **-κρεμάννῠμαι,** Med., *hang up in*, καπνῷ Nic.*Fr.*72.2. **-κυκλέω,** in Pass., *to be introduced* into a speech, of parallels, etc., Aristid.*Rh.*2 p.538 S. **-κύκλιος,** ον, *circular*, of bandages, Sor.*Fasc.*12.512,516 C., Gal.18(1).815.

**ἐπεγνωσμένως,** Adv., (ἐπιγιγνώσκω) = ᾠκειωμένως, Zonar.

**ἐπεγρόμην,** part. **ἐπεγρόμενος,** Ep. aor. Pass. of ἐπεγείρω.

**ἐπεγ-χᾰλάω,** *loose*, δέσμα Nic.*Al.*439. **-χάσκω,** *make mouths at*, in aor. 2 inf. ἐπεγχανεῖν, τινί Ael.*Fr.*69: abs., S.*Fr.*210.49. **-χειρέω,** *attack*, Gal.2.221. **-χέω,** poet. **-χεύω** Nic.*Fr.*72.5:—*pour in upon* or *besides*, A.*Ag.*1137 (lyr.), Philox.2.40; ἄλλην [κύλικα] ἐπ' ἄλλῃ E.*Cyc.*423; *pour in fresh water*, Hp.*Int.*1. **-χῠμᾰτίζω,** *wash out* the throat *afterwards*, *Hippiatr.*22. II. *give a clyster afterwards*, γάλακτι Dsc.5.15. **-χύνω,** late form for **-χέω,** Hero *Spir.*2.28 (Pass.). **-χύτης** [ῠ], ου, ὁ, *cup-bearer*, so called by the Hellespontines, Demetr.Sceps.ap.Ath.10.425c.

**ἐπέδρᾰμον,** v. ἐπιτρέχω. **ἐπέδρη,** ἡ, Ion. for ἐφέδρα.

**ἐπέην,** Ep. for ἐπῆν, 3 sg. impf. of ἔπειμι (A), Il.20.276.

**ἐπεθίζομαι,** *to be accustomed to* a thing, Aristox.*Harm.*p.33 M.

⊛ **ἐπεί,** Conj., both temporal and causal; also **ἐπειδή, ἐπείτε.**

A. Of Time (ἐπειδή is more freq. in this sense in Prose), *after that, since, when*, from Hom. downwds.: I. with Ind., 1. of a definite occurrence in past time, mostly c. aor., ἐπεί ῥ' εὔξαντο *after* they had prayed, Il.1.458; ἐπειδὴ ἐτελεύτησε Δαρεῖος καὶ κατέστη Ἀρταξέρξης *after* D. had died and A. had succeeded, X.*An.*1.1.3: rarely c. impf., ἐπειδὴ εἱστιώμεθ' Ar.*Nu.*1354; ἐ. πόντον εἰσεβάλλομεν E.*IT*260; ἐ. ἠσθένει Δαρεῖος X.*An.*1.1.1: c. plpf., ἐπειδὴ ἐξηπάτησθε.. *after* you had been deceived.., D.18.42; but generally the aor. is found, the plpf. being used only for special emphasis: c. impf. to express an action not yet complete, ἐπεὶ ὑπηντίαζεν ἡ φάλαγξ καὶ ἡ σάλπιγξ ἐφθέγξατο *after* the phalanx began to advance and the trumpet had sounded, X.*An.*6.5.27. 2. with implied reference to some later time, ἐ. or ἐπειδή, = ἐξ οὗ, *from the time when, since*, mostly c. aor., πολλὰ πλάγχθη, ἐ. ἔπερσε Od.1.2; ἐπείτε παρέλαβον τὸν θρόνον, τοῦτο ἐφρόντιζον *ever since* I came to the throne, I had this in mind, Hdt.7.8.α'; ἐπειδήπερ ὑπέστη Th.8.68; δέκατον μὲν ἔτος τόδ' ἐ...ἦραν A.*Ag.*40: sts. c. pres. (used in pf. sense) and pf., ἐ. δὲ φροῦδός ἐστι στρατός *since* the army is gone, S.*Ant.*15; ἐπείτε ὑπὸ τῷ Πέρσῃ εἰσί, πεπόνθασι τοιόνδε *ever since* they have been, *now that* they are.., Hdt.3.117. II. with Subj., ἄν being always added in Att. Prose, and ἄν or κε generally in Poetry: ἐπεί with ἄν becomes ἐπήν (so in Com., Ar.*Lys.*1175, *Av.*983), later ἐπάν (q.v.), Ion. ἐπεάν *Schwyzer* 800 (vi B.C.), Hdt.3.153, al., ἐπήν Hp.*Fract.*6, al., and ἐπειδή with ἄν ἐπειδάν (q.v.); Hom. has ἐπεί κε, ἐπήν (once ἐπεὶ ἄν Il.6.412): 1. referring to future time with fut. apodosis, τέκνα ἄξομεν.. ἐπὴν πτολίεθρον ἕλωμεν *when* we shall have taken the city, Il.4.238; ἐ. κ' ἀπὸ λαὸς ὄληται 11.764, cf. Od.17.23; ἐπεάν περ ἡμίονοι τέκωσι, τότε τὸ τεῖχος ἁλώσεσθαι Hdt.3.153; ταῦτ', ἐπειδὰν περὶ τοῦ γένους εἴπω, τότ' ἐρῶ I will speak of this, *when* I have spoken.., D.57.16, cf. X.*An.*2.3.29; ἐ. ἂν σύ γε πότμον ἐπίσπῃς Il.6.412; χρὴ δέ, ὅταν μὲν τιθῆσθε τοὺς νόμους, ..σκοπεῖν, ἐπειδὰν δὲ θῆσθε, φυλάττειν whenever you are enacting your laws, .. and *after* you have enacted them.., D.21.34. 2. of repeated action, with a pres. apodosis, *whenever, when once*, δαμνᾷ, ἐ. κε λίπῃ ὀστέα θυμός Od.11.221, cf. Il.9.409; ἐπειδὰν ἡ ἐκφορὰ ᾖ.. ἄγουσι *whenever* the burial takes place they bring, Th.2.34; ἐπειδὰν κρύψωσι γῇ.. λέγει *when* they have covered them with earth, ibid.: sts. without ἄν or κε in Poets, ἐ. ἂρ βλέφαρ' ἀμφικαλύψῃ Od.20.86; ἐ. δὴ τόν γε δαμάσσεται.. ὀϊστός Il.11.478, cf. S.*OC*1225 (lyr.), *Ant.*1025. 3. like A. I. 2, δέκα ἡμερῶν ἐπειδὰν δόξῃ within ten days *from* the passing of the resolution, *IG*$1^2$.88.7. III. with Opt. (without ἄν): 1. referring to future time, ἐπειδὴ πρὸς τὸ φῶς ἔλθοι, ὁρᾶν οὐδ' ἂν ἓν δύνασθαι (sc. οὐκ οἴει); *after* he had come into the light.., Pl.*R.*516a: Hom. sts. uses ἐπήν with opt. in same sense as ἐπεί, Il.24.227, Od.2.105 (codd.), etc. 2. more freq. of repeated action, with a past apodosis, ἐ. ζεύξειεν.., δησάσκετο Il.24.14; ἐπειδὴ δέ τι ἐμφάγοιεν, ἀνίσταντο X.*An.*4.5.9; ἐ. πύθοιτο, ἐπῄνει Id.*Cyr.*5.3.55, cf. Th.8.38, Pl.*Phd.*59d, *Prt.*315b. 3. in orat. obliq. after past tenses, representing a subj. in orat. rect., αὐτὸς δὲ ἐπεὶ διαβαίης, ἀπιέναι ἔφησθα (the direct form being ἐπὴν διαβῶ) X.*An.*7.2.27, cf. 3.5.18, *Cyr.*1.4.21; after opt. in a final clause, ἐπορεύοντο, ὅπως ἐπειδὴ γένοιντο ἐπὶ τῷ ποταμῷ.. ἴοιεν Th.7.80. 4. by assimilation to opt. in principal clause, ἦ τ' ἂν.. νῦν μὲν ἀνώγοιμι πτολεμίζειν.. ἐπὴν τεισαίμεθα λώβην Il.19.208; ὃς τὸ καταβρόξειεν ἐπεὶ κρητῆρι μιγείη Od.4.222. 5. ἐπειδάν c. opt. is f.l. in some passages of early authors, as X.*Cyr.*1.3.11, D.30.6 (c. ind., Plb.13.7.8): found in later Gr., Agath.2.5, al., Zos.5.18.10. IV. with Inf., only in orat. obliq., ἐπειδὴ δὲ κατὰ σχολὴν σκέψασθαι, κόπτεσθαι (sc. ἔφη) Pl.*R.*619c, cf. *Smp.*174d, Hdt.4.10, 7.150. V. with other words: 1. ἐ. τάχιστα *as soon as*, freq. separated by a word, ἐ. ἦλθε τάχιστα, .. ἀπέδοτο X.*An.*7.2.6; ἐ. δὲ τάχιστα διέβη Id.*Cyr.*3.3.22; ἐ. θᾶττον Arist.*Pol.*1284$^{a}$40; ἐ. εὐθέως X.*HG*3.2.4; ἐ... αὐτίκα Pi.*N.*1.35; ἐπειδὴ τάχιστα Pl.*Prt.*310c, D.27.16; ἐπειδὰν τάχιστα Hdt.8.144, X.*An.*3.1.9; rarely ἐπειδὴ θᾶττον D.37.41; ἐπειδὰν θᾶττον Pl.*Prt.*325c. b. ἐ. τὰ πρῶτα Il.12.420; ἐ. τὸ πρῶτον A.*Ag.*1287. 2. with emphatic Particles, ἐπεὶ ἄρα *when* then, in continuing a narrative, Il.6.426; ἐπεὶ οὖν *when* then, in resuming a narrative, 1.57, 3.4; ἐπεὶ ὦν Hdt.3.9; ἐπεὶ γὰρ δή Id.9.90, etc.

B. Causal (ἐπεί more freq. in this sense in early Prose: ἐπειδή *whereas* is used in preambles of decrees, *IG*$2^2$.103, etc.; ἐπειδήπερ *inasmuch as*, *Ev.Luc.*1.1), *since, seeing that*, freq. from Hom. downwards: 1. with Ind. (after both present and past tenses), ἐ. οὐδὲ ἔοικε Il.1.119, cf. 153, 278, Pi.*O.*4.16, X.*Mem.*2.3.4; ἐπειδή Th.8.80; ἐπειδὴ οὐκ ἐθέλεις Pl.*Prt.*335c; νίκη δ' ἐπείπερ ἕσπετ', ἐμπέδως μένοι A.*Ag.*854; freq. with past tenses with ἄν, ἐπεὶ οὔποτ' ἂν στόλον ἐπλεύσατ' ἄν S.*Ph.*1037; ἐπεὶ οὔ κεν ἀνιδρωτί γ' ἐτελέσθη Il.15.228, cf. D.18.49; οὐ γὰρ ἂν σθένοντά γε εἷλέν μ'· ἐπεὶ οὐδ' ἂν ὧδ' ἔχοντ' (sc. εἷλεν) S.*Ph.*948: esp. in the sense, *for otherwise*.., Pi.*O.*9.29, S.*OT*433, X.*Mem.*2.7.14, Herod.2.72, etc.: so c. fut., ἐξέστω δὲ μηδενὶ.. τεθῆναι.., ἐ. ἀποδώσει.. *otherwise* he shall pay.., *Rev.Ét.Anc.*4.261 (near Smyrna): c. imper., ἐ. δίδαξον *for* teach me, S.*El.*352, *OC*969, cf. *OT*390, Ar.*V.*73, Pl.*Grg.*473e: with an interrog., ἐ. πῶς ἂν καλέσειας; *for* how would you call him? Ar.*Nu.*688, cf. Pi.*P.*7.5, A.*Ch.*214, S.*Tr.*139 (lyr.); ὦ Ἀλκιβιάδη, ἐπειδὴ περὶ τίνος Ἀθηναῖοι διανοοῦνται βουλεύεσθαι, ἀνίστασαι συμβουλεύσων; Pl.*Alc.*1.106c. 2. c. Opt., ἐ. ἂν μάλα τοι σχεδὸν ἔλθοι Il.9.304, cf. S.*Aj.*916; so after past tenses on the principle of orat. obliq., ἐπείπερ ἡγήσαιντο *since* (as they said) they believed, X.*Mem.*1.4.19. 3. c. Inf. in orat. obliq., ἐ. γιγνώσκειν γε αὐτά Pl.*Prt.*353a, cf. Hdt.8.111, Th.2.93. 4. in elliptical expressions, ἀδύνατός [εἰμι], ἐ. ἐβουλόμην ἂν οἷός τ' εἶναι I am unable (and yet I am sorry), *for* I should like to have the power, Pl.*Prt.*335c; so εἶμι· ἐ. καὶ ταῦτ' ἂν ἴσως οὐκ ἀηδῶς σου ἤκουον ibid. (here the sense may be given by *and yet, although*, cf. ib.333c, 317a, *Ap.*19e, *Smp.*187a, Arist.*EN*1121$^{a}$19); ἐ. ὅ γε ἀποθανὼν πελάτης τις ἦν ἐμός *and yet* (*moreover*) the murdered man was my own hired man, Pl.*Euthphr.*4c. b. sts. after a voc., where 'listen' may be supplied, Ἕκτορ, ἐ. με κατ' αἶσαν ἐνείκεσας Il.3.59, cf. 13.68, Od.3.103, 211. 5. with other Particles, ἐ. ἄρα, ἐ. ἂρ δή *since* then, Od.17.185; ἐ. γε (ἐπεί.. γε Il.1.352, Hes.*Th.*171), more emphatic than ἐ., *since* indeed, E.*Cyc.*181, *Hipp.*955; ἐπειδή γε ib.946, Pl.*Phd.*77d, D.54.29; sts. separated, ἐπειδή.. γε S.*El.*631, Pl.*Phd.*87c; ἐ. γε δή Hdt.3.9, S.*Ant.*923, ἐπειδή γε καί Th.6.18; ἐ. ἦ *since* in truth, ἐ. ἦ πολὺ φέρτερόν ἐστι Il.1.169, cf. 156, Od.9.276; ἐπείπερ (ἐ... περ Il.13.447, Od.20.181) in Trag. and Prose, A.*Ag.*822, S.*OC*75, Pl.*Phd.*114d; ἐπειδήπερ in Com. and Prose, Ar.*Ach.*437, 495, *Nu.*1412, Th.6.18, Pl.*R.*350e; ἐ. τοι *since* surely, S.*OC*433; ἐ. νύ τοι Il.1.416; ἐ. τοι καί E.*Med.*677, Pl.*R.*567e. [ἐ. sts. begins a verse in Hom., Il.22.379, Od.4.13, 8.452, 21.25; sts. coalesces by synizesis with οὐ, οὐδέ, etc., S.*Ph.*446, 948, etc.]

⊛ **ἐπείγω,** Il.12.452, etc., Aeol. **ἐποίγω** Hdn.Gr.2.436: impf. ἤπειγον Pi.*O.*8.47, S.*Ph.*499, Ep. ἔπειγον Od.12.205: aor. ἤπειξα Hp.*Ep.*17, Plu.*Pomp.*21, etc.:—Med. and Pass., Hom. (v. infr.), etc.: fut. Med. ἐπείξομαι A.*Pr.*52: aor. ἠπείχθην Th.1.80, Pl.*Lg.*887c: pf. ἤπειγμαι J.*BJ*1.8.7, Aristid.*Or.*17(15).9, Gal.6.177: the compd. κατ-επείγω is more freq. in Att. Prose:—*press by weight*, ὀλίγον τέ μιν ἄχθος ἐπείγει the weight *presses* lightly *on* him, Il.12.452:—Pass., *to be weighed down*, ἐπείγετο γὰρ βελέεσσι 5.622; θάμνοι.. ἐπειγόμενοι πυρὸς ὁρμῇ *overpowered*, 11.157, cf. 21.362. 2. *press hard* (in pursuit), ἀναγκαίη γὰρ ἐπείγει 6.85, Od.19.73: c. acc., δύω κύνε.. κεμάδ' ἠὲ λαγωὸν ἐπείγετον Il.10.361:—in a current phrase, οὐδεὶς ἡμᾶς τὸ λεγόμενον ἐπείγων διώκει Pl.*Lg.*887b. II. *drive on, urge forward*, ἐρετμὰ.. χερσὶν ἔπειγον Od.12.205; freq. of a fair wind, ἔπειγε γὰρ οὖρος 12.167; ὁππότ' ἐπείγῃ ἲς ἀνέμου Il.15.382; καιρὸς καὶ πλοῦς ὅδ' ἐπείγει κατὰ πρύμναν S.*Ph.*1451 (anap.). III. generally, *urge on, hasten*, ἐπείγετε δ' ὦνον Od.15.445; τὸν οἴκαδ' ἤπειγον στόλον *urged* the homeward course, S.*Ph.*499; ἐ. τινά Id.*OC*1540:—Pass., of a ship, ἐπείγετο χέρσ' ἐρετάων Od.13.115; Διὸς οὔρῳ 15.297, cf. E.*IT*1393, Th.3.49; of persons, θορύβοις ἠπειγμένος J. l.c. 2. Med., *urge on for oneself*, μίμνετ' ἐπειγόμενοι τὸν ἐμὸν γάμον Od.2.97; so τὴν παρασκευήν, τὸν πλοῦν ἐπείγεσθαι, Th.3.2, 4.5, al.: abs., ἐπειγομένων ἀνέμων *by the force of* winds, Il.5.501; ὀπὸς γάλα.. ἐπειγόμενος συνέπηξεν the fig-juice *by its power* curdles the milk, ib.902. 3. Pass., *hurry oneself, haste to do*, c. inf., μή τις.. ἐπειγέσθω οἶκόνδε νέεσθαι Il.2.354, cf. Hes.*Sc.*21, Hdt.8.68.γ', Th.8.46, etc.: abs., *make haste*, ἐπειγέσθω δὲ καὶ αὐτός Il.6.363; ὧραι ἐπειγόμεναι Pi.*N.*4.34; ἐπειχθῆναι πᾶν πρῆγμα τίκτει σφάλματα Hdt.7.10.ζ'; δρόμῳ ἐπείγεσθαι Id.6.112; νυκτὸς ἅρμ' ἐπείγεται A.*Ch.*660; δεῦρ' ἐπείγονται E.*Ion*1258; ὥσπερ τι δεινὸν ἀγγελῶν ἐ. Ar.*Ach.*1070; οὐ τῶν ἐπειγομένων ἀλλὰ τῶν εὖ βουλευομένων Antipho 5.94, cf. Th.8.82; ἐπείγεσθαι ἐπὶ.. Hdt.4.135; ἐς πύλας, πρὸς τὴν γέφυραν, E.*Ph.*1171, Th.6.101;

ἠπείγετο οἴκαδε Pl.*Tht.*142c, etc.: in Hom. mostly in part., like an Adv. with Verbs, ἐπειγομένη ἀφικάνει *in eager haste* she comes, Il. 6.388; ψυχὴ.. ἔσσυτ' ἐπειγομένη 14.519; τάμνον ἐπειγόμενοι 23.119, etc.; so in Att., εἴσω ᾔει ἐπειγόμενος Pl.*Prt.*310b. b. Pass., also, *to be eager for* a thing, esp. in part.: c. inf., πρὸς ἠέλιον κεφαλὴν τρέπε.. δῦναι ἐπειγόμενος *eager for* its setting, Od.13.30, cf. A. *Pr.*52: c. gen., ἐπειγόμενός περ ὁδοῖο *longing for* the journey, Od.1.309, etc.; ἐ. περ Ἄρηος *eager for* the fray, Il.19.142; ἐ. περὶ νίκης 23.437,496. IV. intr., = Pass., *hasten* to a place, Pi.*O.*8.47, S.*El.* 1435, E.*Or.*799, Ar.*Pax*943, etc. 2. *to be pressing, urgent*, ἐν ταῖς ἐπειγούσαις χρείαις Ph.*Bel.*56.47; τὰ ἐπείγοντα *pressing* matters, Plu. *Sert.*3, Aristid.1.119J., cf. *BGU*1141.4 (i B.C.), etc.; χρείαν τινὰ ἐπείγειν λέγων App.*Mith.*79; τῆς ὥρας -ούσης since time *was pressing*, Plu.2.108f; τῶν ἀρχαιρεσίων ἐπειγόντων Id.*Marc.*24. 3. impers., οὐκ ἐπείγει διαριθμεῖν *there's no pressing need* to count, Longin.43.6: part. abs., ἐπεῖξαν *the need being urgent*, Aristid.*Or.*36(48).10.

**ἐπειγωλή**, ἡ, *haste*, *EM*356.34.

**ἐπειδάν**, i.e. ἐπειδὴ ἄν (v. ἐπεί A. II, ἄν B. I. 2), *whenever*, with Subj., of Time, once in Hom., Il.13.285, freq. in Att. 2. for ἐπειδάν c. opt. v. ἐπεί A. III. 5. [-ᾱν is prob.; ἐπεὶ δ' ἄν is to be read in A. *Th.*734, E.*Rh.*469.]

**ἐπειδέ**, once = ἐπειδή before a vowel, *IG*7.15 (Megara, ii B.C.).

**ἐπειδή, ἐπειδήπερ**, v. ἐπεί.

❀ **ἐπεῖδον**, aor. 2, inf. ἐπιδεῖν, with no pres. in use, ἐφοράω being used instead, *look upon, behold, see*, of evils, κακὰ πόλλ' ἐπιδόντα Il.22.61:—Med., ἐπιδόμενοι A.*Supp.*646 (lyr.); ἐπιδέσθαι E.*Med.*1414 (anap.); ἐπιδώμεθα Ar.*Nu.*289 (lyr.). 2. esp. of the gods, *look upon* human affairs, Ζεὺς ἐπίδοι προφρόνως στόλον A.*Supp.*1 (anap.), cf. 145 (lyr.), 1030 (lyr.); νιν Ζεὺς ἐπίδοι κοταίνων Id.*Th.*485 (lyr.); Κύριε, ἔπιδε ἐπὶ τὰς ἀπειλὰς αὐτῶν *Act.Ap.*4.29. 3. *remain seeing*, i.e. *live to see*, τὰ τέκνα Hdt.6.52, cf. X.*Vect.*6.1; *experience*, χαλεπά Id.*An.*3.1.13: with part. added, μηδ' ἐπίδοιμι τάνδ' ἀστυδρομουμέναν πόλιν A.*Th.*220 (lyr.), cf. *Ag.*1539 (lyr.); ἐπιδεῖν ἐρήμην τὴν πόλιν γενομένην Isoc.4.96; τὴν πατρίδα ἐπιδεῖν δουλεύουσαν D.18.205; αὐτὸς λωβηθεὶς καὶ τοὺς αὑτοῦ ἐπιδὼν παῖδας [λωβηθέντας] Pl.*Grg.*473c.

❀ **ἐπεὶ ἦ**, v. ἐπεί B. 5.

**ἐπεικάδες**, ων, αἱ, (εἰκάς) *the days between the 20th and the end* of the month, *EM*131.15; cf. εἰκάς.

**ἐπεικ-άζω**, *surmise, guess*, ἦ καὶ δάμαρτα τήνδ' ἐπεικάζων κυρῶ κείνου; am I right in *surmising* that she is his wife? S.*El.*663; τάσδ' ἐπεικάσας τύχω χοὰς φερούσας; A.*Ch.*14, cf. 567; ὡς ἐπεικάσαι πάθη πάρεστι as one may *read the riddle of* their fates, ib.976; ὡς ἐπεικάσαι as far as *one may guess*, Hdt.9.32; ὅσ' ἐπεικάσαι (Bothe for ὡς) S.*OC* 152 (lyr.); ὥς γ' ἐπεικάζειν ἐμέ Id.*Tr.*1220. **-ασμός**, ὁ, *conjecture*, Gal.14.339.

**ἐπιείκεια, ἐπεικής**, v. ἐπιεικ-.

**ἐπείκελος**, dub. l. for ἐπιείκελος, Opp.*C.*2.167.

**ἐπείκοστον**, τό, a sum *greater by* $\frac{1}{20}$ than another, *PPetr.*2p.156 (ii B.C.):—also **ἐφ-** *PRev.Laws*56.15 (iii B.C.).

**ἐπεικ-τάς**· ὑπόσχεσις, σπουδή, Hsch. **-τέον**, *one must hurry*, Pl.*Lg.*687e. ❀ **-της**, ου, ὁ, *one who urges* or *presses*, *EM*356.34, *Gloss.*; coupled with ἐκβιβαστής, *Cod.Just.*7.51.5.1. **-τικός**, ή, όν, *urgent*, Sch.Il.11.165.

**ἐπεικώς**, Att. part. of ἐπέοικα (q.v.).

**ἐπειλ-έω**, *wind up*, Hero *Aut.*6.2:—Pass., Id.*Bel.*84.10. **-ησις**, εως, ἡ, *winding up*, ἐ. ποιεῖσθαι ib.85.2. II. *rolling*, of a bandage, Sor.*Fasc.*12.506C., al. **ἐπείλικτο, ἐπειλίξας**, v. ἐφελίσσω.

❀ **ἔπειμι** (A), (εἰμί *sum*) inf. ἐπεῖναι: Ep. impf. ἔπεσαν Od.2.344: fut. ἐπέσομαι, Ep. and Lyr. -έσσομαι, 4.756, Pi.*O.*13.99:—*to be upon*, c. dat. loci, κάρη ὤμοισιν ἐπείη Il.2.259; σῆμα δ' οὐκ ἐπῆν κύκλῳ A. *Th.*591; in Prose mostly with Prep., ἐπὶ τοῦ καταστρώματος ἐ. Hdt. 8.118; ἐπὶ [τῷ ποταμῷ] πύλαι ἔπεισι Id.5.52, cf. 7.176; ἐπὶ ταῖς οἰκίαις τύρσεις ἐπῆσαν X.*An.*4.4.2: abs., κώπη δ' ἐλέφαντος ἐπῆεν Od.21.7, cf. 2.344, Il.5.127, A.*Ag.*547, etc. 2. *to be upon, be set upon*, of names, οὐκ ἔπεστι ἐπωνυμίη Περσέϊ Hdt.6.53; so ψεύδεσι σεμνὸν ἔπεστί τι Pi.*N.*7.23; τοῖσι λόγοις σῶφρον ἔ. ἄνθος Ar.*Nu.*1025; *to be attached*, μελέτη δ' ἔπεστι παντί *Anacreont.*58.3; οὔτε τις τάξις οὔτε ἀνάγκη ἔπεστιν αὐτοῦ τῷ βίῳ Pl.*R.*561d; esp. of rewards and penalties, ποινά, κέρδος ἐπέσται, A.*Eu.*543 (lyr.), Ar.*Av.*597; ἔπεστι νέμεσις S.*El.*1467; ἔσχαται τιμωρίαι ἐπὶ ταῖς ἐπαγγελίαις ἔπεισιν Is.3.47, cf. Pl.*Lg.*943d: abs., Ταραντίνων οὐκ ἐπῆν ἀριθμός no count *was taken*, no number *was attached*, Hdt.7.170, cf. 191; *to be at hand, be present*, τίς τέρψις ἐπέσται; S.*Aj.*1216 (lyr.); αἰσχύνη X.*Cyr.*6.2.33; πιεῖν δὲ θάνατος οἶνον, ἣν ὕδωρ ἐπῇ Cratin.273 (s.v.l.); τὰ ἐπόντα *accidents* or *characteristics*, opp. τὸ ὑποκείμενον, Plot.2.4.10. 3. *to be in* one's *possession*, ἀνέρες οἷσιν ἔπεστι μέγα κράτος *h.Cer.*150. 4. *to be imminent*, ἐπόντος τοῦ φόβου τούτου D.21.9; εἰ μηδεὶς ἐπῆν ἀγὼν μηδὲ κίνδυνος ibid. 5. ἔπι for ἔπεστι (v. ἐπί E. II). II. of Time, *to be hereafter, remain*, ἀλλ' ἔτι πού τις ἐπέσσεται Od.4.756; *to be at hand*, οὐδέ τι δειλὸν γῆρας ἐπῆν Hes.*Op.*114; ἐπεσσόμενοι ἄνθρωποι generations *to come*, Orac.ap.Hdt.6.77, Epigr.ap.Aeschin. 3.184; ἐπεσσόμενοι alone, Theoc.12.11. III. *to be set over*, τισί Hdt.7.96, 8.71; ἔπεστί σφι δεσπότης νόμος Id.7.104; τίς δὲ ποιμάνωρ ἔ.; A.*Pers.*241 (troch.), cf. 555 (lyr.). IV. *to be added, be over and above*, of numbers, χιλιάδες ἔπεισι ἐπὶ ταύτῃσι ἑπτά Hdt.7.184, cf. 185; ἐπόντων τεσσάρων *plus* four, Arr.*Tact.*10.8; τὰ ἐπεσόμενα τούτοις (sc. προβάτοις) *Arch.Pap.*1.64 (ii B.C.). V. *to be added* as confirmation, ἔξορκος ἐπέσσεται Pi.*O.*13.99. 2. *belong in addition*, τὰν περὶ αὐτὸ χώραν ἐπείμειν Πριανέων *Schwyzer*289.27 (ii B.C.).

❀ **ἔπειμι** (B), (εἶμι *ibo*) inf. ἐπιέναι, serving in Att. as fut. of ἐπέρχομαι: Ep. 3 sg. impf. ἐπῄιεν Il.17.741; 3 pl. ἐπήϊσαν Od.11.233, ἐπῇσαν 19.445; Att. ἐπῇα, 3 pl. ἐπῇσαν: ἐπιείσομαι, -εισαμένη (qq.v.) belong to a different word: I. *come upon* (in fut. sense, though this is not so fixed in Hom. as in Att.): 1. of persons, *come upon, approach*, Od. 16.42, etc. b. mostly in hostile sense, *come against, attack*, c. dat., Il. 13.482, etc.; τῷ λόφῳ ἐ. Th.4.129; in Prose also with Preps., ἐ. ἐπὶ τὴν Ἑλλάδα, ἐπὶ τοὺς ἀδικοῦντας, Hdt.7.157, Th.1.86 (v.l. πρός), etc.; πρὸς τὸ τεῖχος Id.7.4: abs., Αἰνείαν ἐπιόντα Il.13.477, cf. 5.238; ἐπάγοντες ἐπῇσαν Od.19.445: οἱ ἐπιόντες the *invaders, assailants*, Hdt.4.11, etc.; ὡς ἐπιὼν *by assault*, D.1.21; but ὁ ἐπιών in Trag., = ὁ τυχών, the *first comer*, τό γ' αἴνιγμ' οὐχὶ τοὐπιόντος ἦν ἀνδρὸς διειπεῖν S.*OT* 393, cf. *OC*752. c. *get on the* βῆμα to speak, v.l. for παριέναι in Th.1.72; *come on*, of performers, dub. l. in X.*An.*6.1.11. d. *approach, attack* a question, Arist.*Ph.*186$^a$4. 2. of events, *come upon* or *over* one, *overtake*, c. acc., πρίν μιν καὶ γῆρας ἔπεισιν Il.1.29 (but ἔπειμι γῆρας ἔς τε τὸν μόρσιμον αἰῶνα Pi.*I.*7(6).41); οἷός σε χειμὼν καὶ κακῶν τρικυμία ἔπεισι A.*Pr.*1016: c. dat., *come near*, ὀρυμαγδὸς ἐπῄιεν ἐρχομένοισιν Il.17.741; δεινῶν ἐπιόντων πᾶσι Ἕλλησι *threatening* them, Hdt.7.145: abs., χειμὼν ἐπιών Hes.*Op.*675; νὺξ ἐπῄει A.*Pers.*378, cf. X.*Mem.*4.3.14, *An.*5.7.12; τὸ ἐπιόν the (madness) which *threatens* me, Pl.*Phdr.*238d. b. c. dat. pers., *come into* one's *head, occur* to one, εἰ καὶ ἐπίοι αὐτῷ λέγειν if it so much as *occurred* to him to say.., Id.*R.*388d, cf. 558a; ὅ τι ἂν ἀπὸ ταὐτομάτου ἐπίῃ μοι X.*Mem.*4.2.4; ἃν.. ὑμῖν ἐπίῃ σκοπεῖν D.21.185: abs., τὸ ἐπιόν *what occurs to one*, Pl.*Phdr.*264b. II. of Time, *come on* or *after*: mostly in part. ἐπιών, οὖσα, όν, *following, succeeding, instant*, ἡ ἐπιοῦσα ἡμέρα the *coming* day, Hdt.3.85, Ar.*Ec.*105, Pl.*Cri.*44a; ἡ 'πιοῦσα λαμπὰς θεοῦ E.*Med.*352; ἡ ἐπιοῦσα (sc. ἡμέρα) Plb.2.25.11, Lxx *Pr.*27.1, *Act. Ap.*16.11; τῆς ἐ. νυκτός Pl.*Cri.*46a; τῇ ἐ. νυκτί *Act.Ap.*23.11; ὁ ἐ. βίοτος E.*Or.*1659; τοῦ ἐ. χρόνου Pl.*Lg.*769c; ἐν τῷ ἐ. χρόνῳ X.*Cyr.*2.1.23; ἡ ἐ. ὥρα τοῦ ἔτους D.8.18; εἰς τὴν ἐ. ἐκκλησίαν Id.21.162, *IG* 2$^2$.717.16; εἰς τὴν ἐ. Πυλαίαν D.18.151; τοὐπιόν *the future*, E.*Fr.*1073.6; τῆς ἐ. ἐλπίδος Ar.*Th.*870; περὶ τῶν ἐπιόντων D.*Ep.*4.3; τῶν ἐ. ἕνεκα because of the *consequences*, Id.19.258. 2. generally, *come after, succeed*, κύματα.. βάντ' ἐπιόντα τε S.*Tr.*115 (lyr.); ὁ ἐπιών the *successor*, Id.*OC*1532; αὐτόματα ἔπεισιν ἐκ τῶν ἔμπροσθεν ἐπιτηδευμάτων Pl.*R.*427a; τὰ ἐπιόντα the words *which follow*, Id.*Prt.*344a, cf. *Sph.*257c. 3. rarely, *pass, elapse*, ἐπιόντος τοῦ χρόνου Id.*Ti.* 44b. III. *go over* a space, *traverse, visit*, ἀγρόν Od.23.359; χώρους Hdt.5.74; of an officer, ἐ. πύλας E.*Ph.*1164; τὸ στράτευμα Th.7.78, etc. 2. *go over*, i.e. *count over*, φώκας.. ἀριθμήσει καὶ ἔπεισιν Od.4.411; *think over*, τῇ μνήμῃ ἕκαστα Luc.*Herm.*1; *read*, Hld.2.6.

**ἐπείνυσθαι**, Ion. for ἐφέννυσθαι, *put on* clothes, Hdt.4.64.

**ἐπείξ-ιμος**, ον, *pressing*, ἔργα *POxy.*531.9 (ii A.D.). **-ις**, εως, ἡ, *haste, hurry*, J.*AJ*18.6.5, Plu.*Rom.*29, Ruf.ap.Orib.8.24.23, Aristid. *Or.*48(24).61, Luc.*DMeretr.*10.3, etc. 2. *emergency*, Antyll.ap. Orib.10.23.30. II. *urging, pressing*, *Gloss.*: pl., App.*BC*1.19 (s.v.l.).

**ἐπείπερ** or **ἐπεί περ**, v. ἐπεί B. 1,2,5.

**ἐπεῖπον**, aor. 2, inf. ἐπειπεῖν, pf. ἐπείρηκα Plu.2.1054f: pres. ἐπιλέγω (q.v.):—*say besides* or *afterwards*, Hdt.1.123, Th.1.67, Aeschin. 2.157, etc. 2. ψόγον ἐ. τινί *say* it *of* one, A.*Supp.*972 (anap.), cf. Luc.*Hist.Conscr.*26; σκωπτικόν τι εἴς τινα Id.*Dem.Enc.*33. 3. *quote* as apposite, τὰ ἐξ Ἰλιάδος ἐκεῖνα Ael.*VH*4.18; ἐ. τὸ κοινὸν ἀρχὴ δέ τοι ἥμισυ παντός Luc.*Somn.*3; cf. ἐπιλέγω. 4. *utter, pronounce* a spell, ἐ. ἐπῳδήν Id.*Philops.*35. 5. *make a speech at*, τάφῳ Polem.*Cyn.*2.

**ἐπείρομαι**, inf. -είρεσθαι v.l. in Hdt.7.101, al.: impf. -είρετο Id. 3.22, al.: fut. -ειρήσομαι Id.1.67, al.: used by Att. only in fut. -ερήσομαι Ar.*Lys.*98, *Pl.*32, and aor. -ηρόμην, inf. -ερέσθαι, S.*OC*557 (prob.), Th.8.29, etc.; Ion. ἐπειρέσθαι Hdt.1.19, al.:—*ask besides* or *again*, τοῦτο X.*Cyr.*6.3.10. II. c. acc. pers., *ask* or *question* him *besides*, τι *about* a thing, Ar.*Lys.*98, v.l. in Hdt.7.101; περί τινος Id. 1.158; with relat., ἐ. ὅ τι σιτέεται ὁ βασιλεύς Id.3.22; ὅντινα τρόπον Id.4.161. 2. esp. *inquire of* a god, τὸν θεόν Id.1.19; ἐπήροντο τὸν θεόν, εἰ παραδοῖεν.. Th.1.25; ἐπερησόμενος ψυχὴν ὡς τὸν θεὸν Ar.*Pl.*32; ἔπεμπον τὴν ἐς θεὸν ἐπειρησομένους τὸν χῶρον Hdt.1.67; *question* a person, S.l.c. 3. *ask* the people *for* their opinion, τὴν γνώμην Pl.*Ax.*368d, cf. D.22.5.

**ἐπειρύω**, Ep. and Ion. for ἐπερύω.

**ἐπειρωνεύομαι**, *speak ironically*, App.*BC*4.70, J.*BJ*5.13.1: c. dat., *mock at*, τὸ δαιμόνιον ἐ. ταῖς ἐκ τῶν ἐμῶν σπλάγχνων χοαῖς ib.1.3.6.

**ἐπειρωτάω** or **-έω, ἐπειρώτημα, -ησις**, Ion. for ἐπερ-.

**ἐπεισ-άγω** [ᾰ], *bring in besides* or *over*, esp. of bringing in a second wife, ὁ παισὶν αὑτοῦ μητρυιὰν ἐπεισάγων *Com.Adesp.*110.3; ἐ. [τὴν Κλεοπάτραν] τῇ Ὀλυμπιάδι Satyr.5; ἐ. ἑταίρας εἰς τὴν οἰκίαν (i.e. besides one's wife), And.4.14 (so in Med., γυναῖκα ἄλλην ἐπεισάγεσθαι ἐφ' ὕβρει Δημητρίας *PEleph.*1.8 (iv B.C.)); τινὰς εἰς τὸ δικαστήριον dub. in *CIG*5187a25 (Ptolemais):—Pass., οἱ ἐπεισαχθέντες the *newly made citizens*, D.H.2.56, cf. Luc.*Nav.*33:—Med., *introduce besides*, νέους ἑταίρους Pl.*R.*575d, cf. *Plt.*293d. 2. *bring in* something *new* or *strange*, ἔξωθεν Aeschin.1.166, etc.; ἐ. ἄλλην μηχανήν Plb.32.5.11; νόμον *introduce*, Jul.*Or.*2.88d:—Med., ὕδωρ ἐπὶ τόπους Plb.10.28.3. 3. *bring on besides*, χορείαν ἢ τράπεζαν δευτέραν Antiph.174.1; *bring next upon the stage*, Aeschin.3.231; δρᾶμα Plb. 23.10.12. 4. Med., *draw in*, τὸν οὐρανὸν ἐπεισάγεσθαι ἐκ τοῦ ἀπείρου χρόνου τε καὶ πνοὴν καὶ τὸ κενόν Arist.*Fr.*201. **-ᾰγωγή**, ἡ, *bringing*

*in besides*, ἑτέρων ἰητρῶν Hp.*Praec.*7; esp. of a second wife, J.*AJ*11.6.2; προσώπων ἐ. *introduction of new* characters, D.H.*Vett.Cens.*2.10 (pl.), cf. 3.3 (pl.); κρείττονος ἐλπίδος *Ep.Hebr.*7.19. 2. *means of bringing* or *letting in*, ἐπεσαγωγὰς τῶν πολεμίων Th.8.92. **-αγώγιμος**, ον, *brought in* from abroad, τὰ ἐ. *imported* wares, Pl.*R.*370e. **-ακτέον**, *one must introduce*, Herod.Med. in *Rh.Mus.*58.102. ⊛ **-ακτος**, ον, *brought in from outside*, opp. οἰκεῖος, [Ἔρως] διὰ τῶν ὀμμάτων Pl.*Cra.*420b; *alien*, opp. αὐτόχθων, E.*Ion*590; σῖτος D.18.87, 20.31; τροφή Hdn.8.5.4, cf. *Ostr.*757.4 (ii B.C.); ἡδονή Arist.*EN* $1169^b26$; κακόν *Com.Adesp.*110.5; γάμοι J.*AJ*8.7.5; βασιλεύς Hdn.1.5.5; θύραθεν ἐ., opp. φύσει ὑπάρχον, Arist.*PA*$659^b19$; εἰ ἐπείσακτον τὸ τῆς ἀρετῆς ἦν, καὶ μηδὲν αὐτοῦ φύσει ἡμῖν μετῆν Muson.*Fr.*2 p.6 H.: fem. [ἐπει]σάνκτην (sic) is prob. l. in *SIG*1231 (Nicomedia). 2. *capable of import*, Aristid.*Or.*36(48).17,18. ⊛ **-βαίνω**, *go into upon*, ἵππῳ εἰς θάλασσαν X.*HG*1.1.6; ἐ. ἐς τὴν θάλασσαν *go into* the sea *so as to board* ships, Th.2.90, 4.14. **-βάλλω**, *throw into besides*, ποτῷ E.*El.*498. II. intr., *invade again*, Th.3.13; of a *double attack* of fever, Gal.7.352; simply, *attack*, τῇ ἀγέλῃ Palaeph.1. **-βάτης** [ᾰ], ου, ὁ, *additional passenger, supernumerary on board* ship, E.*Hel.*1550. **-βιάζομαι**, *force one's way in besides, intrude*, ὃς δ' ἂν ἕτερος ἐπεισβιάσηται, Inscrr. on grave-stones, *CIG*3996 (Iconium), etc. **-δέχομαι**, *admit besides*, *Placit.*4.22.2. **-ειμι**, (εἶμι *ibo*) *come in besides*, τῷ οὐρανῷ Arist.*Ph.*$213^b23$; θύραθεν Id.*GA*$736^b28$; *come on* (in battle) *besides*, v.l. in Hdt.7.210; *come next upon the stage*, Aeschin.3.153; *go on into*, X.*Cyn.*10.9; *enter into*, σώματα Hierocl. *in CA*4p.425 M. 2. *come in after*, Hp.*Prorrh.*2.1; ἔξωθεν Pl.*Ti.*81d. b. *impinge*, of external stimuli, Democr.9, Pl.*Ti.*50e, Epicur.*Nat.*84,129 G.; ἀπὸ τῶν ἔξωθεν Id.*Ep.*1p.11 U. **-έλευσις**, εως, ἡ, *additional incursion* (?), Eustr. *in EN*19.34. **-ενεκτέον**, *one must bring in besides*, Stob.2.7.2. **-έρπω**, *enter into*, εἴς τι Iamb.*Myst.*8.6. **-έρρω**, *rush in with ill luck to* one, Poll.9.158, Suid. **-έρχομαι**, *come in besides*, τινί *to* one, Th.8.35; esp. into a family as stepmother, Hdt.4.154; *rush in and attack*, ἐπεισήλθοσαν τῷ Σίμωνι εἰς τὸ συμπόσιον Lxx 1 *Ma.*16.16, cf. *UPZ*13.19 (ii B.C.). 2. *come in after*, Hdt.1.37; κατόπιν τινός Pl.*Prt.*316a; and freq. in Att.; τινί D.H.*Dem.*8. 3. *come into besides*, c. acc., ξένος ἐ. πόλιν E.*Ion*813: c. dat., δόμοις ib.851 (nisi leg. δόμους); εἰς τὸ χωρίον D.47.53; of things, *to be imported*, ἐ. ἐκ πάσης γῆς τὰ πάντα Th.2.38. II. metaph., 1. of customs, *to be introduced later*, Plu.2.676f, etc. 2. *come into* one's *head, occur to* one, c. dat., ib.585f: c. acc., Luc.*VH*2.42. **-ηγέομαι**, *introduce besides into*, τὴν τῶν ἱστίων χρείαν τοῖς ναυτικοῖς D.S.5.7. **-θεσις**, εως, ἡ, *further 'indentation'*, in Kolometry, Sch.Ar.*Eq.*381. II. *insertion*, Anon.*Prog.* in Rh.1.605 W. **-θρῴσκω**, aor. 2 ἐπείσθορε, *spring in after*, *AP*6.219.7 (Antip.).

**ἐπείσιον**, v. ἐπίσιον.

**ἐπεισ-καλέω**, *co-opt*, Decr.ap.Arist.*Ath.*30.4. **-κλητος**, ον, *co-opted*, ibid. II. Subst., ἐπείσκλητος (sc. ἐκκλησία), ἡ, *specially convened meeting*, *Inscr.Magn.*44.10. **-κομίζω**, *bring in besides*, ἕτερον σῶμα ἐ. *CIG*(add.)3882i (Afium Kara Hissar), cf. *Rev.Phil.*36.53. ⊛ **-κρίνομαι** [ῑ], Pass., *to be overcharged with food*, Hp.*Alim.*5. 2. *replace losses*, οὐσία ἀεὶ ῥεῖ τε καὶ ἑτέρα ἀνθ' ἑτέρας ἐπεισκρίνεται S.E.*P.*3.82. ⊛ **-κυκλέω**, *roll* or *bring in one upon another*, 'pile up', τὰ μηδὲν προσήκοντα Luc.*Hist.Conscr.*13; ἀσάφειαν ἡμῖν τοσαύτην S.E.*P.*2.210; πλῆθος σημαινομένων Gal.8.575; ἄλλ' ἐπ' ἄλλοις Longin.22.4:—Pass., ἕτερα ἑτέροις -ούμενα Id.11.1; δ' Ἄττις καὶ ὁ Κορύβας πόθεν ἡμῖν -ήθησαν; Luc.*Deor.Conc.*9, cf. *Philops.*29. **-κύκλησις**, εως, ἡ, = ἀνακύκλησις, ἐπισύναξις, Zonar. **-κωμάζω**, *rush in like disorderly revellers*, Pl.*R.*500b; of tyrants, *Stoic.*3.191: metaph. of arguments, Pl.*Tht.*184a, cf. Luc.*Pseudol.*11: c. acc., Σωφροσύνην καὶ Ἐγκράτειαν -εκώμασαν (nisi leg. -εκόμισαν) Aristox.*Fr.Hist.*15: c. dat., *make an inroad upon*, Κελτοὶ ἐ. τῇ Ἑλλάδι Aristid.*Or.*22(19).8.

**ἐπεισοδ-ιάζω**, *import, introduce* from without, ὁ τῶν αἰσθήσεων ὄχλος ἐπεισωδίασεν [τῇ ψυχῇ] κηρῶν ἀμήχανον πλῆθος Ph.1.134:—Pass., ib.592. **-ιος**, ον, *coming in besides, adventitious*, σύμφυτον .., οὐκ ἐ. Plu.2.451c, cf. 584e; ἐ. ἀκρόαμα Id.*Luc.*40; ἐπιθυμίαι Id.*Cat.Ma.*18; φύκους ἄνθος ἐ. *AP*5.18 (Rufin.). II. **ἐπεισόδιον**, τό, *addition for the purpose of giving pleasure*, Plu.2.629c, 710d; ἐ. γαστρός, of dessert, *AP*6.232.6 (Crin.(?)). 2. in Poetry, *parenthetic addition, episode*: a. in Ep. poems, as the Catalogue in the Iliad, Arist.*Po.*$1459^a36$. b. in Tragedy, the portions of dialogue between two choric songs, ib.$1452^b20$: then of all *underplots* or *parenthetic narratives* in poetry, which might themselves form distinct wholes, ib.$1451^b34$; also in prose speeches, etc., D.H.*Comp.*19, *Isoc.*4, *Th.*7. c. in Comedy, *interlude, intermezzo*, Metag.14. 3. metaph., ἐπεισόδια τύχης Plb.2.35.5; ὅτι μὴ ἐ. τὸ σὸν τῷ παντί Plot.3.3.3. **-ιόω**, *vary by introducing episodes*, Arist.*Po.*$1455^b1$; τὸν λόγον ἐ. ἐπαίνοις Id.*Rh.*$1418^a33$. **-ιώδης**, ες, *episodic, incoherent*, μῦθος Id.*Po.*$1451^b34$: metaph., οὐκ ἔοικεν ἡ φύσις ἐ. οὖσα ὥσπερ μοχθηρὰ τραγῳδία Id.*Metaph.*$1090^b19$, cf. Dam.*Pr.*279. Adv. **-δῶς** Ascl. *in Metaph.*142.28. II. = ἐπεισόδιος I, *adventitious*, οὐ γὰρ ἔξωθεν ἐπίκτητος οὐδ' ἐ. Porph.*Sent.*36; ἐ. καὶ δευτέραν συνεπομένην ὑπόστασιν Iamb.*Protr.*3; ἐ. καὶ συμβεβηκός Dam.*Pr.*14; ἐ. καὶ ἀλλαχόθεν ἐφῆκον Procl.*Inst.*19. **-ος**, ἡ, *coming in besides, approach*, S.*OC*730, *Fr.*273; *entrance from without*, Epicur.*Nat.*21 G., *Placit.*4.22.1; ἀέρος ψυχροῦ Orib.*Fr.*38; ἀθέων λογισμῶν Ph.1.76.

⊛ **ἐπεισ-παίω**, *burst in*, ἐς τὴν οἰκίαν Ar.*Pl.*805; εἰς τὰ συμπόσια *Com.Adesp.*439: abs., Luc.*DMeretr.*15.1. **-πέμπω**, *send in* or *to*, D.C.67.17. **-πηδάω**, *leap in upon*, τοὺς εἰς τὰς τάφρους ἐμπίπτοντας -ῶντες ἐφόνευον X.*Cyr.*3.3.64; τῷ ἄρχειν *usurp*, Philostr.*VA*2.31, cf. Just.*Nov.*42 *Pr.*: abs., Ar.*Eq.*363, D.47.56, D.C.67.17. **-πηδητής**, οῦ, ὁ, *house-breaker, burglar*, Gloss. **-πίπτω**, *fall* or *burst in upon*, c. dat., ναυστάθμοις E.*Rh.*448; ἐ. αὐτοῖς πίνουσι X.*Cyr.*7.5.27: also c. acc., ἐ. πόλιν E.*HF*34: abs., τὰ ἐπεσπίπτοντα Hp.*Vict.*1.10; *burst in*, S.*OC*915, E.*Hec.*1042, J.*BJ*6.9.4. 2. *fall upon*, βρονταὶ καὶ πρηστῆρές τινι ἐπεσπίπτουσι Hdt.7.42. 3. metaph., ἐπεισπίπτει οἰκοτριβὴς δαπάνη Critias 6.14. **-πλέω**, *sail in after*, Th.6.2, X.*HG* 1.1.5; θύννων .. ἐπεισέπλει ὑπογάστρι' Eub.37. II. *sail against, attack*, Th.4.13. **-πνέω**, *breathe in again* (cf. ἐπανάκλησις II), Hp.*Epid.*2.3.7. **-πράττω**, *exact besides*, D.C.74.8. **-ρέω**, *flow in upon* or *besides*, *Trag.Adesp.*89, Ph.*Fr.*73 H., Plu.*Num.*20, Luc.*Alex.*49. **-ροή**, ἡ, *influx*, τῆς νοητῆς λαμπηδόνος *Corp.Herm.*10.4. **-ρύσις**, εως, ἡ, v. ἐπέκρυσις. **-τρέχω**, aor. -έδραμον Jul.*Caes.*309c:—*run in upon* or *after*, τινί l. c.: abs., Ph.2.128. **-φέρω**, *bring in besides* or *next*, [ἄρμενον] Hp.*Art.*4 (Pass.); κακοῦ κάκιον ἄλλο πῆμα A.*Ag.*864; τέκνον δόμοισι Id.*Ch.*649 (lyr.); ἐ. λόγον *bring in a new* argument, Ar.*Th.*1164; in Inscrr. on grave-stones, *bring in another* body, *CIG*3384 (Smyrna), al.:—Med., *bring in for oneself*, μαρτύρια Th.3.53:—Pass., *rush in besides*, Aen.Tact.39.3; τὸ αἰεὶ ἐπεσφερόμενον πρῆγμα whatever *comes upon us, occurs*, Hdt.7.50; ὁ ἐ. [νόμος] the law *newly brought in*, Arist.*Top.*$151^b13$. **-φοιτάω**, *to be in the habit of coming in*, ἔξωθεν Ph.1.615. **-φορέω**, = ἐπεισφέρω, in Pass., ib.468. II. Med., abs., *take food afterwards*, Archig.ap.Orib.8.1.7. ⊛ **-φρέω**, *bring in* or *introduce besides*, πῶς ἐπεσφρῶ τήνδε τῷ κείνης λέχει; E.*Alc.*1056; λέκτροις τ' ἐπεισέφρηκε Id.*El.*1033; ὄφεις ἐπεισέφρησε σπαργάνοις Id.*HF*1267: aor. part. ἐπεισφρείς (as if from ἐπεισπίφρημι) Id.*Fr.*781.50. II. intr., *come in besides*, Suid. **-χέω**, *pour in besides*, φῶς ἐς νοῦν Ph.1.150; ποιότητας τῇ διανοίᾳ ib.194:—Pass., ib.174, al.; of a crowd, *pour in one after another*, J.*BJ*1.18.2, 4.3.3 (v.l. ἐπιχ-).

**ἔπειτα**, Ion. and Dor. **ἔπειτε(ν)** (q.v.), Adv., (ἐπί, εἶτα): I. of mere Sequence, without any notion of cause, *thereupon, thereafter, then*, freq. from Hom. downwds., as Il.1.48, 2.169, etc.: when in strong opposition to the former act or state, with past tenses, *thereafter, afterwards*; with future, *hereafter*, ἦ πέφατ' ἦ καὶ ἐ. πεφήσεται Il.15.140; opp. αὐτίκα νῦν, 23.551; ὃς δ' ἔπειτ' ἔφυ, opp. ὅστις πάροιθεν ἦν, A.*Ag.*171 (lyr.): in Hom. freq. with other Advs., αὐτίκ' ἔ. Il.5.214; αἶψα, ὦκα ἔ., 24.783, 18.527; even ἔνθα .. ἔ. Od.10.297; δὴ ἔ. 8.378: usu. with reference to a former act, *just then, at the time*, 1.106; freq. in narrative, πρῶτα μὲν .., αὐτὰρ ἔ. Il.16.497; πρῶτον μέν .., folld. by ἔ. δέ .., Th.2.55, Pl.*Ap.*18a, etc.; by ἔ. alone, Th.1.33, etc.; by ἔ. δέ .. ἔ. δέ .. ἔ. ..., X.*Cyr.*1.3.14; ἐπεὶ δέ .. ἔ. .. ἔ. .. ἔ. δέ, ib.8.3.24, al.; πρὶν μέν .., ἔ. δέ .. S.*El.*724; ἔ. γε Pl.*Tht.*147c, etc., f.l. in Ar.*Th.*556; κἄπειτα, freq. in Trag., S.*Aj.*61, 305, etc. 2. c. Art., τὸ ἔ. *what follows*, τό τ' ἔ. καὶ τὸ μέλλον καὶ τὸ πρίν Id.*Ant.*611 (lyr.); τά τε πρῶτα, τά τ' ἔ., ὅσα τ' ἔμελλε τυχεῖν E.*IT*1265 (lyr.); οἱ ἔ. *future generations*, A.*Eu.*672; ὁ ἔ. βίος Pl.*Phd.*116a; εἰς τὸν ἔ. χρόνον Id.*Phlb.*39e, X.*Cyr.*1.5.9, *OGI*90.43 (Rosetta, ii B.C.); ἡ ἐς τὸ ἔ. δόξα Th.2.64; ἐν τῷ ἔ. Pl.*Phd.*67d; ἐκ τοῦ ποτὲ εἰς τὸ ἔ. Id.*Prm.*152b. 3. like εἶτα, with a finite Verb after a participle, μειδήσασα δ' ἔ. ἑῷ ἐγκάτθετο κόλπῳ she smiled and *then* placed it in her bosom, Il.14.223, cf. 11.730, etc.: freq. in Trag. and Att., A.*Th.*267, *Eu.*29, Pl.*Phd.*82c: so freq. when part. and Verb are opposed, marking surprise or the like, *and then, and yet, nevertheless*, τὸ μητρὸς αἷμα .. ἐκχέας πέδοι ἔ. δώματ' οἰκήσει πατρός; A.*Eu.*654, cf. 438; χὤταν ἐν κακοῖσί τις ἀλοὺς ἔ. τοῦτο καλλύνειν θέλῃ S.*Ant.*496; ὅστις ἀνθρώπου φύσιν βλαστὼν ἔ. μὴ κατ' ἄνθρωπον φρονῇ Id.*Aj.*761; εἰ πτωχὸς ὢν ἔπειτ' ἐν Ἀθηναίοις λέγειν μέλλω Ar.*Ach.*498, cf. *Av.*29, Pl.*Grg.*519e, *Prt.*319d: adversatively, answering μέν, πολλάκις μὲν ὡρμᾶ .., ἔ .. διεκωλύετο Id.*R.*336b; ἔτι μὲν ἐνεχείρησα .., ἔ .. Id.*Prt.*310c, etc.; also κἄπειτα after a part., Ar.*Nu.*624, *Av.*536; cf. εἶτα I. 2. 4. in apodosi (never at the beginning of the clause; in Hom. freq. strengthd. by other Particles): a. after a Temporal Conj., *then, thereafter*, ἐπεὶ δὴ σφαίρῃ πειρήσαντο, ὀρχείσθην δὴ ἔ. when they had done playing at ball, *then* they danced, Od.8.378; after ἐπεί, Il.16.247; ἐπὴν .. δὴ ἔ. Od.11.121; ὁπότε, Il.18.545; ὅτε, 3.223; ὡς .. ἄρ' ἔ. 10.522; ἦμος .. καὶ τότ' ἔ. 1.478. b. after a Conditional Conj., *then surely*, εἰ δ' ἐτεὸν δὴ .. ἀγορεύεις, ἐξ ἄρα δή τοι ἔ. θεοὶ φρένας ὤλεσαν if thou speakest sooth, *then of a surety* have the gods infatuated thee, 7.360, cf. 10.453, Od.1.290, etc.; so after ἦν, Il.9.394; also when the apodosis takes the form of a question, εἰ μὲν δὴ ἕταρόν γε κελεύετέ μ' αὐτὸν ἑλέσθαι, πῶς ἂν ἔ. Ὀδυσῆος λαθοίμην; how can I *in such a case*? 10.243; when a condition is implied in relat. Pron., ὃν (= εἴ τινα) μέν κ' ἐπιεικὲς ἀκουέμεν, οὔ τις ἔ. τόν γ' εἴσεται 1.547; ὃν (= εἴ τινα) δέ κ' ἐγὼν ἀπάνευθε μάχης ἐθέλοντα νοήσω μιμνάζειν, οὔ οἱ ἔ. ἄρκιον ἐσσεῖται 2.392. II. of Sequence in thought, i.e. Consequence or Inference, *then, therefore*, ξεῖν', ἐπεὶ ἂρ δὴ ἔ. .. μενεαίνεις Od.17.185, cf. Il.15.49, 18.357; οὐ σύ γ' ἔ. Τυδέος ἔκγονός ἐσσι 5.812; rarely at the beginning, ἔπειθ' ἑλοῦ γε θάτερα S.*El.*345. 2. in telling a story, νῆσος ἔ. τις ἔστι *now*, there is an island, Od.4.354, cf. 9.116. 3. in Att. freq. to introduce emphatic questions, *why then* ..? ἔ. τοῦ δέει; Ar.*Pl.*827, cf. *Th.*188, *Nu.*226; mostly to express surprise, or to sneer, *and so forsooth* ..? *and so really* ..? ἔ. οὐκ οἴει φροντίζειν [τοὺς θεοὺς τῶν ἀνθρώπων]; X.*Mem.*1.4.11; so κἄπειτα E.*Med.*1398 (anap.), Ar.*Ach.*126, *Av.*963, X.*Smp.*4.2; freq. with δῆτα added, ἔ. δῆτα δοῦλος ὢν κόμην ἔχεις; Ar.*Av.*911, cf. 1217, *Lys.*985, E.*Alc.*822.

**ἐπείτε** or **ἐπεί τε,** *when* or *since,* Il.11.87,12.393, Hdt.1.14,48, etc.: **ἐπεί τε ἄν, ἐπεί τ' ἄν,** Hdt.1.200,202, *OGI*213.24,35, *SIG*577.30(Milet., iii/ii B.C.).

**ἔπειτε,** Ion. for ἔπειτα, *thereafter,* prob. in Hdt.1.146, 2.52, al., cf. *SIG*²660.2 (Milet., iv B.C.), but ἔπειτεν is Ion. acc. to Ael.Dion.*Fr.*158; Dor. **ἔπειτεν** Pi.*P.*4.211, *N.*3.54, al., Ar.*Ach.*745, *IG*5(1).1390.28 (Andania).

**ἐπέκ,** v. ἐπές.

**ἐπεκ-βαίνω,** *go out upon, disembark,* ἐς γῆν Th.8.105: abs., Id.1.49: c. acc., ἐ. χέρσον, of waves, *go out over, AP*7.393 (Diocl., χέρσῳ cod.), 9.276 (Crin.). **-βάλλω,** *prolong* an incision, Antyll.ap. Orib.45.26.3. II. Geom., *produce,* Archim.*Spir.Praef.* (Pass.); τὸ μῆκος Iamb.*in Nic.*p.57 P. **-βοάω,** *cry out against,* D.C.43.24 codd. **-βοηθέω,** *rush out to aid,* Th.7.53, 8.55. **-δῐδάσκω,** *teach* or *explain besides,* τι Pl.*Prt.*328e; ὡς.. Id.*Euthphr.*7a; ὅπως.. Plu.*Sol.*25; ὁ -διδάσκων λόγος Plb.15.35.7:—Pass., Gal.*Libr.Propr.*1. **-δῐδᾰχή,** ἡ, *added explanation,* Choerob.Rh.22. **-δίδωμι,** *farm out a contract again, IG*7.3073.38 (Lebad.). II. *publish again,* Sch.Il.19.365 (Pass.). **-διηγέομαι,** *explain besides,* Pl.*Phd.*97e. ⊕ **-δῐκέω,** *avenge,* τινί Tz.*H.*10.428. **-δρομή,** ἡ, *sally, sortie,* Th.4.25, Procop.*Vand.*2.8, al.; *raid,* D.C.46.38.

**ἐπέκεινα,** Adv., for ἐπ' ἐκεῖνα, opp. ἐπὶ τάδε (Pl.*Phd.*112b), *on yonder side, beyond,* c. gen., Hecat.ap.Str.12.3.23; τοῦ Ἡρακλείου ἐ. X.*HG*5.1.10; οἱ ἐ. Τίγριδος καὶ Εὐφράτου Hdn.2.8.8; ἐ. ἐλθεῖν Διονύσου *farther than..,* Arr.*An.*5.2.1: metaph., ἐ. τῆς οὐσίας ὑπερέχειν Pl.*R.*509b; ἐλπίδος ἐ. Hld.9.5. 2. with Art., τὸ ἐ., Att. τοὐπ., or τὰ ἐ., Att. τἀπ., the *part beyond,* the *far side,* τὰ ἐ. τῆς Εὐρώπης Hdt.3.115, cf. Th.6.63, etc.; τοὐπέκεινα τῆσδε γῆς *beyond* it, E.*Hipp.*1199; Πίνδου τε τἀπ. A.*Supp.*257, cf. X.*HG*5.1.10: abs., οἱ ἐκ τοῦ ἐ. Id.*An.*5.4.3; ἐν τῷ ἐ. Th.7.58; τῶν νόθων [ἡδονῶν] εἰς τὸ ἐ. ὑπερβὰς Pl.*R.*587c; τὸ ἐ. τοῦ νοῦ Porph.*Sent.*25, Jul.*Or.*4.132c. II. of past Time, οἱ ἐ. χρόνοι the times *beyond* or *before, earlier* times, Isoc.6.41; οἱ ἐ. (sc. τῶν Τρωϊκῶν γενόμενοι) Id.9.6. 2. of future Time, *henceforth,* Lxx 1*Ma.*10.30, Thd.*Su.*64.

**ἐπεκέκλετο,** v. ἐπικέλομαι. **ἐπεκήκατο·** ἐπωνείδιστο, Hsch.

**ἐπέκ-θεσις,** εως, ἡ, *further* ἔκθεσις, Sch.Ar.*Nu.*456. **-θέω,** = ἐπεκτρέχω, Th.4.34, 5.9, X.*HG*5.3.6; ἐς τὰς τάξεις Arr.*An.*5.17.3; τῷ τάγματι Plb.*Fr.*122. **-θύομαι,** *offer sacrifice for,* Arr.*Epict.*2.7.9, Gal.9.833. **-κουφίζω,** *lighten,* τὰς ἐτησίους εἰσφορὰς J.*BJ*1.21.12. **-κρῐσις,** εως, ἡ, *secretion* or *expulsion* of bodies, cj. in Leucipp.ap.D.L.9.32 (ἐπέκρυσιν codd.). **-λέγομαι,** *choose, select,* Procop.*Arc.*6. **-πίνω** [ῐ], *drink off after,* E.*Cyc.*327. **-πλέω,** *sail out against,* v.l. in Th.7.37. **-πλοος,** contr. **-πλους,** ὁ, *sailing out against, attack by sea,* ἐ. ποιεῖσθαι Id.8.20. **-πνέω,** *breathe out twice,* opp. ἐπεισπνέω, Gal.10.700. **-ρηξις,** εως, ἡ, *outbreak, bursting out,* Epicur.*Ep.*2p.54U. **-ροφέω,** *swallow up,* dub. l. in Ar.*Eq.*701; v. ἐκρ-. **-ρῠσις,** εως, ἡ, *influx from without,* Leucipp.ap.D.L.9.32 (nisi leg. ἐπείσρυσις vel ἐπέκκρισις). **-τᾰσις,** εως, ἡ, *extension,* Arist.*Cael.*305ᵇ18; ἔχειν ἐ. to be capable of *extension,* Id.*LI*971ᵇ1. b. of Time, Just.*Nov.*111.1. 2. *explication, evolution,* εἰς ἐνέργειαν καὶ ἐ. προχωρεῖν *Theol.Ar.*14. 3. *stretching* of a rope, Hero *Aut.*2.4; of strands of gut, Ph.*Bel.*58.13; of hernia, κατ' ἐπέκτασιν Heliod.ap.Orib.50.42. 4. οἱ κατ' ἐπέκτασιν παραλελυμένοι patients suffering from *creeping* paralysis, Herod.Med.ap. Orib.10.8.1. II. *lengthening* of a word, Arist.*Po.*1458ᵇ2 (pl.), 1458ᵃ23, A.D.*Pron.*6.14, al.; of a vowel, Id.*Adv.*144.19. **-τᾰτικός,** ή, όν, *lengthening,* Eust.1393.14. ⊕ **-τείνω,** *stretch,* Sor.1.10 (Pass.), al.; *extend,* τὸ αὔταρκες] ἐπὶ τοὺς ἀπογόνους Arist.*EN*1097ᵇ12:—Pass., *to be extended, extend,* Id.*Ph.*217ᵇ9, etc. 2. intr., *extend,* ἐπὶ πλέον Id.*APo.*96ᵃ24; of a people or country, μέχρι.. Str.8.3.11: c. dat., *extend over,* Olymp.*in Mete.*75.12. 3. Pass., *extend beyond,* τῆς οἰκείας ὥρας Thphr.*HP*6.8.4; *reach out towards,* τοῖς ἔμπροσθεν *Ep.Phil.*3.13. 4. Tact., *extend,* τοὺς ἱππέας Ascl.*Tact.*10.20. 5. *expand,* ἓν νόημα Hermog.*Inv.*4.4. II. *lengthen, prolong,* λόγους Plu.2.1147. 2. *pronounce* a syllable *as long,* Arist.*Metaph.*1014ᵇ17. 3. *lengthen* a word, by inserting a vowel or otherwise (as πόληος for πόλεως), ἐπεκτεταμένον, opp. ἀφῃρημένον, Id.*Po.*1457ᵇ35; also by adding a syllable, in Pass., A.D.*Pron.*34.5, al. III. *make more burdensome,* τὰς προσόδους Str.17.1.15. **-τετᾰμένως,** Adv., (ἐπεκτείνω) *vehemently,* θρηνεῖν Sch.A.*Pers.*1051. **-τίνω,** Cret. aor. inf. ἐπεσ-τεῖσαι, *pay up,* τὸ ἁπλόον *GDI*4993 (Gortyn). **-τρέχω,** aor. 2 -έδρᾰμον, *sally out upon* or *against,* πελτασταῖς ἐκ τοῦ τείχους X.*HG*4.4.17: abs., ib.6.2.17: c. acc., *raid,* Paus.1.20.5. **-φέρω,** *carry out,* f.l. for ὑπ- in Plu.*Alex.*26. II. *seek to enforce* a contract, *PEleph.*1.14,16 (iv B.C.). **-φώνησις,** εως, ἡ, *exclamation,* Anon.*Fig.* in *Rhet.Lat.Min.*p.66 Halm. **-χέω,** *pour out upon,* Anon.ap.Suid. s. v. θραυλοτέρας:—Pass., *rush upon,* τοῖς πολεμίοις Lxx *Ju.*15.4, cf. *PTeb.*39.24 (ii B.C.); *to be stretched upon,* τινί Q.S.10.481. **-χράομαι,** *abuse, misuse, PRyl.*75.18 (ii A.D.). **-χωρέω,** *advance next* or *after,* A.*Pers.*401.

**ἐπελ-ᾰσία,** ἡ, *driving away,* 'lifting', [ἵππων] D.S.36.4. **-ᾰσις,** εως, ἡ, *charge,* of cavalry, Arr.*Tact.*16.10 (pl.), al.; ποιεῖσθαι τὰς ἐ. Plu.*Tim.*27, cf. Jul.*Or.*2.60b, Agath.1.14, al.; of elephants, Luc.*Hist.Conscr.*31.

⊕ **ἐπελαύνω,** *drive upon,* τὰς ἁμάξας ἐπελαύνουσι, i.e. *upon* the ice, Hdt.4.28. b. *drive to* a place, ἐπελάντω (non-thematic 3 pl. imper.) βοῦς τρεῖς *SIG*1025.11 (Cos). 2. in Hom., *lay* metal *beaten out into plates over* a surface (cf. ἐλαύνω III. 1), ἐπὶ δ' ὄγδοον ἤλασε χαλκόν Il.7.223; πολλὸς δ' ἐπελήλατο χαλκὸς 13.804, cf. 17.493. 3. metaph., ὅρκους ἐπελαύνειν τινί *force* an oath *upon* one, Hdt.1.146, cf. 6.62. II. *drive* or *ride against,* ἵππον τινί X.*Eq.*8.11; *lead against,* τὴν στρατιήν Hdt.1.164; *push forcibly against,* στέρνα θ' ὁμοῦ καὶ χεῖρας A.R.1.381. 2. intr., *march against,* Hdt.1.17, al.; τινί X.*HG*7.1.21; ἐπὶ Βαβυλῶνα Hdt.3.151, cf. 7.9.α'; ἐπήλασαν οἱ ἱππόται *charged,* Id.9.49, cf. 18, Arr.*Tact.*4.7, al.; τρεῖς [νῆες] ἐπήλασαν περὶ τὸ ἕρμα *drove upon* the rock, Hdt.7.183: c. acc. loci, *march over,* Luc.*Rh.Pr.*5. III. Pass., *to be driven in after,* τὸ -όμενον [τοῦ τομέως] X.*Eq.Mag.*2.3. IV. Med., 3 pl. aor. imper., ἐπελασάσθων οἱ ἁλιασταί let them *impose a fine, IG*5(2).6.23 (Tegea): 3 pl. pres. imper. (non-thematic), ἐπελάσθω (fr. *ἐπελάνσθω) τὰ ἐπιζάμια *Tab.Heracl.*1.127.

**ἐπελαφρ-ίζω,** *lighten, make easy to bear,* ἀτυχήματα, etc., Ph.2.339, al.:—Med., metaph. of persons, ἔχοντες παραμύθιον ἐ. τὰς ἀνίας ib.420; of birds, κακοπαθείας τῷ εὐσεβεῖν ib.200:—Pass., *to be made lighter,* ib.621: metaph., ψυχὴ ἐ. ὑπὸ πενθείας Id.1.351. **-ύνω,** *lighten,* τὸν δεσμόν τινι Plu.2.165e; πόνον J.*AJ*18.1.1, cf. D.Chr.3.123, Max.Tyr.37.5, Hierocl.*in CA*15p.454M.

**ἐπέλδομαι,** v. ἐπιέλδ-.

⊕ **ἐπελέγχω,** = ἐλέγχω, D.L.6.97, *POxy.*64.4 (Pass., iii/iv A.D.).

**ἐπελευθεριάζω,** *act with free will,* Ph.2.328.

⊕ **ἐπελ-εύθω,** aor. 1 ἐπήλευσα, *bring* a child *to* its father, *Leg.Gort.*3.45, al. ⊕ **-ευσις,** εως, ἡ, *coming on* or *to, arrival,* ὄχλων *Cat.Cod. Astr.*7.132, cf. Eust.1574.59; *touching on* a thing, *survey* of it, Id. ad D.P.*Prooem.*p.71B.; so [μέγεθος] ἐν διεξόδῳ καὶ ἐ. καθ' ἕκαστον μέρος αἰσθανόμεθα Plot.2.8.1, cf. Them.*in de An.*30.33. 2. *adventitious impulse,* Chrysipp.*Stoic.*2.282. 3. in Law, *prosecution, PFay.*26.14 (ii A.D.), *POxy.*1638.13 (iii A.D.). **-ευστικός,** ή, όν, *coming on* or *to, touching on* a thing: hence, of casual mention, Eust.ad D.P.*Prooem.*p.69B. Adv. -κῶς Eust.1440.18, 7.26 (Comp.). 2. *of the nature of* ἐπέλευσις 2, κίνησις Chrysipp.*Stoic.*2.282. 3. *occurring casually,* εἶδος ἐν τοῖς λόγοις Str.12.3.27. 4. *liable to prosecution, POxy.*1120.10 (iii A.D.).

**ἐπελήλᾰτο,** 3 sg. plpf. Pass. of ἐπελαύνω. **ἐπέλησε,** v. ἐπιλήθω. **ἐπέλι(γ)ξεν·** ἐπέδραμεν, Hsch.; cf. πελίγξαι. **ἐπελίσσω, ἐπέλκω,** Ion. for ἐφελ-. **ἐπέλλᾰβε,** poet. for ἐπέλαβε, 3 sg. aor. 2 of ἐπιλαμβάνω.

**ἐπελλύχνιον,** τό, *lamp-oil, PRev.Laws* 40.10, 55.9 (iii B.C.).

**ἐπελπίζω,** *buoy up with hope,* αὐτοὺς θειάσαντες ἐπήλπισαν, ὡς λήψονται Th.8.1, cf. Anon.ap.Suid. s. v. Πυθαγόρας, Longin.44.2, Luc.*DMort.*5.2. II. intr., ἐ. τινί *pin one's hopes upon, hope in,* Hld.7.26; ἐπί τινι D.C.41.11: abs., Luc.*Tim.*21; but also, 2. merely, = ἐλπίζω, E.*Hipp.*1011, Ph.1.74, al.; *hope besides,* Th.8.54 (v.l. ἐλπίζων).

**ἐπέλπομαι,** Ep. **ἐπιέλπομαι,** poet. Verb, *have hopes of, hope,* c. inf. fut., μὴ δὴ.. ἐμοὺς ἐπιέλπεο μύθους εἰδήσειν Il.1.545; ἐπιελπόμενος τό γε θυμῷ, νευρὴν ἐντανύειν (fut. inf., v.l. -σειν) Od.21.126; οὐδὲν ἐπελπομένα.. ἐκτολυπεύσειν A.*Ag.*1031 (lyr.): generally, *expect,* Telest.1.1.

**ἐπεμ-βᾰδόν,** Adv. *step upon step, AP*9.668 (Marian.). **-βαίνω,** *step* or *tread upon,* in pf., *stand upon,* c. gen., οὐδοῦ ἐπεμβεβαὼς Il.9.582; σῆς ἐπεμβαίνων χθονὸς S.*OC*924; δίφρου ἐπεμβεβαὼς *mounted on* a chariot, Hes.*Sc.*324; ὄχθων ἐπεμβὰς E.*Ba.*1061 codd.: abs., ἐπεμβεβαὼς Pi.*N.*4.29: also c. dat., *approach, attack,* πύργοις ἐπεμβὰς A.*Th.*634, etc.; τῷ δήμῳ Hyp.*Phil.Fr.*10; ἐ. ἀλλοτρίαις ἕδραις Gal.*UP*14.14: c. acc., ῥάχιν E.*Rh.*783: with a Prep., εἰς πάτραν ὅτι ποτ' ἐπεμβάσῃ Id.*IT*649 (lyr.). 2. *embark* on ship-board, D.50.25. II. c. dat. pers., *trample upon,* ἐχθροῖσιν.. ἐπεμβῆναι ποδὶ S.*El.*456: metaph., παισὶ δ' ἐπεμβαίνειν E.*Hipp.*668; κατ' ἐμοῦ.. μᾶλλον ἐπεμβάσει S.*El.*836 (lyr.); ἁμαρτήμασί τινων Plu.2.59d. 2. τῷ καιρῷ ἐπεμβαίνων *taking advantage of* the opportunity, D.21.203. ⊕ **-βάλλω,** *put on,* πῶμα πίθοιο Hes.*Op.*98; στόμ' ἐ. ἐμοί E.*IT*935; γιγνώσκοντι ἐ. *heap words on* one who already knows, Arist.*Rh.*1406ᵃ34. 2. *throw down upon,* δόμους ἐπεμβαλῶ *will throw* them *on* [the inmates], E.*HF*864: c. acc. loci, ὄχθον ὡς ἐπεμβάλῃ *that* she *may dash* [her] *upon* it (dub. constr.), Id.*IT*290. 3. *intercalate,* Hdt.2.4; *insert,* Pl.*Cra.*399a; πολλὰ ἐπὶ τὰ πρῶτα ὀνόματα ib.414d; of parentheses, Hermog.*Id.*1.12 (Pass.), cf. 1.4, al.; of ingredients in a salad, Gal.6.539: metaph., γῆς σωτῆρα σαυτὸν τῷδ' ἐπεμβάλλεις λόγῳ by this story thou *foistest* thyself *in, intrudest* thyself, as saviour of the land, S.*OC*463: in Inscrr. on grave-stones, *put in another* corpse, *IGRom.*4.1284, al. (Thyatira):—Med., *make fresh additions,* of sculptors, Pl.*Plt.*277a:—Pass., of fruit-trees, *to be engrafted,* Ath.14.653d; cf. ἐπεμβολάς. 4. *thrust on,* X.*Cyn.*10.11. II. intr., *flow in besides,* of rivers, Id.*HG*4.2.11. III. ἐπεμβάλλεται· τρώγει, Hsch. **-βᾰσις,** εως, ἡ, *attack, advance,* D.H.3.19 (pl.). 2. pl., *steps,* τῶν κρηπίδων *IG*2².1671.10,13 (iv B.C.). II. Astrol., *commencement of* χρονοκρατορία, Man.5.80, Ptol.*Tetr.*141, al., Paul.Al.*R.*3. **-βᾰτήρ,** ῆρος, ὁ, = sq.; v. ἐπαμβατήρ. **-βάτης** [ᾰ], ου, ὁ, *one mounted,* ἵππων ἐπεμβάται E.*Ba.*782: abs., *horseman,* Anacr.75.6; also ἁρμάτων ἐ. E.*Supp.*585: abs., ib.685. II. *one who walks on* or *in,* ἐπεμβάται ἴχνεσι κούφοις Orph.*H.*31.3. **-βᾰφίζω,** *bathe again,* Hsch. s. v. κἀπεμβαφίζων: glossed by **-βάπτω. -βῐβάζω,** *put into* a bath *again,* Antyll.ap.Orib.10.13.19. 2. *place on top,* Mich.*in PN*68.5. **-βλέπω,** *gaze at,* τινί prob.l. in D.Chr.4.95. **-βλημα,** ατος, τό, in pl., *the upper* ἀποστηρίγματα (q.v.), Gal.18(2).919. **-βλητέον,** *one must insert,* Pl.*Ti.*51d. **-βοάω,** *raise* a shout, μακρὸν ἐπεμβοάᾳ γλώσσῃ θρόον Nic.*Al.*219. **-βολάς,** άδος, ἡ, of fruit-trees, *grafted,* Arist.*Fr.*274. **-βολέω,** Astrol., =

μεσεμβολέω, *Cat.Cod.Astr.*1.107. **–βολή,** ἡ, *insertion, parenthesis,* Hermog.*Id.*1.1, al., Eust.48.46, etc. 2. *placing over* so as to fasten, Heliod.ap.Orib.48.33.4. **–βόλιμος,** ον, *intrusive,* θεός Lyd. *Mag.*2.3. 2. = ἐμβόλιμος, *intercalary, Gloss.* **–βολος,** ον, = foreg. 2, *CIG*2722.3 (Stratonicea). **–βρίθω** [ι], *bear heavily on,* c. acc., *PFlor.*93.14 (vi A.D.):—Med., *overcome,* ἀηδία ἐ. τινάς *PMasp.*153.13 (vi A.D.). **–βρῑμάομαι,** *to be indignant, rage against,* Sch. rec.A.*Pr.*73. **–μηνος,** ον, *in menstruation,* γυναιξὶν –οις (v.l. ἐπ' ἐμμ.) J.*BJ*6.9.3. ⊛ **–πηδάω,** *trample upon,* τινὶ κειμένῳ Ar.*Nu.*550. II. *make a second throb,* of the pulse, Gal.8.556. **–πίνω** [ῑ], gloss on ἐπεγκανάσσω, Hsch. **–πίπτω,** *fall upon, attack furiously,* ἀλλήλοις Ph.2.109; ποίμναις ἐπεμπίπτειν βάσιν S.*Aj.*42. 2. *fall to, set to work,* Ar.*Pax*471. 3. *fit in,* of cogs, v.l. in Heliod.ap.Orib.49.4.65.

⊛ **ἐπεμφέρω,** *bring in besides, add,* ἀνάγκην τινί Hippodam.ap.Stob. 4.39.26:—Pass., Nic.*Al.*28.

**ἐπέναρ·** εἰς τετάρτην (Lacon.), Hsch.; cf. ἔναρ.

**ἐπενᾰρίζω,** *kill one over another,* S.*OC*1733 (Elmsl. for ἐνάριξον).

**ἐπεν-δίδωμι,** *give over and above,* ἐ. τρίτην *I put in yet a third blow,* A.*Ag.*1386. **–δίημι,** = ἐπαφίημι, Ep. 3 pl. aor. 2 ἐπενδίεσαν, Hsch. **–δῐκάζω,** *contest a claim in court, BGU*1105.31 (i A.D.). **–δῠμα,** ατος, τό, *upper garment,* Aq.*Ex.*28.26, al., f.l. in Plu.*Alex.*32. **–δύνω** [ῡ] or **–δύω,** *put on over,* ἐπὶ τοῦτον ἄλλον κιθῶνα Hdt.1.195:—Med., –σάμενος χιτῶνα J.*AJ*3.7.4; πολλὰ σώματα Aen.Gaz.*Thphr.*p.60 B.:—Pass. (with aor. 2 part. –δύντες J.*AJ*5.1.12), *have on over,* ἐσθῆτας ἐπενδεδυμένοι γυναικείας τοῖς θώραξι Plu.*Pel.*11. ⊛ **–δύτης** [ῠ], ου, ὁ, *robe* or *garment worn over* another, Ps.-Thesp.1, S.*Fr.*439, Lxx 1 *Ki.*18.4; ἐ. χιτών Nicoch.5, cf. Ael.Dion.*Fr.*325, Poll.7.45. **–δῠτοπάλλιον,** τό, = foreg., *CIG*2663 (Halic.). **–δύω,** v. ἐπενδύνω.

**ἐπένε⟨γ⟩ξις,** εως, ἡ, (ἐπενεγκεῖν) *adding, EM*354.30.

**ἐπένερθε,** Adv. *below, Ath.Mitt.*49.15 (Argos).

**ἐπενέχῠρον,** τό, *deed giving security, BGU*993iii 11 (ii B.C.).

**ἐπενήνεον,** impf. of ἐπινηνέω (q.v.). ⊛ **ἐπενήνοθε,** 3 sg. plpf. and pf., thrice in Hom.; of Thersites' head, ψεδνὴ ἐ. λάχνη *a thin coat of downy hair grew thereon,* Il.2.219; of a cloak, οὔλη ἐ. λάχνη *a thick pile was on it,* 10.134: c. acc., of the ambrosial unguent, οἷα θεοὺς ἐ. αἰὲν ἐόντας such as *is on* the gods, Od.8.365, *h.Ven.*62: c. dat., *stick to,* στομίοισι πέριξ ἐ. γαστρός, of leeches when swallowed, Nic.*Al.*509: perh. related to ἐπανθέω. 2. of Time, πουλὺς ἐ. αἰών *had passed,* A.R.4.276. (Cf. κατ–, παρ–; also ἀνήνοθε: ἐπανήνοθε shd. perh. be restored in signf. 1.)

⊛ **ἐπεν-θάπτω,** *bury as well in* a tomb, *Anatolian Studies* 204 (Termessus). **–θεσις,** εως, ἡ, *insertion,* as of a letter, A.D.*Pron.*82.4; of a word, Id.*Synt.*78.24, Phlp.*in APo.*186.26; *application* of a drug, Paul.Aeg.6.42. **–θετικός,** ή, όν, *inserted,* Sch.Il.13.137 (cod. Basil.ap.Valck.Hdt.5.92). **–θήκη,** ἡ, = ἐπένθεσις, Eust.1349.31. **–θρῴσκω,** *leap upon,* (sc. βωμῷ) Pi.*Pae.*6.115; σέλμασι ναῶν A.*Pers.*359; ἐ. ἄνω (sc. τῇ εὐνῇ) S.*Tr.*917; ἐ. ἐπί τινα *leap forth after* or *upon* one, as an enemy, Id.*OT*469 (lyr.). **–θῡμέομαι,** *support, corroborate* a conclusion by additional argument, Hermog.*Inv.*3.9. **–θύμημα** [ῡ], ατος, τό, *added enthymeme* in support of a position, Arist.*Rh.Al.*1438$^{b}$34, Hermog.*Inv.*3.9. **–θύμησις** [ῡ], εως, ἡ, *insertion of a corroborative argument,* Id.*Meth.*5 (pl.), Greg. Cor. in Rh.7.1147 W. (pl.). ⊛ **–ίημι,** *compress* the pulse, Gal.8.887.

**ἐπέννᾰτος** λόγος ratio *of* 10 : 9, Iamb.*in Nic.*p.84 P.

**ἐπεννεᾰκαιδέκᾰτος** [λόγος] ratio *of* 20 : 19, Aristid.Quint.3.1.

**ἐπεννέπω,** *utter over* a victim, ἐπὶ δ' ἔννεπεν εὐχωλῇσιν A.R.4.1596.

**ἐπεννοέω,** *invent in addition,* in Pass., ἐνθύμημα Hermog.*Inv.*3.9.

**ἐπένποι, ἐπενπέτω,** opt. and imper. forms of doubtful origin, *pronounce a sentence* or *inflict a fine, Schwyzer* 409 (Elis).

**ἐπεν-σᾰλεύω,** v. ἐπισαλεύω. **–σείω,** *reduce by succussion,* Hp.*Art.*47. **–τᾰνύω** [ῠ], = ἐπεντείνω, *bind tightly to,* πεῖσμα νεὸς.. ὑψόσ' ἐπεντανύσας Od.22.467. **–τᾰσις,** εως, ἡ, *stretching,* of the τόνοι of an engine, Ph.*Bel.*67.24 (pl.), 25. **–τείνω,** *stretch tight,* ἐπενταθείς *stretched upon* his sword, S.*Ant.*1235. II. intr., *press on amain,* ἐπεντείνωμεν ἀνδρικώτερον Ar.*Pax* 514 (lyr.); *gain strength, increase,* of a report, Thphr.*Char.*8.7. **–τέλλω,** *command besides,* S.*Ant.*218:—Med., *enjoin, PMag.Par.*1.2075.

**ἐπεντεῦθεν,** perh. f.l. for ἀπ–, *henceforward, PMag.Par.*1.2011.

⊛ **ἐπεν-τίθημι,** *insert* a letter, A.D.*Adv.*148.8 (Pass.); a word, Id.*Synt.*88.5; a drug into a cavity, Paul.Aeg.6.14:—Pass., *to be put in besides, CIG*4429 (Seleucia). **–τρίβω** [ῑ], *rub in besides,* Poll.5.102; *inflict,* πληγήν Eust.219.18. **–τρῠφάω,** *treat with wanton insolence,* c. dat., Men.Prot.pp.34, 102 D., cf. Suid. II. *revel in,* διηγήμασι Procop.Gaz.*Ep.*31. **–τρώγω,** *eat besides,* τῶν ὀστέων Ph.2.479. **–τρώματα,** τά, Epicur.*Fr.*413, and **–τρώσεις,** αἱ, Ph.1.115:—*dainties, delicacies,* expld. by Eust.1910.40 (sg.) as ἐρεθισμὸς τρυφητικός, but as τὰ ἐγκοίλια τῆς ἡδονῆς by Ph.: perh. ἐπικεντρώματα.

**ἐπεντύω** and **–ύνω** [ῡν], *set right, get ready,* ἐπέντυε νῶϊν ἵππους Il.8.374; χεῖρα ἐπεντύνειν ἐπί τινι *arm* it for the fight, v.l. in S.*Aj.*451:—Med., *prepare* or *train oneself for* a thing, ἐπεντύνονται ἄεθλα Od.24.89: c. inf., ἐπεντύνοντο νέεσθαι A.R.1.720.

**ἐπεξ-άγω** [ᾰ], *lead out* an army *against* the enemy, Th.2.21. II. *extend, lengthen,* τὴν διήγησιν Plu.2.855c; esp. *discuss at length,* D.C.46.8; περί τινος ἀκριβῶς Id.55.28. 2. seemingly intr. (sc. τάξιν), ἐ. ἀπὸ σφῶν *extend the line of battle* (by taking ground to right or left), Th.5.71; of ships, ἐ. τῷ πλῷ πρὸς τὴν γῆν *extend his line* by sailing towards land, Id.7.52. **–ᾰγωγή,** ἡ, *extension of a line of battle,* τοῦ κέρως Id.8.105. **–ᾰμαρτάνω,** *sin* or *err yet more,* D.H.2.35; δύο ἕτερα Ph.2.346; εἴς τινα against one, J.*AJ*14.16.4. **–ᾰμαρτητέον,** *one must err yet more,* D.22.6. **–ανίστημι,** Pass. with aor. 2 Act. –ανέστην, *rise up, stand up,* Ph.2.582. **–ᾰπᾰτάω,** *deceive yet more,* Mnesim.3.5. **–άπτω,** *kindle,* πῦρ Diog.Oen. 38 (Pass.). **–αρκέω,** *supply in full,* Tz.*H.*12.220. **–αρτίζω,** *equip, furnish, PFay.*95.10 (ii A.D., Pass.). ⊛ **–ειμι,** (εἶμι *ibo*) serving as Att. fut. to ἐπεξέρχομαι, to which it also supplies the impf. –ῄειν, Ion. 3 pl. –ῄϊσαν Hdt.7.223:—*go out against* an enemy, l.c., Th.2.21, etc.; τισί Id.6.97; πρὸς πολεμίους X.*Eq.Mag.*7.3; ἐ. τινὶ ἐς μάχην Th.2.23, etc. 2. *get out, escape,* Arist.*Pr.*937$^{a}$28. II. *proceed against, take vengeance on,* Hdt.8.143; esp. in legal sense, *prosecute,* τινί D.21.216, Men.*Epit.*140; ἐ. τινὶ φόνου *for* murder, Pl.*Lg.*866b, *Euthphr.*4e; ἐ. τινὶ ὑπὲρ φόνου ib.b, cf. e: c. acc. pers., ἐπεξῇμεν τοῦ φόνου τὸν Ἀρίσταρχον Test.ap.D.21.107, cf. Antipho 1.11, etc.: c. dat. rei, *visit, avenge,* τῷ παθήματι Pl.*Lg.*866b (and c. acc., τὸν τῶν πατέρων θάνατον D.S.4.66); also ἐ. δίκῃ, γραφῇ, *prosecute* at law, Pl.*Lg.*754e, *Euthphr.*4c, Aeschin.2.93; *attack,* τῷ λόγῳ μεγαλοπρεπέστερον Pl.*Ly.*215e. III. c. acc., *go over, traverse,* δρυμούς Clearch.37. 2. in writing, *traverse, go through in detail,* σμικρὰ καὶ μεγάλα ἄστεα Hdt.1.5; πάντα Ar.*Ra.*1118; πάσας τὰς ἀμφισβητήσεις Pl.*R.*437a. 3. *go through with, execute,* παρασκευὰς λόγῳ καλῶς μεμφόμενοι ἀνομοίως ἔργῳ ἐπεξιέναι Th.1.84; ἐ. τὰς τιμωρίας ἔτι μείζους Id.3.82. **–ελαύνω,** *send on to the attack,* τοὺς ἱππέας X.*HG*5.3.6. **–έλεγχος,** ὁ, *additional* ἔλεγχος, Pl.*Phdr.*267a, Arist.*Rh.*1414$^{b}$15. **–έλευσις,** εως, ἡ, *visitation, punishment,* Ph.2.569, *POxy.*67.15 (iv A.D.), etc.; *vengeance,* Eust.120.38. II. *traversing of ground* in argument, Eustr.*in EN*316.23. **–ελευστικός,** ή, όν, *avenging,* Eust.18.18. **–έλκω,** *draw off besides,* Hp.*Ulc.*27. ⊛ **–εργάζομαι,** *effect besides,* ἓν δ' ἐπεξειργάσατο D.18.140; *accomplish,* βουλὴ μὲν ἄρχει, χεὶρ δ' ἐ. Ion Trag.63. 2. *slay over again,* ὀλωλότ' ἄνδρ' ἐπεξειργάσω S.*Ant.*1288 (lyr.). 3. *work anew,* ἀγρόν Luc.*Tim.*37. 4. *investigate,* τὴν αἰτίαν A.D.*Synt.*82.7, cf. 122.7. ⊛ **–εργᾰσία,** ἡ, *investigation,* Ptol.*Tetr.*117; *elaboration,* Eustr.*in EN*135.16, Sch.Il.11.226; *carrying into effect* of a law, Just.*Nov.*99 *Pr.* **–εργαστικός,** ή, όν, *conclusive,* –κώτερον τιθέναι τὸν λόγον S.E.*M.*9.144. 2. Adv. Comp. –κώτερον *in greater detail,* ἑρμηνεύει Eust.104.3. **–έρπω,** *creep out into,* c. acc., ἡ ψυχὴ –ουσα τὰ μέρη τοῦ σώματος Hp.*Insomn.*86. **–έρχομαι** (v. ἐπέξειμι), *march out, make a sally,* Hdt.3.54, 6.101, Th.3.26, etc.; ἐ. τινὶ ἐς μάχην Id.5.9; of a message, ἐ. τινί *reach* him, Hdt.8.99 codd. (ἐπεσ– Reiske). 2. *proceed against, prosecute,* τινί Antipho 1.1: generally, τῷ δράσαντι Th.3.38; *attack,* Pl.*Prt.*345d; ἐ. τινὶ φόνου *proceed against* one *for* murder, Id.*Euthphr.*4d; also ἐ. τινὶ δίκην Id.*Lg.*866b; [γραφήν] *follow it up,* Lex ap.D.21.47; ἐ. φόνον Antipho 2.1.2: abs., ἐπεξέρχῃ λίαν thou *visitest* with severity, E.*Ba.*1346: c. acc. pers., *prosecute,* Lys.31.18; *punish,* Plu.*Caes.*69; τὴν πόλιν E.*Andr.*735: c. dat., *take vengeance for,* Nic.Dam.130.18 J. 3. *proceed to an extremity,* κἀπαπειλῶν ὧδ' ἐπεξέρχῃ; S.*Ant.*752; ἐ. πρὸς τέλος ἁπάσης πολιτείας Pl.*Lg.*632c. 4. *follow up,* τῇ παρούσῃ τύχῃ Th.4.14; *pursue, develop,* an argument, τῷ λόγῳ Pl.*R.*361d, *Grg.*492d. II. c. acc., *go through* or *over,* πάντα τῆς χώρης Hdt.4.9; τὸ πᾶν γὰρ ἐ. διζήμενον Id.7.166. 2. *carry out, accomplish,* ἔργῳ τι (opp. ἐνθυμεῖσθαι) Th.1.120; opp. ἐπινοεῖν, ib.70; πᾶν πρὸ τοῦ δουλεῦσαι ἐ. *try* every course, Id.5.100: abs., opp. παραινέσαι, ib.9; νίκην App.*BC*5.91; ἐ. τι εἰς τέλος Luc.*JTr.*17. 3. *discuss, relate* or *examine accurately* or *fully,* οὐδ' εἰ πάντ' ἐ. σκοπῶν S.*Fr.*919, cf. A.*Pr.*870, Th.3.67, Pl.*Lg.*672a; ἀκριβείᾳ περὶ ἑκάστου ἐ. Th.1.22; τι δι' ὀλίγων Pl.*Lg.*778c. **–ετάζω,** *pass in review, feast one's eyes upon,* Men.*Pk.*414. **–ετᾰσις,** εως, ἡ, *fresh review* or *muster,* Th.6.42. **–ευρίσκω,** *devise* or *discover besides,* Hdt.2.160; τι πρὸς ἀσφάλειαν J.*AJ*15.8.5:—Pass., ἐπεξευρημέναι χρεῖαι Arist.*Pol.*1331$^{a}$14. **–ηγέομαι,** *recount in detail,* Plu.*Art.*8, Sch.Ar.*Eq.*714. 2. *explain besides,* Asp.*in EN*48.20, Sch.Il.13.281. **–ηγημᾰτικός,** ή, όν, *epexegetical,* Sch.Pl.*Phd.*64d. **–ήγησις,** εως, ἡ, *detailed account,* Phoeb.*Fig.*1.3, Sch.Il.11.221. 2. *explanation,* Corn.*ND*9.

**ἐπεξῆς,** Ion. for ἐφεξῆς.

**ἐπεξ-ῐακχάζω,** *shout in triumph over,* παιᾶνα A.*Th.*635. **–όδιος,** ον, *of a march* or *expedition*: ἐπεξόδια (sc. ἱερά), τά, sacrifices *before the march of an army,* v.l. in X.*An.*6.5.2. **–οδος,** ἡ, *march out against* an enemy, ἐ. ποιήσασθαι πρός τινα Th.5.8; *sortie,* Aen.Tact.23.1 (pl.), D.C.39.4. II. *attack* for the purpose of revenge, Nic.Dam.130.17 J., Ph.2.314; for punishment, Id.1.283. **–οιωνίζομαι,** *take auguries afresh,* Gal.9.833. ⊛ **–ορκίζω,** *compel to swear a second time,* Plb.15.25.11. **–ορύσσω,** *dig further,* in Pass., *IG*4.823.37 (Troezen). **–ουσιαστής,** gloss on Μάϊος, Philox.Gramm.11.

**ἐπέοικα,** *to be like, suit,* c. dat. pers., ὅς τις οἷ τ' ἐπέοικε Il.9.392: elsewh. impers., *it is fit, proper,* c. dat. pers. et inf., σφῶϊν μέν τ' ἐπέοικε..ἑστάμεν 4.341; νέῳ δέ τε πάντ' ἐπέοικε..κεῖσθαι *'tis a seemly thing* for a young man to lie dead, 22.71, cf. Pi.*N.*7.95: c. acc. pers. et inf., λαοὺς δ' οὐκ ἐπέοικε..ταῦτ' ἐπαγείρειν Il.1.126; ὅν τ' ἐπέοικε βουλὰς βουλεύειν 10.146: with inf. understood, ἀποδάσσομαι ὅσσ' ἐπέοικε [ἀποδάσασθαι] 24.595; οὔτ' οὖν ἐσθῆτος δευήσεαι οὔτε τευ ἄλλου, ὧν ἐπέοιχ' ἱκέτην..ἀντιάσαντα [μὴ δεύεσθαι] Od.6.193. II. part. pl., ἐπεικότα *seemly, fit,* τινί A.*Ch.*669, cf. S.*Ichn.*271. III. *resemble,* c. dat., Arr.*An.*1.12.2, 2.7.8; ἀριθμῷ πάντ' ἐ. Pythag.ap. S.E.*M.*4.2.

**ἐπέπιθμεν,** v. πείθω. **ἐπέπλως,** v. ἐπιπλέω. **ἐπεποίθει,** v. πείθω. **ἐπεπόνθει,** v. πάσχω. **ἐπέπτᾰρε,** v. ἐπι-

παίρω. **ἐπέπτᾰτο,** v. ἐπιπέτομαι. **ἐπέπω,** Ion. for ἐφέπω.

⊕ **ἐπέραστος,** ον, *lovely, lovable*, *Lyr.Alex.Adesp*.4.18, D.S.4.7, Ph. 1.671, Vett.Val.18.29, Luc.*Tim*.17, *Im*.10; ἱερὸς ὁ κόσμος καὶ ἐ. Porph.*Antr*.12; ἐ. ὀφθαλμός Heph.Astr.1.1.

**ἔπεργα,** gloss on ἐπικέλια, Hsch.

⊕ **ἐπεργ-άζομαι,** *cultivate besides, encroach upon*, τὰ τοῦ γείτονος Pl. *Lg*.843c. 2. esp. *encroach upon* sacred ground, Lys.7.24, Aeschin. 3.113; αἴ τις τὰν γᾶν ἐπιεργάζοιτο ἂν Ἀμφικτίονες ἱάρωσαν.. ἀποτεισάτω.. στατῆρας.. καὶ πρασσόντων τὸν ἐπιεργαζόμενον *IG*2[2].1126.15 (Delph.). 3. generally, *cultivate*, Luc.*Tim*.37. 4. *dress* the upper surfaces of blocks of masonry, *IG*1[2].372.86, *SIG*970.11 (Eleusis, iii B.C.), etc. 5. *discuss, inquire into*, Ptol.*Tetr*.117 (nisi leg. ἐπεξ–): c. dat., *work up, pursue in detail*, Men.Rh.p.442S. II. pf. in pass. sense, *to be wrought* or *sculptured upon*, τῷ χαλκῷ Paus.3. 17.3, cf. 8.31.1. **–ᾰσία,** ἡ, *cultivation of another's land, encroachment upon* sacred ground (cf. foreg. 1.2), τῆς γῆς τῆς ἱερᾶς Th.1.139, cf. Pl.*Lg*.843c. II. *right of mutual tillage* in each other's territory, X.*Cyr*.3.2.23. III. *treatment, discussion*, Steph.*in Hp*.1. 107 D. **–αστικός,** prob. f.l. for ἐπηρεαστικός, *AP*5.177 tit. (Mel.).

⊕ **ἐπεργος,** ὁ, *assistant*, *Sammelb*.5680.3 (iii B.C.). 2. ἔπεργον, τό, *work done in addition* to payment of rent, τοῦ μισθώματος καὶ τῶν ἐ. ἁπάντων ἀπότεισμα *IG*12(7).62.15 (Amorgos). 3. as Adj., *useful*, *PSI*6.619.8 (iii B.C.).

**ἐπερεθ-ίζω,** *stimulate, urge on*, Plu.*Eum*.11; ἐ. πηκτίδα χερσίν *touch* the lyre, *AP*9.270 (Marc. Arg.). **–ισμός,** ὁ, *irritation, stimulation*, Plu.2.908e.

**ἐπερ-είδω,** *drive against*, ἐπέρεισε δὲ Παλλὰς Ἀθήνη [ἔγχος] νείατον ἐς κενεῶνα *drove* it *home*, Il.5.856, cf. 17.48; ἐπέρεισε δὲ ἶν' ἀπέλεθρον *put* vast strength *to* it, 7.269, Od.9.538; *thrust* a door *to*, *shut* it *close*, Q.S.12.331; ἐ. γένειόν τινι *lean* it *upon*.., Ael.*NA*5.56: metaph., ἐ. τὸν νοῦν *attend to* a thing, A.D.*Synt*.148.20; τὴν διάνοιαν Plu.2.392b; ἐ. τῷ φιλεῖν ἐμαυτὸν *give* oneself *up to*, ib.463c; *direct*, πρὸς τὴν θεὸν τὸν λόγον Sch.Pi.*N*.7.1:—Med., *rest in* or *upon*, βαυκάλη ἐπὶ διαγωνίων λίθων ἐπηρεισμένη Sor.1.109: metaph., ψυχαὶ –όμεναι πνεύματι Porph.*Abst*.2.38; οὐσίᾳ Plot.6.1.3; ἄλλῳ Id.5.5.7; ἐπ' ἄλλου Iamb.*Comm.Math*.8. 2. ἐ. τὴν φάλαγγά τινι *bring the whole force of* the phalanx *against*, Plu.*Flam*.8: abs., ἐ. τοῖς ἀντιτεταγμένοις Id.*Pyrrh*.21, cf. Arr.*Tact*.16.13:—Med., Ael. *Tact*.14.5. 3. Med., λαίφη προτόνοις ἐπερειδομένας *staying their* sails with ropes, E.*Hec*.112:—Pass., *lean* or *bear upon*, βακτηρίαις Ar.*Ec*.277, cf. Pl.*Lg*.789e: metaph., *lean upon*, ἡμετέρῃ ἐ. Ἑλλὰς ἐφορμῇ A.R.4.204: abs., *resist with all one's force*, Ar.*Ra*.1102. 4. Pass., *to be leaned on*, J.*AJ*9.4.4. b. *to be subject to pressure* or *impact*, Chrysipp.*Stoic*.2.142. II. intr. in Act., τῇ χειρὶ ἐπερείδειν *press heavily* with the hand, Hp.*Art*.11. ⊕ **–εισις,** εως, ἡ, *pressure*, Dsc.5.77, Sor.2.10, Heliod.ap.Orib.10.37.7, Gal.2.386; of the objects of sense, *impact*, Chrysipp.*Stoic*.2.233, al. **–εισμα,** ατος, τό, *support, foundation*, τὰ μαθηματικὰ ἐπὶ ταῖς ἰδέαις ἔχειν τὸ ἐ. Iamb.*Comm.Math*.8. **–εισμός,** ὁ, *impact*, Epicur.*Ep*.1 p.12 U. **–εισтικός,** ή, όν, *for support*, βακτηρία Sch.E.*Hec*.64. II. *pressed home, vigorous*, ἐπιβολή Procl.*in Prm*.p.845 S.

**ἐπερέομαι,** Ion. for ἐπείρομαι, Luc.*Syr.D*.36.

**ἐπερεύγομαι,** Pass., *to be disgorged upon*: of water, *to be poured upon*, ἀκτάς A.R.4.631; δισσὰς ἠπείρους D.P.95.

**ἐπερέφω,** *put a cover upon, roof*, εἴ ποτέ τοι χαρίεντ' ἐπὶ νηὸν ἔρεψα Il.1.39.

**ἐπέρομαι,** v. ἐπείρομαι.

**ἔπερος,** ον, *woolly*, of sheep, *Schwyzer*644.15 (Lydia).

**ἐπερρώπτης·** ὑπηρέτης, Hsch. **ἐπέρτερα·** μείζω καὶ ὑψηλότερα, Id. (leg. ὑπ–).

**ἐπερύω,** Ep. and Ion. **–ειρύω,** *pull to*, θύρην δ' ἐπέρυσσε κορώνῃ Od. 1.441; ἐπὶ στήλην ἐρύσαντες *having dragged* a stone *to the top* [of the tumulus], 12.14; *draw* to one, A.R.3.149:—Med., *draw on one's* clothes, ἐπειρυσάμενον τὴν λεοντέην Hdt.4.8.

⊕ **ἐπέρχομαι,** impf. ἐπηρχόμην Th.4.120 (unless fr. ἐπάρχομαι: Att. impf. is ἐπῇα (but v. ἔρχομαι) and fut. ἔπειμι): aor. 2 ἐπῆλθον, Ep. –ήλῠθον: pf. –ελήλυθα: I. *come upon*: 1. of persons, *approach*, c. dat., Il.12.200,218, etc.; esp. *come suddenly upon*, Od.19.155, Hdt. 6.95: c. acc., ἐ. πόλιν E.*HF*593 codd. (nisi leg. ἐσ–); *come to for advice*, μάντεις, μοῦσαν, Id.*Supp*.155, *Hel*.165, cf. Pl.*Lg*.772d: with Preps., ἐ. ἐς ποταμόν Od.7.280, cf. S.*Aj*.438: metaph., ἐ. ἐς λόγου στάσιν Id.*Tr*.1180; ἐ. ἐς πόλεμον Th.3.47; ἐ. ἐνθάδε Il.24.651. b. freq. in hostile sense, *go* or *come against, attack*, abs., 12.136, al., Th. 1.90, etc.: c. dat., Il.20.91, E.*Ba*.736, Th.6.34, etc.: rarely c. acc., τμήδην αὐχέν' ἐπῆλθε Il.7.262; τὴν τῶν πέλας ἐ. *invade* it, Th.2.39: hence, *visit, reprove*, ταῦτα μέν σε πρῶτ' ἐπῆλθον E.*IA*249, cf. *Andr*. 688: with a Prep., *invade*, ἐπὶ τὴν οἰκίαν *PFay*.12.12 (ii B.C.). c. *come forward to speak*, E.*Or*.931, Th.1.119, Pl.*Lg*.850c; ἐ. ἐπὶ τὸν δῆμον, ἐπὶ τοὺς ἐφόρους, Hdt.5.97, 9.7; ἐπὶ τὸ κοινόν Th.1.90; τοῖς Λακεδαιμονίοις ib.91. d. in Law, *proceed against*, ἐπί τινα *PEleph*.3. 3 (iii B.C.); ἐπί τινα περί τινος *PAmh*.2.96.8 (iii A.D.); τινὶ περί τινος *POxy*.489.11 (ii A.D.); ἐπὶ πιττάκιον *impugn*, *BGU*1167.14 (i B.C.): also in aor. 1 ἐπελεύσασθαι *PStrassb*.35.25 (ii B.C.), etc. (ἐπιπορεύομαι (q.v.) is more common in the pres. in the Hellenistic period.) 2. of events, conditions, etc., *come upon*, esp. *come suddenly upon*, c. acc., μιν.. ἐπήλυθε νήδυμος ὕπνος Od.4.793, al., cf. Hdt.2.141; ἔρως γὰρ ἄνδρας οὐ μόνους ἐπέρχεται E.*Fr*.431: c. dat., τοῖσιν ἐπήλυθε νήδυμος ὕπνος Od.12.311, cf. 5.472; μοι νοῦσος ἐπήλυθεν 11.200; βροτοῖσιν.. ὅταν κλύδων κακῶν ἐπέλθῃ A.*Pers*.600, cf. *Ag*.1256; ἐπῆλθέ μοι πάθος Pl.*Lg*.811d, etc. 3. c. dat. pers., *come into* one's *head, occur to* one, ἵμερος ἐπειρέσθαι μοι ἐπῆλθε Hdt.1.30; ὅ τι ἂν ἐπέλθῃ, Lat. *quicquid in buccam venerit*, Isoc.12.24: impers. c. inf., καί οἱ ἐπῆλθε πταρεῖν Hdt.6.107, cf. S.*Tr*.134 (lyr.); ἐμοὶ τοιαῦτ' ἄττα ἐ. λέγειν Pl. *Grg*.485e, etc.; also ἐπέρχεταί με λέγειν Id.*Phd*.88d. 4. *come in*, of revenues, etc., ἐπερχόμενοι τόκοι, ἐπιβολαί, *BGU*155.11 (ii A.D.), 1049.16 (iv A.D.). II. of Time, *come on*, ἐπήλυθον ὧραι the season *came round again*, Od.2.107, etc.; also, *come on, be at hand*, νὺξ δ' ἄρ' ἐπῆλθε 14.457; γῆρας ἐ. Thgn.528,728; ἕκαθεν ἐπελθὼν ὁ μέλλων χρόνος Pi.*O*.10(11).7; τὸ παρὸν τό τ' ἐπερχόμενον πῆμα and *that which is coming, the future*, A.*Pr*.98. 2. *come in after* or *over* another, of a second wife, Hdt.5.41. III. *go over* or *on* a space, *traverse*, mostly of persons, c. acc., πολλὴν γαῖαν Od.4.268; ἀγρόν 16.27; ἄγκεα πολλά Il.18.321, cf. Od.14.139, Hdt.1.30; *go the round of, visit*, δόμους S.*El*.1297; ναοὺς χοροῖς Id.*Ant*.153 (lyr.); πόλιν, of a god, Maced.*Pae*.29; of an officer, πύλας φυλακάς τ' ἐπῆλθον E.*Ph*. 699; τὰς ξυνωμοσίας ἐπελθών Th.8.54; *walk on* ice, Id.3.23; also of water, ἐπέρχεται ὁ Νεῖλος τὸ Δέλτα *overflows* it, Hdt.2.19, cf. A.*Supp*. 559 (lyr.), Th.3.89. 2. *go through* or *over, discuss, recount*, c. acc., Hes.*Fr*.160.4 codd. Str., Ar.*Eq*.618; *review*, τὰ εἰρημένα περί τινος Arist.*EN*1172[b]8; also ἐ. περί τινος Id.*Ph*.189[b]31, al.; folld. by an interrog., πειρατέον ἐπελθεῖν τίνες.. Id.*Pol*.1289[b]24; πῶς δεῖ.. ἐπέλθωμεν συντόμως ib.1317[a]15. 3. *accomplish*, πολέμῳ καὶ διαχειρίσει πραγμάτων Th.1.97. IV. *come up to, imitate*, πάτρῳ Pi.*P*.6.46.

⊕ **ἐπερωτ-άω,** Ion. **ἐπειρ–,** *consult, inquire of*, c. acc. pers., τὸ χρηστήριον, τὸν θεόν, εἰ.. Hdt.1.53, Th.1.118, etc.; τινὰ περί τινος Hdt. 1.32, cf. Orac.ap.D.43.66; later, ἐν τῷ θεῷ Lxx *Jd*.18.5:—Pass., *to be questioned, asked a question*, Th.5.45, Pl.*Sph*.250a. 2. c. acc. rei, *ask* a question, ταῦτα, τάδε, Hdt.1.30,55, cf. Antipho 1.10; also, *ask about* a thing, [τὰς ναῦς] καὶ τὸν πεζόν Hdt.7.100; σμικρόν τι τῶν ῥηθέντων *call* it *in question*, Pl.*Prt*.329a; ἐ. θυσίαις καὶ οἰωνοῖς ὅ τι χρὴ ποιεῖν *inquire* what.., X.*Oec*.5.19; ἐ. ἐς.. *inquire* about, Lxx *2Ki*.11. 7:—Pass., τὸ ἐπερωτηθέν *the question asked*, v.l. in Pl.*Tht*.146e. 3. c. acc. pers. et rei, ἐ. τοὺς προφήτας τὸ αἴτιον Hdt.9.93 codd.; ἐπηρώτα ὑμᾶς τὸ ἐκ τοῦ νόμου κήρυγμα Aeschin.1.79. 4. abs., *put a question*, esp. of a chairman putting a question to the vote, D.22.9, *SIG*898.17 (Chalcis, iii A.D.), al. 5. in Roman Law, *put a formal question* in *stipulatio*, most freq. in Pass., *POxy*.905.19 (ii A.D.), etc.: also in Act., ib.1273.41 (iii A.D.). b. hence later, *guarantee*, *PLond*.48.9 (vi A.D.). 6. *ask a further question*, *SIG*953.49 (Calymna, ii B.C.), al. **–ημα,** Ion. **ἐπειρ–,** ατος, τό, *question*, Hdt. 6.67, Th.3.53,68, Epicur.*Sent.Vat*.71. 2. *answer to inquiry* put to higher authority: hence, *sanction*, κατὰ τὸ ἐ. τῶν Ἀρεοπαγιτῶν *SIG* 856.6 (ii A.D.), cf. 1008.4 (iii A.D.). 3. = Lat. *stipulatio*, *PCair. Preis*.1.16 (ii A.D.), *Cod.Just*.8.10.12.3 (pl.): hence prob., *pledge*, συνειδήσεως ἀγαθῆς ἐ. εἰς θεόν *1Ep.Pet*.3.21. ⊕ **–ησις,** Ion. **ἐπειρ–,** εως, ἡ, *questioning, consulting*, Hdt.6.67; χρησμῶν Id.9.44, cf. *IG*12 (3).248.3 (Anaphe): pl., Th.4.38. 2. = foreg. 3, *POxy*.1205.9 (iii A.D.), *Cod.Just*.8.10.12.1a. **–ητής,** οῦ, ὁ, *inquirer*, *Gloss*.

⊕ **ἐπές,** Prep. (Arc. for ἐπέκ), c. dat., *as far as relates to*, ταῖς οἰκίαις *SIG*306.9 (Tegea, iv B.C.), cf. *IG*5(2).6.54 (ibid., iv B.C.).

**ἔπεσα,** v. πίπτω. **ἔπεσαν,** Ep. for ἐπῆσαν, 3 pl. impf. of ἔπειμι (A).

**ἐπεσ-βολέω,** *use violent language*, Lyc.130, Max.101. **–βολία,** ἡ, *hasty speech, scurrility*, ἐπεσβολίας ἀναφαίνειν Od.4.159, cf. Man.6. 625, Q.S.1.748: later in sg., Max.65; φοβερῆς ἰὸς –ίης, of Archilochus' satires, *AP*9.185, cf. 7.70 (Jul.). **–βόλος,** ον, (ἔπος, βάλλω) *throwing words about, rash-talking, scurrilous*, λωβητῆρα ἐ., of Thersites, Il.2.275, cf. Them.*Or*.21.262a; νεῖκος ἐ. A.R.4.1727; of satires, ἐ. ἦχος ἀοιδῆς *AP*4.1b.82 (Agath.).

⊕ **ἐπεσθίω,** *eat after* or *with* (cf. ἐπί B. I. 1 d, and v. ἐπιπίνω), κρέασι βοείοις χλωρὰ σῦκ' ἐπήσθιεν E.*Fr*.907; μικρῷ σίτῳ πολὺ ὄψον X.*Mem*. 3.14.3; *eat* cheese *with* wine, Telecl.25, cf. *Com.Adesp*.722. 2. *eat as an antidote*, ὅταν ἔχεως φάγῃ, ἐπεσθίει τὴν ὀρίγανον Arist.*HA* 612[a]24, cf. Thphr.*CP*6.4.7, Trophil.ap.Stob.4.36.28, Dsc.*Eup*.1. 25. II. *eat up*, dub. in Pherecr.156. III. *chew the cud*, Ael. *NA*2.54.

**ἐπέσθω,** Dor. and poet. for foreg., Epich.42.6, Call.*Epigr*.48.

**ἐπεσκεμμένως,** Adv., (ἐπισκέπτομαι) *carefully, circumspectly*, Hierocl.*in CA*10p.436M.

**ἐπεσκοτισμένως,** Adv. *obscurely*, Vett.Val.331.9.

**ἐπεσπευσμένως,** gloss on ἐπιτροπάδην, Hsch. **ἐπέσπον,** aor. of ἐφέπω.

**ἐπέσσηθον·** ἐπέλεκον, ἐπελέπτυνον, Hsch. (v. ἐπισήθω).

**ἐπεσσυμένως,** Adv., (ἐπισεύομαι) *violently*, v.l. in Q.S.3.443. 2. *hastily, promptly*, Aret.*CA*2.3.

**ἐπεστεῖσαι,** v. ἐπεκτίνω. **ἐπεστεώς,** Ion. pf. part. of ἐφίστημι.

**ἐπεστραμμένως,** gloss on ἐπιστροφάδην, Eust.819.52.

**ἐπεσχάρ-ιος** [ᾰ], ον, (ἐσχάρα) *on the hearth*, δαλός *AP*7.648 (Leon.). II. Subst. –ίη, ἡ, *hearth*, ἀελίου, of the earth, dub. in *Epigr.Gr*.149 (Rhenea). **–ωσις,** εως, ἡ, *scarring over*, Orib.*Fr*.143.

**ἐπετειό-καρπος,** ον, *bearing fruit annually*, Thphr.*HP*1.2.2. **–καυλος,** ον, *changing its stalk every year*, ib.6.2.8, 7.2.1.

**ἐπέτειος,** ον, Dor. gen. pl. ἐπετειᾶν A.*Ag*.1015 (lyr.): Ion. **ἐπέτεος** *GDI* iv p.876, v.l. in Hdt.3.89:—*annual*, θυσίαι Id.6.105; ὁ ἐ. καρπός Id.8.108; ὁ ἐ. φόρος the *yearly* revenue, Id.5.49; πρόσοδος Id. 3.89; βύβλον τὴν ἐ. γινομένην Id.2.92; τὸ ὕδωρ τὸ ἐ. the water drawn up by the sun *every year*, ib.25; γενήματα *PTeb*.27.33 (ii B.C.); ἐπέτεια, τά, *yearly additions to treasure*, *IG*1[2].242,244; ἐ.

ἐπικαρπία Pl.*Lg.*955d; ἐ. ἅλοκες A.*Ag.* l. c.; ἐ. νοσήματα *recurring annually*, Pl.*R.*405c: metaph., ἐπέτειοι τὴν φύσιν *changeful* as the seasons, or like birds *of passage*, Ar.*Eq.*518. 2. *lasting for a year*, ἐ. τὰ πολλὰ τῶν ἐντόμων Arist.*Long.*466ᵃ2; τῶν φυτῶν τὰ μὲν ἐπέτειον ἔχει τὴν ζωήν ib.464ᵇ25, cf. Thphr.*HP*1.1.2; ἐ. ψηφίσματα *having force for a year*, D.23.92; τὰ κατὰ τὰς ἀρχάς Plb.6.46.4. 3. *this year's*, ῥόδα Dsc.5.27; = ἐπὶ τοῦ νῦν ἔτους, Hsch.

**ἐπετειο-φορέω**, *bear fruit every year*, Thphr.*CP*1.20.3. **-φόρος**, ον, *fruiting every year*, ibid. **-φυλλος**, ον, *deciduous*, Id.*HP*7.11.3.

**ἐπέτεος**, Ion. for ἐπέτειος.

⊕ **ἐπέτης**, ου, Dor. -ας, ὁ, (ἕπομαι) *follower, attendant*, Pi.*P.*5.4: fem. **ἐπέτις**, ιδος, A.R.3.666.

⊕ **ἐπετήσιος**, ον, = ἐπέτειος, *from year to year, yearly*, καρπός Od.7.118, cf. *PSI*4.320.12 (i A.D.); προστατεία Th.2.80; θυσίαι Jul.*Or.*4.131d; *lasting the whole year*, τελεσφορίη Call.*Ap.*78; ἐγχρονίσας ἐπετήσιον *for a year*, *Epigr.Gr.*815.

**ἐπετίνη**, ἡ, name of a plant, dub. in Thphr.*HP*7.8.1 (prob. πιτυίνη, = χαμαίπιτυς).

**ἐπετινός**, ή, όν, *of the year*, χόρτος *POxy.*1482.12 (ii A.D.).

**ἔπετον**, v. πίπτω.

**ἐπέτοσσε**, poet. aor. (no pres. in use), = ἐπέτυχε, *fell in* or *met with*, c. gen., Pi.*P.*4.25; also in part., ἐπιτόσσαις ῥέζοντας *having come upon* them as they were sacrificing, ib.10.33.

**ἔπεττον**· ἐπιτίνων, Hsch.

**ἐπεύαδε**, Ep. aor. 2 of ἐφανδάνω, Musae.180.

⊕ **ἐπευάζω**, *shout over*, τινά Orph.*H.*79.9.

**ἐπευδοκέω**, *approve*, *PMasp.*151.225 (vi A.D.).

**ἐπευθυμέω**, *rejoice at* a thing, τινί Lxx *Wi.*18.6.

**ἐπευθύνω**, *guide, direct*, X.*Cyn.*5.32; τὸν δρόμον Plu.2.98cf; *direct, administer*, πολίσματα A.*Pers.*860 codd. (lyr.); τὰ κοινά Aeschin.3.158 (v.l.).

**ἐπευκλεΐζω**, *glorify, make illustrious*, πατρίδ' ἐπευκλεΐσας Simon.125.2; πολλά σ' ἔπαινος ἐ. *IG*12(9).1195.1 (Oreus).

**ἐπευκτ-αῖος**, α, ον, = sq., *PMag.Par.*1.271. **-ός**, ή, όν, *longed for, to be longed for*, ἡμέρα Lxx *Je.*20.14.

**ἐπευλαβέομαι**, *shrink from*, c. inf., Lxx 2*Ma.*14.18.

**ἐπευλογέω**, *bless*, Tz.*H.*9.206.

⊕ **ἐπευνάζω**, *sleep on*, βοείαις Nonn.*D.*17.117.

**ἐπεύνακτοι**, ων, οἱ, (εὐνάζω) name for the Helots who were adopted into their lords' places during the Messenian wars, Theopomp.Hist.166:—D.S.8*Fr.*21 writes **ἐπευνακταί**, and seems to identify them with the παρθενίαι (q. v.): Hsch. has ἐνεύνακτοι· οἱ παρθενίαι, and ἐπευνακταί· οἱ συγκοιμηταί.

**ἐπευσχημονέω**, *conduct in due order*, πομπήν *IG*12(8).666.4.

**ἐπευφημ-έω**, *assent with a shout of applause*, c. inf., πάντες ἐπευφήμησαν Ἀχαιοὶ αἰδεῖσθαί θ' ἱερῆα Il.1.22; cf. A.R.4.295: abs., Ph.2.28, Plu.*Galb.*14. II. c. acc. pers., Ἥρην ἐ. *glorify, sing praises to* her, Musae.275. 2. c. acc. et dat. rei, *sing over* or *in furtherance of*, χοαῖσι.. ὕμνους ἐπευφημεῖτε A.*Pers.*620; ἐπευφήμησαν εὐχαῖσιν.. παιᾶνα E.*IT*1403. 3. c. dupl. acc., ἐμὰς τύχας παιᾶν' ἐπηυφήμησεν *sang* a paean *over* my fortunes, A.*Fr.*350.4; folld. by dat., ἐ. παιᾶνα τῇ μῇ συμφορᾷ Ἄρτεμιν *sing* the paean *in praise of* her over my fate, E.*IA*1467. 4. c. acc. et dat., ἐ. νόστον τινί *wish* them *a happy* return, A.R.1.556. 5. c. dupl. acc., *call for the sake of good omen*, Heraclit.*All.*68:—Pass., θεῶν παῖδες οἱ ἥρωες -οῦνται Hierocl.*in CA* 3p.425 M. **-ίζομαι**, *use a euphemism*, Sch.Ar.*Ra.*1421, Hsch. s. v. καταίσια. (Act. only as f.l. for -ησεν, Hld.10.41.) **-ισμός**, ὁ, *shout of approval*, Eust.120.18.

**ἐπευφραίνομαι**, *delight in*, c. dat., Jul.*Gal.*347c, Olymp.*in Phlb.* p.239 S.

**ἐπευφρᾱτίδιος**, ον, *dwelling on Euphrates*, Luc.*Pisc.*19.

**ἐπευχ-άδιος** ᾰ, ον, *votive*, βωμός *JRS*2.93 (Antioch Pisid.). **-ή**, *prayer*, Pl.*Lg.*871c (pl.). 2. [ἐπευχά, = ἐπαρά, *SIG*360.42 (Cherson., iii B.C.). **-ιον**, τό, prop. *praying-carpet* or *rug*: hence, generally, *rug*, Eust.1056.64, Sch.Ar.*Pl.*528. **-ομαι**, *pray* or *make a vow to* a deity, c. dat., θεοῖς, Διί, Od.11.46, Il.6.475, etc.; but in S.*OC*1024, ἐ. θεοῖς *give thanks to* them: c. dat. et inf., *pray to* one *that..*, ἐπεύχετο πᾶσι θεοῖσι νοστῆσαι Ὀδυσῆα Od.14.423, 20.238, cf. S.*Ph.*1470, Ar.*Pax* 1320 (anap.), etc.: without a dat., κατθανεῖν ἐπηυχόμην S.*Tr.*16; ἐ. εὐορκοῦντι εἶναι ἀγαθά Lexap.And.1.98, cf. Aeschin.3.111: c. acc. rei, *pray for*, θανάτου μοῖραν A.*Ag.*1462 (lyr.): c. acc. cogn., ἐ. λιτάς S.*OC*484; τοιαῦτα θεοῖς A.*Th.*280: later, c. acc. pers., ἐ. θεούς Aristaenet.2.2. II. *vow*, c. fut. inf., ἐ. θήσειν τροπαῖα A.*Th.*276. III. *imprecate upon*, μόρον.. Πελοπίδαις Id.*Ag.*1600, cf. 501, *Ch.*112; ἀρὰς τοῖς ἀπειθοῦσιν Pl.*Criti.*119e: c. inf., ἐπεύχομαι αὐτῷ παθεῖν S.*OT*249: abs., *utter imprecations*, μὴ 'πεύξῃ πέρα Id.*Ph.*1286, cf. *Tr.*809: rarely in good sense, ἐ. εὐτυχίαν τινί Plu.*Galb.*18; ἐ. τινὶ εὐτυχεῖν A.*Th.*481. IV. *exult over*, δοιοῖσιν ἐπεύξεαι Ἱππασίδῃσι Il.11.431: abs., 5.119. 2. c. inf., *boast that..*, c. aor. inf., μιγῆναι *h.Ven.*287; fut., A.*Ag.*1262; pres., Id.*Eu.*58, etc.; Ἄργος πατρίδ' ἐμὴν ἐ. (sc. εἶναι) E.*IT*508: c. part., ἐ. ἐκφυγόν *boast* that it has escaped, Pl.*Sph.*235c, cf. E.*Rh.*693 (reading θρασύς).

**ἐπευων-ίζω**, *lower the price of* a thing, D.23.201; ἐ. τοῖς πένησι τὴν ἀγοράν Plu.*CG*5, cf. *Cic.*8, dub. in Luc.*Nigr.*23:—Pass., [ἡ πολιτεία] ὑπὸ τῆς εὐχερείας ἐπευωνίσθη D.C.60.17. **-ισμός**, ὁ, *cheapening*, ἐλαίου *BCH*11.473 (Lydia).

**ἐπευωχέομαι**, Med., *feast upon*, ἐπὶ στρωμάτων D.C.62.15.

**ἐπέφαντο**, 3 sg. plpf. Pass. from φαίνω, Hes.*Sc.*166. **ἔπεφνον**, Ep. redupl. aor. 2 from root of θείνω. **ἐπεφόρβει**, plpf. of φέρβω. **ἐπέφρᾰδον**, Ep. redupl. aor. 2 of φράζω. **ἐπέφῡκον**, Dor. for ἐπεφύκεσαν, 3 pl. plpf. of φύω, Hes.*Op.*149, *Th.*152.

**ἐπέχερον**· ἀκόλουθον, Hsch.

**ἐπεχές**, Adv., = ἐφεξῆς, *following, next*, ἁ ἐ. ἁμέρα, ὁ ἐ. ἐνιαυτός, *IG* 4.841.30,32 (Calauria): Delph. **ἐπεχεῖ** *GDI*2642.47 (ii B.C.).

**ἐπέχυντο**, Ep. 3 pl. aor. 2 Pass. of ἐπιχέω, Hom.

**ἐπέχω**, fut. ἐφέξω (v. infr. IV. 1, 2) and ἐπισχήσω E.*Andr.*160, D.45.88: aor. ἐπέσχον, imper. ἐπίσχες, inf. ἐπισχεῖν; poet. ἐπισχέθοι A.*Th.*453 (lyr.), ἐπέσχεθον A.R.4.1622: pf. ἐπέσχηκα *Supp.Epigr.*1.362.12 (Samos, iv B.C.):—*have* or *hold upon*, θρῆνυν.., τῷ κεν ἐπισχοίης (v.l. ἐπίσχοιας) λιπαροὺς πόδας Il.14.241, cf. Od.17.410; ποτῷ κρωσσὸν ἐ. *hold* it *to* or *for..*, Theoc.13.46; λόγον ζωῆς ἐπέχοντες (sc. κόσμῳ) *holding it out* like a torch, *Ep.Phil.*2.16:—Med., *hold by*, χειρός A.R.4.751. II. *hold out to, present, offer*, οἶνον ἐπισχὼν Il.9.489; ἐπέσχε τε οἶνον ἐρυθρόν Od.16.444; κοτύλην.. ἐπέσχε Il.22.494; εἴ ποτέ τοι.. μαζὸν ἐπέσχον ib.83, cf. E.*Andr.*225; also γάλακτι δ' οὐκ ἐπέσχον οὐδὲ μαστῷ τροφεῖα ματρός I *offered* not mother's food *with* my breast, Id.*Ion* 1492: c. inf., πιεῖν ἐπέσχον Ar.*Nu.*1382: abs., Id.*Pax* 1167:—Med., ἐπισχόμενος (sc. τὴν κύλικα) ἐξέπιεν *having put* it *to his lips*, Pl.*Phd.*117c, cf. Stesich.7, A.R.1.472, Luc.*Tox.*37; ἐπὶ χείλεσι.. μαστὸν ἐπισχομένη Euph.92; *present* a sum of money, τῇ πόλει *Supp.Epigr.* l. c. 2. *extend, spread out*, τὴν πλεκτάνην Arist.*HA*550ᵇ6. 3. simply, *hold*, σκῆπτρα *IPE*2.37 (Panticapaeum); of writings, *contain*, Philostr.*VS*2.24.2, cf. 2.9.1. 4. *enjoin, impose* a task, c. dat. pers., Procop.*Arc.*17, *Vand.*1.8. III. *hold* or *direct towards*, ἔπεχε τόξον σκοπῷ Pi.*O.*2.89; ἄλλῳ ἐπεῖχε τόξα E.*HF*984:—Med., abs., ἐπισχόμενος βάλεν ἰῷ *having aimed at him* he hit him, Od.22.15. b. intr., *aim at, attack*, τί μοι ὧδ' ἐπέχεις; why thus *launch out against* me? 19.71; in tmesi, ἐπὶ αὐτῷ πάντες ἔχωμεν 22.75; ἀλλήλοις ἐ. Hes.*Th.*711; ἄνδρα ἐπέχοντα τῷ Πύρρῳ Plu.*Pyrrh.*16; ἐπέχειν ἐπί τινα Hdt.9.59; τὰς ἐπὶ σφίσι ναῦς ἐπεχούσας Th.8.105; πρός τι Plu.*Ant.*66: c. dat., ἀκτῇσιν ἐπέσχεθον *held straight for* the beach, A.R.4.1766: abs., E.*Ba.*1131. 2. ἐπέχειν τὴν διάνοιαν ἐπί τινι *direct* one's mind to a thing, Pl.*Lg.*926b; τῷ πολέμῳ τὴν γνώμην Plu.*Aem.*8, etc.; also ἐ. ἑαυτόν τινι *attend* to him, Pl.*R.* 99b codd. b. abs., ἐπέχειν (sc. τὸν νοῦν) *intend, purpose*, c. inf., ἐπεῖχε ἐλλάμψεσθαι Hdt.1.80, cf. 153, 6.96: c. dat. rei, *to be intent upon*, ταῖς ἀρχαῖς, διαβάσει, etc., Ar.*Lys.*490, Plb.3.43.2, etc. 3. *stand facing, face* in a line of battle, οὗτοι (sc. οἱ Μῆδοι) ἐπέσχον Κορινθίους Hdt.9.31. IV. *hold back, keep in check*, ἐπέσχε δὲ καλὰ ῥέεθρα Il.21.244; καὶ πῶς ἐπέσχε χεῖρα μαιμῶσαν φόνου; S.*Aj.*50; ἐπισχὼν ἡνίαν ib.847; ἐπίσχωμεν τὸ πλεῖν Id.*Ph.*881; ὀργάς E.*Hel.*1642; οὐκ ἐφέξετε στόμα; Id.*Hec.*1283; χρησμοὺς ἐ. *withhold* them, Id.*Ph.*866; ἐπέχειν τινὰ τῷ ξύλῳ *keep* him *down* with the stick, Ar.*Pax* 1121; τὸ εὐθέως ἐπιχειρεῖν Th.7.33; *confine*, as the earth a corpse, *AP*7.461 (Mel.); ἐ. τῇ χειρὶ τὸ στόμα *cover*, Plu.*Cat.Mi.*28; ἐπέχομεν τὴν ἐκπνοήν Gal.6.172; τὰς διαχωρήσεις ἐ. Id.*Vict.Att.*12:—Med., ἐπισχόμενος τὰ ὦτα Pl.*Smp.*216a:—Pass., τοῦ βάθους ἐπεσχημένου J.*AJ*5.1.3; *to be prevented, hindered*, ὑπό τινος *PFreib.*11.13 (iv A.D.); of the menses, Gal.1.184. b. *stay* or *adjourn* proceedings, τὰ πρὸς Ἀργείους Th.5.46; τὴν ζημίαν καὶ τὴν κατασκαφήν ib.63; τὴν δίαιταν D.21.84; *suspend* payments, in Pass., *PTeb.*337.4 (ii/iii A.D.), cf. *PGiss.*48.11 (iii A.D.). c. ἐ. τινά τινος *stop, hinder from*, E.*Andr.*160, Ar.*Lys.*742, D.S.13.87: c. inf., σε μήτε νὺξ μήτε ἡμέρα ἐπισχέτω ὥστε ἀνεῖναι.. *let* them not *stop* thee so that thou neglect.., Th.1.129; ἐ. τινὰ μὴ πράσσειν τι S.*El.*517, *Ph.*349; κλαυθμυρίζον τὸ βρέφος ἐπισχεῖν μὴ δυνάμεναι Sor.1.88:—Pass., μηδενὸς ἐπεχομένου no *objection being taken*, *PTeb.*327.37 (ii A.D.). d. impers., ἐπέχει *there is a hindrance*, Astramps.*Orac.*97.3. 2. abs., *stay, pause*, Ἀντίνοος δ' ἔτ' ἐπεῖχε Od.21.186; *refrain*, Hdt.1.32, 5.51, 7.139; εἰ δ' ἐφέξετον if you *tarry*, S.*El.*1369, etc.: folld. by a Conj., esp. in imper., ἐπίσχες ἤν.. *wait and see* whether.., E.*Supp.*397; ἐπίσχες ἔστ' ἄν.. προσμάθῃς A.*Pr.*697; ἐ. ἕως.. D.4.1; μέχρι τοσούτου ἕως.. Th.1.90; ἐπίσχες, abs., *hold! stop!* A.*Ch.*896, S.*OC*856, etc.; ἐπίσχετε, μηδὲ συρίξητε Timocl.2.6 D.; ἐπίσχετον, μάθωμεν S.*Ph.*539, cf. E.*Hipp.*567; in part., ἐπισχὼν ὀλίγον χρόνον Hdt.1.132, al.; τὸ ἐπισχεῖν, opp. τὸ παραχρῆμα, Antipho 5.73; οὐ πολὺν χρόνον ἐπισχὼν ἧκεν came *after a* short *interval*, Pl.*Phd.*59e; μικρὸν ἐπισχόντα διεφθείροντο they very *shortly* died, Thphr.*HP*4.4.13, cf. Diocl.*Fr.*43; in Th.2.81 οὐκ ἐπέσχον τὸ στρατόπεδον καταλαβεῖν *did* not *halt* for the purpose of occupying a camp (unless it, = '*had* no *intention* of occupying'). b. c. gen. rei, *stop* or *cease from*, ἐπίσχες τοῦ δρόμου Ar.*Av.*1200; τῆς πορείας X.*Cyr.*4.2.12; τούτου Th.8.31; also ἐ. περί τινος Id.5.32, cf. 8.5: so c. inf., *leave off, cease* to do, X.*Mem.*3.6.10: c. part., *cease* doing, ἀναλῶν οὐκ ἐφέξεις Ar.*Eq.*915 (lyr.), cf. E.*Ph.*449. c. as technical term of the Sceptics, *suspend judgement, doubt*, Str.2.1.11, Ph.1.387, S.E.*P.*1.196; ἐ. ἐν τοῖς ἀδήλοις Plu.2.955c; ⟨πρὸς⟩ τὰ ἄδηλα Arr.*Epict.*1.7.5. 3. Med., *maintain reserve*, ἐπείχετο [ἡ σύγκλητος] κατὰ τοὺς Ἀθηναίους Plb.30.19.17 (s. v.l.). V. *reach* or *extend over* a space, ἑπτὰ δ' ἐπέσχε πέλεθρα Il.21.407; ὁππόσον ἐπέσχε πυρὸς μένος so far as the fire *reached*, 23.238, cf. Hdt.7.19, Th.2.77, f.l. in Hp.*Aër.*5, etc.: aor. Med., ἐπέσχετο he *lay outstretched*, Hes.*Th.*177; βούβρωστις ἐπέσχετο κόσμον *prevailed over..*, *Epigr.Gr.*703.5 (Apollonia); ἀφορία ἐ. τὸν βίον Longin.44.1. VI. *have power over, occupy* a country, οἱ Σκύθαι τὴν Ἀσίην πᾶσαν ἐπέσχον Hdt.1.104, cf. 108, 8.32, Th.2.101, 7.62, etc.; of things, ἐπ' ὀκτὼ μῆνας Κυρηναίους ὀπώρη ἐ. *occupies* or *engages* them, Hdt.4.199; τὴν πόλιν ἐπεῖχε κλαυθμός Plu.*Oth.*17; ὧν τὰς χρόας τὸ

ἡμερινὸν φῶς ἐ. *overspreads*, Pl.*R.*508c: κραυγῆς ἐπεχούσης τὴν ἐκκλησίαν D.S.13.87; πρὸ τοῦ τὰ σώματα τὰς ὠδῖνας ἐπισχεῖν Sor.2.53: generally, *occupy*, τὴν κρατίστην μοῖραν ἐ. *hold* the foremost place, Longin.9.1, cf. 44.12; ὕλης ἐ. τάξιν *Stoic.*3.27; τὴν γῆν κέντρου λόγον ἐπέχουσαν D.L.7.155, cf. *Placit.*3 *Praef.*; τὸν τέλειον ἐ. λόγον Gal.19.160; δίκην ἐπέχειν ἡμᾶς φυτῶν we *are like* plants, Meno *Iatr.* 6.18. 2. abs., *prevail, predominate*, ἣν μὴ λαμπρὸς ἄνεμος ἐπέχῃ Hdt.2.96; σεισμοὶ ἐπέσχον ἐπὶ πλεῖστον μέρος γῆς Th.1.23; πάντῃ ἐπεῖχε γαλήνη Timo 63; [τῶν νεῶν] ἐπὶ πολὺ τῆς θαλάσσης ἐπεχουσῶν *being spread over*.., Th.1.50; τὴν [τύχην].., ἣ νῦν ἐπέχει D.18.253; ἐτησίων ἐπεχόντων Plb.5.5.6. b. of Time, *continue*, τὴν θύραν ἐπεῖχε κρούων Ar.*Ec.*317; ἐπέχων καὶ οὐκ ἀνιεὶς *continuously*, Pl.*Tht.*165e; ἐπὶ πλείους ἡμέρας ὁ σεισμὸς ἐπεῖχεν D.C.68.25; σκότος, νὺξ ἐπέσχε, *came on*, Plu.*Mar.*20, *Crass.*30, etc. VII. Med., fut. ἐπιέξομαι, *meet*, Orac. in *Michel* 855.39 (Magn. Mae.).

**ἐπηβάω**, Ion. for ἐφηβάω, Hdt.6.83.

⊛ **ἐπηβολ-ή**, Dor. ἐπαβολά, ἡ, *part, share*, *Leg.Gort.*5.50, Hsch. **-ία**, ἡ, = συνηβολία, *EM*357.29. ⊛ **-ος** (Aeol. ἐπάβ- dub. in Sapph. *Supp.*10.2), ον, *having reached, achieved*, or *gained* a thing, c. gen., οὐ νηὸς ἐ. οὐδ' ἐρετάων γίγνομαι Od.2.319; τούτων ἐ. Hdt.9.94; ἱματίου ἐ. γενέσθαι *PSI*4.418.22 (iii B.C.); τούτων τῶν θεῶν ἐ. *in possession of*.., Hdt.8.111; τερπνῆς..τῆσδ' ἐ. νόσου A.*Ag.*542; ἐ. φρενῶν, Lat. *compos mentis*, Id.*Pr.*444, S.*Ant.*492; ἐπιστήμης, παιδείας ἐ., Pl. *Euthd.*289b, *Lg.*724b, cf. Hp.*Lex* 2; μήτε πόλεως μήτε πολιτείας Hyp. *Fr.*78; μεγάλων καὶ καλῶν Arist.*EN*1101ᵃ13; νόος οἰκωφελίας αἶσιν ἐπάβολος whose mind is *skilled in* housewifery, Theoc.28.2; τῶν ὄντων ἐ. γενόμενος having become *acquainted with* the true facts, Hld. 10.20: c. inf., *most dexterous at*.., κλέψαι -ώτατος Plu.*Arat.*10. 2. *pertaining to, befitting*, κλήροισιν ἐ. *belonging to* our fields, Nic.*Al.* 232; πάντεσσιν ἐ. ἥνδανε μῆτις A.R.4.1380. II. Pass., *to be reached* or *won*, ἐπήβολος ἅρματι νύσσα Id.3.1272. (ἐφήβολος *CIG* (add.)4303a20 (Myra).)

**ἐπηγκενίδες** [ῐ], αἱ, *long planks* bolted to the upright ribs (σταμῖνες) of the ship, Od.5.253. (Prob. from ἀγκών: ἐπηγανίδες (sic)· ἐπηνύγματα, Hsch.: ἐπητανίδεσσι (ἐπιτανίδες cod.) was read by Rhian.ap. Sch.Od. l.c.)

**ἐπηγορ-εύω**, *say against* one, *cast in* his *teeth*, τινί τι Hdt.1.90 codd.:—also part. -έων (ἐπιγ- cod.) Hsch. (prob. in Hdt. l.c.). **-ία**, ἡ, *accusation, blame*, D.C.55.18, al., Them.*Or.*11.152b; cj. in Pi.*Fr.* 122.

**ἐπηέριος**, ον, *through the air*, φορέεσθαι Q.S.2.573.

**ἐπηετᾰνός**, όν, also η, όν (v. infr.), *abundant, ample, sufficient* (Hom. only in Od.); παρέχουσιν ἐπηετανὸν γάλα θῆσθαι 4.89; πρασιαὶ..ἐπηετανὸν γανόωσαι (as Adv.) 7.128; σῖτον..ἐ. παρέχοιμι 18. 360; πλυνοὶ ἐ. troughs *always full*, 6.86, cf. 13.247; ἐπεὶ οὐ κομιδὴ κατὰ νῆα ἦεν ἐπηετανός 8.233; ἐπηετανὸν γὰρ ἔχεσκον for they had *great store*, 7.99, cf. 10.427; ἐ. βίος Hes.*Op.*31, Pi.*N.*6.10; ἐπηεταναὶ τρίχες *thick, full* fleeces, Hes.*Op.*517; [Ἀμαζόνες] ἐπηετανὸν κομέουσαι A.R.2.1176; ἐπηεταναὶ πλατάνιστοι Theoc.25.20, cf. Orph. *Fr.*280. [In *h.Merc.*113, Hes.*Op.*607, quadrisyll.]

⊛ **ἐπήκοος**, Dor. ἐπάκοος [ᾱ], ον, *listening, giving ear to*, c. gen., ἐμῶν ἔργων A.*Ag.*1420; κακῶν, δίκης, Id.*Ch.*980, *Eu.*732; ἐ. καὶ θεαταὶ δικῶν Pl.*Lg.*767d; λόγων Id.*R.*499a: less freq. c. dat., εὐχαῖς Id. *Phlb.*25b; ἐ. εἶναι γονεῦσι πρὸς τέκνα θεούς Id.*Lg.*931c; ὧν ηὔχοντο τὰ μέγιστα αὐτοῖς οἱ θεοὶ ἐ. γεγόνασι Id.*Mx.*247d; γυναιξὶν *AP*9.303 (Adaeus): abs., *listening to prayer*, of gods, Pi.*O.*14.14 codd., Ar.*Th.* 1157 (lyr.), *BGU*1216.50 (ii B.C.); Ἀσκληπιῷ ἐ. θεῷ *IG*12(8).366 (Thasos); epith. of Artemis, *IG*14.963, 12(9).1262 (Attica), etc. 2. *obedient*, ψυχαί J.*BJ*3.8.5. II. *within hearing, within ear-shot*, εἰς ἐπήκοον στῆσαί τινα, καλέσασθαι, X.*An.*2.5.38, 3.3.1; ἐν ἐπηκόῳ εἶναι, στῆναι, J.*BJ*5.9.3, 3.10.2; ἐξ ἐπηκόου Luc.*Cont.*20; ἐς τὸ ἐπηκοώτατον τοῦ οὐρανοῦ Id.*Icar.*23; ἀναγνῶναι ἐς ἐ. ἅπασι Id.*Symp.* 21. III. Pass., *heard, listened to*, ἃ πᾶς ὑμνεῖ ἐπήκοα γενέσθαι παρὰ θεῶν Pl.*Lg.*931b; ἐ. αἱ τοῦ θεοφιλοῦς εὐχαί Ph.1.296. IV. Subst. ἐπήκοος, Dor. ἐπάκοος, ὁ, *witness* to a transaction, *IG*5(1). 1228 (Taenarum), al., dub. in *Foed.Delph.Pell.*1 *A* 15; ἐπήκοοι *delegates*, *IG*11(4).1065. (Dual ἐπακόω ib.5(1).1230, ἐπάκω 1231, 1233, ἐπάκοε 1232.)

**ἔπηλις** (not ἐπηλίς Hdn.Gr.1.91), ιδος, ἡ, Ion. for ἔφηλις, *cover, lid*, S.*Fr.*1046, Posidipp.41. II. *freckle*, Ael.Dion.*Fr.*57.

**ἐπηλλαγμένως**, Adv., (ἐπαλλάσσω) *crosswise*, Hp.*Oss.*16. II. *changeably*, Hierocl.*Prov.*p.462 B.

**ἐπηλῠγ-άζω** or **-ίζω**, *overshadow, cover*, τινὰς ἱματίοις Ael.*NA*4.7, cf. 3.16, al.:—Med., τῷ κοινῷ φόβῳ τὸν σφέτερον ἐπηλυγάζεσθαι *throw a shade over*, i.e. *disguise, conceal* one's *own* fear by.., Th.6.36; ἐ. τὴν χεῖρα *hold* one's hand *as a shade over one's eyes*, Arist.*GA*780ᵇ 19; and (without χεῖρα) ἐ. πρὸ τῶν ὀμμάτων ib.781ᵇ12, cf. Aristocl. ap.Eus.*PE*14.18; ἐπηλυγισάμενός τινα *putting* him *as a screen before one*, Pl.*Ly.*207b; ἐ. ὕλην Arist.*HA*559ᵃ1, cf. 613ᵇ9; *use as a lurking place*, ὀπήν ib.623ᵃ29:—Pass., *to be concealed*, ὑπὸ τῆς ἀγνωσίας Dam.*Pr.*26; τινί ib.29; *to be suppressed*, Hp.*Mul.*2.156. (Both -άζω and -ίζω are found in codd.) **-αιος**, ον, (ἠλύγη) *shady, dark*, *AB*243, Hsch. **-ισμός**, ὁ, = ἐπισκιασμός, Hsch. s. v. ἠλύγη.

**ἐπῆλυξ**, ῠγος, ὁ, ἡ, *overshadowing*, τὴν πέτραν ἐπήλυγα λαβεῖν take the rock *as a screen*, E.*Cyc.*680.

⊛ **ἔπηλ-ῠς**, ῠδος, ὁ, ἡ, ἔπηλυ, τό, (ἐπήλυθον) *one who comes to* a place, ἔλθετ' ἐπήλυδες αὖθις *come* back *to me* (for they were going away), S. *Ph.*1190 (anap.). II. *incomer, stranger, foreigner*, opp. αὐτόχθων, Hdt.1.78, 4.197; ἄνδρας πολεμίους ἐ. A.*Pers.*243 (troch.), cf. *Th.*34, *Supp.*195, Th.1.29: Adj., ἔ. γένεσις Pl.*Mx.*237b; ἔ. βίος J.*AJ*8.12. 2: also in neut. pl., ἐπήλυδα ἔθνεα Hdt.8.73: neut. sg., ἔπηλυδος γένους D.H.1.60; ὕδωρ ἔπηλυ Paus.2.5.3. **-ῠσία**, Ep. **-ίη**, ἡ, *coming over one*, esp. by spells, *bewitching*, *h.Cer.*228, *h.Merc.* 37. II. *approach*, Διονύσου Nonn.*D.*14.328. ⊛ **-ῠσις**, εως, ἡ, *approach, assault*, Opp.*H.*4.228; πτερύγων *AP*5.267 (Paul. Sil.); βαρβάρων Heph.Astr.1.21. **-ύτης** [ῠ], ου, ὁ, = ἔπηλυς, Th.1.9 codd., f.l. in X.*Oec.*11.4, cf. Poll.3.54, Philostr.*VA*2.9, Procop.*Vand.*2.10: —also ⊛ **-ῠτος**, ον, D.H.3.72, Ph.1.160.

**ἐπημάτιος** [ᾰ], η, ον, (ἦμαρ) *day by day*, A.R.3.895, Opp.*H.*3.229.

**ἐπημοιβός**, όν, late η, όν Opp.*H.*5.135:—*crossing*, ὀχῆες ἐ. (unless = *shifting to and fro*) Il.12.456; τελαμῶνες ἐ. *cross*-belts, Opp.*C.* 1.98. 2. *alternating, serving for change*, χιτῶνες ἐ. Od.14.513; ἀστέρες Arat.190; πρηδόνες Nic.*Th.*365.

**ἐπημύω**, *bend* or *bow down*, ἐπὶ δ' ἠμύει ἀσταχύεσσιν (sc. τὸ λήϊον) Il.2.148, cf. Nic.*Th.*870, Opp.*H.*1.228, *C.*4.123. **ἐπήν**, v. ἐπεί. **ἐπηνέμιος**, ον, *windy*: metaph., *vain*, πλοῦτος Suid.

**ἐπηνύγματα**, v. ἐπηγκενίδες.

**ἐπηόνιος**, ον, (ἠών) *on the shore*, κύκνος *AP*5.124 (Bass.).

**ἐπήορος**, ον, *uplifted*, δούρατα A.R.2.1065, cf. Nonn.*D.*37.47: c. dat., *lifted upon*, καυλοῖσιν ἐ. ἄνθος A.R.3.856, cf. Nonn.*D.*10.205.

**ἐπηπύω**, *shout in applause*, λαοὶ δ' ἀμφοτέροισιν ἐπήπυον Il.18.502: abs., *shout*, Orph.*A.*528.

**ἐπήρᾰνος**, = ἐπήρανος, dub. in Orph.*A.*823, prob. in *Epigr.Gr.* 1013.5 (Memnon).

**ἐπηρᾰσία**, ἡ, = ἐπήρεια, *Supp.Epigr.*2.710.8 (Pednelissus).

**ἐπήρατε**· καλέσατε, Hsch.

**ἐπήρᾰτος**, ον, (ἔραμαι) *lovely, delightsome*, δαίς Il.9.228; εἵματα Od.8.366; freq. of places, [Ἰθάκη] μᾶλλον ἐ. ἱπποβότοιο 4.606; νῆσος Hes.*Fr.*76.4; also καλὸν εἶδος ἐπήρατον Id.*Op.*63; ἐπήρατον ὅσσαν ἱεῖσαι Id.*Th.*67; ἐπήρατον ἴαχον ὄρθιον Sapph.*Supp.*20c.4; κῦδος Alc. *Supp.*23.13; later of persons, ἐ. νεάνιδες A.*Eu.*958 (lyr.); παρθενική A.R.3.1099.

⊛ **ἐπηρε-άζω**, *threaten abusively*, λέγειν ἐπηρεάζοντες Hdt.6.9: c. acc., *speak disparagingly of*, τὴν ἀγαθὴν ἀναστροφήν 1*Ep.Pet.*3.16. II. *deal despitefully with, act despitefully towards*, c. dat. pers., X.*Mem.* 1.2.31; ἐ. μοι συνεχῶς καὶ μικρὰ καὶ μείζω D.21.14, etc.; ἐ. ψηφίσμασι καὶ νόμοις *oppose* them *insolently*, Id.18.320; τινὸς Luc.*Nav.*27; τινά Arist.*Pol.*1311ᵃ37, *Ev.Luc.*6.28, etc.; εἰ δ' ἄν τις..ἐπηρειάζειν δέατοι ἰν τὰ ἔργα *IG*5(2).6.46 (Tegea, iv B.C.): abs., *to be insolent*, Antipho 6.8; ὑψηλὴ ῥὶς ὥσπερ -άζουσα διατετείχικε τὰ ὄμματα X.*Smp.*5.6:—Pass., *to be insulted*, Lys.29.7, D.21.15, D.S.36.11, Ph.2.52, *PGen.* 31.18 (ii A.D.):—later Med. in act. sense, τινί *PLond.*3.846.6 (ii A.D.). III. of the action of disease, διάφορα ἐ. μόρια Steph.*in Hp.* 1.204 D. ⊛ **-ασμός**, ὁ, *despiteful treatment*, defined as ἐμποδισμὸς ταῖς βουλήσεσιν, οὐχ ἵνα τι αὐτῷ, ἀλλ' ἵνα μὴ ἐκείνῳ Arist.*Rh.*1378ᵇ18, cf. 1382ᵃ2, *PTeb.*28.4 (ii B.C.); τύχης ἐ. D.S.20.54. ⊛ **-αστής**, οῦ, ὁ, *insolent person*, Sm.*Ps.*56(57).2, Vett.Val.104.8, *PAmh.*2.134. 12 (ii A.D.). **-αστικός**, ή, όν, *insolent*, *Com.Adesp.*202, Alex. Aphr.*in Metaph.*308.13. Adv. -κῶς Gal.*Anim.Pass.*1.12, al.

⊛ **ἐπήρεια**, ἡ, (ἐπί, ἄρος) *insulting treatment, abuse*, ἐχθροῦ D.18.12, cf. Is.4.5, etc.; περὶ τὸν χορὸν D.21.25; κελεύειν κατ' ἐπήρειαν order *haughtily* or *by way of insult*, Th.1.26; κατ' ἐ. τινος γεγένηταί τι is done to *insult* him, Amips.9; κατ' ἐπήρειαν *BGU*180.8 (ii A.D.); φθόνον τ' ἐ. τε Philem.92.2; ἐν ἐπηρείας τάξει D.18.13; πολλὰ πρὸς ἐπήρειαν καὶ χάριν πράττειν Arist.*Pol.*1287ᵃ38; εἰς ἐ. τὴν ἐμήν ib. 195.20 (ii A.D.); χωρὶς ἐ. *OGI*262.24 (iii A.D.): pl., Man.4.331; λῃστρικαὶ ἐ. Chor. in *Rev.Phil.*1.73; ἐ. δαίμονός τινος his *capricious dealing*, Luc.*Laps.*1, cf. Philostr.*Ep.*18:—later spelt **ἐπήρια**, *BGU* 340.21 (ii A.D.), Melamp.(?) in *PRyl.*28.139 (iv A.D.).

**ἐπηρεμ-έω**, *rest after*, τοῖς καμάτοις Luc.*Am.*45, cf. Paul.Aeg.6.60 (dub.), Marcellin.*Puls.*192. **-ησις**, εως, ἡ, *pause* between systole and diastole of pulse, ib.184, al.

**ἐπηρέσιον**· τὸ προσκεφάλαιον, Hsch. (cf. ὑπ-).

**ἐπήρετμος**, ον, *at the oar*, ἑταῖροι ἦατ' ἐπήρετμοι Od.2.403; ἐ. πόνοι Opp.*H.*4.76. 2. *equipped with oars*, νῆες Od.5.16, 14.224, al.

**ἐπηρεφής**, ές, *overhanging, beetling*, ἐπηρεφέας φύγε πέτρας νηῦς ἐμή Od.10.131, cf. 12.59; κρημνοὶ ἐ. Il.12.54; κότινος Theoc.25.208. II. Pass., *covered, sheltered*, σίμβλοι Hes.*Th.*598; ἐ. φολίδεσσι, of a dragon, A.R.4.144; σπέος πέτρῃσιν ἐ. Id.2.736; νήσους ἐ. δονάκεσσιν Simm.1.8; κόρυμβοι ἐ. πετάλοισι Nic.*Fr.*74.24, cf. Hld.8.14.

⊛ **ἐπήρης**, ες, *equipped*, esp. of ships, πλοῖα Agatharch.83; ἐ. κελήτιον a boat *furnished with oars*, Arr.*An.*5.7.3: generally, ἐ. πτερύγεσσιν Max.415.

**ἐπήριστος** or **-ῐτος**, ον, (ἐρίζω) *contended for*, coined by Eust.725. 16, 1962.7, to expl. Ἐπήριτος (v. Ἐπάριτοι).

**ἐπῆρσε**, Ep. 3 sg. aor. 1 of ἐπαραρίσκω. **ἐπησθεῖεν**, Ion. 3 pl. aor. 1 opt. of ἐφήδομαι.

**ἐπησῠχάζω** (sic), *acquiesce in*, πράσει *PLond.*1.113 (vi A.D.).

**ἐπητᾰνός**, v. ἐπηετανός.

**ἐπήτεια**, ἡ, = ἐπητύς, A.R.3.1007 (pl.).

**ἐπητής**, οῦ, ὁ, *courteous, gentle*, opp. rude and barbarous, Od.13. 332; ἐπητῇ ἀνδρὶ ἔοικας 18.128: pl. ἐπητέες as fem., A.R.2.987 (ἐπήτιδες Lobeck); cf. ἐπητύς.

**ἐπητικός**, ή, όν, *given to following*, Metop.ap.Stob.3.1.115.

**ἐπήτρῐμος**, ον, (ἤτριον) prop. *woven to, closely woven*: hence, generally, *close, thronged*, πυρσοί τε φλεγέθουσιν ἐπήτριμοι torch *upon* torch, Il.18.211; δράγματα..ἐ. πῖπτον ἔραζε ib.552; λίην γὰρ πολλοὶ καὶ ἐπήτριμοι..πίπτουσι too many *one after another*, 19.226, cf. A.R.

1.30, etc.: later in sg., κῦμα Q.S.14.248; ὄχλος Opp.*C*.3.382: neut. pl. as Adv., ib.1.322, al.

**ἐπήτριος·** λόγιος, πανοῦργος, Hsch.

⊛ **ἐπητύς,** ύος, ἡ, *courtesy, kindness,* Od.21.306. (This and ἐπητής perh. from ἕπω; for the form cf. ἐδ-η-τύς.)

**ἐπηῦρον, -όμην,** v. ἐπαυρίσκομαι.

**ἐπηχ-έω,** *resound, re-echo,* E.*Cyc.*426, Pl.*R.*492c: c. acc., ἐπαίνους καὶ ὕμνους Ph.1.348: c. dat., ἐπηχοῦντα [τοῖς κύκνοις] τὰ δένδρα Jul.*Or.*7.236a. II. *accompany* one *in shouting,* E.*IA*1584. **-ησις,** εως, ἡ, *playing upon,* τοῦ αὐλοῦ Callistr.*Stat.*1. 2. abs., *resonance,* St. Byz. s. v. Δωδώνη.

**ἐπηῷος,** ον, (ἠώς) f. l. for ὑπηῷος in Orph.*A.*658.

**ἐπήωρα·** κρεμάμενα, μετέωρα, Hsch. (cf. ἀπήωρος).

⊛ **ἐπί,** Thess. (before τ) ἐτ *IG*9(2).517.14 (iii B.C.), Prep. with gen., dat., and acc., to denote the *being upon* or *supported upon a surface* or *point.*

A. WITH GEN.: I. of Place, 1. with Verbs of Rest, *upon,* καθέζετ' ἐ. θρόνου Il.1.536; ἧστο..ὑψοῦ ἐπ' ἀκροτάτης κορυφῆς 13.12; ἐ. πύργου ἔστη 16.700; κεῖται ἐ. χθονός 20.345: without a Verb expressed, ἔγχεα ὄρθ' ἐ. σαυρωτῆρος (sc. σταθέντα) ἐλήλατο 10.153; ἔκλαγξαν ὀϊστοὶ ἐπ' ὤμων the arrows *on* his shoulders, 1.46; ἐ. γῆς, opp. ὑπὸ γῆς, Pl.*Lg.*728a: also with Verbs of Motion, where the subject rests *upon* something, as *on* a chariot, a horse, a ship, φεύγωμεν ἐφ' ἵππων *on* our chariot, Il.24.356; οὐκ ἂν ἐφ' ὑμετέρων ὀχέων.. ἵκεσθον 8.455; ἄγαγε..δῶρ' ἐπ' ἀπήνης 24.447; ἐπὶ τῆς ἁμάξης.. ὠχέετο Hdt.1.31; ἐπὶ τῶν ἵππων ὀχεῖσθαι X.*Cyr.*4.5.58; οὓς κῆρες φορέουσι..ἐ. νηῶν Il.8.528; πέμπειν τινὰς ἐ. τριήροιν X.*HG*5.4.56, etc.; ἐπ' ὤμου..φέρειν Od.10.170; τὴν κλεῖδα περιφέρειν ἐφ' ἑαυτοῦ to carry the key about *on* his person, Numen.ap.Eus.*PE*14.7; βαδιοῦνται ἐ. δυοῖν σκελοῖν, ἐφ' ἑνὸς πορεύσονται σκέλους, Pl.*Smp.*190d; ἐπ' ἄκρων ὁδοιπορεῖν walk *on* tiptoe, S.*Aj.*1230; of places, *upon,* if the place is an actual *support,* νέρθε κἀπὶ γῆς ἄνω Id.*OT*416; ἐ. τοῦ εὐωνύμου *on* the left, ἐ. τῶν πλευρῶν *on* the flanks, X.*An.*1.8.9, 3.2.36; but most freq., *in,* rarely in Hom., ἐπ' ἀγροῦ *in* the country, Od.1.190; γᾶς ἐ. ξένας S.*OC*1705 (lyr.); νήσου τῆσδ' ἐφ' ἧς ναίει Id.*Ph.*613; ἐ. ξένας δμωὶς ἐπ' ἀλλοτρίας πόλεος E.*Andr.*137 (lyr.); οἱ ἐ. Θρᾴκης σύμμαχοι Th.5.35; τοὺς ἐ. τῆς Ἀσίας κατοικοῦντας Isoc.12.103; ἐπ' οἰκήματος κατίσαι, καθῆσθαι, *in* a brothel, Hdt.2.121.ε', Pl.*Chrm.*163b; τοὺς ἐ. τῶν οἰκημάτων καθεζομένους Aeschin.1.74; ἐ. τῶν ἐργαστηρίων καθίζειν Isoc.7.15; μένειν ἐ. τῆς αὐτῶν (sc. χώρας) remain *in* statu quo, Indut.ap.Th.4.118; οἱ ἐπ' ἐρημίας λῃστεύοντες Jul.*Or.*7.210a; later of towns, ἐπ' Ἀλεξανδρείας *BGU*908.16 (ii A.D.), etc.; sts. also, *at* or *near,* ἐπ' αὐτάων (sc. τῶν πηγῶν) Il.22.153; κόλπος ὁ ἐ. Ποσιδηΐου Hdt.7.115; αἱ ἐ. Λήμνου ἐπικείμεναι νῆσοι *off* Lemnos, ib.6 codd.; τὰ ἐ. Θρᾴκης the Thrace-*ward* region, Th.1.59, cf. *IG*1$^{2}$.45.17, etc.; ποταμοὶ ἐφ' ὧν ἔξεστιν ἡμῖν ταμιεύεσθαι.. *on,* i.e. *near* which.., X.*An.*2.5.18; ἐ. τῶν τραπεζῶν *at* the money-changers' tables, Pl.*Ap.*17c; in Geom., αἱ ἐφ' ὧν ΑΑ ΒΒ [γραμμαί] the lines AA BB, Arist.*EN*1132$^{b}$6, etc.; ἕλιξ ἐφ' ἇς τὰ ΑΒΓΔ a spiral ABCD, Archim.*Spir.*13 (cf. B.I.1k); also ἐ. τοῦ βάτου *in the passage concerning* the bush, *Ev.Marc.*12.26. 2. in various relations not strictly local, μένειν ἐ. τῆς ἀρχῆς remain *in* the command, X.*Ages.*1.37; μένειν ἐ. τινος abide *by* it, D.4.9; ἐ. τῶν πραγμάτων, ἐ. τοῦ πολεμεῖν εἶναι, to be engaged *in..,* Id.15.11, *Prooem.*1; ἐ. ὀνόματος εἶναι bear a name, Id.39.21; ἔχεται πόλις ἐ. νόσου S.*Ant.*1141 (lyr.). b. of ships, ὁρμεῖν ἐπ' ἀγκύρας ride *at* (i.e. *in dependence upon an*) anchor, Hdt.7.188; ἐ. προσπόλου μιᾶς χωρεῖν *dependent upon* an attendant, S.*OC*746. c. with the personal and reflexive Pron., once in Hom., εὔχεσθε..σιγῇ ἐφ' ὑμείων Il.7.195; later mostly with 3rd pers., ἐπ' ἑωυτῶν κεῖσθαι *by* themselves, Hdt.2.2, cf. 8.32; οἰκέειν κώμην Id.5.98; ἐ. σφῶν αὐτῶν αὐτόνομοι οἰκεῖν Th.2.63; ἵζεσθαι Hdt.9.17; ἐφ' ἑαυτῶν πλεῖν Th.8.8; ἐπ' ὑμέων αὐτῶν βαλέσθαι consider it *by* yourselves, Hdt.3.71, etc.; αὐτὴ ἐφ' αὑτῆς σκοποῦσα Th.6.40; ἐφ' ἡμῶν αὐτῶν τὸν ἐξετασμὸν ποιεῖσθαι D.18.16; ἐπ' ἑωυτῶν διαλέγονται speak *in* a dialect of their own, Hdt.1.142; also αὐτοὶ ἐφ' ἑαυτῶν χωρεῖν X.*An.*2.4.10; πράττειν Pl.*Prt.*326d, cf. *Sph.*217c; τὸ ἐφ' ἑαυτῶν μόνον προορώμενοι considering their own *interest* only, Th.1.17. d. with numerals, to denote the *depth* of a body of soldiers, ἐ. τεττάρων ταχθῆναι to be drawn up four *deep,* four *in file,* X.*An.*1.2.15, etc.; ἐ. πεντήκοντα ἀσπίδων συνεστραμμένοι, of the Thebans at Leuctra, Id.*HG*6.4.12; ἐπ' ὀλίγων τεταγμένοι, i.e. *in* a long thin *line,* Id.*An.*4.8.11; οὐκ ἐπ' ὀλίγων ἀσπίδων στρατιὰν παρατεταγμένην Th.7.79; ἐφ' ἑνὸς ἄγειν *in* single *file,* X.*Cyr.*2.4.2, cf. *An.*5.2.6; rarely of the *length* of the line, ἐ. τεσσάρων ταξάμενοι τὰς ναῦς Th.2.90; in X., ἐγένοντο τὸ μέτωπον ἐ. τριακοσίων..τὸ δὲ βάθος ἐφ' ἑκατόν *Cyr.*2.4.2; πλεῖν ἐ. κέρως, ἐ. κέρας, v. infr. C.I.3; ἐ. φάλαγγος γίγνεται τὸ στράτευμα is formed *in* column, *An.*4.6.6, etc. (but in E.*Ph.*1467, ἀσπίδων ἔπι is merely *in* or *under* arms): hence, generally, ἐ. ὀκτὼ πλίνθων τὸ εὖρος eight bricks *wide,* X.*An.*7.8.14. e. c. gen. pers., *before, in presence of,* ἐ. μαρτύρων..πράσσεταί τι Antipho 2.3.8; ἐξελέγχεσθαι ἐ. πάντων D.25.36; so, *before* a magistrate or official, ἐ. τοῦ στρατηγοῦ *POxy.*38.11 (i A.D.), cf. *UPZ*71.15 (ii B.C.), *Ev.Matt.*28.14; γράψομαί σε ἐ. Ῥαδαμάνθυος Luc.*Cat.*18; τινὰ εἰς δίκην καὶ κρίσιν ἐ. τῶν στρατοπέδων προκαλεῖν Jul.*Or.*1.30d; πίστεις δοῦναι ἐ. θεῶν D.H.5.29; but ἐπὶ δικασταῖς is f.l. in D.19.243 (leg. ἔπη). f. with Verbs of perceiving, observing, judging, etc., *in the case of,* ἐπὶ νούσων παντοίων ἐπύθοντο Emp.112.10; δρᾶν τι ἐ. τινος X.*Mem.*3.9.3; αἰσθάνεσθαί τι ἐ. τινος Pl.*R.*406c, etc.; τὴν γνώμην ἔχειν ἐ. τινος Hyp.*Eux.*32; τὰ συμβόλαια ἐ. τῶν νόμων σκοπεῖν D.18.210; ἐπ' αὐτῶν τῶν ἔργων ἂν ἐσκόπει ib.233, cf. 25.2 (v.l.); ἐφ' ἑνός τι παριδεῖν Lycurg.64; τὰς ἐναντιώσεις ἐ. μὲν τῶν λόγων τηροῦντες, ἐ. δὲ τῶν ἔργων μὴ καθορῶντες Isoc.13.7; οὐδεὶς ἐφ' αὑτοῦ τὰ κακὰ συνορᾷ Men.631; ἀγνοεῖν τι ἐ. τινος X.*Mem.*2.3.2; also with Verbs of speaking, *on* a subject, λέγειν ἐ. τινος Pl.*Chrm.*155d, *R.*524e, etc.; ἐπιδεῖξαί τι ἐ. τινος Isoc.8.109; ἵνα τοὺς ἐπαίνους ἐπ' αὐτῶν κοινοὺς ποιήσωμαι D.60.12. 3. implying Motion: a. where the sense of motion is lost in the sense of being supported, ὀρθωθεὶς..ἐπ' ἀγκῶνος having raised himself *upon* his elbow, Il.10.80; ἐ. μελίης..ἐρεισθείς 22.225; τὴν μὲν..καθεῖσεν ἐ. θρόνου 18.389. b. in a pregnant sense, denoting the goal of motion (cf. εἰς A.I.2, ἐν A.I.8), νῆα..ἐπ' ἠπείροιο ἔρυσσαν drew the ship *upon* the land *and left it there,* 1.485; περάαν νήσων ἔπι carry *to* the islands *and leave there,* 21.454, cf. 22.45; ἐ. τῆς γῆς καταπίπτειν X.*Cyr.*4.5.54; ἀναβῆναι ἐ. τῶν πύργων ib.7.1.39; ἐπ' Ἀβύδου ἀφικομέναις Th.8.79 (v.l.); freq. of motion *towards* or (in a military sense) *upon* a place, προτρέποντο μελαινάων ἐ. νηῶν Il.5.700; τρέσσε..ἐφ' ὁμίλου 11.546 (but νήσου ἔ. Ψυρίης νέεσθαι to go *near* Psyria, Od.3.171); ἐπ' οἴκου ἀπελαύνειν, ἀναχωρεῖν, ἀποχωρεῖν, home*wards,* Hdt.2.121.δ', Th.1.30,87, etc.; also with names of places, ἰέναι ἐ. Κυζίκου Hdt.4.14; πλεῖν ἐ. Χίου Id.1.164, cf. 168; ἀποπλεῖν ἐπ' Αἰγύπτου ib.1; ἀπαλλάσσεσθαι ἐ. Θεσσαλίης Id.5.64; ὁ κόλπος ὁ ἐ. Παγασέων φέρων the bay that leads *to* Pagasae, Id.7.193; ἡ ἐ. Βαβυλῶνος ὁδός the road *leading to* B., X.*Cyr.*5.3.45, cf. *An.*6.3.24. c. metaph., ἐ. γνώμης τινὸς γίγνεσθαι come *to* an opinion, D.4.7; ἐπ' ἐλπίδος γενέσθαι Plu.*Sol.*14; ὡς ἐ. κινδύνου as if *to meet* danger, Th.6.34; ἐ. τοῦ ἀλύπως ζῆν *with a view to..,* Pl.*Prt.*358b; cf. infr. B.III.2. II. of Time, *in the time of,* ἐ. προτέρων ἀνθρώπων Il.5.637, 23.332; ἐ. Κρόνου Hes.*Op.*111; ἐ. Κέκροπος, ἐ. Δαρείου, etc., Hdt.8.44, 6.98, etc.; ἐ. τῶν τριάκοντα Lys.13.2; ὀλιγαρχία ἡ ἐ. τῶν τετρακοσίων καταστᾶσα Isoc.8.108; ἐ. τούτου τυραννεύοντος, ἐ. Λέοντος βασιλεύοντος, ἐ. Μήδων ἀρχόντων, etc., Hdt.1.15,65, 134, etc.; ἐ. τῆς ἐμῆς βασιλείας Isoc.3.32; ἐπ' ἐμεῦ *in* my *time,* Hdt.1.5, 2.46, etc.; ἡ εἰρήνη ἡ ἐπ' Ἀνταλκίδου D.20.54, cf. X.*HG*5.1.36; αἱ ἐπ' Ἀσδρούβα γενόμεναι ὁμολογίαι Plb.3.15.5; ἐπ' εἰρήνης *in time of* peace, Il.2.797, 9.403; ἐπ' ἐμῆς νεότητος Ar.*Ach.*211 (lyr.); ἐ. Λάχητος καὶ τοῦ προτέρου πολέμου Th.6.6; ἐπ' ἡμέρης ἑκάστης v.l. for -η -τῃ in Hdt.5.117. b. later ἐ. δείπνου *at* dinner, Luc.*Asin.*3; ἐ. τῆς τραπέζης, ἐφ' ἑκάστης κύλικος, Plu.*Alex.*23; ἐ. τῆς κύλικος, ἐ. τοῦ ποτηρίου, Luc.*Pisc.*34, Plu.*Alex.*53. III. in various causal senses: 1. *over,* of persons in authority, ἐπ' οὗ ἐτάχθημεν Hdt.5.109; οἱ ἐ. τῶν πραγμάτων the public officers, D.18.247; freq. in forged decrees, ὁ ἐ. τῶν ὅπλων στρατηγός ib.38; ὁ ἐ. τῶν ὁπλιτῶν, τῶν ἱππέων, ib.116; ὁ ἐ. τῆς διοικήσεως ib.38 (but cf. C.III.3); τοῦ ἐ. τῶν ὁπλιτῶν is f.l. in Lys.32.5; ὁ ἐ. τῆς χώρας στρατηγός Plu.*Phoc.*32; οἱ ἐ. τῶν σιτοποιῶν καὶ μαγείρων Id.*Alex.*23; ὁ ἐ. τοῦ οἴνου Id.*Pyrrh.*5; ὁ ἐ. τῶν ἐπιστολῶν τοῦ Ὄθωνος, = Lat. *ab epistulis,* his secretary, Id.*Oth.*9; cf. B.III.6. 2. κεκλῆσθαι ἐ. τινος to be called *after* him, Hdt.4.45; ἐ. τινος μετονομασθῆναι Id.1.94: ἐ. τινος τὰς ἐπωνυμίας ἔχειν Id.4.107; ἐ. τινος ἐπώνυμος γίγνεσθαι ib.184; also ἐπ' ὀνόματος καλεῖν Plb.5.35.2. 3. of occasions, circumstances, and conditions, οὐκ ἐ. τούτου μόνον, ἀλλ' ἐ. πάντων, *on* all occasions, D.21.38, cf. 183; ἐφ' ἑκάστων Pl.*Phlb.*25e; ἐφ' ἑκατέρου Id.*Tht.*159c; ἐφ' ἑκάστης μαντείας D.21.54; ἐπ' ἐξουσίας καὶ πλούτου πονηρὸν εἶναι *in..* ib.138; ἐ. τῆς ἀληθείας καὶ τοῦ πράγματος ib.72, cf. 18.17; τὴν ἐ. τῆς πομπῆς καὶ τοῦ μεθύειν πρόφασιν λαβών Id.21.180; ἐ. σχολῆς Aeschin.3.191; ἐπ' ἀδείας Plu.*Sol.*22; ἐπ' ἀληθείας *Ev.Marc.*12.14, *POxy.*255.16 (i A.D.): hence in adverbial phrases, ἐπ' ἴσας (sc. μοίρας) *equally,* S.*El.*1062 (lyr.); ἐ. καιροῦ D.20.90; ἐπ' ἐσχάτων *at* the last, Lxx *De.*17.7 (v.l. ἐσχάτῳ); ἐπὶ τοῦ παρόντος *for* the present, *SIG*543.6 (Epist. Philipp.). 4. *in respect of,* ἐ. τῶν πραγμάτων Arist.*Pol.*1280$^{a}$17, cf. *EN*1131$^{b}$18; *concerning,* τὰ ἐπ' αὐτῶν ἐνεστηκότα *PTeb.*7.6 (ii B.C.).

B. WITH DAT.: I. of Place, *upon,* just like the gen. (hence Poets use whichever case suits the metre, whereas in Prose the dat. is more freq.): 1. with Verbs of Rest, ἕζεο τῷδ' ἐ. δίφρῳ Il.6.354; ἧντ' ἐ. πύργῳ 3.153; στῆ δ' ἐ...νηΐ 8.222; κεῖσθαι ἐ. τινι X.*An.*1.8.27; καίειν ἐ. πᾶσι (sc. βωμοῖς) Il.8.240; ἔβραχε χαλκὸς ἐ. στήθεσσι 4.420; ἐ. χθονὶ δέρκεσθαι 1.88, etc.: also with Verbs of Motion, where the subject rests *upon* something, νηυσὶν ἐπ' ὠκυπόροισιν ἔβαινον 2.351 (v.l. for ἐν); ἐπ' ὤμοις φέρειν E.*Ph.*1131 (but ἐφ' ἵππῳ, ἐφ' ἵπποις and the like are never used for ἐφ' ἵππου, etc.); of places, mostly *in,* ἐ. τῇ χώρῃ Hdt.5.77; τἀπὶ Τροίᾳ πέργαμα S.*Ph.*353; ἐπ' ἐσχάτοις τόποις Id.*Tr.*1100; ἐ. τῇ ψυχῇ δάκνομαι Id.*Ant.*317; also, *at* or *near,* ἐ. κρήνῃ Od.13.408; ἐ. θύρῃσι Il.2.788, etc.; of rivers, etc., *by, beside,* ἐ. ὠκυρόῳ Κελάδοντι.. 7.133, etc.; ἐπ' ἐσχάρῃ Od.7.160; ἐ. νηυσί Il.1.559, etc.; of persons, οὐ τἀπὶ Λυδοῖς οὐδ' ἐπ' Ὀμφάλῃ λατρεύματα *in* Lydia, *in the power of* O., S.*Tr.*356. b. *on* or *over,* ἐπ' Ἰφιδάμαντι *over* the body of Iphidamas, Il.11.261, cf. 4.470; τοιόνδ' ἐπ' ἀνδρὶ κομπάζεις λόγον A.*Ag.*1400; also, *over* or *in honour of,* ἐ. σοὶ κατέθηκε..ἄεθλα Od.24.91; [βοῦς] ἐ. Πατρόκλῳ πέφνεν Il.23.776; κειράμενοι χαίτας ἐπ' Ἀδώνιδι Bion 1.81, cf. Lys.2.80; in Dor. and Aeol. sepulchral Inscrr., *Schwyzer* 348, al. c. in hostile sense, *against,* Hdt.1.61, 6.74,88, S.*Ph.*1139 (lyr.), etc.; *as a check upon,* οἱ πρόβουλοι καθεστᾶσιν ἐ. τοῖς βουλευταῖς Arist.*Pol.*1299$^{b}$37, cf. 1271$^{a}$39; also, *towards, in reference to,* ἐ. πᾶσι χόλον τελέσαι Il.4.178; ἐπ' ἔργοις πᾶσι S.*OC*1268; δικαιότερος καὶ ἐπ' ἄλλῳ ἔσσεαι Il.19.181, cf. S.*Tr.*994 (anap.), etc.; ἐ. τοῖς δυνατοῖς ἔχειν τὴν γνώμην Democr.191; τὸ ἐ. πᾶσιν τοῖς σώμασι κάλλος *extending over* all bodies, Pl.*Smp.*210b; ἡ [παιδεία] ἡ ἐ. σώμασι, ἐ. ψυχῇ, Id.*R.*376e; τἀπὶ σοὶ κακά the ills which lie *upon* thee, S.*Ph.*806: in Att. also, νόμον τίθεσθαι, θεῖναι ἐ. τινι, make a law *for his case,* whether *for* or *against,* Pl.*Grg.*

488d, Lex ap.And.1.87; νόμους ἀναγράψαι ἐ. τοῖς ἀδικοῦσι D.24.5; νόμος κεῖται ἐ. τινι ib.70; τἀπὶ τῷ πλήθει νενομοθετημένα ib.123, cf. 142; τί θεσμοποιεῖς ἐ. ταλαιπώρῳ νεκρῷ; E.*Ph.*1645. d. of accumulation, *upon, after,* ὄγχνη ἐπ' ὄγχνῃ one pear *after* another, pear *on* pear, Od.7.120; ἐ. κέρδει κέρδος Hes.*Op.*644; ἄτῃ ἑτέρα ἐπ' ἄτῃ A.*Ch.*404 (lyr.); πήματα ἐ. πήμασι, ἐ. νόσῳ νόσος, S.*Ant.*595, *OC*544 (both lyr.). e. *in addition to, over and above, besides,* οὐκ ἄρα σοί γ' ἐ. εἶδεϊ καὶ φρένες ἦσαν Od.17.454, cf. 308; ἄλλα τε πόλλ' ἐ. τῇσι παρίσχομεν Il.9.639, cf. Od.22.264; ἐ. τοῖσι *besides,* 24.277; ἐ. τούτοις Him.*Or.*14.10; so of Numerals, τρισχιλίους ἐ. μυρίοις Plu.*Publ.*20, cf. Jul.*Or.*4.148c, etc.; γυναῖκ' ἐφ' ἡμῖν.. ἔχει E.*Med.*694: with Verbs of eating and drinking, *with,* ἐ. τῷ σίτῳ πίνειν ὕδωρ X.*Cyr.*6.2.27; νέκταρ ποτίσαι ἐπ' ἀμβροσίᾳ Pl.*Phdr.*247e; esp. of a relish, κάρδαμον μόνον ἐ. τῷ σίτῳ ἔχειν X.*Cyr.*1.2.11; παίειν ἐφ' ἁλὶ τὰν μᾶδδαν Ar.*Ach.*835: metaph., ἐ. τῷ φάγοις ἥδιστ' ἄν; ἐ. βαλλαντίῳ; Id.*Eq.*707; later ἐ. γογγυλίσι διαβιῶναι live *on* turnips, Ath.10.419a. f. of position, *after, behind,* of soldiers, X.*Cyr.*8.3.16–18. g. *in dependence upon, in the power of,* τὰ δ' οὐκ ἐπ' ἀνδράσι κεῖται Pi.*P.*8.76; ἐ. τινί ἐστι it is *in* his *power* to do, c.inf., Hdt.8.29, etc.; ἐ. σοί ἐστιν ἀναζωπυρεῖν M.Ant.7.2; ἐ. ἑτέροις γίγνεσθαι Th.6.22; ἐ. τῷ πλήθει *in* their *hands,* S.*OC*66, cf. Th.2.84; τὸ ἐπ' ἐμοί, τὸ ἐ. ἐκείνῳ, etc., as far as is *in* my *power,* etc., X.*Cyr.*5.4.11, Isoc.4.142, etc.; τὸ ἐ. τούτοις εἶναι Lys.28.14; ἐ. τοῖς υἱάσι their *property, Leg.Gort.*4.37. h. *according to,* ἐ. τοῖς νόμοις Lex ap.D.24.56; ἐ. πᾶσι δικαίοις ποιούμεθα τοὺς λόγους Id.20.88; ἐ. προφάσει θηρός S.*Tr.*662 codd. (lyr.). i. of condition or circumstances in which one is, ἀτελευτήτῳ ἐ. ἔργῳ Il.4.175, etc.; ἐπ' ἀρρήτοις λόγοις S.*Ant.*556; ἐπ' ἀσφάκτοις μήλοισι E.*Ion* 228 (lyr.); ταύταις ἐ. συντυχίαις Pi.*P.*1.36; ἐπ' εὐπραξίᾳ S.*OC*1554; ἐ. τῷ παρόντι Th.2.36; ἐπ' αὐτοφώρῳ λαβεῖν, v. αὐτόφωρος; also ἐ. τῷ δείπνῳ *at* dinner, X.*Cyr.*1.3.12, Thphr.*Char.*3.2; ἐ. τῇ κύλικι Pl.*Smp.*214b; ἐ. θαλίαις E.*Med.*192 (anap.). k. Geom., of the point, etc., *at* which letters are written, κέντρον ἐφ' ᾧ Κ Hippocr.ap.Simp.*in Ph.*64.14; ἡ [γραμμὴ] ἐφ' ᾗ ΗΚ the line ΗΚ, Arist.*Mete.*375ᵇ22. 2. with Verbs of Motion: a. where the sense of motion merges in that of support, ἐ. χθονὶ βαίνει Il.4.443; θεῖναι ἐ. γούνασιν 6.92; καταθέσθαι ἐ. γαίῃ 3.114; ἱστὸν ἔστησεν ἐ. ψαμάθοις 23.853; ἐ. φρεσὶ θῆκε 1.55; δυσφόρους ἐπ' ὄμμασι γνώμας βαλεῖν S.*Aj.*51, etc. b. in pregnant construction, πέτονται ἐπ' ἄνθεσιν fly *on to* the flowers *and settle there,* Il.2.89; ἐκ.. βαῖνον ἐ. ῥηγμῖνι θαλάσσης Od.15.499; καθεῖσεν ἐ. Σκαμάνδρῳ Il.5.36; ἦλθε δ' ἐ. Κρήτεσσι 4.251, cf. 273; νῆες εἰρύατ'.. ἐ. θινὶ θαλάσσης 4.248. c. rarely for εἰς c. acc., νηυσὶν ἐ. γλαφυρῇσιν ἐλαυνέμεν 5.327, 11.274. d. in hostile sense, *upon* or *against,* ἐ. τινι ἔχειν, ἰθύνειν ἵππους, 5.240, 8.110; ἐ. τινι ἱέναι βέλος, ἰθύνεσθαι ὀϊστόν, 1.382, Od.22.8; ἐ. τοι Ἀκράγαντι τανύσαις Pi.*O.*2.91; ἐ. Τυδεΐδῃ ἐτιταίνετο.. τόξα Il.5.97; ἐφ' Ἕκτορι.. ἀκοντίσσαι 16.358; κύνας.. σεύῃ ἐπ' ἀγροτέρῳ συΐ 11.293; ὡρμήθησαν ἐπ' ἀνδράσιν Od.10.214, cf. E.*Ph.*1379, etc.: also ἐ. τινι τετάχθαι Th.2.70, 3.13; ὅστις φάρμακα δηλητήρια ποιοῖ ἐ. Τηΐοισιν *SIG*37.2 (Teos, v B.C.). II. of Time, rarely, and never in good Att., exc. in sense of succession (infr. 2), ἐ. νυκτί *by* night, Il.8.529; ἐφ' ἡμέρῃ, αἱ δ' ἐ. νυκτί Hes.*Op.*102; ἐπ' ἤματι τῷδε *on* this very day, Il.13.234; ἐπ' ἤματι *for* to-day, 19.229, 10.48, Od.2.284; αἰεὶ ἐπ' ἤματι every day, 14.105; ἐπ' ἡμέρῃ ἑκάστῃ Hdt.4.112, 5.53, cf. D.S.34/5.2.1; ὁ ἥλιος νέος ἐφ' ἡμέρῃ ἐστίν Heraclit.6; ἐ. τρίς *Act.Ap.*10.16, *PHolm.*1.18. 2. of succession, *after,* ἕκτῃ ἐ. δέκα on the 16th of the month, Chron.ap.D.18.155, Decr.ib.181 (δεκάτῃ codd.); τετράδι ἐ. δέκα *IG*1².304.62; πρὸ τῆς ἕκτης ἐ. δέκα ib.2².1361.19; ἐπ' ἐξεργασμένοισι, = Lat. *re peracta,* Hdt.4.164, etc.; ἐ. τινι ἀγορεύειν, ἀνίστασθαι, E.*Or.*898, 902, X.*Cyr.*2.3.7, etc.; ἐ. διεφθαρμένοισι Ἴωσι Hdt.1.170, τὰ ἐ. τούτοισι, = Lat. *quod superest,* Id.9.78, cf. Th.1.65, A.*Ag.*255, etc.; τοὐπὶ τῷδε πῆμα E.*Hipp.*855 (lyr.), etc. 3. *in the time of* (cf. A. II) only in Arc., ἐπὶ Χαιριάδαι *Schwyzer* 665 *A* 21, cf. 666 (Orchom.). III. in various causal senses: 1. of the occasion or cause, τετεύξεται ἄλγε' ἐπ' αὐτῇ *for* her, Il.21.585; ἐ. σοὶ μάλα πόλλ' ἔπαθον *for* thee, 9.492: freq. with Verbs expressing some mental affection, ἐπὶ παντὶ λόγῳ ἐπτοῆσθαι Heraclit.87; μέγα φρονεῖν ἐ. τινι to be proud *at* or *of* a thing, Pl.*Prt.*342d, X.*HG*3.4.11, etc.; χλιδᾶν ἐ. τινι S.*El.*360; ἀγάλλεσθαι, ἀγανακτεῖν ἐ. τοῖς παροῦσι, X.*An.*2.6.26, Isoc.4.122; ὀνομαστὸς ἐ. τινι γεγονέναι X.*Mem.*1.2.61; also ἐφ' αἵματι φεύγειν to be tried *on* a capital charge, D.21.105; πληγὰς λαμβάνειν ἐ. τινι X.*Cyr.*1.3.16; ζημιοῦσθαι ἐ. τινι D.24.122, etc.: in adverbial phrases [δικάσσαι] ἐπ' ἀρωγῇ *with* favour, Il.23.574; δολίῃ ἐ. τέχνῃ Hes.*Th.*540; ἐ. μιῇ αἰτίῃ ἀνήκεστον πάθος ἔρδειν Hdt.1.137, etc.; ἐ. κακουργίᾳ καὶ οὐκ ἀρετῇ *for* malice, Th.1.37; ἐπ' εὐνοίᾳ, ἐπ' ἔχθρᾳ, D.18.273, 21.55; ἐπ' ἀγαθῇ ἐλπίδι *with*.., X.*Mem.*2.1.18, cf. *Ep.Rom.*4.18; ἐφ' ἑκατέροις *in* both cases, Pl.*Tht.*158d, cf. Xenoph.34.4; ἐ. δάκρυσί τινα καταστένειν E.*Tr.*315 (lyr.); ἐ. τῇ πάσῃ συκοφαντίᾳ καὶ διασεισμῷ Mitteis *Chr.*31 vi (ii B.C.), etc. 2. of an end or purpose, υἱὸν ἐ. κτεάτεσσι λιπέσθαι Il.5.154, cf. 9.482; ἐ. δόρπῳ *for* supper, Od.18.44; ἐ. κακῷ ἀνθρώπου σίδηρος ἀνεύρηται Hdt.1.68; ἐ. διαφθορῇ Id.4.164; ἐ. σῷ καιρῷ S.*Ph.*151 (lyr.); ἐ. τῷ κέρδει X.*Mem.*1.2.56; δῆσαι ἐ. θανάτῳ or τὴν ἐ. θανάτῳ, Hdt.9.37, 3.119, cf. 1.109, X.*An.*1.6.10; ἐ. θανάτῳ συλλαβεῖν Isoc.4.154; ἐπ' ἐξαγωγῇ *for* exportation, Hdt.5.6; χρηστηριάζεσθαι ἐ. τῇ χώρῃ *with a view to gaining*.., Id.1.66; ἐ. τούτοις ἐθύσαντο X.*An.*3.5.18; ἐ. τῷ ὑβρίζεσθαι Th.1.38, cf. 34, etc.; τι κακοτεχνεῖν ἐ. αἰσχύνῃ τοῦ ἀνδρὸς *PEleph.*1.6 (iv B.C.). 3. of the condition *upon* which a thing is done, ἐ. τούτοισι *on* these terms, Hdt.1.60, etc.; ἐ. τοῖσδε, ὥστε.. Th.3.114; ἐ. τούτῳ, ἐπ' ᾧτε *on condition that*.., Hdt.3.83, cf. 7.158: in orat. obliq., ἐπ' or ἐφ' ᾧτε folld. by inf., Id.1.22, 7.154, X.*HG*2.2.20; ἐφ' ᾧ μηδὲν κακὸν ποιήσουσιν Th.1.126 (but ἐφ' ᾧ = *wherefore, Ep.Rom.*5.12); ἐπ' οὐδενί *on* no condition, *on* no account, Hdt.3.38; but, *for* no adequate *reason,* D.21.132; ἐπ' ἴσῃ τε καὶ ὁμοίῃ, ἐπὶ τῇ ἴσῃ καὶ ὁμοίᾳ, *on* fair and equal *terms,* Hdt.9.7, Th.1.27; ἐ. ῥητοῖς, v. ῥητός; also of a woman's dowry, τὴν μητέρα ἐγγυᾶν ἐ. ταῖς ὀγδοήκοντα μναῖς D.28.16; γῆμαί τινα ἐ. δέκα ταλάντοις And.4.13; τὴν θυγατέρα ἔχειν γυναῖκα ἐ. τῇ τυραννίδι Hdt.1.60; *on the principle of*.., ἐ. τῷ μὴ λυπεῖν ἀλλήλους Th.1.71. 4. of the price *for* which.., ἔργον τελέσαι δώρῳ ἔ. μεγάλῳ Il.10.304, cf. 21.445; ἐ. τίνι χρήματι; Hdt.3.38; ἐ. πόσῳ; Pl.*Ap.*41a; ἐ. ταλάντῳ χρυσίου Ar.*Av.*154; ἐπ' ἀργυρίῳ λέγειν, πράττειν, D.19.182, 24.200; ἐ. χρήμασι λυμαίνεσθαι Id.19.332; ἐ. πολλῷ ἐρρᾳθυμηκότες Id.1.15; also of money lent *at* interest, δανείζεσθαι ἐ. τοῖς μεγάλοις τόκοις ibid.; ἐ. δραχμῇ δανείζειν lend *at* 12 per cent., Id.27.9; ἐπ' ὀκτὼ ὀβολοῖς τὴν μνᾶν τοῦ μηνὸς ἑκάστου δανείζειν, i.e. *at* 16 per cent., Id.53.13; ἐ. διακοσίαις εἴκοσι πέντε τὰς χιλίας *for* 225 per mille, i.e. 22.5 per cent., Syngr.ap.eund.35.10; also of the security *on* which money is borrowed, δανείζειν ἐ. ἀνδραπόδοις Id.27.27; ἐπ' οἴνου κεραμίοις τρισχιλίοις Id.35.18; ἐ. νηΐ Id.56.3; δανείζειν ἐ. τοῖς σώμασιν Arist.*Ath.*9.1, cf. 2.2, D.H.4.9. 5. of names, φάος καὶ νὺξ ὀνόμασται.. ἐ. τοῖσί τε καὶ τοῖς Parm.9.2; ἐ. τῇ τοῦ οἰκείου ἔχθρᾳ στάσις κέκληται Pl.*R.*470b; so ὄνομα κεῖται ἐ. τινι X.*Cyr.*2.2.12; ὄνομα καλεῖν ἐ. τινι Pl.*Sph.*218c, cf. 244b; πότερον ταῦτα, πέντε ὀνόματα ὄντα, ἐ. ἑνὶ πράγματί ἐστι Id.*Prt.*349b (v. supr. A. III. 2). 6. of persons in authority, ὅς μ' ἐ. βουσὶν εἶσεν who set me *over* the kine, Od.20.209, cf. 221; ποιμαίνειν ἐπ' ὄεσσι Il.6.25; οὖρον κατέλειπον ἐ. κτεάτεσσιν Od.15.89; σημαίνειν ἐ. δμῳῇσι 22.427; πέμπειν ἐ. τοσούτῳ στρατεύματι Th.6.29; ἐ. ταῖς ναυσίν X.*HG*1.5.11; οἱ ἐ. ταῖς μηχαναῖς Id.*Cyr.*6.3.28; οἱ ἐ. ταῖς καμήλοις ib.33; οἱ ἐ. τοῖς πράγμασιν ὄντες D.9.2; ἐ. θυγατρί.. γαμέειν ἄλλην γυναῖκα Hdt.4.154. 7. *in possession of, possessing,* ἐ. τοῖς ἑαυτοῦ μένειν Th.4.105, cf. 8.86; ζῆν ἐ. παιδίοις, τελευτᾶν ἐ. παιδὶ γνησίῳ, Alciphr.1.3, Philostr.*VS*2.12.2; ἐ. παισὶ διαδόχοις Hdn.4.2.1; ἀποθανεῖν ἐ. κληρονόμοις ταῖς θυγατράσι Artem.1.78, cf. *PMeyer*6.22 (ii A.D.); ἐ. μόνῳ παιδὶ σαλεύειν Hld.1.9.

C. WITH ACC.: I. of Place, *upon* or *on to* a height, with Verbs of Motion, ἐ. πύργον ἔβη Il.6.386, cf. 12.375; ἐ. τὰ ὑψηλότατα τῶν ὀρέων ἀναβαίνειν Hdt.1.131; προελθεῖν ἐ. βῆμα Th.2.34; ἀναβιβαστέον τινά, ἀναβαίνειν ἐ. τὸν ἵππον, Pl.*R.*467e, X.*An.*3.4.35; also ἐξ ἵππων ἀποβάντες ἐ. χθόνα Il.3.265; ἐξεκυλίσθη πρηνὴς ἐ. στόμα *upon* his face, 6.43; ἐ. θρόνον.. ἕζετο 8.442; ὤμω.. ἐ. στῆθος συνοχωκότε drawn together *upon* his breast, 2.218; Ὀδυσσῆ' εἷσαν ἐ. σκέπας Od.6.212; θέσθαι ἐ. τὰ γόνατα X.*An.*7.3.23; ἐπ' ἀμφότερα τὰ ὦτα καθεύδειν Aeschin.Socr.54; ἐ. κεφαλήν head-*foremost,* Pl.*R.*553b, Luc.*Pisc.*48 (v. κεφαλή): less freq. than ἐπί with gen. or dat. b. Geom., αἱ ἐ. τὰς ἁφὰς ἐπιζευγνύμεναι εὐθεῖαι *joining* the points of contact, Archim.*Sph.Cyl.*1.8; κάθετος ἐ. perpendicular *to* (v. κάθετος). 2. *to,* ἦλθε θοὰς ἐ. νῆας Il.1.12, etc.; ἐ. βωμὸν ἄγων ib.440; ἴθυσαν δ' ἐ. τεῖχος 12.443; ἐ. τέρμ' ἀφίκετο S.*Aj.*48; ἡ [ὁδὸς] ἐ. Σοῦσα φέρει X.*An.*3.5.15; ἡ ὁδὸς ἡ ἀπὸ τῶν Πυλῶν ἐ. τὸ Ποσειδώνιον Th.4.118; ἐ. τὸ αὐτὸ αἱ γνῶμαι ἔφερον Id.1.79: c. acc. pers., βῆ δ' ἄρ' ἐπ' Ἀτρεΐδην Il.2.18, cf. 10.18, 85, 150, etc.: sts. in pregn. constr. with Verbs of Rest, ἐπιστῆναι ἐ. τὰς θύρας Pl.*Smp.*212d; παρεῖναι ἐ. τὸν τάφον Th.2.34, cf. X.*Cyr.*3.3.12. b. metaph., ἐ. ἔργα τρέπεσθαι, ἰέναι, Il.3.422, Od.2.127; ἰέναι ἐ. τὸν ἔπαινον Th.2.36; ἐ. συμφορὴν ἐμπεσεῖν Hdt.7.88 codd.; also ἐ. τὴν τράπεζαν ἀποδιδόναι, ὀφείλειν, pay, owe *to* the bank, D.33.12, Docum.ap.eund.45.31; ἡ ἐγγύη ἡ ἐ. τὴν τράπεζαν D.33.10; τὸ ἐ. τὴν τράπεζαν χρέως ib.24; also εἰσποιηθῆναι ἐ. τὸ ὄνομά τινος to be entered *under* his name, Id.44.36. c. *up to, as far as* (μέχρι ἐ. X.*An.*5.1.[1]), παρατείνειν ἐπ' Ἡρακλέας στήλας Hdt.4.181; ἐ. θάλασσαν καθήκειν Th.2.27, 97: metaph., ἐ. πεῖραρ' ἀέθλων ἤλθομεν Od.23.248; ἐ. διηκόσια ἀποδιδόναι yield 200-*fold,* Hdt.1.193; in measurements, πλέον ἢ ἐ. δύο στάδια X.*Cyr.*7.5.8, *An.*6.2.2; ὅσον ἐ. εἴκοσι σταδίους ib.6.4.5, cf. 1.7.15: freq. with a neut. Adj. or Pron., τόσσον τίς τ' ἐπιλεύσσει ὅσον τ' ἐ. λᾶαν ἵησιν Il.3.12; ὅσσον ἐφ' 2.616, cf. 15.358; ἐ. τοσοῦτό γε φρονέω,.. ταύτην μηδὲν σίνεσθαι I am prudent *enough,* not to.., Hdt.6.97; ἐ. ὅσον δεῖ Th.7.66; ἐ. πάντ' ἀφῖγμαι S.*OT*265; ἐ. πᾶν ἐλθεῖν X.*An.*3.1.18; ἐ. τὸ ἔσχατον ἀγῶνος ἐλθεῖν Th.4.92; ἐ. μεῖζον χωρεῖν, ἔρχεσθαι, ib.117, S.*Ph.*259; ἐ. μέγα χωρεῖν δυνάμεως Th.1.118; ἐ. μακρότερον, ἐ. μακρότατον, Id.4.41, 1.1, Hdt.4.16, 192; ἐ. σμικρόν, ἐ. βραχύ, a little *way,* a little, S.*El.*414, Th.1.118; ἐπ' ἔλαττον, ἐπ' ἐλάχιστον, Pl.*Phd.*93b, Th.1.70; ἐπ' ὀλίγον, ἐ. πολλά, Pl.*Sph.*254b; ἐ. πλέον *still* more, Hdt.2.171, 5.51, Th.2.51; rarely with Advs., ἐ. μᾶλλον Hdt.1.94, 4.181. d. *before, into the presence of* (cf. A. I. 2e), ἦγον δή μιν ἐ. τὰ κοινά Id.3.156 (but στὰς ἐ. τὸ συνέδριον standing *at the door of* the council, Id.8.79); ἐ. ἡγεμόνας καὶ βασιλεῖς ἀχθήσεσθε *Ev.Matt.*10.18. e. in Military phrases (cf. A. I. 2d), ἐπ' ἀσπίδας πέντε καὶ εἴκοσιν ἐτάξαντο, i.e. twenty-five *in file,* Th.4.93; dub. in X., as ἐ. πολλοὺς τεταγμένοι many *in file, An.*4.8.11 codd.; ἐπ' ὀλίγον τὸ βάθος γίγνεσθαι *Cyr.*7.5.2 codd.; for ἐ. κέρας v. infr. 3. 3. of the quarter or direction *towards* or *in* which a thing takes place, ἐ. δεξιά, ἐπ' ἀριστερά, *to* the right or left, Il.7.238, 12.240, Od.3.171, Hdt.6.33, etc.; ἐ. τὰ ἕτερα or ἐ. θάτερα, Id.5.74, Th.1.87, etc.; ἐ. τὰ μακρότερα, βραχύτερα, *on* the longer, shorter *side,* Hdt.1.50; ἐπ' ἀμφότερα νοέων both *ways,* Id.8.22; ἐπ' ἀμφότερα μαχᾶν τάμνειν τέλος Pi.*O.*13.57, etc.; ἐ. τάδε Φασήλιδος *on* this *side,* Isoc.7.80; ἐ. ἐκεῖνα, v. ἐπέκεινα; ἐφ' ἕν, ἐ. δύο, ἐ. τρία, of space, *in* one, two, three *dimensions,* Arist.*de An.*404ᵇ23, Plot.6.3.13; in Military phrases, ἐ. δόρυ ἀναστρέψαι, ἐ. ἀσπίδα μεταβαλέσθαι, *to* the spear or shield *side,* i.e. *to*

right or left, X.*An.*4.3.29, *Cyr.*7.5.6; ἐ. πόδα ἀναχωρεῖν, etc., retire *on* the foot, i.e. facing the enemy, Id.*An.*5.2.32; so ἐ. κέρας or ἐ. κέρως πλεῖν, etc., sail *towards* or *on* the wing, i.e. *in* column (v. κέρας VII): metaph., ἐ. τὸ μεῖζον κοσμῆσαι, δεινῶσαι, etc., *with* exaggeration, Th.1.10, 8.74, etc.; ἐ. τὸ πλέον ἀγγέλλεσθαι Id.6.34; ἐ. τὸ φοβερώτερον ib.83; ἐ. τὰ γελοιότερα ἐπαινέσαι so as to provoke laughter, Pl.*Smp.*214e; ἐ. τὰ καλλίω, ἐ. τὰ αἰσχίονα, Id.*Plt.*293e; ἐ. τὸ βέλτιον καὶ κάλλιον, ἐ. τὸ χεῖρον καὶ τὸ αἴσχιον, Id.*R.*381b; ἐ. τὸ ἄμεινον Orac.ap.D.43.66. 4. in hostile sense, *against*, ἰέναι ἐ. νέας Il.13.101; ὦρτο δ' ἐπ' αὐτούς 5.590; στρατεύεσθαι or -εύειν ἐ. τινα, Hdt.1.71,77, Th.1.26, etc.; ἰέναι ἐ. φάτιν S.*OT*495 (lyr.); πλεῖν ἐ. τοὺς Ἀθηναίους Th.2.90; πέμπειν στρατηγὸν ἐ. τινας Hdt.1.153; θύεσθαι ἐ. τινα offer sacrifice *on going against*.., X.*An.*7.8.21; ἐφ' ὑμᾶς *to* your *prejudice*, D.6.33, 10.57. 5. of extension *over* a space, πουλὺν ἐφ' ὑγρὴν ἤλυθον *over* much water, Il.10.27: ἐπ' εὐρέα νῶτα θαλάσσης 2.159; ἐ. κύματα 13.27; δρόων ἐπ' ἀπείρονα πόντον 1.350; πλέων, λεύσσων ἐ. οἴνοπα πόντον, 7.88, 5.771; ἐ. πολλὰ δ' ἀλήθην Od.14.120; ἄγουσι..'Ανδρομάχαν..ἐπ' ἅλμυρον πόντον Sapph.*Supp.*20a.7: also with Verbs of Rest, ἐπ' ἐννέα κεῖτο πέλεθρα *over* nine acres he lay stretched, Od.11.577; τόσσον ἐπ' *over* so much, 5.251, cf. 13.114; διώκοντες ἐ. πολὺ *over* a large space, Th.1.50, cf. 62, etc.; ἐ. πλεῖστον ib.4; ὡς ἐ. πλεῖστον 2.34, etc.; freq. to be rendered *on*, δράκων ἐ. νῶτα δαφοινός Il.2.308; ἵππους..ἐ. νῶτον ἐΐσας ib.765; ὅσσα τε γαῖαν ἔπι πνείει 17.447; ἐ. γαῖαν εἰσὶ δύω [γένη] Hes.*Op.*11; ἀοιδοὶ ἔασιν ἐ. χθόνα *Th.*95; ἐ. γᾶν μέλαιναν ἔμμεναι κάλλιστον Sapph.*Supp.*5.2; also, *among*, κλέος πάντας ἐπ' ἀνθρώπους Il.10.213, cf. 24.202,535; δασσάμενοι [κτήματ'] ἐφ' ἡμέας Od.16.385, cf. Pl.*Prt.*322d. II. of Time, *for* or *during* a certain time, ἐ. χρόνον Il.2.299, Od.14.193; πολλὸν ἐ. χρόνον 12.407; παυρίδιον..ἐ. χρόνον Hes.*Op.*133; ἐ. δηρόν Il.9.415; ἐ. πολὺν χρόνον Pl.*Phd.*84c, etc.; ἐπ' ὀλίγον χρόνον Lycurg.7; ἐ. χρόνον τινά, ἐ. τινα χρόνον, Pl.*Prt.*344b, *Grg.*524d; γῆν ἀπεμίσθωσαν ἐ. δέκα ἔτη Th.3.68; ἐ. διετές Lex ap.D.46.20; ἐ. τρεῖς ἡμέρας X.*An.*6.6.36; τὸ ἐφ' ἡμέραν ἀρκέσον enough *for* the day, Id.*Cyr.*6.2.34, cf. D.50.23, Hdt.1.32; ἐ. πολὺ *for* a long time, Th.1.6, etc. 2. *up to, until* a certain time, εὗδον παννύχιος καὶ ἐπ' ἠῶ καὶ μέσον ἦμαρ Od.7.288; οὐδ' ἐ. γῆρας ἵκετ' 8.226. III. in various causal senses: 1. of the object or purpose *for* which one goes, ἀγγελίην ἔπι Τυδῆ στεῖλαν sent him *for* (i.e. *to bring*) tidings of.., Il.4.384 (dub.); ἐ. βοῦν ἴτω let him go *for* an ox, Od.3.421; ἐ. τεύχεα δ' ἐσσεύοντο Il.2.808; ἐλθεῖν πρός τινα ἐπ' ἀργύριον X.*Cyr.*1.6.12; πέμπειν εἴς τινα ἐ. στράτευμα ib.4.5.31; ἴτω τις ἐφ' ὕδωρ ib.5.3.49; ἥκειν ἐ. τοὺς τόκους *for* (i.e. *to demand*) the interest, D.50.61: less freq. c. acc. pers., ἐπ' Ὀδυσσῆα ἤϊε Od.5.149, cf. S.*OT*555; κατῆλθον ἐ. ποιητήν Ar.*Ra.*1418; κατέρχονται ἐ. τὸν Ἀγόρατον Lys.13.23: with acc. of a Noun of Action, ἐξιέναι ἐ. θήραν go out hunting, X.*Cyr.*1.2.9; ἔπλεον οὐχ ὡς ἐ. ναυμαχίαν (v.l. for -χίᾳ) Th.2.83; ἐ. μάχην ἰέναι X.*An.*1.4.12; ἔρχεσθαι, ἵζειν ἐ. δεῖπνον, Il.2.381, Od.24.394; ἐ. δόρπον ἀνέστη 12.439; κληθεὶς ἐ. δεῖπνον Pl.*Smp.*174e, etc.; καλεῖν ἐ. ξείνια Hdt.2.107, 5.18; ἐ. τὴν θεωρίαν *to see* the sight, *Ev.Luc.*23.48, cf. *PTeb.*33.6 (ii B.C.): freq. with neut. Pron. or Adj., ἐ. τοῦτο ἐλθεῖν *for* this *purpose*, X.*An.*2.5.22, cf. Th.5.87; ἐπ' αὐτὸ τοῦτο Pl.*Grg.*447b, etc.; ἐ. τί; *to* what *end?* Ar.*Nu.*256; ἐφ' ὅ τι Id.*Lys.*22,481; ἐφ' ἃ ἤλθομεν *for* which *purpose*, Th.7.15, etc.; ἐπὶ ἶσα *for* like *ends*, Pi.*N.*7.5 (but ἐ. ἶσα μάχη τέτατο, = ἴσως, Il.12.436); ἐ. τὸ βέλτιον *to* a better *result*, X.*An.*7.8.4; ἀναστῆσαί τινα ἐ. χριστὸν Θεοῦ set up *as* God's anointed, Lxx *2Ki.*23.1: after an Adj., ἄριστοι πᾶσαν ἐπ' ἰθύν Il.6.79, cf. Od.4.434; ἄπορος ἐ. φρόνιμα S.*OT*691 (lyr.); χρήσιμος ἐ...οὐδέν D.25.31: after a Noun, ὁδὸς ἐ. τι X.*Cyr.*1.6.21; ὄργανα ἐ. τι ib.6.2.34. 2. *so far as regards*, τοὐπὶ τήνδε τὴν κόρην S.*Ant.*889; ὅσον γε τοὐπ' ἐμέ E.*Or.*1345; τοὐπί σε, τὸ ἐ. σέ, Id.*Hec.*514, X.*Cyr.*1.4.12; τὸ ἐ. σφᾶς εἶναι Th.4.28; ὡς ἐ. τὸ πολὺ *for* the most part, Arist.*Top.*100b29, etc.; ἐ. πᾶν Th.2.51; τὸ πρὸς ἅπαν ξυνετὸν ἐ. πᾶν ἀργόν Id.3.82; κρείσσων ἐπ' ἀρετήν Democr.181; ἐ. μέγα Call.*Dian.*55. 3. of persons set *over* others, ἐ. τοὺς πεζοὺς καθιστάναι ἄρχοντα X.*Cyr.*4.5.58, cf. *HG*3.4.20; στρατηγὸς ἐ. τοὺς ὁπλίτας, ἐ. τὴν χώραν, Arist.*Ath.*61.1, *IG*2².682.24; ἐ. τὸν Πειραιέα Arist.*Ath.* l.c.; ἐ. Ῥαμνοῦντα *IG*2.1206b (cf. A. III. 1); οἱ θεσμοθέται οἱ ἐ. τοὺς νόμους κληρούμενοι D.20.90. 4. *according to, by*, ἐ. στάθμην *by* the rule, Od.5.245, 21.44, etc.

D. Position:—ἐπί may suffer anastrophe (ἔπι) and follow its case, as in Il.1.162; it may likewise follow its Verb, ἤλυθ' ἔπι ψυχή Od.24.20, cf. Il.9.539. II. in Poets it is sts. put with the second of two Nouns, though in sense it also governs the first, ἢ ἁλὸς ἢ ἐ. γῆς Od.12.27, cf. S.*OT*761, *Ant.*367 (lyr.).

E. Abs., used adverbially, without anastrophe, καὶ ἐ. σκέπας ἦν ἀνέμοιο Od.5.443; κτεῖνον δ' ἐ. μηλοβοτῆρας *as well*, Il.18.529; esp ἐ. δέ.. and *besides*.., Hdt.7.65,75, etc.; πολιαί τ' ἐ. ματέρες S.*OT*182 (lyr.). II. ἔπι, for ἔπεστι, *there is*, Il.1.515, 3.45, Od.16.315; οὐ γὰρ ἔπ' ἀνήρ.. *there is* no man.., 2.58; σοὶ δ' ἐ. μὲν μορφὴ ἐπέων 11.367; ἐ. δέ μοι γέρας A.*Eu.*393 codd. (lyr.).

F. Prosody: in ἐπιόψομαι, ι is not elided before a vowel; also in some words where σ or ϝ has been lost, as ἐπιάλμενος, ἐπιείκελος, ἐπιεικής, ἐπιέξομαι (v. ἐπέχω VII), Dor. ἐπιεργάζομαι (v. ἐπεργάζομαι).

G. in Composition: I. of Place, denoting, 1. Support or Rest *upon*, ἔπειμι (A), ἐπίκειμαι, ἐπικαθίζω, ἐπαυχένιος, ἐπιβώμιος, etc. 2. Motion, a. *upon* or *over*, ἐπιβαίνω, ἐπιτρέχω. b. *to* or *towards*, ἐπέρχομαι, ἐπιστέλλω, ἐπαρίστερος, ἐπιδέξιος. c. *against*, ἐπαΐσσω, ἐπιπλέω II, ἐπιστρατεύω, ἐπιβουλεύω. d. *up to* a point, ἐπιτελέω. e. *over* a place, as in ἐπαιωρέομαι, ἐπαρτάω. f. *over* or *beyond* boundaries, as in ἐπινέμομαι. g. implying reciprocity, as in ἐπιγαμία. 3. Extension *over* a surface, as in ἐπαλείφω, ἐπανθίζω, ἐπιπέτομαι, ἐπιπλέω I, ἐπάργυρος, ἐπίχρυσος. 4. Accumulation of one thing *over* or *besides* another, as in ἐπαγείρω, ἐπιμανθάνω, ἐπαυξάνω, ἐπιβάλλω, ἐπίκτητος. 5. Accompaniment, *to, with*, as in ἐπᾴδω, ἐπαυλέω, ἐπαγρυπνέω: hence of Addition, ἐπίτριτος one *and* $\frac{1}{3}$ *more*, $1+\frac{1}{3}$; so ἐπιτέταρτος, ἐπίπεμπτος, ἐπόγδοος, etc. 6. with Adjs., *somewhat, slightly*, as in ἐπίξανθος, ἐπίπικρος. II. of Time and Sequence, *after*, as in ἐπιβιόω, ἐπιβλαστάνω, ἐπιγίγνομαι, ἐπακόλουθος, ἐπίγονος, ἐπιστάτης I. 2. III. in causal senses: 1. Superiority felt *over* or *at*, as in ἐπιχαίρω, ἐπιγελάω, ἐπαισχύνομαι. 2. Authority *over*, as in ἐπικρατέω, ἔπαρχος, ἐπιβουκόλος, ἐπιποιμήν. 3. Motive *for*, as in ἐπιθυμέω, ἐπιζήμιος, ἐπιθάνατος. 4. to give force or intensity to the Verb, as in ἐπαινέω, ἐπιμέμφομαι, ἐπικείρω, ἐπικλάω.

**ἐπιαλές**· τερπνόν, Hsch.; so prob. ἐ]πιαλῆ οἰωνόν *IG*4.760 (Troezen).

**ἐπιάλλομαι**, Ep. for ἐφάλλομαι, aor. 2 part. ἐπιάλμενος Il.7.15, Od.24.320.

**ἐπιάλλω**, fut. ἐπιαλῶ: aor. ἐπίηλα [ῑ]:—*send upon*, ἑτάροις ἐπὶ χεῖρας ἴαλλε *laid* hands *upon* them, Od.9.288; ἐπὶ δὲ Ζεὺς οὖρον ἴαλλεν 15.475; οὗτος γὰρ ἐπίηλεν τάδε ἔργα for this man *brought* these deeds *to pass*, 22.49; also in Com., ἐπιαλῶ (sc. τὸ κέντρον) I *will lay it on*, Ar.*Nu.*1299, cf. *Fr.*552 (dub. l.), Phryn.Com.1 (dub. l.).

**ἐπίαλος**, = sq., Alc.129.

⊛ **ἐπιάλτης**, ου, ὁ, Aeol. for ἐφιάλτης, Alc.129, Macrob.*Somn.*1.3.7.

**ἐπιανδάνω**, v. ἐφανδάνω. **ἐπιανέω**· ἐπιτρέπω, Hsch.

⊛ **ἐπιάομαι**, *cure*, *BCH*25.235 (Amphissa).

**ἐπίαρον**, τό, = ἐφίερον, *sacred penalty*, *SIG*9 (Elis, vi B.C.).

**ἐπῐαύω**, *sleep among*, c. dat., v.l. (ed. Steph. 1566) for ἐνιαύω, Od.15.557. 2. *sleep upon*, ἠϊόσιν *AP*6.192 (Arch.).

**ἐπῐάχω** [ᾰ], *shout out, shout applause* after a speech, ὣς ἔφαθ'· οἱ δ' ἄρα πάντες ἐπίαχον Il.7.403. 2. *shout*, ὅσσον τ' ἐννεάχιλοι ἐπίαχον 5.860.

**ἐπιβάδαι**, f.l. for ἐπίβδαι, Hsch. **ἐπιβάδες** (sc. ἡμέραι), αἱ, gloss on ἐπίβδαι, Sch.Pi.*P.*4.247a.

⊛ **ἐπιβάθρα**, ἡ, *ladder* or *steps to ascend by*: *scaling ladder*, Ph.*Bel.*91.48, Ath.Mech.25.3, J.*BJ*7.9.2, Arr.*An.*4.27.1; *ship's ladder, gangway*, D.S.12.62. 2. metaph., *means of approach, stepping-stone*, Plb.3.24.14 (pl.); ἐ. ἔχειν τὴν Ἄβυδον Id.16.29.2; γάμον ἐ. τισὶ γενέσθαι J.*AJ*11.8.2; τῆς Ἑλλάδος *towards*.., Plu.*Demetr.*8; τῷ ἑξῆς λόγῳ Arr.*Epict.*1.7.22, cf. Plot.1.6.1; εἰς τὸ ἐξευρεῖν Gal.9.149. 3. *platform* for engines of war, J.*BJ*7.8.5; *base, foundation*, γῆ..τοῖς ἐπ' αὐτῆς βεβηκόσιν ἑδραία ἐ. Plot.2.1.7: metaph., γεῦσις ἐ. τῶν αἰσθήσεων Ph.1.665.

⊛ **ἐπίβαθρον**, τό, *fare of an* ἐπιβάτης, *passenger's fare*, καὶ δέ κεν ἄλλ' ἐ...δοίην Od.15.449, cf. D.S.1.96; so of Charon's *fare*, νεὼς Ἀχεροντείας ἐ. Call.*Fr.*110: generally, *rent, payment for* anything, γῆς Plu.2.727f; *toll*, Call.*Del.*22 (pl.). II. τὰ ἐ., of a sacrifice, regarded as a *fare* paid on embarking, A.R.1.421. III. ἐ. ὀρνίθων *roosting-place, perch*, *AP*9.661 (Jul.); ἐ. ἀοιδῆς *stool* for a singer, ib.140 (Claud.), cf. *PLond.*1821.283. 2. = foreg. 1, *PSI*2.171.27 (pl., dub., ii B.C.).

⊛ **ἐπιβαίνω**, rarely -βάω, imper. ἐπίβā Thgn.847, Dor. inf. ἐπιβῆν (infr. IV): fut. -βήσομαι: pf. -βέβηκα: aor. 2 ἐπέβην: aor. 1 Med. ἐπεβησάμην (of which Hom. always uses the Ep. form ἐπεβήσετο, imper. ἐπιβήσεο Il.8.105, al.; later ἐπεβήσατο A.R.3.869, Dor. -βάσατο Call.*Lav.Pall.*65). A. in these tenses, intr., *go upon*: I. c. gen., *set foot on, tread, walk upon*, γαίης, ἠπείρου, Od.9.83, *h.Cer.*127; πόληος, πατρίδος αἴης, Τροίης, Il.16.396, Od.4.521, 14.229; ἀδύτων ἐπιβὰς E.*Andr.*1034 (lyr.); ἐ. τῶν οὔρων *set foot on* the confines, Hdt.4.125, cf. Th.1.103, Pl.*Lg.*778e; τῆς Λακωνικῆς ἐπὶ πολέμῳ X.*HG*7.4.6; πυρῆς ἐπιβάντ' ἀλεγεινῆς, of a corpse, *placed upon*.., Il.4.99; πλατείᾳ τῇ ῥινὶ ἐ. τοῦ χείλους Philostr.*Im.*2.18; also ἐ. ἐπί τινος Hdt.2.107. 2. *get upon, mount on*, πύργων Il.8.165; νεῶν ib.512; ἵππων 5.328, 10.513; δίφρου 23.379; εὐνῆς 9.133; τοῦ τείχεος Hdt.9.70; λέκτρων ἐ. A.*Supp.*39; also ἐ. ἐπὶ νεός Hdt.8.118: freq. in Hom., in aor. Med., ἐπεβήσετ' ἀπήνης Od.6.78, al. b. Archit., *to be superposed*, τὰ ἐπιβαίνοντα πάντα ἐπὶ τοὺς κρατευτάς *IG*7.3073.104, cf. 111 (Lebad.). 3. of Time, *arrive at*, τετταράκοντα ἐ. ἐτῶν Pl.*Lg.*666b; δεκάτω (sc. ἔτεος) ἐ. Theoc.26.29; δωδεκάτου ἐπιβὰς *IG*14.728; τῆς μειρακίων ἡλικίας Hdn.1.3.1. 4. metaph., ἀναιδείης ἐπέβησαν *have trodden the path of* shamelessness, Od.22.424; ἐϋφροσύνης ἐπιβῆτον *enter into* joy, 23.52; τέχνης ἐπιβήσομαι, -βήμεναι, *h.Merc.*166,465; ὁσίης ib.173; εὐσεβίας S.*OC*189 (lyr.); ἐ. δόξης *entertain* an expectation, Id.*Ph.*1463 (anap.); ἐ. σοφίας *undertake* it, Pl.*Epin.*981a; λόγου Luc.*Astr.*8; ἐ. τῆς ἀφορμῆς, τῆς προφάσεως, *seize upon* it, App.*Syr.*2, *Samn.*11, etc.; *preside over*, τῆς ἀνθρωπίνης ψυχῆς Iamb.*Myst.*9.8, al. II. c. dat., *get upon, board*, ναυσὶ Th.7.70; *land on*, ἐ. τῇ Σικελίᾳ D.S.16.66: metaph., ἐ. ἀνορέαις Pi.*N.*3.20; also, *make forcible entry into*, τινὸς οἰκίαις, γῇ, *PHamb.*10.6 (ii A.D.), *PAmh.*2.142.7 (iv A.D.). b. with a Prep., ἐπὶ πύργῳ ἄλλος πύργος ἐπιβέβηκε Hdt.1.181. 2. c. dat. pers., *set upon, assault*, τινὶ X.*Cyr.*5.2.26, Plu.*Cim.*15, etc.; simply, *approach*, dub. in Pi.*Fr.*88.2. 3. *trample on*, λὰξ ἐπίβα δήμῳ Thgn.847. III. c. acc. loci, *light upon*, in Hom. twice of gods *lighting upon* earth after their descent from Olympus, Πιερίην ἐπιβᾶσα, ἐπιβάς, Il.14.226, Od.5.50; so πολλῶν ἐ. καιρὸν *light on* the fit time, Pi.*N.*1.18; then simply, *go on to* a place, *enter* it, γῆν καὶ ἔθνος Hdt.7.50; λειμῶν' S.*Aj.*144 (anap.): with Prep., ἐ. ἐπὶ χώραν Decr.Amphict.ap.D.18.154; εἰς Βοιωτίαν D.S.14.

84. 2. rarely c. acc. pers., *attack*, only poet., S.*Aj*.138 (anap.): metaph., of passion or suffering, Id.*El*.492 (lyr.), *Ph*.194 (anap.). 3. *mount*, νῶθ' ἵππων ἐπιβάντες Hes.*Sc*.286: more freq. with Prep., ἐπὶ τὸν ἵππον Hdt.4.22; ἐπὶ νέα Id.8.120, cf. Th.1.111; but ἐ. ἐπὶ τὸ θῆλυ, of male quadrupeds, *cover* a female, Arist.*HA*539b26; so abs., ib. 574a20, al.: c. dat., Luc.*Asin*.27: c. gen., Horap.1.46, 2.78. 4. ἐ. ἐπὶ τὸ σκέλος *use, put one's weight on*, a broken leg, Hp.*Fract*. 18. 5. with acc. of the Instr. of Motion (cf. βαίνω A. II. 4), ἐπιβῆναι τῷ ἀριστερῷ ἐκείνης τὸν ἐμὸν δεξιόν Luc.*DMeretr*.4.5, cf. *Tox*.48. IV. abs., *get a footing, stand on one's feet*, Il.5.666, Od.12.434; μὴ 'πιβῆν it is forbidden to *set foot* here, *IG*12(3).1381 (Thera). 2. *step onwards, advance*, Τρώων δὲ πόλις ἐπὶ πᾶσα βέβηκε Il.16.69, cf. Hes.*Op*. 679, f.l. in Pi.*N*.10.43; ἐπίβαινε πόρσω S.*OC*179 (s. v. l., lyr.): metaph., *advance in one's demands*, Plb.1.68.8. 3. *mount on a chariot* or *on horseback, be mounted*, Hdt.3.84; *go* or *be on board ship*, Il.15.387, S.*Aj*.358 (lyr.), Hdt.8.90, Th.2.90, etc.

B. Causal in fut. -βήσω Luc.*DMort*.6.4, Ep. inf. -βησέμεν Il.8.197, Hes.*Th*.396, but usu. in aor. 1 Act. (ἐπιβιβάζω, ἐπιβάσκω serve as pres.):—*make* one *mount, set* him *upon*, ὅν ῥα τόθ' ἵππων.. ἐπέβησε Il.8.129; πολλοὺς δὲ πυρῆς ἐπέβησ' ἀλεγεινῆς 9.546; ὥς κ' ἐμὲ.. ἐμῆς ἐπιβήσετε πάτρης Od.7.223; ἐ. τινὰς σκάφεσιν J.*BJ*4.7.6; πλοίων ib. 11.5, cf. Luc. l. c.; ὁπλίτας ὁλκάσιν App.*BC*5.92; τινὰς ἐπὶ τὰς ναῦς ib.2.59: also in aor. 1 Med., νιν ἑῷ ἐπεβάσατο δίφρῳ Call.*Lav.Pall.* 65. b. of things, νευρὰν ἐπέβασε κορώνας *set* the string *on* his bow's tip, B.5.73. 2. metaph. (cf. A. I. 4), εὐκλείης ἐπίβησον *bring to* great glory, Il.8.285; τιμῆς καὶ γεράων Hes.*Th*.396; χαλιφρονέοντα σαοφροσύνης ἐπέβησαν they *bring* him *to* sobriety, Od.23.13; λιγυρῆς ἐπέβησαν ἀοιδῆς Hes.*Op*.659; δουλοσύνας (prob.) E.*Hyps.Fr*.41(64). 86; εἴ σε τύχη.. ἡλικίας ἐπέβησεν *had brought thee to* full age, *IG*2. 2263. 3. [ἠὼς] πολέας ἐπέβησε κελεύθου dawn *sets* them *on* their way, Hes.*Op*.580.

**ἐπιβακχεύω**, *rush on like a bacchanal*, Nicostr.Com.4.

**ἐπιβάλλον**, τό, a kind of *ephemeron* (insect), Sch.[Arr.]*Peripl.M. Eux*.60 (p.417 M.), Sch.Antig.*Mir*.85(92).

⊛ **ἐπιβάλλω**: I. trans., *throw* or *cast upon*, θριξὶ.., ἃς ἐπέβαλλον (sc. πυρί) Il.23.135; ἐπὶ δὲ χλαῖναν βάλεν αὐτῷ Od.14.520, cf. 4.440; ἑωυτὸν ἐς τὸ πῦρ v.l. in Hdt.7.107; φάρη κόραις E.*El*.1221 (lyr.); ἐ. τινὰς ἐπὶ ἁμάξας Th.4.48, cf. Hdt.4.75, 5.112; ἐπιβάλλοντας (sc. χοῦν) *throwing on more and more*, Th.2.76. 2. *lay on*, [ἡμιόνοις] ἐπέβαλλεν ἱμάσθλην Od.6.320; ἐ. πληγάς τινι X.*Lac*.2.8; Ζεὺς ἐπὶ χεῖρα βάλοι A.*Ch*.395 (lyr.), cf. Ar.*Nu*.933 (anap.); ἐ. τὴν χεῖρά τινι Id.*Lys*. 440 (but τῷ καρπῷ τοῦ νοσοῦντος τὴν χεῖρα, of feeling the pulse, Gal. 18(2).40; so τὴν ἁφὴν Id.8.821, Marcellin.*Puls*.119); τὰς χεῖρας τοῖς κατ' Αἴγαιον Plb.3.2.8; Ῥωμαίοις Id.18.51.8; ἐπί τινα *Ev.Matt*.26.50; *impose* as a tax, tribute, τινί τι Hdt.1.106, Th.8.108; as a fine or penalty, ζημίην, φυγὴν ἐ. τινί, Hdt.6.92 (Pass.), 7.3; ἀργύριον Lys.9.6; ἐπιβολὰς Id.20.14, cf. Arist.*Ath*.61.2; λύτρα Lxx *Ex*.21.30 (Pass.); *inflict*, θνατοῖς ἐ. ἀνάλγητα, λύπην, etc., S.*Tr*.128 (lyr.), E.*Med*.1115 (anap.), etc. 3. ἐ. σφρηγῖδα, δακτύλιον, *affix* a seal, Hdt.3.128, 2.38; σφραγῖδ' ἐπί τι Ar.*Av*.559; σύμβολόν τινι ib.1215. 4. *add, contribute*, μικρὸν [ἀληθείᾳ] Arist.*Metaph*.993b2; ἐ. ἐπὶ τὸ ὕδωρ Thphr.*Ign*.49; νέον [φῶς] Pl.*Cra*.409b: metaph., *throw in, mention*, τι dub. in S.*El*.1246 (lyr.) (in Med., "χαίρειν" τεοῖς προθύροις ἐπιβάλλομαι Theoc.23.27); Φαῖστος.. ἐπιβάλλων φησὶ Sch.Pi.*P*.4.28: abs., *bid higher*, Arist.*Pol*.1259a14. 5. *place next in order*, Plb.1.26. 15. 6. *let grow*, κλήματα Thphr.*HP*4.13.5; βλαστοὺς ib.3.5. 1. 7. *let loose*, πρόβατα ἐπὶ κνῆκον *PRyl*.69.6 (i B.C.). 8. causal of ἐπιβαίνω A. III. 3, D.Chr.7.134. II. *throw oneself upon, go straight towards*, c. acc., ἡ δὲ Φεὰς ἐπέβαλλεν Od.15.297: later c. dat. loci, Plb.5.18.3, D.S.1.30, Plot.3.7.12, etc.; νήσοις Rhian.39; εἰς Ἰταλίαν, ἐπὶ τὸν τόπον, Plb.2.24.17, 5.6.6, cf. *PAmh*.2.31.5 (ii B.C.), etc. 2. *fall upon*, ὅπου ἂν ὁ ἥλιος ἐ. Arist.*HA*598a3; esp. in hostile sense, *set upon*, c. dat., ib.623b1, etc.; τοῖς Ἀρβήλοις D.S.17.64: abs., ἐ. λῃστρικῷ τρόπῳ *PRyl*.127.10 (i A.D.); ἐπιβάλλουσαι *jostling, trampling*, Pl.*Phdr*.248a; sens. obsc., Ar.*Av*.1216. 3. (sc. τὸν νοῦν) *set to* a thing, *devote oneself to* it, c. dat., M.Ant.10.30; τοῖς αὐλοῖς D.S.3.59; τοῖς κοινοῖς πράγμασιν Plu.*Cic*.4 (in full τὴν διάνοιαν ἐ. πρός τι D.S.20.43): generally, *give one's attention to, think on*, *Ev.Marc*. 14.72. b. *apprehend*, Epicur.*Fr*.423; *attain by intuition*, c. dat., Dam.*Pr*.54. 4. *fall in one's way*, ὅταν ἐπιβάλλῃ περὶ τῆς τοιαύτης πολιτείας ἡ σκέψις Arist.*Pol*.1266a25; κατὰ τὸν ἐπιβάλλοντα λόγον Id.*GA*716a3. 5. *follow, come next*, Plb.11.23.2; τισί Plu.*Aem*. 33; ἐφ' ὃν ἐπιβαλὼν ἔφη said *thereupon*, Plb.1.80.1; *interrupt*, ἀποκρινομένῳ Thphr.*Char*.7.2. 6. *belong to, fall to the share of*, μόριον ὅσον αὐτοῖσι ἐπέβαλλε Hdt.7.23, cf. Diph.43.16; εἰ μὴ τὸ ὅλον, μέρος γε, ἐπιβάλλει τῆς βλασφημίας ἅπασι D.18.272; ὅσον ἐπιβάλλει αὐτοῖς Arist.*Pol*.1260a19; ἑκάστῳ τῆς εὐδαιμονίας ἐπιβάλλει τοσοῦτον ὅσονπερ ἀρετῆς ib.1323b21; τῶν κτημάτων τὸ ἐπιβάλλον (sc. μέρος) *the portion that falls to one*, Hdt.4.115, cf. Lxx *To*.3.17, 6.12; τὸ ἐ. ἐφ' ἡμᾶς μέρος D.18.254; τὸ ἐ. μέρος τῆς οὐσίας *Ev.Luc*.15.12, cf. *PGrenf*. 1.33.33 (ii B.C.), etc.; *fall due*, of payments, *PLond*.1.3.21 (ii B.C.); τόκον ὃν ἔφη ἐπιβάλλειν αὐτῷ which *was payable by* him, *BCH*6.21 (Delos, ii B.C.). b. part. ἐπιβάλλων, in Law, *next-of-kin*, ὁ ἐ., οἱ ἐ., *Leg.Gort*.7.36, 11.42, al. 7. impers. c. acc. et inf., τοὺς Δελφοὺς δὴ ἐπέβαλλε.. παρασχεῖν *it concerned* them to provide, Hdt.2.180: or c. dat. et inf., ἐπιβάλλει τινὶ ποιεῖν τι Chrysipp.*Stoic*.2.39, al., Plb.18. 51.1; ἐπιβάλλοντος ἡμῖν εὐεργετικοῖς εἶναι Corn.*ND*15; κοινῇ πᾶσιν ἐπιβάλλει *UPZ*112.10 (ii B.C.); καθότι ἐπέβαλλεν ἀνδρὶ καλῷ καὶ ἀγαθῷ *IG*12(7).231.5 (Amorgos): freq. in part., ἐπιβάλλουσαν ἡγεῖσθαι τὴν στρατείαν τινί *incumbent* upon.., Teles p.61 H.; τὸ ἐπιβάλλον Cleanth. *Stoic*.1.128, Arr.*Epict*.2.11.3, etc.; τὰς -ούσας τάσεις τῆς φωνῆς Chrysipp.*Stoic*.2.96; τὸ τῇ φύσει ἐ. Antip.*Stoic*.3.255; *appropriate*, ὑποδοχαί Teles p.41 H.; ἱμάτια *IG*2².1121.15; ἁρμονία Iamb.*Comm. Math*.30; ἡ στέρησις ἐπιβάλλοντός ἐστι παρεῖναι εἴδους τινός a specific form which *ought* to be present, Plot.1.8.11. 8. *shut to, close*, of the larynx, Arist.*PA*664b26. 9. in Logic, λόγοι ἐπιβάλλοντες, -όμενοι, *overlapping* and *overlapped*, of syllogisms in a sorites, Chrysipp.*Stoic*.2.85; so of Time, ἐπέβαλε τοῖς χρόνοις Ἰουλιανῷ Eun.*VS* p.497 B.:—Med., γηραιῷ τῷ Κυρηναίῳ ἐπεβάλετο Anon.*Intr.Arat*. p.326 M. 10. in Alchemy, *make a 'projection'* (cf. ἐπιβολή), Syn.Alch.p.68 B. III. Med., mostly like the intr. usages, but also: 1. c. gen., *throw oneself upon, desire eagerly*, ἐνάρων ἐπιβαλλόμενος Il.6.68; παρθενίας ἐπιβάλλομαι Sapph.102; τοῦ εὖ ζῆν ἐπιβάλλονται Arist.*Pol*.1258a3. 2. c. acc., *put upon oneself*, ἐπιβαλλομέναν.. πλόκον ἀνθέων E.*Med*.840; ἐπιβάλλεσθαι *put on more wraps*, Thphr.*Char*.2.10 (cf. IV. 1); ὕπνον ἡδὺν -όμενος D.Chr.12.51: metaph., *take possession of*, καὶ ἐπὶ κλήρους ἐβάλοντο Od.14.209; αὐθαίρετον δουλείαν ἐπιβαλεῖται *will take upon himself*, Th.6.40. b. of trees, *make fresh growth*, Thphr.*HP*3.5.1. 3. c. acc., also, *attempt, undertake*, ἔργον Pl.*Sph*.264b, *Ti*.48c; μέθοδον Arist.*Pol*. 1260b36: c. inf., Decr.ap.D.18.164, Zeno *Stoic*.1.68, Plb.1.43.2, etc.: abs., πολλῶν -ημένων though many have *made the attempt*, Agatharch.76. 4. c. dat., *put one's hand to*, ἐχέτλῃ *AP*7.650 (Phal.(?)): metaph., *apply* or *devote oneself to*, τόλμῃ καὶ πράξει Plb.5.81.1; ἐγχειρήματι μεγάλῳ D.H.5.25, etc. 5. *arrive at*, [πολίεσσι] Call.*Del*.68; ὅταν ἐπὶ τοὺς χρόνους ἐπιβαλώμεθα D.S.19. 55. 6. ἐπὶ πᾶσι -εβάλοντο *brought up the rear*, Id.18.33. IV. in Pass., *lie upon, be put upon*, ἐπιβεβλημένοι τοξόται archers *with their arrows on the string*, X.*An*.4.3.28, cf. 5.2.12; λάσιον ἐπιβεβλημένος *having* a rough cloak *on*, Theopomp.Com.36; τὸ ἐν ψύχει κεῖσθαι -ημένον Hp.*Epid*.2.3.1, cf. 6.4.14; διφθέραν -ημένη D.Chr.5.25. 2. *to be set over*, ὁ τελώνης ὁ ἐπιβεβλημένος τῷ Ζεύγματι Philostr.*VA*1. 20. 3. Rhet., *ornate* (v. ἐπιβολή), ἰδέα λόγων οὔτ' ἐπιβεβλημένη οὔτ' αὖος Id.*VS*1.20.2.

**ἐπίβαλμα**, ατος, τό, = ὑποπόδιον, Hsch. (leg. ἐπίβαμα). **ἐπίβαλος**, ὁ, *heel*, Id.

**ἐπιβαπτίζω**, metaph., *sink, overwhelm*, J.*BJ*1.27.1, 3.7.15.

**ἐπίβαπτος**, ον, *covered with* (lit. *steeped in*), τινί Thphr.*HP*3.7.4.

**ἐπιβάπτω**, *dip into*, τι ἔς τι Hp.*Morb*.3.16. II. *tan*, Arist.*Pr*. 898b18; *dye*, Alex.Trall.2; *gild* or *silver*, Ps.-Democr.p.46 B.

**ἐπιβάρ-εσις** [ᾰ], εως, ἡ, *burden imposed* on a person, *PLond*.5. 1674.24 (vi A.D.). **-έω**, *weigh down*: hence, *be a burden to*, τινά 1*Ep.Thess*.2.9; *overload*, of food, τὸν ὄγκον Sor.1.108: c. dat., *press heavily upon*, τοῖς ἠτυχηκόσι App.*BC*4.31, cf. 15, 5.107:—Med., *lay a burden on oneself, trouble oneself*, c. inf., *POxy*.1481.12 (ii A.D.):—Pass., with fut. Med. ἐπιβαρήσομαι D.H.4.9, 8.73; ὑπό τινος *SIG* 807.16 (Magn. Mae., i A.D.); ὑπὸ τῶν δανείων *IG*12(5).860.9 (Tenos). 2. Pass., of a bandage, *to be found irksome*, *PMed.Lond*.3. 39. (Cf. ἐπιζαρέω.) **-ής**, ές, *heavy*, Hero *Bel*.102.9. **-ησις**, εως, ἡ, *burden*, *IG*12(5).860.32 (Tenos). ⊛ **-ύνω**, *press heavily on* the enemy, App.*Mith*.25. **-υς**, εια, υ, *oppressive*, εὐωδία Thphr. *HP*3.13.6.

**ἐπι-βᾰσία**, ἡ, = sq., -βασίαν ποιεῖσθαι D.C.80.3, *Fr*.37.2; πρὸς τὴν ὑπατείαν εἰληφέναι Id.37.54: concrete, in pl., ἵνα αἱ ἐ. διὰ [τῆς γεφύρας] διεξίωσιν Id.68.13. 2. ἐ. τῇ δίκῃ, sine expl., Hyp.*Fr*. 242. 3. *wrongful entry*, interpol. in Poll.2.200. **-βᾰσις**, εως, ἡ, *stepping upon*, ἐς τὴν ναῦν Luc.*Nav*.12; *advent*, *Annuario* 6/7.417 (Phaselis); αἱ ἐ. τῆς θαλάσσης *risings*.., Plb.34.9.6. 2. *means of approach, access*, ἔχειν ἐ. *IG*7.167 (Megara); τοῦ νοητοῦ -σεις Plot.6.7. 36; ἐ. τοῦ ἐραστοῦ Them.*Or*.13.163d: hence concretely, *rungs, steps*, Pl.*R*.511b (pl.). 3. ἔς τινα ποιεῖσθαι ἐ. make *a handle against, a means of attacking* one, Hdt.6.61; ἐ. τι τίθεσθαι εἴς τι App.*BC*1.37; *attack*, Luc.*Hist.Conscr*.49; ἀμφισβητούμενον ἢ ἐπίβασιν ἔχον liable *to be impugned*, *IG*2².1051a14. 4. *getting on one's feet*, of a child beginning to walk, Sor.1.114; esp. in recovery after a broken leg, Hp. *Fract*.18 (pl.); τῇ ἐ. χρῆσθαι Id.*Art*.58; *foothold*, in snow, Plb.3.54. 5. 5. *resting of one thing on another*, e.g. of a bone, Hp.*Art*.51. 6. Rhet., κατ' ἐπίβασιν by *gradation*, Longin.11.1. 7. *that on which one stands*, Ph.1.125, 332. 8. *entry* into office, *PLond*.3.1170.3 (iii A.D.). II. of the male, *covering*, Plu.2.754a (pl.). ⊛ **-βάσκω**, causal of ἐπιβαίνω, c. gen., κακῶν ἐπιβασκέμεν υἷας Ἀχαιῶν *lead* them *into* misery, Il.2.234. (Perh. by haplology from ἐπιβιβάσκω.)

**ἐπιβαστάζω**, *weigh in the hand*, E.*Cyc*.379.

**ἐπιβᾰτ-έον**, *one must tread*, ἐπὶ [ἴχνη] Arist.*Mir*.838a34. **-εύω**, *set one's foot upon, occupy*, c. gen., Συρίας Plu.*Ant*.28, cf. Luc.*Cont*. 2: metaph., *take one's stand upon*, τοῦ Σμέρδιος οὐνόματος ἐπιβατεύων *usurping* it, Hdt.3.63, cf. 67, 9.95; τῆς ἡγεμονίας D.C.79.7; τὸ τῆς οὐσίας ἐν -εῦον Dam.*Pr*.88; τούτου ἐ. τοῦ ῥήματος *rely upon*.., Hdt.6.65. II. *to be an* ἐπιβάτης, *passenger* or *soldier on board ship*, ἐ. ἐπὶ [νεῶν] ib.15, al., Luc.*Par*.46; ἐπὶ νηὶ Pl.*La*.183d: c. dat., Ar.*Ra*.48 (with an obscene allusion, cf. ἐπιβαίνω A. III. 3). 2. *mount*, τοῦ θρόνου Philostr.*VS*2.8.2. **-ηγός** (sc. ναῦς), ἡ, *conveying marines*, Ulp.ap.*Dig*.14.1.12. ⊛ **-ήριος**, ον, *fit for scaling*, μηχαναί J.*BJ*3.7.23. 2. *belonging to the entry* of a place, ᾠδή Him.*Ecl*.13. 38. II. a name of Apollo at Corinth, Paus.2.32.2. III. ἐπιβατήριον, τό, *festival to celebrate the advent* of a god, *CIG*4352–5 (Side). 2. ἐπιβατήρια (sc. ἱερά), τά, *sacrifices on disembarkation*, Lib.*Decl*.6.37. 3. λόγος ἐ. speech delivered *on disembarka-*

*tion*, Men.Rh.p.377S., al. ⊛ **-ης**, ου, ὁ, *one who mounts* or *embarks*: 1. ἐπιβάται, οἱ, *soldiers on board ship, fighting men*, opp. the rowers and seamen, *marines*, Hdt.6.12, 7.100, Th.3.95, Plb. 1.51.2, etc. b. *merchant on board ship, supercargo*, D.34.51, 56. 10. c. *passenger* on ship, D.Chr.1.29, al., Plu.*inHes*.8. d. subordinate officer in the Spartan navy, Th.8.61, X.*HG*1.3.17, *Hell. Oxy*.17.4. 2. *fighting man* in a chariot, Pl.*Criti*.119b; on an elephant, Arr.*An*.5.17.3. 3. *rider*, Arist.*EN*1106$^a$20, Luc.*Zeux*. 10. 4. *male quadruped*, *Gp*.16.21.9. 5. *heel*, Hsch. 6. *middle finger*, [Ruf.]*Onom.App*.p.600R. **-ικός**, ή, όν, *of* or *for the* ἐπιβάται, ἡ ἐ. χρεία *their* service, Plb.3.95.5; τὸ ἐ. *the complement of* ἐπιβάται on board ship, Arist.*Pol*.1327$^b$9, Plb.1.47.9 (pl.) (but also, *payment for the* ἐ., *IG*1$^2$.127.20,37, cf. 35). II. ἐπιβατικά, τά, = παρενθήκη II, *EM*357.45, Hsch. **-όριος** ἵππος *stallion*, interpol. in Suid. s.v. κηλώνιον. ⊛ **-ός**, ή, όν (D.C.44.42), *that can be climbed, accessible*, Hdt.4.62; ἐξ ἧς ἐπιβατὸν..τοῖς τότε ἐγίγνετο πορευομένοις there was *a passage* for them, Pl.*Ti*.24e; τὴν Κελτικὴν ἐπιβατὴν ποιῆσαι D.C. l.c.: metaph., χρυσίῳ ἐ. *accessible* to a bribe, Plu.*Dem*. 14. II. παίων ἐ. foot consisting of five long syllables, Id.2.1143b.

**ἐπιβάφια** [βᾰ], τά, in Alchemy, *powders* for gilding and silvering, Zos.Alch.p.218B.

**ἐπίβδᾰ**, ἡ, *the day after a festival*, Sch.Pi.*P*.4.249, *EM*357.54 (pl.); esp. *the day after* the three days of *the Apaturia*, Hsch. s.v. ἐπιβδάαι: proverb., ἕρπειν πρὸς τραχεῖαν ἐπίβδαν come to hard *reckoning* (on the day after the feast, when the guests suffer from excess), Pi.*P*. 4.140; χαῖρε..ταῖς ἐπίβδαις Cratin.323. 2. *new-year's day*, Aristid. *Or*.51(27).26 (pl.).

**ἐπιβδάλλω**, *milk a second time*, Sch.Pi.*P*.4.249.

**ἐπιβεβαι-όω**, *add proof*, Thphr.*CP*5.14.4; *confirm*, ὑποψίαν J.*BJ* 1.22.5; *ratify*, νόμον Plu.*Cat.Mi*.32, cf. *PLond*.3.1157$^v$*b*4 (iii A.D.): —Pass., *to be further confirmed*, Arist.*APr*.47$^a$6. **-ωσις**, εως, ἡ, *further confirmation*, Id.*Rh.Al*.1438$^b$29 (pl.); *guarantee*, *Sammelb*. 5240.17 (i A.D.).

**ἐπιβελτίωσις**, εως, ἡ, *amelioration*, *Gloss*.

**ἐπιβήματα**· εἴδη χορικῆς ὀρχήσεως, Hsch.

**Ἐπιβήμιος**, ὁ, epith. of Zeus at Siphnos, Hsch.

**ἐπιβήτ-ης**, ου, ὁ, *one who sets foot on* or *dwells in*, Orph.*Fr*.353. ⊛**-ωρ**, ορος, ὁ, *one who mounts*, ἐ. ἵππων Od.18.263, Simm.1.3; νεὼς ἐπιβήτορα λαόν, = ἐπιβάτας, *AP*7.498 (Antip.(?)); ἐ. κύκλων, of the Trojan horse, Tryph.307. 2. of male animals, e.g. a boar, συῶν ἐπιβήτωρ Od.11.131; of a bull, Theoc.25.128. II. as Adj., *springing*, Nonn.*D*.20.113. 2. metaph., *at home in, master of* a thing, θηροδιδασκαλίης Man.4.245; *dwelling in*, ὕλης οὐρανίας κτλ. Orph.*Fr*.353.

⊛ **ἐπιβῐ-άζομαι**, *constrain besides*, *CIG*(add.)4325*k* (Olympus), *Rev. Phil*.36.56 (Iconium). **-αστικός**, ή, όν, *exercising constraint*, Epicur.*Nat.Herc*.1420.3.

⊛ **ἐπιβιβ-άζω** (fut. -βιβῶ Lxx*Ho*.10.11, *Hb*.3.15), causal of ἐπιβαίνω, *put* one *upon*, ἐπ' ὀλίγας ναῦς τοὺς ὁπλίτας Th.4.31; τινὰ ἐπὶ τὸ ἴδιον κτῆνος *Ev.Luc*.10.34:—Pass., Apollod.3.1.1. **-άσκω**, = foreg., *put the male to the female*, Arist.*HA*573$^b$1.

**ἐπιβιβρώσκω**, *eat with* a thing, ἐπὶ δὲ γλυκὺ κηρίον ἔβρως (aor. 2) Call.*Jov*.49; ἐπιβεβρωμένος *eaten off at the top*, Gal.14.74; -βρωθέντα *eaten afterwards*, Dsc.*Eup*.2.140.

**ἐπίβῐος**, ον, *surviving*, παιδίον Is.*Fr*.156 (nisi leg. -βιόν).

⊛**ἐπιβῐόω**, only in aor. 2 -εβίων:—*live over* or *after, survive*, ἐπεβίω δύο ἔτη Th.2.65; ἐπεβίων διὰ παντὸς [τοῦ πολέμου] Id.5.26; ἐπιβιόντος..πένθ' ἡμέρας D.41.18, cf. Is.2.45; but αἷς ἄν..ἐπιβιῶ *live to see* married, Pl.*Ep*.361d. (Freq. corrupted to -βιοῦντα, etc. in codd.)

**ἐπιβλᾰβής**, ές, *hurtful*, Aret.*CD*1.2; τῇ ψυχῇ Hierocl.*inCA*13 p.448M.; τὸ ἐ. Procl.*Par.Ptol*.166. Adv. -βῶς Poll.5.135.

**ἐπιβλαί**· περόναι, Hsch.

**ἐπιβλάπτω**, *damage, mar*, εἰς τὸ κάλλος ὑπὸ τῆς λύπης J.*AJ*7.8.5 (Pass., v.l.).

**ἐπιβλάς**· συννεφὲς νιφετῷ, Hsch.; cf. ἐπιβλύξ.

**ἐπιβλαστ-άνω**, *grow* or *sprout on*, τοῖς γεώδεσι Plu.2.325b. II. *grow in addition* or *after*, Thphr.*CP*1.10.6, *HP*7.2.3; τοῖς πρώτοις (sc. φύλλοις) ἀπορρέουσιν ἑτέρων -όντων Plu.2.723f. **-ησις**, εως, ἡ, *after-growth*, Thphr.*HP*3.5.5, *CP*1.10.6, 1.13.6. **-ικός**, ή, όν, *able to grow afresh*, ib.8 (Comp.).

**ἐπιβλασφημέω**, *load with reproaches*, App.*BC*1.115 (Pass.). II. abs., *use blasphemous language*, J.*AJ*20.5.4.

**ἐπι-βλεπτέον**, *one must look at*, Arist.*APr*.45$^b$28. ⊛ **-βλέπω**, fut. -ψομαι, later -ψω Lxx*Le*.26.9:—*look upon, look attentively*, εἴς τινα Pl.*Phd*.63a; ἐπὶ πόλιν Din.1.72; ἐφ' ἑαυτόν v.l. in Arist.*EN*1120$^b$6; πρός τινα Lxx*Ho*.11.4; τινί Luc.*Astr*.20. 2. c. acc., *look well at, observe*, λόγους ἀθρόους Pl.*Lg*.811d; αἰτίαν Arist.*EN*1147$^a$24; κοινωνίαν Id.*Metaph*.991$^a$8: c. acc. dupl., ἄφθαρτον τὸν θεὸν ἐπεβλέψαμεν Phld.*D*.3*Fr*.39; τῆς κατὰ τὴν γαστέρα ταραχῆς -ομένης *being taken into consideration*, Gal.15.673. 3. *face* upwards or downwards, Dsc.5.120. II. *eye with envy*, τύχαις S.*OT*1526. III. Astrol., *to be in aspect with*, Heph.Astr.3.20. **-βλεψις**, εως, ἡ, *looking at*, τοῦ θεάτρου εἴς τινα Plu.*Phil*.11; *view*, ἔργου Id.*Nic*.25, al. 2. of the mind, *inquiry*, Arist.*APr*.45$^b$19, 45$^a$17 (pl.), Epicur.*Ep*.1 p.3U., Porph.*Abst*.1.41. 3. Astrol., *being in aspect*, Procl.*Par.Ptol*.166.

**ἐπιβλήδην**, Adv. *laying on*, ἐλάοντες, of hammers, A.R.2.80.

⊛ **ἐπί-βλημα**, ατος, τό, *that which is thrown over, covering*, Nicostr. Com.15; *coverlet, bedspread*, *IG*12(5).593.4 (Iulis, v B.C.), Gal.14. 638, Sor.1.85; *head-covering*, Gal.*UP*11.12. 2. *tapestry, hangings*, Plu.*Cat.Ma*.4, Arr.*An*.6.29.5. II. *that which is put on, piece of embroidery*, ἐ. ποικίλον *IG*1$^2$.387.28, 2$^2$.1514.31; *mantle*, Lxx *Is*.3.22. 2. *patch*, *Ev.Matt*.9.16, etc. 3. *outer bandage*, Paul. Aeg.6.92. **-βληματικός**, ή, όν, *introductory*, τρόπος Ptol.*Tetr*. 107. **-βλής**, ῆτος, ὁ, *bolt* or *bar fitting into* a socket, Il.24.453; sens. obsc., *AP*5.241 (Eratosth.). II. *cover*, ib.7.479 (Theodorid.). III. ἡ ἐ. (sc. δοκός) *cross-beam*, Lys.*Fr*.175S., *IG*11.144 *A*58 (Delos, iv B.C.), 2$^2$.463.62, 1672.193. **-βλητέον**, *one must apply*, ἀμυχάς Antyll.ap.Orib.7.18.3; ἐμβροχάς Paul.Aeg.3.43; προσθέτοισι ἐς τὴν χώρην Aret.*CA*2.10; *one must make an attempt*, τινί Artem.1.11. 2. -τέον, τό, *accessory reagent*, Ps.-Democr. p.47B. **-βλήτιον**, τό, = ἐπίβλημα I, *SIG*1026 24, al. (pl., Athens, v B.C.). **-βλητικός**, ή, όν, *apprehending directly* (v. ἐπιβολή I. 2b), τρόπος Epicur.*Nat*.28.6; νοήσεις Iamb.*Protr*.4; *quick to apprehend*, τοῦ ἀληθοῦς Alex.Aphr.*in Top*.584.13, cf. Herm.*inPhdr*.p.113A. Adv. -κῶς *by direct apprehension*, Epicur.*Ep*.1 p.12U., Phlp.*in de An*. 547.9, Id.*in APo*.332.14. II. Adv. -κῶς, gloss on ἐπιβλήδην, Sch. A.R.2.80. **-βλητος**, ον, *put upon*, Sm.*Ez*.27.20. II. *imposed, levied*, *Gloss*.

**ἐπι-βλύζω**, *pour forth*, *AP*9.349 (Leon.). **-βλύξ**, Adv. *abundantly, redundantly*, Pherecr.130.4. II. ἐπιβλύξ· συννεφής, Hsch. (-βληξ cod.). **-βλυσμός**, ὁ, *gushing forth*, Aq.*Ge*.2.6, al. **-βλύω**, *flow over*, A.R.4.1238.

⊛ **ἐπιβο-άω**, fut. -βοήσομαι, Ion. and Ep. -βώσομαι (v. infr.):—*call upon* or *to, cry out to*, ἐ. τινὶ ὅτι.. Th.5.65; ἐ. τινί, c. inf., *call on* one to do.., Id.4.28, 7.70: c. acc., *invoke*, θεόν *AP*9.334 (Pers.): abs., of hounds, *give tongue*, X.*Cyn*.6.19; *cry out*, Arr.*Epict*.4.1.14; of *calling upon* the dead at funerals, *BMus.Inscr*.791, al. (Cnidus). 2. *utter* or *sing aloud over*, τινί τι, μέλος χέρνιβι ἐπιβοᾶν Ar.*Av*.898; *shriek out besides*, στέρν' ἄρασσε κἀπιβόα τὸ Μύσιον A.*Pers*.1054 codd. (lyr.); ἔγχει, κἀπιβόα τρίτον παιῶνα Pherecr.131.5. 3. Med., *cry out against*, Luc.*DMeretr*.12.1:—Pass., τὰ ἴδια ἐπιβοώμενος cried out *against* in regard to private matters, Th.6.16. 4. *applaud, acclaim*, Arr.*Epict*.3.23.10, M.Ant.10.34. II. Med., *invoke, call upon*, θεοὺς ἐπιβώσομαι Od.1.378; σὲ γὰρ πρώτην..ἐπιβωσόμεθ' (v.l. for ἐπιδωσόμεθ') Il.10.463; τὸν Ἀπόλλωνα ἐπιβώσασθαι Hdt.1.87; ἐπιβοᾶται Θέμιν E.*Med*.168 (lyr.); θεοὺς..ἐπιβοώμενοι, πατέρων τάφους ἐ., Th. 3.59,67; ὅρκους καὶ πίστεις D.H.11.49; *call to aid*, τὴν ἄλλην στρατιὴν ἐπεβώσαντο Hdt.9.23, cf. 5.1: c. inf., ἐ. [τινὰ] μὴ ἀπολέσαι τὴν πατρίδα Th.8.92. 2. c. acc. rei, *call out*, Id.7.69. **-ή**, ἡ, = ἐπιβόησις, D.L.5.90.

⊛ **ἐπιβοήθ-εια**, ἡ, *coming to aid, succour*, Th.3.51, X.*Cyr*.5.4.47. **-έω**, Dor. -βοᾱθέω, *come to aid, succour*, τινί Hdt.3.146, 7.207, Th.1.73, 4.29, al., *SIG*398.7 (Cos, iii B.C.): abs., Th.3.69, *PPetr*.2 p.143 (iii B.C.), etc. II. *come to aid against*, τινί Th.3.26; ἐπὶ τὸ ἐχόμενον X.*HG*7.5.24. **-ητέον**, *one must take protective measures*, Ath. Med.ap.Orib.*inc*.23.7.

**ἐπιβό-ημα**, ατος, τό, *a call* or *cry to* one, Th.5.65: pl., D.C.42.19, al. **-ησις**, εως, ἡ, *applause*, D.H.*Rh*.7.3: pl., J.*Vit*.48, Plu.*Arat*. 23, D.Chr.40.29, M.Ant.1.16, Charito6.2. 2. *shouting*, Str.10.3. 15. ⊛ **-ητος**, Ion. -βωτος, ον, *cried out against, ill spoken of*, περί τινος Th.6.16; ἐπίβωτος ἀνθρώποις Aeschrio8, cf. Anacr.60. Adv. -τως *notoriously*, Poll.5.160. II. in good sense, *famous*, D.C.60. 28, Themist.*Ep*.11.

**ἐπιβόθριος**, ον, *in* or *at the trench*, Aristid.*Or*.48(24).27.

**ἐπίβοιον**, τό, = τὸ ἐπὶ βοῒ θῦμα, *sacrifice* of a sheep to Pandrosos *after an ox offered* to Athena, Philoch.32, Lycurg.*Fr*.35.

⊛ **ἐπιβόλ-αιον**, τό, *covering, wrapper, garment*, Lxx*Ez*.13.18,21, Herod.Med.in*Rh.Mus*.58.100, Ar.Byz.*Epit*.9.10. ⊛ **-εύς**, έως, ὁ, epith. of Heracles at Thurii, Hsch. ⊛ **-ή**, ἡ, *throwing* or *laying on*, ἱματίων Th.2.49 (pl.); χειρῶν σιδηρῶν, of grappling-irons, Id.7.62 (pl.); τῶν χρωμάτων Luc.*Zeux*.5; σημείων *affixing* of seals, Id.*Tim*. 13; χειρῶν ἐπιβολαὶ ἐγίνοντο *a fray* arose, D.H.10.33. b. χειρῶν ἐπιβολή *massage*, Gal.6.92; without χειρῶν, σκληρὰ ἐ. ib.101, cf. 176. 2. metaph., ἐ. τῆς διανοίας *application* of the mind to a thing, Epicur.*Ep*.1 pp.5,12U. (pl.), Ph.1.230 (pl.), Plot.2.4.10; αἱ ἐ. τῶν νοημάτων Philostr.*VS*2.18; ἐξ ἐπιβολῆς πάνυ very *scrupulously*, Antyll.ap.Orib.45.25.5. b. *act of direct apprehension*, Epicur.*Ep*.1 p.3U.: pl., ib.p.4U.; ἡ ἐκ τῶν ἐ. ταραχή Phld.*D*.1.14; ἐπί τι Epicur. *Fr*.255, cf. Plot.1.6.2; *intuition*, [τῇ ψυχῇ] τὴν ἐπιβολὴν ἀθρόαν ἀθρόων γίνεσθαι Id.4.4.1; [γνῶσις] ἐφάψεται τοῦ ἑνὸς κατὰ ἐπιβολήν Dam.*Pr*. 25bis; opp. συλλογισμός, ibid. c. *conception, notion*, Iamb.*Comm. Math*.1, cf.9, Dam.*Pr*.258 (pl.); *point of view*, ib.201, 396, al.; *doctrine*, ἡ τοῦ Συριανοῦ θαυμασία ἐ. ib.270: pl., *principles*, Ael.*Tact*.21.1. d. *impulse*, *Stoic*.3.41,149; ἐ. φιλοποιίας ib.96. 3. *setting upon* a thing, *design, attempt, enterprise*, v.l. in Th.3.45: c. gen., ἡ ἐ. τῆς ἱστορίας *writing* history, Plb.1.4.2; τῶν ὅλων *acquisition* of empire, Id.1.3.6, cf. 5.95.1; κατασκευασμάτων ἐπιβολαὶ *designs*, Plu.*Per*.12; ἐξ ἐπιβολῆς *designedly*, D.S.13.27. b. of surgical operations, οὐδεμία ὄνησις τῆς ἐ. Philum.*Ven*.4.7; μὴ κατακολουθεῖν ἀδυνάτοις ἐπιβολαῖς Hegetor ap.Apollon.Cit.3. 4. *hostile attempt, assault*, Plb.6.25.7 (pl.), cj. for -βουλάς in Th.1.93. 5. *application* of name to thing, Procl.*in Cra*.p.109P., al. II. *that which is laid on*, ἐπιβολαὶ πλίνθων *courses* of bricks, Th.3.20; βυρσῶν *layers* of hide, Luc.*Nav*.4; *superstructure, gallery*, Ph.*Bel*.80.36 (pl.); λεπιδοειδεῖς ἐπιβολαί the squamous *commissures* of the skull, Gal.10.452. 2. *penalty, fine*, *IG*1$^2$.84.29 (pl.), Ar.*V*.769; ἐπιβολὴν ἐπιβάλλειν Lys.20.14 (pl.), X. *HG*1.7.2, etc.; ἐπιβολὰς ὀφλεῖν And.1.73; ἡ ἐ. τῆς βουλῆς *the penalty imposed* by the council, Aeschin.2.93; ἐξ ἐπιβολῆς in consequence

of infliction of a *fine*, Lys.6.21. **3.** *requisition, number of men required*, Plb.3.106.3; *impost, public burden*, Plu.*Cat.Ma.*18 (pl.), cf. Procop.*Arc.*23; τῆς λαογραφίας *PTeb.*391.19 (i A. D.); *requisition* of corn, *PFay.*81.9 (ii A. D.). **b.** *additional quantity*, *IG*2².1672.285,297. **c.** κατ' ἐπιβολήν τινος *in proportion* to.., *pro rata*, *CPR* 28.17 (ii A. D.), etc. **III.** *a thing put over for shelter* or *protection*, Thphr.*CP*3.16.4. **2.** ἐ. χώματος *embankment*, *PPetr.*3 p.80 (iii B. C.). **3.** *cloak*, *POxy.*298.9 (i A. D.), etc. **IV.** Rhet., = ἐπαναφορά, Phoeb.*Fig.*2.4, Rut.Lup.1.7. **2.** *introduction, approach* to a subject, Hermog.*Id.*1.3; ἐ. τοῦ ῥυθμοῦ ib.2.1. **3.** *power*, '*grasp*', of style or treatment, χάρις καὶ ἐ. D.Chr.18.14; *general survey, consideration*, Ptol.*Tetr.*204; Ἀλεξάνδρου τὴν ἐν ταῖς παρατάξεσιν ἐ. Ael. *Tact.Praef.*6. **4.** '*trimmings*', *ornament*, τὸ ἀφαιρεῖν τὰς ἐ. καὶ αὐτοῖς χρῆσθαι τοῖς ὀνόμασι Aristid.*Rh.*p.522 S. **V.** in Alchemy, '*projection*', i.e. chemical reaction intended to produce transmutation, Syn.Alch.p.58 B. (pl.). **-ος,** ον, f.l. for ἐπήβολος (q.v.), Vett. Val.11.16, 39.35. Adv. -βόλως, = φρονίμως, Hsch.

**ἐπιβομβέω,** *make a booming noise with*, τυμπάνῳ Luc.*DDeor.*12.1. **2.** *ring*, οὔασι Nonn.*D.*40.503. **II.** trans., *cause to sound*, ἠχώ ib.21.230.

**ἐπιβόσκ-ησις,** εως, ἡ, *feeding upon*, Thphr.*CP*5.17.6 (pl.). **-ίς,** ίδος, ἡ, of insects, = προβοσκίς, Arist.*PA*678ᵇ13. **-ομαι,** of cattle, *graze* or *feed upon*, σεύτλοις Batr.54:—Pass., *to be fed upon, eaten down*, τὰ ἐπιβοσκόμενα Thphr.*HP*3.6.3. **2.** *feed on, draw its nutriment from*, αἶαν Nic.*Th.*68: metaph., *devour*, of poison, ib.430; of fire, Hdn.1.14.5. **3.** metaph., *haunt, visit*, θεοὶ ἐ. γῆν Max.Tyr. 19.6. **II.** *feed among*, ποίμνης Mosch.2.82.

**ἐπιβουκόλος,** ὁ, = βουκόλος, Od.3.422, al., usu. in pleon. phrase, βοῶν ἐ. ἀνήρ: without ἀνήρ, 22.292.

**ἐπιβούλ-ευμα,** ατος, τό, *plot, scheme*, Th.3.45, J.*AJ*17.12.2, Plu. *Caes.*4 (pl.), D.C.61.13. **-ευσις,** εως, ἡ, *plotting, treachery*, Pl. *Lg.*872d, prob. in A.*Th.*29. **-ευτής,** οῦ, ὁ, *one who plots against*, ἐ. στρατοῦ S.*Aj.*726. **-ευτικός,** ή, όν, *treacherous*, Ptol.*Tetr.*66. Adv. -κῶς ib.191. ※ **-εύω,** Dor. -βωλεύω *SIG*527.145 (Dreros, iii B. C.):—*plot, contrive against*, c. dat. pers. et acc. rei, ἐ. ⟨κακὸν⟩ πόλει Tyrt.4.8; ἐπανάστασίν τινι Hdt.3.119; θάνατόν τινι ib.122, And.4.15; τοὺς θανάτους τοῖς πέλας Antipho 1.28; κατάλυσιν τῇ τυραννίδι Th.6.54. **b.** c. dat. only, *plot against, lay snares for*, τῇ πόλει A. *Th.*29 codd., *SIG* l.c.; τῷ πλήθει Ar.*Pl.*570, Th.6.60; θεοῖς Pl.*R.* 378c; τῇ πολιτείᾳ D.8.40: c. dat. rei, *tamper with*, σφραγῖδι *Cat.Cod. Astr.*2.193: abs., οὑπιβουλεύων the *plotter*, S.*OT*618, cf. Pl.*Lg.*856c, Arist.*EN*1135ᵇ33: also in aor. 1 Med., *plot*, Arr.*Epict.*4.1.160. **c.** c. acc. rei only, *plan secretly*, τὸν ἔκπλουν Th.7.51; ἀπόστασιν Id.8. 60, etc. **2.** c. dat. rei, *form designs upon, aim at*, πρήγμασι μεγάλοισι Hdt.3.122; ἀνδριάντι Id.1.183; τυραννίδι Pl.*Grg.*473c, etc.; ἔργοις τοιούτοις Lys.28.8. **3.** c. inf., *purpose* or *design to* do, Ἀρίονα ἐκβαλόντες ἔχειν τὰ χρήματα Hdt.1.24; ἐπιχειρήσειν Id.6.137; ποιεῖν Ar.*Pl.*1111; ἐξελθεῖν Th.3.20; καταλῦσαι τὴν δημοκρατίαν Lys.13.12; ἀποκτεινύναι Pl.*R.*566b; also ἐ. ὅπως.. X.*Cyr.*1.4.13: abs., Th.3. 82. **4.** *to be injurious*, δριμύτητα τοῖς ὀφθαλμοῖς -εύουσαν Paul.Aeg. 6.9. **II.** Pass., with fut. Med. -εύσομαι (in pass. sense) X.*Cyr.* 5.4.34: fut. Pass. -ευθήσομαι D.C.52.33: aor. -εβουλεύθην Antipho 4.2.6, Th.1.82, D.22.1, Men.481.15, etc. (but v. supr. 1.1b):—*to have plots formed against one, to be the object of plots*, Antipho l.c.; ὑπό τινος Th.4.60,64, Isoc.4.140; εἰς χρήματα D. l.c. **2.** of things, *to be designed against*, πρᾶγμα.., ὃ τοῖς θεοῖς.. ἐπιβουλεύεται Ar.*Pax* 404: abs., Antipho 2.1.1, Th.3.96; τὰ ἐπιβουλευόμενα *plots*, X.*Eq. Mag.*9.8. **-ή,** ἡ, *plan formed against* another, *plot, scheme*, Hdt. 1.12, Th.4.77,86, Isoc.4.148, etc.; ἐπιβουλὴν ἐπιβουλεύειν Lys.13.18; πρός τινα against one, X.*An.*1.1.8; ἐξ ἐπιβουλῆς *by treachery, treacherously*, ἐξ ἐ. ἀποθανεῖν, ἐξ ἐ. φονεὺς εἶναι, Antipho 2.1.5, 1.3, cf. Th.8.92, X.*An.*6.4.7, etc.; μετὰ ἐπιβουλῆς *designedly*, Pl.*Lg.*867a, al. **-ία,** ἡ, *treachery*, Pi.*N.*4.37, D.S.26.15. **-ος,** ον, *plotting against*, τοῖς καλοῖς Pl.*Smp.*203d: abs., *treacherous*, νόσοι A.*Supp.*587 (lyr.); of persons, X.*Cyr.*1.6.27, Thphr.*Char.*1.7; [θηρίον] (i.e. παῖς) Pl.*Lg.* 808d; δεινὸς καὶ ἐ. a deep *designing fellow*, Lys.*Fr.*75.2; γένος Diph. 66.4; πίθηκον, ἐ. κακόν Eub.115; ζῷα ἐ. Arist.*HA*488ᵇ16,18; τὰ ἐ. τῶν ἀνθρώπων creatures *which prey on* man, Plu.2.727f; τὰ ἐ. τῆς ψυχῆς Porph.*Antr.*34; ἐ. ἀνέμων *PMag.Leid.V.*7.22: Comp. -ότερον, ζῷον Pl.*Tht.*174d: Sup. -ότατος D.Chr.10.7. Adv. -λως, γίγνεσθαι D.H.11.49, cf. Plu.2.715b, etc.; πράσσειν J.*AJ*17.5.7.

**ἐπιβρᾰδ-ύνω,** *tarry* or *loiter at* a place, Luc.*Tim.*46 (nisi leg. ἔτι βρ.). **2.** *to be late* or *in default*, *PFlor.*278 ii 13 (iii A. D.), etc. **II.** trans., *slacken*, opp. ἐπιταχύνειν, τὸν τόνον τῆς ἀπαγγελίας Aristid. *Rh.*p.545 S.; of planetary influence, Vett.Val.219.23; intr., of the pulse, Gal.8.492. **-υς,** εια, υ, *slow, hesitating*, Hsch.s.v. μελλονικιᾶν.

**ἐπιβρᾰχεῖν,** aor. 2 inf. with no pres. in use, *echo, resound*, ἐπέβραχε Q.S.5.498, 8.408; in tmesi, A.R.4.642, Orph.*A.*995.

**ἐπί-βρεγμα,** ατος, τό, *wet application, lotion*, Philonid.ap.Ath.15. 692; *affusion, douche*, Dsc.4.170, Gal.19.720; *decoction*, Ruf.*Ren. Ves.*7.3. **-βρεκτέον,** *one must foment*, Id.*Sat.Gon.*45.

**ἐπιβρέμω,** *make to roar*, τὸ δ' (sc. πῦρ) ἐπιβρέμει ἲς ἀνέμοιο Il.17. 739:—Med., *roar*, χείλεσιν δεινὸν ἐ. χελιδών (comicé) Ar.*Ra.*680 (lyr.), cf. Opp.*C.*4.171. **II.** *roar out*, [ἐπ'] εὐάσμασι τοιάδ' ἐπιβρέμει E.*Ba.*151: abs., *ring*, οὔασιν ἠχῇ Musae.193; στεροπῇσιν Q.S.14.458.

**ἐπιβρέχω,** *pour water on, water*, cj. for ἀποβρίθουσι in Thphr.*HP* 5.3.3; *rain upon*, παγίδας ἐπί τινας Lxx *Ps.*10(11).6. **II.** impers., *it rains*, Simp.*in Epict.*p.92 D.

**ἐπιβρῑθ-ής,** ές, *falling heavy upon*, A.*Eu.*965 (lyr.). ※ **-ω,** *fall heavy upon, fall heavily*, of rain, ὅτ' ἐπιβρίσῃ Διὸς ὄμβρος Il.5.91, 12. 286; in good sense, ὁππότε δὴ Διὸς ὧραι ἐπιβρίσειαν ὕπερθεν when the seasons *weigh down* [the vines], i.e. make the clusters heavy, Od. 24.344; *press down*, μένος τῆς πορθμίδος Ael.*NA*13.19; of winds, Thphr.*Vent.*34; ἐπ' ἄλσεα Q.S.3.326: c. dat., ἐλάτῃσι Id.12.124, cf. 2.371, al.: metaph., μή ποτ' ἐπιβρίσῃ πόλεμος Il.7.343; of persons, ἐπέβρισαν.. ἀμφὶ ἄνακτα *pressed closely, thronged* around him, 12.414, cf. Theoc.22.93, App.*BC*4.25; esp. in Tactics, *exert pressure*, τοῖς σώμασι Ascl.*Tact.*5.2, cf. Arr.*Tact.*12.10; τοῖς πεζοῖς Jul.*Or.*1.36d: generally, ᾗ ἂν ἐπιβρίσῃ Porph.*Abst.*1.43; also of wealth, ὄλβος εὖτ' ἂν ἐπιβρίσαις ἕπηται follows *in full weight*, Pi.*P.*3.106; of love, Opp. *C.*1.392; of wine, ib.4.351; of sleep, *AP*9.481 (Jul.). **II.** trans., *press on*, τὸν κριὸν ἐπὶ τὰ γέρρα J.*BJ*3.7.23; *press home*, ἀκωκὴν ἐ. Opp.*H.*2.467.

**ἐπιβρῑμάομαι,** *to be angry at*, *Gloss.*; cf. ἐπιβρωμάομαι: also ἐπιβριμεῖ (sic)· ἐπιφωνεῖ, Hsch.

**ἐπιβρομέω,** *roar upon* or *over*, of the sea, σπιλάδεσσιν A.R.3.1371; of sea-birds, *scream over*, πελάγεσσιν Id.4.240. **2.** c. acc. cogn., βρύχημα, of lions, Opp.*C.*3.36; κτύπον Nonn.*D.*6.115. **3.** Pass., ὄφρ'.. ἐπιβρομέωνται ἀκουαί *may be filled with the sound*, A.R.4.908.

**ἐπιβροντ-άω,** *thunder in response*, Plu.*Marc.*12: impers., *it thunders as well*, Ps.-Gem.*Calend.*p.183 W. **-ητος,** ον, = ἐμβρόντητος, *frantic*, S.*Aj.*1386.

**ἐπιβροχέω,** *tie with a noose* or *ligament*, τὸ περιτόναιον Gal.14.789.

**ἐπιβροχή,** ἡ, *wetting, bathing*, Gal.14.732, Sor.1.67 (pl.).

**ἐπίβροχος,** ον, *rainy*, ἑσπέρα Lyd.*Ost.*62.

※ **ἐπιβρύκω** [ῡ], *snap at* another, dub. for ἀπο-, Archipp.35. **II.** ἐ. ὀδόντα *gnash* the teeth, *AP*7.433 (Tymn.):—also in form **ἐπιβρύχω,** abs., *gnash the teeth*, Herod.6.13.

**ἐπιβρυχάομαι,** *roar at*, Nonn.*D.*2.245: abs., λέων -ώμενος Aristid. *Or.*28(49).124.

**ἐπιβρύχω,** v. ἐπιβρύκω.

**ἐπιβρύω,** fut. -ύσω [ῠ], *burst over*, as water: of flowers, *burst forth*, Theoc.22.43; ἐ. σκώληξι *to be overrun by*.., Alciphr.1.17.

**ἐπιβρωμάομαι,** *bray at*, λεχώϊσιν Call.*Del.*56 (nisi leg. ἐπεβριμᾶτο).

**ἐπιβρωτέον,** *one must eat afterwards*, Philum.*Ven.*21.4.

**ἐπιβύστρα,** ἡ, *stopper, stoppage*, ὤτων Luc.*Lex.*1.

**ἐπιβύω,** fut. -ύσω [ῡ], *stop up*, εἰ μή.. ἐπιβύσει τις αὐτοῦ τὸ στόμα Cratin.186; τὸ στόμ' ἐπιβύσας κέρμασιν τῶν ῥητόρων Ar.*Pl.*379:—Med., ἐπιβύσασθαι τὰ ὦτα Luc.*Tim.*9, *Pr.Im.*29.

**ἐπιβωθέω,** Ion. for ἐπιβοηθέω (q.v.).

**ἐπιβωμ-ίζω,** *sacrifice at an altar*, *PSI*4.435.8, *PCair.Zen.*34.8 (iii B. C.), cf. Hsch. **-ιος,** ον, *on* or *at the altar*, ψόλος A.*Fr.*24; πῦρ E.*Andr.*1024 (lyr.); βοῦς *AP*9.453 (Mel.); ἐπιβώμια μῆλ' ἐρύσαι drag them *to the altar*, A.R.4.1129; θεοῖς ἐπιβώμια ῥέζειν Theoc.16.26; ἐ. δᾷδες Hld.10.16; ἐπιβώμιος (sc. λόγος), ὁ, Hp.*Ep.*26; Δημοσθένης ἐ. *seated on an altar*, *IG*14.1146. **II.** Subst., *priest of an altar*, *Ath. Mitt.*35.457 (Pergam.). **-ιοστατέω** (as if from a Subst. ἐπιβωμιοστάτης), *stand suppliant at the altar*, E.*Heracl.*44. ※ **-ίς,** = Lat. *altarium*, *Gloss.* **-ίτης** [ῑ], ου, ὁ, *one who attends the altar, a sacrificing priest*, Lysim.ap.J.*Ap.*1.34 (pl.).

**ἐπιβώσομαι,** Ion. for ἐπιβοήσομαι, fut. of ἐπιβοάω, Hom.

**ἐπιβωστρέω,** Ion. and Dor. for ἐπιβοάω, *shout to, call upon*, τινά Theoc.12.35 (nisi leg. ἐπιβῶται).

**ἐπίβωτος,** ον, Ion. for ἐπιβόητος.

**ἐπιβώτωρ,** ορος, ὁ, *shepherd*, ἐπιβώτορι μήλων Od.13.222.

※ **ἐπίγαιος,** ον, *upon the earth*, τὰ ἐ. *the parts on* or *near the ground*, Hdt.2.125; cf. ἐπίγειος.

※ **ἐπιγαιόω,** *make into land*, Zos.2.35.2 (Pass.).

※ **ἐπιγᾰμβρ-εία,** ἡ, *connexion by marriage*, *Peripl.M.Rubr.*16 (-βρίαν codd.), dub. in J.*BJ*1.8.9. **-ευμα,** ατος, τό, = foreg., Sch.E.*Or.* 477. ※ **-ευσις,** εως, ἡ, = foreg., Anon.*in Rh.*78.31 (-γάμευσις codd.). **-ευτής,** οῦ, ὁ, *one connected by marriage*, Aq.*De.*25. 7. **-εύω,** *become son-in-law*, τῷ βασιλεῖ Lxx 1 *Ki.*18.22, cf. Lyd. *Mens.*1.13. **2.** *become father-in-law*, τινί Lxx 1 *Ma.*10.54,56. **II.** ἐ. γυναῖκα *take* a woman *to wife as her husband's next of kin*, ib.*Ge.*38. 8 (v.l.), *Ev.Matt.*22.24. **III.** Med., *intermarry with*, Lxx *Ge.*34. 9, 2 *Ch.*18.1.

※ **ἐπιγᾰμ-έω,** *marry besides*, ἐ. πόσει πόσιν *wed one* husband *after* another, E.*Or.*589; τῇ θυγατρὶ ἐ. τὴν μητέρα *marry* the mother *after* the daughter, And.1.128; ἐ. τέκνοις μητρυιάν *marry and set* a stepmother *over* one's children, E.*Alc.*305, cf. Plu.*Cat.Ma.* 24; ἡ ἐπιγαμηθεῖσα γυνή *the second* wife, D.S.16.93, cf. Plu.*Them.* 32. ※ **-ία,** ἡ, *additional marriage*, Ath.13.560c. **2.** *connexion by marriage*, J.*AJ*17.1.1, al.; πρός τινα Id.*BJ*1.12.13. **II.** *right of intermarriage* between states, ἐπιγαμίας.. καὶ ἐπεργασίας καὶ ἐπινομίας X.*Cyr.*3.2.23; Ἀθαναίοις δόμεν ἐπιγαμίαν Decr.Byz.ap.D.18.91, cf. *GDI*5040 (Hierapytna), Wilcken *Chr.*27 (ii A. D.). **b.** = Lat. *conubium*, *BGU*265.7 (ii A. D.), etc.: generally, *intermarriage*, mostly pl., ἐπιγαμίας ποιεῖσθαι Hdt.2.147; ἀλλήλοις X.*Cyr.*1.5.3, cf. Decr. ap.D.18.187 (sg.); Εὐβοεῦσιν Lys.34.3; παρ' ἀλλήλοις X.*HG*5.2.19; πρὸς ἀλλήλους Arist.*Pol.*1280ᵇ16, Str.5.3.4; ἐπιγαμίαις χρῆσθαι Arist. *Pol.*1280ᵇ36. **-ιος,** ον, *nuptial*, εὐχαί Ph.2.301. **-ος,** ον, *marriageable*, masc. in Hdt.1.196; more freq. as fem., D.40.4, Pl. *Ep.*361d, Men.658, *Epit.*575, etc. **II.** = πατρῷος, Hsch. (fort. ἐπίπαμος· πατρῷος).

**ἐπιγᾰν-όω,** *varnish, glaze*, σιλφίῳ Alex.186.10; cf. ἐπαγάνωσις.

**ἐπιγάνυμαι** [ᾰ], *exult in*, τινί Hsch.

**ἐπιγάστριος,** ον, *over the belly*: τὸ ἐ. the *covering of the abdominal*

*cavity* from thorax to pubes, Ruf.*Onom.*97, Sor.2.55, Gal.17(2).534, Aret.*SA*2.10, Plu.2.559f, *PSI*3.252.37 (iii A.D.): esp. of *the part above the navel*, Poll.2.170, Ps.-Gal.14.705.

**ἐπίγαυρον**· ἰσχυρόν, Hsch.

**ἐπιγαυρόω**, *make proud*, ἑαυτούς Plu.2.78c; τινὰς τιμαῖς καὶ ἀρχαῖς D.C.56.3:—Pass., *to be proud of, exult in*, ἐπιγαυρωθεὶς τῇ ἐντολῇ X. *Cyr.*2.4.30, cf. Them.*Or.*11.143c: abs., Plu.*Oth.*17, 2.760f.

⊕ **ἐπιγδουπέω**, Ep. for ἐπιδουπέω, *shout at* or *in applause*, ἐπὶ δ' ἐγδούπησαν Ἀθηναίη τε καὶ Ἥρη Il.11.45: abs., *sound aloud*, *AP*9.662 (Agath.): c. acc. cogn., καναχὴν ἐ. Nonn.*D.*1.243.

**ἐπιγείζω**, *live on earth*, ψυχὴ ἀνθρωπευομένη καὶ ἄλλως ἐπιγείζουσα Herm.ap.Stob.1.49.68.

**ἐπιγείνομαι**, = ἐπιγίγνομαι, Pi.*P.*4.47 (nisi metri gr. pro ἐπιγενομένων).

**ἐπιγειόκαυλος**, ον, *with procumbent stem*, Thphr.*HP*6.4.5, cj. in 7.8.1.

⊕ **ἐπίγειος**, ον, *on* or *of the earth, terrestrial*, ζῷα Pl.*R.*546a; βροτοί *IG*14.1571; opp. ὑπόγειος, *PMag.Par.*1.3043 (iii A.D.), etc. 2. *creeping*, of plants, Thphr.*HP*3.18.6, 6.2.2, al.; but *land* plants, opp. water-plants, Arist.*PA*681ᵃ21; *living on the ground*, [ὄρνιθες], τετράποδα, Id.*HA*633ᵇ1, *PA*657ᵇ24. 3. neut. pl., ἐπίγεια *ground-floor*, opp. πύργος διώρυφος, *PPetr.*2 p.20 (iii B.C.). II. Subst. ἐπίγειον, τό, misspelling of ἐπίγυον, v.l. in Ar.*Fr.*80,426. (Cf. ἐπίγαιος.)

**ἐπιγειόφυλλος**, ον, *with radical leaves flat on the ground, rosulate*, Thphr.*HP*7.8.3, 9.10.1.

**ἐπιγεισόω**, *put on a coping-stone*, Hsch. s. v. ἐθρίγκωσεν.

**ἐπιγειτνιάω**, *border upon*, Hsch. s. v. ἐπιχωρεῖ.

**ἐπιγελαστάρ**· ὁ καταγελῶν (Lacon.), Hsch.

**ἐπιγελάω**, fut. -άσομαι [ᾰ] Lxx*Pr.*1.26:—*laugh approvingly*, γέλασαν δ' ἐπὶ πάντες Ἀχαιοί Il.23.840, cf. Pl.*Phd.*62a, X.*Ap.*28, etc.; ἐ. χορείαις *smile upon*, Ar.*Th.*979 (lyr.); τινὶ σκώψαντι Thphr.*Char.*2.4: abs., κύματα ἐπιγελᾷ *break with a plashing sound*, Arist.*Pr.*931ᵃ35; στόματα ἐπιγελῶντα, of the mouths of rivers, Str.1.4.2 (s. v.l.); λόγοι ἐπιγελῶντες *pleasant* words, Plu.2.27f. 2. metaph., *sparkle on the surface*, ἐπεγέλασέ τις ὕλη τῷ μίγματι Herm.ap.Stob.1.49.44. II. = ἐπεγγελάω, Lxx*Pr.*1.26, Gal.6.234, Luc.*Bis Acc.*5; τῷ δυστυχοῦντι Chilo ap.Stob.3.1.172.

**ἐπιγεμ-ίζω**, *lay as a burden*, ἐπὶ ὄνους Lxx*Ne.*13.15, cf. *AB* 94. **-ισις**, εως, ἡ, perh. *straining*, spiritus cohibitio κατ' ἐπιγέμισιν vocata, Gal.4.222 Chart.

**ἐπιγέν-ημα**, ατος, τό, *excess of price realized over cost, profit*, *PPetr.* 2 p.2 (iii B.C.); opp. ἔκδεια, *PRev.Laws*17.2 (iii B.C.). **-ής**, ές, *growing after* (opp. συγγενής), φακός Poll.4.194.

⊕ **ἐπιγενν-άω**, *generate after*, *Theol.Ar.*64:—Pass., κοινὸν πάντων εὐτύχημα ἐπεγεννήθη Καῖσαρ *Inscr.Prien.*105.9 (i B.C.), cf. Ath.14. 653d: metaph., *spring up*, Phld.*D.*1.16. **-ημα**, Dor. -ᾱμα (Ps.-Archyt.ap.Stob.3.1.112), ατος, τό, *that which grows upon*: hence, *coating* of the tongue, Hp.*Coac.*225. 2. *superfetation*, Steph.*in Hp.*2.470 D. II. *that which is produced after*, Plu.2.637e, Longin. 6; κατὰ ἐ. *accidental*, opp. congenital, Antyll.ap.Orib.50.2.1. 2. *result, consequence*, Plb.*Fr.*41 (pl.), Phld.*Ir.*p.40 W., al.; ἡ ἑβδόμη ἐ. ἑξάδος Ph.1.237; as philosoph. term of the Stoics, *subsequent manifestation*, *Stoic.*3.19. Chrysipp.ib.3.43. 3. Medic. (καθάπερ ἐν ταῖς ἀρρωστίαις Plb. l. c.), *after-symptom*, Gal.7.43, Erasistr.ap.eund.14. 729; σύμπτωμά ἐστι τοῦ πάθους ἐ. Gal.19.395. **-ημᾰτικός**, ή, όν, *of the nature of an* ἐπιγέννημα, *resulting, consequential*, *Stoic.*3.137; ἐν τῇ ψυχῇ τὸ ἓν οὐκ ἐ. ὡς ἐπὶ τοῦ σώματος Dam.*Pr.*237. Adv. -κῶς Chrysipp.*Stoic.*2.247. **-ησις**, εως, ἡ, *increase of population*, *BGU* 111.21 (ii A.D.), etc. II. *extra growth*, τῶν τοπικῶν σαρκῶν Leonid. ap.Aët.15.5. ⊕ **-ητός**, όν, *formed above, adnate*, ὑδροκήλη, of encysted hydrocele, Heliod.ap.Orib.50.31 tit.; καλοῦσι.. τοῦτο τὸ πάθος "ἐν ἐπιγεν⟨ν⟩ητῷ (sc. χιτῶνι)" Paul.Aeg.6.62 (in tunica superagnata vocamus, Leonid.ap.Aët.14.22).

**ἐπιγεοῦχος**, ὁ, *landowner*, *CPR*36.21 (iii A.D.).

**ἐπιγεραίρω**, *give honour to*, τινά X *Cyr.*8.6.11.

**ἐπιγεύομαι**, *taste of*, τινός cj. in Ael.*NA*4.15.

**ἐπιγεώμοροι**, οἱ, *those next to the* γεωμόροι, *artisans*, *AB*257.

**ἐπιγεωργέω**, *continue cultivating*, *PFrankf.*1.38 (iii B.C.), *PTeb.* 105.50 (ii B.C.).

**ἐπιγηθέω**, *rejoice, triumph over*, ὡς μήτε θεὸς μήτε τις ἄλλος τοῖσδ' ἐπεγήθει A.*Pr.*157; *exult in*, γάμῳ ἐπιγηθήσαντες Opp.*H.*1.570:—also in form -γήθω, τοῖς γινομένοις Simp.*in Epict.*p.88 D.

**ἐπιγηράσκω**, *grow old one upon another*, Jul.*Ep.*180 (citing Od.7. 120).

⊕ **ἐπιγίγνομαι**, Ion. and later -γίνομαι [γῐ], fut. ἐπιγενήσομαι: aor. 2 ἐπεγενόμην: pf. ἐπιγέγονα: I. of Time, *to be born after, come into being after*, ἔαρος δ' ἐπιγίγνεται ὥρῃ (sc. φύλλα, nisi leg. ὥρη) Il.6. 148; of persons, Hdt.7.2; οἱ ἐπιγινόμενοι ἄνθρωποι *posterity*, Id.9. 85; οἱ ἐπιγενόμενοι τούτῳ σοφισταί *who came after* him, Id.2.49; ἀνάγκη τὰ -όμενα κρατεῖν the *new* must prevail over the old, Th.1.71, cf. Pl.*R.*574a; ἀντὶ τῶν ἀποθανόντων ἕτεροι.. [ἐπιγενήσονται] X.*Cyr.*6. 1.12, cf. Th.6.26; τῇ ἐπιγιγνομένῃ ἡμέρᾳ the *following*, the *next*.., Id.3.75; τοῦ ἐπιγιγνομένου θέρους Id.4.52; χρόνου ἐπιγενομένου as time *went on*, Hdt.1.28, cf. Th.1.126 (v.l.); χρόνος.. παρὰ λόγον ἐπιγιγνόμενος Id.4.26; τὰ ἐπὶ τούτῳ ἐπιγενόμενα *that happened after*.., Hdt.8.37. 2. *follow*, of a fleet, Th.3.77. II. of things, *come at the end, come as fulfilment*, c. dat., βουλαῖς οὐκ ἐπέγεντο τέλος Thgn.640; τὸ τέλος, ἡ τελευτὴ ἐ. τινί, Hdt.3.65, 7.157; esp. of sudden changes of weather and the like, *supervene*, καί σφι.. ἅμα τῇ βροντῇ σεισμὸν ἐπιγενέσθαι Id.5.85; πλέουσι αὐτοῖσι χειμὼν.. ἐπεγίνετο Id.8.13, cf. Th.4.3; ἐ. σφι τέρεα Hdt.8.37; νὺξ ἐ. ib.70; νὺξ ἐ. τῷ ἔργῳ Th.4.25; ἄνεμος ἐπεγένετο τῇ φλογί *seconded* the flame, Id.3. 74: abs., τοσαύτη ἡ ξυμφορὰ ἐπεγεγένητο Id.8.96, cf. 1.16; ἐπιγενομένου νότου *Act.Ap.*28.13; τὴν ἐπιγινομένην ἡδονὴν.. τοῖς ἔργοις the *supervening* pleasure, Arist.*EN*1104ᵇ4; μέμψις καὶ μετάνοια ἐ. πράξεσι Plu.*Tim.*36. 2. *come in after*, ἐπὶ τῇ ναυμαχίῃ ἐ. Ἱστιαῖος Hdt.6.27, cf. Ar.*Eq.*136; *come upon, assault, attack*, τινί Th.3.30, 4.93; ἀφυλάκτοις καὶ ἐξαίφνης ἐ. Id.7.32, cf. 3.108; of disease, ἀρρωστία ἐ. D.36.7: freq. in Hp. of additional symptoms, *supervene*, *Aph.*5.2, *Art.*69, al. 3. *befall, come to pass*, Th.5.20. 4. *fall to one, become due*, μισθώσεις ἐ. D.36.9; τὰ ἐπιγινόμενα *the accruing interest*, Arist.*Pol.*1280ᵃ30, cf. *IG*1².236, al., *BGU*8 ii 4 (iii A.D.), etc. 5. *to be incident to*, δόξῃ ἐ. ψεῦδός τε καὶ ἀληθές Pl.*Phlb.* 37b. 6. *to be added*, πρός τι Arist.*Cael.*297ᵃ32.

⊕ **ἐπιγιγνώσκω**, Ion. and later -γῑνώσκω, *look upon, witness, observe*, ἵνα πάντες ἐπιγνώωσι.. μαρναμένους Od.18.30; τινὰ ὀργιζόμενον X. *Cyr.*8.1.33, cf. S.*Aj.*18: rarely c. gen., Pi.*P.*4.279. II. *recognize*, αἴ κέ μ' ἐπιγνώῃ Od.24.217; ὅπως μήτηρ σε μὴ 'πιγνώσεται φαιδρῷ προσώπῳ by thy glad face, S.*El.*1296, cf. Pl.*Tht.*192e (v.l.). 2. of things, *find out, discover*, ἔργον A.*Ag.*1598, cf. Th.1.132, etc.; τὰ γεγονότα Plb.2.11.3; ἐπιγνοίης ἂν αὐτὴν [τὴν σοφίαν].. οἰκείαν γενομένην; *would you recognize* when it became your own?, Pl.*Euthd.*301e; ἐπιγνοὺς ἄνδρα δίκαιον *IG*9(2).313 (Tricca); ἐ. ὅτι.. Arist.*HA*631ᵇ11; τὸν πόλεμον ἐ. τίνα φύσιν ἔχει Plb.1.65.6, cf. *POxy.*930.14 (ii/iii A.D.); ἐ. εἰ.. Lxx *Ge.*37.32, *PFay.*112.14 (i A.D.):—Pass., Phylarch.10 J. b. *find out too late*, ἐπιγνώσῃ τί σπάνις ἐστὶ φίλων *AP*12.186 (Strat.). 3. *learn to know*, θεόν S.*Ant.*960 (lyr.). 4. *take notice of*, Lxx*Ru.*2.10. b. *show favour to*, πρόσωπον ib.*De.*16.19. III. *come to a judgement, decide*, τι περί τινος Th.3.57; τὰ πρόσφορα τοῖς οἰχομένοις Id.2.65; ἐπιγνῶναι μηδέν *come to* no *new resolve*, Id.1.70; ἐ. τι εἶναί τινος *adjudicate* it as his property, D.H.11.52. IV. *recognize, acknowledge, approve*, 1*Ep.Cor.*16.18; ἐ. σε τῆς ἐπιμελείας Chio*Ep.*6. 2. *recognize* an obligation, *undertake* to discharge or deliver, *PLips.*22.14 (iv A.D.), etc.

⊕ **ἐπιγλισχραίνω**, *make still more viscid*, Hp.*Acut.*17.

**ἐπιγλῠκ-αίνω**, *sweeten*, Dion.Byz.2, Gal.14.277, Philum.ap.Orib. 45.29.8. II. intr., *to be sweetish*, Thphr.*CP*6.15.4. **-υς**, εια, υ, *somewhat sweet*, Id.*HP*3.18.10.

**ἐπιγλῠφ-ίς**, = Lat. *cala* (?), *Gloss.* **-ω**, *carve on the surface*, Lxx 1*Ma.*13.29; τύπον δακτυλίῳ Iamb.*Protr.*21.κγ'.

⊕ **ἐπιγλωσσ-άομαι**, Att. -ττάομαι, *utter abuse*, μηδ' ἐπιγλωσσῶ κακά A.*Ch.*1045; περὶ τῶν Ἀθηνῶν οὐκ ἐπιγλωττήσομαι τοιοῦτον οὐδὲν Ar. *Lys.*37. II. c. gen., *vent reproaches against*, ταῦτ' ἐπιγλωσσᾷ Διός A.*Pr.*928. **-ίς**, Att. -ττίς, ίδος, ἡ, *valve which covers the larynx, epiglottis*, Hp.*Cord.*2, Arist.*HA*492ᵇ34, etc. 2. of the *vocal chords*, Gal.8.50.

**ἐπιγναμπτ-ός**, ή, όν, *curved, twisted*, ἕλικες *h.Ven.*87. **-ω**, *curve, bend*, ἆξαι ἐπιγνάμψας δόρυ Il.21.178; ἐπεγνάμπτοντο δὲ κῶπαι A.R. 2.591. II. metaph., *bow, bend to one's purpose*, ἐπέγναμψεν ἅπαντας Ἥρη λισσομένη Il.2.14; ἐπιγνάμψασα φίλον κῆρ 1.569; ἐπιγνάμπτει νόον ἐσθλῶν 9.514:—Med., Nic.*Al.*363.

**ἐπιγνάπτω**, *clean* clothes: *smarten up*, ἑαυτόν Luc.*Fug.*28.

**ἐπιγνᾰφεῖον** and **-ῆϊον**, τό, (γνάφος) *angle-stone of a* γεῖσον, so called from its resemblance to a carding comb, *SIG*245 *G*21,22 (Delph., iv B.C.).

**ἐπίγνᾰφος**, ον, *cleaned*, of clothes, Poll.7.77; cf. δευτερουργός II.

**ἐπι-γνώμας**, α, = ἐπιγνώμων, title of magistrate at Mantinea, *IG* 5(2).269.32 (i B.C.; nom. -γνώμα appears to occur, ib.265.34): **-γνωμονεύω**, *hold this office*, ib.275.7. **-γνώμη**, ἡ, = συγγνώμη, διάγνωσις, Hsch. **-γνωμοσύνη**, ἡ, *prudence*, Lxx*Pr.*16.23. ⊕ **-γνώμων**, ονος, ὁ, ἡ, *arbiter, umpire, judge*, c. gen. rei, Pl.*Lg.*828b, Lxx *Pr.*12.26, *CIG*(add.)3641 *b* 27 (Lampsacus); αἰτιῶν Plu.*Cam.*18; ὀσφρήσιος, of the nose, Hp.*Ep.*23; ἐ. τῆς τιμῆς *appraiser*, D.37.40: abs., Luc.*Deor.Conc.*15. 2. in pl., *inspectors*, Lys.7.25 ap.Harp. (γνώμονας codd.). II. = συγγνώμων, *pardoning*, τινί Mosch.4. 70. III. *acquainted with*, φύσεως, γυναικῶν, Ph.1.29, 2.274; τέχνης S.E.*M.*7.56. **-γνωρίζω**, *make known, announce, signify*, ἀληθῆ εἶναι ταῦτα X.*Cyn.*6.23:—Pass., Sm.*Pr.*20.11. II. *recognize*, J.*AJ*19.3.1. ⊕ **-γνωσις**, εως, ἡ, *recognition*, c. gen., Phld.*Lib.* p.49 O.; σφραγίδων Hdn.7.6.7; [τινῶν] διὰ βοῆς, δι' ὀμμάτων, J.*BJ*6. 2.6; ἐς ἐπίγνωσιν App.*Praef.*13; *recognition* of a mistake, D.S.17. 114; *determination* of a fact, *PTeb.*24.23 (ii B.C.). 2. *knowledge*, τινός Plb.3.7.6, 3.31.4, Attal.ap.Hipparch.1.8.10, cf. Ph.*Bel.*59.2; τοῦ μέλλοντος Ph.2.222; μουσικῆς Plu.2.1145a; θεοῦ Lxx*Pr.*2.5, cf. *Ep. Rom.*10.2, etc.; τὸν θεὸν ἔχειν ἐν ἐπιγνώσει ib.1.28, etc.; λαβὼν κανόνας εἰς ἐπίγνωσιν τῆς ἀληθείας Arr.*Epict.*2.20.21, cf. S.E.*M.*7.259; ἐ. ἐπιστημονική scientific *theory*, *Theol.Ar.*17. II. *decision*, πρὸς -σιν κεκαθίκασιν *SIG*826 *D*16; θεῶν ἐ. Him.*Or.*1.17. **-γνωστέον**, *one must know*, ὅτι.. Nicom.*Ar.*2.6; *one must recognize, discern*, Aristid.Quint.1.21. **-γνωστικός**, ή, όν, *able to discern*, c. gen., Arr. *Epict.*2.3.4. **-γνωστος**, ον, *known*, Lxx*Jb.*18.19. **-γνώωσι**, Ep. 3 pl. aor. 2 subj. of ἐπιγιγνώσκω.

⊕ **ἐπιγογγύζω**, *murmur at*, Hsch. s. v. ἐπιτρύζουσιν.

**ἐπιγομφόω**, *nail, rivet on*, ἀστράγαλον *IG*1².372 *E*.

**ἐπιγονᾰτίς**, ίδος, ἡ, *knee-pan*, Ruf.ap.Orib.25.1.50, Sor.1.103, Gal. 2.303; cf. ἐπιγουνατίς. II. *garment reaching to the knee*, Paus. Gr.*Fr.*144.

⊕ **ἐπιγόνειον**, τό, Egyptian harp, with forty strings arranged in

pairs as in the *μάγαδις*, named from the inventor Epigonus, Juba ap. Ath.4.183c, Poll.4.59.

**ἐπιγονή**, ἡ, *increase, growth*, ἐ. λαμβάνειν become *larger*, Plu.2.506f; μείζονος κακίας Luc.*Tim*.3; ἐνιαυτοῦ αἰγῶν κτλ. ἐ. the year's *produce*, Plu.*Fab*.4; τὴν ἐ. μακαρίαν [γίνεσθαι] *SIG*695.48 (ii B.C.); θρεμμάτων Ph.2.234; ζῴων Porph.*Abst*.1.16; ἐξ ἐπιγονῆς ἐπιγεγενημένοι πῶλοι *BGU*353.14 (ii A.D.). 2. *offspring, breed*, ἵππων D.S.4.15; of men, Lxx 2*Ch*.31.16. II. in Egypt, *descendants of foreign military settlers*, Μακεδών, Ἰουδαῖος τῆς ἐ., Wilcken *Chr*.241 (iii B.C.), Mitteis *Chr*.21.13 (iii B.C.), etc.; later apptly. used in legal fictions of a category of persons, Πέρσης τῆς ἐ. *PStrassb*.83.12 (ii B.C.), *BGU* 1134 (i B.C./i A.D.), etc.

**ἐπίγονος**, ον, *born besides*, of superfetation, Hp.*Vict*.1.31. II. as Subst., ἐπίγονοι, οἱ, *offspring, posterity*, A.*Th*.903 (lyr.); *breed*, of bees, prob. in X.*Oec*.7.34. 2. οἱ Ἐπίγονοι *the Afterborn*, sons of the chiefs who fell in the first war against Thebes, title of Cyclic Epic ascribed to Homer, Hdt.4.32, cf. Pi.*P*.8.42, D.S.4.66, etc. b. of the Heraclids, Hecat.30 J. c. *descendants* of the successors to Alexander's dominions, περὶ Ἀλεξάνδρου καὶ τῶν διαδόχων καὶ ἐ., title of work by Nymphis, Suid. s.v. Νύμφις, cf. D.S.1.3, D.H.1.6, Str.15.3.24; τῷ Ἐπιγόνου κούρῳ, of Antigonus Gonatas, *BMus.Inscr*. 797.8 (Cnidus). d. corps of barbarian youths in Alexander's army, Arr.*An*.7.6.1. e. in Egypt, *belonging to the ἐπιγονή* II, *PSI* 6.588.7 (iii B.C.), *UPZ*14.70 (ii B.C.). 3. *after-born*, i.e. *born after* or *besides the presumptive heir*, Pl.*Lg*.740c, 929d. b. *issue of second marriage*, Poll.3.25.

**ἐπιγουν-ᾰτίς**, ίδος, ἡ, Ion. for ἐπιγονατίς, Hp.*Oss*.17. **-ίδιος** [ῐδ], ον, *upon the knee*, βρέφος ἐ. κατθηκάμενος Pi.*P*.9.62. **-ίς**, ίδος, ἡ, *part above the knee, great muscle of the thigh*, taken as a sign of strength and vigour, κεν..μεγάλην ἐπιγουνίδα θεῖτο he would grow a stout *thigh-muscle*, Od.17.225; οἵην ἐπιγουνίδα φαίνει 18.74, cf. Theoc. 26.34, Alciphr.3.19, Philostr.*Im*.2.24; prob. in this sense in A.R.3.875. II. = ἐπιγονατίς, *knee-pan*, Hp.*Art*.70, 77, Philostr.*Gym*.35; *knee*, Arat.254, 614.

**ἐπιγράβδην**, Adv., (ἐπιγράφω) *scraping the surface, grazing*, Il.21.166. II. *like lines*, Orph.*L*.365.

**ἐπίγραμμ-α**, ατος, τό, *inscription*, E.*Tr*.1191; esp. of the name of the maker on a work of art, or of the dedicator on an offering, Hdt. 5.59, 7.228, Th.6.54, 59. b. *sepulchral inscription in verse, epitaph*, *IG*14.1746, etc. c. *commemorative inscription*, D.20.112: hence, = ἐπιγραφή 1.4, App.*Pun*.94. 2. *short poem*, usu. in elegiac verse, *epigram*, Hieronym.Rhod.ap.Ath.13.604f, Callistr.ap.eund. 3.125c, etc. 3. *title* of a work, Alex.135.4, 10, D.H.*Rh*.8.8, Gal. 6.372, etc.; of a picture, Ael.*VH*9.11. 4. *written estimate* or *demand* of damages, D.38.2; *title* or *label* of a criminal charge, Arist.*Rh*.1374ᵃ1. 5. *mark branded* on a slave's forehead, Herod. 5.79. **-άτιον**, τό, Dim. of ἐπίγραμμα, Plu.*Cat.Ma*.1, Antig.*Mir*. 89. **-ᾰτιστής**, οῦ, ὁ, = sq., Sidon.Apoll.*Ep*.4.1. **-ᾰτογράφος** [γρᾰ], ὁ, *writing epigrams*, prob. in *AP*7.715 (lemma), cf. Sch. Theoc.7.40. **-ᾰτοποιός**, ὁ, *epigrammatist*, Phld.*Po*.5.35.9, D.L. 6.14. **-ᾰτοφόρος**, ὁ, f.l. for -γράφος in *AP*7.715 (lemma), Tz.*H*. 8.425. **-ή**, ἡ, in pl., *markings*, καθ' ὅλον τὸ σῶμα Aët.13.20. **-ος**, *superpositum* (?), *Gloss*.

**ἐπιγρᾰφ-εύς**, έως, ὁ, *inscriber*: at Athens, *registrar* of property, etc. (cf. sq. II. 2), Antipho Soph.112, Poll.8.103, *AB*254, Harp.; prob. for -φῶν in Isoc.17.41. II. = ζωγράφος, Hsch. **-ή**, ἡ, *inscription*, στηλῶν on stones, Th.2.43, cf. Arist.*Mir*.843ᵇ17, J.*AJ*15. 8.1; on a vase, *BCH*6.6 (Delos, ii B.C.); on statues, Plb.5.9.3. 2. *title* of a work, Id.3.9.3, Luc.*Hist.Conscr*.30, etc. 3. *name* of a ship, *OGI*447 (i B.C.). 4. *ascription* of a deed to its author, *credit* or *honour* of a thing, τὴν ἐ. τινος λαβεῖν Plb.1.31.4, cf. *PSI*4.424.9 (iii B.C.); ἀπενέγκασθαι D.S.16.50, cf. Jul.*Caes*.322d. 5. *insertion, interlineation* in a document, *PLond*.2.178.13 (ii A.D.), *PRyl*.316.2 (pl., ii A.D.). II. *description* of parties in pleadings, Is.4.2. 2. *registration of property for taxation*, in pl., Isoc.17.41 codd. (v. foreg.). 3. *impost, tax*, *PSI*5.510.11 (iii B.C.); *assessment*, *POxy*.1445.8 (ii A.D.), etc. 4. *requisition*, ὑποζυγίων *BCH*46.309 (Teos). **-ικός**, ή, όν, *concerning assessments* (?), *IG*11(2).159*A*64 (Delos, iii B.C.). **-ω**, *mark the surface, graze*, ὀϊστὸς ἐπέγραψε χρόα φωτός Il.4.139, cf. 13.553, Poll.4.179; μιν ἐπιγράψας having *put a mark on* the lot, Il. 7.187; ἄκροις δακτύλοις ἐ. *trifle with* dishes, Luc.*Am*.42.—In Hom. the word has not the sense of *writing*. II. *write upon, inscribe*, γράμματα Hdt.3.88; τάδε Id.4.88; ἐ. ὀνομαστὶ τὰς πόλεις Th.1.132, cf. D.59.97; ἐπίγραμμα δ.. προείλεθ' ἡ πόλις αὐτοῖς ἐπιγράψαι Id.18. 289: abs., ἐ. τοῖς ἀναθήμασι *IG*1².76.43; esp. *write* or *place an epitaph* on a tomb, ib.14.1835, al., 7.2543.9:—Med., *have inscribed*, ἐπεγράφου τὴν Γοργόνα Ar.*Ach*.1095 (with play on III. 5); ἐλεγεῖον Th.1. 132:—Pass., of the inscription, *to be inscribed upon*, ἐπιγέγραπταί οἱ τάδε Hdt.5.77, cf. 7.228; τῶν τῷ χρυσέῳ ἐπιγέγραπται "Λακεδαιμονίων" Id.1.51; [ἐπίγραμμα] ὃ Μίδᾳ φασὶν ἐπιγεγράφθαι *over* or *on the tomb of* Midas, Pl.*Phdr*.264c: ἐπιστολὴ -γεγραμμένη *addressed*, of a letter, Plb.16.36.4, cf. Plu.*Cic*.15; also, *to have* something *inscribed upon one*, ἐπεγράφοντο ῥόπαλα, ὡς Θηβαῖοι ὄντες *used to bear* clubs *upon their shields*, X.*HG*7.5.20; so ἀσπὶς ἐπιγεγραμμένη τὰς ὁμολογίας *having* the articles *inscribed upon it*, D.H.4.58. 2. *entitle*, τοῦτο τὸ δρᾶμα Καλλίμαχος ἐ. Εὐνοῦχον Ath.11.496f; αἱ -όμεναι Μαιανδρίου ἱστορίαι *Inscr.Prien*.37.104 (ii B.C.). 3. *sign, append a signature to*, ἄφεσιν *PSI*4.392.6 (iii B.C.); ἐ. τὸν Ἀντώνιον *sign* Antonius' *name*, App.*BC*5.144; αὐτοῦ ποιήματα ἐπέγραψεν (sc. τοῖς Ἑρμαῖς) *inscribed* poems *signed* by himself, Pl.*Hipparch*.228d. 4. *write subsequently*, αἱ ἐπιγραφεῖσαι διαθῆκαι J.*AJ*17.9.4. 5. *write over* an erasure, *POxy*.34.14 (ii A.D.). III. freq. as law-term: 1. *set down* the penalty or damages *in the title* of an indictment (cf. ἐπίγραμμα 4), τί δῆτά σοι τίμημ' ἐπιγράψω τῇ δίκῃ; Ar.*Pl*.480; μέχρι πεντήκοντα δραχμῶν καθ' ἕκαστον ἀδίκημα ἐ. Lex ap.Aeschin.1.38; τὰ ἐπιγεγραμμένα the *damages claimed*, D.29.8, cf. Pl.*Lg*.915a; τιμημάτων -μένων Isoc.16.47:—Med., Lex ap.Aeschin.1.16. b. of a lawgiver, *assign* a punishment, τὰ μέγιστα ἐπιτίμια Aeschin.1.14:—Pass., Din.2.12. c. *make note of, enter*, τὴν πρόφασιν, in inflicting a fine, Arist.*Ath*.8.4. 2. *register* the citizens' names and property, with a view to taxes, *lay a public burden upon* one (cf. ἐπιγραφή II. 2), ἐμαυτῷ.. τὴν μεγίστην εἰσφοράν Isoc.17.41, cf. Arist.*Oec*.1351ᵇ2; ἐ. δήμοις καὶ δυνάσταις στρατιωτῶν καταλόγους Plu.*Crass*.17, cf. *PHib*.1. 44.3 (iii B.C., Pass.), etc.; but ἐ. τινὰ προστίμοις *visit* with penalties, D.S.12.12 (s.v.l.). b. *assess*, τὸ τρίτον μέρος *PEdgar*38.3:—Pass., τὸ τίμημα τὸ -γεγραμμένον τοῖς χρήμασιν Lys.17.7. 3. generally, *register* or *enter in a public list*, ἐπιγράψαι σφᾶς αὐτοὺς ἐπιτρόπους Is.6. 36; ἐ. τινὰ εἰς τοὺς πράκτορας *register* his *name* among the πράκτορες, Decr.ap.And.1.77 (Pass.):—Med., ἐπεγράψαντο πολίτας *enrolled fresh* citizens, Th.5.4; ξένην καὶ ξένον γονέας -ψάμενος D.57.51; πῶς οἷόν τε τῷ ἀνδρὶ δύο πατέρας -ψασθαι; Is.4.4 (later in Act., ἑαυτῷ τινὰ πατέρα -γράφων *claiming* as his father, App.*BC*1.32). 4. Med., ἐπιγράφεσθαι μάρτυρας *cause to be endorsed on a deposition as* witnesses, D.54.31; κλητῆρα οὐδ' ὁντινοῦν ἐπιγραψάμενος Id.21.87; but ἐπιγράφεσθαι τίμημα τῷ κλήρῳ *set one's* valuation on the property, Is.3.2. 5. προστάτην ἐπιγράψασθαι *choose* a patron, *and enter his name as such* in the public register (as μέτοικοι at Athens were obliged to do), Ar. *Pax*684; so prob. ἐπεγράφοντο shd. be restored for -γραφον in Luc. *Peregr*.11; ἐπιγράψασθαί τινα κύριον D.43.15; οἱ τὸν Πλάτωνα ἐπιγραφόμενοι, i.e. the Platonists, Luc.*Herm*.14:—Pass., κύριος ἐπιγεγράφθαι D.43.15, cf. *POxy*.251.32 (i A.D.), al. b. metaph., Ὅμηρον ἐπιγράφεσθαι *attribute* one's fluency to Homer, Luc.*Dem.Enc*.2; πρεσβυτέρους ἐ. χρόνους *claim the authority of* greater antiquity, Id.*Am*. 35. IV. ἐπιγράψαι ἑαυτὸν ἐπί τι *claim credit for*, Aeschin.3.167; ἀλλοτρίοις ἑαυτὸν πόνοις Ael.*NA*8.2, cf. Plu.*Pomp*.31; αὐτὸς ἐ. τὴν νίκην *claim* as his own, J.*AJ*7.7.5:—so Med. and Pass., τοιούτων ῥητόρων ἐπὶ τὰς τοῦ δήμου γνώμας ἐπιγραφομένων *inscribing their names* on.., Aeschin.1.188; ἐπιγράφεσθαι ἀλλοτρίαις γνώμαις D.59.43; τὸν ἐπὶ τοῖς τῆς πόλεως ἀτυχήμασιν ἐπιγεγραμμένον Din.1.29; οἱ ἐπιγεγραμμένοι ἢ φυλάττοντες the parties *whose names were endorsed* upon the συνθῆκαι as securities, Arist.*Rh*.1376ᵇ4; οἱ ἐπιγραφόμενοι τοῖς δόγμασι D.H.6.84; ἡμεῖς δ' ἐσμὲν ἐπιγεγραμμένοι we are merely *the endorsers*, Men.482.8. V. *ascribe to*, τοῖς θεοῖς τὸ ἔργον Hld.8.9 (but θεὸν τῇ πομπῇ Philostr.*VA*8.12):—Med., Φοίβῳ τὰς ἀνίσους χεῖρας *AP*9.263 (Antiphil.). 2. *claim credit for*, τὰ ὑπὸ ἄλλων εὑρημένα J.*AJ*3.4.2; *assume*, προσωνυμίαν Plu.*Demetr*.42; ἐπεγράψατο τὴν ἑαυτοῦ προσηγορίαν Id.*Tim*.36:—Pass., of books, *to be ascribed*, τινί Gal.15.25. 3. *predicate of*, φυγὴν οὐ φυγόντι Philostr.*VS*2. 1.12.

**ἐπίγρῡπος**, ον, *somewhat hooked*, of the beak of the ibis, Hdt.2.76; of the muzzle of the βοῦς ἄγριος, Arist.*HA*499ᵃ7; of horses and men, *somewhat hook-nosed*, Pl.*Phdr*.253d, *Euthphr*.2b, *PPetr*.3 p.7, al. (iii B.C.), etc.

**ἐπιγύᾰλος** [ῠ], ον, *hollow on the surface*, dub. l. in S.*OC*1492 (lyr.).

**ἐπίγυιον** or **ἐπίγῡον**, τό, *stern-cable*, Ar.*Fr*.80, cf. 426: written -γυιον in Aristid.*Or*.23(42).17, Zonar., -γυον in *IG*2².1611.255–8 (iv B.C.), Plb.3.46.3, Harp. s.v. ἐπίγυον (v.l. ἀπόγυιον): scanned ⏑ ⏑ – ⏑ in Ar.

**ἐπιγυμν-άζω**, *exercise excessively*, Philostr.*Gym*.51; *exercise again*, ib.53:—Pass., *take exercise at* or *in*, τοῖσι γυμνασίοισι Hp.*Insomn*.88: abs., dub. in Ph.1.467. **-όω**, *lay bare*, [ὀστοῦν] σμίλῃ Pall. *in Hp. Fract*.12.286C.

**ἐπιγώνιος**, α, ον, *at the angle*, μονάδες Nicom.*Ar*.1.19. II. ἐπιγώνια, τά, *corner-stones* or *-columns*, Aq.*Ps*.143(144).12.

**ἐπιδαίομαι** (A), Pass., (δαίω A) *to be kindled at*: metaph., *delight greedily in*, κίχλης -δαίεται ἦτορ Opp.*H*.4.173, cf. Sch. ad loc.

**ἐπιδαίομαι** (B), (δαίω B) *distribute*, ἐπιδαίομαι ὅρκον dub. sens. in *h.Merc*.383:—Pass., δεκάτη δ' ἐπὶ μοῖρα δέδασται Hes.*Th*.789.

**ἐπιδαίσιος**, ον, (δαίω B) *assigned, allotted*, οἶκος Call.*Jov*.59.

**ἐπίδαιτρον**, τό, *additional dish, dainty*, Philem.ap.Ath.14.646c; = ὄψον, Hsch.

**ἐπιδάκν-ω**, *bite*: hence, of anything pungent, *sting, cause to smart*, ὁ καπνὸς ἐ. τὰς ὄψεις Arist.*Fr*.660; of urine, Ath.1.32e; ἐ. τὴν γεῦσιν Dsc.2.166: metaph., Satyr.*Vit.Eur.Fr*.39 xvi 27:—Med., Nic.*Al*. 19, 121:—Pass., οἱ -όμενοι τὴν κύστιν Dsc.1.112; of hunger, Apollod. ap.Suid. s.v. καρδιώττειν. **-ώδης**, ες, *gnawing*, dub. l. in Philagr. ap.Orib.5.21.10.

**ἐπίδακρ-υς**, υ, *tearful*, Hsch. and Suid. s.v. μυδαλέον. **-ῡσις**, εως, ἡ, *oozing*, of blood, Heliod.ap.Orib.50.52.5. **-ύω**, *weep over* or *for*, πτώματι Ph.2.44; τῇ μνήμῃ τινός Plu.2.583c: abs., Ar.*V*.882, Aeschin.2.85:—Pass., ἐπιδακρυνθέντα· ἐπιγραφέντα (i.e. in a tomb inscription), Hsch. 2. *ooze, exude*, Heliod.ap.Orib.50.49.1.

**ἐπιδᾰλον**· λοιμικόν, Hsch.

**ἐπιδᾱμι-ασταί**, οἱ, *those enjoying the privilege of* ἐπιδαμία (v. ἐπιδημία) at Rhodes, *IG*12(1).157. **-οργέω**, *hold office of* ἐπιδαμιοργός, prob. in *IG*9(1).330.2 (*Supp.Epigr*.2.354). **-οργός**, ὁ, *official* at Delphi, ib.263.35 (iii/ii B.C.), al.; at Sparta, *IG*5(1).5 (iii/ii B.C.); at Ithaca, *SIG*558.30 (iii B.C.); cf. ἐπιδημιουργός.

**ἐπιδάμνᾰμαι**, *subdue*, ἠϊθέους *AP*12.96.5.

**ἐπίδᾱμος, ἐπιδάμιος**, Dor. for ἐπιδημ-.

**ἐπιδᾰνείζω**, *lend money on property already mortgaged*, D.35.22, *PPetr.*3 p.41 (iii B.C.); ἐ. ἐπὶ κτήμασι Arist.*Oec.*1347ᵃ1; ἱερατικὰς προσόδους ἐ. *PGnom.*184 (ii A.D.): Med., *borrow on property already mortgaged*, D.34.6, Syngr.ap.eund.35.11: metaph., ἐπιδανείζεσθαι χρόνον παρὰ τῆς τύχης εἰς ἄδοξον βίον Plu.*Brut.*33.

**ἐπιδᾰπᾰν-άω**, *exhaust, consume as well*, Pall.*Febr.*23. **-ητής**, οῦ, ὁ, *steward, Gloss.*

**ἐπιδασμός**, ὁ, *assessment. PSI*8.901.11 (i A.D.).

**ἐπιδᾰσυς**, εια, υ, *hairy*, Thphr.*HP*3.18.5.

**ἐπιδαψῐλεύω**, intr., *abound, be abundant*, Ister43, Hsch. s.v. Συβαριτικοὶ λόγοι: but more commonly, II. Med., *lavish upon* a person, *bestow freely*, τὰς ἑωυτῶν μητέρας καὶ τὰς ἀδελφεὰς ὑμῖν Hdt. 5.20, cf. Ph.1.400; [τὰν δαπάναν] *Supp.Epigr.*1.327.7 (Callatis, i A.D.); ἐ. τινί τοῦ γέλωτος *give* him *freely of* it, X.*Cyr.*2.2.15: metaph., *illustrate more richly*, Luc.*DMort.*30.2. 2. intr., *to be lavish*, Arist *VV*1250ᵇ25, Ph.2.170; ἔν τινι D.H.*Rh.*6.2, Luc.*Pr.Im.*14.

**ἐπιδέδρομα**, poet. pf. 2 of ἐπιτρέχω.

**ἐπιδεής**, poet. **ἐπιδευής** (q.v.), ές, *in need of*, τινός Pl.*Ti.*33c, v.l. in X.*Cyr.*8.7.12, etc.: pl., -δεέες v.l. in Hdt.4.130: Comp. -έστερος ἐκείνων *inferior to*.., Pl.*Plt.*311b: Sup. -έστατος *most in need*, πλείστων Id.*R.*579e. Adv. -εῶς *inadequately*, Id.*Lg.*899d.

**ἐπιδεῖ**, v. ἐπιδέω (B).

**ἐπίδειγμα**, ατος, τό, *pattern, example*, X.*Smp.*6.6, *PTeb.*25.18 (ii B.C.); σοφίας πλείστης Pl.*Hp.Mi.*368c; προνοίας Gal.*UP*15.4. 2. *display*, ἐ. ἐπιδεικνύναι X.*Cyr.*8.2.15; τὰ τῶν πλουσίων ἐ. *show-pieces, gauds*, Demetr.*Eloc.*108. II. *memorial*, χειμῶνος μεγάλου Epigr. ap.Str.2.1.16.

**ἐπιδείδω**, 3 pl. plpf. (= impf.) ἐπεδείδιον, *fear*, κτύπον Nonn.*D.*28. 330.

**ἐπιδείελος**, ον, *at even, about evening*: neut. pl. ἐπιδείελα as Adv., Hes.*Op.*810, 821 (nisi leg. ἐπὶ δείελα).

**ἐπιδείκ-νῡμι** (-νύω *PPetr.*2 p.110 (iii B.C.)), fut. -δείξω: aor. ἐπέδειξα, Ion. ἐπέδεξα Hdt.2.42:—*exhibit as a specimen*, Ar.*Ach.*765: generally, *display, exhibit*, βίαν Pi.*N.*11.14; τεκμήρια A.*Supp.*53 (lyr.), etc.; ἑωυτόν τινι Hdt.2.42; πᾶσαν τὴν Ἑλλάδα τινί Id.3.135, cf. 6.61; ἐ. τὸ στράτευμά τινι *parade* it before.., X.*An.*1.2.14, cf. *Cyr.*5.5.5; of speeches, compositions, etc., ἐπιδειξάτω τῇ βουλῇ he *shall exhibit* his draft, *IG*1².76.60; ἐ. λόγον Ar.*Eq.*349; ῥαψῳδίαν Pl.*Lg.*658b, cf. Isoc.2.7 (Pass.); σοφίαν Pl.*Euthd.*274a, X.*Smp.*3.3. 2. more freq. in Med., *show off* or *display for oneself* or *what is one's own*, μουσικὰν ὀρθὰν ἐ. *give a specimen of his* art.., Pi.*Fr.*32; ἐμὲ ἐπεδέξατο γυμνὴν *exhibited* me naked, Hdt.1.11; πάντα τὸν στρατόν *showed* all *his* army, Id.7.146; ἐ. τὸν Ἀλέξανδρον *recall* Alexander, Plu.*Pyrrh.* 8; esp. of one's personal qualities, ἐπιδείκνυσθαι τὴν αὑτοῦ δύναμιν And.4.14; σοφίαν, πονηρίαν, Pl.*Phdr.*258a, Isoc.20.4, cf. X.*An.*1.9. 16; ἐπιδείξασθαι αὑτὸν ἀβέβηλον *Inscr.Prien.*113.66 (i B.C.). b. ἐπίδειξαι.. ἅττ' ἐδίδασκες *give a specimen of*.., Ar.*Nu.*935; τὰ γυμνικά *POxy.*42.5 (iv A.D.): abs., *show off, make a display of one's powers*, ἐπεδείκνυντο τοῖς λωποδύταις Ar.*Ra.*771; ὃν.. ἐθεάσασθε ἐπιδεικνύμενον *giving a display* (of fighting in armour), Pl.*La.*179e; of a rhetorician lecturing, Id.*Phdr.*235a; πολλὰ καὶ καλά Id.*Grg.*447a; of epideictic orators, Arist.*Rh.*1391ᵇ26; of a musician, Ael.*VH*9.36: c. part., ἐ. ὑπερθέων Pl.*Lg.*648d. II. *show, point out*, τινὶ τὴν αἰτίαν Id.*Phd.* 100b, cf. Aeschin.1.177; τὴν πονηρίαν Pl.*Prt.*346a; ἐ. αὐτήν, ἥτις ἐστίν Pl.Com.173.5; ἐ. τὸν ἀλεκτρυὸν ὡς ἐτυράννει *show, prove* that.., Ar.*Av.*483, cf. Lys.1.4; ὅτι.. Pl.*R.*391e, etc.: c. part., ἐ. πάντα ἐόντα μεγάλα Hdt.1.30; ἐ. τινὰ φονέα ὄντα *show* that one is a murderer, v.l. in Antipho1.3, cf. Th.3.64 (where perh. ἐπ- '*as an afterthought*'); ἐ. τινὰ δωροδοκήσαντα *prove* that one took bribes, Ar.*Eq.* 832 (anap.); ἐπιδείξω σε ταῦτα ὁμολογοῦντα Pl.*Euthd.*295a, cf. *Chrm.* 158d; ψυχὴν ἐ. πρεσβυτέραν οὖσαν τοῦ σώματος Id.*Lg.*892c; ἐ. αὐτὸν φοβερὸν (sc. ὄντα) καὶ μέγα δυνάμενον And.4.11: c. acc., ἐ. ὅ τι ἂν ἐγκαλῇ ἐναντίον ἀνδρῶν τριῶν *PEleph.*1.7 (iv B.C.), etc.:—Pass., ἐπιδείκνυται αὐθέντης (sc. ὤν) Antipho3.4.9; ἐπεδείχθησαν οὐδὲν βελτίους ὄντες Isoc.4.145, cf. 18.56; κινδυνεύσεις ἐπιδεῖξαι χρηστὸς εἶναι X.*Mem.* 2.3.17 (ἐπιδεῖξαι secl. Cobet). 2. Med., τῆς αἰτίας τὸ εἶδος Pl.*Phd.* 100b; ἔργῳ ἐπεδείκνυτο, ὅτι.. X.*An.*1.9.10, cf. Is.5.30. **-τέον**, *one must display*, τὴν εὐψυχίαν Id.*Cyn.*10.21, etc. 2. *one must point out*, Gal.10.222; *one must prove*, ὅτι.. Porph.*Abst.*3.9. **-τιάω**, Desiderat., *wish to display oneself*, *Com.Adesp.*1008. **-τικός**, ή, όν, *fit for displaying* or *showing off*, ἦθους καὶ πάθους Luc.*Salt.*35; ἡ ἐπιδεικτική *display*, Pl.*Sph.*224b. 2. ἐ. λόγοι speeches *for display*, *set* orations, D.61.2; ἐ. γένος λόγων Arist.*Rh.*1358ᵇ8; ὁ ἐ. *declamatory* speaker, ib.1359ᵃ15, cf. Plu.*Comp.Dem.Cic.*1. Adv. -κῶς, πολεμεῖν Id.*Luc.*11; ἐ. ἔχειν Isoc.4.11: Comp. -ώτερον, γράφειν Plu.2. 28e.

**ἐπῐδεῖν**, v. ἐπεῖδον.

**ἐπιδεινοπᾰθέω**, gloss on ἐπαλαστήσασα, Apollon.*Lex.*

**ἐπίδειξις**, Ion. **ἐπίδεξις**, εως, ἡ, *showing forth, making known*, τοῦτο ἐς ἐ. ἀνθρώπων ἀπίκετο became *notorious*, Hdt.2.46. 2. *exhibition, display, demonstration*, τῆς δυνάμεως Th.6.31; ἐ. ποιεῖσθαι, of a military *demonstration*, Id.3.16; ἐν τοῦτ' ἦν τῆς ἐ. *showing off*, Pl. *Grg.*447c: generally, ἐ. ποιήσασθαι ἥ.. *exhibit* how.., Id.*Phd.*99d; ἐλθεῖν εἰς ἐπίδειξίν τινι come to *display* oneself to one, Ar.*Nu.*269; ἡ ἐ. (sc. τοῦ κάλλους) X.*Mem.*3.11.2; ἐ. ποιήσασθαι τῆς σοφίας Arist. *Pol.*1259ᵃ19. 3. esp. λόγων ἐ. ποιεῖσθαι D.18.280: abs., *set speech, declamation*, Th.3.42; ἐ. ποιήσασθαι Pl.*Grg.*447c, cf. Isoc.4.17, 5.17: pl., *SIG*577.53 (Milet., iii/ii B.C.), 775.3 (Delph., i B.C.). b. name of a trireme at Athens, *IG*2².1623.144. 4. *proof*, Men.161.2 (pl.), *PTaur.*1.1 vii 7 (pl., ii B.C.), etc. II. *example*, ἐπίδειξις Ἑλλάδι *an example* to Greece, E.*Ph.*871; ἐπίδειξιν ποιεῖσθαί τινι ὡς.. *give a sign* or *proof* that.., Aeschin.1.47.

**ἐπιδειπν-έω**, *eat a second meal*, Hp.*VM*10, *Acut.*28. II. *dine, sup off*, Ar.*Eq.*1140, *Ec.*1178 (both lyr.); τῶν πράσων Alex.242. III. *sup at* or *upon*, σκεῦος ᾧ τις ἐ. Artem.1.74. **-ιος**, ον, *after dinner*, ἐ. ἀφῖχθαι Luc.*Lex.*9. II. *convivial*, βασιλεύς Them.*Or.*2.36a (prob.). **-ίς**, ίδος, ἡ, = sq., Ph.2.479 (pl.), Petron.69, Mart.11. 31.7 (pl.); said to be Maced. by Ath.14.658e. **-ον**, τό, *second course, dessert*, ib.664e (pl., s.v.l.).

**ἐπιδεκᾰτ-εία** (-ία Thrasyll. in *Cat.Cod.Astr.*8(3).101), ἡ, Astrol., = καθυπερτέρησις, Vett.Val.102.33. **-εύω**, = καθυπερτερέω, Heph. Astr.1.16, Thrasyll. l.c., Vett.Val.102.27 (Pass.), Porph.*in Ptol.* 188. **-ος**, ον, *containing an integer and one-tenth*: hence ἐ. λόγος ratio *of* 11 : 10, Iamb.*in Nic.*p.54 P. II. *one in ten*: hence Subst. -δέκατον, τό, 1. *tenth, tithe*, Lex ap.And.1.96, X.*HG*1.7.10, Lex ap.D.43.71; ἐ. τόκοι interest *of* 10%, *IG*1².377, Arist.*Rh.*1411ᵃ17, *Oec.*1346ᵇ32. 2. *payment of* 10% *on account*, *IG*11.161 *A* 79 (Delos, iii B.C.). 3. *payment of* 10% as παρακαταβολή (q.v.), ib.5(2).357 (Stymphalus), *PHal.*1.63 (iii B.C.); προδικία ἄνευ ἐπιδεκάτων *IG*12 (8).640 (Peparethus, ii B.C.). 4. *additional, extra payment of one-tenth*, *PHib.*1.32.9 (iii B.C.), *PAmh.*2.33.32 (ii B.C.).

**ἐπιδεκ-τέον**, *one must acquiesce in*, τὸ παραγγελλόμενον Plb.36.5. 4. **-τικός**, ή, όν, *capable of containing* πόλεων Str.3.4.13. 2. *capable of*, c. gen., Chrysipp.*Stoic.*2.64, Phld.*Ir.*p.81 W.; *admitting*, ἄρθρου A.D.*Pron.*63.19; γύμνασμα ἐ. ἠθῶν καὶ παθῶν Theon *Prog.*10; *receptive*, ἐ. αἴτιον, opp. ποιητικόν, Alex.Aphr.*Febr.*25. **-τος**, ον, *accepted*, Sm., Thd.*Is.*60.7; also gloss on ἐπιδεκτικός, Hsch. **-τωρ**, ορος, ὁ, Adj., = -τικός 2, δίκας Aesara ap.Stob.1.49.27.

**ἐπιδελεάζομαι**, in pf. part. Pass., *to be put on as a bait*, D.S.1.35.

**ἐπιδέμνιος**, ον, *on the bed* or *bed-clothes*, ἐπιδέμνιος ὡς πέσοιμ' ἐς εὐνάν E.*Hec.*927 (lyr.).

**ἐπιδέμομαι**, Med., *build upon*, τινί τι Opp.*C.*4.121.

**ἐπιδένδρ-ιος**, ον, *on* or *in the tree*, [σῦκον] Jul.*Ep.*180 p.393b. **-ος**, ον, = foreg., ὄφις Teucr.ap.Boll *Sphaera* p.17.

**ἐπιδέννω**, = ἐπιδέω, Sm.*Is.*1.6 (Pass.).

**ἐπιδεξῐ-ελεύθερος**, f.l. in Pl.*Tht.*175e ap.Suid. s.v. ἀναλαμβάνειν. **-όομαι**, Med., *entertain one another*, Anaximen.ap.D.L.2.4. **-ος**, ον, *towards the right*, i.e. *from left to right*: I. used by Hom. only in neut. pl. as Adv., ὄρνυσθ' ἑξείης ἐπιδέξια rise in order, Od.21.141, cf. Pl.*Smp.*214b; περίθει τὸν βωμὸν ἐ. Ar.*Pax*957; πίνειν τὴν ἐ. (sc. κύλικα) Eup.325, cf. Anaxandr.1.4, Critias33 D.; without idea of motion, ἕστηκεν ἐ. Lys.*Fr.*94; sts. as two words, ἐπὶ δεξιά, opp. ἐπ' ἀριστερά, Il.7.238, cf. Eust. ad Od. l.c.; ἐπὶ δ. χειρός Pi.*P.*6.19, Theoc. 25.18; τὰ ἐπὶ δ., opp. τὰ ἐπ' ἀριστερά, Hdt.2.93, 4.191, 6.33. 2. *auspicious, lucky*, ἀστράπτων ἐ. Il.2.353. II. later as Adj., = δεξιός, *on the right hand*, X.*An.*6.4.1, etc.; τἀπιδέξια *the right side*, Ar.*Av.* 1493 (lyr.); οἱ ἐ. ἄνεμοι Arist.*Pr.*941ᵇ12. 2. *clever, dexterous, tactful*, Aeschin.1.178, Arist.*EN*1128ᵃ17, Thphr.*Char.*29.4; λαβὴ φιλοσόφων ἐπιδέξιος ἡ διὰ τῶν ὤτων Zeno *Stoic.*1.64: c. inf., Arist.*Rh.*1381ᵃ34; ἐ. πρὸς τὰς ὁμιλίας Plb.5.39.6; περί τι Plu.*Aem.*37, D.C.69.10: Sup., Ἀφροδίτην -ωτάτην θεῶν Plu.2.739e: neut. pl. as Adv., ἐπιδέξια *dexterously, cleverly*, Anaxandr.53.5, Nicom.Com.1.27; *elegantly*, ἀναβάλλεσθαι ἐ. Pl.*Tht.*175e: Regul. Adv. -ίως Erasistr.ap.Gal.7.539, Plb.3.19.13, 4.35.7, Corn.*ND*14, Plu.2.439e. 3. *lucky, prosperous*, τύχη D.S.8.4. **-ότης**, ητος, ἡ, *handiness, cleverness, tact*, Pittac.ap.Stob.3.1.172, Aeschin.2.47, Arist.*EN*1128ᵃ17: pl., Plu. 2.441b. II. *position on the right*, Paul.Al.*E.*3.

**ἐπιδεξιπολίης**· ἐκ τῶν δεξιῶν μερῶν περιστρέψας, Hsch.

**ἐπίδεξις**, εως, ἡ, Ion. for ἐπίδειξις.

**ἐπίδερις**, ιδος, ἡ, = ὑποδορίς, Poll.2.174.

⊕ **ἐπιδέρκομαι**, *look upon, behold*, τι, τινάς, Hes.*Op.*268, *Th.*760, etc.; Hom. only as v.l., Od.11.16.

**ἐπιδερκτός**, όν, *to be seen, visible*, τινί Emp.2.7.

**ἐπί-δερμα**, ατος, τό, = sq. II, *Gloss.* **-δερμᾰτίς**, ίδος, ἡ, gloss on λέμμα, *peel*, Erot. II. *skin*, αἰγός Alex.Trall.1.15. ⊕ **-δερμίς**, ίδος, ἡ, *outer skin, epidermis*, Hp.*Nat.Puer.*20, etc. II. *web of water-birds' feet*, Arist.ap.Sch.Il.2.460.

**ἐπί-δεσις**, εως, ἡ, *bandaging*, Hp.*Art.*14, *VC*13, Gal.14.793. 2. *binding*, κεραμίδων *PLond.*1.177.164 (ii A.D.). **-δεσμα**, ατος, τό, = ἐπίδεσμος, Hp.*Fract.*21, *Art.*14, etc. **-δεσμεύω**, *bind up*, *AP* 11.125. **-δεσμέω**, *bind up* or *on*, Pall.*in Hp.Fract.*12.284 C., Paul.Aeg.3.35, *Hippiatr.*11. **-δέσμια**, τά, gloss on δέσματα, Hsch. **-δεσμίς**, ίδος, ἡ, = sq., Gal.14.794, Cass.*Pr.*57. ⊕ **-δεσμος**, ὁ, *upper* or *outer bandage*, Hp.*Off.*9, Ar.*V.*1440, Arist.*HA*630ᵃ6, Ph. *Bel.*96.19: metaph., of fortresses as the '*fetters*' of Greece, Str.9. 4.15: heterocl. pl. ἐπίδεσμα Ael.*NA*8.9:—also **-δεσμον**, τό, Gal.13. 686. **-δεσμοχᾰρής**, ές, *bandage-loving*, of gout, Luc.*Trag.*198.

**ἐπιδεσπόζω**, *to be lord over*, στρατῷ A.*Pers.*241.

**ἐπιδετέον**, *one must bind on*, Antyll.ap.Orib.7.21.9, Gal.18(2).897.

⊕ **ἐπιδετόν**, τό, *application under a bandage*, Hp.*Mul.*1.78.

⊕ **ἐπιδευής**, ές, poet. for ἐπιδεής, *in need* or *want of, lacking*, c. gen., δαιτὸς ἐΐσης, κρειῶν, γάλακτος, etc., Il.9.225, Od.4.87, etc.; βιότου Hes.*Th.*605; λώβης τε καὶ αἴσχεος οὐκ ἐπιδευεῖς *lacking* not scathe nor scorn, Il.13.622; τῶν πάντων ἐπιδευέες (v.l. -δεέες) Hdt.4.130: abs., ὅς κ' ἐπιδευὴς whoever be *in want*, Il.5.481, cf. Parm.8.33. II. *lacking, failing*, ἵνα μή τι δίκης ἐπιδευὲς ἔχησθα that thou may'st have

no point of right *wanting*, Il.19.180: c. gen., βίης ἐπιδευέες *failing* in strength, Od.21.185; ἐ. θέσφατα μαντοσύνης A.R.2.315: as Comp., βίης ἐπιδευέες εἰμὲν ἀντιθέου Ὀδυσῆος *inferior to* Ulysses in strength, Od.21.253, cf. *h.Ap.*338: and abs., πολλὸν δ' ἐπιδευέες ἦμεν far *too weak* were we, Od.24.171: c. inf., τεθνάκην ὀλίγω 'πιδεύης cj. in Sapph.2.15.

⊛ **ἐπιδεύομαι,** Ep. for ἐπιδέομαι (v. ἐπιδέω (B) II), *to be in want of, lack,* c. gen. rei, χρυσοῦ ἐπιδεύεαι Il.2.229, cf. Od.15.371, Nic.*Th.*57; *need the help of,* c. gen. pers., σεῦ ἐπιδευομένους Il.18.77. **II.** *to be lacking in, fall short of,* c. gen. rei, μάχης ἐπιδεύομαι 23.670, cf. 17.142: also c. gen. pers., πολλὸν κείνων ἐπιδεύεαι ἀνδρῶν *fallest* far *short* of them, 5.636; or both together, οὔ τι μάχης ἐπιδευέτ' Ἀχαιῶν 24.385: later c. acc. rei, ἀλκήν A.R.2.1220.—The Act. occurs only in Aeol. fut. inf. ἐπιδεύσην, f.l. in Sapph.2.15 (v. ἐπιδευής).

**ἐπιδεύτερ-ος,** ον, *secondary, of minor rank,* of a dramatist, Suid. s.v. Ἀριστομένης. **-όω,** *repeat, AB*93. **-ωσις,** εως, ἡ, *repetition,* Sm.*Ps.*76(77).11.

**ἐπιδεύω,** *moisten, AP*7.208 (Anyte, tm.):—Pass., αἵματι κρητήρ Orph.*A.*1076.

**ἐπιδέχομαι,** Ion. etc. **-δέκομαι** Hdt. (v. infr.), *Leg Gort.*11.25:—*admit besides* or *in addition,* Hdt.8.75. **2.** *receive besides,* Men. 583. **3.** *receive, welcome,* τινὰς φιλανθρώπως Plb.21.18.3; ἐ. εἰς τὰ οἰκητήρια *POxy.*281.9 (i A.D.). **II.** *take on oneself, undertake,* πόλεμον Plb.4.31.1; τὴν στεφανηφορίαν *Inscr.Prien.*108.255 (ii B.C.), cf. *POxy.*498.6 (ii A.D.), etc.: c. inf., ib.102.7 (iv A.D.): abs., *agree, admit liability, PAmh.*2.31.12 (ii B.C.). **2.** of things, *allow of, admit of,* κατηγορίαν D.10.28; λόγον Arist.*Cat.*$3^{b}2$; τὸ μᾶλλον καὶ τὸ ἧττον ib.$6^{a}19$; ἐναντιότητα ib.$11^{b}1$; τὴν μεσότητα Id.*EN*$1107^{a}8$; τἀκριβές ib.$1094^{b}25$; δόξαν αἰτίας Aeschin.1.48, cf. Hero *Aut.*1.7: c. inf., ὁ χρόνος οὐκ ἐπιδέχεται μακρολογεῖν Din.1.31. **3.** *expect, await,* βαρεῖαν ἐπιδέγμενοι ἀνάγκαν B.16.96. **4.** *accept* a term *as applying to,* ἐπί τινος Ascl.*Tact.*11.2 (v.l. ἐκδ-).

**ἐπιδέω** (A), fut. -δήσω, *bind, fasten on,* τὸν λόφον Ar.*Ra.*1038:—Med., ἐπὶ τὰ κράνεα λόφους ἐπιδέεσθαι *have* crests *fastened* on.., Hdt. 1.171: for Od.21.391, v. πεδάω. **II.** *bind up, bandage.* Hp.*VC*13, *Fract.*21, *Art.*14:—Pass., ἐπιδεδεμένος τραύματα *with one's* wounds *bound up,* X.*Cyr.*5.2.32, al.; ἐπιδεδεμένοι ἀντικνήμιον, χεῖρα, ib.2.3.19.

⊛ **ἐπιδέω** (B), fut. -δεήσω, *want* or *lack of* a number, τετρακοσίας μυριάδας.., ἐπιδεούσας ἑπτὰ χιλιάδων Hdt.7.28: generally, *to be in need of,* Ocell.1.8; τῆς τέχνης ἂν μόνον ἐπιδέοι would *need* nothing *further* but his skill, Pl.*Lg.*709d: impers., ἐὰν δὲ καὶ ἄλλης ἐπιδέῃ βοηθείας D.H.6.63. **II.** Med., *to be in want of,* τινός Hdt.1.32, Pl.*Smp.* 204a, X.*Smp.*8.16, etc.; ἀρχὴν τριάκοντα ἐπιδεομένην ἡμερῶν *lacking* thirty days of its expiry, Pl.*Lg.*766c. **2.** *request, PMag.Lond.* 121.546.

**ἐπίδηλ-ος,** ον, *seen clearly, manifest,* Thgn.442; ἐ. εἶναί τινι Hdt. 8.97; ἐ. ποιεῖν τισί, ἤν.. Ar.*Eq.*38: c. part., ἐ. ἐστι κλέπτων is *detected* stealing, Id.*Ec.*661. **2.** ἐ. μάλιστα γίνεται [ἄνθρωπος] ἀπὸ ἑπταετέος μεχρι τεσσαρεσκαιδεκαετέος *formed,* Hp.*Carn.*13. **II.** *indicative* of a crisis to come, Id.*Aph.*2.24, cf. Gal.17(2).510: so in neut. pl., σῆς ἀρετῆς ἐπίδηλα *as a witness of..*, *IG*12(7).286 (Amorgos). **2.** *distinguished, remarkable,* X.*Oec.*21.10. **3.** *like, resembling,* τινί Ar.*Pl.*368. **III.** Adv. -λως Hp.*Acut.*45, Arist. *Cael.*$297^{b}34$, etc.: Comp. -ότερον Id.*GA*$728^{b}29$, -οτέρως Id.*HA* $604^{a}2$: Sup. -ότατα ib.$510^{a}5$, -οτάτως Id.*GA*$727^{a}23$. (Cf. also ἐπίζηλος.) **-όω,** *indicate* Id.*Mete.*$373^{a}31$; νεύματί τι Philostr.*VA*5.34.

**ἐπίδημα,** ατος, τό, *cushion* (?), dub. in Paul.Aeg.2.48.

**ἐπιδημ-εύω,** = sq., *live among the people, live in the throng,* opp. live in the country, Od.16.28. ⊛ **-έω,** *to be at home, live at home,* opp. ἀποδημέω, Th.1.136, Pl.*Tht.*173e, etc.; παρόντες καὶ ἐπιδημοῦντες Antipho 6.46; ἐ. τρία ἔτη And.1.132; ἐ. Ἀθήνησι *stay at home* at Athens, D.35.16; so ἐν αὐτῇ (sc. τῇ πόλει) ἐ. Pl.*Cri.*52b; opp. στρατεύομαι, Is.9.3. **2.** of diseases, *to be prevalent, epidemic,* Hp.*Prog.*25. **II.** *come home,* X.*Mem.*2.8.1; ἐνθάδε ἐ. Pl.*Smp.* 172c; εἰ νῦν ἐξ ἀγροῦ ἐνθάδ' ἐπιδημεῖ Men.*Georg.*19. **III.** of foreigners, *come to stay in a city, reside in* a place, οἱ -οῦντες ἐν Λακεδαίμονι ξένοι X.*Mem.*1.2.61; ἐ. εἰς Μέγαρα *come* to Megara *to stay* there, D.59.37, cf. Aeschin.2.154; ἐκ Κλαζομενῶν Pl.*Prm.*126b; ἐ. τοῖς μυστηρίοις *to be present at, attend* them, D.21.176; τοὺς ἐπιδημήσαντας ἅπαντας τῶν Ἑλλήνων all *who were present* [at the festival], ib. 217; Φοίβου ἐπιδημήσαντος Call.*Ap.*13: later c. dat., ταῖς Σάρδεσιν Philostr.*VS*1.22.4; also ἐν Μέμφει *UPZ*42.14 (ii B.C.). **2.** abs., *stay in a place, be in town,* ὅσοι ξένοι ἐπιδημοῦσιν Lys.12.35, cf. *Inscr.Prien.*108. 286 (ii B.C.), *Act.Ap.*17.21; Πρωταγόρας ἐπιδεδήμηκεν; Pl.*Prt.*309d: metaph., ἐ. θίασος Μουσῶν Ar.*Th.*40. **3.** ἐ. τινί *visit* a person, *PLond.*2.416.5 (iv A.D.). **-ηγορέω,** *harangue over* a person, App. *BC*1.96. **-ησις,** εως, ἡ, = ἐπιδημία 2, f.l. in Pl.*Ep.*330b. ⊛ **-ητικός,** ή, όν, *staying at home, non-migratory,* ζῷα, opp. ἐκτοπιστικά, Arist. *HA*$488^{a}13$. **II.** ἐπιδημητικά, τά, *expenses of* a governor's *visit, Cod.Just.*12.40.12. ⊛ **-ία,** ἡ, *stay in a place,* Pl.*Prm.*127a; αἱ ἐ. αἱ τῶν συμμάχων X.*Ath.*1.18; of an Emperor, *visit, OGI*517.7 (Thyatira, iii A.D.), Hdn.3.14.1. **2.** ἐ. εἰς.. *arrival* at.. *IG*3.1023. **3.** *prevalence of an epidemic,* νουσήματος Hp.*Nat.Hom.*9; of rain, Ael. *NA*5.13. **4.** Dor. **ἐπιδᾱμία,** ἡ, *right of residence, IG*12(1).43 (Rhodes). **-ιακός,** ή, όν, *epidemic,* νοσήματα Pall.*in Hp.*2.2 D. ⊛ **-ιος,** ον (but α, ον *IG*9(1).333.7 (Locr.)), *among the people,* ἐπιδήμιοι ἁρπακτῆρες plunderers *of one's own countrymen,* Il.24.262; πόλεμος ἐ. *civil* war, 9.64; ἐπιδαμίᾳ δίκᾳ χρήστω *IG* l.c.; ἔφαντ' ἐ. εἶναι σὸν πατέρ' that he was *at home,* Od.1.194; ἐ. ἔμποροι *resident* merchants, Hdt.2.39; οὐδ' εὐνῆς αἰδὼς ἐ. A.R.2.1023: generally, *common, commonplace,* τοῦτο τοὐπιδήμιον Plu.2.735a. **2.** *sojourning among,* ψυχὴ..ἐ. ἄστροις *IG*12(8).609.3 (Thasos); *settling in* a place, A.R.1.827. **3.** of diseases, *prevalent, epidemic,* ἴκτερος Hp.*Int.*37. **4.** ἐπιδήμια θύειν sacrifice *in honour of a visit* or *arrival,* Him.*Ecl.*36.1.

**ἐπιδημιουργ-έω,** *order perfectly,* of the stars, Hp.*Ep.*18 (Pass.). **II.** v. ἐπιδαμιοργέω. **-οί,** οἱ, magistrates sent annually by Doric states to their colonies, Th.1.56. **II.** = δημιουργοί, Procop.*Arc.* 25, al. **III.** v. ἐπιδαμιοργός.

⊛ **ἐπίδημος,** Dor. **-δᾱμος,** ον, = ἐπιδήμιος, Antiph.11; οὐ τυγχάνει ἐ. ὤν not *at home,* Ar.*Fr.*390; ἐπίδᾱμος φάτις Οἰδιπόδα *the popular current* report concerning, S.*OT*495 (lyr.). **2.** *sojourning in* a place, Call.*Dian.*226; Δήλῳ δ' ἦν ἐπίδημος, of Artemis, Id.*Aet.*3.1.26; οἱ ἐπίδᾱμοι *GDI*5040 (Hierapytna), cf. *Milet.*3.149 (ii B.C.). **3.** of diseases, *prevalent, epidemic,* Hp.*Epid.*1.14. **b.** ἐ. βιβλία writings *on epidemic diseases,* Pall. *in Hp.Fract.*12.271 C.

**ἐπιδια-βαίνω,** *cross over after* another, Hdt.4.122, 6.70; ἐ. τάφρον Th.6.101; [ποταμόν] X.*HG*5.3.4, etc.; ἐ. ἐπί τινα, τινί, *cross a river* to attack an enemy, force the passage, Plb.3.14.8, Str.2.5.8, cf. D.C. 60.21. **II.** *pass all bounds,* ταῖς ἐλπίσιν J.*AJ*15.7.9. **2.** *spread,* of diseases, ἄχρι τῆς καρδίας Gal.8.297; ἐπὶ γόνατα Aët.12.2. **-βάλλω,** *criticize,* Philostr.*VS*2.9.3. **-γιγνώσκω,** Ion. **-γῑνώσκω,** *consider afresh,* Hdt.1.133. **-γράφω** [γρᾰ], *pay in addition, PRev.Laws* 34.14 (iii B.C.); -γραφήσω f.l. in Vett.Val.348.11. **-θήκη,** ἡ, *additional will, codicil,* J.*AJ*17.9.4. **II.** *pledge, security,* Lys.*Fr.*110 S.

**ἐπιδιαίρ-εσις,** εως, ἡ, *further incision,* Heliod.ap.Orib.46.8.4, Gal. 1.386. **-ετέον,** *one must make a further incision,* Antyll.ap.Orib. 7.12.3, cf. Gal.17(1).434. **-έω,** fut. -ελῶ *PPetr.*2 p.10 (iii B.C.):—*divide, distribute,* ἑκάστῳ ἄρτους ἑξήκοντα l.c., cf. Plb.1.73.3; κρέα *Schwyzer* 726.33 (Milet., v B.C.); πολίτας ταῖς φράτραις D.H.2.55; τοὺς στρατιώτας εἰς τὴν σατραπείαν D.S.19.44; αὐτοῖς..τοὺς ἱππέας ἐπιδιῄρει *divided and sent against* them, App.*Hisp.*25:—Med., of several, *distribute among themselves,* Hdt.1.150, 5.116. **II.** *make a cross-incision in,* ὑμένα Gal.12.522.

**ἐπιδιαίτησις,** εως, ἡ, *an after-course of dietetic,* Dsc.4.148.3.

**ἐπιδια-κατέχω,** *control afterwards,* Vett Val.246.21. **-κειμαι,** *to be staked upon* a throw at dice, used as Pass. of ἐπιδιατίθημι, Poll. 9.96. **2.** *to be laid upon,* καλάμοις, of vegetables, Sor.1.51. **-κινδῡνεύω,** τινί *share in one's danger,* J.*AJ*14.14.3 (s.v.l.). **-κλύζω,** *rinse out afterwards,* Gal.12.876 (Med.).

**ἐπιδιᾱκονέω,** *render service, PStrassb.*5.11 (iii A.D.).

**ἐπιδια-κρίνω** [ρῑ], *decide as umpire,* Pl.*Grg.*524a, prob. in Id.*La.* 184c. **II.** *confirm a sentence,* D.C.57.20. **III.** *estimate carefully,* Vett.Val.277.17. **IV.** f.l. in Aristid.*Or.*26(14).30 (ἔτι δ. cj. Reiske). **-κρῐσις,** εως, ἡ, *exact estimate,* χρόνων Vett.Val.37. 10 (pl.). **-λείπω,** *allow to elapse,* ὀλίγας ἡμέρας Alex.Trall.1.17.

**ἐπιδιαλλ-ᾰγή,** ἡ, *reconciliation,* dub.l. in J.*AJ*18.9.9 (pl.). **-άσσω,** *bring to reconciliation,* ib.16.6.8.

**ἐπιδια-λύω,** *come as a relief to,* c. acc., Antyll.ap.Orib.6.8.5. **-μένω,** *remain after,* D.L.*Prooem.*11, Dsc.1.12, Artem.1.45; *continue to exist,* Diog.Oen.36. **-μονή,** ἡ, *continued existence, Stoic.* 2.182, M.Ant.4.21. **-νέμω,** *distribute,* ἄρτους ἱερεῦσι Ph.2.240; τινί τι J.*BJ*2.6.3:—Pass., αἱ τρεῖς μναῖ ἐ. τῷ στατῆρι Arist.*Ath.*10. 2. **-νοέομαι,** *think on, devise besides,* Hp.*Praec.*14. **-πέμπω,** *send over besides,* D.C.60.20. **-πλέω,** *sail across after* or *besides,* Id.47.47.

**ἐπιδιαρθρ-όω,** *articulate further,* Procl.*Inst.*177, Ammon.*in Int.* 195.22, Prisc.Lyd.36.8:—hence **-ωσις,** εως, ἡ, Dam.*Pr.*431.

**ἐπιδια-ρρέω,** *flow through* or *melt away besides,* Erot. s.v. ἐπίδυεν. **-ρρήγνῡμαι,** aor. -διερράγην [ᾰ], Pass., *burst at* or *because of* a thing, Ar.*Eq.*701. **-σᾰφέω,** *declare further,* Vett.Val.87.20, al.; *make more explicit,* Hdn.*Fig.*p.95 S.:—Pass., *become clearly understood,* Plb.32.16.5. **-σκευάζω,** *revise again, prepare a new edition of* a work, Hp.*Acut.*3. **-σκοπέω,** *consider further,* D.C. *Fr.*46.2 codd. (nisi leg. ἔτι δια-). **-σύρω** [ῡ], *carry ridicule further,* Sch.Ar.*Pax* 201. **-σχίζω,** *subdivide further, Proll.Hermog.* in Rh.7.214 W. **-τάσσομαι,** *make additions to a will, Ep.Gal.* 2.15. **-τείνω,** *stretch* by inflation *yet further,* Gal.2.17. **2.** intr., *spread far,* of fame or rumour, Plb.31.23.3; *extend* so as to include, ἐπί.. Phld.*Rh.*2.209 S. **-τίθημι,** *arrange besides* or *afterwards,* D.C.62.15:—Med., *deposit as security for* one's doing a given act, Lys.*Fr.*110 S.; ἀργύριον D.33.13; cf. ἐπιδιαθήκη II; also, *stake on* a throw at dice, Poll.9.96; cf. ἐπιδιάκειμαι. **II.** Med., *make a second* or *later will, Pap.Erzherzog Rainer* 723 (ined., cf. Kreller *Erbrechtl.Untersuch.*p.298). **-τρίβω** [ρῑ], *spend time on,* χρόνον τῇ γεύσει Thphr.*Od.*11; *spend,* ἡμέρας τρεῖς J.*AJ*11.5.2, cf. Hdn.2.11.1; ἐπιδιατρίψας *dwelling on it,* Arist.*Mete.*$371^{a}23$. **-φέρομαι,** *go across after,* Th.8.8 (v.l. διαφ-). **-φθείρω,** *destroy, ruin besides,* in Pass., Ph.ap.Eus.*PE*8.14; *become corrupt,* Gal.8.42.

**ἐπιδῐδάσκω,** *teach besides,* X.*Cyr.*1.3.17, *Oec.*10.10, *Sammelb.* 5656.10 (vi A.D.).

**ἐπιδιδῠμίς,** ίδος, ἡ, (δίδυμος II) in Anatomy, *epididymis,* Gal.4.565.

⊛ **ἐπιδίδωμι,** *give besides,* τινί τι Il.23.559, Hdt.2.121.δ', al., E.*Med.*186 (anap.), *Ba.*1128, etc.: abs., Hes.*Op.*396, etc. **b.** of a physician, *administer,* ὅσων τῷ κάμνοντι δεῖ Ph.1.253; *give afterwards,* τροφὴν προδόντες ἐπιδιδόασι τὸν ἐλλέβορον Dsc.4.148. **2.** *give in dowry,* ὅσσ' οὔ πώ τις ἑῇ ἐπέδωκε θυγατρί Il.9.148, cf. Lys.16.10, Pl.*Lg.*944a (Pass.), X.*Cyr.*8.5.19. **b.** esp. *contribute as a 'benevolence',* for the pur-

pose of supplying state necessities, opp. εἰσφέρειν (which was compulsory), Is.5.37; ἐκ τῶν ἰδίων ἐ. Din.1.80; τριήρη ἐπέδωκεν D.21.160; ἐπέδωκα τὰ χρήματα Id.18.113; τὸ κοινὸν ἐπέδωκε τῷ θεῷ *SIG* 489.9 (Delph., iii B.C.); but also, c. *offer money* as a bribe or consideration, X.*Ath.*3.3. 3. *give freely, bestow*, Th.4.11, Ar.*Pax*333; ὑμῖν τῶν ἑαυτοῦ τι Lys.30.26; ἐ. τοῦ ἑαυτοῦ μέρους X.*Cyr.*1.5.1; τὸν ἑαυτοῦ [ζῆλον] εἰς τὴν φιλοδοξίαν *Inscr.Prien.*114.12 (i B.C.). 4. ἐπιδιδόναι ἑαυτόν *give* oneself *up, devote* oneself, τινί to one, Ar.*Th.*213, cf. Luc.*Peregr.*13; εἴς τι *SIG*495.124 (Olbia, iii B.C.), cf. Hdn. 3.4.1; εἰς πᾶν τό σοι χρήσιμον ἐμαυτὸν ἐ. *UPZ*62.9 (ii B.C.); also (sc. ἑαυτὸν) ἐπιδιδόναι εἰς τρυφὴν Ath.12.525e; εἰς ὑπερηφανίαν Nymphis 15; ἐ. ἑαυτὸν τῇ πνεούσῃ Luc.*Herm.*28: abs., ἐπιδόντες ἐφερόμεθα ran *before the wind, Act.Ap.*27.15. 5. *give into* another's *hands, deliver*, ἐπιστολήν τινι D.S.14.47 (dub. l.), *Act.Ap.*15.30; χρηματισμόν Lxx 2*Ma.*11.17; γραμματεῖον Luc.*Peregr.*16: abs., of petitions, freq. in Pap., *BGU*45, etc.; of reports or returns, *POxy.*255.16 (i A.D.), etc.:—Pass., *OGI*515.37 (Mylasa, iii A.D.), Just.*Nov.*53.3.1. 6. ἐ. ψῆφον τοῖς πολίταις *give* them *power to* vote, Plu.*Num.*7. 7. *dictate*, opp. γράφειν, D.Chr.18.18. II. Med., *take as one's witness*, θεοὺς ἐπιδώμεθα '*give each other our* gods', Il.22.254:—in Il.10.463, Aristarch. read σὲ γὰρ πρώτην.. ἐπιδωσόμεθ', perh. in the same sense, though Apollon. and Scholl. explain it by δώροις τιμήσομεν: cf. περιδίδωμι. III. in Prose, freq. intr., *increase, advance*, ἐς ὕψος Hdt.2.13; καθ' ἡμέραν ἐς τὸ ἀγριώτερον Th.6.60; ἐς τὸ μισεῖσθαι Id. 8.83; ἐπὶ τὸ μεῖζον ib.24; ἐπὶ τὸ βέλτιον Hp.*Aph.*1.3, Pl.*Prt.*318a; εἰς ὄγκον πρὸς ἀρετὴν *increase* in virtue Id.*Lg.*913b; πρὸς εὐδαιμονίαν Isoc.3.32: and abs., *grow*, Pl.*Euthd.*271b; *advance, improve*, Th.6.72, 7.8; βελτίων ἔσται καὶ ἐ. Pl.*Prt.*318c, cf. *Cra.*410e, *Tht.*146b, 150d, Isoc.9.68, etc.; ἐ. πάμπολυ [ἡ μάχη] *waxes* great, Pl.*Tht.*179d. 2. = ἐνδίδωμι V, *give in, give way*, ἐ. ἐπίδοσιν τοῖσι ἕλκουσι Hp.*Art.*72, cf. Gal.6.5, Sor.1.103.

**ἐπιδιεξέρχομαι**, *to be excreted afterwards*, opp. προδιεξ–, Gal.16.699.

**ἐπιδιέρχομαι**, *pass along the line*, σύνθημα Poll.1.163.

**ἐπιδιευγάζω**, dub. sens. in *BGU*1143.16 (i B.C.).

**ἐπιδιζήημαι**, *inquire besides, go on to inquire*, Hdt.1.95. 2. *seek for* or *demand besides*, Id.5.106: so **ἐπιδίζομαι** Mosch.2.28.

**ἐπιδιηγ-έομαι**, *relate again, repeat*, Lxx*Es.*1.17, Aristid.*Or.*48(24).35. **-ησις**, εως, ἡ, *after-* or *repeated narration*, Arist.*Rh.*1414ᵇ14, Corn.*Rh.*p.364 H.

**ἐπιδιήκω**, *extend through*, Sor.*Fract.*2.

**ἐπιδιιστάω**, = sq., *dilate*, τὸ στόμα τῆς ὑστέρας Aspasia ap.Aët.16.22.

**ἐπιδιίστημι**, *let an interval elapse*, σύμμετρον ἐπιδιαστήσαντες Philum.ap.Orib.45.29.48. 2. Pass., ἐπιδιίσταμαι *have a second diastole*, of the pulse, Ruf.*Syn.Puls.*8.7. 3. -αμένων τῶν βραχιόνων *getting more separated*, Sor.2.62.

**ἐπιδῐκ-άζω**, *adjudge property in dispute to* one, of the judge, ἐ. κλῆρόν τινι Is.11.26, D.48.26:—Pass., ἐπιδεδικασμένου καὶ ἔχοντος τὸν κλῆρον *having had* it *adjudged to one* and being in possession, Id.43.7: abs., Lexib.16. II. Med., of the claimant, *go to law to establish one's claim*, Pl.*Lg.*874a, *PGnom.*28, 40 (ii A.D.); ἔχω.. τὸν κλῆρον ἐπιδικασάμενος I have obtained it *by a lawsuit*, Is.11.19. 2. c.gen., *sue for, claim at law*, ἐπιδικάζεσθαι τοῦ κλήρου Lys.*Fr.*32, Is.3.41, D. 43.3; ἐ. τῆς ἐπικλήρου *claim the hand of* the heiress, ib.55, cf. And.1.120, Is.10.5; Ἐπιδικαζόμενος, ὁ, title of plays by Philem., Diph., and Apollod.; later ἐ. τῆς ἀρχῆς J.*AJ*19.2.1: metaph., ἐ. τῆς μέσης χώρας Arist.*EN*1107ᵇ31:—Pass., *to be assigned*, of an heiress, D.S.12.18. **-ᾰσία**, ἡ, *process at law to obtain an inheritance*, Is.3.41, 61 (pl.), Lex ap.D.43.16, Ph.2.443; τῆς θυγατρὸς *for* her *hand* as heiress, Is.3.72. **-άσιμος** [ᾰ], ον, *to be claimed as one's right*, J.*AJ*4.2.4; *much sought for*, Luc.*Somn.*9. **-ατοί**, οἱ, *those to whom property is adjudged*, *IG*5(2).159.6 (Tegea, v B.C.).

**ἐπιδῐκεῖν** (cf. δικεῖν), *throw upon*, δίκον φύλλ' ἔπι Pi.*P.*9.124.

**ἐπιδῐκ-έω**, *render justice*, τινί *Schwyzer*366 *A* 23 (Tolophon, iii B.C.). II. = ἐπιδικάζομαι, *Mon.Ant.*23.85 (Adalia). ❋**-ος**, ον, *disputed at law, liable to be made the subject of a process at law* (cf. ἀνεπίδικος), ἐ. τινί ἐστιν ὁ κλῆρος Is.3.3, 43, cf. 11.10; μὴ ἐ. εἶναι τὸν κλῆρον D.44.46. Adv. -κως, ἀνυέσθω Petos.ap.Vett.Val.128.27. II. Subst. ἐπίδικος, ἡ, *an heiress for whose hand her next of kin are claimants at law*, Is.3.64; ἐ. τινα καταλιπεῖν ib.73. 2. generally, *subject to a judicial decision*, δίδωμι ἐμαυτὸν ἐπίδικον τοῖς δημόταις I commit myself *to* the people's *decision*, D.H.7.58 codd.; *disputed*, of territory, πρός τινας Plu.*Cleom.*4; ἐ. νίκη *a disputed* victory, Id.*Fab.*3.

❋**ἐπιδῐμερής**, ές, *containing* $1\frac{2}{3}$, Nicom.*Ar.*1.20, al.

**ἐπιδῑν-εύω**, later form for sq., Opp.*H.*4.218, Hld.3.3. **-έω**, *whirl for* the throw, *swing round* before throwing, ῥῖψ' ἐπιδινήσας Il. 3.378, cf. Od.9.538, etc.:—Med., *turn over in one's mind, resolve*, ἐμοὶ τόδε θυμὸς πόλλ' ἐπιδινεῖται 20.218:—Pass., *wheel about*, as birds in the air, 2.151; Σιληνοὶ.. ὄθμασι δινήθησαν ἔπι Nic.*Al.*33; so ἐπιδινεῖν αὑτούς, of drones, Arist.*HA*624ᵃ24.

**ἐπιδιόγκωσις**, εως, ἡ, *swelling up*, Sor.1.48 (pl.), 2.31.

❋**ἐπιδίομαι**, = -διώκω, inf. -δίεθθαι, part. -διόμενος *GDI*4998 (Gortyn).

**ἐπιδιορθ-όω**, *correct afterwards*, *GDI*5039.9 (Hierapytna, ii B.C.):—Med., ἐ. τὰ λείποντα *to have* deficiencies *set right also, complete* unfinished *reforms*, *Ep.Tit.*1.5; simply, *correct*, Syrian.*in Metaph.*167.11. **-ωσις**, εως, ἡ, *correction of a previous expression*, Hermog.*Id.*2.7, Tib.*Fig.*9. 2. *excusing* of an unpleasant statement (opp. προ–, q.v.), Alex.*Fig.*1.4, Longin.*Rh.*p.194 H. 3. simply, *correction*, Eustr.*in APo.*173.27. **-ωτικός**, ή, όν, *corrective*, Hermog.*Id.*2.4, Alex.Aphr.*in Top.*454.3. Adv. -κῶς Sch.Ar.*Pl.*493.

**ἐπιδιορ-ίζω**, *define* or *determine further*, Arist.*Cael.*303ᵃ13, Gal.7.706, al. **-ιστέον**, *one must define further*, Arist.*Top.*149ᵃ31.

**ἐπιδιουρέω**, *pass along with the urine*, Hp.*Prorrh.*2.4.

**ἐπιδιπλ-ᾰσιάζω**, *make double*, σιτηρέσια v.l. in Hdn.6.8.8:—Pass., J.*AJ*19.1.5. **-οΐζω**, *redouble*: prob. f.l. for ἐπανδιπλάζω, A.*Eu.*1014 codd. (lyr.). **-όω**, *make double*, τὴν δέρριν Lxx*Ex.*26.9; ἐ. τὰ φύλλα *fold* them *double*, *Peripl.M.Rubr.*65. 2. *multiply by two*, Paul.Al.*H.*4:—Pass., Vett.Val.223.34. **-ωσις**, εως, ἡ, *redoubling, double fold*, Ph.2.479 (pl.).

**ἐπιδισκεύω**, *throw away*: hence, *discard*, in Pass., prob. in Phld. *Herc.*1251.17.

**ἐπιδιστ-άζω**, *doubt about* a thing, Thphr.*Od.*45; περί τινος Porph. *Marc.*19. **-ασις**, εως, ἡ, *ambiguity*, v.l. in Gal.6.136.

**ἐπιδίτρῐτος**, ον, *containing* $1\frac{2}{3}$, Nicom.*Ar.*1.21.

**ἐπιδιφρι-άς**, άδος, ἡ, *breastwork of a chariot*, Il.10.475. ❋**-ος**, ον, *on the car*, εἰς ὅ κε δῶρα φέρων ἐπιδίφρια θήῃ Od.15.51, cf. 75. II. *one who sits at his work, plies a sedentary* or *humble trade*, D.H.*Th.*50, *PLond.*5.1708.21 (vi A.D.), Just.*Nov.*90.1 *Intr.*; ἐ. τεχνίτης Iamb. *VP*34.245; τέχνη ἐ. *a sedentary* trade, D.H.2.28; ἐργασία Artem.2.14. 2. Adj., *belonging to daily life*, λέξις, opp. πολιτική, δημηγορική, Phld.*Rh.*1.199 S.

**ἐπίδιχα·** σκύφον τὸν μὴ κενόν, Hsch.

**ἐπιδίψιος**, ον, = δίψιος, Nic.*Th.*436.

**ἐπιδῐ-ωγμός**, ὁ, *continued pursuit*, ἐναντίων Plb.11.18.7. **-ώκτης**, ου, ὁ, *pursuer*, *Gloss.* **-ώκω**, *pursue after*, τινά Hdt.4.1, 160, Lys. 3.35, etc.; *seek for*, Alex.Aphr.*Pr.*1.103. II. *prosecute again*, Is. *Fr.*157. III. *recite afterwards*, *PMag.Leid.V.*11.16. **-ωξις**, εως, ἡ, = ἐπιδιωγμός, Str.10.4.21, Hld.1.32.

**ἐπιδοιάζω**, *entertain doubts over, turn over and over*, πολέας ἐπεδοίασσα βουλάς A.R.3.21; cf. δοιάζω, ἐνδοιάζω.

**ἐπίδοκα·** προσδοκία, Hsch. **ἐπιδοκέω**, f.l. in And.4.29. **ἐπιδοκίδες·** προσδοκίαι, Hsch.

❋**ἐπίδομα**, ατος, τό, *contribution* to a feast, Ath.8.364f (pl.).

**ἐπιδομέω**, v. ἐπιδωμάω.

**ἐπιδονέω**, *sound* or *rattle atop*, Antiph.185.

**ἐπιδοξ-άζω**, *form an opinion about* a thing:—Pass., ἐπιδοξαζόμενον *matter of opinion*, Thphr.*CP*1.5.5. **-ος**, ον, *likely*, of persons, ἐ. γενέσθαι ἐπιεικεῖς *likely* to turn out well, Pl.*Tht.*143d; ἐ. τοῦτο πείσεσθαι *in danger* of suffering.., Hdt.6.12; ἐ. ὢν πάσχειν Antipho 2.1.5, cf. 2.4.9; ἐ. ὢν τυχεῖν being *expected* to gain.., Isoc.6.8; τοὺς ἐ. γενήσεσθαι πονηρούς Id.20.12; ἐπιδοξοτέρου ὄντος (sc. αἱρεθῆναι) App.*BC*1.32: sts. c. fut. part., ἐ. ἦσαν ἐμβαλοῦντες Plu.*Agis* 13; of things, ἐ. ἡ ἀπόστασις παρασχίδων ὀστέων ἀπιέναι Hp.*Fract.*24; ἐ. γενέσθαι Hdt.1.89; πρὸς οὓς ἐ. [ἐστι] πολεμεῖν Arist.*Rh.*1359ᵇ39: abs., ὅσα.. κακὰ ἐπίδοξα καταλαμβάνειν (-λαμβάνει codd.) Hdt.4.11. II. of repute, *glorious*, κῦδος Pi.*N.*9.46; and in late Prose, as Lxx*Si.*3.18, D.S.13.83, Plu.2.239d, etc. Adv. -ξως Lxx 1*Es.*9.45, *IG*12(7).117, 288 (Amorgos), Artem.2.30. **-ότης**, ητος, ἡ, *glory*, Aq.*Za.*6.13, al.

**ἐπιδορᾰτίς**, ίδος, ἡ, *tip, point of a lance, spear-head*, Demad.20, Plb. 6.25.5, al., Corn.*ND*30, Plu.2.217e. II. = σαυρωτήρ (q.v.), *AB* 303. III. *spear-shaft*, gloss on χάρμη, Sch.Pi.*Dith.Oxy.*3.13. IV. *dewlap*, *Gloss.* (nisi leg. ἐπιδορά τις vel ἐπιδορίς).

**ἐπίδορπ-α**, τά, *second course*: hence, of a small offering, Herod. 4.13. **-ίδιος**, ον, = ἐπιδόρπιος, *AP*6.299 (Phan.). **-ίζομαι**, *eat in the second course* or *for dessert*, τι Diph.79, Sophil.4.5: in Poll. 6.102 ἐπιδορπήσασθαι is f.l. for -ίσασθαι, cf. ib.79. ❋**-ιος**, ον (α, ον Ath.4.130c), *for use after dinner*, ὕδωρ (cf. προσδόρπιος) Theoc.13.36; *for dessert*, τράπεζαι Ath. l.c.; also τεῦχος ἐ., of the stomach, Nic.*Al.*21. **-ίς**, ίδος, ἡ, old name for δεῖπνον, Philem.ap.Ath.1.11d. **-ισμα**, ατος, τό, *second course, dessert*, Philippid.20 (pl.), *Com.Adesp.*141 (pl.), Ath.14.664f. **-ισμός**, ὁ, = foreg., *dessert*, Arist.*Fr.*104.

**ἐπι-δόσιμος**, ον, *given over and above*, ἐ. παρὰ τἄλλα τοῦτ' ἔσται Alex.65; ἐ. [δεῖπνα *to which unexpected luxuries have been added*, Crobyl.5. II. *contributed freely*, τριήρης *IG*2².1629.960, cf. 950, *Inscr.Prien.*112.100 (i B.C.). III. ἐπιδόσιμον, τό, *return* handed in, *PLond.*1.131ʳ.348. 2. ἐπιδόσιμος (sc. λόγος), ὁ, *section* of a document, *PRyl.*233.11 (ii A.D.). **-δοσις**, εως, ἡ, *free giving*, ἐν ἐπιδόσει καὶ χάριτι τὴν ἀλλαγὴν ποιοῦνται τούτων Plb.34.8.10. II. *free gift*, esp. *voluntary contribution* to the state, '*benevolence*', *benefaction*, οἱ τὰς μεγάλας ἐπιδόσεις ἐπιδόντες D.18.171; ἐγένοντ' εἰς Εὔβοιαν ἐπιδόσεις παρ' ὑμῖν πρῶται κτλ. Id.21.161, cf. Thphr.*Char.*22.3; ἐπιδόσεις πεποιῆσθαί τισι *Histria*7.23 (i B.C.); *charitable endowment*, *POxy.*705.59 (iii A.D.). 2. *largess* given to soldiers, Lat. *donativum*, Hdn.1.5.1, al. III. *handing in* of a petition, return, etc., *BGU*1193.11 (i B.C.), etc. IV. (ἐπιδίδωμι III) *increase, advance, progress*, ἐ. ἐς πλῆθος τοῦ ῥυφήματος Hp.*Acut.*12; *progress* of disease, Gal.1.198; ἐ. ἔχειν to be capable of *progress* or *improvement*, Pl.*Tht.*146b, *Smp.*175e, cf. Plb.1.20.2; ἐ. λαμβάνειν πρός τι Isoc.15.267, cf. Arist.*Cat.*10ᵇ28; ἐ. ποιῆσαι τοῖς πράγμασι Plb.1.36.2; ἡ ἐ. γίγνεται πρός τι Arist.*EN*1109ᵃ17; τῶν τεχνῶν αἱ ἐ. ib.1098ᵃ25; ἡ τρίτη ἐ. τῆς ὀλιγαρχίας *stage*, Id.*Pol.*1293ᵃ27. b. *devotion, addiction*, τινός to a thing, D.H.*Comp.*4 codd.; ἐ. μὲν εἰς τιμὴν πλούτου.., ὀλιγωρία δὲ τῶν καλῶν Gal.10.172. 2. *giving way, relaxation*, of sinews, Hp. *Art.*8 (pl.); ἐ. ἐπιδοῦναι ib.72. 3. ἐ. αὐτοῦ *self-surrender*, Plot.6.9.11. **-δοτήρ**, ῆρος, ὁ, *giver of more*, τέκνων, opp. ἀφαιρέτης, of

planets, Ptol.*Tetr.*189. **-δοτικός**, ή, όν, *ready to give to those who need*, distd. from μεταδοτικός by Ammon.*Diff.*p.56 V. II. *ready to give way*, Hp.*Mochl.*41.

**ἐπιδουλεύω**, *to be a slave*, παρά τινι Jul.*Ep.*198.

**ἐπιδουπέω**, *make a noise* or *clashing*, ταῖς σαρίσαις Plu.*Eum.*14; ἠχεῖοις Id.*Crass.*23.

**ἐπιδούριτον**· ἐπιπαραστροφίδα, Hsch.

**ἐπιδοχή**, ἡ, *reception in addition*, πολιτῶν Th.6.17 (pl.). II. *undertaking*, *POxy.*102.18, 103.16 (iv A.D.).

**ἐπιδράγματα**, τά, *offerings plucked*, πυρῶν καὶ καρπῶν Orac. in *App.Anth.*p.602 (Tralles).

**ἐπιδρᾰμεῖν, ἐπιδρᾰμέτην**, v. ἐπιτρέχω.

**ἐπιδράσσομαι**, Att. **-ττομαι**, *lay hold of*, τινός Plu.*Alex.*25, Gal. 4.537, etc.; τι Alciphr.3.60: metaph., τινός Phld.*Rh.*2.266 S.; ἀληθείας Jul.*Or.*6.188c; παντὸς πολιτεύματος Plu.2.793c; τὸ ἀκόλαστον ἐ. τινός Id.*Oth.*2.

**ἐπιδράω**, *perform over* a person, of purificatory rites, τινί τι Philostr.*VA*6.5.

**ἐπιδρέπω**, *pluck*, σταφυλήν Hp.*Mul.*1.105.

**ἐπιδρομ-άδην**, Adv., = ἐπιτροχάδην, Orph.*A.*561, *H.*21.5; *rapidly*, Nic.*Th.*481; *cursorily*, ἱστορῆσαι Str.2.1.6. **-έω**, = ἐπιτρέχω, cj. for ἐνι- in Max.282. ❋ **-ή**, ἡ, *running over, inroad*, κυμάτων Arist. *Mu.*400ᵃ26 (pl.); *onward motion*, *IGRom.*4.503.34 (Pergam.). 2. metaph., *brief notice*, Phld.*Rh.*2.268 S.; ἐν τῇ ἐ. τῶν φιλοσόφων in his *summary notice* of them, D.L.7.48; *summary*, προειρημένων λόγων Corn.*Rh.*p.389 H.; ἀποδείξεων Dam.*Pr.*369; ἐπιτομὰς ἢ συνόψεις ἢ ἐπιδρομάς Gal.9.431; ὡς ἐν ἐπιδρομῇ δεδείχθω Iamb.*in Nic.* p.72 P. II. *inroad, raid, attack*, Th.4.34,56; τῷ τειχίσματι ib. 23; ἐξ ἐπιδρομῆς ἁρπαγή plundering by means of *an inroad*, Hdt. 1.6: hence ἐξ ἐπιδρομῆς on *the spur of the moment*, ἐξ ἐ. αἱρέσεις ποιεῖσθαι Pl.*R.*619d; εἰπεῖν Plu.*Ant.*80, cf. Men.*Pk.*148; *cursorily*, μνήμην ποιήσασθαι φαύλως καὶ ἐξ ἐ. D.H.*Pomp.*3 (so κατ' ἐπιδρομήν Aps.*Rh.*p.258 H.); μηδὲν ἐξ ἐ. παθεῖν by *a sudden attack*, D.21. 138, cf. D.H.2.3. III. *office of inspector*, τῆς μητροπόλεως *PFay.* 23.2 (ii A.D.). IV. *a place to which ships run in, landing-place*, Λιβύης.. ἐρήμους ἀξένους τ' ἐπιδρομάς E.*Hel.*404; πλοῦν οὔριον.. Ἰλίου τ' ἐπιδρομάς Id.*IA*1597; τὰς ἐ. τῆς θαλάσσης διαχῶσαι Phalar.*Ep.* 62. V. *flow* of blood (to an atrophied part), Hp.*Off.*24. **-ία**, ἡ, = foreg. II, *assault*, A.R.3.593 (pl.). **-ικός**, ή, όν, *hasty, cursory, summary*, S.E.*M.*5.3 (Comp.). **-ίς**, ίδος, ἡ, *pulley*, *Gloss.* **-ος**, ον, *that may be overrun*, τεῖχος ἐ. a wall *that may be scaled*, Il.6.434 (but τεῖχος ἅρμασιν ἐ. *on which* chariots *can run*, *AP*9.58 (Antip.(?))); ἐ. Ζεφύροισι *overrun* by the W. winds, ib.10.13 (Satyr.), cf. Opp.*H.* 3.635; νησοῖν ἐ. ἐστι θάλασσα Mosch.2.137; τὰ ἐ. καὶ ταπεινά, of countries, Plu.*Eum.*9. 2. metaph., *intelligible*, τοῖς ἀμυήτοις Them.*Or.*13.162c. 3. *fatally easy*, πρᾶγμα Just.*Nov.*72.6. II. Act., *running over, spreading*, of sores, Nic.*Th.*242. 2. metaph., *over-hasty, rash*, γνώμη, ὅρκος, Paus.9.21.6, 33.3. 3. *following freely* or *easily*, A.*Supp.*124 (lyr.); τὸ σὸν κατὰ χεῖρος ἐ. καὶ λεῖον Luc. *Dem.Enc.*10. III. Subst. ἐπίδρομος, ὁ, *cord which runs along the upper edge of a net*, X.*Cyn.*6.9, Poll.5.29, cf. Plin.*HN*19.11; so δι' ὀργάνων ἐπιδρόμων (prob.) by *running ropes*, Plu.*Sert.*22. 2. *a small sail at the stern*, like the *mizzen-sail* of a yawl (or, acc. to Poll.1.91, *the mast of such a sail*), Isid.*Etym.*19.3.3.

**ἐπίδροσος**, ον, *catching the dew*, prob. cj. in Thphr.*HP*7.14.1.

**ἐπιδυσφημέω**, *give an ill name to*, τινά Arist.*EN*1145ᵃ33.

❋ **ἐπιδυσ⟨ω⟩χεῖν**· ἐπιτωθάζειν, Hsch.

**ἐπιδύτης** [ῠ], ου, ὁ, = ἐπενδύτης, Thd.1*Ki.*2.19, *Is.*59.17.

**ἐπιδύω** (**-δύνω** [ῡ] Man.6.642), aor. 2 ἐπέδυν, *set upon* or *so as to interrupt* an action, μὴ πρὶν ἐπ' ἠέλιον δῦναι Il.2.413; ὁ ἥλιος μὴ ἐ. ἐπὶ τῷ παροργισμῷ ὑμῶν *Ep.Eph.*4.26, cf. Lxx*De.*24.15, Ph.2.324.

**ἐπιδωμάω**, *build upon*, pf. Pass. ἐπιδεδώμηται Ph.Byz.*Mir.*4.4: written ἐπιδεδομ- ib.2.3 (teste Bast *Ep.Cr.*p.45); cf. δωμάω, ἐνδώμησις.

**ἐπιδωρέομαι**, *give besides*, Gal.14.305.

**ἐπιδώτης**, ου, ὁ, *the Bountiful*, epith. of gods, esp. Zeus at Mantinea, Paus.8.9.2, cf. Plu.2.1102e:—hence Ἐπιδώτειον, τό, temple at Epidaurus, *IG*4.1492.24.

**ἐπιέβδομος** λόγος ratio *of* 8:7, Ptol.*Harm.*1.15.

**ἐπιεθανίς**· λεπτὸν πρόβατον, Hsch. post ἐπηετα⟨ν⟩ῶν.

❋ **ἐπιείκεια**, ἡ, *reasonableness*, ἔχει τινὰ οὗτος ὁ λόγος ἐπιείκειαν Hp. *Fract.*31. 2. *equity*, opp. strict law, Arist.*Top.*141ᵃ16, etc.; κατ' ἐπιείκειαν, opp. κατὰ τοὺς ὅρκους, Isoc.18.34; ἄκαμπτον εἰς ἐ. Plu.*Cat. Mi.*4. 3. of persons, *reasonableness, fairness*, Th.3.40,48, 5.86, Pl.*Lg.*735a, etc.; ἐ. καὶ πρᾳότης Plu.*Per.*39, cf. 2*Ep.Cor.*10.1; also, *goodness, virtuousness*, Lys.16.11, D.21.207, Arist.*EN*1175ᵇ24: pl., joined with χάριτες, Isoc.4.63, cf. 15.149. II. personified, *Clemency*, Plu.*Caes.*57.

**ἐπιείκελος**, ον, = εἴκελος, *like*, τινί, the masc. freq. in Hom. (esp. in Il.), but only in phrases ἐ. ἀθανάτοισιν, θεοῖς ἐ., Il.1.[265], 4.394, Od.24.36, etc.; so θεοῖς ἐπιείκελα τέκνα Hes.*Th.*968.

**ἐπιεικ-εύομαι**, *to be* ἐπιεικής, Lxx 2*Es.*9.8 (cod. A, cf. Hsch.). ❋ **-ής**, ές, *fitting, meet, suitable*, τύμβον οὐ μάλα πολλὸν.., ἀλλ' ἐπιεικέα τοῖον not very large but *meet* in size, Il.23.246; τείσουσι βοῶν ἐπιεικέ' ἀμοιβήν a *fair* recompense for them, Od.12.382.—Elsewh. Hom. has only the neut. ἐπιεικές, either in the phrase ὡς ἐπιεικές as is *meet*, Il.19.147, 23.537, Od.8.389: or c. inf., ὃν κ' ἐπιεικὲς ἀκουέμεν whom it may be *meet* for you to hear, Il.1.547; ὅπλα.. οἷ' ἐπιεικὲς ἔργ' ἔμεν ἀθανάτων such as is *meet* they should be, 19.21, cf. 23.50, Od.2.207. II. after Hom., 1. of statements, rights, etc., a. *reasonable, specious*, ἡ δὲ τρίτη τῶν ὁδῶν πολλὸν ἐπιεικεστάτη ἐοῦσα μάλιστα ἔψευσται Hdt.2.22; ἐ. πρόφασις Th.3.9; λόγος Pl.*Ti.*67d; ἐπιεικῆ λέγειν Id.*Ap.*34d; ἐ. ὁδός a *tolerable* road, Plu.*Crass.*22. b. opp. δίκαιος, *fair, equitable, not according to the letter of the law*, ἐπανόρθωμα νομίμου δικαίου Arist.*EN*1137ᵇ11, cf. *Rh.*1374ᵃ26; τῶν δικαίων τὰ ἐπιεικέστερα προτιθεῖσι Hdt.3.53; οὔτε τοὐπ. οὔτε τὴν χάριν οἶδεν, μόνην δ' ἔστερξε τὴν ἁπλῶς δίκην S.*Fr.*770, cf. E.*Fr.*645; συγχωρεῖν τἀπιεικῆ τινι Ar.*Nu.*1438; ἐπιεικέστερον ἢ δικαιότερον Antipho 2.2.13; ἐ. ὁμολογία Th.3.4; γνώμη Ar.*V.*1027; τὸ ἐ. καὶ σύγγνωμον Pl.*Lg.* 757e; πρὸς τὸ ἐ., = ἐπιεικῶς 3, Th.4.19. 2. of persons, *able, capable*, παῖς τὰ μὲν ἄλλα ἐ., ἄφωνος δέ Hdt.1.85; οἱ ἐπιεικέστατοι τῶν τριηράρχων X.*HG*1.1.30; τίνες.. τῶν νέων ἐπίδοξοι γενέσθαι ἐ. may be expected to turn out *well*, Pl.*Tht.*143d, cf. *Lg.*957a; τοὺς ἐ. καὶ τοῦ δήμου καὶ τῶν εὐπόρων Arist.*Ath.*26.1. b. in moral sense, *reasonable, fair, good*, ἐ. τὴν ψυχήν, φύσει, Pl.*Smp.*210b, *R.*538c: abs., Th.8. 93, Isoc.1.48, *Ep.Jac.*3.17, etc.; ἐ. ἄνδρες, opp. μοχθηροί, Arist.*Po.* 1452ᵇ34; ἐ. περὶ τὰ συμβόλαια D.34.30; τοὐπιεικές *fairness, goodness*, S.*OC*1127. c. with social or political connotation, the *upper* or *educated classes*, λέγω ἀντικεῖσθαι τοὺς ἐ. τῷ πλήθει Arist.*Pol.* 1308ᵇ27, cf. *Ath.*28.1. III. Adv. **-κῶς**, Ion. **-κέως**, *fairly, tolerably, moderately*, ἐγγλύσσει ἐ. Hdt.2.92; ἐ. δάκνειν, παρρησίαν ἄγειν, Phld.*Lib.*pp.13,45 O.; ἐ. ἔχειν to be *pretty well*, Hp.*Coac.*368; ἐ. ἐξεπίστασθαι Ar.*V.*1249; ἔστι τὸ χωρίον ἐ. ἰσχυρόν *Hell.Oxy.*13.5; ἐ. ἀναίσθητον Arist.*GC*319ᵇ20; ἐ. πλατύ Id.*HA*495ᵇ27, cf. 497ᵃ23; οἱ πυρετοὶ ἐς τεταρταίην ἐ. μεθίστανται *about* the fourth day, Hp.*Coac.* 140, cf. Alex.281; ἐ. τὸ τρίτον μέρος *pretty nearly, about*, Plb.6.26.8; ἐ. οἷοί τε ἦσαν κατέχειν were *fairly well* able.., Pl.*Phd.*117c; ἐ. μὲν.. *perhaps*, Id.*Grg.*493c. 2. *probably, reasonably*, Id.*R.*431e, etc.: Sup. **-έστατα**, γενέσθαι *most suitably*, Id.*Lg.*753b. 3. *with moderation, mildly, kindly*, οὐκ ἐ. ἐντυγχάνων οὐδὲ πρᾴως Plu.*Pyrrh.*23; ἐ. ἔχειν πρός τινα Isoc.15.4: Comp. **-έστερον**, διακείμενοι Id.8.61. 4. *generally, usually*, Plu.*Pel.*18, Jul.*Mis.*348c, Lib.*Or.*11.19, al.

**ἐπιεικοσθέβδομος** λόγος ratio *of* 28:27, Ptol.*Harm.*1.13.

**ἐπιεικοστόμονος** λόγος ratio *of* 22:21, Ptol.*Harm.*2.1.

**ἐπιείκοστος** λόγος ratio *of* 21:20, Ptol.*Harm.*1.15.

**ἐπιεικοστο-τέταρτος** λόγος ratio *of* 25:24, Ptol.*Harm.*2.14. **-τρῖτος** λόγος ratio *of* 24:23, ib.1.15.

**ἐπιεικτός**, ή, όν, *yielding*, Ep. word, in Hom. always with neg., σθένος οὐκ ἐ. *unyielding, dauntless* might, Il.8.32; μένος ἔμπεδον οὐδ' ἐ. Od.19.493; μένος.. ἀάσχετον, οὐκ ἐ. Il.5.892; πένθος ἄσχετον, οὐκ ἐ. *ceaseless*, 16.549. 2. ἔργα γελαστὰ καὶ οὐκ ἐπιεικτά not *tolerable*, Od.8.307; ὀστέον οὐκ ἐ. Opp.*H.*1.526. 3. *permissible*, οὐκ ἐπιεικτὰ ζητῶν Anon.*Incred.*15(14) = Luc.*Astr.*15: c. dat., *befitting*, βροτοῖσιν Man.6.402.

**ἐπιειμένος**, v. ἐπιέννυμι.

**ἐπιείσομαι, ἐπιεισάμενος**, only fut. and aor., *rush, hasten to* or *against*, τοὺς ἄλλους ἐπιείσομαι, ὅν κε κιχείω Il.11.367; ἀγροὺς ἐπιείσομαι ἠδὲ βοτῆρας Od.15.504; ἐπιεισαμένη πρὸς στήθεα χειρὶ παχείῃ ἤλασε Il.21.424 (v.l. ἐπερεισαμένη). (Cf. εἴσομαι II: perh. fut. and aor. of (ἐπι-)(ϝ)ίεμαι.)

**ἐπιεκᾰτοστοεικοστόγδοος** λόγος ratio *of* 129:128, Ptol.*Harm.* 1.10.

**ἐπίεκτος** λόγος ratio *of* 7:6, Ptol.*Harm.*1.15.

**ἐπιέλδομαι**, poet. for ἐπέλδομαι, *desire*, ἐνισπεῖν A.R.4.783.

**ἐπιελίκτωρ**, ορος, ὁ, *one who rolls round*, coined to explain the Homeric ἠλέκτωρ, Sch.Il.19.398.

**ἐπιέλπομαι**, Ep. for ἐπέλπομαι (q.v.).

**ἐπίελπτος**, ον, *to be hoped* or *expected*, Archil.74.5, Opp.*H.*4. 311.

**ἐπιενᾰτος** λόγος ratio *of* 10:9, Ptol.*Harm.*1.15.

**ἐπιενδέκᾰτος** λόγος ratio *of* 12:11, Ptol.*Harm.*2.14.

**ἐπιεννεᾰκαιδέκᾰτος** λόγος ratio *of* 20:19, Ptol.*Harm.*2.1.

❋ **ἐπιέννῡμι**, *put on besides* or *over*, χλαῖναν δ' ἐπιέσσαμεν we *threw* a cloak *over* him, Od.20.143: elsewh. Hom. has only pf. part. Pass. ἐπιειμένος (Aeol. ἐπέμμενος Sapph.70): in metaph. sense c. acc., ἀναιδείην, ἀλκήν, *clad in* shamelessness, strength, Il.1.149, 8.262, etc.; ἐ. ἀχλύν *AP*7.283 (Leon.); λευκοῖσι κόμας ἐ. ὤμοις *covered with* hair *over* her white shoulders, A.R.3.45; χαλκὸν ἐπίεσται *has* brass *upon* or *over it*, Orac.ap.Hdt.1.47:—Med., *put on oneself besides, put on* as an *upper* garment, χλαίνας ἐπιέννυσθαι Hdt.4.64: metaph., ἐπὶ δὲ νεφέλην ἕσσαντο Il.14.350; γᾶν ἐπιεσσόμενος (fut.), i.e. to be buried, Pi.*N.*11.16; so γῆν ἐπιέσασθαι X.*Cyr.*6.4.6; γῆν ἐπιεννύμεθα *AP*7.480 (Leon.), cf. Theoc.*Epigr.*9.4: also, c. acc. rei, ἐπιεσσάμενοι νῶτον κρόκαις *having wrapt one's* shoulders *with* it, Pi.*N.*10.44.— Old Ep. Verb, not found till late (exc. Sapph. l. c.) in the form ἐφέννῡμι, because of the digamma, v. ἕννυμι, καταέννυμι; ἐπιέσασθαι is retained even in X. l. c.; ἐφέσσεσθαι, ἐφέσσατο, A.R.1.691, 1326; ἐφεσσάμενος Theoc. l. c., *AP*7.299 (Nicom.), 446 (Hegesipp.).

**ἐπιεξηκοστοτέταρτος** λόγος ratio *of* 65:64, Ptol.*Harm.*1.11.

**ἐπιεπτᾰκαιδέκᾰτος** λόγος ratio *of* 18:17, Ptol.*Harm.*1.10.

**ἐπιεργάζομαι**, v. ἐπεργάζομαι.

**ἐπίεργος**, ον, perh., = ἔπεργος, θησαυρός *PLond.*2.216.8 (i A.D.).

**ἐπιέτ-εια**, ἡ, *annual college of magistrates*, *IG*5(2).6.61 (Tegea, iv B.C.). **-ής**, ές, *of this year*, ἀγών *SIG*690 (Delph., ii B.C.); χιών v.l. in Plb.3.55.1.

**ἐπιέψεται**, v. ἐφέπω. **ἐπιϝοικία, ἐπίϝοικος**, v. ἐποικ-. **ἔπιζα**· ὄρνεα (Cypr.), Hsch. **ἐπιζάνω**, Ion. for ἐφιζάνω. **ἐπιζάξ**· ἐπὶ τὰ ἀριστερὰ καὶ ἐπ' εὐθείας, Hsch. (with other expll., cf. ἐπιτάξ).

⊛ **ἐπιζᾰρέω,** = ἐπιβαρέω, E.*Rh.*441 (prob., -ζάτει codd.), *Ph.*45 : said to be Arc. by Eust.909.28.

**ἐπιζάφελος** [ᾰ], ον, *vehement, violent,* χόλος Il.9.525. Adv. -λῶς (as if from ἐπιζαφελής, which never occurs, v. Eust.769.22) *vehemently, furiously,* ἐ. χαλεπαίνειν, μενεαίνειν, Il.9.516, Od.6.330; ἐρεείνειν *h.Merc.*487 : also neut. as Adv., ἐπιζάφελον κοτέουσα A.R. 4.1672.

⊛ **ἐπιζάω,** Ion. -ζώω, *survive,* εἰ ἐπέζωσε Hdt.1.120 ; ἂν ὡς ὀλίγιστον χρόνον ἐπιζῴη Pl.*Lg.*661c (-ζώιη cod.), cf. Eus.Mynd.38, etc. : metaph. of envy, Plu.*Num.*22.

**ἐπιζείω,** poet. for ἐπιζέω, Orph.*A.*459.

**ἐπίζεμα,** ατος, τό, *boiling* or *boiled liquid,* Sm.*Ho.*10.7.

**ἐπιζέννῡμι,** = ἐπιζέω, *boil in,* οἴνῳ Gal.13.319 (Pass.).

**ἐπι-ζεύγνῡμι** and -ύω, *join at top,* Hdt.7.36 ; τοὺς κίονας τοῖς ἐπιστυλίοις Plu.*Per.*13 ; τοὺς δακτύλους τῆς ἑτέρας χειρὸς ἐπὶ τὴν ἑτέραν ἐ. Arist.*Pr.*912$^b$14 ; simply, *bind fast,* χεῖρας ἱμᾶσι Theoc.22.3. 2. *join to,* πόλοις..τόνδ' ἐπιζεύξασ' ὄχον A.*Eu.*405 : metaph., ἐπέζευκται κοινὸν ὄνομά [τινι καὶ τινι] Arist.*HA*531$^b$22, cf. *Rh.*1407$^b$19 ; θνητὸν βίον ἀθανάτῳ ἐ. Ph.1.209 ; μηδ' ἐπιζευχθῇς στόμα φήμῃ πονηρᾷ nor *let* thy mouth *be joined* to evil sayings, A.*Ch.*1044 : Math., ἐπεζεύχθω ἀπὸ κτλ. *let* the point A *be joined to* the point B, Arist.*Mete.*376$^a$17. II. *enclose, join up,* of hills, Plb.1.75.4, 3.49.7. III. ἐπεζευγμένον, τό, *minor premise of a disjunctive syllogism,* Chrysipp.ap.S.E.*P.*2.158. **-ζευκτήρ,** ῆρος, ὁ, *strap, trace,* Hsch. **-ζευκτικός,** ή, όν, *connective,* [σύνδεσμος] A.D.*Synt.*272.3, cf. Sch.A.R.1.1349. **-ζευξις,** εως, ἡ, *fastening together, joining,* Thphr.*HP*2.6.1, prob. for ἐπίδεσις in Paul.Aeg.6.97. II. Gramm., *repetition* of a word, Hdn. *Fig.*p.99 S., Phoeb.*Fig.*1.3. III. *addition,* τοῦ τόπου A.D.*Synt.* 336.10, cf. Ptol.*Tetr.*1.

**ἐπιζέφῠρος,** ον, *towards the west, western,* Euph.121 : the Italian Locrians were called **Ἐπιζεφύριοι,** Hdt.6.23, etc., f.l. in Pi.*O.*10.13.

⊛ **ἐπιζέω,** *boil over,* πυρὸς καὶ κλύδωνος ἐπιζέσαντος Plu.2.399d; *bubble up,* πομφόλυγες -ζέουσαι Arr. in Stob.*App.*p.9 G. ; *effervesce,* Dsc. 5.74 : metaph., ἀκούσαντί μοι ἡ νεότης ἐπέζεσε my youthful spirit *boiled over* when I heard, Hdt.7.13 ; οὐ θαυμάσιον ἐπιζεῖν τὴν χολήν Ar.*Th.*468 ; θυμάλωψ ἐπέζεσεν (as if he had said θυμός) Id.*Ach.*321 ; κέντρ' ἐπιζέσαντα of the poison *working out* of the skin, S.*Tr.*840 (lyr.) : c. dat., δεινόν τι πῆμα Πριαμίδαις ἐπέζεσεν E.*Hec.*583. II. Act., *cause to boil, heat,* c. acc., ἐπιζεῖν λέβητα πυρί Id.*Cyc.*392 : metaph., δεινή τις ὀργὴ δαιμόνων ἐπέζεσε τὸ Ταντάλειον σπέρμα Id.*IT*987.

**ἐπίζηλος,** Dor. -ζᾶλος, ον, *enviable, happy,* τύχα B.5.52, cf. A.*Ag.* 939, Ptol.*Tetr.*186 : written ἐπίδηλα in *TAM*2(1).245.12 (Lycia).

**ἐπιζήμι-ος,** Dor. etc. -ζάμιος [ᾱ], ον, *bringing loss upon, hurtful, prejudicial,* Charon 12, Th.1.32, Isoc.2.18, etc.; τινί X.*Mem.*2.7.9, cf. Aeschin.1.45. Adv. -ίως Poll.8.147, D.Chr.14.18. 2. *penal* : ἐπιζήμια, τά, *punishments, penalties,* Pl.*Lg.*784e, 788b ; -ζάμια *Tab. Heracl.*1.127 ; χρησόμεθα ἐπιζημίοις, = ἐπιζημιώσομεν, Epist.Philipp. ap.D.18.157 : sg., -ζάμιον, τό, *fine,* *IG*5(2).6.36 (Tegea), 5(1).1498 (Messenia). II. *liable to punishment,* of persons, Pl.*Lg.*765a ; of acts, Arist.*Pol.*1297$^a$33, cf. *PRev.Laws*7.6 (iii B.C.). **-όω,** *mulct,* στατῆρι κατὰ τὸν ἄνδρα τῆς ἡμέρας X.*HG*5.2.22. **-ωμα,** Dor. -ζᾱμίωμα, ατος, τό, *penalty, Tab.Heracl.*1.155, Poll.8.149. **-ωσις,** εως, ἡ, *infliction of penalties,* Arist.*Ath.*45.1 (pl.).

⊛ **ἐπιζητ-έω,** *seek after, wish for, miss,* τινά Hdt.3.36, Plu.*Sull.*19 ; οὐδὲν ἄλλο χρῆμα οὕτω ἐν βραχέϊ ἐπεζήτησα ὡς.. Hdt.5.24 ; μηδὲν ἐπιζητείτω *let* her *lack* nothing, *PTeb.*416.20 (iii A.D.) ; ἐ. τὸν ἄνθρωπον *make further search for*.., D.18.133 ; τῆς αἰτίας αἰτίαν ἐπιζητούσης *requiring,* Plb.1.5.3, cf. Ph.1.18 : abs., οἱ ἐπιζητοῦντες *the beaters* (for game), X.*Cyr.*2.4.25 :—Pass., τὰ ἐπιζητούμενα περὶ τὴν εὐδαιμονίαν Arist.*EN*1098$^b$22, cf. 1172$^b$35, Diog.Oen.23 ; οἱ -ούμενοι criminals '*wanted*', *POxy.*80.15 (iii A.D.). b. *request,* πρός τινας ὁμολογίαν *Anatolian Studies* 38, cf. *PMasp.*156.16 (vi A.D.). 2. *seek for besides,* μηδ' ἕτερ' ἐπιζήτει καλά Antiph.44.5 ; *inquire further,* περὶ.. Sor.1.2, cf. Gal.16.490. 3. Pass., ἐπιζητεῖται *is matter of question,* ἐ. πότερον.. Arist.*EN*1169$^b$13, cf. Phld.*D.*1.22, *Rh.*1. 194 S., al. 4. *demand, require, PLille*7.6 (iii B.C.) :—Pass., *POxy.* 1194.2 (iii A.D.). **-ημα,** ατος, τό, *requirement, demand,* Phld.*D.* 1.16 (pl.) ; τὰ φυσικὰ ἐ. Id.*Oec.*p.14 J. ⊛ **-ησις,** εως, ἡ, *seeking after, craving,* X.Eph.2.12 ; τροφῆς Gal.19.372 ; δεινὴ τἀνδρὸς ἐ. ἦν he was sorely *missed,* J.*AJ*13.6.3, cf. 4.8.3 ; *desire, craving* (for drink), Herod.Med.ap.Orib.5.30.4 : in pl., *cravings,* Id. in *Rh.Mus.* 58.87. 2. *inquiry, PSI*4.386.40 (iii B.C.), Phld.*Sign.*21, 28 (pl.), J.*Ap.*1.22, Iamb.*Myst.*1.18. 3. *rendering of account for examination,* ἐ. πρός τινας θέσθαι *PLond.*5.1708.158 (vi A.D.). **-ητέος,** α, ον, *to be looked for, required,* Arist.*EN*1094$^b$13 ; *to be sought for,* Chor. in *Rh.Mus.*49.502. **-ητικός,** ή, όν, *apt to crave* or *miss,* τῶν κενώσεων -κὸν γίγνεσθαι τὸ σῶμα Erasistr.(?) ap.Gal.*Consuet.*5. 2. *interrogative,* σύνδεσμος Suid. s.v. μῶν.

**ἐπιζῠγ-έω,** in pass. sense, *to be joined,* Nic.*Fr.*74.22. **-ιον,** τό, = ὑποζύγιον, *IG*5(2).3.13 (Tegea, iv B.C.). II. μέρος τῆς νεώς, Hsch. **-ίς,** ίδος, ἡ, *iron pin* upon which the strands of the torsion-engine were wound, Ph.*Bel.*53.27, Hero *Bel.*83.5. II. *cross-beam,* Apollod.*Poliorc.*172.7.

**ἐπιζυγκ⟨λ⟩-εῖν·** ἐπισκαρδαμύττειν, ἐπιστένειν, ἐπικατακλᾶν, and **-οῦσα·** ἐπικλείουσα, μύουσα, Hsch.

**ἐπίζῠγ-ος,** ον, of tiles, dub. sens. in *Inscr.Délos* 366 *A* 21, 23. **-όω,** *shut to,* τὰς θύρας Artem.1.4, cf. Poll.10.26. **-ωμα,** ατος, τό, *part of the latch of a door, Et.Gud.*288.36.

**ἐπιζώνιον,** τό, *over-girth, Gloss.*

**ἐπι-ζώννῡμι,** *gird on* :—Pass., ἐπεζωσμέναι *with their clothes girt on* so as to leave the breast bare, v.l. for ὑπεζωμέναι in Hdt.2.85 ; ἐπεζωσμένος ἐγχειρίδιον *girt with*.., Plu.*CG*15 codd. ; ταινίαις τὸν χιτῶνα ἐπιζωσθείς Paus.9.39.8. **-ζώστρα,** ἡ, = ζωστήρ, *girdle,* S.*Fr.*342.

**ἐπιζώω,** Ion. for ἐπιζάω (q.v.). **ἐπίηλε** [ῐ], v. ἐπιάλλω. **ἐπιήνδανε,** v. ἐφανδάνω.

⊛ **ἐπίηρα** φέρειν, = ἦρα φέρειν or ἦρα ἐπιφέρειν, bring one *acceptable gifts,* render *service,* ἐπίηρα φέροντα S.*OT*1094 (lyr.), cf. Rhian.1.21 ; ἐπίηρα φέρεσθαι A.R.4.375 ; δέχθαι *AP*13.22 (Phaedim.) ; ἐπίηρα, as Adv., = χάριν, *for the sake of,* Antim.87 ; ὃς κακὰ πόλλ' ὑπέμεινε μιῆς ἐ. θυγατρός *PHamb.*22.2 (iv A.D.). II. sg. ἐπίηρος *pleasant, grateful,* χθών Emp.96.1 ; γέρας Simm.6.3 : Comp. ἐπιηρέστερος Epich. 186. Cf. ἦρα, ἐπιήρανος.

**ἐπιήρᾰνος,** ον, *pleasing, acceptable,* οὐδέ τί μοι ποδάνιπτρα ποδῶν ἐπιήρανα θυμῷ Od.19.343. II. after Hom., *helping, assisting,* Μινύαις ἐπιήρανος Orph.*A.*98 (prob.). 2. *ruling, governing,* Ἀθηνάων ἐπιήρανε *IG*14.1389 ii 1, cf. Nonn.*D.*2.683 ; σοφῶν ἐ. ἔργων Emp.129.3 ; καλῶν ἐ. ἔργων, of Dionysus, Ion Eleg.1.15. 3. *warding off, repelling,* ἐπιήρανος ἀσπὶς ἀκόντων *AP*9.41 (Theon). 4. νεύρων ἐπιήρανος *strengthening, giving tension,* Pl.Com.173.19.

**ἐπίηρος,** ον, v. ἐπίηρα.

**ἐπιθᾰλᾰμ-ιογράφος** [γρᾰ], ὁ, *writer of epithalamia,* Tz. ad Lyc.p.1 S. ⊛ **-ιος,** ον, *belonging to a bridal, nuptial,* ἐπιβουλή Luc.*Salt.*44 ; ἐ. ᾠδαί D.H.*Rh.*4.1. II. Subst. ἐπιθαλάμιος (sc. ὕμνος or ᾠδή), ὁ or ἡ, *bridal song,* sung in chorus before the bridal chamber, Theoc. 18 tit., Luc.*Symp.*40, Him.*Or.*1.1. **-ίτης** [ῑ], ου, ὁ, epith. of Hermes in Euboea, Hsch.

**ἐπιθᾰλασσ-ίδιος,** Att. -ττίδιος, ον, = sq., Th.4.76, X.*HG*3.4.28, Pl.*Lg.*704b, etc.; ἐπιθαλαττιαῖος is prob. f.l. in Str.2.1.16, 3.4. 20. **-ιος,** Att. -ττιος, α, ον Pl.*Lg.*704d, *PRev.Laws*93.5 (iii B.C.), also ος, ον X.*HG*3.1.16 :—*lying* or *dwelling on the coast,* Hdt.1.154 ; τὰ ἐ. Id.5.30 ; ἐ. τῆς Πελοποννήσου Th.2.56 ; *marine,* Epich.90 :—in App.*Hisp.*12 **ἐπιθάλασσος** is prob. f.l.

**ἐπιθαλέωσις,** εως, ἡ, perh. *celebration of the festival of the Corybantes* Θάλειοι, *SIG*1014.95 (Erythrae, iii B.C.).

⊛ **ἐπιθάλλω,** *flourish,* prob. in Nonn.*D.*3.254 (ἔτι θ. codd.).

**ἐπι-θαλπής,** ές, = τερπνός, Hsch. **-θάλπω,** *warm on the surface,* γαῖαν Xenoph.31, cf. Plu.2.780d (Pass.) ; [ᾠά] Ael.*NA*10.35. II. *comfort afterwards, BCH*47.284 (Macedonia, Pass.). **-θαλψις,** εως, ἡ, *warming,* δακτύλων prob. in Paul.Aeg.6.40.

**ἐπιθαλύνω,** *warm, chafe,* dub. in Hsch. (ἐπιθαλάμοντι cod., fort. ἐπιθάλποντι).

**ἐπιθαμβέω,** *marvel at,* Nonn.*D.*1.60.

**ἐπιθᾰνάτ-ιος** [νᾰ], ον, *condemned to death,* D.H.7.35, Lxx *Bel*(ό) 31, 1 *Ep.Cor.*4.9 ; ἐ. μέλος, of Arion, Tz.*H.*1.400. Adv. -ίως, ἔχειν, = ἐπιθανάτως ἔχειν, Ael.*VH*13.27. II. αἱ ἐ. δᾷδες the *funeral* torches, Lib.*Decl.*40.15 ; but ἐ. ἐπιστολή *deadly,* ib.2.28. ⊛ **-ος,** ον, *sick to death, hard at death's door,* D.50.60. Adv. -τως, ἔχειν to be *sick to death,* Poll.3.106. II. *deadly,* ὕβωσις Hp.*Mochl.*36 ; of poisons, Thphr.*CP*6.4.5.

**ἐπιθᾰνής,** ές, = foreg., Ael.*Fr.*102.

**ἐπιθάπτω,** *bury again,* Philostr.*Her.*1.3. II. *bury another in the same grave, CIG*4341 *d* (Attalia), 4366 *k* (Termessus), sqq.

**ἐπιθαρσ-έω,** Att. -ρρέω, *put trust in* or *on,* θεῶν ἀρωγαῖς Plu.*Brut.* 37, cf. S.E.*M.*1.270. II. *take heart to resist,* τοῖς ἐχθροῖς App.*BC* 3.10, cf. Ael.*NA*4.34, 9.1 ; ἐ. τῷ πελάγει *venture on*.., ib.5.56 : abs., *take courage,* D.C.41.50, al. **-ύνω,** Att. -ρρύνω, *cheer on, encourage,* τινά Il.4.183, D.H.10.41, Plu.*Mar.*36.

**ἐπιθαυμάζω,** *pay honour to,* ἐ. τι τὸν διδάσκαλον by giving him a fee, Ar.*Nu.*1147 ; ἐπιθαυμάσας τὸ παράλογον *in wonder at*.., Plu.*Marc.*30 : abs., Arr.*Epict.*1.26.12.

**ἐπιθεάζω,** = ἐπιθειάζω, *invoke the gods against,* τῷ πατρί Pherecr. 118 : abs., ἀγανακτῶν καὶ ἐ. *with imprecations,* Pl.*Phdr.*241b. II. v. ἐπιθειάζω.

**ἐπιθεάομαι,** *survey, examine,* Sch.Ar.*Nu.*499 ; *look at,* τὸν οὐρανόν Agath.5.3 ; *reflect on* a thing, Poll.6.115.

⊛ **ἐπιθέατρον,** τό, *building adjoining a theatre, IG*11(2).287 *A* 94, 120 (Delos, iii B.C.).

**ἐπιθει-άζω,** *call upon in the name of the gods, adjure, conjure,* τοσαῦτα ἐπιθειάσας Th.2.75 ; ἐ. μὴ κατάγειν Id.8.53 ; τῷ λόγῳ Plu.*Them.* 28. II. *inspire,* τινί Id.2.580d, 589d, Max.Tyr.37.5. b. abs., *to be inspired, prophesy,* D.H.1.31 : c. acc. cogn., τοιαῦτα J.*AJ*4. 6.5. 2. *ascribe to divine influence,* τὰς πράξεις Plu.2.579f, cf. Philostr.*VS*1.10 ; *treat with reverence,* Arr.*Epict.*4.1.108, Porph.*Chr.* 39. **-ᾰσις,** εως, ἡ, = sq. 1, Plu.2.1117a (pl.). **-ασμός,** ὁ, *appeal to the gods,* Th.7.75 (pl.). 2. *inspiration,* Poll.1.16, Ph.2. 299. **-αστικός,** ή, όν, *given to appeals to heaven,* in Sup., Plu. *Prov.*2.14. II. *frenzied, inspired,* Hsch. s.v. νυμφόληπτοι.

**ἐπιθέλγω,** *soothe, assuage,* τὴν ὀργήν Plu.2.456a.

**ἐπίθεμ-α,** ατος, τό, = ἐπίθημα, *cover,* Arist.*HA*529$^b$8 (v.l. -θημα), Lxx *Ex.*25.16(17), J.*AJ*3.6.5, *IG*3.14.18, Ruf.ap.Orib.4.2.6, Gal.12. 889. 2. *capital* of a column, Lxx 3 *Ki.*7.4 sq. 3. *remedy for external application,* Ruf.*Ren.Ves.*10, Dsc.*Ther.*19. 4. *addition, POxy.*500.14 (ii A.D.) ; *higher bid, PAmh.*2.85.21 (i A.D.). 5. *shaft* of an arrow, Paul.Aeg.6.88. **-άτιον,** τό, Dim. of ἐπίθεμα 3, *Gloss.* **-ᾰτισμός,** ὁ, = Lat. *augmentum,* ib.

**ἐπίθεος·** σημεῖον ἐν θυτικῇ, Hsch.

**ἐπιθερᾰπ-εία,** ἡ, *care* of a statue, *IGRom.*4.293 *a* i 43, ii 62 (Pergam.). **-ευσις,** εως, ἡ, Rhet., *indignant reiteration of a charge,*

Ps.-Ascon. *in Verr.Act.*i § 27. **-εύω**, *to be diligent about, work zealously for*, τὴν κάθοδον Th.8.47; *court* one's *favour*, ib.84:—Pass., πρός τινος D.C.*Fr.*68.3. **II.** *apply after-treatment*, Hp.*Mochl.*41 (Pass.). **2.** *repeat an application*, *Gp.*17.23.2.

**ἐπιθερμαίνομαι**, Pass., *become feverish*, Hp.*Epid.*1.1, 3.17.ιγ΄. **II.** later in Act., *warm up*, *PHolm.*17.40.

**ἐπιθεσία**, ἡ, *plot*, Aq.*Ps.*34(35).20 (pl.).

**ἐπίθεσις**, εως, ἡ, *setting on its base*, τοῦ ἀνδριάντος *CIG*3124 (Teos). **2.** *laying* or *putting on*, opp. ἀφαίρεσις, Arist.*Juv.*470$^a$11; τῶν χειρῶν *Act.Ap.*8.18, etc.; *application*, περιχρίστων Plu.2.102a, cf. Luc.*DDeor.*13.1 (prob.). **3.** *application of epithets*, τὰς ἐ. ποιεῖσθαι Arist.*Rh.*1405$^b$22. **4.** *imposition of increased burdens*, *Cat.Cod.Astr.*7.134. **II.** (from Med.) *setting upon, attack*, Antipho 2.2.13; ἐ. γίγνεταί τινι X.*An.*4.4.22; ἡ Περσῶν ἐ. τοῖς Ἕλλησι Pl.*Lg.*698b; τῶν ἐ. αἱ μὲν ἐπὶ τὸ σῶμα γίγνονται τῶν ἀρχόντων *attempts*, Arist.*Pol.*1311$^a$31; ἐ. συστῆσαι ἐπί τινα ib.1306$^b$35; ποιεῖσθαι ib.1312$^a$20; λῃστῶν *PPetr.*3p.60 (iii B.C., prob.); κατά τινος D.H.5.7; ἡ διὰ τοῦ πυρὸς ἐ. τοῖς ἔργοις Plb.1.45.2; of disease, *aggravated attack*, Sor.2.49 (pl.). **2.** c. gen., *attempt to gain*, τῆς τυραννίδος D.S.13.92, etc. **3.** *small urn placed on a σορός*, *IGRom.*4.1284 (Thyatira). **4.** *imposture, deception*, Aq.*Pr.*11.1, al. **5.** Pythag. name for *two*, Hsch.

**ἐπιθέσοντας**· ἐποξύνοντας, ἐπιφέροντας, Hsch.

**ἐπιθεσπ-ίζω**, of Triton, *prophesy* or *divine upon*, τῷ τρίποδι Hdt.4.179. **II.** of an oracle, *give sanction*, τινί D.H.2.6; ἐ. βασιλείαν τινί Id.3.35. **III.** *apply a prophecy*, τὰ Τειρεσίου ἑαυτῷ Philostr.*VA*7.4. **-ισμός**, ὁ, *sanction of an oracle*, Arr.*An.*6.19.4.

**ἐπιθετ-έον**, *one must impose*, δίκην Pl.*Grg.*507d; *one must set on*, σφραγῖδα τῷ λόγῳ Jul.*Or.*4.144c; *one must put on, apply*, Herod.Med. ap.Aët.9.2; ἐπίπλασμα Aret.*CA*1.4. **II.** (from Med.) *one must set upon*, τινί Pl.*Sph* 231c; τῷ ἀνδρί Id.*Smp.*217c. ⊛ **-ης**, ου, ὁ, *plotter, impostor*, Luc.*Trag.*172, Sm.*Ps.*1.1, Ptol.*Tetr.*165, Vett.Val.16.11. **II.** *official of a religious association*, *IG*3.1280*a*. **-ικός**, ή, όν, *ready to attack*, θηρίοις X.*Mem.*4.1.3; *enterprising*, στρατηγός ib.3.1.6, Str.3.4.5; ἐπιθετικώτατον περὶ πάσας τὰς πράξεις Arist.*Pol.*1315$^a$11: -κόν, τό, *enterprise*, Corn.*ND*21. **2.** = ἐπιθέτης I, Ptol.*Tetr.*165. **II.** *added*: τὸ ἐ. *the adjective*, A.D.*Synt.*81.17 (pl.); ἐ. σύνταξις, προσηγορίαι, ib.18.7, D.S.4.5. Adv. -κῶς Corn.*ND*35, Sch.Il.13.29: Comp. -ώτερον A.D.*Synt.*81.15. ⊛ **-ος**, ον, *additional*, φυλαί D.H.3.71; esp. at Athens, opp. πάτριος, *relatively modern*, ἑορταί Isoc.7.29; τὰ ἐ., opp. τὰ πάτρια, the *acquired powers* of the Areopagus, Lys.*Fr.*178 S., cf. Arist.*Ath.*25.2, 3.3; so ἐ. ἐξουσία *usurped* authority, Plu.*Cleom.*10: generally, *adventitious*, τὰ μὲν τῶν νόμων ἐπίθετα, τὰ δὲ τῆς φύσεως ἀναγκαῖα Antipho Soph.*Oxy.*1364.25; ἐπιθυμίαι, opp. κοιναί, Arist.*EN*1118$^b$9; ἐ. τῇ φύσει κακά Men.534.13. **2.** *fictitious*, Thphr.*HP*9.8.8; opp. ἀληθινός, D.H.4.70, cf. 68. **3.** of letters, *entrusted for conveyance*, Lys.*Fr.*116 S. **II.** ἐ. [ὄνομα] *adjectival*, D.T.636.9, cf. Plu.*Cor.*11. **III.** Subst. **ἐπίθετον**, τό, *epithet*, Arist.*Rh.*1406$^a$19, D.H.*Comp.*5, A.D.*Synt.*41.15; *adjective*, ib.81.24 (so Adv. -τως, λέγειν indicate *by epithets*, Str.1.2.29, al.). **2.** = ἐπίθημα 5, Aret.*CA*1.1. **3.** ἐπίθετος, ὁ, a throw of the dice, Eub.57.4.

**ἐπιθέω**, *run upon, at* or *after*, Hdt.9.107, X.*Cyn.*6.10: abs., App.*Hisp.*90; ἐ. πρὸς τὴν μάχην Hdn.6.7.8. **2.** metaph., ἡ ἐπιθέουσα εἰς ἀνθρώπους ἀπάτη Plot.2.9.6; *to be diffused over*, πᾶσι τοῖς ἀληθέσι Id.5.3.17, al. **II.** *run upon the surface* of water, Arist.*HA*551$^b$22.

**ἐπιθεωρ-έω**, *examine over again* or *carefully, ascertain*, τι Hp.*Acut.* (*Sp.*)8, Philem.138, D.H.*Rh.*3.2, Plu.*Demetr.*1, Iamb.*Comm.Math.*14:—Pass., Thphr.*Metaph.*34. **b.** *consider next in order*, πάθος Epicur.*Nat.*13 G. **2.** *inspect*, μόσχον Wilcken *Chr.*89.3 (ii A.D.); νεκρόν *POxy.*475.6 (ii A.D.). **3.** *look at, behold*, τινά J.*AJ*15.7.5. **4.** Pass., *to be observed in, to be an aspect of*, ἑκάστῃ οὐσίᾳ Plot.6.6.5. **5.** Astrol., *aspect from the right*, Vett.Val.44.31, Gal.19.541. **-ησις**, εως, ἡ, *contemplation*, τῆς τῶν ὅλων φύσεως M.Ant.8.26. **2.** *inspection*, *CPHerm.*7 ii 23 (iii A.D.). **3.** Astrol., *aspect*, Ptol.*Tetr.*193. **-ητέον**, *one must consider*, πότερον.. Sor.1.97, cf. Gal.8.165, Herod.Med.ap.Orib.7.8.3. **II.** *one must take care*, μή.. Gal.16.134. **-ία**, ἡ, Astrol., *aspecting from the right*, Rhetor.in *Cat.Cod.Astr.*1.155.15.

**ἐπιθήγω**, *whet* or *sharpen yet more*, τὰ κέντρα Ael.*NA*5.16: metaph., *stimulate yet more*, τὰς ἐπιθυμίας Plu.786b.

**ἐπιθήκη**, ἡ, *addition, increase*, Hes.*Op.*380; κἀπιθήκην τέτταρας and 4 loaves (or perh. obols) *over*, Ar.*V.*1391; adponam epithecam insuper, cj. for apo- in Plaut.*Trin.*1025. **II.** *cover* put over a statue, *CPR*27.10 (ii A.D.). **III.** *sum allowed to cover expenses*, *POxy.*1158.24 (iii A.D.), etc.

**ἐπιθηλέω**, = ἐπιθάλλω, Nonn.*D.*3.151.

⊛ **ἐπίθημα**, ατος, τό, *something put on* (cf. ἐπίθεμα): hence, **1.** *lid, cover*, φωριαμῶν ἐπιθήματα *lids* of chests, Il.24.228, cf. Hippon.56, Hp.*Morb.*2.26, Hdt.1.48, Arist.*Ath.*68.3, *IG*2$^2$.1408; ἀσπίδα ἐ. τῷ φρέατι παράθες Ar.*Fr.*295; τοὐπ. τῆς χύτρας ἀφελών Hegesipp.Com.1.13; *slab*, used as the top of a table, Ath.2.49a. **2.** *monument, sepulchral figure*, Is.2.36, Paus.1.2.3. **3.** *head* of a spear, D.S.5.30. **4.** *device* on a shield, Paus.5.25.9. **5.** Medic., *application*, Aret.*CA*1.1, 2.2.

**ἐπιθημᾰτ-ικός**, ή, όν, *concerned with* ἐπιθήματα, -κή (sc. τέχνη) Poll.7.208. **-ουργία**, ἡ, *making of lids* or *covers*, Pl.*Plt.*280d. **-όω**, *put a lid upon*, τι Anticl.13.

**ἐπιθηραρχ-ία**, ἡ, *contingent of four elephants*, Ascl.*Tact.*9, Ael.*Tact.*23. **-ος**, ὁ, *officer commanding such a contingent*, ll. cc.

**ἐπιθιγγάνω**, aor. 2 ἐπέθῐγον, *touch*, Thphr.*Od.*11, Agath.2.24; τῆς κεφαλῆς Plu.*TG*19. **2.** *reach as far as*, ὄψις ἐ. τῆς θαλάσσης Id.2.921d. **3.** c. dat., = ἐφάπτομαι, *IG*5(2).429 (Phigalea).

**ἐπιθλάσας**· συντόμως εἰπών, Hsch.

**ἐπίθλᾰσις**, εως, ἡ, *fracture*, v.l. for περίθλασις, Orib.46.5.2.

⊛ **ἐπι-θλίβω** [ῑ], *press upon the surface*, D.S.3.14; *tread*, ὀπώρην Nonn.*D.*7.91; *crowd round*, App.*BC*4.45: metaph., *repress, check*, Plu.2.782d. **-θλιψις**, εως, ἡ, *pressure on the surface*, Aret.*CA*1.9 (pl.); *crushing*, τοῦ δακτύλου Orib.*Fr.*74.

**ἐπιθοάζω**, *sit as suppliant at an altar*, τάδ' ἐπευχομένη κἀπιθοάζουσ' A.*Ch.*856 (οα in litura); τάδε καὶ θρηνῶ κἀπιθοάζω E.*Med.*1409; cf. θοάζω II; but κἀπιθεάζουσ' *invoking the gods*, and κἀπιθεάζω shd. prob. be read.

**ἐπίθολ-ος**, ον, *turbid*, ὕδωρ Lyd.*Ost.*8. ⊛ **-όω**, *make turbid*, Luc.*Ind.*7, Max.Tyr.33.5: metaph., τὴν φιλίαν Plu.*in Hes.*66; σοφίας κρατῆρα Philostr.*VA*6.11; τῆς ψυχῆς τὰς καθαρότητας Iamb.*VP*24.107; τὸ κρῖνον Agath.3.11:—Pass., *become turbid*, *Placit.*3.5.8, Gal.6.57, Luc.*Lex.*4: metaph., ἡ ψυχὴ -οῦται οὔτε φόβοις οὔτε ἐλπίσιν Artem.4*Prooem.*; τὰ θεωρήματα μηδὲν -ούμενα ὑπ' ἀλλοτρίων δοξασμάτων Iamb.*in Nic.*p.4 P., cf. *Myst.*5.4, Just.*Nov.*22.20.2.

**ἐπιθόρνῠμαι**, *cover*, of the male, βουσί Luc.*Am.*22, etc.; ἐ. ταῖς γεγαμημέναις Philostr.*VA*5.29, cf. *Im.*2.3: abs., Ael.*NA*10.2, al.

**ἐπιθορῠβ-έω**, *shout to*: **1.** in token of approval, X.*HG*2.3.50, Pl.*Prt.*339e, D.H.6.39. **2.** in token of displeasure, X.*HG*1.7.13, Luc.*Asin.*54. **-ως**, Adv. *agitatedly, in turmoil*, διάγειν Vett.Val.184.31.

**ἐπιθράνιον**· μέρος τι τῆς νεώς, Hsch.

**ἐπίθρᾱνοι**, οἱ, *binding timbers* in brick construction, Poll.10.49.

**ἐπιθράσσω**, aor. 1 ἐπιθρᾶξαι· ἐπιθρύξαι, ἐπινύξαι, Hsch.; cf. ἐνθράσσω.

⊛ **ἐπιθραύω**, *break besides*, τρύφος ἄρτου *AP*6.105 (Apollonid.).

**ἐπιθρέξας**, v. ἐπιτρέχω.

**ἐπίθρεπτος**, ον, *well-nourished*, σάρξ Hp.*Prorrh.*2.24.

**ἐπιθρην-έω**, *lament over*, συμφοράς Babr.118.8: abs., τὸ -θρηνεῖν Plu.2.123c, Diog.Oen.61: c. acc. cogn., γοώδες τοῖς εἰρημένοις Hld.10.37. **-ησις**, εως, ἡ, *lamentation over*, Plu.2.611a (pl.). **-ητος**, ον, *lamentable*, Hsch. s.v. περίσφατα.

**ἐπιθρίαμβος** [ῐ], ὁ, *subsequent triumph*, Suid. s.v. θρίαμβος.

**ἐπιθριδάκια** [ᾰκ], τά, (θρίδαξ) *festival of Apollo*, Hsch.

**ἐπίθροισις**, εως, ἡ, prob. f.l. for -θλιψις, Gal.17(1).51.

**ἐπιθρομβόομαι**, Pass., *curdle*, Nic.*Al.*364 (v.l. ἐπιτυρ-).

**ἐπιθρῡλέω**, *disturb with noise*, *EM*456.40. **2.** *proclaim noisily*, Agath.2.2.

**ἐπιθρύπτω**, *enfeeble, enervate*, Philostr.*VA*1.37:—Pass., *practise affectations*, Aristaenet.1.28; ἐπιτεθρυμμένος *effeminate*, Plu.*Dio*17.

**ἐπιθρῴσκω**, *leap upon*, c. gen., νηὸς ἐπιθρῴσκων Il.8.515, cf. E.*Rh.*100: c. dat., *leap* (contemptuously) *upon*, τύμβῳ ἐπιθρῴσκων Μενελάου Il.4.177. **II.** *leap over* a space, τόσσον ἐπιθρῴσκουσι so far *do* [the horses] *spring at a bound*, 5.772; μακρὰ ἐ. Hes.*Sc.*438. **2.** *jut out*, of a rock, Orph.*A.*1266. **III.** *rise*, ὀμίχλη Musae.113.

**ἐπιθυλλίς**, ίδος, ἡ, f.l. for γηθυλλίς in Ath.9.371f, cf. Eust.1155.20.

⊛ **ἐπίθυμα**, ατος, τό, *that which is burnt* in magic, *PMag.Par.*1.1308, al.; *sacrificial victim*, Hsch. s.v. ἱεράθετα.

**ἐπιθυμελίας ἀγῶνα**· τὴν τῶν διαφραγμάτων στάσιν, Hsch.

⊛ **ἐπιθῡμ-έω**, *set one's heart upon* a thing, *long for, covet, desire*, c. gen. rei, Hdt.2.66, A.*Ag.*216, etc.: also c. gen. pers., Lys.3.5, X.*An.*4.1.14 (later c. acc. pers., [Men.] ap.Clem.Al.*Strom.*5.119, *Tab.Defix.Aud.*271.45 (Hadrumetum, iii A.D.)); of political attachments, τῶν ἡμετέρων πολεμίων And.4.28; ὀλιγαρχίας Lys.20.3: c. inf., *desire to* do, πλῶσαι Hdt.1.24; ἀπικνέεσθαι ib.116; περισσὰ δρᾶν S.*Tr.*617, etc.: abs., *desire, covet*, Th.6.92; ὁ ἀεὶ -ῶν Pl.*Prt.*313d, etc.; τὸ ἐπιθυμοῦν τοῦ πλοῦ, = ἐπιθυμία, *eagerness for* it, Th.6.24:—Pass., *to be desired*, τὰ ἐπιθυμούμενα Pl.*Phlb.*35d. **-ημα**, ατος, τό, *object of desire*, Id.*Lg.*687c (sg.), Arist.*EN*1118$^a$13, X.*Hier.*4.7 (pl.). **II.** *yearning, desire*, Hp.*de Arte* 1, Antipho Soph.110, Epicur.*Fr.*141: pl., Philyll.30. **-ησις**, εως, ἡ, *longing, desire*, κακῶν Is.*Fr.*158. **-ήτειρα**, ἡ, fem. of sq., Call.*Dian.*237. **-ητής**, οῦ, ὁ, *one who longs for* or *desires*, νεωτέρων ἔργων Hdt.7.6; [δογμάτων] And.4.6; ἔργων Lys.12.90; τιμῆς, σοφίας, Pl.*R.*475b, etc.; φύσει πολέμου ἐ. Arist.*Pol.*1253$^a$6; κακῶν 1*Ep.Cor.*10.6; ἀλλοτρίων *BGU*531 ii 22 (ii A.D.). **2.** abs., *lover, follower*, X.*Mem.*1.2.60. **b.** *one who lusts*, Lxx *Nu.*11.34. **-ητικός** (hyperdor. **-ᾱτικός** Diotog.ap.Stob.4.7.62), ή, όν, *desiring, coveting, lusting after*, τινός Pl.*R.*475b, al.; τὸ ἐ. *that* part of the soul *which is the seat of the desires and affections*, ib.439e, Arist.*EN*1102$^b$30, etc. Adv. -κῶς, ἔχειν τινός, = ἐπιθυμεῖν, *Hell.Oxy.*16.4, Pl.*Phd.*108a, Isoc.15.244, D.L.8.1; ἐ. διακεῖσθαι Palaeph.23. **-ητός**, ή, όν, *desired, to be desired*, -τὸν τὸ φαινόμενον καλόν Arist.*Metaph.*1072$^a$27, cf. *Rh.*1371$^a$33, etc.; of the *cravings* of pregnant women, Sor.1.53. Adv. -τῶς *EM*148.7. **-ία**, Ion. -ίη, ἡ, *desire, yearning*, ἐ. ἐκτελέσαι Hdt.1.32; ἐπιθυμίᾳ *by passion*, opp. προνοίᾳ, Th.6.13: generally, *appetite*, Pl.*Cra.*419d, etc.; αἱ κατὰ τὸ σῶμα ἐ. Id.*Phd.*82c; esp. *sexual desire, lust*, Democr.234 (pl.), Pl.*Phdr.*232b, etc.; αἱ πρὸς τοὺς παῖδας ἐ. X.*Lac.*2.14. **2.** c. gen., *longing after* a thing, *desire of* or *for* it, ὕδατος, τοῦ πιεῖν, Th.2.52, 7.84, etc.; τοῦ πλέονος Democr.224; τῆς τιμωρίας Antipho 2.1.7; τῆς μεθ' ὑμῶν πολιτείας And.2.10; τῆς παρθενίας Pl.*Cra.*406b; εἰς ἐ. τινὸς ἐλθεῖν Id.*Criti.*113d; ἐν ἐ. τινὸς εἶναι Id.*Prt.*318a, *Tht.*143e; γεγονέναι Id.*Lg.*841c; εἰς ἐ. τινὸς ἀφικέσθαι θεάσασθαι Id.*Ti.*19b; ἐ. τινὸς ἐμβαλεῖν τινί X.*Cyr.*1.1.5;

ἐ. ἐμποιεῖν ἔς τινα an *inclination* towards.., Th.4.81. II. = ἐπιθύμημα, *object of desire*, ἐπιθυμίας τυχεῖν Thales ap.Stob.3.1.172, cf. Lync.ap.Ath.7.295a; ἀνδρὸς ἐ., of woman, Secund.*Sent.*8; πενήτων ἐ., of sleep, prob. in ib.13.

**ἐπιθῡμί-ᾱμα**, ατος, τό, *incense-offering*, S.*OT*913, prob. in *BGU*1.10 (ii/iii A.D.). **-ᾱσις**, εως, ἡ, *offering of incense*, *CIG*3068 *A* 24 (Teos). **-ατρός**, ὁ, *one who burns incense*, ib.2983 (Ephesus). **-άω**, *offer incense*, Plu.*Alex.*25, *CIG*2715.6 (Stratonicea): c. acc., τῷ Βορέᾳ λιβανίδιον prob. in Men.260 (-ίσας codd. Ath.), cf. Plu.2.372d; λιβανωτόν *Milet.*3.145 (iii/ii B.C.), *SIG*694.43 (Pergam., ii B.C.), Artem. 4.2:—Pass., λίβανος ἐπιθυμιαθείς Dsc.1.68.

⊛ **ἐπιθύμιος** [ῠ], ον, = ἐπιθυμητικός, Man.4.565.

**ἐπιθῡμίς**, ίδος, ἡ, *wreath of flowers* for the neck, Hsch. (pl.). II. **ἐπιθῡμίς**, ίδος, ἡ, = θύμος, Ps.-Dsc.3.36.

**ἐπιθῡμόδειπνος**, ον, *eager for dinner*, Plu.2.726a.

**ἐπίθῡμον**, τό, *a parasitic plant growing on thyme*, *Cuscuta Epithymum*, Dsc.4.177, Gal.6.414, 11.875, Artem.1.77.

**ἐπίθῡμος**, ον, *desirous*, *Gloss.*

**ἐπιθύνω**, = ἐπευθύνω, S.*Ph.*1059: Ep. Iterat. -εσκεν A.R.3.1325: c. dat., ἔργοις Man.2.340.

⊛ **ἐπιθύρ-ιος** [ῠ], ον, *over a door*, ἀσπίδες *IG*4.1488.22 (Epid.). II. *fixed on a door*, ἧλοι ib.2².1408.20. III. Subst. ἐπιθύριον, τό, *lintel*, ib.11(2).165.11 (Delos, iii B.C.). ⊛ **-ον**, τό, = foreg. III, *BCH*6.34 (Delos, ii B.C.), *Princeton Exp.Inscr.*1177.

**ἐπι-θῠσιάω**, *offer incense*, Sophr.120. **-θύσιμα** [ῠ], τά, *sacrificial victims*, *IG*2² 1672.295. **-θῦσις**, εως, ἡ, *burning of incense*, *BMus.Inscr.*789 (Cnidus), Ph.Bybl.ap.Eus.*PE*1.10 codd.; λιβανωτοῦ καὶ ἀρωμάτων *OGI*383.142 (pl., Nemrud Dagh, i B.C.). **-θύτης** [ῠ], ου, ὁ, *one who burns incense*, *Gloss.*; so prob. in *CIG*3663 *A* 15 (Cyzicus).

⊛ **ἐπῐθύω**, (θύω A) *sacrifice upon*, *h.Ap.*491 (tm.); *sacrifice besides* or *after*, τέλεον νεαροῖς ἐπιθύσας A.*Ag.*1504; ἐπὶ δ' ἔθυσα μητέρα E.*Or.* 562:—Med., Νέρωνι Γάλβαν ἐ. Plu.*Galb.*14, cf. *Marc.*29, Artem.1.12. II. *burn incense*, Lxx 3 *Ki.*12.33, J.*BJ*7.3.3, D.S.12.11, 18.60, Porph.*Abst.*2.59; λιβανωτόν D.S.18.61, v.l. in Ar.*Pl.*1116: generally, *offer on*, ἐπὶ τοῦ βωμοῦ τὰς δεκάτας D.H.1.40 codd.

**ἐπιθύω**, *rush eagerly at*, ὡς ἂν ἐπιθύσαντες ἑλοίμεθα Od.16.297: c. gen., ἐπιθύουσι βοῶν λίες Euph.35a: c. dat., Opp.*C.*1.281, 385. 2. c. inf., *strive vehemently* to do a thing, ἐρύσσασθαι.. Τρῶες ἐπιθύουσι Il. 18.175; θυμὸς ἐπιθύει κιθαρίζειν *h.Merc.*475; δεδαῆσθαι A.R.2.1154; κύσσαι.. στόμα Id.1.1238:—Med., *rush upon, flood*, Νεῖλος ἐπεθύσατο (sic) αὔλακι γαίης Epic.Anon. in *BKT*5(1).119. (Prob. a compound of ἰθύω [ῠ], with ῡ metri gr.: taken as ἐπῐ-θύω by Epic.Anon. l. c.)

⊛ **ἐπιθώϊος**, ον, (θωή) *under penalty of a fine* for non-attendance, βουλὴ ἀγειρέσθω ἠ δημοσίη ἐ. *Schwyzer*687 *B*6 (Chios, vii/vi B.C.).

**ἐπιθωρᾱκ-ίδιον**, τό, *tunic worn over the* θώραξ, Plu.*Art.*11. **-ίζομαι**, *put on one's armour*, v.l. for θωρακ- (q.v.).

**ἐπιθωτάζω**, = ἐπιχλευάζω, Hsch.; cf. τωθάζω.

**ἐπιθωΰσσω**, *shout* or *call out, give loud commands*, A.*Pr.*73; οὐκ ἀκούσαις ἐπεθώϋξας τοῦτο thou *didst urge* this *upon* not unwilling ears, ib.279; κάλαμος.. κώπαις ἐπιθωΰξει E.*IT*1127.

**ἐπιίδμων**, ον, gen. ονος, = ἐπιΐστωρ, τινός *AP*6.175 (Maced.).

**ἐπιιερουργέω**, *preside at sacrifice*, *Gloss.*

**ἐπιιζάνω**, *sit on*, ἐῇ ἕδρῃ Q.S.6.38.

**ἐπιίζομαι**, Ion. for ἐφέζομαι, Luc.*Epigr.*47.

**ἐπιΐστωρ**, ορος, ὁ, ἡ, *privy to* a thing: c. gen., μεγάλων ἔργων ἐ. *privy to* great works (i.e. the robbery of the mares), Od.21.26; so τεῶν μύθων ἐ. A.R.4.89: abs., ib.16. 2. *acquainted with, practised in*, δίσκων, γεωμετρίης, *AP*11.371 (Pall.), *App.Anth.*7.2 (Euc.); σοφίης *IG*3.946, cf. Doroth. in *Cat.Cod.Astr.*2.172.

**ἐπικαγχάζω**, *laugh loud*, *PMag.Leid.W.*11.50, Hsch.

**ἐπικαγχᾰλάω**, *exult in*, τινί Q.S.1.161; *exult over*, ib.643: abs., Id.2.374.

**ἐπικᾰδεία**, ἡ, (κάδος) *fixing of buckets on* a water-wheel, *PLond.* 3.1177.178, al. (ii A.D.).

**ἐπικαθαιρέω**, *pull down* or *destroy besides*, Th.8.20.

**ἐπικᾰθ-αίρω**, *purge yet more*, Hp.*Judic.*11, Ruf.ap.Orib.7.26.169 (Pass.); of *supplementary menstruation*, Sor.1.28 (Pass.). **-αρσις**, εως, ἡ, *cleaning*, τοῦ ναοῦ *IG*4.1484.109 (Epid.).

**ἐπικαθ-έζομαι**, *sit down upon*, ἐπί τινι Ar.*Pl.*185; [ἐλέφαντι] Gal. *UP*17.1: aor. 1 part. ἐπικαθεσθείς Artem.2.20. II. *to be supported, rest on*, ἐπιζυγίδα -ομένην τῷ διαπήγματι Hero *Bel.*83.11, cf. J.*AJ*8.3.5. **-εύδω**, *sleep upon*, τινί Luc.*Ind.*4; *sit on eggs*, Arist. *HA*542ᵇ20: metaph., *go to sleep over*, i.e. *neglect*, τινί Just.*Nov.*88.2.1. **-έψω**, *boil in as well*, Philum.*Ven.*14.6 (Pass.). **-ηλόω**, *nail fast to*, Apollod.*Poliorc.*146.7 (Pass.). **-ημαι**, Ion. **-κάτημαι**, *sit upon*, τινί Hdt.6.72, Ar.*Eq.*1093; *press upon, be heavy upon*, ἐπί τινι Id.*Ra.*1046: also c. acc., ἐ. καμήλους App.*Syr.*32; πόλις.. λόφον ἐπικαθημένη D.H.1.14: abs., *sit upon* eggs, *incubate*, Arist.*HA*558ᵃ19, 619ᵇ14; of bees, ἐ. ἐπὶ τοῖς κηρίοις ib.625ᵃ5. 2. ἐ. ἐπὶ τῆς τραπέζης (v.l. ἐπὶ τῇ τρ.) *sit at* his counter, of a banker's clerk or money-changer, D.49.17, cf. 33: abs., ὁ ἐπικαθήμενος Id.36.7. 3. of rain, *cling* to a flower, Thphr.*CP*3.24.4. II. *sit down against* a place, *besiege* it, abs., Th.7.27: c. dat., App.*Mith.*78. III. ἐπικαθήμενοι, οἱ, *settlers, residents*, *PTeb.*391.11 (i A.D.). **-ιζάνω**, = ἐπικαθίζω II, ἐπὶ τὴν κεφαλήν Antiph.202.12. **-ίζω**, *set upon*, τινὰ ἐπί τι Hp. *Art.*78: abs., (sc. κλίμακι) ibid.; τινὰ ἐν ἅρματι Lxx 4 *Ki.*10.16; ἐν ὅπλοις ἀφανῶς ἐ. τὸ στρατιωτικόν J.*AJ*18.3.1:—Med., φυλακὴν ἐπεκαθίσαντο *had* a guard *set*, Th.4.130 (ἐπικαθίσταντο Poppo). II. intr., *sit upon*, πειθώ τις ἐπεκάθιζεν ἐπὶ τοῖς χείλεσι Eup.94.5; τοῖς καρχησίοις ἐ. *light upon*, Plu.*Them.*12, cf. Thphr.*CP*6.10.5. 2. *sit down against, besiege*, πόλει Plb.4.61.6. **-ίημι**, *let down, set upon*, τι βακτηρίᾳ Ephipp.14.11; *insert*, Heliod.ap.Orib.44.23.53. 2. *let down, shut*, πύλας App.*Hann.*51. 3. *put down* the foot, Hp. *Art.*60. 4. *incise* or *prick again*, Gal.ap.Orib.7.5.12. **-ικνέομαι**, Dor. 3 sg. fut. -καθιξεῖται, *impose a surcharge* or *penalty*, *IG*5(1).1421.15 (Cyparissia, iv/iii B.C.). **-ισμα**, ατος, τό, = Lat. *insessus*, *Gloss.* ⊛ **-ίστημι**, *set upon, establish*, φυλακάς D.C.41.50; cf. ἐπικαθίζω. 2. *set over*, κριτάς Pl.*Ti.*72b. 3. *establish besides*, τὴν τῶν ἐφόρων ἀρχήν Arist.*Pol.*1313ᵃ27; ἐ. τινὰ στρατηγόν *appoint as successor* in command, Plb.2.19.8, cf. J.*AJ* 7.2.4:—Pass., ἐπικατασταθεὶς στρατηγός Plb.2.2.11, cf. *IG*5(1).1390.12 (Andania). 4. *pay in addition*, *Leg.Gort.*1.47; but simply, *deliver*, σῖτον ἐπὶ τοὺς ὅρμους *PLille*53 (iii B.C.). 5. *perform the manœuvre of* ἀντικατάστασις, Ascl.*Tact.*12.11:—Pass., of troops executing the manœuvre, ib.10.11. **-οράω**, v. ἐπικατεῖδον. **-υγραίνομαι**, *to be kept moist*, Sor.1.44, Orib.*Fr.*144, Paul.Aeg.3.63.

**ἐπικαιν-ίζω**, *renew, restore*, Lxx 1 *Ma.*10.44 (Pass.). **-ουργέω**, *contrive novelties*, Democr.191. **-όω**, *introduce innovations into*, μὴ 'πικαινούντων νόμους A.*Eu.*693 (Steph. for μὴ 'πικαινόντων).

**ἐπικαίνῠμαι**, *surpass, excel* (v. καίνυμαι), πάντας ἐπ' ἀνθρώπους ἐκέκαστο ὄλβῳ τε πλούτῳ τε Il.24.535. II. Pass., *to be adorned* or *furnished with*, ἐπὶ φρεσὶ πευκαλίμῃσι κέκασται 20.35 (unless in signf. 1); οἷς ἐπικαίνυται ἵππος (cj. for ἐπικίνυται) Q.S.12.145.

**ἐπικαιρ-ία**, ἡ, *opportunity*, Hp.*Gland.*4; αἰτίαι περὶ ἀκαιριῶν καὶ ἐ., title of work by Democr., D.L.9.48. ⊛ **-ιος**, ον, = sq., Sup. -ώταται, πράξεις X.*Oec.*5.4, cf. Vett.Val.293.22. Adv. -ίως *conveniently*, ἵδρυται Str.9.2.15, cf. 10.1.7. 2. *important*, τὰ -ώτατα τῆς τέχνης X. *Oec.*15.11; of persons, οἱ ἐ. the *most important persons* of the army, Id.*Cyr.*3.3.12, cf. *HG*3.3.11: c. inf., οἱ θεραπεύεσθαι ἐπικαίριοι those whose cure is *all-important*, Id.*Cyr.*8.2.25. 3. of parts of the body, *vital*, τόποι ἐ. Ti.Locr.102d. **-ος**, ον, *in fit time* or *place*, *seasonable, opportune*, S.*OT*875 (lyr.), Th.6.34; νίκη -οτάτη Id.8.106; of places, -ότατον χωρίον πρὸς τὰ ἐπὶ Θρᾴκης ἀπυχρῆσθαι Id.1.68; τὰ ἐ. *advantageous* positions, X.*Hier.*10.5; τοὺς ἐ. τῶν τόπων D. 18.27, cf. Arist.*Pol.*1331ᵃ21; Κόρκυρα ἐν -οτάτῳ κειμένη Isoc.15.108; τὰ ἐνδεχόμενα καὶ -ότατα Arist.*Rh.*1396ᵇ5; τοῦ πάθους τὸ ἐ. *spontaneous outburst* of passion, Longin.18.2: also c. gen., τρίποδα.. λουτρῶν ἐπίκαιρον, = καιρὸν ἔχοντα λουτρῶν, *convenient for*.., S.*Aj.*1406 (anap.); ἰατὴρ -ότατος *helping in time of need*, Pi.*P.*4.270. Adv. -ως Sm.*Ps.*9.10, Sup. -οτάτως Anon. in *Rh.*132.8. 2. *serious, important*, ἐ. σημεῖα *important* symptoms, Hp.*Epid.*1.25; ἐς τεκμαρσιν Id.*Acut.*1. 3. of parts of the body, *vital*, ἐν τῷ -οτάτῳ ἀφύλακτον X.*Eq.*12.7, cf. Arist.*GA*766ᵃ24; ἐ. τοῦ ζῆν *necessary* for life, ib.719ᵃ16; of wounds, *dangerous*, ἐ. τρῶμα Hp.*Fract.*11; ἕλκος Id. *Acut.*46. Adv. -ρως, τετρῶσθαι Paus.4.8.4. 4. *susceptible* to disorders, Gal.*Nat.Fac.*2.8. II. *for a time, temporary*, opp. ἀΐδιος, Epict.*Gnom.*8; ἡ τῆς δόξης ἐ. εὐδαιμονία Vett.Val.130.30.

⊛ **ἐπικαίω**, *light up* or *kindle on* a place, πῦρ *h.Ap.*491; *burn on an altar*, ὅς μοι πολλὰ βοῶν ἐπὶ μηρί' ἔκηεν Il.22.170, cf. Od.3.9, 17.241. II. *burn on the surface, scorch*, Hp.*Aër.*17 (Pass.); οἱ τὰ σώματα ὑπὸ τῶν ἡλίων ἐπικεκαυμένοι Pl.*Ep.*340d; τῷ χρώματι παρὰ φύσιν -κεκαυμένος Plb.38.8.7, cf. Apollon.*Mir.*23; ἀέρα -όμενον Antipho Soph.26; of lightning, Arist.*Mete.*371ᵇ14; of hot iron, Id.*HA* 631ᵇ26; of cold, Hp.*Aër.*20, Thphr.*CP*2.1.6 (v.l.); of a caustic drug, Dsc.3.35. 2. *burn on the top*, of stumps, Plu.2.529b; of pruning trees by *burning*, Thphr.*HP*6.6.6; *cauterize*, τὰ χείλη τῶν τραυμάτων Aët.13.4, cf. Philum.*Ven.*3.5, al. 3. *brand*, ἵππον *PCair.Zen.*93.4 (iii B.C.).

**ἐπικακτίς**, ίδος, ἡ, prob. f.l. for ἐπιπακτίς, Plin.*HN*13.114, 27.76.

**ἐπικᾰλᾰμ-άομαι**, *glean after* the reapers, Luc.*Tox.*16. **-εια**, τά, *fields whose corn is in stalk*, *PTeb.*115.4, al. (ii B.C.). **-ίς**, ίδος, ἡ, f.l. for ἐπισκαλμίς, Agath.5.22. **-οι πυροί** wheat *in the stalk*, *AB*291 (cf. καλάμη); αἱ ἀπὸ ἐπικαλάμου ἄρουραι fields *whose corn is in stalk*, *POxy.*499.10 (ii A.D.).

**ἐπικᾰλέω**, *summon* a god to a sacrifice or as witness to an oath, etc., *invoke*, θεόν Hdt.2.39, 3.8, al.; ἐπὶ δὲ κάλεσον Ἄρτεμιν Ar.*Lys.* 1280, cf. *Act.Ap.*7.59, etc.; ἐ. θεόν τινι *invoke* a god *over* one, *to be gracious to* him, Hdt.1.199; or, *watch over* his good faith, Id.3.65:—Med., Id.1.87, al., X.*HG*2.3.55, al.; ἐπικαλεσάμενος τὸν θεόν *OGI*194.18 (Egypt, i B.C.). b. *pray for*, πρὸ καιροῦ τὸν θάνατον *PLond.*5.1676.24 (vi A.D.). 2. *invite*, γέροντας ἐπὶ πλέονας καλέσαντες Od. 7.189:—Med., Hdt.1.187, al. II. Med., *call in* as a helper or ally, ἐπικαλεῖσθαί τινα σύμμαχον Id.8.64, cf. Th.1.101: c. inf., Hdt. 1.87; ἐ. τοὺς κεκμηκότας μὴ γενέσθαι Th.3.59; ἐ. ἐκ Θεσσαλίης ἐπικουρίην Hdt.5.63. 2. *call in* as witness, μάρτυρας ἐ. τινάς Antipho 1.30, cf. Pl.*Lg.*664c: c. inf., ἐ. θεοὺς.. καθορᾶν τὰ γιγνόμενα X.*HG*2.3.55: with neut. Adj., ταῦτα ἐ. Hdt.9.62. b. *appeal to*, σύνεσιν καὶ παιδείαν D.18.127 (hence, = Lat. *appello, provoco*, Plu.*Marc.*2; τὸν δῆμον ἀπὸ τῶν δικαστῶν Id.*TG*16; Καίσαρα *Act.Ap.*25.11). 3. *call before one, summon*, of the Ephors, Hdt.5.39. 4. *challenge*, ib.1. III. *call by surname*, Δίων ὃν ἐπεκάλουν Χρυσόστομον Eun. *VS* p.454 B.:—more freq. Pass., *to be called by surname*, ἐπεκλήθησαν Κεκροπίδαι Hdt.8.44; *to be nicknamed*, Ἀριστόδημον τὸν μικρὸν ἐπικαλούμενον X.*Mem.*1.4.2, cf. *HG*2.3.31; also τὸ ὄνομα ἐπικέκληταί σοι Lxx *De.*28.10; ἐπικληθήσεται ἐν αὐτοῖς τὸ ὄνομά μου ib.*Ge.*48.16. IV. *bring as an accusation against*, τινί τι Th.1.139, 4.133, cf. Isoc.12.9; ἐ. τινί, c. inf., *accuse* one of doing, Th.2.27, cf. Antipho 3.1.1; ἐ. τὴν

ἀπόστασιν ὅτι..ἐποιήσαντο Th.3.36; ἐ. τινὶ πάντα ὅσα ἠδίκητο D.C. 37.6; ταῦτ' ἐπικαλεῖς; *is this your charge?* Ar.*Pax*663; ἐ. ἀρχαιότητα *objecting to* its obsoleteness, Pl.*Lg.*657b: abs., ἐπικαλείτω *let him bring his action*, *SIG*45.17 (Halic., v B.C.); ὁ ἐπικαλῶν *the plaintiff*, *PHal.*1.216 (iii B.C.):—Pass., τὰ ἐπικαλεύμενα χρήματα the money *imputed to him*, i.e. *which he was charged with having*, Hdt.2.118; but τὰ ἐπικαλούμενα the *sums claimed*, *PPetr.*2p.108 (iii B.C.), and so in Act. λείαν ἐ. ib.3p.185); περὶ δανείου *PGrenf.*2.31.15 (ii B.C.). 2. c. dat. pers. only, ἐπικαλεῖν τινί *quarrel*, *dispute with*, ἀλλήλοις Pl.*Lg.*766e.

**ἐπικαλλύνω**, *deck out*, Them.*Or.*32.359b; τὴν ἀκοσμίαν τῆς φύσεως Chor.*Zach.*15. **ἐπικαλλωπίζοντες**, *illinentes*, *Gloss.*

**ἐπικάλυμμα** [κᾰ], ατος, τό, *cover*, *veil*, πλοῦτος πολλῶν ἐ. ἐστιν κακῶν Men.90. II. in animals, *covering* of any orifice, of the *gills* of fish, Arist.*HA*505a1, *PA*696b3; of the *opercula* of crabs and other crustacea, Id.*HA*527b26, 541b26, cf. 530a21.

**ἐπικᾰλυπτ-ήριον**, τό, *covering*, Arist.*PA*687b24. **-ος**, ον, *covered*, Thd.*Ez.*27.20. **-ω**, *cover over*, *cover up*, *shroud*, κακὸν δ' ἐπὶ κῶμα καλύπτει v.l. in Hes.*Th.*798; of snow *covering* a track, X. *Cyn.*8.1; ἐ. τὴν ἀπορίαν Pl.*Chrm.*169d; τοὺς ὀφθαλμοὺς Sor.1.106:—Pass., *to be covered over*, *veiled*, ἡ ἐπωνυμία ἐπικεκάλυπται Pl.*Cra.*395b; ἐπικαλύπτεσθαι τὸν νοῦν πάθει ἢ ὕπνῳ *is darkened*, *obscured*, Arist.*de An.*429a7. II. *put as a covering over*, βλεφάρων φᾶρος E.*HF*642 codd. (lyr.):—Pass., τῶν βλεφάρων -κεκαλυμμένων when the eyelids *are drawn down*, Arist.*Sens.*437a25.

**ἐπικάμισον**, τό, = ἐπενδύτης, Tz. ad Hes.*Op.*534, cf. *An.Ox.*3.359.

**ἐπικάμνω**, *suffer at* or *after*, τοῖς παρελθοῦσιν Ael.*VH*14.6.

**ἐπικαμπ-ή**, ἡ, *bend*, *return* or *angle* of a building, Hdt.1.180 (pl.), *IG*$2^2$.1666*B*54. 2. ἐ. ποιεῖσθαι draw up their army *angular-wise*, i.e. with the wings thrown forward at an angle with the centre, so as to take the enemy in flank, X.*Cyr.*7.1.6; ἐς ἐ. τάττειν Arr.*An.*2.9.2, cf. 3.12.2. ✱ **-ής**, ές, *curved*, *curling*, ὠτάρια *BGU*781 ii 4 (i A.D.); [οὐραῖον] Luc.*Gall.*28; ξύλον Plu.*Cam.*32; *convex*, Pall.*in Hp.Fract.* 12.284C.; of hammer-toes, Heph.Astr.1.1. Adv. -πῶς Sch.rec.A. *Th.*384. **-ία**, ἡ, *bend*, *curve*, σπᾶσθαι πρὸς -ίαν *EM*722.35. **-ιος**, ον, = ἐπικαμπής, *curved*, τοῖχοι, τείχη, Ph.*Bel.*80.11, 82.3; ἐ. τάξις an order of battle in which one or both wings *formed an angle* with the centre, being either thrown forwards to attack the enemy in flank (cf. ἐπικαμπή), or backwards so as to meet a flank attack, Plb.6.31. 2, D.S.17.57; also as a march formation, Ascl.*Tact.*11.1. II. Subst. ἐπικάμπιον, τό, = ἐπικαμπή, Arr.*Tact.*26.7; ἐπικαμπίου τάξις Ael.*Tact.*31.4; ἐν ἐπικαμπίῳ, opp. ἐν μετώπῳ, Polyaen.4.3.22, cf. Plb. 5.82.9; also of fleets in naval warfare, Id.1.27.4. 2. of buildings, *wing*, τὸ ἐ. τῆς στοᾶς Plu.2.594b; τῇ ἐξέδρᾳ τῇ ἐν τῷ ἐ. *IG*12(9).234 (Eretria, i B.C.), cf. 12(8).266 (Thasos), *AJA*19.333 (Atalante). 3. ἐπικάμπια, τά, *nodal points* of the moon's orbit, Ptol.*Tetr.*167, Doroth. in *Cat.Cod.Astr.*6.91. **-τω**, *bend into an angle*, τὸν δάκτυλον Arist. *HA*556b17; [κλάδους] χερσί Them.*Or.*21.249a; Archit., *make an angle* or *return*, *IG*$2^2$.1668.75:—Pass., *bend* or *turn*, ἐς τὰ ἀριστερά Hp.*Oss.*10; *arch*, ὀφρὺς ἐπικεκαμμένη Arist.*PA*671b33; of troops, *advance the wings*, *so as to form angles* with the centre and take the enemy in flank, X.*Cyr.*7.1.5, *HG*4.2.20, *An.*1.8.23; τὸ στόμα ἐπικεκαμμένον ἔχουσα [φάλαγξ] Ascl.*Tact.*11.1; also of a fleet, *form a curved line* so as to envelop the enemy, D.C.50.31. 2. Act., ἐ. πρὸς ἔλεόν τινας *move* to pity, Lib.*Decl.*46.13:—Pass., abs., Ctes.*Fr.* 29.56, Lib.*Or.*6.38; πρὸς τὸν ὀδυρμόν Id.*Loc.Comm.*1.31. II. intr., *to be bent*, Arist.*HA*529a12. **-ύλος** [ῠ], ον, *crooked*, *curved*, ὤμους *in* the shoulders, *h.Merc.*90; ἐ. κᾶλα Hes.*Op.*427.

**ἐπίκαμψις**, εως, ἡ, *enveloping movement* in naval warfare, D.C.50. 31. II. *curvature*, [τοῦ ῥάμφους] Ael.*Fr.*76, cf. Paul.Aeg.6. 30. III. *bend* in a road, τῆς ὁδοῦ Nic.Dam.47J.

**ἐπικανθίς**, ίδος, ἡ, = ἐγκανθίς, *Hippiatr.*34, v.l. in Poll.2.71.

**ἐπικᾱπίς** (Dor. for -κηπίς), ίδος, ἡ, *plot by a garden*, *IG*4.823.29 (Troezen).

**ἐπίκᾰρ**, Adv. *head-foremost*, better divisim ἐπὶ κάρ, v. κάρ II.

**ἐπικαρδιάω**, = καρδιάω, Nic.*Al.*19.

✱ **ἐπικαρπ-ία**, ἡ, *produce*, *crop*, ἡ ἐπέτειος ἐ. Pl.*Lg.*955d, cf. *IG*$1^2$. 328.11, *Rev.Ét.Gr.*10.29 (Thespiae, iii B.C.). 2. *harvest-rights*, *Tab.Heracl.*1.108, *BGU*101.19 (ii A.D.); *usufruct*, αἱ ἐκ τῆς γῆς ἐ. D.H.3.58. 3. *revenue* from property, *Leg.Gort.*7.33; τὰς ἐκ ταύτης (sc. τῆς ὠνῆς) ἐπικαρπίας.. ἐνενήκοντα μνᾶς ἐκλέξας having collected 90 minae as the *revenue* from this tax, And.1.92. 4. *profit*, Arist.*Pol.*1258b24; αἱ ἐ. the *profits*, opp. the principal (τὰ ἀρχαῖα), D.27.50; ἐπικαρπίας λαμβάνειν Isoc.8.125; γῆθεν ἀναμένοντι τὴν ἐ. looking to the land for his *profits*, *Com.Adesp.*133.3; ἡ ἐ. τῶν ἁδρῶν the *profits* on the full-grown animals, Antiph.20. 5. *tithe* paid for the pasturage of cattle, Arist.*Oec.*1346a3. 6. metaph., παρρησίας ἐπικαρπίαι D.C.39.10; κινδύνων Onos.34.4; τοῦ πόνου Ael. *NA*2.8. **-ίδιος** [ῐδ], ον, *on fruit*, χνοῦς *AP*9.226 (Zon.). **-ίζομαι**, *draw the nutriment from*, *exhaust*, γῆν, of crops, Thphr.*HP*8.9. 3. **-ιος**, ον, (καρπός I) *bringer* or *guardian of fruits*, epith. of Zeus, Corn.*ND*9, Arist.*Mu.*401a19, Plu.2.1048c, etc.; of Hermes, *IG* 12(7).252 (Amorgos); θεοί Max.Tyr.30.4; *fruit-bearing*, ὧραι Arat. 552. 2. τὸ ἐ. *pedicle* or *fruit-stalk*, Phanias ap.Ath.2.68c, cf. 51c. II. (καρπός II) *on* or *for the wrist*, ἐ. ὄφεις *bracelets* in the shape of snakes, Philostr.*Ep.*22. 2. Subst. ἐπικάρπιον, τό, *part of the hand near the wrist*, Sor.1.84.

**ἐπικαρπολογέομαι**, *glean*, τοὺς ἀμητούς Lxx 4*Ma.*2.9.

**ἐπίκαρπος**, ον, *fruit-bearing*, ἐλαιών *Sammelb.*5126.19 (iii A.D.).

✱ **ἐπικάρσιος**, α, ον, later ος, ον Plb.6.29.1, 6.30.6, Opp.*C.*2.169:— = ἐγκάρσιος, *cross-wise*, *at an angle*, esp. *at a right angle*, as of the *cross-streets* of Babylon, Hdt.1.180; ῥύμη ἐ. πρὸς τὴν..εὐθεῖαν Plb.6.29.1, cf. 6.30.6; τῆς Σκυθικῆς τὰ ἐ. the country *measured along the coast*, opp. τὰ ὄρθια (inwards, at right angles to the coast), Hdt.4.101; opp. κατ' ἰθύ, Q.S.5.81: c. gen., τριήρεας..τοῦ μὲν Πόντου ἐπικαρσίας, τοῦ δὲ Ἑλλησπόντου κατὰ ῥόον *forming an angle* with the current of the Pontus, but.., Hdt.7.36; ἐπικάρσιαι σανίδες *cross*-planks, Plb.1.22. 5; ἐπικάρσιος ἐπείλησις Sor.*Fasc.*12.506C.: neut. pl. as Adv., ἐπικάρσια δὴ προπεσοῦμαι *athwart*, *Com.Adesp.*640. Regul. Adv. -ίως *transversely*, Antyll.ap.Orib.44.8.2, Paul.Aeg.6.40. 2. *striped*, *CPR*21.19 (iii A.D.), etc. II. in Od.9.70 αἱ μὲν [νῆες] ἔπειτ' ἐφέροντ' ἐπικάρσιαι, either (ἐπὶ κάρ), *plunging*, cf. Eust. ad loc., or (as Sch.) = πλάγιαι, i.e. *making leeway*, *drifting*. III. Subst. ἐπικάρσιον, τό, *striped garment*, *Ostr.*64 (ii A.D.), *POxy.*921.14 (iii A.D.).

**ἐπικαρυκεύεται**· ἀρτύει, Hsch.

**ἐπικατα-βαίνω**, *go down to* a place, ἐς Πλαταιάς Hdt.9.25; πρὸς τὴν πόλιν Th.6.97; πρὸς τὴν θάλασσαν Id.7.23,35; *extend downwards*, ὀδύναι ἐς τὰς χεῖρας ἐ. Hp.*Prorrh.*2.40: metaph., [θεοὶ] ψυχῶν προέστησαν -βάντες Dam.*Pr.*130. 2. *go down after* or *against* an enemy, Hdt.8.38, Th.4.11, 7.84. **-βάλλω**, Ep. aor. 2 ἐπικάββαλον, τῷ δ' ἐπὶ φᾶρος κάββαλε A.R.4.187, cf. Q.S.14.583:—*cast over*, ll. cc.; *throw down upon*, ἐ. τὸν οἶκόν τισι, of Samson, J.*AJ*5.8.12, cf. 14. 15.5; *throw down at*, πέτρους D.C.50.33. 2. *let fall down* or *droop at* a thing, τὰ ὦτα X.*Cyn.*4.3. 3. *impose a fine*, *Tab.Heracl.*1.134, where for ἐπικαταβάνοντι Ahrens corrected -βαλίοντι (fut. part.). 4. Pass., *to be distrained upon* by a creditor, Meyer *Juristische Papyri* p.224 (i B.C.). ✱ **-βολή**, ἡ, *distraint*, *PMagd.*31.9 (iii B.C.); ἐ. ποιήσασθαι *PBasel* 7.19 (ii B.C.).

**ἐπικατ-άγνῠμαι**, *to be broken upon*, of eggs, Arist.*Pr.*889b11. II. pf. part. Pass. ἐπικατηγμένος, perh. = ἐπικεκλασμένος, *weak*, *Cat.Cod. Astr.*8(3).188. **-άγω** [ᾰγ], *work out* a calculation, Vett.Val.304. 20. II. usu. in Pass., of ships or persons at sea, *come to land along with* or *afterwards*, Th.3.49, 8.28, J.*AJ*18.7.2, D.Chr.37.4, D.C.42.7, etc.

**ἐπικατα-δαρθάνω**, aor. 2 -έδαρθον, *fall asleep afterwards*, Th.4.133, Pl.*R.*534d. **-δεσμέω**, *swaddle*, σανίσι βρέφη Sor.1.85. **-δέω**, *bind upon* or *to*, Hp.*Epid.*5.58, Luc.*Asin.*16, 34. **-δύνω** [ῡ], *dive after*, Poll.1.108. II. of stars, *set after*, Procl.*Hyp.*5.52; τῷ ἡλίῳ Gem. 9.1:—also Med., -δύομαι Cleom.1.3, Theo Sm.p.138H. **-δυσις**, εως, ἡ, *setting of a star just after sunrise* or *after sunset*, Ptol.*Alm.*8.4, Vett.Val.50.12, etc. II. Astrol., name of eighth τόπος, Antioch. Astr. in *Cat.Cod.Astr.*8(3).117.11. **-θέω**, *run down upon*, *attack*, D.C.40.36. **-θλάω**, *crush*, Sch.Il.19.93.

**ἐπικατ-αιγίζω**, gloss on ἐπαιγίζω, Sch.Il.2.148. **-αιόνησις**, εως, ἡ, *additional fomentation*, Aët.3.172. **-αίρω**, intr., *swoop down upon*, νεκροῖς ὥσπερ ὄρνιν Plu.*Pomp.*31.

**ἐπικατα-καίω**, *burn over*, τοῖς ἀποθανοῦσιν ἱερά Lib.*Decl.*13.59. **-κλάω**, *bend*, Apollon.*Lex.* s.v. ἐπιγνάμψασα, Hsch. s.v. ἐπέγκαψαν. **-κλίνω** [κλῐ], *make bend down upon*, τί τινι *EM*431.4, Sch. Il.2.148. II. *introduce as a concubine*, J.*AJ*1.10.4. **-κλύζω**, *overflow besides*, τὴν Ἀσίην πᾶσαν Hdt.1.107. **-κλώθω**, gloss on ἐπεκλώσαντο, Hsch. **-κοιμάομαι**, *sleep upon*, Hdt.4.172. **-κοιμίζομαι**, gloss on ἐπικαταδαρθάνειν, Sch.Pl.*R.*534d.

**ἐπικατᾰκολουθέω**, *attend to*, φωνῇ Sch.Pi.*O.*6.108: abs., *comply*, *PLille* 4.6 (iii B.C.).

✱ **ἐπικατα-λαμβάνω**, *follow and catch up*, *overtake*, τὰς ναῦς Th.2.90; τινά Id.3.111, Plb.1.66.3, etc.; σελήνη ἥλιον ἐ. Pl.*Ti.*39c: abs., μεταξὺ δὲ ἁμέρα -λαμβάνει *IG*4.952.14 (Epid.):—Pass., Arist.*HA*611b33. b. of fruit which forms before the last year's fruit is ripe, *overtakes* it, Thphr.*HP*2.6.10. 2. *fasten*, *bind on*, κατάπλασμα ταινιδίῳ Gal.13. 357. 3. Gramm. in Pass., of σημεῖα, *to be understood after*, S.E. *M.*8.166. ✱ **-λείπω**, *bequeath in addition*, Ramsay *Studies in the Eastern Rom.Emp.*345. **-ληψις**, εως, ἡ, *overtaking*, Procl.*Hyp.* 4.39.

**ἐπικαταλλᾰγή**, ἡ, *money paid for exchange*, *discount*, Thphr.*Char.* 30.15, *SIG*252.7 (Delph., iv B.C.).

**ἐπικατα-λύω**, *reduce yet further*, τὴν δύναμιν Gal.15.721. **-μένω**, *tarry longer*, X.*Cyr.*1.2.11, *HG*7.4.36. **-μωκάομαι**, = καταμωκάομαι, Poll.8.77; gloss on ἐπιλλίζω, Sch.A.R.3.791. **-ξύω**, *graze*, *scratch*, Apollon.*Lex.* s.v. ἐπιγράβδην. **-πάσσω**, *sprinkle on*, Dsc.*Eup.*2.37 (Pass.). **-πηδάω**, *leap down after*, εἰς τὰ σκάφη J.*BJ*3.10.9. **-πίμπρημι**, *set fire to over*, βουλευτήριόν τινι App.*BC*2.22. **-πίπτω**, *fall upon*, Luc.*Anach.*1; γαίῃ Q.S.3. 399. 2. metaph., *fall to the lot of*, λυγρῷ ἐπικάππεσεν ὄλβος Id.7. 78. **-πλάσσω**, *put on a plaster as well*, Hp.*Fract.*25. **-πλέω**, *bear down upon*, of ships, D.S.16.66, Chariton 8.6. **-πνέω**, *blow against*, *EM*554.1.

✱ **ἐπικατ-ᾰράομαι**, *bring curses*, Lxx *Nu.*5.19,22; *call down curses upon*, λαόν ib.22.17. 2. *curse* (of God), ib.*Ma.*2.2. **-ᾰράσσομαι**, Pass., *fall with a crash*, D.H.10.16, 11.26. **-άρᾱτος** [ᾰρ], ον, *accursed*, Lxx *Ge.*3.14, *Ep.Gal.*3.10,13, *IG*12(9).955 (Euboea); ταῖς ἀραῖς *BMus.Inscr.*918.6 (Halic.).

**ἐπικατα-ρρέω**, *run down*, of humours, from the head to other parts, Hp.*Aër.*3. II. *fall down upon*, νεκροῖς Plu.*Pel.*4. **-ρρήγνῡμι**, *tear*, *rend*, στολάς J.*AJ*2.6.7:—Pass., *fall violently down upon*, τινί D.H.10.16; of rain, Plu.*Mar.*21. 2. Pass., *to be violently purged*, κοιλία -ερρηγνυμένη Gal.16.691. **-ρριπτέω**, *throw down after*, ἑαυτάς X.*An.*4.7.13. **-σείω**, *bring down on*, ἑαυτῷ ἐλέφαντα J.*BJ*1.1.5; ὀρόφους τισί ib.17.6. **-σκάπτω**, *destroy*, τῇ

καλαύροπι τὸ σπήλαιον D.H.1.39; *throw down upon*, ἔτι ζῶντος τὴν γῆν Id.4.48; τὴν πόλιν τισί J.*AJ*13.13.3; *destroy as well*, App.*Ill.*8, al. **-σκευάζω**, *build upon*, πύργους ἐπὶ σκάφη D.C.50.23. 2. *bring about in addition*, πρὸς τῷ πολέμῳ στάσιν ἑαυτοῖς καὶ λιμόν J.*BJ* 4.3.3. 3. Med., *establish by additional arguments*, Arg.D. 46. **-σκοπέω**, *supervise*, Procop.*Goth.*1.7. **-σπάω**, *draw down after*, Arist.*Pr.*901$^a$2:—Pass., *to be drawn in afterwards*, Hp.*Vict.*3. 70. **-σπένδω**, *pour besides as a libation over*, J.*BJ*1.3.6. **-σσω**, late form of ἐπικατάγνυμι, Sch.Od.2.355 (Pass.). **-στᾰσις**, εως, ἡ, in Tactics, wheeling through four right angles and *return to original point*, Ascl.*Tact.*10.1,9. **-στρέφω**, *invert and put over*, ποτήριον σύκοις *Gp.*10.56.6, cf. Dsc.5.79; τῷ Ταντάλῳ ἡ Σίπυλος -εστράφη Sch.S.*Ant.*134. **-σφάζω**, later **-σφάττω** Phld.*Ir.*p.36 W.:—*slay upon* or *over*, τινὰ τῷ νεκρῷ, τῷ τύμβῳ ἑωυτόν, Hdt.1.45; τῇ παρθένῳ Plu.2.772c: without dat., Parth.31.2, Plu.*Cleom.*37; αὑτούς Phld. l.c.:—Pass., τινί J.*AJ*19.1.13. 2. *slay in succession* or *after*, D.H.3.20, App.*Hann.*59,al. **-τέμνω**, *carry the workings of a mine beyond one's boundaries*, D.37.36. **-τρέχω**, *rush down on*, D.H.9.21, D.C.36.32. **-φέρω**, *fell*, *knock down on top of*, Lib. *Descr.*1.7:—Pass., *fall down upon*, τινί J.*AJ*12.9.4. II. Pass., of stars, *follow the sun*, Nech.ap.Vett.Val.279.22, Anon. *in Ptol. Tetr.*22; -φερόμενον, τό, name of eighth τόπος, Thrasyll. in *Cat.Cod. Astr.*8(3).101. III. metaph., *to be brought* or *come to* the use of an expression, ἐπικατενεχθήσεται Aristid.*Rh.*2p.544S. **-φορά**, ἡ, Astrol., name of eighth τόπος, Firm.2.19.9, 7.6.8, al.; cf. ἐπικαταφέρω II. **-φορος**, ον, *prone to*, ἐπί or πρός τι, Terpsicles ap.Ath.9. 391e, Ath.13.608d. ✱ **-χέω**, *pour upon*, Jul.*Mis.*346d. **-χρίω**, in Med., *smear oneself with*, Orib.*Fr.*85. **-ψάω**, *harrow lightly*, χώραν Str.17.3.11. **-ψεύδομαι**, *tell lies besides*, Hdt.3.63, Th.8.74, D.H. 3.2. II. *accuse falsely*, J.*AJ*17.5.5. 2. ἐ. θηλύτητα τῆς ὄψεως *give a false* appearance of femininity, ib.19.1.5. **-ψήχω**, *smooth down*, metaph., τὴν βουλήν App.*BC*2.145 (v.l. -ψύχων).

**ἐπικατ-εῖδον**, aor. 2 (no pres. in use), *look at besides*, τι Hp.*Prog.* 7. **-ειμι**, *go down into*, ἐς τὴν κοιλίαν Th.2.49: abs., of persons, J.*AJ*1.19.3: metaph., *descend in the scale*, Dam.*Pr.*87. **-εράω**, *pour off liquid on* a thing, Heras ap.Gal.13.39, Orib.*Fr.*88. **-εργάζομαι**, dub. sens. in *Tab.Defix.Aud.*83. **-έρχομαι**, = ἐπικάτειμι, Hp.*Nat.Puer.*30. ✱ **-έχω**, *detain*, D.H.9.60, Luc.*Herm.*23, Arg. Cratin. in *POxy.*663.39; *restrain*, ὀργήν D.Chr.3.34.

**ἐπικατηγορ-έω**, *predicate of* a thing *besides*, τί τινος S.E.*M.*9.334; *attribute to . .*, τί τινι Plu.2.1113b; ἐπικλήσει τὸ σχῆμα ἐπικατηγορούσῃ D.H.1.66 (L.Dind. for ἐπικατηγορήσει):—Pass., *to be added to the predicate*, Arist.*APr.*49$^a$25; *to be predicated of*, c. dat., τῷ αὐτῷ ἀριθμῷ ποικίλα Iamb. *in Nic.*p.34P. **-ημα**, ατος, τό, *accusation*, f.l. in Plu. 2.1127d. **-ία**, ἡ, *further predication* or *characterization*, τὰς ἰδιότητας τῶν ἐ. Demetr.Lac.*Herc.*1012.41F., al., cf. S.E.*M.*10.297.

**ἐπικατ-οικέω**, *live at*, *inhabit*, Ceb.15. **-ορθόω**, *adjust again*, ὀστέα Hp.*Fract.*16. ✱ **-ορύσσομαι**, Pass., *to be buried after*, ἐπὶ τῇ ἀπαιδίᾳ Antipho 3.2.10 (sed leg. ἔτι κατ—).

**ἐπικαττύω**, *mend* shoes, Poll.7.82; τὰ σαπρὰ τῶν χιτωνίων Lib. *Decl.*33.10. 2. metaph., *vamp up* old plays, *Com.Adesp.*46.

**ἐπικάτω** [ᾰ], *downwards*, Hsch. s.v. ἐπιπρηνές.

**ἐπικαυλόφυλλος**, ον, *with cauline leaves*, Thphr.*HP*7.8.3.

**ἐπί-καυμα**, ατος, τό, *blister caused by a burn*, Apollod.ap.Sch.Ar. *Pl.*535, Dsc.*Eup.*1.36. 2. *ulcer on the eye*, esp. *the cornea*, Gal.12. 758, 14.774, 19.434. **-καυσις**, εως, ἡ, *burning*, ἐξ ἐ. Str.13.4.11; *scorching*, of the sun's heat, Id.15.1.24. II. *inflammation of the surface*, *scorching up*, joined with ἐρυσίβη, Pl.*Ax.*368c. III. = foreg. 2, Dsc.2.136 (pl.). **-καυστέον**, *one must cauterize*, τὰ δήγματα Aët.13.12. **-καυτος**, *burnt at the tip*, ἀκόντια Hdt.7.71,74.

**ἐπικαχλάζω**, *plash against*, κῦμα πέτραις ἐ. A.R.4.944, cf. Aesop. 381.

✱ **ἐπίκειμαι**, serving as Pass. to ἐπιτίθημι, *to be laid upon*, and so, I. of doors, *to be put to* or *closed* (cf. ἐπιτίθημι II), θύραι δ' ἐπέκειντο φαειναί Od.6.19: metaph., γλώσσῃ θύραι οὐκ ἐπίκεινται Thgn.421. 2. generally, *to be placed*, *lie in* or *on*, c. dat., ἐπισκύνιον ἐπέκειτο προσώπῳ Theoc.24.118; of troops, ὄχθαις Ἴστρου ἐ. Hdn.2.9.1. 3. of islands, νῆσοι ἐπὶ Λήμνῳ (-ου codd.) ἐπικείμεναι *lying off* Lemnos, Hdt. 7.6; so ἐ. τῇ Θρηΐκῃ ib.185; ἐπὶ [τῇ Λακαίνῃ χώρῃ] ib.235, cf. Th.4. 53: abs., αἱ νῆσοι αἱ ἐπικείμεναι the islands *off the coast*, Id.2.14, cf. 4.44; πάσῃ ἐ. τῇ θαλάσσῃ *lies* right *across* the sea, of Crete, Arist. *Pol.*1271$^b$34; ἡ ἐπικειμένη τινὸς γῆ *PTeb.*50.6 (ii B.C.). II. *to be laid upon*, ἐμοὶ σφρηγὶς ἐπικείσθω τοῖσδ' ἔπεσι Thgn.19 (so lit., σφραγὶς οὐκ ἐ. *BGU*361 iii 29 (ii A.D.), etc.); ἐπίκειται ἀγνώμων σῇ κεφαλῇ στέφανος Thgn.1259, cf. X.*Oec.*19.13; ἐ. ἐπί τινος Hero *Spir.*1. 38, al., D.C.67.16: metaph., κρατερὴ δ' ἐπικείσετ' ἀνάγκη Il.6.458, cf. 1*Ep.Cor.*9.16; of a duty, οἷς ἐπέκειτο φροντίζειν Plu.2.786f. 2. *press upon*, *be urgent* in entreaty, Hdt.5.104; *press upon* a retreating enemy, *attack*, Βοιωτοῖσι ib.81; *to be urgent against*, Id.6.49; ἐπεκείμην αὐτοῖς ἐνοχλῶν *PLips.*36.7 (iv A.D.): abs., κἀπικείσομαι βαρύς E. *Rh.*101; κἀπικείμενος βόα Ar.*Eq.*252; Κλέων μ' ὑπεταράττεν ἐπικείμενος Id.*V.*1285; ἐ. λαμπρῶς Th.7.71; πολὺς δ' ἐπέκειτο Theoc.22. 90; of a crowd, ἐ. τινί *Ev.Luc.*5.1. 3. *hang over*, τηλικούτων ἐπικειμένων τῷ μοιχεύοντι κακῶν X.*Mem.*2.1.5; of penalties, θάνατος ἡ ζημίη ἐπίκειται the penalty *imposed* is death, Hdt.2.38, cf. 6. 58, Arist.*Pol.*1297$^a$18; τῷ ἄρξαντι μεγάλα ἐπιτίμια ἐ. Antipho 4.4.7; ζημία . . ἐπέκειτο στατήρ Th.3.70; ὁ ἐπικείμενος κίνδυνος Hdn.1.13. 4. 4. of a name, *to be imposed*, Pl.*Cra.*411c, *Prt.*349c. 5. metaph., σκώμματα ἐπικείμενα *suitable to the purpose*, *pointed*, Longin. 34.2. 6. *to be set in authority*, ἐπὶ τοῦ πυρός *Corp.Herm.*1.13; ἐπικείμενος Ἀλεξανδρείας *PLips.*102 i 8, etc. III. c. acc. rei, esp. in part., κἀπικείμενον κάρα κυνέας head *with* helmet *set thereon*, E.*Supp.* 716 (dub. constr.); ἐ. κυνῆν τῆς κεφαλῆς Hld.5.22; στέφανον ἐπικείμενος *with* a crown *on one's head*, Plu.*Marc.*22; ἅπικας ἐπικείμενοι ταῖς κεφαλαῖς D.H.2.70; σεμνὸν ἐπικειμένη τὸ κάλλος J.*AJ*11.6.9; ἀγγέλου ἢ θεράποντος ἐπικείμενος πρόσωπον Plu.*Lys.*23; ἐπέκειτο ὠτειλάς he *bore* scars *upon* him, App.*Mith.*6; ἱερὰν ἐσθῆτα ἐ. Id.*BC*4. 134; φθίμενος τήνδ' ἐπίκειμαι κόνιν *Epigr.Gr.*622.6; κιθάραν . . κόλλοπας ἐπικειμένην *fitted with* pegs, Luc.*Ind.*10: metaph., οἱ κίνδυνον ἐπικείμενοι *exposed to . .*, App.*BC*4.124.

✱ **ἐπικείρω**, Ep. aor. 1 ἐπέκερσα, *cut off*, *cut down*, πρώτας ἐπέκερσε φάλαγγας Il.16.394; ὄρχους ὀδόντι B.5.108; *cut down* growing corn, τὸν σῖτον ἐ. Thphr.*HP*8.7.4. II. metaph., *cut short*, *baffle*, μάχης ἐπὶ μήδεα κείρει Il.15.467, cf. 16.120.

**ἐπικεκρυμμένως**, Adv., (ἐπικρύπτω) *mysteriously*, Plot.3.9.1, Porph. *Plot.*15.

**ἐπικελᾰδέω**, *shout at* or *to*, esp. *in applause*, *cheer*, ἐπὶ δὲ Τρῶες κελάδησαν Il.8.542.

**ἐπικέλευ-σις**, εως, ἡ, *cheering on*, *exhortation*, Th.4.95, D.H.2. 41. **-σμα**, ατος, τό, = foreg., Hsch. s.v. ἐπιστίγματα. **-σμός**, ὁ, = foreg., Sch.Luc.*Cat.*19. **-στής**, οῦ, ὁ, v.l. for κελευστής, D.S. 20.50. **-στικός**, ή, όν, *cheering on*: τὸ ἐ. the *signal for attack*, Polyaen.5.16.4. **-ω**, *exhort*, *encourage*, *cheer on*, c. dat., ἐπεκέλευσά σοι E.*El.*1224 codd.: abs., Id.*Ba.*1088: c. acc. pers., ἐ. τὸν μὴ διανοούμενον Th.3.82: c. acc. rei cogn., πρὸς τοῖς ἄλλοις κελεύσμασιν ἐ. τόδε "εὖ κύνες" X.*Cyn.*6.20; joined with παρακελεύομαι (which prop. means *cheer* one *on to an act not begun*, ἐ. *to one already begun*), Pl.*Phd.*61a:—Med., τινὶ παραδιδόναι τὴν ἀρχήν Th.4.28: abs., Plu. *Ant.*77. II. *give consent* or *authorization*, *PPetr.*3p.133 (iii B.C.), *PTeb.*201 (i B.C.).

**ἐπικέλια**· ἔπεργα, ἱμάτια, Hsch.

**ἐπικέλλω**, aor. 1 ἐπέκελσα, also ἐπέκειλα *Act.Ap.*27.41: fut. part. acc. ἐπικέλσοντα Numen. (v. infr.):—*bring* ships *to shore*, νῆας ἐπικέλσαι Od.9.148, cf. *Act.Ap.* l.c. 2. abs., *run ashore*, Od.9.138; χέρσῳ ἐ. ἐρετμοῖς A.R.3.575: c. acc., γῆν ἐ. Id.2.352; also of the ship itself, ἡ μὲν ἔπειτα ἠπείρῳ ἐπέκελσεν Od.13.114; of a fish, *rush into* the net, Numen.ap.Ath.7.321b (cj. for ἐπιτέλσωντα).

**ἐπικέλομαι**, *call upon*, στυγερὰς δ' ἐπεκέκλετ' Ἐρινῦς (redupl. aor. 2) Il.9.454; ἐπικεκλομένα Δῖον πόρτιν A.*Supp.*40 (lyr.): c. dat., παιδί A.R.3.85.

**ἐπικεντρ-ίζω**, *apply the spur*, *AP*9.777 (Phil.). II. *graft vines*, *Gp.*5.17.11. **-όομαι**, Astron., *occupy a cardinal point*, -ούμενος cj. for ἐπικεντρόμενος, Antioch.Astr. in *Cat.Cod.Astr.*8(3).115. **-ος**, ον, Astron., *occupying a cardinal point*, Vett.Val.9.19, Man.1.34, Doroth.ap.Heph.Astr.2.5, S.E.*M.*5.40: Comp., Ptol.*Tetr.*79. **-ωσις**, εως, ἡ, *occupation of a cardinal point*, Paul.Al.*P.*1.

**ἐπικεράννῡμι**, *mix in addition*, οἶνον ἐπικρῆσαι (aor. 1 inf.) *mix fresh* wine, Od.7.164, cf. Gal.18(1).169:—Med., Damocr.ap.eund.14.100.

**ἐπίκερας**, τό, = τῆλις, Hp.ap.Gal.19.99.

**ἐπικεραστικός**, ή όν, *tempering the humours*, Gal.6.260; ἀγωγή Alex.Trall.7.7.

✱ **ἐπικερδ-αίνω**, *gain besides*, ἐνιαυτὸν τῇ ἀρχῇ Plu.*Flam.*3. **-εια**, ἡ, = ἐπικέρδια (q.v.), *Peripl.M.Rubr.*49, Philostr.*Her.*19.14: pl., Ph. 2.11. II. *interest*, *PGiss.*53.4 (iv A.D.), etc. **-ής**, ές, *profitable*, *advantageous*, *TAM*2(1).245 (Lycia), Aesop.137, Vett.Val.189. 30, al., Heph.Astr.2.30, App.*BC*1.57. **-ια**, τά, *profit on traffic* or *business*, Hdt.4.152, Philostr.*VS*2.21.2. **-ιον**, *compendium*, *Gloss.*

**ἐπικέρνης**, ου, ὁ, *cupbearer*, Ps.-Callisth.3.31 (v.l.). (Cf. *pincerna.*)

**ἐπικερτομ-έω**, *mock*, used by Hom. only in part., τὸν δ' ἐπικερτομέων προσέφης in *mockery*, Il.16.744, Od.22.194, cf. Luc.*DMort.*14. 5, Hld.8.9; in milder sense, *laughingly*, Il.24.649 (or, *in mockery* of Agamemnon). II. c. acc., ἐπεκερτόμησε he *reproached* him, Hdt. 8.92; τινός *for* a thing, Agath.5.22; *tease*, *banter*, Theoc.20.2, cf. Luc.*BisAcc.*12. **-ημα**, ατος, τό, *sarcasm*, *taunt*, Demetr.*Eloc.* 111. **-ησις**, εως, ἡ, = foreg., Hdn.*Fig.*p.92S., Trypho *Trop.*p.206 S. **-ος**, ον, *mocking*, *cheating*, Q.S.1.136.

**ἐπικεύθω**, *conceal*, *hide*, always with a neg., ἐρέω ἔπος οὐδ' ἐπικεύσω Il.5.816; πρόφρων ὑποθήσομαι οὐδ' ἐπικεύσω Od.5.143; εἰπέ μοι . . νημερτέα μηδ' ἐπικεύσῃς 15.263; μῦθον δέ τοι οὐκ ἐπικεύσω 4.744, cf. 17. 141: and in A.*Ag.*800 (anap.), c. acc., οὔ σ' ἐπικεύσω I *will* not *hide* it *from* thee, cf. A.R.3.332.

**ἐπικέφᾰλ-α**, Adv. *mouth downwards*, of jars, Aët.1.138. **-αιος**, α, ον, *of* or *for the head*, κόσμος Suid. s.v. τιάρα, *EM*758.4. II. Subst. -αιον, τό, = ἐπικεφάλιον, Arist.*Oec.*1346$^a$4, *POxy.*1157.14 (iii A.D.); -αιον τέλος *SIG*1009.4 (Chalcedon, iii/ii B.C.). 2. *list*, *register*, *PTeb.*174 (ii B.C.), etc. 3. measure of weight, = two δίδραγμα, Hero *Mens.*60.4. III. Adv. -αίως *with brief headings*, *summarily*, Gal.17(2).207. **-αιόω**, *add up*, Vett.Val.260.21:—Med., *sum up*, Plb.2.40.4; τὸ ἀρκοῦν Phld.*D.*1.15. II. Pass., *to be summed up*, D.C.52.28. **-ιον**, τό, *poll-tax*, *IGRom.*4.181 (Lampsacus), *IG*12(5).724.11, *POxy.*1438.14 (ii A.D.), Ἀρχ.Δελτ.2. 148 (Beroea, ii A.D.): more freq. in pl., Cic.*Att.*5.16.2, *BGU*833, Wilcken *Chr.*28 (ii A.D.), *POxy.*2131.10 (iii A.D., v.l. -κεφάλαια), etc. **-ον**, τό, *head of battering-ram*, Ath.Mech.23.8. II. *money distributed at so much a head*, *head-money*, *IG*12(5).946.22 (Tenos); = ἐπικεφάλιον, Hsch.

**ἐπικεχοδώς**, ὁ, pf. part. of ἐπιχέζω, used as a mock-name for a bird, *Shitterling*, Ar.*Av.*68.

**ἐπικηδ-εία**, ἡ, (κῆδος) *funeral*, *EM*526.56. **-ειος**, ον (α, ον Lib. *Decl.*40.15), *of* or *at a burial*, *funeral*, ᾠδά E.*Tr.*514 (lyr.), cf. Pl.*Lg.* 800e (pl.); πόνοι E.*Alex.* in *Gött.Nachr.*1922.9; μοῦσα Ael.*NA*5.34; λόγοι D.H.*Rh.*6.1; ἐ., τό, *dirge*, *elegy*, Plu.*Pel.*1, al. (sung before burial, opp. ἐπιτάφιον, Serv. ad Virg.*Ecl.*5.14; opp. θρῆνος, Ptol. Ascal.p.404 H.). **-εύω**, γάμους ἀλλήλοις *form connexions* by marriage, Procop.*Aed.*3.3. II. *bury*, Hsch. s. v. ψέγος. **-ομαι**, *take thought for*, μερόπων Nonn.*D.*7.60: c. inf., Steph.*in Hp.*1.157 D. (fort. ⟨οὐκ⟩ ἐ.).

**ἐπικηκ-άζω**, *revile*, Hsch. in Pass., ἐπεκήκα(σ)το· ἐπωνείδιστο. **-αστος**, ον, = ἐπονείδιστος, Eust.1402.53.

**ἐπικηραίνω**, *to be hostile to* one, Hsch.

**ἐπικήριος**, ον, = sq., Heraclit.ap.Luc.*Vit.Auct.*14.

⊕ **ἐπίκηρος**, ον (α, ον Hsch., hyperdor. -κᾱρος Ecphant.ap.Stob.4.7. 65), (κήρ) *subject to death*, *perishable*, *mortal*, Hp.*Morb.Sacr.*1 (Sup.), Arist.*GA*753ᵃ7 (Comp.); φθαρτή τε καὶ ἐ. [φύσις] Id.*Mu.*392ᵃ34; βίος Call.*Ep.*59; τὸ τῆς φύσεως ἐ. Pl.*Ax.*367b; τὸ θνητὸν καὶ ἐ. Phld. *Mort.*38, etc. b. of plants, *delicate*, Thphr.*HP*6.7.3, 7.5.1. 2. *subject to disaster*, *hazardous*, ἐ. πρᾶγμα ἡ περίφρασις Longin.29.1; κοινωνία Plot.4.4.18: Sup. -ότατος Hsch. Adv., τῆς φιλοσοφίας -ρως διακειμένης Isoc.11.49.

**ἐπικηρόω**, *wax over*, *rub with wax*, Polyaen.2.20.

**ἐπικήρ-υγμα**, ατος, τό, *proclamation*, *Inscr.Prien.*109.162 (pl., ii B.C.). **-ῡκεία**, ἡ, *sending an embassy to treat for peace*, *entering into negotiation*, διὰ τὴν πρὸς Λακεδαιμονίους ἡμῖν ἐ. D.5.18, cf. Plb.14. 2.13, Theopomp.Hist.209 (pl.). **-ύκευμα** [ῡ], ατος, τό, *demand by herald*, E.*Med.*738. ⊕ **-ῡκεύομαι**, Med. (Act. only *AB*141,153), *send a message by a herald*, πρός τινα Hdt.9.87: πρός τινα ὥστε.. Th.7. 49; ὥς τινα ib.48; περί or ὑπέρ τινος, D.S.14.75, Paus.4.8.13; τινὶ εἰ.. *send a message proposing to ask* whether.., Hdt.1.60; ἐ. ταῦτα δι' ἀγγέλων ib.69:—perh. Pass. in Th.8.44 ἐπικηρυκευομένων *messages being sent.* 2. *send ambassadors to treat for peace*, *make proposals for a treaty of peace*, τινί to one, Ar.*Th.*336, Th.4.27; ταῦτά τινι Hdt.4.80, 6.97; ταῦτ' ἐπικηρυκεύομαι Ar.*Th.*1163. 3. of private affairs, *negotiate*, τινί *with* one, D.32.24. II. abs., *go as a herald* or *ambassador*, παρά τινος Plb.21.16.1. **-υκτος**, ον, *denounced*, ᾧ θάνατος ἐ. ἦν App.*Pun.*93. **-υξις**, εως, ἡ, *proclamation of a reward*, Ulp. ad D.19.21. 2. generally, *proclamation*, Ph.*Bel.*98. 36. ⊕ **-ύσσω**, Att. -ττω, pf. -κεκήρυχα D.19.21:—*proclaim*, ἐπικηρυχθεὶς χθονὶ *proclaimed king*, A.*Th.*634; ἐ. πόλεμόν τινι D.C.78.38 (Pass.). 2. esp. of penalties, ἐ. θάνατον τὴν ζημίαν ὃς ἂν.. *proclaim* death as the penalty, X.*HG*1.1.15; ἐ. ἀργύριον ἐπί τινι *set* a price *on* his head, Hdt.7.214 (but ἀργύριον, of a money penalty, Arist.*Oec.* 1351ᵇ31); χρήματά τινι ἐ. D. l. c.; λάφυρον κατά τινων *issue* letters of marque, Plb.4.26.7:—Pass., καί οἱ φυγόντι.. ἀργύριον ἐπεκηρύχθη Hdt.7.213; τὰ ἐπικηρυχθέντα χρήματα the price *set upon one's head*, Nymphod.12, cf. Plu.*Them.*26; but also ὁ ἐπικηρυχθεὶς *the proscribed person*, *outlaw*, D.C.37.10 (pl.). 3. *offer as a reward*, χρημάτων πλῆθος τοῖς ἀνελοῦσι D.S.14.8, cf. D.C.56.43; τὸ -κηρυχθὲν τῷ ἀγαγόντι Plu.*Them.*29: c. inf., τάλαντον δώσειν τῷ ἀπαγαγόντι Lys.6. 18. II. *put up to public auction*, τὰς ὠνάς *PEdgar*64.4 (iii B.C.), cf. *PRev.Laws*48.13 (iii B.C.), *SIG*975.6 (Delos, iii B.C., Pass.), v.l. for ἀποκ. in Plu.*Cam.*8.

**ἐπικίδνημι**, *spread over*, κακοῖς ἐπικίδνατε θυμόν *spread* a brave spirit *over* your ills, Orac.ap.Hdt.7.140:—in Hom. always Pass. (only in Il.), ὕδωρ ἐπικίδναται αἶαν *is spread over* the earth, Il.2.850, cf. A.R.2.978; ὅσον τ' ἐπικίδναται ἠώς far as the morning light *is spread*, Il.7.451, 458; ἐπεκίδνατο οὐρανὸν ἄστρα Q.S.5.347.

**ἐπικῐθάρισμα** [ᾰρ], ατος, τό, *piece performed after a play*, Tertull. *Valent.*33.

**ἐπικίνδῡν-ος**, ον, *in danger*, *insecure*, Hdt.6.86.α'; ἐ. ἦν μὴ λαμφθείη Id.7.239; πρόσοδοι D.36.11; ἐν ἐπικινδύνῳ, opp. ἐν τῷ ἀσφαλεῖ, Th.1.137. 2. *dangerous*, διδάσκαλοι Gorg.*Pal.*4 (Comp.); στρατεῖαι Pl.*R.*467d; ἀρρωστίαι Phld.*Ir.*p.29 W.; δεινὴ καὶ ἐ. ἔρις Pl.*Lg.* 736c, cf. X.*Mem.*4.6.10; -οτέρα πρᾶξις Id.*An.*1.3.19; τινί to one, Hp.*Aph.*4.16, Th.3.54; ἐπικίνδυνόν [ἐστι] *there is danger*, Arist.*HA* 588ᵃ10. 3. Adv. -νως *with danger*, τίκτειν Hp.*Aph.*5.55; *at one's risk*, Th.3.37; *in a precarious* or *critical state*, κεῖσθαι S.*Ph.*502; ἔχειν E.*Fr.*682. **-ώδης**, ες, = foreg., Sch.S.*El.*222.

**ἐπικῑν-έω**, Act. only as f.l. for ἐπινέω (B) or -νηνέω (q.v.), Iamb.*VP* 3.17:—Pass., *to be moved*, ὀσφὺς -κινεῖται Luc.*Asin.*6; *gesticulate at* a thing, v.l. Epict.*Ench.*33.10: metaph., *to be moved*, *zealous*, ἐπί τινι Lxx 1*Es.*8.69(73); also, *to be moved* to passion, τοὺς οὐδ' ἐπικινηθῆναι δυναμένους Phld.*Piet.*21. **-ημα**, ατος, τό, *onward motion*, Procl. *Hyp.*3.53. **-ησις**, εως, ἡ, = foreg., τοῦ ἡλίου Simp.*in Ph.*701. 29. **-ῡμαι**, *move on*, Q.S.12.145 codd.

**ἐπικιρνάω**, = sq., Dsc.*Ther.Praef.*, Alex.Trall.*Febr.*7.

**ἐπικίρνημι**, Ion. for ἐπικεράννυμι, Heraclit.*All.*35, Philum.ap. Orib.45.29.8:—Pass., ἐπικίρναται [ὁ κρητήρ] Hdt.1.51, Plu.2.270a, cf. Heraclit.*All.*40.

**ἐπικιχλίδες**, αἱ, a poem ascribed to Homer, so called because he was rewarded by a present of κίχλαι, *fieldfares*, Clearch.ap.Ath.14. 639a, Menaechm.3 J.

**Ἐπικιχράδας**, title of Zeus at Cos, Hsch.

⊕ **ἐπικίχρημι**, aor. 1 ἐπέχρησα, *lend*, τινὶ τάγματα πρὸς τὸν πόλεμον Plu.*Pomp.*52; ἐπιχρήσας ἑαυτὸν εἰς ἀπαλλοτρίωσιν *CIG*3281 (Smyrna).

⊕ **ἐπικλάζω**, *sound to*, θαλάσσῃ Opp.*H.*5.295; ἐπί οἱ ἔκλαγξε βροντάν *made* thunder *sound in answer to* him, Pi.*P.*4.23.

**ἐπικλαίω**, Att. -κλάω, *weep in answer*, Ar.*Th.*1063; τινί at a thing, Nonn.*D.*30.114.

**ἐπίκλᾱρος**, -κλᾱρόω, Dor. for ἐπικληρ-.

**ἐπί-κλασμα**, ατος, τό, *weakening*, *Gloss.* ⊕ **-κλασμός**, ὁ, = foreg., ib., dub. in *BGU*920.22 (ii A.D.).

**ἐπίκλαυτος**, ον, *tearful*, νόμος Ar.*Ra.*684 (lyr.).

⊕ **ἐπικλάω**, *bend*, in lit. sense only Pass., *bend double*, ἡ δεξιὰ περὶ τὴν κεφαλὴν ἐπὶ τὸ ἄνω ἐπικεκλασμένη Luc.*DDeor.*11.2; ἐπικεκλ. τὸν αὐχένα Id.*Rh.Pr.*11; ὕδωρ ἐπικλώμενον *broken* water, Id.*Tox.*20; ἐπ' ἀλλήλων -κλωμένων τῶν κυμάτων Alciphr.1.1; also, *to be bruised*, Paul.Aeg.6.117. II. metaph., *move to pity*, Plu.*Per.*37; ἐ. τινὰ εἰς οἶκτον Ael.*NA*10.36:—Pass., Th.3.67; ἐ. τῇ γνώμῃ ib.59; ὑπ' εὐνοίης Hp.*Ep.*13; πρὸς οἶκτον Jul.*Or.*2.90d. 2. *shake the resolution of*, τινά Plu.*Oth.*15:—Pass., ἐπικλασθῆναι τῇ γνώμῃ *to be broken in spirit*, *lose courage*, Th.4.37; τὸ ἐπικεκλασμένον τῶν μελῶν *effeminate*, *unmanly* music, Luc.*Demon.*12.

⊕ **ἐπικλεής**, ές, *famous*, A.R.4.1472; ὄνομα *CIG*2613 (Cyprus): Comp., Max.Tyr.29.1. 2. *named*, *called after*, τινί Opp.*H.*2.130. (Ep. acc. ἐπικλέᾶ.)

**Ἐπικλείδια**, τά, festival of Demeter at Athens, Hsch.

**ἐπίκλειθρον**, τό, = ἐπίκλιντρον II, dub. in Gal.*UP*11.13 (vv.ll. ἐπικαίρων, ἐπικλήρων, ἐπικλήθρων): fort. ἐπικλιθρον, cf. ἀνάκλιθρον.

**ἐπικλείω** (A), Ep. -κληΐω, Att. -κλῄω, *shut to*, *close*, τοὺς πρωκτούς Ar.*Pax*101 (anap.); ἐπεκλήϊσσε θύρην Tryph.200:—Med., Luc.*Tox.* 50:—Pass., *to be shut to*, opp. ἀναπτύσσομαι, X.*Eq.*12.6: c. dat., *to be covered* by.., Gal.18(1).429.

⊕ **ἐπικλείω** (B), *extol* or *praise the more*, τὴν γὰρ ἀοιδὴν μᾶλλον ἐπικλείουσι Od.1.351. 2. *relate* or *recount that*.., c. acc. et inf., A.R. 1.18, Opp.*C.*3.78. 3. *call*, *name*, τόν ῥ' ἄνδρες ἐ. Βοώτην Arat.92, cf. A.R.2.1156. 4. *call upon*, *invoke*, Ἀπόλλωνα Id.2.700: c. inf., Κυθέρειαν ἐ. ἀμύνειν Id.3.553.

**ἐπικλέπτοιτο**· ἐπιθυμοίη, Hsch. ⊕ **ἐπικλεσαιδόνα**· ἐπικληδόνα, Id.

**ἐπικλήδην**, Adv., = ἐπίκλην, formed like ὀνομακλήδην, Opp.*C.*1.471.

**ἐπικλῄζω**, = ἐπικλείω (B) 3, Ἀνάφην νῆσον -κλῄζουσι Orph.*A.*1359, cf. Poet.*de herb.*154:—Pass., Poet.ap.D.L.6.100, App.*Syr.*17.

**ἐπικληΐω**, v. ἐπικλείω (A).

**ἐπίκλημα**, ατος, τό, *accusation*, *charge*, S.*OT*227, 529, E.*Or.*570, X. *Oec.*11.4, D.C.*Fr.*23.1.

⊕ **ἐπίκλην**, Adv. *by surname*, *by name*, Pl.*Sph.*221c; ἐπίκλην αἰθὴρ καλούμενος Id.*Ti.*58d; ἑξέως τινος ἐ. λεγομένη called *after*.., Id. *Phlb.*48c; Σαραπίων ἐ. βουκόλος *PLips.*6.7 (iv A.D.), cf. Luc.*Symp.*6, *IG*12(8).529 (Thasos); ὁ τοῦ Αὐγούστου ἐ. λιμήν D.C.75.16. 2. *nominally*, Apollod.3.13.4.—Prop. acc. from an obsolete nom. ἐπίκλη, = ἐπίκλησις, ἐπωνυμία (Hsch.); ἐπίκλην (acc.) ἔχειν, occurs in Pl.*Ti.*38c, *IG*14.1018.6.

**ἐπικληρ-ικός**, ή, όν, *concerning an* ἐπίκληρος, λόγος D.H.*Din.* 12. **-ῖτις**, ιδος, ἡ, = ἐπίκληρος, ἡ, Is.*Fr.*91 S. ⊕ **-ος**, Dor. **-κλᾱρος**, (ὁ only in Thom.Mag.p.138 R.), *heiress*, Ar.*Av.*1653, *V.* 583, And.1.121, Lys.26.12, Pl.*Lg.*630e, Arist.*Ath.*9.2, *Pol.*1270ᵃ27, *IG*2².1165, *Test.Epict.*3.31, etc.; ὥσπερ ἐπικλήρου.. ἀμφισβητήσων ἥκει Lys.24.14. 2. c. dat., ἐ. τῇ ἀρχῇ (so codd.: prob. τῆς ἀρχῆς) *heiress to* the kingdom, D.H.1.70: c. gen., ἐ. οὐσίας μεγάλης Plu. *Cleom.*1. 3. Astrol., perh. f. l. for ἔγκληρος, *Cat.Cod.Astr.*8(4). 225. ⊕ **-όω**, Dor. **-κλᾱρόω**, *assign by lot*, τοῖς χοροῖς τοὺς αὐλητάς D.21.13; ἐ. ταῖς ἀρχαῖς τὰ δικαστήρια Arist.*Ath.*59.5; τὰς διαίτας ib. 53.5; εἰς τὰς φυλὰς τὰ ὀνόματα *OGI*229.52 (Smyrna, iii B.C.); τινὰ ἐπὶ φυλὴν καὶ χιλιαστὺν καὶ ἑκατοστὺν καὶ γένος *Supp.Epigr.*1.352.19 (Samos, iv B.C.); ἐ. τινά c. inf., *appoint* one to do, Call.*Dian.*23:—Pass., *to be assigned by lot*, τῷ μορίῳ ἑκάστῳ Pl.*Lg.*760b, *Inscr.Prien.* 37.103; τῶν δικαστηρίων -κεκληρωμένων *having been settled by lot*, D. 37.39. 2. *have assigned* one *by lot*, ἔθνος D.C.37.50. **-ωσις**, εως, ἡ, *assignment by lot*, *SIG*333.29 (Samos, iv B.C.), *Milet.*3 No. 143.31 (iii B.C.). **-ωτικοὶ** νόμοι laws *governing the treatment of heiresses*, Sch.Patm.D. in *BCH*1.153. **-ωτός**, όν, *assigned by lot*, δικαστήριον *AB*260.

**ἐπί-κλησις**, εως, ἡ, *surname*, *additional name*; used by Hom. only in acc. abs., like ἐπίκλην, and mostly ἐπίκλησιν καλέειν, as Ἀστυάναξ, ὃν Τρῶες ἐπίκλησιν καλέουσιν Astyanax, as they call him *by surname* (his name being Scamandrius), Il.22.506; Ἄρκτος, ἣν καὶ Ἅμαξαν ἐ. καλέουσι which they *call also* the Wain, 18.487, cf. 7.138, 22.29; Τιτῆνας ἐ. καλέεσκεν.. τιταίνοντας ἀτασθαλίῃ μέγα ῥέξαι ἔργον *named* them Titans, *after* their endeavouring.. (ἐπὶ τῷ τιταίνειν), Hes.*Th.* 207; so in Hdt., ἐ. δὲ ἡ κρήνη ἐπικαλέεται Ἡλίου 4.181; Ἀθηναίης ἐ. Ἀσσησίης 1.19; also, *in name only*, *nominally*, [Μενέσθιον] τέκε Πολυδώρη Σπερχειῷ, αὐτὰρ ἐ. Βώρῳ she bare him to Spercheius (really), but *nominally* to Borus, Il.16.177; τὸν τοῦ βουκόλου ἐπίκλησιν παῖδα Hdt.1.114; κατ' ἐ. Apollod.1.3.2; opp. ὄνομα, D.H.5.21. 2. after Hom., in other cases, *surname*, *name*, Th.1.3, etc. 3. *imputation*, *charge*, Id.7.68, *PLille*29.27 (iii B.C.); ἐ. ἔχει κακὸς εἶναι X.*Lac.*9. 4. 4. *title*, D.C.37.6, etc.; βασιλέα ἄξιον τῆς ἐ. Jul.*Or.*2.70c. 5. *announcement* of result of an election, *OGI*458.82 (i B.C., pl.). II. *calling upon*, *invocation*, Ἀφροδίτης Luc.*Salt.*11; δαιμόνων D.C.78.4: abs., *prayer*, ἐ. καὶ εὐχαί Lxx 2*Ma.*15.26; μεμιγμένας ἀπειλαῖς ἐπικλήσεις D.H.5.21. 2. *call* to an office, Astramps.*Orac.*84.9. 3. judicial *appeal*, Vett.Val.281.14; esp. = Lat. *appellatio*, *appeal* to the Tribunes, Plu.*Marc.*2, *Cat.Mi.*33, al. ⊕ **-κλητος**, ον, *called upon*, *called in as ally*, Hdt.5.75, 7.203, Th.4.61. 2. *specially summoned*, σύλλογον ἐ. Περσέων τῶν ἀρίστων ἐποιέετο held a *privy* council, Hdt.7.8 (so Subst. ἐπίκλητος, ἡ, *convocation*, *assembly*, Lxx *Nu.*28.18, al.); ἐπίκλη-

τοι *privy councillors*, among the Persians, Hdt.8.101, 9.42; *committee* of a council, *SIG*353.2 (Ephesus, iv B.C.), Str.14.1.21. 3. *called to* an office, D.H.2.76; ἐ. τῆς συναγωγῆς Lxx*Nu.*1.16. b. *appointed, designated*, πόλεις ib.*Jo.*20.9. 4. *summoned before* a court, *accused*, D.C.78.21. II. *invited in addition, supernumerary guest*, Ar.*Pax* 1266, Plu.2.707a. 2. *alien, foreign*, ὄχλος, opp. ἐπιχώριος, D.H. 6.53. b. *irrelevant*, λοιδορία Plb.8.11.2.

**ἐπικλῑβάνιος** [ᾰ], ον, *at* or *presiding over the oven*, θεά Carnead.ap. S.E.*M.*9.185.

**ἐπικλίν-εια** [κλῐ], ἡ, *inclination, bend*, Heliod.ap.Orib.49.13. 3. 2. *tendency*, πρὸς φθίσιν Gal.17(1).726. **-ής**, ές, *sloping*, χωρίον Th.6.96; λόφοι Plu.*Ant.*45; ἐ. τῷ στάχυϊ καὶ μὴ ὀρθά *inclining, bending*, Thphr.*CP*3.22.1; ἐπικλινές ἐστι τάλαντον Call.*Fr.* 312. 2. *prone, inclined*, πρὸς τὸν Ἄρην Them.*Or.*15.187b; οικείωσις ἐ. πρός τινα Ph.1.252. Adv. -νῶς, ἔχειν πρός τι ib.37, al.

**ἐπικλῑνοπάλη** [ᾰ], ἡ, *wrestling on the couch*, in mal. part., Mart.14. 201.

**ἐπικλίν-της**, ου, ὁ, *moving sideways*, [σεισμοὶ] ἐπικλίνται earthquakes *that move at acute angles*, Arist.*Mu.*396$^{a}$1 (v.l. ἐπικλίται: ἐπικλινίαι (sic) Lyd.*Ost.*53 codd.). ⊛ **-τρον**, τό, *couch, arm-chair*, Ar.*Ec.*907 (lyr.), *Fr.*44, *IG*2$^{2}$.1541.26 (iv B.C.); but, *straight-backed chair*, Gal.18(1).344. II. *back* of a couch or chair, *IG*11(2).144 *A*66, *B*8 (Delos, iv B.C.), *Gp.*13.14.9.

**ἐπι-κλίνω**, *put to, shut* a door: hence, in Pass., once in Hom., ἐπικεκλιμέναι σανίδες *closed* doors, Il.12.121. II. *bend towards*, τὰ ὦτα ἐ. *prick* the ears, X.*Cyn.*6.15; ἐ. αὑτὸν πρός τι *lean* against.., Paus.9.30.10; ξίφει ἑαυτήν Philostr.*Her.*19.11; ἐ. τὸ στόμα *pull* it *open*, Arist.*PA*660$^{b}$22:—Pass., κεραῖαι ἐπικεκλιμέναι spars *leaning on* the wall *and inclined at an angle* to it, Th.2.76. 2. *cause to incline*, πρὸς ταῦτα τὰ πράγματα D.3.8. 3. intr., *lean upon*, τοῖν χεροῖν Pl.*Amat.*132b; *incline towards*, ἐπί τι Chrysipp.*Stoic.*3. 175; πρὸς τὸ χεῖρον Dam.*Pr.*400. 4. = ἐπικατακλίνω, J.*AJ*1.10. 4. III. in Pass., *lie over against* or *near*, Σαλαμῖνος τᾶς ἐπικεκλιμένας ὄχθοις ἱεροῖς (sc. of Attica), E.*Tr.*801 (lyr.), cf. A.R.2.418. IV. Pass., also, *recline upon*, τύλῃ *AP*11.14 (Ammian.). **-κλῐσις**, εως, ἡ, *slope*, ἐδαφῶν Str.1.3.7. II. *inclination towards*, Antip. ap.Stob.4.22.25, Chrysipp.*Stoic.*3.175. III. *lying in bed*, Gal. 18(2).456 (pl.). **-κλῐτέον**, *one must fold in, turn in*, Orib.46.25.5.

**ἐπικλονέω**, *urge violently on*, [τινά] A.R.3.687; δῆριν Q.S.8.426:—Pass., *rush like a tide upon*, of persons, A.R.1.783; of storms, Q.S. 14.501.

**Ἐπικλόπ-ειος**, title of Zeus, Hsch. **-ίη**, ἡ, *trickery*, Nonn.*D.* 8.121. ⊛ **-ος**, ον, *thievish, tricky, wily*, ἠπεροπῆά τ' ἔμεν καὶ ἐ. Od. 11.364; κερδαλέος κ' εἴη καὶ ἐ. 13.291; ἐ. ἦθος, of women, Hes.*Op.*67, cf. A.*Eu.*149 (lyr.); ἐπικλοπώτερον..τὸ θῆλυ Pl.*Lg.*781a; ἐ. λόγοις χρῆσθαι Corn.*ND*16. Adv., Comp. -ώτερον Procop.*Arc.*25, *Goth.*4. 30. 2. c. gen., ἐ. ἔπλεο μύθων *cunning* in speech, Il.22.281; ἐ. ἔπλετο τόξων *cunning* in archery, Od.21.397.

⊛ **ἐπι-κλύζω**, pf. -κέκλῠκα Aeschin.3.173:—*overflow, flood*, ὅθι κύματ' ἐπ' ἠϊόνας (v.l. -όνος) κλύζεσκον Il.23.61, cf. Th.3.89, *PLond.*2.267. 112 (ii A.D.); ἐπέκλυζε τὸ πᾶν..θάλασσα Anon.*Oxy.*1014.16; τοὺς χυμοὺς οἷον ἐπικλύζοντας τὸ δέρμα, in blushing jaundice, Gal.7.267; ἐ. χρυσῷ τὴν λεωφόρον Ps.-Luc.*Philopatr.*21, cf. *Tim.*18:—Pass., *to be overwhelmed*, κύμασι v.l. in Batr.69; πλημυρίσιν Arist.*Mu.*397$^{a}$29. 2. metaph., *deluge, swamp*, πόλιν E.*Tr.*1327 (lyr.), cf. Theoc.25.201; ἐπέκλυσε θυμὸν ἀνίῃ δείματι A.R.3.695; ψυχήν Ph.1.91; ἐ. τινὰ κακοῖς Luc.*Pseudol.*25; φωναῖς ῥητόρων Lib.*Decl.*50.44; τῷ πλούτῳ πάντα Jul.*Or.*1.8b:—Pass., ὑπὸ τῶν δυσπραγιῶν Id.*ad Them.*257c. 3. *sweep away in the flood*, A.R.1.257: metaph., τὸ βασιλικὸν χρυσίον ἐπικέκλυκε τὴν δαπάνην *has merged*, i.e. *liquidated*, the expenses, Aeschin. l.c. 4. Pass., *to be poured over*, Eun.*VS*p.476B. II. intr., *overflow, abound*, D.S.3.47; πλοῦτος -κλύζων Eun.*Hist.*p.257 D., cf. D.H.6.17; τινί with a thing, Id.*Isoc.*14. **-κλῠσις**, εως, ἡ, *overflow, flood*, Th.3.89; ποταμοῦ Thphr.*Fr.*171.11: pl., Them. *Or.*13.167b. **-κλυσμός**, ὁ, = foreg., Poll.1.114, 116, Hld.9.3, Aq. *Jb.*21.17. **-κλυστος**, ον, *flooded*, D.S.1.10, Str.1.2.25.

**ἐπι-κλῠτός**, όν, *famed*, ἐ. ἀνδράσι Φινεὺς ὄλβῳ A.R.2.236. **-κλύω**, *listen to, hear*, c. acc., ἐπεὶ πάντ' αἶνον ἐπέκλυε Νηλεΐδαο Il.23.652, cf. A.R.3.598; σοῦ φωνήμαθ' ὡς ἐπέκλυον βοῶντος S.*Ichn.*39: c. gen., ἐπεὶ δὴ Ζηνὸς ἐπέκλυεν ἀγγελιάων Od.5.150, cf. A.R.1.1240, Eratosth. 19.

**ἐπι-κλώθω**, *spin upon*, ῥάμμα (q.v.) Hermipp.48; elsewh., II. *spin to* one, *assign*, prop. of the Fates who spun the thread of destiny; also of all powers which influence men's fortunes, οὔ μοι τοιοῦτον ἐπέκλωσαν θεοὶ ὄλβον Od.3.208, cf. 4.208, etc.; ὁππότε κεν Μοῖραι ἐπικλώσωσ' (sc. θάνατον) Callin.1.9, cf. Them.*Or.*32.356d:—Med., ὁππότε [θεοὶ] βασιλεῦσιν ἐπικλώσωνται ὀϊζύν Od.20.196, cf. 8.579: sts. c. inf. pro acc., τῷ οἱ ἐπεκλώσαντο θεοὶ οἶκόνδε νέεσθαι 1.17; ὡς γὰρ ἐπεκλώσαντο θεοὶ δειλοῖσι βροτοῖσι, ζώειν ἀχνυμένοις Il.24.525 (here only in Il.):—so in Act., φιτρὸν τὸν Μοῖρ' ἐπέκλωσεν ζωᾶς ὅρον ἔμμεν B.5.143; τοῦτο γὰρ λάχος..Μοῖρ' ἐπέκλωσεν ἐμπέδως ἔχειν A. *Eu.*335 (lyr.); ἐπεὶ τό γε (sc. θανεῖν) Μοῖρ' ἐ. *CIG*3136 (Erythrae), al.—Poet. word, used by Pl.*Tht.*169c τὴν..εἱμαρμένην, ἣν ⟨ἂν⟩ σὺ ἐπικλώσῃς, cf. *Stoic.*2.319, Luc.*Cont.*16, *DMort.*30.2, Jul.*Or.*7. 229c:—Pass., τὰ ἐπικλωσθέντα *its destiny*, Pl.*R.*620e, cf. *Lg.*957e, Plu.2.22b, 114d; ἐξ ἀρχῆς -κεκλωσμένην ἀπόβασιν *Com.Adesp.*295 (troch.). **-κλωσις**, εως, ἡ, *spinning*, τῶν Μοιρῶν *EM*495.25 (pl.). **-κλωσμα**, ατος, τό, *spun yarn*, Diogenian.Epicur.2.53.

**ἐπικνάω**, *scrape* or *grate over*, ἐπὶ δ' αἴγειον κνῆ (impf.) τυρόν Il.11. 639; ἐ. τυρόν, σίλφιον, Ar.*Av.*533 (anap.), 1582; τί τινι ib.1586: Att. inf. ἐπικνῆν *Com.Adesp.*722. 2. *scratch*, τὴν παρειάν Hld.2.8.

**ἐπικνέομαι**, Ion. for ἐφ-.

**ἐπικνήθω**, = ἐπικνάω, Nic.*Th.*698.

**Ἐπικνημίδιοι**, οἱ, name of a tribe of Locrians, who lived *on the slopes of Mount Cnemis*, Str.9.2.42.

**ἐπικνήμιον**, f.l. for ἀντι-, X.*Cyr.*2.3.19.

**ἐπι-κνίζω**, *scratch the surface*, Thphr.*HP*4.2.1, *CP*5.2.4 (Pass.); of the plough, *AP*6.238 (Apollonid.). **-κνῐσις**, εως, ἡ, *scratching on the surface*, Thphr.*CP*5.2.4.

**ἐπικοιλ-αίνω**, *make hollow*, [τὴν ῥάχιν] Sor.1.102. **-ίς**, f.l. for ἐπικυλίς, Poll.2.66. **-ος**, ον, *porous, spongy*, ὀστέον Hp.*VC*1 (Comp.); ἕλκη cj. for ποικίλα in Sor.1.122.

**ἐπικοιμ-άομαι**, *fall asleep after* a thing, Hp.*Aph.*5.27; or, *over* a thing, [τοῖς βιβλίοις] Luc.*Alex.*49: abs., *fall asleep*, δοκεῖς οὐ καθεύδων ἐπικεκοιμῆσθαι Pl.*Euthd.*300a. 2. ἐ. ἐπί τινα *overlay*, Lxx 3*Ki.* 3.19; τῷ αὐτῆς παιδίῳ J.*AJ*8.2.2. II. metaph. in pf. part. Pass., *sleepy* or *negligent about* a thing, Plb.2.13.4. **-ησις**, εως, ἡ, *sleeping upon* one ear, Hp.*Art.*40. **-ητηριάσασθαι**· ὑπηρετικὸν ὄνομα, Hsch. **-ίζω**, *lull to sleep*, Nonn.*D.*4.307.

⊛ **ἐπικοινάομαι**, *consult* an oracle, *GDI*1557, 1563 (Dodona).

**Ἐπικοίνιος**, title of Zeus at Salamis, Hsch.

**ἐπίκοιν-ος**, ον, *common to many, promiscuous*, ἐπίκοινον τῶν γυναικῶν τὴν μεῖξιν ποιεῖσθαι Hdt.4.104, cf. 172, 180; *sharing equally in*, λέκτρων E.*Andr.*124 (lyr.): c. dat., *in common with*, ἀρχὴν ἐ. αὐτῷ ἔχειν D.C.42.44; ἐ. ἀμφοῖν *belonging equally*, Plu.2.368e, cf. 1018f, *BGU* 906.21 (i A.D.): neut. pl. Adv., *in common*, [γυναιξὶν] ἐπίκοινα χρέωνται Hdt.1.216; χρηστήριον, τὸ ἐ. ἔχρησε ἡ Πυθίη Id.6.77 (but ἐχρήσθη ἐπίκοινον χρ. ib.19). Regul. Adv. -νως Orph.*Fr.*256. II. Gramm., *common*, of gender, D.T.634.19, Gell.13.7.3. Adv. -νως A.D.*Conj.* 253.20. III. ἐπίκοινος, ἡ, a game, = ἐπίσκυρος, Sch.Pl.*Tht.*146a, Eust.1601.34, Poll.9.104. ⊛ **-όω**, *communicate*, περί τινος D.C.66.10, etc.:—Med., *consult with*, τινὶ περί τινος Pl.*Prt.*313b; *communicate*, τινί τι D.C.52.21, Procop.*Aed.*2.3. II. Med., *share*, ib.1.4:—Pass., *to be shared with*, γάμους ἀλλήλοις ἐπικοινουμένους Pl.*Lg.* 631d. **-ωνέω**, *communicate with*, τῷ ἔξω χωρίῳ Hp.*Prog.*7; ἀλλήλοις Pl.*Sph.*251d; of troops in order of battle, *to be in touch with*, τοῖς ἄκροις Ascl.*Tact.*1.3; ἐ. πᾶσαι αἱ ἐπιστῆμαι ἀλλήλαις κατὰ τὰ κοινά Arist.*APo.*77$^{a}$26; τίνι οὐκ ἐ. [τὸ μάθημα] τῶν ἐπικαιροτάτων ἐν ἰητρικῇ; Hp.*Fract.*31, cf. Pl.*Grg.*464c: c. dat. pers., D.29.36. 2. *share in* a thing *with* one, τῶν γραμμάτων τί ἐπικοινωνεῖ; what letters has it *in common?* Pl.*Cra.*394c; νόμος οὐδὲν ἐπικοινωνῶν τῷ περὶ τῶν στεφανουμένων νόμῳ *having* nothing *in common with*.., Aeschin.3.44: generally, *share in*, c. gen., Ph.1.561. 3. *to be in partnership with*, c. dat., *POxy.*1280.6 (iv A.D.). **-ωνία**, ἡ, *interrelation*, Pl. *Sph.*252d, Thphr.*Od.*67. **-ωνός**, όν, = κοινωνός, Hp.*Decent.*5.

**ἐπικοίρᾰνος**, ὁ, = κοίρανος, Orph.*A.*294 (better ἔπι κ.).

**ἐπικοιτ-άζομαι**, *pass the night*, Arist.*HA*599$^{a}$30. **-έω**, *keep watch over*, ἐπὶ τῶν ἔργων Plb.21.27.6. **-ιος**, ον, *at bedtime*, ᾆσμα ἐ., of self-examination, Hierocl.*in CA*19 p.460M.

**ἐπικοκκάστρια**, ἡ, *mocker*, ἠχὼ λόγων ἀντῳδὸς ἐ. Ar.*Th.*1059: Ar. Byz.ap.Eust.1761.26 refers it to a verb **ἐπικοκκάζω**: masc. **ἐπικοκκαστής** cj. in Timo 43.

**ἐπικόκκουρος**· ὁ παρατηρητὴς ἐν σταδίῳ (Lacon.), Hsch.

**ἐπικολάπτω**, *carve on stone*, γράμματα *IG*2$^{2}$.1672.6; ὅρον ἐπὶ πέτρας *Inscr.Prien.*37.162 (ii B.C.).

**ἐπικολλ-αίνω**, *smear on*, πηλόν τινι Thphr.*CP*1.6.6. **-ημα**, ατος, τό, *that which is glued on, tessellated work*, Id.*HP*4.3.4 (pl.).

**ἐπικόλπιος**, ον, *in* or *on the bosom*, Ael.*NA*2.50, Nonn.*D.*8.78 codd.

**ἐπικολπόω**, *bend round*, τὰ κέρα, of troops, Agath.3.22.

**ἐπικόλωνος**, ον, *on* or *over a hill*, ὁδός f.l. in D.S.19.19.

**ἐπικομάω**, *wear long hair*, Poll.2.25; ξανθῇ κόμῃ ἐ. Id.4.136.

**ἐπικομίζω**, *bring* or *carry to*, ἐπὶ τοὺς ἔξω τόπους Str.11.2.17, cf. Arist.ap.D.L.5.14 (Pass.):—Med., *bring with one*, τὰ τοῦ Ἰωσήπου ὀστᾶ J.*AJ*2.15.2; τὴν τροφὴν ἑαυτοῖς D.C.50.11, cf. *PLips.*41.10 (iv A.D.).

**ἐπικομμόω**, *adorn with cosmetics*, Them.*Or.*13.167d.

**ἐπικομπ-άζω**, *add boastingly*, E.*HF*981; ἀληθεῖ λόγῳ τι Plu.*Cam.* 22: abs., *boast*, Ph.1.550. **-έω**, = foreg., Th.8.81. 2. *boast of*, τι Id.4.126.

**ἐπικομψεύω**, *deck out*, λόγον J.*AJ*20.12.1 (cod. A).

**ἐπικονέω**, pf. Pass. ἐπικεκόνημαι (-ιμαι cod.)· ἐξέφθαρμαι, ἀπόλωλα, Hsch.

**ἐπικονιάω**, *whitewash*, στοιάν *IG*11(2).229*A*10 (Delos, iii B.C.).

**ἐπι-κόπᾰνον**, τό, *chopping-block, billet*, Men.33, *IG*11(2).199*B*89 (Delos, iii B.C.), Poll.10.101. **-κοπάς** (sc. γῆ), άδος, ἡ, *land cleared of trees*, *PLond.ined.*2316 (iii B.C.). **-κοπή**, ἡ, *cutting close, pollarding*, of trees, Thphr.*CP*5.17.3. 2. *cutting down, felling*, μιᾶς ἐπικοπῆς εἶναι fall by a single *blow*, D.C.38.50, 49.29 (owing to f.l. in Th.5.103). 3. in building, *dressing, trimming* face of blocks of masonry, ἐπικόπτων τὰς ἐπικοπάς *BCH*35.43 (Delos), cf. *IG* 7.3073.71 (Lebad.); ἐ. στρωτήρων ib.4.1484.235 (Epid.). II. *interruption*, Philostr.*VS*2.30. **-κοπος**, ον, of coins, *re-stamped*, *EM* 360.41, Hsch. II. Act., *for cutting*: as Subst., ἐπίκοπον, τό, = ἐπικόπανον, Luc.*DMort.*10.9, Eust.1476.33; *support for cutting upon*, in surgery, Heliod.ap.Orib.44.23.66, Antyll.ib.18, Gal.2.685.

**ἐπικοπρίζω**, *manure*, *Gp.*2.23.5.

**ἐπικόπτ-ης**, ου, ὁ, *satirist, censor*, Timo 60 (v. ἐπισκώπτης). ⊛ **-ω**, pf. -κέκοφα Phld.*D.*1.15:—*strike upon* (i.e. *from above*), *fell*, βοῦν

ἐπικόψων Od.3.443. 2. later, of trees, *lop, pollard*, Thphr.*CP*5.17.3; *cut down* brushwood, *PLond*.3.1170*B*26 (iii A.D.): metaph., *cut short, bring down from high estate*, τοὺς πεφρονηματισμένους Arist.*Pol*.1284b2; φιληδονίαν ἀκόλαστον Plu.2.529b; *check, impede*, πράξεις ib.975b; στάσιν J.*BJ*2.17.4 (Pass., Hp.*Ep*.13); *reprove, censure*, τινά Timo 4, Myro 2 J., Plu.*Cic*.24, Philostr.*VA*5.35, al.; *refute*, Phld. l.c.; δόξας Id.*Po*.5.26. 3. ἐ. χαρακτῆρα *stamp, coin*, Arist.*Oec*.1349b31. 4. *cut anew*, [τὸν] ἀποτριβέντα [μύλον] Str.15.2.2. b. Archit., *dress* blocks of stone, etc., κατὰ κεφαλήν *IG*7.3073.183 (Lebad.), cf. ib.4255.15 (Oropus); πλίνθον *Milet*.7 p.59 (Didyma). 5. Med., *smite one's breast, wail for*, τινά E.*Tr*.627. 6. of disease, *afflict*, βαρύτερον Aret.*SD*2.13. 7. *injure*, αἱ ἡδοναὶ ἐ. τὴν ἰσχύν Philostr.*Gym*.52:—Pass., -κοπεὶς τοὺς ὀφθαλμοὺς ὑπό τινος Id.*VS*2.25.2.

**ἐπικόρμιον**, τό, = ἐπικόπανον, Eust.1476.34: written **ἐπικόρμον** Id.1692.62.

**ἐπίκορον**· ἐπίκοπον, Πάμφιοι (sic), Hsch.

**ἐπίκορρ-ι**· ἐπὶ κονδυλίῳ, Hsch. **-ίζω**, (κόρρη) *strike* or *peck on the head*, Arist.*HA*614a10 (-κορίζω codd.). **-ιστος**, η, ον, *with one's ears boxed* (ἐπὶ κόρρης), Hsch.

**ἐπικορύσσομαι**, *arm oneself against*, τινί Luc.*Alex*.57.

**ἐπικορύφ-ωμα** [ῠ], ατος, τό, gloss on ἐπικτόλωμα, Hsch. **-ωσις**, εως, ἡ, *culmination, terminal number* of an arithmetical series, Nicom.*Ar*.2.3.

**ἐπικός**, ή, όν, *epic*, ποίησις D.H.*Comp*.22; ἐγκώμιον *IG*9(2).531.45 (Larissa); στίχοι Sch.Ar.*Pax*1288; ἐ. κύκλος (v. κύκλος); παροιμίαι Heph.8.6. Adv. -κῶς, = λογίως, Suid. s. v. Μαρῖνος.

**ἐπικοσμ-έω**, *add ornaments to, decorate after* or *besides*, τὰ ἱρά Hdt.1.184; *adorn*, ἄγαλμα, ἕδος, Hyp.*Eux*.24,25; τὴν θεόν *IG*2².1277; [κέρκους] ἐπικεκόσμηκεν ἡ φύσις θριξί Arist.*PA*658a32; ἐ. τινὰς ἐπιγράμμασι *honour* them with.., Hdt.7.228; θεὰν ἐ. *honour, celebrate*, Ar.*Ra*.385; of funeral honours, X.*Cyr*.7.3.11: abs., λέξις -οῦσα Demetr.*Eloc*.106:—Pass., Arist.*Pol*.1263a23; ἱερὸν ἐ. ὅπλοις *SIG*398.9 (Cos, iii B.C.), cf. *Sammelb*.996.4 (i A.D.). **-ημα**, ατος, τό, *ornament*, Asp.*in EN*109.14. **-ησις**, εως, ἡ, *adornment, decoration*, τραπέζης *IG*2².1245; τῆς Ἥρας *BCH*35.285 (Delos); τῶν κοινῶν *IG*2².1228.16. II. *perfecting* of matter by form, Syrian. *in Metaph*.38.21.

**✱ ἐπικοτ-έω**, = κοτέω, ἐπὶ ζαμενὲς κοτέουσα Nic.*Th*.181. **-ος**, ον, *wrathful, vengeful*, στάσις Pi.*Fr*.109.4; μήδεα A.*Pr*.601 (lyr.); ἐπικότους τροφᾶς.. ἀράς *in wrath at* the sons he had bred, Id.*Th*.786 (lyr.). Adv. -τως *wrathfully*, Id.*Pr*.163 (lyr.). II. Pass., *hateful*, S.*Fr*.428.

**ἐπικοττᾰβίζω**, *throw the cottabus on* or *at*, Poll.6.110, prob. f.l. for ἀποκοττ-.

**Ἐπικούρειος**, ον, *of Epicurus, Epicurean*, ἄτομα *AP*11.93 (Lucill.); φιλόσοφος *Act.Ap*.17.18, etc., cf. Str.14.2.20; Ἐπικούρειον, τό, '*utilitarian*' doctrine, Cic.*Fam*.3.9.2; οἱ Ἐ. *the Epicureans*, Luc.*Herm*.16.

**ἐπικουρ-έω**, *to be an* ἐπίκουρος, *act as an ally*, once in Hom., ἑ Μοῖρα ἦγ' ἐπικουρήσοντα μετὰ Πρίαμον Il.5.614, cf. Th.7.57; φίλοις, χθονί, E.*Rh*.937, 956; *render aid*, Foed.ap.Th.5.23, etc. 2. *serve as allies* or *mercenaries*, Isoc.4.168; μισθοῦ ἐ. Pl.*R*.575b. II. generally, *aid* or *help at need*, τινί E.*IA*1452, Ar.*V*.1018, Lys.12.98; [τῇ δικαιοσύνῃ] Pl.*R*.368c; also τῇ ἀναγκαίᾳ τροφῇ ἐ. *provide for* it, Aeschin.1.27; νόσοις ἐπικουρῆσαι *remedy* them, *aid* one *against* them, X.*Mem*.1.4.13; ἐ. τῷ λιμῷ, τῷ γήρᾳ, τῇ πενίᾳ, Id.*Lac*.2.6, 10.2, *Vect*.1.1 (Pass.); ἐσθὴς ἐπικουρεῖ τινι πολλά '*does him yeoman's service*', Id.*Cyr*.6.2.30. 2. c. acc. rei, ἐπικουρεῖν τινι χειμῶνα *keep* it *off from* one, Id.*An*.5.8.25. 3. c. acc. et dat., *furnish, supply*, *POxy*.1630.5 (iii A.D.). **-ημα**, ατος, τό, *protection*, τοῖς ὀφθαλμοῖς χιόνος X.*An*.4.5.13; *remedy*, Gal.6.171: pl., *aids, succours*, τῇ ζωῇ Iamb.*Protr*.20. **-ησις**, εως, ἡ, *succour, protection*, Antipho Soph.*Oxy*.1364.158; τὰς ἐκ τῶ θήω γινομένας ἐ. Euryph.ap.Stob.4.39.27; κακῶν *against* evils, E.*Andr*.28; τῆς ἀπορίας Pl.*Lg*.919b. **-ητικός**, ή, όν, = ἐπικουρικός, Pl.*R*.441a, Aen.Tact.38tit. **✱ -ία**, Ion. -ίη, ἡ, *aid, succour*, Hdt.6.100,108, A.*Pers*.731 (troch.), etc.; ἐπικουρίας δεῖσθαι Th.1.32, X.*Oec*.17.13; τῆς ἐνδείας ἐ. τὸ κέρδος Arist.*EN*1163b4; ἐ. ποιεῖσθαί τινι Th.1.33; ἐ. λαβεῖν, ἔχειν, E.*Or*.266, Pl.*Grg*.492c; ἀπολογίας *towards* one's defence, D.49.50; σκυτίνη 'πικ., = ὄλισβος, Ar.*Lys*.110. II. *auxiliary force*, A.*Supp*.721, Th.7.59 (pl.), Hdt.5.63. 2. *position of the* ἐπίκουροι (in Plato's Republic), Pl.*R*.415c. III. *prayer for aid, entreaty*, *SIG*1015.24 (Halic., iii B.C.). **-ικός**, ή, όν, *serving as* ἐπίκουροι I.3, γένος Pl.*R*.434c, 441a. 2. mostly of troops, *auxiliary, mercenary*, ἐπικουρικὸν μισθώσασθαι Th.4.52; *dependent on* ἐπίκουροι, πράγματα Id.7.48; τὸ ἐ. Ph.2.98. **-ιος**, ον, *succouring*, epith. of deities, Paus.8.41.7. **-ος**, ὁ, *helper, ally*, Hom. only in Il., mostly in pl. of the barbarian *allies* of Troy, Τρῶες.. ἠδ' ἐ. 2.815; Τρῶες καὶ Δάρδανοι ἠδ' ἐ. 3.456, al., cf. Hdt.2.152, 3.91, al. 2. *mercenary troops*, opp. citizen-soldiers, ἐπικούρους προσμισθοῦσθαι Th.2.33, cf. Hdt.1.154, 2.163, 3.145, Lys.12.94, X.*HG*7.1.12, etc.; ἀπὸ Ἀρκαδίας ἐπίκουροι Hermipp.63.18; used as body-guard by tyrants, Hdt.1.64, 6.39, Th.6.55,58. 3. οἱ ἐ. the *guards*, the military class in Plato's Republic, *R*.414b, 415a, 545d. II. as Adj., *assisting, aiding*, c. dat. pers., Ἀφροδίτη ἦλθεν Ἄρῃ ἐπίκουρος Il.21.431; βῆναι ἐ. τινι Pi.*O*.13.97; ταῖς νήσοις ἐ. Ar.*Eq*.1319; τοῖς ἀδικουμένοις ἐ. Th.3.67: c. gen. pers., ἐπίκουρε βροτῶν their *defender*, *h.Mart*.9; τῶν ἀνθρώπων, of Eros, Pl.*Smp*.189d: abs., *patron, protector*, δεσπότης ἐ. X.*Cyr*.7.5.61. 2. c. gen. rei, *defending* or *protecting against*, νόσου E.*Or*.211 (troch.); πῦρ ἐ. ψύχους, σκότους, X.*Mem*.4.3.7; Λαβδακίδαις ἐ. θανάτων *protecting* them *against* deaths, S.*OT*496 (lyr.); πατρὶ αἱμάτων ἐ. E.*El*.138 (lyr.).

**✱ ἐπικουφ-ίζω**, *lighten* a ship by throwing out part of its cargo, Hdt.8.118 (Pass.): metaph., ἐ. ἡ τιμὴ τοὺς πόνους τῷ ἄρχοντι *lightens* his labours, X.*Cyr*.1.6.25; τὰς συμφοράς D.23.70; λειτουργίας *IG*14.1078a; τὴν ταλαιπωρίαν Jul.*adThem*.253b: c. gen. rei, *relieve of* a burden, μόχθου E.*El*.72; τοῦ δέους D.C.43.18:—Med., ταῖς διὰ τὴν ἀρετὴν ἡδοναῖς τὸν πόνον -ίζομαι Lxx 4*Ma*.9.31. II. *lift up, support*, πατρὸς πλευρὰς σὺν ἐμοὶ τάσδ' ἐπικούφιζ' S.*Aj*.1411 (anap.); ἐ. τὴν γῆν *lift up* the soil, X.*Oec*.17.13. 2. metaph., *lift up, encourage*, ἐλπίσι Id.*Cyr*.7.1.18. b. ἐ. νόον ἀνδρὸς *puff up*, in bad sense, Thgn.629. **✱ -ισμός**, ὁ, *relief*, *IGRom*.4.1523.9 (Sardes); τῆς ὀχλήσεως Sor.2.38.

**✱ ἐπικρᾰδ-αίνω**, *wave on high*, πέλεκυν Hld.3.1; *quiver*, τὸ σῶμα πᾶν ἐ. Poll.5.61. **-άω**, = foreg., ἐρετμά A.R.1.552, cf. Opp.*C*.1.91.

**ἐπικράδιον**· ἐπικάρδιον, Hsch.

**ἐπικράζω**, *shout to* or *at*, τινί Luc.*Anach*.16 (pf. part. ἐπικεκρᾱγότες): aor. 1 inf. ἐπικρᾶξαι Ps.-Luc.*Philopatr*.1.

**✱ ἐπικραίνω**, Ep. **-κραιαίνω**, 3 sg. fut. ἐπικρᾱνεῖ dub. in A.*Ag*.1340 codd. (anap.): aor. 1 -έκρᾱνα, Ep. -έκρηνα, -εκρήηνα (v. infr.):—Med., 3 pl. aor. 1 ἐπεκρήναντο Q.S.14.297:—*bring to pass, accomplish*, ἀρὴν πᾶσαν ἐπικρήνειε *may* he *fulfil* it, Il.15.599; οὔ σφιν ἐπεκραίαινε he *fulfilled* it not for them, 3.302, cf. 2.419 (v.l. -δαινε); νῦν μοι τόδ' ἐπικρήηνον ἐέλδωρ *grant* me this prayer, *fulfil* it, 1.455, etc.; μῦθον ἐπεκρήηνε καρήατι by a nod, Call.*Dian*.40; ἐ. τέλος A.*Supp*.624; ἀληθῆ Id.*Th*.887 (lyr.); γάμου πικρὰς τελευτάς Id.*Ag*.744 (lyr.); ποινὰς θανάτων ib.1340 (anap.); χάριν ἀντ' ἔργων ib.1546 (anap.), cf. S.*Ph*.1468 (anap.); τὸ δέον Archyt.ap.Iamb.*Protr*.4:—Pass., χρυσῷ δ' ἐπὶ χείλεα κεκράαντο *were finished off* with gold, Od.4.132, cf. 616.

**ἐπικρανής**· ἐπιμελητής, Hsch. (fort. -κράντης).

**ἐπικρᾱν-ίς**, ίδος, ἡ, *membrane of the brain*, Erasistr.ap.*Placit*.4.5.3, dub. in Gal.2.728 (fort ἐγκρ-). **-ισμα**, ατος, τό, = ἐπίκρανον, Hsch. s. v. ἰανοκρήδεμνος. **-ῖτις**, ιδος, ἡ, pl. -ίτιδες, πλίνθοι *top course* of a wall, *IG*1².372.16, al. **-ον**, τό, *that which is put on the head, head-dress, cap*, E.*Hipp*.201 (anap.), Ph.2.309. II. = κιονόκρανον, *capital*, Pi.*Fr*.88.5, E.*IT*51, *IG*1².313.89, 2².1668.44, etc.

**ἐπίκρᾱσις**, εως, ἡ, (ἐπικεράννυμι) *mixing* of wine, Διοσκούροις *IG* 11(2).159*A*7 (iii B.C.), al.; *tempering*, Diph.Siph.ap.Ath.3.91f; of humours, Herod.Med.ap.Orib.5.30.3, Gal.10.640; φαυλοτήτων Dsc.2.49.

**ἐπικρᾰτ-αιόω**, *add strength to, confirm*, Lxx *Ec*.4.12 (Pass.). **-εια**, ἡ, *mastery*, σωφροσύνη ἐστὶν ἐ. τῶν ἐπιθυμιῶν ib.4*Ma*.1.31; *possession*, X.*Cyr*.5.4.28; *rule*, Plb.12.25.3, etc.; *victory, superiority*, Id.2.1.3. 2. *predominance*, in heredity, *Placit*.5.7.6; διάφορος τῶν χυμῶν ἐ. S.E.*P*.1.80; τὸ κατ' ἐπικράτειαν ὠνομασμένον αἷμα named *from its dominant element*, opp. εἰλικρινὲς αἷμα, Gal.15.74, cf. 5.672, 17(2).216; παρὰ τὰς ἐ. *Placit*.4.9.9: Gramm., *prevalence, authority*, A.D.*Synt*.256.26, al.; numerical *superiority*, ib.326.14. 3. *prevailing opinion*, ἐν τοῖς συμβαίνουσιν.. κατὰ τὴν ἐ... στροβοῦνται Polystr.p.22 W.; αἱ κατ' ἐπικράτειαν δόξαι Epicur.*Nat*.1431.8. II. of a country, *realm, dominion*, ἄπιμεν.. ἐκ τῆς τούτων ἐπικρατείας X.*An*.7.6.42, cf. *Hier*.6.13; ὑπὸ τῇ ἐ. τοῦ χωρίου within *the country subject to* the place, Id.*An*.6.4.4; ἡ Καρχηδονίων ἐ. Pl.*Ep*.349c; of a Roman *province*, Ph.2.518,583 (pl.). **-έω** (Aeol. **-κρετέω** prob. in Alc.82), *rule over*, c. dat., νήεσσιν ἐπικρατέουσιν ἄριστοι Il.10.214; νήσοισιν Od.1.245: abs., *have* or *hold power*, εὖτ' ἂν μηκέτ' ἐπικρατέωσιν ἄνακτες 17.320, cf. 14.60, Archil.69. II. *prevail in battle, be victorious*, ἐπικρατέουσί περ ἔμπης [to them] though they *are victorious* as it is, Il.14.98, cf. Ar.*Lys*.767; ἐ. ἢ ἀπόλλυσθαι *conquer* or die, Hdt.7.104; ἐ. τῇ στάσι Id.1.173; ἐ. τὰ πλείω τοῦ πολέμου *gain the advantage* in most points in the war, Th.4.19. 2. freq. c. gen., *prevail over, get the mastery of* an enemy, ἐ. μάχῃ τῶν Γελῴων Hdt.7.155; τῶν ἐχθρῶν Id.8.94, Lys.34.4; τῆς τινων πονηρίας Id.22.16; ἐ. αὐτῶν (-οῦ codd.) παρὰ τῷ βασιλέϊ, in a suit at law, Hdt.4.65; ἰσχυρὰ ἐ. ἀνδρὸς Ἀνάγκη Philet.8; τοῦ πυρὸς Hdt.1.86; γήρως Pl.*Lg*.752a; ὑμῶν -ήσω τῷ κοάξ Ar.*Ra*.267. 3. rarely c. acc., *master, conquer*, τὰς τῆς φύσεως ἁμαρτίας Isoc.1.52; δύο βασιλέας D.C.36.16:—Pass., -ηθεῖσα (sc. ἡ δεξιά), in left-handed persons, Sor.1.111. 4. c. gen., *become master of*, τῶν πραγμάτων Hdt.4.164; τῆς θαλάσσης Id.1.17, al.; τῶν πολίων, τῶν νεῶν, Id.6.32,115; τῆς ἀναγκαίου τροφῆς, τῆς ἀναβάσεως, Th.1.2, 7.42; τῶν ἐρώτων Pi.*N*.8.5, etc. b. *to be in possession of*, [οἰκίας] *PRyl*.160.3 (i A.D.), etc. 5. generally, *prevail, be superior*, πλήθει Hdt.5.2; πολὺ τῷ ναυτικῷ Th.2.93; τὰ πλείω τῷ πεζῷ Id.7.63; κατὰ θάλασσαν X.*HG*7.1.6: c. inf., *they carried the point that*.., Th.5.46; ἐπεκράτουν μὴ δέχεσθαι τοὺς Ἀθηναίους Id.6.74. b. metaph., *prevail*, τὸ ἀνθρώπινον ἦθος ἐπεκράτει Pl.*Criti*.121b; τὸ δίκαιον Men.*Epit*.16; τὸ ψῦχος, τὸ ὑγρόν, Arist.*Mete*.347b26, *MM*1210a20; τὸ ὄνομα Plb.2.38.1; ὁ λόγος D.S.5.62; ὁ τραχὺς ἦχος Phld.*Po*.994.33. 6. c. part., ἐ. διαιροῦντες *succeed* in keeping it open, Arist.*GA*773a29. **✱ -ής**, ές, *master* of a thing: only Comp. -έστερος, τῇ μάχῃ *superior* in.., Th.6.88; -έστερός τινος γενόμενος having *the upper hand of*.., D.C.55.30; τὸ -έστερον φέρειν Memn.34.3; κατὰ τὸ -έστερον with *success*, D.S.37.2.—Hom. only in Adv. -τέως *with overwhelming might, impetuously*, Il.16.67,81, 23.863 (never in Od.); so Hes.*Sc*.321, A.R.1.367, etc. **-ησις**, εως, ἡ, *mastering, conquest of*, Αἰγυπτίων Th.1.41. II. *supreme power*, ἡ τοῦ Καίσαρος ἐν τῇ Ῥώμῃ D.C.47.21. III. of things, *prevalence*, Gal.4.629, 19.488; ἡ οὐκ ἴση ἐ. Plot.5.7.2; ἐ. αἰθέρος, name given to the *predominance* of πῦρ τεχνικόν at the ἐκπύρωσις, *Stoic*.2.185. **✱ -ητικός**, ή, όν, *astrin-*

gent, Gal.12.361. -ήτωρ, ορος, ὁ, ἀστὴρ *ruling* star, Ps.-Ptol.*Centil.* 25, cf. Vett.Val.132.15, etc.

**ἐπικρᾰτ-ίδες**, ίδων, αἱ, (κράς, κρατός) a kind of *head-dress* (cf. ἐπίκρανον) or *towel*, Hp.*Praec.*10. -ίδιον, τό, Dim. of foreg., = στημονικὸν κάλυμμα [χωρὶς] τῆς κεφαλῆς, Hsch.

**ἐπικρᾰτικός**, ή, όν, (ἐπικεράννυμι) v.l. for ἐπικεραστικός, Gal.6.260, 582, Orib.1.42.3.

⊕**ἐπικρᾰτύνω**, *strengthen*, Hsch.

**ἐπικραυγάζω**, *cry out to* or *at*, Arr.*Epict.*1.21.3, 4.1.19.

**ἐπικρεμάννῡμι** and -ύω, *hang over*, ἄτην τινί Thgn.206 codd.; κίνδυνον Plb.2.31.7; φόβον D.S.16.50. II. Pass., ἐπικρέμαμαι, aor. ἐπεκρεμάσθην, *overhang*, of a rock, *h.Ap.*284; οἰκία ἐπικρεμαμένη τῇ ἀγορᾷ Plu.*Publ.*10: metaph., *hang over, threaten*, θάνατος Simon.39.3; δόλιος αἰών Pi.*I.*8(7).14 (tm.); τιμωρία Th.2.53; ἐπικρεμάμενος κίνδυνος *impending* danger, Id.7.75, cf. 3.40: c.dat.pers., ἐπικρέμαθ' ἧμιν ὄλεθρος A.R.3.483; Ep. 3 pl. impf. ἐπεκρεμόωντο Nonn.*D.*20.173.

**ἐπικρήδιος**, ὁ, a *Cretan dance*, Ath.14.629c.

**ἐπικρήηνον**, -κρήηνε, v. ἐπικραίνω.

**ἐπίκρημνος**, ον, *precipitous, steep*, Pherecyd.82(b) J., Dicaearch.2.6 (v.l. ἀπόκρ-).

**ἐπικρῆναι**· ἑορτὴ Δήμητρος παρὰ Λάκωσιν, Hsch. (leg. -κρήναια). **ἐπίκρηνον**· κεφαλόδεσμον, Id.; cf. ἐπίκρανον.

**ἐπικρηπῖδες**, αἱ, *goloshes*, Thphr.*Char.*2.7 (s.v.l.).

**ἐπικρῆσαι**, v. ἐπικεράννυμι.

**ἐπικρητηρίδιος** ἠθμός strainer *for a mixing bowl*, Demioprat.ap. Poll.10.108.

**ἐπι-κρῐδόν**, Adv., (ἐπικρίνω) *choosing out*, A.R.2.302. ⊕ -κρῖμα, ατος, τό, = Lat. *decretum*, *OGI*453.23 (Aphrodisias, M. Antonius), 669.28 (Egypt, i A.D.); Καίσαρος Epist.ap.J.*AJ*19.6.3. ⊕ -κρίνω [κρῐ], fut. -κρῐνῶ (v. infr.):—*decide, determine*, τι Pl.*Lg.*768a; τὸ πλεῖον καὶ τοὔλαττον D.H.3.29; περί τινος Decr.ap.D.18.38; τοῦ ἐπικρινοῦντος δέοι ἂν Pl.*R.*524e: c. inf., ἐπέκρινε γενέσθαι τὸ αἴτημα αὐτῶν *Ev. Luc.*23.24; ἐ. τί διαφέρει what is the difference, Arist.*de An.*431ᵃ 20; τὸ ἐπικρῖνον *the deciding power*, Id.*Insomn.*461ᵇ25; also, *principle of selection*, rule of life, Epicur.*Nat.*125 G.; *adjudge, inflict*, θάνατόν τινι Lxx *2 Ma.*4.47:—Pass., μέχρις ἂν ἐπικριθῇ αὐτῷ ὑπὸ τῶν ἱερέων ἢ ἀποδοῦναι αὐτὸν ἢ εἰσέρχεσθαι until the judges *determine* whether he shall pay up or enter (without payment), *SIG*1109.71, cf. *PTeb.*284.2 (i B.C.). 2. c. acc. pers., *judge*, τινά Ph.2.380:—Pass., ib.309. II. *select, pick out*, ἐξ ἑαυτῶν τὸν ἄριστον D.S.1.75; ἐ. τινὰ ἴσον ἀδελφοῖς *distinguish, esteem*, Hp.*Jusj.* 2. in Egypt, *select by* ἐπίκρισις II (q.v.), *PGen.*19 (ii A.D.):—Pass., *POxy.*39 (i A.D.). 3. *consider*, πάντα ταῦτα Phld.*Oec.*p.63 J. III. Med., *choose for oneself, pick out*, βοῦν *SIG*1025.17 (Cos, iv/iii B.C.).

**ἐπίκριον**, τό, (ἴκρια) *yard-arm*, Od.5.254, 318, A.R.2.1262, etc.

⊕ **ἐπί-κρῐσις**, εως, ἡ, *determination*, τῶν ἐκλειπτικῶν τηρήσεων Str. 1.1.12; συνημμένων Plu.2.43c (pl.), cf. D.L.9.92, A.D.*Adv.*151.14, Plot.5.3.2; *discrimination* of scents, Dsc.1.14. 2. *verification*, Gal. 17(2).354, cf. 1.117. II. in Egypt, revision of lists and *selection* of privileged persons, *POxy.*288.35 (i A.D.), *PFay.*27.24 (ii A.D.), *BGU*324.2, 19 (ii A.D.), etc. III. *judgement*, Ph.1.38, al.; arbitrator's *award*, *SIG*364.6 (Ephesus, pl.). -κρῐτέον, *one must select*, Ph.1.564. -κρῑτήριον, τό, *court of appeal*, *GDI*5040.67 (Hierapytna), 5024.52 (Gortyn). -κρῐτής, οῦ, ὁ, *adjudicator, arbiter*, τῶν λεγομένων Plb.14.3.7. II. in Egypt, *examining magistrate* (cf. ἐπίκρισις II), *PFay.*27.3 (ii A.D.), *PTeb.*320.2 (ii A.D.). -κρῐτικός, ή, όν, *adjudicatory, determinative*, τινός D.L.9.47, A.D.*Conj.*222.25. -κρῐτος, ον, *approved*, J.*BJ*3.5.5 (v.l. ἔκκριτοι). II. oxyt., ἐπικριτός, ή, όν, *capable of determination* or *resolution*, διαφωνία S.E.*P.*1.170.

⊕ **ἐπίκροκον**· ἐπανθητόν, Hsch.; cf. Lat. *epicrocum*, Paul. ex Fest. p.72 L., etc.

**ἐπικροτᾰλίζω**, = sq., Nonn.*D.*17.29, 37.34.

**ἐπικροτ-έω**, *rattle on* or *over*, τὰ δ' ἐπικροτέοντα πέτοντο ἅρματα flew *rattling over* the ground, Hes.*Sc.*308. 2. c. acc., *strike with a rattling sound, clash*, κύμβαλα Alciphr.1.12; κρόταλα Luc.*Syr.D.* 44; γένειον Opp.*C.*2.244. 3. *clap, applaud*, Men.887, Plu.*Ant.* 12; τινί Luc.*Cont.*8. 4. c. dat. instr., ἐ. ὀδοῦσι *chatter* with one's teeth, Ps.-Luc.*Philopatr.*21; ἐ. τοῖς δακτύλοις *snap* the fingers, Eust. 1602.16: abs., Aristobul.9 J. codd. Ath. -ησις, εως, ἡ, = Lat. *increpatio*, *Gloss.* -ος, ον, *beaten* or *trodden hard*, esp. of ground, ἐν τῷ ἐπικρότῳ ἱππεύειν X.*Eq.Mag.*3.14; ἐ. ποιεῖν Arist.*HA*558ᵃ6: metaph., τὸ ἐ. τῶν λόγων their *sonorousness*, Philostr.*VS*1.25.7.

**ἐπί-κρουμα**, ατος, τό, *beating* with the foot, χθονὸς Ἀργείας S.*Fr.* 287 (anap.). -κρουσις, εως, ἡ, treatment with rods as counter-irritants, Gal.10.998. 2. medical *percussion*, Paul.Aeg.3.69, 6. 51. -κρουσμα, ατος, τό, *forcible blow*, ib.91. -κρουστήριον, τό, *hammer*, *Gloss.* -κρουστικόν, τό, a surgical instrument, = sq., Aët.6.8 (s.v.l.). -κρούστιον, τό, a surgical instrument, perh. *slasher*, *Hermes* 38.282. ⊕ -κρούω, *hammer in*, ἧλον Ar.*Th.*1004, cf. *IG*2².463.64; τὸν ἵππον καὶ τὸν ἄνδρα τὸν -κρούοντα ib.1².374.173; χθόνα βάκτροις *striking* the ground.., A.*Ag.*202 (lyr.); ἐ. τῇ χειρὶ τὸ ξίφος *clap* one's hand *on* one's sword, Plu.*Pomp.*58: metaph., *jeer at*, εἴς τινα Macho ap.Ath.13.579b. II. = ἐπικροτέω 4, Lxx *Je.*31 (48).26. III. Medic., use *percussion*, Aret.*SA*1.6.

**ἐπι-κρύπτω**, poet. aor. 2 ἐπέκρῠφον Q.S.7.235 (v.l. ἀπ-):—*throw a cloak over, conceal*, χεῖρας φονίας A.*Eu.*317 (lyr.); τὴν βούλησιν τοῦ ὀνόματος Pl.*Cra.*421b; f.l. for ἔπη κρύπτειν, E.*Supp.*296:—freq. in Med., *disguise*, κἀπικρύψασθαι κακά S.*Fr.*88.12 (v.l.); τὰς αὐτοῦ τύχας.. τοὐπικρύπτεσθαι σοφόν E.*Fr.*553; ἐ. τὴν αὑτοῦ ἀπορίαν Pl.*La.*196b, cf. *Prt.*346b; τἀληθῆ D.17.17: abs., ἐπικρυπτόμενος *with concealment* or *secrecy*, X.*An.*1.1.6; ἐπικρύπτεσθαί τι τῷ μεγέθει τῶν ἄλλων ἔργων D. 61.45; πρὸς τοὺς πολλοὺς τὴν δεινότητα Plu.*Per.*4; ἐ. τινά τι *conceal* a thing *from* one, Plb.3.75.1; also ἐ. τινὰ ὡς.. Pl.*Tht.*180d; ὅτι οὐχ ὑγιαίνει Id.*R.*476e; *disguise, conceal one's purpose*, τῶν πεντακισχιλίων τῷ ὀνόματι Th.8.92; ἐσθῆτι θεράποντος Plu.*Caes.*38:—Pass., *to be concealed*, Arist.*Pol.*1278ᵃ39. -κρῠφος, ον, *unknown, inglorious*, οἶμος Pi.*O.*8.69, Max.21; *concealed*, πράξεις Plu.*Arat.*10. -κρυψις, εως, ἡ, *concealment*, Str.2.3.8, Plu.*Nic.*23; νούσων *latencies, quiescences*, Aret.*CD*1.5 (pl.).

**ἐπικρώζω**, *caw* or *croak at*, Orac.ap.Ar.*Eq.*1051; τισὶ ὅτι.. Them. *Or.*4.61d.

**ἐπικτάομαι**, *gain* or *win besides*, φίλους A.*Eu.*901; πατρίοισι νόμοισι ἄλλον οὐδένα ἐπικτῶνται Hdt.2.79; ἐ. ἀρχὴν *extend one's* empire, Th.1.144; ἐ. τὰ μὴ προσήκοντα Id.4.61; τριήρεις κέκτησθε πολλὰς καὶ πάτριον ὑμῖν ἐστι ναυτικὸν ἐπικτᾶσθαι *add to those* you have, X.*HG* 7.1.3; τόνδ' ἐ. σύμμαχον *as* an ally, A.*Eu.*671; ξυμμάρτυρας ὔμμ' ἐ. S.*Ant.*846 (lyr.); *acquire additional* property, *PGiss.*108.3 (ii B.C.), etc.:—late in Pass., Agath.1.2, Just.*Nov.*123.4.

**ἐπικτείνω**, *kill besides* or *again*, τὸν θανόντ' ἐ. *slay* the slain *anew*, S.*Ant.*1030; f.l. for ἔτι κτ-, Plu.*Caes.*46.

**ἐπικτένιον**, τό, (κτείς) *tow which remains in the heckle*, ἐ. ὠμοῦ λίνου (v.l. ὠμόλινον) Hp.*Mul.*1.74, cf. Gal.19.99. II. *the pubes*, Hp.*Mul.*1.60. 2. *instep* of the foot, Hsch.

**ἐπικτέρεα**· ἐντάφια, Hsch. (sed cf. κτέρεα).

**ἐπικτερεΐζω**, *perform funeral rites over*, Nonn.*D.*47.241.

**ἐπίκτημα**, ατος, τό, *property held in a foreign country*, Ammon. *Diff.*p.83 V., Ptol.Ascal.p.399 H. II. *acquisition, improvement*, τὸ τῆς τέχνης ἐ. *PMasp.*20.18 (vi A.D.).

⊕ **ἐπικτηνίτης** [νῑ], ὁ, (κτῆνος) *drover*, *PFlor.*126.13 (iii A.D.), *Gloss.*

**ἐπί-κτησις**, εως, ἡ, *further acquisition, fresh gain*, S.*Ph.*1344; χρημάτων Arist.*HA*522ᵃ18: pl., D.H.9.53. -κτητικός, ή, όν, *acquisitive*, Nech.ap.Vett.Val.278.36. -κτητος, ον, *gained besides* or *in addition*, ἐ. γῆ *acquired* land, which was formerly under water, as the Delta of Egypt, Hdt.2.5, cf. 10; property *added to one's hereditary property*, Pl.*Lg.*924a, cf. Lycurg.48; ἐ. γυνὴ *a foreign* wife (like ἐπακτός), or *newly acquired*, Hdt.3.3; ἐ. φίλοι *newly acquired* friends, opp. ἀρχαῖοι, X.*Ages.*1.36; ἐ. δόξα, opp. ἔμφυτος ἐπιθυμία, *acquired* perception, Pl.*Phdr.*237d; τὰ ἐ., opp. τὰ φύσει ὄντα, Id.*R.*618d; opp. σύμφυτα, Arist.*GA*721ᵇ30; τὸ αὐτοφυὲς τοῦ ἐ. αἱρετώτερον Id. *Rh.*1365ᵃ29; γίνεται.. ἐξ ἐπικτήτου, of an *acquired* deformity, Paul. Aeg.6.29; τὰ ἐ. *property acquired after* a certain date, Edict.Aug. in *Notiz.Arch.*4.21, *PGnom.*126 (ii A.D.). Adv. -τως Prisc.Lyd.21.15.

**ἐπικτίζω**, *found in addition* or *anew*, Str.14.1.12, 10.1.10 (Pass.). II. *found in* or *among*, πόλεις ἀγρίοις ἔθνεσι Plu.2.328b codd.

**ἐπικτόλωμα**· ἐπικορύφωμα, Hsch.

**ἐπικτόριον**, τό, *lid* of a pot, Hsch. (leg. ἐπικύθριον, cf. χύτρα).

**ἐπικτός**, = ἐφικτός, prob. cj. for ἑρκτός in Arr.*Ind.*20.11.

**ἐπικτῠπέω**, aor. 1 (v. infr.): aor. 2 ἐπέκτῠπον A.R.1.1136:—*make a noise upon*, τοῖν ποδοῖν ἐπικτυπῶν *stamp on the ground* with the feet, Ar.*Ec.*483; σάκεα ξιφέεσσιν ἐ. *clashed on* their shields with.., A.R. l.c.; σακέεσσιν ἐ. Id.2.1081; *strike*, ἄντυγα Χηλαῖς Nonn.*D.*38.397: abs., *re-echo, respond*, πᾶς δ' ἐπεκτύπησ' Ὄλυμπος Ar.*Av.*780; of a chorus, Plb.30.22.9.

**ἐπικῡδ-αίνομαι**, *exult in*, τινί D.C.71.2. ⊕ -ής, ές, only in Comp. -έστερος (unless the Posit. is to be restored in Sapph.*Supp.*8.11), *glorious, distinguished*, X.*HG*5.1.36; *brilliant, successful*, -έστερα τὰ πράγματα ἐποίησεν Isoc.4.139; -έστεραι ἐλπίδες Plb.16.4.3; and of persons, -έστερος ταῖς ἐλπίσι *more sanguine*, Id.5.69.11, cf. Ph.1. 252, al., Onos.23.2. Adv. Comp. -εστέρως, ἀγωνίζεσθαι Plb.5.23. 2. -ιάω, *vaunt oneself*, τινί A.R.4.383 (nisi leg. ἢ ἔπι κυδιάεις).

**ἐπικυ-έω**, = ἐπικυΐσκομαι, Hp.*Epid.*5.11, Arist.*HA*585ᵃ17:—Pass., ib.11. II. simply, *become pregnant again*, *BGU*1058.30 (i B.C.), al. -ημα, ατος, τό, *a superfetation*, Hp.*Superf.*1, Arist.*GA*773ᵇ 7. -ησις, εως, ἡ, *superfetation*, Id.*Fr.*259, 260 Bonitz; title of treatise by Hp. -ΐσκομαι, *become doubly pregnant*, i.e. *pregnant again before the first foetus is born*, Hdt.3.108, Hp.*Superf.*1, Arist. *GA*773ᵇ28.

**ἐπικυκλ-έω**, intr., *come round in turn upon*, ἐπὶ πῆμα καὶ χαρὰ πᾶσι κυκλοῦσι S.*Tr.*130:—Pass., D.H.*Rh.*10.17. -ησις, εως, ἡ, *return in a cycle*, Alex.Aphr.*de An.*30.26. -ίδιος, epith. of Zeus, Hsch. -ιος, ον, *circular*: ἐ. (sc. πλακοῦς), ὁ, *a round Sicilian cake*, Epich.26 codd. Ath.; of a bandage, *in a circle*, Gal.18(1).820. -ος, ὁ, Astron., *epicycle*, Plu.2.1028b, Theo Sm.p.162 H., Ptol.*Alm.*3.3, Iamb.*VP*6.31 (pl.), etc. -όω, *circle round*, τὸν δῆμον Lyd.*Ost.*8.

**ἐπικῠλίδες**, ίδων, αἱ, *upper eyelids*, Poll.2.66; cf. κύλα.

**ἐπικῠλίκειος** or -ίκιος, ον, *said* or *done over* one's *cups*, λόγοι Ath. 1.2a, Plu.2.1146d, cf. D.L.4.42, Poll.6.108.

**ἐπικῠλινδέω** or -κυλίω (Plb.3.53.4, D.S.19.19), fut. -κυλίσω [ῐ]:—*roll down upon*, πέτρους ἐπί τινας X.*HG*3.5.20; τοῖς ὁδοιποροῦσι πέτρας D.S. l.c., cf. Plb. l.c.:—Pass., τὰ τμήματα τοῦ πελάγους -ισθέντα Ph.2.109; τόκων τόκοις -κυλισθέντων interest *being heaped on* interest, Plu.2.831e; τὸ σιτίον εἰς τὸν στόμαχον -ινδεῖσθαι *is slipped into..*, ib.699c; -ισθεῖσα *overlaying* the infant, Sor.1.106. 2. Pass., *to be applied by rolling*, ταῖς σαρξί Gal.11.757. 3. Pass., *degenerate*, εἰς χρόνια πάθη Id.19.560: metaph., [νοήσεις] δι' ἀρρωστίαν -ούμεναι καὶ ἐπιτρέχουσαι τοῖς εἴδεσιν Dam.*Pr.*88. 4. intr., *roll on*, κύματα Ps.-Luc.*Philopatr.*3.

**ἐπικυλινδρόομαι**, Pass., *to be flattened by rollers*, Thphr.*CP*5.6.7.

**ἐπικύλιον** [ῠ], τό, *upper eyelid* (cf. ἐπικυλίδες), Eust.1951.20.

**ἐπικυλισμός**, ὁ, *turning round*, Sor.2.64, Sm.*Pr.*2.9, Thd.*Pr.*2.15.

**ἐπικυλλόω**, *mould* a cake of dough, prob. for ἐπεκώλυσεν, Hsch.

**ἐπικύλλωμα**, ατος, τό, *lameness*, Eust.1599.13.

**ἐπικῡμ-αίνω**, *flow in waves over*, τῇ θαλάττῃ Philostr.*Im.*2.17: metaph., of hair, ὤμοις καὶ νώτοις Hld.3.4; τοῖς ἱππεῦσιν ἐ. ἡ φάλαγξ Plu.*Alex.*33:—Pass., ὥσπερ ἐν βυθῷ ἄνθρωπος ἐ. Herm.ap.Stob.1.49.45. II. trans., *cause to rise in waves*, τὴν θάλασσαν J.*AJ*4.3.2. **-ατίζω**, *float upon the waves*, Ph.1.455, Ael.*Ep.*18: metaph., -ίζουσα φορὰ τῶν πραγμάτων (cf. foreg.), Ph.1.553; also of persons, ὑπόπτερος ἐ. Id.2.300; of a runner, -ίζων αἴρεται Philostr.*Her.*2.3:—Pass., τοὺς διὰ φιλοκερδίαν τὸν ἅπαντα βίον -ομένους Phld.*Mort.*33; opp. ἐν τῇ γῇ διατρίβειν, Id.*Rh.*2.55S. **-άτωσις** [ᾰ], εως, ἡ, *fluctuation*, τῶν μεταβολῶν M.Ant.9.28 (pl.).

**ἐπικυνέω**, *kiss on the lips*, *EM*361.11.

**ἐπικύπτω**, pf. (v. infr.):—*bend oneself over, stoop over, bow down*, Hp.*Art.*52, Ar.*Th.*239; ὀρθὸς ἕστηκεν, μικρὸν ἐπικύπτων Arist.*HA* 522b18; of the horn of the moon, Thphr.*Sign.*27; ἐ. ἐπί τι *stoop down* to get something, X.*Cyr.*2.3.18; ἐ. ἐς βιβλίον *pore over* a book, Luc.*Herm.*2; *lean upon*, τινί Id.*DMort.*6.2; ἐ. τῷ συνεδρίῳ *bend over towards* it, Id.*JTr.*11: pf. part. ἐπικεκῡφώς *habitually stooping*, Anaxandr.37.

**ἐπικύρβιος**, ον, *registered on* κύρβεις, ἐνέχυρα *IG*12(7).58.5 (Amorgos).

**ἐπικῡρόω**, *confirm, sanction, ratify*, τὴν γνώμην Th.3.71, cf. S.*El.* 793, X.*An.*3.2.32, D.15.34, *SIG*167.20, etc.: c. inf., τίνες..λόγοι καθεῖλον ἡμᾶς κἀπεκύρωσαν θανεῖν; E.*Or.*862:—Pass., πρίν τι ἐπικυρωθῆναι Th.5.45; ἐπικυρωθέντων τῶν νόμων Arist.*Ath.*37.1, cf. *Sammelb.*1161.17 (i B.C.).

**ἐπίκυρτ-ος**, ον, *arched*, S.*Ichn.*294; *round-shouldered*, Πλάτωνος τὸ ἐ. Plu.2.53c. **-όω**, *bend forward*, κάρηνα Hes.*Sc.*234:—Pass., *to be arched*, Luc.*Am.*14.

**ἐπικύρω** [ῡ], Ep. impf. ἐπίκῡρον, Ep. aor. 1 ἐπέκυρσα and ἐπεκύρησα [ῠ] (v. infr.):—*light upon, fall in with*, c. dat., μεγάλῳ ἐπὶ σώματι κύρσας Il.3.23; ἱεροῖσιν ἐπ' αἰθομένοισι κυρήσας Hes.*Op.*755; αἰὲν ἐπ' αὐχένι κῦρε φαεινοῦ δουρὸς ἀκωκῇ (v.l. ἀκωκήν) *kept* always *touching* his neck with.., Il.23.821; ἐπὶ ξίφος αὐχένι κύρσαι *let* his sword *touch* her neck, Q.S.13.394; ἐ. μετατροπίαις Pi.*P.*10.21: c. gen., *meet with, obtain*, ἐπικύρσαις ἀφθόνων ἀστῶν Id.*O.*6.7; μεγάλας ἀγαθᾶς τε..βιοτᾶς ἐπεκύρσαμεν A.*Pers.*853, cf. A.R.3.342.

**ἐπικύρ-ωσις** [ῡ], εως, ἡ, *ratification, confirmation*, χειροτονίας Arist.*Ath.*41.3, cf. D.H.9.51, Just.*Nov.*42.1.1. **-ωτέον**, *one must confirm*, τινὶ τὴν βασιλείαν dub. in J.*AJ*17.9.7.

**ἐπικυστίς**, ίδος, ἡ, = ἐφήβιον, *Gloss.*

**ἐπίκῡφος**, ον, *bent over, crooked*, Lxx 3*Ma.*4.5, Sch.Opp.*H.*1.342, Suid. (Comp.).

**ἐπικύψ** (-κύς cod.)· ἐπικύψας, Hsch.

**ἐπικυψέλιος**, ὁ, (κυψέλη) *guard of beehives*, Πάν *AP*9.226 (Zon.).

**ἐπίκυψις**, εως, ἡ, of the head, *stooping*, Hp.*Epid.*2.1.8, Antyll. and Heliod.ap.Orib.44.8.4 (pl.); *bending forward*, Sor.1.93, prob. cj. in Ruf.*Sat.Gon.*34 (pl.).

**ἐπικωθωνίζομαι**, *go on drinking*, Critias 59 D.

* **ἐπικωκύω**, *lament over*, πατρὸς δαῖτα S.*El.*283; τὸν υἱόν ib.805: abs., Hld.1.13.

**ἐπικωλύω**, *hinder, check*, ἀλλήλους X.*Oec.*8.4; τίς..μ' οὑπικωλύσων τάδε; S.*Ph.*1242; τὸ ἔργον *IG*7.3073.35 (Lebad.); τὸν ἐργώνην ib.45: abs., *to be a hindrance*, Th.6.17:—Pass., *PPetr.*3p.109 (iii B.C.), etc.

**ἐπικωμ-άζω**, *rush on* or *in with a party of revellers*, Plb.26.1.4, Call.*Ep.*43: generally, *make a riotous assault*, ἐπί τινα Ar.*Ach.*982; τινί Men.881; *go careering about*, εἰς τὰς πόλεις Pl.*Lg.*950a; ἐπὶ τὴν οἰκίαν τινός Plu.2.772f: metaph., ἀτύχημα Σπαρτιάταις -εκώμασεν Chor. in *Jahrb.*9.177:—Pass., *to be visited by a reveller*, Plu.*Pyrrh.* 13. **-ασία**, ἡ, *revelling*, *Gloss.* **-αστής**, οῦ, ὁ, *reveller*, Id.

**ἐπικωμ-ιαστικός**, ή, όν, = ἐγκωμ- (q.v.), Arg.Theoc.3. Adv. -κῶς Sch.Pi.*N.*8.1. **-ιος**, α, ον, *of, at*, or *for a* κῶμος or *festal procession*, ὄψ, ὕμνος, Pi.*P.*10.6, *N.*8.50; epith. of Apollo, *IGRom.*4.1539 (Erythrae); ἐπικώμια, τά, = ἐγκώμια, *praises*, Pi.*N.*6.32: sg., -κώμιον *revel*, *Gloss.* * **-ος**, ον, *revelling*, Aristias 3 (L.Dind. for ἐπίκωπος); εἰς οἰκίαν ἐμβαλεῖν ἐ. Plu.2.128d; ἐ. φοιτᾶν Alciphr.1.37.

**ἐπικωμῳδέω**, *make a jest of, caricature*, Pl.*Ap.*31d.

**ἐπικωπ-αστήρ**, ῆρος, ὁ, = sq., *EM*360.44. **-ητήρ**, ῆρος, ὁ, = τροπωτήρ, Hsch. **-ος**, ον, *at the oar, rower*, Men.Eph.ap.J.*AJ*9.14.2. 2. of a boat, *furnished with oars*, κέρκουρος Moschio ap.Ath.5.208f, cf. D.H.3.44, D.S.3.40; *phaselus epicopus, dispatch*-boat, Cic.*Att.*14.16.1, cf. 5.11.4. 3. of a weapon, *up to the hilt, through and through*, Ar.*Ach.*231 (lyr.); cf. ἐπίκωμος.

**ἐπιλᾰβή**, ἡ, *taking hold of, grasping*, πέπλων τ' ἐπιλαβὰς ἐμῶν A.*Supp.*432 (lyr.). 2. *handle, hold*, ἐ. ἔχειν οὐδεμίαν Hp.*Art.*47.

**ἐπιλαγχάνω**, pf. (v. infr. II):—*succeed* another in an office on a vacancy, οὔτε λαχὼν οὔτ' ἐπιλαχών Aeschin.3.62, D.58.29; ἐ. τινὶ βουλῆς *succeed* him in the Council, Pl.Com.167, cf. 166.5. 2. *obtain, have allotted to one*, εὐδαιμονίας Ph.1.629, al. II. *fall to one's lot next*, ἐπιλέλογχε πύματον..γῆρας S.*OC*1235 (lyr.); ἐπιλαχόντα τινὶ πράγματα *PMon.*6.50, cf. 7.45 (vi A.D.).

**ἐπιλᾰδόν**, Adv., = ἰλαδόν, *in troops*, D.P.763.

**ἐπιλάζυμαι**, *hold tight, stop*, ἐ. στόμα, i.e. to be silent, E.*Andr.* 250.—Poet. word for ἐπιλαμβάνω.

**ἐπιλαΐς**, ΐδος, ἡ, name of a bird (v.l. ὑπολαΐς), Arist.*HA*592b22.

**ἐπίλακκος**, ον, *forming a hollow*, τὸ ἐ. μέρος, = βρόχθος, Sch.Theoc. 3.54.

* **ἐπιλᾰλ-έω**, *interrupt in speaking*, Sm.*Ps.*122(123).4. 2. *charm* (v.l. ἐπᾴδω), Lxx *Je.*8.17. 3. Pass., *to be said of..*, ἀλόγοις -εῖται Eust.773.26. **-ημα**, ατος, τό, *incantation*, *PMag.Lond.*121.290.

* **ἐπιλαμβάνω**, *take* or *get besides*, ἐπὶ τοῖς πεντήκοντα ταλάντοις ἑκατόν Arist.*Pol.*1259a28: c. gen. partit., ἐ. τοῦ χρόνου *take a little more* time, M.Ant.1.17; τῆς ἀρχῆς Paus.9.14.5. 2. simply, *take, receive*, *PEleph.*10.1 (iii B.C.), *OGI*179.18 (Egypt, i B.C.), etc. II. *lay hold of, seize, attack*, as a disease, Hdt.8.115, Hp.*Aph.*6.51, Th.2.51; of an enemy, Luc.*Nav.*36:—Pass., ἐπείληπται νόσῳ S.*Ant.*732; τὴν αἴσθησιν ἐπιληφθεὶς *becoming unconscious*, Plu.*Flam.*6; ἐπελήφθη *had an epileptic fit*, Gal.11:859. b. of events, *overtake, surprise*, μή.. χειμὼν τὴν φυλακὴν ἐπιλάβοι Th.4.27; νυκτὸς ἐπιλαβούσης τὸ ἔργον ib. 96; ταχὺ ἐπιλαβὸν γῆρας Pl.*Epin.*974a: impers., ἐπιλαμβάνει, c. acc. et inf., *it befalls* one *that..*, Paus.6.22.4, 7.21.1. 2. *attain to, come within reach of, reach*, X.*An.*6.5.6; ἔτη ὀκτὼ ἐ. πολέμου *live over* eight years, Th.4.133; ἡμέρας ἑπτακαίδεκα τῆς ἑβδόμης ὑπατείας Plu.*Mar.* 46: c. gen. partit., ἐ. τετάρτου μηνός *arrive at*, of the foetus, Arist.*HA* 583b22 (but ἐ. τοῦ ἑνδεκάτου μηνός, of the mother, ib.584a37); ὥστε καὶ τοῦ χειμῶνος ἐ. Thphr.*HP*1.9.6. 3. *seize, stop*, esp. by pressure, τὴν ῥῖνα Ar.*Pl.*703; ἐ. τὸ κλύσμα τῆς ὀπίσω ὁδοῦ Hdt.2.87; ἐ. τὸ ὕδωρ *stop* the water-clock in court, Lys.23.4, Is.3.76; τὸν αὐλίσκον Arist.*Ath.*67.3, cf. *Pr.*866b13, Plb.10.44.12; τὸ στόμα τοῖς ἐπικαλύμμασιν Arist.*HA*527b21. 4. *occupy* space, μηδὲν τῶν τῆς πόλεως.. οἰκοδομήμασι ἐ. Pl.*Lg.*779c (Med.); πλείω τόπον Arist.*Cael.*305b19; πλατύτερον τόπον Plu.*Cat.Ma.*5: metaph., πολὺν χῶρον ἐ. *get over* much ground, *traverse* it rapidly, Theoc.13.65. 5. c. gen., *undertake*, τῆς κινήσεως, τῆς νήξεως, Ael.*NA*5.18, 13.19. 6. c. dat., *assist*, App.*BC*4.96 (nisi leg. ⟨συν⟩επιλ.). 7. intr., *succeed, follow*, Arist.*Pr.*860a7. 8. of food or drink, *take extra*, οἰνάριον Plu.*Cat. Ma.*1; *take after* other food, Dsc.2.112. III. Med. (with pf. ἐπείλημμαι Pl.*Cra.*396d, D.3.27), *hold oneself on by, lay hold of*, c. gen., τῶν νεῶν Hdt.6.113, Th.4.14, etc.; τῶν ἀφλάστων νεὸς Hdt. 6.114; τῶν ἐπισπαστήρων ib.91; τῆς ἴτυος X.*An.*4.7.12; τῶν ἁμαξῶν Plu.*Oth.*3; ὅτου ἐπιλάβοιτο τὰ δρέπανα whomsoever the scythes *caught*, X.*Cyr.*7.1.31; ἐπιλαμβάνεταί μου τῆς χειρὸς τῇ δεξιᾷ Pl.*Prt.*335c; ἐπιλαβόμενός [τινος] τῇ χειρί D.21.60; τῶν τριχῶν by the hair, Aeschin.3.150; μὴ 'πιλαμβάνου *hold* me not! E.*Ph.* 896. 2. *attack*, τινός X.*HG*4.2.22; esp. with words, Pl.*Phdr.* 236b; of things, τῆς θερμασίας πόρων -ομένης Epicur.*Ep.*2p.52U.; of diseases, Luc.*Nigr.*29. 3. *make a seizure of, arrest*, τῶν παίδων D.33.9; *seize* goods in default of payment, Id.21.133. b. *lay hands on in assertion of a claim*, Pl.*Lg.*954c, *POxy.*1707.15 (iii A.D.), etc. 4. *lay hold of, get, obtain*, προστάτεω a chief, Hdt.1.127; προφάσιος ἔς τινα Id.3.36, cf. 6.49; δυνάμιος Id.9.99; καιροῦ Ar.*Lys.* 596; ἐξουσίας, γαλήνης, Pl.*R.*360d, *Plt.*273a, cf. *PTeb.*48.20 (ii B.C.), etc.; ἐ. λογισμῷ, Lat. *ratione assequi*, Pl.*Phd.*79a. 5. of Place, *reach*, δασέος Arist.*HA*629b15; τῶν ὀρῶν Plu.*Ant.*41: metaph., of a state or condition, ἐρημίας ἐπειλημμένοι *having found* an empty field, i.e. an absence of all competitors, D.3.27, cf. Arist.*Pol.*1305b16. 6. *attempt*, πράξεων μεγάλων Plu.*Mar.*7. b. c. inf., *undertake*, γεωργεῖν *IG*7.2446 (Thebes). 7. *touch on*, τινός Pl.*R.*449d. 8. *take up, interrupt* in speaking, Id.*Grg.*506b, *Smp.*214e; *object to*, τοῦ ψηφίσματος X.*HG*2.1.32; ἐ. ὅτι.. *object* that.., Pl.*R.*490c. 9. rarely c. acc., *seize*, τὰς Ἀθήνας (leg. λήψονται) Lycurg.84.

**ἐπιλαμπάδιον**, τό, a surgical instrument used as a *trocar*, *Mulomed. Chironis* 64.

**ἐπίλαμπρ-ος**, ον, *brilliant, illustrious*, Artem.3.61, Sch.Arat.156. **-ύνω**, *make splendid, adorn*, τὴν οἰκίαν, τὸν οἶκον, Phld.*Piet.*74, Plu.*Lys.*30; γένος τιμαῖς D.H.6.41. 2. of sound, *make loud and clear, raise high*, τὸν ἦχον Id.*Comp.*14; τὴν φωνήν, of frogs, Plu.2.912c.

**ἐπίλαμπτος**, ον, Ion. for ἐπίληπτος.

**ἐπι-λάμπω**, *shine after* or *thereupon*, ἠέλιος δ' ἐπέλαμψε *thereupon* the sun *shone forth*, Il.17.650; of the moon, *h.Merc.*141, Plu.2.944d, etc.; ὥς σφι ἡμέρη ἐπέλαμψε Hdt.8.14, cf. 3.135; ἡμέρης ἐπιλαμψάσης when day *had fully come*, Id.7.13; also ἔαρος ἐπιλάμψαντος Id.8. 130. 2. *shine upon* (a place), abs., Hp.*Aër.*6, X.*Cyn.*8.1: c. dat., φλόγες ἐ. ἄκροις τοῖς κέρασι Plu.*Fab.*6; ὁ ἥλιος ἐπέλαμπε τῷ ἔργῳ Id.*Arat.*22, cf. Theo Sm.p.121 H.: metaph., οὗρος..ἐπίλαμψον ἐμῷ ἔρωτι, Κύπρι *AP*5.16 (Gaet.); τοῖς ἀπελπίζουσιν ἐ. *bring* them *new light*, *OGI*194.20 (Egypt, i B.C.), cf. ib.669.7 (ibid., i A.D.). II. trans., *make to shine*, μόχθοι νεότατ' ἐπέλαμψαν μυρίοι (so L.Dind. for μυρίοις) Pi.*Fr.*172 (dub. l.); τὸ ἀγαθὸν πᾶσιν ἐ. τοῖς νοητοῖς ἀλήθειαν Plot.4.7. 10:—Pass., *shine upon*, λόφῳ -ελάμπετο πήληξ A.R.2.920. 2. *illumine*, κολώνας ib.164. **-λαμψις**, εως, ἡ, *shining*, of heavenly bodies, Ph.1.24, al.; ἀστραπῶν Id.2.7 (pl.); *illumination*, Iamb.*Myst.* 5.26, also cj. for ἔκλ. in Hp.*Epid.*6.1.4.

**ἐπιλανθάνω**, v. ἐπιλήθω.

**ἐπιλάρκισμα**, ατος, τό, (λάρκος) *cover of a basket*, *EM*361.22.

**ἐπίλαρχ-ης**, ου, ὁ, *commander of an* ἐπιλαρχία, *PPetr.*3p.21 (iii B.C.). **-ία**, ἡ, *double* ἴλη, i.e. *two* ἶλαι or 128 *horse*, Ascl.*Tact.*7. 11, Arr.*Tact.*18.2.

**ἐπίλᾱσις**, Dor. for ἐπίλησις.

**ἐπιλαφύσσω**, *devour in addition*, Tim.Gaz.*Epit.*103.29.

**ἐπιλε-αίνω**, *smooth over*, Plu.2.74d; τὰ ἄκρα τῶν βλεφάρων, of light sleep, Hld.2.16: metaph., ἐπιλεήνας τὴν Ξέρξεω γνώμην, i.e. *making* it *plausible*, Hdt.7.10; τὸ φαῦλον καὶ ἀγεννὲς τῶν διηγημάτων Jul.*Or.*3.111d. II. *chew*, τροφήν Ph.1.63, al.: metaph., λόγον ib.

180. **-ανσις**, εως, ἡ, *chewing small, rumination*, τροφῆς ib.254: metaph., ἡδονῶν ib.115 (pl.).

**ἐπιλέγδην**, Adv. *by selection*, Eust.955.8.

**ἐπίλεγμα**, ατος, τό, *extract* from a document, *PGrenf.*1.37.15 (ii B.C.).

⊕ **ἐπιλέγω**, *say in connexion with* an action, etc., Hdt.2.35,64, etc.; ποιεῖν τι καὶ ἐπιλέγειν *say while* or *after* doing it, Id.4.65; παίζουσιν ἐπιλέγοντες Id.5.4; ἐ. λόγον τόνδε, ὡς.. Id.2.156,8.49; ἐξηπάτων.. ἐπιλέγων τοιαυτί Ar.*Eq.*418; ἐ. τεκμήρια τὴν ἄλλην αὐτοῦ..παρανομίαν *citing* it as proof, Th.6.28, cf. Alciphr.3.56. 2. *say besides*, ἑκάστῳ "σοὶ μέν κτλ." X.*Cyr.*1.3.7, cf. Arist.*Rh.*1395ᵃ27, Ph.1.512; τὴν αἰτίαν ἐ. Arist.*Rh.*1417ᵃ28:—Med., *repeat*, D.H.*Rh.*11.5:—Pass., [τὰ] ἐπιλεγόμενα Arist.*Rh.*1394ᵃ13. 3. *call by name*, Hdt.5.70; ἐπέλεγον δὲ κιθαρῳδικούς (sc. νόμους) Pl.*Lg.*700b:—Med., A.*Supp.*49 (lyr.):—Pass., *to be surnamed*, J.*AJ*13.10.4. 4. *utter, pronounce* a spell (cf. ἐπεῖπον), ῥῆσιν μυστικὴν Ath.11.496b; ῥῆσίν τινα μακρὰν Luc.*Nec.* 7; τοὺς ἀνθρώπους ἐπιλέγειν τῷ λοιμῷ "φεῦγ' ἐς κόρακας" Arist.*Fr.* 496, cf. *Pr.*926ᵇ23, *EN*1109ᵇ11. 5. *attribute*, τινὶ τὸ καλόν, τὸ χρήσιμον, Id.*Pol.*1323ᵇ12; ἐ. τοῖς εὖ ἔχουσιν ἔργοις, ὅτι.. Id.*EN*1106ᵇ 10. 6. *say against* one, App.*BC*3.18. II. *pick out, select*, Hdt. 3.44,81; ἔκ τινων πεζούς Wilcken*Chr.*11 *A* 35 (ii B.C.):—freq. in Med., τῶν Βαβυλωνίων ἐπελέξατο *he chose him* certain of the Babylonians, Hdt.3.157, cf.6.73, Th.7.19, Arist.*Fr.*151, Wilcken*Chr.*11 *A* 49 (ii B.C.), D.S.3.74:—Pass., ἐπιλελεγμένοι or ἐπειλεγμένοι *chosen men*, X.*Cyr.*3.3.41, Isoc.4.146, *POxy.*1210.4 (i B.C.), etc.; οἱ ἐπιλεγέντες *SIG*577.72 (Milet., iii/ii B.C.). III. Med., *think upon, think over*, ταῦτα Hdt.1.78,2.120, al., cf. Ant.Lib.5.4; μὴ ἐ. not *to care*, Hdt. 7.236, al.; οὐδαμὰ ἐ. μή κοτε.. *to have* no *fear* lest.., Id.3.65, cf. 7. 149: c. inf., πᾶν ἐπιλεγόμενος πείσεσθαι *expecting*.., Id.7.49, cf. 52: rare in Trag., μηδ' ἐπιλεχθῇς 'Αγαμεμνονίαν εἶναί μ' ἄλοχον *deem* me not to be.., A.*Ag.*1498 (anap.). 2. in Hdt. also, *con over, read*, τὸ βυβλίον, τὰ γράμματα, 1.124,125, 2.125, al., cf. Paus.1.12.3, al., Hld.4.8: so in Act., Them.*Or.*11.153a. 3. *recount*, in speaking, τὴν αἰσχύνην καὶ τὸν κίνδυνον D.H.9.57.

**ἐπιλείβω**, also **ἐπιλλ-**, *pour* wine *over* a thing, ἐπὶ δ' αἴθοπα οἶνον λεῖβε Il.1.462; ἐπιλλείβειν ἱεροῖσιν A.R.1.1133: abs., ἀνιστάμενοι δ' ἐπέλειβον Od.3.341.

**ἐπίλειμμα**, ατος, τό, αἰθέρος Sch.Arat.786 (pl., v.l. ἐπιλήμματα, leg. πιλήματα).

**ἐπίλειος**, ον, = ἐπίλεπτος, Steph. *in Gal.*1.272 D.

**ἐπιλειόω**, *smooth off, shave smooth*, τὸ γένειον D.C.48.34 (Med.).

**ἐπιλείπω**, *leave behind*, ἐπὶ δὲ πλεῖον ἐλέλειπτο Od.8.475, cf. X.*An.* 1.8.18 codd.:—Med., *leave behind*, of gleanings, v.l. in Lxx *Ob.*1.5:—Pass., c. gen., *fall short of*, παντὸς ἀριθμοῦ Pl.*Epin.*978b: c. dat., τῇ δυνάμει, τῇ οὐσίᾳ, Arist.*Ath.*20.2, 27.4. 2. *leave untouched*, ὡς οὔτ' ἂν τῶν ἐμῶν ἐπιλίποιμι οὐδὲν οὔτε τῶν φίλων Pl.*Prt.*310e: c. part., μυρία ἐ. λέγων Id.*Phlb.*26b, cf. 52d. II. of things, *fail* one, c. acc. pers., ἥβην.., ἤ μ' ἐπιλείπει Thgn.1131; ὕδωρ [μιν] ἐπέλιπε Hdt.7.21, cf. 2. 174; so τῶν ὄμβρων ἐπιλιπόντων αὐτούς (sc. τοὺς ποταμούς) Id.2.25; γλαῦκες ὑμᾶς οὔποτ' ἐπιλείψουσι Ar.*Av.*1106; ἐπειδὰν αὐτοὺς ἐπιλίπωσιν ἐλπίδες Th.5.103: c. inf., [ὁ νόμος] ἐμοὶ μόνῳ ἐπέλιπε μὴ ὠφελῆσαι Antipho 5.17; ἐπιλίποι ἂν ἡμᾶς ὁ χρόνος time would *fail* me, Isoc.1.11, cf. Lys.12.1, *Ep.Hebr.*11.32; τὸ ὕδωρ ἡμᾶς ἐ. Isoc.15.320; ἐπιλείψει με λέγονθ' ἡ ἡμέρα D.18.296: later, c. dat., Plu.*Cic.*42, Ael.*NA*8. 17. 2. Hdt., freq. of rivers, ἐ. τὸ ῥέεθρον *leave* their stream *unfilled, run dry*, Hdt.7.43,58, al.; without ῥέεθρον, *fail, run dry*, ib. 127; τὰς κρήνας καὶ τὰ φρέατ' ἐπιλείπειν πέφυκεν D.14.30. 3. generally, *fail, be wanting*, ἵνα μὴ ἐπιλίπῃ κατεσθιόμενα Hdt.3.108; σῖτος ἐπιλιπὼν *a deficiency* of it, Th.3.20 codd.; τὰ ἐπιτήδεια ἐ. X.*An.*4.7.1; ὥστε τὸν λόγον μηδέποτε ἐ. Pl.*Prt.*334e; opp. περιγίγνεσθαι, Ar.*Pl.* 554: c. gen., *fall short*, σπουδῆς οὐδὲν ἐ. *Michel* 332.9 (Odessus).

**ἐπιλείχω**, *lick over, lick*, *Ev.Luc.*16.21.

**ἐπίλειψις**, εως, ἡ, *deficiency, lack*, ὀρνίθων Th.2.50; τῆς δυνάμεως Plu.2.695d; τελῶν *CIG*2695*b* (Mylasa).

⊕ **ἐπιλεκτ-άρχης**, ου, ὁ, *commander of a picked band*, Plu.*Arat.*32:—hence **-αρχέω**, *SIG*421.18 (Aetolia, iii B.C.). **-έον**, *one must select*, τόπους Ath.Med.ap.Orib.*inc.*23.8; χῆνας *Gp.*14.22.1; *one must approve*, Just.*Nov.*6.5. **-ης**, ου, ὁ, *collector*, τῶν ἐθνικῶν Eust.367. 23. ⊕ **-ος**, ον, *chosen*, τὸ ἐ. γένος 'Ισραήλ Ph.1.242; ξύλα πρὸς εὐωδίαν ἐ. Ael.*VH*5.6; ἐ. σμύρνα *choice*, J.*AJ*3.8.3; εἰκασίαι Callix.2. 2. esp. of soldiers, οἱ ἐπίλεκτοι X.*An.*3.4.43, *HG*5.3.23, *IG*2².680.12, *IPE*1².352.39 (Cherson.); in Egypt, *OGI*731 (ii B.C.), *UPZ*110.21 (ii B.C.). b. = ἔκτακτος (q.v.), Arr.*Tact.*10.4. c. = Lat. *extraordinarii*, Plb.6.26.6, etc. 2. Adv. **-τως**, = λογάδην, Sch.Th.4.4.

**ἐπιλελογισμένως**, Adv., (ἐπιλογίζομαι) *with consideration*, Phld. *Rh.*1.218 S.

**ἐπίλεξις**, εως, ἡ, *choice, selection*, App.*BC*3.5.

**ἐπίλεπτ-ος**, ον, *somewhat light*, γῆ *Gp.*2.21.3; σιδήρια Arr.*Alan.* 16. **-ουργέω**, *refine still further*, Dam.*Pr.*354, cf. 341 (v.l. **ἐπιλεπτολογέω**). **-ύνω**, *smear over with a thin coat*, τιτάνῳ Poll.7. 124. 2. *sift finely*, Hsch. s.v. ἐπέσηθον.

**ἐπιλέπω**, *strip of bark*, ὄζον ἐ. σιδήρῳ *h.Merc.*109.

**ἐπιλευκ-αίνω**, *to be whitish*, Arist.*PA*676ᵃ32; of a plant, τὴν χρόαν ξανθὸς ἐπιλευκαίνων Thphr.*HP*3.12.9, etc. **-ία**, ἡ, = λεύκη, *leprosy*, Plu.2.670f. **-ος**, ον, *white on the surface, whitish*, Thphr.*HP*3.7.5.

**ἐπιλεύσσω**, *look towards* or *at*, τόσσον τίς τ' ἐπιλεύσσει one can only *see* so far *before* one, Il.3.12.

**ἐπιλήγω**, *end in* or *at*, αἰγιαλῷ J.*BJ*3.9.3, cf. 3.10.7; τῇ τοπαρχίᾳ prob. l., ib.3.3.4.

**ἐπιλήθ-ης**, ες, v.l. for sq., Od.4.221. **-ος**, ον, *causing to forget*, c. gen., φάρμακον.., νηπενθές τ' ἄχολόν τε κακῶν ἐπίληθον ἁπάντων Od.4.221 (Aristarch.; ἐπιλῆθον Ptol.Ascal.); ἴυγγα δέους ἐπίληθον παντός Ael.*NA*15.19, cf. 4.41. ⊕ **-ω**, *cause to forget*, ὁ γάρ τ' [ὕπνος] ἐπέλησεν ἁπάντων *laps one in forgetfulness* of all, Od.20.85; ἡδονὴ σφέας ἐπιλήθουσα τῶν πάρος Aret.*CD*2.12; ἐπιλήσει σε ἀφροδισίων Philostr.*Ep.*68:—Pass., *to be forgotten*, in pf. part. ἐπιλελησμένος Lxx *Is.*23.16, *Ev.Luc.*12.6: fut. -λησθήσομαι Lxx *Wi.*2.4. II. Med., **ἐπιλανθάνομαι**, or more commonly **ἐπιλήθομαι**, Aeol. and Dor. **-λᾱθ-** Alc.*Supp.*25.6, S.*El.*146 (lyr.), fut. -λήσομαι: aor. 2 -ελαθόμην Pl.*Ap.*17a: late aor. 1 -ελήσατο Nonn.*D.*48.969: with pf. Act. λέληθα Hdt.3.46, Pi.*O.*(v. infr.), but more freq. Pass. -λέλησμαι E.*Ba.*188, Ar.*Nu.*631, Lys.26.1, Pl.*Phd.*75d, al.: plpf. -ελελήσμην Ar.*V.*605, Pl.*Phd.*73e, al.:—*let* a thing *escape* one, *forget, lose thought of*, c. gen., ὅπως 'Ιθάκης ἐπιλήσεται (Ep. aor. subj.) Od.1.57; οὐδ' ὁ γέρων δολίης ἐπελήθετο τέχνης 4.455, cf. Hes.*Th.*560; οὐδ' ὡς σχεδίης ἐπελήθετο Od.5.324; γονέων ἐπιλάθεται (Dor.) S.*El.*146 (lyr.), cf. Hdt.4.4, Lys.26.1, etc.; ὑπ' αὐτῶν ὀλίγου ἐμαυτοῦ ἐπελαθόμην Pl.*Ap.* l.c.: prov., Μαλέας δὲ κάμψας ἐπιλάθου τῶν οἴκαδε Str.8.6.20: c. acc., Hdt.3.46, E.*Hel.*265, Ar.*Nu.*631; ὑπὸ χρόνου τι Pl.*Phd.*73e: c. inf., Ar.*V.*853, Pl.*R.*563b, Hyp.*Lyc.*8: c. part., ὀφείλων ἐπιλέλαθα I *forgot that* I owed, Pi.*O.*10(11).3, cf. E.*Ba.*188: with a Prep., ἐ. περὶ τῶν πεπραγμένων And.1.148; περὶ οὗ.., περὶ ὅτου.., Pl.*Prt.*334d, 336d; *leave disregarded, neglect*, πρόσταγμα Ceb.24. 2. less freq., *forget wilfully*, τῶν ἐντολέων μεμνημένος ἐπελανθάνετο Hdt.3.147; ἑκὼν ἐπιλήθομαι Id.4.43, cf. 3.75, Aeschin.1.158.

**ἐπιληΐς**, ίδος, ἡ, (λεία) *obtained as booty* or *plunder, gained in war*, πόλεις X.*HG*3.2.23.

**ἐπιληκέω**, *clap the hands in applause*, or *beat time to* the dancers, Od.8.379.

⊕ **ἐπιλήκητος**· ὁ τετυφλωμένος, Hsch.

⊕ **ἐπιληκῠθίστρια**, Dor. **-λᾱκ-**, ἡ, comic nickname of the muse of Mnasalcas, *the bombastical*, *AP*13.21 (Theodorid.); cf. λήκυθος.

⊕ **ἐπιλήνιος**, ον, (ληνός) *of* or *at a wine-press* or *the vintage*, μέλος Callix.2; ὕμνοι *Anacreont.*57.8; ὄρχησις Longus 2.36; ἐπιλήνια χαίρειν Opp.*C.*1.127; epith. of Dionysus, Orph.*H.*50.1:—also **ἐπιλήναιοι** θεοί Max.Tyr.30.4. II. ἐπιλήνιον, τό, *commission on the vintage*, *PLond.ined.*2135 (iv A.D.). 2. ἐπιλήνια, τά, *vintage-festival*, Ph.1.323, *PFlor.*369.14 (ii A.D.).

**ἐπιληπτ-έον**, (ἐπιλαμβάνω) *one must take into account*, ὁμοιότητα Arist.*Col.*792ᵇ25. **-εύομαι**, = sq., Lxx 1 *Ki.*21.15(16). **-ίζω**, *have an epileptic fit*, Plu.2.290b:—Pass., Alex.Trall.1.15. **-ικός**, ή, όν, *subject to epilepsy, epileptic*, Hp.*Aph.*2.45, Arist.*Pr.*953ᵃ16, Dsc.2.78, al. II. νόσοι, νοσήματα ἐ., *epileptic* complaints, Arist.*EN*1149ᵃ11, 1150ᵇ34. Adv. **-κῶς**, ἀποθνήσκειν, σπᾶσθαι, Hp.*Coac.*339, Agathin. ap.Orib.10.7.10. III. Adv. **-κῶς** *by intuition* or *apprehension*, βλέπειν τὰ πράγματα Gal.5.90. **-ος**, Ion. **-λαμπτος**, ον, *caught* or *detected in* anything, ἐ. ηρέθη S.*Ant.*406: c. part., ἐπίλαμπτος ἀφάσσουσα *caught* in the act of feeling, Hdt.3.69. 2. *culpable, censurable*, πάθος Ph.2.348; βίος Id.2.4, al., cf. Porph.*Chr.*23; of errors in metre, Heph.4.6. 3. *disabled*, ἀνδράποδον Hyp.*Ath.*15 (unless in signf. II); of a hen-partridge, Arist.*HA*613ᵇ18. II. *suffering from epilepsy*, Hp.*Aph.*3.16:—D.25.80 puns on the two senses, τοὺς ἐπιλήπτους φησὶν ἰᾶσθαι, αὐτὸς ὢν ἐ. πάσῃ πονηρίᾳ; so ἐ. ὑπὸ πάθους Plu.2. 798f. **-ωρ**, ορος, ὁ, *censurer*, Ζήνωνος πάντων ἐπιλήπτορος Timo 45.2.

**ἐπίλησις**, Dor. **-λᾱσις**, εως, ἡ, *forgetting, forgetfulness*, καμάτων Pi.*P.*1.46.

**ἐπιλησμ-ονή**, ἡ, *forgetfulness*, Cratin.410 ap.Sch.Ar.*Nu.*788, Lxx *Si.*11.27; ἀκροατὴς -λησμονῆς *Ep.Jac.*1.25:—also **ἐπιλησμονείη** (sic), Hsch., and **ἐπιλήσμη** Alex.315. **-οσύνη**, ἡ, = foreg., Cratin.410 ap.Suid. (v. -λησμονή), *IG*12(8).561 (Thasos), Archig.ap. Gal.8.149, D.C.56.41. **-ων**, ον, gen. ονος, *apt to forget, forgetful*, Cratin.154, Ar.*Nu.*129, al., Lys.12.87, Pl.*R.*486d, etc.: Comp. -έστερος X.*Mem.*4.8.8: c. gen. rei, Id.*Ap.*6: Sup. -έστατος Lys.34. 2, Phalar.*Ep.*30: irreg. Sup. ἐπιλησμότατος (as if from ἐπίλησμος) Ar.*Nu.*790. II. Act., *causing forgetfulness*, ἐ. ἐπῳδή Chio *Ep.*3.6.

⊕ **ἐπι-ληψία**, ἡ, = ἐπίληψις 1.4, *stoppage*, Arist.*Pr.*866ᵇ14. II. = ἐπίληψις II, Hp.*Aph.*3.22 (pl.), Arist.*Fr.*370. **-λήψιμος**, ον, *reprehensible*, Luc.*Rh.Pr.*22, Philostr.*VA*4.42, Max.Tyr.24.6, Hermog. *Inv.*4.13. II. *liable to seizure*, Polem.*Call.*34. **-ληψις**, εως, ἡ, *taking hold of, clasping*, Epicur.*Fr.*141; *taking besides*, τετάρτου τυράννου App.*BC*5.77. 2. in Law, *claiming* property *by seizing*, Pl.*Lg.*954e. 3. *reprehension, censure*, εἰκῇ τὰς ἐ. ποιεῖσθαι Isoc.8. 61; -λήψεως δεόμενος Plu.2.35d; ἔχει ἐπιλήψεις admits *room for censure*, Ath.5.187f. 4. *stoppage*, Mich. in *PN*49.14. II. *epileptic fit*, Hp.*Coac.*587, *Morb.Sacr.*10, Arist.*Pr.*960ᵃ18, etc. (but, *invasion, attack* of disease, Hp.*Morb.*3.16).

**ἐπιλίγδην**, Adv. *grazing*, Il.17.599, Luc.*Nigr.*36. [ἐπῐ-, v.l. ἐπιλλ-, Il. l.c.]

**ἐπιλίζω**, *whizz*, of arrows, Nic.*Fr.*100 (cited as from Men. by *An. Ox.*1.267).

**ἐπιλίημι**· ἐπιτρέπω, Hsch.

**ἐπιλιμνάζομαι**, Pass., *to be overflowed*, Plu.*Caes.*25.

⊕ **'Επιλίμνιος**, ὁ, *by the lake*, title of Poseidon, Hsch.

**ἐπιλιμπάνω**, = ἐπιλείπω, Gramm., *to be wanting*, of a tense, *An. Ox.*4.393, etc.

**ἐπιλῐν-άω**, *visit nets*, Hsch. **-ευτής**, οῦ, ὁ, *one who catches with nets*, prob. in *AP*6.93 (Antip. ⟨Thess.⟩).

**ἐπιλῐπαίνω**, *make fat* or *sleek*, τὸ δέρμα Plu.*Alex.*57.

**ἐπιλῐπᾰρέω**, *make earnest entreaty*, Them.*Or.*34 p.457 D.

**ἐπιλῐπής** (A), ές, = ἐπίλοιπος, Plu.*Sull.*7. II. *defective, wanting*, Interpol. in Sor.2.53, Hsch.

**ἐπιλῐπής** (B), ές, (λίπος) *fatty*, Heliod.ap.Orib.46.22.4.

**ἐπιλιχμάω**, *lick up*, Babr.48.6:—Med., *lick up, devour*, Ph.1.550: metaph., ἐπιθυμία ἐ. τι πυρὸς δίκην ib.305, cf. 527.

**ἐπιλιχνεύω**, *desire eagerly*, Ph.1.38,137.

**ἐπιλλείβω**, v. ἐπιλείβω.

⊛ **ἐπιλλ-ίζω**, (ἰλλός) *make signs to* one *by winking*, οὐκ ἀΐεις ὅτι δή μοι ἐπιλλίζουσιν ἅπαντες Od.18.11; *wink roguishly*, *h.Merc.*387; *look askance*, A.R.1.486: c. dat., *mock at*, Id.4.389: c. acc. et dat., τινὶ κερτομίας Id.3.791. 2. *blink*, when drowsy, Nic.*Th.*163. -ος, ον, *leering, squinting*, Eust.206.29. -όω, = sq., ib.31. -ώπτω, *wink* or *leer*, ἐξ ὀφρύος Plu.2.51c.

**ἐπιλοβίς**, ίδος, ἡ, (λοβός) *lobe of the liver*, *PAmh.*2.14 (iii/iv A. D.), Hsch (-βολίς cod.).

**ἐπιλόγεον** (fort. -λώγεον), *coarse chaff*, Hsch.

**ἐπιλόγ-ευσις**, εως, ἡ, *levying of arrears of taxation*, *PRev.Laws* 19.12 (iii B. C.). -εύω, *levy arrears of taxation*, ib.6.1 (iii B. C.), *PPetr.* 3 p.69 (iii B. C.), etc. -ή, ἡ, *picking out, choice*, τῶν ἀκαθάρτων Lysim.ap.J.*Ap.*1.34, cf. *Cod.Just.*1.5.16.2; *selection*, ἀνδρῶν Plb.7.16.7, etc.; ἵππων Simon *Eq.* tit.; ἡμερῶν Ps.-Ptol.*Centil.*6. -ίζομαι, Att. fut. -λογιοῦμαι Pl.*Ax.*365b: aor. -ελογισάμην X. (v. infr.), D. (v. infr.), -ελογίσθην Hdt. (v. infr.): pf. -λελόγισμαι D.H.3.15:—*reckon over, conclude, consider*, ὅτι.. Hdt.7.177, D.44.34, Pl. l. c., Phld.*Sign.*8, al.; τὰ ἄλλα ὀρθῶς ἐ. D.H. l. c.; *take into account*, οὐδὲν τοῦτο ἐπελογίσαντο X.*HG*7.5.16; οὐκ ἐπιλογίζεται τὸ τέταρτον, of the Egyptian year of 365 days, Procl.*Hyp.*3.56; ἐ. δείγμασιν οὐκ ἀμφιβόλοις *Theol.Ar.*33:—Pass., τὰ βουλαῖς -λογισθέντα Ph.1.428, cf. Phld.*D.*1.15. II. *address the peroration*, πρὸς ὀργὴν ἢ ἔλεον Theodect.ap.Rh.7.33 W. -ικός, ή, όν, *of, belonging to the epilogue* or *peroration*, οἶκτοι Ath.13.590e; ἔννοιαι, νοήματα, Hermog.*Id.*2.9. Adv. -κῶς Arg.Aeschin.3. -ιον, τό, perh. *epilogue*, Phld.*Lib.* p.65 O. -ισις, εως, ἡ, = ἐπιλογισμός, Epicur.*Fr.*423, *Nat.*28.8. -ισμα, ατος, τό, *a reflection*, Id.*Nat.*123G. -ισμός, ὁ, *reckoning, calculation*, Arist.*Pol.*1322$^b$35 codd. (pl.); of dates, D.H.1.74 (pl.); τῆς αἰτίας Plu.2.435b; τῶν φαινομένων Phld.*Sign.*22; ἐξ ἐπιλογισμοῦ Ph.1.168, al., J.*AJ*15.10.2: generally, *reflection, consideration*, opp. ἀπόδειξις, Epicur.*Ep.*1 p.25 U., cf. *Sent.*20, Phld.*Ir.*p.92 W. (pl.); κατ' ἐπιλογισμὸν οὐδένα on no *fixed* or *reasoned principle*, Heph.16.1; μηδεμίαν ἐπιστροφὴν μηδ' ἐ. ἔχων Chrysipp.*Stoic.*3.187; ἐπιλογισμός defined as a *generally accepted inference*, *Stoic.*2.89, cf. Gal. *Sect.Intr.*5, Menodot.ap.eund.*Subf.Emp.*12: practically, = συλλογισμός, ὃ διὰ τοιούτου τινὸς ἐ. συνεβίβαζον οἱ Πυθαγορικοί *Theol.Ar.*47; but perh. of *inductive reasoning*, opp. συλλογισμός, Phld.*Herc.*1003; *higher reasoning*, opp. λογισμός, Plot.1.3.6. 2. *signification*, Iamb. *Protr.*21.ι'. 3. *description, account*, Apollod.*Poliorc.*138.13 (pl.), Erasistr.ap.Gal.8.317. II. *afterthought, later consideration*, opp. προλογισμός, Hierocl. *in CA* 18 p.460 M. ⊛ -ιστέον, *one must reckon*, ὡς.., ὅτι.., Plu.2.40b, S.E.*M.*8.322, Epicur.*Ep.*1p.25U., al. -ιστικός, ή, όν, *able to calculate* or *take into account*, θεωρία ἐ. τῶν ὑπαρχόντων Phld.*Rh.*2.47 S.; τοῦ ἑξῆς Arr.*Epict.*2.10.3; *calculating, prudent*, Ptol.*Tetr.*155. Adv. -κῶς Phld.*Rh.*1.254 S., Gal.18(2).26. II. *inferential, illative*, [σύνδεσμος] A.D.*Conj.*257.18. ⊛ -ος, ὁ, *reasoning, inference*, only Ion., Hdt.1.27; τῆς γνώμης ποιέεσθαι ἐπίλογον give a *reason* for their opinion, Hp.*Nat.Hom.*1. II. *peroration* of a speech, Arist.*Rh.*1414$^b$12, Chrysipp.*Stoic.*2.96, Phld.*Rh.*1.202 S., Longin.12.5, etc. 2. *the concluding portion of a play*, = ἔκθεσις, Sch. Ar.*Ra.*1548: metaph., ἐ. τῆς κοσμοποιίας Ph.1.237. 3. *subjoined* or *explanatory sentence*, Arist.*Rh.*1394$^b$8, cf. *11.—In E.*El.*719 (lyr.), ἐπίλογοι is corrupt.

**ἐπίλογχος** (A), ον, (λόγχη) *barbed*, βέλος E.*Hipp.*221 (anap.).

⊛ **ἐπίλογχος** (B), ὁ, (λαγχάνω) *reserve candidate* for an office, *PRyl.* 77.43, al. (ii A. D.).

**ἐπιλοιβή**, ἡ, *drink-offering*, *Epic.Alex.Adesp.*9 vi 26 (pl.), Orph.*A.* 547,603 (both pl.).

**ἐπιλοιδορέω**, *cast reproaches on*, cj. in Plb.15.33.4:—Med., Suid. s. v. ἐπιτωθάζων.

**ἐπιλοίμια** (sc. ἔπη), τά, (λοιμός) *incantations to drive away pestilence*, Poll.4.53.

⊛ **ἐπίλοιπος**, ον, *still left, remaining*, μῆνας ἑπτὰ τοὺς ἐπιλοίπους Καμβύσῃ ἐς τὰ ὀκτὼ ἔτεα τῆς πληρώσιος Hdt.3.67: freq. in pl., c. gen., αἱ ἐ. τῶν πολίων Id.6.33; τὰ ἐ. τοῦ λόγου Id.4.154; τἀπ. τῶν λόγων S. *Ph.*24, etc.; τἀπίλοιπ' ἄκουσον E.*Tr.*923, cf. Pl.*Cra.*397a; ἡ 'πίλοιπος ὁδός E.*Ph.*842; τί οὖν ἦν ἐπίλοιπον; And.1.87. 2. of Time, *future*, χρόνος Hdt.2.13, Pl.*Lg.*628a, etc.; ἁμέραι ἐ. Pi.*O.*1.33; βίος Antipho *Fr.*67, Lys.2.71, Pl.*Lg.*929e.

**ἐπιλοξόω**, *look askance*, τῇ ἑτέρῃ κούρῃ Herod.4.71.

**ἐπίλουτρον**, τό, *price of a bath*, Luc.*Lex.*2.

**ἐπιλούω**, *bathe*, ἐν ὕδασί τινας Alex.*Fig.*2.21.

**ἐπιλοχᾱγός**, ὁ, *commander of the* λοχαγοί, *PPetr.*3 p.47 (iii B. C.).

**ἐπιλῠγάζω**, -λῠγαῖος, -λῠγίζω, ff.ll. for ἐπηλ-.

**ἐπιλύζω**, Ep. ἐπιλλ-, *have the hiccough besides*, Nic.*Al.*81.

**Ἐπιλύκειον** [ῠ], τό, at Athens, *office of the polemarch* (because built or restored by Epilycus), Arist.*Ath.*3.5.

**ἐπιλῡμαίνομαι**, *infest, ruin*, τὸν ἀνθρώπινον βίον Plu.2.881d.

**ἐπιλῡπ-έω**, *trouble, annoy, offend besides*, τινά v.l. in Hdt.9.50, Lxx 2*Ma.*8.32:—Pass., *to be troubled at*, ἀγαθοῖς ἀλλοτρίοις Iamb.*Protr.* 21.λ'; ὅτι.. S.E.*M.*11.127. -ία, ἡ, *trouble, grief*, *Stoic.*3.25. -ος, ον, (λύπη) *sad*, γένος Ph.2.29; *in low spirits*, Aret.*SA*2.12, *SD*1.6, Ruf.*Fr.*70.21. Adv. -πως *sadly*, ἀπολαύειν Ph.1.136. II. *painful*, ἐπίλυπον ἡ ἀνδρεία Arist.*EN*1117$^a$34; τὸ ἐ. *a thing that causes pain*, ib.1110$^b$19; ἐ. γῆρας Plu.2.13a. Adv. -πως, καταστρέψαι τὸν βίον D.S.17.118.

⊛ **ἐπί-λῡσις**, εως, ἡ, *release from*, ἐ. φόβων δίδου A.*Th.*134 (lyr.): abs., *exemption* from banishment, *SIG*306.51 (Arc., iv B. C.). 2. *solution*, σοφισμάτων S.E.*P.*2.246; *explanation*, 2*Ep.Pet.*1.20, Vett. Val.172.3 (pl.), Hld.1.18, 4.9, Iamb.*Protr.*21 (pl.). 3. *discharge*, of a debt, δοῦναί τισιν ἐ. *PEleph.*27.23 (iii B. C.), cf. *PGrenf.*2.26.27 (ii B. C.). 4. *spell*, *PMag.Leid.W.*25.11, al. 5. Medic., *change of dressing*, Sor.1.28 (pl.), Gal.18(2).838 (pl.), Paul.Aeg.4.48. -λῠτικός, ή, όν, *good at solving difficulties*, [γραμματικοί] οἱ ἐ. καλούμενοι Suid. s. v. Σωσίβιος, cf. Gal.*Subf.Emp.*12. -λῠτος, ον, *manumitted*, *Delph.*3(2).233 (ii B. C.).

**ἐπίλυτρος**, ον, *set at liberty for ransom*, Str.11.2.12.

**ἐπίλυχνος**, ὁ, or -ον, τό, *oil for lamps*, Arist. or Thphr.ap.Ath.4.173f (prob. f.l. for ἔτι λύχνον).

**ἐπιλύω**, *loose, untie*, δεσμά Theoc.*Adon.*42; ἐ. κύνας *let slip* dogs, X.*Cyn.*7.8: generally, *set free, release*, τοὺς κακούργους τῷ πολέμῳ Luc.*Par.*50:—Med., ἐπιλύεσθαί τινα τὸ μὴ οὐχὶ ἀγανακτεῖν Pl.*Cri.* 43c; ἐπιλύεσθαι ἐπιστολάς *open* them, Hdn.4.12.8; Ἐπιλυσαμένη, epith. of various divinities, Hsch. 2. *solve, explain*, πάντα τοῖς μαθηταῖς *Ev.Marc.*4.34:—Pass., S.E.*P.*2.246, Sch.Od.9.106:—Med., J.*AJ*8.6.5, Vett.Val.259.4, Ath.10.45 cf, al.: pf. part. Pass. ἐπιλελυμένος *lucid*, of writings, Vett.Val.329.25. 3. *confute* an accusation, Luc.*BisAcc.*30. 4. Med., *manumit*, *Delph.*3(2).233 (ii B. C.). 5. *release, discharge* a debtor, ἀπὸ τᾶν κοινᾶν ποθόδων ἐπιλυθῆμεν (inf. Pass.) τοὺς ἐρρυτιασμένους *Schwyzer* 104.7 (Troezen, ii B. C.): *pay*, c. dat. pers., ib.12:—Med., *discharge* a debt, δάνειον *PGrenf.*1.26.2 (ii B. C.). II. fut. Med. in pass. sense, *lose strength, give in*, Lys.25.33 (dub. l.).

**ἐπιλωβ-εύω**, (λώβη) *make mockery of* a thing, Od.2.323. -ής, ές, *injurious, mischievous*, Nic.*Th.*35,771. -ητος, ον, *insulted, degraded*, Lyc.1173. -ος, ον, *calamitous*, ἔτος Vett.Val.180.23.

⊛ **ἐπιμάζιος**, ον, (μαζός) = ἐπιμαστίδιος, *AP*9.548 (Bianor), 5.275.5 (Agath.).

**ἐπιμαθής**, ές, v.l. for εὐμαθής, *Cat.Cod.Astr.*8(4).140.

**ἐπιμαιμάω**, *long earnestly after*, τινός Lyc.301.

**ἐπιμαίνω**, *make madly in love with*, τινά τινι Anon.ap.Suid. s. v. Ἀναγυράσιος. II. Pass., with aor. 2 ἐπεμάνην [ᾰ], but also aor. 1 Med. ἐπεμηνάμην Il.6.160, *AP*6.309 (Leon.), Luc.*Syr.D.*21: pf. -μέμηνα:—*to be mad after*, c. dat., τῷ δὲ γυνὴ Προίτου ἐπεμήνατο Il. l. c., cf. Anacr.3, Mosch.*Fr.*2.2, Plu.*Bru.*5; θεὰ ἐ. χώρῳ Call.*Cer.*30; τὰ πρἀγμαθ', οἷς τότ' ἐπεμαίνετο Ar.*V.*744 (lyr.), cf. 1469 (lyr.), Luc. *Am.*22; [ἀστραγάλαις] *AP*6.309 (Leon.): abs., *to be mad, rage*, A. *Ag.*1427, *Th.*155 (both lyr.). 2. *fly madly at, fall upon*, πύργοις *APl.*4.106.

⊛ **ἐπιμαίομαι**, Ep. fut. -μάσσομαι (also perh. in S.*Fr.*55): aor. -εμασσάμην:—*strive after, seek to obtain, aim at*, mostly c. gen., σκοπέλου ἐπιμαίεο *make for* (i. e. *steer for*) the rock, Od.12.220: metaph., ἐπιμαίεο νόστου *strive after* a return, 5.344; δώρων ἐπεμαίετο θυμός his mind *was set upon* presents, Il.10.401; λουτρῶν Theoc.23.57; φυγῆς Timo 5.7: c. dat., *to be set upon*, Orph.*A.*932.—Ep. word, dub. in S. l. c. II. c. acc., *lay hold of, grasp*, ξίφεος δ' ἐπεμαίετο κώπην he *clutched* his sword-hilt, Od.11.531; τῶν ὁπότ' ἰθύσειε.. ἐπὶ χερσὶ μάσασθαι ib.591; χείρ' (i. e. χειρί) ἐπιμασσάμενος *having clutched* [the sword] with my hand, 9.302, cf. 19.480; τὴν ἐπεμάσσατο χειρός *took* her by the hand, A.R.3.106. 2. *touch, handle, feel*, οἰῶν ἐπεμαίετο νῶτα Od.9.441; τὸν δ' ἐπιμασσάμενος προσέφη.. Πολύφημος ib. 446; τὴν (sc. οὐλὴν) γνῶ ῥ' ἐπιμασσαμένη 19.468; ἐπὶ νῶτ' ἐπεμαίετο Hes.*Fr.*166; ἕλκος δ' ἰητὴρ ἐπιμάσσεται ἠδ' ἐπιθήσει φάρμαχ' Il.4.190; ὣς ἄρα μιν.. ῥάβδῳ ἐπεμάσσατ' Ἀθήνη Od.13.429, cf. 16.172; μάστιγι θοῶς ἐπεμαίετ' ἄρ' ἵππους she *touched* the horses sharply with the whip, Il.5.748, etc.; κεφαλὰν ἐπεμάσσατο *stroked*, *AP*7.730 (Pers.): metaph., πυρὸς δ' ἐπεμαίετο τέχνην, Lat. *artem tractavit*, *h.Merc.*108; νόῳ ἐ. ἕκαστα A.R.3.816. III. later abs., of night, *come slowly on*, Orph.*A.*121.

**ἐπίμακρος**, ον, *oblong*, Hp.*Art.*79 (v.l. ὑπόμακρος).

**ἐπιμάλθα** (leg. ἐπιμάλθακα)· ἀγαθά, προσηνῆ· ἢ μαλακά, ἢ ἀσθενῆ λίαν, Hsch.

**ἐπιμανδᾰλωτόν**, τό, (μανδαλωτός) *a lascivious kiss*, like καταγλώττισμα, Ar.*Ach.*1201.

**ἐπιμᾰνής**, ές, *mad after* a thing, τὸ ἐ. εἰς τὰς γυναῖκας Paus.1.6.8; so πρός τινα Ach.Tat.8.1. Adv. -νῶς, ἔχειν πρός τι Ath.7.276e. 2. abs., *raving, mad*, parody of Ἐπιφανής, Plb.26.1$^a$.1; νόσημα Plu.*Dio* 47: Comp. -εστέρα, αἰσχρουργία Luc.*Pseudol.*21.

**ἐπιμανθάνω**, *learn besides* or *after*, opp. προμανθάνω, Th.1.138: c. inf., Hdt.1.131; εἰ.. Id.2.160.

**ἐπιμαντεύομαι**, *prophesy*, c. acc. et inf., App.*BC*4.127; τινί τι ib. 138, Philostr.*VA*5.19.

**ἐπιμαργαίνω**, *to be raving-mad after*, σύες φορυτῷ ἐ. Arat.1123.

**ἐπίμαργος**, ον, *mad after* a thing, Suid.

**ἐπιμάρναμαι**, *go on fighting*, μείζονι πέτρῳ Nonn.*D.*21.8.

**ἐπιμάρπτω**, *clutch*, Hsch.

**ἐπιμαρτῠρ-έω**, *bear witness to* a thing, *depose to*, ἐ. ἡμῖν τὰ ὀνόματα μὴ.. κεῖσθαι Pl.*Cra.*397a; ἐ. τι πρός τινας Plu.*Lys.*22; τὰ χρήματα ἅ κα ἐπιμαρτυρήσωντι of which they *admit the possession*, *Tab.Heracl.* 1.156: c. inf., τῶν πραγμάτων -ούντων τὴν δύναμιν αὐξάνεσθαι Plu. *Sert.*12, cf. 1*Ep.Pet.*5.12; ὅτι.. Luc.*Alex.*42: abs., Plu.*Nic.*6:—

Pass., *to be confirmed by evidence*, S.E.*M*.7.211, Polystr.p.31 W. 2. *bear witness in favour of*, τινί Phld.*Oec*.p.57 J. II. Astrol., *support by aspect*, Vett.Val.111.31, *PMag.Leid.W*.24.16 (ii/iii A.D.). III. in Med., *adjure*, τισὶ μὴ ποιέειν τι Hdt.5.93 (as v.l. for ἐπιμαρτύρομαι). **–ησις**, εως, ἡ, *confirmation, corroboration*, Epicur.*Sent*.24, al.; –ήσεως δεῖσθαι M.Ant.7.62; ἡ ἐκ τῶν φαινομένων ἐ. S.E.*P*.1.181. II. Astrol., *supporting by aspect*, Paul.Al.*O*.4, Ptol.*Tetr*.200. **–ητής**, οῦ, ὁ, *one who calls to witness*, *Gloss*. ✱ **–ία**, ἡ, *a calling to witness*, ἐς ἐ. καταστῆναι Th.2.74; τῶν θεῶν D.C.59.11. II. *supporting by aspect*, ἄστρων Man.2.400 (pl.), cf. 3.314 (pl.), al.

**ἐπιμαρτύρομαι** [ῡ], *call to witness, appeal to*, in case of a treaty, θεούς X.*Cyr*.8.5.25, *An*.4.8.7, etc.; in case of history, Id.*HG*3.4.4: abs., Plb.24.11.8; also, *call* a person *to appear as one's witness*, Ar.*Nu*.495, *V*.1437, etc.; folld. by ὅτι.., *call* bystanders *to witness* that.., D.34.28. 2. *call on earnestly, conjure*, Hdt.5.92.η', Th.6.29. 3. *adduce as evidence, appeal to fact*, ὅτι.. Pl.*Phdr*.244b: c. acc. rei et inf., Plu.*Luc*.35. II. = ἐπιμαρτυρέω I, *PLille* 3.8 (iii B.C.), etc. 2. = ἐπιμαρτυρέω II, Vett.Val.292.10.

**ἐπιμάρτῠρος**, ὁ, *witness to* one's word, etc., Ζεὺς δ' ἄμμ' ἐ. ἔστω Il.7.76; θεοὶ δ' ἐ. ἔστων Od.1.273 (nisi scrib. ἐπὶ μ., et sic Hes.*Sc*.20): fem., Orph.*A*.351. II. Astrol., *supporting by aspect*, Man.6.231 (fem.), Doroth.ap.*Cat.Cod.Astr*.6.113.1.

✱ **ἐπίμαρτυς**, ῠρος, ὁ, = foreg., Ar.*Lys*.1287 (lyr., dat. pl.): acc. –μάρτυρα Musae.1, *Epigr.Gr*.905: pl., nom. –μάρτυρες Call.*Aet*.3.1.48; acc. –μάρτυρας A.R.4.229: in Astrol. sense (v. foreg.), Man.3.285, Doroth.ap.*Cat.Cod.Astr*.6.101.12.

**ἐπιμᾰσάομαι**, *chew*, Alciphr.3.51; *chew after* other food, *Gp*.12.30.9:—Pass., Dsc.3.45.

**ἐπιμαστεύω**, *search for*, Sch.Od.20.377, *EM*361.53.

**ἐπιμαστίδιος**, ον, (μαστός) *on* or *at the breast, not yet weaned*, of infants, A.*Th*.349 (lyr.), E.*IT*231 (lyr.), Nic.Dam.13 J., Luc.*Tox*.61; of birds, γόνος ὀρταλίχων S.*Fr*.793 (anap.).

**ἐπιμάστιος**, ον, (μαστός) = foreg., A.R.4.1734, Poll.2.8.

**ἐπιμαστίω**, *whip* or *beat besides*, Nonn.*D*.1.80, al.

**ἐπίμαστος**, ον, (ἐπιμαίομαι) *sought out, brought in* (like ἐπακτός), ἀλήτης Od.20.377 (variously expld. by Gramm.).

**ἐπιμᾰχ-έω**, (μάχομαι) *stand by, help one in battle*, ὥστε τῇ ἀλλήλων ἐπιμαχεῖν *for* the mutual *defence* of their countries, Th.5.27. **–ία**, ἡ, *defensive alliance*, opp. συμμαχία (both offensive and defensive), Id.1.44, 5.48, D.12.7: metaph. of the state, Arist.*Pol*.1280ᵇ27. **–ιμος**, ον, f.l. for –ος, Arr.*An*.4.25.2. **–ομαι**, *fight after, act as a reserve*, Ael.*Tact*.17, Arr.*Tact*.15.5. **–ος**, ον, *that may easily be attacked, assailable*, of fortified places, opp. ἄμαχος, Hdt.1.84; ἐκ τῆς γῆς ἐ. Th.4.31, cf. 35; τὰ –ώτατα ib.4; τῇ τὸ –ώτατον ἦν τοῦ χωρίου Hdt.9.21, cf. 6.133, X.*An*.5.4.14. II. *contended for, contested*, Hld.8.1. III. *equipped for battle*, Thom.Mag.p.113 R.; epith. of Πλούτων, *GDI*3520 (Cnidus), cf. *SIG*1014.61 (Erythrae, iii B.C.). IV. *ally, helper*, Ph.1.659, Hsch.; ἐ. χωρία *impregnable*, Ph.2.383 (v.l. ἀπο–), cf. Hsch.

✱ **ἐπιμείγνυμι** and **–ύω**, *add by mixing*, μέθυος πολιοῦ ἐπιμείξας Nic.*Th*.582: metaph., ἀθανάταν χάριν Θήβαις –μείξων Pi.*Parth*.2.5; κόλακι.. ἐπέμειξεν ἡ φύσις ἡδονήν τινα *added a mixture of* pleasure to.., Pl.*Phdr*.240b; ἀγλαΐαισιν ἐ. λαόν *make* them *acquainted with* festal enjoyments, Pi.*N*.9.31; ἐμφύλιον αἷμα ἐπέμειξε θνατοῖς *brought* domestic murder *among* them, Id.*P*.2.32; ἐ. τισὶ χεῖρας to fight with them, Id.*N*.3.61. II. intr., *mingle with* others, *have intercourse* or *dealings*, ἀδεῶς Th.1.2; πρός τινας X.*An*.3.5.16; τισί Hld.6.13; χωρίῳ ἐ. *come to* it, Id.5.33; πολλῶν ἐπιμειγνύντων δεῦρο Philostr.*VA* 5.24:—Pass., τοῦ ἠέρος –υμένου τῷ θερμῷ Hp.*Morb*.1.11; ἐπιμείγνυσθαι ἀλλήλοις φιλικῶς X.*Cyr*.7.4.5; παρ' ἀλλήλους Th.2.1: abs., Id.1.146; also ἐ. τισί *join* them, Plu.*Aem*.12; τοῖς πράξεσι *mingle in*.., Id.*Flam*.2; of sexual *intercourse*, ἐ. ἀνδρί D.59.75, cf. Luc.*Am*.22, Artem.1.80. Cf. ἐπιμίσγω.

**ἐπιμειδ-άω**, *smile at* or *upon*, in Hom. always in phrase, τὸν δ' ἐπιμειδήσας προσέφη he addressed him *with a smile*, Il.4.356, al.; in 10.400, of a scornful smile; but ἦκ' ἐπιμειδήσας Hes.*Th*.547: c. dat., *AP*5.345 (Crin.). **–ίᾱσις**, εως, ἡ, *smiling upon*, Plu.2.1009e: pl., –σεις τῆς ψυχῆς ib.1092d. **–ιάω**, *smile at*, X.*Cyr*.2.2.16, A.R.3.129; τῷ λόγῳ Arr.*An*.5.2.3.

**ἐπιμείζων**, ον, gen. ονος, strengthd. for μείζων, *still larger* or *greater*, Democr.211 (sed leg. ἔτι μείζ– vel μέζ–).

**ἐπιμεικτέον**, *one must mix*, Herod.Med.ap.Orib.10.38.2.

✱ **ἐπίμεικτος**, ον, *common to*, Λυδοῖς καὶ Καρσί Str.14.1.38. 2. *mixed*, Nic.*Th*.528, Gal.7.433; φάσηλοι ἐ. ἐκ φορτίδων νεῶν καὶ μακρῶν *combining the features* of.., App.*BC*5.95: ὁ ἐ. (sc. ὄχλος) Lxx *Nu*.11.4. 3. in Metric, of metres in which different feet are combined, Heph.9.1, cf. Sch.adloc. 4. *sociable, gregarious*, Timo 47. 5. Adv. –τως *in combination*, Paul.Aeg.3.48.

**ἐπιμείλια**, v. μείλια.

**ἐπιμειλίσσομαι**, *placate*, τινὰ δώροις J.*BJ*1.20.3:—Act., aor. 1 inf. ἐπιμειλίξαι, prob. for ἐπιμελύξαι· δοῦναι, Hsch.

**ἐπιμειξία**, Ion. –ίη, ἡ, *mixing with* others, *intercourse, dealings*, ἐούσης ἐπιμειξίης πρὸς τοὺς Τεγεήτας Hdt.1.68; ἐπιμειξίᾳ χρῆσθαι πρός.. X.*HG*5.1.1; ἐπιμειξίας οὔσης παρ' ἀλλήλους Th.5.78; ἐπιμειξίαι ἦσαν τοῖς Ἀθηναίοις καὶ Πελοποννησίοις ib.35; ἡ πόλεων ἐ. πόλεσιν Pl.*Lg*.949e; κατὰ τὰς ἐπιμειξίας τὰς τοῖς πολλοῖς Phld.*Ir*.p.73 W.; κατ' ἐπιμειξίαν τοῖς ἄλλοις *in common with*.. opp. ἰδίᾳ, D.L.10.2; of sexual *intercourse*, Vett.Val.48.19 (pl.). 2. *mixture, combination* of elements, Id.162.20, Aret.*SD*2.1, Gal.6.587.

**ἐπίμειξις**, εως, ἡ, = foreg., Thgn.297, Babr.12.23: pl., Chor. in *Rev.Phil*.1.73. (ἐπιμιξ– codd.)

**ἐπιμείρομαι**, *to be assigned by fate*, Vett.Val.346.6.

✱ **ἐπιμελαίνομαι**, *to become black on the surface*, a symptom of mortification, Hp.*Fract*.35; of the tongue, Id.*Morb*.3.6. II. of fruit, *blacken in ripening*, Thphr.*HP*3.15.6.

✱ **ἐπιμέλᾱς**, αινα, ἄν, *blackish*, Thphr.*HP*3.8.7, 6.5.3, etc.

**ἐπιμελεδαίνω**, *attend to*, –ομένη δὲ ὑγιαίνει Hp.*Mul*.1.9 (vv.ll. –μελαινομένη, –μελομένη).

✱ **ἐπιμέλ-εια**, ἡ, written –εα *IG*2².483.24 (iv B.C.), Aeol. gen. –ηΐας ib.12(2).243 (Mytilene); Ion. gen. –λίης Ps.-Hdt.*Vit.Hom*.5 (s.v.l.):—*care bestowed upon* a thing, *attention paid* to it, and abs., *attention, diligence*, Prose word, once in Hdt. (v. infr.), freq. in Th., X., etc.: in pl., *pains*, X.*Cyr*.1.6.4, etc.: c. gen. objecti, ἐ. τοῦ ναυτικοῦ, οἰκείων καὶ πολιτικῶν, Th.2.39,40; τῶν ἔργων Id.3.46; τῶν πραγμάτων And.2.13; τῶν κοινῶν Isoc.7.25; τῶν καμνόντων Pl.*Lg*.720cd (hence, of medical *treatment*, S.E.*P*.2.240); πλήθους γεννημάτων Pl.*Lg*.740cd; also περί τινος τὴν ἐ. ποιεῖσθαι Th.7.56; περὶ τοὺς νέους Lycurg.106; πρὸς τοὺς θεούς, πρὸς τὴν πόλιν, D.22.78, Pl.*Lg*.754b; εἰς τὰ ἀναγκαῖα Posidon.8 J.; ἐπιμέλειάν τινος ποιεῖσθαι, ἔχειν, Hdt.6.105, Th.6.41, Arist.*Pol*.1330ᵇ11, D.61.43, cf. Pl.*R*.451d; opp. ἐπιμελείας τυγχάνειν to *have attention paid* to one, Isoc.6.154, cf. *POxy*.58.22 (iii A.D.), etc.; ἐ. παρὰ τοῦ δαιμονίου Hyp.*Epit*.43; δι' ἐπιμελείας ἔχειν τινά Is.7.14; ἐπιμελείᾳ, κατ' ἐπιμέλειαν, *with diligence*, X.*Cyr*.5.3.47, *HG*4.4.8; δι' ἐπιμελείας θεοῦ ἡ ἀτυχία γίγνεται Antipho 3.3.8; μετὰ πάσης ἐ. X.Eph.2.10. 2. *a commission* or *charge*, Aeschin.3.13, Arist.*Pol*.1299ᵃ20 (pl.); ἡ περὶ τοὺς θεοὺς ἐ. ib.1322ᵇ18, cf. ib.30 (pl.); ἡ τῶν ἐφήβων ἐ., a special office at Athens, Din.3.15; so πρὸς τῇ ἐ. τῶν χρηματιστῶν, = ἐπιμελητὴς τῶν χρ., *POxy*.281.2 (i A.D.). 3. *any employment* or *pursuit*, interpol. in X.*Cyr*.1.6.13, etc.: pl., ἐ. καὶ σπουδαὶ *pursuits* which demand zeal, Arist.*Rh*.1370ᵃ11, cf. *EN*1138ᵇ26. ✱ **–έομαι**, also **–μέλομαι** Hdt.1.98, 2.2,174, al., Th.6.54 (v.l. in 7.39), Lys.7.25 (cod. M), Pl.*Grg*.516b, *PEleph*.13.7 (iii B.C.), *PCair.Zen*.44.17 (iii B.C.), etc.; the contr. form prevails in codd., e.g. Ar.*Pl*.1117, X.*An*.5.7.10, Pl.*Mx*.248e, and in Att. Inscrr. from 380 B.C. (older Att. spellings are ambiguous), and is required by the metre in E.*Ph*.556: fut. ἐπιμελήσομαι Hdt.5.29, Th.3.25, etc.; –μεληθήσομαι v.l. in X.*Mem*.2.7.8, Aeschin.3.27 (Dor. 3 sg. –θησεῖ *IG*12(3).170.25 (Astypalaea), pl. –θησεῦντι ib.12(1).694 (Rhodes)): aor. ἐπεμελήθην Hdt.8.109, Th.8.68, Isoc.4.38, X.*Mem*.1.3.11, etc. (ἐπεμελησάμην only late, *IGRom*.4.684.14 (i A.D.), *SIG*875 (ii A.D.), Gal.*Protr*.9): pf. ἐπιμεμέλημαι Th.6.41: Act. only in *SIG*1044.31 (Halic.):—*take care of, have charge* or *management of*, rare in Poets, as E.*Ph*.556, freq. in Prose: c. gen. objecti, Hdt.1.98, 5.29, Ar.*V*.154, *Pl*.1117, Th.3.25, Isoc.4.38, Pl.*R*.331d, etc.; περί τινος X.*An*.5.7.10; [ὑπὲρ] τῆς στρατηγίας Id.*Cyr*.1.6.12; περί τινα Pl.*Mx*.248e: later, c. dat., παιδίῳ *POxy*.744.6 (i B.C.), cf. *PTeb*.58.62 (ii B.C.): c. acc. et inf., *take care that*.., Th.6.54: c. gen. et inf., X.*Oec*.20.9: folld. by ὅπως with ind. fut. or subj. aor., Foed.ap.Th.4.118, X.*Mem*.2.10.2, etc.: with opt. after an aor., Id.*HG*6.5.37; by ὅπως c. inf., Id.*Cyr*.4.2.37 (s.v.l.); by ὡς with opt. (after past tenses), Id.*An*.1.1.5, etc.; also ἐ. τινὸς ὅπως ἔσται Pl.*Euthphr*.2d; by ἵνα c. subj., *Inscr.Prien*.44.35 (ii B.C.): with neut. Adj. in acc., *take care with respect to* a thing, Th.6.41: c. acc. et dat., τὰ ἄλλα τοῖς πολεμάρχοις X.*HG*5.4.4, cf. *IG*2².233.20 (in E.*Ph*.556 the acc. belongs to ἔχοντες): c. acc. cogn., ἐ. πᾶσαν ἐπιμέλειαν Pl.*Prt*.325c, cf. *IG*2².1261.5: abs., *give heed, attend*, Hdt.2.2. 2. of public commissions, *have charge of, be inspector* or *curator of*, τῶν μοριῶν ἐλαῶν Lys.7.29; τῶν δεκαδέων X.*Cyr*.8.1.14; δρόμου Id.*An*.4.8.25; ὁδῶν (of the Roman *cura viarum*) *CIG*4011 (Ancyra): c. acc. cogn., Pl.*Lg*.812e:—in Att. Inscrr., ἐπιμεληθῆναι (inf. = imper.) is usual of a definite commission, ποιήσεως *IG*2².555, etc. (so –ηθέντων ib.1².70); ἐπιμελεῖσθαι, of matters requiring permanent attention, ib.1².56, etc. 3. *to be engaged in, cultivate* any pursuit, art, etc., δυοῖν τέχναιν D.27.31; τῆς ἀρετῆς X.*Cyr*.7.5.71, cf. *Mem*.4.5.10. **–ημα**, ατος, τό, *care, business*, in pl., Id.*Oec*.4.4, 7.22,37. ✱ **–ής**, ές, *careful* or *anxious about*, ἀγαθῶν Pl.*Smp*.197d; τῶν φιλῶν X.*Mem*.2.6.35, etc.; also ἐ. περὶ τὰ αὑτῶν ἔργα ib.3.4.9. 2. abs., *careful, attentive*, Ar.*Nu*.501, X.*Mem*.2.6.38, etc.: Comp. –εστέρα ψυχή S.*Fr*.472, cf. X.*An*.3.2.30: Sup., Isoc.4.142; –εστέραν ἔχειν ἑτέρου θεραπείαν Men.223.9. Adv. –λῶς *carefully*, X.*Mem*.2.4.2, Pl.*Ti*.88c, Men.*Pk*.32, etc.; Ion. –λέως Hp.*Art*.55; Cret. –λίως *SIG*685.118 (Itanos): Comp. –έστερον X.*Mem*.3.5.14; –έστερα *SIG*785.9; –εστέρως Ath.14.629b: Sup. –έστατα Pl.*Alc*.1.104d. II. Pass., *cared for, an object of care*, οἱ τοῦτ' ἦν ἐπιμελές Hdt.3.40; οἷς ἀγνεῖαι.. ἐπιμελεῖς Pl.*Lg*.909e; τὸ ἐ. τοῦ δρωμένου *the charge* of the execution of orders, Th.5.66: mostly in neut. ἐπιμελές, c. dat. pers., Κύρῳ ἐπιμελὲς ἐγένετο τὰ Κροῖσος εἶπε made him *anxious*, Hdt.1.89, cf. 5.12, 7.37; ἐ. μοι ἦν it was my *business*, Id.2.150: c. inf., οὐδενὶ ἐ. ἦν σκοπεῖν it was no one's *business* to see, Antipho 2.4.6; οἷς ἐ. εἴη εἰδέναι who made it their *business* to know, Th.1.5, cf. D.18.249; ἐ. πεποίημαι εἰδέναι Pl.*Smp*.172c; τοῖς ἄρχουσιν ἐ. ἔστω μή.. Id.*Lg*.932d: c. dat. et gen., οἷς τούτων ἐ. ib.763e, cf. 824; δεῖ περὶ ἀρετῆς ἐ. εἶναι τῇ πόλει Arist.*Pol*.1280ᵇ7. 2. *suitable*, τόπος *POxy*.1412.11 (iii A.D.). **–ησις**, εως, ἡ, *further precaution*, Gal.19.108. **–ητεία**, ἡ, *office of* ἐπιμελητής, *IG*2².1338.30 (pl., i B.C., –ειτ– lap.); *term of such office*, *SIG*825 *A* 5 (Delph., ii A.D.). **–ητέον**, *one must take care of, pay attention*, ἐ. ὅπως.. Pl.*R*.618c; τινός X.*Mem*.2.1.28; περί τι Arist.*Pol*.1334ᵇ31. ✱ **–ητεύω**, *to be an* ἐπιμελητής, *PTeb*.61(*b*).71 (ii B.C.), *IG*3.393, *SIG*829 *A* 7 (Delph., ii A.D.), 855.6 (Ceos, ii A.D.), etc. **–ητής**,

οῦ, ὁ, *one who has charge of* a thing, *manager*, *curator*, τῶν τῆς πόλεως πραγμάτων Ar.*Pl.*907; ὄνων καὶ ἵππων Pl.*Grg.*516a; τῶν εἰς τὴν δίαιταν ἐπιτηδείων X.*Cyr.*8.1.9; also ὁ περὶ τῆς παιδείας ἐ. Pl.*Lg.*951e: abs., φύλαξ καὶ ἐ. X.*Mem.*2.7.14; of a bailiff, Theoc.10.54; of a governor, X.*HG*3.2.11; τῆς Τριφυλίας Plb.4.80.15, cf. Plu.*Alex.*35; Δήλου *SIG*$^2$ 508 (Delos, ii B.C.), etc.; in Salamis, *IG*2$^2$.1008.77, etc. 2. *military commander*, τῆς οὐραγίας Plb.3.79.4. II. as an official title, *curator*, 1. of sacred matters, Lys.7.29; τῶν περὶ τὰ ἱερά Arist.*Pol.*1322$^b$19; μυστηρίων D.21.171, *IG*2$^2$.1672.246, etc.; of the Dionysia, D.21.15; [τῆς πομπῆς] Arist.*Ath.*56.4, *IG*2$^2$.668; of the shrine of Amphiaraus at Oropus, ib.7.4255.32. 2. financial officers at Athens, ib.1$^2$.65.46; of the Eleven, ἐ. τῶν κακούργων Antipho 5.17. 3. of the *chiefs* of the φυλαί or Tribes, D.21.13, *IG*2$^2$.1139, etc.; ἐ. τῆς συμμορίας D.47.22. 4. τῶν νεωρίων Id.22.63, *IG*2$^2$.1629.179; ἐ. ἐμπορίου *clerk* of the market, Din.2.10; ἐ. ἐπὶ τὸν λιμένα harbour-*master*, *IG*2$^2$.1012.19; *inspector* of weights and measures, ib.2$^2$.1013.47; *curator* of the gymnasia, ib.2$^2$.1077.12; of the πρυτανεῖον, ib.3.90; κρηνῶν Arist.*Pol.*1321$^b$26, *Ath.*43.1; ἐ. ὁδοῦ Ἀππίας, = Lat. *curator viae Appiae*, *CIG*4029 (Ancyra, ii A.D.); πυλῶν τε καὶ τειχῶν φυλακῆς Arist.*Pol.*1322$^a$36, cf. *SIG*707.18 (ii B.C.); τῶν ξένων *IG*12(1).49.50 (Rhodes, ii B.C.). 5. title of a magistrate at Epidaurus, Ἀρχ.Ἐφ.1918.117 (ii B.C.), cf. *IG*4.490 (Cleonae), 4.840,841 (Calauria), 4.2 (Aegina). 6. *financial officer* in Egypt, *Arch.Pap.*2.83 (iii B.C.), *PAmh.*2.33.7 (ii B.C.), etc. 7. *deputy* of an Emperor holding honorary local office, *SIG*872 (Eleusis, ii A.D.). **–ητικός**, ή, όν, *able to take charge*, *managing*, X.*Oec.*12.19; ἡ –κή (sc. τέχνη), = ἐπιμέλεια, Pl.*Plt.*275e sq.; αἴσθησις ἐ. τῶν τέκνων Arist.*GA*753$^a$8; τὸ τοῦ ἰδίου σώματος ἐ. M.Ant.1.16. ⊛ **–ήτρια**, ἡ, fem. of ἐπιμελητής, Hsch. s.v. κομίστρια. **–ία**, v. ἐπιμέλεια. **–ομαι**, v. ἐπιμελέομαι.

**ἐπιμέλπω**, *sing to*, Ἀΐδα παιᾶνα A.*Th.*870 (anap.).

**ἐπιμελῳδ-έω**, *sing over* or *at* a person, τοιαῦτα Aristid.*Or.*29(40).30. **–ημα**, ατος, τό, *refrain*, Sch.Theoc.1.64.

**ἐπιμέμβλεται**, late Ep. redupl. form, = *ἐπιμέλει, σοὶ οὐ Τρώων ἐ. thou *carest* not *for* the Trojans, Q.S.3.123; cf. μέμβλεται.

**ἐπιμεμιγμένως**, gloss on ἐπιμίξ, Apollon.*Lex.*

**ἐπιμέμονα**, poet. pf. 2 with pres. sense, *desire* (sc. πορεύεσθαι), S.*Ph.*515 (lyr.); cf. μέμονα.

**ἐπιμεμπτ-έον**, *one must condemn*, Sor.1.28. **–ος**, ον, = sq., of persons or actions, Ph.1.260, Ptol.*Tetr.*157, A.D.*Pron.*86.2, Doroth. ap.Heph.Astr.3.30, App.*BC*2.148, al. 2. *blaming*, Sch.S.*Tr.*446. Adv. –τως Arg.Aeschin.3.

**ἐπιμεμφής**, ές, = ἐπίμομφος II, Nic.*Fr.*74.15, *AP*6.260 (Gem.), Sext.*Sent.*610.

**ἐπιμέμφομαι**, *cast blame upon*, c. dat. pers., ἤ τι κασιγνήτοις ἐπιμέμφεαι Od.16.97, etc.: c. gen. rei, *find fault for* or *because of* a thing, *complain of* it, εὐχωλῆς ἐπιμέμφεται *complains of* a vow [neglected], Il.1.65, cf. 2.225; ἕνεκ' ἀρητῆρος 1.94; ἐ. τινί τινος *blame* one *for* a thing, Luc.*DMort.*27.2; rarely ἐ. τινά τινος, ὧν ἐπιμεμφομένα σε S.*Tr.*122 (lyr.): c. acc., *blame*, νῆσον Call.*Del.*163; γηραλέην χεῖρα *AP*6.83 (Maced.); *find fault*, *complain*, μηδὲν ἐ. Hdt.1.116, etc.; ἐ. ὅτι.. Hp.*Aër.*22. b. c. inf., *to be unwilling*, Hld.1.9. 2. c. acc. rei, *impute as matter of blame*, τὰ Κροῖσος ἐπιμεμφόμενος τῷ Κύρῳ Hdt.1.75, cf. 2.161, etc.

**ἐπίμεμψις**, εως, ἡ, = ἐπιμομφή, ἐπίμεμψιν φέρειν D.H.3.11.

**ἐπιμενετέον**, *one must persist in*, c. dat., Archig.ap.Aët.9.35:— more freq. **–ητέον**, Philum.ib.8.84, Herod.Med.in*Rh.Mus.*58.89, Aët.16.107(97).

**Ἐπιμενίδειος** σκίλλη *Bath asparagus*, *Ornithogalum pyrenaicum*, Thphr.*HP*7.12.1, cf. Plin.*HN*19.93; called Ἐ. φάρμακον 'iron ration' in Ph.*Bel.*88.29 (ἐπιμο[νι]δίου codd.).

**ἐπιμένω**, *stay on*, *tarry*, abs., Il.19.142, Od.17.277; ἐπιμεῖναι ἐς αὔριον 11.351; ἄγε νῦν ἐπίμεινον, Ἀρήϊα τεύχεα δύω do you *wait*, and I will put on my armour, Il.6.340; also ἐ. ἐνὶ μεγάροισιν.. ὄφρα.. Od.4.587; ἐ. ἵνα.. *h.Cer.*160, Ar.*Nu.*196; so ἐ. ἔς τε.. X.*An.*5.5.2: after Hom., *remain in* a place, ἐ. ἐν τῇ πόλει And.1.75, etc.; ἐπὶ τῇ στρατιᾷ X.*An.*7.2.1. 2. abs., *remain in place*, *continue as they are*, of things, Th.4.4, Pl.*Phd.*80c, X.*Cyn.*6.4; *keep one's seat*, of a horseman, Id.*Cyr.*1.4.8; *stay behind* in a place, Str.10.2.24. 3. *continue* in a pursuit, ἐπὶ τῇ ζητήσει, ἐπὶ λόγῳ, Pl.*La.*194a, *Tht.*179e; ἐπὶ τοῖς δοξαζομένοις Id.*R.*490b; ἐπὶ τοῦ κακουργήματος D.24.86; ἐπὶ τῆς πολιορκίας Plb.1.77.1; c. dat., *persist in*, τῇ ἀπονοίᾳ *PTeb.*424.4 (iii A.D.); *continue* treatment, ἐ. βοηθήματι Herod.Med. in *Rh.Mus.*58.83; *cleave to*, μιᾷ γυναικί *PSI*3.158.26 (iii A.D.): also c. part., ἐ. ἐπὶ τῶν ἵππων ὀρθὸς ἑστηκώς Pl.*Men.*93d, cf. *Ev.Jo.*8.7; *spend time over*, ὑποδείγμασι A.D.*Synt.*166.14. 4. *abide by*, ταῖς σπονδαῖς dub. l. in X.*HG.*3.4.6. 5. *endure*, τοῖς συμβεβηκόσι Sor.1.3. II. c. acc., *await*, *be in store for*, τινά E.*Supp.*624 (lyr.), v.l. in Id.*Ph.*223 (lyr.), cf. Pl.*R.*361d: c. aor. inf., ἐ. τι τελεσθῆναι Th.3.2; μὴ 'πιμεῖναι τοὐμὸν ὀξῦναι στόμα not *to wait* so as to.., S.*Tr.*1176: c. fut. inf., Th.3.26.

⊛ **ἐπιμερ-ής**, ές, *superpartient*, of numbers of the form $1 + \frac{2}{x}$, $1 + \frac{3}{x}$, etc., Theo Sm.p.76H., Nicom.*Ar.*1.17, al.; cf. ἐπιμόριος. **–ίζω**, *impart*, *give a portion*, v.l. in Lxx *Jb.*31.2, 39.17. b. Astrol., *assign* a number of years to life, Vett.Val.164.9. 2. *distribute*, τινὰς τοῖς φράτραις D.H.2.50; esp. in Gramm., πρόσωπα A.D.*Synt.*92.21; ἐπιμεριζόμενον ὄνομα *distributive*, D.T.637.15; also γενικὴ –ομένη *partitive* genitive, A.D.*Synt.*35.1:—Pass., *to be distributed*, εἰς πλείονας ἡμέρας Sor.1.21. 3. *mention severally*, *enumerate*, Str.13.1.10, Hdn.*Epim.*157. **–ισις**, εως, ἡ, *distribution*, *Gloss.* ⊛ **–ισμός**, ὁ, *distribution*, Hsch. s.v. ἐπινέμησις; esp. in Gramm., προσώπων A.D.*Synt.*96.1; ἐθνικῶν ib.192.10: abs., *division* of a sentence into words (μέρη λόγου), *parsing*, ib.340.17. b. Astrol., *assignment*, Vett.Val.97.9, Critodem. in *Cat.Cod.Astr.*8(3).102.4. 2. ἐ. τῶν ἀπόρων *allocation of irrecoverable contributions* to wealthier taxpayers, *PFay.*53.5 (ii A.D.), cf. *PAmh.*2.96.8 (pl., iii A.D.), etc. 3. as title of gramm. works: ἐπιμερισμοὶ τῆς Α Ἰλιάδος *parsings* of words in Il.1, *An.Par.*3.294; ἐ. Ὁμήρου κατὰ ἀλφάβητον *parsings* arranged alphabetically, *An.Ox.*1.1; but ἐ. κατὰ ἀλφ. τοῦ Ἡρωδιανοῦ alphabetical *arrangements* of (not 'by') Herodian, title of a spelling-list, Hdn.*Epim.*1, 157; later still ἐ. τῶν ἐννέα μέτρων *analysis*, *digest*, Trichas in Heph. p.365C.; the nature of the lost Ἐπιμερισμοί of Hdn. (*EM*779.27, Sch. Il.4.66) is conjectural. **–ιστής**, οῦ, ὁ, *distributor*, *Gloss.* ⊛ **–ος**· μοιχεύεται, Hsch. **–ότης**, ητος, ἡ, *the quality of being* ἐπιμερής, Iamb. *in Nic.* pp.44,70P.

**ἐπίμεσος**, ον, *middle*, ἡλικία *AB*108; ῥῆμα ἐ. a *middle* verb, *Gloss.*

**ἐπιμεσουράνημα** [ᾰν], ατος, τό, *culmination* of a star just after sunrise or just after sunset, Ptol.*Alm.*8.4.

**ἐπιμεσόω**, *to be at the middle*, ἐπιμεσούσης τῆς ἡμέρας dub. l. in Lxx *Je.*15.9.

**ἐπίμεστος**, ον, *filled up*, *in full measure*, δωσεῖ πάντ' ἐπίμεστα Call.*Cer.*134, Poll.4.170: neut. pl. as Adv., Pherecr.190, Phryn.*PS* p.70B.

**ἐπιμεταλλάσσω**, *die subsequently*, *POxy.*265.30 (i A.D.), etc.

**ἐπιμετα-πέμπομαι**, *send for a reinforcement*, Th.6.21, 7.7. **–φέρω**, *undergo a change*, J.*AJ*19.1.2.

⊛ **ἐπιμετρ-έω**, *measure out to*, οὐκ ἐπιδώσω οὐδ' ἐπιμετρήσω Hes.*Op.*397:—Pass., ὁ ἐπιμετρεόμενος σῖτος the corn *paid by measure* to the Persians, Hdt.3.91. II. *add to the measure*, *give over and above*, ἐ. ὀβολὸν τοῖς ναύταις Plu.*Lys.*4, cf. *Alex.*42; ἄλλα τοσαῦτα [ἔτη] Luc.*DMort.*5.1; ἐ. στρατηγίας χρόνον *prolong* one's magistracy, Plu.*Comp.Ages.Pomp.*3, etc.; *add*, in speaking, πολλά Plb.28.17.2, etc.: c. gen. partit., ἐ. σκωμμάτων *add* some jests, Luc.*Nav.*19; ἐ. τινί *add to* it, ib.18, Plb.3.118.6: abs., 'add insult to injury', Id.5.15.8; so τὸ ἐπιμετροῦν τῆς ἀπεχθείας Id.12.15.12. III. ἐ. τὸν οὐρανόν *measure* it, v.l. in Luc.*Icar.*6. 2. *reduce to measure* or *order*, τὸν ἀνθρώπινον βίον Hierocl. *in CA*20p.462M. IV. intr., ὁ ἐπιμετρῶν λόγος, of *superfluous* additions, Plb.7.7.7, al. **–ησις**, εως, ἡ, *means of measuring*, τοῦ μᾶλλον καὶ ἧττον Dam.*Pr.*50. **–ίδα**· τὸ ἐπίμετρον, ὃ προσάπτεται τῷ χιτῶνι, Hsch. **–ον**, τό, *something added to make good measure*, *excess*, Theoc.12.26, *PTeb.*91.11 (ii B.C.); ἐ. ποιεῖν make *an increase*, Thphr.*CP*4.13.7, Plu.2.676b; πολὺ ποιεῖ τοῦ ψεύδους ἐ. ib.503d; λόγον ἐν ἐπιμέτρῳ διατίθενται *into the bargain*, Plb.6.46.6; ἐξ ἐπιμέτρου λέγειν S.E.*P.*2.47, cf. Gal.8.493.

**ἐπιμήδιον**, τό, an unidentified plant, Dsc.4.19, etc.

**ἐπιμήδομαι**, *imagine* or *contrive* a thing *against* one, δόλον δ' ἐπεμήδετο πατρί Od.4.437, cf. Q.S.14.479.

**ἐπιμήθ-εια**, ἡ, *second thoughts*, *afterthoughts*, opp. προμήθεια, Corn.*ND*18. **–εύομαι**, *think of afterwards* or *too late*, Eust.67.27:— also **–έομαι** Corn.*ND*18.

**Ἐπιμηθεύς**, έως, ὁ, *Epimetheus*, *Afterthought*, brother of *Prometheus*, *Forethought*, Hes.*Op.*85, Pl.*Prt.*320d; Ἐ. ἁμαρτίνοος Hes.*Th.*511; ὀψίνοος Pi.*P.*5.27; τὸ μεταβουλεύεσθαι Ἐπιμηθέως ἔργον, οὐ Προμηθέως Luc.*Prom.Es*7.

⊛ **ἐπιμηθής**, ές, *thoughtful*, Theoc.25.79. Adv. –θέως *carefully*, Herod.3.94.

**ἐπιμήκης**, ες, *longish*, *oblong*, Democr.164, Plb.1.22.6, *Placit.*4.19.3. 2. *long*, μάχαιραι, ταινία, App.*Syr.*32, *Pun.*95, cf. Arist.*Mu.*393$^b$5, Bito 52.3, v.l. in Hdt.7.36: Comp. –έστερος Dsc.1.7, Luc.*DDeor.*10.1; *far-stretching*, *extensive*, τόπος Lxx *Ba.*3.24; ἐ. ἐξ.. ἐπὶ.. *extending* from..to.., App.*Ill.*22; also of Time, Vett.Val.344.5: Sup. –έστατος Hdn.8.1.5; irreg. ἐπιμήκιστος dub. in Ph.1.291.

**ἐπιμηκύνω**, *lengthen*, *prolong*, μάχην Paus.4.10.4.

**ἐπιμηλάδες** αἶγες she-goats *of the flock*, Call.*Ap.*51 codd.

**Ἐπιμηλίδες** Νύμφαι, αἱ, (μῆλα) *protectors of sheep* or *flocks*, Ant.Lib.31.5, Longus 2.39, Alciphr.3.11, Nonn.*D.*14.210, Epic. in *Arch.Pap.*7p.7: **Ἐπιμηλιάδες** in Paus.8.4.2.

**ἐπιμήλιος**, ὁ, *guardian of flocks*, epith. of Apollo at Camirus, Macrob.1.17.45; of Hermes at Coronea, Paus.9.34.3.

**ἐπιμηλίς**, ίδος, ἡ, (μῆλον) *a kind of medlar*, *mespilus germanica*, Dsc.1.118; or *pear*, Pamphil.ap.Ath.3.82d, cf. Hsch. II. = πόρπη, Id.

**ἐπιμηνάω**, 3 pl. pf. –μεμηνάκαντι, = ἐπιμεμενήκασι, they *have been content to wait*, *Schwyzer*91.11 (Argos, iii B.C.).

**ἐπιμηνίδιον**, τό, *monthly allowance*, *PGiss.*16.3 (ii A.D.), *PMich.* in *Class.Phil.*22.250 (pl., ii A.D.), *POxy.*1070.45 (pl., iii A.D.).

**ἐπιμηνι-εία**, ἡ, *the office of* ἐπιμήνιος, *Test.Epict.*4.31, *SIG*241.121 (Delph., iv B.C.). **–εύω**, *hold the office of* ἐπιμήνιος, ib.241.90 (ibid.), 495.180 (Olbia, iii B.C.), *BCH*17.555 (Lampsacus), *Test.Epict.*4.15,35, etc.; τῆς ἐκκλησίας *hold monthly chairmanship*, *SIG*708.2 (Istropolis). ⊛ **–η**, Ion., = ἐπιμηνιεία, ib.58.11 (Milet., v B.C.). ⊛ **–ος**, ον, *monthly*, χρεῶν –ίων τόκοι Hondius *Novae Inscriptiones Atticae* 91; *holding office for a month*, πολέμαρχος, προμνήμων, at Chios, *SIG*402.1, 443.1,2 (iii B.C.); ἐπιμήνιοι, οἱ, *monthly officers*, ib.58.5 (Milet., v B.C.), *OGI*229.30 (Smyrna, iii B.C.): sg., *IG*12(2).645*b*38 (Nesos); ἐ. τῶν ταμιῶν *SIG*426.27 (Bargylia, iii B.C.). 2. *priests who offered the* ἐπιμήνια, Hsch.; ἐπιμηνίους.. οἵτινες ἐχθυσεῦνται τὰ ἱερὰ μετὰ τοῦ ἱερέως *SIG*1106.63 (Cos), cf. 1044.24 (Halic.), *Test.Epict.*2.33. II. ἐπιμήνια, τά, 1. (sc. ἱερά) *monthly offerings*, Hdt.8.41, Inscr.ap.Ath.6.234e. 2. *provisions*, *monthly ration*, *POxy.*531.17 (ii A.D.), etc.; also ἐ. ὀψώνια *PLond.*2.190.16 (iii A.D.); ὁ ἐ. σῖτος Plu.*Flam.*5; ὁ λόγος

ὁ ἐ. the *monthly* account, *SIG*578.54 (Teos, ii B.C.). b. simply, *provisions*, for a ship, Plb.31.12.13, Sor.1.19. 3. *monthly courses of women*, Hp.*Nat.Mul.*13, Sor.1.19 (sg.); ἐπιμήνιον (sc. αἷμα), τό, Dsc.2.79; κάθαρσις ἐπιμηνίων Aret.*SA*1.9.

**ἐπιμηνίω**, *to be angry with*, Πριάμῳ ἐπεμήνιε δίῳ Il.13.460, cf. App.*BC*3.55; τινὶ τῶν γεγονότων Id.*Mith.*55.

**ἐπιμηνῦτής**, οῦ, ὁ, = μηνυτής, τοῦ ἔργου Arr.*An.*3.26.2.

**ἐπιμηρύομαι**, *wind* a layer of gut *on top of* others, Ph.*Bel.*65.43.

**ἐπιμητιάω**, Ep. part. -όωσα, *consider how* to do, c. inf., A.R.3.668.

⊕ **ἐπιμηχᾰν-άομαι**, *devise plans against, take precautions*, Hdt.1.94, 6.91; πᾶν Phld.*Ir.*p.30 W.; δεινόν τινι Luc.*DDeor.*3.1, cf. Q.S.14.427. II. *devise besides*, ἄλλα ἀεὶ καινὰ ἐ. X.*Cyr.*8.8.16; σιτία πονηρά τισι D.Chr.6.11, cf. App.*BC*4.120. **-ημα**, Dor. **-μᾱχάνᾱμα**, ατος, τό, *a means towards* a thing, Hippod.ap.Stob.4.1.94. **-ησις**, εως, ἡ, *device, contrivance*, ἐξ -ήσεως *on purpose, artificially*, Chrysipp.*Stoic.*2.153. **-ητέον**, *one must devise besides*, Herod.Med. in *Rh.Mus.*58.105, Gal.14.169. **-ος**, ον, *craftily devising*, κακῶν ἐπιμήχανε ἔργων *contriver* of ill deeds, Orac.ap.Hdt.6.19.

**ἐπιμῐγή**, ἡ, *intermixture*, S.E.*P.*1.124 (pl.).

**ἐπιμίγνυμι, ἐπίμικτος**, late spellings of ἐπιμείγνυμι, etc. (qq. v.).

**ἐπιμῑμέομαι**, *imitate further*, Thphr.*Metaph.*33.

⊕ **ἐπιμιμνήσκομαι**, fut. -μνήσομαι Hdt.1.5, etc., rarely -μνησθήσομαι (Hdt.2.3, D.19.276): aor. -εμνήσθην Od.1.31, Hdt.1.85, etc., -εμνησάμην Il.17.103, A.*Ch.*623 (lyr.), etc.: pf. ἐπιμέμνημαι, late -μέμνησμαι *POxy.*791 (i A.D.):—*bethink oneself of, remember, think of*, c. gen., ἐπὶ δὲ μνήσασθε ἕκαστος παίδων Il.15.662; κ'.. ἐπιμνησαίμεθα χάρμης we would *think of* battle, 17.103; τοῦ ὅ γ' ἐπιμνησθεὶς Od.1.31, 4.189 (the only parts of the Verb used by Hom.). 2. *make mention of*, ἐπιμνησαίμεθα σεῖο ib.191, cf. Hdt.1.5, 85, A.*Ch.* l. c., S.*Ph.*1400, etc.; οὐ δ' ἐπεμνήσθην 'but, by the way', Herod.5.53, cf. 6.42; also ἐ. περί τινος Hdt.2.101, X.*Cyr.*1.6.12, Pl.*Mx.*239c, etc.: with neut. pron. in acc., τοσαῦτα ἐπιμνησθέντες Hdt.1.14, cf. 2.3; with gen. and acc., τῆς μάχης τε πολλὰ ἐπιμεμνημένοι καὶ τὴν Λήμνου αἵρεσιν Id.6.136; also ἐ. ὅτι.. X.*HG*3.2.8; ἐ. περὶ γυναικῶν, ὡς.. Pl.*Ti.*18c.

**ἐπιμίμνω**, poet. for ἐπιμένω, *abide* or *continue in*, [ἔργῳ] Od.14.66, 15.372.

**ἐπιμίξ**, Ep. Adv. *mixedly, confusedly, pell-mell*, ἐ. ἵπποι τε καὶ αὐτοί Il.11.525, cf. 21.16; ἐ. δέ τε μαίνεται Ἄρης Ares rages *without respect of persons*, Od.11.537; ἐ. κτείνονται Il.14.60: in later Prose, Lxx *Wi.*14.25.

**ἐπι-μιξία, -μιξις**, v. ἐπι-μειξία, -μειξις.

**ἐπιμίσγω**, older poet. and Ion. form (found also in *PRev.Laws* 28.17 (iii B.C.)) of ἐπιμείγνυμι, intr., *have intercourse*, παρ' ἀλλήλους Th.1.13. II. mostly Pass., in Il. always in hostile sense, αἰεὶ μὲν Τρώεσσ' ἐπιμίσγομαι I *have* always *to be dealing with* the Trojans, *am* always *clashing with* them, Il.10.548; ἂψ -ομένων *as the fight was joined* again, 5.505; in Od. of peaceful relations, commerce, etc., οὐδέ τις ἄμμι βροτῶν ἐπιμίσγεται ἄλλος Od.6.205, cf. 241; so in Prose, *have dealings with*, Αἰγύπτῳ, τῇ Ἑλλάδι, Hdt.2.104, cf. 151; ἀλλήλοις X.*Ath.*2.7; πρὸς ἀλλήλους Arist.*Pol.*1327ᵃ39; ἐ. ἐς τὴν ξυμμαχίαν πρός τινας Foed.ap.Th.4.118: abs., Hdt.1.185; ἐ. μηδετέρωσε Foed.ap.Th. l. c.; of sexual *intercourse*, Vett.Val.75.13. 2. of Place, οὐδέ ποτ' ἐς βουλὴν ἐπιμίσγεται οὐδ' ἐπὶ δαῖτας Hes.*Th.*802: later c. acc. loci, *draw nigh to* a place, Call.*Jov.*13. III. Med., *cross*, in breeding, Ἀρκάδας Ἠλείοις Opp.*C.*1.395.

**ἐπιμίσθ-ιος**, ον, *engaged for hire*, χρηματισμός Dam.ap.Suid. s. v. Σεβηριανός, cf. Hsch. s. v. ἐπάρουρος (ἔπταμ- cod.):—pecul. fem. **ἐπιμισθίς**, ίδος, ἑταῖραι *AP*7.403 (Marc. Arg.). **-όω**, *contract for*, in Pass. of bricks, *Michel*1512 (Piraeus, iv B.C.), cf. *IG*12(9).189.30 (Eretria), 11.165.36, 199*A*106 (Delos, iii B.C.), *PPetr.*3 p.109 (iii B.C.); v. l. in Ael.*VH*3.14.

**ἐπιμνημονεύω**, *bear in mind*, *POxy.*264.5 (i A.D.).

**ἐπί-μνησις**, εως, ἡ, *recollection*, Aristeas 154, *EM*357.57. 2. *mention*, Aristeas 31, Orph.*Fr.*49.17. **-μνηστέον**, *one must mention*, Pl.*Ti.*90e.

⊕ **ἐπιμοιρ-άομαι**, *receive by lot, receive as one's share*, c. acc., ἐ. κόνιν *get* earth *enough* for a grave, Moschio Trag.6.31, cf. Ps.-Phoc.99 (ἐπῑ- metri gr.): c. gen., *have a share of*, ταφῆς Ph.2.178. **-ιος**, ον, *fated*, νήματα *AP*7.504 (Leon.). **-ος**, ον, *partaking in*, c. gen., στεφάνων B.1.48, cf. Euryph.ap.Stob.4.39.27.

**ἐπιμοιχ-εύω**, *commit adultery besides*, τινά *with* one, Ps.-Luc.*Philopatr.*6. **-ίδιος**, ον, *adulterine*, Olymp. *in Alc.*p.153 C.

**ἐπιμολεῖν**, aor. 2 inf. of ἐπιβλώσκω, *come upon, befall*, ἐπέμολε πάθος S.*Tr.*855 (lyr.).

**ἐπίμολος**, ὁ, *invader*, γᾶς A.*Th.*629 (lyr.).

**ἐπιμολύνω**, *defile on the surface*, Sor.1.22.

**ἐπιμομφ-ή**, Dor. **-φά**, ἡ, *complaint*, Pi.*O.*10(11).9. **-ος**, ον, *inclined to blame*, φίλοις E.*Rh.*327. II. *blameable, unlucky*, A.*Ag.*553; ἐπίμομφον ἄταν dub. l., Id.*Ch.*830 (lyr.).

**ἐπιμον-ή**, ἡ, *tarrying, delay*, Th.2.18; *residence*, *Sammelb.*5343.42 (ii A.D.). 2. *steadfastness*, Pl.*Cra.*395b, Plu.*Sert.*16; *persistence*, Sor.2.16, 40; of fruit, Thphr.*CP*2.9.8. 3. *staying still, inactivity*, of a patient confined to bed, Phld.*Ir.*p.29 W. 4. Rhet., *dwelling on a point, treating it elaborately*, Longin.12.2, Demetr.*Eloc.*280, Hermog.*Id.*1.11, Alex.*Fig.*1.10, etc. II. ἐν ἐπιμονῇ τινος, of a balance left in the *hands* of the treasurer, *IG*1².423 ii 5. **-ίδιος**, v. Ἐπιμενίδειος. **-ος**, ον, *staying on, lasting long*, Plb.6.43.2; ἐ. ποιεῖν τὸν στρατηγόν *continue* him in his command, ib.15.6; ἐπιμόνους ποιεῖν ἐράνους *delay* their payment, Id.38.11.10; ὁ ὦνος ἐ. ἔστω *Hermes* 17.5 (Delos); κράτησις ἐπίμονος σπέρματος Sor.1.43; ἐ. τινι or ἔν τινι *persevering* in it, Plb.29.26.2, Plu.*Flam.*1; ἐπί τινος *Stoic.*3.32. Adv. -νως *constantly, permanently*, Pl.*Ax.*372a, Ph.1.179; *persistently*, cj. in Gal.19.220: Comp. -ώτερον *more permanently*, *Gp.*2.5.7.

⊕ **ἐπιμορῐ-ασμός**, ὁ, *formation of a number of the form* $1 + \frac{1}{x}$, Iamb. *in Nic.*p.108 P. ⊕ **-ος**, ον, (μόριον) *containing a whole + a fraction with 1 for its numerator* $(1 + \frac{1}{x})$, *superparticular*, ἐ. [ἀριθμοί] Arist.*Pr.*921ᵇ5; λόγοι Ph.2.183 (v. l. for ὑποεπιμερῶν), Plu. *in Hes.*59; of the rhythm of the pulse, Gal.8.516; also ἐπιμόριον, τό, Arist.*Metaph.*1021ᵃ2. Adv. -ίως Nicom.*Ar.*2.20; opp. ἐπιμερής (q. v.), ib.1.20; τῶν ἀριθμῶν οἱ μὲν ἐν πολλαπλασίῳ λόγῳ λέγονται, οἱ δὲ ἐν ἐπιμορίῳ, οἱ δὲ ἐν ἐπιμερεῖ Euc.*Sect.Can.Praef.*, cf. Theo Sm.p.76 H. **-ότης**, ητος, ἡ, *the property of being* ἐπιμόριος, Iamb. *in Nic.*p.44 P.

⊕ **ἐπιμορμύρω** [ῡ], *murmur*, as a wave, D.P.82 (tm.).

**ἐπίμορτος** γῆ *farmed on the métayer system*, Sol.ap.Poll.7.151.

**ἐπιμορφ-άζω**, *pretend*, c. inf., Ph.1.387; ὅτι.. ib.96; ὡς, c. part., ib.193: abs., ib.363. II. c. acc., *simulate*, εὐσέβειαν, τὸ ἀδέσποτον, ib.340, 698:—Med., Hsch. **-όω**, prob. f. l. for foreg., Ph.2.520.

**ἐπιμοτόω**, *apply a* μοτός (q. v.), in imper. Pass. -μοτούσθω, τιλτοῖς Heliod.ap.Orib.44.10.9.

**ἐπιμοχθ-έω**, *work* or *toil at*, Hsch. **-ητος**, ον, *always toilsome*, *CIG*3816 (Dorylaeum). **-ος**, ον, *toilsome*, ἀρετά B.1.71, cf. Man.4.248: gloss on πόνηρος, Sch.Ar.*Pax*383; γῆ Hp.*Ep.*17. Adv. **-θως** *with toil*, App.*Pun.*72; so neut., Lxx *Wi.*15.7.

**ἐπιμοχλεύω**, *bolt, bar*, κλεῖθρα Hld.4.17 (Pass.).

**ἐπιμύζω**, *murmur* or *mutter at* another's words, αἱ δ' ἐπέμυξαν Il.4.20 (also expld. as = ἐμυκτήρισαν, Trypho *Trop.*p.205 S.):—Med., ἐπεμύξατο Hsch.

**ἐπιμῡθ-έομαι**, *say besides*, v. l. for ἀπομ-, Il.9.109. **-εύομαι**, *to be added fabulously*, Arist.*HA*605ᵃ5, Ant.Diog.5. **-ιος**, ον, *coming after the fable*: τὸ ἐ. the *moral*, Luc.*Bacch.*8, Aphth.*Prog.*1, Herm. *in Phdr.*p.92 A.

**ἐπιμυκτηρ-ίζω**, *turn up the nose, mock at*, Men.562.4. **-ισμός**, gloss on ἐπισμυκτόν, Hsch.

**ἐπίμυκτος**, ον, (ἐπιμύζω) *scoffed at*, Thgn.269.

**ἐπιμῠλ-ίδιος**, ον, = sq. 1, δαίμων Hsch. s. v. διαλαός (post διαλυγίσαντες). **-ιος**, ον, *at* or *in the mill*, epith. of Artemis, S.E.*M.*9.185. 2. *of a millstone*, κλάσμα Lxx *Jd.*9.53 (s. v. l.). II. as Subst., 1. ἐπιμύλιον, τό, *the upper millstone*, ib.*De.*24.6. 2. ἐπιμύλιος (sc. ᾠδή), ἡ, *song sung while grinding*, Trypho ap.Ath.14.618d, Ael.*VH*7.4, Hsch. s. v. ἱμαλίς.

**ἐπιμῠλίς**, ίδος, ἡ, *knee-pan*, Hp.*Mochl.*1.

**ἐπίμυξις**, εως, ἡ, (ἐπιμύζω) *sniffing*, Choerob.*Rh.*p.254 S. 2. = στεναγμός, Hsch.

**ἐπιμῠρίζω**, *smear*, τινί with.., Thphr.*Od.*45.

⊕ **ἐπιμύρομαι** [ῡ], *to be washed* by the sea, A.R.1.938; but ῥισὶν ἐπιμύρεται κόρυζα *dribbles*, *An.Ox.*3.220 (ἐπιμυρμύρεται cod.).

**ἐπιμῠσις**, εως, ἡ, *closing*, βλεφάρων Philum.*Ven.*16.3 (pl.), cf. Erot. s. v. καρδαμύσσειν, *EM*490.54; of the *os uteri*, Sor.2.18.

**ἐπιμύσσω**, *laugh at*, cj. in Luc.*DMort.*6.3: aor. 1 ἐπέμυξα Hsch.

**ἐπιμυχθίζω**, gloss on foreg., Hsch.

⊕ **ἐπιμύω**, pf. -μέμῡκα Sor.2.27:—*close* the eyes, τοὺς ὀφθαλμούς D.S.1.48; τὰ βλέφαρα Aret.*SA*1.5; ὄμματα Opp.*H.*2.110: abs., *close the eyes*, Plb.4.27.7, Theoc.21.4 (cj.), Alex.Aphr. *in Sens.*17.14: metaph., *die*, Call.*Ep.*41.5. 2. *wink at*, in token of assent, Ar.*V.*934. II. intr., *close over*, τὰ βλέφαρα τοῖσι ὀφθαλμοῖσι ἐπιμύει *close over* the eyes, Aret.*CA*1.6, cf. *SA*1.5, Sor. l. c.; *close up*, of wounds, Opp.*C.*2.290; ταχὺ τὸν ὄγκον ἐπιμύειν Onos.19.3; ἐπιμύοντας ὀλόσχους, prob. l. for ἐπημ-, Nic.*Th.*870, cf. Sch. ad loc.

**ἐπιμωκάομαι**, *mock at*, Sch.S.*OT*970, Sch.A.R.1.486:—also ⊕ -μωκεύω, v. l. in Luc.*JTr.*16.

**ἐπιμωλέω**, (μῶλος) *claim at law*, *Leg.Gort.*9.28.

**ἐπιμωμ-άομαι**, *find fault with*, τινί D.P.896. **-ητός**, Dor. **-ᾱτός**, ή, όν, *blameworthy*, [ἔρις] Hes.*Op.*13; ἔργον Theoc.26.38. ⊕ **-ος**, ον, *blameworthy*, τὸν βίον Hld.7.2; *blemished*, Artem.5.67: opp. ἄμωμος, Herm.ap.Stob.1.41.1.

***ἐπιναίω**, aor. Pass. ἐπενάσθην, = ἐπῳκίσθη (sic), Hsch.

**ἐπινάσσω**, fut. -ξω, *stuff up, close up*, Hsch.; cf. ἐπινέω (B) fin. II. *pour, heap over*, *Gp.*6.6.2. III. in Pass., *to be blocked*, of too thick milk, Sor.1.87.

⊕ **ἐπινάστιος**, ον, (ναίω) *taken as a stranger into a country, sojourning in a country*, A.R.1.795.

**ἐπιναυμᾰχία**, ἡ, *battle beside the ships*, Ps.-Plu.*Vit.Hom.*192 (pl.).

**ἐπιναυπηγέω**, *build upon the ship*, Poll.1.92 (Pass.). II. *build in addition*, καινὰς τριήρεις Anon.Argent.p.75 Keil.

**ἐπιναύσιος**, ον, (ναυσία) *feeling nausea, sickish*, Plb.31.14.1; *subject to vomiting*, Hp.*Dent.*3.

**ἐπινάχομαι**, Dor. for ἐπινήχ-, Theoc.23.61.

**ἐπινάω**, *send forth emanations* or *influences*, ὁ θεὸς ἀεὶ ἐ. Ascl. *in Metaph.*23.5:—Pass., ἐνέργειαι ἐπινάονται ib.120.2, cf. 186.1.

**ἐπινεάζω**, *take youthful pleasure in*, τινί Poll.10.53.

**ἐπινεᾱνιεύομαι**, *behave like a youth*, in good sense, Poll.3.121; ὁ νοῦς ἐ. καλὴν καὶ ὁσίαν νεανιείαν Ph.1.258; also in bad sense, ἐπινεανιευόμενός φησι *with youthful audacity*, Plu.2.1079d, cf. Ph.1.203, 298. 2. *commit further outrages*, Lib.*Decl.*13.9, 56.

**ἐπινεικής**, ές, *contentious*, Them.*Or.*13.166c.

⊕ **ἐπίνειον**, τό, (ναῦς) *sea-port* where the fleet of a country lies, Hdt.6.116, Th.1.30, 2.84; ἐπίνεια καὶ λιμένας the *harbours* and *roadsteads*, Arist.*Pol.*1327ᵃ33; πολίχνη ᾗ ἐ. καὶ ἀγορᾷ ἐχρῶντο D.H.9.56,

etc. II. Adj. ἐπίνειος, ον, *at a port*, φρουραί, φρούριον, App.*Praef.* 15, *Pun.*100.

**ἐπινείσομαι**, = ἐπινίσσομαι, Hsch.

**ἐπινείφω**, *snow upon*, Thphr.*HP*4.14.6 (Pass.), *CP*5.9.13 (Pass.); θεὸς ἐπινείφει δρόσον (i.e. manna) Ph.2.112· metaph., οἷς δ' ὁ θεὸς ἐπινείφει καὶ ἐπομβρεῖ τὰς ἀγαθῶν πηγάς Id.1.296, cf. 2.383 :—Pass., ἐνθυμήματα *are dropped, distilled into* the mind, Id.1.441. 2. impers., ἐπινείφει *fresh snow falls*, or *it keeps snowing*, X.*Cyn.*8.1.

**ἐπινεμεσάω**, *to be wroth against*, οἴκῳ τινός J.*AJ*13.16.2 (v.l.).

**ἐπινέμ-ησις**, εως, ἡ, *appropriate apportioning* of medical treatment, Hp.*Praec.*8; of a bandage, = ἐπινομή II, Gal.18(1).775. II. (from Med.) *spreading*, πυρός Plu.*Lys.*12, Epicur.*Ep.*2p.40U.; of disease, Antyll.ap.Orib.50.8.3. III. = Lat. *indictio*, *IG*12(9).907.4 (Chalcis, iv A.D.), prob. in ib.7.24 (Megara, v A.D.), Jul.*Ep.*73, Lyd.*Mens.* 3.23, *Cod.Just.*10.16.13.5, etc. **-ητέον**, *one must assign*, Pl.*Lg.* 737c. **-ω**, *allot, distribute*, σῖτον ἑλὼν ἐπένειμε τραπέζῃ Il.9.216, 24.625: c. dat. pers., σῖτον δέ σφ' ἐπένειμε Od.20.254; ἐφ' ἑκατέρῳ τὸ μέρος ἐ. ἑκάτερον Pl.*Plt.*264d. II. *turn* one's cattle *to graze on another's land*, ἐάν τις βοσκήματα ἐπινέμῃ Id.*Lg.*843d; τὰ κτήνη παρὰ τὸν ποταμόν Arist.*Pol.*1305ᵃ26, cf. D.55.11; *enjoy right of pasturage*, *Berl. Sitzb.*1927.7 (Locr., v B.C.). b. ἐ. σῖτον *graze* a crop, Thphr.*HP* 8.7.4. 2. metaph. in Med., *encroach*, of fire, πῦρ ἐ. τὸ ἄστυ *spreads over* the town, Hdt.5.101; πῦρ ἐ. τὴν γραφήν Plu.*Demetr.*22: abs., τὸ πῦρ ταχέως -νέμετο Plb.14.5.7; τὸ πῦρ ἐκώλυσαν.. ἐπινεμηθῆναι D.S.17.26; also of disease, *spread*, τὸ ἐρυσίπελας ταχὺ πάντοθεν ἐπενέμετο Hp.*Epid.*3.4; ἡ νόσος ἐπενείματο Ἀθήνας Th.2.54, cf. Plu. 2.776f: abs., Aret.*SA*1.7: generally, of a piratical force, ἐπενείματο τὴν θάλασσαν Plu.*Pomp.*25; of an army, ἐ. τὴν Γαλατίαν Id.*Caes.*19; of a custom, *spread among*, τινάς Id.*Demetr.*18; *approach*, Μοισᾶν ἀπὸ τόξων Δία.. βέλεσσιν Pi*O.*9.6. b. *feed after*, i.e. *on the leavings of*, τινί Arist.*HA*591ᵇ19. c. *feed on, consume*, κόμην Call. *Dian.*79; δαῖτα Nic.*Al.*510, cf. Plu.2.980d: abs., ib.293a. d. *inhabit*, Luc.*Bacch.*6. 3. metaph. in Pass., *to be encroached upon*, as if by cattle straying over the bounds of their pasture, θῆλυς ὅρος ἐπινέμεται A.*Ag.*485 (lyr.).

**ἐπινεόω**, *renew*, *PMasp.*24*C*44 (Pass., vi A.D.).

**ἐπί-νευμα**, ατος, τό, *nodding* of the head, Gal.5.227 (pl.). **-νευσις**, εως, ἡ, *nodding assent*, τῆς κεφαλῆς Ath.2.66c: abs., *assent*, Καίσαρος J.*AJ*17.9.1; ἡ ἑαυτοῖς ἐ. Polystr.p.16W. II. *inclination* of the head, Gal.2.461; *movement down*, opp. ἀνάνευσις, Ath.Mech.26.2; ἐ. ἐπὶ τὸ ἀριστερὸν πλευρόν, of patients in bed, Philum.(?)ap.Aët.9. 23. **-νευστάζω**, *incline forwards*, opp. ὑπτιάω, of the crescent moon, Arat.789. **-νεύω**, fut. -νεύσω Luc.*Sat.*4, -νεύσομαι Aristaenet.2.1 :—*nod to*, in token of command or approval, *nod assent*, opp. ἀνανεύω, ἐμῷ δ' ἐπένευσα κάρητι Il.15.75; ἐπ' ὀφρύσι νεῦσε Κρονίων 1.528, etc.; ἐπὶ γλεφάροις νεῦσαν Pi.*I.*8(7).49; σὺ.. ἐπένευσας τάδε *did'st approve, sanction* these acts, E.*Or.*284, cf. D.18.324; ἐπένευσεν ἀληθὲς εἶναι he *nodded in sign that* it was true, Aeschin.3.59; σιγῇ δὲ τὰ ψευδῆ.. ἐπινεύουσι they *indicate* falsehoods without speaking, D.21.139: abs., Antipho 2.2.7; Ἑλληνικὸν ἐ. *give* a Greek *nod*, Ar.*Ach.*115: c. acc., *grant* or *promise*, τινά τινι E.*Hel.*681 (lyr.); τι Id.*Ba.*1349; ὑπέρ τινος Plb.21.5.3: c. dat., ἐ. τῇ δεήσει τινός *PGiss.* 1.41 ii 9 (ii A.D.): c. dat. pers., ἐ. τισὶ δεομένοις *SIG*888.13 (Macedonia, iii A.D.): c. dat. pers. et inf., *permit*, κῴδια ἐ. ἡμῖν ἐργάζεσθαι *PPetr.*2 p.108 (iii B.C.). 2. *make a sign* to another to do a thing, *order* him to do, c. inf., ἐπ' ὀφρύσι νεῦσε σιωπῇ.. στορέσαι λέχος Il.9. 620: abs., Od.16.164(tm.), *h.Cer.*169,466, X.*Cyr.*5.5.37. 3. *nod forwards*, κόρυθι ἐπένευε φαεινῇ he *nodded* with his helmet, i.e. it *nodded*, Il.22.314; λόφων ἐπένευον ἔθειραι Theoc.22.186; ἐ. ἐς τὸ κάταντες Luc.*DDeor.*25.2; πέτραι ἐπινενευκυῖαι *overhanging*, Id.*Prom.*1. 4. *incline towards*, εἴς τινα Ar.*Eq.*657. 5. *roll down* an inclined plane, Hero *Aut.*2.1. 6. trans., *elevate, point upwards*, Id.*Bel.*78. 8, 89.14 :—Pass., *to be inclined downwards*, opp. ἐξυπτιάζεσθαι, S.E. *P.*1.120. b. *tilt*, [κεράμιον] *Gp.*7.9. 7. ἐπινενευκὼς σφυγμός, name coined by Archigenes, Gal.8.479.

**ἐπινεφελ-ίς**, ίδος, ἡ, *cloudiness* in the eye, Alex.Trall.2. **-ος**, ον, *clouded, overcast*, Hp.*Epid.*3.2, Pl.Com.65; ἐπινεφέλων ἐόντων the weather being *cloudy*, Hdt.7.37, cf. Arist.*Pr.*939ᵇ15; τὰ ἐ. ib.33; ὅταν ἐπινέφελον ᾖ, opp. αἰθρίας οὔσης, Id.*Mete.*369ᵇ23, cf. *Pr.*939ᵇ39; ἐ. οὖρον *clouded* urine, Hp.*Aph.*4.71, cf. Gal.17(1).494. II. *bringing clouds*, οἱ βορέαι Arist.*Pr.*947ᵇ5.

**ἐπινεφής**, ές, *clouded, dark*, [ἀήρ] Arist.*Pr.*941ᵃ5, Thphr.*CP*5.12.2; ἐπινεφῆ *a clouded sky*, Id.*Vent.*51. II. *bringing clouds*, [ἄνεμος] ib.4.

**ἐπινεφρίδιος**, ον, *upon the kidneys*, δημός Il.21.204.

**ἐπινέφω**, *bring clouds over the sky*, Arist.*Pr.*944ᵇ26; ἐπινέφει ὁ Ζεύς Alex.29; ἐ. [ἄνεμος] Thphr.*Vent.*61: or impers., ἐπινέφει *it is cloudy*, Id.*CP*3.24.4. (In codd. freq. accentuated as if from ἐπινεφέω.)

**ἐπίνεψις**, εως, ἡ, *clouding over*, Arist.*Pr.*944ᵇ25.

**ἐπινέω** (A), *spin to*, esp. like ἐπικλώθω, of the Fates, γιγνομένῳ ἐπένησε λίνῳ *span* for him with her thread at his birth, Il.20.128, 24.210: —Pass., ὁ ἐπινηθεὶς αὐταῖς μόχθος Ael.*NA*7.1, cf. *Fr.*260; ἐπινενησμένα ἐς ἅπαντας Ps.-Luc.*Philopatr.*14.

**ἐπινέω** (B), *heap upon*, γῆν πολλήν Longus 1.31: elsewhere in Ep. form ἐπινηνέω, q.v. II. *heap up* or *load with*, c. gen. rei, ἁμάξας.. ἐπινέουσι φρυγάνων Hdt.4.62: pf. part. Pass., τράπεζαι ἐπινενησμέναι ἀγαθῶν ἁπάντων Ar.*Ec.*838 (-νενασμέναι codd.).

**ἐπινέω** (C), fut. -νεύσομαι, *float on the top*, Alex.33.5; ἐπὶ λεκάνης Ath.15.667e. 2. *swim upon*, τινί Aristid.2.94J.; *swim over*, Arist. *HA*620ᵇ22.

**ἐπίνηθρος**, ὁ, = *iniclaris* (?), *Gloss.*

**ἐπινήϊος**, ον, *on board ship*, *AP*9.82 (Antip. Thess.).

**ἐπινηνέω**, Ep. for ἐπινέω (B), only in impf., *heap* or *pile upon*, c. gen. loci, νεκροὺς πυρκαϊῆς ἐπενήνεον Il.7.428; perh. to be read in Iamb. *VP*3.17. (Fort. -νήεον, cf. νηέω.)

**ἐπινήσιος**, α, ον, *on an island*, ἄκρα *Stad.*182 (s.v.l.).

**ἐπίνητρον**, τό, *distaff*, Poll.7.32, 10.125, *EM*362.20.

**ἐπινήφω**, *to be sober at* or *in*, τῷ βίῳ Plu.2.87e; τῇ πράξει *for* it, Luc.*Am.*45.

**ἐπινήχομαι**, Dor. -νάχ- [ᾱ], *swim upon*, πόντῳ Batr.107, cf. Cerc. 17.11; *flow over*, τοῖς πεδίοις Hdn.8.4.3; παιδὸς ἐπενάχετο φωνά *floated on* the stream, Theoc.23.61; *float*, ὑγρὸν -όμενον ταῖς κρήναις Dsc.1.73, cf. Sor.1.115, Alex.Aphr.*Pr.*1.22; opp. καταδύεσθαι, *Gp.* 7.8.2; of Noah, Ph.1.455; ἀέρι ib.602: metaph., ib.166, Dam.*Pr.* 270. 2. *swim to* or *over to*, c. acc., Call.*Del.*21. 3. *swim against, attack*, ἄλλῳ ἐ. ἄλλος πότμον ἄγων Opp.*H.*2.46.

**ἐπινήχυτος**, ον, = νήχυτος, *abundant*, δῶρα Orph.*A.*39,312.

**ἐπινίκ-ειος** [ῐ], ον, = sq., S.*OC*1088 (lyr.). **-ιος**, ον, *of victory*, ἀοιδαί Pi.*N.*4.78; ὕμνος D.S.5.29; ἀγῶνες ἐ. games *to celebrate victory*, Plb.30.22.1, cf. *IGRom.*4.1268 (Thyatira); ἐ. πομπή, ἑορτή, D.H.3. 41, Plu.*Rom.*29; ἐ. τιμαί the honours *of a triumph*, Id.*Aem.*31; ἡμέρα Id.*Cor.*3; στολή D.C.37.21. Adv. -ίως Hsch. s.v. ἀλαλάζει. II. as Subst., ἐπινίκιον (sc. ᾆσμα, μέλος), τό, *song of victory, triumphal ode*, such as Pindar's, cf. Ath.1.3e; Ζῆνα.. ἐπινίκια κλάζων A.*Ag.*174 (lyr.). 2. ἐπινίκια (sc. ἱερά), τά, *sacrifice for a victory* or *feast in honour of it*, Ar.*Fr.*433, And.4.29, D.21.55, etc.; τὰ ἐ. θύειν Pl.*Smp.*173a, etc.; ἑστιᾶν D.59.33; ἐ. πέμψαι, πεμφθῆναι, of a Roman *triumph*, D.C.36.25, 37.21. b. (sc. ἆθλα) *prize of victory*, S.*El.* 692, D.H.3.27, *IG*7.3195,3196 (Orchom. Boeot.). **-ος**, ον, = foreg., ἄωτος Pi.*O.*8.75, cf. Stratt.40 (dub. l.): Subst. ἐπίνικος (sc. ὕμνος), ὁ, Aristid.*Or.*28(49).34, 61 (pl.).

**ἐπινιπτρὶς** κύλιξ cup handed round at table *after washing hands*, *grace*-cup, Poll.6.31.

**ἐπινίσσομαι**, *go over*, c. gen., πεδίων S *OC*689 (lyr.). 2. c. acc., *come upon, visit*, A.R.4.817, Nic.*Th.*470, *Pae.Delph.*6: abs., Theoc. 8.43, A.R.4.281. (Written with single -σ-, *Pae.Delph.* l.c.)

**ἐπινίφω**, misspelling of ἐπινείφω, q.v.

**ἐπινο-έω**, *think on* or *of, contrive*, τι Hdt.1.48, Hp.*Art.*42,77, Ar. *Eq.*884, Pl.*Lg.*677b; φάρμακον τῇ ψύξει Ael.*NA*9.7, etc.: c. inf., πῶς ἐπενόησας ἁρπάσαι; Ar.*Eq.*1202, cf. *Nu.*1039: abs., *form plans*, opp. δρᾶν, Antipho 3.2.7; opp. ἐπεξελθεῖν, Th.1.70; opp. ἐξεργάσασθαι, Ph.*Bel.*58.43. 2. *have in one's mind, intend, purpose*, ὀλίγον οὐδέν Th.2.8, cf. X.*An.*2.5.4, etc.: c. pres. inf., Hdt.1.27, Ar.*Th.*338, X. *An.*6.4.9, etc.: fut., Hdt.3.134: aor., Id.2.152, 5.24,65, E.*Rh.*195 (lyr., nowhere else in Trag.), Pl.*Ti.*37c:—Pass., Philostr.*Her.*10. 6. 3. *note, observe*, Phld.*Po.*5.11; *perceive*, Plu.*Per.*6. 4. *conceive*, Epicur.*Ep.*1 p.23U.:—Pass., ib.p.6U., S.E.*M.*8.381. II. *invent, contrive*, κατασκευήν Gal.*UP*12.6, etc.:—Med., aor. -ησάμην Luc. *Astr.*17:—Pass., ὀνόματα ὑπὸ τῶν φιλοσόφων ἐπινοηθέντα Id.*Deor. Conc.*13, etc.; but aor. Pass. ἐπινοηθῆναι in act. sense in Hdt.3.122, 6.115, Luc.*Am.*16,31. **-ημα**, ατος, τό, *thought, purpose, contrivance*, Hp.*Art.*42, Antipho Soph.101; esp. in Rhet., Ruf.Rh.p.404 H., Aristid.*Rh.*2p.521S., al. 2. *conception*, Epicur.*Nat.*130,137 G. **-ημᾰτικός**, ή, όν, = ἐπινοητικός, Vett.Val.49.6. **-ήμων**, ον, gen. ονος, = foreg., Id.72.19, Zonar. **-ησις**, εως, ἡ, *thought, conception*, Phld.*Mort.*36. **-ητέον**, *one must contrive, devise means*, c. inf., Nicom.*Harm.*4; τί πρακτέον Hld.10.38; *one must devise* a remedy, Philum.ap.Aët.5.119. **-ητής**, οῦ, ὁ, *inventive person*, περὶ τὰς ἐδωδάς M.Ant.1.16. **-ητικός**, ή, όν, *inventive*, of a writer, Longin.4.1; ἐ. τοῦ διασῴζειν ἑαυτόν Ath.7.310f. 2. *due to reflection*, φάσμα Epicur. *Nat.*362. **-ητός**, ή, όν, *conceivable*, *Vit.Philonid.*p.10C., Phld.*Mus.* p.92K.; *object of thought, existing in the mind*, S.E.*M.*8.38.

**ἐπίνοια**, ἡ, *thinking on* or *of* a thing, *thought, notion*, οὐδ' ἐς ἐπίνοιαν ἰέναι τινός Th.3.46; ὡς.. Id.4.92; οὐδ' ἐπίνοιαν ποιήσασθαί τινος Plb.1.20.12; τὰς ἐ. εἴς τι φέρειν D.H.*Pomp.*1; πάσαις ταῖς ἐ. γίγνεσθαι περί τι Plb.5.110.10; *conception, idea*, ἐναργὴς τοῦ πράγματος ἐ. Epicur.*Fr.*255, cf. Phld.*D.*3.8, al.; κατ' ἐπίνοιαν in *idea*, opp. κατὰ περίπτωσιν (q.v.), *Stoic.*2.29; κατ' ἐ. ψιλὴν ὑφεστάναι ib.159; πᾶσαν ἐ. ἀτοπίας ὑπερβάλλειν Plu.2.1063d. 2. *power of thought, inventiveness*, οἶνον σὺ τολμᾷς εἰς ἐ. λοιδορεῖν; Ar.*Eq.*90, cf. X.*Cyr.*2.3.19; κατὰ τέχνην καὶ ἐ. γίγνεσθαι Thphr.*Od.*7. 3. *invention, device, conceit*, ἐ. ἀστειόταται Ar.*Eq.*539; ζητεῖν καινὴν ἐ. Id.*V.*346; θαυμαστὰς ἐξευρίσκων ἐ. Id.*Eq.*1322, etc.; τέχνης ἐπίνοιαι Arist.*Mu.*399ᵇ 17; πενία ἐπινοιῶν διδάσκαλος Secund.*Sent.*10. 4. *purpose, design*, τίν' ἐ. ἔσχεθες; E.*Ph.*408, cf. *Med.*760 (lyr.); τίς ἐ.; Ar.*Th.*766, cf. *Av.*405 (lyr.); ἥτις ἡ 'πίνοια τῆς ἐγκεντρίδος Id.*V.*1073, cf. *Pl.*45; κατὰ τὴν ἐκφορὰν καὶ τὴν ἐ. *Stoic.*2.128; ἡ ἐ. τῆς καρδίας *Act.Ap.*8.22: pl., ἐξ οἰκείων ἐ., = *sua sponte*, *OGI*580.7 (Cilicia, iv A.D.). II. *afterthought, second thoughts*, ψεύδει γὰρ ἡ 'πίνοια τὴν γνώμην S.*Ant.* 389. III. *intelligence*, κοινὴ ἐ. Plb.6.5.2, cf. Longin.ap.Eus.*PE* 15.20. 2. Psychol., *reflection on experience, retrospection*, Plot.2. 9.1, 6.8.7.

**ἐπινομ-ή**, ἡ, (ἐπινέμομαι) *a grazing over the boundaries*: metaph., ἐ. πυρός *the spread* of fire, Plu.*Alex.*35; of poison, Ael.*NA*12. 32. 2. *right of pasturage*, *Schwyzer* 197.33 (Itanos, iii B.C.). 3. *grazing after* mowing, *POxy.*730.11 (ii A.D.), al. II. pl., *final turns of a bandage*, Heliod.ap.Orib.48.51.2 (pl.), Gal.18(2).563. **-ία**, ἡ, *a grazing over the boundaries*: *right of pasture*, X.*Cyr.*3.2.23 (pl., cf. Poll.7.184), *Berl.Sitzb.*1927.7 (Locr., v B.C.), *IG*9(2).61.7 (Lamia),

5(2).511 (Arc., iii/ii B.C.); ἐ. ἐν τᾷ Δελφίδι SIG534.15 (Delph., iii B.C.). -ιον, τό, *payment for pasturage*, IG5(2).456 (Megalop.), prob. in GDI4647 (Messenia). II. (νόμος) = sq. I, title of work ascribed to Plato, TheoSm.pp.7,84,178 H. -ίς, ίδος, ἡ, *addition to a law, appendix*, name of a work ascribed to Plato; applied to Deuteronomy by Ph.1.495. II. *new-year's gift*, Ath.3.97d. III. *part of a trireme*, Apollonius ἐν Τριηρικῷ ibid.

ἐπινομοθετέω, *make additional laws*, Pl.*Lg*.779d.

ἐπίνομος, ον, *visiting the land*, ἐ. ἡρωΐδων στρατός Pi.*P*.11.7. II. *legal, formal*, App.*BC*3.94 (Sup., s.v.l.). III. Subst. ἐ., ὁ, *possessor of right of pasturage*, *Berl.Sitzb*.1927.8 (Locr., v B.C.). 2. = κληρονόμος, IG9(1).694.36 (Corc.), *Delph*.3(2).243 (ii B.C.), *Schwyzer* 335.18, al., Hsch.

ἐπινοσέω, *to be ill after*, μετὰ τοὺς τόκους Hp.*Epid*.1.16, cf. Phryn. *PS* p.120 B.

ἐπίνοσος, ον, *subject to sickness, unhealthy*, σῶμα Arist.*EN*1113a28, cf. Thphr.*Fr*.20.48 Schneider, D.S.2.48; γενεά Ph.1.516. Adv. -σως *like one who is sick*, διάγειν Hp.*Epid*.1.5, Crates *Ep*.20; ἐ. διακειμένου τοῦ σώματος Sor.1.117, cf. *POxy*.939.21 (iv A.D.). II. *unwholesome*, χωρίον Porph.*Abst*.1.36; θέρος *Gp*.1.12.34; τόπος Hierocl. *Facet*.73; κατομβρία Lyd.*Ost*.37.

ἐπινοσσοποιέομαι, Med., *build their nests upon*, ὄρεσιν Ps.-Democr. *Symp.Ant*.p.6 G.

ἐπίνοστος, ον, *for a return*, ᾠδή Hsch. s.v. ἱμαῖος.

ἐπινοτίζω, *sprinkle on the surface*, Dsc.2.83.2. II. Pass., *perspire slightly*, Philum.ap.Aët.5.78.

ἐπινυκτ-ερεύω, *pass the night at* or *in*, ναυσί Heraclit.*All*.9; of water, *stand for a night*, Plu.2.690c. ⊛ -ίδιος, ον, = sq., Procop.*Aed*. 1.7. -ιος, ον, *by night*, ἐ. μῆλα νομεύων *AP*6.262 (Leon.). -ίς, ίδος, ἡ, *pustule which is most painful by night*, Hp.*Aër*.3, Diocl.*Fr*. 82, Ruf.ap.Orib.44.20.1, Antyll.ib.10.24.10, etc. II. (-νεκτίς cod.)· φυλακὴ δοκοῦντι ἀδικεῖν, Hsch.

ἐπινύμφ-ειος, ον, *bridal*, ὕμνος prob. in S.*Ant*.814 (lyr.): fem. -είη *Supp.Epigr*.2.874 (nisi ἐπὶ νυμφείην). ⊛ -εύομαι, *contract a second marriage*, of a woman, GDI3721.5 (Cos). -ίδιος, ον, *bridal*, Ἀΐδας *AP*7.182 (Mel.).

ἐπινύσσω, *prick on the surface*, Antyll.ap.Orib.10.19.5; -οντες πόνοι *stabbing* pains, Archig.ap.Gal.8.110:—Pass., Sor.*Fract*.24, f.l. in Luc.*Lex*.11.

ἐπινυστάζω, *drop asleep over*, τοῖς σιτίοις Plu.*Brut*.36: abs., Luc. *Bis Acc*.2, Agath.4.18.

⊛ ἐπινωμάω, *bring* or *apply to*, παιῶνα κακῶν τινί S.*Ph*.168 (anap.); σώματα .. ὄμματος αὐγαῖς ἐπενώμας *didst survey* .., E.*Ph*.1564 (anap.). II. *distribute, apportion*, λάχη τὰ κατ' ἀνθρώπους A.*Eu*. 311 (anap.); κλήρους Id.*Th*.727 (lyr.), cf. S.*Ant*.139 (lyr.).

⊛ ἐπινῶς, = λίαν, Suid.; read by Sch. for ἐπιμανῶς in Luc.*VH*2.25.

ἐπινωτ-ιδεύς, έως, ὁ, = νωτιδανός, Epaen.ap.Ath.7.294d. -ίδιος, ον, *on the back*, *AP*6.21.3. ⊛ -ίζω, *attack from behind*, E.*HF*362 (lyr.); = ἐφορμάω, Archipp.5:—Med., *take on one's back*, Paus.Gr.*Fr*. 143. -ιος, ον, *on the back*, Batr.80, Luc.*Am*.26, Alciphr.3. 68. II. ἐπινώτιοι, οἱ, *shoulder-blades*, Poll.2.133 (v.l. ἐπινώτια).

ἐπιξαίνω, *scratch*, τὴν κατάποσιν Sor.1.86.

ἐπιξανθ-ίζω, *brown over by toasting*, πλευρὰ δελφάκεια Pherecr.108. 16 (Pass.). -ος, ον, *inclining to yellow, tawny*, of hares, X.*Cyn*. 5.22; of deer, Poll.5.76; of the open lime-flower, Thphr.*HP*3.10.4, cf. 4.2.7.

ἐπιξενᾰγ-ία, ἡ, = *four* ξεναγίαι, i.e. 2048 *men*, Ascl.*Tact*.6.3, etc. -ός, ὁ, *officer attached to an* ἐπιξεναγία, Ascl.*Tact*.6.3, Ael.*Tact*.16.4, Arr.*Tact*.14.6.

ἐπιξενοδίκη· ἡ συνηγορή, καὶ ἡττηθεὶς ἀπόλλυται, Hsch.

ἐπιξεν-όομαι, Ep. -ξειν- A.R.2.764:—Pass., *to be entertained as a guest, dwell abroad*, Isoc.*Ep*.6.2, Arist.*Pol*.1327a13; πόλει Luc. *Am*.7; *to be on a visit*, εἰς Ὀξύρυγχα Mitteis *Chr*.8.2 (iii B.C.); ἐ. τινί *to be entertained* by one, A.R.l.c., Plu.2.250a; Σοφοκλεῖ ζῶντι Ἀσκληπιὸν ἐ. Id.*Num*.4; παρά τισι *Sammelb*.6262 (iii A.D.). 2. *have hospitable relations with, be intimate with*, ἐπεξενῶσθαι πολλοῖς D.50.56, cf. D.S.1.23; ἡ ἐπιξενωθεῖσα σώμασι μοῖρα *lent to* or *communicated with*, Heraclit.ap.S.E.*M*.7.130. II. as Med., in A.*Ag*.1320 ἐπιξενοῦμαι ταῦτα δ' ὡς θανουμένη *I appeal to thee in* these matters, as one at death's door, cf. S.*Fr*.146. ⊛ -ος, ὁ, = ἐπιχθόνιος, Hsch. 2. *stranger*, *POxy*.480.11 (ii A.D.), etc. -ωσις, εως, ἡ, *hospitable relations*, pl., D.S.31.13, *SIG*888.140 (iii A.D.).

ἐπιξέστ-ης, ου, ὁ, (ἐπιξέω) *workman who dresses blocks of masonry*, IG$2^{2}$.1672.31. -ικῶς, gloss on ἐπιγράβδην, Sch.Il.21.166, Hsch.

ἐπιξέω, *scrape* or *graze on the surface*, Hp.*VC*14 (v.l. for ἐπιξύω), Aret.*CD*1.2; ἅλμασιν ἀκρωνύχοις τὴν πέτραν Hld.5.14: metaph., *polish* a poem, *Vit.Apollon.Rhod.*

⊛ ἐπίξηνον, τό [not -ος, ὁ, as Suid.], (ξηνός) *chopping-block*, Eust. 1443.16; *executioner's block*, A.*Ag*.1277, Ar.*Ach*.318, 355, 359, 365.

ἐπιξηρ-αίνω, *dry on the surface*, Hp.*Fract*.33, Arist.*Pr*.928a9:—Pass., *to be so dried*, Hp.*Prorrh*.2.6; *have an interval of dryness*, Id. *Acut*.28: generally, *to be dried up*, Ruf.*Ren.Ves*.6.5; *to be constipated*, Aret.*CA*1.1. -ᾱσία, ἡ, *dryness on the top*, Hp.*Epid*.6.2.6. -ος, ον, *very dry*, γλῶσσα ib.1.26.β', cf. Aret.*SD*1.15: Comp., *more arid*, Id.*CA*1.1.

⊛ ἐπιξοά, ἡ, Archit., *dressing* of blocks, IG4.1484.84 (Epid.).

ἐπιξυλία, ἡ, *right of cutting timber*, IG5(2).510 (Thisoa, iii/ii B.C.).

ἐπίξυλον· τὸ ἐπὶ παραστροφίδα τοῦ ὑφαινομένου ἱματίου, Hsch.

ἐπίξῡν-ος, ον, poet. for ἐπίκοινος, ἐ. ἄρουρα *a common* field, in which several persons have rights, Il.12.422. -όω, poet. for ἐπικοινόω, *impart* τινί τι Nonn.*D*.26.290:—Med., A.R.3.1162, 4.435.

ἐπιξῠρ-άω, *shave*, ἐπιξύρα τὸν τόπον Cleopatra ap.Gal.12.404. -ητέον, *one must shave*, τὸν τόπον Menemach.ap.Orib.10.15.4.

⊛ ἐπιξύω, *grate over*, τυρὸν ἐπιξυσθέντα Pl.*R*.406a, cf. Arist.*HA*612b 17; *scrape the surface* of the skull, Hp.*VC*14. 2. *skim over*, γαῖαν Arat.650. 3. Pass., *to be carved*, εἰκόνες λίθῳ Procop.*Aed*.1.11.

ἐπιογδοηκοστὸς λόγος ratio *of* 81 : 80, Ptol.*Harm*.1.16.

ἐπιόγδοος λόγος ratio *of* 9 : 8, Porph. *in Harm*.p.310 W.

ἐπιοικοδομά, ἡ, v. ἐποικοδομή. ἐπίϜοικος, v. ἔποικος.

ἐπιοίνιος, ον, *at* or *over wine*, ἆθλον Thgn.971.

ἐπιοινοχοεύω, *pour out wine for*, θεοῖς *h.Ven*.204.

ἐπιοκτωκαιδέκατος λόγος ratio *of* 19 : 18, Ptol.*Harm*.2.1.

⊛ ἐπιοπτ-εύω, *inspect, overlook*, *Schwyzer* 701 *C* (Erythrae, v B.C.). -ης, ου, ὁ, poet. for ἐπόπτης, βοτῶν Hom.*Epigr*.11. -ος, ον, poet. for ἔποπτος, *observed*, Opp.*H*.1.10; *visible*, Arat.25.

ἐπιοραντές· τερπνόν, ἁρπαλέον, Hsch.

⊛ ἐπιορκ-έω, also ἐφιορκέω IG$2^{2}$.1126.9 (Delph. Amphict.), *OGI* 229.69 (Smyrna, iii B.C.), etc.: fut. -ήσω Il.19.188, Ar.*Lys*.914, etc., -ήσομαι (κατ-) D.54.40: aor. ἐπιώρκησα Id.49.67, inf. -ορκῆσαι Hdt. 4.68 (v.l. ἐφ-): pf. ἐπιώρκηκα Pl.*Lg*.948e, X.*An*.3.1.22, Din.1.47 (ἐπιόρκηκα is v.l. in Hdt.l.c.):—*swear falsely, forswear oneself*, οὐδ' ἐπιορκήσω πρὸς δαίμονος Il.19.188: also, c. acc., of things sworn by, τὰς βασιληΐας ἱστίας ἐπιώρκηκε *has sworn falsely by* the royal hearth, Hdt.4.68; θεάς Din.1.47; [θεούς] Ar.*Av*.1609, X.*An*.2.4.7, D.49.67, etc.: mostly abs., Ar.*Eq*.298, 428, *Nu*.402, Pl.*Phlb*.65c, etc.; οὐδὲν ἐφρόντιζ' ἐπιορκῶν D.21.119: c. acc. cogn., ἐ. ὅρκους τινί Id.49.65, cf. Aeschin.1.115; opp. εὐορκέω, Lex ap.And.1.98, Cleanth. *Stoic*.1.131, Chrysipp.ib.2.63, who distinguishes betw. εὐορκεῖν and ἀληθορκεῖν, and betw. ἐπιορκεῖν and ψευδορκεῖν. II. simply, = ὄμνυμι, *swear*, Sol.ap.Lys.10.17. ⊛ -ία, ἡ, *false swearing, perjury*, X.*An*.3.2.4, etc.; ἐ. οἴκαδ' εἰσενέγκασθαι D.19.220: pl., Pl.*Grg*.525a; πρὸς θεούς X.*An*.2.5.21. -ίζω, prob. = ἐξορκ-, *Tab.Defix.Aud*. 41 B 1. -ος, ον, *sworn falsely*, of oaths, εἰ δέ τι τῶνδ' ἐπίορκον Il. 19.264: freq. in the phrase ἐπίορκον ὀμόσσαι take *a false oath*, swear *falsely*, 3.279, 19.260, Hes.*Op*.282, *Th*.232; in full, ἐπίορκον ὅρκον ὤμοσε Ar.*Ra*.150; and so ἐ. ἐπομνύναι (v. ἐπόμνυμι); but in Il.10.332 ἐ. ἐπώμοσε he swore *a bootless oath*, i.e. one which he meant to fulfil, but the gods willed otherwise. II. of persons, *forsworn, perjured*, Hes.*Op*.804, *Schwyzer* 179a (Crete), E.*El*.1355 (anap.), Ar.*Nu*. 399, al.: Sup. -ότατος Antipho 6.48. Adv. -κως Hdn.6.9.2. -οσύνη, ἡ, = ἐπιορκία, *AP*12.250.6 (Strat.). ἐπίορος, v. ἐπίουρος II.

⊛ ἐπιόσσομαι, *have before one's eyes*, ἐπιοσσομένῳ θάνατον καὶ φύζαν ἑταίρων Il.17.381; *gaze on*, A.R.2.28 (tm.); ἐ. αὐγὰς ἠελίοιο, i.e. live, Nic.*Th*.276.

ἐπιουδίς, Adv. *on the floor*, Theognost.*Can*.163. ἐπίουρα, v. οὖρον.

ἐπιούριον, τό, Dim. of sq. II, Hero *Aut*.28.6.

ἐπίουρος, ὁ, = οὖρος (B), *guardian, watcher, ward*, c. gen., ὑῶν ἐ. Od. 13.405; βοῶν Theoc.8.6, 25.1; Οἰχαλίης A.R.1.87; ναυτιλίης v.l. in Id.4.652: less freq. c. dat., Μίνωα τέκε Κρήτῃ ἐ. Il.13.450; κρήνῃ A.R. 3.1180. II. *wooden peg, pin*, IG4.1484.63 (Epid.), Hero *Aut*.16.2, al., *Hippiatr*.26, *Gp*.10.61, prob. l. in Arist.*Pr*.915a11; nickname of Secundus (son of a joiner), Philostr.*VS*1.26: Lat. *epiurus*, Pall.*Agr*. 12.7.15, prob. in Sen.*Ben*.2.12, Aug.*Civ.Dei* 15.27, Isid.*Etym*.19. 19.7: also ἐπίορος, *Ath.Mitt*.51.154 (Delos).

ἐπιούσιος, ον, either, *sufficient for the coming* (and so *current*) *day*, (ἐπιοῦσα (sc. ἡμέρα)), or, *for the day* (ἐπὶ τὴν οὖσαν (sc. ἡμέραν)), ἄρτος *Ev.Matt*.6.11, *Ev.Luc*.11.3; τὰ ἐ. dub. sens. (cf. *Phil.Woch*.47.889) in *Sammelb*.5224.20. (Very rare word in Origen's day, *De Orat*. 27.7.)

⊛ ἐπιόψομαι, fut. (or Ep. aor. subj.), *I will choose*, Il.9.167, Od.2. 294: aor. 1 ind. ἐπιωψάμην *chose*, IG2.948.1 (iv B.C.), cf. Pl.*Lg*.947c (ἐπόψ- codd.), Hsch., Suid.: aor. 1 Pass., τοὺς ἐπιοφθέντας IG2.949.2 (iv/iii B.C.). (From ὀπ- 'choose', cf. Lat. *optare*.)

ἐπίπᾰγος, ὁ, (ἐπιπήγνυμι) *congealed* or *hardened crust on the top of a thing*, Dsc.1.101.2, Aret.*SA*1.9, Gal.*Lex*. s.v. σύναγμα; ἐ. ὑμενώδης *capsule* of lens, Ruf.*Anat*.17; ἁλώδης Plu.2.627f; = γραῦς II, *scum*, Hsch., cf. Gal.6.252.

ἐπίπαγχυ, Adv., strengthd. for πάγχυ, Theoc.17.104, Maiist.13.

ἐπιπᾰθής, ές, *liable to diseases*, *Cat.Cod.Astr*.8(4).132, Paul.Al.*L*. 2: Comp., Id.*O*.

ἐπιπαιᾱν-ίζω, *sing a paean over*, D.S.5.29: c. acc. cogn., πομπήν Plu.*Marc*.22. (The form -παιωνίζω is found in Hsch.) -ισμός, ὁ, *song of victory*, ἐπὶ νίκῃ Str.9.3.10 (v.l. -ωνισμός).

ἐπιπαίζω, *mock at*, τινί Hld.10.13: abs., Alex.172.16, with reference to the preceding line, where ἐπιπαίζεται means *are an after-play*, in allusion to things eaten at a second course. 2. *sport upon*, θαλάττῃ Philostr.*Im*.2.17.

⊛ ἐπίπαιγμα, ατος, τό, = ἐπίπταισμα, πρόσκομμα, Hsch.

ἐπιπαιστικός, ή, όν, (ἐπιπαίζω) *droll*, πρόβλημα Clearch.63.

ἐπιπακτίς, ίδος, ἡ, *rupture-wort*, *Herniaria glabra*, Dsc.4.108 (cf. ἐπικακτίς).

ἐπιπακτόω, *shut close*, τὰς θύρας Ar.*Fr*.721.

ἐπιπᾰλᾰμάομαι, = ἐπιμηχανάομαι, dub. in Luc.*Tox*.16 (v.l. -καλαμ-).

ἐπιπάλλω, *brandish at* or *against*, βέλη A.*Ch*.162 (lyr.).

ἐπιπᾰμᾰτίς, ίδος, ἡ, = ἐπίκληρος, prob. in *Delph*.3(1).294 *V* 7, *GDI* 4969 (Gortyn), cf. Sch.Ar.*V*.581, Hsch.

ἐπιπαμφᾰλάω, *glance over*, A.R.2.127.

**ἐπίπαν** or ἐπὶ πᾶν, v. ἐπί. II. Adj. ἐπίπαντες, v. ἐπίπας.

**ἐπιπάξ·** συντόμως.., ἢ ἐπὶ τὰ ἀριστερά, Hsch. (cf. ἐπιτάξ, ἐπιζάξ).

**ἐπίπαππος,** ὁ, *grandfather's grandfather*, Poll.3.18, Sch.rec.S.*OT* 183; or, *grandfather's father*, Jul.*Or*.2.82b, Hsch.; *grandfather*, Lib. *Or*.1.3, al., prob.l. in *BCH*17.532 (Mysia).

**ἐπιπαραγίγνομαι,** *arrive on the scene*, Satyr.*Vit.Eur.Fr*.39xxi 25, Mitteis *Chr*.8.3 (iii B.C.), etc.; of generals, *succeed in a command*, Plb.1.31.4; of troops, *come up*, ἀτάκτως καὶ σποράδην Id.4.12.7; of events, *come also upon*, τινί Junc.ap.Stob.4.50.27.

**ἐπιπαράγω** [ᾰγ], *bring round upon*, τὴν χεῖρα ἐπὶ τὸ στῆθος Hp. *Mochl*.5.

**ἐπιπαρα-δέχομαι,** Gramm., *take besides*, ἄρθρον A.D.*Synt*.170. 13. **-κειμαι,** *to be adjacent*, Steph. *in Hp*.1.209 D. **-μένω,** *continue to stay with* some one, Phld.*Herc*.1041.1. **-νέω,** *heap up still more besides*, Th.2.77.

**ἐπιπαρᾰριθμέω,** *reckon in comparison*, *PRev.Laws* 76.2 (iii B.C.).

**ἐπιπαρασκευάζομαι,** *provide oneself with besides*, X.*Cyr*.6.3.1.

**ἐπιπάρειμι** (A), (εἰμί *sum*) *to be present besides* or *in addition*, Th. 1.61 codd. (leg. -ιόντας), Luc.*Merc.Cond*.26; *to be present to*, τινί Id. *Symp*.20, Ach.Tat.2.7. 2. Astrol., *occupy a position as well*, Nech. ap.Vett.Val.279.16.

**ἐπιπάρειμι** (B), (εἶμι *ibo*) *march on high ground parallel with* one below, X.*An*.3.4.30, Plb.10.13.3, etc. 2. c. dat., *proceed to attack*, ἐπιπαριὼν τῷ δεξιῷ Th.5.10. 3. *come to one's assistance*, Id.4.108, etc.; εἰ δέοι τι.., ἐπιπαρῇσαν οὗτοι X.*An*.3.4.23; ἐπιπαριόντες ib. 30. 4. *pass along the front of* an army, so as to address it (cf. πάρειμι IV. 2), Th.4.94, 6.67, 7.76; ἐ. κατὰ πρόσωπον Plb.5.83.1. 5. *visit in passing*, Φρυγίαν, Μυσίαν, App.*BC*5.7.

**ἐπιπαρ-εμβάλλω,** *re-form*, ἐ. φάλαγγα Plb.12.19.6. II. intr., *fall into line with others*, Id.3.115.10, 11.23.5. **-έξειμι,** *pass farther along*, of the sun (relatively to the moon), Arist.*Pr*.912$^a$11. **-έρχομαι,** *go past on the way to* a place, παρὰ τὴν ὄχθην D.C.40.35; κατὰ τὰ μετέωρα Id.47.35. 2. Astrol., *intervene as well*, ἐπὶ τόπον Vett. Val.291.9. **-οδος,** ἡ, *second* πάροδος (q.v.), Poll.4.108. **-οινέω,** in Pass., *to be further intoxicated* (with anger), prob. in Phld.*Ir*.p.33 W. **-οξύνω,** *incite still more*, D.C.44.35, Ach.Tat.1.8:—Pass., of persons in fever, *suffer from successive accesses*, v.l. in Hp.*Epid*. 1.2, cf. Gal.7.306; of a sore, *become more inflamed*, Hp.*Prorrh*.1. 162 (dub.). **-ορμάω,** *stir up yet more*, πρὸς τὸν πόλεμον Plu.2.118f.

**ἐπιπαρουσία,** ἡ, *presence* of a planet in a τόπος, *Cat.Cod.Astr*.5(3). 88.5, Paul.Al.*O*.4.

**ἐπιπαρρησιάζομαι,** abs., *apply plain-speaking*, Phld.*Lib*.p.3 O.

⊕ **ἐπίπας,** πασα, παν, = σύμπας, Cret. fem. ἐπίπανσα *Schwyzer* 176.2: pl. ἐπίπαντες ib.198.15 (Crete, ii B.C.), *AP*12.87 (Strat.).

**ἐπιπᾰσῐμάχη** [ᾰχ], ἡ, *general engagement*, *IG*14.1296.

**ἐπί-πασμα,** ατος, τό, *powder for sprinkling*, ῥοὸς Aret.*CA*2.2; ἄρτων Sch.Theoc.15.114, cf. Alex.Trall.*Febr*.3. **-πάσσω,** Att. -ττω, Dor. inf. ἐπιπῆν *IG*4.951.119 (Epid.), cf. πῆν:—*sprinkle upon* or *over*, ἐπ' ἄρ' ἤπια φάρμακα πάσσε Il.4.218, cf. 5.401, *IG*l.c., Euphro11.10; τι ἐπί τι Hdt.4.172; τινί τι Orph.*L*.455, Luc.*DMar*.15.3: c. partit. gen., τῆς εἰρωνείας Id.*Pisc*.22: abs., Theoc.2.18:—Pass., ἐπ' οἶνον ἄλφιτα ἐπιπασθέντα Pl.*R*.405e, cf. *PTeb*.1.19. ⊕ **-παστέον,** *one must sprinkle* or *spread*, Antyll.ap.Orib.7.21.8. **-παστος,** η, ον, *sprinkled over*, ἐπίπασται τευθίδες Philox.2.16. II. ἐπίπαστον, τό, a kind of *cake with comfits* (or the like) *upon it*, Ar.*Eq*.103, 1089, Pherecr.130.3; but (sc. φάρμακον), = ἐπίπασμα, Hp.*Hum*.5, Theoc. 11.2, Aret.*CA*2.2.

**ἐπιπᾰτᾰγέω,** *make a noise with*, κώδωνι καὶ τυμπάνῳ Men.Prot. p.50 D.

**ἐπιπατρόφιον,** τό, *patronymic*, *Schwyzer* 462 *A* 28 (Tanagra, iii B.C.).

**ἐπιπάτωρ** [ᾰ], ορος, ὁ, (πατήρ) *stepfather*, Poll.3.26.

**ἐπιπαφλάζω,** *boil upon* or *over*, κύματα ἐ. αἰγιαλοῖσιν Q.S.11.229, cf. Nonn.*D*.7.34; *boil*, *foam in*, c. dat., ib.1.237.

**ἐπιπᾰχύνω,** *make still thicker*, Alex.Trall.*Febr*.1 and 7.

**ἐπιπεδάω,** f.l. for πεδάω, Corn.*ND*7.

**ἐπιπεδ-ικός,** ή, όν, *two-dimensional*: κύκλοι *two-dimensional* cyclic numbers, Simp. *in Ph*.59.17. **-όομαι,** *to be made plane*, Iamb. *in Nic*.p.27 P., al. ⊕ **-ος,** ον, *on the ground*, *on the ground-floor*, στοαὶ ἐ., opp. ὑπερῷοι, D.H.3.68, cf. *PFlor*.376.7 (iii A.D.); σηκός Aret.*CA*2. 2. II. *level*, *flat*, Pl.*Criti*.112a; χωρίον X.*HG*7.1.29, etc.; οὐκ ἐν ἐπιπέδῳ, ἀλλὰ πρὸς ὀρθίῳ not *on a level*, but.., ib.6.4.14; ἐξ ἐπιπέδου *PThead*.20 i 3 (iv A.D.); = Lat. *de plano*, J.*AJ*19.5.3: irreg. Comp. -πεδέστερος X.*HG*7.4.13. 2. στεγνὰ ἐπίπεδα an accurately fitting *pavement*, *SIG*996.27 (Smyrna, i A.D.). III. in Geom., *plane*, *superficial*, opp. στερεός (solid), Pl.*Phlb*.51c, *Ti*.32a; ἐ. γωνία a *plane* angle, ib.54e; ἡ τοῦ ἐ. πραγματεία *plane* geometry, Id.*R*.528d; μήκους καὶ ἐ. καὶ βάθους one-, *two*-, and three-*dimensional magnitude*, Id. *Lg*.817e; εἰ κῶνος τέμνοιτο ἐπιπέδῳ Democr.155. 2. of numbers, *representing a surface*, Plu.2.367f, Nicom.*Ar*.2.7; ὁ ἰσόπλευρος καὶ ἐ. ἀριθμός a *square* number, Pl.*Tht*.148a. Adv. -δως Nicom.l.c. **-ωσις,** εως, ἡ, *formation of a plane surface*, Iamb. *in Nic*.p.59 P.

**ἐπιπείθ-εια,** poet. -είη or -ίη, ἡ, *confidence*, Semon.1.6, Porph. *Gaur*.6.4. **-ής,** ές, *obedient*, λόγῳ Arist.*EN*1098$^a$4; τινί Hierocl. *in CA*24 p.473 M. **-ομαι,** *to be persuaded*, εἴ τις ἐμοὶ ἐπιπείσεται.. οἴκαδ' ἴμεν Il.17.154; ἐπεπείθετο θυμὸς ἀγήνωρ Od.2.103. 2. *trust to*, *put faith in*, μαρτυρίοισι A.*Ag*.1095 (lyr.), cf. *IG*14.1389 ii 32. 3. *comply with*, *obey*, τινί Il.1.218, Hes.*Sc*.369; εὖ παραινεῖς, κἀπιπείσομαι S.*El*.1472.

**ἐπιπειράομαι,** *do violence to* a woman, c. acc., *Leg.Gort*.2.17, cf. Hsch. ἐπιπείρει (sic)· μοιχεύεται, ἢ μοιχεύει.

**ἐπιπελάζω,** *bring near to*, ξίφος αἵματι σῷ E.*IT*880 (lyr., tm.).

**ἐπιπελανίαι·** ὀλαί, καὶ πόπανα, Hsch.

⊕ **ἐπιπέλομαι,** *come to* or *upon*, οὐδέ τις ἄλλη νοῦσος ἐπὶ στυγερὴ πέλεται.. βροτοῖσι Od.15.408, cf. 13.60: elsewh. only in Ep. aor. 2 part. ἐπιπλόμενος *rolling on*, *approaching*, ἀλλ' ὅτε δὴ ὄγδοόν μοι ἐπιπλόμενον ἔτος ἦλθεν when the eighth *revolving* year had come, 7.261; ἐπιπλομένων ἐνιαυτῶν Hes.*Sc*.87, *Th*.493 (v. ἐνιαυτός); ἐπιπλ. νυκτί, ἐπιπλ. ἠοῦς A.R.2.1231, 4.670, etc.; of persons, Id.3.25, 127; in hostile sense, *attacking*, *assaulting*, Id.1.465; so of a storm, νέφος.. ἐπιπλ. ἄφατον S.*OT*1314 (lyr.). (Cf. περιτέλλομαι, ἐπιτέλλω (B).)

**ἐπίπεμμα,** ατος, τό, *sacrificial cake*, *Inscr.Prien*.362.15 (iv B.C.), al.

**ἐπιπεμπτέον,** *one must send*, Alex.*Fig*.1.1.

⊕ **ἐπίπεμπτος,** ον, Math., $= 1 + \frac{1}{5}$, Nicom.*Ar*.1.22, etc. 2. of loans *bearing interest at the rate of $\frac{1}{5}$ of the principal*, i.e. 20 per cent., ναυτικὸν ἐ. X.*Vect*.3.9. II. = πέμπτος, Eup.65, Lxx *Le*.5.16, al.; τοὐπίπεμπτον *one-fifth* of the votes in a trial, Ar.*Fr*.201.

⊕ **ἐπιπέμπω,** pf. -πέπομφα *POxy*.743.30 (i A.D.):—*send after* or *again*, ἀγγελίας, ἀγγέλους ἐ., c. inf., Hdt.1.160, 4.83 (nisi leg. περι-). 2. *send to*, τοὺς ὁριστὰς ἐπιπέμψαι ὁρίσαι τὰ ἱερά *IG*1$^2$.94; of the gods, *send upon* or *to*, [ὄνειρον] Hdt.7.15; χάριν Pi.*Fr*.75.2 (tm.); ἔρως τινί Pl.*Phdr*.245b (Pass.); esp. by way of punishment, *send upon* or *against*, *let loose upon*, generally of the gods, γένναν ἂν.. Ἅιδας Καδμείοις ἐ. E.*Ph*.811 (lyr.); δέη καὶ κινδύνους τινί Lys.6.20; δεσμοὺς καὶ θανάτους Pl.*Cri*.46c; ἀνάγκην τινά Id.*Phd*.62c; τισὶ πλῆθος ἄρκων Lxx *Wi*.11.17; *send against*, κατασκόπους τοῖς Ῥωμαίοις App.*Pun*. 39; τῇ Καρχηδόνι τινά prob. ib.49, cf. Hdn.3.3.4. II. *send besides*, ἄλλην στρατιάν Th.7.15; πρὸς τὸ στράτευμα ὠφελίαν ἄλλην Id.6. 73. 2. *send* by way of supply, σιτία Ar.*Ec*.235, cf. Plb.6.15.4; digested food, etc., to various parts of the body, Gal.6.301, 427, 15.112.

**ἐπίπεμψις,** εως, ἡ, *a sending to* a place, διὰ τὴν.. ἐπὶ πολλὰ ὑμῶν αὐτῶν ἐ. Th.2.39, cf. Luc.*Phal*.1.3. 2. *visitation*, Epicur.*Ep*.2 p.44 U. (pl.).

**ἐπιπενθεκτος,** ον, = ἐπιπενταμερής, Nicom.*Ar*.1.21.

**ἐπιπεντᾰκοσιοτέταρτος,** ον, $1 + \frac{1}{54}$, Aristid.Quint.3.1.

**ἐπιπεντᾰμερής,** ές, $= 1 + \frac{5}{6}$, Nicom.*Ar*.1.21.

⊕ **ἐπιπεντεκαιδέκᾰτος** λόγος *ratio of* 16 : 15, Porph. *in Harm*.p.310 W.

**ἐπιπεντένᾰτος,** ον, $= 1 + \frac{5}{9}$, Nicom.*Ar*.1.23.

**ἐπιπερι-ελίσσω,** *wrap round a second time*, τι περὶ τὴν κεφαλήν Hp. *Art*.38. **-τρέπω,** *convert to a purpose*, M.Ant.8.35 (s.v.l.).

**ἐπιπερκ-άζω,** *turn dark*, of grapes ripening: ἐπιπερκάζειν τριχί *begin to get a dark* beard, *AP*11.36 (Phil.). **-νος,** ον, *somewhat dark*, of grapes ripening: hence, of the colour of certain hares, X. *Cyn*.5.22, Poll.5.67.

**ἐπιπέσσω,** Att. -ττω, *bake*, ἔλατρα *SIG*57.36 (Milet., v B.C.). II. Pass., *to be concocted*, Gal.*UP*14.11.

**ἐπιπετάννῡμι,** *spread over*, τὰ ὦτα ἐπὶ τὰς ὠμοπλάτας X.*Cyn*.5.10, cf. Aret.*CA*1.10:—Pass., τέφρη ἐπεπέπτατο Q.S.14.25; ἐπίπαγος ἐπιπετάννυται Aret.*SD*2.9.

**ἐπιπέτομαι,** fut. -πτήσομαι Hdt.7.15: aor. ἐπεπτάμην or -όμην (v. infr.); later, also in act. form ἐπέπτην, part. ἐπιπτάς *AP*11.4 7 (Nicarch.), Alciphr.3.59, Porph.*Abst*.1.25:—*fly to* or *towards*, καθ' ὅμιλον ἐπιπτέσθαι μενεαίνων Il.4.126; οἱ.. ἐπέπτατο δεξιὸς ὄρνις 13. 821; ἐ. σοὶ τὠυτὸ ὄνειρον Hdt.7.15; ᾗ 'πέπτετο Ar.*Av*.48; ἀετὸς ἐπιπτόμενος αἴσιος X.*Cyr*.2.4.19. 2. c. acc., *fly over*, πεδία E.*Hel*.1486 (lyr.); γῆν καὶ θάλατταν Ar.*Av*.118; ἐ. ἀρούραις Ael.*NA*17.16: metaph., καινὰ καὶ θαυμαστὰ ἐ. *fly over to*, *run eagerly after*, Ar.*Av*. 1471 (lyr.); ἐπὶ πάντα τὰ λεγόμενα ὥσπερ ἐπιπτόμενοι *flitting* from one to another, Pl.*R*.365a. 3. *fly at* or *on to*, of a male bird, Arist. *HA*564$^b$4.

**ἐπίπετρον,** τό, *a rock-plant*, a kind of *sedum*, Hp.*Ulc*.11 (vulg. ἐπίπτερον), Arist.*PA*681$^a$23, cj. for ἐπίμετρον in Thphr.*HP*7.7.4.

**ἐπίπηγμα,** ατος, τό, in pl., *cross-rods* connecting parts of a torsion-engine, Ph.*Bel*.54.5. II. *second cover*, Heliod.ap.Orib.49.4.39.

⊕ **ἐπιπήγνῡμι** or -ύω, *make to freeze on the top*, X.*Cyn*.5.1:—Pass., with intr. pf. ἐπιπέπηγα, *congeal*, *coagulate*, Thphr.*CP*5.13.2, Gal. 18(1).597. II. Pass., *to be fastened on*, ὀργάνῳ Heliod.ap.Orib. 49.4.39. (Cf. ἐπιπήσσομαι.)

**ἐπιπηδ-άω,** fut. -ήσομαι Pl.*Ly*.216a:—*leap upon*, *rush at*, *assault*, ἀγρίως ἐ. τινί Ar.*V*.705, cf. Pl.l.c., *PTeb*.44.18 (ii B.C.); ἐ. τῷ λόγῳ Plu.2.512d: c. gen., σκάφους J.*BJ*2.21.6; ἐπὶ τὴν τιμωρίαν ib.10; of male animals, ἐπιπηδῶν ὀχεύει Arist.*HA*539$^b$32, cf. Pl.*Phdr*.254a: metaph., *rush in*, *plunge in*, τῇ τέχνῃ Gal.18(1).635. **-ησις,** εως, ἡ, *springing upon*, *assault*, Plu.2.916d (pl.): metaph., ὁρμαὶ καὶ -σεις ib.76c, etc.; of the male animal, ib.768e, 1095a (pl.).

**ἐπιπῆν,** v. ἐπιπάσσω.

**ἐπίπηξ,** πηγος, ὁ, = ἐπίπηγμα, Apollod.*Poliorc*.188.4. 2. *graft*, *Gp*.4.12.8.

**ἐπίπηξις,** εως, ἡ, *bracing up*, *constriction*, τοῦ σώματος Agathin.ap. Orib.10.7.25. II. = ἐπίπαγος, *capsule* of lens, Gal.*Anat.Adm*.10 (Arabic version).

**ἐπιπήσσομαι,** = ἐπιπήγνυμαι I, Dsc.5.101. 2. = ἐπιπήγνυμαι II, Apollon.Cit.3.

**ἐπίπηχυς,** υ, *above the elbow*, Poll.2.140, Hsch.

**ἐπιπῑ-έζω,** *press upon*, ἐπὶ μάστακα χερσὶ πίεζε Od.4.287; λαῖον ἐπὶ στιβαρῷ πιέσας ποδί A.R.3.1335, cf. Dsc.2.4. **-εσμός,** ὁ, *pressing upon*, Gal.8.509, Archig.ap.eund.8.931.

**ἐπίπιθον,** *seria* (= πιθάκνη), *Gloss*.

**ἐπιπικρ-αίνω**, *make still more keen*, δίψαν Hp.*Acut.*62. **-ος**, ον, *somewhat bitter*, Thphr.*HP*6.4.10.

**ἐπιπίλναμαι**, only pres., Ep. for ἐπιπελάζομαι, *come near*, οὔτε χιὼν ἐπιπίλναται Od.6.44 (v.l. ἐπικίδναται); ἐπ' οὐδει πίλναται Il.19.92.

**ἐπιπίμπλημι**, *fill full of*, σπλάγχνων χεῖρ' ἐπιπλῆσαι Ar.*Av.*975.

**ἐπιπίνω** [πῑ], *drink afterwards* or *besides*, Hp.*Acut.*56, Ar.*Pax*712; opp. προπίνω, Ctes.*Fr.*57.25; ἐ. τοῦ οἴνου *drink* some wine *with their food*, Pl.*R.*372b; ὅταν τὸ ὕδωρ πνίγῃ, τί δεῖ ἐπιπίνειν; Arist.*EN*1146ᵃ35: esp. *drink after* eating, κρέ' ἔδων καὶ ἐπ' ἄκρητον γάλα πίνων Od. 9.297; θύννεια.. καταφαγών, κἆτ' ἐπιπιὼν ἀκράτου.. χοᾶ Ar.*Eq.*354, cf. *Pl.*1133, Philem.85.3; ἐ. μετὰ τὸν σῖτον οἶνον X.*Cyr.*6.2.28: abs., τὸ πρῷ 'πιπίνειν Eup.351 (Elmsl. for πρῶτ' ἐπ.).

**ἐπιπιπράσκω**, *sell the right of succession to* a priesthood, *SIG*1014.8 (Erythrae, iii B.C., Pass.); to an inheritance, dub. in *PLond.*1.113 (1).88 (vi A.D.).

**ἐπιπίπτω**, *fall upon* or *over*, ἐπέπιπτον ἀλλήλοις Th.7.84; ἐπί τι X *Oec.*18.7, cf. Thphr.*CP*5.4.5: metaph., ἐπέπεσε μοῖρα Pi.*Pae.*2.64; ἐπί τι Isoc.5.89; διαλογισμοὶ ἐπιπίπτουσί τινι Plu.*Oth.*9. 2. of money, *accrue*, τὸ μέρος ὃ εὑρίσκομες ἐπιπῖπτον ἐπὶ τὸ χρέος τὸ ὀφειλόμενον *SIG*953.66 (Cnidus, ii B.C.). II. *fall upon* in hostile sense, *attack, assail*, τινί Hdt.4.105, Th.3.112; ἀφυλάκτῳ αὐτῷ ἐ. Hdt.9. 116; ἀφάρκτῳ τῷ στρατοπέδῳ Th.1.117; ἀπαρασκεύοις τοῖς ἐναντίοις X.*Cyr.*7.4.3; also ἐς τοὺς Ἕλληνας, v.l. for ἐσ-, Hdt.7.210; of storms, τοῖσι βαρβάροισι ὁ βορῆς ἐπέπεσε ib.189; χειμὼν ἐπιπεσών Pl.*Prt.* 344d; of winds *meeting* one another, Arist.*Mete.*364ᵇ3; of diseases, Hp.*Aër.*3; ἡ νόσος ἐ. τοῖς Ἀθηναίοις Th.3.87; so of grief, misfortunes, etc., οὐχὶ σοὶ μόνᾳ ἐπέπεσον λῦπαι E.*Andr.*1043 (lyr.), etc.; ἐπέπεσε πολλὰ καὶ χαλεπὰ κατὰ στάσιν ταῖς πόλεσι Th.3.82, etc. 2. *come on after*, ἐ. ῥῖγος πυρετῷ Hp.*Aph.*4.46. 3. *accumulate*, πλήθη σίτου ἐπιπεπτωκέναι *PPetr.*2p.62 (iii B.C.).

**ἐπιπίσσω**· ἐπιπάσσω, Hsch.

**ἐπιπίστωσις**, εως, ἡ, *further* πίστωσις, in Rhet., Theod.Byz.ap. Pl.*Phdr.*266e, cf. Herm.*in Phdr.*p.191 A.

**ἔπιπλα**, τά, *implements, utensils, furniture, movable property* (ἡ κούφη κτῆσις, τὰ ἐπιπολῆς ὄντα τῶν κτημάτων, Poll.10.10; σκεύη τὰ μὴ ἔγγεια ἀλλ' ἐπιπόλαια, Hsch.); opp. fixtures, Hdt.1.150,164,7.119, al., S.*Fr.*8, Th.3.68, Is.8.35, X.*Oec.*9.6, Arist.*Pol.*1267ᵇ12, etc.; *fittings* of a ship, *PCair.Zen.*242 (iii B.C.): rarely sg., ἔπιπλον Is.(*Fr.* 28)ap.Poll.10.11, Asp.*in EN*96.30. (The form ἐπίπλοα occurs in Mss. of Hdt.1.94 (cf. Poll.10.10), and late Pap., as *BGU*483.6 (ii A.D.), but ἔπιπλα *PCair.Zen.* l.c., *PGrenf.*1.12.18 (ii B.C.), etc.)

**ἐπιπλᾰδάω**, *to be loose, flabby on the surface*, Ph.2.418 codd.

**ἐπίπλαδον**· φέρεσθαι, Hsch.

**ἐπιπλάζομαι**, fut. -πλάγξομαι: aor. 1 ἐπεπλάγχθην:—*wander about over*, πόντον ἐπιπλαγχθείς Od.8.14; πόντον ἐπιπλάγξεσθαι A.R.3. 1066:—later in Act., Nic.*Al.*127.

**ἐπιπλάζω**, Aeol., = ἐπιπλήσσω, Sapph.17.

**ἐπιπλᾰνάομαι**, = ἐπιπλάζομαι, γῆν Democr.[299]; δακρύων τοῖς ὄμμασιν ἐπιπλανωμένων Hld.7.17, cf. 3.5: abs., κιττὸς ἐπιπλανώμενος Longus 1.2.

**ἐπί-πλᾰσις**, εως, ἡ, *application* of a σικύη, Aret.*CA*2.3; of plasters, ib.1.9 (pl.). **-πλασμα**, ατος, τό, *plaster*, Hp.*Art.*40, Aret.*CA*1.1, Lyc.ap.Orib.9.25.1, etc. **-πλάσσω**, Att. -ττω, *spread* or *plaster on*, γῆν σημαντρίδα ἐπιπλάσας Hdt.2.38; τι ἐπὶ δῆγμα Thphr.*HP*9. 13.3; τί τινι Gal.11.86. II. *plaster up*, τὰ ὦτα Arist.*Pr.*875ᵃ36; τοὺς πόρους Thphr.*Sens.*8. III. *mould upon*, ποτάνοις ἵππον ποτάμιον Plu.2.371d, cf. 362f:—Pass., ναστὸς ἐπιπεπλασμένος *moulded*, *IG*2².1367. IV. Med., *plaster over*, νηδύν Ael.*Fr.*89. **-πλαστέον**, *one must plaster over*, *Gp.*16.18.3. **-πλαστος**, ον, *plastered over*, πρόσωπον Alciphr.3.11; ἐπίπλαστα, τά, *poultices* or *plasters*, Artem.4. 22, Asclep.ap.Gal.12.415. 2. metaph., *feigned, false*, λόγοι J.*BJ*4. 4.3; ὀλοφυρμός, δάκρυα, ib.1.32.2, Luc.*DMort.*27.7; ὑπόκρισις Id.*Am.* 3; φιλία Hdn.3.15.7. Adv. -τως M.Ant.2.16. **-πλαστώδης**, ες, *suitable for a plaster*, Orib.9.55.1.

**ἐπιπλᾰταγέω**, *applaud by clapping*, τινί Theoc.9.22; χεῖρας *Epic. Alex.Adesp.*2.72.

**ἐπιπλᾰτ-ής**, ές, *flat, broad*, only in Adv. -τῶς, Act.7.31. **-ορ**· πλακοῦντος εἶδος, Hsch. **-ύνω**, *expand yet more*, Arist.*Mu.*393ᵃ 20 (Pass.). **-ύς**, ύ, *broad at the top, flat*, ἐπιπλατὺ σφαιροειδές an *oblate* spheroid, Archim.*Con.Sph.Praef.*; λοβοί Thphr.*HP*8. 5.3.

**ἐπιπλεκ-τέον**, *one must weave*, Orph.*Fr.*49.62. ⊛ **-ω**, *wreathe into* a chaplet, *AP*12.256.5 (Mel.); νάρκισσον ὑακίνθῳ Nonn.*D.*10. 338. 2. *bind*, αὐχένα δεσμῷ ib.18.189; *bind upon*, ταρσῷ γυιοπέδην ib.36.365:—Pass., Luc.*Cont.*16. II. metaph., *interweave, combine*, αὐτὰ τῷ τῆς παραλείψεως σχήματι Arist.*Rh.Al.*1438ᵇ5; τὸ διὰ τῶν αὐτῶν ὀνομάτων ἐπιπλέξαι Aristid.*Rh.*2p.544S.; ἐ. ἑαυτοὺς ταῖς προσόδοις *concern* themselves *with*, *PTeb.*6.39 (ii B.C.):—Pass., τὰς ἐπιβολὰς τὰς Ἀννίβου ταῖς.. πράξεσιν ἐπιπεπλέχθαι Plb.4.28.2, cf. Luc.*Dem.Enc.*8; τοῖς Ἕλλησιν ἐ. *to have dealings with*.., Str.14.2. 28; ξένοις ἐπιπλακέντες ἔθεσιν J.*AJ*8.7.5; also, *to have sexual intercourse with*, Posidon.36 J., D.S.36.2a; ἐπιπεπλεγμένος *mixed*, Gal. *Sect.Intr.*6; *complex*, πυρετοί Id.7.432.

**ἐπιπλεοναστέον**, *one must increase the quantity*, Herod.Med.ap. Orib.5.30.39.

**ἐπίπλεος**, έα, Ion. έη, εον, *quite full of*, κρεῶν Hdt.1.119, 3.18; ἀγαθῶν πάντων Id.6.139:—Att. **-πλεως**, ων, Plu.*Ant.*85.

**ἐπίπλευρα**, τά, = τὰ παρὰ τοῖς μαστοῖς ὑπὸ τὰς μασχάλας, Hsch. II. ἐπίπλευρος φέρεται *sideways*, Sch.Nic.*Th.*268.

**ἐπίπλευσις**, εως, ἡ, *sailing against*, ἐ. ἔχειν to have *the power of attacking* (the *weather gage*), opp. ἀνάκρουσις, Th.7.36.

⊛ **ἐπιπλέω**, Ion. -πλώω (both in Hom.), fut. -πλεύσομαι Th.3.16: aor. 1 -έπλευσα ib.80, Ion. -έπλωσα Hdt.1.70: Ep. 2 sg. aor. 2 ἐπέπλως, part. ἐπιπλώς, but (Il.3.47) ἐπιπλώσας:—*sail upon* or *over*, ἐπέπλεον ὑγρὰ κέλευθα Il.1.312, Od.4.842; πόντον ἐπιπλώων 5.284; πόντον ἐπέπλως 3.15; ἐπιπλὼς εὐρέα πόντον Il.6.291; ἐπιπλεῖν ἁλμυρὸν ὕδωρ Od.9.227, etc. II. *sail against, attack by sea*, νηυσὶ ἐ. τινί Hdt.5.86; τῇ Κερκύρᾳ Th.3.76; ἐπὶ τὰς Μινδάρου ναῦς X.*HG*1.5.11, etc.; ἐπὶ τὴν Σαλαμῖνα D.S.20.50: abs., Hdt.1.70, 6.33; also of the ships, Th.3.80: generally, *sail on*, Plb.1.25.4, etc. III. *sail on board* a ship, Hdt.7.98, 8.67, Th.2.66; of commanders, τοὺς ἐπὶ τῶν νεῶν ἐ. στρατηγούς Hdt.5.36; [ναύαρχος] Th.3.16; ξύμβουλος ib.76; ταμίας D.49.14; also ἐ. ταῖς ἐμπορίαις *sail in charge of*, Id.56.8; and ὁ ἐπιπλέων the *supercargo*, Id.32.12; οἱ ἐπιπλεύσαντες ἐπὶ τοῦ ἐλαίου *PCair.Zen.*77.2 (iii B.C.). IV. of a naval commander, *sail past* (in order to address, cf. ἐπιπάρειμι(B)4), τοὺς κυβερνήτας καὶ τριηράρχους Plu.*Lys.*11. V. *sail after*, ἐπὶ παντὶ τῷ στόλῳ Plb.1.50.5; *sail up afterwards*, ib.25.4. VI. *float upon*, ἐπ' αὐτοῦ (sc. τοῦ ὕδατος) Hdt.3.23; ἐπὶ τῆς θαλάσσης Arist.*HA*622ᵇ6; ἐπὶ τῷ ὕδατι Id.*Mete.* 384ᵇ17; *slip, slide upon* ice, Plb.3.55.2,4. VII. *overflow* (of a river), gloss on ἄρδειν, interpol. in App.*BC*2.153; μέχρι ἐπιπλεύσῃ until (the water) *covers* the substance, *PHolm.*21.29.

**ἐπίπλεως**, ων, Att. for ἐπίπλεος (q.v.).

**ἐπίπληγμα**, ατος, τό, gloss on ἔνιγμα, *rebuke*, *Et.Gud.*

**ἐπιπληθύνω**, *increase*, Lxx *Ge.*7.17 (Pass.):—Pass., **-ύνομαι**, *superabound*, χάριτες Demetr.*Eloc.*156.

**ἐπιπλήκτ-ειρα**, ἡ, = fem. of ἐπιπλήκτης, *AP*6.233 (Maec.). **-ἑος**, α, ον, *worthy of reproof*, Ph.1.242. **-ης**, ου, ὁ, (ἐπιπλήσσω) *corrector*, *Gloss.* **-ικός**, ή, όν, *given to rebuking*, D.L.4.63. Adv. **-κῶς** D.S. 17.114, Sch.E.*Med.*967.

**ἐπιπλημμύρω** [ῠ], *overflow*, τι Opp.*H.*1.465:—also **-έω**, τῇ θαλάττῃ Philostr.*Im.*2.17.

⊛ **ἐπίπληξις**, Dor. **-πλαξις**, εως, ἡ, *blame, rebuke*, Ti.Locr.103e (pl.), D.61.18 (pl.); τυγχάνειν τῆς καθηκούσης ἐ. *SIG*630.9 (Delph., ii B.C.); ἐ. ἔχειν incur *criticism*, Aeschin.1.177; ἐ. πρός τι or τινα, Hp. *Decent.*12, Plu.*Sol.*3 (pl.). 2. in strong sense, *punishment*, Lxx 2*Ma.*7.33, *PSI*5.542.30 (iii B.C.), Mitteis*Chr.*31 iii 14 (ii B.C.): pl., of *plagues*, Ph.2.100.

**ἐπιπληρ-όω**, *fill up*, συμπόσιον Ephipp.4 (Casaub., -κληρ- codd. Ath.); κακοῖς ἐ. κακά S.E.*M.*1.68:—Med., οὐδ' ὁπόθεν ἐπιπληρωσόμεθα τὰς ναῦς no resources whence we *shall man* our ships *afresh*, Th.7. 14:—Pass., Gal.15.781. **-ωσις**, εως, ἡ, *refilling, keeping full*, Id. 4.471.

**ἐπιπλήσσω**, Att. -ττω, *strike*, τόξῳ ἐπιπλήσσων Il.10.500; ὑπέρωσιν Nic.*Th.*952. II. *punish, chastise*, esp. with words, *rebuke, reprove*, c. acc. pers., καί μ' οὔ τινά φημι ἄλλον ἐπιπλήξειν Il.23.580, cf. Pl.*Prt.*327a: c. dat., Ἕκτορ, ἀεὶ μέν πώς μοι ἐπιπλήσσεις Il.12.211, cf. Isoc.1.31; ἐμαυτῷ Pl.*Lg.*805b, cf. 1*Ep.Ti.*5.1, etc.; ἐπί τινι for a thing, Pl.*Plt.*286b:—Pass., *to be rebuked*, Id.*Grg.*478e. 2. ἐ. τινί τι *cast* a thing *in* one's *teeth*, Hdt.3.142, 7.136; τὴν.. αὐθαδίαν.. μὴ 'πίπλησσέ μοι A.*Pr.*80; ἐ. τινὶ τοῦτο, ὅτι.. Pl.*Prt.*319d: c. acc. rei only, τί τόδ' ἐπέπληξας; S.*OC*1730 (lyr.): abs., Id.*Aj.*288, X.*Oec.*13.12, etc. III. intr., *fall upon*, ἀρούραις Arat.1095.

**ἐπιπλινθοβολέω**, *lay courses of bricks above*, *IG*2².463.58.

**ἐπίπλοα**, v. ἔπιπλα ad fin.

**ἐπιπλοεντεροκήλη**, ἡ, *hernia of omentum and intestines*, Paul.Aeg. 6.65.

**ἐπίπλοιον**, v. ἐπίπλοον.

**ἐπιπλοκή**, ἡ, *plaiting together*, ῥίζαι κατ' ἐπιπλοκὴν δασεῖαι *matted* roots, Dsc.4.187; ἐπιπλοκαὶ ἀτόμων *entanglements*, Ph.2.489: metaph., τῶν αἰτίων πρὸς ἄλληλα Plot.3.1.2. 2. *union, intercourse*, πρὸς ἀλλήλους Plb.5.37.2; τῶν βαρβάρων Str.14.2.28; εἰς τοὺς τόπους Plb.2.12.7 (but ἐ. εἰς Πελοπόννησον *intermeddling* with the affairs of P., Id.4.3.3): c. dat., Phld.*Ir.*p.47 W.; *connexion* of people with one another, *Stoic.*3.90,161 (pl.); φίλων ἐπιπλοκαὶ ἑστιατικαί friendly *relations*.., ib.254; *sexual intercourse*, D.S.4.9, Plu.*Sol.*20 (pl.), etc. 3. *combination* of styles, in pl., D.H.*Dem.*37, Hermog.*Stat.* 5; *concatenation* of cause with effect, Chrysipp.*Stoic.*2.293,265. 4. *complexity, confusion, muddle*, τοῦ βίου Men.16.8 D.; ἐ. σοφιστικαί *involved arguments*, Alex.Aphr.*in Metaph.*270.30. 5. Gramm., *insertion* of a letter, Ath.7.324d, Hdn.Gr.2.928; *combination*, στοιχείων, λέξεων, A.D.*Synt.*3.11, 4.10. b. *alloying* of metals, Ps.-Democr.p.54 B. c. *mixed nature* of disease, Gal.*Sect.Intr.*6; esp. of fevers, Id.7.370, al. 6. in Metre, *conversion* of rhythms by change in order of syllables, Mar.Vict.p.63 K.; also, *a group of rhythms thus related*, ἐ. δυαδικὴ τετράσημος, τρίσημος, ibid., cf. Juba ib.p.94 K., Sch.Heph.p.110C., al.

**ἐπιπλο-κήλη**, ἡ, *hernia of the omentum*, Gal.7.36:—hence **-κηλικός**, ὁ, *one who suffers from it*, Id.14.789. **-κομιστής**, οῦ, ὁ, *possessing an omentum*, Id.2.556.

**ἐπιπλόμενος**, v. ἐπιτέλομαι. **ἔπιπλον**, τό, v. ἔπιπλα.

**ἐπιπλοόμφαλον**, τό, *umbilical hernia of omentum*, Gal.19.444.

**ἐπίπλοον**, τό, = Homer's δέρτρον, *fold of the peritoneum, omentum*, Hp.*Aph.*5.46, Arist.*HA*495ᵇ29, 519ᵇ7, *PA*677ᵇ12, etc.:—also **ἐπίπλοος**, ὁ, Hdt.2.47; contr. **ἐπίπλους** Epich.80 codd. Ath., Ion Hist. 3; and **ἐπιπόλαιον**, τό, Eub.95.3, Hsch.: **ἐπίπλοιον** Philetaer.17 (s.v.l.).

⊛ **ἐπίπλοος** (A), ον, contr. **ἐπίπλους**, ουν, (ἐπιπλέω) *sailing against*

*the enemy*, νῆες 'ships of the line', Plb.1.50.6, cf. 1.27.5, Ph.*Bel.*104.16. 2. *sailing after*, D.S.20.50.3. 3. *on board ship*: as Subst., = ἐπιβάτης, Arr.ap.Suid., cf. *POxy.*276 (i A.D.), etc. II. for ἐπίπλοα, τά, v. ἔπιπλα ad fin.

**ἐπίπλοος** (B), contr. **ἐπίπλους**, ὁ, *sailing against, bearing down upon, attack* or *onset* of a ship or fleet, Th.2.90, X.*HG*4.3.11, Plu.*Lys.*11, etc.; ποιεῖσθαι ἐπίπλουν, = ἐπιπλεῖν, Th.8.79; ἐ. ἐποιοῦντο τῇ Μιλήτῳ ib.30; ἐπὶ τὴν Σάμον ib.63; τοῖς Ἀθηναίοις Id.3.78; τῇ Πελοποννήσῳ ἑκατὸν νεῶν ἐπίπλουν ἐξαρτύοντες fitting out 100 ships for *the expedition against..*, Id.2.17, cf. 56; ἐ. θέσθαι Plu.*Aem.*9; rarely of friends, *sailing towards, approach*, ἐ. φίλιος Th.8.102.

**ἐπίπλοος** (C), contr. **ἐπίπλους**, ὁ, v. ἐπίπλοον.

**ἐπιπλώω**, Ion. and Ep. for ἐπιπλέω.

**ἐπί-πνευσις**, εως, ἡ, *spasmodic inspiration*, Gal.17(2).750. II. *divine inspiration*, ἐ. θεία Str.10.3.9. **-πνευστικός**, ή, όν, *depending on inspiration*, εἶδος μαντικῆς Sch.A.*Pr.*484. **-πνεύων**· ἐπιβλέπων (Aeol.), Hsch. (citing Alc.66).

⊛ **ἐπιπνέω**, Ep. **-πνείω** (as always in Hom., cf. Call.*Del.*318, A.R.3.937), *breathe upon, blow freshly upon*, περὶ δὲ πνοιὴ..ζώγρει ἐπιπνείουσα Il.5.698; τινί *on* one, Ar.*V.*265; *blow fairly for*, νηῦς.., ἧ.. οὖρος ἐπιπνείῃσιν ὄπισθεν Od.4.357: abs., εἰς ὅ κε..ἐπιπνεύσωσιν ἀῆται 9.139; ἄνεμος..ἥδιστος ἐπέπνει Plu.*Sert.*17, etc. 2. *blow furiously upon*, τινί Hdt.3.26: metaph., μαινόμενος δ' ἐπιπνεῖ..Ἄρης A.*Th.*343 (lyr.), cf. S.*Ant.*136 (lyr.). 3. c. acc., *blow over*, θάλασσαν Hes.*Th.*872; ἀγρούς Luc.*Charid.*1. 4. c. acc. cogn., *blow forth*, πυρὸς σέλας A.R.3.1327. 5. *blow afterwards*, Arist.*Pr.*945$^{b}$1. 6. *blow against*, of one wind *against* another, Thphr.*Vent.*53. II. metaph., 1. *excite, inflame* against, Ἀργείοις Σπαρτῶν γένναν E.*Ph.*794 (lyr.); στρατὸν αἵματι *to* slaughter, ib.789 (lyr.). 2. *inspire into, grant*, Μουσῶν προφῆται ἐπιπεπνευκότες ἡμῖν τὸ γέρας Pl.*Phdr.*262d; ὄλβον Orph.*H.*84.8. 3. *favour*, λαμπρᾶς ἐπιπνεούσης τῆς τύχης, metaph. from the wind, Plb.11.19.5: c. acc., of love, A.R.3.937, Nonn.*D.*3.121: abs., Plu.2.759f. III. Pass., *to be inspired*, ὑπό τινος Longin.13.2; πρὸς αὐτῶν τῶν Μουσῶν Jul.*Or.*2.78b.

**ἐπίπνοια**, ἡ, *breathing upon, inspiration*, ἐ. πραότητος Pl.*Ti.*71c; ἐξ ἐπιπνοίας Διός A.*Supp.*17 (anap.), cf. 43 (lyr.); θείαις ἐ. ib.577 (lyr.); οὐκ ἄνευ τινὸς ἐπιπνοίας θεῶν Pl.*Lg.*811c, cf. *Cra.*399a; μαντικὴν..ἐπίπνοιαν Ἀπόλλωνος θέντες κτλ. Id.*Phdr.*265b; ἐπιπνοίᾳ δαιμονίου ἐνθουσιάζειν Arist.*EE*1214$^{a}$24; ἐ. πρὸς τὸ καλὸν κατασχεθῆναι Plu.*Agis* 7. II. pl., *winds blowing opposite ways*, Thphr.*Vent.*55.

**ἐπίπνοος**, ον, contr. **-πνους**, ουν, *breathed upon*, Poll.5.110. 2. *inspired*, παρά τινος Pl.*Cra.*428c; ἐ. καὶ κατεχομένους ἐκ τοῦ θεοῦ Id.*Men.*99d; ἐ. ἐκ τούτου τοῦ ἔρωτος Id.*Smp.*181c; σὺν τῷ ῥυθμῷ Ael.*NA* 11.10; ἐ. καὶ φοιβόληπτος Plu.*Pomp.*48. Adv. -πνως Poll.1.16.

**ἐπιπόδιος**, α, ον, *upon the feet*, S.*OT*1350 (lyr.).

**ἐπιποθ-έω**, *desire besides* or *yearn after*, c. acc., Hdt.5.93, Ph.2.598; *feel the want of*, Pl.*Lg.*855e; ἐ. τινός Lxx*Ps.*118(119).20; ἐπί τι ib.61(62).11. **-ημα**, ατος, τό, *object of desire*, Aq.*Ps.*139(140).9. **-ησις**, εως, ἡ, *longing after*, τινός 2*Ep.Cor.*7.7, Aq.*Ez.*23.11, Dam.*Pr.*38. **-ητος**, ον, *longed for, desired*, *Ep.Phil.*4.1; *missed, found wanting*, ὅρκοι App.*Hisp.*43. **-ία**, ἡ, = ἐπιπόθησις, *Ep.Rom.*15.23.

**ἐπιποι-έω**, *superadd*, τινί τι Philostr.*VS*2.5.2; *produce*, ξενιτείαν Vett.Val.97.13; τὸ λίαν ἐπιποιεῖν, perh. *exaggeration*, Phld.*Piet.*27. 2. = ἐπιτίθημι V, τὰ δίκαια *Schwyzer*409.4 (Elis). **-ησις**, εως, ἡ, *production*, κάλλους Eust.1843.15,37.

**ἐπιποιμήν**, ένος, ὁ, ἡ, = ποιμήν, θεαὶ δ' ἐπιποιμένες εἰσί Od.12.131.

**ἐπίποκος**, ον, *covered with wool, woolly*, dub. l. in Lxx4*Ki.*3.4, cf. *GDI*3731.6 (Cos).

**ἐπίπολα**, τά, = ἔπιπλα, *GDI*1365 (Dodona).

**ἐπι[πολ]-ᾷ**, = ἐπιπολῆς (cf. ἐπιπολή II), *Mnemos.*42.332 (Argos, iv B.C.). **-άζω**, fut. -άσω Isoc.5.64: pf. ἐπιπεπόλακα Ph.1.365: (ἐπιπολή):—*to be at the top, come to the surface, float on the surface*, ὕλη ἐ. X.*Oec.*16.14; αἱ ἐγχέλεις οὐκ ἐ. Arist.*HA*592$^{a}$10, cf. 547$^{b}$22; ἡ ἀτμὶς ἐ. Id.*Mete.*341$^{b}$11; τὸ ἐπιπολάζον, opp. τὸ ὑφιστάμενον, Id.*Cael.*312$^{a}$6: c. dat., ὕδατι ἐ. ib.311$^{a}$28; [τὸ ἔλαιον] ἐν τῷ ὕδατι ἐ. Id.*Mete.*383$^{b}$25; of birds, *hover over*, Theopomp.Hist.76; of food, *remain crude* in the stomach, Hp.*Vict.*2.54, Arist.*APo.*94$^{b}$12, Gal.6.433, 15.63. II. metaph., *have the upper hand, prevail*, [Epich.]282; Φίλιππος ἐπιπολάζει D.9.25, cf. Isoc.5.64, 8.107; ἐ. ἐν πᾶσι τοῖς πολιτεύμασιν Plb.30.13.2. 2. *to be prevalent, fashionable, current*, τοῖς τηλικούτοις..ὕβρις ἐ. X.*Lac.*3.2; ἐκ τῆς ἐπιπολαζούσης τὰ νῦν λεσχηνείας Pl.*Ax.*369d; αἱ μάλιστα ἐπιπολάζουσαι [δόξαι] Arist.*EN*1095$^{a}$30; ἐπιπολάζοντος τοῦ γελοίου ib.1128$^{a}$12. 3. *to be common, abound*, ὁ χυμὸς ἐπεπόλασεν Hp.*Epid.*1.15; οἱ ἐπιπολάζοντες μύες Arist.*HA* 580$^{b}$14; τὴν..ἄνοιαν ἐ. Alex.45.7 (with play on 1); of habits, Plb.13.3.1, etc.; of poems, Sch.Ar.*Th.*169; γένος -άζον τῷ βίῳ *abounding* in the world, Luc.*Icar.*29. 4. *to be 'uppish'* or *insolent*, D.H.11.6, App.*Mith.*75; ἐ. ὑπεροψίᾳ Id.*BC*3.76: c. dat. pers., *behave insolently to*, Plu.2.634c. III. *wander over*, τὴν Αἴγυπτον Hld.2.25, cf. 8.8. IV. *overflow*, of the sea, Luc.*Asin.*34. 2. ἐ. τῇ ῥητορικῇ *to be engaged upon* it, Id.*Rh.Pr.*26. **-αιόρριζος**, ον, *with roots which run along the surface*, Thphr.*HP*1.6.4, 2.5.1 (Comp.). **-αιος**, ον, *on the surface, superficial*, Hp.*Art.*69 (Comp.); ῥίζα Dsc.4.184, cf. Thphr.*HP*3.6.4 (Sup.), al.; λεπτὸν καὶ ἐ. δέρμα Arist.*Pr.*890$^{a}$13; τραῦμα Luc.*Nav.*37. 2. ὀστέον *shallow* (of the skull), Hp.*VC*21; ὀφθαλμοί, i.e. not deep-set, X.*Smp.*5.5. 3. metaph., *superficial, shallow, commonplace*, παιδεία Isoc.15.190; ἐ. ἡδοναὶ καὶ διατριβαί D.61.56; ἐ. πιθανότης Dsc.*Ther.Praef.*; -ότατος πυρετός *slight* fever, Diocl.*Fr.*107; ἐ. ὕπνος *light* sleep, Luc.*Gall.*25; ἔρως Id.*DMeretr.*8.2; ἐπιστήμης..φύσις (compared to a well) οὐκ ἐ. ἀλλὰ πάνυ βαθεῖα Ph.1.621. b. *on the surface, manifest*: hence, *obvious*, ἐ. λέγομεν τὰ παντὶ δῆλα Arist.*Rh.*1410$^{b}$22, cf. 1412$^{b}$25; ἐπιπολαιότερον τοῦ ζητουμένου Id.*EN*1095$^{b}$24; ἡ -οτάτη..ζήτησις the *most obvious* method of inquiry, Id.*Pol.*1276$^{a}$19; ἐπιπόλαιον τὸ ψεῦδος ib.1282$^{b}$30. II. Adv. -ως *on the surface*, τιτρώσκειν J.*BJ*3.7.22. 2. *slightly*, Hp.*Aph.*2.28; *superficially*, Arist.*Metaph.*987$^{a}$22: Comp. -οτέρως ib.993$^{b}$13. III. ἐπιπόλαιον, τό, v. ἐπίπλοον. IV. ἐπιπόλαια χρήματα, = ἔπιπλα, *Leg.Gort.*5.41, cf. *GDI*5016.15 (Gortyn). **-ἄσις**, εως, ἡ, *being on the surface, coming to the surface*, Hp.*Hum.*3, Arist.*Sens.*440$^{b}$16. **-ασμός**, ὁ, = foreg., ἐ. τῆς ζέσεως Id.*Pr.*930$^{b}$31; λιποθυμώδεις ἐ. *retchings* with faintness, Archig.ap.Orib.8.1.26. 2. metaph., *arrogance, insolence*, D.H.6.65. **-αστικός**, ή, όν, *apt to rise to the surface, floating on the stomach*, of undigested food, Hp.*Acut.*62, Arist.*Pr.*873$^{b}$26. 2. *insolent*: in Adv. -κῶς *violently*, χρώμενος τῇ κραυγῇ Plb.4.12.9. **-έομαι**, v. ἐπιπωλέομαι. **-εύω**, = ἐπιπολάζω I, Ael.*NA*9.61. ⊛ **-ή**, ἡ, (ἐπιτέλλω (B)) pl. Ἐπιπολαί, αἱ, the *Rise*, a triangular plateau near Syracuse which rises from its base (the wall of Achradina) to its apex (Euryalus), Th.6.96, etc. 2. sg., *surface*, *Schwyzer*89.15 (Argos, iii B.C.), Aret.*SD*2.7, Gal.2.626. II. elsewh. only in gen., ἐπιπολῆς, as Adv., *on the top*, Hdt.2.62, Arist.*GA*747$^{a}$5, etc.; κάτω μὲν καὶ ἐ..., ἐν μέσῳ δέ.. X.*Mem.*3.1.7; λίαν ἐ. πεφυτευμένα Id.*Oec.*19.4; ἐ. τὸ σιναρὸν σκέλος ἔχοντα *uppermost*, Hp.*Art.*77; τὰ ἐ. τε καὶ ἐντός Pl.*Phlb.*47c, cf. 46e; of arguments, ἐ. εἶναι to be *superficial*, Arist.*Rh.*1400$^{b}$31; but τὰ παντελῶς ἐ. quite *simple* tasks, D.61.37; πᾶσίν ἐστιν ἐ. ἰδεῖν Arist.*HA*622$^{b}$25, cf. *Rh.*1376$^{b}$14. 2. as Prep., c. gen., *on the top of, above*, τῶν πυλέων Hdt.1.187, cf. Ar.*Ec.*1108, *Pl.*1207. 3. with other Preps., κατύπερθε ἐπιπολῆς τῶν ξύλων Hdt.4.201; ἐξ ἐ. εὑρίσκεσθαι D.S.5.38; οὐκ ἐξ ἐ. ὁ λόγος ἡμῶν καθίκετο made a *deep* impression, Luc.*Nigr.*35, etc. (condemned by Phryn.*PS*p.67 B., Luc.*Sol.*5); δι' ἐ. τῶν λέξεων Seleuc.ap.Ath.9.398a; so ἐν ἐπιπολῇ, = ἐπιπολῆς, Str.12.7.3. **-ῆδες**· περόναι, Hsch. **-ιαῖος**, epith. of Hermes at Rhodes, Gorgon 2; of Zeus at Miletus, Hsch. (prob.).

**ἐπιπολίζω**, *build upon*, Hsch.

**ἐπιπολῐ-όομαι**, *begin to grow grey*, τρίχες ἐ. Arist.*GA*785$^{a}$18. **-ος**, ον, *growing grey, grizzled*, D.54.34.

**ἐπίπολος**, ὁ, = πρόσπολος, *companion*, S.*OT*1322 (lyr.).

**ἐπιπολύ**, Adv. for ἐπὶ πολύ, v. πολύς.

**ἐπιπομπ-εύω**, *triumph over*, ταῖς τῆς πατρίδος συμφοραῖς Plu.*Caes.*56. ⊛ **-ή**, ἡ, *visitation, punishment*, Aristeas 131 (pl.). 2. *enchantment*, Poet.*de herb.*22 (pl.), 165 (pl.), 175, *PMag.Par.*1.2159. **-ός**, ὁ, *one who sends visitations*, *PMag.Leid.V*.7.10.

**ἐπιπον-έω**, *toil on*, X.*Cyr.*5.4.17, *Lac.*2.5, Pl.*Lg.*789e. II. c. dat., *labour on* or *at*, τῇ γῇ J.*AJ*18.8.5, cf. 19.2.5. **-ία**, ἡ, *continued toil*, Hsch. s.v. πονηρία. **-ος**, ον, *painful*, οὖρα f.l. for πέπονα in Hp.*Prorrh.*59 (ap.Gal.); θάνατοι Phld.*Ir.*p.30 W.; ἐπιθυμία Epicur.*Fr.*457; *toilsome, laborious*, λατρεία S.*Tr.*829 (lyr.); ἀσχολία, ἄσκησις, φυλακή, Th.1.70, 2.39, 8.11; γῆρας *wearisome*, Pl.*R.*329d (but in good sense, ἔργα ἐξειργασμένοι καλὰ καὶ ἐ. Id.*Lg.*801e, cf. X.*Cyr.*8.1.29 (Sup.)); βίος ib.2.3.11; μαθήσεις καὶ μελέται Id.*Cyn.*12.15; ἁμέρα day *of sorrow*, S.*Tr.*654 (lyr.): Comp. πρᾶξις -ωτέρα καὶ ἐπικινδυνοτέρα X.*An.*1.3.19; -ώτερον ⟨ἔργον⟩ οὐκ εἴληφ' ἐγώ Alex.195; οὐδὲν διαβολῆς ἐστιν -ώτερον Men.576: Sup. παιδεία -ωτάτη Pl.*R.*450c; τὸ ἐπίπονον *toil*, X.*Cyn.*l.c.; τὰ ἐ. Arist.*EN*1116$^{a}$14; ἐπίπονόν [ἐστι] τὴν δύσκλειαν ἀφανίσαι 'tis *a hard task* to.., Th.3.58. 2. of persons, *laborious, patient of toil*, Ar.*Ra.*1370 (lyr.), Pl.*Phdr.*229d; also, *sensitive to fatigue, easily exhausted*, Thphr.*Sens.*11. 3. of omens, *portending suffering*, X.*An.*6.1.23. II. Adv. -νως *with suffering*, Hp.*Epid.*1.1; *with difficulty*, εὑρίσκεσθαι Th.1.22; ζῆν (opp. τρυφᾶν) Arist.*Pol.*1265$^{a}$34; ἐ. καὶ καλῶς τινα θεραπεύειν Isoc.19.11; βιώσεται X.*Mem.*1.7.2, etc.: Comp. -ώτερον, διακονεῖν Arched.3.8: Sup. -ώτατα, ζῆν X.*Cyr.*7.5.67.

**ἐπιποντία**, ἡ, *Goddess of the Sea*, epith. of Aphrodite in Hsch.

**ἐπιπορ-εία**, ἡ, *coming on the scene*, of marionettes, opp. ἀποπορ., Hero *Aut.*19.1. **-εύομαι**, *travel*, ψυχῆς πείρατα οὐκ ἂν ἐξεύροιο πᾶσαν -όμενος ὁδόν Heraclit.45; *march*, Plb.1.12.4, al.: c. acc., τὴν χώραν *traverse*, ib.30.14: c. dat., τοῖς ἀγροῖς Plu.*Lyc.*28 (s.v.l.); ἐπὶ τοὺς τόπους *PLille*3.78 (iii B.C.). 2. = ἐπιπάρειμι (B) 4, of a general, -όμενος τὰ συστήματα παρεκάλει Plb.11.12.1, cf. 15.10.1, Plu.*Tim.*12; also ἐ. ἐπὶ τὸ πλῆθος *come before* the assembly, Plb.4.9.2; πρός τινα *Ev.Luc.*8.4: metaph., *go* or *run through*, τῇ διανοίᾳ, τῇ ὄψει, Plu.2.470a. 3. Astron., *reach*, τινὶ τῶν κέντρων Ptol.*Tetr.*99: c. acc., ἡλίου τὸν Κριὸν ἐ. *begins to traverse* the Ram, Jul.*Or.*5.172c. 4. ἐ. τὸν ἱστόν, = ἐποίχομαι (q.v.), Ephor.5 J. 5. *take legal proceedings against* a person, *PHib.*1.96.10 (iii B.C.), etc. **-ευσις**, εως, ἡ, *course*, of planets, Ptol.*Phas.*p.11 H.; of the moon, Id.*Tetr.*98. 2. name for *the fifth* τόπος, *Cat.Cod.Astr.*8(4).152.

**ἐπιπορθμεύομαι** (v.l. -πορευ-), *spread*, of a morbid condition, Sch.Nic.*Al.*544.

**ἐπιπορπ-άομαι**, *buckle on oneself, buckle on*, πορφυρίδα Plb.38.7.2. **-ημα**, Dor. **-ᾱμα**, ατος, τό, *garment buckled over the shoulders, cloak, mantle*, part of the dress of a musician, Pl.Com.10, App.*Pun.*109. ⊛ **-ίς**, ίδος, ἡ, = foreg., Call.*Ap.*32; νυμφᾶν *AP*6.274 (Pers.). **-όομαι**, = -άομαι, σάγους D.S.5.30.

**ἐπιπόρρω**, Adv. *yet further*, Arc.190.20, Sch.Pi.*O.*3.79.

**ἐπιπορσ-αίνω**, *prepare for* one, *offer, supply*, Nic.*Fr.*74.54 codd. Ath. **-ύνω**, = foreg., Q.S.7.712.

**ἐπιπορφῠρ-ίζω**, *have a tinge of purple*, Arist.*Col.*796ᵇ14, Thphr. *HP*3.18.2, 6.2.1, al. **-ος**, ον, *with a purple tinge*, ib.4.6.7.

**ἐπιποτάμ-ιος** [ᾰ], α, ον, *on a river*, πόλις Hellanic.54 J. **-ίς**, ίδος, ἡ, *river-nymph*, Sch.Il.20.8.

**ἐπιποτάομαι**, lengthd. for ἐπιπέτομαι, *fly* or *hover over*, τοῖον ἐπὶ κνέφας ἀνδρὶ μύσος πεπόταται A.*Eu.*378; Στυγία τις ἐπ' ἀχλὺς πεπόταται Id.*Pers.*668; γῆν καὶ θάλατταν Ph.2.200. II. *float upon*, ἀέρι Dsc.5.75; τῷ ὑγρῷ Porph.*Antr.*10.

**ἐπιπότια** ᾄσματα (πότος), = σκόλια, Sch.Aristid.p.488 Dind.

**ἐπιποτ-ίζω**, *water*, *PCair.Zen.*286 (iii B.C.). **-ισμός**, ὁ, *watering*, *PHamb.*62.11 (ii A.D.).

**ἐπιπράττομαι**, *exact over and above from*, τινά τι Anon.ap.Suid.

**ἐπιπρείγιστος** (Cret. = ἐπιπρέσβιστος), *next-eldest*, *Leg.Gort.*7.20.

**ἐπιπρέπ-εια**, ἡ, *congruity*, *suitableness*, Arist.*Phgn.*809ᵃ13, Adam. 2.2: in pl., Plb.3.78.2; of literary effect, Phld.*Po.*2.19, 47. II. *appearance*, ἐναντία ἐ. τᾶς ἀλαθινᾶς διαθέσιος Archyt.ap.Stob.3.1.114, cf. Simp.*in Cael.*661.10. ⊛ **-ής**, ές, *becoming*, Diotog.ap.Stob.4.7. 62; τὸ ἐ., = foreg. I, Luc.*Im.*7. **-ω**, *to be conspicuous*, οὐδέ τί τοι δούλειον ἐπιπρέπει εἰσοράασθαι εἶδος καὶ μέγεθος Od.24.252; φυᾷ τὸ γενναῖον ἐπιπρέπει ἐκ πατέρων παισὶ λῆμα Pi.*P.*8.44, cf. Theoc.25. 40, D.H.*Din.*7; ὁ ὀφθαλμὸς ἐ. τῷ μετώπῳ Luc.*DMar.*1.1. II. *beseem*, *suit*, c. dat., Plu.2.794a: impers., ἐπιπρέπει *it is fitting*, c. inf., Xenoph.26.

**ἐπιπρεσβεύομαι**, *go as ambassador*, D.H.2.47. II. *send an embassy*, πρός τινα Id.6.56; τινί Plu.*Sert.*27, *Ant.*68. 2. *send a second embassy*, App.*Gall.*18.

**ἐπιπρηνής**, ές, *sloping downwards*, A.R.1.939; = ἐπὶ στόμα, Hsch.

**ἐπιπρητήν·** αἰγὸς ἡλικία, Hsch.

**ἐπιπρηῠνω**, Ion. for ἐπιπραΰνω, *soothe*, D.P.1052.

⊛ **ἐπιπρίω** [ρῑ], *grind with rage at*, τὸ γένειον *AP*7.531 (Antip. Thess.), cf. Hsch.

⊛ **ἐπιπρό**, Adv. *right through*, *onwards*, A.R.2.133, D.P.276.

**ἐπιπρο-βαίνω**, pf. -βέβηκα, *stretch forward*, *project*, D.P.128, Ruf. *Oss.*37. **-βάλλω**, *throw forward*, ὅπλα ἐπί τινι Simyl.ap.Plu.*Rom.* 17. **-έηκα, -έμεν**, v. ἐπιπροΐημι. **-έχομαι**, *stand forward*, *project*, A.R.4.524. **-θέω**, *run on farther*, Id.1.582, Nic.*Th.*382: *rush into*, κύρτον Opp.*H.*3.379 (nisi divisim). **-ῐάλλω** [ῐ], poet. Verb, *set out* or *place before one*, σφῶιν ἐπιπροΐηλε τράπεζαν Il.11.628. II. *send on one after another*, θεοὺς ἐπιπροΐαλλεν *h.Cer.*326; ἄλλον ἐπ' ἄλλῳ ἰόν Q.S.6.231. **-ΐημι**, poet. Verb, *send forth*, τὸν μὲν νηυσὶν ἐπιπροέηκα..Ἴλιον εἴσω *on board* ship to Ilium, Il.18.58; but κεῖνον.. νηυσὶν ἐπιπροέηκα θοῇσιν, ἐλθεῖν.. *to* the ships, to go.., 17.708; ἄνδρας δὲ λίσσεσθαι ἐπιπροέηκεν ἀρίστους *sent* them *forth* to supplicate, 9.520; Μενελάῳ ἐπιπροέμεν ταχὺν ἰόν (Ep. aor. 2 inf.) *shoot* an arrow *at* him, 4.94; νημερτέα βάξιν ἐ. A.R.4.1185; φρῖκας Nic.*Th.*778; πότμον Orac.ap.Luc.*Alex.*27; λιγὺν οὖρον Orph.*A.*361; τινὰ θαλάσσῃ *into* the sea, A.R.4.1617, etc.; ῥέεθρον θαλάσσῃ, of a river, D.P.49, cf. 794: hence, seemingly intr., νήσοισιν ἐπιπροέηκε (sc. νῆα) he *made straight for* them, Od.15.299.

**ἐπί-προικα·** τὸ δεύτερον ἐπὶ προικὶ δῶρον, Hsch. **-προικος**, ἡ, (προίξ) *woman who inherits a charge upon a property as her dowry*, *AB* 256; but simply, *dowered*, opp. ἄπροικος, Poll.3.35, cf. Hsch.

**ἐπιπρό-κειμαι**, *project*, Sch.Ruf.*Onom.*p.240 R. **-μολεῖν**, aor. 2 inf. of -βλώσκω, *go forth towards*, A.R.3.665, Maiist.27. **-νέομαι**, = foreg., A.R.4.1588. **-νεύω**, *lean forward over*, Nic.*Th.*374, Opp. *C.*4.122. **-πίπτω**, *fall forwards*, A.R.4.1449, Nic.*Al.*496; *project*, Sor.1.69.

**ἐπιπροσ-βάλλω**, *direct one's course to*, Ἀβύδῳ A.R.1.931. **-γίγνομαι**, *to be added besides*, A.D.*Synt.*260.28, Herm.ap.Stob.1.49.69, *POxy.*1725.18 (iii A.D.). **-ειμι**, Astrol., *to be present as well*, Nech.ap.Vett.Val.279.18.

**ἐπίπροσθεν**, rarely **-θε** Antiph.250, *SIG*493.12 (Delos, iii B.C.), Adv.: I. of Place, *before*, ἐ. τίθεσθαι, ποιεῖσθαί τι, put *before one* as a screen, E.*Or.*468, X.*Cyr.*1.4.24; ἐ. γίγνεσθαι to be *in the way*, *intercept the view*, Pl.*Grg.*523d, cf. *Ti.*40c; κώμας καὶ γηλόφους ἐ. ποιεῖσθαι take *cover behind*, X.*Cyr.*3.3.28. 2. c. gen., ἐ. τῶν ὀφθαλμῶν ἔχειν Pl.*Smp.*213a; ταῖς νήσοις οὐδὲν ἐ. τῆς φορᾶς Thphr.*Vent.*30; εὐθὺ οὗ ἂν τὸ μέσον ἀμφοῖν τοῖν ἐσχάτοιν ἐ. ᾖ Pl.*Prm.*137e. II. of Degree, θεῖναί τι ἐ. τινος prefer one *before* another, E.*Supp.*514; ἐ. εἶναί τινος to be *better* than.., Id.*Or.*641; ἐ. τἀσχρὰ..τῶν καλῶν Antiph. l.c.; ἐ. τι θέσθαι τινός J.*AJ*2.4.3; γίγνεται ἐ. τοῦ δικαίου τὰ τριακόσια τάλαντα Id.*BJ*1.6.3. III. of Order, *first*, *prior*, τὰ ἐ. αὐτῶν..τάξαντες αὐτὰ ἐ. ποιησόμεθα Pl.*Lg.*783b,c.

**ἐπιπρόσ-θεσις**, εως, ἡ, *occultation*, Aristarch.Sam.8. ⊛ **-θετέω**, *occult*, τὰ -οῦντα Phld.*Sign.*10. 2. metaph. of nutriment, τροφὴ -ηθεῖσα Hp.*Alim.*4. **-θέτησις**, εως, ἡ, *occultation*, Epicur.*Ep.*2 p.40 U. 2. pl., of *objects casting a shadow* by which measurements are taken, Hero *Deff.*135.8. 3. name of a *bandage*, Nicet.ap.Gal. 18(1).792. ⊛ **-θέω**, *to be before* or *in the way*, Thphr.*Vent.*32; of *occultations* or *eclipses*, Zeno *Stoic.*1.34, Chrysipp.ib.2.199, Procl.*Hyp.* 5.14, al.; but τούτοις ἐ. ⟨ἡ⟩ ἡλίου ἀνταύγεια Ascl.*Tact.*12.10; μηδὲν ἔχειν τὸ -προσθοῦν τοῖς πνεύμασι *protection from* the wind, Ath.Med. ap.Orib.9.12.1: c. dat., Hp.*Medic.*7, etc.; τὸ μέσον ἐ. τοῖς πέρασι *stands before*, *intercepts the view of*, Arist.*Top.*148ᵇ27; ἐ. τοῖς πύργοις *is in a line with* them, *so as to cover* one with the other, Plb.1.47.2: metaph., ἡ ὀργὴ..πολλάκις τοῖς καταλαμβανομένοις -προσθεῖ Chrysipp. *Stoic.*3.95; τὸν χρόνον -προσθοῦντα τῇ γνώσει τῶν πραγμάτων Plu. *Per.*13; *veil*, Longin.32.1:—Pass., *to be occulted*, Theo Sm.p.193 H.: metaph., ὑπὸ τῶν σαρκῶν -ουμένη [ψυχή] Max.Tyr.15.6; περισπασμοῖς Hierocl.p.53 A.; ὑπ' αἰδοῦς Parth.17.3; [τὴν τραγῳδίαν] ὑπὸ τῶν ὀνομάτων ἐπιπροσθουμένην *obscured*, Melanthius ap.Plu.2.41d. **-θησις**, εως, ἡ, *being before*, *covering*, Thphr.*Vent.*30; esp. of *eclipses* or *occultations*, Arist.*Cael.*293ᵇ22, Procl.*Hyp.*5.15, etc.; *superposition* of colour, Arist.*Mete.*342ᵇ9 (pl.); of objects that serve as *cover*, Plb.3. 71.3 (pl.). **-πλέω**, *sail to* or *towards*, τῷ τόπῳ Str.1.3.16. ⊛ **-τίθημι**, *add besides*, Longin.44.1:—Med., corrupt in Artem.4.82. **-φθέγγομαι**, f.l. in Him.*Or.*14.32.

**ἐπιπρόσω**, *in front*, ἡ ἐ. πτέρνη Aret.*SD*2.12.

**ἐπιπρόσωπος**, ον, *with a face represented on it*, φιάλη *Annuario* 4/5. 463 (Halic., iii B.C.).

**ἐπιπροτέρωσε**, Adv. *still farther*, θέειν A.R.2.940.

**ἐπιπρο-φαίνομαι**, Pass., *to appear before one*, of οἰωνοί, A.R.3. 917. **-φέρω**, *move on forwards*, ταρσὸν ποδός Id.4.1519. **-χέω**, *pour forth*, θρῆνον *h.Pan.*18:—Pass., *gush forth*, *burst loose*, Nonn.*D.* 21.69. **-ωθέω**, *push farther forward*, Luc.*Asin.*10.

**ἐπίπρῳρος**, ον, (πρῷρα) *at the prow of a ship*, Hsch.

**ἐπιπταίρω**, *sneeze at*, υἱὸς μοι ἐπέπταρε πᾶσιν ἔπεσσιν he *sneezed* as I spoke the words (a good omen), Od.17.545, cf. *h.Merc.*297, Nonn. *D.*7.107: metaph., *to be gracious to*, *favour*, Ἔρωτές τινι ἐπέπταρον Theoc.7.96; ἀγαθός τις ἐ. ἐρχομένῳ Id.18.16.

⊛ **ἐπίπταισμα**, ατος, τό, *snap of the fingers*, Ar.*Fr.*773 (pl.).

**ἐπιπτάρνυμαι**, = ἐπιπταίρω, Hsch. (glossed by **μετακαλῶ, κατέχω·** ἐπισχετικὸν γὰρ ὁ πταρμὸς πολλάκις).

**ἐπίπτερον**, τό, = φακός, Ps.-Dsc.4.87; cf. ἐπίπετρον.

⊛ **ἐπίπτησις**, εως, ἡ, *flying down upon*, Jul.*Gal.*358e.

**ἐπιπτήσσω**, *crouch for fear*, ἐν τείχει Aristid.ap.Philostr.*VS*2.9.3.

**ἐπιπτίσσομαι**, *to be shelled*, *freed from the husk*, *Gp.*3.7.1.

**ἐπί-πτυγμα**, ατος, τό, (ἐπιπτύσσω) *over-fold*, *flap*, such as covers the orifices in animals, *operculum*, Arist.*PA*679ᵇ18, *HA*526ᵇ29, 528ᵇ 7: pl., *opercula*, of crustaceans, Id.*Resp.*477ᵃ4. **-πτυξις**, εως, ἡ, *application* to one another of vocal cords, Gal.*UP*7.13. ⊛ **-πτύσσω**, *fold up*, *fold*, γραμματεῖον Luc.*Dem.Enc.*25; ἱμάτιον περὶ τὰς ῥῖνας Dam.*Isid.*131: abs., *produce folds*, Gal.11.508:—Pass., *to be folded over*, Hp.*Epid.*6.8.28; of the epiglottis, ἐ. ἐπὶ τὸ τῆς ἀρτηρίας τρῆμα Arist.*HA*495ᵃ28, cf. *PA*664ᵇ28; of the vocal cords, Gal.*UP*7. 13. **-πτῠχή**, ἡ, = ἐπίπτυγμα, *flap*, χιτῶνος J.*AJ*17.5.7, Plu.2. 979c; τοῦ θώρακος Id.*Pomp.*35; αἱ ἐ. τῶν ῥακίων *rags* and tatters, Luc.*DMort.*1.2.

**ἐπιπτύω**, *spit upon*, τινί Call.*Fr.*235, Gal.6.754.

**ἐπί-πτωμα**, ατος, τό, *accident*, *PSI*3.252.28 (iii A.D.). **-πτωσις**, εως, ἡ, *onslaught*, αἰφνίδιον ποιεῖσθαι τὴν ἐ. J.*AJ*18.9.2. 2. *falling upon*, φωνῆς ἐπὶ μίαν τάσιν Nicom.*Harm.*12. b. *falling over* the forehead, τριχῶν Antyll.ap.Orib.44.8.1. 3. *falling to* one, κλήρων Plu.2.740d (pl.). b. *chance*, ἐ. τυχική Phld.*Rh.*1.211 S., cf. Theag. ap.Stob.3.1.117, Str.2.3.7.

**ἐπιπυκνόομαι**, Pass., *to become dense*, Arist.*Col.*794ᵃ14, Sor.2.29.

**ἐπιπυνθάνομαι**, *learn after*, τὰ γεγενημένα D.H.*Th.*29. 2. *inquire again*, Diogenian.3.34.

⊛ **ἐπιπυργῐδία**, ἡ, *on the tower*, epith. of Hecate at Athens, Paus.2. 30.2; of Artemis, ibid., *IG*3.268: so **ἐπιπυργῖτις**, of Athena at Abdera, Hsch.

**ἐπιπῡρέσσω**, aor. 1 -επύρεξα, *have fever afterwards*, Hp.*Prorrh.*1. 15, Gal.18(1).568; after drinking wine, Herod.Med.ap.Orib.5.27.23.

**ἐπιπῡρεταίνω**, = foreg., Hp.*Septim.*3, Aret.*CA*2.2.

**ἐπιπῡριάω**, *foment as well*, Paul.Aeg.3.77; gloss on ἐπιτυφῶσαι, Hsch.

**ἐπίπῡρον**, τό, (πῦρ) *hearth* of an altar, Hero *Spir.*2.21, Hsch. s.v. θυμέλη. II. *brazier* of a censer, *IG*11.199*B*16 (Delos, iii B.C.), al., *PCair.Zen.*13.34 (iii B.C.).

**ἐπίπυρρος**, ον, *reddish*, Arist.*Phgn.*807ᵇ32, Thphr.*HP*4.10.4, *PLond.*3.1207.17 (i B.C.), Poll.5.68.

**ἐπιπυρσεία**, ἡ, *counter-signal by fires*, Polyaen.6.19.2.

**ἐπιπωλέομαι**, *go about*, *go through*, c. acc., ἐ. στίχας ἀνδρῶν, of the general *inspecting* his troops, Il.3.196, etc.; but in 11.264, of *reconnoitring* an enemy.—Them. has **ἐπιπολεῖσθαι** *visit*, Βόσπορον *Or.*6.75c: c. dat., Σύροις ib.11.152b (nisi leg. ἐπιπωλ-).

**ἐπιπωλέω**, *sell the right of succession to* a priesthood, in Pass., *SIG* 1014.85, 107 (Erythrae, iii B.C.).

⊛ **ἐπιπώλησις**, εως, ἡ, *going round*, *visitation*, a name given by Gramm. to the latter half of Il.4, *IG*14.1290.59 (prob.), cf. Str.9.1. 10, Plu.2.29a.

**ἐπίπωμ-α**, ατος, τό, *cover*, Heliod.(?)ap.Orib.49.4.39, Gal.4.636. **-άζω**, *cover with* or *as with a lid*, Hero *Spir.*1 *Praef.*p.150, Simp.*in Cael.*520.15, al., Sm.*Ps.*68(69).16:—Pass., *to be so covered*, Hp. *Loc.Hom.*47, Anthem.p.151 W.—So **ἐπιπωμάννῡμι** Hero *Spir.*1.28 (Pass.). **-ασμός**, ὁ, *covering with a lid* or *cover*, of an arrow, Eust. 1630.63. **-ᾰτίζω**, *cover as with a lid*, *close up*, Arist.*Cael.*294ᵇ15, Thphr.*Ign.*59:—Pass., ib.49; τὸ πῦρ -όμενον σβέννυται Alex.Aphr. *Pr.*1.16; [ἐγχέλεις] ὑπὸ τοῦ θολοῦ τοὺς πόρους -ίζονται Arist.*Fr.*311; of the epiglottis, Gal.14.716. **-ατικός**, ή, όν, *serving to close up the pores*, of oil, Sch.Ar.*Pl.*616. **-άτισις**, εως, ἡ, *covering with a lid*, Phlp.*in APo.*420.13.

**ἐπιπωρ-όομαι**, *become callous on the surface*, Hp.*Art.*29; or *afterwards*, Id.*Fract.*38. **-ωμα**, ατος, τό, *callus formed over* the fracture of bone, Id.*Art.*36. 2. *gouty concretion*, ἀμφὶ τοῖσιν ἄρθροισιν Id. *Prorrh.*2.8. **-ωσις**, εως, ἡ, *formation of a callus*, -ωσιν ποιεῖσθαι Id.*Art.*14; -ώσιες ἄρθρων γίγνονται Aret.*SD*2.12. 2. *callus*, *Placit.*5.13.1 (pl.); of projections on renal stones, Aret.*SD*2.3.

**ἐπιπωτάομαι**, lengthd. form of ἐπιποτάομαι, *AP*9.88 (Phil.).

**ἐπιρραβδ-ίζω**, *smite*, κράδαις καὶ θρίοις Hsch. s. v. κραδίης νόμος. **-οφορέω**, *urge* a horse *by shaking the whip*, X.*Eq.*7.11, Poll.1.220.

**ἐπιρραθυμέω**, *to be careless about* a thing, Luc.*BisAcc.*1.

**ἐπιρραίνω**, aor. 1 -έρρᾱνα, *sprinkle upon* or *over*, ὕδωρ τινί Theoc. 24.98, cf. Arist.*GA*758$^{a}$16; καρποὺς ταῖς κεφαλαῖς D.H.7.72; ἐπὶ τὰ ᾠὰ τὸν θορόν Arist.*HA*567$^{b}$5, cf. Dsc.5.78 (Pass.). II. *besprinkle*, c. acc., Arist.*HA*567$^{b}$9; βωμὸν κατέχριεν ἐπιρραίνων ἑπτάκις Ph.2. 157:—Pass., Arist.*GA*756$^{a}$24.

**ἐπιρρακτός**, ή, όν, *dashed on* or *down*, θύρα ἐπιρρακτή *trap*-door, Plu.2.781e; ποτὸν *forced down* the throat, ib.699d.

⊛ **ἐπίρραμμα**, ατος, τό, *that which is sewn on*, *Gloss.*; dub. cj. for ἐπίρρημα in Poll.4.119 (v. ἐπίρριμμα 1 b).

**ἐπιρραντίζω**, = ἐπιρραίνω, Lxx *Le.*6.27(20) (Pass.), *Hippiatr.*16.

**ἐπιρρᾰπ-ίζω**, *smite*, τινὰ κατὰ κόρρης Aristaenet.1.4; ἐ. τὸ πῦρ *beat* it *out*, D.H.1.59. 2. metaph., *rebuke*, Diog.Bab.*Stoic.*3.221 (Pass.), Sosicr.ap.Ath.10.422c, Herm.*in Phdr.*p.85 A. 3. Pass., *to be checked*, of motion, Olymp.*in Mete.*24.20. **-ιξις**, εως, ἡ, *reproof*, Ion Hist.1. **-ισμός**, ὁ, = foreg., Plb.2.64.4.

⊛ **ἐπιρράπτω**, aor. 2 ἐπέρρᾰφον Nonn.*D.*9.3, al.:—*sew* or *stitch on*, τι ἐπὶ ἱμάτιον *Ev.Marc.*2.21: metaph., δόλον δόλῳ Nonn.*D.*42.315. 2. *sew up*, in Pass., Gal.18(2).579.

**ἐπιρράσσω**, Ep. -ρρήσσω, *dash to*, *shut violently*, *slam to*, θύρην δ' ἔχε.. ἐπιβλὴς.., τὸν τρεῖς μὲν ἐπιρρήσσεσκον Ἀχαιοί, τρεῖς δ' ἀναοίγεσκον Il.24.454, cf. 456; πύλας ἐπιρράξασ' ἔσω (with v.l. ἐπιρρήξασ') S.*OT*1244; τὸ πῶμα prob. in Plu.2.356c; λίθον (at the door of a cave) Id.*Phil.*19:—Pass., *to be dashed to*, of gates, D.H.8.18. 2. *dash against*, ἐ. αὐτοῖς τὴν ἵππον *throw* the cavalry *upon* them, Id. 3.25; ἴχνος κολώναις Nonn.*D.*11.195; *strike*, πέδον ὁπλῇ ib.41. 189. II. intr., *beat upon* one, of a storm, μή τις Διὸς κεραυνὸς ἤ τις ὀμβρία χάλαζ' ἐπιρράξασα; S.*OC*1503; of winds, Arat.292, Opp. *H.*1.634, App.*BC*2.59, Ph.1.507; ἐ. τισί *attack* them, D.S.15.84, cf. D.H.8.67, Ph.2.173, etc.

**ἐπιρραψῳδέω**, *recite in accompaniment*, ἔπη Luc.*Nec.*4; ἐ. ἔπη τινί *upon* him, Philostr.*Her.*2.9.

⊛ **ἐπιρρέζω**, *offer sacrifices at* a place, ὅθι πάντες ἐπιρρέζεσκον ὁδῖται (Ion. impf.) Od.17.211. 2. *sacrifice afterwards* or *besides*, Ζηνὶ χοῖρον Theoc.24.99, cf. *AP*6.157 (Theodorid.); ὄϊν *GDI*3639$^{a}$5 (Cos): abs., *IG*12(1).677.29 (Ialysus).

**ἐπιρρεμβῶς**, Adv. *aimlessly*, *desultorily*, Herm.ap.Stob.1.49.69.

**ἐπιρρεπ-ής**, ές, *inclining the balance*, μνᾶς -έστερον βραχύ rather *more than* a mina *in weight*, Damocr.ap.Gal.13.919. II. *leaning towards*, *prone to*, πρός τι Luc.*Hist.Conscr.*60, Ath.13.576f (Comp.); ἐς τὸ φιλάνθρωπον Hdn.6.9.8; εἰς κακίαν Hierocl.*in CA*3p.425 M.; -εστέρας τὰς γνώμας πρός τινα ἔχειν Hdn.5.8.2: abs., ἐλπίδες -έστεραι *favourable*, Plb.1.55.1. Adv. -πῶς, ἔχειν πρός τι Arr.*Epict.*3.22.1; τῆς τύχης ἐ. κινουμένης Chor.*Milt.*61: Comp. -έστερον S.E.*M.*1.280: Sup. -έστατα Men.Prot.p.119 D. ⊛ -ω, *lean towards*, ὄφρα.. ἡμῖν δ' αἰπὺς ὄλεθρος ἐπιρρέπῃ, metaph. from the balance, Il.14.99: hence, generally, *fall to one's lot*, [ὑμέναιος] ἐ. γαμβροῖσιν ἀείδειν A.*Ag.*707 (lyr.): abs., ib.1042. 2. metaph., *incline*, πρὸς ἔλεον Ph.2.582. II. trans., ἐ. τάλαντον *force down* one scale, Thgn.157. 2. *weigh out to* one, *allot*, esp. of ill fortune, ἐ. μῆνιν πόλει A.*Eu.*888; Δίκα τοῖς παθοῦσι μαθεῖν ἐπιρρέπει Id.*Ag.*251 (lyr.).

**ἐπιρρευμᾰτ-ίζομαι**, *have a further flow* of morbid humours, Gal. 19.664. II. *have a further attack of rheumatism*, Alex.Trall. 12. **-ισμός**, ὁ, *flow* of humours *to* a wound, *Hippiatr.*10; ἰχώρων Harp.Astr. in *Cat.Cod.Astr.*8(3).150.20.

**ἐπίρρευσις**, εως, ἡ, = -ρρυσις, Sch.Opp.*H.*1.116.

⊛ **ἐπιρρέω**, late fut. -ρρεύσω Hero *Spir.*1.9: aor. 1 Act. -έρρευσα Procop.*Aed.*4.6: pf. -έρρευκα Gal.ap.Orib.51.36.17: aor. 2 Pass. -ερρύην Hp.*Nat.Hom.*1, etc.:—*flow upon the surface*, *float*, καθύπερθεν ἐπιρρέει ἠΰτ' ἔλαιον Il.2.754. 2. *flow in besides*, *keep on flowing*, ποταμοῖσι.. ἐμβαίνουσιν.. ἕτερα ὕδατα ἐπιρρεῖ Heraclit.12; ἐπιρρεόντων ποταμῶν (into the sea), Ar.*Nu.*1294; χολὴ πλείων ἐπιρρέουσα Pl.*Ti.*85e; ἄνωθεν ἐπὶ τὰς ἀρούρας ib.22e: metaph. of large bodies of men, *stream on*, ἐπέρρεον ἔθνεα πεζῶν Il.11.724; ἐπιρρεόντων τῶν Ἑλλήνων καὶ γινομένων πλεύνων Hdt.9.38; ἐ. ὄχλος Γοργόνων Pl.*Phdr.* 229d; of a flood of topics, Id.*Tht.*177e; ὄχλος πολὺς ἄμμιν ἐπιρρεῖ Theoc.15.59; of the ἀπόρροιαι of Democritus, Plu.2.733d: c. inf., τὸ πλῆθος τῶν εἰπεῖν ἐπιρρεόντων Isoc.12.95: metaph. also, οὑπιρρέων χρόνος *onward-streaming* time, i.e. the future, A.*Eu.*853; ὄλβου ἐπιρρυέντος if wealth *accumulates*, E.*Med.*1229; ἀγαθῶν ἐπιρρεόντων X. *Ap.*27; πολλὴ αὔξη ὅταν ἐ. πόνων Pl.*Lg.*788d; τὰ ἐπιρρέοντα the *stream* of wealth, Aen.Gaz.*Thphr.*p.27 B. 3. c. gen., [τρίποδες] οἴνου ἐπέρρεον *flowed with* wine, Philostr.*VA*3.27. II. Pass., *to be watered*, ὕδασι Paus.9.8.6.

⊛ **ἐπιρρήγνῡμι**, *rend*, πέπλον δ' ἐπέρρηξ' ἐπὶ συμφορᾷ A.*Pers.*1030 (lyr.); *split*, Heliod.ap.Orib.48.21.3; *break*, νάρθηκας Alciphr.3.51.

**ἐπι-ρρήδην**, Adv., (ἐρέω, ῥηθῆναι) *by name* or *surname*, ἐ. καλέονται Arat.261. II. *explicitly*, *openly*, A.R.2.640; *directly*, τινὰ ἱλάεσθαι ib.847; *clearly*, Arat.191. ⊛ **-ρρημα**, ατος, τό, *that which is said afterwards*: I. in Old Comedy, a *speech*, commonly of trochaic tetrameters, *spoken* by the Coryphaeus *after the Parabasis* (as in Ar.*Nu.*575, *Eq.*565), Hsch., Suid. II. *adverb*, D.H.*Comp.*2, etc.; περὶ ἐπιρρημάτων, title of work by Apollonius Dyscolus. III. *surname*, *nickname*, Macho ap.Ath.13.578d. IV. v. ἐπίρραμμα, ἐπίρριμμα. **-ρρημᾰτικός**, ή, όν, *adverbial*, A.D.*Adv.*169.11, al., Sch.Ar.*Pl.*244, etc. Adv. -κῶς Phryn.*PS*p.10 B., A.D.*Synt.*10.9.

**ἐπίρρηξις**, εως, ἡ, *fissure*, χειλῶν Dsc.2.76; *tearing*, τῆς ἐπιφανείας Paul.Aeg.6.89.

**ἐπίρρησις**, εως, ἡ, *rebuke*, *reproach*, δειλοῦ -ρρησιν μελεδαίνων Archil.8, cf. Plu.2.19c (pl.), Hsch. II. *invocation*, θεῶν Phld.*Piet.* 74 (pl.); *spell*, *charm*, Luc.*Philops.*31, Jul.Afric.*Oxy.*412.46. III. *comment*, Phld.*Rh.*2.55 S.; opp. πρόρρησις, ib.1.31 S.

**ἐπιρρήσσω**, v. ἐπιρράσσω.

**ἐπιρρητέον**, *one must say concerning*, τῷ τοῦ Αἰσχύλου.. ὅτι.. Plu.2.36b.

**ἐπιρρητορεύω**, *declaim over*, τί τινι Luc.*Hist.Conscr.*26; τι κατά τινος Ach.Tat.8.8. II. *introduce besides*, τοὺς ἐπιλογικοὺς οἴκτους Ath.13.59oe.

⊛ **ἐπίρρητος**, ον, *exclaimed against*, *infamous*, τέχναι X.*Oec.*4.2; πλοῦτος Philostr.*VA*7.23. Adv. -τως Poll.3.139. II. ἐ. διαιτητής *agreed upon*, Sch.Patm.D. in *BCH*1.153.

**ἐπιρρῑγέω**, *shiver afterwards*, Hp.*Epid.*1.14:—also -ριγόω, Id. *Prorrh.*1.61.

**ἐπιρρίζ-ιον**, τό, *side-root*, v.l. in Dsc.1.11. **-όω**, prob. f.l. for ἐνριζόω, Nonn.*D.*40.532.

**ἐπίρρικνος**, ον, '*fine*', *wiry*, σκέλη X.*Cyn.*4.1 (περικνά codd.), Poll. 5.58.

**ἐπίρριμμα**, ατος, τό, *winding-sheet*, dub. in Lyd.*Mag.*3.60. b. *slave's outer garment*, dub. cj. in Poll.4.119 (v. ἐπίρραμμα). 2. (ἐπιρρίπτω 1.2) *poultice*, Alex.Trall.8.2 (ἐπιρρίματα codd.), *Febr.*2 (ἐπιρρήματος codd.).

**ἐπιρρίν-ιον** [ῐν], τό, Dim. of sq., Sm.*Ez.*16.12. **-ον**, τό, *nose-ring*, Id.*Jb.*42.11. **-ος**, ον, (ῥίς) *with a long nose*, Heph.Astr.2.2, Ps.-Luc.*Philopatr.*12: so ἐπίρρις, in acc. pl. -ρρινας, *Cat.Cod.Astr.*7.196.4.

⊛ **ἐπιρρῑπίζω**, dub. sens. in Nonn.*D.*30.187 (s. v. l.).

**ἐπιρριπτ-έον**, *one must apply* a plaster, Paul.Aeg.2.47. **-έω**, = sq., only in pres. and impf., X.*An.*5.2.23, Plb.18.46.12, Ph.*Bel.*100. 13, Sor.2.32:—Pass., Ph.*Bel.*99.48, Parth.9.8. 2. intr., *throw oneself upon* the track, X.*Cyn.*6.22. ⊛ **-ω** (ἐπῐρίπτω *AP*5.128 (Autom.)), *cast at*, ὅτε μοι χαλκήρεα δοῦρα Τρῶες ἐπέρριψαν Od.5.310; διώκων ἐ. ἑαυτόν *throws* himself *upon* his prey, Arist.*HA*629$^{b}$20; Βρούτῳ τὴν αὐτοῦ φοινικίδα ἐ. Plu.*Ant.*22; χεῖρα ἐ., Lat. *manum injecit*, *AP*9.84 (Antiphan.): metaph., ἐ. πλάνας τινί A.*Pr.*738; ψευδεῖς αἰτίας ἐ. D.S. 14.12; τὴν μέριμναν ἐπὶ [θεόν] 1 *Ep.Pet.*5.7; *inflict*, πολλὰ σκληρὰ.. ἐπιρριφήσεται, c. dat., Nech. in *Cat.Cod.Astr.*7.146. 2. *apply* a plaster or fomentation, Sor.1.50 (Pass.), 69; σκεπάσματα Dsc.5.88. 3. Pass., -όμενα σκιρρώματα *spreading over the surface*, Id.1.42. 4. *requisition*, ἔργα *PTeb.*5.249 (ii B.C.); ἱερεῖα τρέφειν ib.183. 5. metaph. in Pass., *to be imminent*, οὐ βραχὺς ἐπέρριπτο κίνδυνος Ph.2. 594. II. *throw out opinions*, ἀδιορίστως ἐ. περὶ τῶν λοιπῶν, v.l. for -, Arist.*Metaph.*986$^{a}$34.

**ἐπίρρις**, v. ἐπίρρινος.

⊛ **ἐπίρριψις**, εως, ἡ, *casting upon*, Aq.*Hb.*2.15.

**ἐπιρρόγανον**· ἀπόμακτρον, Hsch. (Prob. -ρροχ-, cf. ῥόχανον.)

**ἐπιρροή**, ἡ, (ἐπιρρέω) *afflux*, *influx*, κακαῖς ἐ. ὕδωρ μιαίνων A.*Eu.* 694; ἐπιρροαῖσιν αἱμάτων Id.*Ag.*1510 (lyr.); δακρύων ἐπιρροαί E.*Fr.* 573; ἐ. αἵματος *determination* of blood *to*.., Hp.*VC*13; opp. ἀπορροή (efflux), Ti.Locr.102b; τῆς τροφῆς Thphr.*CP*5.4.6; κατ' ἐπιρροάν Ti. Locr.101d: metaph., αὔξην τε καὶ ἐ. (sc. νοσημάτων) Pl.*Lg.*783b; ἐ. κακῶν E.*Andr.*349 (pl.); ἀνάμνησίς ἐστιν ἐ. φρονήσεως ἀπολιπούσης Pl. *Lg.*732b. 2. *stream* of a river, A.*Fr.*143 (pl.), A.R.4.623 (pl.). 3. *channel*, *duct*, Hp.*Gland.*12 (pl.). 4. *irrigation*, Ph.1.249.

**ἐπιρροθ-έω**, *shout in answer* or *in approval*, στάσις πάγκοινος ἅδ' ἐπιρροθεῖ A.*Ch.*458 (lyr.); χορὸς.. ἰχθύων ἐπερρόθει S.*Fr.*762, cf. E.*Hec.* 553; ἐ. ὡς.. Id.*Or.*901; ἐ. κτύπῳ *answer to*, *ring with* the sound, A.*Ch.* 427 (lyr.); *applaud*, D.H.6.83. 2. c. acc., λόγοις ἐπιρροθεῖν τινα *rage against*, *abuse* him, S.*Tr.*264. **-ητος**, ον, *blamed*, Hsch. **-ος**, ον, *coming to the rescue*; as Subst., *helper*, τοίη οἱ ἐ. ἦεν Ἀθήνη Il.4. 390; θεά.., μοι ἐ. ἐλθὲ ποδοῖιν 23.770; μακραὶ ἐπίρροθοι εὐφρόναι εἰσίν Hes.*Op.*560; ἐπίρροθοι ἄμμι πέλεσθε A.R.2.1193: also as Adj., μῆτις, πύργος ἐ., ib.1068, 4.1045: c. gen., *giving aid against*, νύκτερον τέλος .. ἀλγέων ἐ. A.*Th.*368 (lyr.); cf. ἐπιτάρροθος. 2. [ὁδὸς] λείη καὶ ἐ. *easy* (?), *AP*7.50 (Archim.). II. ἐ. κακά reproaches *bandied backwards and forwards*, *abusive* language, S.*Ant.*413. 2. δώμαθ' .. ἐ. *full of fault-finding*, Id.*Fr.*583.10.

⊛ **ἐπίρροια**, ἡ, = ἐπιρροή, Thphr.*Sud.*20; τῶν χυμῶν Ael.*NA*12.20: pl., *Placit.*4.22.1, Ph.2.151, Archig.ap.Orib.47.13.12; of rivers, D.S. 5.25: metaph., ἡ ἐ. τῶν ἀγαθῶν Id.33.18.

⊛ **ἐπιρροιβδ-έω**, *croak so as to forbode rain*, of a raven, Thphr.*Sign.* 16. 2. c. acc. cogn., ἐ. ἰὸν λαιμῷ *shoot a whizzing* arrow at.., Q.S. 8.322; cf. ἐπιρροιζέω. **-ην**, Adv. *with noisy fury*, E.*HF*860 (troch.).

**ἐπιρροιζέω**, = ἐπιρροιβδέω, Thphr.*Sign.*16, Arat.969. 2. c. acc. cogn., ἐ. φυγάς τινι *shriek* flight at him, A.*Eu.*424, cf. Lyc.585. II. *make a rustling* or *whirring sound*, Nonn.*D.*48.940, 37.688. III. v. ἐπιρρύζω.

**ἐπιρρομβέω**, *make a buzzing noise*, ἐπιρρόμβεισι δ' ἄκουαι Sapph.2. 11. 2. *swoop down upon*, of an eagle, Sch.Pi.*I.*4(3).77.

**ἐπίρροος**, contr. -ρους, ὁ, *influx*, *redundance*, Hp.*Ulc.*24. 2. *accessory flux*, Orib.8.36.3.

**ἐπίρροπος**, ον, *inclining*, Serapio in *Cat. Cod. Astr.* 1.100.3 (Comp.), Eustr.*in EN*33.16.

**ἐπιρροφ-άνω**, = sq., Hp.*Int.*6. ⊛ **-έω**, Ion. -ρῠφέω, *swallow besides*, Id.*Acut.*24; *take draughts* (of an actor), Arist.*Pr.*948$^{a}$2; ἐπιρροφεῖν τοῦ ὕδατος Plu.*Phoc.*9; τῆς κύλικος Ael.*NA*14.5; ὅταν τὸ ὕδωρ πνίγῃ, τί ἐπιρροφήσομεν; (cf. ἐπιπίνω) Archig.ap.Gal.8.577. II.

*swallow greedily, gulp down*, Clearch.Com.1; ἐ. ἀγαθοῦ δαίμονος Theopomp.Com.76.

**ἐπιρρόχανον**, v. ἐπιρρόγανον.

**ἐπιρρυγχίς**, ίδος, ἡ, (ῥύγχος) *hook of a bird's beak*, Ar.Byz.*Epit.*4.11, Suid.

**ἐπιρρύζω**, *set* a dog *on* one, ἐπί τινα Ar.*V.*705, acc. to Sch. and Hsch. (where also -ρροίζειν); cf. ῥύζω.

⊛ **ἐπιρρυθμίζω**, *remould, amend*, [ποιήματα] Pl.*Lg.*802b; ἐ. ἐς τὸ ἀφελὲς ἑαυτὴν *dress* oneself simply, v.l. in Luc.*Pisc.*12.

**ἐπιρρύομαι**, *save, preserve*, A.*Th.*165 (lyr.).

**ἐπιρρῠπαίνω**, *soil on the surface*, ὥσπερ ἰοῦ -αίνοντος τὴν πολυτέλειαν Plu.2.828a, cf. Philum.*Ven.*3.2 (Pass.). II. Pass., *become foul again*, of a wound, Archig.ap.Orib.46.26.3.

**ἐπιρρύπτω**, *clean*, Herod.Med. in *Rh.Mus.*58.85.

⊛ **ἐπίρρῠσις**, εως, ἡ, = ἐπιρροή, Hp.*Loc.Hom.*21; αἵματος Arist.*PA* 653ᵃ13. II. perh. **ἐπίρρῡσις** (ῥύομαι) *means of saving*, Id.*GA* 745ᵃ28.

**ἐπιρρυσμίζω**, Ion. for ἐπιρρυθμίζω, Hsch.

⊛ **ἐπιρρύσμιος**, η, ον, (ῥυσμός) *in-flowing*, Hsch.; ἐπιρρυσμίη ἑκάστοισιν ἡ δόξις *adventitious*, Democr.7.

**ἐπιρρῠτής**, οῦ, ὁ, = ἐπαρυστρίς, Aq.*Za.*4.2 (pl.).

**ἐπίρρῠτος**, ον, (ἐπιρρέω) *running*, ὕδατα Thphr.*CP*3.8.3, *HP*5.9.5; of food, *infused into* the body, τροφῆς νάματα ἐ. Pl.*Ti.*80d; of sight, *infused* from the sun, Id.*R.*508b; ψυχαί Ti.Locr.99e; ἡδοναὶ δι' αἰσθήσεων ἐπίρρυτοι Max.Tyr.31.7; ἐ. δύναμις, opp. σύμφυτος, Gal.1.319. 2. metaph., *overflowing, abundant*, καρπός A.*Eu.*907. II. Pass., *flowed into, subject to influx*, opp. ἀπόρρυτος, Pl.*Ti.*43a. 2. *overflowed, moist*, πεδίον X.*An.*1.2.22. III. as Subst., perh. *oil-vessel* or *pipe*, ἀλείψασαν δρακτοῖς καὶ ἐπιρύτοις *JRS*16.90, cf. *OGI*479.10 note.

**ἐπιρρῠφέω**, Ion. for -ροφέω (q.v.).

**ἐπιρρωγολογέομαι**, (ῥώξ, ῥάξ) *glean grapes off* the vines, Lxx 4*Ma.*2.9.

**ἐπιρρώννῡμι** and -ύω: aor. ἐπέρρωσα:—*add strength to, strengthen* or *encourage in* a thing, αὗται [αἱ νέες]..σφέας ἐπέρρωσαν Hdt.8.14; τοὺς μὲν ἐξέπληξε, τοὺς δὲ πολλῷ μᾶλλον ἐπέρρωσεν Th.4.36, cf. 8.89; εἰς τὸ ἐπιρρῶσαι αὐτούς X.*HG*7.5.6; ἐ. τινὰ πρὸς τὸν πόλεμον Plu.*Lys.*4; ἐπίρρωσον σαυτήν *collect* your *strength*, Luc.*Tim.*41; ἐ. τὴν γνώμην, τὰ πάθη, Plu.2.62a, 681f. II. Pass. (in which the pf. ἐπέρρωμαι, plpf. ἐπερρώμην serve as pres. and impf.), fut. ἐπιρρωσθήσομαι Luc.*Somn.*18: aor. 1 ἐπερρώσθην (v. infr.):—*recover strength, pluck up courage*, Th.6.93, 7.2; οἱ Κορίνθιοι..πολλῷ μᾶλλον ἐπέρρωντο Id.7.17; ἐς τἆλλα πολὺ ἐπέρρωντο ib.7; ἐπερρώσθη ἄν τις ἰδών X.*HG*3.4.18; ἐπερρώσθησαν ταῖς ὁρμαῖς πρὸς τὸν πόλεμον Plb.1.24.1; τὰς ψυχάς Hdn.3.3.8; κείνοις..ἐπερρώσθη λέγειν (impers.) they *took courage* to speak, S.*OC*661.

**ἐπιρρώομαι**, old Ep. pres.: aor. 1 Med. ἐπερρώσαντο:—*apply one's strength to* a thing, *work lustily at* it, c. dat., [μύλαις] δώδεκα πᾶσαι ἐπερρώοντο γυναῖκες *worked with might and main at* the mill, Od.20.107; ἐπερρώοντ' ἐλάτῃσι A.R.2.661. 2. *move nimbly*, ποσσὶν ἐπερρώσαντο Hes.*Th.*8, cf. A.R.1.385 (tm.): c. acc. cogn., ἐπίρρωσαι δὲ χορείην *urge the rapid* dance, *AP*9.403 (Maec.). 3. *follow rapidly*, ἐπερρώοντο τιθήνῃ Coluth.101. II. *flow* or *stream upon* (one's head), χαῖται ἐπερρώσαντο ἄνακτος κρατὸς ἀπ' ἀθανάτοιο his locks *flowed waving* from his head, Il.1.529; πλοχμοὶ..ἐπερρώοντο κιόντι A.R.2.677.

**ἐπιρρώπια**· ἐπιτελῆ, Hsch. (Prob. ἐπὶ ῥώπια· ἐπ' εὐτελῆ.)

**ἐπίρρωσις**, εως, ἡ, *strengthening*, Ael.*NA*6.1; ῥώμης Lib.*Decl.*48.60. II. Rhet., *intensification*, Longin.11.2.

**ἐπιρρωστέον**, *one must arouse*, πᾶσαν σπουδήν Nicom.*Harm.*1.

**ἐπίρῠτος**, ὁ, or -ον, τό, v. ἐπίρρυτος III.

**ἐπίσαγμα**, ατος, τό, (ἐπισάττω) *pack-saddle*, Lxx *Le.*15.9; *load*, ὄνων Sch.Ar.*Nu.*449: metaph., δεινὸν τοὐπίσαγμα τοῦ νοσήματος the *burden* of the disease, S.*Ph.*755.

**ἐπίσαθρος**, ον, *infirm*, τὰς ὑπάρξεις ἐ. καὶ ἐπικινδύνους ποιεῖν Vett.Val.90.3: Sup., Hsch. s.v. ἐπικηρότατοι.

**ἐπισάλ-εύω**, *ride at anchor off*, τοῖς ἀκρωτηρίοις Philostr.*Her.*19.14: metaph., ἐ. τοῖς ὤμοις (cf. σαλεύω) Arist.*Phgn.*813ᵃ11. II. *float over*, ἡ κόμη ἐπισαλεύει τῷ μετώπῳ Philostr.*Im.*1.23:—Med., Luc.*Am.*40. -**ος**, ον, *tossed on the sea*, πρᾶγμα Secund.*Sent.*17. II. *rough*, ὅρμος *Peripl.M.Rubr.*8, 12; τόπος *Stad.*55.

**ἐπισαλπίζω**, *accompany on the trumpet*, τοῖς ὑμνῳδοῦσιν J.*AJ*9.13.3. II. ἐ. τοῖς κέρασιν *blow* the horns, ib.7.14.5.

**ἐπίσᾱμα**, v. ἐπίσημα.

**ἐπισανδᾰλίς**, ίδος, ἡ, *sandal strap*, *Schwyzer* 462 *B* 29 (Tanagra, iii B.C.).

**ἐπίσαξις**, εως, ἡ, *heaping on* or *up*, τῆς γῆς Thphr.*CP*5.6.3. II. *stuffing, filling*, Erasistr.ap.Gal.7.538.

**ἐπίσαπρος**, ον, *rotten*, dub. l. in Thphr.*HP*3.7.5.

**ἐπισαρκάζω**, *grin, sneer at*, Ph.1.587; τινί Sch.Il.11.110: abs., Sch.S.*El.*1457.

**ἐπισαρκ-ίδιον**, τό, v.l. for ὑποσαρκ- (q.v.) in Hp., Gal.15.891. -**ος**, ον, *covered with flesh*, ὀστέον Hp.*Fract.*18.

**ἐπισάττω**, *pile a load upon*, τι ἐπὶ ὄνους, ἐπὶ καμήλους, Hdt.1.194, 3.9; τι ὄνῳ J.*AJ*1.13.2; ἵππον ἐ. *saddle* it, X.*Cyr.*3.3.27, *An.*3.4.35: c. dupl. acc., *load with*, τὴν ὄνον σῦκα Alciphr.3.20. 2. *heap up*, τὴν ἐπισεσαγμένην γῆν Thphr.*HP*7.2.5. 3. Pass., *to be filled full*, Gal.7.541.

**ἐπισαχθής**· χρεωφειλέτης, Hsch.

**ἐπισβέννῡμαι**, Pass., *go out upon*, τῷ ἄνθρακι Luc.*JTr.*15.

**ἐπίσειον**, v. ἐπίσιον.

⊛ **ἐπίσειστος**, ον, *shaking* or *waving over* the forehead, κόμη Luc.*Gall.*26. 2. ἐπίσειστος, ὁ, a comic *mask with hair hanging on the forehead*, Poll.4.146 sq.

⊛ **ἐπισείω**, Ep. **ἐπισσ-** (as always in Hom.), *shake at* or *against*, τί τινι, esp. with the view of scaring, ὅτ' ἂν..Ζεὺς..αὐτὸς ἐπισσείῃσιν ἐρεμνὴν αἰγίδα πᾶσι Il.4.167, cf. 15.230; ἐπισείουσα τὸν λόφον ἐκπλήττει με Luc.*DDeor.*19.1, cf. 2.2, etc.; τὰ δόρατα Hdn.2.13.4; ἐ. πόλεμον τῇ πατρίδι *stir up*.., J.*BJ*2.17.3; Πέρσας ἐ. *hold* them *out as a threat*, Plu.*Them.*4; but ἐ. τὴν χεῖρα, in token of assent or applause, Luc.*Pr.Im.*4, *Bis Acc.*28; ἐπὶ δ' ἔσεισεν κόμαν E.*IT*1276 (lyr.): abs., τόσσον ἐπισσείει so she *seems to threaten*, of a statue, *AP*9.755:—Pass., κόμαι ἐ. τοῖς κροτάφοις Lib.*Decl.*12.27: metaph., τὸν ἐπισεισθέντα τῶν παθῶν σκηπτόν Ph.1.210. 2. *urge on*, [ἵππον] S.*Fr.*147; ἐ. τινὶ τὰς δρακοντώδεις κόρας *set* them *upon* one, E.*Or.*255; ἐ. πόλιν σοί ib.613; μὴ 'πίσειέ μοι τὸν Μισγόλαν Alex.3; *hurl at*, τινὶ πέτρον Parth.14.4. 3. intr., *assault*, τοῖς τείχεσι D.S.13.94 codd. 4. *shake so as to touch*, Callistr.*Stat.*6, cf. Poll.4.147.

**ἐπισείων**, οντος, ὁ, *streamer* of a ship (cf. παράσειον), Poll.1.90, 91. 2. = μακροπώγων, Id.4.143.

**ἐπισέληνος**, ον, (σελήνη) *moon-shaped*: ἐπισέληνα, τά, *cakes of this shape*, Pl.Com.174.10 (nisi leg. -σέλινα); = πόπανα μηνοειδῆ, Hsch.

**ἐπισεμνολογέω**, *gloss over*, πρᾶξιν Anon.*Prog.* in Rh.1.599 W.

**ἐπίσεμνος**, ον, *rather proud*, *Cat.Cod.Astr.*8(4).137.

**ἐπισεμνύνομαι**, *pride oneself on* a thing, Ph.1.599, al., J.*Ap.*2.3.

**ἐπισεσυρμένως**, (ἐπισύρω II) *carelessly, perfunctorily*, Epict.*Ench.*31, Simp. *in eund.*p.53 D., *EM*191.34.

**ἐπισεύω**, Ep. **ἐπισσ-** (as always in Hom.), *put in motion against, set on*, μή..μοι κῆτος ἐπισσεύῃ μέγα δαίμων Od.5.421; δμῶας ἐπισσεύας 14.399: metaph., τόσα γάρ μοι ἐπέσσευεν κακὰ δαίμων 18.256; ὀνείρατ' ἐπέσσευεν κακὰ δαίμων 20.87; κῆρας *AP*7.439 (Theodorid.). II. mostly Pass., *hurry* or *hasten to* or *towards*, ἐπεσσεύοντο δὲ λαοί Il.2.86; ἔς τινα 13.757; ἐπεσσεύοντο νομόνδε to pasture, 18.575; νῆάδ' (so Aristarch.) ἐπεσσεύοντο Od.13.19; in hostile sense, *rush upon* or *at*, c. dat., νηυσὶν ἐπισσεύεσθαι Il.15.347. 2. freq. in pf. part. Pass. ἐπεσσύμενος, with 3 sg. plpf. ἐπέσσῠτο (used as an aor.): 3 pl. aor. 1 ἐπέσσῠθεν Opp.*C.*4.136:—mostly in hostile sense, *charge*, ἐπέσσυτο δαίμονι ἶσος Il.5.438, al.; τῷ ἐπεσσύμενον βάλε τείχεος ὑψηλοῖο struck him with an arrow from the wall as he *rushed on*, 12.388: c. dat., αὐτῷ μοι ἐπέσσυτο 5.459, cf. 21.227: c. acc., τεῖχος ἐπεσσύμενοι 12.143: c. gen., ἐπεσσύμενος πεδίοιο *rushing, hurrying over* the plain, 14.147, 22.26 (cf. διαπράσσω); also of fire, etc., ἠΰτε πῦρ, τό τ' ἐπεσσύμενον πόλιν ἀνδρῶν..φλεγέθει 17.737; κῦμα δεινὸν ἐπεσσύμενον Od.5.314, cf. 431: also, without any hostile sense, to express rapid motion, c. dat., ὥς οἱ..ὄνειρον ἐπέσσυτο 4.841: c. acc., ὡς πνοιὴ ἐπέσσυτο δέμνια *swept over* them, 6.20: c. inf., ἐπέσσυτο διώκειν he *hasted on* to follow, Il.21.601, cf. A.R.1.758: abs., χερσὶν ἐπεσσύμενος λάβε πέτρης Od.5.428; ἐπεσσύμενος λάβε γούνων 22.310. 3. metaph., *to be in excitement* or *agitation*, εἴ τοι θυμὸς ἐπέσσυται Il.1.173; θυμὸς ἐ. ὄφρ' ἐπαμύνω 6.361: c. inf., μοι ἐπέσσυτο θυμὸς..τέρπεσθαι 9.398.—Ep. word, used occasionally by Trag., only in lyr. (exc. S.*Ichn.*21, 43), πέδον ἐπισύμενος A.*Eu.*786; ἐπέσυτο τάνδε γᾶν..ἄτα E.*Ph.*1065; τείχεα..ἐπέσυτο φλόξ Id.*Hel.*1162; so τίς ὄρεα..τάδ' ἐπέσυτο; Ar.*Fr.*698 (parody of dithyramb).

**ἐπισήθω**, *sprinkle upon*, ψῆγμα χρυσοῦ ταῖς κόμαις J.*AJ*8.7.3: impf. ἐπέσηθον Hsch.

**ἐπισηκρητεύω**, (Lat. *secretum*) *perform secretarial duties as well*, Lyd.*Mag.*3.27.

⊛ **ἐπί-σημα**, ατος, τό, *device* on a coin, Simon.157; on a shield, τοὐπίσημ' A.*Th.*659; ἐ. ἔχων..ἐν μέσῳ σάκει E.*Ph.*1107, cf. 1125: also in form -**σᾱμα**, *Schwyzer* 607 (Thess., v B.C.). ⊛ -**σημαίνω**, Dor. -**σᾱμαίνω** *SIG*953.31 (Calymna, ii B.C.):—*mark*, γράμματα Aen.Tact.31.3 (Med.):—Med., *seal*, μαρτυρίας τᾷ δαμοσίᾳ σφραγῖδι *SIG* l.c.:—Pass., *to have a mark set on one*, κἀπισημανθήσεται κείνου κεκλῆσθαι λαὸς E.*Ion*1593. 2. of a disease, τῶν ἀκρωτηρίων ἀντίληψις αὐτοῦ ἐπεσήμαινεν the seizure of his extremities *set a mark upon* him, Th.2.49:—Pass., ἢν ἅπαξ ἐπισημανθῇ if once he *has the mark* of the disease *upon him*, Hp.*Morb.Sacr.*8. b. *indicate as a symptom*, πολλὰ τοῦ νοσώδους Philostr.*Gym.*30: as a weather-sign, αὐχμούς Id.*Her.*2.9:—Pass., *show symptoms* of disease, Gal.14.661. II. *indicate*, c. acc. et inf., ὁ θεὸς ἐπεσήμαινεν αὐτῷ ὅσιον εἶναι X.*HG*4.7.2. III. intr., *give signs, appear as a symptom in* a case, Hp.*Epid.*1.18; ἄρθρον ἐ. συντεταμένον Id.*Art.*30; of puberty, *show itself*, Arist.*GA*727ᵃ8, 728ᵇ24; of weather-signs, *indicate a change of weather*, Thphr.*Sign.*10, etc.; of omens, τῷ Ῥώμῳ γῦπες ἐ. ἕξ D.H.1.86, etc.; εἰς τὸ δημόσιον Paus.3.12.7; of the gods, δαιμόνιον αὐτοῖς ἐ. D.S.19.103, cf. 5.3, Plu.*Num.*22, *Sull.*14: impers., ἐπισημαίνει *symptoms appear*, Arist.*HA* 572ᵇ32; ἐ. περὶ τοὺς μαστοὺς Id.*GA*728ᵇ29. IV. Med. (pf. Med. in act. sense, Phld.*Mus.*p.82 K., *Ir.*p.5 W., aor. Pass., Id.*Rh.*1.58 S., al.), *assign as a distinguishing mark*, μίαν τινὰ φύσιν Pl.*Phlb.*25a, cf. *Plt.*258c; *distinguish*, τί βούλομαι Id.*Lg.*744a; ἐάν τε ἰάσιμος ἐάν τε ἀνίατος δοκῇ εἶναι Id.*Grg.*526b: abs., D.S.13.28; τοσοῦτον -σημηναμένους having *added* so much *by way of explanation*, Gal.17(1).800. 2. *signify, indicate*, ὃ.."Ὅμηρος ἐπεσ. Pl.*Lg.*681e; ἐ. ἐν τοῖς ὅρκοις ὅτι "οὐκ ἀδικήσω" Arist.*Pol.*1310ᵃ11; τῷ μειδιάματι..τὴν διαμαρτίαν Luc.*Laps.*1; *remark*, "ὀρθῶς" Thphr.*Char.*2.4. 3. *set one's name and seal to* a thing (in token of approbation), ἐπισημαίνεσθαι τὰς εὐθύνας D.18.250: generally, *applaud, signify approval*, Isoc.12.

2, Aeschin.2.49, Men.*Phasm.Fr.*1, etc.: rarely in bad sense, *disapprove*, M.Ant.6.20, App.*BC*5.15; of a historian, Plb.2.61.1. 4. *distinguish* by reward or punishments, ἐπισημαίνεσθαί τινα δώροις Id.6.39.6; τοὺς μὲν χάρισι, τοὺς δὲ κολάσεσιν Id.*Fr.*148; τὰ καλὰ τῶν ἔργων *OGI*116.13 (Delos, ii B.C.), cf. 51.12 (Ptolemais, iii B.C.). **-σήμανσις**, εως, ἡ, *marking*, ἀπὸ ἐπισημάνσεως κεραυνῶν where lightning *has left its mark*, Arist.*Pr.*937ᵇ26. **-σημαντέον**, *one must signify*, Id.*Top.*160ᵃ3, Phld.*Rh.*2.72 S., cf. Antig.Nicae. ap.Heph.Astr.2.18. **-σημαντικός**, ή, όν, *indicative, portending*, Ptol.*Tetr.*94,101, *Cat.Cod.Astr.*4.84.1. ⊛ **-σημᾰσία**, ἡ, *marking, notice*, ἄξιος ἐπισημασίας Plb.39.1.1; τυχεῖν -ασίας Id.30.1.2, cf. Phld. *Rh.*1.12 S., al., etc.; ὑπὸ τοῦ πλήθους ἐ. εὐνοϊκῆς τυγχάνειν Plb.6.6.8; pl., *acclamations*, Cic.*Att.*1.16.11, cf. 14.3.2 (sg.): in bad sense, -ασίας ἔτυχεν ὑπὸ τοῦ δαιμονίου κεραυνωθεὶς D.S.16.83. II. *marking* of letters in a cipher, Aen.Tact.31.3. III. *symptom*, and hence *access* of an illness, Gal.7.426, 10.604, Alex.Aphr.*Pr.*1.130; *signs of the seasons*, Epicur.*Ep.*2 p.43 U., Plb.1.37.4, D.S.1.49, *Placit.*2.19.1 (pl.); *indication of weather to be expected*, Ptol.*Phas.*p.11 H. (pl.), al. 2. pl., *changes in the weather*, *Stoic.*3.184, *Gp.*7.10. ⊛ **-σημειόομαι**, = ἐπισημαίνομαι, *distinguish, observe*, τὸ ἀνίσχον ζῴδιον S.E.*M.*5.68; κρότῳ by applause, Plu.2.235c (nisi leg. -σημην-). 2. *observe, remark*, ὅτι.. Asp.*in EN*139.6, cf. Anon.Lond.21.21. **-σημείωσις**, εως, ἡ, *note* or *comment*, Zeno *Stoic.*1.68. ⊛ **-σημον**, τό, *distinguishing mark, device, badge*, Hdt.1.195; *badge* or *bearing* on a shield, v.l. in Id.9.74; *ensign* or *flag* (or *figurehead*) of a ship, Id.8.88, cf. Hp.*Ep.*17; *device* on a coin, Plu.*Thes.*6; on a signet, *SIG*²588.3 (Delos, ii B.C.); *serial number*, *PPetr.*3p.203 (iii B.C.); ἐπίσημα, τά, *hieroglyphics*, *OGI*56.64 (Canopus, iii B.C.). II. generally, *mark, imprint*, τῶν ὁπλῶν S.*Ichn.*102. **-σημόομαι**, = ἐπισημειόομαι, στεφάνωσίν τινος *IGRom.*4.159.27 (Cyzicus). ⊛ **-σημος**, Dor. **-σᾱμος**, ον, (σῆμα) *serving to distinguish*, τοῖς δ' ὄνομ' ἄνθρωποι κατέθεντ' ἐ. ἑκάστῳ Parm.19.3. II. *having a mark, inscription* or *device on it*, esp. of money, *stamped, coined*, χρυσὸς ἐ., opp. ἄσημος, Hdt.9.41; ἀργύριον Th.2.13; χρυσίον X.*Cyr.*4.5.40, cf. *IG*1².301, al.; so ἀναθήματα οὐκ ἐ. offerings *with* no *inscription on them*, Hdt.1.51; ἀσπίδες ἐ., opp. λεῖαι, *IG*1².280, cf. Men.526. 2. of epileptic patients, *bearing the marks of the disease*, Hp.*Morb.Sacr.*8; of cattle, *spotted* or *striped*, Lxx *Ge.*30.42. 3. *notable, remarkable*, μνῆμ' ἐ. *a speaking* remembrance, S.*Ant.*1258 (anap.); ξυμφοραί E.*Or.*543; εὐνή, λέχος, Id.*HF*68, *Or.*21; τύχη Id.*Med.*544; χαρακτήρ Id.*Hec.*379; τάφος ἐπισημότατος Th.2.43; τιμωρία Lycurg.129; τόποι *IG*12(3).326.42 (Thera, Sup.); of garments, *fine*, *SIG*695.39 (Magn. Mae., ii B.C.); and of persons, ἐ. σοφίην *notable* for wisdom, Hdt.2.20; ἐ. ἐν βροτοῖς E.*Hipp.*103; ἐ. ξένοι Ar.*Fr.*543: in bad sense, *conspicuous, notorious*, ἐς τὸν ψόγον E.*Or.*249; δέσμιος ἐ. *Ev.Matt.*27.16; διὰ δημοκοπίαν Plu.*Fab.*14; ἐπὶ τῇ μοχθηρίᾳ Luc.*Rh.Pr.*25. 4. *significant*, οὐκ ἐ. Artem.1.59, 3.32. III. Adv. -μως Plb.6.39.9, Sm.*Ps.*73(74).4, J.*BJ*6.1.8: Comp. -ότερον Gal.9.762; -οτέρως Artem.2.9: Sup. -ότατα Luc.*Hist.Conscr.*43. **-σημότης**, *nobilitas*, *Gloss.*

**ἐπίσης**, for ἐπ' ἴσης (sc. μοίρας), v. ἴσος.

**ἐπισθένω**, *have strength enough*, c. inf., Q.S.4.567, 14.177.

**ἐπίσθμιος**, ον, *on the neck*: ἐπίσθμιον, τό, *collar*, Hsch.

**ἐπίσιγμα**, ατος, τό, *hounding on* of a dog, prob. l. in S.*Fr.*9 (pl.).

**ἐπισιγίζω**, *hound on, set on*, as a dog, Ar.*V.*704, cf. Hsch. s. v. ἐπιρροίζειν.

**ἐπίσιμον**, f.l. for ἐπίσημον, S.*Ichn.*102.

**ἐπισῑμόω**, *bend inwards*, τὴν προβοσκίδα Ael.*NA*8.10: seemingly intr., *turn aside one's course*, X.*HG*5.4.50.

**ἐπισινής**, ές, (σίνομαι) *liable to be injured by, infested with*, ὄρνισιν ἢ ἄλλοις θηρίοις cj. in Thphr.*HP*8.6.1: abs., Id.*CP*4.10.3 (Comp.). II. Act., *injurious*, τινί ib.2.3.2, *HP*9.8.6; ἐχθροὶ καὶ ἐ. Vett.Val.76. 29. III. abs., *blemished, feeble, diseased*, Chaerem.ap.J.*Ap.*1.32, Vett.Val.18.22, al., *Cat.Cod.Astr.*2.166.13.

**ἐπισίνιος**, ον, *plotting mischief*, Hsch.

**ἐπισίνομαι** [σῑ], aor. 1 -σινάμην, *do hurt to*, Nic.*Al.*413.

**ἐπίσιον** [ῐσῐ], or **ἐπείσιον**, τό, *pubic region*, Hp.*Carn.*14, *Mul.*1.64, 2.113, 120, 177, Arist.*HA*493ᵃ20, Lyc.1385, Gal.*UP*14.13, al., Poll. 2.170, 174, Hsch., Suid., *EM*363.55, Choerob. in *An.Ox.*2.200, cj. in Archil.140. [Both spellings in codd.; also ἐπίσειον, which is disproved by the metre in Lyc. l. c.]

**ἐπίσιστον**, τό, *a cry to urge on dogs*, *AB*252, *EM*363.54.

**ἐπισῑτ-ίζομαι**, fut. Att. -ιοῦμαι Philostr.*VA*6.15, Ion. -ιεῦμαι Hdt. 9.50:—*furnish oneself with food* or *provender*, Id. l. c., Th.8.101, cf. X.*Vect.*4.48; ἐ. ἐκ τῆς κώμης Hdt.7.176; ἐκεῖθεν Th.6.94; εἶχον οὐδὲν ὅτου ἂν ἐπισιτίσαιντο D.50.53, cf. Arist.*Rh.*1411ᵃ9. 2. c. acc. rei, ἐ. ἄριστον *provide oneself with*.., Th.8.95; ἀργύριον ἐ. εἰς τὴν πορείαν X.*An.*7.1.7; κλεψύδραν Philostr.*VS*2.10.1. 3. metaph., ἐ. πρὸς σοφιστείαν *store oneself* for sophistry, Plu.2.78f. II. = παρασιτέω, Pherecr.32. **-ικός**, ή, όν, in neut. -κόν, τό, *provision of food*, *BGU*362 viii 2 (iii A.D.). **-ιος**, ον, (σῖτος) *working for his victuals alone* (without wages), of slaves, Crates Com.33.1, Pl.*R.*420a, Eub. 21; applied to παράσιτοι, Ar.*Fr.*437, Timocl.29. II. ἐπισίτια, τά, *provision-money*, Lys.*Fr.*75 S. **-ισις**, εως, ἡ, = sq. 2, δέκα ἡμερῶν D.S.20.73:—also **-ισμα**, ατος, τό, Polyaen.3.10.11. **-ισμός**, ὁ, *furnishing oneself with provisions, foraging*, X.*HG*3.2.26, *An.*1.5. 9. 2. *stock* or *store of provisions*, ib.7.1.9, D.34.7, J.*BJ*3.5.3, *Ev. Luc.*9.12; ἔχοντες ἐπισιτισμὸν ἡμερῶν μ' Philipp.ap.D.18.157; ἐ. ἀννώνης *OGI*200.15 (Axum, iv A.D.): in pl., Hdn.6.7.1.

**ἐπισίττω**, = ἐπισίζω, Hsch. **ἐπισίφλιον**· αἰσχρόν, μωμητόν, Id.

**ἐπισιωπάω**, *cease speaking at* a point, τὰ ῥήματα οἷς -ησα Philostr. *VA*8.26.

**ἐπισκάζω**, *limp upon*, μηρῷ Lxx *Ge.*32.31(32); πόδεσσι A.R.1.669: abs., τὸ σκέλος ἐ. Hp.*Nat.Mul.*47, cf. *Mul.*2.140, Nic.*Th.*294, Corn. *ND*18: written -σχάζω *BGU*997 ii 5 (ii B.C.).

**ἐπισκαίρω**, *leap, bound*, Ael.*NA*14.8, Nonn.*D.*48.902: c. dat., *leap at* or *on*, Id.2.657, al.: c. acc., Id.22.36 (s. v. l.).

⊛ **ἐπισκαλμίς**, ίδος, ἡ, (σκαλμός) *the part of the rowlock on which the oar rests*, Hsch., Poll.1.87.

⊛ **ἐπισκάπτω**, *dig superficially*, *AP*9.52 (Carph.). II. *harrow in* seed, *Gp.*2.24.1 (Pass.).

**ἐπισκαρδᾰμύσσω**, *wink at*, Hsch. s. v. ἐπιζυγκλεῖν.

**ἐπισκᾰφ-εῖον**, τό, *mattock, hoe*, *BCH*23.566 (Delph., iii B.C.). II. -εῖα, τά, festival at Rhodes, Hsch. (-άφια cod.). ⊛ **-εύς**, έως, ὁ, *one who harrows in the seed*, Id.

**ἐπισκεδάννῡμι**, *scatter* or *sprinkle over*, τι ἐπί τι Pl.*Ti.*85a (Pass.), cf. Alex.186.9:—Pass., *to be sprinkled over*, τινί Plu.*Cat.Mi.*32.

**ἐπισκέλῐσις**, εως, ἡ, (σκέλος) *first spring* or *bound*, in a horse's gallop, X.*Eq.*7.12.

**ἐπισκέλλω**, *dry up*: intr. pf. ἐπέσκληκα Epich.155 codd. Ath.

**ἐπισκεπ-άζω**, *cover over*, τινά Lxx *La.*3.43; *put over*, νεφέλην σεαυτῷ ib.44. **-ής**, ές, (σκέπη) *covered over, sheltered*, Arist.*HA*616ᵇ 14, Thphr.*Vent.*30.

**ἐπισκεπτ-έος**, α, ον, *to be considered* or *examined*, Th.6.18, Pl.*Phd.* 107b (s. v. l.). II. neut. -τέον, *one must consider*, Id.*R.*598d, Aen.Tact.10.20, etc. ⊛ **-ης**, ου, ὁ, *inspector*, *PLond.*3.1171.63 (i B.C.); ἐλαϊκῶν καρπῶν *Sammelb.*4416.8 (ii A.D.): generally, *one who inquires into*, φήμης App.*BC*3.25; = ἐπίσκοπος, *AB*254; = *salutigerulus*, *Gloss.* **-ικός**, ή, όν, *fit for examining*, τινός Arr.*Epict.*1.17. 10; μέθοδος S.E.*M.*5.3. Adv. -κῶς Ptol.*Tetr.*171. ⊛ **-ομαι**, = ἐπισκοπέω, Hp.*Prorrh.*2.1, Men.710, S.E.*M.*5.89, Plu.2.129c, etc. 2. *pass in review*: hence, *number* a host, Lxx 1 *Ki.*15.4. **-ος**, ον, *considered*, *An.Ox.*3.208.

⊛ **ἐπισκέπω**, = ἐπισκεπάζω, Apollod.1.6.2, Longus 1.21, Iamb.*Protr.* 21:—Med., *AP*6.62 (Phil.).

⊛ **ἐπισκευ-άζω**, fut. -σκευῶ *PSI*4.382.3 (iii B.C.):—*get ready*, δεῖπνον Ar.*Ec.*1147 (Pass.); ἐ. ναῦν *refit*, Th.1.29, etc.; ἐ. ἵππους *saddle, equip* them, X.*HG*5.3.1 (s. v. l.):—Med., ἐπισκευάσασθαι ναῦς *have* them *refitted*, Th.7.36; ἐ. ὑποζύγια *have* them *packed, pack* them, X. *HG*7.2.18. 2. τὰ χρήματα ἐφ' ἁμαξῶν ἐπισκευάσαι *pack* them upon .., Id.*Cyr.*7.3.1. 3. Med., *provide oneself with necessaries* for a journey, *Act.Ap.*21.15. II. *make afresh, repair, restore*, τὰ τείχη Th.7.24; τὸν ναόν Inscr.ap.X.*An.*5.3.13; τὰς τριήρεις And.3.14, cf. Lys.*Fr.*34; τὰς ὁδούς D.3.29:—Med., πόλιν παλαιὰν ἐ. διεφθαρμένην Pl.*Lg.*738b:—Pass., *PPetr.*2 pp.34, 62 (iii B.C.). 2. metaph., *reconstruct*, [τὴν διαλεκτικήν] Arist.*Rh.*1359ᵇ15. **-άσιμος** [ᾰ], ον, *needing repair*, *OGI*483.92 (Pergam.). **-αστής**, οῦ, ὁ, *one who equips* or *repairs*, πομπείων D.22.78, etc.; τῶν ἱερῶν Lex ap.Ath.6.235d, Arist.*Ath.*50.1, Ἀρχ.Ἐφ.1923.39 (Oropus, iv B.C.). **-αστικός**, ή, όν, *preparatory*, prob. in Procl.*in Alc.*p.8 C.; *artificial*, χάρις Id.*in Prm.*p.493 S. **-αστός**, ή, όν, *repaired, restored*, ἀθανασία Pl.*Plt.* 270a. ⊛ **-ή**, ἡ, *repair, restoration*, τῶν ἱρῶν Hdt.2.174, cf. 175; τειχῶν D.18.311, etc.; τὰς ἐ. καὶ κατασκευὰς τῶν δημοσίων Plb.6. 17.2. 2. *means of repairing*, Th.1.52. II. pl., *materials for repair* or *equipment, stores*, ἐλέφαντα καὶ μαχαιρῶν λαβὰς καὶ ἄλλας ἐ. D.27.20; χορηγίας καὶ ἐ. Plb.1.72.3. ⊛ **-όω**, = -άζω, *IG*4.558.20 (Argos, ii B.C.), Ἐφ.Ἀρχ.1908.200 (Crete).

⊛ **ἐπίσκεψις**, εως, ἡ, *inspection, visitation*, X.*Oec.*8.15; τῶν ἱερῶν Pl. *Lg.*849a; τῶν ἱππέων Plu.*Crass.*13; ἐν ἐπισκέψει *from the observer's point of view* (opp. ἐν ὑποκειμένοις), Alex.Philalethes ap.Gal.8.726; *visiting* of the sick, Plb.5.56.8, Gal.*Libr.Propr.*1. 2. *investigation, inquiry*, Hp.*Prorrh.*2.4, etc.; ἡ ἐ. ἦν, εἰ.. Pl.*R.*456c: pl., Phld. *Oec.*p.71 J. 3. *numbering, census*, Lxx *Nu.*1.21, al.

**ἐπίσκημμα**, ατος, τό, = ἐπίσκηψις, *Lex.Rhet.Cant.*

**ἐπισκήν-ιος**, ον, *stagy, theatrical*, λέξις Porph.*Chr.*71. 2. ἐπισκήνιον, τό, in a theatre, *the upper story of the* σκηνή, Vitr.7.5.5; but τὸ ἐπὶ τῆς σκηνῆς καταγώγιον, Hsch. **-ος**, ον, *at* or *before the tent*, i. e. *public*, γόοι S.*Aj.*579. 2. οἱ ἐ. *the soldiers quartered* (in the towns), Plu.*Sert.*24, Ἀρχ.Ἐφ.1917.2; cf. sq. II. *on the stage*: ἡ ἐ., as Subst., = ἐπισκήνιον, Vitr.5.6.6. III. *external, adventitious*, ὄχλος D.H.6.53, cf. 9.53. IV. ἐπίσκηνα, τά, festival at Sparta, Hsch. ⊛ **-όω**, *to be quartered in*, ταῖς οἰκίαις Plb.4.72.1; ἐπὶ τὰς οἰκίας ib.18.8: metaph., *dwell upon*, ἡ δύναμις ἐ. ἐπί τινα 2 *Ep.Cor.*12.9.

⊛ **ἐπισκήπτω**, pf. ἐπέσκηφα D.L.1.117:—*make to lean upon*, ἐς δὲ παῖδ' ἐμὸν Ζεὺς ἐπέσκηψεν τελευτὴν θεσφάτων *made* it *fall upon* him, A.*Pers.*740 (troch.); ἐ. χάριν τινί *impose* it *upon*, S.*Aj.*566. 2. intr., *fall upon*, like lightning, πρᾶγμα δεῦρ' ἐπέσκηψεν it *came to* this point, A.*Eu.*482; νόσος ἐπέσκηψεν πολλή (v. l. ἐν-) Plu.*Thes.*15; ᾧ ἂν ἔρως ἐπισκήψῃ Id.2.767d, cf. 701c; αὐτῷ ὁ θάνατος Philum.*Ven.*31. 3. II. *lay it upon* one to do a thing, c. dat. pers. et inf., μοῖρ' ἐπέσκηψε Πέρσαις πολέμους διέπειν A.*Pers.*103 (lyr.), cf. S.*OT*252: folld. by imper., ib.1446: less freq. c. acc. et inf., E.*Alc.*365; τοῖσι πλησιοχώροισι ἐ. κελεύοντας προπέμπειν Hdt.4.33: inf. can freq. be supplied, τοσοῦτον δή σ' ἐπισκήπτω (sc. ποιεῖν) thus much I *command* thee to do, S.*Tr.*1221; so πρὸς δεξιᾶς σε τῆσδ' ἐπισκήπτω τάδε E.*IT*701: pers. is freq. omitted, ἐ. (sc. ὑμῖν) τὸν.. φόνον ἐκπρήξασθαι Hdt.7.158; βάξις ἐπισκήπτουσα.. ἔξω δόμων.. ὠθεῖν ἐμέ A.*Pr.*664; ἐπέσκηψε.. εἷρξαι Αἴαντα S.*Aj.*752, cf. Antipho 1.1; also ἐ. περί τινος E.*IT*1077. 2. esp. *conjure* a person to do a thing, ὑμῖν τάδε ἐπισκήπτω.. μὴ περιιδεῖν

Hdt.3.65; τινὶ πρὸς τῶν θεῶν And.1.32; κλαίοντας, ἱκετεύοντας.. ἐπισκήπτοντας μηδενὶ τρόπῳ τὸν ἀλιτήριον στεφανοῦν Aeschin.3.157, cf. Th.2.73, etc.; of the curses or orders of dying persons, μέμνησθε τὰ ἐπέσκηψε Πέρσῃσι.., μὴ πειρωμένοισι Hdt.3.73, cf. Lys.13.92, D.28.15, 36.32. 3. γᾷ ἐπισκήπτων χέρα *resting* hand *on* earth, i.e. *calling* earth *to witness*, B.7.41: abs., γᾷ -σκήπτων πιφαύσκω Id.5.42. III. as Att. law-term, generally in Med., *denounce* a person, so as to begin a prosecution for perjury (cf. ἐπίσκηψις II), διεμαρτύρησε οὑτοσί..· ἐπισκηψαμένων δ' ἡμῶν.. ἡ.. δίκη τῶν ψευδομαρτυριῶν εἰσῄει, i.e. a διαμαρτυρία was entered..: we *replied by an* ἐπίσκηψις.., and the action for false witness was brought on, Is.5.17; in full, ἐ. τινὶ ψευδομαρτυριῶν D.29.7; ᾗ (sc. τῇ θεῷ) οὐδὲ ψ. θέμις ἐστὶν ἐ. Aeschin.1.130; ἐ. ταῖς μαρτυρίαις D.47.1, cf. Is.3.11; ἐ. [τῇ μαρτυρίᾳ] ὡς ψευδεῖ οὔσῃ *denounce* it as false, Din.1.52:—also in Act., Pl.*Tht.*145c codd., Jul.*Or.*6.186b:—hence Pass., ἐὰν ἐπισκηφθῇ τὰ ψευδῆ μαρτυρῆσαι Pl.*Lg.*937b: generally, πρὸς τῆς θανούσης.. ἐπεσκήπτου *wast denounced, accused*, S.*Ant.*1313:—so in Act., *blame*, τινί Jul.*Or.*7.239a.

**ἐπισκηρίπτω**, = ἐπισκήπτω, Hsch. s. h. v.

**ἐπίσκηψις**, εως, ἡ, *injunction*, τὰς Εὐθυκράτους ἐπισκήψεις Is.9.36, cf. Ph.1.362 (pl.), Plu.*Dio* 11. II. as law-term, *denunciation*, the first step in a prosecution, esp. in a δίκη ψευδομαρτυριῶν, brought against the witness of a διαμαρτυρία (q.v.), τῇ ἐ. τῶν ψευδομαρτυριῶν D.47.51; Charondas πρῶτος ἐποίησε τὴν ἐ. Arist.*Pol.*1274$^{b}$7; τούτων τὰς ἐ. εἶναι theirs shall be the right of ἐ., D.47.72.

⊛ **ἐπισκι-άζω**, *throw a shade upon, overshadow*, τῇ [πτέρυγι] τὴν Ἀσίην Hdt.1.209, cf. Arist.*GA*780$^{a}$30, Thphr.*CP*2.18.3, *Ev.Matt.*17.5: c. dat., Thphr.*Sens.*79, *Ev.Marc.*9.7:—Pass., Ph.1.262, al.; opp. φωτίζειν, S.E.*P.*1.141:—Med., -σκιάζεσθαι τὸν ἥλιον *to ward off* the sun's rays, *Gp.*5.29.3: metaph., *conceal, obscure*, ἀλήθειαν πλάσμασι μυθικοῖς Ph.1.41, etc.; τὰ δεινὰ ἑτέροις ὀνόμασιν ἐ. Junc.ap.Stob.4.50.95; τὴν θωπείαν, τὸν βίον, Luc.*Hist.Conscr.*11, v.l. in *Cal.*1:—Pass., τῇ εὐγενείᾳ Hdn.2.10.3; λαθραῖον ὄμμ' ἐπεσκιασμένη *keeping a hidden* watch, S.*Tr.*914. 2. *darken, obscure*, Ph.2.223 (Pass.): metaph., ἀφροσύνη ἐ. ψυχήν Id.1.685, al. 3. of the Divine presence, *overshadow* for protection, etc., τινί Lxx*Ps.*90(91).4; ἐπὶ τὴν κεφαλήν τινος ib.139(140).8; δύναμις ὑψίστου ἐπισκιάσει σοι *Ev.Luc.*1.35. 4. Pass., *to be weak-sighted*, Vett.Val.111.1. -ασμα, ατος, τό, *shadow thrown in eclipses*, Ptol.*Tetr.*76. -ασμός, ὁ, *shading, covering*, Hsch. II. *weak sight*, Vett.Val.110.36 (pl.), al. -άω, = ἐπισκιάζω, Arat.736, Q.S.2.479; of peacocks, ἑὸν δέμας.. ἐπισκιάουσιν Opp.*C.*2.590. -ος, ον, (σκιά) *shaded, dark*, τόπος Pl.*R.*432c, Arist.*HA*569$^{b}$10; οἴκημα Plu.*Mar.*39; ἀκτῖνες Arat.870: metaph., βίος ἐ. *a retired* life, Lat. *vita umbratilis*, opp. a public life, Plu.2.135b. II. Act., *shading*, c. gen., χεὶρ ὀμμάτων ἐπίσκιος S.*OC*1650. Adv. -ίως Poll.4.51.

⊛ **ἐπισκιρρόομαι**, *become coagulated*, of blood, Poet. *de herb.*33.

**ἐπισκιρτ-άω**, *leap upon*, τινί Nonn.*D.*2.29: metaph., τῷ νεκρῷ Plu.*Dem.*22: abs., ἐπισκιρτῶσιν ἔθειραι, ἴουλος, *AP*5.102 (Rufin.), 12.10 (Strat.). -ημα, ατος, τό, *spring, bound*, Nonn.*D.*19.154.

**ἐπίσκληρος**, ον, *somewhat hard*, κοιλίη Hp.*Prorrh.*1.138: Comp., J.*AJ*17.12.2.

**ἐπισκληρύνομαι**, Pass., *become somewhat hard*, Gal.16.800.

⊛ **ἐπισκοπ-εία**, ἡ, *inspection*, *PTeb.*5.189 (pl., ii B.C.). ⊛ -εύω, = sq., Sm.*Ps.*65(66).7. ⊛ -έω, fut. -σκέψομαι, later -σκοπήσω Babr.103.8: aor. -εσκεψάμην, later -εσκόπησα Luc.*Herm.*44, 59: pf. ἐπέσκεμμαι Hp.*VM*14, Pl.*Epin.*990a; also in pass. sense, Arist.*Cael.*299$^{a}$10, *PA*692$^{a}$18:—*look upon* or *at, inspect, observe*, ἱστορίας καὶ τἆλλα ἔγγραφα *Milet.*3.155 (ii B.C.) (also in Med., ἐ. τὸ περίχωμα *PLille* 1$^{v}$27 (iii B.C.), etc.); *regard*, τἀμ' ἐ. κακά E.*Heracl.*869; of tutelary gods, Θηβαίας ἐπισκοποῦντ' ἀγυιάς, of Bacchus, S.*Ant.*1136 (lyr.); Ἴλιον.. ἐπισκοπεῖ σεμνὸς Ποσειδῶν E.*IT*1414, cf. *Ph.*661 (lyr.); ὦ Δῆμ', ἐναργῶς ἡ θεός σ' ἐπισκοπεῖ Ar.*Eq.*1173, cf. 1186; also of a ruler, ἐ. τὴν πολιτείαν Pl.*R.*506b, cf. X.*Oec.*4.6 (so in Med., θαμὰ ἐπεσκοπεῖτο ἡμᾶς *observed*, Pl.*Ly.*207a): folld. by Relat., ἐ. καὶ ἀναμετρήσαντες ὅσῳ ἐλάσσων ὁ χῶρος γέγονε Hdt.2.109; ἐ. πῶς ἔχει Pl.*Grg.*451c; τόδε ἐπίσκεψαι εἴ τι λέγω Id.*Phd.*87b, cf. X.*Mem.*2.1.22; πότερον.. ἤ.. Pl.*R.*518a; τίς εἴη.. X.*Mem.*3.2.4, cf. *Smp.*1.12; ἐ. μή.. *take care* lest, *Ep.Hebr.*12.15. 2. *visit*, ὦ θάνατε, νῦν μ' ἐπίσκεψαι μολών S.*Aj.*854; *visit* as a friend (ironically), D.9.12; esp. *visit* the sick, X.*Cyr.*8.2.25, *Mem.*3.11.10; of the physician, Hdn.4.2.4:—Med., D.59.56, Gal.11.2, 14.633:—Pass., εὐνὴν ὀνείροις οὐκ ἐπισκοπουμένην *visited* not by dreams, i.e. sleepless, A.*Ag.*13. 3. of a general, *inspect, review*, τὰς τάξεις X.*An.*2.3.2; τὰ ὅπλα Id.*Cyr.*6.3.21, cf. A.*Eu.*296. 4. *consider, reflect, meditate*, ὅ τι ἂν μέλλῃς ἐρεῖν, πρότερον ἐπισκόπει τῇ γνώμῃ Isoc.1.41; also ἐ. πρός τι Pl.*Lg.*924d; περί τινος Id.*Prt.*348d, al., Ceb.35.5; ὑπέρ τινος Plb.3.15.2; σαυτὸν ἐ. ὅστις εἶ X.*Mem.*4.2.24; ἐ. τίς.., ποία τις.. Arist.*Pol.*1274$^{b}$32; πότερον.. ib.1276$^{b}$16:—Med., *examine with oneself, meditate*, Pl.*Phd.*91d; εἰς τὸ ἀληθὲς ἐ. τι Id.*Phlb.*61e, cf. Alex.219.8, Philem.46:—Pass., pf. (v. supr.). 5. *exercise the office of* ἐπίσκοπος, v.l. in 1*Ep.Pet.*5.2. ⊛ -ή, ἡ, *watching over, visitation*, of God, Lxx*Nu.*16.29, *Ev.Luc.*19.44. II. *office of* ἐπίσκοπος, 1*Ep.Ti.*3.1, *Cod.Just.*1.3.35 *Intr.*, etc.: generally, *office*, Lxx*Ps.*108(109).8. 2. = ἐπίσκεψις 3, ib.*Nu.*14.29, al. -ησις, εως, ἡ, *inspection, examination*, Aen.Tact.10.6. -ητέον, *one must consider*, εἰ.. Sch.Luc.*Dem.Enc.*43, cf. Heph.Astr.3.1. ⊛ -ία, ἡ, = εὐστοχία, condemned by Poll.6.205. -ικός, ή, όν, *episcopal*, *Cod.Just.*1.4.29.3. ⊛ -ος (A), ὁ, (σκοπός I) *one who watches over, overseer, guardian*, ἦ γὰρ ὄλωλας ἐπίσκοπος, ὅς τέ μιν αὐτὴν ῥύσκευ (sc. τὴν πόλιν), of Hector, Il.24.729, ἐ.. ὁδαίων Od.8.163; ἐπίσκοποι ἁρμονιάων *watchers over* compacts, of the gods, Il.22.255; νεκροῦ S.*Ant.*217; σῆς ἕδρας Id.*OC*112; ἐ. ὀϊστῶν, of an archer, v.l. in Theoc.24.107; in education, *tutor*, Pl.*Lg.*795d; ἐ. σωφροσύνης καὶ ὕβρεως ib.849a: c. dat., ἀγυιαῖς ἔσσῃ καὶ λιμένεσσιν ἐ. Call.*Dian.*39; esp. of tutelary gods (cf. ἐπισκοπέω), Παλλὰς ἐ. Sol.4.3; Δίκη Pl.*Lg.*872e; Κλειὼ ἐ. χερνίβων Simon.45; Χάριτες Μινυᾶν ἐ. Pi.*O.*14.3; θεοὶ ἐ. ἀγορᾶς A.*Th.*272; πατρῴων δωμάτων ἐ. Id.*Ch.*126; τὸ δεινὸν.. φρενῶν ἐπίσκοπον *guardian* of the mind, Id.*Eu.*518 (lyr.); νυχίων φθεγμάτων ἐ., of Bacchus, S.*Ant.*1148 (lyr); Ἐρινύες *IG*12(9).1179.33 (Euboea, ii A.D.); [Χριστὸς] ἐ. τῶν ψυχῶν 1*Ep.Pet.*2.25: rarely c. dat., πᾶσι γὰρ ἐ. ἐτάχθη.. Νέμεσις Pl.*Lg.*717d. 2. *scout, watch*, c. dat., ἐ. Τρώεσσι, νήεσσιν ἡμετέρῃσιν, *one set to watch* them, Il.10.38, 342. 3. *supervisor, inspector*, sent by Athens to subject states, Ar.*Av.*1023, *IG*1$^{2}$.10, 11; of *municipal officials* at Rhodes, ib.12(1).49.42 (ii/i B.C.): generally, *PPetr.*3 p.75 (iii B.C.), etc. 4. *ecclesiastical superintendent*, ἐπίσκοποι καὶ διάκονοι *Ep.Phil.*1.1, cf. *Act.Ap.*20.28, 1*Ep.Ti.*3.2, etc. -ος (B), ον, (σκοπός II) *hitting the mark, successful*, βάλλειν ἐ. Them.*Or.*11.143a (Sup.); τοξότης Him.*Ecl.*14.3; ἠχή Opp.*C.*1.42; *reaching, touching*, νίκης μὴ κακῆς ἐπίσκοπα A.*Eu.*903; ἄτης τῆσδ' ἐ. μέλος *having regard to* the calamity, S.*Aj.*976: neut. pl. ἐπίσκοπα, as Adv., *successfully, with good aim*, ἐ. τοξεύειν Hdt.3.35, Jul.*Or.*1.11c: regul. Adv. -πως, ἀκοντίζειν ἢ τοξεύειν Alcid.*Soph.*7, cf. Poll.6.205: Comp. -ώτερα, βάλλειν Them.*Or.*8.116b: Sup. -ώτατα Poll.1.215. Cf. εὔστοχος, εὔσκοπος.

**ἐπισκορπίζω**, *scatter over*, Suid. s. v. ἐπικίδναται (Pass.).

**ἐπισκοτ-άζω**, = sq., Hp.*Off.*3. ⊛ -έω, (σκότος) *throw a shadow over*, οἰκίαν ᾠκοδόμησεν τοσαύτην ὥστε πᾶσιν ἐπισκοτεῖν τοῖς ἐν τῷ τόπῳ D.21.158; ἐ. τινὶ τῆς θέας *to be in the way* of his seeing, Pl.*Euthd.*274c, cf. Plu.2.538e; τῷ βωμῷ Judeich *Altertümer von Hierapolis* 339: abs., Plb.24.4, Polyaen.8.23.2; *form a roof*, Hero *Aut.*28.2. 2. metaph., *throw darkness* or *obscurity over*, τῇ κρίσει Sor.*Vit.Hippocr.*13, Arist.*Rh.*1354$^{b}$11; ταῖς τῆς ψυχῆς ἐπιμελείαις Isoc.1.6; τὸ πρὸς χάριν ῥηθὲν ἐ. τῷ καθορᾶν Id.8.10, cf. D.2.20; οἶνος τῷ φρονεῖν ἐπισκοτεῖ Eub.135 = Ophelio 4; ἐ. γὰρ τῷ φρονεῖν τὸ λαμβάνειν Antiph.250; τὸ δ' ἐρᾶν ἐ. ἅπασιν, ὡς ἔοικε Men.48; ἡ ὀργὴ ἐ. τοῖς λογισμοῖς Phld.*Ir.*p.78 W.:—Pass., *to be in the dark* or *in uncertainty*, ἐπισκοτεόμενος τῇ ἀπειρίῃ Hp.*Praec.*8; ἐπισκοτεῖσθαι καὶ κωλύεσθαι Plb.2.39.12; *to be obscured*, ὑπό τινος Id.12.25$^{d}$.7; *to be blinded*, τὰς ὄψεις ὑπὸ θεοῦ J.*AJ*9.4.3, cf. Ph.2.62. -ησις, εως, ἡ, *darkening, obscurity*, of the sun or moon in eclipse, Plu.*Per.*35, *Nic.*23, Ptol.*Tetr.*76, etc.: metaph., οὗ λέγουσιν εἰς -ησιν Plot.2.9.10. -ίζω, = ἐπισκοτέω, Plb.13.5.6 (Pass.), Lib.*Decl.*48.38; *to be overshadowed*, Ps.-Democr.*Symp.Ant.*p.3 G. -ισις, εως, ἡ, and -ισμός, ὁ, = ἐπισκότησις, Procl.*Par.Ptol.*112, 119. -ος, ον, *in the dark, darkened*, ἐπίσκοτον ἀτραπὸν ἐσσυμένα, of the sun, prob. in Pi.*Pae.*9.5, dub. l. in Plu.*Aem.*17.

**ἐπισκύζομαι**, *to be indignant at* a thing, ὄφρα καὶ ἄλλοι ἐπισκύζωνται Ἀχαιοί Il.9.370; μή σοι θυμὸς ἐπισκύσσαιτο ἰδόντι (Ep. aor.) Od.7.306:—Act., aor. ἐπισκύσαι *EM*364.10.

**ἐπισκῠθίζω**, *pour out drink in Scythian fashion*, i.e. with unmixed wine, Hdt.6.84, Chamael.ap.Ath.10.427c.

**ἐπισκυθρωπάζω**, *look gloomy* or *stern*, of hounds, X.*Cyn.*3.5; of men, Plu.2.375a.

**ἐπισκύλλω**, in Pass., aor. 2 part. -σκυλέντες, παροδικῶς *after being* temporarily *distressed*, Vett.Val.171.18.

**ἐπισκύνιον** [ῠ], τό, *skin of the brows* which projects over the eyes and is knitted in frowning (Arist.*GA*780$^{b}$28), πᾶν δέ τ' ἐπισκύνιον κάτω ἕλκεται ὄσσε καλύπτων, of a lion, Il.17.136; δεινὸν ἐ. ξυνάγων, of Aeschylus, Ar.*Ra.*823 (hex.); τοῖον ἐ. βλοσυρῷ ἐπέκειτο προσώπῳ Theoc.24.118, cf. *APl.*4.100; ῥυσὸν ἐ., πολιὸν ἐ., *AP*6.64 (Paul. Sil.), 7.117 (Zenod.); even φαιδρὸν ἐ. ib.12.159 (Mel.); ἐπιστρέψας γυρὸν ἐ., of one who puts on a wise face, ib.11.376.8 (Agath.): in pl., Posidipp.ap.Ath.10.414e: hence, II. *superciliousness*, γυμνώσαντο βίου παντὸς ἐ., of Diogenes, *AP*7.63, etc.; but in Plb.25.3.6, simply, *austerity, gravity of deportment*. III. Adj. ἐπισκύνιος, ον, *supercilious*, Gloss.

⊛ **ἐπίσκυρος**, ὁ, *ball-game* (= ἐπίκοινος III) resembling Rugby football, Hsch., Poll.9.103, Sch.Pl.*Tht.*146a. II. *governor*, Call.*Fr.*231, cf. Hsch.

**ἐπισκῠφισμός**, ὁ, *operation* performed on the scalp for eye-affections, Aët.7.93.

**ἐπί-σκωμμα**, ατος, τό, *jest*, gloss on σιλλοί, *EM*713.7. 2. *term of derision*, Gramm.ap.Gaisf.*Choerob.*1 p.43 (pl.). -σκώπτης, ου, ὁ, *mocker*, v.l. for ἐπικόπτης (q.v.). -σκώπτω, *laugh at, make fun of*, τινά X.*Mem.*4.4.6; τι ib.3.11.16; τινὰ ὡς.., ὅτι.., Pl.*Euthphr.*11c, X.*Smp.*1.5; εἴς τι Plu.*Lyc.*30; *cast in one's teeth*, τινὶ τὴν δεισιδαιμονίαν J.*Ap.*1.22:—Pass., πρός τινων Gal.6.307. 2. abs., *jest, make fun*, Ar.*Ra.*375; ἔφη ἐπισκώπτων X.*Mem.*1.3.7. -σκωψις, εως, ἡ, *mocking, raillery*, Plu.*Ant.*24 (pl.).

⊛ **ἐπισμᾰρᾰγέω**, *rattle* or *echo again*, Opp.*C.*2.78, Q.S.2.546 (ἀπεσμ- codd.), etc.: c. acc. cogn., ἐ. ὕμνον τινί Nonn.*D.*48.965.

**ἐπισμάω**, *rub, smear* something *over* a person, c. acc. pers. et rei, τί γὰρ οὗτος ἡμᾶς οὐκ ἐπισμῇ τῶν κακῶν; Ar.*Th.*389, cf. Cratin.90:

⊛ **ἐπισμήχω** is a less Att. form, Opp.*C.*1.501 (v.l. ἐπισμύχω).

**ἐπισμῠγερός**, ή, όν, *gloomy, sad*, Ἀχλὺς Hes.*Sc.*264; αἶσα A.R.4.1065.—Hom. has only the Adv. -ρῶς, ἀπέτεισεν *sadly* did he pay for it, Od.3.195; ἐ. ναυτίλλεται *at his peril, to his misfortune* doth he sail, 4.672, cf. A.R.1.616.

**ἐπισμυκτόν** (fort. leg. ἐπιμυκτύν)· ἐπιμυκτηρισμόν, Hsch.

**ἐπισμύχομαι** [ῡ], Pass., *to become more and more inflamed* with passion, Zos.4.44.3.

**ἐπισοβέω**, *urge on*, τινά Them.*Or*.4.50b; *push on*, τι Hld.6.11, 4.5; ἐ. κώθωνά τινι *send whizzing at*, Alex.176. II. intr., *glory in*, τιάρᾳ Philostr.*Im*.1.30.

**ἐπίσογκος** [ῐ], ον, (ἴσος, ὄγκος) *of equal bulk*, Str.13.1.67.

**ἔπῐσος**, ον, = ἴσος, Plb.3.115.1, Lxx*Si*.9.10.

**ἐπισοφίζομαι**, *devise in addition*, c. inf., Hp.*Art*.14, Iamb.*VP*18.86.

**ἐπισπάδην** [ᾰ], Adv., (ἐπισπάω) *at one draught*, πίνειν Hp.*Int*.26.

**ἐπισπαίρω**, *pant, struggle*, ἐπί τινι Plu.2.327c.

**ἐπί-σπᾰσις**, εως, ἡ, *drawing in*, τῆς τροφῆς Arist.*Spir*.482ᵃ15, cf. Thphr.*CP*1.17.6, etc.; ἡ ἐ. τοῦ στόματος, in sucking in liquid, Alex. Aphr.*Pr*.2.59. **-σπασμός**, ὁ, *rapid respiration*, Hp.*Epid*.6.5.15. II. *trailing*, of a serpent, Sch.Nic.*Th*.160. III. *inducement* (to inference), *hint*, Phld.*Sign*.13, Demetr.Lac.*Herc*.1055.13 F. IV. *traction* of the foetus, Sor.2.62. V. *suction* of cupping instruments, ib.11. **-σπαστήρ**, ῆρος, ὁ, *latch* or *handle by which a door is pulled to*, Hdt.6.91: spelt **-σπατήρ** *IG*2².1672.123. II. τρίκλωστον ἐπισπαστῆρα βόλοιο, of the fowler's *line*, *AP*6.109 (Antip.). **-σπαστικός**, ή, όν, *drawing to oneself, drawing in*, τοῦ ὑγροῦ Arist.*Pr*.966ᵃ4; ἀτμοὶ ἐ. πρὸς ἑαυτοὺς Str.15.1.38; αἵματος Gal.*Nat. Fac*.2.3: abs. of drugs, Id.11.761, cf. Dsc.2.85,109; ἔμπλαστροι Orib. *Fr*.85; ῥυφήματα ἐ. dub. sens. in Hp.*Acut*.(*Sp*.)2. 2. metaph., *attractive*, Plb.4.84.6, *Stoic*.3.46. Adv. -κῶς, κινεῖν S.E.*P*.3.69. **-σπαστός** or **ἐπίσπαστος**, ή, όν, *drawn upon oneself*, Ἶρος.. ἐπίσπαστον κακὸν ἕξει Od.18.73, cf. 24.462; λύπη Hld.2.6; δεσποτεία D.C.62.3; ἐπισπαστοί, of the suitors in the Od., Paus.8.12.6. II. ἐ. βρόχοι *tight-drawn* nooses, E.*Hipp*.783. ⊛ **-σπαστρον**, τό, *rope for pulling*, D.S.17.90; also, a fowler's *net*, Dionys.*Av*.3.12. 2. = ἐπισπαστήρ I, Poll.10.22. II. *that which is drawn over, curtain, hanging*, Lxx*Ex*.26.36. ⊛ **-σπάω**, *draw* or *drag after* one, Hdt.2.121.δ'; ἦγ' ἐπισπάσας κόμης by the hair, E.*Hel*.116, cf. *Tr*.882, *Andr*.710:—Med., X.*An*.4.7.14:—Pass., ἐπισπασθῆναι τῇ χειρί with the hand, Th.4.130. 2. metaph., *bring on, cause*, τοσόνδε πλῆθος πημάτων A.*Pers*.477. 3. *pull to*, τὴν θύραν X.*HG*6.4.36; cf. ἐπισπαστήρ: ἐπισπασθέντος τοῦ βρόχου *being drawn tight*, D.24.139. 4. *attract, gain, win*, πέποιθα τοῦτ' ἐπισπάσειν κλέος S.*Aj*.769:—freq. in Med., ἐπισπᾶσθαι κέρδος Hdt.3.72; εὔνοιαν Plb.3.98.9; χάριν *SIG*685.40 (Magn. Mae., ii B.C.); ἔχθραν *AP*11.340 (Pall.); *welcome*, Ph.1.384; ἐπισπᾶσθαι πώγωνα *get one* a beard, Luc.*JTr*.16; *induce*, ὕπνον ἐκπώμασιν Lib.*Or*.56.26; *attract*, σίδηρον Phld.*Sign*.1. 5. *draw on, allure, persuade*, τὴν ψυχήν Pl.*Cra*.420a:—Med., ὁ λόγος.. ἂν ἐπισπάσαιτο Th.3.44, cf. 5.111; ἐ. ἡ πέρδιξ [τὸν θηρεύοντα] Arist.*HA*613ᵇ19; θάτερον παρεμπίπτον ἐπεσπάσατο.. τὸ ἕτερον ἐπινόημα *induced, provoked*, Epicur.*Nat*.137 G.: c. inf., *induce* to do, ἐπισπάσασθαι [ἂν] αὐτοὺς ἡγεῖτο προθυμήσεσθαι he thought it would *induce, invite* them to make the venture, dub. l. in Th.4.9; ἐπισπᾶσθαί τινα ἐμπλησθῆναι δακρύων τὰ ὄμματα X.*Cyr*.5.5.10; ἐ. τοὺς πολεμίους ἐφ' ἑαυτόν Plu.*Phil*.18, cf. *Mar*.11, 21, 26; but τοὺς πολεμίους εἰς τόπους *allure, entice*, Plb.3.110.2, etc.:—Pass., ἐπισπώμενον εἰς τἀναντία πολλάκις ἅμα though often he *is being drawn* in opposite directions at once, Pl.*Lg*.863e; φοβοῦμαι μὴ πάντες.. ἐπισπασθῶσιν πέρα τοῦ συμφέροντος [πολεμῆσαι] D.5.19; πολύ τι μᾶλλον ἐπεσπάσμεθα *OGI*223.18 (iii B.C.); ἐπεσπάσθην φιλονεικεῖν Demetr.Lac.*Herc*.1055.23 F. 6. Med., *absorb*, τὰ σιτία -σπᾶται τὴν ὑγρότητα Arist.*Pr*.868ᵇ30; τὰ ἐρινασταʼ [σῦκα] ἐ. τὸν ὀπόν Thphr.*CP*2.9.12; *quaff*, of a drinker, ἀπνευστὶ ἐ. Gal.15.500, cf. Luc. *DDeor*.5.4; of infants, *suck*, γάλα Sor.1.88; of cupping instruments, Hp.*VM*22; *draw in*, πνεῦμα Phld.*D*.3.13:—Pass., of air, *to be sucked in*, Arist.*Pr*.931ᵇ22. 7. Med., *draw in, call in*, Πύρρον Plb.1.6.5; φυλακὴν καὶ βοήθειαν παρά τινος ib.7.6; μάρτυρας -ᾶται τοὺς μουσικούς Phld.*Po*.5.1425.8:—Pass., *to be called in, forced to work*, εἴς τι *PTeb*.27.4 (ii B.C.). 8. in Pass., of the sea, ἐπισπωμένη βιαιότερον *returning with a rush* after having retired, Th.3.89. II. *overturn*: hence proverb., ὅλην τὴν ἅμαξαν ἐπεσπάσω you have '*upset* the apple-cart', Luc.*Pseudol*.32. III. Med., *draw the prepuce forward, become as if uncircumcised*, μὴ ἐπισπάσθω 1*Ep.Cor*.7.18; of the nurse, ἐπισπάσθω τὴν ἀκροποσθίαν Sor.1.113.

**ἐπισπεῖν, ἐπισπών**, v. ἐφέπω (A).

**ἐπισπείρω**, *sow with seed*, ὁδόν Hdt.7.115; *sow upon* or *among*, τι ἐπὶ τὰ ἄνδηρα Thphr.*CP*3.15.4, cf. *HP*7.5.4; τινί τι Id.*CP*.2.17.3 (Pass.): metaph., ἐ. μομφὰν ἀλιτροῖς Pi.*N*.8.39; σοφιστικὰ ζητήματα ταῖς ἐξηγήσεσι Gal.15.519 (v.l.). 2. *sow again, with fresh seed*, Thphr.*CP*2.17.10 (Pass.); *sow after*, ζιζάνια *Ev.Matt*.13.25.

**ἐπίσπεισις**, εως, ἡ, *libation poured over* a sacrifice, Hdt.2.39.

**ἐπί-σπεισμα**, ατος, τό, *a last libation over*: metaph., ἐ. τῶν ἐκκεχυμένων βίων cj. in Demetr.ap.Plu.2.349b. **-σπένδω**, *pour upon* or *over*, esp. as a drink-offering, ἐπὶ τοῦ βωμοῦ οἶνον κατὰ τοῦ ἱρηΐου ἐ. Hdt.2.39; οἶνον ἐ. κατὰ τῶν κεφαλέων Id.4.62; τοῖσι ἱροῖσι Id.7.167; νεκρῷ A.*Ag*.1395; τοιαῖσδ' ἐπ' εὐχαῖς τάσδ' ἐ. χοάς *after* the vows I *pour* these libations, Id.*Ch*.149: abs., Hdt.4.60; οὐδ' ἄν τι θύων οὐδ' ἐπισπένδων ἄνοις A.*Fr*.161; also ἐ. δάκρυ Theoc.23.38. 2. *promise, pledge*, *Leg.Gort*.4.52, 6.11:—Med., *accept in pledge*, ib.6.13, al. II. Med., *make a fresh treaty*, Th.5.22.

**ἐπισπερχ-ής**, ές, *hasty, hurried*, μὴ ἐ. ἀλλ' ἀγαθὸς φαινέσθω Arist. *Phgn*.808ᵃ7, cf. 807ᵇ5. Adv. -χῶς X.*Cyr*.4.1.3: Comp. -εστέρως Aen. Tact.26.10. ⊛ **-ω**, *urge on*, Od.22.451; [ἵππους] κέντρῳ ἐπισπέρχων Il.23.430; [νῆα] ἐρετμοῖς A.R.3.346; τὸ πρᾶγμα κάρτ' ἐπισπέρχει θεός A.*Th*.689; τοὺς ἄλλους τοιαῦτα ἐπέσπερχε Th.4.12: c. inf., *urge* one to do, A.R.1.525, Plu.2.347b. 2. ἐ. ἴχνος *follow close upon* the track, Opp.*C*.4.96: abs., Nic.*Th*.144. II. intr., *rage furiously*, ἐπισπέρχουσιν ἄελλαι Od.5.304, cf. Pi.*Parth*.2.18; εἴ τι ἡ πνὶξ ἐπισπέρχοι Aret.*CA*1.8. 2. *hasten* in flight, Tim.*Pers*.98.

**ἐπισπέσθαι**, v. ἐφέπω (B).

**ἐπισπεύδω**, *urge on, further* or *promote* an object, opp. ἀποσπεύδω, Hdt.7.18; ἐ. τὸ δρᾶν S.*El*.467; τὴν στρατείαν Isoc.4.138, etc.; of persons, *urge on, hasten*, X.*HG*5.1.33; ὀδίταν Theoc.16.93: metaph., οἷς (attracted for οὓς) μὴ φύσις ἐπέσπευσεν whom Nature *has* not *matured quickly*, Pl.*Lg*.810b. II. intr., *hasten onward*, E.*Tr*.1275; πρός τινα X.*Vect*.3.4; ἐ. εἰς ταὐτόν τινι Id.*Smp*.7.4: part. ἐπισπεύδων *in haste*, A.R.3.1389; τὸ -σπεῦδον τῆς πορείας Hld.8.17.

**ἐπισπευστικός**, ή, όν, *urgent*, Eust.831.29.

**ἐπισπῑλόω**, *make spotty*, *Cat.Cod.Astr*.8(4).154.

**ἐπισπλαγχν-ίδιος**, ὁ, apptly. a sacrificial implement, dub. sens. in *IG*11(2).153 (Delos, iii B.C.), *BCH*6.25 (ibid., ii B.C.). **-ίζομαι**, *to have compassion*, Lxx*Pr*.17.5.

**ἐπίσπληνος**, ον, *diseased in the spleen, splenetic*, Hp.*Epid*.7.107.

**ἐπισπόμενος**, v. ἐφέπω (B).

**ἐπι-σπονδή**, ἡ, in pl., *treaty made after another*, Th.5.32. **-σπονδον**, τό, *libation*, οἴνου *Inscr.Prien*.195.26 (iii/ii B.C.). **-σπονδορχηστής**, οῦ, ὁ, = ὑποσπ-, *SIG*1021.28 (Olympia, i B.C.).

⊛ **ἐπισπορ-ά**, ἡ, *second sowing*, Thphr.*CP*2.17.10, *PTeb*.375.14 (ii A.D.). ⊛ **-ία**, Ep. **-ίη**, ἡ, = foreg., Hes.*Op*.446, Poll.1.223. **-ος**, ον, *sown afterwards*, οἱ ἐ. *posterity*, A.*Eu*.673; τὰ ἐ. *secondary crops*, of vegetables, Thphr.*HP*7.1.2, *PTeb*.27.37 (ii B.C.).

⊛ **ἐπισπουδ-άζω**, *urge on, further*, Lxx*Ge*.19.15, *Pr*.13.11 (Pass.). II. intr., *haste* or *make haste in* a thing, Luc.*Pisc*.2. III. *study over*, τι τῷ οἴνῳ Philostr.*VS*2.10.1. **-ασμός**, ὁ, *transport, dispatch*, πυροῦ *PGrenf*.2.23.17 (ii B.C.), cf. *Annales du Service* 13.224 (Crocodilopolis, iii A.D.), prob. in *PStrassb*.93.2 (ii B.C.). ⊛ **-αστής**, οῦ, ὁ, *one who presses on a work*, Lxx*Is*.14.4. II. ἐ. τῆς Θηβαΐδος, name of an official in Egypt, *PBodl.ined*.31218. 2. *transport-master*, *PRyl*.183 (i A.D.).

**ἐπίσπω, -σποιμι, -σπών**, v. ἐφέπω (A).

⊛ **ἔπισσαι**, αἱ, Ion., = ἐπιγινόμεναι τοῖς προγόνοις, Hecat.363 J.; cf. μέτασσαι. ⊛ **ἔπισσον**· τὸ ὕστερον γενόμενον, Hsch.

**ἐπισσείω, ἐπισσεύω**, Ep. for ἐπισείω, ἐπισεύω.

**ἐπίσσοφος**, ὁ, an official at Thera, *Test.Epict*.8.15. (Perh. fr. ψέφω, lit. *supervisor*):—the Verb [**ἐπισ**]**οφεύω** is prob. in *IG*9(1).691.15 (Corc., iii B.C.).

**ἐπίσσῠτος**, ον, (ἐπισεύω, ἐπέσσυμαι) *rushing, gushing*, κλαυμάτων πηγαί A.*Ag*.887; *violent, sudden*, δύαι ib.1150 (lyr.); βίου τύχαι Id. *Eu*.924 (lyr.); φήμα E.*Hipp*.574 (lyr.).

**ἐπίσσωτρον**, τό, Ep. for ἐπίσωτρον (q. v.).

**ἐπίστᾳ**, for ἐπίστασαι, 2 sg. of ἐπίσταμαι.

**ἐπί-σταγμα**, ατος, τό, *anything dropped on* or *in*, Gal.19.118. **-σταγμός**, ὁ, = κόρυζα, Id.13.61, v.l. in Dsc.3.20 (pl.).

**ἐπιστᾰδόν**, Adv., (ἐφίστημι, ἐπιστῆναι) *standing over each in turn* (ἐφιστάμενος ἑκάστῳ *EM*364.35), i.e. *one after another, successively*, νείκεον ἄλλοθεν ἄλλον ἐ. Od.12.392; νώμησεν δ' ἄρα πᾶσιν ἐ. 13.54; *standing by*, A.R.1.293; ἐ. οὐτάζοντες *standing up to* each other, Id.2.84.—The words of Od.16.453, δόρπον ἐ. ὡπλίζοντο, seem to have given rise to the other expl. of the Sch., ἐπισταμένως, ἐμπείρως (as if from ἐπίσταμαι).

**ἐπιστάζω**, *let fall in drops upon* or *into, instil*, τινί τι Arist.*Pr*.871ᵇ18, Orib.46.19.13, cf. Herod.1.81: metaph., ἐ. χάριν *shed* delight or honour, Pi.*I*.4(3).72; ὀλίγον τοῦ μέλιτος Luc.*VH*1.24:—Pass., *to be dropped on*, ἐπειδὰν ἐπισταγῇ ὄνυχι Dsc.2.70, cf. Sor.1.91. II. intr., *bleed at the nose again*, Hp.*Prorrh*.1.148, *Coac*.337.

**ἐπισταθμ-άομαι**, *weigh well, ponder*, A.*Ag*.164 (lyr.). **-εία** or **-ία**, ἡ, *lodging*, ἐ. ποιεῖσθαι παρά τινι take up one's *quarters* with him, D.S.17.47 (v.l. -είαν), cf. 34.17. II. *liability to have persons quartered on one*, Cic.*Att*.13.52.2, Plu.*Sert*.6 (pl.). **-εύω**, *to be billeted* or *quartered upon* another, Id.*Sull*.25; τινί Id.*Demetr*.23, cf. 2.828f. II. Pass., *to have others quartered upon one*, *PPetr*.2 p.36 (iii B.C.), *UPZ* 146 ii 27 (ii B.C.), Plb.21.6.1. 2. *to be assigned as quarters*, οἰκία Plu.*Ant*.9. III. trans., *occupy with*, in metaph. sense, τὰ ὦτα διαλέξεσιν Id.2.778b. **-ησις**, *interpondium*, *Gloss*. ⊛ **-ος**, ον, *quartered on another*, *PPetr*.3 p.41 (iii B.C.); στρατιῶται *SIG*880.61 (Pizus, iii A.D.): neut. pl. as Subst., ἐπίσταθμα, τά, *quarters*, Poll.4.173. II. as Subst., ἐπίσταθμος, ὁ, *quartermaster, satrap*, Isoc.4.120; ἐ. Καρίας ib.162, cf. *AB*253. b. *image placed at a door*, Call.*Epigr*.26, dub. in *POxy*.2146.9 (iii A.D.). 2. = συμποσίαρχος, Plu.2.612c.

**ἐπιστάκτης**, ου, ὁ, *wool used for dropping oil*, Heliod.(?) ap.Orib. 46.19.13.

**ἐπιστᾰλάζω**, = ἐπιστάζω, τι ἐπί τι Mnesith.ap.Orib.*inc*.15.11:—also **-στᾰλάω**, *drop over*, ἱδρὼς.. στήθος ἐ. *AP*9.322 (Leon.).

⊛ **ἐπίστᾰλ-μα**, ατος, τό, (ἐπιστέλλω) *commission*, Thphr.*Char*.5.8. II. *official communication* or *order*, *PFay*.26.4 (ii A.D.), Wilcken *Chr*.42.3, 8 (iv A.D.), *Cod.Just*.7.37.3.1c: pl., of Imperial *letters*, Just. *Nov*.167.1. **-σις**, εως, ἡ, *order*, in pl., Hsch. s. v. ἐπιστολαί. **-τικός**, ή, όν, *epistolary*, ἀπαρέμφατα A.D.*Synt*.239.24, al.; of the dative case, D.T.636.6; ἐ. ὅσα κατὰ ἐντολὰς πρός τινας ποιοῦντες διέπεμπον Procl.*Chr*.ap.Phot.p.322 B.

**ἐπίστᾱμα**, v. ἐπίστημα.

⊛ **ἐπίστᾰμαι**, 2 pers. -ασαι A.*Pr*.376, 982, S.*El*.629, Pl.*Euthd*.296a, but ἐπίστᾳ Pi.*P*.3.80, A.*Eu*.86, 581, ἐπίστῃ Thgn.1085, *PCair.Zen*. 41.19 (iii B.C.), Ion. ἐπίστεαι (ἐξ-) Hdt.7.135; imper. ἐπίστασο ib. 29, 209, A.*Pr*.840, 967, *PCair.Zen*.57.4 (iii B.C.), etc., but ἐπίσταο v.l. in Hdt.7.209, contr. ἐπίστω S.*OT*658, etc.; subj. Ion. ἐπιστέωμαι

Hdt.3.134, Att. ἐπίστωμαι Pl.*Euthd.*296a: impf. ἠπιστάμην A.*Pr.*267, etc.; without augm. ἐπίστατο Il.5.60: Hdt. has ἐπ- 5.42 (v.l. ἠπ-), ἠπ- 3.139; Ion. 3 pl. ἠπιστέατο or ἐπιστέατο 8.132: fut. ἐπιστήσομαι Il.21.320, etc.: aor. 1 ἠπιστήθην Hdt.3.15, Pl.*Lg.*687a. I. *know how to do, be able to do, capable* of doing, c. inf., οὐδέ οἱ ὀστέ' ἐπιστήσονται Ἀχαιοὶ ἀλλέξαι Il.21.320, cf. Od.13.207, Sapph.70, etc.: Hom. has it both of intellectual power, ὅς τις ἐπίσταιτο ᾗσι φρεσὶν ἄρτια βάζειν Il.14.92; ἐπιστάμεναι σάφα θυμῷ Od.4.730; and of artistic skill, ὃς χερσὶν ἐπίστατο δαίδαλα πάντα τεύχειν Il.5.60: freq. in Trag. and Att., οὔπω σωφρονεῖν ἐπίστασαι A.*Pr.*982, cf. 1032, S.*OT* 589; πένεσθαι δ' οὐκ ἐ. δόμος A.*Ag.*962; ἐ... θεοὺς σέβειν E.*Hipp.*996, cf. *Alc.*566; κιθαρίζειν οὐκ ἐ. Ar.*V.*989, cf. Pl.*Smp.*223d, *R.*420e, al.: without inf., σῷζ' ὅπως ἐπίστασαι as best you *can*, A.*Pr.*376, cf. *Eu.* 581. 2. *to be assured, feel sure* that.., τοῦτον ἐπίστανται πλεῖστα εἰδέναι Heraclit.57, cf. Hdt.3.134, 139, 6.139, al.: folld. by ὡς, Id. 1.122. II. c. acc., *understand* a matter, *know, be versed in* or *acquainted with*, πολλὰ δ' ἐπίστατο ἔργα Il.23.705, cf. Od.2.117; Μουσέων δῶρον Archil.1; τὴν τέχνην Hdt.3.130; τὸ μέλλον A.*Pers.* 373; ἐμπειρίᾳ ἐ. τὴν ναυτικήν Th.4.10; τὰς φύσεις ὑμῶν Id.7.14; πάσας τὰς δημιουργίας Pl.*R.*598c; ἔγωγε γράμματ' οὐδ' ἐ. Cratin.122; τὸ μὴ ἐ. γράμματα illiteracy, *PRyl.*73.19 (i B.C.), etc.; ἐ. ἱερατικὰ καὶ Αἰγύπτια γράμματα *PTeb.*291.41 (ii A.D.); ἐ. μύθους τοὺς Αἰσώπου *know* them *by heart*, Pl.*Phd.*61b, cf. *Grg.*484b: also with an Adv., Συριστὶ ἐ. *know* Syrian, X.*Cyr.*7.5.31; with acc. and inf. conjoined, A.*Eu.*276; with inf. to expl. the acc., ἔργον δὲ μοῦνον ἐσθίειν ἐ. Semon.7.24, cf. Archil.65. 2. after Hom., *know* as a fact, *know for certain*, ἐπισταμένοισι εὖ οὐκ ἄν τις λέγοι Hdt.7.8.α', etc.; used convertibly with εἰδέναι, Pl.*Tht.*163b, Arist.*APr.*66b31, *Ph.*184a10; even χάριν ἐ., = χάριν εἰδέναι, Jul.*Or.*8.246c (but sts. εἰδέναι is general, ἐπίστασθαι being confined to *scientific knowledge* (ἐπιστήμη), διὰ τὸ εἰδέναι τὸ ἐπίστασθαι ἐδίωκον Arist.*Metaph.*982b21): freq. strengthd., εὖ ἐ. Hdt. l. c.; σαφῶς ἐ. A.*Pr.*840, etc.: most freq. c. acc., τὰ διαφέροντα ἐ. And.4.19, etc.; also ἐ. περί τινος Hdt.2.3, Th.6.60; περὶ θεῶν E.*Fr.*795.4: folld. by a dependent clause, τί σφιν χρήσηται ἐ. Thgn. 772; ἐ. ὅτι.., or ἐ. τοῦτο, ὅτι.., Hdt.1.3, 156, etc.; ὡς.. A.*Pers.*599; τοῦτ' ἐπίστασ', ὡς S.*Aj.*1370; ἐ. αὐτὸν οἷς ψωμίζεται Ar.*Eq.*715, etc. 3. rarely, *know* a person, Ἀρίγνωτον γὰρ οὐδεὶς ὅστις οὐκ ἐ. Ar.*Eq.*1278, cf. Muson.*Fr.*3 p.12 H., Luc.*Asin.*1; τὸν Ἰησοῦν γινώσκω καὶ τὸν Παῦλον ἐ. *Act.Ap.*19.15; but ὁ παῖς τοὺς τεκόντας οὐκ ἐ. *does* not *know who* they *are*, E.*Ion* 51. III. c. part., in Prose and Trag., *know that* one is, has, etc., εὖ ἐ. αὐτὸς σχήσων Hdt.5.42; ἐσθλὸς ὢν ἐπίστασο S.*Aj.*1399, cf. Th.2.44; also ὡς ὧδ' ἐχόντων τῶνδ' ἐ. σε χρή S.*Aj.*281; ὡς φανέν γε τοὔπος ὧδ' ἐ. Id.*OT* 848: c. dupl. acc., ἑαυτοὺς Φαυστύλου ἠπιστάμεθα παῖδας (sc. ὄντας) Plu.*Rom.*7: c. acc. et inf., S.*Ant.*1092, Lys.*Fr.*53.1. IV. pres. part. ἐπιστάμενος, η, ον, freq. as Adj., *knowing, understanding, skilful*, ἀνδρὸς ἐ. Od.14.359; χαλεπὸν ἐ. περ ἐόντι Il.19.80; καὶ μάλ' ἐ. Od.13.313; even of a dancer's feet, θρέξασκον ἐπισταμένοισι πόδεσσι Il.18.599: also c. gen., φόρμιγγος ἐ. καὶ ἀοιδῆς *skilled, versed in* them, Od.21.406: and c. dat., ἄκοντι Il.15.282: hence, 2. Adv. ἐπιστᾰμένως *skilfully, expertly*, 7.317, Hes.*Th.*87, etc.; εὖ καὶ ἐ. Il.10.265, Od.20.161, Hes.*Op.*107; ἐ. πίνειν Thgn.212; also in Prose, X.*Cyr.*1.1.3, A.D.*Adv.*146.7, Vett. Val.298.2: c. inf., *with knowledge* how to.., Epicur.*Nat.*14.4. (Since ἐφίστημι τὸν νοῦν is used in the sense of ἐπίσταμαι, *attend, observe*, it is prob. that ἐπίσταμαι is merely an old med. form of ἐφίστημι, cf. Arist. *Ph.*247b11 τῷ γὰρ ἠρεμῆσαι καὶ στῆναι τὴν διάνοιαν ἐπίστασθαι.. λέγομεν, and v. ἐπίστασις II. 2.)

**ἐπίσταξις**, εως, ἡ, f.l. for στάξις in Hp.*Prorrh.*1.148.

**ἐπιστᾰσία**, Ion. -ίη, ἡ, = ἐπίστασις II. 2, *attention, care*, ἐ. ποιεῖσθαί τινος Ph.1.192, cf. Phld.*Rh.*2.149 S. (prob.); ἐ. ἔχειν deserve *attention*, Ath.2.66b. 2. *recognition*, ἐς ἐ. τῆς νούσου ἀφικνεόμενοι Aret. *SD*1.6. II. *authority, dominion*, πρὸς τὴν ἐ. αὐτῶν *dominion over* them, Str.8.5.5; τὰς πόλεις ἠλευθέρου τῆς τῶν Καρχηδονίων ἐ. D.S. 20.32: abs., Plu.*Luc.*2, *Nic.*28; ἀρχικὴ ἐ. *Stoic.*3.158, cf. 2.339 (pl.).

**ἐπιστᾰσιάζω**, *to be at variance further*, S.E.*M.*11.37.

**ἐπιστᾰσίδια**, τά, title of work by Archimedes, Tz.*H.*12.974 (cod. Par. in *Rh.Mus.*4(1836).18).

⊕ **ἐπιστάσιον** [ᾰ], τό, *office of* ἐπιστάτης, *IG*2².1635.71, 1651.10, 1672.74.

⊕ **ἐπιστάσιος** [ᾰ] Ζεύς, = Lat. *Jupiter Stator*, Plu.*Rom.*18. (From ἐφίστημι, *he that makes to stand firm.*)

⊕ **ἐπίστᾰσις**, εως, ἡ, (ἐφίστημι) *stopping, stoppage*, [τῆς κοιλίης], οὔρου, Hp.*Coac.*480, *Prorrh.*1.110; ἐ. αἵματος *sluggishness* of the flow of blood, Id.*Insomn.*93, cf. Arist.*GA*718a21; of the growth of trees, Thphr.*CP*2.9.1; πρὸς ἐπίστασιν τῶν ἄλλων as a *deterrent* to others, *PAmh.*2.134.9 (ii A.D.). 2. *violence, vehemence*, ἐπαινεῖ τὴν Ζήνωνος πραγματείαν μετὰ δή τινος λαμπρᾶς ἐ. Procl.*in Prm.*p.604 S. II. (ἐφίσταμαι) *stopping, halt*, τοῦ στρατεύματος X.*An.*2.4.26, cf. Plb.8. 28.13; φροντίδων ἐπιστάσεις *haltings* of thought, *anxious* thoughts, S.*Ant.*225; ἐπιστάσεις καὶ διατριβαί Plu.2.48b (following quot. of S.*Ant.*232); opp. κίνησις, Arist.*de An.*407a33, cf. *LI*969b3. b. ἐπίστασιν ἔχει, πῶς.. there is a *difficulty*, as to how.., Id.*Metaph.* 1089b25. 2. *stopping* to examine a thing, *observation, attention*, τοῦτ' ἄξιον ἐπιστάσεως, εἰ.. Id.*Ph.*196a36; μετὰ ἐ. Plb.2.2.2; μετὰ πολλῆς ἐ. καὶ φιλοτιμίας D.S.29.32; ἄξιος ἐπιστάσεως Plb.11.2.4, Phld. *Rh.*1.31 S.; ἄγειν τινὰ εἰς ἐ. Plb.9.22.7; ἐξ ἐ. ῥητέον *carefully*, Id.3. 58.3; ἐπίστασίν τινων λαμβάνειν Aristeas 256; medical *treatment, care*, πρὸς φλεγμονήν Sor.1.76: generally, *care, attention*, Phld.*Lib.* p.5 O., *Mus.*p.84 K. 3. = ἐπιστασία II, D.S.14.82, Ph.1.143 codd.; κατὰ τὴν ἐ. during his *term as* ἐπιστάτης, *SIG*10 (Samos, vi B.C.); ἐ. ἔργων *superintendence* of works, X.*Mem.*1.5.2; ἡ ἐ. μοι ἡ καθ' ἡμέραν 2*Ep.Cor.*11.28; *oversight* of students, D.H.*Comp.*1. 4. *beginning*, ἐ. ποιεῖσθαι ἀπό.. Plb.1.12.6; ἡ ἐ. τῆς ἱστορίας *introduction*, Id.2.71.7; ἀρχὴ καὶ ἐ. τῆς κατασκευῆς *method of setting about* construction, Ph.*Bel.*50.35. 5. *scum* on urine, Hp.*Aph.*7.35. 6. *position* in rear, τὴν ἐ. ἐπ' ἀλλήλοις ἔχειν one behind the other, of ships, Plb.1.26.12. 7. = μέρος τι τῆς νεώς, Hsch.; cf. ἐπιστατήρ. III. *onset*, Lxx 2*Ma.*6.3; ὄχλου *Act.Ap.*24.12 (nisi leg. ἐπισύστασις). IV. ἐν ἐπιστάσει καὶ ἐν ἀπολογισμῷ, perh. of land *of which the rent has been raised*, *PTeb.*61(*a*).163 (ii B.C.), al. V. Cypr. ἐπισταίς, = ἐπιστασία II, *Inscr.Cypr.*144 H.

⊕ **ἐπιστᾰτ-εία**, ἡ, (ἐπιστατεύω) *authority, rule*, Iamb.*VP*30.174, Porph.*VP*9, *PFay.*104.25 (iii A.D.). II. *office of* ἐπιστάτης, *Klio* 12. 365 (Alexandria, ii B.C.). III. *watchfulness*, Diog.Oen.65. **-έον**, *one must consider*, τι.. A.D.*Synt.*18.22; τῷ "ἐρίπω" ῥήματι, εἰ.. ib.280.16; πρὸς ἕκαστον τῶν λεχθέντων Plot.6.6.12. **-εύω**, = sq., Eus.Mynd.41 codd. Stob., *BMus.Inscr.*1100 (Italy), *CIG*5142 (Cyrene). **-έω**, pf. ἐπεστάτηκα *Michel* 164.10 (Delos):—*to be an* ἐπιστάτης, *to be set over*, ποιμνίοις S.*OT*1028, E.*Fr.*188.4; ἡ ψυχὴ ἐ. τῷ σώματι Pl.*Grg.*465d; ἐπιστήμη ἐ. τῇ πράξει Id.*R.*443e; τῷ τοῦ νομοθέτου ἔργῳ Id.*Cra.*390c, cf. 405d (but τέχνῃ according to art, Id.*Plt.* 293b): abs., Durrbach *Choix d'inscrr. de Délos* 159, *PCair.Zen.*34.7; εἰ μὴ ἐπιστατοῖ τὸ τάττον Plot.4.4.16. 2. c. gen., *to be in charge of, have the care of*, τοῦ ἔργου Hdt.7.22; ἔργων X.*Mem.*2.8.3; ζῴων Id. *Cyr.*1.1.2; τοῦ εἶναι οἵους δεῖ ib.8.1.16; τῆς παιδείας Pl.*R.*600d; οὐκ ὀρθῶς ἂν ἔχοι τὸν χείρω τῶν βελτιόνων ἐπιστατεῖν Id.*Prt.*338b; ὅλων τῶν πραγμάτων Isoc.4.104; τῶν λαῶν σκληρῶς ἐ. Mnaseas 32; ἐ. νοσεόντων Hp.*Praec.*6. 3. *stand by, aid*, οὐ ψεῦδις μάρτυς ἔργμασιν ἐ. Pi.*N.*7.49; Παιὼν τῷδ' ἐπεστάτει λόγῳ A.*Ag.*1248. 4. rarely c. acc., *attend, follow*, τίς γάρ με μόχθος οὐκ ἐπεστάτει; S.*Fr.*150. 5. *stand in the rear rank*, Ascl.*Tact.*10.15. 6. *notice, observe*, Sch.Pi. *O.*3.81. II. at Athens and elsewhere, *to be* ἐπιστάτης or *president* (in the βουλή and ἐκκλησία), freq. at the head of decrees, ἔδοξεν τῷ δήμῳ·.. Νικιάδης ἐπεστάτει Th.4.118, cf. Ar.*Th.*374, Lexap.And.1. 96, *IG*1².10, al., Arist.*Ath.*44.3; in other cities, *SIG*279.1 (Zelea, iv B.C.), *OGI*219.1 (Ilium, iii B.C.), etc.; προέδρων *Inscr.Magn.*2, al.: generally, *preside over*, δικαστηρίων *OGI*556.13 (Tlos). 2. *exercise the office of* ἐπιστάτης III. 2, τοῦ Καίσαρος ναοῦ ib.555.2 (Oenoanda): abs., *SIG*707.21 (Olbia, ii B.C.). **-η**, ἡ, = ἐπιστάτης IV, Sch.Ar. *Av.*437. **-ήρ**, ῆρος, ὁ, = τὸ στόμα τῆς νεώς, Hsch.: and in pl., = οἱ τῶν πλοίων νομεῖς, Id. II. pl., = ἀγορανόμοι, Id. **-ήριος**, ὁ, title of Zeus in Crete, Id. **-ης**, ου, ὁ, (ἐφίσταμαι) *one who stands near* or *by*: hence, like ἱκέτης, *suppliant*, οὐ σύ γ' ἄν.. σῷ ἐπιστάτῃ οὐδ' ἅλα δοίης Od.17.455. 2. in battle-order, *one's rear-rank man*, X.*Cyr.* 3.3.59, 8.1.10, al. b. also, *even numbers* in a λόχος, Ascl.*Tact.*2.3, Arr.*Tact.*6.6. II. *one who stands* or *is mounted upon*, ἁρμάτων ἐ., of a charioteer, S.*El.*702, E.*Ph.*1147; ἐλεφάντων ἐ., of the driver, Plb.1.40.11. 2. *one who is set over, chief, commander*, A.*Th.*816 (815); ὅπλων Id.*Pers.*379; ποιμνίων ἐ. S.*Aj.*27; ἐρετμῶν ἐ. E.*Hel.* 1267; θύματος ἐ. Id.*Hec.*223; but ταύρων πυρπνόων ζεύγλῃσι *mastering* them with.., Id.*Med.*478; ἐνόπτρων καὶ μύρων, of the Trojans, Id.*Or.*1112; ἐ. Κολωνοῦ, of a tutelary god, S.*OC*889; [καιρὸς] ἀνδράσιν μέγιστος ἔργου παντός ἐστ' ἐ. Id.*El.*76; also in Prose, ἐ. γενέσθαι τῶν λόγων ἴσους καὶ κοινοὺς *judges*, And.4.7; ποίας ἐργασίας ἐ.; Answ. ἐ. τοῦ ποιῆσαι δεινὸν λέγειν (where it = ἐπιστήμων) Pl.*Prt.*312d; πραγμάτων Isoc.4.121; ἐπιστάται ἄθλων *stewards* of games, Pl.*Lg.*949a, cf. X.*Lac.*8.4; of a pilot, Id.*Oec.*21.3; *supervisor* of training, Pl. *R.*412a, X.*Mem.*3.5.18 (pl.); ἐ. τῶν παίδων *IG*12(1).43 (Rhodes); τῶν ἐφήβων *Inscr.Prien.*112.73 (i B.C.): voc. ἐπιστάτα, = *Rabbi*, *Ev. Luc.*5.5, al. III. *president* of a board or assembly: at Athens, ἐ. τῶν πρυτάνεων *chairman* of βουλή and ἐκκλησία in cent. v, Arist. *Ath.*44.1, later, *keeper* of Treasury or Archives, *IG*3.841, etc.; ἐ. τῶν προέδρων *chairman* of βουλή and ἐκκλησία from cent. iv, Aeschin. 3.39, D.22.9, etc.; ἐ. ὁ ἐκ τῶν προέδρων *IG*2².204.31 (iv B.C.); in other Greek states, ib.12(1).731 (Rhodes), 12(7).515.116, 125 (Amorgos), etc.; ἐ. τῶν νομοθετῶν ib.2².222; τῶν δικα[στῶν] *LW*1539 (Erythrae). 2. *overseer, superintendent*, in charge of any public building or works, τοῦ νεὼ τοῦ ἐν πόλει, i.e. of the temple of Athena Polias, *IG*1².372; ἱεροῦ *UPZ*42.22 (ii B.C.); ἐ. τῶν ἔργων *clerk* of the works, D.18.114, Lxx *Ex.*1.11 (pl.); τῶν δημοσίων ἔργων Aeschin.3. 14; τοῦ ναυτικοῦ ib.222; τῆς Ἀκαδημείας Hyp.*Dem.Fr.*7; τοῦ Μουσείου *OGI*104.4 (ii B.C.); τῶν κοπρώνων D.25.49. 3. *governor, administrator*, τῆς πόλεως *OGI*254.3 (Babylon, ii B.C.), cf. *IG*12(3). 320.7 (Thera, iii B.C.), *OGI*479.7 (Dorylaeum, ii A.D.); κώμης local *magistrate*, *Arch.Pap.*4.38. 4. = προστάτης, Lat. *patronus*, *IG*14. 1317. IV. in Ar.*Av.*437, = χυτρόπους, Ar.Byz.ap.Eust.1827.45; other explanations, ibid., cf. Sch.Ar. l. c.: τοὐπιστάτου is fr. ἐπίστατος, = πυρίστατος, Anon.ap.Eust.1827.56: dub. sens. in *BpW*1892.514; cf. ἐπίστατον. **-ητέον**, *one must oversee, superintend*, c. dat., Pl.*R.* 377b, 401b: c. gen., X.*Oec.*7.35. **-ικός**, ή, όν, *of* or *for government*: ἡ -κή (sc. ἐπιστήμη) Pl.*Plt.*292b, 308e; δυνάμεις ἐ. τῆς φύσεως Iamb. *Myst.*2.1. 2. *concerning an* ἐπιστάτης, γραφή Arist.*Ath.*59.2. b. -κόν, τό, *tax levied for the support of an* ἐ., *BGU*337.2 (iii A.D.); ἐ. ἱερέων *PFay.*42(*a*) ii 8 (ii A.D.). 3. *careful, attentive*, Syrian.*in Metaph.*13.6. Adv. -κῶς ib.6.6, S.E.*M.*7.182. 4. ἐ. πρός τι *giving an impulse* towards, Phld.*Mus.*p.84 K. 5. *scientific*, κατάληψμα D.L.7.45. II. *steady, calm*, Aët.6.8. Adv. -κῶς, gloss on ἐπισταδόν, Sch.A.R.2.84. **-ις**, ιδος, ἡ, fem. of ἐπιστάτης, οὐ γὰρ

μουσική τούτων ἐ. Aristid.Quint.2.6, cf. Corn.*ND*20, Sch.Ar.*Th.* 380. -ον, τό, *support, stand, SIG*2 *B*4 (Sigeum, vi B.C.), Ar.*Av.* 437, *IG*11(2).161 *C*94 (Delos, iii B.C.), *PGrenf.*1.14.6 (ii B.C.), Hsch. s.v. λάανα; cf. ἐπιστάτης IV. II. ἐπιστᾰτός, v. ἐπιστητός.

**ἐπιστᾰχύω,** (στάχυς) *shoot* or *sprout* forth, prop. of corn: metaph. of the beard, A.R.1.972.

**ἐπιστέαται,** Ion. for ἐπίστανται.

⊛ **ἐπιστεγ-άζω,** *roof over,* οἴκημα δοκοῖς Ctes.*Fr.*20. -η, ἡ, *roof-timber,* Ath.Mech.13.6. -νόω, *close up, block,* τρύπημα Hero*Spir.* 2.37. -ωσις, εως, ἡ, *roofing over, POxy.*1450.8 (iii A.D.).

**ἐπιστείβω,** *tread upon, stand upon,* τόπον S.*OC*56, cf. Nic.*Th.*32, 570; γαῖαν Rhian.1.11; αἰγιαλόνδε Orph.*A.*1120; ἐ. ἔργον *set about,* ib.943.

**ἐπιστείριον·** τὸ τῆς νηός, Suid.

⊛ **ἐπιστείχω,** *approach,* νᾶσον Pi.*I.*6(5).21; ἁλήματα.. ἐ. χθόνα A.*Eu.* 906: abs., τὴν ἐπιστείχουσαν ἡμέραν E.*Fr.*816.7.

**ἐπιστέλλω,** *send to,* γράψας ἐς βυβλίον τάδε ἐπέστειλε ἐς Σάμον Hdt. 3.40; τοῖσι Ἕλλησι Id.7.239; ἤδιω.. ἂν εἶχον ὑμῖν.. ἐπιστέλλειν Th. 7.14; ἐ. ἐπιστολάς τινι D.4.37, cf. Pl.*Ep.*363b; *send a message,* τάδε E.*IT*770; esp. by letter, *write word,* τοιαῦτα Lys.20.27; περί τινος ὡς ἀδικοῦντος Th.8.38; ἐ. ὅτι.. ib.50,99; τὰ ἐπισταλέντα ἐκ τῆς Σάμου the *news received* from Samos, ib.50; τὰ ὑπό τινος ἐπεσταλμένα Plu.*Art.*21. 2. *enjoin, command,* τισί τι Th.5.37; τὸν ἄγγελον ἐπιστείλας ταῦτα ἔπεμψε X.*Cyr.*2.4.32; τινὶ περί τινος ib.4.5.34: c. inf., ἐ. τινὶ ἀπίστασθαι Hdt.6.3; τινὶ ἐκμαθεῖν E.*Ph.*863; ὁ Κῦρος αὐτῷ ἐπέστελλε πρὸς Πέρσας λέγειν X.*Cyr.*4.5.26; also ἐ. τινὰ ποιεῖν τι S.*OT*106, X.*Cyr.*5.5.1: without any case, *give orders* to do, A. *Eu.*205, Th.8.72, etc.; *give orders in writing,* Thphr.*Char.*24.13:— Pass., ἔφη οὐδέν οἱ ἐπεστάλθαι ἄλλο ἢ ἀπαλλάσσεσθαι he *had received orders* to.., Hdt.4.131; καί μοι ἐκ βασιλέος ὧδε ἐπέσταλται Id.6.97; αἷς ἐπέσταλται τέλος to whom the office *has been committed,* A.*Ag.* 908, cf. *Eu.*743; τἀπεσταλμένα Id.*Ch.*779; κατὰ τὰ ἐ. ὑπὸ Δημοσθένους Th.4.8; ἀξιῶ ἐπισταλῆναί τισι c. inf., *PRyl.*121.13 (ii A.D.): with personal construction, ταῦτα ἐπεσταλμένοι *having received* these *instructions,* Th.5.37: in later writers, usu. of *orders given in writing, Act.Ap.*15.20, 21.25, *SIG*837.14 (ii A.D.), etc.; of *orders* for payment, *POxy.*1304 (ii A.D.), etc.

**ἐπιστεν-αγμός,** ὁ, *groaning, Gloss.* -άζω, *groan over,* τινί A. *Pers.*727 (troch.), Plu.*Brut.*51, etc.: abs., E.*IT*283. -ακτος, ον, *uttered in lament over,* Sch.E.*Ph.*1301. -ᾰχίζω, = ἐπιστένω, Hes. *Th.*843 (v.l. -στοναχ-), Nonn.*D.*8.204. -άχω [ᾰ], = ἐπιστένω, τινί A.*Ag.*790 (anap.): aor., ἐπεστενάχησε θανόντι *IPE*2.171 (Panticapaeum): abs., S.*OT*185 (lyr.):—Med., ἐπεστενάχοντο δ' ἑταῖροι Il.4. 154, cf. 19.301 (tm.).

**ἐπίστενος,** ον, *contracted,* Arist.*HA*514$^b$23 (Comp.).

⊛ **ἐπιστένω,** *groan* or *sigh at* or *in answer,* ἐπὶ δ' ἔστενε δῆμος Il.24. 776; ἐπέστενε δ' οὐρανὸς εὐρύς Hes.*Th.*679; *lament over,* τέκνοις E. *Med.*929, cf. Plu.*Caes.*21, etc. 2. c. acc., *lament,* S.*Tr.*947 (lyr.).

**ἐπιστέρησις,** εως, ἡ, *secondary negation* (cancelling a first), *EM* 97.11, *Et.Gud.*51.57.

**ἐπιστεφᾰν-όω,** *deck with a crown,* βωμόν Pi.*O.*9.112; μνάματα *Schwyzer*491 (Thespiae); τινά *IG*3.713.7, Ph.2.6. -ωμα, *corollarium, Gloss.*

**ἐπιστεφ-ής,** ές, Hom. only in phrase κρητῆρας ἐπιστεφέας οἴνοιο bowls *full of* wine, Il.8.232, Od.2.431; ἐγκέρασον Χαρίτων κρατῆρ' ἐ. *Lyr.Alex.Adesp.*19. II. *garlanded,* Εὐμενίδες ναρκίσσου -στεφέες πλοκαμῖδας Euph.94; ὕλης ἀγρίης ἐ., either *full of* jungle or *crowned with..,* Archil.21.2. -ω, in Hom. always in Med., κρητῆρας ἐπεστέψαντο ποτοῖο *filled* them with wine, Il.1.470, Od.1.148, etc. (variously expld., cf. Ath.1.13d, 15.674e, and ἐκστέφω I). II. *to be full of* or *covered with,* τράπεσδαι μακωνίδων ἄρτων ἐπιστέφοισαι Alcm.74 B. III. χοὰς ἐ. τινί *pour* libations *as an honour to* the dead, S. *El.*441. IV. Med., *wreathe,* ἄνθεϊ χαίτην Nonn.*D.*47.11:—also in Act., *crown, surround,* κύμασι Παλλήνην ib.27.158.

**ἐπιστέωνται, ἐπίστη,** v. ἐπίσταμαι.

**ἐπιστηθίδιος,** ον, *on the breast,* τιτθοί *EM*760.48.

**ἐπιστηλόομαι,** *to be set up as a column upon,* θινὸς -ωμένον ἄχθος *AP*7.503 (Leon.).

**ἐπίστημα,** Dor. -ᾱμα, ατος, τό, (ἐφίστημι) *anything set up,* e.g. *monument over* a grave, Pl.*Lg.*958e, Is.*Fr.*159, *IG*12(3).87 (Nisyrus, iii B.C.), D.H.2.67; *ornament on* the prow of ships, D.S.13.3 (nisi leg. ἐπισήμασι).

⊛ **ἐπιστήμη,** ἡ, (ἐπίσταμαι) *acquaintance with* a matter, *understanding, skill,* as in archery, S.*Ph.*1057; in war, Th.1.121, 6.72, 7.62; ἐ. πρὸς τὸν πόλεμον Lys.33.7 (fort. leg. περί); περὶ τὰ μαθήματα Pl. *Phlb.*55d; τοῦ νεῖν Id.*Grg.*511c; ἐπιστήμῃ *skilfully,* οἱ μὴ ἐ. τοὺς ἐπαίνους ποιούμενοι Plot.5.5.13. 2. *professional skill*: hence, *profession,* οἱ τὴν ἰατρικὴν ἐ. μεταχειριζόμενοι *PFay.*106.22 (ii A.D.); ζωγράφος τὴν ἐ. painter *by profession, POxy.*896.5 (iv A.D.). II. generally, *knowledge,* ἐπιστήμῃ σύ μου προὔχοις ἂν S.*OT*1115; πάντ' ἐπιστήμης πλέως full *of knowledge* in all things, Id.*Ant.*721, cf. *Tr.* 338; ἐκ τῆς ἐ. E.*Fr.*522.3; ἐ. δοξαστική, opp. ἀλήθεια, Pl.*Sph.*233c: pl., *kinds of knowledge,* μυρίαι ἀνδρῶν ἐπιστᾶμαι πέλονται B.9.38, cf. Pl.*Smp.*208a. 2. *scientific knowledge, science,* opp. δόξα, Pl.*R.*477b sq., Hp.*Lex*4, Pl.*Plt.*301b, Arist.*APo.*88$^b$30, *EN*1139$^b$18: coupled with ἐμπειρία and τέχνη, Pl.*R.*422c, cf. *Ion*536c, Arist.*Metaph.*981$^a$ 2: pl., *the sciences,* freq. in Pl.(*R.*522c, al.), etc.

**ἐπιστημον-ίζω,** *make wise,* Al.*Is.*52.13 (Pass.). -ικός, ή, όν, *capable of knowledge,* τὸ ἐ. τῆς ψυχῆς Arist.*de An.*431$^b$27; opp. βουλευτικός, Id.*MM*1196$^b$17, cf. *EN*1139$^a$12; θεὸς.. πάντων -ώτατον Id. *Fr.*10 (= S.E.*M.*9.21): Comp. -ώτερος Arist.*Top.*141$^b$16, Ph.*Fr.*70 H. II. *of* or *for science, scientific,* ἀρχαί Arist.*Top.*100$^b$19; ὁ ὁρισμὸς -κός (v.l. -κόν) Id.*Metaph.*1039$^b$32; ἀποδείξεις Id.*APo.*75$^a$30; συλλογισμός ib.79$^b$18; αἴσθησις Phld.*Mus.*p.11 K.; λόγοι Gal.*UP*12. 6; ἐπίγνωσις *Theol.Ar.*17; οὐκ ἦν εὔλογον οὐδ' ἐ. ib.58: Sup. -ώτατον, ἔργον [ὁ κόσμος] Ph.2.217. Adv. -κῶς Arist.*Top.*114$^b$10, Ph.2.417.

**ἐπίστημ-ος,** ον, = ἐπιστήμων, *knowing,* c. gen. rei, Hp.*Epid.*6.8.10. Adv. -μως *skilfully, IGRom.*3.208 (Ancyra). -οσύνη, ἡ, *skill,* περὶ ἐ., title of work by Xenocr. (D.L.4.13). -όω, *make wise,* Aq.*Ps.* 2.10 (Pass.), al. II. *make scientific,* Eustr.*in EN*1.5. -ων, ον, gen. ονος, (ἐπίσταμαι) *knowing, wise, prudent,* ἐ. βουλῇ τε νόῳ τε Od. 16.374; ἄρχοντες X.*Oec.*21.5; ἐπιστήμων γὰρ εἶ, = ἐπίστασαι γάρ, E. *Supp.*843. 2. *acquainted with* a thing, *skilled* or *versed in,* c. gen., κακῶν S.*Fr.*589; τῆς θαλάσσης, τοῦ ναυτικοῦ, Th.1.142, 8.45; τῆς τέχνης Pl.*Grg.*448b; τῶν τόπων *POxy.*1469.12 (iii A.D.); also περί τινος or τι, Pl.*R.*599b, *Sis.*389e: with neut. Adj., τὰ προσήκοντα ἐπιστήμων X.*Cyr.*3.3.9, cf. *Oec.*2.16 (Sup.). 3. c. inf., *knowing how,* λέγειν τε καὶ σιγᾶν Pl.*Phdr.*276a, cf. X.*Oec.*19.16: Comp. -ονέστερος Pl.*Chrm.*174a. Adv. Comp. -ονέστερον X.*Oec.*3.14: Sup. -ονέστατα Pl.*R.*534d. II. *possessed of perfect knowledge,* Id.*Plt.*301b, etc.; opp. δοξαστής, τινός Id.*Tht.*208e; in Arist., *scientifically versed in* a thing, *APo.*74$^b$28, *Cat.*11$^a$33. Adv. -ονως, ἔχειν πρός τι Pl.*Sph.*233c: λέγειν *with science, with art,* Id.*Tht.*207b; εἰπεῖν use *technical* or *scientific* terminology, Aristid.*Or.*26(14).97.

**ἐπιστήρ-ιγμα,** ατος, τό, *support,* Lxx *2Ki.*22.19. -ίζω, *cause to rest on,* ἐπιστηριῶ ἐπὶ σὲ τοὺς ὀφθαλμούς μου ib.*Ps.*31(32).8; *make to lean on,* τί τινι Opp.*C.*4.256; *set over,* Δεῖμον κεραυνῷ Nonn.*D.*2. 417; *confirm,* τινά *Act.Ap.*15.32:—Pass., *to be supported,* ἐν τῷ ὕδατι Arist.*Pr.*933$^a$10; τινί Luc.*Ind.*6; ἐπιστηριχθήσομαι and ἐπεστηρίχθη ἐπὶ [τοὺς κίονας], Lxx *Jd.*16.26, 29, cf. Aq.*Ex.*17.12.

**ἐπιστής,** ῆτος, perh. *prop, Inscr.Délos* 340.11 (ii B.C.). (Gender undetermined.)

**ἐπιστητ-έον,** *one must know,* Sch.D.T.p.316 H., *An.Ox.*3.207. -ός, ή, όν, (ἐπίσταμαι) *that can be scientifically known, matter of science,* Pl.*Tht.*201d, etc.; τὸ ἐ. Arist.*EN*1139$^b$23, al.: Dor. ἐπιστᾱτός Ps.-Archyt.ap.Iamb.*Comm.Math.*8.

**ἐπιστιγμή,** ἡ, *point* or *dot upon* a thing, Aen.Tact.31.2.

**ἐπιστίζω,** *mark with spots on the surface, speckle,* Nic.*Th.*332; νῶτον ἱμάσθλῃ Nonn.*D.*37.410 (s.v.l.):—Pass., *to be spotted* or *speckled,* Thphr.*HP*3.7.5; τῷ νώτῳ οἱ σημεῖα ἐπέστικται Ael.*NA*11. 24; *to be marked with a dot,* ὁ ἐπεστιγμένος Aen.Tact.31.29.—In Moer. and Hsch., ἐπιστίζω, -στιγμα, are for ἐπι-σίζω, -σιγμα.

**ἐπιστίλβω,** *glisten on the surface,* Plu.*Lys.*28, Luc.*Am.*26; ἐπὶ παντὶ τῷ νοητῷ ἐ. Plot.6.7.36.

**ἐπίστιον,** τό, *slip* or *shed* for a ship, νῆες.. εἰρύαται· πᾶσιν γὰρ ἐπίστιόν ἐστιν ἑκάστῳ Od.6.265. (Expld. by Aristarch. (ap.Sch.Il.2.125 ἐπ' ἱστιόν.. ὡσεὶ κατάλυμα παρὰ τῇ νηΐ) as Ion. for ἐφέστιον, cf. sq.; but elsewh. Hom. always uses the form ἐφέστιος; Sch. has ἐποίκιον, νεώριον.., παρὰ τὸ ἱστίον.)

⊛ **ἐπίστιος,** ον, Ion. for ἐφέστιος (q.v.). II. ἐπίστιος, ἡ, = ἀνίσωμα, πίνουσα τὴν ἐ. Anacr.90.4.

**ἐπίστῐχος,** ον, *in a row, EM*634.40, Sch.D Il.11.68, Sch.Opp.*H.* 1.625.

**ἐπιστοβέω,** *scoff at,* A.R.3.663, 4.1725.

**ἐπιστοιβ-άζω,** *pile up,* ξύλα ἐπὶ τὸ πῦρ Lxx *Le.*1.7, *Si.*8.3. -ασις, εως, ἡ, *piling up,* metaph., τῶν παρίσων Eust.774.5.

**ἐπιστοιχειόω,** *furnish the elements* of a compound, Maria ap.Zos. Alch.p.200 B.

**ἐπιστολαγραφεῖον,** v. ἐπιστολογραφεῖον.

**ἐπιστολᾰγράφος** [γρᾰ], ὁ, *royal secretary, BCH*32.431 (Delos, Ptolemaic period), Plb.30.25.16 cod., *OGI*259 (v. *BCH* l.c.); cf. ἐπιστολογράφος.

**ἐπιστολάδην** [ᾰ], Adv. *girt up,* of dress, like ἀνεσταλμένως, Hes. *Sc.*287.

**ἐπιστολαφόρος,** v. ἐπιστοληφόρος.

⊛ **ἐπιστολ-εύς,** έως, ὁ, (ἐπιστολή) *secretary,* τοῦ Αὐτοκράτορος *IG*14. 1085; also in Persia, Suid. s.v. ἐπιστέλλει. II. among the Spartans, *admiral second in command, vice-admiral,* X.*HG*2.1.7, 4.8.11, Plu.*Lys.*7; he carries dispatches, X.*HG*1.1.23. ⊛ -ή, ἡ, (ἐπιστέλλω) *anything sent by a messenger, message, order, commission,* whether verbal or in writing, Hdt.4.10, Th.8.45, etc.; ἐξ ἐπιστολῆς by *command,* Hdt.6.50: used by Trag. always in pl., A.*Pr.*3, *Pers.*783, *Supp.*1012, S.*Aj.*781, *OC*1601, etc.; Πενθέως ἐπιστολαῖς by his *commands,* E.*Ba.*442; τέκνων ἐπιστολὰς ἔγραψεν *commands about* her children, Id.*Hipp.*858. 2. *letter,* ἐ. διαπέμπειν, ἀποδοῦναι, Th.1. 129, 7.10; λύειν Id.1.132; ἐ. ἔδωκεν ἀποδοῦναι Lys.20.27; πέμπειν τινί E.*IT*589 (pl.): in pl. of one letter, like γράμματα, Lat. *litterae,* Id.*IA*111, 314, Th.1.132, etc.; ὁ ἐπὶ τῶν ἐπιστολῶν.. τοῦ Ὄθωνος, Lat. *ab epistulis Othoni,* his *secretary,* Plu.*Oth.*9; νομογραφικὴ ἐ. *BGU*1135.7 (i B.C.). ⊛ -ηφόρος, ὁ, *letter-carrier,* Zoroaster in *Cat. Cod.Astr.*2.193.38:—in form **ἐπιστολᾰφόρος,** *PRyl.*78.24 (ii A.D.), *PLond.ined.*2172 (ii/iii A.D.), *PPetersb.*1 (iii A.D.).

**ἐπιστολιαφόρος,** ὁ, *bearer of dispatches* (v. ἐπιστολεύς II), X.*HG*6. 2.25.

**ἐπιστολίδιον,** τό, = ἐπιστόλιον, *POxy.*1069.14 (iii A.D.), etc.

**ἐπιστολ-ικός,** ή, όν, *suited to a letter,* Arist.*Fr.*670; *in the style of letters,* λόγοι D.H.*Lys.*1.3; as book-title, Gal.8.150, D.L.10.25, prob. cj. in Sor.2.53; χαρακτήρ Demetr.*Eloc.*223, Ap.Ty.*Ep.*19. Adv. -κῶς

Demetr.*Eloc.*233. ⊛ **-ῐμαῖος,** ον, *in* or *of letters*, συνουσίαι Philostr.*VA*4.46; ξυμβουλίαι ib.7.8; γράμματα Ph.2.533; δυνάμεις ἐ. forces *promised by letter* and decreed, but never sent, *paper*-armies, D.4.19.

**ἐπιστόλιον,** τό, Dim. of ἐπιστολή, Epicur.*Fr.*143, *UPZ*69.3,5 (ii B.C.), Plb.31.16.3, Plu.*Ages.*13, M.Ant.1.7, *POxy.*1481.3 (ii A.D.), etc.

⊛ **ἐπιστολογρᾰφ-εῖον,** τό, *registry*, prob. in *UPZ*14.133 (ii B.C.):—also in form **ἐπιστολαγραφεῖον** *PCornell*1.155 (-γράφιον ib. 150). **-ικός,** ή, όν, *used in writing letters*, Porph.*VP*12. **-ος,** ὁ, *letter-writer, secretary*, *OGI*139.14 (Ptol.), 194.24 (i B.C.), *PTeb.*112.87 (ii B.C.), *UPZ*108.34 (i B.C.), *PPar.*70; cf. ἐπιστολαγράφος.

**ἐπιστομ-ᾰτίζω,** = ἐπιστομίζω, Ph.1.85 codd. **-ία,** ἡ, read by Zenod. for ἐπεσβολία, Od.4.159. ⊛ **-ίζω,** Att. fut. -ῐῶ D.7.33: (στόμα):—*bridle, curb*, ἵππον cj. in Ph.1.85; [δελφῖνας] Philostr.*Im.*2.18: metaph., *curb, bridle*, τοὺς ἐχθρούς Ar.*Eq.*845, cf. D.7.33, Aeschin.2.110, *Ep.Tit.*1.11; τὴν Ἰουδαίων νεωτεροποιίαν J.*AJ*17.10.1; *silence* a speaker, Philostr.*VS*2.30, cf. Ph.2.191; οἷον ἐ. καὶ χαλινοῦντες τὸ φιλόφωνον Plu.2.967b:—Pass., ἐπεστομίσθη Pl.*Grg.*482e. II. of flute-players, ἐ. ἑαυτὸν φορβειᾷ καὶ αὐλοῖς *put on the mouthpiece* and flutes, Plu.2.713d; but ὁ αὐλὸς ἐ. Id.*Alc.*2: hence, *gag*, Luc.*Merc.Cond.*7. III. *throw on his face*, τινά Id.*Pr.Im.*10, *Cal.*12. **-ίς,** ίδος, ἡ, = φορβειά II, Hsch. s.v. ἐπίχαλκον. **-ισμα,** ατος, τό, metaph., *curb, restraint*, J.*AJ*19.3.3, 18.9.8. **-όω,** *stop up, close*, Hero *Spir.*1.19:—Pass., ib.33.

**ἐπιστονᾰχ-έω,** = ἐπιστένω, of the waves, Il.24.79. **-ίζω,** = foreg., Nonn.*D.*2.87; v.l. for -στεναχ-, Hes.*Th.*843.

**ἐπιστορέννῡμι** or (Hsch. s.v. ψιάθια) **-στόρνῡμι:** fut. **-στρώσω:** aor. 1 -εστόρεσα or -έστρωσα: aor. Med. -εστορέσαντο Nonn.*D.*24.334:—*strew* or *spread upon*, ἐστόρεσεν δ' ἐπὶ δέρμα *upon* the bed, Od.14.50; ἱμάτιον ἐπὶ τὸ ξύλον Hp.*Art.*75; a barbarous fut., ἐπιστρωννύσω τῇ γῇ νιφετόν, only in Ps.-Luc.*Philopatr.*24. 2. *saddle*, ἐπιστρῶσαι τὸν ὄνον J.*AJ*8.9.1; [ἡ κάμηλος] ἁλουργίδι ἐπέστρωτο Luc.*Prom.Es*4.

**ἐπίστρατα·** ἀποπίπτοντα τῶν πεμμάτων· καὶ ἕρματα, Hsch.

**ἐπιστρᾰτ-άομαι,** = ἐπιστρατεύω, Nonn.*D.*1.267, 48.32, in Ep. 3 pl. impf. ἐπεστρατόωντο. ⊛ **-εία,** Ion. **-ηΐη,** ἡ, *march* or *expedition against*, Hdt.9.3; τῶν Πλαταιῶν *against* Plataea, Th.2.79; σὺν Κύρῳ X.*An.*2.4.1. **-ευσις,** εως, ἡ, = foreg., Hdt.3.4. **-εύω,** *march against, make war upon*, τινί E.*Ba.*784, Ar.*Av.*1522, Th.3.54, etc.; ἐπί τινα Arist.*Oec.*1351$^b$20; ἐπὶ τοὺς Ἕλληνας *IG*2$^2$.680.9; ἐπὶ τὴν Ἑλλάδα And.1.107, cf. Pl.*Mx.*239b; εἰς Θετταλίαν Aeschin.3.83: in Poets c. acc. loci, ἐ. πατρίδα τὴν ταύτης S.*Tr.*362; Εὐβοΐδα χώραν ib.75, cf. E.*Tr.*22; so ἐ. τινά Id.*IA*1154, Th.4.60,92: abs., πολλά A.*Pers.*780; στρατῷ ξύμπαντι S.*Aj.*1056; πεζῷ καὶ ναυσί Plu.*Nic.*7:—Med., with pf. Pass., ἐπιστρατεύεσθαι ἐπ' Αἴγυπτον Hdt.3.107, cf. 6.132: c. dat., E.*Med.*1185, Ar.*V.*11, etc.: c. acc. loci, E.*Ph.*605. **-ηγέω,** *hold office of* ἐπιστράτηγος, *OGI*708.16, etc. **-ηγία,** ἡ, *district in Egypt under an* ἐπιστράτηγος, Dessau *ILS*1409, al. **-ηγος,** ὁ, *viceroy* of one of the three provinces of Egypt formed by Ptolemy V, *OGI*103.4 (ii B.C.), *PGiss.*36.1 (ii B.C.); also under the Romans, Str.17.1.13, *IGRom.*1.1141, al.

**ἐπιστρᾰτοπεδ-εία,** ἡ, *encamping over against*, Plb.1.77.7; ἡ τῶν πολεμίων ἐ. *the fact that* the enemy *was encamped near*, Id.5.76.9. **-εύω,** *encamp over against*, τοῖς Ῥωμαίοις Id.1.19.5; ἐπὶ τὸ ὄρος Id.5.30.4, etc.

**ἐπιστρᾰφής,** ές, = ἐπιστρεφής, Ammon.*Diff.*p.54 V., Ptol.Asc. p.395 H.

**ἐπί-στρεμμα,** ατος, τό, *turn* or *return* of a boundary line, *IG*14.352 i 28 (Halaesa). **-στρεπτέον,** *one must turn back*, πάλιν, in a speech, Aristid.1.99 J.; εἰς ὑγιεινὴν δίαιταν Sor.1.98. II. c. gen., *account must be taken of*, Phld.*Mort.*32. ⊛ **-στρεπτικός,** ή, όν, *reflexive, capable of returning* to its source, δύναμις Procl.*in Prm.*p.607 S.; ἐ. πρὸς ἑαυτό Id.*Inst.*15; κλητικὸν εἰς ἑαυτὸ καὶ ἐ. Herm.*in Phdr.*p.65 A.: Comp., Dam.*Pr.*77. Adv. -κῶς ib.221:—also as gloss on ἐπιστροφάδην, Eust.1956.49. **-στρεπτος** or **-τός,** ον, *to be turned outwards, looked at and admired*, αἰών A.*Ch.*350 (lyr.); ὥραν.. ἐ. βροτοῖς Id.*Supp.*997. II. *that can be turned round, reversible*, Hero *Aut.*15.3, *Spir.*1.28. III. Adv. -τως *diligently*, *Inscr.Perg.*163 *A* i 2. **-στρέφεια,** ἡ, *strictness, severity*, *POxy.*1121.5 (iii A.D.), etc. **-στρεφής,** ές, *turning one's eyes* or *mind* to a thing, *attentive*, ῥήτωρ X.*HG*6.3.7; θεός Plu.2.276a; ἐπιστρεφεῖς πρὸς τὴν θεραπείαν Phld.*Ir.*p.21 W. 2. *exact, strict, severe*, καταγραφαί D.H.10.33 (Comp.); ἀρχή Hdn.7.8.7; δίαιτα Id.5.2.5. Adv. -φῶς, Ion. -φέως, *earnestly, vehemently*, εἴρετο ἐ. Hdt.1.30; ἐ. καὶ ῥητορικῶς φήσουσι Aeschin.1.71; ἐ. πάνυ καὶ θρασέως D.H.7.34: Comp. -έστερον *UPZ*24.24 (ii B.C.), Phleg.*Olymp.Fr.*1, etc.; cf. ἐπιστρέφω II. 5:—ἐπιστρεφῶς is v.l. for ἐπιστρόφως in Eub.150.7 = Ephipp.2.10. II. *flexible, supple*, ἰσχίον Philostr.*Gym.*35: metaph., *modulated, varied*, φωνὴ ἐ., of the nightingale, Arist.*HA*632$^b$24. 2. = ἐπιστρεπτικός, μερισμός Dam.*Pr.*272; νοῦς ib.304. **-στρεφομένως** (-νος cod.), gloss on ἐπιστροφάδην, Hsch. ⊛ **-στρέφω,** pf. ἐπέστροφα Diog. (v. infr. I. 2a):—*turn about, turn round*, νῶτον Orac.ap.Hdt.7.141; δεῦρ' ἐ. κάρα E.*Heracl.*942, cf. X.*Cyn.*10.12; στροφεῖς Hero *Aut.*23.3; ἐ. τὰς ναῦς *tack* (cf. ἐπιστροφή II. 1), Th.2.90; also, *put* an enemy *to flight*, X.*HG*6.4.9; *wheel about*, τοὺς ἱππεῖς Plu.*Sull.*19; *wheel through a right angle*, Ascl.*Tact.*10.5 (Act. and Pass.), etc.; intr., ib.12.11, etc. b. intr., *turn about, turn round*, ἕλκε δ' ἐπιστρέψας Il.3.370; here only in Hom., and perh. trans., *whirl*, but v. Hdt.2.103, S.*Tr.*566; ἀλλὰ πᾶς ἐπίστρεφε δεῦρο Ar.*V.*422; of ships, *put about*, Plb.1.47.8, 50.5; of a wild boar, *turn upon* the hunter, ἐπί τινα X.*Cyn.*10.15; *return*, ἀπὸ τῆς στρατείας Epist. Philipp. in *IG*9(2).517.37 (Larissa), cf. *Ev.Matt.*12.44, etc.; of an illness, *recur*, f.l. for ὑπο-, Hp.*Coac.*124: as Hebraism, c. inf., as periphrasis of πάλιν, ἐπιστρέψει.. εὐφρανθῆναι Lxx *De.*30.9, cf. 2*Es.*9.14, al.; so with καί and finite Verb, ἐπέστρεψεν καὶ ᾠκοδόμησεν ib.2*Ch.*33.3, cf. *Ma.*1.4, al. 2. *turn towards*, νόημα Thgn.1083; ἦθος κατά τινα Id.213; ἐ. τινά *turn* his *attention towards* one, Luc.*Tim.*11; τινὰ πρός τι, εἰς ἑαυτόν, Plu.2.21c, 69f, cf. Hdn.5.3.8; οἱ τὴν Ἑλλάδα ἐπεστροφότες ἐπὶ σοφίαν Diog.*Ep.*34.1; ἐ. πίστιν *press* a pledge *upon* one, S.*Tr.*1182; ἐ. τὴν φάλαγγα *bring* it *into action*, Plu.*Ant.*42: hence, b. intr., *turn* (oneself) *towards*, X.*Eq.*8.12, etc.; ἐ. εἰς or πρὸς ἑαυτόν, of νοῦς, *reflect*, Plot.5.3.1, Procl.*Inst.*15; τὸ ἐπιστρέφον βαθρικόν the steps *leading to* the sarcophagus, Judeich *Altertümer von Hierapolis* 152. 3. *turn* or *convert* from an error, *correct, cause to repent*, Luc.*Hist.Conscr.*5, Plu.*Alc.*16; πλημμελοῦντας Id.*Cat.Mi.*14; *warn*, Philostr.*VS*1.7.1; *coerce*, *Cod.Just.*4.20.15.1. b. Pass., *to be converted, return*, ἐπὶ Κύριον Lxx *De.*30.2; intr., *repent*, ib.*Ju.*5.19, al., *Ev.Matt.*13.15, *Ev.Luc.*22.32, etc. c. Philos., *cause to return* to the source of Being, τινὰς εἰς τὰ ἐναντία καὶ τὰ πρῶτα Plot.5.1.1; τι πρὸς τἀγαθόν Procl.*Inst.*144:—Pass., Plot.1.2.4, 5.2.1; τὸ προϊὸν ἀπό τινος -στρέφεται πρὸς ἐκεῖνο ἀφ' οὗ πρόεισιν Procl.*Inst.*31; πρὸς τὸ ἕν Dam.*Pr.*27:—also intr. in Act., ἐ. εἰς ἑαυτόν Plot.5.3.6; τὸ γεννηθὲν φύσει πρὸς τὸ γεννῆσαν ἐ. Porph.*Sent.*13; οὐδὲν τῶν σωμάτων πρὸς ἑαυτὸ πέφυκεν ἐ. Procl.*Inst.*15. 4. *curve, twist*, ὀδύνη σε περὶ τὰ σπλάγχν' ἔοικ' ἐπιστρέφειν v.l. in Ar.*Pl.*1131; ἐ. ἐπισκύνιον *AP*11.376.8 (Agath.):—Pass., *to be distorted*, ἢν τράχηλος ἐπιστραφῇ Hp.*Aph.*4.35; of hair, *curl*, οἷς ἐπέστραπται τὸ τρίχιον Arist.*Pr.*963$^b$10; ἐπεστραμμένος, of a tree, *crooked*, Thphr.*HP*3.8.4; of fir-needles, *bent*, ib.3.9.6. II. Med. and Pass., esp. in aor. 2 Pass. ἐπεστράφην [ᾰ], also ἐπεστρέφθην Opp.*C.*4.179: Dor. 3 sg. fut. Pass. -στραφησεῖται *GDI*3089.27 (Callatis):—*turn oneself round, turn about*, ἤιε ἐπιστρεφόμενος *constantly turning*, as if to look behind one, Hdt.3.156: and with acc., πολλὰ θάλαμον ἐξιοῦσ' ἐπεστράφη *turned to gaze on* it, E.*Alc.*187; so of a lion retreating, Arist.*HA*629$^b$15; δι' οὗ πάσας ἐπιστρέφεσθαι τὰς περιφοράς by which all the revolving spheres *are turned*, Pl.*R.*616c; δόξα τῇδ' ἐπεστράφη thus *turned about, changed*, S.*Ant.*1111. 2. *go back- and forwards*, πάντῃ *h.Hom.*27.10; κατ' ἄλσος A.*Supp.*508: c. acc., γαῖαν ἐπιστρέφεται *wanders over* the earth, with collat. sense of *observing, studying* it, Hes.*Th.*753, Thgn.648; so ἐ. ὀρέων κορυφάς Anacr.2.4: also c. acc. loci, *turn to* a place, πόθεν γῆς τῆσδ' ἐπεστράφης πέδον; E.*Hel.*83, cf. 89, 768, *Ion*352 (also εἰς χώρας X.*Oec.*4.13): c. acc. cogn., [διεξόδους] ἐπιστρέφεσθαι *walk in*.., Pl.*Phdr.*247a; of the sun, *revolve*, D.P.584. 3. *turn the mind towards, pay attention to, regard* (cf. ἐπιστροφή II. 3), τινός Anacr.96, S.*Ph.*599, Phld.*Lib.*p.15 O., *AP*5.47 (Rufin.); τῶν ἰδίων οὐδὲν ἐ. Thgn.440; εἴς τι Alex.Aphr.*in Sens.*57.18: abs., *return to oneself, pay attention*, ἐπιστραφείς Hdt.1.88; οὐκ ἦλθες,.. οὐδ' ἐπεστράφης E.*Rh.*400; οὐκ ἐπεστράφη, = οὐκ ἐφρόντισε (just above), D.23.136, cf. 10.9, *AP*11.319 (Autom.). b. *conduct oneself, behave*, ἀξίως τᾶς τιμᾶς *SIG*539 *A* 22 (Decr. Amphict., iii B.C.). 4. c. acc., θεοῦ νιν κέλευσμ' ἐπεστράφη *turned against* her, E.*Andr.*101 (lyr.). 5. pf. part. Pass. ἐπεστραμμένος, = ἐπιστρεφής, *earnest, vehement*, λέγειν ἐπεστραμμένα Hdt.8.62; ἀφέλεια -στραμμένη Philostr.*VS*1.7.1. **-στρεψις,** εως, ἡ, *turning, twisting*, ἀγκῶνος Hp.*Art.*18.

**ἐπιστρογγύλλομαι,** Pass., *to be rounded*, Nic.*Th.*514.

**ἐπιστρόγγῠλος,** ον, *rounded, roundish*, f.l. in Arist.*HA*555$^a$29.

**ἐπιστροφ-άδην** [ᾰ], Adv. *turning this way and that way*, κτεῖνε δ' ἐπιστροφάδην Il.10.483; τύπτε δ' ἐ. 21.20, cf. Od.22.308, 24.184 (or perh., = ἐπιστρεφῶς, *earnestly, vehemently*, cf. Hsch.); ἐ. βαδίζειν wander *back- and forwards*, *h.Merc.*210; *on all sides*, Opp.*C.*1.79: Poet. and late Prose, ἐ. κτείνειν, ἀναιρεῖν, Ph.2.33, 320. **-εύς,** έως, ὁ, *turning on a pivot*, a name for *the first of the neck-vertebrae*, Poll.2.131. II. *one who causes to return* to its source, τοῦ γενομένου κόσμου Dam.*Pr.*270. **-ή,** ἡ, *turning about*, τῆς τοῦ ἀτράκτου δίνης Pl.*R.*620e; *twisting*, Thphr.*HP*3.13.3; of strands, Ph.*Bel.*58.15; τῶν σχοινίων Plu.*Alex.*25 (pl.); ἡ εἴσω ἐ. τῶν δακτύλων Philostr.*Im.*1.23. 2. *bending* of a bow, Str.2.5.22. 3. *curve, winding* of a bay, ib.33; of a river, Ptol.*Alm.*8.1. II. intr., *turning* or *wheeling about*, δαΐων ἀνδρῶν ἐπιστροφαί, i.e. hostile men *turning to bay*, S.*OC*1045 (lyr.); *tossing*, of a restless patient, Hp.*Epid.*7.83 (pl.); μυρίων ἐπιστροφαὶ κακῶν *renewed assaults* of ills unnumbered, S.*OC*537 (lyr.), cf. Arr.*An.*7.17.5; esp. in military evolutions, Plb.10.23.3, Plu.*Phil.*7; *wheeling through a right angle*, Ascl.*Tact.*10.4, etc. (but, as a general term, αἱ ἐ. τῶν ἵππων ib.7.2, cf. Arr.*Tact.*16.7); of ships, *putting about, tacking*, Th.2.90,91; ἐξ ἐπιστροφῆς by *a sudden wheel*, Plb.1.76.5, Plu.*Tim.*27; but ἐξ ἐπιστροφῆς παθεῖν to have *a relapse*, Hp.*Coac.*251. 2. *turn* of affairs, *reaction, counter-revolution*, μή τις ἐ. γένηται Th.3.71; *result, end*, Plb.21.32.15 (dub.l.). 3. *attention paid to* a person or thing (ἐπιστρέφω II. 3), ξενοτίμους δωμάτων ἐ. *respect* for guests, A.*Eu.*548; πρὸ τοῦ θανόντος τήνδ' ἔθεσθ' ἐ. S.*OT*134; ὧν ἐ. τις ἦν to whom any *regard* was due, E.*IT*671; so ἐπιστροφῆς ἄξιον X.*HG*5.2.9; παραμυθέεσθαι μετ' ἐπιστροφῆς καὶ ὑποδέξιος Hp.*Decent.*16; ἐ. ποιεῖσθαι Philipp.ap.D.12.1, cf. 19.306, etc.; ἐ. ἔχειν τινός Men.836; περί τινος Chrysipp.*Stoic.*3.187, etc.; ἐπιστροφῆς τυγχάνειν Plb.4.4.4, etc. b. Philos., *turning towards*, πρὸς τὰ τῇδε Plot.4.3.4; ψυχὴ καταδεῖται πρὸς τὸ σῶμα τῇ ἐ. τῇ πρὸς τὰ πάθη τὰ ἀπ' αὐτοῦ Porph.*Sent.*7. 4. *moving up and down in* a place, mostly in pl., πατρῴων δωμάτων ἐπιστροφαί *the range* of them, A.*Th.*648; οἷσιν οὐκ ἐπιστροφαί men who have no *business here*, E.*Hel.*440; βούνομοι ἐ. *haunts* of the grazing herds, A.*Fr.*249; so Κίλιξ δὲ χώρα καὶ Σύρων

ἐπιστροφαί (cj. for Σηρῶν ἐνστροφαί) ib.271. **5.** *intentness, vehemence,* ἐπιστροφὴν εἶχεν ὁ λόγος καὶ ἔρρωτο Philostr.*VS*1.21.5; θρασυτέρᾳ τῇ ἐ. χρήσασθαι ib.2.5.2. **b.** *gravity* of deportment, ἡ ἐ. τοῦ εἴδους Id.*Im.* 2.16. **6.** *correction, reproof,* Plu.2.55b. **7.** *conversion, Act.Ap.*15.3; ἡ πρὸς θεὸν ἐ. Hierocl.*in CA* 24p.473M. **8.** in Philos., *return* to the source of Being, Plot.1.2.4; ἡ ἐ. πρὸς αὐτόν Id.5.3.6, cf. Procl. *Inst.*31; [ἡ ἐ.] τοῦ προελθόντος ἐπάνοδος εἰς τὸ γεννῆσαν Dam.*Pr.*75; ἡ ἐ. τῆς ἐκστάσεώς ἐστιν ἐπανόρθωσις ib.61. **9.** in Logic, *conversion* of a proposition, ἡ σὺν ἀντιθέσει ἐ. *the contraposition,* Suppl.ad Procl. *in Prm.*p.1004S. **-ία,** ἡ, title of Aphrodite, *Verticordia,* Paus.1.40.5. **-ίς** (A), ἴδος, ἡ, *dislocation,* Hsch. **2.** in pl., *curls,* Eust.1561.38. **-ίς** (B), ἴδος, ἡ, = Lat. *anaticula* (part of a door), *Gloss.* **-ος,** ον, *having dealings with, conversant,* ἐ. ἦν ἀνθρώπων Od.1.177; read by Ar.Byz. for ἐπίσκοπος, 8.163; ἐ. τινος *concerned with* or *in* it, A.*Ag.*397 (lyr.). **2.** = ἐπιστρεφής, *curved, winding,* A.R.2.979; ὅρμος D.P.75. **3.** Adv. -φως *diligently, exactly,* Ephipp.3.10, Memn.7.3.

**ἐπιστρώννυμι** or -ύω, v. ἐπιστορέννυμι.

⊛ **ἐπιστρωφ-άω,** Frequentat. of ἐπιστρέφω, only intr., c. acc., *visit* or *frequent* a place, θεοὶ..ἐπιστρωφῶσι πόληας Od.17.486; ἀνέρος, ὅν τε θαμιναὶ ἐπιστρωφῶσι μέριμναι *haunt* him, *h.Merc.*44; γαῖαν Orph.*A.* 830; εἰς γῆν Phryn.Trag.5:—Med., *go in and out of, frequent, haunt,* δῶμ' ἐπιστρωφωμένου A.*Ag.*972; also, *come to,* πόθεν γῆς τῆσδ' ἐ. πέδον; E.*Med.*666. **-ησις,** εως, ἡ, *going to and fro,* κατὰ τὸν σύμπαντα κόσμον Onat.ap.Stob.1.1.39 (pl., -ώσιες codd.).

**ἐπιστύλ-ιον** [ῠ], τό, (στῦλος) *architrave, IG*1².372, *Tab.Heracl.*1.6, *CIG*2751 (Aphrodisias), Plu.*Per.*13, Ph.*Bel.*62.6, Callix.2, Vitr.3.5.8, etc.: also as Adj., ἐπιστύλια ξύλα *IG*1².313.106. **2.** *shelf* with pigeon-holes, Arist.*Ath.*47.5 (pl.). **-ίς,** ίδος, ἡ, = foreg. 1, Ph.1.666. **-ον,** τό, = foreg., *Gp.*14.6.6.

**ἐπιστύφω** [ῡ], *draw up,* of the effect of astringents, Nic.*Al.*79,278; τὰ ἐπιστύφοντα..βρώματα Heraclid.Tarent.ap.Ath.3.120c; τὸν στόμαχον prob. in Plu.2.687d: metaph., of the ears, D.H.*Dem.*38; *reprove,* τὴν ἀπόνοιαν τῶν πλεόνων Alciphr.1.3, cf. Hierocl.*in CA* 19 p.461M. **2.** *apply a second mordant,* as preparation for dyeing, *PHolm.*16.28.

**ἐπίστυψις,** εως, ἡ, *use of astringent remedies,* Plot.4.4.45 (pl.).

**ἐπισυγ-κάμπτω,** *bend together besides,* Hp.*Art.*58. **-κροτέω,** *weld together, combine* in one body, J.*BJ*1.1.6. **-κρούω,** *meet with a check* or *reverse,* D.C.*Fr.*50.2. **-χέω,** in Pass., *to be in confusion,* τὰς περὶ θεοῦ δόξας..ἐπισυγκεχύσθαι Ph.1.320codd. **-χωννύω,** *cover up with earth, Gp.*5.26.2.

**ἐπισυ-ζεύγνῡμι,** *join,* Gal.18(1).741, Sch.Il.2.278. **-ζῠγία,** ἡ, *squadron of* 8 *war-chariots,* = 2 συζυγίαι, Ascl.*Tact.*8, Ael.*Tact.*22.2.

⊛ **ἐπισῡκοφαντέω,** *harass yet more with frivolous accusations,* Hyp. *Fr.*243, Plu.*Ant.*21.

**ἐπισυλ-λαμβάνω,** = ἐπικυΐσκομαι, Orib.22.7.2, Sor.1.23. **-λέγω,** *collect besides* or *after,* Hp.*Off.*11 (Pass.); πᾶσαν τὴν δύναμιν J.*BJ* 1.6.3:—Pass., τὸν -λεγέντα ὀπόν v.l. in Dsc.4.153, cf. Gal.18(1).781. **-ληψις,** εως, ἡ, *second conception, Placit.*5.10.3, Orib.22.7.2. **-λογίζομαι,** *draw a subsequent inference,* A.D.*Conj.*252.5: c. acc. et inf., Iamb.*VP*3.16.

**ἐπισυμ-βαίνω,** *happen besides, supervene,* Arist.*Rh.Al.*1426ᵃ6, *APr.*64ᵇ30; ἐπισυνέβη, c. acc. et inf., J.*AJ*15.7.10; τὰ -οντα ἀρρωστήματα Jul.*Ep.*75b, cf. Herod.Med.ap.Orib.5.30.15. **III.** *come into existence afterwards,* S.E.*M.*9.371, 11.130. **2.** c. dat., ὃ ἂν γενομένῃ τῇ οὐσίᾳ ἐπισυμβῇ Plot.6.3.8. **-βάλλομαι,** f.l. for ἐπὶ νοῦν β., Phylarch.24J. **-μᾰχία,** ἡ, *alliance against a common enemy,* Philipp.ap.D.12.7 codd. (leg. ἐπιμαχία). **-μείγνῡμι,** *add,* Vett. Val.215.6. **-μύω,** *close up,* Thphr.*CP*1.6.3. **-πάρειμι,** Astrol., of planets, *to be present as well,* Nech.ap.Vett.Val.280.5. **-πίπτω,** *collapse, decay,* Ph.2.221, Anon.Lond.27.31; *spring together again,* Str.6.1.12; *contract,* of the heart in systole, Ruf.*Syn.Puls.*3. **II.** *happen besides* or *in addition to,* τοῖς γεγονόσιν J.*AJ*15.10.3; -πίπτουσαι διαστροφαί *casual* distortions, Ptol.*Tetr.*108. **-πλέκω,** *add* a drug to a mixture, Paul.Aeg.4.4:—Pass., *to be combined,* τὸ -όμενον πτωτικόν A.D.*Synt.*124.27. **-πτωσις,** εως, ἡ, *falling together,* Anon.Lond.27.29; *incidence,* ἡ ἔξωθεν ἐ. τῶν πραγμάτων Andronic. Rhod.p.570M. **-φέρω,** *contribute, Theol.Ar.*32. **-φορος,** ον, *contributing their influence, Cat.Cod.Astr.*5(1).180.16.

⊛ **ἐπισυν-άγω** [ᾰ], *collect and bring to* a place, Plb.1.75.2 (Pass.), 5.97.3, Wilcken *Chr.*11 *A* 5 (ii B.C.); *gather together,* Lxx *Ge.*6.16, al., *Ev.Matt.*23.37, etc.:—Pass., *OGI*90.23 (Rosetta, ii B.C.), *Placit.* 3.4.1, Ph.1.338; οἱ -συνηγμένοι ἐν Ξόει Βοιωτοί *Supp.Epigr.*2.871 (Egypt, ii B.C.); *to be combined,* τὰ ἐκ τῶν πληθυντικῶν εἰς τὰ ἑνικὰ -όμενα Longin.24.1; ἐπισυναχθέντες τόκοι *accumulated* interest, *PGrenf.*2.72.8 (iii/iv A.D.), cf. *PFlor.*1.46.14 (ii A.D.); ἐπισυναγόμενος ἀριθμός *counted up,* Ptol.*Tetr.*43. **II.** *bring in,* in a discussion, περιττὸν -ειν καὶ ταύτας Phld.*Acad.Ind.*28. **2.** Astrol., = ἐπισυμφέρω, Vett.Val.288.29. **III.** *conclude, infer,* συλλογιζόμενοι τὸν μεταξὺ χρόνον ἐπισυνάγουσιν ὅτι.. Procl.*Hyp.*5.54. **-αγωγή,** ἡ, *gathering* or *being gathered together,* Lxx 2*Ma.*2.7, 2*Ep.Thess.*2.1, etc. **b.** *collection* of a sum of money, *IG*12(3).1270.11 (Syme, ii/i B.C.). **2.** *collective view, table,* ὁρίων Ptol.*Tetr.*44. **3.** pl., *successive additions,* Id.*Alm.*2.7. **4.** Astrol., *aggregation* of planets in contact, Porph.*in Ptol.*188. **-αθροίζω,** *collect besides,* Hsch. s. v. ἐπαγείρειν. **-αινέω,** *give one's adhesion to,* τινί J.*AJ*5.1.16. **-ακτέον,** *one must connect, link,* τί τινι Dam.*Pr.*83bis. **-ᾰλοιφή,** ἡ, *elision at the close of a verse,* Choerob.*in Heph.*p.226C. **II.** *coalescence of two syllables in one,* Isid.*Etym.*1.35.5. **-αντάω,** *meet at one point,* Theo Sm. p.184H. **-απτέον,** *one must subjoin,* S.E.*M.*10.20. **-απτικός,** ή, όν, *apt to cause a combination,* κακῶν, of the moon, *Cat.Cod.Astr.* 7.115.8. ⊛ **-άπτω,** *join on, subjoin, attach,* τί τινι Hp.*Art.*71, Plb. 3.2.8, Phld.*Vit.*p.43J., cf. D.H.1.87, etc.; *add,* περί τινος S.E.*M.*1.120:—Pass., [λέξεις] A.D.*Synt.*6.28. **2.** = συνάπτειν, μάχην τινί D.S.14.94. **3.** c. dat., *assist, promote,* τῷ τάχει Ph.*Bel.*69.8. **II.** Med., *link oneself with,* τινί Eustr.*in EN*6.18. **-άρχομαι,** *begin together with,* τινί Hippodam.ap.Stob.4.39.26. **-αφή,** ἡ, in Music, *combination of three tetrachords by* συναφή (q. v.), Bacch.*Intr.*84. **II.** Rhet., *subjoining,* Anon.*Fig.*p.146S. **-δεσις,** εως, ἡ, *concatenation,* αἰτιῶν *Placit.*1.28.4, cf. Chrysipp.*Stoic.*2.274; πάντων τῶν ἐν τῷ κόσμῳ M.Ant.6.38. **-δεσμέω,** *act as astringent, Hippiatr.*8,10,34 (v.l. -δεσμεύω). **-δέω,** *bind on top,* Aen.Tact.37.9: metaph., τὴν ἀπορίαν ἐ. μᾶλλον 'tie the knot tighter', Thphr.*CP*2.17.7. **2.** *connect,* as words in a sentence, A.D.*Adv.*133.26:—Med., ἐπισυνδέοιτο ⟨ἂν⟩ τὰ τῆς κοινωνίας Hierocl.p.62A. **II.** *make firm* or *compact,* τὰ σώματα Agathin.ap.Orib.10.7.14. **-δίδωμι,** *rush in together,* of streams, Plu.*Aem.*14. **-ειμι,** (εἶμι *ibo*) *come together again,* ἐκ τῆς φυγῆς D.H.1.63. **-είρω,** *join together besides,* S.E.*M.*1.142. **-έμπτωσις,** εως, ἡ, *succession of words with like terminations and containing the same vowels* (cf. Il.23.116), Eust. 1291.43. **-εργέω,** *contribute,* πρός τι Euryph.ap.Stob.4.39.27, cf. Ocell.4.1, Ptol.*Tetr.*142. **II.** *restrict still further,* τροφῆς πλῆθος Sor.1.56 (-εργεῖν cod.: -έργειν vel -είργειν edd.). **-έχω** γυναῖκα *take to oneself* a wife, Lxx 1*Es.*9.17. **-ήθης,** ες, = συνήθης, Sch.Il.1.35. **-θεσις,** εως, ἡ, *addition,* Vett.Val.280.13, Herm.*in Phdr.*p.107A.; *combination,* S.E.*M.*1.22; τῶν μελῶν Longin.40.1; *complexity,* Marcellin.*Puls.*464. **-θετικός,** ή, όν, *combining*: hence, *eclectic,* of the school founded by Agathinus, Gal.19.353; Leonidas ὁ ἐ. Cael.Aur.*CP*2.1. Adv. -κῶς, κατ' ἐπισύνθεσιν, S.E.*M.*3.40. **-θετος,** ον, *compound*: hence -σύνθετον (sc. μέτρον), τό, *metre composed of* κῶλα *of different* γένη, Heph.15.10. **-θήκη,** ἡ, *additional article to a treaty, Schwyzer*631.4 (Milet. (decree of Methymna), ii B.C.): pl., Plb.3.27.7. **-ίστημι** (also -ιστάω J. *AJ*14.1.3), *cause to coagulate afterwards,* γάλα Sch.Nic.*Al.*373. **2.** *band together,* τινὰς κατά τινος J.l.c.; ἡ φθορὰ ἐ. πλείους τισί Id.*BJ*2.3.4; simply, *incite to conspiracy against,* τινὶ τὸν υἱόν Str.13.4.2. **II.** Pass. with fut. -στήσομαι S.E.*M.*11.119, and aor. 2 and pf. Act.:—*to be collected, gather upon,* c. dat., *Placit.*3.5.10, cf. Procl.*in Prm.*p.645S. **2.** *to be classed along with,* τὸ ποιητικὸν τῆς ἀλγηδόνος ἐπισυστήσεται τῇ ἀλγηδόνι S.E.l.c. **3.** *come into being afterwards,* ib. 3.85: c. dat., μεθέξεσιν Dam.*Pr.*349; *to be made up of,* ἐκ προτέρων τινῶν Iamb.*Comm.Math.*10. **4.** *conspire against, attack* or *resist jointly,* τινί Satyr.*Vit.Eur.Fr.*39x23, *SIG*663.23 (Delos, iii/ii B.C.), Parth.35.2, Socr.*Ep.*15.1, cf. Str.7*Fr.*18: abs., Plu.2.227a; πρὸς τὴν τιμωρίαν τινός D.C.60.21. **b.** *combine to oppose,* εἰ δ' ἄν τις -συνίσταται ταῖς ἐσδόσεσι τῶν ἔργων *IG*5(2).6.15 (Tegea, iv B.C.). **-νέω,** *pile up, lay together,* D.C.40.2. **-οικίζω,** *bring in new colonists,* Str. 5.1.6:—Pass., of a place, *to be colonized anew,* Paus.6.22.5. **-τάσσω,** *contrive against,* διαβολάς τινι J.*BJ*1.28.1. **II.** *bring in as well,* ἑτέραν γυναῖκα ἢ παλλακίδα *PMasp.*6ii 136 (vi A.D.). **-τείνω,** *intensify effort,* Poll.3.121:—Pass., *have a feeling of tightness,* Hp.*Acut.*(*Sp.*) 44. **-τελέω,** *finish completely, PMagd.*2.4 (iii B.C.). **-τέμνω,** *abbreviate,* Sch.Il.2.156. **-τήκω,** *liquefy besides,* Gal.18(2).906:—Pass., of patients, *waste away,* ἐπιξυντακέντες ὤλοντο Aret.*SD*1.14. **-τίθημι,** *add successively,* Archim.*Sph.Cyl.*1.2, Vett.Val.31.25, al., S.E.*P.*2.207, Nicom.*Ar.*1.16:—Pass., Dam.*Pr.*87. **II.** Med., ἐ. τὰ χείλη *close* the edges of a wound, Orib.46.25.6. **III.** Med., ἐπισυντέθειμαι I *have made an* ἐπισυνθήκη, Oikonomos Ἐπιγραφαὶ τῆς Μακεδονίας p.2. **-τρέχω,** *run together* to a place, *Ev.Marc.*9.25. **-ωθέω,** = συνωθέω, Epicur.*Ep.*2 p.47U. (Pass.).

**ἐπισῡρ-ιγμός,** ὁ, *wheezing,* Herod.Med. in *Rh.Mus.*58.86. ⊛ **-ίζω,** = sq., Nonn.*D.*1.71,170. **-ίττω,** *hiss* or *whistle at* a thing, *make a signal by screaming,* Arist.*HA*614ᵇ22.

**ἐπί-συρμα,** ατος, τό, (ἐπισύρω) *anything trailed after* one: *trail* of a snake, Hp.*Ep.*15; *trail* or *track made by dragging* a thing, X.*Cyn.* 9.18. **-συρμός,** ὁ, *laziness, negligence,* εἰς ἐ. καὶ λήθην ἄγειν Plb. 4.49.1, cf. 38.15.10. **II.** *mockery,* Stoic.ap.Stob.2.7.11ᵐ.

**ἐπισυρ-ρέω,** *flow together,* Str.5.3.13, Dsc.4.153; of a crowd, Ph. 2.365: c. dat., D.H.4.55, *Placit.*3.7.3. **-ροια,** ἡ, *conflux,* Ael.*NA* 12.20.

⊛ **ἐπισύρω** [ῡ], *drag* or *trail after* one, τὼ πόδε D.L.1.81; χλαμύδα λαμπράν Posidon.36J.:—Med., ποδήρεις χιτῶνας Luc.*VH*2.46; φελλούς ib.45; φόρτον Porph.*VP*25; γυναῖκας J.*BJ*4.1.10:—Pass., *crawl* or *creep along,* ἐπὶ τῆς γῆς X.*Cyn.*5.13, cf. Ael.*NA*2.23; *to be drawn over, rub against,* μήνιγγι Heliod.ap.Orib.46.19.2; *to be trailed on the ground,* Ph.2.148; *to be protracted,* Just.*Nov.*42.1.2. **2.** *draw gently,* τὸ πνεῦμα Alciphr.3.12. **3.** Med., *draw over oneself,* δέρμα αἰγός Longus 3.24. **b.** *draw up by friction,* Steph.*in Gal.*1.326D. **4.** Pass., *to be impeded* in movements, Aret.*SD*1.7. **II.** c. acc., *do in a slovenly, careless way, slur over, evade intentionally,* τὰ πράγματα Lys.26.3; τὰς πράξεις Plb.29.12.6; γραφήν D.H.1.7 (v.l. ὑπο-); βίον Jul.*Gal.*43b (Pass.): abs., ἐπισύροντες ἐροῦσι D.20.131; ἐπισύρων γέγραφα Jul.*Ep.*4; ἐ. ἐν ταῖς πράξεσι *to be negligent,* M.Ant. 8.51; καταφρονεῖν ὧν οὐκ οἶδεν καὶ ἐπισύρειν Porph.*Abst.*2.53: in this sense freq. in pf. part. Pass., *slurred over, neglected,* Plb.16.20.3; τὸ -μένον [τῶν λέξεων] Phld.*Rh.*1.140S.; γράμματα ἐπισεσυρμένα *slovenly, hastily written,* Luc.*DMeretr.*10.3; φθέγγεσθαι ἐ. τι καὶ συνεχὲς καὶ

ἐπίτροχον Id.*Nav.*2; χρέμπτεσθαι ἐ. Ps.-Luc.*Philopatr.*20; ἐ. καὶ ῥυπαρός *slovenly* and dirty, of a man, D.L.1.81; ἐ. ἤθη *lax* morals, Procl.*in Prm.*p.553 S. Adv. ἐπισεσυρμένως *carelessly*, Epict.*Ench.*31, Sch.Ar.*Ra.*1545.

**ἐπισύ-στᾰσις**, εως, ἡ, *gathering, riotous meeting*, τοῦ ὄχλου *Act.Ap.*24.12 (nisi leg. ἐπίστασις); αἱ τῶν κρατούντων τῆς χώρας βαρβάρων ἐ. *SIG*708.27 (Istropolis, ii B.C.); *insurrection*, Beros.ap.J.*Ap.*1.20, Lxx *Nu.*16.40(17.5): c. gen., *rising against*, τοῦ Κυρίου ib.26.9. 2. *collection*, κακῶν S.E.*M.*11.127; ὑδατίδων Sor.1.58. 3. v.l. for ἐπίστασις, 2*Ep.Cor.*11.28. **-στέλλομαι**, Pass., *to be drawn together, contracted*, of a wasp's waist, Sch.Ar.*Pl.*301: metaph., of style, *to be lowered in tone*, Arist.*Rh.*1404ᵇ17. **-στρέφω**, *collect together*, Lxx *Nu.*16.42(17.7):—Pass., J.*AJ*13.13.3. II. *compress into unity*, Longin.24.1. III. *brace up, restore*, στόμαχον ὑπτιωμένον Sor.1.50(-στροφ[εῖ] cod.). **-σχεσις**, εως, ἡ, *reception*, 1 *Enoch* 22.4.

**ἐπίσυχνος**, ον, neut. as Adv., *generally*, Hp.*Prorrh.*1.140 (v.l. ἐπὶ συχνόν). Adv. -νως Malch.(?)ap.Suid. s. v. Λογγῖνος (ἐπιδείπνως cod. opt., ἐπὶ δείπνῳ Bernh.).

**ἐπισφᾰγίς**, ίδος, ἡ, (σφαγή) *nape of the neck* where the axe strikes the bull, Poll.2.134.

**ἐπισφάζω**, later **-σφάττω**, *slaughter over* or *upon*, esp. of sacrifices at a tomb, κἄμ' ἐπισφάξαι τάφῳ E.*Hec.*505; πρόβατά τινι ἐ. *sacrifice* them *to* the dead, X.*Cyr.*7.3.7 (Pass.). 2. αἷμα μηλείου φόνου ἐ. *shed* the blood of slaughtered sheep *over*, E.*El.*92, cf. 281; αἷμ' ἐπισφάξας νέον Id.*Sthen.*p.44 A.:—Pass., αἷμα ἀρτίως ἐπεσφαγμένον Arist.*Col.*796ᵃ15. II. *kill upon* or *besides*, τρίτον θῦμ' ὡς ἐπισφάξω δυοῖν E.*HF*995, cf. X.*An.*1.8.29 (also ἑαυτὸν ἐπισφάξασθαι ibid.); 'Αντώνιον ἐ. Καίσαρι Plu.*Brut.*18:—Pass., ἐπεσφάγη τοῖς παισίν J.*BJ*5.13.1, cf. Philostr.*VA*4.16. 2. *kill over again*, νεκρούς D.L.2.135. III. *dispatch, strike the death-blow*, Thphr.ap.Porph.*Abst.*2.30, Plu.*Ant.*76: metaph., *talk* one *to death*, Luc.*JTr.*43.

**ἐπίσφαιρα**, ων, τά, *boxing-gloves* used in the σφαιρομαχία, to deaden the blows, Plu.2.825e; so μάχαιραι μετ' ἐπισφαίρων swords *tipped with buttons*, like foils, Plb.10.20.3.

**ἐπισφαίριον**, τό, *tip* of the nose, Gal.18(1).805.

**ἐπισφᾰκελ-ίζω**, *become gangrenous, sphacelate*, Hp.*Art.*14, Aret.*SD*2.9. **-ισις**, εως, ἡ, *necrosis, caries*, τῶν ὀστέων Hp.*Art.*49.

**ἐπισφᾰλ-εια** [ᾰ], ἡ, *precariousness*, τῆς τύχης Plb.38.21.3. **-ής**, ές, (σφάλλομαι) *prone to fall, unstable, precarious*, τὰ μεγάλα πάντα ἐπισφαλῆ Pl.*R.*497d; -εστέρα δύναμις D.2.15, cf. Arist.*EN*1155ᵃ10; ἐπισφαλές [ἐστι] Id.*Pol.*1264ᵇ6; ἐ. φύσει βίος Men.*Epit.*126. II. (σφάλλω) *making to fall, misleading*, εἰς βλάβην Plu.2.653d, etc. 2. *dangerous*, νόσημα Hp.*VM*9; νόσοι Ph.2.413; καιροί Plb.1.66.12: Sup. -εστάτη, χώρα Id.2.29.2; τοῦ ἀγχιβαθοῦς τῶν ἑλῶν 'Ρωμαίοις -σφαλοῦς ἐσομένου Hdn.7.2.5; ἐπισφαλές [ἐστι] παρακοῦσαι Epicur.*Fr.*200. Adv. -λῶς, ἔχειν, διακεῖσθαι, to be *in danger*, Plb.6.25.4, Plu.*Sol.*13; ἐ. βεβηκώς Lxx *Wi.*4.4: Sup. -έστατα, περᾶσαι Plu.*Cat.Mi.*15. 3. *dubious*, Adv. Comp. -έστερον Aristeas314.

**ἐπισφάλλω**, *trip up, make to fall*, J.*BJ*3.7.29, Onos.42.6.

**ἐπίσφατον**· ἐπιμωμητόν, ἢ συνομιλητόν, ἢ ἐπὶ κακῷ ὠνομασμένον, Hsch.; = ἐπιβόητος, Poet.ap.Ammon.*Diff.*p.43 V., *Et.Gud.d.* s. v. διαβόητος; = ἐπιρρητός, *EM*365.11; Eust.1728.12 derives it fr. πεφάσθαι and translates it ὀλέθριος; but cf. περίσφατος.

**ἐπισφάττω**, later form of ἐπισφάζω.

**ἐπισφελίτης** [ῑ], ου, ὁ, (σφέλας) = θρανίτης, Paus.Gr.*Fr.*175.

**ἐπισφετερίζομαι**, *appropriate*, τἀλλότρια Harp. s. v. Σθένελος.

**ἐπισφήκ-ιον**, τό, dub. sens. in *Inscr.Délos* 370.32 (iii B.C.). **-όω**, *bind on* or *to*, Nonn.*D.*9.123:—Med., ib.2.111.

**ἐπίσφην-ος**, ον, *wedge-shaped*, *IG*7.3073.153 (Lebad.). **-όω**, *plug, stop*, Gal.19.654 (Pass.), Sor.2.60 (Pass.). **-ωσις**, εως, ἡ, *stoppage* in difficult labour, Paul.Aeg.3.76.

⊕ **ἐπισφίγγω**, *bind tight, tighten*, κημούς Ph.1.698; νάρθηκας (splints) Gal.18(2).398; πέδιλα ἐ. τοὺς πόδας Luc.*Am.*41; ἐ. τινὰ πήχεσι in the arms, *AP*5.242 (Maced.); ἐ. τοὺς ἀναγωγέας *tie* the shoe-strings *tight*, Ath.12.543f; μοσχεύματα *Gp.*10.12.3: metaph., *shut up tightly*, [θησαυροὺς] κακῶν Ph.1.108; ἐ. τὴν ἀμφισβήτησιν *complicate* it, opp. λύειν, S.E.*M.*2.96; also ἐ. τὴν νήτην *screw* it *tighter, tune* the instrument, Ael.*VH*9.36: metaph., '*screw up*', *intensify*, ὀδύνας (ὠδῖνας cod.) Ph.1.680.

**ἐπισφοδρύνω**, *make rigid, intensify*, Plu.*Cleom.*10; *corroborate, confirm*, Phld.*Sign.*28.

⊕ **ἐπισφρᾱγ-ίζω**, Ep. -σφρηγ-, *put a seal on*, *PRyl.*237.1,2 (Pass., iii A.D.). 2. *confirm, ratify*, θανόντι *APl.*5.366, cf. Vett.Val.354.19:—Med., ἐ. διὰ τῆς συγκλήτου τὴν αὑτοῦ παρανομίαν *get it sanctioned*, Plb.32.6.3; *give one's sanction to*, δόγμα Hierocl.*in CA* 10p.437 M. II. Med., *confirm, ratify*, Pl.*Lg.*855e, 957b, Ph.2.71, etc.; ἐ. τινί τι *give* it him *as a solemn gift*, *GDI*2517.16 (Delph.). 2. *put as a seal upon, impress upon*, [τῇ πολιτικῇ] μίαν ἰδέαν Pl.*Plt.*258c; οἷς -όμεθα τὸ "αὐτὸ ὃ ἔστι" prob. cj. in Id.*Phd.*75d; ἁγνείαν ψυχαῖς Ph.2.381; σιγὴν χείλεσι ἐ. Nonn.*D.*47.218 (but in Hld.6.15 σιγῇ ἐ. τι, and so [ἀριθμῷ] γένη ζῴων -ίζεται *marks with*.., Ph.2.353; -ιζομένην (sc. τέχνην) βεβαιότητι τὰ παθῶν μέτρα Max.Tyr.33.9):—Pass., *to be impressed upon*, τὸ γεγονὸς ἐν ταῖς γνώμαις -ίσθη Plb.15.25.8; *to be marked*, φελλοῖς, of nets, *AP*6.90 (Phil.). **-ισις**, εως, ἡ, = sq., Greg.Cor.*in Hermog.* in Rh.7.1319 W. 2. *cadence* of a verse, Sch.Heph.p.118 C. **-ισμός**, ὁ, *confirmation*, Sch.Hermog. in Rh.7.425 W. ⊕ **-ιστής**, οῦ, ὁ, *one who seals* or *signs*, Luc.*Alex.*23.

**ἐπισφύζω**, *continue to throb*, Gal.4.733.

**ἐπισφύρ-ια** [ῠ], τά, *leg-guards*; in Hom., always of silver, Il.3.331, al. 2. the part *above the ankle-joint, ankle*, *AP*6.206.8 (Antip. Sid.), Opp.*C.*4.438; cf. sq. **-ιος**, ον, (σφυρόν) *on the ankle*, γέρας ἐ., of the *lunula* on the Senators' shoes at Rome, *IG*14.1389 i 31, Philostr.*VS*2.1.8. **-ος**, ον, = foreg., ποδίστρας *AP*6.107 (Phil.).

**ἐπισχάζω**, v. ἐπισκάζω.

**ἐπισχεδί-α**, ἡ, dub. sens. in *PSI*7.858 (iii B.C.). **-άζω**, *say* or *do offhand*, τῷ καιρῷ *make a* suitable *impromptu*, Philostr.*VS*1.2:—Pass., -ασμένα πάντα τῷ καιρῷ Id.*Gym.*54.

**ἐπισχεδόν**, Adv. *near at hand, hard by*, ἐ. ἐρχομένοιο *h.Ap.*3, cf. A.R.2.490: as Prep. c. dat. vel gen., ib.604, 4.948.

**ἐπισχεθεῖν**, poet. aor. 2 of ἐπέχω, *hold in, check*, A.*Th.*453 (lyr.): aor. 1 Pass. ἐπισχεθῆναι Posidon.36 J.

**ἐπισχερώ**, Ep. Adv., (σχερός) *in a row, one after another*, εἰσανέβαινον ἐ. Il.18.68, cf. 11.668, 23.125; ἐ. ἀλλήλοισι A.R.1.528: c. gen., τὸ γὰρ ἦμιν ἐ. ἧεν ἀοιδῆς *the next thing in*.., Id.4.451. II. of Time, τρὶς ἐ. thrice *successively*, Simon.155.5; *by degrees*, Theoc.14.69.

**ἐπι-σχεσία**, ἡ, *thing held out, pretext*, μύθου ποιήσασθαι ἐπισχεσίην Od.21.71. **-σχεσις**, εως, ἡ, (ἐπέχω) *checking, stoppage*, ἐξ ἐπισχέσιος after an *abatement* of fever, Hp.*Epid.*1.7; ἐπισχέσεις γενέσεως Pl.*Lg.*740d; πνεύματος Arist.*Pr.*962ᵃ1; ἀναπνοῆς Gal.7.175; τῆς φωνῆς Plu.*Demetr.*38; πολέμου Id.*Alc.*18; τῶν ἀδικούντων Arr.*Epict.*2.20.23. 2. *delay, reluctance*, ἐπεὶ οὔ τις ἐπίσχεσις οὐδ' ἐλεητύς Od.17.451; ἡ ἐν τῇ Οἰνόῃ ἐ. *delay* or *lingering* there, Th.2.18, cf. *PCair.Zen.*283.5 (iii B.C.). **-σχετέον**, (ἐπέχω) *one must check*, ἱδρῶτας ῥυπισμοῖς (leg. ῥιπ.) Herod.Med.in *Rh.Mus.*58.100. **-σχετικός**, ή, όν, *checking, stopping*, τῆς κοιλίας Erasistr.ap.Ath.15.666a; γαστρός Gal.6.523; ἐπισχετικὸν ὁ πταρμός Hsch. s. v. ἐπιπτάρνυμαι.

**ἐπισχετλιάζω**, *lament over*, Sch.Il.16.686.

**ἐπισχημᾰτίζω**, *make up*, τὸ πρόσωπον εἰς λύπην J.*BJ*2.2.5.

**ἐπι-σχίζω**, *cleave at top*, ἄρουραν A.R.2.662; τὸν φλοιόν Str.16.2.41; *split* the end of a bandage, Sor.*Fasc.*12.514 C., cf. 510 C.:—Pass., Dsc.3.147. **-σχισμα**, ατος, τό, *torn piece, rag*, *EM*555.38 (pl.).

**ἐπισχύω**, (ἰσχύς) *make strong* or *powerful*, τὴν πόλιν X.*Oec.*11.13. II. intr., *to be* or *grow strong*, Thphr.*CP*2.1.4; *prevail*, D.S.5.59, Corn.*ND*7; *to be urgent*, ἐπίσχυον λέγοντες *Ev.Luc.*23.5; ὁ λόγος -ύσει πρὸς συμβουλίαν ἢ διδαχήν Vett.Val.48.6.

⊕ **ἐπίσχω**, redupl. pres. of ἐπέχω, *hold* or *direct towards*, ἐπίσχειν ὠκέας ἵππους Il.17.465; νῶϊν against us, Hes.*Sc.*350; [σελάννα] φάος ἐπίσχει θάλασσαν ἐπ' ἁλμύραν Sapph.*Supp.*25.9. II. *restrain, keep in check*, ἔπισχε μένος Hes.*Sc.*446; τόδε γε [τὸ δέος] οὐδὲν ἐπίσχει Th.3.45, cf. Pl.*Lg.*932e, *Phlb.*45d; τὸ ἐπίσχον *obstruction*, Arist.*Cael.*311ᵃ9: c. gen., ἐπίσχετε θυμὸν ἐνιπῆς καὶ χειρῶν Od.20.266; τινὰ τοῦ θράσους Pl.*Hp.Ma.*298a:—Med., ἐπισχόμεναι ἑανῶν πτύχας *girding up*, *h.Cer.*176; ἐπίσχετ' ὀργῇ χεῖρας Euphro 8.3 (dub.):—Pass., *to be stopped*, ἐπίσχεται τὸ τῆς κοιλίας Thphr.*Sud.*20. III. intr., *leave off, stop, wait*, ἔπισχε *hold!* E.*El.*758. 2. c. gen., *cease from*, τοῦ γράφειν Pl.*Phdr.*257c, cf. *Prm.*152b.

**ἐπισωμᾰτ-όομαι**, Pass., *to be condensed into a mass*, Dsc.5.74. **-ος**, ον, = ἐπίσωμος, in Comp., Id.2.146. **-ωσις**, εως, ἡ, *condensation into a mass*, Zos.Alch.p.107 B.

**ἐπίσωμος**, ον, (σῶμα) *bulky, fat*, *Hippiatr.*9.

**ἐπισωρ-εία**, ἡ, *heaping up*, Nicom.*Ar.*2.15. **-ευμα**, ατος, τό, *heap*, *Gramm.Lat.*4.581 K., *Gloss.* **-ευσις**, εως, ἡ, = ἐπισωρεία, Gal.17(2).413, Sch.Opp.*H.*1.116. **-εύω**, *heap upon*, τινί τι Ath.3.123e; *heap up, accumulate*, διδασκάλους 2*Ep.Ti.*4.3; ἓν ἐξ ἑνὸς Arr.*Epict.*1.10.5; ἀμηχανίας Plu.2.830a:—Pass., Id.*in Hes.*34, Vett.Val.344.12.

⊕ **ἐπίσωτρον**, Poll.1.144, Hsch., Ep. **ἐπίσσωτρον** (as always in Hom.), τό, *metal hoop upon the felloe* (σῶτρον), *tire* of a wheel, Il.23.519: mostly in pl., 5.725, 11.537, al.:—ὀπίσσωτρον is v.l. in Hom. and Hsch.

⊕ **ἐπι-τᾰγή**, ἡ, (ἐπιτάσσω) = -ταγμα, Plb.13.4.3, Lxx 1*Es.*1.18; νόμων ἐπιταγαί D.S.1.70; τὰς ἐ. δυσχερῶς φέροντες Plb.21.6.1; *imposition* of taxes, αἱ ἐ. τῶν εἰσφορῶν D.H.4.19. 2. esp. of oracles or divine commands, κατ' ἐπιταγήν *SIG*1153 (Athens); κατ' ἐ. τοῦ θεοῦ *JHS*26.28, etc.; κατ' ἐ. τοῦ αἰωνίου θεοῦ *Ep.Rom.*16.26, cf. 1*Ep.Cor.*7.6. **-τᾰγίδιον**, τό, *little commission*, *POxy.*2156.16 (iv/v A.D.). **-ταγμα**, ατος, τό, *injunction, command*, *SIG*22.6 (pl., Epist. Darei), etc.; τὸ ὑπὸ τοῦ νόμου ἐ. Pl.*R.*359a; ἐ. ἐπιτάξαι Aeschin.1.3; ἐξ ἐπιταγμάτων And.3.11; ἐξ ἐπιτάγματος D.19.185; κατ' ἐπίταγμα, = κατ' ἐπιταγήν (cf. ἐπιταγή 2), *IG*3.163, 209; τυραννικὸν ἐ. Pl.*Lg.*722e, cf. Hyp.*Dem.Fr.*5, Arist.*Pol.*1292ᵃ20; τὰ ἐ. the *orders* or *demands* of a courtesan, D.59.29. 2. *condition of a treaty*, Plb.1.31.5. 3. Math., ποιεῖν τὸ ἐ. satisfy the *required conditions*, Archim.*Sph.Cyl.*1.2, al. b. *problem*, τά τε θεωρήματα καὶ τὰ ἐ. χρείαν ἔχοντα εἰς.. Id.*Con.Sph.Praef.*; *subdivision of a problem*, Papp.644.9, etc. 4. *tribute*, Lyd.*Mens.*3.23 (pl.). II. *reserve* or *subsidiary force*, Plb.5.53.5, Plu.*Pomp.*69. 2. *detachment of* 8,192 ψιλοί, = *two* στίφη, Ascl.*Tact.*6.3, etc. b. *detachment of* 4,096 *cavalry*, = *two* τέλη, ib.7.11, etc., cf. *PGrenf.*1.18.6 (ii B.C.). **-ταγματικός**, ή, όν, *subsidiary*, of the pronoun αὐτός, A.D.*Pron.*45.12, *Synt.*194.8, cf. Arc.144.7.

⊕ **ἐπιτάδε**, sts. in Mss. for ἐπὶ τάδε, opp. ἐπέκεινα, as Epicur.*Ep.*1 p.17 U.

**ἐπιτᾱδεοτρώκτας**, α, ὁ, (Dor. for ἐπιτηδ–) *one who eats only what is necessary*, Cerc.4.15.

**ἐπί-τᾱδες**, Dor. for ἐπίτηδες. **-τάδιος**· ἐραστής, Hsch. **-τάδευμα**, v. ἐπιτήδευμα.

**ἐπιταινίδιος**, ον, *belonging to a* ταινία, in neut. pl., *SIG*$^2$588.188 (Delos, ii B.C.).

**ἐπιτακ-τέον**, *one must enjoin*, Procl. *in Ti.*1.35 D. **-τήρ**, ῆρος, ὁ, = sq., X.*Cyr.*2.3.4. ⊛ **-της**, ου, ὁ, *commander*, *Gp.*17.2.4: used to transl. Lat. *Imperiosus*, the surname of Manlius Torquatus, Plu. 2.308e. ⊛ **-τικός**, ή, όν, *commanding, authoritative*, Arist.*EN*1143$^a$8; ἡ ἐ. τέχνη the art or faculty *of command*, Pl.*Plt.*260c sq.; so τὸ ἐ. μέρος ib.b. Adv. -κῶς D.S.15.40. **-τος**, ον, *enjoined, prescribed*, μέτρον Pi.*P.*4.236; of the labours of Heracles, Call.*Fr.*7.38 P. 2. ἐπίτακτα, τά, *injunctions, orders*, *IG*5(1).1432 (Messene, i B.C./i A.D.). II. *drawn up behind*, οἱ ἐ. *the reserve* of an army, Th.6.67; ἐ. σπεῖραι Plu.*Sull.*17. **-τωρ**, ορος, ὁ, gloss on σημάντωρ, Hsch., Suid.

**ἐπιτᾰλαιπωρέω**, *suffer* or *labour at*, Th.1.123; πρὸς πολιτικοῖς Pl.*R.*540b; ἔργοις J.*AJ*17.13.3. 2. *labour yet further*, D.H.9.35.

**ἐπιτᾰλάριος** [ᾰρ], ον, *with a basket*, Ἀφροδίτη Plu.2.323a.

⊛ **ἐπίτᾰλον**· πολυχρόνιον, Hsch.

**ἐπίτᾰμα**, ατος, τό, (ἐπιτείνω) *extension*, Plu.2.457c.

**ἐπιτάμνω**, Ion. for ἐπιτέμνω.

**ἐπιτανύω**, = ἐπιτείνω, *stretch*, Hp.*Art.*14; *spread over*, Ζεὺς ἐπὶ νύκτ' ὀλοὴν τάνυσε . . ὑσμίνῃ Il.16.567. 2. *stretch tight*, οὔτοι πόλλ' ἐπὶ τόξα τανύσσεται (fut. Med. in pass. sense) Archil.3; *push home* [a bolt], ἐπὶ δὲ κληῖδ' ἐτάνυσσεν ἱμάντι Od.1.442.

⊛ **ἐπιτάξ**, Adv., (ἐπιτάσσω) *in a row*, Arat.380. II. = συντόμως, *Com.Adesp.*1296; *forthwith, straightway*, cj. in E.*Fr.*292.2. III. *by command* or *pre-arrangement*, Call.*Aet.*1.1.9, dub. in *Iamb.*1.239. (Cf. ἐπιπάξ.)

⊛ **ἐπιταξίδια** (-ίδις cod.)· σιδηραῖ τινες, ὡς ἄγκυραι, Hsch.

**ἐπίταξις**, εως, ἡ, *injunction*, ἡ ἐ. τοῦ φόρου the *assessment* of the tribute, Hdt.3.89: pl., *assessments*, ib.97: *a command, order*, Pl.*Lg.*834d (pl.); κατὰ τὴν τῆς αὑτοῦ ψυχῆς ἐ. ib.687c; κατὰ τὰν ἐ. τῶ Ἀπόλλωνος *Abh.Berl.Akad.*1925(5).21 (Cyrene). 2. *command*, ἄρχοντος ἔργον ἐ. Arist.*Pol.*1326$^b$14, cf. 1325$^a$26; κατ' ἐπίταξιν *imperatively*, Id.*Po.*1457$^a$22. 3. in Tactics, *station on the flanks*, opp. πρόταξις, ὑπόταξις, Ascl.*Tact.*10.1, cf. Ael.*Tact.*24.3.

**ἐπιτάπεινος** [ᾰ], ον, f.l. in Antyll.ap.Orib.9.14.2.

**ἐπιτάρ-αξις** [τᾰ], εως, ἡ, *bewilderment, confusion*, Pl.*R.*518a (pl.). **-άσσω**, Att. **-ττω**, *trouble* or *disquiet yet more*, Hdt.2.139; ἡ κοιλίη ἐπεταράχθη Hp.*Epid.*1.15; πάθει τοὺς λογισμοὺς ἐπιταραττόμενος Plu.2.788e; ᾄδων ἐ. τὰς οἰμωγάς Luc.*DMort.*2.1:—Pass., *to be disarranged*, Sor.1.38. **-ᾰχος**, ον, *liable to disturbance, easily alarmed*, Vett.Val.38.21.

**ἐπιτάρροθος**, ὁ, Ep. for ἐπίρροθος, *helper, defender*, in Hom. always of the gods that help in fight, τινί Il.11.366, Od.24.182; μάχης ἐ. *in* fight, Il.17.339; Δαναοῖσι μάχης ἐπιτάρροθοι 12.180; γράμμα δίκης ἐπιτάρροθον Maiist.59: as fem., τοίη οἱ ἐγὼν ἐπιτάρροθος ἦα Il.5.808, cf. 828; Δίκα . . καλῶν ἐ. ἔργων Terp.6. 2. *master, lord*, Τεγέης Orac.ap.Hdt.1.67; cf. τάρροθος.

**ἐπίταρχον**· ἐπιτάφιον, Hsch.

⊛ **ἐπίτᾰσις**, εως, ἡ, (ἐπιτείνω) *stretching*, [νεύρων] Hp.*Art.*8 (pl.); δέρματος Thphr.*Fr.*172.2; ἐ. καὶ ἄνεσις τῶν χορδῶν *tightening* and slackening, Pl.*R.*349e, cf. Plu.2.99c. 2. *discharge, fire* of artillery, Ph.*Bel.*79.26 (pl.); ἐ. τῶν καταπελτῶν App.*Pun.*93 (pl.). 3. *increase in intensity* or *force*, opp. ἄνεσις, Arist.*Cael.*288$^a$19, al.; ἐπιτάσιες πυρετῶν, opp. ἀνέσιες, Hp.*Acut.*(*Sp.*)54; χειμῶνος Thphr.*Sign.*43; ὄμβρων Plb.4.39.9 (pl.); πόνων Thphr.*Sud.*11, cf. Plu.2.732c sq.; ἐ. εἴς τι λαμβάνειν Porph.*Sent.*32; of style, *intensity*, opp. ἄνεσις, Phld.*Rh.*1.198 S., D.H.*Isoc.*13; *exaggeration*, Longin.38.6; *emphasis*, Hdn.*Fig.*p.91 S.; in Gramm., ἐπιρρήματα ἐπιτάσεως, e.g. λίαν, σφόδρα, D.T.642.13, cf. A.D.*Conj.*223.4. 4. *presence of pitch accent*, opp. ἄνεσις, Phld.*Po.*2.18, *Po.*IVa.4(p.274 H.). 5. *vehemence, asperity*, opp. ἠπιότης, Id.*Hom.*p.33 O.; διαβολῆς Id.*Vit.*p.42 J. 6. = ἐπέκτασις (quod fort. leg.), *Theol.Ar.*55.

**ἐπιτάσσω**, Att. **-ττω**, *put upon* one *as a duty, enjoin*, τι Hdt.5.111, S.*OC*839, etc.; τί τινι, as ἐ. ἄεθλόν τινι Hdt.4.43, cf. 1.155; ἐπέταξε πόνους ἄλλοισιν ἄλλους B.*Fr.*9; ἐπιτάξαντος τᾷ πόλει Γαλλίου σῖτον καὶ Ἀνχαρίου ἱμάτια *SIG*748.25 (I B.C.): c. dat. pers. et inf., *order* one to do, ἐ. τοῖσι μὲν πεζὸν στρατὸν . . παρέχειν Hdt.4.83, cf. 3.159, Ar.*V.*69, And.3.11, etc.: rarely c. acc. et inf., *enjoin* or *order that* . ., X.*Lac.*5.8; with the case omitted, ἐ. ἀποφορὴν ἐπιτελέειν Hdt.2.109, cf. 137: abs., *impose commands*, Th.1.140, al.; τινί on one, S.*Ant.*664:—Pass., *accept orders, submit to commands*, εἰ 'πιταξόμεσθα δή E.*Supp.*521; ἐπιταττόμενος Ar.*V.*686: c. inf., οἱ ἐπιταττόμενοι γαμεῖν Pl.*Lg.*925e: c. acc. rei, ἄλλο τι ἐπιταχθήσεσθε Th.1.140; of things, *to be ordered*, ὁ στρατὸς ὁ -θεὶς ἑκάστοισι Hdt.6.95; so Λακεδαιμονίοις . . ναῦς ἐπετάχθησαν ποιεῖσθαι Th.2.7 s.v.l.; τὰ ἐπιτασσόμενα ἐπετέλεον *orders given*, Hdt.1.115; τἀπιταχθέντα Pl.*Ti.*20b, al.; κατὰ νόμον τὸν ἐπιταχθησόμενον Id.*Lg.*740c; δικαίωσις τοῖς πέλας -ομένη *dictated*, Th.1.141: Math., τὸ ἐπιταχθέν what was *prescribed*, Euc.4.1, al.; πλευρὰς ἔχον ὅσας ἄν τις ἐπιτάξῃ with as many sides as you *please*, Papp.290.26. 2. *use the imperative mood*, εὔχεσθαι οἰόμενος ἐπιτάττει εἰπὼν "μῆνιν ἄειδε θεά" . . τὸ γὰρ κελεῦσαι, φησί, . . ἐπίταξίς ἐστιν Arist.*Po.*1456$^b$16; opp. κελεύειν, *IG*1$^2$.76.33. II. *place next* or *beside*, [Σαγάρτιοι] ἐπετετάχατο ἐς τοὺς Πέρσας Hdt.7.85; ἐπετέτακτο Ἀριστοκράτει Περικλῆς X.*HG*1.6.29:—Med., τοὺς ἱππέας ἐπετάξαντο ἐπὶ τῷ δεξιῷ they *had* the cavalry *placed next*, Th.6.67. 2. *place behind*, ὄπισθεν τοῦ πεζοῦ τὴν ἵππον Hdt.1.80, cf. Pl.*R.*471d (Pass.):—Med., ἐπιτάξασθαι τῇ φάλαγγι λόχους X.*An.*6.5.9:—Pass., τοῖσι μυρίοισι ἐπετέτακτο ἵππος Περσέων μυρίη Hdt.7.41, cf. Plu.*Luc.*31, Ael.*Tact.*29.8, Arr.*Tact.*25.10; Ἀράβιοι ἔσχατοι ἐπετετάχατο Hdt.7.87. b. Gramm., *place after*, in Pass., "αὐτὸς" πάσῃ ἀντωνυμίᾳ -τάσσεται A.D.*Pron.*34.10, cf. *Synt.*138.23. 3. *set in command over*, τινί Arr.*An.*1.24.1:—Pass., οἱ ἐπιτεταγμένοι *set as guards over* the wagons, Th.5.72; ταῖς βασιλικαῖς ἐπιστολαῖς -ταχθεὶς Philostr.*VS*2.24.1, cf. Jul.*Or.*2.63d.

**ἐπιτᾰτικός**, ή, όν, (ἐπιτείνω) *intensive*, τὸ "δα-" ἐ. Sch.Theoc.2.14; of μᾶλλον, A.D.*Conj.*223.4. Adv. -κῶς Sch.S.*OC*632: Comp. -ώτερον Vett.Val.117.36.

**ἐπίταυρον**· ἰσχυρόν, Hsch. (Prob. ἐπίγαυρον, q.v.)

**ἐπιτᾰφ-έω**, *to be present at a funeral*, *SIG*1109.161. ⊛ **-ιος**, ον, (τάφος) *over* or *at a tomb*, ἀγὼν ἐ. *funeral* games, Arist.*Ath.*58.1, D.S.17.117; ἐπιτάφιον (sc. ἀγῶνα) ἀγωνίσασθαι *IG*5(1).660, Plu.*Pyrrh.*31, Luc.*Eun.*4; esp. ἐ. λόγος a *funeral* oration, such as was spoken at Athens over the citizens who had fallen in battle, Pl.*Mx.*236b, D.20.141 (pl.); also ὁ ἐ. (sc. λόγος) Arist.*Rh.*1365$^a$31; title of work by Gorgias; applied to Pl.*Mx.* by D.H.*Comp.*9; ἐ. ἔπαινος Plu.2.218a; ἐ. σοφιστής, of one *who makes such speeches*, Ach.Tat.3.25. II. ἐπιτάφια, τά, = ἐπιτάφιος ἀγών, *IG*2$^2$.1006.22, 12(5).946.16 (Tenos).

**ἐπιτᾰχ-ύνω**, *hasten on, urge forward*, τινὰ τῆς ὁδοῦ Th.4.47; τὸν πόλεμον, τὴν ὁδόν, Plu.*Per.*29, Hdn.2.11.1; τὴν φράσιν *making* it *rapid*, Plu.2.1011e; τὴν σύνθεσιν D.H.*Comp.*20; τῇ Ἑλλάδι τὴν πεπρωμένην Paus.8.51.4:—Pass., ὑπὸ μαστίγων -όμενος Plu.*Ant.*68. **-ῠσις**, εως, ἡ, *hurrying on*, Diotog.ap.Stob.4.7.62.

**ἐπιτέγγω**, *pour liquid upon, moisten*, τί τινι Hp.*Fract.*29, cf. Gal.*UP*14.11, al.; τοὺς ὀφθαλμοὺς δακρύοις Philostr.*VS*2.5.3; ἐ. καὶ μαλάττει Gal.6.122; = ἐπιστάζω, νέκταρ *Anacreont.*53.41.

**ἐπιτέγειος**, ον, *on the roof*, Eust.878.37.

**ἐπίτεγκτος**, ον, as pr. name, Ἥρως Ἐ. *IG*1$^2$.310.82, 3.290.

**ἐπίτεγκτος**, ον, of applications, *capable of being kept moist*, Hp.*Art.*67, Gal.18(1).712.

⊛ **ἐπίτεγξις**, εως, ἡ, *fomentation, embrocation*, Hp.*Fract.*29. II. *moistening*, Id.*Loc.Hom.*17, Gal.10.442; *moisture, humidity*, interpol. in Sor.2.84 (= Aët.16.71).

**ἐπιτεθειασμένως**, Adv. pf. Pass., *enthusiastically*, Poll.1.16.

⊛ **ἐπιτείνω**, Ion. iterat. ἐπιτείνεσκον Hdt.1.186: pf. -τέτακα *PTeb.*19.6 (ii B.C.):—*stretch upon* or *over*, ξύλα ἐπὶ τὴν γέφυραν Hdt. l. c.; ὑπὲρ [τάφρης] Id.4.201:—Hom. only in Pass., ἐπὶ νὺξ ὀλοὴ τέταται δειλοῖσι βροτοῖσι Od.11.19; ἐπὶ πτόλεμος τέτατό σφιν Il.17.736. 2. *stretch as on a frame, tighten, screw up*, esp. of musical strings, ἐ. τὰς χορδάς Pl.*Ly.*209b; ὥσπερ λύραν ἐ. ἕως ἂν ἁρμόσῃ Macho 2.9:—Pass., χορδαὶ -όμεναι Arist.*Pr.*920$^b$3, cf. *GA*787$^b$13, Pl.*Phd.*98c. b. of sounds, *raise* them *to a higher pitch*, ἐ. τὸν φθόγγον καὶ ὀξὺ φθέγγεσθαι Arist.*Phgn.*807$^a$15, cf. 806$^b$27 (Pass.); of pitch accent, Phld.*Po.*2.18 (Pass.). c. metaph., *increase in intensity, augment, heighten*, ἡδονάς Pl.*Lg.*645d; τὰ τιμήματα ἐ. ἢ ἀνιέναι Arist.*Pol.*1308$^b$4; τὰ [τῆς ψυχῆς] γυμνάσια Pl.*R.*498b; ἐ. [τὴν πολιτείαν] Arist.*Pol.*1309$^b$33, cf. 1301$^b$17 (Pass.), *Rh.*1360$^a$25 (Pass.); ἐ. τὴν κρᾶσιν *make* it *stronger*, Plu.2.677f; *heighten* by contrast, τὰ φωτεινὰ καὶ λαμπρὰ τοῖς σκιεροῖς καὶ σκοτεινοῖς ἐ., of painters, ib.57c; τῇ γλυκύτητι τοῦ νουθετοῦντος ἐ. τὸ πικρὸν . . τῆς νουθεσίας ib.67b: abs., *exert oneself greatly*, D.56.13, Arist.*EN*1138$^b$23; *strain matters to an extreme*, Id.*Pol.*1293$^a$26:—Pass., εἰ ἐπιτείνοιντο δυσκατάποτοι if their difficulty in swallowing *increases*, Archig.ap.Gal.12.976; so in pf. part. Pass., *intensified*, ταραχή Epicur.*Ep.*1 p.30 U.; ἐπιτίμησις Phld.*Ir.*p.72 W.: impers., ἐπιτείνεται *increase arises*, Arist.*Cael.*289$^a$3. d. intr., *increase*, of fevers, Hp.*Coac.*114; ἐπέτεινε ὁ λιμός Plu.*Cam.*28; of motion, Arist.*Ph.*238$^a$5. e. intr., *rise*, of price, *PTeb.*8.17 (iii B.C.). 3. *urge on, incite*, τινὰ ποιεῖν τι X.*Eq.Mag.*1.13; τινὰ ἵνα . . *PFay.*112.5 (i A.D.); ἐ. ἑαυτόν *exert* himself, Plu.*Alex.*40. 4. *expedite*, τὰ πράγματα *PTeb.*19.6 (ii B.C.). II. Pass., *suffer more intensely*, τῷ πυρετῷ Hp.*Epid.*5.50; simply, *to be tormented, racked*, ὑπὸ νόσων Pl.*Phd.*86c: then generally, *to be tortured*, ζηλοτυπῶν Luc.*DMeretr.*9.4. 2. *to be on the stretch, screwed up to the uttermost*, αἱ τιμαὶ ἐπετέταντο prices *were 'screwed up'*, D.56.24, cf. Men.Eph. ap.J.*AJ*9.14.2; πολλαπλασίως ταῖς εὐνοίαις ἐπιταθέντες Plb.18.16.3. 3. ἐ. τινί *to be passionately devoted to*, Parth.23.1; also of things, ἐ. [βιβλίοις] Luc.*Ind.*27; εἴς τι D.S.1.37. 4. *hold out, last, endure*, ἐπιταθῆναι πλείω χρόνον, of men, X.*Lac.*2.5, cf. Thphr. *HP*7.10.3.

**ἐπιτειχ-ίζω**, *build a fort* or *stronghold on the frontier* of the enemy's country to serve as the basis of operations *against* him, abs., Th.1.142, 7.47; ἐ. [Δεκέλειαν] τῇ πατρίδι And.1.101, cf. Lys.14.30, Plu.*Alc.*23; ἐ. [ἐν add. codd.] τῷ Φλιοῦντι τὸ . . Τρικάρανον X.*HG*7.2.1, cf. 5.1.2; and in Pass., Δεκελείας ἐπιτετειχισμένης Aeschin.2.76: metaph., ἐ. τυράννους ἐν χώρᾳ *plant* them *like such forts* in a country, D.10.8, cf. 8.36; so τῷ πλούτῳ τὴν ὑπεροψίαν ἐ. Luc.*Nigr.*23; ἐ. [τινὰ] τῇ συνωμοσίᾳ . . πολέμιον Plu.*Brut.*20. **-ισις**, εως, ἡ, *building a fort on the enemy's frontier*, Th.1.142; ἐ. Δεκελείας Id.6.93. **-ισμα**, ατος, τό, *fort* or *stronghold placed on the enemy's frontier*, v.l. in Id.8.95, cf. X.*HG*5.1.2; τινί or ἐπί τινα *against* one, κατασκευάζειν ὑμῖν ἐ. τὴν Εὔβοιαν D.8.66; ἐπὶ τὴν Ἀττικήν Id.18.71; κατὰ τῆς πόλεως D.H.3.43: c. gen., ἔχουσι τοσαῦτ' ἐ. τῆς αὑτοῦ χώρας holding so many *fortresses which command* his country, D.4.5. 2. metaph., τῆς αὐτῆς ἀρχῆς ἐ. πρὸς τὸ μηδ' ὁτιοῦν παρακινεῖν *a barrier* or *obstacle* to . ., Id.15.12; ὥσπερ ἐ. τοῖς υἱοῖς κατάγει τὸν Ἀντίπατρον J.*BJ*1.23.1; τὴν φιλοσοφίαν ἐ. τῶν νόμων *a barrier against*, or *a bulwark in defence of*, the laws, Alcid.ap.Arist.*Rh.*1406$^b$11; ἐ. τῶν ἀνθρωπίνων παθῶν

ἡ ποιητικὴ καθέστηκεν S.E.*M.*1.298. **-ισμός**, ὁ, = -ισις, Th.7.18, X.*HG*5.1.2; τῇ χώρᾳ *against* it, Th.1.122: metaph., ἕτερον κατὰ τῆς πόλεως ἐ. ἐζήτει D.18.87. **-ος**, εος, τό, *wall upon a wall*, Eust.969.5.

**ἐπιτεκμαίρομαι**, *detect* a star *by means of*, ζώνῃ Arat.229; so κείνων (v.l. κείνους) ἧχι κέονται Id.457; *predict*, c. gen., νιφετοῦ Id. 1038, cf. 1129(tm.); *infer, conjecture*, ἐ. οἷος.. Id.142.

**ἐπίτεκν-ος**, ον, *capable of bearing children, fruitful*, Hp.*Aph*.5. 62. **-όω**, *beget afterwards*, J.*AJ*6.5.6.

**ἐπιτεκτ-αίνομαι**, *devise against*, δόλον Opp.*C*.3.405. **-αντῆρες**· οἱ παρασκευασταί, Hsch.

⊕ **ἐπιτέλ-εια**, ἡ, *oversight, command*, prob. f.l. for -μέλεια, Polyaen. 6.9.3 (pl.). II. *fulfilment*, ἐπιτέλειαν ὁ θεὸς ποιήσει τῶν ἀξιουμένων Aristeas 18; καλῶν ἔργων Id.272. ⊕ **-ειος**, α, ον, *bringing to fulfilment*, epith. of Aphrodite, *BCH*49.79 (Delph.); of Zeus, *SIG*961 note 2 (iv B.C.). **-ειόω**, *complete*, esp. a sacrifice, Lycurg.*Fr*.36 (-λεοῦν codd.); τὴν θυσίαν Plu.*Mar*.22; cf. ἐπιτελέωμα. **-είωσις**, εως, ἡ, *after-offering*, esp. in thanksgiving for the birth of a child, Pl. *Lg*.784d. II. *accomplishment, completion*, τῆς εὐχῆς Plu.*Num*. 14, cf. 2.961c; ἐ. τῆς πολιτείας, of the Censorship at Rome, Id.*Cat. Ma*.16, *Flam*.18. **-εσις**, εως, ἡ, *completion*, τοῦ σώματος Arist. *Pr*.894$^{a}$35; θεωριῶν M.Ant.1.16. **-εσμα**, ατος, τό, *that which is completed*, Poll.6.181. **-εστέον**, *one must accomplish*, Isoc.12. 37. **-εστής**, οῦ, ὁ, *accomplisher*, Sch.Lyc.305. **-εστικός**, ή, όν, *capable of effecting one's purpose*, Arist.*Phgn*.813$^{b}$21, cf. Chrysipp. *Stoic*.3.123; *for fulfilment*, ἐ. τῶν εὐχῶν θυσία Hsch. s.v. τελέσσας: Sup., Sch.Il.8.247. II. *capable of celebrating*, μυστηρίων Ptol. *Tetr*.72. **-ευτή**, ἡ, *death*, *Princeton Exp.Inscr*.787[10]. **-έω**, fut. -τελῶ *SIG*229.17 (Erythrae, iv B.C.), Dor. 3 pl. fut. -τελεσσεῦντι *Annuario* 4/5.225.27 (Rhodes, ii B.C.), 3 pl. pf. -τετελέκαντι *SIG*1158.3 (Delph., iii B.C.):—*complete, finish, accomplish*, ἐ. τὰ ἐπιτασσόμενα Hdt.1.115, cf. 51,90; τὰς ἐντολάς ib.157; τὸν προκείμενον ἄεθλον ib. 126; ἀποδείξιας Archyt.4; ἐ. ἔργῳ ἃ ἂν γνῶσιν Th.1.70; ταῦτα τοῖς ἔργοις ἐ. Isoc.2.38; πόλεμον Plb.1.65.2; esp. of *the fulfilment* of oracles, visions, etc., Hdt.1.13 (Pass.), al.; εὐχήν ib.86; ἃ ὑπέσχετο Th.1.138:—Med., τὴν κρίσιν ἐπιτελέσασθαι *get* it *completed*, Pl.*Phlb*. 27c; καλὴν καὶ σεμνὴν πρᾶξιν -τετελεσμένος Plb.15.22.1:—Pass., ὅπως ἂν ἡ εἰρήνη ἐπιτελεσθῇ that it *may be brought to pass*, Decr.ap.D.18. 29; of movements, Hero *Aut*.19.5; [παθήματα] τῇ ἀδελφότητι ἐ. 1*Ep.Pet*.5.9. 2. *bring to perfection*, τὴν γένεσιν Arist.*GA*741$^{b}$5, cf. *HA*539$^{a}$33:—Pass., Id.*GA*758$^{b}$26. 3. Pass. in Logic, of a syllogism, *to be made perfect*, by reduction to the first figure, Id.*APr*. 28$^{a}$5, 41$^{b}$4. II. *discharge* a religious duty, θυσίας Hdt.2.63, Thphr. ap.Porph.*Abst*.2.16, *Inscr.Prien*.108.27 (ii B.C.); τὰ νομιζόμενα τοῖς θεοῖς *PAmh*.2.35.50 (ii B.C.); νηστείας καὶ ὁρτάς Hdt.4.186; λατρείας *Ep.Hebr*.9.6 (so in Med., εὐωχίαν ἐπετελέσατο *Inscr.Prien*.113.61 (i B.C.)): abs., *sacrifice*, τινί Ael.*VH*12.61. 2. *celebrate*, τὴν τοῦ Κυνὸς ἐ. ἐπιτολήν Olymp.*in Mete*.113.14. III. *pay in full*, ἀποφορήν Hdt. 2.109; πεντακόσια τάλαντα βασιλέϊ τὸν ἐπέτειον φόρον Id.5.49, cf. 82, 84; ἐπιμήνια Id.8.41: metaph. in Med., ἐπιτελεῖσθαι τὰ τοῦ γήρως *to have to pay, be subject to*, the burdens of old age, X.*Mem*.4.8.8; ἐ. θάνατον *have to pay the debt of* death, Id.*Ap*.33:—Pass., ἡ δίκη.. τοῦ φόνου..ἐκ Μαρδονίου ἐπετελέετο *was paid in full* by.., Hdt.9. 64. IV. *impose upon*, ἀσεβείας δίκην τινί Pl.*Lg*.910d. **-έωμα**, ατος, τό, *something offered besides the usual sacrifice*, Lycurg.*Fr*. 36. **-ής**, ές, (τέλος) *brought to an end, completed, accomplished*, ποιεῖν τι ἐπιτελές, = ἐπιτελεῖν, Hdt.1.117, 3.141, Hp.*Jusj*., etc.; ἐπιτελῆ ποιῆσαι ἐντολάν τινος *Test.Epict*.1.18; ἐ. ἐγίνετό τι Hdt.1.124, Th.1.141; εὐχαὶ ἐ. γενόμεναι Pl.*Lg*.931e, cf. *SIG*581.5 (ii B.C.); κρίσιν λαμβάνει ὁ πόλεμος ἐπιτελῆ D.H.10.46; of persons, *adult*, Hsch. Ion. Adv. -έως *at last*, Aret.*SA*2.8. II. Act., *effective*, Ant.Lib. 19.3. III. *subject to taxation*, ἔλαιον ἐ. τελῶν *Milet*.3.149.19 (ii B.C.). **-ίζω**, = ἐπιτελέω, in Pass., -ισμένας ἑορτάς *IGRom*.4.1272 (Thyatira).

**ἐπιτέλλω** (A), aor. ἐπέτειλα:—Med., aor. ἐπετειλάμην A.R.3. 264:—Pass., 3 sg. plpf. ἐπὶ..ἐτέταλτο Il.2.643:—*enjoin, prescribe, command*, Hom., etc.—Constr.: c. dat. pers. et acc. rei, ἀλόχῳ δ' ἐπὶ μῦθον ἔτελλεν *spake* a speech of *command* to her, Od.23.349: c. acc. rei only, κρατερὸν δ' ἐπὶ μῦθον ἔτελλε Il.1.25, etc.; μῦθον..ὃν Νέστωρ ἐπέτελλε 11.840; ἐλήθετο συνθεσιάων ἃς ἐπέτελλε..Διομήδης which he *enjoined, prescribed*, 5.320; ἐφετμέων ἃς ἐπέτειλας ib.818; [ἀέθλους] Hes.*Th*.995; so θάνατον ἐπιτέλλειν Pi.*N*.10.77; ἐ. μόχθων τέρματα *fix* them, A.*Pr*.100 (where others take it intr. *arise, appear*): c. dat. pers. only, *give orders to*, ἐπὴν εὖ τοῖς ἐπιτείλω Il.10.63, 13.753, etc.: and so abs., ὁ δὲ σημαίνων ἐπέτελλεν 21.445: c. dat. pers. et inf., *order* him *to* do, 12.84, 21.230; so πέμπων μ' ὧδ' ἐπέτελλε (sc. ποιεῖν) 24.780, cf. 11.765, Od.17.9:—Med., just like Act., ἄλλοισιν δὴ ταῦτ' ἐπιτέλλεο Il.1.295; [νόστον Ἀχαιῶν] ἐπετείλατο Παλλὰς Od.1. 327; ὁ δέ μοι χαλεποὺς ἐπετέλλετ' ἀέθλους 11.622; κραδίῃ ἀνίας A.R. 3.264: c. dat. pers. et inf., Od.21.240: abs., 17.21; ἁγητὴρ υἱῷ ἐπιτελλόμενος Pi.*P*.1.70:—Pass., τῷ δ' ἐπὶ πάντ' ἐτέταλτο ἀνασσέμεν Αἰτωλοῖσι Il.2.643, cf. Od.11.524.—Poet. and later Prose, *BGU*886.2 (Med., ii A.D.), *PThead*.18.4 (iii/iv A.D.).

⊕ **ἐπιτέλλω** (B), Pass., *rise*, of stars, Πληϊάδων..ἐπιτελλομενάων Hes. *Op*.383; Ἀρκτοῦρος..ἐπιτέλλεται ib.567; ἠελίοιο νέον -ομένοιο *h.Merc*. 371: so intr. in Act., Hp.*Int*.39, Democr.14, Arist.*Mete*.345$^{b}$23, Plb. 9.15.9, etc.: the aor. part. ἐπιπλόμενος belongs as much to this verb as to ἐπιπέλομαι (q.v.). 2. metaph. of love, ὡραῖος καὶ Ἔρως ἐπιτέλλεται Thgn.1275. (Hence ἐπιτολή and (later) ἐπιτολή.)

**ἐπιτελουμένως**, Adv. *decisively*, *PMag.Par*.1.2638 (s.v.l.).

⊕ **ἐπιτέμνω**, Ion. -τάμνω, fut. -τεμῶ Antyll. (v. infr.): aor. ἐπέτᾰμον: —*cut upon the surface, make an incision into, gash*, τὸ ἔσω τῶν χειρῶν Hdt.3.8, cf. 4.70; κατὰ μῆκος τὰς σάρκας Id.6.75; φλέβα Hp.*Aër*. 22; ἐ. τὴν σαυτοῦ κεφαλήν Aeschin.2.93:—Med., ἐπεὰν ἐπιτάμωνται τοὺς βραχίονας ἐς τὴν ὁμοχροίην Hdt.1.74; κατά τι in a place, Thphr. *HP*1.8.4. 2. *make a further incision*, opp. τέμνειν, Antyll.ap.Orib. 44.23.2. II. *cut short*, τὰ λοιπὰ τῶν ἐπιχειρημάτων Arist.*SE*174$^{b}$ 29; λέγοντα ἐ. τινά Plb.28.23.3; τὰς προφάσεις Id.35.4.6, cf. 5.58.3; *prune*, Thphr.*HP*6.6.6. 2. *abridge, shorten, epitomize* a book, Plu. *Art*.11:—Med., Luc.*Pr.Im*.16:—Pass., κεφαλαιωδέστατα -τετμημένα Epicur.*Ep*.1p.31 U., cf. Phld.*D*.3.14. 3. *cut off* the view, Man.2.115:—Pass., *to be cut short*, τὰ αὐτοσχέδια ἐ. Ph.2.582.

**ἐπίτεξ**, εκος, ἡ, (τεκεῖν) *at the birth, about to bring forth*, γυνὴ ἐ. ἐοῦσα Hdt.1.111, cf. Hp.*Mul*.1.34, Luc.*Merc.Cond*.34; ὄϊς *GDI*4963 (Gortyn); ἐπίτεξ, οὐκ ἐπίτοκος Thom.Mag.p.124R.; cf. ἐπίτοκος.

**ἐπιτέον**, *one must traverse*, Str.2.5.34 (s.v.l.).

⊕ **ἐπίτερα**· ἐκπιάσματα ἐλαιῶν, Hsch.

**ἐπιτερᾰτεύομαι**, *heighten a marvellous story*, Paus.8.2.7.

**ἐπιτέρεναι**· εἶδος ἄρτων, Hsch.

**ἐπιτερμᾰτίζω**, in Pass., gloss on ἐπικραίνω, Sch.Pi.*O*.6.137.

⊕ **ἐπι-τέρμιος**, ον, (τέρμα) *at the limits*, Hsch.; esp. as epith. of Hermes, Id. **-τερμος**, ον, *adjacent*, *BGU*473.10 (ii/iii A.D.).

**ἐπιτερπ-ής**, ές, *pleasing, delightful*, χῶρος *h.Ap*.413; ἃ καὶ λόγῳ.. ἀκούειν οὐκ ἐπιτερπές Pl.*Phdr*.240e; ἰδεῖν Plu.*Rom*.16; τῶν πεπραγμένων ἐ. αἱ μνῆμαι Arist.*EN*1166$^{a}$25: Sup., τὰ -έστατα Democr.233. Adv. -πῶς, διατίθεσθαι Phld.*Mus*.p.84 K., cf. Plu.*Num*.13. II. *devoted to pleasure* (unless = *pleasant companion*), Id.*Alc*.23. **-νος**, ον, = foreg. 1, in Comp., Thgn.1066. **-ομαι**, Ep. Verb (also in later Prose, Agath.3.21), *rejoice* or *delight in*, ἄλλος ἄλλοισιν ἀνὴρ ἐπιτέρπεται ἔργοις Od.14.228, cf. Hes.*Th*.158; ἵπποις Pi.*O*.5.22; ἀγαθοῖς Thgn.1218; ἐπιτέρπεσθαι θυμόν *h.Ap*.204; Δήλῳ ἐ. ἦτορ ib. 146: c. inf., *AP*9.766 (Agath.).

**ἐπιτεσσαρακοστόπεμπτος** λόγος ratio *of* 46:45, Ptol.*Harm*.1.15.

**ἐπιτεσσαρεσκαιδέκατος** λόγος ratio *of* 15:14, Ptol.*Harm*.1.13.

**ἐπιτεσσερασκαιδεκάτους** τόκους (acc. pl.) interest *at* $7\frac{1}{7}$%, *SIG*364. 90 (Ephesus, iii B.C.).

**ἐπιτετᾰμένως**, Adv., (ἐπιτείνω) *intensely*, ἐ. λευκός Dsc.5.152; θερμαίνειν Id.1.77; *vehemently*, λαλεῖν Phld.*Ir*.p.74 W.; προπίνειν Ath. 2.45d, etc.

⊕ **ἐπιτέταρτος** λόγος ratio *of* 4:3, Theo Sm.p.109 H., Ptol.*Harm*.1. 13, Nicom.*Ar*.1.22.

**ἐπιτετευγμένως**, Adv., (ἐπιτυγχάνω) *successfully*, D.L.2.42, Ach. Tat.*Intr.Arat*.p.79 M.

**ἐπιτετηδευμένως**, Adv., (ἐπιτηδεύω) *deliberately*, D.H.*Comp*.25; κινεῖσθαι Adam.2.38.

**ἐπιτετμημένως**, Adv., (ἐπιτέμνω) *briefly, 'for short'*, ὀνομάζεσθαι Str.4.6.2; *succinctly*, Corn.*ND*35, Ptol.*Tetr*.107, Hld.2.32.

⊕ **ἐπιτετρᾰ-έβδομος**, ον, *containing one plus four-sevenths*, v.l. for τετρακισεφέβδομος, Nicom.*Ar*.1.23. ⊕ **-μερής**, ές, *containing one plus four-fifths*, ib.20, al. ⊕ **-πεμπτος**, ον, = foreg., ib.21.

**ἐπιτετράφαται**, v. ἐπιτρέπω I. 6.

**ἐπιτετῠχημένως**, = εὐτυχῶς, Sch.rec.S.*El*.944.

⊕ **ἐπί-τευγμα**, ατος, τό, (ἐπιτυγχάνω) *a hit*, opp. ἀπότευγμα, Phld.*Rh*. 1.67 S., al.; *success*, D.S.1.27; *'coup'*, Cic.*Att*.13.27.1: pl., ποιητῶν ἀγαθῶν ἐ. D.S.15.6; τὰ περὶ ποιητικὴν ἐ. D.L.8.57; τὰ ἀπὸ τύχης ἐ. J.*BJ*3.5.6; of successful medical diagnoses, Harp.Astr. in *Cat.Cod. Astr*.8(3).137.10. 2. *natural advantage*, τὸ τῆς χώρας ἐ. Agatharch. 89; τὰ τῶν τόπων ἐ. D.S.33.28$^{d}$.2. **-τευκτικός**, ή, όν, *able to attain* or *achieve*, ἕξις ἐ. τῶν βελτίστων Arist.*MM*1199$^{a}$8, cf. Phld.*Vit*.p.24 J.; σύνεσις ἐ. τοῦ μετρίου D.H.*Pomp*.5, cf. Arr.*Epict*.3.12.5. Adv. -κῶς Phld.*Rh*.1.74 S. 2. abs., *successful, effective*, φάρμακον Paul.Aeg. 3.78; ζῆλος Plb.10.22.7. b. Subst. -κόν, τό, *spell, charm for securing success*, *PMag.Leid.W*.8.28 (pl.). II. *advantageous, favourable*, χώρα Plb.2.29.3 (Sup.). **-τευξις**, εως, ἡ, *hitting the mark, attainment*, εὐκαιρία χρόνου ἐ. Pl.*Def*.413c, cf. Arist.*MM*1207$^{b}$16, Phld.*Rh*.1.204 S. (pl.). 2. *success*, App.*Pun*.105. II. *conversation*, f.l. for ἔντευξις in Thphr.*Char*.12.1.

**ἐπιτεύχω**, *make* or *build for*, Ἰλίῳ μέλλοντες ἐπὶ στέφανον τεῦξαι Pi.*O*.8.32.

**ἐπιτεχν-άζω**, *scheme against*, τῇ βουλῇ App.*BC*3.39. II. Med., = sq., Opp.*H*.3.194. **-άομαι**, *contrive for* a purpose or *to meet* an emergency, *invent*, βουλήν Hdt.1.63; τοιόνδε ib.123, 2.2, cf. 119, 121.δ'; πάσας πείρας D.H.4.55. 2. *contrive against*, ἄλλους ἐπ' ἄλλοις πολέμους Id.6.20, cf. Luc.*Bis Acc*.1. **-ημα**, ατος, τό, *contrivance*, Ael.*NA*12.16: pl., *devices*, Ptol.*Alm*.13.2, Jul.*Or*.2. 91c. **-ησις**, εως, ἡ, *contrivance for* a purpose, *invention*, Th.1.71, Arist.*Mu*.398$^{b}$10, Plu.1.296; τολμήματα καὶ -ήσεις παρασχέσθαι εἴς τινα Paus.1.6.6; *artifice*, in speaking, D.H.*Is*.3; *artificial preparation*, ψυχρῶν ὑδάτων Ath.3.124e, cf. Antyll.ap.Orib.10.2.2; αἱ δι' -ήσεως κομμώσεις Ath.13.568a. **-ητός**, όν (ή, όν Philum. (v. infr.)), *artificially made*, Luc.*Prom*.18, *Salt*.27; πυρίαι Philum.ap.Orib.45.29.40.

**ἐπιτεχνολογέω**, *add to the rules of an art*, Alex.Aphr. *in Top*.[518.4].

**ἐπιτηγᾰνίζω**, *fry*, μέλιτι Dsc.*Eup*.2.51.

**ἐπιτηδ-ειόομαι**, *to be made fit* or *capable*, Iamb.*VP*32.228. ⊕ **-ειος**, α, ον: Ion. -εος, έη, εον Hdt.4.158, al. (cf. ἐπιταδεοτρώκτας): Dor. -τάδειος [ᾱ] *SIG*524.36 (Praesus, iii B.C.): regul. Comp. and Sup. -ειότερος, -ειότατος, Th.4.54, 7.86, etc.; -έστερος, -έστατος, Anon. ap.Suid. s.v., Democr.121: Ion. -εότερος, -εότατος, Hdt.9.2, 1.110, al.: (ἐπιτηδές):—*made for an end* or *purpose, fit* or *adapted for*

*it, suitable, convenient*, νομαί ibid., etc. :—Constr.: ἐ. ἔς τι ib.115 (Sup.), etc.; πρός τι Pl.*R*.390b: c. inf., χωρίον -ότατον ἐνιππεῦσαι *most fit* to ride in, Hdt.6.102, cf. 9.2 (Comp.), Th.2.20, Ar. *Pax* 1228, E.*Ba*.508; ἄνδρα -ότατον..δέξαι Hdt.3.134, cf. Ar.*Ec*. 79; so ἐ. τῷ σώματι κινδυνεύειν Antipho 5.63; ἐ. ὑπεξαιρεθῆναι *convenient* to be put out of the way, Th.8.70; τεθνάναι μᾶλλον ἢ σῴζεσθαι And.4.25, cf. Lys.30.24; ἐ. ξυνεῖναι a *fit* person to live with, E.*Andr*.206; also ἐ. ὀστρακισθῆναι *deserving* to be ostracized, And. 4.36; ἐ. πάσχειν D.22.57; ἐκλεγόμενος τὸν ἐ. ἔπαισεν ἄν struck *him who deserved it*, X.*An*.2.3.11; but ἐ. ἐς ὀλιγαρχίαν ἐλθεῖν *likely* or *inclined* to come, Th.8.63; also ὑμῖν ἐπιτήδεόν [ἐστι] οἰκέειν Hdt.4.158, etc. II. *useful, serviceable, necessary*, 1. of things, ὀλιγαρχία ἐ. τοῖς Λακεδαιμονίοις *fit* or *serviceable for*.., Th.5.81; ἐ. τῷ δήμῳ πράττειν Lys.13.51; καταστήσειν ἐς τὸ ἐ. to their *advantage*, Th.4.76; οὐδὲν ηὕροντο ἐ. no *advantage*. Id.1.58; οὐκ ἐ. καταγνῶναί τινος Hdt. 6.97; ἱερὰ οὐκ ἐ., opp. καλά, Id.9.37: esp. as Subst., τὰ ἐ. things *requisite, necessaries*, esp. of *provisions*, Id.2.174, Th.2.23, X.*HG*2.2.2, etc.: also in sg., *what is requisite, needful*, Id.*Vect*.4.38. 2. of persons, *serviceable, friendly*, Hdt.4.72 (Sup.), Th.3.40; τινί to one, Id.4.78, Lys.12.14; ἐ. ποιεῖν τινα And.4.41; ἐ. τῷ πατρὶ *conformable* to his *will*, Hdt.3.52; ἐ. τοῖς πρασσομένοις *favourable* to.., Th. 8.54: also as Subst., *a close friend*, οἱ ἐ. one's *friends*, Id.5.64; Ἀθηναίων ἐ. Id.7.73; μοι ἐ. καὶ φίλος Lys.1.22. 3. c. gen., = ἄξιος, *SIG*1073.19 (Olympia, ii A.D.). III. Adv. -είως, Ion. -έως, *studiously, carefully*, ὑπηρετέεσθαι Hdt.1.108, 4.139. 2. *suitably, conveniently, fitly*, ποιέειν ἐ. Id.9.7.β'; ἐ. σφίσιν αὐτοῖς πολιτεύειν Th.1. 19; *ἐ. ἔχειν Id.5.82: Comp. -ότερον Id.4.54; -οτέρως, διαιτᾶσθαι Hp.*Mul*.1.32. 3. ἐ. ἔχειν τινί to be *on friendly terms* with.., Paus. 3.9.3. ※ **-ειότης**, ητος, ἡ, *fitness, suitableness, convenience* for a purpose, Hp.*Fract*.27; πρός τι Pl.*Lg*.778a, cf. Epicur.*Ep*.1p.9 U.(pl.): *tendency, liability*, Theon Gymn.ap.Gal.6.208. 2. ἐ. πρὸς πόλεμον all *material*, etc., for carrying on war, Plb.2.23.11. 3. *requirement*, ἵνα πρὸς ἑκάστην ἐ. τὸ προσῆκον γένηται Ael.*Tact*.35.1. II. *friendliness, kindness*, πρὸς ἅπαντας Aristid.1.112 J. **-ές**, Adv. *of set purpose, advisedly*, twice in Hom., ἐρέτας ἐ. ἀγείρομεν Il.1.142; μνηστήρων σ' ἐ. ἀριστῆες λοχόωσιν Od.15.28:—later proparox., **ἐπίτηδες**, Hdt.3.130, al., Hp.*VC*11, Ar.*Eq*.893, al., Th.3.112, Pl.*Cri*. 43b, etc.: Dor. **ἐπίτᾱδες** Theoc.7.42: hence, *cunningly, deceitfully*, E.*IA*476; εἰς καιρὸν καὶ ὥσπερ ἐ. *fittingly, as best may be*, Plu.2.577e; cf. ἐξεπίτηδες. **-ευμα**, Cret. **ἐπιτάδουμα** (*SIG*721.12 (Delos (decree of Cnossus), ii B.C.)), ατος, τό, *pursuit, business, custom*, τὰ ἐ. τῆς χώρας Th.1.138, cf. 6.15; μάθημα ἢ ἐ. Pl.*La*.180a; πρὸς τίνα τέχνην ἢ τί ἐ.; Id.*R*.455a, cf. *Euthd*.275b; ἀρετὴ κάλλιστον τῶν ἐ. Isoc.10.54; τὰ καθ' ἡμέραν ἐ. everyday *habits*, Th.2.37, cf. Antipho 3.2.10, etc.; ἐ. πρὸς ὑμᾶς ἄλογον καὶ ἐς τὰ ἡμέτερα ἀξύμφορον Th.1.32; ἐπιτηδεύματα ἀρετῆς, καπηλείας, *practice* of.., Pl.*Lg*.711b, 918a. 2. *habit of life*, Hp.*Epid*.1.23: pl., *ways of living*, Pl.*Phdr*.233d, *Lg*. 793d. **-ευμᾰτικῶς**, Adv. *studiedly*, opp. ἀνεπιτηδεύτως, Phld. *Rh*.1.156S. **-ευσις**, εως, ἡ, *devotion* or *attention to* a pursuit or business, Th.2.36, Pl.*Ax*.369b, etc.; *cultivation of a habit* or *character*, ἐς ἀρετήν Th.7.86; ἀρετῆς Pl.*Lg*.853b; βιότου ἀτρεκεῖς ἐ. scrupulous *refinements*, E.*Hipp*.261 (anap.); τὸ ἐξ -εύσεως, of a *studied* style, D.H. *Lys*.8; of baths, ἐξ ἐ., opp. αὐτοφυῆ, Antyll.ap.Orib.10.2.1; κατ' ἐπιτήδευσιν *as a special study*, opp. κατὰ περίπτωσιν, Gal.2.289; χωρὶς τινος ἐ. Sor.1.59; opp. κρίσις, D.C.63.5. **-ευτέον**, *one must pursue*, Pl.*Lg*. 858d. Adj. -τέος, α, ον, *to be pursued*, Plu.2.10b. **-ευτής**, ὁ, οῦ, *one who practises*, ἀπράγμονος βίου J.*AJ*19.1.5, cf. Ptol.*Tetr*.163. **-ευτικός**, ή, όν, *apt to practise*, ἔργων Andronic.Rhod.p.575 M. **-ευτός**, ή, όν, *artificial, counterfeit*, Sch.Il.5.831. **-εύω**, impf. ἐπετήδευον Pl.*Phd*.64a: aor. ἐπετήδευσα Th.1.37: pf. ἐπιτετήδευκα, Pass. -ευμαι, Pl.*Hp.Ma*.304b, Lys.13.65: (as if a compd. of ἐπί, *τηδεύω, but it is formed directly from ἐπιτηδές):—*pursue* or *practise* a thing, *make it one's business*, c. acc., εὐπαθείας Hdt.1.135, etc.; ἐν τοῖς κακοῖς.. ἀνάγκη κἀπιτηδεύειν κακά S.*El*.309; λαλιάν Ar.*Ra*.1069; εὐσέβειαν Antipho 2.3.11; τὸ δ' ἐπὶ κακουργίᾳ καὶ οὐκ ἀρετῇ ἐπετήδευσαν Th.1.37; τέχνην, μουσικήν, Pl.*Tht*.149a, X.*Ath*.1.13, etc.; ἐ. τι πρός τι *invent* with a view to.., Hdt.6.125:—Pass., *to be practised*, ὅσα κακὰ καὶ αἰσχρά τινι ἐπιτετήδευται Lys.13.65; also, *to be made* so and so *by art*, opp. to being so by nature, Hdt.1.98; of dogs, *to be carefully trained*, πρός τι X.*Cyr*.1.6.40. 2. c. inf.. *take care* to do, *use* to do, Hdt.3.18, 4.170, Pl.*Grg*.524c, Jul.*Or*.1.3d, etc.; also ἐ. ὅπως.. Hdt.3.102. 3. abs. in part., οὐδὲν αὐτοὶ ἐπιτηδεύοντες without any *deliberate purpose* on our part, Speus.ap.*Theol.Ar*.61; ἐπιτηδεύσας *on purpose*, Hld.5. 31. **-έως**, Adv. of ἐπιτήδεος, Ion. for ἐπιτήδειος (q.v.).

**ἐπιτήθη** or -τηθή, ἡ, *great-grandmother*, Theopomp.Com.42. 2. *great great-grandmother*, Poll.3.18.

**ἐπί-τηκτος**, ον, *overlaid with gold*, στέφανον χρυσοῦν, οὐ γὰρ ἐπίτηκτόν τινα Alex.96. 2. *with gold* or *gilded ornaments laid on*, κρατὴρ ὑπάργυρος ἐ. *IG*2².1386.16; στλεγγίδιον ἐ. ib.1544.13. II. metaph., *counterfeit*, ἐπίτηκτα φιλεῖν *AP*5.186 (Mel.); '*veneer*', Cic.*Att*.7.1. 5. **-τήκω**, *melt upon, pour when melted over* a thing, κηρὸν ἐπὶ γράμματα Hdt.7.239; κηρὸν τῷ νεκρῷ Plu.*Ages*.40.

※ **ἐπιτηλίς**, ίδος, ἡ, *horned poppy, Glaucium flavum*, Nic.*Th*.852.

※ **ἐπιτηρ-έω**, *look out* or *watch for*, νύκτα *h.Cer*.244; σιτία Ar.*Ach*. 197; Βορέαν ib.922; καιρόν Plu.*Publ*.17; ἐπετήρουν ἀπιόντας αὐτοὺς Th.5.37; τὴν θεράπαιναν Lys.1.8; ἐ. τὸ βλάβος *watch to detect* it, Ar. *Ra*.1151; ἐ. ὅταν.., ὁπόταν.., Id.*Ec*.633, *Eq*.1031; ὁπότε.. X.*HG* 2.2.16; τί παρ' ὑμῖν ἐψήφισται, τοῦτ' ἐπετήρουν D.19.288: c. inf., ἰδεῖν τι Gal.15.661:—Med., Hld.5.20. II. *keep an eye on*, τινά App.*BC*4.39:—Pass., *to be kept under surveillance*, *POxy*.1413.10 (iii A.D.). 2. *supervise*, *PAmh*.2.77.8 (ii A.D.):—Pass., *PFlor*.1.16 (ii A.D.), etc. **-ησις**, εως, ἡ, *observation*, οὐρανίων Porph.*Abst*.4. 8. 2. *guardianship*, Sch.rec.S.*Ant*.1135. 3. *office of* ἐπιτηρητής 2, *BGU*478.9 (ii A.D.). **-ητέον**, *one must watch for*, τὸν καιρόν τινος Ph.2.305, cf. Heph.Astr.3.1. ※ **-ητής**, οῦ, ὁ, *watcher, scout*, Sch. rec.A.*Th*.36. 2. *superintendent* of taxes, ἐ. ἱερᾶς πύλης (at Elephantine in Egypt) *Ostr*.144 (ii A.D.), cf. 1020, al.; νομῶν *BGU* 478.4 (ii A.D.), *Arch.Pap*.4.143 (ii A.D.); πλοίων *POxy*.2116.1 (iii A.D.). **-ητικός**, ή, όν, *watching for an opportunity*, esp. *to do ill*, Andronic.Rhod.p.572 M., D.L.7.114: c. gen., Plu.2.538d. ※ **-ία**, ἡ, *care*, *Schwyzer*686.4 (Pamphylia).

※ **ἐπιτίθημι**, Pass. mostly furnished by ἐπίκειμαι: A. Act., *lay, put* or *place upon*, of offerings *laid on* the altar, ἐπὶ μηρία θέντες Ἀπόλλωνι Od.21.267, cf. 3.179; λιβανωτόν Ar.*Nu*.426, *V*.96, Antipho 1.18; *set* meats *on* the table, εἴδατα πόλλ' ἐπιθεῖσα Od.1.140, cf. 10.355; πάντ' ἐπιθεῖτε *on* the car, Il.24.264; [νέκυας] ἐπὶ νηυσὶ τιθέντες Od.24.419; τινὶ κύρτον καὶ κώπαν, as a grave-monument, *AP*7.505 (= Sapph.120): Constr. mostly ἐ. τινί τι, τῷ ἰσχυροτέρῳ πλέον βάρος X.*Oec*.17.9, etc.: but also c. gen., ἐ. λεχέων τινά Il.24. 589; ἐ. τι ἐπί τινος Hdt.2.121.δ'; κεφαλὴν ἐπὶ στέρνα τινός X.*Cyr*.7. 3.14: c. acc. only, *put upon, set up*, ἐ. φάρμακα *apply* salves, Il.4.190; δέελον δ' ἐπὶ σῆμά τ' ἔθηκε 10.466; στήλην λίθου Hdt.7.183; φάκελον ξύλων E.*Cyc*.243; ἐ. μνημεῖά τινι to him, Id.*IT*702, cf. *IG*14.446 (Tauromenium), I².1068. 2. *set upon, turn towards*, Ἑκτορέοις ἐπὶ φρένα θῆχ' ἱεροῖσιν Il.10.46; but τῇ δ' ἄρ' ἐπὶ φρεσὶ θῆκε c. inf., *put* it *into* her mind to.., Od.21.1. II. *put on* a covering or lid, ὡς εἴ τε φαρέτρῃ πῶμ' ἐπιθείη 9.314; κεφαλῇ ἐπέθηκε (as v.l. for ἐφύπερθε) καλύπτρην 5.232; λίθον δ' ἐπέθηκε θύρῃσι, i.e. *put* a stone *as a door* to the cave, *put* it *before* the door, 13.370; also, *put* a door *to*, κολλητὰς ἐπέθηκα θύρας 23.194; θύρας ἐπέθηκε φαεινάς 21.45; θυρεὸν μέγαν 9.240 (v. infr. B. II). 2. *set* a seal *on*, *BGU*361 iii 22 (ii A.D.); *apply* a pessary, Hp.*Steril*.214 (Pass.); a cupping instrument, Sor.2.11 (Pass.). III. *put to, add, grant* or *give besides*, ὅσσα τε νῦν ὔμμ' ἐστὶ καὶ εἴ ποθεν ἄλλ' ἐπιθεῖτε Od.22.62, cf. Il.7.364, etc.; κράτος, κῦδός τινι, 1.509 (tm.), 23.400 (tm.), 406 (tm.); ἡμιτάλαντον χρυσοῦ ib.796. 2. of Time, *add, bring on*, ἕβδομον ἦμαρ ἐπὶ Ζεὺς θῆκε Od.12.399; μάλα πολλὰ [ἔτεα] Hes.*Op*.697. IV. *put on* as a finish, χρυσέην ἐπέθηκε κορώνην Il.4.111; περόνην Od. 19.256: metaph., οὐδὲ τέλος μύθῳ ἐπιθήσεις *add* fulfilment, Il.19.107, cf. 20.369; so later ἐ. κεφάλαι' ἐφ' ἅπασι D.21.18; κολοφῶνα ἐ. τῇ σοφίᾳ Pl.*Euthd*.301e; τέλος ἐπιτεθῄκατον ib.272a; πέρας ἐ. τῇ γενέσει Arist.*GA*776$^a$4; πίστιν ἐ. D.12.22, 49.42; ὁ δὲ μισθωσάμενος πίστιν ἐπιθήσει πρὸς τοὺς νεωποίας *SIG*963.34 (Arcesine, iv B.C.); πέρας ἐ. τῷ πράγματι *PGiss*.25.7 (ii A.D.), etc.; ὅρον ἐ. τῷ πράγματι Mitteis *Chr*.87.2 (ii A.D.). V. *impose, inflict* a penalty, σοὶ δέ, γέρον, θωὴν ἐπιθήσομεν Od.2.192; δίκην, ζημίην, ἄποινα ἐ. τινί, Hdt.1. 120, 144, 9.120, etc.; θάνατον δίκην ἐ. τινί Pl.*Lg*.838c; δίκην τὴν πρέπουσαν Id.*Criti*.106b; ἔργων ἀντ' ἀδίκων χαλεπὴν ἐ. ἀμοιβήν Hes.*Op*. 334; τιμωρίαν ὑπέρ τινος D.60.11 (cf. infr. B. IV): so of burdens, grievances, etc., ἐπέθεσαν.. ἐπ' ἄλγεα Τρωσὶ Il.2.39; οἷσιν ἐπὶ Ζεὺς θῆκε κακὸν μόρον 6.357; [ἄτην] οἱ ἐπὶ φρεσὶ θῆκε.. Ἐρινύς Od.15.234; ἀνάγκην ἐ. c. inf., X.*Lac*.10.7; ἐ... μὴ τυγχάνειν *imposing as a penalty* not to.., ib.3.3 (v. infr. B. IV). VI. *dispatch* a letter, ἐ. τι ἐς Αἴγυπτον, ἐς Μυτιλήνην, Hdt.3.42, 5.95; ἐ. [ἐπιστολάς] D.34.28. VII. *give* a name, Hdt.5.68, Pl.*Smp*.205b, etc. VIII. *contribute* (capital) *to* a venture, ἐς πεῖραν *Leg.Gort*.9.44.

B. Med., with pf. Pass. ἐπιτέθειμαι Plu.2.975d, also aor. Pass., *Inscr.Prien*. (v. infr.), etc.:—*put on oneself* or *for oneself*, ἐπὶ στεφάνην κεφαλῆφιν.. θήκατο *placed* a helmet *on his* head, Il.10.30; κρατὶ δ' ἐπὶ.. κυνέην θέτο 5.743, cf. E.*Ba*.702 (tm.), etc.; χεῖρας ἐπ' ἀνδροφόνους θέμενος στήθεσσι *laying one's* hands *upon*.., Il.18.317; κτύπημα χειρὸς κάρᾳ *on one's* head, E.*Andr*.1210 (lyr.). II. *put on* or *to*, as a door, πύλας τοῖς ὠσὶν ἐπίθεσθε Pl.*Smp*.218b; θύρας Orph.*Fr*. 245, al., etc. (v. supr. A. II). III. *apply oneself to, employ oneself on* or *in*, c. dat., ναυτιλίῃσι μακρῇσι Hdt.1.1; τῇ πείρᾳ, τοῖς ἔργοις, Th.7.42, X.*Mem*.2.8.3, etc.; τοῖς πολιτικοῖς Pl.*Grg*.527d: c. inf., *attempt to*.., φιλοσοφεῖν ἐπέθετο Alex.36.3; γράφειν Isoc.5.1, cf. Pl. *Sph*.242b:—Pass., ἐπετέθη πρὸς τὸν πόλεμον *Inscr.Prien*.17.38 (iii B.C.). 2. *make an attempt upon, attack*, τῇ Εὐβοίῃ Hdt.5.31; Ἐφεσίοισι Id.1.26, cf. 102, 8.27; τῷ δήμῳ Th.6.61; τῇ δημοκρατίᾳ X.*Ath*. 3.12; ἐ. τῷ τοῦ δήμου καταλύσει *attempt* it, Aeschin.3.235; τυραννίδι Lycurg.125; ἀρχῇ Plu.2.772d; ἐ. ταῖς ἁμαρτίαις or τοῖς ἀτυχήμασί τινος *take advantage of* them, Isoc.2.3, D.23.70: abs., *make an attack*, κατ' ἀμφότερα Th.7.42, cf. Arist.*Pol*.1302$^b$25. 3. abs., δικαιοσύνην ἐπιθέμενος ἤσκεε he practised justice *with assiduity*, Hdt.1.96, cf. 6. 60. IV. *bring on oneself*, ἐπέθου θύος δημοθρόους τ' ἀρὰς A.*Ag*. 1409. 2. *cause* a penalty *to be imposed*, θάνατον ζημίαν ἐπιθέσθαι Th.2.24; φόβον τινί X.*Cyr*.4.5.41. V. *lay commands on*, τί τινι Hdt.1.111, cf. *OGI*669.61 (Egypt, i A.D.): also c. inf., Hdt.3.63, v.l. in Ath.11.465d. VI. *give* a name, τινί Od.8.554 (tm.), cf. Arist. *Po*.1451$^b$10. VII. *contribute*, πολλοὶ ἐπέθεντο τὰς ἐπιδόσεις εἰς τὴν παρασκευὴν τοῦ πολέμου prob. in *SIG*346.29 (iv B.C.).

**ἐπιτίκτω**, *bring forth after*, Hp.*Superf*.1; τῷ πρώτῳ ἕτερον ἐ. Sor.(?) ap.Orib.22.7.2, cf. Plu.*Phil*.1.

**ἐπιτίμ-αιος** [τῐ], ὁ, (ἐπιτιμάω II. 2) *fault-finder*, nickname of the historian Timaeus, Ister ap.Ath.6.272b, D.S.5.1. ※ **-άω**, Ion. and Delph. **-τιμέω**, Hdt.6.39, *Schwyzer*346.11 (ii B.C.):—*lay a value upon*: hence, 1. *show honour to*, τινά Hdt. l.c. 2. *raise in*

price, οἶνον ἐ. πολύ Diph.32.27: abs., Ael.NA10.50; τὴν αἴτησιν ἐ. raise the demand, Anon.ap.Suid.:—Pass., rise in price, of corn, D.34.39, 50.6, PSI4.356.7 (iii A.D.). II. of judges, lay a penalty on a person, τοῖς ἐξάρνοις ἐ. ταλάντου ἑκάστῳ v.l. in Aeschin.1.113; ἐ. ἀργύριον Hermes17.4 (Delos); but ἐ. τὴν ἀρχαίην δίκην make the original trial the ground of punishment, Hdt.4.43. 2. object to one as blameable, τινί τι Pl.Phdr.237c, Isoc.1.17, etc.:—Pass., Arist.Po.1455$^a$26. b. c. acc. rei only, censure, οὐ τοῦτ' ἐπιτιμῶ D.20.148, cf. Anaxandr.49:—Pass., τὸ..ὑπὸ τῶν πολλῶν ἐπιτιμώμενον X.Mem.1.2.31, cf. Arist.EN1114$^a$29. c. c. dat. only, rebuke, censure, of persons, Lys.24.17; of things, τοῖς ψηφισθεῖσιν Isoc.8.52; τοῖς πεπραγμένοις D.18.64; τοῖς ἀνέμοις Ev.Matt.8.26; τινὶ περί τι Plb.8.9.1; τινὶ ὡς.. D.12.7; τῷ λόγῳ, ὅτι.. Pl.Tht.169d:—Pass., ἐπιτετιμημένος ἐπί τινι Plb.7.12.9. d. abs., λόγῳ καλῶς ἐ. by word, Th.3.38, cf. 4.28; τὸ μὲν ἐπιτιμᾶν..φήσαι τις ἂν ῥᾴδιον εἶναι D.1.16, cf. Arist.Pol.1284$^a$27. -ή, Dor. -ά, ἡ, = ἐπιτιμία I, SIG 254A11, 257.10 (Delph., iv B.C.), 417.12 (ibid., iii B.C.), etc. II. = ἐπιτιμία II, PPetr.3pp.41,48 (pl., iii B.C.). -ημα, ατος, τό, legal penalty, IG1$^2$.75, 11(2).199A65 (Delos, iii B.C.), etc. 2. censure, criticism, Arist.Po.1461$^b$22 (pl.), Plu.2.1110e (pl.). ❀ -ησις, εως, ἡ, castigation, censure, criticism, Th.7.48, Antiph.258, Arist.Rh.1355$^a$24; ἐπιτίμησιν ἐπιτιμᾶν Id.Pol.1340$^b$40: pl., D.S.5.1. II. enhancement in price, σίτου App.BC4.117. 2. Rhet., heightening, by use of a stronger term, Alex.Fig.2.28. -ητέον, one must censure, τινί Arist.Top.118$^a$24, Plb.8.35.2, Ph.2.437, al. II. Adj. -ητέος, α, ον, censurable, Arist.MM1202$^b$22. -ητήρ, ῆρος, ὁ, = sq. II, Opp.H.1.682. -ητής, οῦ, ὁ, estimator, valuer, Antipho5.32, IG1$^2$.75, 2$^2$.1176, 11(2).287A87 (iii B.C.), al.; ἔργων appraiser, overseer (i.e. Zeus), A.Pr.77. II. punisher, chastiser, κολασταὶ κἀπ. κακῶν S.Fr.533; τούτων κολαστὴν κἀπιτιμητὴν E.Supp.255; διακωλυταὶ καὶ ἐ. τῆς..ὁμιλίας Pl.Phdr.240a. -ητικός, ή, όν, censorious, critical, Luc.JTr.23; λόγος ἐ. Pl.Def.416 fin.; σχῆμα D.H.Th.44; ἐμειδίασεν -ητικόν Aristaenet.1.4; προσβλέψας ἡμῖν -κόν τι Gal.8.655. -ητός, όν, liable to penalties, dub. in BGU747 ii 7 (ii A.D.). -ήτωρ, ορος, ὁ, avenger, Ζεὺς ἐ. ἱκετάων τε ξείνων τε, i.e. Zeus ξένιος, Od.9.270. -ία, ἡ, the condition of an ἐπίτιμος, enjoyment of all civil rights and privileges, opp. ἀτιμία, Aeschin.2.88, D.21.106; τὸ συνειλεγμένον εἰς τὴν ἐ. money collected for the recovery of the franchise, Id.18.312; ἡ ἐ. σου οὐδὲν βλαβήσεται POxy.1435.10 (iii A.D.), cf. Schwyzer328.11 (Delph., iii B.C.). II. punishment, penalty, Lxx Wi.3.10, OGI 669.43 (Egypt, i A.D.). III. dignity, respect, ἀξιώματος Artem.1.45; good name, πάντα ποιεῖν ὑπὲρ τῆς ἰδίας ἐ. Ph.2.312. -ιον, τό, mostly in pl., ἐπιτίμια, τά, value, price, or estimate of a thing, i.e., 1. the honours paid to a person, ἔστ' Ὀρέστου ταῦτα τἀπ. S.El.915 (nisi leg. τἀπιτύμβια). 2. assessment of damages, penalty or penalties, ἐ. διδόναι τινί inflict.., Hdt.4.80, cf. E.Hec.1086, etc.; τῶνδε τἀπ. for these things, A.Pers.823; τοῖς ἐ. ἔνοχοι τοῦ φόνου Antipho4.1.4; τὰ ἐκ τῶν νόμων ἐ. Lycurg.4; ἐ. δυσσεβείας the wages of ungodliness, S.El.1382, cf. X.Mem.3.12.3; κρίσεις..μεγάλ' ἔχουσαι τἀπιτίμια D.18.14: in sg., τοὐπιτίμιον λαβεῖν exact the penalty, A.Th.1026; ἐ. ἔπεστί τινι Is.3.47; θάνατον ἔταξε τὸ ἐ. Arist.Oec.1349$^b$30; ἐ. ὀφίλειν τινὶ IG2$^2$.1104; τριπλάσια τὰ ἐ. ἀποτεισάτω PHal.1.208 (iii B.C.), cf. Foed.Delph. Pell.2A21. ❀ -ιος, α, ον, honourable, πόλις IG12(8).528 (Thasos). ❀ -ος, ον, of a citizen, in possession of his rights and franchises (τιμαί), opp. ἄτιμος (q.v.), Ar.Ra.702, And.1.73, Th.5.34, X.HG2.2.11, etc.; χρήματα ἐ. property not confiscated, though the owner was in exile, Lexap.D.23.44. II. valuable, Agath.1.8. 2. subject to penalty: hence, contraband, ἐλαϊκόν PTeb.39.10 (ii B.C.). 3. Subst. ἐπίτιμον, τό, = ἐπιτίμιον 2, SIG685.81 (pl., Crete, ii B.C.), PRev. Laws43.8 (iii B.C., Test.Epict.6.31, PGen.1.30.15 (ii B.C.), etc.

**ἐπιτίνω**, punish, dub. in SIG1208.9 (Thespiae, ii B.C.).

**ἐπιτίτθιος**, ον, at the breast, παῖς AP11.243 (Nicarch.): Subst., ὁ, a suckling, Theoc.24.54.

**ἐπιτιτράω**, aor. 1 inf. ἐπιτρῆσαι, pierce, cut holes in stones, IG11(2).161A55 (Delos, iii B.C.); trepan, Heliod.ap.Orib.46.15.3.

***ἐπιτλάω**, only aor. 2 ἐπέτλην, bear patiently, be patient, τῷ τοι ἐπιτλήτω κραδίη Il.23.591; τῷ τοι ἐπιτλήτω κραδίη μύθοισιν ἐμοῖσιν let it listen patiently to them, 19.220; μυρί' ἐπιτλὰς Nic.Al.241.

**ἐπιτμήγω**, Ep. for ἐπιτέμνω, A.R.4.707.

**ἐπιτμητέον**, one must summarize, Nicom.Ar.2.28.

**ἐπιτοκ-ία**, ἡ, compound interest, Ph.2.285 (pl.); dub. cj. in Thphr. Char.10.2. -ίζω, make liable to a higher rate of interest, SIG364.48 (Ephesus, iii B.C.):—Pass., ib.50. -ιον, τό, = ἐπιτοκία, BGU223.7 (ii A.D.), v.l. in Aesop.177b (p.257 Chambry) (pl.). -ος, ον, (τόκος I) near childbirth, Hp.Superf.17, Antiph.306 (condemned by Phryn. 310), Arist.HA573$^a$2, etc.: heterocl. acc. sg. ἐπίτοκα IG5(1).1390.33 (Andania). 2. fruitful, having borne children, Hp.Epid.6.8.32. II. (τόκος II) bearing interest upon interest, τόκοι ἐ. compound interest, Pl. Lg.842d.

**ἐπιτολή**, ἡ, (ἐπιτέλλω (B)) the rising of a star, ἄστρων E.Ph.1116 (pl.), cf. Archyt.1, Ptol.Alm.8.4: hence, the season of a star's appearance in the heavens, Hp.Aër.2, Thphr.CP2.19.4, etc.; Ἀρκτούρου Th.2.78 (pl.); Κυνός Arist.HA602$^a$26; τῆς Πλειάδος Plb.4.37.2; later of the sun or moon, App.BC5.90, Philostr.VA6.4 (pl.), Artem.1.3 (pl.):—as explained by Gem.13.3, ἐ. = rising (ἀνατολή) of a star as the sun rises or sets (ἐ. ἀληθινή, ἑῴα ἢ ἑσπερία), or just before sunrise or after sunset (ἐ. φαινομένη). 2. rising of the wind, Palaeph.17 (pl., s.v.l.); rise or source of a river, or perh. = ἐπιπολή I. 1, dub.l. in GDI 5075.52 (Latos).

**ἐπιτολμ-άω**, submit or endure to do, σοὶ ἐπιτολμάτω κραδίη καὶ θυμὸς ἀκούειν Od.1.353, cf. Thgn.445: abs., ἐπετόλμησε he stood firm, Od.17.238. 2. dare, venture, abs., Ph.1.594: c. inf., ib.671, al., Gal. 12.710: c. dat., venture upon, τῇ διαβάσει, ἔργῳ, Plu.Phil.10, Ant.69; τῷ δίφρῳ mount it, Philostr.Im.1.11; ἐ. τινί Ruf.Ren.Ves.2.36, Ael. NA7.19, Anon.ap.Suid. s.v. ἀστάθμητον. -ητέον, one must venture, c. inf., Ph.1.2, v.l. in Max.Tyr.24.4: c. dat., Gal.UP14.6, Orib. Fr.138. -ητός, όν, to be ventured, Max.Tyr.24.4 (v.l. -ητέον).

**ἐπιτομ-ή**, ἡ, (ἐπιτέμνω) cutting on the surface, incision, τῆς κεφαλῆς Aeschin.3.51, cf. Ph.Bel.64.1. II. epitome, abridgement, φυσικῶν Arist.Pr.891$^a$7; ἐ. καὶ στοιχείωσις Epicur.Ep.1 p.4 U.; title of works by Chrysippus, etc., Stoic.2.5, etc.; ἐ. κεφαλαιώδεις D.H.1.5, cf. Lxx 2Ma.2.28; ἐν ἐπιτομῇ briefly, Cic.Att.5.20.1; ἐ. τῆς οἰκουμένης, of Rome, Ath.1.20b. III. right of cutting, εἰ δέ κα ἀμπέλους, ἐπιτομὰ ἔστω Supp.Epigr.2.293.11 (Delph., iii/ii B.C.). -ικός, ή, όν, compendious, πραγματεία Gal.9.479 (-ατικ- codd.). Adv. -κῶς Phld.Lib.p.47 O., Theo Sm.p.116 H., Suid. s.v. Εὐτρόπιος. -ος, ον, cut off, ἐ. ξύλα timber cut in short lengths for the joiner, Thphr.HP 5.1.12, cf. 3.13.1 (of bark). 2. short, compendious, ὁδός D.H.1.68, Ph.2.25; τὰ ἐ. τῆς χώρας Paus.10.31.7; ἐπίτομον δείξας ἢ λεωφόρον D.Chr.18.4; περαιώσεις Hld.10.4. 3. abridged, Max.Tyr.31.2, Suid. s.v. Διογενειανός. Adv. -ως Phld.Sign.28: Comp. -ώτερον A D.Pron.3.8, Synt.215.9.

**ἐπιτόν-αιον**, τό, Archit., perh. tie-beam, IG2$^2$.1682.23 (Eleusis, iii B.C.). ❀ -ιον, τό, peg or key by which the strings of an instrument are tuned, ἐ. ψαλτηρίου (-ήριον cod.) prob. in Ath.10.456d: metaph., ἡ συντροφία ὥσπερ ἐ. ἐστι τῆς εὐνοίας Plu.2.3d. 2. pitch-pipe for giving the note to a choir, Et.Gud.d. s.v. ἀπότομον. II. any peg shaped like ἐ. I, Orib.49.4.26, al.; handle of a tap, turn-cock, Hero Aut.13.5, Varro RR3.5.16, Vitr.9.8.11, Ulp.ap.Dig.19.1.17.8; handle of a syringe, Hero Spir.2.18. 2. valve or stop in an organ-pipe, Vitr.10.8.5. 3. pl., sockets in which a roller was set, Bito49.10. -ος, ον, on the stretch, strained, intense, D.S.10.17; of sound, Philostr.VS1.25.7. II. ἐπίτονος (sc. ἱμάς), ὁ, a rope for stretching or tightening, back-stay of a mast (opp. πρότονος), ἐπ' αὐτῷ [ἱστῷ] ἐπίτονος βέβλητο, βοὸς ῥινοῖο τετευχώς Od.12.423 (a στίχος ἀκέφαλος). 2. ἐπίτονοι, οἱ, the great sinews of the shoulder and arm, Pl.Ti.84e, Arist.HA515$^b$9 (sg.); νεύρων ἐπίτονοι Pl.Lg.945c. -όω, brace, 'tune up', Sor.1.25; τὰς ἕξεις ὁ ψυχρὸς οἶνος ἐ. Gal.15.195.

**ἐπιτοξ-άζομαι**, shoot at, τῷ δ' ἐπετοξάζοντο Il.3.79; also in late Prose, Luc.Cal.12, D.C.74.6: abs., Agath.3.22. -εύω, = foreg., τινί D.C.68.31; ταῖς τῶν ὀμμάτων βολαῖς Aristaenet.1.1: abs., Agath. 5.19. ❀ -ίς, ίδος, ἡ, dub. sens. in IG2$^2$.1357 (iv B.C.). 2. = sq., Vitr.10.10.4 codd. -ῖτις, ιδος, ἡ, groove or slot for the arrow in a catapult, Ph.Bel.73.51, 75.2, Hero Bel.77.10, cj. in Vitr.10.10.4.

**ἐπιτοπ-ίζω**, = κατοικίζω, Suid. -ιος, ον, on the spot, Sch.Opp. H.1.596.

**ἐπιτόπως**, Adv. suitably, κείμενοι ἐ., χρηματίζοντες ἐ., of stars, Vett.Val.5.3,7, al.

**ἐπιτόσσαις**, Aeol. part. of ἐπέτοσσε (q.v.).

**ἐπιτρᾰγημᾰτίζω**, serve up as dessert, Arist.(Fr.105)ap.Jul.Ep.180 (Pass.).

**ἐπιτρᾰγ-ία**, ἡ, epith. of Aphrodite, from a she-goat, which was changed into a he-goat (τράγος), Plu.Thes.18, IG3.335. -ίας, ου, ὁ, a kind of fish, which is barren and so grows fat (cf. sq.), Arist.HA 538$^a$14. -οι, οἱ, (τραγάω) the over-luxuriant shoots of a vine, D.H.19.1, Poll.7.152; gloss on ἐπιφυλλίδες, EM367.20. -ῳδέω, make a tragic story of a thing, exaggerate, Thphr.HP9.8.5, D.H.Th.28, Plu.Art.18 (Pass.), Luc.Tox.12; οὐδὲν ἐ. πρὸς σεμνότερον ὄγκον Ph.2.105; descant solemnly upon, τινί Plu.Per.28, Demetr.Eloc.122; lament tragically, Hld.1.3; add to a tragedy, καινὸν ἐπεισόδιον Id.7.6, cf. 2.29.

**ἐπιτρᾰπεζ-ίδιος**· ὁ παράσιτος, Hsch. ❀ -ιος, ον, on or at table, ὕδωρ Luc.Herm.68; λέξις Eust.1561.58; seated on a table, Ἡρακλῆς, of a statuette, Stat.Silv.4.6 tit. II. = foreg., Hsch. s.v. τραπεζῆες. -ος, ον, = foreg. I, τὰ ἐ. σκεύη Thphr.Lap.42. ❀ -ωμα, ατος, τό, a dish set on table, Pl.Com.74, cf. Ath.4.170e.

**ἐπιτρᾰπέουσι**, Ep. 3 pl. pres. for ἐπιτρέπουσι, Il.10.421.

**ἐπιτρᾰχήλιος**, ον, (τράχηλος) on the neck, κόσμος Suid.

**ἐπιτρεπ-τέον**, one must commit, permit, c. dat., X.Hier.8.9, Pl. Smp.213e; τινὶ περί τινος Men.Epit.2; τινί c. inf., Jul.Or.2.85d: also pl., ἐκείνοισι..οὐκ ἐπιτρεπτέα ἐστί Hdt.9.58. -τικός, ή, όν, hortatory, Aristid.2.310 J.; encouraging, γυμνάσιον νεύρων καταλλάξεως ἐπιτρεπτικόν Antyll.ap.Orib.6.35.1. ❀ -ω, Ion. -τράπω [ᾰ] Hdt.3.81: fut. -τρέψω; Dor. 3 pl. -τρέψοντι Pi.O.6.21; Cret. inf. -τραψῆν GDI 5039.21, 5024.12: aor. 1 -έτρεψα Il.10.116, etc.: aor. 2 -έτραπον ib. 59: pf. -τέτρᾰφα Plb.30.6.6:—Med., fut. -τρέψομαι (v.l. -τράψ-) Hdt.3.155: aor. 2 -ετρᾰπόμην Od.9.12:—Pass., fut. -τετράψομαι Pisistr.ap.D.L.1.54: aor. 1 -ετρέφθην Antipho4.3.5; Ion. -ετράφθην, part. -τραφθείς Hdt.1.7: aor. 2 -ετράπην [ᾰ] Th.5.31: pf. (v. infr. I.6):—prop. to turn to or towards, used by Hom. in aor. 2 Med., σοὶ.. θυμὸς ἐπετράπετο εἴρεσθαι thy mind inclined itself to ask, Od.9.12. b. to overturn upon, τινί τι Luc.Lex.8. 2. turn over to, transfer, bequeath, παισὶν ἐπιτρέψειεν ἕκαστος κτήματ' ἐνὶ μεγάροισι Od.7.149. 3. commit, entrust to another as trustee, guardian, or vicegerent, οἱ.. ἐπέτρεπεν οἶκον ἅπαντα 2.226; ἐπιτρέψειας ἕκαστα δμῳάων [ἐκείνῃ] ἥ τις ..ἀρίστη 15.24, cf. Il.17.509; θεοῖσι μῦθον ἐπιτρέψαι leave it to them, Od.22.289, cf. 19.502; so κἀκοισι θῦμον ἐπιτρέπην (Aeol. inf.) Alc.35.1; σμικραῖς ἑαυτοὺς ἐ. ἐλπίσιν E.Fr.921; freq. in Prose, ἐ. τινὶ τὰ

πρήγματα Hdt.6.26; τὴν πόλιν Id.4.202; Νάξον Λυγδάμι Id.1.64; τὰ πάντα Th.2.65; πλεῖστα τῷ ἀλογίστῳ Id.5.99; τὴν ἀρχήν X.*An.*6.1.31, etc.; also a son for education, Pl.*La.*200d: c. dat. et inf., τινά τινι γεροντογωγεῖν Ar.*Eq.*1098: freq. in Att., *refer* a legal issue to any one, τινὶ δίαιταν D.59.45; διάγνωσις -τετράφθω τῷ ἐπιμελητῇ Pl.*Lg.*936a; οἷς (attracted for ἃ) ἂν ἐπιτρέψωσιν οἱ δὲ τάξωσι, τούτοις ἐμμένειν, i.e. acquiesce in the court and abide by its decision, ib.784c (for the constr. cf. And.3.34 fin.). **4.** c. dat. only, *rely upon, leave to,* τοῖσιν γὰρ ἐπετράπομέν γε μάλιστα Il.10.59; ἐπιτρέψαι δὲ θεοῖσιν Od.21.279; ἐ. τῇ ὀλιγαρχίῃ Hdt.3.81; ὥς οἱ (sc. ἰατρῷ) ἐπέτρεψε ib.130: c. dat. et inf., σοὶ ἐπέτρεψεν πονέεσθαι he *left* it to you to work, Il.10.116, cf. 421, Hdt.9.10: freq. in Att., *refer the matter* to a person, *leave it to his arbitration,* Ar.*Ach.*1115, *V.*521, *Ra.*811; τινὶ δικαστῇ to one as a judge, Th.4.83; τῷ ἐν Δελφοῖς μαντείῳ Id.1.28; ἐ. τῷ θεῷ περί τινος Pl.*Grg.*512e, cf. *Alc.*1.117e; ὑμῖν ἐπιτρέπω καὶ τῷ θεῷ κρῖναι Id.*Ap.*35d; Ἀθηναίοις ἐ. περὶ σφῶν αὐτῶν πλὴν θανάτου *to leave* their case to the A. save as to the penalty of death, Th.4.54; περὶ ὧν διαφερόμεθα τοῖς οἰκείοις ἐ. D.27.1:—Pass., δίκης Λακεδαιμονίοις ἐπιτραπείσης Th.5.31. **5.** Med., *entrust oneself, leave one's case to,* τινί Hdt.1.96; διαιτητῇ Id.5.95, cf. X.*An.*1.5.8; also, *to entrust what is one's own to* another, Hdt.3.155,157. **6.** Pass., *to be entrusted,* ᾧ λαοί τ' ἐπιτετράφαται (3 pl. pf. for ἐπιτετραμμένοι εἰσί) Il.2.25; τῇς (sc. Ὥραις) ἐπιτέτραπται μέγας οὐρανός heaven's gate *is committed to* them (to open and to shut), 5.750, cf. Hdt.3.142; ὑπό τινων ἐπιτρεφθῆναι (sc. ἰατρῷ), of a patient, Antipho 4.3.5: c. acc. rei, ἐπιτρέπομαί τι I *am entrusted with* a thing, ἐπιτραφθέντες τὴν ἀρχήν Hdt.1.7; ἐπιτετραμμένοι τὴν φυλακήν Th.1.126. **II.** *give up, yield,* Ποσειδάωνι δὲ νίκην πᾶσαν ἐπέτρεψας Il.21.473; later ἐ. τινί c. inf., *permit, suffer,* Ar.*Pl.*1078, Pl.*Chrm.*171e, etc.: c. acc. et inf., X.*An.*7.7.8; also ἐ. Θηβαίοις αὐτονόμους εἶναι Id.*HG*6.3.9; οὐδενὶ ἐ. κακῷ εἶναι Id.*An.*3.2.31; ἐ. ἀδικέοντι τῷ ἀδελφεῷ Hdt.2.120; μὴ ἐ. τῷ ἀσεβοῦντι Pl.*Euthphr.*5e: abs., *give way,* Pi.*O.*6.21, Ar.*Nu.*799, *Pl.*915, Th.1.71, Pl.*Ap.*35b:—Pass., ἄνευ τοῦ ἐπιτραπῆναι without *leave,* *POxy.*474.40 (ii A.D.). **2.** intr., *give way,* οὐ μὲν ἐπέτρεπε γήραϊ λυγρῷ Il.10.79; *indulge,* μὴ πάντα ἡλικίῃ καὶ θυμῷ ἐπίτρεπε Hdt.3.36; ταις ἡδοναῖς καὶ ἐπιθυμίαις Pl.*Lg.*802c; τῇ ὀργῇ D.H.7.45. **III.** *command,* τὴν μὲν [τάξιν] ἐπὶ τῷ δεξιῷ ἐπέτρεψεν ἐφέπεσθαι X.*An.*6.5.11: elsewh. c. dat., *PLond.*3.1173.3 (ii A.D.), etc.:—Pass., ἐπετράπην ὑπὸ σοῦ *POxy.*51.5 (ii A.D.).

® **ἐπιτρέφω,** fut. -θρέψω Hdt.8.142: pf. -τέτροφα *AP*7.536 (Alc.):—Pass. (v. infr. II, III):—*grow,* in act. sense, κόμην J.*AJ*14.9.4. **2.** *rear upon,* ἐπιτέτροφε τύμβῳ βότρυν *AP* l.c. **3.** generally, *support, maintain,* Hdt.8.142,144; κακὸν τῇ πόλει D.H.10.6; τοῦ ὀμβρίου ὕδατος -ομένου ἀεὶ νέου a fresh *supply* being always *maintained,* Hp.*Aër.*7. **II.** Med., *cause to grow upon,* λασίην βροτοῖς ἐπεθρέψατο χαίτην Man.3.291:—Pass., *form upon,* -όμενος τοῖς σώμασι ῥύπος Gal.10.176; ὅταν σὰρξ ἐπιτραφῇ Id.18(2).780. **III.** Pass., *grow up after,* as posterity, ἐκ τουτέων σφι ἐπετράφη νεότης Hdt.4.3; οἱ ὕστερον ἐπιτραφέντες βασιλέες Id.2.121.α': generally, *grow up as a rival* or *successor,* Id.1.123, D.H.7.9 codd.

® **ἐπιτρέχω,** fut. -δρᾰμοῦμαι X.*Cyn.*9.6, D.17.19: aor. 2 -έδρᾰμον Il.4.524, al. (rarely aor. 1 -έθρεξα 13.409): pf. -δεδράμηκα X.*Oec.*15.6; poet. -δέδρομα Od., etc. (v. infr. II. 2):—Pass., pf. -δεδράμημαι X.*Oec.*15.1:—*run upon* or *at,* mostly for the purpose of attack, abs., ὁ δ' ἐπέδραμεν Il.4.524, cf. 18.527; of dogs, οἱ μὲν κεκλήγοντες ἐπέδραμον Od.14.30; *make an assault upon,* τινί Th.4.32, X.*Cyn.*9.6, ἐπί τινα Id.*HG*5.4.51. **b.** *approach,* εἰς ἃς (sc. μοίρας) ἐπιτρέχει ἡ Σελήνη, τούτοις συνάπτει Serapio in *Cat.Cod.Astr.*8(4).228. **2.** *run after, be eager* or *greedy,* οὔτι ἐπιδραμὼν πάντα τὰ διδόμενα ἐδέκετο Hdt.3.135; συγχωρεῖν ἐπιδραμών *in haste,* Pl.*Lg.*799c; οὐκ ἂν ἡγεῖσθε αὐτὸν κἂν ἐπιδραμεῖν ὥστε γενέσθαι D.27.56: c. dat., *to be greedy for,* App.*Pun.*94. **II.** *run over* a space, τόσσον ἐπεδραμέτην, of horses, Il.23.433, cf. 418,447; *run over* or *graze the surface,* ἀσπὶς ἐπιθρέξαντος ἄϋσεν ἔγχεος 13.409: c. dat., ἀσταχύεσσιν Call.*Aet.*3.1.46. **2.** *to be spread over,* λευκὴ δ' ἐπιδέδρομεν αἴγλη Od.6.45; κακὴ δ' ἐπιδέδρομεν ἀχλύς 20.357: c. dat., τῷ.. ἐπιδέδρομεν ὀδμή Hermipp.82.3 (hex.); ἐπιδέδρομε νυκτὶ φέγγος A.R.2.670; οἱ ἔρευθος ἐπιτρέχει Arat.834, cf. Opp.*C.*3.94; ἐξανθήματα ἐ. τοῖς σώμασιν Plu.2.671a; ὄρεσι.. ἀφ' ἡλίου μορφαὶ ἐ. ib.934f; σημείων τῷ νεκρῷ μοχθηρῶν ἐπιδραμ. Id.*TG*13, etc.: c. acc., οἶδμα ὅταν ἔρεβος ὕφαλον ἐπιδράμῃ when the billow *runs over* the darkness of the deep, S.*Ant.*588 (lyr.); τὴν χώραν, of lava, Arist.*Mir.*$840^{a}5$; ψυχὴν ἐπιδέδρομε λήθη A.R.1.645; Ῥώμην ἐπέδραμε λόγος c. acc. et inf., Plu.*Aem.*25. **3.** of a musician, *run over, play upon,* ἐ. καλάμους χείλεσι Longus 1.24; τὴν σύριγγα τῇ γλώττῃ Alciphr.3.12; τῷ πλήκτρῳ τὰς χορδάς Ath.4.139e. **4.** *overrun,* as an army does a country, ἐ. πεδίον πᾶν Hdt.1.161; τὰς κώμας πάσας Id.8.23; τὴν χώρην πᾶσαν ib.32; τὰ ἔξω Th.4.104. **5.** *run over, treat lightly* or *summarily of,* X.*Oec.*25.1 (Pass.); τῷ λόγῳ ib.6; εὐπόρως ἐ. περί τινος Isoc.*Ep.*9.6; μικρὰ περὶ αὐτῶν D.17.19; τὰς ἀπορίας ἐ. Arist.*Pol.*$1286^{a}7$; Ἡροδότου.. ἡ λέξις.. ῥᾳδίως ἐπιτρέχουσα τοῖς πράγμασιν Plu.2.854e; ἐ. διὰ βραχυτάτων ib.119e; τὸ ἐπιτρέχον σχῆμα Hermog.*Id.*1.11. **6.** of a country, *spread, extend,* ἐπὶ.. D.P.809; μέσην ἐ. νῆσον ib.1092. **7.** τῷ τῆς κώμης -οντι *inspector,* *PFay.*107.7 (ii A.D.): pl., -οντες *POxy.*2121.22 (iii A.D.). **III.** *run close after,* ἅρματα.. ἵπποις ὠκυπόδεσσιν ἐπέδραμον Il.23.504; ἐ. τὰ ἴχνη, of hounds, X.*Cyn.*3.6: c. dat., *follow,* Arat.316; ἐ. τοῖς θήλεσιν, of the male, Plu.2.965e.

**ἐπίτρησις,** εως, ἡ, *trepanning,* Heliod.ap.Orib.46.14.2.

**ἐπιτρῐᾱκοστὸς** λόγος ratio *of* 31:30, Ptol.*Harm.*2.14: so **ἐπιτρῐᾱκοστό-μονος,** 32:31, ibid.: **-δεύτερος, -τριτος, -τέταρτος,** 33:32, 34:33, 35:34, Aristid.Quint.3.1: **-πεμπτος, -όγδοος, -ένατος,** 36:35, 39:38, 40:39, Ptol. l.c., cf. 1.13.

**ἐπιτρῐβή,** ἡ, *irritation, provocation,* Baillet *Inscr. des tombeaux des rois* 1405 (dub. sens.). **II.** *destruction, damnation,* Sch.rec.S.*Aj.*103.

**ἐπιτρίβω** [τρῐ], fut. -ψω Hsch.: pf. -τετρῐφα Ar.*Lys.*952: aor. 2 Pass. ἐπετρίβην [ῐ] Id.*Th.*557, al.: fut. Med. in pass. sense, Luc.*Icar.*33 (v.l. ἐπιτετρίψονται, as in Ar.*Pax* 246):—*rub on the surface, crush,* κἄπνιγε κἀπέτριβεν v.l. in Id.*Nu.*1376, cf. *Ra.*571:—Pass., τυπτόμενον ἐπιτριβῆναι Id.*Nu.*1408; ἐπιτριβόμενος τὸν ὦμον *galled* by the weight, Id.*Ra.*88. **2.** metaph., *afflict, destroy,* [ἥλιος] καίων ἐ. τούς τε ἀνθρώπους καὶ τὴν χώρην Hdt.4.184; γάμον ὅς μ' ἐπέτριψεν Ar.*Nu.*438, cf. 243; ταῦτά με ἐ. πόθῳ Id.*Lys.*888; ὀδύναις τινὰ ἐ. X.*Mem.*1.3.12; ἐ. τοὺς ἀπόρους D.18.104; opp. σῴζειν, Men.*Epit.*550; of an actor, *murder* a part, D.18.180; ἐ. Μένανδρον Plu.2.531b:—Pass., *to be utterly destroyed* or *undone,* Sol.33.7, Ar.*Ach.*1022, *Pax* 246, 369; ἐπιτριβείης *damn you!* Id.*Av.*1530, *Th.*557; ἐπιτριβείην εἴ τι ἐψευσάμην Luc.*DMeretr.*2.3; *to be worried,* Phld.*Ir.*p.27 W.; *to be burdened,* *POxy.*$1252^{v}32$ (iii A.D.), etc. **3.** c. dat., *waste time over,* στοχαστικοῖς Gal.15.172. **II.** Med., *rub paint on one's cheeks,* of women, Phryn.*PS* p.71 B. (cod.), cf. Sch.Ar.*Th.*396 (Act.). **III.** *inflame* by friction, ἐ. τὴν νόσον *aggravate* it, App.*BC*5.59, cf. Gal.19.680; *irritate, excite,* τινά Plb.4.84.8; τινὰ ἐς πόλεμον App.*Mac.*11.7, cf. *PSI*5.452.15 (iv A.D.).

**ἐπιτρῐηραρχ-έω,** *to be trierarch beyond the legal time,* D.50.24,54: -τετριηράρχηκα τέτταρας μῆνας ib.36: Pass., ἐπιτετριηραρχημένων ἤδη μοι δυοῖν μηνοῖν two months *beyond* my *term of office having elapsed,* and my successor not having relieved me, ib.20. **-ημα,** ατος, τό, *burden of a trierarchy continued beyond the legal term,* ib.50.1, 54. **-ος,** ὁ, *trierarch subject to this burden,* *IG*$2^{2}$.1612.136.

® **ἐπιτρῐμερής,** ές, *containing* $1+\frac{3}{4}$, Nicom.*Ar.*1.20.

**ἐπι-τριμμός,** ὁ, (ἐπιτρίβω) *crushing,* Aq.*De.*23.1(2). **-τριπτικός,** ή, όν, (ἐπιτρίβω III) *irritating, exciting,* λόγοι Antyll.ap.Orib.6.6.5. **-τριπτος,** ον, of persons to whom one says ἐπιτριβείης (= ἄξιος τοῦ ἐπιτριβῆναι, *EM*367.1), *accursed, damned,* τοὐπίτριπτον κίναδος the *damned* fox, S.*Aj.*103 (= τὸ ἐξώλες θηρίον, Sch.), cf. And.1.99; ἐ. ψωμοκόλακες Sannyr.10; οὑπίτριπτος the *rogue,* Ar.*Pl.*275, Alex.105, cf. Ar.*Pl.*619; ὦπίτριπτε Ar.*Ach.*557; *rascally,* ῥήτορες Luc.*Tim.*27: Sup., *Com.Adesp.*1348. **2.** ἡ νῦν ἐ. καὶ κατεαγυῖα μουσική the *disreputable* and effeminate music of to-day, S.E.*M.*6.14. (For this sense of a participial formation, cf. οὐλόμενος and ὀνήμενος.)

**ἐπίτρῐτος,** ον (η, ον, v. infr. 4), *containing an integer and one-third* ($1+\frac{1}{3}$), i.e. *in the* ratio *of* 4:3, ἐ. πυθμήν Pl.*R.*546c; ἀριθμοί Ph.2.183; λόγος Id.1.10, al., cf. *PTeb.*72.388 (ii B.C.), etc. Adv. -τως Nicom.*Ar.*2.20. **2.** in Music, ἐ. διαστάσεις, of the interval of the *fourth,* Pl.*Ti.*36a, cf. Plu.2.1138f, Aristid.Quint.3.1; ἐ. ἁρμονία Ph.1.23; ἁ δὲ συλλαβὰ ἐπίτριτον Philol.6. **3.** πούς ἐ., or ἐ., ὁ, a *metrical foot,* of three longs and one short, in which the ratio of θέσις and ἄρσις is 4:3, Sch.Heph.p.112 C.; ἐ. πρῶτος, δεύτερος, τρίτος, τέταρτος, ⏑ – – –, – ⏑ – –, – – ⏑ –, – – – ⏑, Heph.3.3. **4.** in usury, ἐπίτριτον (sc. δάνεισμα), τό, *a loan of which* $\frac{1}{3}$ *is annually paid as interest,* i.e. $33\frac{1}{3}$ *per cent.,* X.*Vect.*3.9; τόκοι ἐ. Arist.*Rh.*$1411^{a}17$; ἑξακόσιαι δραχμαὶ ἐπίτριται 600 drachmae *at* $33\frac{1}{3}$ *per cent.,* Is.*Fr.*79 S. **5.** ἐπίτριτον, τό, tax in Egypt, *PSI*8.902.9 (i A.D.).

**ἐπιτρῐτόω,** *repeat for the third time,* Anaxil.1.

**ἐπίτριψις,** εως, ἡ, *wearing away,* of the action of waves, Lxx *Ps.*92(93).3 (pl.). **II.** *ruin,* ἀνθρώπων prob. in *OGI*669.63 (Egypt, i A.D.).

**ἐπιτρομέω,** *to be in fear of,* τι Q.S.2.474.

**ἐπίτρομος,** ον, (τρέμω) *in fear, alarmed,* Sch.rec.A.*Th.*78.

**ἐπιτροπ-άδην** [ᾰ], Adv., = ἐπιθέτως, *insincerely,* Hsch. **-αῖος,** α, ον, *entrusted to one, delegated,* ἐ. λαβεῖν τὴν ἀρχήν Hdt.3.142; ἐ. ἔχειν τὴν βασιληΐην Id.4.147. **-εία,** ἡ, *charge, guardianship,* τινός *over* one, Pl.*Phdr.*239e, Arist.*Pol.*$1271^{b}25$, Plb.15.$25^{a}$.27, cf. Lys.*Fr.*43; τὴν ἐ. τινὸς λαβεῖν D.H.4.33, etc. **II.** *office of a Roman procurator,* τοῖς κατ' ἐπιτροπείας παρ' ἐμοῦ ἀπεσταλμένοις *PFay.*20.17 (Imperial edict, iii/iv A.D.); τῶν ἐθνῶν Them.*Or.*8.117a (pl.). ® **-εύσιμος,** ον, *subject to wardship,* *BCH*4.453 (cod. Sinait.). **-ευσις,** εως, ἡ, = -εία I, Pl.*R.*554c. **-ευτικός,** ή, όν, *fitted for the office of steward,* X.*Oec.*12.3. **-εύω,** *to be an administrator, guardian,* etc. **1.** abs., Hdt.1.134, X.*Oec.*12.8, 13.1, *IG*3.392, etc.; τινί *for* one, Pl.*Lg.*849b. **2.** c. gen., Λεωβώτεω Hdt.1.65; Αἰγύπτου ἐ. Id.3.15; τοῦ πλήθεος ib.82; Βαβυλῶνος Id.7.62; τινός *PSI*4.281.30 (ii A.D.); χώρας J.*AJ*11.4.6 (Med., v.l. Act.). **3.** c. acc., *govern, manage,* τὴν πατρίδα Hdt.3.36; πόλιν Id.8.127, Pl.*R.*519c; τὸν δῆμον Ar.*Eq.*212, al.; τὴν κτῆσιν Pl.*Lg.*877c:—Pass., *to be managed by bailiffs,* Arist.*Oec.*$1345^{a}8$. **b.** c. acc. pers., ἐ. τινά *to be guardian and regent for* him, Th.1.132, Lys.10.5:—Pass., *to be under guardians,* Is.1.10; ὑπό τινων *SIG*364.58 (Ephesus, iii B.C.), etc.; κακῶς.. ἐπιτροπευθῆναι *to be* ill-*treated by one's guardians,* Pl.*Lg.*928c, cf. D.27.5; αἰσχρῶς -τετροπευμένους ὑπὸ τοῦ πάππου Lys.32.3: metaph., ὁ σοφὸς -εύεται ὑπὸ θεοῦ Porph.*Marc.*16. **4.** in Roman Law, *to be procurator,* *IG*14.911, Plu.2.471a, etc.; τῆς Ἰουδαίας v.l. in *Ev.Luc.*3.1. **b.** *act as agent, represent* a person's interest, Mitteis *Chr.*372 ii 2 (ii A.D.). **II.** = ἐπιτρέπω, *grant, allow,* δίαιταν Is.5.31 codd. ® **-έω,** = foreg., dub. in Pl.Com.265. ® **-ή,** ἡ, *reference,* esp. to an arbiter in decision of a law-suit, ἠξίουν δίκης ἐπιτροπὴν σφίσι γενέσθαι ἢ ἐς πόλιν τινὰ ἢ ἰδιώτην Th.5.41; ἡ ἐ.

τούτῳ πρὸς Παρμένοντα γέγονε D.33.23; εἰς ἐ. ἔρχεσθαι ib.14; ἡ ἐ. ἐγένετό μοι ib.16; τὴν ἐ. λῦσαι ibid.; ἀνέντες τὴν ἐ. having declined it, Th. 5.31. 2. generally, *power to decide*, ἐ. διδόναι τινὶ περί τινος Hp. *Decent.*17, cf. *Schwyzer*195.10 (Crete (from Delos), ii B.C.); διδόναι τῇ συγκλήτῳ τὴν ἐ. Plb.18.39.5; διδόναι ἑαυτοὺς εἰς ἐ., or τὴν ἐ. διδόναι περὶ σφῶν αὐτῶν, Lat. *dedere se in fidem*, to surrender absolutely, Id.2. 11.8, 15.8.14, etc.; ἐ. λαβεῖν εἰς τὸ διαλῦσαι to receive *full powers* to treat, Id.3.15.7, cf. D.H.2.45, D.S.17.47; μετ' ἐξουσίας καὶ ἐ. *Act. Ap.*26.12. II. *guardianship*, Pl.*Lg.*924b, etc.; ἐπιτροπῆς κατάστασις, διαδικασία, Arist.*Ath.*56.6; ἀποχὴ τῆς ἐ. *POxy.*898.24 (ii A.D.); ἐπιτροπῆς δικάζεσθαι, of an action brought by a ward against a guardian, Lys.*Fr.*27; καταγιγνώσκειν τὴν ἐ. D.29.58; ἐπιτροπῆς κρίνειν τινά Plu.2.844c. 2. *office of a Roman procurator*, ἡ τοῦ ἰδίου λόγου ἐ. *BGU*16.8 (ii A.D.): generally, *stewardship*, *PLond.*2.454.10 (iv A.D.). ⊛ -ία, ἡ, metaph., *protection*, dub. in Arist.*EE*1247ᵃ30. -ιάζω (corrupt acc. to Phryn.65) and -ιασμός, *relapse*, *Gloss.*; cf. ὑπο- and ἐπανα-τροπιάζω. ⊛ -ικός, ή, όν, *of* or *for a trustee* or *guardian*, ἐ. νόμοι the laws *of guardianship*, Pl.*Lg.*927e; ἐ. λόγος D.H.*Lys.*20, cf. Hyp.*Or.*65 tit., *BGU*300.24 (ii A.D.), *Cod.Just.*3.10.1.2. 2. of character, εὐεργετικοὺς ἐπιτροπικοὺς χρηστοήθεις *protective, fit to be a guardian* or *trustee*, Ptol.*Tetr.*163. II. *having held the office of procurator*, *Ephes.*3 No.49. ⊛ -ος, ον, (ἐπιτρέπω) *one to whom the charge of anything is entrusted, steward, trustee, administrator*, c. gen. rei, τῶν ἑωυτοῦ Hdt.1.108; τῶν οἰκίων Id.3.63: abs., X.*Oec.*12.3, D.21.78, 27.19, *Ev.Luc.*8.3, etc.; *steward, messman*, X.*Cyr.*4.2. 35: metaph., τῶν [τοῦ Πρωταγόρου] ἐ. Pl.*Tht.*165a. 2. = Lat. *procurator*, Καίσαρος ἐ. Str.3.4.20, Plu.2.813e, etc.; ἐ. Σεβαστοῦ, -τῶν, *OGI*502.10 (Aezani, ii A.D.), 501.2 (Tralles, ii A.D.); ἐ. τῆς Ἠπείρου Arr.*Epict.*3.4.1; τῶν μετάλλων *OGI*678.5 (Egypt, ii A.D.), etc. 3. *governor, viceroy*, οἱ ἐ. τῆς Μέμφιος, Μιλήτου ἐ., Hdt.3. 27, 5.30, cf. 106. 4. *executor*, *PPetr.*3 p.9, al. (iii B.C.). II. c. gen. pers., *trustee, guardian*, Hdt.4.76, Th.2.80, etc.; ἐ. τινι παίδων Hyp.*Epit.*42: abs., Pl.*Lg.*924b, etc.; ὑπὸ ἐπιτρόπους εἶναι *Ep. Gal.*4.2; καθιστάναι ἐ. *PRyl.*153.18 (ii A.D.): metaph., *guardian, protector*, θεὸς ἐ. ἐὼν Pi.*O.*1.106.

**ἐπιτροφή**, ἡ, (ἐπιτρέφω) *sustenance*, *BCH*35.69 (pl., Delos), J.*AJ* 18.9.1.

**ἐπιτροχ-άδην** [ᾰ], Adv. *trippingly, fluently, glibly*: in Hom. only in phrase ἐ. ἀγορεύειν Il.3.213, Od.18.26. II. *cursorily*, D.H. *Amm.*2.2, Man.1.11. -άζω, *run lightly over*: hence, *treat briefly*, ῥαθύμως ἐπιτετροχασμένα D.H.*Th.*16. 2. *trot gently*, *Hippiatr.*33 (p.171.14 O.; ἐντρ- Grynaeus, and so codd. p.164.16 O., al.). -ᾰλος, ον, *quickly passing, 'tripping'*, χρόνοι D.H.*Comp.*18: metaph., *glib, flowing*, ῥύσις τῆς λέξεως Id.*Dem.*40. -ασμός, ὁ, *rapid succession of statements*, as a figure of speech, Phld.*Herc.*862.14 (pl.), Alex. *Fig.*1.17, Phoeb.*Fig.*2.1. -αστέον, verb. Adj. *one must run over*, Nicom.*Harm.*3. -άω, = ἐπιτροχάζω, c. dat., ὕδωρ ἐ. ψαμάθοισι A.R.4.1266: c. acc., σάρκα..-τροχόωσαι σμώδιγγες Nic.*Al.*544: c. gen., κύματος *AP*9.306 (Antiphil.): abs., λοξαὶ ἐπιτροχόωσι κέλευθοι D.P.148; εἶθαρ -τροχάων A.R.4.1606; ῥαθάμιγγες ἐπιτροχόωσ' ὑετοῖο Arat.889. -ίζω, *turbino*, *Gloss.* -ος, ον, *running easily, easily inclined*, ἐπιτροχώτερον ῥέψαι Hp.*Art.*14; περίπατοι ἐ. οἱ μέσοι walks *which break into a run*, Aret.*CD*1.3; βλέφαρον οὐκ ἐ. not very *mobile*, Id.*SD*1.7: metaph., *tripping*, μέλη Hld.4.17; ῥυθμοὶ Aristid. Quint.2.15; *voluble, glib*, στωμύλα καὶ ἐ. λαλεῖν Luc.*DDeor.*7.3; ἐ. καὶ ἀσαφὲς φθέγγεσθαι Id.*Nec.*7. Adv. -ως, φθέγγεσθαι Ael.*NA*7.7.

**ἐπιτρύζω**, *squeak beside* or *over*, πέμφιγες -τρύζουσι θανόντα Euph. 134; τό μοι τελχῖνες -τρύζουσιν *mutter*, Call.*Aet.Oxy.*2079 *Fr.*1.1, cf. Hsch.; μῦς -τρύξας τινί Babr.112.8: abs., [τέττιξ] ἁβρὸν ἐ. *chirps*, *AP*6.54 (Paul. Sil.). (In part perh. f.l. for -τρίζω.)

**ἐπιτρῡπάω**, *bore, pierce*, Philostr.*Im.*1.20 (Pass.).

**ἐπιτρύσσειν**· ἐπίμεινον (Lacon.), Hsch.

**ἐπιτρῡφάω**, *luxuriate, revel in*, δόγμασιν v.l. for ἐντρ- in Ph.2.392.

⊛ **ἐπιτρώγω**, *eat with* or *after*, Luc.*Sat.*21, 28: c. gen. partit., *eat afterwards of*.., χελώνη -τραγοῦσα (aor. 2 part.) ὀριγάνου Ael.*NA*3. 5. II. generally, *eat*, *POxy.*1185.11 (ii/iii A.D.).

**ἐπιτρωπάω**, poet. for ἐπιτρέπω, *allow*, τινί τι or c. inf., Opp.*H.*2. 223, 5.188. 2. *entrust*, κῦδός τινι μέλεσθαι A.R.1.351.

⊛ **ἐπιτυγχάνω**, fut. -τεύξομαι Pl.*R.*431c: aor. 2 ἐπέτῠχον: pf. -τετύχηκα Arist.*Oec.*1352ᵇ5:—prop. *hit the mark*, τοῦ σκοποῦ, opp. ἀποτυγχάνω, Id.*EN*1106ᵇ33; οἱ πολλὰ βάλλοντες ἐπιτυγχάνουσι πολλάκις Plu.2.438a: hence, II. *light* or *fall upon, meet with*, 1. c. dat. pers., Ar.*Nu.*195, 535, Th.3.75; ἐ. γυναικὶ βιαζομένῃ Pl.*Lg.*874c: also c. dat. rei, ἐ. σορῷ Hdt.1.68; ναυσί Th.8.34; βιβλίῳ Luc.*Dem.Enc.* 27; ἐ. [ταῖς θύραις] ἀνεῳγμέναις *to find* them open, Pl.*Smp.*223b. 2. c. gen. pers., μετρίου ἀνδρός Ar.*Pl.*245, cf. Plu.*Art.*12: c. gen. rei, ἐ. ὁλκάδος ἀναγομένης Th.3.3; εὐώνων ἐ. a low market, Arist.*Oec.* l.c. 3. rarely c. acc., τὰς ἁπλᾶς [ἐπιθυμίας] ἐν ὀλίγοις ἐπιτεύξῃ Pl. *R.*431c; ἅττ' ἂν ἐπιτύχῃς Eub.123.5. 4. abs., Ar.*Ra.*570, Th.6. 38; mostly ὁ ἐπιτυχών *the first person one meets, any chance person*, esp. in pl., Hdt.2.2, Antipho 2.1.1: with neg., οὐδὲ φαύλων ἀνδρῶν οὐδὲ τῶν ἐ. Pl.*Cra.*390d; οὐ γὰρ οἶμαι τοῦ ἐ. εἶναι.. Id.*Euthphr.*4a; οὐ περὶ τοῦ ἐ. on no *common matter*, Id.*R.*352d: without the Art., ἐπιτυχόντος ἀνθρώπου λόγος E.*HF*1248, cf. Phot.p.140 R. (= gloss on Eup. 25 D.). III. *attain to, reach, gain* one's end, c. gen. rei, X.*Mem.* 4.2.28, D.48.3; εὐχωλᾶς *Inscr.Cypr.*134 H. (iv B.C.); πολιτείας *BGU* 113.3 (ii A.D.), etc.; τοῦ καλῶς [μειγνύναι] Pl.*Phlb.*61d; ἐ. τοῦ ἀγῶνος *gain* one's suit, D.48.30; *profit by, benefit by*, φιλανθρωπίας *BGU* 522.8 (ii A.D.): abs., οὐ δύνασθε ἐπιτυχεῖν *Ep.Jac.*4.2. 2. c. part., *succeed in* doing, Hdt.8.101, 103 (but ζητέων ἐπιτυγχάνειν *find, light upon* by searching, Hp.*VM*24): so c. inf., Luc.*Nec.*6; γαμβροῦ ὁ ἐπιτυχὼν εὕρεν υἱόν he who *is lucky in* his son-in-law, Democr.272. 3. c. dat. modi, *to be lucky, successful in* a thing, μάχῃ Aeschin.3.165: abs., *to be successful*, Pl.*Men.*97c, Th.3.42, Arist.*Rh.*1354ᵃ9; ἂν ἐπιτύχῃ if she *succeeds*, Men.*Epit.*346; τἆλλα ἐ. X.*HG*4.5.19: also impers., αὐτῷ οὐδὲν ἐπετύγχανε Ant.Lib.41.6. 4. Pass., *turn out well*, αἱ ἐπιτετευγμέναι πράξεις *successful*, Plb.6.53.2, cf. Hipparch.ap. Stob.4.44.81, D.S.1.1, Plu.2.674a; φάρμακον -τετευγμένον *proved* remedy, Heraclid.Tarent.ap.Gal.12.403. IV. c. dat. pers., *converse, talk with* one, Pl.*Lg.*758c.

**ἐπιτῠλίσσω**, Att. -ττω, *roll up*, τι ἐν φύλλοισιν Hp.*Steril.*216. II. *turn over* or *open a book*, D.L.9.114.

**ἐπιτυμβ-ίδιος**, α, ον, (τύμβος) *at* or *over a tomb*, θρῆνοι A.*Ch.*342 (lyr.); τὴν δ' ἐ. τούτῳ θῆκεν χάριν *IG*14.1409.5. II. ἐπιτυμβίδιοι κορυδαλλίδες *frequenting tombs*, or *with tomb-like crests*, or *with tombs in their heads* (v. Ar.*Av.*475), Theoc.7.23, cf. Sch. ad loc. -ιος, ον (also α, ον Plu. (v. infr.)), = foreg. 1, αἶνος, θρῆνος, A.*Ag.*1547 (lyr.), *Ch.*335 (lyr.); εὖχος *APl.*5.368; χοαί S.*Ant.*901; σῆμα *Epigr.Gr.*339.1 (Cyzicus); κρηπίς *AP*7.657.11 (Leon.), cf. Hld.4.8; Ἀφροδίτη ἐπιτυμβία, Lat. *Venus Libitina*, Plu.2.269b; θεοὶ ἐ. *Tab.Defix.*99.9. II. of an old woman 'with one foot in the grave', Alciphr.3.62.

**ἐπιτῠραννέω**, *rule*, ὥσπερ ἐπ' ἀκροπόλει τῆς γενέσεως Porph.*in Ptol.* 192.

**ἐπίτῡρον**, τό, *confection of olives*, Lat. *epityrum*, Cato *RR*119, Plaut. *Mil.*24; commonest in Sicily, Varro *LL*7.86; cf. ἐπίτερα. II. ἐπιτυρά, dub. l. in Hsch. s. v. κάρκαρα (= Semon.33).

**ἐπιτυφλόω**, *stop* the pores, Arist.*Pr.*890ᵇ39 (Pass.); ἐ. τὰ φλεβία Thphr.*Sens.*66. II. *blind*, τὸν νοῦν Phld.*Rh.*1.178 S.

**ἐπιτύφομαι** [ῡ], Pass., aor. 2 -ετύφην [ῠ] Ar.*Lys.*221:—*to be burnt up*, esp. by lightning, Philostr.*VS*1.21.2, cf. *Im.*2.29: metaph., *to be inflamed* by love, τινος *for* one, Ar. l. c.; ἐπιτεθυμμένος *furious*, Pl. *Phdr.*230a.

**ἐπιτῡφῶσαι**· ἐπιπυριάσασα, Hsch.: ἐπιτετυφωμένον ἢ ἐπικεκαυμένον, = Att. ἐπιτεθυμμένον, Moer.p.150 P.

**ἐπιτύχ-ημα** [ῠ], ατος, τό, = ἐπίτευγμα, *EM*548.45. -ής, ές, (ἐπιτυγχάνω) *hitting the mark, successful* (opp. ἀποτυχής, Pl.*Sis.*391c (Comp.)), κότος A.*Supp.*744 Turneb. (lyr.); ἔν τινι Arist.*Div.Somn.* 463ᵇ19, D.S.4.83; κατά τι Plb.5.102.1; ἐς πάντα App.*BC*2.149 (Sup.): c. gen., ἐ. τῶν καιρῶν δόξα *that always hits* the right nail on the head, Isoc.12.30. Adv. -χῶς, εἰπεῖν Pl.*Phlb.*38d; διειλέχθαι Isoc.12.230, cf. Plu.*Mar.*17, Aët.9.28. II. Pass., *easy to hit*, εὔβλητοι καὶ ἐ. App.*Syr.*35. ⊛ -ία, ἡ, *luck, chance*, ὁκόσα -τυχίη ποιέουσιν οἱ ἰητροί Hp.*Morb.*1.1. 2. *success*, opp. ἀποτυχίη, Democr.275; ἐν ταῖς μάχαις Plb.1.6.4; τῶν μαντευμάτων D.H.3.70; ἔργων *OGI*678.2 (Egypt, ii A.D.): pl., Phld.*Po.*2.33; *advantage*, Ph.2.326. b. κατ' ἐπιτυχίαν *casually, by a fortunate coincidence*, Plot.2.3.7. 3. *undertaking*, ματαία ἐ. *BGU*1060.3 (i B.C.).

**ἐπιτωθ-άζω**, *mock, jest*, Pl.*Ax.*364c, Hp.*Ep.*17; *mock at, jeer*, τινα, τινι, App.*BC*2.67, 5.125, cf. Hieronym.Hist.7; τοῖς γινομένοις Men. Rh.p.420 S. -ασμός, ὁ, *mockery, raillery*, Plb.3.80.4, Hld.10.25.

**ἐπίῠδρος**, ον, *capable of irrigation*, κτῆμα *PSI*3.188.7 (vi A.D.).

**ἐπιφᾰγεῖν**, aor. 2 inf. of ἐπεσθίω (q. v.).

⊛ **ἐπιφαιδρύνω**, *make bright* or *clean*, κάρη A.R.4.663:—Pass., Hld. 8.9.

⊛ **ἐπιφαίνω**, aor. 1 (late) -έφᾱνα Lxx *De.*33.2, *Ev.Luc.*1.79:—*show forth, display*, abs., μηδὲ λίην ἐπίφαινε Thgn.359 (s.v.l.); ἐ. προστασίαν ἀξιωματικήν Plb.10.18.8; μηδὲν τεχνικόν D.H.*Amm.*1.10; τὸ ἀγέρωχον, τὴν προαίρεσιν, Plu.*Marc.*1, 2.139d; ἀνθρωπόμορφόν τι Luc.*Alex.* 12; τὸν μισοπόνηρον *play* the μ., Phld.*Ir.*p.74 W.:—Pass., *come into view*, ἠέλιος δ' ἐπέλαμψε, μάχη δ' ἐπὶ πᾶσα φαάνθη Il.17.650; of an enemy, Hdt.2.152, 4.122, Th.8.42, etc.; διὰ τὸ ἐπιφανέντα με κωλῦσαι Test.ap.D.21.22; ἐ. ἐς τὴν Νάξον Hdt.5.30, cf. X.*An.*3.4.13; ἐπιφανῆναι ἐπὶ τὸ ἔργον Id.*Oec.*21.10; ἐπὶ τὰ Δρέπανα Plb.1.49.7; ἐ. τινὶ ἐς οἶκον *to present oneself*, Hdt.4.97; ἐ. τινι *show oneself, appear* to one, Id.1. 24, al.; freq. of dreams and visions, Id.2.91, 3.27; ἐν τῷ ὕπνῳ Id.7. 16; of a divine manifestation, ἐπιφαινομένης αὐτοῖς Ἀρτέμιδος *SIG* 557.5 (Magn. Mae., iii B.C.), cf. *IG*4.951.26 (Epid., iii B.C.); so ἡ χρηστότης ἐπεφάνη τοῦ θεοῦ *Ep.Tit.*3.4; of an Emperor, δήμοις ἑορτάζουσιν ἐπιφανείς Hdn.1.7.2; also ἵνα σφι τιμωρίη..ἐπιφανήσεται Hdt. 8.49; τὰ ἐπιφαινόμενα *symptoms which make their appearance*, Hp. *Aph.*1.12, cf. Sor.1.17, al. 2. c. acc. et inf., *make it manifest that*.., Plu.2.1044d. 3. Pass., lit. *appear upon the surface*, Ti.Locr.101d; ἐ. ταῖς εἰκόσιν ἰδέα Plu.*Arat.*3: metaph., τὸ ἦθος ὡς χρῶμα ταῖς πράξεσιν ἐ. ib.48, cf. *Galb.*23. II. seemingly intr., in Act., *show light, dawn*, ἡμέρας ἐπιφαινούσης Plb.5.6.6 (so ἀνατολῆς ἐπιφαινομένης Id.3. 113.1); ἐπιφᾶναι τοῖς ἐν σκότει καθημένοις *to shine upon*.., *Ev.Luc.* 1.79, cf. Lxx *De.*33.2.

**ἐπίφαλλος**, ὁ, *flute-tune for dancing to*, Trypho ap.Ath.14.618c, cf. Eust.1236.56.

**ἐπιφάν-εια** [ᾰ], ἡ, *appearance, coming into light* or *view*, τῆς ἡμέρας *day-break, dawn*, Plb.3.94.3; in war, *sudden appearance* of an enemy, Aen.Tact.31.8, Plb.1.54.2, Ascl.*Tact.*12.10 (pl.), Onos.22.3 (pl.). 2. esp. of deities appearing to a worshipper, *manifestation*, D.H.2.68, Plu.*Them.*30; *advent*, D.S.2.47; τὰς ὑπ' αὐτῆς (sc. Ἀρτέμιδος) γενομένας ἐναργεῖς ἐ. *SIG*867.35 (Ephesus, ii A.D.); *a manifestation* of divine power, τὰς ἐ. τᾶς Παρθένου *Klio*16.204 (Chersonesus, iii B.C.), cf. Lxx 2 *Ma.*15.27, D.S.1.25. 3. *the first coming* of Christ, 2 *Ep. Ti.*1.10; *the second*, 1 *Ep.Ti.*6.14, al. 4. of the *accession* of Caligula,

Inscr.Cos 391. 5. *appearance, aspect,* οἰκετικὴ ἐ. Myro 2 J.; κατὰ τὴν ἐ., distd. fr. κατὰ τὴν ἔμφασιν, Plb.25.3.6. II. *visible surface* of a body, *superficies,* Democr.155 (pl.), Arist.*Cat.*5a2, *Metaph.*1002a4, *Ph.*209a8, *Sens.*439a31, Euc.*El.*1 *Deff.*, Ph.*Bel.*70.27, Damian.*Opt.* 11; ἡ κατὰ πρόσωπον ἐ. *the front,* Plb.1.22.10; κατὰ τὰς ἐ. μάχεσθαι *to fight in front,* Id.3.116.10; ἐ. ἡ ἐκ δεξιῶν Arr.*Tact.*21.3; αἱ τρεῖς ἐ. τῆς πόλεως its three *visible sides,* Plb.4.70.9; the *surface* or *skin* of the body, D.S.3.29, Pap. in *AJP* 24.327, Gal.16.530, etc.; μυδῶντα τὴν ἐ. Luc.*Philops.*11; τῆς ἔνδον ἐ. τῶν ἐντέρων Gal.18(1).2. 2. *outward show, fame, distinction,* esp. arising from something unexpected, Pl. *Alc.*1.124c; ἐ. ποιεῖν to create a *sensation,* Is.7.13: in pl., Isoc.6.104, D.S.19.1; τὰ πρὸς ἐπιφάνειαν καὶ δόξαν ἀνήκοντα *OGI* 763.19 (Milet., ii B.C.), cf. Arr.*Epict.*3.22.29. **-εια** (sc. ἱερά), τά, *sacrifices in celebration of an* ἐπιφάνεια, Δημήτριος τὰ ἐ. τοῦ ἀδελφοῦ θύων Caryst.10. ⊛ **-ής**, ές, *coming to light, coming suddenly into view, appearing,* of gods, Hdt.3.27, etc.: hence, *present to aid,* θεοὶ -έστατοι D.S.1.17. 2. of places and things, *in full view,* πόλις ἐ. ἔξωθεν, of a place *commanded by another,* Th.5.10, cf. 6.96, 7.19; τινι *to* one, ib. 3; ἔχειν ἐπιφανεῖς θηλάς *visible,* Arist.*HA* 504b23; φλέβες *prominent,* Gal.17(2).209. 3. *manifest, evident,* ὄνειδος Democr.218 (Comp.); ἐκ τῶν ἐπιφανεστάτων σημείων Th.1.21; διὰ τὸ μὴ ἐ. εἶναι Arist.*EN* 1126a23. II. of men, *conspicuous, notable, distinguished* by rank, Hdt.2.89, al.; οἰκίη οὐκ ἐ. ib.172; *notable,* either for good or ill, X. *Mem.*3.1.10, Lys.14.12 (Sup.); ἀνδρείᾳ *for* courage, Th.6.72; πρὸς τὸν πόλεμον Pl.*Lg.*629e; *famous, renowned,* Pi.*P.*7.6 (Comp.), etc.; ἀνδρῶν ἐ. πᾶσα γῆ τάφος Th.2.43; of things, places, etc., χώρα *OGI* 90.46 (Rosetta, ii B.C.); -εστέρα τιμή *IPE* 1².34.22 (Olbia, i B.C.); -έσταται τιμαί *IG* 9(2).1109.10 (Magn. Thess.). 2. of things, *remarkable,* οὗτοί σφεων οἱ -έστατοι νόμοι εἰσί Hdt.5.6; -εστάτη χρεία Plb.1.78.11; -εστάτη μάχη Anon.Hist.*Oxy.*12ii31. 3. as a title of divinities, τῶν -εστάτων θεῶν *IG* 5(1).1179 (Sparta); also of Eastern Kings, e.g. Ptolemy V, *OGI* 90.5 (Rosetta, ii B.C.); Antiochus of Syria, Plb. 26.1a.1, etc. III. Adv. -νῶς *openly, conspicuously,* Th.1.91, 5.105 (Sup.). 2. *with distinction,* λαμπρῶς καὶ ἐ. *IGRom.*4.844 (Phrygia), cf. J.*BJ* 7.3.1: Comp. -έστερον, ζῆν *with greater distinction,* Men. 223.19. **-τος**, ον, *in the light, alive,* S.*Ant.*841 (lyr.); *visible, manifest,* Διοσκούρων ἐ. prob. in Poet.ap.Stob.1.1.31a.

**ἐπιφαρμάσσω**, *apply medicine again to,* ἐ. τὰ σπλάγχνα ἤδη πεφαρμαγμένα Ach.Tat.4.16.

**ἐπίφᾰσις**, εως, ἡ, *becoming visible,* f.l. in Thphr.*Sens.*27 codd. (ἔμφασις Schneider); *outward appearance,* ἐ. βασιλική Plb.4.77.3; κατὰ τὴν ἐ. καταπλαγῆναι by his *outward appearance,* Id.11.27.8; opp. κατ' ἀλήθειαν, Id.14.2.9; but distd. from κατὰ τὴν ἐπιφάνειαν, Id.25.3.6. II. *indication, display,* ἑτοιμότητος, ἀκριβείας, εὐδαιμονίας, Id. 4.11.4, 12.10.4, 31.25.7; ἠθῶν dub. in Phld.*Mus.*p.64 K. (pl.).

**ἐπιφάσκω**, *pretend, profess,* c. inf., εἰδέναι σαφῶς Ph.1.457; ἰᾶσθαι Id.ap.Eus.*PE* 8.14; *act* a part, ἐ. τὸν [σεμνόν] Phld.*Vit.*p.36 J.; τὸν πλούσιον Ph.2.536.

**ἐπιφατνίδιος**, α, ον, (φάτνη) *at the manger,* φορβειά X.*Eq.*5.1.

**ἐπιφάτνιος**· ὁ ἑωσφόρος ἀστήρ, Hsch.

**ἐπίφᾰτος**, ον, *notorious,* S.*Fr.*1048 (codd. Eust., sed leg. ἐπίσφατος). II. (*φένω) = ὀλέθριος, Eust.1728.14 (-σφατος codd.).

**ἐπιφαυλίζω**, *make of small account,* v.l. for -φυλλ- in Lxx *La.*1.22, 2.20.

⊛ **ἐπιφαύσκω**, fut. -φαύσω (v. infr.):—*shine out,* of the sun or moon, Lxx *Jb.*25.5, 31.26: also in pass. form, ib.41.9(10); ἐπιφαύσει σοι ὁ Χριστός *will shine out* for thee, *Ep.Eph.*5.14.

**ἐπιφέρβομαι**, *feed on,* ὁπόσοι γῆν -όμεθα Phanocl.2.2.

**ἐπιφερής**, ές, *prone,* Hsch. s.v. πρωλύθιον.

**ἐπιφέρνια**, τά, *dowry,* Sch.Il.9.147, Eust.1417.14.

**ἐπιφέρω**, fut. ἐποίσω: aor. 1 ἐπήνεγκα: aor. 2 ἐπήνεγκον: Arc. aor. 1 subj. 3 sg. ἐποίσῃ *Schwyzer* 654.21:—Pass., fut. ἐποισθήσεται· ἐπενεχθήσεται, Hsch.:—*bring, put* or *lay upon,* σοὶ.. βαρείας χεῖρας ἐποίσει *will lay* heavy hands *upon* thee, Il.1.89; χεῖρας ἐποίσει Od.16.438; ἐπ' ἀλλήλοισι φέρον πολύδακρυν Ἄρηα Il.3.132, cf. 8.516; ἐπ' ἰχθύσι κῆρα φέρουσα 24.82; so ἐ. δόρυ A.*Eu.*766, cf. E.*Supp.* 1192, Ar.*Av.*344 (lyr.); and in Prose, ἐ. τινὶ πόλεμον *make* war *upon* him, Hdt.5.81, cf. Th.1.141; ὅπλα Id.4.16, 7.18, D.37.36; ἐ. τὸ διάφορόν τισι *to bring* discord *upon* them, Th.7.55; ἐ. δίκην, τιμωρίαν τινί, Pl.*Lg.*943d; ἀμοιβήν τινι Plb.1.84.10: abs., εἰ γὰρ ὧδ' ἐποίσεις if you *shall pursue your attack* thus, Ar.*Eq.*837. b. *inflict,* πληγήν, πληγάς τινι, J.*AJ* 2.14.2, *PTeb.*331.10 (ii A.D.); *vent,* ὀργήν *Ep.Rom.*3.5. 2. *place upon,* esp. of placing offerings on the grave, ἐ. ἀπαρχάς Th.3.58, cf. 2.34; τῷ νεκρῷ στέφανον Plu.*Per.*36; ταφὴν εἴς τινα App.*BC* 1.73; τὰ ἐπιφερόμενα the *offerings,* Isoc.9.1; *lay on, apply,* φάρμακον Pl.*Ep.*354b; ἐ. τὰ στοιχεῖα ἐπὶ τὰ πράγματα Id.*Cra.* 424e. 3. *bring* as a charge *against,* ἐ. τινὶ αἰτίην Hdt.1.68, cf. 26, Antipho 5.38, Pl.*Phd.*98a; ἔγκλημα E.*Or.*766 (troch.); μέμψιν Ar.*Ra.* 1253 (lyr.); ψόγον Th.1.70; ἐ. μωρίην, μανίην τινί, *impute* it *to* him, Hdt.1.131, 6.112; ἀδικίας -ομένης Th.3.42; τὴν Κλεοπάτραν αὐτῷ *cast* Cl. *in his teeth,* D.C.50.1; τι ἐπί τινα Arist.*EN* 1143a27. 4. *bring,* i.e. *confer, impose, upon,* in good or bad sense, ἐ. τιμὰν θνατοῖς Pi.*O.*1. 31; ἐλευθερίαν Th.4.85; δουλείαν Id.3.56. 5. *add to, increase,* ἐ. τὴν ὑπερβολήν ib.82; ὀργὰς ἐπιφέρειν τινί *minister* to his passions, *gratify* him, Cratin.230, Th.8.83 (cf. Sch.); for ἐπὶ ἦρα φέρειν, v. ἦρα. 6. *give* a name *to,* ὄνομα ἐ. τινί Pl.*Plt.*307b, *R.*596a, al., Arist.*Rh.*1408a7, al.; *assign* an attribute to a substantive, τῷ ἀνθρώπῳ χρώματα καὶ σχήματα καὶ κακίας καὶ ἀρετάς Pl.*Sph.*251a. 7. ἐ. ψῆφον *to give* a vote, D.H.2.14. 8. *subjoin, add,* A.D.*Synt.*60.26, al., Demetr.*Eloc.*34, al., Alex.Aphr.*in Sens.*5.9. 9. *adduce, cite,* Εὐριπίδεια D.H.*Comp.*4; παροιμίαν Demetr.*Eloc.*122 (prob.); *produce* proofs, documents, etc., ἀποδείξεις *POxy.*257.19 (i A.D.); κυρία ἡ συγγραφή, ὅπου ἂν -φέρηται *PEleph.*2.16 (iii B.C.). 10. in Logic, *assert as a conclusion* or *inference,* τὸ λῆγον, τὸ λοιπόν, Chrysipp.*Stoic.*2.80; τὸ μὴ ἀκολουθοῦν Str.2.1.21; ὅτι.. ib.27; ὅσα ἐπιφέρουσιν ἄτοπα οἱ Ζήνωνος λόγοι Procl.*in Prm.*p.535 S.:—Pass., τὸ τοῖς ἐξ ὑποθέσεως ληφθεῖσιν ἐπιφερόμενον the conclusion which *follows from* the premises, Chrysipp.*Stoic.*2.89, cf. Arr.*Epict.*1.7.16. 11. ἐπιφέρων, ὁ, a throw at dice, Eub.57.6. II. Med., *bring with* or *upon oneself, bring as a dowry,* τι Lys.19.14, D.40.19; of soldiers, σιτία Plu.*Sert.*13; ὕδωρ Str.3.1.4. 2. *consume* (*eat*) *in addition,* οἱ μὲν πίνουσι μόνον, οἱ δὲ σιτίον -ονται Hp.*Prorrh.*2.3:—Pass., -ομένη τροφή Sor.1.52. 3. *wear* or *carry on one's person,* Hld.8.11. III. Pass., *rush upon* or *after, attack, assault,* ὅς τις.. ἐπὶ νηυσὶ φέροιτο Il.15.743; τισι Th.3.23: abs., X.*Cyr.*2.4.19, etc.; of a ship, *bear down upon* another, Hdt.8.90; θάλαττα μεγάλη ἐπιφέρεται a great sea *strikes the ship,* X.*An.*5.8.20; *inveigh against,* Hdt.8.61: c. inf., *to be eager to* do, Plb.29.24.5. b. of humours etc. in the body, τὸ -όμενον the *accumulation* of milk, Sor.1.77; διαφορεῖν τὸ ἐπενεχθέν disperse the *abscess,* Gal.1.137; cf. ἐπιφορά I.5a. 2. *to be borne onwards,* of a raft, Hdt.2.96; ἐ. ἐπί τι *to be led to* an opinion, Arist. *Sens.*443a22 (s.v.l.). 3. *impend, threaten,* ἐ. κίνδυνος Plb.2.23.7; mostly in part., προδεικνύειν τὰ ἐπιφερόμενα *coming events,* Hdt.1.209, cf. 3.16; ἐ. κακά Antipho 2.1.7; ὑπεικστῆναι τὸν λόγον ἐπιφερόμενον Pl.*Phlb.*43a; τὰ ἐ. *the following* (in speaking or writing), Plb.3.6. 8. 4. of phrases, *to be applied,* ἡ λέξις -φέρεται τοῖς πράγμασιν Plu. 2.41c; but οἱ διὰ μακροῦ -φερόμενοι λόγοι sustained *outbursts,* Demetr. *Eloc.*196. 5. Gramm., *follow,* of letters in a word, D.T.633.2, Heph.1.4, al., etc.

**ἐπίφευκτος**, ον, *to be avoided,* Asp. *in EN* 186.28.

**ἐπιφημητῆρες**· οἱ ἐπευφημοῦντες, κτλ., Hsch. (-τέρ- cod.).

**ἐπίφημι**, *agree, assent,* νόμῳ Emp.9.5: Aeol. aor. inf. Act. ἐπιφάμεναι, = συγκαταθέσθαι, Hsch.

⊛ **ἐπιφημ-ίζω**, *utter words ominous of the event,* ἰόντος αὐτοῦ ἐπὶ τὴν πεντηκόντερον ἐπεφημίζετο (Med.) Hdt.3.124; ἐ. τινὶ πολλὰ καὶ ἄτοπα D.C.39.39. 2. *promise, pledge,* κείνῳ παῖδ' ἐπεφήμισα.. ἐκδώσειν cj. in E.*IA* 130 (anap.); ἡ ἐκ παιδὸς ἐπιφημισθεῖσα τῷ ἀνδρὶ ἑβδόμη ὑπατεία (of Marius) App.*BC* 1.61. II. *apply the name of* A (acc.) *to* B (dat.), where A is usu. a god, *ascribe* or *assign* B *to* A, ἑκάστῃ μοίρᾳ θεόν Pl.*Lg.*771d; ὅσα τις πράττει τοὺς θεοὺς ἐπιφημίζων *in the name of* the gods, D.20.126; ἅπασι τοῖς μεγάλοις ἐ. τὸ δαιμόνιον Plu. *Publ.*23. 2. later the constr. is reversed, τοῖς θεοῖς τι J.*Ap.*2.37; τὴν ἐλαίας γένεσιν.. τῇ Ἀθηνᾷ Max.Tyr.30.5:—Pass., θεοῖς.. παῖδες ἐπεφημίσθησαν D.C.44.37; ὅσα θεῖα Ἐλευσῖνι ἐπιφημίζεται τῇ χώρᾳ Aristid.1.445 J.; μέρη τῆς γῆς Ποσειδῶνι ἐπιπεφήμισται Id.*Or.*46(3). 16. III. *call, name,* c. dupl. acc., τὸ ἀγαθὸν ἐ. λυσιτελοῦν Pl.*Cra.* 417c, cf. *Ti.*73d; ἀέρα ἐ. σκότος Ph.1.6, cf. 2.43, al., Porph.*Abst.*1.7; Ἡλίου -ίζοντας Αἰήτην υἱέα Jul.*Or.*2.82d. 2. with epexegetic inf., τὴν ἔξω φορὰν ἐπεφήμισεν εἶναι τῆς ταὐτοῦ φύσεως the outer revolution he *called* the revolution of the Same, *ordained* that it should be.., Pl.*Ti.*36c: hence, b. c. acc. inf., *allege, declare,* αὐτὸν Ἀσκληπιοῦ θεράποντα εἶναι Ael.*NA* 8.12; πολλὰ ἐ. αὐτῷ δηλοῦν [τὴν ἔλαφον] Plu. *Sert.*11. 3. *bestow* a name *on,* ὀνόματά τισι Ph.1.304, al., D.C.54. 33; πομπῇ ἐπεφήμισαν οὔνομα νηῶν *named* [the fish πομπίλος] *after..,* Opp.*H.*1.187. IV. in later Prose, *dedicate, devote* to a god, Luc.*Sacr.*10; Διὶ ἀγάλματα Max.Tyr.8.8; τοὺς γενομένους τότε παῖδας Ἄρεως ἐ. Str.5.4.12:—Pass., Id.6.2.9, Ph.2.565, Plu.*Cam.*7, etc. **-ισμα**, ατος, τό, *word of ominous import:* of ill omen, Th. 7.75; of good omen, J.*AJ* 17.5.1 (pl.). **-ισμός**, ὁ, *dedication,* Str. 6.2.9. **-ιστέον**, *one must assign, ascribe,* δουλείαν τινί Ph.2.452, cf. 477.

**ἐπιφθάνω** [ᾰ], *reach first,* aor. 2 part. ἐπιφθάς Batr.213: generally, *reach, attain,* ἡλικίαν, Suid. s.v. ἄνηβος; ἐπέφθη τυραννίδι *PLond.*5. 1676.43 (vi A.D.); *arrive,* ὁ Μουκιανὸς οὔπω ἐπεφθάκει D.C.65.18:—Med., *see before* others, ἐπιτέλλουσαν [Αἶγα] Anon.ap.Suid.

**ἐπι-φθέγγομαι**, *utter after* or *in accordance,* A.*Ch.*457 (lyr.); *utter during* or *in connexion with,* φωνὰς ἐπὶ τῇ καθιερώσει Plu.*Publ.*14; μικρὰ ταῖς σπονδαῖς Id.2.15cd. 2. *attach* a name to, *predicate* a quality of, μίαν ἐπ' αὐτοῖς τέχνην ἐπεφθέγξατο Pl.*Phlb.*18d, cf. Plu. 2.1110e. b. *name, call,* ἃ κρίνα, λείρια δ' ἄλλοι -ονται Nic.*Fr.*74. 27. 3. *quote,* τὸ ῥῆμα, ὅτι.. Ph.*Fr.*12 H.; τοῦτο τὸ κοινὸν πᾶσι πράγμασι Plu.2.436d. 4. simply, *utter, pronounce,* Pl.*Cra.*383a:—Pass., Id.*Sph.*257c. II. *respond,* ὁ μὲν ἡγεῖτο λέγων "ἔξω Χριστιανούς", τὸ δὲ πλῆθος -ετο "ἔξω Ἐπικουρείους" Luc.*Alex.*38. **-φθεγμα**, ατος, τό, *refrain,* παιανικὸν ἐ., of the refrain ἰὴ Παιάν, Ath.15. 696f. II. *interjection,* A.D.*Synt.*52.26. **-φθεγματικός**, ή, όν, *containing a refrain,* [σύστημα] Heph.*Poëm.*7.3. **-φθεγξις**, εως, ἡ, *charm, invocation,* Philagr.ap.Aët.12.51; *cry addressed* to dogs, Sch. Ar.*V.*702.

⊛ **ἐπιφθίνω**, *perish upon,* λείρια στήλῃσιν ἐ. Nic.*Fr.*74.70.

**ἐπιφθον-έω**, *grudge* any one's doing a thing, ᾧ δέ κ' ἐπιφθονέοις (sc. ἆσσον ἴμεν) Od.11.149. II. *bear hate* or *a grudge against,* τινι Hdt. 9.79, *PMasp.*154.9 (vi A.D.):—Pass., *to be regarded with jealous hate,* D.H.9.43. **-ος**, ον, *liable to envy* or *jealousy, looked on with jealousy, odious,* αἱ λίην ἰσχυραὶ τιμωρίαι πρὸς θεῶν ἐ. γίνονται Hdt.4.205; γνώμη πρὸς ἀνθρώπων ἐ. Id.7.139; μηδ'.. ἐ. πόρον τίθει A.*Ag.*921; τινι by one, E.*Med.*303, *Supp.*893; εἴ τῳ θεῶν ἐ. ἐστρατεύσαμεν Th.7.77; [πενία] ἥκιστα ἐ. X.*Smp.*3.9; -ώτεραι (sc. αἱ ἐμαὶ διατριβαί) Pl.*Ap.*

37d, cf. R.502d; ἐπίφθονόν ἐστι c. inf., it is invidious, hateful to.., Ar.Eq.1274; εἴ τῳ "μακαρίως" -ώτερον εἰπεῖν Arist.EE1215a10; τὸ ἐ. envy, ἐπὶ μεγίστοις τὸ ἐ. λαμβάνειν Th.2.64. 2. Act., bearing a grudge against, τινι A.Ag.133 (lyr.): abs., malignant, hostile, Id.Eu. 376 (lyr.), Sammelb.3924.35 (i A.D.); τὸ δαιμόνιον.. ἐ. App.Pun.59; ἐ. βλέμμα Hld.4.5. II. Adv. ἐπιφθόνως, διακεῖσθαί τινι to be liable to his hatred, Th.1.75; ἐ. διαπράξασθαί τι in an invidious manner, Id. 3.82; ἥκιστα ἐ. with least invidiousness, X.Cyr.7.5.37. 2. ἐ. ἔχειν πρός τινα to be at enmity with him, ib.3.3.10, 8.2.28.

**ἐπίφθορος**, ον, (φθορά) deadly, φάρμακον Poll.5.132.

**ἐπιφθύζω**, Dor. **ἐπιφθύσδω**, = ἐπιπτύω, spit at, so as to avert a spell of witchcraft, Theoc.7.127, 2.62.

**ἐπιφῐλο-πονέομαι**, Dep., labour willingly and earnestly at, τινι X. Oec.5.5. **-τῑμέομαι**, bestow, κοινὰς δωρεὰς ἐ. [ὁ νομοθέτης] Lib.Decl. 43.29. ⊕ **-τῑμία**, ἡ, endowment, prob. in IG$2^2$.1369 (ii A.D., pl.).

**ἐπίφλεβος**, ον, (φλέψ) with prominent veins, Hp.Epid.6.4.19, Arist. HA493a3, etc.

**ἐπιφλεβοτομέω**, bleed again, Antyll.ap.Orib.7.7.11.

**ἐπιφλεγ-έθω**, = ἐπιφλέγω, Nic.Al.282. **-ής**, ές, (φλέγω) fiery, χρῶμα Arist.Phgn.812a25. **-μα**, ατος, τό, inflammation on the surface, Iamb.Protr.21.κϛ'. **-μαίνω**, suffer from supervening inflammation, Hp.Fract.38, Aret.SA1.9, etc.

**ἐπι-φλέγω**, burn up, πῦρ.. ἐπιφλέγει ἄσπετον ὕλην Il.2.455; ὄφρ' ἤτοι τοῦτον μὲν [νεκρὸν] ἐπιφλέγῃ.. πῦρ 23.52; of an enemy, πάντα ἐπέφλεγον καὶ ἔκειρον Hdt.8.32; ἐ. τὴν πόλιν set fire to it, Th.2.77:—Pass., Nic.Th.188. 2. heat, inflame, τὴν ἐπιφάνειαν Aët.15.20: metaph., inflame, excite, σάλπιγξ αὐτῇ πάντ' ἐκεῖν' ἐπέφλεγεν A.Pers. 395; ἐ. τινὰ αἴθοπι μώμῳ Tim.Pers.222; Ἀννίβας εὐτυχῶν ἐ. τὴν Ἰταλίαν Plu.Cat.Ma.1; with love, Λαῒς ἐ. πόθῳ τὴν Ἑλλάδα Id.2.767f:—Pass., Arist.Phgn.812a27, Ael.NA15.9. 3. illumine, ἥλιος.. ἐ. ἀκτίνεσσιν D.P.1110: metaph., make illustrious, ἐ. πόλιν ἀοιδαῖς Pi. O.9.22. II. intr., to be scorching hot, of the sun, Luc.Anach.25, D.C.59.7: metaph., to be brilliant, εὐφροσύνα τε καὶ δόξ' ἐ. Pi.P.11. 45. **-φλεξις**, εως, ἡ, application of heat, καῦσις κατ' ἐ., opp. caustics, Paul.Aeg.4.5.

**ἐπιφλεύω**, scorch, χεῖρα IG4.955 (Epid.).

**ἐπιφλόγ-ισμα**, ατος, τό, superficial inflammation, Hp.Aph.5.23 (pl.), Erot. s. v. φῷδες (pl.). **-ώδης**, ες, looking as if inflamed, dub. l. in Hp.Coac.456.

**ἐπιφλυγμός**, ὁ, flooding, v.l. for -βλυσμός, Aq.Ge.2.6.

**ἐπιφλυκταινόομαι**, Pass., have pustules on the top, Hp.Epid.4.20.

**ἐπιφλύω** [ῠ], sputter at, τινι A.R.1.481.

**ἐπίφοβος**, ον, frightful, terrible, A.Ag.1152 (lyr.); alarming, γειτνίασις Plu.Pyrrh.7; τινι J.AJ12.7.5. Adv. -βως, τινι App.Syr.35. II. Pass., in fear, timid, Gal.19.707. Adv. -βως, διάγειν Vett.Val.42. 9. 2. risky, θεραπεία Steph. in Hp.1.211 D.

**ἐπιφοινῑκίζω**, get a purple tinge, Arist.Col.796a2.

**ἐπιφοινίσσω**, make red on the surface, Luc.Am.41. II. intr., incline to be red, be reddish, Arist.Phgn.812a33; -φοινίσσον σημεῖον Thphr.Sign.10:—Pass., -ίσσεται τὸ πρόσωπον Arist.Phgn.812a32; -ίσσονται τοὺς ὀφθαλμοὺς ib.37.

**ἐπιφοιτ-άω**, Ion. -έω, come habitually or in addition, πλεῦνος αἰεὶ γινομένου τοῦ ἐπιφοιτέοντος Hdt.1.97; οἱ ἐπιφοιτῶντές τε καὶ οἱ ἀρχὴν ἐλθόντες the subsequent arrivals, Id.9.28; ὁ ἐπιφοιτῶν κέραμος every new wine-jar imported, Id.3.6; ἐ. ἐς.. to go about to different places, Th.1.135; τὴν γῆν δῃοῦν ἐπιφοιτῶντες visiting, invading it, ib.81; τὰς πόλεις Jul.Or.7.221b: c. dat., τοῖς θεάτροις Ael.VH2.13. 2. c. dat. pers., σπάνιος ἐ. σφι visits them rarely, of the Phoenix, Hdt.2.73, cf. Ph.1.265, Palaeph.37, Luc.Am.9, etc. 3. c. acc. pers., of visions, haunt, Hdt.7.16.γ', cf. 15; of a disease, recur, Hp.Coac.316; spread, ἅπασι [τοῖσι νεύροισι], of rheumatic pains, Aret.SD2.12; ἐπεφοίτα πανταχόσε he went round to every ship, Plu.Ant.65. 4. in mal. part., ταῖς θυγατράσι τινός Hdn.5.3.10. **-εύω**, = foreg. 3, ἡ νοῦσος ἐ. ἐς τὸν ἄνθρωπον Aret.CD1.4. **-ησις**, εως, ἡ, a coming upon one, τῶν στρατιωτῶν J.AJ19.3.2; of a god, intervention, manifestation, ib. 17.2.4, Jul.Or.7.221c, Steph. in Hp.1.74 D. 2. frequenting, ἐπὶ τὴν αὐτῷ ποέπουσαν κοινωνίαν Procl. in Prm.p.519 S. **-ος**, ον, coming upon, τινι Man.4.83.

**ἐπιφονεύω**, slay, Sammelb.4309.15 (iii B.C.).

⊕ **ἐπιφορ-ά**, ἡ, (ἐπιφέρω) bringing to or upon: hence, 1. donative, extra pay, in pl., Th.6.31, D.S.17.94; so ἡ ἔξωθεν ἐ. τῆς εὐδαιμονίας Plb.5.90.4. 2. application, ὀνομάτων Pl.Lg.944b, cf.Cra.430d. 3. second course [at dinner], Damox.2.58 (pl.). 4. fine paid by contractor for failure to keep time, BCH35.44 (Delos), cf. Hermes17.5 (ibid.); = καταδίκη, Hsch. (pl.). 5. application, τὴν τῆς αἰσθήσεως ἐ. ποιεῖσθαι to concentrate attention, Plu.2.1144b. b. infliction, πληγῶν POxy. 283.15 (i A.D.). 6. additional payment of φόρος, IG$1^2$.205, al. II. (from Pass.) offering made at the grave, Plu.Num.22. 2. impact, Epicur.Nat.15.26, al.; sudden attack, Plb.6.55.2, etc.; ἐπιφορὰς πρός τινα ποιῆσαι, in controversy, Phld.Lib.p.35 O.; ἐ. ὄμβρων sudden burst of rain, Plb.4.41.7; of wind, Thphr.CP5.12.11; ἡ τοῦ κωρύκου ἐ. Philostr.Gym.57; attack of an orator, opp. ἀπολογία, Id. VS1.25.10 (pl.). 3. vehemence in oratory, Hermog.Id.1.11, al., Philostr.VS1.17.1, al. 4. growth by assimilation of nourishment, Stoic.2.229. 5. Medic., epiphora, persistent flow of tears, as a disease, Dsc.Eup.1.35, Gal.14.749,768 (but non-technically, floods of tears, Plb.15.26.3); deflux of morbid humours, Meno Iatr.5.30, Plu.2.102a (pl.); τοῦ γάλακτος Sor.1.76; ὀχθώδεις ἐ. tuberous eruption, Ruf.ap.Orib.8.24.35. b. attack, πυρετῶν, etc., Vett.Val.3.4 (pl.), al. 6. propensity, -φορὰς ἔχειν πρός τι Men.Rh.p.342 S. III. Rhet., second clause in a sentence, opp. ἀρχή, D.H.Dem. 20. 2. repetition, συνδέσμου Demetr.Eloc.196. 3. succession of clauses ending in the same word, opp. ἐπιβολή, Rut.Lup.1.8. IV. in Stoic Logic, the conclusion of a syllogism, Chrysipp.Stoic.2.80, Crinis ib.3.269, Procl. in Prm.p.534 S. 2. question at issue, τῆς ἐ. ἀπερρυηκέναι Phld.Mus.p.96 K. V. in Gramm., ἔχειν ἐν ἐπιφορᾷ τὸ λλ to have λλ immediately following, Hdn.Gr.2.932. **-έω**, put, pile upon, ἐπιπολῆς τῶν ξύλων χοῦν γῆς ἐ. Hdt.4.201, cf. 8.28; ἐπὶ τὸν ἅλα γῆν ἐ. Id.4.183; ὕλην Id.7.36; τῆς γῆς πολλήν Ar.Pax 167, cf. X.An.3.5.10; [λίθους] ἄνωθεν Ar.Pax 225. 2. bring, offer, Ph.1. 259. ⊕ **-ημα**, ατος, τό, in pl., dishes served up besides or after, dessert, Hdt.1.133, Ar.Fr.774, Archipp.9, etc.: in sg., Eudox.Com. 2, Luc.Lex.8. 2. offering at the grave, Iamb.VP27.122. **-ικός**, ή, όν, (ἐπιφορά II. 3) impetuous, of style, τὸ ἐ. καὶ σφοδρόν Hermog.Id. 2.6; ἐ. σχήματα Aristid.Rh.1 p.494 S.; ἐ. λόγος (viz. D.21) Longin. Fr.18. II. inferential, illative, [σύνδεσμος] A.D.Conj.227.25, al. Adv. -κῶς Sch.D.T.p.65 H. III. (ἐπιφορά III) forming the second or subsequent clause, [ἐκ]φρασις Lesb.Gramm.12. **-ος**, ον, (ἐπιφέρω) carrying towards, εἰ ἄνεμος ἐπεγένετο τῇ φλογὶ ἐπίφορος ἐς [τὴν πόλιν] Th.3.74, cf. 2.77; favourable, of winds, Paus.8.28.4; ἐπιφορώτατος [Ἑρμῆς] A.Ch.813 (lyr.). II. leaning or prone to a thing, ἐ. κάτω ῥέψαι gloss in Hp.Art.14 (Comp.); πρὸς δεισιδαιμονίαν Plu.2.703d; well-suited, εἴς τι Longin.5, Plu.2.623d. Adv. -ρως ἔχειν πρός τι Str.12.3.26. b. of documents, applicable, relating to the matter in hand (cf. ἐπιφέρω I. 9), POxy.266.14, 1282.33 (i A.D.). 2. of ground, sloping, Hp.Ep.17. III. pregnant, Id. Prorrh.1.103; near the time of bringing forth, X.Cyn.7.2; of plants, Thphr.CP3.2.8.

**ἐπιφορτ-ίζω**, load heavily, overload, J.Ap.2.9; ἄμπελον Gp.9.14.6: metaph., τί τινι Phld.Po.5.2; τὴν τέχνην τισί Gal.8.785; ἐ. πλεῖον τῷ πάσχοντι lay a heavier burden upon, Aët.7.91:—Med., X.Eph.5.2: metaph., levy blackmail on, τινι Sch.Ar.Pl.379:—Pass., have excessive burdens laid on one, PSI4.317.6 (i A.D.). **-ισμός**, ὁ, lading, Gloss.

**ἐπίφραγμα**, ατος, τό, (ἐπιφράσσω) covering, lid, Hero Spir.1.5; ἐπιφράγματα· τὰ ὑπὸ τὸ στόμα, Hsch.

**ἐπιφρᾰδ-έως**, Adv., (ἐπιφράζομαι) circumspectly, wisely, Parm.1. 16, A.R.1.1336; carefully, Id.2.1134, 3.83: Comp. -έστερον Hsch. **-μων**· ψευδολόγος, Id.

**ἐπιφράζω**, say besides, Hdt.1.179 (Bekk. ἔτι φράσαι; for ἐπέφραδε v. sub φράζω); ἐπέφρασεν is prob. f.l. for ἐπεφράσατ' in Orph.Fr. 257. II. elsewh. only in Med., mostly aor. 1, and (in same sense) Pass. aor. 1 ἐπεφράσθην: 1. c. inf., think of doing, take into one's head to do, οἷον δὴ τὸν μῦθον ἐπεφράσθης ἀγορεῦσαι Od.5.183; τὸ μὲν οὔ τις ἐπεφράσατ'.., ἐξερύσαι δόρυ Il.5.665. 2. c. acc., devise, contrive, ὑμῖν δ' ἐπιφράσσετ' ὄλεθρον Od.15.444; κακὴν ἐπεφράσατο τέχνην Hes.Th.160 (s.v.l.); ἐπιφράζεται τοιάδε Hdt.6.61; ἀμήχανον ἐξευρεῖν καὶ -φράσασθαι Id.1.48; [γάμον] Theoc.22.166: abs., ὧδε ἐπιφρασθεὶς having come to this conclusion, Hdt.4.200; ἐπιφρασθεῖσα αὐτὴ by her own mother wit, Id.7.239. 3. notice, observe, Ἀλκίνοος δέ μιν οἶος ἐπεφράσατ' ἠδ' ἐνόησεν Od.8.94; ἐ. τινὰ ποιεῦντα Heraclit.5: c. acc., Arr.An.4.8.2, etc.; ὅσσον.. Il.21.410; ὅτι.. Arr.Ind.27.8; ἐ. κατὰ θυμὸν h.Ap.402; recognize, ἵνα μή μιν ἐπιφρασσαίατ' Ἀχαιοὶ Od. 18.94; acquaint oneself with, take cognisance of, ὡς.. ἐπιφρασσαίατο βουλήν Il.2.282, cf. 13.741; ἐ. ὅκως.. imagine how.., Hdt.5.9.

**ἐπί-φραξις**, εως, ἡ, (ἐπιφράσσω) obstruction of the earth, in eclipses, Plu.2.891f, Anaximand.11. **-φρᾰσις**, εως, ἡ, Rhet., specific mention of an individual, a form of pleonasm, Phoeb.Fig.1.3.

**ἐπι-φράσσω**, Att. -ττω, block up, ὕλῃ [τὴν δίοδον] Thphr.HP9.3.2; πόρους Nic.Al.285: metaph., Ph.1.299, al.:—Med., κηρῷ ἐ. τὰ ὦτα stop one's ears, Luc.Im.14:—Pass., to be obstructed, Placit.2.29.1; τὰ τοῦ μέλλοντος ἀκούειν ὦτα ἐπεφράχθη Ph.2.165. **-φραστικῶς**, Adv. descriptively, vividly, Sch.Opp.H.2.331.

**ἐπίφρενα**· ὑποχόνδρια, Hsch.

**ἐπί-φρικτος**, η, ον, bristling on the surface, φολίδεσσι Nic.Th. 157. **-φριξ**· ἡ ἐπανάστασις τῶν κυμάτων, EM800.28. **-φρίσσω**, Att. -ττω, to be rough or bristling on the surface, χαῖται νώτοις ἐπιπεφρίκασιν Emp.83.2; φολίδεσσι D.P.443; Σειληνοὺς πολιῇσιν -φρίσσοντας ἐθείραις cj. in Nonn.D.35.55; esp. of water, νέποδες.. ἐπιφρίσσουσι γαλήνῃ make a ripple on the calm sea, Opp.C.1.384, cf. Orph. A.1149, Poll.1.106.

**ἐπι-φρονέω**, to be shrewd, prudent, only in part. fem. ἐπιφρονέουσα, = ἐπίφρων, Od.19.385 (exc. that Pl.R.424b substitutes it for the Verb in the Hom. phrase ἀοιδὴν μᾶλλον ἐπικλείουσ' ἄνθρωποι). ⊕ **-φροσύνη**, ἡ, thoughtfulness, wisdom, εἰ μὴ ἐπιφροσύνην δῶκε.. Ἀθήνη Od.5.437: in pl., ἐπιφροσύνας ἀνελέσθαι 19.22, cf. Hes.Th.658, A.R.4.1115; observation, Arat.762; prudent reserve, A.R.3.659: also in late Prose, θεία ἐ. Ph.1.203, al.; κατ' ἐπιφροσύνην J.AJ15.11.3; κατὰ τὴν Σεβαστοῦ Καίσαρος ἐ. Onos.Praef.1.

**ἐπίφρουρος**, ον, keeping watch over, metaph., ξίφος ἐ. δέρῃ E.Or. 1575.

**ἐπίφρων**, ον, gen. ονος, (φρήν) thoughtful, οἵ τε δύνανται ἄφρονα ποιῆσαι.. ἐπίφρονα to make the thoughtful thoughtless, Od.23.12; αἰχμητὴν.. καὶ ἐπίφρονα βουλὴν sage in counsel, 16.242; ἐ. Αὐγείαο Theoc.25.29; also ἐ. βουλή Od.3.128, Hes.Th.122; ἐ. μῆτις Od.19. 326, B.15.25.—Ep. and Lyr., never in Il.

**ἐπι-φύλαξ** [ῠ], ᾰκος, ὁ, watchman, Longus 1.21. **-φῠλάσσω**, watch for, πλοῦν Pl.Lg.866d.

**ἐπιφύλιος** [ῠ], ον, (φυλή) *distributed to the tribes*, χθών E.*Ion* 1577.

**ἐπιφυλλ-ίζω**, *glean grapes in a vineyard*: metaph., *deal hardly with*, Lxx *La.* 1.22, 2.20; cf. ἐπιφαυλίζω. **-ίς**, ίδος, ἡ, (φύλλον) *small grapes left for gleaners*, *AP* 6.191 (Corn. Long.), Lxx *La.* 2.20; interpol. in Dsc. 4.142: metaph., of poetasters, Ar. *Ra.* 92, cf. Sch. ad loc., D.H. *Rh.* 10.18.

**ἐπιφυλλόκαρπος**, ον, *with fruit upon the leaves*, Thphr. *HP* 1.10.8, 3.17.4.

**ἐπί-φῠσις**, εως, ἡ, *ongrowth, excrescence*, ἐ. βλεφάρων, = σῦκον II, Hp. *Epid.* 3.7 (pl.); ἐ. σαρκός, of flesh covering the bone, Id. *Fract.* 4; χονδρίων -φύσιες Id. *Art.* 45; ἡ ἐ. τοῦ δέρματος, such as fishes' scales, Mnesith.ap.Ath. 8.357c. 2. Anat., *epiphysis*, Hp. *Art.* 27, *Fract.* 12; opp. ἀπόφυσις (q.v.), Gal. 2.733. 3. *growth*, -φυσιν λαμβάνειν Thphr. *HP* 1.1.2: metaph., *accretion*, Ph. 1.667; λογικῆς φύσεως ib. 636 (pl.). **-φῠτεύω**, *plant over* or *upon* a thing, Ar. *Pax* 168 (anap.): metaph., in Pass., Lxx 4 *Ma.* 15.6. ⊛ **-φύω**, *make to grow, produce on* or *besides*, Thphr. *HP* 1.9.3. II. Pass., with aor. 2 and pf. Act., ἐπέφῡν, ἐπιπέφυκα: —*grow upon*, [τῷ σήματι] ἐπιπέφυκε ἐλαίη Hdt. 4.34; esp. as an excrescence, Arist. *HA* 605ᵃ3; ταῖς ψυχαῖς ἐ. μελανίαι Plb. 1.81.7; ὁ ἐπιπεφυκώς, with or without ὑμήν, *the conjunctiva*, Gal. 7.101, Steph. *in Hp.* 1.88 D.: hence, *adhere, cling closely to* (cf. ἐμφύω), ἀμφοῖν τοῖν χεροῖν with both hands, Plb. 12.10.6, cf. D.S. 36.15; esp. of dogs, ἐ. τοῖς θηρίοις *stick close to* them, *run* them *hard*, Plu. *Luc.* 1: metaph., τοῖς πλείστοις.. οἷον κῆρες ἐπιπεφύκασιν Pl. *Lg.* 937d, cf. Ph. 1.345; *cleave to*, ἀγαθοῖς interpol. in Plu. 2.6c; *attack*, τινι Id. *Pomp.* 51; δόγματι, opp. ὑπερδικεῖν, Id. 2.694e, cf. Jul. *Or.* 2.86b; ἐπιφύντα νέον ἄνδρα an upstart *interloper*, Plu. *Cleom.* 16.

**ἐπιφων-έω**, *mention by name, tell of*, ἐπιφωνεῖν.. ἱερὰν θήκην S. *OC* 1762 (anap.), cf. Aristaenet. 1.14:—Med., Il. Parv. *Fr.* 2. b. *add a title*, Ph. 1.337. 2. *say with respect to*, τινὶ ἐπιφώνημα Plu. *Alex.* 3; εἴς τι Id. *Luc.* 39; ἐπί τινος Apollon. Cit. 3; *apply* a phrase *to*, τινι Ath. 5.178e: freq. of quoted sayings, ἐ. τὸ τραγικὸν κτλ. Ph. 1.127, cf. Plu. *Alc.* 23, al. 3. *call out, proclaim, exclaim*, ἐ. ὡς "εὖ ἡμῖν βεβίωται" Epicur. *Sent. Vat.* 47; ἐπεφώνουν λέγοντες κτλ. *Ev. Luc.* 23.21, cf. *PRyl.* 77.33 (ii A.D.); ἐ. τινὶ καλῶς λέγειν Aristeas 196, cf. Phld. *Herc.* 1251.17, al., *IG* 14.830 (Puteoli, ii A.D.); τῷ παρὰ δεῖπνον ἀκράτῳ προσδιδομένῳ τὸν Ἀγαθὸν ἐπιφωνοῦσι Δαίμονα Philonid. Med.ap. Ath. 15.675b:—Pass., τὸ τοῖς γαμοῦσιν -φωνούμενον "Ταλασίῳ" Plu. *Pomp.* 4. 4. *respond*, in ritual, Lxx 2 *Ma.* 1.23. 5. *subjoin, add as a finishing touch*, Demetr. *Eloc.* 107:—Pass., ib. 110, Hermog. *Inv.* 4.9. **-ημα**, ατος, τό, *a witty saying*, Plu. *Alex.* 3. 2. Rhet., *phrase added by way of ornament* or *as a finishing touch*, Phld. *Rh.* 1.173 S. (dub.), D.H. *Rh.* 10.18, Demetr. *Eloc.* 106, 109, Quint. 8.5.11, Hermog. *Inv.* 4.9, S.E. *M.* 2.57. 3. Gramm., *interjection*, *AB* 100, Hsch. s.v. κόγξ; σίττα· ἐ. αἰξίν, Id. **-ημᾰτικός**, ή, όν, *of the nature of an* ἐπιφώνημα 2, Hermog. *Inv.* 4.9, Eust. 1038.38. Adv. -κῶς Demetr. *Eloc.* 109, Hermog. *Inv.* 1.5 (Comp.). **-ημάτιον**, τό, Dim. of ἐπιφώνημα 2, Arr. *Epict.* 3.23.31. ⊛ **-ησις**, εως, ἡ, *acclamation, cry*, Plu. *Pomp.* 4. II. *added remark*, Ps.-Plu. *Vit. Hom.* 65. III. *uttering* of a spell, Herm.ap.Stob. 1.49.44 (pl.). IV. *address*, Phld. *Lib.* p. 14 O.; πρὸς τοὺς ἀνθρώπους Sch. Opp. *H.* 2.217. **-ητής**, οῦ, ὁ, gloss on λιγύς, Hsch. **-ητικός**, ή, όν: hence -κόν, τό, *an added word*, Sch. Opp. *H.* 1.204.

**ἐπιφώσκω**, = ἐπιφαύσκω, *grow towards daylight, dawn*, *Ev. Matt.* 28.1, *Ev. Luc.* 23.54, *PLond.* 1.130.39 (i A.D.). II. trans., *let shine forth*, φέγγος Poet. *de herb.* 24.

**ἐπιφωτ-ίζω**, *illuminate*, *POxy.* 2146.4 (iii A.D.):—Pass., Plot. 4.3.10, *Corp. Herm.* 13.21. **-ισμός**, ὁ, *illuminating light*, Plu. 2.936b.

**ἐπιχαίνω**, *gape at*, τινι Luc. *Tim.* 18, *Sacr.* 9, al. 2. *desire greedily*, ἐπικέχηνε πᾶσι τοῖς ἐκτός Ph. 1.211, cf. 2.202. II. = ἐγχαίνω, *mock at*, Anon.ap.Suid.

**ἐπιχαιράγᾰθος** [ᾰγ], ον, *taking delight in what is good*, formed as an opp. to ἐπιχαιρέκακος, Eratosth.ap.Str. 1.3.22.

**ἐπιχαιρεκᾰκ-έω**, *rejoice at another's misfortune*, ἀλλήλοις Phld. *D.* 1.11, cf. Ph. 1.314. **-ία**, ἡ, *joy over one's neighbour's misfortune, spite, malignity*, Arist. *EN* 1107ᵃ10, Ph. 2.394, Plu. 2.91b, etc. **-ος**, ον, *rejoicing over one's neighbour's misfortune*, Anaxandr. 59, Alex. 51, Arist. *EN* 1108ᵇ5, Ph. 2.269, Gal. 4.817.

**ἐπιχαίρω**, *rejoice over, exult over*, mostly of malignant joy, c. dat. rei, κακοῖς τοῖς τοῦδε S. *Aj.* 961; ἀτυχίαις τῶν πέλας Men. 673, cf. Arist. *Rh.* 1379ᵇ17: c. dat. pers., D. 21.134; τινὶ τεθνηκότι Plu. *Eum.* 2; ἐπί τινι Phld. *Mort.* 20: abs., Ar. *Pax* 1015 (anap.), D. 9.61: also in aor. 1 Med., ἐπεχήρατο A.R. 4.55:—Pass., Phld. *Mort.* 20. 2. rarely in good sense, ἐπιχαρῆναι (aor. 2 Pass.) *rejoice in* another's *joy*, Ar. *Th.* 314 (lyr.): c. acc., σὲ μὲν εὖ πράσσοντ' ἐπιχαίρω S. *Aj.* 136 (anap.). 3. *take pleasure in*, c. dat., Hld. 6.14.

**ἐπιχαλᾶ**· τὴν τὸ κανοῦν φέρουσαν εἰς τὰς θυσίας θεράπαιναν (-νας cod.), Hsch.

**ἐπιχᾰλαζάω**, *shower hail upon*, τινά Luc. *Tim.* 58.

**ἐπιχᾰλᾰρός**, ά, όν, *somewhat loose*, Hp. *Art.* 50 (Comp.).

**ἐπιχᾰλάω**, fut. -άσω [ᾰ], *loosen, slacken*, τὸ καλῴδιον Plb. 34.3.5; δεσμόν Luc. *Herc.* 3; ἄκρατος ἐ. τόνους ψυχῆς Ph. 2.227. 2. *drop in*, ἔριον εἰς τὴν ἐξέρασιν *PHolm.* 15.39. II. intr., *give way*, δύαισιν οὐδὲν ἐπιχαλᾷς A. *Pr.* 181 (lyr.); ἐπιθυμίαις Ph. 2.298.

**ἐπιχᾰλεπαίνω**, *to be angry at*, Hsch. and Apollon. *Lex.* s.v. ἐπαλαστήσασα.

**ἐπιχαλκ-εύω**, *forge upon* an anvil, μύδρους A. *Fr.* 307; ἐπιχαλκεύειν παρέχοιμ' ἄν, i.e. you can use me as an anvil (I am so hard), Ar. *Nu.* 422; '*drive home*' a point, Arist. *Rh.* 1419ᵇ15 (dub. sens.). II. Pass., *to be wrought upon*, λεπίδες [τοῖς κίοσιν] -κεχαλκευμέναι J. *AJ* 3.6.3. **-ῖται**, οἱ, = ὁπλῖται, Hsch. **-ος**, ον, *covered with copper* or *brass, brazen*, ἀσπίς Hdt. 4.200, Ar. *V.* 18; στόμα, of a flute-player, Alc. Com. 20; ἐπίχαλκος (sc. ἀσπίς), ἡ, Amips. 17. **-όω**, = -χαλκεύω II, in Pass., J. *AJ* 3.6.2 (s.v.l.).

**ἐπιχάραγμα** [χᾰ], ατος, τό, *impression* on a coin, Hsch. s.v. γλαῦκες Λαυριωτικαί.

**ἐπιχᾰράσσω**, Att. -ττω, *cut into*, φύλλον ἐπικεχαραγμένον a *notched* or *serrated* leaf, Thphr. *HP* 6.2.5. 2. *slash through*, κατὰ μίαν ἐπιβολὴν ὅλα τὰ σώματα Heliod.ap.Orib. 47.14.3. II. *impress upon*, βοῦν νομίσμασιν Plu. *Publ.* 11:—Pass., *to be branded*, [ἵπποις] ἐπικεχαράχθαι πρόσωπον Sch. Il. *Oxy.* 1086.30. 2. *impress subsequently*, Ph. 1.64.

**ἐπιχάρ-εια** [χᾰ], ἡ, *charm, attractiveness*, *PMag. Leid. V.* 12 (prob. cj.). **-ής**, ές, *gratifying, agreeable*, τίς ὧδε τλησικάρδιος.., ὅτῳ τάδ' ἐπιχαρῆ; A. *Pr.* 161 (lyr.); πόρνη καλὴ καὶ ἐ. Lxx *Na.* 3.4. II. of a person, *rejoiced at*, πτώματι ἐχθρῶν Lxx *Jb.* 31.29. **-ιεντίζομαι**, *quote as a good joke*, Luc. *Symp.* 12. **-ιεντισμός**, ὁ, *ornamental epithet*, Sch. Opp. *H.* 1.661. **-ίζομαι**, *make a present of*, τινά τινι X. *Eq.* 6.12. 2. intr., ἐπιχάριττα (Boeot. for ἐπιχάρισαι) τῷ ξένῳ *be civil to* him, Ar. *Ach.* 884. ⊛ **-ις**, ὁ, ἡ, neut. ἐπίχαρι, *pleasing, charming*, οὐδ' ἐ. Ἄρης A. *Th.* 910 (lyr.), etc.; ἐ. ἐν ταῖς συνουσίαις X. *Cyr.* 1.4.4; χάρις οὐκ ἐ. Pl. *Lg.* 853d; σιμός, ἐ. κληθεὶς Id. *R.* 474d; θηρίον ἐ., of the hare, X. *Cyn.* 5.33; τὸ ἐ. *pleasantness of manner*, Id. *An.* 2.6.12; *elegance*, of mathematical study, Pl. *R.* 528d: Comp. and Sup. ἐπιχαριτώτερος, -τατος (as if from **ἐπιχάριτος** which is found later, Alciphr. 2.4, Ptol. *Tetr.* 166, prob. in 164), X. *Smp.* 7.5, *Oec.* 7.37. Adv. -τως Id. *Ap.* 4, Isoc. 15.8; Boeot. ἐπιχαρίτως dub. l. in Ar. *Ach.* 867.

⊛ **ἐπίχαρμα**, ατος, τό, *object of malignant joy*, E. *HF* 459, Theoc. 2.20, Posidipp. 42: condemned by Poll. 3.101. II. *malignant joy*, E. *Ph.* 1555 (pl., anap.).

**ἐπιχάροψ**, οπος, ὁ, ἡ, *bluish-eyed*, *Arch. Pap.* 4.142 (ii A.D.).

**ἐπιχάρ-της**, ου, ὁ, *one who rejoices malignantly*, Philonid. 11: condemned by Poll. 3.101. **-τικός**, ή, όν, *expressive of joy*, ἐπιφώνημα *AB* 100. **-τος**, ον, *wherein one feels joy*, ἔργον S. *Tr.* 1262 (anap.); γεραροῖς ἐπίχαρτον A. *Ag.* 722 (lyr.). 2. more freq., *wherein one feels malignant joy*, ἐχθροῖς ἐπίχαρτα πέπονθα Id. *Pr.* 159 (anap.); οἱ δικαίως τι πάσχοντες ἐ. Th. 3.67, cf. D. 45.85; βαρβάροις ἐ. γενόμενος Pl. *Ep.* 356b.

**ἐπιχαρωπός**, όν, *bluish*, dub. l. in *Stud.* 307 (leg. ἐπιχάροπος vel ἐστὶ χ.).

**ἐπιχασμάομαι**, *yawn at* a thing, Hld. 4.5.

**ἐπιχαταί** (χατέω)· ἐνδεεῖς, Hsch.

**ἐπιχαυνόω**, *relax*, τὰς χορδάς Phlp. *in Ph.* 201.30:—Pass., metaph., *to be elated at*, εὐτυχίαις Iamb. *Protr.* 21.κϛ'.

**ἐπιχέζω**, fut. -χεσοῦμαι, *ease oneself upon*, Ar. *Lys.* 440, *Ec.* 640: pf., ἐπικέχοδα Id. *Av.* 68.

**ἐπιχειλής**, ές, (χεῖλος) *on* or *at the lips*, γλῶσσα ἐ. a *ready, chattering* tongue, Poll. 6.120. II. *full up to the rim* (i.e. not quite full, as the rim was deep), of Themistocles, ἐποίησεν τὴν πόλιν ἡμῶν μεστήν, εὑρὼν ἐπιχειλῆ Ar. *Eq.* 814. 2. later, *brim-full*, πίθος ἐ. τῶν ἀγαθῶν Them. *Or.* 13.174d, cf. 8.115a: metaph., πλήρεις καὶ ἐ. ἁμαρτίαι Ph. 1.517. III. *with the lips drawn in*, like old people, Alciphr. 3.55.

**ἐπιχειμ-άζω**, *pass the winter at* a place or *in* an enterprise, Th. 1.89. II. impers., *it is stormy at the same time*, c. dat., Gem. *Calend.* 5:—Pass., -άζεται ὑετῷ ibid. III. trans., *distress*, σεαυτόν Men. 970. **-έριος**, ον, *exposed to stormy weather*, Thphr. *Vent.* 14.

**ἐπιχειρ-έω**, (χείρ) *put one's hand to*, οἱ μὲν δείπνῳ ἐπεχείρεον Od. 24.386, cf. 395; πηδαλίοις Ar. *Eq.* 542. 2. *put one's hand to* a work, *set to work at, attempt*, τῇ διώρυχι Hdt. 2.158; δρησμῷ ἐ. *attempt* an escape, Id. 6.70; τῇ ὁδῷ Id. 7.43, cf. E. *Ba.* 819; τοῖσι βασιληΐοισι Hdt. 3.61; τυραννίδι Id. 5.46; ἔργῳ τοσούτῳ Id. 9.27; λόγοις, τέχνῃ, Pl. *Phdr.* 279a, *Grg.* 521d, etc.; τοῖς ἀδυνάτοις X. *Mem.* 2.3.5, cf. Isoc. 5.41, etc. 3. less freq. c. acc., μεγάλα ἔργα Thgn. 75; δίκαιον πρᾶγμα Pl. *Cri.* 45c, *Phlb.* 57b:—Pass., *to be attempted*, Th. 4.55, 6.31, X. *Cyr.* 6.1.41, etc.; τὸ ἐπιχειρούμενον *the thing attempted*, Pl. *Lg.* 746b. 4. c. inf., *endeavour, attempt* to do, Hdt. 3.38, 65, 9.42, Ar. *Ra.* 81, Th. 2.40, etc.: c. fut. inf., J. *BJ* 6.7.3:—Pass., ἃ τὸ πρῶτον ἐπεχειρήθη πραχθῆναι Pl. *Ep.* 337d, cf. Id. *Ti.* 53a, al. 5. ἐπεχειρήθη c. dat., *an operation was performed*, τῇσιν αἱμορροΐσι Hp. *Epid.* 5.20. II. *make an attempt on, attack*, τινι Hdt. 1.11, 26, 190, Th. 3.94, Ar. *V.* 1030, etc.; πρός τινα Th. 7.21; ἐπί τινα Pl. *Mx.* 241d (but ἐπὶ τὴν τοῦ σώματος διαφθοράν with a view to.., Arist. *Pol.* 1315ᵃ24); εἰς τὰς σατραπείας D.S. 14.80: abs., Hdt. 5.72, 8.108, etc.; κτείνων ἢ ἐπιχειρῶν Lex ap. And. 1.98:—Pass., Th. 2.11. b. sens. obsc., ἐ. μειρακίοις Jul. *Mis.* 359d. III. *attempt to prove, argue dialectically*, Pl. *Tht.* 205a, Hermog. *Inv.* 3.4; περί τινος Arist. *Top.* 101ᵃ30; ἔκ τινος from a topic, ib. 115ᵃ26; ἔς τι D.L. 4.28; ἐ. ὅτι.. Arist. *Top.* 128ᵇ26: abs., Id. *APr.* 66ᵃ34; λογικώτερον ἔστιν ἐπιχειρεῖν ὧδε Id. *Cael.* 275ᵇ12. **-ημα**, ατος, τό, *undertaking, attempt*, esp. of a military *enterprise*, Th. 7.47, X. *HG* 1.2.6, Isoc. 2.8, etc.; μανικὸν ἐ. ἐπιχειρεῖν Pl. *Alc.* 1.113c; πολλὴ μωρία καὶ τοῦ ἐ. Id. *Prt.* 317a. 2. *base of operations against*, κατὰ Κύπρου App. *Syr.* 52. II. in the Logic of Arist., *attempted*, i.e. *dialectical proof*, opp. a demonstrative syllogism (φιλοσόφημα), *Top.* 162ᵃ16, etc.: so in Rhet., [Cic.] *ad Herenn.* 2.2.2, D.H. *Din.* 6, *Is.* 16, Demetr. Lac. 1055.18 F, Hermog. *Inv.* 3.4, Gal. 5.221, etc.; περὶ -ημάτων, title of work by Minucianus. **-ημᾰτικός**, ή, όν, *tentative*, λόγοι Arist. *Mem.* 451ᵃ19. Adv. -κῶς Aristid. *Rh.* 2 p. 540 S.,

Syrian. *in Metaph.*32.3. **-ησις**, εως, ἡ, *an attempt upon, attack*, Hdt.1.11, Th.2.11 (pl.), 4.130; ἡ ἐ. τινος ἐπί τινας *Act.Ap.*12.1 cod. D; τὴν ἐ. μὴ συντάχυνε the *attempt*, Hdt.3.71; ἐκφέρειν τὴν ἐ. Id.8.132; ἐ. ποιεῖσθαί τινος *attempt* a thing, Th.1.70; ἡ ὑμετέρα ἐ. the *attempt* upon you, ib.33; ἡ ἐ. τοῦ σῶσαι Pl.*Alc.*1.115b, cf. *Lg.*631a. II. *dialectical reasoning* (cf. ἐπιχείρημα II), Arist.*Top.*111b16, al.; τὴν ἐ. ποιεῖσθαι κατὰ τὸν εἰκότα λόγον Plb.12.7.4, cf. Phld.*Sign.*29 (pl.), D.H.*Amm.*1.8, Plu.2.698a, S.E.*P.*2.192 (pl.); τὰ ἐφ' ἑκάτερα τὴν ἐ. δεχόμενα things capable of proof or disproof, Hermog.*Prog.*5. **-ητέον** or **-έα**, *one must attempt*, Pl.*Ap.*19a; μείζοσι Isoc.*Ep.*9.18. 2. ἐπιχειρητέα *one must attack*, Th.1.118, 2.3. 3. *one must argue dialectically*, πρός τι to a conclusion, Arist.*Top.*120b8. II. **-ητέος**, α, ον, *to be attempted*, ὅμως δὲ καὶ τοῦτο ἐ. Antipho 2.2.4. **-ητής**, οῦ, ὁ, *an enterprising person*, opp. ἄτολμος, Th.8.96, cf. D.C.59.17: c. gen., *ready to attempt*, παντός Pl.*Ti.*69d. **-ητικός**, ή, όν, *in* or *for attack*, δεινότης Plu.2.978b. II. ἡ -κὴ δύναμις the faculty *of argumentation*, Arr.*Epict.*1.8.7. 2. *attempting to prove*, Ascl.*in Metaph.*224.6, Alex.Aphr. *in Metaph.*176.35. **-ίζω**, *set upon, attack*, Hsch. s. v. ἀλληλίζεσθαι (s.v.l.). II. ἐν ᾗ ἦν ἐπικεχειρισμένος βασιλικῇ γραμματείᾳ while *at his post of* basilicogrammateus, *POxy.*1274.7 (iii A.D.), cf. *Sammelb.*4472.

**ἐπιχειρογρᾰφέω**, *add an attestation to*, σύνταξιν *PSI*5.509.18 (iii B.C.), cf. 515.8 (iii B.C.).

**ἐπίχειρον**, τό, (χείρ) *arm*, Lxx*Je.*31(48).25. II. in pl., **ἐπίχειρα**, τά, prop. *wages of manual labour*: hence, *wages, pay*, 1. of *reward*, Ar.*V.*581, *Trag.Adesp.*116, Theoc.*Ep.*18.8; ἀρετῆς ἐ. Pl.*R.*608c; ironically in D.*Ep.*3.38, Plb.8.12.5, etc.: rarely in sg., Id.38.3.2. 2. more freq. of *punishment*, τοιαῦτα τῆς ὑψηγόρου γλώσσης..τἀπίχειρα γίγνεται A.*Pr.*321, cf. Antipho 1.20, Arr.*Epict.*3.24.24, Ph.1.512, etc.; τῆς προπετείας πικρὰ κομίζονται τὰ. Phld.*Ir.*p.32 W.; ξιφέων ἐ. λαχοῦσα *the wages* of the sword, i.e. slaughter by it, S.*Ant.*820 (lyr.). (Sts. written ἐπιχείρια in codd., vulg. in Hp.*Praec.*1.)

**ἐπιχειρο-νομέω**, *gesticulate*, Ph.1.298, 2.485: metaph., *grasp at*, ταῖς πλεονεξίαις ib.371 (s.v.l.); οἱ ἐπιχειρονομοῦντες, = οἱ ταῖς χερσὶν ὡς νόμοις χρώμενοι, Hsch. **-τονέω**, *sanction* or *confirm by vote*, of the Assembly, ἐπειδὰν ἐπιχειροτονῆτε τὰς γνώμας D.4.30; ἡ εἰρήνη ἡ ἐπιχειροτονηθεῖσα Decr.ap.eund.18.29; incorrectly, ἐπεχειροτόνησεν ἡ βουλὴ καὶ ὁ δῆμος Decr.ib.105. 2. *confirm in office*, τὰς ἀρχὰς Arist.*Ath.*43.4, cf. 37.1; τοὺς προέδρους -τονεῖν the π. shall *confirm* the appointment, Lex ap.D.24.39: hence, of a Roman Tribune, ἐπεχειροτόνησε τῷ Μαρίῳ τὴν στρατηγίαν *got* the Praetorship for him, Plu.*Mar.*35. **-τονία**, ἡ, *voting by show of hands*, Pl.*Lg.*755e; -τονίαν διδόναι, εἰ δοκεῖ..ἢ μή Arist.*Ath.*43.5. 2. *confirmation* of the powers of magistrates, D.58.27 (pl.), Arist.*Ath.*55.4; ἐ. αὐτῶν ἐστι..εἰ δοκοῦσιν καλῶς ἄρχειν ib.61.2. b. ἐ. νόμων *confirmation* of the existing laws, Lex ap.D.24.20.

**ἐπιχερρονησιάζω**, *approach a peninsular form*, dub. in Str.6.3.1 (ἐστὶ δέ τι χερρονησιάζουσα Coraes).

**ἐπιχέω**, fut. -χέω, 2 sg. ἐπιχεῖς Ar.*Pax*169: aor. 1 ἐπέχεα; Ep. aor. 1 ἐπέχευα, inf. ἐπιχεῦαι (v. infr.):—*pour over*, χέρνιβα δ' ἀμφίπολος προχόῳ ἐπέχευε..νίψασθαι Od.1.136, etc.; in full, χερσὶν ὕδωρ ἐπιχεῦαι Il.24.303; χερσὶ δ' ἐφ' ὕδωρ χευάντων Od.4.213, etc.; also οἴνῳ ἐπιχεῖν ὕδωρ X.*Oec.*17.9. 2. metaph., τοῖσι δ' ἐφ' ὕπνον χεῦε Il.24.445; Τρῶες δ' ἐπὶ δούρατ' ἔχευαν 5.618; ἀνέμων ἐπ' ἀϋτμένα χεῦε Od.3.289; θρῆνον *pour* a lament *over* one, Pi.*I.*8(7).64 (tm.); ὀδμὴν A.R.2.191 (tm.); βλασφημιῶν ἐ. (gen. partit.) Luc.*JTr.*35. 3. of solids, *heap up*, θανόντι χυτὴν ἐπὶ γαῖαν ἔχευαν Od.3.258, cf. Il.23.256; ἐπὶ σῆμ' ἔχεεν 6.419:—Med., ὕπερθ' ἐπὶ σῆμα χέεσθαι A.R.3.205. II. *pour in*, ἀπαντλοῦντα καὶ ἐ. Pl.*R.*407d; ἓν ἀγαθὸν ἐπιχέασα, τρί' ἐπαντλεῖ κακά Diph.107 codd. Stob.; *fill* a cup, Ναννοῦς καὶ Λύδης ἐπίχει δύο *AP*12.168 (Posidipp.).

B. Med., *pour* or *throw over oneself*, χύσιν δ' ἐπεχεύατο φύλλων Od.5.487; κατακλιθεὶς ἐπιχείσθω τὴν πέριξ ἄμμον Antyll.ap.Orib.10.8.4; ἐπεχεύατο πήχεε παιδί she *threw her* arms *round* the boy, A.R.1.268; but πολλὴν ἐπεχεύατο ὕλην *for himself*, Od.5.257. 2. *pour itself over*, Q.S.14.604. 3. *anoint oneself*, ἀπὸ δείπνου *Test.Epict.*4.22. II. *have poured out for one to drink*, ἐ. ἄκρατόν τινος *drink* it to any one's health or honour, esp. of lovers' toasts, Theoc.14.18, cf. Antiph.81.2 codd. Ath.; ἔρωτος ἀκράτῳ (gen. partit.) ἐπεχεῖτο Theoc.2.152; also simply ἐπιχεῖσθαί τινος Phylarch.31 J.

C. Pass., *to be poured over*, ἰλύος ἐπιχυθείσης X.*Oec.*17.12: metaph., τοῖς Ἑλληνικοῖς ὀνόμασι τῶν Ἰταλικῶν ἐπικεχυμένων Plu.*Rom.*15. 2. metaph., of a crowd, *stream on* or *in pursuit*, ἐπέχυντο (Ep. aor. 2 Pass.) Il.15.654; ἀνὰ νῆας 16.295; so, *come like a stream over*, τοῖσι ἐναντίοισι ἐπιχυθέντας..μῦς ἀρουραίους Hdt.2.141; τοσούτων μοι πραγμάτων ἐπικεχυμένων Theopomp.Hist.217c. 3. *to be poured in as an addition*, τοῦ νῦν ἐπικεχυμένου λόγου, of the discussion, *that has* now *been started*, Pl.*Plt.*302c; ὁ νυνδὴ λόγος ἡμῖν ἐπιχυθεὶς Id.*Lg.*793b. II. *to be drowned in*, ἰχθῦς νάπυϊ ἐπικεχυμένους Luc.*Asin.*47.

**ἐπιχηρεύω**, *remain in widowhood*, μετά τινος τελευτὴν J.*AJ*20.7.3.

**ἐπιχητία(ς)**· ἐνδεής, Hsch.

**ἐπιχθόνιος**, ον, Ep. Adj., (χθών) *upon the earth, earthly*, freq. in Hom., as epith. of ἄνθρωποι, ἄνδρες, βροτοί, Od.8.479, Il.1.266, 272: abs., ἐπιχθόνιοι *earthly ones, men on earth* (cf. χαμαί), opp. ἐπουράνιοι θεοί, 24.220, cf. Pi.*O.*6.50, B.4.15, etc.; so ἐ. γένος ἀνδρῶν Pi.*Fr.*213.3; ἐ. δαίμονες *who haunt the earth*, Hes.*Op.*123. 2. in pl., *natives* of a country, D.P.459, 1093. 3. *terrestrial*, opp. marine, ἑρπετόν Opp.*H.*2.425.

**ἐπιχιλάδιον**· τὸ χιλιοστόν, Hsch. **ἐπιχιλές**· τὸ ἐλλιπές, Id. **ἐπιχιλοῦντες**· πληροῦντες, Id.; cf. χιλός.

**ἐπιχλευάζω**, *jeer*, abs., Ph.1.193, 426, al.: c. acc., *make a mock of*, τι Plu.*Num.*22; τινα App.*Syr.*53; *mock at*, τινὶ ὅτι.. Plu.2.93b; *say scornfully*, κερδῶ δ' ἐπεχλεύαζεν ὡς.. Babr.82.4, cf. Ph.2.436.

**ἐπιχλῐαίνω**, *warm on the surface* or *slightly*, Luc.*Alex.*21:—Pass., *grow warm*, Hp.*Coac.*611.

**ἐπίχλοος**, ον, (χλόα) *with a green surface*, πέτραι ποιῇσιν ἐ. Opp.*H.*1.131.

**ἐπιχνοάω**, *to be downy on the surface*, ἐθείραις A.R.1.672.

**ἐπίχνοος**, contr. -χνους, ὁ, *a wool-like covering* on the eyes, Hp.*Prorrh.*1.17.

**ἐπι-χόα**· κατάχυσις, Hsch. **-χοάζω**, *pour libations upon*, τοῖς τελευτήσασι Lyd.*Mens.*4.31.

**ἐπιχοή**, ἡ, *alluvial soil*, Str.15.1.16.

**ἐπιχολ-όομαι**, (χολή) *turn into bile*, Gal.15.599. **-ος**, ον, *full of bile, bilious*, πυρετοί Hp.*Fract.*35; *splenetic, ill-tempered*, Philostr.*VS*2.8.2; ταῖς ὀργαῖς Plu.2.129c. II. Act., *producing bile*, ποίη -ωτάτη Hdt.4.58.

**ἐπιχορδίς**, ίδος, ἡ, (χορδή) earlier name for μεσεντέριον (q. v.), Aret.*SA*2.6.

**ἐπιχορεύω**, *dance to* or *in honour of* a thing, Ar.*Pax*1317; *come dancing on*, X.*Smp.*9.4; comically of dishes brought to table, ἄριστον ἐπεχόρευσεν Diph.44.1; εἰς τὸ μέσον ἐ. σαπέρδης Id.64.4. II. *add a chorus* or *choral song*, τοιοῦτό τι Philostr.*VA*5.14.

**ἐπιχορηγ-έω**, *supply, furnish*, Hero *Dioptr.*31; σπέρμα τῷ σπείροντι 2*Ep.Cor.*9.10; ὑμῖν τὸ πνεῦμα *Ep.Gal.*3.5; τὸ ἐοικέναι τοῖς νοητοῖς εἴδεσιν Dam.*Pr.*341; esp. of a husband, *provide for* a wife, ἐ. τῇ γαμουμένῃ τὰ δέοντα *POxy.*905.10 (ii A.D.), cf. 282.6 (i A.D.); conversely, ἐὰν [γυνὴ] ἐ. τῷ ἀνδρὶ αὐτῆς Lxx*Si.*25.22(30):—Pass., τὰ ἀπὸ Λιμυρικῆς -ούμενα *Peripl.M.Rubr.*60; τοῖς παρ' ἑτέρων -ηθεῖσι πλούτοις D.H.1.42; πᾶν τὸ σῶμα διὰ τῶν ἁφῶν..ἐπιχορηγούμενον καὶ συμβιβαζόμενον *Ep.Col.*2.19. **-ημα**, ατος, τό, *an additional supply*, Ath.4.140c (pl.). **-ητέον**, *one must supply*, Sor.1.87. **-ία**, ἡ, *supply, provision*, τῆς ἐ. γενομένης ἐκ τῶν ἱερῶν προσόδων *SIG*818.9 (Ephesus, i A.D.); πᾶν τὸ σῶμα..συμβιβαζόμενον διὰ πάσης ἁφῆς τῆς ἐπιχορηγίας, = διὰ πασῶν τῶν ἐπιχορηγουσῶν ἁφῶν (cf. ἐπιχορηγέω fin.), *Ep.Eph.*4.16; διὰ τῆς ἐ. τοῦ πνεύματος *Ep.Phil.*1.19.

**ἐπιχορῐαμβικὸν** μέτρον, metre in which choriambs and trochees are combined, Heph.14.2, Aristid.Quint.1.28, Sch.metr.Pi.*O.*8, etc.

**ἐπιχορτάζω**, *supply with provender*, Sosith.2.13.

**ἐπιχραίνω**, *colour on the surface*, τὸ σῶμα Luc.*Bis Acc.*6; ἐπικεχράνθαι (vulg. -κεχρῶσθαι) Id.*JTr.*8.

**ἐπίχρᾱσις**, εως, ἡ, apptly. for ἐπίχρησις, *use*, *BCH*6.23 (Delos, ii B.C.).

**ἐπιχράω** (A), (χράω A) *touch on the surface, graze*, c. gen., τάων (sc. Ἁρπυιῶν) ἀκροτάτῃσιν ἐπέχραον..χερσί A.R.2.283: c. acc., τυτθὸν ἐπέχραε δέρμα Q.S.11.480.

**ἐπιχράω** (B), (χράω B), poet. word, only aor. 2 or impf. ἐπέχραον, *attack, assault*, c. dat., ὡς δὲ λύκοι ἄρνεσσιν ἐπέχραον..ὡς Δαναοὶ Τρώεσσιν ἐπέχραον, Il.16.352, 356; μητέρι μοι μνηστῆρες ἐπέχραον *beset* her, Od.2.50. 2. abs., *to be violent, rage*, of the winds, A.R.2.498. 3. c. inf., *to be urgent* or *eager* to do, Id.4.508: c. acc. et inf., [ἀνάγκη] με..νεῖσθαι ἐπέχραε *was urgent* that I should come, Id.3.431.

***ἐπιχράω** (C), *lend besides*, cf. ἐπικίχρημι. II. **ἐπιχράομαι**, *make use of besides*, ἐ. χθονί *to have the use of* it *besides*, E.*Rh.*942; *make use of also*, Ruf.ap.Orib.8.39.2. 2. c. dat. pers., *have dealings with* one, Th.1.41; αἱ ἐπιχρεώμεναι [αὐτῇ] μάλιστα γυναῖκες her most *intimate* friends, Hdt.3.99, cf. Pl.*Lg.*953a.

**ἐπι-χρεία**, ἡ, *use, need*, *PFlor.*207 (iii A.D.); *equipment, stores*, of a ship, *PLond.*3.948.12 (iii A.D.). **-χρειον**, τό, *what is necessary*, τὸ τῆς διατροφῆς ἐ. ib.5.1708.223 (vi A.D.).

**ἐπιχρεμέθω**, *neigh, whinny to*, A.R.3.1260, Q.S.11.328.

**ἐπιχρέμπτομαι**, *punctuate with spitting*, τοῖς λεγομένοις Luc.*Rh.Pr.*19.

**ἐπιχρηματ-ίζω**, *enact a subsequent measure*, *SIG*704 *H* 24 (Epist. Amphict., ii B.C.). **-ισμός**, ὁ, dub. sens. in *IGRom.*4.503 (Pergam.).

**ἐπιχρησιμεύω**, *make more effective*, Paul.Al.*O.*4.

**ἐπιχρησμῳδέω**, *make an oracular pronouncement upon*, τῷ ἑαυτοῦ βίῳ Philostr.*VS*1.8.2: c. acc., ἑαυτοῦ λόγον Id.*VA*5.14.

**ἐπιχρίμπτω**, *bring upon*, νέφος ἐπὶ γαῖαν B.*Fr.*20.3. 2. *attack*, τινα Opp.*C.*2.171. II. Pass., *lean over* or *towards*, A.R.1.1235.

**ἐπί-χρισις**, εως, ἡ, *smearing over*, βελῶν Str.4.4.6 (pl.), cf. Sever. ap.Aët.7.96. **-χρισμα**, ατος, τό, *unguent*, Dsc.1.70.3, cf. Gal.19.382. **-χριστέον**, *one must smear over*, *Gp.*16.18.1, Aët.7.51. **-χριστος**, ον, *smeared on*, φύκη Luc.*Am.*41; φάρμακα Str.11.8.7, cf. Porph.*Abst.*1.27. 2. *rouged, painted*, ἑταίρας ἄνθος Max.Tyr.37.4: metaph., Id.31.6; εὐμορφία Luc.*Tim.*28. **-χρίω** [ῑ], *anoint, besmear*, ἐπιχρίοντες ἀλοιφῇ (sc. τὸ τόξον) Od.21.179; χρῶτ' ἀπονιψαμένη καὶ ἐπιχρίσασα παρειάς 18.172:—Med., χρῶτ' ἀπονίπτεσθαι καὶ ἐπιχρίεσθαι ἀλοιφῇ ib.179. 2. *plaster over*, τινι with a thing, Luc.*Hist.Conscr.*62. II. *lay on* ointment, μετὰ τὸ -χρισθῆναι Zopyr.ap.Orib.14.58.1; κροτάφοις -χριόμενα v.l. in Dsc.3.22; πηλὸν ἐπὶ τοὺς ὀφθαλμούς *Ev.Jo.*9.6, cf. *IG*14.966 (Rome, ii A.D.). 2. abs., *use for anointing*, Call.*Iamb.*1.270. **-χροά**, ἡ, *tinge*, Thphr.*Fr.*159 (pl.).

**ἐπιχρόϊσις,** εως, ἡ, perh. *stains* on clothes, Thphr.*CP*2.5.4 codd. (pl.); cf. ἐπίχρωσις.

**ἐπιχρον-ίζω,** *last long*, Thphr.*Ign.*61; ὅταν [τὸ θερμὸν] -χρονίσῃ Arist.*Pr.*936$^{a}$20; ἐπικεχρονικός *inveterate, chronic*, Gal.11.103:—Pass., ἀὴρ -όμενος ψυχθείς when cooled *in course of time*, Arist.*Pr.* 942$^{a}$33. **-ιος,** α, ον, *lasting for a time, long*, Cic.*Att.*6.9.3. **-ος·** ἐπίχαρτος, Hsch.

**ἐπίχροος,** ον, *coloured*, *Gloss.*

**ἐπίχρυσ-ος,** ον, *overlaid* or *plated with gold*, Hdt.1.50, al., *IG*1$^{2}$.280, X.*Mem.*3.10.14, Longus 1.5, etc.; ὑπάργυρα ἐ. *IG*1$^{2}$.386.7. II. *rich*, prob. for ὑπό-, Hld.2.8. **-όω,** *overlay with gold*, *Gloss.*:—Pass., γρῦπες -κεχρυσωμένοι *BCH*35.260 (Delos, ii B.C.), cf. *Edict. Diocl.Geronthr.*9.22.

**ἐπιχρῴζω,** = ἐπιχρώννυμι, *tinge*, Arist.*Col.*791$^{a}$9; λίτρῳ χαλινά Nic.*Al.*337:—Pass., D.S.2.52.

**ἐπιχρωματίζω,** *render colour*, χρώματα τῶν τεχνῶν τοῖς ὀνόμασι καὶ ῥήμασι with words, Pl.*R.*601a.

**ἐπιχρωματικός,** ή, όν, *partly chromatic*, Ptol.*Harm.*2.1.

**ἐπιχρωνῆν,** dub. l. in Thphr.*Char.*16.2.

**ἐπι-χρώννῡμι** and **-ύω,** fut. -χρώσω: pf. -κέχρωκα Plu. (v. infr.):—*rub* or *smear over, colour on the surface, tinge*, τι Ruf.*Anat.*30, Plu. 2.395e, cf. Plot.4.5.7; τινι with a thing, Luc.*Dom.*8; οὐκ ἄχρι τοῦ ἐπικεχρῶσθαι μόνον, ἀλλ' ἐς βάθος..φαρμάκοις..καταβαφεῖσα Id.*Im.* 16: metaph., ψυχὴ ἐπακτὸν νοῦν ἔχει -χρωννύντα αὐτήν Plot.5.6.4:—Pass., δόξαις ἐπικεχρωσμένοι *merely tinged* with.., Pl.*Ep.*340d. **-χρωσις,** εως, ἡ, *surface-stain*, Plu.2.382c (pl.), Gal.*Phil.Hist.*27 (= Zeno *Stoic.*1.26); cf. ἐπιχρόϊσις.

⊛ **ἐπί-χῠμα,** ατος, τό, (ἐπιχέω) an eye-disease, = ὑπόχυμα, Sch.rec.A. *Pr.*499, Phlp.*in de An.*350.33. II. *extra amount* of oil, *PRyl.*97.5 (ii A.D.). **-χύνω,** late form for ἐπιχέω, Herm.ap.Stob.1.49.69, *JHS*19.73 (Galatia), etc. ⊛ **-χῠσις,** εως, ἡ, (ἐπιχέω) *pouring upon* or *in, influx*, Pl.*Ti.*77d, Arist.*Mete.*356$^{a}$6; ποταμῶν ἐπιχύσεις Ath.8. 331d; τῶν ὄμβρων D.C.41.45: metaph., ἐ. πολιτῶν Pl.*Lg.*740e; τῆς τῶν ἡδονῶν ῥώμης ib.841a. 2. = ὑπόχυσις, Phlp.*in de An.*291.32. 3. = κονίασις, Hsch. II. *toast*, Plb.16.21.12 (pl.); ἐπιχύσεις τινὸς λαμβάνειν, ποιεῖσθαι (cf. ἐπιχέω II), Plu.*Demetr.*25, *Brut.*24. 2. *anointing*, ἐν ταῖς ἐπιχύσεσι *IG*12(1).155.121 (Rhodes). III. *beaker* or *wine-jug*, Men.503, Phylarch.44J., Plaut.*Rud.*1319; ἐ. τοῦ χαλκίου Ar.*Fr.*214. **-χῠτέον,** *one must pour in* or *over*, Dsc.2.76.5; *one must pour in more*, Herod.Med.ap.Orib.10.37. 12. ⊛ **-χῠτήρ,** ῆρος, ὁ, = ἐπίχυσις III, Sm.*Za.*4.2. **-χῠτήριον,** *perfusorium*, *Gloss.* **-χύτης** [ῠ], ου, Dor. **-χύτας,** ὁ, = -χυτήρ, *IG*11(2).161*B*26 (Delos, iii B.C.), *BCH*33.172 (Argos). **-χῠτος,** ον, (ἐπιχέω) *poured over*: as Subst., ἐπίχυτος (sc. πλακοῦς), ὁ, *cake made in a mould* (cf. ἔγχυτος), Nicopho 15. 2. ἐπίχυτον, τό, *coin* or *cast* of silver or lead, Hsch.

**ἐπιχωνεύω,** *remould*, κεράμια *PSI*4.441.7 (iii B.C.); *cast*, *PLeid. X.*21, 84; *cast upon, on top*, Ph.Byz.*Mir.*4.3.

**ἐπιχώνια·** κάρυα, Hsch.

**ἐπιχώννῡμι** and **-ύω,** *heap up*, Ἀρχ.Ἐφ.1923.30 (Oropus, iv B.C.); τὰ περιμήκιστα τῶν ὀρῶν Ph.1.405; νεκρῷ θῖνα γῆς Plu.*Art.*18; τούτοις γῆν ἐπιχώσας *IG*14.1746.13:—Pass., ἐ. τὸ ἔδαφος ἐπὶ τὴν λίμνην Arist. *Mir.*837$^{b}$11; βωμὸς ἐπικεχωσμένος Arg.S.*Ph.* II. *fill up*, τὴν δίοδον Thphr.*HP*9.3.2; τάφρον X.Eph.4.6; τοὺς λιμένας D.S.13.107 codd.

**ἐπιχώομαι,** Dep. *to be angry at*, ἐπεχώσατο μύθοις A.R.3.367.

**ἐπιχωρ-έω,** *yield, give way*, τοῖς ἀπιστοῦσι S.*Ant.*219, cf. Plb.4.17. 8; ἐ. τινὶ πρός τι, of things, *permit* one to do.., Plu.*Dem.*2; ἐ. τῷ ἐπιγράμματι *to be in accordance with*.., Arist.*Mir.*844$^{a}$1; ἐπί τινος ἐπιχωρεῖ πᾶς καιρός any time *will suit*, Ruf.ap.Orib.8.24.59. 2. ἐ. τινί τι *surrender, concede*, τινὶ ἀρούρας *PStrassb.*114.1, cf. Arr.*An.*1. 27.5, Plu.2.422a: c. inf., ἐπικεχώρηταί τινι ποιεῖν τι *IG*2$^{2}$.1012.24: abs., *give one's consent*, *SIG*546*B*3 (iii B.C.), *BCH*6.26 (Delos, ii B.C.). 3. *forgive*, [ἁμαρτήματα] Plu.*Alex.*45, cf. 2.482a. II. *come towards, join* one *as an ally*, Th.4.107; πρός τινα X.*HG*2.4. 34. 2. *to go against, attack*, Id.*An.*1.2.17. 3. *follow after*, προεμβάλλει τοὺς πόδας, καὶ αὐτὸς ἐπιχωρεῖ Paus.9.39.11. 4. *take possession of* an inheritance, *Leg.Gort.*11.6. **-ησις,** εως, ἡ, *concession, permission*, Lxx 2*Es.*3.7, J.*AJ*19.3.3, Arr.*An.*6.25.2; εἰ οὖν τιν' ἐ. ποιεῖ ἔντυχε ἐκείνῳ *PHib.*1.151 (iii B.C.). **-ιάζω,** 1. of persons, *to be in the habit of visiting*, ἐ. Ἀθήναζε Pl.*Phd.*57a; ἐ. τινί *live much with*, Luc.*Pseudol.*19; τοῖς ἄνω πράγμασι *to be occupied with*, Id.*Cont.* 1. 2. of things, *to be customary, be the fashion in* a place, περὶ Ἀθήνας Arist.*Pol.*1341$^{a}$34; μαθήματα τοῖς Ἕλλησιν -άζοντα Stesimbr. 4J.; παρά τισι Plb.6.46.3; τῇ νήσῳ Str.10.5.9:—Pass., *to be the custom* or *fashion*, v.l. in Arist.*Pol.*1335$^{a}$16 (nisi leg. -άζει), cf. Nymphis 9. 3. of vegetables, *acquire the local character*, Diph. Siph.ap.Ath.9.369f. 4. of the sea, *make an inroad*, Polem.*Call.* 25. II. Act., *call in the language of the country*, Βροῦτον τὸν μῶρον Lyd.*Mag.*1.31; also καλεῖν -άζοντες Olymp.*in Mete.*200.20.

**ἐπιχώριος,** α, ον, also ος, ον Pi.*P.*4.80, Ar.*Nu.*601, E.*Ion* 1111, etc.: (χώρα):—*in* or *of the country*, 1. of persons, οἱ ἐ. *the people of the country, natives*, Hdt.1.78, 181, al.; οὑπιχώριοι χθονός S.*OT*939, cf. E.*Ion* l.c.; also of birds, ἐ. ὄρνιθες A.*Supp.*800, cf. 661 (lyr.); οὐ πολλαχοῦ ἐ. Arist.*HA*615$^{a}$14. 2. of things, *of* or *used in the country*, ὑποδήματα Hdt.1.195; κράνεα Id.7.91, cf. Pi.*P.*4.80; τὸν ἐ. τρόπον Ar.*Pl.*47; freq. in neut., τὸ ἐ., τοὐπιχώριον *the custom of the country, fashion*, Id.*Nu.*1173, Th.6.27, etc.; τὰ ἐν Πέρσαις ἐ. X.*Cyr.* 1.4.25, cf. Hp.*Aër.*1: c. dat., *usual*, οἷόν τ' ἐπιχώριον ἀνδράσι γυῖον Emp.62.8; ἐπιχώριον ὂν ἡμῖν c. inf., as it *is the custom of* our *country*, Th.4.17: c. gen., τῆς ἡμετέρας μούσης ἐ. Pl.*Smp.*189b; ἐπιχωρίου ὄντος τοῖς Πέρσαις φιλεῖν it being their *custom* to.., X.*Ages.*5.4; ἐπιχώρια *common things*, Pi.*P.*3.22, cf. Ar.*Pl.*342; καλὰ ἐ. honours *of the country*, Pi.*I.*7(6).2; ἐ. ἁμαρτήματα *against fellow-countrymen*, Pl.*Lg.*730a; ἐπιχώριαι ἐνενήκοντα (sc. δραχμαί) *Michel* 838 (Didyma). Adv. -ίως Ar.*V.*859; *in the language of the country*, D.C.38.13, Lyd. *Mag.*1.7; *in the local dialect*, Gal.14.303.

**ἐπίχωσις,** εως, ἡ, (ἐπιχώννυμι) *a heaping up*, esp. *the choking of a channel*, Plb.4.41.9 (pl.): metaph., *exaggeration*, *Gloss.*

**ἐπιχωστέον,** *one must heap upon*, *Gp.*5.9.7.

**ἐπιψαίρω,** *skim the surface of* a thing, Opp.*H.*4.512.

**ἐπιψᾰκάζω,** old Att. for ἐπιψεκάζω (q.v.).

**ἐπι-ψάλλω,** *play the lyre*, S.*Fr.*60, Poll.4.58 (Pass.); μέλεσι καὶ ῥυθμοῖς Plu.2.713b; *sing*, τοὺς ὕμνους Lxx 2*Ma.*1.30:—Pass., Ph.1. 626. **-ψαλμός,** ὁ, *accompaniment* on a stringed instrument, Ptol.*Harm.*2.12.

**ἐπιψαμμίζω,** *cover with sand*, Hero *Geom.*23.68.

**ἐπι-ψαύδην,** Adv. *grazing*, gloss on ἐπιλίγδην, Sch.Il.17.599, cf. Suid. **-ψαυσις,** εως, ἡ, *touching lightly*, Plu.2.395e (pl.), Ael. *NA*8.7, Ptol.*Harm.*2.1 (pl.). **-ψαύω,** Dor. fut. -ψαυσῶ Archim. *Con.Sph.*30:—*touch on the surface, touch lightly*, c. gen., Hes.*Sc.*217, Hdt.3.87, etc.; *attain*, abs., κατὰ πᾶν τέλος Pi.*I.*4(3).11; ἐ. φιλοτάτων *to aspire to* loves, Id.*P.*4.92; ἐ. τινὸς οὐδὲ κατὰ μικρόν Phan.Hist. 19; γῆς ἐ., of shipwrecked persons, S.*Fr.*636.2: generally, *handle*, κώπης Id.*Ph.*1255; *meddle with*, τάφου Id.*Aj.*1394: metaph., also, *touch lightly upon*, Hdt.2.65. b. Geom., ἡ -ψαύουσα (sc. γραμμή) *tangent*, Archim.*Sph.Cyl.*1.12, etc. 2. c. dat., Q.S.2.456. 3. c. acc., Id.12.551. II. once in Hom., intr. and metaph., ὅς τ' ὀλίγον περ ἐπιψαύῃ πραπίδεσσιν who *can reach* ever so little way by his wits, Od.8.547.

**ἐπιψᾱφίδδω,** Boeot. for ἐπιψηφίζω, *IG*7.504 (Tanagra), al.

**ἐπιψάω,** *stroke*, τὴν κόμην *An.Ox.*3.206.

**ἐπιψέγω,** = ἐπικηδεύω (*bury*), Hsch. s.v. ψέγος.

**ἐπιψεκάζω,** old Att. **-ψᾰκάζω,** *keep dropping*, ἂν..οἱ παῖδες ἡμῖν.. μικραῖς κύλιξι πυκνὰ ἐπιψακάζωσιν, jocosely for ἐπιπίνωσιν, X.*Smp.*2. 26; ἐ. ὀλίγα τινὶ τῶν χαρίτων Luc.*Merc.Cond.*27: abs., ὁ θεὸς ἐπιψακάζει, of small rain, Ar.*Pax* 1141: metaph., θεὸς ἐ. σοφίαν διανοίαις Ph.1.501, cf. 2.383. 2. *sprinkle*, [σπῖνον] Thphr.*Lap.*13; πυρκαϊάν Hld.6.14.

**ἐπίψεκτος,** f.l. for εὐεπίψογος, Heph.Astr.1.1 (= *Cat.Cod.Astr.*8 (2).42).

**ἐπιψέλιον,** τό, *curb-chain*, *AP*6.233.4 (Maec.).

**ἐπιψελλίζω,** *lisp*, Arr.*Epict.*3.24.88.

**ἐπιψεύδομαι,** *lie still more*, X.*Hier.*2.16. II. *attribute falsely*, τι θεοῖσιν A.R.3.381, cf. Ph.2.319, Plu.*Mar.*16, Luc.*Tox.*42. III. *falsify* a number, Plu.*Flam.*9; ὄνομα *call by a wrong* name, Ph.2.398; *feign*, συμφοράν J.*AJ*18.6.8. IV. *deceive*, τινα Herod.6.46.

**ἐπίψηγμα** (better -ψημα), ατος, τό, *scrapings*, ἁλός Dsc.5.110.

**ἐπιψηλᾰφάω,** *feel by passing the hand over the surface*, τι Pl.*R.*360a; ἐ. τινός *feel for* it, Id.*Prt.*310c.

⊛ **ἐπιψηφ-ίζω,** *put to the vote*, in Senate or Assembly, ἐ. τὰς γνώμας Antipho 6.45, etc.; ταῦτα D.22.9: c. inf., *put it to the vote that*.., Th.2.24; of the President in the Amphict. Council, ἐ. τὰς γνώμας Aeschin.3.124. 2. abs., *put the question*, Th.6.14, etc.; οὐκ ἠθέλησεν ἐπιψηφίσαι, of Socrates, X.*Mem.*1.1.18; in the preface to decrees, τῶν προέδρων ἐπεψήφιζε ὁ δεῖνα *IG*2$^{2}$.44, al., cf. Decr.ap.And. 1.77; ἐ. ἐς τὴν ἐκκλησίαν (at Sparta) Th.1.87; ἐ. τῇ ἐκκλησίᾳ Luc. *Tim.*44. 3. ἐ. τινί *to put the question for* or *at the instance of* any one, Hdt.8.61. 4. ἐ. τοὺς παρόντας *to put the question to* them, *take* their *votes*, Pl.*Grg.*474a, cf. 476a. II. Pass., *to be put to the vote*, Aeschin.2.67, 3.126, *Michel* 163.40 (Delos); of an office, *to be voted upon*, Arist.*Pol.*1301$^{b}$25. III. later in Med., of the Assembly itself, or generally of voters, *vote, approve*, τὰ ῥηθέντα D.S.19.61, cf. D.H.6.71, 84, Plu.*Cic.*33 (also in Act., D.H.7.38, Luc.*Charid.*12). 2. ἐ. χρόνον τινί *vote an extension* of command, Plu.*Flam.*7; also στρατιὰν ἄλλην ἐ. πέμπειν v.l. in Th.7.16. 3. Med. in act. sense, *IG* 12(7).239 (Amorgos), 12(9).4 (Carystus), Just.*Nov.*15.6 *Ep.* IV. *confirm*, εὐσέβειαν *IGRom.*3.209.17 (Ancyra, ii A.D.). V. *calculate*, Vett.Val.352.22. **-ῐσις,** εως, ἡ, *calculation, accurate measurement*, Hero *Stereom.*2.69.5. **-ισμός,** ὁ, *confirmatory vote*, τῆς πατρίδος *Arch.Anz.*29.422 (Augusta Traiana). **-ιστής,** οῦ, ὁ, *magistrate who puts a question to the vote*, *BGU*362 xii 2 (iii A.D.).

**ἐπιψῐθῠρίζω,** *whisper in*, οὔασί τινος Nonn.*D.*22.89, cf. Procop. *Arc.*25.

**ἐπιψίσει** (-ψίσῃ cod.)· ἐπιψιεῖ, ἐπιψωμιεῖ, Hsch.

**ἐπίψογος,** ον, *exposed to blame, blameworthy*, X.*Lac.*14.7, Plu. *Comp.Cim.Luc.*1; τὸ ἐ. Max.Tyr.18.9: neut. pl. -ψογα, as Adv., Man.4.506. Adv. -γως *with blame*, λέγεσθαι Plu.*Comp.Dem.Cic.* 3. II. Act., *blaming, censorious*, φάτις A.*Ag.*611.

**ἐπιψοφ-έω,** *rattle at* or *with*, Call.*Dian.*247; *applaud*, Oenom.ap. Eus.*PE*5.33. **-ησις,** εως, ἡ, *increpatio*, *Gloss.*

**ἐπί-ψυξις,** εως, ἡ, *cooling*, Philagr.ap.Orib.5.19.3. **-ψύχω** [ῡ], *cool*, A.R.2.525, Ph.2.345, Plu.*Sert.*8. II. Pass., *take a chill afterwards*, Hp.*Mul.*1.54; but ἐπιψυγῆναι *to be cooled still more*, Gal.11.567.

**ἐπιψωμίζω,** fut. -ιῶ, gloss on ἐπιψίω, Hsch.

**ἐπιωγαί,** ῶν, αἱ (ἰωγή), *places of shelter* for ships, *roadsteads*, Od.5. 404, Opp.*H.*1.602: after Hom. in sg., A.R.4.1640.

**ἐπῐωνικὸν** μέτρον, metre in which Ionics are combined with iambi, Heph.14.3, 5, Aristid.Quint.1.28.

**ἐπιώψατο**, v. ἐπιόψομαι.

**ἔπλε**, for ἔπελε, impf. Act. of πέλω: **ἔπλεο, ἔπλευ, ἔπλετο,** aor. Med. of πέλω. **ἔπληντο**, 3 pl. Ep. aor. 2 Pass. of πελάζω, Il.4.449, 8.63.

**ἐπόγδοος**, ον, 1⅛. Pl.*Ti*.36a,b; ἐ. λόγος the ratio *of* 9:8, Plu.2.367f; ἐ. [τόκος] interest *at the rate of* ⅛ *of the principal*, i.e. 12½%, D.50.17: neut. as Subst., *whole tone* in Music, Philol.6, Hsch.

**ἐπόγκιαι**· αἱ τοῦ πλοίου παραθῆκαι, Hsch.

**ἔπογκ-ος**, ον, *pregnant*, Iambl.*VP*31.194. **-όω**, *stuff*, δορὰν βοὸς χόρτῳ Porph.*Abst*.2.30.

**ἐπογμ-εύω**, (ὄγμος) *trace a furrow*: hence, metaph of dancing, ἐ. κύκλον ὀρχηθμοῖο Tryph.354. **-ιος**, ον, *presiding over the furrows*, Δαμάτηρ *AP*6.258 (Adaeus).

**ἐπόδια, ἐποδιάζω**, Ion. for ἐφοδ-.

⊛ **ἐποδύρομαι** [ῡ], *bewail*, *AP*7.10.7.

**ἐπόζω**, *become stinking*, fut. -οζέσω Lxx *Ex*.7.18, cf. Gal.19.100.

**ἐποίγνυμι** or **ἐποίγω**, v. ἐπῴχατο: but **ἐποίγω**, Aeol. for ἐπείγω, Hdn.Gr.2.436.

**ἐποιδ-αίνω**, *swell up*, Nic.*Al*.477. **-ἀλέος**, α, ον, *swollen*, Hp.*Int*.23. **-έω**, ἐποιδαίνω, Id.*Prorrh*.1.71, Thphr.*HP*3.5.5, 6.4.2. **-ησις**, εως, ἡ, *swelling*, ib.3.5.5. **-ίσκομαι**, Pass., = ἐποιδαίνω, Hp.*Epid*.5.21, Gal.19.429.

⊛ **ἐποίζω**, impf. -ῴζον, *lament over*, τοῖς τεθνηκόσι prob. in A.*Fr*.157.

**ἐποικ-έω**, *go as settler* or *colonist to* a place, *settle in* a place, c. acc., Κυκλάδας E.*Ion* 1583; Βοιωτίαν Str.9.2.25; also ἐν τῇ Ἀσίᾳ X.*Cyr*.6.2.10: abs., Pl.*Lg*.752e. **II.** *to be settled near* or *with hostile views against*, ὑμῖν Th.6.86:—Pass., ἡ Δεκέλεια τῇ χώρᾳ ἐπῳκεῖτο Decelea *was occupied as the seat of offensive operations against* their country, Id.7.27. ⊛ **-ία**, ἡ, = ἀποικία, *IG*9(1).334.1 (in Locr. form ἐπιϝοικία); but f.l. for ἀποικία, App.*BC*2.135. **II.** = ἐποίκιον 1, *Gp*.10.1.1 (pl., s.v.l.). **-ίδιος**, α, ον, *presiding over the house*, of Demeter at Corinth, Hsch. **2.** gloss on ὑπωρόφιος, Sch.Pi.*P*.1.188. ⊛ **-ίζω**, *settle in a colony*, τινὰς πόλεσι App.*BC*1.96, etc.:—Pass., *to be built near*, τεῖχος ἐπὶ τῇ Σηλύῃ -ισμένον D.C.56.12. **II.** = ἐπιτειχίζω, τινί Paus.4.26.6:—Pass., ib.28.1. **III.** *bring into cultivation*, ἔδωκεν.. γῆν ψιλὴν ἀγρὸν ἐποικίσαι *SIG*302 (Gambreum, iv B.C.). ⊛ **-ιον**, τό, *outhouse*, *farmstead*, etc., *IG*9(1).47 (Stiris), *Tab.Heracl*.1.146, *PPetr*.2p.83, 3p.225, al. (iii B.C.), Str.11.3.1, J.*AJ*14.10.6, etc. **II.** *village*, Lxx 1*Ch*.27.25, *PTeb*.382.6 (i B.C./i A.D.), *POxy*.2137.12, 2142.3 (iii A.D.). **-ισις**, εως, ἡ, *settlement of a colony*, App.*BC*5.137. **-ισμός**, ὁ, *settlement*. *Gloss*.

⊛ **ἐποικοδομ-έω**, *build up*, -ήσαντας αὐτὸ (sc. τὸ τεῖχος) ὑψηλότερον Th.7.4, cf. X.*HG*6.5.12, D.55.25: metaph., *pile up*, *use a climax*, Arist.*Rh*.1365ᵃ16, *Rh.Al*.1426ᵇ3. **2.** *build upon*, ἐπὶ κρηπῖδι X.*An*.3.4.11; ἐπὶ κρηπῖδος Pl.*Lg*.736e; ἐπὶ τοὺς τοίχους *OGI*483.117 (Pergam., ii B.C.): metaph., Pl.*Lg*.793c (Pass.); φύσει μαθήματα Ph.1.610; τινὶ εὐτονίαν, ἀσφάλειαν, Arr.*Epict*.2.15.8 (Pass.); ἐπὶ θεμέλιον or θεμελίῳ, 1*Ep.Cor*.3.12, *Ep.Eph*.2.20; θεμελίοις Sor.1.47 (Pass.); τοῖς ἀληθέσιν ἐψευσμένα Paus.8.2.6, cf. Dam.*Pr*.87 (Pass.). **b.** *edify*, ἑαυτοὺς τῇ πίστει *Ep.Jud*.20:—Pass., -ούμενοι ἐν Χριστῷ *Ep.Col*.2.7. **II.** = ἐπιτειχίζω, Plb.2.46.5:—Med., στρατόπεδα πέντε -ησάμενος Arr.*An*.2.1.2. **-ή**, Dor. **ἐπιοικοδομά**, ἡ, *superstructure*, *Tab.Heracl*.1.150. **-ησις**, εως, ἡ, *building up*: metaph., *piling up* of expressions, *climax*, Arist.*GA*724ᵃ29; ἡ τῶν λέξεων ἐ. Longin.39.3. **-ία**, ἡ, = foreg., Haussoullier *Cinquantenaire de l'école des hautes études* p.89 (Didyma, ii B.C.), *SIG*799 ii 4 (Cyzicus, i A.D.), prob. in J.*AJ*19.1.15 (pl.).

**ἐποικονομ-έομαι**, Pass., *to be administered*, Arist.*Oec*.1346ᵃ14 (s.v.l.). **-ητέον**, *one must treat*, Herod.Med.ap.Aët.9.13. **-ία**, ἡ, *apportionment*, ἔργων ἢ παθῶν ἐ. *rhetorical arrangement* of them, Longin.11.2 (nisi leg. ἐποικοδομία).

⊛ **ἔποικος**, ὁ, *settler*, *sojourner*, Pi.*O*.9.69. **2.** *stranger*, *alien*, S.*El*.189 (lyr., as fem.), cf. Pl.*Lg*.742a, *GDI*5048 (Crete). **3.** more freq., *colonist*, Ar.*Av*.1307, *IG*9(1).334.5 (in Locr. form ἐπίϝοικος), ib.1².397; ἐποίκους πέμπειν, ἀποστέλλειν, Th.2.27, Isoc.5.6; esp. of *additional settlers*, ἐ. δέχεσθαι, ἐπάγεσθαι, Arist.*Pol*.1303ᵃ28,37; λαὸν ἔποικον ἄγοις Call.*Aet.Oxy*.2080.69, cf. Ant.Lib.4.4, al. **II.** *neighbouring*, ἔ. Ἀσίας ἁγνᾶς ἕδος A.*Pr*.411 (lyr.). **2.** Subst. *neighbour*, S.*OC*506.

**ἐποικουρέω**, f.l. for ὑπ-, Ph.2.202 (Pass.).

**ἐποικτ-είρω** or **-ίρω**, *have compassion on*, τινα Xenoph.7.3, S.*Aj*.121, *OT*671, etc.: abs., A.*Ag*.1069. (Written -ειρ- Isyll.72; v. οἰκτείρω.) ⊛ **-ίζω**, *compassionate*, c. acc., S.*OT*1296:—Med., *bewail*, *lament*, J.*BJ*1.27.3. **-ιστος**, ον, *pitiable*, A.*Ag*.1221. **-ος**, ον, = *piteous*, φόνος ib.1614.

⊛ **ἐποιμώζω**, *to lament over*, πάθει A.*Ch*.547.

**ἐποίνιος**, ον, (οἶνος) *bacchanalian*, Nonn.*D*.11.301; cf. ἐπιοίνιος.

**ἐποιστ-έον**, *one must charge against*, τινὶ οὐκ ἐ. ἀτοπίαν Plb.12.22.5. **-ικός**, ή, όν, *capable of conferring*, εἶδος ἄδεκτον ἁπασῶν ἐνεργειῶν ὧν ἐποιστικὸν ἄλλῳ Plot.1.1.2. **2.** *productive*, συμπτωμάτων *Stoic*.3.49; συμφορῶν Phld.*Ir*.p.30W., cf. Simp.*in Cat*.224.23.

**ἐποιχνέω**, *ply*, *practise*, μαντοσύναν Aristonous 1.11. **2.** *visit*, *AP*12.131 (Posidipp.), cf. *PBodl.ined*.32471, prob. l. in B.9.1.

⊛ **ἐποίχομαι**, *go towards*, *approach*, μνηστῆρας ἐπῴχετο Od.1.324; αἰτίζειν.. ἐποιχόμενον μνηστῆρας 17.346, cf. 6.282; ἐ. δόμον ἄλλον Thgn.353; [θεοὺς] τραπέζαις ἐ. *draw near to* the gods with sacrificial feasts, Pi.*O*.3.40; εὐεργέταν Id.*P*.2.24. **2.** *approach with hostile purpose*, *attack*, c. acc., Κύπριν ἐπῴχετο νηλέϊ χαλκῷ Il.5.330, cf. 10.487. **II.** *go over*, *traverse*, νηῶν ἴκρια 15.676. **2.** *go round*, *visit in succession*, of one who hands round wine, αὐτοῖσιν θάμ' ἐπῴχετο οἰνοχοεύων Od.1.143; of a general, *pass along* troops, στίχας ἀνδρῶν Il.15.279, cf. 16.155; *inspect*, [φώκας] Od.4.451: abs., *go his rounds*, Il.10.171, 17.215; πάντοσ' ἐποιχόμενος 5.508; πάντῃ ἐ. 6.81, 10.167, etc. **3.** of arrows *visiting* persons with death, τὰ δ' ἐπῴχετο κῆλα θεοῖο πάντῃ ἀνὰ στρατόν 1.383, cf. 50; οἷς ἀγανοῖσι βελέεσσιν ἐποιχόμενος (or -νη) κατέπεφνεν, 24.759, Od.3.280, 5.124, etc. **4.** *go over* or *ply* one's task, ἔργον ἐ. Il.6.492, Od.1.358, 17.227, etc.; δόρπον ἐ. *set about preparing* it, 13.34; freq. of women, ἱστὸν ἐ. *ply* the loom, Il.1.31, Od.5.62, al., cf. Ephor.5J.; ἔργον φυλόπιδος ἐ. Mimn.14.10; φύλοπιν Hes.*Sc*.200 (tm.); [γύας καὶ ἀλωὰς] ἔργοισιν ἐ. *with* labour, Theoc.25.32: c. dat., ἔργῳ ἐ. Q.S.12.343 codd.: abs. in part., with another Verb, *busily*, ἡ μὲν ἐποιχομένη.. ἔντυεν ἵππους Il.5.720.

**ἐποιωνίζομαι**, *forebode*, Hsch. s.v. ἐπιγλωσσῶ.

⊛ **ἐποκέλλω**, = ἐπικέλλω, *run ashore*, νέας, τὴν νέα, Hdt.6.16, 7.182; πλοῖα Th.4.26. **2.** of the ship, *run aground*, *be wrecked*, Id.8.102, Plb.1.20.15; *put in*, Arr.*An*.2.23.3; of tunnies, Arist.*Mir*.844ᵃ30.

**ἐποκλάζω**, *cower with bent knees upon*, τῇ γῇ Hld.4.17.

**ἐποκρῑ-άω**, *to be rough in* or *upon*, χηλαὶ ἐποκριόωσι παγούροις Nic.*Th*.790. **-όεις**, εσσα, εν, *uneven*, *projecting*, στέρνα, of a skeleton, *AP*7.401 (Crin.).

**ἐποκτάμερής**, ές, *in the ratio of* 1⅛:1, Nicom.*Ar*.1.23.

**ἐποκτωκαιδέκατος** λόγος ratio *of* 19:18, TheoSm.p.87H.

**ἐπολβ-ίζω**, *call happy*, τὸν θανόντα Dionys.Trag.3, cf. Nonn.*D*.46.325. **-ος**, ον, *prosperous*, Man.3.112, al.

**ἐπόλιος**, ὁ, a night-bird, perh. = αἰγωλιός, Suid.

**ἐπολισθάνω**, *slip* or *glide upon*, [σανίσιν] J.*BJ*3.7.29; κυλίνδροις ἐς βυθὸν *AP*10.15.3 (Paul. Sil.): metaph., ἐ. ἀμπλακίαις ib.5.277 (Agath.).

**ἔπολμις**, = ἔνολμις (v. ἔνολμος), Hsch.

**ἐπολολύζω**, *shout for joy*, *triumph at*, abs., A.*Ag*.1236 (Med.), Ar.*Eq*.616 (lyr.); τινι *at* or *to* one, A.*Th*.825 (lyr.); τι *over* or *at* a thing, Id.*Ch*.942 (lyr.).

**ἐπολοφύρομαι** [ῡ], *lament over*, τινι J.*BJPraef*.4; πολλὰ ἔργῳ ib.6.4.8.

**ἕπομαι**, v. ἕπω (B).

**ἐπομβρ-έω**, *pour rain upon*:—Pass., *AP*11.365.7 (Agath.). **2.** *pour like rain upon*, τί τινι Ph.1.48, 296. **II.** intr., *gush out over*, *abound as rain*, τὰ -οῦντα Id.1.441. **-ησις**, εως, ἡ, *watering with rain*, Suid. **-ία**, ἡ, *heavy rain*, *abundance of rain*, Hp.*Aph*.3.15 (pl.), D.55.11, etc.: generally, *abundance of wet*, πνευμάτων A.*Fr*.300: opp. αὐχμός, Hp.*Aër*.23, Ar.*Nu*.1120: pl., Arist.*Mete*.360ᵇ6, Thphr.*HP*3.1.5, Str.11.3.4, etc.: metaph., *shower*, χερμάδων Lyc.333; *deluge*, δέλτων Lib.*Ep*.333.5. **2.** *the Deluge*, J.*AJ*1.2.3, al. **II.** *humidity*, of the body, Aret.*SA*2.4, *SD*2.1. **-ίζω**, *water with rain*, Hld.9.9. **-ιος**, ον, = sq., Arist.*HA*601ᵇ10, Thphr.*CP*3.11.5. **-ος**, ον, *very rainy*, ἔαρ, ἔτος, Hp.*Aph*.3.11, *Epid*.3.2; ἔαρ, θέρος, φθινόπωρον, Arist.*HA*601ᵇ26 (v.l. -ιον); χῶραι Thphr.*HP*8.7.6.

**ἑπομένως**, Adv. pres. part. of ἕπομαι, *in a secondary manner*, opp. πρώτως, Arist.*Metaph*.1030ᵃ22, cf. Plu.2.569e: opp. προηγουμένως, Hierocl. *in CA*3p.424M. **II.** *in accordance with*, τῷ νόμῳ Pl.*Lg*.844e, cf. Arist.*de An*.405ᵃ3; τῷ τῆς ἀκολουθίας εἱρμῷ Ph.2.194. **III.** *next* in order, Arist.*GA*736ᵇ13, Plb.4.1.7, Ph.1.560.

**ἐπόμιλλος**, Aeol. for ἐφόμιλος, *Et.Gud*.561.5.

**ἐπομμάδιος**, v. ἐπωμάδιος.

**ἐπόμμᾰσις**, εως, ἡ, Astrol., *aspect*, Gal.19.560.

**ἐπόμνῡμι** or **-ύω** (v. infr. 3), fut. ἐπομοῦμαι Ar.*Lys*.211: aor. ἐπώμοσα:—*swear after*, *swear in accordance* (with an order given), οἱ δ' ἄρα πάντες ἐπώμνυον Od.15.437, cf. Th.2.5. **2.** c. acc. cogn., ἐπίορκον ἐπώμοσε Il.10.332; ὅς κεν τὴν ἐπίορκον.. ἐπομόσσῃ whosoever *swear* a false oath *by* it [the Styx], Hes.*Th*.793, cf. Emp.115.4; also ἐ. ὅρκον τινὶ *swear* an oath *at* his *dictation*, Plu.*Cic*.23:—Med., ἐ. ὅρκον *Stud.Pal*.20.122.16 (v A.D.), etc. **3.** c. acc. pers., ἐ. ἥλιον *to swear by*.., Hdt.1.212; ἐ. τινὰ θεῶν E.*IT*747, cf. Ar.*Nu*.1227, *Schwyzer* 721.5 (iv B.C.), etc.; ἐ. θεοὺς ὡς.. E.*Ph*.433; ἐπομνύω σοι τὴν ἐμὴν καὶ σὴν φιλίαν X.*Cyr*.6.4.6; ἐ. τὴν σὴν (sc. Καίσαρος) τύχην J.*AJ*16.10.8: c. dupl. acc., μή τι θεοὺς ἐπίορκον ἐπόμνυθι Thgn.1195:—Med., ἐπόμνυσθαι Δία f.l. in Jusj.ap.D.24.151; ἐπόμνυσθαι κατά τινος Luc.*Icar*.9, *Cal*.18. **4.** c. acc. rei, *swear to* a thing, Ar.*Lys*.211: abs., Pl.*Lg*.917b. **5.** c. inf., *swear that*, ἐ. θεοὺς μὴ πρότερον ἐκδύσεσθαι.. Hdt.5.106, cf. E.*IT*974, Pl.*Criti*.120a:—Med., ἐπωμόσατο.. εἰδέναι Αἰσχίνην Test.ap.D.18.137; ἐπομνύειν ἦ μὴν c. pres. inf., Plu.*Alex*.47; Ep., ἐ. ἦ μέν.. c. fut. inf., A.R.2.715, etc.; ἐ. ὅτι.. Plu.*Per*.30. **6.** abs. in aor. part., with another Verb, ἐπομόσας εἶπε he said *with an oath*, Hdt.8.5, X.*An*.7.8.2. **II.** Med., = ὑπόμνυσθαι (nisi hoc leg.), Ar.*Pl*.725.

**ἐπομφάλιος** [ᾰ], ον, (ὀμφαλός) *on the navel* or *central point*, βάλεν δεινὸν σάκος.. μέσσον ἐ. *in the centre*, *on the boss* of the shield, Il.7.267; σῦκον ἐ. a fig *with a navel-like stalk*, *AP*6.22 (Zon.). **II.** Subst. ἐπομφάλιον, τό, *the umbilical region*, Parth.35.4, Poll.2.169. **2.** *plaster applied to the navel*, ἐ. καθαρτικά Aët.3.135, cf. Philum.ib.9.25.

**ἐπονείδιστος**, ον, *to be reproached*, *disgraceful*, *shameful*, E.*IT*689; ἐ. εἰρήνη Isoc.12.106 (Comp.), cf. D.19.336; ἀμαθία Pl.*Ap*.29b, etc.; τινι to one, X.*Smp*.8.34; ἐπονείδιστόν ἐστι παρά τισι is *matter of reproach*, D.26.19; ὄνομα τοὐπονείδιστον βροτοῖς the name *of reproach* among men, E.*Fr*.922: Comp., Arist.*EN*1119ᵃ25: Sup., X.*Smp*.8.19. Adv. **-τως** *shamefully*, Pl.*Lg*.633e, Isoc.4.60; also in act. sense, *so as to shame*, ψέγειν Plb.1.14.5.

⊕ **ἐπονήμενοι**, dub. sens. in Alc.*Oxy.*1788*Fr.*15 ii 25, 1789 *Fr.*1 i 5 (v.l. -*νάμ*-).

**ἐπόνησις**, Aeol. -ᾱσις, εως, ἡ, *enjoyment*, συμποσίας v.l. in Alc.46.

⊕ **ἐπονομ-άζω**, *apply* a word (accus.) *as a name* to a thing (dat.), ᾧ γένει κέραμον ἐπωνομάκαμεν to which sort we *have given the name* pottery, Pl.*Ti.*60d; ᾧ τὸ "ἔστιν" ἐπονομάζεις Id.*Tht.*185c; πᾶσι ταὐτὸν ἐ. ὄνομα Id.*Plt.*263c (reversely, τίς Ἀλεξάνδρῳ τὸν ἑαυτοῦ βίον ἐπονομάζει καθάπερ Πλάτωνι; who *dedicates* his life to A., *calls* himself an Alexandrist? Them.*Or.*31.354b):—Pass., τῇ ἀρχῇ ὕβρις ἐπωνομάσθη *the name* insolence *was given to* this rule, Pl.*Phdr.*238a, cf. *Cra.*404b. 2. *call by* a name, ἀπὸ τοῦ θεῖν θεοὺς αὐτοὺς ἐπονομάσαι [φαίνονται] ib.397d; τὰς Μούσας ἀπὸ τοῦ μῶσθαι τὸ ὄνομα τοῦτο ἐ. *called* the Muses *by* this name (viz. Muses), ib.406a; ἐ. αὐτὰ τῇ ἐκείνων ἐπωνυμίᾳ Id.*Phd.*103b; with εἶναι pleon., Id.*Prm.*133d:—Pass., *to be named*, ἀπό τινος after one, Th.6.2, etc.; also τινος, *to be named* the temple *of*.., E.*HF*1329, Pl.*Lg.*738b (but in 626d the gen. depends on ἄξιος); πατρόθεν ἐ. Id.*Ly.*204e; πατρὸς.. δαῖτ' ἐπωνομασμένην, i.e. *called after* Agamemnon (cf. ἐπώνυμος), S.*El.*284; esp. *to be surnamed*, Th.2.29; Ἰουδαῖος ἐπονομάζῃ *Ep.Rom.*2.17. 3. generally, *name, call* so and so, ἀφνειὸν ἐ. τὸ χωρίον Th.1.13; σοφιστὴν ἐ. σεαυτόν Pl.*Prt.*349a, cf. *Phd.*113b, al.; παρακαταθήκην ἐ. D. 28.15. 4. *pronounce* a name, ἐ. τὰ οὐνόματα ἐν τῷ ὕμνῳ Hdt.4.35, cf. 7.117; ἐπονομάζων τινά *uttering* his *name* as he throws the cottabus, Cratin.273, cf. Clearch.Com.1. **-αστέον**, *one must call by a name*, ὅσους θεοὺς οὐρανίους ἐ. Pl.*Lg.*828c. **-αστικῶς**, gloss on ἐπικλήδην Sch.Opp.*H.*1.776.

⊕ **ἐποξ-ίζω**, *turn acid*, Erot. and Suid. s. v. ὀξυρεγμίη. **-ύνω** [ῠ], *hasten*, τὴν πορείαν Lxx 2*Ma.*9.7. 2. *stimulate, excite*, τὸ ἐπιθυμητικὸν πρὸς τὸ ἀκόλαστον Hierocl.*in CA*8 p.431 M. **-υς**, υ, *sharpish in taste*, v.l. for ὕπ-, Hp.*Acut.*59.

**ἐποπάζω**, *bestow besides*, θεὸς δ' ἐπὶ ὄλβον ὀ. Rhian.1.9; ἐπὶ κλέος ὤπασε Μοῖρα *AP*9.521.

**ἐποπίζομαι**, only pres. and impf., *regard with awe, reverence*, Διὸς δ' ἐποπίζεο μῆνιν Od.5.146, cf. *h.Ven.*290, Thgn.1297.

**ἐπόπισθεν**, Adv. *coming after* (better divisim, ἐπ' ὄπ.), Hes.*Fr.* 166.

**ἐποποῖ**, a cry to mimic that of the hoopoe (ἔποψ), Ar.*Av.*58.

**ἐποποι-ία**, Ep. -ίη, ἡ, *epic poetry* or *an epic poem*, Hdt.2.116, Arist. *Po.*1459b8, etc. II. *divination by means of Homeric verses*, *PMag. Berol.*1.328. **-ικός**, ή, όν, *of epic poetry*, σύστημα Arist.*Po.*1456a 11; μίμησις ib.1461b26. **-ός**, ὁ, *epic poet*, Hdt.2.120, Arist.*Po.* 1447b14, Neanth.26 J.: generally, *verse-maker*, Luc.*JTr.*6.

**ἔποπος**, etym. of πόποι, *An.Ox.*4.410.

**ἐποπτάω**, *roast besides* or *after*, Od.12.363, Diph.Siph.ap.Ath.3. 121c; ἐφθὸν ἐποπτᾶν οὔ φασι δεῖν Philoch.171. 2. Pass., *to be burnt*, Paul.Aeg.3.67. II. (as a pun) = ἐπωπάω, *Com.Adesp.*1325.

**ἐποπτ-εία**, ἡ, *highest grade of initiation at the Eleusinian mysteries*, Plu.*Demetr.*26, Sch.Ar.*Ra.*757; ἐ. τινός *initiation into*.., Mich.*in EN* 603.34; ἡ διαλεκτικὴ τῶν ὄντων ἐ. Hierocl.*in CA*26 p.481 M. **-ειρα**, ἡ, fem. of ἐπόπτης I, cj. for ἐποπτετῆρα in Herm.ap.Stob.1.49.44. ⊕ **-εύω**, (ἐπόπτης) *overlook, watch*, of an overseer, ἔργα τ' ἐποπτεύεσκε Od.16. 140, cf. Hes.*Op.*767; Ἑρμῆ.. πατρῷ' ἐποπτεύων κράτη A.*Ch.*1; ἐ. μάχην ib.489; ὁ πάντ' ἐ. τάδε ἥλιος ib.993(985); δίκας Id.*Eu.*224; ἄλλοτε δ' ἄλλον ἐποπτεύει Χάρις φόρμιγγι Pi.*O.*7.11; αἰῶνας -εύουσα χελιδών *IGRom.*4.235 (hex.). 2. *visit, punish*, κότῳ A.*Eu.*220. 3. abs., *keep watch*, οἱ περὶ τοὺς νόμους ἐποπτεύοντες Pl.*Lg.*951d. II. *become an* ἐπόπτης, *be admitted to the highest grade at the mysteries*, Id. *Ep.*333e, Plu.*Demetr.*26: c. acc., *view as an* ἐπόπτης, Pl.*Phdr.*250c: prov., of *attaining to the highest earthly happiness*, ἐποπτεύειν δοκῶ Ar. *Ra.*745. III. *study, meditate on*, c. dat., καθαρῷσιν ἐ. μελέτῃσιν Emp. 110.2. (Cf. ἐπιοπτεύω.) **-ήρ**, ῆρος, ὁ, = sq., of tutelary gods, λιτῶν A.*Th.*640; also ἐ. φρυκτωριῶν Arist.*Mu.*398a31. **-ης**, ου, ὁ, (ἐπόψομαι) *overseer, watcher*, esp. of a god, Πυθῶνος Pi.*N.*9.5, cf. Epich.266; ὁ πάντων ἐ. θεός Lxx *Es.*5.1; title of Poseidon, Paus.8.30.1; of the Sun, *OGI*666.25 (Egypt, i A.D.); δαίμονες ἐ. τῶν ἀνθρωπίνων Ti.Locr. 105a; ὥσπερ ἐπόπτας τῶν στρατηγουμένων D.4.25; ἐ. γῆς καὶ θαλάσσης, of Pompey, *JHS*27.64 (Cyzicus); of Augustus, *IGRom.*4.309 (Pergam.); ἐ. εἰρήνης, of a police *magistrate*, *POxy.*991 (iv A.D.). 2. simply, *spectator*, πόνων A.*Pr.*301. 3. *inspector*, *Cod.Just.*10.16.13 *Intr.* II. *one admitted to the highest grade of the mysteries*, *IG*1².6. 51, Plu.*Alc.*22, etc., cf. ἐφόπται *IG*12(8).205.3 (Samothrace): c. gen., μυστηρίων ἐ. *Michel* 1141 (ibid.); τινος *PMag.Lond.*121.572: metaph., ἐ. τῆς ἐκείνου μεγαλειότητος 2*Ep.Pet.*1.16. **-ικός**, ή, όν, *of* or *for an* ἐπόπτης, τὰ τέλεα καὶ ἐ. the *highest mysteries*, Pl.*Smp.*210a, cf. Philoch. 148, Plu.*Demetr.*26; *esoteric*, διδασκαλίαι Id.*Alex.*7; μέρος φιλοσοφίας Id.2.382d; οἱ -ώτεροι the *more deeply initiated*, Hld.9.9. **-ις**, ιδος, ἡ, fem. of ἐπόπτης, v.l. in Corn.*ND*34; αἱ Ἐπόπτιδες, title of a book by Soranus, Plin.*HN Praef.*33. **-ος**, ον, *visible*, Str.5.3.12.

**ἐποράω**, Ion. for ἐφοράω. **ἐπορβεῖται**· φθονεῖ, Hsch.

**ἐποργάω**, in form ἐποργῶσαι· μηνιῶσαι, Suid.

**ἐποργιάζω**, *revel in* or *among*, πόλεσσι *Anacreont.*13.23.

**ἐποργίζομαι**, *to be wroth at*, τινι Lxx *Da.*11.40: abs., ib.2*Ma.*7.33.

**ἐπορέγω**, *hold out to, give yet more*, εἴ περ ἄν.. Ζεὺς ἐπὶ Τυδεΐδῃ Διομήδεϊ κῦδος ὀρέξῃ Il.5.225:—Med., τιμῆς οὔτ' ἀφελὼν οὔτ' ἐπορεξάμενος Sol.5.2. 2. metaph., [τὸ θεῖον] τισιν ἐ. τὰς μεταδόσεις τῆς ὑπερπλήρους ἀγαθότητος Procl.*Inst.*131. II. Med., *stretch oneself towards*, once in Hom., ἐπορεξάμενος *reaching forward* to strike, Il.5.335; χειρί τινος ἐ. *reach at* a thing, A.R.1.1313; οὐ παλάμῃ ἐπορέχθην Matro *Conv.*70; also χεῖρας τινι ἐ. A.R.2.1212; ἐ. πρός τι Hp. *Epid.*7.11: abs., ib.7.5. 2. ἐ. τινός *yearn for* it, ἀλλοίων ἐ. Emp. 110.6, cf. Pl.*R.*437c, *Tht.*186a. 3. *rise in one's demands*, Hdt. 9.34. **-όρεκτος**, ον, *eager*, πρός τι Sch.Nic.*Th.*75.

**ἐπορέομαι**, = ἐπόρνυμαι, prob. in Emp.137.2.

**ἐπορθιάζω**, *set upright*, ἐ. τὰ ὦτα *prick* the ears, v.l. in Ph.2.4: but mostly of the voice, *lift up at* or *over*, ὀλολυγμὸν τῇδε λαμπάδι A.*Ag.* 29; Ἐρινὺν τήνδε δώμασιν ib.1120: abs., ἐ. γόοις *lift up the voice* in wailing, Id.*Pers.*1050 (lyr.).

**ἐπορθρ-εύω**, *rise early*, Hsch., *EM*368.1:—Med., D.Chr.12.3, Luc. *Gall.*1, Poll.1.71. **-ισμός**, ὁ, *rising early*, τελωνικῶν κεκραγμῶν -ισμοί *morning cries* of noisy tax-gatherers, Plu.2.654f.

**ἐποριγνάομαι**, = ἐπορέγομαι, τινος Them.*Or.*2.33a.

**ἐπορίνω** [ῑ], *urge on*, v.l. in Nic.*Th.*671, Man.6.597.

**ἐπορκιστής**, οῦ, ὁ, = ἐξ- (which is used in Ptol.*Tetr.*182), Procl. *Par.Ptol.*253 (s.v.l.).

**ἐπορμάω, ἐπορμέω**, Ion. for ἐφ-.

**ἐπόρνῡμι** and -ύω, aor. 1 -ῶρσα, poet. Verb, *stir up, arouse, excite*, ὅς μοι ἐπῶρσε μένος who *called up* my might, Il.20.93. 2. *rouse and send against*, ἄγρει μάν οἱ ἔπορσον Ἀθηναίην 5.765, cf. Od.21.100, E.*Cyc.*12: c. inf., οἷόν ἐπόρσειαν πολεμίζειν Ἕκτορι Il.7.42; also of things, τὴν [ὀϊζύν] μοι ἐπῶρσε Ποσειδάων Od.7.271; οἱ ἐπώρνυε μόρσιμον ἦμαρ Il.15.613; ἤ σφιν ἐπῶρσ' ἄνεμον Od.5.109; τῇ τις θεὸς ὕπνον ἐπῶρσε *sent* sleep *upon* her, Od.22.429, cf. Il.12.252 (tm.); λαίλαπας Cerc.5.9. II. Pass., **ἐπόρνῠμαι**, with pf. ἐπόρωρα, later 3 sg. ἐπώρορε Pancr.*Oxy.*1085.15: 3 sg. Ep. aor. 2 Pass. ἐπῶρτο:—*rise against, fly upon* one, c. dat., ἢ καὶ ἐπῶρτ' Ἀχιλῆϊ Il.21.324: abs., ἐπὶ δ' ὄρνυτο δῖος Ἐπειός 23.689, cf. 759, Euph.23: c. acc. cogn., τόνδ' ἐπόρνυται στόλον A.*Supp.*187; of things, c. inf., ὦρτο δ' ἐπὶ.. οὖρος ἀήμεναι Od.3.176; ἐπὶ δίψος ὄρωρεν Nic.*Th.*774.

**ἐπορούω**, Ep. Verb, *spring at*, in hostile sense, τῷ δὲ Μέγης ἐπόρουσεν Il.15.520: abs., ἐπόρουσε κύων ὥς ib.579. 2. Τυδεΐδῃ δ' ἐπόρουσε θεά *sprang to* his side, 5.793; ὅτε οἱ γλυκὺς ὕπνος λυσιμελὴς ἐπόρουσε *came suddenly upon* him, Od.23.343. 3. *spring upon*, c. acc., ἅρμ' ἐπορούσας Il.17.481.

**ἐποροφόω**, *to put on as a roof* or *cover*, τὸν οὐρανόν Heraclit.*All.*48.

**ἐπ-όρυξις**, εως, ἡ, *digging up*, δαπέδου *IG*4.823.51 (Troezen). **-ορύττω**, *dig into*, τὸ τραῦμα Ach.Tat.3.8.

**ἐπορχέομαι**, *dance over* or *at*, ἐπορχούμενος ὗης ἄττης *dancing to the tune of*.., D.18.260: abs., *dance*, Ph.2.485: metaph., *triumph over*, τινι App.*Pun.*66.

⊕ **ἔπος**, older ϝέπος *SIG*9 (v. infr.), etc., εος, τό (Skt. *vácas* 'word', 'hymn', cf. εἶπον): I. *word*, παύρῳ ἔπει in short *utterance*, Pi.*O.* 13.98; ἐπέων κόσμος Parm.8.52, Democr.21; ἔπους σμικροῦ χάριν S. *OC*443; λόγοι ἔπεσι κοσμηθέντες Th.3.67: generally, *that which is uttered in words, speech, tale*, ἔπος ἐρέειν Il.3.83, etc.; φάσθαι Xenoph. 7.3, Parm.1.23, etc.; joined with μῦθος, Od.4.597, 11.561.—Special uses, 1. *song* or *lay accompanied by music*, 8.91, 17.519. 2. *pledged word, promise*, Il.8.8; τελέσαι ἔπος fulfil, keep *one's word*, 14.44, cf. A.*Pr.*1033. 3. *word in season, counsel*, Il.1.216, 2.807, Od.18.166, etc.; freq. in Trag., E.*Hel.*513, etc. 4. *word of a deity, oracle*, Od.12.266, Hdt.1.13, etc. 5. *saying, proverb*, τὸ παλαιὸν ἔπος Id.7.51, cf. Ar.*Av.*507. 6. *word*, opp. *deed*, ἔπε' ἀκράαντα *words* of none effect, opp. ἔτυμα, Od.19.565, cf. E.*HF*111 (lyr.); opp. ἔργον, Il.15.234, Od.2.272, etc., cf. II. 1; αἴτε ϝέπος αἴτε ϝάργον *SIG*9 (Elis, vi B.C.); opp. βίη, Il.15.106; opp. χεῖρες, 1.77 (pl.). 7. *subject of a speech, message*, 11.652, 17.701, S.*OT* 1144, etc. II. later usages, 1. joined with ἔργον or πρᾶγμα Heraclit.1, A.*Pers.*174 (troch.), Ar.*Eq.*39, etc.; ἔργῳ τε καὶ ἔπει Pl. *Lg.*879c; ἅμα ἔπος τε καὶ ἔργον ἐποίεε Hdt.3.134; χρηστὰ ἔργα καὶ ἔπεα ποιέειν Id.1.90. 2. κατ' ἔπος *word by word*, κατ' ἔ. βασανιεῖν φησι τὰς τραγῳδίας Ar.*Ra.*802. 3. πρὸς ἔπος at *the first word*, Luc. *Ep.Sat.*37. b. *word* in exchange for *word*, ἀμείβεσθαι, ἀποκρίνεσθαι, of an oracle, Id.*Alex.*19, *Philops.*38; also ἔ. δ' ἀμείβου πρὸς ἔ. A.*Eu.* 586, cf. Ar.*Nu.*1375, Pl.*Sph.*217d. c. οὐδὲν πρὸς ἔ. to *no purpose*, Ar.*Ec.*751; also, nothing *to the purpose*, ἐὰν μηδὲν πρὸς ἔ. ἀποκρίνωμαι Pl.*Euthd.*295c, cf. Luc.*Herm.*36; τί πρὸς ἔπος; Pl.*Phlb.*18d. 4. ὡς ἔπος εἰπεῖν *almost, practically*, qualifying a too absolute expression, esp. with πᾶς and οὐδείς (not with metaphors), Pl.*Ap.*17a, *Phd.* 78e, *Grg.*456a, al., Arist.*Metaph.*1009b16, *Pol.*1252b29, D.9.47, etc.; opp. ὄντως or ἀκριβεῖ λόγῳ, Pl.*Lg.*656e, *R.*341b; later ὡς ἔ. ἐστὶν εἰπεῖν *POxy.*67.14 (iv A.D.); in Trag., ὡς εἰπεῖν ἔ. A.*Pers.*714 (troch.), E.*Heracl.*167, *Hipp.*1162, once in Pl., *Lg.*967b (s.v.l.). 5. ἑνὶ ἔπει in one *word, briefly*, ἑνὶ ἔπεϊ πάντα συλλαβόντα λέγειν Hdt.3.82. III. of single *words*, esp. with ref. to etymology or usage, Id.2.30, Ar. *Nu.*638, Pl.*Prt.*339a, etc.; ὀρθότης ἐπῶν, = ὀρθοέπεια (q.v.), Ar.*Ra.* 1181; ἄριστ' ἐπῶν ἔχον ib.1161. IV. in pl., *epic poetry*, opp. μέλη (lyric poetry), ἰαμβεῖα, διθύραμβοι, etc., ῥαπτῶν ἐπέων ἀοιδοί Pi.*N.*2. 2; τὰ Κύπρια ἔπεα Hdt.2.117, cf. Th.1.3, X.*Mem.*1.4.3, Pl.*R.*379a, etc.; ἔπεά τε ποιεῖν πρὸς λύραν τ' ἀείδειν Theoc.*Ep.*21.6; νικήσας ἔπος *IG*3.1020; ποητὴς ἐπῶν ib.7.3197.9 (Orchom. Boeot.), cf. *OGI*51.37 (Egypt, iii B.C.). b. generally, *poetry*, even lyrics, Alcm.25 (prob.), Pi.*O.*3.8, etc. c. *lines, verses*, esp. of spoken *lines* in the drama, Ar.*Ra.*862, 956, etc.: sg., *verse, line* of poetry, Hdt.4.29, Pl.*Min.* 319d; *group of verses*, Id.*R.*386c, Hdt.7.143. d. *lines* of writing, μυρίων ἐπῶν μῆκος Isoc.12.136; ἐν ὅλοις ἑπτὰ ἔπεσι παραδραμεῖν, of a historian, Luc.*Hist.Conscr.*28.

**ἐποστρακ-ίζω**, *send potsherds skimming over the water, play at ducks and drakes*, *EM*368.3: hence, -ισμός, ὁ, Poll.9.119.

**ἐπόσχιον**, τό, *offshoot* of a vine, Gal.19.100.

**ἐποτοτύζω**, *cry out, utter lamentably*, ἄλλος ἄλλ' ἐπωτότυζε E.*Ph.* 1038 (lyr.).

**ἐποτρύνω**, *stir up, excite, urge on*, abs., θυμὸς ἐποτρύνει καὶ ἀνώγει Il. 6.439, al.: c. acc. pers., Hdt.7.170, al.; ἐς τὸ πρόσω ἐ. ib.223; ἐπὶ τὰ δεινά Th.1.84 (v.l.); τινὰς ἐς μάχην Plu.*Crass.*23; μαχομένους Id. *Aem.*33: c. inf., ἐ. τινὰ μαχέσασθαι Il.20.171, cf. Hp.*Fract.*22; στείχειν Pi.*N.*9.20; μολεῖν S.*El.*1264 (lyr.); ἔρδειν ὅττι κε κεῖνος ἐποτρύνῃ καὶ ἀνώγῃ [ἔρδειν] Il.15.148: c. dat. et inf., ἑτάροισιν ἐποτρῦναι καὶ ἀνῶξαι.. κατακῆαι *to urge* and order them..to burn, Od.10.531; ἱππεῦσιν ἐπότρυνον.. ἐλαυνέμεν Il.15.258, cf. 16.525, Q.S.8.337; ἑτάροισιν ἐποτρύνας ἐκέλευσεν Od.2.422, cf. 9.488. 2. c. acc. rei, νῶϊν ἐποτρύνει πόλεμον *stirs up* war *against* us, 22.152; also πόλεμον.. ἐ. γίγνεσθαι Th.7.25; ἀγγελίας.. ἐ. Κεφαλλήνων πολίεσσι *send urgent* messages to the cities of the C., Od.24.355; σαλπιγκταὶ ξύνοδον ἐπώτρυνον τοῖς ὁπλίταις *gave the signal for* engagement to the men-at-arms, Th.6.69:—Med., ἐποτρυνώμεθα πομπήν *let us urge on our* escort, Od.8.31:—Pass., *press on, hasten*, A.*Th.*698 (lyr.).

**ἐπουδαῖος**, ον, (οὖδας) *terrestrial*, Hsch.

**ἐπουλ-ίς**, ίδος, ἡ, (οὖλον) *growth on the gum*, Dsc.5.79, Aët.8. 27. **-ος**, ον (proparox.), *frilled, puckered*, of leaves, Thphr.*HP*3. 10.5. **-όω**, *scar over*, Gal.13.449:—Pass., Hp.*Art.*11, Gal.11. 440. ⊛ **-ωσις**, εως, ἡ, *cicatrization*, Id.18(1).723. ⊛ **-ωτικός**, ή, όν, *promoting cicatrization*, Id.11.756.

**ἐπουραῖος**, α, ον, (οὐρά) *on the tail*, δῆγμα *AP*9.252.4.

⊛ **ἐπουράνιος** [ᾰ], ον, Ep. η, ον Arat. (v. infr.), Q.S.2.429:—*heavenly*, in Hom. only of the gods, ἐ. θεός, θεοί, Od.17.484, Il.6.129, al.; εὐσεβέων ἐ. ψυχαί Pi.*Fr.*132.3; πατήρ *Ev.Matt.*18.35; ἡ ἐ. πορεία f.l. in Pl.*Phdr.*256d. 2. pl., as Subst., οἱ ἐ., = θεοί, Theoc.25.5, Mosch. 2.21; opp. ἐπίγειοι, *Ep.Phil.*2.11; so ἤδη ἐ. εἶ Luc.*DDeor.*4.3; τὰ ἐ., = τὰ μετέωρα, v.l. in Pl.*Ap.*19b (ἐ. σώματα 1*Ep.Cor.*15.40). 3. *up to heaven*, ἔπτατ' ἐπουρανίη v.l. in Arat.134.

**ἐπουρέω**, *make water upon*, Pythag.ap.D.L.8.17, Arist.*PA*679ᵃ29.

**ἐπουρ-ιάζω**, (οὖρος) of a fair wind, *waft onwards*, τὰ ἀκάτια Luc. *Hist.Conscr.*45; *swell*, τὴν ὀθόνην Id.*Dom.*12. II. metaph., τὰ ὦτα ἐπουριάσας ἕνεκα πολυπραγμοσύνης περιεργίας *spreading out* his ears to catch gossip, v.l. in Ph.2.4. ⊛ **-ίζω**, = foreg., of the sea, *waft onwards*, Str.3.2.4: metaph., ὥσπερ ἂν λαμπρότερον ἐπουρίσῃ τὸ τῆς τύχης the more freshly the breeze of fortune *blows*, Pl.*Alc.*2.147a (dub. l.); ἀλλ' οὔτι ταύτῃ σὸν φρόνημ' ἐπούρισας *hast turned* thy mind to it, E.*Andr.*610: c. acc. cogn., πνεῦμα αἱματηρὸν ἐ. τινί (of the Erinyes) *send after* him *the gale* of gory breath, A.*Eu.*137. II. intr., *sail with a fair wind*, τρέχε κατὰ τοὺς κόρακας ἐπουρίσας Ar.*Th.* 1226, cf. Epicr.10. ⊛ **-ος**, ον, *blowing favourably*, αὔρα S.*Tr.*954 (lyr.). II. a kind of *fish*, Hsch. **-όω**, *have a fair wind*, Plb.2. 10.6. **-ωσις**, εως, ἡ, dub. in Licymn.ap.Arist.*Rh.*1414ᵇ17, prob. *a speeding onward, as by a gale*: v.l. ἐπόρουσις ap.Sch. ad loc.

**ἐπουσί-α**, ἡ, *surplus*, Gem.18.15, Vett.Val.353.16, etc. **-αστικός**, ή, όν, *denoting material*, of Adjs. in -ειος, *An.Ox.*1.58. **-ώδης**, ες, *added to the essence, non-essential*, Phlp.*in Ph.*38.26; f.l. for ἐπεισοδιώδης, Porph.*Intr.*21.14. II. *symptomatic*, of fever, Alex.Aphr. *Febr.*31, Pall.*Febr.*3.

**ἐπουτίς**· οὐσία (Rhod.), Hsch.

**ἐποφείλω**, *owe still*, φόρους Th.8.5, cf. D.C.51.21:—Pass., τόκος ἐποφειλόμενός τισι Id.42.51.

**ἐποφθαλμ-έω**, = sq., c. dat., Charito 1.7, *PThead.*19.9 (iv A.D.). **-ιάω**, *cast longing glances at, ogle*, τινι Ael.*NA*3.44, cf. *Fr.*81; ἐ. χρήμασι Plu.*Caes.*2; πρὸς τὸν πλοῦτον Id.*Dem.*25; *eye jealously*, τοῖς ἔργοις τινός *POxy.*1630.6 (iii A.D.); v.l. in Hyp.*Fr.*258. **-ίζω**, = foreg., c. dat., Pherecyd.34 J., Plu.*Aem.*30.

⊛ **ἐποφλισκάνω**, *owe still more*, τί τινι Them.*Or.*6.83a, cf. Men.Prot. p.34 D.:—Pass., aor. part. -οφληθείς *PMasp.*168.63 (vi A.D.).

**ἐποφρύδιον**, τό, gloss on ἐπισκύνιον, *Et.Gud.*202.36; cf. ἐποφρύδιον· μέτωπον, Hsch. (-φρυδῶν cod.).

⊛ **ἐποχέομαι**, Pass. with fut. (and in Nonn.*D.*45.322, aor.) Med., *be carried upon, ride upon*, οὐ μὰν ὑμῖν γε (the horses of Achilles) καὶ ἅρμασι δαιδαλέοισιν Ἕκτωρ.. ἐποχήσεται Il.17.449, cf. Arr.*Tact.*17.1; ἐφ' ἵππῳ Paus.6.20.16: abs., κάμηλον ὥστε ἐποχεῖσθαι a camel *to ride on*, X.*Cyr.*7.1.49; of a fractured bone, *rest* or *ride on* the adjoining one, Hp.*Art.*15; com., ἐμβάταις ὑψηλοῖς ἐ. *to be mounted on* high shoes, Luc.*Salt.*27; ἡ κωμῳδία ἀναπαίστοις ἐ. Id.*Prom.Es*6. 2. *float upon*, [ἡ γῆ] ἐ. τῷ ἀέρι *Placit.*3.15.8; *float on the surface*, Gal.7. 604, Aët.5.137. 3. metaph., of a higher power, *transcend* the lower, [θεὸν] -ούμενον τῇ νοητῇ φύσει Plot.1.1.8; θεοὶ τοῖς δαίμοσιν ἄνωθεν -ούμενοι Procl.*in Alc.*p.69 C.; θεία ἀρετὴ ἐπὶ ἀνθρωπίνῃ ἐ. Hierocl.*in CA* 20 p.463 M. b. *to be borne upon, employ as a vehicle or medium*, Plot.4.3.6; τῇ οὐσίᾳ Dam.*Pr.*89, cf. 5. c. *hover over, brood over, play about*, Plot.2.2.3, 2.5.5, 4.3.7.

**ἐποχετ-εία**, ἡ, *watering by sluices*, Str.16.1.10 (pl.). **-ευσις**, εως, ἡ, = foreg., metaph., ἀγαθῶν Procl.*in Alc.*p.2 C. (pl.). **-εύω**, *carry* water *by sluices* or *courses*, Pl.*Grg.*493e; τὸ ἀπορρέον.. δι' ὀχετῶν ἐ. Id.*Criti.*117b; τροφὴν τοῖς φυτευθεῖσι Ph.1.398; ἐ. ἄνθεσιν ὕδωρ Longus 4.4: metaph., ὑφηγήσεις ἐ. ἀκοαῖς Ph.2.359; λόγος οἴνῳ τὸ φιλάνθρωπον ἐπὶ τὴν ψυχὴν.. ἐ. Plu.2.660c, cf. Jul.*Or.*4.137d, Dam. *Pr.*35, etc.:—Pass., *to be so brought*, [αἷμα] ἐκ τῆς καρδίας ἐποχετεύεται καὶ εἰς τὰς φλέβας Arist.*PA*666ᵃ6; [αἱ φλέβες] ἐς ἀλλήλας ἐποχετεύονται *are conducted* one into another, Hp.*Oss.*15: ὕδωρ τὸ Ἰούλιον.. εἰς τὴν πόλιν ἐπωχετεύθη D.C.48.32, cf. 49.42: metaph., ἔλλαμψις ἐκ τῶν πρώτων δυνάμεων ταῖς δευτέραις -εύεται Herm.*in Phdr.*p.145 A.:—Med., *to have* water *brought upon them, to be irrigated*, ἐποχετεύεται τοῖς κοχλίαις τὰ λίαν ἔξαλα Str.17.1.52: metaph., ἐ. ἵμερον *bring the waters of* desire *over oneself, bathe in* them, Pl.*Phdr.*251e.

**ἐποχεύς**, έως, ὁ, (ἐπέχω) *brake*, prob. for ἐποχλεύς (q.v.).

**ἐποχεύω**, of the male animal, *spring upon, cover*, Arist.*GA*741ᵃ 31:—Med., *couple with*, θερμὸν δ' ἐποχεύετο θερμῷ Emp.90 (dub. l.).

⊛ **ἐποχή**, ἡ, (ἐπέχω) *check, cessation*, ἡ κατὰ τὸν πόλεμον ἐ. Plb.38.11.2; μετ' ἐποχῆς with *a check*, Id.10.23.4; ἐποχὰς ποιεῖν.. τῆς προκοπῆς to *check* advance, Plu.2.76d, cf. Plot.6.2.13. 2. *retention*, σπέρματος Gal.8.420; οὔρων Philum.*Ven.*25.2; σκυβάλων Sor.2.20; ἀναπνοῆς (in hysteria) ib.26; γαστρός Gal.6.315; but ἐ. ἐμμήνων *suppression* (not *retention*) of the menses, Sor.2.6, al. II. Philos., *suspension of judgement*, Metrod.*Herc.*831.6, Chrysipp.*Stoic.*2.39, Cic.*Acad.Pr.* 2.18.59, Arr.*Epict.*1.4.11, S.E.*P.*1.10, Gal.1.40, etc. 2. *suspense* of payment, etc., τὰ ἐν ἐποχῇ ἕως ὁρισμοῦ καρπῶν *BGU*599.3 (ii A.D.), cf. *PRyl.*214.34 (ii A.D.), etc. III. *stoppage, pause*, of light during an eclipse, Plu.2.923b. 2. Astron., *position* as referred to celestial or terrestrial latitude and longitude, Ptol.*Alm.*7.4, 12.8; πόλεων ib.2.13 (pl.); ἀστέρων ἐποχαὶ *positions* (longitudes) of stars in a horoscope, Plu.*Rom.*12; αἱ φαινόμεναι τῆς σελήνης ἐ., opp. αἱ οὖσαι, Procl.*Hyp.*4.49. b. *fixed point in time* in reference to which positions are defined and from which their changes are computed, *epoch*, Ptol.*Alm.*3.9; perh. also *position at such a fixed point* (also called *epoch*), ib.3.7. 3. in Musical theory, *period* of vibration, Nicom.*Harm.*3 (pl.).

**ἐποχθίδιος**, α, ον, (ὄχθη) *on* or *of the river-banks*, Νύμφαι *AP*9.556 (Zon.).

**ἐποχθίζω**, *groan* or *grieve for*, ὀδύνῃσι Opp.*H.*5.170.

**ἐποχλεύς**, έως, ὁ, *brake, sprag*, = τροχοπέδη, prob. f.l. for ἐποχεύς, Simarist.ap.Ath.3.99c.

**ἐποχλίζομαι**, *to be bolted*, of doors, Apollon.*Lex.* s.v. ἐπώχατο.

**ἐποχμάζω**, = ἐποχεύω, c. dat., Opp.*C.*1.389.

**ἔποχον**, τό, *saddle-cloth, housing*, X.*Eq.*12.9.

**ἔποχος**, ον, (ἐπί, ϝέχω, cf. Lat. *veho*) *mounted upon*, esp. on horses, chariots, and ships, c. gen. vel dat., ναῶν, ἅρμασιν, A.*Pers.*54, 45 (anap.), cf. S.*Ichn.*181 (lyr.); τῷ ἐ. τοῦ οὐρανοῦ καὶ ἡνιόχῳ Ph.1.486, cf. Lib.*Or.*59.110: metaph., λόγος μανίας ἔ. words *borne on* madness, i.e. frantic words, E.*Hipp.*214 (anap.). 2. abs., *having a good seat* on horseback, X.*Cyr.*1.4.4; ἐπόχους ἡ θήρα ἀποδεικνύει ib. 8.1.35; ἔ. εἶναι to *have a good seat*, Id.*Eq.*8.10, cf. Ar.*Lys.*677; also ἱππασίαις ἔ. *practised in..*, Plu.*Mar.*34. Adv. -χως, ἐγκαθῆσθαι to sit *fast*, Poll.1.209. II. Pass., ποταμὸς ναυσὶ ἔ. *navigable* by ships, Plu.*Mar.*15.

**ἔποψ**, οπος, ὁ, *hoopoe, Upupa epops*, so called from its cry, Epich. 166, Ar.*Av.*226, Arist.*HA*615ᵃ16, Ant.Lib.11.10, etc.; ἐπόπτην ἔποπα τῶν αὐτοῦ κακῶν A.*Fr.*304.

**ἐποψ-άομαι**, (ὄψον) *eat as* ὄψον, ζωμόν Plu.*Lyc.*12. **-ιασμός**, ὁ, sine expl., Suid., *Et.Gud.d.* **-ημα**, ατος, τό, *that which is eaten with bread*, *IG*7.2712.81 (Acraephia). **-ησις**, εως, ἡ, *eating as* ὄψον, Ath.5.186d.

**ἐποψία**, ἡ, *inspection*, Them.*Or.*1.2c, *Cod.Just.*10.16.13*Intr.*

**ἐποψίδιος**, ον, *for eating with bread*, χόνδρος *AP*7.736.8 (Leon.).

**ἐπόψ-ιμος**, ον, (ἐπόψομαι) *that can be looked on*, δεινόν, οὐδ' ἀκουστόν, οὐδ' ἐ. S.*OT*1312. ⊛ **-ιος**, ον, also α, ον Arat.258: (ὄψις):—*full in view, conspicuous*, τόπος S.*Ant.*1110, v.l. in Id.*OC*1600: metaph., *conspicuous, famous*, βωμός *h.Ap.*496: also read by Ar.Byz. for ὑπόψιος, Il.3.42. II. Act., *overlooking all things*, epith. of gods, S. *Ph.*1040; esp. of Zeus, *SIG*1264 (Itanus, iv B.C.), A.R.2.1123, 1133, Call.*Jov.*82, Ant.Lib.6.2. ⊛ **-ις**, εως, ἡ, *view over*, ἐπ' ὅσον ἔ. τοῦ ἱροῦ εἶχε so far as *the view from* the temple reached, Hdt.1.64; ἐκτὸς τῆς ἡμετέρας ἐ. beyond our *range of vision*, Pl.*R.*499d; ἀνώμαλον τὴν ἔποψιν τῆς ναυμαχίας ἐκ τῆς γῆς ἠναγκάζοντο ἔχειν to *view* the sea-fight, Th.7.71; ἔποψίν τινος παρέχειν Plu.*Pomp.*32; καταστὰς εἰς ἔ. τῶν πολεμίων Id.*Luc.*8; ἐν ἐπόψει ἀλλήλοις within *view*, Str.14.5. 16. II. *oversight, superintendence*, ἔ. θεία περὶ τὸν κόσμον Hippod. ap.Stob.4.39.26.

**ἐπόψομαι**, fut. of ἐφοράω. II. v. ἐπιόψομαι. **ἔππᾰσις**, v. ἔμπασις. **ἐπράθην** [ᾱ], aor. 1 Pass. of πιπράσκω. **ἔπρᾰθον**, aor. 2 of πέρθω. ⊛ **ἔπρεσε**, Ep. for ἔπρησε, aor. 1 of πρήθω, Hes.*Th.* 856. **ἐπρήθην**, Ion. aor. 1 Pass. of πιπράσκω. **ἔπρηξα**, Ion. for ἔπραξα, aor. 1 of πράσσω. **ἔπρησα**, aor. 1 of πρήθω.

⊛ **ἑπτά**, οἱ, αἱ, τά, indecl. *seven*, Il.6.421, etc.; as a mystical number, Arist.*Metaph.*1093ᵃ13, etc.; αἱ ἑ. νῆσοι the *seven* largest islands, Alex.268, cf. Arist.*Mir.*837ᵃ31; τὰ ἑ. θεάματα the *Seven* Wonders, Str.17.1.33, cf. D.S.2.11, etc.; οἱ ἑ. σοφισταί the *Seven* Sages, Isoc. 15.109, Aristid.2.311 J.; οἱ ἑ. σοφοί Stob.3.1.172; οἱ ἑ. alone, D.L. 1.40, Lib.*Ep.*286.3. 2. οἱ ἑ., board of magistrates at Olbia, *SIG* 495.2 (iii B.C.); οἱ ἑ. ἄνδρες, = Lat. *septemviri epulones*, D.C.48.32. (I.-E. *septm̥*, cf. Skt. *saptá*, Lat. *septem* (fancifully connected with σέβομαι, Ph.1.30, *Theol.Ar.*43): Hsch. has τεπτά, i.e. ͱεπτά.)

**ἑπτᾰ-βόειος**, ον, *of seven bulls'-hides*, σάκος Il.7.220, 222, etc.; comically, θυμοὶ ἑ. Ar.*Ra.*1017. **-βοιος**, ον, = foreg., ἑ. ἄρρηκτον σάκος S.*Aj.*576. **-βυρσος**, ον, gloss on ἑπταβόειος, Apollon.*Lex.*, Hsch. **-γλωσσος**, ον, *seven-toned*, φόρμιγξ Pi.*N.*5.24. ⊛ **-γράμμᾰτος**, ον, *of seven letters*, Hsch. (glossed by τὸ "ὀργίλον", ἢ "σκληρόν", καὶ "Σάραπιν"). **-γωνικός**, ή, όν, = sq., ἀριθμός Iamb.*in Nic.* p.60 P. **-γωνος**, ον, *heptagonal*, ἀριθμός Nicom.*Ar.*2.7, 11. II. ἑπτάγωνα, τά, certain *musical instruments*, Arist.*Pol.*1341ᵇ41.

**ἑπτᾰδεύω**, *to be a member of a board of seven* (cf. ἑπτά 2), *SIG*1039. 1 (Olbia, iii B.C.).

**ἑπτά-δουλος** [ᾰ], ὁ, *sevenfold-slave*, Hippon.113 B, Herod.5.75. **-δραχμος**, ον, *worth seven drachmae*, Theoc.15.19. **-δρομος**, ον, *having seven laps*, δόλιχος Tz.*H*.6.704.

**ἑπτάδῠμος** [ᾰ], ον, in pl., *seven at a birth*, Arist.ap.Str.15.1.22.

**ἑπτά-ειδος** [ᾰ], ον, *containing seven ingredients*, ἀντίδοτος Paul.Aeg. 3.78.22; cf. ἑξάειδος. **-εικοσαπλᾰσίων**, ον, gen. ονος, *twenty-seven times as great*, Hipparch.ap.Theon.Sm.p.197 H. **-ενος**, ον, = ἑπταετής, Hsch. **-εξ**, *six or seven*, Tz.*H*.11.342. ⊛ **-ετής**, ές, = ἑπτέτης, *seven years old*, v.l. in Hp.*Prog*.19, v.l. for ἑπτέτης in Pl.*Grg*.471c: as fem., *IG*14.1935, Arr.*Ind*.9.1: regul. fem.⊛ **-έτις**, ιδος, ἡ, Amyntas Epigr.*Oxy*.662.30: as Adj., ἑ. ἡλικία Ph.1.393. II. parox. **-έτης**, ες, *of seven years*: neut. ἑπτάετες, as Adv., *for seven years*, Od. 3.304, 7.259. **-ετία**, ἡ, *age of seven years*, εἰς ἑπταετίαν ἀφικέσθαι Pl.*Ax*.366d. 2. *period of seven years*, Ph.1.25, J.*AJ*1.19.6, Plu. *Demetr*.44. **-ζωνος**, ον, *seven-zoned*, of the planetary system, Vett. Val.144.14, Paul.Al.*I*.3, Nonn.*D*.1.241; ἡ ἑ. (sc. σφαῖρα) *PMag.Leid. W*.6.5. **-ήμερος**, ον, *lasting seven days*, D.C.76.1. **-θεος**, ον, *having seven gods*, gloss on the name Ἀρδάβδα, *Peripl.M.Eux*.p.415 M.

**ἑπταῖος**, α, ον, f.l. for ἑπτάκις in Hp.*Nat.Puer*.13.

**ἑπτᾰκαίδεκα**, οἱ, αἱ, τά, indecl. *seventeen*, Hdt.1.50, al.; in Hom., ἑπτὰ δὲ καὶ δέκα Od.5.278, al.

**ἑπτᾰκαιδεκᾰετής**, ές, *of seventeen years*, χρόνος D.S.2.2. 2. (parox.) *seventeen years old*, Plb.4.24.1, Poll.1.55: **-δεκέτης** D.L.5.6.

**ἑπτᾰκαιδεκάκις**, Adv. *seventeen times*, Ptol.*Tetr*.138.

**ἑπτᾰκαιδεκά-μετρος**, ον, *containing seventeen measures*, περίοδος Sch.Ar.*Pax*1320. **-πηχυς**, υ, *seventeen cubits long*, Antig.*Mir*. 91. **-πους**, ὁ, ἡ, neut. -πουν, *seventeen feet long*, Pl.*Tht*.147d.

**ἑπτᾰκαιδεκᾰταῖος**, α, ον, *on the seventeenth day*, Hp.*Aph*.4.36.

⊛ **ἑπτᾰκαιδέκᾰτος**, η, ον, *seventeenth*, Hp.*Aph*.2.24, Th.7.28, etc.; δημαρχικῆς ἐξουσίας τὸ ἑ. *Notiz.Arch*.4.20.

**ἑπτᾰκαιδεκέτης**, ες, v. ἑπτακαιδεκαέτης.

**ἑπτᾰκαιεικοσα-έτης**, ες, *twenty-seven years old*, D.H.4.7, etc. **-πλάσιος** [πλᾰ], ον, *twenty-seven fold*, Pl.*Ti*.35c (v.l. -σιπλ-), *Theol. Ar*.4,41 (v.l. -σιπλ-):—also **-πλασίων**, ονος, ὁ, ἡ, *Placit*.2.21.1.

**ἑπτᾰκαιεικοσέτης**, ες, *twenty-seven years old*, *IG*9(1).873 (Corc., iii B.C.).

**ἑπτᾰκαιεικοσι-μόριος**, ον, *containing a twenty-seventh part*, *Theol. Ar*.4. **-πλάσιος**, ον, v. ἑπτακαιεικοσαπλάσιος.

⊛ **ἑπτᾰκάτιοι** [κᾰ], αι, α, Dor. for ἑπτακόσιοι, *Tab.Heracl*.1.47.

**ἑπτά-καυλος** [ᾰ], ον, *seven-stemmed*, *Theol.Ar*.48. **-κέφᾰλος**, ον, *seven-headed*, δράκοντες Dam.*Isid*.67, cf. *Pr*.265.

**ἑπτάκις** [ᾰ], Adv. *seven times*, Pi.*O*.13.40, Ar.*Lys*.698, etc.:— poet. **ἑπτάκι** Simon.156, A.R.3.861, etc.: also in later Prose, *SIG* 1068.8 (Patmos, iii/ii B.C.), Iamb.*in Nic*.p.17 P.:—Lacon. **ἑπτάκιν** *IG*5(1).213.16 (v B.C.).

**ἑπτᾰκισ-μύριοι** [ῡ], αι, α, *seventy thousand*, Hdt.4.86, Plu.*Demetr*. 28. **-χίλιοι** [χῑ], αι, α, *seven thousand*, Hdt.2.43, etc.; ἑπτασχίλιαι (sic) *PSI*3.250 (iii/iv A.D.).

**ἑπτά-κλῑνος**, ον, *with seven couches* or *beds*, οἶκος Phryn.Com.66, X.*Smp*.2.18; κοιτών Callix.1; and without οἶκος, Tim.Com.1; θὲς ἑπτάκλινον place *seven seats*, Eub.121; τὸ δέρμα κατέχει εἰς ἑ. ἀποταθέν provides sitting-room for *seven*, Arist.*HA*$630^a$22: hence, as a measure of area, Ph.*Bel*.80.48.

**ἑπτᾰκόσιοι**, αι, α, *seven hundred*, Hdt.2.140, etc.

**ἑπτᾰκοσιοστός**, ή, όν, *seven-hundredth*, Archim.*Aren*.1.10, Cleom. 2.1, D.L.1.24.

**ἑπτᾰκότῠλος**, ον, *holding seven cotylae*, λήκυθος Ar.*Fr*.472.

**ἑπτάκτῑς**, ῖνος, ὁ, ἡ, *with seven rays*, of the sun, Jul.*Or*.5.172d, Procl.*in Ti*.1.34 D.

**ἑπτά-κτῠπος**, ον, *seven-toned*, φόρμιγξ Pi.*P*.2.70. **-κωλος**, ον, *of seven members*, περίοδος Sch.Ar.*Ra*.221. **-λοβος**, ον, *with seven lobes*, Ar.Byz.*Epit*.90.16. **-λογχος**, ον, *of seven lances*, i.e. *seven bodies of spearmen*, στόλος S.*OC*1305. **-λόφιον**, = Lat. *septimontium*, *Gloss*. **-λοφος**, ον, *seven-hilled*, ἄστυ, of Rome, Cic.*Att*. 6.5.2, *AP*14.121 (Metrod.), cf. Plu.2.280d. **-μελής**, ές, *having seven members*, Procl.*in Ti*.2.209 D. **-μερής**, ές, *having seven parts*, ψυχῆς τὸ ἄλογον ἑ. Ph.1.45, cf. Procl.*in Ti*.2.209 D. **-μέριον**, τό, dub. sens. in *PMag.Berol*.1.201. ⊛ **-μήκης** κύκλος, dub. sens. in Call.*Iamb*.1.126 (cf. D.S.10.6); perh. referring to the Pythagorean harmony of the planetary spheres. **-μηνιαῖος**, α, ον, *born in the seventh month*, Cic.*Att*.10.18.1, J.*AJ*5.11.4, *Placit*. 5.18.5:—also **-μήνιος**, ον, *Theol.Ar*.48. ⊛ **-μηνος**, ον, παιδίον, βρέφος, τέκνον, *a seven months' child*, Hp.*Septim*.passim; τίκτειν τινὰ ἑπτάμηνον, τίκτειν ἑπτάμηνα [τέκνα], Hdt.6.69, cf. Arist.*HA*$584^a$ 36. II. ἑπτάμηνος, ἡ, *a space of seven months*, *Placit*.5.18.1, cf. *IG*12(1).53 (Rhodes). **-μήτωρ**, ορος, ἡ, *mother of seven children*, Lxx 4*Ma*.16.24. **-μῐτος**, ον, *seven-stringed*, Luc.*Astr*.10; κιθάρη *AP*9.250 (Honest.). **-μναῖος**, α, ον, *weighing seven minae*, Hsch. s.v. μολβίς. **-μοιρία**, ἡ, *arc of seven degrees*, Paul.Al.*H*.1. **-μόριον**, τό, = Lat. *Septempagi*, Plu.*Rom*.25. **-μυξος**, ον, *with seven wicks*, λύχνος *PMag.Lond*.121.593: Subst. -μυξος (sc. λύχνος), ὁ, *seven-branched candlestick*, *JHS*28.195 (Side). **-μῠχος**, ον, *with seven recesses*, σπέος Call.*Del*.65: title of work by Pherecyd.Syr. **-νευρον**, τό, prob. f.l. for ἑπτάπλευρον II, Paul.Aeg.7.17, Apul.*Herb*.1. **-όριον**, τό, = Lat. *septimontium*, *Gloss*. **-ούγκιον**, τό, = Lat. *septunx*, ib. ⊛ **-πάλαιστος** [πᾰ], ον, *seven palms long*, S.E.*M*.9.321:—early Att. **-πάλαστος** *IG*$1^2$.373.237. **-πεκτος**· ἡ βαθείας τρίχας ἔχουσα, Hsch. (-ιος cod.), cf. Suid.; ἡ δυναμένη ἑπτάκις τμηθῆναι, *EM*368. 11. **-πέλεθρος**, ον, *seven plethra large*, Ἄρης Nonn.*D*.36.14. **-πηχυς**, υ, *seven cubits long*, Hdt.1.68, Pl.*Ep*.363a, etc.; *seven cubits tall*, ἀνήρ J.*AJ*18.4.5. **-πλᾰνής**, ές, *with seven revolutions*, v.l. in Secund.*Sent*.1. **-πλᾰσιάζω**, *multiply seven times*, Dam.*Pr*.98, Hero *Geom*.17.7: hence, **-πλᾰσιασμός**, ὁ, ib.33: **-πλᾰσιέφεκτος** λόγος ratio *of* $7\frac{1}{8}$:1, Procl.*Hyp*.4.109. **-πλάσιος** [πλᾰ], α, ον, *sevenfold*, -πλασίῳ φαυλότερος Pl.*Ep*.332a, cf. Iamb.*in Nic*.p.102 P. Adv. -ίως Lxx *Ps*.11(12).6, al. **-πλᾰσίων**, ον, gen. ονος, = foreg., Orib.*Fr*.90, Suid. **-πλευρος**, ον, *having seven ribs*, Arist.*HA* $493^b$15. II. **-πλευρον**, τό, = ἀρνόγλωσσον, Dsc.2.126. **-πλόος**, ον, contr. **-πλοῦς**, οῦν, *sevenfold*, ἑπταπλᾶ ἀνταποδώσει σοι Lxx *Si*.32 (35).13. **-πόδης**, ου, ὁ, *seven feet long*, θρῆνυς Il.15.729; ἄξων Hes. *Op*.424. **-πολις**, ὁ, ἡ, *containing seven cities*: ἑ. μεσάτη ἤπειρος, of Egypt, D.P.251. **-πορος**, ον, *with seven tracks* or *paths*, τείρεα, of the planets, *h.Hom*.8.7; Πλειάς or Πελειάς, E.*IA*7, *Or*.1005 (both anap.); Πληϊὰς ἑ. *Epigr.Gr*.223.4 (Milet.); *seven-mouthed*, of the Nile, Mosch.2.51, D.P.264. **-πους**, ὁ, ἡ, *seven feet long*, σκιά Ar.*Fr*.675, cf. *IG*$1^2$.372.19, Anon.*in Tht*.34.25. 2. *having seven feet*, πολύπους Ael. *Fr*.143. **-πτῠχος**, ον, gloss on ἑπταβόειος, Sch.D Il.7.220. **-πῠλος**, ον, *with seven gates*, epith. of Boeotian Thebes (cf. ἑκατόμπυλος), Il.4.406, Od.11.263, B.18.47, Anaxandr.41.21, cf. A.*Th*.165 (lyr.), S.*Ant*.119 (lyr.). II. ἑ. κλῖμαξ stairway symbolizing the ascent of the soul through the seven planetary spheres, Cels.ap.Orig.*Cels*.6. 22 (prob. for ὑψί-). **-πυργος**, ον, *seven-towered*, of Boeotian Thebes, E.*Ph*.245 (lyr.), etc.: metaph., εὐλογιστία Lxx 4*Ma*.13.7. **-πῠρος**, ον, *with seven flames* or *wicks*, λύχνος *SIG*1106.119 (Cos, iv/iii B.C.).

**ἑπτᾰρουρ-ικὸς** κλῆρος allotment *of seven* ἄρουραι (q.v.), *PTeb*.13 *Intr*. (ii B.C.), cf. 128 (ii B.C.): ⊛ **-ος**, ὁ, *holder of seven* ἄρουραι, ib.60.30 (ii B.C.), etc.: **-ον**, τό, *plot of seven* ἄρουραι, *PFay*.118.25 (ii A.D.).

**ἑπτάρροος**, ον, contr. **-ρους**, ουν, (ῥόος) *with seven channels*, Νεῖλος ἑπτάρους A.*Fr*.300.

**ἑπτάς**, άδος, ἡ, *period of seven days*, Arist.*HA*$553^a$3 (pl.). II. *period of seven years*, *Syria*5.338, etc. III. *the number seven*, *Theol.Ar*.43, Nicom.*Ar*.1.16.

**ἑπτά-σημος** [ᾰ], ον, *of seven times*, in metre, συζυγίαι Heph.11.5, cf. 12.1, Aristid.Quint.1.14. **-στάδιος** [στᾰ], ον, *seven stades long*, διῶρυξ Scymn.649; πορθμός Str.2.5.19; χῶμα J.*AJ*12.2.13: Subst., τὸ ἑ. *space of seven stades*, Str.2.5.22.

**ἑπτάστερος**, ον, *of seven stars*, Eratosth.*Cat*.14, Gal.9.925.

**ἑπτά-στομος**, ον, *seven-mouthed*, πύλαι ἑ., of Boeotian Thebes, E. *Supp*.401; ἑ. πύργωμα, πόλισμα, Id.*Ph*.287, *Ba*.919; πύλαι S.*Fr*.773; of rivers, Str.4.1.8, 7.3.15. **-τάλαντος** [τᾰλ], ον, *weighing seven talents*, λίθος Them.*Or*.23.284b. **-τειχεῖς** ἔξοδοι the *seven* outlets *of the walls* of Thebes, A.*Th*.285. **-τευχος** (sc. βίβλος), ἡ, *book in seven volumes*, Sidon.Apoll.*Ep*.5.15. ⊛ **-τονος**, ον, *seven-toned*, φόρμιγξ Terp.5; γᾶρυς B.*Scol.Oxy*.1361 *Fr*.1.2; λύρα Ion Eleg.3.3; χέλυς E.*Alc*.446 (lyr.). **-φᾰής**, ές, *sevenfold shining*, Orph.*H*.7. 8. **-φάρμᾰκον**, τό, *drug compounded of seven ingredients*, Aët. 15.26. **-φεγγής**, ές, *with seven luminaries*, σφαῖρα Ph.1. 504. **-φθογγος**, ον, *seven-toned*, κιθάρα E.*Ion*881 (lyr.); συμφωνία Nicom.*Exc*.6. **-φυλλος**, ον, *seven-leaved*, κράμβη Hippon. 37. **-φωνος**, ον, *seven-voiced*, στοά, of a colonnade *with a sevenfold echo* at Olympia, Plu.2.502d, Luc.*Peregr*.40, Plin.*HN*36.100.

**ἕπτᾰχᾰ**, Adv. *in seven parts*, Od.14.434:—so **ἑπταχῇ** D.C.55.26: **ἑπταχῶς** Gal.19.280.

**ἑπτά-χορδος**, ον, *seven-stringed*, ἁρμονίαι Arist.*Pr*.$919^b$21, al., cf. Nicom.*Harm*.3. **-χους**, ουν, *holding seven* χόες, Arist.*Ath*.67. 2. **-χρονος**, ον, *of seven times*, πούς Heph.3.3. **-ωρος**, ον, *lasting seven days*, σεληνιακαὶ φάσεις *Theol.Ar*.45.

**ἑπτ-ετηρίς**, ίδος, ἡ, *festival celebrated every seven years*, Arist.*Ath*. 54.7. **-έτης**, = ἑπταετής, *seven years old*, Chionid.3, Ar.*Ra*.422: nom. pl. ἑπτέτεις Pl.*Alc*.1.121e:—fem. **-έτις**, ιδος, Ar.*Th*.480, Luc. *Tox*.61. **-ῆμαρ**, *for a space of seven days*, Orph.*Fr*.47. **-ήμερος**, ον, Ion. for ἑπταήμ-, αἰών *going by 'sevens'*, Hp.*Carn*.19. **-ήρης**, ες, *with seven banks of oars* (sc. ναῦς), Plb.1.23.4, D.S.20.50, Ath.5. 203d. **-ορόγυιος**, ον, (ὄργυια) *seven fathoms long*, πόδες Sapph. 98. **-υσχλος**, ὁ, *sandal laced with seven straps*, Hermipp.67 (pl.), cf. ὕσχλος, ἐννήυσκλοι, πτύσχλοι. **-ώροφος**, ον, *seven stories high*, D.S.14.30 (codd. opt. -όροφος).

**ἔπυδρος**, ον, Ion. for ἔφυδρος, Hdt.4.198.

**ἐπύλλιον**, τό, Dim. of ἔπος, *versicle, scrap of poetry*, Ar.*Ach*.398, *Pax*532, *Ra*.942. II. *short epic poem*, Ath.2.65a.

**ἕπω**, *say, call, name*, ἣν Πέρσειον ἕπουσιν Nic.*Al*.429, cf. 490, *Th*. 508. (Prob. invented by Nic., as pres. of εἶπον.)

⊛ **ἕπω** (A), *to be about, busy oneself with*, τὸν δ' εὗρ' ἐν θαλάμῳ περικαλλέα τεύχε' ἕποντα Il.6.321: elsewh. with Preps., in tmesi, cf. ἀμφέπω, διέπω, ἐφέπω, μεθέπω, περιέπω. (Cf. Skt. *sapati* 'worship', 'tend', *saparyati* 'worship', 'honour', Lat. *sepelio* 'give funeral honours'; not related to ἕπομαι.)

⊛ ***ἕπω** (B), only in Med., **ἕπομαι**, impf. εἱπόμην Il.4.274, al., Hdt.1. 45, Th.3.10, etc., Ep. also ἑπόμην Od.2.413, al.: fut. ἕψομαι Il.10.108, etc.: aor. 2 ἑσπόμην 12.398, al., in moods without ἑ- (v. infr.), imper. σπεῖο 10.285, συνεπί-σπεο *Lyr.Alex.Adesp*.20, inf. σπέσθαι Il.5.423, Od.22.324, part. σπόμενος Call.*Hec*.1.4.7; in Prose in compds., ἐπισπέσθαι Pl.*Phdr*.248c, ἐπι-σπόμενος Th.3.43, etc. (Cf. Skt. *sacate* 'accompany', 'follow', Lat. *sequor*, Lith. *sèkti* 'follow'; ἑσπόμην (Ἀρίσταρχος δασύνει Sch.Il.10.246) fr. ἑ-σπ-όμην, ἑ- (augm.) becoming ἑ- under the influence of ἕπομαι: ἑσπ- does not certainly occur in the moods in Hom.; when found (usu. with v.l. σπ-), it is preceded by an elided vowel, so that σπ- can be read (cf. Ptol.Asc.ap.Sch.Il. l.c.);

Pi.*O*.8.11, 9.83, 10(11).78, *I*.5(4).36 are indecisive (ἑσπ- only cj. in *P*.10.17, *I*.6(5).17); but ἑσποίμην occurs A.R.3.35, ἑσπόμενος 1.103, 470, 3.615, 4.434, Mosch.2.147, pres. indic. ἕσπεται A.R.4.1607, D.P.436,1140, v.l. for ἔρχεται in Od.4.826: pres. part. ἐφεσπόμενος Maiist.46: Skt. has a redupl. pres. stem *sasc(a)-*):—*to be* or *come after, follow*, I. of Persons, whether *after* or *in company with*, abs., ὁ μὲν ἦρχ', ὁ δ' ἅμ' ἕσπετο Il.11.472; ἡγήσατο, τοὶ δ' ἅμ' ἕποντο Od.2.413:—Constr.: c. dat., υἱέϊ σῷ Il.3.174, cf. 9.428, 10.108, etc.: c. acc., Pi.*N*.10.37 (s.v.l.), Luc.*Asin*.51; ἕ. ἅμα τινί Il.2.534, etc.; σοὶ γὰρ ἑψόμεσθ' ἅμα S.*El*.253; with ἅμα doubled, οἵ τοι ἅμ' αὐτῷ Ἴλιον εἰς ἅμ' ἕποντο Od.11.372, cf. 15.541; abs., v. infr. II.2; less freq. ἐπί τινος Apollod.Ath.ap.Ath.7.281f (v. infr. II. 1); ἐπί τινι E.*Alc*.1032, X.*Cyr*.5.2.1, etc.; ἐπὶ βασιλέα against the king, Id. *An*.1.4.14; μετά τινι Il.18.234; μετά τινα 13.492; μετά τινος Ar.*Pl*. 823; σύν τινι Od.7.304, etc.; ὄπισθε Hdt.1.45, etc. 2. *follow*, as attendants, οὐκ οἴη, ἅμα τῇ γε καὶ ἀμφίπολοι δύ' ἕποντο Od.1. 331, cf. 8.46, etc.; also, *escort, attend*, by way of honour, θεοὶ δ' ἅμα πάντες ἕποντο Il.1.424; νέῳ ὧδε θεοὶ πομπῆες ἕπονται Od.3. 376. 3. in hostile sense, *pursue*, Il.11.154, etc.; ἀμφὶ δ' ἄρ' αὐτὸν ἕποντο they *pressed* upon him, ib.474 (never in Od.); οἱ πελτασταὶ εἵποντο διώκοντες X.*An*.5.4.24. 4. *keep pace with*, ὅς καὶ θνητὸς ἐὼν ἕπεθ' ἵπποις ἀθανάτοισι Il.16.154, cf. Od.6.319: metaph. of a man's limbs or strength, γούναθ' ἕποιτο, δύναμις καὶ χεῖρες ἕπονται, they *do his bidding*, Il.4.314, Od.20.237; ἕπεσθαι τοῖς καιροῖς τοῦ πολέμου Plu.*Pomp*.17. 5. *follow* the motions of another, ὁ δ' ἑσπόμενος (better δὲ σπ.) πέσε δουρί, of one from whose body a spear is drawn, Il.12.395; τρυφάλεια ἅμ' ἕσπετο χειρί the helm *went with* his hand, i.e. *came off* in his hand, 3.376; [ἔπαλξις] ἕσπετο, i.e. the battlement *came down*, 12.398. 6. *follow on the track of*, τῷ στίβῳ τῶν ἵππων X.*An*.7.3.43: abs., ἕπεσθε, ὦ κύνες Id.*Cyn*.6.19. 7. *follow, obey*, νόμῳ Hdt.5.18, Th.2.35; τῷ ξυνῷ Heraclit.2; μηνυτῆρος φραδαῖς A.*Eu*.245: abs., Id.*Ag*.1053, Hdt.6.16; *accept an invitation*, X.*Smp*.1.7; ἕ. κακοῖς *submit* to them, S.*Tr*.1074. 8. simply, *come near, approach*, in imper., ἕπεο προτέρω *come on* nearer, Il.18. 387, Od.5.91. 9. *follow up*, esp. *in mind, understand*, ἆρ' ἕπομαί σου τῷ λόγῳ; Pl.*Prt*.319a; οὐχ ἕσπου τοῖς λεχθεῖσιν Id.*Plt*.280b; οὐχ ἕπομαι τοῖς λεγομένοις Id.*Euthphr*.12a. 10. of Time, παραδοῦναι τοῖς ἑπομένοις *to succeeding generations*, Id.*Phlb*.17d. 11. impers., ἕπεται διελθεῖν *it follows* to.., Arist.*EN*1111$^b$5. 12. ἑπόμενα, τά, opp. προηγούμενα, *backward* points, i.e. those lying on the opposite side of the radius vector of a spiral from the direction of its motion, Archim.*Spir*.11*Def*.6. b. Astron., positions *following* in the daily movement of the heavens, *eastward* positions, Hipparch.1.11.5, etc. II. of Things, as of bridal presents, ὅσσα ἔοικε φίλης ἐπὶ παιδὸς ἕπεσθαι *go with* her from the parent's house, Od.1.278, 2.197 (v. supr. 4 and 5). 2. of honour, glory, etc., τούτῳ.. κῦδος ἅμ' ἕψεται Il.4.415; so ἄτη, τιμὴ ἕπεταί τινι, 9.512, 513, ἕπεται παλαιὸς ὄλβος Pi.*P*.5.55; πειθὼ δ' ἕποιτο καὶ τύχη A.*Supp*.523, etc.; ἦ οὐ γιγνώσκεις ὅ τοι ἐκ Διὸς οὐχ ἕπετ' ἀλκή; that no defence *attendeth* thee from Zeus, Il.8.140, cf. Pi.*N*.11.43, A.*Ag*.854. 3. *follow upon* (i.e. *result from*), τῇ ἀχαριστίᾳ ἡ ἀναισχυντία ἕ. X.*Cyr*. 1.2.7, etc.; τὰ ἑπόμενα τῆς τοιαύτης κατακοσμήσεως its *consequences*, Pl.*Plt*.271e, cf. *R*.504b; ἑπόμενος, opp. προηγούμενος, *consequent* (opp. antecedent), Dam.*Pr*.115; τὰ ἑ. [μεγέθη] the *consequents* in a proportion, opp. ἡγούμενα, Euc.5*Def*.11, etc. 4. *follow suit, agree with*, ἕπεται ὁ λόγος.. Κάδμοιο κούραις Pi.*O*.2.22; ἕπεται ἐν ἑκάστῳ μέτρον ib.13.47; ἑπόμενα σωφροσύνῃ things *agreeing with*.., Pl.*Lg*. 632c; ἔργα -όμενα τῇ γραφῇ ib.934c; τὰ τούτοις ἑ. the *like* to these, Id.*R*.406d; ἀναγκαῖα καὶ ἑ. ἀλλήλοις *interdependent*, ib.486e; τὸ πρέπον καὶ ἑπόμενον πάσῃ τῇ πολιτείᾳ Id.*Lg*.835c; of Nymphs, οὔτε θνητοῖς οὔτ' ἀθανάτοισιν ἕπονται they *belong to*.., *h.Ven*.259.

**ἐπῳ-άδιος** [ᾰ], ον, (ᾠόν) *upon the egg, hatched*, Opp.*H*.1.752 (vulg. ὑπῳάδιος). **-άζω**, *sit* or *brood upon eggs*, mostly of birds, Arist. *GA*752$^b$16, al.; also of tortoises, Id.*HA*558$^a$7; bees, ib.554$^a$18; spiders, ib.555$^a$30; crustacea, ib.550$^b$1. II. trans., *hatch, incubate young birds* by artificial heat, D.S.1.74. **-άσις**, εως, ἡ, *sitting on eggs, incubation*, Arist.*HA*563$^a$29. **-ασμός**, ὁ, = foreg., ib.558$^b$ 15, 564$^b$9. **-αστικός**, ή, όν, *fond of sitting*, of birds, ib.560$^a$3 (Comp.).

⊛ **ἐπωβελία**, ἡ, (ὀβελός) *fine of an obol in the drachma*, i.e. *one-sixth of the sum* at which the damages were laid, paid as compensation to the defendant by the plaintiff in case the latter failed to gain one-fifth of the votes, τὴν ἐ. ὀφλεῖν, τῆς ἐ. κινδυνεύειν, D.27.67, 31.14. 2. *added payment of one-sixth* per mensem, as a penalty for failure to discharge debts, Pl.*Lg*.921d. 3. dub. sens. in *PCair.Zen*.15$^r$.44 (iii B.C.).

⊛ **ἐπῳδή**, Ion. and poet. **ἐπαοιδή**, ἡ, *song sung to* or *over*: hence, *enchantment, spell*, ἐπαοιδῇ δ' αἷμα.. ἔσχεθον Od.19.457, cf. Pi.*P*.4. 217; οὐ πρὸς ἰατροῦ σοφοῦ θρηνεῖν ἐπῳδὰς πρὸς τομῶντι πήματι S.*Aj*. 582; of the Magi, Hdt.1.132; μελιγλώσσοις πειθοῦς ἐπαοιδαῖσιν A.*Pr*. 174, cf. S.*OC*1194; ἐπῳδὰς ἐπᾴδειν X.*Mem*.2.6.10 sq.; ἐπῳδαῖς ἀλίσκεσθαι Anaxandr.33.13; οὔτε φάρμακα.. οὐδ' αὖ ἐπῳδαί Pl.*R*.426b; θυσίαι καὶ ἐ. ib.364b; τὰς θυσίας καὶ τελετὰς καὶ τὰς ἐ. Id.*Smp*.202e, etc.: c. gen. obj., *charm for* or *against*.., τούτων ἐπῳδὰς οὐκ ἐποίησεν πατήρ A.*Eu*.649. II. apptly., = ἐπῳδός II, Poet.*Oxy*.661.21 (pl.).

**ἐπώδης**, ες, (ἐπόζω) *rank-smelling*, Hp.ap.Gal.19.100.

**ἐπῳδικός**, ή, όν, *of* or *for an* ἐπῳδός II, *epodic*, τὰ -κά Heph.*Poëm*.4. 1, al. Adv. -κῶς, γεγράφθαι Id.p.62 C.

**ἐπωδίνω** [ῑ], *suffer birth-pangs*, metaph., ἐπωδίνουσι μέριμναι Archyt.Amph.4.

**ἐπῳδ-ιον**, τό, Dim. of ἐπῳδός II, Hsch. s.v. ἐπιρρήματα. **-ός**, όν, (ἐπᾴδω) *singing to* or *over, using songs* or *charms* to heal wounds, ἐπῳδοὶ μῦθοι Pl.*Lg*.903b. b. Subst., *enchanter*, ἐ. καὶ γόης E.*Hipp*. 1038 (but γόης ἐ. *Ba*.234): c. gen., *a charm for* or *against*, ἔθυσεν αὐτοῦ παῖδα ἐπῳδὸν Θρῃκίων ἀημάτων A.*Ag*.1418; ἐ. τῶν τοιούτων *one to charm away* such fears, Pl.*Phd*.78a. c. c. dat., *assisting, profitable*, ἐ. γίγνεσθαι νέοις πρὸς ἀρετήν Id.*Lg*.671a; δυσπραξίᾳ ληφθεὶς ἐ. ἐστι τῷ πειρωμένῳ *Trag.Adesp*.364.4. 2. Pass., *sung to music*, φωναί Plu.2.622d; *fit for singing*, ποιητικὴν ἐ. παρέχειν S.E.*M*.6. 16. b. *sung or said after*, μορφῆς ἐπῳδόν *called after* this form, E. *Hec*.1272. II. in Metre, as Subst., 1. ἐπῳδός, ἡ, Sch.metr. Pi.*O*.4 (ὁ, Gal.*UP*17.3, dub. in D.H.*Comp*.19), *epode, part of a lyric ode sung after the strophe and antistrophe*, ib.26, Gal. l. c., Sch.metr. Pi. l. c., etc. 2. ἐπῳδός, ὁ, *verse* or *passage returning* at intervals, in Alcaics and Sapphics, D.H.*Comp*.19; *chorus, burden, refrain*, Ph. 1.312: metaph., ὁ κοινὸς ἁπάσης ἀδολεσχίας ἐ. the 'old story', Plu.2. 507e. b. *shorter verse of a couplet*, as in the metres invented by Archilochus, Hermog.*Inv*.4.4: hence of short poems written in such metres, ἐπῳδοί Heph.*Poëm*.7.2; ἐπῳδά Plu.2.1141a.

**ἐπωδῡν-ία**, ἡ, *pain, anguish*, Str.15.1.45. **-ος**, ον, (ὀδύνη) *painful*, Hp.*VM*22, *Prog*.7; τραύματα Ar.*Ach*.1205 (lyr.); ζωή Ph.2.579; δάκρυα Plu.2.114c: irreg. Comp. -νέστερος Hp.*Art*.49. Adv. -νως Id.*Epid*.1.26.γ', Ph.1.136.

⊛ **ἐπῴζω**, = ἐπῳάζω, Epich.172, Cratin.108; *cluck*, like a laying hen, Ar.*Av*.266.

**ἐπωθ-έω**, *push on, impel*, ἐπὶ ῥίον ὦσεν ἄναξ *h.Ap*.382, cf. Arist.*Mete*. 370$^b$23, *Pr*.915$^a$2, Arr.*Tact*.16.13; ἐ. ὁρμήν Agatharch.14; παχὺν ἐ. τῷ σιδήρῳ τὸν κοντόν dub. l. in Plu.*Crass*.27. 2. Pass., of tumours, *to be brought to a head*, v.l. in Hp.*Epid*.7.105. **-ίζω**, = foreg., ζέφυρος κύμασι Ps.-Luc.*Philopatr*.3.

**ἐπωκ-ής**, ές, *somewhat sharp* or *acid*, in Comp., φακῇ ἑφθῇ -εστέρῃ τῷ ὄξει Hp.*Int*.21 (v.l.), cf. 22. **-ύνω**, *sharpen, quicken*, τὴν ἐνέργειαν Gal.6.187.

**ἐπώλεθρος**, ον, (ὄλεθρος) *destructive*, Hdn.*Epim*.203.

⊛ **ἐπωλένιος**, ον, *upon the arm*, -ένιον κιθαρίζειν *h.Merc*.433, 510; φορέειν A.R.1.557.

⊛ **ἐπωμ-άδιος** [ᾰ], ον, (ὦμος) *on the shoulders*, πτέρυγας Theoc. 29.29 (v.l. ἐπ' ὀμμασίαις, fort. leg. ἐπομμαδίαις), cf. *APl*.4.108 (Jul.). **-ᾰδόν**, Adv. *on the shoulder*, A.R.1.738, Q.S.13.541, *APl*.4.279. **-ίδιος**, α, ον, *on the shoulder*, φλέψ Hp.*Oss*. 12. II. Subst. -ίδιον, τό, Dim. of ἐπωμίς, *horse's trappings*, App. *Mith*.115. **-ίζομαι**, Med., *put on one's shoulder*, Ps.-Luc.*Philopatr*.4. ⊛ **-ιος**, ον, = ἐπωμάδιος, E.*Hyps.Fr*.32(58).9, Luc.*Am*.44; ἐ. τι ἀνελέσθαι Alciphr.1.1. **-ίς**, ίδος, ἡ, (ὦμος) *the point of the shoulder*, where it joins the collar-bone, Hp.*Art*.1, al., X.*Mem*.3.10. 13, Gal.2.273, etc.; the adjacent part of the collar-bone, Poll.2.133; acc. to Arist.*HA*493$^a$9, *back part of the neck*: pl., Id.*Phgn*.810$^b$ 35. 2. Poet., *shoulder*, Achae.4, Call.*Del*.143, *AP*9.588 (Alc. Mess.). 3. part of a ship, Archimel.ap.Ath.5.209d (s.v.l.). 4. in pl., *leaves of a folding-door*, Lxx*Ez*.41.2. II. *part of the women's tunic that was fastened on the shoulder by brooches, shoulder-strap*, E. *Hec*.558, Chaerem.14.2, Apollod.Car.4, *IG*11(2).287*A*87 (iii B.C.); *tunic* of a rower, E.*IT*1404; the high-priest's *ephod*, Lxx*Ex*.28.6, Ph.2.151, al.

**ἐπωμ-οσία**, ἡ, (ἐπόμνυμι) = ὑπωμοσία, Sch.Ar.*Pl*.725. **-οσις**, εως, ἡ, *swearing to* a thing, Eust.809.32. **-ότης**, ου, ὁ, *additional juror*, *IG*9(1).333.10 (Locr., v B.C.). **-οτικόν**, τό, *oath* (= ὁμοτικόν), Stoic.ap.Rh.2.662, 7.4 W. ⊛ **-οτος**, ον, *on oath, sworn*, ἐ. λέγων S.*Tr*.427; cf. ἐνώμοτος. II. Pass., *witness of oaths*, like ὅρκιος, Ζῆν' ἔχων ἐπώμοτον ib.1188.

⊛ **ἐπώνια**, τά, (ὠνή) *duty on goods sold*, *IG*1$^2$.329.5, Is.*Fr*.43, *PCair. Zen*.206.20, al. (iii B.C.), Poll.7.15: also in sg., ἐπώνιον, τό, *SIG*1014. 5 (Erythrae, iii B.C.), etc. II. *something given into the bargain in a sale*, Phryn.*PS*p.70 B.

⊛ **ἐπωνυμ-ία**, Ion. -ίη, ἡ, (ἐπώνυμος) *derived* or *significant name*, as Ἔπαφος, A.*Supp*.45 (lyr.); Πολυνείκης, Id.*Th*.829 (lyr.); ἐ. ποιεῖσθαι ἀπό or ἐπί τινος, Hdt.2.42, 1.94; ὅθεν ἔθεντο τὰς ἐ. Id.4.45; ἔχειν ἐ. ἐπί τινος ibid.; καλεῖσθαι ἐ. ἐπί τινος Id.1.14; κατὰ τὴν ἐ. τινὸς κληθῆναι Id.1.173; ἐ. ἔχειν ἀπό τινος, Id.4.15, Pl.*Criti*.114a; ἐ. ἀπό τινος ἔχειν, ἐγκαταλιπεῖν, λαβεῖν, Hdt.7.121, Th.2.102, Pl.*Phdr*.238c; τῆς θεοῦ ἐπωνυμίας ἄξιος the *name derived* from her, Id.*Lg*.626d; τὴν τῇδε ἐ. αὐτοῦ its *namesake* here, Id.*Phdr*.250e; ἐ. ἀφ' ἑαυτῶν παρέχεσθαι Th.1.3; but ἐ. σχεῖν χώρας to have *the naming* of it, i.e. have it *named after* one, ib.9; ἐ. τινὶ Μαργίτην τίθεσθαι *as a nickname*, Aeschin.3.160; προσείληφε τὴν ἐ... συκοφάντης Id.2.99; ἔχουσα τὴν ἐ. τὴν τοῦ ὃ ἔστιν Pl.*Phd*.92d: folld. by inf., ἐ. ἔχει σμικρός τε καὶ μέγας εἶναι he has *the name of* being, ib.102c; ἀποβαλεῖν τὴν ἐ. τὸ.. καλὸς κἀγαθὸς κεκλῆσθαι X.*Oec*.12.2; ἐ. ἔχοντος Θασίου εἶναι Hdt.2. 44: acc. as Adv., Ὀλυμπίῳ ἐπωνυμίην θύειν *by surname*, ibid.; ἀπὸ τῆς κυψέλης ἐ. Κύψελος οὔνομα ἐτέθη Id.5.92.ε'. 2. generally, *name, title*, θεῶν -ίαι Id.2.4, cf. Pl.*R*.394a, *PHal*.1.251 (iii B.C.), etc.; συγγραμμάτων Sor.*Vit.Hippocr*.13. ⊛ **-ιον**, τό, *surname*, Plu. 2.560e; ἐ. παιδικόν Id.*Pyrrh*.1; = Lat. *cognomen*, D.H.5.19. **-ιος**, α, ον, poet. for sq. I. 3, *called after* or *by the name of*, τινος Pi.*P*.1.30, v.l. in Hdt.2.112; ἐπωνυμίαν χάριν νίκας Pi.*O*.10(11).78. ⊛ **-ος**, ον (for the form cf. ἀν-ώνυμος), *given as a significant name*, τῷ δ' Ὀδυσεὺς ὄνομ' ἔστω ἐπώνυμον Od.19.409 (cf. ὀδυσσάμενος τόδ' ἱκάνω ib.407); Ἀλκυόνην καλέεσκον ἐπώνυμον, οὕνεκ'.. Il.9.562, cf. *h.Ap*. 373; Κύκλωπες δ' ὄνομ' ἦσαν ἐπώνυμοι, οὕνεκα.. Hes.*Th*.144; τῷ μὲν

ἐπώνυμον ἦεν [Χρυσάωρ], ὅτ᾽.. ib.282; when the reason is omitted, the name is itself significant, Ἀρήτη δ᾽ ὄνομ᾽ ἐστὶν ἐπώνυμον ('the Desired') Od.7.54; κάρτα δ᾽ ὢν ἐ., πομπαῖος ἴσθι, of Hermes, A.*Eu.*90; Ζεὺς ἀλεξητήριος ἐ. γένοιτο may he become a defender *according to his name*, Id.*Th.*9, cf. 405; ἐπωνύμῳ δὲ κάρτα Πολυνείκει λέγω ib.658; ὦ Πολύνεικες ἔφυς ἄρ᾽ ἐ. *rightly* wert thou *named*.., E.*Ph.*1494 (anap.). 2. *surnamed*, Ἀθηναίῃ ἐ. Κραθίῃ Hdt.5.45; πολλῶν ὀνομάτων ἐ., of Aphrodite, S.*Fr.*941.2; τόδ᾽ ἐπώνυμον this is her *proper name* (sc. Αἴγλα), Isyll.47. 3. freq. c. gen., *named after* a person or thing, ἐμοῦ δ᾽.. ἐπώνυμον γένος Πελασγῶν A.*Supp.*252, cf. *Pr.*850, S.*OC*65; ἐ. ὄρνιχος *called after* it, Pi.*I.*6(5).53, cf. Hdt.7.11, S.*Fr.*323, Euph.34.3; τῇ Ἀρτέμιδι, ἧς ἐστιν ἐ. ἡ φρατρία *Rev. Épigr.*1.239 (Naples, ii A.D.); ἔνθεν ἔστ᾽ ἐ. A.*Eu.*689; ἐ. δεῖπνα Θυέστου E.*Or.*1008 (anap.); πόλεις ἐ. βασιλέων Plu.*Comp.Thes.Rom.*4; ἐ. τοῦ θανάτου τινὸς γενέσθαι Id.*Flam.*21; ἐ. ἐπί τινος Hdt.4.184; ἔκ τινος D.P.779; ἀπό τινος Scymn.547: c. dat., Ὀδυσσεύς εἰμ᾽ ἐ. κακοῖς S.*Fr.*965 (s.v.l.); πόλιν ποιεῖν ἐ. τινι Pl.*Lg.*969a; φυλὴν ἐ. ἐποίησαν Ἀττάλῳ Plb.16.25.9; ἐ. ἑαυτῷ D.H.1.9; χῶραι ἐ. *local names* of places, Plb.5.21.7; = Lat. *cognomen*, D.H.5.25 codd.; τῆς πράξεως ἐ., of Mummius, i.e. *Achaïcus*, Plu.*Mar.*1; *title*, D.C.72.22. Adv. -μως *by being named after*, ἔκ τινος Ath.3.121a; ἐ. τῇ γεννώσῃ χώρᾳ Dsc.3.23. II. Act., *giving one's name to* a thing or person, αὐτό μοι σύ, παῖ, λαβὼν ἐ. (sc. τὸ σάκος) *which gives* thee *thy name* (of Eurysaces), S.*Aj.*574; τοῦ ἐ. τῆς πόλεως Διονύσου *SIG*762.13 (Dionysopolis, i B.C.). 2. at Athens, οἱ ἐ. (sc. ἥρωες) the heroes *who gave their names to the Attic* φυλαί, Decr.ap.And.1.83, Isoc.18.61, D.21.103, etc. b. ἄρχων ἐ. the first Archon, *who gave his name to the current year*, *IG*3.81, al., Poll.8.89; also of the Spartan Ephors, Paus.3.11.2; of the Roman *consules ordinarii*, *IG*14.1389 i 34, Hdn.1.16.3; οἱ τὰ ἐ. ἄρξαντες App.*Syr.*51; ἄρξαντα τὴν ἐ. ἀρχήν *SIG*872.6 (Eleusis, ii A.D.).

**ἔπωπα**· ἀλεκτρυόνα (-ωνα cod.) ἄγριον, Hsch. (leg. ἔποπα).

**ἐπωπ-άζω**, = sq., Hsch. **-άω**, (ὠπάομαι) = ἐφοράω, *observe, regard*, πολλὰ A.*Ch.*693; πάντα φρενὶ Id.*Eu.*275 (lyr.); *guide, direct*, γλῶσσαν καὶ στόμ᾽ ἐπωπᾷ [Πειθώ] ib.971. ⊛ **-ετής**, οῦ, ὁ, epith. of Zeus at Athens, Hsch. **-εύς**, έως, ὁ, *inspector*, dub. in Agatharch.26 (κοπεῦσι Müller). II. a divinity (perh. Zeus), *Schwyzer*720.24 (Theb.ad Mycalen, iv B.C.). **-ή**, ἡ, *look-out place, observation-post*, A.*Supp.*539 (pl., lyr.). **-ίς**, ίδος, ἡ, *watcher* (Lacon.), Hsch. II. epith. of Demeter at Sicyon, Id.

**ἐπωπίς**, ίδος, ἡ, (ἕπομαι) *attendant, companion*, Lyc.1176 (v.l. ἐπ- = foreg., cf. *EM*368.32).

**ἐπωρεύει**· ὡραῖα συντελεῖ, Hsch. **ἐπωριάζω**, (ὥρα) *to be concerned about* a thing, Id. (Cf. εὐωριάζω.)

**ἐπωροφ-ία**, ἡ, *roof*, *IG*1$^2$.372.81, 373.243. **-ίς**, ίδος, ἡ, = foreg., ib.11(2).287*A*62 (Delos, iii B.C.), *Inscr.Délos* 290.171 (iii B.C.).

**ἐπωρυδόν**· ἐπιρρεόντως, Hsch. (fort. ἐγὼ ῥυδόν, cf. Od.15.426).

**ἐπωρύω** [ῠ], *howl at*, *AP*9.311 (Phil.):—in Med., Lxx *Za.*11.8.

**ἔπωσις**, εως, ἡ, *pushing* or *'spooning' stroke*, opp. ἄπωσις, Arist.*Ph.*243$^a$18.

**ἐπωστρίδες**· αἱ κατὰ Σάμον ταῖς γυναιξὶ τὴν δεξιὰν χεῖρα ἐπέχουσαι κατὰ τὴν ὀσφύν, Hsch.

**ἐπωτειλόομαι**, Pass., *to be scarred over*, Aret.*SD*2.4.

⊛ **ἐπωτίδες**, αἱ, (οὖς) *beams projecting like ears on each side of a ship's bows*, whence the anchors were let down, *cat-heads*, used also as an armament, E.*IT*1350, Th.7.34,36, Str.3.1.4, D.S.17.115: later in sg., App.*BC*5.107.

**ἐπωφέλ-εια**, ἡ, *help, advantage*, Democr.278. **-έω**, *aid, succour*, τινα S.*El.*578, *Ph.*905; τινὰ οὐδέν Id.*El.*1005, E.*Or.*955, cf. Ar.*Nu.*1442; τινι S.*OC*441, E.*Andr.*677: abs., Pl.*Lg.*843c; ἐν πολέμῳ Seleuc.ap.Ath.15.697d:—Pass., *receive aid*, Phalar.*Ep.*137.—In S.*OC*541 (lyr.), ἐδεξάμην δῶρον, ὃ μήποτ᾽.. ἐπωφέλησα πόλεος ἐξελέσθαι, the Sch. takes ἐπωφέλησα as, = ὤφελον, *would that* I never had received: -ήσας cj. Jebb. **-ημα**, ατος, τό, *help, store*, βορᾶς S.*Ph.*275. **-ής**, ές, *helpful, useful*, Sever.*Clyst.*p.17 D., Poll.5.136, *Cod. Just.*1.2.17.1; ἡμῖν Hierocl.*in CA*11 p.441 M. Adv. -λῶς Poll.5.135, Vett.Val.165.18, Them.*Or.*21.252a, 22.278c. **-ία**, ἡ, = ἐπωφέλεια, *AP*6.33 (Maec.). **-ιμος**, ον, = ἐπωφελής, ἔργα *Carm.Aur.*6.

**ἐπῴχατο**, Ep. 3 pl. plpf. Pass., πᾶσαι γὰρ [πύλαι] ἐπῴχατο all *were shut to*, Il.12.340 (= ἐπικεκλιμέναι ἦσαν, ἐπέκειντο, Aristarch., who derived it from ἐποίγω, prob. rightly, cf. προσοίγνυμι; = ἐπωχλισμέναι ἦσαν *were bolted*, Apollon.*Lex.*, reading ἐπώχατο; πάσας γὰρ ἐπῴχετο Zenod., vulg.).

**ἔπωχρος**, ον, *yellowish*, of a bone, Hp.*VC*19: of the complexion, *sallow*, Aret.*SD*2.5.

**ἔρα**, ἡ, *earth*, Erot.s.v. ἔρπει, Sch.Il.*Oxy.*221 x 28, *EM*369.24, Hsch. (also expld. as, = κοιλία), cf. Str.16.4.27:—Adv. **ἔραζε**, Dor. **ἔρασδε**, *to earth*, κατὰ δὲ πτερὰ χεῦεν ἔραζε Od.15.527; ἀπὸ δ᾽ εἴδατα χεῦεν ἔ. 22.85, cf. Hes.*Op.*421,473; so νιφάδες δ᾽ ὡς πῖπτον ἔ. Il.12.156; οὑμὸς δὲ πότμος.. κυρῶν ἄνω ἔ. πίπτει A.*Fr.*159; ὄρπακες βραβύλοισι καταβρίθοντες ἔρασδε Theoc.7.146; *on the ground*, θάλλειν Mosch.2.66.

**ἔραδος**· παρὰ τὸ ἐρίζειν· παιδίονα, νεῖκος, συνδρομή, λοιδορία, ἀνεξικακία, Hsch.

⊛ **ἔραμαι**, 2 sg. Ep. ἔρασσαι or ἔρᾶσαι Theoc.1.78, 3 sg. ἔρᾶται Id.2.149 (with unexpld. ᾱ); 2 pl. ἐράασθε Il.16.208; 3 sg. subj. Aeol. and Dor. ἔρᾶται Sapph.*Supp.*5.4, Pi.*P.*4.92; opt. ἐραίμαν ib.11.50; impf. ἠράμην [ᾰ] Sapph.33, Thgn.1346, etc.: fut. ἐρασθήσομαι A.*Eu.*852: aor. ἠράσθην Alcm.33, Hdt.1.8,96, E.*Med.*700, *IG*1$^2$.920.2, poet. ἐράσθην Phoen.1.19; poet. aor. Med. ἠρᾱσάμην Il.16.182, Hermesian.7.49,96 (Ep. and Lyr. ἠράσσατο Il.20.223, Archil.26, Nicaen.1.5; ἐράσσατο Hes.*Th.*915, Pi.*P.*2.27): pf. ἤρασμαι Parth.2.3: **ἐράω** (q.v.) supplies the pres. and impf. in Prose. I. *love*, c. gen. pers., prop. of the sexual passion, as always in Hom.; mostly of the man, ὥς σεο νῦν ἔραμαι Il.3.446, cf. 16.182, 20.223, etc.; λέχους E.*Med.*491; τῆς ἑωυτοῦ γυναικός Hdt.1.8; but of the woman, ἡ.. ἠράσσατ᾽ Ἐνιπῆος Od.11.238: c. acc. cogn., ἐ. μέγαν γ᾽ ἔρωτα E.*Med.*697. II. of things, *desire passionately, lust after*, ὃς πολέμου ἔραται ἐπιδημίου Il.9.64; φυλόπιδος.. ἧς τὸ πρίν γ᾽ ἐράασθε 16.208; ἐρασθεὶς τυραννίδος Hdt.1.96; τῶν ἀπεόντων Pi.*P.*3.20; καλῶν ib.11.50; γῆς τῆσδε A.*Eu.*852; κείνων ἔραμαι E.*Alc.*866 (anap.); θανάτου ἔρανται Aret.*CA*2.5. 2. c. inf., *desire eagerly*, οὐκ ἔραμαι πλουτεῖν Thgn.1155; ἤρατο ἐπιψαύειν Pi.*P.*4.92; ἔραται γλῶσσα μέλιτος ἄωτον [προχέειν] Id.*Pae.*6.58; ἔραμαι πυθέσθαι S.*OC*511 (lyr.); λαβεῖν τι E.*Med.*700; φαγεῖν Ar.*Fr.*51 (lyr.).

**ἔρανα**· ἐκ συνεισφορᾶς δῶρα κτλ., Hsch. **ἐράναι**· βωμοί, Id.

**ἐρᾰν-άρχης**, ου, ὁ, *president of an* ἔρανος, *collector of contributions to it*, *BGU*1133.5 (i B.C.), D.L.6.63, Artem.1.35 (pl.), Harp. s.v. πληρωτής:—hence **-αρχέω**, *hold this office*, *IG*11(4).1223 (Delos). **-έμπολος**, ὁ, *trader on borrowed capital*, Hsch., Phot., Suid. **-εστάς**, ὁ, = ἐρανιστής, *Schwyzer*427.3 (Dyme). **-ησις**, v. ἐράνισις. **-ίζω**, *lay under contribution*, c. acc. pers., τοὺς φίλους D.*Ep.*3.38, cf. D.L.6.63 (pun on ἐναρίζω). 2. *collect by way of contribution*, στεφάνους Aeschin.3.45; ἐ. φίλον παρὰ φίλοις Pl.*Lg.*915e: abs., Thphr.*Char.*1.5; τισι for their benefit, *IG*7.411.7 (Oropus): metaph., *bring together, combine*, εἰς ὅλον *AP*9.13$^b$ (Antiphil.), cf. 11 (Phil.), Ael.*VH*12.1; ἠράνισαι (2 sg. pf. Pass.) νεφέλαις *art swollen up* with.., *AP*9.277 (Antiphil.):—Med., *collect for oneself, borrow*, τροφὴν παρ᾽ ἑτέρων Plu.2.1058d, cf. Poll.4.43; πανταχόθεν ἡδονὴν ἐρανίζεσθαι Luc.*Vit. Auct.*12, cf. *Salt.*49; λόγους εἰς εὐωχίαν Hld.5.16, cf. Men.Rh.p.433 S.: abs., D.L.9.50; *beg one's bread*, *BCH*48.517 (Palestine). II. *assist by contributions*, πολλοῖς (πολλοὺς cod.) Antipho 2.2.12; τούτους (v.l. -οις) Ph.1.635:—Pass., *to be so assisted*, ἐρανισθεὶς πρὸς τῶν φίλων D.L.8.87. 2. metaph., of '*log-rolling*', ἐφ᾽ οἷς -ίζει τοῖς περὶ αὐτόν D.39.18. **-ικός**, ή, όν, *of* or *for an* ἔρανος, ἐ. δίκη an action *arising out of the matters of an* ἔρανος, Arist.*Ath.*52.2, cf. Poll.8.37; ἐ. συγγραφή *BGU*1165.30 (i A.D.); νόμος ἐ. ibid.; ἐ. λόγος a speech (of Dinarchus) *on these matters*, D.H.*Din.*12; ἀκροάσεις ἐ. lectures *paid for by fees*, Posidon.36 J. **-ιον**, τό, Dim. of ἔρανος, Hsch. **-ισις**, εως, ἡ, *collecting of contributions, contributing*, Pl.*Lg.*915e. II. (written ἐράνησις) *feeding, maintenance*, προβάτων *PMasp.*141$^v$ *b* 11 (vi A.D.). **-ισμός**, ὁ, = foreg. I, D.H.6.96. **-ιστής**, οῦ, ὁ, *member of* or *contributor to an* ἔρανος I, Pherecyd.11 J. (pl.); ἑστιᾶν ἐρανιστάς to give a club-dinner, Ar.*Fr.*408, Arist.*EN*1123$^a$22; *member of an* ἔρανος III, *IG*2$^2$.1265 (pl.), 11(4).1223 (Delos, pl.), etc.

**ἐραννός**, ή, όν, (ἔραμαι) *lovely*, in Hom. only of places, Il.9.531, Od.7.18, al., Ar.*Lys.*1297 (lyr.), Theoc.28.21, Mosch.3.89: after Hom., generally, ἐ. Ἀοῦς φάος B.16.42; ὕδωρ Simon.45; φιλότης D.P.777; φηγός, ἄλσος, Orph.*A.*991, 987; seldom of persons, Ἑκάτη Id.*H.*1.1 codd. (ἐρεμνὴν Wiel); τὸ ἐ., in Neo-Platonic Philos., the *Beatific Vision*, Anon.*in Prm.*2.30.

⊛ **ἔρᾰνος**, ὁ, *meal to which each contributed his share, picnic*, εἰλαπίνη ἠὲ γάμος; ἐπεὶ οὐκ ἔρανος τάδε γ᾽ ἐστίν Od.1.226, cf. 11.415: metaph., Pl.*Smp.*177c. 2. generally, *feast, festival*, Pi.*O.*1.38; πολύθυτος ἔ. Id.*P.*5.77; *wedding-banquet*, ib.12.14, Pherecyd.11 J.; ἔρανον εἰς θεοὺς.. ἐποίεις E.*Hel.*388. II. *loan* raised by contributions for the benefit of an individual, bearing no interest, but recoverable at law, in instalments, παρὰ τῶν φίλων ἔ. συλλέξαι Antipho 2.2.9, cf. Thphr.*Char.*22.9; κομισόμενος τὸν ἔ. recover the *loan*, Arist.*Ph.*196$^b$34; ἔ. εἰσενεγκεῖν τινι Thphr.*Char.*15.7, Philem.213.14; ἔ. τινι εἰς τὰ λύτρα εἰσφέρειν D.53.8; ἔ. εἰς ἐλευθερίαν Id.59.31, cf. *GDI*2317 (Delph.), al.; ἔ. ἀναλαμβάνειν *BGU*1165.16 (i B.C., with mention of interest); ἔ. εἰκοσίμνως Lys.*Fr.*19; πεντακοσιόδραχμος *SIG*1215.5 (Myconos); διτάλαντον εἶχες ἔ. [δωρεὰν] παρά τινων D.18.312: in pl., *debts* thus contracted, Ar.*Ach.*615 (prob.), Hyp.*Ath.*9; τοὺς ἐ. διενεγκεῖν pay off such *debts*, Lycurg.22; ἐράνους λέλοιπε he has left *repayment-instalments* unpaid, D.27.25; ἔ. συνεφήβοις ἀπενεγκεῖν (cf. infr. III) Luc.*DMeretr.*7.1. 2. metaph., τοὐράνου γάρ μοι μέτεστι· καὶ γὰρ ἄνδρας εἰσφέρω (spoken by Lysistrata), Ar.*Lys.*651; δεῖ τοῖς γονεῦσι τὸν ὡρισμένον ἐξ ἀμφοτέρων ἔ. καὶ παρὰ τῆς φύσεως καὶ παρὰ τοῦ νόμου δικαίως φέρειν D.10.40, cf. 21.101, Isoc.10.20, Pl.*Lg.*927c; κάλλιστον ἔ. [τῇ πόλει] προϊέμενοι Th.2.43, cf. X.*Cyr.*7.1.12, Ph.2.553, etc.: generally, *favour, service*, esp. one which brings a return, κάλλιστον ἔ., δοὺς γὰρ ἀντιλάζυται E.*Supp.*363; ἔ. ἀντιλαμβάνειν Arist.*Pol.*1332$^b$40; ἀποδοῦναι Alex.280; ironically, τὸν αὐτὸν ἔ. ἀποδοῦναι 'pay him back in his own coin', D.59.8. III. *a permanent association* apparently religious in character (cf. ἐρανιστής), *IG*12(1).155.12 (Rhodes, ii B.C.), 2$^2$.1369 (Athens, ii A.D.); ἔ. συνάγειν Μηνὶ Τυράννῳ ib.3.74; καλεῖται ὁ αὐτὸς καὶ ἔ. καὶ θίασος Ath.8.362e; functioning as a *friendly society*, Plin.*Ep.Trai.*92; it could apparently lend to a non-member, ὅρος χωρίων ὑποκειμένων τῷ ἐ. καὶ τῷ ἀρχεράνῳ *SIG*1198 (Amorgos, iii B.C.), cf. *BGU*1133-6 (i B.C.).

⊛ **ἐραπίδα**· ὃ ἡμεῖς ἐλαπέδα, Hsch. **ἔρασδε**, Dor. for ἔραζε (q.v.).

**ἐρᾰσί-μολπος** [ῐ], ον, *delighting in song*, of Thalia, Pi.*O.*14.15. **-πλόκᾰμος**, ον, *decked with love-locks*, Ibyc.9, Pi.*P.*4.136. **-πτερος**, ον, *of amorous wing*, Nonn.*D.*10.256.

**ἔρᾰσις**, εως, ἡ, (ἔραμαι) *love*, as etym. of ἥρως, *EM*437.38, etc.

⊛ **ἐρᾰσιχρήμᾰτος**, ον, *loving money*, X.*Mem.*1.2.5, Philostr.*VS*2.29.

⊛ **ἐράσμιος**, ον, also η, ον Anacr.20:—*lovely, pleasant*, Semon.7.52; τὴν ψυχὴν ἐ. X.*Smp.*8.36: Comp., Them.*Or.*17.216a: Sup. -ώτατον,

ψυχῆς ἦθος X.*Mem*.3.10.3; τὸ ἐ. Plot.1.3.2; *beloved, desired*, πόλει A.*Ag*.605; ταῖς ἀγέλαισιν Mosch.3.20; ἐ. ἄγειν τινά treat *affectionately*, J.*AJ*19.6.1: neut. as Adv., ἐράσμιον ἀνθήσασα *AP*7.219 (Pomp. Jun.).

**ἐραστ-εύω**, = ἐράω (A), ἐραστεῦσαι γάμων A.*Pr*.893 (lyr.). ⊛ **-ής**, οῦ, ὁ, (ἔραμαι) *lover*, prop. c. gen. pers., Ar.*Eq*.732, etc. **b.** *admirer*, Pl.*Men*.70b, *Ly*.222a, *Prt*.317c. **2.** metaph., c. gen. rei, τυραννίδος Hdt.3.53; τῆσδε τῆς γνώμης *an adherent* of.., S.*OT*601; πολέμων E.*Heracl*.377 (lyr.); παίδων *eager for* children, Id.*Supp*.1088; πραγμάτων, = πολυπράγμων, Ar.*Pax*191, *Nu*.1459; τοῦ πονεῖν *fond* of work, Id.*Pl*.254; λόγων, νοῦ καὶ ἐπιστήμης, Pl.*Phdr*.228c, *Ti*.46d; ἐπαίνου X.*Cyr*.1.5.12, cf. Plu.*Cam*.25, etc.; also ἐ. περὶ τὸ καλὸν καὶ τῆς Ἀφροδίτης καλῆς οὔσης Pl.*Smp*.203c: as fem., ἐρασταὶ αὐτοῦ πολλαὶ πόλεις Philostr.*VS*1.25.1; ἐ. γυνή Luc.*Philops*.15. **-ικός**, ή, όν, *loving*, καλῶν *Cat.Cod.Astr*.2.176. ⊛ **-ός**, ή, όν, = ἐρατός, *beloved, lovely*, in Prose the usual form, Pl.*Smp*.204c, *Phdr*.250d; also in [Simon.]178.1; τόνδε δρόμον ποίησεν ἐραστόν $IG1^2$.817: Comp., *AP*12.197 (Strat.). **-ρια**, ἡ, fem. of ἐραστής, *lover*, Eup.414; ἀλλοτρίων λεχέων Perict.ap.Stob.4.28.19, cf. Ael.*NA*3.40. **-ριάω**, *to be amorous*, Phot.

**ἔρᾱται**, 3 sg. subj. (also ind. in Theoc.) of ἔραμαι; but **ἐρᾶται**, ind. Pass. of ἐράω.

**ἐρατεινεύειν** (**-τειχεύειν** Phot.)· στρατεύεσθαι, ἢ δυσφορεῖν, Hsch.

⊛ **ἐρᾰτεινός**, ή, όν, *lovely*, in Hom. mostly of places, Il.2.532, 5.210, al.; also of things, ἠνορέη, φιλότης, 6.156, Od.23.300; ὕδωρ Pi.*O*.6.85; εὐναί Id.*Fr*.122.7: rarely of persons, and then mostly of women, ἐγείνατο παῖδ' ἐρατεινήν Od.4.13, cf. *h.Cer*.423, Hes.*Th*.136, 909; ὁμηλικίη ἐ. her *lovely* companions, Il.3.175; of Polyphemus, οὐδ' ἄρ' ἔμελλ' ἑτάροισι φανεὶς ἐ. ἔσεσθαι a *welcome, glad* sight to my comrades, Od.9.230.—Ep. and Lyr. word: epith. of ὕδατα, Hp.*Aër*.5.

**ἐρᾰτίζω**, Ep. form of ἔραμαι, used by Hom. always in phrase, κρειῶν ἐρατίζων *greedy after* it, Il.11.551, 17.660, *h.Merc*.64, 287. **II.** *love*, Ζεὺς ἐράτιζε τριηκοσίους ἐνιαυτούς Call.*Fr*.20.

**ἐρᾰτο-γλέφᾰρος**, ον, *with lovely eyes*, Λατοῦς ἔρνος Limen.26 (prob.). **-πλόκᾰμος**, ον, = ἐρασιπλόκαμος, Orph.*H*.44.2.

⊛ **ἐρᾰτός**, ή, όν, (ἔραμαι) *lovely*, of places and things, δῶρ' ἐρατὰ .. χρυσέης Ἀφροδίτης Il.3.64; ἔργ' ἀνθρώπων Hes.*Th*.879; φιλότης ib.970; χέλυς, φωνή, πόλις, *h.Merc*.153, 426, *h.Ap*.477; βᾶμα *beloved* footfall, Sapph.*Supp*.5.17; χῶρος Archil.21.4; ἔπεα Alcm.45; ὄψ B.16.129; νίκα Corinn.*Supp*.1.24; αἰδώς, κῶμοι, Pi.*P*.9.12, *I*.2.31; ὠδίς Id.*O*.6.43: Sup., παίδων -ώτατον ἄνθος *AP*12.151: used by Trag. in Lyr., στήθεα A.*Th*.864 (anap.); λέχος E.*Heracl*.915; μολπαί Id.*El*.718 (s.v.l.); ὕμνοι Ar.*Th*.993; of persons, φυὴν ἐρατή Hes.*Th*.259, 355; νέοι ἄνδρες ἐ. Thgn.242; παῖς Pi.*O*.10(11).99: neut. as Adv., ἐρατὸν κιθαρίζειν *h.Merc*.423, 455. **2.** *beloved*, ἀνδράσι μὲν θηητὸς ἰδεῖν ἐ. δὲ γυναιξί Tyrt.10.29.—Ep. and Lyr. word.

**ἐρᾰτό-στομος**, ον, *lovely-mouthed*, *Lyr.Adesp*. in *Philol*.80.333. **-χροος**, ον, *fair of complexion*, *AP*5.75 (Rufin.).

**ἐρᾱτύω**, Dor. for ἐρητύω, B.16.12, S.*OC*164; ἐράτοθεν· ἀνεπαύσαντο, Hsch. (prob. Cypr. for ἐρήτυθεν Il.2.99).

**Ἐρᾰτώ**, οῦς, ἡ, *Erato, the Lovely*, one of the nine Muses, Hes.*Th*.78, etc.: Pythag. name for *two*, *Theol.Ar*.11. **2.** one of the Oceanides, Hes.*Th*.246.

**ἐρᾰτ-ώνῠμος**, ον, *of gracious fame*, κόρα B.16.31; ἀοιδά cj. in Stes.44. **-ῶπις**, ιδος, ἡ, *of lovely look*, *IG*14.1356.8, v.l. in Hom.*Epigr*.1.2.

**ἔραυνα**, later form for ἔρευνα, *POxy*.67.18 (iv A.D.), Ph.1.485 (Pap.):—also **ἐραυν-άω** Lxx 1*Ch*.19.3 (v.l.), 1*Ep.Cor*.2.10, al., *POxy*.294.9 (i A.D., Pass.), Ph.1.484 (Pap.): **-ησις**, *PMasp*.166.21 (vi A.D.): **-ητής**, *PFay*.104 (iii A.D.), *POxy*.1651.18 (iii A.D.): ⊛ **-ητικόν**, τό, *examination-dues*, ib.1650.6, al. (i/ii A.D.).

**ἐραχάται**, οἱ, *binders of sheaves*, and **ἔραχος**, τό, *sheaf* (Boeot.), Hsch. (Perh. cf. ἔρχατος.)

⊛ **ἐράω** (A), used in Act. only in pres. and impf. (which in Poetry are ἔραμαι, ἠράμην), Ion. **ἐρέω** Archil.25.3: impf. ἤρων Hdt.9.108, E.*Fr*.161, Ar.*Ach*.146:—Pass., ἀντ-ερᾶται X.*Smp*.8.3; opt. ἐρῷο Id.*Hier*.11.11; inf. ἐρᾶσθαι Plu.*Brut*.29, etc.; part. ἐρώμενος (v. infr.):—also **ἐράομαι**, 3 sg. ἐρᾶται Plu.2.753b, Philostr.*Gym*.48 (ἐράασθε v. sub ἔραμαι): all other tenses will be found under ἔραμαι:—*love*, c. gen. pers., prop. of the sexual passion, *to be in love with* (οὐκ ἐρᾷ ἀδελφὸς ἀδελφῆς .. οὐδὲ πατὴρ θυγατρός X.*Cyr*.5.1.10), ἤρα τῆς .. γυναικός Hdt.9.108, etc.: c. acc. cogn., ἐρᾶν ἔρωτα E.*Hipp*.32, Pl.*Smp*.181b: abs., ἐρῶν *a lover*, v.l. in Pi.*O*.1.80 (pl.), S.*Fr*.149.8 (pl.); opp. ἡ ἐρωμένη *the beloved one*, Hdt.3.31, S.E.*P*.3.196; [ὁ] ἐρώμενος X.*Smp*.8.36, Pl.*Phdr*.239a, cf. Ar.*Eq*.737 (pl.); τὸν ἐρώμενον αὐτοῦ, Lat. *delicias ejus*, Arist.*Pol*.1303$^b$23. **2.** without sexual reference, *love warmly*, opp. φιλέω, οὐδ' ἤρα οὐδ' ἐφίλει Pl.*Ly*.222a:—and in Pass., ὥστε οὐ μόνον φιλοῖο ἂν ἀλλὰ καὶ ἐρῷο X.*Hier*.11.11, cf. Plu.*Brut*.29; κινεῖ [τὸ οὗ ἕνεκα] ὡς ἐρώμενον Arist.*Metaph*.1072$^b$3. **II.** c. gen. rei, *love* or *desire passionately*, τυραννίδος Archil.25.3; τερπνότατον τοῦ τις ἐρᾷ τὸ τυχεῖν Thgn.256; μάχης ἐρῶν A.*Th*.392; μόνος θεῶν γὰρ Θάνατος οὐ δώρων ἐρᾷ Id.*Fr*.161; ἀμηχάνων ἐρᾷς S.*Ant*.90; πατρίδος ἐρᾶν E.*Ph*.359; οὗ ἐπιθυμεῖ τε καὶ ἐρᾷ Pl.*Smp*.200a: and c. inf., *desire* to do, A.*Fr*.44.1; θανεῖν ἐρᾷ S.*Ant*.220; ἀποθανεῖν ἐρῶντες Hp.*de Arte* 7; φαγεῖν Ar.*Ach*.146; πληροῦσθαι Pl.*Phlb*.35a.

**ἐράω** (B), *pour forth, vomit*, ἐρᾶσαι· κενῶσαι, Hsch.: usu. in compds., ἀπὸ σφαγὴν ἐρῶν A.*Ag*.1599, cf. ἀπ-, ἐξ-, κατ-, κατεξ-, μετ-, συν-εράω.

**ἔρβως** (i.e. ἔρϝως)· εὐρώς, Hsch.

**ἐργάδεις**, f.l. for Ἀργαδεῖς in Plu.*Sol*.23 codd. (corr. Cobet).

⊛ **ἐργάζομαι**, Il.18.469, etc., Cret. **ϝεργάδδομαι** *Schwyzer*181 v 5: fut. -άσομαι Thgn.1116, etc., Dor. ἐργαξοῦμαι Theoc.10.23, ἐργῶμαι *PCair.Zen*.107.4 (iii B.C.), Lxx *Ge*.29.27, al., *IG*7.3073.12 (Lebad., ii B.C.) (but Hsch. ἐργᾷ· ἐργάζει): aor. εἰργασάμην, Ion. ἐργ- Hdt.2.115, A.*Th*.845 (lyr.), etc., 3 pl. opt. ἐργασαίατο Ar.*Av*.1147, *Lys*.42; Dor. ἠργάξαντο *SIG*248 *M* (Delph., iv B.C.): pf. εἴργασμαι, Ion. ἔργ- Hdt.2.121.ε', A.*Fr*.311, etc.—These tenses are used both in Med. and Pass. signfs.: for other Pass. tenses, v. infr. III:—Att. Inscrr. of cent. iv have ἠργαζόμην, ἠργασάμην, (ἐξ-) $IG2^2$.1585.11, 1669.10, al., but εἴργασμαι ib.1666 *A* 27; so also ἠργάσατο ib.7.424 (Oropus, iv B.C.), εἰργασμένος ib.3073.51 (Lebad., ii B.C.), ἐξήργασατο *UPZ*19.8 (ii B.C.), εἴργασμαι *PCair.Zen*.146.3 (iii B.C.); but this rule is often broken in later Pap., Inscrr., and codd.:—*work, labour*, esp. of husbandry, Hes.*Op*.299, 309, Th.2.72, etc.; but also of all manual labour, of slaves, ἐ. ἀνάγκῃ Od.14.272; of quarrymen, Hdt.2.124, etc.; τὴν οὐσίαν οὐ δικαζόμενον ἀλλ' ἐργαζόμενον κεκτημένον Antipho 2.2.12; ἐ. ἐν τοῖς ἔργοις in the mines, D.42.31: c. dat. instr., χαλκῷ with brass, Hes.*Op*.151; also of animals, βοῦς ἐργάτης ἐργάζεται S.*Fr*.563; of birds *working* to get food, Arist.*HA*616$^b$35; of bees, ib.625$^b$22; of Hephaestus' self-acting bellows, Il.18.469; τὸ χρῆμ' ἐργάζεται the matter *works*, i.e. *goes on*, Ar.*Ec*.148; ὁ ἀὴρ ἐργάζεται *produces an effect*, Thphr.*CP*5.12.7; οὐχ ὁμοίως ἐργάσεται τὸ θερμόν ib.6.18.11. **II.** trans., *work at, make*, ἔργα κλυτά, of Athena, Od.20.72, cf. 22.422; ἀγάλματα, ὕμνους, Pi.*N*.5.1, *I*.2.46; τρίποδα, Νίκην, *SIG*34 (Delph., v B.C.); ἁμαξίδας Ar.*Nu*.880; οἰκοδόμημα Th.2.76; εἰκόνας, ἀνδριάντας, καλὰ ἔργα, Pl.*Cra*.431c, X.*Mem*.2.6.6, Pl.*Men*.91d; κηρόν, σχαδόνας, of bees, Arist.*HA*627$^a$6, 30; μέλι Sor.*Vit.Hippocr*.11; *make* so and so, ξηρὸν ἐ. τινά Luc.*DMar*.11.2; μέγαν Ael.*VH*3.1. **2.** *do, perform*, ἔργα ἀεικέα Il.24.733; ἔργον ἐπ' ἔργῳ ἐ., of husbandmen, Hes.*Op*.382, cf. 397; ἐργασίας ἐ. Arist.*EN*1121$^b$33, cf. X.*Oec*.7.20; ἐναίσιμα, φίλα ἐ., Od.17.321, 24.210; θαυμαστά Pl.*Smp*.213d; περὶ θεοὺς ἄδικον μηδέν Id.*Grg*.522d; ἐ. πρᾶγμα, opp. βουλεύειν, S.*Ant*.267, cf. *OT*347; τὸ ἔργον Κυρίου 1*Ep.Cor*.16.10: c. dupl. acc., *do* something *to*.., τά περ νῦν ἐ. [ὁ ἥλιος] τὸν Νεῖλον Hdt.2.26, etc.; chiefly in bad sense, *do* one ill, *do* one a shrewd turn, κακὰ ἐργάζεσθαί τινα S.*Ph*.786, Th.1.137, etc.; so οἷά μ' εἰργάσω, τί μ' ἐργάσει; S.*Ph*.928, 1172 (lyr.), etc.; μὴ δῆτα τοῦτό μ' ἐργάσῃ Id.*El*.1206; αἴσχιστα ἐ. τινά Ar.*V*.787; less freq., ἀγαθὰ ἐ. τινά Hdt.8.79, cf. Th.3.52, Pl.*Cri*.53a; πολλὰ καὶ καλὰ τὴν Ἑλλάδα Id.*Phdr*.244b; seldom τινί τι Ar.*V*.1350; οἷν ἐμοὶ δυοῖν ἔργ' ἐστὶ κρείσσον' ἀγχόνης εἰργασμένα S.*OT*1374. **b.** *perform* rites, τὰ ἱερὰ ἐ. 1*Ep.Cor*.9.13. **c.** in Law, ζημίαν ἐ. *do* damage, Is.6.20, cf. Hyp.*Ath*.22. **3.** *work* a material, ὅπλα .. οἷσίν τε χρυσὸν ἐργάζετο Od.3.435; ἐ. γῆν *till* the land, Hdt.1.17, etc.; ἐ. [ἀγροὺς] ἐργάταις X.*Cyr*.1.6.11; γῆν καὶ ξύλα καὶ λίθους Id.*HG*3.3.7; [ἀργυρῖτιν] Docum.ap.D.37.28; ἐ. θάλασσαν, of traders, D.H.3.46; γλαυκὴν ἐ., of fishers, Hes.*Th*.440. **4.** *earn by working*, χρήματα Hdt.1.24, Ar.*Eq*.840, etc.; καινὸν βίον ἐκ τοῦ δικαίου And.1.144, cf. Hes.*Op*.43; ἀργύριον ἀπὸ σοφίας Pl.*Hp.Ma*.282d; μισθοῦ τὰ ἐπιτήδεια X.*Mem*.2.8.2. **5.** *work at, practise*, μουσικήν, τέχνας, etc., Pl.*Phd*.60e, *R*.374a, etc.; ἐπιστήμας X.*Oec*.1.7; ἀρετὴν καὶ σωφροσύνην v.l. in Isoc.13.6; δικαιοσύνην, ἀνομίαν, *Act.Ap*.10.35, *Ev.Matt*.7.23. **6.** abs., *work at a trade* or *business, traffic, trade*, ἐν [γναφείῳ] Lys.23.2; ἐν ἐμπορίῳ καὶ χρήμασιν D.36.44; ἐν τῇ ἀγορᾷ Id.57.31 (also οἱ τὴν τετράγωνον (sc. ἀγοράν) ἐργαζόμενοι those who *trade in* the square, *BCH*8.126 (cf. *Glotta*14.73)); κατὰ θάλατταν D.56.48; τούτοις .. ναυτικοῖς ἐ. *trade* with this money on bottomry, Id.33.4; δὶς ἢ τρὶς ἐ. τῷ αὐτῷ ἀργυρίῳ Id.56.30; ταῦτα ἐ. thus he *trades*, Id.25.82; οἱ ἐργαζόμενοι *traders*, Id.34.51; οἱ ἐν Δήλῳ ἐ., = Lat. *qui Deli negotiantur*, *CIG*2285*b*; esp. of courtesans, σώματι ἐ., Lat. *quaestum corpore facere*, D.59.20; ἐπὶ τέγους ἀπὸ τοῦ σώματος Plb.12.13.2; ἀπὸ τῆς ὥρας Alexis Sam.ap.Ath.13.572f, Plu.*Tim*.14. **7.** *cause*, κολακείην Democr.268; πημονάς S.*Ant*.326; πόθον τινί D.61.11; σύριγγας ἀνιάτους Paul.Aeg.6.44. **III.** Pass., rarely in pres. and impf., D.H.8.87 (ἐξ-), Hyp.*Eux*.35: fut. ἐργασθήσομαι S.*Tr*.1218, (ἐξ-) Isoc.*Ep*.6.8: pf. εἴργασμαι (v. infr.): aor. 1 εἰργάσθην Pl.*R*.353a, Thphr.*HP*6.3.2, etc. **1.** *to be made* or *built*, ἔργαστο τὸ τεῖχος Hdt.1.179; ἐκ πέτρας εἰργασμένος A.*Pr*.244; οἰκοδόμημα διὰ ταχέων εἰργ. Th.4.8; λίθοι εἰργ. *wrought* stones, Id.1.93; γῆ εἰργ. X.*Oec*.19.8; θώρακας εὖ εἰργ. Id.*Mem*.3.10.9. **2.** *to be done*, A.*Ag*.354, 1346, E.*Hec*.1085; εἰργασμένα *things done, deeds*, Hdt.7.53 (ἐργ-), E.*Ion*1281, cf. S.*OT*1369.

**ἐργᾰθεῖν**, Ep. **ἐεργᾰθεῖν**, Att. **εἰργᾰθεῖν**, poet. aor. 2 inf. of εἴργω, *sever, cut off*, ἀπὸ δ' αὐχένος ὦμον ἐέργαθεν Il.5.147; ἀπὸ πλευρῶν χρόα ἔργαθεν 11.437. **II.** *hold back, check*, S.*El*.1271, E.*Ph*.1175, A.R.3.1171.

**Ἐργαῖος**· ἀέριος Ζεύς, Hsch.

**ἐργᾰλ-εῖον**, Ion. **-ήϊον**, Cret. **ϝεργαλεῖον** *Schwyzer*180, τό, (ἔργον) *tool, instrument*, Hdt.3.131, Th.6.44, Pl.*Plt*.281c, etc. **-ίδιον**, τό, Dim. of foreg., *PMasp*.1.24, 273 (vi A.D.).

**ἐργᾰλοθήκη** (leg. ἐργαλειο-), ἡ, *case for instruments*, gloss on σουγλάριον, Hsch.

**ἔργανα**, τά (also γέργανα, i.e. ϝέργ-), = ἐργαλεῖα, Hsch. **ἐργανεῖον** (-λεῖον cod., extra ordinem), τό, = ἐργαστήριον (Tarent.), Id.

⊛ **ἐργάνη** [ᾰ], ἡ, *worker*, epith. of Athena, τὴν Διὸς γοργῶπιν Ἐ. S.*Fr*.844.2, cf. $IG1^2$.561, 2.1434, al., 4.990 (Epid.), Ael.*VH*1.2, Paus.1.24.3, prob. l. for ἐργάτις in *APr*.461: Delph. **ϝαργάνα** *Schwyzer* 319(1) (vi/v B.C.); cf. ὀργάνη. **II.** = ἐργασία, *PPetr*.2 p.60 (iii B.C.), Hsch.

**ἐργᾰσ-είω**, Desiderat. of ἐργάζομαι, *long to do, be about to do*, ὡς

ἐργασείων οὐδέν S.*Tr.*1232; τί δ' ἐργασείεις; Id.*Ph.*1001. ❀ -ία, Ion. -ίη, Cret. Ϝεργασία *Leg.Gort.*8.44, ἡ, (ἐργάτης) *work, business*, ἐργασίην φεύγουσα *h.Merc.*486, etc.; opp. ἀργία, X.*Mem.*2.7.7; ἐ. ἀγαθή productive *labour*, Id.*Vect.*4.29; ἐργασίᾳ ἐγχειρεῖν, of bees, Arist. *HA*625ᵇ24; ἡ περὶ τὴν θάλατταν ἐ., of seamen, Pl.*R.*371b; μὴ γενομένης ἐργασίας if no *work* was done, D.27.20; δὸς ἐργασίαν, c. inf., Lat. *da operam ut*.., *Ev.Luc.*12.58, cf. *OGI*441.109 (*SC. de Stratonicensibus*, i B.C.): pl., τὰς ἐν ὑπαίθρῳ ἐ. ἐργάζεσθαι X.*Oec.*7.20; ἐ. ἀνελεύθεροι Arist.*EN*1121ᵇ33, cf. Epicur.*Fr.*196 (dub.). 2. *function*, ἥπατος Aret.*SD*1.15. II. *working at, making, manufacture*, ἱματίων, ὑποδημάτων, etc., Pl.*Grg.*449d, *Tht.*146d, etc.; ἡ τῆς ἐσθῆτος ἐκ τῶν ἐρίων ἐ. X.*Oec.*7.21; *making up* of a prescription, Hp.*Ulc.*14: metaph., Πέργαμος ἀμφὶ τεαῖς χερὸς ἐργασίαις ἁλίσκεται Troy is (i.e. is doomed to be) taken in the part *wrought by* thy *hands*, Pi.*O.*8.42; ἐ. ἡδονῆς *production* of pleasure, Pl.*Prt.*353d; ἐ. χρημάτων money-*making*, Arist.*EN*1160ᵃ16 (but *administration* of property, *Leg.Gort.* l.c.). 2. *working* of a material, ἡ ἐ. τοῦ σιδήρου Hdt.1.68; χαλκοῦ, ἐρίων, ξύλων, Pl.*Chrm.*173e; τῶν χρυσείων μετάλλων Th.4.105, cf. Hyp.*Eux.*36; πίττης Thphr.*HP*9.2.6: most commonly, *tillage* of the ground, ἐ. γῆς, χώρας, Ar.*Ra.*1034 (pl.), Isoc.7.30, etc.; ἐ. κήπων Pl. *Min.*316b; ἐ. περὶ τὴν τροφὴν *preparation* (i.e. mastication and digestion) of food, Arist.*Juv.*469ᵃ3; *treatment* of silphium, Thphr.*HP*6.3.2. 3. generally, *trade, business*, X.*Mem.*3.10.1; ἐπὶ τῆς ἐργασίας ὢν τῆς κατὰ θάλατταν engaged in *trade* by sea, D.33.4; ἡ ἐ. τῆς τραπέζης the banking *business*, Id.36.6; ἐ. χρυσοχοϊκή, ἀρωματική, *PLond.*3.906.6 (ii A.D.), *PFay.*93.7 (ii A.D.); βαφεῖς τὴν ἐ. dyers by *trade*, *PTeb.*287.3 (ii A.D.); esp. of *a courtesan's trade*, Hdt.2.135, D.18.129; of sexual *intercourse*, Arist.*Pr.*876ᵃ39. b. ἐὰν ἐργασίαν εὕρῃ ὁ οἰκέτης if a slave brings in *earnings*, Hyp.*Ath.*22. 4. *practising, exercising*, τῶν τεχνῶν Pl.*Grg.*450c; Κύπριδος *AP*5.218 (Paul. Sil.); ἀκαθαρσίας *Ep.Eph.*4.19. 5. *work of art, production*, τετράγωνος ἐ., of the Hermae, Th.6.27 (non legit Sch.); τῶν τειχῶν αἱ ἐργασίαι the fortification *works*, Id.7.6. 6. literary *execution*, ἐ. ποιητική Phld. *Po.*5.11; *elaboration* of a topic, Sch.Pi.*P.*2.24. 7. *production* of a play, Arg.Men.*Oxy.*1235.108. III. *guild* or *company* of workmen, ἡ ἐ. τῶν βαφέων Judeich *Altertümer von Hierapolis* 50; ἐριοπλυτῶν ib. 40; ἐ. θρεμματική dub. sens., ib.227. -ίμη, ἡ, *poor kind of myrrh*, Dsc.1.64.2. ❀ -ιμος, ον, *to be worked, that can be worked*, Alc.ap. Sch.Gen.Il.21.319, Plu.2.701c; ξύλα, opp. καύσιμα, Poll.7.109; σκεῦος ἐ. δέρματος Lxx *Le.*13.49; mostly of land, ἐ. χωρία *tillable* land, Pl.*Lg.*639a, 958d, Arist.*Pr.*924ᵃ1 (sg. in *PHal.*1.103 (iii B.C.)); τὰ ἐ. X.*Cyr.*1.4.16, etc.; τὰ τεμένη, ὅσα.. θεμιτόν ἐστιν ἐ. ποιεῖν to bring *into cultivation*, *IG*2.1059.17 (iv B.C.); ἡ ἐ. (sc. γῆ) Thphr.*HP* 6.3.5. 2. ἐ. ἡμέρα a *work*-day, Lxx 1*Ki.*20.19. 3. ἐ., τό, *cost of manufacture*, ἄρτων *UPZ*149.25, cf. 20 (ii B.C.). II. Act., *working for a livelihood*, τὸ ἐ. the *working people*, App.*BC*3.72; esp. of courtesans, Artem.1.78. 2. *active*, θρασύτης Orph.*H.*60.7. -ις, εως, ἡ, *perpetration*, φόνου Sch.E.*Med.*864. -τέον, *one must till the land*, X.*Eq.Mag.*8.8. II. τοὔργον ἔστ' ἐ. it *must be done* or *one must do* it, A.*Ch.*298, cf. E.*Med.*791, X.*Oec.*7.35; τὰ ἔργα.. ὡς ἔστιν ἐργαστέα ib.13.3; ὅτ' ἦν ἐ. when it was *necessary to act*, S.*Tr.* 688. -τήρ, ῆρος, ὁ, *workman*, esp. *in husbandry*, X.*Oec.*5.15; of a smith, Orph.*H.*66.4. ❀ -τηριακός, ή, όν, *practising a handicraft*, ἄνθρωποι Plb.38.12.5: -κοί, οἱ, *work-people*, D.S.31.25. -τηριάρχης, ου, ὁ, *foreman of a workshop*, *CIG*4968 (Egypt), *Anatolian Studies* 30 (Ephesus). -τηρίδιον, τό, Dim. of ἐργαστήριον, *BGU* 1127.9 (i B.C.). ❀ -τήριον, τό, *any place in which work is done*: *workshop, manufactory*, Hdt.4.14, Lys.12.8, *IG*2².1013.9; attached to a mine, ib.1582.58, al., D.37.4, Is.3.22; butcher's *shop*, Ar.*Eq.*744; perfumer's *shop*, Hyp.*Ath.*6; barber's *shop*, Plu.2.973b; μισθώσασθαι ἐ. πρὸς ἄνοιξιν καπηλείου *POxy.*2109.31 (iii A.D.); euphem. for *a brothel*, D.59.67, Alciphr.*Fr.*5.1. 2. metaph., τὴν πόλιν ὄντως εἶναι πολέμου ἐ. X.*HG*3.4.17; λόγων ἐ. Lib.*Or.*55.34. b. of persons, *gang*, συκοφαντῶν ἐ. D.39.2, 40.9; πειρατικὸν ἐ. Hld.5.20. c. as Adj., φάρμακον ἐ. τινός Sch.S.*Tr.*846. ❀ -τής, οῦ, ὁ, = ἐργάτης, A.D. *Adv.*135.4, *IGRom.*4.1209 (Thyatira); = Lat. *negotiator*, *SIG*1229.1 (Hierapolis); v.l. in J.*AJ*18.1.1, Gal.*Thras.*33. -τικός, ή, όν, *able to work, working, industrious*, Hp.*Prorrh.*2.4 (Comp.), Pl.*Men.* 81e (v.l.), X.*Mem.*3.1.6; οἱ ἐ. the *working men*, Plb.10.16.1: Comp., Phld.*Oec.*p.32 J. 2. *skilled in producing*, c. gen., φωνῆς Epicur. *Sent.Vat.*45: generally, *productive*, σωφροσύνης Phld.*Mus.*p.24 K.; ὑγιείας *Gp.*11.2.6; ἡ ἐ. (sc. τέχνη) the *art of manufacturing*, c. gen., ἐρεοῦ προβλήματος, στήμονος καὶ κρόκης, Pl.*Plt.*280e, 281a; τὸ τῆς τροφῆς ἐ. the organ *that prepares* food, the mouth, Arist.*Pol.*1290ᵇ 27. II. *of a workman*, ἱμάτια *Lex.Mess.* in *Rh.Mus.*47.412 (nisi ἐργατ-legend.). -τῖναι· αἱ τὸν πέπλον ὑφαίνουσαι, Hsch. (cf. *IG*2². 1034, *EM*149.21, Suid. s.v. Χαλκεῖα). ❀ -τρα, τά, *reward of labour, wage-cost*, χλαμύδος *PEdgar*65.89 (iii B.C.). II. name of an object belonging to an οἰνοχόη, φιάλη, etc., *IG*2².830.85, 1640.16, *BCH*32.6 (Delos, iv B.C.). -τρίς, ίδος, ἡ, = ἐργάτις, Hsch. s.v. καιρωστρίδες.

ἐργᾰτ-εία, ἡ, *labour, work, handicraft*, in pl., Lxx *Wi.*7.16, *BGU* 1159.9 (i B.C.). 2. *gang of workmen*, ibid., *POxy.*1450.6 (iii A.D.). II. Ἐργάτ(ε)ια, τά, festival of Heracles in Laconia, Hsch. -εύομαι, *work hard, labour*, Lxx *To.*5.5, D.S.20.92:— Act., -εύω *UPZ*110.102 (ii B.C.). -ης, ου, ὁ, *workman*, *Hermes* 17.5 (Delos), *Ev.Matt.*10.10, etc.; esp. *one who works the soil, husbandman*, γῆς ἐ. Hdt.4.109, 5.6; οἱ ἐ. οἱ περὶ γεωργίαν D.35.32: abs., S.*OT*859, E.*El.*75, etc.: also with Subst., ἐ. ἀνήρ Theoc.10.9, D. 59.50; οὑργάτης λεώς the *country*-folk, Ar.*Pax* 632; of animals, βοῦς ἐ. a *working* ox, Archil.39, S.*Fr.*563; ἐ. σφῆκες Arist.*HA*627ᵇ32; also ἐ. θαλάττης, of a fisher, Alciphr.1.11; ἐ. λίθων a stone-*mason*, Luc.*Somn.*2. b. in the religious sense, 2*Ep.Ti.*2.15, 2*Ep.Cor.*11. 13 (pl.). 2. Adj. *hard-working, strenuous*, ἐ. στρατηγός X.*Cyr.*1.6. 18; σώφρων κἀ. Ar.*Ach.*611; opp. ἀργός, Pl.*Euthd.*281c; φειδωλὸς καὶ ἐ. Id.*R.*554a. II. *one who practises* an art, τῶν ἐν πολέμῳ X.*Cyr.*4. 1.4; ἐ. δίκης, of a judge, Lyc.128: abs., *practitioner* in some special branch of surgery, e.g. lithotomy, ἐ. ἄνδρες Hp.*Jusj.* III. *doer*, ἄσημος οὑργ. τις ἦν S.*Ant.*252; τῶν καλῶν X.*Mem.*2.1.27; ἀνομίας Lxx 1*Ma.*3.6; τῆς ἀδικίας *Ev.Luc.*13.27. IV. *producer*, τῶν ἐν τῷ κόσμῳ γινομένων Heraclit.75; [Αἰὼν] θείας φύσεως ἐ. *SIG*1125.12 (Eleusis). V. a sort of *capstan* or *windlass*, Bito 58.12, Vitr.10. 2.7, al., Orib.49.4.1. -ήσιος, α, ον, = ἐργάσιμος, χώρα dub. in Plu. *Cat.Ma.*21 (v.l. ἔργα πίσσια). ❀ -ικός, ή, όν, = ἐργαστικός, opp. ἐργατῶν ἄρχων, Pl.*Plt.*259e; *like a workman*, γυνὴ ἐ. Luc.*Somn.*6; *hard-working*, Pl.*Men.*81e (with v.l.); δοῦλοι Plu.*Cat.Ma.*4; ἐ. καὶ γεωργικός D.H.*Rh.*11.6; ἐ. κτήνη, ὄνος, *PFay.*111.6 (i A.D.), *PSI* 1.38.5 (ii A.D.); τὸ ἐ. Hp.*Aër.*24: Comp. -ώτερος, Sup. -ώτατος, of bees, Arist.*HA*624ᵇ29, 622ᵇ19; ποταμὸς ἐ., of the Nile, Hdt.2.11. Adv. -κῶς, πρός τι *advantageously* for.., Plu.*Cam.*16. -ίνης [ῑ], ου, ὁ, = ἐργάτης, esp. *husbandman*, Theoc.10.1, A.R.2.376 (pl.); ἐ. ἄνδρες Theoc.21.3, *AP*11.58 (Maced.); βοῦς ἐ. A.R.2.663 (pl.), *AP* 6.228 (Adaeus). II. c. gen., *making* a thing or *practising* an art, μέλιτος ὁ χρυσὸς ἐ. *AP*5.239 (Maced.); Κύπριδος ib.274 (Paul. Sil.). -ις (parox.), ιδος, fem. of ἐργάτης, *workwoman*; of the *worker* bees, Arist.*HA*627ᵃ12, *Lyr.Alex.Adesp.*7.12; μάθε ὡς ἐ. ἐστὶν [ἡ μέλισσα] Lxx *Pr.*6.8a; ἐ. βοῦς *AP*9.741. 2. Adj. *laborious, industrious*, γυναῖκες οὕτω ἐ. Hdt.5.13; γλῶσσαν μὲν ἀργὸν χεῖρα δ' εἶχεν ἐργάτιν S.*Ph.*97; βιοτὰ *APl.*1.15.6. 3. *working for hire*, Μοῖσ' οὐ πω ἐ. ἦν Pi.*I.*2.6; of a courtesan, Archil.184. II. c. gen., *working at* or *producing*, μνήμην ἁπάντων μουσομήτορ' ἐργάτιν A.*Pr.* 461 (ἐργάνην Stob.); νέκταρος ἐ., of bees, *AP*9.404.8 (Antiphil.); νήματος ἠλακάτα ib.6.174 (Antip. (Sid.)); σελίδων, of poetesses, ib.9. 26.8 (Antip. Thess.); Κύπριδος, of courtesans, ib.5.244.8 (Maced.); rare in Prose, πόλις ἐ. τῶν ἀγαθῶν D.H.2.76.

ἐργᾰτοκῠλίνδριος τόπος place *for a windlass* (cf. ἐργάτης v), Bito 55.5.

ἐργατώδης, f.l. for ἐργώδης, Marcellin.*Puls.*150.

ἐργατῶνες, Att. ἐρχατῶνες, *shelters* for slaves in country districts, Hsch.: but ἐργάτωνες, in Crete, *undertakers*, Id.

ἐργεπείκτης, ου, ὁ, (ἐπείγω) *taskmaster*, Eust.583.16.

ἐργεπιστᾰσία, ἡ, *superintendence of works*, *CIG*2779 (Aphrodisias, pl.), *IGRom.*4.861 (Laodicea ad Lycum, pl.), Keil-Premerstein *Erster Bericht* 16.

ἐργεπιστᾰτ-έω, *to be superintendent of works*, *OGI*510.12 (Ephesus), *IGRom.*4.1352 (Lydia), 818 (Hierapolis), Sch.Ar.*Pax* 605. ❀ -ης, ου, ὁ, *superintendent of works*, Epich.212, Artem.4.31, *IG*3.486 (ii A.D.), 12(5).253 (Paros).

ἐργέτην· ἐργασίαν, Hsch. **ἔργετος·** φραγμός, Id.

ἔργμα (ἔργμα Pi.*N.*4.6), ατος, τό, poet. for ἔργον, *work, deed, business*, *h.Hom.*27.20, 32.19, Thgn.29, Archil.70, Sol.4.11, Pi.*N.* l.c., A.*Th.*556, *Eu.*501 (lyr.); ἔργμασιν ἐν πολέμου Epigr. (= *IG*1².394) ap.Hdt.5.77: rare in Prose, as Democr.43, Perict.ap.Stob.4.28.19, Procl. *in Prm.*p.590 S.

❀ ἔργμα, ατος, τό, (εἴργω) *fence, guard*, Arist.*PA*658ᵇ18; τάφου S. *Ant.*848 (lyr.); *obstacle*, Hp.*Steril.*213; *means of hindering*, δυνάμεως Hierocl. *in CA* 24 p.473 M.

ἐργνύω, = εἴργω, *enclose*, Hsch.; cf. καθειργνυμι.

❀ ἐργοδιωκτ-έω, *to be a taskmaster*, Lxx 2*Ch.*8.10. -ης, ου, ὁ, *taskmaster*, *PPetr.*2 p.6 (iii B.C.), Lxx *Ex.*3.7, Ph.2.86.

ἐργοδοσία, ἡ, *letting out work*, *Arch.Anz.*1904.8 (Milet.).

ἐργοδοτ-έω, *let out work*, opp. ἐργολαβέω, Apollod.Com.20, *CIG* 2826.5 (Aphrodisias). ❀ -ης, ου, ὁ, *one who farms out work*, X.*Cyr.* 8.2.5, *CIG*3467.22 (Sardes); un-Attic, acc. to Phryn.326; incorrectly used of *workmen*, Aret.*SD*1.6.

ἐργολάβ-εια [ᾰ], ἡ, = ἐργολαβία II, τῶν μειρακίων *making profit out of* them, Alciphr.1.34. ❀ -έω, *contract for the execution of work*, opp. ἐργοδοτέω, *CIG*3467.24 (Sardes) (also in Med., Polyaen.6.51): c. acc., ἐ. ἀνδριάντας X.*Mem.*3.1.2, cf. Philoch.97; τὸ ἱερὸν ἢ δαμόσιον ἔργον *SIG*²940.7 (Cos, i B.C.); τὸ ἰατρικὸν ἔργον *BCH*25.235 (Amphissa); τὸ μακρὸν τεῖχος Plu.*Per.*13: c. inf., *SIG*²588.220 (Delos, ii B.C.), *IG*12(8).640.6 (Peparethus, ii B.C.). II. *make profit out of*, τὰ ἰατρικά Phld.*Rh.*1.329 S.; so of Sophists, ἐ. τὰ μειράκια Alciphr.3.55: so abs., freq. in Oratt., σοφιστὴς ἐργολαβῶν Aeschin.2.112, cf. D.22. 49; ἔν τινι in a matter, Aeschin.3.33; τινι for one, D.25.47; ἐπί τινα or κατά τινος against one, Aeschin.1.173, D.*Ep.*3.34. -ία, ἡ, *contract for the execution of work*, πρὸς ἐργολαβίαν γεγράφθαι [λόγους] Isoc.5.25: pl., *Ath.Mitt.*51.29 (Samos), Plu.*Cat.Ma.*19. II. *profit-making*, ἐργολαβίας ἕνεκεν παραμένειν ἐν τῷ μαθήματι D.S.2.29, cf. Lib.*Decl.*23.20. ❀ -ος, ὁ, *contractor*, Pl.*R.*373b, *IG*9(1).694.32 (Corc.); τοῦ ἀγάλματος *for making* it, Plu.*Per.*31; ἐ. δικῶν brief-*mongers*, i.e. advocates, Them.*Or.*21.260b; but, *collusive plaintiff*, Paul.Al.*O.*2. II. Adj. *for gain, gainful*, v.l. in Plb.20.12.1.

ἐργο-λήπτης, ου, ὁ, = foreg., Teleclid.56. -μίσης [ῑ], ου, ὁ, *one who hates work*, Hdn.Gr.2.685. -μωκεύω, *flatter, wheedle*, *Gloss.*:—Med., = *assentior, ancillor*, prob. in Dosith.p.430 K. (= p.95 T.):—hence -μωκία, -μωκος, *Gloss.*; -μωκέω, = ἐμπαίζω, Hsch.

❀ ἔργον, Dor. Ϝέργον *IG*4.800 (vi B.C.), Elean Ϝάργον *SIG*9 (vi B.C.), τό: (ἔρδω, OE. *weorc* (neut.) 'work', Avest. *varəza*-):—

*work*, Il.2.436, etc.; ἔ. οὐδὲν ὄνειδος, ἀεργίη δέ τ' ὄνειδος Hes.*Op*.311; πλεόνων δέ τε ἔ. ἄμεινον Il.12.412; ἔ. ἐποίχεσθαι 6.492; νῦν ἔπλετο ἔ. ἅπασι 12.271; esp. in pl., ἄλλος ἄλλοισιν..ἐπιτέρπεται ἔργοις Od.14.228; ἐπὶ ἔργα τράποντο Il.3.422; ἔργων παύσασθαι Od.4.683; τὰ σ' αὐτῆς ἔργα κόμιζε see to thine own *tasks*, Il.6.490: esp. in the following relations, **1.** in Il. mostly of *works* or *deeds* of war, πολεμήϊα ἔ. Il.2.338, al., Od.12.116; ἔργον μάχης Il.6.522; alone, ἀτελευτήτῳ ἐπὶ ἔργῳ 4.175, cf. 539; ὑπέσχετο δὲ μέγα ἔργον 13.366; ἐπ' αὐτῷ δ' ἔργον ἐτύχθη ἀργαλέον 4.470; later, ἔργον..Ἄρης κρινεῖ A.*Th*.414; ἐν τῷ ἔ. during the *action*, Th.2.89, cf. 7.71; τὸ ἐν Πλαταιαῖς ἔ. Pl.*Mx*.241c; τῶν πρότερον ἔ. μέγιστον ἐπράχθη τὸ Μηδικόν Th.1.23; ἔργου ἔχεσθαι to engage in *battle*, ib.49. **2.** of peaceful *contests*, κρατεῖν ἔ. Pi.*O*.9.85; ἔργου ἔχεσθαι Id.*P*.4.233; also ἔργα θῆκε κάλλιστ' ἀμφὶ κόμαις placed [the reward of] noble *deeds* about his hair, Id.*O*.13.38. **3.** of *works of industry*, **a.** of *tillage*, *tilled lands*, ἀνδρῶν πίονα ἔ. Il.12.283, etc.; ἔργ' ἀνθρώπων 16.392, Od.6.259; βροτῶν 10.147; οὔτε βοῶν οὔτ' ἀνδρῶν φαίνετο ἔργα ib.98; ἔργα alone, 16.140, etc.; Ἔργα καὶ Ἡμέραι—the title of Hesiod's work; πατρώϊα ἔ. their father's *lands*, Od.2.22; οὔτ' ἐπὶ ἔργα..ἴμεν will neither go to our *farms*, ib.127, cf. 252; Ἰθάκης..ἔργα *the tilled lands* of Ithaca, 14.344; ἀμφὶ..Τιταρησσὸν ἔργ' ἐνέμοντο inhabited *lands*, Il.2.751; τὰ τῶν Μυσῶν ἔ. Hdt.1.36; so later, *PBaden* 40.5 (ii A.D.): generally, *property*, *wealth*, *possessions*, θεὸς δ' ἐπὶ ἔργον ἀέξῃ Od.14.65, cf. 15.372. **b.** of women's *work*, weaving, Il.9.390, etc.; ἀμύμονα ἔ. ἰδυίας ib.128; ἔργα ἐργάζεσθαι Od.22.422, 20.72. **c.** of other *occupations*, θαλάσσια ἔ. fishing, 5.67; a seaman's life, Il.2.614: periphr., δαιτὸς..ἔργα *works* of feasting, 9.228; φιλοτήσια ἔ. Od.11.246; ἔργα γάμοιο Il.5.429; ἔργα Κυπρογενοῦς Sol.26; Ἀφροδίτης *h.Ven*.1; also τέκνων ἐς ἔ. A.*Ag*.1207: abs., ἔργον Luc.*DDeor*.17.1, *AP*12.209 (pl., Strat., s.v.l.); also ἔργα ἰσχύος καὶ τάχους X.*Cyr*.1.2.12; φίλα ἔργα μελίσσαις, of flowers, Theoc.22.42; of *mines*, etc., ἔ. ἀργυρεῖα X.*Vect*.4.5, D.21.167, etc.; ἔργα πίσσια dub. l. in Plu.*Cat.Ma*.21. **4.** *deed*, *action*, ἔργ' ἀνδρῶν τε θεῶν τε Od.1.338; θέσκελα ἔ. Τρώων Il.3.130; ἀήτυλα ἔ. 5.876; καρτερά, ἀεικέα ἔ., ib.872, 22.395; παλίντιτα, ἄντιτα ἔ., Od.1.379, 17.51; ἔργα ἀποδέκνυσθαι Hdt.1.16, cf. Pl.*Alc*.1.119e, D.C.37.52; opp. ἔπος, *deed*, not word (v. ἔπος II.1); opp. μῦθος, Il.9.443, 19.242, A.*Pr*.1080 (anap.), etc.; opp. λόγος, S.*El*.358, E.*Alc*.339; ἔργῳ, opp. λόγῳ, freq. in Att., etc., Th.2.65, etc.: so in pl., λόγῳ μὲν..τοῖσι δ' ἔργοισιν S.*OC*782, cf. E.*Fr*.360.13; λόγοισιν εἴτ' ἔργοισιν S.*OT*517; opp. ῥήματα, Id.*OC*873; opp. ὄνομα, E.*IA*128 (anap.), Th.8.78, 89; in many phrases, πέπρακται τοὔργον A.*Pr*.75, cf. *Ag*.1346; χωρῶ πρὸς ἔργον S.*Aj*.116; τὸ μὲν ἐνθύμημα χαρίεν.., τὸ δὲ ἔ. ἀδύνατον its *execution*, X.*An*.3.5.12; ἐν ἔργῳ χέρνιβες ξίφος τε ready for *action*, E.*IT*1190; ἡ κατάρα ὑπὸ τοῦ δαίμονος εἰς ἔ. ἤγετο Jul.*Or*.7.228b. **II.** *thing*, *matter*, πᾶν ἔ...ὑπείξομαι in every *point*, Il.1.294; ἃ Ζεὺς μήδετο ἔ. 2.38, etc.; πάρος τάδε ἔ. γενέσθαι 6.348, etc.; ὅπως ἔσται τάδε ἔ. 2.252, Od.17.78, etc.; μέμνημαι τόδε ἔ. Il.9.527; ἄκουε τοὔργον S.*Tr*.1157, cf. *OT*847, *Aj*.466; in bad sense, *mischief*, *trouble*, of disease, αἰτίη τοῦ ἔ. Aret.*SA*1.9; μέγα ἔ. a serious *matter*, Od.4.663, Th.3.3. **2.** μέγα ἔ., like μέγα χρῆμα, χερμάδιον λάβε χειρὶ Τυδεΐδης, μέγα ἔ. a monstrous *thing*, Il.5.303, cf. 20.286; φυλόπιδος μέγα ἔ. a *mighty* call to arms, 16.208. **III.** Pass., *that which is wrought* or *made*, *work*, οἷ' ἐπιεικὲς ἔργ' ἔμεν ἀθανάτων, of the arms of Achilles, Il.19.22; ἔ. Ἡφαίστοιο metal-*work*, Od.4.617; πέπλοι.., ἔργα γυναικῶν Il.6.289, Od.7.97, cf. 10.223; ὕφασμα, σῆς ἔ. χερός A.*Ch*.231; κολεόν..λώτινον ἔ. Theoc.24.45; of a wall, Ar.*Av*.1125; of a statue, X.*Mem*.3.10.7: in pl., of siege-*works*, ἔ. καὶ μηχαναί Plb.5.3.6; of a *machine*, Apollod.*Poliorc*.157.4, al., Ath.Mech.15.2, al.; of public *buildings*, *Mon.Anc.Gr*.18.20; of an author's *works*, D.H.*Comp*.25; τὸ περὶ ψυχῆς ἔργον Ἀριστοτέλους *AP*11.354.8 (Agath.). **2.** *result of work*, *profit* or *interest*, ἔργον [χρημάτων] *interest* or *profit* on money, Is.11.42, cf. D.27.10. **IV.** special phrases: **1.** ἔργον ἐστί, **a.** c. gen. pers., it is his *business*, his *proper work*, ἀνδρῶν τόδ' ἐστὶν ἔ. A.*Ch*.673; ὅπερ ἐστὶν ἔ. ἀγαθοῦ πολίτου Pl.*Grg*.517c; of things, φραδέος νόου ἔργα τέτυκται it is *a matter* (which calls) for a wary mind, Il.24.354; *function*, ἅπερ νεῶν ἄμεινον πλεουσῶν ἔργα ἐστίν Th.2.89; οὐ θερμότητος ἔργον ψύχειν Pl.*R*.335d; τοῦτο ἑκάστου ἔ. ὃ ἂν ἢ μόνον τι ἢ κάλλιστα τῶν ἄλλων ἀπεργάζηται ib.353a; ἔργα τοῦ ἐγκεφάλου *functions*, Gal.16.518: c. dat. pers., οἷς τοῦτο ἔ. ἦν X.*Cyr*.4.5.36, cf. 6.3.27: with the possessive Pron., σὸν ἔ. [ἐστί] c. inf., A.*Pr*.635; ἐμὸν τόδ' ἔ. κρῖναι Id.*Eu*.734; σὸν ἔ., θῦε θεοῖς Ar.*Av*.862; ὑμέτερον ἐντεῦθεν ἔ. Id.*Pax*426: with Art., νῦν ἡμέτερον τὸ ἔ. Hdt.5.1. **b.** c. gen. rei, *there is need* of.., τί δῆτα τόξων ἔ.; E.*Alc*.39; πολλῆς φυλακῆς ἔ. [ἐστί] Pl.*R*.537d: esp. with neg., οὐδὲν..ὀδόντων ἔ. ἐστ' Ar.*Pax*1310; οὐ δόλου νῦν ἔ. Id.*Pl*.1158, cf. E.*Hipp*.911: c. dat. pers., ἐπέδρης μὴ εἶναι ἔ. τῇ στρατιῇ Hdt.1.17: with Art., οὐκ ἂν μακρῶν λόγων ἡμῖν τόδ' εἴη τοὔργον S.*El*.1373: with a part. added, οὐδὲν ἦν ἔ. αὐτοῦ κατατείνοντος Plu.*Publ*.13: also c. inf., οὐδὲν ἔ. ἑστάναι there is no *use in* standing still, Ar.*Lys*.424, cf. *Av*.1308; οὐδὲν ἔ. ταῦτα θρηνεῖσθαι S.*Aj*.852, cf. 12. **c.** c. inf., *it is hard work*, *difficult* to do, πολὺ ἔ. ἂν εἴη διεξελθεῖν X.*Mem*.4.6.1; πολὺ ἔ. ἦν τῷ νομοθέτῃ πάντα γράφειν Lys.10.7; ἔ. ἐστὶν εἰ ἐροῦμεν D.24.51; ἔ. εὑρεῖν πρόφασιν Men.76; also μέγα ἔ. ταῖς..ἐπιθυμίαις καλῶς χρῆσθαι Pl.*Smp*.187e; χαλεπὸν ἔ. διαιρεῖν Ar.*Ra*.1100 (lyr.): also in gen., πλείονος ἔ. ἐστὶ..μαθεῖν Pl.*Euthphr*.14b: rarely with a part., οὐδὲν ἔ. μαχομένῳ Philippid.15.3; ἔ. [ἐστί] c. acc. et inf., *it can scarcely happen* that.., ἔ. ἅμα πάντας ὀργισθῆναι καὶ ἁμαρτεῖν Arist.*Pol*.1286a35. **2.** ἔργον παρασχεῖν τινί give one *trouble*, Ar.*Nu*.523, cf. *AP*9.161 (Marc. Arg., punning on Hesiod's Ἔργα); ἔργον ἔχειν take *trouble*, c. part., X.*Cyr*.8.4.6; c. inf., Id.*Mem*.2.10.6. **3.** ἔ. γίγνεσθαι τῆς νόσου to be its *victim*, Anon.ap.Suid. s.v. ἄτολμοι; κτεινόμενος ὑμέτερον ἔ. εἰμί Plu.*Eum*.17; τῆς ὑμετέρας γέγονεν ἔ. ὀλιγωρίας Luc.*Dem.Enc*.29. **4.** ἔ. ποιεῖσθαί τι to make a matter *one's business*, *attend to* it, Pl.*Phdr*.232a, X.*Hier*.9.10; so ἐν ἔργῳ τίθεσθαι Ael.*VH*4.15. **V.** = ἐργασία III, τὸ ἔ. βαφέων *CIG*3498 (Thyatira).

**ἐργο-ποιία**, ἡ, *method*, *proceeding*, Ath.Mech.38.2. **II.** *manufacture*, *Gloss*. **-πονέομαι**, *work hard*, Artem.3.6. ⊛ **-πόνος**, ὁ, *husbandman*, *AP*11.9 (Leon.); *hunter*, Opp.*C*.1.148; *fisher*, Nic.*Th*.831; ἐ. ἐλέφαντος *a worker in*.., Man.1.298: as Adj., *laborious*, Coluth.195 (fem.); in bad sense (cf. πόνηρος, πανοῦργος), Rhetor. in *Cat.Cod.Astr*.7.198. **-στόλος**, ον, = ἐργεπιστάτης, Charito 4.2, *CIG*3700 (Cyzicus). **-τεχνίτης** [ῑ], ου, ὁ, *skilled craftsman*, *expert*, Orph.*Fr*.180, Iamb.*Myst*.9.2 (pl.).

**ἐργότρυς**, ὁ, (ὀτρύνω) = ἐργεπείκτης, Hsch.

**ἐργο-φόρος**, ον, *worker* bee, Ael.*NA*5.42. **-χειρον**, τό, *manual labour*, *PMasp*.23.20 (vi A.D.), *PLond*.4.1708.56 (vi A.D.), etc.

**ἐργύλον**· στάτην (Ion.), Hsch.

⊛ **ἔργω**, Ep. and Ion., and **ἐέργω**, Ep. for Att. **εἴργω** (or **εἵργω**, v. infr.), which occurs once in Hom., τῆλέ με εἴργουσι ψυχαί Il.23.72 (s.v.l.): impf. εἶργον Th.1.106, (ἐξ-) Hdt.5.22: fut. ἔρξω (ξυν-) S.*Aj*.593, εἴρξω or εἵρξω Id.*Ph*.1407, E.*El*.1255, Th.4.9: aor. 1 ἔρξα Od.14.411, v.l. for εἶρξα in Hdt.3.136, εἶρξα E.*Ba*.443, Philipp.ap.D.12.2, etc.: aor. 2 εἰργάθον (v. ἐργαθεῖν):—Med. and Pass., pres., Il.17.571, Hdt.5.57, etc.: fut. ἔρξομαι S.*OT*890 (lyr.), εἴρξομαι X.*An*.6.6.16, Aeschin.3.122: aor. 1 ἔρχθην Il.21.282, Hp.*Mul*.1.4, εἵρχθην Lycurg.112, D.59.66: pf. ἔργμαι *h.Merc*.123, Ep. 3 pl. ἔρχαται Od.10.283; εἶργμαι Ar.*Av*.1085, εἷργμαι X.*HG*5.2.31; Ep. part. ἐεργμένος Il.5.89: plpf., Ep. 3 pl. ἔρχατο 17.354, ἐέρχατο Od.10.241. (εἵργω, = *shut in*, εἴργω, = *shut out*, acc. to Eust.1387.3; cf. the compds. ἀπείργω, καθείργω, but ἄφ-ερκτος occurs A.*Ch*.446 (lyr.); the aspirate was always used in Att. acc. to Tz. in *An.Ox*.3.352, but v. κατείργω: at Heraclea it occurs in ἀφ-, ἐφ-, and συν-hέργω (qq.v.): ϝεργ-, cf. Skt. *vrajás* 'enclosure', and perh. Lat. *urgeo*; ἐ- is prothetic in Ep. ἐ-ϝέργω):—*bar one's way* either *by shutting in* or *shutting out*: **I.** *shut in*, *shut up*, ἐρχθέντ' ἐν ποταμῷ Il.21.282; *pen*, ἐνὶ Κίρκης ἔρχαται ὥς τε σύες Od.10.283; [ἄρνες] διακεκριμέναι ἕκασται ἔρχατο 9.221; τὰς μὲν ἄρα ἔρξαν κατὰ ἤθεα κοιμηθῆναι 14.411; ὅσσους Ἑλλήσποντος ἐντὸς ἐέργει *encloses*, Il.2.845 (so ἔνδον εἵρξας Ar.*Ach*.330); ἂψ ἐπὶ νῆας ἐέργε [φάλαγγας] *drove* them to the ships *and shut* them *up* there, Il.16.395, cf. 12.219, Th.1.106; *shut up*, θανόντων ψυχάς Thgn.710; esp. in prison, Hdt.3.136, Philipp.ap.D.12.2, Lycurg.112 (Pass.), D.59.66, etc.; of things, θύραι δόμον ἐντὸς ἔεργον Od.7.88; σύμπαντα ἐντὸς μιᾶς ὁμοιότητος ἕρξας *having included*.., Pl.*Plt*.285b:—Pass., σάκεσσι γὰρ ἔρχατο πάντῃ *were fenced in*, *secured*, Il.17.354; γέφυραι ἐεργμέναι *well-secured*, *strong-built*, *compact*, 5.89: Medic., of discharges, *to be retained*, Hp.*Mul*.1.4, 8; ἐὰν ἡ τοῦ βλεφάρου θρὶξ εἱρχθῇ if the eyelash *is caught* (in the loop), Paul.Aeg.6.13 (fort. εἱρθῇ, vel ἐρθῇ, cf. ἐρτός). **II.** *shut out*, Il.23.72, Th.4.9, etc.; ἀμφὶς ἐέργει Il.13.706 (v. ἀμφίς A.II); κλήθροις ἂν εἰργοίμεσθα E.*Hel*.288. **2.** c. gen., *shut out* or *keep away from*, ὡς ὅτε μήτηρ παιδὸς ἐέργῃ μυῖαν Il.4.131, cf. Od.12.219; τῶν μὲν πάμπαν ἔεργε..θυμόν Hes.*Op*.335, cf. Parm.1.33; ἔργειν τινὰ σιτίων Hdt.3.48:—freq. in Pass., [μυῖα] ἐργομένη χροός Il.17.571; εἴργεσθαι ἱερῶν, νομίμων, ἀγορᾶς, *to be excluded from participation in*.., Isoc.4.157, Antipho 6.36, Lys.6.24; but εἰργόμενον θανάτου καὶ τοῦ ἀνάπηρον ποιῆσαι *short of*, *excluding* death and maiming, Aeschin.1.183: with Preps., ἔ. [βέλος] ἀπὸ χροός Il.4.130; τινα ἀπὸ τιμῆς Od.11.503; [ἀηδὼν] ἀπὸ χλωρῶν πετάλων ἐργομένα A.*Supp*.63 (lyr.); ἐκ τῶν Ἑλληνίδων πόλεων X.*An*.6.6.16, etc.: rarely c. dat. pers., εἴργειν..μητρὶ πολέμιον δόρυ *to keep* it *off* from her, A.*Th*.416:—Med., *keep oneself*, *abstain*, *withdraw from*, c. gen., πόλιος Hdt.4.164; τῶν ἀσέπτων ἔρξεται S.*OT*890 (lyr.); γελώτων Pl.*Lg*.732c, etc.; ἔργετο [τοῦ ἄλσεος] he *kept away from* it, i.e. *spared* it, Hdt.7.197. **3.** *hinder*, *prevent from* doing, abs., Thgn.686, Pl.*Lg*.784c: c. dupl. acc., ἀλλ' ἡμᾶς τουτό γε μηδὲν..εἴρξῃ Id.*Sph*.242a, cf. Ar.*V*.334 (lyr.):—Pass., οὐδὲν εἴργεται nothing *is barred*, i.e. all things are permitted, S.*Tr*.344; εἴργου *stop! cease!* Id.*OC*836. **b.** c. inf., mostly with μή or μὴ οὐ added, οὐ νὺξ ἔργει μὴ οὐ κατανύσαι Hdt.8.98; εἴργει τόνδε μὴ θνήσκειν νόμος E.*Heracl*.963, cf. A.*Ag*.1027 (lyr.): c. inf. only, κακὸν δὲ ποῖον εἶργε τοῦτ' ἐξειδέναι; S.*OT*129; εἵρξω πελάζειν Id.*Ph*.1407 (troch.); οὐδὲν εἴργει..τελειοῦσθαι τάδε Id.*Tr*.1257: with the Art., εἰργαθεῖν τὸ μὴ οὐχ ἑλεῖν E.*Ph*.1175; also εἰργ. ὥστε.. or ὥστε μή.., c. inf., X.*HG*7.2.13, *An*.3.3.

***ἔργω**, *do work*, v. ἔρδω.

**ἐργώδης**, ες, *difficult*, *troublesome*, ἐ. φαρμακεύεσθαι *hard* to purge, Hp.*Aph*.2.37, cf. X.*Mem*.2.6.9; ἐ. αἱ φαρμακεῖαι Hp.*Aph*.4.5; of persons, Thphr.*Char*.6.10; θυγάτηρ κτῆμ' ἐστὶν ἐργῶδες πατρί Men.60; πολέμιος Plu.*Marc*.30; ἐργῶδές [ἐστιν] c. inf., Arist.*EN*1171a5, Philippid.9.9, cf. Sosip.1.24: Comp. -έστερον Arist.*EN*1102a25, Luc.*Halc*.4: Sup. -έστατος X.*Mem*.1.3.6. Adv. -δῶς *with difficulty*, ὑγιάζεται Hp.*Aph*.6.6, cf. Thphr.*HP*9.16.5, Ph.*Bel*.84.12.

**ἐργων-έω**, *contract for a work*, *Hermes* 17.4 (Delos), *IG*11(2).150*A*14 (ibid., iii B.C.), 7.3073.92 (Lebad., ii B.C.). **-ης**, ου, ὁ, (ὠνέομαι) *a contractor*, *Hermes* 17.4 (Delos), *IG*11(2).150*A*9 (ibid., iii B.C.), 7.3073.4 (Lebad., ii B.C.), *SIG*495.135 (Olbia, iii B.C.): Dor. **-ας** *IG*4.1508 (Epid., iii B.C.). **-ία**, ἡ, = ἐργολαβία, Plb.6.17.5, *IG*5(2).6.42 (Tegea, iv B.C.), 7.3073.25 (Lebad., ii B.C.).

⊛ **ἔρδω**, impf. ἔρδον Il.11.707, Ion. ἔρδεσκον 9.540, Hdt.7.33: fut.

ἔρξω Od.11.80, Hes.*Op.*327, A.*Pers.*1059 (lyr.), S.*Ph.*1406 (troch.): aor. ἔρξα Od.8.490, Hdt.5.65; and so in A.*Th.*923 (but ἦρξεν *Ag.*1529 codd.): pf. ἔοργα Il.5.175, etc.; 3 pl. ἔοργαν Batr.179: plpf. ἐώργειν, 3 sg. ἐώργει Od.4.693, 14.289, ἐόργεε Hdt.1.127: pf. part. Pass. ἐργμένος B.12.207: aor. 1 part. Pass. ἐρχθείς ib.65. (Aspirated acc. to Sch.Ar.*Ach.*329, and so freq. in codd. of Hom., cf. Thgn.690, Epic. ap.Pl.*Euthphr.*12a: fr. ϝέργ-yω (through ϝέρζω, cf. ἔργον: impf. ϝέρδον Sol.ap.Arist.*Ath.*12.3: aor. 1 ἔϝερξα *Inscr.Cypr.*146 H.: written βέρξῃ in *Schwyzer* 183 (Crete, iii/ii B.C.), cf. ϝηρόντων (imper.) *GDI*5013 ii 10, ϝήροντι ib.4987 a 2):—poet. and Ion. Verb, *do*, ὅσσ' ἔρξαν τ' ἔπαθόν τε Od.8.490; ἔρξον ὅπως ἐθέλεις Il.4.37; ἔρξον ὅπῃ.. νόος ἔπλετο 22.185; εἰ δέ κεν ὣς ἔρξῃς 2.364; εὖ ἔρξαντα 5.650, cf. *Inscr.Cypr.* l.c.; οὔτε εὖ ἔρδων οὔτε κακῶς Thgn.368; αἴ τις τούτων τι ϝέρκσαι *Leg Gort.*10.30; opp. πάσχω, ἔρξαι τε καὶ παθεῖν Pi.*P.*8.6; παθεῖν ἔρξαντες prob. in A.*Ag.*1658 (troch.): freq. c. acc., ἔ. ἔργα βίαια, μέγα ἔργον, Od.2.236, 19.92; ἔ. φίλα, ἐσθλά, πολλά, etc., 15.360, Il.2.272, 9.320, etc.: sts. c. dat. pers., ὃς δὴ πολλὰ κάκ' ἀνθρώποισιν ἐώργει Od.14.289; μὴ Νυκτὶ.. ἀποθύμια ἔρδοι Il.14.261, cf. Mosch.4.93 codd.: more freq. c. dupl. acc., ὅ με πρότερος κάκ' ἔοργε Il.3.351; κακὰ πολλὰ ἔοργε Τρῶας 5.175, cf. 9.540, A.*Pers.*236 (troch.), etc.; ἀνήκεστον πάθος ἔ. τινά Hdt.1.137; also εὖ ἔ. τινά Thgn.105, 955, Semon.7.80, etc.; κακῶς Hdt.6.88, E.*Med.*1302: without an Adv., ἔ. τινά *to do* one *harm*, S.*Ph.*683 (lyr.): less freq. with Subst. alone as object, ἔ. πήματα A.*Pers.*786; προσωφέλησιν S.*Ph.* 1406 (troch.); ἔρδοι τις ἣν ἕκαστος εἰδείη τέχνην *let* him *practise*.., Ar. *V.*1431; also φάρμακα ταῦτ' ἔρδοισα χερείονα μήτε τι Κίρκας Theoc.2.15:—Pass., τὸ καλῶς ἐργμένον B.12.207; εὖ ἐρχθέντος ib.65. 2. *offer* a sacrifice (cf. ῥέζω), not in pf. and plpf.; ἔρδομεν ἀθανάτοισι τεληέσσας ἑκατόμβας Il.2.306; ἔ. ἱερὰ καλά Hes.*Th.*417; σφάγια θεοῖσιν ἔρδειν A.*Th.*231; Διὶ θυσίας Hdt.1.131:—Pass., θυσίη ἐρδομένη ὧδε Id.4.60; θανόντεσσιν ἐρδόμενον μέρος Pi.*O.*8.78: abs., *offer sacrifice*, ἔρδειν.. ἱεροῖς ἐπὶ βωμοῖς Hes.*Op.*136, cf. Porph.*Abst.*2.59.—Found in late Ion. Prose, Aret.*CA*2.3. (ῥέζω is another form of this verb.)

⊛ **ἐρέα**, ἡ, *wool*, = ἔριον, Callix.2, Str.4.4.3, Isig.ap.Sotion.p.183 W.; but ἐρεῶν *PHib.*1.115.20 (iii B.C.), *PCair.Zen.*176.322 (iii B.C.) may be gen. pl. of ἐρεοῦς.

**ἐρέας**, v. *ἐρής.

**ἐρεβεννός**, ή, όν, Ep. Adj., (Ἔρεβος) *dark, gloomy*, νύξ Il.8.488, Hes. *Op.*17, etc.; ἀήρ Il.5.864; νέφεα 22.309. (Never in Od.; cf. ἐρεμνός.)

**Ἐρέβεσφιν, Ἐρέβευσφιν**, v. Ἔρεβος.

**ἐρεβίνθ-ειος**, ον, *of the* ἐρέβινθος *kind*, Διόνυσος ἐ., proverb of any *worthless* article, Zen.3.83. **-η**, ἡ, = ἐρέβινθος, *EM*569.14. **-ιαῖος**, α, ον, *of the size of an* ἐρέβινθος, Dsc.5.137, 152. **-ινος**, η, ον, = ἐρεβίνθειος, Hsch., Phot., Suid. ⊛ **-ιον**, τό, Dim. of ἐρέβινθος, *POxy.*1837.15 (pl., vi A.D.), *Stud.Pal.*20.75. **-οπώλης**, *cicerarius*, *Gloss.* ⊛ **-ος** (proparox.), ὁ, *chick-pea, Cicer arietinum*, κύαμοι ἢ ἐ. Il.13.589, cf. Pl. *R.*372c; eaten as dessert, Xenoph.22.3, Ar.*Pax* 1136, Crobyl.9, etc.; χρύσειοι ἐ. Sapph.30; κριὸς ἐ., of a special variety, Sophil.8, cf. Thphr. *HP*8.5.1. II. metaph., of the *membrum virile*, Ar.*Ach.*801, *Ra.* 545 (lyr.); cf. κριθή IV. (Cf. ὄροβος, Lat. *ervum*.) **-οφόρος**, ον, *bearing chick-pea*, [γῆ] *PLond.ined.*2361 (iii B.C.). **-ώδης**, ες, *like chick-peas*, φύλλον Thphr.*HP*6.5.3.

**ἐρεβοδιφάω**, *grope about in Erebos*, ὑπὸ τὸν Τάρταρον Ar.*Nu.*192.

**ἐρεβόθεν**, *from nether gloom*, E.*Or.*178.

**Ἔρεβος**, τό: Att. gen. Ἐρέβους Ar.*Av.*694, Ion. Ἐρέβευς Il.8.368, Od.11.37, Ἐρέβεσφιν or Ἐρέβευσφιν, Hes.*Th.*669, *h.Cer.*349, ἐξ Ἐρέβ- Il.9.572: no dat. or pl. occurs:—*Erebos*, a place of nether darkness, forming a passage from Earth to Hades, Il.16.327, Od.10.528, al., Hes.*Th.*515, etc.; rare in Prose, Pl.*Ax.*371e, Plu.2.953a, 1130d: metaph., ἔ. ὕφαλον *the darkness* of the deep, S.*Ant.*589 (lyr.); of a riddle, ἀξυνέτοις ἔ. *AP*7.429 (Alc.). II. personified, Hes.*Th.* 125. (Skt. *rájas*, Goth. *riqis*, ONorse *røkkr* 'darkness'.)

**Ἐρεβόσδε**, Adv. *to* or *into Erebos*, Od.20.356.

**Ἐρεβοφοῖτις**, ἡ, *she that walks in Erebos*, Sch.Il.19.87.

**ἐρεβ-ώδης**, ες, *dark as Erebos*, θάλασσα *Lyr.Adesp.*132 (= *Trag. Adesp.*377), cf. Apollod.1.1.2, Ph.Bybl.ap.Eus.*PE*1.10. ⊛ **-ῶπις**, ιδος, ἡ, *gloomy-looking*, Orph.*L.*544.

⊛ **ἔρεγ-μα**, ατος, τό, *bruised corn*, Thphr.*CP*4.12.12 (pl.); φακῶν ἐρέγματα Erot. ⊛ **-μῖνος**, η, ον, *made of bruised beans*, ἄλευρον Dsc.3.80.3, Orib.4.8.7. ⊛ **-μός**, ὁ, = ἔρεγμα, Gal.6.533, Archig.ap.eund. 12.812, *PTeb.*9.10 (ii B.C.), *PHolm.*23.37, 39; = ὁ δίχα διῃρημένος κύαμος, Erot. II. = ἐρυγμός, *Mim.Oxy.*413.19, Moer.p.158 P., *EM*371.20.

⊛ **ἐρεείνω**, (ἐρέω A) *ask, inquire*: c. acc. pers., *ask of* one, *question* him, Od.7.31, 5.85, *h.Merc.*487, etc.: c. acc. rei, *ask about* a thing, Il.6.145, etc.: c. dupl. acc., ἐ. τινά τι Od.1.220, 4.137; ἐ. ἀμφὶ ξείνῳ *ask* about one, 24.262:—Med., ἐρεείνετο μύθῳ 17.305: *search after*, ἐρεείνειν τινά Batr.52. 2. *visit* a place, D.P.713. 3. *ask for*, τι *h.Merc.* 533. II. *say, speak*, ib.313.—Ep. word, used in hex. by Theopomp. Com.30; ἐὰν μὴ μεῖζον ἅτερος θατέρου ἐρεείνῃ, Spartan saying in Plu. 2.228e codd. (ἐρατέημεν Id.*Lyc.*19 codd.: leg. μέσδων.. ἐρᾶτε ἦμεν.)

**Ἐρεθειμιάζω**, v. Ἐρεθίμιος.

**ἐρεθίζω**, Ep. inf. -ιζέμεν Il.4.5: impf. ἠρέθιζον S.*Ant.*965 (lyr.), Ep. ἐρ- Il.5.419: fut. -ίσω Gal.1.385, -ιῶ Hp.*Mochl.*2, Plb.13.4.2: aor. 1 ἠρέθισα D.H.3.72; poet. ἐρ- A.*Pr.*183 (lyr.), inf. ἐρεθίξαι *AP*12.37 (Diosc.): pf. ἠρέθικα Aeschin.2.37:—Pass., aor. 1 ἠρεθίσθην, part. ἐρεθισθείς Hdt.6.40, D.H.4.57: pf. ἠρέθισμαι Hp. (v. infr.), etc.: (ἐρέθω):—*rouse to anger, rouse to fight*, Il.1.32; κερτομίοις ἐπέεσσι 5.419; κύνας τ' ἄνδρας τε, of a lion, 17.658; ἐ. τοὺς Πέρσας Hdt.3.146; φιλαύλους τ' ἠρ. Μούσας S.*Ant.*965 (lyr.); ὥσπερ σφηκιὰν ἐ. τινά Ar. *Lys.*475; χεῖρον.. ἐρεθίσαι γραῦν ἢ κύνα Men.802; πὺξ ἐ. *challenge to* a boxing-match, Theoc.22.2; *provoke to curiosity*, μητέρα σήν Od.19.45: generally, *excite, chafe*, φρένας ἐ. φόβος A.*Pr.*183 (lyr.); of physical *irritation*, Hp.*Mochl.*2; βῆχες βραχέα -ουσαι *causing* brief *irritation*, Id.*Aph.*4.54: metaph., ἐ. πλανάτας χοροῖσιν E.*Ba.*148 (lyr.); ἐ. μάγαδιν *to touch* it, Telest.4; φλόγα Hld.8.9; τὸ φονικὸν καὶ θηριῶδες Plu.2.822c; *incite* to rivalry, 2*Ep.Cor.*9.2:—Pass., *to be provoked, excited*, ὑπό τινος Hdt.6.40, cf. Ar.*V.*1104; ἠρεθισμένος *under provocation*, Men.574; ὀργῇ χεῖρας -ισμένας Euphro 8.3; of love, τοῖς νέοισιν -ισμένος Timocl.30; of fire, φέψαλος.. -όμενος.. ῥιπίδι Ar. *Ach.*669 (lyr.); αἰθὴρ -έσθω βροντῇ A.*Pr.*1045 (anap.); πνεῦμα ἠρεθισμένον, of one who has run till he is out of breath, E.*Med.*1119; ἕλκος ἠρεθισμένον *irritated*, Hp.*Fract.*27, cf. 31, Plb.1.81.6; ὀσμὴ -ισμένη Eub.75.9; ἐπὶ τὴν ὕβριν ἠρεθίσθαι Luc.*Am.*22. II. abs., *to be quarrelsome* or *perverse*, Ph.1.359.

**Ἐρεθίμιος**, ὁ, epith. of Apollo in Rhodes, *SIG*724 (i B.C.):—hence **Ἐρεθίμια**, τά, his festival, prob. in *IG*12(1).735: **Ἐρεθειμιάζω**, *belong to a guild of worshippers of* Ἀ.Ἐ., Inscrr. in *Hermes* 61.477; cf. Ἐρεθύμιος, Ἐρυθίβιος, Ἐριδίμιος.

**ἐρέθ-ισμα**, ατος, τό, *provocation*, App.*Sam.*3; χορῶν ἐ. Ar.*Nu.*312 (pl.); συμποσίων ἐ., of Anacreon, Critias 1 D.; φύσας ἄγειν κάτω-ίσμασι, i.e. by purging, Aret.*CA*2.5. **-ισμός**, ὁ, *irritation*, Hp.*Acut.*43; ἐ. κνησμώδης Thphr.*Sud.*16; ῥῖγος καὶ ἐ. Lxx *De.*28.22, *IG*12(9).1179: in pl., *stimulating treatment*, Hp.*Aph.*1.20; -ισμοὶ πρὸς ἀφροδίσια Porph.*Abst.*1.47. II. *provocation*, Phld.*Ir.*p.54 W. (pl.), D.H.10.33. 2. *rebelliousness*, Lxx *De.*31.27; *perverseness*, Ph.1.359. **-ιστέον**, *one must irritate*, Pl.*Ti.*89b; *one must stimulate* bowel-action, Gal.6.413, Aët.4.20, Paul.Aeg.1.24. **-ιστής**, οῦ, ὁ, *rebellious* or *perverse person*, Lxx *De.*21.18, Ph.1.359, Hsch. s.v. ἔριθος. **-ιστικός**, ή, όν, *of* or *for irritation*, σημεῖον Hp.*Acut.*48: c. gen., *provocative*, ὀρέξεως Diph.Siph.ap.Ath.3.120e. Adv. -κῶς Sch.Il.16.36. **-ιστός**, ή, όν, *easily provoked*, '*touchy*', Phld.*Lib.* p.42 O.

**Ἐρεθύμιος**, epith. of Apollo in Lycia: also **Ἐρεθύμια**, τά, festival in his honour, Hsch.; cf. Ἐρεθίμιος.

**ἐρέθω**, impf. ἤρεθον Mosch.3.84, Theoc. (v. infr.), Ep. ἐρέθεσκον A.R. 3.618, 1103:—poet. form of ἐρεθίζω, in Il. *stir to anger, provoke*, μή μ' ἔρεθε, σχετλίη 3.414; ὅτ' ἄν μ' ἐρέθῃσιν ὀνειδείοις ἐπέεσσιν 1.519; in Od. of all sources of *disquiet*, ὀδυνάων.., αἵ μ' ἐρέθουσι 4.813; μελεδῶναι 19.517: c. inf., *h.Hom.*8.14: c. acc. rei, ἤρεθον ᾠδάν they *raised* a song, Theoc.21.21 codd.; ἐ. ἐρωμανίην *increase* it, *AP*5.255 (Paul. Sil.). II. *explore, search*, ἰλυούς v.l. for ἐρέοντες in Nic.*Th.*143.

**ἐρειγμός**, ὁ, v.l. for ἐρεγμός in Gal.6.533.

⊛ **ἐρείδω**, Ep. impf. ἔρειδον Il.13.131: fut. ἐρείσω Call.*Del.*234, Aristid. *Or.*17(15).10 codd.: aor. 1 ἤρεισα S.*Ant.*1236, Pl.*Phdr.*254e, *Ti.*91e; Boeot. 3 sg. εἵρισε Corinn.*Supp.*1.32; Ep. ἔρεισα (ἐπ-) Il.7.269: pf. ἤρεικα (συν-) Hp.*Morb.Sacr.*7, (προσ-) Plb.5.60.8; but ἐρήρεικα Dsc.*Eup.*1.84, (προσ-) Plu.*Aem.*19:—Med., fut. ἐρείσομαι (ἀπ-) Arist.*Pr.*885$^b$29, Plb.15.25.25: aor. 1 ἠρεισάμην Hes.*Sc.*362, (ἀπ-) Pl. *R.*508d; Ep. ἐρ- Il.5.309:—Pass., 3 fut. ἐρηρείσεται Hp.*Mul.*2.133: Ep. aor. 1 ἐρείσθην Il.7.145: pf. ἐρήρεισμαι Hdt.4.152, Hp.*Art.*78 (but 2 sg. ἠρήρεισθα Archil.94 is from ἀραρίσκω); also ἤρεισμαι Ti. Locr.98e (ἐρήρ- ib.97e), D.S.4.12, Paus.6.25.5; Ion. 3 pl. pf. ἐρηρέδαται Il.23.284, 329, Ep. ἐρήρειται A.R.2.320: plpf. ἠρήρειστο Il.4.136; 3 pl. ἐρηρέδατο Od.7.95, ἠρήρειντο A.R.3.1398:—Hom. uses the augm. only in ἠρήρειστο, Hes.*Sc.*362 in ἠρείσατο.—Ep., Ion., and poet. Verb, also found in Pl. and later Prose:—*cause to lean, prop*, δόρυ ..πρὸς τεῖχος ἐρείσας Il.22.112; θρόνον πρὸς κίονα μακρὸν ἐρείσας Od.8.66; πύργῳ ἔπι προὔχοντι.. ἀσπίδ' ἐρείσας Il.22.97; [νέκυας] ἀλλήλοισιν ἔ. *piling* them *against* each other, Od.22.450; ἐρείσατε.. πλευρὸν ἀμφιδέξιον S.*OC*1112; πρὸς στέρν' ἐρείσας (sc. τοὺς παῖδας) E.*HF* 1362, cf. *Ba.*684; τὰ ἰσχία πρὸς τὴν γῆν Pl.*Phdr.*254e; ἐ. τινὰ εἰς ἕδραν E.*Heracl.*603; τὰς κεφαλὰς εἰς γῆν Pl.*Ti.*91e; ἐς χεῖρας ἐ. τι Theoc.7.104; ἐ. τὴν κεφαλὴν ἐπὶ γῆς Pl.*Ti.*43e; τὸ γόνυ κατὰ τοῦ ἰσχίου Plu.*Flam.*20; βόῳ ἔνι κἄλπιν A.R.1.1234: generally, *fix firmly, plant*, ἄγκυραν χθονί Pi.*P.*10.51; εἰς γῆν ἐ. ὄμμα E.*IA*1123, cf. Aristid.*Or.*17(15).10; ἐπὶ χθονὸς ὄμματ' A.R.1.784; ἐ. πόδας ἐς βένθος *plant* the foot *firm*, ib.1010: metaph., ἐ. τὰν γνώμαν *fix* one's mind *firmly* on a thing, Theoc.21.61. 2. *prop up, support, stay*, ἀσπὶς ἄρ' ἀσπίδ' ἔρειδε, κόρυς κόρυν, ἀνέρα δ' ἀνήρ, of close ranks of men-at-arms, Il.13.131; ἐπ' ἀσπίδος ἀσπίδ' ἔρεισον Tyrt.11.31; πέλτην ἐρεῖσαι E.*Rh.*487; κίον' οὐρανοῦ τε καὶ χθονὸς ὤμοιν ἐ. A.*Pr.*352. 3. *press hard, attack*, τινα Pi.*O.*9.32: sens. obsc., ἐ. γυναῖκα Ar.*Ec.*616, *Fr.*74. 4. *push, thrust*, ὅπῃ κέ τις.. ἐρείδῃ Emp.12.3; ἔπη.. ἤρειδε κατὰ τῶν ἱππέων *hurled forth*.., Ar.*Eq.*627; ὁ χορὸς ἤρειδεν ὁρμαθοὺς μελῶν τέτταρας Id.*Ra.*914:—Med., ἔπος πρὸς ἔπος ἠρειδόμεσθ' Id.*Nu.* 1375. 5. *infix, plant in*, πλευραῖς ἔγχος S.*Ant.*1236; ἀνταίαν πληγήν *inflict* it, E.*Andr.*844 (lyr.):—Pass., ἄλγημα ἐρηρεισμένον *fixed* pain, Gal.8.385. 6. *press down, depress*, πλάστιγγα τοῦ βίου S.*Fr.* 576.5. 7. of wagers or matches, *match, set* one pledge *against* another, Theoc.5.24. II. intr., *press hard*, ἀμφ' αὐτῷ πελεμίξαι ἐρείδοντες βελέεσσιν Il.16.108; εἴς τινα Ar.*Nu.*558; νέφος ἐ. ἐπὶ γῆν Plu. *Num.*2; πνεῦμα κατὰ τῆς σχεδίας Id.*Crass.*19; of an illness or pain, *settle upon* a particular part, νόσος ὁμότοιχος ἐ. A.*Ag.*1004 (lyr.), cf. Ruf.ap.Orib.45.30.27, Gal.11.61; *exert pressure*: hence, *rest*, ἐπὶ τὸ ἔδαφος Hero *Aut.*2.7. 2. *set to work, fall to*, esp. of eating, ἔρειδε Ar.*Pax* 31, cf. 25 (where, acc. to Sch., it is metaph. from rowers); ἐρείδετον Id.*Fr.*493. 3. *become fixed*, πρῷρα ἐρείσασα *Act.Ap.*27.

41. III. Med. and Pass., *prop oneself, lean upon*, τῷ ὅ γ' ἐρεισάμενος (sc. σκήπτρῳ) Il.2.109; ἔγχει ἐ. 14.38; ἐπὶ μελίης.. ἐρεισθεὶς 22.225: c. gen., ἐρείσατο χειρὶ παχείῃ γαίης *leant* with his hand *against* the earth, 5.309: abs., ἐρεισάμενος βάλε *having planted himself firm, taken a firm stand*, 12.457, cf. 16.736; of one fallen, ὁ δ' ὕπτιος οὔδει ἐρείσθη 7.145, 11.144; οὔδεϊ.. σφι χαῖται ἐρηρέδαται their hair *rests on* the ground, 23.284; γόνατος κονίαισιν ἐρειδομένου *set, planted* in.., A.*Ag*.64 (anap.); τοῖσι γούνασι ἐρηρεισμένοι Hdt.4.152; ταῖς χερσὶν ἐπὶ δόρατι ἠρεισμένος Paus.6.25.5, cf. Corn.*ND*9; *press closely, be tight*, of bandages, Hp.*Off*.8; τοὺς ὀδόντας ἐρήρειστται *has* her teeth *clenched*, Hp.ap.Erot. (ξυνερήρ. codd. Hp.). 2. *to be fixed firm, planted*, ἔγχος διὰ θώρηκος ἠρήρειστο *had been fixed*, Il.3.358, etc.; λᾶε ἐρηρέδαται *stand firmly fixed*, 23.329; θρόνοι περὶ τοῖχον ἐρηρέδατ' Od.7.95; ἁ γᾶ ἐρήρειστα: ἐπὶ τᾶς αὐτᾶς ῥοπᾶς Ti.Locr.97e: abs., δίκας ἐρείδεται πυθμήν *is set firm*, A.*Ch*.646 (lyr.); opp. πλανᾶσθαι, Arist.*GA*$720^a$12; ἐρηρεικός, of a bone *stuck* in the throat, Dsc.*Eup*.1.84. 3. ἐρείδεσθαι ναυαγίαις *to be driven ashore* in shipwreck, Pi.*I*.1.36. IV. Med., 1. in recipr. sense, *struggle* one with another, Il.23.735 (v.l. ἐρίζεσθον). 2. c. acc., *support* or *set firmly for oneself*, πλησίον ἠρείσαντο καρήατα Simon.172; βάκτρῳ δ' ἐρείδου.. στίβον E.*Ion* 743; ἐπὶ γαῖαν ἴχνος *AP*12.84 (Mel.); ἐπὶ τοίχῳ λίθον Theoc.23.49; ἐπὶ χειρὶ παρειήν A.R.3.1160; χεῖρας σκηπανίῳ *AP*6.83 (Maced.); ἐπὶ σκίπωνος τὸ γῆρας ib.7.457 (Aristo); ἐς πόλον ἐκ γαίης μῆτιν ἐ. *to raise one's* thoughts.., ib.9.782 (Paul. Sil.).

**ἐρεικ-αῖον** (sc. μέλι), τό, *heather honey*, Plin.*HN*11.41. **-η**, ἡ, *heath*, *Erica arborea*, A.*Ag*.295, Eup.14.4, Theoc.5.64, Thphr.*HP*1.14.2, Dsc.1.88.—The Inscr. quoted s.v. ἐρεικόεις proves that ἐρείκη is correct; ἐρίκη [ῐ] is the later spelling, v. ἐρείκινος. **-ηρὸν κολλούριον** eye-salve *made with* ἐρείκη, Sever.ap.Aët.7.103. **-ινος**, η, ον, *of* ἐρείκη, ξύλα, φυτά, *BGU*731 ii 8 (ii A.D.), *PStrassb*.29.11 (iii A.D.): written ἐρικ-. **-ιον**, τό, *crumbly pastry*, = ἴτριον, Gal.19.100. II. ἐρίκια, τά, *heath-plants*, *PLond*.3.905 (ii A.D.). **-ίς**, ίδος, ἡ, (ἐρείκω) *pounded barley, groats*, mostly in pl., written ἐρικ-, Gal.19.100:—Cret. **-άς**, ἡ, Hsch. **-ίτας** [ῑ] ἄρτος bread *of groats*, Seleuc.ap.Ath.3.114b (ἐρικ-). **-όεις**, εσσα, εν, *heathery*, pr. n. **Ἐρεικοῦς** λόφος *Schwyzer*720 (Theb. ad Mycalen, iv B.C.): **Ἐρεικοῦσσα**, one of the Aeolian Isles (N. of Sicily), Str.6.2.11, St. Byz. s.v., Sch.Ar.*Pl*.586: **Ἐρεικώδης** Sch.A.R.3.41. **-της**, v. ἐρέκτης. ⊛ **-τός**, ή, όν, *bruised, pounded*, πυρός (ὥστε δύο ἐξ ἑνὸς γεγονέναι) Paus.Gr.*Fr*.177: also ἐρικτά, τά, *barley-broth*, Hp.*Mul*.2.118, Hsch., Suid. **-ω**, A.*Pers*.1060: aor. 1 imper. ἔρειξον Ar.*Fr*.22, part. ἐρείξας Hp.*Morb*.2.67, *Nat.Mul*.32 (ἐρίξας *Mul*.2.113 codd.): aor. 2 ἤρικον Il.17.295, (δι-) Alex.Aet.3.21 (tm.):—Med., aor. 1 ἐρειξάμην Porph.*Abst*.2.6:—Pass., pf. ἐρήριγμαι (v. infr.):—*rend*, ἤρεικον χθόνα *rent* it with the ploughshare, Hes.*Sc*.287; πέπλον ἐ. A.*Pers*.1060 (lyr.): in this sense Hom. has only Pass., ἐρεικόμενος περὶ δουρί Il.13.441. 2. *bruise, pound*, of pulse, Ar.*Fr*.22, cf. Dieuch.ap.Orib.4.6.4; κάχρυς, ζειάς, Hp.*Morb*.2.67, *Mul*.2.113, *Superf*.34; κριθαὶ ἐρηριγμέναι Id.*Nat.Mul*.103; κύαμοι ἐρηρ. Arist.*HA*$595^b$7; ἐρειχθείσης τῆς κνήκου Diocl.*Fr*.140; ναῦς πρὸς ἀλλήλαισι πνοαὶ ἤρεικον *shattered* them, A.*Ag*.655; of pain, ὀδύναι μιν ἤρικον S.*Fr*.152 (lyr.). II. intr., aor. 2 ἤρῐκον *to be rent* or *shattered*, ἤρικε.. κόρυς περὶ δουρὸς ἀκωκῇ Il.17.295.

**ἐρεινοῦς**, ῆ, οῦν, *woollen*, *PGrenf*.2.111.13 (v/vi A.D.).

**ἔρειξις**, εως, ἡ, (ἐρείκω) *pounding, grinding*, Suid. II. = ἐσχισμένη γῆ, *EM*372.17.

**ἐρειοί**, οἱ, dub. l. in Theoc.15.50.

**ἐρειοῦς**, v. ἐρεοῦς.

**ἐρείπ-ιον**, τό, (ἐρείπω) *fallen ruin, wreck*, Arist.*Rh*.$1413^a$6, Aristid.*Or*.49(25).42, Opp.*H*.5.324: generally in pl., ναυτικὰ ἐ. *wreckage*, A.*Ag*.660, *Fr*.274, E.*Hel*.1080; θραύμασίν τ' ἐρειπίων A.*Pers*.425; *ruins*, οἰκημάτων, [τειχέων], Hdt.2.154, 4.124; δόμων E.*Ba*.7; ἐρείπια alone, ἐν τοῖς Κιμωνίοις ἐ. Cratin.151; ἐ. χλανιδίων *fragments* of garments, *Trag.Adesp*.7; πέπλων E.*Tr*.1025; νεκρῶν ἐ. *dead carcasses*, S.*Aj*.308, E.*Fr*.266.—Poet. and later Prose (exc. Arist. and Hdt. ll. cc.), D.H.1.14, *CIG*2700e (Mylasa), Paus.10.38.13, Aristid. l.c., etc. **-ιος**, ον, *falling, ruinous*, οἰκία Ph.1.197, cf. 2.436; ἐρείπιος γῆ· ἡ χέρσος, Suid. **-ιώδης**, ες, *ruinous*, *Gloss.* **-ιών**, ῶνος, ὁ, *heap of ruins*, dub. in *CIG*2554.113 (Crete), dub. in Lyd.*Mag*.3.71. **-οτόπιον**, τό, *heap of ruins*, Sch.Opp.*H*.1.54. ⊛ **-ω**, Ep. impf. ἔρειπον Il.12.258 (v. sub fin.): fut. ἐρείψω S.*OC*1373, X.*Cyr*.7.4.1: aor. 1 ἤρειψα Hdt.1.164, (ἐξ-) Pi.*P*.4.264: intr. in aor. 2 ἤρῐπον (v. infr. II), and pf. ἐρήρῐπα (κατ-) Il.14.55:—Med., aor. 1 ἠρειψάμην (ἀν-) only f.l., v. *ἀνερείπομαι: aor. 2 ἠριπόμην (in pass. sense) *AP*9.152 (Agath.):—Pass., aor. 1 part. ἐρειφθείς S.*Aj*.309; ind. ἠρίφθην Arr.*An*.1.21.4 codd., (κατ-) ib.2.22.7: aor. 2 ἠρίπην [ῐ] (v. infr.): pf. ἐρήριμμαι ib.1.21.6; ἤρειμμαι (κατ-) *IG*12(3).326.20 (Thera, ii A.D.): plpf. ἐρήριπτο (κατ-) Arr.*An*.1.19.2; cj. for ἠρείπετο in Plu.*Brut*.42; Ep. ἐρέριπτο Il.14.15; late Prose ἠρήριπτο Agath.1.10.—Poet. Verb (also in Hdt., X., Plb. and later Prose):—*throw* or *dash down, tear down*, ἔρειπον ἐπάλξεις Il.12.258; ἔρειπε δὲ τεῖχος Ἀχαιῶν 15.361; ὄχθας καπέτοιο.. ποσσὶν ἐρείπων ib.356; προμαχεῶνα ἕνα τοῦ τείχεος ἐ. Hdt.1.164 (v. sub fin.); πόλιν.. ἐρείψεις S.*OC*1373: metaph., λαοὺς διχοστασίαις ἤρειπον B.10.68; [Λαβδακίδας] ἐρείπει θεῶν τις some god *casts* them *down*, S.*Ant*.596 (lyr.):—Pass., *to be thrown down, fall in ruins*, ἐρέριπτο δὲ τεῖχος Ἀχαιῶν Il.14.15; τῆς μὲν ἐρειπομένης (sc. γαίης) Hes.*Th*.704; τῶν πύργων ἐρειπομένων Plb.1.42.10; ἐν δ' ἐρειπίοις νεκρῶν ἐρειφθεὶς ἕζετο S.*Aj*.309 (v.l. ἐρεισθείς); ἐρείπεται κτύπος.. Διόβολος the thunder *comes crashing down*, Id.*OC*1462 (lyr.); ἐρείπεσθαι εἴς τινα *to fall* upon.., Plu.*Alex*.33: aor. 2 part. Pass. ἐριπέντι *fallen*, Pi.*O*.2.43 (v.l. -όντι, cf. A.D.*Synt*.280.21). II. intr., aor. 2 ἤρῐπον, Ep. ἔρῐπον, *fall down*, ἤριπε δ' ἐξ ὀχέων Il.5.47, etc.; γνὺξ δ' ἔριπε *fell* on his knee, ib.68; ἐν κονίῃ, ἐν κονίῃσι, ib.75, 11.743; of trees, ἡ δ' ἐκ ῥιζέων ἐριποῦσα 21.243: hence, of a warrior, ἤριπε δ' ὡς ὅτε τις δρῦς ἤριπεν 13.389; ἀπ' οὐρανοῦ ἤριπεν ἀστὴρ ἐν πόντῳ Theoc.13.50: metaph., δείματι ἤριπεν her heart *sank* with terror, Simon.37.3; where this tense is apptly. trans., as in Hdt.9.70, Paus.10.32.6, ἤρειπον may be restored.

**ἔρ-εισις**, εως, ἡ, *propping up, shoring up*, οἰκίας *BCH*35.243 (Delos, ii B.C.). 2. *resting, supporting*. ἡ ἐπ' ἐδάφους ἔ. τοῦ ποδός Aristeas 69. 3. *pushing against, thrusting*, τοῦ πέτρου D.H.*Comp*.20; τοῦ χείλους Ath.11.488e. 4. *leverage*, Menesth.ap.Erot. s.v. ἄμβην. **-εισμα**, ατος, τό, *prop, stay, support*, σκῆπτρα, χειρὸς ἐρείσματα E.*HF*254; ἀμφὶ βάκτροις ἔρεισμα θέμενος, = ἐρεισάμενος, ib.108: in pl., *stays* of a house, Pl.*Lg*.793c; *props* to keep a boat on shore upright (cf. ἕρμα), Theoc.21.12; ἁμμάτων ἐ. *strong* knots, E.*HF*1036 (lyr.); of the legs *which support* the body, Arist.*PA*$689^b$19, *IA*$708^b$15; of the framework of the body, Id.*PA*$655^a$25, cf. *HA*$532^b$3; of food, ἀμβροσία γαστρὸς ἔ. λεπτῆς *Arch.Pap*.8.256. 2. metaph., of a person, Θήρων' ἔ. Ἀκράγαντος *pillar* of Agrigentum, Pi.*O*.2.6; Ἑλλάδος ἔ. κλειναὶ Ἀθᾶναι Id.*Fr*.76, cf. Luc.*Dem.Enc*.10, *Tim*.50; ἔ. Ἀθηνῶν, of the (future) tomb of Oedipus, S.*OC*58. b. of good fortune, εἰς ἀπροσδόκητον ἔ. καταντῶσιν Vett.Val.333.30. II. *contusion*, Hp.*Fract*.11. **-εισμός**, ὁ, = foreg. 1, Aq.*Is*.3.1. **-ειστικός**, ή, όν, *pushing, thrusting*, κινήσεις Ruf.*Anat*.68; δένδρον Hdn.Gr.ap. Orion.61.24.

**ἐρείψιμος**, ον, *thrown down, in ruins*, στέγος E.*IT*48.

**ἐρειψῐπύλας** [ῠ], α, ὁ, *overthrowing gates*, B.5.56.

**ἔρειψις**, εως, ἡ, *throwing down, ruin*, *IG*$2^2$.463.104.

**ἐρειψίτοιχος** [ῐ], ον, *overthrowing walls*, δωμάτων A.*Th*.883 (lyr.): perh. to be read in B.12.167.

⊛ **ἐρέκτης**, ου, ὁ, *one who splits* beans, Orion 54.8 (fort. leg. ἐρείκτης).

**ἐρεμν-αῖος**, η, ον, = sq., Q.S.2.510. **-ός**, ή, όν, (*ἐρεβ-νός, cf. Ἔρεβος) *murky, black, dark*, ἐρεμνὴν γαῖαν ἔδυτε Od.24.106, cf. *h.Merc*.427; ἐρεμνῇ νυκτὶ ἐοικώς Od.11.606, cf. Sapph.*Supp*.1.18; ἐρεμνῇ λαίλαπι ἶσοι Il.12.375; ἐ. αἰγίς 4.167, Hes.*Sc*.444; ἕσπερος A.R.4.1289; ἐρεμνῇ ψακάδι φοινίας δρόσου, of bloodshed, A.*Ag*.1390; ἐ. αἷμα S.*Aj*.376 (lyr.); Ἅιδου μυχοί prob. in E.*Heracl*.218: metaph., ἐ. φάτις a *dark, obscure* rumour, S.*Ant*.700; ἔρος ἐ. Ibyc.1.

**ἐρεό-ξῠλον**, τό, *cotton*, *PLond*.3.928.1 (ii A.D.); cf. ἐριόξυλον. **-πώλης**, ου, ὁ, *wool-seller*, *POxy*.1669.5 (iii A.D.); cf. ἐριοπώλης.

⊛ **ἐρεοῦς**, ᾶ, οῦν, (ἐρέα) contr. from ἐρέεος, *of wool, woollen*, *IG*$1^2$.386.18, Pl.*Plt*.280e, al., *PCair.Zen*.54.37 (iii B.C.), *PPetr*.2 p.108 (ii B.C.); τὰ ἐρεᾶ *PCair.Zen*.295 (iii B.C.); τελαμῶνες Sor.1.83; v.l. for ἐριοῦς, Dsc.1.19:—also written **ἐρειοῦς**, ᾶ, οῦν, ἐσθής *IG*11(2).161*B*62 (Delos, iii B.C.); cf. χιθῶνα ἐριοῦν *BGU*816.18 (iii A.D.). (Cf. ἐρέα fin.)

⊛ **ἐρέπτομαι**, *feed on*, c. acc., only in pres. part., mostly of granivorous animals, λωτόν, κρῖ λευκόν, πυρὸν ἐρεπτόμενοι, Il.2.776, 5.196, Od.19.553, al.; of men, λωτὸν ἐ. 9.97, *AP*9.618; βότρυν ib.7.20; of fish, δημὸν ἐ. *feeding on* the fat of a carcase, Il.21.204.—Ep. Verb, used burlesquely by Ar.*Eq*.1295, ἐρεπτόμενον τὰ τῶν ἐχόντων:—Act., ἐρέπτω *eat*, Nonn.*D*.40.306; also causal, = τρέφω, Hsch.

⊛ **ἐρέπτω**, = ἐρέφω, *crown*, στεφάνοισι ποίας Pi.*P*.4.240, cf. B.4.16, Opp.*C*.4.262, etc.: metaph., λαῶν γενεὰν ἐ. ἄνθεσιν εὐνομίας Pi.*Pae*.1.9:—Med., κεφαλὴν ἀνθέμοις ἐρέπτομαι Cratin.98. II. *pluck*, ἄνθος cj. in Nonn.*D*.47.466.

**ἐρέριπτο**, v. ἐρείπω. **ἔρερον**, = εἴρερον, Hsch. s.v. εἰς ἔρερον. **ἐρέσθαι** and **ἔρεσθαι**, v. ἔρομαι. **ἐρεσία**, ἡ, = εἰρεσία, *Gloss.* ⊛ **ἐρεσιμήτρην**· τὴν γεωμετρίαν, Hsch. **ἐρεσκίη**· θρησκ⟨ε⟩ία, Id. **ἐρεσμεῖ**· καταπνεῖ (fort. -πλεῖ), Id. **ἐρεσμεί**· κώπη, Id. **ἐρεσμίονες**· αἱ χεῖρες, Id.

⊛ **ἐρέσσω**, Plu.2.1128c, *Pomp*.73, *Cic*.47, rarely **-ττω**, Luc.*Cont*.1, al. (earlier ἐλαύνω): Ep. impf. ἔρεσσον Od.11.78: aor. ἤρεσα A.R.1.1110, (δι-) Od.12.444, ἤρεσσα (δι-) 14.351: (ἐρέτης):—*row*, ἄνδρας ἐρεσσέμεναι μεμαῶτας Il.9.361; οἱ δὲ προπεσόντες ἔρεσσον Od.9.490, 12.194; ἐρετμόν, τῷ καὶ ζωὸς ἔρεσσον 11.78; πομπίμοις κώπαις ἐ. S.*Tr*.561; ἤρεσαν ἐς λιμένα A.R.1.1110; of birds flying, πτεροῖς ἐ. E.*IT*289: abs., Id.*Ion*161 (lyr.); [ναυτίλος] οὖλος ἐρέσσων ποσσίν Call.*Ep*.6.5. II. trans., *speed by rowing*: metaph., γόων.. ἐρέσσετ'.. πόμπιμον χεροῖν πίτυλον *ply* with your hands *the measured* stroke of lamentation, A.*Th*.855 (cf. ἔρεσσ' ἔρεσσε καὶ στέναζ' Id.*Pers*.1046):—Pass., ναῦς ἠρέσσετο ib.422, cf. *Supp*.723, A.R.1.633; of birds, πτερύγων ἐρετμοῖσιν ἐρεσσόμενοι A.*Ag*.52. 2. generally, *put in quick motion, ply*, τὸν πόδα E.*IA*138 (anap.), *AP*10.22 (Bianor); γεωτόμον ὅπλον ib.101 (Id.): metaph., τοίας ἐρέσσουσιν ἀπειλὰς.. καθ' ἡμῶν S.*Aj*.251 (lyr.); ἐ. μῆτιν Id.*Ant*.158 (anap.):—Pass., of a bow, *to be plied, handled*, Id.*Ph*.1135 (lyr.); of Io, οἴστρῳ ἐρεσσομένα *driven onward*, A.*Supp*.541 (lyr.). III. *row through, traverse*, in Pass., νήεσσιν ἐρέσσεται.. ὕδωρ *AP*4.$3^b$.30 (Agath.).

**ἐρεσ-χελία**, ἡ, = φλυαρία, *EM*371.1, Suid. s.v. Ἀδάμ; = *decudia* (?), *Gloss.*; *quarrel*, *PMonac*.1.23 (vi A.D., -χειλία Pap.). **-χηλέω** (freq. with v.l. **-χελέω**), used only in pres., *talk lightly, to be jocular*, παίζειν καὶ ἐ. Pl.*R*.545e, cf. *Lg*.885c, Luc.*DMort*.16.3, etc.: c. inf., *discuss jocularly whether*.., Philostr.*VA*2.14. II. trans., *quiz, banter*, τινα Pl.*Phdr*.236b; τι Ath.6.223e, etc.; *tease, worry*, Ael.*NA*3.37, 15.22, Luc.*Musc.Enc*.10: c. dat. pers., ὁ λόγος ἐ. νῷν Pl.*Phlb*.53e. 2. c. acc. cogn., προφάσεις, πολέμου ἀφορμάς ἐ., *find trifling* excuses or occasions, App.*Pun*.74, *Mith*.64; cf. ἐρίσχηλος.

**ἐρετ-αίνω,** = ἐρέσσω, Hsch. **-άνης·** ναύτης, Id. **-ή·** ἐπιθυμητή, Id. ⊛ **-ης,** ου, ὁ, mostly in pl., *rowers*, Od.1.280, al., A.*Pers.*39(anap.), Hdt.6.12, Th.1.31, etc.: sg., Ar.*Eq.*542: metaph., κυλίκων ἐρέται, of tipplers, Dionys.Eleg.5.2. II. in pl., also, *oars*, *AP*6.4.6 (Leon.). (Root *erə*-, cf. Skt. *aritár*- 'rower', ἁλι-ήρης, τρι-ήρης, etc.) **-ικός,** ή, όν, *of* or *for rowers* or *rowing*: ἡ -κή (sc. τέχνη) the *art of rowing*, Pl.*Lg.*707a; ἐ. πληρώματα crews *of rowers*, Plu.*Pomp.*25; ἐρετικόν, τό, *crews*, App.*Hann.*54 (but, *service as a rower*, *PGnom.*143); ἐ. αὐλήματα Poll.4.56. **-μίον,** τό, Dim. of sq., cj. in *Com.Adesp.*607. ⊛ **-μόν,** τό, *oar*, poet. for κώπη, πῆξαί τ' ἐπὶ τύμβῳ ἐρετμόν Od.11.77, cf. 23.276, Pi.*P.*4.18, E.*El.*433(lyr.), etc.; εὐῆρες ἐ. Od.11.121,129, etc.: pl., εὐήρε' ἐ. ib.125; ἐρετμοῖσι φρύξουσι Orac. ap.Hdt.8.96, cf. E.*IA*1388(troch.), *IT*1485: metaph., πτερύγων ἐ. A.*Ag.*52(anap.). II. = τὸ ἀνδρεῖον αἰδοῖον, Hsch. (A fem. form ἐρετμαῖς = κώπαις is found in Hsch.) ⊛ **-μός,** ὁ, *rowing*, Hdn.*Epim.*36. **-μόω,** *furnish with oars, set to row*, χέρας E.*Med.*4; but χεῖρας ἐ. *lay* their hands *to the oar*, Orph.*A.*358; *use* their hands *as oars*, *swim*, Nonn.*D.*7.185. 2. ἐ. πορείην *pursue* a course, ib.33.191, al. 3. *traverse* as if with oars, ib.14.4:—Pass., ἀὴρ ἐρετμώθη πτερύγεσσιν ib.6.388.

⊛ **ἔρετο·** ὠρυήθη, Hsch.

⊛ **Ἐρέτρια,** Ep. (metri gr.) **Εἰρέτρια,** ἡ, Il.2.537:—*Eretria*, *IG*1$^2$.304.17, Th.8.60, Hdt.6.43, etc.:—hence **Ἐρετριεύς,** έως, ὁ, *an Eretrian*, Hdt.5.99, al., etc.: pl. Ἐρετριῆς *IG*2$^2$.43.85 (iv B.C.); Ἐρετριεῖς ib.12(9).207.5 (iii B.C.), etc.; acc. Ἐρετριᾶς ib.188; gen. Ἐρετριῶν ib.1$^2$.49.12, al., Ἐρετριέων ib.12(9).187.13, etc.; written Ἐρετρειέων ib.201.7 (acc. sg. contr. Ἐρετρῆ prob. in Crates Theb.2):—Adj. ⊛ **Ἐρετρικός,** ή, όν, *Eretrian*, Hdt.6.101, etc.; οἱ Ἐ. the disciples of the *Eretrian* Menedemus, Str.9.1.8 (v.l. **Ἐρετριακοί,** as in D.L.1.18, etc.). ⊛ **Ἐρετριάς** (sc. γῆ), άδος, ἡ, *a kind of clay*, Hp.*Morb.*3.16, Dsc.5.152.

**ἐρετριάζει·** σκώπτει, παίζει, Hsch.

**ἐρευγ-μᾰτώδης,** ες, *causing eructation*, κρέα Hp.*Acut.*(*Sp.*)49. **-μός,** ὁ, *eructation*, Id.*Coac.*138 (pl.), Arist.*Pr.*895$^b$15. **-μώδης,** ες, v.l. for ἐρευγματώδης, Hp.*Vict.*2.42.

**ἐρεύγομαι** (A), also **ἐρυγγάνω** (q.v.), fut. ἐρεύξομαι Hp.*Mul.*1.41: aor. 1 ἠρευξάμην Procop.*Goth.*2.4: aor. 2 ἤρῠγον Arist.*Pr.*895$^b$22, Nic.*Al.*111:—*belch out*, *disgorge*, c. acc., ἐρευγόμενοι φόνον αἵματος Il.16.162; ἰόν Nic.*Th.*232: abs., *belch*, ἐρεύγετο οἰνοβαρείων Od.9.374, cf. Hp.*Morb.*2.69, Arist.*Pr.*895$^b$12. 2. metaph., of volcanoes, ἐρεύγονται πυρὸς παγαί Pi.*P.*1.21, cf. Procop.*Goth.*4.35; of a river, *discharge itself*, ἐς τὴν θάλασσαν App.*Mith.*103, cf. Alc.*Supp.*11.3: c. acc. cogn., ἐρεύγονται σκότον..νυκτὸς ποταμοί, of the rivers of hell, Pi.*Fr.*130.8; κόλπος ἀφρὸν ἐρευγόμενος D.P.539, cf. Lxx *Le.*11.10; ἵππος ἐρεύγεται ἄνδρα, as the description of a Centaur, *APl.*4.115. 3. *blurt out* (cf. ἐξερυγγάνω), *belch forth*, *utter*, ἡμέρα τῇ ἡμέρᾳ ἐρεύγεται ῥῆμα Lxx *Ps.*18(19).2; ἐρεύξομαι κεκρυμμένα *Ev.Matt.*13.35. (Cf. Lat. *ērūgĕre*, Lith. *riáugėti* 'belch'.)

**ἐρεύγομαι** (B), aor. 2 Act. ἤρῠγον, *bellow*, *roar*, ἤρυγεν, ὡς ὅτε ταῦρος ἤρυγεν Il.20.403; τόν γ' ἐρυγόντα λίπε..θυμός ib.406; ὅσον βαθὺς ἤρυγε λαιμός *roared* to the full depth of his throat or voice, Theoc.13.58; of the sea, ἀμφὶ δέ τ' ἄκραι ἠϊόνες βοόωσιν ἐρευγομένης ἁλὸς ἔξω the headlands echo to the *roar* of the sea, Il.17.265; κῦμα..δεινὸν ἐρευγόμενον Od.5.403; ἐρεύγεται ἤπειρόνδε ib.438 (cf. βοάω I.2):—so in later Gr., λέων ἐρεύξεται Lxx *Ho.*11.10, *Am.*3.8; σκύμνος ἐρευγόμενος ib.1*Ma.*3.4; with v.l. ὠρύομαι, ib.*Ez.*22.25; cf. προσερεύγομαι. (Cf. Lat. *rūgio* 'roar'.)

**ἐρευθ-ᾰλέος,** η, ον, (ἔρευθος) *ruddy*, Nonn.*D.*12.329,359. ⊛ **-έδᾰνον,** τό, *madder*, *Rubia tinctorum*, Hdt.4.189; of the wild form, *Rubia tinctorum*, Thphr.*HP*9.13.6, Dsc.3.143 (ἐρευθέδανος ῥίζα Ps.-Dsc. ibid.): hence, *dye* made therefrom, *PHolm.*26.36. **-έω,** *to be red*, Luc.*Ner.*7; *to be flushed*, *BGU*928.14 (iii A.D.). **-ήεις,** εσσα, εν, *red*, A.R.1.727, Nic.*Th.*899 (v.l. -ιόεις). **-ημα,** ατος, τό, *redness*, Gal.19.433. **-ής,** ές, = ἐρευθήεις, ὕδωρ Str.16.4.20; σελήνη Arat.784, cf. Opp.*C.*3.94. **-ιάω,** *become red*, Hp.*Mul.*2.112, Opp.*H.*3.25. **-ιόεις,** v. ἐρευθήεις. ⊛ **-ος,** εος, τό, *redness*, *flush*, Hp.*Epid.*1.26.ε', Plu.2.48c; of dye, A.R.1.726; [ἡδονὴ] ἔρευθος εἰργασμένη with *painted* cheeks, Ph.2.266. **-ω,** aor. 1 inf. ἐρεῦσαι Il. (v. infr.):—*make red*, *stain with red*, αἵματι γαῖαν 11.394; γαῖαν ἐρεῦσαι αὐτοῦ ἐνὶ Τροίῃ 18.329; βωμὸν φόνοισι Pythag.ap.S.E.*M.*9.128:—Pass., *to be* or *become red*, Sapph.93, Hp.*Epid.*2.3.1, *Morb.Sacr.*15, Theoc.17.127; [ἀστὴρ] καλὸν -όμενος A.R.1.778. II. intr. in Act., ἔρ[ευθε φώτων αἵμα]τι γαῖα B.12.152; τὸ πρόσωπον ἐ. Hp.*Morb.*4.38. (ONorse *rjóða*, OE. *réodan* 'redden', OE. *réad* 'red'; v. ἐρυθρός.)

**ἐρευκτικός,** ή, όν, (ἐρεύγομαι A) *promoting eructation*, Dsc.1.70.3.

**ἔρευν-α,** ης, ἡ, *inquiry*, *search*, ἔ. τινός *search* for.., S.*OT*566, cf. *Ichn.*92; οὐδ' ἦξας εἰς ἔ. ἐξευρεῖν γονάς; E.*Ion*328; ἔ. ποιεῖσθαι τῶν οἰκιῶν Arist.*Oec.*1351$^b$34, cf. *PTeb.*38.19 (ii B.C.); v. ἔραυνα. II. *exploratory operation*, Herod.Med.ap.Orib.50.46.2. **-άς,** άδος, ὁ, = Lat. *quaestor*, Lyd.*Mag.*1.25 (pl.); = Lat. *quaesitor*, ib.2.29. **-άω,** also -ίω *GDI*5075.35 (Crete), and **ἐραυνάω** (q.v.):—*seek* or *search for*, *search after*, *track*, ἴχνι' ἐρευνῶντες κύνες ἤϊσαν Od.19.436; μετ' ἀνέρος ἴχνι' ἐρευνῶν Il.18.321; τεύχε' ἐ. Od.22.180; τὴν σοφὴν εὐβουλίαν A.*Pr.*1038; θεῶν βουλεύματ' Pi.*Fr.*61; νεκρούς E.*Med.*1318; κακούργους X.*Cyr.*1.2.12; ἄν τινα οἴωμαι σοφὸν εἶναι Pl.*Ap.*23b, cf. 41b; τὸ γραμματεῖον D.25.61; ὧν..ἂν θεὸς χρείαν ἐρευνᾷ the things whereof he *seeks after* the use, i.e. whatever things he finds serviceable, S.*OT*725. 2. *search*, *explore* a place, Hdt.5.92.δ', Sor.*Vit.Hippocr.*3; τεναγέων ῥοάς Pi.*N.*3.24; ὄρος Theoc.25.221; τοὺς ὑπόπτους τῶν τόπων Ael.*Tact.*17: abs., εὑρήσεις ἐρευνῶν thou wilt find *by searching*, Pi.*O.*13.113, cf. S.*Ant.*268; εἰσβάντες εἰς τὸ πλοῖον ἠρεύνων Antipho 5.29. 3. *inquire after*, φάτιν E.*Hel.*662 (lyr.); παίδων ἐρευνῶν σπέρμ' ὅπως γένοιτό μοι Id.*Med.*669; *examine into* a question, ib.1084 (anap.), cf. Pl.*Tht.*200e, al.:—also in Med., διάνοια πᾶσαν φύσιν -ωμένη ib.174a; οἰκημάτιον X.Eph.2.10. 4. c. inf., *seek* to do, Theoc.7.45. **-ητέον,** *one must inquire*, ποῖα.. X.*Smp.*8.39; εἰ.. Ph.2.27. **-ητήρ,** ῆρος, ὁ, = sq., Nonn.*D.*2.25. **-ητής,** οῦ, ὁ, *searcher*, *inquirer*, Clearch.25, Parth.1.1: c. gen., τῶν ἐλέγχων, τῶν ἀδήλων, J.*AJ*7.5.5, *BJ*1.30.7; διόπται καὶ ἐ. *spies*, D.C.78.14; *inspector*, *customs-officer*, *UPZ*149.15 (iii/ii B.C.); cf. ἐραυνητ-ής, -ικόν. **-ήτρια,** ἡ, fem. of foreg., Corn.*ND*1.

**ἔρευξις,** εως, ἡ, (ἐρεύγομαι A) *eructation*, Hp.*Epid.*1.23 (pl.), Aret.*SA*2.3 (pl.).

**ἐρεύω,** = ἐρευνάω, Eust.670.65, Hsch.:—hence **ἐρευτής,** οῦ, ὁ, = ἐρευνητής, *exactor*, *collector of state-debts*, *SIG*527.132 (Dreros, iii B.C.), *GDI*5073.18 (Cnossus, ii B.C.). (Cf. ἐρέω (A).)

⊛ **ἐρεφύλλινον** ἄνθος, dub. sens. in *PMag.Leid.W.*1.23.

**ἐρέφω,** impf. ἤρεφον Ar.*Fr.*73, poet. ἔρ- Pi.*O.*1.68, also **ἐρέπτω** (q.v.): fut. ἐρέψω Ar.*Av.*1110: aor. 1 ἤρεψα D.19.265 (nowhere else in Att. Prose), Ep. and Lyr. ἔρεψα Hom., Pi.*O.*13.32:—**Med.,** fut. ἐρέψομαι E.*Ba.*323: aor. 1 ἠρεψάμην A.R.2.159, etc., (κατ-) Ar.*V.*1294:—**Pass.,** Corn.*ND*17: pf. ἤρεπται Philostr.*VA*1.25: (cf. ὄροφος, ἐρέπτω):—*cover with a roof*, καθύπερθεν ἔρεψαν..ὄροφον λειμωνόθεν ἀμήσαντες, i.e. they *thatched* [the hut] with reeds Il.24.450, cf. Od.23.193; τὰς..οἰκίας ἐρέψομεν πρὸς αἰετόν Ar.*Av.*1110, cf. *Fr.*73; ἤρεψε τὴν οἰκίαν ξύλοις D. l.c.:—Pass., τὰ βασίλεια χαλκῷ ἤρεπται Philostr. l.c. 2. *cover with a crown*, *crown*, δύο δ' αὐτὸν ἔρεψαν πλόκοι σελίνων Pi.*O.*13.32; [κρατήρων] κρᾶτ' ἔρεψον καὶ λαβάς S.*OC*473:—Med., *crown oneself*, κισσῷ E.*Ba.*323; στεφάνῳ κόμαν B.8.24; δάφνῃ μέτωπα *one's* forehead, A.R.2.159:—Pass., στεφάνοισι χαίταν ἐρεφθείς B.12.70. 3. *wreathe as with garlands*, ναὸν κρανίοις Pi.*I.*4(3).54: generally, *cover*, λάχναι νιν μέλαν γένειον ἔρεφον Id.*O.*1.68.

**Ἐρεχθεύς,** έως, Ep. ῆος, ὁ, an ancient hero of Attica, first in Il.2.547, Od.7.81:—hence **Ἐρέχθειον,** τό, *Temple of Erechtheus* at Athens, Paus.1.26.5, Plu.2.843e: **Ἐρεχθεῖδαι,** οἱ, *members of the Erechtheid tribe*, *SIG*911.17: hence, a name of the Athenians, Pi.*I.*2.19, E.*Med.*824 (-εῖδαι, lyr.), etc.: sg. in Ar.*Eq.*1015,1030:—**Ἐρεχθηΐς,** ΐδος, contr. **-ῄς,** ῇδος, fem. Adj. *of Erechtheus*, θάλασσα Ἐ. a fountain at Athens *sacred to him*, Apollod.3.14.1: also a name of one of the Attic Tribes, *IG*1$^2$.929, D.21.68, etc. II. name of Poseidon at Athens, Plu.2.843b, Lyc.158,431; Ποσειδῶνι Ἐρεχθεῖ *IG*1$^2$.580.

**ἐρεχθῖτις,** ιδος, ἡ, = ἀριστολοχεία στρογγύλη, Ps.-Dsc.3.4; = ἠριγέρων, ib.4.96.

⊛ **ἐρέχθω,** *rend*, *break*, δάκρυσι καὶ στοναχῇσι καὶ ἄλγεσι θυμὸν ἐρέχθων Od.5.83:—Pass., ἐρεχθομένην ἀνέμοισι, of a ship, *buffeted* by the winds, Il.23.317: metaph., ὀδύνῃσιν ἐρεχθομένη *h.Ap.*358; πρήξεσιν οὐχ ὁσίαις ἐ. Procl.*H.*7.38.

**ἐρεχμός,** ὁ, Aeol. for ἐρεγμός, *EM*371.19.

**ἐρέψιμος,** ον, *of* or *for roofing*, δένδρα ἐ. Pl.*Criti.*111c; ὕλη Thphr.*HP*4.2.8.

**ἔρεψις,** εως, ἡ, *roofing*, Thphr.*HP*5.6.1, *Supp.Epigr.*3.147 (iii B.C.); *style of roof*, Plu.*Per.*13, *Ant.*45, etc.

**ἐρέω** (A), Ep. Verb, = ἐρεείνω, ἔρομαι, ἐρωτάω, *ask*, *inquire*, c. acc. rei, *about* a thing, ἐρέων γενεήν τε τόκον τε Il.7.128, cf. Od.21.31; *seek for*, Ὕλαν A.R.1.1354. 2. c. acc. pers., *question*, μάντιν ἐρείομεν (v. infr.) ἢ ἱερῆα Il.1.62; ἀλλήλους ἐρέοιμεν Od.4.192; ὅπως ἐρέοιμι ἑκάστην 11.229. 3. c. acc. rei, *search*, *explore*, ἰλυούς Nic.*Th.*143 (v.l. ἐρέθοντες). (Prob. ἐρε(ϝ)-, cf. ἐρευτής: ἐρείομεν perh. metri gr. for ἐρέ(ϝ)-ο-μεν, pres. subj. of non-thematic stem.)

**ἐρέω** (B), Ion. for ἐρῶ, I *will say*; v. ἐρῶ.

**ἐρέω** (C), Ion. for ἐράω (A).

**ἐρημ-άζω,** (ἐρῆμος) *to be left lonely*, *go alone*, ἐρημάζεσκον (Iterat.) Theoc.22.35, cf. *AP*7.315 (Zenod. or Rhian.):—also in Med., Satyr.*Vit.Eur.Fr.*39xxi8. ⊛ **-αῖος,** η, ον, poet. for ἐρῆμος, *desolate*, *solitary*, Mosch.3.21, A.R.2.672, etc.; *silent*, νύξ Emp.49; *deserted*, νεοσσοί A.R.4.1298: c. gen., *reft of*, *AP*9.439 (Crin.). **-άς,** άδος, ἡ, pecul. fem. of ἐρῆμος, Man.6.67. **-η** (sc. δίκη), ἡ, v. ἐρῆμος III.

**Ἐρημήσιος,** ὁ, epith. of Zeus at Lesbos, Hsch.

**ἐρημ-ία,** ἡ, I. of places, *a solitude*, *desert*, *wilderness*, Hdt.3.98, A.*Pr.*2, etc.; ἡ Σκυθῶν ἐ. Ar.*Ach.*704; ἀφίκετ' εἰς ἐ. Id.*Lys.*787; ἕρπει εἰς τὰς ἐρημίας to *solitary places*, Arist.*HA*610$^b$24, etc. II. as a state or condition, *solitude*, *loneliness*, ἐρημίαν ἄγειν, to keep *alone*, E.*Med.*50; μονάδ' ἔχουσ' ἐ. Id.*Ba.*609 (troch.); ἐρημίας τυχών Id.*El.*510; ἐν ἐρημίᾳ ἐλοιδοροῦντο Antipho 2.1.4; of persons, *isolation*, *destitution*, S.*OC*957, Lys.18.25; πολλὴν ἡμῶν ἐ. καταγνόντες Is.1.2; δι' ἐρημίαν from *being left alone*, Th.1.71, cf. 3.67; ἐρημίας ἐπειλημμένοι D.3.27; εὑρετικὸν εἶναί φασι τὴν ἐ. Men.39. b. of places, *desolation*, ἐρημίᾳ δοῦναί τι E.*Tr.*97; ἐρημία..πόλιν ὅταν λάβῃ ib.26; ἀτριβὴς ὑπ' ἐρημίας Th.4.8. 2. c. gen., *want of*, *absence*, φίλων X.*Mem.*2.2.14; ἀρσένων, βροτῶν, ἀνδρῶν, E.*Hec.*1017, *Ba.*875 (lyr., pl.), Th.6.102; λύχνων Ar.*Av.*1484 (lyr.), etc.; δι' ἐρημίας πολεμίων πορευόμενος *without finding* any enemy, X.*HG*3.4.21; τὴν ἐ. τῶν κωλυσόντων ὁρῶν seeing that there would be *none* to hinder him, D.4.49; ἐ. σώματος, = κενόν, Zeno *Stoic.*1.26; even ἐ. κακῶν *freedom from* evil, E.*HF*1157. **-ικός,** ή, όν, *of* or *for solitude*, *living in a desert*, Lxx *Ps.*101(102).7. **-ίτης** [ῑ], ου, ὁ, *of the desert*, ὄνος ib.*Jb.*11.12.

**ἐρημο-βάτης** [ᾰ], ου, ὁ, *traveller in deserts*, *Cat.Cod.Astr.*8(4).151.

**-βόας**, *bubo*, *Gloss.* **-δίκιον** [ῐκ], τό, = δίκη ἐρήμη, *Cod.Just.*3.1.13.3, *Gloss.* **-θωκος**· ἐρημολόγος, Hsch. **-κόμης**, gen. ου, *void of hair*, κρατός *AP*6.294(Phan.); κόρση ib.7.383 (Phil.). **-λάλος** [ᾰ], ον, *chattering in the desert*, μοῦσα (of the τέττιξ) ib.196 (Mel.). **-λόγος**, gloss on ἐρημόθωκος, Hsch. **-νόμος**, ον, *haunting the wilds*, θεαί A.R.4.1333; θῆρες *AP*6.184(Zos.); also in late Prose, ζῷα ἐ. Agath.2.24. II. ἐρημόνομος, ον, *desolate*, λόχμη, πόντος, Nonn.*D*.37.12, 47.510. **-πλάνος** [ᾰ], ον, *wandering alone*, Orph.*H*.39.4 (ἐρημοπλάνα codd.); noted as διθυραμβῶδες by Demetr. *Eloc.*116. **-ποιός**, όν, *making desolate*, gloss on ἐρημωτής, Suid., cf. *PMag.Leid.V.*15.23. **-πολέω**, *play the hermit*, Eustr. *in EN* 7.10. **-πολις**, ι, gen. ιδος, *reft of one's city*, E.*Tr.*603 (lyr.).

⊛ **ἐρῆμος**, ον, fem. ἐρήμη Od.3.270, S.*OC*1719(lyr.), *Ant.*739, *Tr.*530 (lyr.), and in the phrase δίκη ἐρήμη (v. infr. III): Att. **ἔρημος**, ον, acc. to Hdn.Gr.2.938: Comp. -ότερος Th.3.11, Lys.29.1, etc.: Sup. -ότατος Hdt.9.118:—*desolate, lonely, solitary*, 1. of places, ἐς νῆσον ἐρήμην Od.3.270; χῶρος Il.10.520; τὰ ἐ. τῆς Λιβύης the *desert parts*.., Hdt.2.32, cf. Th.2.17; ἡ ἐρῆμος (sc. χώρα) Hdt.4.18; ἡ ἐρήμη Ael.*NA* 7.48: pl., ib.3.26; *empty*, πνύξ Ar.*Ach.*20. 2. of persons or animals, τὰ δ' ἐρῆμα φοβεῖται (i.e. the sheep), Il.5.140; Ξέρξην ἔ. μολεῖν A. *Pers.*734(troch.); ἧσθαι δόμοις ἔ. Id.*Ag.*862; πόρτις ἐρήμα S.*Tr.*530 (lyr.); ἔ. κἄφιλος Id.*Ph.*228; τὸν θεὸν ἔ. ἀπολιπόντε Ar.*Pl.*447; freq. of poor, friendless persons, And.4.15, etc.; ἐρημότεροι, opp. δυνατώτεροι, Th.3.11; οὐκ ὢν οὔτε τῶν ἐρημοτάτων οὔτε τῶν ἀπόρων κομιδῇ D. 21.111; εἰς ὀρφανὰ καὶ ἔ. ὑβρίζειν Pl.*Lg.*927c; ὄρνιθες *solitary, not gregarious*, Plu.*Caes.*63: neut. as Adv., ἔρημα κλαίω I weep *in solitude*, E.*Supp.*775; ἔρημον ἐμβλέπειν to look *vacantly*, Ar.*Fr.*456. 3. of conditions, πλάνος S.*OC*1114. II. c. gen., *reft of, void* or *destitute of*, [χώρη] ἐ. πάντων Hdt.2.32; ἀνθρώπων Id.4.17, cf. 18; ἀνδρῶν Id.6.22, S.*OT*57; Ἀθηναίων Hdt.8.65; στέγαι φίλων ἔ. S.*El.* 1405; Πειραιᾶ ἔ. ὄντα νεῶν Th.8.96; τῇ ἦν ἐρημότατον τῶν πολεμίων (sc. τὸ τεῖχος) Hdt.9.118; [τὰ γεγραμμένα] ἀπόντος τοῦ γράψαντος ἔρημα τοῦ βοηθήσοντός ἐστιν Isoc.*Ep.*1.3; θεῶν ἔρημα εἶναι πάντα Pl.*Lg.* 908c. 2. of persons, *bereft of*, συμμάχων Hdt.7.160; πατρός S. *OC*1719(lyr.); πατρὸς ἢ μητρός Pl.*Lg.*927d; πρὸς φίλων S.*Ant.*919; so ἔ. οἶκος a house *without heirs*, Is.7.31. 3. with no bad sense, *wanting, without*, ἐσθὴς ἐρῆμος ὅπλων Hdt.9.63; *free from*, ἀνδρῶν κακῶν ἔρημος πόλις Pl.*Lg.*862e. III. ἐρήμη, rarely ἔρημος (with or more commonly without γραφή, δίκη, δίαιτα), ἡ, an *undefended* action, *in which one party does not appear*, and judgement goes against him *by default*, ἤλπιζε..τὴν γραφὴν..ἐρήμην ἔσεσθαι would be *undefended*, Antipho 2.1.7; ἐρήμῃ δίκῃ θάνατον καταγιγνώσκειν τινός Th.6.61; δίκην εἷλον ἐρήμην I got *judgement by default*, D.21.81; ἐρήμην αὐτὸν λαβόντες..εἷλον Lys.20.18; τὴν ἔρημον δεδωκότα having given *it by default* in one's favour, D.21.85; ἔρημον ὦφλε δίκην he let it go *by default*, ib.87, cf. Antipho 5.13; ἐρήμην τινὸς καταγνῶναι τὴν δίαιταν D.33.33; ἐρήμην καταδιαιτῆσαί τινος Id.40.17; γενομένης ἐρήμου κατὰ Μειδίου Test.ap.eund.21.93; ἐρήμην κατηγορεῖν to accuse *in a case where there was no defence*, Pl.*Ap.*18c, cf. D.21.87; ἐρήμην or ἐξ ἐρήμης κρατεῖν, Luc.*Anach.*40, *JTr.*25; ἁλῶναι Id.*Tox.*11, etc. 2. *unclaimed, vacant*, Arist.*Ath.*43.4, *EN*1125$^{b}$17, Is.3.61. 3. for ἐρήμας τρυγᾶν v. sub τρυγάω.

**ἐρημο-σκόπος**, ὁ, *one who keeps watch negligently*, Anon.ap.Suid. **-σύνη**, ἡ, *solitude*, *AP*9.4(Cyllen.), 665(Agath.). ⊛ **-τελωνία**, ἡ, *tax for maintenance of desert-police*, *PLond.*2.88 (ii A.D.), etc. **-φίλης** [ῐ], ου, ὁ, *loving solitude*, *AP*9.396(Paul. Sil.), *APl.*4.256. **-φύλαξ** [ῠ], ακος, ὁ, *desert-policeman*, *PCair.Zen.*172.25 (iii B.C.), etc.:—hence ⊛ **-φῠλᾰκία**, ἡ, *maintenance of this force*, *PFay.*68 (ii A.D.), etc.

⊛ **ἐρημ-όω**, *strip bare, desolate, lay waste*, ἱερὰ θεῶν Th.3.58; τὴν χώραν And.3.21; πλοῦτον Lxx *Si.*21.4; ὁ κτίζων καὶ ἐρημῶν θεός *POsl.* 1.105:—Pass., ἐρημωθείσης Κρήτης Hdt.7.171; πόλεις ἠρημώθησαν Th.1.23; μιᾷ ὥρᾳ ἠρημώθη ὁ τοσοῦτος πλοῦτος *Apoc.*18.17. II. *bereave* one *of* a thing, c. dupl. acc., ἐ. τινὰ εὐφροσύνας μέρος Pi.*P.*3. 97: c. acc. et gen., ἀνδρῶν ἐ. ἑστίαν Id.*I.*4(3).17; ἐ. ναυβατῶν ἐρετμά *to leave* the oars *without* men, E.*Hel.*1609; ἑαυτὸν ἐρημοῖς (sc. φίλων) Pl.*Alex.*39:—Pass., *to be bereft of*, ἀνδρῶν Hdt.1.164; συμμάχων Id. 7.174; Μίλητος Μιλησίων ἠρήμωτο Id.6.22; ἄρσενος θρόνου A.*Ag.* 260; πατρός E.*Andr.*805; τὰ ἐρημούμενα φυλακῆς *left without*, X.*Eq. Mag.*4.18. 2. *set free, deliver from*, Διὸς ἄλσος ἠρήμωσε λέοντος E. *HF*360(lyr.); Ἀσίαν Περσικῶν ὅπλων Plu.*Cim.*12:—Pass., πνεῦμα ὀσμῶν ἐρημωθέν *being free from*.., Pl.*Ti.*66e. III. *abandon, desert*, ἑὸν χῶρον Pi.*P.*4.269; τάξιν ἠρήμου θανών A.*Pers.*298, cf. E.*Andr.*314, Pl.*Lg.*865e; ἐ. Συρακούσας *to evacuate* it, Th.5.4; τόνδ' ἐρημώσασ' ὄχον *having left* it *empty*, by stepping out of it, A.*Ag.*1070:—Pass., [πόλιν] ἐρημοῦσθαι ὑπὸ τῶν πατρικίων D.H.11.9. IV. *leave alone, keep isolated*, A.*Supp.*516, E.*Med.*90:—Pass., ὄνοι ἐρημωθέντες τοῦ ὁμίλου *being isolated from*.., Hdt.4.135. **-ωσις**, εως, ἡ, *making desolate*, Lxx *Le.*26.34, al., Heph.Astr.1.21; χωρίου Arr.*An.*1.9.7; βδέλυγμα τῶν ἐ. Lxx *Da.*9.27, cf. *Ev.Matt.*24.15. **-ωτής**, οῦ, ὁ, *desolator*, θῆρα Μακηδονίας *AP*6.115 (Antip.).

**ἐρηρέδᾰται, -ατο**, v. ἐρείδω. **ἐρήριμμαι**, v. ἐρείπω. **ἐρήρισται**, v. ἐρίζω.

***ἐρής** (nom. not found), *son, child*, gen. pl. ἐρέων, dat. pl. ἔρεσσι Puchstein *Epigr.Gr.*p.76; acc. pl. ἐρέας, dat. pl. ἐρέεσφι, = τέκνα, τέκνοις (Thess.), Hsch.

⊛ **ἐρητύω**, Dor. **ἐρᾱτύω**, impf. ἐρήτυον (without augm.) Il.18.503, Ion. -ύεσκον A.R.1.1301, Q.S.11.341: fut. -ύσω A.R.1.296, (κατ-) S.*Ph.*1416(anap.): aor. 1 opt. ἐρητύσειε Il.1.192, imper. ἐρήτυσον E. *Ph.*1260, Iterat. ἐρητύσασκε Il.2.189, 11.567, Theoc.25.75:—Pass. (v. infr.). [ῠ before a vowel, unless it be a long syll., as ἐρητῡοντο μένοντες Il.8.345 (exc. ἐρατύει [ῠ] S.*OC*164(lyr.)); long before σ, and in 3 pl. aor. 1 Pass. ἐρήτῡθεν.]:—Ep. Verb (used twice in Trag.), *restrain, check*, κήρυκες δ' ἄρα λαὸν ἐρήτυον Il.18.503; ἐρητύσασκε φάλαγγας 11.567; ἐπέεσσιν ἐρήτυε φῶτα ἕκαστον 2.164, cf. Od.9.493; ἐρητύσειέ τε θυμόν Il.1.192; πολλὰ κέλευθος ἐρατύει a long road *parts* us, S.*OC* l. c. (ἐρατύοι Musgr.):—Med., ἐρητύοντό τε λαόν Il.15.723:—Pass., παρὰ νηυσὶν ἐρητύοντο μένοντες 8.345; ἐρητύετ' ἐν φρεσὶ θυμός 9.462; ἐρήτυθεν (3 pl.) δὲ καθ' ἕδρας 2.99, 211. 2. later c. gen., *to keep away from*, τέκνα δεινῆς ἁμίλλης E.*Ph.*1260; [κύνας] ὑλαγμοῦ Theoc.25.75; τινὰ κακότητος A.R.1.296:—Pass., c. inf., ναυτιλίης ..ἐρητύοντο μέλεσθαι Id.2.835. 3. c. inf., *prevent*, ἐ. τινὰ μίμνειν Nonn.*D*.14.63.

**ἔρι**, τό, indecl. form of ἔριον, *wool*, Philet.19.

**ἐρῐ-**, insepar. Particle, like ἀρι-, used as a prefix to strengthen the sense of a word, *very, much*; mostly Ep. and Lyr.

**ἐρι-αύχην**, ενος, ὁ, ἡ, *with arched neck*, opp. βυσαύχην, ἐριαύχενες ἵπποι Il.10.305, al., never in Od. **-αχθής**, ές, (ἔριον, ἄχθος) *laden with wool, woolly*, or (ἐρι-, ἄχθος) *heavy-laden*, ποίμνη Max.520. **-βόας**, ου, ὁ, *loud-shouting*, of Bacchus, Pi.*Fr.*75.10; of Hermes, *AP*15. 27.5 (Besant.).

**ἐρίβοια**· νύξ· καὶ μεγάλως τιμωμένη, Hsch.

**ἐρί-βομβος**, ον, *loud-buzzing*, μέλισσαι Orph.*Fr.*154, 189. **-βους**, etym. of Ἠερίβοια, Eust.562.40. **-βρεμέθων**, οντος, = sq., prob. in *Hymn.Is.*166. **-βρεμέτης**, ου, Ep. εω, ὁ, *loud-thundering*, Ζεύς Il.13.624; of Aeschylus, Ar.*Ra.*814(hex.); Διόνυσος D.P.578, etc.; *loud-roaring*, λέοντες Pi.*I.*4(3).46; *loud-sounding*, αὐλός *AP*6.195 (Arch.). **-βρεμής**, ές, = ἐρίβρομος, τρίπους ib.344. **-βρῑθής**, ές, *very heavy*, Opp.*H.*5.636. **-βρομος**, ον, *loud-shouting*, of Bacchus, *h.Bacch.*56, Anacr.11, Panyas.13.2; *loud-roaring*, λέοντες Pi.*O.*11(10).21; χθών, νεφέλα, Id.*P.*6.3, 11. **-βρύχης** [ῡ], ου, Ep. εω, ὁ, = sq., ταῦρος Hes.*Th.*832; σῦς B.5.116; πόντος, λέων, Opp.*H.*1.476, 709. ⊛ **-βρῡχος**, ον, *loud-bellowing*, λέων Q.S.3.171; *loud-braying*, of the trumpet, *AP*6.159(Antip. Sid.). **-βῶλαξ**, ᾰκος, ὁ, ἡ, *with large clods*, of rich, loamy soil: hence, *very fertile*, once in Od., ἐριβώλακος ἠπείροιο 13.235; freq. in Il., ἐν Φθίῃ ἐριβώλακι 1. 155, etc.; γαῖα Orph.*L.*655; πόλεως ἐ. Cratin.56. **-βωλος**, ον, = foreg., Od.5.34, Il.21.154, al.; ἄρουραι *h.Cer.*471. **-βωτος** (-βωλος cod.), = μεγαλόψοφος (i.e. ἐριβόητος), Hsch. **-γάστωρ**, ορος, ὁ, ἡ, *pot-bellied*, μόσχοι Nic.*Al.*344. **-γδουπέω**, *rattle loud*, coined by Sch. Il.6.507. **-γδουπος**, ον, = ἐρίδουπος (q. v.), *loud-sounding, thundering*, in Hom. epith. of Zeus, Διὸς υἱὸν ἐριγδούποιο Il.5.672; ἐ. πόσις Ἥρης Od.15.112; exc. in Il.11.152 ἐ. πόδες ἵππων; so after Hom., Ναΐδων ἐ. στοναχαί Pi.*Dith.Oxy.*2.12; καλαῦροψ *APl.*4.74; βοείη Nonn.*D.*18.105. **-γηθής**, ές, *very joyful*, Orph.*L.Prooem.* 24. **-γηρυς**, ὁ, ἡ, *loud-speaking*, Hsch. **-γληνος**, ον, *with large eye-balls, full-eyed*, Opp.*C.*1.310.

⊛ **ἔριγμα**, ατος, τό, (ἐρείκω) *bruised beans*, φακῶν ἢ ἐρεβίνθων Hp. *Coac.*621 (pl.):—also ⊛ **ἐρίγμη**, ἡ, Sch.Ar.*Ra.*508.

**ἐρῐδ-αίνω**, impf. ἠρίδαινον Babr.68.3: Ep. aor. 1 ἐρίδηνα A.R.1.89:—Med., Q.S.5.105: Ep. aor. 1 inf. ἐρῑδήσασθαι Il.23.792 (with vv. ll., dub.); elsewh. Hom. uses only pres.: (ἐρίζω):—*wrangle, quarrel*, μετ' ἀνδράσι Od.21.310; αὔτως γάρ ῥ' ἐπέεσσ' ἐριδαίνομεν Il.2.342; νῦν δὲ περὶ πτωχῶν ἐ. Od.18.403; εἰ δὴ σφὼ ἕνεκα θνητῶν ἐ. Il.1.574; εἵνεκα τῆς ἀρετῆς ἐ. we *strive* (as for a prize) for her excellence, Od.2.206: c. dat., Εὖρός τε Νότος τ' ἐριδαίνετον ἀλλήλοιιν..πελεμιζέμεν Il.16.765, cf. A.R.1.89; also ἀντία πάντων..ἐριδαινέμεν οἷος Od.1.79; τι in a thing, Call.*Dian.*262; of war, first in A.R.2.986, etc.:—Med., ποσσὶν ἐριδήσασθαι *compete in* the foot-race, Il.23.792.—Ep. word: also c. acc., τεθυμωμένον ἄνδρα μὴ ἐριδαίνειν (fort. -δμαίνειν) Demetr.Byz. ap.Ath.10.452d; Luc.*Pisc.*6 may be a reminiscence of A.R.1. 89. **-άντης**, ου, ὁ, *wrangler*, Timo 28.2: Ion. gen. pl. ἐριδαντέων Democr.150: Dor. **Ἐριδάντας**, epith. of Heracles at Tarentum, Hsch.

**ἐρί-δηλος**, ον, = ἀρίδηλος, Hdn.*Epim.*185.

**ἐριδίαν**· ἅμαξα, Hsch.; cf. ἐριωδία.

**Ἐριδίμιος**, ὁ, epith. of Zeus at Rhodes, Hsch. (Cf. Ἐρεθίμιος.)

**ἐριδῑνής**, ές, (δῖνος) *whirling, eddying swiftly*, Tryph.231 (v.l. περιδ-).

⊛ **ἐρίδιον**, τό [-ῑδ- Luc.*Ocyp.*89], Dim. of ἔριον, Heliod.ap.Orib.46. 19.4, Sor.1.82, Luc. l. c., Arr.*Epict.*3.22.71, *PMeyer*20.36 (iii A.D.).

**ἐριδμαίνω**, = ἐρεθίζω, *to provoke to strife, irritate*, σφήκεσσιν ἐοικότες..οὓς παῖδες ἐριδμαίνωσιν Il.16.260. II. intr., = ἐριδαίνω, *contend*, A.R.3.94; of friendly rivalry, Mosch.2.69; διά τι *APl.*4.297; ἐριδμαίνεσκε χροιῆς ὕπερ Nic.*Al.*407; περὶ νίκης Nonn.*D.*37.490: c. inf., φιλήματος ἄκρα φέρεσθαι Theoc.12.31. 2. c. dat., *contend against*, Nonn.*D.*7.355, al.

**ἐρί-δμᾱτος**, ον, (δέμω) *strongly-built*, i.e. *immovable, unconquerable*, ἔρις ἐ. A.*Ag.*1461(lyr.). **-δουπος**, ον, = ἐρίγδουπος, in Hom. always of things and places, ἀκταί, ποταμοί, Il.20.50, Od.10.515; αἴθουσα Il.24.323, Od.20.176; *resounding*, ἀκοή Emp.4.11. **-δωρος**, ον, *rich in gifts, abundant*, ὀπώρη Opp.*C.*3.504. **-έμπορος**, ὁ, *wool-merchant*, *PTeb.*103.26 (i B.C.), *Sammelb.*3965.

⊛ **ἐρίζω**, Dor. 3 pl. ἐρίζοντι Pi.*N.*5.39; Ep. inf. ἐριζέμεναι, -έμεν, Il. 1.277, 23.404: impf. ἤριζον D.9.11, Dor. ἔρισδον Theoc.6.5, Ep. ἔριζον Il.2.555, Ion. ἐρίζεσκον Od.8.225, Crates Theb.1.3: fut. ἐρίσω *Ev.Matt.*12.19, (δι-) App.*BC*5.127 codd., Dor. ἐρίξω Pi.*Fr.*11: aor. 1 ἤρῐσα Hes.*Th.*928, Lys.2.42, poet. ἔρισα Pi.*I.*8(7).30, ἔριξα Id.*Pae.* 6.87; Ep. opt. ἐρίσσειε Il.3.223; Dor. part. ἐρίξαντες *Tab.Heracl.*2. 26: pf. ἤρῐκα Plb.3.91.7:—Med., Ep. impf. ἐρίζετο Hes.*Th.*534: aor.

subj. ἐρίσσεται Od.4.80:—Pass., Ep. pf. ἐρήρισμαι (in act. sense), v. infr.: (ἔρις):—*strive, wrangle, quarrel*, διαστήτην ἐρίσαντε Il.1.6, etc.; τὸ δίκαιον οὐκ ἔχει λόγον δυοῖν ἐρίζειν S.*El.*467: c. dat., Hes.*Th.* 928, Pi.*Pae.*l.c., etc.; ἀλλήλοις Od.18.277; ἀντιβίην τινί Il.1.277; ἀντία τοῖς ἀγαθοῖς Pi.*P.*4.285; πρὸς θεόν ib.2.88; πρός τινα περί τινος Plu.*Tim.*14; ὅς ποτ' Ἀθαναίαν ἔριν ἤρισε Theoc.5.23; πρὸς πᾶν τὸ λεγόμενον Hdt.7.50; περί τινος about a thing, Il.12.423, al.; περὶ μικρῶν ἀκριβῶς ἐ. Isoc.2.39: folld. by a relat., ἐ. ὅστις ἀρείων Theoc.5.67; ὁπότερος γενναιότερος Pl.*Ly.*207c: c. inf., *contend* that.., ἤριζον οἱ πολλοὶ οὐ λυσιτελήσειν τὴν πάροδον D.9.11: abs., of *sophistical disputations*, opp. διαλέγεσθαι, ἀμφισβητεῖν, Pl.*R.*454a, *Prt.*337b, cf. CratesTheb.1.3; of political *discord*, c. dat., Foed.ap.Th.5.79. 2. *rival, vie with, challenge*, οὐκ ἂν ἔπειτ' Ὀδυσῆΐ γ' ἐρίσσειε βροτὸς ἄλλος Il.3.223; ἐπεὶ σφισιν οὔ τις ἔριζεν Od.8.371: c. acc. rei, *rival* or *contend with* one *in* a thing, οὐδ' εἰ.. Ἀφροδίτῃ κάλλος ἐρίζοι Il.9.389, cf. Od.5.213, Hes.*Sc.*5: c. dat. rei, δρηστοσύνῃ οὐκ ἄν μοι ἐρίσσειε βροτὸς ἄλλος in service, Od.15.321; ποσί Il.13.325; γνώμῃ καὶ πλήθει καὶ ἀρετῇ ἐ. τινί Lys.2.42; ἐρίσσειαν περὶ μύθων Il.15.284; ἀθανάτοισιν ἐρίζεσκον περὶ τόξων Od.8.225; τῷ Διῒ πλούτου πέρι Hdt.5.49: c. inf., ἐρίζετον ἀλλήλοιιν χερσὶ μαχέσσασθαι Od.18.38; ἴσα δὲ πίνειν οὔτις οἱ ἀνθρώπων ἤρισεν Phalaec.ap.Ath.10.440e; πρὸς θεούς Pl.*R.*395d; Νέστωρ οἶος ἔριζε N. alone *rivalled* (him), Il.2.555, cf. X.*Cyn.*1.12. II. Med., like Act., ᾧ [τόξῳ] οὔ τίς τοι ἐρίζεται Il.5.172; μοι ἐρίσσεται.. κτήμασιν Od.4.80; ἐρίζετο βουλὰς Κρονίωνι Hes.*Th.*534, cf. Pi.*I.*4(3).29: also in pf. Pass., τῷ οὔ τις ἐρήρισται κράτος Hes.*Fr.*195. 2. Pass., ταχυτὰς ποδῶν ἐρίζεται *there are contests in* fleetness of foot, Pi.*O.*1.95.

**ἐρί-ζωος**, ον, = πάνυ ζῶν, Hsch. **-ήκοος**, ον, (ἀκοή) *sharp of hearing*, λεπτῆς ἀϋτῆς Orph.*L.*468. **-ηρά**, ἡ, (ἔριον) *tax on wool*, *Arch.Pap.*1.552. **-ηρος**, ον, as epith. of ἑταῖρος, perh. *faithful, trusty* (μεγάλως τιμώμενοι κτλ., Hsch.), ἐ. ἑταῖρος, in sg., only in Il. 4.266: elsewh. always in heterocl. pl. ἐρίηρες ἑταῖροι, acc. ἐρίηρας ἑταίρους or ἑτάρους ἐρίηρας, Od.9.100, Il.3.47, etc.; parodied by Cratin. 143; ἐρίηρος ἀοιδός *loyal* to his master's house, Od.1.346, al. **-ηχής**, ές, (ἠχέω) *loud-sounding*, Opp.*H.*3.213.

**ἐριθάκη**, ἡ, *bee-bread*, Arist.*HA*554ᵃ17, 627ᵃ22, Varr.*RR*3.16, Plin. *HN*11.17. 2. *soft parts* of crustaceans, *entrails* of pigs, Hsch.

**ἐρῑθάκίς**, ίδος, ἡ, = ἔριθος (ἡ), *a female day-labourer*, Theoc.3.35.

⊛ **ἐρίθᾰκος**, ὁ, *robin-redbreast, Erithacus rubecula*, Arist.*HA*592ᵇ22, *Gp.*15.1.22, etc.; cf. ἐριθεύς, ἐρίθυλος: —the bird described as imitative by Porph.*Abst.*3.4 must be different.

**ἐρῑθᾰκώδης**, ες, *full of* ἐριθάκη 2, γραῖαι Epich.61.

**ἐρι-θᾰλής**, ές, (θάλλω) = ἐριθηλής, Limen.6, Hsch. II. Subst. **ἐριθαλές**, τό, *stone-crop, Sedum altissimum*, Plin.*HN*25.160; cf. ἐριθαλίς· εἶδος δένδρου, Hsch.; dub. l. in Ps.-Dsc.4.88. **-θαλλος**, ον, *growing luxuriantly, flourishing*, of plants and trees, Simon.54 (s.v.l.).

**Ἐριθάσεος**, ὁ, title of Apollo in Attica, *IG*2².1362 (iv B.C.): written Ἐρισαθεύς in cod. Hsch. (post ἐριθαλεῖς).

**ἐρῑθ-εία**, ἡ, *labour for wages*, Hsch. (pl.), Suid. II. *canvassing for public office, intriguing*, Arist.*Pol.*1302ᵇ4, 1303ᵃ14 (pl.). 2. *selfish* or *factious ambition*, ζῆλος καὶ ἐ. *Ep.Jac.*3.14; οἱ ἐξ -είας *Ep. Phil.*1.17; pl., *intrigues, party squabbles*, *Ep.Gal.*5.20. ⊛ **-εύομαι**, Dep., (ἔριθος) *serve, work for hire*, Lxx *To.*2.11:—so in Act., Hld.1.5. II. of public officers or characters, *canvass, intrigue for office*, οἱ ἐριθευόμενοι Arist.*Pol.*1303ᵃ16; cf. ἐξεριθεύομαι. 2. later Act., generally, *compete with*, τινι Sch.S.*Aj.*833: abs., *indulge in petty intrigue*, Eust.1162.23. **-εύς**, έως, ὁ, = ἐρίθακος, Thphr.*Sign.*39, Arat 1025. ⊛ **-ευτός**, Cret. **-εοτός**, ή, όν, *corrupt*, δίκα *SIG*526.26 (Itanos, iii B.C.).

⊛ **ἐρίθεχνα**, τά, *for wool-work* (?), ἔρια κηρίθεκνα ϝεργαλεῖα dub. in *Schwyzer*180 (Crete): more prob. χηρίτεχνα, = χειρίτεχνα.

**ἐρῑθηλής**, ές, (θάλλω) *very flourishing, luxuriant*, of plants, μυρίκης τ' ἐριθηλέας ὄζους Il.10.467; ἔρνος.. ἐριθηλὲς ἐλαίης 17.53; δάφνης ἐριθηλέος ὄζον Hes.*Th.*30; of gardens, ἀλωάων ἐριθηλέων Il.5.90; γαῖα A.R.2.723: metaph., εὐνομία *APl.*4.72.5, cf. Orph.*Fr.*142, 206.

**Ἐρίθιος**, ὁ, epith. of Apollo in Cyprus, Ptol.Heph.ap.Phot.*Bibl.* p.153 B.

⊛ **ἔρῑθος**, ὁ, ἡ, *day-labourer, hired servant*; of *mowers* or *reapers*, Il. 18.550, 560; later ἔριθοι, αἱ, *spinsters* and *weavers, workers in wool* (prob. because popularly derived from ἔριον), D.57.45, Theoc.15.80; ἐρίων ἔριθοι *PHib.*1.121.34 (iii B.C.); of spiders, πάντα δ' ἐρίθων ἀραχνᾶν βρίθει S.*Fr.*286, cf. Philostr.*Im.*2.28. II. metaph., *servant, minister*, τλήμων γαστρὸς ἔριθος, = *crepitus ventris*, *h.Merc.*296; Ἔρις .. Νίκης κασιγνήτη καὶ ἔ. Timo 21.2; ὕπνον νυκτὸς ἔ. Epic.Anon. in *BKT*5(1)p.70.

**ἐρίθυλος**, ὁ, = ἐρίθακος, Sch.Ar.*V.*922.

**ἐρί-θῡμος**, ον, *high-spirited*, Q.S.1.742, Orph.*Fr.*270. **-θυρίς**, Aeol. **ἔρθυρις**· ἡ μεγάλη θυρίς, *EM*377.35.

**ἐρικάνην**· φραγμόν, Hsch.:—also **ἐρικέα**· φράγματα, and **ἐρίκεος**· φραγμοῦ, Id. (Perh. to be connected with ἐρκάνη, ἕρκος.)

**ἐρῑκεῖν**, v. ἐρείκω. **ἐρικευθές**· πυθμήν, Hsch.

**ἐρίκ-η**, **-ηρόν**, etc., later spellings of ἐρείκ-η, -ηρόν, etc.

**ἐρι-κλάγκτης**, ου, ὁ, (κλάζω) *loud-sounding*, γόος Pi.*P.*12.21. **-κλαυτος**, ον, *much-weeping*, γονεῖς *AP*7.560 (Paul. Sil.); πένθος *Epigr.Gr.*406.8 (Iconium). II. Pass., *much-wept, bewailed*, Opp. *H.*2.668 (-κλαυστ-), Epic.Anon. in *BKT*5(1) p.85. **-κλῠτός**, όν, *much-renowned*, cj. for ἀγακλυτός, Orph.*A.*1030.

**ἐρῑκόεις**, later spelling of ἐρεικόεις.

**ἐρικός**, ή, όν, *woollen*, *PRev.Laws* 103.2 (iii B.C.).

**ἐρικτέᾰνος**, ον, *wealthy*, Opp.*C.*1.312.

**ἐρικτός**, ή, όν, v. ἐρεικτός.

⊛ **ἐρί-κτῠπος**, ον, *loud-sounding*, of Poseidon, Hes.*Th.*456, 930. **-κῡδής**, ές, *very famous, glorious*, of gods and their descendants, Il. 14.327, Od.11.576, 631; of their gifts, θεῶν ἐ. δῶρα Il.3.65, 20.265; ἥβη ἐ. 11.225, Hes.*Th.*988; νίκα B.12.190: generally, ἐ. δαίς *a splendid* banquet, Il.24.802, Od.3.66, al.; of places and men, ἄστυ Orac.ap.Hdt.7.220; θεῶν ἐ. οἶκοι Theoc.17.108; φῶτες Orph.*L.*302: Sup. -έστατος, Ἰάμβλιχος Eun.*VS* p.461 B. **-κύμων** [ῡ], ον, (κύω) *big with young*, ἐ. φέρματι γένναν A.*Ag.*119 codd. recc. (ἐρικύματα cod. Med.). **-λαμπέτις**, ἡ, pecul. fem. of sq., Max.103. **-λαμπής**, ές, *bright-shining*, σοφίη Procl.*H.*4.13.

**ἐρίμη**· ἔξοδος, Hsch. (Cf. ἐξίθμη, ἐρμή.)

**ἐρι-μύκης** [ῡ], ου, ὁ, = sq., ταῦρος Call.*Fr.*13ᵇ (dub. l.). **-μῡκος**, ον, (μυκάομαι, μέμυκα) *loud-bellowing*, βοῶν ὑπὸ πόσσ' ἐριμύκων Il.20.497, cf. 23.775, Od.15.235, Hes.*Op.*790; ὀλολυγά *AP*6.219.17 (Antip.).

**ἐρῑν-άζω**, aor. 1 inf. ἐρινάξαι and ἐρινάσαι, Hsch.:—*hang fruiting branches of the wild fig* (ἐρινεός) *near the cultivated fig* (συκῆ) in order that the gall-insect (ψήν) which lives in the wild fruit may carry pollen to the σῦκον, Thphr.*CP*2.9.5:—Pass., τὸ ἐρινασμένον *the fig subjected to caprification*, Id.*HP*2.8.3. II. *gather wild figs*, Poll. 7.143. **-άς**, άδος, ἡ, = ἐρινεός, Nic.*Th.*854. II. = ὄλυνθος, Amer.ap.Ath.3.76e (ἐρίνακας codd.), Hsch. **-άς**· νέας βοῦς, Id. **-ασμός**, ὁ, *caprification*, Thphr.*CP*2.9.5, *HP*2.8.1. **-αστός**, ή, όν, *subjected to caprification*, Id.*CP*2.9.12. **-εόν**, τό, *fruit of the* ἐρινεός, Hp.*Loc.Hom.*47: pl., ἐρινεά *PCair.Zen.*33.12 (iii B.C.), v.l. in Arist.*HA*557ᵇ28. **-εός**, ὁ, *wild fig-tree, Ficus Caprificus*, Il.6.433, al., Hes.*Fr.*160, Arist.*HA*557ᵇ25, Thphr.*HP*2.2.4: Att. **ἐρινεώς** Lync.ap.Ath.3.75d; ἐρινεῶν ἕνα χαλκοτόν *BCH*35.16 (Delos). 2. = ἐρινεόν, Arist.*HA*557ᵇ25, Dsc.1.128. 3. = ἔρινος, v.l. in Diocl.*Fr.*149 (= Sch.Nic.*Th.*647). II. Adj. **ἐρινεός**, ά, όν, contr. **-οῦς**, ῆ, οῦν, *of the wild fig-tree*, ἐρινεὸν σῦκον, = ἐρινεόν, Arist. *HA*554ᵃ15; ἐρινῶν σύκων Ath.3.76c (quoting ἐρινοῖς fr. Epich.128); κράδαις ἐριναῖς E.*Fr.*679.

⊛ **ἐρίνεος** [ῐ], α, ον, Ion. also **εἰρίνεος**, η, ον, *woollen*, κιθών, εἵματα, πῖλοι εἰρ., Hdt.1.195, 2.81, 4.73; τρυχία, προσκεφάλαιον, Hp.*Art.*78, *Fract.*16 (ἐρ- codd., but εἰρ- *Acut.*21); cf. Att. ἐρεοῦς.

**ἐρῑν-εώδης**, ες, *full of wild fig-trees*, Str.13.1.35. **-εώς**, εώ, ὁ, v. ἐρινεός I. 1. **-όν**, τό, *wild fig*, ἐρίν' ἀπέδοτο, σῦκα πωλεῖν ὀμνύων Alex.128.8, cf. Thphr.*HP*2.8.2, v.l. in Arist.*HA*557ᵇ28: read by Aristarch. in Od.5.281. **-ός**, ὁ, = ἐρινεός, *wild fig-tree*, Stratt.42, Theoc.25.250, Lyc.741, *IG*11(2).287*A*153 (Delos, iii B.C.), *Inscr. Délos*353*A*37 (iii B.C.), v.l. in Arist.*HA*557ᵇ31. 2. = ἐρινόν, *a wild fig*, πέπων ἐ. S.*Fr.*181; ὀπόεντας ἐ. Nic.*Al.*319.

**ἔρινος**, ὁ, a plant like *basil*, Nic.*Th.*647, cf. Diocl.*Fr.*149. 2. = ἐπιμήδιον, Ps.-Dsc.4.19, v.l. for ἐχῖνος, Dsc.4.141, cf. Paul.Aeg.7.3.

⊛ **Ἐρῑνύς** (so, not Ἐριννύς, in best codd. and Inscrr., cf. *Tab.Defix.*108 (iii/ii B.C.), *IG*12(3).367 (Thera); later Ἐρεινύας ib.12(9).1179.34 (Euboea, ii A.D.)), gen. ύος, ἡ: pl. Ἐρινύες, acc. Ἐρινῦς Od.2.135, etc.; gen. pl. Ἐρινύων trisyll., E.*IT*931, 970. [ῡ in trisyll. cases (nom. sg. -ῦς E.*Med.*1389 (anap.), but acc. sg. -ὺν ib.1260 (lyr., s.v.l.)), ῠ in quadrisyll.]:—*the Erinys*, an avenging deity, ἠεροφοῖτις Ἐ. Il.9.571, 19.87; δασπλῆτις Ἐ. Od.15.234: more freq. in pl., μήτηρ στυγερὰς ἀρήσετ' Ἐρινῦς 2.135, etc.; Γαῖα.. γείνατ' Ἐρινῦς Hes.*Th.*185; later three in number, μίαν τριῶν Ἐ. E.*Tr.*457 (troch.), cf. Apollod.1.1.4, etc.; avengers of perjury, homicide, unfilial conduct, etc., Il.19.259, 9.454; upholders of the natural and moral order, ἥλιος οὐχ ὑπερβήσεται μέτρα· εἰ δὲ μή, Ἐρινύες μιν Δίκης ἐπίκουροι ἐξευρήσουσιν Heraclit.94; Ἐρινύες ἔσχεθον αὐδήν (sc. of the horse of Achilles, as rebuking presumption), Il.19.418: com., Ἐρινύων ἀπορρώξ, of Timon, Ar.*Lys.*811 (lyr.). II. in less personal sense, *guilt, punishment invoked* upon the guilty, freq. c. gen., μητρὸς Ἐρινύες *curses from* one's mother, Il.21.412, Od.11.280; τείσαιτο ἐρινῦς πατρὸς παίδων τε Hes. *Th.*472; ἱδρύσαντο Ἐρινύων τῶν Λαΐου τε καὶ Οἰδιπόδεω ἱρόν Hdt.4. 149; Ἀρά τ' Ἐρινὺς πατρὸς ἡ μεγασθενής A.*Th.*70, cf. S.*OC*1434, etc.; later in Prose, ξενικαὶ Ἐ. Pl.*Ep.*357a; ἐρινῦς καὶ ποινὰς τῶν δι' ἐκεῖνον ἠτυχηκότων Plb.23.10.2; of persons in whom such powers are embodied, νυμφόκλαυτος Ἐ. A.*Ag.*749 (lyr.); ἔτεκε νύμφα δόμοις Ἐ. S.*Tr.*895 (lyr.), cf. E.*Med.*1260 (lyr.), etc.; φρενῶν Ἐρινύς *frenzy* of the soul, S.*Ant.*603 (lyr.); Ἐρινὺν ἐπορθιάζειν raise a *Fury-song*, A.*Ag.*1119. III. epith. of Demeter in Arcadia, Antim.28, Call. *Fr.*207, Paus.8.25.6. IV. = Ἀφροδίτης εἴδωλον, Hsch. (Derived from Arc. ἐρινύειν, = θυμῷ χρῆσθαι, by Paus. l.c.)

**ἐρῑνύω**, v. foreg. ad fin.

**Ἐρῑνῠώδης**, ες, *like the* Ἐρινύες, Plu.2.458c; συκοφαντίαι ib.602e.

**ἐρίξας**, v. ἐρείκω. **ἐριοῖ**· ἐργάζεται, Hsch.

⊛ **ἐριο-κάρτης**, ου, ὁ, (κείρω) *shearer*, *PFlor.*71.438, al. (iv A.D.); perh. cf. ἐριωκαίτης, ἐριωκέδης, *PTeb.*401.1, 16 (i A.D.). **-κόμος**, ὁ, = ἐριουργός, Hdn.*Philet.*p.449 P.; cf. εἰροκόμος.

⊛ **ἔριον**, τό, Ion. **εἴριον** *GDI* iv p.876 (Chios, iv B.C., also written ἔρια ibid.), Hdt., Hp., and always in Hom. (indicating ἐρϝ-) exc. gen. ἐρίοιο in Od.4.124:—*wool*, Il.12.434, Od. l.c., Pl.*Smp.*175d; ἐρίῳ στέψαντες, i.e. with woollen fillets, Id.*R.*398a, etc.: freq. in pl., Il. 3.388, Od.18.316; εἴρια ῥυπαρά, ἔρια οἰσυπηρά, greasy wool, Hp. *Fract.*21, Dsc.2.74; ἔρια καθαρά *PCair.Zen.*12.62 (iii B.C.); τἄρια, crasis for τὰ ἔ., Ar.*Ra.*1387; οὖλα ἔρια ib.1067; ἔ. πεπταμένα outspread *flocks of wool*, Id.*Nu.*343; ἐρίων τάλαντον Id.*V.*1147; τὰ Μιλήσια ἔ. Eub.90.3, cf. Amphis 27.1; ἔρια ἀπὸ ξύλου *cotton*, Hdt.3.

47, cf. 106; τὸ ἔ. [τῆς ἀράχνης] a spider's *web*, Philostr.*Im.*2.28; τὰ ἐκ τῆς θαλάττης ἔ., of the *byssus* of the pinna, Alciphr.1.2. (ἔρια *Schwyzer* 180 (Crete) without initial ϝ-; Lat. *vervex* perh. not cogn.)

⊛**ἐριό-ξῠλον**, τό, *cotton*, Ulp.ap.*Dig.*32.70.9; cf. ἐρεόξ-. **-πλύτης** [ῠ], ου, ὁ, (πλύνω) *wool-cleaner, fuller*, Dsc.2.163, *BGU* 118 iii 7 (ii A.D.); ἡ ἐργασία τῶν ἐ. *IGRom.*4.821 (Hierapolis). **-πωλέω**, *sell* or *deal in wool*, Poll.7.28. ⊛ **-πώλης**, ου, ὁ, *a dealer in wool*, Critias 70 D., Poll.7.28, *PLips.*14.6 (iv A.D.); cf. ἐρεοπώλης. **-πωλικῶς**, Adv. *like a wool-dealer, roguishly*, Ar.*Ra.*1386. **-πώλιον**, τό, *woolshop*, in pl., Zeno *Stoic.*1.58, J.*BJ*5.8.1. **-ραβδιστής**, οῦ, ὁ, *wool-beater*, *Stud.Pal.*4 p.70 (i A.D.). **-στεπτος**, ον, (στέφω) *wreathed in wool*, κλάδοι A.*Supp.*22 (anap., Auratus for ἱεροστ-).

**ἐριούνης**, ὁ, v. sq.

⊛**ἐριούνιος** and **ἐριούνης**, ὁ, Ep. epith. of Hermes, of uncertain meaning, σῶκος ἐριούνιος Ἑρμῆς Il.20.72; Ἑρμείας ἐριούνιος 24.457, 679; ἐριούνης Ἑρμείας 20.34, Od.8.322; Διὸς ἐριούνιος υἱός *h.Merc.* 28; θεῶν ἐριούνιε δαῖμον ib.551: abs., ἐριούνιος, i.e. Hermes, Il.24. 360,440; Ἑρμῆς ἐ., opp. δόλιος, Ar.*Ra.*1144, cf. *EM*374.24; also in later Prose, θεοί Ant.Lib.25.2. II. as Adj., ἐ. νόος Orph.*L.*199.

**ἐριουργ-εῖον**, τό, *wool-factory*, Poll.7.28. **-έω**, *work in wool*, X.*HG*5.4.7, *Lac.*1.3, etc. **-ία**, ἡ, *wool-working*, Poll.7.28, Sor.1. 4 (pl.). **-ικός**, ή, όν, *for wool-work*, [σφόνδυλος] ib.110. ⊛ **-ός**, όν, *working in wool*, D.C.79.7: as Subst., *wool-worker*, Gal.10.11, *PRyl.*94.14 (i A.D.), Ath.14.618e; ἡ ἱερὰ φυλὴ τῶν ἐ., at Philadelphia, *IGRom.*4.1632.28.

**ἐριοῦς**, v. ἐρεοῦς.

**ἐριο-ῠφάντης**, ου, ὁ, *weaver of wool*, *PTeb.*5.239 (ii B.C.). **-φόρος**, ον, *wool-bearing*, δένδρον *cotton*-tree, *Gossypium arboreum*, Thphr. *HP*4.7.7 (pl.); ἐ. βολβός, *Pancratium maritimum*, ib.7.13.8.

**ἐριπεῖν**, v. ἐρείπω. **ἔριπες**· δαλοί, Hsch. **ἐρίπεσθαι**· φθίνειν (φθονεῖν cod.), Id.

**ἐρίπλευρος**, ον, *with sturdy sides, stout*, φυά Pi.*P.*4.235.

⊛ **ἐρίπνη**, ἡ, (ἐρείπω) *broken cliff, crag*, in pl., E.*El.*210 (lyr.), A.R.1. 581, 2.1247, etc.: sg., Nic.*Th.*22; any *sheer ascent*, ἐπάλξεων ἐρίπναι E.*Ph.*1168.

**ἐρίπνοος**, ον, *blowing strongly*, Lyr. in *Philol.*80.338.

**ἐριπόω**, = ἐρείπω, *EM*374.32.

⊛ **ἐριπτοίητος**, ον, *much scared*, Nonn.*D.*28.13.

**ἐρίπτω**, = ἐρείπω, *EM*374.34, Sch.Il.14.15.

**ἔρις** (A), ιδος, ἡ, acc. ἔριν Od.3.136, etc.; also ἔριδα, usu. in Ep.: pl. ἔριδες, later ἔρεις *Ep.Tit.*3.9, etc.:—*strife, quarrel, contention*: I. in Il., mostly of *battle-strife*, αἰεὶ γάρ τοι ἔ. τε φίλη πόλεμοί τε μάχαι τε 1.177; μεμαυῖ' ἔριδος καὶ ἀϋτῆς 5.732, cf. 13.358; κακὴ ἔ. 3.7; ἔ. πτολέμοιο 14.389, al.; reversely, ἔριδος νεῖκος 17.384; ἔριδα ξυνάγοντες Ἄρηος 5.861; ἔριδι or ἐξ ἔριδος μάχεσθαι, 1.8, 7.111; ἔριδι ξυνιέναι 20.66, 21.390; later, τὰν Ἀδράστου τάν τε Καδμείων ἔριν Pi.*N.*8.51; ἔρις ἐνόπλιος Gorg.*Fr.*6 D. II. generally, *quarrel, strife*, ἔρις θυμοβόρος Il.20.253, etc.: less freq. in pl., ἔριδας καὶ νείκεα ib.251: freq. of political or domestic *discord*, φόνοι, στάσεις, ἔρις, μάχαι S.*OC*1234 (lyr.); ἔριδες, νείκη, στάσις,.. πόλεμος Ar.*Th.*788; ἔριδος ἀγών S.*Aj.* 1163 (anap.); ὅταν φίλοι φίλοισι συμβάλωσ' ἔριν E.*Med.*521; ἔριν περί τινος ἐκφυγεῖν Pl.*Lg.*736c; λύειν, κατασβέσαι, E.*Ph.*81, S.*OC*422; γενέσθαι ἔριν πρὸς σφᾶς αὐτούς Th.6.31: with Preps., ἐς ἔριν ἐλθεῖν τινι Hdt.9.33, cf. Ar.*Ra.*877 (hex.); ἀφῖχθαι, ἐμπεσεῖν, E.*IA*319 (troch.), 377; ἐν πολλῇ ἔριδι εἶναι Th.2.21; ἐν ἔριδι εἶναι πρὸς ἀλλήλους Id.6.35; ὑπὲρ τοῦ μέλλοντος δι' ἐρίδων ἦν Plu.*Caes.*33: c. inf., εἰσῆλθε τοῖν τρὶς ἀθλίοιν ἔρις.. ἀρχῆς λαβέσθαι S.*OC*372. 2. *wordy wrangling, disputation*, ἐκ τῆς ἔριδος.. ἐμάχοντο Hdt.1.82; κοινὸν λόγον δώσοντες ἀλλήλοις ἔριν E.*Ba.*715; ἐγένετο ἔρις τοῖς ἀνθρώποις μὴ λοιμὸν ὠνομάσθαι ἀλλὰ λιμόν Th.2.54; ἦν ἔρις καὶ ἄγνοια εἴτε.. Id.3.111; μεστὸς ἐρίδων καὶ δοξοσοφίας Pl.*Phlb.*49a, cf. *Ti.*88a; ἡ περὶ τὰς ἔριδας φιλοσοφία Isoc.10.6; ἔριδος ἕνεκα Pl.*Sph.*237b; cf. ἐριστικός. III. Personified, *Eris*, a goddess who excites to war, Ἔ. κρατερή Il.20.48; ἐν δ' Ἔ. ἐν δὲ Κυδοιμὸς ὁμίλεον, ἐν δ' ὀλοὴ Κήρ 18.535; Νὺξ.. Ἔριν τέκε καρτερόθυμον Hes.*Th.*225: hence, as goddess of *Discord*, at the marriage of Peleus and Thetis, Coluth.39, al. 2. as a principle of nature, πάντα κατ' ἔριν γίνεσθαι Heraclit.8: pl., Emp.124.2. IV. *contention, rivalry*, freq. in Od., ἔργοιο in work, 18.366; ὅς τις ἔριδα προφέρηται ἀέθλων for prizes, 8.210; ἔρις χερσὶ γένηται 18.13; ἔριδα προφέρουσαι in eager *rivalry*, 6.92; ἔριν στήσαντες ἐν ὑμῖν 16.292: in later Poets, *contest*, καλλονᾶς, μελῳδίας, E.*IA*1308, *Rh.*923; ὅπλων ἔριν ἔθηκε συμμάχοις Id.*Hel.*100; ἔριν ἔχειν ἀμφὶ μουσικῇ Hdt.6.129; Ἥρα Παλλάδι τ' ἔριν μορφᾶς ἁ Κύπρις ἔσχεν E.*IA*183; ἔριν ἐμβάλλειν τισὶ πρὸς ἀλλήλους ὅπως.. X.*Cyr.*6.2.4; εἰς ἔριν ὁρμᾶσθαι ταύτης τῆς μάχης πρὸς τοὺς πεπαιδευμένους ib.2.3.15; εἰς ἔριν συμβάλλειν τινὰς περὶ ἀρετῆς Id.*Lac.*4.2; κατ' ἔριν τὴν Ἀθηναίων out of *rivalry with*.., Hdt.5.88, cf. Pl.*Criti.*109b; ἔβα Πινδάροιο (leg. -οι) ποτ' ἔριν Corinn. 21; Διὸς βρονταῖσιν εἰς ἔριν κτυπῶν in *rivalry with*.., E.*Cyc.*328; in good sense, ἔρις ἀγαθῶν A.*Eu.*975 (lyr.), cf. Hes.*Op.*24.

**ἔρις** (B), = ἶρις, Att., acc. to Hsch. s.v. ἔριδας.

**ἐρίς**, ἡ, perh. *wool-worker*, *PLond.ined.*2172 (ii A.D.).

**Ἐρισαθεύς**, v. Ἐριθάσεος.

**ἐρῑσάλπιγξ**, ιγγος, ὁ, ἡ, *loud-trumpeting*, name of a bird in Sch. Ar.*Av.*884: in Hsch. ἠρισάλπιγξ.

**ἐρισθενής**, ές, *very mighty*, epith. of Zeus, Il.13.54, Od.8.289, Hes. *Th.*4, etc.; also of Poseidon, Id.*Cat.Oxy.*1358 *Fr.*2.27; of men, A.R.1.41, etc.; of the Furies, Orph.*H.*69.7; ἐ. ἕρμα πόληος *Epigr. Gr.*452.11 (Syria); ἐ. θέμεθλα *AP*9.808.6 (Cyrus).

**ἐρισία**, ἡ, = ἔρις, Theognost.*Can.*87.

**ἐρίσκηπτον**, τό, (ἔρις (B), σκήπτω) = ἐρυσίσκηπτρον, Hsch., prob. cj. in Plu.2.664f; *erisceptron* is v.l. in Dsc.1.4, *aerisceptron* in 1.20.

**ἔρισμα**, ατος, τό, (ἐρίζω) *cause of quarrel*, Il.4.38. II. ἐρίσμασιν· εἰρεσίαις, Hsch.

**ἐρισμάρᾰγος** [μᾰ], ον, *loud-thundering*, epith. of Zeus, Hes.*Th.*815, *IGRom.*4.360.13 (Pergam.), etc.; θάλασσα Musae.318; ἀστραπή Luc. *Tim.*1.

**ἐρισμός**, ὁ, = ἔρις, Timo 28.3.

**ἐρί-σπορος**, ον, *well-sown*, αἶα Opp.*C.*2.119. **-στάφῠλος** [ᾰ], ον, of wine, *made of fine grapes*, Od.9.111,358. II. *rich in grapes*, of Lesbos, Archestr.*Fr.*56.9; of Bacchus, *AP*9.580.6, Nonn.*D.*12. 251. **-στέφᾰνος**, ον, *eminently crowned*, epith. of Rhea, *Rev.Ét. Gr.*19.268 (Aphrodisias).

**ἐριστήρ**· μαρσίππιον (-ίππιος cod.), σάκκος, ἢ ἕρκτης καὶ πράκτης, Hsch. (leg. ἐρκτήρ).

**ἐριστ-ής**, οῦ, ὁ, (ἐρίζω) *wrangler*, Lxx *Ps.*138(139).20 (pl., v.l.). **-ικός**, ή, όν, *eager for strife* or *battle*, Sch.E.*IA*588. 2. *involving a contest* (or perh. *debate*), παιδιαί Arist.*Rh.*1371ᵃ1. II. esp. *fond of wrangling* or *arguing, captious*, Pl.*Ly.*211b, etc.; ὁ ἐ. ἐστί πως οὕτως ἔχων πρὸς τὸν διαλεκτικὸν ὡς ὁ ψευδογράφος πρὸς τὸν γεωμετρικόν Arist.*SE*171ᵇ35; οἱ Ἀκαδημιακοὶ τῶν ἄλλων ἐριστικώτεροι Luc.*Pisc.* 43: Sup. **-ώτατος** D.L.2.134; Ἐριστικοί, οἱ, nickname of the Megarian school, ib.106; ἡ **-κὴ** τέχνη *sophistry*, Pl.*Sph.*231e, al.; τὸ **-κόν**, defined as τὸ ἔντεχνον καὶ περὶ δικαίων.. καὶ ἀδίκων ἀμφισβητοῦν ib.225c; τὰ ἐ. Arist.*Rh.*1402ᵃ3; ἐ. συλλογισμός, λόγος, *sophism, fallacy*, Id.*Top.*100ᵇ23, *Metaph.*1012ᵃ19 (pl.); τέχνη ἐριστικῶν, a work of Protagoras, D.L.9.55. Adv. **-κῶς** Pl.*R.*454b, Arist. *Ph.*186ᵃ6. **-ός**, ή, όν, *that may be contested*, τὰ δὲ τοῖς δυνατοῖς οὐκ ἐριστὰ πλάθειν such *contests* cannot *be waged* with the powerful, so as to engage with them, S.*El.*220 (lyr.).

**ἐρισύβη**, ἡ, = ἐρυσίβη, Lxx *De.*28.42, Hsch.

**ἐρι-σφάρᾰγος** [φᾰ], ον, *loud-roaring*, of Poseidon, *h.Merc.*187; of Zeus, Pi.*Fr.*15, B.5.20; *loud-voiced*, of men, Plu.2.698e. **-σφηλος**, ον, *overthrowing much*, of Heracles, Stesich.82.

**ἐρίσχηλος**, ον, = λοίδορος, ἐρισχήλοις κορυνήταις Parth.*Fr.*18; cf. ἐρεσχηλέω.

**ἐρι-ταρβής**, ές, *very timid*, Hsch. ⊛ **-τῑμος**, ον, *highly-prized, precious*, of gold, Il.9.126; of the Aegis, 2.447; τρίποδες *h.Ap.*443, Ar.*Eq.*1016; of persons, Man.3.324; Μοῖραι dub. cj. in *Epigr.Gr.* 248.9; in later Prose, φιλοσοφία Them.*Or.*2.54d; iron., δουλείη *IG* 14.1363. II. as Subst., a fish, prob. a kind of *sardine*, Dorio and Epaenet.ap.Ath.7.328f, Diph.Siph.ib.355f, *PLips.*92.3 [*Arch. Pap.*4.482] (ii/iii A.D.). **-τμητος**, ον, *well-cut*, ἱμάντες Opp.*C.* 4.106.

**ἐριφέας**· χίμαρος, Hsch.

**ἐριφεγγής**, ές, *very brilliant*, Procl.*H.*3.13(7), Man.6.22.

⊛ **ἐρίφειος**, ον, (ἔρῐφος) *of a kid*, Pherecr.130.9, Antiph.222.7, X.*An.* 4.5.31; ζωμός Dieuch.ap.Orib.4.6.1: **Ἐρίφιος**, epith. of Dionysus at Metapontum, Apollod.ap.St.Byz. s.v. Ἀκρώρεια, cf. Hsch.

**ἐριφιήματα**· ἔριφοι (Lacon.), Hsch.

**ἐρίφιον**, τό, Dim. of ἔρῐφος, Athenio 1.30, *Ev.Matt.*25.33, Gal.8. 443, *PLond.*1.113.4, etc. II. = *rubus agrestis*, *Gloss.*

**ἐρι-φλεγής**, ές, *much-flaming*, Nonn.*D.*26.33. **-φλοιος**, ον, *with thick bark*, δρύες, Pergamene wood, Agathocl.ap.Eust.994.42.

⊛ **ἔρῐφος**, ὁ (ἡ, Alc.*Supp.*24.1, *GDI*5029 (Crete)), *kid*, ἀρνεσσιν.. ἢ ἐρίφοισι Il.16.352, cf. 24.262, Od.9.226, Alc. l.c., Orph.*Fr.*32c, etc. II. Ἔριφοι, οἱ, the constellation *Haedi*, Democr.14, Theoc. 7.53 (cf. Sch. ad loc.), Arat.158, Eratosth.*Cat.*13, Chio *Ep.*4.1, Ptol. *Alm.*7.5, etc.

**ἐρῐφοστάσιον** [ᾰ], τό, *fold, pen for kids*, *Gloss.*

**Ἐριφύλλιος**, ὁ, epith. of Apollo and Hermes, Hsch.

**ἐρίφυλλος**, ον, *with many* or *large leaves*, Hsch.

**Ἐριχθόνιος**, ὁ, an Attic hero, A.*Fr.*368, E.*Ion*21, Arist.*Fr.*637, etc.: **Ἐριχθονίδαι**, = Ἐρεχθεῖδαι, *IG*3.771.

**ἐρίχρῡσος**, ον, *rich in gold, wealthy*, βασιλῆες *AP*9.785.

**ἔριψ**· σωμάτιον, Hsch.

**ἐριώδης**, ες, Ion. εἰρι-, *like wool, woolly*, Hp.*Art.*49, Arist.*HA*630ᵃ 30, Thphr.*HP*3.7.4; κιρσοί Orib.45.18.28.

**ἐριωδία**· ἄμαξα, Hsch.; cf. ἐριδίαν, ἐρωδία.

**ἐριώδῡνος**, ον, (ὀδύνη) *very painful*, Max.161, Hsch.

**ἐριώδων**, οντος, ὁ, ἡ, (ὀδούς) *with large teeth*, Hsch.

**ἐριώλη** (on the accent, v. Hdn.Gr.1.324), ἡ, *whirlwind, hurricane*, A.R.1.1132 (prob. cj.), 4.1778; applied to Cleon, Ar.*Eq.*511, with pun on ἔριον, ὀλλύναι, *V.*1148, cf. Dionys.Trag.12.

**ἐριώπης**, ου, ὁ, fem. **-ῶπις**, ιδος, (ὤψ) *large-eyed, full-eyed*, in fem., Hom.*Epigr.*1.2: fem. acc. ἐριώπεα Max.545 (s.v.l.); ἐρίωπα Id.32.

**ἑρκάζειν**· σκώπτειν, Hsch.

**ἑρκάνη**, ἡ, (ἕρκος) *fence, enclosure*, Ael.Dion.*Fr.*179; *stall, pen*, Them.*Or.*23.292a.

**ἑρκατή**· φυλακή, Hsch. **ἕρκατος**· φραγμός, Id.

**ἑρκ-εῖος** (freq. written ἕρκειος in codd.), ον, also α, ον A.*Ch.*653:—*of* or *in the* ἕρκος or *front court*, Ζεὺς Ἑ., as the household god, Od.22. 335, Hdt.6.68, S.*Ant.*487, E.*Tr.*17, Cratin.Jun.9, Pl.*Euthd.*302d, Arist.*Mu.*401ᵃ20: abs., Ἑρκεῖος, ὁ, Paus.4.17.4; also βωμὸς ἑ. Pi. *Pae.*6.114. 2. Ἑρκεῖοι, οἱ, = Lat. *Penates*, D.H.1.67. 3. πύλαι, θύρα ἑ., the gates, door *of the court*, A.*Ch.*561, 571, 653; πρὸς κίον' ἑρκείου στέγης S.*Aj.*108; ἐφ' ἑρκείῳ πυρᾷ E.*Tr.*483. **-ίον**, τό, *fence, enclosure*, αὐλῆς Il.9.476, Od.18.102; ἐξ ἑρκίων καὶ ἐξ οἰκίας ἐκπετόμενος Thphr.*Sign.*53; later, *dwelling*, A.R.2.1073. ⊛ **-ίτης**

[ῑ], ου, ὁ, name for a *farm-slave*, Amer.ap.Ath.6.267c. (Written ἐρκῆται in Hsch.)

**ἑρκο-θηρικός**, ή, όν, (θήρα) *of* or *for netting* or *fishing with nets*, Pl.*Sph.*220c: **-θηρευτικός**, Poll.7.139: Subst. **-ρευτής**, οῦ, ὁ, ib. 137. **-πεζα**, ἡ, *thorn-hedge*, Hsch., Phot. (Cf. ἅρπεζα.)

**ἕρκος**, εος, τό, *fence, enclosure* (πᾶν ὅσον ἂν ἕνεκα κωλύσεως εἴργῃ τι περιέχον Pl.*Sph.*220b) round gardens and vineyards, Od.7.113, Il. 5.90, 18.564; esp. round the court-yards of houses, Od.21.238 (pl.), al.; ὑπὲρ ἕρκος ὑπερθορεῖν Sol.4.29, Hdt.6.134: pl., S.*Aj.*1274; also, *the place enclosed, court-yard*, στὰς μέσῳ ἕρκεϊ Il.16.231, cf. Od.8.57 (pl.), etc.; Κίσσιον ἕρκος, i.e. Susa, A.*Pers.*17 (anap.); ποῖον γαίας ἕ.; what city? E.*Heracl.*441; ἕ. ἱερόν sacred *enclosure*, S.*Tr.*607; shell of the pinna, Plu.2.980b. 2. *wall for defence*, ἕρκεϊ χαλκείῳ Il.15.567; ἕρκος.. ἐκ ναυηγίων περιεβάλοντο Hdt.7.191, cf. 9.99. 3. periphr., ἕ. ὀδόντων the *fence* (consisting) of the teeth, mostly in phrase, ποῖόν σε ἔπος φύγεν ἕ. ὀδόντων; Il.4.350, cf. Sol.27.1; ἀμείψεται ἕ. ὀδόντων Il.9.409, Od.10.328; κάρχαρον ἕ., without ὀδόντων, Opp.*H.*1. 506; ἀγγέων ἕρκεσι, = ἄγγεσι, Pi.*N.*10.36; μέλαν ἕ. ἅλμας, i.e. the sea, Id.*Dith.Oxy.*1.16, cf. *P.*2.80 (= ἐπιφάνεια, Sch.); σφραγῖδος ἕ., i.e. a seal, S.*Tr.*615. 4. metaph., *defence*, ἕ. ἀκόντων, of a shield, *a defence against* javelins, Il.15.646; ἕ. βελέων 5.316; ἕ. ἰωχμοῖο, of the lion's skin, Theoc.25.279; ἕρκεσιν εἴργειν κῦμα θαλάσσας A. *Pers.*89 (lyr.). b. of persons, ἕ. Ἀχαιῶν, of Ajax, Il.3.229; of Achilles, Pi.*Pae.*6.85; of soldiers, ἕρκος πολέμοιο a *defence against* war, Il.4.299; of Achilles, ἕ. Ἀχαιοῖσιν..πολέμοιο 1.284; of Clytaemnestra, γαίας μονόφρουρον ἕ. A.*Ag.*257 (lyr.): abs., Pi.*P.*5.113, etc. 5. *a net, toils*, for birds, Od.22.469: mostly in pl., σπίζ' ὅπως ἐν ἕρκεσιν S.*Fr.*431, cf. Ar.*Av.*528 (anap.), Pherecr.209, Arist. *HA*617$^b$24; for deer, Pi.*N.*3.51; *coils* of a lasso, Hdt.7.85: metaph., τῆς Δίκης ἐν ἕρκεσιν A.*Ag.*1611, cf. S.*Aj.*60, E.*Med.*986 (lyr.); λέκτρων ἔχεσθαι φιλτάτοις ἐν ἕρκεσι Id.*Ba.*958, cf.*Hymn.Is.*158; χρυσοδέτοις ἕρκεσιν..γυναικῶν, of Eriphyle's necklace, S.*El.*838 (lyr.).

**ἑρκοῦρος**, ον, *watching an enclosure*, *AP*12.257 (Mel., ὀρκοῦρος cod.).

**ἑρκτή**, ἡ, Ion. for εἱρκτή. **ἑρκτήρ**, v. εἱρκτήρ.

**ἑρκτός**, ή, όν, = ῥεκτός, *feasible*, Arr.*Ind.*20 (fort. leg. ἐπικτόν).

**ἕρκτωρ**, ορος, ὁ, (ἔρδω) *a doer*, κακῶν Antim.*Eleg.*5.

**Ἑρκῦνα** or **-υννα**, ἡ, title of Demeter at Lebadea, Lyc.153:— hence **Ἑρκύνια** (-κήνια cod.), τά, festival of Demeter, Hsch.

⊕ **ἕρμα**, ατος, τό, *prop, support*: in pl., of the *props* used to keep ships upright when hauled ashore, νῆα..ἐπ' ἠπείροιο ἔρυσσαν ὑψοῦ ἐπὶ ψαμάθοις, ὑπὸ δ' ἕρματα μακρὰ τάνυσσαν Il.1.486, cf. 2.154: metaph., of men, ἕ. πόληος *prop* or *stay* of the city, 16.549, Od.23.121, *Epigr.Gr.* 452.11 (Syria); τοῦτο..οἷον ἕ. πόλεως κεῖσθω as *a foundation* for the city, Pl.*Lg.*737b; ὥσπερ ἕ. τῆς πολιτείας βέβαιον Plu.2.814c; ἕ. ἐχέγγυον [ἑταιρίας] D.C.*Fr.*40.15; ὥσπερ ἕρματος ἀεὶ δεόμενοι τῆς τροφῆς Gal.19.208. 2. *sunken rock, reef*, Alc.*Supp.*26.6, Hdt.7.183, Th. 7.25, E.*Hel.*854; ἄσημα ἕ. Anacr.38; ἄφαντον ἕ. A.*Ag.*1007 (lyr.), cf.*Eu.*564 (lyr.); ἕ. ὕφαλα D.H.1.52; ἕ. γῆς ἁπαλόν a soft *bank* of mud, App.*BC*5.101. 3. *cairn, barrow*, πρὸς ἕρμα τυμβόχωστον..τάφου S.*Ant.*848 (lyr., nisi leg. ἔργμα); Ἑρμᾶν ἀφετήριον ἕρμα starting-post, *AP*9.319 (Philox.); ἕρματα τῶν θεμελίων *ruins* of the foundations, D.S.5.70. 4. *that which keeps a ship steady, ballast*, Plu.2. 782b; of *stones* with which cranes and bees were supposed to steady themselves in their flight, Arist.*HA*597$^b$1, 626$^b$25; μετὰ τῶν γεράνων ἀναχωρῶ πάλιν, ἀνθ' ἕρματος πολλὰς καταπεπωκὼς δίκας Ar.*Av.*1429: metaph., τῆς ψυχῆς ἐχούσης ἕ. Chrysipp.*Stoic.*2.299; τὸ ἀπὸ τῆς φρονήσεως ἕ. Socr.ap.Stob.3.3.61; οἷον ἕ. τὴν τῶν γερόντων ἀρχὴν θεμένη Plu.*Lyc.*5; οὔτε τι ἕ. ἐν τῇ ψυχῇ ἔχει D.C.46.3; also λαβοῦσα ἕ. Δῖον having *conceived* by Zeus, A.*Supp.*580 (lyr.); so perh. μελαινέων ἕρμ' ὀδυνάων *freight* of dark pains, Il.4.117 (athetized by Aristarch.). II. (εἴρω A) in pl., ἕρματα *ear-rings*, 14.182, Od.18.297; *band, noose*, Ael. *NA*17.35; a serpent's *coils*, ib.37.

⊕ **ἑρμᾰγέλη**, ἡ, *a herd of Hermae*, *AP*11.353.6 (Pall.).

⊕ **Ἑρμάδιον**, τό, Dim. of Ἑρμῆς I. 2, Keil-Premerstein *Dritter Bericht* 117, Suid. II. Dim. of Ἑρμῆς I. 1, Luc.*Cont.*1.

⊕ **ἑρμάζω**, (ἕρμα) *steady, support*, Hp.*Art.*44. II. ἑρμάσαι· ἐλαφρῶς περιελίξαι, Hsch.

**Ἑρμ-άθήνη**, ἡ, *terminal bust* (cf. Ἑρμῆς I. 2) *with head of Athena*, Cic.*Att.*1.1.5, 1.4.3; so of busts with heads of other divinities, of Eros, -έρως, Plin.*HN*36.33 (pl.); of Heracles, -ηρακλῆς, Cic.*Att.*1. 10.3, *Milet.*1(7) No.305; of Pan, cf. Ἑρμόπαν. (Cic.*Att.*1.4.3 appears to explain *Hermathena* as a Janus-like bust of Hermes and Athena; this is perh. a pun, but cf. Ἑρμῆς I. 2.)

**Ἑρμαΐζομαι**, *imitate Hermes*, Eust.10.25.

⊕ **Ἑρμᾰϊκός**, ή, όν, *of Hermes*, σειρά Marin.*Procl.*28; *of the planet Mercury*, σφαῖρα Procl.*in Alc.*p.113C.; so in Astrol., Ἑ. ἔργα *Cat. Cod.Astr.*2.203; Ἑ. πράξεις ib.8(4).238, cf. Sch.Ptol.*Tetr.*77; also of certain ζῴδια, Jul.Laod. in *Cat.Cod.Astr.*5(1).187. Adv. -κῶς Eust. 808.19. II. pl., = sq. I. 1, *Cat.Cod.Astr.*1.150.

⊕ **ἕρμ-αιον**, τό, prop. *gift of Hermes*, i.e. *unexpected piece of luck, godsend, wind-fall, treasure-trove* (cf. Ἑρμῆς II), S.*Ant.*397; ἕ. ἂν ἦν τινι c. inf., Pl.*Phd.*107c, *R.*368d; ἕ. ἂν εἴη ἡμῖν, εἰ.. Id.*Smp.*176c; ἑρμαίῳ ἐντετυχηκέναι Id.*Grg.*486e; ἕ. ἡγήσασθαι, ποιεῖσθαί τι, Id.*Smp.* 217a, *Grg.*489c; νομίζειν D.38.6. 2. = ἕρμαξ, Sch.Od.16.471. 3. *barrow, tomb*, *Papers of Amer. School* 3 Nos.501, 585 (Tymandos). 4. = ἠρύγγη, Ps.-Dsc.3.21; = ἀλόη, ib.22. II. Ἕρμαια (sc. ἱερά), τά, *festival of Hermes*, Pl.*Ly.*206d, Aeschin.1.10, *IG*2$^2$.1227 (ii B.C.), Durrbach *Choix d'inscrr. de Délos* 117 (ii B.C.). 2. Ἕρμαιον, τό, *temple of Hermes*, *SIG*546*B*6 (Melitaea, iii B.C.), *Schwyzer* 709 (Ephesus, iii B.C.), al. (Prop. neut. of Ἑρμαῖος, but as Subst. proparox., Hdn.Gr.1.369.) **-αῖος**, α, ον, *called after Hermes*, Ἑ. λόφος, in Ithaca, Od.16.471 (expl. as = ἕρμαξ by Sch. ad loc.); Ἑ. λέπας Λήμνου A.*Ag.*283, cf. S.*Ph.*1459 (anap.). 2. *of Hermes*, Λύρη, the constellation *Lyra*, Arat.674; Ἑρμαῖος, ὁ (sc. μήν), month at Argos, etc., Polyaen.8.33; in Boeotia, *IG*7.289, al.; in the Aetolian league, *GDI*1745, al.; cf. Ἑρμαιών. 3. *gainful*, δαιμόνων δόσις A. *Eu.*947. 4. fem. **Ἑρμαΐς**, ίδος, ἡ, κρήνη Hp.*Ep.*17. **-αϊσταί**, οἱ, *worshippers of Hermes*, *IG*12(1).162 (Rhodes), *Inscr.Cos* 156; = Lat. *Mercuriales*, *SIG*726.1 (Delos, i B.C.). (Written Ἑρμαιισταί, *Exploration archéologique de Délos* 7(1).118.) ⊕ **-αιών**, ῶνος, ὁ, name of a month at Halicarnassus, *SIG*45.4 (v B.C.); in Ceos, *IG*2$^2$.1128.

**ἕρμακον**· ὄρνεον, Hsch.

**ἑρμάν**, f.l. for ἕρμα, Phot., Harp. **Ἑρμάν**, v. Ἑρμῆς.

**Ἑρμάνουβις** or **-ης** [ᾰ], ιδος, ὁ, Graecized form of Anubis, Plu.2. 375e, Porph.ap.Eus.*PE*3.11, *AP*11.360.

**ἕρμαξ**, ᾰκος, ἡ, (ἕρμα) *heap of stones, cairn*, Nic.*Th.*150; λιθακές τε καὶ ἕρμακες Epic. in *Arch.Pap.*7.10. II. = ἕρμα I. 2, Hsch.

**Ἑρμάριον**, τό, Dim. of Ἑρμῆς, etym. of ἁρμάριον, *EM*146.56.

**ἑρμ-ᾰσις**, εως, ἡ, (ἑρμάζω) *supporting*, Erot. s. v. ἥρμοσται: Dor. **ἕρμασσις**, αὐλῶν *IG*4.823.41 (Troezen). **-ασμα**, ατος, τό, *prop, support*, Hp.*Off.*25. **-ασμός**, ὁ, *supporting*, Id.*Fract.*29.

⊕ **ἑρμᾰτ-ίζω**, = ἑρμάζω, *support by means of a sling*, τῆς κνήμης ἡρματισμένης Hp.*Fract.*23. II. (ἕρμα I. 4) *steady as by ballast*, ἑ. ἑαυτοὺς λιθιδίοις Plu.2.967b:—Med., *ballast themselves*, λιθιδίοις ib.979b: —Pass., τοῖς ἀξιολόγοις ἀγαθοῖς ἡρματίσθαι Phld.*Mort.*18. 2. trans. in Med., νύμφας ἐς οἴκους ἑρματίζονται *they take* brides into *their* houses *as ballast*, E.*Fr.*402.8, cf. Lyc.1319. **-ικός**, ή, όν, *on a firm base*, κράββατος *PGen.*68.10 (iv A.D.). **-ίτης** [ῑ], ου, ὁ, *serving as ballast*, πέτρος Lyc.618.

**Ἑρμ-αφρόδῑτος**, ὁ, *Hermaphrodite*, or *person partaking of the attributes of both sexes*, so called from Hermaphroditus, son of Hermes and Aphrodite, D.S.4.6, Luc.*DDeor.*23.1, Ptol.*Tetr.*124, Gal.4. 619. 2. as Adj., ἑ. πάθος Leonid.ap.Paul.Aeg.6.69.

**Ἑρμάων**, **Ἑρμέας**, **Ἑρμείας**, v. Ἑρμῆς.

**Ἑρμεῖον**, τό, *shrine of Hermes*, or perh. = ἕρμαξ I, Str.8.3.12 (pl.).

**Ἑρμέρως**, ωτος, ὁ, v. Ἑρμαθήνη.

⊕ **ἑρμή**· ἔξοδος, Hsch. (Cf. ἐξίθμη, ἐρίμη.)

**Ἑρμῄδιον**, τό, Dim. of Ἑρμῆς, Ar.*Pax*924: as term of endearment, ὡρμῄδιον ib.382. (-ίδιον codd. Ar.)

⊕ **ἑρμην-εία**, ἡ, (ἑρμηνεύω) *interpretation, explanation*, Pl.*R.*524b (pl.), *Tht.*209a, Epicur.*Nat.*28.1; esp. of thoughts by words, *expression*, Diog.Apoll.1, X.*Mem.*4.3.12; χρῆσθαι τῇ γλώσσῃ πρὸς ἑρμηνείαν Arist.*PA*660$^a$35, cf. *de An.*420$^b$19, *Resp.*476$^a$19, Hermog.*Inv.*1.1, etc.; *mediation*, Pl.*Epin.*984e; *style*, D.H.*Comp.*1, al., Demetr.*Eloc.* 1, etc.; *an expression*, ἡ ἀκόλουθος ἑ. Sch.Pi.*O.*3.1: also in pl., αἱ Πλατωνικαὶ ἑ. Plato's *gifts of style*, D.H.*Pomp.*1.2. 2. in Music, *expression*, Plu.2.1138a, 1144d. 3. *translation*, Aristeas 3, Ph.2. 141; ἑ. τῶν Ῥωμαϊκῶν *POxy.*1201.12 (iii A.D.); ἑ. ἔχειν to *mean when translated*, Ph.1.232, Porph.*Plot.*17. **-ευμα**, ατος, τό, *interpretation, explanation*, in pl., E.*Ph.*470, *HF*1137, Ph.2.300. 2. *symbol, monument*, Νηρῇδος γάμων E.*Andr.*46. **-ευματικὰ** βιβλία *glossaries, Gloss.* ⊕ **-εύς**, έως, ὁ, *interpreter*, esp. of foreign tongues, *dragoman*, Hdt.2.125, 154, al., X.*An.*1.2.17, *PCair.Zen.*65 (iii B.C.), *PTheb.Bank* 9.1 (ii B.C.), etc. b. *court interpreter*, *POxy.*237 vii 37 (ii A.D.), etc. 2. *matrimonial agent, go-between*, Ptol.*Tetr.* 181. 3. *broker, commissionaire*, *POxy.*1517.6 (iii A.D.), etc. II. *interpreter, expounder*, Pi.*O.*2.85, A.*Ag.*616, 1062, etc.; ἑρμηνῆς τῶν θεῶν, of poets, Pl.*Ion* 534e; λόγος τῶν νόμων ἑ. Id.*Lg.*907d; σιωπὴ δ' ἄπορος ἑ. λόγων E.*Fr.*126. 2. applied to planets, D.S.2. 30. **-ευσις**, εως, ἡ, *style, expression*, Longin.*Rh.*p.187 H. 2. *interpretation*, D.C.66.1. **-ευτέον**, *one must express*: ἑ. προσφόρως *one must use* the appropriate *style*, Demetr.*Eloc.*120. 2. *one must interpret*, Sch.rec.A.*Pr.*226. **-ευτής**, οῦ, ὁ, = ἑρμηνεύς, Pl. *Plt.*290c, Lxx *Ge.*42.23, Poll.5.154. **-ευτικός**, ή, όν, *of* or *for interpreting*: ἡ -κή (sc. τέχνη) Pl.*Plt.*260d; διάλεκτος ἑ. τινός Id.*Def.* 414d; λόγος Ph.1.58; ἑ. δύναμις power *of expression*, gift *of style*, Luc.*Hist.Conscr.*34, Theod.(?)ap.Nicol.*Prog.*p.2 F. **-εύτρια**, ἡ, fem. of ἑρμηνευτής, Sch.E.*Hipp.*589. ⊕ **-εύω**, Dor. **ἑρμᾱνεύω** *SIG*1168.88 (Epid.), *interpret* foreign tongues, X.*An.*5.4.4; *translate*, D.H.*Th.*49, etc.; ἀπὸ Ῥωμαϊκῶν *PRyl.*62.30 (iii A.D.):—Pass., Ἑλληνιστὶ D.H.2.12, cf. Lxx *Jb.*42.17, etc. II. *explain, expound*, S.*OC*398, E.*Fr.*636.5, etc.; ὑμῖν ταῦτα Antipho 3.2.1; ὅ τι λέγει Philyll.11; τὰ τῶν ποιητῶν Pl.*Ion* 535a:—Med., Id.*Epin.*985b:— Pass., Arist.*SE*166$^b$11. 2. *put into words, express*, Th.2.60, Pl. *Lg.*966b, etc.; τι διά τινος Hermog.*Id.*2.5; τι πεζῶς Id.*Meth.*30:— Pass., D.H.*Comp.*25. 3. *describe, write about*, τὸν Νεῖλον Demetr. *Eloc.*121. III. abs., *speak clearly, articulate*, Hp.*Epid.*5.74.

**Ἑρμηρακλῆς**, έους, ὁ, v. Ἑρμαθήνη.

⊕ **Ἑρμῆς**, οῦ, ὁ, nom. Ἑρμῆς Od.5.54, etc.: acc. Ἑρμῆν 8.334, etc., Ion. Ἑρμέην Hdt.5.7, late Ἑρμῆ *CIG*5094 (Nubia): dat. Ἑρμῇ Od.14. 435, Ἑρμέᾳ Il.5.390: voc. Ἑρμῆ *h.Hom.*18.12, A.*Pers.*629, *Eu.*90: Ep. gen. Ἑρμέω *h.Merc.*413, *h.Ven.*148, Hdt.5.7, etc.; lengthd. Ἑρμείω Il.15.214:—Ep. nom. **Ἑρμείας**, Od.1.42, al., *IG*5(2).558 (Arc.), acc. -αν Od.1.38, 5.28, al.; later **Ἑρμείης**, Call.*Dian.*69, etc.; gen. Ἑρμείαο Od.12.390, 15.319, Ἑρμεία *AP*7.480 (Leon.); dat. Ἑρμείᾳ *IG*1$^2$.631 (vi B.C.); voc. Ἑρμεία Od.5.29, al.:—Boeot. and Dor. nom. **Ἑρμᾶς**, gen. ᾶ, Corinn.*Supp.*2.57, Pi.*P.*2.10, etc., voc. Ἑρμᾶ A.*Fr.*384, acc. Ἑρμᾶν ib.273: also **Ἑρμάων** [ᾱ], Hes.*Fr.*23, Bion *Fr.*7.

8, *AP*4.3b.64 (Agath.):—contr. **Ἑρμάν** (not -ᾶν), ᾶνος, Call.*Fr.*32 P., *IG*5(2).360, al. (Arc.), ib.5(1).1390.33 (Andania, i B.C.), *Supp.Epigr.* 2.165 (Laconia): Thess. dat. Ἑρμαίου *IG*9(2).716 (dub.), Ἑρμάου ib. 715, al., Ἑρμάο ib.471, Ἑρμᾶ ib.356: Cret. acc. Ἑρμάον *Schwyzer* 179a:—*Hermes*, son of Zeus and Maia, Od.5.28, 14.435, Hes.*Th.* 938, etc. **2.** *pillar surmounted by bust*, at Athens and elsewhere, And.1.37, Th.6.27, etc.; τῶν ἱερῶν Ἑρμῶν *IG*12(8).188.14 (Samothrace); as a decorative piece, with two faces, Keil-Premerstein *Dritter Bericht* 117: Ἑ. τρικέφαλος, τετρακέφαλος, Hsch. **3.** ὁ τοῦ Ἑρμοῦ ἀστήρ the planet *Mercury*, Pl.*Ti.*38d, *Epin.*987b, Arist.*Mete.* 342$^{b}$33, *Metaph.*1073$^{b}$32, Thphr.*Sign.*46, etc.: later Ἑρμῆς, ὁ, in same sense, *Placit.*2.32.1, Plu.2.1028b, Cleom.2.7: hence, Ἑρμοῦ ἡμέρα D.C.37.19. **4.** Ἑρμαῖ· παραφυάδια δένδρων ἄχρηστα, Hsch. **5.** *cake* in the shape of a κηρυκεῖον, *Schwyzer* 694 (Chios, iv B.C.), Hsch. **II.** prov. and phrases: **1.** Ἑρμῆν ἕλκειν to *make a last effort*, from the parting cup at a feast being drunk *to Hermes*, Stratt.22. **2.** κοινὸς Ἑρμῆς *shares in your luck!* Arist. *Rh.*1401$^{a}$21, Thphr.*Char.*30.9, Men.*Epit.*67, etc. **3.** ἐν τῷ λίθῳ Ἑρμῆς, of the actual potentially in the material, Arist.*Metaph.*1002$^{a}$ 22, 1017$^{b}$7. **4.** Ἑρμῆς ἐπεισελήλυθε '*Hermes* is come in', a saying used when conversation suddenly ceased, Plu.2.502f. **5.** τὸ Ἑρμοῦ ῥαβδίον, like 'Fortunatus' cap', Arr.*Epict.*3.20.12. **6.** Ἑρμοῦ βοτάνιον, Ἑρμοῦ πόα, = λινόζωστις, Dsc.4.189, Plin.*HN*25.38.

**ἑρμητής,** οῦ, ὁ, = Ἑρμῆς I. 5, *GDI* iv p.883 (Erythrae).

**Ἑρμίδιον,** v. Ἑρμήδιον.

⊛ **ἑρμίν** (Hdn.Gr.2.431) or **ἑρμίς** (Philem.226), ῖνος, ὁ, = ἕρμα, *bedpost*, Od.8.278, 23.198, Herod.3.16.

**ἑρμογλῠφ-εῖον,** τό, *statuary's shop*, Pl.*Smp.*215b. **-εύς,** έως, ὁ, *carver of Hermae*: generally, *statuary*, Luc.*Somn.*2, Plu.2. 580e. **-ικός,** ή, όν, *of* or *for a statuary*: ἡ -κὴ τέχνη *the art of a statuary*, Luc.*Somn.*7. **-ος,** ὁ, = ἑρμογλυφεύς, ib.2, Porph. *Hist.Phil.Fr.*11, Iamb.*VP*34.245.

**Ἑρμο-δάκτῠλον,** τό, a plant, in two varieties, *Colchicum luteum* and *autumnale*, [Gal.]14.760, Alex.Trall.11. ⊛ **-κοπίδης,** ου, ὁ, (κόπτω) *a Hermes-mutilator*, in pl., Ar.*Lys.*1094, Plu.*Alc.*20. **-λογέω,** *build with loose stones*, τάφον *AP*7.554 (Phil.). **-μᾰχέω,** *fight with* Ἑρμαῖ I. 4, as a game, Hsch. s. v. Ἑρμαῖ.

**Ἑρμόπᾱν,** ᾶνος, ὁ, a deity partaking of the attributes of Hermes and Pan, Hdn.Gr.1.13, Porph.ap.Eus.*PE*3.11: a Hermes-Heracles-Pan statue is described (but not named) in *APl.*4.234 (Phld.).

**ἔρνατις·** ἀναδενδράς, Hsch.

**ἐρνεσίπεπλος** [ῐ], ον, *wrapt in foliage*, Orph.*H.*30.5.

**ἐρνίον,** τό, Dim. of ἔρνος II, *Lyr.Alex.Adesp.*4.17.

**ἐρνοκόμος,** ον, *tending young plants*, Hsch.

**ἐρνόομαι,** Pass., *shoot up*, Ph.2.402.

⊛ **ἔρνος,** εος, τό, *young sprout, shoot*, ὁ δ' ἀνέδραμεν ἔρνεϊ ἶσος shot up like *a young plant*, Il.18.56, cf. Od.14.175; οἷον δὲ τρέφει ἔ. ἀνὴρ ἐριθηλὲς ἐλαίης Il.17.53, cf. Od.6.163; σκιεροῖσιν ὑφ' ἔρνεσιν (sic codd. Ath.) οἰναρέοις Ibyc.1.5; ἔ. δάφνης, δόνακος, ὕλας, E.*Med.*1213, *Hel.* 183 (lyr.), *Ba.*876 (lyr.). **2.** in pl., *wreaths* worn by victors in games, Pi.*N.*11.29, *I.*1.29. **II.** metaph., *scion, offspring*, Id.*N.*6. 37 (pl.), B.5.87, A.*Ag.*1525 (lyr.), *Eu.*661, 666, S.*OC*1108 (pl.), *Sammelb.*4229.10; Ἡρακλέος ἱερὸν ἔ. Theoc.2.121; ἔ. τῆς νηδύος E.*Ba.* 1306; [κεράων] ἔ., periphr. for κέραα, Opp.*C.*2.210; of Delos, as *having sprung out of the sea*, Pi.*Fr.*87.2. **2.** *fruit*, of the apple of Discord, Coluth.60, al.

**ἐρνύγας** (acc. pl.), poet. coined word for κέρατα, Arist.*Po.*1457$^{b}$ 35: perh. cf. sq.

**ἔρνυτας·** ἔρνη, βλαστήματα, κλάδοι, Hsch.

**ἐρνώδης,** ες, *like a young sprout*, Dsc.1 *Praef.*8, *Gp.*10.22.5 (Sup.).

**Ἐρξείης** or **Ἐρξίης,** ὁ, Greek equivalent of Darius, either *doer* (cf. ἐρξίας, ὁ πρακτικός *EM*376.52) or *restrainer* (εἴργω), Hdt.6.98.

**ἔρξω, ἔρξα,** v. ἔρδω.

**ἐρόδανα·** ἔργον ἐρινάξει, Hsch.

⊛ **ἐρόεις,** εσσα, εν, (ἔρος) poet., *lovely, charming*, Ἀλίη Hes.*Th.*245, cf. *h.Ven.*263, *h.Merc.*31; βῶμος Sapph.54, cf. Ar.*Av.*246 (lyr.); Νημερτής Emp.122.4; Ἑλένης τύπος *APl.*4.149 (Arab.).

**ἔρομαι** (not found in pres. ind. (exc. 2 sg. ἔρεαι Orac. in Certamen *Prooem.*), its place being taken by ἐρέω (A), ἐρωτάω); Ion. and Ep. **εἴρομαι** Il.1.553, Od.1.284, al.: impf. (= aor.) εἰρόμην Il.1.513, Pi.*O.*6. 49, Hdt.2.44, etc.: fut. ἐρήσομαι S.*OT*1166, Ar.*Nu.*1409, Pl.*Prt.*355c; Ion. εἰρήσομαι Od.4.61, 7.237, Hdt.1.67 (ἐπ-): aor. 2 ἠρόμην Sapph. 1.15, E.*Ion*541, Th.3.113, etc.; imper. ἐροῦ S.*El.*563, E.*Or.*763 (troch.), etc., Ep. ἔρειο Il.11.611; subj. ἔρωμαι Od.8.133, Pl.*R.*538d, etc.; εἴρωμαι Od.16.402, Hdt.4.76; opt. ἐροίμην Od.1.135, 3.77, etc.; inf. ἐρέσθαι in Hom. always in the phrase μεταλλῆσαι καὶ ἐρέσθαι 3.69, al. (exc. in 1.405) (ἔρεσθαι is freq. in codd., as Lys.12.24, E.*El.*548, cf. Hdn.Gr.1.466); part. ἐρόμενος Ar.*Eq.*574, Th.4.40:—Ep. and Ion. also **ἐρέομαι** in subj. ἐρέωμαι Od.17.509, inf. ἐρέεσθαι 6.298, 23.106, Hp.*Prorrh.*2.41, impf. ἐρέοντο Il.1.332, 8.445; ἐπ-ειρεόμενος is v.l. in Hdt.3.64:—*ask, inquire*, mostly folld. by indirect question, εἴροντο.. ὅττι ἑ κήδοι Od.9.402, etc.; ἤρετο ὅτι θαυμάζοι Th.3.113; τὸν ξεῖνον ἐρώμεθα εἴ τιν' ἄεθλον οἶδε Od.8.133, etc.; ἠρόμην ὅπου.. Pl.*R.*327b; διὰ τί.. Id.*Prt.*355c, etc.: folld. by a direct question, ἤρετο Ξενοφῶντα, εἰπέ μοι, ἔφη, ὦ Ξενοφῶν, οὐ σὺ ἐνόμιζες..; X.*Mem.*1.3.8; ἐρομένου δὲ τοῦ Ἀγησιλάου, ἆρ' ἂν ἐν καιρῷ γένοιτο, εἰ..; Id.*HG*4.3.2, cf. *Cyr.*1.4.19. **2.** c. acc. objecti, *learn by inquiry*, ἐρέεσθαι δώματα πατρός Od.6.298; *ask after* or *for*, εἰρόμεναι παῖδας Il.6.239; εἴρεαι Ἕκτορα δῖον 24.390; θεῶν εἰρώμεθα βουλάς Od.16.402. **3.** c. acc. pers., *question*, Il.1.332, etc., Hdt.1.32, Lys.12.24; εἴρετο δ' ἡμέας, ὦ ξεῖνοι, τίνες ἐστέ; Od.9.251; ἀλλήλους εἴροντο τίς εἴη καὶ πόθεν ἔλθοι 17. 368, cf. E.*Or.*763 (troch.), etc.; in later Prose, Jul.*Or.*7.229b. **4.** c. acc. pers., *petition*, Ar.*Eq.*574. **5.** c. dupl. acc., *to ask* one *about* a thing, τὸ μέν σε πρῶτον..εἰρήσομαι.., τίς πόθεν εἰς ἀνδρῶν; Od.7. 237, cf. 19.509; ἐρήσομαί σε τουτί· παῖδά μ' ὄντ' ἔτυπτες; Ar.*Nu.* 1409. **6.** freq. τινὰ περί τινος, as ἵνα μιν περὶ πατρὸς..ἔροιτο Od.1. 135, 3.77, cf. Hdt.4.76, al., E.*El.*548; also οἱ δέ μιν ἀμφὶ δίκας εἴροντο Od.11.570; ἀμφὶ πόσει εἴρεσθαι 19.95. (Ion. εἰρ- Att. ἐρ- from ἐρϝ- (aor. stem), cf. ἐρέ(ϝ)ω, ἐρευτής: pres. ἐρέ(ϝ)ομαι: ἐροίμην and similar forms in Hom. are variously expld. or emended.)

**ἐρόντι·** μάλα, λίαν, πάνυ, Hsch.; perh. cf. ἐρρεντί.

⊛ **ἔρος** (A), ὁ, acc. ἔρον, dat. ἔρῳ: poet. form of ἔρως:—*love, desire*, οὐ..θεᾶς ἔρος οὐδὲ γυναικός Il.14.315, cf. Od.18.212; freq. in phrase αὐτὰρ ἐπεὶ πόσιος καὶ ἐδητύος ἐξ ἔρον ἕντο Il.1.469, al.; ἱμερτῶν ἔργων ἐξ ἔρον ἱέμενον Thgn.1064; ἔρος λυσιμελής Hes.*Th.*910, cf. Ibyc.1.6, etc.: used by Trag. in lyrics, S.*El.*197, E.*Med.*152, and by E. in dialogue, *Hipp.*337, *El.*297, al.; also in late Prose, ἔρῳ φέρεσθαι Luc. *Asin.*33. **II.** as pr. n., *Eros*, the god of love, Hes.*Th.*120, Alcm. 36, Sapph.74, Theoc.29.22.

**ἔρος** (B), τό, *wool*, only in Ion. form εἶρος (q. v.). but cf. ἔπερος, εὔερος.

**ἐροτή,** ἡ, = ἑορτή, *POxy.*2084.26 (iii A.D.); Cypr. acc. to Hsch.: **ἔροτις** Aeol. (acc. to Eust.1908.57), E.*El.*625: also in Dor. Inscrr., *IG*4.583.6 (Argos), *SIG*1009.5 (Chalcedon); θεοῖς ὧνπερ ἔην ἔ. *IG*11 (4).1150 (Delos).

**ἔρουα·** πορεύου, ἀναπαύου (Cypr.), Hsch. (cf. ἐρωέω).

**ἔροψ,** a bird, Hsch.

**ἑρπάκανθα** [ᾰκ], ἡ, = ἄκανθος, Ps.-Dsc.3.17.

**ἐρπεδό⟨ε⟩σσα·** ἐπίπεδος, Hsch. (Cf. ἀρπεδόεις.)

**ἑρπετό-δηκτος,** ον, *bitten by a reptile*, Dsc.3.68, Crateuas *Fr.*5. **-εις,** εσσα, εν, *of reptiles*, γένος Opp.*C.*2.274.

**ἑρπετόν,** Aeol. perh. **ὄρπετον** (q. v.), τό, (ἕρπω) *beast* or *animal which goes on all fours*, Od.4.418; πᾶν ἑ. πληγῇ νέμεται Heraclit.11; ἑρπετὰ ὅσσα τρέφει μέλαινα γαῖα Alcm.60.3; ὄφις καὶ σαύρας καὶ τὰ τοιαῦτα τῶν ἑρπετῶν Hdt.4.183; τοῖς μὲν ἄλλοις ἑρπετοῖς πόδας ἔδωκεν.., ἀνθρώπῳ δὲ καὶ χεῖρας X.*Mem.*1.4.11; ἑρπετά, opp. πετεινά, Hdt.1.140, cf. Theoc.15.118, A.R.4.1240: generally, ἑ. οὐδὲ γυνή Call.*Jov.*13; πυκινώτατον ἑ., of a hound, Pi.*Fr.*106; of insects, Semon.13, Nic.*Fr.* 74.46. **II.** *creeping thing, reptile*, esp. *snake*, E.*Andr.*269, Theoc. 24.57; περὶ κιναδέων τε καὶ ἑ. Democr.259; ἑρπετά τε καὶ δάκετα ⟨πάντα⟩ Ar.*Av.*1069; of the monster Typhoeus, with a *snake's* body, Pi.*P.*1.25. **2.** as Adj., *creeping*, κακὸν ἑ. πρᾶγμα *POxy.*1060.7 (vi A.D.); τὰ ἑ. θηρία Philum.*Ven.*10.1.

**Ἑρπετοσῖται,** οἱ, name of a tribe of *snake-eaters*, Porph.*Chr.*69.

⊛ **ἑρπετώδης,** ες, *snake-like*, προβολή, of the elephant's trunk, Aret. *SD*2.13.

**ἑρπηδών,** όνος, ἡ, *a crawling*, Nic.*Al.*418, ubi Sch. male ἑρπυδόνα.

**ἕρπηλα,** a kind of *shell-fish*, Numen.ap.Ath.7.306c (v. l. ἕρπιλαν); ἑρπήλας δολιχήποδας Id.ap.eund.7.305a (v. l. ἕρπηνας).

**ἑρπηνώδης,** ες, *of the nature of* ἕρπης, Ph.2.205, Antyll.ap.Orib.10. 34.6.

**ἕρπης,** ητος, ὁ, (ἕρπω) *shingles*, Hp.*Prorrh.*2.11 (pl.); ἕ. ἐσθιόμενοι Id.*Aph.*5.22:—also **ἑρπήν,** ῆνος, ὁ, Ph.2.64; **ἑρπήνη,** ἡ, *EM*377. 7. **II.** ἕρπης, ητος, ὁ, name of an animal (snake?), Plin.*HN*30. 116, prob. in Philum.*Ven.*19.1 (ὅπητες cod.).

⊛ **ἑρπηστ-ήρ,** ῆρος, ὁ, v.l. for ἑρπυστήρ, Orph.*L.*49, Opp.*C.*3.110, 411. ⊛ **-ής,** οῦ, ὁ, = ἑρπετόν, Nic.*Th.*9, etc.; of a mouse, *AP*9.86 (Antiphil.). **b.** *guinea-worm*, *Hippiatr.*58. **2.** Adj. *creeping*, ἑρπηστὴν πόδα, κισσέ, χορεύσας *AP*11.33 (Phil.). **-ικός,** f.l. for ἑρπυστικός (q. v.).

**ἕρπιλα,** v. ἕρπηλα.

**ἕρπις,** ὁ, Egypt. word for *wine*, Hippon.51.2, f.l. for ὄλπιν in Sapph.51, cf. Tz. ad Lyc.579.

**ἕρπνουν,** etym. of τερπνόν coined by Pl.*Cra.*419d.

**ἑρπτόν,** τό, = ἑρπετόν, Arist.ap.Eust.481.36.

**ἑρπύζω,** impf. εἵρπυζον Q.S.13.93: pres. only in Hom.: aor. 1 ἑρπύσαι in Att. (v. ἕρπω):—*creep, crawl*, in Hom. always of persons weighed down by age or deep distress, ἑρπύζοντ' ἀνὰ γουνόν Od.1. 193; ἑρπύζων παρὰ θῖνα 13.220, cf. Il.23.225, A.R.4.1289; of quadrupeds and children, Nic.*Al.*542; χρόνος ἑρπύζων *AP*6.19 (Jul.); of ivy, ib.7.22 (Simm. Theb.).

**ἑρπυλλ-άριον,** τό, Dim. of ἕρπυλλος, Damocr.ap.Gal.14.192. **-ῐνος,** η, ον, *made of tufted thyme*, στέφανος Eub.99; μύρον Antiph. 106.7, cf. Gal.12.512. **-ιον,** τό, = ἕρπυλλος, Aret.*CD*1.3 (ἕρπυλον Hude, and so *Hippiatr.*54). **-ίς,** ίδος, ἡ, *grasshopper*, Hsch. **-ος,** ὁ, poet. also ἡ, Theoc.*Ep.*1, *AP*4.1.54 (Mel.), Pancr.ap.Ath.15. 677f:—*tufted thyme*, *Thymus Sibthorpii*, Cratin.98, Ar.*Pax*168, Thphr.*HP*1.9.4, al., *CP*2.18.2, Dsc.3.38.

**ἑρπ-ύσιμος,** *reptabundus*, *Gloss.* **-ῠσις,** εως, ἡ, (ἑρπύζω) *creeping*, Sch.D.P.121. **-υσμός,** ὁ, = foreg., Suid.; also, = ἡ φωνὴ τῶν χοίρων, Hsch. **-υστάζω,** = ἑρπύζω, Apollon.*Lex.* s. v. ἄταλλε. ⊛ **-υστήρ,** ῆρος, ὁ, = ἑρπηστής, *a reptile*, Opp.*C.*3.110 (v. l.). **2.** Adj. *creeping*, ὄφεις ἑ. ib.411 (v. l.), Orph.*L.*49 (v. l.). ⊛ **-υστής,** οῦ, ὁ, *a crawling child*, *AP*9.302 (Antip.). **-υστικός,** ή, όν, *creeping*, ζῷα ἑ. *serpents*, Arist.*HA*487$^{b}$21; of squirrels, etc., Id.*PA*688$^{a}$9: Medic., ἑρπυστικά (sc. ἕλκη), τά, *spreading ulcers*, Hp.*Ulc.*3, *Coac.*618, etc. (Freq. written ἑρπηστ-, cf. Max.Tyr.13.7, etc.)

⊛ **ἕρπω,** impf. εἷρπον Od.12.395 codd., E.*Cyc.*423, etc., ἧρπον *IG*4. 951.86 (Epid.): Dor. fut. ἑρψῶ Theoc.5.45, 18.40, Att. only in compd.

ἐφέρψω, later ἑρπύσω (διεξ–) Arist.*Mu.*$398^{b}33$ : aor. ἧρψα (ἐξ–) Lxx *Ps.*104(105).30 ; Att. εἵρπῠσα Ar.*V.*272 : (cf. Lat. *serpo*) :—*move slowly, walk*, ἥμενος ἢ ἕρπων Od.17.158 ; ὅσσα τε γαῖαν ἔπι πνείει τε καὶ ἕρπει Il.17.447 ; ἔργα ζωοῖσιν ἑρπόντεσσί θ' ὁμοῖα Pi.*O.*7.52 ; ἕρπον (εἷρπον codd.) ῥινοί *began to move*, Od.12.395 ; of infants, A.*Th.*17 ; of a lame man, S.*Ph.*207 (lyr.) ; ἕ. ἐξ εὐνῆς Ar.*V.*552 ; ἕρπον τοῖς ὀδοῦσι θηρίον an animal that *walks* on its teeth, *Carm.Pop.*35. **2.** simply, *go, come*, in Dor. dialects, where the aor. is ἔμολον, ἦνθον, etc., εἰς τὸ ἱερόν *IG*4.951.86 (Epid.), cf. *GDI*5040.39 (Crete), *BMus. Inscr.*968*A*6 (Cos), etc., cf. καθέρπω: also freq. in Trag., A.*Pr.*810, etc. ; ἕρπεθ' ὡς τάχιστα S.*OC*1643 ; Θησεὺς ὅδ' ἕρπει E.*HF*1154 ; ἕρπειν ἐς μῦθον, πρὸς ᾠδάς, Id.*Hel.*316, *Cyc.*423 ; ἕρπε δεῦρο *come* hither, Id.*Andr.*722 : and c. acc. cogn., ἐξόδους ἕ. κενάς S.*Aj.*287 ; κέλευθον Id.*Ph.*1223 ; εὐθεῖαν ἕρπε τήνδε A.*Fr.*195. **b.** of things, events, etc., ἕρπει ἄντα τῶ σιδάρω τὸ καλῶς κιθαρίσδην Alcm.35 ; βότρυς ἐπ' ἦμαρ ἕρπει S.*Fr.*255 ; ἥβη ἕρπουσα πρόσω Id.*Tr.*547 ; of a tear *stealing* from the eye, Id.*El.*1231 ; πρὸς τὸν ἔχονθ' ὁ φθόνος ἕρπει Id.*Aj.*157 ; τὸ ἐς αὔριον αἰεὶ τυφλὸν ἕρπει Id.*Fr.*593 ; τοῦτο γὰρ ἀθάνατον φωνᾶεν ἕρπει this (word) *goeth forth* undying, Pi.*I.*4(3).40 ; ὁ πόλεμος ἑρπέτω *let* it *take its course*, Ar.*Eq.*673, *Lys.*129 ; of *coming* events, εἰ δὲ δαίμων γενέθλιος ἕρποι Pi.*O.*13.105, cf. *N.*4.43, 7.68 ; of calamities, *come suddenly* on one, S.*Ant.*585, 618 (both lyr.), *Aj.*1087.

**ἐρρ–**, see also ἐνρ–.

**ἔρρα·** ζιζάνια, Hsch. (leg. αἶρα).

**ἐρραγέως·** ταχέως, Hsch. (Fort. ἐμμαπέως.) **ἐρράδᾰται**, v. ῥαίνω.

**ἔρραος**, ὁ, *ram*, Lyc.1316. **2.** *wild boar*, Call.*Fr.*335 : **ἐρράς**, Hsch.

**ἐρραστωνευμένως**, Adv. *carelessly*, Thom.Mag.p.325 R.

**ἐρράπτω**, = ἐνράπτω, Hp.*Art.*37, D.S.5.52, Ael.*NA*2.22 (Pass.) :— Med., Aristid.*Or.*41(4).3. **ἐρρέθην**, v. ἐρῶ.

**ἔρρειθρος**, ον, *canalized*, Hero *Geom.*23.68.

**ἐρρεντί**, Adv. (said to be formed from a part. ἐρρείς, as if from ἐρρῶ (*ἔρρημι), = ἔρρω), of unknown meaning, Alc.130 ; perh. cf. ἐρόντι.

**ἐρρετός·** φθόρος, Hsch. ; cf. ἔρρω. **ἐρρηγεῖα**, v. ῥήγνυμι. **ἐρρήεις**, = ἐρσήεις, Hsch.

**ἐρρήθην**, v. ἐρῶ, εἰπεῖν.

**ἐρρηνοβοσκός**, όν, = προβατοβοσκός, S.*Fr.*655.

**ἐρρη-φορέω**, = ἀρρηφορέω, *IG*3.916, **al.** **–φόρος**, = ἀρρηφόρος, ib.902. (Cf. ἐρση-φορία, –φόρος.)

**ἔρρῑγα**, pf. of ῥιγέω.

**ἔρρῑνον**, τό, (ἐν, ῥίς) *sternutatory medicine*, Antyll.ap.Orib.8.13. 1. **II.** as Adj., ἕ. ἄλευρον Archig.ap.Aët.6.28 ; ἕ. φάρμακα Gal. 11.769, 12.30, al. :—written **ἔνρινον**, Paus.Gr.*Fr.*166.

**ἔρριψις**, εως, ἡ, *prostration*, Hp.*Hum.*4, *Epid.*6.1.15 : also expld. as *restlessness* or *morbid fears*, cf. Gal.7.592, Diocl.*Fr.*192 : v.l. ἔριψις ; cf. ἔρειψις.

**Ἔρρος·** ὁ Ζεύς, Hsch. (Perh. cf. Ἕρσος.)

**ἔρρους**, ουν, (ἐν, ῥόος) *irrigated*, Hero *Geom.*23.68.

**ἐρρυθμισμένως**, Adv. pf. part. Pass., (ῥυθμίζω) *gracefully*, ἀναθορεῖν D.C.79.16.

**ἔρρυθμος**, ον, = ἔνρυθμος (q.v.).

**ἔρρυσος**, ον, *somewhat wrinkled, subrugose*, Dsc.3.105.

⊛ **ἔρρω** (A), Locr. **ϝέρρω** (v. infr.), fut. ἐρρήσω *h.Merc.*259, Ar. (v. infr.) : aor. 1 ἤρρησα Id.*Ra.*1192 : pf. ἤρρηκα (εἰσ–) Id.*Th.*1075 :— *go slowly* : ἔρρων *limping*, of Hephaestus, Il.18.421 ; ἥ μ' οἴῳ ἔρροντι συνήντετο met me *wandering* alone, Od.4.367. **II.** *go* or *come to one's own harm*, ἐνθάδε ἔρρων Il.8.239, 9.364 ; ὑπὸ γαίῃ ἐρρήσεις *h.Merc.* l.c. ; ἄτιμος ἔρρειν A.*Eu.*884 ; ὡς Πόλυβον ἤρρησεν he *went with a murrain* to Polybus, Ar.*Ra.*1192, cf. *Lys.*336 (lyr.). **2.** mostly in imper., ἔρρε *away! begone!* Il.8.164, Thgn.601 ; ἔρρ' οὕτως Il.22.498 : pl., ἔρρετε 24.239, A.R.3.562 : 3 sg., ἐρρέτω *away with him, let him go to ruin*, Il.20.349, Od.5.139 ; ἀσπὶς ἐκείνη ἐρρέτω Archil.6.4 ; in a legal formula, αὐτὸς μὲν ϝερρέτω *Berl.Sitzb.*1927.8 (Locr., v B.C.), cf. *Schwyzer*415 (Elis, v B.C.) ; ϝάρρην ib.409 ; ἐρρέτω Ἴλιον *perish* Troy! S.*Ph.*1200 (anap.) : with a Prep., ἔρρ' ἐκ νήσου θᾶσσον Od.10.72 ; ἔρρ' ἀπ' ἐμεῖο Theoc.20.2 ; ἔρρ' ἐκ προσώπου Herod. 8.59 ; in Att. strengthd., ἔρρ' ἐς κόρακας *go hang!* Ar.*Pl.*604 (anap.), Pherecr.70.5, etc. ; ἐς κόρακας ἔρρειν φασὶν ἐκ τῆς Ἀττικῆς Alex.94.5 ; ἔρρε εἰς ὄλεθρόν τε καὶ Ἄβυδον Lys.*Fr.*5a : opt. ἔρροις *AP*5.2 (Antip. Thess.) : part., ἔρρων νυν αὐτὸς χὴ ξυνοικήσασά σοι..γηράσκετ' E.*Alc.* 734 : fut., οὐκ ἐρρήσετε; οὐκ ἐς κόρακας ἐρρήσετε; Ar.*Lys.*1240, *Pax* 500 ; εἰ μὴ 'ρρήσεθ' Id.*V.*1329 (lyr.). **3.** of persons and things, *to be clean gone, perish, disappear*, ἔρρων ἐκ ναός A.*Pers.*964 (lyr.) ; ἔρρει πανώλης ib.732 (troch.) ; ἄφαντος ἔρρει S.*OT*560, cf. Pl.*Lg.*677c ; ἔρρει ταῦτα ἐκ τῆς αὐτῶν χώρας Id.*Phlb.*24d ; ἔρρειν ἐκ τῆς τοῦ εἶναι ἕδρας Plot.3.7.4 ; ἔρρει τὰ κᾶλα the ships *are lost*, Hippocr.ap.X.*HG*1.1. 23 (prob.) ; ἔρρει πᾶσ' Ἀφροδίτα A.*Ag.*419 (lyr.) ; ἔρρει τὰ θεῖα the honour due to the gods *is gone*, S.*OT*910 (lyr.) ; ἔρρει δέμας φλογιστόν Id.*El.*57 ; ἔρρεις μάτην E.*Hel.*1220 ; θανόντας ἔρρειν Id.*Supp.* 1113 ; ἐξ οἵων καλῶν ἔρρεις from what fortunes *hast* thou *fallen*, Id. *IT*379 ; ἔρρει τὰ ἐμὰ πράγματα X.*Smp.*1.15, cf. *Cyr.*6.1.3.

**ἔρρω** (B), Aeol. for εἴρω, *EM*90.12.

**ἔρρωγα**, pf. of ῥήγνυμι.

⊛ **ἐρρωμένος**, η, ον, pf. part. Pass. of ῥώννυμι : generally used as Adj., *in good health*, D.2.21, etc. ; ἐρρωμένος ὤν, opp. ἀσθενέστερος, Lys.24.7 ; *powerful, influential, formidable*, ἐρρωμένη τέχνης δύναμις Pl.*Phdr.*268a ; μηχαναί Hero *Aut.*21.2 (sed leg. αἰρομένας) : irreg. Comp., τειχομαχίη ἐρρωμενεστέρη Hdt.9.70 ; οἱ –έστεροι τῶν ἀνθρώπων Pl.*Grg.*483c ; ἐρρωμενεστέραις ταῖς γνώμαις X.*Cyr.*3.3.31 ; τὸ φύσει –έστερον Pl.*Smp.*181c : Sup. –έστατος And.4.37, Pl.*R.*477d. Adv. ἐρρωμένως *stoutly, manfully, vigorously*, A.*Pr.*65, 76, Ar.*V.*230 ; ἐσθίειν Critias *Fr.*32 D. ; χωρεῖν X.*Ages.*2.11 : Comp. –έστερον Pl. *Hp.Ma.*287a, –εστέρως Isoc.4.163 : Sup. –έστατα Pl.*R.*401d.

**ἐρρώμην**, v. ῥώννυμι. **ἐρρώοντο, ἐρρώσαντο**, v. ῥώομαι. **ἔρρωσο**, v. sub ῥώννυμι. **ἐρσαῖος**, α, ον, = ἐρσήεις, Hsch.

**ἐρσενικός**, ή, όν, = ἀρρενικός, *PPetr.*3 pp.14, 173 (iii B.C.).

**ἔρσεο·** διεγείρου, and **ἔρση·** ὁρμήσῃ, Hsch.

⊛ **ἕρση**, ἡ : Ep. **ἐέρση**, later **ἀέρση** *PLit.Lond.*60 (Posidipp.) : Aeol., Dor. **ἐέρσᾱ** Sapph.*Supp.*25.12 (αδερσα ( = ἀ δ' ἐέρσα) Pap.), **ἔερσᾰ** Pi. *N.*3.78, cf. Hdn.Gr.2.90 : Cret. **ἄερσα** Hsch. : **ἔρσα** Alcm.48, **ἕρσα** Theoc.20.16 :—*dew*, Il.23.598, etc. ; τεθαλυῖά τ' ἐέρση (v.l. θ' ἐέρση) abundant *dew*, Od.13.245 ; θῆλυς ἐ. 5.467, Hes.*Sc.*395 : pl., *raindrops*, κατὰ δ' ὑψόθεν ἧκεν ἐέρσας αἵματι μυδαλέας Il.11.53 ; στιλπναὶ δ' ἀπέπιπτον ἕ. (sc. τῆς νεφέλης) 14.351, cf. Theoc.2.107 ; χλωραῖς ἐ. Pi.*N.*8.40 : generally, of any *liquid*, ἄνθεμον ποντίας ὑφελοῖσ' ἐέρσας from the *water* of the sea, ib.7.79 ; *foam*, ib.3.78 ; γλυκερὴ ἐέρση, of *honey*, Hes.*Th.*83. **II.** metaph., of *young and tender animals*, χωρὶς δ' αὖθ' ἕρσαι (this form only here in Hom.) Od.9.222, cf. Hsch. ; esp. of *kids born in winter*, Id. (Cf. Skt. *varṣám* 'rain'.)

⊛ **ἑρσήεις**, Ep. **ἐερσ–** (Dor. **ἐρσάεις** *Hymn.Is.*167), εσσα, εν, *dewy*, λωτόν θ' ἑρσήεντα Il.14.348 ; λειμών *AP*9.668.3 (Marian.) : metaph., of a corpse, οἷον ἐερσήεις κεῖται *fresh*, Il.24.419 ; νῦν δέ μοι ἑρσήεις καὶ πρόσφατος..κεῖσαι ib.757.

⊛ **ἔρσην**, ενος, ὁ, Aeol., Dor., Ion., for ἄρσην, *IG*12(2).73.3 (Mytil.), 4.952.132 (Epid.), *BMus.Inscr.*968*B*13 (Cos), *Leg.Gort.*10.49, Hdt. 1.109, 192, etc. ; also *PHib.*1.32.11, al. (iii B.C.) : Comp. ἐρσεναίτερος *Schwyzer*424.2 (Elis, iv B.C.).

**ἐρσηφορία, –φόρος**, = ἀρρηφορία, –φόρος, Sch.Ar.*Lys.*643 (written ἐρσε–), *IG*3.318, 319 ; cf. ἐρρηφορέω, ἐρσοφόρος.

**ἔρσις**, εως, ἡ, (εἴρω A) *a binding, band*, Suid., etc., v.l. in Th.1.6.

**Ἕρσος**, ὁ, epith. of Apollo in Attica, *IG*1².783 ; perh. cf. Ἔρρος.

**ἐρσοφόρος**, = ἀρρηφόρος, τῶν ἁγιωτάτων μυσταρίων prob. in *IG*12 (2).255 (Mytil.) ; cf. ἐρρηφορέω, ἐρσηφορία.

**ἕρσω**, (ἕρση) *bedew, moisten*, like ἄρδω, Nic.*Th.*62, 631 (both Pass.).

**ἐρσώδης**, ες, = ἑρσήεις, ἀήρ Thphr.*CP*3.2.6.

**ἔρτις·** κρημνός, Hsch.

**ἐρτός**, ή, όν, (εἴρω A) *threaded, passed through*, βρόχος Heracl.ap. Orib.48.1.1.

**ἐρῠγ-άζομαι**, = sq., Sor.1.108 (ῥυγιάζεσθαι cod.). **–άω**, *belch*, *Gp.*17.17.1.

**ἐρυγγάνω**, Prose and Att. form of ἐρεύγομαι (A), *belch*, Hp.*Vict.*3. 76, Cratin.58 : c. acc., [Βάκχιον] ἐ. E.*Cyc.*523, cf. Eup.198 ; σκοροδάλμην Luc.*Alex.*39 : metaph., δάνει' ἐρυγγάνων Diph.43.21 :—also in Med., c. acc., Hp.*Vict.*3.75.

**ἐρῠγ-ή**, ἡ, *belching*, Sch.Ar.*Pax* 528, Aret.*SD*1.5, Gal.1.629. **II.** *bellowing*, Hsch. **–ήτωρ**, ορος, ὁ, *bellower*, Id. **–μα**, ατος, τό, = ἐρυγή 1, Hp.*Morb.*2.66. **–μαίνω**, *bellow*, Hsch. **–μᾰτώδης**, ες, *causing eructation*, νοῦσος Hp.*Morb.*2.69. **–μηλος**, η, ον, (ἐρῠγεῖν) *loud-bellowing*, ταῦρος Il.18.580. **II.** ἐρυγμήλη, ἐπίθετον ῥαφανίου, ἴσως ἀπὸ τῆς ἐρυγῆς, *EM*379.27, cf. Hsch. (ἐρυγηλή cod.). **–μός**, ὁ, = ἐρυγή 1, Arist.*Pr.*$908^{a}3$ (pl.), al., Thphr.*Od.*59 (pl.).

⊛ **ἐρῠθ-αίνω**, aor. ἐρύθηνα A.R.1.791, Lxx *Wi.*13.14 :—Pass., Hom. (v. infr.), etc. :—poet. and later Prose word for ἐρυθραίνω, ἐρεύθω, *dye red*, αἷμα πέπλον ἐρύθηνεν A.R.4.474 ; φύκει –ήνας χρόαν Lxx l.c. ; *make to blush*, A.R.1.791 :—Pass., *to be dyed red*, ἐρυθαίνετο αἵματι γαῖα Il.10.484, cf. 21.21 : c. gen., Nonn.*D.*11.92 (s.v.l.) ; *blush scarlet*, *AP*12.8 (Strat.) :—Pass., also in later Prose, Arr.ap.Stob.1. 31.8, Poll.2.87. **–ημα**, ατος, τό, *redness* or *flush upon the skin*, Hp.*Aph.*7.49, Th.2.49 (pl.) ; ἐ. προσώπου *blush*, E.*Ph.*1488 (lyr.), Hp.*Acut.*(*Sp.*)6 (pl.) ; ἐ. ῥόδων φέρειν Aristaenet.1.10 : abs., *redness*, X.*Cyn.*5.18 ; *blush*, Chaerem.1.4. **II.** concrete, ἐρύθημα ἱματίων *scarlet* garments, Lxx *Is.*63.1.

**ἐρυθίβη, –ιος**, said to be Rhodian for ἐρυσίβ-η, –ιος (q.v.).

**ἐρῠθῖνος**, ὁ, = ἐρυθρῖνος, Henioch.3.3, D.L.8.19, Opp.*H.*1.97.

**ἐρυθράδιον**, τό, = ἐρυθρόδανον, Sch.Nic.*Th.*74.

**Ἐρυθραί**, αἱ, *Erythrae* in Ionia, Hdt.1.142, etc. ; locat. Ἐρυθρᾶσι *IG*1².10.14 :—hence **Ἐρυθραϊκὸν** σατύριον, *Serapias cordigera*, Dsc. 3.128, Plin.*HN*26.97 :—but **Ἐρυθριὰς** γῆ is f.l. for Ἐρετριάς, Heras ap.Gal.13.545.

**Ἐρυθραϊκός**, ή, όν, *of the Red Sea*, κυβερνήτης *OGI*674.10 (i A.D.).

**ἐρυθρ-αίνω**, *paint red, rouge*, πρόσωπον Perict.ap.Stob.4.28.19 ; παρειάς Hdn.5.6.10 :—Pass., *become red*, Thphr.*HP*3.12.5, Sor.1. 108 ; *blush*, X.*Cyr.*1.4.4, Arist.*EN*$1128^{b}13$. **II.** intr., *to be red*, Id.*Pr.*$890^{a}8$ ; ἡ τέρμινθος.. χλοερὸν ἐνέγκασα [καρπὸν] μετὰ ταῦτα ἐρυθραίνει Thphr.*HP*3.15.3. **–αῖος**, α, ον, = ἐρυθρός, πόντος, θάλασσα, D.P.597, 958, etc. ; κάλαμος Id.1127. **II.** *of* or *from Erythrae*, Hdt.1.18, etc. **–ᾰνός**, όν, κισσός *red-berried* ivy, Plin. *HN*24.82. **–ημα**, ατος, τό, = ἐρύθημα (perh. f.l.), Poll.6.180, v.l. in Lxx *Is.*63.1. **–ίας**, ου, ὁ, *of ruddy complexion*, opp. ὠχρίας, Arist.*Cat.*$9^{b}31$, *PPetr.*3 p.30 (iii B.C.). **–ίᾱσις**, Ion. **–ίησις**, εως, ἡ, *ruddiness, blushing*, Hp.*Decent.*5, Hsch. s.v. λατραπία. **–ιάω**, Ep. part. –ιόων Musae.161 : impf. ἠρυθρίων Luc.*Laps.*1, etc. : aor. 1 ἠρυθρίᾱσα Pl.*Ly.*204c, etc. : pf. ἠρυθρίᾱκα *PTeb.*37.10 (i B.C.) (v. ἀπηρυθριᾱκότως) :—*blush, colour up*, Pl.*Prt.*312a, D.18.128 ; ἀστεῖόν γε..ὅτι ἐρυθριᾷς Pl.*Ly.*204c : c. part., *blush at* doing, Dromo 1 ; ὅστις δ' ἐρυθριᾷ..πρὸς τοὺς ἑαυτοῦ γονέας, οὐκ ἔστιν κακός Antiph.261, cf. Men.782, Diph.135 ; also ἐ. τινά *to blush before* one, Aristaenet.1.13, Lyd.*Mag.*3.38 ; τὴν ἀρχήν ib.50 : c. inf., Ph.2.310, Chor. in Lib.4. 775 Reiske. **2.** *to be inflamed*, Aret.*SA*1.8.

⊛ **ἐρυθρῖνος,** also **ἐρυθῖνος** (q.v.), ὁ, a hermaphrodite fish, prob. *Serranus anthias,* Arist.*HA*538$^a$20. 2. a sea-fish, prob. *Pagellus erythrinus,* Speus.ap.Ath.7.300e, Hierocl. *in CA*26 p.480 M., etc.

**ἐρυθρίς,** = foreg., *Gloss.*

**ἐρυθρο-βἄφής,** ές, *red-dyed,* Eust.6.8. **-βωλος,** ον, *with red earth,* Sch.D.P.183. **-γραμμος,** ον, *with red lines,* Arist.*Fr.*294, cf. Ath.7.321e. **-δάκτῠλος,** ον, *red-fingered,* criticized as unpoet., Arist.*Rh.*1405$^b$21.

**ἐρυθρόδᾰν-ον,** τό, = ἐρευθέδανον, Dsc.3.143: **ἐρυθρόδανος,** ἡ, Plin. *HN*24.94 (v.l.); cf. ἐρυθρύδανον. **-όω,** *dye with madder, dye red,* LXX *Ex.*25.5, 26.14. **-ωσις,** εως, ἡ, *dyeing scarlet,* Zos.Alch.p.220 B.

**ἐρυθρο-ειδής,** f.l. for ἐλυτρο- (q.v.). **-κάρδιος,** ον, *with red pith,* Thphr.*HP*3.12.3. **-κομίς,** ίδος, ἡ, *with red down,* a kind of pomegranate, Plin.*HN*13.113. **-λευκος,** ον, *reddish-white,* Gal.17(1).835, Hsch. s. v. φλογόλευκον. **-μέλας,** αινα, αν, *blackish-red,* Philem.Lex.ap.Ath.14.652f.

**ἐρυθρόνιον,** τό, = σατύριον, Ps.-Dsc.3.128.

**ἐρυθρό-ξανθος,** ον, *reddish-yellow,* Aët.12.13. **-ποίκῐλος,** ον, *spotted with red,* συνόδοντες Epich.69. **-πους,** ὁ, ἡ, neut. πουν, *red-footed,* πελειάς Arist.*HA*544$^b$4. II. a bird, prob. *the redshank, Totanus calidris,* Ar.*Av.*303. **-πρόσωπος,** ον, *of a ruddy look,* Anon.ap.Suid. s. v. Ἁρμάτος.

⊛ **ἐρυθρός,** ά, όν, [ῠ by nature, Ar.*Ach.*787, al.: hence the later Comp. and Sup. are perh. -ώτερος, -ώτατος, as in Pl.*Ti.*83b, *Epin.* 987c; but the metre requires -ότερος in Anaxandr.22, Dromo 1, cf. Choerob. *in Theod.*2.76]:—*red,* νέκταρ ἐ. Il.19.38, Od.5.93; χαλκός Il. 9.365; χρυσὸν ἐ. ἰδεῖν Thgn.450; κῆρυξ ἐ., a ship painted with vermilion, Orac.ap.Hdt.3.57; -ότερον κόκκου Dromo l.c.; ἐ. πέλανος, of blood, A.*Eu.*265 (lyr.); ἐρυθρά, τά, *red pimples, eruption,* Hp.*Liqu.*6; but ἐ. διελθόντα *red* motions, Id.*Coac.*178. 2. ἐρυθρά, ἡ, = μελισσόφυλλον, Ps.-Dsc.3.104; ἐρυθρός, ὁ (sc. ῥοῦς), fruit of the ῥοῦς βυρσοδεψική, Dsc.1.108. 3. ἐρυθρόν, τό, ᾠοῦ *yolk,* Sor.1.124, Orib.*Syn.*5.13. II. Ἐρυθρὴ θάλασσα in Hdt. *the Indian Ocean,* in which the Red Sea (Ἀράβιος κόλπος) is sts. included (of the existence of the Persian Gulf he was ignorant), 1.180, 2.11,158, 4.42, al.; πόντος Ἐ. Pi.*P.*4.251—later the *Red Sea* only, *OGI*69,186,190, al.: also of the *Persian Gulf,* X.*Cyr.*8.6.20, D.S.2.11; *Peripl.M.Rubr.* prob. mentions Zanzibar and China; used of remote and unknown places, μόνον οὐκ ἐπὶ τὴν Ἐ. θάλατταν πρεσβείας πέμπειν D.19.304: really ἡ Ἐρύθρα θάλασσα sea *of Erythras,* acc. to Agatharch.5. (Lat. *rubro-* fr. **rudhro-,* cf. Skt. *rudhirá-*; v. ἐρεύθω.)

**ἐρυθρότης,** ητος, ἡ, *redness, ruddiness,* τῆς χρόας Gal.1.582, cf. Phlp. *in Cat.*148.5.

**ἐρυθρό-χλωρος,** ον, *pale-red,* Hp.*Epid.*6.3.13 (vulg. -χολος: al. -χροος, acc. to Gal.17(2).66). **-χροος,** ον, contr. -χρους, ουν, *red-coloured,* ὑπόδεσις D.C.43.43. **-χρως,** ωτος, ὁ, ἡ, = foreg., Cratin.221.

**ἐρυθρύδανον,** τό, = ἐρυθρόδανον, *PSI*5.489 (iii B.C.).

**ἐρυθρώδης,** ες, = ἐρυθροειδής, Ath.3.76b.

⊛ **ἐρύθω,** = ἐρεύθω, *Hymn.Is.*147.

**ἐρῠκᾰνάω,** poet. for ἐρύκω, *restrain, withhold,* κεῖνον ἐρυκανόωσ' ἀέκοντα Od.1.199: c. inf., *from* doing, Q.S.12.205: also Ep. impf. ἐρύκανε (from **ἐρῡκάνω**) Od.10.429, cf. Orph.*A.*647.

**ἐρυκτῆρες,** οἱ, *a class of freedmen* at Sparta, Myro 1 J.

**ἐρύκω** [ῡ], Il.24.658, Hdt.4.125, S.*Tr.*121 (lyr.), etc., rare in Prose, X.*An.*3.1.25, Plb.*Fr.*45: Ep. inf. ἐρυκέμεν Il.11.48: fut. ἐρύξω Od.7. 315, al. (not later): aor. 1 ἤρυξα A.*Th.*1081 (anap.), (ἀπ-) X.*An.*5.8. 25; Ep. ἔρυξα Il.3.113, Od.17.515, etc.: Ep. aor. 2 ἠρύκᾰκον Il.5.321, 20.458, ἐρύκᾰκον 11.352, etc., inf. ἐρῡκακέειν 5.262, Od.11.105:—Med., Il.12.285:—Pass., v. infr. II: cf. ἐρυκάνω, -ανάω: (perh. akin to ἐρύω B):—*keep in, curb, restrain,* ἵππους Il.11.48, etc.; λαὸν ἐρυκάκετε *keep* them *back* (from flight or fighting), 6.80, cf. 24.658; but λαὸν ἔρυκε *kept* them *in their place,* 23.258; αἰθὴρ ὄμβρον ἐρύκει *forces* it *back,* Emp. 100.18; θυμὸν ἐρυκακέειν *to curb* desire, Od.11.105; πολύστονον ἐρύκεν (inf.) ὕβριν B.16.41; ἕτερος δέ με θυμὸς ἔρυκεν another mind *checked* me (opp. ἀνῆκεν), Od.9.302; ἐρυκέμεν εὐρύοπα Ζῆν *to restrain* him, Il.8.206; γυίων πίστιν ἐ., i.e. to mistrust, Emp.4.13; ἔρυκέ μιν ἔνδοθεν αἰδώς A.R.3.652: c. gen., μηδέ μ' ἔρυκε μάχης *keep* me not *from* fight, Il.18. 126; ἀλλά τις θεῶν.. Ἅιδα σφε δόμων ἐρύκει S.*Tr.*121; μηδέ σ' Ἔρις ἀπ' ἔργου θυμὸν ἐρύκοι Hes.*Op.*28: c. inf. praes., *hinder from* doing, Pi.*N.* 4.33; aor., E.*HF*317; fut., ἄλλον ἀναστήσεσθαι ἐρύξω A.R.1.346: c. acc. et inf., ἤρυξε πόλιν μὴ 'ναπραπῆναι A.*Th.*1081; ἐ. τἆλλα ἰχθύδια μὴ διαρπάσωσι.. Arist.*HA*621$^a$24. 2. abs., *hinder,* ἐρύκακε γὰρ τρυφάλεια Il.11.352; ἐρυκέμεν *to stay* [their flight], 21.7. 3. *hold in check, keep off* the enemy, εἴ κεν ἐρύξομεν ἀντιάσαντες Il.15.297, cf. Od.22.138; so τὰ δ' οὐ μένος ἀμὸν ἐρύξει Il.8.178; ἐ. τοὺς ἐπιόντας Hdt.4.125, cf. 5.15, etc. 4. *detain* a guest, ξείνισ' ἐνὶ μεγάροισιν ἐείκοσιν ἤματ' ἐρύξας Il.6.217, cf. Od.17.408, al.; also, *detain* by force, *confine,* [πόντος] πολέας ἀέκοντας ἐρύκει Il.21.59, cf. Od.1.14, 7.315, etc.; ἔρυξον ἐνὶ μεγάροισι γυναῖκας *keep* them *close,* 19.16; of the dead, ἤ μιν ἐρύξει γῆ φυσίζοος ἤ τε κατὰ κρατερόν περ ἐρύκει Il.21.62; σφωε δόλος καὶ δεσμὸς ἐρύξει Od.8.317; ὅσσ' ἔτι Νεῖκος ἔρυκε Emp.35.9:—Med., κῦμα δέ μιν (sc. χιόνα).. ἐρύκεται Il.12.285. 5. *ward off,* θεοῦ δ' ἠρύκακε δῶρα (sc. ἄκοντα) 21.594; ἅ κέν τοι λιμὸν ἐρύκοι Od.5. 166; κακόν, τό οἱ οὔ τις ἐρύκακεν Il.15.450; ἐ. ψευδέων ἐνιπάν Pi.*O.* 10(11).5; τὰ μὴ καλὰ νόσφιν ἐ. Theoc.7.127; ἀπ' ἐμαυτοῦ τὰ κακὰ X. *An.*3.1.25; τὸν πόλεμον ἀπὸ τῆς Μακεδονίας Plb.*Fr.*45. 6. *keep away,* ὀλίγος δ' ἔτι χῶρος ἐρύκει Il.10.161. II. Pass., *to be held back, detained,* δηθ' ἐνὶ νήσῳ ἐρύκεαι Od.4.373, cf. 17.17. 2. abs., *hold back, keep back,* μή μοι ἐρύκεσθον, says the driver to his horses, Il. 23.443. 3. *to be kept away,* τοῦ Ἀσωποῦ (v.l. ἀπὸ τοῦ Ἀ.) Hdt.9. 49. 4. ἀνέδην ὅδε χῶρος ἐρύκεται this place *is* remissly *guarded,* i.e. *is free* or *open* to all, S.*Ph.*1153 (lyr., dub. l.).

⊛ **ἔρῠμα,** ατος, τό, (ἐρύω B) *fence, guard,* ἔ. χροός, of defensive armour, Il.4.137; of a cloak, Hes.*Op.*536; θώρακας, ἐρύματα σωμάτων X.*Cyr.*4.3.9; ἔ. νιφετοῦ *a defence against..,* Call.*Fr.*142; τὸ ἔ. τοῦ τείχεος the *defence given by* it, Hdt.7.223,225; περιβαλέσθαι ἕρκος, ἔ. τῶν νεῶν Id.9.96, cf. Th.8.40; ἔ. Τρώων *the wall* of Troy, S.*Aj.*467; ἔ. λίθοις ὤρθωσαν *a breast-work,* Th.6.66; ἔ. τειχίζεσθαι, τειχίζειν, Id. 1.11, X.*HG*2.3.46; also of a river or trench used as a military *defence,* Id.*An.*2.4.22. 2. *safeguard* or *defence,* ἔ. χώρας, of the Areopagus, A.*Eu.*701; παῖδας ἔ. δώμασι E.*Med.*597; ἔ. πολεμίας χερός *against..,* ib.1322; ἔ. χθονὸς ὄφρα βάλοιτο Call.*Hec.*1.2.8.

**ἐρῠμάτιον,** τό, Dim. of foreg., Luc.*DMeretr.*9.5.

**ἐρυμνάομαι,** Pass., *to be defended,* Anon.ap.Suid.

**ἐρυμνόνωτος,** ον, *with fenced back,* of a crab, f.l. for τερεμνό-, *AP* 6.196 (Stat. Flacc.).

**ἐρυμν-ός,** ή, όν, Comp. -ότερος, Sup. -ότατος, *AP*7.138 (Acerat.), 599 (Jul.): (ἐρύω B):—*fenced, fortified, strong,* by art or nature, Γλήχωνά τ' ἐρυμνήν Hes.*Fr.*38, cf. Th.5.65, Plb.1.30.8, Plu.*Cam.*9, etc.; ἐ. δώματα E.*Hel.*68; κεῖναι μὲν πύργοισι.. ἐρυμναί, Δῆλος δ' Ἀπόλλωνι Call.*Del.*23; τὰ ἐρυμνὰ *strong positions,* X.*An.*5.7.31, etc.; τόποι οἱ ἐ. Arist.*Pol.*1330$^b$18; τὸ ἐ. Onos.42.15; of hills, *steep, sheer,* Ὄθρυς A.R.2.514, etc. Adv. Comp. -οτέρως Arist.*Pol.*1331$^a$30. **-ότης,** ητος, ἡ, *strength* or *security* of a place, X.*Cyr.*6.1.23; τῶν τειχῶν Arist.*Pol.*1330$^b$37; αἱ ἐ. τῶν Ἄλπεων *the difficulties of passing* them, Plb.3.47.9, etc. **-όω,** *fortify, make strong,* Agath.2.4, *EM*378. 31:—Pass., μερόπεσσιν -ώθησαν ἀγυιαί Nonn.*D.*6.386 (s. v.l.).

**ἐρυμνῶδις** (sic)· λύπην καὶ φλεγμονὴν παρέχων, ἢ ὑπερήφανον, Hsch. (cf. Lat. *aerumnosus*). **Ἐρυμός·** Ζεύς, καὶ ζυγός, καὶ ζεύγλη, Id. (cf. ῥυμός). **ἐρύμυλον·** τὸν μεγάλως μυκώμενον ταῦρον (leg. ἐρύγμηλον), Id. **ἐρυνόν·** σκοτεινόν, ἠσφαλισμένον, Id. (confusion of ἐρεμνόν and ἐρυμνόν).

**ἔρυξις,** εως, ἡ, = ἔρευξις, Hp.*Epid.*6.8.8.

**ἐρῠσαιθρον,** *apiastrum, Gloss.*; cf. *olusatrum.*

**ἐρῠσάρμᾰτες,** acc. -ᾰτας, nom. and acc. pl., with no sg. in use, *chariot-drawing,* ἵπποι Il.15.354, 16.370, Hes.*Sc.*369.

**ἐρῠσῖβ-άω,** *suffer from rust,* Thphr.*CP*4.14.2. **-η** [ῑ Orph.*L.* 600], ἡ, *rust,* in corn, Pl.*R.*609a; αὐχμοὶ καὶ ἐ. Arist.*HA*553$^b$20: pl., Pl.*Smp.*188b, X.*Oec.*5.18, Thphr.*CP*3.22.1, etc. II. title of Demeter in Lydia, *Et.Gud.*210.25. **-ιος,** ὁ, *averting rust,* epith. of Apollo at Rhodes, Str.13.1.64 (in alleged Rhod. form ἐρυθίβιος, from ἐρυθίβη: v.l. ἐρεθίβιος, etc., cf. Ἐρεθίμιος). **-όω,** *affect with rust,* Thphr.*CP*3.24 fin.:—Pass., = ἐρυσιβάω, ib.22.2, Ath.Med.ap.Orib.1. 2.12, etc. **-ώδης,** ες, *affected with rust,* ἄνθη, ὕλη, Arist.*HA*605$^b$ 18, 626$^b$23; *liable to mildew,* Thphr.*HP*8.3.2; χῶραι Id.*CP*3.24.4.

**ἐρῠσίθριξ** ἵππων ψήκτρη comb *for drawing through the hair, curry-comb, AP*6.246 (Phld. or Marc. Arg.).

**ἐρύσῐμον** [ῠ], τό, *hedge-mustard, Sisymbrium polyceratium,* Thphr. *HP*8.3.1, Dsc.2.158: **εἰρύσιμον** in Nic.*Th.*894, Orph.*A.*917; cf. ῥύσιμον. 2. as Adj., ἐρύσιμον· ἑλκύσιμον, Phot.

**ἐρῠσί-νηϊς,** ΐδος, ἡ, either *preserving ships* or *checking ships* (cf. ἰσχάς), ἄγκυρα *AP*6.90 (Phil.). **-πελας,** πέλατος, τό, *erysipelas,* Hp.*VM*19 (pl.), *Prog.*23, *Aph.*5.23, Gal.10.949, Orib.45.1.3 (pl.), *Gp.* 12.23.5 (pl.), etc. **-πελᾰτώδης,** ες, *of the nature of* ἐρυσίπελας, οἴδημα Hp.*VC*20; φλεγμοναί Dsc.1.26; διάθεσις Ruf.ap.Orib.8.24.16. Adv. -δῶς, ἔχειν Gal.18(1).448. ⊛ **-πτολις,** ὁ, ἡ, (ἐρύω B) *protecting the city,* epith. of Athena, Il.6.305 codd. (ῥυσ- Sch.), *h.Hom.*11.1, 28.3.

**ἔρυσις,** εως, ἡ, (ἐρύω A) *a drawing,* νεῶν Max.Tyr.19.4 (pl.).

**ἐρυσί-σκηπτρον,** τό, a plant, = ἀσπάλαθος, Thphr.*Od.*57, Dsc.1. 20; = κύπερος, ib.4; also, = ἄκανθα λευκή, Ps.-Dsc.3.12; = ἱερὰ βοτάνη ib.4.60; cf. ἐρίσκηπτον. **-χαιος,** ον, expl. as, = *carrying a shepherd's staff,* Alcm.24.4; but prob. = *inhabitant of* Ἐρυσίχη in Acarnania, cf. Hdn.Gr.ap.Bgk.ad lcc. **-χθονίδαι,** οἱ, name of an Athenian γένος, *SIG*728 D[1] (i B.C.). ⊛ **-χθων,** ὁ, ἡ, gen. χθονος, *tearing up the earth,* of an ox ploughing, Strato Com.1.19.

**ἐρυσμός,** ὁ, *safeguard* against witchcraft, *h.Cer.*230. II. a vegetable, the seed of which was eaten by women in childbirth, Paus. Gr.*Fr.*182.

**ἔρυσος,** ὁ, *basket,* Hsch.

**ἐρυστός,** ή, όν, *drawn,* κολεῶν ἐρυστὰ.. ξίφη S.*Aj.*730.

**ἐρῠτήρ,** ῆρος, ὁ, *that which draws up,* ἐ. φάρυγγος, of a strip of papyrus used to induce vomiting, Nic.*Al.*363.

**ἐρύφαξε·** κατεπάτησεν, ἐτόξευσεν, Hsch.

⊛ **ἐρύω** (A), Il.4.467, al., Ion. εἰρύω, Dor. ϝερύω (v. infr.): Ep. inf. εἰρύμεναι [ῠ] Hes.*Op.*818: impf. εἴρυον Mosch.2.14, ἔρυον Il.12.258, ἐρύεσκον Nonn.*D.*43.50: fut. ἐρύω Il.11.454, al., ἐρύσω Opp.*H.*5.375; Ep. ἐρύσσω Orph.*L.*35, Nonn.*D.*17.183: aor. εἴρυσα Od.2.389, Hdt. 2.136 (in Hdt. εἴρυσα takes the place of εἵλκυσα), ἔρυσα Il.5.573; εἴρυσσα 3.373, Od.8.85; lengthd. ἐρύσασκε (ἐξ-) Il.10.490; imper. εἴρυσον S.*Tr.*1033 (hex.), Dor. ϝερυσάτω (dub. sens.) *BCH*50.15 (Delphi, iv B.C.); subj. ἐρύσω Il.17.230, εἰρύσω Hp.*Morb.*2.8, etc.; 2 sg. ἐρύσσῃς Il.5.110; Ep. 1 pl. ἐρύσσομεν (for -ωμεν) 14.76, 17.635; opt. ἐρύσαιμι 8. 21, εἰρύσαιμι Timo 59; inf. ἐρύσαι, ἐρύσσαι, Il.17.419, 8.23, εἰρύσαι Hp. *Morb.*1.29, (δι-, ἐξ-) Hdt.7.24, 1.141; part. ἐρύσας Il.23.21, ἐρύσαις Pi. *N.*7.67, εἰρύσας Hdt.4.10, ἐρύσσας A.R.3.913.—Ion., Dor., and poet. Verb:—*drag, draw,* implying force or violence, νῆα.. εἰς ἅλα, ἅλαδε, ἠπειρόνδε, Il.1.141, Od.2.389, 10.423; ἐπ' ἠπείροιο on land, 16.325,359; [δόρυ] ἐ. ἐπ' ἄκρης, of the Trojan horse, 8.508; freq. of the dead,

νεκρόν, νεκροὺς ἐ., of the friends, *drag* them *away*, *rescue* them, Il.5.573, 16.781; of the enemy, *drag* them *off for plunder*, *ransom*, etc., 4.467, al.; τρὶς ἐρύσας περὶ σῆμα (sc. Ἕκτορα) 24.16; of dogs and birds of prey, *drag and tear*, οἰωνοὶ ὠμησταὶ ἐρύουσι 11.454, etc.; *drag away*, *carry off violently*, Od.9.99: c. gen. partit., διὰ δώματ' ἐ. . ἢ ποδὸς ἢ καὶ χειρός 17.479; ἐ. τινὰ κουρίξ by the hair, 22.187; also, *pull down*, *tear away*, κρόσσας μὲν πύργων ἔρυον Il.12.258, cf. 14.35. **2.** simply, *draw*, *pull*, δόρυ ἐξ ὠτειλῆς 16.863; φάρμακον ἐκ γαίης Od.10.303; ἐξ οὐρανόθεν πεδίονδε Ζῆν' Il.8.21; κίον' ἀν' ὑψηλὴν ἐρύσαι Od.22.176; φᾶρος..κὰκ κεφαλῆς εἴρυσσε *drew* it *over* his head, 8.85; ἄλλον μὲν χλαίνης ἐρύων, ἄλλον δὲ χιτῶνος *pulling* or *plucking* him by.., Il.22.493; νευρὴν ἐπὶ τῷ ἐ. *drawing* the bowstring at him, 15.464; ἐ. τόξον Hdt.3.30, 4.10; εἴρυσον ἔγχος *draw* thy sword, S.*Tr*.1033 (hex.); *attract*, *absorb*, [ὑγρόν] Hp.*Loc.Hom*.14: c. gen. partit., τῆς χολῆς Id.*Morb*.1.29; ἐπί τινι κλῆρον ἐ. *draw* lots for.., Call.*Jov*.62; ἐκ ποδὸς ἐ. *to put* aside, Pi.*N*.7.67; ὅππη ἐμὸν νόον εἰρύσαιμι Timo l. c.; also πλίνθους εἰρύσαι *make* bricks, Hdt.2.136.

**B.** Med. **ἐρύομαι**, Ion. **εἰρύομαι** [ῠ], fut. inf. ἐρύεσθαι Il.14.422, al., ἐρύσσεσθαι v. l. in Od.21.125, Il.21.176: aor. 1 εἰρύσσατο 22.306, ἐρύσαντο 1.466, etc.; subj. ἐρύσωμαι A.R.1.1204; opt. ἐρύσαιο, –αίατο, Il.5.456, 298; inf. ἐρύσασθαι 22.351; part. ἐρυσσάμενος 1.190, εἰρυσάμενος (ἐπ–) Hdt.4.8:—*draw for oneself*, ἐρυσαίμεθα νῆας *launch us* ships, Il.14.79; [ἵππον] ἐς ἀκρόπολιν ἐ. Od.8.504; ξίφος, ἄορ, μάχαιραν ἐρύεσθαι, *draw one's* sword, Il.4.530, 21.173, 3.271; ἄορ ἐκ κολεοῖο Theoc.22.191; δόρυ ἐξ ὠτειλῆς εἰρυσάμην Od.10.165; of meat on the spit, ἐρύσαντό τε πάντα they *drew* all *off*, Il.1.466, etc.; ἐρύσσασθαι μενεαίνων in his anxiety *to draw* [the bow], Od.21.125; βύρσαν θηρὸς ἀπὸ μελέων Theoc.25.273; simply, *wrench*, ὅταν ἱστὸν ἀνέμοιο καταΐξ..ὑπὲκ προτόνων ἐρύσηται A.R.1.1204. **2.** of captives, χρυσῷ ἐρύσασθαι *weigh* against gold (cf. ἕλκω): hence, *ransom*, Il.22.351 (cf. ἀντερύομαι). **3.** *draw towards oneself*, ἔθεν ἆσσον ἐρύσσατο Od.19.481. **b.** *assimilate*, *retain*, γονήν, τροφήν, Hp.*Mul*.2.166, 171. **II.** *draw out of* the press, ἐρύσασθαί τινα μάχης Il.5.456; esp. of friends *dragging away* the body of a slain hero, οὐδέ κε..ἐκ βελέων ἐρύσαντο νέκυν 18.152; of enemies, 14.422, 17.161: c. dat., *in spite of*, *from*, 5.298, 17.104.

**C.** Pass., pf. εἴρῡμαι, plpf. 3 pl. εἰρύατο [ῡ Il.14.30, al., ῠ 4.248], εἴρυντο (v. infr.): aor. ἐρύσθην or εἰρ–, Hp.*Epid*.5.47, *Mul*.1.36:—*to be drawn ashore*, *drawn up in line*, of ships, εἴρυντο νέες ταχὺν ἀμφ' Ἀχιλῆα Il.18.69; εἰρύατο νῆες θῖν' ἔφ' ἁλὸς πολιῆς 14.30, cf. 4.248. **2.** *to be drawn*, *attracted*, of moisture, Hp. l. c.; *to be contracted*, ἐς τοὔπισθεν ἐρυσθείς, of tetanic convulsions, Id.*Epid*.5.17; τὴν γνάθον ἐρυσθεῖσα ib.4.36. (ϝερῠ–, ϝρῡ–, cf. ῥῡ-τήρ (βρύτηρ), ῥῦ-μα, ῥῡ-μός.)

⊛**ἐρύω** (B), only in Med. **ἐρύομαι**, redupl. non-thematic pres. 3 pl. εἰρύαται [ῠ] Il.1.239, *h.Cer*.152, [ῡ] Od.16.463; inf. εἴρυσθαι 3.268, 23.151 (from *se-srū*–, v. infr.); impf. εἴρῡτο Il.16.542, 24.499, Od.23.229, Hes.*Sc*.138, εἴρυντο Il.12.454, εἰρύατο [ῠ] 22.303: from unredupl. stem **ῥῡ**– (*srū*–), non-thematic 3 pl. impf. ῥύατ' [ῡ] 18.515, Od.17.201, inf. ῥῦσθαι Il.15.141, iterat. ῥύσκευ 24.730: thematic pres. **ῥύομαι** [ῠ] Od.14.107, 15.35, Il.9.396, 10.259, 417, Hes.*Sc*.105; with ῡ, ῥύομ' Il.15.257, ῥύοιτο 12.8, ῥύοισθε 17.224; impf. ῥύετ' [ῡ] 16.799: ῡ in Trag. (E.*HF*197, al., also A.*Eleg*.3), but ῠ in Id.*Th*.303 (lyr.), 824 (anap.): thematic impf. ἐρύετο [ῡ] Il.6.403; non-thematic ἔρῡτο 4.138, 5.23, al., ἔρῡσο 22.507 (ἔρῡτο as aor. 2 S.*OT*1351 (lyr.)): pres. inf. ἔρυσθαι Od.5.484, 9.194, al.; later pres. ind. ἔρῡται A.R.2.1208: fut. ἐρύσσεται Il.10.44, ἐρύεσθαι [ῠ] 20.195, ῥύσομαι [ῡ] Hes.*Th*.662, Hdt.1.86, A.*Th*.91 (lyr.); 3 pl. ῥυσεῦνται Call.*Lav.Pall*.112: aor. 1 εἰρῠσάμην (from *e-serŭ*–) Il.4.186, 20.93, 21.230; opt. ἐρύσαιτο [ῠ] 24.584; ind. also ἐρρύσατο [ῡ] Od.1.6, al., ἐρύσατο [ῡ] Il.5.344, al., once with ῥῠ, ῥῠσάμην 15.29: from the redupl. pres. εἴρῡμαι are formed fut. ind. 3 pl. εἰρύσσονται 18.276, 1 pl. εἰρῠόμεσθα 21.588: aor. 1 inf. εἰρύσσασθαι 1.216; opt. εἰρυσσαίμην 8.143, 17.327, Od.16.459:—later Pass., aor. ἐρρύσθην *Ev.Luc*.1.74, 2*Ep.Ti*.4.17, Hld.10.7: for ἔρῦτο and ἐρυσσάμενοι as Pass., v. infr. 4:—*protect*, *guard*, of armour, [πήληξ] κάρη ῥύετ' Ἀχιλλῆος Il.16.799; [κυνέη] εἴρυτο κάρη Hes.*Sc*.138; ῥύεται δὲ κάρη Il.10.259, etc.; μίτρης..ἣ οἱ πλεῖστον ἔρυτο 4.138, cf. 23.819; ἄστυ δὲ πύργοι ὑψηλαί τε πύλαι σανίδες τ'..εἰρύσσονται 18.276, cf. 12.454; ἀμφὶ δὲ τάφρον ἤλασαν, ὄφρα σφιν νῆας..ῥύοιτο ib.8; οἶος ἐρύετο Ἴλιον Ἕκτωρ 6.403, cf. 22.507, 24.499; οἵ με πάρος γε εἰρύατο 22.303; ὅς σε πάρος περ ῥύομ' 15.257, cf. A.*Th*.91 (lyr.), etc.; καὶ πῶς βέβηλον ἄλσος ἂν ῥύοιτό με; Id.*Supp*.509; Λυκίην εἴρυτο δίκῃσί τε καὶ σθένεϊ ᾧ Il.16.542; ἀριστήων οἵ τε πτολίεθρα ῥύονται 9.396; [ἔλαφον] ὕλη εἰρύσατο 15.274; of warders or watchmen, 10.417; σῦς τάσδε φυλάσσω τε ῥύομαί τε Od.14.107; νῆα, νῆας ἔρυσθαι, 9.194, 10.444, 14.260, 17.429; εἴρυσθαι μέγα δῶμα 23.151; ἣ νῶϊν εἴρυτο θύρας, of a female slave, ib.229; ἐπέτελλεν..εἴρυσθαι ἄκοιτιν 3.268; αὖλιν ἔρυντο, of dogs, Theoc.25.76; ἔτι μ' αὖτ' εἰρύαται οἴκαδ' ἰόντα *lie in wait for* me, Od.16.463; χαλεπόν σε θεῶν..δήνεα εἴρυσθαι *to discover* them, 23.82 (here perh. a difft. word, cogn. with ἐρευνάω, cf. Pi.*Fr*.61); φρεσὶν εἰρύσσαιτο *keep* in his heart, *conceal*, Od.16.459; οἵ τε θέμιστας πρὸς Διὸς εἰρύαται *maintain* them, Il.1.239: hence, *support*, *hold in honour*, with notion of obedience, οὐ σύ γε βουλὰς εἰρύσαο Κρονίωνος 21.230; ἔπος εἰρύσσασθαι 1.216. **2.** without any notion of defence, merely *cover*, ὡς ῥύσαιτο περὶ χροῒ μήδεα φωτός Od.6.129; φύλλων χύσις ἦλ θα πολλὴ ὅσσον τ' ἠὲ δύω ἠὲ τρεῖς ἄνδρας ἔρυσθαι 5.484. **3.** c. acc. rei, *keep off*, *ward off*, ἀλλ' οὐκ οἰωνοῖσιν ἐρύσσατο κῆρα μέλαιναν by no augury *could* he *ward off* black death, Il.2.859; ἡ δ' (sc. ἀσπὶς) οὐκ ἔγχος ἔρυτο 5.538, 17.518, Od.24.524; ἀλλὰ πάροιθεν εἰρύσατο ζωστήρ Il.4.186. **4.** *thwart*, *check*, *curb*, much like ἐρύκω, Διὸς νόον εἰρύσσαιτο 8.143; μὴ ὁ μὲν κραδίῃ χόλον οὐκ ἐρύσαιτο 24.584; Ἠῶ ῥύσατ' ἐπ' Ὠκεανῷ Od.23.244; νῆά τ' ἔρυσθαι A.R.3.607; so prob. in Τρωΐας ἶνας ἐκταμὼν δορί, ταί νιν ῥύοντό ποτε (*thwarted* him) μάχας..ἔργον..κορύσσοντα Pi.*I*.8(7).57; νόστον ἐρυσσάμενοι *having been balked of* their return (Med. in pass. sense, cf. ἐστεφανώσατο, κατασχόμενος), Id.*N*.9.23 (v. l. ἐρεισ–):—Pass., ἡ δ' ἔρῦτ' εἰν Ἀρίμοισι Hes.*Th*.304. **5.** *rescue*, *save*, *deliver* (not in Att. Prose exc. Th.5.63); μετὰ χερσὶν ἐρύσατο Φοῖβος Ἀπόλλων Il.5.344, cf. 11.363; πῶς ἂν..εἰρύσσαισθε Ἴλιον; 17.327; Ποσειδάων..Νέστορος υἱὸν ἔρυτο 13.555; βουλῆς..ἥ τίς κεν ἐρύσσεται ἠδὲ σαώσει Ἀργείους 10.44; ἀλλ' Ἥφαιστος ἔρυτο σάωσε δέ 5.23; ὁ δ' ἐρύσατο καί μ' ἐλέησεν Od.14.279; ἐρρύσατο καὶ ἐσάωσεν Il.15.290; ἀρήξω τὸν ἱκέτην τε ῥύσομαι A.*Eu*.232; πατρίδα ῥυομένους Id.*Eleg*.3; ῥύου με κἀκφύλασσε S.*OC*285, cf. Hdt.7.217, 8.114: freq. folld. by a Prep., οὐ γάρ κεν ῥύσαιτό σ' ὑπὲκ κακοῦ Od.12.107; Ζεῦ πάτερ, ἀλλὰ σὺ ῥῦσαι ὑπ' ἠέρος υἷας Ἀχαιῶν Il.17.645, cf. 224; ἐκ..πόνων ἐρρύσατο Pi.*P*.12.19; ῥύσασθαί μιν ἐκ τοῦ παρεόντος κακοῦ Hdt.1.87; ὡς ἂν ἀλλὰ παῖδ' ἐμὴν ῥυσώμεθ' ἀνδρῶν ἐκ χερῶν μιαιφόνων E.*Or*.1563: ἀπὸ φόνου S.*OT*1351 (lyr.); ἀπὸ τοῦ πονηροῦ *Ev.Matt*.6.13: c. gen., ῥ. τινὰ τοῦ μὴ κατακαυθῆναι Hdt.1.86; κακῶν μυρίων E.*Alc*.770; τόξων Id.*Ion* 165 (lyr.); πολέμου καὶ μανιῶν ῥ. Ἑλλάδα Ar.*Lys*.342: c. inf., ῥ. τινὰ θανεῖν E.*Alc*.11; τινα μὴ κατθανεῖν Id.*HF*197, cf. *Or*.599, Hdt.7.11; also, *save from an illness*, *cure*, Id.4.187: generally, Id.3.132. **6.** *set free*, *redeem*, τὸν ἔνθεν ῥυσάμην I *set him free* from thence, Il.15.29; ἐκ δουλοσύνης Hdt.5.49, 9.90; δουλοσύνης ib.76; μάντιν Ἠλεῖον..ἀπημελημένον ἐν τοῖσι ἀνδραπόδοισι ἐρρύσατο Id.3.132; but χρυσῷ ἐρύσασθαι Il.22.351 seems to come from (ϝ)ερύω (v. ἐρύω (A) B.I.2). **b.** metaph., *redeem*, *compensate for*.., ἔργῳ γὰρ ἀγαθῷ ῥύσεσθαι τὰς αἰτίας (v.l. λύσεσθαι) Th.5.63; ταῦτα πάντα κατθανοῦσα ῥύσομαι my death *will redeem* (*purchase*) all this, E.*IA* 1383 (troch.); ῥ. καμάτους *Epigr.Gr*.853.6:—double sense in S.*OT* 312, 313 ῥῦσαι σεαυτὸν καὶ πόλιν, ῥῦσαι δ' ἐμέ, ῥῦσαι δὲ πᾶν μίασμα τοῦ τεθνηκότος *redeem* (*deliver*) thyself and the state and me, and *redeem* the pollution from the dead (the μίασμα being thought of as an unpaid debt). (ἐρῠ– ῥῡ– from *serŭ*– *srū*–, cogn. with Lat. *servare*, v. οὖρος 'guard', ἔρυμα, ἐρυμνός.)

**ἔρφος**, εος, τό, *a skin*, = στέρφος, τέρφος, Nic.*Al*.248, *Th*.376.

**ἐρχανήεις**, εσσα, εν, *like a fence*, πυλών Hsch.; cf. ἐρκάνη, ἔρχατος.

**ἔρχᾰται, ἔρχᾰτο**, Ion. pf. and plpf. Pass. of ἔργω.

***ἐρχᾰτάομαι**, Pass., *to be kept* or *shut up*, ἐν δὲ ἑκάστῳ [συφεῷ] πεντήκοντα σύες..ἐρχατόωντο Od.14.15. (Lengthd. fr. ἔρχατο.)

**ἔρχᾰτος**, ὁ, *fence*, *enclosure*, *hedge*, Hsch.; cf. ἕρκατος.

⊛**ἔρχομαι** Il.13.256, etc. (Act. ἔρχω as barbarism, Tim.*Pers*.167): impf. ἠρχόμην Hp.*Epid*.7.59, Arat.102, (δι–) Pi.*O*.9.93; freq. in later Prose, Lxx *Ge*.48.7, *Ev.Marc*.1.45, Luc.*Jud.Voc*.4, Paus.5.8.5, etc.; in Att. rare even in compds., ἐπ-ηρχόμην Th.4.120 (perh. fr. ἐπάρχομαι), προσ– ib.121 (perh. fr. προσάρχομαι), περι– Ar.*Th*.504 cod.: from ἐλυθ– (cf. ἐλεύθω) come fut. ἐλεύσομαι, Hom., Ion., Trag. (A.*Pr*.854, *Supp*.522, S.*OC*1206, *Tr*.595), in Att. Prose only in Lys.22.11, freq. later, D.H.3.15, etc.: aor., Ep. and Lyr. ἤλῠθον Il.1.152, Pi.*P*.3.99, etc., used by E. (not A. or S.) in dialogue (*Rh*.660, *El*.598, *Tr*.374, cf. Neophr.1.1); but ἦλθον is more freq. even in Hom., and is the only form used in obl. moods, ἐλθέ, ἔλθω, ἔλθοιμι, ἐλθεῖν, ἐλθών; Ep. inf. ἐλθέμεναι, –έμεν, Il.1.151, 15.146 (indic. never ἐλυθ– unaugmented unless ἐξ-ελύθη Il.5.293 has replaced ἐξ-έλυθε); Dor. ἦνθον Epich.180, Sophr.144, Theoc.2.118; imper. ἐνθέ Aristonous 1.9; part. ἐνθών *IG*9(1).867 (Corc., vi B. C.), (κατ–) *Schwyzer* 657.4 (Arc., iv B. C.); subj. ἔνθῃ *Berl.Sitzb*.1927.164 (Cyrene); Lacon. ἔλσῃ, ἔλσοιμι, ἐλσών, Ar.*Lys*.105, 118, 1081; later ἦλθα Lxx 2*Ki*.24.7, *Ev.Matt*.25.36, *BGU*530.11 (i A. D.), *IG*14.1320, etc.; 3 pl. ἤλθοσαν Lxx *Jo*.2.22, al., *PTeb*.179 (ii B. C.), etc.; ἤλυθα *IG*14.1971, Nonn.*D*.37.424, (ἐπ–) *AP*14.44: pf. ἐλήλῠθα (not in Hom.) A.*Pr*.943, etc.; sync. pl. ἐλήλῠμεν, –υτε, Cratin.235, Achae.24, 43; Ep. εἰλήλουθα, whence 1 pl. εἰλήλουθμεν Il.9.49, Od.3.81, part. εἰληλουθώς 19.28, 20.360; once ἐληλουθώς Il.15.81, part. κατ-εληλευθυῖα *Berl.Sitzb*.1927.166 (Cyrene); Cret. pf. inf. ἀμφ-εληλεύθεν, v. ἀμφέρχομαι: Boeot. pf. διεσσ-είλθεικε *Schwyzer* 485.2 (Thesp., iii B. C.), part. κατηνθηκότι ib.657.39 (Arc., iv B. C.): plpf. ἐληλύθειν Ar.*Eq*.1306; Ion. ἐληλύθεε Hdt.5.98; Ep. εἰληλούθει Il.4.520, εἰληλούθειν Call.*Fr*.532.—In Att. the obl. moods of pres., as well as the impf. and fut. were replaced by forms of εἶμι *ibo* (q. v.): in Lxx and Hellenistic Greek the place of the compounds, esp. ἐξ–, εἰσ-έρχομαι, is commonly taken by ἐκ–, εἰσ-πορεύομαι, etc., the fut., aor., and pf. being supplied as before by ἐλυθ– (ἐλθ–): **I.** *start*, *set out*, ἦ μέν μοι μάλα πολλὰ..Λυκάων ἐρχομένῳ ἐπέτελλε when I *was setting out*, Il.5.198, cf. 150; τύχησε γὰρ ἐρχομένη νηῦς a ship *was* just *starting*, Od.14.334; ἐς πλόον ἐρχομένοις (v. l. ἀρχ–) Pi.*P*.1.34. **2.** *walk*, = περιπατέω, χαμαὶ ἐρχομένων ἀνθρώπων Il.5.442; σὲ δ' ἐρχόμενον ἐν δίκᾳ πολὺς ὄλβος ἀμφινέμεται *walking* in justice, Pi.*P*.5.14: the two foreg. rare signfs. belong only to the pres. ἔρχομαι. **II.** (much more freq.) *come* or *go* (the latter esp. in Ep. and Lyr.), ἦλθες thou *art come*, Od.16.461, etc.; χαίροισ' ἔρχεο *go* and fare thee well, Sapph.*Supp*.23.7, cf. Il.9.43, Od.10.320, 1.281; ἀγγελίην στρατοῦ..ἐρχομένοιο 2.30, cf. 10.267; πάλιν ἐλθέμεν, αὖτε εἰλήλουθα, 19.533, 549; οἶκον ἐλεύσεται ib.313; οἴκαδε 5.220; ἐς οἴκους A.*Pers*.833: as a hortatory exclamation, ἀλλ' ἔρχευ, λέκτρονδ' ἴομεν Od.23.254, cf. 17.529. **III.** c. acc. cogn., ὁδὸν ἐλθέμεναι *to go* a journey, Il.1.151; ἄλλην ὁδόν, ἄλλα κέλευθα ἤλθομεν Od.9.262; τηϋσίην ὁδὸν ἔλθῃς 3.316: freq. in Trag., A.*Pr*.962, *Th*.714 (also κατὰ τὴν αὐτὴν ὁδόν Pl.*Lg*.707d); νόστιμον ἐλθεῖν πόδα (v. l. δόμον) E.*Alc*.1153; ἀγγε-

λίην, ἐξεσίην ἐλθεῖν, *go* on an embassy, Il.11.140, Od.21.20. 2. c. acc. loci, *come to, arrive at*, rare in Hom., ’Αΐδαο δόμους ἔρχεαι Il. 22.483; ἔρχεσθον κλισίην 1.322: freq. in later Poets, Pi.*P*.4.52, S. *Tr*.259, etc.; *traverse*, ὁ ἥλιος ἔρχεται τῆς Λιβύης τὰ ἄνω Hdt.2.24: c. acc. pers., αἴ κέν τι νέκυς (acc. pl.) ᾐσχυμμένος ἔλθῃ Il.18.180; σὲ δ', ὦ τέκνον, τόδ' ἐλήλυθεν πᾶν κράτος S.*Ph*.141 (lyr.). 3. c. gen. loci, ἔρχονται πεδίοιο *through* or *across* the plain, Il.2.801; but also, *from* a place, γῆς τινος S.*OC*572. 4. c. dat. pers., *come to*, i.e. *come to aid* or *relieve* one, rare in Hom., Od.16.453; freq. later, Pi.*O*.1.100, Th.1.13, etc.; ἀποροῦντι αὐτῷ ἔρχεται Προμηθεὺς ἐπισκεψόμενος τὴν νομήν Pl.*Prt*.321c; also in hostile sense, ἔρχομαί σοι *Apoc*.2.5. IV. c. fut. part., to denote the object, ἔρχομαι ἔγχος οἰσόμενος I *go to* fetch.., Il.13.256; ἔρχομαι ὀψομένη 14.301: freq. in Trag., μαρτυρήσων ἦλθον A.*Eu*.576; ἐκσώσων E.*Med*.1303. 2. in Hdt. like an auxiliary Verb, ἔρχομαι ἐρέων, φράσων, I *am going to* tell, 1.5, 3.6, al.; σημανέων 4.99; μηκυνέων 2.35: rare in Att., ἔ. κατηγορήσων, ἀποθανούμενος, Pl.*Euthphr*.2c, *Thg*.129a; ἔρχομαι ἐπιχειρῶν σοι ἐπιδείξασθαι, for ἔ. σοι ἐπιδειξόμενος, Id.*Phd*.100b; οὐ τοῦτο λέξων ἔρχομαι, ὡς.. X.*Ages*.2.7. 3. c. part. pres., aor., or pf., in Hom., to show the manner of moving, ἄγγελος ἦλθε θέουσα she *came* running, Il.11.715, al.; μὴ πεφοβημένος ἔλθῃς lest thou *come thither* in full flight, 10.510; ἦλθε φθάμενος he *came* first, 23.779; κεχαρισμένος ἔλθοι Od.2.54. 4. aor. part. ἐλθών added to Verbs, οὐ δύναμαι.. μάχεσθαι ἐλθών *go and* fight, Il.16.521; κάθηρον ἐλθών *come and* cleanse, ib.668; λέγοιμ' ἂν ἐλθών A.*Supp*.928; δρᾶ νυν τάδ' ἐλθών S.*Ant*.1107. V. of any kind of motion, ἐξ ἁλὸς ἐλθεῖν *to rise* out of the sea, Od.4.448, al.; ἐπὶ πόντον *to go* over it, 2.265; with qualifying phrase, πόδεσσιν ἔ. *to go* on foot, 6.40 (but πεζὸς εἰλήλουθα *have come* as a foot-soldier, Il. 5.204); of birds, 17.755, etc.; of ships, 15.549, Od.14.334; of spears or javelins, freq. in Il.; of natural phenomena, as rivers, 5.91; wind and storm, 9.6, Od.12.288; clouds, Il.4.276, 16.364; stars, *rise*, Od. 13.94; time, εἰς ὅ κεν ἔλθῃ νύξ Il.14.77, cf. 24.351; ἐπὴν ἔλθῃσι θέρος Od.11.192; ἔτος ἦλθε 1.16; of events and conditions, εἰς ὅ κε γῆρας ἔλθῃ καὶ θάνατος 13.59, cf. 11.135; of feelings, *go*, ἦ κέ μοι αἰνὸν ἀπὸ πραπίδων ἄχος ἔλθοι Il.22.43; ἀπὸ πραπίδων ἦλθ' ἵμερος 24.514; of sounds, etc., τὸν.. περὶ φρένας ἤλυθ' ἰωή 10.139; Κύκλωπα περὶ φρένας ἤλυθεν οἶνος Od.9.362; without φρένας, περὶ δέ σφεας ἤλυθ' ἰωή 17.261, cf. 16.6; of battle, ὁμόσ' ἦλθε μάχη Il.13.337; of things sent or taken, ὄφρα κε δῶρα ἐκ κλισίης ἔλθῃσι 19.191, cf. 1.120; so later, esp. of danger or evil, c. dat., εἰ πάλιν ἔλθοι τῇ 'Ελλάδι κίνδυνος ὑπὸ βαρβάρων X.*HG*6.5.43; ἦλθεν αὐτῷ Ζηνὸς βέλος A.*Pr*.360; μηδ' ὑπ' ἀνάγκας γάμος ἔλθοι Id.*Supp*.1032 (lyr.), cf. *Pers*.436; of reports, commands, etc., Id.*Pr*.663, Th.8.19; τοῖς 'Αθηναίοις ὡς ἦλθε τὰ γεγενημένα *came to* their *ears*, ib.96; τὰ ἐρχόμενα ἐπ' αὐτόν that which *was about to happen* to him, *Ev.Jo*.18.4; of property, which *comes* or *passes* to a person by bequest, conveyance, gift, etc., τὰ ἐληλυθότα εἴς με ἀπὸ κληρονομίας *BGU*919.7 (ii A.D.); ἔ. εἴς τινα ἀπὸ παραχωρήσεως, κατὰ δωρεάν, *PLond*.3.1164e6 (iii A.D.), *PMasp*.96.22 (vi A.D.):—Geom., *pass, fall*, ἔ. ἐπὶ τὸ αὐτὸ σαμεῖον *pass* through the same point, Archim.*Aequil*.1.15; ὅπου ἂν ἔρχηται τὸ ἕτερον σαμεῖον wherever the other point *falls*, ib.2.10.

B. Post-Homeric phrases: 1. ἐς λόγους ἔρχεσθαί τινι *come* to speech with, Hdt.6.86.α', S.*OC*1164 codd.; so ἐς ὄψιν τινὶ ἐλθεῖν Hdt. 3.42. 2. εἰς χεῖρας ἐλθεῖν τινι (v. χείρ); so ἐς μάχην ἐλθεῖν τινι Id. 7.9.γ'; εἰς ὀργάς τισιν Pl.*R*.572a. 3. ἐπὶ μεῖζον ἔ. increase, S.*Ph*. 259; ἐπὶ μηδέν Id.*Fr*.871.8, *El*.1000; ἐπὶ πᾶν ἐλθεῖν try everything, X.*An*.3.1.18. 4. ἐς τὸ δεινόν, ἐς τὰ ἀλγεινὰ ἐλθεῖν, *come* into danger, etc., Th.3.45, 2.39; εἰς τοσοῦτον αἰσχύνης ἐληλύθατον ὥστε.. Pl.*Grg*.487b, etc.; εἰς τὸ ἔσχατον ἀδικίας Id.*R*.361d; ἐπ' ἔσχατον ἐλθεῖν ἀηδίας Id.*Phdr*.240d; ὅσοι ἐνταῦθα ἦλθον ἡλικίας *arrived* at that time of life, Id.*R*.329b; ἐς ἀσθενὲς ἔ. *come* to an impotent conclusion, Hdt.1.120; ἐς ἀριθμὸν ἐλθεῖν to be numbered, Th.2.72; εἰς ἔρωτά τινος ἐλθεῖν Anaxil.21.6; εἰς ἔλεγχον Philem.93.3, etc.; εἰς ἑαυτὸν ἐλθεῖν *come* to oneself, *Ev.Luc*.15.17, Arr.*Epict*.3.1.15. 5. παρὰ μικρὸν ἐλθεῖν c. inf., *come within a little of, be near* a thing, E. *Heracl*.296 (anap.); παρ' ὀλίγον ἐλθεῖν Plu.*Pyrrh*.10; παρὰ τοσοῦτον ἡ Μυτιλήνη ἦλθε κινδύνου so narrow was her escape, Th.3.49; παρ' οὐδὲν ἐλθόντες τοῦ ἀποβαλεῖν Plb.1.45.14; παρ' οὐδὲν ἐλθ. ἀπολέσθαι Plu. *Cam*.8. 6. with διά and gen., periphr. for a Verb, e.g. διὰ μάχης τινὶ ἐλθεῖν for μάχεσθαί τινι Hdt.6.9, E.*Hel*.978, Th.4.92; διὰ πυρὸς ἐλθεῖν τινι rage furiously against.., E.*Andr*.488 (lyr.); but οἱ διὰ πάντων τῶν καλῶν ἐληλυθότες *who have gone* through the whole circle of duties, have fulfilled them all, X.*Cyr*.1.2.15; διὰ πολλῶν κινδύνων ἐλθόντες Pl.*Alc*.2.142a. 7. ἔ. παρὰ τὴν γυναῖκα, παρὰ 'Αρίστωνα, of sexual intercourse, *go in to* her, *to* him, Hdt.2.115, 6.68; πρός τινα, of marriage, X.*Oec*.7.5. 8. ἔ. ἐπὶ πόλιν *attack*, Th.2.11. 9. ἔ. ἐς *depend* upon or *be concerned* with, τό γ' εἰς ἀνθρώπους ἐλθόν Aristid. 1.149 J.; τοῖς λογισμοῖς εἰς ἑαυτοὺς ἐρχόμενοι D.S.13.95; ὅσα εἰς ἀρετὴν ἔρχεται Lib.*Or*.22.18; τῶν πραττομένων οὐκ ὀλίγον εἰς ἐκεῖνον ἤρχετο ib.14.31.

**’Ερχομενός**, ὁ or ἡ, = ’Ορχομενός, Hes.*Fr*.38, *IG*7.3171, etc.

**ἕρψις**, εως, ἡ, (ἕρπω) *creeping*, Pl.*Cra*.419d, Arist.*PA*639$^{b}$3.

⊛ **ἐρῶ**, Att. fut. of εἴρω (B), Th.6.9, A.*Eu*.45, Ar.*Ra*.61, etc., Ion. and Ep. **ἐρέω** (later as pres., Nic.*Th*.484, Ath.9.400a, Gal.15.878, al.); opt. ἐροίην X.*Cyr*.3.1.14, Lib.*Or*.1.87: impf. ἤρεον (v. l. εἴρεον) Hp.*Epid*.2.2.9: pf. Act. εἴρηκα A.*Pr*.821, Ar.*Ra*.558, etc.: plpf. εἰρήκειν Plu.2.184d:—Pass., pf. εἴρημαι Il.4.363, Ar.*Lys*.13, etc.; Ion. 3 pl. εἰρέαται Hdt.7.81, contr. εἰρῆται *Schwyzer* 811.17 (Oropus, iv B.C.); part. εἰρημένος, Cret. ϝερημένος *Supp.Epigr*.2.509, Arg. ϝεϝρημένος *Schwyzer* 98 (Mycenae): plpf. εἴρητο Il.10.540, Hdt.8. 27, etc.: aor. 1 Pass. ἐρρήθην Pl.*Lg*.664d, later ἐρρέθην Arist.*Cat*. 11$^{b}$12, al.; Ion. εἰρέθην Hdt.4.77, 156: fut. ῥηθήσομαι Th.1.73, Pl. *R*.473e, Isoc.8.73, D.27.53: more freq. εἰρήσομαι, mostly in 3 sg. -ήσεται Il.23.795, Pi.*I*.6(5).59, S.*Ph*.1276, etc.; part. -όμενος Hp. *Art*.53.—Hom. uses only fut. ἐρέω, 3 sg. pf. and plpf. Pass., with part. εἰρημένος, aor. part. ῥηθείς in the phrase ἐπὶ ῥηθέντι δικαίῳ (v. infr.), and fut. Pass.—The place of the pres. εἴρω (q.v.) is supplied by φημί, λέγω or ἀγορεύω; εἶπον serves as aor. (ϝερε-: ϝρη-, cf. ῥήτρα, ῥητός, Lat. *verbum*, Engl. *word*.) I. I *will say* or *speak*, c. acc. rei et dat. pers., Il.1.297: abs., οὐδὲ πάλιν ἐρέει he *will say* nothing against it, 9.56; ἐν δ' ὑμῖν ἐρέω among you, ib.528, cf. Od. 16.378: freq. in Att., ἐρεῖν τι πρός τινα Pl.*R*.520a (Act.), 595b, *Tht*. 179a (both Pass.); τι περί τινος Id.*Phlb*.29d, etc.: c. acc. pers., *speak of*, κακῶς ἐρεῖν τινα Thgn.796, E.*Alc*.705: and c. dupl. acc., ἐρεῖ δέ μ'.. τάδε ib.954, cf. Pl.*Cri*.48a:—Pass., μῦθος.. εἰρημένος ἔστω Il.8. 524; εἰρημένα μυθολογεύειν Od.12.453; λίαν εἰρημένος too *true*, A.*Pr*. 1031; ἐπὶ ῥηθέντι δικαίῳ after justice *has been pronounced*. Od.18. 414; ἐπὶ τοσοῦτον εἰρήσθω περί τινος *let* this *suffice*, Arist.*EN*1117$^{b}$ 21. II. I *will tell, proclaim*, ἔπος Il.1.419, etc.; 'Ηὼς.. Ζηνὶ φόως ἐρέουσα *announce* it, 2.49; ἐρέω τιν' ὑμῖν αἶνον Archil.89.1. 2. *tell, order*, c. dat. pers. et inf., X.*HG*3.2.6, etc.: c. acc. et inf., Id.*Cyr*.8. 3.6:—Pass., εἴρητο συλλέγεσθαι τὸν στρατόν *orders had been given*.., Hdt.7.26, etc. III. Pass., *to be mentioned*, οὗτοι μὲν οἱ παραθαλάσσιοι.. εἰρέαται Id.4.181, cf. Arist.*Mu*.393$^{b}$27. 2. *to be specified, agreed, promised*, εἰρημένος μισθός Hes.*Op*.370, Hdt.6.23; εἰρημένον, abs., *when it had been agreed*, Th.1.140; κὰ(τ) τὰ ϝεϝρημένα *Schwyzer* l. c.

**ἐρωγάς**, = sq., Hsch.

**ἐρωδία·** ἅμαξα, Hsch.; cf. ἐριδίαν, ἐριωδία.

**ἐρῳδιός**, ὁ, *heron*, Il.10.274, Epich.46, Semon.9, Ar.*Av*.886, Call. *Aet.Oxy*.2080.64, Clitarch.22 J., Ant.Lib.7.7, etc.:—also **ῥῳδιός**, Hippon.63, and **ἀρῳδιός** (q.v.):—Aristotle mentions three kinds: ὁ πέλλος, prob. *common heron, Ardea cinerea*; ὁ λευκός, *egret, A. alba, gazetta*; ὁ ἀστερίας, *bittern, A. stellaris, HA*609$^{b}$21: the ἐρῳδιός in Il. l. c. (cf. Ael.*NA*1.1) was prob. a *shearwater*. (ἐρωδιός freq. in codd., even in Pap. of Call. l. c. (ii A.D.), but ἐρῳδιός (with ωι and oxyt.) Hdn.Gr.2.924 and codd. Hom.)

**ἔρωες**, οἱ, coined as etym. of ἥρωες by Hierocl. *in CA*3 p.424 M.

**ἐρω-έω**, (ἐρωή) Ep. Verb, *rush, rush forth*, αἷμα κελαινὸν ἐρωήσει περὶ δουρί Il.1.303, Od.16.441; ἠρώησαν ὀπίσσω, of horses, they *started back*, Il.23.433; *escape harm*, Nic.*Th*.117. 2. c. gen. rei, *draw back* or *rest from*, ἐρωῆσαι πολέμοιο Il.13.776, cf. 17.422; ἐρωήσουσι δὲ χάρμης 14.101; ἐρώησαν καμάτοιο *h.Cer*.301; οἴνου Epic. in *Arch.Pap*. 7.4; [νεφέλη] οὔ ποτ' ἐρωεῖ (sc. σκοπέλου) the cloud never *fails from* it, never *leaves* it, Od.12.75; ἴθι νῦν κατὰ λαὸν 'Αχαιῶν, μηδ' ἔτ' ἐρώει (sc. τοῦ ἰέναι) Il.2.179: c. acc., *leave, quit*, Theoc.13.74, 24.101. II. trans., *drive* or *force back*, once in Hom., τῶ κε καὶ ἐσσύμενόν περ ἐρωήσαιτ' ἀπὸ νηῶν Il.13.57; χεῖρας ὑσμίνης Theoc.22.174; ῥόον Call. *Del*.133; θηρὸς ὀλοὸν κέρας Id.*Fr*.249; δρόμον ἐλεφάντων cj. in Nonn. *D*.36.188: c. acc. et inf., 'Αχαιοὺς ἐ. κορέσασθαι Q.S.3.520.—Dub. in late Prose, Ant.Lib.7.3. ⊛ **-ή**, ἡ, Ep. Noun (Hom. only in Il.), *quick motion, rush, force*, ἀνδρὸς ἐ. Il.3.62, cf. 14.488; mostly of things, δουρὸς ἐ. 15.358; βελέων ἐ. 4.542; λείπετο δουρὸς ἐ. a spear's *throw* behind, 23.529, cf. 21.251; λικμητῆρος ἐ. *the force* or *swing* of the winnower's (shovel), 13.590; ἐκτὸς ἐρωῆς πετράων A.R.4.1657; πυρός *AP*9.490 (Heliod.). 2. *impulse, desire*, περὶ Κύπριν ἐ. ib.10. 112, cf. Procl.*H*.3.10; γαστρὸς ἐ. Opp.*C*.3.175. II. c. gen. rei, *drawing back from, rest from*, πολέμου δ' οὐ γίγνετ' ἐ. Il.16.302, 17. 761; μάχης Theoc.22.192; δακρύων Mosch.4.40: abs., *escape*, D.P.601.

**ἐρωμᾰν-έω**, *to be mad for love*, Opp.*C*.3.368, Nonn.*D*.1.136, al., *AP*5.266.10 (Agath.). **-ής**, ές, *maddened by love*, διάθεσις πρὸς μειράκιον D.S.30.22, cf. Nonn.*D*.16.10, al. 2. *exciting mad love*, φίλτρα Orph.*H*.55.14 (ἐρωτομ- codd.). **-ία**, Ep. **-ίη**, ἡ, *mad love*, *AP*5.46 (Rufin.), 219 (Agath.), 254 (Paul. Sil.).

⊛ **ἐρωμένιον**, τό, *a little love, darling*, *AP*11.168 (Antiphan.).

⊛ **ἔρως**, ωτος, ὁ, acc. ἔρων for ἔρωτα Alex.Aet.3.12, *AP*9.39 (Musicius): in Ep. and Lyr. usu. **ἔρος** (q.v.): (ἔραμαι, ἐράω A):—*love*, mostly of the sexual passion, θηλυκρατὴς ἔ. A.*Ch*.600 (lyr.); ἐρῶσ' ἔρωτ' ἔκδημον E.*Hipp*.32; ἔ. τινός *love for* one, S.*Tr*.433; παίδων E. *Ion*67: generally, *love of* a thing, *desire for* it, πατρῴας γῆς A.*Ag*.540; δεινὸς εὐκλείας ἔ. Id.*Eu*.865, etc.; ἔχειν ἔμφυτον ἔρωτα περί τι Pl.*Lg*. 782e; πρὸς τοὺς λόγους Luc.*Nigr.Praef*.; ἔρωτα σχὼν τῆς 'Ελλάδος τύραννος γενέσθαι Hdt.5.32; ἔ. ἔχει με c. inf., A.*Supp*.521; θανόντι κείνῳ συνθανεῖν ἔρως μ' ἔχει S.*Fr*.953; αὐτοῖς ἦν ἔρως θρόνους ἐᾶσθαι Id.*OC*367; ἔ. ἐμπίπτει μοι c. inf., A.*Ag*.341, cf. Th.6.24; εἰς ἔρωτά τινος ἀφικέσθαι, ἐλθεῖν, Antiph.212.3, Anaxil.21.5: pl., *loves, amours*, ἀλλοτρίων Pi.*N*.3.30; οὐχ ὅσιοι ἔ. E.*Hipp*.765 (lyr.); ἔρωτες ἐμᾶς πόλεως Ar.*Av*.1316 (lyr.), etc.; of dolphins, πρὸς παῖδας Arist.*HA*631$^{a}$ 10: generally, *desires*, S.*Ant*.617 (lyr.). 2. *object of love* or *desire*, ἀπρόσικτοι ἔρωτες Pi.*N*.11.48, cf. Luc.*Tim*.14. 3. *passionate joy*, S.*Aj*.693 (lyr.). II. pr. n., *the god of love*, Anacr.65, Parm.13, E.*Hipp*.525 (lyr.), etc.; ῎Ε. ἀνίκατε μάχαν S.*Ant*.781 (lyr.): in pl., Simon.184.3, etc. III. at Nicaea, a *funeral wreath*, *EM*379. 54. IV. name of the κλῆρος 'Αφροδίτης, *Cat.Cod.Astr*.1.168; = third κλῆρος, Paul.Al.*K*.3; one of the τόποι, Vett.Val.69.16.

**’Ερωτάριον**, τό, Dim. of ἔρως II, *a little Cupid*, *BCH*29.543 (Delos), *AP*11.174 (Lucill.).

⊛ **ἐρωτ-άω**, Ep. and Ion. **εἰρωτάω**, contr. in Hom. and best codd. of Hdt., as 3.119, 4.145, al.: impf. ἠρώτων Hp.*Epid*.7.3, (ἐπ-) Th.7.10,

etc.; εἰρώτα Od.15.423; Ion. εἰρώτευν Hdt.1.158, part. -τεῦντας v.l. in 3.62 (elsewh. εἰρώτων 3.140): fut. -ήσω Hp.*VM*15, Pl.*R.*350e, etc.: aor. 1 ἠρώτησα X.*Cyr.*4.5.21, S.*Tr.*403, etc.: pf. ἠρώτηκα Pl.*Phlb.* 18a:—used in Att. to supply the defective tenses of ἔρομαι:—*ask*, τινά τι something *of* one, ἅ μ' εἰρωτᾷς Od.4.347; εἰρωτᾷς μ' ὄνομα κλυτόν 9.364; ὅσ' ἂν σ' ἐρωτῶ S.*OT*1122; οὐ τοῦτ' ἐρωτῶ σ' Ar.*Nu.*641:—Pass., *to be asked*, τι Pl.*Lg.*895e, X.*Cyr.*1.4.3. **2.** ἐ. τι *ask about* a thing, A.*Pr.*228, Pl.*R.*508a; τι περί τινος Id.*Tht.*185c; ἐ. ἐρώτημα *to ask* a question, Id.*R.*487e; τὰς πύστεις ἐρωτῶντες εἰ.. *putting* the question, whether.., Th.1.5:—Pass., τὸ ἐρωτηθέν, τὸ ἐρωτώμενον ἀποκρίνασθαι, to answer the *question*, Th.3.61, X.*Mem.*4.2.23, etc.; τὰ ἔμπροσθεν ἠρωτημένα Pl.*Lg.*662e:—Pass., also with person as subject, ἐρωτηθεὶς τὸ καλόν *asked about* beauty, Id.*Hp.Ma.*289c. **3.** folld. by indirect question, εἰρώτα.. τίς εἴη καὶ πόθεν ἔλθοι Od.15.423; ἐ. εἰ.. or ἤν.. *to ask* whether.., Hp.*Steril.*230, cf. Th.8.53; ἐ. ἦ.. A.*Th.*181; αἰτίαν καθ' ἥντινα Id.*Pr.*228; πότεροι.. Ar.*Ach.*648; τοῦτο πρῶτον ἠρώτα, πότερον.. X.*An.*3.1.7; ἐ. πῶς δεῖ ποιεῖν Id.*Mem.*1.3.1. **II.** *question* a person, εἰρωτᾷς μ' ἐλθόντα θεὰ θεόν Od.5.97; ἐ. καὶ ἐλέγχειν Antipho 6.23; τινα ἀμφί τινος E.*Ion* 236 (lyr.):—Pass., *to be questioned*, ἐρωτᾶσθαι θέλω Id.*IA*1130. **b.** of sentries, *challenge*, Aen.Tact.22.12; τὸ ἐρωτώμενον the *password*, Id.26.9. **2.** in Dialectic, opp. demonstration, *question* an opponent *in order to refute him from his answers*, Arist.*APr.*24$^a$24; τι ib.42$^a$39; hence later, *submit, set forth, propound* an argument, λόγον Gal.5.257:—Pass., ὁ λόγος.. ἠρωτῆσθαι φαίνεται Arr.*Epict.*2.19.1; ἐρωτηθέντος τοῦ σοφίσματος S.E.*P.*2.237. **III.** later, = αἰτέω, *beg, entreat*, ἐ. τινὰ τὰ εἰς εἰρήνην LXX 1*Ki.*30.21, al.; ἐρωτᾶτε τὰ εἰς εἰρήνην τὴν Ἱερουσαλήμ ib.*Ps.*121(122).6; ἅ σε ἐρωτῶ *PMag. Par.*1.272; ἐ. τινὰ ποιεῖν τι *POxy.*292.7 (i A.D.), *Ev.Luc.*8.37, etc.; ἐ. τινὰ ἵνα.. ib.7.36; ὅπως.. ib.7.3, al., *PMag.Leid.W.*16.13; ἐ. τὸν πατέρα περὶ ὑμῶν *Ev.Jo.*16.26. (Perh. from ἐρ(ϝ)ωτάω, cogn. with ἐρ(ϝ)έσθαι (v. ἔρομαι).) **-ημα**, ατος, τό, *that which is asked, question*, Th.3.54, etc.; ἡ πρὸς τὸ ἐ. ἀπόκρισις ib.60; τὰ ἐ. τοῦ ξυνθήματος *asking for* the password, Id.7.44; ἐ. περί τινος Pl.*Prt.*336d; ἐ. ἐρέσθαι, Id.*Phlb.*42e; διπλᾶ ἔστρεφε τὰ -ήματα Id.*Euthd.*276d. **2.** in Stoic terminology, a question requiring the answer 'Yes' or 'No', opp. πύσμα, Chrysipp.*Stoic.*2.61. **II.** in Dialectic, *question inviting an answer which may help to refute an opponent*, Arist.*APr.*64$^a$36 (pl.), *APo.*77$^a$36, al. **-ηματίζω**, = ἐρωτάω II. 2, Id.*Top.*155$^b$4. **-ηματικός**, ή, όν, *interrogative*, ὄνομα D.T.636.11; χρεῖαι Hermog.*Prog.*3. Adv. -κῶς Theo *Prog.*4, Sch.Ar.*Nu.*1225, etc. **-ησις**, εως, ἡ, *questioning, interrogation*, Hp.*Steril.*213, Pl.*Prt.*312d, al., X.*Cyr.*8.4.13, al.; ἐ. ποιήσασθαι Isoc.8.58; τινος *about* a thing, Pl.*Tht.* 147c; ἐρωτήσεως [ἐπιρρήματα] *interrogative* adverbs, D.T.642.12. **II.** ἐ. ἀντιφάσεως ('Is A B or is it not B?') Arist.*APr.*24$^a$25, $^b$10; v. ἐρώτημα II. **III.** *proposition, matter submitted*, δηλοῖ τὴν ἐ. φόβον ἔχειν *Cat.Cod.Astr.*1.103. **-ητέον**, verb. Adj. *one must ask*, ἐρώτημα Arist.*APo.*77$^b$7. **-ητικός**, ή, όν, *skilled in questioning*, Pl. *Cra.*398e. **II.** ἡ -κή (sc. τέχνη) *the art of putting questions*, Arist. *SE*172$^a$16; ἐ. λόγοι ib.183$^b$38; v. ἐρωτάω II. 2.

**ἐρωτ-ιάς**, άδος, ἡ, pecul. fem. of ἐρωτικός, Νύμφαι *AP*9.627 (Marian.). **-ιάω**, *to be lovesick*, Hp.*Ep.*19 (*Hermes* 53.69), Ach.Tat. 6.20, Aen.Gaz.*Thphr.*p.24 B. **-ῐδεύς**, έως, ὁ, *a young Eros*: pl., ἐρωτιδεῖς *Anacreont.*25.13. **-ίδια** (sc. ἱερά), τά, *festival of Eros* at Thespiae, Ath.13.561e, Sch.Pi.*O.*7.154: also **-ίδαια** *IG*5(1).656, **-ίδεια** ib.659, 7.48, etc.

**ἐρωτίζω**, = ἐρωτάω, Hsch. s.v. ἠρώτιζον.

⊕ **ἐρωτ-ικός**, ή, όν, *of* or *caused by love*, ὀργή, λύπη, Th.6.57, 59; ἐ. ξυντυχία a *love*-affair, ib.54; ἐ. λόγος a discourse *on love*, Pl.*Phdr.* 227c; ἐ. μέλος a *love* song, Bion 2.2; περὶ ἐ. αἰτίαν Arist.*Pol.*1303$^b$22; ἐ. ἀρετή Phld.*D.*3*Fr.*76; ἐ. δυνάμεις Ph.2.481; δεινὸς περὶ τὰ ἐ. Pl.*Smp.*193e, al.; τοῖς περὶ τὰς γυναῖκας ἐρωτικοῖς ἔνοχος Plu.*Cim.* 4; also, = Ἐρωτίδια, Plu.2.748f; ἡ -κή (sc. φιλία), Arist.*EN*1164$^a$3. **II.** of persons, *amorous*, Pl.*R.*474d, Arist.*EN*1156$^b$1, Theoc. 14.61, etc.; περὶ τὰ εὐμορφότατα Luc.*Dom.*2: Comp. -ώτερος X. *Smp.*4.62: generally, *fond of* a thing, πρὸς χρυσίον Plu.*Dem.*25; τὰ τοῦ σώματος -ικὰ πρὸς πλησμονὴν καὶ κένωσιν the *cravings* of the body, Pl.*Smp.*186c. Adv. -κῶς, περιαλγήσας Th.6.54; ἐ. μεταχειρίζεσθαί τινα Lys.*Fr.*1.5; ἐ. διατίθεσθαι Pl.*Smp.*207b; ἐ. ἔχειν τοῦ Σωκράτους ib.222c; τοῦ ποιεῖν τι X.*Cyr.*3.3.12: Sup. -ώτατα, ἔχειν τοῦ ἔργου Id. *Hier.*1.21. **-ιον**, τό, = Ἐρωτάριον, *IG*11(2).161*B*118 (Delos, iii B.C.), Luc.*Philops.*14. **II.** *charming, sweet child*, Aristaenet.1.19. **2.** = ἐρώμενον (Tarent.), Hsch. ⊕ **-ίς**, ίδος, ἡ, *loved one, darling*, Theoc.4.59. **II.** as Adj., ἐρωτίδες νῆσοι islands *of love*, *AP*7.628 (Crin.). **-ίσκος**, ὁ, = ἐρωτάριον, *Schwyzer* 462 *B* 54 (Tanagra, iii B.C.), *Gloss.*

**ἐρωτο-γράφος** [ᾰ], ον, *for writing of love*, μέτρον *AP*7.421.10 (Mel.). **-δῐδάσκᾰλος**, ὁ, ἡ, *teacher of the art of love*, Ath.5.219d. **-εις**, εσσα, εν, *loving*, Hdn.*Epim.*206. **-ληπτος**, ον, *love-smitten*, Procop. *Arc.*1; ἔς τινα ib.4. **-μᾰνέω**, = ἐρωμανέω, Stoic.ap.Stob.2.7.5$^{b9}$ (dub.), Poll.3.68. **-μᾰνής**, ές, = ἐρωμανής, cj. in Stoic.ap.Stob.2.7. 5$^{b9}$, Orph.*H.*55.14 codd., Ath.13.599e, Aristaenet.1.27, etc. Adv. -ῶς Zonar. **-μᾰνία**, ἡ, = ἐρωμανία, *raving love*, Plu.2.451f. **-παίγνιον**, τό, in pl., title of *amatory poems* by Laevius, Gell.2.24.8. **-πλάνος** [ᾰ], ον, *beguiling love*, φθόγγος *AP*7.195 (Mel.). **-πλοέω**, *sail on love's ocean*, ib.5.155 (Id.). **-τόκος**, ον, *producing love*, μῦθοι Musae. 159; πρόσωπον Nonn.*D.*4.129; Κυθερείη Procl.*H.*2.13:—fem. **-τόκεια**, ἡ, Ἀφροδίτη *PMag.Par.*1.2557. **-τρόφος**, ον, *the nurse* or *mother of love*, i.e. Aphrodite, Orph.*A.*478, cf. 868.

**ἐρωτύλος**, ὁ, Dor. word, *a darling, sweetheart*, Theoc.3.7. **II.** as Adj., ἐρωτύλα ἀείδειν sing *love-songs*, Bion *Fr.*7.10, cf. 13: dub. as epith. of Ἔρος, *PMag.Lond.*121.471 (-τυλλ- Pap.). **III.** name of a very small star, *AP*9.614 (Leont.). **IV.** name of a gem, Ps.-Democr.ap.Plin.*HN*37.160.

⊕ **ἐς**, Ion., old Att., Dor. form of εἰς: all compounds must be sought under εἰσ-, except a few words which appear only in the form ἐσ-. **II.** Arc., = ἐκ, *IG*5(2).6.49 (Tegea, iv B.C.), al.; also Delph., *BCH*23.611, and Arg., *IG*4.492 (Mycenae, vi B.C.); v. ἐκ init.

**ἐσαπλῶς**, perh. = ἁπλῶς, dub. in Diogenian.Epicur.2.50.

**ἐσάχρι**, Adv., (εἰς ἄχρι) *as far as*, c. gen., A.R.1.604, *APl.*4.307 (Leon.); ἐ. τούτων τῶν χρόνων Ezek.*Exag.*5.

**ἐσαώρας**· εἰς καιρούς, Hsch.

**ἔσβηνες**· εἶδος ποτηρίου (Tarent.), Hsch. **ἔσγονος**, v. ἔκγ-. **ἐσδέλλω**, v. ἐκβάλλω. **ἐσδοκά**, v. ἐκδοχή. **ἔσδοσις**, **-δοτήρ**, v. ἐκδ-. **ἐσδραμύλιξον**· εἴσδραμε, Id. **ἐσδύομαι**, v. ἐκδύω I. 3. **ἐσεργνύναι**, Ion. for εἰσείργειν, *shut in, enclose*, Hdt.2.86. **ἐσηλῠσίη**, ἡ, = εἰσέλευσις, *AP*9.625 (Maced.).

**ἔσθαι**, aor. 2 inf. Med. of ἵημι, and pf. Pass. of ἕννυμι.

**ἐσθ-έω**, (ἐσθής) *clothe*: only pf. and plpf. Pass., mostly in part. ἠσθημένος, Ion. ἐσθημένος, *clothed* or *clad*, τι *in* a thing, ἐσθῆτα ἐσθημένος Hdt.6.112: c. dat., ῥάκεσι ἐσθημένος Id.3.129; ἠσθημένοι πέπλοισι E.*Hel.*1539; Πελοποννησιακῶς ἠσθημένος Pythaen.6: 3 pl. pf. ἤσθηνται Ael.*Fr.*121: 3 sg. plpf. ἤσθητο Id.*VH*12.32; ἠσθῆσθαι Id. *NA*16.34. **-ημα**, ατος, τό, *garment*, always in pl. in Trag., *clothes, raiment*, as A.*Pers.*836, *Ag.*562, S.*El.*268, cf. Th.3.58, etc.: later in sg., Ael.*VH*1.2, Jul.*Or.*2.85a.

**ἔσθην**, 3 dual plpf. Pass. of ἕννυμι, Il.18.517.

**ἐσθής**, ῆτος, Dor. ἐσθάς, ᾶτος, Pi.*P.*4.79, 253, ἡ, acc. ἐσθήν *SIG* 1215.7 (Myconos, iii/ii B.C.): (ἕννυμι):—*clothing, raiment*, χαλκόν τε χρυσόν τε ἅλις ἐσθῆτά τε δόντες Od.5.38; χρηστηρία ἐ. *the dress* of prophetesses, A.*Ag.*1270; Ἀργολὶς ἐ. Id.*Supp.*237; μετρίᾳ ἐσθῆτι χρήσασθαι to *dress* simply, Th.1.6: καθαρὰ ἐ., = Lat. *toga pura*, Nic. Dam.*Fr.*127 J.; τὴν ἐσθῆτα μεταβαλεῖν, = Lat. *mutare vestem*, put on mourning, D.C.37.33 (but τὰς ἐσθῆτας μεταβαλέσθαι Plu.*Pomp.*59): in pl., of *the clothes of several* persons, A.*Th.*872 (anap.); *of one*, E. *Hel.*421: abstract pl., πλούτους καὶ τρυφὰς καὶ ἐσθῆτας Pl.*Alc.*1.122c, cf. cj. in Arist.*Rh.*1386$^a$32, dub. in Pl.*Grg.*465b. **II.** collectively, *clothes*, ἐσθῆτα ἔσφερον εἴσω, i.e. *the clothes* just washed, Od.7.6; ἔντυνον εὐνὴν ἐσθῆτος μαλακῆς 23.290; τὰ ἐσθῆτος ἐχόμενα εἶχον κατηρείκοντο Hdt.3.66, cf. X.*An.*3.1.19: rarely in later Gr., Plu.*CG*2, *PThead.*49.4 (iv A.D.), *POxy.*2110.5 (iv A.D.). **III.** metaph., ἐ. τῆς πόλεως, of walls, Demad.*Fr.*4.

**ἔσθησις**, εως, ἡ, (ἐσθέω) *clothing, raiment*, dub. l. in Arist.*Rh.*1386$^a$32, cf. Poll.10.51: pl., Ath.1.18e, *Act.Ap.*1.10: dat. pl., ἐσθήσεσι Ph.2.158, Str.3.3.7, v.l. in *Ev.Luc.*24.4.

**ἔσθι**, = ἴσθι, v. εἰμί A.

⊕ **ἐσθίω** (cf. ἔσθω, ἔδω, the latter of which is the radic. form, and supplies fut. and pf. of ἐσθίω), impf. ἤσθιον Hes.*Op.*147: fut. ἔδομαι (old pres. subj. of non-thematic stem) Il.4.237, Ar.*Pax*1357 (lyr.), etc.; ἐδοῦμαι late, (προκατ-) Luc.*Hes.*7, etc.: pf. ἐδήδοκα Ar.*Eq.*362, X.*An.*4.8.20; opt. ἐδηδοκοίη Cratin.320; Ep. part. ἐδηδώς, -υῖα, Il.17. 542, *h.Merc.*560: plpf. ἐδηδόκειν Luc.*Gall.*4 (v.l.):—Med., aor. 1 ἠδεσάμην (κατ-) Gal.5.752:—Pass., ἐσθίομαι Od.4.318, Thphr.*HP*1.12.4, Luc.*Cyn.*11, etc.: aor. 1 ἠδέσθην v.l. in Hp.*Vict.*2.54, Arist.*Pr.*908$^a$29, (ἀπ-, κατ-) Pl.Com.138, 35: pf. ἐδήδεσμαι (κατ-) Pl.*Phd.*110e, ἐδήδεμαι (ἀπ-) Arist.*HA*591$^a$5 (v.l.); Ep. 3 sg. ἐδήδοται Od.22.56.—The aor. 2 and later also the fut. are supplied by φαγ- (v. φαγεῖν); in Ion. and Hellenistic Greek the pf. is βέβρωκα βέβρωμαι, aor. Pass. ἐβρώθην; in late Greek the pres. is τρώγω:—*eat*, ἐσθιέμεν καὶ πινέμεν Od.2.305, 21.69; τὰ ἐσθίοντα ἐν στρατιᾷ the *ration-strength*, X.*Cyr.*1.6. 17: usu. c. acc., κρέα ἤσθιον Od.20.348, cf. S.*Fr.*671 (from a satyric drama), E.*Cyc.*233: c. gen., ἐ. τινός *eat of..*, X.*HG*3.3.6, etc.; of animals, *devour*, ἤσθιε δ' ὥς τε λέων ὀρεσίτροφος Od.9.292; χρόα γῦπες ἔδονται Il.4.237, cf. Hes.*Th.*524, 773, Semon.9, etc.; *consume*, βίοτον καὶ κτήματ' ἔδονται Od.2.123:—Pass., ἐσθίεταί μοι οἶκος my house *is eaten up*, I am *eaten* out of house and home, 4.318; ὅσσα τοι ἐκπέποται καὶ ἐδήδοται 22.56. **2.** metaph., πάντας πῦρ ἐσθίει the fire *devours* all, Il.23.182; of an *eating* sore, A.*Fr.*253:—Pass., ὀδόντες ἐσθιόμενοι *decayed* teeth, Thphr.*Char.*19.3; ἐσθιόμενα *eroded* parts of the bowel, Hp.*Epid.*4.20. **3.** *fret, vex*, ἐ. ἑαυτόν Ar.*V.*287 (lyr.); ἐ. τὴν χελύνην ὑπ' ὀργῆς *to bite* the lip, ib.1083; ἐ. καρδίαν Pythag.ap. Plu.2.12e. **4.** *take in one's mouth*, γλῶτταν αὐλοῦ Philostr.*Im.*1.20.

**ἐσθλαί**· ξύλινα παίγνια,.. (Cypr.), Hsch.

**ἐσθλοδότης**, ου, ὁ, *giver of good*, Man.2.142.

⊕ **ἐσθλός**, ή, όν, Aeol. ἔσλος Sapph.28, Alc.96: Dor. **ἐσλός**, ά, όν, Pi.*P.*8.73, etc. (never in B.); Arc. **ἐσλός** *Inscr.Olymp.*266 (v B.C.): Comp. and Sup. -ότερος, -ότατος, *AP*9.156 (Antiphil.), 6.240 (Phil.):—poet. Adj., = ἀγαθός, *good* of his kind, ἐ. ἐν σταδίῃ Il.15.283: later c. inf., A.R.1.106, etc.: hence **I.** of persons, *brave, stout*, ἐσθλὸν ἐνὶ προμάχοισι Il.4.458, etc.; opp. δειλός, Hes.*Op.*214; *noble*, opp. κακός, οὔ τινα γὰρ τίεσκον.. οὐ κακὸν οὐδὲ μὲν ἐ. Od.22.415; πένιχρος οὐδεὶς πέλετ' ἔσλος οὐδὲ τίμιος Alc.49; τόκηες Id.*Supp.*25.12; εἴτ' εὐγενὴς πέφυκας εἴτ' ἐσθλῶν κακή S.*Ant.*38; ἐσθλοῦ πατρὸς παῖς Id. *Ph.*96; ἀπ' ἐσθλῶν δωμάτων E.*Andr.*772 (lyr.), etc.; of horses, *well-bred*, Il.23.348. **2.** morally *good, faithful*, φίλος S.*OT*611; εἰς ἡμᾶς γεγώς Id.*El.*24; τινι Naumach.ap.Stob.4.23.7; κύνα ἐσθλὴν ἐκείνῳ, πολεμίαν τοῖς δύσφροσιν A.*Ag.*608. **3.** like ἐΰς and φίλος, weakened almost to a possess. pron., ἐσθλὸν ἀνεψιὸν ἐξεναρίξας Il.16.

573, cf. 5.469, Od.3.379. II. of things, *good* of their kind, φάρμακα, κτήματα, κειμήλια, Il.11.831, Od.2.312, Il.9.330, etc. 2. of mind, qualities, etc., νόος Od.7.73; βουλή Il.9.76; ἔπος 1.108; κλέος 5.3, Pi.*P.*4.175: freq. in neut. pl., μυρί'.. ἐσθλὰ ἔοργε Il.2.272; ἔσθλ' ἀγορεύοντες, κακὰ δὲ φρεσὶ βυσσοδόμευον Od.17.66; ἔσλων ἢ κάλων Sapph.28, cf. *Supp.*2.4. 3. *fortunate, lucky,* ὄρνιθες Od. 24.311; ὕπαρ 19.547; χάρματα Pi.*O.*2.19; γάμοι E.*IA*609; τύχη S.*OC*1506; ἀράσαντο πάμπαν ἔσλα τῷ γάμβρῳ Sapph.51.4; ἐσθλόν, τό, *good luck, prosperity,* opp. κακόν, Il.24.530; παρὰ καὶ κακῷ ἐσθλὸν ἔθηκεν Od.15.488; ἐσλὸν βαθὺ Pi.*O.*12.12. 4. Subst. ἐσθλά, τά, *goods,* πυρὴν ἐμπλησέμεν ἐσθλῶν Od.10.523; εἴ τις ἐσλὰ πέπαται Pi. *P.*8.73. 5. ἐσθλόν [ἐστι] c. inf., *it is good, expedient to..,* Il.24. 301: also pl., οὐ γὰρ ἐσθλὰ.. κερτομέειν Archil.64.—Poet. word, used by X.*Cyr.*1.5.9, Chrysipp.*Stoic.*3.60, Luc.*Syr.D.*19 (Ion.), etc.

**ἐσθλότης,** ητος, ἡ, *goodness,* Chrysipp.*Stoic.*3.60 (pl.).

⊕ **ἔσθος,** εος, τό, rare form for ἔσθημα, Il.24.94, Ar.*Av.*943 (lyr.); τὸ ἔ. (with hiatus, i.e. ϝέσθος) in the mouth of a Laconian, Id.*Lys.* 1096; cf. βέστον *EM*195.45, γεστία Hsch.

**ἔσθω,** Ep. inf. ἐσθέμεναι Od.7.220: impf. ἦσθον 6.249, Matro *Conv.* 115:—poet. form of ἐσθίω, *eat,* ἔσθειν καὶ πίνειν Od.5.197, cf. 7.220; ἐσθέμεναι κειμήλιά τε πρόβασίν τε, i.e. *eat up* chattel and cattle, i.e. all one has, 2.75; of worms or animals, *feed on, devour,* Il.24.415, Od.13.409: also in Trag., Com., and later Poets, A.*Ag.*1597, Archipp.20, Philippid.9.5, Python 1.13, Call.*Iamb.*1.270, Matro l.c.: sts. in later Prose, Lxx *Le.*17.10, 19.26, Plu.2.101d codd.; in Cos, *Arch.f.Religionswiss.*10.402 (iii B.C.):—Pass., Lxx *Le.*17.13.

**ἐσία,** ἡ, v.l. for ἐσσία in Pl.*Cra.*401c.

**ἐσία,** ἡ, (ἵημι) *a mission, embassy,* Suid., etc.; cf. ἐξ-εσίη.

**ἐσιάλλοντι·** ἐκτείνουσιν, ἐκπέμπουσιν, Hsch.; cf. ἰάλλω.

**ἐσιέμεναι,** fem. pres. part. Med. of εἰσίημι, Od.22.470.

**Ἐσιῆς,** = Egyptian *ḥsy, praised,* used of the dead, *Jahrb.*32.201 (Memphis), *PMag.Lond.*46.259, 262, *PMag.Par.*2.1.

**ἐσικνέομαι, ἐσίπταμαι,** v. sub εἰσ-.

**ἔσις,** εως, ἡ, (ἵημι) *a sending forth, EM*469.49. 2. (ἵεμαι) *an aiming at,* coined by Pl.*Cra.*411d, 420a: but the compd. ἔφεσις is found. II. (ἕζω) *a sitting,* Hellad.ap.Phot.*Bibl.*p.535 B.

**ἐσιώθην·** ἐσώθη, Hsch.

**ἐσκάλισις,** εως, ἡ, prob. *packing in a wooden crate* (cf. κᾶλον), *IG*4. 1485.85 (Epid.); cf. παρκάλισις and perh. διακάλισις, unless all three words belong to καλινδέω (καλίω).

**ἐσκατάμιζεν·** ἐσκάριζεν, Hsch. ⊕ **ἔσκε,** v. ἔστε.

**ἐσκεθῆν,** Arc. aor. inf., perh. = ἐκ-σχεθεῖν, fr. ἐξέχω, *keep out, exclude, Schwyzer*665 $C^4$ (iv B.C.).

**ἐσκεμμένως,** Adv. pf. part. Pass., *deliberately,* D.24.157, Lib.*Ep.* 61.7.

**ἐσκιχρέμεν,** Dor. pres. inf. of ἐσκίχρημι, *lend out,* [ἀργύριον] *Schwyzer*617 (Dodona, iii B.C.).

**ἔσκληκα,** intr. pf. of σκέλλω.

**ἔσκλητος,** ἡ, Dor., = ἔκκλητος, *an assembly of Notables* at Syracuse, Hsch., cf. *IG*14.612 (Rhegium).

**ἔσκον,** Ep. and Ion. impf. of εἰμί *sum* (q.v.).

**ἐσλιήνω,** Boeot., = ἐκλειαίνω, *cancel* a debt, aor. 1 imper. ἐσλιανάτω *IG*7.3172.73 (Orchom., iii B.C.), *Supp.Epigr.*3.342.28 (Thisbe, iii B.C.); ἐσλιήνει (3 sg. pres. subj.) τὰν οὐπεραμερίαν ib.30.

**ἐσλός,** Dor. for ἐσθλός (q.v.).

**ἔσμα,** ατος, τό, = μίσχος, *stalk, pedicle,* Arist.*Fr.*271.

**ἔσμιον·** νόστιμον, Hsch.

**ἐσμονῶ·** ἐξελεύσομαι, Hsch. (fort. ἐσμολίω, Boeot.(?) fut. of ἐκμολεῖν).

**ἑσμός,** ὁ, (ἕζομαι) *that which settles,* esp. *a swarm of bees,* Hdt.5.114, Pl.*Lg.*708b, X.*HG*3.2.28; ἑ. λαμβάνειν Plu.*Dio* 24; of wasps, καθ' ἑσμοὺς in *swarms,* Ar.*V.*1107. 2. *any swarm* or *flock,* ἑ. ὑβριστής, of men, A.*Supp.*30 (anap.); ἑ. ὡς πελειάδων ἵζεσθε ib.223; γυναικῶν Ar.*Lys.*353, etc.; [τεχνιτ]ῶν *Pae.Delph.*14; στρατιᾶς *Epigr.Gr.*985 (Philae). 3. (ἵημι) of things, ἑσμοὶ γάλακτος *streams of milk,* E.*Ba.* 710; ἑ. μελίσσης γλυκύς, i.e. honey, Epin.1.7; ἑ. νούσων A.*Supp.* 684 (lyr.); λόγων Pl.*R.*450b; πληγῶν Ph.2.95; παθῶν Porph.*Abst.* 1.34. 4. = ὁδός, Hsch.; πατρίδος καλῆς τὸν ἐπάξιον ἑ. ἐλέσθαι *Arch. Pap.*1.220 (ii B.C.). (ἐ– freq. in codd., but cf. Ar.*V.* l.c., Eust.178.16.)

**ἑσμοτόκος,** ον, *producing swarms of bees, AP*6.239 (Apollonid.).

**ἑσμοφύλαξ** [ῠ], ᾶκος, ὁ, *watcher of a swarm of bees, Gp.*15.2.9.

**ἐσόβδην,** Adv., v. sub ὄβδη. **ἔσοπτρον,** v. εἰσ–. **ἔσοπτρος,** ὁ, = foreg., Orph.*Fr.*31 i 30. **ἐσοῦ,** late form of σοῦ, v. σύ. **ἐσοῦμαι,** Dor. for ἔσομαι, fut. of εἰμί *sum.*

**ἐσπαρμένως,** Adv., (σπείρω) gloss on σποράδην, Hsch.

**ἑσπέρα,** Ion. -έρη, ἡ, prop. fem. of ἕσπερος: I. (sc. ὥρα), *evening,* ἑσπέρας *at eve,* Pi.*P.*4.40, Eup.322, Pl.*Phd.*59e, al.; τῆς ἑσπέρας Alex.125.7; also ἑσπέρην Hp.*Mul.*2.121; ἀπὸ ἑσπέρας εὐθύς just at *nightfall,* Th.3.112; ἄκρᾳ σὺν ἑσπέρᾳ Pi.*P.*11.10; πρὸς ἑσπέραν towards *evening,* Ar.*V.*1085, X.*HG*1.1.30, *Ev.Luc.*24.29; εἰς ἑσπέραν Pl.*Smp.*223d; ἐπειδὴ ἑσπέρα ἦν ib.220c; ἐπεὶ πρὸς ἑσπέραν ἦν X.*HG*4.3.22; ἑσπέρας γιγνομένης Pl.*R.*621a; περὶ ἑσπέραν βαθεῖαν late in *the evening,* Plu.2.179e: metaph., ὁ βίος ἑσπέραν ἄγει life is wearing to its *eve,* Alex.228; ἑ. βίου Anon.ap.Arist.*Po.*$1457^b24$: pl., διχομήνιδες ἑσπέραι *evenings* when the moon is full, Pi.*I.*8(7).47. 2. *night,* μίαν ἑ. αὐλισάμενος J.*BJ*5.2.1. II. (sc. χώρα) *the west,* πρὸς ἑσπέραν φέρει E.*Or.*1260; ἡ πρὸς ἑσπέρην [χώρη] Hdt.1.82, cf. 3. 115; τὸ πρὸς ἑσπέρης Id.8.130, 132, 4.38; τὰ πρὸς ἑσπέραν Th.6.2; τὴν ἀνατολὴν ποιεῖσθαι ἀφ' ἑσπέρας Arist.*Mete.*$345^a3$, cf. $344^b34$; τὰ πνεύματα πνεῖ τῆς δείλης ἀπὸ τῆς ἑ. Thphr.*Vent.*47: metaph. in political sense, τὰ προφαινόμενα ἀπὸ τῆς ἑ. νέφη Plb.5.104.9, cf. 9.37.10: Ἑ., ἡ, the *Western Empire,* Agath.4.29, 5.16.

**ἐσπεράσαι,** v. ἐκπεράω.

⊕ **Ἑσπερ-ία** (sc. χθών), ἡ, *the Western land,* of Italy, Agathyll.ap. D.H.1.49; of Spain, Suid. s.v. Ἰβηρία. **–ικός,** ή, όν, = sq.: Ἑ. μῆλον, = κίτριον, Juba 24. ⊕ **–ῖνός,** ή, όν, = –ιος, X.*Lac.*12.6, *AP*5. 201 (Asclep. or Posidipp.), Ptol.*Alm.*8.4, D.C.69.18; θυσία Lxx 4*Ki.* 16.15, al.: Ἑσπέρινος, ὁ (sc. μήν), name of month in Doris, *GDI*2172 (Erineos). **–ιον,** *citreum, Gloss.* ⊕ **–ιος,** α, ον, and ος, ον E.*HF* 395 (lyr.): (ἕσπερος): I. of Time, *towards evening,* Hom., esp. in Od., usu. with Verbs, ἑ. δ' εἰς ἄστυ.. κάτειμι Od.15.505; ἑσπερίους ἀγέρεσθαι ἀνώγει 2.385; ἀπονέεσθαι ἑ. 9.452; ἑ. φλέγειν Pi.*N.*6.38; ἑσπερίῃσι (sc. ὥραις) *at eventide,* Opp.*C.*1.138, cf. Man.2.422; ἄχρι ἑσπερίου (sc. χρόνου) Arist.*HA*$619^b21$ (v. ἀκρέσπερος); ἑ. ἀοιδαί songs sung *at even,* Pi.*P.*3.19: in late Prose, ἑσπέριος [γένεσις] Vett.Val. 72.21. II. of Place, *western,* ἠὲ πρὸς ἠοίων ἢ ἑ. ἀνθρώπων Od.8.29, cf. E.l.c.; ἔριφοι Theoc.7.53; ἅλς Arat.407, cf. Call.*Fr.*443; τὰ ἑ. *the western parts,* Th.6.2, Plu.*Ant.*30; ἀφ' ἑσπερίης (sc. χώρης) from *the west, IG*14.1020. III. Ἑσπέριος, ὁ, = Ἕσπερος, the star, Gal. 17(1).16. (ϝεσπ–, cf. ϝεσπάριοι, of the *Western* Locrians, *IG*9(1).334 (v B.C.), Lat. *vesper.*) **–ίς,** ίδος, pecul. fem. of ἑσπέριος, *western,* ἅλμη Nonn.*D.*6.219. II. as Subst., *night-scented stock, Matthiola tristis,* Thphr.*CP*6.17.3, Plin.*HN*21.39; = *citreum, Gloss.* 2. as pr. n., Ἑσπερίδες, αἱ, *the Hesperides, daughters of Night,* who dwelt in an island, *on the western verge of the world,* and guarded a garden with golden apples, Hes.*Th.*215, E.*Hipp.*742 (lyr.), D.S.4.27, etc.: hence Ἑσπερίδων μῆλα *quinces,* Pamphil.ap.Ath.2.82d. 3. Ἑ. νῆσοι, = Κασσιτερίδες, D.P.563. **–ισμα,** ατος, τό, (*ἑσπερίζω) *supper,* Philem.Lex.ap.Ath.1.11d. ⊕ **–ίτης** [ῑ], ου, ὁ, fem. **–ῖτις,** ιδος, *western,* χώρα D.L.4.27; λίμνη Suid. **–όθεν,** Adv. *from the west,* Arat.891.

**ἑσπερόμορφος,** ον, *dark, shadowy,* Tz.*H.*11.224.

**ἕσπερος,** ον (v. sub fin.), *of* or *at evening,* [ἀστὴρ] ἕ. the *evening-star,* Il.22.318; opp. ἑῷος ἀστήρ, *AP*7.670 (Pl.); prov., οὐθ' ἕσπερος οὐθ' ἑῷος οὕτω θαυμαστός Arist.*EN*$1129^b28$: as Subst., without ἀστήρ, E.*Ion* 1149, Bion *Fr.*8.1; ἕσπερε πάντα φέρων ὅσα φαίνολις ἐσκέδασ' αὔως Sapph.95; esp. of the planet Venus, Eratosth.*Cat.*43, Cic.*ND*2.20. 53; also ἕ. σελάνας φάος Pi.*O.*10(11).73; ἕ. θεός the god *of darkness,* i.e. Hades or death, S.*OT*178 (lyr.); like ἑσπέριος, joined with a Verb, *h.Hom.*19.14; ἕ. γίγνεται, of the planet Venus, Ti.Locr.96e. 2. as Subst., *evening,* μέλας ἐπὶ ἕσπερος ἦλθε Od.1.423; μένον δ' ἐπὶ ἕσπερον ἐλθεῖν waited the coming on of *evening,* 4.786; ποτὶ ἕσπερον at *eventide,* Hes.*Op.*552: also heterocl. pl., ποτὶ ἕσπερα Od.17.191; ὑφ' ἕσπερα *AP*5.304: fem., ἐρεμνὴ ἕσπερος A.R.4.1290: metaph. of age, τί δ' ἕσπερός ἐστι γυναικῶν; *AP*5.232 (Maced.). II. *western,* τόποι A.*Pr.*350; ἀγκῶνες S.*Aj.*805; ὠκεανὸς D.P.63; ἕ. (sc. γῆ) *the west country,* ἀφ' ἑσπέρου Call.*Del.*174; πρὸς ἑσπέρου D.P.335; ἑσπέρου κέρας, promontory in Africa, Ptol.*Geog.*4.6.2: as Adj., ὁ Ἥλιος..-ον κύκλον διανύων Nech.ap.Vett.Val.151.29. (ϝέσπ–, cf. Ἑσπέριος fin.)

**ἐσπευσμένως,** Adv., (σπεύδω) *with eager haste,* D.H.*Dem.*54, J.*AJ* 5.6.3, Arr.*Epict.*1.20.12.

**ἐσπίφρημι,** in inf. -πιφράναι, *insert,* Arist.*HA*$541^b11$.

⊕ **ἕσπομαι,** later Ep. form of ἕπομαι (q.v.).

**ἑσπόμην,** inf. σπέσθαι, aor. 2 of ἕπομαι.

**ἔσπον,** aor. 2 of ἐνέπω: only in 2 pl. in the formula ἔσπετε νῦν μοι, Μοῦσαι *tell* me now, ye Muses, Il.2.484, al.; later ἔσπετε νῦν μοι ὅσοι πολυπράγμονές ἐστε σοφισταί Timo 1. (Prob. fr. ἔν-σπ-ετε (v.l. in Il. l.c.); σπ– (cf. ἐνι-σπ-εῖν) is the weak form of seqᵘ, cf. Lith. *sekù* 'say', Lat. *in-sece.*)

**ἐσπουδασμένως,** Adv. pf. part. Pass., *seriously, in earnest,* Pl.*Sis.* 390c; *zealously,* Str.10.3.5, J.*AJ*16.7.1; *hastily,* Hld.1.27.

**ἐσπρεμμίττεν,** Cret., = ἐκπρεμνίζειν, *GDI*5027 (Gortyn).

**ἔσρος,** (ἐσ-ρέω) coined as etym. of ἔρως by Pl.*Cra.*420b.

**ἔσσα,** Ep. aor. 1 Act. of ἕννυμι, inf. ἕσσαι: part. aor. 1 Med. **ἑσσάμενος.** II. **ἔσσαι,** = ἕσαι, aor. 1 inf. of ἵζω. **ἔσσα,** Aeol. and Dor. fem. part. of εἰμί *sum.*

**ἔσσᾱμον,** τό, = ἔνσημον, *standard, Inscr.Magn.*26.23.

**ἐσσεδάριος,** ὁ, = Lat. *essedarius, gladiator who fought in a car, Rev. Ét.Anc.*29.46 (Smyrna), *CIG*2889 (Miletus), *IG*12(8).547 (Thasos).

**ἐσσεῖται,** Ep. and Dor. 3 sg. fut. of εἰμί *sum.* **ἔσσευα,** Ep. aor. 1 Act. of σεύω.

**ἐσσῆαι·** ἐκχέαι, Hsch.

⊕ **ἐσσήν** (A), ῆνος, ὁ, *priest of Artemis* of Ephesus, in pl., *SIG*352.6 (iv B.C.), 363.10 (iii B.C.), Paus.8.13.1. II. *king,* θεῶν ἐ. Call.*Jov.* 66; Μυρμιδόνων ἐ. Id.*Aet.*1.1.23 (expld. as = οἰκιστής by Hdn.Gr.2. 923): prop. *king bee* (i.e. *queen bee*), acc. to *EM*383.31. (ἐσσήν in Call.*Aet.*1.1.23 (Pap.), perh. because of supposed connexion with ἑσμός, ἕσσαι, or ἡσσάω.)

**ἐσσήν** (B), ῆνος, ὁ, transliteration of Hebr. *ḥōšen,* worn by Jewish priests, J.*AJ*3.7.5, 3.8.9, where it is said to mean λόγιον, by which word it is rendered in Lxx *Ex.*28.15.

⊕ **ἐσσηνεύω,** *hold office of* ἐσσήν (A), *BMus.Inscr.*578 c 7 (Ephesus); cf. ἐσσίνευσεν.

⊕ **ἐσσηνία,** ἡ, *term of office as* ἐσσήν (A), Ἀρχ.Δελτ.7.258 (Ephesus, ii A.D.).

⊕ **ἐσσήτιοι·** μάντεις, Hsch. **ἐσσί,** Ep. and Dor. 2 sg. of εἰμί *sum.*

**ἐσσία,** ἡ, Pythag. Dor. for οὐσία, Pl.*Cra.*401c. **ἔσσιμος,** v. ἔνσιμος.

**ἐσσίνευσεν·** ἐσίμηνεν, Hsch. (fort. ἐσσήν–· ἐσήμ–).

⊕ **ἐσσίταλα·** πρόσοδος, ἐμπολή, Hsch. (cf. ἐξίταλα).

**ἔσσο**, 2 sg. plpf. Pass. of ἕννυμι, Il.3.57, Od.16.199. **ἔσσομαι**, Ep. and Aeol. fut. of εἰμί *sum*. **ἐσσόν**· ἱμάτιον, Hsch. **ἐσσόομαι**, Ion. for ἡσσάομαι.

**ἐσσόριον**, τό, = ἐνσόριον, *CIG*3270 (Smyrna).

**ἔσσῠμαι**, pf. Pass. of σεύω.

**ἐσσύμενος** [ῠ], η, ον, Ep. and Lyr. part. Pass. of σεύω (in sense and accent pres., but redupl. as if pf.), *hurrying, eager, impetuous*, Il.6.518, Pi.*P*.4.135; *eager, yearning for*, c. gen., πολέμου, ὁδοῖο, Il.24.404, Od.4.733: also c. inf., πολεμίζειν, ἀλύξαι, Il.11.717, Od.4.416, cf. 15.73; ἐλαύνειν Pi.*Fr*.107.5. II. Adv. ἐσσυμένως *furiously, eagerly*, ἐμάχοντο, δόρπον ἕλοντο, Il.15.698, Od.14.347, cf. Pi.*Fr*.166, *APl*.4.43.

**ἔσσῠο, ἔσσῦτο**, 2, 3 sg. plpf., or Ep. aor. 2 Pass. of σεύω. **ἐσσυρευτόν**· βλοσυρόν, δοκερόν, Hsch. **ἐσσύτερον**· ἰσχυρότερον, Id. **ἔσσωμαι**, pf. Pass. of ἐσσόομαι, v. ἡσσάομαι. ⊛ **ἔσσων**, ον, Ion. for ἥσσων. **ἔστα**· ἐνδύματα, Id.; cf. ἔστη. **ἔστᾰκα**, trans. pf. of ἵστημι (q. v.); but **ἕστᾱκα**, Dor. for ἕστηκα. **ἐστάλᾰτο**, Ion. 3 pl. plpf. Pass. of στέλλω, Hes.*Sc*.288. **ἑστάμεν, -άμεναι** [ᾰ], Ep. pf. inf. of ἵστημι: but II. **ἕστᾰμεν**, 1 pl. ind. **ἕσταν, ἑστᾰότες**, v. ἵστημι. **ἑστᾰότως**, Adv. *standing still, quietly*, v. l. for ἑσταότος, Il.19.79. ⊛ **ἕστᾰσαν**, 3 pl. plpf. of ἵστημι, *they stood*, Hom.: but **ἔστᾰσαν**, for ἔστησαν, 3 pl. aor. 1, *they set* or *placed*, Il.12.56 (Aristarch., codd. aliq.), 2.525, Od.3.182, al. (but the v. l. ἵστασαν is to be preferred). **ἑστᾶσι, ἑστᾶτε, ἑστᾰτον**, v. ἵστημι.

⊛ **ἔστε**, Dor. **ἔστε** *EM*382.8, v. l. in Theoc.5.22, al., cf. Eust.161 fin. (written εστε in *IG*14.352 ii 60 (Halaesa)); Locr. **ἔντε** ib.9(1).334.15; Delph. ἕντε *Schwyzer* 323 *B*44 (also εἴστε, v. infr.); Boeot. **ἔττε** *IG*7.3054.7 (Lebad.): from ἐνς (= εἰς) with suffix -τε as in ὅ-τε, and so **εἴστε** *SIG*241.69 (Delph., iv B. C.). (ἔσκε Archil.14, *AP*7.727 (Theaet.) may be f. l.).—Found in post-Homeric Ep., Ion., Trag., X., *POxy*. 2120.7 (iii A. D.), etc. (it is f.l. in Pl.*Smp*.211c). I. CONJUNCTION, = ἕως: 1. *up to the time that, until*, a. with aor. ind., of actual occurrence in past time, ἅτερ γνώμης τὸ πᾶν ἔπρασσον ἔ. δή σφιν ἀντολὰς ἐγὼ ἄστρων ἔδειξα A.*Pr*.457, cf. S.*Ant*.415, *Aj*.1031, *El*.753; ἔ. περ A.R.2.285; παίουσι τὸν Σωτηρίδαν ἔστε ἠνάγκασαν πορεύεσθαι X.*An*.3.4.49, cf. 2.5.30. b. with aor. subj. and ἄν, of future time, after primary tenses, ἐγὼ δὲ τὴν παροῦσαν ἀντλήσω τύχην ἔστ' ἂν Διὸς φρόνημα λωφήσῃ χόλου A.*Pr*.378, cf. 697, *Eu*.449; τῇδε μενέομεν ἔστ' ἂν καὶ τελευτήσωμεν Hdt.7.141, cf. 158; περιμένετε ἔστ' ἂν ἐγὼ ἔλθω X.*An*.5.1.4; ἔντε, ἔντε κ' ἀποτείσῃ, *IG*9(1).334.15, *Schwyzer* 323 *B*41 (v/iv B. C.); ἔστε κε indef., *until such time as*.., Theoc.5.22; χιμάρῳ δὲ καλὸν κρέας ἔστε κ' ἀμέλξῃς Id.1.6, cf. 6.32; also after historical tenses, ἐδέοντο Εὐρυβιάδεω προσμεῖναι ἔστ' ἂν αὐτοὶ τέκνα τε καὶ τοὺς οἰκέτας ὑπεκθέωνται Hdt.8.4, cf. X.*HG*3.1.15, *An*.4.5.28: retained in orat. obliq., αὐτὸς ἔφη παραμενεῖν ἔστ' ἂν τοὺς βότρυς ποιήσωσι γλεύκος Longus 4.5: ἄν omitted, ἀρήγετ' ἔστ' ἐγὼ μόλω S.*Aj*.1183; cf. ἄν (A) B. I. 2. c. with aor. opt. after historical tenses (representing ἔστ' ἄν with subj.), ἐπιμεῖναι ἐκέλευσαν ἔστε βουλεύσαιντο X.*An*.5.5.2; ἀνέμενεν αὐτοὺς ἔστ' ἐμφάγοιέν τι he always waited *until*.., Id.*Cyr*.8.1.44; in orat. obliq., ὅτι.. δέοιτο ἂν αὐτοῦ μένειν ἔστε σὺ ἀπέλθοις ib.5.3.13. d. with aor. inf., in orat. obliq. and the like for opt., ἔστε αὐτὴν νέμεσθαι Κρῆτας, = ἔστε αὐτὴν νέμοιντο Κρῆτες, Hdt.7.171; freq. in later writers, ἔστε Δαρεῖον γνῶναι, = ἔστε Δαρεῖος γνοίη, Arr.*An*.2.1.3; ἔστε παρελθεῖν ib.4.7.1, cf. Ael.*HA*2.11; for ἔστ' ἄν with subj., Arr.*Cyn*.2.4, 25.2, 31.5. e. with impf. ind., ἔστ' ἀφίκανεν A.R.4.849. 2. *so long as, while*, a. with impf. ind. of actual occurrence in past time, ἔστε μὲν.. ἔπινον, ἡδὺ τέως ἐδόκει Thgn.959; ἔστε μὲν αἱ σπονδαὶ ἦσαν, οὔποτε ἐπαυόμην X.*An*.3.1.19, cf. *Mem*.1.2.18, Arr.*An*.2.11.6. b. with pres. subj. and ἄν, of future time, ἔστ' ἂν ἀοιδάων ᾖ γένος Ἑλλαδικῶν Xenoph.6.4; οὐ μὲν δὴ λήξω ἔστ' ἄν.. λεύσσω.. τόδ' ἦμαρ S.*El*.105 (anap.), cf. E.*Alc*.337; ἔστ' ἄν περ ἐπιδεικνύηται X.*Eq*.11.9; ἔστ' ἂν ἔκδημος (sc. ᾖ) χθονὸς Θησεύς, ἄπειμι E.*Hipp*.659: so with pf. subj., = pres., ὑμῖν Λακεδαιμόνιοι ἐπαγγέλλονται γυναῖκας ἐπιθρέψειν, ἔστ' ἂν ὁ πόλεμος ὅδε συνεστήκῃ Hdt.8.142; of present time, Emp.42.2. c. with pres. opt. after historical tenses (representing ἔστ' ἄν with subj.), ἐδόκει τοῖς στρατηγοῖς βέλτιον εἶναι τὸν πόλεμον ἀκήρυκτον εἶναι, ἔστ' ἐν τῇ πολεμίᾳ εἶεν X.*An*.3.3.5; τοσοῦτον χρόνον ζῆν ἔστε νικῴη.. ib.1.9.11. d. with aor. subj. and ἄν, ἔστ' ἂν πολεμίους δείσωσι κελευόμενα πάντα ποιοῦσι Id.*Mem*.3.5.6. II. ADV. *even to*, a. of Space, *up to*, βόθροι ἐγίγνοντο μεγάλοι ἔστε ἐπὶ τὸ δάπεδον Id.*An*.4.5.6, cf. 4.8.8, Arr.*An*.1.28.3; ἔστ' ἐπὶ πᾶχυν Theoc.7.67. b. of Time, ἔστε ἐπὶ κνέφας Arr.*An*.7.25.2; ἔστε ἐς.., κατὰ.., *IG*14.352 ii 60, i 65 (Halaesa); εἴστε εἰς Θεύχαριν ἄρχοντα *SIG*241.69 (Delph., iv B. C.); ἔστε πρὸς τὸ ἐφηβικὸν Luc.*Nav*.3. III. PREPOSITION, c. acc.. a. of Space, *up to*, ἔστε τὸν ὅρον, ἔστε καὶ τὰν φάραγγα, *Schwyzer* 289.166, 169 (ii B. C.); παρατείνει ἔστε τὴν θάλασσαν Arr.*Ind*.2.2 (⟨ἐπί⟩ Hercher). b. of Time, *until, up to*, ἔ. καὶ τὸν νῦν χρόνον *Schwyzer* 289.113; ἔ. καὶ τὰν τριακάδα τοῦ Ἀλσείου *SIG*1023.25 (Cos, iii/ii B. C.).

**ἔστεισις**, Arc., = ἔκτεισις (q. v.).

**ἐστεκνόομαι**, Cret., = ἐκτ-, *bring forth issue*, *Leg.Gort*.8.24.

**ἐστενωμένως**, Adv., (στενόω) *in brief compass*, Eustr. *in APo*.199.2.

**ἔστη**· στολή (Cypr.), Hsch.; cf. ἐσθής.

**ἕστηκα, ἑστήξω** and **ομαι, ἔστησα, ἔστην, ἑστηώς**, v. ἵστημι.

**ἑστηκότως**, Adv. *firmly*, ἑ. καὶ βεβαίως Phld.*Rh*.1.70S.

**ἐστήκω**, v. sub στήκω.

**ἐστηριγμένως**, Adv. *firmly*, Sch.Opp.*H*.2.395. **ἑστηῶσι**, v. ἵστημι.

⊛ **ἑστία**, ἡ, Ion. **ἱστίη** (as always in Hom. (exc. in ἀνέστιος, ἐφέστιος) and Hdt., cf. *Schwyzer* 687.1 (Chios, vii/vi B. C.), *IG*12(5).554 (Ceos), and v. ἐφέστιος; ἑστίῃ is f. l. in Hes.*Op*.734); Boeot. **ἱστία** (Ἱ.) *IG*7.556 (Tanagra); also Coan, *SIG*1025.29, and Arc., ib.559.55; Locr. **ἱστία** *IG*9(1).334.7; both forms in Cretan, Ἑστία *SIG*527.15 (iii B. C.), Ἱστία *GDI*5079.7, al.:—*hearth of a house*, in Hom. only in solemn appeals, ἴστω νῦν Ζεὺς πρῶτα θεῶν.. ἱστίη τ' Ὀδυσῆος Od.14.159, al., cf. Hdt.4.68, S.*El*.881; καθῆσθαι παρ' ἑστίᾳ, of suppliants, Pi.*Fr*.81; ἐπὶ τὴν ἑστίαν καθίζεσθαι Th.1.136; ἡ δορύξενος ἑ. S.*OC* 633; ἑ. μεσόμφαλος A.*Ag*.1056; ἐν στέγῃ τις ἥμενος παρ' ἑστίᾳ Id.*Fr*.362.3. 2. *the house itself, home*, Pi.*O*.1.11, *P*.11.13: freq. in Trag., as A.*Ch*.264, etc.; διξὰς ἱστίας οἰκέε Hdt.5.40; καταλείποντα ἐν τᾷ ἱστίᾳ παῖδα ἡβάταν, of a colonist, *IG*9(1).334 (Locr., v B. C.): metaph., of *the last home, the grave*, τὰν χθόνιον ἑ. ἰδεῖν S.*OC*1726 (lyr.). 3. *household, family*, οἱ πολλοί, πλὴν ὀγδώκοντα ἱστιέων κτλ., Hdt.1.176; ἱστίη οὐδεμία νομιζομένη εἶναι Γλαύκου Id.6.86.δ'. 4. *altar*, like ἐσχάρα, A.*Th*.275, *Eu*.282; βούθυτος ἑ. S.*OC*1495 (lyr.); γᾶς μεσσόμφαλος ἑ., of the Delphic shrine, E.*Ion*462 (lyr.); Πυθόμαντις ἑ. S.*OT*965; βωμός, ἑ. χθονός (as a sanctuary) A.*Supp*.372 (lyr.); ἡ κοινὴ ἑ. the public *altar*, serving as a sanctuary to refugees, *IG*2[2].1029, Arist.*Pol*.1322$^b$28; πολιτικὴ ἑ. App.*Pun*.84:—ἡ κοινὴ ἑ. also of *the public table*, ἐδέξαντο τοὺς πρεσβευτὰς ἐπὶ τὴν κοινὴν ἑ. Plb.29.5.6, cf. *IG*5(1).961 (Cotyrta), 7.21 (Orchomenus in Boeotia), Poll.9.40; μυηθεὶς ἀφ' ἑστίας, of a class of public initiates at Eleusis, Is.*Fr*.84, cf. *IG* 2.1355, al.; so ὁ ἀφ' ἑ. παῖς Porph.*Abst*.4.5; simply ὁ ἀφ' ἑ., ἡ ἀφ' ἑ., Ἐφ.Ἀρχ.1894.176, 1885.146. 5. metaph., of places which are to a country as the hearth to a house, as a metropolis, Plb.5.58.4; ἑ. καὶ μητρόπολις D.S.4.19; of Delos, ἱστίη ὦ νήσων Call.*Del*.325:—Pythag., of the *central fire* of the universe, Philol.7, etc., cf. Alex.Aphr. *in Metaph*.38.23; of the earth, E.*Fr*.944; of the heart in the body, Arist.*PA*670$^a$25; μίαν, ἰδίαν ἑ. ἤθους οὐκ ἔχειν, Plu.2.52a, 97a; of the liver as *focus* of a fever, Gal.15.742. II. as pr. n. **Ἑστία**, Ion. **Ἱστίη, Ἑστίη**, *h.Hom*.24.1, v. l. in Hes.*Th*.454:—*the hearth-goddess*, *h.Ven*.22, Hes.*Th*. l. c., Pi.*N*.11.1, etc., cf. *h.Hom*.24, 29, Orph.*H*.84, D.S.5.68; Ἑ. βουλαία *IG*12(5).732 (Andros), Aeschin. 2.45, App.*Mith*.23; Ἑ. πρυτανεία *IG*12(5).659 (Syros); worshipped as ἡ κοινὴ Ἑ. by the Getae, D.S.1.94, cf. Hdt.4.127: prov., ἀφ' Ἑστίας ἄρχεσθαι to begin from *the beginning*, Ar.*V*.846, Pl.*Euthphr*.3a; ἀπ' ἄλλης Ἑ. καὶ ἀρχῆς τὰς πράξεις προχειρίζεσθαι Str.1.1.16 (also ἐξ ἑ. ἄρχεσθαι Hsch.); ἡ Ἑ. γελᾷ, of the *fire* crackling, Arist.*Mete*.369$^a$32. 2. = Lat. *Vesta*, Str.5.2.3, Plu.*Rom*.2, etc. 3. title of a priestess, *IG*9(1).486 (Acarnania); ἑ. πόλεως, as an honorary title, ib.5(1).583 (Sparta). [ῑ in Od. in the appellat. 14.159, ῐ in *h.Hom*. in pr. n.; in Hes. the reverse: ῐ always in Com. and Trag.] (Etymological connexion with Vesta is doubtful; the dialects never have ϝ-, exc. in the pr. n. ϝιστίαν (gen. sg. masc.) *IG*5(2).271.18 (Mantinea); cf. γιστία.)

**Ἑστιαῖον**, τό, *temple of Vesta*, D.C.*Fr*.6.2, al. II. Ion. **Ἱστιήϊα**, τά, *funds of the temple of* Ἱστίη, *SIG*57.40 (Miletus, v B. C.).

**Ἑστιαῖος**, ὁ (sc. μήν), name of month in Cyprus, *Hemerolog.Flor.* (-έος).

**ἑστί-ᾱμα**, ατος, τό, (ἑστιάω) *banquet*, τὰ Ταντάλου θεοῖσιν ἑ. E.*IT* 387: metaph., ἐμπιπλὰς ὀργὴν κακῶν ἑστιαμάτων Pl.*Lg*.935a. **-αρχέω**, *to be* ἑστιάρχης, Luc.*Am*.10. **-άρχης**, ου, ὁ, *the master of a feast*, Plu.2.643d, prob. in *CIG*2052.4 (Apollonia in Thrace).

**Ἑστιάς**, only pl. **Ἑστιάδες**, αἱ, *Vestal virgins*, D.H.2.64, Plu.*Ant*. 21; Ἑ. παρθένοι Id.*Num*.13.

**ἑστίᾱσις**, εως, ἡ, *feasting, banqueting, entertainment*, Th.6.46 (pl.), Pl.*R*.612a (pl.), D.19.234; λόγων ἑ. a *banquet* of speeches, Pl. *Ti*.27b; ἑ. συμφορητός, = ἔρανος, Arist.*Pol*.1286$^a$29. II. *public dinner given by a citizen to his fellow-citizens*, as a λειτουργία, ib.1321$^a$37.

**Ἑστιασταί**, οἱ, association of *worshippers of Hestia* at Rhodes, *IG*12(1).162.8.

**ἑστιατήρ**· ὁ δοκιμαζόμενος, Hsch.

**ἑστιᾱτ-ήριον**, τό, *banqueting-hall*, *Rev Épigr*.1.239 (Naples, ii A. D.), Philostr.*VS*2.23. ⊛ **-ικός**, ή, όν, *convivial*, ἐπιπλοκαί Antip. *Stoic*.3.254. II. Subst. -ικόν, τό, *fund for public banquets* at Delos, *Inscr.Délos* 320 *B*77 (iii B. C.). ⊛ **-ορία**, ἡ, *allowance of food*, Lxx 4*Ki*.25.30. 2. *feast*, ib.*Da*.5.23; ἑ. γερδίων *PTeb*.584 (ii A. D.). ⊛ **-όριον**, later -ειον, τό, = ἑστιατήριον, *IG*11(2).144 *A*68 (Delos, iv B. C.), Theopomp.Hist.32, *Bull.Soc.Arch*.5.126 (iii B. C.), *Sammelb*.6596 (ii B. C.), D.H.2.23, *SIG*1109.141 (Athens, ii A. D., -είου): Ion. **ἱστιητόριον** Hdt.4.35: Rhod. **ἱστιατόριον** *IG*12(1).677 (iii B. C.). **-ορίς**, ἡ, *Areca nut* (kernel of the palm *Areca Catechu*), Plin *HN*24.165 (v. l.). **-ωρ**, ορος, ὁ, *one who gives a banquet, host*, Pl.*R*.421b, *Ti*.17a, Charond.ap.Stob.4.2.24, Ph.2.70, Them.*Or*.24.301a. 2. at Athens, *the citizen on whom the liturgy of* ἑστίασις (q. v.) *fell*, D.20.21, 39.7. b. at Delphi, *manager of the commissariat* at the Pythais, *SIG*711 *D*[2]17, al. (ii B. C.). 3. metaph., ἑ. τοῦ λόγου Philostr.*VA*6.10. II. *guest*, Posidon.9J. III. **ἱστιάτορες**, οἱ, *office-bearers of a religious association* (ὀργεῶνες), *IG* 2[2].1259 (iv B. C.); = ἐσσῆνες (A) 1, at Ephesus, Paus.8.13.1.

**ἑστιᾶχος**· οἰκουρὸς κτλ., Hsch. (cf. ἑστιοῦχος).

**ἑστιάω**, Ion. and Dor. **ἱστιάω**, impf. εἱστίων Lys.19.27, Ion. 3 sg. ἱστία Hdt.7.135: fut. ἑστιάσω [ᾱ] Antiph.68.1: aor. 1 εἱστίασα X.*Cyr*. 1.3.10, Is.8.18, inf. ἑστιᾶσαι Ar.*Nu*.1212 (later ἡστίασεν *SIG*1104.26 (Athens, i B. C.), ἱσστίασεν ib.714.31 (Eretria, ii B. C.)): pf. εἱστίακα D.21.156:—Med. and Pass., v. infr.: (ἑστία):—*receive at one's hearth* or *in one's house*, ξένους Lys.12.8; *entertain, feast*, τινα Hdt. l. c., Ar.*Nu*.1212; ἐν δόμοισιν ξένον E.*Alc*.765; ἑ. τινὰ ἰχθύσι on fish, Pl.*R*.404b; at Athens, ἑ. τὴν φυλήν (cf. ἑστίασις) D.21.156; τὴν πόλιν Arist.*EN*1122$^b$23; of the dining-room, ὁ ἀνδρὼν ὁ..

ἑστιῶν αὐτούς Ael.*VH*8.7. 2. abs., *give a feast*, ἑ. μεγαλοπρεπῶς ib.12.51; οἱ ἑστιῶντες *entertainers*, Pl.*Grg.*518d; τὸν ἱστιῶντ' ἐπαινέω Epich.35.4. 3. c. acc. cogn., Ζεὺς..Πέλοπι ἔρανον ἱστιῶν Id. 87; γάμους ἑ. *give a* marriage *feast*, E.*HF*483, Ar.*Av.*132; ἑ. νικητήρια X.*Cyr.*8.4.1; ἐπινίκια D.59.33; δεκάτην ὑπέρ τινος Id.40.28; γενέθλια Luc.*Herm.*11: and c dupl. acc., ἅμα θύσαντα τὰ ἱερὰ ἑστιᾶσαι ἐκεῖνον Antipho 1.16; θεσμοφόρια ἑ. τὰς γυναῖκας Is.3.80; τὴν γενέθλιον ἑ. τινά Luc.*Dem.Enc.*26, cf. *Symp.*2: c. dat., Eup.59. 4. metaph., ἑ. τινὰ λόγων καλῶν Pl.*R.*571d, cf. Luc.*Philops.*39; ἑ. τὰς ἀκοάς, τὴν ὄψιν, Ael.*VH*3.1, *NA*17.23, etc. II. Pass., with fut. Med. ἑστιάσομαι Pl.*R.*345c, *Tht.*178d; later ἑστιαθήσομαι Sch.Ar. *Ach.*977: aor. 1 εἱστιάθην Pl.*Phdr.*247e, (συν-) D.19.190; later ἑστιάσασθαι S E.*M.*8.186: pf. εἱστίαμαι Pl.*R.*354a, Ion. inf. ἱστιῆσθαι Hdt. 5.20:—*to be a guest, be feasted*, Id. l. c., Pl.*R.*372c; ἑ. παρὰ ἀνδρὶ φίλῳ Antipho 1.26: c. acc. rei. *feast on*.., ἑ. ἐνύπνιον *have a* visionary *feast*, 'feast with the Barmecide', Ar.*V.*1218; ἑ. γῆν, τὰ ὄντα, Pl.*R.*612a, *Phdr.*247e: c. dat., εὐωδίᾳ X.*Smp.*2.3; λόγοις Ath.7.275b: metaph., ταῦτά σοι εἱστιάσθω ἐν τοῖς Βενδιδείοις Pl.*R.*354a.

**ἔστιοι**, = νεκροί, at Clitor in Arcadia, *AB*1096.

**ἑστιόομαι**, Pass., (ἑστία) δῶμ' ἑστιοῦται the house *is founded* or *established* (by children), E.*Ion* 1464 (lyr.).

**ἑστιοπάμων** [ᾰ], ονος, ὁ, *householder*, Dor. and Aeol., Poll.1.74, 10.20.

**ἕστιος**, α, ον, *of the* ἑστία, θεοί, ἐσχάρα, Hld.1.30, 4.18. II. Ἑστιος, ὁ (sc. μήν), name of month in Magnesia, *IG*9(2).1117.11.

**ἑστιουχ-έω**, (ἔχω) *preside over the home* or *state*, ἄρχοντες ἑ. πόλεως καὶ πολιτῶν σωτηρίας Charond.ap.Stob.4.2.24. ❋ **-ος**, ον, *guarding the house*, Δήμητερ ἑστιοῦχ' Ἐλευσῖνος χθονός *guardian of*.., E.*Supp.* 1, cf. Ar.*Av.*866, Pl.*Lg.*878a. 2. *having an altar* or *hearth*, γαῖα, πόλις, αὐλά, A.*Pers.*511, S.*Ant.*1083, E.*Andr.*283 (lyr.). 3. *on the hearth* or *altar*, ἑ. ψόλος A.*Fr.*281.2 (prob.); πῦρ Plu.2.158c. II. *entertainer, feaster, host*, Ar.*Fr.*776, Ph.1.389.

**ἑστιῶτις**, ιδος, ἡ, *of* or *from the house*, αὔρα S.*Tr.*954 (lyr.).

**ἕστο**, v. ἕννυμι.

**ἐστοχασμένως**, Adv. pf. part. Pass., *hitting the mark*: c. gen., ἐ. τοῦ σκοποῦ Hld.7.5: abs., Ptol.*Tetr.*9.

**ἐστραμμένως**, Adv., (στρέφω) *in a varied manner*, Thom.Mag. p.294 R.

**ἐστρίς**, Adv. *until three times, thrice*, Pi.*O.*2.68, *Pae.Erythr.*tit. p.140 P.: better written divisim.

**ἐστυμμένως**, Adv., (στύφω) *tightly*, Eust.155.19.

**Ἐστρῆνες**· Σειρῆνες, Hsch.

**ἐστώ**, οῦς, ἡ, Dor. for οὐσία (*substance*), opp. μορφή, Archyt.ap. Stob.1.40.2, Philol.6. II. Pythag., *dyad*, Phot.*Bibl.*p.143 B.

❋ **ἔστωρ**, ορος, ὁ, *peg at the end of the pole*, passing through the yoke and having a ring (κρίκος) affixed, prob. for passing the inside reins through, Il.24.272 (v.l. ἕκτορι), Aristobul.7 J.

**ἐσύνηκεν**, aor. 1 with double augm. of συνίημι.

**ἐσύστερον**, Adv. for εἰς ὕστερον, *hereafter*, Od.12.126, Hdt.5.41: better written divisim.

**ἔσφᾰλα**, Dor. for ἔσφηλα, aor. 1 of σφάλλω.

**ἐσφαλμένως**, Adv., (σφάλλω) *erringly, amiss*, *AP*15.38 (Cometas), Sch.Th.1.140.

**ἐσφέρω, ἐσφορά**, v. εἰσ-.

**ἐσφιγμένως**, Adv., (σφίγγω) *tightly*, Dosith.p.412 K.

**ἐσ-φλᾰσις**, εως, ἡ, *contused fracture* of the skull *with depression*, Hp.*VC*6: **-φλάω**, in Pass., *to be so fractured*, ibid.

**ἐσχάζοσαν**, Alexandr. for ἔσχαζον, Lyc.21, cf. Choerob.*in Theod.* 2.64.

❋ **ἐσχάρ-α**, Ion. **-άρη** [ᾰ], ἡ, Ep. gen. and dat. ἐσχαρόφιν (ἀπ' ἐσχ- Od.7.169, ἐπ' ἐσχ- 5.59, 19.389):—*hearth, fire-place*, like ἑστία, Hom. (esp. in Od.), ἡ μὲν ἐπ' ἐσχάρῃ ἧστο Od.6.52; ἧσται ἐπ' ἐσχάρῃ ἐν πυρὸς αὐγῇ ib.305; of suppliants, ἕζετ' ἐπ' ἐσχάρῃ ἐν κονίῃσι 7. 153. 2. *pan of coals, brazier*, Ar.*Ach.*888, *V.*938, cf. Poll.10.94, 95. 3. Τρώων πυρὸς ἐσχάραι *watch-fires* of the camp, Il.10.418. II. *sacrificial hearth* (hollowed out in the ground and so dist. from βωμός, structural altar, St.Byz. s. v. βωμοί, Phot.; used esp. in hero-worship, Neanth.7 J.), Od.14.420, S.*Ant.*1016: but freq. used generally, *altar of burnt-offering*, πρὸς ἐσχάραν Φοίβου A.*Pers.*205; ἐπ' ἐσχάρᾳ πυρός Id.*Eu.*108; ἠμένας ἐπ' ἐσχάραις ib.806; Πυθικὴ E.*Andr.* 1240; at Eleusis, D.59.116, cf. Lycurg.*Fr.*37; Ἡρακλειδῶν ἐ. *IG*2. 1658 (iv B.C.); so βώμιοι ἐσχάραι structured *altars*, E.*Ph.*274; sometimes movable, X.*Cyr.*8.3.12, Callix.2, *PCair.Zen.*13(iii B.C.). III. *fire-stick* (bored with the τρύπανον, q. v.), Thphr.*HP*5.9.7, *Ign.* 64. IV. *platform, stand, basis*, Ph.*Bel.*92.13, Ath.Mech.32.10, Vitr.10.11.9. 2. *grating*, Lxx *Ex.*27.4, al. V. Medic., *scab, eschar* on a wound caused by burning or otherwise, τὰς ἐκπτώσιας τῶν ἐ. Hp.*Art.*11, cf. Pl.Com.184.4, Arist.*Pr.*863ᵃ12, Dsc.1.56, Gal.10. 315, etc. VI. in pl., = τὰ χείλη τῶν γυναικείων αἰδοίων, Ar.*Eq.* 1286. **-άδιν**, *landica*, Gloss. **-εῖον**, τό, *platform, scaffolding*, *IG*2².1672.308. **-εύς**, έως, ὁ, *a ship's cook*, Poll.1.95, Them. *Or.*15.195b. **-εών**, ῶνος, ὁ, = ἐσχάρα 1, Theoc.24.48, *AP*7.648 (Leon.). 2. *forge*, Nonn.*D.*14.22, al. **-ίδιον**, τό, Dim. of ἐσχαρίς, *IG*11(2).164*B*17 (Delos, iii B.C.). **-ινθον**, τό, a dance at Sparta, Poll.4.104. **-ιον**, τό, Dim. of ἐσχάρα: 1. *pan of coals*, Ar.*Fr.*516 (pl.). 2. *stand, platform*, Plb.9.41.4 (pl.), D.S. 20.91. 3. *cradle for launching ships*, Callix.1. 4. *eschar*, Archig.ap.Orib.51.42.3. **-ιος**, ον, *of* or *on the hearth*, πῦρ *AP*7.210 (Antip.). ❋ **-ίς**, ίδος, ἡ, *brazier*, Alex.250, Plu.*Crass.*16, etc.; ἐ. χρυσῆ *CIG*2859 (Branchidae); ἐ. ἀργυρᾶ *IG*12(8).51.22 (Imbros, ii B.C.); used in fishing by night, Ael.*NA*2.8. ❋ **-ίτης** [ῑ] (sc. ἄρτος), ὁ, *bread baked over the fire*, Antidot 3, Crobyl.2, Lxx 2*Ki.*6.19, J.*AJ*7.4.2.

**ἐσχᾰρόπεπτος**, ον, *grilled*, Hp.*Epid.*4.41.

**ἔσχᾰρος**, ὁ, *a fish*, = κόρις, perh. a kind of *sole*, Archipp.24 (prob. l.), Mnesim.4.44, Dorio ap.Ath.7.330a (written ἐσχαρός in Hsch.).

**ἐσχᾰρόφῐν**, Ep. gen. and dat. sg. of ἐσχάρα.

**ἐσχᾰρ-όω**, (ἐσχάρα v) *form an eschar*, of ointments, Orib.50.8.2:— Pass., *come to an eschar*, ἠσχαρωμένα ἕλκη Dsc.4.171. II. *ulcerate*, τὴν ὑστέραν Sor.2.12: abs., *to be caustic*, Dsc.5.75. **-ώδης**, ες, *scab-like*, Poll.4.204, Gal.19.434. **-ωμα**, ατος, τό, *scab, eschar*, *Hippiatr.*81. **-ών**, ῶνος, ὁ, (ἐσχάρα 1) *place for a hearth*, *IG*11(2).144 *A* 61 (Delos, iv B.C.), Roussel *Cultes Égyptiens* 222. **-ωσις**, εως, ἡ, *formation of an eschar*, Arist.*Pr.*863ᵃ14, Heliod.ap.Orib.45.19.1, Sor. 2.41. **-ωτικός**, ή, όν, *tending to form an eschar*, Dsc.2.73; φάρμακα *caustics*, Lycus ap.Orib.8.25.24, Gal.10.324.

**ἐσχᾰτ-άω**, (ἔσχατος) *to be at the edge*, Hom. (only in Il.) always in Ep. part., εἴ τινά που δηΐων ἕλοι ἐσχατόωντα *straying about the edge* of the camp, Il.10.206; Ἀνθηδών, Μύρσινος ἐσχατόωσα, *lying on the border*, 2.508, 616; ἕσπερος ἐ. the *extreme* west, Call.*Del.*174, cf. Theoc.7.77; κάρηνον ἐ. *sinciput*, Arat.207: with a Verb, τεχθήσεται ἐσχατόωσα *at last*, Man.4.459. **-εύω**, *to be at the end*, τὰ ἐσχατεύοντα τῶν δένδρων the parts *farthest off*, i.e. the branches, Thphr. *CP*5.1.3, cf. Plu.2.366b; -εύοντες τόποι Arist.*Cael.*298ᵃ14; *to be at the extremity*, τῆς Ἀρκαδίας Plb.4.77.8. II. *to be the lowest* or *meanest*, τῶν διδασκόντων Phld.*Rh.*2.54 S. **-ιά**, Ion. **-ιή**, ἡ, *farthest part, edge, border*, esp. of a place, Ep., Ion., Lyr., and sts. in Trag. (lyr.); νήσου ἐπ' ἐσχατιῆς Od.5.238; ἀγροῦ ἐπ' ἐσχατιήν (v.l. -ῆς) on *the edge* of the land, 4.517, cf. 5.489 (v.l. -ῆς, -ῇ); simply ἐπ' ἐσχατιῇ, -ῆς, *on the edge* or *shore*, 9.182, 280; ἐπ' ἐσχατιῇ λιμένος at *the mouth* of the harbour, 2.391; ἐσχατιῇ πολέμοιο on *the skirts* of battle (i.e. *farthest parts* of the field), Il.11.524, cf. 20.328; ἐσχατιῇ *round the edge* [of the funeral pile], 23.242; ἐσχατιαῖς, for ἐν ἐ., *on the outskirts*, S.*Ph.*144 (anap.); also, of parts of the body, καρδίης ἡ ἐ. Hp.*Cord.*4; γένυος Arat.57: metaph., *the extremity, highest point*, ὄλβου πρὸς ἐσχατιαῖς (v.l. -ιάς) Pi.*I.*6(5).12; πρὸς ἐσχατιὰν ἀρεταῖσιν ἱκάνων Id.*O.*3.43; τὸ μηδαμῶς ὂν ἐ. τῆς πρώτης αἰτίας Dam.*Pr.*441; μέχρι τῶν ἐ. Ph.1.685. 2. *border* of a country, ἐσχατιῇ Γόρτυνος Od.3.294; ναῖον δ' ἐσχατιὴν Φθίης Il.9 484; ἐσχατιῇ alone, Od.14.104; ἀν' ἐσχατιήν Archil.89.4: pl., αἱ ἐ. τῆς οἰκεομένης *the extremities* of the world, Hdt.3.106; also, *borders, frontier-land*, τῆς Αἰτωλίδος Id.6.127: abs., Id.3.115, 116, X.*HG*2.4.4, etc.: in Attica, *a boundary estate*, i.e. one at the sea-side or the foot of the mountains (cf. *AB*256), Aeschin.1.97, D.42.5, *IG*2².1594 (iv B.C.), Alciphr.3.34, cf. *IG*12(5).872.82 (Tenos): pl., ib.88. 3. of Time, ἀν' ἐσχατιάν *at last*, Pi.*P.*11.56: so dat., ἐσχατιῇ Nic.*Th.*437. 4. in pl., = δύσεις, Arat.574. **-ίζω**, *to be last, to come too late*, Lxx 1*Ma.*5.53: c. inf., ἐ. παραγενέσθαι ib.*Jd.*5.28 cod. A. **-ιος**, α, ον, poet. for ἔσχατος, Nic.*Th.*746, *AP*7.555 (Joann. Poet.), Opp.*C.*1. 124. **-ιώτης**, ου, ὁ, fem. **-ῶτις**, ιδος, *on the frontier*, as pr. n. of one from Ἐσχατιά (in Tenos), *IG*12(5).872, al.

**ἐσχᾰτό-γηρως**, ων, *in extreme old age*, D.S.15.76, Str.14.1.48, M. Ant.9.33: gen. sg. -γηρως Mitteis *Chr.*31 vii 29 (ii B.C.), v.l. in Lxx *Si.* 42.8: as fem., Poll.2.18: **-γηρος**, ον, Lxx *Si.* l. c., Ruf.*Fr.*64:—later **-γέρων**, οντος, ὁ, Procop.*Arc.*9.

**ἐσχᾰτόεις**, in acc. ἐσχατόεντα, f.l. for ἐσχατόωντα, D.P.65.

**ἐσχᾰτοκόλλιον**, τό, *end* of a papyrus roll, Mart.2.6.3; cf. πρωτόκολλον.

❋ **ἔσχᾰτος**, η, ον, also ος, ον Arat.625 (prob. fr. ἐκ, ἐξ, perh. **eghsкατος* (cf. ἐχθός) like ἔγ-κατα): I. of Space, as always in Hom., *farthest, uttermost, extreme*, θάλαμος ἐ. the *hindmost* chamber, Od.21. 9; ἔσχατοι ἄλλων *at the end of the lines*, Il.10.434, cf. 8.225; ἔσχατοι ἀνδρῶν, of the Aethiopians, Od.1.23; οἰκέομεν.. ἔσχατοι 6.205; ἐσχάτη τῶν οἰκεομένων ἡ Ἰνδική Hdt.3.106, cf. Th.2.96, etc.; τὸ ἔ. τῆς ἀγορᾶς X.*HG*3.3.5; ὑπ'.. ἐσχάτην ὁπλὴν S.*El.*720; τάξις ἐ. the *farthest part of* the army, Id.*Aj.*4: pl., ἔσχατα γαίης Hes.*Th.*731; τὰ ἐ. τῶν στρατοπέδων Th.4.96; ἐπ' ἔσχατα χθονός S.*Fr.*956; αἱ ἐπ' ἔσχατα τοῦ ἄστεως οἰκίαι Th.8.95; ἐξ ἐσχάτων ἐς ἔσχατα ἀπικέσθαι from *end* to *end*, Hdt.7.100, cf. X.*Vect.*1.6; παρ' ἔσχατα λίμνης Pl.*Phd.*113b, cf. Th.3. 106:—in various senses, *uppermost*, ἐ. πυρά S.*El.*900; *lowest, deepest*, ἀΐδας Theoc.16.52; ἅλς *AP*13.27 (Phal.); *innermost*, σάρκες S.*Tr.* 1053; *last, hindmost*, ἤλαυνε δ' ἔ. Id.*El.*734; ἐπ' ἐσχάτῳ at the *close* of a document, *PTeb.*68.54 (ii B.C.), etc. 2. of Degree, *uttermost, highest*, τὸ ἔ. κορυφοῦται βασιλεῦσι Pi.*O.*1.113; ἀνορέαι ἔ. Id.*I.*4(3). 11; σοφία Lib.*Or.*59.88; of misfortunes, sufferings, etc., *utmost, last, worst*, πόνος, ἀδικία, κίνδυνοι, Pl.*Phdr.*247b, *R.*361a, *Grg.*511d; ὀδύναι αἱ ἔ. Id.*Prt.*354b; δῆμος ἔ. *extreme* democracy, Arist.*Pol.*1296ᵃ2. b. Subst., τὸ ἔ., τὰ ἔ., *the utmost*, ἐς τὸ ἔ. κακοῦ ἀπιγμένοι Hdt.8.52; τετρῦσθαι ἐς τὸ ἔ. κακοῦ Id.1.22; without Art., ἐπ' ἔσχατα βαίνεις S. *OC*217 (lyr.); προβᾶσ' ἐπ' ἔσχατον θράσους Id.*Ant.*853 (lyr.); ἐπ' ἔ. ἐληλυθὼς ἠλιθίας Pl.*Phdr.*240d, cf. *R.*361d, etc.; ὃ πάντων κακῶν ἔσχατόν ἐστι, τοῦτο πάσχει Id.*Phd.*83c; οἱ τὰ ἔ. πεποιηκότες X.*Cyr.*8.8.2; ζημιοῦσθαι πᾶσι τοῖς ἐ., Lat. *extremis suppliciis*, Pl.*Plt.*297e; ἔσχατ' ἐσχάτων κακά *worst of possible* evils, S.*Ph.*65, cf. Philem.178; εἰς τὰ ἔ. ἐληλυθὼς *UPZ*60.12 (ii B.C.): Comp. οὔτε γὰρ τοῦ ἐσχάτου -ώτερον εἴη ἄν τι Arist.*Metaph.*1055ᵃ20: Sup. -ώτατος f.l. in X.*HG*2.3.49, cf. Phryn.51; τὰ -ώτατα Phld.*Hom.*p.32 O. 3. of Persons, *lowest, meanest*, D.S.8.18, D.C.42.5, Alciphr.3.43: prov., οὐδείς, οὐδ' ὁ Μυσῶν ἔ., i.e. *the meanest* of mankind, Magnes 5, cf. Philem.77; in

Pl.*Tht.*209b it seems to mean the *remotest* of mankind, cf. πρὸς ἐσχάτην Μυσῶν v.l. in *App.Prov.*2.85 (παρὰ τοῖς ἐ. τῆς Μυσίας Apostol.8.1); similarly οὐδὲ τὸν ἔσχατον Καρῶν Plu.2.871b. **4.** of Time, *last*, ἐς τὸ ἔ. to the *end*, Hdt.7.107, Th.3.46; ἔ. πλόος, ναυτιλίαι, *the end of* it, Pi.*P.*10.28, *N.*3.22; ἐσχάτας ὑπὲρ ῥίζας over *the last* scion of the race, S.*Ant.*599 (lyr.); ἔ. Ἑλλήνων, Ῥωμαίων, Plu.*Phil.*1, *Brut.*44: neut. ἔσχατον, as Adv., *for the last time*, S.*OC*1550; *finally, best of all*, 1*Ep.Cor.*15.8; *at the latest*, ἔ. ἐν τρισὶ μησίν *SIG*1219.11 (Gambreion, iii B.C.), cf. *Inscr.Prien.*4.45 (iv B.C.); εἰς τὴν ἐσχάτην at the *last*, Lxx *Ec.*1.11; ἐπ' ἐσχάτῳ ib.2*Ki.*24.25, al.: Subst. ἐσχάτη, ἡ, *end*, οὐχ ἕξεις ἐ. καλήν Astramps.*Orac.*21.4, cf. 40.3. **5.** in the Logic of Arist., τὰ ἔ. are the *last* or *lowest species*, *Metaph.*1059$^{b}$26, or *individuals*, ib.998$^{b}$16, cf. *APo.*96$^{b}$12, al.; τὸ ἔ. ἄτομον *Metaph.*1058$^{b}$10. **b.** ὁ ἔ. ὅρος the *minor* term of a syllogism, *EN*1147$^{b}$14. **c.** *last step* in geom. analysis or *ultimate condition* of action, τὸ ἔ. ἀρχὴ τῆς πράξεως *de An.*433$^{a}$16. **II.** Adv. -τως *to the uttermost, exceedingly*, πῦρ ἐ. καίει Hp.*de Arte*8; ἐ. διαμάχεσθαι Arist.*HA*613$^{a}$11; ἐ. φιλοπόλεμος X.*An.*2.6.1; φοβοῦμαί σ' ἐ. Men.912, cf. Epicur.*Ep.*1 p.31 U. **b.** -τως διακεῖσθαι to be *at the last extremity*, Plb.1.24.2, D.S.18.48; ἔχειν *Ev.Marc.*5.23; ἀπορεῖν Phld.*Oec.*p.72 J. **2.** so ἐς τὸ ἔ., = ἐσχάτως, Hdt.7.229; εἰς τὰ ἔ. X.*HG*5.4.33; εἰς τὰ ἔ. μάλα Id.*Lac.*1.2; τὸ ἔ. *finally, in the end*, Pl.*Grg.*473c; but, τὸ ἔ. *what is worst of all*, ib.508d.

**ἔσχεθον**, v. sub ἔχω.

**ἐσχηματισμένως**, Adv. pf. part. Pass., *by the possession of form*, Syrian.*in Metaph.*113.29. **II.** *figuratively*, Aps p.331 H., Sch. Ar.*Pl.*23; *artificially, disingenuously*, of argument, Herm.*in Phdr.* p.84 A.; *fraudulently*, Just.*Nov.*6.5.

**ἔσχων**, impf. of *σχάω, = σχάζω (q.v.).

**ἔσω**, Adv. related to ἐς as εἰς to εἴσω (qq.v.): Comp., ἐσωτέρω τῆς Ἑλλάδος Hdt.8.66: Sup., ὡς ἐσωτάτω τῆς μασχάλης Hp.*Art.*7; τὰ ἔ. Id.*Oss.*9, cf. Corn.*ND*28.

**ἔσωθεν** (**εἴσωθεν** only in Hp.*Art.*46 codd.), rarely **ἔσωθε** E.*Heracl.*42: Adv.: *from within*, Hdt.7.36, 8.37, Aen.Tact.32.7, etc. **2.** *within, inside*, Hdt.1.181, 2.36, A.*Ag.*991 (lyr.), S.*Tr.*601: c. gen., ἔσωθεν ἄντρων E.*Cyc.*516 (lyr.); ἔσωθε ναοῦ Id.*Heracl.* l.c.

**ἐσωπή**, ἡ, (ὤψ) *appearance, look*, Opp.*H.*4.358.

**ἐσωρῆ⟨σ⟩αι**· ὑπουργῆσαι τοὺς αὐτούς, Hsch.

⊛ **ἐσώτατος**, η, ον, Sup. of ἔσω, *innermost*, opp. ἐξώτατος, Ph.2.147, *Fr.*67 H., Sch.Pi.*N.*1.61: Comp. **ἐσώτερος**, α, ον, *Act.Ap.*16.24; εἰς -ώτερον *PMagd.*29.10 (iii B.C.); cf. ἔσω.

**ἐσωτεριαῖος**, α, ον, *inner*, λίθοι for an *inner* wall, *POxy.*498.14 (ii A.D.).

**ἐσωτερικός**, ή, όν, *inner, esoteric*: ἐσωτερικά, τά, of certain Stoic doctrines, Gal.5.313; ἐ. μαθήματα Iamb.*Comm.Math.*18; of persons, -κοί, οἱ, the disciples of Pythagoras, Id.*VP*17.72; μέμνησο τὸν μὲν ἐ., τὸν δὲ ἐξ. καλεῖν (of Aristotle), Luc.*Vit.Auct.*26. (Prob. coined to correspond with ἐξωτερικός (q.v.).)

**ἐσωτέρω**, Comp. of ἔσω (q.v.).

⊛ **ἐσωτικός**, ή, όν, *internal*: -κόν, τό, *household, family*, *Rev.Arch.*20(1912).258 (Thrace).

**ἐσώφωτον**, τό, *hollow, interior space*, Hero *Stereom.*1.41.2.

⊛ **ἐτάζω**, aor. 1 ἤτασα (v. infr.), *examine, test*, mostly in compd. ἐξετάζω (for which it is v.l. in Hdt.3.62, ap.*AB*96), cf. παρετάζω; τοὺς ἀδικέοντας Democr.266; ἐτάζει (etym. of ἔτος) Pl.*Cra.*410d; freq. in Lxx, ὁ ἐτάζων καρδίας 1*Ch.*29.17; ἐτάζουσι Polusap.Stob.3.9.51: aor. 1 inf. ἐτάσαι Aristid.1.460 J. (prob. l.): c. dupl. acc., ἥν με Μουσάων ἐτάσῃς χάριν *AP*7.17 (Tull. Laur.); *reveal, unmask*, τινα ib.12.135 (Asclep.):—Pass., Lxx *Wi.*6.7, al. **2.** *visit, try, afflict*, τινα μεγάλοις ἐτασμοῖς ib.*Ge.*12.17. (Fr. ἐτός (B) as δοκιμάζω fr. δόκιμος.)

**ἑταίρ-α**, Ion. -η, ἡ, v. sub ἑταῖρος II. **-εία**, ἡ, also **ἑταιρία**, E.*Or.*1072, 1079, Th.3.82, Pl.*R.*365d, D.10.259, Arist.*Pol.*1272$^{b}$34, al.; Ion. **-ηΐη**: (ἑταῖρος):—*association, brotherhood*, τῶν ἡλικιωτέων Hdt.5.71; ἑ. ποιεῖσθαι Isoc.3.54 (pl.); μαρτύρων συνεστῶσ' ἑ. D.21.139; αἱ βόες νέμονται καθ' ἑταιρείας Arist.*HA*611$^{a}$7; of a *social group* in Crete, *Leg.Gort.*10.38. **2.** at Athens and elsewhere, *political club* or *union for party purposes*, Eup.8.6 D., *Com.Adesp.*22.31 D., Th.3.82, Lys.12.55, Isoc.4.79 (pl.); -ίας συνάξομεν Pl.*R.*365d; σπουδαὶ ἑταιριῶν ἐπ' ἀρχάς Id.*Tht.*173d; at Carthage, τὰ συσσίτια τῶν ἑ., compared to the φιδίτια at Sparta, Arist.*Pol.*1272$^{b}$34, cf. 1305$^{b}$32. **3.** = Lat. *collegium*, ἑταιρία Ἰουλιανή, = *collegium Lupercorum Juliorum*, D.C.44.6. **II.** generally, *friendly connexion, friendship, comradeship*, Simon.118, S.*Aj.*683, E.*Or.*1072, *AP*7.51 (Adaeus); opp. ἔχθρα, D.29.23. **III.** = ἑταίρησις, And.1.100, v.l. in D.S.2.18: Anaxil.21.3 combines signfs. II and III. **-εῖος**, α, ον, Ion. **-ήϊος**, η, ον, (ἑταίρειος Hdn.Gr.1.137):—*of* or *belonging to companions*: Ζεὺς ἑ. *presiding over fellowship*, Hdt.1.44, Diph.20, D.Chr.1.39, etc.; so, of God, Ph.2.452; φόνος ἑ. the murder *of a comrade*, *AP*9.519 (Alc. Mess.). **II.** *amorous*, ἑ. φιλότης *h.Merc.*58; στόλος *AP*9.415 (Antiphil.). **III.** ἑταιρεῖον, τό, *house of a* ἑταίρα, Sch. Ar.*Eq.*873. **-ειώτης**, ου, ὁ, *member of a* ἑταιρεία, Hdn.*Epim.*37. ⊛ **-εύομαι**, Pass., *prostitute oneself*, D.S.12.21, Theopomp. Hist.217$^{c}$. ⊛ **-έω**, *keep company with*, Aeschin.1.13, Phoenicid.4.2; τινι *with* a man, And.1.100, etc.; φιλία ἑταιροῦσα *meretricious* friendship, Plu.2.62d; οἱ πολλοὶ αὐτῶν ἡταιρήκασιν Lys.14.41; οὐκέτι φαίνεται μόνον ἡταιρηκώς, ἀλλὰ καὶ πεπορνευμένος Aeschin.1.52. **II.** Med., = ἑταιρεύομαι, of men, Theopomp.Hist.217$^{b}$; of women, Plu.*Ant.*18. **-ηΐη, ἑταιρήϊος**, η, ον, Ion. for ἑταιρεία, ἑταιρεῖος, α, ον. **-ησις**, εως, ἡ, *unchastity*, Aeschin.1.13, D.22.21, Ph.2.381, etc. **-ία**, ἡ, v. ἑταιρεία. **-ίδεια** (sc. ἱερά), τά, *the festival of* Ζεὺς ἑταιρεῖος at Magnesia, Hegesand.25. **-ίδιον**, Dim. of ἑταίρα, Ph.ap. Eus.*PE*8.14 (pl.), Plu.2.808e, Hld.7.10. ⊛ **-ίζω**, *to be* ἑταῖρος or *comrade* to any one, c. dat., ἀνδρὶ ἑταιρίσσαι Il.24.335; of the Graces, *h.Ven.*96. **2.** trans. in Med., *associate with oneself, choose for one's comrade*, ἤ τινά που Τρώων ἑταρίσσαιτο Il.13.456, cf. Call.*Dian.*206, Naumach.ap.Stob.4.23.7. **b.** *win over*, App.*Hann.*32, *BC*3.21. **II.** = ἑταιρεύομαι, *to be a courtesan*, in Act., Luc.*DMeretr.*7.3; of a man, Sch.Ar.*Th.*261:—Med., Ath.13.593b, *Cat.Cod.Astr.*8(4).169. **2.** *associate with* ἑταῖραι, *Com.Adesp.*1012. ⊛ **-ικός**, ή, όν, *of* or *befitting a companion*: ἡ ἑταιρική *companionship*, Arist.*EN*1157$^{b}$23; in full, ἑ. φιλία ib.1161$^{b}$12. Adv. -κῶς, προσφέρεσθαι Id.*EE*1243$^{a}$5. **2.** τὸ ἑταιρικόν, = ἑταιρεία I. 2, Th.8.48; ἑ. συνάγειν Hyp.*Eux.*8; τὰ ἑταιρικά *factions, clubs*, Plu.*Lys.*5, D.C.37.57; = Lat. *collegia*, Id.38.13. **b.** *ties of party*, opp. τὸ ξυγγενές, Th.3.82. **3.** ἵππος -κή horse-*guards* of the Macedonian kings, Plb.16.18.7, D.S.17.37, Arr.*An.*3.16.11. **II.** *of* or *like a* ἑταίρα, *meretricious*, γυνή Plu.2.140c, etc.; τὸ ἑ. the *custom of* ἑταῖραι, Alciphr.2.1; *concerning* ἑταῖραι, λόγοι D.H.*Lys.*3: so Adv. -κῶς *meretriciously*, κεκοσμημένοι Zeno *Stoic.*1.58, Luc.*Bis Acc.*20, Plu.*Pomp.*2. **2.** ἑ. (sc. τέλος), τό, *tax on courtesans*, *Ostr.*83 (ii B.C.); τελώνης ἑταιρεικοῦ (sic) Ἀφροδίτη *Arch.Pap.*6.219 (Elephantine, ii B.C.). **-ίς**, ίδος, ἡ, = ἑταίρα, v.l. in X.*HG*5.4.6, cf. Ph.1.40, *AP*6.208 (Antip. Thess.); περὶ τῶν Ἀθήνησι Ἑ., title of several works, Ath.13.567a:—not good Att., acc. to Thom.Mag.p.129 R. **-ισμα**, ατος, τό, = ἑταιρικὸν τέλος, *PGrenf.*2.41 (i A.D., pl.). **-ισμός**, ὁ, (ἑταιρίζω II) *harlotry*, Clearch.6, *OGI*674.17 (Egypt, i A.D.). **-ιστής**, οῦ, ὁ, *lewd man*, Poll.6.188:—fem. ⊛ **-ίστρια**, = τριβάς, Pl.*Smp.*191e, Luc.*DMeretr.*5.2, Tim.*Lex.*

⊛ **ἑταιροποιέομαι**, *make friends*, Sch.Il.12.310.

**ἑταῖρ-ος**, Ep. and Dor. also **ἕτᾰρος**, Cleobul.ap.D.L.1.93, A.*Pers.*988 (lyr.), ὁ:—*comrade, companion*, in Hom. esp. of the followers of a chief, *comrades-in-arms*, Il.1.179, al.; *messmate*, 17.577; *fellow-slave*, Od.14.407, al.: joined with ἀνήρ, 8.584, Hdt.5.95, Antipho 1.18; later, as a term of address, φίλ' ἑταῖρε Thgn.753, cf. Pl.*Grg.*482a; ὦταῖρε Scol.ap.Ar.*V.*1238, cf. *Ev.Matt.*20.13, al.: c. gen., δαιτὸς ἑταῖρε *partner* of my feast, *h.Merc.*436; νυκτὸς ἑ. ib.290; πόσιος καὶ βρώσιος ἑταῖροι mess*mates*, Thgn.115; ἑ. ἐν πρήγματι Id.116. **2.** metaph., of things, ἐσθλὸς ἑταῖρος, of a fair wind, Od.11.7, 12.149; φθόνος κενεοφρόνων ἑ. Pi.*Fr.*212; γέλως ἑ. ὕβρεων Plu.2.622b: c. dat., βίον..τὸν σοφοῖς ἕταρον *AP*7.470 (Mel.). **3.** *pupil, disciple*, e.g. of Socrates, X.*Mem.*2.8.1, al., cf. Arist.*Pol.*1274$^{a}$28; Λεύκιππος καὶ ὁ ἑ. αὐτοῦ Δημόκριτος Id.*Metaph.*985$^{b}$4: pl., *fellow-pupils*, Poll.4.45. **4.** of political *partisans* (cf. ἑταιρεία I. 2), Lys.12.43, Th.8.48; οἱ περὶ αὐτὸν ἑ. his *club-mates*, D.21.20. **5.** *members of a religious guild*, *OGI*573.1 (Cilicia, Jewish). **6.** rarely of *lovers*, Semon.7.49, Ar.*Ec.*912 (lyr.). **7.** ἑταῖροι, οἱ, the *guards*, i.e. the *cavalry* of the Macedonian kings, Theopomp.Hist.217, Anaximen.Lamps. ap.Harp. s.v. πεζέταιρος, Arr.*An.*3.16.11, etc.; to be distinguished from the king's immediate *retinue* (cf. supr. I), Theopomp. l.c., Arr.*An.*2.12.6, al.; of the *Comites* of the Roman Emperor, Βαρβίλλῳ τῷ ἐμῷ ἑτέρῳ (sic) *PLond.*1912.105 (Epist. Claudii), cf. *SIG*798.6 (Cyzicus, i A.D., pl.). **8.** as Adj., *associate of*, τὸ ἐπιθυμητικὸν ἡδονῶν ἑ. Pl.*R.*439d: Sup., τοῖς σεαυτοῦ ἑταιροτάτοις your *closest companions*, Id.*Grg.*487d, cf. *Phd.*89e, D.Chr.1.44; σαργῶν γένος πέτρῃσιν ἑ. *constant to* the rocks, Opp.*H.*4.267: abs., of animals, *gregarious*, Id.*C.*2.325. **II. ἑταίρα**, Ion. **ἑταίρη**, Ep. **ἑτάρη** [ᾰ], ἡ, *companion*, Ἔρις..Ἄρεος..κασιγνήτη ἑτάρη τε Il.4.441; Λάτω καὶ Νιόβα μάλα μὲν φίλαι ἦσαν ἑ. Sapph.31, cf. 11; φύζα, φόβου κρυόεντος ἑ. Il.9.2; φόρμιγξ..ἣν ἄρα δαιτὶ θεοὶ ποίησαν ἑ. Od.17.271, cf. *h.Merc.*478; Νίκην, ἣ χορικῶν ἐστιν ἑ. Ar.*Eq.*589; μιμητική..τῷ ἐν ἡμῖν ἑ. καὶ φίλη ἐστί Pl.*R.*603b; Ποσειδάωνος ἑ., of a submerged city, Call.*Del.*101. **2.** *courtesan*, Hdt.2.134, Ar.*Pl.*149, Ath.13.567a, 571d, etc.; opp. πόρνη (a common *prostitute*), Anaxil.22.1; opp. γαμετή, Philetaer.5; Ἀφροδίτη ἑ. Apollod.Hist.17. **-οσύνη**, ἡ, = ἑταιρεία, Paul.Al.*D.*3. **-όσυνος**, η, ον, *friendly, a friend*, *AP*12.247 (Strat.). **-ότης**, *contubernium*, *Gloss.* **-οτρόφος**, ον, *keeping mistresses*, Man.4.313, Jul.*Gal.*238e.

**ἔταλον**, τό, (ἔτος) *yearling*, *Schwyzer*644.18 (Aegae, iv/iii B.C.); also **ἔτελον**, ib.252.11 (Cos, iii B.C.).

**ἐτάλασσας**, v. sub *τλάω.

**ἐτανόν**· ἀληθῶς, σφόδρα, Hsch.; cf. ἐτεός. **2.** ἐτανός *yearly*, coined by Tz. ad Hes.*Op.*31.

**ἕταρος, ἑτάρη**, v. ἑταῖρος I and II. **ἔτας**, v. ἔτης.

**ἔτ-ᾰσις**, εως, ἡ, (ἐτάζω) *trial, affliction*, Lxx *Jb.*10.17. ⊛ **-ασμός**, ὁ, = foreg., ib.*Ge.*12.17 (pl.). **-αστής**, οῦ, ὁ, = ἐξεταστής, *CIG* (add.)3641 *b*42 (Lampsacus), Suid. s.v. δοκιμαστῆρες.

**ἐταυτῶς**· ἀληθῶς, Hsch. ⊛ **ἐτέα**, ἡ, prob., = ἰτέα, Theognost.*Can.*7. **ἐτεῇ**, v. ἐτεός.

**ἔτειος**, α, ον (ος, ον E.*Fr.*330 (s.v.l.)), (ἔτος) *yearly, annual*, ἄεθλα Pi.*I.*4(3).67; δασμός E.*Rh.*435; *of the year*, ὧραι Thphr.*Od.*68; μεταλλαγαί E.*Fr.*330 (prob.); ἐτεία, ἡ, *yearly board of officials* or *the term of such a board*, *SIG*559.45 (Magn. Mae., iii B.C., but Arc.): neut. pl. ἔτεια, as Adv., Lyc.721. **2.** *lasting a year*, φρουρά A.*Ag.*2. **II.** *of one year, yearling*, X.*Cyn.*5.14; βρέφος Poll.2.8.

**ἔτελις**, ὁ, a fish, Arist.*HA*567$^{a}$20. **ἔτελον**, v. ἔταλον.

**ἔτεμεν**· ἤμελγεν, Hsch.; cf. τέμνοντα.

**Ἐτεοβουτάδης**, ου, ὁ, *a genuine son of Butes*, one of the family which supplied the hereditary priests of Athena Polias, Alex.201, D.21.182, cf. Harp.

**ἐτεοδμώς**, ῶος, ὁ, *honest slave*: καί κ' ἐτεοδμώων read by Ptol. Ascal. for καί κέ τεο δμώων in Od.16.305.

⊛ **Ἐτεόκρητες**, οἱ, *true Cretans*, Od.19.176, *POxy.*1241 v 27.

**ἐτεόκρῖθος** (sc. κριθή), ἡ, *genuine, good barley*, Thphr.*CP*3.22.2.

⊛ **ἐτεός**, ά, όν (not found in masc.), *true, genuine*, πόλλ' ἐτεά Il.20.255; ἢ ἐτεὸν Κάλχας μαντεύεται 2.300; εἰ ἐτεόν περ whether it be *true* indeed, 14.125; εἰ δὴ ῥ' ἐ. γε καὶ ἀτρεκέως ἀγορεύεις 15.53. II. ἐτεόν, as Adv., *in truth, verily*, εἰπέ μοι εἰ ἐ. γε φίλην ἐς πατρίδ' ἱκάνω Od.13.328, cf. Il.8.423; εἰ ἐ. . . μιμνήσκομαι *rightly*, Theoc.25.173. 2. in Ar. (not in other Com.) interrog., *really, indeed*, οὐκ ἀκούσεσθ' ἐ. . .; *Ach.*322, cf. 609; ἐ. ἡγεῖ γὰρ θεούς; *Eq.*32, cf. 733; in asking for information, τί οὖν τοῦτ' ἐστὶν ἐ.; *Nu.*93, cf. *V.*8; τί δὲ τοῦτ' ἐγέλασας ἐ.; *Nu.*820; cf. ἐτός (B). 3. fem., ἐτεή, ἡ, *reality*, [ἄνθρωπος] ἐτεῆς ἀπήλλακται Democr.6; dat. ἐτεῇ, as Adv., *in reality*, νόμῳ γλυκύ, νόμῳ πικρόν, ἐτεῇ δ' ἄτομα καὶ κενόν Id.125; ἐ. οὐδὲν ἴσμεν Id.7.

**ἑτεράλκ-εια**, ἡ, *varying fortune of battle*, coined by Eust.662.46. **-έομαι**, *to be conquered*, Sch.Il.15.738. **-ής**, ές, *giving strength to the other side*, μάχης ἑτεραλκέα νίκην victory in battle *inclining to the other side*, Il.16.362; σῆμα τιθεὶς Τρώεσσι, μ. ἑ. ν. a sign that victory *was changing sides*, 8.171; ἵνα δὴ Δαναοῖσι μ. ἑ. ν. δῷς *inclining to their side*, 7.26; without μάχης, δίδου ἑτεραλκέα νίκην 17.627, Od.22.236; Ἄρης ἑ. A.*Pers.*952 (lyr.): in late Prose, ἑ. νίκη Ps.-Luc.*Philopatr.*8, Ael.*Fr.*135. 2. Act., ἑ. δῆμος a body of men *which decides the victory*, Il.15.738; λύσις ἑ. κήδευς Nic.*Th.*2; ποδῶν ἑ. ταρσῷ, of a lame man, Nonn.*D.*9.230. II. *inclining first to one side then to the other, doubtful*, μάχη Hdt.9.103; μόθου ἑ. κλωγμῷ Orac.ap.Luc.*JTr.*31. Ion. Adv. -αλκέως, ἀγωνίζεσθαι *with varying fortune*, Hdt.8.11.

**ἑτερ-αριθμὸς** [ἄ], ον, *of different number*: τὸ ἑ. *change of number*, as a figure of speech, Phoeb.*Fig.*1.5. **-αχθέω**, = ἑτεροκλινέω, Phryn.*PS*p.68 B. **-εγκεφᾰλάω** or **-έω**, *to suffer in half the brain, to be half-mad, crazy*, Ar.*Fr.*778. **-ειδής**, ές, = ἑτεροειδής, *illusory*, ἄλην ἑ. λεύσσων Nic.*Al.*84. **-ήμερος**, ον, *on alternate days, day and day about*, ζώουσ' ἑτερήμεροι, of the Dioscuri, Od.11.303, cf. Ph.2.189, Jul.*Or.*4.147a; ἑ. ὁ βίος τῶν ἀσκητῶν Ph.1.643; of an intermittent fever, Orph.*L.*633. **-ήρης**, ες, (*ἄρω) = ἀμφήρης, Max.165.

**ἑτέρηφι**, Ep. dat. fem. of ἕτερος.

**ἑτερο-βάρεια** [βᾰ], ἡ, *weighing down to one side*, Hsch., Suid. s. v. κατὰ πρόσκλισιν. **-βᾰρής**, ές, *weighing down one side*, Eust.1316.26. **-γᾰμία**, ἡ, *second marriage*, Tz. ad Lyc.1317. **-γάστριος**, ον, *by another mother*, opp. ὁμογάστριος, Tz. ad Hes.*Op.*374. **-γενέω**, *differ in kind*, Nicom.*Ar.*1.10. **-γενής**, ές, *of different kinds*, τὰ ἑ. Arist.*Cat.*1ᵇ16; of animals, Id.*HA*601ᵃ25; ἑ. ζῷα Ph.2.370; ᾠά *Gp.*14.7.28; ἐξ ἑτερογενῶν σωμάτων ὑπάρξαι, of Centaurs, D.S.4.8; μόρια, i.e. not paired, Gal.*UP*16.14. 2. *of different kind* or *race*, Demetr.Lac.1012.36 F., D.T.635.7; [ἑτερότης] ἑ. καὶ ἀλλόφυλος πρὸς αὐτήν Dam.*Pr.*308; simply, *different*, πράξεις D.S.1.9. Adv. -νῶς, διαφέρειν ἀλλήλων S.E.*M.*7.361, cf. Nicom.*Ar.*1.10. 3. *of diverse materials*, of a garment, Sm.*De.*22.11: generally, *complex*, opp. ὁμογενής, Demetr.Lac.1429.2 F. II. Gramm., *of different gender*, A.D.*Conj.*243.1 (s. v. l.); -γενές, τό, *change of gender* in a *constructio ad sensum*, Phoeb.*Fig.*1.5. ⊛ **-γλαυκος**, ον, *with one eye grey*, Arist.*GA*779ᵇ4. **-γλωσσος**, Att. **-ττος**, ον, *of other* (i.e. *foreign*) *tongue*, Plb.23.13.2, Str.8.1.2; ἐν ἑτερογλώσσοις λαλεῖν *by men of foreign tongue*, 1*Ep.Cor.*14.21, cf. Onos.26.2, Aq.*Is.*33.19. 2. *of diverse tongues*, ζῷα Ph.1.406. **-γνάθος**, ον, *with one side of the mouth harder than the other*, [ἵπποι] X.*Eq.*1.9, al.; glossed by ἀπειθής, ἡ ἀπλήστος, Phot. **-γνης**, ητος, ὁ, = ἑτερογενής, Hdn.Gr.1.83. **-γνωμοσύνη**, ἡ, *difference of opinion*, J.*AJ*10.11.7, Hsch. s. v. διχόνοια. **-γνώμων**, ον, gen. ονος, = ἀλλογνώμων, τόποι Vett.Val.79.18; τὰ ἐς θεὸν -γνώμονες Agath.4.2, cf. 3.12. **-γονος**, ον, = ἑτερογενής, Hippiatr.11, Hsch. s. v. ἀμφίσγονοι. **-δίδακτος** [ῐ], ον, *taught by another*, opp. αὐτοφυής, Olymp. *in Alc.*p.11 C. **-δῐδασκᾰλέω**, *teach differently, teach false doctrine*, 1*Ep.Ti.*1.3. **-δοξέω**, *hold an erroneous opinion*, Pl.*Tht.*190e; *differ in opinion*, περί τινος Ph.1.508. **-δοξία**, ἡ, *a taking one thing for another, error of opinion*, Pl.*Tht.*193d. 2. *difference of opinion*, Ph.*Fr.*72 H. (pl.). **-δοξος**, ον, *differing in opinion*, Luc.*Eun.*2. 2. *holding opinions other than the right, heterodox*, Ph.1.403, al., Arr.*Epict.*2.9.19, J.*BJ*2.8.5; [ἰατρός] Sor.1.52, cf. Gal.9.670. Adv. -ξως *in heterodox manner*, τῆς μουσικῆς ἀκροᾶσθαι Philostr.*VS*2.1.11. **-δῠνᾰμία**, ἡ, *shifting of strength*, Sch.Il.7.26. **-δύνᾰμος** [ῠ], ον, *of different power* or *faculty*, Porph.*Sent.*33 (prob. l.). **-εθνής**, ές, *of another tribe, foreign*, Str.8.1.2, Ph.2.400. **-είδεια**, ἡ, *numerical diversity*, *Theol.Ar.*8. ⊛ **-ειδής**, ές, *of another kind*, Arist. *HA*508ᵇ11, f.l. in *Placit.*2.30.5; *of diverse kinds*, Ph.*Fr.*29 H. 2. *having the form of diversity*, Dam.*Pr.*303; opp. ταυτοειδής, ib.340. Adv. -δῶς ib.55. **-ζηλος**, ον, *zealous for one side*. Adv. -λως *unfairly*, Hes.*Th.*544. II. *zealous in another pursuit*, *AP*11.216 (Lucill.). 2. *of different tastes*, S.E.*M.*7.56. **-ζῠγέω**, *draw unequally*, Apollon.*Lex.* s. v. ἰσοφόροι: c. dat., ἑ. ἀπίστοις *to be yoked in unequal partnership* with unbelievers, 2*Ep.Cor.*6.14. **-ζῠγία**, ἡ, *inclination to one side*, of the balance, Sch.Luc.*Lex.*3. **-ζῠγος**, ον, *unevenly yoked*, of *animals of diverse kind*, Lxx *Le.*19.19, cf. Ph.2.369; of vases, *not pairs*, *PCair.Zen.*38.12 (iii B.C.). 2. of the balance, *leaning to one side*, Ps.-Phoc.15. II. *yoked with another*, i.e. *double*, Nonn.*D.*10.348. III. Gramm., *differently formed*, A.D.*Adv.*171.17. Adv. -γως *in a different declension*, Hdn.Gr.ap. Eust.113.35; also τὰ ἑ. λεγόμενα (e.g. σπουδαῖος, as Adj. of ἀρετή) Procl. *in Cra.*p.40 P. **-ζυξ**, ῠγος, ὁ, ἡ, *yoked singly, without its yokefellow*, metaph., μήτε τὴν πόλιν ἑτερόζυγα περιιδεῖν γεγενημένην Cimon ap.Plu.*Cim.*16. II. = foreg. II, Nonn.*D.*5.148. **-θᾰλής**, ές, *flourishing on one side*: of children of the same father, but different mothers, *Cat.Cod.Astr.*8(3).110, Eust.1283.2, Tz. ad Hes.*Op.*374. **-θρησκος**, ον, *practising a false religion*, interpol. in Suid. s. v. θρῆσκος. **-θροος**, ον, *speaking different tongues*, Nonn.*D.*36.426, al. 2. *sounding different from before*, ib.9.256, al. 3. *of twofold sounds*, ἠχώ ib.42.255.

**ἑτεροῖ-ος**, α, ον, Ep. **-οῖῖος**, η, ον, D.P.1180:—*of a different kind, diverse*, Hdt.1.99, al.; τὰ ἑ. οὐκ ἀλλοῖα; Pl.*Prm.*161a, al.; τί φαίνεται ἑτεροῖον διανοηθεὶς ὁ ἰητρὸς ἤ . .; Hp.*VM*7; ἑ. τινός ib.9; *unusual, strange*, Id.*Acut.*6; φωναί Phld.*Po.*994 *Fr.*10. Adv. -οίως, διαιτηθῆναι Hp.*Acut.*39, cf. Gal.2.219. II. *diversified, differentiated*, κόσμος, ἀριθμός, Dam.*Pr.*194, 204. III. *different from what should be, untoward*, ἤν τι ἑ. ἀποβαίνῃ Luc.*JTr.*32. **-ότης**, ητος, ἡ, *difference in kind*, Pl.*Prm.*160d, Ph.1.5; ἡ ἑτερότης ἄρα ἑτεροιότης Dam.*Pr.*440. **-όω**, *make of different kind, alter*, Hp.*Acut.*37, Plu.2.559c; ἐς τοιήνδε ἕξιν τὸν ἄνθρωπον Aret.*SD*2.1:—Pass., Hdt.2.142, 7.225, Hp.*VM*14, *Fract.*15, Ph.2.93; τὸ -ούμενον τῆς πτώσεως A.D.*Synt.*96.4. II. Pass., *to be differentiated*, Dam.*Pr.*220. **-ωσις**, εως, ἡ, *alteration*, Diog.Apoll.5 (pl.); opp. φορά, Arist.*Ph.*217ᵇ26, cf. *Mu.*400ᵃ24 (pl.); ἀέρος Epicur.*Ep.*2 p.43 U. (pl.); (sc. ψυχῆς) of sensation, Chrysipp.*Stoic.*2.23; τῆς οὐσίας, τοῦ τέλους, τοῦ περιέχοντος, Plu.2.430c, A.D.*Pron.*18.15, M.Ant.4.39: Ἑτεροιούμενα, τά, *mythological transformations*, title of work by Nicander, Ant.Lib.1, etc. **-ωτικός**, ή, όν, *alterative*, ἡ τερατολογουμένη -ωτική, of Chrysippus' theory of sensation (cf. ἑτεροίωσις), *Stoic.*1.108.

**ἑτερό-καρπος**, ον, *bearing different fruit*, of grafts, Hp.*Nat.Puer.*26. **-κῑνησία**, ἡ, *motion externally caused*, Procl. *in Alc.*p.225 C. **-κίνητος** [ῐ], ον, *moved by external force, incapable of self-motion*, opp. αὐτοκίνητος, Id.*Inst.*14, Simp. *in Epict.*p.10 D., Dam. *Pr.*18, al., Syrian. *in Metaph.*23.21. Adv. -τως Simp. *in Epict.*p.4 D. **-κλῐνέω**, *lean on one side*, Anon.*Intr.Arat.*p.98 M., Sm.*Ps.*16(17).11, Phryn.*PS*p.68 B.; cf. -κλονέω. **-κλῐνής**, ές, *leaning to one side, uneven*, Hp.*Art.*24; of a building, D.C.57.21; τὰ ἑ. τῶν χωρίων *sloping* ground, X.*Cyn.*2.7. Adv. -νῶς *one-sidedly*, Sor.2.62; ἑ. ἔχειν πρὸς ἡδονήν to have *a propensity* to it, Arr.*Epict.*3.12.7. **-κλῐτος**, ον, (κλίνω) *irregularly inflected*, of nouns, as γυνή, γυναικός, A.D.*Synt.*102.12, etc.; of Verbs, as ἔσθω, ἔφαγον, Id.*Pron.*13.2. Adv. -τως Eust.113.41. **-κλονέω**, *shake to one side*, Opp.*C.*4.204 (v. l. -κλινέω). **-κοπία**, ἡ, *exercise in which two parties are engaged*, Cael.Aur.*TP*5.11.133 (*hatero-* codd.). **-κρᾱνία**, ἡ, *pain on one side of the head* (cf. ἡμικρανία), Archig.ap.Gal.8.94, Aret.*CD*1.2, etc. (also **-κράνιον**, τό, Gal.14.400). Adj.⊛ **-κρᾱνικός**, ή, όν, *liable to such pain*, Antyll.ap.Orib.10.19.1. **-κτῠπος**, ον, *repeating sound*, Ἠχώ Nonn.*D.*39.347. **-κωφέω**, *to be deaf of one ear*, Lxx *Si.*19.27 (nisi leg. ἐθελο-). **-κωφος**, ον, *deaf on one side*, Cyrill.ap.Valck.*Anim-adv. ad Ammon.*p.65. **-λογία**, ἡ, *different*, i.e. *false, speech*, Sm.*Ps.*138(139).4. **-μαλλος**, ον, *woolly, shaggy on one side*, Str.5.1.12: also **-μαλλής**, ές, Hsch. s. v. καυνάκαι. **-μάσχᾰλος** χιτών, ὁ, a frock *with* only *one hole for the arm*, i.e. *only coming over one shoulder*, worn by slaves, opp. ἀμφιμάσχαλος, Poll.7.47, Sch.Ar.*Eq.*878. **-μεγεθέω**, *increase on one side*, Artem.1.31. **-μέρεια**, ἡ, *inclination to one side*, Suid., Phot. s. v. κατὰ πρόσκλισιν. **-μερής**, ές, *leaning to one side, one-sided*, βίος Crito ap.Stob.3.3.64. Adv. -ρῶς *one-sidedly* (i.e. not in equal proportions), Speus.ap.*Theol.Ar.*61 (nisi leg. -ρεῖς). 2. τὸ ἑ. *separation*, Porph.ap.Stob.1.49.25ᵃ. **-μετρία**, ἡ, *difference of metre*: **-μετρος**, ον, *of different metre*, both in Heph.*Poëm.*p.74 C. ⊛ **-μήκης**, ες, *with sides of uneven length*, i.e. *oblong*, X.*Eq.*7.14; ἑτερόμηκες, τό, *oblong rectangle*, Arist.*Cat.*11ᵃ10, *de An.*413ᵃ17, Euc.1 *Def.*22. 2. of numbers, *not square*, i.e. produced by the multiplication of two *unequal* factors, as 6 = 3 × 2, Pl.*Tht.*148a, Plu.2.367f; opp. ἰσόπλευρος (both of line and number), Arist.*APo.*73ᵇ1. **-μηκικὸς** λόγος the ratio *of the sides of a rectangle*, Iamb. *in Nic.* pp.72, 94 P. **-μήτριος**, ον, *born of another mother*, Sch.Lyc.19 (ed. Bachm.). **-μήτωρ**, ορος, ὁ, ἡ, = foreg., Sch.A.R.4.223.

**ἑτερομοιότης**, ητος, ἡ, *identity in diversity*, Procl.*Theol.Plat.*1.21.

**ἑτερο-μόλιος** δίκη, (μολεῖν) a trial *in which only one of the two parties appears*, Zen.3.88, Eust.999.63, Hsch. (-μυνος cod.). (Perh. rather to be connected with *μωλέω, as in Cret. ἀμφιμωλέω etc.) **-μορφος**, ον, *of different* or *diverse form*, Ael.*NA*12.16, Ph.1.655; opp. ἀνθρωποειδής, Ptol.*Tetr.*145; so of monstrosities, Alex.Aphr.*Pr.*2.47: hence **-μορφία**, ἡ, *monstrosity*, of the Minotaur, Isid.*Etym.*11.3.9. **-ούσιος**, ον, *differing in substance*, Porph.*Sent.*35. Adv. -ίως ib.37:—also in form **ἑτερούσιος**, ψυχὴν ἐν ἀλλοτρίῳ πράγματι καὶ ἑτερουσίῳ συνδεδεμένην ib.32, cf. Iamb.*Myst.*1.19. **-πάθεια** [πᾰ], ἡ, (παθεῖν) *counter-irritation*, Dsc.2.154. **-πᾰχής**, ές, *of unequal thickness*, ξύλα Apollod.*Poliorc.*164.8. **-πλᾰνής**, ές, *wandering hither and thither*, ὄθμα Nic.*Al.*243. ⊛ **-πλᾰτής**, ές, *with unequal sides*, of beams, Apollod. *Poliorc.*161.12: **-πλᾰτέω**, *vary in breadth*, Hero *Mens.*59. **-πλευρος**, ον, *with two visible faces*, λίθοι *SIG*247 ii 70 (Delph., iv B.C.); cf. ἀτερόπλευρος. II. *with unequal sides*, Scymn.267. **-πλοκος**, ον, *irregularly combined*, Diom.p.481 K. **-πλοος**, ον, contr. **-πλους**, ουν, *lent on bottomry with the risk of the outward*, but not of the homeward, *voyage*, ἀργύριον D.34.30; δανείσαντες ἑ. τἀργύριον εἰς Ἀθήνας Id.56.29; τὰ ἑ. (sc. ἀργύρια) Id.34.8. **-πνοοι** αὐλοί, οἱ, *uneven, double* flutes, *Anacreont.*2 B.4 (dub. l.). **-ποδέω**, (ἑτερόπους) *go lame of one foot*, *Hippiatr.*109. **-ποιός**, όν, *making different*, Iamb.*Myst.*1.18; *creating difference*, Dam.*Pr.*192, al.; δύνα-

μις, opp. ταυτοποιός, Procl. *in Cra.* p.20P.; ἡ κίνησις ἐκστατικὴ ἐστι καὶ ἑ. Simp. *in Epict.* p.99D. **-πορπος**, ον, (πόρπη) *clasped on one side*, of a woman's dress, Call.*Fr.*225. **-πους**, ὁ, ἡ, gen. ποδος, *with uneven feet, halting*, Alciphr.3.27, Philostr.*VS*1.21.1, *Hippiatr.*13. **-πρόσωπος**, ον, *of another person*: σχῆμα ἑ. when a statement is made *in the words of another*, Phoeb.*Fig.*1.5, cf. Choerob.Rh. p.256S. Adv. -πως, ἀνατίθησι *Proll.Hermog.* in Rh.7.7W. **-πτολις**, ὁ, ἡ, *of another city*, Erinn.5; *of various cities*, λαός Nonn.*D.*26.41. **-πτωτος**, ον, *having cases formed from different stems*, e.g. μέγας, μεγάλου, A.D.*Pron.*11.4. II. **-πτωτον**, τό, *change of case*, as a figure of speech, Phoeb.*Fig.*1.5. **-ρρέπεια**, ἡ, *leaning to one side*, Poll.8.14. **-ρρεπέω**, *lean on one side*, Plu.2.1026e. **-ρρεπής**, ές, Act., *making now one side and now another preponderate*, Ζεύς A.*Supp.*403 (lyr.). II. *inclining to one side or the other*, of patients in the crisis of a disease, Hp.*Acut.*(*Sp.*)21. 2. *one-sided*, ἑ. ζήτημα where the *weight* of evidence *preponderates*, Hermog.*Stat.*1. III. Adv. -πῶς v.l. in Poll.8.13. **-ροπία**, ἡ, = ἑτερορρέπεια, Id.4.172. **-ροπος**, ον, *inclined to one side*, ἡ κλῖμαξ ἑ. ἐπὶ γῆν ἀφίξεται will come down *on one corner, unevenly*, Hp.*Art.*43; ἑ. ἐπάρματα swellings *on one side*, Id.*Epid.*1.1; φλεγμοναί ibid.; τὰ ἑ., of crippled limbs, Id.*Off.*23. 2. *inclining to one side or the other*, θεῶν ἑ. δῶρα gifts *that may prove either good or evil*, Rhian.1.2. II. Adv. -πως Poll.4.172, Gal.8.430, Aspasia ap.Aët.16.72. **-ρρυθμος** (Ion. **-ρρυσμος** Hsch.), ον, *of different rhythm*: hence, of the pulse, *having a false rhythm*, i.e. unsuitable to the patient's age, Gal.8.516, al.

⊛**ἕτερος**, α, ον, only Att.-Ion. with ἑ-, Dor. **ἅτερος** [ᾰ] *IG*4.914.9 (Epid.), etc. (and Att. in crasis, v. infr.), Aeol. **ἄτερος** Alc.41.5, etc.:—but **ἅτερος** [ᾱ], Att. crasis for ὁ ἕτερος, *Com.Adesp.*14.23D., al., Ion. **οὕτερος** (fr. ὁ ἕτ-) Hdt.1.34, etc., Dor. **ὥτερος** Theoc.7.36; neut. θάτερον A.*Ag.*344, And.2.7, etc., Ion. τοὔτερον Hdt.1.32: pl. ἅτεροι, for οἱ ἅτεροι, Arist.*Pol.*1255$^a$20; θἄτερα S.*El.*345, Th.1.87, etc.; gen. θατέρου S.*Ph.*597, etc., Ion. τοὐτέρου Semon.7.113, Dor. θατέρω Ti.Locr.94a, θωτέρω Epich.71 (dub. l.); dat. θατέρῳ A.*Pr.*778; fem. nom. ἡτέρα *IG*2$^2$.1498.76, 1615.14,87 (iv B.C.), S.*OC*497, Ar.*Lys.*85, 90 codd., Paus.Gr.*Fr.*82; dat. θητέρᾳ S.*OT*782, *Tr.*272, E.*Hipp.*894, Ar.*Av.*1365, etc., cf. Paus.Gr. l.c. (in Mss. sts. θατέρᾳ), Ion. τἠτέρῃ Phoen.5.2.—Later masc. and fem. θάτερος, θατέρα, even with the Art., Men.846, Chrysipp.ap.Paus.Gr.*Fr.*82, Lyc.590, Polem.*Cyn.*4, Luc.*DMort.*26.1 (condemned in *Pseudol.*29), *Gp.*14.20.2, etc.; τῶν θατέρων Iamb. *in Nic.* p.83P.; θάτερον acc. sg. masc., E.*Ion*[849]. I. *one* or *the other of two*, usu. c. Art. exc. in Poets; freq. of natural pairs, σκαιῇ (sc. χειρὶ) ἔγχος ἔχων, ἑτέρηφι δὲ λάζετο πέτρον Il.16.734; τῇ ἑτέρῃ μὲν..τῇ δ' ἑτέρῃ.. 14.272, cf. X.*Cyn.*10.11; χειρὶ ἑτέρῃ with *one* hand, Il.12.452, Od.10.171 (but χεὶρ ἑτέρη commonly of the *left* hand, v. infr. IV.1); ἑτέρῳ διὰ κροτάφοιο Il.4.502; χωλὸς δ' ἕτερον πόδα 2.217, cf. Ar.*Ec.*162, Din.1.82; ἀμφότεραι αἱ γνάθοι, ἢ ἡ ἑτέρα X.*Eq.*1.9; ἐκκοπεὶς τὸν ἕ. τῶν ὀφθαλμῶν D.H.5.23; εἰς γόνυ θάτερον Philostr.*Im.*2.20; of pairs in general, Il.5.258, etc.; τὴν ἑ. πύλην *one of the* two gates, Hdt.3.156; ὁ ἕ. τῶν στρατηγῶν Th.4.43; τὸ ἕ. τοῖν δυοῖν τειχοῖν Id.7.24: freq. of alternatives presented, τῶνδε τὰ ἕ. ποιέειν Hdt.4.126; ἑλοῦ γε θάτερ', ἢ..ἢ.. S.*El.*345; τοῖνδ' ἑλοῦ δυοῖν πότμοιν τὸν ἕ. E.*Ph.*952; δυοῖν ἀγαθοῖν τοῦ ἑτέρου τεύξεσθαι Th.4.28; δυοῖν θάτερα, ἢ..ἢ.. Pl.*Tht.*187c; ὅταν δυοῖν καλοῖν θάτερον κάλλιον ᾖ, ἢ τῷ ἑτέρῳ τούτοιν ἢ ἀμφοτέροις ὑπερβάλλον κάλλιόν ἐστιν Id.*Grg.*475a: in pl., *one of two parties* or *sets*, Od.11.258; τῶν ἕτεροί γε παῖδα κλαύσονται *one set* of parents, either mine or thine, Il.20.210; δώῃ δ' ἑτέροισί γε νίκην 7.292; ἑτέροισι δὲ κῦδος ἔδωκαν 13.303: freq. with neg., οὐδ' ἕτεροι 11.71. 2. in double clauses ἕτερος (in Prose always ὁ ἕτερος) is generally repeated; ἑ. μὲν δουρὶ.., τῷ δ' ἑ. 21.164; τὸν ἕ., ἕ. δὲ.. Od.5.266; ἕ. λευκόν, ἑτέρην δὲ μέλαιναν Il.3.103, etc.: but sts. omitted in one clause, [ἕτερος μὲν] κακῶν, ἕ. δὲ ἑάων 24.528, cf. 7.420, *IG*2$^2$.1388.46 (prob.), etc.; ἡ μὲν.., ἡ δ' ἑτέρη Il.22.149, *IG*1$^2$.76.50; ἕ..., ὁ δὲ.. Od.8.374; answered by ἄλλος, ἕτερον μὲν κεύθῃ ἐνὶ φρεσίν, ἄλλο δὲ εἴπῃ Il.9.313, cf. Od.7.123; reversely ἄλλῳ ὀρχηστύν, ἑτέρῳ κίθαριν [ἔδωκε] Il.13.731, cf. Pl.*R.*439b, *Tht.*186e; τότε μὲν ἕτερα.., τότε δὲ ἄλλα.. Pl.*Alc.*1.116e; ὁ ἕτερος.., ὁ λοιπός.. X.*An.*4.1.23; ἕτερα.., τὰ δὲ.. S.*OC*1454 (lyr.); later μίαν μὲν..ἑτέραν δέ A.D.*Synt.*172.5; τὴν μίαν..τὴν δ' ἑτέρην *AP*9.680. 3. repeated in the same clause, ἐξ ἑτέρων ἕτερ' ἐστίν *one* building follows on *another*, Od.17.266; (ἀ) δ' ἀτέρα τὰν ἀτέραν κύλιξ ὠθήτω let *one* cup push on *the other*, Alc.41.5; ἢ θάτερον δεῖ δυστυχεῖν ἢ θάτερον *one party* or *the other*, E.*Ion*[849]; ἕτεροι ἑτέρων ἠξίωσαν ἄρχειν Th.2.64; ἕτερος ἀφ' ἑτέρου θεραπείας ἀναπιμπλάμενοι ἔθνῃσκον ib.51; εἴ τίς τι ἕτερος ἑτέρου προφέρει Id.7.64; ξυμμειγνυμένων ἑτέρων ἑτέροις Ar.*Av.*701; συμφορὰ ἑτέρα ἑτέρους πιέζει *one* calamity oppresses *one, another others*, E.*Alc.*893 (lyr.); ἑτέρᾳ δ' ἕτερος ἕτερον ὄλβῳ καὶ δυνάμει παρῆλθεν Id.*Ba.*905, cf. S.*OC*231 (anap.); ἄλλη δ' εἰς ἑτέρην ὀλοφύρετο A.R.1.250. 4. = δεύτερος, *second*, ἡ μὲν.., ἡ δ' ἑτέρη.., ἡ δὲ τρίτη.. Od.10.352sq., cf. Il.16.179, al., X.*Cyr.*2.3.22; ἡ ἑ. πρότασις the *minor* premiss, Arist.*EN*1143$^b$3: without Art., ἕ. τέρας Hdt.7.57; προσαγορεύεις αὐτὰ ἑτέρῳ ὀνόματι you call them further by a *new* name, Pl.*Phlb.*13a; cf. IV.1b. b. with Pronouns of quantity, ordinals, etc., τόσσοι δ' αὖθ' ἕτεροι ποταμοί as many *more*, Hes.*Th.*367; ἕτερον τοσοῦτον as much *again*, Hdt.2.149; ἑτέρου τοσούτου χρόνου for as long *again*, Isoc.4.153; ἕ. τοιαῦτα *other things* of like kind, Hdt.1.120,191; ἑτέρῳ τοιῶνδε (sc. ἀνθρώπων) ἄρχεις ib.207; τῷ αὐτῷ τρόπῳ..τῷ ἑτέρῳ in the same way *over again*, Id.2.127; ἄλλα τε τοιαῦθ' ἕτερα μυρία Ar.*Fr.*333.4; χιλίας ἑτέρας [δραχμάς] D.58.6; δεύτερον, τρίτον ἕ. δικαστήριον, Id.23.71,74; ἕ. ἐγώ, of a friend, Pythag.ap.Iamb. *in Nic.* p.35P.; ἕτεροι αὐτοί *second* selves, Arist.*EN*1161$^b$28; εὕρηκε τὸν ἕ., τὸν σέ Men.474. II. without Art., *another*, of many, with a sense of *difference*, Il.4.306, Od.7.123, Ar.*Ach.*422, *Lys.*66, etc.; ἕ. αὖ τις Id.*Eq.*949; ἕ. αὖ Id.*Pax*295, etc.; ἕτερα ἄττα Pl.*Tht.*188b; repeated ἑτέραν χἀτέραν τρικυμίαν Men.536.8: with neg., οἷα οὐχ ἕτερα [ἐγένετο] such as none *like them* had happened, Th.1.23; ναυμαχία.. οἵα οὐχ ἑτέρα τῶν προτέρων Id.7.70; οὐδεμιᾶς ἧσσων μᾶλλον ἑτέρας ib.29 (s.v.l.); οὐχ ἕτερον ἀλλά.. *none other than*, Plu.2.671b, cf. *UPZ* 71.9 (ii B.C.). b. οἱ ἕ. *the rest*, Hdt.4.169. c. ὁ ἕ. '*one's neighbour*', ἀγαπᾶν τὸν ἕ. *Ep.Rom.*13.6, cf. *Ep.Gal.*6.4. III. *of another kind, different*, ἕ. δέ με θυμὸς ἔρυκεν Od.9.302; τὸ μὲν ἕ., τὸ δὲ ἕ., i.e. they are *different*, Pl.*Men.*97d, cf. *R.*346a; ἕ. τε καὶ ἀνόμοιον Id.*Smp.*186b; τὸ δὲ ταὐτὸν ἕ. ἀποφαίνειν καὶ τὸ θάτερον ταὐτόν Id.*Sph.*259d; ἕ. ἤδη ἦν καὶ οὐχ ὁ αὐτός D.34.12; ἑτέραν ἔδωκεν παντὶ τῷ κόσμῳ ὄψιν *OGI*458.7 (i B.C.); ἕ. εὐαγγέλιον *Ep.Gal.*1.6: coupled with ἄλλος, χἀτέρους ἄλλους πόνους and other *different* toils, E.*Supp.*573 (s.v.l.), cf. *Or.*345 (dub.l.); Ῥόδον καὶ ἄλλας ἑτέρας πόλεις D.15.27; ἕτερον τό τ' ἀλγεῖν καὶ θεωρεῖν ἔστ' ἴσως Philem.75.7; ἕτερα φρονῶν καὶ δημηγορῶν Din.1.17: c. gen., *other than, different from*, φίλους.. ἑτέρους τῶν νῦν ὄντων Th.1.28, cf. Pl.*Prt.*333a, D.10.44, etc.; ἕτερον, ἕτερα ἤ.., E.*Or.*345, X.*Cyr.*1.6.2; παρὰ ταῦτα πάντα ἑτερόν τι Pl.*Phd.*74a; ἕτερα πολιτείας εἴδη παρὰ μοναρχίαν Arist.*Pol.*1294$^a$25, cf. 1286$^b$21. 2. *other than should be*, euphem. for κακός, παθεῖν μὲν εὖ, παθεῖν δὲ θάτερα S.*Ph.*503; ἀγάθ' ἢ θάτερα, ἵνα μηδὲν εἴπω φλαῦρον D.22.12: abs., δαίμων ἕ. Pi.*P.*3.34; λέκτρα, συμφοραί, E.*Med.*639 (lyr.), *HF*1238; ἐὰν τὰ ἕ. ψηφίσωνται οἱ δικασταί D.48.30; πλέον θάτερον ἐποίησαν did more *harm* (than good), Isoc.19.25, cf. Pl.*Phd.*114e, *Euthd.*280e, Aristid.2.117J. IV. Special Phrases: 1. elliptical, mostly in dat. fem., a. τῇ ἑτέρᾳ (sc. χειρί), Ep. ἑτέρῃ or ἑτέρηφι, *with one hand* (v. sub init.); *with the left hand*, Od.3.441, Il.22.80, Theoc.24.45: hence prov., οὐ τῇ ἑτέρᾳ ληπτός not to be caught with *one* hand, Pl.*Sph.*226a; ἐκ δ' ἑτέρης A.R.1.1115, *AP*9.650 (Leont.). b. θατέρᾳ (sc. ἡμέρᾳ) *on the morrow*, S.*OT*782, E.*Rh.*449; τῆς ἑτέρας Pl.*Cri.*44a; but τῇ ἑτέρᾳ *on the following* (i.e. *the third*) day, X.*Cyr.*4.6.10. c. (sc. ὁδῷ) *in another* or *a different way*, καὶ τῇδε φῦναι χἀτέρᾳ S.*OC*1444; *another way*, τρέπεσθαι Ar.*Nu.*812; ἑτέρᾳ πῃ Id.*Eq.*35; τότ' ἄλλοσ'.., θατέρᾳ δὲ.. S.*Tr.*272; θατέρᾳ.., θατέρᾳ.. *in one way.., in the other..*, Henioch.5.16; ἑτέρηφι Hes.*Op.*216: acc. ἑτέραν ἐκτρέπεσθαι Luc.*Tim.*5. 2. adverb. with Preps.: a. ἐπὶ θάτερα *to the one* or *the other side, one* or *the other way*, ἐπὶ μὲν θάτερα.., ἐπὶ θ. δὲ.. Hp.*Art.*7; τότε μὲν ἐπὶ θάτερα, τότε δ' ἐπὶ θ. Pl.*Sph.*259c: also with another Prep., ἐς τὰ ἐπὶ θάτερα *to* or *on the other side*, Th.1.87; ἐκ τοῦ ἐπὶ θάτερα *from the other side*, Id.7.37; ἐκ μὲν τοῦ ἐπὶ θ., ἐκ δὲ τοῦ ἐπὶ θ. Pl.*Prt.*314e: c. gen., ἐς τὰ ἐπὶ θ. τοῦ ποταμοῦ Th.7.84; εἰς τἀπὶ θ. τῆς πόλεως X.*HG*6.2.7; τὸ ἐπὶ θάτερον τῆς ῥινός Hp.*Art.*35. b. κατὰ θάτερα *on the one* or *other side*, κατὰ θ. ἀστός D.57.30; ψόφου κατὰ θ. προσπεσόντος Plu.*Brut.*51, etc.; but καθ' ἕτερα *at other points*, Th.7.42. V. Adv. **ἑτέρως** *in one* or *the other way*, opp. ἀμφοτέρως, Pl.*Tht.*181e; ἑ. τε καὶ ἑ., = ἀμφοτέρως, Id.*Phdr.*235a; τοῦ σκέλους ἑ. ἔχειν, = ἑτεροσκελὴς εἶναι, Philostr.*VA*3.39. 2. *differently*, rarely in Poetry, οὐχ ἑ. τις ἐρεῖ Theoc.*Ep.*10.3; ἑ. ἔχειν to be *different*, Ar.*Pl.*371: freq. in Prose, ὡς ἑ. *in the other way* (cf. ὡς), ἣν ἡ ἑτέρη γνάθος ἐκστῇ ὡς ἑ. χρὴ τὴν ἐπίδεσιν ἄγειν Hp.*Art.*34, cf. Pl.*Sph.*266a, etc.; ἐάν τε καλῶς, ἐάν θ' ὡς ἑ. D.18.85, cf. 212: c. gen., *differently from*, ἑ. πως τῶν εἰωθότων Pl.*Plt.*295d; ἑ. ἤπερ.. Ael.*NA*12.28. 3. *otherwise than should be, badly, wrongly*, once in Hom., ἑ. ἐβόλοντο Od.1.234; εἰ καὶ ἑ. τοῦτο ἀπέβη *SIG*851.10 (Marc. Aur.); εἴ τι ἑ. φρονεῖτε *Ep.Phil.*3.15.

**ἑτερο-σήμαντος**, ον, *of different signification*, Eust.1411.43. Adv. -τως Sch.Hes.*Sc.*354. **-σκελής**, ές, *with uneven legs*, Hippiatr.13; of a triangle, *scalene*, Poll.4.161. ⊛**-σκιος**, ον, (σκιά) *throwing a shadow only one way* (at noon), of those who live north and south of the tropics, Posidon.ap.Str.2.5.43, Cleom.1.7. **-σσυτος**, ον, *darting from the other side*, Nonn.*D.*38.244. **-στοιχος**, ον, *belonging to the other series*, Hsch., Phot. **-στομος**, ον, *one-edged*, πέλεκυς Poll.1.137. II. ἑ. φάλαγξ a marching formation in which the λοχαγοί of the leading κέρας are on the r., those of the rear κέρας on the l., or vice versa, Ascl.*Tact.*10.22, etc. Adv. -μως ib.11.4. **-στροφος**, ον, *consisting of two different strophes*, Heph.*Poëm.*5.3, Sch.Ar.*Nu.*263. **-σφυκτος**, ον, *having one wrist-pulse different from the other*, Marcellin.*Puls.*147:—hence **-σφυξία**, ἡ, Gal.18(2).301. **-σχημάτιστος**, ον, *differently formed*: τὸ ἑ. *change of grammatical form*, as a figure of speech, Phoeb.*Fig.*1.5. **-σχήμων**, ον, *of varying shape*, φύλλα Thphr.*HP*1.10.1; *altered in shape, distorted*, Luc.*Hist.Conscr.*51. Adv. -μόνως Vett.Val.333.20:—later **-σχημος**, ον, *irregular*, διαλείμματα Heliod.ap.Orib.48.20.15. **-ταγής**, ές, *belonging to a different series* or *order*, opp. ὁμοταγής, Procl.*Inst.*21, Dam.*Pr.*38.

⊛**ἑτερότης**, ητος, ἡ, *otherness, difference*, λέγω γένους διαφορὰν -τητα Arist.*Metaph.*1058$^a$8, cf. *Ph.*201$^b$20, Epicur.*Nat.*49G., etc.; opp. ταυτότης, Plu.2.1013a, etc.: pl., Phld.*Rh.*1.8S. 2. *civil discord*, ἑ. καὶ διαφορά Plu.*Num.*17.

**ἑτερο-τράχηλος** [ᾰ], ον, *with neck turned to one side*, of Alexander, Tz.*H.*11 No.368 tit. **-τροπος**, ον, *of different sort* or *fashion*, κακόν Ar.*Th.*724; γαλεῶν ἑ. φῦλα Opp.*H.*1.379; *various*, τύχης ἑ. ὁρμή *AP*9.768 (Agath.), cf. Nonn.*D.*2.669, 7.7.

**ἑτερ-ούας**, ὁ, ἡ, τό, *one-eared, one-handled*, An.Ox.2.7, Eust. 870.2. **-ουΐς**, ΐδος, ἡ, *vessel with one handle*, Hsch.

**ἑτερούσιος**, v. ἑτεροούσιος.

**ἑτεροφᾰνής**, ές, *diverse in appearance*, Gal.18(1).777.

**ἑτεροφθαλμ-ία**, ἡ, *difference of the two eyes*, *Hippiatr*.13, Dem. Ophth.ap.Simon.Jan. s.v. ethereoftalmia. ❀ **-ος**, ον, *one-eyed*, D. 24.141, Arist.*Metaph*.1023ᵃ5; ἑ. γενομένη ἡ Ἑλλάς, metaph., of the proposed destruction of Athens, Leptinesap.Arist.*Rh*.1411ᵃ5, cf. Demad.65 B., Plu.2.803a. II. *with different-coloured eyes*, *Gp*. 16.2.1.

**ἑτερο-φορέομαι**, Pass., = ἑτερορρεπέω, Tim.*Lex*. s.v. ταλαντοῦσθαι. **-φρονέω**, *to be distraught*, Epicur.*Sent.Vat*.17. **-φροσύνη**, ἡ, *difference of opinion, discord*, Iamb.*VP*7.34. **-φρων**, ον, gen. ονος, *thinking strangely, raving*, Tryph.439; λύσσα *AP*1.19 (Claudian.), cf. Nonn.*D*.9.49. **-φυής**, ές, *of different nature*, Anon.*in Cat*. 61.8. **-φῦλος**, ον, *of another race* or *breed*, Ael.*NA*16.27, Scymn. 101; opp. πολίτης, Iamb.*VP*16.69: generally, *differing in kind*, πρός τι Dam.*Pr*.74; *of different kinds*, Simp.*in Ph*.890.16. **-φυτον** δένδρον, τό, a *grafted* tree, Jul.*Ep*.180. **-φωνέομαι**, *to be different in sound*, Eust.1626.3. **-φωνία**, ἡ, *diversity of note*, ἑ. καὶ ποικιλία τῆς λύρας Pl.*Lg*.812d; περὶ ἑτεροφωνίας τῶν ὁμογενῶν, title of work, Thphr.*Fr*.181. **-φωνος**, ον, *of different voice*: hence, *foreign*, A.*Th*. 170(lyr.). II. *discrepant*, opp. σύμφωνος, Porph.*Chr*.15. **-χηλος**, ον, *with unequal hoofs*, *Hippiatr*.109. **-χροέω**, *to be of different colour*, *AB*386; *to be discoloured*, of bones, Orib.46.11.7. **-χροια**, ἡ, *difference of colour*, Hierocl.p.21 A., Xenocr.28, Gal.14. 325. **-χροιος**, ον, = ἑτερόχρους, Polem.*Phgn*.9. **-χροιότης**, ητος, ἡ, *difference of colour*, Pyrrhoap.D.L.9.86. **-χρονος**, ον, *of different times*: τὸ ἑ. *a change of tense*, as a figure of speech, Phoeb.*Fig*. 1.5. **-χροος**, ον, contr. **-χρους**, ουν, *of different colour*, Thphr.*CP* 5.3.2; *of varied colours*, χορὸς ὀρνίθων Nonn.*D*.5.186: heterocl. dat. and acc. ἑτερόχροϊ, -χροα, ib.12.305, 5.58. II. *piebald*, βοῦς Porph. *Abst*.4.7. **-χρωμᾰτέω**, = ἑτεροχροέω, *Gp*.2.6.37. **-χρωμος**, ον, = ἑτερόχροος, *Hippiatr*.14. **-χρως**, ωτος, ὁ, ἡ, = ἑτερόχροος, Poll.9.98. II. ἑτερόχρωτες ὕπνοι sleep *with one of different sex*, Luc.*Am*.42.

❀ **ἑτέρσετο**, v. τερσαίνω.

**ἑτέρ-ωθεν** (or **-θε** Hes.*Sc*.281, cf. A.D.*Adv*.194.4), Adv. *from the other side*, Il.1.247,al.; ἐκ δ' ἑτέρωθεν v.l. in Theoc.22.91. 2. in pregnant sense with Verbs of rest, *on the other side, opposite*, ἕστηκ' Il.3.230, cf. 6.247. II. *from another quarter, from outside*, Lys. 17.4, Pl.*Lg*.702c, Arist.*EN*1121ᵃ34, Bato 5.9. ❀ **-ωθι**, Adv. *on the other side*, ἔνθεν.., ἑ. δὲ.. Od.12.235: in later Prose, Ph.1.301, Jul.*Or*.2.69a. II. = ἄλλοθι, *elsewhere*, Il.5.351, 15.348, Od.4.531, Pl.*Prm*.146c, etc.; οὐδαμόθι ἑ. nowhere *else*, Hdt.3.113; ἑ. πανταχοῦ anywhere *else*, Antipho 6.39; λέγει ἑ. ὅτι *in another passage*, Ph.1.372, cf. Hdt.9.58: c. gen., ἑ. τοῦ λόγου *in another part* of my story, Id.6.19; ἑ. που τοῦ σώματος Arist.*PA*663ᵇ3. III. *at another time*, τότε μὲν.., ἑ. δὲ.. Hdt.3.35. ❀ **-ώνιος**, ον, *another's property*, Eust.1214.27, cf. Hsch. **-ωνῠμέω**, Math., *to have a different denominator*, Nicom.*Ar*.1.17. **-ώνῠμος**, ον, *with different designation*, Simp.*in Cat*.38, Procl.*in Prm*.p.955 S. II. *with different denominator*, Nicom.*Ar*.1.13,al. **-ωνῠμία**, ἡ, *difference of name*, Eust.304.24. **-ωσε**, Adv. *to the other side*, Il.4.492, Od.16. 179; ἔνθεν μὲν.., ἑ. δὲ.. Pl.*Sph*.224a; *on one side*, ἑ. κάρη βάλεν Il. 8.306, cf. Od.22.17. 2. in pregnant sense with certain Verbs, *on the other side*, οἱ δ' ἑ. καθῖζον Il.20.151; κἂν ἑ. πατάξῃ τις D.4.40. II. = ἄλλοσε, *elsewhither, aside*, ἑ. λιασθεὶς Il.23.231; κύνες ἑ. φόβηθεν Od.16.163, etc.; ἑ. τρέχων Ar.*Ach*.828; also εἰς ἑ. A.R.4.1315. 2. *elsewhere*, Luc.*Charid*.22.

**ἑτέρωτα**, Aeol. for ἑτέρωθι, Sapph.1.5, cf. A.D.*Adv*.194.5.

**ἔτετμε**, v. τέτμον.

**ἐτέτυμον**· ἀληθές, ἢ ἀληθῶς, Hsch. **ἐτεωνέω**· ἀληθεύω, and **ἐτεώνια**· ἀληθῆ, Id.; cf. ἐτεός.

**ἐτήρ**, ῆρος, ὁ, *one year old*, ἐτῆρας ἀμνοὺς θεοῖς ἔρεξ' ἐπακτίοις S.*Fr*. 751 (v.l. εὐείρας).

**ἐτηρίς**, ίδος, ἡ, *term of years*, Hierocl.*Facet*.62.

**ἔτης**, ὁ, Elean ϝέτας (v. infr.), in Hom. always in pl. **ἔται**, οἱ:—*clansmen*, i.e. *kinsmen and dependents of a great house*, ἀμύνων σοῖσιν ἔτῃσι Il.6.262; δαινύντα γάμον πολλοῖσι ἔτῃσιν Od.4.3; παῖδάς τε κασιγνήτους τε ἔτας τε Il.6.239, cf. Od.15.273; ἔται καὶ ἀνεψιοὶ Il.9. 464; ἔτας καὶ ἑταίρους 7.295; γείτονες ἠδὲ ἔται Od.4.16. II. later, *citizen*, ἔταις ἁμαχανίαν ἀλέξων τεοῖσιν Pi.*Pae*.6.10, cf. Epic. in *Arch. Pap*.7.4; τὼς ἔτας καττὰ πάτρια δικάζεσθαι Foed.Lac. in Th.5.79: in sg., *a private citizen*, opp. those who hold office, πρός σε.. ὡς ἔτην λέγω A.*Supp*.247; οὔτε δῆμος οὔτ' ἔτης ἀνὴρ Id.*Fr*.377; ἀρχῷ, φωτὶ δ' οὐκ ἔτῃ πρέπων E.*Fr*.1014; αἴτε ϝέτας αἴτε τελεστά *SIG*9.8 (Olympia, vi B.C.), cf. 141.12 (Corc. nigra, iv B.C.), *Mus.Belg*.16.70 (Athens, ii A.D.), *IG*5(2).20 (Tegea). (On the breathing, see Hdn.Gr.2.55.)

**ἐτησ-ίαι**, οἱ, gen. ἐτησίων Hdn.Gr.1.425: (ἔτος):—with or without ἄνεμοι, *periodic winds*, esp. those blowing from north-west during the summer, Hdt.2.20, 6.140, cf. Hp.*Aër*.10, D.4.31, Arist.*Mete*.361ᵇ35; of the *southerly monsoon* in the Indian Ocean, Arr.*An*.6.21.1; Εὖροι ἐ. Posidon.ap.Str.3.2.5. II. sg., as nickname of Antipater, who reigned for forty-five days, *King of the Dog-days*, *PCair.Zen*.19.6 (iii B.C.), Porph.*Fr.Hist*.4.6. ❀ **-ιάς**, άδος, poet. fem. of sq., epith. of αὔρη, Nonn.*D*.12.286. ❀ **-ιος**, ον, and in Hp. η, ον: (ἔτος):—*lasting a year*, πένθος οὐκ ἐ. E.*Alc*.336; προστασία f.l. in Th.2.80; ἐτησίους ἄρχειν to govern *for a year*, D.C.60.24. 2. *annual*, ὧραι Plu.2.993e; θυσίαι Th.5.11, etc., cf. *SIG*1024.24 (Myconus); φόρος *IG*7.2227 (Thisbe); ἐτήσιοι πρόσιτ' ἀεί Cratin.23; βορέαι ἐ., = ἐτησίαι, Arist.*Pr*.940ᵃ35; ἐ. πνεύματα Arr.*Ind*.21.1. Adv. -ίως Sch.Lyc. 107: neut. as Adv., τρυγόωσιν ἐτήσιον *AP*5.226 (Maced.).

❀ **ἐτητῠμ-ία**, poet. -ίη, ἡ, *truth*, Call.*Aet*.3.1.76, *AP*9.771 (Jul.), Max.462, Orph.*Fr*.280.7. ❀ **-ος**, ον, poet. redupl. for ἔτυμος, *true*, οὐκ ἔσθ' ὅδε μῦθος ἐ. Od.23.62; ἐ. ἄγγελος ἐλθών Il.22.438; ἐτήτυμα μυθησαίμην Hes.*Op*.10; τοῦτ' ἀγόρευσον ἐτήτυμον tell me this *true*, Od.1.174; τοῦτ' ἐ.; c.inf., is this *true*, that..? A.*Pers*.737 (troch.); εἰ λέγεις ἐτήτυμα S.*Ph*.1290; τὸ δ' ἐ. but *the truth* is.., Ar.*Pax* 119. 2. of persons, *truthful*, οὐ ψευδόμαντις.., ἀλλ' ἐ. E.*Or*.1667; ἐ. στόμα Id.*IT*1085. 3. *genuine, real*, κείνῳ δ' οὐκέτι νόστος ἐ. for him there remains no *true, real* return, Od.3.241; ἀλάθεια, κλέος, Pi.*O*.10(11). 54, *N*.7.63; ἐ. Διὸς κόρα A.*Ch*.948; παῖς ἐ. γεγώς S.*Tr*.1064; χρυσός Theoc.12.37: in late Prose, Them.*Or*.22.279d. II. as Adv., in neut. ἐτήτυμον, *truly, really*, Od.4.157, Il.13.111, 18.128, Archil.62: regul. Adv. -μως A.*Ag*.167 (lyr.), 682 (lyr.); ὡς ἐ. S.*El*.1452.

❀ **ἔτι** [ĭ], Adv.: I. of Time, 1. of the Present, *yet, still*, ἔ. μοι μένος ἔμπεδον Il.5.254; ἔ. τυτθὸν ἐόντα 6.222; εἰ Ζεὺς ἔ. Ζεύς S.*OC*623; ἔτ' ἐκ βρέφεος *ever* since babyhood, *AP*9.567 (Antip.); ἔ. καὶ νῦν Il. 1.455; ἔ. καὶ ἐκ παρόντων v.l. in Th.7.77; ἔτ' ἂν ἐκ τῶνδε θεὸς χρῄζων θείη A.*Ch*.340; ἔ. καὶ νυνί Pl.*Smp*.215d; νῦν ἔ. ζεῖ A.*Th*.708 (lyr.), cf. *Ag*.818. 2. of the Past, mostly with impf., ἀήθεσσον γὰρ ἔτ' αὐτῶν Il.10.493, cf. Hdt.9.102, Th.5.111, etc.: with aor., Pl.*Prt*.310c, etc.; ἔ. πρότερον, πρόσθεν, Th.8.45, Pl.*Sph*.242d: with the sense, *already*, γεγονέναι ἔ. οὐχ ἧττον ἢ εἶναι Id.*Men*.97a. 3. of the Future, *yet, longer*, ἄλγε' ἔδωκεν.. ἠδ' ἔ. δώσει Il.1.96, cf. 5.465: c. opt., ἔ... φιλέοι Od.15.305: c. imper., μή τις ἔ... ἔστω 2.230; *hereafter*, A.*Pr*.907, S.*El*.66, Ar.*V*.758 (anap.), etc. 4. with a neg., no *longer*, οὐδὲ.. ἔ. παρέμειναν D.H.5.46; v. οὐκέτι, μηκέτι. II. of Degree, *still, besides*, ἐς δεκάτην γενεὴν ἕτερόν γ' ἔ. βόσκοι *another* (and another and so on), Od.14.325; ἔτ' ἄλλο Hes.*Op*.157, cf. Il.6.411, Od.11.623, S.*Ant*.218, etc.; τίν' οὖν ἔτ' ἄλλον..; A.*Ch*.114; πρὸς τοῖσδ' ἔ., πρὸς τούτοις ἔ. (cf. προσέτι), S.*Ph*.1309, Ar.*Nu*.720 (anap.); ἔ. τε and *besides, nay more*, Pl.*Phdr*.279a; ἔ. τοσόνδε this *further* point, Id.*Tht*. 184b; ἔ. δὲ καί Th.1.80, etc.; πρῶτον μὲν.., ἔπειτα δὲ.., ἔ. δὲ.. X.*An*.6.6.13; ἔ. καί alone, τά τε εἴδωλα, ἔ. καὶ τὰ γεγραμμένα Pl. *Sph*.239d; ἔτι καὶ ἔ. ἀεί *Theol.Ar*.30. 2. freq. to strengthen a Comp., ἔ. μᾶλλον *yet* more, Il.14.97, 362; μᾶλλον ἔ. Od.18.22; ἔ. καὶ μ. Pi.*P*.10.57; καὶ ἔ. καὶ μᾶλλον Ael.*NA*16.24; ἔ. πλέον Hdt.7.6; πλέον ἔ. Th.1.80; παῖς τε κἄτι τοῦδ' ἀνούστερος A.*Pr*.987; πότμῳ τῷ νῦν.. κἄτι τοῦδ' ἐχθίονι S.*OT*272, cf. *El*.559, 1189. 3. with the Posit., ἔ. ἄνω *yet* higher up, X.*An*.7.5.9; ἔ. μάλα Ar.*Pax* 53, 462, *Ra*. 864. (Skt. *áti* 'beyond', Lat. *et*, Goth. *iþ* 'but', 'however'.)

**ἔτλην**, ης, η, aor. 2 of *τλάω.

**ἐτν-ηρός**, ά, όν, (ἔτνος) *like soup*, ἕψημα Phaeniasap.Ath.9.406c. **-ήρῠσις**, εως, ἡ, (ἀρύω A) *soup-ladle*, Ar.*Ach*.245, *Fr*.779. **-ίτης**, Dor. **-ίτας** [ῑ], ἄρτος, ὁ, = λεκιθίτης, Eucrat.ap.Ath.3.111b, Seleuc. ib.114b.

**ἐτνοδόνος**, ον, *soup-stirring*, τορύνα *AP*6.305 (Leon.), 306 (Aristo).

**ἔτνος**, εος, τό, *thick soup* made with pease or beans, Ar.*Ach*.246, *Ra*.62, 506, Pl.*Hp.Ma*.290d; ἔ. πίσινον Ar.*Eq*.1171; φάκινον Hp. *Acut*.(*Sp*.)53; κυάμινον Gal.*Vict.Att*.53; as poultice, τὸ ἔτνος τὸ ἐκ τῶν κυάμων Lycusap.Orib.9.35.1. (ἔτνος from a false deriv. from ἔω, *EM*387.9, etc.)

**ἑτοιμ-άζω**, pf. ἡτοίμακα Plb.3.72.6: pf. Pass. ἡτοίμασμαι both in med. and pass. sense (v. infr.): (ἕτοιμος):—*get ready, prepare*, ἐμοὶ γέρας αὐτίχ' ἑτοιμάσατ' Il.1.118; [νέας] Hdt.6.95; στρατιώτας *Act. Ap*.23.23; ὁδὸν Lxx *Is*.40.3, al.; ἔγκλημα μικρὸν αἰτίαν τε S.*Tr*.361; δῶμα E.*Alc*.364; βουλὴν Id.*Heracl*.472; δάκρυα δ' ἑτοιμάζουσι *to those furnishing* them, Id.*Supp*.454; ἀργύριον ῥητὸν Th.2.7, etc.; ἑαυτὸν ἵνα.. *Apoc*.8.6. II. Med., *cause to be prepared*, ὄφρ' ἱρὸν ἑτοιμάσσαιατ' Ἀθήνῃ Il.10.571; ἑτοιμάσσαντο δὲ ταύρους Od.13.184, cf. Hdt. 8.24; ἑτοιμασάμενος ἃ δεῖ *Inscr.Prien*.55.34 (ii B.C.). 2. with pf. Pass. ἡτοίμασμαι, *prepare for oneself*, τἄλλα ἡτοιμάζετο *made his* other *arrangements*, Th.4.77; ὅπως ἑτοιμάσαιντο τιμωρίαν Id.1.58; πλείονα ἡτοιμασμένος X.*Cyr*.3.3.5; τροφὴν ἡτοιμασμένοι D.23.209; τὰ πρὸς τὸν βίον Epicur.*Sent.Vat*.30, cf. Metrod.*Fr*.53. 3. *prepare oneself, make oneself ready*, c. inf., X.*Ap*.8; πρὸς τὴν χειμασίαν Plb. 3.105.11. III. Pass., *to be prepared*, ἔλεγε ἡτοιμάσθαι *that preparations had been made*, Th.6.64, cf. 7.62, etc.; ἑ. τι *to be prepared with*.., Plb.8.30.7. **-ᾰσία**, ἡ, *readiness*, πρὸς τὰς ὑπουργίας Hp. *Decent*.12; εἰς ἑ. ὑμῶν παρέχειν to place at your *disposal*, J.*AJ*10.1. 2. II. *preparation*, ἀρμένων Aen.Tact.21.1, cf. Lxx *Ps*.9.38(10. 17); τροφῆς ib.*Wi*.13.12; *equipment*, ἐν -σίᾳ εὐαγγελίου *Ep.Eph*. 6.15.

❀ **ἑτοιμό-δακρυς**, υ, gen. υος, *easily moved to tears*, Eust.115.30. **-εγρήγορος** ὕπνος *light* sleep, Steph.*in Hp*.1.146 D. **-θάνᾰτος** [θᾰ], ον, *ready for death*, Str.15.1.59. **-κόλλιξ**, ῑκος, ὁ, *one who gives rolls freely*, *Com.Adesp*.1094. **-κοπία**, ἡ, *officiousness*, Hp.*Praec*. 12 (s.v.l.). **-λόγος**, ον, *talkative*, Phot. s.v. εὑρεσίλογος. **-μεμφής**, ές, *ready to censure*, Eust.873.3. **-πειθής**, ές, *ready to obey*, Hdn.*Epim*.38. **-πτωτος**, ον, *inclined to fall*, gloss on ἀκροσφαλής, *AB*367. **-πωλεῖον**, τό, *cook-shop where dressed meats are sold*, *BGU* 1647.6 (ii A.D.). **-πώλης**, ου, ὁ, *one who keeps such a shop*, Demetr. Astrol. in *Cat.Cod.Astr*.1.106. **-πωλις**, ιδος, ἡ, = -πωλεῖον, *Gloss*.

❀ **ἑτοῖμος**, ον, also fem. ἑτοίμη Il.9.425, Hp.*Art*.66, -μᾶ S.*El*.1079 (lyr.), etc.:—in v B.C. and later **ἕτοιμος**, η, ον, or ος, ον, cf. Hdn.Gr. 2.938:—*at hand, ready, prepared*, ὀνείαθ' ἑτοῖμα προκείμενα Od.14.453,

etc.; τὶν δ' αἶνος ἑτοῖμος Pi.*O.*6.12; [τὰ κρέα] εἶχε ἕτοιμα Hdt.1.119, cf. 3.123; ἑτοιμοτάταν ἐπὶ δαῖτα Theoc.13.63, cf. E.*Cyc.*357 (lyr.); ἑ. χρήματα money *in hand*, Hdt.5.31; ἐξ ἑ. *in ready money*, *POxy.*2106.23 (iv A.D.); ἑ. ἀεὶ παρακείμενον ἐκμαγεῖον Pl.*Ti.*72c; ἑ. ποιήσασθαι to make *ready*, Hdt.1.11; ὡς ἑτοῖμα ἦν Th.2.3; ἐπειδὴ αὐτῷ ἑ. ἦν ib.98; ἐξ ἑτοίμου *at once and without hesitation, immediately, offhand*, ἐξ ἑ. λαμβάνειν Isoc.5.96; ἐξ ἑ. ὑπακούειν X.*Oec.*14.3; ἐξ ἑτοιμοτάτου διώκειν Id.*Cyr.*5.3.57; ἐξ ἑ. φίλον εἶναι Id.*Mem.*2.6.16; γίνεται ταῦτα ἐξ -οτάτου are *most likely to attack*, Hp.*Prog.*24; ἐν ἑτοίμῳ ἐστί Epicur.*Ep.*3p.62U., cf. Theoc.22.61; ἐν ἑ. ἔχειν Plb.2.34.2, 2*Ep.Cor.*10.6, etc.; ἑτοιμότερα γέλωτος λίβη tears *that came more readily than*.., A.*Ch.*448; τὰ ἑ. *that which is ready to hand*, ἐπὶ τὰ ἑ. μᾶλλον τρέπονται Th.1.20; τὰ ἑ. βλάψαι ib.70; τοῖς ἑ. περὶ τῶν ἀφανῶν.. κινδυνεύειν Id.6.9. 2. of the future, *sure to come, certain*, αὐτίκα γάρ τοι ἔπειτα μεθ' Ἕκτορα πότμος ἑ. Il.18.96; χώλωσις ἑτοίμη τοῖσι περιγινομένοισι Hp.*Art.*66; also, *easy to be done, feasible*, ἐπεὶ οὔ σφισιν ἦδε γ' ἑτοίμη (sc. μῆτις) Il.9.425; ἑ. [ἐστι] τὸ διαφθαρῆναι *imminent*, Plu.2.706c: c. inf., ἑ. μᾶλλόν [ἐστι] ἀπεχθάνεσθαι Pl.*R.*567a, cf. E.*HF*86; οὐ γάρ τι ἑ. μεταπεῖσαι it is not *easy*.., Paus.2.23.6. 3. of the past, *carried into effect, realized*, ταῦτα ἑ. τετεύχαται Il.14.53; ἠδ' ἄρ' ἑτοῖμα τέτυκτο and this promise has been *made good*, Od.8.384. II. of persons, *ready, active, zealous*, ἑ. ἦν ἐμοὶ σειραφόρος A.*Ag.*842; τινι *in* or *for* a thing, Pi.*O.*4.16; ἐς τι for a thing, Hdt.8.96; πρός τι X.*Mem.*4.5.12: c. dat. pers., *ready to assist* or *go with* him, etc., Pi.*N.*4.74, Hdt.1.70: c. inf., *ready to* do, ib.42,113, al.; ἐπιστενάχειν πᾶς τις ἑ. A.*Ag.*791; χωρεῖν ἑ. S.*Aj.*813, cf. *Ant.*264, Antipho 6.23, Ar.*V.*341 (lyr.); ὑπακούειν ἑτοιμότεροι *too ready*.., Th.4.61; θηρία ἑ. διαμάχεσθαι Pl.*Smp.*207b: c. Art., τὸ μὴ βλέπειν ἑτοίμα S.*El.*1079 (lyr.); ἦν ἕτοιμος, abs., he was *ready*, Hdt.1.10; ἑ. ἔχειν τινός Id.3.45; ἑ. ποιέεσθαί τινας Id.5.86. 2. of the mind, *ready, bold*, λῆμα Ar.*Nu.*458 (lyr.); ἡ γνώμη Th.4.123; τὸ ἑ. *readiness, resolution*, E.*Or.*1106; τὸ ἑ. τῆς γνώμης Philostr.*Her.*8.1; τὰ θερμά τε καὶ ἑ. τῶν θηρίων Id.*VA* 7.14. III. Adv. -μως *readily, willingly*, Th.1.80; ἑ. ἔχω τελευτᾶν I am *ready* to die, Demad.4, cf. D.18.161, *PAmh.*2.32.6 (ii B.C.), *Act.Ap.*21.13; ἑ. ἥκειν X.*An.*2.5.2; διδόναι *IG*2[2].956.24; ἑ. παρορᾷς *evidently*, Pl.*Hp.Ma.*300c: Comp. ἑτοιμότερον Is.4.14, -οτέρως Alex. Trall.12: Sup. -ότατα Pl.*Plt.*290a.

**ἑτοιμότης**, ητος, ἡ, *readiness*, πρὸς τὸ ποιεῖν ὁτιοῦν D.54.36; λόγων ἑ. *power* of speaking *offhand*, Plu.2.6e, cf. *Cam.*32: pl., M.Ant.4.12; of things, ἑ. κτήσεως Phld.*Oec.*p.46 J.; *aptitude*, Ph.1.392. II. *predisposition*, Plot.6.1.8; in Medic. sense, Gal.7.291.

**ἑτοιμο-τόμος**, ον, *ready to cut*, χεῖρες *AP*9.282 (Antip. Thess.). **-φθαρτος**, ον, *easily decomposed*, Steph. *in Hp.*1.102 D.

⊛ **ἔτος**, εος, τό, irreg. dat. ἔτῃ *IG*2.1059.18:—*year*, τῶν προτέρων ἐτέων in bygone *years*, Il.11.691; τόδ' ἐεικοστὸν ἔ. ἐστὶν ἐξ οὗ.. 24.765, cf. Od.2.89, 19.222; ὅτε.. ὀγδόον μοι ἐπιπλόμενον ἔ. ἦλθε 7.261; ἑ. ἐνιαυτῶν, v. ἐνιαυτός; ἑκάστου ἔτους Pl.*Phd.*58b; ἀν' ἕκαστον ἔ. Thphr.*HP*4.4.4; ἀνὰ πᾶν ἔ. *AP*9.430 (Crin.); ἀνὰ πάντα ἔτεα Hdt. 8.65; δι' ἔτους πέμπτου every fifth *year*, Ar.*Pl.*584; κατὰ ἔ. every *year*, Th.4.53, D.S.3.2, *Ev.Luc.*2.41, etc. (freq. καθ' ἔ., as *PPetr.*3p.34 (iii B.C.) and later); ἔ. εἰς ἔ. *year* after *year*, S.*Ant.*340 (lyr.); δι' ἔτους *annually*, Ph.1.19,378; εἰς ἔ. Theoc.*Ep.*13.4; εἰς ἔ. ἐξ ἔτεος Id.18.15; ἔ. ἐξ ἔτους Lxx *Le.*25.50; παρὰ ἔ. every other *year*, Paus.9.32.3 (but πὰρ ϝέτος *yearly*, *Tab.Heracl.*1.101); πάλαι πολλὰ ἤδη ἔτη Pl.*Ap.*18b; τρίτῳ ἔτει Th.1.101; τρίτῳ ἔτεϊ πρότερον Hdt.6.40; τρίτῳ ἔτεϊ τούτων in the third *year* after this, ibid., etc.; freq. in acc., ἔ. τόδ' ἤδη δέκατον.. βόσκων now for these ten *years*, S.*Ph.*312; τύραννος ἐγεγόνει ἤδη χιλιοστὸν ἔτος Pl.*R.*615c, cf. D.3.4, 33.23; of a person's age, γεγονὼς ἔτη τρία ἀπολείποντα τῶν ἑκατὸν Isoc.12.270; οἱ ὑπὲρ τὰ στρατεύσιμα ἔτη γεγονότες X.*Cyr.*1.2.4, cf. 13, etc.; without γεγονώς, τοὺς ὑπὲρ τετταράκοντα ἔτη Id.*An.*5.3.1; οἱ μέχρι τετταράκοντα ἐτῶν ib.6.4.25, etc.: in gen., ἐπειδὰν ἐτῶν ᾖ τις τριάκοντα Pl.*Lg.*721b; μυρίων ἐτῶν *within a period* of 10,000 *years*, Id.*Phdr.*248e; ὥρα ἔτους, v. ὥρα I. 2. *regnal year*, τὸ πέμπτον ἔ. Δομιτιανοῦ *POxy.*477.8 (ii A.D.). (ϝέτος *SIG*9.2 (Olympia, vi B.C.), *Berl.Sitzb.*1927.8 (Locr., v B.C.), *Inscr.Cypr.*135.1 H., *Tab.Heracl.* l.c.; cf. Lat. *vetus.*)

**ἐτός** (A), Adv. *without reason, in vain*, only with neg., οὐκ ἐτὸς *no wonder*, Ar.*Ach.*411, al., Philetaer.5, Anaxil.30, Pl.*R.*414e, 568a; οὐκ ἐτὸς ἄρ' ἦσθα δεινὴ καὶ σοφή Ar.*Ec.*245, cf. *Pl.*404.

⊛ **ἐτός** (B), ή, όν, = ἐτεός, *true*, Hsch., perh. to be read in Crates Com.8: neut. pl. ἐτά *truly*, Call.*Fr.anon.*283.

**ἑτός**, ή, όν, verb. Adj. of ἵημι, *sent*, only in compds., as ἀν-ετός, ἀφ-ετός. **ἔτρᾰγον**, aor. 2 of τρώγω. ⊛ **ἔττακαν**· ἔστησαν, Hsch. **ἔττε**, v. sub ἔστε.

**ἐττημένος**, η, ον, perf. part. Pass. of *ττάω (cf. δια-ττάω), *sifted*, Pherecr.211; ἐττησμένα Hsch.

**ἐτῠμ-ηγορέω**, *derive*, ἀπὸ αἰτίας ὄνομα Procl. *in Cra.*p.43P. **-ηγορία**, ἡ, = ἐτυμολογία, ib.p.45 P. (pl.). **-ηγόρος**, ον, (ἀγορεύω) *speaking truth*, Orph.*A.*4, 1178.

**ἐτῠμόδρῡς**, ῠος, ἡ, *true oak, Quercus Robur*, Thphr.*HP*3.8.2,7.

**ἐτῠμολογ-έω**, *argue from etymology*, Diogenian.Epicur.2.18, Gal. 5.214. II. *analyse a word and find its origin*, Πλάτων -λογῶν τὸν οἶνον Ath.2.35b, cf. Corn.*ND*32; ἐ. τι ἀπό τινος ib.1, Str.1.2.34; ἔκ τινος *An.Ox.*3.220; παρά τι *EM*220.37; πρός τι Phlp. *in de An.*92.4:—Pass., -εῖσθαι ταῖς Ἑλληνικαῖς φωναῖς Str.13.1.52. **-ία**, ἡ, *etymology*, Id.16.4.29, D.H.*Comp.*16, A.D.*Adv.*153.13, Ph.1.354, etc. **-ικός**, ή, όν, *belonging to* ἐτυμολογία, Eust.1799.25; -κά, τά, title of work by Chrysipp. (*Stoic.*2.9, al.); ἡ -κή *the science of etymology*, Varro *LL*7.109; τὸ -κόν *an etymological dictionary*, *EM*212.13 (pl.), Sch.Il.13.130 (pl.), etc. Adv. -κῶς Eust.396.15. **-ος**, ον, *studying etymology*: as Subst., ἐ., ὁ, *etymologist*, *EM*199.24, Varro *LL*6.39.

**ἔτῠμος**, ον, also η, ον S.*Ph.*205 (lyr.) (only in neut. in Hom.):—poet. Adj. *true*, ψεύσομαι, ἦ ἔτυμον ἐρέω; Il.10.534; φάμ' ἔτυμον S.*Ant.*1320 (lyr.), cf. Call.*Fr.*1.39P.; ψεύδεα πολλὰ λέγων ἐτύμοισιν ὁμοῖα Od.19.203, cf. Hes.*Th.*27, Thgn.713; οἵ ῥ' ἔτυμα κραίνουσι those [dreams] have *true* issues, Od.19.567; γνώσει τάδ' ὡς ἔ. A.*Pr.*295 (anap.); ἔ. λόγος Stesich.32, Pi.*P.*1.68; ἔ. ἄγγελος, φήμη, φάτις, A.*Th.*82 (lyr.), E.*El.*818, Ar.*Pax*114 (anap.); βάλλει μ' ἐτύμα φθογγά S.*Ph.*205 (lyr.); πάθεα A.*Eu.*496; τέχνη Dor.ap.Pl.*Phdr.*260e; ὡς ἔτυμ' ἑστάκαντι how *natural*.., Theoc.15.82. 2. neut. ἔτυμον, as Adv., ἀλλ' ἐτυμόν τοι ἦλθ' Ὀδυσεύς Od.23.26; οὔ σ' ἔτυμόν γε φάμεν πεπυσθαι Il.23.440; ὡς ἔτυμον *AP*7.352: regul. Adv. -μως Xenoph. 8.4, Pi.*O.*6.77, A.*Th.*918 (lyr.), B.12.228, etc.; ὡς ἐτύμως A.*Eu.*534 (lyr.). II. ἔτυμον, τό, as Subst., *the true sense* of a word *according to its origin*, its *etymology*, D.S.1.11, Plu.2.278c, Ath.13.571d. Adv. -μως *etymologically*, Arist.*Mu.*400[a]6, Str.9.2.17, Ph.1.30: Comp. -ώτερον *EM*526.2: Sup. -ώτατα Nicom.*Ar.*2.27.—Never in Att. Prose; in later writers only in signf. II, exc. in Pl.*Ax.*366b.

**ἐτῠμότης**, ητος, ἡ, *true meaning* of a word, Str.5.4.10, 8.3.19, Plu. 2.638e.

**ἐτῠμώνιον**· ἀληθές, Hsch.

**ἐτωσιοεργός**, όν, *working in vain* or *sluggishly*, Hes.*Op.*411.

**ἐτώσιος**, ον, (ἐτός A) Ep. Adj. *to no purpose, fruitless*, βέλος ὠκὺ ἐ. ἔκφυγε χειρός Il.14.407; ἐτώσια πίπτει ἔραζε [βέλεα] 17.633; τὰ δὲ πάντα ἐ. θῆκεν Ἀθήνη made them *fruitless*, Od.22.256; δῶρα δ' ἐ. ταῦτα χαρίζεο 24.283; *useless, unprofitable*, ἐ. ἄχθος ἀρούρης Il.18.104; ἐ. πόλλ' ἀγορεύειν Hes.*Op.*402; ἔργον ἐ. λιπεῖν to leave it *undone*, ib. 440; ἐτώσια χερσὶ προδεικνύς, i. e. making *mere* feints, not real blows, Theoc.22.102: masc., first in Id.25.236 (οἰστός): fem., Orph.*L.*539: neut. ἐτώσιον, as Adv., Id.*A.*700; pl., ἐτώσια γηράσκοντας A.R. 2.893, cf. Theoc.1.38: regul. Adv. -ίως Sch.Ar.*Ec.*246.

⊛ **εὖ**, Ep. also ἐΰ Od.1.302, etc., cf. A.D.*Adv.*200.20: Adv. (prop. neut. of ἐΰς):—*well*, opp. κακῶς (as in Th.4.63), Hom., etc. I. of knowledge or action, *well, thoroughly, competently*, εὖ μέν τις δόρυ θηξάσθω, εὖ δ' ἀσπίδα θέσθω Il.2.382; εὖ καὶ ἐπισταμένως κέασαν ξύλα Od. 20.161; τὴν πόλιν κοσμέων καλῶς τε καὶ εὖ Hdt.1.59; τὸ πρᾶγμα βασανίσας καλῶς τε καὶ εὖ Pl.*Euthd.*307b, etc.; τόξων ἐῢ εἰδώς *cunning* with the bow, Il.2.718, etc.; εὖ τόδ' ἴσθι A.*Pers.*173 (troch.); εὖ γὰρ σαφῶς τόδ' ἴστε ib.784; εὖ οἶδ' ὅτι parenthetic in colloquial speech, σὺ γὰρ εὖ οἶδ' ὅτι οὐ πράγματ' ἄγεις Ar.*Pax*1296, cf. D.14.2, etc.; εὖ οἶδα, in answers, Dioxipp.4; εὖ μήδεο consider *well*, Il.2.360; εὖ λέγεις *well* spoken! Pl.*Ap.*24e, cf. D.5.2, etc.: with λέγω omitted, οὐδὲ τοῦτ' εὖ Ἐρατοσθένης Str.1.3.1. 2. *morally well, kindly*, εὖ ἔρδειν, = εὐεργετεῖν, Il.5.650; εὖ εἰπεῖν τινα to speak *well* of him, Od.1.302; εὖ δρᾶν εὖ παθών S.*Ph.*672, etc. 3. with passive or intransitive Verbs, *fortunately, happily, in good case*, εὖ ζώουσι Od.19.79; εὖ οἴκαδ' ἱκέσθαι *safely*, Il.1.19, cf. Od.3.188; τοῦ βίου εὖ ἥκειν Hdt.1.30; εὖ φρονῶν in one's *right* mind, A.*Pr.*387, etc. (but εὖ φρονεῖν εἴς τινας, τὰ σά, to be *well-disposed* towards, And.2.4, S.*Aj.*491); standing last for emphasis, ἄνδρες γεγονότες εὖ Hdt.7.134; νόμους μὴ λύειν ἔχοντας εὖ Id.3.82; τελευτήσει τὸν βίον εὖ Id.1.32, cf. Th.1.71, Arist. *EN*1124[b]13, etc.: separated from its Verb, εὖ πρᾶγμα συντεθέν D. 18.144. II. coupled with other Adverbs, esp. when qualifying nouns, adjectives, and adverbs, εὖ μάλα Od.4.96, etc.; ἡ ἀορτὴ εὖ μάλα κοίλη Arist.*HA*514[b]22; εὖ μάλα πᾶσαι *h.Ap.*171; εὖ μάλα πολλά Heraclit.35; εὖ μάλα πρεσβύτης Pl.*Euthphr.*4a; μάλα εὖ καὶ κομψῶς Id.*Sph.*236d; εὖ καὶ μάλα Id.*Smp.*194a (sed cf. *CQ*15.4); κάρτα εὖ Hdt.3.150; εὖ.. πάνυ or πάνυ εὖ, Ar.*Pl.*198, Pl.*Men.*8cb; εὖ σφόδρα Nicostr.8, Philem.75.4; εὖ κἀνδρικῶς, εὖ κἀνδρείως, Ar.*Eq.*379 (lyr.), *Th.*656; καλῶς τε καὶ εὖ (v.supr.I.1); εὖ τε καὶ καλῶς Pl.*R.*503d. III. as Subst., τὸ εὖ the *right*, the *good cause*, τὸ δ' εὖ νικάτω A.*Ag.*121; τὸ γὰρ εὖ μετ' ἐμοῦ Ar.*Ach.*661; the *Good*, final cause, τὸ εὖ τεκταινόμενος ἐν πᾶσιν τοῖς γιγνομένοις Pl.*Ti.*68e; τοῦ εὖ ἕνεκα Arist.*Sens.*437[a]1, cf. eund.*Metaph.*1092[b]26: in Art, *perfection, the ideal*, τὸ εὖ διὰ πολλῶν ἀριθμῶν γίνεται Polyclit.2. IV. as the Predicate of a propos., τί τῶνδ' εὖ; A.*Ch.*338 (lyr.), cf. 116; εὖ εἴη may it be *well*, Id.*Ag.*216 (lyr.); εὐορκεῦντι μέμ μοι εὖ εἶμεν or εἴη, *SIG*953.9 (Calymna, ii B.C.), *PEleph.*23.19 (iii B.C.); εὖ σοι γένοιτο *well* be with thee, E.*Alc.*627, cf. *Fr.*707. V. Interjection, *well done!* to cheer on dogs, εὖ κύνες X.*Cyn.*9.20; *ahoy! ho! Lyr.Alex.Adesp.*20.11; cf. εὖγε. VI. in Compds., implying *abundance* (εὐανδρία), *prosperity* (εὐδαίμων, opp. κακοδαίμων), *ease* (εὔβατος, opp. δύσβατος): compounded only with Nouns and Adjs. (hence εὖ πάσχω, εὖ ποιέω are better written divisim, but εὐποιητικός implies εὐποιέω: v. ἀντευποιέω); εὐδοκέω is exceptional. (Replaced by καλῶς in later Gr., exc. in set phrases.)

**εὗ**, enclit. εὑ, Ion. and Ep. for οὗ (οὑ), gen. of reflex. Pron. of 3rd pers., Il.20.464; for αὐτοῦ, Hdt.3.135. II. for αὐτοῦ, Il.14.427, 24.293. III. apptly. for ἑῷ, *Trans.Am.Phil.Ass.*57.202 (Laodicea Combusta).

**εὖα**· ἐπιφημισμὸς ληναϊκὸς καὶ μυστικός, Hsch. II. for acc. sg. εὔαν, v. εὔας. III. εὐά· τράγου φωνῆς μίμημα Anon.ap.Suid.

**εὐαγγελ-έω**, = εὐαγγελίζομαι, Pl.ap.Phryn.235 (prob. referring to *R.*432d, *Tht.*144b, where codd. and edd. have εὖ ἀγγέλλω). **-ία**, ἡ, *good tidings*, Lxx 4*Ki.*7.9, J.*AJ*18.6.10. ⊛ **-ίζομαι**, impf., Paus. 4.19.5: fut. part. -ιούμενος J.*AJ*6.4.2, 18.6.10, Luc.*Icar.*34: aor. (v. infr.):—Act., only in later Gr., Lxx 1*Ki.*31.9, *Apoc.*10.7, *PGiss.*27.6 (ii A.D.): plpf. εὐηγγελίκειν dub. in D.C.61.13: (εὐάγγελος):—

*bring good news, announce them*, λόγους ἀγαθοὺς φέρων εὐαγγελίσασθαί τινι Ar.*Eq.*643, cf. Phryn.Com.44, D.18.323; τὴν εὐτοκίαν Sor.1.70; εὐτυχίας τῇ πατρίδι Lycurg.18; πρός σε ταῦτα Men.*Georg.*83; also τινά τι J.*AJ*18.6.10, Alciphr.3.12, Hld.2.10; εὐ. ὅτι.. Thphr.*Char.*17.7; τινι ὅτι.. Luc.*Philops.*31: c. acc. et inf., Plu.*Mar.*22:—Act., εὐ. τὰ τῆς νίκης *PGiss.* l.c.; τισιν ὡς.. Polyaen.5.7:—Pass., *receive good tidings*, ἐν ᾗ -ίσθη ἡ πόλις ἡμέρᾳ *AJA*18.323 (Sardes, i B.C.). II. *preach* or *proclaim as glad tidings*, τὴν βασιλείαν τοῦ Θεοῦ *Ev.Luc.*4.43, etc.; εἰρήνην ὑμῖν *Ep.Eph.*2.17, etc. 2. abs., *proclaim glad tidings*, πτωχοῖς Lxx *Is.*61.1, cf. *Ev.Luc.*4.18, etc.: c. acc., *preach the glad tidings of the gospel to*, τὸν λαόν ib.3.18; κώμας τῶν Σαμαρειτῶν *Act.Ap.*8.25:—so in Act., *Apoc.*10.7; τινι Lxx 1*Ki.*31.9:—Pass., *have the gospel preached to* one, *Ev.Matt.*11.5, *Ep.Hebr.*4.2,6; also of the gospel, *to be preached*, *Ev.Luc.*16.16, *Ep.Gal.*1.11. ⊛ **-ιον, τό,** *reward of good tidings*, given to the messenger, εὐαγγέλιον δέ μοι ἔστω Od.14.152; οὐ..εὐ. τόδε τείσω ib.166; ἀπολήψῃ τὸ εὐ. Plu.*Demetr.*17: in Att. always in pl., εὐαγγέλια θύειν to make a thank-offering for *good-tidings*, Isoc.7.10, Men.*Pk.*415; εὐ. θύειν ἑκατὸν βοῦς τῇ θεῷ Ar.*Eq.*656; ἐβουθύτει ὡς εὐ. X.*HG*4.3.14; εὐαγγελίων θυσίαι Aeschin.3.160; εὐ. στεφανοῦν, ἀναδῆσαί τινα, to crown one for *good news brought*, Ar.*Eq.*647, *Pl.*765; ἐστεφανωμένη ἐπ' εὐαγγελίοις Plu.*Sert.*11, cf. *Supp.Epigr.*1.362.7 (Samos, iv B.C.). II. *good tidings, good news*, in pl., Lxx 2*Ki.*4.10, Cic.*Att.*2.3.1, 13.40.1, *Inscr.Prien.*105.40 (i B.C.): sg., J.*BJ*2.17.4, Luc.*Asin.*26, App.*BC*3.93, *Sammelb.*421 (iii A.D.). 2. in Christian sense, *the gospel*, *Ep.Gal.*1.11, etc.

⊛ **Εὐαγγέλιος,** ὁ, *giver of glad tidings*, epith. of Zeus, Aristid.*Or.*53 (55).3. II. (sc. μήν) month in an Asiatic calendar, *Hemerolog.Flor.*

**εὐαγγελ-ιστής,** οῦ, ὁ, *bringer of good tidings*: hence, *evangelist, preacher of the gospel*, *Act.Ap.*21.8. II. *proclaimer of oracular messages*, *IG*12(1).675 (Rhodes). ⊛ **-ος,** ον, (ἀγγέλλω) *bringing good news*, πῦρ A.*Ag.*21; ἐλπίδες ib.262, etc.; σωτηρίων πραγμάτων εὐ. ib.646; Φήμη εὐ. *IG*14.1120; ῥινός Opp.*H.*5.237; title of Hermes, Hsch.

**εὐάγ-εια** [ᾱ], ἡ, (εὐᾱγής) *brightness, clearness, alertness*, [τῆς ψυχῆς] Iamb.*VP*24.107: pl., ἀγχίνοιαί τε καὶ ψυχῆς εὐάγειαι ib.17.74: prob. cj. ib.3.13. **-έω** [ᾰ], (εὐᾰγής A) *to be pure, holy*, E.*Ba.*1008 (lyr.); αὐτὸς δ' εὐαγέοιμι καὶ εὐαγέεσσιν ἅδοιμι Theoc.26.30, cf. Orph.*Fr.*222; εὐαγέων καὶ εὐαγέεσσι μελοίμην Call.*Del.*98. II. in Pass., *to be purified*, *IG*12(1).677 (Rhodes).

**εὐᾰγής** (A), ές, (ἄγος A) *free from pollution, pure*: 1. of persons, *guiltless*, ὁ δὲ ἀποκτείνας τὸν ταῦτα ποιήσαντα..ὅσιος ἔστω καὶ εὐ. Lex ap.And.1.96, cf. Porph.*VP*15; εὐαγεστάτων ἱππέων, v.l. for εὐγενεστάτων, D.H.10.13; of bees, *chaste* (cf. Virg.*G.*4.198), *AP*9.404.7 (Antiphil.). 2. of actions, *holy, lawful*, τίς οἶδεν εἰ κάτωθεν εὐαγῆ τάδε; S.*Ant.*521; εὐαγές ἐστι τὸ ἀποκτεῖναι D.9.44, cf. Arist.*Fr.*538, App.*BC*2.148; τοῦτο δ' οὐκ εὐαγές μοι ἀπέβη *well-omened, favourable*, Pl.*Ep.*312a. Adv. εὐαγέως, ἔρδειν *h.Cer.*274, 369, cf. A.R.2.699, *POxy.*1203.5 (i A.D.), etc.; οὐκ εὐαγῶς Ph.2.472: Sup. -έστατα Jul.*Or.*7.230d. 3. of offerings or services, *undefiled*: hence, *lawful*, ἐλέφας..οὐκ εὐ. ἀνάθημα Pl.*Lg.*956a; θυηλαί A.R.1.1140, etc.; ὕμνοι *AP*7.34 (Antip. Sid.); λύσις a solution *free from defilement*, S.*OT*921; οὐκ εὐ. ἀπολογίαι Porph.*Abst.*2.10. (Εὐhάγης as pr. n., *IG*12(9).56.118 (Styra, v B.C.).)

**εὐᾰγής** (B), ές, (ἄγνυμι) = καλῶς κεκλασμένος, Suid., cf. *EM*266.3.

⊛ **εὐᾱγής,** ές, (v. fin.) *bright, clear*, εὐᾱγέος ἠελίοιο (cf. ἀγής II) Parm.10.2; καθαρὰ καὶ εὐαγέα, of the sun and heavenly bodies, Hp.*Insomn.*89, cf. Democr.ap.Thphr.*Sens.*73,78; λευκῆς χιόνος..εὐαγεῖς βολαί E.*Ba.*662; εὐαγέστερον γίγνεσθαι, opp. σκοτωδέστερα φαίνεσθαι καὶ ἀσαφῆ, Pl.*Lg.*952a; εὐαγέστατος, opp. θολερώτατος, of air, Id.*Ti.*58d; χεύων ὁλκὰν εὐαγῆ *Lyr.Alex.Adesp.*35.19; σὺν..εὐαγεῖ (also εὐαγεῖ, εὐαυγεῖ) Ὑγιείᾳ *Pae.Erythr.*15, al.; ὀφθαλμοί Aret.*SA*2.4, Adam.1.13. 2. metaph., *alert*, ἄνθρωποι Hp.*Vict.*2.62 (v.l. γίνεται εὐαγής (sc. ἥ τε ὄψις καὶ ἡ ἀκοή), cf. εὐαγέα (v.l. εὐπαγέα) καὶ εὐήκοα ibid.). II. *far-seen* or *conspicuous*, πέτρα Pi.*Pae.Fr.*19.25; ἕδραν παντὸς εὐαγῆ στρατοῦ a seat *in full view* of the army, A.*Pers.*466; ἔστην θεατὴς πύργον εὐαγῆ λαβών E.*Supp.*652. (ᾱ Parm. l.c., *Lyr.Alex.* l.c., *AP*6.204 (Leon., s.v.l.).—Perh. fr. εὐ-ᾱυγής (ἄυγή lengthd., cf. εὐᾱγορέω, εὐᾱής, etc.), as ἑᾱτοῦ fr. ἑᾱυτοῦ: εὐαυγ- is a correction in Pi. l.c., v.l. in *Pae.Erythr.* l.c., and may be the original spelling; cf. εὐαυγής.)

**εὐάγητος,** ον, = εὐᾱγής, *bright*, φύσιν εὐ., of clouds, Ar.*Nu.*276 (lyr.). (ᾱ, which prohibits the other expl. given by Sch., = εὐκίνητος.—The sense *ductile*, from ἡγέομαι, is very dub.)

**εὐάγκᾰλος,** ον, (ἀγκάλη) *easy to bear in the arms*, ἄχθος οὐκ εὐάγκαλον A.*Pr.*352; τόξον E.*Fr.*785 (Nauck ἄγκυλον); φόρτος, of Anchises, Ael.*Fr.*148, cf. Porph.*Abst.*1.45: metaph., λόγοι Them.*Or.*18.219d; *pleasant to embrace*, Luc.*Am.*25.

**εὐάγκεια,** poet. fem. of sq., Πίνδον ἀν' εὐάγκειαν Call.*Cer.*83. (Formed like Κυπρογένεια.)

⊛ **εὐαγκής,** ές, (ἄγκος) *with sweet glades*, Pi.*N.*5.46.

**εὔαγλις,** ἡ, *consisting of many* or *fine cloves* (ἄγλιθες), of a head of garlic, Nic.*Al.*432 (cod. opt., melius εὐάγλις).

**εὐᾰγόραστος,** ον, *easily bought, cheap*, Hsch. s.v. εὔωνον.

**εὐᾱγορέω, εὐᾱγορία,** Dor. for εὐηγ-.

**εὐάγρ-ευτος,** ον, = εὔαγρος, Sch.Opp.*H.*4.587. ⊛ **-έω,** *to have good sport*, *AP*6.304.8 (Phan.), Antig.Car.ap.Ath.7.297f: c. acc., εὐαγρεῖν ἠέρα γαῖαν ὕδωρ *AP*6.12 (Jul.). **-ής,** ές, = εὔαγρος, Opp.*H.*3.49, 4.157. **-ία,** poet. **-ίη,** ἡ, *good sport*, Plb.8.29.6, *AP*6.187 (Alph.), 9.268 (Antip. Thess.). **-ος,** ον, (ἄγρα) *lucky in the chase*, S.*OC*1088 (lyr.), *AP*6.34 (Rhian.); *affording good sport*, ib.9.555 (Crin.); epith. of Pan, *Sammelb.*4031, 4053; of Ares, *BMus.Inscr.*1064 (Egypt).

**εὐᾰγωγ-ία,** ἡ, *good education*, ἡ Ἐπικράτους εὐ. τοῦ ἀδελφοῦ Aeschin.2.151, cf. Simp.*in Epict.*p.19 D., al. II. *easiness of being led*, ψυχῆς πρὸς λόγους Pl.*Def.*413b, cf. Them.*Or.*13.175c: abs., *docility*, Arist.*VV*1250$^{b}$32; κουφότης καὶ εὐ. Philostr.*VA*6.13. ⊛ **-ος,** ον, *easily led, ductile*, ἐπί τι, εἴς τι, τινι πρός τι, Pl.*R.*486d, X.*Oec.*12.15, Arist.*Pol.*1327$^{b}$38; πρὸς πᾶν Plb.11.29.9; εἰς ἀκολασίαν S.E.*M.*6.34; τινι *by* a master, Pl.*Lg.*671b; πόλις -οτέρα ὑπὸ τῶν τυχόντων Isoc.*Ep.*2.15; εὐάγωγόν ἐστι πᾶς ἀνὴρ ἐρῶν Men.352. 2. *easily purged*, -ότατος χυμός Gal.15.78. II. metaph., *easily managed*, of the Nile, Isoc.11.13; of horses, *docile*, Poll.1.195; of the voice, *easily trained*, Id.2.117; δακτύλων τὸ εὐ., of a statue, Luc.*Im.*6; of land, *easily cultivated*, Str.5.3.12; *commodious*, ἐνδιαιτήσεις Ph.1.334. III. Adv. *-γως in an accommodating spirit*, Cic.*Att.*13.23.3.

**εὐάγων** [ᾰ], ωνος, ὁ, ἡ, *of successful contests*, τιμά Pi.*N.*10.38.

**εὐαδές·** εὔπνουν, and **εὐαδής·** εὐήνεμος, οἱ δὲ εὐαής, Hsch. (cf. S.*Ph.*828 (lyr.)). II. **εὐαδέα** (accus.?) dub. l. in Hp.*Decent.*4 codd.

**εὐᾰδίκητος** [ῐ], ον, (ἀδικέω) *liable to wrong*, And.4.15, Luc.*Tim.*32, Hipparch.ap.Stob.4.4.4. II. Medic., *easily injured*, Sor.1.47, 106, Ath.Med.ap.Orib.*inc.*21.16, Gal.10.542.

**εὔαδον,** v. ἁνδάνω.

**εὐᾱερ-ία,** ἡ, *freshness of air*, prob. in Callix.1, cf. Ptol.*Tetr.*86; *fineness of weather*, Plu.2.787e, Eust.1505.19: Ion. **εὐηερίη,** v. εὐήρεια. ⊛ **-ος,** ον, *with fresh, good air*, τὸ εὐ. Str.3.2.13, cf. Herod.Med. in *Rh.Mus.*58.73, Orib.9.20.1.

**εὐάζω,** *cry* εὐαί, in honour of Bacchus, S.*Ant.*1134 (lyr.), E.*Ba.*1034 (lyr.); Διονύσῳ *AP*9.363.11 (Mel.), cf. D.S.4.3, Callistr.*Stat.*2: c. acc. cogn., μελῳδὸν εὐ. χορόν Sopat.10:—Med., Βάκχιον -ομένα E.*Ba.*68 (lyr.).

⊛ **εὐᾱής,** ές, (ἄημι) *well ventilated, fresh, airy*, χώρῳ ἐν εὐαεῖ Hes.*Op.*599 (εὐᾰέϊ codd., Rzach). II. Act., of a wind, *favourably blowing, fair*, opp. δυσαής, Hdt.2.117, E.*Hel.*1504 (lyr.); ἀνέμων εὐαέσσιν ῥοθίοις prob. in E.*Fr.*773.36 (lyr.): metaph., *favourable*, Ὕπνε.., εὐαὲς ἡμῖν ἔλθοις [with ᾰ] S.*Ph.*828 (lyr., s.v.l.).

⊛ **εὔαθλος,** ον, *successful in contests*, Pi.*I.*6(5).3. II. *happily won*, γέρα *APl.*5.363.

⊛ **εὐαί** (εὐαΐ Hdn.Gr.1.503), a cry of joy like εὐοῖ, Ar.*Lys.*1294 (lyr.), etc.; εὐαὶ σαβαῖ Eup.84.

**εὐαιμ-ία,** ἡ, (αἷμα) *goodness of blood*, Gal.7.564. **-ορράγητος** [ρᾰ], ον, *easily bleeding*, Id.19.457, Leonid.ap.Aët.15.5, Paul.Aeg.6.30. **-ος,** ον, *full-blooded*, in Comp., μόριον Gal.17(2).423, cf. 11.290.

**εὐαίν-ετος,** ον, (αἰνέω) *much-extolled*, μέριμνα B.18.11; ἵππος Antim.25. **-ητος,** ον, = foreg., Ὀρφεύς Pi.*P.*4.177.

**εὐαίρετος,** ον, (αἱρέω) *easy to be taken*, χώρη Hdt.7.130; λαγώς Poll.5.50, cf. X.*Mem.*3.1.10.

**εὐαισθ-ησία,** ἡ, *quick sensibility, vigorous capacity of sensation*, Pl.*Ti.*76d, Arist.*PA*656$^{a}$16, *Stoic.*3.32, Aristeas 259, Ph.1.104, al., Gal.*UP*8.6, Iamb.*Protr.*2. **-ητέω,** *have keen perceptions*, Tz.*H.*4.451. **-ητικός,** ή, όν, = sq., Gal.16.360; δύναμις *sensory* faculty, Steph.*in Gal.*1.234 D. **-ητος,** ον, (αἰσθάνομαι) *with quick senses* or *keen perceptions*, περί τι Pl.*Lg.*812b; ἐλέφας εὐ. ζῷον Arist.*HA*630$^{b}$21: Comp. -ότερος Pl.*Ti.*75c; τῆς καρδίας τὴν ὑπερῴαν -οτέραν ἔχειν Plu.2.14d: Sup. ὁ ἄνθρωπος -ότατος τῶν ἄλλων ζῴων Arist.*PA*660$^{a}$20; τὸ εὐ., = εὐαισθησία, Gal.10.387. Adv. -τως, ἔχειν τινός have *keen perceptions* of.., Pl.*Lg.*670b, cf. 661b: Comp. -οτέρως, ἔχειν περὶ ὥρας καὶ μηνῶν καὶ ἐνιαυτῶν Id.*R.*527d. II. of things, *easy to perceive*, Arist.*Cael.*289$^{a}$7 (Comp.), Plu.2.956f.

**εὐαίων,** ωνος, ὁ, ἡ, *happy in life*, of persons, E.*Ion* 126 (lyr.), Call.*Del.*292, etc.; *happy, fortunate*, βίοτος A.*Pers.*711, S.*Tr.*81; πλοῦτος S.*Fr.*592.3 (lyr.); [Ὕπνος] Id.*Ph.*829 (lyr.); πότμος E.*IA*550 (lyr.).

**εὐάκεστος** [ᾰ], ον, (ἀκέομαι) *easy to remedy*, ἁμαρτάδες εὐακεστότεραι Hp.*Acut.*39.

**εὐᾰκής,** ές, = foreg., -έστερόν [ἐστι] Ruf.(?)ap.Orib.*inc.*4.54. Ion. Adv. -ακέως *by an easy process of healing*, Aret.*CA*2.2.

**εὐᾱκοέω, εὐάκοος,** ον, v. εὐηκ-.

**εὐᾰκόνητος,** ον, *well-whetted*, gloss on εὐήκης, Sch.Nic.*Al.*411.

**εὐάκουστος** [ᾰ], ον, = εὐήκοος I. 3, Ἡρακλῆς *IG*14.904.

**εὐάκτῑν,** ῑνος, ὁ, ἡ, *with beautiful rays*, Hdn.Gr.1.18.

**εὐᾰλαζόνευτος,** ον, *easy to pretend about*, Arist.*Rh.*1390$^{b}$21.

**εὐᾱλάκᾰτος** [ᾰκ], ον, Aeol. for εὐηλ-, Theoc.28.22.

**εὐαλδής,** ές, (ἀλδαίνω) *well-grown, luxuriant*, φῦκος, χιλός, *AP*9.325, *IG*14.1389 ii 24. Ion. Adv. -έως Hp.*Lex* 2. II. Act., *fertilizing*, Ἱππουκρήνη Arat.217, cf. Plu.2.664c: Comp. -έστερα [ὕδατα] ib.912f.

**εὐαλθής,** ές, (ἀλθαίνω) *easily healed*, Hp.*Art.*39: Comp., ib.68: Sup., Antyll.ap.Orib.45.16.4. II. Act., *healing*, Nic.*Al.*326, 622.

**εὐάλιος,** ον, Dor. for εὐήλιος.

**εὐαλλοίωτος,** ον, (ἀλλοιόω) *easily changed*, Gal.*UP*8.6, al., Paul.Aeg.1.50.

**εὐαλσής,** ές, (ἄλσος) *with beautiful groves*, prob. in Str.3.3.1.

**εὐάλφῐτος,** ον, *of good meal*, *AP*7.736 (Leon.).

**εὐαλῶς·** εὐχερῶς θηρώμενος, Hsch. (leg. -άλωτος vel -αλής).

**Εὐᾰλωσία,** ἡ, (ἅλως) *filling the threshing-floor*, of Demeter, Hsch.

**εὐάλωτος** [ᾰ], ον, *easy to be taken* or *caught*, X.*Cyn.*9.9, Pl.*Phdr.*240a, Demetr.Com.Vet.4; ὑπὸ πάντων διὰ κολακείας εὐ. Plu.*Crass.*6; οὔτε ὑφ' ἡδονῆς οὔτε ὑπὸ δέους εὐ. Id.*Sert.*10; εὐ. εἰς δεισιδαιμονίαν,

πρὸς ἡδονάς, *easily led away* to.., ib.11, Id.2.256e; εὐ. εἰς τὸ μιμεῖσθαι *easily led* to imitate, ib.334d: Comp. -ωτότερος Ph.2.132, Luc. *Abd.*28 (εὐαλούστερος is corrupt in Alciphr.2.1): Sup. -ότατος Ph.1.458, D.C.60.2. Adv. -τως Ph.1.129. II. Medic., *easily affected*, Sor.1.47; παλμῷ Gal.7.599; but also, *easily cured*, ὑπὸ τῆς τέχνης Alex.Trall.1.11.

**εὐᾱμερία, -άμερος**, Dor. for εὐημ-.

⊛ **εὐάμπελος**, ον, *with fine vines*, E.*Fr.*530.3, Str.3.3.1, al.: epith. of Dionysus, *AP*9.524.6.

**εὐάμπυξ**, ῦκος, *with fair fillet*, Μοῖσαι Pi.*Dith.Oxy.*1.13.

**εὐάν** [ᾱ] (εὔαν D.T.642.18, Hdn.Gr.1.503, 2.12), *euhan*, a cry of the Bacchanals, cf. εὐοῖ, E.*Tr.*326, Luc.*Trag.*38.—Acc. to Hsch., an Indian name for *ivy*, which was sacred to Bacchus.

**εὐανά-βλαστος**, ον, *shooting up freely*, θαλλοί Sch.Opp.*H.*2.491. **-γνωστος**, ον, *easy to read aloud*, Arist.*Rh.*1407$^{b}$11, Phld. *Rh.*1.199 S.

**εὐανάγωγος** [ᾰγ], ον, *easy to expectorate*, Dsc.3.36, Gal.14.271.

**εὐανα-διδάκτως**, Adv., gloss on εὐανακλήτως, Suid., Zonar.926. **-δοτος**, ον, *easy to digest*, Ath.1.26a, Diph.Siph.ap.eund.8.356b (v.l. εὐαπόδοτον), Dsc.2.85, Iamb.*VP*3.13. **-κλητος**, ον, *easy to call out*, of the names of dogs, X.*Cyn.*7.5. II. *easy to recall*, πρὸς τὸ κοινὸν συμφέρον Plu.*Cim.*17; εὐ. ἑαυτὸν παρέχειν Id.*TG*2. Adv. εὐανακλήτως, διακεῖσθαι πρός τινα M.Ant.1.7. 2. *easily cured*, Aret.*SD*1.7. ⊛ **-κόμιστος**, ον, *easy to bring back*, Plu.2.458e; *easily restored*, of health, Gal.6.297. **-ληπτος**, ον, *easy to recover*, Str.1.2.16; *easily reparable*, Hp.*Epid.*6.4.7; *easily, comfortably suspended*, of fractured limbs in a sling, Id.*Fract.*47 (Sup.). Adv. -τως Id.*Off.*9. II. Act., *easily taking in, of good capacity for*, ἀρετῆς Stob.2.7.11$^{m}$. **-λῠτος**, ον, *easily analysed*, Simp.*in Cat.*217.18. Adv. -τως ib.212.16. **-λωτος**, ον, dub. l. in Antyll.ap.Orib.10.2.2 (εὐανάδοτος Daremb.). **-μνηστος**, ον, *easily remembering*, Hierocl.*in CA*8 p.432 M. **-πειστος**, *credulus*, *Gloss.* **-πνευστος**, ον, *easy to repeat in a breath*, ἡ ἐν κώλοις λέξις Arist.*Rh.*1409$^{b}$14. **-σειστος**, ον, *easily excited*, πρὸς τοῦ πάθους Phld.*Ir.*p.38 W.

**Εὐάνασσα**, ἡ, epith. of Demeter, Hsch.

**εὐανά-στροφος**, ον, *ready to turn back, cautious*, Ptol.*Tetr.*159. **-σφαλτος**, ον, *quickly recovering*, Hp.*Alim.*28; ὕπνοι *from which one wakes easily*, Ruf.(?)ap.Orib.*inc.*4.55. **-τμητος**, ον, *easy to dissect*, Gal.2.454. **-τρεπτος**, ον, *easy to upset*, *actiones* Cic.*Att.*2.14.1, cf. Heph.Astr.*Praef.*; *easily refuted*, Iamb.*Protr.*21.κʹ. 2. Medic., '*shaky*', Gal.18(1).605; but τὸ τῆς σαρκὸς εὐ. *mobility*, Id.*UP*1.7. **-τροφος**, ον, *well-fed*, Sch.Lyc.307.

**εὐανδρ-έω**, *abound in men*, Aristeas 108, Str.1.2.40, Ph.1.641; εὐ. πολλῇ ἡλικίᾳ Plu.*Cat.Ma.*26:—Med., Scymn.252, Ocell.4.4. II. *to be in full vigour*, πλήρωμα, φάλαγξ εὐ., Plu.*Cam.*8, App.*Syr.*37. **-ία**, ἡ, *abundance of men*, esp. *of good men and true*, οὐδὲ εὐ. ἐν ἄλλῃ πόλει ὁμοία X.*Mem* 3.3.12, cf. D.H.1.16, Str.16.2.13, Plu. *Per.*19. II. *physical fitness*, as a subject of a contest, Din.*Fr.*16.2, *IG*2$^{2}$.956.48, al.; εὐανδρίᾳ νικᾶν And.4.42: so in pl., ἐν ταῖς εὐανδρίαις Ath.13.565f; πληρωμάτων εὐανδρίαις *by the crews being able-bodied men*, Plu.*Pomp.*24. 2. *manliness*, E.*El.*367; ἡ δ' εὐανδρία διδακτός Id.*Supp.*913; παρασκευάζειν πρὸς εὐανδρίαν to train to *manly spirit*, Antig.Rexap.D.L.7.7. **-ος**, ον, (ἀνήρ) *abounding in good men and true*, Σπάρτα Tyrt.15.1; χώρα, γᾶ, Pi.*P.*1.40, E.*Tr.*229 (lyr.), Ar.*Nu.*300 (lyr.), etc.; εὐανδροτάτη πόλις Plu.2.209e. II. *prosperous to men*, συμφοραί A.*Eu.*1031.

**εὐάνεμος** [ᾱ], Dor. for εὐήνεμος.

**εὐάνετος**, ον, (ἀνίημι) *easy to dissolve*, Dsc.5.124.

**εὐάνθ-εμον**, τό, *a plant like camomile*, Hp.*Mul.*1.78 (v.l. βοάνθεμον). **-εμος**, ον, *flowery, blooming*, φυά Pi.*O.*1.67; ἥβη *AP*7.602 (Agath.); ἶρις ib.4.1.9 (Mel.). **-έω**, *to be flowery* or *blooming*, Luc. *VH*2.6 (dub.): metaph., *to be overgrown, hypertrophied*, Hp.*Nat.Mul.*8 (ἐκθέωσι Littré fr. Erot.), v.l. in *Mul.*2.135; but later, *to be flourishing, prosperous*, *BGU*1080.24 (iii A.D.). ⊛ **-ής**, ές, *blooming, downy*, πυκάσαι τε γένυς εὐανθέϊ λάχνῃ Od.11.320. II. *rich in flowers, flowery*, ἀγροί Thgn.1200; κόλποι λειμώνων Ar.*Ra.*373 (lyr.); τόπος Pl.*Smp.*196b; *decked with flowers*, στόλος Pi.*P.*2.62, cf. Sapph.78; *freely flowering*, Thphr.*HP*6.2.3. 2. *flowered, gay-coloured, gay, bright*, χρῶμα Pl.*Phd.*110c, cf. Arist.*Col.*792$^{a}$15, 794$^{b}$5 (Comp.); θρόμβοι αἵματος Hp.*Coac.*621, cf. 575; στρωμναί Ph.1.639 (Sup.); ἐσθής Luc.*Rh.Pr.*15; βαφαί Ael.*NA*16.41; πορφύρη *AP*6.250 (Antiphil.); λίθος Jul.*Or.*2.51a; τὸ εὐ. τοῦ ὄρνιθος its *bright colours*, Ath. 9.399a; *pink, flushed*, σῶμα Sor.1.100. III. metaph., *blooming, fresh, goodly*, ὄλβος Pi.*I.*5(4).12; of persons, ἁλικία ib.7(6).34, cf. *O.*6.84, Ar.*Nu.*1002; εὐ. ὀργά a *goodly, noble* temper, Pi.*P.*1.89: ἐν ἅλμῃ.. εὐανθεστέρᾳ in *fresher* brine, Sotad.Com.1.21: Sup. -εστάτη ἡλικία Plu.2.120a.

⊛ **εὐάνιος** [ᾰ], ον, (ἀνία) *taking trouble easily*, Hsch. (also glossed by πειθήνιος, i.e. εὐάνιος [ᾱ], Dor. for εὐήνιος).

**εὐᾱνορία**, ἡ, Dor. for εὐηνορία.

**εὐαντ-έω**, *meet graciously*, c. dat., Call.*Dian.*268. **-ης** (or -ής), ες, = sq., opp. δυσάντης, A.R.4.148. ⊛ **-ητος**, ον, (ἀντάω) *accessible, gracious*, θεός *BMus.Inscr.*1012 (Chalcedon, i B.C.); Μήτηρ θεῶν *IG* 3.134, *Bull.Soc.Arch.*4.188 (ii B.C.). II. *acceptable*, ἄγρη Opp.*C.*2.488, cf. *H.*2.149.

**εὐαντόλως**, *correpte*, *Gloss.* (dub. l.).

**εὐάντυξ**, ὔγος, ὁ, ἡ, of a chariot, *with beautiful rail*, Suid., Phot. (but cf. εὐάξων).

**εὐάνωρ** [ᾱ], ορος, ὁ, ἡ, Dor. for εὐήνωρ. **εὐαξής**, v. εὐαυξής.

**εὐάξιος**, ον, *valuable, considerable*, *PFlor.*37.7 (v/vi A.D.).

**εὐάξων**, *with beautiful axles*, gloss on εὐάντυξ, Suid., Phot.

**εὐαπάλλακτος**, ον, *easy to get rid of*, ἵππος (i.e. *finding a ready sale*) X.*Eq.*3.1; -ότερον πάθος Arist.*Pr.*883$^{a}$18, cf. Ruf.ap.Orib.6.38.19, Max.Tyr.13.3. Adv. -τως, ἔχειν to be *easy to evacuate*, of a position, Aen.Tact.16.18.

**εὐαπαντ-ησία**, ἡ, *affability*, Chrysipp.*Stoic.*3.60 (pl.). **-ητος**, ον, *affable, courteous*, τινι *IG*4.1.26 (Aegina, ii B.C.); φιλανθρωπίᾳ Lxx 2*Ma.*14.9.

**εὐαπάρτιστος**, ον, *well-finished, perfect*, Sch.E.*Hipp.*362.

**εὐᾰπάτητος** [πᾱ], ον, *easy to cheat*, Pl.*Phdr.*262b (Comp.); οἱ ἀγαθοὶ εὐ. Bias ap.Stob.3.37.36, cf. Arist.*Insomn.*460$^{b}$9, al. II. Act., *cheating readily*, τὸ θῆλυ -ότερον Id.*HA*608$^{b}$12.

**εὐαπήγητος**, ον, Ion. for εὐαφήγητος.

**εὐαπό-βᾰτος**, ον, *easy to disembark on*, νῆσος -ωτέρα Th.4.30. **-βλητος**, ον, *easily lost*, Alex.Aphr.*Quaest.*122.8, Simp.*in Epict.* p.52 D., *in Ph.*274.29. **-δεικτος**, ον, *easily demonstrated*, Ph.*Bel.*62.27. **-δεκτος**, ον, *acceptable*, Ptol.*Tetr.*44, Sch.Il.2.235. **-δοτος**, ον, *easy of digestion*, f.l. for εὐανάδοτος (q.v.). 2. *easy of solution* or *explanation*, πράγματα Str.2.4.5, cf. S.E.*M.*8.85. **-κρῐτικός**, ή, όν, *ready at answering questions*, Chrysipp.*Stoic.*2.42. **-κρῐτος**, ον, *easy to expound by answers*, Sor.1.1 (s.v.l.). II. Act., in Adv. -τως, ἔχειν πρός τινας to have *an easy answer*.., Artem.4.63. **-κύλιστος** [ῠ], ον, *easy to roll off*, Gal.*UP*7.15, 10.6. **-λόγητος**, ον, *easy to excuse*, Str.10.3.1, Plu.*Agis* 17, Hierocl.*in CA*19 p.461 M. **-λῠτος**, ον, *easy to be separated from*, ὀστέων Hp.*Mochl.*1; ἀπό τινος Id.*Art.*14: abs., Arist.*HA*530$^{a}$6; *easily uprooted*, Thphr.*HP*1.3.1. II. *easily solved*, of a question, Phld.*Sign.*11, Demetr.Lac.1055.23 F., A.D.*Pron.*30.13. **-νιπτος**, ον, *easy to wash off*, Sch.D.T.p.204 H. **-πνοος**, ον, *easily evaporating*, Thphr.*Od.*42. **-πτωτος**, ον, *easily falling off*, Id.*CP*2.9.3. **-ρρῠτος**, ον, *easily flowing away*, Hp.*Fract.*28; *too fluid*, Gal.12.389. II. *easily slipping off*, of bandages, Id.18(2).765. **-σβεστος**, ον, *easy to extinguish*, Artem.1.74. **-σείστως**, Adv. *so as to be easily shaken off*: hence, *insecurely*, καταλαμβάνειν Chrysipp.*Stoic.*2.90. **-σπαστος**, ον, *easy to be torn from*, ἀλλήλων [τὰ ᾠά] Arist.*HA*550$^{a}$12. **-τείχιστος**, ον, *easy to wall off, blockade*, Th.6.75, X.*HG*2.4.31. **-φυκτος**, ον, *easily escaping, slippery*, τὸ ἐν τοῖς λόγοις εὐ. Sch.Ar.*Ra.*848.

**εὐαρδής**, ές, *well-watered*, γῆ Agath.5.12.

**εὔαρ**, etym. of ἔαρ, coined by Hellad.ap.Phot.*Bibl.*p.535 B.

**εὐάρεσκος**, v. sub εὐάρεστος.

**εὐαρεστ-έω**, *to be well pleasing*, τῷ Κοινῷ τῶν Δελφῶν *SIG*611.19 (ii B.C.), cf. Lxx *Ge.*5.22, al., D.S.14.4: abs., Ph.1.102; εὐαρέστησεν *it seemed good, it was resolved*, *IG*14.757.8 (Naples, i A.D.):—Pass., *to be well pleased, satisfied*, τινι *with* a thing, Ph.*Bel.*55.23; τῇ νήσῳ, τῇ ἡγεμονίᾳ, D.S.3.55, 20.79; θυσίαις *Ep.Hebr.*13.16. 2. Medic., in Pass., *to be benefited, get relief*, of patients, Herod.Med. in *Rh.Mus.*58.72,79. II. intr., = Pass., Lysipp.7, Apollon.Perg.*Con.*1 *Praef.*, D.H.11.60, Hierocl.*in CA*11 p.442 M. **-ημα**, ατος, τό, *individual taste, preference*, Herod.Med.ap. Orib.5.27.6. **-ήριος**, ον, *propitiatory*, θυσίαι v.l. for ἀρεστ-, D.H.1.67. **-ησις**, εως, ἡ, *being well pleased*, πρὸς τὴν κοινὴν εὐ. *to please* the public, D.H.10.57, cf. Hierocl.p.52 A.; ἢ διὰ φόβον ἢ δι' εὐ. from fear or *favour*, J.*AJ*12.6.2: pl., Ph.1.290. II. *satisfaction*, Aq., Sm., Thd.*Ex.*29.18. III. Medic., *relief, benefit*, Herod.Med. in *Rh.Mus.*58.71, Sor.1.32, Philum.ap.Orib.8.45.7. **-ητέον**, *one must be content with*, τοῖς ἐν τῷ κόσμῳ πραττομένοις Ph.2.413. **-ία**, ἡ, = εὐαρέστησις, Hierocl.*in CA*11 p.442 M.: in pl., *individual tastes, predilections*, Phld.*Rh.*1.152 S. **-ικός**, ή, όν, *easily contented*, διάθεσις εὐ. πρὸς πᾶν τὸ συμβαῖνον M.Ant.9.6. **-ος**, ον, (ἀρέσκω) *well-pleasing, acceptable*, Cleanth.3.6; τινι Lxx *Wi.*4.10, Ph.2.69, 2*Ep.Cor.*5.9, etc.; τισι *Ath.Mitt.*15.134 (Nisyrus); παρά τινι Lxx *Wi.*9.10; ἐν τοῖς ἀναλώμασι *Inscr.Prien.*114.15 (i B.C.): abs., ἀποδημία εὐ. Ph.2.77; θέλημα τοῦ θεοῦ *Ep.Rom.*12.2; χρῆσις *pleasant*, Herod.Med.ap.Orib.5.27.20; σύμμαχοι prob. in *PHib.*1.15.26 (Comp., iii B.C.); τὸ εὐ. Ph.1.585. Adv. -τως, ἔργον συνετέλεσεν *IG*12(8).640.10 (Peparethus, ii B.C.): Comp. -οτέρως, διακεῖσθαί τινι X.*Mem.*3.5.5 (εὐαρεσκοτέρως codd.); -τως ἱερησάμενος *SIG*708.20 (Istropolis, ii B.C.), cf *IPE*1$^{2}$.94 (Olbia); λατρεύειν τῷ θεῷ *Ep.Hebr.*12.28. II. *choice*, οἶνος, πυρός, *PStrassb.*1.9 (vi A.D.), *PFlor.*30.30 (iv A.D.). III. *according to taste*, λαχανόσπερμον λαμβάνειν εὐ. *PFay.*90.17 (iii A.D.).

**εὐάρητος** ὄνειρος· εὔτακτος, Hsch.

**εὐᾰρίθμητος**, ον, *easy to count*, i.e. *few in number*, Hp.*Acut.*3, Pl. *Ap.*40d, *Smp.*179c; τὸ πλῆθος οὐκ εὐ. ἦν J.*AJ*2.15.1; ὀλίγα καὶ εὐ. Jul.*Or.*3.102c.

**εὐαρίστως**, Adv., later spelling of εὐαρέστως, *IPE*1$^{2}$.107 (Olbia).

**εὔαρκτος**, ον, (ἄρχω) *easy to govern, manageable*, of a horse's mouth, A.*Pers.*193.

**εὐάρμᾰτος**, ον, (ἅρμα) *with beauteous car*, Θήβα S.*Ant.*845 (lyr.). 2. *victorious in the chariot-race*, Pi.*P.*2.5, *I.*2.17.

**εὐαρμοστ-έω**, *to be well tempered* or *composed*, Hp.*Praec.*9; *to be of convenient size*, Ph.*Bel.*53.29; *suit, agree with*, c. dat., Dieuch.ap. Orib.4.7.25. **-ία**, ἡ, *happy adaptation, suitableness*, μὴ μόνοις τοῖς λεγομένοις, ἀλλὰ καὶ ταῖς τούτων εὐ. συμπείθειν Isoc.15.189; εὐ. ψυχῆς πρὸς τὰς ἡδονάς Pl.*Def.*411e, cf. Ph.2.79, etc. II. of men's dispositions and tempers (with metaphor from music), Pl.*R.*400d, *Prt.*326b, etc.; εὐ. τρόπων D.61.19; εὐ. πρὸς ἔντευξιν Pl.*Pomp.*1; of political *concord*, κοινὸν ἀγαθὸν εὐ. τις Ecphant.ap.Stob.4.7.64. **-ος**, ον, (ἁρμόζω) *well-joined, harmonious*, κάλαμοι E.*El.*702 (lyr.); μέλος,

ὄνομα, Pl.*Lg*.655a,*Cra*.405a. **II.** of men, *well-tempered*, Hp.*Epid.* 2.6.1; *accommodating, harmonious*, πρὸς ἅπαντα τὴν ἕξιν τῆς ψυχῆς εὐ. ἔχειν Isoc.12.32; εὐ. ἑαυτὸν ἐν πᾶσι παρέχων Pl.*R*.413e: Comp. and Sup., Id.*Prt*.326b, *R*.412a; τὸ εὐ., = εὐαρμοστία, Ph.1.5. Adv. -τως, ἔχειν πρός τι Isoc.11.12, cf. Ruf.ap.Orib.7.26.135; ἀπηκριβῶσθαι Ph.1.33.

**εὔαρνος**, ον, *rich in sheep*, *AP*6.108 (Myrin.); *in lambs*, ὄϊς ib.7.657.9 (Leon.).

**εὐάροτος** [ᾰ], ον, (ἀρόω) *well-ploughed* or *easy to be ploughed*, A.R.2.810; ὀργάς *AP*6.41 (Agath.); αὖλαξ ib.9.347 (Leon.):—also **-ἀροτρίαστος**, ον, *EM*141.2.

**εὐάρτυτος**, ον, (ἀρτύω) *well-seasoned*, χοιρίον Ath.4.165b; ἅλες Orib.*Fr*.80; ὀσμή Archig.ap.Gal.13.175.

**εὐαρχ-ία**, ἡ, *good government*, *PMasp*.2iii9 (vi A.D.), *EM*390.38; gloss on εὐηγεσία, Sch.Od.19.114. **-ίζω**, in fut. -ιῶ, = ἄρξομαι, Hsch.: also aor. 1 Med. -ίσασθαι· ἀπάρξασθαι, Id. **-ισμός**, ὁ, *good discipline*, Lyd.*Mens*.4.4. **II.** = Lat. *strena*, *Gloss.* **-ος**, ον, *governing well*, Luc.233. **2.** *easily governed*, Arist.*Oec*.1344$^b$14. **II.** *beginning well*, λόγος Luc.*Lex*.1; *making a good beginning*, of one's first customer in the market, *AP*6.304 (Phan., s.v.l.).

**εὐάς**, = Lat. *ovatio*, Plu.*Marc*.22; cf. εὐαστής II.

**εὐάς**, άδος, ἡ, *one who cries* εὐαί, i.e. *a Bacchanal*, κούρη Orph.*H*.49.1: as Subst., Philostr.*Im*.1.19. **2.** as Adj., ὁ, ἡ, *Bacchic*, φωνή Nonn.*D*.19.110. **II.** Εὔας, ὁ, a name of Bacchus, Hsch.

**εὐάσκεται**· εὐωδεῖται, Hsch.

**εὔ-ασμα**, ατος, τό, *a Bacchanalian shout*, in pl., E.*Ba*.129, 151 (both lyr.). **-ασμός**, ὁ, *the cry of* εὐαί, Hermesian.7.18, Str.4.4.6, Plu.*Marc*.22, *Ant*.75 (pl.).

**εὐάστ-ειρα**, ἡ, fem. of εὐαστήρ, Orph.*H*.51.8, 69.1. **-ερος**, ον, (ἀστήρ) *rich in stars*, Arat.237. **II.** *fair star*, of the moon, Orph.*H*.9.3.

**εὐαστήρ**, ῆρος, ὁ, = sq., Orph.*H*.30.1, Epic.*in Arch.Pap*.7.4; Βάκχος *AP*9.246 (Marc.Arg.). **-ής**, οῦ, or parox. **εὐάστης**, ου, ὁ, (εὐάζω) *one who cries* εὐαί, *a Bacchanal*, Orph.*H*.54.5, *APl*.1.15, etc. **2.** εὐ. θεός, = Βάκχος, *Ath.Mitt*.27.94 (Pergam., ii B.C.). **II.** ὁ εὐ. θρίαμβος, = Lat. *ovatio*, D.H.5.47 (nisi leg. οὐαστής). **-ικός**, ή, όν, *Bacchanalian*, ἐπίρρημα, ἀναφώνημα, A.D.*Adv*.121.21, Hsch. s.v. εὔασμα.

**εὐάτριος** [ᾱ], ον, Dor. for εὐήτριος.

**εὐαυγής**, ές, *bright, shining*, v.l. in Pi.*Pae.Fr*.19.25, v.l. in *Pae.Erythr*.15, al.: Sup. -έστατος v.l. in Arist.*Mu*.397$^a$16; cf. εὐαγής.

**εὐαυγία**, ἡ, *illumination*, Iamb.*Protr*.21.κδ'; cf. εὐάγεια.

**εὐαυξής**, ές, *easily elongated, elastic*, Arist.*HA*493$^a$30; *increased in growth*, in Comp. -έστερος Id.*PA*673$^b$34; *quick-growing*, Thphr.*CP* 1.8.4: Comp., *Gp*.10.57.9 (v.l. -όтερον); *tall*, Suid. s.v. βλωθρή: Sup., Gal.*UP*11.14. (εὐαξ- Suid., Hsch. s.v. εὐαλδῆ, v.l. in Arist. *PA* l.c., Thphr. l.c. (codd. Urb., Med.), *Gp*.l.c., εὐαυξ- v.l. ib.10.13.3: prob. εὐάξ- from εὐαυξ-, cf. εὐαγής.)

**εὐαφαίρετος**, ον, *easy to disperse*, Thphr.*Od*.42.

**εὐάφεια** [ᾰφ], ἡ, *softness to the touch*, Heraclid.Cum.5; -είας χάριν Heliod.ap.Orib.49.8.3, cf. Antyll.ib.45.2.1, Gal.12.844.

**εὐαφήγητος**, Ion. **εὐαπ-**, ον, *easy to describe*, Hdt.7.63, D.C.42.26.

**εὐαφήδισεν**· ἄφρων τις ἐν αὐταῖς ἰσχυρόν, Hsch.

**εὐαφής**, ές, (ἁφή) *soft*, of seeds ready to germinate, Thphr.*CP*2.17.10; σπλήν Aret.*SD*1.14; of tumours, = εὐείκτος, Paul.Aeg.6.3: metaph., *susceptible*, νοῦς Plu.2.588e. Adv. Sup. -εστάτως, σκευαζομένη ἔμπλαστρος Aët.16.47. **II.** Act., *having a gentle, delicate touch*, ἀνήρ Aret.*CA*2.9; τὸ εὐαφὲς τῶν δακτύλων Luc.*Im*.14; σπόγγοι Paul.Aeg.4.21: Sup. τὸ -έστατον Ph.*Fr*.14 H.: metaph., εὐ. μετάβασις an *easy, unforced* transition, Luc.*Hist.Conscr*.55. Adv. -ῶς, Ion. -έως, *gently*, Id.*Harm*.1, Aret.*CA*1.6: metaph., δεικνύναι point out *gently*, M.Ant.11.18.4.

**εὐάφίη**, ἡ, Ion. for εὐάφεια, *AP*5.34 (Rufin.), 293.16 (Agath.).

**εὐάφιον**, τό, *mild ointment*, Asclep.ap.Gal.13.314.

**εὐαφόρμως**, Adv. *opportunely*, Sch.S.*OC*111, Ulp.ad D.21.143, 19.188.

**εὐαφρόδιτος**, prob. f.l. for ἐπαφρ-, *Cat.Cod.Astr*.7.221.

**εὐαχής, εὐάχητος**, Dor. for εὐηχ-.

**εὐβαλκής**, ές, dub. sens., of a form of ἀγών, *IG*5(1).267, al. (Sparta). (Perh. for εὐϝαλκής (ἀλκή) with secondary ϝ.)

**εὐβάστακτος**, ον, *easy to carry* or *move*, μηχανή Hdt.2.125, cf. Arist.*Rh*.1373$^a$32, *Pol*.1257$^a$34; ἐλαφροὶ καὶ εὐ. Corn.*ND*30; τοῖς ὠταρίοις by the ears (handles), Demoph.*Sim*.3. **II.** *well-supported*, Hp.*Fract*.30 (dub. sens.).

**εὔβᾰτος**, ον, (βαίνω) *accessible, passable*, οὐ γὰρ εὔ. περᾶν A.*Pr*.718; ποιεῖν τι εὔ. τινί Pl.*Lg*.761a: Comp. -ώτερος X.*HG*4.6.9. **II.** of dwarf fig-trees, in Comp., *more accessible* or *manageable*, Thphr.*HP* 2.6.12.

**εὐβαφής**, ές, *well steeped* or *dyed*, Herm.ap.Stob.1.49.44 (dub. l.); *vivid*, of the colours of plants, Sabin.ap.Orib.9.17.2. **II.** Adv. -βαφῶς prob. f.l. for εὐαφῶς in Herod.Med. in *Rh.Mus*.58.72:—so εὐβαφία, ἡ, f.l. for εὐάφεια, ib.87; εὐβαφῶν (σπόγγων) f.l. for εὐαφῶν, Paul.Aeg.4.21.

**εὔβιος**, ον, = sq. I, Arist.*HA*620$^a$21 (Sup.). **II.** = sq. II, *Supp.Epigr*.2.530.1 (Puteoli, ii/iii A.D.).

**εὐβίοτος** [ῐ], ον, *easily finding their food*, of certain animals, Arist.*HA*609$^b$19, 615$^a$18. **II.** *leading an honest life, respectable*, D.C.52.39, prob. in Antioch.Astr. in *Cat.Cod.Astr*.1.110: written -βίωτος in *IG*5(2).491 (Megalopolis, ii/iii A.D.).

**εὔβλαπτος**, ον, *easily hurt*, Arist.*GA*719$^a$34, *Gp*.9.9.10.

**εὐβλαστ-έω**, *grow vigorously*, Thphr.*CP*1.20.5; *germinate well*, of seeds, ib.4.7.2, cf. 4.3.3; *strike readily*, of cuttings, ib.3.7.11. **-ής**, ές, *growing vigorously*, ib.1.8.1. **II.** Act., *making to grow luxuriantly*, ib.2.3.3. **-ία**, ἡ, *vigorous growth*, ib.1.20.5, al. (Sts. written -βλάστεια.) **-ος**, ον, = εὐβλαστής I, Ph.2.56, al.

**εὐβλέφᾰρος**, ον, *with beautiful eyelids*, Δίκη *AP*14.122.

**εὔβλητος**, ον, *easily hit, exposed to blows*, App.*BC*2.79; τοῖς πολεμίοις Id.*Syr*.35.

**εὐβοήθητος**, ον, *easily assisted* or *defended*, χώρα Arist.*Pol*.1327$^a$3, cf. 21. **2.** of diseases, *easily cured*, Hp.*Acut.*(*Sp.*)8 (Comp.), Arist.*Pr*.862$^b$6.

**εὐβόητος**, ον, = εὔφημος, Hsch. s.v. ἐν εὐφήμῳ.

**Εὔβοια**, gen. ας, Ion. ης, ἡ, *Euboea*, Il.2.535, etc.: **Εὐβοίηθεν**, poet. -θε, *from Euboea*, Call.*Del*.197: **Εὐβοεύς** (not Εὐβοιεύς *EM*389.10, and so gen. pl. Εὐβοέων *SIG*419.4 (Delphi, iii B.C.), al., but Εὐβοιέων ib.417.4 (ibid., iii B.C.), al., where οι may be short as in βοιηθέω), έως, ὁ, acc. Εὐβοᾶ, pl. -οᾶς (in codd. often -οέας, cf. Th.4.92) A.D. *Pron*.99.22:—*a Euboean*, Hdt.8.4, etc.:—Adj. **Εὐβοϊκός**, ή, όν, *Euboean*, Id.3.89 (v.l. -εικός), etc. (perh. trisyll. in A.*Fr*.356, E.*Hel*.767); -βοϊκή, ἡ, = ἀκτῆ, Ps.-Dsc.4.173; -κόν, τό, *sweet chestnut*, Thphr.*HP*1.11.3, 4.5.4: masc. **Εὐβοΐτης**, ου, ὁ, Str.10.1.14: fem. **Εὐβοΐς**, gen. Εὐβοΐδος, Hdt.3.89, D.S.12.11; Εὐβοΐς, ἡ, = Εὐβοϊκόν, D.Chr.7.74; contr. forms Εὐβοΐδα, etc., S.*Tr*.74, E.*Heracl*.83 (lyr.), *El*.442 (lyr.), A.*Fr*.30, Ion Trag.18; lengthd. **Εὐβοιΐς** S.*Tr*.237, 401, *Fr*.255.

**εὐβολ-έω**, *make a good throw* with the dice, Luc.*Am*.16. **-ος**, ον, *throwing luckily* (with the dice), Μίδας ἐν κύβοισιν εὐβολώτατος Eub.58, cf. Poll.9.94, Suid. s.v. Μίδας: generally, *lucky*, ἄγρη Opp.*H*.3.71, Hld.5.18. Adv., ἦν γὰρ -λως ἔχων he was *in luck*, cj. Pors. for εὐβούλως, A.*Ch*.696: Comp., πεσσοὶ -ώτερον πίπτοντες Aristaenet.1.23.

**εὐβοσία**, ἡ, *good pasture*, ἡ χώρα ἔχει πολλὴν εὐ. Arist.*HA*522$^b$22, cf. 575$^b$32; *good culture*, Thphr.*HP*1.11.4. **2.** *good living*, Arist.*GA*726$^a$6. **3.** *good condition*, τοῦ σώματος ib.774$^b$25. **4.** *abundance, plenty*, ἐν εὐ. ὑπάρχειν *Inscr.Prien*.108.48 (ii B.C.); ἄφθονον -βοσίαν γενέσθαι St.Byz. s.v. Ἀζανοί; ἵνα ὁ δῆμος ἐν εὐβοσίᾳ διαγένηται *Supp.Epigr*.1.366.49 (Samos, iii B.C.); ἐξ ἁλός *AP*11.199 (Leon.). **II.** divinity worshipped in Asia Minor, *Zeitschr.f.Numism*.7.223 (coin of Hierapolis); Σεβαστὴ Εὐ., of a deified Empress, *IGRom*.4.654 (Acmonia): also spelt Εὐποσία (q.v.):—hence **Εὐβοσιάρχης**, ου, ὁ, official title (like Εὐθηνιάρχης), *Papers of Amer. School* 3 No.317; cf. Εὐποσιάρχης.

**εὐβόστρῠχος**, ον, *of beautiful locks*, αἴγλη *AP*5.250 (Iren.), cf. Poll.2.27.

**εὐβοτ-έομαι**, *furnish good pasture*, Str.11.3.2. **-ος**, ον, (βόσκω) *abounding in pasture*, Od.15.406 (or, *with fine oxen*, cf. βοτόν (Addenda)); τοῖς ζῴοις πᾶσιν εὔβοτον Pl.*Criti*.111a, cf. Ph.1.669, Plu.*Cam*.16: Sup., Scymn.607, prob. in E.*Fr*.1083.6. **II.** *well-fed, thriving*, ἀμνός Theoc.5.24.

**εὔβοτρυς**, υ, gen. υος, *rich in grapes*, S.*Ph*.548, *AP*9.668.9 (Marian.): **εὐβότρυος**, ον, f.l. in *Anacreont*.4.17.

**εὐβουλ-εύς**, έως, ὁ, like εὔβουλος, *he of good counsel*, epith. of Zeus, D.S.5.72; of Dionysus, Orph.*H*.30.6: acc. εὐβουλῆ Plu.2.714c: Εὐ. alone, = Πλούτων, Nic.*Al*.14, Orph.*Fr*.237, Hsch. **-ία**, ἡ, *good counsel, soundness of judgement, prudence*, A.*Pr*.1035, 1038, S.*Ant*.1050, Th.1.78, Isoc.9.46, Arist.*EN*1142$^b$6, etc.; περί τινος Pl.*Prt*.318e: pl., αἱ τῶν προγόνων εὐ. Aeschin.2.75. **II.** Pythag. name for *three*, *Theol.Ar*.14. **-ος**, ον, *well-advised, prudent*, Thgn.329, Hdt.8.110, Pi.*O*.13.8, B.14.37, Th.1.84, Pl.*R*.428b, Arist.*EN*1141$^b$13: Comp., *Ar.Pax*689: Sup., And.1.140. Adv. -λως (v. εὔβολος): Comp. -ότερον D.C.43.16: Sup. -ότατα *Gp*.5.16.1.

**εὐβρᾰχής**, or **-βρεχής**, ές, *well steeped* or *soaked*, Nic.*Al*.298.

**εὐβρῑθής**, ές, *laden with fine* yarn, σπάθαι *AP*6.288.7 (Leon.).

**εὔβροχος**, ον, *well-noosed, well-knit*, ἅμμα *AP*6.179 (Arch.).

**εὔβρωτος**, ον, *good to eat*, Str.17.1.51; πρὸς ξηροφαγίαν Ath.3.113b.

**εὐβύριος**, ον, = εὔοικος, Euph.128; said to be from a Messapian word, *EM*389.24.

**εὔβυρσος**, ον, *with beautiful hide* or *skin*, Sch.A.R.3.1299.

**εὔβωλος**, ον, (βῶλον) *fertile* (v. sub εὔπωλος).

**εὐβωλοστρόφητος**, ον, *easy to plough*, Eust.385.36, 1431.53.

**εὐγᾱθής, εὐγάθητος**, Dor. for. εὐγηθ-.

**εὔγαιος**, ον, freq. v.l. for εὔγειος.

**εὐγάλακτος** [γᾰ], ον, *yielding much* or *good milk*, αἴξ Alciphr.3.21; τροφός Orib.*Eup*.1.1 (Sup.); νομή Gal.19.121: heterocl. nom. pl. εὐγάλακτες, = εὔτροφοι, Hsch. **II.** εὐγάλακτον, τό, a plant, = γλαύξ, Plin.*HN*27.82.

**εὐγάληνος** [ᾰ], ον, *very calm*, Lyc.20. Adv. -νως Sch.A.R.4.1776.

**εὐγᾰμ-έω**, *marry happily*, Heph.Astr.1.1. **-ία**, ἡ, *happy marriage*, ib.1.20, Paul.Al.*M*.3, Poll.9.160. **-ος**, ον, *happily married*, of persons, Heph.Astr.1.1, Paul.Al.*N*.4, Nonn.*D*.1.27; also εὐνή, ὕδωρ, Id.13.352, 20.144.

**εὖγε** or **εὖ γε**, Adv. *well, rightly*, in replies confirming or approving what has been said: as σοὶ γὰρ χαρίζομαι. Answ. εὖγε σὺ ποιῶν Pl.*R*.351c; εὖγ', εὖγε ποιήσαντες Ar.*Pax*285; εὖγε, εὖγε, ὦ κύνες, ἕπεσθε X.*Cyn*.6.19; εὖ γοῦν θέγοις ἂν χερνίβων E.*Or*.1602; εὖγε μέντἂν διετέθην Ar.*Av*.1692. **2.** without a Verb, *good! well said! well done!* Pl.*Grg*.494c, al.; doubled εὖγ', εὖγε Ar.*Eq*.470; εὖγ',

εὖγε, νὴ Δί', εὖγε Id.*Ec.*213; εὖγ', ὅτι ἐπείσθης Id.*Nu.*866: c. gen., εὖγε τῆς προαιρέσεως Luc.*Vit.Auct.*8.

**εὔγειος,** *ον,* (γῆ) *of* or *with good soil,* Thphr.*HP*4.11.1, D.S.5.40, Dsc.1.64; εὔγειος (sc. γῆ or χώρα), ἡ, *fertile land,* Thphr.*CP*5.13.2 (pl.), *Gp.*2.21.1; cf. εὔγεως. **II.** metaph., ψυχή Ph.1.651.

⊛ **εὐγένεια,** poet. **εὐγενία** (q.v.), ἡ, *nobility of birth,* A.*Pers.*442, E.*Fr.*53, al., Isoc.3.42, Arist.*Rh.*1390$^{b}$16, etc.; ἐμῶν εὐ. παίδων, = ἐμοὶ εὐγενεῖς παῖδες, E.*Tr.*583 (lyr.): pl., Pl.*Euthd.*279b, *R.*618d; *pure breeding,* of animals, Onos.1.21. **2.** = γενναιότης, *nobleness* of mind, Plu.*Dem.*24, *Ant.*86, Ael.*VH*12.1, D.Chr.52.16, etc. **3.** bodily *excellence,* ἡ ἐν τοῖς σώμασιν εὐ. Plu.*Rom.*6, cf. Gal.*UP*10.6; of materials, χαλκοῦ Philostr.*VA*3.54: generally, *excellence,* Lib.*Or.*49.27. **4.** of style, *elevation, nobility,* Longin.34.2; ποιημάτων D.H.*Comp.*18. **5.** as a title, ἡ εὐ. σου *PGen.*1.50.14 (iv A.D.).

⊛ **εὐγένειος,** Ep. **ἠϋγέν-,** *ον,* (γένειον) of a lion, *well-maned,* λέων.. ἠϋγένειος Od.4.456; λίς Il.15.275; of Pan, *well-bearded, h.Hom.*19.39; of men, Pl.*Euthphr.*2b, Luc.*Icar.*10.

**εὐγεν-έτης,** *ου,* Dor. **-τας,** ὁ, = sq., used by E. in lyr., *Ion* 1060, al., cf. Tim.*Pers.*219, *AP*12.195 (Strat.):—fem. **-έτειρα,** ib.9.788, *IG*14.192 (Syracuse); also **-έτις,** prob. in *IG*5(1).259 (Sparta). ⊛ **-ής,** *ές,* in Hom. **εὐηγενής** (q.v.), and in *h.Ven.*94 **ἠϋγενής**: (γένος):—*well-born,* A.*Pers.*704 (troch.), S.*OC*728, etc.; εὐ. δόμος E.*Ion* 1540; τὸ μὲν ἐστίχθαι εὐγενὲς κέκριται being tattooed is esteemed *a mark of nobility,* Hdt.5.6. **2.** in Trag. etc. with the connotation *noble-minded, generous* (more prop. γενναῖος, cf. Arist.*Rh.*1390$^{b}$22), S.*Ant.*38, *Ph.*874, etc.; διαφέρει φύσις γενναίου σκύλακος..νεανίσκου εὐ. Pl.*R.*375a. **3.** of animals, *high-bred,* ἵππος Thgn.184, S.*El.*25; λέων A.*Ag.*1259; ὄρνιθες Plb.1.58.7; of plants, *of a good sort,* Ael.*VH*2.14; ῥόαι Eriph.2.11; πυροί Gal.11.120; βλαστοί *Gp.*5.37.2: so in Comp., Eub.44; φλέβες καὶ ἶνες Thphr.*HP*5.1.7 (s.v.l., cf. εὐτενής); χαλκός S.*Fr.*864 (v.l.): metaph., of a wife, ὥσπερ εὐγενῆ χώραν ἐντεκνώσασθαι παρασχεῖν Plu.*Cat.Mi.*25. **4.** of outward form, *noble,* δέρη, πρόσωπον, E.*Hel.*136, *Med.*1072; of style, τὸ εὐ. τῆς λέξεως Ael.*NA Epil.*; εὐ. ῥυθμοί D.H.*Comp.*18. **II.** Adv. *-νῶς nobly, bravely,* κατθανοῦμεν E.*Cyc.*201, cf. *Tr.*727; εὐτυχεῖν Plu.2.7f. ⊛ **-ία,** ἡ, = εὐγένεια, E.*HF*696 (lyr.), *AP*7.337.6; *eugenia,* a kind of vine, Plin.*HN*14.25. **-ίζω,** *ennoble,* πόλιν Philem.180, cf. Lib.*Eth.*17.4. **-ιος**· εὐγενής, καὶ εἶδος ἀμπέλου, Hsch. **II.** **-ιον,** τό, name of a kind of *laurel, Gp.*11.3.4. **-ίς,** *ίδος,* fem. of εὐγενής, J.*AJ*7.3.3, *CIG*3200 (Smyrna), *Cat.Cod.Astr.*8(4).159; = Lat. *Matrona,* Lyd.*Mens.*3.22, cf. Hdn.Gr.1.95.

**εὐγεφύρωτος** [ῡ], *ον, easy to bridge over,* τόπος Plb.3.66.5.

**εὐγεώργ-ητος,** *ον, easy to cultivate,* Sch.S.*Ant.*569:—also **-ος,** *ον,* Scyl.24.

**εὔγεως,** *ων,* = εὔγειος, Str.7.4.6, Plu.*Sull.*16, Ael.*NA*5.56, App.*BC*4.102 codd.

**εὐγηθ-ής,** Dor. **εὐγᾱθ-,** *ές, joyous, cheerful,* E.*HF*793 (lyr.). **-ητος,** Dor. **εὐγάθ-,** *ον,* = foreg., Id.*IT*212 (lyr.).

**εὐγηρ-έω,** *grow old happily, Stoic.*3.156. **-ία,** ἡ, *green old age,* Arist.*Rh.*1361$^{b}$26, *Stoic.*3.24, Plu.2.111b, *Cat.Cod.Astr.*8(4).167; χλόης Ph.2.163.

**εὔγηρυς,** *υ, sweet-sounding,* ἀοιδά Ar.*Ra.*213 (lyr.), cf. Opp.*H.*5.617.

**εὐγήρως,** *ων, enjoying a green old age,* Arist.*Rh.*1361$^{b}$28, Call.*Ep.*41.6, *Epigr.Gr.*223.2 (Milet.), Ph.1.515, al.: nom. pl. εὔγηροι Hp.*Vict.*1.32, Arist.*HA*615$^{a}$33: neut. εὔγηρα Hp.*Art.*58.

**εὐγλάγ-ετος** [ᾰ], *ον,* = sq., Luc.*Trag.*110. ⊛ **-ής,** *ές,* Nic.*Th.*617; and **εὔγλᾰγος,** *ον,* Lyc.307:—*abounding in milk*: metapl. dat. εὔγλαγι *AP*9.744 (Leon.).

**εὔγληνος,** Ep. also **ἐΰ-,** *ον, bright-eyed,* of wild beasts or fish, Lyc.597, Opp.*C.*3.97, Marc.Sid.59.

**εὔγλυπτος,** *ον, well-carved,* μέταλλον *AP*7.363:—also **εὐγλύφᾰνος** [ῠ], *ον,* Nonn.*D.*34.228; **εὐγλῠφής,** *ές,* κάλαμοι *AP*6.63.4 (Damoch.).

**εὐγλωσσ-ία,** Att. **-ττία,** ἡ, *glibness of tongue, fluency of speech,* E.*Fr.*206.4, Ar.*Eq.*837, Ps.-Ptol.*Centil.*38, Iamb.*Protr.*20. **II.** *sweetness of song,* Ael.*NA*17.23. **-ος,** Att. **-ττος,** *ον,* Cret. **-γλωθος** *GDI*5112 (Phaestos, iii/ii B.C.):—*good of tongue, eloquent,* A.*Supp.*775: τὸ Νεστόρειον εὔ. μέλος E.*Fr.*899.1; *glib of tongue, voluble,* Ar.*Nu.*445 (anap.). **2.** *sweet-sounding,* of the Attic dialect, *AP*9.188, cf. Gal.8.586; τὸ εὔ. *that which is pleasant to the ear,* D.H.*Comp.*1. **3.** = εὔφημος, *GDI* l.c. **II.** Act., *loosing the tongue, making eloquent,* οἶνος *AP*9.403 (Maec.).

**εὐγλωττ-έω,** gloss on εὐστομέω, Thom.Mag.p.160 R. **-ίζω,** *make sweet-voiced,* ὁπόσα -ίζοι τοὺς χαραδριούς Philostr.*VA*6.36.

**ἐϋγλώχῑν,** *ῖνος,* ὁ, ἡ, *keen-pointed,* Opp.*H.*5.439, Q.S.8.406.

**εὖγμα,** *ατος,* τό, (εὔχομαι) *boast, boasting,* κενὰ εὔγματα εἰπών Od.22.249. **II.** in pl., *prayers, wishes,* A.*Pr.*584 (lyr.), *Th.*267, *Ch.*463 (lyr.), S.*Ant.*1185, Ar.*Th.*354 (lyr.), Call.*Lav.Pall.*139.

**εὐγμᾰλέος,** *α, ον, to be prayed for,* prob. in Hsch., Phot.

**εὔγναμπτος,** Ep. **ἐΰγν-,** *ον, well-bent, well-twisted,* κληῖσιν ἐϋγνάμπτοις Od.18.294; χαλινοί Opp.*H.*5.498; περόναι A.R.3.833; ἄγκυρα Orph.*A.*498, etc. **εὐγνάπτοις**· καλῶς κατεσκευασμένοις, Hsch. (v.l. in Od.18.294).

**εὔγνητος,** *ον,* = εὐγενής, Philox.1.

⊛ **εὐγνωμ-ονέω,** *have good sense* or *feeling, show a reasonable* or *conciliatory spirit,* Arist.*Rh.Al.*1420$^{a}$16, Epicur.*Sent.Vat.*62, Plu.*Num.*12, etc.; opp. κακοδαιμονᾶν, Id.*Luc.*4; πρὸς τοὺς ἐχθρούς D.S.13.22. **II.** *reward, repay,* τοὺς ἱερέας Lib.*Decl.*34.26, cf. *PAmh.*2.142.17 (iv A.D.); εὐ. τὴν ἀντίδοσιν *make* a return gift *in token of gratitude,* Him.*Or.*8.7. **-ονία,** ἡ, = sq., *PLond.*2.1000.6 (vi A.D.). ⊛ **-οσύνη,** ἡ, *considerateness, courtesy,* Aeschin.3.170, Procl.*in Prm.*p.551 S.; *a reasonable spirit,* Arist.*MM*1198$^{b}$34, Anon.Hist.Alex.Magn.p.825 J., v.l. in Luc.*JConf.*7. **2.** *prudence,* Plu.*Them.*7, etc. **-ων,** *ον,* gen. *ονος,* (γνώμη) *of good feeling, considerate, reasonable,* And.2.6 (Comp.), X.*Mem.*2.8.6; φιλάνθρωπος καὶ εὐ. ψυχή Aeschin.1.137; τὸ μὲν κρῖναι τοῦ εὐγνώμονος, τὸ δὲ δὴ πράττειν κατὰ τὴν κρίσιν τοῦ ἐπιεικοῦς Arist.*MM*1199$^{a}$2; πολέμιοι -έστεροι Plb.2.57.8; ψεῦδος -έστερον Luc.*VH*1.4: metaph., of a game, εὔ. εἰς τὰς ἄλλας πράξεις *not interfering with* them, Gal.*Parv.Pil.*2; παθεῖν εὐγνώμονα to be *indulgently* treated, D.S.13.23: Sup., ὡς -εστάτων τυγχάνειν D.*Ep.*3.45. **2.** *sensible, prudent,* Aeschin.3.170, etc.; εὐ. ὁ μὴ λυπεόμενος ἐφ' οἷσιν οὐκ ἔχει, ἀλλὰ χαίρων ἐφ' οἷσιν ἔχει Democr.231; τὸ λέγειν πρὸς μὴ παρόντας οὐκ εὔ. φαίνεται Plu.2.420f. **3.** εὔγνωμον τὸ πόνημα is an offering *of gratitude, APl.*4.41 (Agath.). **II.** Adv. *-νως considerately, kindly,* τοῖς πλήθεσι προσφέρεσθαι D.S.19.9, cf. Plu.*Ant.*63; *reasonably, BGU*1011.16 (ii B.C.), Luc.*Tox.*5. **2.** *gratefully,* Plu.*Sull.*10, Ael.*NA*2.8. **3.** *prudently,* χρῆσθαι ἑαυτῷ X.*Ages.*2.25.

**εὔγνωστος,** *ον, well-known, familiar,* E.*Or.*[1394], Lys.17.4, Pl.*Sph.*218e; opp. ἄγνωστος, Epicur.*Nat.*28.5. **2.** *easy to discern,* S.*Aj.*704 (lyr., with v.l. -γνωτος); τὰ εὔ. καὶ εὐμαθῆ X.*Oec.*20.14: Sup., Arr.*Tact.*2.1; εὔγνωστον..πότερος ἡμῶν ἐσθ' ὁ πονηρός D.29.1; ὅτι.. Lys.17.4. Adv. *-τως,* κρίνειν Theo Sm.p.65 H.

**εὔγομφος,** *ον, well-nailed, well-fastened,* πύλαι E.*IT*1286:—also **εὐγόμφωτος,** *ον,* Opp.*H.*1.58.

**εὐγον-έω,** *to be fruitful,* of flocks, Thphr.*CP*1.14.1. **-ία,** ἡ, *fruitfulness,* Pl.*R.*546a, X.*Lac.*1.6, Ph.2.390, etc.; opp. ἀγονία, Iamb.*Comm.Math.*15. **-ος,** *ον, productive,* v.l. in E.*Hec.*581 (Sup.); τὸ εὔγονον *productive power,* J.*BJ*4.8.3 codd. (sed leg. εὔτονον).

**εὐγραμμᾰτία,** ἡ, *calligraphy,* Gal.14.587.

**εὐγράμμᾰτος,** ὁ, *a good writer,* Heph.Astr.1.1.

**εὐγραμμ-ία,** ἡ, *good design,* of figures in tapestry, Callix.2. **-ος,** *ον, well-designed,* γραφαί D.H.*Is.*4; *well-drawn,* Luc.*JTr.*33; *of graceful contour,* εὔ. τῇ συστάσει, of a person, Str.4.5.2; ὀφρύων τὸ εὔ. their *fine lines,* Luc.*Im.*6. Adv. *-γράμμως,* of architecture, Lyd.*Mag.*3.70. **II.** *well-defined,* περίοδοι D.H.*Dem.*40; so τὸ εὔ. Id.*Comp.*23. **III.** masc., *a good writer,* Man.5.245.

**εὐγρᾰφής,** *ές,* (γράφω) *well-painted, AP*6.221 (Leon.). **II.** Act., *writing well,* κάλαμος ib.6.66.6 (Paul. Sil.), cf. 65.10 (Id.).

**εὐγρᾰφία,** poet. **-γρᾰφίη,** ἡ, *skill in painting, Epigr.Gr.*841 (Thrace, ii A.D.).

**εὐγύᾰλος** [ῠ], *ον, well arched* or *rounded,* Tryph.537, Nonn.*D.*13.68 codd. (εὐρυάλῳ Ludwich).

**εὔγυιος,** *ον, with fine limbs, stalwart,* νέοι B.10.10.

⊛ **εὔγῡρος,** *ον, tortuous* (= γυρός, q.v.), πάλη *APl.*3.25 (Phil.).

**εὐγων-ία,** ἡ, *regularity of angles,* prob. cj. in E.*Ion* 1137. **-ιος,** *ον, with regular angles,* X.*Oec.*4.21, Arist.*Pr.*912$^{b}$15; *with perfect angles, four square,* of blocks, *IG*2$^{2}$.1666*A*64, etc.; *right-angled,* Gal.18(2).856.

**εὐδαίδᾰλος,** *ον, beautifully wrought,* νᾶα B.16.88; ναόν Id.*Fr.*11.3.

**εὐδαιμον-έω,** pf. εὐδαιμόνηκα Arist.*Metaph.*1048$^{b}$26: (εὐδαίμων):—*to be prosperous, well off,* Hdt.1.170, Th.8.24, etc.; τι in respect to.., Hdt.2.177, S.*Ant.*506, etc.; οὔτις ἀνδρῶν εἰς ἅπαντ' εὐ. E.*Fr.*45; ἔν τινι Luc.*DMort.*24.3; εὐδαιμονοίης E.*El.*231, *Ph.*1086: dual, εὐδαιμονοῖτον Id.*Med.*1073; parodied by Ar.*Ach.*446, 457. **II.** *to be truly happy,* εὐδαιμονοῦσιν ἄνθρωποι ὀρθοσύνῃ καὶ πολυφροσύνῃ Democr.40, cf. Arist.*Pol.*1339$^{b}$19, Diog.Oen.25, etc. **-ημα,** *ατος,* τό, *piece of good luck,* Luc.*Im.*22, *Stoic.*3.136 (pl.). **-ησις,** *εως,* ἡ, *possession of* εὐδαιμονία, Eustr.*in EN*91.27. **-ία,** Ion. **-ίη,** ἡ, *prosperity, good fortune, opulence, h.Hom.*11.5, Pi.*N.*7.56, Hdt.1.5,32, Hp.*Ep.*11 (v.l.), etc.; χρημάτων προσόδῳ καὶ τῇ ἄλλῃ εὐ. Th.2.97; of countries, Hdt.5.28, 7.220, etc.; μοῖρ' εὐδαιμονίας Pi.*P.*3.84: pl., E.*IA*591 (anap.), Pl.*Phd.*115d. **2.** *true, full happiness,* εὐ. οὐκ ἐν βοσκήμασιν οἰκεῖ οὐδ' ἐν χρυσῷ Democr.171; εὐ. ψυχῆς, opp. κακοδαιμονίη, Id.170, cf. Pl.*Def.*412d, Arist.*EN*1095$^{a}$18, Zeno *Stoic.*1.46, etc. **b.** personified as a divinity, *SIG*985.8 (Philadelphia). **-ίζω,** *call* or *account happy,* εὐδαιμόνιζε παῖδα σήν E.*Tr.*268, cf. X.*Mem.*2.7.7, Arist.*EN*1096$^{a}$2, etc.; τὴν πόλιν Isoc.8.83: c. gen. rei, οὐ..μοίρας εὐδαιμονίσαι πρώτης for his eminent fortune, S.*OC*144, cf. Pl.*R.*516c, al.; αὐτὸν εὐδαιμονιεῖ τῆς περιουσίας D.21.109, cf. 19.67; εὐ. τινὰ ὑπέρ τινος X.*An.*1.7.3 (s.v.l.); ἐπί τινι D.18.260; διά τι Luc.*Nigr.*23:—Pass., διά τι Pl.*R.*465d, al. **-ικός,** *ή, όν, tending* or *conducive to happiness,* Arist.*EN*1176$^{b}$16, *Rh.*1367$^{b}$13; τὰ εὐ. *the constituents thereof,* X.*Mem.*4.2.34; τελετὴ καλή τε καὶ εὐ. Pl.*Phdr.*253c. **2.** of persons, *likely to be happy,* Ar.*Ec.*1134, Arist.*EN*1099$^{b}$3; οἱ εὐ. philosophers *who make happiness the chief good,* D.L.1.17; esp. of Anaxarchus, Clearch.14; so also εὐ. αἵρεσις Gal.*Phil.Hist.*4. Adv. *-κῶς,* πράττειν, διάγειν, Ar.*Pax* 856 (lyr.), X.*HG*3.2.9. **-ισμα,** *ατος,* τό, *that which is thought to be a happiness,* Pl.*Ep.*354c. **II.** *congratulation,* App.*BC*4.16. ⊛ **-ισμός,** ὁ, *thinking* or *calling happy, predication of happiness,* Arist.*Rh.*1367$^{b}$34, *EN*1127$^{b}$18, Plu.*Pel.*34, etc.: pl., ὕμνοι καὶ εὐ. Ph.1.312, al. **-ιστέον,** *one must pronounce happy,* Arist.*EN*1100$^{a}$10. **2.** *-έος, α, ον, to be called happy,* Arr.*An.*1.12.2.

⊛ **εὐδαιμ-οσύνη,** ἡ, = εὐδαιμονία, Archyt.ap.Stob.3.1.112,114, Perict.ib.4.28.19, X.Eph.1.16. ⊛ **-ων,** *ον,* gen. *ονος, blessed with a good genius*: hence, *fortunate,* τάων εὐδαίμων τε καὶ ὄλβιος *happy in respect to* them (the days), Hes.*Op.*826; εὐ. καὶ ὄλβιος Thgn.1013; εὐ. καὶ ὑμνητός Pi.*P.*10.22: freq. in Trag., A.*Pr.*647, *Pers.*768, S.*Ant.*582, etc.: c. gen. rei, *happy in* or *on account of..,* Hes. l.c.; εὐ. τοῦ τρό-

που Pl.*Phd.*58e; ironically, εὐ. εἶ, ὅτι οἴει.. Id.*R.*422e; τὸ εὐδαιμον, = εὐδαιμονία, Th.2.43. Adv. -μονως E.*Or.*601, Ar.*Pl.*802, Arist.*Pol.* 1281$^a$2, etc.: Comp. -έστερον, διάγοντες X.*An.*3.1.43: Sup., πόλις -έστατα διάξει Pl.*Lg.*710b. 2. of outward prosperity, *wealthy*, οἱ εὐδαίμονες αὐτῶν Hdt.1.133, cf. 196, 5.8, Th.1.6, etc.; ἐν πολλοῖς χρήμασιν εὐδαίμονες ὄντες Lys.32.17; οἱ πλούσιοι καὶ εὐ. Pl.*R.*406c; οἰκία μεγάλη τε καὶ εὐ. Id.*Prt.*316b; αἱ Ἀθῆναι μεγάλαι τε καὶ εὐδαίμονες Hdt.8.111; Εὐβοίῃ, νήσῳ μεγάλῃ τε καὶ εὐ. Id.5.31; Κυράνα Pi.*P.*4.276, etc.; πόλις εὐ. Gorg.*Fr.*10 D.; Ἀραβία εὐ. *Peripl.M Rubr.*26; γῆ ἀρόσαι οὐκ εὐ. Philostr.*Im.*2.24; opp. εὐτυχής, ὄλβου δ' ἐπιρρυέντος εὐτυχέστερος ἄλλου γένοιτ' ἂν ἄλλος, εὐδαίμων δ' ἂν οὔ E.*Med.* 1230. 3. *truly happy*, βίος Pl.*Phlb.*11d; ὁ εὖ ζῶν μακάριός τε καὶ εὐ. Id.*R.*354a, cf. 580b (Sup.), Arist.*EN*1098$^b$21, etc.

**εὐδάκρῡτος**, ον, (δακρύω) *tearful, lamentable*, A.*Ch.*181.

**εὐδάκτῠλος**, ον, *with beautiful fingers*, Alciphr.3.67.

**Εὐδαλαγῖνες**· αἱ Χάριτες, Hsch. ❀**εὐδάμνας**· εὐδάμαστος, *easily subdued*, Id.

**Εὐδάνεμος** [ᾰ], ὁ, *Storm-stiller*, a hero worshipped at Eleusis, Arr.*An.*3.16.8; = ἄγγελος, Hsch.: also in pl., Εὐδανέμων βωμός, at Athens, Arr. l. c., cf. D.H.*Din.*11. (Εὐδ. codd. Arr.)

**εὐδάνει**, prob. f.l. for ἐνδαύει, Lyc.1354.

**εὔδαος**, ον, dub. sens. in *Sammelb.*5199.2.

**εὐδάπᾰνος** [δᾰ], ον, (δαπάνη) *lavish of expense, liberal*, ἐλευθεριότης εὐ. εἰς τὰ καλά Arist.*VV*1250$^a$13; τὸ εὐ. Plu.*Sol.*3: Sup., D.C.44.39. II. *of moderate expense, cheap*, D.H.2.23, D.C.52.30, Porph.*Abst.*2.14.

**εὐδαρκής**· εὐόφθαλμος, Hsch. (prob. f.l. for εὐδρακής or εὐδερκής).

❀**εὐδείελος**, ον, *clear, distinct*, Hom. (only in Od.), usu. of Ithaca, 2.167, 9.21, etc.: generally, ἤ πού τις νήσων εὐδείελος 13.234; *far-seen*, Κρόνιον Pi.*O.*1.111; ἄστυ Orac.ap.Eus.*PE*6.7. II. *open to the sun, sunny*, χθὼν Ἰαολκοῦ Pi.*P.*4.76; Κρίσῃ *h.Ap.*438; ὅσσα φύει εὐ. αἶα Euph.50. (In signf. 1 perh. fr. δέελος (dub. l.), δῆλος (*δεάλος?): the alternative expl. from δείλη (cf. supr. II) given by ancient Gramm., e.g. Apollon.*Lex.* and Str.9.2.41, does not suit signf. 1, but suits the forms.)

**εὐδεινός**, ή, όν, later contr. of εὐδιεινός, Orph.*H.*22.5 codd.: Comp. -ότερος *An.Ox.*2.207; also εὐδινή (v.l. -διεινή) Str.6.3.9, cf. *OGI* 194.22 (Egypt, i B.C.), Hsch.

**εὐδειπν-ία**, ἡ, *feast offered to departed souls*, Harmod.1; cf. sq. II. -**ος**, ον, *with goodly feasts*, δαῖτες εὔ. *well-appointed, sumptuous* feasts, E.*Med.*200 (anap.). II. epith. of departed souls to whom offerings were made (cf. foreg.), παρ' εὐδείπνοις ἔσῃ ἄτιμος ἐμπύροισι κνισωτοῖς χθονός A.*Ch.*484; taken by some Gramm. as applied to the festival itself, Hsch., Phot., *EM*42.3.

**εὔδεκτος**, ον, *capacious*, σῶμα *IG*11(4).1247 (Delos, iii/ii B.C.).

❀**εὔδενδρος**, ον, *well-wooded, abounding in fair trees*, ἄλσος Pi.*O.*8.9; μάτηρ (sc. Γαῖα) Id.*P.*4.74; τέμενος Simon.13; χόρτοι E.*IT*134 (lyr.), etc.: also in Prose, Hp.*Aër.*12 (Sup.), Str.2.3.4, Ph.2.117.

❀**εὐδερκής**, ές, *seeing brightly, bright-eyed*, Max.151, 263.

**εὐδέρμᾰτος**, ον, (δέρμα) *with good, stout hide*, Sch.A.R.2.125.

**εὐδές** (post εὐετηρία)· εὔυπνον, εὐήνεμον, Hsch. (fort. εὐαές).

**εὐδέψητος**, ον, (δεψέω) *well-tanned*, δέρματα Hp.*Art.*30 (Sup.), cf. Gal.18(1).436.

**εὔδηλος**, ον, *quite clear, abundantly manifest*, A.*Pers.*1005 (lyr.), etc.; εὔ. [ἐστὶ] κελεύων *may be seen* bidding.., Ar.*Ach.*1130 (sed cod. R ἔνδηλος); ῥυθμός *easily distinguishable*, Arist.*Pr.*882$^b$9; εὔ. γράμματα *plainly legible*, *POxy.*1100.3 (iii A.D.); εὔδηλόν [ἐστιν] ὅτι.. Pl.*Plt.*308d; φιλόσοφός τις εἶ—εὔδηλον Alex.135.11; ἐν εὐδήλῳ [ἐστί] Hp.*de Arte*9. Adv. -λως Plu.*Thes.*3.

**εὐδία**, Ion. -ίη, ἡ, *fair weather*, εὐδία ἐκ χειμῶνος Pi.*I.*7(6).38, cf. Antipho 2.2.1, Hp.*Insomn.*89; ἐν εὐδίᾳ χειμῶνα ποιεῖν X.*HG*2.4.14; ὅταν εὐ. γένηται Arist.*HA*551$^a$3; εὐδίας (gen.) *in fine weather*, ib.597$^b$13: pl., ἔν γε χειμῶσιν καὶ ἐν εὐδίαις Pl.*Lg.*961e; εὐδιῶν οὐσῶν Arist.*HA*626$^a$4. 2. metaph., *tranquillity, peace*, Pi.*O.*1.98, *P.*5.10, A.*Th.*795, X.*An.*5.8.20; τὴν Αἴγυπτον εἰς εὐδίαν ἀγαγεῖν *OGI*90.11 (Rosetta, ii B.C.), cf. Herod.1.28; εὐ. καὶ διαγωγὴ ἄλυπος Polystr. p.17 W.; of the mind, Protag.9; σαρκὸς εὐ. *good condition* of.., Plu.2.126c; εἰς ἔμ' εὐδίαν ἔχων being *at ease* so far as I am concerned, S.*Ichn.*346. [On the prosody, v. εὔδιος.]

**εὐδιά-βᾰτος**, ον, *easy to cross*, ποταμός X.*HG*4.2.11, Colot.ap.Plu.2.1117d, cf. Polyaen.2.2.1. -**βλητος**, ον, = εὐδιάβολος, Arist.*EE* 1237$^b$23, Chrysipp.*Stoic.*3.77, S.E.*M.*3.160, Ptol.*Tetr.*2: Sup., Eus.Mynd.47. -**βόητος**, ον, *readily talked about*, Ptol.*Tetr.*172. -**βολος**, ον, *easy to misrepresent*, Pl.*Lg.*944b; εὐδιάβολα τὰ τοιαῦτα πρὸς τοὺς πολλούς Id.*Euthphr.*3b. Adv. -λως, ἔχειν D.61.17. -**γνωστος**, ον, *easy to distinguish*, Gal.14.63 (Sup.), Nicom.*Harm.*2.

**εὐδιάγωγος** [ᾰ], ον, *cheerful*, Dsc.4.60 (Comp.); *pleasant*, ἀνάπαυλαι Ph.1.52, etc.

**εὐδιάζω**, *calm, still*, χειμῶνας Ph.2.567 (metaph.):—in Med., = εὐδιάω, βίος ἀσαλεύτῳ ἡσυχίᾳ εὐδιαζόμενος Pl.*Ax.*370d. II. intr. in Act., *to be calm*, εὐδιαζούσας ἡμέρας Antig.*Mir.*150.

**εὐδιά-θετος**, ον, *well-arranged*. Adv. -τως J.*BJ*3.5.2. 2. *easily affected*, ὑπὸ τῶν ἔξωθεν A.D.*Synt.*291.15. II. *well-disposed*, of persons. Adv. -τως, = εὐγνωμόνως, Hsch. III. *easy to dispose of* (in marriage), Id. s. v. οὐκ εὐ.; also of arguments or objections, Them. *in APo.*62.33. -**θρυπτος**, ον, *easily crushed*, Phlp. *in de An.*360.15.

**εὐδίαιος** or **ἰαῖος**, ὁ, *hole in a ship*, for letting off the bilge-water, Plu.2.699f, Poll.1.92, Hsch., Suid. II. **εὐδίαιον**, τό, *the end of a clyster-pipe*, Paul. ex Fest.p.69 L.; εὔδιον Poll.4.181. 2. = γυναικεῖον μόριον, Hsch. 3. = πρωκτός, Id. III. as Adj., εὐδιαῖος, α, ον, *caught in fair weather*, τριγόλας Sophr.67.

**εὐδιαίρετος**, ον, *easy to divide*, Arist.*Ph.*215$^b$11 (Comp.); *easy to tear, destroy*, Thphr.*HP*7.13.1, Arist.*PA*654$^a$30, etc.; *easy to take to pieces*, of a machine, Ph.*Bel.*56.35.

**εὐδιαίτερος**, α, ον, irreg. Comp. of εὔδιος (q.v.).

**εὐδῐαίτητος**, ον, *easy to decide*, Str.8.1.1, Gal.2.881.

**εὐδίαιτος** [ῐ], ον, *living temperately*, opp. πολυδάπανος, X.*Ap.*19, cf. Poll.6.27, etc.

**εὐδιακόμιστος**, ον, *easy to convey through* or *across*, Hsch. s.v. ἀγχίπους.

**εὐδιάκονος** [ᾱ], *serving well*, Hsch. s. v. ἀκόμης.

**εὐδιά-κοπος**, -**κοπτος**, ον, *easy to cut through*, Plb.3.46.4, 55.1. -**κόσμητος**, ον, *easy to arrange*, Id.8.34.9. ❀-**κρῐτος**, ον, *easy to distinguish*, A.D.*Adv.*164.12, Gal.1.317. 2. *easy to explain, clear*, σαφὴ καὶ εὐ. Just.*Nov.*166*Pr.*, cf. Sch.Il.24.23. -**λειπτος**, ον, *intermittent*, πῦρ Ps.-Plu.*Vit.Hom.*105 (s.v.l.).

**εὐδιάλλακτος**, ον, *easy to reconcile, placable*, D.H.4.38, Plu.2.332d. Adv. -τως Id.*Caes.*54, M.Ant.1.7 (v.l. εὐαναδιδάκτως codd. Suid.).

**εὐδιά-λογος**, = εὐόμιλος, Suid., Zonar. -**λῠτος**, ον, *easy to undo* or *open*, of traps, Str.6.2.6. 2. *easy to dissolve* or *break up*, gloss on ὑποψάθυρος, Gal.16.762: metaph., φιλίαι Arist.*EN*1156$^a$19, cf. Ph.1.379; Ἑλλάς Plu.*Phil.*8. 3. *easy to solve* or *refute*, D.H.*Rh.*9.5, Hermog.*Meth.*22. 4. *easy to dissolve*, and so *to digest*, Hices.ap.Ath.3.87e. II. *easy to reconcile*, Plb.29.11.5.

**εὐδῐάναξ** [ᾰν], ακτος, ὁ, *ruler of the calm*, Luc.*VH*1.15.

**εὐδιανέμητος**, ον, *divisible*, *Gloss.*

**εὐδιανόητος**, ον, *of good understanding*, Sm.1*Ki.*25.3.

**εὐδιᾱνός**, ή, όν, = εὔδιος, ψυχρᾶν εὐδιανὸν φάρμακον αὐρᾶν a *warm* remedy for chill airs, i.e. a warm cloak, Pi.*O.*9.97, cj. in *P.*5.10.

**εὐδιά-πλαστος**, ον, *easily moulded, plastic*, of water, Olymp.Alch. p.82 B. -**πνευστος**, ον, = sq., Thphr.*Od.*39, Ath.1.26e, Ath. Med.ap.Orib.1.2.2. II. Act., *perspiring freely*, ib.9.5.3, Gal.6.407. -**πνοος**, ον, contr. -**πνους**, ουν, *easily transpiring*, τὸ ὑγρόν Arist.*PA*671$^a$32. -**πτωτος**, ον, *prone to error*, ὁρμή Porph.*Marc.*22.

**εὐδιάρθρωτος**, ον, *well-articulated*, of style, Eust.106.12, al.

**εὐδιά-σειστος**, ον, *easily shaken*, ἀνέμῳ *EM*104.5, cf. Hsch. s. v. ῥαδινόν, etc. II. *easy to disprove*, A.D.*Pron.*4.23. -**σκέδαστος**, ον, *easily spread*, of a plaster, Orib.9.37.7. II. *easily dispersed*, ἡδονή Eus.Mynd.63. -**σπαστος**, ον, *easily torn asunder*, χάραξ Plb.18.18.9. -**φθαρτος**, ον, *easily spoiled*, Pl.*Lg.*845d. ❀-**φθορος**, ον, *easily destroyed*, ὀλιγαρχία Arist.*Pol.*1306$^a$10; [ἔντομα] Id.*PA*682$^b$16; of papyrus rolls, *Arch.Pap.*6.101 (i A.D.). II. *easily corrupted*, Arist.*Ath.*41.2 (Comp.); *easily going bad*, of food, Xenocr.ap.Orib.2.58.145, Dsc.1.105.

**εὐδιαφορ-έω**, = εὐφορέω, κατὰ τὴν γέννησιν *Gp.*19.6.12. -**ησία**, ἡ, *freedom of perspiration*, Sor.1.29. -**ητος**, ον, *easily carried off by perspiration* or *secretion*, Dsc.ap.Ath.1.10c, Phlp. *in de An.*443.27. 2. *easily distributed* or *digested*, of foods, Gal.6.661, Xenocr.2, *PGoodsp.Cair.*2 i 11 (ii A.D.). 3. *easily evaporated*, ὕδωρ Olymp. *in Mete.*299.8. II. Act., *easily perspiring*, Gal.15.583.

**εὐδιά-χῠτος**, ον, *easily dissolved*, φάρμακα ὑπὸ τῶν κοιλιῶν Arist.*Pr.*864$^a$29; γῆ Thphr.*CP*3.2.6. 2. *easily diffused*, ἀήρ *Placit.*4.13.11. 3. *flexible*, Sch.Pi.*P.*1.17. II. *easily relieved*, τὴν ὄρεξιν εὐ. ἔχειν Epicur.*Sent.*26. -**χώρητος**, ον, of food, *easy to digest and pass*, Xenocr.31, cf. Ruf.*Interrog.*40: Comp., Arist.*Pr.*927$^b$22.

❀**εὐδιάω**, Ep. part. εὐδιόων, (εὔδιος) *to be fair* or *calm*, of sea and weather, κόλπος A.R.2.371; [ἄνεμος] Opp.*H.*3.58; πάντῃ Διὸς -όωντος Arat.899; of persons, *to enjoy such weather*, A.R.2.903.

❀**εὐδίδακτος** [ῐ], ον, *docile*, D.S.2.29.

**εὐδιεινός**, ή, όν, = εὔδιος, χειμών Hp.*Aph.*3.12 (v.l.), Plu. *in Arat.*7 (Comp.); γαλήνη Pl.*Lg.*919a; τροπαί Arist.*HA*542$^b$5; ὁ ζέφυρος Id.*Pr.*943$^b$21, etc.; ἐν εὐδιεινοῖς in *sheltered spots*, X.*Cyn.*5.9, Arist.*HA*548$^b$21, cf. *Mete.*347$^a$23 (Comp.), Thphr.*HP*3.2.5. Adv. -νῶς *calmly, gently*, ἱλαρῶς καὶ εὐ. παρακελεύειν Hp.*Decent.*16; later contr. εὐδεινός (q.v.).

**εὐδιέξοδος**, ον, *easily going out*, Hp.*Flat.*8; εὐ. κοιλίη an *easy* evacuation, Id.*Salubr.*5.

**εὐδίετος**, ον, (διίημι) *easily melting*, Dsc.1.19.

**εὐδιήγητος**, ον, *easy to tell*, Isoc.19.28, Procop.*Aed.*4.1, etc.

**εὐδῐκ-ία**, Ion. -ίη, ἡ, (δίκη) *righteous dealing, righteousness*, εὐδικίας ἀνέχῃσι Od.19.111; εὐδικίῃ *righteously*, A.R.4.343; σύντροφος εὐδικίης *IG*3.1151; ὃς εὐδικίης ἀγανῇσι σῶσε..πόλιας *Epigr.Gr.*915, cf. *BCH*50.444 (Thespiae, iv A.D.): also in late Prose, Phld.*Hom.*p.43 O., Ph.1.664, Plu.2.781f. -**ος**, ον, *righteous*, *BCH*23.302 (Termessus): as pr. n., *IG*1$^2$.393 (vi B.C.), etc.

**εὐδῑν-ής**, ές, = sq., χοροῦ κύκλος Orac.ap.Porph.*Plot.*22 (acc. -δίνεα codd.). -**ητος**, ον, *easily turning*, τρύπανα *AP*6.205.7 (Leon.). II. *well-rounded*, Nonn.*D.*6.109. -**ός**, όν, v. εὐδεινός.

**εὐδιόδ-ευτος**, ον, = sq., Plu. *in Hes.*13. -**ος**, ον, *easy to go through, permeable*, χώρα Thphr.*HP*1.7.1; *permeable* by the breezes, ἕξις τῆς σαρκός Arist.*Pr.*887$^b$24. II. *easily passing through*, πρὸς τοὺς πόρους Thphr.*Od.*60; τροφή Aret.*CA*2.6.

**εὐδιοίκητος**, ον, *easy to assimilate* or *digest*, Herod.(?)Med. in *Rh.Mus.*58.112, Ath.Med.ap.Orib.1.9.2, Xenocr.33, Alex.Aphr. *in Top.*153.6, Gal.14.736. II. *well-ordered*, ἁρμονία (of structure and function) Antyll.ap.Orib.6.10.4. III. as a complimentary term of address, *POxy.*1413.32 (iii A.D.).

**εὔδιον**, τό, v. εὐδίαιος II.

**εὐδιοποιέω**, *clear the sky*, Gloss.

**εὐδί-οπτος**, ον, *easy to see through*, Arist.*PA*658$^a$5, *Pr.*932$^b$8 (Comp.), cf. Thphr.*Sens.*80; τὸ εὐ. τῆς θαλάσσης Arist.*GA*779$^b$31. **-όρθωτος**, ον, *easy to remedy* or *correct*, νοῦσοι Hp.*de Arte* 13; συμφορά D.H.10.42. II. *easily repaired*, Apollod.*Poliorc.*139.7. **-όριστος**, ον, *easy to define*, Arist.*de An.*421$^a$7; *easy to distinguish*, Gal.7.778.

* **εὔδιος**, ον, *calm, fine, clear*, of air, weather, sea, ἄνεμος X.*HG*1.6.38 (Comp.); εὔδια πάντα Theoc.22.22; ἁλὸς ἄκραι A.R.1.521, etc.; *warm, mild*, χειμών Hp.*Aër.*10; *peaceful*, εὐ. καὶ γαληνὸς βίος Ph.1.411; of persons, *mild, gracious*, εὐδίjα *the Gracious one*, Inscr. Cypr. in *Berl.Sitzb.*1911.639, cf. Opp.*H.*4.29; τὸ εὔδιον τοῦ προσώπου M.Ant.6.30: neut. εὔδιον, εὔδια, as Adv., Opp.*C.*1.44, *AP*10.14.1 (Agath.): Comp. -αίτερος X.l.c.: Sup. -εστάτη [χώρη] Hp.*Aër.*12. II. *in fine weather*, κέπφοι εὔδιοι ποτέονται Arat.916; *bringing fine weather*, Orph.*H.*38.24. (For εὔδιϝος, cf. Ζεύς.) [ῑ in εὐδία, εὔδιος, exc. metri gr., Orph. l.c., Arat. l.c.]

**εὐδίπλωτος**, ον, *easily folded*, Eust.1056.65.

**εὔδιφρος**, ον, *with beautiful chariots*, of Elis, Nonn.*D.*37.139.

**εὔδμητος**, Dor. **-δμᾱτος**, ον, *well-built*, βωμός Il.1.448; πύργοι Hes.*Sc.*242; κολώνα Pi.*P.*12.3; ἀγυιαί A.R.1.317. (Always in Ep. form ἐΰδμ-, exc. in Od.20.302 ὁ δ' εὔδμητον βάλε τοῖχον.)

**εὐδοκ-έω**, *to be well pleased* or *content*, Plb.2.49.2, al.; ἐάν.. Id.29.12.8: c. part., Id.15.36.6: c. dat., *to be content with, find pleasure in* a person or thing, Id.18.52.5, D.S.17.47, D.H.8.74; τῇ ἀδικίᾳ 2*Ep. Thess.*2.12; ἔν τινι Lxx *Is.*62.4, al., 2*Ep.Cor.*12.10, al.; εἴς τινα 2*Ep. Pet.*1.17; ἐπί τινι Lxx *Ju.*15.10: also c. acc., τινα ib.*Ge.*33.10; [ἐγγύους] *SIG*672.27 (Delph., ii B.C.); ἡ γῆ -ήσει τὰ σάββατα Lxx *Le.*26.34. 2. *consent, approve*, c. dat., τοῖς γεγραμμένοις *PLond.*3.1168.15 (i A.D.), al.; τῇ δημοσιώσει *POxy.*1273.40 (iii A.D.); also ἐπί τινι *PTeb.*317.33 (ii A.D.), al.: freq. abs. in legal documents, *PRyl.*120.24 (ii A.D.), etc. 3. c. inf., *consent, agree to do*, Plb.1.78.8, al. (and c. acc. et inf., *consent* that.., Id.1.8.4, Lxx 2*Ma.*14.35); *to be ready, willing*, *PGrenf.*1.1.17 (ii B.C.), 1*Ep.Thess.*2.8. b. *determine, resolve*, *Ev.Luc.*12.32, etc. 4. *to be content, happy*, Phld.*D.*1.1:—also in Med., τῆς εὐδοκουμένης ζωῆς Id.*Mort.*36. 5. Med., = Act. in signf. 1, ἐπί τινι Plb.1.8.4; τινι Id.3.31.6, D.S.15.16 codd.; περί τινος Phld.*Rh.Supp.*p.44 S. II. Pass., *to be favoured*, i.e. *prosper*, Lxx 1*Ch.*29.23: c. dat., *find approval with*, τισι Plb.1.88.4, al. 2. *to be approved*, ὑπό τινων *BGU*1157.12 (i B.C.). III. of persons or things, *to be well-pleasing* or *acceptable, find favour with*, τινι Plb.20.5.10, Max.Tyr.32.5; τὰ -οῦντα ἑαυτῷ Phld.*Rh.Supp.*p.54 S. IV. c. acc. et gen., *deem worthy of*, τινα τιμῆς *PLond.*1.3.6 (ii B.C.). **-ησις**, εως, ἡ, *satisfaction, approval*, Plb.16.20.4, D.S.15.6, D.H.3.13, S.E.*M.*7.200; *consent, concurrence*, *POxy.*1273.39 (iii A.D.); ἔλαβον -ησιν *SIG*685.108 (Crete, ii B.C.). **-ητός**, ή, όν, *well-pleasing, acceptable*, Sm.*Ps.*67(68).31, D.L.2.87. Adv. -τῶς *with good repute*, *Vit.Philonid.*p.9 C. **-ία**, ἡ, = εὐδόκησις, esp. of God, Lxx 1*Ch.*16.10, al., *Ev.Luc.*2.14, al.; *good will*, *Ep.Phil.*1.15; *contentment*, Phld.*Piet.*25. 2. *object of desire*, Lxx *Ps.*144.16, *Si.*18.31. 3. v.l. for εὐδοκιμίη in Hp.*Praec.*6.

* **εὐδοκῐμ-άζω**, *choose, select*, *PThead.*19.17 (iv A.D.). (Incorrect form.) **-έω**, impf. ηὐδοκίμουν Pl.*Grg.*515e: aor. ηὐδοκίμησα X.*Cyr.*7.1.46, D.7.20: pf. ηὐδοκίμηκα Ar.*Nu.*1031: the augm. is omitted in Ion., Hdt.3.131, 7.227, and freq. in codd. of Att., etc., as Ar. l.c., X.*HG*6.1.2, etc.:—*to be of good repute, highly esteemed, popular*, Thgn.587, E.*Fr.*546 (lyr.), Ar. l.c., Pl.*Grg.* l.c., etc.; εὐ. ἐνθυμήματι *gain credit by*.., X.*HG*4.5.4; εὐ. ἔν τινι *to be distinguished* in a thing, Hdt.1.59, Th.2.37; ἐπὶ σοφίᾳ ἐν πᾶσι τοῖς Ἕλλησιν Pl.*Hp.Ma.*291a, cf. Isoc.3.30; ἐπὶ τῶν λόγων D.*Prooem.*9; τὰ ἄλλα D.C.60.8; περί τι Pl.*R.*368a, etc.; παρὰ τοῖς ἀνθρώποις ἔκ τινος Isoc.11.28, cf. Plu. *Dio* 34; ἀπό τινων Eus.Mynd.55; ἀπ' ἀρετῆς ἐκ γένους ἀλλ' οὐκ ἐκ τοῦ προστυχόντος εὐ. D.C.*Fr.*57.48; ἐς φήμην Id.*Fr.*54.7; εὐ. μάλιστα τῶν Πρωταγόρου μαθητῶν Pl.*Prt.*315a; διὰ πάντων τῶν βασιλέων Hdt.6.63; εὐ. παρὰ βασιλεῖ *to have influence* with him, Id.8.87, cf. Lys.25.24, etc.:—later in Med., *Com.Adesp.*110.4. 2. of wine, meats, etc., *to be highly esteemed, popular*, εὐ. σφόδρα Alex.282, cf. Philem.122; σκῶπες σφόδρα εὐ., i.e. their flesh, Arist.*HA*618$^a$3; so of things generally, θεάματα κατὰ τὰς τέχνας -οῦντα Isoc.4.45, cf. 9.11; παρὰ τοῖς Ἕλλησι -δοκιμῶν νόμος D.21.50, cf. Arist.*EN*1181$^a$16; of popular arguments, Id.*Rh.*1400$^b$25; of physicians and medical treatments, Gal.10.390, Herod.Med. in *Rh.Mus.*58.112; ἐκ τούτων ἡ νῦν εὐ. σοφία *AP*11.157 (Ammian.):—also in Pass., ἀκρόαμα -ούμενον Plu.*Galb.*16; *to be recognized, approved*, *PTeb.*25.16 (ii B.C.). 3. of money, *to be genuine*, Lxx *Ge.*43.23. II. in Med., *hold in honour*, D.S.4.24 codd. * **-ησις**, εως, ἡ, *good repute, reputation, credit*, mostly in pl., Pl.*R.*358a, 363a, Luc.*Pisc.*25: sg., Them.*Or.*29.347c. **-ία**, ἡ, = foreg., Pl.*Phlb.*58d (pl.); v.l. in Hp.*Praec.*6. **-ίζω**, *nobilito*, Gloss. * **-ος**, ον, *in good repute, honoured, famous, glorious*, στρατιά A.*Pers.*858 (lyr.); θανάτου μέρος E.*Heracl.*621 (lyr.); εὐ. εἴς τι, πρός τι, in Sup., Pl.*Ap.*29d, *Lg.*878a; ἐπί τινι Plu.*Lys.*22; ἐν πᾶσιν Pl.*Lg.*631b; τὴν πατρίδα ἐν τῇ Ἑλλάδι -ωτέραν ποιεῖν X.*Mem.*3.7.1.

**εὐδοκουμένως**, Adv. pres. part. Med. of εὐδοκέω, *satisfactorily*, c. dat., Plb.18.51.10, D.S.28.11.

**εὐδόμητος**, ον, formed to expl. εὔδμητος, Eust.782.24.

**εὔδομος**, Boeot. for ἕβδομος, *BCH*21.558 (Thespiae).

**εὐδοξ-έω**, *to be in good repute, to be honoured, famous*, E.*Rh.*496, X.*Mem.*3.6.16, D.20.142, Ph.2.61, etc.; τὰ πολλὰ X.*HG*1.1.31. **-ία**, ἡ, *good repute, honour*, Simon.4.6, Pi.*P.*5.8, E.*Tr.*643, Isoc.11.29, etc., cf. Arist.*Rh.*1361$^a$25; *virtue, excellence*, Pi.*N.*3.40: in pl., D.18.322. 2. *approval*, μετ' εὐδοξίας πλήθους ἀριστοκρατία Pl.*Mx.*238d. II. *good judgement*, opp. ἐπιστήμη, Id.*Men.*99b. **-ος**, ον, (δόξα) *of good repute, honoured*, Thgn.195, Pi.*P.*12.5, Th.1.84 (Sup.), etc.; Νίκη Simon.145, cf. Pi.*P.*6.17; εὔ. παρά τισι Pl.*Lg.*773a; νέες εὐδοξόταται '*crack*' ships, Hdt.7.99. Adv. -ξως *remarkably*, '*famously*', Pl.*Hp.Ma.*287e; *with distinction*, στεφανῶσαί τινα Man.1.102.

**εὔδουλος**, ον, *good to one's slaves*, Achae.32, Pherecr.212.

**εὐδρᾰκής**, ές, (δέρκομαι) *sharp-sighted*, S.*Ph.*847 (lyr.).

* **εὐδρᾰν-εια** [δρᾰ], ἡ, (δραίνω) *bodily strength and health*, Lxx *Wi.*13.19, Hsch. **-ής**, ές, *vigorous*, Phot.

**εὐδρομ-έω**, *to be fleet of foot*, Men.681, Plu.*Phil.*18: metaph., *go off well*, Philostr.*Im.*1.30; *to be successful*, S.E.*M.*10.36. **-ία**, Ion. -ίη, ἡ, *swiftness*, πλόου Hp.*Ep.*14. **-ίας**, poet. -ίης, ου, ὁ, *rapid swimmer*, of a fish, Eratosth.12 codd. * **-ος**, ον, *running well, swift*, κλωστήρ *AP*6.160 (Antip. Sid.); Ἄρτεμις Orph.*H.*36.6; of pulleys, Gal.18(1).521: metaph. in Sup. -ώτατος, πρὸς ἀρετήν Max.Tyr.16.8. 2. *easily traversed*, ὄρη Id.26.2 (Sup.), cf. Poll.1.186. II. in Medic. sense, *lively*, σῶμα Plu.2.715e; = εὐδιαχώρητος, τροφαί Aret.*CA*2.6.

**εὔδροσος**, ον, *with plenteous dew, abounding in water*, παγαί E.*IA*1517 (lyr.); τόποι Ar.*Av.*245 (lyr.); νασμοί Aristonous 1.42.

* **εὐδυκήμερος**· εὔστοχος, Hsch.

**εὐδύνᾰμος** [ῠ], ον, *mighty*, Sch.Pi.*O.*1.165.

**εὐδύνᾰτος** [ῠ], ον, = foreg., Orph.*H.*29.20, al.

**εὐδυσώπητος**, ον, *soon put out of countenance*: *easily worked upon by entreaty*, Plu.2.528e, dub. in *PMed.Lond.*155 iii 33.

**εὕδω**, impf. ηὗδον Pl.*Smp.*203b, E.*Rh.*763, 779, εὗδον Il.2.2, Theoc.2.126; Ep. iter. εὕδεσκε Il.22.503: fut. εὑδήσω A.*Ag.*337: aor. εὕδησα (καθ-) Hp.*Int.*12:—*sleep*, Il.2.19, Hdt.1.34, etc.: c. acc. cogn., ὁππότ' ἂν αὖτε εὕδησθα γλυκὺν ὕπνον Od.8.445; ὕπνον οὐκ εὐδαίμονα E.*HF*1013; γλυκερὸν καὶ ἐγέρσιμον ὕπνον Theoc.24.7; μακρὸν ἀτέρμονα νήγρετον ὕπνον Mosch.3.104; ὕπνῳ γ' εὕδοντα *slumbering* in sleep, S.*OT*65; εὕδειν.. παρὰ χρυσέῃ Ἀφροδίτῃ Od.8.337, cf. 342; ξὺν ὁμήλικι εὕδειν Thgn.1063; ὅλην διατελεῖν νύκτα εὕδοντα Pl.*Lg.*807e; of the *sleep of death*, Πρόμαχος δεδμημένος εὕδει ἔγχει ἐμῷ Il.14.482; οὑμὸς εὕδων.. νέκυς S.*OC*621. II. metaph., *rest, be still*, ὄφρ' εὕδῃσι μένος Βορέαο Il.5.524; εὑδέτω πόντος εὑδέτω δ' ἄμοτον κακόν Simon.37.15, cf. A.*Ag.*566; πόλεμον εὕδοντ' ἐπεγείρει Sol.4.19; εὕδουσιν ὀρέων κορυφαί Alcm.60.1; οὔπω κακὸν τόδ' εὕδει E.*Supp.*1147 (lyr.); εὕδει χάρις *sleeps, ceases*, Pi.*I.*7(6).17; οὔποθ' εὕδει λυπρά σου κηρύγματα E.*Hec.*662; of the mind or heart, *to be at ease*, πυκνῆς ἀκούσαι ψακάδος εὑδούσῃ φρενί S.*Fr.*636, cf. Theoc.2.126; of persons, *take one's ease, be inactive*, κεἰ βραδὺς εὕδει S.*OC*307; Γοργίαν ἐάσομεν εὕδειν we will let him *rest*, Pl.*Phdr.*267a. (καθεύδω is generally used in Att. and later Prose, exc. Pl. ll.cc., X.*Cyn.*5.11.)

**εὐδώρητος**, ον, *abundantly given*, Opp.*H.*4.359.

**εὔδωρος**, poet. ἐΰδ-, ον, *generous*, Opp.*H.*2.39.

**Εὐδωσώ**, ἡ, title of Aphrodite at Syracuse, Hsch.

**εὐέᾱνος**, ον, *richly robed*, Mosch.4.75, Max.477, 562: pr. n. Εὐ[ε]ανο[ν], = Εὐηνόν (acc.), dub. in B.*Scol.Oxy.*2081(*e*).

* **εὐέγρετος**, ον, (ἔγρομαι, ἐγείρω) *easily aroused, stimulated*, πρὸς διδασκαλίαν v.l. in Hierocl. in *CA*18 p.432 M.

**εὐεγχής**, ές, *with mighty spear*, Ἄρης B.12.147.

**εὔεδνα**· ἀγλαΐα, Hsch.

**εὔεδρος**, ον, (ἕδρα) *on stately throne*, of gods, A.*Th.*96, 319 (both lyr.). 2. εὐ. καθέδρα a *firm* seat on horseback, etc., Anon.ap. Suid.; τὸ εὔ. Ph.1.21; *well-poised*, Apollod.*Poliorc.*157.3. Adv. -ρως, = βεβαίως, Hsch., Phot. 3. of ships, = εὔσσελμος, Theoc.13.21. 4. *well-fitting*, of building materials, D.H.*Comp.*6. Adv. -ρως, = εὐθέτως, Hsch. II. Pass., *easy to sit*, ἵππος X.*Eq.*1.12 (Comp.). III. *in a right* or *lucky place*, εὐέδρος ὄρνις a bird of augury *appearing in a lucky quarter*, Ael.*NA*16.16.

* **εὐέθειρα**, fem. Adj. *beautiful-haired*, κούρα Anacr.76; Ἶσις *Sammelb.*4127.21.

**εὐέθωκεν** (i.e. ἐϝέθωκεν)· εἴωθεν, Hsch.

**εὐειδ-εια** or **-ία**, ἡ, *good looks*, Lesb.Rh.2.7, Corn.*ND*15 (v.l. εὐήθεια). **-ής**, ές, *well shaped, comely*, γυνή Il.3.48; prop. of female beauty (v. Eust. adloc.), cf. Hes.*Th.*250, Thgn.1002, Pi.*I.*8(7).31, B.12.102, Hdt.1.196 (Sup.), al., Pl.*Cri.*44a, X.*Mem.*3.11.4; of males, Hdt.1.112, 6.32 (Sup.), A.*Pers.*324, E.*Hel.*1540, X.*HG*5.3.9: generally, *beautiful*, χρωτὸς εὐειδὴς φύσις E.*Alc.*174; τὸ εὐ. *beauty of face*, Cret. usage mentioned by Arist.*Po.*1461$^a$14.

**εὐείκαστος**, ον, *easy to conjecture*, Hsch. II. *good at guessing*, Ptol.*Tetr.*155.

* **εὐεικτος**, ον, *pliant, tractable*, D.C.69.20 (Zonar., εὔοικτος (q.v.) codd.); *soft, yielding*, τὰ εὐ. Alex.Aph.*Pr.*2.23, cf. Heraclit.*All.*51 (εὐθικτος codd.); of abscesses, Paul.Aeg.4.18: Comp. -ότερος, gloss on λειότερος, Sch.Orib.49.3.5. Adv. -τως (-τῶς cod.) f.l. for εὐεκτικῶς, Hsch.

**εὐείλατος**, v. εὐίλατος.

**εὐείλητος**, ον, *well rolled up, tight*, gloss on οὖλος, Eust.1056.65.

**εὐειλος**, ον, (εἵλη) *sunny, warm*, Ar.*Fr.*780; χωρία Arist.*HA*597$^b$7, Thphr.*HP*4.1.1, al.

**εὐειμᾰτέω**, *to be well-dressed*, Antiph.54, Arist.*Rh.Al.*1420$^a$17, Gerhard *Phoinix* p.6, Sotad.9.3 (v.l. εὐειμονῆς).

**εὐείμων**, ον, gen. ονος, *well-dressed*, A.*Pers.*181: Sup. -ειμονώτατος Max.Tyr.3.10.

**εὔειρος**, ον, (εἶρος, ἔριον) *with* or *of good wool, fleecy*, Hp.*Mul.*2.187

(Sup.), AP7.657 (Leon.):—Att. **εὔερος** (cf. Phryn.122) S.Tr.675 (Lob. for εὐείρῳ); εὐερόν τ' ἄγραν (Schneidew. for εὐκερῶν τ') Id.Aj.297; εἴ τινα πόλιν φράσειας ἡμῖν εὔερον Ar.Av.121; γλῶσσαν εὐέρων βοτῶν Cratin.175: heterocl. acc. pl. εὔειρας v.l. for ἐτῆρας, S.Fr.751.

**εὐείσβολος**, ον, easily invaded, Aen.Tact.16.16. 2. easy of entrance, στόμα λιμένος Str.17.1.6.

⊕**εὐέκ-βᾰτος**, ον, easy to get out of, πύαλος Hp.Acut.65. **-κάθαρτος** [κᾰ], ον, easily cleared up, prob. in Phld.Herc.1251.4. **-καρτέρητος**, ον, easy to endure, Id.D.1.12: written for εὐεγκ. **-καυστος**, ον, = sq., Corn.ND32. **-καυτος**, ον, easily flaring up, Gal.11.405. **-κρῐτος**, ον, of food, easy to excrete, Hp.Acut.10, Diph.Siph.ap.Ath.2.62f, Dsc.2.9, Xenocr.33, Gal.6.503. **-νιπτος**, ον, easy to wash out, of a colour, Poll.1.44. **-πλήρωτος**, ον, easily fulfilled or realized, Phld.D.1.13. **-πλῠτος**, ον, = εὐέκνιπτος, Poll.1.44. II. Act., purging, relaxing, v.l. for εὐέκκριτος in Hp.Acut.10. **-ποίητος**, ον, easy to turn to account, i.e. assimilate, of food, Ath.Med.ap.Orib.1.2.2. **-πόρθητος**, ον, easily sacked, in Comp., Apollon.Lex. s.v. ἀλαπαδνότεροι. **-πτωτος**, ον, prone to failure, Ptol.Tetr.161. **-πύρωτος** [ῠ], ον, easily heated, Str.12.8.17, Eust.346.25. **-ρυπτος**, ον, easy to wash out, Poll.1.44.

**εὐεκτ-έω**, to be in good condition, τῷ σώματι Ceb.16, cf. Ph.1.611, Gal.UP1.21, Aesop.185, etc.; ὅταν ἢ ζῷον ἢ δένδρον εὐεκτῇ Plu.2.919c. **-ης**, ου, ὁ, (ἔχω) of a good habit of body, opp. καχέκτης, Plb.3.88.2, D.L.2.22: as Adj., ἀθληταί Ph.1.583. **-ία**, ἡ, = εὐεξία, Archyt.ap.Stob.3.1.110, 112. **-ικός**, ή, όν, in good case, healthy, σώματα Pl.Lg.684c, cf. Ph.2.84, Gal.6.662; of persons, Arist.EN 1176a15. 2. conducive to εὐεξία, wholesome, Id.Top.105a31, EN 1129a20. Adv. -κῶς Gal.8.106, Hierocl.in CA16 p.456M.; also glossed by σχετικῶς, Suid. **-ός**, όν, = εὐέκτης, Sch.E.Hipp.109 (Comp.). Adv. -τῶς, gloss on λίπα, Sch.DIl.10.577, Zonar., prob. for εὐκτεῶς, = ὑγιῶς, Hsch. (cf. εὐεστότερος).

**εὐέκ-φορος**, ον, bringing forth timely births, γυναῖκες Arist.HA584b7. II. easy to pronounce, Phld.Po.1676.8:—hence **-φορία**, ἡ, ibid. **-χόλωτος**, ον, easily made bilious, Philagr.ap.Paul.Aeg.7.6.

**εὐέλαιος**, ον, rich in olive-trees or oil, Str.5.4.3.

**εὐέλᾰτος**, ον, gloss on εὐήλατος, Hsch.

**εὐέλεγκτος**, ον, easy to refute or detect, of persons or arguments, Pl.Tht.157b, Arist.Rh.1418b19. 2. easy to test, Pl.Ap.33c.

**εὐελίδης**· αὐθάδης, Hsch.; also epith. of Zeus in Cyprus, Id. **εὐελιέστερα**· εὐάγωγος, Id.

**εὐέλικτος**, ον, easily rolling, Eust.229.36, Poll.2.117.

**εὐέλιον**· ἐλλιπὲς ἐν ἱερείῳ, Hsch.

**εὐελκής**, ές, easily healing, favourable for healing, of the constitution, opp. δυσελκής, Hp.Acut.46, Gal.10.386.

**εὔελκτος**, ον, easy to draw, Gal.11.402.

**εὔελον**· εὐήλιον, Hsch. (Fort. εὔε(ι)λον, sed cf. ἕλα.)

**εὔελπ-ις**, ὁ, ἡ, neut. εὔελπι, gen. ιδος, hopeful, cheerful, Th.4.10, 62, X.An.2.1.18, etc.; ἐν τοῖς δεινοῖς Th.1.70; περὶ τῆς ψυχῆς Pl.Hp.Mi.364a; πρὸς τὸν θάνατον Id.Ap.41c, cf. Luc.Demon.6, D.C.57.19; τοῦ κρατήσειν D.S.30.16. 2. c. acc. et fut. inf., εὔελπίς εἰμί σ' ἰσχύσειν A.Pr.509; εὔελπις σωθήσεσθαι in good hope to be saved, Th.6.24: c. acc. et pres. inf., Pl.Phd.63c; τὸ εὔελπι hopefulness, Plu.2.1101d, D.C.42.1, etc.; εὔ. λαλιά cheerful talk, Plb.1.32.6. II. Pass., well hoped of, the subject of hope, LxxPr.19.15(18): Medic., of a patient, Aret.SD1.13. **-ιστία**, ἡ, hopefulness, sanguine temper, confidence, περὶ τοῦ μέλλοντος Epicur.Sent.Vat.39, cf. Plb.11.3.6, Phld.Oec.p.73J., Cic.Att.2.17.2; τινος Ph.1.502, Perict.ap.Stob.4.28.19; θάρρος καὶ εὐ. Procl.in Cra.p.88P.

**εὐέμ-βᾰτος**, ον, easy to get into, πύαλος Hp.Acut.65; ψυχὴ οὐδενὶ τῶν τοιούτων βουλευμάτων εὐ. ChioEp.16.2; τινι εὐ. ἀπολιπεῖν τὴν ἀκρόπολιν ib.15.3. **-βλητος**, ον, easy to put in, of dislocated joints, Hp.Art.71. **-βολος**, ον, exposed to invasion, χώρα Arist.Pol.1331a4. II. = foreg., Hp.Fract.42.

**εὐέμετος** or **εὐήμετος**, ον, (ἔμετος) vomiting readily, Hp.Art.40 (εὐημέτης, εὐήμετος codd.):—also **-εμής** or **-ημής**, ές, Id.Mul.2.125, Aph.4.6, Dsc.2.169 (Comp.); ὅπως εὐεμὲς ᾖ (cod. Urb.) that vomiting may be easy, Thphr.HP9.10.2.

**εὐέμ-πρηστος**, ον, easily set on fire, dub. in Diog.Oen.8. **-πτωσία**, ἡ, liability, proneness to a thing: hence, evil proclivity, Stoic.3.102: in Medic., an illness to which people are commonly liable, such as colds, Posidon.ap.Gal.5.434, Stoic.3.103 (pl.). **-πτωτος**, ον, easily falling into: hence, prone, liable, εἴς τι Posidon.ap.Gal.5.434; εἰς ὀργὴν Stoic.3.110: Comp., εἰς τὰς ὀργάς Phld.Ir.p.97W.; ἐπί τι Id.Rh.Supp.p.26S.: abs., Ptol.Tetr.164. Adv. -τως Gal.5.448, Dsc.Ther.Praef.; εὐ. ἔχειν πρός τι Phlp.in de An.53.15. **-φρακτος**, ον, easily obstructed, Gal.6.497.

**εὐέν**, an exclamation like εὐάν, εὐοῖ, Hdn.Gr.1.503 (nisi leg. εὐαί).

**εὐέν-δοτος**, ον, easily yielding, γῆ Str.16.1.9; βύρσα Hippiatr.8. 2. morally weak, Ph.2.269, al.; τὸ εὐ. Id.1.153. **-τευκτος**, ον, affable, Id.2.187, Poll.5.138. Adv. -τως ib.139. **-τρεπτος**, ον, reverend, σεμνοὶ καὶ εὐ. Ptol.Tetr.159. **-τροπος**, reverens, Gloss.

**εὐεξ-άγωγος** [ᾰ], ον, easy of export, Str.5.2.5. **-άλειπτος** [ᾰ], ον, easy to wipe out, X.HG2.3.53 (Comp.), Sch.D.T.p.505H. **-ανάλωτος** [νᾰ], ον, easy of digestion, Hp.Alim.49. **-απάτητος** [πᾰ], ον, easily deceived, ὑπό τινος Pl.R.409a, cf. X.Eq.Mag.7.15, Corn.ND25. **-απτος**, ον, easily kindled or lighted, M.Ant.9.9, Gal.7.342, al. **-άρτῡτος**, ον, easy to get ready, Ph.Bel.56.34. **-έλεγκτος**, ον, easy to refute, Pl.Hp.Ma.293d. **-έλικτος**, ον, skilful in manœuvre, Str.3.3.6. **-έλκυστος**, ον, easily extracted, Heraclid.Tar.ap.Gal.12.692. **-έταστος**, ον, easy to criticize, Arist.de An.408a10. **-ής**, f.l. for εὐαξής, Phot. s.v. εὐαλδεῖ (cf. Hsch.): Comp. -έστερος f.l. for εὐαξέστερος, Aët.6.58; v. εὐαυξής.

**εὐεξία**, ἡ, (εὐέκτης) good habit of body, good health, Hp.Aph.1.3 (pl.); σαρκός E.Fr.201; εὐ. τῶν σωμάτων καὶ καχεξία Pl.Grg.450a, cf. Arist.EN1129a19, Top.105a31; εὐ. πολιτική bodily vigour required of a citizen, Id.Pol.1335b6; ὑγίεια καὶ εὐ. Pl.R.559a: pl., εὐεξίαι τῶν σωμάτων Id.Prt.354b, cf. Aeschin.1.189, Plb.1.57.1, v.l. in Isoc.4.1; περὶ εὐεξίας (opp. ὑγίεια, as temporary high condition to permanent health), title of work by Gal.4.750, 1.408, Thras.12; νικᾶν εὐεξίαν, εὐεξίᾳ, SIG1060 (iv/iii B.C.), 1061 (ii B.C.). II. generally, vigour, good condition, ὑγίεια καὶ κάλλος καὶ εὐ. ψυχῆς Pl.R.444d; τῆς πολιτείας Plb.20.4.1; φωνῆς Plu.2.804b, etc. 2. skill, ability, περὶ τὸ ἐπιτάδουμα SIG721.12 (Delos, ii B.C.); εὐ. ἐν τοῖς πολεμικοῖς Plb.3.6.12.

**εὐεξίλαστος** [ῑ], ον, placable, Sch.A.R.4.148.

**εὐέξοδος**, ον, easy to get out of or escape from, ἔστι δ' οὐκ εὐέξοδον A.Pers.688; εὐ. χώρα, opp. δυσέμβολος, Arist.Pol.1326b41, cf. 1330b2. II. Act., easily escaping, ὕδωρ Id.Pr.874a32.

**εὔεξος**· εὐφυής, Hsch.

**εὐεπ-άγωγος** [ᾰ], ον, easy to lead on, πρός τι Plb.31.8.5. **-αίσθητος**, ον, easily feeling, sensitive, Hp.Mul.1.38. **-ακολούθητος**, ον, easy to follow, of a train of argument, Arist.Rh.1357a11. **-ανόρθωτος**, ον, easy to correct, σώματα Hp.de Arte11.

**εὐέπεια**, Ion. and poet. εὐεπίη (q.v.), ἡ, (εὐεπής) beauty of language, eloquence, Pl.Phdr.267c; ἐν ταῖς ὁμιλίαις Ph.2.79; εὐέπειαι λόγων Pl.Ax.369d; esp. with ref. to sound, euphony, D.H.Comp.23, al.: coupled with καλλιλογία, Id.Dem.25. II. welcome words, S.OT932 (cf. εὐεπής II).

**εὐεπ-εκτᾰτος**, ον, naturally lengthened, cj. in A.D.Pron.99.2. **-έραστος**, ον, v. εὐεπηρέαστος. **-ήβολος**, ον, cf. εὐεπίβολος. **-ήκοος**, ον, responsive, ὕλη Steph.in Hp.1.173D. **-ηρέαστος**, ον, exposed to harm, Arr.Epict.4.1.111 (Sup.), Vett.Val.49.4; ὑπό τινος Gal.6.124; πρὸς τὰς νόσους Sor.1.109; liable to wanton damage, κώμη prob. in SIG888.16 (Thrace, iii A.D., εὐεπεράστῳ lapis).

**εὐεπής**, ές, (ἔπος) melodious, φωνή X.Cyn.13.16; euphonious, λέξις D.H.Comp.22; ἁρμονία -εστέρα ibid. Adv. -πῶς, κῶλα εὐ. συγκείμενα ibid.: Sup., ποίησις -έστατα ἔχουσα D.Chr.52.15. 2. eloquent, εὐ. ἐν τῷ λέγειν Hsch. s.v. λιγύς. 3. making eloquent, inspiring, ὕδωρ, of Helicon, AP11.24 (Antip.). II. Pass., well-spoken, acceptable, λόγος Hdt.5.50.

**εὐεπί-βᾰτος**, ον, easy to ascend, λόφος Str.5.3.7; τεῖχος Polyaen.6.5; καταρράκται App.BC5.82 (Comp.). II. easy of attack, τόποι Ph.Bel.94.40: metaph., Id.1.459, Luc.Cal.19. **-βλεπτος**, ον, easily seen, manifest, Poll.1.172, dub. in Epicur.Nat.2.6, Phld.D.3 Fr.36. **-βλητος**, ον, easily grasped, Simp.in de An.259.28. **-βολος**, ον, hitting the mark: hence, shrewd, intelligent, Vett.Val.38.1, al., Ptol.Tetr.57, v.l. in S.E.M.7.322: also spelt εὐεπήβ-. Adv. -λως Sch.Ptol.Tetr.99, Simp.in Ph.738.4. **-βούλευτος**, ον, exposed to treachery or stratagem, χώρα Str.2.3.4, cf. Ph.2.552, Vett.Val.236.27: Comp., X.Cyr.8.4.3, Onos.36.6, D.C.38.31. **-βουλος**, ον, fond of plotting or intriguing, Ptol.Tetr.162. **-γνωστος** or **-γνωτος**, ον, easy to recognize or understand, Sor.1.58, Artem.4.84, Cat.Cod.Astr.1.114; αἰτίαι Corn.ND9: Comp., a more skilled recognizer, cj. in Hp.Ep.22. **-δεκτος**, ον, easily receiving, τινος Sch.A.R.1.1005. **-δοτος**, ον, = εὐένδοτος, Antyll.ap.Orib.45.15.5. **-δρομος**, ον, easily scaled, γεώλοφον Agath.2.2; assailable, χωρία τοῖς βαρβάροις Id.5.14: metaph., φιλοσοφία εὐ. σοφισταῖς Them.Or.20.235d.

**εὐεπίη**, ἡ, Ion. for εὐέπεια, Hp.Decent.3, AP6.322 (Leon.), IG14.1089, 2012 Cb4.

⊕**εὐεπί-θετος**, ον, easy to set upon or attack, τινι Th.6.34, D.C.50.32 (Comp.); τόποι Plb.4.19.12; εὐεπίθετον ἦν..τοῖς πολεμίοις was easy for them to make an attack, X.An.3.4.20 (but εὐ. τοῖς ἐχθροῖς exposed to assault by.., Antip.Stoic.3.255); εὐ. ὁ μεθύων Arist.Pol.1314b34; εὐ. τοῖς..ἀμφισβητητικοῖς Pl.Plt.306a. Adv. εὐεπιθέτως, ἔχειν to be exposed, Aen.Tact.23.4. **-κλειστος**, ον, gloss on εὐκλήϊς, Sch.Il.24.318. **-ληπτος**, ον, open to censure, Plb.29.5.1. **-λόγιστος**, ον, easily inferred, S.E.M.1.297, Gal.18(2).27. **-μεικτος**, ον, accessible, χώρα πᾶσα εὐ. Str.11.2.2; of men, τὸ εὐ. πρὸς ἀλλήλους Id.11.4.6, cf. Poll.5.138. Adv. -τως ib.139. **-νόητος**, ον, fertile in devices, 'sharp' in business, Vett.Val.44.22. **-πόλαστος**, ον, tending to return or be vomited, Sor.1.109. **-σημος**, ον, easily distinguished, Sch.DIl.23.240. **-στρεπτος**, ον, easily turned, ἐπὶ τὸ χεῖρον App.Pun.50. **-στροφος**, ον, easily twisted, EM616.7. II. beautifully curved, of a dome, Agath.5.9. **-τακτος**, ον, submissive, εἴς τι AP11.73 (Nicarch.). **-τευκτος**, ον, easily hitting the mark, successful, περί, πρός, εἴς τι, Vett.Val.39.20, 40.36, 45.10; ἐν μάχαις Malch.p.391D.; opportune, βοήθημα Sever.Clyst.p.34D. **-τήδευμα**, ατος, τό, act embodying good conduct, cj. in Stoic.ap.Stob.2.7.11e (pl.). **-φορία**, ἡ, 'embarras de richesse', in respect of plurality of causes, S.E.P.1.181. **-φορος**, ον, inclined, prone, πρός τι Corn.ND35; εἴς τι Sch.Ar.Pl.990: Comp., Phld.Lib.p.43O.; esp. of authors who are fond of particular phrases, freq. in Gramm., ἐπί.. Sch.S.Aj.693: c. inf., Sch.E.Ph.4. Adv. -ρως v.l. in Sch.Pi.P.4.207; εὐ. ἔχειν πρός τι Str.1.2.20. II. leading easily, ὁδὸς ἐπί τινα D.H.10.46. ⊕ **-χείρητος**, ον, easy to be attacked, Str.5.3.7, Poll.1.172. Adv. -τως Hierocl.in CA10p.436M. 2. easy to be attempted or proven, πρόβλημα Arist.APr.42b29, cf. Top.111a11 (Comp.). 3. insidious, Ph.2.107 (Comp.). II. readily attempting, D.L.4.30. **-ψογος**, ον, open to censure, διὰ γυναῖκα Heph.Astr.1.1.

**εὐέργ-εια,** Ion. -είη, ἡ, = sq. I, *AP*15.34 (Arethas). **2.** *ease* of a surgical operation, Orib.45.18.14. ⊛ **-εσία,** Ion. **-εσίη,** ἡ, *well-doing*, opp. κακοεργίη, Od.22.374; opp. κακότης, Thgn.548, etc. **II.** *a good deed, kindness*, εὐεργεσίας ἀποτίνειν Od.22.235, cf. Hes.*Th.*503 (pl.); ἡ ἐξ Ἱστιαίου εὐ. done by him, Hdt.5.11; ἐκτίνειν Id.3.47 (pl.); εὐεργεσίας ἀποδέξασθαι ἔς τινας ib.67; καταθέσθαι ἔς τινα Th.1.128; εὐ. πεποιημέναι ἔς τινα Hdt.4.165; προέσθαι X.*An.*7.7.47; προσφέρειν Pl.*Grg.*513e; opp. εὐ. ἀπολαβεῖν Isoc.14.57; εὐ. ὀφείλεταί μοι Th.1.137, cf. 32; ἀντ' εὐεργεσίης for *service done*, Simon.97.6, Theoc. 17.116, cf. B.1.47 (pl.), *IG*1².108; ἀπ' εὐεργεσίας καθίστασαν τοὺς βασιλεῖς Arist.*Pol.*1286ᵇ10: c. gen., εὐ. τῆς πόλεως *good service done* the state, Pl.*Lg.*850b: pl., *public services*, τὰς τῶν προγόνων εὐεργεσίας Lys. 14.24, etc. **2.** ψηφίζεσθαί [τινι] εὐεργεσίαν to vote him *the title of* εὐεργέτης (q.v.), D.20.60, cf. *IG*2².29, etc.; κείσεταί σοι εὐ. ἐν τῷ ἡμετέρῳ οἴκῳ ἐς αἰεὶ ἀνάγραπτος Th.1.129, cf. X.*HG*1.1.26, etc. **III.** Εὐεργεσία, personified, = Lat. *Liberalitas*, D.C.71.34. **2.** epith. of Hera at Argos, Hsch.

**Εὐεργέσια,** τά, festival of Ptolemy Euergetes at Delos, *SIG*²588. 54 (ii B.C.).

⊛ **εὐεργέτ-εια,** ἡ, = εὐεργέτις, *UPZ*81 ii9,10 (iv B.C.). **-έω,** the augm. εὐηργ- is sts. found, esp. in codd., as impf. εὐηργέτουν X.*Ap.* 26: aor. εὐηργέτησα Ar.*Pl.*835, v.l. in Din.1.16, but ηὐεργέτησα Lys. 9.14: pf. εὐηργέτηκα v.l. in Lycurg.140: pf. Pass. εὐηργέτημαι X. *Mem.*2.2.3, *SIG*798.5 (Cyzicus, i A.D.), but Inscrr. and Pap. have εὐεργέτηκα *IG*2².573 (iv B.C.), εὐεργέτημαι *PLond.*2.169.26 (i A.D.), εὐεργετήθην *IG*7.2808 (Hyettus, iii A.D.), ηὐεργετημένοι *PTeb.*326.16 (iii A.D.):—*to be a benefactor*, S.*Ph.*670, *IG*2².786, etc.; [Ἰησοῦς] διῆλθεν -τῶν *Act.Ap.*10.38. **2.** *to be proclaimed as* εὐεργέτης I. 2, *JHS*10.76 (Patara, i A.D.). **II.** c. acc. pers., *do good services* or *show kindness to* one, τοὺς θανόντας εἰ θέλεις εὐεργετεῖν A.*Fr.*266.1, cf. *Eu.*725, E.*Ion*1540, Lys.l.c., etc.; ὁ νόμος βούλεται -τεῖν βίον ἀνθρώπων Democr.248; εὐ. τὸν δῆμον *IG*2².791.25, etc.; τὸν θεὸν εὐεργετηκότες *SIG*417.13 (Delph., iii B.C.): c. acc. cogn., εὐ. τινὰ τὴν μεγίστην εὐεργεσίαν Pl.*Ap.*36c, cf. *R.*615b; ὅ τι ἂν ἡμᾶς εὐεργετήσῃς ib.345a; μεγάλως or μεγάλα εὐ., X.*Cyr.*8.2.10,12: c. dat. rei, χρήμασιν εὐ. ib.2:—Pass., *have a kindness done one*, εὐεργεσίαν εὐεργετηθεὶς Pl.*Grg.*520c; μείζω εὐηργετημένοι X.*Mem.*2.2.3; καί τι εὐεργέτηται ὑπ' ἐμοῦ Pl.*Cri.*43a; ἀντὶ πολλῶν καὶ μεγάλων ὧν εὐεργετήθη παρὰ τοῦ θεοῦ *IG*7.2808 (Hyettus, iii A.D.); εὐεργετούμενος εἰς χρήματα Pl.*Smp.*184b. **-ημα,** ατος, τό, *service done, kindness*, πρός τινα X.*Cyr.*8.2.2, cf. Hp.*Ep.*25 (pl.), etc.: pl., X.*Cyr.*5.5.34, Isoc.4.34, Arist.*EN*1161ᵃ16, *IG*2².808, etc. ⊛ **-ης** (Thess. **εὐϝεργέτας** *IG*9(2). 257.5 (v B.C.)), ου, ὁ, *benefactor*, Pi.*P.*2.24, S.*Ant.*284; τινι to one, Hdt.6.30, E.*HF*1252: more commonly c. gen., τῆς γῆς Id.*Rh.*151, cf. Pl.*Cra.*403e, etc. **2.** as an honorary title, εὐ. βασιλέος ἀνεγράφη was registered as the King's *benefactor*, Hdt.8.85, cf. 3.140; πρόξεινος καὶ εὐ. Id.8.136, cf. *IG*1².82, X.*HG*6.1.4, etc.; μέγιστος εὐ. παρ' ἐμοὶ ἀναγεγράψῃ Pl.*Grg.*506c, cf. Lys.20.19, etc.; οἱ ἐξουσιαστοὶ αὐτῶν εὐ. καλοῦνται *Ev.Luc.*22.25: conferred on kings and emperors, as Antigonus, *Inscr.Prien.*2.6 (iv B.C.); ὁ παντὸς κόσμου σωτὴρ καὶ εὐ., of Trajan, *IG*12(1).978 (Carpathos); σὺ ὁ εὐ., mode of address to a superior, *POxy.*38.13 (i A.D.), 486.27 (ii A.D.), etc. **II.** as Adj., *beneficent, bountiful*, ἀνήρ Pi.*O.*2.94, cf. *P.*4.30. **-ητέον,** *one must show kindness to*, τοὺς φίλους X.*Mem.*2.1.28. **-ητικός,** ή, όν, *beneficent*, v.l. in Arist.*EN*1171ᵇ16, cf. *Gloss.* **-ία,** ἡ, = εὐεργεσία II, *Philol.*71.39 (Delph., iii B.C.). **-ικός,** ή, όν, *productive of benefit, beneficent*, ὠφέλιμα καὶ εὐ. Arist.*Rh.*1388ᵇ12, cf. Phld.*Piet.*11, etc.; δόξα εὐ. a reputation *for beneficence*, Arist.*Rh.*1361ᵃ28; ἀρετὴ δύναμις εὐ. πολλῶν καὶ μεγάλων ib.1366ᵃ38: c. gen. pers., φιλανθρωπία ἕξις εὐ. ἀνθρώπων Pl.*Def.*412e; τὸ εὐ. *beneficence*, D.S.1.25: Comp., τὸ -ώτερον Hdn.6.9.8; of persons, *beneficent, bountiful*, εὐεργετικὸν (v.l. -ητικὸν) εἶναι καλὸν Arist.*EN*1171ᵇ16, etc.; εὐ. χρηστὸς φιλάνθρωπος Muson.*Fr.*8 p.39 H.: Sup. **-ώτατος,** εἰς τοὺς Ἕλληνας Plb.7.8.6. Adv. **-κῶς,** διακείμενος *OGI*90.11 (Rosetta, Ptol. V), cf. *IG*5(2).266. 13 (Mantinea, i B.C.). ⊛ **-ις,** ιδος, (parox.) fem. of εὐεργέτης, E. *Alc.*1058: as Adj., εὐ. ψυχή Pl.*Lg.*896e; ἀρετή Ph.2.164:—also -ισσα, ἡ, Demitsas Μακεδ. No.421 (Thessalonica, ii A.D.).

⊛ **εὐεργ-έω,** *cultivate land well*, *BGU*1118.27, al. (i B.C.). ⊛ **-ημα,** ατος, τό, late form, = εὐεργέτημα, *JHS*22.366 (dub. l.). **-ής,** ές, (ἔργον) *well-wrought, well-made*, of chariots, εὐεργέος ἔκπεσε δίφρου Il.5.585; of ships, μία δ' ἤγαγε νηῦς εὐ. 24.396, and freq. in Od., cf. *IG*1².74.27; πηδάλιον Hes.*Op.*629; of garments, ἀμφ' ὤμοισιν ἔχουσ' εὐεργέα λώπην Od.13.224; of gold, *wrought*, χρυσοῦ.. εὐεργέος ἑπτὰ τάλαντα 24.274. **2.** *well-done*: hence in pl., εὐεργέα, = the Prose εὐεργεσίαι, *benefits, services*, οὐκ ἔστι χάρις μετόπισθ' εὐεργέων 22.319, cf. 4.695; also ἀθάνατοι χαίρουσι βροτῶν εὐεργέσι τιμαῖς *Milet.*1(7). 205b (ii A.D.). **3.** = εὐεργός II. 2, τῷ ψυχρῷ Olymp.*in Mete.*313. 9. **4.** *easy*, of a surgical operation, Antyll.ap.Orib.45.2.6. **5.** *effective*, τὴν εὐώνυμον χεῖρα -εστέραν Sor.2.61. **-ία·** τορύνη, εὐπιστία, Hsch. (cf. εὔργη and εὐοργία). **-ός,** όν, *doing good* or *well, upright*, of women, Hom., only in Od., in phrase καὶ ἥ κ' εὐεργὸς ἔῃσιν 11.434, al. **2.** *serviceable*, πρὸς τὴν χρῆσιν Arist.*PA*660ᵃ10, cf. Zeno *Stoic.*1.28; χάρτη εὐ. εἰς ἀπογραφὴν (of τὸ ἡγεμονικόν) *Stoic.* 2.28. Adv. **-γῶς,** ἔχειν πρός τι Arist.*Mete.*377ᵇ25. **3.** Astrol., = ἀγαθοποιός, Man.3.63, al. **II.** Pass., *well-wrought, well-tilled*, γῆ *Gp.*2.46.2. **2.** *easy to work*, [ὕαλος] Hdt.3.24; ὕλη Arist.*Ph.*194ᵃ 34; ξύλον Thphr.*HP*3.9.6 (Comp.); ἔρια Luc.*Fug.*12; *easily reaped*, λᾷον Theoc.10.43.

**εὐερέθιστος,** ον, *easily excited, irritable*, Str.14.2.24; μέρη Ruf.ap. Orib.8.39.1; διαθέσεις Antyll.ap.eund.10.13.6; *easily provoked*, εἰς ὀργάς Plot.1.8.14.

**εὐερία,** ἡ, *fineness of wool, fleeciness*, Pl.Com.169.

**εὐέριος,** ον, = εὔερος, Phot. s. v. εὔειρον: condemned by Phryn.122.

**εὐέρκ-εια,** ἡ, *security*, Pl.*Lg.*778c, 779b. **-ής** (Cret. **ουερκής** *Hymn.Curet.*10), ές, (ἕρκος) *well-fenced, well-walled*, αὐλή Il.9.472, Od.21.389; οἶκος Pi.*Pae.*4.45; ἄλσος Id.*O.*13.109; πόλις A.*Supp.* 955; ἀκρόπολις J.*AJ*15.11.4; χώρα εὐ. πρὸς τοὺς πολεμίους Pl.*Lg.* 760e; ὑποδοχή ib.848e: Sup., -έστατοι πράξεις ὡσανεὶ πόλεις Ph.1. 681; *secure*, θύραι δ' εὐερκέες εἰσί Od.17.267 (v.l. εὐεργέες). Adv. **-κῶς** Plu.2.503c. **2.** *girding in, surrounding*, of nets, Opp.*H.* 4.655.

**εὐέρκτης,** ου, ὁ, poet. for εὐεργέτης, *AP*9.92 (Antip. Thess.), *BCH* 23.302 (Termessus): pl., as a title of rank, *Arch.Pap.*1.220 (ii B.C.).

**εὐερμ-έω,** *to be favoured by Hermes, to be fortunate*, Poll.5.135 (Phot. wrongly εὐερνῶ). **-ής,** ές, (Ἑρμῆς) *fortunate*, Vett.Val.14. 24, Hsch. **-ία,** ἡ, *good luck*, Ael.*NA*5.39, Poll.5.135.

**εὐερνής,** ές, (ἔρνος) *sprouting well, flourishing*, δάφνα E.*IT*1100 (lyr.); of a kind of Cassia, Dsc.1.13; δένδρον -έστατον Ph.1.629; of men and animals, *well-grown*, Posidon.*Fr.*28 J. (Comp.), Str.11.4. 3, *Epigr.Gr.*314.10 (Smyrna): Comp. -έστερα, νήπια Gal.17(1).826; of countries, *rich in plants*, εὔβοτος καὶ εὐ. Str.16.1.24.

**εὔερος,** ον, Att. form of εὔειρος (q.v.).

**εὐερωτητικός,** ή, όν, *good at questioning*, Chrysipp.*Stoic.*2.42.

**εὐέστιος,** ον, (εὐεστώ) *prosperous*, of Delos, Call.*Del.*325; γῆρας Id.*Epigr.* in *Berl.Sitzb.*1912.548.

**εὐεστότερος,** ον, Comp. (no Posit.), *in better case, healthier*, Aët.5. 53; cf. sq. (Fort. εὐεκτότερος.)

**εὐεστώ,** οῦς, ἡ, (εὖ, ἑστώ, v. sub εὖ) *well-being*, title of work by Democr. (of Happiness as the Supreme Good), *prosperity*, ἐν τῇ παρελθούσῃ εὐεστοῖ Hdt.1.85; ἐν εὐ. φίλῃ A.*Th.*187, *Ag.*929; χαίρουσαν εὐεστοῖ πόλιν ib.647, cf. Call.*Aet.*4.1.7.

⊛ **εὐετηρία,** ἡ, (ἔτος) *a good season* (for the fruits of the earth), X. *HG*5.2.4, etc.: in pl., ἐν ταῖς εὐ. Arist.*GA*760ᵇ3. **2.** *thriving*, Pl. *Smp.*188a; of cattle, Arist.*HA*574ᵃ14, al. **3.** generally, *prosperity, plenty*, ἡ ἐκτὸς εὐ. Id.*EN*1098ᵇ26, cf. 1155ᵃ8, *Pol.*1306ᵇ11, *SIG* 799.16 (Cyzicus, i A.D.), etc.: personified, Εὐ. *IG*12(2).262 (Mytil.), *Ath.Mitt.*37.288 (Pergam., ii A.D.), etc.; as name of a trireme, *IG*2². 1607.6.

**εὐετία,** poet. -ίη, ἡ, = foreg., *AP*14.121.4 (Metrod.).

**εὐεύρετος,** ον, (εὑρίσκω) *easy to find*, χώρα εὐεύρετος ἑκάστοις a place *in which it will be easy to find* everything, X.*Oec.*8.17, cf. *Mem.*3.1.10.

**εὐέφικτος,** ον, *easy to find in use, current*, ἡ τοῦ ἄρθρου παράθεσις, ἡ εἰς τὸ πληθυντικὸν μετάθεσις, A.D.*Synt.*44.26, 185.21, prob. in Phld. *Rh.*2.254, cf. 1.63 S.

**εὐεφόδευτος,** ον, *easily approached* or *comprehended*, λόγος Iamb. *in Nic.*p.95 P.

**εὐέφοδος,** ον, *easy to come at* or *attack, assailable, accessible*, of places, X.*Cyr.*2.4.13, Plb.1.26.2, etc. **II.** *easily conducted*, ζήτησις S.E.*M.*7.25.

**εὐέψητος,** ον, *readily cooked*, Thphr.*CP*4.12.12, Dsc.1.128, *Gp.*2. 25.1 (Comp.).

**εὐζηλ-ία,** ἡ, *good, correct style* (cf. ζῆλος), ἡ ἐν τοῖς λόγοις εὐ. καὶ καθαριότης Plu.*Lyc.*21. ⊛ **-ος,** ον, *in good style* (cf. ζῆλος), οὐκ εὐ. ἀναχρονισμός Eust.361.24. Adv. **-λως,** μελετᾶν *AP*11.144 (Cereal.). **II.** *enviable*, Nic.*Al.*9.

**εὐζήτητος,** ον, *readily ascertained*, Gal.10.590.

**εὔζυγος,** Ep. ἐΰζ-, ον, (ζυγόν III) of ships, *well-benched*, Od.13.116, 17.288, A.R.1.4; ἅρμα θαλάσσης Opp.*H.*1.190; εὐσδύγων prob. in Alc.*Oxy.*1233 *Fr.*4.9.

**εὔζυμος,** ον, *well-leavened*, Gal.14.46.

⊛ **εὔζυξ,** ῡγος, ὁ, ἡ, *well-matched*, μαζοί *AP*5.55 (Diosc.).

**εὐζω-έω,** *live well*, M.Ant.3.12. ⊛ **-ΐα,** ἡ, *well-living*, Arist.*EN*1098ᵇ 21, Hierocl. *in CA Praef.*p.416 M., al.; *civil well-being*, *PMasp.*19.28, al. (vi A.D.); also, *means of subsistence*, *PLond.*5.1708.20 (vi A.D.): trisyll., metri gr., ἱερὸν εὐζῴας ἄωτον Pi.*P.*4.131: pl. -ζωΐαι, opp. κακοζωΐαι, Herm. *in Phdr.*p.179 A. **-ῗτον·** καλῆς ζωῆς, Suid., Phot.

**εὔζωμον,** τό, *rocket, Eruca sativa*, Thphr.*HP*1.6.6, al., *CP*2.5.3, *PCair.Zen.*292.15 (iii B.C.), Dsc.2.140, *POxy.*1088.15 (i A.D.), Ael. *NA*6.46, Gal.1.681. (Prop. neut. of **εὔζωμος,** ον, *making good broth.*)

**εὐζων-ία,** ἡ, *marauding by light-armed men*, used for Heb. *Gad* (Phoen. deity, = Τύχη) by Aq.*Ge.*30.11, with ref. to the play on *gādh* (quasi 'marauding band') ib.49.19:—hence -ίζω, ibid.

**εὔζωνος,** Ep. ἐΰζ-, ον, (ζώνη) *well-girdled*, Hom. (only in Il. and *h.Cer.*), as epith. of women, Il.1.429, *h.Cer.*255, al. **2.** later, of men, *girt up for exercise, active*, μῆκος δ' ὁδοῦ εὐζώνῳ ἀνδρὶ πέντε ἡμέραι ἀναισιμοῦνται Hdt.1.72; τριήκοντα ἡμερέων εὐζώνῳ ὁδός ib.104, cf. 2. 34, Th.2.97; of light troops, X.*An.*5.4.23, Plb.3.35.7, Plu.*Demetr.* 9; of ὁπλῖται without their heavy shields, X.*An.*7.3.46: generally, *well-equipped*, Lxx *Jo.*4.13; also εὔ. τῇ κεφαλῇ πυκτεύειν Philostr.*Im.* 2.19; later, of ships, Max.Tyr.1.3. Adv. **-νως** Alciphr.3.55. **3.** of a garment, *well-girded*, dub. in S.*Fr.*342. **4.** metaph., *unencumbered*, πενία Plu.*Pel.*3; εὔ. καὶ ἐλεύθερος βίος D.C.56.6. **5.** in Lit. Crit., *work-a-day, unpretending*; in depreciatory sense, *cheap*, τὸ εὔ. καὶ οἷον εὐτελὲς εἶδος τοῦ λόγου Hermog.*Id.*2.10; τὸ εὔ. χωρὶς εὐτελείας ib.11; ἐκπίπτειν τῷ λόγῳ εἰς τὸ -ότερον ib.1.5.

**εὔζωος,** ον, (ζωή) *living long, tenacious of life*, Thphr.*CP*4.4.10 (Comp.), 5.4.3.

**εὔζωρος,** ον, *quite pure, unmixed*, of wine, Hp.*Morb.*3.14, E.*Alc.*

757, Ar.*Ec.*227: Comp. -ότερος, εὐζωρότερον.., ὦ παῖ, δός Diph.58, cf. Cratin.412, Eup.382; also κέρασον εὐζωρέστερον Antiph.139; πίνειν.. κύλικας εὐζωρεστέρας Eub.150.8 (= Ephipp.3.11), cf. *Lyr. Adesp.*p.681 Bgk.

**εὔζωστος**, ον, (ζώννυμαι) *easily girt, convenient for girding*, ἢ εὐζωστότατος αὐτὸς ἑωυτοῦ ἐστι Hp.*Art.*14; gloss on εὔζωνος, Sch.D Il.1.429.

**εὐηγενής**, ές, Ep. for εὐγενής, *h.Ven.*229, Theoc.27.43, *IG*14.1389 i 29 (cf. εὐηφενής).

**εὐηγεσία**, ἡ, (ἡγέομαι) *good leadership*, ἐξ εὐηγεσίης Od.19.114.

**εὐηγής**, ές, = εὐαγής, dub. l. in Aret.*CD*1.13.

**εὐηγορ-έω**, Dor. εὐᾱγ-, *speak well of, praise*, Pi.*I.*1.51 (Pass.). ⊛ -ία, ἡ, *good words, praise*, Call.*Lav.Pall.*139. -ος, ον, (ἀγορεύω) *speaking well* or *auspiciously*, Eub.71 codd. Ath.

**εὐήδεια**, ἡ, prob. f.l. for εὐείδεια, Corn.*ND*15.

**εὐήδονος**, ον, *attractive*, ὀφθαλμός Heph.*Astr.*1.1.

**εὐήδυντος**, ον, *palatable*, Orib.*inc.*13.34. **εὐηερίη**, v. εὐαερία.

**εὐήθ-εια**, poet. also εὐηθία, Ion. -ίη, ἡ, *goodness of heart, guilelessness*, generally in ironical sense, πάνυ γενναίαν εὐ. Pl.*R.*348c, cf. D. 24.52, *Com.Adesp.*773; δι' εὐηθίην by his *good nature*, Hdt.3.139. 2. in bad sense, *simplicity, silliness*, ἐς τοσοῦτο εὐηθίης ἀνήκει τοῦτο Id.7. 16.γ', cf. 1.60; κουφόνους εὐηθία A.*Pr.*385; ἀνωφελὴς εὐηθία.. γυνή E.*Hipp.*639; πολλῆς -είας, ὅστις οἴεται Th.3.45; -ειάν τινος καταγιγνώσκειν Lys.26.2. ⊛ -ης, ες, (ἦθος) *good-hearted, simple-minded, guileless*, Pl.*R.*349b; of swans, Arist.*HA*615ᵃ33; -έστεροι, opp. πανουργότατοι, Lys.3.44; τὸ εὔηθες, = εὐήθεια, Th.3.83. b. of a courtesan, *of easy virtue*, Archil.19. 2. in bad sense, *simple, silly*, πρῆγμα εὐηθέστατον Hdt.1.60; μῦθος, λόγος, Id.2.45, Pl.*Lg.*818b (Sup.); ἥψατο πρῶτον τοῦ -εστάτου attacked the *silliest* argument first, Arist.*Rh.*1418ᵇ23; κακοήθης δ' ὢν τοῦτο παντελῶς εὐήθης φήθης D.18. 11; τὸ τῶν προβάτων ἦθος εὐ. Arist.*HA*610ᵇ23: as Subst., *simpleton*, X.*HG*2.3.16; εὐηθές [ἐστι] c. inf., it is *simple, foolish, absurd*, Arist. *Metaph.*1062ᵇ34, cf. Democr.67; λίαν εὐ. Arist.*APo.*88ᵇ17. 3. metaph., of wounds or illnesses, *mild, easily treated*, opp. κακοήθης (malignant), Hp.*VM*8: Comp., Id.*Prorrh.*1.98: Sup., Id.*Prog.* 20. b. [τρώματα] ἐν χωρίοισι εἶναι εὐήθεσι.. φαινόμενα *innocent* (not dangerous), Id.*Prorrh.*2.12; cf. εὐχερής III. 2. II. Adv. -θως, ἔχω Pl.*Phd.*100d, cf. Arist.*Metaph.*1024ᵇ32: Comp. -έστερα, τοῦ δέοντος Pl.*Plt.*276e: Sup. -έστατα E.*Andr.*625 (εὐήθης and -εια discussed by Gal.18(2).236–8). -ία, Ion. -ίη, = foreg. (q.v.). -ίζομαι, Med., *to act like an* εὐήθης, *play the fool*, πρὸς ἀλλήλους Pl.*R.*336c; *to be merry, jest*, Philostr.*VA*8.7. -ικός, ή, όν, *like an* εὐήθης, *good-natured*, ironically, Pl.*R.*343c, *Chrm.*175c. 2. *simple, foolish*, εὐηθικώτερόν ἐστι ἢ ὥστε.. Arist.*Ph.*218ᵇ8, cf. Iamb.*Myst.*3.17. Adv. -κῶς Ar.*Nu.*1258, Arist.*GA*757ᵃ2; εὐ. ἔχειν Pl.*Hp.Ma.*301d.

**Εὐήϊος**, = Εὔιος, Ph.2.559.

**εὐήκης**, ες, (ἀκή A) *well-pointed*, αἰχμῆς.. εὐήκεος Il.22.319; *keen-edged*, φάσγανα A.R.2.101, Phanocl.1.8; ξυρόν Nic.*Al.*411.

**εὐηκής**, ές, (ἄκος) *healing*, βάξις Emp.112.11.

**εὐηκο-έω**, *to be* εὐήκοος, *listen and obey willingly*, c. gen., τῶν κρινόντων Jusj.ap.Stob.4.1.48. -ΐα, ἡ, *ready obedience*, D.S.17.55. II. *readiness to hear prayer*, Eun.*VS*p.458 B., Procl.*in Cra.*p.72 P., Marin.*Procl.*1, 34(pl.). ⊛ -ος, Dor. εὐάκ- [ᾱ], ον, (ἀκοή) *hearing well* or *easily*, Hp.*Aph.*3.17 (Comp.). 2. *hearing willingly, obedient*, Arist.*EN*1102ᵇ27 (Comp.). 3. *inclined to give ear*, of the gods, θνατοῖς *AP*9.316.5 (Leon.), cf. *IG*12(2).101,105 (Mytil.); written εὐήκοος, *Sammelb.*4607.5: generally, *inclined*, πρὸς μεταβολὴν Thphr.*CP* 2.14.5 (Sup.). Adv. -όως, διακεῖσθαι πρός τι Plb.27.7.7. II. Pass., *easily heard, audible*, Arist.*Top.*107ᵇ2; -ώτερα τὰ τῆς νυκτ's Id.*Pr.* 899ᵃ19. 2. *pleasant to the ear, agreeable*, τὸ εὐ. Demetr.*Eloc.*48, al.

⊛ **εὐηλάκατος** [ᾰκ], Aeol. εὐᾱλ-, ον, *possessing a fine distaff*, of women, Theoc.28.22.

**εὐήλᾰτος**, ον, (ἐλαύνω) *easy to drive* or *ride over*, πεδία *fit for cavalry operations*, X.*Cyr.*1.4.16, cf. *HG*5.4.54; ἡ τῆς ἀρετῆς [ὁδὸς] τὰ πρῶτα οὐκ εὐήλατά κως παρέχειν δοκέει Eus.Mynd.63. II. *well-ground*, ἄλφι Antim.64; *well-hammered*, ἄκμων Euph.51.10.

⊛ **εὐῆλιξ**, ῐκος, ὁ, ἡ, (ἡλικία) *of good stature*, Polem.*Phgn.*5; Στάτιος (στάτης cod.) ὁ εὐῆλιξ εἴρηται Lyd.*Mag.*1.23.

**εὐήλιος**, Dor. εὐάλ- [ᾱ], ον, *sunny, genial*, χώρη Hp.*Aff.*60, cf. E. *Hipp.*129 (lyr.), X.*Oec.*9.4; ἁμέραι Ar.*Ra.*242 (lyr.); εὐάλιον πῦρ *the sun's heat*, E.*IT*1138 (lyr.); εὐ. οἰκία Arist.*Oec.*1345ᵃ32; ἐν εὐηλίῳ *in a sunny spot*, Id.*HA*616ᵇ14; τὸ μετόπωρον εὐ. Philostr.*VA*4.17. Adv. -ίως *in sunlight*, A.*Eu.*906. II. of persons, *fond of the sun, fond of basking*, Philostr.*VA*6.4.

**εὐημερ-έω**, (εὐήμερος) *spend one's days cheerfully*, S.*El.*653; ταῖσι Θήβαις εἰ.. εὐημερεῖ καλῶς τὰ πρὸς σέ though your relations with Thebes *are all fair weather*, Id.*OC*616; τὸ εὐημεροῦν τῆς πόλεως the *prosperous* class, Arist.*Pol.*1308ᵇ24; πόλεις εὐημεροῦσαι ib.1322ᵇ38; εὐ. καὶ τροφὴν ἄφθονον ἔχειν *thrive*, Id.*HA*573ᵇ22; opp. χαλεπῶς ἔχειν, ib.597ᵇ10; εὐ. τοῖς σώμασι Id.*GA*775ᵇ16. 2. *to be successful* in a thing, τὴν ἐκκλησίαν -ήσας ᾤχόμην φέρων Aeschin.2.63; καθ' ὑπερβολὴν εὐ. Thphr.*Char.*21.11; τῆς Λεαίνης παρὰ τῷ Δημητρίῳ -ούσης Macho ap.Ath.13.577d; of physicians, *to be successful* with a remedy, Gal.12.749: c. acc., τοὺς Ἐπιγόνους εὐημερήκει, of a dramatist, Ath.13.584d; of an actor, εὐ. ἐπὶ τραγῳδίας Suid. s.v. σαυτὴν ἐπαινεῖς; ἀκρόαμα εὐημεροῦν Plu.2.521f: generally, *have good luck*, ἐν ἅπασιν Philem.79.3, cf. *Com.Adesp.*110.8. -ημα, ατος, τό, *a success*, usu. in the military sense, Plb.3.72.2, *OGI*299.7 (Pergam., pl.), Cic. *Att.*5.21.2, D.S.13.17, Ph.2.120: pl., *successes*, *Inscr.Prien.*109.90 (ii B.C.), 111.130 (i B.C.): generally, *strokes of good fortune*, Epicur. *Fr.*488; σωματικὰ εὐ. bodily *excellencies*, Vett.Val.161.16. ⊛ -ία, Dor. εὐᾱμ-, ἡ, *fine weather*, εὐημερίας οὔσης X.*HG*2.4.2; γενομένης Arist.*HA*569ᵇ10: pl., ib.542ᵇ28. II. *prosperity, health and wealth*, E.*El.*197 (lyr.); ἡ ἐκτὸς εὐ. Arist.*EN*1178ᵇ33; *happiness*, Pherecr.213; *joy of living*, ἐνούσης τινὸς εὐ. ἐν [τῷ ζῆν] Arist.*Pol.* 1278ᵇ29; personified, Εὐ. Alex.161, *Schwyzer*462 *A*6 (Tanagra, iii B.C.); -ίας ἡμέραν ἐπιτελεῖν to keep a day of *rejoicing*, Alciphr.1. 21; *good living*, Phld.*Acad.Ind.*p.59 M., al.: pl., ἁδραὶ εὐ. *PRyl.* 233.16 (ii A.D.). 2. *thriving condition, healthiness*, τοῦ σώματος Arist.*HA*543ᵇ26; πρὸς εὐ. καὶ πρὸς ὑγίειαν with a view to.., Id. *Oec.*1345ᵃ26. 3. *honour and glory*, Pi.*I.*1.40; *piece of good luck*, Cic.*Att.*9.13.1, Plu.2.498c; *military success*, Plb.7.9.10; εὐ. ἐμπορικαί *success* in trade, Hippod.ap.Stob.4.1.94; of virtuosi, ἡ παρὰ τοῖς θεάτροις εὐ. Ath.14.631f. ⊛ -ος, Dor. εὐάμ- [ᾱ], ον, (ἡμέρα) *of a fine* or *prosperous day*, εὐ. φάος a *happy* day, S.*Aj.*708 (lyr.). 2. *bright, happy*, εὐάμεροι μολπαί E.*Fr.*773.47 (lyr., nisi leg. -αμερίαι); χρόνῳ δ' ἐξέλαμψεν εὐ. Id.*Hyps.Fr.*41(64).62 (lyr.); πρόσωπον Ar.*Av.* 1322 (lyr.); μοῖρα Pl.*Ti.*71d (perh. with play on ἥμερος); τὸ εὐ. *a prosperous life*, Ph.1.515.

**εὐήμετος**, **εὐημής**, v. sub εὐέμετος, εὐεμής.

**εὐημονία**, ἡ, (ἥμων) *skill in throwing* or *hitting*, glossed by ἐμπειρία, Hsch.

**εὐηνεμ-ία**, ἡ, *fair wind*, Luc.*Lex.*15. -ος, Dor. εὐάν- [ᾱ, exc. in *AP*9.555 (Crin.)], ον, *well as to the winds*, i.e., I. *serene, calm*, πόντου χεῦμα E.*Fr.*316; πλόος εὐ. a *fair* voyage, Theoc.28.5. b. epith. of Zeus at Sparta, Paus.3.13.8. 2. *sheltered from the wind*, λιμένες E.*Andr.*749 (and perh. also λίμνα S.*Fr.*371 (lyr.)); χώρα Luc.*Abd.*27. II. *open to the wind*, [ὡς πῦρ] ἐν εὐανέμοις βάσσαις (cf. εὔπνοος II) S.*Aj.*197 (lyr.), cf. Orib.9.20.1.

**εὐήνιος**, ον, (ἡνία) *obedient to the rein*, ἅρμα Emp.4.5; ὀχήματα Pl. *Phdr.*247b; ἵπποι -ώτατοι Id.*R.*467e; of persons, *tractable, docile*, Id.*Lg.*730b; τὸ ἀγαθὸν εὐ. ὄν Porph.*Abst.*2.39; of a disease, *easily yielding*, Hp.*Virg.*1; cf. εὐάνιος. Adv. -ίως *patiently, tractably*, Pl. *Sph.*217d, Plu.2.9b; ζῆν Arr.*Epict.*4.7.12.

**εὐηνορία**, Dor. -ᾱνορία, ἡ, (εὐήνωρ) *manliness*, E.*HF*407 (lyr.): pl., Pi.*O.*5.20.

**εὐήνῠτος**, ον, (ἀνύω) *easy to achieve*, Hsch.: **εὐήνυστος**, Zonar.

⊛ **εὐήνωρ**, Dor. εὐάνωρ [ᾱ], ορος, ὁ, ἡ, Hom. (only in Od.), prob. '*the joy of men*', φέρον δ' εὐήνορα οἶνον 4.622; φέρον δ' εὐήνορα χαλκόν 13. 19. II. later, of communities, etc., *well-manned, abounding in brave men*, Pi.*O.*1.24, 6.80, etc.; λαός Id.*N.*10.36; ἵππος, of the Trojan horse, Tryph.468.

**εὐηπελ-ής**, ές, *prosperous*, Hsch. (glossed by πρᾶοι, wh. however belongs to εὐήνιοι; perh. fr. *ἄπελος 'strength', cf. ONorse *afl* 'strength'; v. ἀναπελάσας, ἀνηπελίη, κακηπελίη, νηπελέω, ὀλιγηπελέω). -ία, ἡ, *prosperity*, Call.*Cer.*136, Hsch.

**εὐήρᾰτος**, ον, (ἔραμαι) *lovely*, σταθμοί Pi.*O.*5.9; φιλοφροσύναι ib. 6.98; κάλλος Telest.1.6.

**εὐήρεια**· εὔπλοια, εὐχέρεια, Hsch., cf. *EM*390.50. (Leg. εὐηερίη (= εὐαερία), cf. the corrupt gloss εὐηχερία· εὐηρία, εὔπλοια, Hsch.)

**εὐήρετμος**, ον, (ἐρετμόν) *well fitted to the oar*, σκαλμός A.*Pers.* 376. 2. *well-rowed*, πλάτα S.*OC*716 (lyr.); ναῦς E.*Ion*1160.

**εὐηρημένοι**· τετορνημένοι, Hsch.

**εὐήρης**, ες, (ἀραρίσκω) *well-fitted*, Hom. (only in Od.) always of the oar, *well-poised, easy to handle*, λαβὼν εὐ. ἐρετμόν 11.121; οὐδ' εὐήρε' ἐρετμά ib.125, al.; νεὼς εὐ. πίτυλος the plash *of the well-poised oars*, E.*IT*1050; σκάφη Plu.*Ant.*65; *well-knit*, γυῖα Nic.*Th.*81: generally, ὄργανα εὐ. πρὸς τὴν χρείαν *well-fitted for*.., Hp.*Medic.*2; εὐ. τεύχη Orac.ap.Paus.4.12.4; εὐήρεας ἵππους, = εὐαγώγους, Hsch.: fem. εὐήρις, pr. n. in Paus.1.27.4 (s.v.l.).

**εὐήροτος**, ον, (ἀρόω) *easy to cultivate*, πεδίον Str.9.4.5 (s.v.l.), cf. Poll.1.227: irreg. Sup. εὐηρότατον Hsch. (glossed by εὐδιον), Suid.

**εὐήρῠτος**, ον, (ἀρύω A) *good to draw*, ὕδωρ *h.Cer.*106.

**εὐήτριος** (A), Dor. εὐάτρ-, ον, (ἤτριον) *with good* or *fine thread, well-woven*, A.*Fr.*47; ὕφασμα Pl.*Plt.*310e; ὑφὴ (v.l. ὑφαί) D.H.*Comp.*23; ἱμάτιον Luc.*Lex.*9; αἱ εὐ. σινδόνες, of cotton, Str.15.1.20. II. Act., *well-weaving*, τὰν πέπλων εὐάτριον ἐργάτιν.. κερκίδα *AP*6.289 (Leon.).

**εὐήτριος** (B), ον, (ἦτρον), = εὐκοίλιος, Hsch.

**εὐηφεν-έω**, *to be wealthy, prosperous*, Epic.*Oxy.*1794.13. -ής, ές, (ἄφενος) *wealthy*, Il.11.427, 23.81 (vulg. εὐηγ-): as pr. n., *IG*12 (8).376.14 (Thasos).

**εὐήχ-εια**, ἡ, *euphony*, Phld.*Po.*994.24. -έομαι, *to be euphonious*, ib.18. -ής, Dor. εὐᾱχ-, ές, *well-sounding, tuneful*, ὕμνος Pi.*P.*2. 14; ὑμέναιος Call.*Del.*296; ὄργανον Plu.2.437d; *euphonious*, Phld. *Po.*2.3. -ητος, Dor. εὐάχ- [ᾱ], ον, = foreg., ὕμνοι E.*Ion*884 (lyr.); *loud-sounding*, πόντος Id.*Hipp.*1272 (lyr.). -ος, ον, = εὐηχής, *euphonious*, Phld.*Po.*994.24, v.l. in D.H.*Comp.*14, cf. Longin.24.2; *melodious*, of the voice, Ath.3.80d; εὐ. φωνητήρια ὄργανα Ph.1.511; ἀρτηρίαν εὐ. παρασκευάζειν Dsc.2.27; κύμβαλα Lxx *Ps.*150.5: neut. pl. εὔηχα as Adv., κελαδεῖν Ps.-Luc.*Philopatr.*3: regul. Adv. -ήχως Thom.Mag.p.223 R.

**εὐθάλᾰμος** [θᾰ], ον, *blessing wedlock*, Ἀφροδίτη Nonn.*D.*2.324.

**εὐθάλασσος** [θᾰ], ον, *lying well by the sea*, Philostr.*VS*2.1.3. 2. δῶρον εὐ. the gift *of sea-power*, S.*OC*711 (lyr., with allusion to θάλασσα 3). II. *a 'good sailor'*, Alciphr.2.4.

⊛ **εὐθάλ-εια** [θᾰ], ἡ, *bloom, flower* of a thing, εὐδαιμοσύνας Archyt.ap. Stob.3.1.107: εὐθαλία τῶν καρπῶν *EM*442.13. -έω, *bloom, thrive*, Nic.*Fr.*74.16, Plu.2.28e, *POxy.*729.22 (ii A.D.), Q.S.4.423: metaph., Them.*Or.*27.339c. -ής, ές, *blooming, flourishing, thriving*,

Αἴγυπτος A.*Fr.*300.5; γῆρας Men.*Mon.*388: ἄνηθον Mosch.3.100, cf. *AP*9.3 (Antip.), Orph.*A.*912; Χάριτες *AP*7.600 (Jul.): later in Prose, δένδρον *SIG*889.9 (Arcesine, iii A.D.); εὐθαλέστερα παιδία Sabin.ap.Orib.9.17.3; ζῷα εὐθαλῆ *POxy.*902.15 (v A.D.): metaph., τὸ εὐ. [τῆς ψυχῆς] Ph.1.512; πτερὰ εὐ. τῆς ψυχῆς Them.*Or.*21.251b.

**εὐθᾱλής,** ές, Dor. Adj. *flourishing, thriving,* τύχα Pi.*P.*9.72; πέδον B.8.5; εὐκάρπεια E.*Tr.*217 (lyr.); καρποί Ar.*Av.*1062 (lyr.); φύλλα *AP*9.313 (Anyte); εὐθηλής is cj. ib.247 (Phil.), *h.Mart.*9:—also **-θᾰλος,** ον, *thriving well,* v.l. in *EM*197.34.

**εὐθαλπής,** ές, *warming well, genial,* θέρος Q.S.4.541.

**εὐθᾰνᾰσία,** ἡ, *easy, happy death,* Posidipp.18, August.ap.Suet. *Oct.*99, Ph.1.182. **2.** *noble death,* Cic.*Att.*16.7.3.

**εὐθᾰνᾰτ-έω,** *die a noble death, Stoic.*3.156, Plb.5.38.9, J.*AJ* .4.5. **-ος,** ον, *dying easily* or *happily*: εὐ. θάνατος, = εὐθανασία, Men. 23, cf. Paul.Al.*M.*3. Adv. -τως Cratin.413, Men.481.16.

**εὐθάρσ-εια,** ἡ, *good courage,* App.*BC*3.91: -ία, Pl.*Def.*412a. **-έω,** *to be of good courage,* And.2.16: prob. to be written divisim in A.*Th.* 34, *Supp.*1015. **-ής,** ές, *of good courage, h.Mart.*9 (v.l.), A.*Ag.* 930, *Supp.*249, E.*El.*526; ἐν τοῖς δεινοῖς X.*Ages.*11.10; πρὸς κίνδυνον D.S.11.35; τὸ εὐθαρσῆ εἶναι Andronic.Rhod.p.575 M.: Comp. -έστερος Diph.111, Plu.2.69a; of *bolder* interpreters, Ph.1.606: Sup. -έστατος X.*HG*7.1.9. Adv. -ῶς, ἔχειν πρός τι Arist.*EN*1115$^{a}$21. **2.** *safe, secure,* τὰ δεινὰ καὶ τὰ εὐ. X.*Eq.Mag.*4.11.

**εὐθέᾱτος,** ον, (θεάομαι) *easy to be seen,* Poll.5.150.

**εὐθεῖ·** ἥρει, Hsch. **εὐθεῖα,** ἡ, v. εὐθύς A.3.

**εὐθεῖν·** ἐλθεῖν (Cret.), Hsch. **εὐθεῖος,** = εὐόμιλος, Zonar.

**εὐθέμῑτος,** ον, *just, righteous,* σαδράπαι Ἀρχ.Ἐφ.1927.27 (Aranda).

**εὐθένεια,** ἡ, *supply, provisioning,* ὀμνύω..ἔχειν παρ' ἐμαυτῷ χοίρους..εἰς τὴν εὐθένιαν (or -ίαν) τῆς..πόλεως *BGU*649.16 (ii A.D.); εἰς εὐθένειαν τῶν..στρατιωτῶν..οἴνου ξέστας ib.974.6 (iv A.D.), cf. *PGoodsp.Cair.*11.5 (iv A.D.), *POxy.*1412.6 (iii A.D.), 1261.7 (iv A.D.), *PLond.*3.1245.5 (iv A.D.); πᾶσαν εὐθένειαν *supplies* of all kinds, *POxy.*1252$^{v}$.14 (iii A.D., but εὐθηνιαρχικός ib.17); [ᾠὰ] πρὸς διάπρασιν καὶ εὐθένιαν (or -ίαν) τῆς..πόλεως ib.83.11 (iv A.D.), cf. *PSI* 4.309 (iv A.D.); ἐραυνηταῖς εὐθεν[ίας] *PFay.*104.18 (iii A.D.); ἐπὶ τῶν μερισμῶν τῶν σπερμάτων καὶ τῆς εὐθενίας *PTeb.*397.19 (ii A.D., but κοσμητεύσας εὐθηνίας ib.15,28); εὐθενίας ἔπαρχος, = Lat. *praefectus annonae, IG*14.1072 (Rome, ii A.D.); εὐθενείας ἔ. ib.917 (iii A.D.). **II.** *welfare, prosperity, abundance,* Poll.9.160; gloss on εὔσοια, Sch.S.*OC*390, v.l. in Arist.*Rh.*1360$^{b}$16, *HA*602$^{a}$15, al.; *good* physical *condition,* τοῦ σκήνεος εὐθένεια cj. for εὐσθ- in Democr.57.

®**εὐθενέω,** *thrive, flourish,* of animals and plants, μῆλα..εὐθενοῦντα A.*Eu.*944 (lyr.); καρπόν τε γαίας καὶ βοτῶν..ἀστοῖσιν εὐθενοῦντα ib. 908, cf. Thphr.*CP*2.4.5, 5.11.3; μή τιν' οἶκον εὐθενεῖν A.*Eu.*895 (Scalig. for εὐσθ-); εὐθενούντων τῶν πραγμάτων D.18.286; also of men, τοὺς στρατιώτας..εὐθενεῖν Id.8.20; ἡ Λοκρὶς εὐθηνεῖ (leg. εὐθενεῖ) τῷ ζεφύρῳ Thphr.*Vent.*44, cf. Plu.*Publ.*11, Ael.*NA*5.13. **II.** Pass. in same sense, [οἱ Λακεδαιμόνιοι] εὐθενήθησαν Hdt.1.66 codd. (elswh. εὐθηνέω in codd. Hdt.); τὴν πόλιν εὐθενεῖσθαι D.19.231 (s.v.l.). (εὐθηνέω (q.v.) is freq. v.l.; εὐθενέω (Att. acc. to Zonar.) is required by metre in A.*Eu.*895 (cj.), Cratin.327, and is found in best codd. of D., Arist. (v.l. in *PA*680$^{a}$28, *HA*601$^{b}$9, *Mete.*352$^{a}$6, al., εὐσθεν- v.l. in *EN*1100$^{a}$6, *GA*775$^{a}$29, etc.), cod. Urb. of Thphr. *CP*5.11.3, al., Aristid.*Or.*46(3).42, v.l. in Ael.*VH*13.1, etc.)

**εὐθενής·** εὐπαθοῦσα· ἰσχυρά, Hsch.: Sup. -έστατος, οἶκος *PIand.*62.9 (vi A.D.).

**εὐθενία,** ἡ, = εὐθένεια II (q.v.), from which it cannot be distd. after ii B.C.: Ion. **εὐθενίη** (–⏑⏑–) Epigr. in *Rev.Phil.*19.178 (i B.C.), *Epigr.Gr.*1036.19 (Nicomedia); εὐθενία is v.l. in Arist.*Rh.*1360$^{b}$16, *HA*602$^{a}$15 (v.l. εὐσθένεια, εὐθένεια), Porph.*Gaur.*16.2.—From ii A.D. εὐθένεια and εὐθενία begin to be confused with εὐθηνία.

®**εὐθενιᾰκός,** ή, όν, *for food-supply,* εἴδη -κά *provisions, Stud.Pal.* 20.84.3 (iii A.D.).

**εὐθενιαρχέω,** = εὐθηνιαρχέω, *PSI*6.705 (iii A.D.).

**εὐθερᾰπ-ευσία,** ἡ, *ease of treatment,* Heliod.ap.Orib.46.22.11. **-ευτος,** ον, *easy to cure,* Hp.*Coac.*501 (Comp.), Thphr.*HP*9.16.6, etc.: Comp., Phld.*D.*1.24. **2.** *easy to help* or *remedy,* D.C.38.24. **II.** *easily won by kindness* or *attention,* X.*Cyr.*2.2.10.

**εὐθέριστος,** ον, *easily harvested*: εὐθέριστον, τό, *a kind of balsam,* Plin.*HN*12.114, prob. in Dsc.1.19.

**εὐθέρμαντος,** ον, *easy to warm,* Thphr.*CP*4.7.3 (Comp.).

**εὔθερμος,** ον, *very warm,* Hp.*Nat.Puer.*24 (Comp., nisi leg. ἔνθ-).

**εὔθερος,** ον, *pleasant in summer, sunny,* Poll.5.108 codd. (fort. εὐάερος).

**εὐθεσία,** ἡ, *good condition, habit of body,* Hp.ap.Gal.19.101; ἐνιαυτὸς εὐθεσίης a year *of plenty,* ibid.

**εὐθέσμως,** Adv. *lawfully,* ἄλοχον λάβε *AP*9.444 (Eratosth.).

**εὐθετ-έω,** *to be suitable, convenient,* εὐθετεῖ πᾶσι χρῆσθαι for all to use, Thphr.*HP*5.7.4; εὐ. εἴς τι D.S.2.41,48; *to be timely, opportune,* Orph.*Fr.*272; of an epithet, *to be suitable,* Sch.Il.*Oxy.*1086.110; so of food, Diocl.*Fr.*141; of bandages, Gal.18(1).789, al.; λιμένας.. ταῖς μακραῖς ναυσὶν εὐθετοῦντας D.S.5.12: f.l. in Thphr.*HP*1.1.3 codd. **II.** trans., *set in order,* ἕκαστα Luc.*DDeor.*24.1 (v.l. for εὐθετίσαντα), cf. *SIG*1240 (ii A.D.); [τὰς τρίχας] Ar.*Fr.*782; *adorn,* εὐ. ἑαυτήν D.C.51.13; *lay out* a corpse, Id.40.49, cf. Phryn.*PS* p.71 B. **-ησις,** εως, ἡ, *prosperity,* Eust.1383.13. **-ίζω,** *set in order, arrange orderly,* Hes.*Th.*541; χελιδὼν..καλιὴν ηὐθέτιζεν Babr.118.2; τὰς κόμας Luc.*Ind.*29, etc.:—Med., ὀστέον εὐθετισάμενος Hp.*Fract.*8, cf. 16. **II.** in Pass., *to be suitably employed,* εἴς τι A.D.*Adv.*140.11, *Synt.*169.19. **-ισμός,** ὁ, *convenience, propriety,* Id.*Adv.*144.19, *Synt.*309.12; *orderly arrangement,* Simp.*in Ph.*487.29, *in Cat.*336.38. ® **-ος,** ον, (τίθημι) *well-arranged, conveniently placed,* ὀστέα Hp.*Off.*15: Comp. -ώτερος Id.*Fract.*4; ἐν εὐ. τόπῳ in a *suitable* place, Ἀρχ.Δελτ.7.200 (Ephesus). **b.** of the ashes of a corpse, *easily stowed,* A.*Ag.*444 (lyr.); so of the corpse, *laid out* for burial (cf. εὐθετέω), *Supp.Epigr.*1.449 (Phrygia, iii A.D.); εὔ. σάκος, ἀρβύλαι, *well-fitting, ready for use,* A.*Th.*642 (Sch., εὔκυκλον cod. Med.), *Fr.*259; εὔ. εἴς τι D.S.2.57; πρός τι Id.5.37; εὔθετόν ἐστι c. inf., it is *convenient..,* Id.21.21; καιρὸς εὔ. Lxx *Ps.*31(32).6, D.S.5.57. **2.** of persons, *well-adapted,* εἰς τοὺς τραγῳδοὺς εὔ., οὐκ εἰς τὸν βίον Philem.105.5; εἰς, πρὸς φιλίαν, Phld.*Ir.*p.46 W., *Lib.*p.45 O.; εἰς τὴν βασιλείαν τοῦ θεοῦ *Ev.Luc.*9.62; πράγματι for a business, Nicol.ap.Stob.3.1.40; πρός τι Plb.25.3.6, etc.; *quick, able,* κατὰ τὰς ἐντεύξεις τοῖς ὄχλοις εὔ. D.S.33.22: abs., εὔθετοι *fit and proper persons, PTeb.*27.44 (ii B.C.), etc. Adv. -τως, ἔχειν Hp.*Fract.*23; πρός τι D.S.33.4.

**εὐθεώρητος,** ον, *easily seen* or *observed,* Arist.*HA*578$^{a}$20, Thphr. *HP*1.1.1 (Comp.); τινι D.S.19.37. **2.** *easy to perceive,* Arist.*Rh.* 1376$^{b}$31; εὐθεώρητόν ἐστι περί τινος it is *easy to conduct an inquiry* about.., Id.*GA*724$^{a}$17; οὐκ ἔστιν εὐ. ποτέρως.. Id *SE*180$^{b}$3; τίνες εἰσὶ καὶ πόσαι.. Iamb.*Comm.Math.*24: c. acc. et inf., Phld.*Herc.*1251.7.

**εὐθέως,** Adv. of εὐθύς (q.v.).

**εὐθηγής,** ές, *sharpening well, AP*6.63 (Damoch.).

**εὔθηκτος,** ον, *well sharpened, keen,* Lyc.1105, Nonn.*D.* 7.121.

**εὐθηλ-έομαι,** Pass., (εὐθηλής) *to be well-suckled, fatted up,* χοῖρος A.*Fr.*309.1:—also in Act., [παιδία] εὐθηλέοντα, = εὐθαλῆ, Democr. 276. **-ήμων,** ον, gen. ονος, = sq., μόσχος *AP*6.263 (Leon.). **-ής,** ές, v. εὐθᾱλής. **-ία,** ἡ, gloss on εὐθηνία, Suid. **-ος,** ον, (θηλή) *with distended udder,* E.*IA*579 (lyr.), *Ba.*737, *AP*9.224 (Crin.); εὐ. μαστὸς θεᾶς Lyc.1328.

**εὐθήμελκτος,** ον, = νεήμελκτος, Aët.9.42; cf. εὐθυμελγής.

®**εὐθημ-ονέομαι,** Dep. *keep in order, manage,* Pl.*Lg.*758b:—Act., intr., *to be in good order,* Simp.*in Ph.*1067.24; trans. in Tz.*H.*1.367. **-οσύνη,** ἡ, *habit of good management, tidiness,* Hes.*Op.* 471, X.*Cyr.*8.5.7, Ael.*NA*9.17, Dam.*Isid.*231. **II.** *good order,* of the course of nature, Plot.4.4.6, 6.8.17. **III.** personified, Orph. *Fr.*336. **-ων,** ον, gen. ονος, (τίθημι) *tidy in habits,* of animals, Arist.*HA*616$^{b}$23, 618$^{b}$30. **2.** *harmonious,* ἀοιδή A.R.1.569. **II.** Act., *setting in order,* c. gen., δμῳαὶ..δωμάτων εὐ. A.*Ch.*84.

**εὐθηνέω,** *thrive, flourish,* εὐθηνέειν Αἴγυπτον Hdt.2.91,124 codd., cf. X.*Ath.*2.6 codd.; κτήνεσιν εὐθηνεῖ (sc. ὁ ὄλβιος) *h.Hom.*30.10; πρόβατα εὐθηνεῖν may their sheep *thrive, SIG*526.42 (Crete, iii B.C.); τὰ κτήνεα εὐθηνεῖν εἰκός prob. in Hp.*Aër.*12 (εὐθύνειν codd.), cf. *Epid.* 6.4.20 (εὐθυνεῖ vulg., εὐθενεῖ Gal.); freq. in Lxx (*Jb.*21.9, al.), cf. *BGU*1118.30 (i B.C.), al., Ph.1.211, 2.429:—Pass., Αἴγυπτος καρποῖς ἀφθόνοις εὐθηνεῖτο *POxy.*1381.238 (ii A.D.). (εὐθηνέω—Ion. acc. to Zonar.—is freq. v.l. for εὐθενέω (q.v.) and is required by metre in *h.Hom.* l.c.)

**εὐθήνησις,** εως, ἡ, = sq., Phld.*Lib.*p.11 O. (s.v.l.).

®**εὐθηνία,** ἡ, *prosperity, plenty,* Lxx *Ge.*41.29, al., Ph.2.1, al.; ὅπως οἱ ἄλλοι ἐν εὐθηνίᾳ ὦσι *OGI*90.13 (Rosetta, ii B.C.); ὑπηρετεῖν τῇ τε εὐθηνίᾳ καὶ τῇ εὐδαιμονίᾳ ib.669.4 (Egypt, i A.D.); τῶν τὰς καλὰς ἀγόντων ἡμέρας εὐθηνία, description of Isis, *POxy.*1380.135 (ii A.D.); πάντα τὰ πρὸς εὐθηνίαν τῆς χώρας *Peripl.M.Rubr.*48; σώματος *good condition,* Andronic.Rhod.p.573 M. **2.** personified as a goddess, *Abundance, Plenty, IG*4.676 (Thyreatis), *J. of P.*11.144 (Anazarba), prob. in *CIL*10.1624 (Puteoli). **3.** generally, *abundance,* φρονήσεως Ph.1.618; τῶν ἀναγκαίων Id.*Fr.*109 H.; v.l. in Arist.*Rh.*1360$^{b}$16, al. **II.** like Lat. *annona, corn-supply,* εἰς εὐθηνίαν σιτωνίας *SIG*783.16 (Mantinea, i B.C.); ἡ ἀπὸ σιτίων φερομένη εὐθηνία Plu.2.307d; εὐθηνίας ἐπιμελητής *IG*4.795 (ii A.D.); γεναμένῳ ἀγορανόμῳ καὶ ἐπὶ τῆς εὐθηνίας Mitteis *Chr.*227.9 (ii A.D.), cf. *PFlor.* 382.76 (iii A.D.), *OGI*705 (Alexandria, ii A.D., εὐθυνίας lapis); κοσμητεύσας εὐθηνίας (v. εὐθένεια). **2.** *a largess of corn,* εὐθηνία ἔτους τρίτου, personified on coins of Alexandria, *B.Mus.Cat.* No.1164: so in pl., χρήματα πολιτικὰ ἐς εὐθηνίας ἢ νομὰς ἀθροιζόμενα Hdn.7.2.5.

**εὐθηνιάρχ-ης,** ου, ὁ, *commissioner of food-* (esp. *corn-*) *supply, BGU*556 ii 12, *POxy.*1412.1 (both iii A.D.):—hence **-έω,** ib.908.19 (ii A.D.), 2108.3 (iii A.D.), *BCH*12.84 (Zeus Panamaros). **-ία,** ἡ, *CPHerm.*716 (iii A.D.). **-ικός,** ή, όν, στέφανος *POxy.*1252$^{v}$.17 (iii A.D.).

**εὐθηνός,** όν, *thriving, flourishing,* καρποί Lyd.*Ost.*38, cf. Hdn.*Epim.* 175; εὔθυνος, v.l. in *EM*197.34, should perh. be εὐθηνός (εὔθηνος?).

**εὐθήξ,** ῆγος, ὁ, ἡ, (θήγω) = εὔθηκτος, Theognost.*Can.*40:—hence **εὐθηξία,** ἡ, *EM*256.18.

**εὐθήρ-ᾱτος,** ον, *easy to catch* or *win,* Διὸς ἵμερος οὐκ εὐ. ἐτύχθη A. *Supp.*87; ἔτ' εὐ. *AP*12.105 (Asclep.), cf. Corn.*ND*28; στέφανος Plb. 31.25.3; εὐ. ὑπὸ τῶν τοιούτων Arist.*EN*1110$^{b}$14:—Ion. **εὐθήρητος,** v.l. **-ευτος,** Opp.*H.*5.426. **-ία,** ἡ, *success in sport,* Ael.*NA*10.48 (pl.), Poll.1.108. **II.** metaph., of the 'battue' of Persians at Marathon, Agath.2.10. **-ος,** ον, (θήρα) *lucky* or *successful in hunting,* E.*Ba.* 1253; εὔθηρος ὀρνέων ἴρηξ Babr.72.21 (cj.); of Pan, *AP*6.185 (Zos.); εὔθηροι, οἱ, club of *sportsmen* at Pergamum, *Ath.Mitt.*33.409; εὐ. ἄγρη *successful* sport, *AP*6.27 (Theaet.), cf. 253 (Crin.); τὸ εὔ. *good sport,* Ph.2.114; εὔ. κάλαμοι *successful* fishing-rods, *AP*6.89 (Maec.); *successful as bait,* Ael.*NA*12.42. **II.** (θήρ) *abounding in game, good for hunting,* ὄρος Str.14.1.12; βίον *AP*6.268 (Mnasalc.); εὔ. καὶ εὐίχθυς Aristid.*Or.*44(17).16.

**εὐθής, ές,** only in later Lxx translators for εὐθύς A, Lxx 1 *Ki*.29.6, *Ps*. 118(119).137; βιβλίον τοῦ εὐθοῦς the Book of the *Righteous* (*Jashar*), ib.2*Ki*.1.18: neut. pl. εὐθεῖα ib.2*Es*.19.13, cf. interpol. in Thom. Mag. p.165 R., Suid. s. v. εὐθυγενής.

**εὐθήσαυρος,** ον, *well-stored, precious,* ἔλαιον *AP*6.300 (Leon.).

**εὐθικός,** ή, όν, (εὐθύς) *straight,* κίνησις S.E.*M*.10.51.

**εὐθικτ-έω,** *find the range,* of artillery, Apollod.*Poliorc*.144.11. **-ος,** ον, (θιγεῖν) *touching the point, clever, quick,* εὔ. τὴν διάνοιαν Arist.*HA* 616ᵇ22; εὔ. πρὸς τὰς ἀποκρίσεις *quick* in repartee, Ath.13.583f; εὔ. νοῦς, γνώμη, προσβολή, Ph.1.54,240,286; *witty,* Plb.18.4.4, *AP*6.322 (Leon.): f.l. for εὔεικτος, Heraclit.*All*.51 codd. Adv. -τως Lxx 2*Ma*. 15.38, Hdn.4.7.2.

**εὐθιξία,** ἡ, *cleverness, tact,* Ph.1.54,157,593, Anon.ap.Suid.

**εὔθλαστος,** ον, (θλάω) *easily indented* or *bruised,* Arist.*Mete*.386ᵃ26, Hero *Spir*.1 *Praef*., *Gp*.9.17.3.

**εὐθλίζοντι** (dat. sg.), prob. f.l. for ὑελίζοντι, Hermes Trism. in *Rev. Phil*.32.264.

**εὐθνήσιμος,** ον, *in* or *with easy death,* A.*Ag*.1293.

**εὔθοινος,** ον, *eating hugely,* of Hercules, Plu.2.267f. II. εὔ. γέρας *a sumptuous* offering, A.*Ch*.257.

**εὐθορύβητος** [ῠ], ον, *easily confounded,* πρός τινα before . ., Plu.*Nic*.2.

**εὔθραυστος,** ον, (θραύω) *easily injured* or *broken,* Arist.*GA*775ᵃ9 (v.l. εὔφθαρτον), Plu.2.174d, Apollod.*Poliorc*.185.15.

**εὔθρεπτος,** ον, *well-reared, EM*28.41 (Comp.).

**εὔθριγκος,** ον, *well-coped,* of high walls, E.*Hel*.70.

**εὔθριξ,** Ep. **ἐΰθρ-,** τρῐχος, ὁ, ἡ, *with beautiful hair,* Eub.104 (lyr.); in Il. always of horses, *with flowing mane,* ἵππους 23.13,301; of dogs, X.*Cyn*.4.6; of birds, *well-plumed,* Theoc.18.57. 2. *fleecy, thick,* λῆνος Nic.*Al*.452. II. *attached to a stout line,* of a fish-hook, *AP* 9.52 (Carph.).

❋**εὔθρονος,** Ep. **ἐΰθρ-,** ον, *with beautiful seat* or *throne,* ἐΰθρονος Ἠώς Il.8.565, Od.6.48, al.; Ἀφροδίτα Pi.*I*.2.5; Ὧραι Id.*P*.9.60, cf. B.15. 3, etc.

**εὔθροος,** Ep. **ἐΰθρ-,** ον, *loud-sounding,* Opp.*C*.3.285, *AP*6.39 (Arch.).

**εὐθρῠβής,** ές, = εὔθρυπτος I, Dsc.1.70, 5.124.

**εὐθρύλλητος,** ον, = πολυθρυλ(λ)ητος (in bad sense), Vett.Val.187. 4, 199.2.

**εὔθρυπτος,** ον, (θρύπτω) *easily broken,* αὐχήν Arist.*PA*694ᵇ29; *easily dispersed,* ἀήρ Id.*de An*.420ᵃ8, cf. Democr.ap.Thphr.*Sens*.73; of earth, *crumbling,* Str.12.8.17, Plu.*Sert*.17; of the fleshy parts of fish, Id.2.916b. II. metaph., *enervated,* Gal.1.186, Sor.1.25.

**εὐθύ,** neut. of εὐθύς, used as Adv.; v. εὐθύς B.

**Εὐθυαῖος,** ὁ (sc. μήν), name of a month in the Aetolian Calendar, *IG*9(1).379 (Naupactus), *GDI*1950 (Delph.), etc.

**εὐθῠβολ-έω,** *throw forward,* τὸν γόνον *Placit*.5.9.2:—Pass., S.E. *M*.5.58. II. intr., *dart* or *go right forward,* τοῦ σπέρματος -οῦντος εἰς [τὴν μήτραν] *Placit*.5.14.2. 2. metaph., *hit the mark,* ἔχων τὸν νοῦν εὐθιξίᾳ πρὸς τὴν θεραπείαν -οῦντα Anon.ap.Suid. s. v. εὐθιξία, cf. Ph.2. 176. **-ία,** ἡ, *direct throw,* Plu.*Nic*.25. **-ος,** ον, (βάλλω) *throwing straight*: hence, *hitting the mark, accurate, exact,* prob. for εὐθύβουλος in Aristox.ap.Stob.1.7.18; ἀπόκρισις, στοχασμοί, Ph.1.617, 2.126; ὄνομα εὐ. the *exact* name, Id.1.73 (Sup.), al.: Comp., Id.1.618: Sup., Id.1.300; τὸ εὐ., = foreg., Id.2.465. Adv. -λως Id.1.99, al., Procl. *in Prm*.p.872 S.: in the lit. sense, *in a direct course,* εὐ. περαιωθῆναι τὸ πέλαγος Hld.5.22.

**εὐθῠ-γένειος,** ον, *with straight beard,* Polem.*Phgn*.67. **-γενής,** prob. f.l. for -τενής in Suid., Phot. **-γλωσσος,** Att. **-ττος,** ον, *straightforward, plain-spoken,* Pi.*P*.2.86, Dam.*Isid*.23, Procop.*Arc*. 29. **-γνωμίας,** ου, ὁ, *witness who gives direct evidence,* Phot. **-γνωμος,** ον, *straightforward,* Democr.181. **-γραμμᾰτίζω,** *reduce to a rectilinear figure,* ὁ κύκλος -ίζεται Phlp.*in APr*.477.2. **-γραμμικός,** ή, όν, *rectilinear,* ἀριθμός Iamb.*in Nic*.p.56 P. Adv. -κῶς, στίχος εὐ. ἐκκείμενος ib.p.96 P. **-γραμμος,** ον, = foreg., Arist.*Cael*.286ᵇ13, al.; γωνία Oenopides ap.Procl.*in Euc*.p.333 F., cf. Euc.1.44; τὸ εὐ. (with or without σχῆμα) *rectilinear figure,* Arist.*APr*.69ᵃ31, *Pr*.913ᵇ 18, Thphr.*HP*1.12.1.

**εὐθυδήμονα** (leg. εὐθύδημον)· ἁπλοῦν πολίτην, E.*Fr*.227.

**εὐθῠ-δίκαι** [ῐ], in pl., = εὐθύδικοι, of the Eumenides, A.*Eu*.312 (lyr., s. v. l., -δίκαιοι Herm.; cf. ὀρθοδίκαιος). **-δικία,** ἡ, *direct trial,* on the merits of the case, without exceptions or technical pleas, εὐθυδικίας ἀποδέχεσθαι Is.7.3; εἰσιέναι D.34.4; also εὐθυδικίᾳ εἰσιέναι, εἰσελθεῖν, Id.45.6, Is.6.43; τὸν ἐξ εὐθυδικίας λόγον συνίστασθαι Mitteis *Chr*. 31 vi 13 (ii B.C.). **-δίκος,** ον, *righteous-judging,* B.5.6, A.*Ag*.761 (lyr.), *AP*6.346 (Anacr.). II. εὐθύδικον, τό, = εὐθυδικία, *IG*5(2). 357.25 (Stymphalus, iii B.C.). **-δρομέω,** of ships, *run a straight course,* Ph.1.131,327, *Act.Ap*.16.11: metaph., of persons, Agath.2. 21. **-δρόμος,** ον, *running a straight course,* ἄνεμοι Plb.34.4.5; νῆες Orph.*H*.22.10. **-έντερος,** ον, *with straight intestines,* Arist.*HA*507ᵇ 34. **-έπεια,** ἡ, *straight speaking,* Adam.1.11, Hsch. (pl.). **-επής,** ές, (ἔπος) *plain-spoken,* Adam.1.16. **-εργής,** ές, *accurately wrought,* Luc. *Hist.Conscr*.27 (nisi leg. εὐεργής). **-ζωμον,** τό, *extemporized broth,* coined by Eust.1191.14. **-θάνατος** [θᾰ], ον, *quick-killing, mortal,* πληγή Plu.*Ant*.76. **-θριξ,** τρῐχος, ὁ, ἡ, *with straight hair,* Arist.*GA* 782ᵇ34, Poll.2.22. **-καίνα·** ἡ σχοῖνος, διὰ τὸ εὐθέως κτείνειν, καὶ δύναται εἶναι **εὐθυκταίνα,** Hsch.; cf. καίνω. **-καυλος,** ον, *with a straight stalk,* Thphr.*HP*6.4.5 (Comp.). **-κρέων·** παχύς, Hsch. **-κτέανον·** ἰθὺ πεφυκυῖαν, εἰς ὀρθόν, Id. (-κτέσαν cod., cf. ἰθυκτέανον, εὐκτέανος.) **-ληπτος,** ον, *easy to get at, to procure,* Anon.ap.Suid. **-λογία,** ἡ, = εὐθυέπεια, Polem.*Phgn*.15. **-λόγος,** ον, gloss on εὐθυρρήμων, Suid.

**εὐθῠμᾰχ-έω,** *fight fairly,* Hsch. s. v. Θετταλὸν σόφισμα. **-ης,** ου, Dor. **-χᾱς,** ὁ, *fighting openly,* Pi.*O*.7.15. **-ία,** ἡ, *fair fight,* Plu. *Sert*.10. ❋ **-ος** [ᾰ], ον, = εὐθυμάχης, Simon.137.

**εὐθυμελγής,** ές, = νεήμελκτος, Aët.3.38.

**εὐθῠμετρ-ία,** ἡ, *survey,* κώμης *PTeb*.12.6 (ii B.C.), etc. **-ικός,** ή, όν, *linear,* '*running*', opp. στερεός, πόδες *Supp.Epigr*.2.568.12 (Didyma, ii B.C.), cf. Hero *Geom*.3.19. II. *linear,* of number, [ἀριθμός] Theo Sm.p.95 H., cf. Iamb. *in Nic*.p.57 P.; ἑβδομάς *Theol. Ar*.44.

❋ **εὐθῡμ-έω,** *to be of good cheer,* E.*Cyc*.530, *AP*5.100, *Ep.Jac*.5.13: fem. dat. pl. pres. part. εὐθυμεύσαις Theoc.15.143; περὶ τῆς κριθῆς εὐθύμει *do not be anxious* about . ., *PAmh*.2.133.4 (ii A.D.). II. trans., *cheer, delight,* τινα A.*Fr*.350.4, cf. Democr.279:—Pass., *to be cheerful,* Id.3, X.*HG*7.4.36; ἐπί τινι Id.*Cyr*.4.1.19; ἐν ταῖς ἀτυχίαις Arist.*Rh*.1379ᵇ 18; πάντα -εῖσθαι χρή Aret.*CA*1.1. **-ητέον,** *one must be cheerful,* X.*Ap*.27. ❋ **-ία,** ἡ, *cheerfulness, contentment,* Pi.*I*.1.63, *Pae*.1.2, B.16.125, X.*Cyr*.4.5.7, Philem.96.4, Men.231, etc.: in pl., Pi.*O*.2. 34, X.*Cyr*.1.3.12, Arist.*Pr*.954ᵃ25; περὶ εὐθυμίης, title of works by Democritus and Hipparchus Pythagoreus. II. Εὐ. personified, Pi.*Fr*.155, Memn.4.2, *LW*45 (Erythrae). **-ος,** ον, *kind, generous,* ἄναξ Od.14.63. II. *cheerful,* Democr.174, X.*Cyr*.6.4.13 (Comp.), Pl.*Lg*.792b; συμπόσια εὔ. Ion Eleg.1.14; φέρειν γῆρας εὔ. εἰς τελευτάν Pi.*O*.5.22; of horses, *spirited,* X.*Eq*.11.12 (Sup.); τὸ εὔ., = εὐθυμία, Plu.2.1106c, D.C.42.1. Adv. -μως *cheerfully,* Batr.159, A.*Ag*. 1592: Comp. -ότερον X.*Cyr*.2.2.27: Sup. -ότατα ib.3.3.12.

**εὔθῡνα** (v. infr.), ἡ, gen. εὐθύνης, acc. εὔθυναν, nom. pl. εὔθυναι: (εὐθύνω):—*setting straight, correction, chastisement,* Pl.*Prt*.326e (pl.); *calling to account, POxy*.1203.9 (i A.D.), etc. II. esp. at Athens, *public examination of the conduct of officials,* held on the expiration of their term of office (dist. fr. λόγος '*rendering of accounts*', οὔτε χρήματα διαχειρίσας τῆς πόλεως δίδωμι λόγον αὐτῶν, οὔτε ἀρχὴν ἄρξας οὐδεμίαν εὐθύνας ὑπέχω αὐτῆς Lys.24.26; λόγον διδόντων τῶν χρημάτων . . καὶ εὐθύνας διδόντων *IG*1².91.27), used in sg. by Ar.*V*.571, Lys.10. 27, al.; ἡ εὐ. βλάβη τις δικαία ἐστίν Arist.*Rh*.1411ᵇ20: more freq. in pl., *IG*l.c., Ar.*Eq*.825 (anap.), etc.; πρεσβείας εὔθυναι *an account* of one's embassage, D.19.82; [τῆς στρατηγίας] ἔμ' ἀπαιτεῖς εὐθύνας Id. 18.245; opp. εὐθύνας διδόναι Ar.*Pax*1187, And.1.90; ὑποσχεῖν Lys.30. 3; κατηγορεῖν [τινος] εἰς τὰς εὐ. Antipho6.43; τὰς εὐ. κατηγορεῖν, ἐπὶ τὰς εὐθύνας ἐλθεῖν, D.19.81,2; εὔθυνάν τινι ἐμβαλέσθαι Arist.*Ath*.48.4, cf. Decr.ib.39.6; εὐθύνας or εὔθυναν ὀφλεῖν to be convicted, or accused, of malversation, And.1.73, Lys.10.27; κλοπῆς ἕνεκα Aeschin.3.10; εὐθύνας ἀποφυγεῖν, διαφυγεῖν, to be acquitted thereof, Pl.*Lg*.946d, 947e; τῆς εὐθύνης ἀπολύειν τινά Ar.*V*.571: metaph., τὰς εὐ. τὰς τοῦ βίου *the accounts rendered* of your life, Alex.262.8, cf. Ph.2.214, al. (On the accent see Hdn.Gr.1.257.37: the later form εὐθύνη, nom. pl. εὐθῦναι is sts. found in codd. of early writers, as Lys.10.27, Pl.*Prt*. 326e, but shd. prob. be corrected.)

**εὐθυνία,** freq. f.l. for εὐθηνία, as Aët.5.94: so perh. **εὔθυνος** in *EM* 197.34 for εὔθηνος.

**εὐθύνομος** [ῠ], ον, = εὐθύδικος, Simon.93.

**εὐθῦν-ος,** ὁ, *corrector, chastiser, judge,* A.*Pers*.828, *Eu*.273 (lyr.). II. at Athens and elsewhere, *public examiner* (cf. εὔθυνα), *IG*1².188, Decr.ap.And.1.78, Pl.*Lg*.945a sq., Arist.*Pol*.1322ᵇ11, *Ath*.48.4, *SIG* 38.3 (Teos, v B.C.); official of a guild, *Supp.Epigr*.2.458 (Moesia, ii/iii A.D.), etc. **-σις,** εως, ἡ, (εὐθύνω) *straightening,* opp. κάμψις, Arist. *Mete*.386ᵃ7, *IA*708ᵃ24; τῆς ῥινός Gal.18(1).481. **-τέον,** *one must correct,* τοὺς Εὐκλείδου ὅρους Iamb. *in Nic*.p.26 P. **-τήρ,** ῆρος, ὁ, *corrector, chastiser,* ὕβριος Thgn.40. 2. *one who levels* or *straightens,* θριγκῶν Man.4.293. 3. as Adj., εὐθυντὴρ οἴαξ the *guiding* rudder, A. *Supp*.717. **-τηριαῖος,** α, ον, *belonging to the* εὐθυντηρία (cf. sq. II. 1 b), *Milet*.7.59 (Didyma). **-τήριος,** α, ον, *making straight*: *directing, ruling,* σκῆπτρον A.*Pers*.764. II. Subst. εὐθυντηρία, ἡ, *the part of a ship wherein the rudder was fixed,* E.*IT*1356. b. *base, plinth, socle* of a wall, *IG*2².1668.16, *BCH*26.43 (Delph.), *IGRom*.4.293a i 38 (Pergam., ii B.C.); εὐ.· τὸ ἐν τῷ ἐδάφει σύμπαγμα ὑπὸ τῶν ἀρχιτεκτόνων, Hsch. 2. -τήριον, τό, *rule, norm,* γνώμων καὶ εὐ. *Theol.Ar*.59. **-τής,** οῦ, ὁ, = εὔθυνος, Pl.*Lg*.945b,c; δῆμος εὐθυντὴς χθονός cj. Markl. for αὐθέντης, E.*Supp*.442. **-τικός,** ή, όν, *of* or *for the conduct of* εὔθυνα (q.v.), εἶδος δικαστηρίων Arist.*Pol*.1300ᵇ19; λόγος εὐ. D.H.*Din*. 11. **-τός,** ή, όν, *capable of being straightened,* Arist.*Mete*.385ᵇ27. ❋ **-ω,** (εὐθύς) = the Homeric ἰθύνω (which is a freq. v.l., as in A.*Pers*.773): —*guide straight, direct,* οἰωνὸν γνώμῃ στομίων ἄτερ εὐθύνων Id.*Pr*.289; εὐ. ἡνίας Ar.*Av*.1739 (lyr.); [ἅρματα] Isoc.1.32; εὐ. δόρυ *steer* the bark *straight,* E.*Cyc*.15; εὐ. πλάτην Id.*Hec*.39; ὁ εὐθύνων *the helmsman, Ep.Jac*.3.4; εὐ. ἀγέλας *lead* or *drive* them, X.*Cyr*.1.1.2; εὐ. χερσί *manage, guide* him, S.*Aj*.542; εὐ. πόδα E.*Heracl*.728, etc. 2. metaph., *direct, govern,* Κύρου δὲ παῖς . . ηὔθυνε στρατόν A.*Pers*.773; πᾶσαν εὐθύνων πόλιν S.*Ant*.178, cf. 1164, E.*Hec*.9, Pl.*Min*.320d. 3. *make straight, straighten,* opp. κάμπτειν, πτέρυγας Arist.*IA*709ᵇ10:— Pass., Id.*Mete*.385ᵇ32. II. *make* or *put straight,* εὐ. δίκας σκολιάς *make* crooked judgements *straight,* Sol.4.37; εὐ. λαοῖς δίκας Pi.*P*.4. 153; εὐ. οὖρον *send a straight* fair wind, Id.*O*.13.28; εὐ. ὄλβον Id.*P*. 1.46; ὥσπερ ξύλον διαστρεφόμενον . . εὐ. ἀπειλαῖς καὶ πληγαῖς Pl.*Prt*. 325d, cf. 326e. III. *examine the conduct of* an official, Id.*Plt* 299a; εὐ. τὰς ἀρχάς Arist.*Pol*.1271ᵃ6, 1274ᵃ17, al.:—Pass., c. gen., -όμενος τῆς ἐφορείας Id.*Rh*.1419ᵃ31. 2. c. gen. criminis, *call to account for* . ., τινα κλοπῆς Plu.*Cic*.9:—Pass., τῶν ἀδικημάτων ηὐθύνθη

Th.1.95; οἱ -όμενοι *the culprits*, Mitteis *Chr.*31 iii 10 (ii B.C.), cf. *Notiz. Arch.*4.21 (Cyrene, i B.C.): c. dat., εὐ. φόνῳ *PTeb.*14.4 (ii B.C.); *to be mulcted, punished*, ἐπί τινι D.C.*Fr.*90, al.: abs., *IG*1².41.6; ἑκατὸν δραχμῇσι ib.4.15, al. 3. generally, *refute or censure*, τοὺς λόγους τινός Phld.*Piet.*67; τὴν Φιλίστου διάλεκτον Plu.*Nic.*1:—Pass., *to be refuted*, δι' αὐτῶν τῶν φαινομένων Phld.*Sign.*30, cf. Plot.3.6.13; but also, *to be critically examined*, Id.4.6.13. 4. *examine by torture*, Procop.*Goth.*3.32 (Pass.). IV. intr., *serve as* εὔθυνος, Pl.*Lg.*946d.

**εὐθῠ-ονειρία**, ἡ, *vivid dream*, Arist.*Div.Somn.*463ᵃ25, *Gp.*2.35.4 (pl.). ⊛ **-όνειρος**, ον, *dreaming vividly*, Arist.*Div.Somn.*463ᵇ16, cf. Plu.2.437f. ⊛ **-ορϝία**, v. εὐθυωρία. **-ορον**· τόπος ἐπ' εὐθείας ἔχων τὸν ὅρον, *EM*391.48, Phot. **-πλοέω**, *sail straight*, ἐπί τι Str.11.2.3, cf. Arr.*Cyn.*25.8: metaph., Cerc.5.16. **-πλοια**, ἡ, *straight voyage*, in dat. -πλοίᾳ Str.3.3.1, prob. l. in Id.6.3.7. **-πλοκία**, ἡ, (πλοκή) *straight weaving, evenness of texture*, Pl.*Plt.*283a, 311b. **-πλοος**, ον, contr. **-πλους**, ουν, *sailing straight*, Str.6.3.7 (dub. l.). **-πνοος**, ον, contr. **-πνους**, ουν, *straight-blowing*, Pi.*N.*7.29; ἄνεμοι Arist.*Mu.*394ᵇ35. II. *breathing freely*, Hp.*Epid.*6.2.19. **-πομπός**, όν, *guiding straight*, αἰών Pi.*N.*2.7.

**εὐθυπορ-έω**, *go straight forward*, πότμος εὐθυπορῶν (metaph. from a ship) *unswerving* destiny, A.*Ag.*1005 (lyr.); of motion, Arist.*IA* 710ᵃ7; opp. ἀνακάμπτειν, of ἀπόδειξις, Id.*deAn.*407ᵃ29: c. acc. cogn., εὐ. ὁδόν, δρόμον, *hold a straight* course, Pi.*O.*7.91, *I.*5(4).60. II. *have a straight grain*, of trees, Thphr.*CP*1.8.4. **-ία**, ἡ, *straightness of course*, Pl.*Lg.*747a, Arist.*Aud.*802ᵃ30. II. *straightness of grain* in wood, Thphr.*HP*5.6.2. **-ικός**, ή, όν, *moving in a straight line*: -κά, τά, Phlp.*in Mete.*12.33. ⊛ **-ος**, ον, *going straight*, of colour, Democr.ap.Thphr.*Sens.*73; τάσις, opp. μεταληπτική, Gal.10.443: metaph., *straightforward*, ἦθος Pl.*Lg.*775d. II. *with a straight passage*, κέρας Arist.*Aud.*802ᵇ11; *with straight grain*, of wood, Thphr.*CP*5.17.3 (Sup.).

**εὐθύρῖνος**, ον, = εὔθυρριν, *PLips.*2.6 (i A.D.), 5 ii 7 (iii A.D.), in gen. sg. -ρίνου.

**εὐθυρρημ-ονέω**, *speak in a straightforward manner*, '*call a spade a spade*', ὁ σοφὸς -ήσει Zeno *Stoic.*1.22; *utter off-hand*, Plu.*Demetr.*14. **-οσύνη**, ἡ, *plainness of speech*, Phld.*Rh.*2.281 S., M.Ant.11.6, S.E.*M.*2.22. **-ων**, ον, gen. ονος, (ῥῆμα) *plain-spoken*, Cic.*Fam.*12.16.3 (Comp.), Poll.5.119. Adv. -μόνως Id.4.24. II. gloss on εὐθύγλωσσος, Sch.Pi.*P.*2.157.

**εὐθύ-ρριζος**, ον, *straight-rooted*, Thphr.*HP*1.7.2. **-ρρῖν** (or **εὔθυριν**), ῖνος, ὁ, ἡ, *straight-nosed*, *PAmh.*2.51.23 (i B.C.), *BGU*93 ii 11 (ii B.C.), al.; nom. **-ρρις** (v.l. -ριν) Poll.2.73.

**εὔθυρσος**, ον, *with beautiful shaft*, νάρθηξ E.*Ba.*1158 (lyr.).

⊛ **εὐθύς**, εῖα, ύ, Ion. and Ep. **ἰθύς** (q.v.: so always in Hom. and Hdt.), *straight, direct*, whether vertically or horizontally, opp. σκολιός, καμπύλος, Pl.*Tht.*194b, *R.*602c, etc.; κατὰ τὸ εὐθὺ ἑστάναι stands still with reference to *the vertical*, of a spinning top, ib.436e; εὐ. πλόος, ὁδοί, Pi.*O.*6.103, *N.*1.25, etc.; εὐθυτέρα ὁδὸς X.*Cyr.*1.3.4; ὁδοὺς εὐθείας ἔτεμε Th.2.100; ῥόμβος ἀκόντων Pi.*O.*13.93; εὐθεῖα (sc. ὁδῷ) *by the straight road*, Pl.*Lg.*716a; εὐθεῖαν ἕρπε A.*Fr.*195; τὴν εὐ. E.*Med.*384; ἐπ' εὐθείας D.S.19.38, Ascl.*Tact.*2.6, Plot.2.1.8; so also εἰς τὸ εὐ. βλέπειν X.*Eq.*7.17, etc.; πλήρης τοῦ εὐθέος tired *of going straight forward*, ib.14; ἡ ἐς τὸ εὐ. τῆς ῥητορικῆς ὁδὸς the *direct* road to.., Luc.*Rh.Pr.*10; κατ' εὐθύ on *level ground*, Lxx 3*Ki.*21.23; but ἡ κατ' εὐ. τάσις *in the direct line*, Apollon.Cit.2; *on the same side*, Gal.8.62; also, opp. εἰς τὸ ἐντός, Plot.6.7.14. 2. in moral sense, *straightforward, frank*, of persons, εὐθὺν χρὴ τὸν ἑταῖρον ἔμμεν καὶ μὴ σκολιὰ φρονεῖν *Scol.*16; κοινᾶνι παρ' εὐθυτάτῳ Pi.*P.*3.28; ῥῆτραι Tyrt.4.6; τόλμα Pi.*O.*13.12; δίκα Id.*N.*10.12; κρῖνε δ' εὐθεῖαν δίκην A.*Eu.*433, cf. 'Αρχ.'Εφ.1911.134 (Gonni); ὁ εὐθὺς λόγος E.*Hipp.*492; τὸ εὐ. τε καὶ τὸ ἐλεύθερον Pl.*Tht.*173a; ἀπὸ τοῦ εὐθέος λέγειν to speak *straight out*, Th.3.43; ἐκ τοῦ εὐ. ὑπουργεῖν *outright, openly, without reserve*, Id.1.34; ἐκ τοῦ εὐ., opp. δι' αἰνιγμάτων, Paus.8.8.3: in fem., τὴν εὐθεῖαν τινι συνειπεῖν Plu.*Cic.*7; ἁπλῶς καὶ δι' εὐθείας Id.2.408e; ἀπ' εὐθείας ib.57a, *Fab.*3; κατ' εὐθεῖαν *by direct reasoning*, Dam.*Pr.*432; μηδὲν ἐξ εὐθείας παρέχει (an amulet) does no good *directly*, Sor.2.42. 3. εὐθεῖα, ἡ, as Subst., a. (sc. γραμμή) *straight line*, Arist.*APr.*49ᵇ35, al., Euc.1 *Def.*7, al.; ἐπ' εὐθείας εἶναι lie in a *straight line*, Archim.*Con.Sph.*7, al.; ἐπὶ τὴν αὐτὴν εὐ., ἐπὶ τῆς αὐτῆς εὐ. ἐκτείνειν, in the same *line*, Plb.3.113.2,3; ἐπὶ μίαν εὐ. ib.8: Comp., εὐθυτέρα ἡ γραμμὴ γίνεται Arist.*Mech.*855ᵃ24. b. (sc. πτῶσις) *nominative case*, D.T.636.5, A.D.*Pron.*6.11, etc.; κατ' εὐθὺ in *the nominative*, Arist.*SE*182ᵃ3.

B. as Adv., **εὐθύς** and **εὐθύ**, the former prop. of Time, the latter of Place, Phryn.119, etc. I. **εὐθύ**, of Place, *straight*, usu. of motion or direction, εὐθὺ Πύλονδε *straight to*.., *h.Merc.*342; εὐθὺ πρὸς τὰ νυμφικὰ λέχη S.*OT*1242; εὐ. [τὴν ἐπὶ] Βαβυλῶνος *straight towards*.., X.*Cyr.*5.2.37: and so c. gen., εὐ. τῶν κυρηβίων, εὐθὺ Πελλήνης, Ar.*Eq.*254, *Av.*1421; εὐ. τοῦ Διὸς Id.*Pax*68; εὐ. τοὐρόφου Eup.47; εὐ. τῆς σωτηρίας Ar.*Pax*301, cf. Th.8.88, etc.; ἀποθανούμενος ἥει εὐ. τοῦ δαιμονίου *in opposition to*.., Pl.*Thg.*129a (s.v.l.); cf. ἰθύς. b. νῆσον οἰκεῖ εὐθὺ Ἴστρου *opposite*.., Max.Tyr.15.7. 2. = ἁπλῶς, *simply*, καλεῖν Thphr.*HP*3.8.2, cf. 9.13.2. 3. rarely of Time, Philoch.144, Arist.*Rh.*1414ᵇ25, *UPZ*77.27 (ii B.C.), *PGrenf.*1.1.24 (ii B.C.), Aristeas 24, Luc.*Nav.*22. II. **εὐθύς**, 1. of Time, *straightway, forthwith*, Pi.*O.*8.41; ὁ δ' εὐ. ὡς ἤκουσε A.*Pers.*361; ὁ δ' εὐ. ἐξῴμωξεν S.*Aj.*317; τὸ μὲν εὐ. τὸ δὲ καὶ διανοούμενον Th.1.1, cf. 5.3, 7.77; joined with other adverbial words, τάχα δ' εὐ. ἰὼν Pi.*P.*4.83; εὐ. κατὰ τάχος Th.6.101; εὐ. παραχρῆμα (v. sub παραχρῆμα); εὐ. ἀπ' ἀρχῆς Ar.*Pax*84 (anap.); εὐ. ἐξ ἀρχῆς X.*Cyr.*7.2.16; ἐξ ἀρχῆς εὐ. Arist.*Pol.*1287ᵇ10; εὐ. κατ' ἀρχὰς Pl.*Ti.*24b; ἀφ' ἑσπέρας εὐ. ἤδη Luc.*Gall.*1; εὐ. ἐκ νέου, ἐκ παιδός, *even* from one's youth, Pl.*R.*485d, 519a; εὐ. ἐκ παιδίου X.*Cyr.*1.6.20: with a part., εὐ. νέοι ὄντες Th.2.39; εὐ. ἥκων X.*An.*4.7.2; εὐ. ἀπεκτονώς D.23.127; τοῦ θέρους εὐ. ἀρχομένου *just* at the beginning of summer, Th.2.47; ἀρξάμενος εὐ. καθισταμένου [τοῦ πολέμου] from the *very* beginning of the war, Id.1.1; εὐ. ἀποβεβηκότι *immediately* on disembarking, Id.4.43; εὐ. γενομένοις at *the moment of* birth, Pl.*Tht.*186b: metaph., *at once, naturally*, ὑπάρχει εὐθὺς γένη ἔχον τὸ ὄν Being falls *at once* into genera, Arist.*Metaph.*1004ᵃ5, cf. *Po.*1452ᵃ14: with Subst., ἡ τῶν Ἰταλιωτῶν εὐθὺς φυγή Hdn.8.1.5. 2. less freq. in a local relation, ὑπὲρ τῆς πόλεως εὐ. *just* above the city, Th.6.96; παρ' αὐτὴν εὐ. ὁ ἔσπλους ἐστίν *directly* past it (the mole), Id.8.90; ἐγγύτατα τούτου εὐ. ἐχομένη *immediately* adjoining this, ibid., cf. Theoc.25.23; εὐ. ἐπὶ τὴν γέφυραν Foed.ap. Th.4.118, cf. X.*Cyr.*7.2.1,2, 2.4.24, *Ages.*1.29; τὴν εὐ. Ἄργους κἀπιδαυρίας ὁδόν the road *leading straight to* Argos, E.*Hipp.*1197 (condemned by Phot.); εὐ. Λυκείου Pherecr.110, cf. Arist.*HA*498ᵃ32, etc. 3. of Manner, *directly, simply*, v.l. in Pl.*Men.*100a. 4. like αὐτίκα II: *for instance, to take the first example that occurs*, ὥσπερ ζῷον εὐθὺς Arist.*Pol.*1277ᵃ6, cf. *Cael.*284ᵇ10, etc.; οἷον εὐθύς Cleom.1.1, D.Chr.11.145.

C. regul. Adv. **εὐθέως**, used just as εὐθύς, S.*Aj.*31, *OC*994, E.*Fr.*31, Pl.*Phd.*63a, etc.; αἰσθόμενος εὐθέως *as soon as* he perceived, Lys.3.11; ἐπεὶ εὐθέως ᾔσθοντο X.*HG*3.2.4; εὐθέως παραχρῆμα Antipho1.20, D.52.6. 2. = εὐθύς B. II. 4, οἷον εὐθέως as *for example*, Plb.6.52.1, 12.5.6 (dub. sens. in Hp.*Art.*55); so εὐ. alone, Ph.2.589. (εὐθέως is the commoner form in later Greek, *PCair.Zen.*34.17 (iii B.C.), etc.)

**εὐθύσᾰνος** [ῠ], ον, *well-fringed*, ζώνη *AP*6.202 (Leon.).

**εὐθυσία**, ἡ, *auspicious sacrifice*, Phld.*Oec.*p.33 J. (pl.).

**εὐθῠ-σκόλιος**, ον, *slightly curved*, Orib.45.18.33. **-σκοπέω**, *look straight at*, Plu.2.737a. **-σκόπος**, ον, *seeing straight*, Hsch. s.v. οὐκ εὐθυσκόπου.

**εὐθυσμός**, ὁ, (εὐθύνω) *straightness*, trans. of Hebr. *Shur*, Ph.1.576.

**εὐθῠ-στομος**, ον, *talking plainly*, *EM*191.32, Sch.Luc.*JTr.*27; f.l. for εὔστομος, Poll.5.60. **-τενής**, ές, (τείνω) *straight*, ὁδός Ph.1.456, cf. Dion.Byz.3; πλοῦς Iamb.*VP*3.16; εὐ. τὴν τρίχα Ael.*NA*4.34: Medic., τομή Antyll.ap.Orib.44.8.1. Adv. -νῶς ib.9, Ph.1.338, Gal.18(1).797.

⊛ **εὐθύτης** [ῠ], ητος, ἡ, (εὐθύς) *straightness*, opp. καμπυλότης, Arist.*Cat.*10ᵃ12; opp. περιφέρεια, Id.*Mete.*385ᵇ30; εὐ. τριχῶν, opp. οὐλότης, Id.*GA*782ᵃ3; ἡ εὐ. τῆς τάσεως the *direction*.., Gal.6.193. II. *righteousness*, Lxx *Jo.*24.14, al.

**εὐθῠ-τοκία**, ἡ, *simple interest*, *IG*12(5).860.25 (Tenos), 5(1).1146.37 (Gythium). **-τομέω**, *make a straight incision*, Antyll.ap.Orib.44.8.23:—hence **-τομία**, ἡ, ib.4, al. **-τομος**, ον, *cut straight, straight*, ὁδός Pi.*P.*5.90. **-τονος**, ον, opp. παλίντονος, term applied to the lighter torsion-engines, τὰ εὐ. ὄργανα Hero *Bel.*74.5, 104.4; καταπάλται Ath.Mech.14.6. **-τράχηλος** [ᾰ], ον, *with a straight neck*, of the bladder, Sor.1.18. **-τρεχής**, ές, *running in a straight line*, *IG*2².463.73. **-τρητος**, ον, *bored straight through*, [ὀστᾶ] Gal.*UP*8.7, cf. Ruf.ap.Orib.8.24.62, Antyll.ib.8.13.1. **-τρῐχος**, ον, = εὔθυθριξ, Arist.*HA*629ᵇ35, Polem.*Phgn.*57. **-τρῡπος**, ον, = εὐθύτρητος, Democr.ap.Thphr.*Sens.*73. **-φερής**, ές, *running in a straight line*, Pl.*Lg.*815b. **-φλοιος**, ον, *straight-barked*, name of a kind of oak, Thphr.*HP*3.8.2. **-φορέομαι**, Pass., *to move in a straight line*, Procl. *in Prm.*p.906 S. **-φορία**, ἡ, *motion in a straight line*, Arist.*Ph.*227ᵇ18. **-φρων**, ον, gen. ονος, (φρήν) *whole-hearted, sincere*, A.*Eu.*1040, f.l. in ib.1034 (both lyr.). **-φυής**, ές, *straight grown*, opp. παρεστραμμένος, cj. Scalig. in Thphr.*HP*4.2.6. **-χαλκος**, ον, *payable on demand in cash* (copper), *POxy.*1482.15 (ii A.D.). **-ωνυξ**, υχος, ὁ, ἡ, or **-ώνῠχος**, ον, *with straight nails* or *talons*, Arist *HA*517ᵃ33, 600ᵃ19, 633ᵇ2. **-ωρέω**, *go straight forward*, v.l. for εὐθυπορέω, Id.*Pr.*905ᵇ6. ⊛ **-ωρία**, ἡ, *straight course* or *direction*, Pl.*R.*436e, *Ti.*45c, Arist.*de An.*406ᵇ31; κατ' εὐθυωρίαν *longitudinally*, Id.*PA* 654ᵃ17; also ἀντικροῦσαι κατ' εὐ. to oppose *directly*, Id.*Rh.*379ᵃ11; κατ' εὐ. νοῆσθαι, opp. κατ' ἀναλογίαν, Ti.Locr.94b; ἄπειρα εἰς εὐ. *in an infinite series*, Arist.*Metaph.*994ᵃ2: εὐθυωρίᾳ ἐπὶ θάλασσαν *SIG*685.65 (Itanos, ii B.C.), cf. ib.421.48 (Thermon, iii B.C.); ἀν εὐθυωρείαν (sic) *Tab.Heracl.*1.65; also Arc. εὐθυορϝίαν *BCH*39.55 (Orchom. Arc., iv B.C.); cf. ἰθυωρίη. ⊛ **-ωρος**, ον, *in a straight direction*: mostly in neut. εὐθύωρον as Adv., = εὐθύς, εὐ. ἄγειν X.*An.*2.2.16, Ael.*NA*11.16; ὁρᾶν ib.7.5: as Adj., εὐθύωρον τὴν ἀναχώρησιν ἐποιήσαντο Anon.ap.*EM*391.42, cf. Procop.*Aed.*2.2.

⊛ **εὐθώρηξ**, ηκος, ὁ, ἡ, *well-mailed*, *AP*9.389 (Trajan), Nonn.*D.*15.156; μύες Marcell.Sid.30.

**εὔια**· δέδια, Hsch.

**εὐιάζω**, = εὐάζω, S.*Ichn.*221, E.*Cyc.*495 (lyr.).

**εὐιακός**, ή, όν, *Bacchic*, θίασοι *APl.*4.289:—fem. ⊛ **εὐιάς**, άδος, *AP* 9.603 (Antip.); οἴνη *IG*3.779.

**εὐίᾱτος**, Ion. -ητος, ον, (ἰάομαι) *easy to heal* or *remedy*, Arist.*EN* 1121ᵃ25, Thphr.*HP*5.4.5, Porph.*Abst.*1.56, freq. in Comp., Hp.*Art.*14, X.*Eq.*4.2, etc.

**εὐιδε** (i.e. ἔϝιδε), Aeol., = εἶδε, v. *εἴδω A.

**εὐίδρως**, ωτος, ὁ, ἡ, *easily perspiring*, Thphr.*Sud.*20: but neut. **εὔιδρον**, ib.19:—also **εὐίδρωτος**, ον, Gal.6.222: pl. εὐίδρωτα Arist.*Pr.*867ᵇ35.

**εὐιερία**, ἡ, *sanctity, sacredness*, *Sammelb.*1007 (i A.D.).

⊛ **εὐίερος** [ῐ], ον, *fit for sacrifice*, πέλανοι *Pae.Oxy.*675.14; θύματα *IG*

5(1).1390.70 (Andania, i B.C.); θυηπολίαι *AP*6.231 (Phil.): generally, *holy*, θυμέλαι *Ath.Mitt.*17.272 (iii A.D.); βοαί Orac. in *Milet.*7.64 (ii/iii A.D.).

**εὐϊκέτευτος**, ον, *open to entreaty*, gloss on εὐάντητος, *EM*388.40.

⊛ **εὐιλασία**· εὐπειστία, prob. in Hsch., cf. *Gloss.*

**εὐϊλάσιμος**, ον, = sq., prob. l. in *Sammelb.*4116.5.

⊛ **εὐΐλᾰτ-ος** [ῑ], ον, (ἵλημι) *very merciful*, of deities, *PCair.Zen.*34.19 (iii B.C.), *IG*3.73, *GDI*3543 (Cnidus), etc.; εὐ. ἐγένου αὐτοῖς Lxx *Ps.*98(99).8; also τυχεῖν εὐϊλάτου τοῦ βασιλέος *PPetr.*2 p.45 (iii B.C.); later written εὐειλ- *GDI*3536 (Cnidus), *UPZ*109.6 (i B.C.):—hence -εύω, *to be merciful*, Lxx *De.*29.20(19), al.

**εὔϊνος**, ον, (ἴς) *with stout fibres*, ξύλον Thphr.*HP*3.10.1, *Ign.*72.

⊛ **Εὔιος** (**Εὔϊος** *EM*391.15, cf. Lat. *Euhius*), ὁ, name of Bacchus, from the cry εὐαΐ, εὐοῖ, in lyr. passages, S.*OT*211, E.*Ba.*157, Ecphantid.3, etc.; Εὔιος, = Βάκχος, E.*Ba.*566, 579. II. εὔιος, ον, as Adj., *Bacchic*, πῦρ S.*Ant.*964; τελεταί E.*Ba.*238; ἀγάλματα Id.*Tro.*451 (troch.).

**εὔιππος**, Ep. **ἐΰιππ-**, ον, of persons, *delighting in horses*, *h.Ap.*210, Hes.*Cat.Oxy.*1358.21, Pi.*O.*3.39: Sup., X.*HG*4.2.5, etc. 2. of places, *famed for horses*, Pi.*P.*4.2, S.*OC*668 (lyr.).

**εὔιστος** πόθος, ὁ, desire *of knowledge*, Epigr.ap.Plu.2.14c (leg. εὐκταῖον).

**εὐίσχιος**, ον, *with beautiful hips*, γυνή *Inscr.Prien.*317, cf. *AP*5.115 (Marc. Arg.); of a horse, *with fine quarters*, *Hippiatr.*115; βόες Hsch. s. v. κάμινοι.

**εὔιχθυς**, υ, *abounding in fish*, θάλασσα D.S.11.57, cf. Ath.8.360e, Aristid.*Or.*44(17).16, Philostr.*VA*3.55.

⊛ **εὐϊώτης**, ου, ὁ, (εὔιος) *Bacchic*, χοροί *Lyr.Alex.Adesp.*22:—fem. **εὐϊῶτις**, ιδος, οἴνη Moschio Trag.6.11.

**εὐκᾰής**, ές, (καίω) *easily burnt*, Dsc.4.150, Sch.A.R.1.434 (Sup.).

**εὐκαθ-αίρετος**, ον, *easy to conquer*, Th.7.18 (Comp.); *easily exhausted*, δυνάμεις Herod.Med.ap.Orib.5.30.11; *unstable*, τύχη, πρᾶγμα, Vett.Val.175.30, 212.21. **-εδρος**, ον, gloss on εὔσσελμος, Hsch., Sch.Od.2.390, etc.; on εὔζυγος, Sch.A.R.1.4. **-εκτος**, ον, *easy to keep under* or *restrain*, X.*Cyr.*7.5.69 (Sup.). **-οσίωτος**, ον, *consecrated*, *IG*14.455 (Catana, v A.D.).

**εὐκαιρ-έω** (late, acc. to Phryn.103), *have opportunity, leisure* or *time*, *PSI*4.342.2 (iii B.C.), Plb.20.9.4, 1*Ep.Cor.*16.12, etc.: c. inf., οὐδὲ φαγεῖν ηὐκαίρουν *Ev.Marc.*6.31, cf. Plu.2.223d, Luc.*Am.*33; τοῦ διαβῆναι *PEleph.*29.7 (iii B.C.). II τινι or εἴς τι, *devote one's leisure* to a thing, εὐ. τοῖς ἀθανάτοις ἑαυτοῦ Clio *Ep.*16.6; εὐ. εἰς οὐδὲν ἕτερον ἤ.. *Act.Ap.*17.21. III. *enjoy good times, prosper*, Plb.4.60.10; τοῖς βίοις Id.32.5.12: in this sense also εὐκαιρέομαι, Posidon.59 J. 2. *to be timely*, Phld.*Rh.*2.64 S., Epicur.(?) *Oxy.*215 ii 2. **-ή**, ἡ, *favourable opportunity*, dub. in *POxy.*123.3 (iii/iv A.D.). **-ημα**, ατος, τό, *seasonable, opportune act*, *Stoic.*3.136 (pl.). **-ία**, Ion. -ίη, ἡ, *good season, opportunity*, τὴν εὐ. διαφυλάττειν Isoc.12.34; ἀπολαύειν τῆς εὐ. Phld.*D.*3 *Fr.*89; εὐκαιρίαν ζητεῖν ἵνα.. *Ev.Matt.*26.16; εὐ. τοῦ ἐλθεῖν *PMich.* in *Class.Phil.*22.250 (ii A.D.); *leisure*, Hp.*Ep.*17, 23; κατὰ πολλὴν εὐ. καὶ σχολήν D.H.*Comp.*23—a usage condemned by Phot. and Suid. s. v. σχολή. II. *appropriateness*, opp. ἀκαιρία, Pl.*Phdr.*272a; μεταφορᾶς, στίχων, Plu.2.16b, 736f. 2. *convenient situation*, τῶν πόλεων Plb.16.29.3, cf. 4.44.11, Ph.1.4. 3. *opportune supply*, ὑδάτων, of rainfall or irrigation, Thphr.*CP*3.23.4 (pl.), D.S.1.52. III. *wealth, prosperity*, αἱ τῶν βίων εὐ. Plb.1.59.7, cf. 13.9.2 (cj.), etc.; εὐ. οὐκ ἔχει he has no *property*, *BGU*665 ii 4 (i A.D.). **-ος**, ον, *well-timed, seasonable*, λόγος Philem.113; θάνατος *Com.Adesp.*116; ὕδατα (rainfall) Thphr.*HP*8.7.6; *nihil -ότερον epistula tua*, Cic.*Att.*4.7.1: c. inf., χῶ τι σοι λέγειν εὔκαιρόν ἐστι S.*OC*32, cf. Epicur.*Nat.*28.4; -ότερον ἔσται διελθεῖν J.*AJ*12.9.7; τὸ εὔκαιρον, = εὐκαιρία, D.H.*Din.*7; τὸ μέτριον καὶ τὸ εὔ. ἐν ἡδοναῖς Aristo *Stoic.*1.86; εὔκαιρον ἀείσας *in season*, Pl.*Epigr.*5.5. II. of places, *convenient, well situated*, τόποι *PPetr.*2 p.28 (iii B.C., Sup.), cf. Plb.4.38.1 (Sup.), D.S.1.63, etc. III. *rich, wealthy*, dub. l. in St.Byz. s. v. Χαττηνία. IV. Adv. -ρως *seasonably, opportunely*, Hp.*Medic.*3, Nico 1, *PCair.Zen.*38.28 (iii B.C.), al., etc.; εὐ. χρῆσθαί τινι Isoc.5.143; εὐ. ἔχειν πρός τι Id.11.12, Arist.*HA*582ᵃ28; *favourably, propitiously*, *PCair.Zen.*46 (iii B.C.), *POxy.*2086ʳ.6 (ii A.D., εὐκερως Pap.): Comp. -ότερον Pl.*Phd.*78a: Sup. -ότατα Plb.5.63.13. 2. οὐκ -ρως ἔχειν to have no *leisure*, Id.5.26.10.

**εὐκάκωτος** [ᾰ], ον, *easily affected* by disease, Aët.12.19; to be read for εὐπαθής in Gal.19.208.

**εὐκαλλώπιστος**, ον, *beautifully adorned*, Hsch. s. v. κοσμιωτάτη, Phot. s. v. κεκομψευμένος.

**εὔκᾱλος**, **εὐκᾱλία**, Dor. for εὐκηλ-.

**εὐκάμᾰτος** [κᾰ], ον, *of easy labour, easy*, κάματος E.*Ba.*66 (lyr.). 2. εὐ. στέφανοι crowns *won by noble toils*, *APl.*4.335. 3. *easily enduring fatigue*, Philostr.*Gym.*42. 4. *laborious*, ἄγρη Nonn.*D.*5.483; *caused by toil*, ἱδρῶτες Id.25.28.

⊛ **εὐκᾱμία**· ἡσυχία, ἤτοι εὐφημία (Dor.), *EM*392.5 (i.e. εὐκᾱλία, = ἡσυχία, and εὐκᾱμία (fr. κημός), = εὐφιμία, cf. Hsch. s. v. εὐκαλεία, εὐκηλρία).

**εὐκάμπ-εια**, ἡ, *flexibility*, of the body, Antyll.ap.Orib.6.35.1. ⊛ **-ής**, ές, (κάμπτω) *well-bent* or *curved*, δρέπανον Od.18.368; κληῗδ' εὐκαμπέα 21.6; χαλάσασ' εὐκαμπέα τόξα *h.Hom.*27.12; ἄροτρον, ἅρπη, Max.458, A.R.3.1388; εὐκαμπὴς τὰ κέρατα Luc.*DMar.*15.2; τὸ εὐ. τῶν μελῶν Id.*Im.*14. II. *flexible*, φλοιός Thphr.*HP*3.10.4; κλάδοι Str.15.1.20; κατασκευάζειν τὸ κέρας εὐ. Plu.*Sull.*17; of timber, Orib.9.19.2 (Comp.); πῦον *slippery*, Aret.*SD*1.10. (εὐκαμπὲς ἄγκιστρον *AP*6.4 (Leon.) is corrupt: εὐκᾰπές (κάπτω) *easily swallowed*, Salm.) **-ος**, ον, = sq., Hp.*Art.*60 (v.l. -πτοι). **-τος**, ον, *flexible*, Sapph.*Supp.*5.13, Arist.*PA*692ᵃ2.

**εὐκαμψία**, ἡ, *flexibility*, of the voice, Arist.*GA*786ᵇ10.

**εὐκᾰπής**, v. εὐκαμπής.

**εὐκάρδιος**, ον, (καρδία) *stout-hearted*, S.*Aj.*364 (lyr.), *Ph.*535, Chrysipp.*Stoic.*2.247, etc.; of a horse, *spirited*, X.*Eq.*6.14. Adv. -ίως *with stout heart*, E.*Hec.*549, D.H.5.8, J.*AJ*12.9.4, *BJ*7.8.7. II. *good for the stomach*, Diocl.*Fr.*120 (Comp.), Ruf.ap.Orib.5.11.3 (Sup.), Xenocr.8. 2. *good for the heart, restorative, cordial*, Hp.*Aff.*41, 54, Alex.Trall.*Febr.*4.

**εὐκάρπ-εια**, ἡ, = εὐκαρπία, in dat. -είᾳ (-ίᾳ codd.), E.*Tr.*217 (lyr.); cf. παγκάρπεια. **-έω**, *bear good fruit* or *crops*, Hp.*Ep.*10, Thphr.*CP*1.20.5, *HP*2.7.7, Str.5.2.7, *BGU*1040.5 (ii A.D.). **-ησις**, εως, ἡ, f.l. for ἐκκάρπησις, Gal.6.665. **-ία**, ἡ, *fruitfulness*, *IG*1².76.45, Arist.*Fr.*252, Thphr.*CP*2.1.2; cf. εὐκάρπεια. **-ος**, ον, *fruitful*, of women, *h.Hom.*30.5; of trees, corn, land, Pi.*P.*1.30, *N.*1.14, *Pae.*2.26, etc.; of sheep, Palaeph.18; φυτά, ζῷα, Ocell.4.9; [χώρη] -οτάτη Hp.*Aër.*12; εὔ. θέρος S.*Aj.*671: metaph., -οτάτη ἀρετή Ph.1.647. II. Act., *fruitful, fertilizing*, ἀήρ Thphr.*CP*2.3.3; epith. of Aphrodite, S.*Fr.*847; of Dionysus, *AP*6.31; of Demeter, ib.7.394 (Phil.).

**εὐκάρφωτος**, ον, gloss on εὐγόμφωτος, Sch.Opp.*H.*1.58.

**εὐκατά-βλητος**, ον, *easily overthrown*, Eust.1055.51. **-γέλαστος**, ον, *exposed to ridicule*, Alex.Aphr.*Pr.*1.80. ⊛ **-γνωστος**, ον, *blameworthy*, Mitteis *Chr.*31 viii 11 (ii B.C.), *EM*400.6.

**εὐκατ-άγωγος** [ᾰγ], ον, *easy to wind up*, of a torsion-engine (cf. καταγωγίς), Ph.*Bel.*53.33. 2. *good for landing in*, λιμήν Eust. ad D.P.195. **-αγώνιστος**, ον, *easily conquered*, Plb.9.4.8, Luc.*Tyr.*22.

**εὐκατά-καυστος**, ον, *easily burnt*, gloss on εὐκατάπρηστος, Suid., Phot. **-κλαστος**, ον, gloss on εὐκέατος, Sch.Od.5.60. **-κόμιστος**, ον, *easy to be transported*, ὕλη Str.12.3.12. **-κράτητος** [κρᾰ], ον, *easy to hold* or *defend*, Plb.4.56.9.

**εὐκάτακτος**, ον, (ἄγνυμι) *easily broken, fragile*, τὸ εὐ. Ph.2.309, Artem.1.66 (-εακτον codd.).

**εὐκατά-ληκτος**, ον, *with a good termination*, Eust.1613.33. **-ληπτος**, ον, *easy to apprehend* or *recognize*, Erot.*Praef.*, Heliod.ap.Orib.46.28.3, Artem.1.1ᵃ, etc. II. Adv. -τως, ἔχειν to be *easily bandaged by* κατάληψις (q. v.), Hp.*Off.*9. III. *easy to capture*, of cities, Hsch. s. v. διατειχίζειν.

**εὐκατάλλακτος**, ον, *easily appeased, placable*, opp. μνησίκακος, Arist.*Rh.*1381ᵇ5, cf. *Vit.Philonid.*p.3 C., Lxx 3*Ma.*5.13. Adv. -τως, ἔχειν πρός τινας Sch.S.*Aj.*1345.

**εὐκατά-λῠτος**, ον, *easy to overthrow*, X.*HG*3.5.15 (Comp.). **-μάθητος** [μᾰ], ον, *easy to understand*, Hp.*Acut.*28, Gal.7.463. **-μάχητος** [μᾰ], ον, *easily conquered*, Sch.Th.6.17. **-μικτος**, *affabilis*, *Gloss.* **-νόητος**, ον, *easy to observe* or *understand*, Plb.18.30.11, Ptol.*Tetr.*30. **-πάλαιστος** [πᾰ], ον, *easy to throw in wrestling*, *EM*400.5. **-παυστος**, ον, *easily pacified*, Gal.1.334, Paul.Aeg.1.66. **-πληκτος**, ον, *easily scared*, Lib.*Arg.D.Prooem.*11. **-ποτος**, ον, *easily swallowed*, Philum.ap.Aët.9.19. **-πρακτος**, ον, *easily accomplished*, Poll.9.161. **-πράϋντος** [πρᾱ], ον, *placable*, *Gloss.* **-πρηστος**, ον, *easily kindled* or *set on fire*, ὕλη Ph.*Fr.*103 H., Suid.

**εὐκατᾰρίθμητος**, ον, *easily counted*, Gal.7.463.

**εὐκατά-σειστος**, ον, *easily shaken* or *thrown down*, Eust.969.61. **-σκεπτος**, ον, *convenient for inspection*, Hp.*Fract.*30, Gal.2.700. ⊛ **-σκεύαστος**, ον, *easily constructed*, Ph.*Bel.*60.51: Comp., ib.61.6. 2. *well-made*, ἅρμα Sch.E.*Hipp.*1226. **-στᾰτος**, ον, *well-fixed, firmly established*, διάθεσις Alex.Aphr.*Pr.*1.87, cf. Asp. *in EN*106.11; τὰ τοῦ τόνου εὐ. γίνεται A.D.*Adv.*157.16. **-στροφος**, ον, *brought to a good conclusion, well-turned*, of a period: only in Adv. -φως, ἀπηρτίσθαι Demetr.*Eloc.*10. **-σχετος**, ον, *easily held fast*, Hp.*Fract.*22 (Comp.). **-τακτος**, ον, *easy to set in order*, Ptol.*Geog.*1.1. **-τρόχαστος**, ον, *easily overrun* or *attacked*, Str.14.5.6; of writers, *open to attack, incorrect*, Id.1.2.2:—also **-τροχος**, Hsch. **-φερής**, ές, = εὐκατάφορος, Id. s. v. ὑγρός. **-φθορος**, *corruptibilis*, *Gloss.* **-φορία**, ἡ, *propensity, proclivity*, *Stoic.*3.25 (pl.). **-φορος**, ον, *prone towards*, πρός τι Arist.*EN*1109ᵃ15, Plu.2.503c. **-φρόνητος**, ον, *easy to be despised, contemptible*, ὑπό τινος X.*HG*6.4.1, cf. *Cyr.*8.3.1, D.4.18, Men.*Sam.*297, Arist.*Pol.*1312ᵇ24, etc.; *negligible*, πᾶσα ἀλγηδὼν εὐ. Epicur.*Sent.Vat.*4, cf. Phld.*D.*1.25, al.; esp. in Lit. Crit., D.H.*Comp.*3, Longin.3.1, Demetr.*Eloc.*4, etc. Adv. -τως Plu.*Demetr.*16. **-φρόνιστος**, ον, *well-considered*, dub. l. in Ph.1.664. **-ψευστος**, ον, *safe to tell lies about*, Str.1.2.19.

**εὐκατ-έργαστος**, ον, *easy to work*, χώρα Thphr.*CP*4.7.3 (Comp.); ἔρια Gal.18(2).525; of food, *easy of digestion*, X.*Mem.*4.3.6 (Comp.), Diph.Siph.ap.Ath.2.91e, Dsc.2.90, Sor.1.49. 2. *easy of accomplishment*, D.*Ep.*1.6 (Comp.), Arist.*Rh.*1363ᵃ31; εὐκατεργαστότερόν ἐστι c. inf., X.*HG*6.1.12. 3. *easy to subdue* or *conquer*, D.H.3.20; πᾶσιν Plu.*Pyrrh.*19. **-ηγόρητος**, ον, *easy to blame, open to accusation*, Antipho Soph.51, Th.6.77, Plb.4.29.3. **-οίκητος**, ον, *convenient for dwelling in*, gloss on εὔκτιτος, Sch.E.*Or.*1621. **-οπτος**, ον, *easily seen, conspicuous*, χῶρος Aen.Tact.27.2: c. dat., τοῖς ἀθανάτοις εὐ. Satyr.*Vit.Eur.Fr.*39 ii 22. **-όρθωτος**, ον, *easily effected*, πολιορκία D.S.34/5.2.45; χειρουργία Heliod.ap.Orib.44.23.23. Adv. -τως Sch.A.R.1.246.

**εὔκαυστος**, ον, *easily burning*, Thphr.*Ign.*72 (Comp.), Sch.Ar.*Pax* 1134 (Sup., εὐκαστοτα cod.): -**καυτος**, Phot. s. v. πισσοκωνήτῳ πυρί.

**εὐκέαστος**, ον, (κεάζω) *easily cleft* or *split*, Eust.1241.48.

**εὐκέᾰτος**, ον, poet. for foreg., κέδρου τ' εὐκεάτοιο Od.5.60; ἐρινεοῦ εὐ. Theoc.25.248.

**εὐκέλᾰδος**, ον, *well-sounding, melodious*, λωτός E.*Ba.*160 (lyr.); χοροί Ar.*Nu.*312 (lyr.); μολπά *AP*7.194 (Mnasalc.); κιθάρης γῆρυς *Not.Scav.*1912.459 (Ostia), cf. Epic. in *Arch.Pap.*7.8.

**εὔκεντρος**, ον, *pointed*, βέλος *AP*9.339 (Arch.).

**εὐκένωτος**, ον, *easily evacuated*, Gal.10.626.

**εὐκεραΐστος** [ᾰ], ον, *easily disabled*, δύναμις, to be read in Gal.19.207.

**εὐκέρᾱος**, ον, *with beautiful horns*, Mosch.2.52; Διόνυσος *AP*9.827 (Ammon.).

**εὐκερᾱσία**, ἡ, = εὐκρασία, *well-tempered constitution*, *PMag.Leid.W.*17.35.

⊛ **εὐκέραστος**, ον, *well-mixed, well-tempered*, ἀήρ Plu.2.922e; ἦχος D.H.*Comp.*22.

**εὐκερδής**, ές, *gainful*, Opp.*C.*1.37.

**εὐκερμᾰτέω**, (κέρμα) *to be rich in money*, Eub.144; condemned by Phryn.339.

**εὔκερως**, ων, contr. for εὐκέραος, ἄγρα S.*Aj.*64; [τράγος] Herod.8.17: neut. pl., τὰ εὔκερω Max.Tyr.35.7: acc. pl. εὐκέρωτας *Gp.*18.1.3:—poet. **ἠΰκερος**, Μήνη Doroth.ap.Heph.Astr.3.30.

**εὐκέφᾰλος**, ον, *with a good head*, Arr.*Cyn.*4.4 (del. Hercher), Poll.2.43, *Hippiatr.*115.

⊛ **εὐκηλήτειρα**, ἡ, (κηλέω) *she that lulls* or *soothes*, παίδων εὐ. Hes.*Op.*464.

**εὐκηλία**, Dor. **-κᾱλία**, ἡ, *quiet*, Hsch.

**εὔκηλος** (A), ον (cf. Hdn.Gr.1.161), Dor. **εὔκᾱλος**, (v. ἕκηλος) *free from care, at one's ease*, εὔκηλος τὰ φράζεαι ἅσσ' ἐθέλησθα Il.1.554; εὗδον δ' εὔκηλοι Od.14.479, cf. S.*El.*241 (lyr.); ἡμεῖς μὲν.. πολέας τελέοντες ἀέθλους.., ὁ δ' εὔκηλος.. Od.3.263; εὔκηλοι πολέμιζον Il.17.371; εὔκηλος τότε νῆα θοὴν.. ἐλκέμεν ἐς πόντον, i.e. *without fear*, Hes.*Op.*671, cf. *h.Merc.*480; εὔ. τέρπου φρένα Pherecr.152. 2. in Alexandr. and later Ep. of things, νὺξ εὔ. *still, silent*, Theoc.2.166; πτέρυγες εὔ. *steady, even*, A.R.2.935; αὖραι εὔ. Opp.*H.*4.415. Adv. -λως A.R.2.861.

**εὔκηλος** (B), ον, (καίω) *easily burning*, or (cf. εὐκέατος) *easily split*, Ion Trag.28.

**εὐκήπευτος**, ον, *easy to cultivate*, Thphr.*HP*7.7.2 (cod. Urb.).

**εὐκῑν-ησία**, ἡ, *ease of motion, mobility*, Antyll.ap.Stob.4.37.16; μελῶν Herod.Med.ap.Orib.5.27.20; τροχιλιῶν Orib.49.4.34; πυρός Simp.*in Cael.*662.20; βάσεως Artemo 12; *mobility* of troops, Plb.8.26.3, D.S.3.49 (pl.): generally, Dam.*Pr.*287. 2. *mobility* of mind, τῆς ψυχῆς αἱ εὐ. Epicur.*Ep.*1 p.20 U., cf. Phld.*Ir.*p.72 W., Ath.Mech.32.1. **-ητος**, ον, *easily moved, agile*, Hp.*Aph.*3.17, Pl.*Ti.*58e; -ότατον εἶδος ib.56a; -ότερον ψυχὴ σώματος Arist.*MM*1199$^b$32; -ότατον τὸ σφαιροειδές Id.*de An.*405$^a$12, al.; of persons, Id.*HA*491$^b$13; *mobile*, of troops, Plb.1.40.7. 2. *easily moved, changeable*, Arist.*Cat.*8$^b$35; τὸ εὐ. *fickleness*, Hdn 7.7.1. Adv. -τως D.S.20.95. 3. *easily moved, inclinable*, πρὸς ἀρετήν, πρὸς ὀργήν, Arist.*Cat.*13$^a$27 (Comp.), *Rh.*1379$^a$26; πρὸς ἀδικίαν Zaleuc.ap.Stob.4.2.19. 4. = εὐέλεγκτος, Arist.*Metaph.*991$^a$16. 5. of language, *flowing, graceful*, Phld.*Po.*994.35.

**εὔκισσος**, ον, *ivied*, Ἑλικών *AP*7.407 (Diosc.).

**εὐκίων** [ῐ], ον, gen. ονος, *with beautiful pillars*, αὐλαί E.*Ion* 185 (lyr.), cf. *AP*7.648.7 (Leon.).

**εὔκλᾰδος**, ον, *with fine boughs*, Quint.*Ps.*47(48).3; gloss on εὔκνημος, Sch.Nic.*Th.*648; on εὔπτορθον, Suid.

**εὔκλαστος**, ον, (κλάω) *easily broken*, Dsc.4.146, Ath.Mech.18.1; gloss on εὐκέατος, Sch.Od.5.60.

⊛ **εὐκλεής**, ές, acc. sg. *εὐκλεέα, contr. εὐκλεᾶ Pi.*P.*12.24 (-έα codd.), shortened εὐκλεᾰ Id.*N.*6.29, S.*OT*161 (lyr., s.v.l.), disyll., B.5.196; dat. *εὐκλεέϊ, shortened εὐκλεΐ Pi.*N.*2.24: acc. pl. *εὐκλεέας, contr. ἐϋκλεῖας Il.10.281, Od.21.331, shortened εὐκλέᾰς Id.*O.*2.90, Simon.95.1; later poet. εὐκλειής *Epigr.Gr.*946 (Tralles), ἐϋκλειής A.R.1.73; gen. εὐκλειοῦς *Arch.Pap.*1.220 (ii B.C.): (κλέος):—*of good report, famous*, freq. of persons, Od. l. c., etc.; also of things, οὐ μὰν ἧμιν ἐϋκλεὲς ἀπονέεσθαι Il.17.415; ὀϊστοί Pi.*O.*2.90, cf. *N.*6.29, etc.; εὐκλέα γλῶσσαν a song *that tells of his glory*, B. l.c.; γόος εὐκλεὴς.. Ἀτρείδαις A.*Ch.*321 (lyr.); βίου πονηροῦ θάνατος -έστερος Id.*Fr.*90; -έστατος βίος E.*Alc.*623, etc.: in Prose, of persons, X.*Vect.*6.1 (Comp.), *HG*7.2.20 (Sup.), Pl.*Mx.*247d; δόξα εὐ. Id.*Smp.*208d; later πόσῳ εὐκλεέστερον..; c. inf., Muson.*Fr.*19 p.109 H.; εὐ. θάνατος Ph.2.574 (Sup.). Adv. -εῶς, Ep. -ειῶς, ὀλέσθαι ἐϋκλειῶς πρὸ πόληος Il.22.110, cf. *AP*6.332.8 (Hadr.); εὐκλεῶς ἀπολέσθαι, κατθανεῖν, A.*Pers.*328, *Ag.*1304: Sup. εὐκλεέστατα X.*Eq.Mag.*1.1. II. Εὐκλῆς, Orphic title of Hades, *IG*14.641 (Thurii).

⊛ **εὐκλειᾰ**, ἡ, -κλεία metri gr., A.*Th.*685: Ep. **ἐϋκλείη** Il.8.285, Od.14.402; **εὐκλείη** *IG*14.1663:—*good repute, glory*, τὸν.. ἐϋκλείης ἐπίβησον Il. l.c., cf. Antipho Soph.49, Th.2.44, X.*An.*7.6.33, Pl.*Mx.*247a, *Ep.*354b, A.R.1.141, etc.; λιπὼν.. εὔκλειαν ἐν δόμοισι A.*Ch.*348 (lyr.); στέφανος εὐκλείας S.*Aj.*465, E.*Supp.*315; ἄγαλμα εὐκλείας S.*Ant.*703. II. Εὐ. personified, B.12.183, *IG*3.277. 2. title of Artemis in Boeotia, etc., Plu.*Arist.*20, Paus.9.17.1,2:—hence **Εὔκλεια**, τά, festival at Delphi, *Schwyzer* 323 *D*7 (Delph., v/iv B.C.): **Εὔκλειος**, ὁ, epith. of Zeus, B.1.6; (sc. μήν) name of month, e.g. at Corcyra, *IG*9(1).694.51, al.; at Tauromenium, ib.14.430 ii 9.

**εὐκλεΐζω**, *bring honour to*, Sapph.118.6; *praise*, Tyrt.12.24: Dor. aor. 1 εὐκλέϊξα Pi.*P.*9.91, B.6.16; πατέρα εὐκλείζων (trisyll.) ἐνὶ δήμῳ *IG*1².1085.

**ἐϋκλειής**, Adv. **ἐϋκλειῶς**, Ep. for εὐκλεής, εὐκλεῶς.

**εὔκλεινος**, ον, *much-famed*, Arist.*Fr.*640(40).

**εὔκλειστος**, ον, (κλείω) *well-shut*, Eust.1937.61, Hdn.*Epim.*178.

**ἐϋκληΐς** [ῑ], ῖδος, ἡ, Ep. for foreg., *well-closed, close-shut*, θύρη.. ἐϋκληῗς, ἀραρυῖα Il.24.318 Aristarch. (ἐῢ κληῗσ' (dat. pl.) Trypho).

**εὐκληματέω**, *grow luxuriantly*, of vines, Lxx *Ho.*10.1, Ph.1.681, Phlp.*in GA*43.26.

**εὐκληρ-έω**, *to be fortunate*, Teles p.60 H.: c. acc. cogn., [κλῆρον] *AP*11.128 (Pollian.). **-ημα**, ατος, τό, *a piece of good fortune*, Antiph.317, Teles p.26 H., D.S.18.13, Str.5.3.7. (εὐκλήρωμα is f.l. in *AB*77.) **-ία**, ἡ, *good luck in drawing lots*, Lib.*Decl.*16.30. 2. generally, *good fortune*, φύσεως D.H.3.14, cf. Ael.*NA*1.54. **-ος**, Dor. **-κλᾶρος**, ον, *fortunate*, Lxx *De.*4.20, *APl.*4.296 (Antip.), Ael.*Fr.*288: euphem. of the dead, *BGU*1209.5 (i B.C.).

**εὔκλωνος**, ον, *with fine twigs*, πενταπέτηλον Androm.ap.Gal.14.40.

**ἐΰκλωστος**, ον, *well-spun*, χιτών *h.Ap.*203; λίνον, νῆμα, *AP*6.33 (Maec.), 284.

**εὔκμητος**· εὐπαγής, Hsch.

⊛ **ἐϋκνήμῑς**, ῖδος, ὁ, ἡ, *well-greaved*, freq. in nom. and acc. pl. ἐϋκνήμιδες, ἐϋκνήμιδας, in Il. always epith. of Ἀχαιοί 1.17, al.; in Od. also of ἑταῖροι, 2.402, 9.550: gen. sg. as fem., -κνήμῑδος Ἰτώνης Poet.ap. *EM*519.1. II. *with goodly spokes*, ἀπήνη Nonn.*D.*7.140.

**εὔκνημος**, ον, *with beautiful ankle*, πούς *AP*5.202 (Asclep.); *with handsome legs*, of a statue, Plin.*HN*34.82; of men, Herm.ap.Stob.1.49.45; *with strong calves*, *UPZ*121.6 (ii B.C.). II. as Subst., a plant in Nic.*Th.*648, *Al.*372.

**εὔκνιστος**, ον, (κνίζω) *ticklish, irritable*, Man.5.337.

**εὐκοίλιος**, ον, *easing the bowels*, Diocl.*Fr.*126, Plu.2.137a, Dsc.2.120, Diph.Siph.ap.Ath.9.371b (Comp.):—hence Subst. **-κοιλιότης**, ητος, ἡ, Paul.Aeg.3.77.

**εὐκοινόμητις**, ὁ, ἡ, *deliberating for the public weal*, ἀρχά A.*Supp.*700 (lyr.).

**εὐκοινων-ησία**, ἡ, *good fellowship*, *Stoic.*3.64, M.Ant.11.20. **-ητος**, ον, *easy to deal with*, εἰς χρήματα Arist.*EN*1121$^a$4, cf. Them.*Or.*22.269c.

**εὐκολία**, ἡ, (εὔκολος) prop. *contentedness with one's food*, Plu.2.461c; ἡ περὶ τὴν δίαιταν εὐ. Id.*Caes.*17: but, in earlier authors, 2. of the mind, *contentedness, good temper*, Pl.*Alc.*1.122c, etc.; ὀλιγόδεια καὶ εὐ. Ph.2.457. 3. of the body, *ease and lightness in moving*, εὐ. καὶ εὐχέρεια Pl.*Lg.*942d: metaph., εὐ. πρὸς τὴν ποίησιν *facility* in verse-making, Plu.*Cic.*40; εὐ. πρήξιος *AP*7.694 (Adaeus).

**εὐκολίδες**· [εὐ] τῆς εὐκολίας ποιητικαί, Hsch.

**Εὐκολίνη**, ἡ, epith. of Hecate, Call.*Fr.*17 P.

**εὐκόλλ-ητος**, ον, *well soldered*, *POxy.*1449.24 (iii A.D.). **-ος**, ον, (κόλλα) *gluing well, sticky*, ἰκμάς *AP*6.109 (Antip.).

**εὔκολος**, ον, (κόλον): I. of persons, *easily satisfied, contented with one's food*, Ἑρμείας *AP*9.72 (Antip.); εὐ. τῇ διαίτῃ Plu.*Lyc.*16; τὸ εὔκολον τῆς διαίτης Id.*Galb.*3: but, in earlier authors, 2. of the mind, opp. δύσκολος, *easily satisfied, contented, good-natured*, ὁ δ' εὔ. μὲν ἐνθάδ', εὔ. δ' ἐκεῖ, of Sophocles, Ar.*Ra.*82, cf. Arist.*Rh.*1381$^a$31: Sup., Max.Tyr.26.2: c. dat., εὐ. πολίταις *at peace with* them, Ar.*Ra.*359; εὐ. ἑαυτῷ Pl.*R.*330a; εὐ. πρὸς τοὺς συνήθεις Plu.*Fab.*1: c. inf., εὐ. φέρειν ἧτταν Id.2.629a. Adv. -λως *calmly*, εὐχερῶς καὶ εὐ. ἐξέπιεν Pl.*Phd.*117c, cf. Isoc.9.3 (v.l. -κλεῶς); εὐ. φέρειν τι Arist.*EN*1100$^b$31, cf. Anaxandr.53.4; εὐ. ἔχειν Lys.4.9; εὐθύμως καὶ εὐ. ζῆν X.*Mem.*4.8.2; *carelessly*, διειλέχθαι Pl.*Sph.*242c: Comp. -ώτερον, ἀποθανούμεθα Plu.2.235c; -ωτέρως Steph.*in Gal.*1.294 D.; also -ώτερον κρατῆσαι *more easily*, Polyaen.5.13.2. 3. *ready, agile*, *AP*5.205.2 (Leon.); of soldiers, ἐλαφροί, εὐ., εὐχερεῖς Poll.1.130; τὴν ἀναπνοὴν οὐκ εὐ. Aret.*SD*1.15. 4. rarely in bad sense, *easily led, prone*, πρὸς ἀδικίαν Luc.*Merc.Cond.*40; -ώτεροι ταῖς ὀργαῖς Plu.2.463d; τὰ ἀνόητα καὶ εὐ. Philostr.*VA*3.28. II. of things, *easy*, οὐ γὰρ εὐκόλῳ ἔοικεν Pl.*R.*453d, cf. *Prm.*131e: Sup. -ώτατοι Id.*Lg.*779e; *easy to understand*, Lxx 2*Ki.*15.3. Adv. Comp. -ώτερον *more easily*, Ph.2.211. 2. *lithe*, εὐ., ὑγρομελής, of the pyrrhich, Poll.4.96. III. epith. of Hermes at Metapontum, Hsch.; of Asclepius at Epidaurus, *IG*4.1260.

⊛ **εὔκολπος**, ον, *with beautiful bays*, Archestr.*Fr.*9.3. 2. *in goodly folds*, of a net, *AP*6.28 (Jul.).

**εὐκόλυμβος**, ον, *diving well*, Heph.Astr.2.2, Sch.Lyc.387.

**εὐκόμης**, ου, ὁ, (κόμη) = εὔκομος, Poll.2.24, 5.83, Max.Tyr.3.8.

**εὐκομῐδής**, ές, (κομιδή) *well cared for*, νομαί Hdt.4.53 (Sup.), cf. Hsch.

⊛ **εὐκόμιστος**, ον, (κομίζω) = foreg., Poll.9.161, Eust.1560.6. 2. *easily extracted*, Sor.2.62; *easily carried off*, App.*Mith.*90.

**εὔκομος**, ον, (κόμη) *lovely-haired*, of goddesses and noble ladies, Ep. and Lyr. form **ἠΰκομος**, Il.1.36, Hes.*Th.*241, Pi.*O.*6.91, *P.*5.45; Σελήνη Epimenid.2: in Prose, Philostr.*Ep.*29; *well fleeced*, εὔκομα μῆλα *AP*9.363.20 (Mel.); *with goodly foliage*, δένδρεσιν ἠϋκόμοισιν Emp.127.2, cf. Alex.Aphr.*Pr.*2.51.

**εὔκομπος**, ον, *loud-sounding*, εὔκομποι πληγαὶ ποδός, in dancing, E.*Tr.*152 (lyr.).

**εὔκονος** (sc. ἄρτος), ὁ, *bread made with bran*, Amerias and Timachidas ap.Ath.3.114e.

**εὐκοπ-έω**, *enjoy an easy life*, διὰ ὅλου βίου *PSI*4.286.38 (iii/iv A.D.). **-ία**, ἡ, *ease, facility*, D.S.1.36, 3.17, Lxx 2*Ma.*2.25; ἐν πάσῃ εὐ. *PMag.Par.*1.159. **-ος**, ον, *easy*, Plb.18.18.2: mostly in Comp., -ωτέρα σκευασία Dsc.1.39; -ώτερόν [ἐστι] c. inf., *Ev.Matt.*9.5, 19.24, etc. Adv. -πως Hp.*Epid.*2.6.31, Ar.*Fr.*783, D.S.3.24, Ph.*Bel.*56.16: Comp. -ώτερον Antip.*Stoic.*3.256.

**εὐκόρῠθος**, ον, (κόρυς) *with beautiful helmet*, Opp.*C.*1.363.

**εὐκόρῠφος**, ον, (κορυφή) *with handsome head*, Herm.ap.Stob.1.49.45: metaph., of sentences, *well wound up, ending well*, D.H.*Dem.* 40, 43.

**εὐκοσμ-έω**, *behave orderly*, LXX 1*Ma.*8.15. **-ητος**, ον, *well-adorned*, *h.Merc.*384. **-ία**, ἡ, *orderly behaviour, good conduct, decency*, E.*Ba.*693, X.*Cyr.*1.2.3, Arist.*Pol.*1299$^b$16, etc.; τῆς εὐ. τῆς περὶ τὸ θέατρον *IG*$2^2$.354.16 (iv B.C.); εὐ. τοῦ θεάτρου ib.$2^2$.223*B*8; εὐ. ἡ κατὰ τὸ ἱερόν *SIG*1007.24 (Pergam., ii B.C.); εὐκοσμία τῶν παίδων Pl.*Prt.*325d; ὁ ἐπὶ τῆς εὐκοσμίας καὶ τῶν παρθένων *CIG*3185.19 (Smyrna); ὁ ἐπὶ τῆς εὐ. ἄρχων *IGRom.*4.582 (Aezani). **-ίως**, Adv. *decently*, περιστέλλεσθαι Anon.Hist.*Oxy.*218ii 9. **-ος**, ον, *behaving well, orderly, decorous*, Sol.4.33, Th.6.42 (Comp.); οὐκ εὔκοσμον αἴρονται φυγήν A.*Pers.*481; τὸ εὔ., = εὐκοσμία, Th.1.84; ὁ εὔ., official title at Pergamum, *IGRom.*4.353$^b$3 (ii A.D.); at Athens, *SIG*1109.94, 136 (ii A.D.). 2. *well-adorned*, τοῖχοι γραφῇσιν εὔκοσμοι Aret.*CA*1.1. II. Adv. -μως *in good order*, Od.21.123, Hes.*Op.*628: Sup. -ότατα X.*Cyr.*2.4.1. 2. *ornamentally, gracefully*, ξεῖν A.R.1.1120; διαλέγεσθαι Plu.*Dem.*11.

**εὔκουρος**, ον, (κείρω) *well-shorn*, Hegem.ap.Ath.15.698e.

**εὐκράδαντος** [κρᾰ], ον, (κρᾰδαίνω) *well-poised*, gloss on ῥαδαλός, *EM*701.53.

**εὐκρᾰδής**, ές, (κράδη) εὐκραδέος..συκέης *a fine fig-tree*, Nic.*Al.*347 (v.l. εὐκραδέης, εὐκραδίης).

**εὐκρᾰδίως**, = εὐκαρδίως, *App.Anth.*3.292.

**εὐκρᾱής**, Ep. **ἐϋκρ-**, ές, = εὔκρατος (v.l. for ἀκραής in Od.14.299, Hes.*Op.*594); of winds, *gentle*, A.R.2.1228, 4.891; ἀήρ Thphr.*CP*1.11.6, 2.3.3 (nisi leg. εὐκράς); *temperate*, neither too dry nor too wet, τόποι Arist.*Mete.*352$^a$7; of love, Opp.*H.*4.33. II. = εὐκράς (A) 2, Poll.6.23 (interpol.). III. Adv. -αῶς prob. cj. for εὐκραής in Aristaenet.1.3.

**εὐκραίρης**, ητος, ὁ, ἡ, = sq., Max.84.

**εὔκραιρος**, Ep. **ἐΰκρ-**, ον, also η, ον, (κραῖρα) *with fine horns*, esp. of oxen, βουσὶν ἐϋκραίρῃσιν *h.Merc.*209; εὐκραίρῳ βοτὰ A.*Supp.*300. 2. of ships, *with beautiful beak*, Opp.*H.*2.516, Tryph.213.

**εὐκράς** (A), ᾶτος, ὁ, ἡ, = εὔκρατος, *temperate, of even temperature*, κρήνη εὐκρὰς πρὸς χειμῶνα καὶ θέρος Pl.*Criti.*112d; of climate, Thphr.*HP*7.1.4: metaph., ἔστιν οἷς βίος ὁ μικρὸς εὐκρὰς ἐγένεθ' E.*Fr.*504; ἡδονή ib.197. 2. *mixed for drinking*, οἶνος Poll.6.23. 3. of persons, *mixing readily with*, οὐ πολλοῖς εὐ. *AP*12.105 (Asclep.). (εὔκρας E.*Fr.*197, Poll.)

**εὐκράς** (B), κρᾶτος, ὁ, ἡ, = εὐκέφαλος, Hsch.

**εὐκρᾱσία** (late -**κρᾱσίη** Man.5.59), ἡ, *good temperature, mildness*, τῶν ὡρῶν Pl.*Ti.*24c; τοῦ ἀέρος Plb.34.8.4: abs., Arist.*Pr.*860$^b$12; ἐν ταῖς εὐκρασίαις *in good climates*, Thphr.*CP*3.21.1. 2. of persons, εὐ. τοῦ σώματος *good temperament*, Arist.*PA*673$^b$25, cf. *GA*744$^a$30, Zeno *Stoic.*1.37, Gal.6.31, etc.

**εὐκρᾱτό-μελι**, ιτος, τό, *honey-wine*, Ruf.*Fr.*117, Choerob. *in Theod.* 1.344. **-ποσία**, ἡ, *drinking of* εὔκρατον, Alex.Trall.5.5.

**εὔκρᾱτος**, Ion. **εὔκρητος**, ον, (κεράννυμι) *well-tempered, temperate*, E.*Fr.*772; ἐγκέφαλος Democr.ap.Thphr.*Sens.*56; ἀήρ Pl.*Ax.*371d; ὥρα Arist.*GA*752$^b$30; εὔκρατον ποιεῖ τὴν θερμότητα Id.*PA*652$^b$26; of countries, D.S.1.10; τόποι Ath.Med.ap.Orib.9.12.5 (Sup.); οἰκήσεις Plb.34.1.8 (Comp.); οἶκος Aret.*CA*1.1; of the *temperate* zone, *Stoic.*2.195, etc.; μεῖξις Chrysipp.ib.219; of liquids, *tempered, lukewarm*, ὕδωρ *IG*5(1).1390.108 (Andania), cf. Gal.6.101, etc.; of wine, *mixed for drinking*, Arist.*Pr.*874$^a$28. 2. metaph., *temperate, mild*, ὀλιγαρχία Id.*Pol.*1320$^b$21; τὸ εὔ. τοῦ ἤθους M.Ant.1.15; Κύπρις *AP* 6.208 (Antip.Thess.): in Astrol., of beneficent planetary influences, Gal.9.911. 3. in Lit. Crit., εὔ. ἁρμονία, ἑρμηνεία, *mixed* style, D.H.*Comp.*21 (v.l. κοινή), *Dem.*3; συνθήκη ὀνομάτων Luc.*Hist.Conscr.* 46. II. of persons, εὔκρητοι πρὸς ἅπαντας (cf. εὐκράς (A) 3) Hp.*Decent.*3. III. Adv. -τως *temperately*, ἀνδρείως καὶ εὐ. Phld.*Herc.* 1251.14; *temperately*, Gal.1.342. 2. εὐ. ἔχειν to be *temperate*, of climate, Cleom.1.2; to be *lukewarm*, Artem.1.64.

**εὐκρᾱτόω**, *temper*, in Pass., Sch.Hes.*Th.*p.461 G., Sch.Lyc.177 (-τυνθῆναι codd., Scheer).

**εὐκρᾰτῶς**, Adv. (Adj. -κρᾰτής is not found) *firmly, fast*, ἔχειν τι Arist.*Pr.*875$^a$22; cf. δυσκρατής.

**εὔκρεκτος**, ον, (κρέκω) *well-struck, well-sounding*, of stringed instruments, φόρμιγξ A.R.4.1194. 2. *well-woven*, of the threads of the warp, μίτοι *AP*6.174 (Antip. (Sid.)).

**ἐϋκρήδεμνος**, ον, *with beauteous fillet*, Nonn.*D.*26.338.

**εὔκρημνος**, ον, *with fair cliffs*, Opp.*C.*3.251.

**εὔκρηνος**, Ep. also **ἐΰκρ-**, ον, (κρήνη) *well-watered*, πέτρη *APl.*4.230 (Leon.); *with fair fountains*, πτολίεθρον Call.*Aet.*3.1.72.

**ἐϋκρηπῖς**, ῖδος, ὁ, ἡ, *well-based*, Nonn.*D.*40.258.

**εὔκρητος**, ον, Ion. for εὔκρατος.

**εὔκρῑθος**, ον, (κριθή) *rich in barley*, ἀλωά Theoc.7.34; ἄρουρα *AP*6.258.6 (Adaeus).

**εὐκρίν-εια** [ῐ], ἡ, (εὐκρῐνής) *clear-sightedness*, Pl.*Def.*414a. 2. *distinctness of outline*, Diocl.*Fr.*141. 3. *limpidity* of style, εὐ. καὶ καθαρότης Hermog.*Id.*1.2, cf. 4. 4. *clear distinction*, προσώπων καὶ πραγμάτων Procl.*in R.*1.15 K. **-έω**, *keep distinct, keep in good order*, τοὺς στρατευσομένους δεῖ εὐκρινεῖν X.*HG*4.2.6 (nisi leg. διευκρ-); τὰ εὐκρινοῦντα τὴν σύγχυσιν Hermog.*Id.*1.4, cf. 11. II. *judge fit, decide*, *PCair.Zen.*150.22 (iii B.C.). **-ής**, ές, (κρίνω) *well-separated*, X.*Eq.Mag.*3.3; *well-opened*, στόματα (sc. τῆς μήτρας) Hp.*Mul.*1.17 (s. v.l., cf. III). II. *distinct, clear*, τῆμος δ' εὐκρινέες τ' αὖραι καὶ πόντος ἀπήμων then the winds are *regular, steady*, Hes.*Op.*670; ἡ διάγνωσις εὐ. γενήσεται Is.10.2; οὐκ εὐκρινές ἐστι πρὸς τὴν ἀκοὴν there is no *clear discernment*, Arist.*Pr.*903$^a$17. Adv. -νῶς, ἔχειν Pl.*Sph.*242c; εὐκρινέστερον ἰδεῖν Id.*R.*564c; οὐκ εὐκρινῶς εἴτε..εἴτε.. without *distinction*, Str.16.4.20, cf. 6.1.11. 2. of literary style, *pellucid*, opp. ἀμφίβολον, Phld.*Po.*1676.8; τὸ καθαρὸν καὶ εὐ. Hermog.*Id.*1.1; of authors, such as Critias and Xenophon, ib.2.11, 12. III. *well-arranged, in good order*, Hp.*Mul.*1.17 (if σώματα be read); πάντα..εὐκρινέα ποιέεσθαι Hdt.9.42. Adv. -νῶς, κεῖσθαι X.*Oec.*8.19. 2. of bandages, *simple, not creased*, Hp.*Off.*10, cf. Gal. 18(2).776. Adv. -νῶς ib.725; Ion. -νέως Hp.*Off.*3. IV. *having had a favourable crisis, convalescent*, σωμάτιον Isoc.*Ep.*4.11, cf. Hsch.; but, *indicating a good crisis, favourable*, of symptoms, Hp.*Coac.*604, Antyll.ap.Orib.9.4.2: metaph., Men.*Pk.*163. 2. of illnesses, *easily brought to a crisis*, Hp.*Aph.*3.8, *Epid.*2.1.5 (Sup.). 3. = νεκρός, Hsch.: Att. use. acc. to *EM*392.32. **-ητος**, ον, *highly sensitive*, prob. f.l. for εὐκίνητος, Aret.*SD*1.6.

**εὔκρῐτος**, ον, (κρίνω) *easy to decide*, οὐκ εὔ. τὸ κρῖμα A.*Supp.*397; εὔ. [ἐστιν] ὅτι.. it is *easily discerned, manifest*, Pl.*Plt.*272c, cf. d; εὔκριτ' ἐστί Men.*Epit.*136; ἴχνη *distinct*, Poll.5.66. 2. Medic., *having a good crisis*, νόσημα Hp.*Aph.*1.12; κρίσιες -ώτεραι Id.*Acut.* 14. Adv. -τως, opp. ἀνακρίτως, Pall.*in Hp.*2.181 D.

**ἐϋκρόκᾰλος**, ον, *pebbly*, Nonn.*D.*15.95.

**εὐκρότᾰλος**, Ep. **ἐϋκρ-**, ον, *accompanied by castanets*, χορεῖαι *AP* 9.139 (Claudian.); *lively, rattling*, πλατάγη ib.6.309 (Leon.).

**εὐκρότητος**, ον, *well-hammered, well-wrought*, πρόχους S.*Ant.*430; Δωρίς E.*El.*819.

**εὔκροτος**, ον, *well-sounding*, ἀνάπαιστα Alciphr.3.43. Adv. -τως Sopat. in Rh.8.14 W. II. Adv. -τως, = εὐκροτήτως, applied to the elements in the body, Meno *Iatr.*19.27.

**εὔκρυπτος**, ον, *easy to hide*, Hp.*Fract.*18 (Comp.), A.*Ag.*623.

**εὐκρῠφής**, ές, = foreg., Arist.*HA*623$^a$28.

**εὐκτάζομαι**, Frequentat. of εὔχομαι, Hsch., Phot.

**εὐκταῖος**, α, ον, (εὔχομαι) Att. Adj. (used chiefly by Trag., cf. ἀραῖος): 1. *of* or *for prayer, votive*, Ἅιδου..εὐκταίαν χάριν A.*Ag.* 1387; τρίτην Διὸς σωτῆρος εὐκταίαν λίβα Id.*Fr.*55; εὐχαί Ar.*Av.* 1060; ἐπῳδαί Pl.*Lg.*906b; εὐ. [νύμφα] *devoted*, E.*IT*213 (lyr.); πανηγύρεις εὐ., Lat. *ludi votivi*, D.C.58.12: εὐκταῖα, τά, *votive offerings, vows, prayers*, A.*Supp.*631 (lyr.), S.*Tr.*239. 2. epith. of gods, *invoked in* or *by special prayer*, πατρὸς εὐκταίαν Ἐρινύν, πατρόθεν εὐκταία φάτις, of the curse *invoked by* Oedipus, A.*Th.*723, 841 (both lyr.); Θέμις εὐκταία E.*Med.*169 (anap.); τοῖσι δυστυχοῦσιν εὐκταία θεός Id.*Or.*214. 3. generally, *prayed for, desired*, ἠώς, λιμένες, *AP*6.242 (Crin.), 9.41 (Theon); γάμος γὰρ..εὐκταῖον κακόν Men.*Mon.*102, cf. Epicur.*Sent.Vat.*35; *desirable*, f.l. for εὐκτέον in Pl.*Lg.*687e: Sup., τήβεννος (of the *latus clavus*), *AJA*18.323 (Sardes, i B.C.); ἴασις Gal. 7.738, cf. Luc.*Tyr.*17. Adv. -αίως, ἔχειν Sch.Pi.*P.*5.159; δέχεσθαί τινα J.*BJ*7.2.1.

**εὐκτέᾰνος** (A), ον, (κτέανον) *wealthy*, A.*Pers.*897 (lyr.), *AP*9.442 (Agath.).

**εὐκτέᾰνος** (B), ον, = εὐκτήδων, Thphr.*HP*3.9.3 (Comp.); δρῦς Plu.*Marc.*8.

**εὐκτέον**, (εὔχομαι) *one must pray for* or *desire*, Pl.*Lg.*687e, Heraclit.*Ep.*7.8; θεῷ τὰ ἄξια θεοῦ prob. cj. in Porph.*Marc.*12: abs., Max. Tyr.11.4.

**εὐκτήδων**, ον, gen. ονος, *straight-grained*, of wood, Thphr.*HP*5.1.11.

**εὐκτημοσύνη**, ἡ, *wealth*, Poll.6.196.

**ἐϋκτήμων**, ον, gen. ονος, (κτῆμα) *wealthy*, Pi.*N.*7.92; εὐκτ- Paul. Al.*M.*2.

**εὐκτήριος**, α, ον, *of* or *for prayer*, οἶκος *Cod.Just.*1.2.15 *Intr.* II. Subst. εὐκτήριον, τό, *oratory*, Just.*Nov.*131.7 *Intr.*, *Rev.Bibl.*1911.287 (Jericho, vi A.D.).

**εὔκτητος**, ον, *honestly acquired*, πλοῦτος Crates Theb.10.9, cf. Paul. Al.*N.*4; τἀγαθὸν εὔ. Phld.*Sto.*339.4.

**εὐκτικός**, ή, όν, (εὐκτός) *expressing a wish*, in Gramm., ἐπίρρημα A.D.*Synt.*248.6, cf. Ph.1.541: -κή, ἡ (with or without ἔγκλισις), the *optative* mood, A.D.*Synt.*245.27, D.T.638.7, etc. Adv. -κῶς *in the optative*, Suid. s. v. ἀγαπῴην. 2. *expressing a prayer* or *vow*: -κόν, τό, *utterance in the form of a prayer* or *wish*, *Stoic.*2.61 (pl.); εὐ. ὕμνοι Men.Rh.p.333 S.: so -κά, τά, Procl.*Chr.*ap.Phot.*Bibl.*p.320 B.; but, *liturgy*, Philostr.*VA*6.40, S.E.*M.*8.72. Adv. -κῶς *in the form of a prayer*, Theon *Prog.*5.

**ἐϋκτίμενος** [ῐ], η, ον, (κτίζω) = εὖ ναιόμενος, *good to dwell in*, epith. of cities, ἐϋ. πτολίεθρον Il.2.501, etc.; πόλις B.5.149; of anything on which man's labour has been bestowed, νῆσον ἐϋκτιμένην ἐκάμοντο wrought it *so as to be good to dwell in*, Od.9.130; ἐϋ. ἐν ἀλωῇ on a *well-made* threshing-floor, Il.20.496, 21.77; the same phrase, of a garden, *well-wrought*, Od.24.226. (εὐκτ- in *h.Ap.*36, B. l.c.)

**εὔκτιστος**, ον, poet. **ἐΰκτ-**, (κτίζω) = foreg., Sch.Hes.*Sc.*270.

**ἐΰκτῐτος**, ον, = ἐϋκτίμενος, of places, Il.2.592, = *h.Ap.*423, cf. D.P. 552; πόλις Hes.*Fr.*81.5; μέγαρα B.3.46. (Glossed by εὐκατοίκητος (q. v.).)

**εὐκτός**, ή, όν, (εὔχομαι) *wished for, desired*, ὄφρ' ἔτι μᾶλλον Τρωσὶ μὲν εὐκτὰ γένηται that *what they wish for* may happen, Il.14.98; τὰ δ' εὐκτὰ παρὰ θεῶν ᾐτησάμην S.*Fr.*843. 2. *to be wished for*, εὐκτὸν ἀνθρώποισι E.*Ion*642, cf. Isoc.12.243, Men.*Georg.*82; εὐ. ὁ τῷ βατράχῳ βίος Theoc.10.52; εὐκτότατος γάμος Eup.383: εὐκτόν ἐστι c. inf., E.*Heracl.*458, X.*Mem.*1.5.5. II. *vowed, dedicated*, ἴουλος *AP*10.19 (Apollonid.).

**εὐκτῠπέων,** ουσα, ον, (κτυπέω) *clattering,* Q.S.5.21.

**εὐκῠβέω,** (κύβος) *to be lucky with the dice,* Amphis 11.

**εὐκυκλής,** ές, = sq., Ἀληθείη Parm.1.29.

**εὔκυκλος,** ον, *well-rounded, round,* in Il. always of ἀσπίς, 5.453, 797, al., A.*Th.*590; εὔ. ἕδρα Pi.*N.*4.66; σφαίρη Parm.8.43; στεφάναι X.*Cyn.*9.12; εὔκυκλον ποιεῖν Pl.*Ti.*40a; ὀφθαλμοὶ σελήνης -ότεροι Alciphr.*Fr.*5. 2. in Od. as epith. of ἀπήνη, *well-wheeled,* 6.58, 70; ὄχοι A.*Pr.*710; ἀντίπηξ E.*Ion* 1391. 3. of bandages, *in horizontal circles, orbicular,* Heliod.ap.Orib.48.61 tit., Gal.18(1).786. II. *moving in a circle, circling,* χορεία Ar.*Th.*968 (lyr.). Adv. -λως Orph. *L.*135.

**εὐκύκλωτος,** ον, *well-rounded,* Eub.56.4, Aristopho 14.

**εὐκύλῐκος** [ῠ], η, ον, (κύλιξ) *suited to the wine-cup,* λαλιή *AP*7.440.8 (Leon.).

**εὐκύλιστος** [ῠ], ον, *easily rolled,* Hero *Aut.*2.4, Phlp.*in Ph.*647.2. Adv. -τως Hero *Aut.*11.11.

**εὐκύμαντος** [ῠ], ον, *easily made to undulate,* ἐποχαί Nicom.*Harm.* 3 (Comp.). II. metaph., *strong-surging,* εἰς θυμόν Eust.1392.49.

**εὔκωπος,** ον, *well-equipt with oars,* Opp.*H.*5.242; gloss on εὐσελμος, Hsch.

**εὐλάβ-εια** [λᾰ], ἡ, Ion. -ίη Thgn.118, Agatho in *PLG* ii p.268 B.:— *discretion, caution,* Thgn. l.c., Agatho l.c., etc.; ἐσῴζετ' ἂν τὴν -ειαν S.*El.*994; personified in E.*Ph.*782; ἡ εὐ. σῴζει πάντα Ar.*Av.*376; εὐλάβειαν ἔχειν μή.., = εὐλαβεῖσθαι μή.., Pl.*Prt.*321a; so εὐ. αὕτη.. τὸ μὴ νέους..γεύεσθαι *caution to prevent* their tasting, Id.*R.*539b; εὐλαβείας οὐ μικρᾶς δεῖται, εὐ. ἐστὶ πολλῆς, D.19.262, Arist.*Pol.*1269$^{a}$14; εὐ. ποιητέον περί τινας ib.1315$^{a}$17; δι' εὐλαβείας ἔχειν ἀλλήλους D.H. 5.38; ἐπ' εὐλαβείᾳ..προείρηται by way of *caution,* Pl.*R.*539d; ἐπ' εὐ. in A.*Ag.*1024 is f.l. for ἐπ' ἀβλ., cf. Sch. ad loc. 2. c. gen., *caution* or *discretion in* a thing, πολλὴ εὐ. τούτων ποιητέα Antipho 3.3. 11; εὐλάβειαι πληγῶν *avoidance of..,* Pl.*Lg.*815a; τῶν αἰσχρῶν Arist.*EN*1121$^{b}$24; ηὐλάβεια τῶν ποιουμένων S.*OC*116; εὐλάβειαν τῶνδε προυθέμην Id.*El.*1334; ἡ τῶν περιεχόντων εὐ. *careful employment of..,* Phld.*D.*3*Fr.*32. 3. *reverence, piety,* πρὸς or περὶ τὸ θεῖον, D.S.13.12, Plu.*Num.*22 (but also πρός τινα Ph.2.581): abs., *godly fear, Ep.Hebr.*5.7, 12.28; *religious scruple,* οὐδεμίαν εὐ. προορωμένων *UPZ*42.21 (ii B.C.). b. as title, ἡ σὴ εὐ. your *reverence, PFlor.* 73.7 (vi A.D.). 4. in bad sense, *over-caution, timidity,* Plu.*Fab.*1, 2. 432e; εὐλαβίη γὰρ ἀπειρίη Aret.*CA*1.2. ⊛ **-έομαι,** impf. ηὐλαβούμην v.l. in E.*Or.*748 (troch.), 1059, εὐλ- Aeschin.1.25: fut. -ήσομαι Pl. *R.*410a, Arist.*EN*1127$^{b}$6; also -ηθήσομαι Lxx *De.*2.4, al., D.L.7.116, Gal.5.249: aor. ηὐλαβήθην (or εὐλ-) Pl.*Phd.*89c:—*to be discreet, cautious, beware,* folld. by μή or ὅπως μή with subj., εὐ. μὴ φανῇς κακὸς γεγώς S.*Tr.*1129, cf. E.*Hipp.*100, Ar.*Eq.*253, Pl.*Phd.*89c, etc.: by fut. ind., ὅπως μὴ..οἰχήσομαι ib.91c (om. cod. B): c. inf., εὐλαβουμένῳ πεσεῖν S.*OT*616; εὐ. λέγειν Pl.*Phd.*101c: with μή inserted, εὐ. μὴ σῴζειν φίλους E.*Or.*1059, cf. Ar.*Lys.*1277, Cydias 1. 2. *take care,* ὅπως κατοίσεις Ar.*Ach.*955; εὐ. περί τι Pl.*Lg.*927c, *Ion* 537a; περί τινος Id.*Lg.*691b; ἀμφί τινι Luc.*Gall.*21: abs., εὐλαβήθηθ' S.*OT*47; εὐλαβούμενος ἠρόμην Pl.*Prt.*333e, cf. 316d; εἰ μηδὲν εὐλαβηθέντα τἀληθὲς εἰπεῖν δέοι *without reserve,* D.18.159; *take precautions,* Arist. *Pol.*1303$^{b}$27. 3. *incur risk,* εὐλαβήθη περὶ καθαιρέσεως δόξης Vett. Val.231.19, cf. 209.11. II. c. acc., *have a care of, beware of,* εὐλαβοῦ στρόμβον..μή σ' ἀναρπάσῃ A.*Fr.*195; εὐ. τὴν κύνα *'ware* the dog, Ar.*Lys.*1215; εὐ. πενίαν Pl.*R.*372c; τὸν φθόνον D.18.305; τὸ ψεῦδος Arist.*EN*1127$^{b}$6; τοὺς ὑβρίζεσθαι νομίζοντας Id.*Pol.*1315$^{a}$27; τὰς μυίας Id.*HA*611$^{b}$11. 2. *reverence, pay honour to,* τὸν θεόν Pl. *Lg.*879e; τὸν δῆμον Plu.*Per.*7; in Lxx, *fear* God, *Na.*1.7; εὐ. ἀπὸ τοῦ ὀνόματος Κυρίου *Ze.*3.12; μηδὲν -ούμενον, ὡς οἱ πολλοὶ λέγουσιν, ὅτι ..δεῖ.. Sor.1.49. 3. *watch for, await quietly,* καιρόν E.*Or.*699. 4. *put out of harm's way,* τὰ κοῖλα γαστρός Id.*Ph.*1411. III. later in Act., εὐλαβεῖν τινα *beware of, BGU*665.4 (i A.D.); cf. εὐλάβησον, -ῆσαι, Phot. **-ής,** ές, (λαβεῖν) *taking hold well, holding fast, clinging,* metaph., πενία Luc.*Tim.*29: lit. in Adv. εὐλαβῶς, κατέχειν Ael.*NA*3.13, 6.55 (Sup.): but mostly, II. metaph., *undertaking prudently, discreet, cautious,* Democr.91, Pl.*Plt.*311a, al.; τὸ εὐλαβές, = εὐλάβεια, ib. b; εὐλαβὴς περί τι Plu.*CG*3; τὸ πρὸς τὰ μεγάλα τῶν τετολμημένων εὐ. Hdn.2.8.2; εὐ. ἀπό τινος *keeping* from.., Lxx *Le.* 15.31. Adv. -βῶς Pl.*Sph.*246b; εὐ. διακείμενος D.S.13.12, etc.: Comp. -εστέρως E.*IT*1375; -έστερον διακεῖσθαι πρός τι Plb.1.18. 1. 2. *reverent, pious,* Lxx *Mi.*7.2 (v.l. εὐσεβής), *Ev.Luc.*2.25, *Act. Ap.*2.5, etc.: Sup. -έστατος, as title, Dionys.*Ep.*71, Procop.Gaz.*Ep.* 126. III. Pass., *easy to get hold of,* κέρκος Luc.*Lex.*7. 2. *cautiously undertaken* or *effected,* μετάβασις Pl.*Lg.*736d; ἡδοναί Plu.*Per.* 15 (ἀβλ- Reiske). **-ητέον,** *one must beware of,* c. acc., Pl.*R.*608a, *Grg.*527b, cf. 480e, Epicur.*Fr.*465, Dsc.*Eup.*2.160, etc. **-ητέος,** *verecundus, Gloss.* **-ητικός,** ή, όν, c. gen., *careful to avoid,* Pl.*Def.* 412a; ὀρθοῦ ψόγου Stoic.ap.Stob.2.7.5$^{b2}$. **-ίη,** Ion. for εὐλάβεια.

**εὐλάζω,** (εὐλή) = σκωληκιάω, Hsch.

**εὐλᾶϊγξ,** ὁ, ἡ, gen. ιγγος, poet. for εὔλιθος, τράπεζα *AP*9.767 (Agath.); σορός ib.7.605 (Jul.), cf. Coluth.46, Nonn.*D.*5.134.

**εὐλάκα,** ἡ, Dor. word, ἀργυρέᾳ εὐλάκᾳ **εὐλαξεῖν** (Lacon. fut. inf.), *should plough* with silver *ploughshare,* intimating that there would be a dearth, corn being worth its weight in silver, Orac.ap.Th.5.16 (v.l. εὐλάχα, Phot.).—Neither Verb nor Noun occurs elsewh. (Cf. αὖλαχα, αὖλαξ.)

**εὔλᾰλος,** ον, *sweetly-speaking,* Lxx *Si.*6.5; epith. of Apollo, *AP*9. 525.6; of the Argo, Orph.*A.*244: metaph., of a wine-jar, *AP*9. 229 (Marc. Arg.). II. = εὔγλωσσος II, Lxx *Jb.*11.2.

**εὐλαμπής,** ές, *bright-shining,* Max.582, Max.Tyr.17.10 (Sup.); ὀφθαλμοί Adam.1.8; τὸ εὐ. ib.19:—also **εὔλαμπρος,** ον, v.l. for εὔχαλκος in Antiph.208.2.

**εὐλάχᾰνος** [λᾰ], ον, *fruitful in herbs, AP*7.321.6; τόποι *Gp.*12. 3.3.

**εὐλεί-αντος** and **εὐλέαντος,** ον, (λεαίνω) *easily triturated,* Xenocr.42; τροφή Arist.*PA*674$^{b}$33: Comp., Antyll.ap.Orib.10.13.12: **-ωτος,** ον, *easily powdered,* Gal.12.189, Asclep.ap.eund.13.678.

**εὔλειμος,** ον, = sq., E.*Ba.*1084 codd. (prob. ὕλιμος).

**εὐλείμων** (ἐῠ-), ον, gen. ονος, *with goodly meadows,* οὐ γάρ τις νήσων ἱππήλατος οὐδ' εὐ. Od.4.607, cf. *h.Ap.*529, Hes.*Fr.*134.

**εὔλεκτρος,** ον, *bringing wedded happiness,* of Aphrodite, S.*Tr.*515 (lyr.), *AP*5.244 (Maced.). 2. *a beauteous bride,* S.*Ant.*796 (lyr.).

**εὔλεξις,** ι, ὁ, ἡ, *with good choice of words,* ridiculed by Luc.*Lex.*1, *Rh.Pr.*17.

**εὐλέπιστος,** ον, *easily peeled* or *shelled,* βάλανος Dsc.4.157.

**εὐλεχής,** ές, = εὔλεκτρος, θάλαμος *AP*7.649 (Anyte); Κύπρις *APl.* 4.182 (Leon.).

⊛ **εὐλή,** ἡ, *worm, maggot,* the larva of the fly (rarely in sg., *AP*7. 472.10 (Leon.)), different fr. ἕλμινς; Hom. only in Il., of worms bred in flesh, 19.26, 24.414, al.; ὑπ' εὐλέων καταβρωθῆναι Hdt.3.16, cf. 4.205, Hp.*Mul.*1.75, Pl.*Ax.*365c, Arist.*HA*506$^{a}$30:—of common worms, Orph.*L.*600.

**εὔληκτος,** ον, *soon ceasing,* Luc.*Trag.*324.

**εὐλημᾰτέω,** (λῆμα) *to be of good spirit,* A.*Fr.*106.

**εὐληνής,** ές, *fleecy, EM*393.6, Hsch.

**εὔληπτος,** ον, *easily taken hold of,* οὐδ' εὔληπτον εἶναι τὸ ὕδωρ J.*AJ* 1.16.2, cf. Gal.*UP*11.5 (Sup.). Adv., τὸ ἔκπωμα εὐληπτότατα ἐνδιδόναι to give it *so that one can most easily take hold of it,* X.*Cyr.*1.3.8: metaph., εὐ. τὰ τῆς διατριβῆς Iamb.*VP*7.33. 2. *easy to be taken* or *reduced,* νησιῶται Th.6.85; ἧττον εὐ. πόλις D.H.3.43; εὐ. ὀργή, κόλαξι, Ph.2.590, Plu.2.66b; *easy to gain* or *obtain,* Luc.*Merc.Cond.*10; *easy to apprehend,* τοῖς ἀκούουσι Iamb.*Protr.*4.

**εὔληρα,** ων, τά, *reins,* Il.23.481, Q.S.4.508, 9.156; Dor. **αὔληρα** Epich.178 (for ἀϝληρα, cf. ἀβληρά Hsch.):—hence **εὐληρωσίων** (εὐληροσιῶν cod.)· πληγῶν, Id. (Cf. ταυληρόντα.)

**εὔλητο·** ἐπέφυρτο, ἐτετάρακτο, Hsch. (Perh. for ἑόλητο.)

⊛ **εὐλίβᾰνος** [ῐ], ον, *rich in frankincense,* Aristonous 1.23, Orph.*H.* 55.17.

**εὔλῐθος,** ον, *of goodly stone,* ἄντρον Orph.*H.*59.4; *made of fair stones,* J.*BJ*5.5.6.

**εὐλίμεν-ος** [ῐ], ον, (λιμήν) *with good harbours,* ἀκταί E.*Hel.*1463; [πόλις] εὐλιμενωτέρα Pl.*Lg.*705a, cf. 704b,d; εὐ. ἁλὸς οἶκοι Archestr. *Fr.*26: c. gen., ἱερὸν παντὸς κύματος εὐλίμενον *App.Anth.*3.81 (Posidipp.):—also -λῐμήν, -ένος, πορθμοί Procop.*Aed.*1.5. **-ότης,** ητος, ἡ, *good harbourage,* Men.Rh.p.352 S.

**εὔλιμνος,** ον, (λίμνη) *abounding in lakes,* Arist.*HA*601$^{b}$22.

**εὔλῐνος,** ον, *spinning well,* epith. of Ilithyia, Olen ap Paus.8.21.3.

⊛ **εὐλῐπής,** ές, (λίπος) *very fat,* Lyc.874. 2. *rich in resin,* πεύκη Epigr.ap.Philostr.*Her.*19.17.

**εὐλῐτάνευτος** [ᾰ], ον, (λιτανεύω) *easily entreated,* Sch.A.R.1.1141.

⊛ **εὐλογ-έω,** impf. εὐλόγουν or ηὐλ- Ar.*Ec.*454, Isoc.12.206: fut. -ήσω E.*Hec.*465 (lyr.): aor. εὐλόγησα or ηὐλ- Lxx *Ge.*1.22, al.: inf. εὐλογῆσαι Ar.*Eq.*565: pf. εὐλόγηκα Lxx *Nu.*23.11:—Pass., with fut. Med. εὐλογήσομαι (v.l. -ηθήσομαι, as always in Lxx, 2*Ki.*7.29, al.) Isoc.9.5: aor. εὐλογήθην Phalar.*Ep.*119.3 (opt.): pf. εὐλόγημαι Lxx *Ru.*2.19:—*speak well of, praise,* πόλιν A.*Ag.*580; πατέρα τὸν ἁμόν S.*Ph.*1314, cf. Ar.*Eq.* l. c., E.*Hec.* l. c., al., Isoc. ll. cc.; *deliver a panegyric upon,* Arist.*Rh.Al.*1426$^{a}$3: with neut. Adj., εὐ. καὶ δίκαια κἄδικα Ar.*Ach.*372, cf. *Ec.*454; θεοὶ εὐλογοῦσί τινα honour him, E. *Supp.*927:—Pass., ἐπαινοῖς εὐλογούμενον πέδον S.*OC*720; τὸν ἐν Δωδῶνι δαίμον' εὐλογούμενον Id.*Fr.*461. II. of God or men, Lxx *Ge.*35.9, al., *Act.Ap.*3.26, al.: freq. in pf. part. Pass. εὐλογημένος, as Lxx *De.*28.3, *Ev.Luc.*1.28. 2. *bless, praise* a god, *OGI*73 (Egypt), cf. εὐ. τὴν Εἶσιν (sic) *CIG*4705c (ibid.); σου τὰς δυνάμεις Buresch *Aus Lydien* 113; so in Lxx and NT, *Jo.*22.23, al., *Ep.Jac.*3.9. 3. also, apptly. by a Hebr. euphemism, *curse,* Lxx 3*Ki.*20(21).10, cf. *Jb.*2.5. **-ητός,** ή, όν, *blessed,* ib.*Ge.*9.26, al., Ph.1.453, *Ev.Luc.* 1.68, *Ep.Rom.*1.25, etc. ⊛ **-ία,** ἡ, *good* or *fine language,* Pl.*R.*400d, Luc.*Lex.*1. 2. *plausibility,* ἔχει τινὰ εὐλογίαν Thphr.*CP*6.31.1; *habet* εὐλογίαν Cic.*Att.*13.22.4, cf. *Ep.Rom.*16.18; ἡ τοῦ δόγματος εὐ. prob. in Phld.*Sign.*27; ἡ εὐ. τῶν πραγμάτων Id.*Herc.*1251. 8. II. *praise, eulogy,* Pi.*N.*4.5, Th.2.42; ὑμνῆσαι δι' εὐλογίας E. *HF*356 (lyr.); ἄξιος εὐλογίας Ar.*Pax* 738: pl., Pi.*I.*3.3, 6(5).21, Pl. *Ax.*365a; *good fame, glory,* ἀγήραντος εὐ. Simon.100, cf. Pi.*O.*5.24; εὐλογίαν φέρει *Lyr.Alex.Adesp.*21.10; ἔχειν εὐ. τινὰ πρός τινα *POxy.* 65.4 (iii/iv A.D.). 2. esp. *praise* to God, Lxx *Si.*50.20(22), *Apoc.* 7.12, *OGI*74 (Egypt). III. *act of blessing,* opp. κατάρα, Lxx *Ge.* 27.12, *Ep.Jac.*3.10. 2. *blessing called down* or *bestowed,* Lxx *Pr.* 10.22, 1*Ep.Pet.*3.9. 3. *gift, bounty,* Lxx *Jo.*15.19, 4*Ki.*5.15, 2*Ep. Cor.*9.5; ὁ σπείρων ἐπ' εὐλογίαις ἐπ' εὐλογίαις καὶ θερίσει *bountifully,* ib. 6, cf. Ph.1.129. **-ίζω,** = εὐλογέω, v.l. in Lxx *To.*4.12:—Pass., v.l. in Ph.1.395. **-ιμος,** *benedictus, Gloss.* **-ιστέω,** *act rationally, prudently,* Diog.Bab.*Stoic.*3.219, Antip.ib.253, Ph.1.395; ἔν τινι D.L.7.88, Arr.*Epict.*2.23.35; πρός τι Plu.*Oth.*13, etc. II. = εὐλογέω II, *bless,* Ph.1.125, 130, al. **-ιστία,** ἡ, *circumspection, prudence,* Pl.*Def.*412e, *Stoic.*3.64, Antip.ib.253, Phld.*D.*3*Fr.*81, Plu.2.103a, M.Ant.4.26, Phalar.*Ep.*119.4. II. = εὐλογία III, *blessing,* Ph.1.597, al. **-ιστος,** ον, *easily computed,* hence of ratios,

*simple*, Arist.*Sens.*439b32; opp. περιττός, Id.*Metaph.*1092b27; πληθύς D.H.4.15. 2. *well-weighed*, αἰτίαι Id.1.4; *well-calculated, reasonable*, ὁδός Id.5.55; *rational*, ἐκλογή Antip.*Stoic.*3.253, Chrysipp.ib. 46; λόγος Phld.*Rh.*2.160S.; τῶν ἀλγεινῶν ὑπομονή Hierocl. *in CA* 11 p.441 M. 3. *probable*, Phld.*Lib.*p.27 O. 4. *blessed*, Ph.1.46, al. II. Act., *calculating well* or *rightly*: hence, *prudent, circumspect*, ἀνδρὸς τὸ κρατέειν (sc. θυμοῦ) εὐλογίστου Democr.236, cf. Arist. *Rh.*1385b27, Plb.10.2.7, Phld.*Ir.*p.81 W., etc.: Sup., Ph.1.644; τὸ εὐ., = εὐλογιστία, Arr.*Epict.*1.11.17, Ps.-Dsc.1.103. Adv. -τως *rationally*, opp. ἀλογίστως, Epicur.*Ep.*3 p.66 U.; *prudently, wisely*, κεχρῆσθαι τοῖς καιροῖς Plb.18.33.7 (Sup.); εὐ. φέρειν D.H.4.21, cf. Arr.*Epict.* 3.2.2, M.Ant.8.32.

**εὐλογοποιέω**, *excuse*, Sch.E.*Hec.*1187, Eust.1233.54.

**εὔλογος**, ον, *reasonable, sensible*, νουθετήματα A.*Pers.*830; οὐκ εὐλόγῳ ἔοικεν Pl.*R.*605e; εὔ. ὀργή Phld.*Ir.*p.45 W.; εὔλογόν [ἐστι] c. inf., *it is reasonable that..*, Pl.*Cra.*396b, Arist.*Pol.*1286b15, etc.; -ώτερόν [ἐστι] Id.*EN*1102b2: Sup., Id.*Cael.*286b34. 2. *reasonable, fair*, πρόφασις Th.3.82, D.18.152, etc.; τὸ εὔ. *a fair reason*, Th. 4.87. 3. *probable*, c. dat. et inf., Hp.*de Arte* 7 (Comp.), cf. Sphaer. *Stoic.*1.141, Cic.*Att.*14.22.2; διὰ σημείων εὐ. Phld.*Lib.*p.30 O.; ἐκ τῶν εὐ. *in all probability*, Plb.10.14.6, cf. Plu.*Them.*13; ἐκτὸς τῶν εὐ. πίπτειν to be beyond *all probability*, Arist.*Metaph.*1060a18: Comp., Pl.*Ep.*352a: Sup., Cic.*Att.*13.6.4. Adv. -γως Phld.*Lib.*p.33 O. 4. *suitable, conformable*, c. dat., Plot.6.5.10. 5. *creditable*, κατορθώσασι εὔ. [ἐστί] Ar.*Ra.*736. 6. *eloquent*, v.l. for ἱκανός, Lxx *Ex.* 4.10, whence Ezek.*Exag.*113, Ph.2.93, 1.166 (interpr. as *reasonable*). II. Adv. -γως *with good reason, reasonably*, A.*Th.*508, *Supp.*47 (lyr.), *Fr.*6, Ar.*V.*771, Lys.12.7; εὐ. ἄπρακτοι ἀπίασιν Th. 4.61; εὐ. φέρειν (Abresch εὐλόφως, q.v.) E.*Fr.*175; εὐ. ἔχειν Pl. *Phd.*62d; εὐ. φθονεῖν τινι Alex.219.1; τοῖς εὐ. καὶ τοῖς κακῶς ἔχουσι Men.48; freq. like εἰκότως, at the close of a sentence, implying assent, Arist.*EN*1153b15, 1162b6: Comp. -ωτέρως Isoc.6.28; -ώτερον Plb.7.7.7. 2. εὐ. τινὰ ἐπιδέξασθαι (v.l. ἐνδόξως) *honourably*, Lxx 1*Ma.*12.43.

**εὐλογοφᾰνής**, ές, *seeming probable*, Doxop. in Rh.2.316 W., Sch. S.*OC*761.

**εὐλογχ-έω**, *to be lucky*, prob. in Hsch. for εὐλογεῖν· εὐμοιρεῖν. -**ος**, ον, (λέλογχα) *fortunate, propitious*, Democr.166.

✱**εὐλοιδόρητος**, ον, *open to reproach*, Men.439, Plu.2.757a.

**εὐλοκοπέομαι**, *to be eaten of worms*, Artem.5.81.

**εὔλοφος**, ον, *well-plumed*, κυνῆ S.*Aj.*1286, cf. *Fr.*341; κράνος Hld. 7.5. II. *taking the yoke well, strong, patient*, opp. δύσλοφος, νῶτον Lyc.776; αὐχήν Dam.*Isid.*89. Adv. -φως, ὑποφέρειν τι Phld.*Mort.* 35; φέρειν Dam.*Isid.*190, Eust.1653.6; ἀγωνίζεσθαι Anon.ap.Suid.

**εὐλοχία**, ἡ, *glorious progeny*, *Hymn.Is.*156.

✱**εὔλοχος**, ον, *helping in childbirth*, of Artemis, E.*Hipp.*166 (lyr.); Εἰλήθυια Call.*Ep.*54.

**εὐλύγιστος**, ον, (λυγίζω) *flexible*, *EM*530.56, Eust.73.19.

**εὐλύρ-ας** [ῠ], α, ὁ, = εὔλυρος, epith. of Apollo, Sapph.*Supp.*20c.5, B.*Scol.Oxy.*1361 *Fr.*12, E.*Alc.*570 (lyr.), Ar.*Th.*969 (lyr.), Limen. 4. -**ία**, ἡ, dub. l. in *PMag.Leid.V.*8.8 (fort. εὐμυρία, = -μοιρία). -**ος**, ον, (λύρα) *skilled in the lyre*, of Apollo, E.*Fr.*477; of the Muses, Ar. *Ra.*229 (lyr.); of a harper, *IG*14.1663.

**εὐλῠσία**, ἡ, *suppleness, ease of movement*, D.L.6.70, Muson.*Fr.*19 p.107 H.; εὐ. κοιλίας *a healthy motion* of the bowels, Cic.*Fam.*16. 18.1. II. *release, redemption*, opp. στένωσις, *PFlor.*296.21 (vi A. D.).

✱**εὐλῠτ-έω**, *discharge* a debt, prob. in Hsch. s. v. καταθεῖναι τὴν τιμήν. -**ησις**, εως, ἡ, *discharge of a debt*, *BMus.Inscr.*4.481*.307 (Ephesus). ✱-**ος**, ον, (λύω) *easy to untie* or *loose*, X.*Cyn.*6.12; ὑποδέσεις D.S.15.44; *loose*, θύραι στροφὰς ἔχουσαι εὐ. Id.3.22. 2. *easy to relax, relaxed*, διαχωρήσιες Hp.*Prog.*18, cf. Arist.*Pr.*876b31. 3. *loosely knit, supple*, of joints, Id.*Phgn.*809b26 (Comp.), 811a1; *loose*, of a machine, Hero *Aut.*26.3. 4. *soluble, easily dissolved*, Dsc.5.159; σπλὴν *friable*, Aret.*SD*1.14; *soft, yielding*, of the *os uteri*, Hp.*Mul.* 2.115: hence metaph., *easily dissolved* or *broken*, στέργηθρα E.*Hipp.* 256 (anap.); of engagements, X.*HG*5.2.19; of health, Gal.5.443; of problems, *easy to solve*, Arist.*GA*755b23, Just.*Nov.*97.6 *Intr.* 5. *easily released*, of the foetus, εὐ. πρὸς τὸν τόκον Hp.*Septim.*4 (Comp.): so metaph., στόμα εὔ. πρὸς λοιδορίαν Thphr.*Char.*6.10. b. *free from burdens, at ease*, Jul.*Caes.*315b. II. Adv. -τως *easily, freely*, οὖρα οὐκ εὐ. ἰόντα Hp.*Coac.*446; εὐ. στρέφεσθαι Hero *Aut.*18.1; εὐ. [πέλτην] μεταφέρειν D.S.5.34; *loosely*, ἐναγκυλίζεσθαι Plb.27.11.5. ✱-**όω**, aor. 1 imper. εὐλύτωσον· ἀπάλλαξον, Hsch.

**εὔλωστοι** (-λαστ- cod.)· εὐφυεῖς, Hsch.; cf. λωστός, λῷμα.

✱**εὐμάθ-εια** [μᾰ], ἡ, *readiness in learning, docility*, Pl.*R.*490c, Arist. *Rh.*1362b24, Call.*Fr.*32 P., etc.: pl., Ph.1.326: also in poet. form **εὐμαθία**, Pl.*Chrm.*159e, *Men.*88a: Ion. -ίη *AP*6.325 (Leon. Alex.), al. -**ής**, ές, (μαθεῖν) *ready* or *quick at learning*, opp. δυσμαθής, Pl. *R.*486c, al.; τινος Id.*Ep.*344a; πρός τι D.24.17 (Comp.). Adv. -θῶς, παρακολουθεῖν Aeschin.1.116: Comp. -έστερον Pl.*Lg.*723a. II. Pass., *easy to learn* or *know, intelligible*, A.*Eu.*442, Arist.*Rh.*1409b4; εὐ. φώνημα *well-known*, S.*Aj.*15; εὔγνωστα καὶ εὐ. X.*Oec.*20.14, cf. S.*Tr.*614: Comp., διήγησις Plb.14.12.5. -**ία**, -**ίη**, v. εὐμάθεια.

**εὐμάκης** [ᾱ], ες, v. εὐμήκης.

**εὐμάλακτος** [μᾰ], ον, *easily moulded*, Dsc.1.97; gloss on εὐστρεπτος, Eust.1453.3. II. Gramm., *liquid*, of consonants, *EM*700.24.

**εὔμαλλος**, ον, *of fine wool*, μίτρα Pi.*I.*5(4).62.

**εὐμᾶλος**, Dor. for εὔμηλος.

**εὐμάρᾰθος** [μᾰ], ον, *abounding in fennel*, *AP*9.318 (Leon.).

**εὐμάραντος** [μᾰ], ον, *soon withering*, Artem.1.77.

**εὐμάρ-εια** [ᾰ], ἡ, (Ion. dat. -έῃ is found in Hdt.2.35 codd., cited by Greg.Cor.p.521 S., Suid.), also -ία Pl.*Ly.*204d, but Ion. acc. -ίην only as v.l. for -είην in Hdt.4.113:—*easiness, ease, opportunity*, τινι *for doing* a thing, E.*Fr.*181; but more commonly τινος, S.*Ph.*284, 704 (lyr.); εὐ. φυγῆς Anon.ap.Suid.; τῆς ζητήσεως Arist.*Pol.*1276a 24. 2. *ease of movement, dexterity*, χεροῖν E.*Ba.*1128, cf. Arist. *Mu.*398b35. 3. of internal condition, *ease, comfort*, εὐμαρείᾳ χρώμενος πολλῇ S.*Tr.*193; but also εὐμαρείῃ (-έῃ codd.) χρᾶσθαι euphem. for *alvum exonerare, to ease oneself*, Hdt.2.35, cf. 4.113; εὐ. παρασκευάζειν to provide *easy* or *ready means*, Pl.*Lg.*738d; πρὸς τὰς ἐκ Διὸς ὥρας εὐ. μηχανᾶσθαι *provision for, protection against*, Id.*Prt.* 321a; εὐ. ἐστί c. inf., it is *easy* to.., Id.*Ly.* l. c., X.*Oec.*5.9; δι' εὐμαρείας *easily*, Luc.*Am.*13; κατὰ πολλὴν εὐ., μετὰ πάσης εὐ., Ph.2. 428, 1.670; πρὸς εὐμάρειάν τινος for his *convenience*, Luc.*Hipp.*5; ἐν πάσῃ εὐ. εὐθὺς γίνεται M.Ant.4.3. ✱-**έω**, *have abundance*, πάντων B.1.65. ✱-**ής**, ές, *easy, convenient*, most commonly of things, εὐμάρεα προλέξαις Alc.*Supp.*22.7; εὐ. χεῖρωμα an *easy* prey, A.*Ag.* 1326; δυστυχούντων γ' εὐμαρὴς ἀπαλλαγή Id.*Supp.*339; ἔνθεσις Pherecr.108.6: Comp., Ph.1.19, Ascl.*Tact.*7.3; εὐμαρές [ἐστι] c. inf., *'tis easy*, Sapph.*Supp.*5.5, Thgn.845, Simon.125.5, Pi.*P.*3.115, *N.*3.21, E.*Alc.*492; so ἐν εὐμαρεῖ [ἐστι] Id.*IA*969, *Hel.*1227, *Fr.* 382.10; [Ἡράκλειαν] ἐξ εὐμαροῦς ἔλαβεν Phleg.*Mir.*3. b. *easy to obtain, abundant, cheap*, σῖτος *IG*12(5).714.15 (Andros, iv B. C., Comp.). 2. rarely of persons, *bringing ease*, χρόνος γὰρ εὐ. θεός S.*El.*179 (lyr.); *gentle*, Aret.*SD*1.6: Comp. -έστερος *more 'in touch'*, Hp.*Decent.*13. II. Adv. -ρῶς, poet. -ρέως, *easily, readily*, πείθομαι B.5.195, cf. A.*Fr.*366, Pl.*Criti.*112e, *Lg.*706b, Luc.*Am.*53, Sor.1.33, etc.; τλήσεται εὐ. *AP*5.245 (Paul. Sil.): Comp. -έστερον *Trag.Adesp.*383, Hdn.8.7.6: Sup. -έστατα Ph.2.419; εὐμαρέως τοι χρῆμα θεοὶ δόσαν οὔτε τι δειλὸν οὔτ' ἀγαθόν Thgn.463. (From μάρη = χείρ (cf. εὐχερής) Sch.Il.15.137.) [ᾰ, for καταφαγῆμεν εὐμᾶρέα shd. be read in Epich.42.] -**ίη**, ἡ, v. εὐμάρεια.

**εὔμᾰρις** [later ᾰ (v. infr.)], ιδος, ἡ, acc. εὔμᾰριν A.*Pers.*660 (lyr.); but acc. pl. εὐμᾰρίδας (sic) Lyc.855 (on the accent, v. Hdn.Gr.1.99): —*an Asiatic shoe* or *slipper* (made of deerskin, Poll.7.90), βαρβάροις ἐν εὐμάρισι E.*Or.*1370 (lyr.); κροκόβαπτον..εὔμαριν ἀείρων A. l. c.; βαθύπελμος εὔμᾰρις *AP*7.413 (Antip.), cf. Lyc. l. c. (Prob. a foreign word.)

**εὐμᾰρότης**, ητος, ἡ, = εὐμάρεια, Callistr.*Stat.*3.

**εὐμάχᾰνος** [μᾱ], ον, Dor. for εὐμήχανος.

**εὔμᾰχος**, ον, *easy to fight against, assailable*, Max.Tyr.26.2 (Sup.).

**εὐμεγέθης**, ες, *of good size, large*, Ar.*Pl.*543, Eub.110; ἀστράγαλος Aen.Tact.31.17; ποταμὸς μάλα εὐ. X.*HG*5.2.4; *tall*, γυνή *AP*5.37 (Nicarch.), cf. *PLips.*1.3 (ii B. C.), etc. 2. *considerable, weighty, important*, μαρτυρία D.23.16; πρᾶγμα Ph.2.196.

**εὐμέζεος** (-μάξεως cod.)· εὐφυής (ἐφυεὶς cod.) τοῖς αἰδοίοις, Hsch.

**εὐμεθόδευτος**, ον, = sq. II, Ptol.*Alm.*1.10; *having a good method*, ἰατρός Steph. *in Hp.*2.317 D.

**εὐμέθοδος**, ον, *easily compassed* or *discovered*, Archim.*Spir.Praef.*; *well-arranged*, τὸ εὐ. Lyd.*Mag.*3.53, Olymp. *in Alc.*p.131 C., Alex. Trall.*Praef.* Adv. -δως Id.1.11, Aristaenet.1.13, Hierocl. *in CA Praef.*p.416 M. II. of persons, *scientific*, ἰατρός Alex.Trall.1.12.

**εὐμέθυστος**, ον, *easily made drunk*, *Gp.*7.34.2.

**εὐμειδής**, ές, *smiling, propitious*, A.R.4.715, Call.*Dian.*129.

**εὐμείλικτος**, ον, *easily appeased*, Corn.*ND*12:—also **εὐμειλής**, ές, and **εὐμ⟨ε⟩ίλιχος**, ον, Hsch.

**εὐμέλαθρος**, ον, *with fair halls*, *Trag.Adesp.* in *Gött.Nachr.*1922. 25.

**εὐμέλᾰνος**, ον, *well-blackened, inky*, βροχίς *AP*6.295.4 (Phan.).

**εὐμέλ-εια**, ἡ, *melody*, D.S.4.84, Plu.2.456b, etc. 2. *melodious language*, Longin.28.2; v. l. for ἐμμ-, D.H.*Comp.*18; εὐ. φωνῆς Phld.*Rh.*1.196 S. -**ής**, ές, *melodious*, μουσική Arist.*Pol.*1341b26, Sopat.10; opp. ἐμμελής (metrical), D.H.*Comp.*11, etc.: generally, *agreeable*, συμπόσια Pl.*Ax.*371d. Adv. -λῶς *gracefully*, Machoap. Ath.13.577d. II. *with stout limbs*, Ael.*Fr.*110.

**εὐμελῐτέω**, *to have a good stock of honey*, Arist.*HA*625a24, Thphr. *HP*6.2.3.

**εὐμένεια**, ἡ, poet. -ία Pi.*P.*12.4:—*goodwill, favour*, ἡμῖν..παρὰ τῶν θεῶν..εὐ. εἴη Hdt.2.45, cf. S.*OC*631, E.*Hel.*313, X.*Ap.*7, Pl. *Smp.*197d, etc.; ἡ πρὸς τὸ θεῖον εὐ. the *favour* of the gods (v. πρός) Th.5.105; ἡ συναντωμένη τισὶν εὐ. παρὰ τοῦ δαιμονίου *SIG*601.14 (Teos, ii B. C.); ἐπ' εὐμενείᾳ to gain *favour*, Luc.*Tox.*1; σὺν εὐμενίᾳ *kindly*, Pi. l. c. II. of smell, *pleasantness*, Thphr.*CP*6.14.12.

✱**Εὐμέν-ειος**, α, ον, Adj. of Εὐμένης, pr. n. of two kings of Pergamum, στρατιῶται Polyaen.4.6.13. II. -**εια**, τά, festival in honour of Eumenes II of Pergamum, at Pergamum, *OGI*267.34; at Aegina, ib.329.40; at Sardes, ib.305.9. -**ειος**, ὁ (sc. -μήν), name of month at Pergamum, ib.338.2. -**έτης**, ου, ὁ, poet. for εὐμενής, *well-wisher*, χάρματα δ' εὐμενέτῃσι Od.6.185, *IG*12(8).23 (Lemnos, ii A. D.):—fem. ✱-**έτειρα**, Hsch. -**έω**, *to be gracious*, Ps.-Phoc.142, Opp.*C.*1.9, etc.; τινι *to* one, A.R.2.260, Theoc.17.62. II. c. acc., *deal kindly with*, ἀνεψιόν Pi.*P.*4.127 (s. v. l.); but also, 2. Pass., of benefits *graciously bestowed*, *IPE*I².362.12 (Cherson.). -**ής**, ές, (μένος) *well-disposed, kindly*, τινι *to* one, epith. of gods, *h.Hom.* 22.7 (not in Il. or Od.), Pi.*P.*2.25, A.*Supp.*686 (lyr.), cf. X.*HG*6.4. 2; ἵλεως καὶ εὐ. Id.*Cyr.*1.6.2, Theoc.5.18; Ἑρμῆς *IGRom.*1.1228 (Egypt, ii A. D.); τὸ τῶν θεῶν εὐ. D.4.45. 2. of men, A.*Pers.*175

(troch.), *Supp.*488 (Comp.); πόλει S.*Ant.*212, etc.; εὐ. πρός τι *well-disposed* for it, Plu.*Luc.*42; τὸ εὐ., = εὐμένεια, Pl.*Lg.*792e; ξεῖνος δὲ ξείνῳ.. -έστατον πάντων Hdt.7.237: in Dor. Prose, *Schwyzer* 84 (Argos, v B.C.). **3.** of actions, etc., εὐμενεῖ τύχᾳ, νόῳ, Pi.*O.*14.15, *P.*8.18; εὐ. ὀλολυγμός *signifying goodwill, friendly*, A.*Th.*268. **4.** of places and things, γῆ εὐ. ἐναγωνίσασθαι *favourable* to fight in, Th.2.74; εὐμενεῖ ποτῷ (of a river) *kindly, bounteous*, A.*Pers.*487; of the air, *mild, soft*, Thphr.*CP*2.1.6; so of medicines, *beneficial*, ὑποχονδρίῳ καὶ σπλάγχνοισιν Hp.*Acut.*59, cf. Aret.*CA*1.3; but also *agreeable*, [κόμμι] -έστερον κόλλης Hp.*Art.*33; of a road, *easy*, X.*An.*4.6.12 (Comp.). **II.** Adv. -νῶς, Ion. -έως, A.*Ag.*952, Pl.*Phd.*89a, A.R.2.1275, etc.: Comp. -έστερον E.*Hel.*1298, Pl.*Lg.*718d; also -εστέρως Isoc.4.43, D.H.*Rh.*5. **-ία**, ἡ, v. εὐμένεια. **-ίδες** (sc. θεαί), αἱ, strictly *the gracious goddesses*, euphem. of *the* Ἐρινύες or Furies, name of play by A.; ὥς σφας καλοῦμεν Εὐμενίδας, ἐξ εὐμενῶν στέρνων δέχεσθαι τὸν ἱκέτην S.*OC*486; ὀνομάζειν γὰρ αἰδοῦμαι θεὰς Εὐμενίδας E.*Or.*38; distd. from the σεμναὶ θεαί by Philem.217. **-ίζομαι**, *propitiate*, ἥρωας X.*Cyr.*3.3.22, cf. Ael.*NA*7.44; τινα διά τινος App.*BC*4.54. **-ικός**, ή, όν, *like the* εὐμενής, of persons, Arist.*VV*1251b32; διόρθωσις Plb.12.7.6. **-ισταί**, οἱ, *guild of worshippers of Eumenes*, *Ath.Mitt.*27.172.

**εὐμερδής**· εὔρωστος, Hsch.; cf. εὐσμερδής.

**εὐμέριστος**, ον, (μερίζω) *easily divided*, Thphr.*CP*6.10.8. **2.** *easily calculated*, Hp.*Septim.*3.

**εὐμετα-βλησία**, ἡ, *changeableness*, Sch.Th.3.37. **-βλητος**, ον, (μεταβάλλω) *easily changed, changeable*, Arist.*Rh.*1373a30, M.Ant.5.33, etc.; of food, *easy of digestion*, Hp.*Alim.*49; τὸ εὐ., = foreg., Aesop.367, Iamb.*Protr.*21.κϛ′. Adv. -τως Sch.Th.3.37. ⊛ **-βολος**, ον, = foreg., *changeable*, of things and persons, Gorg.*Hel.*13, Pl.*R.*503c, X.*HG*2.3.32, Arist.*EN*1100b3, etc.; εὐ. ἐστὶν.. βίος Diph.118; ἀνὴρ εὐ. γλώσσῃ Lxx *Pr.*17.20; τὸ εὐ., = εὐμεταβλησία, M.Ant.4.3; τὸ εὐ. τῆς τύχης Diogenian.Epicur.2.60. **-γνωτος**, ον, *fickle*, Vett.Val.304.28 (nisi leg. -γνωστος).

**εὐμετάγωγος** [ᾰ], ον, *easy to put aside, get rid of*, Gal.19.558; *easily moved*, Antyll.ap.Orib.45.2.2.

**εὐμετά-δοτος**, ον, *readily imparting, generous*, 1*Ep.Ti.*6.18, Vett.Val.46.24, al., Herm.*in Phdr.*p.94A.; τὸ εὐ. *generosity*, M.Ant.1.14. **II.** Pass., *easily imparted*, μυστήρια Sch.Ar.*Pl.*1014; of leprosy, *contagious*, Paul.Aeg.4.1. Adv. -τως Hsch. s.v. εὐσυναλλάκτως. **-θετος**, ον, *easily changing*, πρὸς ἔλεον Plu.2.799c; *changeable, fickle*, Id.*Dio*53, Vett.Val.243.30, App.*Mac.*16. **II.** *portable*, Gal.11.215. **-κίνητος** [ῑ], ον, *easily moved* or *changed*, ἐπὶ τὸ χεῖρον Arist.*Metaph.*1019a28; τὸ εὐ. *caprice*, M.Ant.1.16. **-κόμιστος**, ον, *ready to migrate*, Sch.Th.1.2. **2.** *portable*, Aët.1.39. **-κύλιστος** [ῠ], ον, *easy to roll over*, τὸ τῆς βάσεως (sc. τῆς τύχης) εὐ. Gal.*Protr.*2. **-νόητος**, ον, *inconstant, fickle*, Vett.Val.11.17, al. **-πειστος**, *easy to persuade*, Arist.*EN*1151b6, Them.*Or.*7.98b. **-ποίητος**, ον, *easily altered*, ὑπὸ φύσιος καὶ ὑπὸ τύχης Hp.*Decent.*13. **-πτωτος**, ον, *unstable*, παιδία Thphr.*Sens.*45; τὸ τῆς τύχης εὐ. D.S.9.10, cf. Secund.*Sent.*9. Adv. -τως v.l. in Arr.*Epict.*2.22.8. **-ρρευστος**, ον, *easily diverted from its course*, χυμός Aët.5.57 (-ρυστός ed.). **-στᾰτος**, ον, *unsteady, changeable*, Plu.2.5d. **-τρεπτος**, ον, *revocable*, gloss on παλινάγρετον, Sch.Il.1.526, cf. Suid. s.v. ἀβέβαιος. **2.** τὸ εὐ. *easy convertibility*, Gal.6.825. **-φορος**, ον, *easily moved*: *moving quickly*, ὀφθαλμοί *EM*255.52; gloss on θοός, Sch.A.R.1.741. **-χείριστος**, ον, *manageable*, of persons, Isoc.*Ep.*2.20, Pl.*Phdr.*240a, X.*An.*2.6.20; of things, Onos.6.5; λόγος -ότερος Isoc.*Ep.*9.2; σώματα εὐ. τῇ τέχνῃ Max.Tyr.10.3; χρεία εὐ. πρὸς τὸ ζῆν Arist.*Pol.*1257a37. **2.** *easy to cope with*, ἰσχύς Th.6.85, cf. X.*HG*5.2.15; of persons, D.H.8.6 (Comp.). **II.** in Act. signf., Adv. -τως *handily, adroitly*, τῇ ἀσπίδι χρῆσθαι Philostr.*Gym.*19, cf. Eustr.*in EN*343.32.

**εὐμετρ-ία**, ἡ, *good measure* or *proportion*, Aret.*CA*2.3; θεία εὐ. Hierocl.*in CA*23p.468M., cf. Longin.*Proll.Heph.*5. **2.** *excellence of metre*, Eust.1414.9. **-ος**, ον, *well-measured, well-calculated*, σφενδόνα A.*Ag.*1010 (lyr.); *well-proportioned*, v.l. for ἔμμητρον, Theoc.25.209. **2.** *of moderate size* or *proportions*, οἶκος Aret.*CA*1.1. Adv. -ως ib.1.6, Sor.1.86. **3.** *excellent in metre*, [λέξις] εὐ. καὶ εὔρυθμος D.H.*Comp.*25; opp. κακόμετρος, Phld.*Po.*1676.8.

⊛ **εὐμήκης**, Dor. **εὐμάκης** [ᾱ], ες, (μῆκος) *tall*, Pl.*Prm.*127b, Thphr.*HP*3.9.2, Theoc.14.25; *long*, ξυστοί Jul.*Or.*2.60a: Comp. -έστερος Arist.*PA*696a17: Sup. -έστατος *PPetr.*2p.14 (iii B.C.), Str.5.2.5. **2.** *considerable, great*, τύχαι E.*IA*595 (anap.). **3.** εὔμηκες, τό, kind of *balsam*, Plin.*HN*12.114.

**εὔμηλος**, Dor. **εὔμᾱλος**, ον, *rich in sheep*, Od.15.406, *h.Ap.*54, Pi.*O.*6.100, Simon.103, Theoc.22.157, etc.

**εὔμηρος**, ον, *with beautiful thighs*, Poll.2.187, 9.162.

**εὐμήρῡτος**, ον, (μηρύω) *easy to spin out*, Luc.*Fug.*12.

**εὔμητις**, ιδος, ὁ, ἡ, *wise, prudent*, Opp.*H.*5.97, *AP*9.59.8 (Antip. ⟨Thess.⟩), prob. in Phld.*Rh.*2.14S.

**εὐμηχάν-ημα** [χᾰ], ατος, τό, *ingenious contrivance*, dub. in Chrysipp.ap.*EM*701.25 (cf. *Stoic.*2.318). **-ία**, Dor. **εὐμᾱχ-**, ἡ, *skill in devising means*, c. inf., Pi.*I.*4(3).2, *Pae.*7*Fr.*16.11; = εὐπορία, *Stoic.*3.64, Plu.*Tim.*16; *inventive skill*, Andronic.Rhod.p.578M., Luc.*Phal.*1.12. **-ος**, Dor. **εὐμάχ-** [μᾱ], ον, **I.** of persons, *skilful in contriving, inventive*, opp. ἀμήχανος, A.*Eu.*381 (lyr.), Pl.*Prt.*344d, etc.: c. gen., εὐμήχανος λόγου Id.*Cra.*408b; ἁλίων εὐ. ἔργων Opp.*H.*4.593: with a Prep., εὐ. πρὸς τὸν βίον, of birds, *full of devices* for supporting life, Arist.*HA*614b34, cf. 616b34: Sup., of the bee, *Gp.*15.3.1; ἔν τινι D.S.20.92: τὸ εὐ., = foreg., Plu.2.830c. Adv. -νως Ph.1.170, Plu.*Per.*31, Aristaenet.2.15, etc. **II.** Pass., of things, *skilfully contrived, ingenious*, ἐκ τῶν ἀμηχάνων πόρους εὐμηχάνους πορίζων Ar.*Eq.*759 (-ος πορίζειν Bentl.); ἐπίνοιαι Pl.*R.*600a.

**εὔμικτος**, ον, *social*, Them.*Or.*22.270d. **2.** of a road, *frequented*, v.l. for εὐεπίμικτος, Poll.3.96.

**εὐμίμητος** [ῑ], ον, *easily imitated*, Pl.*R.*605a.

**εὐμιξία**, ἡ, *happy union*, *Sammelb.*5656.7 (vi A.D.).

**εὐμίσητος** [ῐ], ον, *well-hated*, in Sup., X.*Cyr.*3.1.9, Longin.*Rh.*p.198H.

**εὔμῑτος**, ον, *with fine threads*, εὐμίτοις πλοκαῖς, i.e. τὸν μίτον εὖ πλέκουσα, E.*IT*817.

**εὔμιτρος**, ον, *with beautiful* μίτρα (q.v.), Mosch.4.98.

**ἐϋμμελίης**, ὁ, (εὖ, μελία) *armed with good ashen spear*, ἐϋμμελίω (Ion. gen.) Πριάμοιο Il.4.47, al.; Πάνθου υἱὸς ἐϋμμελίης 17.9, cf. Od.3.400, Hes.*Sc.*368, etc.: Dor. gen. ἐϋμμελία *APl.*1.6.

**εὔμναστος**, ον, Dor. for εὔμνηστος.

**εὐμνημόνευτος**, ον, *easy to remember*, Pl.*Ti.*18c, d, D.56.45, Aen.Tact.24.14, Ath.7.277c, etc.: Comp. -ότερος Arist.*Rh.*1367a26: Sup., ib.1409b6. **II.** *at one's fingers' ends*, ἔστω σοι εὐ. φάρμακα Hp.*Decent.*9.

**εὐμνήμων**, ον, gen. ονος, in Adv. Comp. -εστέρως, ἔχειν to be *easier to remember*, X.*Ages.*11.1.

⊛ **εὔμνηστος**, Dor. **-μναστος**, ον, *well-remembering, mindful*, τινος S.*Tr.*108 (lyr.); χρηστήριον Boeo 1.

**εὐμογία**, poet. **-ίη**, ἡ, *industry*, Aglaïas 4.

**εὐμοιρ-ᾱτέω**, = sq., Ti.Locr.99e. **-έω**, *to be well off for*, c. gen., Hp.*Ep.*27, Phalar.*Ep.*53 (v.l. for εὐπορεῖν), Anon.*Fig.*p.156S.; εὐμοίρει, in Epitaphs, *IG*14.2387, etc. ⊛ **-ία**, ἡ, *happy possession* of a thing, σώματος, φωνῆς, Luc.*Eun.*8, *Salt.*72; εὐ. τῆς αἱρέσεως *excelling*, Id.*Rh.Pr.*8; φύσεως εὐ. Ph.1.238, al.: abs., D.H.*Rh.*5.3; *good fortune*, Plu.2.14c, etc. **-ίτης** [ῑ], ου, ὁ, = μακαρίτης, of the dead, *IG*14.555 (Catana), 2300 (Comum, v A.D.). ⊛ **-ος**, ον, *well-endowed by fortune*, B.5.1; opp. ἄμοιρος, Pl.*Smp.*197d, cf. Ph.1.282, Call.*Del.*295, *AP*6.278 (Rhian.), Luc.*JConf.*19. Adv. -ρως, ἀποθανεῖν J.*AJ*8.12.6; βιώσασα *IG*12(5).319 (Paros): Comp. -ότερον, ἀποθνήσκειν App.*Hann.*29.

**εὐμολπ-έω**, *sing well*, *h.Merc.*478. **-ία**, ἡ, *sweet song*, Hsch.: title of poem by Musaeus, Paus.10.5.6. ⊛ **-ος**, ον, *sweetly singing*, *AP*9.396 (Paul. Sil.): as pr. n. in *h.Cer.*154, etc.

**εὐμορφία**, ἡ, *beauty of form*, Democr.294, E.*Tr.*936, Pl.*Smp.*218e; σώματος Id.*Lg.*716a; λόγων εὐμορφίαι E.*Cyc.*317, cf. *AP*9.400 (Pall.); εὐμορφίαι τῶν ὄψεων J.*AJ*10.10.1; χολῆς λοβοῦ τε.. εὐ. *symmetry* in the σπλάγχνα, A.*Pr.*495; αἱ ἐκ τῶν διδασκαλείων εὐ. *elegances* of the School (in Rhet.), Epicur.*Fr.*50.

**εὐμορφολογέω**, gloss on ἀστειορρημονέω, Zonar.

⊛ **εὔμορφ-ος**, ον, *fair of form, comely, goodly*, Sapph.76 (Comp.), Hdt.1.196, A.*Ag.*416, 454 (both lyr.); σῶμα.. εὔ. ἰδεῖν S.*Fr.*88.10: γαμεταί, ἀνδράποδα, D.H.11.2, Ph.2.478 (Sup.): metaph., εὔ. κράτος A.*Ch.*490. **-ότης**, ητος, ἡ, *comeliness*, Sch.Opp.*H.*1.505. **-όω**, *become beautiful*, dub.l. in Vett.Val.344.9.

**εὐμουσ-ία**, ἡ, *sense for beauty and art*, πραγμάτων εὐ. E.*Fr.*188, cf. Ps.-Plu.*Vit.Hom.*92; *skill in music*, Men.Rh.p.443S. **II.** *good music*, κινεῖ ἡμᾶς ἡ εὐ., ἐνοχλεῖ δ' ἡ ἀμουσία *Placit.*4.20.2; *sweetness of song*, Arg.Theoc.5. **-ος**, ον, *skilled in the arts*, esp. *in poetry, music, and dancing*, Man.4.60, 5.269; but usu., **2.** *musical, melodious*, μολπά E.*IT*145 (lyr.); τιμαί Ar.*Th.*112 (lyr.); παιδιά Luc.*Am.*53; χεύματα *AP*9.661 (Jul.). Adv. -σως *gracefully*, Corn.*ND*14, Plu.2.1119d.

**εὔμοχθος**, ον, *laborious*, γυμνάς (= γυμνάσιον) *Epigr.Gr.*239, cf. *IG*3.758a.

**εὔμῡθος**, ον, *eloquent*, *AP*4.3b.61 (Agath.).

**εὔμῡκος**, ον, *loud-bellowing*, *AP*6.255 (Eryc., dub.l.); βουκόλια ib.9.104 (Alph.).

⊛ **εὔμωλος**, ον, (μῶλος) = ἀγαθὸς πολεμιστής, εὔοπλος, Hsch. (-μολ- cod.): Sup. -ότατον, = ἁπαλόν, νεώτατον, Id.

**εὐνάεις**, εσσα, εν, v. εὐνάων.

⊛ **εὐνάζω**, fut. -άσω [ᾰ] Od.4.408, X.*Cyn.*9.3; Dor. εὐνάξω Pi. (v. infr.): aor. ηὔνᾰσα E.*Rh.*762, εὔνασα Simon.184.10, A.R.3.1000:—Med., v. infr.:—Pass., Od.5.65: aor. 1 ηὐνάσθην or εὐν-, Pi.*P.*3.25, E.*Ion*17, 1484, (ξυν-) S.*OT*982; Ep. 3 pl. εὔνασθεν (κατ-) Il.3.448: pf. ηὔνασμαι (κατ-) E.*Rh.*611: (εὐνή):—mostly poet., cf. εὐνάω: **1.** *lay* or *place in ambush*, ἔνθα σ' ἐγὼν.. εὐνάσω ἑξείης Od.4.408. **2.** *put to bed, put to sleep*, οὔ σε παιηόνων ἄδορπον εὐνάξομεν Pi.*Pae.*6.128, cf. A.R.4.1060, etc.; of animals, *lay* their young *in a form*, X.*Cyn.*9.3: metaph., of death, *lay asleep*, S.*OT*961, cf. *Tr.*1042 (lyr.), E.*Rh.*762; so βάρβιτον οὐδὲ θανὼν εὔνασεν εἰν Ἀΐδῃ Simon. l.c.; *calm, soothe*, εὐνάζειν.. βλεφάρων πόθον S.*Tr.*106 (lyr.); χόλον A.R.3.1000:—Pass., *go to bed, sleep*, Hom., only in Od., ἐν προδόμῳ εὐνάζετο δῖος Ὀδυσσεύς 20.1; εὐνάζοντο κατὰ μέγαρα 23.299, cf. Hes.*Op.*339, etc.; σκληρῶς εὐ. X.*Cyn.*12.2; also ἔνθα δέ τ' ὄρνιθες.. εὐνάζοντο there they *used to roost*, Od.5.65; of sexual intercourse, παρ' ἀνδράσιν εὐνάζεσθαι ib.119; so θεαῖς εὐνάζεται *h.Ven.*190; θεῷ E.*Ion*17; εὐνάσθη ξένου λέκτροισιν Pi.*P.*3.25; εὐνάσθην ὑπὸ σπαργάνοις Id.*Fr.*193; γάμοις.. βασιλικοῖς εὐνάζεται E.*Med.*18; Φοίβῳ κρυπτόμενον λέχος ηὐνάσθην Id.*Ion*1484 (lyr.); of animals, Arist.*HA*609b23:—so in Med., κούρῳ παρθένος εὐνάσατο Call.*Aet.*3.1.1. **3.** *give in marriage*, τέκνα E.*Fr.*17. **4.** of pain, *lull, deaden*, τὴν ταλαιπωρίην Aret.*CA*2.1:—Pass., σὺ γάρ μ' ἀπ' εὐνασθέντος ἐκκινεῖς κακοῦ S.*Tr.*1242.

⊛ **εὐνᾰής**, ές, *fair-flowing*, B.8.42, 1.75 (p.439J.).

❋ **εὐναῖος**, α, ον, (εὐνή) *in one's bed* or *couch*, εὐ. [λαγώς] a hare *in its form*, X.*Cyn*.5.9; εὐ. [ἴχνη] traces *of the form*, ib.7, cf. S.*Fr*.174, *Ichn*. 226, Stratt.3 (dub. l.). 2. mostly of the marriage-bed, εὐ. δάμαρ, γαμέτας, A.*Fr*.383, E.*Supp*.1028 (lyr.); Κύπρις Id.*Andr*.179; εὐ. γάμοι A.*Supp*.332; ἄτα εὐ., of Helen, E.*Andr*.104 (eleg.); λέχος Critias 2.6 D.; θάλαμοι *BCH*29.412 (Callatis). 3. *keeping one's bed*, λύπᾳ εὐναίᾳ δέδεται ψυχά E.*Hipp*.160 (lyr.); εὐ. πτέρυγες *brooding*, of a bird on the nest, *AP*9.95 (Alph.). 4. εὐναία, ἡ, *a nest* (v. sub καρφηρός); but εὐναῖα, τά, *bed*, is f.l. in Orph.*L*.223. 5. personified, Εὐναίη, ἡ, *the Spirit of Repose*, Emp.123.1. II. (εὐνή II) *of* or *for anchorage*: hence, generally, *steadying, guiding a ship*, πηδάλια E.*IT*432 (lyr.). 2. as Subst., εὐναία, = εὐνή II, *an anchor*, λίθος εὐναίης A.R.1.955: in pl., ib.1277.

**εὐνάν**, ᾶνος, ὁ (masc. acc. to Lupercus, sine expl., fem. acc. to others, = γυνή), Pi.*Fr*.303.

**εὐν-άσιμος**, ον, *good for sleeping in*: εὐνάσιμα, τά, *convenient sleeping-places*, X.*Cyn*.8.4. **-αστήρ**, ῆρος, ὁ, (εὐνάζω) = εὐνητήρ, Lyc. 144:—fem. **εὐνάστειρα**, metaph., Androm.ap.Gal.14.36. II. *serving as an anchor*, λίθος Opp.*H*.3.373. **-ᾱτήρ, -ᾱτειρα, -ᾱτρια, -ᾱτωρ**, v. εὐνητ-. ❋**-ᾱτήριον**, τό, *bed-chamber*, A.*Pers*.160 (troch.), S.*Tr*.918 (pl.); *marriage-chamber*, E.*Or*.590. (**εὐναστήριον** is a later form found in codd. of S. and E. ll. cc.) **-άω**, fut. -ήσω *AP*10.12: aor. 1 εὔνησα Od.4.440:—Pass., aor. 1 εὐνήθην v. infr., etc.: pf. εὔνημαι *AP*7.397 (Eryc.): (εὐνή):—poet. Verb, = εὐνάζω, rare in Trag.: 1. *lay* or *place in ambush*, ἑξείης δ' εὔνησε [ἡμᾶς] Od. l. c. 2. *lay asleep, lull to sleep*, φρουρὸν ὄφιν A.R.4.87: metaph., τῆς δ' εὔνησε γόον Od. 4.758; κάματον, ἐλπίδας, χόλον, *AP*10.12, 4.3b.41 (Agath.), Nonn.*D*. 13.276:—Pass., *make one's couch*, prob. in S.*Aj*.604 (lyr.); *lie asleep*, esp. of death, εὐνήθης ὕπνον ὀφειλόμενον *AP*7.78 (Dionys. Cyz.), cf. 397 (Eryc.); πόλλ' ἐν κακοῖσι θυμὸς εὐνηθεὶς ὁρᾷ S.*Fr*.661; of a dog, *to lie kennelled*, Id.*OC*1571 (lyr.):—Hom. only in aor. Pass., of the winds, παύσασθαι δ' ἐκέλευσε καὶ εὐνηθῆναι Od.5.384; elsewh. of sexual intercourse, 10.296, al.; φιλότητι or ἐν φιλότητι εὐνηθέντε, Il. 3.441, 14.314, cf. 331, al.: c. dat. pers., *to be bedded with*.., θεὰ βροτῷ εὐνηθεῖσα, γυνὴ θεῷ εὐνηθεῖσα, 2.821, 16.176; παρ' ἀνδράσιν εὐνηθεῖσαι Hes.*Th*.967. II. Med., *stupefy* with narcotics, Aret.*CA*2.5.

**εὐνάων**, ουσα, ον, (νάω) *fair-flowing, liquid*, ἀπ' εὐνάοντος οὐρανοῦ dub. l. in A.*Fr*.44 (v.l. εὐνήεντος).

**εὐνεικής**, ές, *easy to decide*, of a suit: hence, *easy to interpret*, of an oracle, Antim.75.

❋ **εὐνέτης**, ου, ὁ, (εὐνή) = εὐναστήρ, E.*Or*.1392 (lyr.), *AP*9.241 (Antip. ⟨Thess.⟩):—fem. **εὐνέτις**, ιδος, Hp.*Epid*.7.42, A.R.4.96, etc.

**εὔνεως**, ων, (ναῦς) *well furnished with ships*, Max.Tyr.5.5, 31.7.

**εὐν-ή**, ἡ, Ep. gen. sg. and pl. εὐνῆφι, -φιν Od.2.2, al.:—*bed*, εὐνῇ ἔνι μαλακῇ Il.9.618, etc.; ἔβη εἰς εὐνήν Od.1.427, etc.; ὄρνυτ' ἄρ' ἐξ εὐνῆφιν Od.2.2, al.: in Cret. Prose, εὐνά *Schwyzer*180. 2. *bedding*, dist. fr. λέχος (the bedstead), λέχος πόρσυνε καὶ εὐνήν Od.3.403; ἐκθεῖσαι πυκινὸν λέχος ἐμβάλετ' εὐνήν 23.179; cf. ἐνεύναιος. b. esp. of soldiers in the field, Th.3.112, 4.32, 6.67, Pl.*R*.415e, A.*Ag*.559, E.*Rh*.1 (anap.). 3. εὐναὶ νυμφάων their *abode*, Il.24.615; of animals, συφεοὺς δυοκαίδεκα ποίει.. εὐνὰς συσί Od.14.14; *lair* of a deer, 4.338, Il.11.115; [νεβρὸν] ἐξ εὐνῆφι θορόντα 15.580; *form* of a hare, X.*Cyn*. 6.16; *nest*, S.*Ant*.425; κριοῦ εὐναί, a place in Colchis where the ram of Phrixus rested, A.R.4.116. 4. *marriage-bed*, μεμνημένος οὔτε τι σίτου οὔτ' εὐνῆς Il.24.130; εὐνῆς ἐπιβήμεναι 9.133; ἐξ εὐνῆς ἀνστᾶσα 14.336; usu. with some word added to denote this, ἔτλην ἀνέρος εὐνήν 18.433; ἀνδρὸς ἐν εὐνῇ ἤθελον εὐνηθῆναι Od.4.333; ἀπανήνασθαι θεοῦ εὐνήν 10.297; ἐμίγην φιλότητι καὶ εὐνῇ Il.3.445, etc.; ζαλωτὸν ὁμόφρονος εὐνᾶς Pi.*O*.7.6; εὐναὶ ἀνανδρώτοισι S.*Tr*.109 (lyr.); εὐναὶ γαμήλιοι, νυμφίδιοι, κρύφιαι, E.*Med*.1027, *Alc*.886 (anap.), *El*.720 (lyr.); without such a word, Διὸς εὐναί Pi.*P*.2.27; ἄλλην τιν' εὐνὴν ἀντὶ σοῦ στέργει πόσις; E.*Andr*.907, cf. *Hipp*.1011; of Pyrrha and Deucalion, ἄτερ εὐνᾶς κτισσάσθαν λίθινον γόνον Pi.*O*.9.44; ὅσιος ἀπ' εὐνᾶς E.*Ion*150 (lyr.). 5. *one's last bed, the grave*, ἔνθα σ' ἔχουσιν εὐναί A.*Ch*.318 (lyr.); εἰς εὐνὴν πατρὸς S.*El*.436; Ἄϊδος εὐνάς *Epigr.Gr*.431 (Antioch.) (so some take Τυφωέος εὐναί in Il.2.783). II. pl. εὐναί, *stones thrown out from the prow and used as anchors*, ἐκ δ' εὐνὰς ἔβαλον, κατὰ δὲ πρυμνήσι' ἔδησαν Il.1.436, = Od.15.498; ὕψι δ' ἐπ' εὐνάων ὁρμίσσομεν we will let the ships ride *at anchor* in deep water, Il.14.77; εὐνὰς δ' ἔνθ' ἔβαλον κατὰ βένθεος Q.S.12.346; even of iron anchors, Sch.Il.1.436.—Rare in early Prose, X.*Mem*.3.11.8: in pl., Th. ll. cc., Pl.*Prt*.321a, *R*.415e, *Plt*.272a. **-ῆθεν**, Adv. *from, out of bed*, Od. 20.124, A.R.2.197. **-ημα**, ατος, τό, (εὐνάω) *marriage*, E.*Ion*304 (pl.).

**εὔνησος**, ον, *with beautiful islands*, πόλις Nonn.*D*.41.15.

**εὐν-ητήρ**, Dor. **-ᾱτήρ**, ῆρος, ὁ, (εὐνάω) *a bedfellow, husband*, A.*Pers*. 137 (lyr.); of fish, Opp.*H*.4.383:—fem. **-ήτειρα** (Dor. form used by Trag.), θεοῦ μὲν εὐ. *partner of* his *bed*, A.*Pers*.157 (troch.); εὐ. Διὸς λεχέων Id.*Pr*.895 (lyr.), cf. Theoc.*Syrinx*1: metaph., εὐνήτειρα νὺξ ἔργων *that makes* works *cease*, A.R.4.1058. II. χιτὼν εὐνητήρ a *night*-shirt, *Com.Adesp*.920. **-ήτης**, ου, Dor. **-ᾱτας**, ὁ, = εὐνητήρ, E.*Med*.159 (lyr.), cf. Hsch.:—fem. **-ήτρια**, S.*Tr*.922 codd. (leg. -ᾱτρια). **-ήτωρ**, Dor. **-ᾱτωρ**, ορος, ὁ, = εὐνητήρ, A.*Supp*.665 (lyr.), E.*Ion*912 (lyr.), *HF*27, 97.

**εὔνια**, ων, τά, *beds*, ἐξ εὐνίων ἀναπηδᾶν App.*BC*5.117, Anon.ap. Suid.

**εὐνίκητος** [ῑ], Dor. **-ᾱτος**, ον, *easily overcome*, Gal.1.338 (Sup.); ταῖς πρὸς ἄνδρα κοίταις Myia *Ep*.1.

**εὖνις** (A), ὁ, ἡ, acc. εὖνιν, gen. εὔνιδος and εὔνιος Hdn.Gr.2.641, nom. pl. εὔνιδες and εὔνιες (v. infr.):—*reft of, bereaved of*, c. gen., ὅς μ' υἱῶν .. εὖνιν ἔθηκε Il.22.44; ψυχῆς τε καὶ αἰῶνός σε.. εὖνιν ποιήσας Od.9. 524; βραχίονες εὔνιδες ὤμων *lacking*.., Emp.57.2; εὔνιες ἀνδρείων ἀχέων *free from*.., Id.147.2; γέννας εὖνιν πατρός A.*Ch*.247, cf. 794 (lyr.); εὖνιν ἔθηκ' ἀρετῆς *IG*14.2100: abs., *bereaved of children*, πολλὰς Περσίδων.. ἔκτισσαν εὔνιδας ἠδ' ἀνάνδρους A.*Pers*.289 (lyr.).

❋ **εὖνις** (B), ιδος, ἡ, (on the accent cf. Hdn.Gr.1.95), = εὐνέτις, *bedfellow, wife*, S.*Tr*.563, E.*Or*.929, *IA*397 (troch.), 807, *AP*9.355 (Leon. Alex.).—Masc. in *EM*393.38.

**ἐΰννητος**, ον, Ep. for εὔνητος (νέω), *well spun* or *woven*, οἱ δὲ χιτῶνας εἵατ' ἐϋννήτους Il.18.596, cf. 24.580; πέπλοι λεπτοὶ ἐΰννητοι Od.7.97.

**εὐνο-έω**, *to be well-inclined* or *favourable*, c. dat., τοῖσι ἐμοῖσι πρήγμασι Hdt.7.237; τινι S.*Aj*.689, Lys.13.13, Ar.*Nu*.1411, X.*Oec*.12.5, etc.: ὀμνύω.. εὐνοήσειν Καίσαρι *OGI*532.9 (Galatia, Aug.); τῷ ἀντιδίκῳ *be at peace with*, *Ev.Matt*.5.25: abs., Hdt.9.79; ὁ εὐνοῶν one's *well-wisher*, Arist.*EE*1241ᵃ11:—Med., Phalar.*Ep*.119:—Pass., *to be kindly* or *affectionately treated*, dub. l. in Men.1087; ὑπὸ γυναικὸς Vett. Val.68.3; *to be liked*, ὑπὸ θεῶν καὶ ὑπὸ γυναικῶν Heph.Astr.1.1. **-ημα**, f.l. for εὐνόμημα (q. v.). **-ησις**, εως, ἡ, f.l. in Artem.2.12. **-ητικός**, ή, όν, *kindly disposed*, πρὸς ἑαυτό Hierocl.p.41 A. Adv. *benevolently*, διακεῖσθαι πρὸς ἀλλήλους Stoic.ap.Stob.2.7.11ⁱ. **-ητος**, ον, *easily understood*, Iamb.*Protr*.21. II. *intelligent*, οἰκονόμος Vett.Val.45. 28. 2. *well-disposed*, τινι Anon.*in Rh*.88.29.

**εὐνόθευτος**, ον, *easily adulterated*, ἔλαιον Corn.*ND*20.

**εὔνοιᾰ**, ἡ, Ion. **εὐνοίη** (εὐνοίαν is f.l. in Hdt.3.36), poet. **εὐνοΐη** *IG*14.815: (εὔνοος):—*goodwill, favour* (dist. fr. φιλία, Arist.*EN*1155ᵇ33, 1166ᵇ30), κατὰ εὐνοίην Hdt.6.108; δι' εὐνοίας Th.2.40; δι' εὔνοιαν Pl.*Prt*.337b; εὐνοίας ἕνεκα Docum.ap.D.18.54, etc.; εὐνοίας ἕνεκα τῆς εἰς τὸν δῆμον *IG*2².212.32, etc.; κατ' εὔνοιαν κρίνειν *partially*, Antipho 3.4.1; κατ' εὔνοιαν φρενῶν A.*Supp*.940; μετ' εὐνοίας And.1.9, Pl.*Phdr*.241c, D.18.276, *Ep.Eph*.6.7; ὑπ' εὐνοίας D.2.9; εὐνοίῃ τι ποιῆσαι Hdt.7.239; εὐνοίᾳ λέγειν S.*Ph*.1322; εὐνοίᾳ μᾶλλον ἢ ἐλέγχῳ τὰ γιγνόμενα δοκιμάζειν Lys.31.22; εὐνοίᾳ τῇ σῇ *for the love* of you, Pl.*Grg*.486a: with objective gen., ἐπ' εὐνοίᾳ χθονὸς *for love* of fatherland, A.*Th*.1012; εὐνοίᾳ τῇ ἑαυτοῦ Pl.*Grg*.485a; ἕνεκα τῆς τῶν Ἑλλήνων εὐνοίας *goodwill towards* them, X.*An*.4.7.20; [εὔνοιαν] ἔχειν εἴς τινα Docum.ap.D.18.54; πρός τινα Pl.*R*.470a; πρὸς τὸν δῆμον *IPE*1². 32.7 (Olbia), etc.; εὐ. παρὰ τῶν θεῶν D.2.1; εὔνοιαν ἔκ τινων κτᾶσθαι X.*Cyr*.8.2.22; εὔνοιαν παρασχεῖν to show *favour*, S.*Tr*.708; ἔργῳ δεικνύναι Antipho 5.76; εὔνοιαν ἔχειν to *wish heartily* that.., Th.2.11; ὡς ἑκατέρων τις εὐνοίας.. ἔχοι Id.1.22; ἡ εὐ. παρὰ πολὺ ἐποίει τῶν ἀνθρώπων μᾶλλον ἐς τοὺς Λακεδαιμονίους Id.2.8: in pl., *impulses of kindness, favours*, τοῖς ἥσσοσιν γὰρ πᾶς τις εὐνοίας φέρει A.*Supp*.489; Ἀρτέμιδος εὐνοίαισι Id.*Th*.450; ταῖς εὐ. μεθ' ὑμῶν ἦσαν Isoc.14.15; but, *acts of kindness, favours*, D.S.15.9. II. *gift* or *present in token of goodwill*, D.19.282: pl., *benevolences*, Id.8.25. [εὔνοια as dactyl, *Arch.Pap*.1.220 (twice, ii B. C.).]

**εὐνο-ΐζομαι**, = εὐνοέω, Arist.*EE*1241ᵃ8. **-ϊκός**, ή, όν, *well-disposed, kindly, favourable*, εὐνοϊκωτέρους ὑπάρχειν τινί D.57.1, cf. Amphis 1: Sup. -ώτατος, περὶ τοὺς οἰκείους Lib.*Decl*.49.16. Adv. εὐνοϊκῶς, ἔχειν τινί X.*HG*4.4.15; πρός τινα Id.*Mem*.2.6.34, Arist. *Rh.Al*.1436ᵇ18; εὐ. διακεῖσθαι πρός τινα Isoc.12.237; πρὸς τὴν πόλιν *SIG*810.25 (Nero); εὐ. ἀκοῦσαι Hyp.*Lyc*.19; εὐ. προσδέχεσθαι D.18. 7: Comp. -ωτέρως Id.51.2; -ώτερον Lib.*Decl*.49.31: Sup. -ώτατα X.*Cyr*.8.4.1.

**εὐνόιος**, ον, = foreg., φίλοι καὶ εὐ. *SIG*559.52 (Magn. Mae., iii B. C.), cf. *IGRom*.4.247.34 (Assos). Adv. -οίως *Sammelb*.5294.9 (iii A. D.).

**εὐνομ-έομαι**, fut. -ήσομαι Hdt.1.97, Pl.*R*.380b: aor. 1 εὐνομήθην Hdt.1.66, ηὐν- Th.1.18: pf. εὐνόμημαι Epimenid.ap.D.L.1.113:—*have good laws, be well-ordered*, Hdt. ll. cc., Th.1.18, etc.; [πόλις] μέλλει εὐνομήσεσθαι Pl. l. c.; πόλις -ουμένη D.24.139, cf. Arist.*Rh*.1354ᵃ20, *Pol*.1294ᵃ3; οἰκία οὐκ εὐ. Aeschin.1.171; ἰσχύσετε, ὅταν εὐνομῆσθε when you *observe the laws*, ib.5. (Act. only in pres. part. εὐνομοῦσα Pl.*Lg*.927b.) **-ημα**, ατος, τό, *law-abiding, virtuous action*, Chrysipp.*Stoic*.3.73: pl., *Stoic*.3.136. ❋ **-ία**, Ep. and Ion. **-ίη**, ἡ, *good order*, ἀνθρώπων ὕβριν τε καὶ εὐνομίην ἐφορῶντες Od.17.487; ἐν εὐ. εἶναι Xenoph.2.19; μετέβαλον ὧδε ἐς εὐ. Hdt.1.65, cf. 2.124: pl., εὐνομίῃσι πόλιν κάτα.. κοιρανέουσ' *h.Hom*.30.11, cf. Pl.*Sph*.216b; ἀπόλεμος εὐ. Pi.*P*.5.67, cf. *AP*6.195 (Arch.); Καίσαρος εὐ. ib.236 (Phil.); εὐνομίαν διὰ τῆς μουσικῆς εἰσδέχεσθαι Pl.*R*.425a; οὐκ ἔστι εὐνομία τὸ εὖ κεῖσθαι τοὺς νόμους, μὴ πείθεσθαι δέ Arist.*Pol*.1294ᵃ3, cf. 1280ᵇ6, Pl. *Def*.413e; οἱ ἐπὶ τῆς εὐνομίας, title of officials in Crete, *GDI*5075.35 (Latos). 2. *loyalty to divine law*, εὐνομίᾳ σέβων μεγίστᾳ S.*Aj*.713 (lyr.). 3. personified as daughter of Themis, Hes.*Th*.902, cf. Pi.*O*.9.16, 13.6, B.12.186, D.25.11, *Lyr.Adesp*.140.6, *IG*2.1598; title of a poem by Tyrtaeus, cf. Arist.*Pol*.1307ᵃ1, Str.8.4.10. 4. *observance of the laws of art*, εὐ. μουσική Longus 2.35. II. (εὔνομος II) *diligence in foraging*: metaph., of bees, Philostr.*Im*.2.2; *regularity in pasturing*, of sheep, Longus 1.5. ❋ **-ος**, ον, (νόμος) *under good laws, well-ordered*, πόλις Pi.*I*.5(4).22, Pl.*Ti*.20a (Sup.); Σκύθαι A.*Fr*.198; ἄνδρες Pl.*Lg*.815b; πολιτεία Zeno *Stoic*.1.27 (Sup.). 2. of things, ἔρανος -ώτατος Pi.*O*.1.37; μοῖρα εὐ., = εὐνομία, Id.*N*.9. 29. II. (νομή) of places, *good for pasture*, Longus 4.4 (Sup.).

❋ **εὔνοος**, ον, Att. contr. **εὔνους**, ουν, dat. εὔνῳ Th.4.87: pl. εὖνοι, also heterocl. εὔνοις (contr. from εὔνοες) Lys.8.19, Philem.222, *IG*2². 505.10, al.: gen. pl. εὐνόων Th.6.64 codd., εὔνων edd.:—*well disposed, kindly, friendly*, ἀνὴρ φίλος καὶ εὐ. Hdt.5.24; ἐνυπνίων κριτὴς A.*Pers*. 226 (troch.); τινι to one, Hdt.7.173, al., S.*Ph*.1351, etc.; τῷ δήμῳ And.4.16, *IG*2².808.10, etc.; τῇ πόλει *SIG*572.5 (Nisyros, iii B. C.),

etc.; οἱ ἐμοὶ εὖνοι my *well-wishers*, X.*Ap*.27; τὸ εὔνουν, = εὔνοια, S.*El*. 1203, Th.4.87, al.; opp. δυσμενής, X.*Cyr*.8.3.5; dist. fr. φίλος, Arist. *EN*1156ᵃ2: Comp. εὐνούστερος Lys.27.13, etc.; Ion. εὐνοέστερος Hdt. 5.24, Herod.6.72; also εὐνοώτερος Philox.Gramm.ap.*EM*394.13: Sup. εὐνούστατος S.*Aj*.822, Ar.*Eq*.874, etc.; εὐνοέστατος *EM*394.5. 2. of things, τὴν πάροδον ἵν' ἔχῃς.. εὐνουστέραν *more favourable*, Dionys. Com.3.17. Adv. εὐνόως *IG*7.1 (Megara, iv/iii B.C.), etc.; ἔχειν πρός τινα Plu.*Galb*.8, cf. Aristeas 242; διακείμενος Phld.*Lib*.p.38 O.; contr. εὔνως, χρῆσθαί τινι M.Ant.3.11: Comp. -νούστερον, ἔχειν τινί Arr. *Epict*.4.6.7: Sup. -νούστατα, διακεῖσθαι πρός τινα D.S.19.6.

**εὔνοστος**, ἡ, *Good Yield, tutelary genius of corn-mills*, Eust.214.18, 1383.42, Hsch., Suid. s.v. προμυλαία, *EM*394.3. II. εὐνόστου λιμήν, a harbour of Alexandria, harbour *of happy return*, Str.17.1. 6,10.

**εὐνουχ-εῖον**, τό, a kind of *lettuce*, = ἀστυτίς, Plin.*HN*19.127. **-ίας**, ου, ὁ, *like a eunuch, impotent*, Hp.*Aër*.22, Arist.*GA*746ᵇ24. II. metaph., of *a melon without seeds*, opp. σπερματίας, Pl.Com.64.4; εὐ. κάλαμοι reeds *without inflorescence*, Thphr.*HP*4.11.4. **-ίζω**, *castrate*, τινα *Ev.Matt*.19.12 (Act. and Pass.), Luc.*Sat*.12, etc.; γυναῖκας Xanth.19: metaph., γῆν Philostr.*VA*6.42; φάρμακον Archig. ap.Orib.8.2.8:—Pass., Gal.4.570, D.C.68.2. **-ισμός**, ὁ, *castration*, Gal.4.576: **-ιστής**, οῦ, ὁ, *castrator*, *Gloss*. **-ιστέον**, *one must defertilize*, τοὺς μόσχους *Gp*.17.8.2.

**εὐνουχοειδής**, ές, *like a eunuch*, Hp.*Aër*.22 (Sup.):—also **εὐνουχώδης**, ες, Philostr.*VS*1.25.9, Aët.16.26, Suid. s.v. ἄρρεν.

⊛ **εὐνοῦχος**, ὁ, (εὐνή, ἔχω) *castrated person, eunuch*, employed to take charge of the women and act as *chamberlain* (whence the name, ὁ τὴν εὐνὴν ἔχων), Hdt.3.130, al., Ar.*Ach*.117, X.*Cyr*.7.5.60, etc. 2. of animals, Philostr.*Her*.1.3, Sch.Par.A.R.1.585. 3. of dates, *without stones*, Arist.*Fr*.267:—Pythag. name for θρίδαξ, Lycus ap. Ath.2.69e. II. as Adj., *watching the bed, sleepless*, λαμπάδες εὐνούχοισιν ὄμμασιν S.*Fr*.789.

**εὖντα**, Dor. for ἐόντα, neut. pl. of part. ὤν, Theoc.2.3.

**εὔνυμφος**, ον, *of a fair bride*, λέχος *Cat.Cod.Astr*.2.175.

**εὐνώμας**, α, ὁ, (νωμάω) = εὐκίνητος, *mobile*, αἰὲν εὐνώμᾳ χρόνῳ by the *ceaseless* march of time, S.*Aj*.604 (lyr., s.v.l., cf. εὐνάω I. 2).

**εὔνωτος**, ον, *stout-backed*, Arist.*Phgn*.809ᵇ28.

**εὔξαντος**, ον, (ξαίνω) *well-carded*, of wool, *AP*6.282 (Theod.).

⊛ **εὔξενος**, Ion. **εὔξεινος**, ον, *kind to strangers, hospitable*, ἀνδρῶνας εὐ. δόμων *the guest*-chambers, A.*Ch*.712; λιμὴν εὐξεινότατος ναύταις E. *Hipp*.157 (lyr.). Ep. Adv. ἐϋξείνως A.R.1.963, 1179. II. πόντος εὐ. *the Euxine*, now *the Black Sea*, Hdt.1.6, al., E.*IT*125 (lyr., codd., sed leg. Ἀξείνου); and so εὐ. (leg. ἄξ–) οἶδμα Id.*HF*410 (lyr.); εὐ. πέλαγος Pi.*N*.4.49; ὁ Εὔξεινος alone, Str.11.1.5; cf. ἄξενος: εὔξεινος is a euphemism, like Εὐμενίδες.

**εὔξεστος**, Ep. **ἐΰξεστος**, η, ον, but ος, ον Od.15.333: (ξέω):—*well-planed, well-polished*, of carpenters' work, ῥυμός, ἀπήνη, φάτνη, Il.24. 271, 275, 280; χηλός Od.13.10; ἄκοντες 14.225; τράπεζαι 15.333; τὸ εὔξεστον Luc.*Hist.Conscr*.27.

**εὐξήραντος**, ον, *easily drying* or *evaporating*, Arist.*GA*782ᵇ4, *Long*. 466ᵃ26.

**εὐξόανος**, ον, *skilled in sculpture*, Man.4.569.

**εὔξοος**, Ep. **ἐΰξοος**, ον, gen. ἐΰξου Il.10.373:— = εὔξεστος, ἅρμα, δίφρος, Il.2.390, Od.4.590; δόρυ Il.10.373; σκέπαρνον ἐΰ. an axe *of polished metal* or *haft*, Od.5.237. II. *easy to polish*, εὐξοώτερα Thphr.*HP*5.6.4.

**εὐξυλεία**, ἡ, *abundance of timber*, name of a field, *IG*9(1).61.26 (Daulis).

**εὐξυλή**, prob. f.l. for εὔχυλα or εὐαυξῆ, Thphr.*CP*1.20.3.

**εὐξυλοεργός**, όν, *skilled in carpentry*, πελεκήτορες Man.4.324.

**εὔξυλος**, ον, *furnishing handsome timber*, Thphr.*HP*4.4.6; *abounding in timber*, App.*Hann*.58.

**εὐξύμβλητος, εὐξύμβολος, εὐξυνεσία, εὐξύνετος**, Att. for εὐσ–.

**εὔξυστος**, ον, (ξύω) *easily scraped* or *rasped*, Hp.*VC*19.

**εὐογκ-ία**, Ion. **-ίη**, ἡ, *being moderate in bulk*, εὐ. ἀσφαλέστερον μεγαλογκίης Democr.3. **-ος**, ον, *of good size, bulky, massive*, Hp. *Art*.23; κοιλίη Id.*Prog*.11; οὐδ' ἄγαν εὐ. E.*Fr*.688.3; εὐ. εἶναι γαστρὶ μὴ πληρουμένῃ Trag.*Adesp*.546.5; εὐ. φωνή *a full, rich* voice, opp. ψιλή, Philoch.66: Comp., -ότεραι ἀπὸ τῶν ἰσχίων Sor.2.53: metaph., *weighty, important*, opp. εὐτελής, Arist.*Rh*.1408ᵃ12: Comp., Phld.*Po*. 2.38. II. *of moderate* or *convenient bulk, compact*, Aen.Tact.29.6 (Comp.), 31.23 (Sup.), Arist.*Mete*.380ᵃ5 (Comp.), *GA*766ᵇ20, Mnesith.ap.Ath.7.357f, etc.; *portable*, Thphr.*HP*9.16.8; τὰ εὐ. τῶν ἀναθημάτων Plu.2.969e; στρατόπεδον *of manageable size*, Polyaen.5.16.1: metaph., τῆς λέξεως τὸ εὐ. *compact, concise*, of γνῶθι σεαυτόν, Plu.2.511b. Adv. -κως, διάγειν preserve *a moderate embonpoint*, Diocl.*Fr*.141.

**εὐοδ-έω**, *have a free course* or *passage*, of running water, D.55.10; of bodily secretions, Arist.*GA*725ᵃ35, etc.; of trees, *have root-room*, Thphr.*HP*1.6.4:—impers. in Pass., εὐοδεῖται *there is a free passage*, Arist.*GA*739ᵃ35. 2. metaph., *fare well, prosper*, εὐοδῶν πορεύομαι Theopomp.Com.74, cf. Ph.1.430, Procl.*Hyp*.4.31; κατὰ τὸν βίον Herm.*in Phdr*.p.155 A.; τέχναι, ψυχὴ εὐ., Ph.1.687, 240; εὐώδει σοι τὰ πράγματα ib.145; ἀπόδειξις -οῦσα πρὸς τὰ συμπεράσματα Dam.*Pr*. 376; [ἡ ἀρετή].. προϊοῦσα εὐοδεῖ M.Ant.6.17; εὐόδει, on a gravestone, *IG*12(7).449. ⊛ **-ία**, ἡ, *a good journey*, καὶ σοὶ δ' εὐοδίης τρίβον ὄλβιον εὔχομαι εἶναι *Arch.Pap*.1.221 (ii B.C.): hence εὐοδίαν ἀπὸ στόματος χέειν *good wishes for one's success*, A.*Fr*.36; personified, *OGI*77 (Alexandria, iii B.C.): metaph., κατ' εὐοδίαν Phld.*Rh*.2. 27 S.: c. gen., εὐ. τοῦ ἐλθεῖν *a good opportunity* of coming, *PMich*. in *Class.Phil*.22.250 (ii A.D.). II. *success*, Demetr.Lac.1012.47 F., 1429.2 F. III. *permeability*, τῶν πόρων Sor.1.86. **-ιάζω**, *pass, insert in the right way*, [καθετῆρα] Paul.Aeg.6.59:—Subst. **-ιασμός**, ὁ, ibid. **-ιος**, *boni itineris*, *Gloss*.

**εὐοδμία, εὔοδμος**, v. εὐοσμία, εὔοσμος.

**εὔοδ-ος**, ον, *easy to pass*, of mountains, X.*An*.4.8.10; of a road, *easy to travel*, ὁδὸς.. εὐοδωτάτη τοῖς ὑποζυγίοις ib.4.2.9; οὐκ εὔοδα ἔσται ὑμῖν Lxx *Nu*.14.41. Adv. -όδως, πορεύεσθαι ib.*Pr*.24.64 (30. 29). 2. metaph., *free from difficulty, simple*, Epicur.*Fr*.18, Ptol. *Alm*.1.2 (Comp.). Adv. *simply, readily*, νοεῖσθαι Phld.*D*.3.11: Sup. -ώτατα, τῷ τῆς ἀνδρείας ὀνόματι προσαγορεύεσθαι ib.*Fr*.81. 3. *favourable*, πρός τι Mnesith.ap.Ath.3.92c; ὁ εὔοδος θεός, of Pan, *CIG* 4705*b*, cf. *OGI*38 (Egypt, iii B.C.), al., *Epigr.Gr*.826, etc. **-όω**, *help on the way*, c. dat. pers., σφῷν δ' εὐοδοίη Ζεύς S.*OC*1435 (nisi leg. σφώ): c. acc. pers., Lxx *Ge*.24.27, *PSI*4.299.14: abs., τὸ εὐοδοῦν Thphr.*CP*5.6.7. 2. Pass., *have a prosperous journey*, Lxx *Da*.8.11, al., *Ep.Rom*.1.10; of things, *prosper, be successful*, ὡς Κλεομένεϊ εὐωδώθη τὸ πρῆγμα v.l. in Hdt.6.73; θησαυρίζων ὅ τι ἂν εὐοδῶται, = εὐπορῇ, 1*Ep.Cor*.16.2, cf. *Act.Ap*.11.29. **-ωσις**, εως, ἡ, *successful progress*, Protag.Astrol. in *Cat.Cod.Astr*.8(2).119, Asp.*in EN*386.25.

**εὐοῖ** (εὐοῖ A.D.*Synt*.320.1, cf. Lat. *euhoe*), exclamation used in the cult of Dionysus, Ar.*Lys*.1294 (lyr.), etc.; cf. εὐαί, εὐάν: εὐοῖ σαβοῖ D.18.260: as an interjection, ἀναταράσσει—εὐοῖ—μ' ὁ κισσός S.*Tr*.219 (lyr.).

**εὐοίκ-ητος**, ον, *favourably placed*, τόπος Philoch.76: gloss on εὔπωλος, Eust.1431.54. 2. *comfortable*, of a house, Alex.Aphr.*in Top*.269.16. **-ονόμητος**, ον, *well arranged*, only in Adv. -τως Sch. E.*Or*.470. 2. *easy to digest*, Diph.Siph.ap.Ath.2.54d: Comp., Id.ib.3.80c, Eust.866.21. **-ος**, ον, *with good houses*, gloss on εὐβύριον, *EM*389.24. 2. *convenient to inhabit, comfortable*, κύρτος Opp.*H*.3.370. II. *good economist*, D.C.44.39 (Sup.). 2. *kind to servants* (οἰκέται), Achae.32.

**εὐοικτος**, ον, *compassionate*, αὐτοκράτωρ D.C.69.20 (-εικτος Zonar.; fort. εὔθικτος).

**εὐοιν-έω**, *abound in good wine*, Str.11.10.1, Max.Tyr.30.4. **-ία**, ἡ, *abundance of good wine*, Str.2.1.14, Horap.2.92, St.Byz. s.v. Λάμψακος (cj.), Eun.*VS*p.467 B. (cj.). **-ιστος**, ον, *of good wine*, ἐπιλοιβαί dub.l. in Orph.*A*.603. **-ος**, ον, *abounding in wine*, Λέσβος Hermesian.7.55, cf. Str.5.4.2; σταφυλή *AP*6.300.5 (Leon.): Sup., Max.Tyr.3.10.

**εὐοιώνιστος**, ον, *of good omen*, D.S.33.28ᵃ, Sch.Luc.*JTr*.47, prob. in Phryn.*PS*p.71 B.

**εὔολβος**, ον, *wealthy, prosperous*, βασιλεῖς E.*IT*189 (lyr.); πάτρα *IG*7.530 (Tanagra); βίος, οἶκοι, Orph.*H*.29.19, Man.3.46.

**εὐολίσθ-ητος**, ον, *easily slipping, unsteady*, Iamb.*Protr*.21.κ'. **-ος**, ον, *slippery*, *Placit*.1.4.2; κόπρος Alex.Aphr.*Pr*.1.90; πηλαμύς Xenocr. ap.Orib.2.58.142, cf. Apollod.*Poliorc*.149.3, Hierocl.*in CA*16 p.456 M. II. metaph., *unsteady*, ἡλικία Ph.2.463.

**εὐόλκιμος**, ον, (ὁλκή) *easily drawn, ductile, sticky*, Hp.*Art*.36.

**εὐόμαλος**, ον, *level*, πεδία Agath.3.19.

**εὐομβρ-ία**, ἡ, *abundance of rain*, Lyd.*Ost*.38. **-ος**, ον, *abounding in rain*: *well-watered*, Str.4.1.7.

**εὐομιλ-ητος** [ῐ], ον, *affable*, πρὸς πᾶσαν ἀπάντησιν *SIG*708.16 (Istropolis, ii B.C.). **-ία**, ἡ, *charm of conversation, wit*, Charis.pp.33. 12, 549.10 K. **-ος**, ον, *sociable*, *Com.Adesp*.1015, Vett.Val.40.4, M.Ant.1.16, Hld.3.10, Dam.*Isid*.49, Agath.1.13.

**εὐόμματος**, ον, *keen-sighted*, *EM*284.8.

**εὐομολόγητος**, ον, *easy to concede, indisputable*, Pl.*R*.527b.

**εὔομφος**, ον, Arc. for εὔοσμος, Timachidas ap.Ath.15.683c (εὐόμφαλον codd.). εὔομφα· ὀνόματα, Hsch.

**εὐόνειρος**, ον, *having auspicious dreams*, Str.16.2.35; *bringing such dreams*, νύξ Hld.3.5; εὐ. καὶ ἄλυπα, opp. φοβερόν, Plu.2.83d.

⊛ **εὐόνυξ**, υχος, ὁ, ἡ, *with strong claws*, Marc.Sid.34.

**εὐοπλ-έω**, *to be well-equipped*, *AP*12.120 (Posidipp.), Ph.1.20, Hld.8.16, Arr.*Tact*.5.3. ⊛ **-ία**, ἡ, *a good state of arms and equipments*, X.*Hier*.9.6; as a subject of competition, *IG*2².956.58. ⊛ **-ος**, ον, (ὅπλον) *well-armed, well-equipped*, Ar.*Ach*.592; λόχος, πόλις, X. *HG*4.2.5 (Sup.), *Hier*.11.3; τῶν ζῴων τὰ ἄρρενα -ότερα Arist.*HA*538ᵇ 4. II. (ὁπλή) *with good hoofs*, Poll.1.194.

**εὔοπτος**, ον, (ὁράω, ὄψομαι) *open to view*, οὐκ ἐν εὐόπτῳ οἰκέουσιν αἱ νοῦσοι Hp. *de Arte*11; *conspicuous*, Lxx *Ep.Je*.60, Longus 4.3. 2. *attractive, good-looking*, Muson.*Fr*.21 p.116 H. (Sup.), *EM*276.36, *Cat.Cod.Astr*.8(2).59. II. (ὀπτάω) *well-cooked*, τροφή Ath.Med. ap.Orib.*inc*.23.3.

**εὐόρατος**, ον, (ὁράω) = foreg. I, Eust.86.42.

**εὐοργ-ησία**, ἡ, *gentleness of temper*, E.*Hipp*.1039, *Ba*.641 (troch.). **-ητος**, ον, *good-tempered*, ἤθεα Hp.*Aër*.12 (Comp.); εὐ. πρὸς τὸ πρέπον Gorg.*Fr*.6 D.; τοῖς κόλαξι.. εὐόργητος Eub.25; τὸ εὐ. καὶ πρᾶον Arist.*MM*1186ᵃ23, cf. Plu.2.413c. Adv. -τως, προσομιλεῖν τῷ πολέμῳ *with good temper*, opp. ὀργισθείς, Th.1.122. ⊛ **-ία**· ἀπιστία (sic), Hsch. (cf. εὐεργία). ⊛ **-ος**, ον, (ὀργή) = εὐόργητος, Id. perh. from Archil., cf. *PLG*2 p.439 B.).

**εὐόρεκτος**, ον, *appetizing*, τὸ ἥδιον εὐορεκτότερον Plu.2.663f, cf. Dsc.5.13. II. *with a better appetite*, Gal.18(2).299.

**εὐόριστος**, ον, *easily bounded* or *limited*, Arist.*Mete*.360ᵃ23; τὸ εὐ., opp. τὸ δυσόριστον, ib.378ᵇ24, *GC*329ᵇ31; μέτρον ἀριθμῷ οὐκ εὐ. Herod. Med.ap.Orib.6.25.4.

**εὐορκ-έω**, *swear truly, take a true oath*, opp. ἐπιορκέω, Gorg.*Fr*. 15 D., Isoc.1.23, Iamb.*VP*28.144, etc.; *keep one's oath* when taken,

Lex ap.And.1.98; *τινι* to one, Th.5.30; [*τὴν ψυχήν*] *by* one's soul, E.*Or.*1517 (troch.); *εὐορκοῦντες κρίνειν* X.*HG*1.7.25. II. Act., *keep one's oath by*, *τινας* Sch.A.R.2.259:—Pass., *ἡ θεὸς εὐορκεῖτο* Call.*Aet.*3.1.42. **-ησία,** *ἡ*, *fidelity to one's oath*, Alexand.Com. 2. **-ία,** *ἡ*, = foreg., Pi.*O.*2.66 (pl.), App.*Pun.*63, Hierocl. *in CA* 2 p.422 M. II. in pl., *oaths taken with a good conscience*, Lib.*Or.*59.122. **-ος,** *ον*, *keeping one's oath, faithful to one's oath*, *ἀνδρὸς δ' εὐόρκου γενεὴ μετόπισθεν ἀμείνων* Hes.*Op.*285, cf. 190, Orac.ap.Hdt.6.86.γ', Ar.*Pl.*61, X.*HG*2.4.42, etc.; *εἴς τινα* E.*Med.*495. II. of oaths, *εὔορκα ἀντομωμοκώς* Antipho 1.8; [*διομόσασθαι*] *εὐορκότερα* Id.6.16; *ψηφίσασθαι* Is.2.47; *γνῶναι* D.18.249; *εὐορκοτέραν θήσεσθε τὴν ψῆφον* Id 29.4, cf. 21.24; *εὐορκοτάτην ⟨τὴν⟩ ψῆφον ἐνεγκεῖν* Lycurg.13: Sup., Lys.19.11; *in accordance with* one's *oath, no breach of oath*, *εὔορκόν* [*ἐστι*] Foed.ap.Th.5.18, cf. 23,29; *εὔορκα ταῦθ' ὑμῖν ἐστι* D.21.34 (v.l. *ἔνορκα*): so in Adv., *τάδ' εὐόρκως ἔχει* A.*Ch.*979; *εὐ. θέσθαι τὴν ψῆφον* Arist.*Rh.Al.*1433$^a$1. **-ωμα,** *ατος, τό*, *faithful oath*, A.*Ch.*901 (pl.). **-ωτος,** *ον*, = *εὔορκος*, Poll.1.39.

**εὐόρμ-ητος,** *ον*, gloss on sq., Sch.A.R.4.900. **-ος,** *ον*, *with good mooring-places*, *ἐν δὲ λιμὴν εὔορμος* Od.4.358, 9.136, Hes.*Sc.*207, cf. Il.21.23; *γῆ* S.*Ph.*221; *εὐορμότατοι λιμένες* Ph.2.567. 2. *well-moored*, *εὐόρμων..πρυμνήσια νηῶν* *AP*10.4 (Marc. Arg.).

**εὐορν-ῑθία,** *ἡ*, *good augury*, S.*Fr.*1049. **-ις,** *ῑθος, ὁ, ἡ*, *of good augury*, *τύχη* *Trag.Adesp.*343; *οἰωνοί* D.H.2.73. II. *abounding in birds*, epith. of Tanagra in *AP*7.424 (Antip. Sid.).

**εὐόροφος,** *ον*, *well-roofed*, *AP*9.59.5 (Antip. ⟨Thess.⟩).

**εὐόρπηξ,** *ηκος, ὁ, ἡ*, *with fine branches*, Nonn.*D.*21.298.

**εὐοσμέω,** *smell well, be fragrant*, Thphr.*CP*6.16.1, cj. in E.*Ba.*235.

**εὐοσμία,** *ἡ*, *fragrance, perfume*, S.*Fr.*370 (pl.), Thphr.*CP*6.14.4:—but **εὐοδμία,** Id.*Od.*51, Antipho Soph.8; this form is stated to be poet., Ion., and Aeol. by Poll.2.75.

**εὔοσμος** or **εὔοδμος,** *ον*, (*ὀδμή, ὀσμή*) *sweet-smelling, fragrant*. *εὔοδμον ἔαρ* Pi.*Fr.*75.15; *εὐόδμοισι προσθετοῖσι* Hp.*Loc.Hom.*47; *εὔοσμον μύρον* Achae.17, cf. E.*Ba.*235; *εὐόδμοισι σελίνοις, νέκταρος εὐόδμοιο*, Theoc.3.23, 17.29; v.l. for *εὐώδης* in D.P.937; *εὔοδμος τῇ ὀσφρήσει* Thphr.*HP*9.13.3: Comp. and Sup., Id.*CP*6.16.1.

**εὐοσφρ-αντικωτάτη,** gloss on *εὐρινοτάτη*, Hsch. **-ητος,** *ον*, *keen-scented*, gloss on *εὔρινος*, *EM*765.53.

**εὐόφθαλμος,** *ον*, *with beautiful eyes*, X.*Cyr.*8.1.41 (Comp.), *BGU* 316.14 (iv A.D.). 2. *keen-eyed*, X.*Smp.*5.5 (Sup.). II. *pleasing to the eye*, Aristox.*Fr.Hist.*15, *Cat.Cod.Astr.*8(4).240: metaph., *fair only to the eye, specious*, *εὐόφθαλμον ἀκοῦσαι μόνον* Arist.*Pol.*1268$^b$24. Adv. *-μως* Antipho *Fr.*59.

**εὔοφρυς,** *υ*, *with fine eyebrows*, Philostr.*Her.*19.9, *AP*5.75 (Rufin.).

**εὐοχέω,** *guide well*, in Pass., of an elephant, Suid.; of horses, f. l. for *εὐωχέομαι*, X.*Eq.Mag.*8.4.

**εὐοχθ-έω,** *to be in plenty, to be in good case*, Hes.*Op.*477, Rhian.1.9. **-ος,** *ον*, *with goodly banks, fertile, rich*, *γῆ* Hom.*Epigr.*7.2; also *εὔοχθοι δαῖτες* B.*Fr.*18.4; *βορά* E.*Ion* 1169.

**εὔοχος,** *ον*, (*ἔχω*) *holding firmly*, *δεσμός* Hp.*Art.*43. II. *easy to maintain*, *σχῆμα* Id.*Fract.*47 (Sup.).

**εὐοψ-έω,** *abound in fish*, Str.4.1.8, 14.2.21. **-ία (A),** *ἡ*, (*ὄψον*) *abundance of ὄψα* (q.v.), i.e. fish in Alciphr.3.3, but pork in Plu.*Fr. inc.*145. **-ία (B),** *ἡ*, (*ὄψις*) *good looks*, Alex.38. **-ος,** *ον*, *abounding in ὄψα*, esp. fish, *ἀγορά* Anaxandr.33.10, Timocl.11.1; *χωρίον* Archestr.*Fr.*50 B., cf. Str.10.2.21; *ἡ θάλασσα τῆς γῆς -οτέρα* Plu.2.667c, etc. **-ωνία,** *ἡ*, = *εὐοψία* (A), Alex.316.

⊛ **εὐπᾰγής,** *ές*, (*πήγνυμι*) of the body or limbs, *compact, firm*, Pl.*Lg.*775c, X.*Cyn.*4.1, 5.30, Philostr.*Gym.*34; *παιδάριον* Plu.*Lyc.*16; of things, *σχαλίδες* X.*Cyn.*2.7; *βάκτρον* Theoc.25.208; of blood, *readily coagulating*, Aret.*SD*2.4: Comp., Ph.1.418; *firm in texture, well-woven*, *BGU*1564.10 (ii A.D.): metaph., *sound, solid*, of style, Phld.*Po.*994.34,35. Adv. *-γέως* Opp.*H.*3.401.

**εὐπάθ-εια** [*πᾰ*], Ion. **-είη,** *ἡ*, (*εὐπᾰθής*) *comfort, ease*, X.*Ages.*9.3; *οὐ καρτερίαν τὴν ἀρετὴν ἀλλ' εὐ. νομίζειν* ib.11.9, cf. Plu.2.132c: esp. in pl., *enjoyments, luxuries*, *ἐν εὐπαθείῃσι εἶναι* *enjoy oneself, make merry*, Hdt.1.22,191, 8.99; *εὐπαθείας ἐπιτηδεύειν* Id.1.135; also, *delicacies, dainties*, *εὐπαθείας ἐκ τῆς ἀγορᾶς πολυτελεῖς πορίζεσθαι* X.*Ap.*18, cf. Pl.*R.*404d. 2. pl. in Stoic Philos., *innocent emotions*, opp. *πάθη*, *Stoic.*3.105, al. 3. = *τὸ εὖ πάσχειν*, *receipt of benefits*, Arist.*EN* 1159$^a$21. 4. *sensitiveness* to impressions, Alex.Aphr.*Pr.*2.53; to disease, Gal.8.205, al.; *passivity*, Plu.2.589. **-έω,** *enjoy oneself, make merry*, *πίνειν καὶ εὐπαθέειν* Hdt.2.133,174; *indulge oneself, live comfortably*, Pl.*R.*347c; of the soul, *τρέφεται καὶ εὐπαθεῖ* Id.*Phdr.*247d; opp. *δυστυχέω*, D.C.56.45. 2. *receive benefits*, *ὑπό τινος* from one, Plu.2.176b (better divisim). **-ής,** *ές*, (*πάθος*) *enjoying good things, easy, luxurious*, *βίος* Crates Com.16. II. *easily affected*, *ὑπὸ τοῦ ἀέρος* Arist.*Pr.*887$^b$23 (Sup.); *εἰς τὸ πάσχειν* Thphr.*CP*5.14.7 (Comp.); *τὸ εὐ. τῆς φύσεως* Alex.Aphr.*Pr.*2.53; *εὐ. τῷ ἀέρι* Plu.2.949e (Comp.); *πρὸς τὸ πῦρ* Id.*Alex.*35; *τροφῆς -έστατον ὑπὸ πέψεως* Id.2.661c; *-έστερος οἶνος* *Gp.*5.45.1; *susceptible* to disease, Aret.*SD*1.11; of persons, *susceptible*, *πρὸς τὸ φαινόμενον αἰσχρόν* Plu.2.528d; [*τάξεις*] *-έστεραι πρὸς τὰς τῶν πολεμίων ἐπιφανείας* Onos.6.3. **-ητικός,** *ή, όν*, *easily contracted*, *νοσήματα* *Cat.Cod.Astr.*8(4).174. **-ητος,** *ον*, = *εὐπαθής* II, *Corp.Herm.*10.10.

⊛ **εὐπαιδ-ευσία,** *ἡ*, *goodness of education*, E.*Fr.*1100, Men.*Mon.*653, Aret.*SD*1.6; *culture, scholarship*, *ἐπιστολαὶ -ευσίας μεσταί* Philostr.*VS*1.18.4. **-ευτος,** *ον*, *well-educated, well-trained*, Hp.*Art.*43, cf. E.*Or.*410; *τῶν ἄλλων -ότατοι* Phld.*Piet.*65; *docile*, of an elephant, Philostr.*VA*2.11; *εὐπαίδευτόν ἐστι* it is *a thing easily learnt*, c. inf., Hp.*Art.*1; *εὐ. ἐπιστολή* a *scholarly* letter, D.H.*Pomp.*1.1. Adv. *-τως* Aret.*CD*1.3: Comp. *-ότερον* Athenocles ap.Ath.5.177e.

**εὐπαιδία,** *ἡ*, *a goodly race of children*, A.*Fr.*350 (pl.); *τέρπεται δ' εὐπαιδίᾳ* E.*Supp.*490; *εὐπαιδίαν ἔχοντ'* *blest* in his *children*, Id.*Ion* 678 (dochm.); *ὦ μακάριε τῆς εὐπαιδίας* Ar.*V.*1512; *τῆς..ἡμετέρας εὐ.* Isoc.11.41, cf. 9.72; *τὰ τῆς εὐ. δίκαια*, = Lat. *jus trium liberorum*, *POxy.*1264.18 (iii A.D.).

⊛ **εὔπαις,** *παιδος, ὁ, ἡ*, *blest with children*, i.e. *with many* or *with good, fine children*, *h.Hom.*30.5, Hdt.1.32, E.*Hec.*810; *'Ασκληπιός* Ar.*Pl.*639 (lyr.); *βιοτά* E.*Ion* 491 (lyr.); *'Αθῆναι* *AP*6.330 (Aeschin.); but *Λατοῦς γόνος εὔπαις* her *noble son*, E.*HF*689, *IT*1234 (both lyr.).

**εὔπακτος,** Dor. for *εὔπηκτος*, B.16.82, etc.

**εὐπάλαιστος** [*πᾰ*], *ον*, *easy to overcome in wrestling*, [Epich.]254.

**εὐπάλαιστρος** [*πᾰ*], *ον*, *skilful in contest*, metaph., *τὸ κατὰ τὰς εἰρωνείας εὐ.* Longin.34.2.

**εὐπάλᾰμος** [*πᾰ*], *ον*, *handy, skilful, ingenious*, of persons, Phoronis *Fr.*2, Nonn.*D.*5.216, al.: more freq. in the abstract, *inventive*, *μέριμνα* A.*Ag.*1531 (lyr.); *Ἔρως* Orph.*H.*58.4; *σοφίη* *IG*14.967. 2. *skilfully wrought*, *ὕμνοι* Cratin.70, cf. Nonn.*D.*17.146, al. b. *easily manipulated*, Ph.*Bel.*60.47.

⊛ **εὐπᾰλής,** *ές*, (*πάλη*) *easy to wrestle with*: hence, *easy of accomplishment*, *ἄεθλοι* A.R.2.618. Adv. *εὐπαλέως* Id.4.193. II. (*πάλλω*) *easily handled*, *θύρσος* S.*Ichn.*220.

**εὐπάξ,** *ᾶγος, ὁ, ἡ*, Dor. for *εὐπηγής*, *εὐπᾶγι κύκλῳ* cj. for *εὐπαγεῖ*, E.*Or.*1428 (lyr.).

**εὐπαράγωγος** [*ᾰγ*], *ον*, *easy to bring into place*, *ὀστέα* Hp.*Fract.*6; *flexible*, *αὐχήν* Aret.*SD*1.8. II. *easy to lead by the nose, easy to lead astray*, Ar.*Eq.*1115 (lyr.); *ἐλπίς* Pl.*Ti.*69d; *credulous*, *νόσος* Philostr.*VA*7.39. 2. Act., *seductive, alluring*, *λόγος, πλάσματα*, Ph.1.268, 2.481.

**εὐπαράδεκτος,** *ον*, *easily received, acceptable*, *ἐπίνοιαι* Plb.10.2.11 (Comp.), cf. Phld.*D.*1.24 (Comp.): in Gramm., *admissible*, A.D.*Pron.*89.7, al.; opp. *ἀπόβλητος*, Id.*Synt.*164.25; *easy to admit*, *σαφὲς καὶ εὐ.* Plot.6.4.1. II. *receiving readily*, [*λάκκοι*] *εὐ. ὕδατος* Ph.1.572: metaph., [*εὐφυΐα*] *εὐ. σπερμάτων ἀρετῆς* ib.136; *εὐ. πρὸς τὰ θεωρήματα* ib.572.

**εὐπαραίτητος,** *ον*, *placable*, Plu.*Phoc.*29, *Dio* 47; *ἐπί τινι γενέσθαι* D.C.42.18 (*ἀπ-* codd.). 2. *easily disposed of*, *τρόπος* S.E.*P.*2.204. 3. *furnishing a good ground of excuse*, D.L.3.78 (s.v.l.).

**εὐπαράκλητος,** *ον*, *easily influenced*, *πρός τι* Pl.*Ep.*328a, cf. Aristaenet.2.1.

**εὐπαρᾰκολούθ-ητος,** *ον*, *easy to follow*, of a narrative, argument, etc., Plb.4.28.6, Hero *Bel.*73.12, D.H.*Pomp.*6.2; *τοῦ εὐ. ἕνεκα* Arist.*EN*1108$^a$19. Adv. *-τως* D.H.*Th.*37. II. Act., *quick to follow*, Hsch. **-ος,** *ον*, = foreg. II, *Et.Gud.*220.3.

**εὐπαρα-κόμιστος,** *ον*, *easy to steer*, *πρὸς τὴν γῆν* Plu.*Luc.*13; *εὐ. ὁ πλοῦς ἐπὶ τὰ στενά* Plb.4.44.6: metaph., *easy to bring over*, *λογισμῷ πρὸς τὸ συμφέρον εὐ.* Plu.2.597b. II. [*πόλις*] *εὐ. πρὸς τὰς παραπομπὰς τῆς ὕλης* *conveniently situated for the supply* of wood, Arist.*Pol.*1327$^a$10. **-κρουστος,** *ον*, *easy to set aside, refute*, *συνηγορία* A.D.*Pron.*6.20. **-ληπτος,** *ον*, *readily applicable*, Eust.746.44.

**εὐπαράλλακτος,** *ον*, *subject to change, unstable*, *κάλλος εὐ. κτῆμα* Secund.*Sent.*14.

**εὐπαρα-λόγιστος,** *ον*, *easily cheated* or *misled*, *εὐ. πᾶς ὄχλος* Plb.11.29.9, cf. Phld.*Ir.*p.38 W., J.*AJ*4.6.11, Hierocl. *in CA*13 p.448 M.: Sup., Plb.5.75.2. **-μύθητος** [*ῡ*], *ον*, *easily appeased*, *θύμασιν καὶ εὐχαῖς* Pl.*Lg.*888c. 2. *admitting of easy consolation*, *θάνατος* Plu.2.110e, Onos.42.21, cf. Vett.Val.286.16; *εὐ. τὸ δεινόν* Luc.*DDeor.*11.2 (dub. l.), cf. Hld.4.5. 3. *easily proved*, S.E.*M.*10.212.

**εὐπάρᾱος** (so, without iota, codd.), *ον*, Dor. for *εὐπάρειος*, Pi.*P.*12.16.

**εὐπαρά-πειστος,** *ον*, *easily persuaded*, *φίλοις* X.*Ages.*11.12 (Sup.). **-πλους,** *ουν*, *easy to coast along*, Str.17.3.22. **-τήρητος,** *ον*, *noticeable*, *σολοικισμός* [Hdn.Gr.] post *Lex.Vind.*p.307 N. **-τρεπτος,** *ον*, *easy to turn from his opinion*, Poll.8.12. **-τύπωτος** [*ῠ*], *ον*, *easily misled by false impressions*, *αἰσθητήρια* M.Ant.5.33. **-φορος,** *ον*, *easily distracted*, Hsch. **-χώρητος,** *ον*, *readily admissible*, Archim.*Quadr.Praef.*

**εὐπάρεδρος,** *ον*, *constantly attending*, *τὸ εὐ. τῷ Κυρίῳ* *constant waiting* on the Lord, 1*Ep.Cor.*7.35 (v.l. *εὐπρόσ-*), cf. Hsch., Suid.

**εὐπάρειος** [*ᾰ*], *ον*, *with fair cheeks*, Poll.2.87, 9.162: Dor. **-αος** (q.v.).

**εὐπαρ-είσδῠτος,** *ον*, *easily accessible*, Hp.*Art.*30 codd.: sed leg. **-έκδυτος,** *slipping out of place easily*. II. *easily inserted*, Paul.Aeg.6.114. **-ηγόρητος,** *ον*, *easily alleviated*, *πάθη* Ptol.*Tetr.*153; *easily consoled*, *εὐ. τὴν ψυχήν* Vett.Val.166.8. Adv. *-τως* dub. l. in Phalar.*Ep.*10.

⊛ **εὐπάρθενος,** *ον*, *famed for fair maidens*, Tryph.51, Nonn.*D.*39.188. II. *εὐ. Δίρκα* Dirce, *happy maid!* E.*Ba.*520 (lyr.), cf. *AP*6.287 (Antip.), Nonn.*D.*16.311; cf. *εὔπαις*.

**εὐπαρ-όδευτος,** *ον*, *easy to pass by, ignore*, *κάλλος οὐκ εὐ.* *striking* beauty, Malch.p.393 D. **-οδος,** *ον*, *easy of access*, Str.3.2.11 (Comp.). 2. *easy of introduction*, Sever.*Clyst.*p.37 D. **-οιστοι·** *εὐπαράγωγοι*, Hsch. ⊛ **-όξυντος,** *ον*, *easily provoked, irritated*, *ὑπὸ κακῶν* Plu.*Ant.*73. **-όρμητος,** *ον*, *easily excited*, *πρός τινας* Arist.*Rh.*1379$^a$17. **-οχος,** *ον*, *submissive*, of a mare, *Hippiatr.*14.

**εὐπαρρησίαστος,** *ον*, *speaking with bold freedom*, Heph.Astr.1.1; *a fit subject for free speech*, Vett.Val.241.12.

**εὐπάρῠφος,** *ον*, *with a fine purple border*, *περίζωμα* Plu.*Aem.*33: as Subst., *εὐπάρυφος*, *ἡ*, *a fine garment*, Nicostr.Com.9, Hdn.1.16.3: neut.

pl. εὐπάρυφα, τά, Lxx *Es.*23.12. 2. of persons, *wearing such a garment*, εὐ. τις *a grandee*, Ph.2.346 (pl.), Plu.2.57a, cf. Luc.*Somn.* 16, *Demon.*15, Alciphr.3.42. 3. metaph., *pompous*, διηγήματα Plu.2.547e; but εὐ. λόγοι *equivocal, lascivious* stories, Ath.10.453a.

❀ **εὐπάτειρα** [ᾰ], ἡ, = sq., Men.616 (with v.l. εὐπατέρεια), Choerob. in *An.Ox.*2.196, Theognost.*Can.*99, Gramm. in Reitzenstein *Gesch.d. Gr.Etym.*p.306, *Et.Gud.*, *EM*318.55; cf. ἀπάτειρα.

**εὐπᾰτέρεια**, ἡ, (πατήρ) *daughter of a noble sire*, epith. of Helen, Il. 6.292, Od.22.227; of Tyro, 11.235; ἑταῖραι Mosch.2.29, cf. A.R.1. 570, *AP*9.688. 2. of places, *belonging to a noble father*, αὐλά E. *Hipp.*68 (lyr.).

**εὐπᾰτόριον**, τό (v.l. -ος, ὁ), *Agrimonia Eupatorium* (so called from Mithridates *Eupator*), *agrimony*, Dsc.4.41. 2. = πράσιον, Ps.-Dsc. 3.105.

❀ **εὐπᾰτρίδης**, ου, Dor. -δας, α, ὁ, (πατήρ) *of good* or *noble sire, of noble family*, of persons, used by Trag. in lyr., S.*El.*162, E.*Alc.*920 (anap.), *Hipp.*152, etc.; εὐ. οἶκοι Id.*Ion* 1073: also in later Prose, Muson.*Fr.* 13^B p.69 H. II. Εὐ., οἱ, at Athens, the *old aristocracy*, opp. ἀγροῖκοι (or γεωμόροι Plu.*Thes.*25) and δημιουργοί, Arist.*Ath.*13.2, cf. *Scol.*14, Isoc.16.25, X.*Smp.*8.40; πένητας Εὐπατρίδας οὐδεὶς ὁρᾷ Alex. 90.3; but τὰ τῶν Εὐ. πάτρια sacred traditions of the *Eup.*, Ath.9.410a and ἐξηγητὴς ἐξ Εὐ. *IG*3.267,1335, refer to a particular family of that name. 2. at Rome, *Patricians*, Plu.*Publ.*18, *Fab.*16, etc.

**εὐπᾰτρις**, ιδος, ἡ, fem. of foreg., *born of a noble sire*, E.*IA*1077 (lyr.); τίς ἂν εὐ. ὧδε βλάστοι; S.*El.*1081 (lyr.); ἐλπίδων.. εὐπατρίδων of hopes *derived from those of noble birth*, dub. cj. ib.858 (-ιδᾶν vel -ιδῶν codd.). 2. at Rome, αἱ εὐπάτριδες ἀρχαί *magistratus patricii*, D.C.46.45: γυνὴ εὐ., = Lat. *patricia*, Id.72.5 (here acc. sg. -ίδα, but cf. κακόπατρις, ὁμόπατρις).

❀ **εὐπάτωρ** [ᾰ], ορος, ὁ, ἡ, = foreg., A.*Pers.*970, Ael.*Fr.*292. II. *a good father*, dub. in Man.4.86.

**εὐπέδῑλος**, ον, *well-sandalled*, Ἶρις Alc.13 B (-πέδιλλ- Ahrens).

**εὐπέδιος**, ον, *with level* or *good soil*, Q.S.11.125, perh. f.l. for εὐρυπέδοιο:—fem. **εὐπεδιάς**, άδος, Sch.Ar.*Lys.*88.

**εὔπεζος**, ον, (πέζα) *with beautiful feet*, Poll.2.192.

**εὐπείθ-εια**, ἡ, *ready obedience*, Zeno *Stoic.*1.56, Ti.Locr.104b, Str. 7.4.8, Lxx 4 *Ma.*5.16, Plu.*Dio*4, etc.; also εὐπειθία or εὐπείθια *IG*5(1). 548 (Sparta, ii A.D.); Ion. -πειθείη Eus.Mynd.ap.Stob.4.5.29 (v.l. -πειθίη). -έω, *to be disposed to obey*, Charond.ap.Stob.4.2.24. II. *comply* with an order, *OGI*665.5 (Egypt, i A.D.). III. v.l. for εὐπιθέω (q.v.). ❀ -ής, ές, (cf. εὐπιθής) *ready to obey, obedient*, τινι Pl.*Phdr.*254a; τοῖς νόμοις -έστατος Id.*Lg.*715c, cf. 890c: c. gen., τῶν νόμων ib.632b; -έστατοι πρὸς ἀρετήν ib.718c; εἴς τι Id.*Phdr.*271d; *compliant*, εὐ. γεγονέναι *BGU*1104.23 (i B.C.), Lxx 4 *Ma.*12.6, etc.; of things, as of the voice, *under control*, Arist.*Aud.*802^a6; ὕλη (material) εἰς ἅπαν εὐ. Gal.6.3; of food, Plu.2.669b. Adv. -θῶς ib. 981a. II. Act., *persuasive*, of a rein, εὐπειθεῖ δεσμῷ Opp.*C.*1.313; dub. l. in A. (v. εὐπιθής).

**εὔπειστος**, ον, (πείθομαι) of persons, *easily persuaded*, Arist.*EN* 1151^b10. 2. *easy to demonstrate*, Id.*LI*969^b22; *easy to convince people of*, S.*Aj.*151 (anap., v.l. εὔπιστ-).

**εὔπεκτος**, ον, = εὔποκος, Hsch.

**εὐπελᾰγής**, ές, *lying fairly by the sea*, Orph.*A.*167.

**εὐπελέκητος**, ον, *easy to work with the axe*, Thphr.*HP*5.6.4 (Comp.).

**εὐπελής**, ές, (πέλω) *easy*, dub. in Orac.ap.Eus.*PE*5.23.

**εὐπέμπελος**, ον, only in A.*Eu.*476 ἔχουσι μοῖραν οὐκ εὐπέμπελον (sc. Εὐμενίδες), acc. to Sch. *placable, gentle*, opp. δυσπέμφελος; perh. *easily sent away, dismissed* (πέμπω).

**εὔπεμπτος**, *missilis*, Gloss.

**εὐπένθερος**, ον, *with a good father-in-law*, Theoc.18.49

**εὐπέπαντος**, ον, *well-ripened*: *mellow*, of scents, Thphr.*Od.*39.

**εὔπεπλος**, Ep. ἐΰ-, ον, *with beautiful peplos, beautifully robed*, of women, Il.5.424, Od.6.49, Hes.*Th.*273; οὐρανοῦ θυγάτηρ Pi.*Pae.Fr.* 16.10, cf. B.8.61. II. εὔπεπλον, τό, = δαφνοειδές, Ps.-Dsc.4.146.

**εὐπεπτ-έω**, *have a good digestion*, Hp.*Dent.*4, Gal.12.288. ❀-ος, ον, *easy of digestion*, opp. δύσπεπτος, Hp.*Acut.*15 (Sup.), Arist.*EN* 1141^b18, Gal.6.577 (Comp.):—Act., *having a good digestion*, Ruf.ap. Orib.8.47.7, Ath.Med.ap.Orib.9.5.6 (Comp.). 2. *easy of coction*, of a humour, Gal.1.280 (Sup.).

**εὐπέραντος**, ον, *well-finished, distinctly outlined*, Eust.1613.35:— also -περάτωτος [ᾰ], ον, ib.36.

**εὐπέρᾱτος**, ον, *easy to pass*, ποταμός Str.15.1.26 (Comp.), cf. Eust. 892.28.

**εὐπερι-άγωγος** [ᾰ], ον, *easily turned round*, Luc.*Musc.Enc.*3. -αίρετος, ον, *easily stripped off*, φλοιός Thphr.*HP*5.1.1. -βλεπτος, *conspicuus, perspicuus*, Gloss. -βλητος, ον, *well-dressed*, Simp. *in Cat.*270.24, Anon.*in Cat.*51.2. -βολος, ον, gloss on εὐερκής, Hsch. -γραπτος, ον, = sq. 2, Luc.*JTr.*33; σάρξ Theon Gymn. ap.Gal.6.91. -γρᾰφος, ον, *easy to trace* or *sketch out*, Str.2.1. 22, 5.1.2. 2. *with a good outline* or *contour*, Luc.*Am.*14, Ael. *NA*10.13; τοῦ ποδὸς τὸ μὴ εὐ. Luc.*Dom.*7. 3. Adv. -φως *by easy definition*, ὅρῳ ὑποπεσεῖν Iamb.*VP*29.159. 4. *concise*, διαλογισμός Epicur.*Ep.*2 p.35 U. -θραυστος, ον, *easy to break*, τὸ θυμικόν Plu.2.458e. -κάλυπτος [ᾰ], ον, *easy to conceal*, δυσπραξία Trag. *Adesp.*547.10. -κοπτος, ον, *suffering importunity readily*, εὐ. τὰς ἐντεύξεις *waiving ceremony* in his address, Plb.11.10.3. -κτητος, ον, *easily acquiring possessions*, Paul.Al.*M.*3, *N.*4. -ληπτος, ον, *easily embraced*, Hippiatr.14. 2. metaph., *limited*, ὑποθέσεις Plb.7. 7.6. II. *easy to comprehend*, ἀνθρώπῳ Porph.*Abst.*3.4. -νόητος, ον, *well-considered*, στίχος *Epigr.Gr.*1096.9 (Stratonicea). -οπτος, ον, *easily slighted, despicable*, ἀρχή Plb.*Fr.*157. -όριστος, ον, *well-defined*, Str.2.1.30; gloss on εὐδείελος, Apollon.*Lex.* ❀ -πᾰτος, ον, *allowing one to walk easily*, Luc.*Trag.*324. -σπαστος, ον, *easy to pull away*, X.*Cyn.*2.7. -σταλτος, ον, *lightly clad* for exercise, Eust.198.43. -στᾰτος, ον, *easily besetting*, ἁμαρτία *Ep. Hebr.*12.1; perh. *leading to distress*, cf. περίστασις; εὐπερίστατον, = εὔκολον, εὐχερῆ, Hsch. -στολος, ον, *circumspect, wary*, Ptol. *Tetr.*164. -στρεπτος, ον, *easily turned* or *wheeled about*, *EM*728. 42, Sch.Opp.*H.*4.294. -στροφος, ον, = foreg., Ascl. in *Metaph.* 5.8. 2. *wriggling*, τὸ τοῦ δράκοντος εὐ. Eust.229.37, cf. Hsch. s.v. ἀγχίστροφος. -τρεπτος, ον, *easy to turn over*, λίθος Seleuc. ap.Ath.4.155e; *supple*, κάμψις Gal.*UP*2.4. II. *easily refuted* or *reversible*, Luc.*JTr.*50. -φρόνητος, ον, *contemptible*, Suid. s.v. ἐκ παντὸς ξύλου. -φωρος, ον, *easily detected*, τοῖς πολεμίοις Plu. 2.238f. -χῠτος, ον, *easily diffused*, ib.954d, Herm.ap.Stob.1.49. 44. -ψογος, ον, *open to blame*, διὰ γυναῖκα Heph.Astr.1. 1. -ψυκτος, ον, *easily cooled*, Sor.1.99, Philum.ap.Aët.9.21, Cass. *Pr.*2.

**εὐπέτᾰλος**, ον, *with beautiful leaves, leafy*, δάφνα Pi.*Parth.*2.69; κισσός Ar.*Th.*1000 (lyr.); λεύκη *AP*4.1.19 (Mel.). II. as Subst., εὐπέταλον, τό, = δαφνοειδές, Dsc.4.146, cf. Ruf.ap.Orib.7.26.39. 2. εὐπέταλος, ὁ, a precious stone, Orph.*L.*230, Plin.*HN*37.161.

**εὐπέταστον**· πλατύ, εὐρίπιστον, Hsch.

**εὐπέτ-εια**, Ion. -είη, ἡ, *ease*, δι' εὐπετείας *easily*, E.*Ph.*262; μετ' εὐπετείας γίγνεσθαι Pl.*Ti.*64d; κατὰ πολλὴν εὐπέτειαν D.H.6.52: pl., εὐπετείας διδόναι give *facilities*, grant *indulgences*, κακίας πέρι Pl.*R.* 364c. 2. *easiness of getting* or *having*, γυναικῶν Hdt.5.20; τροφῆς X.*Oec.*5.5; τῶν προθυμουμένων Pl.*Lg.*718d; ἀγορᾶς Plu.*Nic.*20. 3. *easy decline, degeneration*, Hp.*Nat.Hom.*12. -ής, ές, (πίπτω) prop. of dice, *falling well*: metaph., *favourable, fortunate*, A.*Supp.*1011: Gramm., τὸ εὐ. *good cadence*, v.l. for εὐεπές, D.H.*Comp.*22: generally, *easy, without trouble*, ὁδός, πρόσοδος, Pl.*Sph.*218d (Comp.), X. *Cyr.*5.2.3 (Sup.), etc.; πάντα δ' εὐπετῆ θεοῖς E.*Ph.*689 (lyr.); οὐδὲν εὐ. τῶν μεγάλων Pl.*R.*365c: c. inf., εὐπετὴς χειρωθῆναι Hdt.3.120, 145; ὀφθῆναι, εἰσακοῦσαι, Pl.*Sph.*254a, *R.*494d; also εὐπετές [ἐστι] *it is easy to*.., πολλοὺς εὐπετέστερον διαβάλλειν ἢ ἕνα Hdt.5.97, cf. A. *Supp.*995, X.*Cyr.*4.3.13. 2. Adv. -τῶς, Ion. -τέως, *favourably, fortunately*, εὐπετῶς ἔχειν A.*Ag.*552; οὐ χαλεπῶς, ἀλλ' εὐ. *easily*, Hdt.3.69, cf. 1.189, al.; εὐ. φυλάξασθαι Antipho 3.4.7; ἔχειν τι X. *An.*2.5.23; with numerals, ἑξακοσίους ἀμφορέας εὐ. χωρέει it *easily* holds 600 amphoreis, i.e. *full* 600, Hdt.4.81; τὸ πλάτος γίνεται τεσσέρων εὐ. δακτύλων comes to *full* four fingers, Id.1.193: Comp. -εστέρως Id.3.143; also -έστερον, φέρειν τὸ νόσημα Hp.*Prog.*6. II. of garments and arms, *easy to wear, light*, σάγοι, θυρεοί, Plb.2.28. 7, Plu.*Phil.*9. 2. of wine, *easily affected*, Arist.*Pr.*907^b16 (Comp.). III. of persons, *contented, accommodating*, E.*Cyc.*526; *accommodating*, εὐ. ἦθος D.H.*Pomp.*4.2. Adv. -τῶς, φέρειν S.*Fr.* 585; *readily*, Id.*Ichn.*242 (lyr.).

**εὐπέτης**, ες, (πέτομαι) *flying well*, Eust.899.55.

**εὔπετρος**, ον, *of good hard stone*, *AP*6.306.8 (Aristo).

**εὐπεψία**, ἡ, *digestibility*, Arist.*PA*650^a11, 677^b31, Gal.16.245, etc.

**εὐπηγής**, ές, = sq., once in Hom., ξεῖνος μέγας ἠδ' εὐπηγής *well-built, stout*, Od.21.334; μῆτραι Hp.*Mul.*1.47; δικλίδες A.R.3.236: Dor. perh. **εὐπᾱγής**, v. εὐπάξ.

**εὔπηκτος**, ον, (πήγνυμι) *well put together, well-built*, ἐνὶ μεγάρῳ εὐ. Il.2.661; μυχῷ κλισίης 9.663; μυχῷ θαλάμων εὐ. Od.23.41; σύριγγα ἐκ καρῶ εὐπάκτοιο of *well-moulded, compact*, wax, Theoc.1.128 (s.v.l.); *firm*, of bandaging, Gal.18(2).904. II. of fluids, *easily congealed* or *frozen*, Arist.*Long.*466^a31, 467^a8. 2. Act., εὐ. ἀήρ Thphr.*CP*5.14.3 (Comp.).

**εὐπήληξ**, ηκος, ὁ, ἡ, *with beautiful helmet*, *AP*6.120 (Leon.). 2. *with fine crest*, ταὼς Babr.65.1a.

**εὔπηνος**, ον, (πήνη) *of fine texture*, ὑφαί E.*IT*312, 814.

**εὐπηξία**, ἡ, (εὔπηκτος) *compactness*, [τραχήλου] Adam.2.21.

**εὔπηχυς**, υ, *with beautiful arms*, χεῖρες E.*Hipp.*200 (anap.); epith. of Athena, Rhian.1.14.

❀ **εὐπῖδαξ**, ᾰκος, ὁ, ἡ, *abounding in fountains*, *AP*6.253.1 (Crin.).

**εὐπῐθ-έω**, = εὐπειθέω, of an instrument, v.l. in Hp.*Mul.*2.133. ❀ -ής, ές, = εὐπειθής 1, οὐ πείσεις νιν, οὐ γὰρ εὐπιθής A.*Pr.*335: here and in *Ag.*274, *Ch.*259, *Eu.*829, *Supp.*623 cod. Med. has -πειθ-, but -πῐθ- is required by the metre in *Pr.*l.c. and is possible elsewh. (but in *Ag.*982 (-πιθ- codd.) the metre perh. favours -πειθ-); the sense is sts. Act., ὀνείρων φάσματ' εὐπ(ε)ιθῆ σέβεις; *Ag.*274; σῆμα τ' εὐπ(ε)ιθῆ βροτοῖς *Ch.*259; perh. also θάρσος εὐπ(ε)ιθές *Ag.*982 (lyr.); δημηγόρους.. εὐπ(ε)ιθεῖς στροφάς *Supp.*623 (s.v.l.); sts. Pass., σὺ δ' εὐπ(ε)ιθὴς ἐμοὶ *Eu.*829, cf. *Pr.* l.c.

❀ **εὐπίλητος** [ῑ], ον, *well-compressed, dense*, dub. l. in Arist.*Sens.* 438^a15 (Comp.).

**εὐπῑν-εια** [ῑ], ἡ, perh. *elegance* of style, Longin.30.1; cf. sq. II. 2. εὐπινείας χάριν for *embellishment*, Heliod.ap.Orib.49.4.42. -ής, ές, (πῖνος) *neat, tidy*, οὐδ' ἐρημίᾳ γυναικὸς οἶκος εὐπινὴς οὐδ' ὄλβιος E. *Melanipp.Capt.Fr.*6.11 (s.v.l.); so perh. Cratin.414. II. *bright, decorative*, τὸν χαλκὸν.. ἔφασαν.. λειότερον, εὐπινέστερον, δυσωτότερόν τε εἶναι τοῦ σιδήρου (therefore preferable in machine-construction) Heliod.ap.Orib.49.3.5 (Comp.), cf. 7: hence metaph., of the style of ancient writers, *elegant, simple, quaint*, Caesar mihi irridere visus est 'quaeso' illud tuum, quod erat εὐπινὲς et urbanum, Cic.*Att.* 12.6.3 (Adv. -νῶς ib.15.17.2); as v.l. for ἀπηνής, ἁρμονία D.H.*Comp.*

22. (εὐπινής· εὐειδής, πίνος γὰρ τὸ εἶδος, *Et.Gud.d*, *EM*395.4: εὐπινές· τὸ ἀφελὲς καὶ μὴ λίαν τετημελημένον, ἀλλὰ μέτριον πίνον ἔχον, Phot.)

**εὔπιστ-ία**, ἡ, *pious belief*, prob. cj. in Jul.*Or*.4.153a. **-ος**, ον, (πίστις) *trustworthy, trusty*, of persons, X.*Cyr*.1.2.12 (Sup.); δῆμος *BCH*37.124 (Abdera, ii B.C.); εὔπιστα *things easy to believe* S.*Aj*.151 (anap., v.l. εὔπειστα). II. Act., *easily believing, credulous*, Men. 380, Arist.*Rh*.1389$^a$18. Adv. εὐπίστως, ἔχειν Ar.*Th*.105. III. *readily obeying*, Euc.ap.Stob.3.6.63 (sed leg. εὔπειστος).

**εὐπίων** [ῑ], ον, gen. ονος, *very fat*: *very rich*, φόρτος *AP*7.654 (Leon.).

**εὐπλᾰδής**, ές, *pliant, ductile*, ὕλη Iamb.*Comm.Math*.4; cf. πλαδαρός.

**εὐπλᾰνής**, ές, *successfully tracking* Opp.*C*.4.365.

**εὐπλαστ-ία**, ἡ, *credibility in fiction*, Eust.990.42. **-ος**, ον, *easy to mould* or *put into shape*, of a broken nose, Hp.*Art*.39 (Sup.); φύσει πούς εὔ. Aristaenet.1.12. 2. *easy to mould, ductile*, εὐπλαστότερον κηροῦ Pl.*R*.588d, cf. Ael.*NA*17.9, Dsc.4.75; φύσις (of sea-water) Arist.*GA*761$^a$34 (Comp.); ἦθος Pl.*Lg*.666c (Comp.); of men, *impressionable*, Arist.*Po*.1455$^a$33.

**εὐπλᾰτής**, ές, *of a good breadth*, λόγχη X.*Cyn*.10.3.

**ἐύπλειος**, η, ον, *well filled*, κὰδ δ' ἄρα πήρην θῆκεν ἐϋπλείην Od.17.467.

**εὐπλεκής**, Ep. **ἐϋπλ-**, ές, = sq., θύσανοι.. πάντες ἐϋπλεκέες Il.2.449; δίφροι (cf. sq.) 23.436, Hes.*Sc*.306; σπυρίδες *AP*6.28 (Jul.); of cords, Opp.*H*.5.379: metaph., ἀοιδαί Pi.*Pae*.3.12.

❋**εὔπλεκτος**, Ep. **ἐϋπλ-**, ον, also η, ον Nonn.*D*.13.200 (cj. for ἀπλ-): (πλέκω): —*well-plaited, well-twisted*, σειρὰς τ' εὐπλέκτους Il.23.115; ἐϋπλέκτῳ ἐνὶ δίφρῳ a chariot *with sides of wicker* or *basket-work*, ib. 335; of nets, E.*Ba*.870 (lyr.); of hair, *AP*5.286.6 (Agath.).

**εὔπλευρος**, ον, *with strong lungs*, Arist.*HA*587$^a$3, *Phgn*.810$^b$12.

**εὐπληθής**, ές, *luxuriant*, Thphr.*HP*4.11.4 (Comp.).

**εὔπληκτος**, ον, *easily struck*, so as to sound, Plu.2.721f.

**εὐπλήρωτος**, ον, *easily filled*: *full*, Gal.1.329, al., Alex.Trall.1.11.

**εὐ-πλοέω**, *have a good voyage*, Ps.-Hdt.*Vit.Hom*.18, Teles p.25 H., Euryph.ap.Stob.4.39.27, D.Chr.63.2, Heph.Astr.3.30; εὐπλοεῖτε, as a wish, *IG*14.933; εὐπλόι (= -ει) ib.2409, cf. 2472 (Arelate). 2. *prosper, receive promotion*, μέχρι τῶν Σεβαστείων χαρακτήρων *SIG* 783.24 (Mantinea, i B.C.). ❋**-πλοια**, poet. **-οίη**, ἡ, *a fair voyage*, εἰ δέ κεν εὐπλοίην δώῃ.. ἐννοσίγαιος Il.9.362; εὔπλοιαν ἔπραξαν A.*Supp*. 1045 (lyr.); εὐπλοίας τυχών S.*OT*423, etc. (εὐπλοΐη is required by the metre in *AP*9.9 (Polyaen.), 107 (Leon. or Antip. Thess.), *BMus. Inscr*.1012 (Chalcedon); **εὐπλωΐα** *Cat.Cod.Astr*.2.169.) II. **Εὔπλοια**, a name of Aphrodite, *IGRom*.3.921 (Cilicia), *IPE*1.94 (Olbia), Paus.1.1.3; on a lamp dedicated to Helioserapis, *IG*14.2405.48 (Puteoli). III. dub. sens. in *PCair.Zen*.15$^r$.40 (iii B.C.).

**ἐϋπλοκᾰμ-ίς**, ῖδος, Ep. fem. of sq., ἐϋπλοκαμῖδες Ἀχαιαί Od.2.119, 19.542. **-ος**, Ep. **ἐϋπλ-**, ον, *with goodly locks, fair-haired*, epith. of goddesses and women, in Hom., etc., esp. of Eos and Artemis, Od.5.390, 20.80, cf. B.3.34, etc.; later also of boys and men, Mosch. 1.12, Orph.*L*.439; εὐ. κόμαι *goodly* tresses, E.*IA*790 (lyr.): metaph., ἐϋπλοκάμου πολιῆς ἁλός Archil.11, cf. Opp.*C*.2.131; of the tentacles of polypi, ib.3.182.

**ἐΰπλοκος**, ον, (πλέκω) = εὔπλεκτος, Opp.*H*.3.75, *AP*6.174 (Antip. ⟨Sid.⟩).

**εὔπλοος**, ον, contr. **-πλους**, ουν, (πλέω) *good for sailing, fair*, εὔ. πλόος, = εὔπλοια, Erinn.1. II. of a person, *having a fair voyage*, εὔπλοος ὅρμον ἵκοιτο Theoc.7.62 (-πλοον codd.), cf. *BGU*665 ii 7 (i A.D.).

**εὔπλουτον κανοῦν**· εὖ ἔχον πλούτου, διὰ τὰς ἐπ' αὐτῷ ὀλάς· πλοῦτον γὰρ ἔλεγον τὴν ἐκ τῶν κριθῶν καὶ τῶν πυρῶν περιουσίαν, Hsch.

**ἐϋπλῡνής**, ές, (πλύνω) *well-washed, well-cleansed*, φᾶρος Od.8.392, 425, 13.67, 16.173.

**εὔπλωτος**, ον, *favourable to sailing*, κῦμα *AP*10.25 (Antip.).

**εὐ-πνοέω**, = εὔπνοος εἰμι, Arist.*Pr*.896$^a$32. II. *respire freely*, ὅταν εὐπνοῇ ὅλον τὸ σῶμα Philistion *Fr*.4. **-πνοια**, ἡ, *easiness of breathing*, Hp.*Prog*.5, Arist.*Pr*.960$^b$24, al.; ἡ τῆς ζωῆς εὔ. Chrysipp. *Stoic*.2.238. II. *free blowing*, ἀνέμων D.S.2.40. 2. *airy situation*, Arist.*Pr*.909$^b$5; ἐν εὐπνοίᾳ Thphr.*CP*6.16.5; εὔπνοιαι εὐήλιοι dub. l. in Dsc.3.119. III. *fragrance*, *AP*12.7 (Strat., in poet. form ἐϋπνοΐη). **-πνοος**, ον, contr. **-πνους**, ουν, Ep. **ἐΰπνοος**, (πνέω) *breathing well* or *freely*, Hp.*Prog*.15, *Epid*.4.26 (Comp.), Max.Tyr. 30.6 (v.l. ἄϋπνος). 2. causal, *making one breathe freely, relieving oppression of the breath*, λουτρόν Hp.*Acut*.66. 3. *sweet-smelling*, λείρια Mosch.2.32; ῥόδον *IG*14.2040.3. II. *affording a free passage to the air*, μυκτῆρες X.*Eq*.1.10 (Comp.); ὁ ⌊περὶ τὴν κεφαλ⌋ὴν τόπος εὔ. Arist.*PA*653$^b$2, cf. 673$^b$23 (Sup.); κάλαμοι Longus 2.35; νεφέλαι εὔ. αὔραις Orph.*H*.21.6. 2. *open to the winds, airy*, οἰκία εὔπνους μὲν τοῦ θέρους, εὐήλιος δὲ τοῦ χειμῶνος Arist.*Oec*.1345$^a$31; τόποι Id.*Pr*.869$^a$34 (Comp.); δένδρα Thphr.*CP*1.15.4; τὸ εὔ. τοῦ τόπου Pl.*Phdr*.230c. III. *good to breathe, fresh and pure*, of the air, Thphr.*CP*1.13.8, Str.3.2.13: Comp. εὐπνοώτερος X. l. c., Hp. *Epid*.4.26; also εὐπνούστερος ib.7.39, Arist.*Pr*.960$^b$22, Gal.5.911: Sup. -ούστατος Arist.*PA*673$^b$23.

❋**εὐποδία**, ἡ, (εὔπους) *goodness of foot*, X.*Eq*.1.3, Poll.1.194.

**εὐποιέω**, freq. written in codd. for εὖ ποιέω, as Hp.*Loc.Hom*.46, etc.

**εὐποίημα**, ατος, τό, *benefaction*, *PLond*.5.1729.21 (pl., vi A.D.).

**εὐποιητικός**, ή, όν, *disposed to do good, beneficent*, εἰς or περὶ χρήματα, Arist.*Rh*.1381$^a$20, 1366$^b$16; τινος towards one, ib.1379$^b$32, Porph.*Abst*.3.26; τὸ εὐ. *beneficence*, Arist.*Rh*.1371$^b$3, Antip.*Stoic*.3. 249. 2. Astrol., *beneficent*, of planetary influences, opp. κακοποιητικός, ἰδιοτροπία Ptol.*Tetr*.210.

**εὐποίητος**, ον (v. infr.), *well-made, well-wrought*, ἔν τε θρόνοις εὐ. Od.20.150; εὐποιητόν τε πυράγρην 3.434; ἅρμα B.5.177, cf. Hes.*Sc*. 64, A.R.3.871, etc.: fem. -τῇσι, -τάων, Il.5.466, 16.636 (nisi scrib. divisim, cf. Sch.Il. ll. cc.).

❋**εὐποιΐα**, ἡ, *beneficence*, *Ep.Hebr*.13.16, *Inscr.Perg*.333, Luc.*Abd*. 25, D.L.10.10, Procl.*in Alc*.p.121 C.; τῆς εἴς τινας εὐ. *IG*3.1054:—in form **εὐποΐα**, εἰς πλῆθος *Inscr.Prien*.112.19 (i B.C.): in pl., ib.113. 76 (i B.C.), Ph.1.582, Hierocl.p.59 A.

**εὐποίκιλος**, ον, *variegated*, ἄνθος *AP*6.154 (Leon. or Gaet.).

**εὐποιός**, όν, (ποιέω) = εὐποιητικός, Hsch.

**εὔποκος**, ον, *fleecy*, νομεύματα A.*Ag*.1416, cf. *Hymn.Curet*.48.

**εὐπολέμ-ητος**, ον, *easy to be conquered*, Poll.1.158. ❋**-ος**, ον, *good at war, successful in war*, Νίκη *h.Mart*.4; πόλις X.*Vect*.4.51 (Comp.), *Oec*.4.3; of warriors, *APl*.4.331 (Agath.). Adv. -μως *skilfully*, of an officer, D.C.78.38.

**Εὐπολίδειος**, ον, *in the style of Eupolis*, D.H.*Rh*.11.10; **-ειον** (sc. μέτρον), τό, *metre invented by him* Heph.16.5.

**εὔπολις**, ιδος, ὁ, ἡ, *abounding in cities*, Poll.9.27.

**εὔπομπος**, ον, *well-conducting, conducting to a happy issue*, S.*OT* 697 (lyr.); εὐπόμπῳ τύχῃ (in allusion to Hermes πομπαῖος) A.*Eu*.93.

**εὔπονος**, ον, *toilsome*, φυλακαί Aristonous 1.38.

**εὐπόρευτος**, ον, *easy to travel*, ὁδός Ceb.16. II. *easily passing*, Sch.Lyc.686.

❋**εὐπορ-έω**, fut. -ήσω: aor. εὐπόρησα: pf. εὐπόρηκα Diph.43.19, etc., ηὐπ- Pl.*Hp.Ma*.297e, Plu.2.403f:—*prosper, thrive*, εὐποροῦσι γὰρ οἱ ὀλίγοι *are wealthy*, Arist.*Pol*.1280$^a$4, cf. *SIG*344.116 (Teos, iv B.C.); εὐ. ἀπὸ τῶν πονηροτάτων X.*Mem*.2.7.4; οἱ εὐποροῦντες Amphis 15.6; of things, ὅθεν ὁ πόλεμος εὐπορεῖ from which sources war *is successfully maintained*, Th.6.34. b. c. gen. rei, *have plenty of, abound in*, χρημάτων Lys.19.25, Antiph.228.2; σίτων X.*HG*1.6.19; ῥημάτων, ὀνομάτων, λόγων, Pl.*Ion* 536c, *Sph*.267d, *Smp*.209b; ἐφοδίων Plu.*Them*. 10; εὐ. ἵππων *gain possession of*.., X.*HG*1.1.10; εὐ. τῆς ἀληθείας *attain* it, Arist.*Metaph*.996$^a$16; also εὐ. ἔν τινι Antipho 5.66; τοῖς ἀναγκαίοις Plb.1.17.2. 2. *find a way, find means*, abs., ὡς ἕκαστοι ηὐπόρησαν Th.6.44, cf. Pl.*Grg*.478a: c. inf., *to be able to* do, ἐπιχειρεῖν Arist. *Top*.102$^a$13 (also τοῦ πολλὰ λέγειν Pl.*Phdr*.235a); also εὐπορῶ ὅτι λέγω I *have plenty* to say, Id.*Ion* 532c: c. part., Id.*Lg*.654b; τοῦτο εὐ. *to be provided with an answer* on this point, Id.*Euthd*.279a; οὐκ εὐ. ὅπῃ.. not *to know how* to do, Id.*Smp*.219e; μᾶλλον εὐ. πρὸς τὴν γνῶσιν Arist.*PA*644$^b$28. II. c. acc. rei, *supply* or *furnish*, τἀργύριον Is.7.8; δέκα μνᾶς τινι D.33.7; *procure*, ἄλλοθεν χρήματα Id.40.36; ὅθεν σιτοπομπίας εὐπόρησε τοῖς στρατιώταις Id.23.155; *bring forward*, ἀποδείξεις D.S.2.31; *find available*, μὴ -ήσας πλοῖον (leg. πλοίων) *POxy*. 1068.3 (iii A.D.):—hence in Pass., = intr. Act., *have plenty of, abound in*, τινος Arist.*Oec*.1347$^b$4; μαθητῶν *Act.Ap*.11.29; τινι Plb.5.43.8; *obtain the use of*, πλοίου *PFlor*.367.8 (iii A.D.): abs., οἱ εὐπορούμενοι *SIG*495.66 (Olbia, iii B.C.), cf. Luc.*BisAcc*.27, *PMag.Par*.1.3125:—εὐπορηθέν in strict pass. sense, *being furnished*, Ps.-Plu.*Vit.Hom*. 210. III. as Philos. term, opp. ἀπορέω, *have one's doubts resolved, gain clear knowledge*, Pl.*Men*.80c, Arist.*Metaph*.995$^a$27; εὐ. περί τινος Id.*de An*.403$^b$21. **-ημα**, ατος, τό, *advantage, help*, Alcid.*Soph*.26 (pl.). **-ησις**, εως, ἡ, in pl., *facilities*, Phld.*Rh*.2.217 S. **-ητέον**, *one must have plenty*, καθαρσίων Ph.5p.147 C. **-ητος**· ὁ καλῶς διοικῶν, Hsch. ❋**-ία**, ἡ, (εὔπορος) *ease, facility*, of doing a thing, c. inf., Emp.100.5; ναῦς εὐ. ἦν ποιεῖσθαι Th.4.52: abs., ὅτε πολλὴ ὑμῖν εὐ. φαίνεται X.*An*.7.6.37: c. gen. rei, *easy means of providing*, τοῦ βίου Pl.*Prt*.321e; τοῦ καθ' ἡμέραν Th.3.82; also εὐ. ἐν τῇ τέχνῃ, ἐκ τῆς τέχνης, Lys.24.5; εὐ. τῆς τύχης Th.3.45; εὐπορίαν τῇ βδελυρίᾳ τῇ ἑαυτοῦ τοὺς συμμάχους ποιεῖσθαι to make them *a means of satisfying* his brutal passions, Aeschin.1.107; ἡ παρ' ἀλλήλων εὐ. mutual *assistance*, Isoc.6.67. 2. *plenty, abundance*, opp. πενία, Democr. 101; χρημάτων X.*HG*4.8.28; ἀγαθῶν Arist.*Metaph*.1091$^b$26; ἡ περὶ τὸν βίον εὐ. Isoc.1.2; ἡ περὶ τὴν οὐσίαν εὐ. Arist.*Pol*.1326$^b$34: abs., *welfare*, X.*Cyr*.3.3.7; opp. ἀπορία, Arist.*Pol*.1279$^b$27: in pl., *advantages*, Isoc.15.253, D.5.8; εὐπορίαι προσόδων Arist.*Pol*.1293$^a$3; ἀρουραίη εὐ. rustic *wealth*, *AP*9.373.6; μιῆς ὄϊος καὶ βοὸς εὐ. *consisting of* one sheep or ox, ib.149 (Antip.); ἡ Εὐ. θεά *SIG*1111 (Piraeus, iii A.D.). II. opp. ἀπορία, *solution of doubts* or *difficulties*, Pl.*Phlb*. 15c; opp. ἀμηχανία, X.*Oec*.9.1; ἡ ὕστερον εὐ. λύσις τῶν πρότερον ἀπορουμένων Arist.*Metaph*.995$^a$29; *resourcefulness*, Hp.*Off*.7. **-ίζω**, *supply, provide means for*, ἐνεργείαις Gal.18(2).722 (dub. l.). **-ιστία**, ἡ, *ease of procuring* a thing, Epicur.*Fr*.470. **-ιστος**, ον, (πορίζω) *easy to procure* or *secure*, Id.*Ep*.3p.63 U., *Sent*.21, *Fr*.469, Dsc.*Eup. Praef*.: Sup., ἀμπεχόνη, οἰκία, Ph.2.424, cf. Phld.*D*.1.15; *feasible*, Cic.*Att*.7.1.7; εὐπόριστα (sc. φάρμακα), τά, *common, family medicines*: title of work by Dsc., Orib.*Eup.Praef*. (called περὶ ἁπλῶν φαρμάκων in codd. of Dsc.*Eup*.); also, *ordinary food*, opp. *game out of season*, Plu.*Luc*.40, *Pomp*.2. II. Act., *providing one's subsistence with ease*, Ptol.*Tetr*.155. **-ος**, ον, *easy to pass* or *travel through*, ἄτης.. πέλαγος οὐ μάλ' εὔ. A.*Supp*.470; ὁδός Pl.*R*.328e; τὰ εὔ. *open ground*, X.*Eq.Mag*.4.4; εὔπορον ἦν διιέναι Th.4.78, cf. X.*An*.3.5.17; εὔ. ποιεῖν τὰ ὦτα to *open* one's ears, Luc.*Lex*.1; μήτρα *lax*, Sor.1.34. 2. *easily got, easily done, easy*, τὰ μέγιστα.. σφι εὔπορά ἐστι Hdt.4.59; πολλά τοι θεὸς κἀκ τῶν ἀέλπτων εὔπορ' ἀνθρώποις τελεῖ E.*Fr*.100; παρ' ἐμοῦ δ' ἔστιν ταῦτα εὔ. Ar.*Pl*.532, cf. Pl. *R*.404c; φιλία.. εὔ. εἴη Ar.*Lys*.1266; τὴν κατὰ θάλασσαν ἔφοδον -ωτέραν Th.1.93; πλεῖστον.. μέλι καὶ -ώτατον Pl.*R*.564e; τὸ εὔ., = εὐπορία, εὑρίσκειν τὸ εὔ. Hp.*Art*.78; διὰ τὸ εὔ. τῆς ἐλπίδος Th.8. 48; εὔπορόν ἐστι it is *easy*, c. inf., X.*An*.3.5.17, D.3.18, etc.; ἐν

εὐπόρῳ κεῖται c. inf., Str.10.3.8: Comp. -ώτερον Pl.*R.*404c. **II.** *ready, glib*, γλῶττα Ar.*Eq.*637. **2.** of persons, *full of resources* or *devices, ingenious, inventive*, opp. ἄπορος, E.*Fr.*430 (Sup.); εἰ οὖν τις ..-ώτερος ἐμοῦ Pl.*Phd.*86d; εὔ. ἐν τοῖς ἀπόροις Alex.234.5; -ώτεροι πρὸς ἅπαν ἔργον Pl.*Prt.*348d: c. inf., χρήματα πορίζειν -ώτατον γυνή Ar.*Ec.*236; ἐς τὴν δίαιταν -ώτατοι Id.*V.*1112. **III.** *well-provided with, rich in*, πόλιν τοῖς πᾶσιν -ωτάτην Th.2.64; τὰ περὶ τὸν βίον -ώτεροι Isoc.8.19; τίς -ώτερος χρημάτων; D.Chr.3.132: abs., *fertile*, γῆ Poll.1.186; *well-furnished*, πράγματ' -ώτερα D.19.89; *well off, wealthy*, οἱ εὔ. Id.1.28, etc.; opp. οἱ ἄποροι, Arist.*Pol.*1279b8, etc.; *persons of substance*, capable of bearing taxation, *SIG*344.115 (Sup., Teos, iv B.C.); εὔ. καὶ ἐπιτήδειος *POxy.*1187.11 (iii A.D.), etc. **IV.** Adv. -ρως *easily*, X.*Cyr.*1.6.9, etc.: Comp. -ώτερον Pl.*Smp.*204e. **2.** *in abundance*, εὔ. ἔχειν πάντα Th.8.36; οὐκ εὔ. ἔχω I don't feel *well*, Luc.*Lex.*2 codd. (εὐφ- Cobet). **3.** *resourcefully*, Hp.*Off.*7.

**εὐπόρφῠρος**, ον, *of bright purple colour*, v.l. in Lxx *Ez.*23.12.

**εὐποσία**, ἡ, *abundance*, *IPE*1$^2$.140,141 (Olbia); θεὰ Εὐ. Judeich *Altertümer von Hierapolis* 26.

**εὐποσιάρχης**, ου, ὁ, = εὐβοσιάρχης (q. v.), *CIG*3385.2 (Smyrna), *IG*12(8).526 (Thasos), *Supp.Epigr.*1.332 (Tomi):—hence **-αρχέω**, *LW*53 (Erythrae).

**εὐπότιστος**, *riguus*, *Gloss.*

**εὐποτμ-έω**, *to be lucky, fortunate*, Plu.*Aem.*26. **-ία**, ἡ, *good fortune*, Xanth.10, Plu.*Arist.*24, Luc.*DDeor.*15.1, Ael.*NA*11.40. **-ος**, ον, *happy, prosperous*, αἰών A.*Ag.*246 (lyr.); δύνασις -οτάτα μελέων S.*Fr.*568, cf. Plu.2.58d (Comp.); of trees, *flourishing*, Sever.ap.Orib. 9.17.2 (Comp.). Adv. -μως Epist.Anaximen.ap.D.L.2.4, Muson. *Fr.*17 p.93 H.

⊛ **εὔποτος**, ον, (πίνω) *easy to drink, pleasant to the taste*, ῥέος A.*Pr.*676, 812; ὕδωρ Ath.Med.ap.Orib.*inc.*23.15; of milk, A.*Pers.*611. **II.** *good to drink from*, ἐκπώματα Eratosth.ap.Ath.11.482b (Sup.). **III.** *accustomed to drink*, Aret.*CA*2.3.

⊛ **εὔπους**, ὁ, ἡ, πουν, τό, gen. ποδος, *with good feet*, of horses and dogs, X.*Eq.*1.3, *Cyn.*3.2; of a bird, εὔπους καὶ κακόπτερος Arist.*HA*617b4; *fleet of foot*, Δηώνη Call.*Fr.*48. **II.** *with good feet, flowing*, ἁρμονία *AP*6.54 (Paul. Sil.).

**εὐπρᾱγ-έω**, = εὖ πράσσω, *do well, be well off, flourish*, Th.2.60, 6.16, X.*Ap.*27, etc. **-ημα**, ατος, τό, *a success*, in war, in pl., App.*Pun.*4, *BC*1.51: generally, Sch.Pi.*I.*3.1. **-ία**, Ion. εὐπρηγίη, ἡ, Eus.Mynd.59:—*welfare, success*, Pi.*O.*8.14, *P.*7.16, Antipho 2.4.9, Th.5.46, etc.: pl., Id.1.84, 4.17, Pl.*Lg.*732c, Isoc.9.42. **II.** *well doing*, opp. mere success, Pl.*Alc.*1.116b, *Euthd.*281b; περὶ αὐλημάτων εὐ. ib.279e, cf. *Prt.*345a; *good deeds, services*, Arist.*Rh.*1367a4 (pl.); cf. εὐπραξία.

**εὐπρακτ-έω**, *prosper*, Vett.Val.198.28. **-ος**, Ep. -πρηκτος, ον, *easy to be done*, X.*An.*2.3.20 (Comp.); οὐκ εὔπρηκτα κέλευθα Opp.*H.* 5.63. **II.** *well-to-do, prosperous*, Vett.Val.72.11, Man.1.352.

**εὐπραξία**, Ion. εὐπρηξίη, ἡ, = εὐπραγία, Hdt.7.49, 8.54, A.*Th.*224, S.*OC*1554, etc.: pl., E.*Ion* 566; also in codd. of Th.1.33, 3.39 (-πραγία Phot.): both forms in Arist., -πραγία *Pol.*1325a22, -πραξία *EN*1098b22. **2.** epith. of Artemis at Tyndaris, *IG*14.375. **II.** *good conduct*, X.*Mem.*3.9.14, Arist.*EN*1140b7.

⊛ **εὔπραξις**, εως, ἡ, poet. for εὐπραξία, A.*Ag.*255 (lyr.. sed scrib. divisim).

**εὐπρᾶτος**, ον, gloss on εὔωνος, Hsch.

**εὔπρεμνος**, ον, *with good stem*, δρῦς *AP*6.221.10 (Leon.); εὐπρέμνοις· εὐστελεχέσιν, Hsch.

**εὐπρέπ-εια**, ἡ, *goodly appearance, comeliness*, εὐπρεπείᾳ προέχειν Th.6.31; opp. ἀπρέπεια, Pl.*Phdr.*274b, al.; *majesty*, εὐ. τῆς δόξης Lxx *Je.*23.9, cf. *Ep.Jac.*1.11; *dignity*, *SIG*880.19 (Pizus, iii A.D.); ἐστεφάνωσε ἁ πόλις..-είας καὶ εὐνοίας ἕνεκα τᾶς ἐς τὰν πόλιν *IG*4.1418 (Epid., iv B.C.). **II.** *speciousness, plausibility*, εὐπρεπείᾳ λόγου Th. 3.11, 82; ἔχει..εὐπρέπειαν μᾶλλον ἢ ἀλήθειαν Pl.*Euthd.*305e; *pretext*, c. inf., Plu.*Pyrrh.*23. **-έω**, *to be seemly, acceptable*, Aq.*Pr.*2.10. **-ής**, ές, (πρέπω) *well-looking, comely*, of outward appearance, σχῆμα -έστατον Hdt.1.60, cf. 2.37; [κόσμος] εὐ. A.*Pers.*833; εὐ. ἰδεῖν *fair* to look on, Ar.*Th.*192, X.*Mem.*2.1.22; εἶδος -εστάτη E.*Hec.*269 (v.l. ἐκπρ-); τὴν ὄψιν D.40.27; κοσμοῦντες..οἰκοδομήμασιν -έστερα Pl.*Lg.*761c. **2.** *decent, seemly*, ἄνδρα δ' -έστερον (sc. ἐξελθεῖν ἐστι) A.*Ch.*664, etc.; οὐ γὰρ εὐ. λέγειν E.*Or.*1145; λόγος ἐμοὶ οὐκ -έστερος λέγεσθαι Hdt.2.47; νόσημα ῥηθῆναι οὐκ εὐ. Isoc.12.267; τελευτὴ -εστάτη a *most glorious* end, Th.2.44. **3.** *specious, plausible*, opp. ἀληθής, E.*Tr.*951; σκῆψις -εστάτη Hdt.3.72; εὐ. αἰτία Th.6.76; εὐ. δειλία cowardice *veiled under a fine name*, Id.3.82; μετ' ὀνόματος εὐ. ibid.; ἀπάτη εὐπρεπεῖ Id.4.86; ἐκ τοῦ εὐ. *in pretence*, Id.7.57; τὸ εὐ. τοῦ λόγου, = εὐπρέπεια II, Id.3.38, 44; εὐ. ἦν πρὸς τοὺς πλείους Id.8.66. **II.** Adv. -πῶς, Ion. -πέως, οὐκ ἔχειν -έως ἐκλιπεῖν τὴν τάξιν Hdt.7.220, cf. A.*Ag.*616, etc.; *with a good pretext*, Th.6.6: Comp. -πέστερον E.*Rh.*841; -πεστέρως *Gloss.*: Sup. -πέστατα Th.8.109. **-ίζω**, in Pass., *to be acceptable*, Aq.*Ps.*140(141).6.

**εὔπρεπτος**, ον, *conspicuous*, A.*Supp.*722.

**εὐπρηγίη**, v. εὐπραγία. **εὐπρηξίη**, Ion. for εὐπραξία.

**εὔπρηστος**, ον, (πρήθω) *well-blowing, strong-blowing*, εὔπρηστον ἀϋτμὴν ἐξανιεῖσαι, of bellows, Il.18.471.

**εὐπριστία**, ἡ, *the being skilfully sawn*, ξύλων Sch.Il.8.93.

**εὔπριστος**, ον, *easily sawn*, Thphr.*HP*5.6.3, f.l. for καπυρόν in Hp.*VC*19.

**εὐπρο-αίρετος**, ον, *having a good moral purpose*, Ptol.*Tetr.*158, Vett.Val.82.11, al. Adv. -τως, ζῶντες Artem.2.37. **-ιρον**, (πρῳρ- cod. extra ordinem)· εὐπρόσωπον, εὐκέφαλον, Hsch.; cf. προίρης. **-ορᾶτος**, ον, *easily foreseen*, *Gloss.*

**εὐπροσ-αγκάλιστος**, gloss on εὐάγκαλος, Hsch. **-δεκτος**, ον, *acceptable*, *Ep.Rom.*15.16, 31; τοῖς πολλοῖς Plu.2.801c; εὐχή, θυσία, Porph.*Marc.*24, Sch.Ar.*Pax* 1054; ὥσπερ οὐκ εὐ. (sc. ὄν) c. inf., Phld.*Rh.Supp.*p.78. **-δόκητος**, ον, *well-expected*, Iamb.*Protr.*20. **-εδρος**, ον, v.l. for εὐπάρεδρος (q. v.). **-ηγορία**, ἡ, *affability*, Isoc.1.20. **-ήγορος**, ον, *easy of address*, i.e. *affable, courteous*, ἐν -οισίν ἐστί τις χάρις; E.*Hipp.*95; εὐ. φρήν Id.*Alc.*775; γῆρας *Trag.Adesp.* 552, cf. Trag. in *Gött.Nachr.*1922.31; τῷ λόγῳ εὐ. Isoc.1.20; οὐκ εὐ. ἆται miseries that forbid *my being spoken to*, E.*HF*1284: Sup. -ώτατος J.*AJ*19.1.13. Adv. -ρως D.H.*Rh.*5.4. **-θετος**, ον, *easily assimilated*, τροφή Hp.*Alim.*49; of medicines, Gal.14.267. **-ῐτος**, ον, *easy of access*, of places, Str.12.3.11, Luc.*VH*2.44. **2.** of persons, *accessible, affable, agreeable*, Gal.*Anim.Pass.*8, Alex.Aphr. *in Top.* 531.21, Man.5.288, *Gp.*2.44.2. Adv. -τως Poll.5.139.

**εὐπρόσκοπος**, ον, *far-seeing, cautious*, τὸ τῶν ἠθῶν εὐκινητότερον καὶ πολυτροπώτερον καὶ -πώτερον Ptol.*Tetr.*173; cf. ἀπρόσκοπος (B. **II.** *easily taking offence*, ἀθύμῳ καὶ ἀσθενικῷ καὶ εὐπροσκόπῳ καὶ πρὸς πάντας δυσαρέστῳ ib.207; cf. ἀπρόσκοπος (A).

**εὐπροσ-όδευτος**, ον, *income-producing*, of flowers, *Gp.*10.1.3. **-οδος**, ον, of persons, *accessible*, πᾶσιν Th.6.57, X.*Ages.*9.2, Plu.*Publ.* 4. **2.** of places, *easily accessible*, in Sup., X.*HG*6.5.24, *An.*5.4.30; ἔνθα ᾤετο εἶναι -ώτατον ὅσα δεῖ προσκομίζεσθαι *the readiest way of approach* for.., Id.*Cyr.*6.1.23, cf. Aen.Tact.22.15. **II.** Act., *approaching easily, manageable*, νῆες Ph.*Bel.*104.16. **-οιστος**, ον, *easy of approach*: generally, *easy*, ἔκβασις E.*Med.*279. **-όμῑλος**, ον, *pleasant, nice to deal with*, dist. fr. εὐόμιλος, Phryn.*PS* p.68 B. (= *Com.Adesp.*1015): Sup. -ότατος Suid. **-όρμιστος**, ον, *easy to land on*, νῆσος D.S.5.13, cf. Poll.1.100. **-ρητος**, ον, = εὐπροσήγορος, condemned by Id.5.138. **-φθέγκτοις**· εὐήχοις, Hsch. **-φορος**, ον, *easily uttering, fluent*, ἐν τῇ Ῥωμαίων φωνῇ Hdn.8.3.7. **II.** *easily assimilated, nutritious*, of food, Xenocr.9. **-φῠτος**, ον, *easily growing to*, τῷ ὁμοίῳ τὸ ὅμοιον Thphr.*CP*1.6.2.

**εὐπροσωπ-έω**, *make a good show*, *PTeb.*19.12 (ii B.C.), *Ep.Gal.*6.12. ⊛ **-ία**, ἡ, *fair appearance*, D.H.3.11. **-ίζομαι**, Pass., = εὐπροσωπέω, Al.*Ps.*140(141).6.

**εὐπροσωποκοίτης**, ὁ, *lying so as to present a fair face*, τύχαι εὐ. (metaph. from the dice), A.*Ch.*969 Franz (lyr.).

⊛ **εὐπρόσωπος**, ον, *fair of face*, Cratin.304, Anaxandr.9.5; μειράκιον Ar.*Pl.*976, cf. *Ra.*412 (lyr.), X.*Mem.*1.3.10 (Sup.); *with glad countenance*, S.*Aj.*1009; comice, λοπάς Eub.44.1. **2.** metaph., *fair in outward show, specious*, ὑπεκρίναντο..εὐπρόσωπα Hdt.7.168; οὐκ εὐ. φροιμίοις E.*Ph.*1336; λόγους εὐ. καὶ μύθους D.18.149; εὐ. ἡ τοιαύτη νομοθεσία Arist.*Pol.*1263b15: Comp., Aristid.1.429 J. Adv. -πως Philostr.*VS*1.18.4, Aristaenet.1.9, Jul.*Or.*7.224b. **3.** perh. *possessing legal personality*, Antig.ap.Plu.2.458f (with pun on signf. 1).

**εὐπροφάσιστος** [ᾰ], ον, *with good pretext, plausible*, αἰτία Th.6.105; ἀφορμαί Ptol.*Tetr.*2; -ιστον (sc. ἐστί) c. inf., App.*BC*3.76; εὐπροφάσιστα ἀδικεῖν Ph.2.496. Adv. -τως Ptol.*Tetr.*6, Vett.Val.286.14. **2.** *easily admitting of pretexts*, App.*Pun.*64.

**εὐπρόφορος**, ον, *easy to pronounce*, D.H.*Comp.*12. Adv. -ρως, dub. sens., *PMag.Leid.V.*8.26.

**εὐπροχώρητος**, ον, *progressing easily*, Ptol.*Tetr.*157.

**εὐπρυμν-ής**, ές, *well-steering, well-governing*, εὐπρυμνῆ φρενὸς χάριν A.*Supp.*989 (s. v.l.). **-ος**, ον, *with goodly stern* or *poop*, νῆες Il. 4.248, B.12.150, cf. Hp.*Ep.*14, E.*IT*1000, 1357; πλᾶται Id.*IA*723.

**εὔπρῳρος**, ον, *with goodly prow* or *head*, πλάτα E.*IA*765 (lyr.); cf. εὐπρωιρον.

**εὔπταιστος**, ον, *easily stumbling*: metaph., *unreliable*, of words as compared with facts, Hp.*Praec.*2.

**εὔπτερος**, ον, *well-winged, well-plumed*, of birds, S.*OT*175 (lyr.); αὐχένες, δέμας, E.*Ion* 1200, 1203; φαρέτρα v.l. in Bion 1.82 (Tricl.): metaph., εὐ. γυναῖκες *high-plumed* dames, Ar.*Nu.*800. **II.** εὔπτερον, τό, = ἀξίαντον, Ps.-Dsc.4.134; = τριχομανές, ib.135.

**εὐπτέρῠγος**, ον, = foreg. 1, Opp.*C.*3.125; of ships, *AP*10.6 (Satyr., dub. l.).

**εὐπτησία**, ἡ, *expertness in flying*, Artem.5.69, Max.Tyr.31.2.

**εὐπτόητος**, ον, *easily scared*, πρὸς ἅπαν Plu.2.642a, cf. Sch.A.*Th.*78.

**εὐπτόλεμος**, ον, poet. for εὐπόλεμος, *AP*4.3b.22 (Agath.); Ep. ἐϋπτ- Q.S.5.320.

**εὔπτορθος**, ον, *finely branching*, of horns, *APl.*4.96.4.

**εὐπῡγία**, ἡ, *fine shape in the hinder parts*, Alex.98.11.

**εὐπυγμέω**, *to be in vigorous health*, *PLond.*3.1244.7 (iv A.D.).

**εὔπῡγος**, ον, (πυγή) *well-shaped in the hinder parts*, Herm.ap.Stob. 1.49.45 (Comp.), Poll.2.184.

**εὐπυνδάκωτος** [ᾰ], ον, *well-bottomed*, of a cup, Luc.*Lex.*13.

**εὔπυργος**, ον, *well-towered*, of fortified towns, Τροίην εὔ. Il.7.71, cf. Hes.*Sc.*270, B.5.184, *AP*9.62 (Even.): poet. ἠΰπυργος prob. in Pi. *N.*4.12.

**εὔπῡρος**, ον, *fertile in corn*, Poll.9.162.

**εὐπῡροφόρος**, = foreg., Str.5.4.2 (s. v. l.).

**εὐπύρωτος**, ον, (πυρόω) *easily set fire to*, Thphr.*CP*1.22.5.

**εὐπώγων**, ωνος, ὁ, *well-bearded*, Arist.*Phgn.*808a23, *AP*9.99 (Leon.), 744 (Id.).

**εὔπωλος**, ον, *abounding in foals* or *horses*, in Hom. as epith. of Troy, Ἴλιον εἰς εὔ. Il.5.551, al.; αὔχημα εὔιππον, εὔπωλον the glory of noble steeds and *their offspring*, S.*OC*711 (lyr.).

**εὔπωνος** ὄμβρος· εὔποτος, Hsch.; cf. πώνω, γακουπώνης.

**εὐραί**, αἱ, f.l. for θύραι, Poll.1.146. II. **εὖραι**· αὖραι, Hsch.

**εὐρακύλων**, ωνος, ὁ, name of a north-east wind, = Lat. (Vulg.) *euroaquilo*, ἄνεμος τυφωνικὸς ὁ καλούμενος εὐ. *Act.Ap.*27.14, with many vv. ll., including εὐροκλύδων.

**εὐράξ**, Adv. *on one side, sideways*, στῆ δ' εὐ. σὺν δουρί Il.11.251, 15.541, cf. Lyc.920. II. εὐ. πατάξ, an exclamation in Ar.*Av.*1258, to frighten away birds.

**εὔραπτος**, ον, *well-sewn*, *Gloss.*: gloss on ἐϋρραφής, Sch.Od.2.354.

**εὐράχαντες**· ἥκοντες· ῥαχίας γὰρ ἐκάλουν τοὺς τραχεῖς καὶ παρήκοντας τόπους, *EM*395.21, Phot.

**εὔρειθρος**, ον, = ἐΰρρεής, Man.1.141.

**εὐρεῖος**, α, ον, (Εὖρος) *easterly*, A.*Supp.*871 (lyr.) cod. Med.

**εὐρείτης**, v. ἐϋρρείτης.

* **εὐρέκτης**, ου, ὁ, (ῥέζω) *beneficent*, *IGRom.*4.854 (Laodicea ad Lycum).

* **εὕρεμα**, ατος, τό, later form of εὕρημα, v.l. in Hp.*Vict.*1.2, *SIG* 1012.11 (Cos, ii/i B.C.), *PMag.Leid.W.*7.34, Str.16.2.24, *AP*7.411 (Diosc.), Babr.*Prooem.* ii 2.

**εὑρεσι-έπεια**, v. εὑρησι-. **-κάκος**, ον, *inventive of evil*, Sch.E.*Med.*407. **-λογέω, -λογία, -λογος**, v. εὑρησιλογέω, etc.

**εὑρέσιος** Ζεύς, ὁ, = *Jupiter Inventor*, D.H.1.39.

**εὕρεσις**, εως, ἡ, *a finding, discovery*, Pl.*R.*336e, *Cra.*436a; οὐχ εὕ. τοῦτ' ἔστιν, ἀλλ' ἀφαίρεσις Men.*Epit.*102. II. of writings, *invention, conception*, παρασκευήν, ἣν οἱ παλαιοὶ καλοῦσιν εὕρεσιν, opp. χρῆσις, D.H.*Dem.*51, cf. *Stoic.*2.96.

**εὑρεσίτεχνος** [ῐ], ον, *inventor of arts*, Orph.*H.*32.14.

**εὑρέσφι**· γυναιξίν, Hsch. (cf. ἔορ, ἔορες).

**εὑρετ-έος**, α, ον, *to be discovered, found out*, Th.3.45. **-ής**, οῦ, ὁ, *an inventor, discoverer*, Pl.*La.*186e, Isoc.2.17, *SIG*728*K*3 (Delph., i B.C.), etc.; cf. εὑρέτις. **-ικός**, ή, όν, *inventive, ingenious*, Pl.*Smp.*209a: Comp. in Id.*Plt.*286e, 287a; ἰατρός Gal.7.212: Comp., Procl. *in Alc.*p.177 C.; εὑρετικὸν εἶναί φασι τὴν ἐρημίαν Men.39: c. gen., λόγων D.H.*Lys.*15; also, *able to make discoveries from*.., οὗ ἔμαθεν Pl.*R.*455b, cf. Andronic.Rhod.p.578 M. II. *concerned with inquiry or discovery*, λόγος, opp. ἀποδεικτικός, Gal.4.650. **-ις** (parox.), ιδος, fem. of εὑρετής, S.*Fr.*101 (v.l. εὑρετής), Secund.*Sent.* 10 (v.l. εὑρετής); acc. εὑρέτιν D.S.1.25 (this form determines the accent; for the acc. of εὑρετίς would be εὑρετίδα). * **-ός**, ή, όν, *discoverable*, Hp.*Vict.*1.2; τὰ μὲν διδακτὰ μανθάνω, τὰ δ' εὑρετὰ ζητῶ S.*Fr.*843; εὑρετὰ ἀνθρώποις X.*Mem.*4.7.6.

**εὕρετρα**, τά, *reward given to finder* of lost property, Ulp. in *Dig.* 47.2.43.

* **εὑρέτρια**, ἡ, = εὑρέτις, D.S.5.67, *POxy.*1380.185 (ii A.D.).

**εὔρηκτος**, ον, *easy to break*, Aret.*CD*1.13, Orib.49.3.8.

* **εὕρημα**, ατος, τό, later εὕρεμα (q.v.), (εὑρίσκω) *invention, discovery, thing discovered not by chance but by thought*, Hp.*VM*4; ἀριθμῶν καὶ μέτρων εὑρήματα S.*Fr.*432; πολλῶν λόγων εὑρήμαθ' E.*Hec.*250, cf. Ar.*Nu.*561, Pl.*Tht.*150d, al.; τύμπανα, Ῥέας.. εὑ. E.*Ba.*59, cf. *HF*188; τὰ τῶν ἰατρῶν εὑ. D.26.26; opp. ὑπηρέτημα, Antipho 1.15. 2. c. gen., *invention for* or *against* a thing, *remedy*, τῆσδε συμφορᾶς E.*Hipp.*716. 3. *excuse*, εἰς συκοφαντίαν *POxy.*472.33 (ii A.D.). II. *that which is found unexpectedly*, i.e. much like Ἕρμαιον (q.v.), *piece of good luck, windfall*, Hdt.7.155; εὑ. εὕρηκε ib.10.δ', 8.109; εὑ... κάλλιστον εὕρηκ' E.*Heracl.*533; εὑ... οἷον ηὕρηκας τόδε Id.*Med.*716, cf. 553; εὑρήμασι πλούσιος ἐγένετο Hdt.7.190; εὑ. γίγνεται τόδε E.*El.*606; ἐκείνοις δὲ δυστυχοῦσι εὑ. εἶναι διακινδυνεῦσαι Th.5.46; εὑ. ἐδόκει εἶναι X.*An.*7.3.13, cf. Is.9.26, Herod.6.30, etc. 2. of a child, *foundling*, εὑ. δέξατ' ἐκ Νυμφᾶν S.*OT*1106 (lyr.), cf. E.*Ion*1349. III. (in form εὕρεμα) *sum realized* by a sale, *SIG*1012.11 (Cos, ii/i B.C.); cf. ἀφ-, ὑπερεύρεμα.

**εὑρημοσύνη**, ἡ, *fluency, eloquence*, Poll.2.128.

**εὑρήμων**, ον, gen. ονος, (ῥῆμα) *fluent, eloquent*, Poll.2.128, Hsch.

**εὐρήσει**· λοιδορήσει, Hsch.; cf. εὐρητοῖς.

**εὑρησῐ-επής**, ές, *inventive of* ἔπη, *creative in poetry*, Pi.*O.*9.80; in bad sense, *coiner of phrases*, Ar.*Nu.*447 (anap.):—later **εὑρεσιέπεια**, glossed by εὑρεσιλογία, Suid.: pl., Hsch. **-λογέω**, *invent ingenious arguments, explanations*, or *pretexts*, Plb.26.1.2, al., Phld.*Rh.*1.207 S., Str.13.1.69, Ph.1.314, al., Plu.2.31e, Porph.*Antr.*36; ταῦτα Plu.2.625c. * **-λογία**, ἡ, *skill in finding arguments*, esp. *perverse* or *sophistical ingenuity*, Plb.18.46.3, D.S.1.37, Ph.1.628, 698, Plu.2.1033b, Arr.*Epict.*2.20.35: pl., Plb.12.26ᶜ.4, 29.1.2: -ίαν ἔχειν, of a phenomenon, admit of *an ingenious explanation*, Str.17.1.34. **-λογος**, ον, *ingenious in argument, sophistical*, Corn.*ND*31: Sup., D.L.4.37.—εὑρησι- is freq. in Pap. in this group of words, e.g. *PRein.*14.23, 15.21 (ii B.C.), Phld.*Rh.*1.207 S., etc.; εὑρεσι- first in Pap. of iv A.D., *POxy.*71 i 9 (corr. fr. εὑρησι-), *PMasp.*153.32 (vi A.D.), etc., f.l. in Plb.18.46.3, Ph. ll. cc. (εὑρησ- v.l. 1.628), etc.

**εὕρησις**, εως, ἡ, worse form of εὕρεσις, Apollod.3.3.1.

**εὐρητοῖς**· τοῖς ἀτιμήμασιν, Hsch.; cf. εὐρήσει.

**εὔρητος**, ον, (ῥηθῆναι) *easy to tell*, Ael.*NA*17.23.

**εὑρήτωρ**, ορος, ὁ, = εὑρετής, v.l. for εἰδήμονα, *AP*9.505.4.

**εὔριζος**, Ep. ἐΰρρ-, ον, *well-rooted*, Nic.*Fr.*74.17 codd. Ath. (dub. l.), cf. Lxx *Ps.*47(48).3.

**εὖριν**, late form of εὖρις (q.v.).

**εὔρῖνος** (A), Ep. ἐΰρρ-, ον, (ῥίς) = εὖρις, Babr.43.8, Opp.*C.*2.456, Ael.*NA*2.15, Heph.Astr.1.1 (admitted by *EM*765.53, Suid., in S.*Aj.* 8): Sup. in Hsch.

**εὔρῖνος** (B), Ep. ἐΰρρ-, ον, *of good leather*, A.R.3.1299, *AP*14.55.9.

**εὐρῑπῐδ-ἀριστοφᾰνίζω**, *write in the style of Euripides and Aristophanes*, Cratin.307. **-ειος**, α, ον, *of* or *like Euripides*, Εὐ. τι συμβήσεται Pl.*Tht.*154d; τὸ Εὐ. *the saying of Euripides*, Plu.*Pyrrh.* 14. II. τὸ Εὐ. (sc. μέτρον) an asynartete verse so called, Heph. 15.16. **-ης**, ου, ὁ, *Euripides*, n. pr. II. nickname given to the *cast 40* of the dice, from one Euripides who held office with the Forty at Athens, Diph.73.3, cf. Ath.6.247a, Poll.9.101. **-ικῶς**, Adv. *like Euripides*, Sch.Ar.*Eq.*18. **-ιον**, τό, *little Euripides*, term of endearment, Ar.*Ach.*404, 475.

**Εὐρῑπική** σχοῖνος, name of a kind of reed, Dsc.4.52, *Eup.*1.26, Plin.*HN*21.119.

**εὐρίπιστος** [ρῐ], ον, (ῥιπίζω) *easily fanned into flame*, Cic.*Att.*14.5.2. II. *unstable*, Alex.Aphr. *in Sens.*26.21, Hsch. s.v. γάγγαλος.

* **εὔρῑπος**, ὁ, *any strait* or *narrow sea, where the flux and reflux is violent*, X.*HG*1.6.22, Arist.*HA*544ᵃ21, 548ᵃ9, *Mu.*396ᵃ25; esp. *the strait which separates Euboea from Boeotia*, *h.Ap.*222, Hdt.5.77, etc., cf. Str.9.2.8: prov. of *an unstable, weak-minded* person (cf. Poll.6.121), πλείους τραπόμενος τροπὰς τοῦ Εὐρίπου Aeschin.3.90; μεταρρεῖ ὥσπερ Εὔριπος Arist.*EN*1167ᵇ7; ἄστατα καὶ ἀβέβαια Εὐρίπου τρόπον Hipparch.ap.Stob.4.44.81; Εὔριποι γενόμενοι Lib.*Ep.*907. II. generally, *canal, ditch*, etc., *SIG*799.7 (Cyzicus, i A.D.), Babr.120.2, *AP*14.135.2 (Metrod.), D.H.3.68. 2. the *Spina* in the Circus, Lyd.*Mens.*1.12. III. *ventilator, fan*, ἐξ εὐρίπου τινὸς αὔραν εἰσπνεῖν ἐπιτεχνώμενον Gal.10.649. (εὖ, ῥιπή, ῥιπίζω.)

**εὐρῑπώδης**, ες, *like a Euripus*, τόποι Arist.*GA*763ᵇ2. II. *living in such a place*, Id.*HA*621ᵇ23.

**εὖρῖς**, ινος, ὁ, ἡ, *with a good nose*, i.e. *keen-scented*, κυνὸς.. ὥς τις εὔρινος βάσις S.*Aj.*8 (v. εὔρινος), cf. Nic.*Fr.*98; of Cassandra, εὖρις.., κυνὸς δίκην A.*Ag.*1093; late Ep. dat. pl. ἐΰρρίνεσσι Opp.*C.*4.357.

* **εὑρίσκω**, impf. ηὕρισκον or εὑρ- S.*OT*68, etc.: fut. εὑρήσω *h.Merc.* 302, Th.7.67, etc.: aor. 2 εὗρον Il.1.498, etc., later ηὗρον or εὗρον E.*Med.*553, etc.; 3 pl. εὕροσαν Lxx *De.*31.17, *BGU*1201.16 (i A.D.); imper. εὑρέ Hdn.Gr.2.23; Ep. inf. εὑρέμεναι Od.12.393: later aor. 1 εὕρησα Man.5.137; εὗρα v.l. in *Ev.Luc.*8.35, *Act.Ap.*5.10, (ἐν-) *PGen.*3.19 (ii A.D.): pf. εὕρηκα S.*OT*546, etc., pf. imper. 2 sg. εὕρηκε Nausicr.1 D.:—Med., fut. εὑρήσομαι Hdt.9.6, Lys.13.9, etc.: aor. 2 εὑρόμην Hom., Att. ηὑρ- or εὑρ- A.*Pr.*269, Th.1.58, etc.: aor. 1 εὑράμην Hes.*Fr.*116.3 (testes omnes), Str.12.34.4, Iamb.*VP*35.255, *AP*9.29 (Antiphil.), Epigr.ap.Paus.6.20.14, *Ep.Hebr.*9.12, *IG*3.900 (ii A.D.):—Pass., fut. εὑρεθήσομαι S.*OT*108, E.*IA*1105, Isoc.9.41: aor. 1 ηὑρέθην or εὑρέθην S.*Aj.*1135, etc.: pf. ηὕρημαι or εὑρ- A.*Pers.*743 (troch.), etc.—Hom. has only aor. Act. and Med., exc. ἐϋ' εὑρίσκω (v.l. ἐφευρίσκω) Od.19.158. (Earlier Att. Inscrr. have ηὑρέθην, ηὕρημαι, as *IG*2².1636.32, al., *Epigr.Gr.*35 (iv B.C.): εὑρέθην *SIG*679.80 (Magn. Mae., ii B.C.): the augm. is seldom found in Papyri, ηὕρισκεν *PPetr.* 3 p.101 (iii B.C.); never in those of Men. or Phld.):—*find*, εὗρεν δ' εὐρύοπα Κρονίδην ἄτερ ἥμενον ἄλλων Il.1.498, etc.; εὕρημα εὑ., v. εὕρημα. 2. c. part., *find that*.., εὑρίσκε Λακεδαιμονίους.. προέχοντας Hdt.1.56, cf. 1.5:—and in Pass., ἢν εὑρεθῇς μὴ δίκαιος ὤν S.*Tr.*411, cf. *OT*839, *OC*946: with part. omitted, ὅταν τοὺς θεοὺς εὕρω κακούς (sc. ὄντας) Id.*Ph.*452; εὑρίσκει τοσαῦτα ἔτη (sc. ὄντα) Th.5.26; θῆλυς εὕρημαι (sc. ὤν) S.*Tr.*1075; ἄνους ηὑρέθη Id.*Aj.*763. 3. c. inf., εὑρίσκε πρῆγμά οἱ εἶναι.. *found* that the thing for him was.., Hdt.1.79:—Med., εὑρίσκεται (sed leg. εὑρίσκέ τε) ταῦτα καιριώτατα εἶναι ib.125:—Act., also, *find means, be able*, οὐχ εὑρίσκει χρήσασθαι Arr.*Epict.*2.12.2. 4. εὑ. ὅπως.. *to find* by what means.., Th.7.67:—Med., c. inf., *find out* or *discover how to*.., ηὕρετο.. παύειν E.*Med.*196 (anap.). 5. Pass., εὑρέθη ὅτι.. *it was found that*.., Lxx 1 *Es.*2.22(26). 6. *befall*, of evils, τινα ib.*Ge.*44.34, *De.*31.17. II. *find out, discover*, οὐδέ τι μῆχος εὑρέμεναι δυνάμεσθα Od.12.393; οὐδέ τι τέκμωρ εὑρέμεναι δύνασαι 4.374, cf. Il.7.31; εὑ. ὁδόν Pi.*P.*10.29; ἐξ ἀμηχάνων πόρον A.*Pr.*59; μηχανὴν σωτηρίας Id.*Th.*209; πημάτων ἄρηξιν S.*El.*875; τινα ἐμοῦ βελτίονα Ar.*Pl.*104, etc.: abs., εὕρηκα Archim.ap.Plu.2.1094c:—Med., εὕρετο τέκμωρ Il.16.472; ὄνομ' εὕρεο *think of* a name to give him, Od.19.403; εἴ τιν' ἑταίροισιν θανάτου λύσιν.. εὑροίμην 9.422. 2. c. inf., *get a chance of, be able*, ἵνα εὕρωμεν ἐπιστολὴν γράψαι *BGU*822.28 (ii/iii A.D.), cf. 17, 20, *PGrenf.*1.64.3 (vi A.D.), etc. III. *devise, invent*, ὀχήματα A.*Pr.*468, etc.; προφάσιν Antipho 5.65:—Med., τὰ δ' ἔργα τοὺς λόγους εὑρίσκεται deeds *make themselves* words, S.*El.*625. IV. *get, gain*, ἀρετάν, δόξαν, Pi.*O.*7.89, *P.*2.64; τὰ χρήματ' ἀνθρώποισιν εὑρίσκει φίλους S.*Fr.*88; ἐξ ὀλβίων ἄζηλον εὑροῦσαι βίον Id.*Tr.*284, cf. E.*Med.*1107 (anap.); δεινὰ δ' εὑροῦσαν πρὸς αὐθαίμων πάθη S.*OC*1078 (lyr.); ἀφ' ὧν ὄνασιν εὕρωσι Id.*El.*1061; μέγ' εὑρεῖν κέρδος ib.1305; εὑ. σωτηρίαν τῷ ἀνθρώπῳ Pl.*Prt.*321c; εὑ. μητρὶ φόνον *bring about* murder, E.*El.*650: abs., *acquire wealth*, Lxx *Le.*25.47:—Med., *find* or *get for oneself, bring on oneself*, οἷ.. αὐτῷ πρώτῳ κακὸν εὕρετο Od.21.304 (so in Act., μή πού τις ἐπίσπαστον κακὸν εὕρῃ 24.462); αὐτὸς ηὑρόμην πόνους A.*Pr.*269; μοῖραν ηὕρετ' ἀσφαλῆ Id.*Ag.*1588, cf. *Th.*880 (lyr.): so in pf. Pass., μέγα πένθος ηὕρηται S.*Aj.*615 (lyr.); εὑρήσεται τιμωρίην *will get for himself, obtain*, Hdt.3.148, cf. 9.26; ἀλεωρήν Id.9.6; κλέος Pi.*P.*3.111; ἄδειαν εὑρόμενος And.1.15; ἀτέλειαν D.20.1; εὑρίσκεσθαι ὠφελίαν ἀπό τινος Th.1.31; τι παρά τινος *IG*1².108.47, Lys.13.9; εὑ. παρά τινος c. inf., *procure* from him that.., Hdt.9.28; δεηθέντες οὐκ ἐδύναντο εὑρέσθαι Lys.14.20. V. esp. of merchandise, etc., *fetch, earn* money, εὑροῦσα πολλὸν χρυσίον *having fetched* a large sum, Hdt.1.196; ηὗρε πλέον ἢ ἐνενήκοντα τάλαντα X.*HG*3.4.24, cf. *Vect.*4.40; οἰκία εὑρίσκουσα δισχιλίας (sc. δραχμάς) Is.8.35; ἐγδίδομεν.. τοὺς θριγκούς.. ὅτι ἂν εὕρωσιν for what they *will fetch*, *IG*7.3073.7 (Lebad.); ἐρωτᾶν τί εὑρίσκει what it *will fetch*, Thphr.*Char.*15.4. 2.

of the sum or bid which *secures* an article or contract, οἰκέτην.. ἀποδίδοται τοῦ εὑρόντος sells *for what he will fetch*, X.*Mem*.2.5.5; τοῦ ἤδη εὑρίσκοντος ἀπεδίδοτο Aeschin.1.96, cf. *SIG*966.37 (Attica, iv B.C.), 581.99 (Rhodes-Hierapytna, ii B.C.); ἐκτιθέτωσαν τὸ εὑρίσκον ἐφ' ἡμέρας δέκα the *highest* or *winning* bid, *PRev.Laws*48.16 (iii B.C.), cf. *UPZ*112 vi9 (iii B.C.); προσέβαλον αὐτῷ τοῦ εὑρίσκοντος ἀνὰ [x] ἱερεῖα [x] I have placed at his disposal [x] pigs at the *current price* of [x], *PCair.Zen*.161.5 (iii B.C.), cf. *UPZ*114(1).24 (ii B.C.).

* **εὐροέω,** (εὔροος) *flow well* or *abundantly*, Thphr.*CP*5.6.4. II. metaph., *go on well, be favourable*, ὅταν δ' ὁ δαίμων εὐροῇ A.*Pers*.601; τῶν πραγμάτων αὐτῷ εὐροούντων Plb.4.48.11; τῆς τύχης εὐροούσης D.S.2.45; of men, *to be prosperous*, Arr.*Epict*.1.1.22, 3.10.10. III. *to be fluent, speak successfully*, Plu.*Alex*.53.

**εὐροή,** ἡ, = εὔροια I, αἵματος Aret.*CA*2.3.

**εὐρόθιος,** ον, *rushing rapidly*, κεραυνοί Orph.*H*.19.7 (s.v.l.).

**εὔροια,** ἡ, *good flow, free passage*, ὑδάτων Pl.*Lg*.779c; τῶν φλεβῶν Arist.*Somn*.457ᵃ26. II. *flow of words, fluency*, εὔροιά σε εἴληφεν Pl.*Phdr*.238c; σὺν εὐροίᾳ σχεδιάσαι Philostr.*VS*1.8.4. III. *prosperous course*, Pl.*Lg*.784b; πραγμάτων Plb.2.44.2, etc.; *abundance*, τῶν πάντων Clearch.8. 2. εὔροια βίου *happy life*, Zeno *Stoic*.1.46, Cleanth.ib.126, Chrysipp.ib.3.4, al.

**εὐροίζητος,** ον, *loud-whizzing*, of an arrow, *APl*.4.104 (Phil.).

**εὐρο-κλύδων,** v. εὐρακύλων. **-νοτος,** ὁ and ἡ, *a wind between* Εὖρος *and* Νότος, *SSE*., Arist.*Mete*.363ᵇ22 (pl.), *Mu*.394ᵇ33, Agathem.2.7, *IG*14.1308, Gal.16.400.

**εὔροος,** Ep. **ἐΰρροος,** ον, contr. **εὔρους,** ουν, *fair-flowing*, Σκάμανδρος Il.7.329; ποταμός 21.130; Σπερχειός S.*Ph*.491; Εὐρώτας E.*Hec*.650 (lyr.); in Prose, *flowing well*, *IG*7.4255.17 (Oropus, iv B.C.), Pl.*Ti*.77d. II. Medic., of the body, *with the pores and passages open*, Hp.*Aph*.2.9; σῶμα Arist.*HA*581ᵇ19; τὰ ὑγρά, αἷμα, Aret.*SA*1.10, Gal.15.843: Comp. εὐροώτερος Hp.*Mul*.1.1; εὐρούστερος Gal.16.360. Adv. -ρόως, ῥυῆναι Aret.*CA*1.7. III. of words, etc., *fluent, glib*, στόματα v.l. in E.*Fr*.439; λέξις D.H.*Comp*.23; ποικιλία -ρωτέρα v.l. ib.19. IV. *prosperous, successful*, οἷς ἂν εὔ. ᾖ γένεσις Pl.*Lg*.740d; βίος Archyt.ap.Stob.2.31.120, M.Ant.2.5: Sup. -ρούστατος Max.Tyr. 27.8. Adv. -ρόως, βιώσεσθαι, διεξάγειν, Arr.*Epict*.1.4.27, 3.22.45; βιοῦν S.E.*M*.11.110; contr. εὔρως Poll.4.23.

* **εὔροπος,** ον, (ῥοπή) *easily inclining*, εὔ. ἅμμα an *easy-sliding* noose, *AP*9.543 (Phil.). Adv., οὐκ εὐρόπως εἶχεν it was not *easy*.., Antipho 5.76.

**Εὖρος,** ὁ, *the East wind* (later, as dist. fr. ἀπηλιώτης, *ESE*.), Il.2.145, Arist.*Mete*.363ᵇ21, *Mu*.394ᵇ20, *IG*14.1308, etc. (Connected with ἠώς by Gell.2.22.7, with αὔρα by Vitr.1.6.11. Possibly from εὔω, because *parching*.)

**εὖρος,** εος, τό, *breadth, width*, mostly abs., εὖρος *in breadth*, opp. μῆκος or ὕψος, Od.11.312, Hdt.1.93, 178, al.; ποταμὸς εὖρος πλέθρου X.*An*.1.4.4 (τὸ εὖρος πλέθρου ib.1.4.9); εἰς εὖρος E.*Cyc*.390; ἐν εὔρει A.*Th*.763 (lyr.).

**ἐΰρρᾰπις,** ιδος, ὁ, ἡ, *with beautiful staff*, Nonn.*D*.4.1.

**ἐΰρρᾰφής,** ές, (ῥάπτω) *well-stitched*, ἐϋρραφέεσσι δοροῖσι Od.2.354, 380; ἐϋρραφέος παρὰ μηροῦ D.P.940; γενύων σφίγκτωρ *AP*6.233 (Maec.).

**ἐϋρρεής,** ές, (ῥέω) *fair-flowing*, Hom. (only in Il.) always in Ep. gen. ἐϋρρεῖος (for -ρεέος) ποταμοῖο, Il.6.508, al.; εὐρεῖος Πείροιο Hes. *Fr*.74 (v.l. εὐρῆος codd. Str.).

**ἐϋρρείτης,** ου, ὁ, (ῥέω) = foreg., Σατνιόεντος ἐϋρρείταο Il.6.34; Αἴγυπτον ἐϋρρείτην Od.14.257; Σιμόεντι ἐπ' εὐρείτᾳ E.*Tr*.810 (lyr.); εὐρείτας οἶνος Philox.16: **ἐΰρρειτος,** η, ον, prob. in Orac.ap.Paus.5.7.3.

**ἐΰρρην,** Ep. for *εὔρην, *abounding in sheep*, A.R.1.49.

**ἐΰρρηνος,** ον, = foreg., A.R.3.1086. 2. *of a good sheep*, κόρση Orac. in *AP*14.149.

**ἐΰρρηχος,** ον, (ῥηχός) *very prickly*, παλίουρος Nic.*Th*.868.

**ἐΰρρῑν, ἐΰρροος,** Ep. for εὔριν, εὔροος.

**εὐρῠ-άγυιᾰ** [ᾰγ], fem. Adj. used only in nom. and acc., *with wide streets*, Τροίη Il.2.141, al.; Ἀθήνη Od.7.80; Μυκήνη Il.4.52; πτόλις εὐ. Od.15.384; χθὼν εὐρυάγυια, = εὐρυόδεια (q.v.), *h.Cer*.16; εὐ. δίκα, i.e. *public*, Terp.6. **-αίχμας,** Dor. gen. α, ὁ, *far-stretching with the spear, far-conquering*, στρατός Pi.*Fr*.173. **-ᾱλος,** ον, (ἅλως) *with wide threshing-floor, broad*, χῶρος Opp.*H*.1.62; νέφεα dub. in *AP*7.748 (Antip.Sid.):—in Nonn.*D*.4.409, etc. (cj. in 13.68), also **εὐρυάλως,** ωος. II. **Εὐρύαλος·** ὁ Ἀπόλλων, Hsch. * **-ᾱναξ,** ακτος, ὁ, *wide-ruling*, Ζεύς B.5.19:—fem. **-άνασσα,** ἡ, Call.*Cer*.122. **-βάλινδος,** epith. of Dionysus, Hsch. * **-βᾰτος,** ον, *wide-stepping*, Ζεύς Ar.*Fr*.184, with a play on II. 2. *spacious*, Q.S.2.283 (v.l. for ἠλίβ-), Nonn.*D*.28.79. II. pr. n. (later -της Alciphr.3.20, v.l. in Harp.), a proverbial cheat, Pl.*Prt*.327d, D.18.24, Aeschin.3.137; the betrayer of Croesus, Ephor.58 J., D.S.9.32:—hence **-βᾰτεύομαι,** *cheat like Eurybatus*, Diogenian.4.76, Suid. **-βίας,** Ion. and Ep. **-βίης** (Dor. gen. -βία prob. in B.10.52), ὁ, = εὐρυσθενής, Hes.*Th*.931, *h.Cer*.294, Pi.*O*.6.58, *Pae*.6.103, al., B.10.52, A.R.4.1552; φθόνος εὐ. B.15.31; εὐ. ταῦρος *Supp.Epigr*.2.518 (Rome, iv A.D.). **-βόας,** ου, ὁ, *far-shouting, loud-shouting*, Lib.*Decl*.43.74. **-γάστωρ,** ορος, ὁ, ἡ, *big-bellied*: metaph., of the sea, Orac.ap.Apollod.2.8.2. **-γένειος,** ον, *broad-chinned*, Opp.*C*.2.104; *broad-bearded*, Nonn.*D*.18.345. **-δαμηνός,** epith. of Zeus, *JHS*18.96. **-δίκεια,** τά, *festival of Eurydice* at Cassandrea, Polyaen.6.7.2. **-δίνης** [ῑ], Dor. **-νᾱς,** ὁ, *wide-eddying*, Ἀλφεός B.3.7, 5.38. **-εδής,** ές, *broad-seated, spacious*, -εδοῦς.. χθονός Simon.5.17 (v.l. -όδου); cf. εὐρυόδεια, εὐρώδης. **-ζῠγος,** ον, *broad-throned, wide-ruling* (cf. ὑψίζυγος), Ζεύς Pi.*Fr*.14. **-θέμειλος,** ον, *with broad foundations*, of Ἀιδης, *IG*14.1015 (-μιλος lapis); also (with v.l. -θέμεθλον) βρέτας Call.*Dian*.248.

**εὐρυθμ-ία,** ἡ, *rhythmical order* or *movement*, κατὰ ῥυθμὸν εὐρυθμίαν παραδιδόναι Pl.*R*.522a, cf. *Prt*.326b; αἱ περὶ τὴν λέξιν εὐ. *the measured cadences* of language, Isoc.5.27; ἡ κυκλικὴ εὐ. τῶν περιόδων D.H. *Pomp*.6.10. 2. *harmony* between the orator and his hearers, Plu.2.45e. 3. of persons, *gracefulness*, Pl.*R*.400d; ἡ δ' εὐ. τό τ' ἦθος Damox.3.7; εὐ. τῶν σωμάτων *graceful movement*, Plu.2.8c, cf. Quint.1.10.26, Luc.*Salt*.8. 4. εὐ. χειρέων *delicacy* of touch, in a surgeon, etc., Hp.*Decent*.8, cf. Plu.2.67e. **-ίζω,** *shape* (by massage), κρανίον Sor.1.102. **-ιστος,** ον, *easily shaped*, Gal.7.677. * **-ος,** ον, Ep. ἐΰρρ– Man.1.60:—*rhythmical*, μουσικὴ εὔ., distd. fr. εὐμελής, Arist.*Pol*.1341ᵇ26; λέξις Id.*Rh*.1409ᵃ21; opp. ἔνρυθμος, D.H.*Comp*.11, 25; εὔ. κρούματα Ar.*Th*.121 (lyr.); εὔ. πούς *moving in time, keeping time*, ib.985 (lyr.); προβήματα Id.*Pl*.759; μέλος Pl.*Lg*.655a; κίνησις ib.795e; σφυγμὸς εὔ. a *regular* pulse, Gal.19.409. Adv. -μως, καὶ μουσικῶς εἰπεῖν Isoc.13.16; φέρεσθαι Plu.2.45e. 2. of persons, *orderly, graceful*, Pl.*Prt*.326b (Comp.), *R*.413e, etc.; εὔ. βακτηρία '*the nice conduct of* a cane', Antiph.33.4. Adv. -μως *gracefully*, E.*Cyc*.563; πέμπειν εὐ. τὸν κότταβον Pl.Com.47. 3. *well-proportioned, well-fitted*, both of the armour and the body, X.*Mem*.3.10.10 (Comp.), 11; τὸν πόδα -ότερον τοῦ ὑποδήματος Thphr.*Char*.2.7; εὔ. ὀρνίθιον Arist.*HA*592ᵇ24; φύλλα Thphr.*HP*3.18.7 (Comp.), cf. 12.9. 4. of surgical operations, in Adv., *neatly*, Hp.*Off*.4.

* **εὐρυθμο-κάρηνος** [ᾰ], ον, *broad-headed*, σιγύνη Opp.*C*.1.152; Πίθος Nonn.*D*.20.127. * **-κερως,** ωτος, ὁ, ἡ, *with spreading horns*, of deer and oxen, Opp.*C*.2.293, v.l. in Mosch.2.153.

**Εὐρυκλῆς,** έους, ὁ, name of a famous ventriloquist: hence as appellat., *ventriloquist*, Ar.*V*.1019, Pl.*Sph*.252c (cf. Sch. ad loc.), Plu.2.414e.

**Εὐρυκλύδων,** ωνος, ὁ, = Τυφῶν, *EM*772.31; cf. Εὐρακύλων.

**εὐρυκόας·** μεγαλόνους, μέγα ἰσχύων, εὐήκοος, κτλ., Hsch.

**εὐρῠ-κοίλιος,** ον, *hollow*, of the right ventricle of the heart, Hp. *Cord*.4; *with wide cavity*, of the caecum, Ruf.ap.Orib.7.26.25. **-κολπος,** ον, = εὐρύστερνος, χθών Pi.*N*.7.33. * **-κόωσα,** (κοάω, = κοέω) epith. of night, variously expld. by Hsch. (-κόωσα perh. = -μέδουσα). 2. of the sea-goddess Ceto, Euph.112. **-κρείων,** οντος, ὁ, *wide-ruling*, Il.1.102, al., shd. be written divisim. **-λείμων,** ον, gen. ωνος, *with broad meadows*, Λιβύα Pi.*P*.9.55. **-μέδων,** οντος, ὁ, = εὐρυκρείων, of αἰθήρ, Emp.135.1; Ποσειδάν Pi.*O*.8.31; γόνον εὐ. Κρόνου, i.e. Chiron, Id.*P*.3.4:—in Hom. only as pr. n.; so also fem. **Εὐρυμέδουσα.** **-μενής,** ές, *broad and strong*, τεῖχος, Φᾶσις, Orph. *A*.987, 1052. **-μέτωπος,** ον, *broad-fronted*, of oxen, Il.10.292, al., Hes.*Th*.291, Strato Com.1.20.

**εὐρυμνάσαι·** ἐρευνῆσαι, Hsch., *EM*397.11.

**εὐρῠ-νεφής,** ές, *lord of spreading clouds*, Ζεύς B.15.17. **-νοος,** ον, *broad-minded*, ῥήτρη Diosc. in *PLit.Lond*.98 ii 1.

**εὐρυντέον,** *one must dilate*, τοὺς πόρους Antyll.ap.Orib.6.10.12.

**εὐρύνω,** (εὐρύς) *make wide* or *broad*, εὔρυναν ἀγῶνα *cleared* the arena (for dancing), Od.8.260; τὸ μέσον εὐ. *leave a wide space* in the middle, Hdt.4.52; εὐ. τοὺς μυκτῆρας *dilate* them, X.*Eq*.1.10; αὔλακας εὐ. Theoc.13.31; *widen* a wound, ὄνυξι App.*BC*2.99; στήθεα Opp.*C*.3.442:—Pass., *to be widened, become wider*, Ph.2.112, D.P.92, Luc. *Electr*.6; γῆς -ομένης ὑπὸ πνευμάτων καὶ ὑδάτων, of the formation of valleys, Ocell.3.4. 2. metaph., *extend*, ξενίου δαίμονος ἐργασίην *AP*7.698 (Christod.).

* **εὐρύ-νωτος** [ῠ], ον, *broad-backed*, φῶτες S.*Aj*.1251. **-όδειά,** ἡ, (ὁδός) fem. Adj. used only in gen., *with broad ways*, in Hom. always of the earth (as εὐρύπορος of the sea), χθονὸς εὐρυοδείης Il.16.635, Od.3.453, etc. II. epith. of Demeter at Scarpheia, Hsch. (Derived fr. ἕδος by *EM*396.24; cf. εὐρυεδής.)

**εὐρυοδίνης,** f.l. for ἀργυροδίνης in Orac.ap.Str.1.3.8, 12.2.4.

**εὐρύοδος,** ον, v. εὐρυεδής.

**εὐρύοπᾰ,** ὁ, Ep. epith. of Zeus, used as nom. in fifth foot, Od. 14.235, al., cf. Pi.*Pae*.6.134, 8.24; as voc. (only once in Hom.), εὐρύοπα Ζεῦ Il.16.241; εὐρύοπα Κρονίδης Orac.ap.Hdt.8.77, cf. *h.Hom*. 23.4; also as acc. (as if from nom. εὐρύοψ), εὐρύοπα Ζῆν Il.8.206, al.; εὗρεν δ' εὐρύοπα Κρονίδην I.498, cf. 24.98; Ζῆνα.. εὐρύοπα κρείοντα *h.Hom*.23.2; later, of a mortal, κῆρυξ εὐ. *BMus.Inscr*.902 (Halic., iii B.C.). [ᾰ by nature, freq. ᾱ by position.] (Derived by the Greeks from ὀπ–, ὄψομαι, *wide-eyed* (cf. ἥλιος εὐ. Orph.*L*.701) or from ὀπ– 'voice' (cf. ϝέπος, ὄψ (A), *vox*), *far-sounding*, i.e. *thundering* (cf. χορὸς εὐρύοπα κέλαδον φθεγγόμενος *Lyr.Adesp*.93, cf. Sch.Il.1.498): prob. cogn. with Skt. *urūcī* 'wide', epith. of Heaven-and-Earth, etc., fem. of *uru-vyác-* or **uru-ác-*.)

**εὐρῠ-πέδῑλος,** ον, *broad-sandalled*: *broad*, ὁπλή Opp.*C*.1.288. **-πεδος,** ον, *with broad surface, spacious*, γαῖα *Lyr.Adesp*.138.3, *AP*7.748 (Antip. Sid.). **-πορος,** ον, *with broad ways*, in Hom. always of the sea (as εὐρυόδεια of the earth), *where all may roam at will*, μέγα κῦμα θαλάσσης εὐρυπόροιο Il.15.381, cf. Od.4.432, 12.2, A. *Pers*.108. **-πρωκτία,** ἡ, *the character of a* εὐρύπρωκτος, Ar.*Ach*. 843, *V*.1070 (both lyr.), al. * **-πρωκτος,** ον, *wide-breeched*, i.e. *pathicus*, Id.*Ach*.716, *Nu*.1090: Comp., Eub.120.7.

**εὔρυπτος,** ον, (ῥύπτω) *easy to wash out*, Poll.1.44.

**εὐρῠ-πύλής,** ές, *with broad gates*, ἀν' εὐρυπυλὲς Ἄϊδος δῶ Il.23.74, cf. Od.11.571. **-ρέεθρος,** ον, *with broad channel, broad-flowing*, Il.21.141; cf. sq. **-ρέων,** ουσα, ον, *broad-flowing*, shd. be written divisim, Il.2.849, etc.

* **εὐρύς,** εὐρεῖα, εὐρύ, Ion. fem. εὐρέᾰ (not εὐρέη) Hdt.1.178, cf. Theoc.

7.78; Aeol. fem. εὔρηα Alc.*Supp.*12.5: gen. εὐρέος, είας, έος: acc. sg. εὐρύν, (in Hom.) sts. εὐρέα (v. infr.): gen. εὐρέος as fem., Asius 13, Opp.*C.*3.323: so nom. pl. εὐρέες *AP*9.413 (Antiphil.):—*wide, broad*, οὐρανὸν εὐρύν Il.3.364, al.; εὐρεῖα χθών 4.182, al.; εὐρέα πόντον 6.291; εὐρέα κόλπον 18.140, al.; εὐ. σχεδίη Od.5.163; ὦμοι Il.3.210, Od.18.68, al. (Comp. εὐρύτερος δ' ὤμοισιν ἰδὲ στέρνοισιν ἰδέσθαι Il.3.194); μετάφρενον 10.29; σάκος 11.527; τεῖχος 12.5; ὁδὸς εὐρυτέρη 23.427; εὐρὺν ἀγῶνα (v. ἀγών); κατά, ἀνά, μετὰ στρατὸν εὐρὺν Ἀχαιῶν, 1.229, 384, 478: freq. in Ep. and Lyr., rare in Trag. (exc. in lyr.); in iambic trimeters, E.*Fr.*921; ποιεῖν τὸν δῆμον εὐρὺν καὶ στενόν Ar.*Eq.*720; not common in Prose (never in Papyri), εὐ. τάφρος Hdt.1.178; κόθορνοι εὐρύτατοι *loose* boots, Id.6.125; οἰκίαι X.*An.*4.5.25; οὔτ' εὐρεῖα οὔτε στενὴ διαφυγή Pl.*Lg.*737a; φλέβες εὐρύτεραι, opp. λεπτότεραι, Diog.Apoll.6, cf. Pl.*Ti.*66d; πόροι Thphr.*CP*3.11.2; κατὰ στενότερα καὶ εὐρύτερα Pl.*Phd.*111d. 2. *far-reaching, far-spread*, κλέος εὐρύ Od.23.137; κληδών Simon.84.6; εὐ. ἐλπίδες Pl.*Epigr.*7. II. as Adv.: the neut. εὐρύ is used as positive, Pi.*O.*13.24; cf. εὐρυκρείων, εὐρυρέων: Comp. εὐρυτέρως, ἔχειν Ar.*Lys.*419. (Skt. *urú-* 'wide', Comp. *várīyān*.)

**εὐρῠ-σάκης** [ᾰ], ες, *with broad shield*: only as name of Ajax' son, S.*Aj.*575, Plu.*Sol.*10:—hence **Εὐρυσάκειον**, τό, his shrine, *IG*2².1232.22, Hyp.*Fr.*35. **-σθενής**, ές, *of far-extended might, mighty*, in Hom. always of Poseidon, Il.7.455, 8.201, Od.13.140; of Zeus, B.18.17; Apollo, Pi.*I.*2.18; Telamon, Id.*N.*3.36; Himera, Id.*O.*12.2; ἀρεταί, πλοῦτος, ib.4.12, *P.*5.1.

**εὐρυσμᾰτώδης**, ες, *like a dilatation*, βρογχοκήλη Paul.Aeg.6.38.

⊕ **εὐρύ-σορος** [ῠ], ον, *with wide bier* or *tomb*, σῆμα *AP*7.528 (Theodorid.). **-στερνος**, ον, *broad-breasted*, Γαῖ' εὐ. Hes.*Th.*117; οὐρανός *APl.*4.303, Orph.*L.*645; Ἀθάνα Theoc.18.36: later in Prose, Gal.4.629; of Poseidon, Corn.*ND*22. **-στήθης**, ες, = foreg., Arist.*HA*632b11. **-στιχαιός**, f.l. for Ἐρυσίχαιος, *EM*180.27. **-στομία**, ἡ, *broadness of pronunciation*, Eust.11.43. **-στομος**, ον, *wide-mouthed*, μῆτραι Hp.*Mul.*1.48, cf. X.*Eq.*10.10, Ath.10.453a. **-τενής**, ές, *wide-extended*, Nonn.*D.*21.328.

**εὐρύτης** [ῠ], ητος, ἡ, (εὐρύς) *width* or *breadth*, Hp.*Acut.*(*Sp.*)9. II. *broadness* of sound, Sch.Th.1.72.

**εὐρύτῑμος** [ῠ], ον, *honoured far and wide*, Ζεύς Pi.*O.*1.42.

**εὔρῠτος**, ον, (ῥέω) *full-flowing*, κρήνη E.*IA*420.

**εὐρύ-τρητος**, ον, *with wide holes*, ἠθμός Dsc.1.66. **-τρῦπος**, ον, (τρυπάω) = foreg., f.l. for εὐθύ- in Democr.ap.Thphr.*Sens.*73.

**Εὐρῠφάεσσα** [φᾰ], ης, ἡ, *Far-shining*, wife of Hyperion and mother of Helios, *h.Hom.*31.2, 4.

**εὐρῠ-φᾰρέτρης**, Dor. **-τρᾱς**, ὁ, *with wide quiver*, of Apollo, Pi.*P.*9.26: acc. sg. -φάρετρᾰν Id.*Pae.*6.111; εὐρυφάρετρ' Ἄπολλον Id.*Fr.*148. **-φλεβος**, ον, *with wide veins*, Gal.6.30. **-φυής**, ές, *broad-growing, broad-eared*, in reference to the manner in which the grains of barley (κρῖ) are set on the stalk, Od.4.604. **-φωνία**, ἡ, *broadness of sound*, Eust.39.42. **-φωνος**, ον, gloss on Τηλεβόαι, Id.1396.3. **-χᾰδής**, ές, (χανδάνω) *wide-gaping, wide-mouthed*, of cups, *AP*6.305 (Leon.), Luc.*Lex.*7. **-χαίτης**, Dor. **-τᾱς**, ὁ, *with wide-streaming hair*, of Dionysus, Pi.*I.*7(6).4. **-χανδής**, ές, = εὐρυχαδής, Eust.870.55. **-χᾰνής**, ές, = foreg., γαστήρ Opp.*H.*3.344; of a wounded man, Nonn.*D.*22.242. ⊕ **-χορος**, ον, *with broad places, spacious*, Μυκαλησσός, Λακεδαίμων, Il.2.498, Od.15.1, etc.; Ἑλλάς Il.9.478; πτόλις, of Troy, Sapph.*Supp.*20a.12; Ἀσία, Λιβύα, Pi.*O.*7.18, *P.*4.43; Ἄργος B.9.31; ἀγυιαί Pi.*P.*8.55, E.*Ba.*87 (lyr.), Orac.ap.D.21.52; οἶκος *AP*6.319 (Nicod.). (Prop. *with broad dancing-places*, cf. χορός; then a conventional epithet, perh. connected by poets with χῶρος.)

**εὐρῠχωρ-έω**, *enlarge*, Sm.*Ps.*17(18).37. **-ής**, ές, = εὐρύχωρος, Hp.*VM*22 (dub. l.), Paus.3.19.1: Comp. -έστερος Arist.*HA*508a28: Sup. -έστατος Id.*PA*668b16. **-ία**, Ion. -ίη, ἡ, *open space, free room*, ἐν τῇ λοιπῇ εὐ. τῆς θήκης Hdt.4.71; πολλὴν εὐ. ἔχειν D.19.272; εὐ. ποιεῖτε τῷ θεῷ *Carm.Pop.*7; -ίας σε δεῖ *Com.Adesp.*46 D.; ἡ ἄνω εὐ., of a dislocated joint, Hp.*Art.*11 (in later Medic., of bodily *orifices*, Sor.1.58 (pl.); ἡ ἀκουστικὴ εὐ., *meatus auditorius*, ib.10); ἐν εὐ. εἶναι to have *plenty of room*, Pl.*Tht.*194d: prov., ἕκητι Συλοσῶντος εὐρυχωρίη Heraclid.*Pol.*34, Zen.3.90: pl., Pl.*Lg.*804c (εὐρυχώρια, τά, codd.), Aen.Tact.1.9, 2.1. 2. *an open field* for battle, X.*Cyr.*4.1.18, *HG*7.4.24; ἐν εὐρυχωρίῃ ναυμαχέειν to fight *with plenty of sea-room*, Hdt.8.60.β', cf. Th.2.83, al. 3. metaph., *free space, room for doing* a thing, τῆς ἀποδείξεως Pl.*Min.*315d; εὐ. τινὸς διδόναι, παρέχειν, Plu.2.48f, 828d. **-ος**, ον, *roomy, wide*, Arist.*PA*675b27; πεδίον D.S.19.84; ναῦς Max.Tyr.1.3; τὰ εὐ. *wide spaces*, Aen.Tact.2.2, Ph.*Bel.*92.47.

**εὐρώγης**, ες, (ῥώξ) *of fine grapes*, πεντάς *AP*6.190 (Gaet.).

⊕ **εὐρώδης**, ες, poet. for εὐρύς, S.*Aj.*1190 (lyr., s.v.l.; εὐρυεδῆ cj. Musgr.).

**εὐρωεία**, ἡ, perh. = εὐρωΐα (q.v.), *Sammelb.*4324.7.

**εὐρώεις**, εσσα, εν, (εὐρώς) *mouldy, dank*, οἰκία.. εὐρώεντα, of the nether world, Il.20.65; εἰς Ἀΐδεω δόμον εὐρώεντα Od.10.512, 23.322, cf. Hes.*Op.*153; πείρατα, of Tartarus, Id.*Th.*739; εὐρώεντα κέλευθα Od.24.10; ὑπὸ ζόφῳ εὐρώεντι *h.Cer.*482; τάφον εὐρώεντα S.*Aj.*1167 (anap.); later, *dank, slimy*, ἰλύς, πηλός, Opp.*H.*1.781, 2.89. (Expld. as = εὐρέα or πλατέα, ἀναπεπταμένα (cf. εὐρύς) by Apollon.*Lex.*, Hsch., *EM* 397.57, and possibly so used in late Poets, κόλπος θαλάσσης Opp.*H.*5.3, βέρεθρον Nonn.*D.*26.107; of a monster's throat, ib.25.476.)

**εὐρωΐαν**· εὐεξίαν, ὑγίειαν, Hsch.; cf. εὐρωεία.

⊕ **Εὐρωπαῖος**, α, ον, *European*, ἔθνη D.H.1.2; Ion. **Εὐρωπήϊος**, η, ον, Hdt.7.73:—later **Εὐρώπειος**, η, ον, γαίη D.P.152:—fem. **Εὐρωπίς**, ίδος, St.Byz.

⊕ **Εὐρώπη**, ἡ, *Europa, Europe*, as a geog. name, first in *h.Ap.*251, Pi.*N.*4.70, A.*Fr.*191, Hdt.1.4, al. II. fem. pr. n. in Hes.*Th.*357, Hdt.1.2, etc.:—also **Εὐρώπεια**, ἡ, Mosch.2.15.

**Εὐρωπία**, ἡ, = Εὐρώπη I, S.*Fr.*39, E.*Fr.*381. II. *broad surface*, Ἀχελῴου κρανᾶν Pi.*Fr.*249b Schroeder.

**εὐρῶπις**· ἡ πατρίς, Hsch.

**εὐρωπός**, ή, όν, = εὐρύς, E.*IT*626, Opp.*H.*3.20, 4.526.

**εὐρώς**, ῶτος, ὁ, *mould, dank decay*, Thgn.452, Simon.4.4, B.*Fr.*3.8, E.*Ion* 1393, Pl.*Ti.*84b, Arist.*GA*784b10, Theoc.4.28, Call.*Fr.*313, Ph.2.461; εὐρὼς ψυχῆς Plu.2.48c; εὐρῶτι γήρως τὰς τρίχας βεβαμμένος *Com.Adesp.*53 D.

**εὐρωστ-έω**, *to be robust*, Poll.3.121, *POxy.*1493.8 (iii/iv A.D.), prob. in Gal.13.194; ἐὰν εὐρωστῇ σοι τὰ πράγματα Ph.2.403. II. *display moral strength*, πρὸς τὰς ἀλγηδόνας Phld.*Piet.*33b. **-ία**, ἡ, *stoutness, strength*, Arist.*Mir.*830a9, D.S.17.88, *PRyl.*235.8 (ii A.D.); τῆς ψυχῆς Plu.*Cat.Mi.*44; personified, Εὐ. *Ath.Mitt.*32.308 (Pergam.). **-ος**, ον, (ῥώννυμι) *stout, strong*, ἱππεῖς X.*HG*4.3.6, cf. Aen.Tact.1.7, *PCair.Zen.*56.1 (iii B.C.), etc.; στόμα Arist.*HA*617b3; εὔρωστος τὸ σῶμα X.*HG*6.1.6; τῷ σώματι Isoc.15.116 (Sup.); τὰς ψυχάς Arist.*Phgn.*810a25. Adv. -τως X.*Ages.*2.24; εὐ. τὸν βίον διάξετε Antiph.1 D.

**εὐρωστόψῡχος**, ον, *stout-hearted*, *Et.Gud.* s.v. Αἴθιοψ: perh. corrupted to εὐροστουχε (voc.) in *PMag.Par.*1.2231.

**Εὐρώτας**, α, ὁ, *Eurotas*, the chief river of Laconia. II. *pudenda muliebria*, with allusion to εὐρύς, *AP*5.59 (Rufin.).

**εὐρωτιάω**, (εὐρώς) *to be* or *become mouldy, decay*, Thphr.*CP*1.6.8, Luc.*Nec.*15, etc.; βίος εὐρωτιῶν the life of '*the great unwashed*', Ar.*Nu.*44.

⊕ **ἐΰς**, ὁ (v. εὖ), *good, brave, noble*, Ep. word freq. in nom., ἐῢς πάϊς Ἀγχίσαο Il.2.819, etc.; once in acc. ἐΰν 8.303; neut. always ἠΰ (v. ἠΰς) (εὖ only as Adv.): irreg. gen. sg. ἑῆος, παιδὸς ἑῆος 1.393; υἱέος ἑῆος 15.138, 24.422, 550; ἀνδρὸς ἑῆος 19.342; φιλότητι καὶ αἰδοῖ φωτὸς ἑῆος Od.14.505; always at end of verse (exc. in Od.15.450): freq. with v.l. ἑοῖο, as Il.18.71: irreg. gen. pl. ἐάων *good things, good fortune*, 24.528; θεοὶ δωτῆρες ἐάων Od.8.325; δῶτορ ἐάων ib. 335, *h.Hom.*18.12, 29.8, cf. Hes.*Th.*46, 111. ((1) ἑῆος: for this form Zenod. read ἑοῖο; but ἑῆος (= ἀγαθοῦ, Sch.Il.15.138) became, like ἐσθλός (v. ἐσθλός I.3) and φίλος, almost a possess. Pron. of 1st, 2nd, and 3rd pers., and may be retained. Some Gramm. wrongly took εηος to be a form of ἑός ('his') and conversely gave to ἑός ('his') the signf. 'good' (Anon.ap.A.D.*Synt.*156.1, *EM*307.33, 318.1): hence the erroneous forms ἑῆος, ἑάων (but ἐῢς rightly), *Lex. de Spir.* pp.194, 196, 198, freq. in codd. The reading ἑῆος (ἐῆος) is well attested only where a substituted ἑοῖο would have had to mean *my* or *thy*: where the reference is to the 3rd pers. we find υἱὸς ἑοῖο, πατρὸς ἑοῖο, παιδὸς ἑοῖο almost without v.l., Il.13.522, al. (v.l. ἑῆος Il.14.9, 18.71, 138). (2) The origin of the forms ἑῆος ἐάων and the variation ἐϋ- : ἠϋ- are obscure: ἐάων perh. had ϝ-, Il.24.528.)

**εὖσα**, Dor. fem. part. of εἰμί (*sum*), Theoc.2.76, (παρ-) 5.26; but **εὖσα**, aor. 1 of εὕω.

**εὐσᾰβέω**, = εὐσεβέω, *Schwyzer*418.15 (Elis).

**εὐσάλευτος** [ᾰ], ον, (σαλεύω) *easily shaken*, πράξεις Ph.1.96.

**εὔσᾰλος**, ον, *with a good roadstead*, ἐμπόριον *Peripl.M.Rubr.*24.

**εὔσαμα**· ἀναφώνημα βακχικόν, κτλ., Hsch. (fort. εὔασμα).

**εὔσανα**, τά, = ἐγκαύματα, Poll.6.91, Hsch.; also, = εὔστραι, Id.

**εὐσᾰνίδωτος** [ῐ], ον, (σανίς) gloss on εὔσελμος, Hsch. (-όντου cod.).

**εὐσαρκ-έω**, *to be fleshy*, Sch.Ar.*Pl.*561. **-ία**, ἡ, *fullness of flesh, good condition*, Hp.*Art.*53, Arist.*HA*493b22, Ph.1.666; coupled with κάλλος, Phld.*Mort.*29: pl., Antyll.ap.Stob.4.37.16; of fruit, Thphr.*CP*1.9.2. **-ος**, ον, (σάρξ) *fleshy, in good condition*, Hp.*Aph.*4.7, X.*Lac.*5.8, Arist.*HA*583a9, Phld.*Mort.*30, etc.; of meat, Amphis 16; opp. σαρκώδης on the one hand, and ἄσαρκος on the other, Gal.6.30. **-όω**, *make* εὔσαρκος, Id.10.998. **-ωσις**, εως, ἡ, = εὐσαρκία, Hp.*Acut.*(*Sp.*)29.

**εὔσβεστος**, ον, *easily quenched*, θερμασία ἔμφυτος Gal.17(2).548; ὑπεκκαύματα ἡδονῶν Ph.2.63.

⊕ **εὐσέβεια**, ἡ (cf. εὐσεβία), *reverence towards the gods* or *parents, piety* or *filial respect*, εὐ. εἰς θεοὺς καὶ γονέας Pl.*R.*615c, etc.; μιαίνων εὐσέβειαν Ἄρης A.*Th.*344 (lyr.); εὐ. Ζηνός *towards* him, S.*El.*1097 (lyr.); πρὸς εὐσέβειαν, = εὐσεβῶς, ib.464; εὐ. πρός, περὶ τοὺς θεούς, Pl.*Smp.*193d, Isoc.12.124, cf. 10.58; πρὸς ἀδελφόν D.C.48.5; ἡ πρὸς τὸ θεῖον εὐ. *Inscr.Prien.*117.63 (i B.C.), etc.; τὴν εὐ. τῶν πραχθέντων Antipho 3.2.12: pl., *acts of piety*, Arist.*Rh.Al.*1423b28. 2. *loyalty*, ἡ ὑμετέρα πρός με εὐ. *PLond.*3.1178.14 (Claudius); ἡ εἰς με εὔνοια καὶ εὐ. *SIG*814.2 (Nero). 3. = Lat. *Pietas*, App.*BC*2.104, Mitteis *Chr.*71.12 (v A.D.), Orph.*Fr.*159, etc. 4. *credit* or *character for piety*, εὐσέβειαν οἴσῃ S.*El.*968.

⊕ **Εὐσέβεια**, τά, games in honour of Antoninus Pius, at Puteoli, *IG* 3.129, 14.737.8, 7.49.23:—also **Εὐσέβειος** ἀγών *Annuario*6/7.447: **Εὐσέβειος**, ὁ (sc. μήν), month named after Antoninus Pius, *BGU* 741.51 (ii A.D.): **Εὐσεβείωνες**, οἱ (sc. θεοί), *patrons of* εὐσέβεια, *Supp. Epigr.*3.545.

⊕ **εὐσεβ-έω**, *live* or *act piously* or *reverently*, abs., Thgn.145, *Berl. Sitzb.*1927.8 (Locr., v B.C.), S.*Aj.*1350, etc.; εἴς τινα towards one, Id.*Ant.*731; περί τινα E.*Alc.*1148; περὶ θεούς Pl.*Smp.*193a; πρὸς τὸν θεόν Men.*Mon.*567; πρὸς θεοὺς *AP*10.107 (E.); εὐ. τὰ πρὸς θεοὺς S.*Ph.*1441; τὰ περὶ τοὺς θεοὺς Isoc.3.2; of outward acts of service, θύουσα καὶ εὐσεβοῦσα τοῖς θεοῖς *PRyl.*112(a).4 (iii A.D.); εὐ. θεούς *to reverence* them, A.*Ag.*338 (nisi leg. εὖ σέβειν); εὐσεβήσασαν τὴν θεόν *BCH*44.77 (Lagina):—Pass., εὐσεβεῖσθαι *to be reverenced*, Antipho

3.3.11, Ph.2.201; of a duty, *to be reverently discharged*, Pl.*Ax.* 364c. **-ημα**, ατος, τό, *deed of piety*, Demetr.*Eloc.*281. ⊛ **-ής**, ές (dat. pl. -σεβέοις *IG*5(1).1390.5 (Andania)), (σέβω) *pious, religious*, opp. δυσσεβής (q.v.), Thgn.1141, Hdt.2.141, Pi.*O.*3.41; τρόπος Ar.*Ra.* 457 (lyr.): not common in early Prose, Gorg.*Fr.*6 D., Pl.*Phlb.*39e; *dutiful*, esp. *discharging sacred duties*, πρός or ἔς τινα, A.*Supp.*340, E. *El.*253; ἀνὴρ εὐ. (v.l. εὐλαβής) κατὰ τὸν νόμον *Act.Ap.*22.12; εὐ. καὶ φοβούμενος τὸν θεόν ib.10.2: c. acc. modi, -εστέρα χεῖρα *more righteous* in act, A.*Ch.*141; εὐσεβεῖς κἀξ εὐσεβῶν βλαστόντας S.*El.*589; ὁ τῶν εὐσεβῶν χῶρος, of a place in the nether world, Pl.*Ax.*371c; ἐν εὐσεβέων (sc. χώρῳ) Call.*Ep.*12, cf. *Sammelb.*2048 (ii B.C.). b. Astrol., αἱ τῶν εὐσεβῶν μοῖραι *Cat.Cod.Astr.*8(4).227. 2. as epith. of Emperors, = *Pius*, *IGRom.*3.91 (iii A.D.), al., *PGrenf.*1.49.28 (iii A.D.), *PHamb.*1.13.2 (iii A.D.), etc.; esp. of Antoninus Pius, *IGRom.*3.1293, al. b. of taxes, etc., due to the Emperor, *BGU*917.15 (iv A.D.), etc. 3. metaph., of a piece of land, *dutiful*, i.e. *productive*, ἀγρὸν -έστερον γεωργεῖν οὐδ' ἕνα οἶμαι Men.*Georg.*35. II. of acts, things, etc., *holy, sacred*, ταὐτὰ μοὐστὶν εὐσεβῆ θεῶν πάρα A.*Ch.*122; εὐ. χρηστήριον E.*El.*1272; ἐν εὐσεβεῖ [ἐστι] c. inf., Id.*Hel.*1277; τὸ εὐ., = εὐσέβεια, S.*OC*1125, E.*Tr.*43; τὸ ὑμέτερον εὐ. Antipho 5.96; τοὐμὸν εὐ. E.*Hipp.*656; τι τῶν ἐν ἀνθρώποις εὐσεβῶν παραβαίνειν Philipp.ap. D.18.157. III. Adv. εὐσεβέως, Att. -βῶς, Pi.*O.*6.79, etc.; εὐσεβῶς ἔχει, for εὐσεβές ἐστι, S.*OT*1431, D.19.212: Comp. -έστερον X.*Mem.* 4.3.16: Sup. -έστατα Isoc.4.33. **-ία**, Ion. **-ίη**, ἡ, poet. for εὐσέβεια, Thgn.1142 codd., Pi.*O.*8.8, S.*Ant.*943 (lyr.), *OC*189 (lyr.); personified, Emp.4.5, Critias 6.22, *Epigr.Gr.*1055 (Syria), etc.

⊛ **εὔσειστος**, ον, *liable to earthquakes*, Str.10.1.9.

**εὐσέλᾱος**, ον, *bright-shining*, or **εὐσέλᾱνος** (Dor. for -σέληνος), ον, *moon-lit*, εὐσέλανον δῖον οἶκον *Lyr.Adesp.*79C (εὐσέλαον Διὸς οἶκον cj. Salm.): **εὐσέληνος**, ον, *of the bright moon*, φέγγος E.*Rh.* (spurious prologue).

⊛ **εὔσελμος**, Ep. **ἐΰσσελμος**, ον, (σέλμα) *well-benched* or *-decked*, Hom. always in Ep. form, νηός, νῆες, Il.2.170, Od.2.390, al., cf. Stes.32, E. *Rh.*97; cj. in Id.*IT*1383.

**εὔσεπτος**, ον, (σέβω) *reverent*, S.*OT*864 (lyr.).

**εὐσήκωτος**, ον, *well-poised*, κανών Bito 65.10.

**εὐσήμ-αντος**, ον, *easily remarked* or *observed*, Ptol.*Alm.*5.12 (Comp.). II. *easily designated*, *PMeyer* 20.46 (iii A.D.). **-είωτον**, *bene clavatum*, *Gloss.* **-ία**, ἡ, *good prognostic*, Hp.*Epid.*6.2.17 (-είη Gal.ad loc.). 2. *favourable omen*, Arist.*Ath.*44.4. 3. generally, *favourable sign*, *PMasp.*9ii 28 (vi A.D.). ⊛ **-ος**, Dor. **-σᾱμος**, ον, *of good signs* or *omens*, φάσμα ναυβάταις E.*IA*252 (lyr.), cf. Plu.*Caes.*43; ἱερά Philostr.*VA*8.7.12; [πῦρ] ib.1.31. II. *easily known by signs, conspicuous*, εὔσημον γὰρ οὐ μὲ λανθάνει [τὸ πλοῖον] A.*Supp.*714; καπνῷ δ' ἁλοῦσα.. εὐ. πόλις Id.*Ag.*818; σημεῖα Hp.*Mochl.*16; τόπος *Annuario* 4/5.225 (Rhodes, ii B.C.); ἴχνη Thphr.*CP*6.19.5 (Comp.); οὐκ εὔσημον, ὅθεν.. *not easy to distinguish*, ib.3.8.2; *legible, clear*, ὅπως -σαμοτέρα ὑπάρχῃ ἁ ἀναγραφά *SIG*1023.96 (Cos, iii/ii B.C.); εὐ. γράμματα *OGI*665.12 (Egypt, i A.D.); εὐ. προσαγόρευσις Men.381; of sound, *distinct*, βοαί S.*Ant.*1021; ἦχοι Phld.*Po.*2.16 (Sup.); *well-marked*, βραχίων Philostr.*Gym.*35; οὐλὴ εὔσημος *PPetr.*1 p.54 (iii B.C.). 2. *clear, intelligible*, λόγον εὐ. δοῦναι 1*Ep.Cor.*14.9; διδασκαλία Erot.*Prooem.*, Heliod.ap.Orib.48.20.7. 3. *evident*, τισι Phld.*Ir.* p.91 W., cf. Porph.*Abst.*3.5. 4. εὔσημα, τά, = Lat. *insignia*, f.l. for σύσσημα, D.S.36.2. 5. of garments, *with fine edging*, *BGU*1564. 11 (ii A.D.). II. Adv. **-μως** *clearly, distinctly*, ἔχειν Arist.*Mete.* 363ᵃ27; μεμνῆσθαι Str.10.2.23; προσανένεγκε *POxy.*1188.5 (i A.D.): Sup. -ότατα Plu.2.1022a. **-ων**, dub. in Heph.Astr.1.1.

**εὔσηπτος**, ον, (σήπω) *easily putrefying* or *decaying*, Arist.*GA*785ᵃ2, *Pr.*861ᵃ38, Dsc.2.160: Comp., Plu.2.912c.

**εὐσηψία**, ἡ, *readiness to decay*, Thphr.*HP*8.9.1.

**εὐσθέν-εια**, ἡ, *strength, firmness*, Democr.57 codd. (εὐθ- Dind.), Thphr.*CP*3.1.6, 2.1 (v.l. εὐθ-), Ph.2.548 (v.l. εὐθηνία); ἡ πρὸς τὴν πύρωσιν εὐ., of scents, Thphr.*Od.*19. **-έω**, *to be strong, healthy*, Hp.*Morb.Sacr.*10 (prob. l.), E.*Cyc.*2, Arist.*Pr.*862ᵃ11, 925ᵃ3 (v.l. εὐθενέω); f.l. for εὐθενεῖν, A.*Eu.*895; so prob. in D.C.53.8. **-ής**, Ep. **ἐϋσθ-**, ές, (σθένος) *stout*, εἶδος Il.Pers.6, cf. Ph.*Bel.*56.31, Q.S.14. 633; *strong, firm*, σίδηρος *APl.*4.323 (Mesom.): irreg. Sup. -ώτατος Ps.-Luc.*Philopatr.*28. Adv. -νῶς Gal.17(2).185, f.l. in Ph.1.264.

**εὐσίδηρος** [ῑ], ον, *well-ironed*, i.e. *bound with iron*, Sch.Hes.*Sc.*270.

**εὐσίπυος** [ῐ], ον, (σιπύα) *with full bread-basket*, *AP*6.288.10 (Leon.).

⊛ **εὐσῖτ-έω**, *to have a good appetite*, Hp.*Aph.*2.31; f.l. for συσσ-, Pyrgio 1; *to be well fed*, f.l. in Thphr.*HP*4.8.13. **-ία**, ἡ, *hearty appetite*, Aret.*SD*1.16. **-ος**, ον, *with good appetite*, Hp.*Coac.*124; εὐ. πολλῶν σιτίων Aret.*SD*1.16. 2. *easy to feed*, ζῷον Philostr.*VA* 1.41. 3. *well-provided with food*, κῶμαι ib.1.21. II. *producing a hearty appetite*, εὔσιτον οἱ πόνοι Ruf.ap.Orib.*inc.*6.33: Comp. and Sup., Id.ib.7.26.77, 5.11.3. III. = εὔκριθος (q.v.), Sch.Theoc.7.34.

**εὔσκαλμος**, ον, *well-tholed*, ναῦς prob. in *AP*7.215 (Anyte).

**εὐσκάνδιξ**, ῐκος, ὁ, ἡ, *abounding in chervil*, πρηών *AP*9.318 (Leon.).

**εὔσκαρθμος**, Ep. **ἐΰσκ-**, ον, (σκαίρω) *swift-springing, bounding*, ἵπποι Il.13.31; νῆες Q.S.14.10; Πάν *AP*6.32 (Agath.).

**εὐσκάριστος** [ᾰ], ον, (σκαρίζω) gloss on foreg., Sch.Il.13.31, *EM* 398.23.

**εὔσκᾰφος**, ον, (σκάπτω) *easy to dig*, Hsch. s.v. λάχεια.

**εὐσκέδαστος**, ον, (σκεδάζω) *easy to disperse*, Gal.10.842, al.

**εὐσκέπαστος**, ον, *well-covered, well-protected*, Th.5.71 (Sup.); τὸ εὐ. *good shelter*, D.C.49.30.

**εὐσκεπής**, ές, (σκέπας) = foreg., τῶν ἔξω πνευμάτων *from*.., Thphr. *Vent.*24; τοὺς εὐ. καὶ εὐηλίους [τόπους] *sheltered* and *sunny*, Id.*HP*4. 1.1, cf. *CP*1.13.11.

**εὔσκεπτος**, ον, *easy to examine*, σκέψις Pl.*Phlb.*65d.

**εὐσκευέω**, *to be well equipped*, S.*Aj.*823.

**εὔσκευος**, ον, *well-wrought*, δέμας, of a statue, dub. in *App.Anth.* 1.193 (Egypt).

**εὐσκί-αστος** [ῐ], ον, *well-shaded, shadowy*, S.*OC*1707 (lyr.). **-ος**, ον, (σκιά) = foreg., Ἀχέροντος ἀκτά Pi.*P.*11.21; ἐν εὐσκίοις δρόμοισιν Ἀκαδήμου θεοῦ Eup.32; οἰκία X.*Oec.*9.4; ἄλσος Theoc.7.8.

**εὐσκόπελος**, ον, *rocky*, Pisand.ap.St.Byz. s.v. Νιφάτης.

**εὔσκοπος**, Ep. **ἐΰσκ-**, ον, (σκοπέω) *keen-sighted, watchful*, ἐΰσκοπος Ἀργεϊφόντης Il.24.24, Od.7.137; of Artemis, 11.198 (cf. II); of Heracles, Theoc.25.143; of Pan, Orph.*H.*11.9; of men, *AP*11.112 (Nicarch.). 2. *far-seen*, of stars and light, Ar.*Ec.*2 (v.l.), A.R.4. 1716; of places, *commanding a wide view*, τὰ -ώτατα X.*Cyr.*6.3.2, cf. Arist.*HA*628ᵃ11 (nisi leg. εὐσκεπῆ), Plu.*Cat.Ma.*13. II. (σκοπός) *shooting well, of unerring aim* (as some explain Od.11.198), of Apollo, Orac.ap.Hdt.5.61; Βριτόμαρτις Call.*Dian.*190; τόξοις πρόσωθεν εὐσκόποις χειρουμένη A.*Ch.*694; εὐσκοπώτερα βάλλειν Hld.9.5. Adv. -πως, βάλλειν Ph.2.355: metaph., ἐξομοιοῦν Id.1.681; εὐ. ἔχειν τῶν ἀποκρίσεων Philostr.*VS*2.1.9.

**εὔσκυλτος**, *agilis, mobilis*, *Gloss.*

**εὐσκωμμοσύνη**, ἡ, *quickness in jesting* or *repartee*, Poll.5.161.

**εὐσκώμμων**, ον, gen. ονος, (σκῶμμα) *of ready wit*, esp. in *bantering* or *repartee*, Poll.5.161, Lib.*Decl.*15.25. Adv. -μόνως Poll.5.161.

**εὔσμαλον**· εὔχαρι, Hsch. **εὐσμερδής**· εὔρωστος, Id.; cf. σμερδαλέος.

**ἐΰσμηκτος**, ον, *well-cleaned*, σίδηρος Max.285.

**ἐΰσμηνος**, ον, *forming fine swarms*, μέλισσα Nonn.*D.*7.332.

**ἐϋσμῆριγξ**, ιγγος, ὁ, ἡ, *with beautiful tresses*, Ἠώς Nonn.*D.*11.388.

**εὐσμίλευτος** [ῑ], ον, *well chiselled*, Hsch. (εὐσμήλωτα cod.).

⊛ **εὔσοια**, ἡ, *happiness, prosperity*, S.*OC*390 (Sch.), *Fr.*122.

**εὔσοος**, ον, *safe and well, happy*, εὔσοα τέκνα Theoc.24.8: **εὔσως**, Bato 5.10 is corrupt; cf. εὔσους· ὁ διευτυχῶν, καὶ ἥρως ἐγχώριος, καὶ εὐκίνητος, εὔφορος (cf. σεύω), Hsch.

**εὐσότρου**· εὐδρόμου, Hsch. (leg. ἐϋσσώτρου).

**εὐσπάθητος** [ᾰ], ον, *closely woven*, Hsch. s.v. τρίμιτον: prob. l. for εὐσπάρτεος, Id. **εὐσπαλές** (-εύς cod.)· εὐτελές, Id. ⊛ **εὐσπάρτεος** ἱστός· οὗ μήτε ἀραιὸς μήτε πυκνὸς ὁ στήμων τυγχάνει, Id.

**εὐσπειρής**, ές, *well-coiled*, δράκων *AP*6.206 (Antip. Sid.):—also ⊛ **εὔσπειρος**, ον, *well-wreathed*, κόρυμβοι ib.219.3 (Antip.).

**εὐσπλαγχν-ία**, ἡ, *good heart, firmness*, E.*Rh.*192, *PMasp.*97 *D*69 (vi A.D.). **-ος**, ον, *with healthy bowels*, Hp.*Prorrh.*2.6. II. *compassionate*, Lxx *Prec.Man.*7, *Ep.Eph.*4.32, 1*Ep.Pet.*3.8, *PMag. Leid.V.*9.3, *PMasp.*20.11 (vi A.D.).

**εὔσπολον**· εὐείμονα, εὐσταλέα, Hsch.

**εὔσπορος**, Ep. **ἐΰσπ-**, ον, *well-sown*, γύαι Ar.*Av.*230 (lyr.); Αἴγυπτος *APl.*4.295. 2. *rich in seed*, ἀνθέμιον cj. in *AP*4.1.36 (Mel.). II. *favourable to seed*, of Hermes, dub. cj. in Herm.ap.Stob.1.5.14.

**ἐΰσσελμος**, **ἐΰσσωτρος**, Ep. for εὔσελμος, εὔσωτρος.

⊛ **εὐστάθ-εια** [ᾰ] (also **-ία** *IPE*1².91.11 (Olbia, ii/iii A.D.), poet. **-ίη** *AP*12.199 (Strat.)), ἡ, *stability, tranquillity*, coupled with εὐνομία, Ph. 1.248; κατὰ τὰς πόλεις ib.680; ὑπὲρ εὐσταθείας τῆς πόλεως *IPE*1².94. 11 (Olbia); τὴν Αἴγυπτον ἐν εὐ. διάγουσαν *OGI*669.4 (Egypt, i A.D.); εὐστάθειαν τῷ Βακχείῳ *SIG*1109.15 (ii A.D.). 2. esp. of *bodily health*, εὐ. σαρκός Epicur.*Fr.*8, 424, Olympic.ap.Gal.10.56. 3. of persons, εὐσταθίη ἡ ἐν ἑωυτῷ *self-possession*, Hp.*Decent.*12; *stedfastness, tranquillity*, Phld.*Mus.*p.33 K., Ph.1.231, al.; ἐν βουλαῖς Plu.2.342f, al.; τῆς ψυχῆς Ath.Med.ap.Orib.*inc.*21.20, cf. Ptol.*Tetr.*11; *steadiness*, ὁρμῶν *Stoic.*3.65. **-έω**, *to be steady, stable*, ὅταν πολῖται εὐσταθῶσι δαίμονες *are favourable*, E.*Rh.*317; εὐ. ταῖς διανοίαις D.H.6.51; εὐστάθει *rest in peace!* in an epitaph, *IG*14.1464; *to be calm, tranquil*, of the sea, Luc.*VH*1.30; οὐκ εὐ. οἱ ὄρνιθες Plu.2.281b. 2. *enjoy sound, stable health*, εὐ. καὶ ὑγιαίνειν Epicur.*Fr.*68, cf. 413, Sor.1.87, Herod. Med.ap.Orib.7.8.1. 3. of cities or countries, *enjoy tranquillity*, εὐσταθοῦσα βασιλεία *OGI*56.19 (Canopus, Ptol. III); τὴν πόλιν εὐ. *SIG* 708.37 (Istropolis, ii B.C.), cf. App.*Hisp.*9. **-ής**, ές, Ep. **ἐϋστ-**, as always in Hom., (ἵσταμαι) *well-based, well-built*, περὶ τοῖχον ἐϋσταθέος μεγάροιο Il.18.374, al.; ἐντὸς ἐϋσταθέος μεγάρου, ἐκτὸς ἐϋ. θαλάμου, Od. 20.258, 23.178. II. metaph., *steadfast, tranquil*, ψυχαί Democr. 191; ἀνήρ Plu.2.44a; οἱ -έστεροι Hdn.2.6.5; γνώμη Aret.*SA*1.10; -έστεροι γνώμῃ ib.2.3; περὶ τῆς εὐσταθοῦς τῶν θεῶν διαγωγῆς dub. in Phld.*D.*3 tit. 2. of the body, *sound, healthy*, σαρκὸς εὐσταθὲς κατάστημα Epicur.*Fr.*68, Metrod.*Fr.*5; of persons, *healthy, sound*, Ath. Med.ap.Orib.*inc.*7.1. 3. εὐ. νοῦσοι *easily cured, not serious*, Hp.*Aph.* 3.8; καῦσοι Id.*Epid.*1.1. 4. of weather, *steady, settled, calm*, θέρος ib. 3.15; Ζέφυρος A.R.4.821. 5. generally, *steady, quiet*, βίος Hierocl. p.53 A.; ἁρμονία D.H.*Dem.*36; in political sense, *firmly established*, μοναρχία Phld.*Hom.*p.31 O. III. Adv. -θῶς, ἔχειν Sor.1.40, cf. D.L.7.182, Asp.in *EN*115.3; στρατοπεδεῦσαι App.*Hisp.*25, al.: Sup. -έστατα Id.*BC*2.115; Aeol. -θέως *IG*12(2).243 (Mytilene).

**εὐσταθμ-ία**, ἡ, f.l. for εὐστομία, Orib.45.29.22. ⊛ **-ος**, ον, *accurately measured*, dub. in *PTeb.*5.85 (ii B.C.), v.l. in Lxx *Si.*26.18(23); *of full weight*, νομίσματα *Cod.Just.*10.27.2.6. Adv. -μως, ἴσον *precisely equal in weight*, Hp.*Mul.*1.1: Comp. -ώτερον *BKT*3 p.15.

**εὐστάλ-εια** [ᾰ], Ion. **-ίη**, ἡ, *simple arrangement*, Hp.*Art.*82. 2. *orderliness*, ἐπιθυμιῶν καὶ φόβων Phld.*Oec.*p.65 J. 3. of troops, *light equipment*, Plu.*Sert.*12. **-ής**, ές, (στέλλω) *well-equipped*, στόλος A. *Pers.*795; of troops, *light-armed*, εὐσταλεῖς τῇ ὁπλίσει Th.3.22; ἱππεὺς

-έστατος X.*Eq.*7.8, etc.; ὁπλισμὸς -έστερος D.H.7.59; τὸ εὐσταλὲς πρὸς πόλεμον, = εὐστάλεια, Hdn.3.8.5. 2. *convenient, neat,* Hp.*Fract.* 37 (Comp.), prob. in Id.*Mochl.*1; *convenient to handle, manageable,* σωμάτιον Id.*Superf.*7 (Comp.); πλοῦς οὔριός τε κεὐσταλής a fair and *easy* voyage, S.*Ph.*780. 3. *compact,* εὐ. τὸν ὄγκον Plu.*Mar.*34; σώματα Id.2.353a; εὐ. δίαιτα *light* diet, Philum.ap.Orib.45.29.8. 4. *correct in habit and manners, well-behaved,* κόσμιος καὶ εὐ. ἀνήρ Pl.*Men.* 90a, cf. Diod.Com.2.17; *orderly,* ἱερουργίαι Plu.*Sol.*12; in dress, *neat, trim,* Luc.*Tim.*54. II. Adv. -λῶς, Ion. -λέως, of dress, *well girt up,* Hp.*Off.*3, Opp.*C.*1.97; of light-armed troops, κούφως καὶ εὐ. ἐκτρέχειν Hdn.4.15.1. 2. of bandaging, *compactly,* Hp.*Off.*9 (Sup.), *Mochl.*1 codd. 3. *decently, in order,* ταφῆναι Phld.*Mort.*31.

**εὐστάφῠλος** [ᾰ], Ep. ἐϋστ-, ον, *rich in grapes,* epith. of Dionysus, *IG*7.3098 (Lebad.); εὐ. ἐνὶ Νάξῳ *PSI*7.845.16 (v/vi A.D.).

**εὔστᾰχυς,** υ, *rich in corn,* *AP*6.36 (Phil.): Ep. ἐΰστ- Orac.ap. Hld.2.26; σπόρος, γῆ, Ph.2.14, 21: metaph., *blooming, fruitful,* ἡλικίη *AP*7.589 (Agath.); τεκέων εὐ. ἀνθοσύνην ib.5.275 (Id.). 2. νάρδος εὐ. *with a fine spike,* Nic.*Th.*604.

**εὐστεγής,** ές, *well-covered,* Sch.Lyc.350.

**εὐστείλ(ε)ος,** ον, *with a good haft* or *handle,* Hsch.

❋ **ἐϋστείρη,** fem. Adj. *with good keel,* ἐϋστείρης.. νηός A.R.1.401.

❋ **εὔστεκτος,** ον, *guarded, self-controlled,* Call.*Iamb.*1.300.

**εὐστελέχης,** ες, quoted as compound of στέλεχος, Hdn.Gr.2.687.

**εὔστερνος,** ον, *broad-chested,* Man.4.96; δαμάλεις *Gp.*17.2.1: metaph., χοάνοισι, of the earth, Emp.96.1.

**εὐστέφᾰνος,** Ep. ἐϋστ-, ον, epith. of Artemis, Il.21.511; of Aphrodite, Od.8.267, al., Hes.*Th.*196, al.; of Demeter, *h.Cer.*224, Hes. *Op.*300; of a Nereid, Id.*Th.*255 (expld. by Sch. as *well-girdled,* = εὔζωνος). 2. εὐ. θεῶν θυσίαι *graced with beauteous garlands,* Ar. *Nu.*309 (lyr.); θυμέλαι *IG*5(1).734 (Sparta); λειμῶνες εὐ. *crowned with flowers,* Opp.*C.*1.462. II. of cities, *crowned, circled with walls and towers,* of Thebes, Il.19.99, Hes.*Sc.*80, *Th.*978; Mycenae, Od.2.120; εὐ. ἀγυιαί Pi.*P.*2.58; Κρότων D.P.369.

**εὐστεφής,** ές, (στέφος) = foreg., Orac.ap.Amm.Marc.31.1.5, Max. 529.

**εὐστήρικτος,** ον, *firm, fixed,* Sch.rec.A.*Th.*312.

**εὐστῐβής,** ές, (στείβω) *well-trodden,* αἰθυίαις λέπας *AP*6.23.

**εὔστικτος,** ον, *variegated,* Opp.*C.*1.336.

**εὔστιπτος,** Ep. ἐΰστ-, ον, *closely-woven* or *well-fulled,* φᾶρος A.R. 2.30.

**εὐστῐχία,** poet. -ίη, ἡ, in poetry, *good ordering of lines,* σχεδίου *IG*14.2012 *Cb*6.

**εὔστολος,** ον, = εὐσταλής I. 1, ναῦς S.*Ph.*516 (lyr.); ὁλκάς A.R.1. 603. 2. = εὐσταλής I. 4, Πλάτων Luc.*Epigr.*45 (acc. to Planudes).

**εὐστομᾰχ-έω,** *have a good appetite,* Phld.*Sign.*38. -ία, ἡ, *wholesomeness* of food, Hices.ap.Ath.7.298b, Aët.9.30, Paul Aeg.2. 49; f.l. for εὐστομία, Dsc.2.16. -ος, ον, *equable, tranquil.* Adv. εὐστομάχως, *ferre* Cic.*Att.*9.5.2; ἀπορέγχειν *AP*11.4 (Parmen.). II. *good for the stomach, wholesome,* Diocl.*Fr.*125, Dsc.1.117, Sor.1.94, Hices.ap.Ath.15.689c, Gal.6.593: Sup., lemma ad Ath.7.310a.

**εὐστομ-έω,** *to be* εὔστομος, *sing sweetly,* of the nightingale, S.*OC* 18, cf. Ael.*NA*1.20, Philostr.*VS*2.10.5; *speak finely,* Luc.*Trag.*181; *employ euphonious words,* Dam.*Pr.*81. 2. generally, = εὐφημέω, A.*Ch* 983(997), Ar.*Nu.*833. -ία, poet. -ίη, ἡ, *goodness of sound, euphony,* Pl.*Cra.*404d, D.H.*Comp.*7, etc.; *sweet singing,* Ael.*NA*17. 23; *beauty of language,* D.H.*Lys.*12, *Dem.*13, etc.; δάκρυσον νεότητα καὶ εὐ. *Syria* 5.337 (Sidon). II. *pleasantness to the mouth, goodness of taste,* Thphr.*CP*6.16.2, Dsc.2.16: pl., Plu.2.687d; f.l. for εὐστομαχία, Hices.ap.Ath.7.310f. III. *skill with the mouth,* of a flute-player, Philostr.*VA*5.21. -ος, ον, (στόμα) *with mouth of good size,* of dogs, X.*Cyn.*4.2; of horses, εὐ. τῷ χαλινῷ *well-bitted,* opp. ἄστομος, Plu.2.39a. 2. *with large mouth,* of cups, Luc.*Lex.* 7; of a harbour, Poll.1.100. 3. *easy to keep open,* of a vein, Aret. *CA*2.2. II. *speaking well, eloquent,* *AP*14.10.8 (Comp.), Ptol. *Tetr.*166; *making eloquent,* λάγυνος *AP*9.229 (Marc. Arg.). Adv. -μως *with clear utterance,* Ael.*NA*4.42: Sup. -ώτατα ib.13.18; *melodiously,* ib.1.43; ᾖδον Aristaenet.2.19. 2. like εὔφημος, *avoiding words of ill omen,* and so, *keeping silence,* περὶ μὲν τούτων.. μοι.. εὔστομα κείσθω on these things.. let me keep *a religious silence,* Hdt. 2.171, cf. Ael.*NA*14.28, Porph.*Abst.*2.36; εὔστομ' ἔχε *peace, be still!* S.*Ph.*201 (lyr.). III. *pleasant to the mouth, palatable,* Thphr.*HP* 2.6.10 (Comp.), 4.3.4, Sor.1.94, Dsc.1.110 (Comp.).

❋ **εὔστοργος,** ον, *contented*: Sup. -ότατος Suid. s.v. ἀπαθέστατα (misquoting M.Ant.1.9).

❋ **εὐστόρθυγξ,** Ep. ἐϋστ-, υγγος, ὁ, ἡ, *consisting of a fine branch,* κορύνα *AP*6.35 (Leon.); Πρίαπος ib.232 (Crin.).

❋ **εὐστόν** or **εὔστόν,** τό, (εὕω) *victim whose skin is singed,* *SIG*1037.5 (Milet., iv/iii B.C.).

**εὐστοχ-έω,** pf. inf. εὐστοχηκέναι D.S.2.31:—*hit the mark, succeed,* opp. ἁμαρτάνω, Plb.1.14.7, etc.: c. gen., εὐ. πάσης περιστάσεως, τῶν καιρῶν, τῆς ἐλπίδος, *to hit* them *exactly,* Id.2.45.5, 28.3.6, 32.3.10; τῆς εἰσβολῆς τοῦ λιμένος Str.17.1.6; περί τι Id.5.3.8: c. acc., θηρίον Apollod.1.7.4: abs., Plb.9.12.1; ἐν ἅπασιν J.*BJ*1.15.1; *guess aright,* Plu.2.617d:—Pass., impers., Antyll.ap.Orib.44.23.44; εὐστοχηθεῖσα χάρις blessing *seasonably granted,* J.*AJ*15.9.2. -ημα, ατος, τό, *lucky hit,* D.L.5.34. -ία, Ep. -ίη, ἡ, *skill in shooting at a mark, good aim,* ἐπὶ τόξων εὐστοχίᾳ γάνυται E.*IT*1239 (lyr.), cf. Call. *Dian.*217, Pancrat.*Oxy.*1085.8; χερὸς εὐ., periphr. for *a bow,* E.*Tr.* 812 (lyr.): in later Prose, D.S.5.18: pl., Id.3.25: metaph., εὐ. καιροῦ Plu.2.74d. II. metaph., *sagacity, shrewdness,* Arist.*EN*1142b2, Plb.18.33.7; χειρῶν εὐ., of artists, D.H.*Comp.*25, cf. *APl.*4.310 (Damocharis), etc.; εὐ. μνήμης Ph.*Fr.*11 H. ❋ -ος, ον, *well-aimed,* τῷδ' ἂν εὐστόχῳ πτερῷ (Elmsl. for πέτρῳ) E.*Hel.*76; ἀκόντιον X.*Eq.*12.13 (Sup.); πληγή Plb.6.25.9. II. *aiming well,* ὅσοι δὲ τόξοις χεῖρ' ἔχουσιν εὔ. E.*HF*195; λόγχαις..-ώτατοι Id.*Ph.*140, cf. *Fr.*321 (Comp.); εὔ. τὴν τοξικὴν Luc.*Nav.*33. Adv. -χως, βάλλειν X.*Cyr.*1.4.8; εὐστοχα βάλλειν, τοξεύειν, Parth.15.1, Luc.*Nigr.*36: Sup. -ώτατα D.C. 67.14. 2. metaph., *making good shots,* i.e. *guessing well, hitting the right nail on the head,* Arist.*Div.Somn.*464a33; *shrewd,* Id.*Rh.* 1412a12, Ephipp.14.1, cj. in Luc.*Epigr.*45; βουλευτήριον *Com.Adesp.* 201; εὔστοχόν τι ἔνεστι τοῖς κακοῖς Pl.*Lg.*950b; εὔ. ἐν ἀπαντήσεσιν *ready* at repartee, D.L.6.74. Adv. -χως Pl.*Lg.*792d, Arist.*PA*639a5, Phld.*Rh.*2.108 S. 3. *successful,* ἄγρη Opp.*H.*3.280; εὐχαί *AP*9. 158.8.

**εὔστρα** or **εὔστρα** (*EM*398.31), ἡ: (εὕω):—*place for singeing slaughtered swine,* Ar.*Eq.*1236 (pl.). II. *roasted barley,* from which ἄλφιτα were made, Paus.Gr.*Fr.*184, cf. *EM*90.31. 2. a kind of *pulse,* *PTeb.*9.14, 11.9 (ii B.C.).

**εὐστρᾰφής,** ές, (στρέφω) = sq., Ammon.*Diff.*p.54 V., Sch.Il.*Oxy.* 1086.111.

❋ **εὔστρεπτος,** Ep. ἐΰστρ-, ον, *well-twisted,* of leathern ropes, ἐϋστρέπτοισι βοεῦσι Od.2.426. II. *well-plied, nimble,* πόδες *AP*9. 533; πρόσωπον *turning hither and thither,* Nonn.*D.*3.180.

**ἐϋστρεφής,** ές, (στρέφω) *well-twisted,* of a bow-string, ἐϋστρεφέα νευρήν Il.15.463; of a lyre-string, ἐϋστρεφὲς ἔντερον οἰός Od.21.408; πεῖσμα ἐϋ. 10.167; ὅπλῳ ἐϋστρεφεῖ 14.346; ἐϋστρεφέεσσι λύγοισι 9.427; v. εὔστροφος. II. *shapely,* ὦμοι Simm.1.10 (s. v. l.).

❋ **εὐστροφάλιγξ** [ᾰ], ιγγος, ὁ, ἡ, *curly,* of hair, *AP*6.219.18 (Antip.).

**εὐστροφία,** ἡ, *suppleness, versatility,* ἔν τινι Chrysipp.*Stoic.*3.178, cf. Porph.*Abst.*3.23; τὸ μετ' εὐστροφίας ὀξὺ πρὸς τὰς ἀπαντήσεις Plu. 2.510f, cf. 975a, Lxx *Pr.*14.35.

**εὔστροφος,** Ep. ἐΰστρ-, ον, *well-twisted,* ἐϋστρόφῳ οἰὸς ἀώτῳ with *well-twisted* wool (i.e. a sling), Il.13.599, 716 (ἐϋστρεφεῖ Aristarch.). II. *easily turned, manageable,* νῆες E.*IA*293 (Sup., lyr.); *turning easily on a pivot,* Hero *Aut.*26.2: metaph., ζῷον, of man, Pl. *Criti.*109c; πρὸς τὰς ἀπαντήσεις εὐ. λόγος Plu.2.803f; τὸ εὐ. τοῦ φθέγματος Philostr.*VS*2.10.5. Adv. -φως, τέθριππον ἕλκων *APl.*4.385, cf. Alex.Trall.1.16.

❋ **εὔστρωτος,** Ep. ἐΰστρ-, ον, (στρώννυμι) *well spread with clothes,* λέχος *h.Ven.*157, cf. *h.Cer.*285, Nonn.*D.*18.164.

**εὔστῡλος,** ον, *with goodly pillars,* ναοί E.*IT*128 (lyr.). II. *with columns at the best distances,* Vitr.3.3.1.

❋ **εὐσύγ-κρῐτος,** ον, either *well-compounded, well-constituted,* or *discriminating,* Diog.Oen.1, 2. -κρυπτος, ον, *well-covered,* Hp.*Fract.* 4, Aret.*SD*1.8. -χώρητος, gloss on ἐπιεικτός, Sch.D Il.8.32.

**εὐσύϊνος,** = οἰσύ-, *IG*5(1).1390.23 (Andania, i B.C.).

**εὐσῡκοφάντητος,** ον, *exposed to calumny,* Plu.2.707f.

**εὐσύλληπτος,** ον, *easily taken* or *caught,* Horap.1.54 (Comp.). II. Act., *receptive,* τοῦ σπέρματος *Gp.*17.1 (Comp.): abs., *conceiving easily,* Gal.19.153, S.E.*M.*5.60, Ptol.*Tetr.*72; τὸ εὐ., of the earth, Corn. *ND*28.

**εὐσυλλόγιστος,** ον, *well-concluded, conclusive,* εὐσυλλογιστότερα.. τἀληθῆ Arist.*Rh.*1355a38. 2. *easily inferred,* ἔκ τινων πόσον.. Plb. 12.18.8, cf. 8.37.1.

**εὐσυμ-βίβαστος** [ῐ], ον, *probable, consistent,* Eust.247.29. -βίωτος [ῐ], ον, *easy to live with,* Vett.Val.42.19. -βλητος, old Att. εὐξ-, ον, = sq. I, τέρας Hdt.7.57; ἥδ' οὐκέτ' εὐξύμβλητος ἡ χρησμῳδία A.*Pr.*775. -βολος, old Att. εὐξ-, ον, *easy to divine* or *understand,* εὐξ. τόδ' ἐστὶ παντὶ δοξάσαι A.*Ch.*170, cf. D.C.40.17. II. *easy to deal with, honest, upright,* X.*Mem.*2.6.5; εὐξ. δίκαι suits *which afford easy arbitration,* A.*Supp.*701 (lyr.). Adv. εὐξυμβόλως Poll.5.139. 2. *readily contributing one's* συμβολή, Antipho Soph.74. III. *affording a good omen, auspicious,* πρός τι Plu.*Demetr.*12, cf. Ael.*NA*3.9, Hld.9.25. Adv. -λως Sch.Pi.*I.*6(5).67. -βουλος, ον, *giving good counsel,* Hdn.Gr.2.791, Tz.*H.*6.839. -μέτρως, Adv. *in suitable proportions,* Archig.ap.Orib.8.2.32. -περίφορος, ον, *easy to live with, accommodating,* D.L.7.13. -πλήρωτος, ον, *easily filled up, attained,* πέρας Epicur.*Ep.*3 p.65 U. -πτωτος, ον, *collapsing easily,* Anon.Lond.27.26. -φύτος, ον, *easily growing together,* Thphr.*CP*3.7.10.

**εὐσυν-άγωγος** [ᾰγ], ον, *easily collected together,* τόπος τοῖς πεμπομένοις εὐ. a place *convenient for collecting* imports, Arist.*Pol.*1331b 2. -άλλακτος, ον, *easy to deal with,* πρὸς ἀκρόασιν Plu.2.42f, cf. Ptol.*Tetr.*165, Vett.Val.116.32. Adv. -τως Lxx *Pr.*25.10. -αλλαξία, ἡ, *fair dealing,* *Stoic.*3.64, 67. -άντητος, ον, gloss on εὐάντητος, Sch.Opp.*H.*2.149. -άρμοστος, ον, *easily fitted together,* Arist.*GA*718a29. -δεξίαστος [ῐ], ον, *loyal to pledges given,* Ptol. *Tetr.*165. ❋ -δετος, ον, *readily combining,* τὰ φῶτα *Cat.Cod.Astr.*8 (4).119. -ειδησία, ἡ, *conscientiousness, integrity,* *PSI*5.452.26 (iv A.D.). ❋ -είδητος, ον, *with a good conscience,* M.Ant.6.30. II. *honest,* πρᾶγμα *Sammelb.*4426.12 (iii A.D.).

**εὐσυνεσία,** old Att. εὐξ-, ἡ, *shrewdness,* Critias *Fr.*73 D., Arist. *EN*1143a10.

**εὐσύνετος,** old Att. εὐξ-, ον, *quick of apprehension,* Arist.*EN*1143a 11; -ώτεροι εἰς ταῦτα ib.1181b11: c. gen., γνώμης θείας Porph. ad Il. p.324 S. Adv. -τως Suid. s. v. ἀστικῶς: Comp. -ώτερον Th.4. 18. II. *easily understood,* ξυνετοῖς E.*IT*1092 (lyr.); διανόημα Phld.*Po.*2.40; κέντροις εὐσυνέτοις Epigr.Astrol.*Oxy.*464.42 (iii A.D.).

**εὐσυν-ήγορος**, ον, *skilled in advocacy*, Hdn.Gr.2.791, al. **-θεσία**, ἡ, *good arrangement* of words, Eust.85.34. II. *observance of treaties*, Ph.2.267. **-θετέω**, *keep faith*, opp. ἀσυνθετέω, Chrysipp. *Stoic.*2.63, Plu.*Rom.*5; ἐν πᾶσι Plb.21.42.5, cf. *PTeb.*61(*a*).32 (ii B.C.); πρός τινα Procop.*Vand.*2.2. II. *grant*, τί τισι *PPetr.*2 p.22 (iii B.C.). ※ **-θετος**, ον, *easy to compound into a word*, λόγος Arist.*Rh.* 1406$^a$36. Adv. -τως *suitably*, ἐκλέγεσθαι Eust.2.22; prob. in *PLit. Lond.*170 (i A.D.). 2. *easy to put together* or *construct*, Ph.*Bel.*56. 34, Apollod.*Poliorc.*155.16. II. of persons, in act. sense, *constructive, inventive*, εἰς τὸ νοῆσαι Man.5.272. 2. *easy to deal with*, Ptol.*Tetr.*165. **-θεώρητος**, ον, *easy to observe*, Epicur.*Nat.*28. 9. ※ **-οπτος**, ον, *easily taken in at a glance, seen at once*, Isoc.15. 172, Aeschin.3.118, Thphr.*HP*1.9.5: μέγεθος Arist.*Po.*1451$^a$4; πλῆθος, χώρα, Id.*Pol.*1327$^a$1; τάφοι ἀλλήλοις εὐ. *within easy sight of* each other, ib.1274$^a$37; δύναμις εὐ. τοῖς ἐκ τῆς πόλεως Plb.5.24.6. II. metaph., *easily taken in by the mind*, of a poem, Arist.*Po.*1459$^a$33; λέγω δὲ περίοδον λέξιν ἔχουσαν.. μέγεθος εὐ. Id.*Rh.*1409$^b$1; of the facts of a case, ib.1414$^a$12, cf. *Pol.*1323$^b$7; of a falsity or error, *easily seen* or *detected*, Id.*Sens.*441$^a$10. Adv. -τως Id.*Mir.*838$^b$10. **-τακτος**, ον, *well-arranged*, τάξις Arr.*Tact.*16.10. 2. *with good syntax, easy*, ἑρμηνεία Eust.66.36. Adv. -τως Id.336.4. **-τέλεστος**, ον, *easily brought to a conclusion*, Vett.Val.212.17. **-τριπτος**, ον, *easily broken*, Plb.9.19.7.

**εὐσύστᾰτος**, ον, *of proper consistency*, Crito ap.Gal.13.884; ἔμβρυα εὐ. Antyll.ap.Orib.6.31.5 codd. (nisi leg. ἀσύστ-). II. *easy to make friends with*, Vett.Val.39.14.

**εὐσύστροφος**, ον, *alert*, opp. ἀσύστροφος, Olymp.*in Grg.*p.258 J.

**εὔσφαιρος**, ον, *fair and round*, of pearls, Tz.*H.*11.490; ζῷα ib.7. 726.

**εὔσφυκτος**, ον, (σφύζω) *with a good pulse*, Gal.9.802 (Comp.), Aret. *CA*2.4.

**εὐσφυξία**, ἡ, *goodness, healthiness of pulse*, Aret.*CA*1.4.

**εὔσφῠρος**, Ep. **ἔϋσφ-**, ον, *with beautiful ankles*, of women, Hes. *Sc.*16, *Th.*254, Theoc.28.13, etc.; πούς E.*Hel.*1570.

**εὔσχετος**, ον, (σχεῖν) *easily kept in its place*, Hp.*Off.*15.

**εὐσχημάτιστος** [ᾰ], ον, *well-formed*, Eust.1570.47.

**εὐσχημον-έω**, *to behave with decorum*, Pl.*Lg.*732c, Men.*Mon.*646, Phld.*Rh.*2.281 S., *PSI*5.541.5. **-ημα**, ατος, τό, *decorous act*, *Stoic.* 3.136. ※ **-ίζω**, *train, educate*, *GDI*1708.14 (Delph.).

※ **εὐσχημ-ος**, ον, = εὐσχήμων, *EM*398.19; ῥυθμοί v.l. in D.H.*Comp.* 17. Adv. -μως v.l. in E.*Hec.*569. **-οσύνη**, ἡ, *gracefulness, elegance*, Pl.*Smp.*196a, X.*Cyr.*5.1.5; *decorum*, Arist.*EN*1128$^a$25; *refinement*, Id.*Pol.*1329$^b$28; βίου, ῥημάτων, Pl.*R.*588a, *Lg.*627d (but also κίβδηλος εὐ. a spurious *respectability*, Id.*R.*366b). 2. of the body, 1*Ep.Cor.*12.23; ἡ τοῦ σώματος εὐ. *IGRom.*4.1029.35 (Astypalaea, i B.C.). II. *proper treatment, adequate maintenance*, *IG*9(1).189 (Tithora). ※ **-ων**, ον, gen. ονος, (σχῆμα) *elegant in figure, mien and bearing, graceful*, opp. ἀσχήμων, Pl.*R.*413e, al.; ἀλεκτρυών Cratin. 108; τὰ εὐ. ἡμῶν (sc. μόρια) 1*Ep.Cor.*12.24: Comp. -έστερος *more respectable*, Pl.*R.*554e: Sup. -έστατοι, πονεῖν ἵπποι X.*Eq.*11.12. 2. in bad sense, *with an outside show of goodness, specious in behaviour*, εἴς τινα E.*Med.*584. II. of things, *decent, becoming*, λόγοι Id.*Hipp.* 490, D.60.9; πρᾶγμα οὐδαμῶς εὔσχημον λέγειν Aeschin.3.162; λέγειν εὐσχήμονα Arist.*EN*1128$^a$7; τὸ εὔσχημον *decorum*, Pl.*R.*401c, *Lg.* 797b. Adv. -μόνως *with grace and dignity, like a gentleman*, Ar.*V.* 1210, X.*Cyr.*1.3.8, Arist.*EN*1101$^a$1; ζῆν Phld.*Herc.*1251.18: Comp. -έστερον, ἔχειν Pl.*Epin.*981a; τι φέρειν D.60.35: Sup. -έστατα *IG* 2$^2$.1034.11. 2. later also, *noble, honourable*, in rank (condemned by Phryn.309), *Ev.Marc.*15.43, *Act.Ap.*13.50, J.*Vit.*9, Vett.Val.66. 7, al.; ἡ εὐ. *the noble lady*, *PFlor.*16.20 (iii A.D.). b. title of a village magistrate, in pl., εὐ. κώμης *BGU*147 (ii/iii A.D.): sg., ἡ οἰκία τοῦ εὐ. *PRyl.*236.15 (iii A.D.).

**εὐσχῐδής**, Ep. **ἐϋσχ-**, ές, = sq., Opp.*C.*2.211; κάλαμοι *AP*6.68 (Jul. Aegypt.).

**εὔσχιστος**, ον, *easy to split*, Thphr.*HP*5.6.3, Dsc.5.127. 2. *well-split*, of a pen, *AP*6.227 (Crin.).

**εὐσχολ-έω**, *to have abundant leisure*, Phld.*Rh.*1.377 S., D.S. 10.7, M.Ant.11.18: c. inf., J.*AJ*5.2.5; εἴς τι Id.*BJ*3.7.29; τινος *for* a thing, Luc.*Am.*33; εἰ -εῖτε ἐπαινέσαι με Muson.*Fr.*48 p.130 H. **-ία**, ἡ, *leisure*, Aq., Thd.3*Ki.*6.17, Longus 3.13. **-ος**, ον, *unoccupied*, esp. *by war*, Plb.4.32.6; *leisured, leisurely*, ἀναχώρησις Phld.*Oec.*p.64 J.; εὐ. τὴν ψυχήν Hierocl.ap.Stob.4.22.24 (corr. Gaisf.): Comp. -ώτερος Teles p.47 H., M.Ant.4.24.

**εὐσωμᾰτ-έω**, *to be well-grown, to be strong and lusty*, E.*Andr.*765, Ar.*Nu.*799; ἀλεκτορίδες τὸν χειμῶνα οὐ πάνυ εὐσωματοῦσι Orib.1.3.5; of trees, εὐ. τοῖς μεγέθεσι Plu.2.641a. **-ία**, ἡ, *strength* or *good habit of body*, Poll.2.235. **-ος**, ον, *well-grown*, ibid. **-ώδης**, ες, = sq., Arist.*Pr.*869$^b$14 (Comp.).

**εὔσωμος**, ον, *sound in body*, *EM*105.46. **εὐσωπία**· ἡσυχία, Hsch.

**εὔσως**, ων, = εὔσοος (q. v.).

**εὔσωτρος**, Ep. **ἐΰσσ-**, ον, *with good felloes*, i.e. *with good wheels*, ἀπήνη Hes.*Sc.*273 (v.l. Il.24.578).

**εὐτᾰκής**, ές, (τήκω) *easy to soften by heat*, Luc.*Herm.*61.

**εὐτακτ-έω**, *to be orderly, behave well*, Th.8.1, X.*Mem.*4.4.1, etc.; of soldiers, *obey discipline*, ib.3.5.21; εὐ. πρὸς ἀρχήν *to be obedient* towards.., Plu.*Cam.*18; *to be continent*, Epict.*Ench.*29.2, D.L.4.42, *AP*5.39.7 (Nicarch.). II. Act., *pay regularly*, τοὺς φόρους *PHib.* 1.35.6 (iii B.C.), cf. *POxy.*1471.16 (i A.D.); τὰ ὀψώνια *PSI*4.350.2 (iii B.C.), etc.:—Pass., ὅπως οἱ μισθοὶ τοῖς παιδευταῖς εὐτακτέωνται *SIG* 672.10 (Delph., ii B.C.), cf. *BGU*1107.11. III. Pass., *to be reduced to order*, ὑπὸ τοῦ διανοητικοῦ ὡς ὑπό τινος ἰσότητος Nicom.*Ar.*1.23; -ουμένη ἀπόβασις, def. of εἱμαρμένη, *Theol.Ar.*60: c. acc. cogn., τὸν τοῦ νοῦ λόγον -ούμενος Iamb.*VP*15.66. **-ημα**, ατος, τό, *act of orderly behaviour*, *Stoic.*3.136. ※ **-ος**, ον, (τάσσω) *well-ordered, orderly*, πόλις Ar.*Av.*829; σιωπή Posidon.24 J.; βίος Men.*Mon.*298; εὐ. τὸν βίον, τὴν δίαιταν, Plu.2.749d, D.L.2.25; περὶ τὸν βίον Hp. *Medic.*1. 2. esp. of soldiers, etc., *orderly, well-disciplined*, Ar.*V.* 424, Th.2.89, *IG*7.1.7 (Megara, iv B.C.), etc.; πορεία Th.7.77: Comp., X.*An.*3.2.30; *well-behaved*, Epicur.*Fr.*217; name of a category of ἔφηβοι, *IGRom.*4.482 (Pergam., i B.C.); κατὰ χρόνους εὐτάκτους at *regular* intervals, Sor.1.19. II. Adv. -τως *in an orderly manner*, Hp.*Epid.*1.6, Epicur.*Fr.*127, etc.; *in order*, A.*Pers.*399, Ar.*Nu.*964; *regularly*, of payments, *PTeb.*5.55 (ii B.C.), *BGU*1147.12 (i B.C.): Comp. -ότερον D.45.77; -τέρως X.*Eq.Mag.*2.7.

**εὐτᾰμίευτος**, ον, *easily regulated* or *graduated*, Arist.*GA*787$^b$5, Hp. *Art.*33,38. 2. *easily stored*, i.e. *lasting*, of perfumes, Thphr.*Od.*13.

**εὐταξία**, ἡ, *good arrangement*, τῶν φλεβῶν, of a gem, *AP*9.695 (pl.); τῶν τῆς ψυχῆς μερῶν πρὸς ἄλληλα Pl.*Def.*411d; ψυχῆς πρὸς ἡδονάς ibid.e; *good condition*, ὅπλων καὶ ἵππων X.*Mem.*3.3.14. 2. *good order, discipline*, Th.6.72; *orderly behaviour*, Pl.*Alc.*1.122c, etc.; as a subject of competition, *SIG*1061.4 (Samos, ii B.C.), cf. *IG*2$^2$.417; in a state, *orderliness, order*, ἡ εὐνομία εὐταξία Arist.*Pol.*1326$^a$30, cf. 1321$^a$4; ὁ αἱρεθεὶς ἐπὶ τὴν εὐ. *IG*7.4254. 3. *moderation in diet*, Erasistr.ap.*Placit.*5.30.3. 4. *continence*, Gal.8.451. II. Stoic term, *practical judgement, tact*, *Stoic.*3.64, al.

**εὐτάρακτος** [τᾰρ], ον, *easily disturbed*, Plu.*Arat.*10.

※ **εὔταρσος**, ον, *delicate winged*, ἰξύς (of the grasshopper) *AP*7.213 (Arch.). 2. *of delicate ankles*, ἀστράγαλοι ib.6.254 (Myrin.).

※ **εὖτε**, Ep., Ion., and poet. Adv. (rare in Trag., never in Com. or Att. Prose): I. of Time, *when*, 1. with ind., of a definite occurrence in past time, εὖτέ μιν προὔπεμψεν *when* he sent him, Il.8. 367, cf. 11.735, 23.85, E.*Ion*888 (lyr.): with impf., ἤκουσας.. εὖτε ὁρμῶμεν Hdt.7.209, prob. in B.3.25: freq. with a corresp. Particle in apodosi, τῆμος δὴ Od.13.93; δὴ τότε γε 22.182; καὶ τότε δὴ ῥα 24. 147; τόφρα δέ 20.73; δέ Il.23.62, Od.17.359; δ' ἄρα 20.56: the clause with εὖτε may stand last, Il.5.396, 6.515, Pi.*O.*3.28. 2. with subj., εὖτ' ἄν (like ὅταν), a. referring to future time, οὔ τι δυνήσεαι χραισμεῖν, εὖτ' ἂν πολλοὶ πίπτωσι *when* many shall be falling, Il.1.242, cf. 2.34, A.*Pers.*230 (troch.). b. with pres. in apod., *whenever, so often as*, ἥμισυ ἀρετῆς ἀποαίνυται, εὖτ' ἄν μιν κατὰ δούλιον ἦμαρ ἕλῃσιν *whenever* it comes upon him, Od.17.323, cf. 320, Hdt.6. 27, A.*Ag.*12: in orat. obl. (for opt. after past tense), Pi.*O.*6.67: ἄν is sts. omitted, εὖτ' ἔρδωμεν *whenever* we offer, Od.7.202, cf. Hes.*Th.* 28, B.1.73, A.*Th.*338 (lyr.), A.R.2.801, *AP*14.45. 3. with opt., *whenever, as often as*, with impf. in apodosi, εὖτε μάχοιτο *whenever* he fought, Hes.*Sc.*164, cf. *h.Hom.*18.8, B.12.118, A.*Ag.*565, A.R.2. 471. II. causal, *since*, with aor. ind., S.*Aj.*716 (lyr.), *OC*84, *Ph.* 1098 (lyr.). III. Adv. of Comparison, for ἠΰτε, *as*, twice in Il., εὖτ' ὄρεος κορυφῇσι κτλ. 3.10; τῷ δ' εὖτε πτερὰ γίγνετ' 19.386 (so Aristarch., but with vv.ll. ὥστε, αὖτε): freq. in Q.S., 1.549, al.

**εὐτειχ-εος**, ον, (τεῖχος) *well-walled*, Τροίη Il.1.129, etc. **-ής**, ές, Pi.*O.*6.1, *N.*7.46, E.*Andr.*1009 (lyr.); prop. oxytone, cf. Hdn. Gr.2.37,687; but acc. εὐτείχεα (Id.2.99) Il.16.57. **-ητος**, ον, (τεῖχος) = εὐτείχεος, Φρυγίη *h.Ven.*112. **-ιστος**, ον, *well-fortified*, f.l. for ἀτ-, Plb.3.90.8. **-ος**, ον, = εὐτείχεος, Max.Tyr.27.3 (Sup.), A.D.*Synt.*187.11, al.

**εὐτέκμαρτος**· καλῶς τυπούμενος, Hsch.

※ **εὐτεκν-έω**, *to be happy in children*, E.*Fr.*520, *Stoic.*3.156, Plu.2. 278b. ※ **-ία**, poet. **-ίη**, ἡ, *blessing of children*, εὐτεκνίας κύρσαι E.*Ion* 470 (lyr.); εὐτεκνίᾳ δυστυχίαν.. καθελεῖν Id.*Supp.*66 (lyr.), cf. Arist. *Rh.*1361$^a$1, *EN*1099$^b$3, *Stoic.*3.24, *IG*9(1).979; εὐ. παίδων Epigr.ap. Plu.*Fr.*22.7; *fruitfulness*, *IG*14.1615. II. personified, Εὐτεκνεία (sic) *Syria*6.295 (Philippopolis). [-τεκ- in ll. cc. poet., and Theoc. 18.51.] **-ος**, ον, *blest with children*, Sup. -ωτάτη E.*Hec.*581, etc.; of Priam, ib.620 (Sup.); εὐ. βοῦς (i.e. Io) A.*Supp.*275; πατρίς E. *HF*1405; εὐ. χρησμοί oracles *that give promise of fair children*, Id.*Ion* 423; εὐ. ξυνωρίς a pair *of fair children*, Id.*Ph.*1618: Comp. -ότερος D.S.4.74: Sup. -ώτατος ll. cc. II. of animals, *kind to their young*, Arist.*HA*563$^b$6, 614$^b$33. **-όω**, *make people happy in their children*, εἰς τέκνα *Cat.Cod.Astr.*7.217.

※ **εὐτέλ-εια**, Ion. **εὐτελείη** or **εὐτελίη** (v. infr. II. 2), ἡ, *having little to pay, cheapness*, πρὸς εὐτελείην τῶν σιτίων to procure *cheapness* of .., Hdt.2.92; εἰς εὐτέλειαν *cheaply*, i.e. *vilely*, εἰς εὐ. χηνὶ συγγεγραμμένῳ Ar.*Av.*805; κρέα δὲ τίνος ἥδιστ' ἂν ἐσθίοις; Answ. εἰς εὐτέλειαν *the cheapest*, Antiph.20; μᾶζα πρὸς εὐτέλειαν ἐξωπλισμένη Id.226. 2. *meanness, shabbiness*, εὐσέβειαν καὶ οὐκ εὐ. ὑμῖν ἀνέγραψε Lys.30.21; εὐ. οἴκου καὶ ἀμορφία Luc.*Dom.*14. II. *thrift, economy*, ἐπ' εὐτελείᾳ *economically*, Ar.*Ra.*406 (lyr.); φιλοκαλοῦμεν μετ' εὐτελείας *without extravagance*, Th.2.40; ἐς εὐ. ξυντετμῆσθαι to be cut down *to an economical standard*, Id.8.86; ἐς εὐ. σωφρονίσαι ib.1: in pl., *economies*, ταῖς εὐτελείαις οἱ θεοὶ χαίρουσι Antiph.164.1. 2. Εὐτελίη personified, Εὐ., κλεινῆς ἔκγονε Σωφροσύνης Crates Theb. 12. ※ **-ής**, ές, (τέλος) *easily paid for, cheap*, Hdt.2.86 (Comp. and Sup.), Pl.*Cri.*45a, etc.; *slight, easy*, Id.*Lg.*649d; τὰ εὐ. ἐν χειρουργίᾳ *simple* methods of treatment, *BKT*3 p.24; εὐτελέστερα δὲ τὰ δεινά the danger would be *more cheaply met*, Th.8.46 codd. (dub.). Adv. -λῶς *at a cheap rate*, X.*Smp.*4.49; ἀγόρασον εὐ. Ephipp.15.1: Comp. -έστερον X.*Cyr.*8.3.46; -εστέρως *Gloss.*: Sup. -έστατα, σκευά-

σαι *IG*1².44.9; f.l. for εὐσταλέστατα, Hdn.2.11.1. 2. *mean, paltry, worthless*, of persons, σηματουργὸς δ' οὔ τις εὐ. ἄρ' ἦν A.*Th*.491; of character, Arist.*Pol*.1272ᵇ41; opp. σεμνότερος, Id.*Po*.1448ᵇ26 (Comp.); ὅστις -έστατος Eup.189; παιδισκάριον Men.338; ἀνόητος, εὐ. ὑπερβολῇ Id.615; so of things, εὐ. βίος *shabby*, Pl.*Lg*.806a; of land, *depreciated in value*, *PTeb*.61(*b*).30 (ii B.C.); -εστέρα ἄσκησις *paltry, requiring no exertion*, X.*Eq.Mag*.1.16; τἄλλα δὲ..-έστατα Pl.Com. 174.11, cf. Epin.1.4. II. *thrifty, frugal*, δίαιτα X.*Mem*.1.3.5; δεῖπνον Plu.2.150c (Comp.). **-ίζω**, *disparage*, ib.1073c, Luc. *Pr.Im*.13, *Anacreont*.27A.10; *make disreputable*, *Cat.Cod.Astr*.8(4). 205. **-ισμός**, ὁ, *disparagement*, Longin.11.2 (pl.). **-ιστής**, οῦ, ὁ, *disparager*, Phld.*Vit*.p.42 J.

**εὐτενής**, ές, = εὔτονος, cj. for εὐγενής in Thphr.*HP*5.1.7 and Plu. *Fr*.12.2. II. of stones, *squared*, *IG*2².1666 A 29, al., 7.4255.20.

**Εὐτέρπη**, ἡ, *the Well-pleasing*, name of a Muse, Hes.*Th*.77, etc.: Pythag. name for *eight*, *Theol.Ar*.55.

**εὐτερπής**, ές, *delightful, charming*, ἄνθος, φωνή, Pi.*O*.6.105, *AP*9. 364 (Nestor).

**εὔτευκτος**, ον, = εὔτυκτος, τάφος *Epigr.Gr*.238 (Smyrna).

**εὐτέχν-ητος**, ον, *skilfully wrought*, *AP*6.260 (Gemin.). **-ία**, ἡ, *skill in art*, Str.1.2.33, D.H.*Dem*.35, Luc.*Herm*.20, *APl*.4.142. 6. **-ος**, ον, *skilfully wrought*, ναυτικόν Hp.*Ep*.14. 2. *skilful*, of persons, σκυτοτόμοι *AP*6.206 (Antip. Sid.), cf. *Epigr.Gr*.979 (Philae, i B.C.). 3. Adv. -νως, = ἐπισταμένως, Sch.Opp.*H*.3.536.

**εὔτηκτος**, ον, *easily melted* or *dissolved*, Arist.*Pr*.865ᵇ1 (Comp.), *de An*.422ᵃ19, Lxx *Wi*.19.21, Man.6.524: hence **εὐτηξία**, ἡ, *fusibility*, Arist.*Mir*.834ᵃ7.

**εὐτῐθάσευτος** [ᾰ], ον, *easily tamed*, Str.15.1.43.

**εὐτῑμώρητος**, ον, *easily punished*, Ptol.*Tetr*.157.

**εὐτίνακτος** [ῐ], ον, *easily shaken*, Hsch. s. v. κροτητά.

⊛ **εὐτλήμων**, Dor. -τλάμων [ᾱ], ον, gen. ονος, *much-enduring, steadfast*, εὐτλήμονι δόξῃ A.*Pers*.28 (anap.).

**εὔτμητος**, Ep. **ἐΰτμ-**, ον, (τέμνω) *well-cut*, ἱμάντες Il.10.567, Theoc. 25.102; τελαμών Il.7.304. 2. *easily cut*, σώματα Aret.*CD*1.2.

**εὔτοιχος**, ον, *with good walls*, Man.4.151.

**εὐτοκ-έω**, *bring forth easily*, Hp.*Superf*.2, Cic.*Att*.10.18.1. 2. *to be prolific*, of trees or animals, Thphr.*CP*1.14.1, Ph.1.249, al.: metaph., ib.520:—Pass., *to be brought forth easily*, Corn.*ND*34. **-ία**, ἡ, *easy delivery*, Call.*Ep*.54, *AP*9.268 (Antip. Thess.), Sor.1.70, Plu. *Rom*.21; τρισσῇ εὐ. *three children happily born*, *AP*9.349 (Leon.). 2. *fertility*, γυναικῶν Ph.1.183; of crops, ib.301. **-ιος**, ον, *aiding in childbirth*, φάρμακον Aët.1.115. **-ος**, ον, *bringing forth easily*, Arist. *HA*576ᵃ22 (Comp.), 573ᵃ9 (Sup.), Chrysipp.*Stoic*.2.212 (Sup.). 2. = εὔτεκνος I (which is v.l.), Ph.1.274; *fertile*, Hp.*Nat.Mul*.16.

**εὐτολμ-έω**, *to be daring enough*, ἀδικεῖν D.C.55.16. **-ία**, ἡ, *courage, boldness*, E.*Med*.469, Arist.*Rh.Al*.1423ᵇ3, *VV*1250ᵇ5: pl., D.S.17.10, Ph.2.382. **-ος**, ον, *brave-spirited, courageous*, εὐ. ψυχῆς λῆμα Simon.140; ἀπ' εὐ. φρενός A.*Ag*.1302; of men, v.l. in X.*An*.1.7.4, etc.: Comp., Ph.2.122: Sup., ib.68, D.H.6.14, etc.: usu. in good sense, εὔ. εἶναι κρῖνε, τολμηρὸς δὲ μή Men.*Mon*.153, but iron., εὔ. ἰατρός Gal.15.913; κύνες Opp.*C*.3.383; εὔ. ἄκεα *heroic* remedies, Aret.*CD*1.2; so εὔτολμόν ἐστι c. inf., Id.*CA*2.1; τὸ εὔ. πρὸς τοὺς κινδύνους Andronic.Rhod.p.576 M. Adv. -μως Tyrt.15, A. *Ag*.1298, D.S.17.34: Comp. -ότερον Plu.*Sol*.14, Aret.*CA*1.1: Sup. -ότατα Ph.2.461. II. in bad sense, *daring, audacious*, *Anatolian Studies* 204 (Termessus).

**εὔτομος**, ον, *well-divided, regular*, of a city, Arist.*Pol*.1330ᵇ23. II. *well-cut*, of a gem, *POxy*.1449.14 (iii A.D.).

⊛ **εὐτον-έω**, *have power* or *faculties*, Hp.*Ep*.16, 17; *have power* or *means* to do, εἰπεῖν τι Plu.2.531b, cf. 533c; παρέχειν τι *IG*14.830.10 (Puteoli, ii A.D.), cf. Wilcken *Chr*.176.18 (i A.D.); τοῦ μηδὲν αὐτῶν λυθῆναι *SIG*1109.30, cf. 49 (ii A.D.). ⊛ **-ία**, ἡ, *tension, vigour*, D.S.5.39; σκελῶν ib.34: esp. in Stoic philos. (cf. τόνος), Chrysipp.*Stoic*.2.146, etc.; ὁ ἐν τῇ ψυχῇ τόνος λέγεται ὡς εὐ. καὶ ἀτονία ib. 3.123, cf. Phld.*Ir*.p.69 W.; εὐ. ψυχῆς, of courage, *Stoic*.3.66, cf. 73: generally, *vigour* of character, Plu.*Phoc*.3, 2.456f, *BGU*786 ii 1 (ii A.D.); also, *vigour* of style, D.H.*Vett.Cens*.2.3, Hermog.*Id*.1.11, Aps.p.282 H. b. Medic., *tension*, Ruf.*Sat.Gon*.46 (pl.); also μαλθακὴ εὐ. gentle *force*, Hp.*Ep*.15. c. *elasticity*, Ph.*Bel*.71.33. **-ος**, ον, (τείνω) *well-strung, vigorous*, of men's bodies or limbs, Hp.*Aph*.3. 17, Arist.*IA*710ᵃ31, Luc.*Anach*.24, *AP*12.216 (Strat.): Comp., Men. 693; of men, -ώτεροι τοῖς σώμασι D.S.4.3; τὸ εὔ., = εὐτονία, Pl.*Lg*. 815a, etc.: esp. in Stoic philos. (cf. τόνος), Chrysipp.*Stoic*.3.121, 123; of engines, Plb.8.5.2 (Comp.); of the wind, D.S.1.41; of wine, Arist.*Mir*.832ᵃ11; τὸ εὔ., name of an eyesalve, Aët.7.115; εὔ. πληγή Hero *Bel*.74.12. b. *distended*, εὐτόνῳ φλεβί (sens. obsc.) Neophr.(?) *Medea* in *PLit.Lond*.77 *Fr*.2.7. c. *elastic, yielding*, -ώτερος χαλκοῦ χρυσός Porph. ad Il.20.259. 2. *active, energetic*, πρόνοια *POxy*. 1468.7 (iii A.D.); προσοχή Iamb.*Protr*.21.κα' (Sup.); of persons, -ώτατος εἶναι c. part., *OGI*315.52 (Pessinus, ii B.C.). 3. of an orator, *forcible*, εὐ. τῇ φράσει D.H.*Vett.Cens*.5.4; τῆς λέξεως τὸ εὔ. ib.3.2, cf. Phld.*Po*.5.5. 4. Adv. -νως *with might and main, vigorously*, Ar. *Pl*.1095, X.*Hier*.9.6, Arist.*Pr*.885ᵃ6, Ph.1.311, *Ev.Luc*.23.10: Comp. -ώτερον, τοῦ δέοντος ἀφιᾶσι Luc.*Nigr*.36. 5. *strenuously*, Phld. *Herc*.1251.23, *Po*.2 p.274 H. 6. *peremptorily*, -ώτερον ἐπιστεῖλαι, γράψαι, *PLille* 1.3 i 14 (iii B.C.), *PPetr*.2 p.22, 3 p.132 (cf. p. x) (iii B.C.). II. of the voice, *well-pitched*, Arist.*GA*786ᵇ8. (Sts. as v.l. in codd. for ἔντονος, Plb.1.c.; εὔτονος is perh. f.l. for ἔντονον in S. *Fr*.966.) **-όω**, '*tone up*', *brace*, τὴν δύναμιν Gal.14.252.

**εὐτοξ-ία**, ἡ, *skill in archery*, Hdn.1.15.2 codd. (dub. l.). **-ος**, ον, *with good arrows*, φαρέτρη *APl*.4.214 (Secund.).

**εὐτόρν-ευτος**, ον, = sq. 1, *AP*5.134. **-ος**, ον, *well-turned, rounded, circular*, E.*Tr*.1197, Lyc.664. 2. *easy to turn*, of wood, Thphr. *HP*5.6.4 (Comp.), 5.6.2 (Sup.).

⊛ **εὐτράπεζος**, ον, *with good table, hospitable*, ἀνδρῶνες A.*Ag*.244 (lyr.); of persons, Plu.*CG*19. 2. *luxurious*, βίος E.*Fr*.670.2; of men, Eriph.6; *dainty, sumptuous*, ἀγορά Plu.2.667c.

⊛ **εὐτρᾰπελ-εύομαι**, *to be witty, ready*, Plb.12.16.14, D.S.38/9.7; cj. Dind. for εὐτραπεζευόμενοι, Eust.1053.18. **-ία**, ἡ, *ready wit, liveliness*, Hp.*Decent*.7, Pl.*R*.563a, Posidipp.28.5, Cic.*Fam*.7.32.1, D.S.15.6: pl., *pleasantries*, Demetr.*Eloc*.177; defined by Arist. as πεπαιδευμένη ὕβρις, *Rh*.1389ᵇ11, cf. *EN*1108ᵃ24; ἡ περὶ τὰς παιδιὰς καὶ τὰς ὁμιλίας εὐ. Plu.*Ant*.43. 2. rarely in bad sense, = βωμολοχία, *Ep.Eph*.5.4. **-ίζομαι**, = Lat. *jocor*, Dosith.p.431 K.:—hence **-ισμός**, ὁ, *Et.Gud*.505.55. **-ος**, ον, (τρέπω) *easily turning* or *changing*, of the Athenians, Ael.*VH*5.13; *nimble*, of apes, Id.*NA*5. 26; in earlier Gr. always metaph., λόγος εὐ. *a dexterous, ready* plea, Ar.*V*.469 (lyr.). Adv. -λως *dexterously, readily, without awkwardness*, Th.2.41. 2. of persons, *ready with an answer* or *repartee, witty*, Arist.*EN*1108ᵃ24, 1128ᵃ10; εὐ. παρὰ τὰς συνουσίας Plb.23.5.7; τίτθη εὐ. Jul.*Or*.7.227a: Sup., Plb.9.23.3. b. in bad sense, *jesting, ribald*, Isoc.7.49; εὐτράπελόν ἐστι c. acc. et inf., it is *ludicrous* that.., Plu.2.1062b. 3. *tricky, dishonest*, v.l. in Pi.*P*.4.105; εὐ. κέρδη *time-serving* arts, of flatterers, ib.1.92.

**εὐτρᾰφ-έω**, *to be well-nourished, thrive*, Thphr.*CP*4.10.1 (nisi leg. -τροφεῖ). **-ής**, ές, (τρέφω) *well-fed, thriving, fat*, Hp.*Aër*.12, E. *Med*.920, *IT*304, Arist.*HA*546ᵃ15, etc.; *large, well-grown*, of peppercorns, Gal.6.270 (Sup.); *luxuriant*, of hair-growth, Id.1.326 (Sup.); τὸ εὐτραφές, = εὐτροφία, Polyaen.7.36. Adv. -φῶς, Ion. -φέως, ἔχειν *to be fat*, Hp.*Septim*.8, cf. Philostr.*VS*2.1.7. II. Act., *nourishing*, ὕδωρ A.*Th*.308 (Sup., lyr.); γάλα Id.*Ch*.898, Philostr.*VA*3.9; v.l. in Thphr.*CP*1.18.1. **-ητος**, ὁ, *epicure*, *EM*122.31. **-ία**, Ion. **-ίη**, ἡ, *good husbandry*, *Epigr.Gr*.1036 (Nicomedia).

**εὐτράχηλος** [ᾰ], ον, *with fine neck*, Tim.Gaz.ap.Ar.Byz.*Epit*.81.8, *Hippiatr*.115.

**εὐτρεπ-ής**, ές, (τρέπω) *readily turning*: hence generally, *prepared, ready*, εὐτρεπὲς ποιεῖσθαί τι E.*Ba*.440; τοὐμὸν εὐ. πάρα ib.844; εὐτρεπῆ..τὸν κοντὸν ποιοῦ Epicr.10.4; δεῖπνον εὐ. Antiph.80.12; ἄριστον Men.*Pk*.117; τούτων -πῶν γενομένων Plb.6.26.10; also of persons, εἰδὼς εὐτρεπεῖς ὑμᾶς D.4.18; συνήγοροι..καθ' ἡμῶν εὐ. Id.21.112, cf. *Com.Adesp*.15.19 D.; εὐ. πρός τι D.H.2.3, Ph.1.174. Adv. εὐτρεπῶς, ἔχειν to be *in a state of preparation*, D.1.21. ⊛ **-ίζω**, Att. fut. -ιῶ: pf. εὐτρέπικα *AP*9.316.8 (Leon.):—*make ready*, ξίφος A.*Ag*.1651; ἃ χρή E.*IT*470; πάντα D.1.13, cf. 3.13, 4.16, Men.*Sam*.6; τὰ τείχη *to restore* them, X.*HG*2.2.4; τὴν σύριγγα *lubricates* the windpipe, Hp.*Cord*.2:—Med., *get ready for oneself*, or something *of one's own*, Th.4.123, 2.18, Ph.1.619:—Pass., *to be prepared, made ready*, E. *IA*1111, Ar.*Pl*.626; [ναῦς] ἱστίοις -ομένη Arist.*Fr*.11; σφαγαῖσιν ηὐτρεπισμένος *ready for*.., Lyc.614, cf. Aen.Tact.18.1, Jul.*Mis*.362b; *to be performed, executed*, Phld.*Po*.5.21. 2. Medic., *treat*, Hp. *Loc.Hom*.1, al.; dub. in Thphr.*Char*.13.9. II. *win over, conciliate*, τινά τινι X.*HG*4.8.12:—so in Med., ib.6: pf. Pass., in med. sense, ἅπαντας ηὐτρέπισται D.18.175. **-ισμός**, ὁ, *preparation*, Simp.*in Ph*.793.7, Suid. **-ιστέον**, *one must treat*, of a doctor, Hp. *Loc.Hom*.30; *one must prepare*, Hld.4.15. 2. Adj. -ιστέος, α, ον, Poll.10.76. **-ιστής**, οῦ, ὁ, *one who gets ready*, Sch.rec.S.*El*.72.

**εὔτρεπτος**, ον, *easily changing*, Arist.*Mu*.400ᵃ23, Plu.*Mar*.21; ζωή Man.4.532; ὕδατα Plu.2.912b. 2. Medic., of diseases, *mild*, Gal.15.590; but εὔ. ἐς συγκοπὴν *easily turning* to.., Aret.*CA* 1.1. b. of the skin, *sensitive*, Menemach.ap.Orib.10.15.3. 3. *ready, inclined*, τὸ εὔ. πρὸς μεταβολάς Plu.2.978f. 4. *versatile*, Poll.6.121, cj. in Man.4.86. 5. Adv. -τως v.l. for εὐτρεπῶς, J. *Vit*.61.

**εὐτρεφής**, Ep. **ἐϋτρ-**, ές, (τρέφω) *well-fed*, ὄϊες ἐΰ. Od.9.425; αἰγὸς ἐΰ. 14.530; σαρκὸς εὐτρεφέστατον πάχος E.*Cyc*.380 (prob. l.), cf. Pl. *Lg*.835d. II. *nourishing*, Thphr.*CP*1.18.1 (v.l. εὐτραφοῦς).

**εὐτρήρων**, ωνος, ὁ, ἡ, *abounding in doves*, Nonn.*D*.13.62.

**εὐτρήσιος**, prob. = *muliebria passus, pathicus*, Eup.56.

**εὔτρητος**, Ep. **ἐΰτρ-**, ον, (τετραίνω) *well-pierced*, λοβοί Il.14.182; χόανα Hes.*Th*.863; δόνακες *APl*.1.8 (Alc.); *with many orifices*, φλέβια Thphr.*Sens*.56; *porous*, σπόγγος Q.S.9.429; πέδον *AP*6.21.5.

⊛ **εὐτρίαινα** [ῐ], ὁ, acc. -τρίαιναν, *with goodly trident*, epith. of Poseidon, Pi.*O*.1.73.

**εὐτρῖβής**, ές, *well-rubbed, powdered fine*, Dsc.5.121, as v.l. for εὐθρυβής, cf. Nic.*Al*.328, 405: heterocl. dat. ἐΰτριβι (as from εὔτριψ), ib.44.

**εὔτριπτος**, ον, (τρίβω) *easy to pound*, Democr.ap.Gal.14.130; *friable*, Dsc.2.24, Gal.13.124.

⊛ **εὔτρῐχος**, ον, = εὔθριξ, γενειάς E.*HF*934 (s.v.l.).

**εὐτριψία**, ἡ, *sensitiveness to friction*, Cass.*Pr*.68.

**εὐτροπ-έομαι**, Pass., *to be easily dealt with*, ὑπό τινος Apollod. *Poliorc*.138.5. **-ία**, ἡ, (εὔτροπος) *versatility*, ἡ περὶ τὸ ἦθος εὐ. Plu. 2.500d. II. *good disposition*, ἤθεος Democr.57; πρὸς τὰς ὑφηγήσεις Ph.2.399. III. in reading aloud, *expression*, Aët.16.67.

**εὔτροπις**, ιδος, ὁ, ἡ, *with good keel*, gloss on ἐΰστείρης, Sch.A.R.1. 401.

⊛ **εὔτροπος**, ον, (τρέπω) *versatile*, etym. of εὐτράπελος, Arist.*EN*1128ᵃ 10. II. (τρόπος) *morally good*, Sch.Od.1.1; of diseases, *mild*,

Hp.*Hum.*13; εὔτροπος ἀνθρώποισι δαίμων dub. sens. in *PHib.*1.2.6 (cf. Epich.258). Adv. -πως, gloss on εὐοργήτως, Sch.Th.1.122.

**εὐτρόσσεσθαι·** ἐπιστρέφεσθαι (Paphian), Hsch.

**εὐτροφ-έω,** *thrive, flourish,* Arist.*GA*765ᵇ26, Thphr.*HP*8.8.4, etc.:—also Med. or Pass., Id.*CP*4.1.4. **-ής,** ές, = εὐτραφής, Hp.*Dent.*29 (s. v. l.). **-ία,** ἡ, *good nurture, thriving condition,* τῶν σωμάτων, τῶν ψυχῶν, Pl.*Prt.*351a,b, cf. Arist.*HA*542ᵃ28, Thphr.*HP*5.2.2, Orph.*Fr.*49 vi 89: pl., Ph.2.1, Antyll.ap.Stob.4.37.16. **-ιάω,** gloss on μυσιάω, Hsch. **-ος,** ον, *nourishing, healthy,* χώρα Thphr.*CP*1.14.1; ἔαρ Opp.*C.*3.180. II. Pass., *well-nourished, thriving,* of trees, D.S.17.89; of children, Hp.*Dent.*1, Orph.*Fr.*49 vi 88: Comp., Hp.*Dent.*13, Ath.Med.ap.Orib.9.5.6: metaph., of diseases, Luc.*Abd.*27.

***εὐτρόχᾰλος,** Ep. ἐΰτρ-, ον, (τρέχω) *running well, quick-moving,* ποταμός Opp.*C.*2.131; μέλισσα *APl.*4.36 (Agath.); ἀοιδή A.R.4.907; γλῶσσα *IG*5(1).264 (Sparta, Aug.). II. *well-rounded,* σφαῖρα, κύκλος, A.R.3.135, Man.2.130; λίνον Nic.*Al.*134; ἐϋτροχάλῳ ἐν ἀλωῇ on the *rounded* threshing-floor, Hes.*Op.*599, 806.

***εὔτροχος,** Ep. and Lyr. ἐΰτρ-, ον, poet. metapl. acc. ἐΰτροχα *An. Ox.*1.271: (τροχός):—*well-wheeled,* ἐΰτροχον ἅρμα καὶ ἵππους Il.8.438, Hes.*Sc.*463; ἅμαξαν ἐΰ. Od.6.72, Il.24.150, etc.; σατίναι εὔ. Sapph.*Supp.*20a.13; εὔ. κύκλος E.*Ion* 19. II. (τρέχω) *smoothly-running,* Pl.*Ti.*37c; *running easily,* of a cord put through loops, X.*Cyn.*2.4; εὔ. γλῶσσα a *ready, glib* tongue, E.*Ba.*268; γλῶσσα εὔ. ἐν τῷ διαλέγεσθαι Plu.*Per.*7; of style, D.H.*Comp.*20; τὸ τῆς φύσεως, τῆς διανοίας εὔ., Ph.1.240, Dam.*Isid.*80, cf. 32; τὸ σφαιροειδὲς ἡμῶν οὐκ εὔ. Plot.2.2.2. Adv. -χως, ἀναγινώσκειν to read *fluently,* Ph.1.303. III. *well-rounded, round,* τεῖχος *IG*14.1389 ii 13.

**εὐτρύγητος** [ῡ], ον, *convenient for the vintage,* of low vines, Thphr.*CP*3.7.4 (Comp.).

**εὐτρύπητος** [ῡ], ον, *easily pierced,* Sch.Orib.4 p.531 D. (Comp.).

**εὐτρῠφάλειος** [ᾰ], gloss on εὐκόρυφος, Sch.Opp.*C.*1.362.

**εὔτρωτος,** ον, *easily wounded,* Gal.*UP*1.2.

***εὐτῠκ-άζομαι,** *make ready*: εὐτυκάζου (εὐτύκαζον cod.)· εὔτυκτον ἔχε, ἕτοιμον, Hsch.: hence restored by Dind. for ..τυκάζου in A.*Th.*149 (lyr.). **-ής,** ές, *easily worked,* and Adv. -ῶς· ῥᾳδίως, Hsch. **-ίζω,** = εὐτυκάζομαι, Id., *EM*399.17. **-ος,** ον, rare form for sq., *well-built,* εὐτύκους δόμους A.*Supp.*959 (Porson). II. *ready,* γλῶσσα ib.994: c. inf., πᾶς τις ἐπειπεῖν ψόγον.. εὔτυκος ib.974 (anap.); ὑμνεῖν B.8.4; ἐς χορόν Pratin.Lyr.2; πῦρ εὔ. ἔστω Theoc.24.88; ἃ θεὸς εὔ. ἕρπει (fort. ἕρπειν) Call.*Lav.Pall.*3; [κρέα] v.l. in Hdt.1.119.

**εὔτυκτος,** ον, (τεύχω) *well-made, well-wrought,* κυνέη Il.3.336, etc.; ἱμάσθλη 8.44, etc.; κλισίη 10.566, Od.4.123; κυνέα B.17.50; κρέα εὔ. ποιήσασθαι to get meat *ready for eating,* v.l. in Hdt.1.119.

**εὐτύπωτος** [ῠ], ον, *easily taking an impression,* κηρός Gal.*UP*6.13, cf. Id.1.322, Phlp.*in de An.*605.16, Eust.633.23, prob. in Plu.2.660c.

**εὐτύχ-εια** [ῠ], ἡ, poet. for εὐτυχία, S.*Fr.*1050. II. Εὐτύχεια, τά, festival in honour of Eutyches, *SIG*²588.55 (ii B.C.): sg., Εὐτύχειον, τό, fund devoted to its maintenance, *Inscr.Délos* 370.44 (iii B.C.). **-ευδοξέω,** *enjoy fame and fortune, PTeb.*418.19 (iii A.D.). ***-έω,** impf. ηὐτύχουν or εὐτ- S.*Fr.*107.10, etc.: fut. -ήσω E.*Or.*1212: aor. 1 ηὐτύχησα or εὐτ- ib.542, etc.: pf. ηὐτύχηκα or εὐτ- Pl.*Lg.*811c, etc.: 3 pl. plpf. ηὐτυχήκεσαν D.18.18:—Pass., aor. 1 εὐτυχήθην Hdn.2.8.3, 2.9.3: pf. εὐτύχημαι Th.7.77, etc.:—*to be prosperous, fortunate,* Pi.*O.*7.81, *I.*3.1, etc.; οἱ εὐτυχοῦντες *people in prosperity,* Antipho 2.4.9; εὐ. τινός *to be well off for* a thing, Luc.*Charid.*23; εἰ μνήμης εὐτυχῶ if I remember rightly, Ath.2.58c: c. dat., τῷ πολέμῳ Hdt.1.171, cf. S.*El.*68; τῷ βίῳ Men.655: more freq. c. acc. rei, τοὺς ἄλλους πολέμους Hdt.1.65; τὰ πάντα Id.3.40, cf. S.*OT*88; ἐς τέκνα E.*Or.*542, *Ion* 567; ἔν τινι X.*HG*7.1.5: c. part., *to succeed in* doing, E.*Or.*1212, cf. X.*HG*7.1.11: later c. inf., Plu.2.333e, Vett.Val.241.11, Longus 4.19, D.L.9.100: c. acc. cogn., εὐ. εὐτύχημα X.*An.*6.3.6; εὐτύχει at the close of letters, Pl.*Ep.*321c; εὐτυχεῖτε Ep.Philipp.ap.D.18.78, Septimius Severus in *IG*12(7).243.30; εὐτύχει on gravestones, *CIG*4346 (Side), 4837 (Egypt); ἀλλ' εὐτυχοίης *fare thee well!* A.*Ch.*1063, S.*OT*1478, E.*Med.*688. 2. of things, *turn out well, prosper,* βρότεια πράγματ' εὐτυχοῦντα A.*Ag.*1327; πόνου τοι χωρὶς οὐδὲν εὐτυχεῖ S.*El.*945; τὰ εὐτυχοῦντα Id.*Fr.*681; τὰ πολλὰ.. εὐτυχοῦντα *if they succeed,* Th.3.39, cf. 4.79:—also in Pass., ἱκανὰ τοῖς πολεμίοις ηὐτύχηται Id.7.77; τὰ τῆς μάχης εὐτυχεῖτο Plu.*Num.*12: ταῦτα αὐτοῖς ἐς κάλλος εὐτύχηται Gal.*Protr.*12; ἄπιστον τὸ -ούμενον Alciphr.2.3; of a person, εὐτυχηθεὶς Iamb.*VP*2.9. II. Act., *obtain, attain to,* παρὰ τῶν Σεβαστῶν στέφανον *Ephes.*3 No.70, cf. Sch.Pi.*P.*9.173, *PMasp.*23.23 (vi A.D.). ***-ημα,** ατος, τό, *piece of good luck, success,* E.*Ph.*1356, Pl.*Smp.*217a, Men.5.3 D., etc.; εὐτυχεῖν εὐ. X.*An.*6.3.6. ***-ής,** ές, *successful, fortunate,* of persons and events, Hdt.1.32, etc.: Comp., S.*Aj.*550: Sup., Pl.*Lg.*877e; opp. ὄλβιος, Hdt. l.c.; opp. εὐδαίμων, E.*Med.*1229 (Comp.); εὐτυχεῖ πότμῳ A.*Pers.*709 (troch.); εὐτυχῆ κλύουσα πρᾶξιν S.*Tr.*293: c. dat., εὐ. ἱκέσθαι τινί to come *with blessings* to him, Id.*OC*308; δαίμων δὲ τοῖς μὲν εὐτυχὴς καθ' ἡμέραν Id.*El.*999; τὸ εὐτυχές, οἳ ἄν.. Th.2.44. II. Adv. -χῶς Pi.*N.*7.90, A.*Pers.*325, etc.; Ion. -χέως Hdt.3.39: Comp. -έστερον E.*Heracl.*247 (v.l. -ρος); πράττειν Pl.*Euthd.*280a: Sup. -έστατα Men.*Sam.*44:—εὐτυχῶς Ἀμμαίῳ at close of letter, D.H.*Amm.*2 fin. **-ησις,** εως, ἡ, in pl., *lucky strokes of fortune,* Phld.*Rh.*2.217 S. **-ία,** Ion. -ίη, ἡ, *good luck, success,* Pi.*O.*6.81, Hdt.1.32, Th.7.77, etc.; τὴν ἀτυχίαν εἰς εὐ. αἰτοῦμαι μεταστῆναι Antipho 2.4.4; defined, Arist.*Rh.*1361ᵇ39; ἐπ' εὐτυχίᾳ, -ίαισιν, E.*IT*1490 (anap.), Ar.*Ec.*573 (lyr.); πολλῇ εὐ. χρῆσθαι Pl.*Men.*72a; κατά τινα θείαν εὐ. Id.*Lg.*798b; ἡ κατὰ πόλεμον εὐ. Th.1.120: pl., *pieces of good luck, successes,* Id.2.44.

**εὐύᾰλος,** ον, *of good glass,* φιάλαι *AP*11.55, acc. to Planudes (Pall.).

**εὔυγρος,** ον, *very moist,* Vett.Val.9.24.

**εὐυδρ-έω,** *to abound in water,* Str.8.6.8. **-ία,** ἡ, *abundance of water,* Id.5.1.12. **-ος,** ον, (ὕδωρ) *well-watered, abounding in water,* ἄστυ Simon.96; ἀκτά Pi.*P.*1.79; Μαραθών Call.*Hec.*1.1.8; νάπη Nic.*Al.*622; γῆ ποιώδης καὶ εὔ. Hdt.4.47; χῶρος -ότερος Id.9.25; [ὄρη] -ότερα *Gp.*2.6.5 (v.l. ἐν-). 2. of a river or spring, *with beautiful water,* Κάσας B.10.119; Εὐρώτας E.*IT*399 (lyr.); Κασταλὶς *Pae.Delph.*5; so prob. εὔυδρον ποτόν (vulg. ἔνυδρον τόπον) Polyzel.2.

**εὐυμν-ία,** ἡ, gloss on εὐμολπία, Hsch. (ἐν- cod.). ***-ος,** ον, *celebrated in many hymns, h.Ap.*19, Call.*Ap.*31, etc.: Sup., Id.*Fr.*36. II. *used in beautiful hymns,* ῥήματα Id.*Epigr.* in *Berl.Sitzb.*1912.548. [The penult. short in Epich.91.]

***εὐυπάντητος,** ον, *easily approached,* Dumont-Homolle *Mélanges d'Archéologie* 459 (Apollonia in Thrace).

**εὐυπέρ-βᾰτος,** ον, *easily stepped over*: of a socket, *out of which the end of a bone easily slips,* Hp.*Art.*8. II. *easy of access, PFay.*110.9 (i A.D.), *POxy.*1272.16 (ii A.D.). **-βλητος,** ον, *easily surpassed,* Arist.*EN*1123ᵃ17.

**εὔυπνος,** ον, *sleeping well* or *soundly,* Hp.*Dent.*15, cj. in Max.Tyr.30.6: Comp., Gal.18(2).299, etc. II. Act., *granting good sleep,* of Zeus at Delphi, Hsch.

**εὐυπό-δητος,** ον, of a sandal, *easy to bind under the foot,* Tz. ad Lyc.853. **-κρῐτος,** ον, *playing one's part well,* Vett.Val.48.1; also εὐ. συμβίωσις, of marriage, Id.119.33. **-ληπτος,** ον, *easy to take up, light,* Heph.Astr.2.2. II. in Comp., *more easily enclosed,* v.l. in Arist.*Sens.*438ᵃ15, cf. Alex.Aphr.*in Sens.*26.20, 36.1. III. *enjoying a good reputation, Cod.Just.*1.4.26 *Intr.*, Just.*Nov.*128.18.

**εὐύποπτα** σώματα persons *believed to be dangerously ill,* Aët.5.78.

**εὐυποχώρητος,** ον, *easily yielding,* σώματα Herm.ap.Stob.1.49.69.

**εὐύφ-αντος** [ῠ], ον, (ὑφαίνω) = sq., Suid. **-ής,** ές, (ὑφή) *well-woven,* στολή Tim.*Pers.*180; λαίφεα *AP*10.2 (Antip. Sid.); ἱμάτιον Herm. *in Phdr.*p.192 A., *BGU*1564.10; πέπλος v.l. in S.*Tr.*602.

**εὐφαής,** ές, (φάος) *very bright,* Nonn.*D.*8.111.

**εὐφάλαρα·** λαμπρά, Hsch., *EM*399.32.

**εὐφαμέω, εὔφᾱμος,** Dor. for εὐφημ-.

**εὐφαντ-ᾰσίωτος,** ον, *gifted with a vivid imagination,* Vett.Val.47.1, Quint.6.2.30; πρᾶξις *Cat.Cod.Astr.*8(4).209; also in bad sense, *fantastic, fanciful,* Vett.Val.150.12. **-αστος,** ον, *imaginative,* Phlp. *in de An.*155.30, Platon.*Diff.Com.*15. II. *easily imagined,* Procl. *in Prm.*p.518 S.

**εὔφαπτον·** ὑπὸ θεοῦ κατεχόμενον, Hsch.

***εὐφᾰρέτρης,** ου, Dor. -ας, α, ὁ, *with beautiful quiver,* Ἀπόλλων S.*Tr.*208 (lyr.), Maced.*Pae.*1.

**εὐφάρμᾰκος,** ον, *abounding in drugs,* ὄρος Thphr.*HP*9.10.3.

**εὐφέγγ-εια,** ἡ, *brilliancy,* Iamb.*Protr.*21.ιε'. **-ής,** ές, *bright, brilliant,* ἡμέρα.. εὐ. ἰδεῖν A.*Pers.*387, cf. B.18.26; Ἄρκτος A.R.3.1195; σελάνα B.8.29, cf. Plu.2.161e; πεύκη, of a torch, *AP*7.407.5 (Diosc.); τὸ εὐ. Luc.*Hipp.*8. 2. *shiny,* τοῖχοι Suid. s. v. δύο τοίχους.

**εὐφεροσύνη,** etym. of εὐφροσύνη, coined by Pl.*Cra.*419d.

**εὔφηβος,** written for ἔφηβος, *IG*3.1104 (ii A.D.).

**εὐφημ-έω,** Dor. εὐφᾱμέω, (εὔφημος) *use words of good omen,* opp. δυσφημέω: I. *avoid all unlucky words,* during sacred rites: hence, as the surest mode of avoiding them, *keep a religious silence,* φέρτε δὲ χερσὶν ὕδωρ εὐφημῆσαί τε κέλεσθε Il.9.171, cf. Call.*Ap.*17, 18, etc.; mostly imper., εὐφήμει, εὐφημεῖτε, *hush! be still!* Ar.*Nu.*297, *Ach.*241, al.; οἱ δὲ ἀμβώσαντες μέγα εὐφημέειν μιν ἐκέλευον Hdt.3.38; εὐφημεῖν χρὴ τὸν πρεσβύτην Ar.*Nu.*263; εὐφήμει τοῦτό γε, ἦν δ' ἐγώ Pl.*Euthd.*301a, cf. *R.*329c; οὐκ εὐφημήσεις; Id.*Smp.*214d:—Pass., εὔφημον εἴη τοὔπος εὐφημουμένῃ *since you have been spoken fair,* A.*Supp.*512. II. *shout in triumph,* Id.*Ag.*596, *Eu.*1035 (lyr.), Ar.*Pl.*758, D.S.5.49. 2. c. acc., *honour by praise, speak well of,* θεούς Pl.*Epin.*992d, cf. X.*Smp.*4.49:—Pass., *to be called by a mild name,* πολιτεία.. εὐφημούμενος λῆρος D.S.37.17; also, *to be honoured,* Hp.*Ep.*27, *CIG*4389 (Isauria); *to be applauded,* Ph.2.589; πρὸς πάντων -ηθεὶς Hdn.2.3.11; ὑπὸ ὄχλων Vett.Val.38.25. III. *sound triumphantly,* κέλαδος Ἑλλήνων πάρα.. ηὐφήμησεν A.*Pers.*389; ὀλολυγμὸς εὐφημῶν Id.*Ag.*28. **-ητέον,** *one must use words of good omen,* ἐπί τισι Ph.2.257. **-ητικός,** ή, όν, *of happy significance,* ἀντίφρασις Eust.763.37. **-ία,** ἡ, *use of words of good omen,* opp. δυσφημία: I. *abstinence from inauspicious language, religious silence,* εὐφημίαν ἴσχε, = εὐφήμει, S.*Tr.*178; εὐ. ἐσχηκέναι πρός τινα Pl.*Lg.*717c; εὐφημία 'στω, εὐφημία 'στω, as a proclamation of *silence* before a prayer, Ar.*Th.*295, cf. *Av.*959; so εὐφημίαν.. κηρύξας ἔχω S.*Fr.*893; Ταλθύβιος.. εὐφημίαν ἀνεῖπε καὶ σιγὴν στρατῷ E.*IA*1564; μετ' εὐ. διδάσκειν Pl.*Lg.*949b; ἐν εὐ. χρὴ τελευτᾶν Id.*Phd.*117e; πρὸς εὐφημίαν τρεπέσθω Luc.*Laps.*17. II. in positive sense, *auspiciousness,* λόγων εὐ. E.*IA*608, Aeschin.1.169; πᾶσαν εὐ. παρειχόμην D.*Ep.*2.19; esp. *a fair* or *honourable name* for a bad thing, *euphemism* (as Εὐμενίδες, εὐφρόνη, etc.), δι' εὐφημίας Pl.*Lg.*736a; εὐφημίας ἕνεκα Aeschin.3.92, cf. Plu.2.449a. 2. f.l. for εὐφωνία, Demetr.*Eloc.*175. III. *prayer and praise, worship,* offered to the gods, E.*IA*1469; = εὐχή, Pl.*Alc.*2.149b; εὐξάμενον μετ' εὐφημίας Din.2.14: pl., Pi.*P.*10.35. 2. *honour, good repute* enjoyed by men, Phld.*Ind.Sto.*16, 20; ἀθάνατος εὐ. D.S1.2; opp. δυσφημία, 2*Ep.Cor.*6.8; ἀδιάλει-

πτος Plu.2.121e; ἡ ὕστερον εὐ. D.Chr.31.20; τὴν παρὰ πᾶσιν ἀγαθὴν εὐ. good *repute*, *IG*12(5).860.39 (Tenos, i B.C.); ἡ ἐκ τῶν ξένων εὐ. *OGI* 339.30 (Sestos, ii B.C.); *panegyric*, Jul.*Or*.3.106a, Lib.*Or*.62.3; ἡ εὐ. σου, as a form of address, *PLond*.3.891.9 (iv A.D.); αἱ εὐ. *plaudits, acclamations* in a local senate, *POxy*.2110.2 (iv A.D.). **-ίζομαι,** *use words of good omen*, A.D.*Pron*.10.22, Hsch. s.v. εὐοίαιον, *EM* 388.43. **-ισμός,** ὁ, *use of an auspicious word for an inauspicious one*, e.g. Εὐμενίδες for Ἐρινύες, εὐφρόνη for νύξ, etc., Eust.1398.52, Demetr.*Eloc*.281; κατ' εὐφημισμόν Corn.*ND*21, Hermog.*Prog*. 7, Palaeph.51, Olymp.*in Mete*.105.19; ἀπ' εὐφημισμοῦ Phld.*Piet*. 111. ❋ **-ος,** Dor. **εὔφᾱμος,** ον, (φήμη) *uttering sounds of good omen*, ἀετός Arist.*HA*618$^{b}$31: usu. in derived senses, I. *abstaining from inauspicious words*, i.e. *religiously silent*, εὔφημον.. κοίμησον στόμα A.*Ag*.1247; γλῶσσαν εὔ. φέρειν Id.*Ch*.581; so perh. εὔ. γόοι Id.*Fr*.40; εὐφάμου στόμα φροντίδος ἱέντες moving the lips of *reverent* thought, i.e. keeping a holy silence, S.*OC*132 (lyr.); so ὑπ' εὐφήμου βοῆς, i.e. in silence, Id.*El*.630; εὔφημα φώνει, = εὐφήμει, Id.*Aj*.362, 591, E.*IT*687; εὔφημος ἴσθι S.*Fr*.478; εὔ. πᾶς ἔστω λαός Ar.*Th*.39 (anap.). 2. *mild, softening* (cf. εὐφημία II. 1, εὐφημισμός), ἐν -οτάτοις ὀνόμασι..κατονομάζειν Pl.*Alc*.2.140c; πρὸς τὸ -ότατον, Lat. *in meliorem partem*, Luc.*Prom.Es* 3. Adv. Comp. -ότερον Eust.1398.49. 3. *fair-spoken*, εἰς τὸ δαιμόνιον Phld.*Piet*.18. II. in positive sense, *fair-sounding, auspicious*, μῦθοι Xenoph.1.14; ἦμαρ A.*Ag*.636; ἔπος Id.*Supp*.512; εὔφημοι κέλαδοι E.*Tr*.1072 (lyr.); εὔφαμον δ' ἐπὶ βωμοῖς μοῦσαν θείατ' ἀοιδοί A.*Supp*.694 (lyr.); Μούσης ἀνοίγειν..εὔφημον στόμα Ar.*Av*.1719; εὔ. πόνοι *pious, holy*, E.*Ion*134 (lyr.); δόμοι Id.*Andr*.1144; ᾠδῆς γένος, ἐρωτήματα, Pl.*Lg*.800e, *Hp.Ma*.293a, cf. *Ep.Phil*.4.8; πλοῦς Iamb.*VP*3.16 (Sup.). Adv. -μως *with* or *in words of good omen*, *h.Ap*.171 (dub. l.), A.*Eu*.287, *IG*1$^{2}$.108.55, Pl.*Phdr*. 265c: Comp. -ότερον Aristaenet.2.9. III. *laudatory*, λόγοι εὔ. *panegyrics*, Plb.31.3.4. (Also f.l. for εὔχυμος Aët.5.58, for εὔφιμος Nic.*Al*.275.)

❋ **εὔφθαρτος,** ον, *easily destroyed, perishable*, Arist.*Cael*.280$^{b}$25, 305$^{a}$6 (Comp.), Plb.2.35.6, M.Ant.2.12. 2. *easily corrupted*, Gal.8. 34. II. *easy of digestion*, Diph.Siph.ap.Ath.2.68f.

**εὐφθογγ-έω,** gloss on εὐστομέω, Sch.S.*OC*18. ❋ **-ος,** ον, *well-sounding, cheerful*, λύρη Thgn.534; κελάδους -οτέρους A.*Ch*.341 (anap.); σύριγγες E.*Tr*.127 (lyr.); *sweet-voiced*, of birds, Str.15.1. 69: Sup., Id.6.1.9.

**εὐφῐλ-ής,** ές, *well-loved*, χείρ A.*Ag*.34. II. Act., *loving well*, ποίμνης τοιαύτης οὔτις εὐ. θεῶν Id.*Eu*.197. **-ητος,** η, ον, *well-beloved*, only in Id.*Th*.107 (lyr.).

**εὐφῐλό-παις,** παιδος, ὁ, ἡ, *the children's darling*, of a lion's whelp, A.*Ag*.721 (lyr.). **-τίμητος** [τῐ], ον, *properly made an object of ambition*, δαπανήματα Arist.*EN*1122$^{b}$22.

**εὔφῑμος,** ον, *well-bitted, well-bridled*, Hdn.*Epim*.178 (hence **εὐφῑμία,** v. εὐκαμία). II. *astringent, styptic*, Nic.*Al*.275.

**εὔφλαστος,** ον, *easily crushed*, Sch.Lyc.26.

**εὐφλεβής,** ές, = εὔτονος I. 1b, κέρας Neophr.(?) *Medea* in *PLit.Lond*. 77 *Fr*.2.19.

**εὔφλεκτος,** ον, *easily set on fire*, X.*Cyr*.7.5.22, Arr.*An*.2.19.1.

**εὐφορβ-ία,** ἡ, *high feeding*, σφαδᾴζεις πῶλος ὣς εὐφορβίᾳ S.*Fr*. 848. **-ιον,** τό, *spurge, Euphorbia resinifera*, Dsc.3.82, Gal.13. 270; freq. also, *its resinous juice*, S.E.*P*.1.93, *Edict.Diocl*.32. 70. **-ος,** ον, (φέρβω) *well-fed*, Orph.*Fr*.285.65.

**εὐφορ-έω,** *bear well, be productive*, Hp.*Ep*.10, *Ev.Luc*.12.16, Ph.2. 64, al.: metaph., λόγος εὐ. πλημμύραις ῥημάτων καὶ ὀνομάτων Id.1. 690 (ἐμφ- cod.): c. acc., εὐ. σταφυλάς Gal.1.547. II. of ships, *have a prosperous voyage*, Luc.*Lex*.15. **-ητος,** ον, *endurable*, τινι A.*Ch*.353 (lyr.). **-ία,** ἡ, *power of enduring easily*, Hp.*Fract*.35; *contentment*, Phld.*Lib*.p.17 O. 2. *sense of well-being* in disease, τοῦ νοσοῦντος Herod.Med. in *Rh.Mus*.58.106, cf. Gal.11.10, 14.615, Orib.*Syn*.6.6. II. *fertility*, Ph.2.57, al.: in pl., γαστέρων εὐφορίαι Hp.*Epid*.6.7.2; *periods of productivity*, Chrysipp.*Stoic*.2.337; ψυχῶν εὐφορίαι ibid.; *abundant produce*, καρπῶν, οἴνου, Xenag.3, Alciphr. 1.24; ἐλαίου *IG*2$^{2}$.1100.59; σίτου Ἀρχ.Ἐφ.1913.7 (Nisyros, iii B.C.). III. *grace of movement*, in dancing, Poll.4.97.

**εὐφόρμιγξ,** ιγγος, ὁ, ἡ, *with beautiful lyre*: *playing beautifully on it*, Λύκειος *AP*7.10. II. Pass., of lyrical music, *beautifully played* or *accompanied*, Opp.*H*.5.618.

**εὔφορος,** ον, (φέρω) *well* or *patiently borne*, πόνοι Pi.*N*.10.24. 2. *easy to bear* or *wear, manageable, light*, ὅπλα X.*Cyr*.2.3.14 (Sup.); δόρυ Id.*Eq*.7.8 (Sup.); ἔκπωμα Critias *Fr*.34 D. (Sup.); σφενδόνη Luc. *Dom*.7; *ductile*, of clay, Ph.1.418 (Sup.); of wines, -ώτατοι κεφαλῇ καὶ πέψεσιν Ruf.ap.Orib.6.38.15. 3. *easily borne, spreading rapidly*, of diseases, Luc.*Abd*.27; of persons, εὔ. πρὸς ἡδονὰς λόγων Longin.44.1. II. of the body, *active, vigorous, healthy*, Phoc.3.4; εὔ. ἔχειν τὸ σῶμα Arist.*HA*575$^{a}$33; but, *capable of graceful movement*, in dancing, -ώτερον τὸ σῶμα ἕξειν X.*Smp*.2.16. 2. *able to endure, patient*: in Adv. -ρως, τλῆναι S.*Ph*.872; ὀχεῖν Democr.173: Comp. -ώτερον, φέρειν Hp.*Fract*.18: Sup. -ώτατα, φέρειν *Aph*.1.13; τὰ κρύη καὶ τοὺς χειμῶνας εὐ. ἔχειν Plu.2.651c. 3. of animals and plants, *productive, fertile*, Arist.*HA*538$^{a}$1, Thphr.*CP*1.17.10; χώρα Ph.2.297 (Sup.); ἀγρός Plu.2.59a: c. gen., ὀπώρας Hdn.1.6.1; πυρετῶν Gal.7.334: metaph., εὔ. γνῶσις Phld.*Hom*.p.62 O. (dub.); πόλις εὔ. πρὸς ἀνδρῶν ἀρετήν *rich* in manly virtue, D.H.*Rh*.3.3. 4. *easily able* to do, c. inf., Aret.*SD*1.2. 5. Adv. -ρως *easily*, εὐ. καὶ μετὰ ῥαστώνης ἐνεργεῖν Ph.2.283; ἐς τὸ πάθος ἐκφερόμενος App.*BC*2.146 (Sup.); εὐφόρως ἔχειν τῆς γλώττης to have a *ready* tongue, Philostr. *VS*1.25.5; εὐφόρως ἔχειν to feel *well*, Gal.11.28: with no Verb expressed, κοιλίαι τοῖσι πλείστοισι πάνυ εὐφόρως Hp.*Epid*.1.3, cf. Gal. 17(1).209: Comp. -ωτέρως, περιγίνεσθαι Hp.*Art*.69.—An irreg. Comp. εὐφορέστερος in Aret.*CA*1.4.

**εὔφορτος,** ον, *well-freighted, well-ballasted*, νᾶες *AP*12.53 (Mel.): metaph., *agreeable, gracious*, opp. βαρὺς ἐπὶ ταῖς εὐπραγίαις, [στρατηγός] Onos.42.24; μέλη Opp.*C*.1.85, cf. 4.447.

**εὐφρᾰδ-εια** [ᾰ], ἡ, *correctness of language*, Phld.*Rh*.1.165 S., S.E. *M*.1.98. ❋ **-ής,** ές, (φράζω) *expressing oneself correctly* or *accurately*, Simp.*in Ph*.968.30, Suid. Ep. Adv. -έως *eloquently*, πεπνυμένα πάντ' ἀγορεύειν Od.19.352. 2. Pass., *well-expressed*, λόγος Lyd.*Mens*.4. 64, cf. Sch.Il.14.382 (Comp.), etc. **-ίη,** ἡ, Ion. and poet. for εὐφράδεια, *IG*14.1294.

❋ **εὐφραίνω,** Ep. **ἐϋφρ-,** fut. Att. εὐφρᾰνῶ A.*Ch*.742, etc., Ion. and Ep. εὐφρανέω Il.5.688, ἐϋφρανέω 7.297: aor. 1 εὔφρᾱνα or ηὔφρ- Simon. 155.12, Pi.*I*.7(6).3, E.*Or*.217, etc.; Ep. εὔφρηνα Il.24.102, subj. ἐϋφρήνῃς 7.294:—**Pass.,** with fut. Med. εὐφρᾰνοῦμαι X.*Smp*.7.5; Ion. 2 sg. εὐφρανέαι (v.l. -έεαι) Hdt.4.9; also Pass. εὐφρανθήσομαι Ar.*Lys*. 165, Aeschin.1.191, Men.*Pk*.68: aor. 1 εὐφράνθην or ηὐ- Pi.*O*.9.62, Ar. *Ach*.5: (εὔφρων):—*cheer, gladden*, εὐφρανέειν ἄλοχον Il.5.688; ἐϋφραίνοιτε γυναῖκας Od.13.44; ἀνδρὸς ἐϋφραίνοιμι νόημα 20.82; εὐ. θυμόν τινος Pi.*I*.7(6).3; νόον, φρένα, A.*Ch*.742, *Supp*.515; [τινὰ] ἐπέεσσι Il. 24.102; τινὰ δι' ἀρετήν Pl.*Mx*.237a; τινά τι Agatho 12; πλεῖστα X. *Mem*.2.4.6. II. Pass., *make merry, enjoy oneself*, εὐφραίνεσθαι ἕκηλον Od.2.311, cf. Hdt.4.9, *Ev.Luc*.16.19, etc.; τινι *at* or *in* a thing, Pi.*P*.9.16, Ar.*Nu*.561, Pl.*Lg*.796b; ἐπί τινι Ar.*Ach*.5, X.*Smp*.7.5, Aeschin.1.191; ἔν τινι X.*Hier*.1.16; διά τινος ib.8; ἀπό τινος ib.4.6: c. part., εὐφράνθη ἰδών *was rejoiced at* seeing, Pi.*O*.9.62, cf. Men.*Pk*. 68; εἰ πεπαυμένος μηδέν τι μᾶλλον ἢ νοσῶν εὐφραίνεται S.*Aj*.280, cf. E.*Med*.36; τὰ ἐμὰ εὐ. *enjoy a pleasure* in my stead, Luc.*DMar*.13.2.

**εὐφράν-της,** ου, ὁ, *one who cheers*, *EM*436.3. **-τικός,** ή, όν, *cheering*, ὀφθαλμῶν Ath.13.608a. 2. of persons, *cheery*, Vett.Val. 9.3, al.: Comp. -ώτερος *more cheered* by good fortune, *Cat.Cod.Astr*. 8(4).238. **-τοποιός,** όν, = foreg. 1, Sch.Ar.*Pax*519. ❋ **-τός,** ή, όν, *pleasant*, dub. in Gal.5.88: Εὐφραντά, τά, title of work by Timocrates, D.L.10.6, cf. Sch.E.*Hec*.100, al. 2. *cheered, delighted*, Sch. rec.A.*Pr*.536.

**εὐφρᾰσία,** ἡ, *good cheer*, ἡ ἐν τῇ ψυχῇ εὐ. Epict.*Gnom*.19, cf. Melamp.p.24 D., al., *PFlor*.391.1, al. (iii A.D.), *PRyl*.28.47, al. (iv A.D.), Hsch. s.v. δαῖτος.

**εὔφραστος,** ον, (φράζω) *easy to make intelligible*, Arist.*Rh*.1407$^{b}$12; *distinct*, ὀπωπή D.P.171.

❋ **εὐφρονέων,** Ep. **ἐϋφρ-,** *with kind* (or *prudent*) *mind*, ὅ (or ὅς) σφιν ἐϋφρονέων ἀγορήσατο καὶ μετέειπεν Il.1.73, al.; fem. -έουσα A.R.3. 998: pl. -έοντες Man.1.233. (The Verb -φρονέω is not found; perh. better divisim.)

❋ **εὐφρόνη,** ἡ, (εὔφρων) *the kindly time*, euphem. for νύξ, *night*, chiefly poet., Hes.*Op*.560, Pi.*N*.7.3, etc.: also in Ion. and late Prose, Heraclit.26, 57, Hdt.7.12, 56, al., Hp.*Mul*.1.1, Jul.*Or*.2.85b; ἄστρων εὐ., = ἀστερόεσσα εὐ., S.*El*.19; εὐφρόνης, = νυκτός, *by night*, Epist.Anaximen. ap.D.L.2.4; κατ' εὐφρόνην A.*Pers*.221 (troch.), S.*El*.259. II. = εὐφροσύνη, Hsch., cf. E.*Hel*.1470 codd. (lyr., sed leg. εὐφροσύναν).

**εὐφρονίδης,** ου, ὁ, *son of Night*, *Epigr.Gr*.1029.6 (Cius).

❋ **εὐφροσύνη,** Ep. **ἐϋφρ-,** ἡ, (εὔφρων) *mirth, merriment*, γέλω τε καὶ εὐφροσύνην παρέχουσαι Od.20.8, cf. 10.465, etc.; esp. of a banquet, *good cheer, festivity*, οὐ..τί φημι χαριέστερον εἶναι ἢ ὅτ' ἐϋφροσύνη μὲν ἔχῃ κατὰ δῆμον ἅπαντα κτλ. 9.6, cf. *h.Merc*.449, 482, etc.; κρατὴρ μεστὸς ἐϋφροσύνης Xenoph.1.4: pl., σφισι θυμὸς αἰὲν ἐϋφροσύνῃσιν ἰαίνεται is cheered *with glad thoughts*, Od.6.156; *festivities*, A.*Pr*. 539, E.*Ba*.377 (both lyr.), etc.: chiefly poet., used by X.*Cyr*.8.1.32, *Ages*.9.4 (pl.): in sg., Id.*Cyr*.3.3.7, Pl.*Ti*.80b; ἡ χαρὰ καὶ ἡ εὐ. Epicur.*Fr*.2: also in later Prose, Lxx *Ge*.31.27, al., *Act.Ap*.2.28, Diogenian.Epicur.4.50, *PLips*.119 ii 1 (iii A.D.), etc.; εὐ. ψυχῆς οἶνος πινόμενος Lxx *Si*.34.28 (31.36). II. pr. n., *Euphrosyne*, one of the Graces, Hes.*Th*.909, etc.

**εὐφρόσῠνος,** η, ον, also ος, ον dub. in *AP*5.39.6 (Nicarch.), *IGRom*. 4.416 (Pergam.):—poet. and later Prose for εὔφρων, *cheery, merry*, Ptol.*Tetr*.166, Vett.Val.15.5, *Sammelb*.411 (iii/iv A.D.). Adv. -νως *in good cheer*, Thgn.766. II. Act., *cheering, making cheerful*, Dsc.4.127; νύξ Orph.*H*.3.5, etc. 2. εὐφρόσυνον, τό, = βούγλωσσον, Plin.*HN*25.81.

**εὔφρουρος,** ον, (φρουρά) *watchful*, κομιδή Opp.*H*.5.621.

**εὔφρων,** Ep. **ἐΰφρ-,** ον, both in Hom.: (φρήν):—*cheerful, merry*, of persons, εἴ πέρ τις..δαίνυται εὔφρων Il.15.99, etc.; θυμός Od.17.531; ἶλαι Pi.*N*.5.38. Adv. -νως *with good cheer*, Id.*P*.10.40, etc. 2. Act., *cheering, making glad* or *merry*, οἶνος Il.3.246; οἶμος Pi.*Pae*. 6.115; εὔφρων πόνος εὖ τελέσασι A.*Ag*.806 codd.; ὦ φέγγος εὖφρον ib.1577; βοαὶ εὔφρονες Ἀργείοις S.*Aj*.420 (lyr.): neut. pl., εὔφροσιν δεδεγμένη, = εὐφροσύναις, A.*Eu*.632 (s.v.l.). II. *kindly, gracious*, θεὸς εὐ. εἴη εὐχαῖς Pi.*O*.4.14, cf. A.*Pers*.772, S.*Aj*.705 (lyr.), A.R.4. 1411, etc.; γαῖαν ἀνθρώποισι καὶ εὔφρονα μήλοις Pi.*O*.7.63; εὐ. ἥδ' ὁμιλία A.*Eu*.1030; ψῆφον δ' εὔφρον' ἔθεντο Id.*Supp*.640 (lyr.); v.l. for ἐπίφρονος in Theoc.25.29. Adv. -νως A.*Ag*.351, al. 2. *of sound mind, reasonable*, ἄνδρες Xenoph.1.13. III. = εὔφημος, πῶς εὔφρον' εἴπω; A.*Ch*.88; οὐδ' αὖ τόδ' εὖφρον Id.*Supp*.378.

**εὐφῠ-ής,** ές, (φυή) *well-grown, shapely*, μηροί Il.4.147; πτελέη 21. 243; κλάδος, of ivy, E.*Fr*.88; πρόσωπον Id.*Med*.1198; ὀδόντες Alex. 98.20; μαζοί *AP*5.55 (Diosc.); *suitably formed*, πόδες Arist.*PA*691$^{b}$15; χορείας εὐφυὴς βάσις *well-ordered, graceful*, Ar.*Th*.968 (lyr.). II.

*of good natural disposition*, X.*Mem*.1.6.13, al., Arist.*EN*1114b8, Thphr.*Char*.29.4; of horses and dogs, X.*Mem*.4.1.3 (Sup.), Jul. *Or*.2.87a. **2.** *naturally suited* or *adapted*, πρός τι Pl.*R*.455b; πρὸς τὰς τέχνας Isoc.4.33 (Sup.); εἴς τι Pl.*Prt*.327b(Sup.); οὐκ εὐ. λέγειν Aeschin.1.181; εὐ. τὰ σώματα καὶ τὰς ψυχάς Pl.*R*.409e; -έστατος τὴν γνώμην Isoc.9.41: rarely in bad sense, εὐ. πρὸς ἀγονίαν Arist.*GA* 748b8. Adv., εὐφυῶς ἔχει c. inf., Id.*Pol*.1321a9; εὐ. ἔχειν πρὸς.. ib. 1303b8: Comp. -έστερον, ἔχειν D.61.42; also -εστέρως Hierocl. p.27 A. **3.** of place, *well situated*, Arist.*PA*666a14 (Sup.); of time, καιρὸς εὐ. πρὸς σωτηρίαν Plb.1.19.12. Adv. -ῶς, κεῖσθαι πρός.., Arist. *Pol*.1327a33. **III.** *naturally clever*, like εὐτράπελος, euphem. for βωμολόχος, Isoc.7.49, 15.284; σοφιστὴς εὐ. Alex.36.4, cf. 135.13; εὐφυὴς *a man of genius*, Arist.*Po*.1455a32, cf. *Rh*.1390b28; opp. γεγυμνασμένος, ib.1410b8; of hounds, Id.*HA*608a27 (Comp.). Adv. εὐφυῶς *cleverly, skilfully*, Pl.*R*.401c; κολακεύειν Antiph.144.2; ὀψοποιεῖν Alex.24.1. **-ία**, ἡ, *natural goodness of growth* or *shape, shapeliness*, δακτύλων Hp.*Off*.4, cf. *Art*.82; εὐ. καὶ ὥρα Plu.*Sol*.1; ἡ τῶν ζῴων εὐ. Porph.*Abst*.3.24. **II.** *good natural parts*, and morally, *goodness of disposition*, freq. in both senses at once, Arist.*EN*1114b 12, *Rh*.1362b24, etc.; defined as τάχος μαθήσεως, Pl.*Def*.413d. **2.** of places, *fertility, favourable situation*, etc., εὐ. πρός τι Thphr.*CP*1.2.3; ἡ τῶν τόπων εὐ. Plb.2.68.5.—εὐφύεια is cited from Alex.317, and is found in Pap., as Anon. *in Tht*.4.43, al.

**εὐφύλακτος** [ῠ], ον, *easy to keep* or *guard*, A.*Supp*.998; εὐ. ἡ καρδία *well-guarded*, Arist.*PA*670a26; εὐφυλακτότερον τὸ ὕδωρ τοῦ ἀέρος *more easily confined*, Id.*Sens*.438a15, cf. *PA*656b2 (Sup.); ἐν εὐφυλάκτῳ εἶναι to be *on one's guard*, E.*HF*201; -ότερα αὐτοῖς ἐγίγνετο it was *easier* for them *to keep a look-out*, Th.8.55; ὅπως εὐφύλακτα αὐτοῖς εἴη Id.3.92, cf. Plu.*Rom*.18. **II.** (φυλάττομαι) *easy to guard against*, Arist.*SE*174b35 (Comp.), D.C.57.1.

**εὔφυλλος**, ον, *leafy*, Νεμέα Pi.*I*.6(5).61; δάφνα E.*IT*1246 (lyr.).

**εὐφύσητος** [ῡ], ον, gloss on εὔπρηστος, Sch.Il.18.471; *easily blown away*, *EM*273.35.

**εὔφῠτος**, ον, (φυτόν) *well-planted*, Poll.1.228.

**εὐφων-έω**, *have a good voice*, Phld.*Rh*.1.367 S. ⊛ **-ία**, ἡ, *goodness of voice*, X.*Mem*.3.3.13, Arist.*Pr*.903b27; τόλμα καὶ εὐ., of an orator, Plu.2.838e. **2.** *excellence of tone*, of horns, Arist.*Aud*.802b2. **II.** *euphony*, D.H.*Comp*.25, Quint.1.5.4, Demetr.*Eloc*.68. **-ος**, ον, *sweet-voiced, musical*, Πιερίδες Pi.*I*.1.64; χορός A.*Ag*.1187; *sweet-toned*, λύρα Arist.*Metaph*.1019b15; τὸ βαρὺ ἀπὸ τοῦ ὀξέος -ότερον Id. *Pr*.920a23; εὔ. θαλίαι *accompanied with sweet songs*, Pi.*P*.1.38. **2.** *loud-voiced*, of a herald, Ar.*Ec*.713, X.*HG*2.4.20, cf. D.19.126; οἱ -ότατοι Hdn.2.6.4. **3.** *euphonious*, Democr.18b, D.H.*Comp*.12, Demetr.*Eloc*.70; -ότατον τὸ ᾱ D.H.*Comp*.14. **4.** Adv. -νως Poll. 2.113: Comp. -οτέρως Demetr.*Eloc*.255; -ότερον Plu.2.1132b: Sup. -ότατα, ᾄδειν Philostr.*VA*4.42.

**εὐφώρᾱτος**, ον, *easy to detect*, Gal.13.333; διαφορά Plu.2.63c; συκοφαντία Lib.*Decl*.49.79: Comp., Gal.6.95: **Εὐφωρατ**[.] dub. in *Lyr Alex.Adesp*.19 tit.

⊛ **εὐχαίτης**, ου, ὁ, *with beautiful hair*, Γανυμήδης Call.*Ep*.53; epith. of Hades, *Ath.Mitt*.24.257(Thrace); of horses, *with beautiful mane*, Poll. 5.83; of plants, *with beautiful leaves*, λωτός *AP*4.1.51 (Mel.); κισσός ib.9.669 (Marian.): also **εὔχαιτος**, ον, σώματα Herm.ap.Stob.1.49.60.

**εὐχαιτίας**, ου, ὁ, v.l. for foreg., D.S.20.54.

**εὐχάλῑν-ος** [ᾰ], ον, *well-bridled*, S.E.*M*.1.169. **-ωτος**, ον, (χαλῑνόω) = foreg., Hdn.*Epim*.178.

**εὔχαλκος**, ον, *wrought of fine brass* or *well-wrought in* (or *pointed with*) *brass*, στεφάνη Il.7.12; ἀξίνη 13.612; μελίη 20.322; τρίποδες Od.15.84; κράνος A.*Th*.459; ὅπλα Id.*Pers*.456.

**εὐχάλκωτος**, ον, (χαλκόω) = foreg., κρεάγρα *AP*6.305.5 (Leon.).

**εὐχανδής**, ές, *spacious*, Man.6.463; νηδύς Nic.*Al*.63.

**εὐχᾰράκτ-ηρος**, *bene figuratus, formosus*, Gloss. ⊛ **-ος**, ον, *clearly stamped*, νομισμάτια *PLips*.13.10 (iv A.D.).

**εὐχάρ-εια** [χᾰ], ἡ, *grace, charm*, Simp. *in Epict*.p.119 D.; cf. εὐχαρίη II. **-ής**, ές, = εὔχαρις, Men.Rh.p.406 S.; v.l. for εὔχαρις, Lxx *Wi*.14.20. **-ίζω**, *render thanks*, τόπῳ *Sammelb*.4563. **-ίη**, ἡ, = εὐχαριστία, Ἀθήναιον 7.210 (Patrae). **II.** = εὐχάρεια, *urbanity*, Hp. *Praec*.10 (v.l. εὐχαριστίη). ⊛ **-ις**, neut. εὔχαρι, gen. ιτος, *charming, gracious*, esp. in society, Democr.104, Pl.*R*.486d, 487a, X.*Cyr*.7. 4.1; ἀστεῖοι καὶ εὐ. ib.2.2.12; εὔ. κατὰ τὰς ἐντεύξεις, ἐν ταῖς ὁμιλίαις, Plb.22.21.3, 23.5.7; τὸ εὔ. *urbanity*, X.*Ages*.8.1, 11.11, M.Ant.1.16. 5; of Aphrodite, *gracious*, E.*Heracl*.894 (lyr.), *Med*.631 (lyr.); of animals, Arist.*HA*592b24: Comp. -ιτώτερος Plot.3.6.6: Sup. -ιτώτατος, ἐς τὸν δῆμον App.*BC*2.26. **II.** of places, *pleasant*, Arist.*Pol*. 1331a36. **-ισμα**, *corollarium*, Gloss.

⊛ **εὐχᾰριστ-έω**, *bestow a favour on, oblige*, τῷ δήμῳ τῷ Δηλίων *IG*11 (4).665 (Delos, iii B.C.); τινι *PPetr*.2 p.4 (iii B.C.), *PHib*.1.66.5 (iii B.C.). **2.** *to be thankful, return thanks*, Decr.ap.D.18.92, *IPE*1². 352.14 (Chersonesus, ii B.C.); τοῖς Ἀθηναίοις Posidon.36 J., cf. Phld. *Ir*.p.92 W., al.; ἐπί τινι or περί τινος *for* a thing, Plb.4.72.7, D.S.16. 11, etc.; esp. to the gods, ἐπὶ τῷ ἐρρῶσθαί σε τοῖς θεοῖς εὐ. *UPZ*59.10 (ii B.C.), cf. Lxx *Ju*.8.25, 1*Ep.Cor*.1.4, etc.:—Pass., *to be thanked*, ηὐχαρίστηται κεραυνοῖς Hp.*Ep*.17; *to be received with thanks*, 2*Ep. Cor*.1.11. **3.** *pray*, τῷ θεῷ περί τινος *PLond*.2.413, 418 (iv A.D.). **-ήριος**, ον, *expressive of gratitude*, ὁλοκαύτωμα εὐ. τινός Ph. 2.157; εὐχαί *PMasp*.6.6 (vi A.D.): as Subst., εὐχαριστήρια (sc. ἱερά), τά, *thank-offering*, τοῖς θεοῖς θύειν εὐ. Plb.5.14.8, cf. Sch.Pi.*P*.7.9; *mission of thanks* to the Senate, D.S.29.11: sg., Ἀσκληπιῷ καὶ Ὑγείᾳ .. εὐχαριστήριον (sc. ἀνέθηκεν) *IG*12(3).1086 (Melos), cf. 3.132*l*, *IPE* 1².162.2, *OGI*699 (Egypt), Lxx 2*Ma*.12.45. **-ητέον**, *one must give thanks*, τινι Ph.1.273; ὑπέρ τινος ib.533. ⊛ **-ητικός**, ή, όν, = -ιστικός, λόγος, ὕμνος, ib.177, 371. Adv. -κῶς ib.273 (v.l. -ιστικῶς). ⊛ **-ία**, ἡ, *thankfulness, gratitude*, Decr.ap.D.18.91, *Stoic*.3.67, Phld.*Ir*.p.93 W.; τοῦ δήμου *OGI*227.6 (Didyma, iii B.C.); πρός τινα D.S.17.59, *PLond*.3.1178.25 (ii A.D.); πρὸς τὸν θεόν Plb.1.36.1; ἀπόντι μᾶλλον εὐ. ποίει Men.693. **2.** *giving of thanks*, εἰς εὐ. θεοῦ *SIG*798.5 (Cyzicus, i A.D.), cf. Ph.1.60, Lxx *Wi*.16.28, *Corp.Herm*.1.29, etc.: pl., ποιεῖσθαι -ίας 1*Ep.Ti*.2.1. **-ικός**, ή, όν, *of gratitude*, ὕμνοι Ph. 2.109; εὐχή *JHS*37.101 (Lydia, ii A.D.). Adv. -κῶς Ph.1.59. ⊛ **-ος**, ον, *agreeable*, τινι τέχνῃ X.*Oec*.5.10 (Comp.); λόγοι Id.*Cyr*.2.2.1 (Sup.); -ότατα καὶ πιθανώτατα εἴρηκε Plb.12.28.11; εὐχάριστα *acceptable gifts*, *AJA*30.249 (Cypr.). Adv. -τως, τελευτᾶν τὸν βίον to die *happily*, Hdt.1.32. **II.** *grateful, thankful*, X.*Cyr*.8.3.49 (Sup.), *Inscr. Prien*.103.8 (ii/i B.C.), *Ep.Col*.3.15, etc. Adv. -τως, διακεῖσθαι πρός τινα D.S.1.90; ἀποδιδόναι Ph.1.520; τῶν γεγονότων μνημονεύειν Plu.2. 477f. **III.** *beneficent*, θεοί *UPZ*41.13 (ii B.C.); title of Ptolemy V, *OGI*90.5 (Rosetta); τὸ τῆς ψυχῆς εὐ. D.S.18.28; βεβαιωτὴς (-ότης codd.) εὐχάριστος, of God, Ph.1.128 codd. (ἰσχυρότατος cj. Cohn).

⊛ **εὐχάρῑτος**, ον, freq. v.l. for foreg., as in Arist.*HA*592b24.

**εὐχάροπος** [ᾰ], ον, strengthd. for χάροπος, *Gp*.14.16.2.

**εὐχατῆσαι**· ἐπικαυχήσασθαι, Hsch. **εὐχατότερον**· πλουσιώτερον, Id.

**εὐχείμερος**, ον, (χεῖμα) *healthy* or *convenient to winter in*, πόλεις Arist.*Pol*.1330a41. **II.** Act., *bearing the winter* or *the cold well*, ὄϊες Id.*HA*596b4 (Comp.).

**εὐχείμων**, prob. f.l. for λευχ-, Suid.

**εὐχεῖον**, τό, *house of prayer, synagogue*, *PLond*.3.1177.60 (iii A.D.).

**εὔχειρ**, χειρος, ὁ, ἡ, *quick* or *ready of hand, handy, dexterous*, Pi.*O*. 9.111; σὺν νόῳ εὔχειρες Hp.*Art*.33, cf. S.*OC*472.

**εὐχειρία**, Ion. -ίη, ἡ, *manual dexterity, skill*, ἀνόητος εὐ. Hp.*Art*. 35, cf. Ruf.ap.Orib.*inc*.20.1; in flute-playing, Poll.4.72; in battle, Plb.11.13.3, 16.10.1, *Fr*.158 (pl.), Hdn.1.17.12, etc. (Sts. confused in codd. with εὐχέρεια.)

**εὐχείρωτος**, ον, (χειρόω) *easy to master* or *overcome*, A.*Pers*.452, X.*HG*5.3.4, etc.; *easy to train*, τῷ νομοθέτῃ Arist.*Pol*.1332b9; simply, *easy*, Porph.*Abst*.3.4. (Comp. εὐχειρότερος D.C.37.7, and Sup. εὐχειρότατος X.*Cyr*.1.6.36, *Oec*.8.4, Thphr.*HP*4.14.7, are ff.ll. for -ωτότερος, -ωτότατος.)

⊛ **εὐχέρ-εια**, ἡ, *tolerance of* or *indifference to* evil, μὴ ἡμῖν πολλὴν εὐχέρειαν ἐντίκτωσι τοῖς νέοις πονηρίας Pl.*R*.392a; *licentiousness*, A. *Eu*.494 (lyr.); ἡ τῆς πράξεως εὐ. Aeschin.1.124; *unscrupulous conduct*, ἡ πρὸς τὸν δῆμον εὐ. Plu.*Demetr*.11; *looseness*, περὶ τὰς γυναῖκας, περὶ τοὺς ὅρκους, Id.*Lyc*.15, *Lys*.8; *recklessness*, πρὸς τὸν ὅρκον εὐ. καὶ ταχύτης Id.2.271c; *hastiness*, Ph.2.276; πρὸς ὀργήν Luc.*Prom*.9; of a historian, *irresponsibility*, εὐ. καὶ τόλμα καὶ ῥᾳδιουργία Plb.12. 25e.2, cf. 16.18.3; εἰκαιότης καὶ εὐ. Ph.1.193; of an artist, *uncritical facility*, ἐν τῷ ποιεῖν εὐ. καὶ ταχύτης Plu.*Per*.13. **II.** *indifference to danger* or *hardship*: hence, *coolness, fortitude*, ἀνδρεία καὶ εὐ. (ironical) Pl.*R*.426d; εὐκολία καὶ εὐ. Id.*Lg*.942d, cf. *Alc*.1.122c; περὶ τὰς κυνηγίας εὐ. καὶ τόλμα Plb.22.3.8; cf. εὐχειρία. **III.** *ease, agreeableness*, κατὰ τὴν προφοράν Phld.*Po*.994.`; *comfort*, ὁδὸς πρὸς εὐχέρειαν ὡδοποιημένη *OGI*175.9 (Egypt, ii B.C.); περὶ τὰς δυστοκίας τῶν γυναικῶν τῇ εὐχερείᾳ.. βοηθεῖν to minister to the *comfort* (or promote the *fortitude*) of women.., Arist.*HA*587a11 (cf. εὐχερής II). **IV.** *dexterity, skill*, εὐ. Πραξιτέλους Luc.*Am*.11 (nisi leg. εὐχειρία). ⊛ **-ής**, ές, *tolerant of* or *indifferent to evil, unpleasantness* or *inaccuracy, not squeamish*, ἡ ὗς -έστατον πρὸς πᾶσαν τροφὴν ζῴων ἐστίν Arist. *HA*595a18; οὐδενὸς γὰρ πώποτε ἀπέβαλεν ὀσπρίου λέπος· οὕτως ἐκεῖνός ἐστιν εὐ. ἀνήρ Alex.266.8, cf. Aristopho12.5, S.*Ph*.519, 875; of lizard-eaters, λίαν εὐχερεῖς Menesth.ap.Orib.2.68.13; εὐ. βίος of the swineherd, Pl.*Plt*.266d; τὸ εὐ. τῶν ὀνομάτων the *loose* use of names, Id. *Tht*.184c. Adv. -ρῶς, φέρειν τὴν ὠχρότητα, i.e. gloss it over, Id.*R*. 474e, cf. *Tht*.154b; εὐ. ἔχειν πρὸς τὴν ἀνθρωποφαγίαν Arist.*Pol*.1338b 21; -ρῶς ὥσπερ θηρίον ὕειον ἐν ἀμαθίᾳ μολύνηται Pl.*R*.535e: Comp. -έστερον, πρὸς πᾶν βρῶμα ἔχειν X.*Lac*.2.5; ἄλλο μικρῷ μεῖζον -έστερον κινοῦσιν *more readily, with fewer qualms*, Arist.*Pol*.1307b5, cf. Din. 1.55. **2.** *unscrupulous, reckless*, D.21.103, Arist.*Metaph*.1025a2. Adv. -ρῶς *heedlessly, recklessly*, ὦ λέγων εὐχερῶς ὅτι ἂν βουληθῇς D.18. 70, cf. 264. **II.** *indifferent to danger* or *suffering, cool, unconcerned, unflinching*, τῆς πολεμικῆς χρείας τῆς κατ' ἄνδρα.. εὐχερεῖς καὶ πρακτικοί *cool* and efficient in individual fighting, Plb.4.8.9; εἰς εὐχερῆ τῆς ἀποτέξεως ὑπομονήν Sor.1.46 (cf. εὐχέρεια II). Adv. -ρῶς καὶ εὐκόλως ἐξέπιεν drank the hemlock *coolly* and good-humouredly, Pl.*Phd*.117c. **III.** *easy*, εὐχερές ἐστι c. inf., Batr.62; τὰ λαχανευόμενα μεταφυτεύεται πρὸς εὐχερῆ τελείωσιν Sor.1.87: Comp., ib.108. Adv. -ρῶς, τοῦ γινομένης εὐχερῶς ἀποξύνεται τὸ γάλα Id.1.115, cf. *PLond*.2.401.24 (ii B.C.): Sup. -έστατα, τρέπονται (sc. εἰς φυγήν) D.S.31.38. **2.** σπασμοὶ εὐχερέες, i.e. *not dangerous*, Hp.*Prorrh*.1. 119 (cf. Gal.16.773); cf. εὐήθης I. 3. **3.** c. dat., *suitable, adapted*, θαλάσσα.. μεγάλαις ναυσὶν οὐκ εὐ. App.*BC*2.84.

**εὐχετάομαι**, Ep. for εὔχομαι, only in pres. and impf. (without augm.):—*pray*, θεοῖσι.. μεγάλ' εὐχετόωντο ἕκαστος Il.8.347, 15.369; Κρονίωνι.. εὐχετάασθαι 6.268; πάντες δ' εὐχετόωντο θεῶν Διὶ Νέστορί τ' ἀνδρῶν 11.761, cf. Od.8.467. **II.** *boast, profess*, c. inf., τίνες ἔμμεναι εὐχετόωντο; Od.1.172, etc.; with inf. omitted, A.R.1.189, Orph.*A*.289; *brag*, ἵνα μή τις.. εὐχετόῳτ' ἐπέεσσι Il.12.391; οὐ μὲν καλὸν ὑπέρβιον εὐχετάασθαι 17.19; μὰψ αὔτως εὐχετάασθαι 20.348; κταμένοισιν ἐπ' ἀνδράσιν εὐχετάασθαι *to glory* over them, Od.22.412.

**εὐχέτης**, ου, ὁ, *one who prays*, Eust.1725.57, Zonar.

**εὐχετιάζον**· ηὔχοντο, Hsch.

⊛ **εὐχή**, ἡ, (εὔχομαι) *prayer* or *vow*, once in Hom. (cf. εὖχος, εὐχωλή), ἐπὴν εὐχῇσι λίσῃ Od.10.526, cf. Hes.*Th*.419, Thgn.341, Hdt.1.31, etc.; θεὸς εὔφρων εἴη..εὐχαῖς Pi.*O*.4.15; εὐχὰς ἀνασχεῖν τινι S.*El*.636; εὐχὴν ἐπιτελέσαι, Lat. *vota persolvere*, Hdt.1.86; εὐχὰς ἀποδιδόναι X.*Mem*.2.2.10; εὐχὴν ἀνέστησεν *SIG*1142 (Phrygia, i/ii A.D.); εὐχῇ χρῆσθαι, Lat. *votis potiri*, Pl.*Lg*.688b; κατὰ χιλίων..εὐχὴν ποιήσασθαι χιμάρων to make *a vow* of a thousand goats, Ar.*Eq*.661; ἐν θεῶν εὐχαῖσι S.*OT*239, etc.; εὐχαὶ πρὸς θεούς Pl.*Lg*.70?b; εὐχὰς εὔχεσθαι τοῖς θεοῖς D.19.130; εὐχὰς εὔξεται ὑπὲρ τῆς πόλεως *Inscr.Prien*.174.18 (ii B.C.); εὐχὰς ποιεῖσθαι Th.6.32, Arist.*Mu*.400$^{a}$17; εὐχὴν ἀποθύειν Diph.43.10; κατ' εὐχήν, ἐξ εὐχῆς, Lat. *ex voto*, Call.*Ep*.48, *AP*6.357 (Theaet.); ἔχειν εὐχήν to be under *a vow*, *Act.Ap*.18.18. **2.** *wish* or *aspiration*, opp. reality, εὐχαῖς ὅμοια λέγειν to build '*castles in the air*', Pl.*R*.499c, cf. 540d; μὴ εὐ. δοκῇ εἶναι ὁ λόγος ib.450d; κατὰ τὴν τῶν παίδων εὐ. like a boy's *wish*, Id.*Sph*.249d; εὐχῆς ἄξια things *to be wished*, but not expected, Isoc.4.182; πολιτεία ἡ κατ' εὐχὴν γινομένη the *ideal* state, Arist.*Pol*.1295$^{a}$29, cf. 1288$^{b}$23; ζῆν κατ' εὐχήν ib.1260$^{b}$29. **3.** *prayer for evil*, i.e. *curse*, *imprecation*, πατρὸς κατ' εὐχάς A.*Th*.820, cf. E.*Ph*.70.

**εὐχήμων**, ον, gen. ονος, *to be wished for*, Hsch.

**εὔχῑλος**, ον, *rich in fodder*, κάπη Lyc.95. **II.** of a horse, *feeding well*, X.*Eq*.1.12 (Comp.), cf. Arist.*PA*675$^{b}$15 (Comp.).

**εὐχίμᾰρος** [ῐ], ον, *rich in goats*, *AP*6.108 (Myrin.).

**εὐχίον**, τό, Dim. of εὐχή, dub. in *IG*14.622 (Rhegium).

⊛ **εὔχλοος**, ον, contr. **-χλους**, ουν, (χλόη) *fresh and green*, epith. of Demeter, S.*OC*1600, cf. Nonn.*D*.41.15.

**εὔχλωρος**, f.l. for ἔγχλωρος (Coraes), Thphr.*HP*3.5.2.

⊛ **εὔχομαι**, impf. εὐχόμην (Att. ηὐ-) Il.3.275, etc.: fut. εὔξομαι Ar.*Av*.622 (anap.), etc.: aor. 1 εὐξάμην (Att. ηὐ-) Il.8.254, etc.: 2 sg. subj. εὔξεαι Od.3.45: (augm. ηὐ- only Att. acc. to Hdn.Gr.2.789, Moer.175):—*pray*, θεοῖς Il.3.296, Hdt.8.64, Th.3.58, etc.; ἀγάλμασι Heraclit.5; ἀνέμοισι Hdt.7.178; Ἀργείοισι A.*Supp*.980: c. acc. cogn., εὐχὰς εὔ. τοῖς θεοῖς D.19.130; εὐχὰς ὑπέρ τινος πρὸς τοὺς θεοὺς εὔ. Aeschin.3.18; εὔ. ἔπος *to utter* it *in prayer*, Simon.37.19, Pi.*P*.3.2, A.*Supp*.1059 (lyr.); μεγάλα, μέγα εὔ., *pray* aloud, Il.3.275, Od.17.239; πολλὰ Ποσειδάωνι 3.54: later, c. acc., Ἄρτεμιν εὔ. *AP*9.268 (Antip. Thess.): abs., Il.7.298, A.*Ch*.465 (lyr.), Ar.*Fr*.39 D. (lyr.), etc. **2.** c. acc. et inf., *pray that*, Od.15.353, 21.211, Hdt.1.31; of an unrealizable wish (cf. εὐχή 2), Arist.*EN*1118$^{a}$32, cf. Macho ap.Ath.8.341d: c. inf. alone, εὔ. θάνατον φυγεῖν Il.2.401; τί δοκέεις εὔχεσθαι ἄλλο ἢ..λαβεῖν; Hdt.1.27; οἶκον ἰδεῖν Pi.*P*.4.293, etc.; τοῖς θεοῖς c. acc. et inf., Pl.*Phd*.117c; also εὔ. τοὺς θεοὺς δοῦναί μοι *pray* that the gods may give, Ar.*Th*.351, X.*An*.6.1.26; πρὸς τοὺς θεοὺς διδόναι Id.*Mem*.1.3.2; ταῖς Μούσαις εἰπεῖν Pl.*R*.545d, etc.; later εὔ. ἵνα Aristeas 45, D.H.9.53, Arr.*Epict*.2.6.12; ὅπως *Wien.Stud*.44.159. **3.** c. acc. obj., *pray for*, *long* or *wish for*, χρυσόν Pi.*N*.8.37, etc.; εὐχόμενος ἄν τις ταῦτα εὔξαιτο Antipho 6.1; εὔ. τινί τι *pray for* something *for* a person, S.*Ph*.1019; κακόν τινι Lys.21.21; also, *pray for* a thing *from*.., τοῖς θεοῖς πολλὰ ἀγαθὰ ὑπέρ τινος X.*Mem*.2.2.10; τοῖς θεοῖς πολυκαρπίαν ib.3.14.3; δεινὸν κατά τινος Luc.*Abd*.32. **II.** *vow* or *promise to* do.., c. fut. inf., εὔχομαι ἐξελάαν κύνας Il.8.526; θεοῖσι..ἑκατόμβας ῥέξειν Od.17.50, cf. Il.4.101, Pl.*Phd*.58b, *IG*1$^{2}$.108.55, 2$^{2}$.112.6 (iv B.C.): c. aor. inf., εὔχετο πάντ' ἀποδοῦναι *claimed* (the right) to pay in full, Il.18.499 (unless in signf. III. 3): c. pres. inf., ηὖξω θεοῖς..ἂν ὧδ' ἔρδειν τάδε; A.*Ag*.933, cf. S.*Ph*.1032 codd. **2.** c. acc. rei, *vow* a thing, πολλῶν πατησμὸν εἱμάτων A.*Ag*.963; ἱερεῖον Ar.*Av*.1619; [λύχνον] περὶ παιδός Call.*Ep*.56.3. **3.** εὔ. κατά τινος of the thing vowed (as though on the altar), εὔ. τοῖς θεοῖς κατὰ ἑκατόμβης Plu.*Mar*.26, cf. 2.294b; κατὰ νικητηρίων D.*Ep*.1.16. **III.** *profess loudly*, *boast*, *vaunt*, οὕτω φησὶ καὶ εὔχεται, οὕνεκ' Ἀχιλλεὺς νηυσὶν ἔπι γλαφυρῇσι μένει Il.14.366; εὑρεῖν Emp.2.6: mostly, not of empty boasting, but of something of which one has a right to be proud, ταύτης τοι γενεῆς τε καὶ αἵματος εὔχομαι εἶναι Il.6.211, cf. 8.190; πατρὸς δ' ἐξ ἀγαθοῦ καὶ ἐγὼ γένος εὔχομαι εἶναι 14.113, cf. Pl.*Grg*.449a: rarely without inf., ἐκ Κρητάων γένος εὔχομαι (sc. εἶναι) Od.14.199; τὸ πατρόθεν ἐκ Διὸς εὔχονται Pi.*O*.7.23, cf. *P*.4.97; πόρτις εὔχεται βοός (sc. εἶναι) A.*Supp*.314; ἔνθεν εὔχομαι γένος E.*Fr*.696; but also, **2.** *boast vainly*, *brag*, εὔχεαι αὔτως Il.11.388: c. inf., εὔ. δῃώσειν S.*OC*1318. **3.** simply, *profess* or *declare*, ἱκέτης δέ τοι εὔ. εἶναι Od.5.450; οὔτ' ὦν ἀκοῦσαι οὔτ' ἰδεῖν εὔχοντο Pi.*O*.6.53; τίς χθὼν εὔχεται ἥδε [εἶναι]; A.R.4.1251; cf. supr. II. 1. **IV.** Pass., ἐμοὶ μετρίως ηὖκται I *have prayed* sufficiently, Pl.*Phdr*.279c: pf. inf., ταῦτα μὲν ηὖχθαι *IG*2$^{2}$.112.12 (iv B.C.); ἡ πανήγυρις ἡ..εὐχθεῖσα *vowed*, D.C.48.32: but plpf. (or non-thematic preterite) ηὔγμην in act. sense, S.*Tr*.610; so εὖκτο Thebaïs *Fr*.3. (Cf. Skt. *óhate* 'to (be able to) boast that one is', 'to brag', Avest. *aog*- 'declare solemnly'.)

**εὔχορδος**, ον, *well-strung*, λύρα Pi.*N*.10.21.

⊛ **εὔχορος**, v. ἠΰχ-.

**εὔχορτος**, ον, of pasture, *fattening*, τοῦτο (sc. τὸ χωρίον) Arist.*HA*595$^{b}$26; εὔχορτα πεδία Poetae ap.Poll.7.184: neut. pl. -χορτα *pastures*, *IGRom*.4.1349 (Lydia).

**εὖχος**, εος, τό, (εὔχομαι) poet. Noun: **I.** *thing prayed for*, *object of prayer*, εὖχος δοῦναι, ὀρέξαι, πορεῖν τινι, Il.5.285, 22.130, Od.22.7, S.*Ph*.1203; εὖχος ἀρέσθαι to obtain *it*, Il.7.203; ἑλεῖν Tyrt.12.36, Pi.*P*.5.21; Τεῦκρον..εὖχος ἀπηύρα took *it* away from him, Il.15.462. **II.** *boast*, *vaunt*, μέλεον δέ οἱ εὖχος ἔδωκας 21.473; εὖχος ἔργῳ καθελών Pi.*O*.10(11).63, al.; of persons, Ἀνάκρεον, εὖ. Ἰώνων *AP*7.27 (Antip. Sid.). **III.** later, *vow*, *votive offering*, Pl.*Epigr*.5.3.

**εὔχρεως**, ων, f.l. for χρυσέῳ, Antim.*Eleg*.4.

**εὐχρημᾰτ-έω**, *to be wealthy*, Poll.3.109, 6.196. **-ία**, ἡ, *wealth*, ibid. **-ιστος**, ον, *good man of business*, Vett.Val.38.35, Ptol.*Tetr*.162. **2.** *richly endowed*, ὑπὸ θεῶν Heph.Astr.1.1. **-ος**, ον, *wealthy*, Poll.3.109.

**εὐχρημονέω**, = εὐχρηματέω, Pl.Com.ap.Poll.6.196.

**εὐχρηστ-έω**, *to be serviceable*, τινι for a thing, Plb.12.18.3; εἴς τι Dsc.1.7; ἐπί τινι Ruf.ap.Orib.8.39.5, etc.; τινι to a person, *SIG*618.13 (Heraclea ad Latm., ii B.C.): abs., Chrysipp.*Stoic*.3.184, Diog.Bab.ib.3.233, *Michel* 163.22 (Delos). **2.** *lend*, *advance*, *UPZ*123.26, *Inscr.Prien*.108.109 (ii B.C.). **II.** Pass., εὐχρηστεῖσθαι διά τινα *to receive assistance* through his means, D.S.5.12; ὑπό τινος Plu.2.185e. **2.** *to be in common use*, of words, Eust.964.21, etc. **-ημα**, ατος, τό, *advantage received*, *Stoic*.3.23. ⊛ **-ία**, ἡ, *ready use*, σκευῶν Arist.*Oec*.1345$^{b}$1, cf. Ph.*Bel*.72.7; *utility*, *serviceableness*, Chrysipp.*Stoic*.3.168; πρός τι Plb.9.7.5. **2.** *service rendered*, πλείστην εὐ. τῇ ἐπαρχείᾳ παρέξεσθαι *Inscr.Prien*.105.25 (i B.C.). **II.** *credit*, D.S.1.79. ⊛ **-ος**, ον, also -η, ον Orph.*Fr*.272: (χράομαι):— *useful*, *serviceable*, ἔν τινι Hp.*Fract*.16 (Sup.); πρός τι Pl.*Lg*.777b, X.*Mem*.3.8.5, etc.; εἴς τι D.S.5.40 (Sup.); of persons, c. dat., *PPetr*.3 p.153 (iii B.C.); τῷ δήμῳ *Inscr.Prien*.102.5 (ii/i B.C.); σκεῦος εὔ. τῷ δεσπότῃ 2*Ep.Ti*.2.21; εὔχρησται ἡμέραι, in astrology, Orph.*Fr*.272. Adv. -τως Chrysipp.*Stoic*.2.334; εὐ. ἔχειν πρός τι Plb.3.73.5, Ael.*Tact*.3.2. **II.** *easy to execute*, διίππευσις ib.18.4. **-ότης**, ητος, ἡ, *serviceableness*, Simp.*in Ph*.373.26 (pl.).

**εὐχρηστόψῡχος**, ον, *having useful moral qualities*, *Cat.Cod.Astr*.8(3).188.

**εὐχρόαστος**, ον, f.l. for εὔχρηστος in X.*Eq*.1.17.

**εὐ-χροέω**, *to be of a good, healthy look*, Hp.*Morb*.2.1, Ar.*Lys*.80, Gal.17(2).215. **-χροής**, ές, rare poet. form for εὔχροος, δέρμα βόειον εὐχροές Od.14.24. **-χροια**, Ion. -οίη, ἡ, *goodness of complexion*, *fresh and healthy look*, Hp.*Coac*.67, Arist.*HA*584$^{a}$14, Thphr.*Sud*.39, Dsc.*Eup*.1.105, Aret.*SA*2.4. **-χροος**, ον, contr. **-χρους**, ουν, Ion. **-χροιος**, ον, (χρόα) *well-coloured*, *of good* or *healthy complexion*, Hp.*Aph*.3.17, X.*Lac*.5.8, etc.; κριὸν εὔχρουν *IG*5(1).1390.67 (Andania, i B.C.): Comp. -οώτερος X.*Cyr*.8.1.41; -ούστερος Arist.*Pr*.863$^{b}$1: Sup. -ούστατος ib.960$^{b}$5. **2.** in Music, εὔχροα χρώματα Philoch.66.

**εὔχρῡσος**, ον, *rich in gold*, of the Pactolus, S.*Ph*.394 (lyr.); Σάρδεις Max.Tyr.27.3 (Sup.).

**εὔχρωμος**, ον, = εὔχρως, *Gloss*. Adv. -μως '*safe and sound*', *PRyl*.237.8 (iii A.D.); also in an epitaph, ζήσας εὐχρώμως *Rendic.d.Pontif.Accad.Rom.Ser*.iii vol.3.192.

**εὔχρως**, ων, = εὔχροος, Ar.*Eq*.1171, *Th*.644, Theopomp.Com.24, X.*Oec*.10.5: pl., εὔχρω Arist.*PA*677$^{a}$23; *ruddy*, Thphr.*HP*.3.9.7; *bright-coloured*, ib.7.3.1. **2.** of music, = εὔχροος, condemned by Pl.*Lg*.655a. (Only used in nom. and acc.)

⊛ **εὐχρωτέω**, imper. -χρώτ⟨ε⟩ι, in an epitaph, = ὑγίαινε, χαῖρε, etc., *IG*14.2305.

**εὐχῡλ-ία**, ἡ, *goodness of flavour*, Hices.ap.Ath.3.87c, Xenocr.ap.Orib.2.58.57; *wholesomeness of juice*, Sor.1.53. **-ος**, ον, *juicy*, *succulent*, Thphr.*CP*6.11.15 (Comp.), Archig.ap.Gal.12.460, etc.; of meat, Alex.189, Diph.Siph.ap.Ath.2.62c, Hices.ib.7.282d: metaph., Phld.*Po*.1676 *Fr*.11. Adv. -λως Hp.*Mul*.1.17.

⊛ **εὐχῡμ-ία**, ἡ, = εὐχυλία, Hp.*Loc.Hom*.10 (dub. l.), Thphr.*CP*6.11.4. **II.** Medic., *healthy state of the humours*, Gal.11.491, al. **2.** of food, *faculty of producing such a state*, Id.6.749. **-ος**, ον, *well-flavoured*, Posidon.3 J.; πρὸς τὴν ἐδωδὴν εὔ. Arist.*GA*763$^{b}$7: Comp., Plu.2.690a. **II.** *productive of healthy humours*, *wholesome*, Hp.*Aff*.55, Gal.17(2).876. **III.** *plump*, *in good condition*, Ptol.*Tetr*.144.

**εὔχῠτος**, ον, *easily dissolved*, Dsc.5.153; ἔς τι Aret.*CD*1.3; gloss on ἑανοῦ, Sch.D Il.18.612.

⊛ **εὐχωλ-ή**, ἡ, (εὔχομαι) Ep. form of εὐχή, *prayer*, *vow*, οὔτ' ἄρ' ὅ γ' εὐχωλῆς ἐπιμέμφεται οὔθ' ἑκατόμβης Il.1.93, cf. 65; θυέεσσι καὶ εὐχωλῇς ἀγανῇσι 9.499, cf. Od.13.357; εὐχωλέων οὐκ ἔκλυε Φοῖβος Hes.*Sc*.68; also in *Inscr.Cypr*.94 H. and Ion. Prose, Hdt.2.63, Protag.A 1 Diels, Luc.*Syr.D*.28, 29. **2.** *votive offering*, *Sammelb*.1719, al. **II.** *boast*, *vaunt*, πῇ ἔβαν εὐχωλαί, ὅτε δὴ φάμεν εἶναι ἄριστοι Il.8.229; *shout of triumph*, ἔνθα δ' ἅμ' οἰμωγή τε καὶ εὐχωλὴ πέλεν ἀνδρῶν 4.450. **2.** *object of boasting*, *glory*, κὰδ δέ κεν εὐχωλὴν Πριάμῳ καὶ Τρωσὶ λίποιεν Ἀργείην Ἑλένην 2.160, cf. 4.173; ὅ μοι..εὐ. κατὰ ἄστυ πελέσκεο 22.433. **-ῐμαῖος**, α, ον, *bound by a vow*, *under a vow*, Hdt.2.63; used as translation of Celtic *soldurii*, Nic.Dam.*Fr*.80 J. **2.** εὐ. θέαι, = Lat. *ludi votivi*, D.C.79.9. **II.** = εὐκταῖος, *yearned*, *longed for*, Poll.5.130.

**εὐχώρητος**, ον, *giving free passage*, φλέβες, ἀρτηρίαι, Steph. *in Hp*.2.373 D. **II.** *easily accommodated*, *EM*285.16.

**εὐχώριστος**, ον, (χωρίζω) *easy to separate*, Thphr.*CP*4.6.8, Nicom.*Harm*.2.

**εὐψάμᾰθος** [ψᾰ], ον, *sandy*, *AP*6.223 (Antip.).

**εὐψηλάφητος** [ᾰ], ον, gloss on εὐαφής, Suid.; on εὔθικτος, *EM*391.30. Adv. -τως, gloss on εὐθίκτως, Hsch.

**ἐϋψήφις**, ῑδος, ὁ, ἡ, *with many pebbles*, *shingly*, Nonn.*D*.10.163.

⊛ **εὔψοφος**, ον, *well-sounding*, cj. in D.Chr.12.36.

**εὔψυκτος**, ον, *easy to cool* or *chill*, Arist.*Sens*.444$^{a}$12, *Pr*.887$^{b}$31 (Comp.), Gal.1.329.

**εὐψῡχ-έω**, *to be of good courage*, *Ep.Phil*.2.19, J.*AJ*11.6.9, *BGU*1097.15 (i A.D.), Poll.3.135. **II.** εὐψύχει *farewell!* a common inscr.

on tombs, *IG*12(2).393 (Mytilene), etc. 2. εὐψυχεῖν, = χαίρειν, in a letter of condolence, *POxy.*115.1 (ii A.D.). -ής, ές, (ψῦχος) *agreeably cool*, τὸ τῆς πόλεως εὐ. Hdn.6.6.4: Comp., Id.1.12.2, Antyll.ap. Orib.9.13.1: written -ψῦγής, Aët.5.74. -ία, ἡ, *good courage, high spirit*, A.*Pers.*326, E.*Med.*403, Th.1.121, etc.; *goodness of soul*, opp. κακοψυχία, Pl.*Lg.*791c. ⊛ -ος, ον, (ψυχή) *of good courage, stout of heart*, θράσος A.*Pers.*394; ἀνήρ E.*Rh.*510, etc.: Comp., Philostr. *VA*6.20; τὸ.. ἐς τὰ ἔργα εὔψυχον Th.2.39, cf. 43, 4.126; -ότατοι πρὸς τὸ ἐπιέναι Id.2.11. Adv. -χως X.*Eq.Mag.*8.21. II. (ψύχω) *cooling*, Thphr.*CP*5.14.1 (Comp.).

**εὕω**, aor. 1 εὗσα (v. infr.), *singe*, esp. of singeing off the bristles of swine before they are cooked, εὗσέ τε μίστυλλέν τε καὶ ἀμφ' ὀβελοῖσιν ἔπειρεν Od.14.75, cf. 426, 2.300; σύες εὕόμενοι τανύοντο διὰ φλογὸς Il.9.468; so of the Cyclops, πάντα δέ οἱ βλέφαρ' ἀμφὶ καὶ ὀφρύας εὗσεν ἀϋτμή Od.9.389: metaph., of a shrewish wife, ἄνδρα.. εὕει ἄτερ δαλοῦ Hes.*Op.*705 (αὔει codd. Stob.). (Sts. εὔω in codd., v.l. Il.9.468 (cf. *EM*401.24), Od.2.300 (cf. *EM*398.34), Hes. l. c.: but v. ἀφ-εύω, ἐφ-εύω; cf. Lat. *uro* fr. *eus-ō.)

**εὐωδ-έω**, *to be fragrant*, Hdn.*Epim.*250. ⊛ -ης, ες, (ὄδωδα) *sweet-smelling, fragrant*, ἐν θαλάμῳ εὐώδεϊ Il.3.382; ἔλαιον Od.2.339; κυπάρισσος 5.64: Comp. -έστερος Pl.*Hp.Ma.*290e, Arist.*Pr.*877b25: Sup. -έστατος Hdt.3.112; ἄδυτον Pi.*O.*7.32, cf. *B.*13.40, etc.; ὀδόντες Hp.*Mul.*2.185; opp. δυσώδης, Arist.*de An.*421b23; εὐῶδες ὄζειν Id. *Pr.*906b14; of wines, *having a bouquet*, *PTeb.*120.62 (i B.C.), etc. -ία, Ion. -ίη, ἡ, *sweet smell*, Hdt.4.75, X.*Smp.*2.3, etc.; esp. of sacrifices, ὀσμὴ -ίας LxxGe.8.21: metaph. in *Ep.Eph.*5.2: in pl., Pl.*Ti.* 65a: in pl., also, *fragrant substances*, D.S.1.84. -ιάζω, *have a sweet savour, 'bouquet'*, οἶνος -άζων Lxx*Za.*9.17: c. acc. cogn., ὀσμὴν εὐ. *emit a sweet* savour, ib.*Si.*39.14:—Pass., *to be fragrant*, Str.15.2.3, Dsc.2.76.8. -ίζομαι, *perceive a sweet smell*, S.E.*M.*7.293; ὑπό τινος ib.11.227.

**εὐώδῑν**, ῖνος, ὁ, ἡ, *happy as a parent, fruitful*, Opp.*C.*3.19; νηδύς *AP*6.201 (Marc. Arg.); epith. of Demeter, Max.529; εὐ. ἐς ζῴων γένεσιν Ael.*NA*13.5; of women, *easily delivered*, ib.4.29. II. Pass. *happily born*, Coluth.281, Nonn.*D.*14.148.

**εὐώλενος**, ον, *fair-armed*, Pi.*P.*9.17 codd.: δεξιά E.*Hipp.*605.

**εὐωμοσία**, ἡ, *observance of an oath*, Hdn.*Epim.*205.

**εὐώμοτος**, ον, (ὄμνυμι) *observing oaths*, Poll.1.39.

**εὐων-έω**, *buy cheaply*, *PGiss.*79 iii 15 (ii A.D.). -ητος, ον, *well-bought, cheap*, τὸ εὐ. Str.5.1.12. -ία, ἡ, *cheapness*, Plb.2.15.4, *PGiss.*79 iii 14 (ii A.D.). ⊛ -ίζω, *hold cheap*, Aq.*Ps.*11(12).9 (Pass.).

**Εὐώνιος**, ὁ (sc. μήν), name of a month at Halos, *GDI*1461.

**εὔωνος**, ον, *of fair price, cheap*, Hp.*Nat.Mul.*59 (Sup.), Epich.42.10, Pl.*Euthd.*304b (Sup.), D.18.89 (Comp.), *PCair.Zen.*48.5 (iii B.C.), etc.; ἀείσιτος Epich.34; φίλοι X.*Mem.*2.10.4 (Sup.); θάνατος *AP*11.169 (Nicarch.); of persons, εὐ. εἰς ὅ τι μισθοῖντο App.*BC*2.120: irreg. Comp. -νέστερος Epich.121. Adv. -νως, Sup. -ότατα *IG*12(3).169 (Astypalaea). [εὐ- short in Hippon.22 B.]

**εὐωνύμ-ιος** [ῠ], α, ον, dub. cj. in Corinn.19. ⊛ -ος (A), ον, (ὄνομα) *of good name, honoured*, Hes.*Th.*409, Pi.*O.*2.7, etc.; εὐ. χάρις the honour *of a good name*, Id.*P.*11.58; δίκη.. μὴ εὐ. not *creditable*, Pl.*Lg.* 754e. 2. *expressed in well-chosen terms*, λόγος Luc.*Lex.*1. II. *having an auspicious name* or *sound*, ἀριστοκρατία Pl.*Plt.*302d; πρόσρημα D.C.52.4. 2. *prosperous, fortunate*, δίκα, πόδες, Pi.*N.* 7.48, 8.47, cf. Eust.895.37. 3. epith. of Artemis, Ἀρχ. Ἐφ. 1914.20 (Gonni, iv/iii B.C.). III. euphem. (like ἀριστερός) for *left, on the left hand* (because *bad* omens *came from the left*), ὠλένη εὐ. S.*Tr.*926; ἐξ εὐωνύμου χειρὸς Hdt.7.109; ἐξ εὐωνύμου (sc. χειρός) Id.1.72; κατὰ τὰ εὐ. X.*Lac.*11.10; εἰς τὰ εὐ. παρεκκλίνειν Arist.*PA* 666b7; ἐπὶ τὰ εὐ. ἀνακλίνεσθαι Id.*HA*498a11; ἐξ -ωνύμων *Ev.Matt.* 20.21; as military term, τὸ εὐ. κέρας Hdt.6.111, Th.5.67, etc.; τὸ εὐ. (without κέρας) Th.4.96. 2. euphem. of *bad* omens, opp. οἱ δεξιοὶ φύσιν, A.*Pr.*490, cf. *SIG*1167.3 (Ephesus, vi/v B.C.). 3. Astron., *southerly*, Cleom.1.1. -ος (B), ἡ, *spindle-tree, Euonymus europaeus*, Plin.*HN*13.118; τὸ εὐ. δένδρον Thphr.*HP*3.18.13.

**εὐώπιον**, = πυρὰ παρθενική, at Troezen, Hsch.

**εὐῶπις**, ιδος, ἡ, (ὤψ) *fair-eyed*, or *fair to look on*, εὐώπιδα κούρην Od. 6.113, 142, *h.Cer.*333, cf. S.*Tr.*523 (lyr.), *Pae.Erythr.*13, Call.*Dian.* 204; εὐ. Σελάνα Pi.*O.*10(11).74: in later Prose, of Hera, Max.Tyr. 14.6.

**εὐωπός** (A), όν, = εὐώψ, E.*Or.*918, D.P.1075, Babr.124.9; εὐ. πύλαι *friendly* gates, E.*Ion*1611 (troch.): in later Prose, Max.Tyr.8.3. II. *seeing well*, Arist.*GA*780b36; εὐ. ὄμμα, of a snake, Ael.*NA*8.12.

**εὐωπός** (B), ὁ, a sea-fish, Opp.*H.*1.256.

**εὐωρέω**, (εὔωρος I) *to be negligent*, Hsch.

⊛ **εὐωρία**, ἡ, (ὥρα) *fineness of the season*, Longus 1.9. II. (ὥρα) *freedom from care*, *Sammelb.*4324.7.

**εὐωριάζω**, = εὐωρέω, S.*Fr.*561, prob. for ἐξωρ- in A.*Pr.*17 (cf. Hsch. and Phot.).

**εὔωρος**, ον, (ὤρα) *careless, neglectful*, οὐδέ τοι εὔωροι θυέων Euph. 129. II. (ὥρα) εὔωρος γῆ *fruitful* land, Hsch.; εὔωρος γάμος, Lat. *maturae nuptiae*, S.*Fr.*200.

**εὐωχ-έω**, fut. -ήσω Thphr.*Char.*8.3: aor. 1 -ησα Metag.14, etc.:— Med. and Pass., Aeol. part. εὐωχήμενος Alc.*Supp.*23.5: fut. Med. -ήσομαι Ar.*Ec.*717, Pl.*R.*372b: aor. 1 εὐωχησάμην Luc.*Sat.*11: but fut. Pass. εὐωχηθήσομαι *IG*12(5).946.8 (Tenos): aor. 1 εὐωχήθην (v. infr.): pf. εὐώχημαι Hp.*Steril.*220, Ar.*Lys.*1224:—the augm. is never found (it is cj. in Pl.*Grg.*522a): (εὖ, ἔχω, cf. Ath.8.363b):— *entertain sumptuously*, c. acc. pers., Hdt.1.126, 4.73, 95, E.*Cyc.*346, Ar.*V.*341, etc.; of animals, *to feed well*, θηρίον Pl.*R.*588e; τὰς ὗς Arist.*HA*595a24:—Med. and Pass., *fare sumptuously, feast*, εὐωχήμενος Alc. l. c.; εὐωχέονται Hdt.5.8; ὡς ἔθυσαν καὶ εὐωχήθησαν Id.1.31; εὐωχημένοι, εὐωχηθέντες, *after dinner*, Ar.*Lys.*1224, *Ec.*664: c. acc. cogn., *feast upon, enjoy*, κρέα εὐωχοῦ X.*Cyr.*1.3.6, cf. Hp.*Steril.* l. c., Plb.8.24.13; εὐωχεῖσθαι ἐπινίκια *to hold a feast* of triumph, Luc. *Nav.*39; εὐ. γάμους, ἑορτήν, Hld.7.26, 8.7; of animals, *eat their fill*, X.*An.*5.3.11, *Eq.Mag.*8.4; καχρύων ὀνίδιον εὐωχημένον *having eaten its fill of* barley, Ar.*V.*1306. II. metaph., of other luxuries, εὐωχοῦντες [αὐτοὺς] ὧν ἐπεθύμουν Pl.*Grg.*518e; πολλὰ καὶ ἡδέα.. ηὐώχουν ὑμᾶς ib.522a (εὐ- codd.); so εὐωχεῖν τινα καινῶν λόγων *to entertain* him *with* them, Thphr.*Char.*8.3:—Med., *relish, enjoy*, c. gen., εὐωχοῦ τοῦ λόγου Pl.*R.*352b. III. Act. in med. sense, And.*Fr.*1. -ητέον, *one must feast*, λόγοις τὰς ἀγαθὰς ψυχάς Max.Tyr.28.5. -ητήριον, τό, *banqueting-house*, Greg.Cor.p.527 S. -ητής, οῦ, ὁ, *a reveller, guest*, Sch.rec.A.*Pr.*1022. -ητικός, ή, όν, *festive*, Gloss. ⊛ -ία, ἡ, *good cheer, feasting*, Ar.*Ach.*1009 (lyr.), *Ra.*85, Hp.*Aff.*27, etc.; ποιεῖν τὴν εὐ. to hold the *wake*, *CIG*3028 (Ephesus): in pl., *festivities*, Ar.*Fr.*216, Pl.*R.*320a, al. 2. generally, *supply of provisions* for an army, Plb.3.92.9; *plenty*, σίτου Ruf.ap.Orib.6.38.10. II. metaph., λόγων εὐωχίαι *feasts* of reason, *AP*4.3.6 (Agath.). -ιάζω, = εὐωχέω, v. l. in Lib.*Descr.*9.5. -ιαστικός, ὁ, translation of Lat. *Cibullius*, Lyd.*Mens.*4.1.

**εὐώψ**, ῶπος, ὁ, ἡ, (ὤψ) *fair-eyed* or *fair to look on*, παρειά S.*Ant.*530 (anap.); εὐῶπα πέμψον ἀλκάν send *goodly* aid, Id.*OT*189 (lyr.).

**ἔφᾱ**, Dor. for ἔφη, v. φημί. **ἐφαάνθη**, Ep. for ἐφάνθη, v. φαίνω. **ἔφᾱβος, ἐφᾱβικός**, Dor. for ἐφηβ-.

⊛ **ἐφαγιστεύω, ἐφαγνίζω**, v. ἀφ-.

**ἐφαιμάσσω**, *make bloody*, Orib.46.24.3, Cleopatra ap. Gal.12. 404:—Pass., Cass.*Pr.*57.

**ἐφαιμορρᾰγέω**, *have secondary haemorrhage*, Heliod.ap.Orib.50. 52.1:—also -αιμορροέω, Id.ib.50.51.1.

**ἐφαιρέω**, *take hold on, overspread*, ἐπὶ χλόος εἷλε παρειάς A.R.2. 1216. II. Med. -αιρέομαι, aor. 2 -ειλόμην, *choose as successor*, D.C.49.43:—Pass., *to be chosen* or *appointed to succeed* another, ἄρχειν Th.4.38, cf. *IG*9(1).694.93 (Corc.). 2. ὅσσουν ἐφάνγρενθεὶν κινες Thess. for ὅσων ἐφαιροῦνται (= κατηγοροῦσι) τινες whomsoever any persons *accuse*, ib.9(2).517.41 (Larissa, iii B.C.).

**ἐφᾰκέομαι**, v. ἐπᾰκέομαι.

**ἐφάλιος** [ᾰ], ον, (ἅλς B) = ἔφαλος, Phot., Suid.

⊛ **ἐφάλλομαι**, fut. -αλοῦμαι Lxx 1*Ki.*10.6: Ep. aor. 2 ἔπαλτο, part. ἐπάλμενος, ἐπιάλμενος (v. infr.): regul. aor. 2 inf. -αλέσθαι *IG*4.951. 27 (Epid., iv B.C.):—*spring upon*, so as to *attack*, c. dat., Ἀστεροπαίῳ ἔπαλτο Il.21.140, cf. 13.643; Τρώεσσιν ἐπάλμενος 11.489, etc.; ἐπάλμενος ὀξέϊ δουρὶ ib.421, cf. Od.14.220: without hostile sense, c. gen., ἵππων ἐπιάλμενος *having leaped upon* the chariot, Il.7.15; κύσσε.. μιν .. ἐπιάλμενος Od.24.320; of fame, ἐς Αἰθίοπας ἔπαλτο Pi.*N.*6.50: rare in Prose, ἐπὶ τὸν οὐδὸν ἐ. (a Homeric reminiscence) Pl.*Ion*535b; ἐπὶ τὰν χῆρα *IG* l. c.; ἐπί τινας *Act.Ap.*19.16; ἵπποις Plu.2.139b; θαλάττης Alciphr.1.10; ζῴῳ, in hostile sense, Philum.*Ven.*33.3; εἰς τοὔπίσω ἐ., of an exercise, Gal.6.145: metaph., of the spirit of prophecy, Lxx l. c.

**ἔφαλμος**, ον, *steeped in brine, salted*, βρώματα Plu.2.687d: **ἔφαλμα**, ατος, τό, in Thphr.*CP*5.9.6, is prob. corrupt.

⊛ **ἔφᾰλος**, ον, (ἅλς B) *on the sea*, of seaports, Κήρινθόν τ' ἔφαλον Il.2. 538, cf. 584, S.*Aj.*190 (lyr.); οἰκία Philostr.*Im.*1.12; ἡ ἐ. (sc. γῆ) *the coast*, Luc.*Am.*7.

**ἐφᾱλόω**, Dor. for ἐφηλ-, Hsch.

**ἔφαλσις**, εως, ἡ, *bouncing on* to a surface, Arist.*Pr.*913b30 (s. v. l.).

**ἐφάμαν** [φᾰ], Dor. for ἐφάμην, v. φημί.

**ἐφᾰμαρτάνω**, causal, *seduce to sin*, Lxx*Je.*39(32).35. II. abs., *miss one's aim*, Tryph.*Trop.*p.194 S.

**ἐφᾰμαρτέω**, = ἐφομαρτέω, Herod.5.43; read by Aristarch. in Il. 12.412, al.

**ἐφάμαρτος** [ᾰμ], ον, *sinful*, Eust.1365.40. **ἐφαμάω**, v. ἐπαμάομαι.

**ἐφάμερος, ἐφᾰμέριος**, Dor. for ἐφημ-.

**ἐφάμιλλος** [ᾰ], ον, (ἅμιλλα) *a match for, equal to, rivalling*, ἐ. γίγνεσθαί τινι X.*Mem.*3.3.12, Isoc.1.12 codd.; ἀρχὴ ἐ. ταῖς μεγίσταις Plb. 32.8.3; τὸ ἐ. *equality, evenness*, Plu.2.153f. Adv. -λως, ἀγωνίσασθαι Id.*Cleom.*39, cf. Aristaenet.1.2. II. Pass., *regarded as an object of rivalry* or *contention*, ἐφάμιλλον τῆς εἰς τὴν πατρίδα εὐνοίας ἐν κοινῷ πᾶσι κειμένης D.18.320; ἐφάμιλλον ποιεῖν τι Id.20.102; νίκην ἐ. ποιεῖν Plu. 2.214d; ὅπως ἐφάμιλλον ᾖ πᾶσι.. φιλοδοξεῖν *IG*2².1227.20, cf. 1292.18.

**Ἐφάμιος**, epith. of Zeus, Hsch.

**ἔφαμμ-α**, ατος, τό, = ἐφαπτίς, Plb.2.28.8. -ᾰτίζω, *bind upon* or *together*, Orib.49.22.23, cj. in Sor.*Fasc.*48. -ίζω, in Pass., *become covered with sand*, *PTeb.*60.42 (ii B.C.). -ος, ον, *sandy*, Thphr. *CP*2.4.4, etc. (nisi leg. ὕφαμμος).

**ἔφαν**, Ep. for ἔφασαν, v. φημί.

**ἐφανδάνω**, Ep. ἐπιανδάνω, *please, be grateful to*, c. dat., ἐμοὶ δ' ἐπιανδάνει οὕτως Il.7.407; βουλήν, ἥ ῥα θεοῖσιν ἐφήνδανε ib.45; τοῖσιν δ' ἐπιήνδανε μῦθος Od.16.406: aor. ἐπεύαδεν Musae.180: c. inf., A.R. 3.950, Orph.*A.*773.

**ἐφάπᾰλος** [ᾰπ], ον, *somewhat tender*, φυτόν *Gp.*10.78.3.

**ἐφάπαξ** [ᾰπ], Adv. *once for all*, Eup.175, *Ep.Rom.*6.10, *Ep.Hebr.* 7.27, etc. II. *at once*, 1*Ep.Cor.*15.6.

**ἐφαπλ-όω**, *spread* or *unfold over*, ἄωτον Orph.*A.*1336: c. gen., λέων .. γυῖα γῆς ἐφαπλώσας Babr.95.2; στήθεος ἐφαπλώσας.. ὄχθης Nonn. *D.*15.9: c. dat., δίκτυα νεπόδεσσιν ἐ. ib.20.385; ἐρετμοῖς χεῖρας Orph.

*A*.457 : metaph., ἐ. τὸ ἀγαθὸν διὰ τοῦ κόσμου Hierocl. *in CA* 21 p.467 M. :—Pass., τοὺς ἐμπροσθίους πόδας ἐφηπλῶσθαι ταῖς χερσί *to have* the skin of the front feet *spread over* the hands, Longus 1.20 ; σκότος ἐφήπλωται v.l. in Plu.2.167a. **-ωμα**, ατος, τό, *anything spread over, rug, cloak*, Eust.1347.40. **-ωτέον**, *one must spread over*, κατά τινων ὀθόνιον Sor.2.11.

❀ **ἐφαπτίς**, ίδος, ἡ, *soldier's upper garment*, *PMagd.*13.6 (iii B.C.), Plb.30.25.10, Callix.2, Anon.ap.Suid.: Astron., the *cloak* of the figure Sagittarius, Ptol.*Tetr.*25 (pl.), Heph.Astr.1.3 (pl.). 2. *ephod*, J.*AJ* 3.7.7. II. *woman's garment*, Str.7.2.3.

❀ **ἐφάπτ-ω**, Ion. **ἐπάπτω**, *bind on* or *to*, πότμον ἐφάψαις ὀρφανόν *having fixed* it as his doom, Pi.*O.*9.60 ; τί δ᾽.. ἐγὼ λύουσ᾽ ἂν ἢ ᾽φάπτουσα προσθείμην πλέον; what should I gain by undoing or *by making fast* [Creon's command]? v.l. in S.*Ant.*40 ; ἔγνω.. τοὔργον κατ᾽ ὀργὴν ὡς ἐφάψειεν τόδε he knew that she *had made fast* (i.e. perpetrated) the deed, Id.*Tr.*933 :—Pass., 3 sg. pf. and plpf. ἐφῆπται, -το, *is* or *was hung over* one, *fixed as* one's *fate* or *doom*, c. dat. pers., Τρώεσσι κήδε᾽ ἐφῆπται Il.2.15, cf. 6.241 ; Τρώεσσιν ὀλέθρου πείρατ᾽ ἐφῆπται 7.402, cf. Od.22.41 ; ἐφῆπτο ib.33 ; ἀθανάτοισιν ἔρις καὶ νεῖκος ἐφῆπται Il.21.513. II. Med., aor. 1 ἐφηψάμην, 3 sg. ἐφάψατο Pi.*P.*8.63 ; *lay hold of*, once in Hom., ἐπὴν χείρεσσιν ἐφάψεαι ἠπείροιο Od.5.348, cf. Thgn.6, A.*Supp.*412, etc.; ἱκέτης ἔφαψαι πατρός S.*Aj.*1172, etc. ; ξίφους E.*El.*1225 (lyr.); *partake of* food, Iamb.*VP*3.17 ; *treat*, ἰατρῶν δίκην ἐ. Philostr.*VA*8.7 ; ἐπεί γε τοῦδ᾽ ἐφάπτομαι τόπου *reach* it, E.*Hel.*556 ; σκοπιᾶς ἐφάψασθαι ποδοῖν Pi.*N.*9.47. b. Geom., *touch*, Euc. 3 *Def.*3, etc.; in Arist., of a circle, *pass through* angular points, *Mete.* $376^b$9 ; of a point, *lie on* a circle as locus, ib.$376^a$6. c. as law-term, c. gen., *claim as one's property*, S.*OC*859, Pl.*Lg.*915c, *GDI*1883.17 (Delph.), *Milet.*3 No.140.29 : c. dat., *GDI*1780.8 (Delph.). d. generally, *lay violent hands upon*, τοίχου, ἱματίου, Pl.*R.*574d. 2. *lay hold of* or *reach* with the mind, *attain to*, τοῦ ἀληθοῦς Id.*Smp.*212a ; ἐ. τινὸς μνήμῃ, αἰσθήσει, Id.*Phdr.*253a, *Phd.*65d ; ἐ. ἀμφοῖν τῇ ψυχῇ Id.*Tht.*190c (c. acc., dub. in *Lg.*664e) ; ἐ. λόγων *touch upon, meddle with*, Pi.*O.*9.12 ; ζητημάτων Pl.*Lg.*891c ; *apply oneself to*, ἐξηγήσεως Gal.16.558. 3. c. dat. rei, *apply oneself to*, ἔπεσι, τέχναις, κελεύθοις ζωᾶς, Pi.*O.*1.86, *P.*8.63, *N.*8.36. 4. c. gen. rei, εἴδεος ἐπαμμένος *possessing* a certain degree of beauty, Hdt.1.199, 8.105 ; τὰ ἐν τῷ μέσῳ ἁπάσης ταύτης τῆς ἕξεως ἐφαπτόμενα [σώματα] bodies *possessing* all these qualities in moderation, Pl.*Lg.*728e ; θηριώδους καὶ ἀλόγου μᾶλλον ἢ λογικῆς ἐφάπτεσθαι δοκεῖ φωνῆς, of the sibilant *s*, D.H.*Comp.*14. 5. *follow, come next*, f.l. for ἐφεψάσθω, Theoc.9.2. III. Pass., *to be kindled*: hence, *blush*, Id.14.23. **-ώδης**, ες, *like an* ἐφαπτίς, Phot. s. v. σπολάς. **-ωρ**, ορος, ὁ, also ἡ, *laying hold of, seizing*, ῥυσίων A.*Supp.*728. II. *one who strokes* or *caresses*, ib.312, 535 (lyr.) (with ref. to the name Ἔπαφος).

**ἐφαρδμόν**· ἀρδευτὸν πεδίον, Hsch. ❀ **ἐφαρίξαντο**· ἐψήσαντο, Id. (fort. ἐψαφίξαντο· ἐψηφίσαντο).

❀ **ἐφαρμ-ογή**, ἡ, *adjustment*, πρός τι Plu.2.780b : Geom., of figures, *coincidence*, Cleom.2.5, Simp. *in Cael.*184.21 ; *adjustment of claims*, Hero *Metr.*3 *Praef.* II. *agreement*, τῶν προλήψεων ταῖς οὐσίαις Arr. *Epict.*1.22.2. III. *union*, Plot.6.9.11. ❀ **-όζω**, Att. **-όττω**, Dor. **-όσδω** Theoc.1.53. I. intr., *fit on* or *to*, πειρήθη δ᾽ ἕο αὐτοῦ ἐν ἔντεσι .. εἰ οἷ ἐφαρμόσσειε Il.19.385 (unless trans.). 2. *to be adapted* or *capable of adaptation to*, τινι Arist.*APo.*$88^a$33, *Pol.*$1276^b$25, al.; ἐπί τινος Id.*Ph.*$201^b$14, al.; ἐπί τι ib.$228^b$25, al.; ὁ.. μάλιστ᾽ ἂν ἐφαρμόσας πολίτης ἐπὶ πάντας τοὺς.. πολίτας Id.*Pol.*$1275^a$33 : abs., ὁ λόγος οὐκ ἐ. Id.*Cael.*$308^b$2, etc.; *tally*, Id.*Resp.*$474^a$10 : Geom., *coincide*, ἐπί τι Euc. 1.4, Archim.*Con.Sph.*18 : c. dat., ibid., Papp.244.9 :—Pass., c. dat., Plot.4.4.23. 3. *befit, suit*, [οἴνῳ] ἐφαρμόζουσιν ἀοιδαί Panyas.14.2 ; *to be applicable*, of a test, ἐπί τινος Arist.*Pol.*$1275^b$32. II. trans., *fit* one thing *on to* another, οἱ χροΐ κόσμον Hes.*Op.*76 ; τοὔνομ᾽.. ἐλεγείῳ Critias 4 D.; σχοίνῳ [τοὺς ἀνθέρικας] Theoc.1.53 :—Med., ζεῦγλαν ἐφηρμόσατο *AP*9.19 (Arch.). b. Geom., in Pass., of a figure, *to be applied to* another figure, ἐπί τι Euc.1.4, Archim.*Aequil.Prooem.* ; γραμμὴ γραμμῇ Plot.2.7.1. 2. *suit, accommodate*, τὰς δαπάνας ταῖς προσόδοις X.*Ages.*8.8 ; τοὺς λόγους τοῖς προσώποις D.H.*Lys.*13 ; λόγῳ μέλη καὶ μέτρα καὶ ῥυθμούς, Plu.2.769c, cf. Orph.*A.*1001 ; *apply*, τι ἐπί τι Arist.*APo.*$75^b$4 ; *refer*, τι ἔς τινα Luc.*Pisc.*38 ; λόγων τε πίστιν .. ἐφαρμόσαι *to add fitting* assurance, S.*Tr.*623 :—Med., χάρματι καὶ λύπῃ μέτρον ἐφηρμόσατο *AP*9.768 (Agath.), cf. 10.26 (Luc.) :—Pass., *adapt oneself to*, τινι Epic.ap.Clearch.47, cf. Antig.*Mir.*25. **-οσις**, εως, ἡ, = ἐφαρμογή, τόπων καὶ τάξιος Ti.Locr.95c, cf. Procl.*Hyp.*3.13. **-οστέον**, *one must adapt*, τινί τι Plb.1.14.8, Plu.2.34f, Luc. *Hist.Conscr.*6.

**ἐφάρξαντο**, Att. for ἐφράξαντο.

**ἐφαρπάζω**, perh. by mistake for ἀφαρπ-, *Sammelb.*4315.4.

**ἐφαύριον**, = ἐπαύριον, *PHamb.*27.4 (iii B.C.), *PTeb.*119.17 (ii B.C.).

**ἔφαψις**, εως, ἡ, *touching, caressing*, A.*Supp.*45 (lyr.), Sch.A.R.1.842. 2. *knot*, Paul.Aeg.6.51.

**ἐφέασθεν**· ἐγέλασαν, διεχύθησαν, Hsch.

**ἐφεβδομᾰτικός**, ή, όν, *presiding over the week*, θεοί *PLeid.W.*1.34, 2.10.

**ἐφέβδομος**, ον, *containing* 1 + 1/7, Theo Sm.p.77 H., Iamb. *in Nic.* p.84 P., Hero *Stereom.*1.20.2, al.; cf. ἐπιέβδομος.

**ἐφεγρήσσων**· ὁ ἀγρυπνῶν, Hsch. **ἐφεδές**· ἐπίπεδον, ταπεινόν, χαμαί, Id. **ἐφεδέτα(ι)**, title of officials at Samos, Id.

❀ **ἐφέδρ-α**, Ion. **ἐπέδρη**, ἡ, *sitting by* or *before* a place : hence, *siege, blockade*, Hdt.1.17 ; ἐπέδρην ποιήσασθαι Id.5.65 ; *observation* of a besieged place, Ath.Mech.18.14 (pl.). 2. *sitting upon*, Pl.*Plt.*288a. II. *stable*, Phleg.*Mir.*3. 2. *base*, Hero *Spir.*1.30. 3. *surface* of a threshold, *Rev.Phil.*44.249 (Didyma, ii B.C.). III. a plant, = ἵππουρις, Hsch., Plin.*HN*26.36, Ps.-Dsc.4.46. **-άζω**, pf. part. ἐφηδρακώς, *set* or *rest upon*, τί τινι S.E.*P.*2.211, Hld.1.2. II. *support*, τὴν βάσιν τοῦ πρεσβύτου Id.7.8 :—Pass., Sor.1.70. ❀ **-ᾶνον**, τό, *that on which one sits*, οἷον ἐ. γλουτός Arist.*HA* $493^a$23 : pl., Ruf.*Onom.*116, Poll.2.184. 2. *seat*, Phryn.Trag.7 (s. v. l.). 3. ἐφέδρανον ὄργανον apparatus *for persons under operation to sit on*, Orib.49.2.1, 49.4.68. II. = ἐφέδρα III, Ps.-Dsc.4.46. **-εία**, ἡ, *a sitting upon*, ἐπὶ δένδρεσι Arist.*HA*$614^b$6 ; ἡ ἐπὶ τοῖς ᾠοῖς ἐ. Id.*IA*$713^a$21. II. *sitting by, waiting for one's turn*, of pugilists, etc., *drawing 'byes'*, Pl.*Lg.*819b. 2. in war, *reserve*, Plb.1.9.2, D.S.17.12, D.H.9.57 (pl.) : but in pl., *observation-posts*, Ath.Mech.16.4. III. *lying near, protection*, ἡ τῶν πολεμίων ἐ. Plb.23.16.2 ; *station, post*, τῷ φυγόντι ἐξ ἐ. Id.1.17.11 ; *lying in wait*, Plu.*Flam.*8, Onos.14.1. IV. *watchfulness* against symptoms of disease, περὶ ἐ., title of work by Antonius the Epicurean, Gal.5.1. (Sts. written -ρία.) ❀ **-εύω**, (ἔφεδρος) *sit upon, rest upon*, ἄγγος ἐφεδρεῦον κάρᾳ E.*El.*55 ; *sit on* eggs, Arist.*HA*$564^a$11. 2. *occupy* land, *PStrassb.*114.3. II. *lie by* or *near, lie in wait*, of an enemy watching for an opportunity of attack, Th.4.71, 8.92 ; ὅταν εἰδῶσιν ἐφεδρεύουσαν τὴν δύναμιν Isoc.8.137 ; ἐ. τινί *keep watch over*, as a prisoner, E.*Or.*1627 : generally, *watch for*, τοῖς .. ἀγαθοῖς ἐφεδρεύων ἕτερος καθεδεῖται D.5.15 ; τοῖς καιροῖς τινος Id.8.42, cf. *PBaden* 39 iii 7 (ii A.D.), Him.*Or.*2.26 ; τοῖς ἀτυχήμασί [τινος] Arist.*Pol.*$1269^a$38 ; τοῖς ἐσομένοις Hld.4.17 : metaph., of disease, *lie in wait*, Hp.*Ep.*19 (*Hermes* 53.64) ; but, *to be associated with* other diseases, Id.*Flat.*6. 2. of a third combatant, *draw a 'bye'*, Luc. *Herm.*40. 3. in war, *form the reserve*, Plb.18.32.2. 4. *watch over, protect*, τῇ τοῦ σίτου κομιδῇ Id.5.95.5. III. *halt*, Plu.*Pyrrh.*32, etc. **-ευσις**, εως, ἡ, *lying in wait*, v.l. in Aq.*Jb.*37.3 (pl.). **-ήσσω**, poet. for ἐφεδράζω, *sit upon*, ἕδρης Coluth.256 ; ἅρμασι Nonn. *D.*20.36. 2. *sit by*, τινι *AP*7.161 (Antip. Sid.) : abs., Coluth. 69 :—also **-ιάω**, Id.15. **-ίζω**, *sit* or *ride upon*, in a game wherein the loser carried the winner on his back, Ἐφεδρίζοντες, title of play by Philemon. **-ισμός** or **-ιασμός**, ὁ, *the game itself*, Poll.9.118, Hsch. **-ιστήρ**, ῆρος, ὁ, *one who plays the game*, Id. :—also **-ίτης** [ῑ], ου, ὁ, Phot. s. v. παλαστή. **-ος**, ον, (ἕδρα) *sitting* or *seated upon*, c. gen., λεόντων ἔφεδρε, of Cybele, S.*Ph.*401 (lyr.) ; ἵππου E.*Ion* 202 (lyr.) ; γῆς ἐ. στρατός Id.*Rh.*954. 2. ἔφεδρον, τό, *firm seat, bench*, Hp.*Fract.*8. 3. ἔφεδρον, τό, = ἵππουρις, prob. in Dsc.4.46, Plin.*HN*26.133. II. *sitting by, at*, or *near*, τῶν πηδαλίων, of a helmsman, Pl.*Plt.* 273e : also c. dat., σκηναῖς E.*Tr.*139 (anap.) : abs., ξύνεστιν ἔφεδρος lies *close at hand*, S.*Aj.*610 (lyr.). 2. *posted in support* or *reserve*, ἐφέδρους ἱππότας .. ἱππόταις ἔταξε posted horsemen *to support* horsemen, E.*Ph.*1095, cf. Plb.8.31.6, Onos.21.6, al. 3. *lying by and watching, waiting on*, τῶν καιρῶν, τοῖς καιροῖς, Plb.3.12.6, *Fr.*160, cf. Call.*Del.* 125 ; ἔ. βίου *waiting upon* his life, i.e. *for* his death, Men.663 ; χαλεπώτατοι ἔ., of debtors in a city, Aen.Tact.14.1. 4. the third competitor in contests, *who sits by to fight the conqueror*, Pi.*N.*4.96, E.*Rh.*119, Ar. *Ra.*792, cf. Luc.*Herm.*41 sq. ; πρὸς βασιλέα τὸν μέγιστον ἔφεδρον ἀγωνιζόμεθα X.*An.*2.5.10 ; καθάπερ ἐ. ἀθλητῇ Plu.*Sull.*29 ; Κράσσος, ὃς ἔ. ἦν ἀμφοῖν Id.*Caes.*28 ; ἔ. τοῦ ἀγῶνος Id.*Pomp.*53 ; μόνος ὢν ἔφεδρος δισσοῖς, i.e. one *against* two, with no one to take his place if beaten, A.*Ch.*866 (anap.). 5. generally, *one who waits to take another's place, a successor*, ἔ. βασιλεύς Hdt.5.41 ; ἔ. τινός Luc.*Gall.*9.

**ἐφέζομαι**, chiefly used in part. and 3 sg. impf. ; inf. ἐφέζεσθαι Od. 4.717 ; imper. ἐφέζεο *AP*15.13 (Const. Sic.) :—*sit upon*, c. dat., δενδρέῳ ἐφεζόμενοι Il.3.152 ; πατρὸς ἐφέζετο γούνασι 21.506 ; δίφρῳ ἐφέζεσθαι Od.4.717, cf. 509 ; ἔνθα δ᾽ ἄρ᾽ αὐτὸς ἐφέζετο 17.334 ; ὄχθῳ A.*Av.*774 (lyr.) : also c. gen., Pi.*N.*4.67, A.R.3.1001 ; ἐπὶ νώτοις Mosch.2.125 ; εἰς αὐλιν *AP*5.236.10 (Agath.) : also c. acc., Εὐρώταν ἐφεζόμεναι E.*Hel.*1492 (lyr.) ; τύχῃ .. ναῦν θέλουσ᾽ ἐ. A.*Ag.*664. 2. *sit by* or *near*, c. acc., οὐδ᾽ ἔχων μύσος .. τὸ σὸν ἐφεζόμην βρέτας prob. for ἐφεζομένη, Id.*Eu.*446. Cf. ἐφίζω.

**ἐφέηκα**, Ep. for ἐφῆκα, v. ἐφίημι.

**ἐφείκοστα**, τά, *additional tax of* 1/20, *PRev.Laws* 34.3 (iii B.C.).

**ἐφείω**, Ep. aor. 2 subj. 1 sg. of ἐφίημι.

**ἐφεκᾰτέρωθεν**, *on either side*, Ph.*Bel.*95.10 (s. v. l.).

**ἐφεκκαιδέκᾰτος**, ον, *containing the ratio* 17 : 16, Theo Sm.p.69 H., Aristid.Quint.3.1 ; cf. ἐφεξκαιδέκατος.

**ἐφεκ-τέον**, (ἐπέχω) *one must suspend judgement*, περί τινος S.E.*P.* 2.94, *M.*8.160, cf. D.L.9.81. **-τικός**, ή, όν, *able to check* or *stop*, κοιλίας Diph.Siph.ap.Ath.8.355e, Mnesith.ap.eund.2.57d ; ἱδρώτων Dsc. 1.30 ; ἀφροδισίων *Gp.*12.27.3 (Comp.) ; σηπεδόνων Dsc.5.109. II. *practising suspense of judgement*, of the Sceptics, *Stoic.*2.37, Gell.11.5.6, Philostr.*VS*1.8.4, D.L.*Prooem.*16, Syrian. *in Metaph.*73.16. Adv. **-κῶς** Arr.*Epict.*1.14.7. III. Geom., ἐ. τόπος *immobile* locus, opp. διεξοδικός (q. v.), Apollon.Perg.*Fr.*22. **-τός**, ή, όν, *to be held back*: τὰ ἐφεκτά subjects *on which to suspend the judgement*, S.E.*P.*3.55.

❀ **ἔφεκτος**, ον, *containing* 1 + 1/6, Vitr.3.1.6 ; τόκος ἔ. *when* 1/6 *of the principal was paid as interest*, = 16⅔ %, D.34.23 : ἔφεκτον, τό, *charge of* 1/6 on payments for grain-transport, *PLond.ined.*2093 (iii B.C.).

**ἐφέλης**· ἐπίαλτος, Hsch. ; Aeol. acc. ἐφέλην Id. s. v. ἐπιάλης.

**ἐφελίσσω** (only in form ἐπε(ι)λ- ; aor. 1 part. ἐπειλίξας dub. in D.23.161 (iii p.lxxxviii Blass), but found in Gal.18(2).7) :—*roll up*, τὸ μεταξὺ τοῦ βιβλίου, i.e. *skip*.., Gal. l. c. :—Med., *wriggle behind one*, οὐρήν Nic.*Th.*220 :—Pass., *to be rolled up*, ἐπείλικτο ὥσπερ τὰ βιβλία Paus.4.26.8.

**ἐφελκ-ίς**, ίδος, ἡ, *scab of a sore* or *wound*, Aret.*SD*2.3, Gal.8.6, al., Archig.ap.eund.12.679. **-όομαι**, Pass., *break out into sores*, Hp. *Epid*.6.8.21.

**ἐφελκ-τικός**, ή, όν, *attractive*, Eust.1765.9; φάρμακον *Hippiatr*.20; τὸ ἤλεκτρον ἐ. τῶν ἀχύρων Phld.*Sign*.1. **-υσις**, εως, ἡ, *attraction*, Asp. *in EN*160.5. **-υσμός**, ὁ, = foreg., Eust.52.24; *suction*, Sor.1.118; opp. διωσμός, Paul.Aeg.6.88. **-υστής**, οῦ, ὁ, = βοηθός, Phot., Suid. **-υστικός**, ή, όν, *drawing on, attractive*, τὰς ψυχάς Hippod.ap.Stob.4.1.94; τὸ ε̄.. γίνεται ἐ. τοῦ ν̄ Choerob. *in Theod*.2.38, cf. *EM*431.22, Eust.52.22. Adv. -κῶς Sch.Luc.*VH* 2.25. II. in later Gramm., Pass., *attracted, suffixed*, τὸ ν̄ ἐφελκυστικὸν γίνεται *EM*438.50, cf. Sch.D.T.p.465 H. ⊛ **-ω**, Ion. **ἐπ-**, fut. ἐφέλξω E.*HF*632: aor. 1 inf. -ελκῦσαι Thphr.*Char*.30. 10:—Med., fut. -ελκύσομαι A.D.*Synt*.50.21: aor. 1 part. -ελκυσάμενος Thphr.*CP*5.1.10: (Hom. only in Med. and Pass., v. infr. II, III):—*drag* or *trail after* one, ἐ. τὰς [οὐράς], of long-tailed sheep, Hdt.3.113; ἵππον ἐκ τοῦ βραχίονος ἐ. *to lead* a horse by a rein upon the arm, Id.5.12; ναῦς ὣς ἐφέλξω *will take in tow*, E. l.c., cf. Th.4.26; ἐ. ξύλον, of a log tied to the leg, Polyzel.3; τὰ ὀπίσθια σκέλη ἐφέλκουσιν ἐπὶ τὰ ἐμπρόσθια *drag forward*, in the disease of horses called εἰλεός, Arist.*HA*604ᵇ1; τὰς ὁπλὰς καὶ τὰ ἰσχία ἐ. *draw* them *up*, ib.18, cf. *Hippiatr*.121. 2. *bring on, bring in its train* (v. infr. III.4), πολλὰς ἐφέλκων ξυμφορὰς E.*Med*.552, cf. *Ion* 1149, *HF* 776 (lyr.); ἄλλην αἴσθησιν μετὰ τοῦ λογισμοῦ Pl.*Phd*.05e:—Med., *AP*10.37 (Luc.). 3. *draw* or *drink off*, E.*Cyc*.151. 4. ἐ. πλείους ἡμέρας *delay* for several days, Thphr.*Char*. l. c.:—Pass., τὰ ἐφελκόμενα *arrears* of payment, *PPetr*.3p.151 (iii B.C.), cf. *PSI*4. 350.4 (iii B.C.), *UPZ*50.33 (ii B.C.); ἐφέλκεται τῷ Φιλίππῳ he *is in arrears* of tax-payments to P. (the tax-collector), *PPetr*.2p.108 (iii B.C.). II. Pass., ἐφελκομένοισι πόδεσσιν with feet *trailing after* him, of one who is dragged lifeless away, Il.23.696; τὸ δ' ἐφέλκετο μείλινον ἔγχος 13.597; ὁ λίθος ὄπισθε ἐπελκόμενος *dragging behind* (the boat), Hdt.2.96; of camels, Id.3.105; also οἱ ἐπελκόμενοι *the stragglers* of an army, Id.4.203; -ομένη προθυμία *lagging, tardy*, Plb.9.40.2. 2. *to be attracted*, ῥείθροισιν *h.Hom*.19.9; μηδὲ.. τούτῳ ἐφέλκεσθαι *be* not *led away* by this argument, Th.1.42. III. Med. like Act., *drag after one*, χωλαίνει καὶ ἐφέλκεται (sc. τὸν πόδα) Pl.*Lg*.795b, cf. Antip.*Stoic*.3.256; τἄλλα Pl.*R*.544e. 2. *draw to oneself, attract*, αὐτὸς γὰρ ἐφέλκεται ἄνδρα σίδηρος the very sight of iron (i.e. arms) *draws* men *on*, i.e. *tempts* them *to use them*, Od. 16.294, 19.13; ὕδωρ ἐπ' ἑωυτὸν ὁ ἥλιος ἐ. Hdt.4.50; ἐ. τινὰ πρός τι Plb.9.1.3; of flowers, ἠϊθέας -όμεναι χροιῇσι Nic.*Fr*.74.65; κάλλεϊ.. πάντας ἐ. *APl*.4.288 (Leont.). 3. *draw* or *pull to*, τὴν θύραν ἐφελκύσασθαι Luc.*Am*.16; προστίθησι τὴν θύραν καὶ τὴν κλεῖν ἐφέλκεται Lys.1.13; ἐ. ὀφρῦν to frown, *AP*7.440 (Leon.); ἐ. κατὰ τῆς κεφαλῆς τὸ ἱμάτιον Plu.*Caes*.66, cf. *Pomp*.79. 4. *bring on* consequences, πόλλ' ἐφέλκεται φυγὴ κακὰ E.*Med*.462; ὁ καὶ σίδηρον ἀγχόνας τ' ἐ. Id.*Fr*.362.26, cf. Hp.*Decent*.1; κινδύνους Isoc.*Ep*.4.6; τοὔμπαλιν οὗ βούλονται ἐ. X.*Cyr*.8.4.32. 5. *claim for oneself, assume*, ἀλλότριον κάλλος Pl.*Grg*.465b; Μοῦσαν ὀθνείην *AP*9.434 (Theoc., = p.xvi W.). 6. *drag behind one as inferior*, i.e. *surpass*, τινὰ κάρτεϊ A.R.1.1162. 7. Gramm., *attract to the close of a word*, τὸ νῦ διὰ εὐφωνίαν Demetr.*Eloc*.175, cf. Eust.52.19. 8. ἐ. ἆσθμα *draw* a *deep* breath, Philostr.*Im*.2.22.

**ἐφέλκωσις**, εως, ἡ, (ἐφελκόομαι) *ulceration*, Hp.*Epid*.6.7.2 (pl.), Gal. 18(2).789.

**ἔφελξις**, εως, ἡ, *a dragging after* one, τοῦ πεπηρωμένου μορίου Arist. *IA*708ᵇ10.

**ἐφέμεν**, Ep. for ἐφεῖναι, aor. 2 inf. of ἐφίημι. **ἐφενάπται**· ἐπακολουθῆσαι (Lacon.), Hsch. (fort. ἐφέψασθαι). **ἐφέννυμι**, v. ἐπιέννυμι.

⊛ **ἐφεξῆς**, Ion. **ἐπεξῆς**, poet. **ἐφεξείης** Orph.*A*.327, 357:—Adv. *in order, in a row, one after another*, ἵζεσθαι Hdt.5.18; χωρεῖν E.*Hel*. 1390; ἑστάναι Ar.*Ec*.842, etc.; ἵστασθ' ἐ. πάντες *all in a row*, Id.*Fr*. 66; ἐ. ἐπὶ κέρως τεταγμέναι Eub.67.4, Xenarch.4.6; φάλαγγα βάθος ἐ. X.*HG*7.5.23; τὰ ἐ. λεγόμενα Pl.*Sph*.261d; ἵν' ἐ. ἡμῖν ὁ λόγος ἴῃ Id. *Plt*.281d; τὰς πράξεις ἐ. διελθεῖν Isoc.4.26; ἐ. ἀποκρίνεσθαι *in a connected manner*, Ruf.*Interrog*.2: c. Art., ᾗα τὰς ἐ. [πολιτείας] ἐρῶν Pl. *R*.449a, cf. *Lg*.696e; ἡ ἐ. γωνία the *adjacent* angle, Euc.1.14; αἱ ἐ. τομαὶ *adjacent* sections, of branches of a hyperbola and its conjugate, Apollon.Perg.*Con*.2.19; γραμμαὶ ἐ. κείμεναι a *series* of straight lines, Archim.*Spir*.10; ἡ ἐ. [οἰκία] *next door*, Men.*Inc*.2.31; τὸ ἐ. ῥητέον Pl.*Phdr*.239d, cf. Arist.*Cael*.281ᵃ28, etc. 2. c. dat., *next to*, Pl. *Prm*.149a, al.; τὸ ἐ. τούτοις Id.*Phlb*.34d; ἐ. τοῖς εἰρημένοις Arist. *Pol*.1294ᵃ32: rarely c. gen., [γωνίας] Pl.*Ti*.55a. II. *successively, continuously*, esp. with πᾶς, ἐ. πάντας X.*Oec*.12.10; δῃοῦν πᾶσαν τὴν γῆν ἐ. Id.*HG*4.6.4; τὴν Ἑλλάδα πᾶσαν ἐ. ἁρπάζειν D.8.55; μὴ τοῖς αἰτίοις, ἀλλὰ πᾶσιν ἐ. ὀργίζεσθαι Id.*Prooem*.38.2. 2. less freq. of Time, τρεῖς ἡμέρας ἐπεξῆς Hdt.2.77, cf. Lys.19.52; ἐ. τέτταρες Ar. *Ra*.915; δὶς ἐ. Call.*Ep*.37. 3. *thereupon, immediately afterwards*, εὐθὺς ἐ. D.18.31; εἰσελθὼν οἴκαδε καὶ ἐ. οὑτωσὶ καθεζόμενος Id.21. 119.

**ἔφεξις**, εως, ἡ, (ἐπέχω) = ἐπισχεσία, *excuse, pretext*, τοῦ δ' ἔφεξιν; = τίνος χάριν; Ar.*V*.338 (troch.), cf. E.*Fr*.599 (tragic use, acc. to Sch. Ar. l.c.). II. *checking, stopping*, *IG*12(9).207.10 (Eretria).

**ἐφεξκαιδέκατος**, ον, = ἑκκαιδέκατος, λόγος Plu.2.1021e.

**ἐφεπτακαιδέκατος**, ον, *containing* $1+\frac{1}{17}$, λόγος Plu.2.1021d, Aristid. Quint.3.1.

⊛ **ἐφέπω**, Ep. impf. ἔφεπον, iterat. ἐφέπεσκον, Il.16.732, Od.12.330: fut. ἐφέψω Il.21.588: aor. 2 ἐπέσπον A.*Pers*.552 (lyr.) (the only place in Trag.), inf. ἐπισπεῖν, part. ἐπισπών (v. infr. III):—*ply, wield*, ἔγχος Pi.*P*.6.33. 2. c. dat. pers., *apply, direct towards* or *against*, Πατρόκλῳ ἔφεπε κρατερώνυχας ἵππους Il.16.732, cf. 724. 3. *ply, belabour, lay on to*, [ἵππους] μάστιγι 24.326; of warriors, *belabour, harass* the enemy, 11.177, 22.188; σφεδανὸν ἔφεπ' ἔγχεϊ 21.542: c. acc. loci, ὣς ἔφεπε κλονέων πεδίον 11.496; of hunters, *beat, drive*, κορυφὰς ὀρέων Od.9.121 (but ἄγρην ἐφέπεσκον,.. ἰχθῦς ὄρνιθάς τε *plied* (ἐνήργουν Sch.) the chase, (hunting) fish and birds, 12.330): abs. metaph., *punish*, παραιβασίας Hes.*Th*.220. II. *ply* or *practise* a pursuit, ἄλλοι δ' ἐπὶ ἔργον ἔποιεν Od.14.195; πόλεμον ἐ. Simon.142.2 (codd. *AP*); τερπωλὰς καὶ θαλίας Archil.13; συμποσίας Pi.*P*.4.294; ὅσια καὶ νόμιμα Ar.*Th*.675; πολλὰ ἐπέπουσι (v.l. ἐφ-) Hdt.7.8.α'; τὰν Φιλοκτήταο δίκαν ἐ. *practising* his way, Pi.*P*.1.50. 2. *govern, administer*, Θήβας A.*Pers*.38 (anap.), cf. 552; πόλιας θνητῶν v.l. in Simon.142.2; Ζεὺς ὥρην ἐφέπων Man.3.32; *face* (*ply, cope with*) a task, οὐδέ κ' Ἀθήνη τοσσῆσδ' ὑσμίνης ἐφέποι στόμα Il.20.359; τοσσούσδ' ἀνθρώπους ἐφέπειν καὶ πᾶσι μάχεσθαι ib.357; μαιμώων ἔφεπ' ἔγχεϊ *faced* (*plied*) them with his spear, 15.742. 3. c. acc. loci, *haunt, frequent*, of gods, nymphs, etc., γαῖαν καὶ βένθεα λίμνης Hes. *Th*.366, cf. Pi.*P*.1.30, *Pae.Delph*.7; of birds, A.R.2.384; γῆν καὶ θάλασσαν Luc.*Trag*.267; *visit*, σῴζων ἐφέποις ἡμᾶς Aristonous 1. 47. 4. *molest, follow* a woman, Herod.2.47; cf. ἐφέπειν (-έπτειν cod.)· ἐπακολουθεῖν, Hsch. III. *come upon, encounter, face*, πότμον ἐπίσπῃς, etc. Il.6.412, etc.; θάνατον καὶ πότμον ἐ. Od.24.31; θανεῖν καὶ πότμον ἐ. Il.7.52, Od.4.562, etc.; κακὸν οἶτον ἐ. 3.134; ὀλέθριον ἦμαρ ἐ. Il.19.294; ἐ. αἴσιμον ἦμαρ 21.100; reversely, αἰὼν ἔφεπε μόρσιμος Pi.*O*.2.10.—The Act. is rare in Att. (v. supr.).

B. Med., ἐφέπομαι (in later Poets ἐφέσπομαι Maiist.46, Naumach. ap.Stob.4.23.7, Nonn.*D*.16.401, ἐπιέσπομαι Opp.*C*.3.272): impf. ἐφειπόμην: fut. ἐφέψομαι S.*Ant*.636, ἐπιέψομαι A.R.2.18: aor. 2 ἐφεσπόμην (but 3 pl. ἐπέσποντ(ο) Pi.*P*.4.133), imper. ἐπίσπου, inf. ἐπισπέσθαι: also aor. 1 imper. ἐφεψάσθω (v.l. ἐφαψ-) Theoc.9.2:—*follow, pursue*, once in Hom. in hostile sense, ληϊστῆρσιν ἐπισπόμενος Ταφίοισιν Od.16.426, cf. Hdt.1.103, 3.54, Th.4.96, etc. II. *follow, attend*, λαῶν ἔθνος ἐπισπόμενον ἑοῖ αὐτῷ Il.13.495; ἐπισπέσθαι ποσὶν *attend* on foot, i. e. keep up with, 14.521, cf. Hdt.3.14, 31, al.; εἰ μή οἱ τύχη ἐπίσποιτο if fortune *attend* him not, Id.1.32, etc.; ᾧ χάρις ἐφέσπετο Ar.*V*.1278: abs., opp. ἡγεῖσθαι, Th.3.45. 2. *obey, attend to*, ἐπισπόμενοι θεοῦ ὀμφῇ Od.3.215; ἐπισπόμενοι μένεϊ σφῷ *giving the reins to* their passion, 14.262; τῇ γνώμῃ τινὸς ἐ. Hdt.7.1c.γ'; βουλῇ.. ἐπισπέσθαι πατρὸς A.*Eu*.620; [γνώμαις], βουλεύμασι, τῷ δικαίῳ, S.*Ant*. 636, *El*.967, 1037: abs., ὁ ἐπισπόμενος, opp. ὁ πείσας, Th.3.43; also, *agree, approve*, εἰ δὲ.. ἐπὶ δ' ἕσπωνται θεοὶ ἄλλοι Od.12.349, cf. Pi.*P*. 4.133. 3. *follow* an argument, μόγις πως ἐ. Pl.*Lg*.644d, cf. *Tht*. 192e, etc.

**ἐφέργω**, *confine*, ὕδωρ *Tab.Heracl*.1.131.

**ἐφερμήν-ευσις**, εως, ἡ, *explanation*, Procl. *in Prm*.p.494 S. **-ευτέον**, *one must explain*, ib.p.670 S. ⊛ **-ευτικός**, ή, όν, *explanatory*, Phlp. *in APo*.359.31, Eust.777.57, Sch.rec.Theoc.2.48. **-εύω**, *interpret*, τί τινι Philostr.*VA*3.25: abs., τοῦ -οντος δεῖσθαι Philostr. Jun.*Im*.8, cf. Phlp. *in APo*.435.30.

**ἐφερπύζω**, later pres. for sq., Nic.*Fr*.74.41, *AP*9.231 (Antip. [Sid.]), Orph.*L*.707, etc.

**ἐφέρπω**, fut. -ψω A.*Eu*.500 (lyr.): aor. 1 ἐφείρπυσα Ar.*Pl*.675 (ἐφερπύσας is f. l. for -ποίσας in Theoc.22.15):—*creep upon*, ἐπὶ [χύτραν] Ar. l. c. II. poet., *come on* or *over, come gradually* or *stealthily upon*, τινα A.*Eu*.314 (anap.); ἐπ' ὅσσοισι νὺξ ἐφέρπει E.*Alc*.269 (lyr.): abs., μηδ' ἐφερπέτω νόσος A.*Eu*.943 (lyr.). 2. abs., *go forth, proceed*, ib.500 (lyr.): esp. in part., *coming on, future*, χρόνος ἐφέρπων Pi.*O*. 6.97; ἐφέρποισα κρίσις Id.*Fr*.131.5; τᾶς -ούσας νυκτὸς during the *following* night, *IG*4.952.15 (Epid.).

**ἐφεσίαν**· ἀντιποίησιν, ἐπιθυμίαν, Hsch.

**ἐφέσιμος** δίκη, ἡ, *suit in which there was the right of* ἔφεσις or *appeal* to another court, Poll.8.62, Gal.10.19, Luc.*Pr.Im*.15; γνῶσις ἐ. D. 7.9; κρίσις Arist.*Ath*.45.2; τὰ ἐ. D.C.52.33. II. (ἐφίεμαι) *accessible*, μὴ πᾶσιν ἀλλ' ἑνὶ τὴν ἀρχὴν ἐ. εἶναι J.*AJ*19.4.3.

⊛ **ἔφεσις**, εως, ἡ, (ἐφίημι) *throwing* or *hurling at, shooting*, ἡ τοῖς βέλεσιν ἔ. Pl.*Lg*.717a. 2. (ἐφίημι A. IV) as law-term, *appeal to a judicial tribunal* from a lower tribunal, *IG*1².39.74; from an administrative decision, ἡ εἰς τὸ δικαστήριον ἔ. Arist.*Ath*.9.1, cf. 45.2, 55.2; from the vote of a δῆμος, D.57.6; also of appeals to a popular assembly, ἀπὸ βουλῆς ἐπὶ δῆμον Poll.8.62; ἐπὶ τὸν δῆμον ἀπὸ τῶν πατρικίων D.H.6.58; πρὸς τὸν Ἐρχιέων δῆμον Id.*Is*.14. 3. *permission, licence*, *Sammelb*.6236.39 (Theadelphia, i B.C.). II. (ἐφίεμαι) *aiming at a thing, appetite, desire*, τινος Archyt.ap.Stob.2.31.120, Pl.*Lg*.864b, Arist.*EN*1114ᵇ6, Gal.*Nat.Fac*.3.6, Plot.5.5.12, etc.: abs., Pl.*Def*. 413c; ἐφέσεις καὶ διώξεις Plu.2.468c. 2. *attempt upon*, c. gen., ἔ. τῆς ἀρχῆς ποιήσασθαι D.C.71.23, cf. 43.38.

⊛ **Ἔφεσος**, ἡ, *Ephesus*, Hdt.1.142, etc.:—Adj. **Ἐφέσιος**, α, ον, γράμματα *a magic* formula, Plu.2.706e, Eust.1864.16 (also **Ἐφεσήϊα**, γρ. Anaxil.18.7 anap.)): **Ἐφεσία**, ἡ, = ἀριστολόχεια στρογγύλη, Ps.-Dsc. 3.4; = ἀρτεμισία, ib.113 ⊛ **Ἐφέσια**, τά, festival of Artemis at Ephesus, Th.3.104 (also Ἐφέσεια, τά, *OGI*10.10): **Ἐφεσηονίκης** [ῑ], ὁ, victor in these games, *Ephes*.2.72 (iii A.D.): **Ἐφεσίς**, ίδος, ἡ, in pl., title of poem by Aeschrio, Sch.Lyc.688.

**ἐφεσπερ-εία**, ἡ, *keeping awake in the evening*, Suid. **-εύω**, *keep awake in the evening*, Poll.1.71. ⊛ **-ος**, ον, (ἑσπέρα) *western*, νομὸς prob. in S.*OC*1059 (lyr.).

**ἐφέσσαι, ἔφεσσαι, ἐφέσσεσθαι,** v. ἐφίζω. **ἐφέστα**· τὸ ἑσπερινὸν δίκτυον, Hsch.

**ἐφεστι-άζομαι,** *feast, make merry,* Hsch., Phot., Suid. * **-ος,** Ion. **ἐπίστιος,** ον, Hdt. (v. infr.), **ἐφ[ίστιος]** prob. in *SIG*1218.17 (Iulis, v B.C.): (ἑστία):—*at one's own fireside, at home,* ἀπολέσθαι ἐ. Od.3.234; Τρῶες, ἐ. ὅσσοι ἔασιν as many as are in *their own homes,* opp. ἐπίκουροι, Il.2.125: with Verbs of motion, ἀλλ' ἐμὲ.. ἐφέστιον ἤγαγε δαίμων (i.e. ἐπὶ τὴν ἑστίαν) Od.7.248; ἦλθε.. ἐ. 23.55, cf. E.*Rh.*201; ἐφέστιον πῆξαι.. σκῆπτρον (i.e. ἐπὶ τῇ ἑστίᾳ) S.*El.*419; of suppliants who claim protection by *sitting by the fireside,* ἐπίστιος ἐμοὶ ἐγένεο Hdt.1.35; ἱκέτης καὶ δόμων ἐ. inmate of the temple, A.*Eu.*577, cf. 669; κάθησθε δωμάτων ἐ. Id.*Supp.*365; τόνδ' ἐ. θεῶν ib.503, cf. S.*OT*32; *guest,* ἐλθόντ' ἐς δόμους ἐφέστιον Id.*Tr.*262; freq. in A.R., ἐ. ἐν μεγάροισιν 1.909, 3.1117, etc.: c. dat. pers., ἐ. ἀθανάτοισιν *dwelling with* them, 3.116, cf. 4.518: c. dat. loci, πηγῇσιν ἐ. Ἀσωποῖο 1.117. II. generally, *of* or *in the house* or *family,* πόνοι.. δόμων ἐφέστιοι A.*Th.*853 (lyr.); θύματα Id.*Ag.*1310; μίασμα Id.*Eu.*169 (lyr.); ἀλαλαγαί S.*Tr.*206 (lyr.); περιστερὰ οἰκέτις ἐ. τε Id.*Fr.*866; εὐναί E.*El.*216; ἐ. δόμοι the chambers *of the house,* A.*Th.*73: Ion. ἐπίστιον, τό, *household, family,* Hdt.5.72,73; later ἐφέστιον, τό, D.H.1.24, *POxy.*2106.18 (iv A.D.). III. θεοὶ ἐ. *the household* gods, to whom the hearth was dedicated, Hierocl.p.54 A.; Ζεὺς ἐπίστιος or ἐφέστιος as *presiding over hospitality,* Hdt.1.44, S.*Aj.*492; ἐ. ἵδρυμα ἐν οἰκίᾳ ἔχων, a living image *by the hearth,* Pl.*Lg.*931a. IV. ἐπίστιος, ἡ, v. ἐπίστιος II.

**ἐφεστρίδιον,** τό, Dim. of sq., Luc.*Merc.Cond.*37, *DMort.*10.4, al.

**ἐφεστρίς,** ίδος, ἡ, (ἐφέννυμι) *upper garment, wrapper,* X.*Smp.*4.38; a philosopher's *mantle,* Ath.3.98a; soldier's *cloak,* Plu.*Luc.*28; πᾶσα ἡ σύγκλητος μελαίναις ἐ. χρώμενοι Hdn.4.2.3, cf. 7.11.2,3; also a woman's *robe,* *AP*9.153 (Agath.), etc. 2. χλαμὺς ἐ. Ath.5.215c. II. *coverlet,* Poll.6.10, 10.42, Hsch.

* **ἐφέτειος,** ον, = ἐπέτειος, *of one year's standing,* ἐφηβεύσαντες *BCH* 11.86 (Apollonis); of animals, *yearling, Arch.Pap.*5.394 (ii A.D.).

**ἐφετ-έον,** (ἐφίημι) *one must allow,* τινι c. inf., Cic.*Att.*9.4.2, cf. J.*AJ* 4.8.23. **-ηρία,** ἡ, dub. sens., *IG*1².313.122, 314.136 (pl.). * **-ης,** ου, ὁ, *commander,* in pl., A.*Pers.*79 (lyr.). II. **ἐφέται,** οἱ, at Athens, *the Ephetae,* a court which tried cases of homicide under the ἄρχων βασιλεύς, *IG*1².115, Decr.ap.And.1.78, prob. in Arist.*Ath.*57.4, Lex ap.D.23.37, Harp. III. *judge of appeals,* Just.*Nov.*49 *Pr.* 2. **-ικός,** ή, όν, (ἐφίεμαι) *actuated by desire,* Thphr.*Metaph.*9. 2. Gramm., *expressive of desire,* ῥήματα Choerob. *in Theod.*2.212, al. II. ἐ. χρόνοι periods *within which appeals may be lodged,* Just.*Nov.*49.1 *Intr.* **-ίνδα** παίζειν, Adv., play at *catch-ball* (with play on ἔφεσις 1.2), Cratin.415.

* **ἐφετινός,** ή, όν, *yearling,* of animals, *PMasp.*141 vi 9, al. (vi A.D.). II. *of the present year,* χόρτος *POxy.*1482.12 (ii A.D.).

**ἐφετ-μή,** ἡ, (ἐφίημι) poet. word, *command, behest,* Il.14.249; θεῶν ὤτρυνεν ἐφετμή 21.299: freq. in pl., *behests,* esp. of the gods or one's parents, 5.508, Pi.*O.*3.11, etc.; Θέτις δ' οὐ λήθετ' ἐφετμέων παιδὸς ἑοῦ Il.1.495, cf. Pi.*P.*2.21, A.*Ch.*300, E.*IA*634; *demands, prayers,* Pi.*I.*6(5).18. * **-ός,** ή, όν, (ἐφίεμαι) *desirable,* θεῖόν τι καὶ ἐ. Arist.*Ph.*192ᵃ17, cf. Plu.2.374d; ἐφετόν, τό, *object,* τὸ γνωστὸν ἐ. ἐστι τοῦ γνωστικοῦ Dam.*Pr.*27; οἰκεῖον ἐ. ib.12. II. ἔφετο[ς] perh. for ἐφ' ἔτος, = ἐπ' ἔτος, *this year's,* *IG*5(2).433.7 (Megalop., ii B.C.); [τῷ πρὸ τοῦ ἐ]φ' ἔτος ἐνιαυτῷ *SIG*742.56 (Ephesus, i B.C.).

**ἐφευάζω,** = ἐπευάζω, Plu.*Marc.*22.

* **ἐφεύρ-εμα,** ατος, τό, *discovery, invention,* in pl., Sch.E.*Hec.*627; *artifices, tricks,* *IG*2².1119.4 (iii A.D.). **-εσις,** εως, ἡ, *discovering, discovery,* Sch.D.T.p.31 H., Just.*Nov.*84.1.1 (pl.), David *Proll.*44.8. **-ετής,** οῦ, ὁ, *inventor, contriver, Anacreont.*36.3; κακῶν *Ep.Rom.*1.30:—fem. **-έτρια,** Sch.Opp.*H.*1.354. **-ετικός,** ή, όν, *inventive,* Sch.Od.1.349. **-ημα,** ατος, τό, = ἐφεύρεμα, Sch.D.T.p.108 H. (pl.), Sch.E.*Hec.*626 (pl.). **-ησις,** εως, ἡ, = ἐφεύρεσις, Sch.Ar.*Pl.*1160 (pl.). * **-ίσκω,** Ion. ἐπ-, fut. ἐφευρήσω: aor. 2 ἐφηῦρον or ἐφεῦ-; Aeol. ἐπεύρ[οι] Sapph.*Supp.*4.9: pf. ἐφηύρηκα S.*El.*1093 (lyr.), Euphro 1.17, etc.:—*find* or *discover, find anywhere,* εἴ που ἐφεύροι ἠϊόνας λιμένας τε Od.5.439, cf. 417, Pl.*Phdr.*266a: usu. c. part., ὃν δ' αὖ.. βοόωντα ἐφεύροι Il.2.198; δαινυμένους δ' εὖ πάντας ἐφεύρομεν Od.10.452; τὴν γ' ἀλλύουσαν ἐφεύρομεν ἀγλαὸν ἱστόν we *discovered* her undoing it, 24.145, cf. S.*El.*1093 (lyr.), Pl.*Plt.*307c; Κύπρι.. σε πικροτάταν ἐπεύροι prob. in Sapph. l. c.:—Pass., μὴ ἐπευρεθῇ πρήσσων Hdt.9.109; κλέπτων ὅταν τις.. ἐφευρεθῇ S.*Fr.*930; δρῶν ἐφευρίσκῃ (2 sg.) Id.*OC*938; ἐφηύρημαι κακός (sc. ὤν) Id.*OT*1421, cf. *Ant.*281; δειλὸς ὢν ἐφηυρέθης E.*Supp.*319. 2. *discover besides,* v.l. for ἔθ' εὑρ. in Od.19.158; ταῖς ἀρχαίαις τέσσαρας χορδὰς Paus.3.12.10. 3. *bring in besides,* ὅσα δ' ἂν ἐφευρίσκῃ [τὰ τέλη] X.*Vect.*4.40. II. *find out, invent,* of arts, [τέχναν] Pi.*P.*12.7 (Med. μῆτιν -ευρομένοις ib.4.262); σοφῶς ἐφεῦρες ὥστε μὴ θανεῖν E.*Alc.*699. 2. *find out, discover,* ἐφεῦρε δ' ἄστρων μέτρα καὶ περιστροφὰς S.*Fr.*432.8; χρόνου διατριβὰς ib.479, cf. Cratin.140; ἴδιόν τι Euphro 1.17; δσίαν ἐπίνοιαν *SIG*799.5 (Cyzicus, i A.D.).

**ἐφεύω,** *cook together with,* Nic.*Fr.*79.

**ἐφεψιάομαι,** *mock* or *scoff at,* τεθνεῶτί γ' ἐφεψιόωνται ἅπαντες Od.19.331, cf. 370.

**ἐφέψω,** *boil over again,* Philoch.171:—Pass., -εψομένου ὕδατος *boiling over,* Pall.*Febr.*12.

**ἐφήβαιον,** τό, *pubes,* Dsc.1.3, Gal.8.4; *hair of the pubes,* Suid. s.v. βλήχων: more freq. in pl., -βαια γυναικεῖα Heraclid.Syrac.ap.Ath.14.647a, etc.

**ἐφήβ-αρχος,** ὁ, (ἔφηβος, ἄρχω) *overseer of the youth,* a magistrate in several Greek cities, *OGI*339.42 (Sestos), *IG*12(2).134 (Mytilene, in form **ἐφάβ-**), 12(3).524 (Thera), *SIG*798.23 (Cyzicus), etc., cf. Arr.*Epict.*3.1.34, 7.19: **-αρχέω,** *hold this office,* *CIG*1957*g* (Beroea), *OGI*583.10 (Cyprus), *Not.Arch.*4.189 (Cyrene, iii A.D.). **-άω,** Ion. ἐπ-, *come to man's estate, grow up to manhood,* Hdt.6.83, A.*Th.*665, E.*Fr.*559, X.*Cyr.*6.1.12. * **-εία,** ἡ, *youth, adolescence,* περὶ Ἐπικούρου -είας D.L.10.4. 2. *ephebic training,* *IG*2².1028.42, *SIG*1109.130, etc. 3. *body of* ἔφηβοι, prob. in Str.5.4.7. **-εῖον,** τό, *principal court* in the παλαίστρα, Vitr.5.11.2. **-ειος,** α, ον, *youthful,* ἀλικία *AP*7.427.12 (Antip. Sid.); ἀκμαί *Epigr.Gr.*231 (Cnios). * **-εύω,** *to be an* ἔφηβος, *arrive at man's estate,* Str.14.1.18, Paus.7.27.5, Artem.1.54; οἱ ἐφηβεύσαντες *those who have undergone the ephebic training,* *IG*2².665, etc., cf. Hp.*Ep.*25; τὸ ἐφηβεῦον, = οἱ ἔφηβοι, Hld.7.8. **-ία,** ἡ, = ἐφηβεία 1, Artem.1.54 codd. II. = ἐφηβεία 3, Lxx 2*Ma.*4.9. * **-ικός,** ή, όν, Dor. **ἐφᾱβ-,** ά, όν, *of* or *for an* ἔφηβος, ἆθλα Theoc.23.56. II. τὸ ἐφηβικόν, 1. = ἐφηβεία 1, Luc.*Nav.*3. 2. *part of the theatre assigned to the youths,* Poll.4.122; **-κὸς** τόπος Sch.Ar.*Av.*795. **-ιος,** α, ον, = foreg. 1, τὴν πρωτότμητον τρίχα τὴν -ίην κεῖρας *IG*12(5).173 iv (Paros). 2. **ἐφήβια,** τά, *celebration on reaching adolescence,* *EM*532.2. II. *pubic,* ossa Cael.Aur.*CP*3.140. * **-ος,** hyperdor. **ἔφᾱβος,** ὁ, (ἥβη) *one arrived at adolescence* (i.e. the age of 18 years, Poll.8.105, Harp. s.v. ἐπιδιετές; in Persia 16 or 17 years, X.*Cyr.*1.2.8), Lycurg.76, Arist.*Ath.*42.2, *IG*2².1156, al., *SIG*959.12 (Chios), etc.; εἰς τοὺς ἐφήβους ἐγγραφῆναι Pl.*Ax.*366e; ἐξ ἐφήβων ἐστὶ καὶ ἤδη εἴκοσι ἐτῶν Teles p.50 H.: generally, *boy,* καλὸς ἐστιν ἔ. ὁ σός *PLit.Lond.*52. 2. *young girl,* Hsch. II. *kind of cup,* Steph.Com.1.5, Philem.Lex.ap.Ath.11.469a. III. *throw of the dice,* *AP*7.427.5 (Antip. Sid.). IV. a woman's *shoe,* Herod.7.61. **-οσύνη,** ἡ, *age of an* ἔφηβος, *adolescence,* *AP*6.282.6 (Theod.). * **-οτης,** *pubertas,* Gloss.

* **ἐφηβοφύλαξ** [ῠ], ακος, ὁ, title of official at Pergamum, *IGRom.*4.396.

* **ἐφηγ-έομαι,** *lead to* a place: c. dat. pers., esp. as Att. law-term, *lead the magistrate to a place where a criminal lay concealed,* whom the informer durst not seize himself, D.22.26, cf. 26.9, Poll.8.50. * **-ησις,** εως, ἡ, *action against one who harboured a criminal,* or *concealed public property,* *AB*187, Phot., *EM*403.23, Suid., Zonar.

**ἐφήδομαι,** *exult over,* τινι X.*HG*5.3.20, D.Chr.11.64, etc.; Θηβαίοις.. ἐφησθῆναι παθοῦσιν D.18.18; ἐπ' ἐχθρῷ D.C.*Fr.*109.16: abs., X.*Ages.*7.5; οὐκ ἐπιτήδειος ὁ καιρὸς -ησθῆναι D.15.21: rarely in good sense, Aristaenet.1.12.

**ἐφηδύνω,** *sweeten, give a relish to, season,* τὴν τροφήν Plu.2.668d; οἶνον κινναμώμοις ib.693c; τὸ ἀτερπὲς Ruf.ap.Orib.7.26.118: metaph., λόγους τὴν διατριβὴν ἐ. Plu.2.514f; ὁ Εὐριπίδης τὸ αὐτὸ ἑτέρως -ύνας Longin.15.6, cf. 34.2 (Pass.), Pythag.ap.Porph.*Abst.*3.26. 2. *soothe, win over,* τινὰ πειθοῖ Ph.1.566, cf. 2.268.

**ἐφήκω,** fut. -ξω S.*El.*304:—*to have arrived,* Id.*Aj.*34, *Ant.*1257 (anap.), etc.; ἐπειδὴ ἡ ἡμέρα ἐφῆκε Th.8.67. 2. ὅσον ἂν ἡ μόρα ἐφήκῃ so far as it *reaches,* so much space as it *occupies,* X.*Lac.*12.5.

**ἐφῆλιξ,** Dor. **-ᾶλιξ,** ῐκος, ὁ, ἡ, *adolescent,* νεότας *AP*7.427.5 (Antip. Sid.).

* **ἔφηλις,** Ion. ἐπ- (q.v.), ιδος, also **ἐφηλίς,** ίδος, ἡ: (ἧλος):—*rivet, burr* or *clinch* to secure a nail, Ph.*Bel.*63.50, *IG*11(2).165.13 (Delos, iii B.C.). II. in pl., *rough spots which stud the face* (from ἧλος), or, acc. to others, *freckles* (from ἥλιος), Hp.*Prorrh.*2.23, *Alim.*20, *Mul.*2.215, Thphr.*HP*9.20.3, Sor.1.44 (sg.), etc.: acc. pl. ἐφήλεις Dsc.1.123. 2. in sg., = λέπρα, ἐ. ἀργινόεσσα, λεύκη, Nic.*Th.*333, 858.

**ἔφηλος,** ον, (ἧλος) *nailed on* or *to,* Suid. II. *with a white speck on it,* ὀφθαλμός Ael.*NA*15.18; ὀφθαλμοῖσιν ἔφηλος Call.*Fr.anon.*106; of persons suffering from the complaint, Lxx *Le.*21.20.

**ἐφηλότης,** ητος, ἡ, *white speck on the eye,* S.E.*M.*7.233.

**ἐφηλ-όω,** *nail on,* in Pass., Apollod.*Poliorc.*158.8, Ath.Mech.25.3: metaph., τῶνδ' ἐφήλωται τορῶς γόμφος διαμπάξ the bolt is *driven home,* i.e. it *is irrevocably fixed,* A.*Supp.*944; cf. ἐφαλόω. **-ώδης,** ες, gloss on φολλικώδεα, Erot. **-ωτός,** ή, όν, *nailed on,* Hero *Aut.*2.2.

* **ἔφημαι,** pf. Pass. used as a pres., (cf. ἧμαι) *to be seated on, sit on,* κληΐδεσσιν ἐφήμενοι Od.12.215; [θρόνῳ] 6.309; πύλῃσιν Nic.*Al.*507: c. gen., πόντου θινὸς ἐφήμενος S.*Ph.*1124, cf. Lyc.367; *to be seated at* or *in,* δόμοις, τάφῳ, A.*Ag.*1217, *Ch.*501: c. acc., βρέτας ἐφήμενος Id.*Eu.*409; τάφον Id.*Fr.*157 (ἐφιμένη cod. Hsch.): βωμία ἐφημένη, = βωμῷ ἐ., E.*Supp.*93. II. *act as assessor* (cf. ἔφεδρος), Παλλὰς οἵ τ' ἐφήμενοι A.*Eu.*629. III. ἐπήμενοι dub. sens. (or from ἐφίημι?) in Alc.*Supp.*4.14.

**ἐφημερ-ευτήριον,** τό, *guard-room, lock-up,* *PPetr.*2 p.26 (iii B.C.). **-ευτής,** οῦ, ὁ, in pl., title of those who *took their turn of serving* their equals at a Jewish festival, Ph.2.481. **-εύω,** *keep guard by day,* Plb.21.27.6, *IGRom.*1.817 (Callipolis); ἐπὶ τῶν πυλῶν *SIG*731.14 (Tomi, i B.C.): c. dat., τοῖς κινδύνοις D.S.11.8 codd. II. τῶν νυνὶ ἐφημερευόντων *those cleaners who are now taking their turn of service* in the temple, *UPZ*7.6 (ii B.C.); cf. ἐφημερία. **-έω,** *to be president for the day,* prob. in *IG*14.830.20 (Puteoli, ii A.D.). * **-ία,** ἡ, *division* of the priests *for the daily service of the temple,* Lxx 1*Ch.*23.6, *Ne.*23.30, *Ev.Luc.*1.5. 2. the *service* itself, Lxx 1*Es.*1.16. **-ῐνός,** ή, όν, = sq., Alex.262.9, Ph.2.395, *POxy.*924.2 (ἐπιημ-, iv A.D.). **-ιος,** Dor. **ἐφᾱμ-,** ον, also α, ον Pi.*N.*6.6: (ἡμέρα):—*on, for* or *during the day,* οὔ κεν ἐφημέριός γε βάλοι κατὰ δάκρυ παρειῶν Od.4.223; *by day,* opp. μετὰ νύκτας, στάθμα Pi. l.c. 2. *for a day only,* ἐφημέρια φρονέοντες taking no thought for the morrow, Od.21.

85; κῆδος ἐ. *short-lived*, Thgn.656; of men, ἐφημέριοι *creatures of a day*, A.*Pr*.547 (lyr.), Ar.*Av*.687; θνατά τε καὶ ἐφαμ. ζῷα Ti.Locr. 99d. 3. *for the day, daily*, ἀμβροσία Plu.2.938b; λάτρις ἐ. *hired by the day*, Thgn.486; μισθὸς *AP*7.634 (Antiphil.). -ίς, ίδος, ἡ, *diary, journal*, esp. *a military record*, as kept by Alexander's staff, Ath.10. 434b, Plu.*Alex*.23, Arr.*An*.7.25.1; of Caesar's *commentarii*, Plu. *Caes*.22; of office *registers*, *BGU*1168.10 (i B.C.). 2. *day-book, account-book*, *PCornell*1.2 (iii B.C.), *PCair.Zen*.176.357 (pl., iii B.C.), Plu.2.829c, D.L.6.86; εἰς τὰς ἐ. φιλοσοφεῖν to profess philosophy for the *ledger*, Plu.2.999a. II. = ἐφημερία, J.*Vit*.1: pl., Id.*AJ*7.14. 7, 12.6.1. -όβῐος, ον, *living for the day, from hand to mouth*, χειροτέχνης Ph.2.389, cf. Ptol.*Tetr*.160. -ον, τό, *short-lived insect, the may-fly, Ephemera longicauda*, Arist.*HA*490ᵃ34, 552ᵇ23. II. *a poisonous plant, Colchicum autumnale*, Thphr.*HP*9.16.6, Nic.*Al*. 250; = κολχικόν, Dsc.4.83. 2. *Polygonatum multiflorum*, ib. 84. ❋-ος, ον, Dor. ἐπάμ- Pi.*P*.8.95, *Fr*.182 (ἐφαμ- *I*.7(6).40, *Fr*.157): (ἡμέρα):—more common form of ἐφημέριος, esp. in Prose, *living but a day*: hence, *short-lived*, τερπνὸν Id.*I*. l.c.; τύχαι E.*Heracl*.866, Diph.45; ὄλβος οὐ βέβαιος, ἀλλ' ἐ. E.*Ph*.[558]; ἐ. σώματα καὶ χρήματα ἡγεῖσθαι Th.2.53; χρῆσις Arist.*Pol*.1252ᵇ16; ἐ. καὶ προπετῆ βίον Men.382; τὸ ἐ. Arist.*EN*1096ᵇ5; ἐ. πᾶν τὸ τῶν πολλῶν ἀγαθὸν Epicur. *Fr*.489. 2. of men, ἐφήμεροι *creatures of a day*, Pi.*P*.8.95, Semon. 1.3, A.*Pr*.83; ὦ τάλας ἐφάμερε Pi.*Fr*.157; ὦφήμερε Ar.*Nu*.223; ὦ φίλοι καὶ ἀτεχνῶς ἐ. Pl.*Lg*.923a. II. *for the day, daily*, πυρετὸς Hp.*Aph*.4.55; τροφή D.H.8.41, *Ep.Jac*.2.15, Vett.Val.62.17, cf. D.S.3.32 (pl.); γυμνασία Ascl.*Tact*.1.4; πράξεις Luc. *Pseudol*.17; δαπάνη Plu.*Per*.16, etc.: neut. pl. as Adv., *once a day*, Orib.*Eup*.1. 9. III. φάρμακον ἐ. *killing on the same day*, Plu.*Them*.31. -ούσιος, ον, = ἐφημερόβιος, Procl.*Par.Ptol*.225.

**ἐφημίαι**· ἀγροί, καὶ βελτίονα φήμης, Hsch.

**ἐφημῐόλιος**, ον, less correct form of ἡμιόλιος, v.l. in Theo Sm.p.77 H., Bacch.Sen.p.106 Bellermann.

**ἐφημῐσυς**, υ, *half as much again*, *POxy*.1668.10 (iii A.D.).

**ἐφημοσύνη**, ἡ, (ἐφίημι) *command, behest*, οὐδ' ὣς Μενελάου ἐφημοσύνης ἀμέλησε Il.17.697, cf. Od.12.226, Pi.*P*.6.20, S.*Ph*.1144 (lyr.): pl., A.R.1.33. **ἔφησθα**, = ἔφης, v. φημί.

**ἐφησῠχάζω**, *remain quiet*, Plb.2.64.5 (v.l. ἀφ-), Ph.2.65 (v.l. for ἡσ-); ὀλίγον χρόνον Hld.4.11; μικρὸν -ησυχάσας τοῖς εἰρημένοις Id. 6.7; ἀπὸ τῆς αἰώρης Aret.*CD*1.8. 2. *acquiesce in*, τῇ δικαιολογίᾳ *PLond*.5.1708.261 (vi A.D.); τοῖς κρινομένοις Just.*Nov*.123.21 *Intr*. II. Act., *pass over in silence, omit*, τὰ πλήθη τῶν ἄλλων Ph. 2.3 (v.l. for ἀφ-).

**ἐφθᾰλέος**, α, ον, (ἕψω) *cooked*, Hsch., Phot., Suid.

**ἐφθαρμένως**, Adv. pf. Pass., (φθείρω) *corruptly*, *Theol.Ar*.43.

❋**ἐφθέος**, α, ον, (ἕψω) *to be boiled*, opp. ὠμός, Nic.*Al*.392.

**ἐφθήμερος**, ον, *lasting seven days*, ἀνοχαί Plu.2.223a.

**ἐφθημῐμερής**, ές, *containing seven halves*, i.e. 3½: esp. in metre, -μερές, τό, *a measure of three feet and a half*, such as the first 3½ feet of a Hexameter or Iambic Trimeter, Heph.7.3, Sch.Ar.*Pl*.302 (pl.), etc.; ἐ. τομή a caesura after such a phrase, Aristid.Quint.1.25.

**ἐφθίατο**, v. φθίνω.

**ἐφθονημένως**, Adv. pf. Pass., (φθονέω) *grudgingly*, Vett.Val.301.6.

**ἐφθοπώλιον**, τό, *place where dressed meat is sold, cook-shop*, Posidipp.21.

❋**ἐφθός**, ή, όν, verb. Adj. of ἕψω, *boiled*, of meat or fish, Hdt.2.77, Hp.*VM*13, E.*Cyc*.246, Ar.*Pax*717, Ecphantid.1, Pl.*R*.404c, etc.; of vegetables, Antiph.6; of water, Arist.*Mete*.380ᵇ10; of a hot bath, ἐφθόν [με]..πεποίηκεν Antiph.245. 2. ἐφθὸς χρυσὸς *refined* gold, Simon.64. II. metaph., *languid, unnerved*, Hp.*Epid*.4.16.

**ἐφθότης**, ητος, ἡ, *languor*, Hp.*Acut*.49.

**ἐφθόω**, *roast, boil*, Suid. **ἐφιάλλω**, v. φιάλλω.

**ἐφῐαλτ-εία**, ἡ, a herb (= ἐφιαλτία) used as a *preventive of nightmare*, Poet. *de herb*.162 (ἐφιάλτιον cod.). ❋-ης, ου, ὁ, Aeol. ἐπιάλτης Alc.129, also ἐπίαλος ibid.:—*nightmare*, conceived as a throttling demon, Phryn.Com.1, Dsc.3.140 (pl.), Artem.2.37, Ruf.ap.Orib. 7.26.177, Str.1.2.8; pr. n. of one of the Aloidae, Il.5.385, Od.11. 308, Pi.*P*.4.89 ('Επ- acc. to Sch.Od. l.c., cf. A.D.*Synt*.179.22), and Att. pr. n., cf. Ael.Dion.*Fr*.381, *IG*1².950.92, etc. (Identified with ἠπιόλης by A.D.*Fr*.8.12 (or Apollodorus, v. Sophr.68 note); ἐπιάλτης is expld. as ῥιγοπύρετον by Suid.; popularly connected with ἐφάλλομαι, Sch.B Il.5.385, or ἐφιάλλω, *EM*403.32; cf. *incubo*.) -ία, ἡ, = γλυκυσίδη, Aët.1.84; = ἐφιαλτεία (q.v.). -ικός, ή, όν, *suffering from nightmare*, Orib.*Syn*.8.2, Paul.Aeg.3.15. -ιον, τό, = δρακοντία μικρά, Ps.-Dsc.2.167.

**ἐφιδρόω**, Ion. ἐπιδρ-, *perspire in addition to* or *after*, πυρετῷ Hp. *Epid*.1.3 (as v.l. for ὑφ-); *perspire slightly over the whole body* or *on the upper part only*, Id.*Prorrh*.1.4, al., Gal.16.513:—Pass., *perspire consecutively*, Antyll.ap.Orib.9.23.6.

**ἐφίδρ-ῡσις**, εως, ἡ, *planting firmly*, in pl., of the feet, Ph.1.125. -ύω, *place* or *set upon*, φύσις ἐ. πάντα γαστρί ib.116:—Med. with pf. Pass., *place oneself upon, mount*, ib.21, al.: metaph., λόγος ἐ. θυμῷ ib.114.

**ἐφίδρωσις**, εως, ἡ, *superficial perspiration*, Plu.*Brut*.25 (pl.), Gal. 16.601.

**ἐφιδύειν**· ὀκνεῖν, Hsch. ❋**ἐφιδύη**· ὄκνος, Theognost.*Can*.7.30.

**ἐφιελίς**, ίδος, ἡ, = κάλυξ, part of a priest's crown, J.*AJ*3.7.6 (fort. φιελίς).

**ἐφιέρ-εια**· τὰ ἐπὶ τοῖς ἱερείοις ἀποθυόμενα, Hsch. ❋-ον, τό, *sacrificial cake*, *IG*3.74 (pl.):—also -ος, ὁ, Poll.6.76. II. v. ἐπίαρον.

**ἐφιζάνω**, Aeol. impf. ἐπίσδανον Alc.*Supp*.28.7:—Hom. only in Il., always in impf., *sit at* or *in*, δείπνῳ, αἰθούσῃσιν, 10.578, v.l. in 20. 11; *sit upon*, ὕπνος ἐπὶ βλεφάροισιν ἐφίζανεν 10.26; νώτοισιν ἐφίζανε Mosch.2.108: c. acc., θῶκον A.R.1.667: later also in pres., χείλεσι ἀφρὸς ἐ. Aret.*SA*2.12; ἐ. τις ὥρα καὶ ῥυτίδι πρώτῃ Philostr.*Im*.2.1, cf. Porph.*Antr*.19 · abs., *form a deposit*, Dsc.5.75.

**ἐφίζω**, Dor. **ἐφίσδω** Theoc.5.97: I. causal, in Ep. aor. ἐφέσσαι, ἐφέσσασθαι:—*set upon*, once in Hom. in Act., τούς μ' ἐκέλευσα Πύλονδε καταστῆσαι καὶ ἐφέσσαι *set* me *ashore*, Od.13.274:—more freq. in Med., γούνασιν οἷσιν ἐφεσσάμενος *having set* [me] *on* his knees, 16.443: fut. ἐφέσσεσθαι Il.9.455: imper., με νηὸς ἔφεσσαι Od.15.277; ἐς Λιβύην μ' ἐπὶ νηὸς ἐφέσσατο 14.295 (Rhianus: ἐέσσατο codd.):—Med. also, *reduce* a dislocation, Hp.*Mochl*.25. II. intr., *sit at* or *by*, abs., *sit*, Hom. only in Od., always in impf., ἐφῖζε Od.3.411, 19.55; ἔνθα..ἐφίζεσκε 17.331: later in pres., βαρὺς δ' ἐφίζει A.*Supp*. 651 (lyr.); ὥρα ἐφίζοισα γλεφάροις *sitting upon*, Pi.*N*.8.2; ὕπνος.. βλεφάροισιν ἐφίζων Mosch.2.3; πρὸς ὄμμ' ἀχλὺς ἐφίζει Critias 6.11 D.; ἀμφὶ μήλοις Nic.*Al*.478; τηνεὶ γὰρ ἐφίσδει (Dor.) Theoc.5.97.

❋**ἐφίημι**, Ion. ἐπ-, Dor. 3sg. ἐφίητι Pi.*I*.2.9, Ion. 3pl. ἐπιεῖσι Hdt.4. 30: fut. ἐφήσω Od.13.376: aor. 1 ind. ἐφῆκα, Ep. ἐφέηκα 9.38, Ion. ἐπῆκα Hdt.5.63; in other moods aor. 2 forms were used, imper. ἔφες Il.5. 174; Ep. subj. ἐφείω 1.567, 2 sg. ἐφῇς S.*El*.554, opt. ἐφείην Il.18.124; Ion. inf. ἐπεῖναι Hdt.2.100; part. ἐφείς S.*Aj*.495 (v.l.), etc.:—Med., pres. inf. ἐφίεσθαι Antipho 5.79; part. ἐφιέμενος Od.13.7: fut. ἐφήσομαι Il.23.82: aor. 2 ἐφεῖτο S.*Ph*.619:—Pass., pf. ἐφέωται and ἐφεῖται Hsch.: [ἐφῑημι Ep., ἐφῐημι Att.; yet Hom. always uses ἐφιείς, ἐφίει, ἐφιέμενος with ῑ, exc. ἐφίει Od.24.180]:—*send to* one, Πριάμῳ..Ἶριν ἐφήσω Il.24.117; μ' ἐφέηκε..καλέειν *sent* me to call, A.R.1. 712. 2. in Hom., c. inf., *set on, incite* to do, ἠλεός, ὅς τ' ἐφέηκε πολύφρονά περ μάλ' ἀεῖσαι Od.14.464; so ἐ. τινὰ ἐχθοδοπῆσαι, χαλεπῆναι, στοναχῆσαι, Il.1.518, 18.108,124. 3. of things, *throw* or *launch at* one, ὅς τοι πρῶτος ἐφῆκε βέλος 16.812; ἄλλοις ἐφίει βέλεα Od.24.180, etc.; [ἔγχος], μελίην, Il.20.346, 21.170; οἰστὸν ἐπί τινι E.*Med*.632 (lyr.); χεῖράς τινι to *lay* hands *on* him, μνηστῆρσιν ἀναιδέσι χεῖρας ἐφήσω Od.20.39, cf. Il.1.567, etc. 4. of events, destinies, etc., *send upon* one, τοῖσιν ἀεικέα πότμον ἐφῆκε 4.396, etc.; Ἀργείοισι πολύστονα κήδε' ἐφῆκεν 1.445, cf. 21.524; μνηστήρεσσιν ἄεθλον τοῦτον ἐφήσω Od. 19.576; νόστον.., ὅν μοι Ζεὺς ἐφέηκε which he *hath laid upon* me, 9. 38; so πάντ' ἐφήσω μόρον A.*Eu*.502 (lyr.); τέκνοις ἀρὰς ἐ. Id.*Th*.786 (lyr.). 5. *send against*, in hostile sense, τῷ στρατοπέδῳ τὴν ἵππον Hdt.5.63; τὴν ἵππον ἐπὶ τοὺς Ἕλληνας Id.9.49; ἡνίοχοι ἐφίεσαν ὠκέας ἵππους Hes.*Sc*.307; στρατὸν ἐς πεδία E.*Heracl*.393. 6. *let in*, freq. of water, ἐπεῖναι τὸν ποταμὸν ἐπὶ τὴν χώρην Hdt.7.130, cf. 2.100; τὸ ὕδωρ ἐπὶ τὴν ἔσοδον Id.7.176; also ἐ. ἀκτῖνα Θήβαισι E.*Ph*.5; ἀγέλας ἐπὶ τὰ χωρία X.*Cyr*.1.1.2; ἄγαν ἐφῆκας γλῶσσαν *did'st let loose*, E. *Andr*.954; ὀργὴν τινι ἐ. Pl.*Lg*.731d. 7. *throw into*, ἐς λέβητ' ἐφῆκεν ἕψεσθαι μέλη E.*Cyc*.404. II. *let go, loosen*, esp. the rein, ἐ. καὶ χαλάσαι τὰς ἡνίας τοῖς λόγοις Pl.*Prt*.338a; οὐρίᾳ ἐφέντα (abs.) ibid.; πᾶσαν ἐφεὶς ὀθόνην [τῷ ἀνέμῳ] *AP*10.1 (Leon.), cf. A.R.2.934. b. *give up, yield*, τινὶ τὴν ἡγεμονίαν Th.1.95; πάντ' ἐφέντες ἡδονῇ E.*Fr*. 564; *allow*, τἆλλα τοῖς δούλοις Arist.*Pol*.1264ᵃ21. c. c. inf., *permit, allow*, τινὶ ὀνειδίσαι Hdt.1.90, cf. 3.113; σοί γ' ἐφῆκα πᾶν λέγειν S.*El*. 631; ἢν ἐφῇς μοι (sc. λέγειν) ib.554, cf. 556,649: c. acc. et inf., τοὺς νεωτέρους ἐ. διώκειν X.*Cyr*.4.2.24 (v.l. for ἀφ-):—Pass., ἐφεθήσεταί τινι c. inf., Luc.*Pr.Im*.24. d. *command*, Pi.*I*.2.9 (v.infr.B). 2. *give up, leave as a prey*, ἐφῆκεν ἐλλοῖς ἰχθύσιν διαφθοράν S.*Aj*.1297, cf. 495 (v.l.); τὴν ἀποσκευὴν ἐ. τοῖς στρατιώταις διαρπάσαι D.S.14.75; intr. (sc. ἑαυτόν), *give oneself up to*, ἰσχυρῷ γέλωτι Pl.*R*.388e; [παιδιᾷ] Id.*Ti*.59c. III. *put* the male *to* the female, ἐπῆκε ὀχεῦσαι τὸν ἵππον Hdt.3.85, cf. 4.30, Arist.*HA*630ᵇ33. IV. as law-term, *leave* to another to decide, *refer*, δίκας ἐ. εἴς τινας D.40.31; εἰς δικαστήριον ibid.; ἐ. τινὰ εἰς τὸ δικαστήριον *refer* him to.., Id.34.21; (sc. ἑαυτόν) *appeal*, εἰς τοὺς δικαστάς Id.29.59; ἐπί τινα Luc.*BisAcc*.4; εἰς ἕτερον δικαστήριον Id.*Herm*.30; ἀπό τινος D.C.64.2: abs., Id.37.27.

B. Med., *lay one's command* or *behest upon*, ὑμέων δ' ἀνδρὶ ἑκάστῳ ἐφιέμενος τάδε εἴρω Od.13.7, cf. Il.23.82, 24.300; ἐπιστολὰς ἅς σοι πατὴρ ἐφεῖτο A.*Pr*.4; πρός τι τοῦτ' ἐφίεσαι; S.*OT*766: c. inf., ἐ. τινὶ ἀγγεῖλαι Id.*El*.1111, cf. Ar.*V*.242; χαίρειν τἄλλ' ἐγώ σ' ἐ. I *bid* thee have thy will, S.*Aj*.112, cf. A.*Ch*.1039: abs., ὡς ἐφίεσαι Id.*Pers*.228 (troch.), cf. E.*IT*1483; ἐ. ἐς Λακεδαίμονα *send orders to*.., Th.4.108. 2. *allow* or *permit* one to do, κάρα τέμνειν ἐφεῖτο τῷ θέλοντι S.*Ph*.619; f.l. for ὑφ- in X.*An*.6.6.31, etc. II. c. gen., *aim at*, καλῶν Isoc.2.25; ἀγαθοῦ τινος Arist.*EN*1094ᵃ2, etc.; in fighting, τῶν προσώπων, τῶν ὄψεων, Plu.*Pomp*.71, *Caes*.45. 2. *long for, desire*, τί μοι τῶν δυσφόρων ἐφίῃ; S.*El*.143 (lyr.); τί..ἐφίεσαι φιλοτιμίας; E.*Ph*.531; τῶν ἀλλοτρίων Antipho 5.79; τῶν κερδῶν, ἀρχῆς, Th.1.8,128; τῶν ἐν Σικελίᾳ ἀγαθῶν Id.4.61; ἰσότητος Arist.*Pol*.1302ᵃ25: c. gen. pers., X.*Mem*.4.1.2: c. inf., ὧν..σου τυχεῖν ἐφίεμαι ἄκουσον S.*Ph*.1315; ἐ. ἄρξειν Th.6.6 codd. (leg. ἄρξαι): c. acc. et inf., S.*OT*1055.

**ἐφῑκάνω** [ᾰ], = sq., χαλεπὸν δ' ἐπὶ γῆρας ἱκάνει Od.11.196; ὅσον τ' ἐπὶ θυμὸς ἱκάνοι Parm.1.1.

❋**ἐφικνέομαι**, Ion. ἐπ-, fut. ἐφίξομαι Xenoph.6.3: aor. 2 ἐφῐκόμην, Ep. -ῑκόμην Il.13.613: pf. ἐφῖγμαι D.25.101: I. *reach at, aim at*, c. gen., of two combatants, ἅμα δ' ἀλλήλων ἐφίκοντο Il.13.613; simply, *reach* or *hit* with a stick, εὖ μάλα μου ἐφικέσθαι πειράσεται Pl.*Hp.Ma*.292a; ὅσων ἂν ἐφικέσθαι δυνηθῶσιν Isoc.12.227; ἐφῖκται πάντων ἡ τούτου κακοπραγμοσύνη D.25.101, cf. Plu.2.267c, etc.; σφενδόνη οὐκ ἂν ἐφικοίμην αὐτόσε Antiph.55.20; τὰ βέλη ἐ. τῆς πρὸς τὸν σκοπὸν Luc.*Nigr*.36. 2. *reach, extend*, ὅσον ὁ ἥλιος ἐ. Thphr.*HP*1.

7.1, etc.; ἐφ' ὅσον ἀνθρώπων μνήμη ἐ. X.*Cyr*.5.5.8; ἐ. ἐπὶ τοσαύτην γῆν τῷ ἀφ' ἑαυτοῦ φόβῳ *to reach* by the terror of his name over.., ib.1.1.5; ἐ. ἐς τὸ λεπτότατον *to reach* to the smallest matter, Luc.*JConf*.19; ὅπου μὴ ἐ. ἡ λεοντῆ, προσραπτέον..τὴν ἀλωπεκῆν Plu.2.190e; c. part., ἐ. φθεγγόμενον Id.*TG*18; ἐ. βλέποντα μέχρι τινός D.Chr.62.1. 3. metaph., *hit, touch the right points*, ἐ. ἐξαριθμούμενος Plb.1.57.3; τὰ ἄλλα λέγων ἐπίκεο ἀληθέστατα Hdt.7.9. 4. *reach, attain to*, τῆς ἀρετῆς Isoc.1.5; ἀνδραγαθίας Aeschin.3.189; τοῦ τριηραρχεῖν D.20.28, cf. 122; τῷ λόγῳ τῶν ἐκεῖ κακῶν Id.19.65: c. inf., ἐ. τῷ λόγῳ διελθεῖν *to be able to*.., Plu.2.338c, cf. Plb.1.4.11, *Inscr.Prien*.105.47 (i B.C.): abs., *succeed in one's projects*, App.*Mith*.102; of a poison, *reach* a vital part, *take effect*, ib.111. II. c. acc., *to come upon*, like ἐφικάνω, εἴ σε μοῖρ' ἐφίκοιτο Pi.*I*.5(4).15: c. dupl. acc., ἐπικέσθαι μάστιγι πληγὰς τὸν Ἑλλήσποντον *to visit* it *with* blows, Hdt.7.35. III. c. acc., *befit, be suitable to* (cf. ἱκνέομαι III), Hp.*Fract*.17.

**ἐφικτός**, ή, όν, *easy to reach, accessible, attainable*, v.l. for ἀνυστόν in Parm.4.7; οὐκ..ἐν ὀφθαλμοῖσιν ἐφικτόν Emp.133.1; οὔτε τέχνη οὔτε σοφίη ἐφικτόν, ἢν μὴ μάθῃ τις Democr.59; ἐλπίδες ἐφικταί Id.58, cf. Plb.12.25$^{i}$.9, Phld.*Herc*.1457.11; τὸ μέσον ἐπίπαν ἐ. Arist.*PA*666$^{a}$15; ἐφικτὸς εἰκότι λόγῳ Plu.*Thes*.1. II. ἐφικτόν ἐστι it is *possible*, c. inf., Plb.9.24.5; καθόσον ἐφικτόν to the best of one's *power*, Arist.*Mu*.391$^{b}$3; ὡς οὐκ ἦν ἐφικτὰ αὐτοῖς Ael.*NA*5.7; οἱ ἐν ἐφικτῷ τόποι *within reach*, Thphr.*Lap*.25, cf. *Ign*.70; ἐν ἐφικτῷ τῆς ἐλπίδος, τοῦ φιλῆσαι, Plu.2.494e, 496c; εἰς ἐφικτὸν προελθοῦσα coming *within reach*, D.H.2.38. III. Act., *attacking*, Ποιναί *Trag.Adesp*.256.

**ἐφῑμείρω**, strengthd. for ἱμείρω, c. acc., Nic.*Fr*.74.42: c. gen., *AP*5.268 (Agath.), Nonn.*D*.14.355: c. inf., ἐ. θεὸς εἶναι Musae.80:—Med., in tmesi, ἐφ' αἵματος ἱμείρονται Arat.975.

⊛ **ἐφίμερος** [ῐ], ον, *desired, delightful*, φιλότης Hes.*Sc*.15, *Th*.132; χῶρος Archil.21; ὕμνος Thgn.993, Theoc.1.61; φάτις A.*Ch*.840; ἡ τέκνων ὄψις ἐ. προσλεύσσειν ἐμοί S.*OT*1375; τὴν ἐ. κόμην Anaxil.38; ἐ. ἀνδράσιν ἄγρη Opp.*H*.4.110.

**ἔφιξις**, εως, ἡ, *reaching the mark*, τὴν ἔ. ποιεῖσθαι, of projectiles, Ph.*Bel*.81.33.

⊛ **ἐφι-ορκέω**, = ἐπιορκέω, *IG*2$^{2}$.1126 (Decr. Amphict.), 5(1).1390.6 (Andania, i B.C.), *PTeb*.78.17 (ii B.C.), etc. **-ορκία**, = ἐπιορκία, Lxx *Wi*.14.25.

⊛ **ἐφιππ-άζομαι**, *ride a tilt at*, λόγοις Cratin.358. 2. *ride upon*, ἐπὶ δελφῖνος Luc.*DMar*.6.2; sens. obsc., Artem.1.79. 3. abs., *ride*, Palaeph.52, Jul.*Or*.2.60a. **-αρχία**, ἡ, *double* ἱππαρχία, consisting of 1024 horse, Ascl.*Tact*.7.11, Arr.*Tact*.18.4, Suid. s.v. ἐφίππων. **-αστήρ**, ῆρος, ὁ, = ἐπιβήτωρ, Apollon.*Lex*. s.v. ἐπιβώτορι. **-εύω**, *ride against, attack with cavalry*, τινι D.S.17.19. II. *ride upon*, Babr.76.15. b. *cover* the female, Opp.*C*.1.390. **-ιος**, ον, *for putting on a horse*, κασᾶς X.*Cyr*.8.3.6, *PLond*.2.402 ii 5 (ii B.C.); πῖλος Plu.*Art*.11; ἐ., τό, *saddle-cloth*, Antiph.109, X.*Eq*.7.5, Epict.*Fr*.18 (pl.); *saddle*, Luc.*Nav*.30, *Hist.Conscr*.45: pl., Hor.*Epist*.1.14.43. II. ἐφίππιος (sc. δρόμος), ὁ, *horse-course*, a course of a certain length so called, Pl.*Lg*.833b. (-ειος codd. Plu.*Art*. l.c., Epict. l.c., etc., but -ῐος Antiph. l.c., Hor. l.c.) **-ίς**, ίδος, ἡ, prob. = ἐφίππιον, gloss on ἱπνή (Sicel word), Hsch. **-ος**, ον, *on horseback, riding*, Eup.27; ἔ. εἰς τὸν τόπον ἠνέχθη Plu.2.306f; ἔ. ὄντες, opp. ὁπλιτεύοντες, Lys.14.10 (as v.l.); ἀνδριὰς ἔ. *an equestrian* statue, Plu.*Publ*.19; ἔ. εἰκὼν χαλκῆ Id.*Fab*.22 (so, with εἰκών omitted, *PSI* 3.204.6 (ii A.D.)); βίος Philostr.*Her*.19.19. 2. κλύδων ἔ. a rushing wave *of horses*, S.*El*.733.

**ἐφίπταμαι**, late pres. of ἐπιπέτομαι, Mosch.1.16, Arist.*Mir*.841$^{b}$31, J.*AJ*1.10.3, 3.1.5, Plu.*Cleom*.39, Porph.*Abst*.1.25.

**ἐφίσδω**, Dor. for ἐφίζω. **ἐφίσης**, = ἐπ' ἴσης, v. ἴσος.

⊛ **ἐφιστάνω**, late form for ἐφίστημι, *set over*, τινά τινι Plu.2.233e. II. *stop, check*, v.l. in Dsc.4.16. 2. *attend to* a thing, c. dat., Plb.5.35.6; *consider carefully*, πῶς.. Id.11.2.5; εἰ.., ὅτι.., Arr.*Epict*.1.26.16, 2.18.31; *note*, of a commentator, Ammon. *in APr*.68.10. 3. *attack*, c. dat., Simp. *in Ph*.795.17.

**ἐφίστασις**, εως, ἡ, incorrect form for ἐπίστασις II. 5, in pl., Erot. s.v. ἐπαναιώρημα.

**ἐφιστάω**, = ἐφιστάνω II. 1, Dsc.2.32.

⊛ **ἐφίστημι**, Ion. ἐπ-: A. causal in pres., impf., fut., and aor. 1 (also in the later pf. and plpf. ἐφέστᾰκα, ἐφεστάκειν [ᾰ], v. infr. II. 1, VI. 2): I. *set, place upon*, τεῖχος τείχει Th.2.75; τι ἐπί τινος Pl.*Criti*.116a; τι ἐπί τινι X.*HG*3.1.7; ὅρους ἐπὶ οἰκίαν D.41.6: metaph., ἐ. τὴν ἐκεῖ μοῖραν βίῳ Pl.*R*.498c; ἀνάγκην τινί D.H.1.16. II. *set over*, μ' Ἀπόλλων τῷδ' ἐπέστησεν τέλει A.*Ag*.1202; φύλακ' ἐπέστησεν βοΐ Id.*Supp*.303; ἐ. τινὰ ὕπαρχόν τισι Hdt.5.27; τινὰ παιδαγωγόν τινι Pl.*Alc*.1.122b, cf. X.*Lac*.2.1; τινὰ πεντηκοντόρῳ Id.*An*.5.1.15; τινὰ τοῖς πράγμασι Isoc.2.27; τὸν νόμον Arist.*Pol*.1292$^{b}$28; ἐπὶ [συμμάχων] τινά Plb.2.65.9; ἐφεστάκει τινὰς πρὸς χρείαν Id.10.20.5; κύνα ἐπὶ ποίμνην D.26.22; τινὰ ἐπὶ τὰς εὐθύνας Id.18.112: c. inf., βουλὴν ἐπιμελεῖσθαι τῆς εὐκοσμίας Isoc.7.37:—Pass., *to be appointed, instituted*, *PTeb*.61(*b*).358 (ii B.C.), etc. 2. *bring in*, ἡ τύχη ἐπιστήσασα Ῥωμαίους Plb.15.20.6; Φίλιππον ἐ. τοῖς πράγμασι *to let* him *have a hand in* the business, D.19.34. 3. *bring in, cause, occasion*, κατάπληξίν τισι D.S.14.62; κίνδυνον, ἀγῶνά τινι, App.*Hann*.55, *Syr*.10; ἡ τύχη λοιμικὴν διάθεσιν ἐπέστησε Γαλάταις Plb.2.20.7. III. *set up, establish*, ἀγῶνα Hdt.1.167, 6.38: c. acc. et inf., *ordain, prescribe*, ὁ νόμος ἐφίστησι τὰ λοιπὰ κρίνειν τοὺς ἄρχοντας Arist.*Pol*.1287$^{a}$26; ἐπιστήσατε quid facere debeamus, Plin.*Ep*.6.31.12. IV. *set by* or *near to*, ἐπιστήσαντες κύκλῳ τὸ σῆμα ἱππέας Hdt.4.72; esp. *place in rear*, of troops, τὴν φάλαγγα τούτοις κατόπιν ἐ. Plb.1.33.6, cf. 1.26.14. V. *stop, cause to halt*, ἐπιστῆσαι τὸ στράτευμα X.*Cyr*.4.2.18; τὴν ὁδόν, τὴν πορείαν, D.S.17.112, Plu.*Cim*.1; τοὺς ἱππέας τοῦ πρόσω Arr.*An*.5.16.1; ἐ. τὴν ὁρμήν *check* it, Plb.16.34.2; τὴν διήγησιν *interrupt* it, Id.7.11.1; *check*, ἔμμηνα Dsc.1.125, cf. *POxy*.1088.20 (i A.D.): abs., ἐπιστήσας (sc. ἑαυτόν) *having halted*, X.*An*.1.8.15:—Pass., *to be checked, stopped*, *PPetr*.2 p.62 (iii B.C.); ἐὰν ἐφίστηται ἡ κοιλία Sor.1.122. VI. ἐφίστημι τὴν διάνοιαν κατά τι, περί τινος, *fix one's mind upon it, attend* to it, Isoc.9.69, Arist.*Metaph*.987$^{b}$3, Thphr.*Char.Prooem*., etc.; τὴν σκέψιν περί τινος Arist.*Metaph*.1090$^{a}$2; τὸν λόγον Id.*Juv*.470$^{b}$5; τὸν νοῦν τινι D.S.12.1; αὑτὸν ἐπιστήσας ἐπί τι Arist.*Top*.135$^{a}$26: ἐπιστῆσαι abs., *give attention*, τούτοις ἐπιστήσαντες Id.*Mu*.391$^{a}$26; περί τινος Id.*GC*315$^{b}$18; περί τι Id.*HA*487$^{a}$13; ἐπί τι Plb.1.65.5, etc.; ἐπιστήσασι μᾶλλον λεκτέον one must speak *with* more *care and accuracy*, Arist.*Pol*.1335$^{b}$3, cf. *EN*1144$^{a}$22; πότερον..ἢ Jul. *ad Them*.265b; ὅτι.. Sor.1.97 (hence ἐπίσταμαι, ἐπιστήμη, qq.v.). 2. c. acc. pers., *arrest the attention of*, Plu.*TG*17, cf. 2.17e, Gal.18(2).105; ἐπιστῆσαί τινα ἐπί τι *call* his *attention* to, Plb.2.61.11, cf. 4.34.9; τοῦ καιροῦ τοῦ κατὰ τὴν διήγησιν ἐφεστακότος ἡμᾶς ἐπί τι *having led* us to.., Id.10.21.2, cf. 31.23.1: hence, *object*, Plot.1.4.5.

B. intr. in Med. and Pass., ἐφίσταμαι, aor. 1 ἐπεστάθην [S.]*Fr*.[1127.5], E.*Hipp*.819, *IT*1375, etc., with pf., plpf. (Aeol. plpf. 3 sg. ἐπήστᾱκε *Schwyzer*646.16 (Cyme, ii B.C.): Dor. plpf. 3 pl. ἐφεστάκεον [ᾱ] *SIG*241.146 (Delph., iv B.C.)), and aor. 2 Act.: (the causal tenses are not found in Hom., the Med. or Pass. only in impf. ἐφίστατο Il.11.644; elsewh. always aor. 2 or pf. Act. with Ep. inf. ἐφεστάμεναι Od.24.380):—*stand upon*, τεῖχος..ῥύατ' ἐφεσταότες Il.18.515; πύργῳ ἐφεστήκει 6.373; δίφρῳ ἐφεσταότος 17.609, etc.; ἐπέστη βηλῷ ἔπι λιθέῳ 23.201; ἡ..ἐπισταθεῖσα ὀρθή Arist.*Metaph*.1051$^{a}$28; ἐπὶ τὰς..σχεδίας Plb.3.46.8. 2. *to be imposed upon*, μόχθων τῶν ἐφεστώτων ἐμοί S.*Tr*.1170. 3. *stand on the top* or *surface*, τὸ ἐπιστάμενον [τοῦ γάλακτος], i.e. *cream*, Hdt.4.2; λιπαρότητες ἄνω ἐφιστάμεναι Hp.*Prog*.12; ἐ. καθάπερ ὀρρὸς [γάλακτι] Dsc.1.72; of vapour, *form*, Arist.*Juv*.469$^{b}$31. II. *to be set over*, ἐφίσταται πύλαις A.*Th*.538; οἷός τε πολλοῖς προβατίοις ἐφεστάναι Ar.*V*.955; οἷοι νῷν ἐφεστᾶσι σκοποί S.*Aj*.945; ἄρχοντες ἐφ' ἑκάστῳ μέρει ἐ. X.*Hier*.9.5; ἐπί τινος Pl.*R*.460b; ἐπὶ τῆς πολιτείας D.19.298: rarely c. gen., τὸν ἐπεστεῶτα τῆς διώρυχος Hdt.7.117; ὅσοι θεοῦ χρημάτων ἐφέστασαν E.*Andr*.1098: abs. in part., ὁ ἐφεστηκώς the *person in authority*, the *officer in command*, X.*Oec*.21.9; οἱ ἐφεστῶτες, Ion. οἱ ἐπεστεῶτες, Hdt.2.148, S.*Aj*.1072, X.*Mem*.3.5.19. III. *stand by* or *near*, ὡς πυκνοὶ ἐφέστασαν ἀλλήλοισιν Il.13.133; ἐπ' ἄκρῳ χείλει ἐφεσταότες, ἐ. παρὰ τάφρῳ, 12.52, 199; θύρῃσιν ἐφίστατο 11.644; ἐπὶ τὰς πύλας, ἐπὶ τὰς θύρας, Hdt.3.77, Pl.*Smp*.212d; ἐπὶ τοῖς προθύροις Id.*Phlb*.64c; esp. of dreams or visions, *appear to*, εὕδοντι ἐπέστη ὄνειρος Hdt.1.34, cf. 7.14; ὄναρ κεφαλῆφιν ἐπέστη Il.10.496; ἐπιστᾶσα τῆς νυκτός Isoc.10.65; ἄγγελος ἐπέστη αὐτοῖς *Ev.Luc*.2.9: abs., *stand by*, Hdt.3.78; πολλῶν ἐφεστώτων App.*Syr*.10; ἤμην ἐφεστώς *Act.Ap*.22.20; οἱ λέβητες ἐπεστεῶτες Hdt.1.59; ὁ ἀντίδικος ἐφέστηκε Pl.*Tht*.172e, cf. Aeschin.3.79; without hostile sense, ἐπέστης S.*OC*558, cf. *Ev.Luc*.2.38, etc.; of troops, *to be posted after* or *behind*, κατόπιν ἐ. τοῖς θηρίοις Plb.16.18.7. 2. in hostile sense, *stand against*, τὰ φρονέοντες ἐφέστασαν ἀλλήλοισιν Il.15.703, cf. 5.624; ἔνθα μένος πνείοντες ἐφέστασαν Od.22.203, cf. 24.380; *appear before*, of an army, ἐπὶ τῇ πόλι Hdt.4.203; ἐπὶ τὸ βασίλειον Isoc.9.58; *come upon suddenly* or *by surprise*, Th.8.69; ἐξαίφνης ἐπιστὰς τοῖς γιγνομένοις Isoc.8.41, cf. D.6.5, Luc.*DDeor*.17.1; εἰς τοὺς ὄχλους Isoc.18.9; so of events, etc., αἰφνίδιος αὐτοῖς ἐ. ὄλεθρος 1*Ep.Thess*.5.3, cf. *Ev.Luc*.21.34; διὰ τὸν ἐφεστῶτα ζόφον Plb.18.20.7; διὰ τὸν ὑετὸν τὸν ἐφεστῶτα *Act.Ap*.28.2. 3. metaph., of events, *spring upon* one, *occur*, πρίν μοι τύχη τοιάδ' ἐπέστη S.*OT*777, cf. Th.3.82; in pf., *impend, be at hand*, τὸν ἐφεστηκότα κίνδυνον τῇ πόλει D.18.176; ὁ καιρὸς..ἐφέστηκε 2*Ep.Ti*.4.6; περὶ τοῦ βασιλέως..ὁ λόγος ἐφέστηκε νῦν Arist.*Pol*.1287$^{a}$2, cf. *Metaph*.999$^{a}$25; of a more remote future, *to be in store, lie in wait for*, κῆρες ἐφεστᾶσιν θανάτοιο Il.12.326. IV. *halt, stop*, as in a march, ἄλλοτε καὶ ἄλλοτε ἐφιστάμενος X.*An*.2.4.26 (cf. A.V); ἐπιστὰς περιέμεινα Pl.*Smp*.172a: c. gen., ἐ. τοῦ πλοῦ Th.2.91. V. *fix one's mind on, give one's attention to*, σφαγῇ E.*Andr*.547; τῇ τρύγῃ *PFlor*.236.4 (iii A.D.); ἐπί τι Isoc.10.29, D.18.60; τοῖς πράγμασιν..ἐπιστάντες Id.4.12; ἐπιστάς abs. (sc. τοῖς πράγμασι), Id.18.233; διὰ ταῦτ' ἐγρήγορεν, ἐφέστηκεν Id.6.19.

C. aor. 1 Med. in causal sense, *set up*, τὰς θύρας X.*Ages*.8.7; *set, post*, φρουροὺς ἐπεστησάμην Id.*Cyr*.8.2.19; τέλος ἐπιστήσασθαι, Lat. *finem imponere*, Pl.*Lg*.802a: pres. is once so used, τοῦ με τήνδ' ἐφίστασαι βάσιν; why dost thou *cause* me *to halt?* S.*Tr*.339. 2. ἐπιστησάμενος, intr., *having been* ἐπιστάτης, *IGRom*.4.1265 (Thyatira).

**ἐφίστιος**, v. ἐφέστιος.

⊛ **ἐφιστορέω**, *inquire* or *search further*, Hsch.

**ἔφλᾰδον**, v. φλάζω.

**ἐφοδ-εία**, ἡ, (ἐφοδεύω) *going the rounds, visiting sentries*, Plb.6.35.8: pl., Ph.*Bel*.93.5, Polyaen.7.14.2:—written -ία, D.S.20.16. 2. *making a round of visits*, *SIG*656.26 (Abdera, ii B.C.). II. *inspectorate*, *PTeb*.96.2 (i B.C.). **-ευτέον**, *one must examine*, τὰ καθ' ἕκαστα Str.14.1.4, cf. S.E.*P*.2.198; περί τινος Iamb. *in Nic*.p.58 P. ⊛ **-ευτής**, οῦ, ὁ, *one who goes the rounds: spy*, Aq.*Ge*.42.9. **-ευτικῶς**, Adv. *by tracing an argument, advancing to a conclusion*, S.E.*M*.8.308, *P*.2.142. **-εύω**, *go the rounds*, X.*HG*2.4.24, 5.3.22, Ph.*Bel*.80.38; κώδωνι Plu.*Arat*.7: c. acc., *visit, inspect*, ἔ. φυλακάς Plb.

6.35.11; τὰ ἔργα *PTeb.*13.3 (ii B.C.); τὴν πόλιν *SIG*731.16 (Tomi, i B.C.); τὰ ὅπλα καὶ τὰ τείχη Plu.2.781d; *make a tour of*, τὰ μαγειρεῖα Thphr.*Char.*6.9: generally, *make a tour of inspection*, X.*Cyr.*8.6.16; of the γυναικονόμος, Timocl.32.2:—Pass., ἐφοδεύεται *the rounds are made*, Ar.*Av.*1160. **2.** rarely c. dat., *superintend, watch over*, ἀγῶσιν A.*Ch.*728 (anap.). **3.** *visit as a spy, spy out*, Lxx *De.*1.22, al.: metaph., of a geographer, *explore*, Str.8.6.4, 17.1.1:—Pass., περιγεγραμμένων τῶν μεταρσίων ἐφοδευθήσεται καὶ τὰ πρόσγεια *Placit.*3.8.2. **4.** metaph., of reasoning, *carry on methodically*, λόγον Sor.2.25, cf. S.E.*M.*8.222, Ptol.*Tetr.*103, Max.Tyr.16.8. **-ηγέω**, *act as guide*, Suid. **-ια**, τά, v. ἐφόδιον. **-ιάζω**, Ion. **ἐποδ-**, *furnish with supplies for a journey*, ἀποπέμπουσι ἐποδιάσαντες ἐς Ἀθήνας Hdt.9.99; τινα Plu.*Cat.Mi.*65: c. dupl. acc., ἐφόδιον -ιάσεις αὐτόν Lxx *De.*15.14: metaph., of Philosophy, ἐ. τινὰ πρὸς τὴν στρατείαν Plu.2.327e:—Med., *supply oneself*, ἐκ τῆς πόλεως Plb.18.20.2:—Pass., *to be supplied with*, τι Lxx *Jo.*9.12; λαμπρῶς -ασθείς J.*BJ*2.7.1: metaph., Ph.1.535; διὰ τὸ μὴ ἐφωδιάσθαι ἀπὸ φυσιολογίας Theo Sm. p.188 H. **2.** generally, *supply* or *furnish with* a thing, αὐτοὺς ἀλκῇ καὶ ὅπλοις D.S.5.34; also ταῦτά σοι ἐφωδίασα Apollod.*Poliorc.*138.1. **3.** *reduce to system*, Ptol.*Tetr.*9. **4.** = *impetum facio, irruo*, *Gloss.* **II.** Med., c. acc. rei, πενταδραχμίαν ἑκάστῳ ἐφοδιασάμενος *having seen* that five drachmae *were paid* to each, X.*HG*1.6.12. **2.** metaph., *maintain, promote*, ἀργίαν Plu.*Sol.*23; τὴν ἀπείθειαν Id.*Cor.*16. **-ιασμός**, ὁ, gloss on ἐπισιτισμός, Hsch. **-ιαστής**, οῦ, ὁ, Dor. **-τάς**, ᾶ, *traveller* (?), *IG*9(2).1358 (Lamia); = *invasor*, *Gloss.* **-ικός**, ή, όν, *appertaining to method*, [λόγος], title of work by Archimedes, Hero *Metr.*1.32. Adv. -κῶς *systematically*, Ptol.*Tetr.*106. **2.** *of an inspector*, λειτουργίαι *PTeb.*32.4 (ii B.C.), etc.; μέτρῳ ἐφοδικῷ dub. in ib.208 (i B.C.). **-ιον**, τό, mostly in pl. **ἐφόδια**, Ion. **ἐπόδια**, τά (v. infr.), *supplies for travelling, money and provisions*, esp. *of an army*, ἐπόδια δοῦναι, λαβεῖν, Hdt.4.203, 6.70; δι' ἀπορίαν ἐφοδίων τοῖς στρατευομένοις D.3.20; of an ambassador's *travelling-allowance*, ἐφόδι' οὐκ ἔχω Ar.*Ach.*53, cf. Men.*Pk.*160; ἐφόδι' ἀναλίσκειν D.19.311, cf. *BCH*6.25 (Delos, ii B.C.): sg. in *PSI* 4.363.17 (iii B.C.): generally, *ways and means, maintenance*, ἐφόδια τῷ γήρᾳ ἱκανά D.49.67, cf. Ar.*Pl.*1024; τὰ τῆς φυγῆς ἐ. Aeschin.1.172, Plu.*Arat.*6; τὰ ἐ. τοῦ πολέμου the *sinews* of war, Arist.*Rh.*$1411^{a}12$; ἐφόδια τοῖς ἵπποις And.4.30; of public money, οὐδὲ μιᾶς ἡμέρας ἐφόδι' ἐστὶν ἐν τῷ κοινῷ D.23.209; in phys. sense, τὰ ἐν σώματι ὑπάρχοντα ἐ. Arist.*Pr.*$871^{b}24$. **2.** less freq. in sg., εὐσεβὴς βίος μέγιστον ἐ. Epich.[261]; ἀργύριόν τι ῥητὸν ἔχοντας ἐ. Th.2.70; οὐκ ἔχων.. εἰ μὴ παῖδα καὶ ὅσον ἐ. X.*An.*7.3.20; χιλίας λαβόντες δραχμὰς ἐφόδιον παρ' ὑμῶν D.19.158, cf. *SIG*390.58 (iii B.C.): metaph., εἰς τὴν εὔνοιαν Hyp.*Epit.*27; ἡ χρηστότης.. θαυμαστὸν ἐ. βίῳ Men.472, cf. 360, 792; πρὸς εὔνοιαν Phld.*Lib.*p.18 O.; τὴν Ἰλιάδα τῆς πολεμικῆς ἀρετῆς ἐ. νομίζων Plu.*Alex.*8; τὴν σωφροσύνην ἐ. εἰς τὸ γῆρας ἀποτίθεσθαι Id.2.8c; ἐ. παιδείας ὁ πλοῦτος Artem.4.67. **3.** metaph., = ἀφορμή, D.34.35, Hyp.*Eux.*19; εἰς τὸ ἐπιβουλεύειν Sor.1.3. ❋ **-ιος**, ον, *for a journey*, εὐχαί *EM*348.43. **II.** *on the road, accessible*, *BGU*1116.8 (i B.C.). **-ος** (A), ον, *accessible*, f.l. for εὐεφ-, Th.6.66 (in Sup. -ώτατος), Polyaen.1.49. **-ος** (B), ὁ, *one who goes the rounds*, X.*Cyr.*8.6.16, Plb.6.36.6. **2.** *inspector*, *PTeb.*30.27 (ii B.C.). ❋ **-ος** (C), ἡ, *approach*, Th.4.129, 6.99 (pl.); αὐτόθεν ἐπὶ τοὺς πολεμίους X.*An.*4.2.6; εἰς τὸν λόφον ib.3.4.41; *entrance* to a holy place, *Jahresh.*18 *Beibl.*23 (Cilicia, ii A.D.); ἔφοδον θύειν sacrifice *on arrival*, *GDI* 2501.34 (Delph.). **b.** ἔφοδοι θαλάττης *advance* of the tides, Thphr.*Metaph.*29. **c.** in argument, *method of reasoning*, ἡ ἀπὸ τῶν καθ' ἕκαστον ἐπὶ τὰ καθόλου ἔ. Arist.*Top.*$105^{a}14$; τὰ ἀκόλουθα, τὰ ἑξῆς τῆς ἐ., Ph.1.572, 598; ἐξ ἐναργέος ἐφόδου, i.e. from the clear teaching of experience, Hp.*Praec.*1. **d.** Archit., *course* of masonry, *IG*$2^{2}$.244.98 (iv B.C.), 5(2).33 (Tegea, iii B.C.). **2.** *means of approach*, Plb.1.13.9; *right of access*, δίδοσθαί τινι τὴν ἔ. ἐπὶ τοὺς πολλούς Id.4.34.5; ἐπὶ τὰς ἀρχὰς καὶ τὸν δῆμον *SIG*278.12 (Priene, iv B.C.), cf. *IG*11(4).547 (Delos, iii B.C.); *access for traffic and intercourse, communication*, ἔφοδοι παρ' ἀλλήλους Th.1.6; πρὸς ἀλλ. Id.5.35; *right of importation*, τῶν ἐπιτηδείων X.*HG*2.4.3. **b.** pl., natural *passages*, e.g. nostrils, Hp.*Epid.*6.2.16. **3.** *attempt, plan, method*, ib.6.5.1, Arist.*EE*$1230^{a}35$, Thphr.*Sens.*60; ἔ. τῆς ἐξηγήσεως Plb.3.1.11; *method of procedure*, Vett.Val.24.12; σοφιστικοῖς λόγοις καὶ ἐφόδοις χρησάμενοι Id.334.9. **II.** *attack, onslaught*, A.*Eu.*375 (lyr., pl.), Th.1.93, etc.; τοῦ στρατεύματος X.*An.*2.2.18; ἔφοδον ποιεῖσθαι Th.2.95; δέξασθαι Id.4.126, Pl.*Phd.*95b; γνώμης μᾶλλον ἐφόδῳ ἢ ἰσχύος Th.3.11; ἐξ ἐφόδου τρέψασθαι at *the first assault*, Plb.1.36.11, cf. *OGI* 654.4 (Egypt, i B.C.), etc.; τῇ πρώτῃ ἐφόδῳ ἁλῶναι D.H.4.51; αὐτῇ ἐ. τρεψόμενοι τοὺς πολεμίους Id.3.4; of ships, εἰς τὴν ὁδὸν καὶ εἰς τὴν ἔφοδον dub.l. in Plb.3.25.4 codd. (leg. ἄφ-); νυκτιπόλοι ἔφοδοι of *the haunting powers of darkness*, as subject to Persephone, E.*Ion* 1049 (lyr.). **2.** *attack* or *access* of fever, Hp.*Prog.*20; *afflux* of heat or cold, Id.*Vict.*1.32 (pl.). **3.** Rhet., *artful exordium*, D.H.*Is.*3 (pl.), *Lys.*15; = *insinuatio*, [Cic.] *ad Herenn.*1.4.6, cf. Aphth.*Prog.*13, etc. **III.** *proceedings* in a law-court, *suit*, *PHib.*1.96.10 (iii B.C.), etc.

**ἐφοίτη**, Dor. 3 sg. impf. of φοιτάω.

**ἐφόλκ-αιον**, τό, (ἐφέλκω) prob. *lading-plank*, ξεστὸν ἐ. Od.14.350. **-ή**, ἡ, *tension, pull*, Sor.2.62. ❋ **-ιον**, τό, *small boat towed after a ship*, Moschio ap.Ath.5.208f, Plu.*Pomp.*73, Philostr.*VA*4.32: pl., Str.2.3.4. **2.** generally, *appendage*, *AP*7.67 (Leon.), Plu.*Pomp.*40; of a verse or phrase, Aristid.2.23 J., 330 J.; = sq. 2, Men.*Pk.*380. **3.** *rudder*, Hsch. ❋ **-ίς**, ίδος, ἡ, = foreg. 1, Ach.Tat.3.3, Philostr.*VA*4.9. **2.** = foreg. 2, *burdensome appendage*, τινι E.*Andr.*200, cf. *HF*631, 1424 (pl.), Ael.*Fr.*110. **-ός**, όν, *drawing on, enticing*, ἐφολκὰ λέγειν Th.4.108: c. gen., παιδὸς ἐφολκόν Call.*Fr.*291; ἐ. εἰς παρρησίαν Ael.*VH*8.12; ὅσα κυνὶ ὀρέγεται ἐ. εἰς τὴν ἑαυτοῦ φιλίαν Id.*NA*7.10. **II.** *requiring to be drawn on, laggard*, Ar.*V.*268; μὴ πρόλεσχος μηδ' ἐ. ἐν λόγῳ not eager to begin, nor yet *lagging, tedious* in reply, A.*Supp.*200.

❋ **ἐφομαρτέω**, *accompany, come on* (*with*), abs., Il.8.191, 12.412, 23.414 (ἐφαμ- Aristarch.), Nic.*Al.*479: c. dat., A.R.1.201: rare in Prose, as Arr.*An.*1.19.2.

**ἐφομῑλέω**, *live with* or *among*, c. acc., dub. in Hermesian.7.51: c. dat., Nonn.*D.*5.410.

**ἐφόνιον**, τό, *saddle for an ass*, *PCair.Zen.*355.86 (iii B.C.).

**ἐφοπλίζω**, *get ready*, of meals, δόρπον, δεῖπνον ἐ., Il.23.55, Od.19.419; δαῖτα γέρουσιν ἐφοπλίζωμεν Il.4.344:—Med., δόρπα τ' ἐφοπλισόμεσθα *we will get ready our* suppers, 8.503, 9.66. **2.** *fit out, equip, make ready*, ἡμιόνους καὶ ἅμαξαν ἐφοπλίσαι Od.6.37, cf. 57, 69, Il.24.263; [νῆα] ἐφοπλίσσαντες Od.2.295: c. inf., A.R.4.1720. **3.** *arm against*, τινά τινι Opp.*C.*3.244:—Med., Ἔρων ὔμμιν ἐφοπλίσομαι *AP*9.39 (Music.), cf. *APl.*4.151.9. **II.** Med. in prop. sense, *arm oneself*, ἐς ἀγῶνα Opp.*H.*5.617; *get ready to attack*, λαγωοῖς Id.*C.*3.86.

**ἐφόρ-ᾱσις**, εως, ἡ, *observation*, ἡ τῶν θεῶν ἐ. Porph.*Marc.*21. **-ᾱτέον**, *one must observe*, Heph.Astr.3.4. ❋ **-ᾱτικός**, ή, όν, *fit for overlooking*, ἔργων X.*Oec.*12.19. **-άω**, Ion. 3 sg. ἐπορᾷ, inf. ἐπορᾶν, Hdt.1.10, 3.53: Aeol. pres. part. ἐπόρεις (ἐφορεῖς cod.) *Lyr.Adesp.*61: impf. ἐφεώρων, Ion. 3 sg. ἐπώρα Hdt.1.48: fut. ἐπόψομαι Od.19.260, A.*Ag.*1642, etc.: aor. 1 ἐπόψατο Pi.*Fr.*88.6 (but ἐπεῖδον (q.v.) generally used as aor. 1):—Pass., Dor. aor. 1 inf. ἐποφθῆμεν Diotog. ap.Stob.4.1.96: (ἐπιόψομαι (q.v.), ἐπιώψατο are from a difft. root):—*oversee, observe*, of the sun, πάντ' ἐφορᾷς καὶ πάντ' ἐπακούεις Il.3.277, cf. Od.11.109, S.*El.*824 (lyr.); ὁπόσας ἐφορᾷ φέγγος ἀελίου E.*Hipp.*849 (lyr., codd.); of the gods, *watch over, visit*, Ζεὺς.. ὅς τε καὶ ἄλλους ἀνθρώπους ἐφορᾷ Od.13.214; θεοὶ.. ἀνθρώπων ὕβριν τε καὶ εὐνομίην ἐφορῶντες 17.487; Ζεὺς πάντων ἐφορᾷ τέλος Sol.13.17; σὲ γὰρ θεοὶ ἐπορῶσι Hdt.1.124; Ζεὺς ὃς ἐφορᾷ πάντα S.*El.*175 (lyr.); Δίκην πάντα τὰ τῶν ἀνθρώπων ἐφορᾶν D.25.11 (later c. gen., χώρα ἧς ὁ Ἥλιος ἐφορᾷ *UPZ*14.30 (ii B.C.), etc.); λιμὸς μαλθακόν σφ' ἐπόψεται A.*Ag.*1642; of men, τὰ πρήγματα ἐπορᾶν τε καὶ διέπειν Hdt.3.53; [τὰς πόλεις] Eup.290; πάντ' ἐφορῶν καὶ διοικῶν D.3.34; οὐ ῥᾴδιον ἐφορᾶν πολλὰ τὸν ἕνα Arist.*Pol.*$1287^{b}8$; ἀρχὴ ἐφορῶσα περὶ τὰ συμβόλαια ib.$1321^{b}13$; of a general going his rounds, Th.6.67, X.*Cyr.*5.3.59; *visit* the wounded, αὐτόπτης ἐ. ib.5.4.18; δαῖτα ἐποψόμενος *attend* it, Pi.*O.*8.52 (s.v.l.):—Pass., of insane persons, δοκοῦσιν ὑπό τινων μειζόνων ἐφορᾶσθαι δυνάμεων Paul.Aeg.3.14. **2.** *look upon, behold*, ἐποψόμενος Τιτυόν Od.7.324; ἕκαστα τῶν συγγραμμάτων *inspect* them, Hdt.1.48: freq. c. part., ἐπόψεαι.. φεύγοντας Il.14.145; κτεινομένους μνηστῆρας Od.20.233; ἐπορᾷ μιν ἐξιόντα Hdt.1.10; ἐ. τοὺς φίλους εὐδαίμονας γενομένους X.*Cyr.*8.7.7, etc.; cf. ἐπεῖδον: esp. of evils, ἐποψόμενος Κακοΐλιον Od.19.260, al.; Ἀγαμέμνονός σέ φημ' ἐπόψεσθαι μόρον A.*Ag.*1246; τὰ μέλλοντ' οὐδεὶς ἐ. S.*Tr.*1270 (anap.), cf. Ar.*Th.*1048 (lyr.):—Pass., ὅσον ἐφεωρᾶτο τῆς νήσου as much of it as *was in view*, Th.3.104. **3.** Astrol., = ἐπιβλέπω III, *Cat.Cod.Astr.*1.126.

**ἐφορ-εία**, ἡ, (ἐφορεύω II) *office of ephor*, X.*Lac.*8.3, Lys.*Fr.*315 S.; with v.l. **ἐφορία**, Arist.*Pol.*$1270^{b}7$, *Rh.*$1419^{a}31$. **II.** (ὅρος) *frontier*, Hecat.217 J. **-εῖον**, τό, *office* or *court of the ephors*, X.*Ages.*1.36, Plu.2.232f. **-εύω**, = ἐφοράω, c. acc., A.*Supp.*627 (anap.), 677 (lyr.), *Eu.*531 (lyr.); χώρας Id.*Pers.*7 (anap.); περί τινος Luc.*Charid.*10. **II.** *to be ephor*, Th.8.6, X.*HG*1.3.1, *Abh.Berl.Akad.*1925(5).8 (Cyrene), *Tab.Heracl.*1.122. **-ικός**, ή, όν, *of* or *for the ephors*, δίφροι X.*Lac.*15.6.

**ἐφόριος**, α, ον, (ὅρος) *bordering on*, Ῥωμαίων App.*BC*5.9; *on the border* or *frontier*, ἀγορὰ ἐ., where the people of adjacent states met for market and other purposes, *IG*$1^{2}$.115.27 (= D.23.37); ἐ. πόλεις Aristid.*Or.*26(14).81; στήλη Poll.9.8; δένδρα prob. in *Ostr.Strassb.*772 (ii A.D.). **II.** ἐφόρια, τά, *boundaries*, *PFay.*23(*a*).5 (ii A.D.).

❋ **ἐφορμ-αίνω**, *rush on*, δρόμῳ A.*Pers.*208, cf. Orph.*H.*33.5, 74.7; τινι *upon* or *against* one, Opp.*C.*3.367. **-άω**, Ion. **ἐπ-**, *stir up, rouse against* one, οἵ μοι ἐφώρμησαν πόλεμον Il.3.165; ὅς μοι ἐφορμήσας ἀνέμους Od.7.272; ἐπορμῆσαι τοὺς λύκους *set* them *on*, Hdt.9.93; ᾧ καὶ Ζεὺς ἐφορμήσῃ κακά S.*Fr.*680; σῦν Ant.Lib.2.2: c. dupl. acc., ναύτας ἐφορμήσαντα.. τὸ πλεῖν *having urged* them *on* to sail, S.*Aj.*1143: c. acc. et inf., Orph.*L.*26. **II.** intr., *rush upon, attack*, τινι E.*Hipp.*1275 (lyr.), Plu.*Pomp.*19, etc.; ἐπί τινα D.C.36.24: abs., Plb.8.6.1: c. inf., *desire*, Opp.*H.*2.94, Orph.*L.*34; f.l. for ἀφορμ- in X.*HG*1.6.21.—This use is more freq. in Pass. (v. infr.). **III.** Pass. and Med., *to be stirred up*: c. inf., *to be eager* or *desire* to do, θυμὸς ἐφορμᾶται πολεμίζειν ἠδὲ μάχεσθαι Il.13.74, cf. Od.1.275, 21.399, etc.: abs., *rush furiously on*, ἔγχει ἐφορμᾶσθαι Il.17.465: mostly in aor. part. Pass., ἐφορμηθείς 6.410, etc.; ἄκοντι ἐφορμαθείς Pi.*N.*10.69; ἐφορμηθέντες ἐξ ἑνὸς ῥόθου A.*Pers.*462: without hostile sense, *spring forward*, τρὶς μὲν ἐφωρμήθην Od.11.206, cf. Hes.*Op.*459: c. acc., *rush upon, make a dash at*, ὥς τ' ὀρνίθων.. αἰετὸς αἴθων ἔθνος ἐφορμᾶται Il.15.691, cf. 20.461; so ἐφορμήσεσθαι ἀέθλους Hes.*Sc.*127: rarely (if ever) found in Prose, dub.l. in Th.6.49. **-έω**, Ion. **ἐπ-**, *lie moored at* or *over against* a place, *blockade* it, λαθὼν τοὺς ἐπορμέοντας having escaped *the blockading fleet*, Hdt.8.81, cf. Th.8.75, X.*An.*7.6.25; πεζῇ τε καὶ ναυσὶν ἐ. Th.4.24: c. dat., ἐ. τῷ λιμένι Id.7.3, cf. 3.31; ἐπὶ τῇ Μιλήτῳ Id.8.30; ἐπὶ τῷ λιμένι X.*HG*6.2.7; ἐπὶ τοῦ στόματος Plb.

1.46.5: c. acc., ἐ. ναυσὶ τὴν ἀκτήν App.*BC*5.72: generally, *lie by and watch*, S.*OC*812; ἐ. τοῖς καιροῖς D.3.7; *rely on*, εἰκόσι καὶ πιθανοῖς Ph. 2.413, al.:—Pass., *to be blockaded*, Th.1.142, 8.20. **-ή**, ἡ, *way of attack*, μία δ' οὐ γίγνετ' ἐφορμή only *room* for one *to attack*, Od.22. 130, cf. A.R.4.148, Opp.*H*.4.623; *assault, attack*, πόλεις ἐφορμαῖς λαβεῖν Th.6.90; *enterprise*, A.R.4.204. **-ησις** (A), εως, ἡ, (ἐφορμέω) *lying at anchor so as to watch* an enemy, *blockading*, Th.2.89, 8.15; *means of so doing*, Id.6.48; ἐ. παρασχεῖν Id.3.33. **-ησις** (B), εως, ἡ, (ἐφορμάω) *onset, attack*, ἐχθρῶν Ph.2.174; κατ' ἐχθρῶν ib.296: pl., App.*BC*5.106. 2. *approach*, Hld.8.9. **-ητικός**, ή, όν, *capable of urging on*, Max.Tyr.7.8, v.l. for ἐξορμ- in Poll.4.86. **-ίζω**, (ὅρμος) *bring* a ship *to her moorings, bring to shore*, in Med., ἀμφὶ ταύτην θῖνα *AP*7.636 (Crin.):—Med. and Pass., *come to anchor*, ἐς [λιμένα] Th.4.8:—in Med. also, = ἐφορμέω, -ορμιούμενος τοῖς πολεμίοις App.*BC*5.108. II. intr. in Act., *seek refuge in*, [ἔλαφοι] ποταμοῖσιν ἐφώρμισαν *AP*9.244 (Apollonid.), cf. 254 (Phil.). **-ος** (A), ον, *at anchor*, αἱ νῆες.. ἔφορμοι οὖσαι Th.3.76 (s. v. l.); τὸ πλοῖον ἔφορμον ποιήσω *Mim.Oxy*.413.194 (ii A.D.). **-ος** (B), ὁ, = ἐφόρμησις, τοὺς ἐ. ποιεῖσθαι Th.3.6, cf. 4.27; ἐς ἔ. πλεῖν ib.32.

⊛ **ἔφορος**, ὁ, (cf. ἐπίουρος) *overseer, guardian, ruler*, στρατιᾶς A.*Pers*. 25 (anap.); χώρας S.*OC*145 (lyr.); σφαγίων E.*Rh*.30 (lyr.); τῶν παίδων Pl.*Phdr*.265c; καρπῶν, οἰάκων, Aristid.*Or*.41(4).10, 42(6).4; ὁ τῆς γενέσεως ἔ. θεός Procl.*in Ti*.1.53 D., al.: as fem., Ael.*Fr*.160: later in neut. pl., ἔφορα Iamb.*Myst*.4.1. II. at Sparta, ἔφοροι, οἱ, *the ephors*, Hdt.1.65, 6.82, 9.76, Pl.*Lg*.692a, Arist.*Pol*.1265$^b$ 39, 1272$^a$5; also, title of magistrates at Heraclea, *Tab.Heracl*.1. 1, al.; at Thera, *Test.Epict*.4.1; in the Eleuthero-Laconian cities, *IG*5(1).1110, al.; also of officials of corporations, ib.209.8 (sg.), 26.4 (pl.).

**ἐφοστρίδες**· εἶδος ἱματίου, Hsch. (nisi leg. ἐφεστρ-).

**ἐφυβρ-ίζω**, *insult over* one, ἐφυβρίζων ἕλετο Il.9.368: c. dat., S. *Aj*.1385: c. acc., τὴν ἀμαθίαν ὑμῶν Plu.2.579c, cf. *APl*.1.4 (also Med., μὴ 'φυβρίζεσθαι νεκρούς E.*Ph*.1663): with neut. Adj., πολλὰ ἐ. τινά Id.*Heracl*.947; τὰ δεινὰ πόλει Id.*Ph*.179; εἰς ἀδελφὸν οἷ' ἐφύβρισας Id.*Andr*.624; ἐφύβριζον ἄλλα τε καὶ εἰ.. they *gave vent to insulting language*, asking especially whether.., Th.6.63. II. *exult maliciously*, S.*Aj*.955 (lyr.). **-ιστήρ**, ῆρος, ὁ, *insulting*, ἴαμβοι v.l. in *AP*7.352. ⊛ **-ιστής**, οῦ, ὁ, *insolent person*, Ptol.*Tetr*.165. ⊛ **-ιστος**, ον, *wanton, insolent*, Vett.Val.71.18; τυραννίς Hdn.2.4.2, 6.1.2; ἐφύβριστα πάσχειν Id.2.7.3: c. dat., ἐ. ἀναστροφῇ *revelling in*.., Man.4. 312. Adv. **-τως** Plu.*Art*.30, Hdn.2.13.11. II. Pass., *contemptible*, Lxx *Wi*.17.7. Adv. **-τως**, κατέστρεψε τὸν βίον Posidon.7 J.

**ἐφυγρ-αίνομαι**, Pass., *become moist*: of the bowels, *to be relaxed*, Hp.*Epid*.1.10. **-ος**, ον, *moist on the surface*, Arist.*Pr*.935$^a$28; ὀμφαλοί ib.896$^a$17: Comp., τὰ -ότερα Thphr.*CP*2.4.7.

**ἐφυδάτιος** [ᾰ], η, ον, *in* or *of the water*, Νύμφη ἐφυδατίη A.R.1. 1229.

**ἐφυδρ-εύω**, *water*, τι Thphr.*HP*2.7.1. ⊛ **-ιάς**, άδος, ἡ, *of the water*, Νύμφαι Alex.Aet.3.22, *AP*9.327 (Hermocr.), 329 (Leon.). **-ίς**, *water-spider*, *Gloss*.; ἐφυδρίδες is prob. f.l. in Artem.2.38marg. **-ος**, Ion. ἔπ-, ον, (ὕδωρ) *moist, rainy*, of the west wind, Od.14.458; ἡμέρα Aristid.*Or*.48(24).50. 2. *abounding in water*, [γῆ] ἔπυδρος πίδαξι Hdt.4.198, cf. Hp.*Aër*.1, Arist.*Mete*.347$^a$31, Dsc.1.15. 3. *living on the water*, νῆτται Philostr.*Im*.1.9 (cf. ἐπίυδρος).

**ἐφ' ὕδωρ** (not ἐφύδωρ), ὁ, *keeper of the water-clock* (κλεψύδρα) in the Athen. law-courts, Poll.8.113 (but ἐφ' ὕδωρ *under water, submerged*, *CPR*32.11 (iii A.D.)).

**ἐφυλακτέω**, *bark at*, τινι Plu.2.551c.

**ἐφυμν-έω**, *sing* or *chant at* or *after*, οὐ γὰρ ὡς φυγῇ παιᾶν' ἐφύμνουν A.*Pers*.393; *chant* or *utter over*, τί οὖν μ' ἄνωγας τῆδ' ἐφυμνῆσαι χθονί; Id.*Eu*.902, cf. *Ch*.386 (lyr.); κακὰς πράξεις ἐφυμνήσασα τῷ παιδοκτόνῳ S.*Ant*.1305; τὸ πάτριον μέλος ἐ. Pl.*Lg*.947c, cf. *Smp*.197e; later of orations, etc., ἐ. τῇ θυσίᾳ Philostr.*VS*1.25.3; τίνι μύθων φῆμαι θαυμαστότερα ἐφύμνησαν; Aristid.*Or*.22(19).2:—Pass., Pl.*Lg*.799a; [ἐπῳδὸν] ἐφυμνεῖσθαι καλόν Ph.1.313. 2. of music, *sound in accord*, ἐφυμνεῖ πηκτίδος συγχορδίᾳ S.*Fr*.412. II. *sing a dirge* or *mournful strain*, Id.*OT*1275. III. *sing of, descant on*, Δία Id.*Ant*. 658. **-ιάζω**, *sing as the refrain*, Eratosth.ap.Sch.Pi.*O*.9.1 (Pass.). ⊛ **-ιον**, τό, *burden, refrain*, of a hymn, A.R.2.713, Call. *Ap*.98, *Sos*.8.4, Ph.1.535, Ath.15.701c, Sch.Pi.*O*.9.1.

⊛ **ἐφύπερα** [ῠ], τά, *upper floor*, *BGU*1247.11 (ii B.C.).

⊛ **ἐφύπερθε** [ῠ], before a vowel **-θεν**, Adv. *above, atop*, στορέσαι ἐ. Il. 24.645, cf. 9.213; κεφαλή τ' ἐ. τε χαῖται Od.4.150, cf. Il.14.184; *from above*, Od.9.383, Theoc.23.59: c. gen., Simon.183.7: Geog., *above*, c. gen., A.R.2.393.

**ἐφυπν-όω**, *sleep meantime*, Hsch. **-ώττω**, *go to sleep over*, τοῖς Ὁμήρου ποιήμασιν Jul.*Ep*.190.

**Ἐφύρα** [ῠ], Ion. **-ρη**, ἡ, *Ephyra*, old name of Corinth, Il.6.152; also perh. of other cities in Elis and Thesprotia, Sch.Od.1.259, 2. 328:—hence **Ἐφύρ-ηθεν**, A.R.4.1212: **-ηνδε**, Call.*Del*.42.

**ἐφυστερ-έω**, *to be late, in arrear*, ὅσα ἐφυστερήκει τοῖς καιροῖς J. *AJ*19.1.5, cf. 18.9.3; *to be deferred*, Sor.1.21, Gal.7.471: c. gen., *to be left behind by*, τοῦ ἡλίου Alex.Aphr.*in Mete*.31.28. **-ητικός**, ή, όν, '*postponing*', of increasingly rare attacks of fever, Gal.19. 201. **-ίζω**, *come later, come after*, τὰ ἐφυστερίζοντα, = αἱ ὑστεροῦσαι πόλεις, Th.3.82, cf. D.H.*Th*.29; *to be deferred, overdue*, Gal.7.471.

**ἐφυφαίνω**, *weave in* or *upon*, ἐπὶ μήτιν ὑφαίνων Opp.*C*.3.415.

**ἐφυφή**, ἡ, *woof*, opp. στήμων, Pl.*Lg*.734e.

**ἐφύω** [ῡ], *rain upon*: impers. ἐφύει, c. dat., Thphr.*HP*4.14.8, etc.: abs., *it rains after*, Id.*CP*6.17.7:—pf. part. Pass. ἐφυσμένος *exposed to rain*, X.*Cyn*.9.5.

**ἐφ' ᾧ, ἐφ' ᾧτε**, i.e. ἐπὶ τούτῳ ὥστε, v. ἐπί B. III. 3.

**ἐφώδει**· ἐπέληγε (Lacon.), Hsch. **ἐφώσια**· τὰ νομιζόμενα, Id.

**ἐφώριος**, ον, (ὥρα) *mature*, *AP*9.563 (Leon.).

**ἔχᾰδον**, v. χανδάνω.

**ἐχέβιον**, τό, = μεσάβιον, Poll.1.252.

**ἐχέβωμον**, τό, *altar-base* or *chapel containing an altar*, *IG*12(5).595 *B* 24, *Mus.Belg*.25.108 (Iulis).

**ἐχέγγυος**, ον, *having given* or *able to give security, trustworthy, secure*, δόμοι E.*Med*.387; λόγος Id.*Andr*.192; ποιεῖν δόσιν ἐ. Id.*Ph*. 759; ζημία ἐ. a penalty *to be relied on* (for the prevention of crime), Th.3.46; φρουρά D.H.2.37: Comp. **-ώτερος** Them.*Or*.26.321d: Sup. **-ώτατος**, μάρτυς Ath.9.398f; τὸ τῆς φρουρᾶς ἐ. *security*, Hdn.2.13.8; ἐ. πρὸς ἀσφάλειαν, εἰς σωτηρίαν, Plu.2.59f, 1055b: c. gen., σωφροσύνης τρόπος οὗτος ἐ. *AP*10.56.11 (Pall.); ἀπορρήτων ἐ. *safe to be entrusted with* secrets, Plu.*Publ*.4; ἀξίωμα ἐ. πρὸς ἡγεμονίαν *equal to* command, Id.*Per*.37, cf. Hdn.3.13.4: c. inf., *sufficiently strong* to.., Plu.*Aem*. 8, 2.923c; οὐκ ἐ. πρὸς τὸ ἀριθμεῖν not *sufficient justification* for counting.., Longin.ap.Porph.*Plot*.20. II. Pass., *having received a pledge, secured against danger*, ἱκέτης S.*OC*284.

**ἐχε-γλωττία**, ἡ, *tongue-truce*, '*linguistice*', coined by Luc.*Lex*.9, after ἐκεχειρία (*armistice*). **-γνᾰθον**, τό, *bit*, dub. in *PStrassb*.37.9 (ii A.D.). **-δερμία**, ἡ, *being hide-bound*, of horses, *Hippiatr*.26; = Lat. *coriago*, Veget.*Mulom*.2.118. **-δημία**, ἡ, = *Academia* (after Echemos, king of Arcadia), coined by Dicaearch.ap.Plu.*Thes*.32. **-θῡμος**, ον, *a master of one's passions, under self-control*, Od.8.320:—Subst. **-θῡμία** is v.l. for -μυθία in Ph.2.267.

**ἐχείδιον**, τό, Dim. of ἔχις, *little adder*, Suid. s. v. ἔχις; cf. ἐχίδιον.

**ἐχε-κήλης**, (κήλη) *ruptured*, Hsch. **-κολλος**, ον, *glutinous, sticky*, Hp.*Art*.33 (Comp.); πηλός Plu.2.966d; τὸ ἐχέκολλον ib.735f; ἐχέκολλον μάλιστα ἡ πεύκη *takes glue* best, Thphr.*HP*5.6.2. Adv. **-λως** Dsc.5.153. **-κτέᾰνος**, ον, *with great possessions*, Rhian.1.7, Nonn.*D*.11.37. ⊛ **-μῡθέω**, *to hold one's peace*, Ph.1.309, al., J.*BJ* 1.24.1, Luc.*DDeor*.21.2; τὰ ἀπόρρητα καὶ ἐχεμυθούμενα *things unspoken*, Iambl.*Protr*.21; a Pythagorean word, εἰ δύνανται ἐ. Id.*VP* 20.94. **-μῡθία**, ἡ, *silence, reserve*, ἡ Πυθαγόρειος ἐ. Plu.*Num*.8, cf. 2.728d, Ph.2.267 (v.l. -θυμία), Alciphr.2.55, Ath.7.308d, Iamb.*VP* 6.32, etc. **-μῡθος**, ον, *taciturn*, in Sup., Suid. ⊛ **-νηΐς**, ΐδος, contr. **-νῇς**, ῇδος, ἡ, (ναῦς) *ship-detaining*, ἄπλοιαι A.*Ag*.149 (lyr.); ἄγκυρα *AP*6.27.5 (Theaet.); γαλήνη Nonn.*D*.13.114. II. a small fish, supposed to have the power of *holding ships back*, Arist.*HA*505$^b$19, Opp.*H*.1.212, Plin.*HN*9.79; in form **ἐχεναΐς**, = Lat. *remora*, Donat. ad Ter.*Andr*.739, *Eun*.302. **-νίκειον** [νῑ], τό, *endowment created by Echenice*, *Inscr.Délos*370.42:—hence **-εια**, τά, *festival maintained thereby*, ib.366*A* 133 (iii B.C.).

**ἐχεόδηκτος**, ον, *bitten by a viper*, Str.13.1.14codd., Dsc.2.120, Philum.*Ven*.17.11.

**ἐχε-πάμων** [ᾰ], ον, gen. ονος, *holding property*: hence, *heir* or *representative*, *IG*9(1).334.16 (Locr.). **-πευκής**, ές, (πευκ-, cf. *pungo*) *sharp, piercing*, βέλος Il.1.51, 4.129: expld. by Eust., etc., as *bitter*, and so later σμύρνη Nic.*Th*.600; σικύοιο ῥίζα ib.866, cf. Orph.*L*.475. **-πικρος**, ον, = foreg., Eust.42.33. **-πωλος**, ον, *having horses*, Hsch., Suid. **-ρρημοσύνη**, ἡ, (ῥῆμα) = ἐχεμυθία, Iamb.*VP*34.246. **-σᾶμία**· ὅτε θέρους ὄντος ψεκάσῃ ἢ βροντήσῃ, Hsch. (i.e. a sign which causes public business to be suspended, cf. διοσημία). **-σαρκος**, ον *clinging close to the body*, χιτών Ath.13. 590f.

**ἔχεσκον**, v. ἔχω.

**ἐχέστονος**, ον, *bringing sorrows*, ἰός Theoc.25.213.

**ἐχέτης**, ου, ὁ, = ὁ ἔχων, *man of substance*, Pi.*Fr*.304.

**ἐχέτλ-η**, ἡ, (ἔχω) *plough-handle*, Hes.*Op*.467, A.R.3.1325, *AP* 7.650 (Phalaec.), D.S.9.7, Alciphr.3.19, Luc.*JTr*.31:—hence **-εύω**, *plough*, Hsch. **-ήεις**, εσσα, εν, *of an* ἐχέτλη, γόμφος *AP*6.41 (Agath.). **-ιον**, τό, *hold* of a ship, Nic.*Th*.825.

⊛ **ἐχετογνώμονες**, οἱ, *sluices* or *penstocks to hold up the water at a certain height*, Abyd.8.

**ἐχέτρωσις**, εως, ἡ, *Bryonia cretica*, Hp.*Nat.Mul*.33, Gal.19.101, cj. in Dsc.4.182.

**ἔχευα**, ας, ε, Ep. aor. 1 of χέω, Hom.:—Med., ἐχεύατο Il.5.314.

**ἐχε-φρονέω**, *to be prudent*, *APl*.4.332.6 (Agath.). ⊛ **-φροσύνη**, ἡ, *prudence, good sense*, *AP*9.767 (Agath.). ⊛ **-φρων**, ον, gen. ονος, (φρήν) *sensible, prudent*, ἀνὴρ ἀγαθὸς καὶ ἐ. Il.9.341, cf. Od.13.332; freq. as epith. of Penelope, 4.111, etc.; later of animals, σκύλακες Nonn.*D*.16.226: late in Prose, Syn.Alch.p.65 B. Adv. **-νως** D.S. 15.33.

**ἐχήνια**, τά, *part of a bridle* or *bit*, *IG*2$^2$.1388.74, 1464.13.

**ἔχης**, ητος, ὁ, = ἐχέτης, Hdn.*Epim*.38, *EM*404.23.

**ἔχησις**, εως, ἡ, *having*, Alex.Aphr.*in Metaph*.417.27.

**ἐχθ-αίρω**, Dor. 3 pl. -οντι Theoc.24.29: impf. ἤχθαιρον E.*Supp*. 879: aor. 1 ἤχθηρα Il.20.306, A.*Pers*.772, etc.; Dor. ἤχθᾱρα Timocr. 1.4:—Med., Ep. aor. 1 ἐχθήρατο in act. sense, Nic.*Al*.618, cf. ἀπεχθαίρω:—Pass., S.*Aj*.458: fut. Med. ἐχθαροῦμαι in pass. sense, Id.*Ant*.93: (ἔχθος):—*hate, detest*, ἵν' ἐχθήρειε γέροντα Il.9.452, cf. Od.4.692; ὄφρα σε Λιμὸς ἐχθαίρῃ, φιλέῃ δὲ.. Δημήτηρ Hes.*Op*.300 (cf. Cratin.317); Θεμιστοκλῆ' ἤχθαρε Λατώ Timocr.1.c., cf. Ion Trag. 44, parodied by Ar.*Ra*.1425: c. acc. cogn., ἔχθος ἐχθήρας μέγα S. *Ph*.59: with acc. pers. added, οὐδ' αὖ τοσοῦτον ἔχθος ἐχθαίρω σε I *do* not *bear* thee so great *hatred*, Id.*El*.1034:—Pass., *to be hateful*,

θεοῖσι A.*Supp.*754, cf. S.*Aj.*458: abs., A.*Ch.*241: fut. Med., ἐχθαρῇ μὲν ἐξ ἐμοῦ S.*Ant.*93:—Med. in act. sense, Nic.*Al.*618.—Poet. word, used by Hp.*Ep.*17, Arist.*EN*1126ᵇ24, 1180ᵃ22, and late Prose, Parth. 36.2, Str.17.2.3, Ph.2.543,555 (c. inf., ἅ τις παθεῖν ἐχθαίρει (v.l. ἐχθραίνῃ) Id.ap.Eus.*PE*8.7), Plu.*Rom.*17, D.C.37.38, etc. (ἐχθραίνω is f.l. in E.*Med.*555, etc.) **-αρτέος**, α, ον, *to be hated*, S.*Aj.* 679.

**ἔχθαρ**, τό, = ἔχθος, Theognost.*Can.*79.

**ἐχθέγιον**, τό, dub. sens. in *BGU*950.4 (Byz.).

⊛ **ἐχθές**, Adv. = χθές, *yesterday*, Ar.*Nu.*175, *Th.*616, etc.; ἀπ' ἐ. *AP* 11.35 (Phld.); μέσφα τό γ' ἐ. Theoc.2.144; οὐ γάρ τι νῦν γε κἀ. today or *yesterday*, S.*Ant.*456; οὐκ ἐ. οὐδὲ πρῴην Antipho *Fr.*58; ἐ. καὶ τρίτης [ἡμέρας] Lxx *Ru.*2.11, cf. M.Ant.10.7. (ἐχθές is commoner than χθές in Com. and Lxx. is the only form used in *NT*, and freq. in papyri of all periods, *PSI*4.442.21 (iii B.C.), etc.; cf. χθές.)

**ἐχθεσινός**, ή, όν, = χθεσινός, *yesterday's*, διαγωγή *AP*10.79 (Pall.), cf. Dosith.p.397 K.

**ἐχθέω**, v. ἔχθω (A).

**ἔχθημα**, ατος, τό, = μίσημα, S.*Fr.*651.

**ἐχθιζινός**, ή, όν, = ἐχθεσινός, Men.303.

**ἐχθ-ίζομαι**, *incur odium*, Phot. ⊛ **-ιστος**, η, ον, Sup. of ἐχθρός, *most hateful*, Ἀχιλῆϊ Il.2.220; ἐ. δέ μοί ἐσσι θεῶν 5.890, etc.; τὸν θεοῖς ἐ. θεόν A.*Pr.*37; ἐ. ὁρᾶν S.*Aj.*818; ἐ. γεγώς E.*Med.*467. 2. *most hostile*, τῶν ἡμῖν ἐχθίστων Th.2.71; ὡς δὲ ἐχθροὶ καὶ ἐ., πάντες ἴστε Id.7.68: c. gen., οἱ ἐκείνου ἐ. his *bitterest enemies*, X.*An.*3.2.5: Luc. has also ἐχθίστατος *Trag.*246. **-ίων**, ον, gen. ονος, Comp. of ἐχθρός, *more hateful*, A.*Pers.*438, S.*OT*272, E.*El.*222, Ar.*Av.*370, Th.4.86, Pl.*Ly.*214c. Adv. ἐχθιόνως, ἔχειν X.*Smp.*4.3.

**ἐχθο-δᾰπός**, όν, *foreign*, *hostile*, φῶτες *IGRom.*4.360.38 (Pergam., ii A.D.): perh. formed fr. ἐχθός, cf. ἀλλοδαπός, ἡμεδαπός, etc. **-δοπέω**, *show enmity towards, engage in hostility with*, ὅ τέ μ' ἐχθοδοπῆσαι ἐφήσεις Ἥρῃ Il.1.518. **-δοπός**, όν, *hateful*, φώς S.*Ph.*1137 (lyr.); πόλεμος Ar.*Ach.*226 (lyr.); τοῖα.. ἀνεστέναζες.. ἐχθοδόπ' Ἀτρείδαις S.*Aj.*931 (lyr.); τῆς δ' οὐ ἐχθοδοποῦ γεγονυίας πολλοῖς, ἴσως δὲ.. ἑτέροις προσφιλοῦς Pl.*Lg.*810d; of a drug, Pl.Com. 196; ἐ. ὄμματα A.R.4.1669. (Perh. by assimilation fr. ἐχθοδαπός 'foreign', 'hostile' (q.v.).)

**ἔχθοι**, Adv. *outside*, *IG*4.1484.66 (Epid.).

**ἔχθος**, εος, τό, *hate*, Διὸς ἔχθος ἀλευάμενος Od.9.277: and in pl., ἔχθεα λυγρά Il.3.416, cf. Pi.*P.*2.55; ἴδια, κοινὰ ἔχθεα, Hdt.3.82; κατὰ ἔχθος τινός *hatred for* one, Id.9.15, cf. Th.1.103, 7.57; ἔχθει c. gen., A.*Supp.*332, Th.1.95; ἐς ἔχθεα ἀπικνέεσθαί τινι to incur his *enmity*, Hdt.3.82; εἰς ἔχθος ἐλθεῖν τινι E.*Ph.*879; ὑπ' ἔχθους Plu.*Publ.*9. II. ὦ πλεῖστον ἐ. *object of* direst *hate*, A.*Pers.*284.—In Prose ἔχθρα is more freq.

**ἐχθός**, Adv. = ἐκτός, *outside*, τᾶς ϝοικίας *Schwyzer* 323 C 35 (Delph., iv B.C.). 2. *except*, προξένω ib.363.11 (Locr., v B.C.).

**ἐχθόσδῐκος** δίκα suit *with a foreigner*, *IG*5(2).357.26 (Stymphalus, iii B.C.).

⊛ **ἔχθρ-α**, Ion. **ἔχθρη**, ἡ, *hatred, enmity*, Hdt.5.81, Pi.*P.*4.145, etc.: in philos. sense, = νεῖκος 1.5, Plot.3.2.2; ἐ. τινός *hatred for, enmity to* one, Antipho 2.4.1, Th.3.10; κατ' ἔχθραν τινός Ar.*Pax* 133; ἐ. ἔς τινα Hdt.1.5, Th.2.68; εἰς θεόν *Ep.Rom.*8.7; πρός τινα A.*Pr.*491 (pl.), Th.2.68; δι' ἔχθρας μολεῖν, ἀφῖχθαί τινι, to be *at feud* with one, E.*Ph.* 479, *Hipp.*1164; δι' ἔχθρας οὐδετέρῳ γενήσομαι Ar.*Ra.*1412; εἰς ἐ. βάλλειν τινά A.*Pr.*390; εἰς ἐ. ἐλθεῖν D.21.62; καταστῆσαί τινας εἰς ἔχθραν τῷ δήμῳ X.*HG*3.5.9; πολλὴν εἰς ἔχθραν ἀλλήλοις καὶ πολλῶν πέρι καθίστανται Pl.*Plt.*307d, cf. Isoc.9.67; πρὸς ἔχθραν from *personal enmity*, D.18.141; ἐ. συμβάλλειν, συνάπτειν τινί, to engage in *hostility* with.., E.*Med.*45, *Heracl.*459; ἐ. τισὶν ἄρασθαι D.21.132; καταλλάσσεσθαι τὰς ἐ. Hdt.7.145; λύσασαν ἐ. τὴν πάρος E.*Tr.*50; τὰς μεγάλας ἐ. διαλύεσθαι Th.4.19; πρὸς ἀλλήλους ἐ. ἀνείλοντο Is.1.9; διαλλαχθῆναι τῆς ἐ. And.2.26: prov., Ἐμπεδοκλέους ἐ., of undying *hatred*, Lys. *Fr.*261 S. **-αίνω**, impf. ἤχθραινον X.*Ages.*11.5: aor. 1 ἤχθρηνα Max.67, -ᾱνα Ph.2.394; later form of ἐχθαίρω (q.v.): (ἐχθρός):—*hate*, τινα X.l.c.; τι Ph.2.297; οἱ ἐχθράναντες *one's enemies*, ib.394:—Pass., ὑπό τινων Phld.*Mort.*20; also ἐ. τινί *to be at enmity with*, Lxx *Nu.*25.18, al., Ael.*NA*5.2. II. *make hateful* or *hostile*, τινά τινι Max. l.c. **-ασμα**, ατος, τό, = ἔχθρα, Hsch. **-εύω**, *to be at enmity with*, τινι Lxx *Ex.*23.22, al., Phld.*Rh.*2.134 S., Tz.*H.*1. 671. ⊛ **-ία**, ἡ, late form of ἔχθρα, Lxx *Ge.*26.21. **-ικός**, ή, όν, *hostile*, interpol. in Hermog.*Id.*1.8, cf. Astramps.*Onir.*1.

**ἐχθρο-δαίμων**, ον, gen. ονος, *hated of the gods*, S.*OT*816. **-ειδῶς**, Adv. = ὑπόπτως, Hsch. **-λέων**, οντος, ὁ, *opponent-lion*, *IG*2.2836 (εἰχθρ- lapis). **-ξενος**, ον, *hostile to strangers, inhospitable*, ναύταισι A.*Pr.*727, cf. *Th.*606, 621; δόμοι E.*Alc.*558. **-ποιέω**, *make hostile*, App.*BC*5.60, cf. Hsch.:—Pass., Ptol.*Tetr.*191. **-ποιός**, όν, *causing enmity*, δαίμονες Charond.ap.Stob.4.2.24, cf. App.*BC*1.54.

**ἐχθρός**, ά, όν, (ἔχθος) *hated, hateful*, of persons and things, freq. from Hom. downwds. (Hom. has it only in this pass. sense); ἐ. γάρ μοι κεῖνος ὁμῶς Ἀΐδαο πύλῃσι Od.14.156, Il.9.312; ἐχθρὸν δέ μοί ἐστιν c. inf., 'tis *hateful* to me to.., Od.12.452; θεοῖσιν ἐ. Hes.*Th.* 766, Thgn.601, Ar.*Eq.*34; ὁ θεοῖσιν ἐ. Pl.Com.74, etc.; cf. θεοισεχθρός. II. Act., *hating, hostile*, first in Hes. and Pi. (v. infr. III), τινι D.10.11, X.*Ages.*6.1, etc.: c. gen., ὕβριος ἐχθρὰν ὁδὸν *averse from* insolence, Pi.*O.*7.90: abs., ἐ. γλῶσσα A.*Ch.*309 (anap.); ὀργαί Id.*Eu.*937 (anap.), etc.; ἀστέρες Vett.Val.143.5. III. as Subst., ἐχθρός, ὁ, *enemy*, where the act. and pass. senses freq. coincide, Hes.*Op.*342, Pi.*P.*2.84, etc.; ἀνὴρ ἐ. Hdt.1.92; ὁ Διὸς ἐ. A.*Pr.*120 (anap.); ἐχθροῖς ἐχθρὰ πορσύνων Id.*Ag.*1374; εἴ..τινα ἴδοι ἐχθρὸν ἑαυτοῦ Th.4.47; οἱ ἐμοὶ ἐ. Id.6.89, etc.—Acc. to Ammon.*Diff.*p.63 V., ἐχθρός is *one who has been* φίλος, *but is alienated*; πολέμιος *one who is at war*; δυσμενής *one who has long been alienated and refuses to be reconciled*. IV. regul. Comp. ἐχθρότερος D.*Prooem.*40.3, *AP*5. 160 (Hedyl. or Asclep.); Sup. -ότατος Pi.*N.*1.65, S.*OT*1346 (lyr.), D.19.300: but more freq. irreg. ἐχθίων, ἔχθιστος (qq.v.). V. Adv. ἐχθρῶς, μισοῦντες Pl.*Lg.*697d, etc.: Comp. -οτέρως D.5.18: Sup. -ότατα Id.23.149.

**ἐχθρόφρων**, ον, gen. ονος, *hostile in disposition*, *EM*245.23.

**ἐχθρωδ-έω**, *to be hostile*, πρός τινας Suid. s.v. Ἐμπεδοκλέους ἔχθρα. **-ης**, ες, *hostile*, Sch.Opp.*H.*1.685: Comp. -έστερος Sch. E.*Hec.*745, *Or.*614. Adv. -δῶς, διαθεῖναί τινα πρός τινας J.*BJ*1.24.2; ἐ. ἔχειν τινί D.C.43.10, cf. Nic.Dam.57 J., Sch.E.*Med.*290.

**ἐχθῦσαι**· ἐξεμέσαι, and ⊛ **ἔχθυσῃ**· ἐκφυσήσῃ, Hsch.

**ἐχθυσία**, v. ἐκθυσία.

⊛ **ἔχθω** (A), *hate*, οὐ δικαίως θάνατον ἔχθουσιν βροτοί A.*Fr.*353; ἔχθεις S.*Ph.*510 (lyr.), E.*Med.*117 (anap.); ἔχθει S.*Aj.*459: c. dupl. acc., ταῦτά τοί σ' ἔχθει πόσις E.*Andr.*212:—Hom. only in Pass., καὶ ἐχθομενός περ Ἀθήνῃ Od.4.502; οὐ γὰρ ὀΐω πάγχυ θεοῖς..[αὐτὸν] ἔχθεσθαι ib. 756; ἥ τοι ἐμοὶ ῥήγεα σιγαλόεντα ἤχθεθ' 19.338; ἤχθετο πᾶσι θεοῖσι 14. 366; κολοσσῶν ἔχθεται χάρις ἀνδρί A.*Ag.*417 (lyr.); σωφρονοῦντι δ' ἤχθετο E.*Hipp.*1402.—Only pres. and impf., exc. pf. part. Pass. ἠχθημένος Lyc.827: the forms ἔχθει (imper.) Thgn.1032, ἤχθεε Hermesian.7.39 are corrupt.

**ἔχθω** (B), = ἔξω, *except*, c. gen., *Schwyzer* 323 C 43 (Delph., iv B.C.).

**ἐχίδιον**, τό, *young viper*, Arist.*HA*558ᵃ29 (v.l. ἐχίδνιον); cf. ἐχείδιον.

⊛ **ἔχιδν-α**, ἡ, (ἔχις) *viper*, Hdt.3.108, S.*Tr.*771, Pl.*Smp.*218a, etc.; prob. of a *constrictor snake*, *Act.Ap.*28.3: metaph., of a treacherous wife or friend, A.*Ch.*249, S.*Ant.*531; ἱματισμένη ἐ., of woman, Secund.*Sent.*8; γεννήματα ἐχιδνῶν *brood of vipers*, term of reproach, in *Ev.Matt.*3.7. II. pr. n. of a monster, Hes.*Th.*297, S.*Tr.* 1099. **-αῖος**, α, ον, *of* or *like a viper*, χόλος *AP*7.71 (Gaet.). 2. *snaky*, κόρυμβος Nonn.*D.*14.216. II. pr. Adj. Ἐχιδναῖος, α, ον, *born of Echidna*, δάκετον Call.*Fr.*161. **-ήεις**, εσσα, εν, = foreg., Nic.*Th.*209; δίφρος ἐ. *drawn by vipers*, Nonn.*D.*13.191.

**ἐχιδνο-ειδής**, ές, *snake-like*, *Gloss.* **-κέφᾰλος**, ον, *snake-headed*, Sch.E.*Ph.*1136. **-κομος**, ον, *snaky-haired*, Nonn.*D.*1. 173. **-λογέω**, *collect vipers*, Eust. ad D.P.376. **-τοκος**, ον, *born of a viper*, Anon.*Prog.*9 in Rh.1.626 W. **-φᾰγία**, ἡ, *eating of vipers*, Dsc.*Eup.*1.227.

**ἐχιδνώδης**, ες, = ἐχιδνοειδής, Sch.E.*Ph.*1136.

**ἐχίειον** [ῐ], τό, = ἔχιον II, Nic.*Th.*65, 637. II. Adj. -ειος, α, ον, = ἐχιδναῖος, Tz.*H.*12.840.

**ἐχιεύς**, έως, ὁ, *a young viper*, pl. ἐχιῆες Nic.*Th.*133.

**Ἐχῖναι**, ῶν, αἱ, *islands in the Ionian sea*, Il.2.625, E.*IA*286 (lyr.), etc.:—commonly called Ἐχινάδες, αἱ, Hdt.2.10, Th.2.102, etc.

**ἐχῖναῖος**, ον, = ἐχιδναῖος, dub. in Nic.*Th.*230.

**ἐχῖνᾰλώπηξ**, εκος, ὁ, *hedgehog-fox*, St.Byz. s.v. Ἀζανοί.

**ἐχινέα**, ἡ, a kind of *vase*, *BCH*35.286 (Delos, ii B.C.), *Ath.Mitt.* 33.377 (Pergam.), *Chron.Lind.*B.101; contr. ἐχινῆ (q.v.).

⊛ **ἐχινέες**, οἱ, *kind of mouse with rough bristling hair*, in Libya, Hdt. 4.192 (v.l. ἐχῖνες): acc. pl. ἐχῖνας Arist.*Mir.*832ᵇ3.

**ἐχινῆ** (sc. δορά), ἡ, *hedgehog's skin*, Hdn.Gr.1.334. II. ἐ. στρατιωτική, prob. = ἐχινέα, *IG*11(2).161 B 125 (Delos, iii B.C.).

**ἐχίνιον**, τό, = ἱπποφαές, Ps.-Dsc.4.159.

**ἐχινίς**, ίδος, ἡ, = ἐχῖνος II. 1, Hp.*Nat.Mul.*32.

**ἐχινίσκος**, ὁ, Dim. of ἐχῖνος, *hollow of the ear*, Poll.2.86. II. Dim. of ἐχῖνος II, Id.10.95.

**ἐχινο-μήτρα**, ἡ, *the largest kind of sea-urchin*, *Echinus melo*, Arist. *HA*530ᵇ6. ⊛ **-πους**, ποδος, ὁ, *kind of prickly-plant*, *Genista acanthoclada*, perh. the same as ἔχιον, Eleg.ap.Plu.2.44e (pl.), cf. Hsch. s.v. λυκόφανον, *EM*405.12.

⊛ **ἐχῖνος**, ὁ (on the accent, v. Hdn.Gr.1.183), *hedgehog* (prop. ἐ. χερσαῖος, as in Thphr.*Sign.*30), *Erinaceus europaeus*, Archil.118, Emp. 83, Ar.*Pax*1086, Ion Trag.38, S.*Ichn.*121, etc. 2. *sea-urchin*, Epich.53, Archipp.24; ἐ. θαλάττιος Pl.*Euthd.*298d. II. *large wide-mouthed jar*, Hp.*Mul.*2.172, *Steril.*230, Ar.*V.*1436, Eup.415, Men.*Epit.Fr.*10, Erot., Hsch., Poll.6.91. 2. *vase* in which the notes of evidence were sealed up by the διαιτηταί, in cases of appeal from their decision, D.45.17, 48.48, Arist.*Ath.*53.2, Thphr.*Char.*6. 8. III. hard *case* of beech-mast, chestnuts, etc., Id.*HP*3.10. 1, Xenocr.43, Hsch. 2. *neck-vertebra* of the κεστρεύς, Dorio ap. Ath.7.306f. IV. *third stomach of ruminating animals*, Arist.*PA* 676ᵃ11, 674ᵇ15, *HA*507ᵇ6, Antig.*Mir.*17; βοῶν ἐ. Call.*Fr.*250; also, *gizzard* of graminivorous birds, Ael.*NA*14.7. V. pl., *sharp points* at each end of a bit, X.*Eq.*10.6, Poll.1.148; but = τῶν ὑποστομίων τὰ κοῖλα, ib.184. VI. Archit., *cushion of the Doric and Tuscan capital* (prob. from its form), Vitr.4.3.4, 4.7.3. 2. = οἱ τῶν τειχῶν ἀγκῶνες, Hsch. VII. a kind of *cake*, Lync.ap.Ath.14.647a, Hsch. VIII. a plant, v.l. ἔρινος (q.v.), Dsc.4.141, Gal.11.880, Paul.Aeg.7.3. (Cf. OHG. *igil*, Slav. *ježĭ*, Lith. *ežỹs*.)

**ἐχινώδης**, ες, *prickly, like a hedgehog*, Arist.*Mir.*832ᵇ3, cf. Ar.Byz. *Epit.*109.9: generally, *rugged*, Str.12.3.11.

⊛ **ἐχιόδηκτος**, ον, = ἐχιδνόδηκτος, Dsc.1.13, al., *Gp.*12.30.1; v.l. for ἐχεό-, Str.13.1.14.

**ἔχιον**, τό, (ἔχις) a plant, *Echium plantagineum*, Dsc.4.27 (*echios* Plin.*HN*25.104). II. = ὠκιμοειδές, Dsc.4.28, Sch.Nic.*Th.*637.

⊛ **ἔχῐς** [Nic.*Th.*223, -ῑς metri gr. *IG*2.1660], εως, ὁ (ἡ Opp.*C.*3.439), gen. pl. ἔχεων Pl.*Euthd.*290a: gen. sg. ἔχιος Nic.*Th.*130: pl., dat. ἐχίεσσι ib.826; gen. ἐχίων ib.653; acc. ἔχιας ib.9, but ἔχεις Thphr. *Char.*1.7:—*viper*, Pl.*Smp.*217e, Arist.*HA*$511^{a}16$, etc.: metaph., συκοφάντης καὶ ἔ. τὴν φύσιν D.25.96; ὥσπερ ἔ. ἢ σκορπίος ἠρκὼς τὸ κέντρον ib.52; cf. ἔχιδνα. II. = ἔχιον II, Nic.*Th.*541, 636, Plin. *HN*22.50.

**ἐχίτης** [ῑ], ου, ὁ, a kind of *stone*, Plin.*HN*37.187, *Gloss.*

⊛ **ἔχμα**, ατος, τό, (ἔχω) *that which holds*; and so, I. *hindrance, impediment*, Il.21.259 (pl.). 2. c. gen., *bulwark, defence against*, ἐπηλυσίης *h.Merc.*37; βολάων A.R.4.201. II. *holdfast, stay*, ἔχματα πέτρης *the grip* of the rock (viz. the river-bed), Il.13.139; ἔχματα πύργων *buttresses* of the fortifications, 12.260; ἔχματα νηῶν *props* or *cradles* for the ships, 14.410; ἔχματα γαίης, of the earth which *holds fast* the roots of a tree, A.R.1.1200; ἔχματα γούνων, of muscles, Nic.*Th.*724:—also **ἐχμός**, ὁ, Eust.1411.24.

**ἐχμάζω**, *hold fast, hinder*, Eust.904.4, Sch.E.*Or.*265, Hsch.; cf. ὀχμάζω.

⊛ **ἐχομένιον**, τό, *coriander*, *POxy.*729.31 (ii A.D.), 1279.17 (ii A.D.).

**ἐχομένως**, Adv. pres. part. of ἔχομαι, = ἐφεξῆς, prob. in Epicur. *Ep.*2 p.40 U., cf. Apollod.3.1.1, Ph.1.84, A.D.*Pron.*101.6, Bito 57.1, Petos.ap.Vett.Val.332.32, etc.; ἐ. τινός *next after* him, D.L.4.23.

⊛ **ἐχόντως**, Adv. pres. part. of ἔχω, in phrase ἐ. νοῦν, = νουνεχόντως (q.v.), Pl.*Lg.*686e; ἐχόντως ἑαυτὸν τὸν νοῦν Id.*Phlb.*64a.

**ἐχυρῆσαι**· τῷ διὰ χειρὸς ὅρκῳ συνθέσθαι, καὶ κρατηθῆναι, Hsch.

⊛ **ἐχῠρ-ός**, ά, όν, (ἔχω) = ὀχυρός, *strong, secure*, λιμήν, χωρία, Th.4.8, X.*Cyr.*2.4.13; ἀπὸ ἐχυροῦ ποθέν Th.1.90; ἐν τῷ ἐχυρῷ εἶναι to be in *safety*, Id.7.77; ἐν -ωτάτῳ ποιεῖσθαί τι X.*Cyr.*1.6.26. 2. of arguments, etc., *strong*, λόγος Th.3.83; ἐλπίς Id.7.41; ἐχυρὰ παρέχεσθαι to give *good reasons*, Id.1.32; τὴν τόλμαν..-ωτέραν παρέχεσθαι Id.2.62; -ωτέρα δύναμις Id.1.42; τοῦτο ὁ φόβος ἐχυρὸν παρεῖχε Id.3.12; ἀποδείξεις -ώταται Ph.1.420. 3. of persons, ἐ. πρὸς τοὺς καλοὺς *proof* against, Plu.*Sol.*1. II. Adv. -ρῶς Th.5.26: Comp. -ώτερον Id.8.24. (ὀχυρός is v.l. in A.*Pers.*78, 89 (lyr.), and is the usual form in Plb., exc. 2.30.6; but ἐχυρός is usual in Ph., as 1.257, al.) **-ότης**, ητος, ἡ, *strength*, ἐν οἰκοδομίαις Ph.2.116, cf. 120, 1.478 (ἐχ- Pap.), 688, J.*AJ*15.11.4. (ὀχυρότης is a v.l. and shd. be preferred in Plb.1.57.6, but for καὶ ὀχ- (v.l. καὶ ἰσχ-) in Ph.1.644 καὶ ἐχ- shd. be restored.) **-όφρων**, ον, gen. ονος, (φρήν) *strong-minded*, Hsch. **-όω**, *make secure, fortify*, Phot., Suid.; ἐχυρῶσαι is v.l. for ὁρίσαι, Isoc.5.122.

⊛ **ἔχω** (A), 2 sg. ἔχεισθα cj. in Thgn.1316 (ἔχοισθα cod.), ἔχῃσθα cj. in Sapph.21 (ἔχεισθα cod.); 2 sg. subj. ἔχῃσθα Il.19.180: impf. εἶχον, Ep. ἔχον Od.2.22, al., Ion. and poet. ἔχεσκον Il.13.257, Hdt.6.12, *Epigr.Gr.*988.6 (Balbilla): fut. ἕξω, Ep. inf. ἑξέμεναι Call.*Aet.*3.1.27 (of duration) or σχήσω (of momentary action, esp. in sense *check*, v. infr. A.II.9, not found in Att. Inscrr. or *NT*); 2 sg. σχήσησθα *h.Cer.*366 codd.: aor. 1 ἔσχησα f.l. in Nonn.*D.*17.177, also ἔσχα *IG*3.1363.6, 14.1728, 3 pl. μετ-έσχαν ib.12(7).271.12 (Amorgos, iii A.D.): aor. 2 ἔσχον, imper. σχές S.*El.*1013, E.*Hipp.*1353 (anap.) (σχέ only in Orac.ap. Sch.E.*Ph.*638 (dub. l.), sts. in compds. in codd., as πάρασχε E.*Hec.*842, κάτασχε Id.*HF*1210); subj. σχῶ Il.21.309, etc.; opt. σχοίην Isoc. 1.45, in compds. σχοῖμι (as μετάσχοιμι S.*OC*1484 (lyr.), κατάσχοιμεν Th.6.11); 3 pl. σχοίησαν Hyp.*Eux.*32, σχοῖεν Th.6.33; inf. σχεῖν Il. 16.520, etc., Ep. σχέμεν 8.254 (in Alexandr. Gr. 3 pl. impf. and aor. 2 εἴχοσαν *AP*5.208 (Posidipp. or Asclep.), v.l. in *Ev.Jo.*15.22, ἔσχοσαν Scymn.695): for the poet. form ἔσχεθον, v. *σχέθω: pf. ἔσχηκα Pl.*Lg.*765a, εἴσχηκα in Inscrr. of iii/i B.C., *SIG*679.54, etc.; Ep. ὄχωκα is dub., v. συνόχωκα:—**Med.**, impf. εἰχόμην Pi.*P.*4.244, etc.: fut. ἕξομαι Il.9.102, etc.; σχήσομαι ib.235, Ar.*Av.*1335, more freq. in compds. (ἀνα-) A.*Th.*252, (παρα-) Lys.9.8, etc.: pf. Pass. παρ-έσχημαι in med. sense, X.*An.*7.6.11, etc.: aor. 2 ἐσχόμην Hom., Hdt.6.85, rare in Att. exc. in compds.; imper. σχέο Il.21.379, σχέσθε 22.416, later σχοῦ in compds. (ἀνά-) E.*Ion*947, etc.; inf. σχέσθαι Od.4.422, Hes.*Fr.*79:—Pass., fut. Med. ἐν-έξομαι in pass. sense, E.*Or.*516, D.51.11, later σχεθήσομαι Gal.*UP*15.3, freq. in compds. (συ-) Phld.*Ir.*p.83 W., (ἐν-) Plu.2.980f, (ἐπι-) S.E.*P.*1.186: aor. 1 ἐσχέθην Arr.*An.*5.7.4, 6.11.2, Aret.*SA*2.5, (κατ-, συν-) Plu.*Sol.*21, Hp.*Int.*45 vulg.: fut. Med. σχήσομαι in pass. sense, Il.9.235 (dub.), 655, 13.630: aor. 2 Med. in pass. sense, ἐσχόμην Il.17.696, al., Hdt.1.31 (σχέτο Il.7.248, 21.345), part. σχόμενος Od.11.279, prob. in Isoc.19.11, (κατα-) Pi.*P.*1.10, Pl.*Phdr.*244e, Parth.33.2 (s.v.l.): pf. ἔσχημαι Paus.4.21.2; also in compds., freq. written -ίσχημαι, -ήσχημαι in codd. of late authors. (I.-E. *seĝh-* (cf. Skt. *sáhate* 'overpower', Goth. *sigis* 'victory', Gr. ἑχ- dissim. fr. ἑχ-), reduced form *sĝh-* (σχ-), whence redupl. ἴσχω (= *si-sĝh-o*) (q.v.): cf. ἕκ-τωρ, ἕξω, ἕξις; but *h*έχ- *IG*1$^{2}$.374.161, al., is a mere error (ἔχ- ib.1$^{2}$.116.4, 16).)

**A.** Trans., *have, hold*: **I.** *possess*, of property, the most common usage, Od.2.336, 16.386, etc.; οἵ τι ἔχοντες the *propertied class*, Hdt.6.22; ὁ ἔχων a *wealthy man*, S.*Aj.*157 (anap.); οἱ ἔχοντες E.*Alc.*57, Ar.*Eq.*1295, *Pl.*596; οἱ οὐκ ἔχοντες the *poor*, E.*Supp.*240; κακὸν τὸ μὴ 'χειν Id.*Ph.*405; ἔχειν χρέα *to have* debts *due to one*, D.36.41, cf. 37.12; *to have received*, θεῶν ἄπο κάλλος ἐ. *h.Ven.*77; τι ἔκ τινος S.*OC*1618; παρά τινος Id.*Aj.*663; πρός τινος X.*An.*7.6.33, etc.; ὑπὸ..θεοῖσι *h.Ap.*191; πλέον, ἔλασσον ἔ. (v. h. vv.): in aor., *acquire, get*, ὄνομα E.*Ion*997: also fut. σχήσω, δύναμιν Th.6.6; λέχος E.*Hel.*30, cf. Pi.*P.*9.116:—Pass., *to be possessed*, ἔντεα..μετὰ Τρώεσσιν ἔχονται Il.18.130, cf. 197. **2.** *keep, have charge of*, ἔχον πατρώϊα ἔργα Od.2.22; κῆπον 4.737; Εἰλείθυιαι..ὠδῖνας ἔχουσαι Il.11.271; πύλαι.., ἃς ἔχον Ὧραι 5.749, 8.393; τὰς ἀγέλας X.*Cyr.*7.3.7; διαιτητῶν ἐχόντων τὰς δίκας *having control of*, D.47.45; *to be engaged in*, φυλακὰς ἔχον *kept* watch, Il.9.1, 471; σκοπιὴν ἔχεν Od.8.302; ἀλαοσκοπιὴν εἶχε Il.10.515, 13.10; σκοπιὴν ἔ. τινός *for* a thing, Hdt.5.13; δυσμενῶν θήραν ἔχων S.*Aj.*564, etc.; ἐν χερσὶν ἔ. τι (v. χείρ). **b.** metaph., of a patient, οὐκ ἔχει ἑωυτόν *is* not *himself*, Hp.*Int.*49. **3.** c. acc. loci, *inhabit*, οὐρανόν Il.21.267; Ὄλυμπον 5.890; *haunt*, [Νύμφαι] ἔχουσ' ὀρέων αἰπεινὰ κάρηνα Od.6.123; Βρόμιος ἔχει τὸν χῶρον A.*Eu.*24; esp. of tutelary gods and heroes, Th.2.74, X.*Cyr.*8.3.24; of men, πόλιν καὶ γαῖαν Od.6.177, 195, etc.; Θήβας ἔσχον (ἔσχεν codd.) *ruled* it, E.*HF*4; ἔχεις γὰρ χῶρον *occupiest* it, S.*OC*37, cf. Od.23.46; in military sense, ἔ. τὸ δεξιόν (with or without κέρας) Th.3.107, X.*An.*2.1.15; of beasts, τὰ ὄρη ἔ. Id.*Cyn.*5.12. **4.** *have to wife* or *as husband* (usu. without γυναῖκα, ἄνδρα), οὕνεκ' ἔχεις Ἑλένην καί σφιν γαμβρὸς Διός ἐσσι Od.4.569, cf. 7.313, Il.3.53, etc.; ἔσχε ἄλλην ἀδελφεήν Hdt.3.31, cf. Th.2.29; νυμφίον Call.*Aet.*3.1.27; also of a lover, Th.6.54, *AP*5.185 (Posidipp.), etc.; ἔχω Λαΐδα, ἀλλ' οὐκ ἔχομαι Aristipp.ap.D.L.2.75, cf. Ath.12.544d:—in Pass., τοῦ περ θυγάτηρ ἔχεθ' Ἕκτορι Il.6.398. **5.** *have in one's house, entertain*, Od.17.515, 20.377, *h.Ven.*231, 273. **6.** pres. part. with Verbs, almost, = *with*, ἤϊε ἔχων ταῦτα Hdt.3.128, cf. 2.115; ὃς ἂν ἥκῃ ἔχων στρατόν Id.7.8.δ', cf. X.*Cyr.*1.6.10.—Prose use. **7.** of Place, ἐπ' ἀριστερὰ ἔ. τι *keep* it on one's left, i.e. to keep to the right of it, Od.3.171; ἐπ' ἀριστερὰ χειρὸς ἔ. 5.277; ἐν δεξιᾷ, ἐν ἀριστερᾷ ἔ., Th.3.106; τοὺς οἰκέτας ὑστάτους ἔ. X.*Cyr.*4.2.2: but in aor., *get*, περιπλώοντες τὴν Λιβύην τὸν ἥλιον ἔσχον ἐς τὰ δεξιά Hdt.4.42. **8.** of Habits, States, or Conditions, bodily or mental, γῆρας λυγρὸν ἔ. Od.24.250; ἀνεκτὸν ἔχει κακόν 20.83; ἕλκος Il.16.517; λύσσαν 9.305; μάχην ἔ. 14.57; ἀρετῆς πέρι δῆριν ἔ. Od.24.515; ὕβριν ἔ. *indulge in*.., 1.368, etc.; ['Αφροδίτην] 22.445; [φρένας] ἔ. Il.13.394, etc.; βουλήν 2.344; τλήμονα θυμόν 5.670; τόνδε νόον καὶ θυμὸν ἐνὶ στήθεσσιν ἔχοντες 4.309, cf. Od.14.490 (for later senses of νοῦν ἔχειν, v. νοῦς); ἄλγεα Il.5.895, etc.; ἄχεα θυμῷ 3.412; πένθος μετὰ φρεσὶν 24.105; πένθος φρεσίν Od.7.219; πόνον..καὶ ὀϊζύν Il.13.2, Od.8.529; οὐδὲν βίαιον Hdt.3.15; πρήγματα ἔ. Id.7.147, cf. Pl.*Tht.*174b, etc.: in periphrastic phrases, ποθὴν ἔ. τινός, = ποθεῖν, Il.6.362; ἐπιδευὲς ἔ. τινός, = ἐπιδεύεσθαι, 19.180; ἔ. τέλος, = τελεῖσθαι, 18.378; κότον ἔ. τινί, = κοτεῖσθαι, 13.517; ἐπιθυμίαν τινός E.*Andr.*1281; φροντίδα τινός Id.*Med.*1301; ἡσυχίην ἔ. *keep* quiet, Hdt.2.45, etc. (fut. ἡσυχίαν ἕξειν D.47.29, but οὐκ ἔσθ' ὅπως..ἡ. σχήσει *will* not *keep* still *for a moment*, Id.1.14); αἰτίαν ἔ. *to be* accused, X.*An.*7.1.8; ὑπό τινος A.*Eu.*99 (but μομφὴν ἔ., = μέμφεσθαι, E.*Or.*1069, A.*Pr.*445): in aor., of entering upon a state, ἔσχεν χόλον *conceived* anger, B.5.104; ἔχειν τι κατά τινος *have* something against somebody, *Ev.Matt.*5.23, *Ev.Marc.*11.25, *Apoc.*2.4; ἔχω τι πρός τινα *Act.Ap.*24.19; ἔχειν πρός τινα 2*Ep.Cor.*5.12; ἕξει πρὸς τὸν Θεόν *JRS*14.85 (Laodicea):—these phrases are freq. inverted, οὓς ἔχε γῆρας Il.18.515; οὐδὲ Ποσειδάωνα γέλως ἔχε Od.8.344; ἀμηχανίη δ' ἔχε θυμόν 9.295; θάμβος δ' ἔχεν εἰσορόωντας Il.4.79; σ' αὔτως κλέος ἐσθλὸν ἔχει 17.143; Διὸς αἴσῃ, ἥ μ' ἕξει παρὰ νηυσί 9.609 (unless the antecedent is τιμῆς in l.608); ὥς σφεας ἡσυχίη τῆς πολιορκίης ἔσχε Hdt.6.135; ὄφρα με βίος ἔχῃ S.*El.*225 (lyr.): c. dupl. acc., φόβος μ' ἔχει φρένας A.*Supp.*379; also of external objects, αἴθρη ἔχει κορυφήν Od.12.76; μιν ἔχεν μένος ἠελίοιο 10.160; σε οἶνος ἔχει φρένας 18.331; ἔχῃ βέλος ὀξὺ γυναῖκα, of a woman in travail, Il.11.269; λόγος ἔχει τινά c. inf., the story *goes, that*.., S.*OC*1573 (lyr.); and so in later Gr., Plu.*Dem.*28, Ph.1.331, Ael.*VH*3.14, *NA*5.42, Ath.13.592e; ὡς ἡ φάτις μιν ἔχει Hdt.7.3, cf. 5, 26, 9.78 (but also ἔχει φάτιν Διονυσοφάνης θάψαι Μαρδόνιον Id.9.84; [Κλεισθένης] λόγον ἔχει τὴν Πυθίην ἀναπεῖσαι Id.5.66); ὡς ἂν λόγος ἔχῃ πρὸς ἀνθρώπους, ὅτι.. Plu.*Alex.*38:—Pass., ἔχεσθαι κακότητι καὶ ἄλγεσι Od.8.182; κωκυτῷ καὶ οἰμωγῇ Il.22.409; ὀργῇ Hdt.1.141; νούσῳ Hp.*Epid.*5.6; ἀγρυπνίῃσι Hdt.3.129; ὑπὸ πυρετοῦ Hp.*Aph.*4.34; ὑπὸ τοῦ ὕδρωπος Id.*Prorrh.*2.6, ἐν ἀπόρῳ Th.1.25; ἐν συμφοραῖς Pl.*R.*395e. **9.** *possess mentally, understand*, ἵππων δμῆσιν Il.17.476; τέχνην Hes.*Th.*770; πάντ' ἔχεις λόγον A.*Ag.*582, cf. E.*Alc.*51; ἔχετε τὸ πρᾶγμα S.*Ph.*789; ἔχεις τι; *do you understand?* Ar.*Nu.*733: imper. ἔχε *attend! listen!* Pl.*Alc.*1.109b; ἔ. οὖν ib.129b: with imper., ἔχ', ἀποκάθαιρε Ar.*Pax*1193; ἔ. νυν, ἄλειψον Id.*Eq.*490; ἔχεις τοῦτο ἰσχυρῶς; Pl.*Tht.*154a; *know of* a thing, μαντικῆς ὁδόν S.*OT*311; τινὰ σωτηρίαν; E.*Or.*778 (troch.). **10.** *keep up, maintain*, καναχὴν ἔχε *made* a rattling noise, Il.16.105, 794; βοὴν ἔχον, of flutes and lyres, 18.495. **11.** *involve, admit of*, τά γ' αἰσχρὰ κἀνθάδ' αἰσχύνην ἔχει E.*Andr.*244, cf. Th.1.5; βάσανον Lys.12.31; ταῦτ' ἀπιστίαν, ταῦτ' ὀργὴν ἔχει D.10.44; ἀγανάκτησιν, κατάμεμψιν, Th.2.41; τὰ ἀόρατα νοσήματα δυσχερεστέραν ἔχει τὴν θεραπείαν Onos.1.15. **12.** of Measure or Value, τὸ Δαμαρέτειον..εἶχε 'Αττικὰς δραχμὰς δέκα D.S.11.26; ἔχει τὸ Εὐβοϊκὸν τάλαντον 'Αλεξανδρείους δραχμὰς ἑπτακισχιλίας App.*Sic.*2.2; χοῖρος ἔχων τὸ ὕψος δύο καὶ ἡμίσους πήχεων Ptol.Euerg.9. **b.** Geom., ἡ ἔχουσα τὰ κέντρα the (straight line) *containing* the centres, Archim.*Aequil.*1.6; ὁ κύκλος ἔχων τὸ πολύγωνον the circle *containing* (*circumscribing*) the polygon, Id.*Sph.Cyl.*1.23. **13.** c. dupl. acc., 'Ορφέα ἄνακτ' ἔχειν E.*Hipp.*953; Ζῆν' ἔχειν ἐπώμοτον S.*Tr.*1188; παιδιὰν ἔ. τὸν ἐκείνου θάνατον Seleuc. Alex.ap.Ath.4.155e. **II.** *hold*: **1.** *hold*, ἔ. χερσίν, ἐν χερσίν, μετὰ χερσίν, etc., v. χείρ; μετὰ γαμφηλῇσιν ἔ. Il.13.200; πρόσθεν ἔ. ἀσπίδα ib.157; ὑψοῦ, πασάων ὑπέρ, ὄπιθεν κάρη ἔ., 6.509, Od.6.107, Il.23.136; ἔ. τινί τι *to hold* it for him, as his helper, 9.209, 13.600; *uphold*, οὐρανὸν..κεφαλῇ τε καὶ ἀκαμάτῃσι χέρεσσι Hes.*Th.*517, 746; ἔχει δέ τε κίονας, of Atlas, Od.1.53; ἐπ' ὤμων πατέρα S.*Fr.*

373. **2.** *hold fast*, χειρὸς ἔχων Μενέλαον *holding* him *by* the hand, Il.4.154, cf. 16.763, 11.488 (v. infr. C.I); ἔ. τινὰ μέσον *grip* one by the middle, of wrestlers, Ar.*Nu.*1047; ἔχομαι μέσος Id.*Ach.*571, cf. *Eq.*388, *Ra.*469: metaph., ἔ. φρεσί *keep* in one's mind, Il.2.33; νῷ ἔ. τινά Pl.*Euthphr.*2b, cf. *R.*490a. **3.** of arms and clothes, *bear, wear*, εἷμα δ' ἔχ' ἀμφ' ὤμοισι Il.18.538, cf. 595; παρδαλέην ὤμοισιν ἔ. 3.17; σάκος ὤμῳ 14.376; κυνέην κεφαλῇ Od.24.231; τάδε εἵματ' ἔχω 17.24, cf. 573, etc.; στολὴν ἀμφὶ σῶμα E.*Hel.*554, cf. X.*Cyr.*1.4.26, etc.; πολιὰς ἔχω I am grey-haired, Aeschin.1.49: abs., as a category, Arist.*Cat.*$2^a$3. **4.** of a woman, *to be pregnant*, Hdt.5.41, Hp.*Epid.*4.21, Arist.*Pol.*$1335^b$18; in full ἐν γαστρὶ ἔ. Hdt.3.32; also πρὸς ἑωυτῇ ἔχειν Hp.*Epid.*1.26.ιγ'. **b.** παῖδα ἔσχεν she *had*, i.e. *bore*, a child, Nic.Dam.11 J. **5.** *support, sustain*, esp. an attack, c. acc. pers., Il.13.51, 20.27; cf. B.I.1, C.III. **6.** *hold fast, keep close*, ὀχῆες εἶχον [πύλας] 12.456; θύρην ἔχε μοῦνος ἐπιβλής 24.453. **7.** *enclose*, φρένες ἧπαρ ἔχουσι Od.9.301; σάρκας τε καὶ ὀστέα ἶνες ἔ. 11.219; τοὺς δ' ἄκραντος ἔχει νύξ A.*Ch.*65 (lyr.); of places, *contain*, θηρῶν οὓς ὅδ' ἔχει χῶρος S.*Ph.*1147 (lyr.), cf. X.*Cyn.*5.4; [τεῖχος] νῆας ἐντὸς ἔχον Il.12.8; ὅσσους Κρήτη ἐντὸς ἔχει *h.Ap.*30. **8.** *hold* or *keep in a certain direction*, ὀϊστὸν ἔχε *aimed* it, Il.23.871; more fully χεῖράς τε καὶ ἔγχεα.. ἀντίον ἀλλήλων 5.569; of horses or ships, *guide, drive, steer*, πεδίονδ' ἔχον ὠκέας ἵππους 3.263, cf. 11.760; φόβονδε 8.139; τῇ ῥα.. ἔχον ἵππους 5.752, etc.; παρὲξ ἔχε δίφρον Hes.*Sc.*352; ὅπῃ ἔσχες.. εὐεργέα νῆα Od.9.279; παρὰ τὴν ἤπειρον ἔ. νέας Hdt.6.95, etc.: abs., τῇ ῥ' ἔχε that way he *held his course*, Il.16.378, cf. 23.422; Πύλονδ' ἔχον I *held on* to Pylos, Od.3.182, cf. S.*El.*720: metaph., ἐπὶ ῥητορείαν ἔσχε Hsch.Mil.(?) ap.Sch.Pl.*R.*600c; also (esp. in fut. σχήσω, aor. 2 ἔσχον), *put in, land*, νέες ἔσχον ἐς τὴν Ἀργολίδα χώρην Hdt.6.92; σχεῖν πρὸς τὴν Σαλαμῖνα Id.8.40; ἐς Φειάν, τῷ Δήλῳ, κατὰ τὸ Ποσειδώνιον, Th.2.25, 3.29, 4.129; τάχ' οὖν τις ἄκων ἔσχε S.*Ph.*305; ποῖ σχήσειν δοκεῖς; Ar.*Ra.*188; ἔχε.. ἀρὰν ἐπ' ἄλλοις *point* it against others, S.*Ph.*1119 (lyr.); ὄμμ' ἔ. *to turn* or *keep* one's eye *fixed*, Id.*Aj.*191 (lyr.); ἐπὶ ἔργῳ θυμὸν ἔ. Hes.*Op.*445; ἄλλοσ' ὄμμα θητέρᾳ δὲ νοῦν ἔ. S.*Tr.*272; τὸν δὲ νοῦν ἐκεῖσ' ἔχει E.*Ph.*360; δεῦρο νοῦν ἔχε *attend to* this, Id.*Or.*1181; πρός τινα or πρός τι τὸν νοῦν ἔ., Th.3.22, 7.19; so πρός τινα τὴν γνώμην ἔ. Id.3.25. **9.** *hold in, stay, keep back*, ἵππους Il.4.302, 16.712; *check, stop*, [τινα] 23.720, etc. (σχήσω is usu. fut. in this sense, τὸ πεπρωμένον οὐ σιδάρεον σχήσει τεῖχος Pi.*Fr.*232, cf. Il.11.820, Ar.*Lys.*284, D.19.272, but ἕξω Il.13.51); χεῖρας ἔχων Ἀχιλῆος *holding* his hands, 18.33; but οὐ σχήσει χεῖρας *will* not *stay* his hands, Od.22.70; ἔ. [δάκρυον] 16.191; ἔ. ὀδύνας *allay, assuage* them, Il.11.848; ἔσχε κῦμα Od.5.451; σιγῇ μῦθον 19.502 (so εἶχε σιγῇ καὶ ἔφραζε οὐδενί Hdt.9.93); ἐν φρεσὶ μῦθον Od.15.445; στόμα σῖγα, ἐν ἡσυχίᾳ, E.*Hipp.*660, *Fr.*773.61 (lyr.); πόδα Id.*IT*1159; πόδα ἔξω or ἐκτός τινος ἔχειν, v. πούς:—Pass., οὖρα σχεθέντα Aret.*SA*2.5. **10.** *keep away from*, c. gen. rei, τινὰ ἀγοράων, νεῶν, Il.2.275, 13.687; γόων S.*El.*375; φόνου E.*HF*1005: c. inf., ἦ τινα.. σχήσω ἀμυνέμεναι Il.17.182; *stop, hinder from* doing, τοῦ μὴ καταδῦναι X.*An.*3.5.11, cf. *HG*4.8.5; ἔσχον μὴ κτανεῖν E.*Andr.*686, cf. Hdt.1.158, etc.; μὴ οὐ τάδ' ἐξειπεῖν E.*Hipp.*658; ὥστε μή.. X.*An.*3.5.11; τὸ μὴ ἀδικεῖν A.*Eu.*691, cf. Hdt.5.101: also c. part., ἔ. τινὰ βουθυτοῦντα S.*OC*888 (troch.); μαργῶντα E.*Ph.*1156. **11.** *keep back, withhold* a thing, ὅς οἱ χρήματα εἶχε βίῃ Od.15.231, cf. D.30.14; Ἕκτορ' ἔχει.. οὐδ' ἀπέλυσεν Il.24.115, cf. 136; αὐτὸς ἔχε *pray keep* it, a civil form of declining, E.*Cyc.*270. **12.** *hold in guard, keep safe*, Il.24.730; of armour, *protect*, 22.322. **13.** with predicate, *keep* in a condition or place, εἶχον ἀτρέμας σφέας αὐτούς Hdt.9.54, cf. 53, Ar.*Th.*230; ἔ. ἑωυτοὺς κατ' οἴκους Hdt.3.79; σαυτὸν ἐκποδὼν A.*Pr.*346, cf. X.*Cyr.*6.1.37; σῖγα νάπη φύλλ' εἶχε E.*Ba.*1085; τοὺς στρατιώτας πολὺν χρόνον πειθομένους ἔ. X.*Cyr.*7.2.11. **14.** *hold, consider*, τινὰ θέᾳ ἰκέλαν Sapph.*Supp.*25.3 (dub.), cf. E.*Supp.*164; τινὰ ὡς προφήτην *Ev.Matt.*14.5; τινὰ ὅτι προφήτης ἦν *Ev.Marc.*11.32; ἔχε με παρῃτημένον *Ev.Luc.*14.18, cf. *POxy.*292.6 (i A.D.). **III.** c. inf., *have means* or *power* to do, *to be able*, c. aor. inf., Il.7.217, 16.110, etc.: c. pres. inf., Od.18.364, etc.; πόλλ' ἂν λέγειν ἔχοιμι S.*Ph.*1047: sts. with inf. omitted or supplied from context, ἀλλ' οὔ πως ἔτι εἶχε he *could* not, Il.17.354; οἷά κ' ἔχωμεν so far as we *be able*, Od.15.281; ἐξ οἵων ἔχω S.*El.*1379; ὅσον εἶχες E.*IA*1452; ὡς ἔχω Id.*Hec.*614. **b.** *have to face, be obliged*, παθεῖν Porph.*Chr.*63; εἰ ἕξω βλαβῆναι Astramps.*Orac.*p.5 H.; βάπτισμα ἔχω βαπτισθῆναι *Ev.Luc.*12.50. **2.** after Hom., οὐκ ἔχω, folld. by a dependent clause, I *know* not.., οὐκ εἶχον τίς ἂν γενοίμαν A.*Pr.*905, cf. Isoc.12.130; οὐδ' ἔχω πῶς με χρὴ.. ἀφανίσαι S.*OC*1710; οὐκ ἔχων ὅ τι χρὴ λέγειν X.*Cyr.*1.4.24; οὐκ ἔχω ποῖ πέσω S.*Tr.*705; ὅπως μολούμεθ' οὐκ ἔχω Id.*OC*1743; the two constructions combined, οὐ γὰρ εἴχομεν οὔτ' ἀντιφωνεῖν οὔθ' ὅπως.. πράξαιμεν Id.*Ant.*270. **IV.** impers. c. acc., *there is*.. (as in Mod. Gr.), ἔχει δὲ φυλακτήριον πρὸς τὸ μή σε καταπεσεῖν *PMag.Par.*1.2505, cf. 1262, 1840.

**B.** intrans., *hold oneself*, i.e. *keep*, so and so, ἔχον [οὕτως], ὥς τε τάλαντα γυνή (sc. ἔχει) *kept balanced*, like the scales which.., Il.12.433; ἕξω δ' ὡς ὅτε τις στερεὴ λίθος I *will keep unmoved*, as a stone.., Od.19.494, cf. Il.13.679, 24.27; νωλεμέως ἐχέμεν 5.492; ἔγχος ἔχ' ἀτρέμας it *kept* still, 13.557; σχὲς οὗπερ εἶ *keep* where thou art, S.*OC*1169; ἕξειν κατὰ χώραν Ar.*Ra.*793, cf. Hdt.6.42, X.*Oec.*10.10; διὰ φυλακῆς ἔχοντες *to keep* on their guard, Th.2.81; ἔχε ἠρέμα *keep* still, Pl.*Cra.*399e, etc.; ἔχε δή *stay now*, Id.*Prt.*349e, *Grg.*460a, etc.; ἔχ' αὐτοῦ D.45.26. **2.** *hold fast*, οὐδέ οἱ ἔσχεν ὀστέον Il.16.740; cf. A.II.6. **3.** c. gen., *keep from*, πολέμου Th.1.112 (cf. C.IV). **4.** with Preps., *to be engaged* or *busy*, ἀμφί τι A.*Th.*102 (lyr.), X.*An.*5.2.26, etc.; περί τινας Id.*HG*7.4.28. **II.** simply, *be*, ἑκὰς εἶχον Od.12.435; ἔ. κατ' οἴκους Hdt.6.39; περὶ πολλῶν ἔ. πρηγμάτων Id.3.128; ἀγῶνα διὰ πάσης ἀγωνίης ἔχοντα *consisting* in.., Id.2.91; ἔ. ἐν ἀνάγκαισι E.*Ba.*88 (lyr.); ὅπου συμφορᾶς ἔχεις Id.*El.*238; ἐκποδὼν ἔχειν Id.*IT*1226, etc. **2.** freq. with Advbs. of manner, εὖ ἔχει Od.24.245, etc.; καλῶς ἔχει, κακῶς ἔχει, *it is, is going on* well or ill, v. καλός, κακός (but fut. σχήσειν καλῶς *will turn out* well, D.1.9, cf. 18.45; εὖ σχήσει S.*Aj.*684); οὕτως.. σχεῖν *to turn out, happen* thus, Pl.*Ap.*39b; οὕτως ἔχει so *the case stands*, Ar.*Pl.*110; οὕτως ἐχόντων, Lat. *cum res ita se habeant*, X.*An.*3.2.10; ὡς ὧδ' ἐχόντων S.*Aj.*981; οὕτω χρὴ διὰ στέρνων ἔχειν Id.*Ant.*639; οὕτως ἔ. περί τινος X.*Mem.*4.8.7, cf. Hdt.6.16; πρός τι D.9.45; τῇδ' ἔ. S.*Ph.*1336; κοσμίως ἔ. Ar.*Th.*854; ἥδιον ἔ. πρός τινας D.9.63; ὡς εἶχε just as he *was*, Hdt.1.114; ὥσπερ εἶχε Th.1.134, X.*HG*4.1.30; ὡς ἔχω how I *am*, Ar.*Lys.*610; ὥσπερ ἔχομεν Th.3.30; τἀναντία εἶχεν D.9.41; ἀσφαλέως, ἀναγκαίως ἔχει, = ἀσφαλές, ἀναγκαῖόν ἐστι, Hdt.1.86, 9.27; καλῶς ἔχει *no, I thank you*, v. καλός. **b.** c. gen. modi, εὖ ἔ. τινός *to be well off for* a thing, *abound in* it; καλῶς ἔ. μέθης *to be* well off for drink, i.e. *to be* pretty well drunk, Hdt.5.20; σπόρου ἀνακῶς ἐ. *to be* busy with sowing, Id.8.109; εὖ ἐ. φρενῶν, σώματος, E.*Hipp.*462, Pl.*R.*404d; εὖ ὥρας ἔχον χωρίον Poll.5.108; cf. ἥκω; so ὡς ποδῶν εἶχον as fast as they could go, Hdt.6.116, 9.59; ὡς τάχεος εἶχε ἕκαστος Id.8.107; ὡς.. τις εὐνοίας ἢ μνήμης ἔχοι Th.1.22; ὡς ὀργῆς ἔχω S.*OT*345, cf. E.*Hel.*313, 857, etc.; πῶς ἔχεις δόξης; Pl.*R.*456d; οὕτω τρόπου ἔχεις X.*Cyr.*7.5.56; μετρίως ἔ. βίου Hdt.1.32; ὑγιεινῶς ἔ. αὐτὸς αὑτοῦ καὶ σωφρόνως Pl.*R.*571d; οὐκ εὖ σεαυτοῦ τυγχάνεις ἔχων Philem.4.11: also c. acc., εὖ ἔ. τὸ σῶμα καὶ τὴν ψυχήν Pl.*Grg.*464a, cf. X.*Oec.*21.7: c. dat., οὕτως ἐχόντων τούτων τῇ φύσει D.18.315; πῶς ἔχετε ταῖς διανοίαις Lycurg.75; τῇ λέξει κακῶς ἔ. Isoc.9.10. **III.** of direction, *hold* or *turn* towards, v. supr. A.II.8. **2.** *stand up, jut out*, κίονες ὑψόσ' ἔχοντες Od.19.38; δι' ὤμου ἔγχος ἔσχεν Il.13.520. **3.** *lead towards*, ὁδοὶ ἐπὶ τὸν ποταμὸν ἔ. Hdt.1.180, cf. 191, 2.17; ἔ. εἴς τι *to be directed, point* towards, ἔχθρης ἐχούσης ἐς Ἀθηναίους Id.5.81; τὸ ἐς τοὺς Ἀργείους ἔχον *what concerns* them, Id.6.19; ταῦτα ἐς τὴν ἀπόστασιν ἔχοντα ib.2, etc.; of Place, *extend, reach to*, ἐπ' ὅσον ἔποψις τοῦ ἱροῦ εἶχε Id.1.64. **4.** ἐπί τινι ἔ. *have* hostile *feelings* towards.., Id.6.49, S.*Ant.*987 (lyr.). **IV.** after Hom., ἔχω as auxiliary, c. aor. part. giving a perfect sense, κρύψαντες ἔχουσι Hes.*Op.*42; ἀποκληΐσας ἔχεις Hdt.1.37; ἐγκλῄσασ' ἔχει Ar.*Ec.*355, cf. *Th.*706; freq. in S., θαυμάσας ἔχω *OC*1140, cf. *Ant.*22, al.: also in late Prose, ἀναλώσας ἔχεις Aristid.*Or.*18(20).1; ὅς σφε νῦν ἀτιμάσας ἔχει E.*Med.*33: less freq. c. pf. part., S.*OT*701, *Ph.*600, X.*An.*1.3.14, 4.7.1: rarely c. pres. part., πατρίδα καταστένουσ' ἔχεις E.*Tr.*318 (lyr.), cf. X.*Cyn.*10.11. **2.** part. ἔχων, with pres., adds a notion of duration to that of present action, τί κυπτάζεις ἔ.; why do you *keep* poking about there? Ar.*Nu.*509; τί δῆτα διατρίβεις ἔ.; why then *keep* wasting time? Id.*Ec.*1151; τί γὰρ ἕστηκ' ἔ.; ib.853, cf. *Th.*473, 852: without interrog., φλυαρεῖς ἔ., ἔ. φλυαρεῖς, you *keep* chattering, Pl.*Grg.*490e, *Euthd.*295c; κακοῦν ἔχοντ' αὐτὸν ἀποκτιννύναι D.23.35 (and so possibly ἐνεργεῖ ἔ. Arist.*Metaph.*$1072^b$23); παίσδεις ἔ. Theoc.14.8: so in later Prose, παίζεις ἔ. Luc.*Icar.*24; but ῥιπτεῖς ἔ.; do you throw away the prize *when it is in your grasp?* Aristid.1.443 J.

**C.** Med., *hold oneself fast, cling closely*, τῷ προσφὺς ἐχόμην Od.12.433, cf. Il.1.513, etc.; πρὸς ἀλλήλῃσιν Od.5.329: mostly c. gen., *hold on by, cling to*, [πέτρης] ib.429; χερσὶν ἀώτου 9.435; βρετέων A.*Th.*98 (lyr.); ἐξόμεσθά σου Ar.*Pl.*101; τῆς πληγῆς ἔχεται *claps his hand on* the place struck, D.4.40. **2.** metaph., *cleave, cling to*, ἔργου Hdt.8.11, X.*HG*7.2.19; γεωργίας *BGU*7.6 (iii A.D.); τῶν πραγμάτων Jul.*Or.*1.19a; βιοτᾶς, ἐλπίδος, E.*Ion*491, *Fr.*409; τῆς αὐτῆς γνώμης Th.1.140; *lay hold on, take advantage of*, τῶν ἀγαθῶν ἔχεο Thgn.32; προφάσιος ἔχεσθαι Hdt.6.94; *fasten upon, attack*, D.18.79; *lay claim to*, ἀμφοτέρων τῶν ἐπωνυμιέων Hdt.2.17; *to be zealous for*, [μάχης] S.*OC*424; ἀληθείας Pl.*Lg.*709c; κοινῇ τῆς σωτηρίας X.*An.*6.3.17, etc. **3.** *come next to, follow closely*, ib.1.8.4; ἕπεσθαι ἐχομένους ὅτι μάλιστα τῶν ἁρμάτων Id.*Cyr.*7.1.9; of peoples or places, *to be close, border on*, c. gen., Hdt.4.169, Th.2.96, etc.; freq. in part., τὴν ἐχομένην [τῶν νεωρίων] στοάν Aen.Tact.11.3; οἱ ἐ. the *neighbouring* people, Hdt.1.134; ὁ ἐχόμενος the *next* man, Aen.Tact.22.27; of Time, τὸ ἐχόμενον ἔτος the *next* year, Th.6.3; ὁ ἐ. διαλογισμός *PRev.Laws*16.15 (iii B.C.); τὰ ἐχόμενα τούτοις *what follows*, Pl.*Grg.*494e (without τούτοις Isoc.6.29). **4.** *depend*, ἔκ τινος Od.6.197, 11.346: c. gen., σέο δ' ἕξεται Il.9.102. **b.** *to be connected with* by etymology, τὸ θύειν τοῦ θυμιᾶν εἴχετο Porph.*Abst.*2.59. **5.** *pertain to*, ὅσα ἔχεται τῶν αἰσθήσεων Pl.*Lg.*661b; ἃ διδασκάλων εἴχετο Id.*Prt.*319e; ὅσα τέχνης ἔχεται Id.*Men.*94b, etc.: esp. in Hdt. in periphrases, τὰ τῶν ὀνειράτων, καρπῶν ἐχόμενα, 1.120, 193; ὀρνίθων ἢ ἰχθύων 2.77; σιτίων, ἐσθῆτος, 3.25, 66. **II.** *bear* or *hold for oneself*, κρήδεμνα ἄντα παρειάων σχομένη before her cheeks, Od.1.334; ἀσπίδα πρόσθ' ἔσχετο *his* shield, Il.12.294, cf. 298, 20.262. **III.** *maintain oneself, hold one's ground*, 12.126; ἔχεο κρατερῶς 16.501. **2.** c. acc., *keep off from oneself, repel*, 17.639 (unless σχήσεσθαι is Pass., cf. 9.235). **IV.** *keep oneself back, abstain* or *refrain from*, ἀϋτῆς, μάχης, 2.98, 3.84; βίης Od.4.422; ἐχώμεθα δηϊοτῆτος ἐκ βελέων Il.14.129; τῆς ἀγωγῆς Hdt.6.85; τῆς τιμωρίης Id.7.169; τῶν ἀθίκτων S.*OT*891 (lyr., s.v.l.): c. inf., A.R.1.328; οὐκ ἂν ἐσχόμην τὸ μὴ ἀποκλῇσαι S.*OT*1387; κακῶν ἄπο χεῖρας ἔχεσθαι *to keep one's* hands from ill, Od.22.316; Μενέλεω σχέσθαι χέρα E.*Rh.*174: abs., σχέο, σχέσθε, *hold! cease!* Il.21.379, 22.416. **V.** Pass. of ἔχω B.I, ἐπὶ ξυροῦ ἀκμῆς ἔχεται ἡμῖν τὰ πρήγματα *are balanced* on.., Hdt.6.11.

⊛ **ἔχω** (B), *bear, carry, bring*, imper. ϝεχέτω *Schwyzer* 686.24 (Pam-

phyl., iv B.C.): 3 sg. aor. 1 ἔϜεξε *brought as an offering*, *Inscr.Cypr.* 66 H. (Cf. Skt. *váhati*, Lat. *veho*, ΓαιάϜοχος.)

**ἐψάλᾰται**, Ion. 3 pl. pf. Pass. of ψάλλω.

**ἑψ-ᾰλέος**, η, ον, (ἕψω) *boiled, fit for boiling*, Nic.*Al.*552. **-ανδρα**, ἡ, (ἀνήρ) *cooking up men*, epith. of Medea, from her renewing old Aeson, *AP*15.26.5 (Dosiad.). **-άνη**, ἡ, (ἕψω) = ἑψητήριον, Hsch. **-ᾰνός**, ή, όν, *boiled*, Hp.*Mul.*2.117, Arist.*Pr.*923ª17, Dsc. 2.107; ῥαφανῖδες Polyaen.4.3.32; ἑψανά, τά, = ἑψήματα, Diocl.*Fr.* 120: sg., *BGU*1120.14 (i B.C.).

**ἑψεῖνα**, τά, dub. sens. in *PLond.*3.1177.217 (ii A.D.).

**ἕψεμα**, ατος, τό, late form of ἕψημα, Lxx 4*Ki.*4.38,39.

**ἐψευσμένως**, Adv. pf. part. Pass., (ψεύδομαι) *falsely, wrongly*, Pl. *Lg.*897a, Str.1.2.30, etc.

**ἑψέω, ἑψάω**, v. ἕψω.

**ἕψ-ημα**, ατος, τό, *anything boiled*: in pl., *vegetables fit for kitchen use*, Pl.*R.*372c,455c, Diocl.*Frr.*119,141, D.S.1.80, etc. 2. *mash*, Thphr.*HP*4.4.10. II. *must boiled down to one third part*, Hp. *Vict.*2.52, Pl.Com.149, *PPetr.*3 p.310 (iii B.C.), Dsc.5.6. **-ημᾰτώδης**, ες, *like* ἕψημα, ὀσμή Id.1.26. **-ησις**, εως, ἡ, *boiling*, Hp.*VM* 5; ἡ ἕ. τῶν κρεῶν Hdt.4.61, cf. *SIG*57.34 (Milet., v B.C.); λινῶν *PTeb.*406.22 (iii A.D.); *smelting* of ore, Thphr.*HP*5.9.1; *concoction, softening*, Gal.13.415, Aret.*SA*2.6: pl., Pl.*Plt.*303e. **-ητεῖς**· τὰ μικρὰ ἰχθύδια, Hsch. **-ητέον**, *one must boil*, Dsc.2.76, Sor.1.51, *Gp.*18.16.1. **-ητήρ**, ῆρος, ὁ, *dish* or *pan for boiling*, *AP*6.305 (Leon.). **-ητήριον**, τό, = foreg., Hsch. **-ητής**, οῦ, ὁ, *one who smelts* ore, Agatharch.28. **-ητικός**, ή, όν, *of* or *for boiling*, *Gloss.* ❀ **-ητός**, ή, όν, *boiled*, ὄξος X.*An.*2.3.14; ὕδατα Nic.*Al.*111; ἑψητός (sc. οἶνος), ὁ, *must*, *Gp.*7.12.23, al. II. ἑψητοί, ῶν, οἱ, *small fish boiled for eating*, Ar.*V.*679, Nicopho 18, Arist.*HA*569ª20: sg., Archipp.16, Eub.93, Posidipp.3, *PCair.Zen.*83.3 (iii B.C.), cf. Gal. 19.102; cf. ἑψητεῖς.

**ἑψί-α** [ῐ], Ion. -ίη, ἡ, *amusement*, S.*Fr.*3; *plaything*, Nic.*Th.*880: pl., ἕψια, τά, *EM*406.8; ἕψεια, Hsch. (Etym. uncertain: derived by Hsch. from ἕπομαι, by *EM* from ἔπος. The connexion with Lat. *jocus* is doubtful.) **-άομαι**, (ἑψία) Ep. Verb, *amuse oneself*, θύρησι καθήμενοι ἑψιαάσθων Od.17.530; ἑψιάασθαι μολπῇ καὶ φόρμιγγι 21. 429; ἀμφ' ἀστραγάλοισι.. ἑψιόωντο A.R.3.118, cf. 1.459, Call.*Dian.* 3, *Cer.*39, Nonn.*D.*10.326 (ἐψιόωντο, as if from ἔπος, Philon.(?) ap. Sch.A.R.3.118; but cf. ἀφεψιάομαι). **-άτιμον**· γυμναστικόν, παιγνιῶδες, Hsch.

**ἑψιέω**, f.l. in A.*Fr.*51; v. ἐμψίω.

**ἑψικός**, ή, όν, *for boiling*, dub. in *PLond.*2.429.13 (iv A.D.).

**ἐψῑλωμένως**, Adv. pf. part. Pass., (ψιλόω) *in an expressionless tone*, ἐκφέρειν, of reciters or rhapsodes, Phld.*Rh.*1.200 S.

**ἐψιμῠθισμένως**, Adv. pf. part. Pass., (ψιμυθίζω) *with paint* or *cosmetics*, Sch.Ar.*Pl.*1064.

**ἑψόπωλις**, *popina*, *Gloss.*; cf. ὀψοπώλιον.

**ἕψω**, impf. ἧψον Ar.*Ra.*505, al.: fut. ἑψήσω Nicoch.15, Men.260: aor. ἥψησα Hdt.1.119 (v.l. ἕψ-), Ar.*Fr.*4, Pl.*Euthd.*301d, etc.; cf. συν-έψω: pf. ἥψηκα Ph.2.245:—**Med.**, imper. ἕψου A.*Fr.*310: fut. ἑψήσομαι Pl.*R.*372c:—**Pass.**, ἕψεται Antiph.217.4, part. ἑψόμενος Pi. *N.*4.82, Hp.*Int.*44: fut. ἑψηθήσομαι Gal.13.398: aor. ἡψήθην Hdt.4. 61, Plu.2.690c, etc., part. ἑψηθείς Dsc.5.85, *Eup.*1.139 (v.l. ἑφθέντες): pf. ἡψημένος D.S.2.9, ἑψ- Arist.*Pr.*884ᵇ14, Hp.*Mul.*1.78.—**ἕψω** is Att. acc. to Hdn.Gr.1.456: **ἑψέω** is dub., imper. ἕψεε v.l. in Hp.*Acut.* (*Sp.*)63, impf. ἥψεε v.l. ἕψεε Hdt.1.48; elsewh. in Hdt. and Hp. the uncontracted forms are found: **ἑψάω** is a late form, Olymp. *in Mete.*315.8, al.:—*boil, seethe*, of meat and the like (never in Hom., where meat is roasted, v. ὀπτάω), Hdt.1.48, al., Hp.*VM*3, Pl.*Euthd.* 301c, etc.; ἕ. χύτραν '*to keep* the pot *boiling*', Ar.*Ec.*845, Pl.*Hp.Ma.* 290d; prov. of useless labour, λίθον ἕψεις Ar.*V.*280 (lyr.), Pl.*Erx.* 405b: c. gen. partit., ἥψομεν τοῦ κορκόρου we *boiled some* pimpernel, Ar.*V.*239:—Med., ἕψου μηδὲ λυπηθῇς πυρί A.*Fr.*310:—Pass., *to be boiled*, of meat, Hdt.4.61, etc.; of liquids, *boil*, Arist.*Mete.*379ᵇ28, Plu.2.690c. 2. *digest*, τὰ σιτία Hp.*Acut.*28. 3. of metals, *smelt, refine*, ἑψόμενος χρυσός Pi.*N.*4.82. 4. Med., ἑψήσασθαι κόμην *dye* it, Poll.2.35:—also in Act., Phot., Hsch. (ἐψεῖν cod.). 5. metaph., γῆρας ἀνώνυμον ἕψειν *cherish* an inglorious old age, Pi.*O.*1.83.

**ἕω**, Ion. subj. pres. of εἰμί (*sum*). **ἕω**, Ion. subj. aor. 2 of ἵημι. 2. gen. and acc. of ἕως (A), *the dawn.* **ἑώα**· ἡ τοῖς προβάτοις περιτιθεμένη διφθέρα, Hsch.; cf. ὅα, ὤα, also ὑποδίφθερος. **ἔωγα, ἔωγμαι**, v. οἴγνυμι. **ἔωθα, ἐώθεα**, v. ἔθω.

❀ **ἕωθεν**, Ep. ἠῶθεν (q.v.), Adv., (ἕως (A)) *from morn*, i.e. *at earliest dawn*, Pl.*Phd.*59d, etc.; ἕ. εὐθύς Ar.*Pl.*1121, Eub.119.8. 2. αὔριον ἕ. to-morrow *early*, X.*Cyr.*4.2.6, Pl.*La.*201c; so ἕωθεν alone, Ar.*Ach.*278, etc.; τό γ' ἕωθεν Arist.*HA*546ª22.

❀ **ἑωθινός**, ή, όν, (ἕως (A)) *in the morning, early*, ὁ ἥλιος ὁ ἑ. Hdt.3.104; ἑωθινὸς εἶδον στρατόν S.*Fr.*502; οὔσης.. ἐκκλησίας ἑ. Ar.*Ach.*20; πότοι Bato 5.3; τὸ ἑ., as Adv., *early in the morning*, Hdt.l.c., Hp. *Aër.*6; ἐξ ἑωθινοῦ, = ἕωθεν, Ar.*Th.*2, Pl.*Phdr.*228b, etc.; ἐξ ἑ. μέχρι δείλης X.*HG*1.1.5; εὐθὺς ἐξ ἑ. Alex.257.4; περὶ τὴν ἑ. φυλακήν about the *morning* watch, Plb.3.67.2; ὑπὸ τὴν ἑ. (alone) ib.43.1, cf. Lxx 1*Ma.*5.30; ἑ. φυλακῆς Plu.*Pomp.*68; προσειπεῖν τὸ ἑ. to wish one *good morning*, Luc.*Laps.*1, cf. Macho ap.Ath.13.580d (dub. l.); ἑ. δίκαι, prov. for *business soon transacted*, *AB*258. 2. *eastern*, ἔθνος D.P.697: Comp. -ώτερος Str.11.2.2: Sup. -ώτατος Id.4.5.1.

**ἑώϊος**, ον, also α, ον, poet. for ἑῷος, epith. of Apollo, A.R.2.686, 700. 2. *eastern*, ἄκρη D.P.111.

**ἐῴκει**, v. ἔοικα.

**ἑωλ-ίζω**, (ἕωλος) *keep till next day*, τὰ κρέα Gal.16.761, cf. Ruf.ap. Orib.4.2.8. II. Pass., *to be* or *become stale*, of grain, Gal.6. 518. 2. in good sense, *to be capable of being kept till next day*, ib. 713. **-ισμός**, ὁ, *keeping till next day*, of food, Ruf.ap.Orib.4.2. 7 (pl.).

**ἑωλο-κρᾰσία**, ἡ, (κρᾶσις) *mixture of dregs, heel-taps*, etc., with which the drunken were dosed at the end of a revel by their stronger-headed companions: metaph., ἑωλοκρασίαν τινά μου τῆς πονηρίας κατασκεδάσας having discharged *the stale dregs* of his rascality over me, D.18.50, cf. Harp., Luc.*Symp.*3; also, = κραιπάλη, ἐμμένει τὸ.. δυσάρεστον, ὥσπερ ἑ. τις ὕβρεως ἢ ὀργῆς Plu.2.148a. **-νεκρός**, ὁ (cf. sq. 1)· ὁ πρὸ πολλοῦ τεθνηκώς, Suid.

❀ **ἕωλος**, ον (prob. from ἕως (A), ἠώς), *a day old, kept till the morrow, stale*, of bread, Hp.*Aff.*52, Antyll.ap.Orib.4.11.2; of meat and fish, ἕωλοι κείμενοι δύ' ἡμέρας ἢ τρεῖς Antiph.161.6; αὔριον ἕωλον τοῦτ' ἔχων [τὸ τέμαχος] Axionic.6.15; πρόσφατον καὶ νέον ὕδωρ τὸ ὑόμενον, ἕ. δὲ καὶ παλαιὸν τὸ λιμναῖον Arist.*Fr.*215; ἕ. νεκρός Luc.*Cat.*18; ἕ. ἡμέρα the day *after a feast*, esp. after a wedding, when the scraps were eaten, Axionic.8.6; ἕ. θρυαλλίς a *stinking* wick (after the lamp has been blown out), Luc.*Tim.*2. 2. of actions, etc., *stale, out of date*, τἀδικήμαθ' ἕ... ὡς ὑμᾶς καὶ ψυχρ' ἀφικνεῖται D.21.112; ῥαψῳδίαι, πράγματα, Plu.2.514c,674f; ἕωλόν ἐστι τὸ λέγειν ib.777b, cf. Luc.*Pseudol.*5; δόξα J.*BJ*4.6.2 (Comp.); σοφισμάτια Porph.*Abst.*1.3; *old-fashioned*, φιλοτιμία prob. in Phld.*D.*1.1; later, of legal instruments, *out-of-date, expired*, γράμμα *PSI*5.452.22 (iv A.D.), cf. *PLond.*1.77.60 (vi A.D.); of payments, *in arrear*, *Sammelb.*1093.3, 1090.5 (ii A.D.). 3. of money, *lying without use, hoarded*, Philetaer.7.7. 4. of persons, *coming a day too late*, Plu.*Nic.*21; of things, *belated*, προθυμία Procop.*Goth.*4.23. 5. *on the day after a debauch*, i.e. *suffering from its effects*, Plu.2.128d; ἕ. ταῖς μνήμαις ib.611f.

**ἐώλπει**, v. ἔλπομαι.

**ἔωμεν** (v.l. ἕομεν), subj. form for ἧομεν (cf. ἄω c), ἐπεί χ' ἔ. πολέμοιο when we *have had our fill* of war, Il.19.402.

**ἐών**, Ep. and Ion. part. of εἰμί (*sum*). **ἐώνημαι, ἐωνήμην**, v. ὠνέομαι. **ἐῳνοχόει**, v. οἰνοχοέω. **ἔῳξα**, v. οἴγνυμι.

**ἑῷος**, α, ον, A.*Pr.*25, etc.; also ος, ον E.*Ph.*169 (lyr.), D.H.1.12, dub. in Gem.*Calend.*p.220 M.: poet. **ἑώϊος**, Ion. and in Hom. **ἠοῖος** (qq.v.): (ἕως (A)):—*in* or *of the morning*, πάχνην ἑ. ἥλιος σκεδᾷ the *morning* rime, A.l.c.; ἑ. φθέγματ' ὀρνίθων S.*El.*18, etc.; ἑ. ἀστήρ, = Ἑωσφόρος, E.*Fr.*929, cf. Pl.*Epigr.*15; οὔθ' ἕσπερος οὔθ' ἑ. οὕτω θαυμαστός Arist.*EN*1129ᵇ28; ἑ. ἐξαναστῆναι to get up *early*, E.*El.*786. 2. *eastern*, τεῖχος X.*HG*4.4.9; τὰ ἑ. *eastern parts*, Luc.*Cont.*5; ἐξ ἑῴας (sc. χώρας) Arist.*Pr.*946ᵇ14; κατὰ τὰς ἑῴας Id.*Mu.*394ª11 (perh. *in the morning*). b. ἑῴα, ἡ, = *Oriens*, the *Eastern provinces* of the Roman Empire, ὁ τὴν ἑῴαν ἐπιτροπεύων Philostr.*VS*2.1.13; ἀρχὸς ἑῴας, = Lat. *magister militum per Orientem*, *IG*14.1073; ὕπαρχος ἑῴας, = Lat. *praefectus praetorio Orientis*, *AP*9.690 (v A.D.).

❀ **ἑώρα**, v. αἰώρα, cf. Ael.Dion.*Fr.*23: pl., of a festival in honour of Erigone, Arist.*Fr.*515 (αἰ- codd.). **ἑωρέω**, = αἰωρέω, prob. in S. *OC*1084 (lyr.), cf. Hsch., Dosith.p.431 K. **ἑώρημα**, = αἰώρημα, Sch.Ar.*Pax*77. **ἑωρίζεται**· μετεωρίζεται, ἀναπατεῖ, Hsch.

**ἔωρτο**, v. ἀείρω. **ἕως** (A) ἡ, Att. form of the Ion. ἠώς (q.v.).

❀ **ἕως** (B), Ep. **εἷος, ἧος** (v. sub fin.), Dor. **ἇς**, Aeol. **ἆς** (qq.v.), Boeot. **ἇς** *IG*7.3303, al., and **ἅως** ib.2228,3315. A. Relat. Particle, expressing the point of Time up to which an action goes, with reference to the end of the action, *until, till*; or to its continuance, *while*: I. *until, till*, 1. with Ind., of a fact in past time, θῦνε διὰ προμάχων, ἧος φίλον ὤλεσε θυμόν Il.11.342, cf. Od.5.123; ἕ. ἀπώλεσέν τε καὐτὸς ἐξαπώλετο S.*Fr.*236, cf. A.*Pers.*428, Pl.*Chrm.*155c, etc.; for πρίν, μὴ πρότερον ἀπελθεῖν ἕως ἀποκατέστησε τὰ πράγματα D.S.27.4: with impf. with ἄν in apodosi, of an unaccomplished action, ἡδέως ἂν Καλλικλεῖ διελεγόμην, ἕ. ἀπέδωκα I would have gone on conversing *till* I had.., Pl.*Grg.*506b, cf. *Cra.*396c. 2. ἕ. ἄν or κε with Subj. (mostly of aor.), of an event at an uncertain future time, μαχήσομαι.. ἧός κε τέλος πολέμοιο κιχείω *till* I find, Il.3.291, cf. 24.183, A.*Pr.*810, etc.: ἄν is sts. omitted in Trag., ἕ. μάθῃς S.*Aj.*555; ἕ. κληθῇ Id.*Tr.*148; ἕ. ἀνῇ τὸ πῆμα Id.*Ph.*764: so freq. in later Gr., *UPZ*18.10 (ii B.C.), *PGrenf.* 2.38.16 (i B.C.), *Ev.Marc.*14.32, Vett.Val.68.18, etc.; ἕ. οὗ γένηται Gem.8.32. 3. ἕ. with Opt. (mostly of aor.), relating to an event future in relation to past time, ὦρσε.. Βορέην, ἧος ὁ Φαιήκεσσι.. μιγείη caused it to blow, *till* he should reach.., Od.5.386, cf. 9.376, Ar.*Ra.*766, Pl.*Phd.*59d; ἕως δέοι βοηθεῖν Th.3.102, cf. Lys.13.25: ἄν or κε is added to the Opt. (not to ἕως), if the event is represented as conditional, ἕ. κ' ἀπὸ πάντα δοθείη *till* (if possible) all things should be given back, Od.2.78; οὐκ [ἂν] ἀποκρίναιο, ἕ. ἂν σκέψαιο Pl.*Phd.*101d, cf. S.*Tr.*687 codd., Isoc.17.15, *IG*2².1328 (ii B.C.). b. in orat. obliq., ἔδωκεν.. ἕ. ἀνὴρ εἶναι δοκιμασθείην D.27.5. c. by assimilation to an opt. with ἄν, [λόγον] ἂν διδοίης ἕ. ἔλθοις Pl.*Phd.*101d. 4. c. subj. or opt., expressing purpose, *in order that*, Od.4.800, 6.80, 19.367; πορεύου εἰς Διονυσιάδα.. ἕως τὸν ἐκεῖ ἐλαιῶνα ποτίσῃς *PFay.*118.12 (ii A.D.); σπούδασον ἕως οὗ ἀγοράσῃ κτλ. *POxy.*113.25 (ii A.D.); χρυσίον ἐδανισάμην ἕως ὅτε δυνηθῶ ἀγοράσαι ib.130.13 (vi A.D.). 5. with Inf. in orat. obliq., ἐντειλάμενος διεκπλέειν ἕ... ἀπικνέεσθαι Hdt.4.42: otherwise only in later Gr., ἕ. ἐλθεῖν ἐς.. Lxx *Ge.*10.19, cf. *PLond.*1. 131ʳ251 (i A.D.), D.H.9.4 (v.l.), Anon.ap.Suid. s.v. λυσσώμενον. 6. with Advbs. of Time and Place, ἕ. ὅτε *till the time when*, c. ind., v.l. for ἔστε in X.*Cyr.*5.1.25; ἕ. οὗ, f.l. for ἐς οὗ, Hdt.2.143: freq. in later Gr., Gem.l.c., *Ev.Matt.*1.25, etc.; ἕ. ὅτου ib.5.25, etc.; ἕ. πότε; *how long?* ib.17.17, *Ev.Jo.*10.24; ἕ. τότε Lxx *Ne.*2.16; ἕ. ὀψέ *till* late,

f.l. for ἐς ὀψέ, Th.3.108; ἕ. ἄρτι 1Ep.Jo.2.9; ἕ. ὧδε *as far as* this place, *Ev.Luc.*23.5. b. with Preps., of Time, ἕ. πρὸς καλὸν ἑῷον ἀστέρα *AP*5.200; of Place, ἕ. εἰς τὸν χάρακα Plb.1.11.14; ἕ. πρὸς τὸν Καύκασον D.S.2.43; ἕ. ἐπὶ τὴν θάλασσαν *Act.Ap.*17.14. II. as Prep., 1. of Time, c. gen., *until*, ἕως τοῦ ἀποτεῖσαι *until* he has made payment, Lex ap.Aeschin.1.42, cf. Lxx *Ge.*3.19, etc.; ἕ. τελειώσεως Epicur.*Ep.* 2p.38 U.; ἕ. ὡρισμένων χρόνων Phld.*D.*1.7; ἕ. τινός *for* a time, Parth. 9.2, etc.; ἕ. τοῦ νῦν *Ev.Matt.*24.21; ἕ. Ἰωάννου ib.11.13. b. of Place, ἕ. τοῦ γενέσθαι.. *up to the point where*.. Arist.*PA*668$^b$2, cf. *HA*630$^b$27, Plb.9.36.1; *as far as*, ἕ. Σάρδεων *Ath.Mitt.*44.25 (Samos, iii B.C.); ἕ. τοῦ Ἀρσινοΐτου νομοῦ *PTeb.*33.5 (ii B.C.); ἕ. Φοινίκης *Act. Ap.*11.19: so c. gen. pers., ἦλθον ἕ. αὐτοῦ *Ev.Luc.*4.42, cf. Lxx 4*Ki.* 4.22. c. of Number or Degree, ἕ. τριῶν πλοίων Docum.ap.D.18.106; διδόναι ἕ. ταλάντων ἑκατόν Lxx 1*Es.*8.19(21); οὐκ ἔστιν ἕ. ἑνός ib.*Ps.* 13.3; οὐκ ἔχομεν ἕ. τῆς τροφῆς τῶν κτηνῶν *PTeb.*56.7 (ii B.C.); ἐᾶτε ἕ. τούτου *Ev.Luc.*22.51; μαχοῦμαι ἕ. ζωῆς καὶ θανάτου *OGI*266.29 (Pergam., iii B.C.); ἕ. μέθης Corn.*ND*30. 2. rarely c. acc., ἕ. πρωΐ Lxx *Jd.*19.25; ἕ. μεσημβρίαν *PLond.*1.131$^r$346,515 (i A.D.); ἕ. τὸ "βωμῷ" *down to* the word "βωμῷ", Sch.Pi.*O.*6.111. III. *while, so long as*, c. ind., ἦος ἐνὶ Τροίῃ πολεμίζομεν Od.13.315, cf. 17.358,390; ἕ. δ' ἔτ' ἔμφρων εἰμί A.*Ch.*1026, cf. *Pers.*710 (troch.); ἕ. ἔτι ἐλπὶς [ἦν] Th.8.40; ἕ. ἔτι νέος εἶ Pl.*Prm.*135d: in this sense answered in apodosi by τῆος, Od.4.90, Il.20.41; by τόφρα, Od.12.327, Il.18.15; by τόφρα δέ, 10.507; by δέ alone, 1.193, Od.4.120 codd. b. ἕ. ἄν c. subj., when the whole action is future, οὔ μοι.. ἐλπίς, ἕ. ἂν αἴθῃ πῦρ A.*Ag.* 1435; λέγειν τε χρὴ καὶ ἐρωτᾶν, ἕως ἂν ἐῶσιν Pl.*Phd.*85b; οὐδὲν ἔστ' αὐτῷ βεβαίως ἔχειν ἕ. ἂν ὑμεῖς δημοκρατῆσθε D.10.13. c. ἕως c. opt. in a Conditional relative clause, φήσομεν μηδὲν ἂν μεῖζον μηδὲ ἔλαττον γενέσθαι ἕ. ἴσον εἴη αὐτὸ ἑαυτῷ Pl.*Tht.*155a.

B. in Hom. sts. Demonstr., = τέως, *for a time*, ἦος μὲν.. ὄρνυον· αὐτὰρ ἐπεί.. Il.12.141; ἦος μὲν ἀπείλει..· ἀλλ' ὅτε δή.. 13.143, cf. 17. 727,730, Od.2.148; ἦος μὲν.. ἕποντο.. αὐτὰρ ἐπεί.. Il.15.277; *all that time*, Od.3.126, cf. Hdt.8.74. (ἕως, as iambus, only once in Hom., Od.2.78; as a monosyll., Il.17.727, dub.l. in Od.2.148; when the first syllable is to be long codd. Hom. have εἵως or ἕως (never εἷος or ἦος, Ludwich *WkP*1890.512, exc. ειος v.l. (*PFay.*160) in Il.20.41), 3.291, 11.342, al.; εἵως (or ἕως) is found even when the metre requires a trochee, 1.193, al.; comparison of Dor. ἇς (from *ἇος) with Att.-Ion. ἕως points to early Ion. *ἦος (cf. Skt. *yāvat* 'as great as, as long as, until') and this should prob. be restored in Hom.; cf. τέως.)

**ἔωσα**, v. ὠθέω. **ἔωσι**, Ion. for ὦσι, 3 pl. pres. subj. of εἰμί (*sum*).

**ἕωσπερ**, strengthd. for ἕως, Th.7.19, Pl.*Phdr.*243e, v.l. in D.25. 70, etc.

⊛**Ἑωσφόρος**, Dor. **Ἀωσφόρος**, ὁ, *Bringer of morn, the Morning-star*, Il.23.226, Hes.*Th.*381, Pi.*I.*4(3).24; = ἕσπερος and Ἀφροδίτης ἀστήρ, Ibyc.42, Pl.*Ti.*38d, Eudox.*Ars* 5.2, *Placit.*2.15.4. (Trisyll. in Hom. and Pi., quadrisyll. in Hes. (s.v.l.): Ἀεσφόρος (cf. ἐασφόρος) is cj. in Pi. l.c.)

**ἑωυτοῦ, ἑωυτέων**. Ion. for ἑαυτοῦ, etc.

# F

F F (ϝ), also ⊏, sixth letter of the oldest Gr. alphabets, pronounced like Engl. *w*, *IG*9(1).334 (Locr., v B.C.), 4.333, 14.2420, Alcm. 23.6, Sapph.*Supp.*1.6, Corinn.ib.1.29, etc.; it was written in many dialects until ii B.C. (and pronounced even later); in others (incl. Ion. and Att.) it died out (with the sound) before the date of the earliest Inscrr., surviving only as a numeral, = 6, in the form ⊏, *SIG* 46.106 (Halic., v B.C.), *IG*1$^2$.760 (Athens, v B.C.), *PCair.Zen.*13.4 (iii B.C.), *BMus.Cat.Coins*, Egypt Pl.XVI 4 (200/199 B.C.), later in the form ϛ, ib.Egypt Pl.XXX 5 (47 B.C.), *PMag.Lond.*121.770 (iii A.D., Pl.61) and medieval Mss. Its name was ϝαῦ (cf. Semitic *wāw*) acc. to Varro and Didymus (v.Varro *LL* p.209 G.-S.), later δίγαμμα (q.v.). (Words with initial ϝ will be found under the second letter.)

# Z

Z ζ, ζῆτα (q.v.), τό, indecl., seventh (later sixth) letter of Gr. alphabet (cf. *IG*14.2420): as numeral ζʹ = ἑπτά and ἕβδομος (ςʹ, i.e. ϝ, ϝαῦ, the digamma, being retained to represent ἕξ, ἕκτος), but ͵ζ = 7,000.

Zeta, being a double consonant (pronounced either as *zd* or as *dz* acc. to dialect and date), made a short vowel at the end of the foregoing syllable long by position; exc. before pr. names, which could not otherwise come into the hexam., ἄστυ Ζελείης Il.4.103, 121; ὑλήεσσα Ζάκυνθος *h.Ap.*429, etc.: afterwds. pronounced as Engl. *z*, cf. ζμῆνος *PCair.Zen.*151.4 (iii B.C.), ζμύρνης ib.9 (iii B.C.), ἀμφιζβήτησιν Mitteis *Chr.*31 viii 6 (ii B.C.), cf. Ael.Dion.*Fr.*187; sts. σζ was written, ἐνδέσζμους *IG*2$^2$.1672.308 (iv B.C.), θυσιάσζειν *IG* 3.73.

**ζά** [ᾰ], Aeol. for διά, rarely as Prep., ζὰ τὰν σὰν ἰδέαν Theoc.29.6, cf. *IG*12(2).484.3 (Mytil.); ζὰ νυκτός ap.Jo.Gramm.*Comp.*3.3; ζὰ χῶρις ἔχην Sapph.*Oxy.*1787 *Fr.*3 ii 18; ζαβάλλω, ζάημι, etc. 2. as Prefix (cf. διά), *very*, in Ep. Adjs., ζαής, ζάθεος, ζάκοτος, etc.; cf. ζαμενέω, ζάπλουτος, ζάφελος.

⊛**ζᾶ**, = γῆ, *Inscr.Cypr.*135.8 H.; but ζαν, dub. sens. in the phrase ὑϝαις ζαν, ib.10 (fort. = διὰ βίου).

**ζαβάλλω**, Aeol. for διαβάλλω, = ἐξαπατῶ, Hsch., *EM*406.42.

**ζάβατος**, ον, Aeol. for διαβατός, Sapph.158. 2. = πίναξ ἰχθυηρός (Paph.), Hsch. (cf. γαβαθόν, καβάθα).

**ζαβλεμένως**· μεγάλως πεποιθώς, Hsch.; cf. βλεμεαίνω, ἀβλεμέως.

**ζάβοτος**, ον, (βόσκω) = πολύφορβος, πολύκτηνος, Hsch.

**ζαβρός**, όν, for ζάβορος (?), = πολυφάγος, Hsch., Phot., Suid.

⊛**ζάγκλη**, ἡ, = sq., Nic.*Al.*180. II. an ancient name of Sicilian Messene, from the shape of the natural mole which forms the harbour, Th.6.4, etc.

**ζάγκλον**, τό, *reaping-hook, sickle*, Sicilian for δρέπανον, Th.6.4, cf. Call.*Aet.Oxy.*2080.73. (ζάγκλιον, = σκολιόν, acc. to Str.6.2.3.)

**ζάγρα**, ἡ, and Dim. **ζάγριον**, τό, a term of abuse, Timostr.4.

**Ζαγραῖος**, ὁ, epith. of Dionysus, Orph.*Fr.*210.

**Ζαγρεύς**, έως, ὁ, son of Zeus and Persephone, slain by the Titans and resuscitated as Dionysus, πότνια γῆ, Ζαγρεῦ τε θεῶν πανυπέρτατε πάντων Alcmaeonis *Fr.*3 (*EGF* p.77), cf. E.*Fr.*472.11 (anap.), Call.*Fr.* 171, Nonn.*D.*10.294; identified with Ἅιδης by A.*Fr.*228. (Glossed by μεγάλως ἀγρεύων *Et.Gud.*227.37.)

**ζάγρη**· βόθρος, λάπαθον, Hsch. **ζάγρος**, α, ον, *barefoot*, Zonar., interpol. in Suid.

**ζάδηλος**, ον, for διάδηλος, of a sail *with holes in it*, Alc.18.7.

**ζαελεξάμαν**, = διελεξάμην, *I discoursed with*, τινι Sapph.87 (with vv.ll.; ζὰ δ' ἐλ. cj. Ahrens).

**ζαζαῖος**· εἶδος ἰχθύος, Opp.ap.Cyr. in *An.Par.*4.182; ζάζεος Cyr. ap.Schmidt Hsch. s.v. ζαιός.

⊛**ζάημι**, = διάημι, part. ζαέντες, Hsch.: 3 sg. ζάει Id.: but **ζάει**· βινεῖ, Id. is connected with βία (q.v.).

⊛**ζαής**, ές, (ζα-, ἄημι) Ep. Adj. *strong-blowing, stormy*, ἄνεμος ζαής Il.12.157, Od.5.368, prob. cj. in Hes.*Th.*253; ὦρσεν ἔπι ζαῆν ἄνεμον Od.12.313 (cf. Hdn.Gr.2.154,923); ζαοῦς Νότου *AP*9.290 (Phil.).

⊛**ζάθεος** [ᾰ], α, ον, also ος, ον E.*Tr.*256 (lyr.), 1075 (lyr.); poet. Adj. (used by Trag. only in lyrics):—*very divine, sacred*, of places favoured by the gods, Il.1.38, al. (not in Od.), *h.Ap.*223; ζ. Πύλος, Ἰσθμός, Pi.*P.*5.70, *I.*1.32, cf. B.2.7; νᾶσος Id.5.10; Πέλοπος δάπεδα Id.10.24; ἔναυλοι E.*Ba.*121 (lyr.), etc.; Ὤλενος A.*Fr.*284; of things, ἄνεμοι Hes.*Th.*253; χρόνος Pi.*Pae.*6.5; κλῇδες, σελᾶναι, E.*Tr.* ll. cc.; ποταμοί Ar.*Nu.*283 (lyr.); μολπαί Id.*Ra.*385; τιμαί Castorio 1; later of persons, Ἀπόλλων *AP*9.525.7. Adv. -έως Hdn.Gr.1.514.

**ζαθερής**, ές, (θέρος) *scorching*, καῦμα *AP*6.120 (Leon.).

**ζαιός**· εἶδος ἰχθύος, Hsch., cf. Plin.*HN*9.68 (v. ζαζαῖος).

**ζακαλλής**, ές, (κάλλος) *very beautiful*, Hsch. **ζακελτίδες**, v. ζεκ-.

⊛**ζακορ-εύω**, *to be a* ζάκορος, *IG*3.162.12, *CIG*2298 (Delos). **-ίσου** (gen. sg.), name of a kind of balsam, scanned as four long syllables, Aglaïas 23 (ζακορύτιον Polydorus ap.Sch.). **-ος**, ὁ and ἡ, *attendant in a temple* (more honourable than νεωκόρος acc. to Philem.Lex. (cf. *Philol.*57.353 sqq.) in Reitzenstein *Gesch.d.Gr.Etym.*p.394), ζ. Ἀφροδίτης Hyp.*Fr.*178; θεῶν Plu.*Cam.*30; Δηοῦς *IG*3.713.1: abs., Anon.*Oxy.*218 ii 14; τὰς ἱερείας καὶ τὰς ζ. *IG*1$^2$.4.14 (v B.C.), cf. ib.7. 1883 (Thespiae), Men.126,311, *IG*12(2).484.21 (Mytil., late), Plu. *Sull.*7, etc.

**ζάκοτος** [ᾰ], ον, *exceeding wroth*, Il.3.220, Theoc.25.83; of things, ἔγχος Pi.*N.*6.53; ὕδωρ Id.*Pae.*9.18.

⊛**ζακρυόεις**, εσσα, εν, (κρυόεις) *very numbing, freezing*, θάνατος Alc. *Supp.*12.8.

**ζάκτι**· κρίμνον ἐν ἔτνει (-νοῦ ἐν ἔθνει cod.) ἑφθῷ, Hsch.

**ζακυνθίδες**, αἱ, = κολοκύνται, *from Zacynthus*, Hsch., cf. *AB* 261. **ζάλ**· μέγα, ἰσχυρόν, πολύ, Hsch. **ζάλα**· θόρυβος, Id. **ζαλαγεῦσα**, f.l. for λαλ- or σαλ-, *AP*9.412 (Phld.). **ζᾰλαίνω**, = μωραίνω, Hsch., *EM*406.43. **ζάλακες**· ἐχῖνοι, Hsch. **ζαλαύδα**· κινοῦ, Id.

⊛**ζαλάω**, in Ep. part. ζαλόωσα.. χάλαζα *driving* hail, Nic.*Th.*252.

**ζαλέγομαι**, v. διαλέγομαι, ζαελεξάμαν.

**ζαλεία**, ἡ, = δάφνη Ἀλεξανδρεία, Dsc.4.145.

**ζάλευκος** [ᾰ], ον, *very white*, f.l. in Orac.ap.Zos.2.6 (πάνλευκος ap. Phleg.*Macr.*4).

**ζαλέω**, v. ζηλέω.

**ζάλη** [ᾰ], ἡ, *squall, storm, driving rain*, A.*Ag.*656, S.*Aj.*352 (lyr.), etc.; κονιορτοῦ καὶ ζάλης ὑπὸ πνεύματος φερομένου Pl.*R.*496d; ζάλη πνευμάτων by a *storm* of winds, Id.*Ti.*43c; χειμὼν καὶ ζ. Hp.*Insomn.* 89; ζ. ἀνέμων Plu.2.993e; βέλεσι πυρπνόου ζάλης, of the fiery rain from Aetna, A.*Pr.*373: metaph., ζάλαι *storms, distresses*, Pi.*O.*12. 12; ἡ τοῦ βίου ζ. Procop.Gaz.*Ep.*47; λογισμῶν ζάλαι *Cat.Cod.Astr.* 2.211; οἶκος ζ., of women, Secund.*Sent.*8.

⊛**ζαλλεύω**, Aeol. imper. 3 pl. ζαλλευόντον dub. sens. in Alc.*Oxy.* 1789 *Fr.*1 i marg. (= *Fr.*12 Lobel).

**ζαλμός**, ὁ, Thracian word for a *skin*, Porph.*VP*14.

**ζάλος** [ᾰ], ὁ, *mud*, ζ. ἰλυόεις, = βορβορῶδες κῦμα, Nic.*Th.*568; ζάλον (ζαλόν cod.)· πηλόν, Hsch.: metaph., Lib.*Ep.*1144.

**ζᾶλος, ζᾶλόω, ζᾶλωτός**, Dor. for ζῆλος, etc.

**ζάματος**, = ζάβατος 2, Hsch.: **ζαμάτιον**, τό, = τρύβλιον, Id. **ζαμελής**· μέγα μέλος ἔχων, Id.

**ζᾰμεν-έω**, *to put forth all one's fury*, Hes.*Th.*928. ⊛**-ής**, ές, (μένος) poet. Adj. *very strong, mighty, raging*, *h.Merc.*307 (in Sup. ζαμενέστατε); Κένταυρος, ἅλιος, Pi.*P.*9.38, *N.*4.13, cf. *Sammelb.*

5829.8: once in Trag., ζ. λόγος word *of violence* or *enmity*, S.*Aj*.137 (anap.); also in late Ep., ζ. χόλος Opp.*C*.3.448: neut. as Adv., ἐπὶ ζαμενὲς κοτέουσα Nic.*Th*.181:—in form **ζᾱμενός**, ή, όν, Orac.ap. Porph.*Plot*.22 codd., Hsch.

**ζαμερίτας**, α, ὁ, Dor. word for μακαρίτης, Phot.

**ζαμῆται**· μεγαλουργοί, Hsch. ⊛ **ζαμίλαμπις**, a kind of *stone*, Orph.*L*.263 (s.v.l.).

**ζᾱμία, ζᾱμιόω**, etc., Aeol., etc., for ζημ-.

**ζᾱμιοργία**, Elean for δημιουργία, *Schwyzer* 409.6 (vi B.C.).

**Ζάν, Ζανός**, ὁ, Dor. and Ion. for Ζήν, Ζηνός, v. Ζεύς.

**ζάνεκέως** or **ζάνεκῶς**, Adv., Aeol. for διανεκῶς, cj. in Corinn.9; cf. αἰζηνεκές· διηνεκές, αἰώνιον, Hsch. **ζανίδες**· ἡγεμονίδες, Id.

⊛ **ζάπεδον** [ᾰ], τό, = δάπεδον, Xenoph.1.1, *IG*12(5).215 (Paros).

**ζάπῑμελος** [ῑ], ον, *very fat*, Hsch.

**ζαπληθής**, ές, (πλήθω) *very full*, ζ. γενειάς *a thick, full* beard, A. *Pers*.316; ζ. στόμα Μούσης *full-sounding*, *AP*7.75 (Antip.).

⊛ **ζάπλουτος**, ον, *very rich*, Hdt.1.32, E.*Andr*.1282, Lib.*Decl*.30.12, Jul.*Ep*.89b.

**ζᾰπότης**, ου, ὁ, *toper*, Hsch.

**ζάπῡρος** [ᾰ], ον, (πῦρ) *very fiery*, ἕλικες στεροπῆς A.*Pr*.1084 (anap.); πωτήματα Orac.ap.Porph.ap.Eus.*PE*6.3.

**ζαργάνη**, = ταινία, Sch.Opp.*H*.1.100.

**ζάρηκες** (-ικές cod. extra ordinem)· ἐπίθετον πελαγῶν (-αργῶν Mus.), Hsch.

**ζάρος**, ὁ, a bird of prey, Sch.E.*Ph*.45.

**ζαροῦν**· καθεύδειν, Hsch. **ζαρτός**· ζωμὸς τριπτός, Id. **ζᾰτεύω, ζατρεῖον**, Dor. for ζητ-. **ζατήσασθαι**· αἰσθέσθαι, Id.; cf. ζατόω. **ζατός**, v. ζητός.

**ζατόω**, = φράζω, *EM*408.11, cf. Hsch.:—Med. with aor. Pass., = αἰσθάνομαι, Id. s. v. ἐζατώθη, ἐζατωσάμην. **ζατράπης**, v. σατράπης.

**ζατρεφής**, ές, (τρέφω) Ep. Adj. *well-fed, fat, goodly*, ταύρων ζατρεφέων Il.7.223; φώκας ζατρεφέας Od.4.451.

**ζατρίκιον**, τό, *the game of chess*, Sch.Theoc.6.18. (From Skt. *catur-aṅga-* 'four members', through Pers. and Arab.)

**ζαυκίτροφος**, ον, (σαυκρός) *tenderly reared*, Hsch. (ζακκί- cod.).

**ζᾰφεγγής**, ές, *very bright*, Id. **ζᾰφελής**, ές, *violent*, with Adv. -λῶς, Id.; cf. ἐπιζαφελῶς; = πάνυ ἀφελής, Suid.:—also **ζάφελος**, ον, Nic. *Al*.556, *EM*408.17.

**ζαφλεγής**, ές, Ep. Adj. *full of fire*, of men at their prime, ἄλλοτε μέν τε ζαφλεγέες τελέθουσιν.. ἄλλοτε δὲ φθινύθουσιν ἀκήριοι Il.21.465; of *fiery* horses, *h.Hom*.8.8. II. *shining, bright*, ἄστρα Orac.ap. Eus.*PE*3.15; σέλας Nonn.*D*.2.26.

**ζαφοίταισα**, v. διαφοιτάω.

**ζαφόρος**, ον, = πολυφόρος, Hsch.:—hence **ζαφορέω**, *to be fertile*, prob. l. Id. **ζάχμα** (ζαγμά cod.)· ἡνία, Id.

**ζάχολος** [ᾰ], ον, (χολή) = ζάκοτος, *AP*9.524.7.

**ζαχρᾱής**, ές, prob. = ζαχρηής, Epic.in *Arch.Pap*.7 p.6.

**ζαχρειής**, v.l. for ζαχρηής. Adv. ζαχρειές *violently*, Nic.*Th*.290.

⊛ **ζαχρεῖος**, ον, (χρεία) *very needy*: c. gen., ζ. ὁδοῦ *one who wants to know* the way, *asks eagerly after* it, Theoc.25.6.

**ζαχρηής**, ές, used only in pl., *attacking violently, furious, raging*, μένος Βορέαο καὶ ἄλλων ζαχρηῶν ἀνέμων Il.5.525 (-χρει- most codd.); of warriors, ζαχρηεῖς.. κατὰ κρατερὰς ὑσμίνας 12.347, cf. 13.684; cf. ζαχραής, ζαχρειής. (From ζα- and χράω (B); cf. ἐπιχράω (B).)

**ζάχρῡσος**, ον, *rich in gold*, Θρῃκία, ἐμπολά, E.*Alc*.498, *IT*1111 (lyr.): in late Prose, Lib.*Or*.11.140.

**ζάχῠτος** [ᾰ], ον, = διάχυτος, Nonn.*D*.19.347.

**ζάψ**, ή, *surf*, καρίδας ἢ ζ. ἐκφέρει κιχθύδια Cratin.Jun.13, cf. Euph. 3, Simm.11; πόντου.. περιστείνει ἁλυκὴ ζ. Dionys.Iamb.ap.Clem.Al. *Strom*.5.8.47 (who says some took ζ. = πῦρ).

**ζάω**, v. ζῶ.

**Ζβελσοῦρδος**, ὁ, divinity worshipped in Thrace, *Rev.Ét.Gr*.26. 247:—also in forms Ζβερθοῦρδος, Ζβελθι- or Ζβερθι-οῦρδος, etc.

**ζβίχ** (ζαβίχ cod.)· λευκόν, Hsch. (hence κνὰξ ζβὶχ λευκόν cj. Salm. in Thespis 4; cf. κναξζβί).

**-ζε**, inseparable Suffix, denoting *motion towards*:—prop. representing -σδε, as in Ἀθήναζε, Θήβαζε, θύραζε for Ἀθήνασδε, Θήβασδε, θύρασδε: but sts. found with sg. Nouns, as ἔραζε, χαμᾶζε, Ὀλυμπίαζε, Μουνυχίαζε, cf. A.D.*Adv*.194.18.

⊛ **ζέα**, ή, = ζειά, D.H.2.25, Dsc.2.89 (v.l. ζειά): nom. sg. **ζέη** *PPetr*. 2 p.69 (iii B.C.). 2. = λιβανωτὶς κάρπιμος, Dsc.3.74. II. *the roof of a horse's mouth*, *Hippiatr*.1,8. (With ζέα I, cf. Skt. *yávas* (masc.), Lith. *javaĩ* (masc. pl.) 'corn'.)

**ζεγέριες**, οἱ, a Libyan word, = βουνοί, but used as a name for a kind of *mouse*, Hdt.4.192; **ζεγερίαι**, Hsch.

⊛ **ζειά**, ή, usu. in pl. ζειαί (sg., v. infr.), *one-seeded wheat, Triticum monococcum*, used as fodder for horses, Hom. only in Od.; πὰρ δ' ἔβαλον ζειάς, ἀνὰ δὲ κρῖ λευκὸν ἔμειξαν 4.41, cf. 604; in Il. ὄλυραι, e.g. ἵπποι.. κρῖ λευκὸν ἐρεπτόμενοι καὶ ὀλύρας 5.196, 8.564; ἀπὸ ὀλυρέων ποιεῦνται σιτία (sc. οἱ Αἰγύπτιοι), τὰς ζειὰς μετεξέτεροι καλέουσι Hdt. 2.36, cf. Eup.14D., X.*An*.5.4.27, Str.15.1.18, Asclep.ap.Gal.13.257: in sg., ζειὰ ἁπλῆ Dsc.2.89 (v.l. ζέα), = Gal.6.517. 2. *rice-wheat*, in sg., Thphr.*HP*8.9.2, al. (where ὄλυρα is a cultural variety); ζ. δίκοκκος, *Triticum dicoccum*, Dsc. l. c. (v.l. ζέα), Gal. l. c.

**ζειγάρη**· τέττιξ παρὰ Σιδήταις, Hsch.

**ζείδωρος**, ον, *zea-giving* (Plin.*HN*18.82, *EM*410.6), as epith. of the earth, ζείδωρος ἄρουρα Il.2.548, Od.3.3, Hes.*Op*.173; ζ. ἀρδμός Nonn.*D*.26.185: c. gen., ζ. ὀπώρης ἀχράς *AP*9.4 (Cyllen.): also in late Prose, Hld.9.22 (ζε(*F*)έ-δωρος, cf. ζέα). II. some authors derived it from ζάω, = βιόδωρος (so expld. by Hsch.), *life-giving*, Ἀφροδίτη Emp.151; Ἥλιος Nonn.*D*.12.23, cf. 22.276. **ζείζιν**, *mamma, Gloss*.

**ζειλίαυρος**, = ἀναγαλλὶς κυανῆ, Ps.-Dsc.2.178. **ζεῖνος**, v. ζῆνος.

**ζείνυμεν** (-αμεν cod.)· σβέννυμεν, Hsch. **ζειπίτις**· ὁ περιχύτης, Id. (ζειποίτης Gramm. in Reitzenstein *Ind.Lect.Rost*.1892/3 p.10).

**ζειρά**, ή, *a wide upper garment*, girded about the loins and falling over the feet, worn by Arabians, Hdt.7.69; by Thracians, ib.75, X.*An*.7.4.4: ζιραί Hsch.; but ζειρά is prescribed by Gramm. in Reitzenstein *Ind.Lect.Rost*.1892/3 p.10.

**ζειρατείς**· ἱμάτιόν τι Σύρων, Hsch. **ζειρεῖν**· ἀρωματοποιεῖν, Id. **ζειρόν**· ποικίλον, Id. **ζεῖρος**, a kind of *grape*, Id.

**ζειροφόρος**, ον, *wearing a* ζειρά, Ἀΐδης Antim.88. II. ζειροφόρους· ζωνοφόρους, Hsch. (χων- cod.).

**ζείω**, late Ep. for ζέω, A.R.1.734, Call.*Dian*.60.

**ζεκαμναία**, ά, Elean for δεκα-, *sum of ten minae*, *Schwyzer* 409.7 (vi B.C.).

**ζεκελτίδες** (v. l. ζακ- as in Hsch.), αἱ, Boeot. for γογγυλίδες or κολοκύνται, Nic. etc. ap.Ath.9.369a.

**ζελᾶς**, ὁ, gen. and dat. ζελᾶ, Thracian word, = οἶνος, Choerob.*in Theod*.1.145: but dat. τῷ ζῆλα Eup.(*Fr*.355) ibid., cf. Hsch. s. v. ζίλαι, Phot. s. v. ζειλα (sic).

**ζέλκια**· λάχανα (Phryg.), Hsch. (ζέλμια poscit ordo): ζέλκεια· λάχανα παρὰ Φρυξὶ τὰ παρ' ἡμῖν λεγόμενα Φρύγια Gramm. in Reitzenstein *Ind.Lect.Rost*.1892/3 p.9.

**ζέλλω**, aor. 2 ἔζελον, Arc. for βάλλω, Hsch., *EM*408.42.

**ζέμα**, ατος, τό (ζέω) *fermentation*, Herasap.Gal.13.1044: metaph., *lewdness*, Lxx *Jd*.20.6. II. *boiling*, ἐνδοὺς ζέμα bringing it to *the boil*, Herasap.Gal.13.548; δὸς ζέμα keep it on *the boil*, Orib.*Fr*.113; ὄρνις ἀπὸ ζέματος a *boiled* fowl, Alex.Trall.*Febr*.1. 2. *that which is boiled, decoction*, Dsc.*Alex*.7, *Gp*.8.37.3:—also **ζέμμα**, Lxx *Ez*.24.13.

**ζέμελεν**· βάρβαρον ἀνδράποδον (Phryg.), Hsch.

**ζέννῡμι**, = ζέω, Philagr.ap.Orib.5.17.7, *PHolm*.15.22 (Pass.), al.:—Pass., Dsc.2.70, Alex.Aphr.*Pr*.1.104.

**ζεο-ποίιον**, τό, *mill for grinding* ζέα, prob. in *AB*261. **-πῡρον**, τό, (ζέα, πυρός) a variety of *Triticum monococcum*, Gal.6.515.

**ζέρεθρον**, τό, Arc. for βέρεθρον, βάραθρον, Str.8.8.4.

**ζέρνα**, ή, = κύπειρος, *Gp*.2.6.23.

**ζεσελαιοπαγής**, ές, *cooked in boiling oil*, Philox.3.18.

**ζέσις**, εως, ή, (ζέω) *seething, effervescence, boiling*, Pl.*Ti*.66b, Ocell. 2.9, etc.; χολῆς Gal.16.577; οὔρων ib.661; ὅταν ἑψηθῇ μέχρι ζέσεως up to *boiling heat*, Plu.2.690c: metaph., ζ. τῆς ψυχῆς Pl.*Cra*.419e; [ὀργή] ζ. τοῦ περὶ καρδίαν αἵματος Arist.*de An*.403$^a$31.

⊛ **ζεστάκρατα**, τά, (ζεστός, ἄκρατον) *hot wine*, Pall.*in Hp*.2.162 D.

**ζεστολουσία**, ή, *washing in hot water*, Theon ap.Gal.6.208, 212.

**ζεστός**, ή, όν, (ζέω) *seethed, boiled*, κρέα ζ. καὶ ὀπτά App.*Hisp*. 85. II. *hot*, ὕδωρ Nic.*Fr*.70.11, Dsc.1.33, Sor.1.50; ὕδατα ζ., of hot springs, Str.12.8.17; opp. χλιαρός, S.E.*P*.1.101; ψάμμος D.L.6. 23; λίθος Ps.-Plu.*Fluv*.1.2; εἰ δὲ -οτέρας κράσεως δέοιντο if they want the oil-bath *hotter*, Herod.Med.ap.Orib.10.37.12: metaph., χλιαρὸς εἶ καὶ οὔτε ζ. οὔτε ψυχρός *Apoc*.3.15.

**ζεστότης**, ητος, ή, *heat*, Paus.10.11.4.

⊛ **ζετραία**, ή, Thracian for χύτρα, Poll.10.95.

**ζευγάριον** [ᾰ], τό, Dim. of ζεῦγος, *a puny pair* or *team*, esp. of oxen, Ar.*Av*.582; ζ. βοεικόν Id.*Fr*.109; βοοῖν ib.387, cf. *PCair.Zen*.251.7 (iii B.C.).

**ζεύγελα**· διάβροχα ξύλα· καὶ τῶν βοῶν ἢ ἡμιόνων ζευκτά· καὶ τέμαχος ἐκ πλευρᾶς ἡλισμένης, Hsch.

**ζευγελάτης** [ᾰ], ου, ὁ, = ζευγηλάτης, Hsch.

**ζευγηλ-ᾰσία**, ή, *the driving a yoke of oxen*, Eust.361.13. **-ᾰτέω**, *drive a yoke of oxen*, X.*An*.6.1.9, *Dialex*.7.2. **-άτης** [ᾰ], ου, ὁ, *the driver of a yoke of oxen, teamster*, S.*Fr*.616, X.*An*.6.1.8, *PFay*.112.6 (i A.D.), *Dialex*.7.2: pl., D.S.31.24:—a fem. **-ᾰτρίς**, ίδος, S.*Fr*.878.

**ζευγίζω**, *yoke in pairs, unite*, in Pass., *PGrenf*.1.1.1 (ii B.C.), Lxx 1*Ma*.1.15, Aq.*Nu*.25.3.

⊛ **ζευγίον**, τό, = ζυγόν III.2, *IG*11(2).287*A* 51 (iii B.C.), 12(5).872.37 (iii B.C.).

**ζευγίππης**, ου, ὁ, in pl., dub. l. in D.S.19.106 (leg. ζευγίτας).

**ζευγίς**, ίδος, ή, *rope*, *BGU*544.5 (ii A.D.).

**ζευγίσιον**, τό, *rating of the* ζευγῖται, ζ. τελεῖν Arist.*Ath*.7.4, cf. Poll.8.130.

**ζευγίτης** [ῑ], ου, ὁ, fem. **ζευγῖτις**, ιδος, (ζεῦγος) *yoked in pairs*, ζευγίτιδες ἵπποι Call.*Ap*.48; ἡμίονοι ζευγῖται D.S.17.71; of soldiers, *in the same rank*, Plu.*Pel*.23; κάλαμος ζ. a reed *of which were made the mouthpieces of the double flutes* (ζεύγη), Thphr.*HP*4.11.3. II. ζευγῖται, οἱ, the third of Solon's four classes of Athenian citizens, so called from *their being able to keep a team* (ζεῦγος) *of oxen*, Arist.*Pol*. 1274$^a$20, *Ath*.4.3, Lex ap.D.43.54, *IG*1$^2$.45.40, etc.

**ζεύγλᾱ**, ή, poet. for sq., ἄτης E.*Fr*.285.10, cf. *Lyr.Alex.Adesp*.11. 8, *AP*9.19 (Arch.), Choerob.*in Theod*.1.304.

⊛ **ζεύγλ-η**, ή, *loop attached to the yoke* (ζυγόν), through which the beasts' heads were put, χαίτη ζεύγλης ἐξεριποῦσα παρὰ ζυγόν Il.17. 440; ἔζευξα.. ἐν ζυγοῖσι κνώδαλα ζεύγλαισι δουλεύοντα A.*Pr*.463; ὑποδύντες ὑπὸ τὴν ζ. Hdt.1.31; βόας ζεύγλᾳ πέλασσεν Pi.*P*.4.227; ὑπάγειν τοὺς ἵππους τῇ ζ. Luc.*DMar*.6.2. 2. = ζεῦγος I.1, *BGU*1507 (iii B.C.).—Not found in good Att. Prose. II. *cross-bar* of the double rudder, E.*Hel*.1536. **-ηθεν**, Adv., for ἐκ τῆς ζεύγλης, A.R.3.1319. **-ηφι**, Ep. gen. or dat. of ζεύγλη, Call.*Dian*.162.

**ζευγλόδεσμον**, τό, = ζυγόδεσμον, Hsch.

⊛ **ζεῦγμα**, ατος, τό, (ζεύγνυμι) *that which is used for joining, band, bond*, τὸ ζ. τοῦ λιμένος the *barrier* of ships moored across the mouth of the harbour, Th.7.69, cf. 70, D.S.13.14:—written **ζεογμα**, *Rev. Phil.*50.70 (Didyma, ii B.C.). **2.** *bridge of boats*, *AP*9.147 (Antag.); τὰ ζ. τῶν ποταμῶν D.H.9.31, cf. Plu.2.174e, etc.; *pier* or *platform formed by lashing several vessels together*, Plb.3.46.2, Plu.*Marc.*14, 15. **3.** *canal-lock*, *PPetr.*2 p.123, 3 p.210 (iii B.C.): metaph., ζεύγματ' ἀνάγκης *the bonds* of necessity, E.*IA*443. **II.** Gramm., *zeugma*, a figure of speech, wherein two subjects are used jointly with the same predicate, which strictly belongs only to one, Alex. *Fig.*2.17.

⊛ **ζευγματικόν**, τό, *lock-toll*, *PLond.*3.1157.6, al. (iii A.D.), *POxy.*2129.4, al. (iii A.D.).

**ζεύγνῡμι**, ζεύγνῡσι A.*Pers.*191, (ὑπο–) Pl.*Plt.*309a; 2 pl. imper. ζεύγνῠτε E.*Rh.*33 (lyr.); inf. -ύναι (μετα–) X.*Cyr.*6.3.21, Ep. ζευγνῦμεν Il.16.145; part. ζευγνύς Hdt.1.206, 4.89; impf. 3 pl. ἐζεύγνῠσαν Id.7.33, Ep. ζεύγν– Il.24.783: also **ζευγνύω** Hdt.1.205, Plb.5.52.4, etc.: impf. ἐζεύγνυον Hdt.4.89 (Ep. ζεύγν– v.l. Il.19.393): fut. ζεύξω Pi.*I.*1.6, etc.: aor. 1 ἔζευξα Od.3.478, etc.: late pf. ἔζευχα (ἐπ–) Philostr.*VA*2.14:—Med., Ep. impf. 3 dual ζευγνύσθην Il.24.281, 3 pl. ἐζεύγνυντο Od.3.492: fut. ζεύξομαι E.*Hec.*469 (lyr.), etc.: aor. 1 ἐζευξάμην Hdt.3.102, E.*Ion* 901 (lyr.):—Pass., fut. ζευχθήσομαι (δια–) Gal.9.938: aor. 1 ἐζεύχθην Pi.*O.*3.6, Hdt.7.6, A.*Ag.*842, Pl.*Plt.*302e: more commonly aor. 2 ἐζύγην [ῠ] Pi.*N.*7.6, E.*Supp.*822 (lyr.), (συ–) Pl.*R.*546c: pf. ἔζευγμαι Il.18.276: plpf. ἔζευκτο Hdt.4.85.—Usu. in aor. Act. in Hom.: the simple Verb is rare in Att. Prose:—*yoke, put to*, ὑπ' ὄχεσφιν ἵππους Il.23.130; ὑφ' ἅρμασιν ἵππους 24.14; ὑπ' ἀμάξῃσιν βόας ἡμιόνους τε ib.783; κἄζευξα πρῶτος ἐν ζυγοῖσι κνώδαλα A.*Pr.*462:—Med. (esp. in Od.), ἵππους ζεύγνυσθαι *put to one's* horses, Od.3.492, al.: abs., ζευγνύσθην Il.24.281; ζεύξομαι ἆρα πώλους E.*Hec.*469 (lyr.); καμήλους Hdt.3.102; of riding horses, *harness, saddle and bridle*, ζεῦξαι Πάγασον Pi.*O.*13.64, cf. Ar.*Pax*128, 135; of chariots, *put to, get ready*, ζ. ἅρμα, ὄχους, Pi.*P.*10.65, E.*Andr.*1020 (lyr.):—Med., τέθριππα Id.*Alc.*428. **2.** *bind fast*, ἀσκοὺς δεσμοῖς X.*An.*3.5.10:—Pass., φάρη.. ἐζευγμέναι πόρπαισιν *having* them *fastened*.., E.*El.*317. **3.** metaph., πότμῳ ζυγεὶς *in the yoke of* fate, Pi.*N.*7.6; ζυγεὶς ἐν ἅρμασι πημάτων A.*Ch.*795 (lyr.); ἀνάγκῃ ζυγείς S.*Ph.*1025; ζεύχθη *was tamed*, Id.*Ant.*955 (lyr.); θεσφάτοις.. ζυγεὶς E.*Supp.*220; ὁρκίοισι ζ. Id.*Med.*735; μοναρχία ζευχθεῖσα ἐν γράμμασιν ἀγαθοῖς Pl.*Plt.*302e:—Med., τόνδ' ἐν ὅρκοις ζεύξομαι E.*Supp.*1229. **II.** *join together*, σανίδες.. μακραὶ εὔξεστοι ἐζευγμέναι *well-joined*, Il.18.275 (elsewh. in Hom. only in signf. I); ζεῦξαι ὀδόντας, in setting a fractured jaw, Hp.*Art.*32; τὼ πόδε ζευγνύντες, of sculptors who made their statues with *joined* feet, Hld.3.13. **2.** *join in wedlock*, ἐπειδὰν εὐφρόνη ζεύξῃ μία *yokes* her *in wedlock*, S.*Fr.*583.11; of the parents or authors of the marriage, τίς ταύτην ἔζευξε; E.*IA*698; ζ. τὴν θυγατέρα τινί App.*BC*2.14, cf. Ath.12.554d:—in Med., of the husband, *wed*, ἄκοιτιν ζεύξασθαι E.*Alc.*994 (lyr.); παρθένειον ἐζεύξω λέχος Id.*Tr.*676 (so in Act., γάμοις ἔζευξ' Ἀδράστου παῖδα I *married* his daughter, Id.*Ph.*1366; ὁ Σεμέλην ζεύξας γάμοις Id.*Ba.*468):—Pass., *to be married*, ἐζευγμένη, opp. κόρη, S.*Tr.*536; γάμοις ζευχθῆναι or ζυγῆναι, Id.*OT*826, E.*IA*907, etc.; ἐν γάμοις Id.*El.*99; ἐς ἀνδρὸς εὐνάν Id.*Supp.*822 (lyr.): metaph., ζ. μέλος ἔργμασι Pi.*N.*1.7, cf. *I.*1.6. **3.** *join* opposite banks *by bridges*, ποταμὸν ζεῦξαι Hdt.1.206; τὸν Ἑλλήσποντον Id.7.33, Lys.2.29; μηχαναῖς ἔζευξεν Ἕλλης πορθμόν A.*Pers.*722 (troch.):—also in Med., ζεύγνυσθαι τὸν Βόσπορον Hdt.4.83 (v.l. -νύναι):—Pass., Id.7.6, 34; διῶρυξ ἐζευγμένη πλοίοις X.*An.*1.2.5; but also, **b.** γεφύρας ζεῦξαι Hdt.1.205, cf. 4.85, 118, al. **4.** *furnish* ships *with cross-benches* (ζυγόν III), Hes.*Fr.*76.6; but ζεύξαντες τὰς παλαιὰς [ναῦς] ὥστε πλωΐμους εἶναι *having strengthened* them *with thwarts*, Th.1.29, cf. Sch. ad loc. **5.** *pair* or *match* gladiators, Arr.*Epict.*1.29.37. **6.** *join* issue at law, in Pass., [δίκαι] ὑπέρ τινος ἐζευγμέναι *SIG*742.44 (Ephesus, i B.C.). (Cf. Skt. *yunákti*, pl. *yuñjánti* 'yoke', Lat. *jungo, jugum*.)

**ζευγοποιία**, ἡ, *the making of mouthpieces for double flutes*, Thphr. *HP*4.11.6.

⊛ **ζεῦγος**, εος, τό, (ζεύγνυμι) *yoke of beasts, pair* or *team of mules, oxen* or *horses*, Il.18.543, *IG*5(2).3.1 (Arc., iv B.C.), etc.; ζ. ἵππων And.4.26. **2.** *carriage drawn by a yoke of beasts, a chariot*, ζεύγεϊ κομίζεσθαι Hdt.1.31; ἐπὶ ζευγέων ἐλάσασαι ib.199; ἐπὶ ζεύγους ἄγειν And.1.45; τῷ ζεύγει ὃ ἦγεν τὴν γυναῖκα Hyp.*Lyc.*5; *wagons*, ζεύγεσι τοὺς λίθους ἄγουσι *SIG*124 (iv B.C.); βοεικά Th.4.128; *racing-car*, = τέθριππον, Id.5.50; ζ. τέθριππον A.*Fr.*346; ἢ συνωρίδι ἢ ζεύγει νενίκηκεν Pl.*Ap.*36d (but = συνωρίς, Plu.2.146d); ζ. μίσθιον a hired *chariot*, Id.*Ant.*6; λευκὸν ζ. *with* white *horses*, D.21.158. **II.** *pair* or *couple* of any things, ἰρήκων, αἰγυπιῶν, Hdt.3.76; πεδέων ib.130; Ἀτρειδᾶν A.*Ag.*44 (anap.); ἐμβάδων Ar.*Eq.*872, cf. Herod.7.51; ἐνωτίων *BGU*1050.9 (Aug.), etc.; κεράμου *IG*$1^{2}$.313.23, al.; [κεράμων] *SIG*245 Gi36 (Delph., iv B.C.); θυρῶν *IG*$1^{2}$.313.110; ταῶν Antiph.205; καλλιπύγων Cerc.14: abs., *married couple*, τὸ ζ., ὃ καλεῖται θῆλυ καὶ ἄρρεν X.*Oec.*7.18; τὸ ἐρωτικὸν ζ. Luc.*Am.*11; κατὰ ζεῦγος in *pairs*, Plu.2.93d; ἐς ζεύγεα Luc.*Syr.D.*12. **2.** *mouthpiece of a double flute*, Thphr.*HP*4.11.4, 6. **3.** ζ. ἱματίων *suit* of clothes, *BGU*814.9 (iii A.D.). **III.** incorrectly also of *more than two things* or *persons joined together*, ζ. τριπάρθενον three maiden sisters, of the Graces, E.*Fr.*357; so ζ. τρίδουλον Ar.*Fr.*576; ζ. νεκρῶν, where parents and children are spoken of, E.*HF*454. **IV.** = Lat. *jugerum*, *Cod.Just.*10.27.2.8.

**ζευγοτροφ-έω**, *keep a yoke of beasts*, Poll.8.132. **-ος, ον,** *keeping a yoke of beasts*, *IG*$2^{2}$.1576.73 (iv B.C.), Plu.*Per.*12.

**ζευγοφορέομαι**, Pass., *to be drawn by a yoke of oxen*, cj. in Ph. Bybl. ap. Eus.*PE*1.10 (ζυγ- codd.).

**ζευγῶχος**, ὁ, (ἔχω) *owner of a* ζεῦγος, *IG*4.742.8 (Hermione).

**ζεύκ-τειρα**, ἡ, fem. from sq., of Aphrodite, Orph.*H.*55.3. **-τήρ**, ῆρος, ὁ, *one who yokes* or *joins*: hence Adj. ζ. ἱμάντες the straps *of the yoke*, J.*AJ*12.4.6, cf. Hsch. s.v. ζεύγλας. **-τήριος**, α, ον, *fit for joining* or *yoking*, γέφυρα γαῖν δυοῖν ζ. A.*Pers.*736 (troch.); πάτερ.. Μαινάδων ζευκτήριε Id.*Fr.*382. **II.** as Subst., ζευκτήριον, τό, = ζυγόν, *yoke*, Id.*Ag.*529, *POxy.*934.5 (iii A.D.); ζευκτηρία, ἡ, = ζεύγλη II, *Act.Ap.*27.40. **-τὴς** λαοῦ, gloss on ζευξίλεως, Hsch. (prob. for ζευκτὸς λαός cod.); = *junctor*, *Gloss.* **-τικός**, ή, όν, = εὐναῖος, of Aphrodite, Sch.Opp.*H.*4.156; = ζευκτήριος, ἡνίαι *Gloss.*

**ζευκτός**, ή, όν, (ζεύγνυμι) *yoked, harnessed*, Plu.2.278b, etc.; *joined in pairs*, κάλαμοι Pl.*Epigr.*24.4; στίχος ἡρῴῳ ζ. ποδί, of the pentameter, *AP*7.9 (Damag.). **2.** *joined*, πορθμὸς γεφύρᾳ ζευκτός Str.10.2.8. **II.** ζευκτόν, τό, = ζεῦγος I.2, Sor.1.49, prob. in Aët.9.30.

**ζεύμαν**· τὴν πηγήν (Phryg.), Hsch.

**ζευξίγᾰμος** [ῐ], ἡ, *she that yokes in marriage*, epith. of the planet Venus, *Cat.Cod.Astr.*1.173.

**Ζευξιδία**, epith. of Hera at Argos, *EM*409.28.

**ζευξίλεως** [ῐ], ω, ὁ, *subjugator of men*, of a king, S.*Fr.*133.

**ζεύξιππος**, *desultor, junctor*, *Gloss.*

⊛ **ζεῦξις**, εως, ἡ, (ζεύγνυμι) *yoking* or *manner of yoking* oxen, ζεύξι τοιαύτῃ χρεώμενοι Hdt.3.104. **II.** *bridging*, τοῦ Βοσπόρου Id.4.88; τοῦ Ἑλλησπόντου Id.7.35.

⊛ **Ζεύς**, ὁ, nom. Il.1.175, al., once written Ζηύς *IG*12(3).1313 (Thera), but Ζεύς ib.1316, al.; Boeot. Δεύς (q.v.); voc. Ζεῦ Il.1.503, etc.; gen. ΔιϜός *BMus.Inscr.*952 (Cephallenia, vi B.C.), Διός Il.1.63, etc.; dat. ΔιϜί *Schwyzer* 80 (Argive, from Olympia, v B.C.), Διί Il.1.578, al., *IG*$1^{2}$.80.12 (v B.C.), etc., contr. Δί [ῑ] Pi.*O.*13.106, *SIG*9, 35 (Elis, vi B.C., Syrac., v B.C., from Olympia); late Δεί *JHS*32.167 (Pisidia), etc.; acc. Δία, rarer than Διός, Διί in Hom. (Il.1.394, al.), freq. later (cf. Skt. *dyaús*, gen. *divás*, loc. *diví* 'sky', 'heaven', 'day', loc. also *dyávi*, = Lat. *Jove*, acc. *dyā́m*, = Lat. *diem*, = Gr. Ζῆν (v. infr.)): also nom. **Ζήν** prob. in A.*Supp.*162 (lyr.); gen. dat. acc. Ζηνός, Ζηνί, Ζῆνα, Il.4.408, 2.49, 14.157, al., freq. in Trag. (Com. only in Trag. phrases); Coan Ζηνί *SIG*1025.24 (iv/iii B.C.); acc. Ζῆν (Ζῆν' Aristarch.) Il.8.206, 14.265, 24.331, Hes.*Th.*884, at end of verse, before vowel in next verse (stem Ζην- prob. originated in acc. sg.); Cret. Ττηνός, Ττηνί, *GDI*5024.23, 77, Τῆνα, Τηνί, ib.5039.11, 5145.12, Δῆνα *SIG*527.17 (iii B.C.); nom. Δήν Hdn.Gr.2.911:—Dor. and Att.-Ion. forms with α (of doubtful origin), nom. **Ζάν** Pythag. ap. Porph.*VP*17, Ar.*Av.*570; gen. Ζανός *Schwyzer* 696 (Chios, iv B.C.), Cerc.1.7, Philox.2.10, *IG*5(1).407 (Sparta, ii A.D.); Ζανός and Ζανί, *Lyr.Adesp.*82A, B (Ionic); acc. Ζᾶνα Call.*Fr.*10.6 P., cf. Euhem.24 J. (*FGrH* 63); nom. **Ζάς** Pherecyd.Syr.1, 2 (Ζής ap. Hdn.Gr. l.c.), Ζάς Ζαντός Choerob. *in Theod.*1.116; **Δάν** (q.v.); **Τάν** Head *Hist.Num.*$^{2}$469 (Crete); nom. **Δίς** Rhinth.14, Hdn.Gr. l.c.:—obl. cases Ζεός, Ζεΐ, Ζέα, cited by S.E.*M.*1.177, 195; Ζεῦν f.l. for Ζῆν' Aeschrio 8.5: the pl. Δίες, Δίας, Διῶν, Διοί, Ael.Dion.*Fr.*127; τοὺς κτησίους Δίας Ath. 11.473b; Δίες καὶ Ζῆνες *Stoic.*2.191; Elean Ζᾶνες Paus.5.21.2:—*Zeus*, the sky-god, ὕει μὲν ὁ Ζ. Alc.34, cf. *SIG*93.34 (v B.C.), Thphr. *Char.*14.12, etc.; Ζεῦ ἄλλοι τε θεοί Il.6.476; ὦ Ζεῦ καὶ πάντες θεοί, ὦ Ζεῦ καὶ θεοί, X.*Cyr.*2.2.10, Ar.*Pl.*1, etc.; Ζεῦ Ζεῦ A.*Ch.*246, Ar.*V.*323 (lyr., prob. l.); ὦ Ζεῦ βασιλεῦ τῆς λεπτότητος τῶν φρενῶν Id.*Nu.*153; in oaths, οὐ μὰ Ζῆνα, twice in Hom., Il.23.43, Od.20.339: freq. in Com. and Prose, οὐ μὰ Δία Ar.*V.*193, Pl.*R.*426b (c. Art., μὰ τὸν Δί', οὐ Ar.*V.*169, al.); ναὶ μὰ Δία Id.*Ach.*88, X.*Mem.*2.7.14; νὴ τὸν Δία or νὴ Δία, Ar.*V.*217, *Eq.*319, etc.; cf. νηδί; πρὸς τοῦ Διός Id.*Av.*130; πρὸς Διός X.*An.*5.7.32; οὐ τὸν Δία alone, Ar.*Lys.*986: prov. of enormous wealth, τῷ Διὶ πλούτου πέρι ἐρίζειν Hdt.5.49. **II.** of other deities, Ζ. καταχθόνιος, = Πλούτων, Il.9.457; Ζ. χθόνιος S.*OC*1606, *SIG*1024.25 (Myconos, iii/ii B.C.); of non-Greek divinities, Ζ. Ἄμμων Pi.*P.*4.16, etc.; freq. of Semitic Baalim, Ζ. Βεελβάσωρος, etc., *OGI*620 (Gerasa, i A.D.)), etc.; Ζ. Ὠρομάσδης, = Pers. *Ahuramazda*, ib.383.41 (Nemrud Dagh, i B.C.). **III.** of persons, ὁ σχινοκέφαλος Ζ., iron. of Pericles, Cratin.71; in flattery of kings, Hdt.7.56 (of Xerxes); Ξέρξης ὁ τῶν Περσῶν Ζ. Gorg.*Fr.*5a D.; [ἱερεὺς] Σελεύκου Διὸς Νικάτορος *OGI*245.10 (ii B.C.); of the Roman emperors, Opp.*C.*1.3; Νέρων Ζ. Ἐλευθέριος *IG*7.2713.41 (Acraephiae), etc.; Ζῆνα τὸν Αἰνεάδην *AP*9.307 (Phil.). **IV.** Διὸς ἀστήρ the *planet Jupiter*, Pl.*Epin.*987c, Arist.*Mete.*$343^{b}30$, etc.; so Ζεύς *Placit.*2.32.1, Cleom.2.7; Διὸς ἡμέρα a day of the week, D.C.37.19. **V.** Pythag. name for the *monad*, *Theol.Ar.*12.

**ζεύσασθαι**· γεύσασθαι, Hsch.

**ζεφῠρ-ήϊος**, ον, = ζεφύριος, Nonn.*D.*48.517. **-ηΐς**, ΐδος, pecul. fem. of ζεφύριος, ἀκτή Posidipp. ap. Ath.7.318d codd. (-ίτιδος Valck.). **2.** *of the god Zephyros*, γενέθλη Nonn.*D.*37.335, cf. 47.341. **-ίη** (sc. πνοή), ἡ, = Ζέφυρος, *the west wind*, Od.7.119. [Ζεφ- long metri gr.] **-ικός**, ή, όν, = sq., Arist.*Mete.*$364^{a}20$, Thphr.*HP*8.7.7. ⊛ **-ιος**, ον, sts. also α, ον (cf. Ζεφυρίη), *of the West* or *west wind, westerly*, Id.*CP*2.3.1; τοῖς ζ. (sc. ἀνέμοις) *at the period of west winds*, Arist.*HA*$618^{a}7$; *western*, τοῖχος *Inscr.Délos* 290.166 (iii B.C.), cf. *IG*12(5).126 (Paros, ii B.C.). **II.** ᾠὸν ζ. *wind*-egg, also ἀνεμιαῖον, ὑπηνέμιον, Arist.*HA*$560^{a}6$, *GA*$749^{b}1$. **III.** Ζ. ἄκρα or Ζεφύριον, τό, name of a cape in Cyprus, Str.14.6.3, Ath.7.318d: Ζεφύριον, τό, cape in S. Italy, Str.6.1.7. **-ίτης** [ῑ], ου, ὁ, = foreg. I, epith. of the month of March, Lyd.*Mens.*4.152: fem. ⊛ **-ῖτις**, ιδος, ἡ, = foreg. I, αὖραι Orph.*H.*81.1; = foreg. III, epith. of Aphrodite, as worshipped in Cyprus, Call.*Ep.*6; cf. ζεφυρηΐς I.

⊛ **Ζέφῠρος**, ὁ, any *westerly wind*, Βορέης καὶ Ζ., τώ τε Θρῄκηθεν ἄητον Il.9.5: coupled with Νότος, 21.334; opp. Εὖρος, Od.5.332, 19.206; Ζ. δυσαής, ἔφυδρος, 5.295, 14.458; ψυχρός Arist.*Pr.*946ᵃ17; but εὐδιεινὸς καὶ ἥδιστος ib.943ᵇ21; ὁπότε νέφεα Ζ. στυφελίξῃ Il.11.305; ἅμα πνοιῇ Ζεφύροιο θέοιμεν, of horses, 19.415; later, *the due West wind*, opp. ἀπηλιώτης, Arist.*Mete.*363ᵇ12, cf. *Mu.*394ᵇ26; but rather *north-west* in Id.*Pol.*1290ᵃ19. (Prob. cogn. with ζόφος. cf. ζοφόπνοια.)

⊛ **ζέω**, contr. 3 sg. ζεῖ even in Il.21.362; later Ep. **ζείω** Call.*Dian.* 60, subj. ζείῃσι Epic. in *Arch.Pap.*7 p.7; in late Prose **ζέννυμι** (q.v.): impf. ζέε Il.21.365, ἔζεε Hes.*Th.*695, ἔζει S.*OC*434: fut. ζέσω (ἐξανα-) A.*Pr.*372: aor. ἔζεσα Hdt.7.188, cf. ἐπιζέω; Ep. ζέσσα Il.18.349:—Pass., aor. ἐζέσθην (ἀπ-) Dsc.1.3, (ἐν-) Aret.*CA*1.2: pf. ἔζεσμαι *Gp.*10.54.3:—*boil, seethe*, of water, ἐπεὶ δὴ ζέσσεν ὕδωρ ἐνὶ ἤνοπι χαλκῷ Il.18.349, Od.10.360; ὡς δὲ λέβης ζεῖ ἔνδον as the kettle *boils*, Il.21.362, cf. E.*Cyc.*343; rarely of solids, *to be fiery hot*, χθὼν ἔζεε Hes.*Th.*695, 847; χαλκός Call. l. c. 2. *ferment*, Hp.*VM*11; γλεύκους ζέοντος Dsc.5.8. 3. metaph., *boil* or *bubble up*, τῆς θαλάσσης ζεσάσης Hdt.7.188; αἷμα διὰ χρωτὸς ζέσσ' *AP*7.208 (Anyte); οἶνος ζεῖ Pl.*Lg.*773d. b. of passion, ὁπηνίκ' ἔζει θυμός S.*OC*434, cf. Pl.*R.*440c, etc.; τὸ ζέον τῆς μάχης Hld.1.33. 4. c. gen., *boil up* or *over with* a thing, λίμνη ζέουσα ὕδατος καὶ πηλοῦ Pl.*Phd.*113a; πίθος ζ. [οἴνου] Thphr.*HP*9.17.3; πεδία ζείοντ' Ἀγαρηνῶν *boiling, teeming with..*, *APl.*4.39 (Arab.); of persons, ζ. σκωλήκων Luc.*Alex.*59: c. dat., ζ. φθειρί Id.*Sat.*26; ζ. φλογμῷ Lyc.690; θάλαττα αἵματι καὶ ῥοθίῳ ζέουσα Aristid.1.142 J. II. causal, *make to boil, boil*, τοὶ δὲ λοετρὰ πυρὶ ζέον A.R.3.273; θυμὸν ἐπὶ Τροίῃ πόσον ἔζεσας; *AP*7.385 (Phil.). 2. *exhale*, ἀϋτμήν (v.l. -μῇ) A.R.1.734. (ζέ(σ)-ω, cf. ζεσ-τός, Skt. *yásati* 'boil', OHG. *jësan* 'ferment', 'foam', Engl. *yeast*.)

**ζῆ, ζῆθι**, imper. of ζῶ (q.v.). **ζηβήνη**, v. ζιβύνη.

**ζηλ-αῖος**, α, ον, (ζῆλος) *jealous*, *AP*9.524.7. **-άς**, *paelex*, *Gloss.* **-ευτής**, οῦ, ὁ, = ζηλωτής in vulgar language, Eust.1527.34. ⊛ **-εύω**, = ζηλόω, Democr.55 (v.l.), Simp.*in Epict.*p.56 D. **-έω**, = ζηλοτυπέω, etym. of ζηλήμων, Eust.70.30:—in Dor. form **ζᾱλέω**, *to be zealous for*, τὰ τᾶς αὐτοσαυτοῦ πατρίδος *SIG*734.7 (Delph., i B.C.). **-η**, ἡ, *female rival*, X.Eph.2.11, Aristaenet.1.25 codd.

**ζηλημ-οσύνη**, ἡ, poet. for ζῆλος, Q.S.13.388 (pl.). **-ων**, ον, gen. ονος, (ζηλέω) *jealous*, σχέτλιοί ἐστε, θεοί, ζηλήμονες ἔξοχον ἄλλων Od.5.118; and late Ep., as Call.*Dian.*30, Opp.*C.*3.191, Musae.36, 37; μῆνις *AP*3.7 (Inscr. Cyzic.).

⊛ **ζηλο-δοτήρ**, ῆρος, ὁ, *giver of bliss*, *AP*9.524.7. **-μᾰνής**, ές, *mad with jealousy*, κόλασμα ib.5.217 (Agath.), cf. Nonn.*D.*41.211.

⊛ **ζῆλος**, ου, ὁ, later εος, τό, *Ep.Phil.*3.6 codd. opt.; Dor. **ζᾶλος** *IG*12(5).891, etc.:—*jealousy* (= φθόνος), Hes.*Op.*195, S.*OT*1526: coupled with φθόνος by Democr.191, Lys.2.48, Pl.*Phlb.*47e, 50c, *Lg.* 679c (pl.); εἰς ζῆλον ἰέναι Id.*R.*550e: more usu. in good sense, *eager rivalry, emulation*, Id.*Mx.*242a, Arist.*Rh.*1388ᵃ30. 2. c. gen. pers., *zeal for* one, ξυναίμων S.*OC*943; κατὰ ζῆλον Ἡρακλέους in *emulation* of him, Plu.*Thes.*25; ζ. πρός τινα Luc.*Dem.*57: abs., *passion*, *PGrenf.*1.1.13 (ii B.C.). 3. c. gen. rei, ζῆλον.. γάμων ἔχουσα causing *rivalry* for my hand, E.*Hec.*352; ζ. ἀζήλων καὶ φόβον ἀφόβων Phld.*Oec.*p.66 J.; ζ. τῶν ἀρίστων *emulous desire* for.., opp. φυγὴ τῶν χειρόνων, Luc.*Ind.*17; ἀνδραγαθίας Plu.*Cor.*4; so ζ. πρός τι Phld.*Rh.*2.53 S., Plu.*Per.*2; ζ. περὶ τὰ στρατιωτικά Str.14.2.27: pl., *ambitions*, Phld.*Rh.*2.54 S. 4. *fervour, zeal*, Lxx 4*Ki.*19.31, al., 1*Ep.Cor.*14.1, al.; *indignation*, ζ. πυρός *Ep.Hebr.*10.27. 5. personified as son of Styx, brother of Βία, Κράτος, Νίκη, Hes.*Th.* 384. II. *pride, honour, glory*, S.*Aj.*503; ζ. καὶ χαρά D.18.217; τὸν αὐτὸν ἔχει ζῆλον ὁ στέφανος, ib.120; ζῆλον καὶ τιμὴν φέρει τῇ πόλει Id.23.64, cf. 18.273, 60.33. III. *spirit*, τῆς πολιτείας Plb.4.27.8: pl., *tastes, interests*, τοῖς ἀπὸ διαφόρων ἐπιτηδευμάτων, βίων, ζήλων, ἡλικιῶν, Longin.7.4. 2. esp. in Lit. Crit., *style*, τοῦ Ἀσιανοῦ λεγομένου ζήλου Str.14.1.41, cf. Plu.*Ant.*2.

**ζηλοσύνη**, ἡ, poet. for ζῆλος, *h.Ap.*100.

**ζηλοτῠπ-έω**, *to be jealous of*, c. acc., ζηλοτυπῶν με καὶ φθονῶν Pl.*Smp.*213d; τὴν αὑτοῦ γυναῖκα Ath.12.532a, cf. *POxy.*472.11 (ii A.D.); ζ. δούλην ἐπὶ τῷ ἀνδρί in regard to her husband, Plu.2.267d: c. dat., *emulate*, ζ. τινὶ ἐπαινουμένῳ Demetr.*Eloc.*292:—Pass., ἡ -ουμένη μεμοιχεῦσθαι Ph.1.141. 2. *envy*, Cic.*Att.*13.18.2 (Pass., ib.13.1); ζ. τινά τινος Jul.*Or.*5.167c. II. c. acc. rei, *regard with jealous anger*, τὰ γιγνόμενα Aeschin.1.58. 2. *pretend to, affect*, κάθαρμα ζηλοτυποῦν ἀρετήν Id.3.211; *imitate, follow*, τὴν Θάλητος δόξαν Suid. s. v. Φερεκύδης:—Pass., ἡ ζηλοτυπουμένη τυραννίς Plu.*Arat.*25. **-ία**, ἡ, *jealousy, rivalry, envy*, Aeschin.3.81, *Com.Adesp.*16.20 D.; ζ. καὶ φθόνος τῆς δόξης Plu.*Per.*10; ἡ κατὰ τὴν τέχνην ζ. Luc.*Cal.*2; ζ. πρός τινα Plu.2.276b; θυσία ζηλοτυπίας Lxx *Nu.*5.15: pl., Phld.*Rh.*2.139 S. **-ος**, ον, (τύπτω) *jealous*, Ar.*Pl.*1016, Men.*Pk.*409, J.*AJ* 5.8.2, etc.; title of mime by Herodas; ζ. δύναι *AP*5.151 (Mel.); τὸ ζ. Phld.*Hom.*p.41 O. Adv. -πως Str.14.1.20; ζ. ἔχειν διὰ τὸν ἔρωτα J.*BJ*1.22.3; πρός τινα Aeschin.Socr.*Oxy.*1608.83: Sup. -ώτατα, διατεθῆναι πρός τινα Ael.*VH*12.16. 2. *eager*, πρὸς τὴν τῶν ἀρρένων συνουσίαν Ptol.*Tetr.*62.

⊛ **ζηλ-όω**, (ζῆλος): I. c. acc. pers., *vie with, emulate*, τινα Th.2.37, Pl.*R.*553a, *Michel* 1007.29 (Teos, ii B.C.):—Pass., Phld.*Rh.*1.125 S., etc.: c. acc. rei, Th.2.64; in bad sense, *to be jealous of, envy*, ζηλοῖ δέ τε γείτονα γείτων Hes.*Op.*23, cf. *h.Cer.*168, 223, Theoc.6.27; τὴν αὐτοῦ γυναῖκα Lxx *Si.*9.1: abs., *to be jealous*, 1*Ep.Cor.*13.4; ζηλώσαντες *through jealousy*, *Act.Ap.*7.9. b. c. acc. pers., *to be jealous for*, Lxx *Nu.*11.29. 2. *esteem* or *pronounce happy, admire, praise*, τινά τινος one for a thing, S.*El.*1027, Isoc.4.91; ζηλῶ σε τῆς εὐβουλίας Ar.*Ach.*1008 (lyr.); τῆς εὐγλωττίας Id.*Eq.*837; τῆς εὐτυχίας τὸν πρέσβυν Id.*V.*1450 (lyr.); τοῦ πλούτου X.*Smp.*4.45; τινὰ ἐπί τισι *IG* 12(5).860.47 (Tenos, i B.C.): more rarely, ζ. τινά τι S.*Aj.*552; ζ. σε οὐθούνεκα.. A.*Pr.*332; τὴν πόλιν, ὅτι.. X.*HG*6.5.45; πολλά σε ζηλῶ βίου, μάλιστα δ' εἰ.. S.*Fr.*584: c. part., σε ζ. θανόντα πρὶν κακῶν ἰδεῖν βάθος A.*Pers.*712 (troch.), cf. E.*Or.*521: iron., ζηλῶ σε happy in your ignorance! Id.*Med.*60; ὑμῶν οὐ ζηλοῦμεν τὸ ἄφρον Th.5.105:—Pass., *to be deemed fortunate*, ὑπό τινων Pl.*Phdr.*232a. II. c. acc. rei, *desire emulously, strive after, affect*, ὁ μὲν δόξης ἐπιθυμεῖ καὶ τοῦτ' ἐζήλωκε D.2.15; ἀρετήν Id.20.141; ἀστρολογίαν Epicur.*Ep.*2 p.53 U.; μάθησιν *PSI*1.94.9 (ii A.D.); πίστιν *Cod.Just.*1.1.3.2:—Pass., ἡ ἀρετὴ ὑπὸ πάντων τῶν ἀνθρώπων ζηλοῦται Lys.2.26; τὰ ζηλούμενα Arist.*Rh.* 1360ᵇ34. III. also of persons, *pay zealous court to*, *Ep.Gal.*4.17:—Pass., ib.18. **-ωμα**, ατος, τό, *that which is emulated*: *object of envy* or *ambition*, Phld.*Rh.*2.27 S.: in pl., *high fortune*, E.*IT*379; ζ. τυραννικά D.H.7.55. II. in pl. also, *emulous efforts, rivalries*, νέων ζ. Aeschin.1.191, *AP*7.219 (Pomp. Jun.), cf. D.19.260. 2. *emulation*, ζήλωμα τῆς τῶν Ῥωμαίων ἀρετῆς App.*BC*5.113: pl., Lyc. 355, Max.Tyr.7.7. **-ωσις**, εως, ἡ, *emulation, imitation*, τῶν βαρβάρων Th.1.132; μεγάλων συγγραφέων μίμησις καὶ ζ. Longin.13.2, cf. Max.Tyr.7.9. II. *zealous pursuit*, αἱ πολύτροποι τοῦ βίου ζ. Ph. 1.362; *custom, fashion*, ἀρχαιότροποι ζ. ib.468. III. *jealousy*, Lxx *Nu.*5.14. **-ωτέος**, α, ον, *to be emulated*, D.L.5.74. II. ζηλωτέον *one must emulate* or *copy*, Plb.4.27.8, Plu.2.12a; νέοις ζ. τοὺς γέροντας Id.*Fr.inc.*2. 2. *one must strive after*, πραότητι Ath. Med.ap.Orib.*inc.*21.18. **-ωτής**, οῦ, ὁ, *emulator, zealous admirer* or *follower*, μιμητὴς καὶ ζ. τῆς πατρῴας ἀρετῆς Isoc.1.11; ζ. καὶ ἐρασταὶ τῆς Λακεδαιμονίων παιδείας Pl.*Prt.*343a; τῆς ἡλικίας τοῦ μειρακίου Aeschin.2.166; τῶν καλῶν βουλευμάτων ib.171; τῆς αὐτῆς αἱρέσεως *SIG*675.27 (Oropus, ii B.C.); μαθήσεως Phld.*Rh.*2.262 S.; πνευμάτων 1*Ep.Cor.*14.12; τῶν ἀγαθῶν τῶν εἰς τὴν πόλιν μαρτυρουμένων *IG*7.2712.99 (Acraephiae): c. gen. pers., τοῦ Διός Muson.*Fr.*8 p.37 H.; τῷ πράτῳ θεῷ Sthenid.ap.Stob.4.7.63 (nom. sg. ζηλωτάς codd.); Θουκυδίδου, Ἀντισθένους, Luc.*Hist.Conscr.*15, *Herm.*14; perh. *champion*, Epicur.*Nat.*70 G. 2. *jealous*, θεὸς ζ. Lxx *Ex.*20.5. II. *zealot*, used to translate Κανανίτης or Καναναῖος, *Ev.Luc.*6.15, *Act.Ap.*1.13, J.*BJ*4.3.9; τῶν πατρίων ἐθῶν Id.*AJ*12.6.2; τῶν νόμων Lxx 2*Ma.* 4.2. **-ωτικός**, ή, όν, *emulous*, Arist.*Rh.*1388ᵃ36, Ptol.*Tetr.*167; περί τι Arist.*Rh.*1388ᵇ9; λόγος Ph.1.135. **-ωτός**, ή, όν, also ός, όν E.*Andr.*5, *Med.*1035; Dor. **ζᾱλ-** Simon., Pi. (v. infr.):—*enviable*, of things, σοφία Pl.*Hp.Mi.*368b; καλὰ καὶ ζ. ἐπιγράμματα D.22.72: Comp., Isoc.6.95; ζηλωτὸν ὁ πλοῦτος Lycurg.*Fr.*97. 2. *to be deemed happy, to be envied*, of persons, Thgn.455, S.*Ant.*1161; τινι by one, A.*Pers.*710 (troch.), E.*Med.*1035, Pl.*Smp.*197d, etc.; ὑπό τινος Isoc.5.69: c. gen. rei, θῆκέ μιν ζαλωτὸν ὁμόφρονος εὐνᾶς Pi.*O.*7.6; ζ. τῆς εὐνοίας Plu.*Pomp.*61: c. dat., Id.*Luc.*38. 3. of conditions, *enviable, blessed*, αἰών Simon.71, E.*Med.*243; πότμος Arist.*Fr.*675; ζηλωτότατος βίος Ar.*Nu.*464 (lyr.); γάμος Plu.2.289b, etc.

⊛ **ζημία**, Dor. **ζᾱμία** (*SIG*239 *D* iii 5 (Delph., iv B.C.), etc., later **σαμία** *Delph.*3(1).342 (ii B.C.), cf. ταμία, ἀττάμιος), ἡ, *loss, damage*, Epich. 148; opp. κέρδος, Lys.7.12, Pl.*Lg.*835b, Arist.*EN*1132ᵇ12; ζημίαν or -ίας λαβεῖν to sustain *loss*, S.*Fr.*807, D.11.11; ζ. ποιεῖν Ar.*Pl.*1124; ζ. ἐργάζεσθαι Is.6.20 (unless insignf. I.2); ζ. φέρειν τῇ πόλει Pl.*Lg.*l.c.; ζ. εἶναι νομίζειν consider *as loss*, Isoc.3.50, Is.7.23; ζ. πλείονα ὑπομένειν τῆς τιμῆς *PFlor.*142.8 (iii A.D.). 2. ζ. ἐργάζεσθαι, of a slave, be guilty of a *delict*, Is.6.20 (v. supr.), Hyp.*Ath.*22. II. *penalty* in money, *fine*, ζημίην ἀποτίνειν Hdt.2.65, cf. *PHal.*1.195 (iii B.C.); ἐκτίνειν Pl.*Lg.*774e; ἱρὴν ζ. ὀφείλειν Hdt.3.52; ζ. καταβάλλειν D.24.83, cf. *SIG* l.c.; μετὰ.. χρημάτων ζημίας Pl.*Lg.*862d; ζ. ἐπέκειτο στατήρ Th.3.70; ζημίαν ὀφείλειν τάλαντον Plu.*Lys.*27; τῆς ζ. ἀφεθῆναι Id.*Arist.*4. 2. generally, *penalty*, ζ. ἐπιτιθέναι τινί Hdt.1.144; ζ. ἔπεστί τινι Id. 2.136; πρόσκειταί τινι X.*Vect.*4.21; γλώσσῃ ζ. προστρίβεται A.*Pr.* 331, cf. 384; with the penalty added, θάνατον ζ. ἐπιθέσθαι, προθεῖναι, τάξαι, to make death *the penalty*, Th.2.24, 3.44, D.20.135; θάνατος ἡ ζ. ἐπίκειται Hdt.2.38, cf. 65; but ἐφ' οἷς.. θάνατος ἡ ζ. Pl.*Prt.*325b: in pl., θανάτου ζημίαι πρόκεινται Th.3.45 (v.l.): c. gen. criminis, ζ. ἀδικίας *penalty for..*, Pl.*Tht.*176d, cf. *Lg.*860e (pl.). b. simply, *expense*, *SIG*717.81 (ii/i B.C.), *PLond.*5.1660.10, 1674.23 (pl., vi A.D.). III. of what is bought too dearly, *a bad bargain, a dead loss*, X.*Mem.*2.3.2: usu. with Adj., φανερὰ ζᾱμία Ar.*Ach.*737; καθαρὰ ζ., λαμπρὰ ζ., Alciphr.3.21, 38, cf. Alex.56.6.

**ζημιάζω**, *damno*, *Gloss.*

**ζημιο-πρακτέω**, *exact punishment from*, τινὰ τὰ μὴ καθήκοντα *PTaur.*7.7 (ii B.C.). **-ψῡχος**, *damnatissimus*, *Gloss.*

⊛ **ζημι-όω**, fut. -ώσω Lys.1.48: aor.1 ἐζημίωσα E.*Or.*578, Th.2.65, etc.: pf. ἐζημίωκα D.21.49:—Pass., fut. ζημιωθήσομαι Lys.29.4, Is.10.16, X.*Mem.*3.9.12; more freq. Med. ζημιώσομαι in pass. sense, Hdt. 7.39, And.1.72, Th.3.40, Isoc.18.37, D.1.27, Arist.*Pol.*1320ᵃ10: aor. ἐζημιώθην Pl.*Lg.*855b, Isoc.15.160: pf. ἐζημίωμαι Din.3.16, Arist.*Rh.* 1372ᵇ8:—*cause loss* or *do damage to, penalize*, πόλιν Lys.30.25; τοσαύτας ἡμέρας ζημιοῦν τινα *to cause* one *the loss of..*, Ael.*VH*3.23: c. Adj. neut., μηδὲν μηδένα Pl.*Lg.*846a; οὐδὲν ζ. τὸ κοινόν Isoc.6.5; πλείω ζ. σαυτὸν ἤ.. X.*Cyr.*3.1.30:—Pass., μεγάλα ζημιώσεται *will suffer* great *losses*, Th.3.40; πολλά Pl.*Lg.*916e: abs., Id.*Grg.* 490c. II. *fine, mulct* in a sum of money, c. dat. rei, ζ. τινὰ χιλίῃσι δραχμῇσι Hdt.6.21, cf. 136; χρήμασιν Th.2.65; μναῖς τρισί Pl.*Lg.* 936a; also ζ. τινὰ ἕως τριάκοντα μνᾶς Lycurg.*Fr.*40 (dub. l.); τινά τινος *deprive* of.., Lyd.*Mag.*2.19:—Pass., *to be fined* or *amerced* in a thing, c. dat. rei, χρήμασι Antipho 2.4.7; δραχμῇ τῆς ἡμέρας Pl.*Lg.*

766d; *μέχρι τοσούτου* ib.855b: also, c. acc. rei, *ταῦτα* ib.774b; ζ. *τριάκοντα λίτρας* Arist.*Fr.*476; *suffer financial loss*, *PFlor.*142.8 (iii A.D.): hence metaph., *τοῦ ἑνὸς τοῦ περιέχεαι μάλιστα τῇ ψυχῇ ζημιώσεαι* *wilt lose*, Hdt.7.39; *τὴν ψυχὴν αὐτοῦ Ev.Matt.*16.26; *ἑαυτόν Ev.Luc.*9.25; *τὰ κέρατα* Ael.*NA*10.1. 2. generally, *punish*, *τὴν θάλασσαν* Hdt.7.35; *σφέας* Id.9.77; *τινὰ θανάτῳ* Id.3.27; *τινὰ φυγῇ, πληγαῖς*, Th.4.65, 8.74:—Pass., *ζημιοῦσθαι ζημίαις ἐσχάταις* Lys.31.26; *θανάτῳ* Antipho 3.3.9, *PTeb.*5.92 (ii B.C.); *θανάτῳ καὶ πᾶσι τοῖς ἐσχάτοις* Pl.*Plt.*297e; *χρήμασιν καὶ ἀτιμίᾳ* Id.*Lg.*721b. **-ώδης**, ες, *causing loss, ruinous*, Id.*Cra.*417d, *Lg.*650a, X.*Mem.*3.4.11. Adv. -δῶς, censured by Poll.8.147. **-ωμα**, ατος, τό, (ζημιόω) *penalty, fine*, Luc.*Prom.*13, *Sammelb.*5174.13 (vi A.D.), etc.; *τῆς ἀταξίας* for their disorder, X.*HG*3.1.9; *-ώματα ἔστω ἀστυνόμοις* let them have *the right of imposing penalties*, Pl.*Lg.*764c. 2. *loss*, opp. *λῆμμα*, *BGU*419.13 (iii A.D.); *injury, damage*, ζ. *προστρίβεσθαί τινι* D.C.52.33. **-ωσις**, εως, ἡ, *infliction of penalties*, Arist.*Pol.*$1300^{b}22$ (pl.). **-ωτής**, οῦ, ὁ, *one who punishes*, Sch.rec.A.*Pr.*77; *executioner*, Eust.1833.53. **-ωτικός**, ή, όν, *likely to suffer loss*, Vett.Val.67.19, al.

**Ζήν**, v. Ζεύς. **Ζήνιον** ὕδωρ (cf. foreg.), *rain*-water, *PMag.Par.*1.225.

**Ζηνοδότειος**, α, ον, *of the School of Zenodotus*, D.L.2.15.

**Ζηνοδοτήρ**, ῆρος, ὁ, *giver of Zeus*, i.e. of his counsel, *AP*9.525.7.

**Ζηνοποσειδῶν**, ὁ, *Zeus-Poseidon*, a divinity worshipped in Caria, Macho ap.Ath.8.337c, cf. 2.42a, *CIG*2700 add. (Mylasa); Dor. **Ζᾱνοποτειδάν** *GDI*5163*b*12 (ibid.).

**ζῆνος**, η, ον, perh. = ζέϊνος, *made of spelt* (ζέα), *UPZ*94.1, al. (ii B.C.).

**Ζηνόφρων**, ον, gen. ονος, (Ζήν, φρήν) *knowing the mind of Zeus*, epith. of Apollo as revealing Zeus' will in oracles, *AP*9.525.7.

**Ζηνώνειος**, ον, *of Zeno*, αἵρεσις D.L.1.19; τὸ Ζ. Ph.2.460; Ζ., ὁ, *Stoic philosopher*, D.L.7.5:—also **Ζηνωνικός**, Dor. **Ζᾱν-**, ή, όν, ἔρως Cerc.9.16.

**ζῆσις**, εως, ἡ, *vitalization*, Dam.*Pr.*83bis.

**ζῆτα**, τό, indecl., *the letter* ζ, Pl.*Cra.*419b, etc.; of the *sixth* book of the Iliad, *POxy.*930.15 (ii/iii A.D.), *Epigr.Gr.*1095. (Semitic *zayin*, influenced by the names of the following letters, Gr. ἦτα, θῆτα.)

**ζητᾰρετησιάδης**, ου, ὁ, *virtue-seeker*, Epigr.ap.Hegesand.2.

**ζητ-εύω**, poet. for sq., Hes.*Op.*400, *h.Ap.*215, *h.Merc.*392: Dor. **ζᾱτεύω** Alcm.33.8. **-έω**, Dor. part. **ζάτεισα** Theoc.1.85: impf. ἐζήτουν, Ep. 3sg. ζήτει Il.14.258 (nowh. else in Hom.): aor.1 ἐζήτησα Isoc.16.14: pf. ἐζήτηκα Din.2.19:—Med., aor. 1 ἐζητησάμην (ἀν-) Longus *Prooem.*2:—Pass., fut. ζητηθήσομαι S.E.*P.*1.60, *M.*8.16; but ζητήσομαι in pass. sense, ib.1.28, Gal.1.649:—*seek, seek for*, ἐμὲ δ' ἔξοχα πάντων ζήτει Il. l.c.; ζ. πημάτων ἀπαλλαγάς A.*Pr.*318, cf. 264; εὑρήσεις ζητῶν Ar.*Pl.*105; μὴ ζητῶν without *seeking*, X.*Ages.*8.1; τὸ ζητούμενον ἁλωτόν *what is sought for* may be found, S.*OT*110. 2. *inquire for*, τὰ πινάκια καὶ τὰ γραμματεῖα $IG1^2$.91.11; τοὺς ἄρχοντας X.*An.*2.3.2: with relat. clause, ὅτου δέοιτο ὁ Κῦρος Id.*Cyr.*8.5.13. 3. *search after, search out*, τὸν αὐτόχειρα S.*OT*266; μεγάλοις μηνύτροις ἐζητοῦντο οἱ δράσαντες Th.6.27; of huntsmen, ζ. τὸν λαγώ X.*Cyn.*6.25. 4. *search* or *inquire into, investigate, examine*, of philosophical investigation, ζ. τὰ θεῖα X.*Mem.*1.1.15; ζ. καὶ ἐρευνῶ κατὰ τὸν θεόν Pl.*Ap.*23b; ζητουμένης ἀρετῆς ὅ τι ἐστίν Id.*Men.*79d; τὸ ζητούμενον the *matter of inquiry*, the *question*, Id.*Tht.*201a, Arist.*Top.*$110^{a}7$, Str.2.1.18, A.D.*Adv.*188.13; also of judicial *inquiry*, ζ. περὶ ἀδικημάτων Din.1.8; ζήτησιν τὴν ὑπέρ τινος ζ. ib.10; ἔνοχος εἶναι τοῖς ζητουμένοις ib.55: generally, ζ. πότερον.. ἤ Pl.*Phlb.*27c; ζ. πρὸς ἐμαυτόν Luc.*Lex.*17. 5. *require, demand*, τῶν πράξεων παρὰ τοῦ στρατηγοῦ τὸν λόγον ζητοῦντες D.4.33: metaph., ὁ περικράνιος ὑμὴν.. τὴν ἐπιδιαίρεσιν ζ. *requires* the opening up of the wound, Heliod.ap.Orib.46.7.3. II. *seek after, desire*, ἀμήχανα E.*Alc.*203; ἐμοὶ ζητῶν ὄλεθρον S.*OT*659; of natural tendencies, ὁ θερμὸς ὕφαμμον χώραν ζητεῖ Thphr.*HP*8.11.8:—Pass., ζητούμενος *sought after, in great demand*, *PMag.Par.*1.3086, 3114. 2. c. inf., *seek to* do, ἐκμαθεῖν τι ζ. Hdt.3.137, A.*Pr.*776; μεταλαβεῖν Ar.*Pl.*370, cf. Pl.*Prt.*322b, *Men.*90e, *SIG*372.7 (Samothrace, iii B.C.): c. fut. inf., ζητεῖς ἀναπείσειν Ar.*Pl.*573 codd. (sed leg. -πείθειν): c. acc. et inf., *seek* or *desire that*, Pl.*R.*443b, *Chrm.*172c. III. *have to seek, feel the want of*, ἵνα μὴ ζητέοιεν σιτία Hdt.1.94; Νέρωνα Plu.*Galb.*8:—Pass., ζητούμενος οἷς ἀπέλειπες *Epigr.Gr.*215.3 (Rhenea). **-ημα**, ατος, τό, *that which is sought*, Hp.*VM*3; οὐ ῥᾴδιον ζ. *a thing* not easy *to find*, of Pentheus' mutilated limbs, E.*Ba.*1139; δυσνοούμενον ζ., of God, Secund.*Sent.*3. II. *inquiry, question*, S.*OT*278, *Act.Ap.*15.2, al.; esp. of a philosophic nature, τὸ περὶ νόμους ζ. Pl.*Lg.*631a; τὰ περὶ φύσεως ζ. ib.891c; ποιητικῶν ζ. λύσεις Metrod.*Herc.*831.13; also τοῦτ'..οὖ τυγχάνει ζ. Pl.*Cra.*421a; ἐκεῖνό γ' ἦν τὸ ζ. πρῶτον, πότερον.. Id.*Sph.*221c; *search*, σῶμα μυρίοις ζητήμασιν εὑρών E.*Ba.*1218; μητρός *after* her, Id.*Ion* 1352. 2. *official* or *judicial inquiry*, *POxy.*97.14 (ii A.D.). III. in pl., *claims*, *PRyl.*117.14 (iii A.D.); *subjects of dispute*, *SIG*785.8 (i A.D.), *Act.Ap.*25.19. **-ημάτιον**, τό, Dim. of foreg. II, Arr.*Epict.*2.16.20, Lib.*Decl.*46 *Pr.*2. **-ηματικός**, ή, όν, = ζητητικός 2, Sch.Pl.p.212H.

**Ζητήρ**, epith. of Zeus in Cyprus, Hsch.

**ζητ-ήσιμος**, ον, *to be searched*, τὰ ζ. *places to be beaten* for game, X.*Cyn.*6.6. **-ησις**, εως, ἡ, *seeking, search for*, κατ' Εὐρώπης ζήτησιν ἐκπλῶσαι Hdt.2.44; κατὰ βίου τε καὶ γῆς ζ. Id.1.94, cf. 2.54; ἀνδρὸς κατὰ ζήτησιν in *quest* of him, S.*Tr.*55; ἡ ζ. τῶν δρασάντων Th.8.66; ζ. ἐπιστήμης Pl.*Tht.*196d, etc.; τῆς τροφῆς Th.8.57; τῆς ἀληθείας Id.1.20. 2. *searching, examining*, ζήτησιν ἐποιέετο τῶν νεῶν *searched* the ships, Hdt.6.118, cf. Lys.12.30, Aeschin.1.43. 3. *inquiry, investigation*, esp. of a philosophic nature, Pl.*Cra.*406a, *Ap.*29c, al.; περὶ τῆς τοῦ παντὸς φύσεως Id.*Ti.*47a; ζ. τοῦ μέλλοντος διὰ ὀρνίθων ποιεῖσθαι *inquire into* the future by augury, Id.*Phdr.*244c: in pl., Id.*Phd.*66d, Phld.*Rh.*1.276S., 2.185S. 4. *judicial inquiry*, Din.1.10, *POxy.*237 vi 7 (ii A.D.), etc.: pl., *suits, controversies*, *OGI*629.9 (Palmyra, ii A.D.). **-ητέος**, α, ον, *to be sought*, S.*Aj.*470, Ar.*Th.*604, etc. II. ζητητέον, *one must seek*, Id.*Nu.*761, Sannyr.8; ἥ τινα ἑτέραν [δύναμιν]..ἡμῖν ζ. Pl.*Phlb.*58d. **-ητήριον**, τό, = βασανιστήριον, Anon.ap.Suid. ⊛ **-ητής**, οῦ, ὁ, *seeker, inquirer*, τινος Pl.*R.*618c; φαῦλος ζ. Id.*Chrm.*175e. II. ζητηταί, οἱ, at Athens, *commissioners to inquire into extraordinary offences* or *to recover moneys owing to the State*, And.1.14 (sg.), Lys.21.16, D.24.11, Pl.Com.125 (sg.). **-ητικός**, ή, όν, *disposed to search* or *inquire*, Pl.*Men.*81e, Ptol.*Tetr.*6; τινος *into* a thing, Pl.*Ax.*366b; περί τι Id.*R.*528c. 2. οἱ ζ. διάλογοι Plato's dialogues *of search* or *investigation*, opp. οἱ ὑφηγητικοί, Thrasyll.ap.D.L.3.49; τὸ ζ. ἔχουσι πάντες οἱ τοῦ Σωκράτους λόγοι are *devoted to search* or *inquiry*, Arist.*Pol.*$1265^{a}12$. Adv. -κῶς Procl.*in Prm.*p.515S. 3. οἱ ζητητικοί, a name given to *the Sceptics*, D.L.9.69; ἡ ζητητική *their philosophy*, ib.70; ἡ ζ. ἀγωγή S.E.*P.*1.7. **-ητός**, ή, όν, *sought for*, τινι S.*OC*389.

**ζητός**, Arc. **ζατός**, = ζητητός, *IG*5(2).4.22 (Tegea, iv B.C.).

**ζήτρ-ειον** or **-εῖον**, τό, *a place of punishment for slaves* at Chios, Eup.19D., Theopomp.Com.63, cf. *EM*411.33, Eust.837.44: **-ιον**, prob. in Herod.5.32, cf. Choerob.ap.*EM* l.c.: metaph. in dat. pl. -ίοις, 'treadmills', dub. in Phld.*Oec.*p.44J.:—the forms **ζώστειον**, Ar.*Fr.*93; **ζώντειον** or **-εῖον**, Poll.3.78, Zonar.; **ζώτειον**, *EM*414.40 are incorrect. **-εύω**, in Dor. form **ζατρ-**, = ἐν μυλῶνι βασανίζω, *EM*408.12. **-ός**, ὁ, *executioner*, Hsch.

**ζήτωρ**, ορος, ὁ, = ζητητής, Hsch., Phot.

**ζιβύνη**, ἡ, = σιβύνη, Lxx *Is.*2.4, Ph.*Bel.*92.44, Porph.ap.Eus.*PE*3.12: **ζηβήνη**, Hsch.:—Dim. **ζιβύννιον**, τό, Id.

⊛ **ζιγγίβερις**, εως, *Edict.Diocl.*32.68 (*Delph., Clit.*), ὁ, ἡ (both in *Edict.Diocl.* l.c.); or **ζιγγίβερι**, τό, Dsc. (codd. opt.) and Gal. ll. cc.:—an Arabian spice-plant, the root of which was used in medicine, prob. *ginger*, Dsc.2.160, Gal.6.572, 11.880. (Perh. fr. Malay *inchi-ver* (*inchi* = root) through Skt. *śṛṅgaveram* and a Prakrit *singaber.*)

**ζίγγος**, ὁ, *humming* of bees, etc., Hsch.

**ζιγγόω**, *drink* (Cilician word), Nicostr.Com.38.

**ζίγλας**· κῶλα, Hsch.

**ζιγνίς**, ίδος, ἡ, a kind of *lizard*, Arist.*HA*$604^{b}24$ (v.ll. δειμνύς, ζιγνύς, διγνύς, ζίγνης).

**ζιγνῶσαι**· σκυθρωπάσαι, *EM*411.52, Hsch. (ζικν- cod.).

**ζιζάνιον**, τό, a weed that grows in wheat, = αἶρα II, prob. *darnel, Lolium temulentum*, *Gp.*2.43, *EM*411.46: pl., *Ev.Matt.*13.25, *Gp.*10.87.1. (Cf. Sumer. *zizân* 'wheat'.)

**ζιζουλά**, τό, *jujube*, Alex.Trall.6.5; cf. sq. and Ital. *giuggiola, zizzola.*

**ζίζῠφον**, τό, a tree, the fruit of which is *the jujube, Zizyphus vulgaris*, *Gp.*10.3.4; *ziziphus*, Colum.9.4.3: gen. pl. *zizuforum*, *Edict.Diocl.*6.56.

**ζίκαιος**, Elean for δίκαιος, *Schwyzer* 409 (vi B.C.):—also perh. written **ζικέα**, epith. of Nemesis, *BMus.Inscr.*1079 (Egypt (?)).

**ζίλαι**, v. ζελᾶς. **ζινίχιον**, τό, *shoe-latchet*, Suid. **ζιτᾶνα**· καταπύγονα, Hsch. **ζίφυιος**, Elean for δίφ-. **ζίω**, = ζητέω, *EM*411.51: ζίεται· ζητεῖται, ibid., Hsch. **ζμαράγδινος**, v. σμαρ-. **ζμάω**, v. σμάω. **ζμῆμα**, v. σμῆμα. **ζμιρριεῖα**, τά, *emery*, *IG*12(8).51.20 (Imbros, ii B.C.); cf. σμύρις. **ζμύρνη, ζμύρνινος**, etc., v. σμύρν-. **ζόα, ζόη, ζοΐα**, v. ζωή. **ζόασον**· σβέσον, Hsch. **ζοός**, v. ζωός. **ζορκάς**, άδος, and ζόρξ, ζορκός, ἡ, v. δορκάς. **ζούγωνερ**, Lacon. for ζύγωνες, *ploughing oxen*, Id. **ζουΐον ἢ ζοῦον**· θηρίον, ἢ ἐρυσίπελας, Id. (Prob. Thess. for ζῷον.) **ζούσθω**· ζωννύσθω, Id. (Prob. Thess.)

**ζόφ-εος**, α, ον, v.l. for sq., νύξ Nic.*Al.*501. ⊛ **-ερός**, ά, όν, (ζόφος) *dusky, gloomy*, Χάος Hes.*Th.*814; οἴκημα Hp.*Acut.*(*Sp.*)18, cf. Hierocl.p.33A.; opp. λαμπρός, of the air, *misty*, Chrysipp.*Stoic.*2.140, cf. Luc.*Nigr.*4; τὴν θάλασσαν ζοφερὰν διαφαίνεσθαι Arist.*Mir.*$843^{a}25$; τὸ ζοφερόν Hp.*Virg.*1, Arist.*de An.*$426^{b}2$. 2. metaph., ζ. φροντίδες *AP*5.296.8 (Agath.). **-ιος**, ον, = ζόφεος, ζοφερός, ib.7.377 (Eryc.).

**ζοφο-δορπίδας**, α, ὁ, *supping in the dark* or *in secret*, of Pittacus, Alc.37B, cf. Plu.2.726a: **-δορπίας** in Theognost.*Can.*20, Zonar.; **-δερκίας**, Hsch., Suid. **-είδελος**, ον, *dusky, gloomy*, Nic.*Th.*657. ⊛ **-ειδής**, ές, *dark-coloured*, Hp.*Mul.*1.11; of the colour of an elephant, Aret.*SD*2.13. **-εις**, εσσα, εν, = foreg., Nic.*Th.*775, *Al.*474, Orph.*H.*78.4. **-μηνία**, ἡ, (μήνη) = σκοτομηνία, Hsch., Gramm. in Reitzenstein *Ind.Lect.Rost.*1892/3 p.10. **-πνοια**, ἡ, = ἡ ἀπὸ δύσεως πνοή, Sch.Il.21.334.

⊛ **ζόφος**, ὁ, *nether darkness*, ἱεμένων Ἔρεβόσδε ὑπὸ ζόφον Od.20.356, cf. 11.155, Il.21.56, *Ep.Jud.*6; Ἀΐδης δ' ἔλαχε ζόφον ἠερόεντα obtained *the realms of gloom* for his share, Il.15.191, cf. Od.11.57, *h.Cer.*402, 446, etc.; γῆς ὑπὸ ζόφον A.*Pers.*839. 2. generally, *gloom, darkness*, Hes.*Sc.*227, Plb.18.20.7, Arist.*Mu.*$400^{a}8$, *Ep.Hebr.*12.18, Plu.*Alc.*28, Luc.*DMort.*15.2; χειμέριος ζ. *the gloom* of winter, Pi.*I.*4(3).18: metaph., τῆς ψυχῆς..ζ. Plu.2.48c. II. *the dark quarter*, i.e. *the West*, ἤδη γὰρ φάος οἴχεθ' ὑπὸ ζόφον Od.3.335; οὐ γὰρ ἴδμεν ὅπῃ ζ. οὐδ' ὅπῃ ἠώς 10.190; ποτὶ ζόφον, opp. πρὸς ἠῶ τ' ἠέλιόν τε, Il.12.240, Od.13.241, 9.26 (*the North* acc. to Str.10.2.12); Γαδείρων τὸ πρὸς ζόφον to *the west* of..., Pi.*N.*4.69.—Poet. and later Prose. (Prob. cogn. with ζέφυρος.)

**ζοφ-όω**, *darken*, Hld.2.15:—Pass., *to be* or *become dark*, γήρᾳ κανθὸν ἐζοφωμένος *AP*6.92 (Phil.); τὴν ὄψιν ἐζοφωμένος Ps.-Luc.*Philopatr.*

4. -ώδης, ες, = ζοφοειδής, οὖρον Hp.*Coac.*570; θάλαττα Arist.*Pr.* 944$^b$22; ἀήρ ib.946$^a$34 (Sup.), cf. Vett.Val.312.32; [σελήνη] Thphr. *Sign.*12; Βόσπορος Str.1.2.9; Εὖρος App.*Hann.*20; *opaque*, Cleom. 1.4. -ωσις, εως, ἡ, *a darkening*, ἀέρος Sch.E.*Ph.*1534.

**ζόω**, v. ζῶ.

**ζῠγάδην** [ᾰ], Adv., (ζυγόν) *jointly, in pairs*, Ph.1.237, al., Phot., Suid.

**ζῠγάδιον**, τό, a kind of *shoe*, prob. in Suid. s. v. ξυρίδες.

**⊛ ζύγαινα** [ῠ], ης, ἡ, *the hammer-headed shark*, Epich.59, Arist.*HA* 506$^b$10, Philotim.ap.Gal.6.727, Ael.*NA*9.49, Opp.*H.*1.367.

**ζῠγάρχ-ης**, ου, ὁ, *leader of a line of horsemen*, Ascl.*Tact.*7.9, Ael. *Tact.*19.8:—hence -έω, Ascl. l. c. -ία, ἡ, *detachment of two chariots*, ib.8, Ael.*Tact.*22.2.

**⊛ ζῠγάστριον**, τό, Dim. of sq., Poll.7.79, 10.138.

**⊛ ζύγαστρον** [ῠ], τό, *chest, box* (κιβωτός, κυρίως δὲ ξυλίνη σορός, παρὰ τὸ ἐζυγῶσθαι, Phot.), S.*Tr.*692, E.ap.Phot., X.*Cyr.*7.3.1. 2. at Delphi, = γραμματοφυλάκιον, *SIG*241.49,146 (iv B.C.), *Delph.*3(2). 205 (iii B.C.), Phot. 3. in pl., *fastenings*, λάρνακος Sch.Theoc. 7.78.

**ζυγαστροφέω**, doubtful word in Sophr.90.

**ζῠγ-έω**, *march in line*, opp. στοιχεῖν (in file), Ascl.*Tact.*2.6, al. 2. *form a line*, of contingents, Plb.3.113.8. -ή, ἡ, *pair*, *PSI*3.225.4 (vi A.D.); *faggot*, ib.5.481.4 (v/vi A.D.). -ηδόν, Adv. *in pairs*, Hld.10.27.

**ζῠγηφόρος**, ον, poet. for ζυγοφόρος (q. v.), A.*Fr.*326, E.*Rh.*303.

**ζῠγία**, ἡ, *maple, Acer campestre*, Thphr.*HP*3.3.1, 5.3.3, Dicaearch. 2.2, Plin.*HN*16.67.

**ζῠγ-ιατής**, *jumentarius*, Gloss. -ίζω, = ζευγ-, Suid. -ικός, ή, όν, (ζυγός) *of* or *for a balance*, τὰ -κά Nicom.*Harm.*2. -ιμος, ον, = ζύγιος I, βοῦς Plb.34.8.9. -ινος, η, ον, *of the tree* ζυγία, Thphr. *HP*5.3.3. -ιον, τό, = ζυγόν III. 1, ὑπὸ τὰ ζ. Callix.1, cf. Aq., Sm. *Pr.*11.1. ⊛ -ιος, α, ον, also ος, ον E. (v. infr.), *IG*2$^2$.1604.71 (iv B.C.): (ζῠγόν):—*of* or *for the yoke*, esp. (sc. ἵππος) *draught-horse*, opp. σειραφόρος, E.*IA*221 (lyr.), Ar.*Nu.*122: c. gen., θηρῶν ζυγίους ζεύξασα σατίνας having yoked cars to *teams* of beasts, E.*Hel.*1310: as Subst., κατασκευάσαι.. ὁδὸν ζυγίοις πορευτήν *Milet.*3 No.149.45 (ii B.C.). II. epith. of Hera as patroness of marriage, A.R.4.96, Musae.275; also of other divinities, as Aphrodite, *IG*3.171, cf. *AP* 7.555 (Joann.), Hsch. III. ζύγιος, ὁ, = ζυγίτης, Poll.1.87,120; κώπη ζ. *IG*2$^2$. l. c., Polyaen.5.22.4 (pl.). IV. *of full weight*, νομίσματα *Stud.Pal.*20.121.18 (v A.D.). -ίς, ίδος, ἡ, = ἕρπυλλος, Dsc. 3.38, Philin.ap.Ath.15.681f. -ίσκον, τό, Dim. of ζύγιον, *IG*2$^2$. 1549.9. -ίτης [ῑ], ου, ὁ, *the rower who sat on the mid-most of the three banks*, like μεσόνεος, Sch.Ar.*Ra.*1106.

**ζῠγῖτις**, ιδος, fem. of ζύγιος II, Nicom.ap.Phot.*Bibl.*p.144 B.

**ζυγκλεῖ**· μύει, ὁρμᾷ, σκυθρωπάζει, Hsch.

**ζῠγο-δέσμιον**, τό, Dim. of sq., *PLond.*1821.113. -δεσμον, τό, (ζυγόν I) *yoke-band*, i. e. a band for fastening the yoke to the pole, ζ. ἅμα ζυγῷ ἐννεάπηχυ Il.24.270, cf. *PFay.*121.5 (i/ii A.D.); of the Gordian knot, Plu.*Alex.*18, etc.: pl., ζυγόδεσμα Procl.*H.*1.31, *AP* 9.155 (Agath.), 741, etc.:—also -δεσμος, ὁ, Artem.2.24, Them.*Or.* 2.30b. -δέτης, ου, ὁ, (δέω A) = foreg., Hsch. -ειδής, ές, *like a yoke*, ὀστᾶ Gal.14.721. -εις· βούτυρος, Cyr. (ζυγήσεις· βότρυς Hsch.). -κέφᾰλον, τό, *tax on land at so much a jugum*, *CIG*2712. 5 (Mylasa, v A.D.), Just.*Nov.*17.8. -κρούστης, ου, ὁ, *one who uses a false balance*, Artem.4.57. -λωρον, τό, = ζυγόδεσμος, Sch.rec.A. *Pers.*188. ⊛ -μᾰχέω, *struggle with one's yoke-fellow*, ἵπποι ἐν ἅρματι ζ. App.*Syr.*33. 2. generally, *struggle, quarrel*, τινι *Com.Adesp.* 207, cf. Hyp.*Fr.*245, Procop.Gaz.p.141 B.; πορνοβοσκοῖς.. διὰ βίου ζ. Phld.*Herc.*223.8; περί τινος D.39.6; πρὸς τὴν τύχην Men.673; πρὸς οἰκέτην Plu.*Cat.Ma.*21, cf. Chor. in *Hermes* 17.235; ὑπὲρ ὀνόματος Gal. 10.963. -μᾰχία, ἡ, *quarrelling, strife*, Aristaenet.1.2.

**⊛ ζῠγόν**, τό, also **ζυγός**, ὁ (in various senses), *h.Cer.*217, Pl.*Ti.*63b, Theoc.30.29, Lxx *Ge.*27.40, al., Plb.4.82.2, *Ev.Matt.*11.29, Jul.*Or.*5. 173a, etc.: rarely in pl., ζυγοί Lxx *Pr.*11.1, Sch.Th.1.29: Delph. **δυγός** (q. v.). I. *yoke* of a plough or carriage, ζ. ἱππεῖον Il.5.799, 23.392; ὑπὸ ζυγὸν ἤγαγεν ἵππους 5.731, cf. Od.3.383; ἐπὶ ζυγὸν αὐχένι θεῖναι βουσί Hes.*Op.*815, cf. 581; ὑπὸ ζυγόφιν (i. e. ζυγοῦ) λύον ἵππους Il.24.576: prov., τὸν αὐτὸν ἕλκειν ζ. 'to be in the same boat', Aristaenet.2.7, Zen.3.43; ταὔτ' ἐμοὶ ζ. τρίβεις Herod.6.12. 2. metaph., ἐπὶ ζυγὸς αὐχένι κεῖται *h.Cer.*217; ἐχθροῖσιν ὑπὸ ζυγὸν αὐχένα θήσω Thgn.1023; ἐπαυχένιον λαβεῖν ζ. Pi.*P.*2.93; δούλιον ζ. *the yoke* of slavery, Hdt.7.8.γ', A.*Th.*75 (pl.), 471. etc.; δουλείας, ἀνάγκης ζ., S.*Aj.*944, E.*Or.*1330; ὑπὸ ζυγῷ λόφον δικαίως εἶχον S.*Ant.*291; ἐπιτιθέναι τινὶ ζυγὰ τοῦ μή.. so as to prevent.., X.*Cyr.*3.1.27; ζυγῷ ζυγῆναι Pl.*R.*508a; ἄγειν ὑπὸ τὸν ζ. τινάς Plb.4.82.2, cf. D.H.3.22; ὑπὸ τὸν ζ. ὑπαγαγεῖν D.C.*Fr.*36.10; ζυγὸν ὑποστῆναι D.H.10.20. II. *cross-bar* of the φόρμιγξ, Il.9.187. 2. ζυγὸς ἡ τῆς ἀμπέλου πρὸς τὴν χάρακα συζυγία *Gp.*5.29.6. III. in pl., *thwarts* or *benches joining* the opposite sides of a ship, Od.9.99, 13.21, Hdt.2.96: rarely in sg., θοὸν εἰρεσίας ζυγόν S.*Aj.*249 (lyr.): metaph., of the seat of authority compared to the helmsman's seat, ἐς τὸ πρῶτον πόλεος ζ. E.*Ion* 595; ἐπεὶ δ' ἐπὶ ζυγοῖς καθέζετ' ἀρχῆς Id.*Ph.*74; σὺ ταῦτα φωνεῖς νερτέρᾳ προσήμενος κώπῃ, κρατούντων τῶν ἐπὶ ζυγῷ δορός; while on the *main thwart* sits authority, A.*Ag.*1618; also of a coachman's *seat, box*, *PMasp.*303.15 (vi A.D.). 2. in pl., *panels* of a door, *IG*1$^2$.372. 199, 2$^2$.1457.14, 1672.155; cf. ζεύγλιον. IV *beam of the balance*, ζυγὸν ταλάντου A.*Supp.*822 (lyr.), cf. Arist.*Mech.*850$^a$4: hence, *the balance itself* (cf. πῆχυς IV), αἴρειν τὸν ζυγόν Pl.*Ti.*63b; ἐν πλάστιγγι ζυγοῦ κεῖσθαι Id.*R.*550e; ζυγῷ or ἐν τῷ ζ. ἱστάναι, Lys.10.18, Pl. *Prt.*356b; ζυγὸν ἱστάναι D.*Prooem.*55: in pl., Id.25.46, *SIG*975.39 (Delos, iii B.C.): prov., ζ. μὴ ὑπερβαίνειν Pythag.ap.D.L.8.18. b. the constellation *Libra*, Hipparch.3.1.5, Ph.1.28, Man.2.137, etc.; ζ. Ἀφροδίτης Porph.*Antr.*22. V. καρχασίου the *yard-arm* at the mast head, Pi.*N.*5.51, cf. Ach.Tat.5.16. VI. *cross-strap* of a sandal, Ar.*Lys.*417, Poll.7.81; ζυγός, ὁ, Phot. VII. *pair*, κλεινὸν ζυγόν, of persons, E.*Hel.*392; κατὰ ζυγά *in pairs*, Arist.*HA* 544$^a$5, Theoc.13.32. VIII. *rank* or *line* of soldiers, opp. *file* (στοῖχος), ἐν τῷ πρώτῳ ζ. ἐμάχοντο τέσσαρες Th.5.68; ὁ ζυγός Polyaen.4.4.3 (τὰ ζυγά 2.10.4); κατὰ ζυγόν *line with line*, Plb.1.45.9; κατ' ἄνδρα καὶ ζ. Id.3.81.2; esp. *front rank*, Ael.*Tact.*7.1, Arr.*Tact.*8.1; also of the Chorus, Poll.4.108. IX. ζυγὰ ἢ ἄζυγα *even* or odd, a game, Sch.Ar.*Pl.*817. X. measure of land, *SIG*963.13 (Amorgos, iv B.C.).

**ζῠγοποι-έω**, *make yokes*, wrongly cited by Poll.7.115 fr. Ar.*Pl.* 513. ⊛ -ός, ὁ, *maker of yokes*, Pherecr.130.

**ζῠγός**, ὁ, v. sub ζυγόν.

**ζῠγοσταθμ-έω**, = ζυγοστατέω, Tz.ad Lyc.270, 275 (both Pass.). -ος, ὁ, *balance*, Plu.2.928b.

**⊛ ζῠγοστᾰσ-ία**, ἡ, *weighing*, *PGrenf.*2.46$^a$8 (ii A.D.). ⊛ -ιον, τό, *weigh-house*, *CIG*3705 (Apollonia ad Rhyndacum), *JRS*2.87 (Antioch in Pisidia): pl., *IGRom.*4.657 (Acmonia); -στασίου [τέλος] *weighing*-toll, *BGU*337.20 (ii/iii A.D.). 2. *zygostasii munus*, office of ζυγοστάτης, *Cod.Just.*11.28.1.

**⊛ ζῠγοστᾰτ-έω**, *weigh by the balance, weigh*, ὥσπερ ἐν τρυτάνῃ Luc. *Hist.Conscr.*49; τινὰς πρὸς τὸν Τιμάρχου βραχίονα Alciphr.2.2. b. *act as libripens*, Mitteis *Chr.*316 ii 4 (ii A.D.). II. Pass., *to be in equilibrium*, Plb.6.10.7; ἐζυγοστατεῖτο αὐτοῖς ὁ πόλεμος Id.1.20. 5. -ημα, ατος, τό, *balance*, Eust.665.29. ⊛ -ης, ου, Dor. -ᾱς, ὁ, *public weigher*, *Cod.Just.*10.73.2 (iv A.D.), Artem.2.37: metaph., ὀρθὸς ὢν ζ., of Zeus, Cerc.4.33.

**ζῠγό-ταυρον**, τό, *yoke, pair of oxen*, *PFlor.*167.3, 256.3 (iii A.D.). -τράχηλον [ᾰ], τό, *neck-piece of yoke*, *PLond.*3.1177.190 (ii A.D.). -τρῡτάνη [ᾰ], ἡ, *balance*, Phot. s. v. ζυγός.

**ζῠγουλκός**, όν, *drawing the yoke*, βόες Moschio Trag.6.26.

**ζῠγόφιν**, Ep. gen. of ζυγόν, Il.24.576; ὑπὸ ζ. Poet.ap.D.Chr.32.85.

**ζῠγοφορ-έω**, *weigh*, in Pass., Hsch. II. v. ζευγοφορέομαι. -ος, ον, *bearing the yoke*, πῶλος E.*HF*121 (lyr., -ηφόρος codd.); ἵπποι Plu. 2.524a: elsewh. in poet. form **ζυγηφόρος** (q. v.).

**ζῠγόω**, (ζυγόν) *yoke, join together*, [σκέλη] Sor.1.84; ζ. κιθάραν *put the cross-bar to* the lyre, Luc.*DDeor.*7.4, *DMar.*1.4; κανόνες ἐζυγωμένοι δύο Agatho 4.2, cf. Lxx *Ez.*41.26. 2. *close*, χείλη ῥαφαῖς Paul.Aeg.6.67 (prob.); *shut off*, Hp.*Cord.*12 (Pass.). 3. metaph., *bring under the yoke, subdue*, A.*Fr.*115.

**ζύγρα**, ἡ, dialectic form for διύγρα (sc. χώρα), *marsh-land*, Eust. 295.28.

**ζυγωγόν**, glossed ἧπαρ, dub. l. in *PLond.*1821.50 (prob. ζυγωτόν = συκωτόν).

**ζῠγ-ώδης**, ες, f. l. for ζυγάδην (wh. is restored fr. Lyd.*Mens.*2.12), Ph.1.22. -ωθρίζω, *weigh, examine*, Ar.*Nu.*745, acc. to Sch.: but acc. to Poll.10.26 from **ζύγωθρον** (*the bar of a door*), *lock up*. -ωμα, ατος, τό, *bolt, bar*, Plb.7.16.5. b. *cross-rod*, Apollod.*Poliorc.*177. 8. II. = ζυγόν III. 1, Sch.Th.1.29. III. *arcus zygomaticus*, which connects the cranial with the facial bones, Gal.2.437,746, Poll.2.85; cf. ζυγοειδής. IV. = ζυγόν II, Ptol.*Alm.*7.5. V. *canal-lock*, *PFlor.*273.20 (iii A.D.). -ωσις, εως, ἡ, (cf. ζυγόν IV) *a balancing*, κατὰ τὴν ζύγωσιν, of heavy oars, Callix.1. -ωτός, ή, όν, (ζυγόω) *yoked*, ἅρματα ζ. S.*El.*702.

**ζύθιον**, τό, Dim. of ζῦθος, = ἀλφίτου πόσις, Hsch. (ἡ ἐξ ἀ. π. Gramm. in Reitzenstein *Ind.Lect.Rost.*1892/3 p.12.)

**⊛ ζῡθοπώλης**, ου, ὁ, *beer-seller*, *POxy.*85 iv 4 (iv A.D.):—fem. only in form **ζυτόπωλις** (q. v.).

**ζῦθος**, ου, ὁ (also -ος, τό, Thphr. (v. infr.), D.S. (v. infr.)), an Egyptian kind of *beer*, brewed with barley, Thphr.*CP*6.11.2, Dsc.2. 87, Str.17.1.14, D.S.1.34, etc.; cf. ζῦτος. 2. *beer* of northern nations, Posidon.15 J., Str.3.3.7, D.S.5.26. (The word was used in Egypt acc. to Thphr. l. c., etc.: written ζυτο- (q. v.) in the older Pap.: freq. accented ζύθος in codd., but ζῦθος Phot., ζῡ- in verse, Poet.ap.D.Chr.32.82, Colum.10.116.)

**ζύμ-η** [ῡ], ἡ, *leaven*, Arist.*GA*755$^a$18, Lxx *Ex.*12.15; *beer-yeast*, *PTeb.*375.27 (ii A.D.), etc.: metaph., of *corruption, falsehood*, *Ev. Matt.*16.6, etc. (ζῡ-μᾱ or ζῡσ-μᾱ, cf. Skt. *yauti* 'mix', Skt. *yūs*, Lat. *jūs* 'soup', Lett. *jaut* 'stir dough', *javs* 'dough'.) -ήεις, εσσα, εν, *leavened*, ἄρτος Hsch. -ίζω, *to be like leaven*, τὴν ὀσμήν Dsc.2. 80. -ίτης ἄρτος [ῑ], ὁ, *leavened* bread, Cratin.99 (prob. l.), Hp. *Vict.*2.42, 3.75, X.*An.*7.3.21, Lxx *Le.*7.3(13), Sor.1.94, Philostr.*Im.* 2.26. -ίωσις, εως, ἡ, = ζύμωσις, subject of lost work by Zos. Alch.p.216 B.

**ζῡμοειδής**, ές, = ζυμώδης, Sch.Orib.4 p.526 D.

**⊛ ζῡμ-ουργός**, ὁ, *maker of leaven*, *PAmh.*2.128.29 (ii A.D.), *PFay.* 333 (ii A.D.). ⊛ -όω, (ζύμη) *leaven*, μικρὰ ζύμη ὅλον τὸ φύραμα ζ. 1 *Ep. Cor.*5.6:—Pass., *to be leavened, ferment*, Lxx *Ex.*12.34,39, Plu.2. 659b, etc.; of digestion, τὰ μέλανα -οῦται Hp.*Acut.*61; [κοιλίη] ἐζυμωμένη *in a ferment*, Id.*VM*11. 2. *cause to effervesce*, γῆν Gal.10. 964, Aët.1 *Praef.*:—Pass., ζυμουμένη [χύτρα] Alex.124.8. -ώδης, ες, *like leaven*, Arist.*GA*755$^a$23. -ωμα, ατος, τό, *fermented mixture*, Pl.*Ti.*74d; ζύμωμα χθονός, of a fungus, Nic.*Al.*521, cf. 525 cum Sch. ad loc. -ωσις, εως, ἡ, *fermentation*, Pl.*Ti.*66b, Plu.2.659b, Gal.16.

661; ἥπατος ζύμωσις *a swelling* of the liver, Hp.*Epid.*4.8. **-ωτικός**, ή, όν, *causing to ferment*, τινος Diocl.*Fr.*118. **-ωτός**, ή, όν, *fermented, leavened*, Lxx*Ex.*13.7, al.

**ζῦτᾶς**, ᾶ, ὁ, *brewer*, *BGU*1087 ii 2 (iii A.D.).

**ζυτηρά**, ἡ, *tax on brewing*, *PCair.Zen.*176.30 (iii B.C.), *PTeb.*40.4 (ii B.C.).

**ζῦτο-ποιέω**, *brew beer*, *PCair.Zen.*199.9 (iii B.C.). **-ποιΐα**, ἡ, *brewing*, *Ostr.Fay.*10.4 (i A.D.). **-ποιός**, ὁ, *brewer*, *PPetr.*3p.85 (iii B.C.), al., *PTeb.*5.173 (ii B.C.), etc. **-πώλιον**, τό, *beer-shop*, *PCair.Zen.*189.6 (iii B.C.), al., *PRyl.*127.12 (i A.D.). **-πωλις**, ιδος, ἡ, *woman who sells beer*, *BGU*38.18 (ii/iii A.D.).

**ζῦτος**, ὁ, = ζῦθος, *PCair.Zen.*176.4 (iii B.C.), al., *PPetr.*3p.327 (iii B.C.), *UPZ*149.14 (iii/ii B.C.), *PMag.Par.*1.908, *OGI*200.16 (Axum, iv A.D.):—also **ζῦτος**, εος, τό, *PHib.*1.113.6 (iii B.C.), Glauc.ap. *POxy.*1802.42.

**ζῦτουργεῖον**, τό, *brewery*, *PPetr.ined.* iii No.124 (iii B.C.), v. indicem.

⊛ **ζῶ** (contr. fr. ζώω: ζάω only in Gramm., *EM*410.38), ζῇς (Choerob. *in Theod.*2.28), ζῇ, ζῆτε (but ζῇς, ζῇ acc. to Anon.ap.*EM*410.48, Sophronius ap.Choerob. *in Theod.*2.416); imper. ζῆ S.*Fr.*167, E.*IT* 699, ζῆθι (as if from ζῆμι, cf. *EM* l.c.) Pherecr.11 D., Men.*Mon.* 191, *AP*10.43, σύ-ζηθι Philem.ap.*Et.Gen.* s.v. ζῆ; opt. ζῴην; inf. ζῆν: impf. ἔζων S.*El.*323, Ar.*Ra.*1072; ἔζην in most codd. of D.24.7 is a form suggested by ἔζης, ἔζη; 3 pl. ἔζων Ar.*V.*709, Pl.*Lg.*679c: fut. ζήσω Ar.*Pl.*263, Pl.*R.*465d, Men.*Mon.*186, [Epich.]267, ζήσομαι Hp.*Nat.Puer.*30, D.25.82, Arist.*Pol.*1327b5: aor. 1 ἔζησα Hp. *Prog.*1, *AP*7.470 (Mel.), Plu.2.786a, etc.: pf. ἔζηκα Arist.*Metaph.* 1048b25, D.H.5.68, etc.: but in Att. aor. and pf. are mostly supplied from βιόω. Exc. part. ζῶντος, Il.1.88, Hom. always uses the Ep. Ion. Lyr. pres. **ζώω** (also in Pi.*O.*2.25, Hdt.7.46, al., Diog.Apoll.4, Herod.2.29, *IG*12(8).600.9 (Thasos), and Trag. (in lyr.), S.*El.*157, *OC*1213, cf. *BCH*47.95 (Cavalla), *Bull.Soc.Arch.Bulg.*7.13 (Macedonia); subj. ζώῃ *IG*12(8).262.12 (Thasos, v B.C.), cf. *Schwyzer*339, al. (Delph.), contr. ζῷ *Berl.Sitzb.*1927.161 (Cyrene); Cret. δώω *Leg. Gort.*4.21, al.); inf. ζωέμεναι, -έμεν, Od.7.149, 24.436: impf. ἔζωον 22.245, Hes.*Op.*112, Hdt.4.112; Ion. ζώεσκον Hes.*Op.*90, Bion 1.30: aor. 1 ἔζωσα (ἐπ-) Hdt.1.120; inf. ζῶσαι *IG*11(4).1299 (Delos): pf. part. ἐζωκότα *BMus.Inscr.*1009 (Cyzicus); inf. ζόειν Semon.1.17: impf. ζόεν *AP*13.21 (Theodorid.). (Root gʷiē-, gʷiō- also in βίος and ὑγιής (q.v.).)

I. prop. of animal life, *live*, Hom. (v. infr.), etc.; also of plants, τὸ ζῆν κοινὸν εἶναι φαίνεται καὶ τοῖς φυτοῖς Arist.*EN*1097b33; ἐλέγχιστε ζωόντων vilest *of living men*, Od.10.72; ζώειν καὶ ὁρᾶν φάος ἠελίοιο Il. 24.558; ζῶντος καὶ ἐπὶ χθονὶ δερκομένοιο 1.88, cf. Od.16.439; ζῶν καὶ βλέπων A.*Ag.*677; ζώει τε καὶ ἔστιν Od.24.263; ζώντων καὶ ὄντων D. 18.72; τοῦ εἶναί τε καὶ ζῆν ἕνεκα Pl.*R.*369d; ζῶσα πόλις καὶ ἐγρηγορυῖα Id.*Lg.*809d; ζῶν καὶ ἔμψυχος Id.*Phdr.*276a; ῥεῖα ζώοντες *living* at ease, of the gods, Il.6.138, al.; ζῶν κατακαυθῆναι to be burnt *alive*, Hdt.1.86: c. acc. temp., ζ. ἤματα πάντα *h.Ven.*221, etc.; ὀλίγα ἔτεα Hdt.3.22: c. dat. modi, δμῶες.. ἄλλα τε πολλὰ οἷσίν τ' εὖ ζώουσι whereby men *live* in comfort, Od.17.423, cf. D.60.5; κοράκων πονηρίᾳ Ar.*Th.*868; ἐπὶ τοῖς αἰσχίστοις ἔργοις, ἐπὶ τοῖς παροῦσιν ἀγαθοῖς, And.1.100, Isoc.10.18; also ζῆν ἀπό τινος *to live on* a thing, Thgn. 1156, Hdt.1.216, 2.36, 4.22, Ar.*Pax*850, etc.; ἔκ τινος Id.*Ec.*591, D. 57.36, 1*Ep.Cor.*9.14: c. part., ζῆν συκοφαντῶν And.1.99; ἐργαζόμενοι Arist.*Pol.*1292b27: c. dat. commodi, ζῆν ἑαυτῷ *for* oneself, dub. l. in E.*Ion*646, cf. Ar.*Pl.*470, Men.507; τὸ ζῆν, = ζωή, A.*Pr.*681, Pl. *Phd.*77d (without Art. εἰς ἕτερον ζ. Id.*Ax.*365d); διὰ παντὸς τοῦ ζῆν *Ep.Hebr.*2.15; also, *a living*, τὸ ζ. οὐκ ἔχομεν *OGI*515.57 (Mylasa, iii A.D.); ζήτω ὁ βασιλεύς *long live* the king, Lxx 1*Ki.*10.24; βασιλεῦ, εἰς τὸν αἰῶνα ζῆθι ib.*Da.*3.9; asseverations, ζῶ ἐγώ, καὶ ζῶν τὸ ὄνομά μου, καί.. ib.*Nu.*14.21; ζῇ κύριος, εἰ.., ὅτι.., ib.1*Ki.*19.6, 29.6; ζῇ ἡ ψυχή σου, εἰ οἶδα ib.17.55. 2. = βιόω, *live, pass one's life*, c. acc. cogn., ζώεις δ' ἀγαθὸν βίον Od.15.491; ζ. βίον μοχθηρόν S.*El.*599, cf. E.*Med.*249, Ar.*V.*506, etc.; ζόην τὴν αὐτήν Hdt.4.112, cf. Pl.*R.*344e; τὸν βίον ἀσφαλῶς Philem.213.5; ἥδιστον ἀνθρώπων βίον S.*Fr.*583.4; νυμφίων βίον Ar.*Av.*161; also ζ. ἀβλαβεῖ βίῳ S.*El.*650, cf. *Tr.*168; εὖ ζῆν Id.*Ph.*505; κακῶς Id.*OC*799; ζ. δοῦλος Id.*OT*410; ἐκ τῶν ἄλλων ὧν ἔζης from the other *acts of your life*, D.21.134; ποιεῖσθαι φθόνον ἐξ ὧν ζῇς ib.196. 3. aor. 1 ἔζησα, causal, *quicken*, ἐν τῇ ὁδῷ σου ζῆσόν με Lxx*Ps.*118(119).37, al. II. *live* in the fullest sense, δι' ὧν ζῆν ἐπιστάμεθα X.*Mem.*3.3.11, etc.; βιοὺς μὲν ἔτη τόσα, ζήσας δὲ ἔτη ἑπτά D.C.69.19; in religious or mystical sense, *Ep.Rom.*7.9, al., cf. Ramsay *Cities and Bishoprics* 2 p.565 (Phryg.); θεὸς ζῶν Lxx*De.*5. 26(23), etc.: freq. metaph. of things, *to be in full vigour*, ὄλβος ζώει μάσσων Pi.*I.*3.5; ἄτης θύελλαι ζῶσι A.*Ag.*819; ζῶντι χρώμενος ποδί S.*Fr.*790; [μαντεῖα] αἰεὶ ζῶντα περιποτᾶται Id.*OT*482; ἀεὶ ζῇ ταῦτα [νόμιμα] Id.*Ant.*457; τὰς ξυμφορὰς τῶν βουλευμάτων ζώσας μάλιστα *have* most *living power*, Id.*OT*45; λόγια ζῶντα *Act.Ap.*7.38; χρόνῳ τῷ ζῶντι καὶ παρόντι S.*Tr.*1169; ζῶσα φλόξ *living* fire, E.*Ba.*8; ὕδωρ ζῶν *spring* water, Lxx*Nu.*5.17 (and metaph., *Ev.Jo.*4.10); ζώσης φωνῆς Cic.*Att.*2.12.2.

**ζωαγρία**, ἡ, = ζωγρεῖον, Ael.*NA*13.10.

**ζωάγρια**, ων, τά, (ζωός, ἀγρέω, orig. *ransom paid for a prisoner taken alive*) *reward for life saved*, ζωάγρι' ὀφέλλεις Od.8.462; δῶρα λάμψονται ζωάγρια Κροίσου Hdt.3.36; Θέτι.. ζωάγρια τίνειν Il.18.407, cf. Call.*Fr.*162, *AP*6.220.15 (Diosc.); rare in Prose, Demetr.Lac. *Herc.*1014.49; also, *offerings* to Aesculapius and other gods *for recovery from illness*, *IG*14.967a5: c. gen., νούσων ibid.; ζ. ἀποθύειν Ael.*NA*11.31: sg. in Orac.ap.Plu.*Arat.*53:—a form **ζώγρια**, τά, Suid.:—Adj. **ζωάγριος**, ον, ζ. μοι χάριτας ὀφλήσεις you will owe me thanks *for a life saved*, Babr.50.15.

**ζωαλκής**, ές, *life-preserving*, χείρ, of Παιάν, *IG*14.1015.

**ζῳάριον**, τό, Dim. of ζῷον, *Sammelb.*5224.57, Sch.A.R.1.1265, 3.276.

**ζωάρκεια**, ἡ, *means of subsistence*, Sch.E.*Hec.*362: **ζωαρκία**, Anon. *Prog.* in Rh.1.599 W.: **ζωαρκέω**, *support life*, Gramm. in Reitzenstein *Ind.Lect.Rost.*1892/3 p.10.

**ζωαρκής**, ές, *life-supporting*, αὐγή *Milet.*6.18 (ii A.D.), cf. Procl.*H.* 1.2, Nonn.*D.*25.178; χρεία *PLond.*5.1729.17, al. (vi A.D.); τὰ ζ. *the necessaries of life*, Phot.

**ζῴαρχος**, ον, *commander of one elephant*, Ascl.*Tact.*9.1, Ael.*Tact.* 23.1.

**ζωγάνης**, ὁ, *slave-king* at festival in Babylon, Beros.3.

**ζώγη**, a kind of *plant*, Hsch.

**ζωγλύφος** [ῠ], = ζῳογλ-, Mitteis *Chr.*129.15 (ii B.C.); recommended by Philem.Lex. (cf. *Philol.*57.353 sqq.) in Reitzenstein *Gesch.d.Gr. Etym.*p.394.

**ζωγονέω**, = ζῳογονέω, of a *living* tree, *POxy.*1188.4 (i A.D.):—Pass., S.E.*M.*1.264 (s.v.l.).

**ζωγορίτης**· ὁ ὀπὸς τοῦ ὀποβαλσάμου, Hsch.

**ζωγράφ-εῖον**, τό, *painter's studio*, Plu.2.471f. **-έω**, *paint from life, paint*, τινα Pl.*R.*598b, etc.:—Pass., Id.*Cra.*434b: metaph., ἡδοναὶ.. ἐζωγραφημέναι Id.*Phlb.*40b; ὀνείρους ζ. Porph.*Chr.*23. II. *adorn with paint*, τὰς ληκύθους Ar.*Ec.*996; τὰς ὀφρῦς ἀσβόλῳ Alex. 98.16, cf. Nicostr.ap.Stob.4.23.62. III. generally, *adorn*, κῆπον σὺν τοῖς φυτοῖς *Arch.Pap.*2.449. ⊛ **-ημα**, ατος, τό, *a picture*, Pl.*Phlb.* 39d, *Cra.*430b sq. ⊛ **-ητός**, ή, όν, *painted, parti-coloured*, Hsch. s.v. ποικίλον. ⊛ **-ία**, ἡ, *art of painting*, Democr.28a, Pl.*Phdr.*275d, X.*Mem.*1.4.3: metaph., φυσικὴ ζ. Secund.*Sent.*14. II. *painting*, τῶν παρειῶν v.l. in Philostr.*Ep.*22 (cod. Barocc.50); τοῦ στύλου *IGRom.*1.1272 (Egypt, ii A.D.). 2. metaph., ἐπὶ σκιᾷ (sc. οὐσίᾳ) ζωγραφία καὶ τὸ φαίνεσθαι Plot.6.3.8. **-ίδες**, *picturae*, *Gloss.* **-ικός**, ή, όν, *skilled in painting*, Pl.*Tht.*145a, X.*Smp.*4. 21: ἡ -κή (sc. τέχνη) *the art of painting*, D.S.14.46; *connected with painting, used by painters*, γένη *BGU*10.11 (ii A.D.); ἀσβολή Dsc.5. 162. Adv. -κῶς S.E.*M.*11.255. ⊛ **-ος**, ὁ, (ζωός or ζωή, γράφω) *one who paints from life* or *from nature*, Hdt.2.46, Pl.*Grg.*448c, 453c, *Lg.*656e, etc.: metaph., πολιτειῶν ζ. Id.*R.*501c: generally, *painter*, Luc.*Herod.*4, *Epigr.*41. (ζωγρ- without iota, *PSI*4.346, 407 (iii B.C.), *SIG*682.3 (ii B.C.), Pap. in *Abh.Berl.Akad.*1904(2).6 (ii B.C.), *EM* 412.53: so ζωγραφία *SIG*960.13 (ii B.C.), Phld.*Rh.*2.166 S.)

**ζωγρ-εία**, v. ζωγρία. **-εῖον** (sts. written **ζώγριον** as in Porph. *Gaur.*14.4), τό, *place for keeping animals, a menagerie*, Str.12.3.30 (pl.), Epict.*Gnom.*62 (pl.), Porph.*Sent.*28; *cage*, Aq.*Je.*5.27; *trap*, Onos.11.3; *fish-pond*, Plu.2.89a, Ael.*NA*11.34, Xenocr.34. II. pl., ζωγρεῖα, τά, = ζωάγρια, Hld.8.17. **-εύς**, έως, ὁ, dub. l. (for ζῷον?) in Gal.4.497 (*BpW*36.799). **-εύω**, = ζωγρέω, Polyaen.4. 3.27 (Pass.). ⊛ **-έω**, (ζωός, ἀγρέω) *take, save alive, take captive* instead of killing, ζώγρει, Ἀτρέος υἱέ, σὺ δ' ἄξια δέξαι ἄποινα Il.6.46, cf. 10.378, Hdt.1.86, etc.; εἷλε.. καὶ ἐζώγρησε Id.3.52; τοὺς μὲν ἀπέκτειναν, τινὰς δὲ καὶ ἐζώγρησαν Th.2.92; πλὴν ὅσον ἐκ τριῶν νεῶν οὓς ἐζώγρησαν Id.7.23; πλὴν μηδαμῇ μηδαμῶς ζωγροῦντας provided that they do not *spare* him *alive*, Pl.*Lg.*868c; opp. διαφθείρειν, ἀποκτεῖναι, Plb.3.84.10, Lxx*Nu.*31.18: metaph., ἀνθρώπους ἔσῃ ζωγρῶν *Ev.Luc.* 5.10; of ships, ἃς ἐζώγρησεν αὐτάνδρους Charito 7.6:—Pass., Hdt.1. 66, 5.77. II. *restore to life and strength, revive*, περὶ δὲ πνοιὴ Βορέαο ζώγρει ἐπιπνείουσα Il.5.698 (quoted by Aret.*CA*2.3); *preserve alive*, ζώγρει, δέσποτ' ἄναξ, τὸν σὸν ναετῆρα *Epigr.Gr.*841.7 (Thrace, ii A.D.). **-ία**, Ion. -ίη, ἡ, *taking alive*, ζωγρίῃ λαβεῖν or αἱρέειν, = ζωγρεῖν, Hdt.6.28, 37; συλλαβεῖν *SIG*700.30 (Macedonia, ii B.C.) ζωγρίᾳ ἐγκρατὴς or κύριος γενέσθαι τινός, Plb.1.9.8, 1.79.4; ζωγρίᾳ ἀνάγεσθαι or εἰσανάγεσθαι, Str.11.11.6, Plb.1.82.2; ζ. ἀποβαλεῖν τινα to lose him *by his being captured*, ib.15.2, Str.8.4.2; ζ. ἁλῶναι Plb.5. 86.5. **-ια**, τά, v. ζωάγρια. **-ιον**, τό, v. ζωγρεῖον. **-ίας**, ου, ὁ, *one taken alive*, ζωγρίαν συλλαμβάνειν, ἑλεῖν τινα, Ctes.*Fr.*29.3, 9, Zos.1. 51; οὐ κατελίπομεν ζωγρίαν Lxx*De.*2.34; ζωγρίας ἐλήφθη D.S.25.10; ζωγρίας ἔλαβε δισχιλίους ibid.; ζωγρίαι ἑάλωσαν Memn.56.3.

**ζώγρος**, ὁ, late form for ζωγρεῖον, *cage*, Phlp. *in de An.*106.12, Sch. Nic.*Th.*825. II. **ζῶγρον**· ἐγρήγορον, Hsch.

**ζωγύς**, v. ζωτύς.

**ζῳδαρίδιον**, τό, Dim. of ζῷον, *tiny figure*, Hero *Spir.*2.34 (p.312. 10 S.), *Wiener Denkschr.*47(4).59.

**ζῳδάριον**, τό, = foreg., Dim. of ζῷον, *animalcule*, as *a grub*, Alex. 140, Arist.*HA*557b1, etc. II. = ζῴδιον I, *IG*2².1491.4, *Inscr.Délos* 298 A 31 (iii B.C.), *SIG*²588.31 (Delos, ii B.C.), Hero *Spir.*2.34, *PMag. Leid.V.*10.1.

⊛ **ζῳδι-ακός**, ή, όν, (ζῴδιον) *of* or *for* ζῴδια, ζῳδιακός (with or without κύκλος), ὁ, *the Zodiac*, Eudem.ap.Theon.Sm.p.198 H., Phld.*Mus.*p.100 K., Cleom.1.4, al., D.S.2.31, etc.; also ἡ ζῳδιακή (sc. ὁδός) Man.4. 168. Adv. -κῶς Ptol.*Tetr.*18, Vett.Val.22.12, *PMich.* in *Class.Phil.* 22.13. **-άρχης**, ου, ὁ, = ζῳδιοκράτωρ, Dam.*Pr.*132.

**ζῳδιο-γλύφος** [ῠ], ον, (γλύφω) = ζῳογλύφος, Plu.2.712e. **-κράτωρ** [ᾰ], ορος, ὁ, *divinity presiding over the zodiac*, Dam.*Pr.*131, 351.

⊛ **ζῴδι-ον**, τό, Dim. of ζῷον II, *small figure, painted* or *carved*, Hdt. 1.70, *IG*1².374.288, 11(2).161 B 74 (Delos, iii B.C.), Plu.2.673f; *statuette*, *OGI*717.6 (Egypt, iii A.D.); of large figures, ζ. πηχῶν ἑκκαίδεκα D.S.1.47. II. Astron., *sign of the Zodiac*, διὰ μέσων τῶν ζ. Arist.*Metaph.*1073b20; ὁ κύκλος ὁ τῶν ζ. Id.*Mete.*343a24, cf. Plb.9.15.

7, Zeno *Stoic.*1.34, Hipparch.2.1.3, al., Gem.1.3, Autol.1.10, etc. :—also **ζῴδιον**, τό, Arat.544, Man.1.309, al. **-οποιός**, *signarius*, *Gloss.* **-οφόρος**, *signifer*, ib. ⊛ **-ωτός**, ή, όν, (ζῴδιον) = ζῳωτός, Poll.7.55, Hsch.

**ζώζω**, late spelling of σῴζω, *UPZ*81 ii 19, *Sammelb.*1060, etc.

**ζώειος**, α, ον, *animal*, opp. ἀνθρώπειος, ἵππειος, Dam.*Pr.*85.

⊛ **ζωή** (ζωιή (prob. an error) *SIG*577.34 (Milet., iii/ii B.C.)), Dor. **ζωά**: Ion. and poet. **ζόη**, Hdt.1.32, Herod.10.4, S.*Fr.*556, etc. (v. infr.), cf. *IG*9(1).86 (Hyampolis), Dor. **ζόα**: Aeol. **ζοΐα** Theoc. 29.5: ἡ:—*living*, i.e. one's *substance*, *property*, ἦ γάρ οἱ ζ. γ' ἦν ἄσπετος Od.14.96; τοὶ δὲ ζωὴν ἐδάσαντο ib.208; κατὰ ζωὴν φαγέειν 16.429; τὴν ζόην ποιέεσθαι or καταστήσασθαι ἀπὸ or ἐκ.. to get one's *living by*.., Hdt.8.105, cf. 2.36, Arist.*HA*608$^b$21; ἐξ ἁλὸς Theoc.*Beren.* 2. 2. after Hom., *life*, *existence*, opp. death, Tyrt.15.5, Pi.*N.*8.36, etc.; θανάτου πέρι καὶ ζωᾶς ib.9.29; οὐδὲν γὰρ ἄλγος οἷον ἡ πολλὴ ζόη S.*Fr.*556; ζόας (ζωᾶς codd.) βιοτά E.*HF*664 (lyr.); τοῦ βίου ζωή Pl. *Ti.*44c; ὁ τῆς ζ. χρόνος *SIG*1210 (Calymna), etc.: as a term of affection, ζωή *my life!* Juv.6.195: pl., ζόαι A.*Fr.*99.13; ζωαί Lxx*Ps.*62(63). 3(4); μετὰ τὴν μίαν ζ. πολλαὶ ζ. Dam.*Pr.*100; αἱ τῆς ψυχῆς ζ. καὶ δυνάμεις Iamb.*Comm.Math.*3. 3. *way of life*, ζόην ἔζωον τὴν αὐτὴν Hdt. 4.112, cf. 114. II. ζωή, = γραῦς II, *the scum on milk*, Eust.906.52; ζόη· τὸ ἐπάνω τοῦ μέλιτος, Hsch. [The form ζόη (paroxyt.) is required by the metre in trimeters in S.*Fr.*556, E.*Hec.*1108, and in lyrics S. *Fr.*592, E.*Med.*976, al., ζωή never: ζόη in other Poets, Call.*Fr.*114, Theoc.*Ep.*18.9, Herod.10.4.] (For the root, cf. ζῶ: fancifully connected with ζέω and ζητέω, Dam.*Pr.*81: in signf. II ζόη prob. fr. ζέω.)

**ζῳηδόν**, Adv., (ζῷον) *in the manner of beasts*, Plb.6.5.9.

**ζωηρός**, ά, όν, (ζωή) *living* and *giving life*, Suid.

**ζωητός**, ή, όν, *capable of being vitalized*, Dam.*Pr.*83 bis.

**ζωηφόρος**, ον, *life-bringing*, Them.*Or.*19.228d, Sch.Il.8.70; ζ. γραμμὴ [χειρός] line *of life*, in palmistry, *Cat.Cod.Astr.*7.238.

**ζωθάλμιος**, ον, (ζωή, θάλλω) *giving the bloom and freshness of life*, Pi.*O.*7.11.

⊛ **ζωθαλπής**, ές, (θάλπω) *warming* or *cheering life*, Nonn.*D.*1.454:—fem. **ζωθαλπις**, ιδος, ib.16.397 (v.l. -πέες).

**ζωθήκη**, ἡ, *small room wherein to rest by day*, opp. *dormitorium* (the bedroom), Plin.*Ep.*2.17.21; *zothecula*, ib.5.6.38. II. *niche* in a wall, prob. in Apollod.*Poliorc.*145.1 (pl.); used as a *chapel*, *Supp.Epigr.*2.849 (Alexandria); Lat. *zotheca*, Dessau *ILS*5449, al.

**ζωΐδιον**, τό, v. ζῴδιον ad fin.

**ζωϊκός**, ή, όν, (ζῷον) *of* or *proper to animals*, ἡ ζ. φύσις Arist.*PA* 645$^a$6, cf. 681$^b$4; ἡ ζ. ἱστορία a history *of animals*, ib.668$^b$30: περὶ ζωϊκῶν, title of lost work by Aristotle, Ath.7.328f. 2. *animal*, ψυχή, σῶμα, Porph.*Gaur.*1.2, 13.4; ζ. ἄνθρωπος Dam.*Pr.*200.

**ζώϊον**, τό, poet. for ζῷον, Semon.13.

⊛ **ζωϊτός** or **-τόν**, or ζωτ-, dub. sens. in *BCH*8.307 (Delos, iv B.C.).

⊛ **ζωκτήρ**, ῆρος, ὁ, dub. l. in *PLond.*2.236.8 (iii A.D., fort. ζωστήρ).

**ζῶμα**, ατος, τό, (ζώννυμι) *loin-cloth*, *drawers*, worn next the body in a boxing contest, ζ. δέ οἱ πρῶτον παρακάββαλεν Il.23.683; in war, 4.216; ἐπόμην σάκος οἷον ἔχων καὶ ζ. φαεινόν Od.14.482; ζώματα καὶ κυπάσσιδες Alc.15.6. 2. = ἔνδυμα, πεζοφόροις ζ. A.*Fr.*246. 3. *band* used in surgery, Hp.*Art.*14. II. = ζώνη, *woman's girdle*, ἔλυσε ζ. παρθένω Alc.*Supp.*8.10, cf. S.*El.*452, *IG*2$^2$.1514.15, Ar.*Fr.* 320.7, Men.432, *AP*6.272 (Pers.).—A non-Att. form **ζῶσμα** (v. Thom.Mag.p.165 R.) in Str.7.2.3, Sor.*Fasc.*45, al., Ach.Tat.1.1, 3. 21, Hld.3.1.

**ζωμάλμη**· ζωμὸς ἅλμης Θασίας, Sch.Suid. s.v. Θασίαν.

**ζωμ-άριον**, τό, Dim. of ζωμός, Democr.ap.Gal.14.94. ⊛ **-άρυστρον** [ᾰ], τό, = ζωμήρυσις, Sch.Ar.*Ach.*244 (v.l. -ος, ἡ); spelt **-ιστρον**, *POxy.*1289.3 (v A.D.). **-ευμα**, ατος, τό, *soup*, ζωμεύματα put by way of joke for ὑποζώματα νεώς (v. ὑπόζωμα fin.), Ar.*Eq.*279. **-εύω**, (ζωμός) *boil into soup*, κρεάδια ἐζωμευμένα Id.*Fr.*591, cf. Phryn.*PS* p.68 B.:—Pass., Hp.*Int.*35, Dsc.*Eup.*2.122: **-ευτός**, ή, όν, Orib.*Fr.* 119 (-ιστούς in Paul.Aeg.5.13 codd.). **-ήρῠσις**, εως, ἡ, (ἀρύω A) *soup-ladle*, Antiph.249, Philem.Jun.1.6, Anaxipp.6.1, *IG*2$^2$.1416 (iv B.C.), Ath.3.126d, *AP*6.101 (Phil.). **-ίδιον**, τό, Dim. of ζωμός, a *little sauce*, Ar.*Nu.*389.

**ζωμίλη**, ἡ, = ἄνηθον, Hsch., Phot.

**ζωμ-ίον**, τό, Dim. of ζωμός, *PTeb.*112.75 (ii B.C.). **-ιστός**, v. ζωμευτός.

**ζωμοποι-έω**, *make into soup* or *sauce*, Xenocr.54 (Pass.). **-ός**, όν, *making sauce*, Plu.2.218c. II. *serving to flavour soup*, of mushrooms, Dsc.4.82.

⊛ **ζωμός**, Dor. **δωμός** (q.v.), ὁ, *soup* or *sauce* to eat with meat, fish, etc., Ar.*Eq.*1174, *Pax*716, al.; οἱ ζ. οἱ τῶν πιόνων *soups* made from animals with soft fat (πιμελή), Arist.*HA*520$^a$8, cf. *PA*651$^a$29; ζ. μέλας black *broth* of the Spartans, Matro *Conv.*94, cf. Plu.*Lyc.*12: metaph., *bloodshed*, Thphr.*Char.*8.7. 2. Com. name for *fat*, *greasy fellow*, λιπαρὸς περιπατεῖ Δημοκλῆς, ζ. κατωνόμασται Anaxandr.34.5, cf. Aristopho 4.3. 3. in Alchemy, *wash*, Ps.-Democr.Alch.p.48 B., Zos.Alch.p.169 B.

**ζωμοτάρῑχος** [ᾰ], ὁ, *stewed salt-fish*, as a nickname, Alex.42.

**ζων-αῖοι**, οἱ, an order of divine beings (cf. ζώνη IV), Dam.*Pr.*130; ζ. κόσμος the world over which they preside, ib.206. Adv. **-ως** ib. 131. ⊛ **-άριον**, τό, Dim. of sq., Anon.*in Rh.*114.19, Hdn.*Epim.* 41. ⊛ **-η**, ἡ, (ζώννυμι) *belt*, *girdle*: I. prop. *the lower girdle worn by women* just *above the hips*, περὶ δὲ ζώνην βάλετ' ἰξυῖ Od.5.231, 10. 544, cf. Il.14.181, Hdt.1.51, etc.—Phrases: 1. λῦσε δὲ παρθενίην ζ. unloosed her maiden *girdle*, of the bridegroom, Od.11.245, cf. *Lyr. Alex.Adesp.*11.18, Plu.*Lyc.*15:—Med., of the bride, μούνῳ ἐνὶ ζώναν ἀνέρι λυσαμένα *AP*7.324 (hence ζώνη, abs., of *marriage*, E.*IT*204 (lyr.); of *sexual intercourse*, Philostr.*VA*7.6): but also, b. ζ. λῦσαι to loose *the girdle* for childbirth, Hyp.*Fr.*67; later λύσασθαι or ἀπολύσασθαι, Call.*Del.*209, Opp.*C.*3.56; so ζώναν κατατίθεσθαι Pi.*O.*6. 39. c. of men on a march, ζ. λύσασθαι to slacken one's *belt*, i.e. rest oneself, Hdt.8.120; ζ. ἀναλύεσθαι Call.*Del.*237. 2. of pregnant women, τέκνων ἤνεγχ' ὑπὸ ζώνην βάρος A.*Ch.*1000; πῶς γάρ σ' ἔθρεψεν ἐντὸς.. ζώνης; Id.*Eu.*608; τοῦτον.. ἔφερον ζώνης ὕπο E.*Hec.* 762; also ὑπὸ ζώνῃ θέσθαι to *conceive*, *h.Ven.*255. 3. prov., εἰς ζώνην δεδόσθαι to be given *for girdle-money* (as we should say, *pin-money*), of Oriental queens who had cities given them for their small expenses, X.*An.*1.4.9; ἣν [χώραν] καλεῖν.. ζ. τῆς βασιλέως γυναικός Pl.*Alc.*1.123b. II. man's *belt* (more freq. ζωστήρ), ἡ ζ. τοῦ Ὠρίωνος the three stars that form the *belt* of Orion, Arist.*Mete.* 343$^b$24; the *belt* of barbarians, in which they wore the dagger, X.*An.*1.6.10, 4.7.16, Theopomp.Hist.39a, Luc.*Anach.*33, Pl.*Hp.Mi.* 368c. b. belt used as a *purse*, *PRyl.*127.32 (i A.D.), *Ev.Matt.*10. 9, Plu.2.665b; ζ. χρυσίου Luc.*Fug.*31. 2. *part round which the girdle passed*, *waist*, Ἄρεϊ ζώνην ἴκελος Il.2.479 (misunderstood by Paus.9.17.3), cf. Il.11.234, Orph.*Fr.*168.28, Hp.ap.Erot. (also expld. as = ὀσφύς). 3. = Lat. *cingulum*, *belt* worn by Roman civil and military officers, [Demod.]5; = ἀξίωμα, Suid.; οἱ ὑπὸ ζώνην *soldiers*, Anon.ap.eund.s.v. αὐθεντήσαντα, cf. *Cod.Just.*1.5.12.6.11, Just.*Edict.* 13.26, *PLond.*5.1680.21 (vi A.D.). III. *anything that goes round like a belt*, Plu.2.935a, Luc.*Musc.Enc.*3; of the *girdle* of ocean, Porph. *Chr.*69. 2. *one of the zones of the terrestrial sphere*, *Stoic.*2.195, Posidon.ap.Str.2.2.2, *Placit.*2.12.1 (pl.), etc.; ζ. διακεκαυμένη, εὔκρατος, Str.1.2.24, 1.4.6. b. *one of the planetary spheres*, οἱ μὲν [τῶν πλανητῶν] ὑψηλὴν ζ. φέρονται οἱ δὲ ταπεινήν Diog.Oen.8, cf. Vett.Val.26.18, *Corp.Herm.*1.25. c. Astrol., = ζῴδιον, Porph. *in Ptol.*186. 3. in Archit., = διάζωμα, *frieze*, Paus.5.10.5. 4. Lat. *zona*, in Medic., *shingles*, Scrib.Larg.63, 247; cf. ζωστήρ III. 3. 5. *stripes* on fish, Ael.*NA*3.28, al. IV. pl., an order of divine beings presiding over, or *engirdled with* cosmic *zones*, opp. ἄζωνοι, Dam.*Pr.*96, Procl.*in Prm.*p.494 S. **-ιαῖος**, α, ον, *as thick as a girdle*, πάχος Ath.Mech.38.3. **-ιον**, τό, Dim. of ζώνη, Ar. *Lys.*72, Arist.*Mir.*832$^b$23, *AP*5.157 (Asclep.), Plu.2.154b.

**ζωνιοπλόκος**, ον, *plaiting* or *embroidering girdles*, Thom.Mag. p.168 R.

**ζωνῖτις**, ιδος, ἡ, *in belts* or *seams*, καδμεία Dsc.5.74; cf. ζώννυμι III. 2.

⊛ **ζώννῡμι** (ὑπο-ζωνύναι *IG*1$^2$.73.9), (παρα-) Pl.*R.*553c; **ζωννύω** Hp. *Mul.*1.68: impf. ἐζώννυον *Ev.Jo.*21.18: fut. ζώσω Lxx*Ex.*29.9, *Ev. Jo.* l.c.: aor. 1 ἔζωσα Od.18.76, Hp.*Art.*14: pf. ἔζωκα Paus.8.40.2, (δι-) D.H.2.5:—Med. (v. infr. II):—Pass., aor. 1 ἐζώσθην (δι-) Thphr.*Sign.*22: pf. ἔζωμαι (δι-) Th.1.6 ap.Phot., Suid. s.v. σέσωται, 3 sg. ἔζωται (δι-) *IG*2$^2$.1491.36, (ὑπ-) ib.1621.68, ἔζωσται Hp.*Art.* l.c.; also in med. sense (v. infr.): rare in Att., even in compds.:—*gird*, esp. *gird round the loins* for a pugilistic conflict (v. infr.), ἄγον ζώσαντες ἀνάγκῃ Od.18.76 (here only Act. in Hom.); ζῶσέ [μιν].. Ἀθήνη Hes.*Op.*72; ζ. τινά *hug* him in wrestling, Paus.8.40.2; ζ. γαῖαν, of Ocean, *AP*9.778 (Phil.); ζ. νῆα ὅπλῳ, = ὑποζώννυμι II, A.R.1.368: c. dupl. acc., ζ. τινὰ ζώνην Lxx*Le.*8.7, cf. 1*Ki.*17.39. II. Med., **ζώννῠμαι**, *gird oneself*, esp. of athletes, γυμνός, ζωννυμένων τῶν πρὶν ἐνὶ σταδίῳ *IG*7.52.6 (Megara, iv B.C.); τὼ δὲ ζωσαμένω βήτην ἐς μέσσον ἀγῶνα Il.23.685, cf. 710; ζώννυνταί τε νέοι καὶ ἐπεντύνονται ἄεθλα Od.24.89; Ὀδυσσεὺς ζώσατο μὲν ῥάκεσιν περὶ μήδεα 18.67, cf. Parth. 10.2. 2. generally, *gird up one's loins* for battle, ζώννυσθαι ἄνωγεν Ἀργείους Il.11.15; ζώννυσθαι [ζωστῆρι] 10.78: c. acc., ὅθι ζωννύσκετο μίτρην 5.857 (vulg.); ζώσατο δὲ ζώνην 14.181 (vulg.); χαλκὸν ζώννυσθαι 23.130; ἐς γόνυ μέχρι χιτῶνα ζώννυσθαι Call.*Dian.*12; χιτῶνα εἰς μηρὸν ἔζωστο Plu.*Ant.*4; for labour, Hes.*Op.*345; ἐπὶ βουσίν A.R.1.426, etc.; ζώννυσθαι τὰς κοιλίας ζώναις Theopomp.Hist. 39a. III. Pass., *to be fixed by means of girths*, Lxx 1*Ma.*6.37. 2. *to be formed in belts* or *seams*, καδμεία ἐζωσμένη (ἐξωσμ- codd.) prob. in Ps.-Democr.Alch.p.45 B. (cf. ζωνῖτις). (ζω(σ)- from I.-E. *yōs-*, cf. Lith. *júosti* 'to gird', *júostas*, Avest. *yāsta-*, = ζωστός 'girt'.)

**ζωνο-γάστορες** (-γάστριαι cod.)· οἱ τὰς γαστέρας ζωννύμενοι, Hsch.: ζωνογάστωρ· ὁ τὴν γαστέρα ζωννύμενος, Gramm. in Reitzenstein *Ind. Lect.Rost.*1892/3 p.11, cf. Hsch. s.v. μεσογάστορα. **-δρακοντις** [ᾰ], *girdled with snakes*, epith. of the moon, *PMag.Par.*1.2864. **-ειδής**, ές, *like a belt* or *girdle*, Apollon.*Lex.* s.v. ἵρεσσιν ἐοικότες, Eust. 1068.24. Adv. **-δῶς** *in belts*, Olymp.*in Mete.*191.21.

**ζωνός**, f.l. for εὔζωνος, Arist.*Phgn.*810$^b$4.

**ζωνοφόρος**, ον, *wearing a belt*, *PRain.* in *Wiener Denkschr.*42(2).4.

**ζώντειον** or **ζωντεῖον**, v. ζητρεῖον.

**ζώντως**, *vivide*, *Gloss.*

**ζῳο-γενής**, ές, *of animate kind*, *mortal*, opp. ἀειγενής, Pl.*Plt.*309c. **-γλύφος** [ῠ], ὁ, *sculptor*, *AP*12.56 (Mel.), 57 (Id.); cf. ζῳγλύφος.

**ζῳογον-έω**, *propagate* or *engender living creatures*, of inanimate substances, ἡ φύσις ζ. Thphr.*CP*3.22.3, cf. *HP*8.11.2 (so in Med., Id.*CP*3.24.3), Arist.*Mir.*835$^b$26; of animals, *breed*, like ζῳοτοκέω, D.S.1.88, Plu.2.494c:—Pass., Arist.*Mir.*832$^a$14: generally, *engender* [στοιχεῖον] ἕκαστον ἀπὸ ἑτέρου -εῖται Vett.Val.162.17. II. *to be viviparous*, Thphr.*HP*7.14.3; *produce alive*, Luc.*Am.*19; ζ. παρθένον, of Zeus, *producing* Pallas *alive* from his head, Id.*DDeor.*8, cf. D.S.1.23. 2. *make alive*, *quicken*, τι Thphr.*CP*4.15.2:—Pass., Arist.*Fr.*311, Isid.ap.Ath.2.93f: metaph., σωφροσύνη ζ. τὸ φρονοῦν Ph.2.378, cf. 435. 3. = ζωγρέω, *preserve alive*, Lxx*Ex.*1.17, 1*Ki.*

27.9; κύριος θανατοῖ καὶ ζ. ib.2.6, cf. *Ev.Luc.*17.33:—Pass., *Act.Ap.*7.19. **-ησις**, εως, ἡ, *creation of life*, *Theol.Ar.*46. **-ητικός**, ή, όν, *capable of generation*, ib.49; σύλληψις Aët.1.142. **-ία**, ἡ, *production of animals*, Pl.*Epin.*980c, Ph.1.14; *of living things*, Dam.*Pr.*284; *breeding of worms*, Thphr.*CP*5.9.3; *generation*, Sor.1.2. **-ικός**, ή, όν, = ζωογονητικός, Ph.2.148, Procl.*Inst.*155; νοῦς Dam.*Pr.*272. Adv. -κῶς Procl.*in Alc.*p.52 C. ⊛ **-ος**, ον, *producing animals*, *generative*, Aret.*SD*2.5, Orph.*H.*38.3; name of Apollo, *AP*9.525.7; *producing life*, Procl.*Inst.*155; θεός Jul.*Or.*5.175c, Dam.*Pr.*267; ῥοίζημα ib.282; ῥαθάμιγγες Procl.*H.*1.10.

**ζωο-γράφος** [ᾰ], ον, poet. for ζωγρ-, Theoc.15.81 (v.l. ζῳο-). **-δοτήρ**, ῆρος, ὁ, *giver of life*, Orph.*Fr.*65:—fem. **-δότειρα**, Hsch. **-δότης**, ου, ὁ, = foreg., Vett.Val.124.31, Them.*Or.*15.198b. **-δότιον**, τό, = μελίλωτον, Ps.-Dsc.3.40. **-ειδής**, ές, (ζῳο-) *like an animal*, *Gp.*10.9.4. **-θετέω**, (τίθημι) *make alive*, -οῦσα φύσις Archel.ap.Antig.*Mir.*19. **-θηρία**, ἡ, (ζῳο-) *chasing living creatures*, Pl.*Sph.*223b. **-θηρικός**, ή, όν, (ζῳο-) *of* or *for* ζῳοθηρία, ib.221b: ἡ -κή (sc. τέχνη) = ζῳοθηρία, ib.220a, 222a. **-θῠτέω**, *sacrifice live victims*, Thphr.(?) ap.Porph.*Abst.*2.26. **-κέφᾰλος**, ον, (ζῳο-) *animal-headed*, Anon. post Max.p.111 L. **-μορφος**, ον, (ζῳο-) *in the shape of an animal*, Plu.*Num.*8.

⊛ **ζῷον**, τό, *living being*, *animal*, Hdt.5.10 (of bees), Ar.*V.*551, *Pl.*443, etc.; πᾶν ὅ τι περ ἂν μετάσχῃ τοῦ ζῆν ζῷον ἂν λέγοιτο Pl.*Ti.*77b; ζῷα, opp. φυτά, Id.*Phd.*70d, 110e, etc.; ζ. θαλάττιον, χερσαῖον, Phld.*Rh.*1.98 S.; contemptuously, ὅπως ἡ χώρα τοῦ τοιούτου ζῴου καθαρὰ γίγνηται may be free from this kind of *animal* (i.e. beggars), Pl.*Lg.*936c; ζ. πονηρόν, of women, Secund.*Sent.*8. II. in art, *figure*, *image*, not necessarily of animals (cf. ζῴδιον), ζῷον δέ οἱ ἐνῆν, ἀνὴρ ἱππεύς Hdt.3.88: mostly in pl., ζῷα ἐς τὴν ἐσθῆτα ἐγγράφειν Id.1.203, cf. 2.4,124,148, Pl.*R.*515a, etc.; ζῷα γράψασθαι τὴν ζεῦξιν τοῦ Βοσπόρου to have *pictures* of the bridging of the Bosporus painted, Hdt.4.88; cf. ζωγραφέω: ζῷα ποιεῖν Plu.*Per.*13. III. *sign* of the Zodiac, Man.2.166.—The word is post-Hom., no generic word used for *animal* being found till after the middle of the fifth cent. B.C. (ζώϊον Semon.13, whence Att. ζῷον by contraction: ι is found in $IG1^{2}$.372.42, al., 11(2).161 *B*76 (Delos, iii B.C.), Phld.*Rh.*2.166 S., and in codd. opt. in the Noun; the Adj. ζωός (q.v.) had no ι: for the compds. (exc. ζωγλύφος, ζωγράφος) decisive evidence is lacking: ζῳάγρια with ι was read by Aristarch. in Il.18.407.)

**ζωόνῠχον**, τό, a name of the plant λεοντοπόδιον, Ps.-Dsc.4.133.

⊛ **ζῳοπλαστ-έω**, *mould to the life*, *make into statues*, analogous to ζωγραφέω, Lyc.844 (ζωο- codd.). II. *work into life-shape*, ζ. θνητὰ γένη Ph.1.13. ⊛ **-ης**, ου, ὁ, *the Creator*, ib.184. II. *a moulder of creatures*, *sculptor*, etc., Id.2.211. **-ία**, ἡ, *artistic representation*, Eust.1157.25.

**ζωοποι-έω**, = ζωογονέω I, Arist.*HA*$555^{b}9$; = ζωογονέω II. 2, Id.*GA*$730^{a}2$, Thphr.*CP*3.22.4: metaph., D.S.2.52. II. *make alive*, θανατῶσα καὶ ζ. Lxx 4*Ki.*5.7, cf. *Ev.Jo.*5.21; *bring to life*, νεκρά Luc.*VH*1.22, cf. Sch.E.*Alc.*122; *endow with life*, ἑαυτό Dam.*Pr.*78, al., cf. Procl.*Inst.*25:—Pass., ib.209. 2. *preserve alive*, Lxx *Jd.*21.14. **-ησις**, εως, ἡ, *making alive*, ib.2*Es.*9.8. **-ητικός**, ή, όν, *generative*, *Theol.Ar.*31; τὸ ζ. Diocl.*Fr.*172; *vitalizing*, θερμότης Steph.*in Hp.*1.132 D. **-ία**, ἡ, = ζωογόνησις, Thphr.*CP*5.18.2, Dam.*Pr.*100. **-ός**, όν, *creative of life*, Thphr.*CP*2.9.6, Procl.*Inst.*145, Porph.ap.Eus.*PE*3.11, Dam.*Pr.*80, al.: c. gen., ζ. τῆς ὅλης γενέσεως ib.283; ζ. τὸ ὕδωρ καὶ γόνιμον Sch.E.*Ph.*347.

⊛ **ζῳο-πώλης**, ου, ὁ, *selling animals*, esp. for sacrifice, Hsch. ⊛ **-πωλις** (sc. ἀγορά), ἡ, *beast-market*, Id. (nisi leg. -πώλιον).

⊛ **ζωός** (without ι, cf. *Schwyzer*436.2 (Crimisa, v/iv B.C.), Cret. **δωός** *Leg.Gort.*3.41, Cypr. pr. n. Ζωϝόθεμις *Schwyzer*684 (v B.C.)), ή, όν, (ζῶ) *alive*, *living*, Pi.*P.*4.209, Hdt.2.70, etc.; οὐ..ζωοῦ οὐδὲ θανόντος Od.17.115; ζωὸν ἑλεῖν τινα to take prisoner, Il.6.38; ζωὸν λαβεῖν X.*HG*1.2.5; cf. ζωγρέω: metaph., ζωὸν δὲ φθιμένων..κλέος A.*Eleg.*3.—Also **ζώς** Il.5.887, 16.445, Hdt.1.194, *JRS*15.145,148 (Cotiaeum) (ζῶς Ptol.Ascal., ζώς Hdn.Gr.2.53; on the other cases, ib.712); **ζοός** Archil.63, Epich.189, *Berl.Sitzb.*1927.161 (Cyrene), Theoc.2.5 (ζόος in Epich. l. c., Hdn.Gr.2.947).

**ζῳοστάσιον** [ᾰ], τό, (ἵστημι) *stall* or *stable*, Eust.531.17 (pl.).

**ζωοτάμον**, f.l. in Orph.*A.*315 codd. (ζῶα ταμών Lobeck).

**ζῳότης**, ητος, ἡ, *animal nature*, Demetr.Lac.*Herc.*1055.15, Plu.2.1001b, A.D.*Pron.*6.24, Gal.19.163, Porph.*Gaur.*16.5; *vitality*, Dam.*Pr.*58.

**ζωοτοκ-έω**, *to be viviparous*, opp. ᾠοτοκέω, Arist.*Pol.*$1256^{b}13$; τὰ -οῦντα *viviparous* animals, Id.*GA*$732^{b}8$: generally ζωοτοκεῖ ἀήρ Ph.1.263:—Pass., *to be born alive*, Arist.*PA*$693^{b}23$. **-ία**, ἡ, Id.*GA*$754^{b}29$. ⊛ **-ος**, ον, opp. ᾠοτόκος, Id.*HA*$489^{a}34$, al., Ph.1.502; [βόες] *bringing forth live* calves, Theoc.25.125. 2. *life-giving*, Nonn.*D.*26.191, al.

**ζῳοτροφ-εῖον**, τό, *place for keeping animals*, *Gloss.* **-έω**, *breed* or *have parasitic animals*, Thphr.*CP*2.17.8: generally ἀὴρ ζ. μᾶλλον γῆς Ph.1.641. II. *keep animals*, Id.2.233. **-ία**, ἡ, *feeding of animals*, Pl.*Plt.*261e. **-ικός**, ή, όν, *connected with the feeding of animals*, ib.263e: ἡ -κή (sc. τέχνη), = ζῳοτροφία, ib.267b. **-ος**, ον, *nourishing animals*. Max.Tyr.39.4, 41.5.

**ζῳοτύπος** [ῠ], ον, *modelling animals from life*, Nonn.*D.*5.527, Man.4.343: generally, *modelling to the life*, of a sculptor, *AP*15.1.

**ζῳοφᾰγ-έω**, *live on animal food*, Arist.*HA*$590^{b}1$. **-ία**, ἡ, *a living on animal food*, ib.$628^{b}13$, Porph.*Abst.*2.27, 4.21. **-ος**, ον, *carnivorous*, opp. καρποφάγος, Arist.*Pol.*$1256^{a}25$, cf. *PA*$696^{b}29$.

**ζωόφθαλμον**, τό, = ἀείζωον τὸ μέγα, Dsc.4.88. 2. = *leaf-rosette*, Plin.*HN*25.160.

**ζωοφορ-έω**, of animals, *bring forth alive*, Arist.*HA*$638^{a}31$; of plants, *bear fruit*, *Gp.*5.13.1. **-ος**, ον, *life-giving*, *IG*3.171; ἄνεμοι *AP*9.765 (Paul. Sil.). II. **ζῳοφόρος**, ον, *bearing animals*: and so, 1. *bearing the figures of animals*, *sculptured*, πίνακες D.S.18.26; Lat. *zophorus*, as Subst., *frieze*, Vitr.3.5.10. 2. ὁ ζ. κύκλος, = ὁ ζῳδιακός, Arist.*Mu.*$392^{a}11$, *Corp.Herm.*13.12, etc.; without κύκλος, Ph.2.153, *AP*14.124; σφαῖρα ἡ ζ. (ζωηφ- cod.) Ph.2.294.

**ζωοφῠτ-έω**, *put forth live shoots*, *flourish*, *PCair.Zen.*72.4 (iii B.C.), Apollod.Hist.ap.Ath.15.682d, *PMasp.*104.6 (vi A.D.). II. *produce alive* or *endow with life*, Ph.2.372: with v.l. **ζωοφυεῖν**, ib.294. **-ος**, ον, = ζώφυτος II, μέρη Plu.2.701c. II. **ζωόφῠτον**, τό, *zoöphyte*, S.E.*P.*1.41 codd. 2. = ἀείζωον τὸ μέγα Ps.-Dsc.4.88.

**ζῳόω**, *fashion into an animal*, pf. inf. Pass. ἐζῳῶσθαι Alex.Aphr.*in Top.*137.26.

**ζωόω**, *impregnate*, ζωοῦσα θορή Aret.*SD*2.5:—Pass., Porph.*Gaur.*1.1, 3.1. 2. *quicken*, *make alive*, Lxx *Ps.*79(80).18; *endow with life*, ἑαυτὸ οὐσιοῖ καὶ ζωοῖ Dam.*Pr.*80, Phlp.*in GC*200.6:—Pass., Hp.*Alim.*38, Gal.19.174,180, Phlp.*in GC*151.5, Id.*in de An.*64.7, al.; θηρίον ζωωθὲν τὸ σῶμα Plot.1.1.10, cf. 4.4.28; [γῆ] ἐζωωμένη Id.6.7.12. II. Pass., of putrescent plants, *breed worms*, Thphr.*CP*5.18.2 (nisi leg. ζῳο-).

**ζώπισσα**, ἡ, *pitch and wax from old ships*, or *pine-resin*, Dsc.1.72.

**ζωπονέω**, *represent alive*, *AP*9.742 (Phil.).

**ζωπύρα**, ἡ, a plant, = κλινοπόδιον, Hsch.; *zopyrontion*, Plin.*HN*24.137.

**ζωπύρειος**, ἡ, medicine named after the physician Zopyrus, Orib.*Fr.*125, cf. Gal.14.205, Paul.Aeg.7.11.

**ζωπῠρ-έω**, (ζώπυρον) *kindle into flame*, *cause to blaze up*, ζ. τοὺς ἄνθρακας Men.71; τὸ πνεῦμα ζ. Thphr.*Ign.*27:—in Pass., *to be quickened by fire*, of the foetus, Hp.*Vict.*1.9. 2. metaph., μέριμναι ζωπυροῦσι τάρβος A.*Th.*290 (lyr.); ζωπυρουμένας φρενός Id.*Ag.*1034 (lyr.); τῆς φύσεως τὸ ζωπυροῦν Arist.*PA*$670^{a}25$, cf. Plu.2.940c; ζ. τινά *to provoke* him, Ar.*Lys.*682 (lyr.); ζ. τρυφήν *increase* it, Plu.*Lyc.*9; in Magic, *quicken*, *fill with power*, *PMag.Leid.V.*10.7 (Pass.). II. intr., *burst into flame*, ἣν ἡ θέρμη ζωπυρῇ Aret.*SD*1.8. **-ημα**, ατος, τό, = ζώπυρον I, gloss on φεψάλυξ, Sch.Ar.*Lys.*107. **-ητέον**, *one must kindle*, Ph.1.187. **-ιον**, τό, = κλινοπόδιον, prob. in Dsc.3.95 (from the name of the physician Zopyrus). II. **ζωπύρια**, τά, *bellows*, Phot., Suid. (nisi leg. ζωπυρεῖα). **-ίς**, ίδος, ἡ, *kindling up*, *reviving*, Jul.*Or.*5.172b. **-ον**, τό, *spark* or *hot coal*, used to kindle *a fire*: hence metaph., σμικρὰ ζ. τοῦ τῶν ἀνθρώπων διασεσωσμένα γένους (of the survivors of the flood), Pl.*Lg.*677b, cf. Luc.*Tim.*3; so [τὸ βαρὺ καὶ κοῦφον] οἷον ζ. ἄττα κινήσεως Arist.*Cael.*$308^{a}2$; βραχέα τινὰ ζ. τῆς Λυκούργου νομοθεσίας Plu.2.240a; ζ. τι πρὸς σωτηρίαν βίου Max.Tyr.2.4; ζώπυρα τῆς ἰδίας σωτηρίας Ph.2.519; ζ. φιλανθρωπίας *flashes* of humanity, Nic.Dam.*Fr.*127 J. II. Act., *pair of bellows*, Ephor.42 J. **-ος**, ον, *glowing*, of desire, θερμὸν καὶ ζ. Philostr.*VA*1.34. 2. *restorative*, ἔχει τι ζ. ὁ τοῦ προσώπου περισπογγισμός Sor.2.28. ⊛ **-ωσις**, εως, ἡ, *kindling*. Max.Tyr.9.7.

⊛ **ζωροποτ-έω**, *drink neat wine*, Call.*Fr.*109, *AP*11.25 (Apollonid.). **-ης**, ου, ὁ, *drinking neat wine*, Hedyl.ap.Ath.11.497d; οἴνου Man.4.300; ὀφθαλμοὶ..κάλλεος ἀκρήτου ζωροπόται *AP*5.225 (Paul. Sil.).

⊛ **ζωρός**, όν, *pure*, *sheer*, prop. of wine without water, like ἄκρᾱτος, ζ. μέθυ A.R.1.477; πόμα *AP*12.50 (Asclep.); πότος Hippoloch.ap.Ath.4.129d: abs., ζωρός (sc. οἶνος) *AP*6.105 (Apollonid.), etc.: Comp., ζωρότερον δὲ κέραιε mix the wine *more pure*, i.e. add less water, Il.9.203, cf. Arist.*Po.*$1461^{a}14$; κεράσας ζωρότερον Ὁμηρικῶς Ephipp.10; so later -ότερον πίνειν Hdt.6.84; and in the sense drink *hard*, ζ. πιεῖν Thphr.*Char.*4.6, cf. Ael.*VH*13.4, Luc.*Tim.*54, etc.; πίνειν -οτέρῳ χρώμενον οἰνοχόῳ Antiph.149; ζωρὸν δέπας a cup *of sheer wine*, *AP*11.28 (Marc. Arg.); ζωρὸν πέλαγος a sea *of wine*, ib.7.457.6 (Aristo); ζωρότερον κισσύβιον ib.5.288.4 (Agath.); of drugs, Luc.*DMort.*7.1, *Nav.*45; διδόναι τι ζωρότερον ἐσθίειν Hp.*Nat.Mul.*69; -ότερον γάλα Ruf.*Fr.*118: metaph., ζωροτάτη μανίη *AP*7.30 (Antip. Sid.). (In Philum.*Ven.*2.3, 4.2 ζωρός is opp. ἄκρατος, and so perh. in Emp.35.15, but the reading is doubtful.)

**ζωρύα**, ἡ, perh. = *pipe for running water*, (ζωός, ῥέω) *IG*4.823.46 (Troezen); cf. ὑδρορύα.

**ζῶρυξ**, = διῶρυξ, *PMeyer*20.18 (iii A.D.), *Stud.Pal.*20.70.25 (iii A.D.).

**ζώς**, rarer form for ζωός (q.v.).

**ζώσιμος**, ον, (ζῶ) *viable*, Alex.Aphr.*Pr.*2.47; *likely to survive*, Aët.13.22, Horap.1.38. II. *pertaining to this life*, τὰ ζ. prob. in Phld.*Herc.*1251.9.

**ζῶσις**, εως, ἡ, (ζώννυμι) *girding on*, *cincture*, σάκκων Lxx *Is.*22.12.

**ζῶσμα**, v. ζῶμα. **ζώστειον**, v. ζήτρειον.

⊛ **ζωστήρ**, ῆρος, ὁ, (ζώννυμι) in Il. always *a warrior's belt*, prob. of leather covered with metal plates, ὅθι ζωστῆρος ὀχῆες χρύσειοι σύνεχον 4.132; δαιδάλεος, παναίολος, ib.135,186; φοίνικι φαεινός 7.305, cf. Hdt.9.74, S.*Aj.*1030; of an Amazon, Pi.*Fr.*172: in Od., a swineherd's *belt*, 14.72, cf. Theoc.7.18, 26.17. II. later, = ζώνη, *a woman's girdle*, Paus.1.31.1: metaph., of the encircling sea, νῆσοι.., ἃς..ζ. Αἰγαίου κύματος ἐντὸς ἔχει *AP*9.421 (Antip. Thess.); ὠκεανὸς ἀτλαντικὸς ζ. Secund.*Sent.*2. III. *anything that goes round like a girdle*: 1. *stripe marking certain height in the ship*, Hld.1.1. 2. *grass-wrack*, *Posidonia oceanica*, Thphr.*HP*4.6.2, Plin.*HN*13.135. 3. = ζώνη III.4, ib.26.121. IV. name of a

cape on the west coast of Attica, Hdt.8.107, Hyp.*Fr.*67, etc. 2. epith. of Apollo at Zoster, *AB*261 (sed leg. Ζωστήριος). V. ζωστῆρες Ἐνυοῦς, of warriors, Call.*Ap.*85. VI. name of a πηγή in the Chaldaean system, Dam.*Pr.*96.

⊛ **Ζωστήριος**, *α, ον, of* Ζωστήρ (a place on the west coast of Attica), Ζωστήριος Ἀπόλλων *IG*I$^2$.324.70, Euph.95b, Paus.1.31.1, cf. foreg. IV. 2; Ζωστηρία, epith. of Athena, *Schwyzer*319 (Delph., vi/v B.C.), *IG* I$^2$.324.97 (v B.C.), Paus.9.17.2, St.Byz. s.v. Ζωστήρ, Hsch. (-στειρα cod.); Ἀθηνᾶ ζωστῆρα (sic) *AB*261. 2. ζωστήριον, τό, = ζωστήρ, dub. in *PLond.*2.402.8 (ii B.C.), cf. *Gloss.*

**ζωστηροκλέπτης**, *ου, ὁ, one who steals belts*, Lyc.1329.

**ζώστ-ης**, *ου, ὁ, one who girds*, *Gloss.* **-ός**, *ή, όν, girded*, ὑπένδυμα Plu.*Alex.*32, cf. X.Eph.1.2, Hsch. s.v. ζῶστρα. ⊛ **-μα**, *ἡ, head-band, fillet*, Theoc.2.122 (pl.). **-ρίς**, *cingulum*, *Gloss.* **-ρον**, *τό, belt, girdle*, Od.6.38 (pl.).

**Ζωτεάτας**, epith. of Apollo at Argos, Hsch.: **Ζωτελιστής**, epith. of Apollo at Corinth, Id.

**ζώτειον**, *τό*, v. ζήτρειον.

**ζωτικός**, *ή, όν*, (ζῶ) *fit for giving* or *maintaining life*, ἐπιθυμία Pl. *Ti.*91b; δυνάμιες Ti.Locr.100d, cf. D.S.2.51 (Sup.), Gal.15.506; πνεῦμα LXX *Wi.*15.11; ἰκμάς Corn.*ND*2; φῶς Porph.*Marc.*13; τὸ ὑγρὸν -ώτερον τοῦ ξηροῦ Arist.*GA*761$^a$27, cf. 733$^a$11; [ἔαρ] -ωτάτη ὥρα Thphr.*CP*1.13.4. II. *full of life, alive*, Pl.*R.*610e, Thphr. *HP*1.14.2, Porph.*Gaur.*16.3,5; τὰ τήθυα ζωτικώτερα τῶν σπόγγων *more like animals*, Arist.*PA*681$^a$10; τὰ -ώτατα μέρη (of the body) Plu.2.130b. Adv. -κῶς, ἔχειν to be *fond of life*, Id.*Cat.Mi.*70. 2. *characteristic of life, vital*, τὸ αὐτὰ ὑφ' αὑτῶν κινεῖσθαι ζωτικόν Arist. *Ph.*255$^a$6; τόνος, πνεῦμα, φύσις, *Stoic.*2.235, 241, 272; κίνησις Herm. ap.Stob.1.41.7, cf. Plot.6.7.5 (Comp.), Porph.*Sent.*37; κατὰ τὸ ζ. Procl.*Inst.*189. Adv. -κῶς ib.39, Dam.*Pr.*79, Herm.ap.Stob.l.c. 3. ζ. χρόνος duration *of life*, Vett.Val.132.4; of works of Art, *true to life*, τὸ ζ. φαίνεσθαι πῶς ἐνεργάζῃ τοῖς ἀνδριᾶσιν; X.*Mem.*3.10.6; -ώτατα ἐξεργάσασθαι Plu.2.668d.

**ζωτύς** (or **ζωγύς**)· θώραξ, Hsch.

**ζῳύλλιον**, *τό*, = sq., Tz.*H.*9.957.

**ζῳύφιον** [ῠ], *τό*, Dim. of ζῷον, ζῴδιον, Ath.5.210c, Gal.6.666, Hsch., cj. for ζωόφυτα in S.E.*P.*1.41.

**ζωφορ-ία**, Ion. -ίη, *ἡ, the sun's progress through the zodiac*, Man. 4.510. **-ος**, *ον*, (φέρω) = ζωοφόρος (q.v.).

**ζωφῠτ-έω**, *thrive, flourish*, of trees or plants, *POxy.*1188.3 (i A.D.), cf. *PLond.*2.214 (iii A.D.); ζωφυτοῦν ἄλσος *BCH*44.79 (Lagina). ⊛ **-ος**, *ον*, (φύω) *giving life to plants, fertilizing*, αἷμα A.*Supp.*857; γῆ Plu. *Rom.*20. II. Pass., *spring from the earth*, τὰ ζ. *plants*, Diusap. Stob.4.21.16.

**ζώω**, Ep. and Ion. for ζῶ.

**ζῳ-ώδης**, *ες, like an animal, animal*, κάλλος Democr.105; δαίμων Posidon.ap.Gal.5.469; βίος Plu.2.8a, Aret.*SD*1.5; αἰσθήσεις Ph.2. 22 (Sup.), cf. M.Ant.7.55; ἐνέργειαι Dam.*Pr.*102; ἡδονή Marin.*Procl.* 4; of persons, *brutish*, Aret.*SD*1.7; but ἐς χροιὴν ζ. *like a living person* (of one dead), Id.*SA*2.11. **-ωδία**, *ἡ, animal nature*, Iamb. *Protr.*21.ιϛ'.

⊛ **ζώωσις**, *εως, ἡ*, (ζωόω) *making alive*, [Gal.]19.174.

**ζῳωτός** (with ι, Inscrr., v. infr.), *ή, όν*, also *ός, όν* Charesap.Ath. 12.538d: (ζῷον):—*adorned with figures*, φαρέτρα *IG*11(2).161 *B* 100 (Delos, iii B.C.); χιτών Callix.2; ἐφαπτίς Plb.30.25.10; σκύφος *OGI* 214.54 (iii B.C.); αὐλαῖαι Chares l.c.

# H

**H η, ἦτα** (q.v.), *τό*, indecl., eighth (later seventh) letter of the Gr. alphabet; as numeral η', = ὀκτώ and ὄγδοος, but ͵η, = 8,000. In most local alphabets of v B.C. and earlier it represents *h*, in others (incl. the Ion. = later general Gr. alphabet) one of the long *ē* sounds (cf. βῆ βῆ). Described by E.*Fr.*382.5, Agatho 4.2.

⊛ **ἤ** (A), Ep. also **ἠέ** (in signf. A.II ἤ (or ἠέ) folld. by ἦ (or ἦε), v. infr.), Conj. with two chief senses, Disj. (*or*) and Comp. (*than*).

A. Disjunctive, *or*, ἐγὼ.. ἢ ἄλλος Ἀχαιῶν Il.2.231, cf. 397, 800, 4.142, 7.236, al.; θεόσυτος ἢ βρότειος ἢ κεκραμένη A.*Pr.*116. 2. ἢ.. ἤ *either.. or*, ἢ νῦν δηθύνοντ' ἢ ὕστερον αὖτις ἰόντα Il.1.27, cf. 151, 5.484, etc.; so ἢ.. ἤτοι.. Pi.*N.*6.4, *Fr.*138; ἤτοι.. ἤ.. A.*Ag.*662, S. *Ant.*1182, Th.2.40, etc. (in Classical Gr. the alternative introduced by ἤτοι is emphasized, later no distn. is implied, *Ep.Rom.*6.16; ἤτοι.. ἢ.. ἤ.. *PTeb.*5.59 (ii B.C.)); ἤ repeated any number of times, ἐγὼ δέ κεν αὐτὸς ἕλωμαι ἢ τεὸν ἢ Αἴαντος ἰὼν γέρας ἢ Ὀδυσῆος Il.1.138, cf. Od.15.84, S.*Ant.*707; ἤ is prob. wrongly accented in codd. of Il.2.289, Od.3.348, 19.109, v. ἦ Adv. I.3: ἢ πόλις βροτός θ' ὁμοίως A.*Eu.*524 (lyr.) is exceptional. 3. *or else, otherwise*, εἰδέναι δεῖ περὶ οὗ ἂν ᾖ ἡ βουλή, ἢ παντὸς ἁμαρτάνειν ἀνάγκη Pl.*Phdr.*237c; μή με λυπεῖτε, ἢ φεύξομ' ἐκ τῆς οἰκίης Herod.5.74; ζῶντα κακῶς λέγειν ἐκώλυσε.., ἢ τρεῖς δραχμὰς ἀποτίνειν ἔταξε Lex Sol.ap.Plu.*Sol.*21, cf. 24, *IG*I$^2$.94.10, Them.*Or.*21.260a. II. in Questions or Deliberations in Disj. form (the accentuation is ἢ (ἠέ) folld. by ἦ (ἦε), Hdn. Gr.2.24, al., A.D.*Conj.*224.28): 1. Direct questions, a. introduced by ἢ (ἠέ), ἢ δολιχὴ νοῦσος ἦ Ἄρτεμις ἰοχέαιρα.. κατέπεφνεν; Od.11.172; ἤ τι κατὰ πρῆξιν ἦ μαψιδίως ἀλάλησθε..; 3.72, cf. 1.408, 16.462, Il.6.378, 15.735, 16.12, etc. b. without an introductory Particle, θεός νύ τις ἦ βροτός ἐσσι; art thou a goddess *or* a mortal? Od.6.149, cf. 1.226, 4.314, 372, 643, 20.130, 21.194, Il.10.63, 425, 534, 15.203: accented ἦ, Hdn.Gr.2.145, al., but ἤ freq. in codd. of Hom. and always in codd. of later writers: ἤκουσας ἢ οὐκ ἤκουσας ἢ κωφῇ λέγω; A.*Th.*202; ἄρτι δὲ ἥκεις ἢ πάλαι; Pl.*Cri.*43a; κακουργεῖν δεῖ ἢ οὔ; ib.49c; preceded by πότερον, πότερον δοκεῖ σοι κάκιον εἶναι, τὸ ἀδικεῖν ἢ τὸ ἀδικεῖσθαι; Id.*Grg.*474c, etc. 2. Indirect questions, freq. epexegetic of a preceding question and identical in form with direct questions. a. εἴπ' ἄγε,.. ἤ ῥ' ἐθέλει.., ἦ ἀπέειπε.. Il.9.674; ὄφρα δαῶμεν ἢ ἐτεὸν Κάλχας μαντεύεται ἦε καὶ οὐκί 2.300; διάνδιχα μερμήριξεν ἢ ὅ γε.. ἐναρίζοι ἦε χόλον παύσειεν 1.190; later with εἰ.. ἤ A.*Ch.*890, *Ag.*478, S.*OC*80, etc.; πότερον or πότερα.. ἤ.. Id.*Pers.*148, 352, *Ag.*630, etc.; sts. εἴτε.. ἤ E.*El.*897; ἢ.. εἴτε S.*Aj.* 177. b. without introductory Particle, οὐδέ τι οἶδα ζώει ὅ γ' ἦ τέθνηκε Od.11.464, cf. Il.10.546, Od.24.238.

B. Comparative, *than, as*, after a Comp., Il.11.162, etc.: after positive Adjs. which imply comparison, ἄλλος, ἕτερος ἤ.., S.*OT*595, *Tr.*835 (lyr.); ἐναντίος ἤ Pl.*Grg.*481c; ἴδιόν τι πάσχειν πάθος ἢ οἱ ἄλλοι ibid.: after Advbs. or adverbial phrases, πλήν, πρίν, πρόσθεν, χωρίς (qq.v.), ἀλλά (v. ἀλλ' ἤ); τῇ ὑστεραίᾳ ἤ.. Id.*Cri.*44a (f.l. in *Smp.*173a); ἐν τῷ πέμπτῳ καὶ δεκάτῳ ϝέτει ἀπὸ τῶ ποτεχεῖ ϝέτεος ἢ Ἀριστίων ἐφορεύει *Tab.Heracl.*1.121; παρὰ δόξαν ἢ ὡς αὐτὸς κατεδόκεε Hdt.1.79, cf. 8.4; διαφερόντως ἤ.. Pl.*Phd.*85b; οὐδ' ὅσον ἤ.. not so much *as*.., not more *than*.., Theoc.9.21: after Verbs implying comparison, βούλεσθαι ἤ.. to wish *rather than*.., v. βούλομαι IV, αἱρέω B.II. 1b; so φθάνειν ἤ.. to come sooner *than*.., Il.23.445, Od.11.58; ἐπιθυμεῖν ἤ.. X.*Cyr.*1.4.3; δέχεσθαι ἤ.. Lys.10.21: less freq. after a word not implying comparison, δίκαιον ἡμέας ἔχειν.. (sc. μᾶλλον) ἤ περ Ἀθηναίους Hdt.9.26; ἐμοὶ πικρὸς.. ἢ κείνοις γλυκύς S.*Aj.*966 (s.v.l.); δεδικαιωμένος ἢ ἐκεῖνος *Ev.Luc.*18.14. 2. joining two Comparatives which refer to the same subject, πάντες κ' ἀρησαίατ' ἐλαφρότεροι πόδας εἶναι ἢ ἀφνειότεροι Od.1.165; ταχύτερα ἢ σοφώτερα Hdt.3.65; μανικώτεροι ἢ ἀνδρειότεροι Pl.*Tht.*144b, cf. Ar.*Ach.*1078. 3. rarely after a Sup., πλεῖστα θωμάσια ἔχει Αἴγυπτος ἢ ἄλλη πᾶσα χώρη Hdt.2.35 (s.v.l.); πίθοιτό κεν ὔμμι μάλιστα ἢ ἐμοί A.R.3.91. 4. ἢ οὐ is used when a neg. precedes, οὐδέν τι μᾶλλον ἐπ' ἡμέας ἢ οὐ καὶ ἐπ' ὑμέας Hdt.4.118, cf. 5.94, Th.2.62, etc.: after an implied neg., ὠμὸν.. πόλιν ὅλην διαφθεῖραι μᾶλλον ἢ οὐ τοὺς αἰτίους Id.3.36. 5. freq. omitted with numerals after πλείων, ἐλάττων, μείων, ἔτη.. πλείω ἑβδομήκοντα v.l. in Pl.*Ap.*17d; οὐ μεῖον πεντακοσίους X.*An.*6.4.24: sts. with an inf. or conditional clause, τί γὰρ ἀνδρὶ κακὸν μεῖζον ἁμαρτεῖν E.*Alc.* 879; τίς εὐπραξία σπανιωτέρα.., εἰ [δύναμις] πάρεστιν (for ἢ δύναμιν παρεῖναι); Th.1.33. 6. pleon. with a gen., τίς ἂν αἰσχίων εἴη ταύτης δόξα, ἢ δοκεῖν.. Pl.*Cri.*44c, cf. Lys.10.28. 7. the Disj. and Comp. uses are found together in Il.15.511 βέλτερον, ἢ ἀπολέσθαι ἕνα χρόνον ἠὲ βιῶναι, ἢ δηθὰ στρεύγεσθαι ἐν αἰνῇ δηϊοτῆτι better, *either* to die once for all *or* win life, *than* long to toil in battle. [ἢ οὐ, ἢ οὐκ combine by Synizesis into one syll. in Trag. and Com., A.*Pr.*330, S.*Aj.*334, Ar.*Lys.*128; so usually in Ep., Od.1.298, al.; ἢ αὐτός Hes.*Fr.*194; ἢ εἰ Alex.201.]

**ἤ** (B), an exclamation expressing disapproval, ἢ ἢ σιώπα Ar.*Nu.* 105; ἢ ἤ· τί δρᾷς; E.*HF*906 (lyr.), cf. Suid. 2. to call attention, ποῦ Ξανθίας; ἢ Ξανθία where 's Xanthias? *hi*, Xanthias! Ar.*Ra.*271.

⊛ **ἤ** (or **ἦ**) (C), Cypr. for *if*, *Inscr.Cypr.*135.6 H. 2. Cret. for *when, after*, ἤ κ' ἀποστᾶ μωλῆν *after* retiring, he shall take proceedings, *Leg.Gort.*1.52; ἐν ταῖς τριάκοντα ἤ κα ϝείποντι within 30 days *from the time of* their proclamation, ib.8.18.

⊛ **ἦ**, Adv., never in the form ἦε (ἠέ):

I. to confirm an assertion, *in truth, of a surety*, ἦ ὀλίγον οἷ παῖδα ἐοικότα γείνατο Τυδεύς Il.5.800, etc.; ironically, 1.229, al.; with concessive force, *it is true that*..: hence, *although*.., ἦ καὶ γένει ὕστερος ἦεν 3.215: freq. strengthd. by the addition of one or two other Particles, as ἦ ἄρα Od.24.193; ἦ ἄρα δή Il.13.446; ἦ ῥα 4.82; ἦ ῥά νυ 6.215; ἦ γάρ 1.78; ἦ γάρ τοι Od.16.199; ἦ δή Il.2.272; ἦ δή που 21.583; ἦ δῆτα S.*OT*429; ἦ θην Il.20.452; ἦ κάρτα S. *El.*1279; ἦ μάλα Il.3.204; ἦ μάλα δή 5.422; ἦ μήν and ἦ μέν (v. infr.); ἦ νυ Il.22.11; ἦ τάχα Od.18.73; ἦ τε 13.211: and to express doubt, ἦ που, v. ἦ που and ποῦ: esp. ἦ μήν used in oaths and asseverations, Il.2.291, 7.393, A.*Pr.*73, 168, etc.; also ἦ μάν Il.2.370, 13.354, Sapph.*Supp.*23.5; ἦ μέν Od.10.65 (later εἶ μήν, v. εἶ): c. inf. in orat. obliq., after Verbs of swearing, etc., σὺ δὲ σύνθεο, καί μοι ὄμοσσον, ἦ μέν μοι πρόφρων ἔπεσιν καὶ χερσὶν ἀρήξειν Il.1.77: ἦ μέν also in Ion. historical Prose, Hdt.4.154, 5.93, al.; ἐγγυᾶσθαι, ἦ μὴν παραμενεῖν Pl. *Phd.*115d; ἐγγυητὰς καταστῆσαι ἦ μὴν ἐκτείσειν Lex ap.D.24.39: with other Particles, ἦ μὲν δή Il.2.798, Od.18.257, al.; ἦ δὴ μάν Il.17. 538. 2. in the combinations ἐπεὶ ἦ, ὅτι ἤ and τί ἤ; A.D.*Conj.*255. 5, *Synt.*307.19 (cf. Hdn.Gr.1.520), recognizes an 'expletive' ἠ (παραπληρωματικὸς σύνδεσμος) perispom. after ἐπεί, barytone after ὅτι or τί. It is prob. the same as the affirmative ἦ (cf. A.D.*Conj.* l.c.), and occurs in the same combinations, ἐπεὶ ἦ πολύ.. Il.1.169, al.; ἐπεὶ ἦ μάλα ib.156, Od.10.465; ἐπεὶ ἦ καί.. Il.20.437, Od.16.442. Trypho took τίη as one word, and this can be supported by τί ἢ δὲ σύ.. Il.6.55, but A.D.(*Conj.* l.c.) infers from the accent of ὅτι ἤ that τί ἤ was two words. The Attic accentuation is said by Eust.45 init., 118.39, 907.14 to be τιή, ὁτιή (qq.v.). 3. this ἦ (or ἤ) is prob. to be recognized in ὥς τε γὰρ ἦ Il.2.289, ὥς τέ τευ ἦ Od.3.348, 19.109, where codd. have ἤ (in Od.3.348 ἠδέ (cj. Bekker) shd. perh. be read for ἠέ).

II. in Questions not involving alternatives: 1. Direct

questions, a. epexegetic of a preceding question, suggesting the answer to it, *τίπτ' εἰλήλουθας; ἦ ἵνα ὕβριν ἴδῃ Ἀγαμέμνονος;* why hast thou come? *is it* that thou mayst see..? Il.1.203, cf. 5.466, 7.26, Od.4.710, 13.418, 17.376, B.17.5; *τί δῆτα χρῄζεις; ἦ με γῆς ἔξω βαλεῖν;* S.*OT*622, cf. E.*Or.*1425 (ἤ codd.): *τίς σοι διηγεῖτο; ἦ αὐτὸς Σωκράτης;* Pl.*Smp.*173a (perispom., cod. B): on the accent, Hdn. Gr.2.112. b. not epexegetic of a preceding question, *ἦ σύ γ' Ὀδυσσεύς ἐσσι πολύτροπος;* art thou the wily Odysseus? Od.10.330, cf. Il.11.666, 15.504; *ἦ οὐκ ὀτρύνοντος ἀκούετε..Ἕκτορος;* do you not hear..? ib.506, cf. Od.16.424; *ἦ τὸ πλοῖον ἀφῖκται;* Pl.*Cri.*43c; *ἦ οὐ δοκεῖ καὶ σοὶ οὕτω;* don't you think so too? Id.*Grg.*479b (perispom., cod. T); *ἦ βούλει συλλογισώμεθα αὐτά;* shall we work them (the consequences) out? ib.479c (perispom., cod. T); *ἦ τορῶς λέγω;* A.*Ag.*269; *ἦ κἀν δόμοισι τυγχάνει τανῦν παρών;* S.*OT*757: freq. with other Particles, *ἦ ἄρ..;* Od.20.166, Il.19.56; mostly *ἦ ῥα..;* 5.421, 762, Od.4.632; also in Trag. (in lyr.), A.*Pers.*633, S.*Aj.*172, 955: esp. to mark the first of several questions, Pi.*I.*7(6).3 sqq.; *ἦ ἄρα δή..;* Il.13.446; *ἦ ῥά νυ..;* 4.93; *ἦ νυ..;* 15.128; *ἦ ταῦτα δή..;* S.*Ph.*565, *El.*385; *ἦ ταῦτα δῆτα..;* Id.*OT*429; *ἦ γάρ..;* A.*Pr.*745, 757, S.*OT*1000: in Att. Prose, *ἦ γάρ;* standing alone, *is it not so?* Pl.*Tht.*160e, *Grg.*449d, 468d; *ἦ καί..;* A.*Ag.*1207, 1362:—ἦ usu. begins the sentence, except that the vocative may precede, as in Il.5.421, 762, Od.4.632, S.*OC*863, 1102, or ἀλλά, as in A.*Ag.*276, *Ch.*774:—by Crasis ἦ combines with ἄρα in Att. and the *κοινή* to ἆρα (q.v.), in all other dialects (cf. A.D.*Conj.*223.24) to ἦρα (q.v.), but ἆρα is found in Pi.*P.*4.78 (ἄρα codd.), al., Archil.86, 89. 2. Indirect questions, *οἴχετο πευσόμενος μετὰ σὸν κλέος ἦ που ἔτ' εἴης* Od.13.415 (v.l. εἰ, which alone has Ms. authority in Il.1.83, Od.19.325); *ὄφρα καὶ Ἕκτωρ εἴσεται ἦ καὶ ἐμὸν δόρυ μαίνεται ἐν παλάμῃσιν* Il.8.111 (v.l. εἰ); *ἀλλ' ἄγε μοι τόδε εἰπὲ..ἦ καὶ Λαέρτῃ αὐτὴν ὁδὸν ἄγγελος ἔλθω;* Od.16.138 (v.l. εἰ); *ἀμφίστασθαι ἦ κα πεφυτεύκωντι πάντα κὰτ τὰν συνθήκαν* they shall investigate *whether..* *Tab.Heracl.*1.125; *μαντεύσασθαί οἱ..ἦ λώϊόν οἵ κα εἴη* Isyll.34; *διαψαφίξασθαι ἦ δοκεῖ αὐτὸν στεφανῶσαι* *IG*12(3).170.12 (Astypalaea): accented ἤ in codd. Hom., but it shd. perh. be perispom.

**ἦ,** for ἔφη, 3 sg. impf. or aor. 2 of ἠμί (q.v.). **ἦ,** for ἦν, Att. contr. from Ion. ἔα, impf. of εἰμί (*sum*).

**ἧ,** Adv. of Place, *where*, *Berl.Sitzb.*1927.170 (Cyrene), *Leg.Gort.*6.31.

⊛ **ᾗ,** dat. sg. fem. of relat. Pron. ὅς, ἥ, ὅ, in adverb. sense, 1. of Place, *which way, where, whither*, relat. to τῇ, Il.13.53, 15.46; also in Trag. and Att., S.*El.*1435; *τῇδε..ᾗ* A.*Ch.*308; *ἐκείνῃ..ᾗ* Pl.*Phd.*82d; Dor. ᾇ *SIG*56.28 (Argos, v B.C.). II. of Manner, *how, as*, *ᾗ καὶ Λοξίας ἐφήμισεν* A.*Ch.*558; *ᾗ νομίζεται* S.*OC*1603; *ᾗ βούλονται* Th.8.71, etc.:—not in Hom., unless we read *ᾗ θέμις ἐστί* for *ἣ θέμις*, v. *θέμις*. 2. *wherefore*, Th.1.25, 2.2, al. 3. *in so far as*, *διαφέρειν τὰ ἑκούσια τῶν ἀκουσίων ᾗ ὁ μὲν..τῷ δέ..* X.*Mem.*2.1.18, cf. Pl.*Men.*72b; *ῥήτορες ᾗ ῥήτορες* Phld.*Rh.*2.265 S.; *ᾗ ἄνθρωπος qua* man, Arist.*EN*1096$^{b}$2. III. with Sup., *ᾗ ἐδύνατο τάχιστα as* quickly *as* he could, X.*An.*1.2.4, etc.; *ᾗ δυνατὸν μάλιστα* ib.1.3.15; *ᾗ ἄριστον* Id.*Cyr.*2.4.32, etc.; *ᾗ ῥᾷστά τε καὶ ἥδιστα* Id.*Mem.*2.1.9; *ᾗ ἂν δύνωμαι τάχιστα* Id.*Cyr.*7.1.9.

**ἦα, ἦεν,** 1 and 3 sg. Ep. impf. of εἰμί (*sum*). **ᾖα,** contr. for ἤϊα, Ion. impf. of εἶμι (*ibo*). **ᾖα,** *τά*, contr. from ἤϊα (q.v.).

**ἠἄρινός,** v. ἐαρινός.

**Ἥατος,** ὁ (sc. μήν), name of month at Heraclea Trachinia, *GDI*1895.

**ἠβαιός,** ά, όν, Ion. (Cypr. acc. to *AB*1095) for βαιός, *small*, usu. with neg. *οὐδέ*, *οὔ οἱ ἔνι φρένες, οὐδ' ἠβαιαί* no sense is in him, no not *the least*, Il.14.141, cf. Od.21.288; *οὔ οἱ ἔνι τρίχες, οὐδ' ἠβαιαί* no not even *a few*, 18.355; also *ἠβαιὴν οὔτι κατὰ πρόφασιν* Call.*Fr.*540: rarely without neg., [*πηλαμύδες*] *καὶ ἠβαιαί περ ἐοῦσαι* Opp.*H.*4.514. II. often in neut. as Adv., *οὐδ' ἠβαιόν* not *in the least*, not *at all*, Il.2.380, Od.3.14, etc., cf. Phylarch.(?)84J.: rarely without a neg., *ἠβαιὸν ἀπὸ σπείους a little* from the cave, Od.9.462.

**ἡβ-άσκω,** Incept. of ἡβάω, *come to puberty*, Hp.*Aph.*3.28, X.*An.*4.6.1; *παῖς ἡβάσκων ἄρτι* ib.7.4.7; of women, *become marriageable*, Ruf.ap.Orib.*inc.*2.2. 2. metaph., *νῦν ἔθ' ἡβάσκει κακόν* (read by Gal. for *ἡβᾷ σοι*) E.*Alc.*1085; *ἡμῖν ἡβάσκει πενίη* *AP*6.30 (Maced.); *ποιητικὴ οὔπω ἡβάσκουσα* Philostr.*Her.Praef.* 3. *reach*, or *show the outward signs of, manhood*, Aristaenet.1.11, Philostr.*Im.*2.7. ⊛ **-άω,** Cret. **ἡβίω** *Leg.Gort.*7.41, al., Aeol.(?) **ἀβάω** Hdn.Gr.2.16, Alc.*Supp.*7.11 (dub.); Ep. opt. *ἡβώοιμι*, part. *ἡβώων* (v. infr.): impf. ἥβων Ar.*V.*357: fut. *-ήσω* (ἐφ-) X.*Cyr.*6.1.12, Dor. ἡβάσω [ᾱ] *AP*7.482: aor. 1 ἥβησα Od.1.41, Hes.*Op.*132, Pl.*Ap.*41e: pf. ἥβηκα (παρ-) Hdt.3.53, etc.: (ἥβη):—*attain* or *have attained puberty*, *ὅταν ἡβήσαι τε καὶ ἥβης μέτρον ἵκοιτο* Hes.*Op.*132; *ἡβῶσιν ὀψέ* Hp.*Aër.*4; *ἐπειδὰν ἡβήσωσι* Pl.*Ap.* l.c.; of women, *γυνὴ τέτορ' ἡβώοι* (sc. ἔτη) four years *past puberty*, Hes.*Op.*698; *ἡβάσεις ἥβαν* *AP* l.c.; *ἡβᾶν ἐπὶ διετές*, v. sub *διετής*; *ὀμόσαι Χαλκιδέων τοὺς ἡβῶντας ἅπαντας* all the *adults*, *IG*1$^{2}$.39.32, cf. Ar.*Ra.*1055, Th.4.132. 2. *to be in the prime of youth*, *εἴθ' ὣς ἡβώοιμι, βίη τέ μοι ἔμπεδος εἴη* Od.14.468, al.; *ἀνὴρ οὐδὲ μάλ' ἡβῶν* not even *in the prime of life*, Il.12.382, cf. Od.23.187, A.*Ch.*879; *γέροντα τὸν νοῦν, σάρκα δ' ἡβῶσαν φέρει* Id.*Th.*622; *ἡβᾶν σθένος to be young* and strong, E.*HF*436 (lyr.); *ἥβων I was young*, Ar.*V.*357; *ἡ. τὰς αἰσθήσεις*, of an old man, Philostr.*VS*1.9.3; of plants, *ἡμερὶς ἡβώωσα a young, luxuriant* vine, Od.5.69, cf. Simon.183.3, Longus 4.5; *ἡβῶντ' ἀρτίως οἰνίσκον* (*παρὰ προσδοκίαν* for *νεανίσκον*) Cratin.183. 3. metaph., *to be fresh, vigorous*, *ἡβώοις, φίλε θυμέ* Thgn.877 (dub. l.); *ἀεὶ γὰρ ἡβᾷ τοῖς γέρουσιν εὖ μαθεῖν* 'tis always *youth* for old men to learn, i.e. 'tis never too late to learn, A.*Ag.*584 (nisi leg. ἥβη): *ἡβᾷ δῆμος εἰς ὀργὴν πεσών* the people *rages like a passionate youth*, E.*Or.*696, cf. *νεανικός*; *ἄγγελον..γέρονθ', ἡβῶντα δ' εὐγλώσσῳ φρενί exulting*, A.*Supp.*775; also of things, *γάμοι, ἔαρ ἡ.*, Opp.*H.*1.474, 2.252. 4. *to have the outward signs of puberty*, Arist.*GA*746$^{b}$23; *γένυς ἡβᾷ* *AP*12.31 (Phan.). ⊛ **-η,** Dor. **ἥβα,** Aeol. **ἄβα** Alc.101, ἡ: (v. sub fin.):—*youthful prime, youth*, *νεηνίῃ ἀνδρὶ ἐοικώς, πρῶτον ὑπηνήτῃ, τοῦ περ χαριέστατος ἥβη* Od.10.279, cf. Il.24.348; *καὶ δ' ἔχει ἥβης ἄνθος ὅ τε κράτος ἐστὶ μέγιστον* 13.484, cf. Hes.*Th.*988; *ἐρικυδής* Il.11.225, Hes. l.c.; *πολυήρατος* Od.15.366, etc.; *ἥβης μέτρον ἱκέσθαι* or *ἱκάνειν*, = ἡβάσκειν, 11.317, 18.217, etc.; *ἥβην πολυήρατον ἱκόμεθ'* 15.366, cf. Il.24.728; *ἥβης ἀπόνασθαι, ταρπῆναι*, 17.25, Od.23.212; *ἐφ' ἥβης* Ar.*Eq.*524; *θρέψασθαί τινα πρὸς ἥβην* until *manhood*, Pl.*Mx.*238b; *μέχρι ἥβης* Th.2.46. b. *strength and vigour of youth*, [*δίσκον*] *ἀφῆκεν..πειρώμενος ἥβης* Il.23.432; *ἥβῃ τε πεποίθεα χερσί τ' ἐμῇσι* Od.8.181, cf. 16.174; *ἥβης ἀκμή* S.*OT*741: in pl., *καρποτρόφοι νεάνιδες ἧβαι* E.*Ion* 477 (lyr.). c. as a legal term, ἥβη was *the time before manhood*, at Athens sixteen years of age, *AB*255.15; fourteen acc. to *EM*359.17, Harp. s.v. *ἐπιδιετές*; at Sparta eighteen, *τὰ δέκα ἀφ' ἥβης* (sc. ἔτη), i.e. men of twenty-eight, X.*HG*2.4.32, 3.4.23; *τὰ τετταράκοντα ἀφ' ἥ.* ib.6.4.17; of women, *ἐπεὶ δ' ἐς ἥβην ἦλθεν ὡραίαν γάμων* E.*Hel.*12. d. of oxen, *ἥβης μέτρον ἔχοντε* Hes.*Op.*438; of the *fresh* skin of a snake, Nic.*Th.*138. 2. metaph., *cheer, merriment*, Pi.*P.*4.295; *δαιτὸς ἥβη* E.*Cyc.*504 (lyr.); also *youthful fire, spirit*, Pi.*P.*6.48. 3. *body of youth*, A.*Pers.*512, 733, *Ag.*109 (lyr.), etc. 4. *the pubes*, Hp.*Epid.*3.4, Ar.*Nu.*976, Theopomp.Com.37, Arist.*HA*493$^{b}$3, al. II. a kind of *vine*, Hsch.; Dor. ἆβαι (pl.) v.l. in Theoc.5.109. III. pr.n., Ἥβη *Hebe*, Il.4.2, Od.11.603, Hes.*Th.*950; later allegorized as *goddess of youth*. (Cf. Lith. *jėgà* 'power'.) ⊛ **-ηδόν,** Adv. *from the youth upwards*, *ἅπαντες ἡβηδόν* Hdt.1.172, cf. 6.21, Luc.*Vit.Auct.*14, al.; *ἄξιον Ἐφεσίοις ἡ. ἀπάγξασθαι* Heraclit.121; *τοὺς ἄνδρας ἡ. ἀποσφάξαι* D.S.3.54, cf. D.H.2.16, al. **-ησις,** εως, ἡ, *pubescence*, *περὶ τὸ ἦτρον* Sor.1.24. **-ητήρ,** ῆρος, ὁ, = ἡβητής, *AP*5.276 (Eratosth.), 6.76 (Agath.), Coluth.71. **-ητηρία,** ἡ, *the age of* ἥβη, *IG*12(9).916.22 (Chalcis). **-ητήριον,** τό, *a place where young people meet*, for exercise and amusement, Plu.*Pomp.*40, 53, Ath.10.425e, D.C.61.17, Hsch. **-ητής,** οῦ, ὁ, Dor. **ἡβᾱτάς** *IG*9(1).334 (Locr., v B.C.), *Berl.Sitzb.*1927.160 (Cyrene), **ἀβᾱτάς** only in Call. (v. infr.); Thess. **εἰβᾱτάς** (q.v.): (ἡβάω):—*in one's prime, adult*, *κοῦροι ἡβηταί* *h.Merc.*56, cf. Call.*Lav.Pall.*109; *βραχιόνων ἡβητὴν τύπον* E.*Heracl.*858. **-ητικός,** ή, όν, *youthful*, *λόγοι* X.*HG*5.3.20; *ἡλικία* Id.*Lac.*4.7, Gal.17(2).791. **-ήτωρ,** ορος, ὁ, = ἡβητήρ, *κίχλαι* Matro *Conv.*78. **-ικός,** ή, όν, = ἡβητικός, *ἡλικία* Gal.16.655 (with v.ll.), Steph. *in Hp.*2.373 D.

**ἠβολεῖν·** *ἀργεῖν*, Hsch.

**ἤβολον** *ἦμαρ· καθὸ ἀπα⟨ν⟩τῶσιν εἰς ταὐτόν, ἢ εὔκαιρον, ἱερόν*, Hsch. (= Call.*Fr.anon.*170).

**ἡβυλλιάω,** Comic Dim. of ἡβάω, *to be in the bloom of youth*, Ar.*Ra.*516, Pherecr.108.29.

⊛ **ἠγάθεος** [ᾰ], η, ον, Dor. **ἀγάθ-,** *most holy*, of places immediately under divine protection, *Πύλος, Λῆμνος*, Il.1.252, 2.722; *Πυθώ* Hes.*Th.*499, Pi.*P.*9.71; *χῶρος, ἄντρον*, A.R.3.981, 4.1131. (ἀγα-, θεός with Epic metrical lengthening.)

**ἠγᾰλέος,** α, ον, (ἄγνυμι) *broken in pieces*, Call.*Fr.anon.*91.

**ἠγάνεα·** *πέμματα τὰ ἀπὸ τηγάνου*, Hsch.; cf. ἤγανον. **ἠγανές·** *καθαρόν, νέον*, and **ἠγάν⟨ε⟩ος·** *νεανίσκος*, Id.

⊛ **ἤγᾰνον,** τό, Ion. for τήγανον, Anacr.26.

⊛ **ἡγέμαχος·** *πολέμαρχος*, Hsch., cf. *EM*299.43.

⊛ **ἡγεμόν-εια,** ἡ, fem. of ἡγεμονεύς, = ἡγεμόνη, Orph.*A.*909. **-ευμα,** ατος, τό, *leading*: but in E.*Ph.*1492 *ἁγεμόνευμα νεκροῖσι*, = ἡγεμὼν νεκρῶν, cf. Sch. ad loc. **-εύς,** έως, ὁ, Dor. **ἁγ-** *IG*5(1).540 (iii A.D.), Ep. for ἡγεμών, acc. ἡγεμονῆα, -ῆας, Opp.*C.*1.224, *AP*14.72.11, Man.1.36, etc.; of a Roman *governor*, *IG*14.1437, *Supp.Epigr.*1.405 A 2 (Samos). **-εύω,** Dor. **ἁγ-,** *lead the way*, *προτὶ Ἴλιον* Il.16.92; *πρὸς δώματα, ἀγορήνδε, λέχοσδε, δεῦρο*, Od.3.386, 8.4, 23.293, 17.372; *πρόσθ' ἡγεμόνευεν* 22.400, 24.155; *αὖλιν ἐφ' ἡμετέρην* Theoc.25.60; *ἐπιθυμίας καὶ ἔρωτος ἡγεμονεύσαντος* Pl.*Smp.*197a: c. dat. pers., Od.3.386, 8.4, Hes.*Th.*387, etc.; *τῇ ἴμεν, ᾗ κεν δὴ σὺ..ἡγεμονεύῃς* Il.15.46; *ὁδὸν ἡ. to lead* the way, *ἐγὼ δ' ὁδὸν ἡγεμονεύσω* Od.6.261, cf. Parm.1.5: twice in Hom., c. dat. et acc., *τοῖσι γέρων ὁδὸν ἡγεμόνευε* Od.24.225; *ὕδατι ῥόον ἡ. make* a course for the water, Il.21.258. II. *lead* in war, *rule, command*, once in Hom., c. dat., *Τρωσὶ μὲν ἡγεμόνευε..Ἕκτωρ* 2.816: elsewh., c. gen., *Λοκρῶν δ' ἡ. Αἴας* ib.527, cf. 552, Hdt.7.99, 160, etc.; *ἡγεμόνων ἡ.* X.*Ages.*1.3, etc.; *ἡ. τῆς σκέψεως to take the lead* in it, Pl.*Prt.*351e: abs., *to have* or *take the command*, Hdt.8.2; *ἡ. ἐν πόλει* Pl.*R.*474c:—Pass., *to be ruled*, *ὑπό τινος* Th.3.61.—Signf. II never occurs in Od., and signf. I rarely in Il. III. *to be governor*, *τῆς Συρίας* *Ev.Luc.*2.2: abs., *PTeb.*302.7 (i A.D.), *IGRom.*3.162 (Ancyra, ii A.D.), etc. ⊛ **-έω,** *have authority*, *ἔν τινι* Pl.*Ti.*41c, 70c; *have the primacy*, Id.*Lg.*631c. ⊛ **-η,** Dor. **ἁγ-** *JHS*13.353 (Aetol.), fem. of ἡγεμών:—*queen*, epith. of Artemis, Call.*Dian.*227, Ant.Lib.4.5; *Ἄρτεμις Ὀρθωσία Ἡ.* *IG*2.1663c; of Aphrodite, Hsch.; at Athens, one of the Charites, Paus.9.35.2; *flagship*, Hsch. **-ητ̄ς,** ῖδος, ἡ, poet. for ἡγεμονίς, Man.4.98. **-ία,** ἡ, *leading the way, going first*, Hdt.2.93; *τῇ τῶν δυναστευόντων ἡ.* by their *example*, Pl.*Lg.*711c. II. *authority, rule*, of dynasties or nations, Hdt.1.7, 3.65, etc.; of a general or officer, Th.4.91; *ἐν ἡγεμονίαις* Id.7.15; *ἡ ἡ. τῶν Ἰώνων τοῦ πολέ-*

μου Hdt.6.2; ἡ κατὰ πόλεμον ἡ., τῶν πολεμικῶν ἡ ἡ., Arist.*Pol.* 1285ᵇ9,18; αἱ ἡ. τῶν στρατοπέδων Pl.*Euthd.*273c; τῶν ὀπισθοφυλάκων X.*An.*4.7.8; ἡ. δικαστηρίου *presidency* in a court, Aeschin.3.14; *headship* of a philosophical school, Phld.*Acad.Ind.*p.59 M. 2. *political supremacy*, ἡ ἡ. τῆς Ἑλλάδος X.*HG*7.1.33; παρ' ἑκόντων τῶν Ἑλλήνων τὴν ἡ. ἐλάβομεν Isoc.8.30; ἡ ἡ. κατὰ θάλατταν Id.12.67, cf. Arist. *Ath.*23.2; ἡ ἐν Ἀρείῳ πάγῳ βουλὴ οὐδενὶ δόγματι λαβοῦσα τὴν ἡ. ib.1, cf. *Pol.*1304ᵃ23; *political leadership* of an individual, ib.1296ᵃ39; γένος ὑπερέχον πρὸς ἡ. πολιτικήν ib.1288ᵃ9. b. = Lat. *imperium*, Plu. *Mar.*36, D.C.60.17, etc.; Αἴγυπτον δήμου Ῥωμαίων ἡγεμονίᾳ προσέθηκα *Mon.Anc.Gr.*15.1; τοῖς καλοῖς τῆς ἡ. νόμοις Ath.Mech.39.7; τριῶν τῶν μεγίστων ἡ. Plu.*Luc.*30; *reign of an Emperor*, *Ev.Luc.*3.1; *office of prefect*, *POxy.*237 v6 (ii A.D.), al. III. *military unit, regiment*, *IG*2².657 (pl.), *PRein.*9.13 (ii B.C.), Plu.*Cam.*23 (pl.); but αἱ μείζονες ἡ. the higher *commands*, Ael.*Tact.*10.4. IV. *chief thing, principal part*, ἡ. τῆς τέχνης Diph.17.5. V. *a principality*, Lxx *Ge.*36.30; *a Roman governorship*, ἡ Ἰλλυρίδος ἡ. Hdn.6.7.2, cf. 7.5.2; *tenure of office of a governor*, *PRyl.*77.36 (ii A.D.); ἡ Ἡ. the *Government*, *PGrenf.*2.73.11 (iii A.D.). -ίδης, ου, ὁ, = ἡγεμών, Lxx 2*Ma.* 13.24. ❋ -ικός, ή, όν, *of* or *for a leader, ready to lead* or *guide*, πρός τι X.*Mem.*2.3.14 (Comp.); πρὸς τὰ πονηρὰ Id.*Cyr.*2.2.25; κλῆμα -ώτατον τῆς ἀμπέλου *Gp.*4.13.4: ἡ. τόπος *vital* spot, Vett.Val.38.13. II. *capable of command, authoritative*, ψυχὴ ἐν τοῖς ἥλιξι ἡ. X.*Smp.*8.16; ἡ. φύσις Philol.11; ἡ. τὴν φύσιν Pl.*Phdr.*252e; ἡ. τέχναι Id.*Phlb.*55d; οἱ κατ' ἀρετὴν ἡ. πρὸς πολιτικὴν ἀρχήν Arist.*Pol.*1288ᵃ12; τὸ ἄρρεν.. τοῦ θήλεος -ώτερον ib.1259ᵇ2; -ωτάτη [ἐπιστήμη] Id.*Metaph.*996ᵇ 10; ἡ. καὶ πολιτικὸς βίος (sc. τῆς πόλεως) Id.*Pol.*1327ᵇ5; ζῴδια, viz. Aries, Leo, Sagittarius, *Cat.Cod.Astr.*1.165, Ptol.*Tetr.*34; ἡγεμονικόν, *authoritative*, of knowledge, Pl.*Prt.*352b; τὸ ἡγεμονικόν *the authoritative part of the soul* (reason), esp. in Stoic philosophy, Zeno *Stoic.*1.39, etc.; but also, *the governing part* of the universe, of the aether or sun, Chrysipp.*Stoic.*2.186,192, Cleanth.ib.1.112. Adv. -κῶς *like a leader*, opp. δεσποτικῶς, Arist.*Fr.*658; ἡ. καὶ βασιλικῶς Plb.2.64.6, cf. Procl.*in Alc.*p.52C.: Comp. -ώτερον *more like an Emperor*, J.*AJ*19.4.2. 2. = Lat. *consularis*, Plu.*Pomp.*26. 3. *of* or *belonging to the prefect of Egypt*, ὑπηρέτης *CPR*18.35 (ii A.D.); πλοῖα *POxy.*2116.1 (iii A.D.). 4. -κά, τά, *payment to a* ἡγεμών, ἐδίδοτο Κλέωνι ἐν Ἀλεξανδρείᾳ ἡ...καὶ σῖτος ἀκόλουθος *PLond.ined.* 2089 (iii B.C.). -ιος, ον, *guiding*, epith. of Hermes, as *the guide* of departed souls, cf. ψυχοπομπός, Ar.*Pl.*1159, *IG*2².1496.85, Corn. *ND*16. -ίς, ίδος, ἡ, fem. of ἡγεμών, *imperial*, πόλεις Str.8.6.10, cf. *CIG*2721 (Stratonicea); γῆ App.*BC*2.65: metaph., δικαιοσύνη ἡ ἐν ἀρεταῖς ἡ. Ph.2.5; αἰσθήσεων ἡ. ὅρασις Id.2.24.

**ἡγεμόσυνα** (sc. ἱερά), τά, *thank-offerings for safe-conduct*, X.*An.* 4.8.25.

❋ **ἡγεμών**, Dor. ἁγ-, Aeol. ἀγίμων *IG*12(2).164 (Mytil.), al., όνος, ὁ; also ἡ, Pi.*I.*8(7).22, A.*Supp.*722, Aeschin.1.171, X.*Oec.* (infr. II):— *one who leads*; and so, I. in Od., *guide*, 10.505, 15.310, Hdt.5. 14, S.*Ant.*1014, Pl.*Men.*97b; ἡγεμόνες γενέσθαι τινὶ τῆς ὁδοῦ Hdt.8. 31, cf. E.*Hec.*281, X.*Mem.*1.3.4; ἡ. ποδὸς τυφλοῦ E.*Ph.*1616; ἡγεμόνες τοῦ πλοῦ Th.7.50; of a charioteer, S.*OT*804. 2. *one who does a thing first, shows the way* to others, τοῖς νεωτέροις ἡ. ἠθῶν χρηστῶν γίγνεσθαι Pl.*Lg.*670e; πατέρες τῆς σοφίας καὶ ἡ. Id.*Ly.*214a; πόνους τοῦ ζῆν ἡδέως ἡγεμόνας νομίζετε X.*Cyr.*1.5.12; τῆς εἰρήνης ἡ. D.18.24; [ἀχαριστία] ἐπὶ πάντα τὰ αἰσχρὰ ἡ. X.*Cyr.*1.2.7: abs., of choir-*leaders*, *Mnemos.*47.253 (Argos, ii/i B.C.). II. in Il., *leader, commander, chief*, opp. λαοί, πληθύς, 2.365, 11.304: c. gen., ἡγεμόνες Δαναῶν, φυλάκων, etc., 2.487, 9.85, cf. Hdt.6.43, 7.62, al.; στρατηγὸς καὶ ἡ. τῶν Ἑλλήνων πρὸς τὸν βάρβαρον ib.158; ἡ. τῶν πολεμίων Id.9.33; ἔχοντες ἡγεμόνας τῶν πάνυ [στρατηγῶν] Th.8.89; = λοχαγός, Arr.*Tact.* 5.6; ἡ. τῶν ἐν προχειρισμῷ *PAmh.*2.39 (ii B.C.); *chief, sovereign*, Pi.*I.* 8(7).22, etc.; ἡ. γῆς τῆσδε S.*OT*103, cf. *OC*289; πάντων..καὶ αὐτοῦ βασιλέως ἡ. X.*HG*3.5.14: ἡ. συμμορίας D.21.157; of the *queen*-bee and *queen*-wasp, regarded by Arist. as males, Arist.*HA*553ᵃ25, 629ᵃ3 (but ἡ τῶν μελισσῶν ἡ. X.*Oec.*7.32, cf. 38); ὁ ἡ. τῶν προβάτων, of the bell-wether, Arist.*HA*573ᵇ24; τῶν βοῶν ib.575ᵇ1; νέμειν τὰ κρέα τοῦ ἡγεμόνος βοὸς *SIG*1044.36 (Piraeus, iv B.C.), cf. X.*HG*6.4. 29. b. ἡ. χοροῦ *leader* of a chorus, Poll.4.106; παῖδες ἡ. *IG*7.3196 (Orchom. Boeot.); *president* of a gymnasium, ib.3.1086, al. c. *a Roman Emperor*, Str.4.3.2, Plu.*Cic.*2, al.; as translation of *princeps*, *Mon.Anc.Gr.*7.9; ἡ. νεότητος, = Lat. *princeps juventutis*, ib.18; *a provincial governor*, Str.17.3.25, *Ev.Matt.*27.2, *Act.Ap.*23.24: freq. of the *praefectus Aegypti*, *PRyl.*119.4 (i A.D.), etc.; ἡ. ἀμφοτέρων, i.e. of Upper and Lower Egypt, *POxy.*39.6 (i A.D.): ἡ. Κύπρου *Tab. Defix.Aud.*25.13 (iii A.D.). 2. as Adj., ἀνήρ Pl.*Criti.*119a; [ναῦς], of the flagship, A.*Supp.*722; ἡ. τῆς φυλῆς κορυφαῖος D.21.60 (s.v.l.); ἡ. πόδες Arist.*HA*490ᵇ5, *IA*713ᵇ32: as neut., ἡγεμόσι μέρεσι Pl.*Ti.* 91e. III. in Prosody, = πυρρίχιος, D.H.*Comp.*17, *Dem.*47. IV. ἡγεμόνες, Dor. ἁγ-, αἱ, in Architecture, *coping-tiles* of the roof, *IG*2². 463.70, 1627.303, 4.1484.100 (Epid.). V. a kind of fish, = ἡγητήρ 2, Plu.2.980f.

❋ **ἡγέομαι**, Dor. ἁγ- (irreg. pres. part. ἁγώμενος *Hymn.Curet.*4), impf. ἡγούμην Il.12.28, etc., Ion. -εύμην Hdt.2.115, ἡγέοντο Id.9.15: fut. ἡγήσομαι Il.14.374, etc.: aor. 1 ἡγησάμην Od.14.48, etc.: aor. 1 ἡγήθην in pass. sense, *PGiss.*48.20 (iii A.D.) (cf. περιηγ-): pf. ἥγημαι Hdt.1.126, 2.115, ἅγημαι Pi.*P.*4.248:—*go before, lead the way*, ὣς εἰπὼν ἡγεῖθ', ἡ δ' ἕσπετο Παλλὰς Ἀθήνη Od.1.125; ἂν παῖς ἡγήσαιτο νήπιος 6.300, etc.; πρόσθεν δὲ..Ἶρις ἡγεῖτ' Il.24.96; ἡγοῦ πάροιθε E. *Ph.*834; ἡ. ἐπὶ νῆα Od.13.65; ἐς τεῖχος Il.20.144; κλισίηνδε Od.14. 48, cf. Hdt.2.93, etc.; ἡγησόμενος οὐδεὶς ἔσται X.*An.*2.4.5: Astron., *precede* in the daily movement, Autol.2.3, al. b. c. dat. pers., Τρωσὶ ποτὶ πτόλιν ἡγήσασθαι Il.22.101; ἐκ Δουλιχίου..ἡγεῖτο μνηστῆρσι Od.16.397; οἱ γὰρ βλέποντες τοῖς τυφλοῖς ἡγούμεθα Ar.*Pl.*15; ἡ. τοῖς πολίταις πρὸς ἀρετήν X.*Ages.*10.2. c. with ὁδόν added, ὁδὸν ἡγήσασθαι *to go before* on the way, Od.10.263; ἡ. τινὶ τὴν ὁδόν Hdt.9.15. d. c. acc. loci, ἥ οἱ..πόλιν ἡγήσαιτο who *might guide* him to the city, Od.6.114, cf. 7.22, 15.82; ἡ. βωμοὺς ἀστικούς A.*Supp.*501. e. ἅρματα ἡ. *drive* chariots, Philostr.*Im.*2.23. f. of logical priority, *to be antecedent*, opp. ἕπεσθαι, *Stoic.*2.71, 88, S.E. *M.*8.110, al., Dam.*Pr.*241, Phlp.*in GC*195.13, *in Ph.*496.14. g. ἡγούμενον, τό, the *leading principle*, the *main thing*, Ph.*Bel.*62.14, cf. Sosip.1.47. 2. c. dat. pers. et gen. rei, *to be* one's *leader in* a thing, θεῖος ἀοιδός..ἡμῖν ἡγείσθω..ὀρχηθμοῖο Od.23.134; ἡ. τινὶ σοφίας, ᾠδῆς, Pi.*P.* l. c., Pl.*Alc.*1.125d; ἀλήθεια δὴ πάντων μὲν ἀγαθῶν θεοῖς ἡγεῖται πάντων δὲ ἀνθρώποις Id.*Lg.*730c; ἡ. τοῦ χοροῦ Πέρσαις X.*Cyr.*8.7.1, cf. Call.*Del.*313: c. gen. rei, ἁ. νόμων *to lead* the song, Pi.*N.*5.25; φρόνησις ἡ. τοῦ ὀρθῶς πράττειν Pl.*Men.*97c; ἡ. παντὸς καὶ λόγου καὶ ἔργου X.*Mem.*2.3.15: also, τὸ ὀρθῶς τοῖς τοιούτοις χρῆσθαι ἐπιστήμη ἦν ἡγουμένη Pl.*Euthd.*281a. 3. c. dat. rei, *to be leader in*.., κερδοσύνῃ, νηπιέῃσι ἡ. τινί, Il.22.247, Od.24.469. 4. c. acc. rei, *lead, conduct*, ἡ. τὰς πομπάς D.21.174; τὴν ἀποδημίαν (v.l. for ᾐτήσατο) Dinon 7; τὰς τύχας E.*Supp.*226: with adverbial acc., ἡ γλῶσσα πάνθ' ἡγουμένη S.*Ph.*99. 5. part. ἡγούμενος, η, ον, as Adj., σκέλη ἡγούμενα, opp. ἑπόμενα, the *front* legs, Arist.*IA*713ᵇ6; ὁ ἡ. πούς the *advanced* foot, Id.*Fr.*74. II. *lead, command* in war, c. dat., νῆες θοαί, ᾗσιν Ἀχιλλεὺς ἐς Τροίην ἡγεῖτο Il.16.169, cf. Od.14.238; οὐ γὰρ ἔην ὅς τίς σφιν ἐπὶ στίχας ἡγήσαιτο *might lead* them to their ranks, Il.2.687; ἡ. Τρώεσσιν ἐς Ἴλιον 5.211; ἡ. Μήοσιν 2.864; λόγχαισιν E.*Ba.*1360; ἑτέροις Lys. 31.17, cf. X.*An.*5.2.6; ἐν ταῖς στρατείαις, αἷς ἡγεῖται βασιλεύς Isoc. 12.180: also generally, πόλει E.*Fr.*282.24; but usu. c. gen., Σαρπηδὼν δ' ἡγήσατ'..ἐπικούρων Il.12.101; ἡγήσατο λαῶν 15.311, cf. 2. 567, al.; ἡ. τῆς ἐξόδου Th.2.10; ἡγούμενος τῶν ἡδονῶν ἀλλ' οὐκ ἀγόμενος ὑπ' αὐτῶν Isoc.9.45: abs., *to be in command*, Id.16.21, etc. 2. *rule, have dominion*, c. gen., τῆς Ἀσίης, τῆς συμμαχίης, Hdt.1.95, 7. 148; οἱ Θεσσαλίης ἡγεόμενοι Id.9.1: abs., οἱ ἡγούμενοι *the rulers*, S. *Ph.*386, cf. A.*Ag.*1363; ἡ. ἐν τοῖς ἀδελφοῖς *leading men*, *Act.Ap.* 15.22; ἡ. σχολῆς *to be the head* of a philosophical school, Phld.*Acad. Ind.*p.107 M., al. 3. as official title, ἡγούμενος, ὁ, *president*. συνόδου *PGrenf.*2.67.3 (iii A.D.); γερδίων ib.43.9 (i A.D.); ἱερέων *PLond.* 2.281.2 (i A.D.): abs., *PFay.*110.26 (i A.D.). b. of Roman governors, ἡ. ἔθνους, = Lat. *praeses provinciae*, *POxy.*1020.5 (ii/iii A.D.); ἡ. τῆς Γαλατίας Luc.*Alex.*44. c. of subordinate *officials*, ἡ. τοῦ στρατηγοῦ *POxy.*294.19 (i A.D.); κώμης *PRyl.*125.3 (i A.D.). d. *abbot*, Just.*Nov.*7.1, al.: fem. -μένη *abbess*, ibid. 4. ἡγούμενος as Adj., *principal*, πυλὼν *PFlor.*382.15 (iii A.D.), *POxy.*55.9 (iii A.D.). III. post-Hom., *believe, hold*, Hdt. (usu. in pf. ἥγημαι, 3 pl. ἡγέαται), etc.; ἡ. τι εἶναι Id.1.126, al.; ἡγεῖσθε δὲ [θεοὺς] βλέπειν.. πρὸς τὸν εὐσεβῆ βροτῶν S.*OC*278, cf. Th.2.89, Ar.*Nu.*1020 (lyr.), etc. 2. with an attributive word added, ἡ. τινὰ βασιλέα *hold* or *regard* as king, Hdt.6.52; μηδ' αὐθαδίαν εὐβουλίας ἀμείνον' ἡγήσῃ ποτέ A.*Pr.*1035; ἅπαντας ἐχθροὺς τῶν θεῶν ἡγοῦ πλέον Id.*Ch.*902, cf. 905; ἡ. τἄλλα πάντα δεύτερα *to hold* everything else secondary, S.*Ph.*1442; οὐκ αἰσχρὸν ἡγῇ..τὰ ψευδῆ λέγειν; ib.108, cf. *Ant.*1167; τὰς τούτων ἀπορίας ἀντιπάλους ἡ. τῷ ἡμετέρῳ πλήθει Th.4.10; περὶ πολλοῦ ἥγημαι μὴ ξεινοκτονέειν Hdt.2.115; περὶ πλείονος Isoc.19.10; περὶ πλείστου Th.2.89; περὶ οὐδενός Lys.7.26; παρ' οὐδέν Decr.ap.D.18.164: c. part., πᾶν κέρδος ἡγοῦ ζημιουμένη φυγῇ E.*Med.*454. 3. esp. of belief in gods, τὴν μεγίστην δαίμονα ἥγηνται εἶναι Hdt.2.40, cf. 3.8; ἡ. θεοὺς *to believe in* gods, Ar.*Eq.*32, E.*Hec.*800, *Ba.*1326; δαίμονας ἡ. Pl.*Ap.*27d. 4. ἡγοῦμαι δεῖν *think* fit, *deem* necessary, c. inf., And.1.23, D.1.20: without δεῖν, παθεῖν μᾶλλον ἡγησάμενοι ἢ.. Th.2. 42 (s.v.l.); ἡγησάμην διατάγματι αὐτοὺς σωφρονίσαι *Inscr.Magn.*114 (ii A.D.); ἡγήσατο ἐπαινέσαι Pl.*Prt.*346b. IV. pf. in pass. sense, τὰ ἁγημένα, = τὰ νομιζόμενα, Orac.ap.D.43.66; ἡγεόμενον *being led*, Hdt.3.14 (ἀγόμενον Dind.): hence act. form ἡγέω, Hdn.Gr.2.950. (*sāg-*, cf. Lat. *praesagio*.)

❋ **ἠγερέθομαι**, Ep. form of ἀγείρομαι (Pass.) *gather together, assemble*, only 3 pl. pres. and impf., and inf., ἀμφὶ δέ μιν..ἀγοὶ ἠγερέθονται Il. 3.231, cf. *h.Ap.*147; ἀμφ' Ἀτρεΐωνα ἀολλέες ἠγερέθοντο Il.23.233; περὶ δ' ἐσθλοὶ ἑταῖροι ἀθρόοι ἠγερέθοντο Od.2.392; ἀμφ' αἷμα..ἀολλέες ἠγερέθοντο 11.228; σφιν ἐπέφραδον ἠγερέθεσθαι Il.10.127 Aristarch. (ἠγερέεσθαι codd.): subj. ἠγερέθωνται Opp.*H.*3.360.

**ἤγερθεν**, Ep. 3 pl. aor. 1 Pass. of ἀγείρω.

❋ **ἡγεσία**, ἡ, (ἡγέομαι) = ἥγησις, Hsch. (ἡγεσκίης· ὁδηγησίας cod.).

**ἡγεσίλαος, ἡγησίλεως** [ῑ], v. ἀγησίλαος.

❋ **ἡγέτης**, ου, ὁ, Dor. ἁγ- (ἀγ-), (ἡγέομαι) *leader*, voc. ἡγέτα ὁδοῖο *Epigr.Gr.*1035.13 (Pergam.); ἀγέτα κώμων Orph.*H.*52.7 codd.; ἁ. θηροσύνας *AP*6.167 (Agath.):—fem. **ἀγέτις**, ιδος, ib.7.425 (Antip. Sid.).

❋ **ἡγηλάζω**, Ep. collat. form of ἡγέομαι, *guide, lead*, κακὸς κακὸν ἡγηλάζει Od.17.217; but κακὸν μόρον ἡ. *lead* a wretched life, 11. 618; βίοτον βαρὺν ἡ. A.R.1.272; ἱερὸν γόον Orac.ap.Zos.1.57: for Arat.893, v. ὑφηνηλάζω.

**ἡγηλάτέω**, prob. f.l. for ἀγ-, Them.*Or.*4.56c.

**ἥγ-ημα**, ατος, τό, *that which guides*, *Inscr.Perg.*246.27. II. (ἡγέομαι III) *thought, purpose*, Lxx *Ez.*17.3. -ησίπολις [σῐ], εως, ὁ, *leader of the state*, D.L.2.131. -ησις, εως, ἡ, *command*, Lxx *Jd.*5.15 (v.l.), 1*Ma.*9.31. -ήτειρα, ἡ, fem. of ἡγητήρ, Pl.*Epigr.*5.7, Opp.

C.1.253. —ητέον, *one must lead*, X.*HG*4.7.2, *Eq.Mag*.4.3. II. *one must hold, consider*, Pl.*R*.361a, Plb.1.35.9, Hierocl.p.63 A., etc. —ητήρ, Dor. ἁγ–, ῆρος, ὁ, = ἡγητής, *a guide*, S.*OC*1521; σοφίης ἐὸν ἡγητῆρα his *guide* to philosophy, *IG*3.947. 2. the *pilot-fish*, Opp.*H*.5.70. 3. = ἡγήτωρ, *a leader*, ἁ. ἀνήρ Pi.*P*.1.69. —ητηρία (sc. παλάθη), ἡ, *mass of dried figs, borne in procession at the Attic* Πλυντήρια, in memory of the discovery of this food, *which was considered the first step in civilized life*, Ath.3.74d, Porph.*Abst*.2.7, Hsch., Phot.: —ητορία, *EM*418.49: —ήτρια, Eust. 1399.29. —ητής, οῦ, ὁ, = ἡγητήρ, *a guide*, νόσφιν ἡγητῶν A.*Supp*. 239. —ητικός, Dor. ἁγ–, ή, όν, = ἡγεμονικός, *authoritative, leading*, τοὔνομ' οὐχ ἁ. *Com.Adesp*.in *Gött.Nachr*.1922.28; opp. ἀπορητικός, Procl.*in Prm*.p.483 S.; dub. sens. in Vett.Val.15.16. ⊛ –ήτωρ (Dor. ἁγ– Ibyc.*Oxy*.2081(*f*)*Fr*.4), ορος, ὁ, *leader, commander, chief*, Τρώων, φυλάκων, Il.3.153, 10.181; ἡγήτορες ἠδὲ μέδοντες *chiefs in war* and leaders in council, 2.79, etc.; ἡ. ὀνείρων, of Hermes, *h.Merc*. 14. II. title of chief priest of Aphrodite in Cyprus, *BMus.Inscr*. 975.10 (Amathus), cf. Hsch. s. v. ἀγήτωρ.

**ἡγιασμένως**, Adv. pf. Pass., (ἁγιάζω) *in holy manner*, Al.*Ps*.133 (134).2.

**ἠγμένως**, Adv. pf. Pass., (ἄγω) *reasonably*, Suid. (prob. l.).

**ἡγνευμένως**, Adv. pf. Pass., (ἁγνεύω) *purely*, Poll.1.32.

**ἠγόν** (ἦγον cod.)· κατεαγός, Hsch.; cf. ἠγαλέος.

**ἠγορόωντο**, Ep. and Ion. lengthd. for ἠγορῶντο, v. ἀγοράομαι.

⊛ **ἡγός**, ὁ, = ἡγεμών, *EM*390.36; = εὐδαίμων (Ionic), ib.37.

**ἡγούμενος**, ὁ, v. ἡγέομαι II. 3.

⊛ **ἤγουν**, Conj., (ἤ γε οὖν) *that is to say, or rather*, to define a word more correctly, freq. in glosses, cf. Eust.50.15, Lyd.*Mens*.4.23, etc.: sts. introduced into the text, κακὰ πάντα [ἤγουν τήν τε ἀπεψίην] καί.. Hp.*Acut*.(*Sp*.)49 (ii 491 L.); διὰ ξηρότητα [ἤγουν χαυνότητα] τῆς γῆς X.*Oec*.19.11: in late Prose, *or at any rate*, *PMasp*.328 i 20 (vi A. D.), al.: generally, *or*, *POxy*.941.5 (vi A. D.).

**ἡδᾰνός**, ή, όν, = ἡδύς, etym. of ἑδανός, Eust.974.53.

⊛ **ἠδέ**, *and*, prop. correlative to ἠμέν: ἠμέν.., ἠδέ.., *both.., and..*, Il.7.302, etc. II. without ἠμέν, *and*, ἡγήτορες ἠδὲ μέδοντες 2.79, cf. 1.41, 96, 251, etc.: sts. with τε before it, σκῆπτρόν τ' ἠδὲ θέμιστας 9.99; Ἕκτορ τ' ἠδ' ἄλλοι 12.61; Ἥρη τ' ἠδὲ Ποσειδάων καὶ Παλλὰς Ἀθήνη 1.400; αὐτός τ' ἀναχάζομαι ἠδὲ.. 5.822, cf. Pi.*O*.13.44; also μέν.., ἠδέ.. Od.1.240, 12.381, etc.; μέν τε.., ἠδέ.. Orph.*H*.14.9; παίδων ἠδ' ἀλόχων καὶ κτήσιος ἠδὲ τοκήων Il.15.663; ἠ. καί *and* also, 1.334, Od.2.209, 4.235, 1.240; ἠδ' ἔτι καί Il.1.455, 2.118; ἠδέ τε *AP* 9.788.9.—The Trag. use ἠ. in anapaestics and lyrics, A.*Pers*.16, 289, etc.; and (less freq.) in iamb., as Id.*Ch*.1025, *Eu*.414, S.*Fr*.386, 549, E.*Hec*.323, *HF*30: twice found in Com., Eup.14 (anap.), Alex.133.6 (trim., s. v. l.). Not in Att. Prose; used by Hp. (= ἔτι δέ) acc. to Gal.19.102, cf. Aret.*CD*2.7; ἀτὰρ ἠδέ ib.1.3.

**ᾔδεα, ᾔδειν**, v. *εἴδω.

**ἠδελφισμένως**, Adv. pf. Pass., prop. *with brotherly likeness*: metaph., ἠ. ἐν γαστρὶ ἐχούσῃ *just as if*.., Hp.*Mul*.1.3: abs., *in like manner*, ib.2.205.

**ἡδέως**, Adv. of ἡδύς, v. ἡδύς III.

⊛ **ἤδη**, Adv.: 1. *already, by this time*, νὺξ ἤ. τελέθει 'tis *already* night, Il.7.282; ἤ. Τρώεσσιν ὀλέθρου πείρατ' ἐφῆπται ib.402: with numerals, ἤ. γὰρ τρίτον ἐστὶν ἔτος Od.2.89; τρίτην ἤ. ἡμέραν Pl.*Prt*. 309d; ἔτος τόδ' ἤ. δέκατον S.*Ph*.312; ἦν δ' ἦμαρ ἤ. δεύτερον ib.354; τελοῦντες ἕκτον ἕβδομόν τ' ἤ. δρόμον Id.*El*.726; ἤ. γὰρ πολὺς ἐκτέταται χρόνος Id.*Aj*.1402. 2. *forthwith, immediately*, φρονέω δὲ διακρινθήμεναι ἤ. Ἀργείους καὶ Τρῶας Il.3.98; λέξον νῦν με τάχιστα, ὄφρα καὶ ἤδη.. ταρπώμεθα κοιμηθέντες Il.24.635, cf. Od.4.294; ἤ. νῦν.. μεγάλ' εὔχεο Il.16.844; στείχοις ἂν ἤ. S.*Tr*.624; ἤδη.. στέλλεσθε; Id.*Ph*.466; μετὰ τοῦτ' ἤ. Ar.*Th*.655; ἤ. ποτέ *now at length*, Mitteis *Chr*.87.8 (ii A. D.); on the verso of a letter, *urgent, immediate*, *PCair. Zen*.154 (iii B. C.); ἤ ἤ. ταχὺ ταχύ *PMag.Osl*.1.319. 3. opp. to the future or past, *actually, now*, οὐκ ὄναρ, ἀλλ' ὕπαρ ἤ. Od.20.90; τοῖς μὲν γὰρ ἤ., τοῖς δ' ἐν ὑστέρῳ χρόνῳ S.*OC*614; οἱ μὲν τάχ', οἱ δ' ἐσαῦθις, οἱ δ' ἤ. E.*Supp*.551; οὐ τάχ', ἀλλ' ἤ. Ar.*Ra*.527; ἡ ἤ. χάρις *present* favour, D.23.134; τὸ ἤ. κολάζειν X.*An*.7.7.24. 4. of logical proximity, ἤ. γὰρ ἂν προστίθεσθαι Pl.*Tht*.201e; τὰ ἐκ τούτων ἤ. συγκείμενα ib.202b; πᾶς ἤ. ἂν εὕροι Id.*R*.398c; ἂν σὺ ὁμολογήσῃς, ταῦτ' ἤ. ἐστὶν αὐτὰ τἀληθῆ Id.*Grg*.486e; τοῦτο τοὔπος δεινὸν ἤ. Ar.*Ach*.315; τὰ πάντα τὰ πράγματα διαφθείραντα ταῦτ' ἐστὶν ἤ. D.19.19. b. καὶ ἤ. *and further, as well*, ἐμέ τε καὶ σὲ καὶ τἄλλ' ἤ. Pl.*Tht*.159b, cf. S.E.*P*.1.53, 219, etc. c. *for instance*, Aen.Tact.4.1, 10.25. d. *only then, then and not before*, τότ' ἤδη A.*Pr*.911, Isoc. 12.25, *Ep*.6.9; ἐνταῦθ' ἤ. Aeschin.3.140; κακοπαθοῦντες ἤ. τῶν λόγων ἅπτονται Th.1.78. 5. with Sup., ὦ πάντων ἀνδρῶν ἤ. μάλιστα.. κτησάμενε *up to this time*, Hdt.8.106; μέγιστος ἤ. διάπλους Th.6.31: with Comp., ἤδη.. λόγου μέζων Hdt.2.148. II. joined with other words of time, ἤ. νῦν *now already*, Il.1.456, A.*Ag*.1578; νῦν ἤ. Od.23.54, S.*Ant*.801 (anap.); ἤ. ποτέ Il.1.260, S.*Aj*.1142, Ar.*Nu*.346; ποτ' ἤ. A.*Eu*.50; ἤ. πώποτε Eup.214, Pl.*R*.493d; πάλαι ἤ. S.*OC*510 (lyr.); ἤ. τότε *even then*, Pl.*R*.417b; ἐπεὶ ἤ. Od.4.260; εἰ ἤ. Il.22.52; τὸ τηνίκ' ἤ. S.*OC*440; τὸ λοιπὸν ἤ. Id.*Ph*.454; ἄλλοτε ἤ. πολλάκις Pl.*R*.507a; ἤ. γε even *now*, D.19.52. III. of place, ἀπὸ ταύτης ἤ. Αἴγυπτος after this Egypt begins, Hdt.3.5, cf. 2.15, 4.99, E.*Hipp*.1200; Φωκεῦσιν ἤ. ὅμορος ἡ Βοιωτία ἐστίν Th.3.95. (In general, cf. Arist.*Ph*.222[b]7.)

**ᾔδη, ᾔδης, ᾔδησθα**, v. *εἴδω. **ἥδιστος, ἡδίων**, Sup. and Comp. of ἡδύς.

⊛ **ἥδομαι**, Boeot. ϝᾱδ– [ᾱ] Corinn.in *BKT*5(2).34, Dor. ἁδ– [ᾱ], Aeol. ἄδ– [ᾰ] Sapph.*Supp*.24.10: fut. ἡσθήσομαι S.*OT*453, Pl.*Phdr*. 233e, etc.: aor. 1 ἥσθην (post-Homeric, v. infr.), also ἡδέσθην (sic) Hsch., Med. ἡσάμην Od.9.353: (*swād-*, cf. ἁνδάνω, ἡδύς):—*enjoy oneself, take one's pleasure*, once in Hom., Od. l. c.; freq. in Hdt. and Att.:—Constr.: 1. with part., ἥσατο πίνων Od. l. c.; ἥσθη ἀκούσας he *was glad* to have heard, Hdt.3.34; ἥδοι' ἄν.. ἰδοῦσα A.*Pr*.758, cf. S.*Ph*.882; δρῶντες ἂν ἡδώμεθα (sc. δρῶντες) Id.*Aj*.1085; οἶ' ἄν.. ἡσθείη λαβὼν Id.*El*.1325; ἡ. θωπευομένους Ar.*Ach*.635, etc. 2. c. dat., ἥδεσθαί τινι *to delight in* or *at* a thing or person, Hdt.1.69, al., Th.1.120, etc.; ἅπαντες ἡδόμεσθά σοι Ar.*Eq*.623 (lyr.): in aor., ironically, ἥσθην ἀπειλαῖς I *am amused* at your threats, ib.696, cf. *Nu*.174: once c. gen., πώματος ἥσθη he *enjoyed* the draught, S.*Ph*.715 (lyr.). 3. c. acc. and part., ἥσθην πατέρα τὸν ἁμὸν εὐλογοῦντά σε I *am pleased to hear* you praising him, ib.1314; δόμους ἥδεται πληρουμένους E.*Fr*.328. 1. 4. with neut. Adj., ἕτερον ἥσθην Ar.*Ach*.13; τοῖα θ' ἥδομαι Id. *Ra*.748 (cod. R); ἥσθην βαιά Id.*Ach*.2; βραχέα ἡσθεῖσα Th.3.40: c. acc. cogn., ἡδονὰς ἥδεσθαι Pl.*Phlb*.63a, etc. 5. folld. by a Prep., ἥδεσθαι ἐπί τινι X.*Cyr*.8.4.11, Pl.*Phlb*.48b, etc.; ὑπέρ τινος Lys.2.26; but πρὸς ὀλίγον ἡσθεὶς ναυτιᾷ for a little time, Arr.*Epict*.4.9.4. 6. ἥδομαι ὅτι.. Ar.*Nu*.773. 7. abs., ὡς ἥδομαι καὶ χαίρομαι κεὐφραίνομαι Ar.*Pax* 291, cf. Plu.2.440a, etc.; esp. in part., as Adj., *glad, delighted*, ἡδομένᾳ ψυχᾷ, φωνᾷ, E.*Fr*.754 (lyr.), Ar.*Av*.236 (lyr.); τὸ ἡδόμενον Plu.2.1025e, 1101f: freq. in dat., ἡδομένοισι ἦν τὸ γινόμενον they were *pleased at*.., Hdt.8.10, cf. 9.46; ἐὰν ὑμῖν ἡδομένοις (sc. ᾖ) Antipho 6.8, cf. Pl.*Phd*.78b, *La*.187c; τὸ ἡδόμενον κατὰ σάρκα Epicur. *Sent*.4. II. Act., ἥδω *please, delight*, c. acc. pers., aor., ἧσε Anacr.148: so later pres., ἥδει Muson.*Fr*.18[B]p.103 H.; ἥδομεν Men. *Mon*.38: aor. 1 ἧσα Ephipp.6.5 (s. v. l.), Ael.*NA*10.48, Hld.10.32, *AP*7 lemma (λαλῆσαι f. l. for ἀλλ' ἧσαι); τὰ ἥδοντα *joys, pleasures*, opp. τὰ λυποῦντα, Antipho Soph.*Oxy*.1364.116, cf. Pl.*Ax*.366a, Diog. Oen.29; τὸ ἧδον S.E.*M*.7.203.

**ἡδομένως**, Adv. of foreg., *with joy, gladly*, πράττειν τι X.*Cyr*.8.4.9.

⊛ **ἡδονή**, Dor. ἁδονά (or in Trag. chorus ἡδονά S.*OT*1339), ἡ, (ἥδομαι) *enjoyment, pleasure*, first in Simon.71, S. l. c., Hdt.1.24, al.; prop. of sensual pleasures, αἱ τοῦ σώματος or περὶ τὸ σῶμα ἡ., X.*HG* 4.8.22, 6.1.4; αἱ κατὰ τὸ σῶμα ἡ. Pl.*R*.328d; σωματικαὶ ἡ. Arist.*EN* 1151[a]13; αἱ περὶ πότους καὶ περὶ ἐδωδὰς ἡ. Pl.*R*.389e; but also ἀκοῆς ἡ. Th.3.38; ἡ ἀπὸ τοῦ εἰδέναι ἡ. Pl.*R*.582b; of *malicious pleasure*, ἡ ἐπὶ τοῖς τῶν φίλων κακοῖς, ἐπὶ ταῖς λοιδορίαις ἡ., Id.*Phlb*.50a, D.18.138; ἡδονῇ ἡσσᾶσθαι, ἡδοναῖς χαρίζεσθαι, to give way *to pleasure*, Th. l. c., Pl.*Lg*.727c; κότερα ἀληθείῃ χρήσομαι ἢ ἡδονῇ; shall I speak truly or *so as to humour you?* Hdt.7.101; εἰ ὑμῖν ἡδονὴ τοῦ ἡγεμονεύειν ib.160; ἡ. εἰσέρχεταί τινι εἰ.. one feels *pleasure* at the thought that.., Id.1.24; ἡδονὴν ἔχειν τινός to be *satisfied with*.., S.*OC* 1604; ἡδονὴν ἔχει, φέρει, Pherecr.145.2, Alex.263.6; ἡδονὴ ἰδέσθαι (like θαῦμα ἰδέσθαι), of a temple, Hdt.2.137: with Preps. in Adv. sense, δαίμοσιν πρὸς ἡδονήν A.*Pr*.494; ὃ μὲν ἔστι πρὸς ἡ. D.18.4; πρὸς ἡ. λέγειν to speak so *as to please another*, S.*El*.921, Th.2.65; δημηγορεῖν D.4.38; οὐ πρὸς ἡ. οἱ ἦν τὰ ἀγγελλόμενα Hdt.3.126; πάντα πρὸς ἡ. ἀκούοντας D.8.34; later πρὸς ἡδονῆς εἶναί τινι Parth.8.8, Lib. *Or*.12.1; καθ' ἡδονὴν κλύειν S.*Tr*.197; καθ' ἡδονήν [ἐστί] μοι c. inf., A.*Pr*.263; καθ' ἡ. τι δρᾶν, ποιεῖν, Th.2.37, 53; καθ' ἡδονὰς τῷ δήμῳ τὰ πράγματα ἐνδιδόναι ib.65; ἐν ἡδονῇ ἐστί τινι it is *a pleasure* or *delight* to another, Hdt.4.139; folld. by inf., E.*IT*494; by acc. et inf., Hdt.7.15; ἐν ἡδονῇ ἔχειν τινά to take *pleasure* in them, Th.3.9; ἐν ἡδονῇ ἄρχοντες, opp. οἱ λυπηροί, Id.1.99; μεθ' ἡδονῆς Id.4.19; ὑφ' ἡδονῆς S.*Ant*.648, etc.; ὑπὸ τῆς ἡ. Alex.24, 110.23: as dat. modi, ἡδονᾷ *with pleasure*, S. *OT*1339 (lyr.), cf. Hdt.2.137 (f. l.). 2. concrete, *a pleasure*, S.*El*. 873 (pl.), Ar.*Nu*.1072 (pl.); ἡδοναὶ τραγημάτων *sweetmeats*, Sopat. 17. 3. pl., *desires after pleasure, pleasant lusts*, X.*Mem*.1.2.23, *Ep.Tit*.3.3, al. II. in Ion. Philosophers, *taste, flavour*, usu. joined with χροιή, Diog.Apoll.5, Anaxag.4 (pl.), cf. Arist.*PA*660[b]9, Thphr. *HP*4.4.7, Lxx *Nu*.11.8, Eudem.ap.Ath.9.369f, Mnesith.ap.eund.8. 357f.

**ἡδονικός**, ή, όν, *of* or *for* ἡδονή, *pleasurable*, Chrysipp.Tyan.ap.Ath. 14.647d; βίος ἡ. Arist.ap.D.L.5.31. II. οἱ ἡ. the *voluptuaries*, of the Cyrenaic school of philosophers, Ceb.13, Ath.13.588a; ἡ ἡ. αἵρεσις Gal.*Libr.Propr*.16; ἐπὶ σωφροσύνης οὐχὶ ἡ. λέγεται ὁ ὑπερβάλλων ἀλλ' ἀκόλαστος Asp.*in EN*53.19. Adv. –κῶς Procl.*in Prm*. p.521 S.

**ἡδονο-κρᾰσία**, ἡ, *rule of pleasure*, Aristeas 278. —πληκτος, Dor. ἁδονόπλακτος, ον, *pleasure-struck*, Cerc.6.10:—also –πλήξ, ῆγος, ὁ, ἡ, φύσις Timo 58.4.

⊛ **ἦδος**, εος, τό (Aeolic, acc. to Hdn.Gr.2.904), *delight, pleasure*, οὐδέ τι δαιτὸς ἐσθλῆς ἔσσεται ἦ. Il.1.576; ἀλλὰ μίνυνθα ἡμέων ἔσσεται ἦ. 11.318; ἀλλὰ τί μοι τῶν ἦ.; what *delight* have I therefrom? 18.80; αὐτὰρ ἐμοὶ τί τόδ' ἦ.; Od.24.95, cf. Theoc.16.40, A.R.3.314.—In this sense almost confined to Ep. and nom. sg.; in late Prose, πρὸς τὸ ἦ. Alex.Aphr.*Pr*.1.20. II. = ὄξος, *vinegar*, used as a flavouring, τοῦτο μόνον Ἀττικοὶ τῶν ἡδυσμάτων ἦ. καλοῦσι Ath.2.67c, cf. Poll.6.65, Eust.1417.19, prob. l. in Antiph.134.4:—Dor. form **ἆδος** (in both senses), *EM*18.12, Hsch. s. v. γᾶδος.

**ἦ δ' ὅς**, for ἔφη ἐκεῖνος, v. ἠμί.

**ἡδοσύνη**, ἡ, = ἡδονή, Dor. ἁδοσύνᾱ, Hsch.

**ἡδύ-βιος** [ῠ], ον, *sweetening life*: τὰ ἡ. a name of certain *cakes*, Chrysipp.Tyan.ap.Ath.14.647c. II. *living pleasantly*, Ptol.*Tetr*. 162, Vett.Val.18.29, Sch.Ar.*V*.504. —βόης, Dor. ἁδῠβόας, ου, ὁ, *sweet-sounding*, ἁδυβόα.. αὐλῶν πνεύματι E.*Ba*.127; ἡ. κόσσυφος *AP* 9.396 (Paul. Sil.); δόναξ *APl*.4.231 (Anyte). —γαιον, τό, = σι–

κυον, Heraclid.Tarent.ap.Ath.2.74b(ἡδυνέον isf. l. in Hsch.). -γάμος, ον, *sweetening marriage*, κέρδος *AP*5.242(Maced.). -γελως, ωτος, ὁ, ἡ, *sweetly laughing*, *h.Hom*.19.37, *AP*5.134. -γλωσσία, ἡ, *sweetness of tongue*, *PMag.Leid.V*.20. -γλωσσος, Dor. ἁδ-, ον, *sweet-tongued*, βοά Pi.*O*.13.100. -γνώμων, ον, gen. ονος, (γνώμη) *of pleasant mind*, opp. ἡδυσώματος, X.*Smp*.8.30. -δειπνος, ον, *dainty-supping*, name of a parasite, Alciphr.3.68 tit. -επής, Dor. ἁδ-, ές, *sweet-speaking*, Il.1.248; Ὅμηρος Pi.*N*.7.21, cf. *AP*9.525.8, etc.; *sweet-sounding*, λύρα Pi.*O*.10(11).93; ὕμνος Id.*N*.1.4: voc., ὦ Διὸς ἁδυεπὲς φάτι S.*OT*151: poet. fem. pl., ἡδυέπειαι Μοῦσαι Ὀλυμπιάδες Hes.*Th*.965,1021: sg., -έπεια σῦριγξ Nonn.*D*.10.390. -θροος, ον, contr. -θρους, ουν, *sweet-strained*, Μοῦσα E.*El*.703 (lyr.); Διόνυσος *AP*9.524.8: Dor. ἁδ-, κίθαρις *Pae.Delph*.13. -καρπος, ον, *with sweet fruit*, Pherecyd.178 J.; δένδρον Thphr.*HP*4.4.5. -κρεως, ων, gen. ω, *of sweet flesh*, Arist.*HA*564ᵃ3, al.: Comp. -κρεώτερος Id. *GA*786ᵃ15. -κωμος, ὁ, name of a kind of αὔλησις, Trypho ap. Ath.14.618c; of a dance, Poll.4.100. -λάλος [ᾰ], ον, = ἡδυλόγος, φθόγγοι *IG*12(7).95.4 (Amorgos).

⊛ Ἡδύλειος [ῠ], α, ον, *of* or *connected with Hedylus*, κύλιξ *IG*11(2).154 *B*50 (Delos, iii B.C.).

⊛ ἡδῠλ-ίζω, (ἡδύλος) *flatter, wheedle*, Men.28. ⊛ -ισμός, ὁ, *flattering*, Eust.1417.21, Phot.

ἡδῠλογ-έω, *speak sweet things*, τινι Phryn.Com.3.4. ⊛ -ία, ἡ, *jesting*, in pl., Ath.4.164e. -ος, Dor. ἁδ-, Aeol. ἀδ-, ον, *sweet-speaking, sweet-voiced*, Sapph.*Oxy*.1787 *Fr*.11.4; σοφία Cratin.238, Timo 67.4; λύραι μολπαί τε Pi.*O*.6.96; Χάρις *AP*5.136 (Mel.); γλῶσσα ib.7.159 (Nicarch.). 2. of persons, *flattering, fawning*, E.*Hec*. 132 (anap.): as Subst., *jester*, Ath.4.165b. (In signf. 1 proparox., in 2 parox.)

ἡδύλος [ῠ], η, ον, Dim. of ἡδύς, only as pr. n. (exc. A.D.*Adv*.172.1, *EM*742.52).

⊛ ἡδῠ-λύρης [ῠ], ου, ὁ, *singing sweetly to the lyre*, Πίνδαρος *AP*11.370 (Maced.): Dor. ἀδυλύρας, epith. of Apollo, *Philol*.71.6 (Argos, iv B.C.). -μανής, ές, *full of sweet frenzy*, Nonn.*D*.7.269. -μέλεια, ἡ, *sweetness of melody*, Vett.Val.3.20 (pl.). -μελής, Dor. ἁδ-, Aeol. ἀδ-, ές, *sweet-singing*, χελιδοῖ Anacr.67, cf. Sapph.122 (Comp.), Pi.*N*.2.25; *sweet-sounding*, ξόανα S.*Fr*.238, etc.: poet. fem., ἡδυμέλεια σῦριγξ Nonn.*D*.29.287. -μελι, = μελισσόφυλλον, prob. in Ps.-Dsc.3.104. -μελίφθογγος, ον, *of honey-sweet voice*, Σιμωνίδης *AP* 9.571 (acc. to Planudes). -μῐγής, Dor. ἁδ-, ές, *sweetly-mixed*, χόνδρος ib.7.736 (Leon.).

ἥδῠμος, Dor. ἅδ- ον, poet. for ἡδύς, *sweet, pleasant*, usu. epith. of sleep (v. νήδυμος, for which it is v.l. in Il.2.2, Od.4.793, 12.311, cf. Hsch. s.v. νήδυμος), *h.Merc*.241, 449, Antim.74, Simon.79, A.R.2.407; λόγοι Epich.179; οἶνος Orph.*Fr*.261: irreg. Sup. -έστατος Alcm. 137.

ἡδυν-τέον, *one must season*, Alex.186.4. -τήρ, ῆρος, ὁ, *seasoning*, ἅλες Eratosth.ap.Hsch., Poll.6.71. -τήριος, α, ον, *sweetening, soothing*, Sch.E.*Hec*.535. -τικός, ή, όν, *fit for seasoning*, Arist.*Pr*.923ᵃ29. II. -κή τέχνη *an art of seasoning*, Pl.*Sph*. 223a. -τός, ή, όν, *seasoned*, πίσσα, στέαρ, Hp.*Mul*.1.88, 2.205. -ω, aor. 1 ἥδυνα Pl.*Tht*.175e, Diph.24:—Pass., aor. 1 ἡδύνθην Antiph.90: pf. ἥδυσμαι Pl. (v. infr.), inf. ἡδύνθαι Phot.: (ἡδύς):—*season* a dish, c. acc., [κόκκυγας] Epich.164; ὄψον Pl.*Tht*. l. c.; κρόμμυον.. οὐ μόνον σῖτον ἀλλὰ καὶ ποτὸν ἡδύνει X.*Smp*.4.8; *make pleasant*, γεῦσιν, οἴνους, Thphr.*Od*.9,10; even of salt (cf. ἡδονή II), Arist.*Mete*.359ᵃ 34. II. metaph., ἡ. θῶπας λόγους Pl.*Tht*. l. c.; ὁ ποιητὴς ἡ. τὸ ἄτοπον Arist.*Po*.1460ᵇ2:—Pass., τὴν ἡδυσμένην μοῦσαν παραδέξῃ ἐν μέλεσιν Pl.*R*.607a, cf. Arist.*Po*.1449ᵇ28, *Pol*.1340ᵇ17, D.H.*Comp*. 25; τοὺς λόγους ἡδύνεσθαι ἄν τι ὑπὸ τῶν φθόγγων X.*Smp*.6.4. 2. *delight, coax, gratify*, κόλαξ ἥδυνέ τινα λόγῳ Diph.24; ἡ. τὴν ἀκοήν D.H.*Comp*.14:—Pass., Timo 17.

ἡδύ-οδμος [ῠ], Dor. ἁδ-, ον, = ἡδύοσμος, οἶνος Hp.*Mul*.1.34; ἔαρ Simon.74. -οινία, ἡ, *sweetness of wine*, Hp.*Morb*.4.34, *Gp*.5.2. 19. -οινος, Dor. ἁδ-, ον, *producing sweet wine*, ἄμπελοι X.*An*.6.4.6; -ότερος καρπός Thphr.*CP*3.15.1. 2. *containing sweet wine*, λεπαστή Apolloph.6. II. ἡδύοινοι, οἱ, *dealers in sweet wine*, X.*Vect*.5.3. -όνειρος, ον, *causing sweet dreams*, ἰσχάδες Hermipp.63.16. -οσμος, ον, *sweet-smelling, fragrant*, στρώματα Ar.*Fr*.695. II. ⊛ ἡδύοσμον, τό, = μίνθη, *green mint, Mentha viridis*, Thphr.*HP*7.7.1, Str.8.3.14; ἡ. ἄγριον *wild mint, M. longifolia*, Dsc.3.34. [As trisyll., *AP*11.413 (Ammian.).] -όφθαλμος, ον, *sweet-eyed*, Hsch. s. v. μελίγληνος.

ἡδῠπάθ-εια [πᾰ], ἡ, *pleasant living, luxury*, X.*Cyr*.7.5.74, Hp.*Ep*. 17, Plu.2.6b, al., Sor.1.34, Luc.*DMort*.10.8: in pl., Ath.4.165e, Just.*Nov*.105.1; title of work by Archestratus, Ath.1.4e. -έω, *live pleasantly, enjoy oneself*, X.*Cyr*.1.5.1, Jul.*Mis*.342b; ἡ. ἀπό τινος X.*Oec*.5.2. -ημα, ατος, τό, *enjoyment*, σαρκός *AP*9.496 (⟨Ath.⟩). -ής, ές, (παθεῖν) *living pleasantly, enjoying oneself, luxurious*, Antiph.91, Aristox.*Fr.Hist*.15.

ἡδύ-πνευστος, ον, = ἡδύπνοος, *AP*5.117 (Marc. Arg.). -πνοΐς, ΐδος, ἡ, *ox-tongue, Helminthia echioides*, Plin.*HN*20.75; to be restored in Hsch. for ἡδυπνοΐδης. ⊛ -πνοος, Dor. ἁδ-, ον, contr. -πνους, ουν, *sweet-breathing*, αὖραι E.*Med*.840 (lyr.); of musical sound, Pi.*O*.13. 22, *I*.2.25; of auspicious dreams, S.*El*.480 (lyr.). 2. *sweet-smelling, fragrant*, λεπαστή Telecl.24 (lyr.); χῶρος *AP*9.564 (Nic.); κρόκος *IG*14.607e (Carales); ὅρμος (necklace) Dsc.1.99. 3. v. ἡδύχρους II. -πολις, Dor. ἁδ-, ὁ, ἡ, *dear to the people*, S.*OT*510 (lyr.). -πορφύρα [ῠ], ἡ, a kind of πορφύρα, Arist.*Fr*.304. -πότης, ου, *fond of drinking*, epith. of Dionysus, *AP*9.524.8, cf. Hedyl. ap.Ath.4.176d, Man.4.493. II. *furnishing sweet drink*, ἄμπελος Nonn.*D*.12.249. ⊛ -πότις, ιδος, ἡ, *something that makes drink taste pleasant*, name of a cup, Epig.5, *IG*11(2).110.26 (Delos, iii B.C.), *SIG*² 588.7 (ib., ii B.C.), Semusap.Ath.11.469c:—Dim. -ποτίδιον, *IG*7.303 (Oropus, iii B.C.), 11(2).203*B*29 (Delos, iii B.C.):—also -πότιον, Cratin.Jun.14 (s. v. l.), *IG*2².1534.220 (iii B.C.), al. ⊛ -ποτος, ον, *sweet to drink*, οἶνος Od.2.340, 3.391, etc.; also of a cup, ἡ. κύλιξ *Philol*. 72.547 (Olbia, v B.C.). -πρόσωπος, ον, *of sweet countenance*, χόνδρος Matro *Conv*.102. -ραβδον, τό, = κιννάμωμον, Hsch.

⊛ ἡδύς, ἡδεῖα, ἡδύ, ἡδὺς ἀϋτμή (as fem.) once in Hom., Od.12.369: Dor. ἁδύς [ᾱ], Boeot. neut. ϝαδού (written γάδου) cj. in Corinn.17 (cf. pr. n. ϝαδιούλογος *IG*7.2788.3), Elean βάδύς (q. v.): irreg. acc. ἁδέα for ἡδύν Theoc.20.44, for ἡδεῖαν ib.[8], Mosch.3.82: Ion. fem. ἡδέα, Dor. ἁδέα: Comp. ἡδίων [ῑ], Sup. ἥδιστος Od.13.80, etc.; also ἡδύτερος Thphr.*HP*3.2.1, Ps.-Phoc.195, *AP*9.247 (Phil.); ἡδύτατος ib.11.298. 7, Plu.2.98e. I. *pleasant* to the taste, δεῖπνον Od.20.391; of wine, 3.51, 9.197, etc.; to the smell, ἀμβροσίην.. ἡδὺ μάλα πνείουσαν 4.446; ὀδμὴ δ' ἡδεῖα ἀπὸ κρητῆρος ὀδώδει 9.210; to the hearing, δίδου δ' ἡδεῖαν ἀοιδήν 8.64; αὐδή Hes.*Th*.40; feelings or states, ἡ. ὕπνος Il.4.131, Od.1.364, al.; κοῖτος 19.510; ἡδὺ μάλα κνώσσουσα 4.809; ἡδὺς μῦθος, opp. ἀλγεινός, S.*Ant*.12: c. inf., φέγγος ἥδιον δρακεῖν A.*Ag*.602; ἡδὺς ἀκοῦσαι [λόγος] Pl.*Men*.81d, cf. Ar.*V*.503; later ἡ. ἀκουσθῆναι D.H.*Comp*.9; εἰ.. τόδε πᾶσι φίλον καὶ ἡδὺ γένοιτο Il.4.17, cf. 7.387: c. inf., οὐκ ἂν ἐμοί γε μετὰ φρεσὶν ἡδὺ γένοιτο ζωέμεν Od.24.435; ἁδύ τι θαρσαλέαις τὸν μακρὸν τείνειν βίον ἐλπίσι A.*Pr*.536, etc.; so οὔ μοι ἥδιόν ἐστι λέγειν I had *rather* not.., Hdt.2.46: neut. as Subst., τὸ δι' ἀκοῆς τε καὶ δι' ὄψεως ἡδύ Pl.*Hp.Ma*.298a; μεμιγμένον τῷ σεμνῷ τὸ ἡ. D.H.*Comp*.1; τὰ ἡ. *pleasures*, Th.5.105, Pl.*Grg*.495a, etc.: neut. as Adv., ἐπ' αὐτῷ ἡδὺ γέλασσαν *merrily*, Il.2.270, etc.; ἁδὺ δὲ καὶ τὺ συρίσδες *sweetly*, Theoc.1.2. II. after Hom., of persons, *welcome*, S.*OT*82, *Ph*.530 (Sup.), *El*.929; ironically, ἥδιστος.. δεσμώτης ἔσω θακεῖ Id.*Aj*.105; like εὐήθης, *innocent, simple*, ὡς ἡ. εἶ Pl.*Grg*.491e, Plu.*Art*.17, etc.: Sup., ὦ ἥδιστε *my good friend* (iron.), Pl.*R*.348c, al. 2. *well-pleased, glad*, ἡδίους ἔσεσθ' ἀκούσαντες D.23.64; ἡδίους ταῖς ἐλπίσιν Plu.*Cam*.32; τὴν γνώμην ἡδίω πρὸς τὸ μέλλον ποιεῖν to open *a pleasanter* view of the future, Id.*Fab*.5. III. Adv. ἡδέως *pleasantly, with pleasure*, καθεύδειν Pl.*Cri*.43b; εὕδειν S.*Tr*.175; δρᾶν Id.*Ant*.70; δρᾶν τινα E.*IA*1122; βίοτον ἄγειν Id.*Cyc*.453; λαβεῖν, δέχεσθαι, Ar.*Eq*.440, X.*Mem*.1.2.4; ἡ. ἂν ἐροίμην I would *gladly* ask, should *like to* ask, D.18.64; ἡ. ἔχειν τι to be *pleased* or *content* with, E.*Ion*647 (but ἵν' ἡ δόκησις Ξοῦθον ἡ. ἔχῃ ib.1602); οὐδὲ πότων ἡ. εἶχον had no *inclination* to drink, Hp.*Epid*.3.13; τινος, of a person, Macho ap.Ath.13.577e; ἡ. ἔχειν πρὸς ἅπαντας to be *suave, courteous* towards.., Isoc.1.20; τινι D.5.15; ἡ. ἔχειν, of things, to be *pleasant*, E.*IA*483; ἡ. ἔμοιγε κἀλγεινῶς ἅμα S.*Ant*.436; iron., ἡ. γε '*prettily* said', Pl.*Hp.Ma*.300c: Comp. ἥδιον Lys.7.40, Pherecr.67, etc.: Sup., ἥδιστα μεντἂν ἤκουσα Pl.*Tht*.183d, etc. 2. in Hom. neut. ἡδύ as Adv. (v. supr.), cf. ἥδομαι. [ἥδῐον E.*Supp*.1101 (s. v. l.), Ar. *V*.298 (lyr.), Alex.25.6, but ἡδίον(α) [ῑ] E.*Cyc*.251, etc.] (Skt. *svādús*, Lat. *suāvis*.)

ἡδύσᾰρον, τό, *axe-weed, Bonaveria Securidaca*, Dsc.3.130.

ἥδυσμα, ατος, τό, (ἡδύνω) *relish, seasoning, sauce*, Ar.*Eq*.678, *V*. 496, Pl.*R*.332d, X.*Mem*.3.14.5, Thphr.*CP*6.4.6, etc.; of vinegar, Ath.2.67c: metaph., οὐ.. ἡδύσματι χρῆται ἀλλ' ὡς ἐδέσματι τοῖς ἐπιθέτοις Arist.*Rh*.1406ᵃ19; ἡ μελοποιία μέγιστον τῶν ἡ. Id.*Po*.1450ᵇ16, cf. Jul.*Or*.7.207b: in pl., *spices, aromatics*, Hp.*Mul*.2.202, Dsc.1.61, Plu.2.995c.

ἡδυσμάτιον, τό, Dim. of foreg., Telecl.1.11.

ἡδυσματο-θήκη, ἡ, *spice-box*, Poll.10.93. -ληρος, ον, *absurdly dainty*, ὀψάρια Archestr.*Fr*.45.18.

ἡδυσμός, ὁ, (ἡδύνω) *a sweet savour, sweetness*, Lxx *Ex*.30.34.

ἡδύστομος, *jocosus*, *Gloss*.

ἡδυσώμᾰτος [ῠ], ον, *of sweet form*, opp. ἡδυγνώμων, X.*Smp*.8.30.

ἡδύτεραι· αἱ τρυγόνες, Hsch.

ἡδύτης [ῠ], ητος, ἡ, (ἡδύς) *sweetness*, Sch.Ar.*Av*.222.

ἡδῠ-τόκος, ον, *producing sweets*, Nonn.*D*.3.150. -φαής, Dor. ἁδ-, ές, *sweet-shining*, ἤλεκτρος D.P.317; πλινθίς *AP*6.295 (Phan.). -φάρυγξ [ᾰ], υγγος, ὁ, ἡ, *sweet to the throat*, prob. in Philox.2.18. -φθογγος, ον, *sweet-voiced*, τέττιγες Hsch. s. v. ἠχηταί. -φρων, ονος, ὁ, ἡ, *sweet-minded*, *AP*9.525.8. -φωνία, ἡ, *sweetness of sound*, Babr.9.3, Alciphr.3.12, etc. ⊛ -φωνος, Dor. ἁδ-, Aeol. ἀδ-, ον, *sweet-voiced*, Sapph.61; ὄρτυξ Pratin.Lyr.4, cf. Aristaenet.1.10. ⊛ -χᾰρής, ές, *sweetly joyous*, *AP*3.18 (Inscr. Cyzic.). ⊛ -χροος, ον, contr. -χρους, ουν, *of sweet complexion*, πρόσωπα *IG*14.2040.7; ἡδύχρουν μύρον a *fragrant* perfume, Dsc.1.58; τὸ ἡ. Androm.ap.Gal.14.52, Alex.Trall.7.3; *hedychrum*, Cic.*Tusc*.3.19. 46. II. ἡδύχρους, also ἡδύπνους, ὁ, a lamb not yet weaned, Phot.

ἧδω, v. ἥδομαι II. ἡδώ· ἶρις, ἤγουν τόξον, Hsch. ⊛ ἠέ, v. ἤ, *or, whether*. ἠέ, exclam. *ah!* A.*Th*.966, 980, *Supp*.831 (all lyr.). ἦε, ἤει, v. εἰμι (*ibo*). ἠείδης, ἠείδη, v. εἴδω. ἠέλιος, ὁ, v. ἥλιος. ἠελιῶτις, v. ἡλιώτης.

ἠερέθομαι, Ep. for ἀείρομαι, only in 3 pl. pres. and impf., *hang floating* or *waving in the air*, αἰγίδα.., τῆς ἑκατὸν θύσανοι.. ἠερέθονται Il.2.448; of a flight of locusts, 21.12; of flying-fish, Opp.*H*.1.435; ἐξ χεῖρες ἑκάστῳ -ονται A.R.1.944: metaph., ὁπλοτέρων ἀνδρῶν φρένες ἠερέθονται young men's minds *turn with every wind*, Il.3.108.—The form ἀερέθονται in Hsch., cf. *EM*421.6.

⊛ ἠέριος, η, ον, (ἦρι) *early, at* or *with early morn*, ἠερίη δ' ἀνέβη μέγαν οὐρανόν Il.1.497, cf. 557, 3.7 (Sch. ἐαριναί), Od.9.52, A.R.3.417. II.

later, (ἠήρ) *misty, dimly seen,* Arat.349, A.R.1.580, 4.1239. 2. *high in air,* ἠ. Γεράνεια Simon.114; of birds, Opp.*C.*1.380, *H.*3.203; of flying-fish, ib.1.430; ἄγραι *AP*6.180 (Arch.), cf. Nonn.*D.*7.315, al. 3. *airy, air-like,* πῦρ Hp.*Vict.*1.10.

**ἠερο-δίνης** [ῑ], εω, ὁ, *wheeling in mid air,* αἰετός *AP*9.223 (Bianor). **-ειδής**, ές, Ion. and Ep. for ἀερ-, which is not found, *misty, cloudy, dark* (esp. in Od.), ἐπ' ἠεροειδέα πόντον Od.2.263, etc.; σπέος ἠ. 12.80, cf. 13.103; πέτρη, of Scylla's cave, 12.233: neut. as Adv., *in the far distance, dimly,* ὅσσον δ' ἠεροειδὲς ἀνὴρ ἴδεν Il.5.770: ἠ. νεφέλη Hes. *Th.*757; πνοιαί Orph.*H.*38.22.—Ep. word, ἠ. αὐγαί Arist.*Col.*792ᵇ8: Comp., ὕδωρ πάντων -έστερον Arr.*Ind.*6.3. **-εις**, εσσα, εν, Ion. and Ep. for ἀερόεις (q.v., cf. cj. in Telest.1.12) *cloudy, murky,* Τάρταρος Il.8.13, al., cf. Hes.*Th.*119; ζόφος Il.15.191, etc.; ἠερόεντα κέλευθα *the murky* road (i.e. death), Od.20.64; later ἠ. ἴασπις D.P. 724; μόλυβδος Man.6.391; *livid,* χροιή Nic.*Th.*257. II. epith. of ὄναγρος, = ταχύς, acc. to Sch., Opp.*C.*3.183. ⊛**-θεν**, Ion. and Ep. for ἀερ-, *from air,* *APl.*4.107 (Jul.). **-μήκης**, ες, Ep. for ἀερ-, *high as heaven,* Orph.*A.*924. ⊛ **-μικτος**, ον, (μείγνυμι) *mingling with air,* φωναί Id.*Fr.*297ᵇ2 (in form ἀερό-). ⊛**-μορφος**, ον, (μορφή) *air-formed,* αὖραι Id.*H.*81.6, cf. 16.1. **-πλαγκτος**, ον, *wandering in mid air,* ib.7.8, Man.4.509. ⊛**-ποιταν·** ἐπιτιμῶσαν, and **-πομπα·** κατὰ τὸν ἀέρα φαινόμενα, Hsch.

**ἠέροπος**, ὁ, Ion. for ἀέροψ, Ant.Lib.18.3.

**ἠερο-φεγγής**, ές, *shining in the air,* Ζεύς Orph.*H.*20.2. **-φοίτης**, ου, ὁ, = ἠερόφοιτος, Ion Lyr.10, Orph.*L.*45, Nonn.*D.*24.79, al. **-φοῖτις**, ιδος, ἡ, *walking in darkness, coming unseen,* Ἐρινύς Il.9.571, 19.87. II. *air-traversing,* of the moon, Orph.*H.*9.2; μέλισσα Ps.-Phoc.171. **-φοιτος**, ον, (φοιτάω) *air-wandering,* φύσις, of birds, ib.125; οἶστρος Orph.*A.*47; of cuttle-fish, Opp.*H.*3.166 (cf. ἠέρα τεμνουσι 1.427); of the moon, Max.485, etc. **-φωνος**, ον, *sounding through air, loud-voiced,* κήρυκες Il.18.505 (s.v.l., ἱεροφώνων cj. Ahrens); γέρανοι Opp.*H.*1.621.

**ἠερτίζω**, = ἀερτάζω, Hsch. ⊛ **ἠήν**, exclam., = ἤ ἤ, Men.*Per.* 15. **ἠήρ**, v. ἀήρ.

**ἠθάδιος** [ᾰ], ον, poet. for ἠθάς, Opp.*C.*1.448.

**ἠθαῖος**, α, ον, Dor. for ἠθεῖος, Pi.*I.*2.48.

**ἠθᾰλέος**, η, ον, (ἦθος) *accustomed,* εὐναί Opp.*C.*2.307; [ταῦροι] ib. 88, cf. *Epigr.Gr.*1035.23 (Pergam.).

**ἠθάνιον**, τό, Dim. of ἠθμός, Hellanic.53 J.; cf. ἠθήνιον.

⊛**ἠθάς**, άδος, ὁ, ἡ, (ἦθος II) *accustomed to* a thing, *acquainted with* it, c. gen., ἠ. εἰμί πως τῶν τῆσδε μύθων S.*El.*372; θήρης Opp.*H.*4.122; τῶν χωρίων Ael.*NA*7.6: c. dat., πέτραις ib.9.36. 2. abs., *inured, accustomed,* Hp.*Mul.*1.1; τῶν γὰρ ἠθάδων φίλων νέοι.. εὐπιθέστεροι E. *Andr.*818; of animals, *tame,* [ὄρνιθες] ἠ. *domestic* fowls, Ar.*Av.*271; of decoy-birds, Plu.*Sull.*28; ἠ. σκόμβροι Ael.*NA*14.1. II. of things, *usual, customary,* νίκη *APl.*5.354; πάδαν *AP*9.264 (Apollonid. or Phil.): as neut., τὰ καινά γ' ἐκ τῶν ἠθάδων ἡδίον' ἐστί E.*Cyc.*250; τοῖς ἠθάσι λίαν τοῖς τ' ἀρχαίοις ἐνδιατρίβειν Ar.*Ec.*584, cf. 151.

**ἠθεῖος**, also **ἠθαῖος**, α, ον, *trusty, honoured,* term of address used to express respect, ἠθεῖε Il.6.518, al., Hes.*Sc.*103: periphr., ἠθείη κεφαλή Il.23.94; ἀλλά μιν ἠθεῖον καλέω Od.14.147; ξεῖνον ἐμὸν ἠθαῖον Pi.*I.*2.48; ἠθαῖοι *trusty friends,* Antim.22. (Cf. ἦθος.)

**ἤθεος**, ὁ, ἡ, Att. for ἠίθεος (q.v.).

**ἠθ-έω**, aor. 1 ἤθησα (ἤθισα codd.), gloss on ἦσα, v. ἤθω:—Med., aor. 1 ἠθησάμην Nic.*Al.*324: (ἤθω):—*sift, strain,* Nic.l.c.:—Pass., *to be strained,* τὸ ἠθούμενον Pl.*Cra.*402d; [οἶνος] ἠθημένος Epil.6; χρυσὸς ἠθημένος διὰ πέτρας *filtered through,* Pl.*Ti.*59b: metaph., ἐκ τετρημένης [τὴν ῥῆσιν] ἠθεῖ *lets it trickle out,* Herod.3.33. **-ημα**, ατος, τό, *that which is sifted* or *strained,* Dieuch.ap.Orib.4.7.26. **-ήνιον·** ἠθάνιον, Hsch. **-ησις**, εως, ἡ, *riddling,* λίθων *IG*4.1485.124 (Epid.); prob. l. for ἤθισις, Arist.*Pr.*870ᵇ18. **-ητήρ**, ῆρος, ὁ, = ἠθμός, Marc.Sid.76. **-ητήριον**, τό, = ἠθμός, Str.3.2.9. **-ητικός**, ή, όν, *capable of being strained,* Thphr.*CP*6.16.6.

**ἠθῐκ-εύομαι**, *speak ethically,* Phoeb.*Fig.*1.1, Sch.Il.7.408. ⊛**-ός**, ή, όν, (ἦθος II) *moral,* opp. διανοητικός, Arist.*EN*1103ᵃ5, al.; τὰ ἠθικά *a treatise on morals,* Id.*Pol.*1295ᵃ36, cf. Democr.4ᵃ; οἱ ἠ. λόγοι Phld. *Herc.*1251.13; τὸ ἠ. φιλοσοφίας, opp. φυσικόν, διαλεκτικόν, D.L. *Prooem.*18; ἡ ἠ. φιλοσοφία Str.1.1.18; ἡ ἠ. alone, Ph.1.370. II. *showing moral character, expressive thereof,* λέξις Arist.*Rh.*1408ᵃ11; πῶς.. τοὺς λόγους ἠ. ποιητέον ib.1391ᵇ22, cf. 1395ᵇ13; ἠ. τραγῳδία Id. *Po.*1456ᵃ1; ἡ Ἰλιὰς παθητικόν, ἡ δὲ Ὀδύσσεια ἠ. ib.1459ᵇ15; ἠ. μέλη, ἁρμονίαι, Id.*Pol.*1341ᵇ34, 1342ᵃ3 (Sup.); οὐκ ἔστιν ὁ αὐλὸς ἠθικόν, ἀλλὰ.. ὀργιαστικόν ib.1341ᵃ21; ἠ. γραφεύς, ἀγαλματοποιός, ib.1340ᵃ38; ἠθικὴ ἡ ἐν ὀφθαλμοῖς *the expression of character* by the eyes, Philostr. *Gym.*25. Adv. -κῶς, λεκτέον (opp. ἀποδεικτικῶς) Arist.*Rh.*1418ᵃ39; ἠ. μειδιάσας laughing *expressively,* Plu.*Brut.*51; ἐπικροτεῖν τὸ μετακάρπιον Aristaenet.1.27; *in character,* Demetr.*Eloc.*216; *naturally,* ib.297. 2. *tactful,* Plu.2.73f (Comp.). Adv. -κῶς Id.*Alex.*52.

**ἤθῐσις**, v. ἤθησις. **ἠθμάριον**, τό, Dim. of ἠθμός, Hsch.

**ἠθμοειδής**, ές, *like a strainer, perforated,* Hero *Spir.*1.8, Plu.2.699a; κοιλίαι Aret.*SD*2.3. II. τὸ ἠ. ὀστοῦν the *ethmoid* or *perforated* bone at the root of the nose, Gal.*UP*11.12: more freq. in pl., τὰ -ειδῆ, with or without ὀστᾶ, ib.8.7; ἠ. δεξαμεναί, of the kidneys, prob. in Ph.2.244 (αἰμο-, ἰσθμο- codd., cf. Gal.*Nat.Fac.*1.15). Adv. -δῶς Ruf.*Anat.*52.

⊛**ἠθμός**, *SIG*2 (Sigeum, vi B.C.), Hdn.Gr.1.543, in codd. usu. (but perh. wrongly) **ἠθμός**, ὁ, (ἤθω) *strainer, colander,* *SIG* l.c., E.*Fr.* 374, *IG*2².1416.11, 4.39.20, Gal.*Nat.Fac.*1.15; esp. *wine-strainer,* Pherecr.41; part of an eel-trap, Arist.*HA*534ᵃ22; of the eyelashes, X.*Mem.*1.4.6; prov., τῷ ἠθμῷ ἀντλεῖν, of fruitless toil, Arist.*Oec.* 1344ᵇ25. II. ἠ. σχοίνινος, = κημός III, Cratin.132, cf. *AP*9.482.23 (Agath.). III. *sluice* or *weir* (?), *IG*11(2).287 *A* 75 (Delos, iii B.C.).

**ἠθμώδης**, ες, = ἠθμοειδής, Sch.Ar.*V.*99.

**ἠθογρᾰφ-έω**, *paint* or *describe character,* Marcellin.*Vit.Thuc.*50. **-ος**, ὁ, *painter of character,* Arist.*Po.*1450ᵃ28.

**ἠθολογ-έω**, *express characteristically,* γονέων πάθη Lxx 4*Ma.*15.4:—Pass., κωμῳδία -ουμένη comedy *of manners,* Longin.9.15. **-ία**, ἡ, *painting of character,* esp. by mimic gestures (cf. χαρακτηρισμός), Posidon.ap.Sen.*Ep.*95.65, Quint.1.9.3, Suet.*Gramm.*4 (pl.). **-ος**, ον, *painting character* by mimic gestures (cf. βιολόγος), of dramatic and mimic performers, D.S.20.63, Cic.*Orat.*2.59.242, Ath.1.20a; of Socrates, Timo 62.

**ἠθονόη**, coined as etym. of Ἀθηνᾶ, Pl.*Cra.*407b.

⊛**ἠθοποι-έω**, *mould the character of* a person, τὸν θεατήν Plu.*Per.*2; τὴν ψυχήν S.E.*M.*6.30. II. *express* or *delineate character,* D.H. *Lys.*19: c. acc., τὸ σχῆμα τῆς γυναικός Aps.p.322 H. **-ητικός**, ή, όν, *expressive of character.* Adv. -κῶς Eust.1955.54. **-ία**, ἡ, *formation of character,* Str.2.5.26 (pl.), Gal.15.97. II. *delineation of character,* Phld.*Po.*5.9 (pl.), Str.14.1.41, D.H.*Lys.*8, *Isoc.*11 (pl.), Hermog.*Prog.*9, Aphth.*Prog.*11, etc. **-ός**, όν, *forming character,* ἠ. τὸ θερμόν Arist.*Pr.*955ᵃ32; μέλη S.E.*M.*6.36; παιδεύσεις Plu.*Them.* 2; τὸ ἠ., = foreg. I, Id.2.660c.

⊛ **ἦθος**, εος, τό (cf. ἔθος), *an accustomed place*: hence, in pl., *haunts* or *abodes* of animals, μετά τ' ἤθεα καὶ νομὸν ἵππων Il.6.511; [σύας] ἔρξαν κατὰ ἤθεα κοιμηθῆναι Od.14.411; of lions, Hdt.7.125; of fish, Opp.*H.*1.93; of *the abodes of men,* Hes.*Op.*167, 525, Hdt.1.15, 157, A.*Supp.*64 (lyr.), E.*Hel.*274, Pl.*Lg.*865e, Arist.*Mu.*398ᵇ33; ἔλεγον ἐξ ἠθέων τὸν ἥλιον ἀνατεῖλαι away from his *accustomed place,* Hdt. 2.142; of plants, Callistr.*Stat.*7: metaph., with play on signf. II, Pl.*Phdr.*277a. II. *custom, usage*: in pl., *manners, customs,* Hes.*Op.*137, *Th.*66, Hdt.2.30, 35, 4.106, Th.2.61; τρόποι καὶ ἤθη Pl. *Lg.*896c; ἐθρέψω Ξέρξην ἐν τοῖς αὐτοῖς ἠ. ib.695e; φθείρουσιν ἤθη χρήσθ' ὁμιλίαι κακαί *PHib.*1.7.94 (E.*Fr.*1024 = Men.218); τοῖς ἤθεσιν ἁπλοῦς D.S.5.21. 2. *disposition, character,* ἐπίκλοπον ἦθος Hes.*Op.* 67, 78; ἠ. ἐμφυές Pi.*O.*11(10).21; ἀκίχητα ἠ., of Zeus, A.*Pr.*187; τοὐμὸν ἠ. παιδεύειν S.*Aj.*595; ὦ μιαρὸν ἠ. Id.*Ant.*746; τὸ τῆς πόλεως ἠ. Isoc.2.31; βελτίων τῆς πόλεως τὸ ἠ. D.20.14; esp. *moral character,* opp. διάνοια, Arist.*EN*1139ᵃ1; as the result of habit, τὸ πᾶν ἠ. διὰ ἔθος Pl.*Lg.*792e, cf. Arist.*EE*1220ᵃ39; ἠ. ἀνθρώπῳ δαίμων Heraclit.119; ἠ. πηγὴ βίου Stoic.ap.Stob.2.7.1; τῆς ψυχῆς, τῆς γνώμης, Pl.*R.*400d, D.61.16: freq. opp. πάθος, Arist.*Rh.*1356ᵃ23 (pl.), etc.; ἠθῶν τε καὶ παθῶν μίμησις D.H.*Pomp.*3; τὸ ἠ. πρᾶος Pl.*Phdr.*243c: less freq. in dat., ἀγοραῖος τῷ ἠ. Thphr.*Char.*6.2, cf. *Inscr.Magn.*164.3 (i/ii A.D.): pl., *traits, characteristics,* Pl.*R.*402d, Arist.*EN*1144ᵇ4 (in sg., τὸ τῆς ἀνδρείας ἠ. Pl.*Lg.*836d): seldom in pl., of an individual, στερρὸν τὰ ἤθεα Hp.*Ep.*11; ἱερὸς κατὰ τὰ ἤθη Ath.1.1e. b. of outward *bearing,* ὡς ἱλαρὸν τὸ ἠ. X.*Smp.*8.3; ὑγρότης ἤθους Lycurg.33; ὑψηλὸς τῷ ἠ. Plu.*Dio* 4: in pl., of facial expression, ὀφθαλμῶν ἤθη Philostr.*Gym.* 25. c. in Rhet., *delineation of character,* ἠ. ἔχουσιν οἱ λόγοι ἐν ὅσοις δήλη ἡ προαίρεσις Arist.*Rh.*1395ᵇ13; ἠ. ἐμφαίνειν Phld.*Rh.*1.200 S.; esp. opp. πάθος, Longin.9.15, etc.; κατ' ἠ. λέγεσθαι, opp. κατὰ πάθος, D.H.*Comp.*22, cf. *Lys.*19: in pl., πραγμάτων καὶ ἠθῶν Phld.*Po.*5.5; ἐν πάθεσι καὶ ἤθεσιν Demetr.*Eloc.*28, etc.; so of works of art, ἡ Ζεύξιδος γραφὴ οὐδὲν ἔχει ἠ. Arist.*Po.*1450ᵃ29; πάθος καὶ ἠ. καὶ σχημάτων χρῆσις Ael.*VH*4.3; πολλὰ ἤθη ἐπιφαίνει Philostr.*Her.*2.10; also of Music, S.E.*M.*6.49. d. *dramatis persona,* εἰσάγει ἄνδρα ἢ γυναῖκα ἢ ἄλλο τι ἠ. Arist.*Po.*1460ᵃ11, al. 3. also of animals, ἠ. τὸ πρὸς τοκέων (prob. l. for ἔθος) A.*Ag.*727, cf. E.*Hipp.*1219, Pl.*R.*375e, Arist. *HA*487ᵃ12 (pl.); τὸ ἠ. ἀσθενής, of a bird, ib.615ᵃ18; of things, *nature, kind,* παρὰ δ' ἠ. ἑκάστῳ (to each of the four elements) Emp. 17.28; τοῦ πυρετοῦ Gal.7.353. 4. ἐν ἤθει *tactfully* (cf. ἠθικός II. 2), προσφέρεσθαι τοῖς ἁμαρτάνουσιν Plu.2.73e, cf. Herm. *in Phdr.*p.195 A.; διὰ μέτριον ἦθος, of the expression δοκεῖ μοι, Steph. *in Hp.*1.59 D.

**ἠθροισμένως**, Adv. pf. part. Pass. of ἀθροίζω, gloss on ἀγεληδόν, Hsch.

**ἤθω**, collat. form of ἠθέω (q.v.), aor. 1 ἦσα, Hp.ap.Gal.19.103.

⊛**ἠΐ**, Boeot. for αἰεί (= ἀεί), *Schwyzer* 462 *A* 25 (Tanagra, iii B.C.), Hdn.Gr.1.497.

⊛**ἤϊα** (A), contr. **ἦα**, τά, *provisions for a journey,* Ep. word, Hom. mostly in Od., δεῦτε, φίλοι, ἤϊα φερώμεθα 2.410, cf. 289; καί νύ κεν ἤϊα πάντα κατέφθιτο 4.363; ἐξέφθιτο ἤϊα πάντα 12.329; ἐν δὲ καὶ ἦα κωρύκῳ [ἔθηκε] 5.266, cf. 9.212: generally, [ἔλαφοι] παρδαλίων τε λύκων τ' ἤϊα πέλονται *food* for wolves, Il.13.103; ἤϊα κριθάων, = ἄλευρα, Nic.*Al.*412. II. ὡς δ' ἄνεμος.. ἠΐων θημῶνα τινάξῃ καρφαλέων, i.e. a heap of *husks* or *chaff* (= ὀσπρίων καλάμαι acc. to Eratosth.ap.Eust.1445.42), Od.5. 368; τὴν γαστέρ' ἤων κἀχύρων σεσαγμένος Pherecr.161. (Etym. uncertain: not related to the sg. ἤϊον which is glossed by παρειάν, γνάθον, Hsch.; cf. εἰαί, εἶοι.) [ῐ, but ῑ Od.2.289, 410, Il.13.103.]

**ἤϊα** (B), Ion. for ᾖειν, impf. of εἶμι (*ibo*).

⊛ **ἠίθεος** [ῐ], contr. **ἤθεος** (v. infr.), Dor. **ἄθεος** Cerc.9.11, but Aeol. (?) **ἠΐθεος** Sapph. (v. infr.): ὁ:—*unmarried youth* (ἠίθεον ἢ καὶ γεγαμηκότα ἄπαιδα Pl.*Lg.*877e), Sapph.*Supp.*20a.18 (pl.); παρθένος ἠ. τε joined, Il.22.127, al.; χοροὺς παρθένων τε καὶ ἠιθέων Hdt.3.48, cf. Plu. *Thes.*15; including παρθένοι, B.16 tit., cf. 43, al.; of the θεωροί sent to Delos, Arist.*Ath.*56.3; οὐ γάρ ἐστιν ἤθεος E.*Ph.*945; of animals, *unmated,* Pl.*Lg.*840d: later as Adj., παῖδες ἠίθεοι Plu.*Thes.*17; ἠϊθέοισιν ἐφήβοισιν *IG*3.1151. 2. ἠίθεοι, οἱ, *ghosts of those who die unmarried,* *Tab.Defix.Aud.*52.7. II. rare as fem., ἠϊθέη, = παρθένος,

Nic.*Fr.*74.64, *AP*9.241 (Antip.⟨Thess.⟩); κόρη ἤθεος Eup.332. III. metaph. as Adj., νοῦς Porph.*Marc.*33. (ἠιθ– shd. be read as ἠθ– in Prose.)

**ἠικανός**· ὁ ἀλεκτρυών, Hsch. **ἤϊκτο**, v. ἔοικα. **ἤϊξε**, v. ἀΐσσω.

**ἠϊόεις**, εσσα, εν, (ἠΐα A) Ep. word of doubtful meaning, ἐπ' ἠϊόεντι Σκαμάνδρῳ Il.5.36; perh. connected by later poets with ἠϊών, hence ἠ. Πάνορμος Q.S.1.283; κόλλουρος *haunting the shore*, Marc.Sid.22: but perh. also with ἠΐα (A), χήνεσιν ἠϊόεν πεδίον κάτα βοσκομένοισιν Q.S.5.299; derived from ἴον by *EM*423.14.

**ἤϊον**, Ep. for ἤεσαν, 3 pl. impf. of εἶμι (*ibo*); also 1 sg., Luc.*Syr.D.* 24. II. Ion. impf. of ἀΐω, read by Zenod. for ἔκλυον, Od.2.42. III. v. ἠΐα (A) fin.

⊛ **ἤϊος**, ὁ, epith. of Phoebus, ἤϊε Φοῖβε Il.15.365, 20.152, *h.Ap.*120. (Prob. from the cry ἤ, ἤ, cf. ἰήϊος.)

**ἠϊόω**, (ἠΐα A) *provide with food*, in Pass., Hsch.

**ἠϊών**, Trag. ἠών E.*Or.*994, Dor. ἀϊών Pi.*I.*1.33, A.*Ag.*1158 (lyr.), ᾀών Mosch.3.37 (cj.): όνος, ἡ:—*shore, beach*, ὅθι κύματ' ἐπ' ἠϊόνος κλύζεσκον Il.23.61; ἀμφὶ δέ τ' ἄκραι ἠϊόνες βοόωσιν 17.265; ἂμ πέτρῃσι καὶ ἠϊόνεσσι καθίζων (Ep. dat.) Od.5.156, cf. Hdt.2.113, 8.96, E.*Tr.* 827 (lyr.), X.*HG*1.1.5, Sotion p.191 W., D.C.59.25. 2. after Hom., in pl., of other *banks*, as of a lake, Pi.*I.*1.33; of a river, A.*Ag.* l.c., A.R.2.659, 4.130, D.H.4.27. 3. metaph., of the *lower part of the face*, over which the tears flow, Hsch. (pl.): sg., = πᾶσα ἡ τῶν ὀφθαλμῶν περιγραφή, Poll.2.71.

**ἦκα**, Adv.: I. of Place or Motion, *slightly, a little*, ἦκ' ἐπ' ἀριστερά *a little* to the left, Il.23.336; ἦ. παρακλίνας κεφαλήν Od.20.301: hence, generally, *softly, gently*, ἦ. ἐλάσαι 18.94, cf. 92; ἀπώσατο ἦ. γέροντα Il.24.508; ἦ. μάλα ψύξασα 20.440; ἦ. κιόντας Od.17.254; ἦ. βιησάμενος Nic.*Al.*226. II. of Sound, *softly, low*, ἦ. πρὸς ἀλλήλους ἀγόρευον Il.3.155; ἦ. μύρεσθαι, μάλ' ὁμαδῆσαι, A.R.3.463, 565. III. of Sight, *softly, smoothly*, ἦ. στίλβοντας ἐλαίῳ with oil *soft*-shining, Il.18.596; ἦκ' ἐπιμειδήσας *soft*-smiling, Hes.*Th.*547; ἦ. μέλαν *slightly* black, Opp.*C.*3.39. IV. of Time, *by little and little*, *AP*5.278 (Paul. Sil.), Opp.*H.*2.67. (Perh. connected with Lat. *sēg-nis* (for *sēc-nis*): but Hsch. has γάκα (i.e. ϝᾶκα)· ἡδέως; cf. ἥσσων, ἥκιστος, ἥκιστος, ἠκαῖον, ἤκαλος, ἠκαλέον.)

**ἧκα**, aor. 1 of ἵημι.

**ἠκάδα**· ἠνδρωμένην γυναῖκα, Hsch. **ἠκαῖον**· ἀσθενές, Id. **ἤκαλος**, ον, = ἀκαλός, Call.*Fr.*27 P.:—also **ἠκαλέον γελόωσα**· πράως, οὐκ ἐσκυθρωπακυῖα, Hsch. **ἤκᾰχε**, v. ἀχεύω, ἀχέω (A) II. 1.

**ἤκεστος**, η, ον, (Ep. for *ἄκεστος, from κεντέω) *untouched by the goad*, of young heifers reserved for sacrifices, βοῦς..ἤνις ἠκέστας Il. 6.94, 275, 309:—also **ἠκέστης**· ἀδάμαστος, Suid.

**ἠκή**, ἡ, Ion. for ἀκή (A), ἀκωκή, Hsch.: hence, *edge, meeting-point*, κύματός τε κἀνέμου Archil.43.

⊛ **ἠκής**, ές, *sharp*, Hsch.

**ἤκιστος**, η, ον, Sup. Adj. of Adv. ἦκα, ἤκιστος ἐλαυνέμεν *the gentlest* or *slowest* in driving, Il.23.531 (ἥκ– Eust.1314.27, *EM*424.27; cf. sq.).

**ἥκιστος**, η, ον, prob., like foreg., Sup. of ἦκα, *least*, ὁ δ' ἥκιστ' ἔχων μακάρτατος S.*Fr.*410. 2. c. inf., *worst* at.., ἥ. θηρᾶν, κρυμῷ ὁμιλεῖν, Ael.*NA*9.1, 4.31 (cf. foreg.). II. mostly as Adv., ἥκιστα *least*, Hp.*Acut.*68, S.*Ph.*427, etc.; οὐκ ἥ. ἀλλὰ μάλιστα Hdt.4.170; ὡς ἥ. *as little as possible*, Th.1.91. 2. in reply to a question, *not at all*, S.*OT*623, E.*HF*299, etc.; ἥκιστά γε S.*OT*1386, Pl.*Phdr.*276c; ἥ. πάντων Ar.*Pl.*440. 3. οὐχ ἥ., freq. in litotes, *above all, more than all*, A.*Ch.*116; οἵ τε ἄλλοι καὶ οὐχ ἥ. Ἀθηναῖοι Pl.*Prt.*324c, cf. *Tht.* 177c, *Smp.*178a, al.; ἐπὶ πολλῶν μέν.., οὐχ ἥ. δὲ ἐν τοῖς παροῦσι πράγμασι D.2.1, cf. Th.7.44, etc.: c. gen., οὐχ ἥ. Ἀθηναίων σέ, ἀλλ' ἐν τοῖς μάλιστα Pl.*Cri.*52a.

**ἠκρῑβωμένως**, Adv. pf. part. Pass. of ἀκριβόω, *exactly*, Aristeas 310, Eust.1406.29 (ed. Rom.).

⊛ **ἥκω**, Il.5.478: impf. ἧκον (v. infr.): fut. ἥξω (v. infr.); Dor. ἡξῶ Theoc.4.47, Call.*Fr.*1.65 P. (in Dor. and Hom. more commonly ἵκω): all other tenses late; aor. 1 part. ἥξας Paus.2.11.5, Gal.6.56, 10.609: pf. ἧκα Philostr.*VA*3.24, Scymn.62, 1 pl. ἥκαμεν *UPZ*72. 9 (ii B.C.), *CIG*4762 (Egypt, i A.D.), Dor. ἥκαμες f.l. in Plu.2.225b, 2 pl. ἥκατε *PGrenf.*2.36.18 (i B.C.), 3 pl. ἥκασι Lxx 4*Ki.*20.14, *Ev. Marc.*8.3; inf. ἡκέναι *UPZ*6.30 (ii B.C.): plpf. ἥκεσαν J.*AJ*19.1.14: —Med., pres. subj. ἥκηται Aret.*SD*2.1: fut. ἥξομαι v.l. in M.Ant. 2.4:—*to have come, be present*, prop. in a pf. sense, with impf. ἧκον as plpf., I *had come*, and fut. ἥξω as fut. pf., I *shall have come*, μάλα τηλόθεν ἥκω Il.5.478, cf. Od.13.325, Pi.*O.*4.12 (ἵκω codd. vett.): impf. ἧκον A.*Pr.*661, Th.1.91, al., Pl.*R.*327c, Hdt.8.50, etc.: fut. ἥξω A.*Pr.* 103, al., E.*Andr.*738, Ar.*Pax* 265, Orac.ap.Th.2.54, etc.; ἧκε imper., S.*Aj.*1116, Ar.*Pax* 275, X.*Cyr.*4.5.25; ἡκέτω E.*Rh.*337:—Constr. mostly with εἰς, Hdt.8.50, A.*Ch.*3, etc.; παρά τινα Hdt.7.157, Th.1. 137; πρός τινα A.*Ch.*659; πρὸς δαίμονα S.*Fr.*770; esp. in worship, ἥκω πρὸς τὴν κυρίαν Ἶσιν *OGI*186.6 (Egypt, i B.C.), cf. *Ev.Jo.*6.37; πρὸς πόλιν S.*OC*734; ἐπί τινα *to set upon, attack*, Pl.*R.*336b, Aeschin. 2.178; but ἥ. ἐπὶ τὸ στράτευμα *to have come to fetch* the army, X. *An.*7.6.2; οἱ ἐπὶ ταῦθ' ἥκοντες D.18.28; ἐπ' ὀλέθρῳ E.*IA*886 (troch.); περὶ σπονδῶν X.*An.*2.3.4: c. acc., ἥξεις ποταμόν A.*Pr.*717, cf. 724, 730; ἥ. δῆμον τὸν Λυρκείου S.*Fr.*271.6, cf. E.*Ba.*1; ἥκουσιν αὐτῷ ἄγγελοι X.*Cyr.*5.3.26; ἐς ταὐτὸν ἥ. *to have come* to the same point, to agree, E.*Hec.*748, *Hipp.*273: with Adv. of motion, ἥ. ἐνθάδε, δεῦρο, S.*Ph.*377, D.19.58; βῆναι κεῖθεν ὅθενπερ ἥκει S.*OC*1227: c. neut. Pron., αὐτὰ ταῦτα ἥκω παρά σε Pl.*Prt.*310e; ἐρωτώμενοι ὅ τι ἥκοιεν for what they *had come*, X.*HG*4.5.9: c. acc. cogn., ὁδὸν μακρὰν ἥκειν Id.*Cyr.*5.5.42: c. inf., μανθάνειν γὰρ ἥκομεν we *are here* to learn, S. *OC*12. 2. *to have reached a point*, ἐς τοσήνδ' ὕβριν ib.1030; εἰς τοῦτο ἀμαθίας E.*Andr.*170; εἰς τοσοῦτον ἀμαθίας Pl.*Ap.*25e; εἰς ὅσον ἡλικίας Id.*Chrm.*157d, etc.; πρὸς γάμων ἀκμάς S.*OT*1492; ὁρᾷς ἵν' ἥκεις; ib.687, etc.; Geom., *pass* through a point, διὰ τῶν πόλων Autol.*Sph.*10, cf. Archim.*Con.Sph.*9. b. διὰ μάχης, δι' ὀργῆς ἥκειν, A.*Supp.*475, S.*OC*905; cf. διά A. IV. c. with an Adv. folld. by gen., οὕτω πόρρω σοφίας ἥκεις Pl.*Euthd.*294e; εὖ ἥκειν τινός *to be* well *off for* a thing, *have plenty of* it, τοῦ βίου, χρημάτων, Hdt.1.30, 5.62; ἑωυτῶν Id.1.102; θεῶν χρηστῶν Id.8.111; πιθανότητος Demetr.Magn. ap.D.H.*Din.*1; οὐκ ὁμοίως ἥ. τινός not *to be* equally *well off* in respect of.., Hdt.1.149; πῶς ἀγῶνος ἥκομεν; how *have* we *sped* in the contest? E.*El.*751; ὧδε γένους ἥ. τινί *to be* this *degree* of kin to him, Id.*Heracl.*213; ὡς δυνάμεως ἥκεις Paus.4.21.10; ἐς μῆκος εὖ ἥκων Ael.*NA*4.34: abs., εὖ ἥκειν *to be flourishing*, Hdt.1.30: rarely c. gen. only, σὺ δὲ δυνάμιος ἥκεις μεγάλης thou *art in* great power, Id.7.157 (nisi leg. μεγάλως). 3. *to have come back, returned*, D.20.73; from exile, And.2.13; αὐτίκα ἥξω I *shall be back* in a moment, X.*An.*2.1.9; ἧκέ νυν ταχύ *come back* soon, Ar.*Pax* 275; ἄψορρον ἥξεις A.*Pr.* 1021; ἄψορρον ἥξομεν πάλιν S.*El.*53. 4. c. part., ἥκω φέρων I *have come* bringing (i.e. with), Id.*OC*579, cf. 357, Ar.*Pax* 265, Eup.22 D., Pl.*Grg.*518d; ἧκεν ἄγων Id.*Phd.*117a; ἕτερόν τι ἥκεις ἔχων Id.*Grg.* 491c, etc.: c. fut. part., like ἔρχομαι, ἥκω φράσων, ἀγγελῶν, etc., I *am going*, I *intend* to say, E.*Ph.*706, 1075, etc. 5. *to have come to be*, θεοῖς ἔχθιστος ἥκω S.*OT*1519 (troch.), cf. *Aj.*636 (lyr.), *El.*1201, etc.; *take one's origin*, ἀπὸ πολιτειῶν τοιούτων ἥκετε, ἐν αἷς.. Th.4.126. II. of things, in various uses: of meats, *to have come to table*, Alex.132; ὡς τὰ περιφερόμενα ἧκε πρὸς ἡμᾶς X.*Cyr.*2.2.3; of reports, ἐμοὶ ἀγγελίη ἥκει παρὰ βασιλέος Hdt.8.140.α', cf. S.*OC*1177; of events, πῆμα ἥκει τινί A.*Pr.*103, cf. Ar.*Ra.*606, etc.; ἐπ' ἀνδρὶ ἥκει βίου τελευτή S. *OC*1472; ἵν' ἥκει τὰ μαντεύματα what they *have come to*, Id.*OT*953; ὡς αὐτὸν ἥξοι μοῖρα ib.713 codd.; ἥξει πόλεμος Orac.ap.Th.2.54; ἐς αὐτὸν ἥξει τὸ δεινόν Id.6.77; of Time, ἥκει ἦμαρ, νύξ, A.*Ag.*1301, E.*IT*42; ἥκει ὑμῖν ὁ καιρός Lys.12.79; τὸ μέλλον ἥξει A.*Ag.*1240. 2. *concern, relate to*, ποῖ λόγος ἥκει; to what *do* the words *relate?* E.*Tr.*154 (lyr.); εἰς ἔμ' ἥκει..τὰ πράγματα Ar.*Pl.*919; εἰς ἐμὲ τὸ ἐλλεῖπον ἥξει *will fall* upon me, X.*Cyr.*1.5.13: freq. in part., τὰ εἰς τοὺς κινδύνους ἥκοντα Antipho 5.81; τὰ εἰς πλοῦτον ἥ. Pl.*Erx.*392d; τὰ πρὸς ἔπαινον, εἰς φιλανθρωπίαν ἥ., Plb.12.15.9, 28.17.2, etc. 3. *depend upon*, ὅσα τῆς Φωκέων σωτηρίας ἐπὶ τὴν πρεσβείαν ἧκε D.19.30; τό γε ἐπ' αὐτοὺς ἧκον μέρος Ph.2.21; ὅσα γ' εἰς βούλησιν ἥκειν τὴν ἐμήν Hld.4.7. 4. c. inf., ἧκέ μοι γένει..πενθεῖν *it has come* to me by birth.., my birth lays it on me.., S.*OC*738, cf. *Ichn.*356; καλῶς αὐτοῖς κατθανεῖν ἧκον βίου *it being well for them at their age to die*, E.*Alc.*291. 5. c. part., ὃ καὶ νῦν ἥκει γινόμενον which *commonly* happens even now, Plb.24. 9.11 codd. (v.l. γενόμενον). (Prob. from same root as ἵκω.)

**ἦλ, ἦλι**, apoc. for ἧλος, or for ἥλιος, Euph.153a, b.

**ἠλαιθερής**, ές, = ἡλιοθερής, *EM*425.9: Comp., prob. in Hsch.

**ἠλαίνω**, Ep. for ἀλαίνω, *wander, stray, flit about*, ἠλαίνοντι Theoc. 7.23 (ἠλαίνονται codd., but cf. Gal.12.361): metaph., *wander in mind*, Call.*Dian.*251.

**ἠλάκᾰτα** [ᾰκ], ων, τά, only in pl., *wool on the distaff*, ἠλάκατα στρωφῶσ' ἁλιπόρφυρα Od.6.53, 306, cf. 7.105; ἠ. στροφαλίζετε 18.315; ἠ. ἀνελισσομένης Alex.Aet.3.4.

**Ἠλακάτεια**, τά, festival at Sparta, Sosib.18 (–ατοία cod. Hsch.).

⊛ **ἠλᾰκάτη** [κᾰ], ἡ (so in Att. Inscrr., $IG2^2$.1517.209, but **ἠλεκ–** $SIG^2$ 588.17 (Delos, ii B.C.), *AJA*17.162 (Cyrene), *Sammelb.*5873, cf. Hsch.; v. ἠλεκάτιον), Dor. **ἠλᾰκάτᾱ** E.*Or.*1431 (lyr.), Aeol. **ἀλᾰκάτᾱ** Theoc.28.1 (ᾱλ– also in χρυσᾱλάκατος, εὐᾱλάκατος, Dor. ἠλ– is dub.):—*distaff*, Od.4.135, 1.357, Il.6.491, E. l.c., etc.; ἡ ἠ. [τοῦ ἀτράκτου] *the stalk* of the spindle, Pl.*R.*616c: metaph., γηραιῇσι.. ἠλακάτῃσι with *the fate* of old age, *IG*14.1389 i 18. II. of *distaff-shaped* objects: 1. *one joint of a reed* or *cane*, Thphr.*HP*2.2.1; *a reed*, = δόναξ, Hsch.; ὥσπερ ἠ., of the pistil of the citron-flower, Thphr.*HP*1.13.4, cf. 4.4.3. 2. in Compds. (e.g. χρυσηλάκατος), *arrow*, Hsch. 3. *the upper part of the mast*, which was made to turn round, A.R.1.565 (v. Sch.), Ath.11.475a. 4. *windlass*, Sch.Th.7.25 (v.l. ἠλεκ–). 5. the constellation *Coma Berenices*, Sch.Arat.146.

**ἠλᾰκᾰτῆνες**, ων, οἱ, large sea-fish, prob. of the *tunny* kind, Men. *Kol.Fr.*7, Mnesim.4.35, Mnaseas 33. (Sg. only in Hdn.Gr.2.923.)

**ἡλάμην, ἥλατο**, v. ἅλλομαι.

**ἠλαξός** and **ἠλαξόος**, sine expl., *EM*425.5 (perh. ἡ λαξός, misunderstood).

⊛ **ἡλάριον**, τό, Dim. of ἧλος, *small nail*, *POxy.*1658.11 (iv A.D.), Suid. s.v. ἧλος.

**ἤλᾰσα**, v. ἐλαύνω.

**ἠλασκάζω**, lengthd. form of ἠλάσκω, ὑπὸ πτόλιν ἠλασκάζων Il.18. 281: c. acc. loci, *h.Ap.*142 codd. II. *shun, flee from*, c. acc., ἐμὸν μένος ἠλασκάζει Od.9.457 (v.l. ἠλυσκάζει).

⊛ **ἠλάσκω**, Ep. form of ἀλαίνω (cf. ἠλαίνω), *wander, stray, roam*, [ἔλαφοι] αὔτως ἠλάσκουσαι ἀνάλκιδες Il.13.104; [μυῖαι] κατὰ σταθμὸν ποιμνήϊον ἠλάσκουσιν 2.470; of persons, Emp.121.4, D.P.675.

**Ἠλειᾰκός** or **Ἠλιᾰκός**, ή, όν, (Ἦλις) *of* or *from Elis*: τὰ Ἠλιακά *the Antiquities of Elis*, Paus.5 tit.; οἱ Ἠλειακοί *philosophers of the school of Elis*, disciples of Phaedo, Str.9.1.8, D.L.*Prooem.*17, 2.105, 126.

**ἠλεκάτιον** [ᾰ], τό, Dim. of **ἠλεκάτη** (v. ἠλακ–), *BCH*35.286 (Delos, ii B.C.).

**ἠλέκτρῑνος**, η, ον, Dor. **ἀλ–**, *made of* ἤλεκτρον, Luc.*VH*1.20, Hld. 3.3. II. *shining like it*, ὕδωρ Call.*Cer.*29.

**ἠλεκτρίς**, ίδος, ἡ, fem. of ἠλέκτωρ, epith. of the Moon, Orph.*H.*9. 6. II. Ἠλεκτρίδες νῆσοι *amber* islands, at the mouth of the Po, Str.5.1.9, cf. Plin.*HN*4.103.

**ἤλεκτρον**, τό, and **ἤλεκτρος**, ὁ or ἡ (gender indeterminate in Hom., Hes., and Pl., neut. in Hdt.3.115, Thphr.*HP*9.18.2, Ti.Locr.102a, masc. in S.*Ant.*1038 codd., Eust. ad D.P.293, fem. in Ar.*Eq.*532, Alex. Aphr.*Pr.Praef.*), *amber* (cf. Ἠλεκτρίδες), [ὅρμος] μετὰ.. ἠλέκτροισιν (i.e. *pieces of amber*) ἔερτο Od.15.460, cf. 18.296, Hdt.3.115, Pl.*Ti.* 80c, Phld.*Sign.*1, D.L.1.24, etc.; ἠλέκτρου λιβάδες A.R.4.606. II. *an alloy of gold and silver*, χρυσοῦ τ' ἠλέκτρου τε καὶ ἀργύρου ἠδ' ἐλέφαντος Od.4.73, cf. Hes.*Sc.*142, Hom.*Epigr.*15.10, Pytheas ap.Ath. 11.465d; τἀπὸ Σάρδεων ἤ. S.*Ant.*1038 (cj.): in pl., of the pegs of a lyre, ἐκπιπτουσῶν τῶν ἠλέκτρων Ar.*Eq.*532. (The two senses are difficult to distinguish in early Poetry; cf. Paus.5.12.7, Plin.*HN*33. 80, 37.31. The word is connected with ἠλέκτωρ.)

**ἠλεκτρό-ομαι**, Pass., *become electrum*, Zos.Alch.p.180 B. **-φαής**, ές, *amber-gleaming*, αὐγαί, of the tears of the Phaethontiades, E.*Hipp.* 741 (lyr.). **-φόρος**, ον, *amber-bearing*, δένδρα, δάκρυον, Tz.*H.*4. 381, 690.

**ἠλεκτρώδης**, ες, *amber-like*, κοιλίης ταραχή Hp.*Epid.*4.38; βάλανοι Philostr.*VA*1.21.

**ἠλέκτωρ**, ορος, ὁ, *the beaming sun*, τεύχεσι παμφαίνων ὥς τ' ἠλέκτωρ Il.6.513; ὥς τ' ἠλέκτωρ Ὑπερίων 19.398; *fire* as an element, ἠ. τε χθών τε καὶ οὐρανὸς ἠδὲ θάλασσα Emp.22.2: gen. ἠλέκτωρος Choerob. *in Theod.*1.301 H.: dat. ἠλέκτωρι Epic. in *Arch.Pap.*7.4: hence acc. ἠλέκτωρα has been restored in Euph.110.

**ἠλέμᾰτος**, Dor. and Aeol. ἀλέματος, ον, *idle, vain*, Sapph.*Supp.* 15.5, Alc.*Supp.*23.4; ὦ τᾶς ἀλεμάτω ψυχᾶς prob. l. in Theoc.15.4 (ἀδεμ-, ἀδαμ- codd.); of a person, Timo 34.3, cf. 66.4 (cj.); βροντή Sotad.2; χειρὸς ἐκηβολία *AP*6.75 (Paul. Sil.); φαντασίη ib.11.350 (Agath.). Adv. -τως *idly*, A.R.4.1206; *in vain*, Call.*Cer.*91: so neut. pl. ἠλέματα Opp.*H.*4.590.

**ἠλεός**, ή, όν, *distraught, crazed*, φρένας ἠλεέ Od.2.243; in shorter form φρένας ἠλέ (perh. replacing Aeol. ἄλλε, written αλε), Il.15.128; ἠλεὰ ῥέξας Call.*Fr.*174, cf. 173: neut. pl., as Adv., *foolishly*, *AP*7. 639 (Antip.), Call.*Aet.*3.1.66: Aeol. ἆλλος prob. in Sapph.35, 110, dub. in ἀλλοφρονέω, ἀλλοφάσσω; cf. ἀλοσύνα (s.v. ἠλοσύνη). 2. Act., *distracting, crazing*, οἶνος Od.14.464. II. ἀλεός [ᾰ], is cited from A. (*Fr.*410) by Hsch. (ἀλαιός cod.), cf. Hdn.Gr.2.909, *EM*59. 45; cf. ἀλεόφρων· ὁ παράφρων ibid.: ἀλ(ε)ώσσειν· μωραίνειν, Hsch.

**ἠλέσθην**, v. ἀλέω (A). **ἠλεύατο**, 3 sg. 1 aor. of ἀλέομαι.

**ἠλήλατο, ἠλήλαντο**, v. ἐλαύνω. **ἦλημα**, v. βήλημα.

**Ἡλιάδης**, ου, ὁ, *child of the Sun*, Luc.*Am.*2; οἱ Ἡλιάδαι, an ancient family in Rhodes, Str.14.2.8, D.S.5.56.

**ἡλιάζομαι**, fut. -άσομαι (v. infr.): aor. 1 inf. -άσασθαι Ar.*Eq.*798: —*sit in the court* Ἡλιαία, *be a Heliast*, Id.*Lys.*380 (-άξεις, -άζεις codd., -άζει Cobet), *V.*772 (with a play on the word, ἡλιάσει πρὸς ἥλιον), Lex ap.D.24.50.

**ἡλιάζω**, *bake in the sun*, [μάζας] Str.16.4.13, cf. Dieuch.ap.Orib.4. 8.1:—Pass., *bask in the sun*, Arist.*HA*611ᵇ14; *ferment*, -άζεται ἡ β̄ ληνός *BGU*1551.1, 10 (iii B.C.); πολλάκις ὁ οἶνος -αζόμενος τελειοῦται τῇ κράσει καὶ τῇ δυνάμει Anon.*Incred.*17. II. Pass., = ἐξηλιάζομαι, Lxx *2Ki.*21.14.

**ἡλιαία**, ἡ, at Athens, *public place* or *hall*, in which the chief law-court was held, ἐν ἡλιαίᾳ Ar.*Eq.*897; ἀναβὰς εἰς τὴν ἡ. τὴν τῶν θεσμοθετῶν prob. in Antipho 6.21, cf. *IG*1².39.75, 63.14. 2. *supreme court* at Athens, Lex Solonis ap.Lys.10.16, Lex ap.D.21.47, Paus.1.28.8, etc. II. = ἁλία (A) (q.v.). III. ἡλιαίη, = ἀλέα (B), Hsch.

**Ἡλιαῖα**, τά, *festival of Helios*, Jul.*Or.*4.156c.

**ἡλιᾰκός**, Dor. ἁλιακός, ή, όν, *of the sun, solar*, Zeno *Stoic.*1.34; φάντασμα, εἴδωλον, Demetr.Lac.*Herc.*1013.17; κύκλος ἡ. *the sun's orbit, the ecliptic* (v. ἐκλειπτικός), D.S.1.98; ἡ. (sc. κύκλος), ὁ, Cleom. 1.4, etc.; φῶς ἡ. Ph.2.254, al.; ἔκλειψις ἡ. D.L.1.23; ἐνιαυτός Gem. 8.47, *Placit.*2.32.3; ἔτος, στέφανος ἁ., at Rhodes, Com.*Adesp.*336.4, 6; κάνθαρος ἡ. *dung*-beetle (v. ἡλιοκάνθαρος), *PMag.Par.*1.751; τροχίσκος ἡ. (magical remedy), Nech.ap.Harp.Astr. in *Cat.Cod.Astr.*8(3). 135; ἡλιακή (sc. περίοδος), ἡ, *solar year*, Plu.*Caes.*59. Adv. -κῶς Procl.*in Prm.*p.631 S.

**ἡλιανθές**, τό, *laudanum-plant, Cistus laurifolius*, Ps.-Democr.ap. Plin.*HN*24.165.

**ἡλιάς**, άδος, ἡ, fem. of ἡλιακός, ἀκτίς Orac.ap.Luc.*Alex.*34; Ῥόδος Id.*Am.*7. II. Ἡλιάδες, αἱ, *daughters of the Sun*, who were changed into poplars and wept amber, Parm.1.9, A.R.4.604, Str.5.1.9; ἡ Ἡλιὰς αἴγειρος Philostr.*VA*5.5. III. ἡλιάδες· αἱ κατάχρυσοι κλῖναι, Hsch.

**ἡλίᾰσις** (A), εως, ἡ, = ἡλίωσις, *exposure to the sun*, Gal.4.807 (pl.), D.C.59.7, *Gp.*7.1.3.

**ἡλίᾰσις** (B), εως, ἡ, *sitting in the* Ἡλιαία, Jusj.ap.D.24.150.

**ἡλιαστ-ήριον**, τό, *place for sunning oneself*, Str.17.1.44, Gal.18(1). 518; *place for drying fruit*, etc., *PRyl.*206.48 (iii A.D.), *POxy.*1631. 17 (iii A.D.), etc. **-ής**, οῦ, ὁ, (ἡλιαία 2) *Heliast*, Ar.*V.*206, 891, *Eq.* 255, *IG*1².63.14, etc. II. *fuller*, = Lat. *lutor*, *Gloss.* **-ικός**, ή, όν, *of, for*, or *like a Heliast*, γέρων Ar.*V.*195; ὀβολός Id.*Nu.*863; ὅρκος Lex ap.D.24.21, Hyp.*Eux.*40.

**ἡλῐ-αυγής**, ές, (αὐγή) *gleaming like the sun*, *EM*425.24. **-άω**, *to be like the sun*, κόμαι ἡλιῶσαι *Anacreont.*16.5, cf. Hld.3.4, Philostr. *VA*7.42. II. Act., *expose to the sun*, τὰς σταφυλὰς Arist.*Pr.*926ᵇ38.

**ἠλῐβάτας** [βᾰ], ὁ, *haunting the heights*, τράγος Antiph.133.3, cf. Anaxil.12 (-βάτους codd.):—hence **-βᾰτέω**, *haunt the heights*, Sch. Il.15.273.

**ἠλίβᾰτος** [ῐ], Dor. ἀλ-, ον, *high, steep*, always in Hom. as epith. of πέτρη or πέτραι, Il.15.273, al., cf. Hes.*Th.*675, 786, Thgn.176, Pi. *O.*6.64, A.*Supp.*352 (lyr.), E.*Supp.*80 (lyr.), Theoc.26.10, etc.; ὄρος, ἄκρη, ἐρίπναι, A.R.2.169, 361, 1248; of the Olympian throne of Zeus, Ar.*Av.*1732; of trees, *h.Ven.*267 (so prob. in Hes.*Sc.*422).—Also in X. and later Prose, πέτραι ἠ. *An.*1.4.4; τόποι Plb.4.41.9; πέτρος Str.17.1.50; δένδρα Agatharch.97; πῦρ Hanno *Peripl.*16; σταυρός Epigr.ap.Plu.*Flam.*9. II. *deep, abysmal*, ἄντρῳ ἐν ἠ. Hes.*Th.* 483; Τάρταρος ἠ. Stes.83; ἠ. ὑπὸ κευθμῶσι E.*Hipp.*732 (lyr.); πελάγεσσιν ἐν ἠ. Opp.*H.*3.171: metaph., κακὸν ἠ. Damox.2.22; εὐήθεια Porph.*Abst.*1.12. III. in later Poets (perh. from a misunderstanding of [Κύκλωψ] ἠ. πέτρην ἐπέθηκε θύρῃσιν Od.9.243), *huge, enormous*, μέλεα Opp.*H.*5.66; σχεδίη Q.S.11.312; so in Prose, κῦμα, σκιαί, Plu.2.163c, 935f. (Etym. dub., cf. ἄλιψ· πέτρα, Hsch.)

**Ἡλίεια**, only in Rhod. form Ἁλίεια, τά, *festival of the Sun*, *SIG* 724 (Rhodes, ii/i B.C.), al.; written Ἅλεια in Ath.13.561e, Ἁλίων (gen.) in Aristid.*Or.*25(43).32, ἀλιειτα (for Ἁλίεια τά..) in *Com. Adesp.*336.

**ἤλῐθα**, Adv. *very much, exceedingly*, ληΐδα.. συνελάσσαμεν ἤ. πολλήν Il.11.677, cf. Od.5.483; ἄστρα ἤ. μυρία Man.2.3; καθαρὴν γλάγεος πόσιν ἤ. πίνειν Nic.*Al.*423, cf. A.R.3.342 (expl. by Sch. as, = ἀθρόως), 4.177, 1265. II. *in vain, to no purpose*, Call.*Lav.Pall.*124, A.R. 2.283; ἔβρασεν ἤ. νηδὺς πνεύματα Nic.*Al.*25, cf. 140. (Prob. connected with ἠλεός in both uses.)

**ἠλῐθῐ-άζω**, *speak* or *act idly, foolishly*, Ar.*Eq.*1124. **-ος**, Dor. ἀλ-, α, ον, also ος, ον Hdt.1.60: (ἤλιθα II):—*idle, vain*, χόλος Pi.*P.* 3.11; βέλος A.*Ag.*366 (anap.); ὁδός Theoc.16.9. II. *foolish, silly*, εὐήθη Hdt.1.60; ἠλίθιον θάρρος θαρρεῖν Pl.*Phd.*95c; νόμος *PThead.*25. 7 (iv A.D.); freq. of persons, E.*Cyc.*537, Ar.*Ach.*443, etc.: Comp. -ώτερος X.*Smp.*3.6: Sup. -ώτατος Ar.*Ec.*765; ἠλίθιόν [ἐστι] c. inf., Arist.*Pol.*1286ᵃ12, prob. in Antiph.58; also ἠλιθίων ἐστί is the mark *of a fool*, Phld.*Po.*5.32. Adv. -ίως, διακεῖσθαι Lys.1.10; οἰόμενοι Pl. *Tht.*180d, cf. Theoc.10.40: Comp. -ώτερον Jul.*Gal.*89a: neut. ἠλίθιον as Adv., Ar.*Nu.*872. 2. *without sense*, of the dead, *Tab.Defix. Aud.*43.7. **-ότης**, ητος, ἡ, *folly, silliness*, Cratin.188, Pl.*R.*560d, al., Phld.*Rh.*1.249 S., etc.; γνώμης Them.*Or.*1.11d. **-όω**, *make foolish, distract*, φρένας A.*Pr.*1061 (anap.). **-ώδης**, ες, *like a fool*, Philostr.*VS*2.1.10. **-ώνη**, ἡ, *one who makes foolish* or *distracts*, epith. of the Ἐρινύες, *Tab.Defix.*108.

**ἠλῐθοποιός**, όν, gloss on ἠλεός, Sch.Od.14.464.

**ἡλῐκί-α**, Ion. -ίη, Dor. ἁλικία, ἡ, (ἧλιξ) *time of life, age*, ἥν πως ἡλικίην αἰδέσσεται ἠδ' ἐλεήσῃ γῆρας Il.22.419; γηραιὸν μέρος ἁλικίας Pi.*P.*4.157; παρὰ τὸν ἁλικίας ἐοικότα χρόνον Id.*O.*4.29; τήνδ' ἡ. ἀστῶν, i.e. their old *age*, A.*Pers.*914: acc. used adverbially, *in age*, νέος ἡλικίην Hdt.3.134; ἐτέων ἐὼν ἡλικίην πέντε καὶ τριήκοντα Id.1.26, cf. X.*Cyn.*2.3: so in dat., ἡλικίᾳ ἔτι τότε ὢν νέος Th.5.43; προεληλυθότες ταῖς ἡ. X.*HG*6.1.4; also ὑπὸ τῆς ἡ. from our *age*, Pl.*La.*180d; αἱ δι' ἡλικίαν ἄτοκοι Id.*Tht.*149c; οἱ ἐν τῇ αὐτῇ ἡ. Th.1.80; τὸ ἀχρεῖον τῆς ἡ. Id.2.44; ὅταν.. τοῦ γεννᾶν ἐκβῶσι τὴν ἡ. Pl.*R.*461b; πόρρω τῆς ἡ. to an advanced *age*, Id.*Grg.*484c; προήκων ἐς βαθὺ τῆς ἡ. Ar. *Nu.*514; προϊούσης τῆς ἡ. Pl.*Phdr.*279a; ὁ παρ' ἡλικίαν νοῦς beyond *one's age*, Men.*Mon.*690: in pl., ἐν ἁπάσαις ταῖς ἡ. Pl.*R.*412e, cf. *Lg.* 625b, al. 2. *prime of life, manhood*, ἐν ἁλικίᾳ πρώτᾳ Pi.*N.*9.42; αὐτὴ ἡ ἡ. τῶν νέων κατέκρινε Antipho 4.4.2; ἡλικίαν ἔχειν, εἰς ἡ. ἐλθεῖν, ἀφικέσθαι, Pl.*Euthd.*306d, *Tht.*142d, *Men.*89b; ἡλικίην ἔχειν c. inf., to be *of fit age* for doing, Hdt.1.209, cf. Pl.*Tht.*146b; ἡλικίας μετέχειν Th.7.60; οἱ ἐν τῇ ἡλικίᾳ men *of military age*, Id.8.75; ἐν ἡλικίᾳ στρατεύεσθαι D.4.7; ἐστρατευμένος ἁπάσας τὰς ἐν ἡλικίᾳ στρατείας Id.21.95; οἱ τῆς ἡ. ἐντὸς γεγονότες Lys.2.50; ἡ καθεστηκυῖα ἡ. maturity, Th.2.36, cf. *IG*12(7).239.21 (Amorgos); of women, *womanhood, marriageable age*, Hp.*Prorrh.*2.30, D.59.22; αἱ ἐν ἡ. γυναῖκες Pl.*R.*461b; τὴν ἡλικίαν τὴν ἑαυτοῦ καταμεμψάμενος Is.7.14: in pl., οἱ ταῖς ἡ. οὐ καλῶς κεχρημένοι Aeschin.1.194. 3. *youthful passion*, ἡλικίῃ καὶ θυμῷ ἐπιτρέπειν Hdt.3.36; εἴκειν Id.7.18. 4. *maidenhood*, τὴν ἡ. οὐ καλῶς διαφυλάξασαν Aeschin.1.182. II. as collective Noun, = οἱ ἥλικες, *those of the same age, comrades*, ὃς ἡλικίην ἐκέκαστο ἔγχεϊ Il.16.808, cf. Pi.*P.*1.74; esp. *those of military age*, τῆς ἡ. ἀπούσης ἐν ταῖς ναυσί Lys.2.49, cf. Th.3.67, 8.1, etc.; also, *men of any age*, παίδων τε καὶ ἀνδρῶν καὶ πάσης ἡ. Pl.*Lg.*959e. III. *time*, ταῦτα ἡλικίην ἂν εἴη κατὰ Λάϊον about the *time* of Laius, Hdt.5. 59, cf. 60, 71; ἡ. τετρακοσίοισι ἔτεσι.. πρεσβυτέρους Id.2.53. IV. *age, generation*, ἐπὶ τῆς νῦν ἡ. Isoc.4.167; πρὸ τῆς ἡμετέρας ἡ. Din. 1.38; εἰς τὴν νῦν ζῶσαν ἡ. D.60.11; πολλαῖς ἔμπροσθεν ἡ. Plu.*Per.* 27, cf. D.L.5.37. V. of the body, *stature*, as a sign of age, Hdt. 3.16, Pl.*Euthd.*271b, D.40.56; τῇ ἡ. μικρός *Ev.Luc.*19.3 (but προσθεῖναι ἐπὶ τὴν ἡ. πῆχυν ἕνα add a cubit to one's *age* (cf. πήχυιος), *Ev. Matt.*6.27); ἄνδρας ἡμισταδιαίους τὰς ἡ. Luc.*VH*1.40; *height* of a pillar, Id.*Syr.D.*28. **-άζομαι**, Pass., *assume this* or *that quality*, dub. in Herm.ap.Stob.1.49.69. **-ώτης**, ου, ὁ, Cret. ϝαλικιώτας (written βαλικιώτης), Hsch.:—*equal in age, comrade*, Hdt.5.71, Ar.*Nu.* 1006, And.1.48; ἡ. τινί Lys.20.36; ἐμὸς ἡ. Pl.*Ap.*33d; ἡ. καὶ ἑταῖροι Id.*Smp.*183c, al.: c. gen., ἡ. τῶν λόγων Him.*Or.*12.4:—fem. **-ῶτις**, ιδος, Plu.2.554a, Luc.*DMar.*15.2; ἡ. ἱστορία *contemporary* history, Plu.*Per.*13; πράξεις ἡ. D.S.1.58: c. dat., *contemporaneous with*, ib.9: c. gen., Max.Tyr.3.2, Them.*Or.*4.58b.

**ἡλίκος** [ῐ], η, ον, *as big as*, πόσος τις; μικρός, ἡλίκος Μόλων Ar.*Ra.* 55; τί τοσοῦτον ὕβρισεν, ἡλίκον..; D.21.147; τηλικοῦτος, ἡ. οὐδείς πω βασιλεύς Id.1.9. 2. of age, *as old as*, ἄνδρα.. ἡλίκον Θουκυδίδην Ar. *Ach.*703; τοῖσιν ἡλίκοισι νῷν, = τηλίκοις ἡλίκοι νώ, Id.*Ec.*465; οἱ ἡλί-

κοι ἐγώ, = τηλίκοι ἡλίκοι ἐγώ, Pl.*La.*180d: rare in Trag., ὁρᾷς μὲν ἡμᾶς, ἡλίκοι.. *of what various ages..*, S.*OT*15. 3. in indirect questions, *how big, how great*, Thphr.*Char.*23.2, Crates Theb.18, etc.; ὁρῶν ἡ. ἐστὶ Φίλιππος D.6.6, cf. Pl.*Chrm.*154b; freq. in expressions of wonder, θαυμάσι' ἡλίκα *extraordinarily great*, D.19.24; θαυμαστὸν ἡλίκον Id.24.122; μέγιστα ἡλίκα Luc.*Merc.Cond.*13; also, *how small*, ἰδοὺ ἡλίκον πῦρ ἡλίκην ὕλην ἀνάπτει *Ep.Jac.*3.5; ἂν ἴδω γὰρ ἡλίκον ἰχθὺν ὅσου τιμῶσι Antiph.166.6, cf. Luc.*Herm.*5. 4. in exclamations, ἡλίκον λαλεῖς Men.*Sam.*40. (Compd. of *yo-*, relat. Pron. stem (cf. ὅς), and *-āli-* (cf. ἧλιξ), with suffix *-κο-*; cf. πηλίκος, τηλίκος.)

**ἡλῐκοσοῦν**, strengthd. for ἡλίκος, *however so great*, Plot.1.4.7.

⊛ **ἧλιξ**, Dor. **ἅλιξ**, Aeol. **ἄλιξ** Sapph.119, ῐκος, ὁ, ἡ:—*of the same age*, καταίθουσα παιδὸς.. δαλὸν ἥλικ', of Meleager's torch, A.*Ch.*608; δρῦς A.R.2.479; Πηλῆος.. ἡ. χαίτην Tryph.637: mostly in pl., βόες .. ἥλικες ἰσοφόροι Od.18.373; ἅλικες οἷα παρθένοι Pi.*P.*3.17; ἄνδρες ἡ. Ar.*V.*245; ὑφ' ἡλίκων νεανίδων Id.*Th.*1030(lyr.); ἐν ἅλικι χρόνῳ in *equal* time, B.7.45. 2. Subst., *fellow, comrade*, οἱ ἥλικες Hdt.1.34, 2.32; ἥλικές θ' ἥβης ἐμῆς A.*Pers.*681; τὸν ἥλικα τόνδε Ar.*Ach.*336 codd. (sed leg. ὁμήλικα); μετὰ τῶν ἡ. Antipho 3.2.3; prov., ἧλιξ ἥλικα τέρπει Pl.*Phdr.*240c, cf. Arist.*EN*1161$^b$34. (Fr. ϝᾶλιξ, cf. βαλικιώτης: compd. of *swo-* 'one's own' (cf. ϝός, Lat. *suus*) and *-āli-* 'size', 'growth' (cf. Lat. *alo, aequ-āli-s*, Gr. ὁμ-ᾶλι-ξ), with suffix *-κ-*.)

**ἡλιό-βᾰτος**, ον, coined as etym. of ἠλίβατος, *EM*427.45. **-βλητος**, ον, = ἡλιόβολος, πλάκες E.*Ba.*14; of a tree, *sun-scorched*, Ael.*NA*8.26. **-βολέομαι**, Pass., *to be sun-struck*, Zen.5.53. **-βολος**, ον, *exposed to the sun, sunny*, of places, Thphr.*CP*4.12.3. ⊛ **-δρόμος**, ὁ, *sun's messenger*, ἡ. Διός Ramsay *Cities and Bishoprics* 2 p.566 (Acmonia); title of a grade of initiates in Mithras-worship, Cumont *Mystères de Mithra* 1.317. **-δύσιον** [ῠ], τό, *sunset*, Vett.Val.362.34. **-ειδής**, ές, *like the sun, bright and beaming*, Pl.*R.*509a, Gal.5.635, Plot.1.6.9; ἀήρ Arist.*Fr.*42; [σῶμα] Porph.*Sent.*29: Sup. -ειδέστατος Pl.*R.*508b, Gal.*UP*3.10. **-θαλπής**, ές, *warmed by the sun*, gloss on ἐλαθερής, Hsch. **-θερέω**, *to sun oneself*, Gal.6.137. ⊛ **-θερής**, ές, (θέρω) *warmed in the sun*, *EM*58.1. **-καής**, ές, (κάω, καίω) *sunburnt*, Luc.*Lex.*2; ὄστρακον v.l. in Dsc.2.2: -καές, τό, name of a *powder*, Orib.*Fr.*115. **-κᾰΐα**, ἡ, *sun-burning, exposure to the sun*, D.L.7.1 (pl.), Paul.Aeg.3.6 (pl.), Phlp.*in Ph.*60.13, *in GC*148.14. **-καλλίς**, ίδος, ἡ, = ἡλιανθές, Plin.*HN*24.165. ⊛ **-κάμῑνος** [ᾰ], ὁ, *a room exposed to the sun*, for winter use, Plin.*Ep.*2.17.20, *IGRom.*4.1431.43 (Smyrna). **-κάνθᾰρος**, ον, *the dung-beetle* or *scarab*, Alex.Trall.*Febr.*7. **-καυστος**, Dor. ἀλ-, ον, (καίω) = ἡλιοκαής, Theoc.10.27, Dsc.2.2. **-καυτέω**, *to be sunburnt*, Alex.Aphr.ap.Simp.*in Ph.*968.25. **-κεντρίς**, ίδος, ἡ, a kind of *fly*, *Gloss.* **-κόμας**, ου, ὁ, *with hair like the sun*, Eust.976.53. **-κτῠπος**, ον, *sunburnt*, A.*Supp.*155 (lyr.) (ἡδιόκτυπον cod. Med.). **-μᾰνής**, ές, *sun-mad, mad for love of the sun*, epith. of the cicada, Ar.*Av.*1096 (lyr.). **-μαντεία**, ἡ, *magical invocation of the sun*, *PMag.Leid.W.*4. **-μορφος**, ον, *sun-shaped*, Castorio 1.

**ἡλιόομαι**, Pass., *live in the sun, be exposed to the sun*, ἡλιωμένος, opp. ἐσκιατροφηκώς, Pl.*R.*556d; of places, ὅπως ἡ γῆ ἡλιωθῇ Thphr.*CP*3.4.1, cf. *HP*1.10.3; τὰ ἡλιούμενα *parts exposed to the sun*, X.*Oec.*19.18; -ούμενος ἀήρ Ath.Med.ap.Orib.9.5.1. 2. *to be sun-struck*, ἡλιοῦσθαι τὴν κεφαλήν Hp.*Aër.*3; or *sunburnt*, Muson.*Fr.*19 p.107 H. 3. *to be illuminated by the sunlight*, Arist.*de An.*419$^b$31, *Pr.*913$^a$22:—late in Act. **ἡλιόω**, *place in the sun*, Aët.1.102,112, al.

**ἡλιοπάλιος** or -ον, name of a plant or stone, *PMag.Berol.*2.18 (perh. *sun-opal*, cf. ὀπάλλιος).

**ἡλιό-πεπτος**, ον, *ripened in the sun*, σταφὶς *Hippiatr.*58. **-πλήξ**, πλῆγος, ὁ, ἡ, *sunburnt*, Call.*Iamb.*1.219. **-πους**, ποδος, ὁ, = ἡλιοτρόπιον, Ps.-Dsc.4.190.

⊛ **ἥλιος**, ὁ, Ep. **ἠέλιος**, as always in Hom. (exc. in the late passage Od.8.271) and Hes., cf. Hp.*Alim.*42: Dor. **ἀέλιος** [ᾱ] Pi.*P.*4.144, Call.*Cer.*92, *Lav.Pall.*89, and lyr. in Trag., S.*Ant.*809, E.*Ph.*175, al., but **ἅλιος** [ᾱ], S.*Tr.*96, E.*Alc.*395 (ἀέλιος S.*Tr.*835): Cret. **ἀβέλιος** (i.e. ἀϝ-), Hsch.: Aeol. **ἀέλιος** Sapph.79 (= *Oxy.*1787*Fr.*1.25), *Supp.*25.7; **ἄλιος** Sapph.69 (s.v.l.): Arc. **ἀέλιος** (or ἀ-) *IG*5(2).4.12 (Tegea, iv B.C.):—*sun*, Il.7.421, etc.; ὁρᾶν φάος ἠελίοιο *to see the light of life, live*, 18.61, etc.; ὑπ' ἠελίῳ τε καὶ οὐρανῷ ἀστερόεντι ναιετάουσι 4.44; γυνή.. ἀρίστη τῶν ὑφ' ἡλίῳ E.*Alc.*151; οὐκέτ' ἔστιν ὑφ' ἀλίῳ ib.395; also ὑπὸ ἡλίου ἑωρᾶσθαι Th.2.102; οἱ ὑπὸ τοῦτον τὸν ἥλιον ἄνθρωποι D.18.270; τριῶν τῶν ὑπὸ τὸν ἥ. μεγίστων ἡγεμονιῶν Plu.*Luc.*30: prov., οὐδ' ὁ ἥ. εἴσεται Hld.7.21; ὥσπερ σελήνη γ' ἡλίῳ (sc. ὅμοιος) a pale reflection, *Com.Adesp.*5.15 D. 2. to determine the cardinal points, πρὸς ἠῶ τ' ἠέλιόν τε towards the *East*, opp. πρὸς ζόφον: εἴτ' ἐπὶ δεξί' ἴωσι πρὸς ἠῶ τ' ἠέλιόν τε, εἴτ' ἐπ' ἀριστερὰ τοί γε ποτὶ ζόφον ἠερόεντα Il.12.239, cf. Od.9.26; ὅσσοι ναίουσι πρὸς ἠῶ τ' ἠέλιόν τε, ἠδ' ὅσσοι μετόπισθε ποτὶ ζόφον 13.240; πρὸς ἠῶ τε καὶ ἡλίου ἀνατολάς, opp. πρὸς ἑσπέρην, Hdt.7.58; τὰ πρὸς ἠῶ τε καὶ ἥλιον ἀνατέλλοντα Id.4.40; οἱ ἀπὸ ἡλίου ἀνατολέων Αἰθίοπες *the eastern..*, Id.7.70. 3. *day*, S.*El.*424; *a day*, Pi.*O.*13.37, Hp.*Alim.*42, E.*Hel.*652 (pl.), Ps.-Luc.*Philopatr.*4,26, etc.; later, *year*, Herod.10.1. 4. *sunshine, sun's heat*, ἐπὶ τοῖς ὄρεσιν Pl.*Phd.*116e; ἡ. πολύς Luc.*Nav.*35, cf. *Herm.*25; πολὺν τὸν ἡ. ἐμφαίνειν, of a sunburnt person, Id.*Ind.*3, cf. *Rh.Pr.*9: pl., *sunbeams*, Thphr.*Sign.*22, Ael.*NA*16.17; *hot sunny days*, Th.7.87. 5. metaph., *sunshine, brightness*, ψυχῆς Plu.2.994e, cf. Artem.2.36, etc.; of a person, Ἑλλάνων δόξης δεύτερον Ἀέλιον *IG*14.1188; of Ptol. VI, *UPZ*15.33; νέος Ἥ., of Nero and Caligula, *SIG*814.34, 798.3. II. as pr. n., *Helios, the sun-god*, Od.8.271, etc.; νὴ τὸν Ἥ. Men.*Sam.*108; ὑπὸ Δία Γῆν Ἥλιον, in manumission-formula, *POxy.*48.6, 49.8 (i A.D.), *IG*9(1).412 (Aetolia), *IPE*2.54.10 (iii A.D.); [Ἥλιος] δούλους ἐλευθέρους ποιεῖ Artem.2.36; identified with Apollo, *Carm.Pop.*12, E.*Fr.*781.11; with Dionysus, D.Chr.31.11, etc. 2. Ἡλίου ἀστήρ, of the planet *Saturn*, v.l. in Pl.*Epin.*987c, cf. D.S.2.30, Theo Sm.p.130 H. (I.-E. *sāwelios*, cf. Cret. ἀβέλιος, Lith. *sáulė*, Lat. *sōl*.)

**ἡλιοσέληνος**, ὁ, *sunstone*, imitatur quodammodo congressum solis et lunae, figuratque colore, Procl. *de sacrificio et magia* 101 (Kroll *Analecta Gr.*, Greifsw.1901 p.8).

⊛ **Ἡλιο-σέρᾱπις**, ιδος, ὁ, *an Egyptian divinity*, *IG*14.2405.48 (Puteoli). **-σκόπιος**, ον, *looking to the sun*: ἡ. τιθύμαλλος *sun-spurge, Euphorbia helioscopia*, Dsc.4.164, cf. Ruf.ap.Orib.7.26.39 (v.l. -σκόπος), Plin.*HN*26.69. **-σκόπος**, ὁ, a Hermetic plant, *Cat.Cod.Astr.*8(2).163. **-στᾰσία**, ἡ, *solstice*, *Gloss.* **-στερής**, ές, *depriving of sun*, i.e. *shading from the sun*, epith. of the Thessalian hat, S.*OC*313. **-στῐβής**, ές, *sun-trodden*, ἀντολαί A.*Pr.*791. **-τρόπιον**, τό, *heliotrope*, Thphr.*HP*7.3.1, Gal.19.732; ἡ. τὸ μέγα, *Heliotropium villosum*, Dsc.4.190; ἡ. τὸ μικρόν, *H. supinum*, ib.191. 2. = *Croton tinctorius*, *PHolm.*8.3, al. II. *sun-dial*, Moschio ap.Ath.5.207f, *IG*11(2).287 *A*117 (Delos, iii B.C.), Plu.*Dio* 29, Sch.Ar.*Av.*998, etc. III. *green stone streaked with red, blood-stone*, Plin.*HN*37.165, Herm.Trism. in *Rev.Phil.*32.258. **-τρόπιος**, ον, belonging to foreg. 1, ξύλον *Theb.Ostr.*144.1 (i A.D.). II. v. Ἀλιοτρόπιος. **-τροπος**, ὁ, = ἡλιοτρόπιον 1, Ps.-Dsc.4.190.

**ἡλιοῦχος**, ον, *possessing sun*, *PMag.Par.*1.3228 (s.v.l.).

**ἡλιο-φεγγής**, Dor. ἀλ-, ές, *shining like the sun*, Philod.Scarph.136. **-φυές**, τό, = κλύμενον, Ps.-Dsc.4.13. **-φυτον**, τό, = μίλαξ τραχεῖα, ib.4.142.

**ἡλιόω**, v. ἡλιόομαι.

**ἡλίσκος**, ὁ, Dim. of ἧλος, *little nail*, Ar.*Fr.*314.

**ἡλῐτε**, v. ἀλιταίνω.

**ἡλῐτενής**, ές, *lofty*, πέτρα Suid.; cf. ἠλίβατος.

⊛ **ἡλίτης** [ῑ], ου, ὁ, (ἥλιος) = ἡλιοειδής, λίθος Dam.*Isid.*233; helitis (leg. -es) lapis, Procl. *de sacrificio et magia* 91 (Kroll *Analecta Gr.*, Greifsw.1901 p.8).

**ἡλῖτις**, ιδος, ἡ, (ἧλος) *of* or *like nails*, ἡ. λεπίς iron *that scales off from nails*, Dsc.5.78, Aët.2.58.

**ἡλῐτο-εργός**, όν, *missing the work, failing in one's aim*, *AP*7.210 (Antip.), dub. l. in Alc.*Oxy.*1360*Fr.*6. **-μηνις**· ὁ μάτην ἐγκαλῶν, Hsch.: acc. sg. -μηνιν Epic. in *Arch.Pap.*7.5. **-μηνος**, ον, *missing the right month*, i.e. *untimely born*, Il.19.118, Tryph.556, Plu.2.358e, *AP*12.228 (Strat.).

**ἡλιφάρμᾰκος**, ἡ, *a plant useful to staunch blood*, Timag.ap.Stob.4.36.19. **ἠλίφατος**, variant for ἠλίβατος, Hsch.

**ἧλιψ**, ῖπος, ὁ, *a Dorian shoe* (cf. ἀνήλιπος), Sch.Theoc.4.56.

**ἡλῐ-ώδης**, ες, = ἡλιοειδής, εἴδωλον Chaerem.14.14; μῆλα Philostr.*Im.*1.6; κόμη Anon.ap.Eust.432.26. **-ών**, ῶνος, ὁ, month at Termessus, Lanckoroński *Städte Pamphyliens und Pisidiens* 2.34. **-ωπός**, όν, *lit by the sun's eye*, οὐρανός Ζεὺς S.*Fr.*26 (= E.*Fr.*p.531 N.), 470. **-ωσις**, εως, ἡ, (ἡλιόομαι) *exposure to the sun*, Hp.*Epid.*7.82, Thphr.*CP*6.16.5, Sor.2.38, S.E.*P.*3.16. **-ωτέος**, α, ον, *needing exposure to the sun*, Philostr.*Gym.*58. **-ώτης**, ου, ὁ, fem. **-ῶτις**, poet. **ἠελιῶτις**, ιδος, (ἥλιος) *of the sun*, ἀκτῖν' ἐς ἡλιῶτιν S.*Tr.*697; ἠελιῶτις αἴγλη *AP*7.601 (Jul.Aeg.); αὐγαί Paul.Al.*M.*3; οἱ ἡλιῶται *the inhabitants of the sun*, Luc.*VH*1.17. II. ἡλιῶτις, ἡ, Ion. name for *the dawn*, *EM*440.55.

**ἤλκησε**, v. ἑλκέω.

**ἡλληγορημένως**, Adv. pf. part. Pass., (ἀλληγορέω) *allegorically*, Tz.ad Hes.*Op.*56.

**ἡλό-κεντρον**, τό, *spur*, *Gloss.* **-κοπέω**, = Lat. *clavo*, Dosith.p.435 K., *Gloss.*; ὑποδήματα -κεκοπημένα *hob-nailed* shoes, Gal.13.326. **-κοπική** τέχνη *nail-smith's* trade, *BGU*1124.11 (i B.C.). **-κόπον**, τό, = Lat. *forma clavaris*, *Gloss.* ⊛ **-κόπος**, ὁ, (κόπτω) *nail-smith*, *BGU*1028.19 (ii A.D.), Judeich *Altertümer von Hierapolis* 133; = Lat. *clavarius, clavifixor, clavorum faber*, *Gloss.*

**ἧλον**, τό, = βράβιλον or κοκκύμηλον, Seleuc.ap.Ath.2.50a.

**ἡλο-παγής**, ές, (πήγνυμι) *fixed with nails*, Man.1.149. **-πληκτος**, ον, *hurt by a nail*, *Hippiatr.*34. **-ποιός**, ὁ, *nail-smith*, Lat. *clavarius*, *Gloss.*

⊛ **ἧλος**, Dor. **ἆλος**, *IG*4.1484.62 (Epid.), *SIG*245 i 69 (Delph., iv B.C.), Pi. (v. infr.), Aeol.(?) ϝάλλοι (pl.) written γάλλοι, Hsch.: ὁ:—*nail-head, stud*, as an ornament, σκῆπτρον χρυσείοις ἥλοισι πεπαρμένον Il.1.246, cf. 11.633; ἐν δέ οἱ [τῷ ξίφει] ἧλοι χρύσειοι πάμφαινον ib.29, cf. Ath.11.488b,c: hence, of the stars, *Placit.*2.14.3. 2. after Hom., *nail*, Pi.*P.*4.71: ἧλοι σιδηροῖ καὶ ξύλινοι X.*Cyn.*9.12, etc.; of shoe-nails, Thphr.*Char.*4.13: prov., ἥλῳ ἐκκρούειν τὸν ἧλον Luc.*Laps.*7; ἥλῳ ὁ ἧλος (sc. ἐκκρούεται) Arist.*Pol.*1314$^a$5, etc. 3. = Lat. *acutus* (= *spur*), *Gloss.* II. *wart, callus*, Thphr.*Ign.*37, Nic.*Th.*272; ἧλοι καὶ τύλοι Dsc.1.104, cf. Asclep.ap.Gal.13.647; also on plants, esp. the olive, Thphr.*HP*4.14.3.

⊛ **ἧλος**, ὁ, *barren spot*, Hsch.

**ἡλός**, supposed nom. of the voc. ἠλέ, v. sub ἠλεός.

⊛ **ἡλοσύνη**, ἡ, = ἠλιθιότης, Nic.*Al.*420: Aeol. **ἀλοσύνα** Theoc.30.12; cf. ἆλλος (s.v. ἠλεός).

**ἡλόω**, *sharpen*, ἡλοῦσιν αὐτὸ (sc. τὸ κοντάριον) ξυλοπυρίας (sic) Anon. *in Rh.*236.18. II. Pass., *become callous*, ἡλωμέναι ἐξοχαί Gal.17(1).902.

**ἧλπετο**, v. ἔλπομαι.

**ἠλσάμην**, = ἠλασάμην, (ἐλαύνω) Ibyc.55; διηλσάμην is prob. l. in Semon.17.

**ἠλῠγ-άζω**, (ἤλυξ) *overshadow*, only in compd. ἐπηλ– (q.v.). **–αῖος**, α, ον, *shadowy, dark*, Suid. **–η** [ῠ], ἡ, *shadow*, Erot. s.v. ἐπηλυγάζονται, Hsch. s.v. ἠλυγισμένος: metaph., δίκης ἠ. *the 'fog'* of a lawsuit, Ar.*Ach.*684; cf. ἤλυξ. **–ίζω**, = ἠλυγάζω, in pf. part. Pass. ἠλυγισμένος, Hsch.

**ἤλῠθον**, v. ἔρχομαι. **ἤλυξ**, ῠγος, ὁ, = ἠλύγη, Choerob. *in Theod.* 2.400; ἠλύγων ὀρέων· ἐν σκότῳ κατεχομένων, Hsch. (leg. –αίων). **ἤλυξα**, v. ἀλύσκω. **ἠλῠσίη**, ἡ, = ἤλυσις, ὁδός, Id., cf. *EM*497.9.

**Ἠλύσιον** [ῠ] πεδίον, τό, *the Elysian* fields, Od.4.563, A.R.4.811, Str.1.1.4, Plu.*Sert.*8, etc.: in pl., *IG*14.1973; χῶρος Ἠλύσιος ib.2012 *Ca*8; λειμών Luc.*JConf.*17; ἐν Ἠλυσίῳ alone, *IG*14.1750. **II.** ἠλύσια, τά, = ἐνηλύσια (q.v.), Polem.Hist.93.

**Ἠλύσιος**, α, ον, *Elysian*, αὖραι *IG*14.1389i22; χοροστασίαι ib.58.

**ἤλῠσις**, εως, ἡ, = ἔλευσις, *step, gait*, βραδύπουν ἤ. προτιθεῖσα E.*Hec.*67; πυκνὴν βαίνων ἤ. Id.*Ph.*844; πικρὰν διώκων ἤ. Id.*HF*1041.

**ἠλυσκάζω**, v. ἠλασκάζω. **ἦλφον**, v. ἀλφάνω. **ἤλω**, v. ἁλίσκομαι. **ἠλώμην**, v. ἀλάομαι.

**ἡλωτός**, ή, όν, (ἡλόω) *nailed, nail-shaped*, Paul.Aeg.6.66.

**ἧμα**, ατος, τό, (ἵημι) *that which is thrown, dart, javelin*, ἥμασιν ἔπλευ ἄριστος best *at darting*, Il.23.891: hence ἥμων (q.v.). **II.** Ϝῆμα, v. εἶμα.

**ἠμᾰθόεις**, εσσα, εν (or –όεις, εν if Πύλος (q.v.) be fem.), Ep. for ἀμ–, (ἄμαθος) *sandy*, epith. of the Elean Pylos, Πύλον ἠμαθόεντα Od.1.93, al., Hes.*Sc.*360: generally ἠμαθόεσσα ἠϊών A.R.1.932. (Deriv. from the name of a river by Str.8.3.14.)

❀ **ἧμαι**, ἧσαι, ἧσται E.*Alc.* (v. infr.) (but κάθ-ηται, v. κάθημαι), ἧσθον *h.Ap.*456, ἥμεθα, ἧστε, ἧνται Call.*Fr.*122, Ep. εἵαται Il.10.100, ἕαται 3.134 (κατέαται Hdt.1.199); imper. ἧσο Hom., ἧσθω (καθ–) A.*Pr.*916; subj. and opt. only in compd. καθ–; inf. ἧσθαι; part. ἥμενος: impf. ἥμην, ἧσο, ἧστο (but ἐκάθητο, καθ-ῆτο, v. κάθημαι), dual ἥσθην (ἑήσθην Orph.*A.*815), pl. ἥμεθα (ἥμεσθα E.*IA*88), ἧσθε Cratin.142, ἧντο, Ep. εἵατο Il.7.61, ἕατο ib.414, ἐκατέατο Hdt.8.73 (v.l. ἐκαθ–): (I.-E. *ēs–*, cf. Skt. *āste* (= ἧσται) 'sits'; aspirate borrowed from ἵζω, ἕζομαι; Ep. εἵαται εἵατο fr. ἥαται ἥατο (which shd. perh. be restored) through ἕαται ἕατο):—*to be seated, sit*, Il.1.498, etc.: freq. with collat. sense, *sit still, sit idle*, 2.255, 18.104, etc.; ἧσθαι ἐν εἰρήνῃ Callin.1.4; κατ' οἴκους ἐκτὸς ἡμένῳ πόνων E.*Fr.*10; of an army, *encamp*, Il.15.740, 24.542; πόλιν ἀμφὶ 18.509; πρόσθε τειχέων E.*Supp.*664; of a spy, *lurk*, Il.18.523: metaph., πρὸς ἐμᾷ ψυχᾷ θάρσος ἧσται c. acc. et inf., E.*Alc.*604 (lyr.); *lie hid*, ἥατ' ἐνὶ Τρώων ἀγορῇ κεκαλυμμένοι ἵππῳ, i.e. in the wooden horse, Od.8.503, cf. 512; of magistrates, ἐν ἀρχαῖς ἥμενοι E.*Andr.*699; δαιμόνων σέλμα σεμνὸν ἡμένων A.*Ag.*183 (lyr.); later, of things, *lie*, ἱρὸν ἧσται Hdt.9.57; ἐπὶ στέγος ἱερὸν ἧνται κάλπιδες Call.*Fr.*122, cf. Luc.*Syr.D.*31; ἡμένῳ ἐν χώρῳ (or χόρτῳ) in *a low* place, Theoc.13.40:—Constr.: mostly with Preps., ἐνὶ δίφρῳ Il.16.403, cf. A.*Pr.*368, etc.; ἐπὶ κορυφῇς Il.14.158; ἐπ' ἐσχάραις A.*Eu.*806; παρὰ κλισίῃ Il.1.330, etc.; ἀνὰ Γαργάρῳ 15.153: c. dat., Οὐλύμπῳ 13.524, cf. 21.389, etc.; ἐρετμοῖς at the oar, E.*Cyc.*16; ἀνορόφοις πέτραις Id.*Ba.*38: rarely c. acc., A.*Ag.*183 (v. supr.); Σιμόεντος κοίτας E.*Rh.*547: c. part.. τίη.. ἧσ' ὀλιγηπελέων; Il.15.245; ὀδυρόμενος, ἀλλοφρονέων, Od.14.41, 10.374; πεφυλαγμένος ἧσο Orac.ap.Hdt.7.148; ἐκπεπληγμένη S.*Tr.*24.

❀ **ἡμαιθον**, τό, *half-obol*, or *two-obol piece* at Cyzicus, Herod.3.45, Phoen.2.3, cf. Hsch.

❀ **ἦμαρ**, Dor. and Arc. **ἆμαρ**, ατος, τό, = ἡμέρα, *day*, the prevailing form in Hom., νύκτες τε καὶ ἤματα Od.11.183; νύκτας τε καὶ ἦμαρ by night and *day*, Il.5.490, Od.24.63 (where sg. ἦμαρ is used as pl., as in ποσσῆμαρ, ἐννῆμαρ, ἐξῆμαρ); ἆμαρ ἢ νύκτες Pi.*P.*4.256; ἦμαρ alone, *by day*, Hes.*Op.*176 (but τὸ ἠ. *on that day*, *JHS*12.234 (Cilicia)); μέσον ἠ. mid*day*, Il.21.111, cf. Pi.*P.*9.113, etc.; δείελον ἠ. evening, Od.17.606; ἤματι χειμερίῳ on a winter's *day*, Il.12.279, cf. 16.385. **2.** used in Ep. with Adjs., of a state or condition, αἴσιμον, ὀλέθριον, μόρσιμον, νηλεὲς ἠ., *the day* of destiny, of death, Il.8.72, 19.294, Od.10.175, Il.11.484; ἐλεύθερον, δούλιον, ἀναγκαῖον ἠ., *the day* of freedom, of slavery, 6.455, 463, 16.836; νόστιμον ἠ. Od.1.9, al.; ἠ. ὀρφανικόν Il.22.490. **II.** with Preps., ἐπ' ἤματι *day by day, daily*, Od.12.105, 14.105 (αἰὲν ἐπ' ἤματι S.*OC*688); *in a day, within a day's space*, Il.10.48, 19.229, Od.2.284; ἐπ' ἄματι *at the close of day*, Theoc.24.139; ἐπ' ἆ. *by day*, S.*OT*199; ἐπ' ἠ. *for a day*, Id.*Fr.*255.3, E.*Ph.*401; ἐπ' ἆμαρ ἕκαστον, ἆμαρ ἐπ' ἆμαρ, Theoc.17.96, 11.69; ἠ. ἐπ' ἠ. ἀεὶ *AP*9.499; κατ' ἠ. *day by day*, S.*Ph.*798, E.*Hec.*628; κατ' ἠ. αἰεὶ S.*OC*682 (lyr.); ἀεὶ κατ' ἠ. E.*Tr.*392; ἀεὶ τὸ κατ' ἠ. Id.*El.*145 (lyr.); τὸ κατ' ἦμαρ *the needs of the day, one's daily bread*, S.*Ph.*1089, *Fr.*593 (lyr.); but κατ' ἆ. also, *this day, to-day*, Id.*OC*1079, cf. *Aj.*753; τὸ μὲν παρ' ἆ., τὸ δὲ *on one day, and on the next*.., Pi.*P.*11.63; παρ' ἠ. *on the morrow*, S.*OC*1455 (lyr.); παρ' ἠ. ἡμέρα day *after day*, Id.*Aj.*475; ἐν ἄματα πάντα *in perpetuity*, *IG*5(2).5 (Tegea); without ἐν, ib.262.22 (Mantinea).

**ἡμαρτημένως**, Adv. pf. part. Pass. of ἁμαρτάνω, *faultily*, ἡγεῖσθαι Pl.*Men.*88e; ἠ. ἔχειν Id.*Lg.*670c, Iamb.*VP*33.233.

**ἠμάτιος** [ᾰ], η, ον, (ἦμαρ) poet. for ἡμερήσιος, *by day*, ἠματίη μὲν ὑφαίνεσκεν μέγαν ἱστόν, νύκτας δ' ἀλλύεσκεν Od.2.104, cf. 19.149; ἠμάτιαι σπεύδουσι [μέλισσαι] Hes.*Th.*597; ἠ. φέγγος, i.e. the sun, *AP*9.651 (Paul. Sil.). **2.** *day by day, daily*, Il.9.72.

**ἤμβροτον**, Ep. aor. 2 of ἁμαρτάνω.

❀ **ἡμεδᾰπός**, ή, όν, (ἡμεῖς) *of our land* or *country, native*, opp. ἀλλοδαπός, χαρακτὴρ Ar.*Pax* 220; νόμισμα ἡ. *IG*1².91.4; στρατιή Call.*Fr.*152: of a person, Pl.*Thg.*124d, Luc.*Phal.*1.11; ἡ ἡμεδαπή (sc. γῆ) *IG*1².115.30; of the Roman empire, opp. to barbarian lands, Hdn. 1.1.4. (ἡμεδ– = Skt. *asmad*–, stem of 1st pers. pl. pron.; for the termin. –απος, cf. ἀλλοδαπός.)

**ἡμέδιμνον**, τό, = ἡμιμέδιμνον, in pl., *IG*2².1675.265, *SIG*1027.11 (Cos); also **ἡμέδιμνος**, ὁ, *IG*14.423 i 34 (Tauromenium), Did. in *Gramm.Lat.*3.412 K.; **ἡμίδιμμνον**, τό, *SIG*998.8 (Epid., v B.C.).

**ἡμεῖς**, v. ἐγώ. **ἡμεκτέω**, v. περιημεκτέω.

**ἠμελημένως**, Adv. pf. part. Pass. of ἀμελέω, *in a state of neglect*, διάγειν Isoc.*Ep.*8.10; ἠ. ἔχειν X.*Mem.*3.11.4; ἐς προῦπτον κίνδυνον ἐκπέμπεσθαι Arr.*Ind.*20.3; *with studied neglect*, ἑαυτὴν ἠ. πως κοσμήσασα D.C.51.12; *carelessly*, Max.Tyr.28.5.

**ἤμελλον**, v. μέλλω.

**ἠμέν**, Ep. Conj., correl. to ἠδέ (from ἦ and μέν, δέ), *both*.. and.., ἠ. νέοι ἠδὲ γέροντες Il.2.789, etc.; ἠ. ἀνακλῖναι πυκινὸν νέφος ἠδ' ἐπιθεῖναι 5.751; sts. καί is added to ἠδέ, ἠ. θεὸν ἠδὲ καὶ ἄνδρα 5.128; ἠ. δέμας ἠδὲ καὶ αὐδήν Od.2.268; ἠ. δή ποτ' ἐμεῦ πάρος ἔκλυες.. ἠδ' ἔτι καὶ νῦν μοι.. ἐπικρήηνον ἐέλδωρ Il.1.453: rarely folld. by δέ or τε, ἠ... πολλοὶ δέ.. 12.428; ἠ. ὅσοι χαλεποί.. οἵ τε φιλόξεινοι Od.8.575: more freq. by καί, Il.15.664, 670, Hes.*Op.*339.

❀ **ἡμέρα**, Ep. and Ion. **ἡμέρη** *IG*12(5).1 (Ios), Dor. **ἁμέρα** ib.5(1).213.43, al., 1390.109, 1432.25, *Test.Epict.*4.12, *Michel*995*A*32, etc., Locr. **ἀμάρα** *IG*9(1).334.42 (aspirated perh. only in Att. and West Ion., cf. ἐπάμερος Pi., etc., αὐθημερόν *IG*7.235.18 (Oropus), etc.; usu. unaspirated in early Att. Inscrr., *IG*1².49.6, al.; aspirated in codd. even in dialects: original ἀμέρα prob. took aspirate from ἑσπέρα): ἡ:—*day*, less freq. than ἦμαρ in Hom., ἠ. ἥδε κακὸν φέρει Il.8.541, 13.828; τίς νύ μοι ἡ. ἥδε; Od.24.514; νύκτες τε καὶ ἡ. 14.93; μῆνές τε καὶ ἡ. ib.293; νοῦσοι ἐφ' ἡμέρῃ αἱ δ' ἐπὶ νυκτὶ Hes.*Op.*102; ἡ σήμερον ἡ., v. σήμερον: ἅμα ἡμέρᾳ or ἅμα τῇ ἡμέρᾳ *at daybreak*, X.*An.*6.3.6, Aeschin.3.76; ἅμ' ἡμέρῃ διαφωσκούσῃ Hdt.3.86; ἡ. διέλαμψεν, ἐξέλαμψεν, ὑπέφαινε, Ar.*Pl.*744, *Pax*304, X.*Cyr.*4.5.14; τῆς ἡ. ὀψὲ late *in the day*, Id.*HG*2.1.23. **2.** sts. like Ep. ἦμαρ, with Adjs. to describe *a state* or *time of life*, ἐπίπονος ἁ. *a life* of misery, S.*Tr.*654 (lyr.); λυπρὰν ἄγειν ἡ. E.*Hec.*364; ἐχθρὰ ἡ. Id.*Ph.*540; παλαιὰ ἁ. old *age*, S.*Aj.*623 (but θεία ἡ. Id.*Fr.*950 is dub. l.); τερμία ἁ. Id.*Ant.*1330 (lyr.); αἱ μακραὶ ἁμέραι length of *days*, Id.*OC*1216 (lyr.); νέα ἁ. youth, E.*Ion*720 (lyr.); so τῇ πρώτῃ ἡ. Arist.*Rh.*1389ᵃ24; ἐπὶ τῇ τελευταίᾳ ἡ. at the close of *life*, ib.1389ᵇ33, cf. S.*OT*1529; ζωὴν βλέπουσιν ἡ. look *life*-like, Herod.4.68. **3.** poet. for *time*, ἡ. κλίνει τε κἀνάγει πάλιν ἅπαντα τἀνθρώπεια S.*Aj.*131; ἐς τόδ' ἡμέρας Id.*OC*1138: pl., ἐν ἡμέραις τινὸς *in the days* of.., Lxx 1*Ch.*4.41, etc.; ἡ. ἀρχαῖαι ib.*Ps.*142(143).5. **4.** *birthday*, D.L.4.41. **5.** *a fixed day*, τακτὴ ἡ. *Act.Ap.*12.21; ῥητὴ ἡ. Luc.*Alex.*19; ἡ. ἔστησαν ἀρχαιρεσιῶν D.H.6.48, cf. *Act.Ap.*17.31; ἡ. Κυρίου Lxx *Jl.*2.1, cf. 2*Ep.Pet.*3.12, etc.; ἡ. κρίσεως *Ev.Matt.*10.15: so abs., ὑπὸ ἀνθρωπίνης ἡμέρας a human *tribunal*, 1*Ep.Cor.*4.3; ἡμέραι καὶ ἀγῶνες *Jahresh.*23 *Beibl.*93 (Pamphyl.). **6.** in pl., *age*, προβεβηκὼς ἐν ταῖς ἡ. *Ev.Luc.*1.7, cf. Lxx *Ge.*47.8, etc. **II.** abs. usages, **1.** gen., τριῶν ἡμερέων *within* three *days*, Hdt.2.115, cf. Th.7.3; ἡμερῶν ὀλίγων *within* a few *days*, Id.4.26, etc.; ἄλλης ἡ. another *day*, S.*El.*698; τῆς αὐτῆς ἡ. Isoc.4.87; μιᾶς ἁμέρας *IG*5(1).213.43 (Sparta, v B.C.); ἡμέρας *by day*, opp. νυκτός, S.*Fr.*65; οὐθ' ἡμέρας οὔτε νυκτὸς Pl.*Phdr.*240c; τοὺς.. τῆς ἡ. ἄρτους δ̄ *daily*, *UPZ* 47.21 (ii B.C.); δὶς τῆς ἡμέρης ἑκάστης twice every *day*, Hdt.2.37; δὶς τῆς ἡ. Pl.Com.207; πεντάκις τῆς ἡ. Men.326; κατεσθίω.. τῆς ἡ. πένθ' ἡμιμέδιμνα five *every day*, Pherecr.1. **2.** dat., τῇδε θἡμέρᾳ, = σήμερον, S.*OT*1283; τῇ τόθ' ἡ. Id.*El.*1134. **3.** acc.. πᾶσαν ἡ. any *day*, i.e. soon, Hdt.1.111, 7.203; τὴν μὲν αὐτίχ' ἡ. S.*OC*433; ὅλην τὴν ἡ. Eup.233; τρίτην ἡ. ἥκων two *days* after one's arrival, Th.8.23; οὐδεμίαν ἡ. ὑπεύθυνος εἶναί φημι D.18.112; πέντε ἡμέρας during five *days*, Th.8.103; τὰς ἡ. in the *daytime*, X.*Cyr.*1.3.12; τὴν ἡ. *daily*, Lxx *Ex.*29.38. **III.** with Preps., μίαν ἀν' ἁμέραν on one *day*, Pi.*O.*9.85; ἀνὰ πᾶσαν ἡ. every *day*, Hdt.7.198; ἀφ' ἡμέρας τῆς νῦν from this *day*, S.*OT*351; but ἀφ' ἡμέρας γίνεσθαι ἐν τῷ Μουσείῳ *from early in the day*, Plb.8.25.11; δι' ἡμέρης, Att. –ρας, the whole *day* long, Hdt.1.97, 2.173, Pherecr.64, Ar.*Ra.*260 (lyr.); διὰ τρίτης ἡ. every other *day*, Hdt.2.37; διὰ πολλῶν ἡ. at a distance of many *days*, Th.2.29; δι' ἡμερῶν τινων Thphr.*HP*4.3.6; εἰς ἡμέραν *yearly*, Lxx *Jd.*17.10; ἐν ἡμέρῃ *in a single day*, Hdt.1.126, cf. Men.*Pk.*377; ἐν ἡ. μιᾷ S.*OT*615; τῇδ' ἐν ἡ. Id.*OC*1612; ἐν ἐκείνῃ τῇ ἡ. *Ev.Jo.*14.20; ἐν ὑστεραίσιν ἡ. A.*Ag.*1666; ἐν ὀκτὼ ἡ. Lys.20.10; but ἐν τρισὶν ἡ. *within* three *days*, *Ev.Jo.*2.19; ἐξ ἡμέρας by *day*, οὔτε νυκτὸς οὔτ' ἐξ ἡ. S.*El.*780; ἡμέραν ἐξ ἡμέρας *day* after *day*, Henioch.5.13, Lxx *Ge.*39.10, 2*Ep.Pet.*2.8 (but ἐξ ἡμερῶν εἰς ἡμέρας Lxx 2*Ch.*21.15); ἐπ' ἡμέρην ἔχειν, ἐφ'–ραν χρῆσθαι, *sufficient for the day*, Hdt.1.32, Th.4.69; τὸ γὰρ βρότειον σπέρμ' ἐφ' ἡ. φρονεῖ A.*Fr.*399; τῆς ἐφ' ἡ. βορᾶς E.*El.*429; but τοὐφ' ἡμέραν *day by day*, Id.*Cyc.*336: c. dat., ἐπ' ἡμέρῃ ἑκάστῃ (v.l. –ρης –της) every *day*, Hdt.5.117; ὁ ἥλιος νέος ἐφ' ἡμέρῃ Heraclit.6; καθ' ἡμέραν *by day*, A.*Ch.*818 (lyr.); καθ' ἡ. τὴν νῦν *to-day*, S.*OC*3, *Aj.*801; but καθ' ἡ. commonly means *day by day*, *IG*1².84.40, etc.; καθ' ἡ. ἀεὶ [S.]*Fr.*1120.4: with Art., τὸν καθ' ἡ. βίον Id.*OC*1364; ἡ καθ' ἡ. ἀναγκαία τροφή Th.1.2; τὰ καθ' ἡ. ἐπιτηδεύματα Id.2.37; τὸ καθ' ἡ. ἀδεὲς Id.3.37, etc.; τὸ καθ' ἡ. *every day*, Ar.*Eq.*1126 (lyr.), etc.; also τὰ καθ' ἑκάστην τὴν ἡ. ἐπιτηδεύματα Isoc.4.78; μετ' ἡμέρην *in broad daylight*, opp. νυκτός, Hdt.2.150, cf. Ar.*Pl.*930; opp. νύκτωρ, Aeschin.3.77; μεθ' ἡμέρας *some days* after, Lxx *Jd.*15.1; ἡμέραν παρ' ἡμέραν γιγνομένη *day* following on *day*, Antipho 5.72; but παρ' ἡμέραν *every other day*, Dsc.3.137, Luc.*DDeor.*24.2; παρ' ἡ. ἄρχειν Plu.*Fab.*15; καθ' ἡμέραν εἰώθειν ὀργίζεσθαι, νῦν παρ' ἡμέραν, εἶτα παρὰ δύο, εἶτα παρὰ τρεῖς Arr.*Epict.*2.18.13; πρὸ ἡμέρας before *day-break*, Diph.22; but πρὸ ἁμερᾶν δέκα ἢ κα μέλλωντι ἀνα-

γινώσκεν *GDI*5040.42 (Crete); πρὸ ἡμερῶν ἑπτὰ εἰδυῶν Ὀκτωμβρίων *SIG*646.2 (Thisbe, ii B.C.); γίγνεται, ἔστι πρὸς ἡμέραν, towards *day*, near *day*, X.*HG*2.4.6, Lys.1.14; also, *for the day, daily*, Charito 4.2. IV. as pr. n., *the goddess of day*, Hes.*Th*.124. 2. v. ἥμερος II.

**ἡμεραῖος**, α, ον, *of the daytime*, ἡμεραίας (sc. ὥρας) *PLips*.40iii 5 (iv A.D.). II. *a day long*, πλοῦς Scyl.69.

**ἡμεράλωψ** [ᾰ], ὁ, ἡ, the contrary of νυκτάλωψ (q.v.), Gal.14.768 (from Dem.Ophth., cf. Simon.Jan. s.v. *nictilopa*).

**Ἡμερασία**, ἡ, (ἥμερος) epith. of Artemis in Arcadia, Paus.8.18.8: -άσια, τά, her festival, *IG*5(1).1387.5 (Thuria, iii B.C.); Ἡ. τὰ ἐν Λούσοις *Ath.Mitt*.49.118 (Aegium in Achaea).

**ἡμέρ-ευσις**, εως, ἡ, *spending of the day*, Aq.*Ps*.1.2. **-εύω**, *spend the day*, ἐν τόπῳ ἐρήμῳ X.*HG*5.4.3; ἐν τῇ ἀγορᾷ D.44.4; πρὸς πῦρ X.*Oec*.4.2; ἐν πόνοισιν E.*Fr*.525 codd.: abs., *to travel the whole day*, A.*Ch*.710. 2. *pass one's days*, ἔκηλα ἡ. S.*El*.787:—Med., δίαιταν ἥντιν' ἡμερεύεται dub. l. in E.*Fr*.812.6. 3. *work by day*, *PLond*.3.1177.78 (ii A.D.). ※ **-ήσιος**, Dor. ἁμ-, α, ον, also ος, ον Plb.9.13.6, Str.7.1.5, Gem.18.4: (ἡμέρα):—*of the day*, τὰ ἡ. Hp.*Mul*.1.11; ὕπνοι Democr.212; ἡ. φάος light *as of the day*, A.*Ag*.22; θεοί *PMag.Leid.W*.2.10. II. *a day long*, ἡ. ὁδός a *day's* journey, Hdt.4.101, Pl.*R*.616b; ἡ. λόγος a speech *lasting a whole day*, Isoc.15.320; ἁ. χρόνος Ti.Locr.97c, etc.; ζωή Plu.2.111c. III. *of* or *for a day*, ἀνωμαλία Gem. l. c.; μισθός *PFay*.91.23 (i A.D.); τὸ ἡ. (sc. μίσθωμα) *a day's wages*, Suid.; πεντακοσίους γράφει στίχους ἡμερησίους 500 lines *every day*, D.L.7.181. Adv. -ίως *daily*, *POxy*.83.12 (iv A.D.), prob. in *PGrenf*.2.67.11 (iii A.D.). 2. ἡ. μνημόσυνον *calendar*, *Epigr.Gr*.1096.1 (Stratonicea). 3. ἡμερησία, ἡ, *day-book*, *BGU*12.32, 870.3 (ii A.D.). **-ία**, Dor. ἁμ- (sc. ὥρα), ἡ, = ἡμέρα, S.*Aj*.208 (s.v.l.).

**ἡμερίδης**, ου, ὁ, (ἥμερος) of wine, *mild, mellow*, Plu.2.663d, 692e. 2. epith. of Dionysus, as patron of the *cultivated* vine (ἡμερίς), ib.451c, 994a.

**ἡμερ-ίδιον**, τό, Dim. of ἡμέρα, *Gloss*. ※ **-ινός**, ή, όν, *of day*, φῶς Pl.*R*.508c; *by day*, opp. νυκτερινός, πυρετός Hp.*Epid*.1.5; ἄγγελος ἡ. *day*-messenger, X.*Cyr*.8.6.18; cf. ἡμεροδρόμος; ἡ. θεωρίαι Plb.9.14.6; βοηλάται *PLond*.3.1177.153 (ii A.D.). II. ἡ. σῖτα, in Ar.*Pax* 163 (anap.), is expl. by Sch., θνητά, ἐπίγεια (v.l. ἡμερίων); ἰχθύς ἡ. is dub. in Ephipp.5.2 (anap.). ※ **-ιος**, Dor. ἁμ-, ον, used by Trag. in lyr., *lasting but a day*, γέννα, αἷμα, E.*Ph*.130, 1512; οὔτε θεῶν γένος οὔθ' ἁμερίων.. ἀνθρώπων S.*Aj*.398, cf. *Ant*.789; κάματος *Hymn.Is*.87: abs., ἡμέριοι *mortals*, Orac.ap.D.S.7.12, Opp.*H*.2.669, *AP*7.372 (Loll. Bass.); ἡ. μισθός *PMasp*.164.6 (vi A.D.). II. *daily*, κύκλος Ph.1.92 (nisi leg. ἡμερ(ήσ)ιος).—Poet. Adj., for in X.*Oec*.21.3 ἡμερινός should be read.

**ἡμερίς**, ίδος, fem. of ἥμερος: as Subst., ἡμερίς (sc. ἄμπελος), ἡ, *the cultivated vine*, opp. ἀγριάς, Od.5.69, Simon.183, Opp.*C*.3.458, Jul.*Or*.7.221b, etc.; distd. from ἀμπελίς, Ar.*Ach*.997: metaph., ἡ ποιητικὴ ἡ. τῶν Μουσῶν Plu.2.15e. 2. = ἡμερόδρυς, Thphr.*HP*3.8.2.

**ἡμερό-βιος**, ον, *living for a day*: τὸ ἡ., = τὸ ἐφήμερον, *an insect*, esp. *may-fly*, Thphr.*Metaph*.29, Plin.*HN*11.120; of Diogenes, *living from hand to mouth*, Satyr.ap.Porph.*Abst*.p.270 N. **-γράφος** [ᾰ], ὁ, *one who keeps a diary*, Marin.*Procl*.37. **-δᾰνειστής**, οῦ, ὁ, *one who lends on daily interest*, D.L.6.99, 100. **-δοτος**, ον, *bestowed for a day*, Theognost.*Can*.136 (but Ἡρόδοτος ib.84). **-δρομέω**, *to be a* ἡμεροδρόμος, Str.5.4.13, Luc.*DDeor*.24.1. **-δρόμης**, Dor. (?) -ας, ου, ὁ, *long-distance runner, courier*, Hdt.6.105, *SIG*303 (Olympia, iv B.C.). **-δρόμιον**, τό, *astrological calendar*, title of work by Pappus, *Cat.Cod.Astr*.1.69. **-δρόμος**, ον, *taking a day to traverse*, χώρα Tim.*Pers*.41. 2. -δρόμος, ὁ, = ἡμεροδρόμης, Hdt.9.12, Pl.*Prt*.335e, Arist.*Mu*.398ᵃ30, D.S.15.82: metaph., of the *sun*, prob. in *PMag.Par*.2.190, cf. Hsch. **-δρῦς**, υος, ἡ, *nut-gall oak, Quercus infectoria*, Id. **-ειδής**, ές, *of the form of day*, φάντασμα Epicur.*Fr*.294 (p.353 U.); τὸ τῆς φιλοσοφίας ἡ. Iamb.*Protr*.21.κθ'. **-θαλλής**, ές, (θάλλω) *gently-sprouting*, *AP*9.374 (nisi leg. -θηλέσι). **-θηρικός**, ή, όν, *of* or *for the hunting of tame beasts*: ἡ -κή sc. τέχνη) *the art of hunting them*, Pl.*Sph*.222c. **-καλλές**, οῦς, τό, *Martagon lily, Lilium Martagon*, Cratin.98.5, Thphr.*HP*6.1.1, 6.6.11, Dsc.3.122:—also **ἡμεροκατάλλακτον**, τό, ibid. **-κλέπτης**, ου, ὁ, *one who robs by day*, *Gloss*. **-κοίτης**, ου, ὁ, a fish, = ἀνωδόρκας, Opp.*H*.2.199, 224. **-κοιτος**, Dor. ἁμ-, ον, *sleeping by day*, epith. of a thief, Hes.*Op*.605, Opp.*H*.2.408; ἁμεροκοίτοι βλαχαλτεκέων, for ἁμεροκοίτων, E.*Cyc*.58. ※ **-λεγδόν**, Adv., (λέγω) *by count of days*, A.*Pers*.63 (anap.); λογεῦσαι *PRev.Laws*4.1 (iii B.C.); *in the form of a diary*, ἡ. *perscripta omnia*, Cic.*Att*.4.15.3. 2. *to the very day*, Arist.*HA*575ᵃ27. **-λογέω**, *to count by days*, τὸν χρόνον Hdt.1.47. **-λόγιον**, τό, *calendar*, Plu.*Caes*.59 (v.l. -λογεῖον):—also **-λογικά**, τά, Ptol.*Phas*.p.11 H. II. -λόγιον, τό, = μέρος τι τῶν περὶ τὴν κύστιν, Hsch. **-μαντεία**, ἡ, *divination by day*, *PMag.Lond*.121.155. **-μᾰχία**, ἡ, *battle by day*, Aristid.2.314 J. (s.v.l.). **-νύκτιον**, τό, = νυχθήμερον, Vett.Val.314.21, Phlp.ap.Simp.*in Ph*.1179.17, Phlp.*in Ph*.711.12, al., *Cat.Cod.Astr*.8(3).113, *EM*540.21. **-πῖτυς**, υος, ἡ, *cultivated pine*, Hsch. s.v. μήκωνες. **-ποιέω**, = ἡμερόω, Id. s.v. ἐξημερῶσαι: **-ποιός**, όν, *Gloss*. **-πόσιον**, τό, *day's portion of wine*, *BMus.Inscr*.1006 (Cyzic., i A.D.).

※ **ἥμερος**, Dor. ἅμ-, in codd. of Pi. (v. infr.) and A. (v. infr.), but ἡμ- *Tab.Herad*.1.172, ον, also α, ον Hdt.5.82, Pi.*N*.9.44, etc. (v. infr. II). 1. *tame*, of animals, χῆνα φέρων.. ἥμερον ἐξ αὐλῆς Od.15.162; ἡ. ζῷα Pl.*Phdr*.260b; κρέα θήρεια καὶ τῶν ἡ. X.*Cyr*.1.3.6. 2. of plants and trees, *cultivated*, ἐλαίη Hdt.5.82; δένδρεα Id.4.21, 8.115; καρπός Pl.*Criti*.115a, cf. *Ti*.77b; τροφή, of corn, Corn.*ND* 2. 3. of countries, *cultivated, reclaimed*, ἡμερωτέρη χώρη Hp.*Aër*.12; so ἡμερώταται ὁδοί *smooth, easy* roads, Pl.*Lg*.761a. 4. of men, *civilized, gentle*, Hdt.2.30 (Comp.), Pi.*P*.1.71, 3.6; ἄνδρες οὕτως ἡ. καὶ φιλάνθρωποι D.21.49, cf. Phld.*Ir*.p.88 W. (Sup.); ἁμέροις χερσίν, αἰὼν ἁ., Pi.*N*.8.3, 9.44; οἶκος ἅ. ἀστοῖς Id.*O*.13.2; so of a lion, ἐν βιότου προτελείοις ἅμερον A.*Ag*.721; κρατηθεὶς -ώτερος φανεῖ ib.1632, cf. Pl.*Prt*.326b, Isoc.9.67. Adv. -ρως Plb.5.54.9: Comp. -ωτέρως Pl.*Lg*.867d: Sup. -ώτατα D.C.57.18. 5. Medic., of tumours, *benign*, opp. κακοήθης, Leonid.ap.Aët.15.5. II. Ἡμέρα, ἡ, title of Artemis in Arcadia, B.10.39, Call.*Dian*.236, *IG*5(2).398 (Lusi).

**ἡμεροσκοπ-εῖον**, τό, *place for watching by day*, Aen.Tact.6.6, Str.3.4.6. **-έω**, *keep day-watch*, Aen.Tact.6.1. **-ία**, ἡ, *watching by day*, [Id.]6.tit. ※ **-ος**, ον, *watching by day*, φύλαξ Ar.*Av*.1174: as Subst., *day-watcher*, Hdt.7.183, 192, S.*Ant*.253, X.*HG*1.1.2, Aen.Tact.6.1, al.: metaph., πιστὸν ἡ. ὀφθαλμὸν ἔξω A.*Th*.66.

**ἡμερότης**, ητος, ἡ, (ἥμερος) *cultivation*, of a country, Hp.*Aër*.12. 2. of men, *gentleness*, Pl.*R*.410d, Ephor.31(b) J., Epicur.*Sent.Vat*.36, Phld.*Hom*.p.32 O., D.S.32.27, etc.; of animals, Arist.*HA*588ᵃ21. II. as a title, *Clemency*, ἡ ἡμετέρα ἡ. Just.*Nov*.115 *Pr*.

**ἡμεροτοκέω**, *produce eatable fruits*, Ph.1.402: metaph., ib.455.

**ἡμεροτροφίς**, ίδος, ἡ, *feeding for the day*: = χοῖνιξ, Heraclid.Lemb.5.

※ **ἡμερούσιος**, α, ον, *daily*, *Gloss*. Adv. -σίως *PSI*4.287.12 (iv A.D.), etc.

**ἡμερο-φᾰής**, ές, *shining by day*, ἄστρον Theano *Ep*.10:—also **-φᾰνής**, ές, Pl.*Def*.411b, Arist.*Top*.142ᵇ1. **-φαντος**, ον, *appearing by day*, ὄναρ A.*Ag*.82 (lyr.). **-φῠλᾰκέω**, *to be a day-watcher*, App.*BC*4.62. **-φύλαξ** [ῠ], ᾰκος, ὁ, = ἡμεροσκόπος, X.*HG*7.2.6, Ph.2.236, *Ostr.Strassb*.534.1 (ii A.D.). **-φυλλος**, ον, = ἥμερος, ἐλαία Isyll.20 (Dor. with ἡμ-). **-φωνος**, ον, *heralding the day*, epith. of the cock, v.l. for ἱμερό-, Simon.80 B.

**ἡμερ-όω**, (ἥμερος) *tame, make tame*, 1. prop. of wild beasts, Arist.*HA*488ᵃ29 (Pass.), *Gp*.16.21.2; but simply, *to be pacified*, Pl.*R*.493b (Pass.); δώροις Id.*Lg*.906d. 2. of plants and trees, *reclaim, cultivate*, ἡ. ἐξ ἀγρίων Hp.*Aër*.12, cf. Thphr.*CP*2.14.1, 5.15.6; also of land, Crates Com.55. 3. of countries, *clear* them of robbers and wild beasts, as Hercules and Theseus did, ναυτιλίαισι πορθμὸν ἁμερώσαις Pi.*I*.4(3).57; χθόνα ἀνήμερον τιθέντες ἡμερωμένην A.*Eu*.14; or *to cultivate* them, Thphr.*CP*5.15.6, al. 4. of men also, *civilize, humanize*, λόγῳ Pl.*R*.554d; ἁρμονίᾳ τε καὶ ῥυθμῷ ib.442a; δίκη πάντα ἡμέρωκεν τὰ ἀνθρώπινα Id.*Lg*.937e; τὸ θυμούμενον Eus.Mynd.1:—Pass., ὑπὸ παιδείας Pl.*Lg*.935a. b. *tame by conquest, subdue*, ἡμερώσας δὲ Αἴγυπτον ἐξυβρίσασαν Hdt.7.5:—Med., πᾶν ἔθνος ἡμερούμενος βασιλεῖ Id.5.2, cf. 4.118:—Pass., πόθεν σου ὁ ὀφθαλμὸς ἡμέρωται; whence that *crest-fallen* look? *Mim.Oxy*.413.153. **-ωλίας**· τοὺς ἐν αὐλῇ διακόνους, Hsch. **-ωμα**, ατος, τό, *cultivated plant*, Thphr.*CP*5.6.8 (pl.), prob. in *HP*1.7.1 (pl.). **-ωρέω**, = ἡμεροφυλακέω, Hsch., Phot.:—Subst. **-ωρία**, ἡ (-ῳα cod.), Id. **-ωσις**, εως, ἡ, *a taming, reclaiming*, τῆς χώρας (by clearing it of wild beasts), D.S.1.24; *cultivation*, of lands, Thphr.*CP*2.4.3; of men, *civilizing*, Plu.*Num*.6 (pl.), Scymn.187. **-ωτής**, οῦ, ὁ, *tamer, civilizer*, of Hercules, Max.Tyr.3.7.

**ἧμες**, Dor. for ἦμεν, 1 pl. impf. of εἰμί (*sum*).

**ἡμετέρειος**, ον, = ἡμεδαπός, Anacr.71, Anaxandr.9.

※ **ἡμέτερος**, Dor. ἁμέτ-, Aeol. ἀμμέτ-, α, ον, (ἡμεῖς) *our*, Il.2.374, etc.; εἰς ἡμέτερον (sc. δῶμα) Od.2.55, 17.534; so ἡμέτερόνδε 8.39, 15.513; ἐφ' ἡμέτερ' ib.88, Il.9.619; ἐν ἡμετέρου Hdt.1.35, 7.8.δ'; ἡ ἡ. (sc. χώρα) Th.6.21, etc.; τὸ ἡ. *our case*, Pl.*Ti*.27d; τὸ ἡ. γέλωτ' ἂν πάμπολυν ὄφλοι Id.*Lg*.778e, etc.; τὰ ἡ. φρονεῖν to take *our part*, X.*HG*6.3.14, etc.; ἄνδρες ἡ. they are *in our power*, Pl.*R*.556d, cf. X.*Cyr*.2.3.2; ἡ. κέρδη τῶν σοφῶν, = ἡμῶν τῶν σοφῶν, Ar.*Nu*.1202; ἡμέτερον αὐτῶν [οἰκοδόμημα], = ἡμῶν αὐτῶν, Pl.*Grg*.514b; representing an objective gen., τὸ ἡ. δέος fear *of us*, Th.1.77; εἰς τὴν ἡ. διδασκαλίαν *Ep.Rom*.15.4. II. sts. for ἐμός, Od.11.562, al., Theoc.2.31, etc.; τὰ ἡ. *my* property, *PRyl*.114.18 (iii A.D.); so in Imperial titles, as ἡ ἡ. ἡμερότης Just.*Nov*.115 *Pr*.

**ἠμί** (v. sub fin.), I *say*, the 1st pers. of pres. being used in Att. dialogue in emphatic repetitions, παῖ ἠμί, παῖ boy I *say*, boy! Ar.*Nu*.1145, *Ra*.37; otherwise only in 3 sg. ἠσί Hermipp.1, Aeol. ἦσι Sapph.97, Dor. ἠτί Alcm.139. II. impf. ἦν, 3 sg. ἦ (the only part used by Hom., chiefly in Il., always at the end of a speech), ἦ, καὶ ἐπ' ἀργυρέῃ κώπῃ σχέθε χεῖρα he *spake* and.., Il.1.219, etc.; ἦ ῥα, καὶ ἀμπεπαλὼν προΐει.. ἔγχος 3.355, etc.; rarely with the subject expressed, ἦ ῥα γυνὴ ταμίη 6.390, cf. Theoc.22.75: freq. in Att. in the phrases ἦν δ' ἐγώ *said* I, Pl.*R*.327c, etc.; ἦ δ' ὅς *said* he, Cratin.192, etc.; ἦ δ' ὃς λέγων Ar.*V*.795; ἦ δ' ἡ Pl.*Smp*.205c; with the subject repeated, ἦ δ' ὃς ὁ Γλαύκων Id.*R*.327b, etc.; later without ὅς, ἦ δ' ὁ Νεῖλος Philostr.*VA*6.16. (Cf. Lat. *aio, ad-agium*: ἦ fr. *ἠκτ, hence ἠμί etc. on analogy of φῇ: φημί, etc.)

**ἡμῐ-**, insep. Prefix, used in compos., *half-*. (Cf. Skt. *sāmi-*, Lat. *sēmi-*.)

**ἡμι-άγρυπνος**, ον, *half-awake*, Agath.4.19. **-αλφα**, τό, *half-alpha*, a musical note, ⅄, ⊬, Alyp.4, al.

**ἡμιαμβεῖον**, τό, *half-iambic line*, i.e. catalectic dimeters, in pl., Cleanth.*Stoic*.1.129, *Anacreont*.tit.

**ἡμιαμβικός**, ὁ, *writer of such verses*, dub. in Sch.Nic.*Th*.377.

**ἡμι-αμφόρειον**, τό, *half-ἀμφορεύς*, *IG*11(2).161 *A* 121 (Delos, iii B.C.), J.*BJ*2.21.2. **-ανδρος**, ὁ, *half-man, eunuch*, Hippon.114, Luc.*DDeor*.23.1. **-άνθρωπος**, ὁ, = foreg., Id.*Deor.Conc*.4. ※ **-ἀρού-**

ριον, τό, *half an aroura*, *BGU*417 (ii/iii A.D.); as a measure, *produce of half an aroura*, χόρτου ἡ. *PSI*4.368 (iii B.C.). **-άρρην**, ενος, ὁ, = ἡμιάνθρωπος, v.l. in Ctes.*Fr.*29.5, Theopomp.Hist.101. **-αρτάβιον** [ᾰβ], τό, *half an* ἀρτάβη, *PRyl.*167.17 (i A.D.), *POxy.*708.6 (ii A.D.). **-άρτᾰβος**, ον, *of half an* ἀρτάβη, μέτρον ib.1031.22 (iii A.D.). **-άρτιον**, τό, *half-loaf*, Epich.52, Sophr.27, 28. **-ασσάριον**, τό, *half-as*, Lat. *semissis*, Plb.2.15.6, Head *Hist.Num.*$^{2}$ 601. **-άστᾰτον**, τό, *the half-indefinite*, a figure of speech expressing certainty as to the genus but doubt as to the species (e.g. Virg.*Aen.*8.352), Sacerd.p.469 K. **-αστρᾰγάλιον** [ᾰλ], τό, *creature with only one* ἀστράγαλος, Arist.*HA*499$^{b}$25 (v.l. **-αστράγαλος**). **-βάρβᾰρος**, ον, *half-barbarous*, Str.13.1.58, Philostr.*VS*2.1.13. **-βᾰφής**, ές, *half-dipped*, *half-dyed*, Nonn.*D.*1.358. **-βῐος**, ον, *half-alive*, Man.2.358. **-βρᾰχής** or **-βρεχής**, ές, *half-watered*, γῆ Thphr.*CP*3.23.1; *sodden*, θέρμοι *AP*11.413 (Ammian.). **-βρᾰχυς**, εια, υ, in prosody, *half of a short*, ἡμιβράχεια (sc. προσῳδία) Sch.D.T.p.207 H.: pl., ἡμιβράχεα, τά, ib.p.208 H. **-βροτος**, ον, *half-man*, ἵππος ἡ. a centaur, Opp.*C.*2.7. **-βροχος**, ον, = ἡμιβρεχής, Thphr.*HP*3.1.6, 8.6.1. **-βρώς**, ῶτος, ὁ, ἡ, = sq., Antiph.89, *AP*6.57 (Paul. Sil.). **-βρωτος**, ον, *half-eaten*, X.*An.*1.9.26, Axionic.8.2, Nic.*Th.*919, etc. **-γᾰμος**, ον, *half-married*, i.e. *a concubine*, Philostr.*VS*1.21.4. **-γένειος**, ον, *but half-bearded*, of a youth, Theoc.6.3. **-γενής**, ές, *intermediate*, *equivocal*, Pl.*Ti.*66d; of fruits, *half-formed*, Thphr.*HP*1.14.1. **-γραμμον**, τό, (γράμμα II.5) *half a scruple*, *Hippiatr.*22. **-γρᾰφος**, ον, *half-written*, Men.1014. **-γυμνος**, ον, *half-naked*, Luc.*DMar.*14.3, Arr.*Ind.*24.8. ⊛ **-γύναιξ** [ῠ], αικος, ὁ, ἡ, *half-woman*, Simon.179.9, Suid. s.v. ἄρρεν:—also **-γύναιος** [ῠ], ον, Id. s.v. Πολύευκτος. **-δᾰής**, ές, (δαίω A) *half-burnt*, νηῦς Il.16.294; Φαέθων A.R.4.598. II. (δατέομαι) *half-divided*, *half-mangled*, σκύβαλον *AP*9.375; χειρὸς βάρος Nic.*Al.*55 (cf. ἡμιδεής). **-δάϊκτος** [ᾰ], ον, (δαΐζω) *half-slain*, Opp.*C.*2.281, *H.*5.669. **-δακτῠλιαῖος**, α, ον, *half a finger long*, S.E.*M.*10.137. **-δακτύλιον** [ῠ], τό, *half-finger's breadth*, *IG*$2^{2}$.1013.25, 5(1).1390.16 (Andania, i B.C.), Plb.6.23.11, Ph.*Bel.*65.3, Plu.2.935d. **-δᾰμής**, ές, *half-slain*, Opp.*H.*1.716 (v.ll. ἡμιθανής, ἡμιδαής). **-δᾰνάκη** [νᾰ], ἡ, *half-*δανάκη, prob.l. in Theon *Prog.*13:—Dim. **-ιον**, τό, Hsch. **-δᾰπής**, ές, expld. by ἡμιτελής, Phot., Suid. **-δᾱρεικόν**, τό, *half-daric*, X.*An.*1.3.21, prob. in *SIG*276.13 (Delphi, iv B.C.). ⊛ **-δεής**, ές, (δέω B) *wanting half*, *half-full*, X.*An.*1.9.25, *AP*5.182 (Posidipp.), *PSI*4.428.24, cj. for -δαής in Nic.*Al.*55; ἐξ ἡμιδεοῦς γέμοντα ἤδη *from being only half-full..*, Them.*Or.*18.222b. **-δελτα**, τό, *half-delta*, a musical note, Λ, Alyp.4, al. **-δέξιον**, τό, *dactylic trimeter*, Sacerd.pp.514, 544 K. **-διμνον**, v. ἡμέδιμνον. **-διπλοΐδιον**, τό, *a woman's dress folded at the top so as to fall half-way down the figure*, Ar.*Ec.*318, cf. *EM*430.46. **-δουλεία**, ἡ, *half-slavery*, Chrysipp.*Stoic.*2.284. **-δουλος**, ον, *half-slave*, E.*Andr.*942, Chrysipp.*Stoic.*2.284. **-δραχμον**, τό, *half-drachma*, Poll.6.160; τέταρτον ἡ. *IG*$1^{2}$.373.18: as an apothecaries' weight, Gal.13.674, al. **-δωδέκατον**, τό, = ἡμίχουν, Hsch. **-ειλος**, ον, (εἴλη) *half-exposed to the sun*, Thphr.*HP*3.23.1. **-εκταΐδιον**, τό, Dim. of sq., dub. in *IG*9(2).1222. **-έκτεων**, gen. -εω, τό, *half-*ἑκτεύς, acc. sg. -εων (written -εον) ib.$1^{2}$.76.7; gen. -εω ib.$2^{2}$.1356; but -έου Ar.*Nu.*643; nom. -έον ib.645, *Mémoires présentés à l'Acad. des Inscr.*1923.2 (iv B.C.); written -ειον ibid.; pl. -εια *IG*$2^{2}$.1672.15, 268, al.; -έα prob. cj. in Pl.Com.174.12: Ion. pl. -εκτῆ *Milet.*7.27. (Accent doubtful, parox. in codd.; -ειον, -εια may have short ει as in εἰάν, etc.) ⊛ **-εκτον**, τό, *half-*ἑκτεύς, D.34.37, Thphr.*HP*2.6.2, *IG*3.98, etc.; *a vessel containing thus much*, Hp.*Steril.*230 (-εκτέον ap. Erot.). II. ἡ. χρυσοῦ, = 8 obols, Crates Com.20, cf. *SIG*45.26 (Halic., v B.C.), *IG*$1^{2}$.310.118 (cf. p.303). **-εκφᾰνής**, ές, *half-brilliant*, of stars of the lesser magnitudes, Ptol.*Alm.*7.1. **-έλλην**, ηνος, ὁ, ἡ, *half-Greek*, Luc.*Salt.*64. **-επές**, τό, *half-hexameter*, Mar. Vict.p.73 K., Sacerd.p.544 K. **-έργαστος**, ον, *half-wrought*, *half-completed*, ὕλη Gal.5.538:—also **-εργής**, ές, Luc.*Astr.*5, and **-εργος**, ον, ἔμβρυον Hp.*Mul.*1.78; [αἷμα] Gal.5.535; of buildings, *IG*$1^{2}$.372.5; τεῖχος ἡ. μετῆκε Hdt.4.124, cf. Th.7.2, J.*AJ*14.16.2, Plu.2.841d. **-έτης**, ες, (ἔτος) *of half a year*, ἡμιέτες, καὶ ἡ. χρόνος Poll.1.54. **-εφθος**, ον, (ἕψω) *half-boiled*, Hp.*Art.*63, Lxx *Is.*51.20, Dsc.*Eup.*1.84, Gal.6.725: generally, *half-cooked*, even by roasting or frying, of Empedocles in Luc.*DMort.*20.4; v.l. for ἡμίοπτος, Id.*Gall.*2. **-ζύγιος** [ῠ], ον, *forming half a pair of scales*, Arist.*Mech.*853$^{b}$26. **-ζωνον** (-ζώνιον cod.), *semicinctum*, *Gloss.* **-ζως**, *half-alive*, Hdn.*Epim.*239. ⊛ **-θᾰλής**, ές, (θάλλω) *half-green*, στέφανοι *AP*7.465 (Heraclit.). ⊛ **-θᾰνής**, ές, *half-dead*, Str.2.3.4, Lxx 4*Ma.*4.11, *Ev.Luc.*10.30, *AP*11.392 (Lucill.), *PAmh.*2.141.13 (iv A.D.). ⊛ **-θέα**, Ep. **-θέη**, ἡ, *demigoddess*, Call.*Aet.*3.1.71: gen. pl. -θεάων *IG*14.1389 i 57. **-θέαινα**, ἡ, *demigoddess*, Opp.*C.*3.245. **-θεος**, Aeol. **αἰμί-** Alc.*Supp.*8.13, Dor. **ἁμί-** Theoc.18.18 codd., **ἡμίσῐος** Alcm.23.7: ὁ:—*demigod*, ἀνδρῶν ἡρώων θεῖον γένος, οἳ καλέονται ἡμίθεοι Hes.*Op.*160, cf. *h.Hom.*31.19, 32.19, Pi.*P.*4.184, Pl.*Ap.*28c, Isoc.9.70, etc.; once in Hom. (if genuine), ἡμιθέων γένος ἀνδρῶν Il.12.23. II. Pythag. name for *five*, *Theol.Ar.*32. **-θηλυς**, υ, *half-woman*, Ἄττις *Anacreont.*11.2. **-θηρ**, ηρος, ὁ, ἡ, *half-beast*, Apollod.1.6.3, Philostr.Jun.*Im.*4. **-θῆτα**, τό, *half-theta*, a musical note, ⌒, Alyp.13. **-θνής**, ῆτος, ὁ, ἡ, = ἡμιθανής, Ar.*Nu.*504, Th.2.52, Plb.14.5.7, Gal.10.1021; of fear, Aeschin.3.159; ὕπνος βαθὺς καὶ ἡ. Philostr.*VA*2.36. **-θνητος**, ον, *half-mortal*, of the Dioscuri, Lyc.511, cf. Gal.17(1).235. 2. *half-dead*, Lxx *Wi.*18.18. **-θραυστος**, ον, *half-broken*, E.*HF*1096, Lyc.378, *AP*9.568.5 (Diosc.). ⊛ **-θωράκιον** [ᾱ], τό, *front plate of the* θώραξ, *SIG*421.40 (Aetolia, iii B.C.), Plu.2.596d. **-ϊουδαῖος**, ὁ, *half-Jew*, J.*AJ*14.15.2. **-ιππος**, ὁ, coined on analogy of ἡμίονος, Sch.D.T.p.167 H. **-κάδιον** [ᾰ], τό, *half-*κάδος, Philoch.155a, *IG*14.422 iii 81 (Tauromenium), *BGU*1095.16 (i A.D.). **-κᾰκος**, ον, *half a villain*, S.*Fr.*1051, Alex.10, Oenom.ap.Eus.*PE*5.24. Adv. -κως, ἐβοσκόμην Ar.*Th.*449. **-κᾰλάθιον** [λᾰ], τό, *half a basket*, ἀνθράκων *IG*11(2).161 *A* 109 (Delos, iii B.C.); ἰσχάδων *Inscr.Magn.*116.38. **-καυστος** (so Thphr.*Lap.*53, Charito 1.3) or **-καυτος**, ον, *half-burnt*, Ael.*VH* 13.2, D.C.50.35, Jul.*Or.*1.27d. **-κενος**, ον, *half-empty*, S.E.*M.*5.77, Poll.5.133. **-κεντρος**, ον, *half-way between cardinal points*, prob. in Jul.Laod. in *Cat.Cod.Astr.*5(1).190. **-κερᾰμία** and **-κέρᾰμον**, *urna*, *Gloss.* **-κεραύνιος**, ὁ, name of a *bandage*, Gal.12.496 Chart. **-κεφάλαιον** [ᾰ], τό, less Att. form for ἡμίκρανον (i.e. ἡμίκραιρα), acc. to Phryn.303: **-κεφάλιον** and **-λον**, *Gloss.*; = *sinciput*, Dosith.p.389 K. **-κίριον**, τό, *cloth* or *sackcloth of half size*, *PCair.Zen.*69.10 (iii B.C.). **-κλάδευτος** [ᾰ], ον, *half-pruned*, *Gloss.* **-κλαστος**, ον, (κλάω) *half-broken*, Plu.2.306b, 317d. **-κλειστος**, ον, *half-shut*, prob.l. for ἡμικλεῖς in Anon.ap.Suid. **-κλήριον**, τό, (κλῆρος A) *half the inheritance*, Is.7.6, D.48.20; pleon., τοῦ κλήρου τὸ ἡ. Is.11.24. II. *half a* κλῆρος, *PPetr.*3 p.245 (iii B.C.), *PMagd.*1.6 (iii B.C.), *Schwyzer* 734.4 (Zelea). **-κλίβᾰνος** [ῑ], ὁ, *half-share in a bakehouse*, *PLond.*5.1724.33 (vi A.D.). **-κλῖνον**, τό, *half-sized couch*, *IG*11(2).147 *B* 14 (Delos, iv B.C.). **-κόγγιον**, τό, *half-congius*, Dsc.ap.Gal.19.776. ⊛ **-κόλλιον**, v. -κόριον. **-κοπος**, ον, *half-mangled*, gloss on ἡμιδαμής, Sch.Opp.*H.*1.716; expld. by ἡμίπλευρος, Hsch. II. **-κοπον**, τό, *half-carcase*, *Sammelb.*4630.16 (ii A.D.), *PSI*6.683.33 (ii A.D.). **-κόριον**, τό, *half-*κόρος, a dry measure, Hsch. (-κόλλιον cod.):—also **-κορος**, ὁ, Aq., Sm., Thd.*Hos.*3.2. **-κόσμιον**, τό, *half the universe*, Cleom.1.9, 11. **-κοτύλη** [ῠ], ἡ, *half-*κοτύλη, *POxy.*1142.2 (iii A.D.), v.l. in Hp.*Nat.Mul.*107, Hero *Spir.*2.30. **-κοτῠλίειος**, α, ον, *holding half a* κοτύλη, *PCair.Zen.*89.6 (iii B.C.), al. **-κοτύλιον** [ῠ], τό, *half-*κοτύλη, Hp.*Nat.Mul.*47, 107, Arist.*HA*573$^{a}$7, Dieuch. ap.Orib.4.7.37, etc., dub. in *IG*$1^{2}$.842 *A* 2. **-κουρος**, ον, *half-sheared*, *PHib.*1.32 (iii B.C.). **-κραιρα**, ἡ, *half the head* or *face*, Ar.*Th.*227, Amips.7, Crobyl.6; ἡμίκραιραν χορδῆς *IG*$2^{2}$.1356. 2. = sq., Gal.12.591, al. ⊛ **-κρᾱνία**, ἡ, (κράνιον) *pain on one side of the head* or *face*, ib.592:—also ⊛ **-κράνιον**, τό, *PMag.Lond.*121.199, *Arch.f. Religionswiss.*24.176 (Carnuntum). **-κρᾱνικός**, ή, όν, *of* or *like* ἡμικρανία, ἀλγήματα Gal.12.594; πάθος Aët.6.49; οἱ ἡ. *persons suffering therefrom*, Gal.8.206, Paul.Aeg.3.5; φάρμακα remedies *for* ἡ., Gal.12.592. ⊛ **-κρᾱνον**, τό, = ἡμίκραιρα I, Alex.Trall.1.12. **-κρής**, ῆτος, ὁ, *half a Cretan*, Lyc.150. **-κύᾰθος** [ῠ], ὁ, *half-*κύαθος, Thessal. in *Cat.Cod.Astr.*8(3).149, Aret.*CA*2.2, Gal.19.770. **-κυκλικός**, ή, όν, = sq., Sch.Pl.*Alc.*1.129c. **-κύκλιος**, ον, (κύκλος) *semicircular*, Sch. A.R.4.1613:—also **-κυκλος**, ον, στοά Philostr.*Im.*1.12, cf. Hld.8.14. II. as Subst., **-κύκλιον**, τό, *semicircle*, Arist.*APo.*41$^{b}$17, *Ph.*264$^{b}$24; *hemisphere*, Ach.Tat.*Intr.Arat.*27, Heph.Astr.2.11; of a tactical formation, κατὰ τὸ ἡ. Onos.21.5. 2. *a place for public entertainment* or *meeting*, Plu.*Alc.*17, *Nic.*12; *place of assembly* at Samos, Porph.*VP*9. 3. *semicircular seat*, *armchair*, Cic.*Lael.*1.2, Poll.6.9. 4. *semicircular dial*, Vitr.9.8.1. 5. *semicircular statue-base*, *IG*11(2).287 *B* 73 (Delos, iii B.C.), *BCH*29.543 (ibid.); *drum of a half-column*, *Rev.Phil.*43.182 (Didym.). 6. *barrel-vault*, Ph.*Bel.*87.12. 7. *theatrical machine*, described by Poll.4.127, 131. **-κυκλιώδης**, ες, *semicircular*, γραμμή Str.13.1.34:—also **-κυκλώδης**, Hsch. s.v. ἡμίαρτον: **-κυκλοειδής**, ές, Heliod.(?) ap.Orib.46.11.34. Adv. **-κυκλοειδῶς** Tz. ad Hes.*Op.*450. **-κυκλος**, ον, v. ἡμικύκλιος. ⊛ **-κύλινδρος** [ῠ], ὁ, *half-cylinder*, D.L.8.83:—Dim. **-κυλίνδριον**, τό, Porph.*Abst.*4.7, Eutoc. ad Archim.*Sph.Cyl.*2. 2. as Adj., *semicylindrical*, πύργοι Ph.*Bel.*84.25 (s.v.l.). **-κῠνες**, οἱ, *half-dogs*, name of a fabulous nation, elsewh. κυνοκέφαλοι, Hes.*Fr.*62, Simm.1.9. **-κυπρον**, τό, (κύπρος II.2) *a measure*, Hippon.24; said to = $\frac{1}{2}$ μέδιμνος, Hsch. **-κώνιον**, τό, *half-cone*, Euc.*Opt.*30. **-κῳον**, τό, *half a* κῷον, *Sammelb.*4425 vii 12 (ii A.D.). **-λᾰγος**, ὁ, *half-hare*, i.e. *rabbit*, *Edict.Diocl.*4.33. **-λάμιον**· μέρος Μεσσαπίων, Hsch. **-λαμπρος**, ον, *at half brilliancy*, φῶς Sch.Arat.733. **-λάσταυρος**, ὁ, *half a rogue*, Men.1014. **-λέπιστος**, ον, *half-peeled* or *shelled*, Str.17.1.34. **-λεπτος**, ον, *half-hatched*, *Anacreont.*25.10. **-λευκος**, ον, *half-white*, Luc.*Prom.Es* 4. **-λιτριαῖος**, α, ον, *weighing half a pound*, βῶλοι Str.3.2.8. ⊛ **-λίτριον**, τό, *half-pound*, Epich.9, *POxy.*1051.12 (iii A.D.), Archig.ap.Orib.8.1.27. ⊛ **-λιτρον**, τό, in Sicily, *half-obol*, Arist.*Fr.*510. 2. *half-pound*, Asclep.ap.Gal.13.445, al. **-λουτος**, ον, *half-washed*, Cratin.416. **-λοχία**, ἡ, *half-*λόχος, Suid. s.v. διμοιρίτης:—also **-λόχιον**, τό, Ascl.*Tact.*2.2, Ael.*Tact.*5.2. **-λοχίτης** [ῑ], ου, ὁ, *leader of a* ἡμιλοχία, Ascl.*Tact.*2.2, Ael.*Tact.*5.2, Suid. l.c. **-μᾰθής**, ές, *half-learned*, Philostr.*VS*2.5.4, Poll.6.160. **-μᾰνής**, ές, *half-mad*, Aeschin.1.171, Luc.*Deor.Conc.*4. **-μάραντος** [μᾰ], ον, *half-withered*, Id.*Tox.*13, Alciphr.3.62. **-μάσητος** [μᾰ], ον, *half-chewed*, Crates Com.49. **-μέγιστον**, τό, *half-mina*, Hsch. **-μέδιμνον**, τό, *half-*μέδιμνος, Pherecr.1, D.55.24, Dicaearch.Hist.23:—also **-μέδιμνος**, ὁ, *SIG*945.3 (Assos, iv B.C.), Poll.4.168; cf. ἡμέδιμνον. **-μεθής**, ές, *half-drunk*, *AP*6.251 (Phil.). **-μέθῠσος**, ον, (μεθύω) = foreg., Poll.6.160. **-μείλιον**, τό, *half a mile*, *BCH*37.149 (Trajanopolis, ii/iii A.D.). **-μέριστος**, ον, *divided in half*, gloss on ἡμιδάϊκτος, Sch. Opp.*H.*2.287. **-μεστος**, ον, *half-full*, Poll.5.133. ⊛ **-μετρον**, τό, gloss on ἡμικάδιον, Suid. **-μηδος**, ὁ, *half a Mede*, Oenom.ap.Eus.*PE*5.21. **-μηνιαῖος**, α, ον, (μήν) and **-μήνιος**, ον, *half-monthly*,

Gloss. **-μιτρον**, τό, *half-mitra* (v. μίτρα), Poll.10.191, Hsch. ❋ **-μναῖον**, τό, *half-mina*, *IG*1².371.7, X.*Mem*.2.5.2, Pl.*Lg*. 774d, etc.:—the form **-μνεα** (pl.) is found in Plu.*Lyc*.12 codd., Porph.*Abst*.4.4 codd.: sg. **-μνοῦν** Asclep.ap.Gal.13.746. **-μόδιον**, τό, *half a modius*, *Gp*.7.24.2. **-μοιριαῖος**, α, ον, *equal to half a degree*, μέγεθος Cleom.2.2. **-μοίριον**, τό, *half a part*, Hp.*Ulc*. 12. II. *half a degree*, Cleom.2.1, Ptol.*Alm*.1.10, al. **-μόριον**, τό, sine expl., Poll.6.160 (v.l. -μοίριον). **-μόχθηρος**, ον, *half-evil*, *half a villain*, Pl.*R*.352c, Ph.2.346; *half-bad*, of things, Gal.6.;6. **-μυ**, *half-μυ*, ˧, a musical note, Alyp.4, al.

❋ **ἡμίνα**, ἡ, (ἥμισυς) *half*, *Leg.Gort*.2.49, *SIG*525.13 (Gortyn, iii B.C.), prob. in Hsch. s.v. ἰνιμίνα. II. a Sicil. measure, = κοτύλη, Epich. [290], Sophr.105; ἡ. βασιλική, = ἡμικοτύλιον, Aristid.*Or*.49(25).32, cf. *IG*7.2712.66 (Acraeph.). (Hence Lat. *hemīna*; Italic and properisp. acc. to Theognost.*Can*.101, but prob. orig. Greek.)

**ἡμί-ναυλον**, τό, *half-freight*, *PGoodsp.Cair*.30xli 19 (ii A.D.), *PFay*. 104.7 (iii A.D.). **-ναυον**, τό, prob. an Egyptian measure of length, *PCair.Zen*.383 (iii B.C.). **-νεοτελής**, ές, gloss on νεοτελής, Herm.*in Phdr*.p.159 A. (s.v.l.). **-νηρος**, ον, contr. for ἡμινέαρος, *half-fresh*, and so of fish, *half-salted*, Xenocr.77, Ath.3.118f. ❋ **-ξέστον**, τό, *half-ξέστης* (Alexandrian, acc. to Diph.Siph.ap.Ath.3. 121b), Dsc.1.25, *Hippiatr*.100, Sch.Ar.*Pl*.436. **-ξηρος**, ον, *half-dry*, *PFlor*.118.3 (iii A.D.), *AP*9.137 tit., Suid. s.v. λαιψηρόν. **-ξύρητος** [ῠ], ον, (ξυράω) *half-shorn*, D.L.6.33. ❋ **-όγδοον**, τό, = *two* χόες, Hsch. ❋ **-οβόλιον**, τό, *half-obol weight*, Paul.Aeg. 3.29; in form **-οβελιν**, on coins of Aegium, Head *Hist.Num*.² 413. ❋ **-όδελος**, ὁ, = ἡμιωβέλιον, dub. in *GDI*2562.26 (Delph., iv B.C.). **-όδιον**, *semita*, *Gloss*. **-όδιος**, ον, prob. f.l. in Arist. *Oec*.1352ᵇ26.

**ἡμιολ-ιασμός**, ὁ, *multiplying by one and a half*, Antipho Soph. 75. **-ίζω**, *increase by one half*, χρέος *Schwyzer* 418.8 (Elis). ❋ **-ιος**, α, ον, hyperdor. ἀμ-, ον, (ὅλος) *containing one and a half*, *half as much or as large again*, Pl.*Tht*.154c; περίμετρος Plb.6.32.7; ηὔξησε τὰ δόρατα ἡμιολίῳ μεγέθει D.S.15.44: c. gen., τὰς περόνας ἡμιολίας..τοῦ τότε κατεστεῶτος μέτρου *half as large again as*.., Hdt.5.88; [γωνία] ἀμιόλιος τᾶς μέσας Ti.Locr.98a; [ὁ γνήσιος ἀετὸς] ἡ. τῶν ἀετῶν Arist.*HA* 619ᵃ13; neut., *half as much again*, ἡμιόλιον οὗ πρότερον ἔφερον X.*An*.1. 3.21; ἡμιόλιον ὀφλέτω ὅ τι συλάσαι let him be fined *half as much again* as the amount he seized, *IG*9(1).333.5 (Locr., v B.C.); of numbers, *half as many again*, ποιήσας ἡμιολίους τοὺς ναύτας ἢ πρόσθεν Plb.10. 17.12. II. *in the ratio of one and a half to one* (3:2), as in musical sounds, ἡμιολίαι διαστάσεις Pl.*Ti*.36a; τὸ δι' ὀξειᾶν ἡ. Philol.6; ἡ ἡμιολία *this ratio*, τὴν ἡ. τοῦ τιμήματος Pl.*Lg*.956d; ἀποτίνειν τὴν φέρνην σὺν τῇ ἡ. Mitteis *Chr*.280.15 (ii B.C.). Adv. **-ίως** Nicom.*Ar*.2.20, Procl.*in Ti*.2.223 D. III. ἡμιολία ναῦς *a light vessel with one and a half banks of oars*, D.S.19.65; also ἡμιολία alone, Thphr.*Char*.25.2, D.S.16.61, *Mus.Belg*.14.20 (but **-ίους** Plb.5.101.2, **-ιον** Hsch.), etc.; used by pirates, Thphr.*Char*.l.c.; ἡ. λῃστρικαί Arr.*An*.3.2.5, etc.; expld. by δίκροτος (q.v.) ναῦς, Hsch. IV. τροχαϊκὸς ἡ. (sc. στίχος) trochaic verse *consisting of a metre and a half*, Heph.15.2. **-ίς**, ίδος, ἡ, = ἡμιολία ναῦς, Poll.1.82.

**ἡμιόλκιον**, τό, (ὁλκή) *half-drachm*, Archig.ap.Orib.8.46.16.

**ἡμιον-άγριον**, τό, *mule* (produce of ὄναγρος), *PEdgar* 13.3 (iii B.C.). **-ειος**, α, ον, Ion. **-εος** Hdt.1.188:—*of, belonging to a mule*, ἅμαξα ἡ. *drawn by mules*, Od.6.72, Il.24.189; ζυγὸν ἡ. ib.268; κόπρος ἡμιονείη, = ἡμιονίς, Pamphoap.Philostr.*Her*.2.19, cf. Suid. s.v. II. ἡμιόνειος πόα, = ἡμιόνιον I, Dsc.*Eup*.2.100. **-ηγός** (**-ᾱγός** *Gloss*.), ὁ, *muleteer*, *PLond.ined*.2358 (iii B.C.), *Rev.Phil*.50.67 (Didyma, ii B.C.), Str.14.2.24. ❋ **-ικός**, ή, όν, = ἡμιόνειος, ζεῦγος X.*An*.7.5.2; ὁδὸς ἡ. a road *only fit for mules*, Str.6.3.7; ἡ. ἅρμα *drawn by mules*, *BGU*814.6 (iii A.D.). **-ιον**, τό, *milt-wort*, *Asplenium Ceterach*, Thphr.*HP*9.18.7, Plin.*HN*27.34; = ἄσπληνος, Dsc.3.134. II. Dim. of ἡμίονος, Str.5.3.6 (s.v.l.). III. a kind of *bird*, Hsch. **-ίς**, ίδος, ἡ, *mule-dung*, Hp.*Nat.Mul*.90. ❋ **-ίτης** [ῑ], ου, ὁ, *muleteer*, *PCair.Zen*.4.69 (iii B.C.). **-ῖτις**, ιδος, ἡ, *of* or *for a mule*, ἵππος ἡμιονῖτις a mare *in foal of a mule*, Str.5.1.4. II. ἡμιονῖτις, ιδος, ἡ, *mule-fern*, *Scolopendrium Hemionitis*, Dsc.3.135. **-όκουρος**, ὁ, *mule-clipper*, *Gloss*. **-ος**, ἡ, Il.2.852, Pi.*O*.6.22, *Rev.Phil*. 50.67 (Didyma, ii B.C.), etc.; ὁ, Il.17.742, Pl.*Ap*.27e, etc.: Aeol. **αἰμί-** Sapph.*Supp*.20a.14:—*half-ass*, i.e. *mule*, Il.10.352, al., Arist. *HA*576ᵇ11, etc.; ταλαεργός Il.23.654: prov., γνοίης ὅσσον ὄνων κρέσσονες ἡμίονοι Thgn.996; ἐφ' ἡμιόνων on a car drawn by mules, Il.24. 702; εἰς ἡμιόνους ποιεῖν to write an ode on *a team of racing-mules*, Arist.*Rh*.1405ᵇ26: prov., ἐπεὰν ἡμίονοι τέκωσι, i.e. never, Hdt.3. 153: metaph., ἡ. βασιλεύς, i.e. half-Mede, half-Persian, Orac.ap.Hdt. 1.55. 2. ἡ. ἀγροτέρα *wild ass, onager*, Il.2.852; αἱ ἐν Συρίᾳ καλούμεναι ἡ. Arist.*HA*491ᵃ2, cf. 580ᵇ1, al. II. as Adj., βρέφος ἡμίονον *a mule*-foal, Il.23.266.

**ἡμί-οπλος**, ον, *half-armed*, *Gloss*. ❋ **-οπος**, ον, (ὀπή) *with half its holes*, ἡ. αὐλοί flutes *with only three holes*, Anacr.20; ἡ. (without αὐλός), ὁ, used metaph. of *something small*, A.*Fr*.91. II. ἡμίοπον· ἥμισυ, Gal.19.102. ❋ **-οπτος**, ον, *half-roasted*, Alex.175, Luc.*Gall*.2 (v.l.), Hld.2.19. **-ουγκιαῖος**, α, ον, = Lat. *semuncialis*, *Gloss*. ❋ **-ούγκιον**, τό, *half* οὐγκία *or ounce*, Lat. *semuncia*, Epich.8:—written **-ούγγιον** in Gal.13.558. **-πᾰγής**, ές, *half-congealed*, *half-hardened*, Pl.*Ti*.59e,60d; δρόσος Arist.*Mu*.394ᵃ26; ᾠὰ ἡ. *half-hard, medium-boiled* eggs, Hp.*Acut*.(*Sp*.)53: metaph., ἡ. σοφία Ph.1.322. **-πᾰθής**, ές, *half-suffering*, μέρεα Aret.*SD*1. 7. **-πᾰχής**, f.l. for κνημοπαχής, Thphr.*CP*3.4.3. **-πέλεκκον**, τό, *half-axe*, i.e. *one-edged axe* (the πέλεκυς being double-edged), Il.23.851,858,883. **-πέ(πε)ιρος**, ον, *half-ripe*, Hsch. s.v. βλῆσα. **-πεπτος**, ον, *half-ripened*, Plu.*Caes*.69; *half-digested*, τροφή Gal.11.666, al. **-πέπων**, ον, gen. ονος, *half-ripe*, Herod.Med.ap. Orib.5.31.6. **-πέρσης**, ου, ὁ, *half a Persian*, Oenom.ap.Eus.*PE* 5.21. **-πήχειον**, τό, *half-cubit*, S.E.*M*.7.105:—also **-πήχιον**, τό, Hipparch.3.5.6, Theo Sm.p.53 H. **-πηχῦαῖος**, α, ον, *half a cubit long*, Dsc.3.129, *Gp*.10.4.1. **-πηχυς**, υ, *of half a cubit*, διάστημα S.E.*M*.10.132: as Subst., δύο -πήχεα ib.127; *half a cubit high*, ἄνθρωπος Phld.*Sign*.2. **-πλεθρον**, τό, *half-πλέθρον*, Hdt.7. 176, X.*An*.4.7.6. **-πλεκτος**, ον, *half-plaited*, Philyll.31. **-πλευρος**, v. ἡμίκοπος. **-πλεως**, ων, *half-full*, Poll.5.133. **-πληγής**, ές, *half-struck*, Olymp.*in Mete*.200.15. **-πληγία**, ἡ, *paralysis*, Paul.Aeg.3.16. **-πλήξ**, ῆγος, ὁ, ἡ, *half-felled*, of a tree, *cleft*, [πεύκη] A.R.4.1683. **-πλήρης**, ες, *half-full*, κύστιες Aret.*CA*1. 6. **-πλήρωτος**, ον, *half-manned*, [πλοῖα] Poll.1.121; *half-full*, Id.5.133. **-πλίνθιον**, τό, (πλίνθος) *half-plinth, brick* (two of which formed a plinth), ἡμιπλίνθια χρυσοῦ *ingots* of gold, Hdt.1.50, cf. *IG*1².314.82:—also **-πλινθος**, ὁ, *Gloss*. **-πνικτος**, ον, (πνίγω) *half-choked*, *Gloss*. **-πνοος**, ον, contr. **-πνους**, ουν, *half-breathing, half-alive*, Batr.252, Gal.*UP*6.3. **-ποδιαῖος**, α, ον, *half a foot broad* or *high*, Apollod.*Poliorc*.146.7, Bito 45.4. **-πόδιον**, τό, *half-foot*, *IG*1².372.49,163, al., Thphr.*HP*7.2.7, Plb.6.23.2, *Hermes* 17.4 (Delos): **-πόδιος**, v.l. in *Gp*.4.12.2. **-ποίητος**, ον, *half-made*, Poll.6.160. **-πολον**, τό, *half the sphere*, Hsch. **-πόνηρος**, ον, *half-evil*, Arist.*EN*1152ᵃ17, *Pol*.1315ᵇ10. **-πους**, ποδος, ὁ, *half foot*, Apollod.*Poliorc*.178.3. **-πτωτος**, ον, (πίπτω) *half-fallen*, Suid. s.v. ἐρείπιον. **-πύργιον**, τό, *half-tower*, Philostr.*VS*2.1. 11. **-πῡρος**, ον, (πῦρ) *half of fire*, Arist.*Mu*.395ᵃ23, Cleom.2.4, Plu.2.928e. **-πύρωτος** [ῠ], ον, *half-burnt*, *AP*7.401.5 (Crin.).

**ἡμιρόδιον**, τό, *half a* ῥοδία (q.v.), Roussel *Cultes Égyptiens* 236 (Delos, ii B.C.).

**ἡμι-ρρᾰγής**, ές, *half-broken*, πίνακες Aristid.*Or*.25(43).32. ❋ **-ρρήνιον**, τό, *half-grown sheep*, Michel 995 *D* 33:—fem. **-ρρηνιαία**, ἡ, ib. 35 (Delph.). **-ρρομβιαῖος**, α, ον, *like a* ἡμιρρόμβιον, Gal.18(1). 788. **-ρρόμβιον**, τό, = ἡμίτομος II.2b, Heliod.ap.Orib.48.20.13, Gal. 18(1).797,838. ❋ **-ρρόπως**, Adv. *half turning the scale*, i.e. *lightly, gently*, opp. ἀθρόως, Hp.*Epid*.2.1.7. **-ρρῠπος**, ον, *half-dirty*, εἴριον Id.*Mul*.2.205. ❋ **-σάκιον**, τό, (σάκος or σάκκος) *half-sack*, σησάμων Poll.10.169.

**ἡμῐσάκις**, Adv. *half a time*, Iamb.*in Nic*.p.14 P., al.; δὶς καὶ ἡ. two and *a half times*, Papp.556.16.

**ἡμι-σάλευτος** [ᾰ], ον, (σαλεύω) *half-shaken*, Hsch. **-σᾰπής**, ές, (σήπομαι) *half-putrid*, Hp.*Morb*.1.31, Gal.7.301, al.

**ἡμίσεια**, ἡ, **ἡμίσεον**, τό, **ἡμίσεος**, **ἥμισος**, v. ἥμισυς.

**ἡμισελήνιον**, τό, *half the apparent breadth of the moon*, Ptol.*Alm*. 9.10.

**ἡμῐσύελπις**, ιδος, ὁ, ἡ, *half-hopeful*, f.l. in Luc.*Cal*.10.

**ἡμίσ-ευμα** [ῐ], ατος, τό, *a half*, Lxx *Nu*.31.36; παραλληλογράμμου *Theol.Ar*.39; name of a tax on vines, *PSI*4.434.4 (sg., iii B.C.), *Raccolta Lumbroso* 123 (pl., iii B.C.). **-ευτής**, οῦ, ὁ, gloss on ἡμιτιεύς, Hsch. **-εύω**, (ἥμισυς) *halve*, Lxx *Ps*.54(55).24, Aq.*Ge*. 33.1. 2. *boil down to one half*, *Hippiatr*.2.

**ἡμῐσιάζω**, *halve*, Asclep.*Tact*.12.11: **-σειάζω**, Hero *Geom*. 7.4 (Pass.), al.

**ἡμί-σικλον**, τό, *half-σίκλος*, J.*AJ*7.13.1: **-σίκλιον**, Hsch. **-σιος**, v. ἡμίθεος. **-σκουτον**, τό, *half-σκοῦτα*, Hero *Mens*.14. **-σοφος**, ον, *half-wise*, Luc.*Herm*.15, *Bis Acc*.8. **-σπάθιον** [ᾰ], τό, *half-spatula*, Heliod.ap.Orib.44.14.4, 23.66, Leonid.ap.Paul.Aeg.6. 78. **-σπαστος**, ον, *half pulled down*, Str.17.3.12; *half torn away*, *AP*10.21 (Phld.). **-σπῐθᾰμιαῖος**, α, ον, *of half a span*, σπλῆνες πλάτος -ιαῖοι Hp.*Fract*.29. **-σπίθᾰμος** [πῐ], ον, = foreg., Ph.*Bel*. 56.4. **-σπονδος**, ον, *half bound by treaty*, Poll.6.30. **-στᾰδιαῖος**, α, ον, *of half a stadium*, Luc.*VH*1.40, etc. **-στάδιον** [ᾰ], τό, *half-stadium*, Plb.3.54.7, Str.17.1.48, Ath.Mech.8.8. **-στᾰτήρ**, ῆρος, ὁ, = sq., prob. in *IG*12(3).1638 (Thera). **-στάτηρον** [ᾰ], τό, *half-στατήρ*, *IG*1².917 (prob.), *SIG*218.25 (Olbia, iv B.C.), *Schwyzer* 701 (Erythrae, v B.C.), Arist.*Fr*.529, cf. Hsch. s.v. ἡμίχα. **-στίχιον** [τῐ], τό, *half-line, half-verse*, D.H.*Comp*.26, Hipparch.1.4.9, S.E.*M*. 1.165, Iamb.*VP*29.162. **-στρᾰτιώτης**, ου, ὁ, *half-soldier*, Luc. *Bacch*.3 codd. (dub.l.). **-στρόγγῠλος**, ον, *half-round*, Id.*Ocyp*. 97. **-στρόφιον**, τό, f.l. for στροφεῖον, Poll.4.127.

**ἡμῐσύ-δουλος** [ῠ], ὁ, *half a slave*, Man.4.600. **-θλαστος**, ον, *half-crushed*, Hsch.

**ἡμισύνθεσις**, εως, ἡ, *half-set*, *POxy*.741.15 (pl., ii A.D.).

❋ **ἥμῐσυς**, εια, υ, gen. ἡμίσεος Hdt.2.126, Th.2.78, 4.83, X.*Oec*.18.8, Pl.*Smp*.205e, *IG*2².1612.267, D.23.213, etc. (ἡμίσεως is sts. a v.l., as in Th.ll.cc., and is found in later writers, as Dsc.2.70); also as fem., Th.4.104; later contr. ἡμίσους D.H.4.17, Plu.*Mar*.34, etc. (as fem., Lxx 3*Ki*.16.9): nom. and acc. pl. masc., Ion. ἡμίσεες, -εας, Il. 21.7, Hdt.9.51, Att. ἡμίσεις Th.3.20, Pl.*Tht*.154c (ἡμίσεας is preferred by Phryn.*PS*p.73 B.): neut. pl. ἡμίσεα Th.4.16, Pl.*R*.438c, later ἡμίση D.36.36 (cod. S), al., *IG*2².1678.23, Thphr.*Char*.30.16, *IG*12 (5).872.107 (Tenos), *SIG*²588.4 (Delos, ii B.C.), etc.: Ion. fem. ἡμίσεᾰ Hdt.5.111 (hyperion. -σέη Luc.*Syr.D*.14), acc. pl. -έας Hdt.8.27, also acc. sg. ἡμίσεαν *IG*2.1055.16, 1059.14, gen. ἡμισέας Pl.*Men*.83c: **ἥμυσυς** (assim.), *Rev.Phil*.54.192 (Erythrae, v B.C.), *IG*2².43 *A* 45 (iv B.C.), *PEleph*.20.40 (iv B.C.), *IG*11(2).161 *A* 23 (Delos, iii B.C.), *UPZ* 54.6 (ii B.C.), etc.: neut. **ἥμισον**, τό, *Berl.Sitzb*.1927.8 (Locr., v B.C.),

SIG1011.7 (Chalcedon, iii/ii B.C.), ib.671 *A* 13 (Delph., ii B.C.), *BGU* 183.41 (i A.D.): pl. ἥμισα *SIG*56.7 (Argos, v B.C.); also ἥμισσον, τό, ib.306.14 (Arc., iv B.C.), 1009.20 (Ephesus, iii/ii B.C.): pl. ἥμισσα ib. 240 *P* (Delph., iv B.C.): acc. pl. τοὺς ἡμίσους *Not.Arch.*4.20 (Cyrene, Aug.):—*half*, I. as Adj., ἡμίσεες λαοὶ *half* the people, ἡ. δ' ἄρα λαοὶ ἐρητύοντο.. ἡ. δ' ἀναβάντες ἐλαύνομεν Od.3.155 sq., cf. Il.21.7 (elsewh. Hom. uses only neut. ἥμισυ as Subst. (v. infr. II)); τοὺς ἡμίσεας ἀποστέλλειν Hdt.9.51, cf. Th.3.20, X.*Cyr.*2.1.6, etc.; ἥμισυς λόγος *half the tale*, A.*Eu.*428 (λόγου cod. Med.); τὸ ἥμισυ τεῖχος Th.2.78; ὁ ἡ. ἀριθμός Pl.*Lg.*946a: c. gen., like a Comp., τὸ ὕψος ἥμισυ ἐτελέσθη οὗ διενοεῖτο *half of* what he intended, Th.1.93: metaph., οὐδ' ἂν ἥμισυς ἑαυτοῦ γένοιτο πρὸς ἀρετήν Pl.*Lg.*647d (οὐ δι' ἥμισυν stands for οὐ διὴμ. '*half-and-half*', ib.806c). 2. in Prose also with the Subst. in gen. and giving its gender and number to ἥμισυς, τῶν νήσων τὰς ἡμισέας Hdt.2.10; τῶν ἀνδραπόδων τὰ ἡμίσεα Id.6.23; αἱ ἡμίσειαι τῶν νεῶν *half of* the ships, Th.8.8; οἱ ἡμίσεις τῶν ἄρτων X.*Cyr.*4.5.4; ὁ ἥμισυς τοῦ ἀριθμοῦ Pl.*Phd.*104a; τοῦ χρόνου D.20.8: abs., οἱ ἡ. *half* of them, Th.3.20. II. as Subst. in neut., ἡ. τιμῆς, ἐνάρων, ἀρετῆς, Il.9.616, 17.231, Od.17.322; τὸ μὲν.., τὸ δ' ἡ. Il.13.565; πλέον ἡ. παντός Hes.*Op.*40, Pl.*R.*466c; ὑπὲρ ἡ. πάντων X.*Cyr.*3.3.47; ἡ. οὗ δεῖ Pl.*Phd.*77c, etc.; ἐν ἡμίσει τῆς νυκτός at *mid*night, Lxx *Jd.*16.3: usu. c. Art., τὸ ἡ. τοῦ στρατοῦ Th.4.83, etc.; also τὤμισυ Hes.*Op.*559, *Schwyzer*701 (Erythrae, v B.C.); θἤμισυ Ar.*Lys.*116: indecl., ἀπὸ τοῦ ἡ. Lxx *Ex.*30.15; τῷ ἡ. φυλῆς ib.*Nu.*32.33: pl., τῆς χορείας τὰ ἡμίσεα Pl.*Lg.*672e; ἄρτων ἡμίσεα X.*An.*1.9.26; ῥαφανίδων τὰ ἡ. Thphr. l.c.: after Numerals, ἐν δυοῖν καὶ ἡμίσει ἡμέρας *IG*$2^2$.1673.73; δεκατεττάρων καὶ ἡμίσους Str.2.5.39; μνῶν.. δώδεκα καὶ ἡμίσους D.H.4.17; τετραποδίαν μίαν καὶ ἥμισυ *IG* $1^2$.373.28; without καί, μυριάδων ἑπτὰ ἡμίσους Plu.*Mar.*34: indecl., τριῶν ἥμισυ σταδίων Str.8.6.21, cf. *PTeb.*110.5 (i B.C.), Plu.*Cat.Mi.* 44, etc.: as Adv., ἡ. μὲν νύμφην.., ἡ. δ' αὖτε ὄφιν Hes.*Th.*298, cf. Pi.*N.*10.87: so in pl., τὰ μὲν ἡμίσεα φιλόπονος, τὰ δὲ ἡ. ἄπονος Pl.*R.* 535d: with Preps., οὐδ' εἰς ἡ. not *half*, Ar.*Th.*452: regul. Adv. ἡμισέως *half-done*, Pl.*R.*601c. b. ἥμισυ, τό, = ἡμίεκτον, Hsch. 2. fem., ἡ ἡμίσεια (sc. μοῖρα), τῇ ἡμισείᾳ τῆς γῆς Th.5.31; ἡ ἡ. τοῦ τιμήματος Pl.*Lg.*956d; οὐ γὰρ ἐφ' ἡμισείᾳ χρηστὸν εἶναι δεῖ *by halves*, D. 19.277; ἐξ ἡμισείας Luc.*Cat.*1, Artem.1.26, S.E.*M.*10.145. (ἡμισυ-fr. ἡμιτυ-, ἡμισσο- fr. ἡμιτϝο-, cf. ἡμίτεια, ἡμιτύεκτον; enlarged fr. ἡμι-.)

ἡμισύ-τρῐτον, τό, *a third half*, i.e. *one and a half*, Archil.167. -χοῖνιξ, ικος, ἡ, = ἡμιχοῖνιξ, Hdn.Gr.2.261. -χοιρος, sine expl., ibid.

⊛ ἡμι-σφᾰγής, ές, *half-slain*, *Gloss.* -σφαίριον, τό, *hemisphere*, Alex.261.7, Pl.*Ax.*371b, Hero *Spir.*1.8, Porph.*Antr.*24, etc.: dual in Ph.2.155. ⊛ -σφήκιον, τό, dub. sens. in *BCH*35.243 (Delos, ii B.C.). -σχετος, ον, *half-related* (cf. ἄσχετος 3), σχέσις Olymp. *in Phd.*p.19 N.; τὸ ἡ. τῆς προνοίας Dam.*Pr.*131. Adv. -τως ibid. -σχοινον, τό, *half a schoenus*, *Tab.Heracl.*1.29, al., *AB* 263. -ταινίδιον, τό, *half a* ταινία, *PSI*7.858.9 (iii B.C.). -τᾰλαντιαῖος, α, ον, *in which the prize is half a talent*, ἀγών *CIG*2810.19 (Aphrod.), *IGRom.*4.161 (Cyzicus). -τάλαντον [τᾰ], τό, *a half-talent*, as a weight, χρυσοῦ Il.23.751, cf. *IG*$1^2$.371.6; πένθ' ἡμιτάλαντα Is.7.44; τρίτον ἡμιτάλαντον *two talents and a half*, ἕνατον ἡ., = 8½, Hdt.1.50, 51, cf. Poll.9.54, *EM*744.25. -τάρῑχος [ᾰ], ον, *half-salted*, = ἡμίνηρος, Archestr.*Fr.*38.7, Ael.*NA*13.2.

⊛ ἡμίτεια, ἡ, prob. = ἡμίεκτον, *SIG*998.9 (Epid., v B.C.), *IG*11(2). 147 *A* 8 (Delos, iv/iii B.C.).

ἡμιτέλ-εια, ἡ, (τέλος) *remission of half the tribute*, ἡ. τῶν κακῶν ἐδέδοτο Luc.*Nec.*14. -εστος, ον, (τελέω) *half-finished*, Th.3.3, dub. in D.H.1.59, etc.; of a lady's hair, *half-done*, Aeschin.Socr.18; of a child, Nonn.*D.*1.5. -έω, *complete one-half of*, χρόνον *Ath.Mitt.* 25.412 (Pergam.). -ής, ές, (τέλος) *half-finished*, δόμος ἡ. a house *but half complete*, i.e. childless, Il.2.701; βίος Str.7.3.3, cf. Luc. *DMort.*19.1; Ὀλύμπιον Dicaearch.1.1; ἡ. θάλαμος *AP*7.627 (Diod.); ἡ. νίκη D.H.2.42; φωναί Id.*Comp.*14; ἐνέργειαι Aret.*SD*1.7; of a child, Luc.*Sacr.*5; οὐδὲν ἡμιτελὲς καταλείπειν X.*Cyr.*8.1.3; ἡ. ἀφιέναι D.H.*Th.*9; ἡ. ἀνήρ, opp. τελείως ἀγαθός, X.*Cyr.*3.3.38; ἡ. περὶ λόγους D.H.*Dem.*23; ἡ. τὴν ἀρετήν Ph.2.199. Adv. -λῶς Longin. ap.Porph.*Plot.*19.

ἡμι-τεσσέριον, τό, a liquid measure, οἴνου *Inscr.Prien.*362.16 (iv B.C.). ⊛ -τέταρτον, τό, a weight, = ⅛ μνᾶ, *Ann.dell' Inst.*37.201. 2. = ¾, ἡ. ὕδρευμα *PFlor.*50.99. -τετράγωνος [ᾰ], hyperdor. ἀμ-, ον, *forming half a square*, of the isosceles right-angled triangle, Speus. ap.*Theol.Ar.*63, Ti.Locr.98a,b, Simp. *in Cael.*638.3. -τέχνιον, τό, *half* (i.e. *trivial*) *art*, Sch.D.T.p.110 H.

ἡμιτιεύς· ἡμισευτής, Hsch.: ἡμίτιον· τετράχουν, Id.

ἡμι-τμής, ῆτος, ὁ, ἡ, = ἡμίτομος I, Man.4.6. -τμητος, ον, (τέμνω) gloss on ἡμιδαΐκτος, Sch.Opp.*H.*2.287. -τομίας, ου, ὁ, (τομή) *half an eunuch*, Sch.Theoc.3.4. -τομος, ον, (τέμνω) *cut in two*, ξύλα *IG*$1^2$.313.98; ἄντυξ Mosch.2.88. 2. of the moon, *half-full*, *Theol. Ar.*12. II. as Subst., -τομος, ὁ, a kind of *cup*, Pamphil.ap.Ath.11. 470d. 2. -τομον, τό, *half*, Hdt.7.39, 9.37, *Inscr.Délos* 298 *A* 182 (iii B.C.), *AP*9.137; κύκλου Ael.*NA*15.4; ἡμίτομα ᾠῶν Alex.261.10: —also -τόμιον, τό, *flat side of a half-bean*, Dsc.2.105, v.l. in Luc. *VH*2.38. b. *lozenge-shaped bandage*, = ἡμιρρόμβιον, Hp.*Off.*7, Gal. 18(2).732. -τονιαῖος, α, ον, *consisting of a semitone*, Aristox.*Harm.* p.52 M., Theo Sm.p.53 H.; ὑπεροχή Ptol.*Harm.*2.9. -τόνιον, τό, *semitone*, Philol.6, Aristox.*Harm.*p.21 M., al., D.H.*Comp.*11, Arr. *Epict.*2.11.2, etc. II. *half the skein* or *bundle of gut* in a torsion-engine, Ph.*Bel.*68.46, Hero *Aut.*2.6. 2. *one of the two frames containing the* τόνος in such an engine, Id.*Bel.*90.4. -τρής, ῆτος, ὁ, ἡ, *half-bored*, Choerob. *in Theod.*1.185. ⊛ -τρῐβής, ές, (τρίβω) *half worn out*, χλαμύς *PCair.Zen.*92.5 (iii B.C.), cf. *CPR*27.8 (ii A.D.), Sch.Ar.*Pl.*729. II. *blunt*, ξοΐς *BCH*35.43 (Delos); λείστριον ib. 8.323 (ibid.). -τρίγωνος [ῐ], hyperdor. ἀμ-, ον, *forming half a triangle*, τρίγωνον, of the triangles made by drawing a perpendicular from an angle of an equilateral triangle, Speus.ap.*Theol.Ar.*63: neut. as Subst., Ti.Locr.98a, Simp. *in Cael.*561.13. ⊛ -τρῐταῖος, α, ον, *half every three days*, τρόπος ἡ., *of a semi-tertian* fever, Hp.*Epid.*1. 2, Gal.17(1).233: -τριταϊκός, ἡ, όν, Ptol.*Tetr.*199. -τρῖτον, τό, *the sixth part* (of a mina), Inscr. on a weight, *CIG*8535. -τριψις, εως, ἡ, *half-massage*, Gal.18(2).873.

ἡμίτρωτος, ον, gloss on ἡμιδαής, Sch.Opp.*H.*1.716.

⊛ ἡμιτύβιον [ῠ], τό, *linen cloth, towel, napkin*, Sapph.116, Hp.*Art.* 37, Ar.*Pl.*729; of a kind of material, *Michel*832.23 (Samos, iv B.C.). (Egypt. acc. to Poll.7.71:—in codd. sts. ἡμιτύμβιον, as in Aret.*CD* 1.3, v.l. in Lib.*Decl.*26.42, which is interpr. by Suid., *a half* (i.e. *small*) *grave*; but prob. this form is due to the copyists, who wished to find a meaning in the word.)

ἡμιτύεκτον, τό, = ἡμιέκτεων, *GDI*4957 *a* 4 (Crete).

ἡμι-τύλιον [ῠ], τό, *half a* τύλη, *BGU*40.12 (pl., iii A.D.). -τυμπάνιστος [ᾰ], ον, sine expl. (cf. ἀποτυμπανίζω), Poll.6.160; = ἡμιθανής, Hsch. (-στής cod.). -ύπνος, ον, *half-asleep*, *Gloss.* -ύφαντος [ῠ], ον, *half-woven*, Aen.Tact.29.6. -υφής, ές, = foreg., *IG*$2^2$.1522. 26, 1524.213, etc. -φᾰής, ές, *half-shining*, = ἡμιφανής, λάρναξ *AP* 7.478 (Leon., sed leg. ἡμιχανεῖ). -φάλακρος [φᾰ], ον, *half-bald*, ib.11.132 (Lucill.). ⊛ -φᾰνής, ές, (φαίνομαι) *half-visible*, Str.17.1. 32. -φάριον [ᾱ], τό, (φᾶρος) *half-robe*, Aristaenet.1.4, Suid., Hsch. -φᾶτος, ον, *half* (cf. δίφατος), Id. -φαυλος, ον, *half-knavish*, Luc.*BisAcc.*8. -φαυστος, ον, *half-lit*, Poll.6.160. -φι, τό, *half-*φῖ, Ϸ, a musical note, Gaud.*Harm.*21, 22. -φλεκτος, ον, *half-burnt*, App.*BC*5.88, Luc.*DDeor.*13.2; by love, Theoc.2.133; *half-cooked*, Hp.*Epid.*2.6.29. -φόριον, τό, *half-subscription*, *SIG* 1109.40 (Athens, ii A.D.). -φόρμιον, τό, *half a* φορμός, Demioprat. ap.Poll.10.169. -φρακτος, ον, *half-fenced*, Id.6.160. -φυής, ές, (φυή) *half-grown*, Men.1014. -φωνος, ον, *half-pronounced*, λέξις Aristaenet.1.10. 2. Subst. ἡμίφωνον, τό, *a semi-vowel*, as ρ σ, Arist.*Po.*$1456^b27$, Phld.*Po.*2.16, D.H.*Comp.*14, D.T.631.16, etc. II. *half able to speak*, Gal.*UP*6.3; *half-vocal*, of certain signs of the Zodiac, *Cat.Cod.Astr.*1.166, Vett.Val.5.24:—hence -φωνία, ἡ, Steph. *in Hp.*1.184 D. -φωσώνιον, τό, a kind of *garment*, Ar.*Fr.*784; cf. φώσσων.

ἡμίχα· ἡμιστάτηρα, Hsch. ἡμιχανής, ές, *half-open*, v. ἡμιφαής.

ἡμί-χῐον, τό, a measure, *half a* χοῦν, *PCair.Zen.*12.17 (iii B.C.), etc. -χλωρος, ον, *half-green*, *Gloss.* ⊛ -χοαῖος, α, ον, *holding a half-*χόος, Thphr.*HP*9.6.4. -χοεῖος, α, ον, = foreg., *PCair.Zen.* 353.16 (iii B.C.). -χοινίκιον [ῐκ], τό, *half-*χοῖνιξ, Hp.*Nat.Mul.*50, *IG*$2^2$.1013.21, Dieuch.ap.Orib.4.7.18. -χοίνῐκος, ον, *holding a half-*χοῖνιξ: τὸ ἡ. *a half-*χοῖνιξ, Thphr.*HP*8.4.5, Dsc.5.72. -χοῖνιξ, ῐκος, ἡ, *half-*χοῖνιξ, v.l. in Hp.*Nat.Mul.*50, *Morb.*3.17. -χοιρον, τό, = ἡμισύχοιρος, Hsch. s.v. δέλιχρα. -χολώδης, ες, *half-bilious*, dub. l. in Hp.*Epid.*7.29. ⊛ -χοον, τό, *half-*χόος, Id.*Int.*42 (in pl. ἡμίχοα, as *SIG*1027.15 (Cos), Arist.*HA*$627^b3$); also ἡμίχα *IG*11(2). 199 *B* 80 (Delos, iii B.C.); -χόεα Hp.*Morb.*3.17: contr. -χουν Arist. *Ath.*69.2, *IG*$1^2$.188.22, *PAmh.*2.93.12 (ii A.D.). -χόριον, τό, *half-chorus, semi-chorus*, Poll.4.107, Sch.Ar.*Eq.*586. -χρηστος, ον, *half-good*, Arist.*Pol.*$1315^b9$. ⊛ -χρύσους [ῡ], ὁ, *half-stater*, Anaxandr.5: -χρῡσος *CIG*2855.31 (Milet., ii B.C.), *Annuario*6/7.407. -χώνη, ἡ, *half-*χώνη, Kretschmer *Gr.Vaseninschr.*p.143. -χώριον, τό, *half of an office* or *liturgy jointly undertaken*, *POxy.*1413.1 (iii A.D.). -χωστος, ον, (χώννυμι) = Lat. *semirutus*, *Gloss.* -ψίλιον [ψῐ], τό, ψιλή *of half size*, *PSI*7.858.3 (iii B.C.), *PLond.ined.*2095 (iii B.C.). -ψυκτος, ον, *half-dried*, Str.15.1.18:—also -ψῡγής, ές, κόνυζα *Gp.*2.27.9; *half-cooled*, κλίβανα Dsc.3.86, cf. Paul.Aeg.3. 54. -ψῡχος, *semianimis*, *Gloss.* -ωβελιαῖος, α, ον, *costing* or *worth half an obol*, *PCair.Zen.*19.5 (iii B.C.):—less correctly written -ωβολιαῖος, κρέα Ar.*Ra.*554; *as large as a half-obol*, X.*Mem.*1.3.12. (-βελιαῖος shd. prob. be restored.) -ωβέλιον, τό, *half-obol*, *IG*$1^2$. 6.90, Eup.154, Aeschin.Socr.41, Arist.*Rh.*$1374^b26$, *IG*11.(2).287 *A* 40 (Delos, iii B.C.), etc.:—less correctly -ωβόλιον, X.*An.*1.5.6 codd., Arist.*Fr.*589 codd. Poll., Thphr.*Char.*6.9, Dsc.4.175: -ώβολον Thphr. *Lap.*46 (-ος cod.), Sor.1.63 (v.l.), Hdn.*Epim.*204: Dor. ⊛ -ωδέλιον, τό, *GDI*2562.26 (Delph.), *IG*14.2406.77: Boeot. ἑμνιωβέλιον, τό, *Supp. Epigr.*3.356.5,7 (Acraeph., iii B.C.). -ωρία, ἡ, (ὥρα) *half-hour*, Dam.*Pr.*389. -ωριαῖος, α, ον, *lasting half an hour*: neut. as Subst., Phlp. *in Ph.*802.15. -ώριον, τό, = ἡμιωρία, Men.1015, Str.2. 5.36, Hipparch.2.4.2, Cleom.1.6, *Apoc.*8.1 (v.l. ἡμίωρον), Dsc.1.33.

ἧμμαι, v. ἅπτω.

ἥμορος, ον, = ἄμοιρος, Hsch., Phot.:—fem. ἡμορίς, ίδος, A.*Fr.* 165: ἡμόριξεν· ἄμοιρον ἐποίησεν, Hsch. (ἥμορος Ion. form = Aeol. ἄμμορος (q. v.).)

ἦμος, Dor. ἆμος, Adv. of Time, correl. to τῆμος, *at which time, when*, in Hom., freq. in protasi with τῆμος, τῆμος ἄρα.., τῆμος δή.., etc., in apodosi (v. τῆμος); ἆμος.., τᾶμος.. Theoc.13.25; ἦ..., δὴ τότε Il.1.475, al.: folld. by δὴ τότ' ἔπειτα Od.17.1; by καὶ τότε δή Il.8.68; by καὶ τότ' ἔπειτα 1.477; by καὶ τότε δὴ ῥα 16.779; by ἄρα or ῥα alone, Od.2.1, 19.428, cf. S.*Aj.*935 (lyr.); by τηνικαῦτα Hdt.4. 28; by τότε S.*Tr.*155: rarely without some particle in apodosi, as Od. 3.491, E.*Hec.*915 (lyr.); ἦ. ὅτε A.R.4.267, 452, 1310, Orph.*A.*120, *IG* 14.1389 i 25, etc.: rarely with Subj., without ἄν, ἦ. δ' ἥλιος.. οὐρανὸν ἀμφιβεβήκῃ Od.4.400; ἦ. ἥλιος δύνῃ Hp.*Mul.*1.23, cf. *Prorrh.*2.

4 (v.l.). 2. with pres., *while, so long as*, S.*Tr*.531 : or impf., Id. *OT*1134.

**ἡμοσύνη**, ἡ, (ἧμων) *skill in throwing* or *shooting*, Hsch.

**ἡμῠόεις**, εσσα, εν, *drooping*, v.l. in Nic.*Th*.626.

**ἡμύω**, aor. ἤμυσα (v. infr.) : pf. part. ἡμυκώς Sch.Nic.*Th*.626 ; cf. ὑπ-εμνήμυκε :—Ep. Verb, *bow down, sink*, Hom., only in Il., ἑτέρωσ' ἤμυσε κάρη πήληκι βαρυνθέν 8.308 ; ἤμυσε καρήατι, of a horse, 19.405 ; of a corn field, ἐπί τ' ἠμύει ἀσταχύεσσιν 2.148 : metaph., of cities, *totter, fall*, τῶ κε τάχ' ἠμύσειε πόλις Πριάμοιο ἄνακτος ib.373 ; rare in Trag., χρόνῳ δ'.. ἤμυσε στέγος S.*Fr*.864 ; later, simply, *fall, perish*, οὔνομα δ' οὐκ ἤμυσε Λεωνίδου *AP*7.715 (Leon.). II. trans., *cause to fall, ruin*, πόλιν Musae.*Fr*.22. (In Hom. ῠ in pres., ῡ in aor. I ; but ῡ in pres. κατ-ημύουσιν A.R.3.1400, cf. Opp.*H*.1.228, Nic.*Al*.453 ; ῠ in aor., *AP*9.262 (Phil.), but ῡ ib.7.715 (v. supr.) ; cf. ἀμύω, ἐπημύω.)

**ἠμφισβητημένως**, Adv. pf. part. Pass., (ἀμφισβητέω) *in a questionable manner*, [διαλέκτους] προσφέρεσθαι dub. in Phld.*Rh.Supp*.p.56 S.

**ἡμωδίαν**· αἱμωδίαν and **ἡμωδίασαν**· ἐνάρκησαν (ἠνάρχ- cod.), αἱμωδίασαν, Hsch. ; Att. acc. to Moer.

**ἧμων**, v. ἀμάω (A).

**ἧμων**, ονος, ὁ, (ἵημι) *thrower, darter*, ἡ. ἄνδρες Il.23.886.

**ἤν** (A), contr. fr. εἰ ἄν and ἐάν (q.v.).

**ἤν** (B), Interject. *see there!* ἤν, οὐχ ἡδύ; Ar.*Eq*.26 ; ἤν, μεθίεμεν Id. *Pl*.75 ; ἀλλ' ἤν χιτών σοι Men.148 ; ἤν, τότε βακχίαζε.. χθών Philod. Scarph.14 ; also ἢν ἰδού Pratin.Lyr.1.15, Ar.*Ra*.1390, Herod.1.4, Luc.*DMort*.10.10, Anach.1, Alciphr.*Fr*.6.6, cf. Theoc.8.26 ; folld. by καὶ δή, E.*HF*867, Ar.*Pax*327 :—also **ἠνίδε** (i.e. ἢν ἴδε) Pl.*Epigr*. 20, Theoc.2.38, Call.*Del*.132 ; with τοι, Theoc.1.149, 3.10.

❀ **ἦν**, ον, v. φημί, εἰμί (*sum*). **ἦνα**, inf. ἦναι, v. αἴνω.

**ἠναγκασμένως**, Adv. pf. part. Pass., (ἀναγκάζω) *perforce*, D.H. *Pomp*.3 (dub. l.).

**ἠναντιωμένως**, Adv. pf. part. Pass., (ἐναντιόομαι) *in opposite ways*, διακεῖσθαι Phld.*Mus* p.103 K.

**ἤνεγκα, ἤνεγκον, ἤνεικα**, v. φέρω. **ἦνεκα**, v. αἰνέω.

**ἠνεκής**, ές, *bearing onwards*, i.e. *far-stretching*, ἠνεκέεσσι τρίβοις Nic.*Al*.592. Adv. -κέως *continuously, without break*, τὸ πάντων νόμιμον.. ἠ. τέταται Emp.135.2 : neut. ἠνεκές as Adv., Arat.445, Call. *Aet*.1.2.8 ; of Time, ἠνεκὲς αἰέν Emp.17.35, cf. Nic.*Al*.517, etc. (Found in early Ep. only in compds., such as διηνεκής.)

**ἠνέμιον**, τό, = ἀνεμώνη, v.l. for ἠρέμιον in Dsc.2.176.

**ἠνεμ(ο)ειδές**· ἠχῶδες, Hsch.

❀ **ἠνεμό-εις**, Dor. ἀνεμόεις [ᾱ], εσσα, εν, (ἄνεμος) *windy, airy*, δι' ἀέριας ἠνεμοέσσας Od.9.400 ; προτὶ Ἴλιον ἠνεμόεσσαν Il.3.305, etc. ; πτύχας ἠνεμοέσσας Od.19.432, cf. Tyrt.2.3, Pi.*O*.4.8, E.*Heracl*.781 (lyr.) ; of Places, Call.*Del*.11, D.P.472 ; οὔρεα ἠ. Id.1129. 2. of motion, *rapid, rushing*, αἰγίδες A.*Ch*.592 codd. (lyr.) ; αὔρα S.*Tr*.953 (lyr.) ; λαγωός Nic.*Th*.453 ; πέτευρον Man.6.444 ; ἀνεμόεν φρόνημα *high-soaring, airy* thought, S.*Ant*.354 (lyr.). 3. *stirred, waved by the wind*, ἐρινεός Il.22.145 ; *filled by the wind*, ἱστίον Pi.*P*.1.92. ❀ **-φοιτος**, ον, *walking on the wind*, βροντή Nonn.*D*.2.24 ; ψυχή ib.37.85.

**ἤνετο**, v. ἄνω (A), = ἀνύω. **ἦνθον**, ες, ε, Dor. for ἦλθον, v. ἔρχομαι.

**ἡνία** (A), Dor. ἀνία, ίων, τά (v. sub fin.), *reins*, Il.5.226, Od.3.483, Hes.*Sc*.95, Pi.*P*.4.18, *I*.1.15 : rare exc. in Poets, ἐφ' ἡνία, = ἐφ' ἡνίαν (v. sq.), Ael.*Tact*.19.12. II. sg., ἡνίον, τό, *bit*, Poll.1.148. (I.-E. *nsiyo*-, cf. Skt. *nāsyam* 'nose-rein', Ir. *éssi* 'reins'.)

❀**ἡνία** (B), Dor. ἀνία, ἡ, post-Hom., = foreg., *bridle, reins*, in pl., Pi. *P*.5.32, A.*Pers*.193, etc. ; πρὸς ἡνίας μάχεσθαι Id.*Pr*.1010 ; εἰς τοὐπίσω ἑλκύσαι τὰς ἡ. Pl.*Phdr*.254c : less freq. in sg., Ἥλιε.. ἐπισχὼν χρυσόνωτον ἡ. S.*Aj*.847 ; ἡ. χαλᾶν E.*Fr*.409 : the sg. for *one rein*, ἔπειτα λύων ἡ. ἀριστερὰν S.*El*.743. 2. metaph., Ἔρως.. ἡνίας ηὔθυνε παλιντόνους Ar.*Av*.1739 ; δυοῖν γυναικοῖν ἄνδρ' ἕν' ἡνίας ἔχειν E.*Andr*.178 ; ἐφεῖναι καὶ χαλάσαι τὰς ἡ. τοῖς λόγοις Pl.*Prt*.338a ; παραλαβοῦσαι τῆς πόλεως τὰς ἡ. Ar.*Ec*.466 ; τούτῳ παραδώσω τῆς πυκνὸς τὰς ἡ. Id.*Eq*. 1109 ; γαστρὸς πᾶσαν ἡ. κρατεῖν Men.*Mon*.81 ; τῷ δήμῳ τὰς ἡ. ἀνεὶς Plu.*Per*.11 ; ἐνδιδόναι τοῖς βουλήμασι τὰς ἡ. D.H.7.35 ; παρὰ τὴν ἡ. πράττειν Philostr.*Im*.2.18 ; πρὸς ταῖς ἡ., of high officials, *BCH*32.431 (Delos) ; ἐπὶ τῶν ἡ. Lxx 1 *Ma*.6.28. 3. as a military term, ἐφ' ἡνίαν wheeling *to the left* (*the left being the bridle hand*), Plb.10.23.2, Ascl. *Tact*.10.2, Polyaen.4.3.21 ; [τὸν ἵππον] περισπάσας ἐφ' ἡνίαν τῷ χαλινῷ Plu.*Marc*.6 ; ἐξ ἡνίας, opp. ἐκ δόρατος, Plb.11.23.6. II. *any leather thong*, esp. *sandal-thong*, ἡνίαι Λακωνικαί Ar.*Ec*.508.

**ἡνια**, τά, gen. pl. ἡνίων, = τῶν κεκομμένων, Hp.ap.Gal.19.103 ; cf. ἦνα.

**ἠνιγμένως**, Adv. pf. part. Pass., (αἰνίσσομαι) *as in a riddle, obscurely*, Plot.6.2.22.

**ἠνίδε**, v. ἤν (B).

❀ **ἡνίκᾰ** [ῑ], Dor. ἁνίκα Pi.*P*.4.24, al., Theoc.5.41 ; Aeol. ἄνικα Id. 29.33 :—Adv. of Time, relat. to τηνίκα, *at the time when*, usu. with past tenses of ind., Od.22.198 (nowhere else in Hom.), Pi. l.c., S. *Aj*.1144, al., Th.7.73, Ar.*Nu*.607, Lys.19.4, Pl.*Grg*.509e, D.21.78, etc. ; ἡνίκ' ἐχρῆν δύνειν, νῦν ἄρχεται ἠδύνεσθαι Timo 17 : with pres. ind., ἡνίκαπερ X.*Cyr*.8.8.9 : μετὰ τὴν ζωὴν.. ἡνίκ' οὐκ εἰσίν Phld.*Mort*. 36 ; rarely *while*, ἡ. ἦν ἔτ' ἐν φάει E.*Ion*726. 2. ἡνίκ' ἄν, like ὅταν, with Subj., of fut. time, *whenever*, S.*Ph*.880, *OT*1492 : to denote repeated occurrence in pres. time, Id.*Ph*.310, Ar.*Pax*1179, X.*Cyr*.1. 2.4, etc. ; ἄν shd. be restored in A.*Fr*.304.7 ; ἄν goes with Verb in ἡνίκ' ἂν ὠφέλει *when* it would have been to his advantage, D.29.16 ; but ἡνίκ' ἂν ἀνέβη ἡ νεφέλη, of repeated occurrence, Lxx *Ex*.40.36(30). 3. with opt. in orat. obliq., or to denote an uncertain or repeated occurrence in past time, *whenever*, S.*Ph*.705 (lyr.) : also in orat. obliq., of future time, ἡνίκα.. ἀπείη *when* he should have been absent, Id.*Tr*.164 ; but ἡνίκ' ἂν ἡμεῖς μὴ δυναίμεθα, with implied protasis, D.4.31 ; and so ἡνίκ' (ἂν) καταλαμβάνοιμι, εἰ τυγχάνοιμι X.*Oec*.11.14. 4. c. gen., ἡ. τοῦ χρόνου *at which point* of time, Ael.*NA*12.35. 5. ἡ. χρὴ φλεβοτομεῖν *in which case*.., Orib.*Syn*.6.13. 6. after Verbs of knowing or remembering, οὐ μνημονεύεις.. ἡνίκα.. ; S.*Aj*.1273 ; οἶδ' ἡνίκ' Αἴας εἷλκε Κασάνδραν E.*Tr*.70, cf. Ar.*Ec*.815.

**ἡνίον**, τό, v. ἡνία, τά.

**ἡνιο-ποιεῖον**, τό, *saddler's shop*, X.*Mem*.4.2.8. ❀ **-ρράφος** [ᾰ], ὁ, *saddler*, Gloss.

**ἡνιοστροφ-έω**, *guide by reins, drive*, ἅρμα E.*Ph*.172. **-ος** (parox.), ὁ, *charioteer*, S.*El*.731. II. ἡνιόστροφος, ον, Pass., *guided by reins*, ἡνιοστρόφου δρόμου A.*Ch*.1022 (sed leg. ἡνιοστροφῶ).

❀ **ἡνιοχαράτης**, ὁ, *riding-master* (Lacon.), Hsch.

**ἡνιοχ-εία** (-ία v.l. in Pl.*Thg*.123d), ἡ, *chariot-driving*, Id.*Grg*. 516e, al. : pl., Id.*Lg*.795a ; ἡ. ἁρμάτων Hdn.1.13.8 : generally, *conduct, management*, τῆς μηχανῆς Plu.2.966f. ❀ **-εύς**, έως, Ep. ῆος, ὁ, poet. for ἡνίοχος, ὑπὸ δ' ἔστρεφον ἡνιοχῆες Il.5.505 ; θρασὺν Ἕκτορος ἡνιοχῆα 8. 312, cf. *APl*.5.337 ; *the constellation Auriga*, Nonn.*D*.1.178, al. **-ευτικός**, ή, όν, = ἡνιοχικός, ἀρετή Sch.Pi.*O*.10(11).83. Adv. -κῶς *Et.Gud*. 672.29. ❀ **-εύω**, Dor. ἀν-, poet. form of ἡνιοχέω, *act as charioteer*, ὁ μὲν νόθος ἡνιόχευεν Il.11.103, cf. 23.641, Od.6.319 : metaph., *direct, guide*, πηδαλίῳ.. ἀνιόχευεν Alex.Aet.2 : c. gen., τῆς ἐμῆς ψυχῆς ἡ. Anacr.4 : c. acc., χορὸν ἡ. *IG*3.82a. ❀ **-έω**, Lacon. ἀνιοχίω (v. ἀνιοχίων), prose form of ἡνιοχεύω, *hold the reins*, ἀνωτέρω,.. κατωτέρω ταῖς χερσίν higher up or lower down, i.e. longer or shorter, X.*Eq*.7.10 : c. acc., *drive*, ἅρματα Hdt.4.193 ; λέοντας Luc.*DDeor*.12.2 : metaph., Μουσῶν στόμαθ' ἡνιοχήσας Ar.*V*.1022 ; τὴν διάνοιαν Luc.*Am*.37 ; ἔθνεα.. φρεσὶν ἡ. *Epigr.Gr*.922 (Emesa) ; τῆς ἱερᾶς κεφαλῆς τῆς πάντα -ούσης Lib.*Ep*987.5 ; βασιλεύει καὶ ἡ. Plu.2.155a : rarely c. gen., συνωρίδος Pl.*Phdr*.246b :—Pass., *to be guided*, ib.253d, X.*Cyr*.6.1. 29 : metaph., of the months, *AP*7.482. **-η**, ἡ, fem. of ἡνίοχος, a name of Hera, Paus.9.39.5. **-ησις**, εως, ἡ, = ἡνιοχεία, Pl.*Phdr*. 246b, D.Chr.36.42 ; νεφέλης ὀπισθοφυλακούσης Ph.2.174. **-ητικός**, ή, όν, = sq., Procl.*in Prm*.p.520 S. (v.l. -οχικός). **-ικός**, ή, όν, *of* or *for driving*, εἶδος Pl.*Phdr*.253c sq. ; χιτὼν ἡ. a *driver's* coat, Callix.2 ; στολή Jul.*Or*.3.122c : ἡ -κή (sc. τέχνη) *the art of driving*, Pl.*Ion* 538b. Adv. -κῶς Eust.1303.35. **-ος**, Dor. and Aeol. ἀν- Pi.*P*.5.50 (v.l. ἁν- as in *N*.6.66, but cf. ἀνιοχίω), Sapph.*Supp*.20a.19, ὁ : (ἡνία, ἔχω) :— *one who holds the reins, driver, charioteer*, Il.8.89, etc. : sts. opp. παραιβάτης, 23.132 ; ἡ. θεράπων 5.580, 8.119 ; παρεβεβήκεε δέ οἱ ἡ. Hdt.7.40. 2. generally, *chariot-driver*, as in the games, etc., Pi. *P*.5.50, Ar.*Pax*905 (pl.), X.*HG*3.2.21, Pl.*Phdr*.254b, *PPetr*.3p.180 (pl., iii B.C.), etc. ; ὑποπτέρων ἵππων ἡ. Pl.*Criti*.116e. b. *rider*, Thgn. 260. 3. ὁ ἡ. τῆς νεώς *the helmsman*, Poll.1.98. 4. metaph., *one who guides, governs*, χειρῶν καὶ ἰσχύος ἀ. Pi.*N*.6.66 ; παλαισμοσύνας δεξιὸς ἡ. Simon.149 ; ἡ. τέχνης τραγικῆς *IG*2.2263 (iv B.C.) ; παντοίης ἀρετῆς ib.7.2539.2 (Thebes) ; ἡ. κιθάρας, of a harper, Epigr.ap.St. Byz. s.v. Μίλητος : fem., αἰγίδος ἡ., of Athena, Ar.*Nu*.602 ; in Prose with οἷον prefixed, Pl.*Plt*.266e, etc. ; of love, Plu.2.759d, Hermesian.7.84. 5. as Adj., *guiding*, γνώμη *Carm.Aur*.69 ; ἄνεμοι Man.5.153. II. ἡνίοχοι, οἱ, at Athens, a class of rich citizens *who had to furnish chariots* for public service, Ael.Dion.*Fr*.196, Phot. III. in pl., also, = ἔκφοροι (ἔκφορος III), Id. IV. *the constellation Auriga*, Arat.156, Eudox.ap.Hipparch.1.2.10, etc.

**ἠνίπαπε**, v. ἐνίπτω.

***ἦνις**, ἡ, epith. of cows, of uncertain meaning (*yearling*, fr. ἔνος (c), acc. to *EM*432.2, Hsch.), used by Hom. only in acc. sg. and pl. : gen. ἤνιος A.R.4.174 :—βοῦς.. ἤνις ἠκέστας Il.6.94, 275, 309 ; βοῦν ἦνιν εὐρυμέτωπον ἀδμήτην 10.292, Od.3.382. (ἦνιν codd. and Ptol. Oroandae ap.Hdn.Gr.2.71 ; ἧνιν Tyrannio ibid. : perh. a stem in ῑ.)

**ἡνίσκος**, ὁ, Dim. of ἡνία (B) II, *small thong* or *strap*, cj. in Herod. 7.22.

**ἦνον**, v. ἄνω (A), = ἀνύω.

❀ **ἠνορέη**, Dor. ἀνορέα, ἡ, (ἀνήρ) poet. word for ἀνδρεία, *manhood, prowess*, ἠνορέῃ πίσυνοι καὶ κάρτεϊ χειρῶν Il.8.226 ; κάρτεΐ τε σθένεΐ τε πεποιθότας ἠνορέῃ τε 17.329 ; ἱπποσύνῃ τε καὶ ἠνορέηφι πεποιθώς 4.303 ; ἀλκῆ τ' ἠνορέῃ τε κεκάσμεθα Od.24.509 ; ἀνορέας οὐκ ἀμπλακών Pi.*O*. 8.67 ; *manly beauty*, ἡ. ἐρατεινήν Il.6.156 ; ὕδατος ἡ. its *strength*, Epigr.ap.Ael.*NA*10.40 ; *force*, πολλάκι τοι ῥέα μῦθος, ὅ κεν μόλις ἐξανύσειεν ἠνορέη, τόδ' ἔρεξε A.R.3.189 : in pl., *triumphs of manhood*, Pi.*N*.3.20. (Perh. fr. *ἀνορία with Aeol. -ρε- fr. -ρι-.)

**ἦνοψ**, οπος, ὁ, ἡ, perh. *gleaming*, ἤνοπι χαλκῷ Il.16.408, 18.349, Od.10.360 ; οὐρανός Call.*Fr.anon*.24 ; πυρός ib.28. (Expld. as, = ἄν-οψ, *not to be looked at, dazzling*, by Scholl. in Lexx., but Ϝῆνοψ is prob. in Hom.)

❀ **ἤνπερ**, related to εἴπερ, as ἤν (ἐάν) to εἰ, X.*An*.3.2.21.

**ἤνσει**, Lacon. 3 sg. impf. of ἀνθέω, Ar.*Lys*.1258.

**ἤνυστρον**, τό, *fourth stomach of ruminating animals*, Arist.*PA* 674b15, *HA*507b9 (not the *first stomach*, as Poll.2.204, Hsch.) ; as a dish, Ar.*Eq*.356, 1179, Alex.273 : pl., Diox.1 :—written **ἔνυστρον** in Lxx *De*.18.3, *Ma*.2.3, ἐν- condemned by Phryn.140.

**ἠνώγεα, ἠνώγει**, v. ἄνωγα.

**ἡνωμένως**, Adv. pf. part. Pass., (ἑνόω) *in one word* (e.g. καλὸς κἀγαθός), Procl.*in Prm*.p.525 S. ; *in a unity*, Id.*in Euc*.p.138 F., Dam.*Pr*. 1 ; *together*, Hero *Geom*.12.53.

**ἠνώχλουν**, v. ἐνοχλέω. **ἦξα**, v. ἀΐσσω, ἄσσω :—but ἦξα, v. ἄγνυμι.

**ἦξις**, εως, ἡ, (ἥκω) *coming*, v.l. for ἴξις in E.*Tr*.396 ap.*AB*99.

**Ἠοῖαι**, αἱ, title of a poem of Hesiod, of which each section began ἢ οἵη, Paus.9.31.5, Ath.10.428b.

**ἠοῖος**, α, ον, Ion. **ἠοῖος**, Dor. **ἀοῖος**, = ἑῷος, *of the morning*, ἀστήρ Ion Lyr.*Fr.*10; ἠοῖαι σαίρεσκον Euph.53.2; ἡ ἠοίη (sc. ὥρα) *the morning*, πᾶσαν δ' ἠοίην.. Od.4.447, cf. Hsch. 2. *toward the dawn, eastern*, ἠὲ πρὸς ἠοίων ἢ ἑσπερίων ἀνθρώπων Od.8.29; πρὸς θαλάσσης ἠοίης Hdt.4.100; πρὸς τοὺς ἠ. τῶν Λιβύων ib.160; πρὸς ἠοίην (sc. γῆν) towards *the East*, Call.*Del.*280. (Cf. ἠῷος.)

**ἤομεν**, 1 pl. impf. of εἶμι (*ibo*).

**ἠονή**, coined (fr. ὄνησις) as etym. of ἡδονή, Pl.*Cra.*419c.

**ἠόνιος**, η, ον, contr. from ἠϊόνιος, *on the shore*, σῶμα *AP*7.383(Phil.); ψάμμος ib.365 (Zonas or Diod.).

**ἠπᾰνάω** and -έω, *to be in want*, Hsch.: ®**ἠπᾰνία**, ἡ, *want*, Id., *EM* 433.17, prob. l. in *AP*5.238(Paul. Sil.).

**ἠπ-άομαι**, *mend, repair* (rare word for the common ἀκέομαι), τὰ ῥαγέντα τῶν ἱματίων Gal.*Thras.*25: abs., Id.*UP*3.1:—Med., aor. 1 inf. ἠπήσασθαι Hes.*Fr.*172; κόσκινον Ar.*Fr.*227; ῥαγὲν ἱμάτιον Gal.*Thras.* 5: pf. part. Pass., ἱμάτια ἠπημένα Aristid.2.307 J., cf. *BCH*51.326.

**ἧπαρ**, ᾰτος, τό, (v. sub fin.) *liver*, Od.9.301, Gal.2.575, etc.; of various animals, as a favourite dish, κάπρου Ar.*Fr.*318.5; καπρίσκου Crobyl.7; [ἐρίφου] Euphro 1.23; εἰ μὴ σὺ χηνὸς ἧπαρ ἔχεις Eub.101, cf. Ath.3.106fsq., Poll.6.49; φασγάνῳ οὖτα καθ' ἧπαρ Il.20.469; παῖσαι ὑφ' ἧπαρ or πρὸς ἧπαρ, S.*Ant.*1315, E.*Or.*1063; ὑφ' ἧπαρ πεπληγμένη S.*Tr.*931; ὑφ' ἥπατος φέρειν, of *pregnant* women, E.*Supp.*919 (lyr.): as the seat of the passions, anger, fear, etc., A.*Ag.*432 (lyr.), 792 (anap.), *Eu.*135, E.*Supp.*599 (lyr.); χολὴν οὐκ ἔχεις ἐφ' ἥπατι Archil.131; χωρεῖ πρὸς ἧπαρ..δύη S.*Aj.*938; τήκειν ἧ. Call.*Aet.Oxy.* 2079.8, cf. *Fr.*222; of love, χαλεπὸς γὰρ ἔσω θεὸς ἧπαρ ἄμυσσεν Theoc. 13.71; τὸ μὲν θυμοειδὲς περὶ τὰν καρδίαν, τὸ δ' ἐπιθυματικὸν περὶ τὸ ἧπαρ Ti.Locr.100a, cf. Plu.2.450f. II. *fruitful land*, Agroetas ap. Sch.A.R.2.1248. III. = ἥπατος, Plin.*HN*32.149. (I.-E. *yēqʷr̥t*, cf. Lat. *jecur*, Skt. *yákr̥t*.)

**ἠπᾰτ-ηρός**, ά, όν, = ἡπατικός, δυσεντερία Steph. *in Hp.*1.130 D., Paul.Aeg.3.42. **-ιαῖος**, α, ον, = ἡπατικός I, λοβός Hp.*Oss.* 18. **-ίας**, ου, ὁ, = ἡπατικός I, λοβοί Poll.2.215. **-ίζω**, *to be liver-coloured*, Dsc.3.22, Aët.16.104(94). 2. *suffer from hepatic dropsy*, Diocl.*Fr.*46 (prob. l.). **-ικός**, ή, όν, *of the liver*, πάθος Plu.2. 733c; τὸ ἡπατικόν *divination from the liver*, Sch.rec.A.*Pr.*484. II. *suffering from liver-complaint*, Dsc.2.70, Philagr.ap.Orib.5.19.7, *POxy.*1088.48; διάθεσις Dsc.1.109. 2. *for liver-complaint*, φάρμακον Gal.11.749. **-ιον**, τό, Dim. of ἧπαρ, a common dish at Athens, Ar.*Fr.*506, Alc.Com.25, Alex.110.16, *PLond.*3.1259.36(iv A.D.), etc. **-ῖτις**, ιδος, ἡ, *of* or *in the liver*, δυσεντερία Gal.18(1). 145; ἡ ἡ. (sc. φλέψ) the *vena cava ascendens*, Hp.*Oss.*10, Diog.Apoll. 6, Arist.*HA*512$^a$6. 2. *liver-coloured*, ἀλόη *Gp.*6.6.2, Alex.Trall. 7.6; *hepatitis* [*gemma*], Plin.*HN*37.186. II. as Subst., *liver-wort*, = εὐπατώριον, Ps.-Dsc.4.41.

**ἡπᾰτοειδής**, ές, *liver-like*, τῷ χρώματι Dsc.5.85.

**ἥπᾰτος**, ὁ, a fish of uncertain kind, Eub.61, Arist.*HA*508$^b$19, Speus.ap.Ath.7.300e, Philotim.ap.Gal.6.720.

**ἡπᾰτοσκοπ-έω**, *inspect the liver for soothsaying*, Lxx *Ez.*21.21 (26). **-ία**, ἡ, *inspecting of the liver*, Hdn.8.3.7. **-ικός**, ή, όν, *connected with soothsaying*, τέχνη Phleg.*Macr.*4, cf. Jul.*Gal.*298b. **-ος**, ον, *inspecting the liver, soothsaying*, Artem.2.69; ἡ. ἱερά, Hsch. s.v. ῥυτά.

**ἡπᾰτουργός**, όν, *liver-destroying*, epith. of Perseus, who killed the sea-monster by leaping down its throat sword in hand, Lyc.839.

**ἡπᾰτοφᾰγέομαι**, Pass., *to have one's liver eaten*, ὑπὸ γυπῶν S.E.*M.* 1.286. **ἤπᾰφε**, v. ἀπαφίσκω.

**ἠπεδᾰνός**, ή, όν, *weakly*, Il.8.104; *halting*, of Hephaistos, Od.8. 311; ἄνδρες, χέρες, A.R.2.800, 3.82; λέων Babr.*Fab.Hex.*9; νόος Man.2.160; in Ion. Prose, ἠ. πῦρ *a slight, trifling* fever, Hp.*Mul.*1.4; of a child, *weakly*, ib.27; τὰ ἠ. ib.78; ἠ. ὕπνος *light, slight*, dub. in Ion Trag.4; of ghosts, prob. cj. in Euph.134. 2. c. gen., *void of*, φάμας ἔσσεαι ἠπεδανά *AP*9.521. II. Act., *weakening*, δεῖμα Orph. *L.*382, cf. *Fr.*142. (Derived by Gramm. fr. ἀ- priv., πέδον, cf. *EM* 433.26, and v. νηπεδανός: better fr. ἀ- and πούς, Hsch.; for the termination perh. cf. οὐτιδ-ανός.)

**ἠπειγμένως**, Adv. pf. part. Pass., (ἐπείγω) *hurriedly*, Hsch.

**ἠπειρογενής**, ές, (γενέσθαι) *born* or *living in the mainland*, ἔθνος, of the Lydians and Ionians, A.*Pers.*42.

**ἠπειρόθεν**, Adv. *from the mainland*, Arat.1094.

®**ἤπειρ-ος**, Dor. ἄπ- [ᾱ], ἡ, *terra firma, land*, opp. *the sea*, Od.3.90, 10.56, Il.1.485, Hes.*Op.*624, etc.; κατ' ἤπειρον by *land*, Hdt.4.97, 8. 66; μήτ' ἐν θαλάττῃ μήτ' ἐν ἠπείρῳ Ar.*Ach.*534, cf. Timocr.8: hence, even of an island, ἤπειρόνδε Od.5.56; but, II. esp. *the mainland of Western Greece*, opp. the neighbouring islands, Od.14.97, al.; ἤπειρόνδε 18.84, cf. Th.3.114 (so as pr. n., Pi.*N.*4.51, X.*HG*6.1.7, etc.): generally, *mainland*, opp. islands, Hdt.1.148,171, al., Th.1.5, Philostr.*VA*1.20, etc. III. later, *a continent*, esp. of Asia, Hdt.1.96, 4.91, A.*Pers.*718 (troch.), X.*HG*3.1.5, D.60.11, etc.; ῥεῖθρον ἠπείροιν (-ων codd.) ὅρον, of the Tanais or Phasis, A.*Pr.*790; so δισσαὶ ἄπειροι, i.e. Europe and Asia, S.*Tr.*101 (lyr.); τὼ δύ' ἠπείρω Id.*Fr.*881; ἐφ' ἑκατέρας τῆς ἠ. Isoc.4.35; ἤ. δοιαί, δίδυμαι, ἀμφότεραι, Mosch. 2.8, *AP*7.18 (Antip. Thess.), 240 (Adaeus), Lib.*Ep.*783.3; ῥίζαν ἀπείρου τρίταν, of Libya, Pi.*P.*9.8. IV. *plain*, opp. mountain, ἤπειρόνδε A.R.2.734,976. V. in Egypt, *land above inundation-level*, *PGiss.*48.8 (iii A.D.); more freq., γῆ ἤ. *PLond.*3.1201.2 (ii B.C.), etc. (Fr. ἄπερ-yος, cf. Germ. *Ufer*.) **-όω**, *to make into mainland*, opp. θαλαττόω, Arist.*Mu.*400$^a$28; βυθόν *AP*9.670:—Pass., *to become so*, Th.2.102, Ph.2.511. **-ώτης**, ου, ὁ, fem. **-ῶτις**, ιδος, *landsman*, Luc.*Ind.*19; ἄγειν ἀπειρώταν [ἰχθύν] to treat it *as a landsman*, Theoc.21.58 (prob. l.); ἵπποι Philostr.*Im.*1.30. II. Subst. -ώτης, ὁ, *dweller on the mainland*, opp. νησιώτης, Hdt.6.49, cf. 1.171, Isoc.4.132: fem. Adj., αἱ ἠπειρώτιδες Αἰολίδες πόλιες, opp. to those in islands, Hdt.1.151, cf. 7.109, Th.1.5, al.; also ἠ. ξυμμαχία alliance *with a military power*, opp. ναυτική, ib.35, cf. 4.12; πόλεις τῇ παρασκευῇ ἠπειρώτιδας Id.6.86. III. *Asiatic*, ψυχή E.*Andr.*159: Subst. fem., ib.652. 2. Ἠπειρώτης, ου, ὁ, *an Epirote*, Arist.*Fr.*494. **-ωτικός**, ή, όν, *continental*, ἔθνη X.*HG*6.1.12, Arist.*Pol.*1338$^b$22. 2. *of a landsman*, βίος Max.Tyr.19.7, cf. 8.9, al. II. *of Epirus*, πᾶν τὸ Ἠπειρωτικόν Th.3.102; Ἠ. [μῆλα] Dsc.1.115.

®**ἤπερ**, poet. ἠέπερ, (ἤ) *than at all, than even*, after a Comp., v. ἤ (A).

**ᾗπερ**, *in the same way as*, v. ὅσπερ II. 4.

**ἠπερόπ-ευμα**, ατος, τό, *cozener*, γυναικῶν Critias 1.3 D. ®**-εύς**, έως, Ep. ῆος, ὁ, = ἠπεροπευτής, ἠπεροπῆά τ' ἔμεν καὶ ἐπίκλοπον Od.11. 364; of Bacchus, *AP*9.524.8; of dreams, A.R.3.617. **-ευτής**, οῦ, ὁ, *a cheat, deceiver*, of Paris (cf. sq.), γυναιμανές, ἠπεροπευτά (Ep. voc.) Il.3.39, cf. *h.Merc.*282, etc. ®**-εύω**, Ep. Verb, used only in pres. and impf., *cheat, cajole*: c. acc. pers., esp. of *seduction*, γυναῖκας ἀνάλκιδας ἠπεροπεύεις Il.5.349; τά τε φρένας ἠπεροπεύει θηλυτέρῃσι γυναιξί Od.15.421; so of Aphrodite, τί με ταῦτα λιλαίεαι ἠπεροπεύειν; Il.3.399: generally, 23.605, Od.14.400, 15.419; ἐμὰς φρένας 13.327, Hes.*Op.*55. **-ηΐς**, ΐδος, ἡ, pecul. fem. of ἠπεροπεύς, ἠ. τέχνη *cheating* arts, [Hom.] ap.Str.1.2.4, etc.

**ἤπ-ησις**, εως, ἡ, *mending*, Eust.1647.60: **-ητής**, οῦ, ὁ, *repairer, mender*, Batr.184, *POxy.*2149.21 (ii/iii A.D.), v.l. in X.*Cyr.*1.6.16; condemned by Phryn.73; προστάτης τῶν ἠ. *Sammelb.*3939, cf. 3962: —fem. **-ήτρια**, ἡ, *needlewoman*, *UPZ*91.16 (ii B.C.), *POxy.*1679.5 (iii A.D.), Hsch. (-πίτ- cod.) (Dor. **ἀπήτρια** Id.): **-ητήριον**, τό, *needle*, Ael.Dion.*Fr.*29, *Gloss.* ®**-ητρον**, τό, in pl., *mender's wages*, *POxy.* 736.10 (i B.C./i A.D.), *PTeb.*120 *Intr.* (i B.C.).

**ἠπῐαίνω**, (ἤπιος) *mitigate*, prob. in Arist.*Mu.*397$^b$1.

**ἠπῐᾰλ-έω**, *have a fever* or *ague*, Ar.*Ach.*1165 (lyr.), Arist.*Pr.*947$^b$ 21. **-ης**, ητος, ὁ, = ἐφιάλτης, *nightmare*, personified in Sophr.68: acc. Ἠπιάλητα Id.70: -όλης Hdn.Gr.2.518; cf. sq. **-ος**, ὁ, *ague*, Thgn.174, Gal.7.347; ἠ. πυρετός Hp.*Superf.*34, Dsc.4.68; ἠ. πυρετοῦ πρόδρομος Ar.*Fr.*332: in pl., ἠ. καὶ πυρετοί Hp.*Aër.*3: metaph., ἀηδόνων ἠ. *ague* to nightingales, Com. name of a bad poet, Phryn. Com.69. II. = foreg., *nightmare*, Ar.*V.*1038, as expld. by Did. ap.Sch. (but coupled with πυρετοί). **-ώδης**, ες, *like the ἠπίαλος, aguish*, πυρετοί Hp.*Epid.*4.20.

**ἠπιάργυρον**· τὸ βάλσαμον, Hsch.

**ἠπιάω**, aor. 1 Pass. ἠπιήθη, = ἐταπεινώθη, Hsch. (s.v.l.).

**ἠπῐο-δίνητος** [δῑ], ον, *softly-rolling*, βλέφαρα *AP*5.249 (Paul. Sil.). ®**-δωρος**, ον, *soothing by gifts, bountiful, fond*, μήτηρ Il.6.251; Κύπρις Stesich.26; Μοῦσαι Opp.*H.*4.7, etc. **-δώτης**, ου, ὁ, *giver of* ἤπια (φάρμακα), of Asclepius, Orph.Εὐχή 37. **-θῡμος**, ον, *gentle of mood*, *APl.*4.65, Orph.*H.*59.15.

**ἠπιόλης** and **ἠπ-**, ου, ὁ, v. ἠπιάλης and ἠπίολος.

**ἠπιόλιον**, τό, Dim. of ἠπίαλος, Hsch.

**ἠπίολος**, ὁ, *moth*, Arist.*HA*605$^b$14 (v.l. ἠπιόλης).

**ἠπιό-μοιρος**, ον, *of kindly fate*, Castorio 1 codd. Ath. (sed leg. ἡλιόμορφος, q.v.). **-μῡθος**, ον, *soft-speaking*, Max.68.

®**ἤπῐος**, α, ον, also ος, ον Hes.*Th.*407, E.*Tr.*53, etc. I. of persons, *gentle, kind*, πατὴρ ὣς ἤπιος αἰεί Il.24.770, cf. Od.2.47,234; of a monarch, ἀγανὸς καὶ ἤ. ib.230, 5.8, cf. 14.139; ἡνίοχος Il.23.281: c. dat. pers., ἐθέλω δέ τοι ἤπιος εἶναι 8.40, cf. Od.10.337, etc.; ἤ. ἀνθρώποισι καὶ ἀθανάτοισι θεοῖσι Hes.*Th.*407; ἠπιώτερος τοῦ πατρός Hdt. 5.92.ζ'; of the gods, σωτῆρας..ἠπίους θ' ἡμῖν μολεῖν S.*Ph.*738; θεὸς ἀνθρώποισιν -ώτατος E.*Ba.*861, cf. Ar.*V.*879 (lyr.); ἐχίδνης οὐδὲν -ωτέρα E.*Alc.*310; οὐδέ πω ἤπιος *appeased*, Id.*Med.*133: later in Prose, 1*Ep.Thess.*2.7, 2*Ep.Ti.*2.24. 2. of feelings, words, etc., εἴ μοι κρείων Ἀγαμέμνων ἤπια εἰδείη had *kindly feeling* towards me, Il.16.73; δμῶς δέ τοι ἤπια οἶδε Od.13.405, cf. 15.557; ἤ. δήνεα οἶδε Il.4.361; μῦθος ἤ. Od.20.327; ὀργαί, φρένες, E.*Tr.*53, *Fr.*362.6; πρὸς τὸ -ώτερον καταστῆσαί τινα Th.2.59. 3. of heat and cold, *mild, less intense*, τὸ πνῖγος -ώτερον γέγονεν Pl.*Phdr.*279b, cf. *Ti.*85a (Comp.); ἠπιώτεραι αἱ θέρμαι, of a fever, Hp.*Epid.*7.1; τὰ τοῦ πυρετοῦ ἤπια ib.5.73; αἰθέριον πῦρ ἤ. ὄν Parm.8.57; of river-currents, -ώτερα ῥεύματα Meno *Iatr.*16.26. II. Act., *soothing, assuaging*, φάρμακα Il.4.218, 11. 515; opp. ἰσχυρά, Hdt.3.130, cf. 7.142 (Comp.); ἀκέσματα A.*Pr.*482; φύλλα S.*Ph.*698 (lyr.); ποτήματα *soft* drinks, opp. φαρμακώδη καὶ δριμέα, Sor.2.44: Sup., Phld.*Ir.*p.44 W. 2. ἤπιον ἦμαρ c. inf., a day *favourable* for beginning a thing, Hes.*Op.*787. III. Adv. -ίως Hdt.7.105,143, S.*El.*1439 (lyr.); ἠ. ἀμείψασθαι Hdt.8.60; χρήσετ' αὐτῇ σοι τότ' ἠ. Men.*Epit.*495: Comp. -ωτέρως, ἔχειν πρός τινα D.56. 44; -ώτερον καὶ κηδεμονικώτερον Phld.*Piet.*65: Sup. -ωτάτως Hsch.

**ἠπιότης**, ητος, ἡ, *gentleness*, Epicur.*Fr.*462, Hecat.Abd.ap.J.*Ap.* 1.22, Lxx *Es.*3.13(13.2), Phld.*Hom.*p.33 O., Ph.2.267.

**ἠπιό-φρων**, ονος, ὁ, ἡ, *gentle-minded*, ἠ. φιλότητος..ὁρμή Emp.35. 13; Αἴγινα B.12.78; Ἀσκληπιός *IG*3.171. ®**-χειρ**, χειρος, ὁ, ἡ, *with soothing hand*, *AP*9.525.8, prob. in Orph.*H.*23.8, 84.8.

**ἠπιόω**, intr., *feel easier*, ἠπίωσε τῷ σώματι Hp.*Epid.*5.20 (nisi leg. ἠπίως ⟨εἶχ⟩ε):—Pass., *to be softened*, ἠπιοῦσθαι ὑπὸ τῆς μουσικῆς Phld. *Mus.*p.33 K.: aor. ἠπιώθην Sch.Il.1.146.

**ἠπίταδες**· ἐπίτηδες, Hsch.

**ἡπλωμένως**, Adv. pf. part. Pass., (ἁπλόω) gloss on ἐκτεταμένως, prob. in Hsch.

**ἦπου** or **ἦ που**, *I ween*, ἦ που σοφὸς ἦν ὅστις ἔφασκεν.. Ar.*V.*725; ἦ που νέος γ' ὢν ἦσθ' ὑβριστής Id.*Th.*63, cf. Il.3.43, 16.830; ironical,

S.*Aj.*1008, E.*Med.*1308; χαλεπὸν πόλιν κατασκευάσασθαι, ἦ που δὴ.. *much more..*, Th.1.142; so ἦ που alone, Lys.30.17, Pl.*Phd.*84d; ἦ πού γε Isoc.1.49; also ἦ που δή.. *much less*, prob. in Th.8.27; also ἦ πού γε δή Id.6.37: and with a neg., ἦ που..γε..οὐ δεῖ χρήσασθαι And.1.86. II. to make a hesitating suggestion, *surely..?* Od. 13.234, A.*Pr.*521, Ar.*Pl.*970.

**ἠπύη**· φωνή Hsch. (fort. ἠπύει· φωνεῖ).

**ἠπύτᾰ** [ῠ], ὁ, Ep. for ἠπύτης (which is not found), (ἠπύω) *calling, crying*, ἠπύτα κῆρυξ the *loud-voiced* herald, Il.7.384; ἠ. σῦριγξ the *shrill* pipe, Q.S.6.170; πόντος Opp.*C.*2.136.

**ἠπύω**, Dor. and Arc. ἀπύω [ᾱ], *IG*5(2).6.3 (Tegea, iv B.C.), and Trag. (who use the Verb only in lyr., exc. aor. 1 ἤπῡσα E.*Rh.*776): [ῠ in pres., exc. in Mosch. (v. infr.); ῡ in fut. and aor.]:—*call to*, c. acc., ἔνθ' ποιμένα ποιμὴν ἠπύει Od.10.83, cf. 9.399; ἀλλά με Πυθὼ.. ἀπύει Pi.*P.*10.4; *invoke*, ἄπυεν Εὐτρίαιναν Id.*O.*1.72, cf. *P.*5.104; ἰαλέμῳ τοὺς θανόντας ἀπύεις E.*Tr.*1304: c. dupl. acc., τί με τόδε χρέος ἀπύεις; why *callest* thou *on* me for this? Id.*Or.*1253: c. dat. pers., ἤπυσα δ' αὐτοῖς μὴ πελάζεσθαι *called to* them not.., Id.*Rh.*776. 2. abs., of the wind, *roar*, οὔτ' ἄνεμος τόσσον περὶ δρυσὶν ὑψικόμοισι ἠπύει Il.14.399; of the lyre, *sound*, ἐν δέ τε φόρμιγξ ἠπύει Od.17.271; *sing*, Λυδίοις ἀπύων ἐν αὐλοῖς Pi.*O.*5.19: c. acc. cogn., μέλος ἠπύοντες Mosch. 2.124. 3. *utter, speak*, πατρὸς ὄνομ' ἀπύεις A.*Pr.*593; τί ποτ' ἀπύσω; E.*Hec.*154; ἀπύσατ' ἀντίφων' ἐμῶν στεναγμάτων Id.*Supp.*800; πρὸ σοῦ γὰρ ἀπύω (Com. for ὑλακτῶ) Ar.*Eq.*1023. 4. folld. by an interrog., τίς ἂν ἀπύοι εἰ..; *would tell* whether..? S.*Aj.*887; ἀπύσει τίς ὅδε..; E.*Ba.*984 (nisi leg. ἀπύσει· τίς..;). II. Med., *summon, prosecute*, ἀπυέσθω ὁ ἀδικήμενος τὸν ἀδικέντα *IG* l. c.

**ἦρ**, contr. for ἔαρ. **ἦρ**, v. ἦρα (B).

**ἦρᾰ**, 3 sg. impf. of ἐράω. II. Boeot. for ἦρω, 2 sg. aor. 1 Med. of αἴρω, Ar.*Ach.*913 (v.l. ἦρω).

**ἦρα** (A), 1 sg. aor. 1 of αἴρω:—but ἦρα', i.e. ἤραο, Ep. for ἤρω, 2 sg. aor. 1 Med. of αἴρω, Od.24.33. II. contr. fr. ἦ ἄρα in dialects other than Att., as Sapph.102, Alc.94, Alcm.61, Pi.*P.*9.37, B.5. 165, Sophr.1 D., Hp.*Prorrh.*1.117,120,121 (ἄρα ibid.), Herod.4.21, 5.14, Call.*Fr.*1.51 P., cf. A.D.*Conj.*223.25.

⊛**ἦρα** (B), acc. sg., = χάριν, *service, gratification*, θυμῷ ἦ. φέροντες Il. 14.132; μητρὶ φίλῃ ἐπὶ ἦ. φέρων 1.572, cf. 578; ἐπ' Ἀτρεΐδῃ Ἀγαμέμνονι ἦ. φέροντες Od.3.164; λαοί.. ἐφ' ἡμῖν ἦ. φέρουσιν 16.375; ἐπ' Ἴρῳ ἦ. φέρων 18.56; ἦ. κομίζειν Orph.*L.*761. II. later c. gen., = χάριν, *for the sake of, on account of, for*, ἦ. πάλας B.10.21; ἦ. φιλοξενίης Call.*Fr.*41, cf. Dosiad.*Ara* 18; τίνος ἦ.; *wherefore?* *APl.*4.299. (Hdn.Gr.1.398 rightly makes it acc. of a Subst. ἦρ; Aristarch. took ἐπίηρα as one word, Sch.Il.1.572, Apollon.*Lex.*, but there is no ἐπί in Il.14.132, and ἐπίηρα (q.v.) in later poets proves nothing for Hom.:—prob. (ϝ)ῆρα, perh. cogn. with ONorse *værr* 'snug', 'comfortable', OHG. *alawāri* 'friendly' (Germ. *albern*), Goth. *unwērjan* (= ἀγανακτεῖν), Gr. ἐρίηρος, βρίηρον.)

⊛**Ἥρα**, Ion. Ἥρη, ἡ, *Hera*, Il.16.432, etc.; νὴ τὴν Ἥραν, an oath of Athen. women, X.*Mem.*1.5.5. 2. applied to the Empresses of Rome, as Ζεύς to the Emperors, *IG*9(2).333 (Thess.), *CIG*3956[b] (add.). 3. Pythag. name for *nine*, *Theol.Ar.*58. 4. the planet Venus, Arist.*Mu.*392[a]28, Ti.Locr.96e. (Perh. connected with ἥρως and Lat. *servo*, cf. Ἡρϝαῷοι, = *inhabitants of Heraea*.)

**ἠραινεῖ** (sic)· ληρεῖ, Hsch.; cf. ἤρης.

⊛**Ἡραῖος**, α, ον, *of Hera*, Ἥραιον or Ἡραῖον (sc. ἱερόν), τό, *temple of Hera*, Hdt.1.70, Th.3.68, Duris60 J., etc.: Ἡραῖα (sc. ἱερά), τά, *her festival*, Ἡ. τὰ ἐν Ἄργει *SIG*1064.9 (Halic.), cf. Paus.2.24.2; epith. of Zeus, Διὶ Ἡραίῳ χοῖρος *IG*1[2].840.21. II. Ἡραῖος, ὁ (sc. μήν), a month at Delphi, *GDI*1693, al.; at Olus, ib.5075: Aeol. Ἥραος *OGI*265.15 (Temnos, from Pergam.):—also Ἡραιών, ῶνος, at Tenos, *IG*12(5).875.23; and Magnesia, *SIG*589.13.

**ἠραιωμένως**, Adv. pf. part. Pass., (ἀραιόομαι) gloss on ἀποκριδόν, Sch.Opp.*H.*1.547.

**ἤρακεν**· ἡνίασεν, Hsch.

⊛**Ἡρακλέης**, contr. -κλῆς, ὁ, the former in Ep., Pi., Hdt., and E. *Heracl.*210, *Ion*1144, *HF*924; the latter also in E., S., and Att. Prose: the orig. forms of the obl. cases Ἡρακλέεος, -κλέεϊ, -κλέεᾰ nowhere appear in use; but in Att. the contracted forms Ἡρακλέους Ar. *Nu.*1050, Ἡρακλέει E.*Heracl.*8,988, Ar.*Av.*567, Ἡρακλέᾱ Id.*V.*757 (anap.) (also in *h.Hom.*15.1, Hes.*Sc.*448, Theoc.24.1); in Ion. and Ep., Ἡρακλῆος, -κλῆϊ, -κλῆα (-κλῆϊ Pi.*I.*5(4).37, -κλῆος dub. in E. *Heracl.*541):—these forms are still further shortd., Ἡρακλέος Hdt.2. 42 (v.l. -έους), Pi.*O.*3.44 (scanned ⏑ ⏑ – *P.*10.3), E.*HF*806 (lyr.), Ἡρακλέϊ Hdt.2.145, Theoc.25.71; Ἡρακλέᾰ Hdt.2.42sq., Pi.*O.*10(11). 16, *AP*9.391 (Diotim. or Call.) (scanned – ⏑ – S.*Tr.*233, Ar.*Th.*26); again contr. Ἡρᾰκλῆ S.*Tr.*476 cod. A, interpol. in Pl.*Phd.*89c, Ael. *VH*1.24; Ἡρακλεῖ B.8.9, Th.7.73: irreg. acc. Ἡρακλῆν A.R.2.767, dub.l. in Theoc.13.73; contr. Ἡρακλῆν v.l. in Paus.8.31.3 and Epigr. ap.Alcid.*Od.*24, *BGU*166.12 (ii A.D.): voc. Ἡράκλεες Archil.119, Pi. *N.*7.86, E.*HF*175; Att. Ἡράκλεις Pl.*Euthd.*303a, etc., later Ἥρακλες Orph.*H.*12.1 [ᾰ], *AP*9.468 [ᾱ], Gramm.ap.Lib.*Ep.*255: pl. Ἡρακλέες Pl.*Tht.*169b (but Ἡρακλεῖς Hdn.Gr.1.424), acc. -έας Ar.*Pax* 741: dual Ἡρακλέε Philostr.*VA*5.5: (Ἥρα, κλέος):—*Heracles*, Il.14. 266, etc.; Ἡρακλέος στῆλαι (v. Ἡράκλειος), prov. of going to the farthest point, Pi.*O.*3.44; Ἡρακλέους ὀργήν τιν' ἔχων a temper *like Heracles*, Ar.*V.*1030, *Pax*752; prov. of close friendship, ἄλλος Ἡρακλῆς, ἄλλος αὐτός (Mss. οὗτος) Arist.*EE*1245[a]30; but ἄλλος οὗτος Ἡρακλῆς 'a second *Heracles*', Id.*MM*1213[a]13, Varr.*Sat.Men.*tit.: voc. Ἡράκλεις as an exclamation of surprise, anger, or disgust, Ar.*Ach.*284, *Nu.*184. 2. the planet Mars, Arist.*Mu.*392[a]25, Ach. Tat.*Intr.Arat.*17. [ᾰ, long by position in Ep. and E., as *Heracl.* 123.]

⊛**Ἡρακλεῖδαι**, οἱ, *the Heraclidae* or *descendants of Heracles*, Hdt.1.7, etc.; title of play by Euripides.

⊛**Ἡράκλειος**, α, ον, also ος, ον S.*Tr.*51; Ep. -ήειος, in Ion. Prose -ήϊος, η, ον:—*of Heracles*, βίη Ἡρακληείη, i.e. *Heracles himself*, Il. 11.690, al., Theoc.25.154, etc.; Ἡ. στῆλαι the opposite headlands of Gibraltar and Apes' Hill near Tangier, Hdt.2.33, 4.8 (where -κλέων is the best reading); στᾶλαι Ἡ. Pi.*I.*4(3).12. Adv. -είως *like Heracles*, Luc.*Peregr.*33. II. Ἡράκλειον or -εῖον, Ion. -ήϊον (sc. ἱερόν), τό, *temple of Heracles*, Hdt.2.44, al.; also, *a huge drinking-cup*, such as Heracles used, Ath.11.469c. 2. Ἡράκλεια (sc. ἱερά), τά, *his festival*, Ar.*Ra.*651, *IG*3.129; Ἡ. θύειν D.19.86, etc. 3. Ἡρακλεία, ἡ, *frothy poppy, Silene viscosa*, Thphr.*HP*9.12.5, 9.15.5, Dsc.4.66. b. title of poem by Rhianus. III. νοῦσος Ἡρακλείη *epilepsy*, Hp.*Mul.* 1.7, cf. Gal.17(2).341; but Ἡ. πάθος *elephantiasis*, Aret.*SD*2.13. IV. Ἡράκλεια λουτρά *hot* baths, Ar.*Nu.*1051, ubi v. Sch. (also Ἡρακλέους κοῖται soft bedding, Megaclid.ap.Ath.12.512f). V. λίθος Ἡρακλεία or Ἡράκλεια, ἡ, *the magnet*, Pl.*Ti.*80c, *Ion*533d, Epicur.*Fr.*293; from Heraclea in Lydia, acc. to Hsch. 2. πάνακες Ἡράκλειον *opopanax*, Zopyr.ap.Orib.14.62.1. VI. Ἡράκλειος, ὁ (sc. μήν), a month at Delphi, *GDI*1685, al.; at Halicarnassus, *SIG*1015.1.

⊛**Ἡρακλείτ-ειος**, α, ον, *of Heraclitus*, ἥλιος Pl.*R.*498b; Ἡ., οἱ, *his disciples*, Id.*Tht.*179e, D.L.9.6. **-ίζω**, *to be a follower of Heraclitus*, Arist.*Metaph.*1010[a]11. **-ιστής**, οῦ, ὁ, *follower of Heraclitus*, D.L. 9.15.

**Ἡρακλεών**, ῶνος, ὁ, name of month at Stratonicea, *BCH*11.226; at Lagina, ib.44.70.

**Ἡρακλεώτης**, ου, ὁ, *a man of Heraclea*, Arist.*Pol.*1327[b]14, *IG*2[2]. 1271 (-ειώτης ib.1[2].145):—Adj. **Ἡρακλεωτικός**, ή, όν, *of Heraclea*, Arist.*HA*525[b]5; ἅμμα Heracl.ap.Orib.48.8.1; [καρύα] Thphr.*HP* 1.10.6, 3.6.5, cf. Zopyr.ap.Orib.14.50.2; ἀμύγδαλα Diocl.*Fr.*126; ὀρίγανος -κή Philum.*Ven.*16.9; but σκύφος Ἡρακλεωτικός is said to derive its name directly from *Heracles*, Ath.11.500a:—fem. also ⊛-ῶτις Thphr.*HP*3.3.8, al.

**Ἡρακληΐς**, ΐδος, ἡ, *Heracleid*, a poem *on Heracles*, Arist.*Po.*1451[a] 20; cf. καρύα.

**Ἡρακλῆς**, ὁ, contr. from Ἡρακλέης (q.v.).

**Ἡρακλίσκος**, ὁ, Dim. of Ἡρακλῆς, title of Theoc.24:—a form **Ἡρακλεΐσκος** mentioned as dub. by Choerob. in *An.Ox.*2.268.

**ἠράνθεμον**, τό, = ἀνθεμίς, Dsc.3.137.

**ἠρᾰνος**, ὁ, *keeper*, μήλων A.R.2.513; Ἡσίοδος πάσης ἠ. ἱστορίης Hermesian.7.22; Μουσαῖος Χαρίτων ἠ. ib.16; ἦραν' ἁλίων μυχῶν Simm.13; glossed by βασιλεὺς ἢ βοηθός, *EM*436.28, cf. Hsch.: ἠρανέων· βοηθῶν, χαριζόμενος, Id. (Cf. ἐπιήρανος II.)

**Ἥραος**, v. Ἡραῖος II.

**ἤραρε**, v. ἀραρίσκω. **ἠρασάμην**, v. ἔραμαι. **Ἡράσιος**, ὁ (sc. μήν), name of month at Sparta, Hsch. **ἤρᾰτο**, 3 sg. aor. of ἄρνυμαι, Hom. II. 3 sg. impf. of ἔραμαι, Thgn.1346, Pi.*P.*3. 20. **ἠρᾶτο**, v. ἀράομαι. **ἠρᾶτον**· τὸν ἠρέα στράτιον, Hsch.

⊛**ἠρέμᾰ** (ἠρέμας before a vowel in A.R.3.170), Adv. *gently, softly*, ἥσυχος, ἠ., said as to a horse, Ar.*Pax*82 (anap.); ψήχειν ἠ. τὸν βουκέφαλον Id.*Fr.*42; ἠ. ἐπιγελάσαι Pl.*Phd.*62a; ἔχε ἠ. keep *still*, Id.*Cra.* 399e; ἠ. ἠρόμην Id.*Prt.*333e. b. on the stage, *aside, in a stage-whisper*, Sch.E.*Hec.*1023, *Or.*671, Sch.A.*Ch.*46. 2. *slightly*, ἠ. ῥιγοῦν Pl.*Tht.*152b; ἀγανακτεῖν Id.*Phlb.*47a; δάκτυλοι.. ἠ. διηρθρωμένοι Arist.*HA*517[a]32: sts. with an Adj., ἐν ἠ. προσάντει Pl.*Phdr.* 230c; ἠ. λευκός Arist.*Mete.*375[a]21; ἠ. θερμός Id.*GC*326[a]12; ἠ. παθητικός ib.328[b]7; ἠ. ὅμοιος Id.*Top.*117[b]23; ἠ. ψεκτός Id.*EN*1126[b]8; ἠ. καὶ γελοῖον *rather* ludicrous, dub. in Luc.*Merc.Cond.*28 codd. 3. *slowly*, περιφέρεσθαι Pl.*R.*617a.

**ἠρεμ-άζω**, *to be still, silent*, esp. from grief, Lxx 2 *Es.*9.3. **-αῖος**, α, ον, *quiet, gentle*, λῦπαι, ἡδοναί, Pl.*Lg.*734a; γένεσις Id.*Plt.*307a; πῦρ ἠ. a *slight* fever, Hp.*Mul.*1.38; σμικρὰ καὶ ἠ., opp. μεγάλα καὶ σφοδρά, Pl.*Lg.*733c: Comp., πόλιν -οτέραν ποιεῖν Plu.*Sol.*31: irreg., ἠρεμέστερος X.*Cyr.*7.5.63, Thphr.*Vent.*29. Adv. -αίως, = ἠρέμα, X. *Eq.*9.5, *Cp.*12.14.1: Comp. -αίτερον (v.l. -αιότερον) Arist.*Mete.*368[a] 12; -εστέρως ἔχειν X.*Cyr.*3.1.30. **-αιότης**, ητος, ἡ, *tranquillity*, Hp.*Praec.*2. **-εί**, v. ἠρεμί.

⊛**ἠρεμ-έω**, hyperdor. ἀρεμ- Ti.Locr.95d:—*to be still, keep quiet, be at rest*, opp. κινέομαι, Hp.*Fract.*6, Arist.*Ph.*238[b]23, al., Aristox.*Harm.* p.12 M.; τὸ ἠρεμοῦν, opp. τὸ κινούμενον, Pythag.ap.Arist.*Metaph.* 986[a]24; of the object of knowledge, Pl.*Phd.*96b, Arist.*APo.*100[a]6; ἐν τοῖς νόμοις ἠρεμοῦντες διαμένειν X.*Ages.*7.3; *acquiesce* in a verdict, Pl.*Lg.*956d; ἠ. τῇ διανοίᾳ Arr.*Epict.*2.21.22: acc. to Stoics, only of animate beings, *Stoic.*2.161. 2. *to be unmoved, remain fixed*, μόνος οὗτος ἠ. ὁ λόγος Pl.*Grg.*527b, cf. *Lg.*891a. 3. c. inf., *refrain from* doing.., Luc.*Jud.Voc.*4 (s.v.l.). **-ητέον**, *one must keep quiet*, Ph.1.89, Archig.ap.Gal.13.168. ⊛**-ησις**, hyperdor. ἀρέμ-, εως, ἡ, Ti.Locr.104b:—*rest*, opp. κίνησις, Arist.*Ph.*251[a]26, al.; ἡ νόησις ἔοικεν -ήσει μᾶλλον ἢ κινήσει Id.*deAn.*407[a]32; ἐν ἀρεμήσει, of ἐπιθυμία, Ti.Locr.l.c. **-ί** [ῐ], Adv. for ἠρέμα, Ar.*Ra.* 315, v.l. in Aristaenet.1.22 (-μεί Theognost.*Can.*165). **-ία**, ἡ, *rest*, opp. κίνησις, Arist.*Ph.*202[a]4; ἐν ἠ. εἶναι Id.*Metaph.*988[b]4, cf. Aristox.*Harm.*p.12 M., Sor.1.46. 2. of the mind, *quietude*, ἠ. ψυχῆς περὶ τὰ δεινά Pl.*Def.*412a, cf. Arist.*deAn.*426[a]27 (pl.); ἐπὶ πολλῆς ἠ. ὑμῶν leaving you entirely *at rest*, v.l. for ἐρημίας, D.13.8 (ἠρεμίη κοίτης is perh. a mistake for ἐρημίη, *Epigr.Gr.*321.11). **-ίζω**,

*bring to rest, stop,* ἵππον X.*Eq.*7.18 ; ὁρμήν Arist.*EE*1224ᵇ8 :—Pass., Id.*APo.*87ᵇ9, *Ph.*238ᵇ25, al. ; καθίσταται καὶ -ίζεται is calmed and *brought to rest,* ib.248ᵃ2. II. intr., = ἠρεμέω, X.*Lac.*1.3. **-ιος,** α, ον, = ἠρεμαῖος, Procl.*in Prm.*p.803 S. II. -ιον, τό, = ἀνεμώνη, Dsc.2.176 (v.l. ἠνέμιον). **-ισις,** εως, ἡ, *tranquillizing,* πράϋνσις ἠ. ὀργῆς Arist.*Rh.*1380ᵃ8 (-ησις codd.). **-ισμα,** ατος, τό, *point of rest,* Simp.*in Ph.*1311.32. **-ος,** ον, later form for ἠρεμαῖος, *quiet,* ἠ. καὶ ἡσύχιος βίος 1*Ep.Ti.*2.2, cf. *OGI*519.10 (iii A.D.), Procl.*in Prm.*p.536 S.; ἠ. πούς Luc.*Trag.*207 ; ἤρεμον ἑαυτὸν παρέχειν *IPE*1².40.24(Olbia, ii/iii A.D.); -ώτερος ἐπισπασμός *gentler* traction, Sor.1.73. 2. τὸ ἠ. *smoothness,* of pigments, Thphr.*Lap.*62. 3. Adv. -μως *quietly,* Asp.*in EN*120.13. (Cf. Lith. *rìmti* 'grow still', Goth. *rimis* (= ἡσυχία), Skt. *ramṇāti* 'set at rest'.) **-ότης,** ητος, ἡ, = ἠρεμία, ψυχῆς Cleonid.*Harm.*13.

⊛ **ἠρεσίδες,** αἱ, *priestesses of Hera* at Argos, *EM*436.49 (which derives the word from Ἥρα or ἀρύω).

**ἤρευν,** Ion. impf. of αἱρέω, Hes.*Sc.*302. **ἠρήρει,** v. ἀραρίσκω. **ἠρήρειντο, ἠρήρειστο,** v. ἐρείδω. **ἤρης**· ἄφρων, Hsch.

⊛ **-ήρης,** an Adj. termin., 1. from ἀραρ-εῖν, ἀραρ-ίσκω, as in θυμαρής, φρενήρης, χαλκήρης, εὐήρης. 2. from ἐρε- (ἐρέ-της), as in ἀμφήρης, ἁλιήρης, τριήρης, etc. 3. prob. from (ϝ)ηρ- (cf. ἦρα B) in pr. n. Περιήρης, Διώρης (fr. Διοήρης).

⊛ **ἦρι,** Ep. Adv. (Boeot. acc. to *AB*1095) *early,* ἠ. μάλ' Il.9.360 ; μάλ' ἠ. Od.20.156 ; ἠῶθεν δὲ μάλ' ἠ. 19.320 ; *in the morning,* μαντεύεσθαι *Schwyzer* 789 (Cumae). (ἄ(γ)ερι, cf. ἠέριος, ἄριστον.)

**ἠρι-γένεια,** ἡ, (ἦρι, γενέσθαι) *early-born, child of morn,* epith. of Ἠώς, Od.4.195, etc.: also abs., = Ἠώς, 22.197, 23.347 ; καθαρᾶς ἅπερ ἠριγενείας as at clear *morn,* Theoc.24.39 ; γενέθλιον ἠριγένειαν a birthday *morning, AP*9.353 (Leon. Alex.) ; later, epith. of the Moon, *Hymn. Mag.*5.3. 2. in later Ep., *a day,* Nonn.*D.*38.271, Q.S.10.478. II. (ἔαρ) *bearing in spring,* λέαινα A.*Fr.*426 (nisi leg. ἠυγ–). ⊛ **-γένειον,** τό, = περιστερεὼν ὕπτιος, Ps.-Dsc.4.60 ; = ἠρύγγιον, Hsch. **-γενής,** ές, = ἠριγένεια, epith. of Ἠώς, A.R.3.1224 : abs., = Ἠώς, Id.2.450 ; *a day,* Orph.*Fr.*275. **-γέρων,** οντος, ὁ, *early-old,* name of groundsel, from its hoary down, *Senecio vulgaris,* Thphr.*HP*7.7.1, Dsc.4.96.

**Ἠρῐδᾰνός,** ὁ, *Eridanus,* a legendary river, Hes.*Th.*338, Hdt.3.115 ; later identified with the *Po,* E.*Hipp.*737 (lyr.), etc. II. a river in Attica, Call.*Fr.*100e, Paus.1.19.5.

**ἠρι-εργής,** ὁ, (ἠρίον) *grave-digger,* Hsch. **-εύς,** έως, ὁ, *a corpse,* Id.

**Ἠρικᾰπαῖος** or **Ἠρικεπ-,** ὁ, a bi-sexual Orphic divinity, Ἠ. πρωτόγονος Orph.*Fr.*167a.1, cf. *H.*6.4, *Fr.*60, al.; epith. of Dionysus, Hsch.

**ἤρικε,** v. ἐρείκω.

**ἠρινό-θερμον**· τὸ ἄνθεμον, Hsch. **-λόγος,** ον, *talking in spring,* τέττιξ, Id.

⊛ **ἠρῐνός,** ή, όν, (ἦρ) = ἐαρινός, ἄνεμος Sol.13.19 ; φύλλα Pi.*P.*9.46 ; κάλυκες Cratin.98 ; λειμών E.*Supp.*448 ; φθέγματα Ar.*Av.*683 (lyr.) ; χρόνος X.*HG*3.2.10 : neut. as Adv., *in spring,* γῆ τ' ἠρινὸν θάλλουσα E.*Fr.*316.3 ; ὅταν ἠρινὰ . . χελιδὼν κελαδῇ Ar.*Pax* 800.

**ἠρίον,** τό, *mound, barrow, tomb,* ἔνθ' ἄρ' Ἀχιλλεὺς φράσσατο Πατρόκλῳ μέγα ἠ. Il.23.126, cf. *SIG*11 (Delph.), *IG*12(1).168 (Rhodes), A.R.1.1165, etc. ; ἠρία νεκύων, Κορύθοιο, Theoc.2.13, Nic.*Fr.*108 ; εἵσατο βωμόν . ., ἠ. ὄφρα γένοιτο *Epigr.Gr.*411 (Patara) ; κατὰ χθονὸς ἠρία τεῦχον *AP*7.180 (Apollonid.), cf. *Epigr.Gr.*214.1 (Rhenea) ; in Prose, Arist.*Ath.*55.3, D.57.67, prob. in Din.2.17, cf. Lycurg.109, Plu.*TG*9, etc.: metaph., ἠρία τῶν ψυχῶν τὰς βίβλους Them.*Or.*4.59d. (Derived from ἔρα by Harp., etc. : ⌊ϝ⌋ηρίον prob. in Hom.)

**ἠρι-πόλη,** ἡ, (πολέω) *early-walking* : hence, *dawn, AP*5.227 (Paul. Sil.), 253 (Id.). **-σάλπιγξ,** v. ἐρι-.

**ἠρίσκος,** ὁ, perh. Dim. of ἦρος, *IG*11(2).199 *B* 35 (Delos, iii B.C.).

**ἠρίστριον,** τό, *spring-garment,* formed like θερίστριον, Hsch.

**ἠρίφακον**· θαμνίσκον (Lacon.), Hsch.

**ἠρμένως,** Adv. pf. part. Pass., (αἴρω) *loftily,* Poll.9.147.

**ἡρμοσμένως,** Adv. pf. part. Pass., (ἁρμόζω) *fitly,* D.S.17.19.

**ἠροάνθια,** τά, a feast of the Peloponnesian women *at which they wore spring flowers,* Phot. : **ἠροσάνθεια,** Hsch.

**ἠροικάκαι**· κοιλώματα τῆς γῆς, Hsch.

**ἡροϊκός,** ή, όν, in late Poets for ἡρωϊκός, Man.1.13, *IG*12(7).125 (Amorgos).

**ἦρος,** ὁ, dub. sens. in *IG*11(2).144 *A* 72 (Delos, iv B.C.) ; ἦρον ὠνουμένων ἔδωκεν . ., τὸν ἦρον ἐνδήσαντι . ., τέλος ἐν Πάρῳ τοῦ ἤρου, ib.203 *A* 39,40 (iii B.C.) ; cf. ἠρίσκος.

**Ἡροφάνεια,** τά, festival at Megara, *IG*7.48 (ii B.C.).

**ἠρόχια**· τὰ Θεοδαίσια· οἱ δὲ ἑορτήν. οἱ δὲ ἱερά, Hsch.

**ἡρπαγμένως,** *raptim, Gloss.* **ἦρσα,** v. ἀραρίσκω.

**ἠρύγγ-ιον,** τό, v. ἤρυγγος. **-ίς,** ίδος, ἡ, *of* or *belonging to the* ἤρυγγος, ῥίζαι Nic.*Al.*564. **-ος,** ἡ, *eryngo, Eryngium creticum,* Id.*Th.* 645, 849 : more freq. as Dim., **ἠρύγγιον,** τό, *E. campestre,* Thphr. *HP*6.1.3, Plu.2.700d, 776f (both forms in Dsc.3.21, ἠρύγγιον also = ἀλόη, Ps.-Dsc.3.22) :—also **ἠρύγγη,** ἡ, Plin.*HN*22.18, Phot. ; = πόλιον, Hp.ap.Erot. (perh. to be read in *Ulc.*11) ; **ἠρυγγίτης** [ῑ], ου, ὁ, Plu.2.558e, Suid. II. **ἤρυγγος,** ὁ, *goat's beard,* Arist.*HA*610ᵇ 29 (s.v.l.).

**ἤρυγε,** v. ἐρεύγομαι. **ἠρύκακε,** v. ἐρύκω.

⊛ **ἦρυς** or **ἠρύς,** ἡ, fem. of ἥρως, *Glotta* 15.306 (Lilybaeum, ii B.C.).

**ἥρῳ,** poet. dat. sg. of ἥρως : **ἥρω,** gen. and acc. of same.

**ἡρώασσα,** ἡ, Cret., = ἡρωΐνη, *GDI*4952 (Dreros).

**ἡρώειον,** τό, = ἡρῷον (q.v.).

**ἡρω-ίαμβος** [ῐ], ὁ, *poem consisting of hexameters and iambics,* Tz. *H.*4.868. **-ίζω,** *write heroic verse* or *an epic poem,* Eust.4.1 :

⊛ **-ισμός,** ὁ, *worship of heroes, IG*12(2).29 (Mytil., spelt **-οισμός**) :—hence **-οϊσταί,** οἱ, *IG*2².1339 (i B.C.) ; **-ωισταί** *Annuario* 4/5.482 ; **-ωιασταί** *BCH*50.15 (Delph., iv B.C.), 22.255 (Acraephia) : later **ἡρωστής** (q.v.). ⊛ **-ικός,** ή, όν, *of the heroes,* κατὰ τοὺς ἡ. χρόνους (cf. ἥρως I. 1) Arist.*Pol.*1285ᵇ4 ; ἡ χλαῖνα ἡ. φόρημα Ammon.*Diff.* p.140 V. 2. *of* or *for a hero, heroic,* φῦλον Pl.*Cra.*398e ; ἡ. σώματα *of heroic stature,* Phld.*Po.*2.43 ; ἀρετή Arist.*EN*1145ᵃ20 ; ἡρωϊκὰ φρονεῖν Luc.*Am.*20. Adv. -κῶς *like a hero,* τελευτῆσαι τὸν βίον D.S. 2.45 ; cf. ἡροϊκός. II. in Metre, ἡ. στίχος *heroic verse, hexameter,* Pl.*Lg.*958e ; μέτρον Arist.*Po.*1459ᵇ32 ; εἰς τὴν ἡ. τάξιν ἐπανῆχθαι to be brought into an *Epic* poem, D.60.9. Adv. -κῶς, τὴν τραγῳδίαν ἀναγνῶναι D.T.629.18. ⊛ **-ίνη** [ῑ], ἡ, fem. of ἥρως, *heroine,* Theoc. 13.20, 26.36, Call.*Del.*161, D.P.1022, Luc.*Nec.*15, D.C.48.50 : contr. **ἡρῴνη,** Ar.*Nu.*315, *IG*14.1389i55, 2².1358.8, al. ; **ἡροῖνα** ib.12(2). 228 (Mytil.). II. *a deceased woman* (cf. ἥρως II), *CIG*2259 (Samos), *IG*3.889 ; of a deified Empress, Jul.*Caes.*334b. **-ιος,** α, ον, = ἡρωικός, ἀρεταί Pi.*O.*13.51 ; πομπαί Id.*N.*7.46 [ῳ]. ⊛ **-ίς,** ίδος, ἡ, = ἡρωΐνη I, Id.*P.*11.7, Call.*Fr.*126. 2. = ἡρωΐνη II, *IG*12(7).51 (Amorgos), *Rev.Phil.*36.55 (Iconium), *AJP*48.33 (Apamea). II. as fem. of ἡρωικός, τιμαί A.R.1.1048 ; ἀοιδή *Epic, AP*9.504. 2. (sc. ἐννεετηρίς) *nine-yearly festival* at Delphi, Plu.2.293c. ⊛ **-ΐσσα,** contr. **ἡρῷσσα,** = ἡρωΐνη, A.R.4.1309, 1358, *IG*5(1).610 (Sparta), al., 12(5).325 (Paros), *AP*6.225 (Nicaen.). **-ϊστής,** v. -ίζω.

**Ἥρων,** ωνος, ὁ, name of a god, *BCH*24.374 (Bithynia), *Annales du Service* 20.238 (Theadelphia), etc. ; also **Ἥρως,** ωος, ὁ, *Epigr.Gr.*841 (Thrace), Call.*Ep.*26.

⊛ **ἡρώνα,** ἁ, perh. *service, office,* ἐπιτελέσσαντα ταὶς ἡρώναις παίσαις (acc. pl.) dub. in *IG*12(2).242 (Mytil.).

**ἡρωο-γονία,** ἡ, a poem of Hesiod, Procl.*Vit.Hes.*p.8 G. **-λογέω,** (λέγω) *tell of heroes,* Str.11.6.3. **-λογία,** ἡ, *tale of heroes,* title of work by Anaximander, Ath.11.498b.

⊛ **ἡρῷον,** Ion. **-ώϊον,** τό, 1. (sc. ἱερόν or ἕδος) *shrine of a hero,* Hdt. 5.47, 67, Th.2.17, etc. ; θηρῷον, i. e. τὸ ἡρῷον, Ar.*V.*819. 2. *tomb, IG*12(7).478 (Amorgos), *IGRom.*4.799 (Apamea, iii A.D.), etc. : in form **ἡρώειον,** *CIG*4418 (Cilicia), etc. 3. (sc. μέτρον) *hexameter,* Plu.*Num.*4, etc. 4. **ἡρῷα** (sc. ἱερά), τά, *festival of a hero,* δειπνεῖν Id.2.811d, cf. *IG*2².974.

⊛ **ἡρῷος,** α, ον, contr. for ἡρώϊος (q.v.) ; ὁ ἡ. (sc. ῥυθμός) *the heroic measure, hexameter,* Pl.*R.*400b, cf. Arist.*Rh.*1408ᵇ32 ; ἡ. ⌊μέτρον⌋ Id. *Po.*1460ᵃ3 ; πούς ἡ. *dactyl, AP*7.9 (Damag.), etc.

**ἡρώπτει**· σκώπτει, Hsch. ; cf. ἠρόπτω· σκώπτω (v.l. κόπτω), *EM* 437.27.

⊛ **ἥρως,** ὁ (also ἡ in signf. III), gen. ἥρωος (ἥρως codd. in Od.6.303, fort. leg. ἥρωος), *IG*2².1641.6 (iv B.C.), etc.; also ἥρω D.19.249, *IG*2. 1191 (iii B.C.), Paus.10.4.10 : dat. ἥρωϊ, mostly in form ἥρῳ Il.7.453, Od.8.483, Pl.Com.174.18, Orac.ap.D.43.66 : acc. ἥρωα Pl.*Lg.*738d, *IG*3.810 (ἥρωα *Epigr.Gr.*774 (Priene)) ; usu. in form ἥρω *IG*2.1058.25 (iv B.C.), Pl.*R.*391d, A.R.2.766, etc., also ἥρων Hdt.1.167 :—Plur., nom. ἥρωες (ῶ Pi.*P.*4.58), rarely contr. ἥρως, as in Ar.*Fr.*304 : dat. ἥρωσιν A.*Fr.*55, Ar.*Av.*1485 ; ἡρώεσσι Sophr.154 : acc. ἥρωας (ῶ Pi.*P.*1.53), rarely ἥρως, as in A.*Ag.*516, Luc.*Dem.Enc.*4 :—*hero,* ἥρωες Δαναοί, Ἀχαιοί, Il.2.110, 19.34 ; στίχας ἀνδρῶν ἡρώων Od.1. 101 ; ἡρώων ἀγοράς, of the Phaeacians, 7.44 ; ἥρῳ Δημοδόκῳ 8.483 ; οἱ ἡγεμόνες τῶν ἀρχαίων μόνοι ἦσαν ἥρωες, οἱ δὲ λαοὶ ἄνθρωποι Arist.*Pr.* 922ᵇ18, but cf. Il. cc. 2. *the Fourth Age of men,* between δαίμονες and ἄνθρωποι, Hes.*Op.*172, cf. Pl.*Cra.*398c. 3. *heroes, as objects of worship,* ἡ. ἀντίθεοι Pi.*P.*1.53, 4.58 ; ἡ. θεός, of Heracles, Id.*N.*3.22 ; but [Ἡρακλεῖ] τῷ μὲν ὡς Ὀλυμπίῳ θύουσι, τῷ δὲ ἑτέρῳ ὡς ἥρωι ἐναγίζουσι Hdt.2.44 ; Σίσυφος ἡ. Thgn.711 ; twice in A., *Ag.*516, *Fr.*55 ; once in E., *Fr.*446 (lyr.) ; οὔτε θεοὺς οὔθ' ἥρωας αἰσχυνθεῖσα Antipho 1.27 ; esp. of *local deities,* founders of cities, patrons of tribes, etc., Hdt.1.168, Th.4.87, Pl.*Lg.* l. c., Arist.*Pol.*1332ᵇ18, etc. ; at Athens, ἡ. ἐπώνυμοι *heroes* after whom the φυλαί were named, Paus.1.5.1, 2, cf. Hdt.5.66 ; of historical persons to whom divine honours were paid, as Brasidas at Amphipolis, Th.5.11, cf. Hdt.5.114, 7.117 : hence, = Lat. *divus,* ἥρωα ἀπεδείξατε [τὸν Αὔγουστον] D.C.56.41 ; also, = *Lares,* D.H.4.14 ; ὁ κατ' οἰκίαν ἡ., = *Lar familiaris,* ib.2. II. later, = μακαρίτης, *deceased,* Alciphr.3.37, Hld.7.13 : pl., *PMag.Par.*1.1390 : freq. in Inscrr., ἥρως χρηστέ, χαῖρε *IG*9(2).806, cf. 14.223, etc. ; even of women, ib.9(2).961 (Larissa), al. ; θεοῖς ἥρωσι, = *Dis Manibus,* ib.14. 1795 (Rome), etc. ; ὑβρίσαντας τοὺς ἥρωας τῶν τέκνων ἡμῶν *SIG*1243. 23 (Acraeph.). III. ἡ. ποικίλος, = στιγματίας, Hsch., Phot. IV. βοῦς ἡ., = ἡγεμών, *IG*2².1126.32. V. v. Ἥρων.

**ἡρῷσσα,** v. ἡρωΐσσα. ⊛ **ἡρωστής,** = ἡρωϊστής, Keil-Premerstein *Dritter Bericht* 117 (Tire).

**ἡρωφόρος,** ον, *bearing heroes, EM*230.40.

**ἧς,** Dor. and Aeol. 3 sg. impf. of εἰμί (*sum*). **ἧς,** gen. sg. fem. of ὅς. II. Dor. for εἷς, *one.* **ἧσα,** aor. 1 of ἅδω ; but, II. **ἧσα,** aor. 1 of ἥδω. **ἦσαν,** Att. for ᾔδεσαν, 3 pl. plpf. (used as impf.) of οἶδα. II. Att. for ᾔεσαν, 3 pl. impf. of εἶμι (*ibo*). **ἥσατο,** v. ἥδομαι.

**ἥσθημα,** ατος, τό, (ἥδομαι) = ἡδονή, Eup.131.

**ἡσιεπής,** (ἵημι) *throwing words,* i. e. *babbler, EM*669.7.

⊛ **Ἡσίοδος,** ὁ, *Hesiod,* Pi.*I.*6(5).67, etc. ; Aeol. **Αἰσ-** *EM*452.37 :—Adj. **Ἡσιόδειος,** α, ον, Pl.*Lg.*658d, Plu.2.657d.

**ἦσις,** εως, ἡ, (ἥδομαι) = τέρψις, Suid. ; but ησει, = ἦσαν (3 pl. impf. of εἰμί), *PLond.*3.1170ᵛ387, al. (iii A.D.) ; ησιν, = ἦσαν, Bell *Jews and Christians in Egypt* 1914.16 (iv A.D.) ; also ησει, perh. = ἦσαν (3 pl. impf. of εἰμί), *Sammelb.*7194ʳ14 (ii A.D.).

**ἥσιχερ**· δαψιλής, Hsch.; cf. ἀσιχέρ.

**ἡσκημένως**, Adv. pf. part. Pass., (ἀσκέω) *in a practised manner*, Poll.1.157.

**ἦσμεν**, Att. for ᾔδειμεν, v. *εἴδω. **ἧσο**, v. ἧμαι.

**ἧσσα**, Att. ἧττα, ης, ἡ, *defeat, discomfiture*, Th.5.12,7.72, Pl.*Lg.* 638b; πολέμου in war, Id.*La.*196a; ἧττα.. πολέμου καὶ δικῶν καὶ ἀγορῶν Aeschin.3.111, cf. Plu.2.840c; μὴ δι' ἧτταν, ἀλλὰ διὰ προαίρεσιν Arist.*EN*1150ᵃ24; ἧτταν προσίεσθαι to let oneself be *conquered*, X.*Cyr.*3.3.45: c. gen. rei, *yielding* or *giving way to* a thing, ἡδονῶν, ἐπιθυμιῶν, Pl.*Lg.*869e(pl.); ἡ ἐν τοῖς τοιούτοις ἧ. καλή D.*Ep.*3.45; ἡ ὑπὸ τῶν λιπαρούντων ἧ. Plu.*Brut.*6.

❀ **ἡσσ-άομαι**, Att. ἡττ-, S.*Fr.*936, Th.3.57: fut. ἡσσηθήσομαι E.*Hipp.* 727, 976, ἡττ- Lys.20.32, X.*Cyr.*3.3.42: fut. Med. ἡττήσομαι in pass. sense, Lys.28.9, X.*An.*2.3.23: aor. ἡσσήθην E.*Andr.*917, etc.: pf. ἥσσημαι S.*Aj.*1242, E.*Alc.*697: plpf. ἥττητο D.19.160: Ion. ἑσσόομαι, part. ἑσσούμενος Hdt.1.82: impf. ἑσσοῦτο (without augm.) Id.7.166, 8.75: aor. ἑσσώθην Id.2.169, etc.: pf. ἕσσωμαι Id.8.130 (and v.l. in 7.9.β'), Herod.8.19: (ἥσσων):—*to be less* or *weaker than, inferior to*, c. gen. pers., E.*Alc.*697: c. gen. pers. et part., ἡττᾶσθαί τινος εὖ ποιοῦντος X.*An.*3.2.23, cf. *Cyr.*5.4.32; ἡττᾶσθαί τινός τινι ib.8.2.13; ἔν τινι in a thing, ib.3.3.42, etc.: c. gen. rei, τὸ μὴ δίκαιον τῆς δίκης -ώμενον E.*Ion* 1117: c. neut. Adj. in acc., ὃ ἡττῷτο wherein he *had proved inferior*, X.*Cyr.*1.4.5. **2.** as a real Pass., *to be defeated, discomfited*, ὑπό τινος Hdt.3.106, And.4.28, Th.2.39; ὑπ' ἔρωτος, ὑπ' ἔχθρας, Pl.*Phdr.*233c, *Plt.*305c, etc.; πρὸς τἀφροδίσια Id. *Lg.*650a: c. gen. pers., E.*Hec.*1252, Ar.*Av.*70, Th.3.57, etc.: c. gen. rei, τοῦ κόπου γὰρ ἕσσωμαι Herod. l.c.: c. dat. modi, ἑσσωθῆναι μάχῃ ὑπό τινων Hdt.5.46, etc.; τοῖς ὅλοις D.9.64, etc.; also c. acc., μάχην Isoc.5.47, D.19.320; ἀγῶνα D.C.63.9: c. dat., τῷ θυμῷ *to be broken* in spirit, Hdt.8.130; ἑσσωθέντες τῇ γνώμῃ πρὸς Κύρου Id.9.122; ἡ. περί τι Pl.*Sph.*239b: abs., οἱ ἡσσώμενοι, opp. οἱ κρατοῦντες, A.*Th.* 516, cf. Hdt.7.9.β'; τὴν γνώμην αὐτῶν οὐχ ἡσσῆσθαι Th.6.72. **3.** as law-term, *to be cast in a suit*, S.*Aj.*1242, Ar.*Pl.*482, etc.; ἡττ. ἐν τοῖς δικαστηρίοις X.*Mem.*4.4.17; δίκην, παραγραφήν, Pl.*Lg.*880c, D.45. 51. **4.** *give way, yield*, c. gen. pers., οἱ φύσαντες ἡσσῶνται τέκνων S.*Fr.*936; εἰ παθών γε σοῦ τάδ' ἡσσηθήσομαι E.*Hipp.*976; *give way, be a slave to* passion and the like, νηδύος ἡσσημένος Id.*Fr.*282.5; τοῦ παρόντος δεινοῦ Th.4.37; τῶν φόβων Pl.*Lg.*635d; ἡδονῆς X.*Ages.*5.1; ὕπνου Id.*Cyr.*1.5.11; [χρημάτων] Lys.28.9; τῆς τούτων παρασκευῆς ib. 11; θνητοῦ κάλλους Isoc.10.60; πικροῦ ἔρωτος E.*Hipp.*727: c. gen. pers., *to be in love with*.., Plu.2.771f; of other things, ἡττ. τοῦ ὕδατος X.*HG*5.2.5; τοῦ δικαίου ib.5.4.31; τῆς ἀληθείας D.18.273; τὸ δίκαιον ἡττ. τοῦ φθόνου D.25.75. **5.** c. dat., *to be overcome by*.., ἀκοῆς ἡδονῇ ἡσσώμενοι Th.3.38, cf. 7.25; ὕπνῳ Ael.*NA*13.22; τοῖς δικαίοις Plu. *Cat.Mi.*16. **II.** later in Act. ἡττάω, *overcome*, τινα Corn.*ND*9, Arr.*Epict.*2.22.6, al.: aor. 1 ἥττησα, τὰς ψυχὰς τῶν ὑπεναντίων Plb.1. 75.3; ταῖς ψυχαῖς τοὺς ὑπεναντίους Id.3.18.5, cf. Heraclit.*Incred.*16; *defeat*, τοὺς Λακεδαιμονίους ἀπὸ κράτους ἡττηκότες D.S.15.87. **-ητέος**, α, ον, neut. pl. ἡσσητέα *one must be beaten*, γυναικός *by* a woman, S. *Ant.*678, cf. Ar.*Lys.*450.

**ἡσσόνως**, Adv. of sq., J.*AJ*17.5.5, 18.2.4, 19.1.15, prob. in Hp. *Art.*69.

**ἥσσων**, ἧσσον, gen. ονος; Att. ἥττων, Ion. ἕσσων (not ἕσσων) Hdt. (v. infr.), Democr.50, Hp.*VC*2: formed from ἧκα (prop. ἡσσ-, cf. ἥκιστος), but in sense Comp. of κακός, μικρός: **I.** c. gen. pers., *inferior*; esp. in force, *weaker*, αἴθ' ὅσον ἥ. εἰμὶ τόσον σέο φέρτερος εἴην Il.16.722; of horses, 23.322, al.; ῥώμῃ ἥσσονες τῶν Περσέων Hdt.8. 113, cf. 9.62; γυναικῶν ἥσσονες S.*Ant.*680; Κύπριδος E.*Andr.*631; ἔς τι in a thing, Hdt.3.102: c. inf. modi, ἥσσ. τινὸς θέειν *not so good* at running, ib.105; οὐδενὸς ἥσσ. γνῶναι *second* to none in judging, Th.2.60; ἱππεύειν ἥττ. τῶν ἡλίκων *inferior* to them in riding, X.*Cyr.* 1.3.15. **2.** abs., οἱ ἥσσ. *the weaker party*, A.*Supp.*203, 489; οὐχ ἥσσους γενέσθαι to have the best of it, Th.4.72; τὸ λαμβάνειν τὰ τῶν ἡττ. X.*An.*5.6.32: c. dat. modi, ἥσσονες ναυμαχίῃ Hdt.5.86: c. acc. modi, τὸν νοῦν ἥσσ. S.*El.*1023, cf. X.*Cyr.*1.4.4; of things, τὸν ἥττω λόγον κρείττω ποιεῖν 'to make *the worse* appear the better cause', Pl.*Ap.*18b, cf. Ar.*Nu.*114: pl., οἱ ἥττους λόγοι ib.1042, Isoc.15.15; τὸ ἧσσ. ἀδικίᾳ νέμεις E.*Supp.*379(lyr.). **b.** *less, fewer*, ἵνα πλείω μὲν ἀκούωμεν, ἥττονα δὲ λέγωμεν Zeno *Stoic.*1.68. **II.** c. gen. rei, *giving way* or *yielding to* a thing, *a slave to*.., τοῦ τῆσδ' ἔρωτος εἰς ἅπανθ' ἥσσ. S.*Tr.*489; τῶν αἰσχρῶν Id.*Ant.*747; ὀργῆς Id.*Fr.*929; γάμων E.*IA*1354; κέρδους Ar.*Pl.*363; ἡδονῶν Pl.*Prt.*353c; γαστρὸς ἢ οἴνου ἢ ἀφροδισίων ἢ πόνου ἢ ὕπνου X.*Mem.*1.5.1; χρημάτων Democr. l.c., Theopomp.Hist.121: generally, *unable to resist*, τοῦ πεπρωμένου E.*Hel.*1660; νόσων καὶ γήρως Lys.2.78; οἱ ἥττους τῶν πόνων [ἵπποι] X.*Eq.Mag.*1.3, 2.78. **III.** neut. ἧσσον, ἧττον, as Adv., *less*, ὀλίγον δέ τί μ' ἧσσ. ἐτίμα Od.15.365, cf. E.*Hipp.*264 (anap.); ἧσσόν τι Th. 3.75; ἧσσ. ἑτέρων Id.1.84; ὁμοίως τε τρωθεὶς καὶ ἧσσ. Hp.l.c.: mostly with Verbs, but also with Adjs., ἀριστοκρατίαι.. αἱ μὲν ἧττ., αἱ δὲ μᾶλλον μόνιμοι Arist.*Pol.*1307ᵃ14, cf. *Mete.*340ᵇ8: with a Comp., ἧττ. ἀκριβέστερον Id.*Pr.*957ᵇ8; ἧττ. εὐληπτοτέραν D.H.3.43 codd.: with neg., οὐχ ἧσσ., οὐδ' ἧσσ., not a whit *less, just as much*, A.*Ch.*181, 708, Th.1.8; οὐδὲν ἧσσ., μηδὲν ἧσσ., S.*Aj.*276, 1329; for τὸ μᾶλλον καὶ ἧττ., v. μάλα.

**ἡστ-ικός**, ή, όν, (ἥδομαι) *pleasing, agreeable*, πάθος S.E.*M.*6.33. Adv. -κῶς, opp. ἀλγεινῶς, ib.10.225. ❀ **-ός**, ή, όν, = foreg., Simp. *in de An.*266.25, al., Hsch., Suid.

❀ **ἡσυχ-άζω**, fut. -άσω Th.2.84, *AP*5.132 (Maec.), -άσομαι Luc. *Gall.*1: aor. ἡσύχασα Th.1.12: (ἥσυχος):—*keep quiet, be at rest*, σὺ δ' ἡσύχαζε A.*Pr.*329, cf. 346; ἡ ἀπορία τοῦ μὴ ἡσυχάζειν the difficulty of *finding rest*, Th.2.49; οἱ πολέμιοι ἡσύχαζον X.*An.*5.4.16; ἀνάγκη τὸ ἡσυχάζον ἑστάναι Pl.*Prm.*162e; τοὺς [νόμους] οὐκ ἐῶν ἡσυχάζειν ἐν τιμωρίαις Luc.*Abd.*19; ἡ. πρὸς μίαν θύρην, of a lover, *AP*5.166 (Asclep.); ὁ διαλεκτικὸς ἡσυχάσει S.E.*P.*2.239: freq. in part., ἡσυχάζων προσμενῶ S.*OT*620, cf. E.*Or.*134; ὥστε μὴ ἡσυχάσασα αὐξηθῆναι *by resting from war*, Th.1.12; ἡσυχαζουσῶν τῶν νεῶν ib.49; μόλις ἡσυχάσαντες Id.8.86; ἡσυχάζουσαν ἔχων τὴν διάνοιαν Isoc.5.24; τὸ ἡσυχάζον τῆς νυκτός *the dead* of night, Th.7.83; ἡ. ἀπό τινος *keep away* from.., *AP*5.132 (Maec.): c. dat., *suspend work on*, *PFay.*117.23 (ii A.D.); ἀλλ' ἡσύχαζε only *be tranquil, calm thyself*, E.*HF*98, *IA* 973. **b.** ὁ -άζων, with or without λόγος, a fallacy, Chrysipp.*Stoic.* 2.8 (pl.), Gell.1.2.4 (pl.). **II.** trans., *bring to rest*, ἡσυχάσας τὼ δύο εἴδη, τὸ τρίτον δὲ κινήσας Pl.*R.*572a. **b.** abs., *impose silence*, D.C.69.6. **2.** *leave unspoken*, ἃ χρὴ λέγειν Ph.1.254, cf. 2.268; τὰς ἀπειλάς J.*AJ*7.7.3. **III.** Pass. in impers. sense, ἡσυχάζεται ἐπὶ τῆς γῆς *there is quiet*, Lxx *Jb.*37.17. **-αῖος**, Dor. ἀσῠχ-, α, ον, = ἥσυχος, βάσις S.*OC*197 (lyr.); ἐλάσεις X.*Eq.*9.6; *gentle*, Pl.*Plt.*307a; of persons, E.*Med.*808; *at rest*, of the embryo, Pl.*Lg.*775c; τὸ ἡ. *peace, tranquillity*, S.*Fr.*941.6; τὸ ἡ. ἀργὸν E.*Fr.*552.4: neut. as Adv., ἡσυχαῖον κράζειν, ᾄδειν, Thphr.*Sign.*52, 53; λύχνος καιόμενος -αῖον prob. in ib.54. **-αίτερος, -τατος**, irreg. Comp. and Sup. of ἥσυχος (q.v.). **-αστέον**, *one must keep quiet*, Ph.1.2. **2.** ἡσυχαστέος, α, ον, *to be kept secret, unsaid*, Id.2.5. **-αστής**, οῦ, ὁ, *hermit*, Just. *Nov.*5.3. **-αστικός**, ή, όν, *soothing*, τρόπος, of music, Aristid. Quint.1.19; ἦθος μελοποιίας Cleonid.*Harm.*13. **-άστρια**, ἡ, *she who soothes*, gloss on εὐκηλήτειρα, Hsch., Suid., cf. *EM*59.35. **-άω**, Ep. part. ἡσυχόωσα, gloss on γαληνιόωσα, Sch.Opp.*C.*1.115. ❀ **-ῇ** (with ι *PHib.*1.73.6 (iii B.C.), *PCair.Zen.* (v. infr.)), Dor. -ᾷ, Adv. *stilly, quietly, softly, gently*, Pi.*P.*11.55, etc.; ἡ. κατακεῖσθαι Ar.*Pl.*692; μετέρχεσθαί τινα E.*Hipp.*444; ἔχ' ἡ. keep *quiet!* Pl.*Hp.Ma.*298c; ἡ. ἔχειν τὴν οὐράν to keep it *still*, X.*Cyn.*3.4; ἡ. γελάσαι Pl.*Phd.*115c; κοσμίως πάντα πράττειν καὶ ἡ. Id.*Chrm.*159b, etc.; ἡ. ἀναμιμνήσκεσθαι to recollect *quietly, at one's ease*, Aeschin.2.35; εὐσεβεῖν E.*Fr.* 286.9. **2.** *by stealth, secretly*, Plu.*Alc.*24, Th.8.69, Plot.2.9. 18. **3.** *to some extent*, Men.*Her.*20; *slightly*, φύλλον περικεχαραγμένον ἡ. Thphr.*HP*3.14.1; βηχίον ἡ. ξηρὸν Hp.*Epid.*4.27; ὀξὺς Theoc. 14.10 (prob. l.); ὑπόσιμος *PCair.Zen.*76.11 (iii B.C.); μακροπρόσωπος *PStrassb.*87.11 (ii B.C.); ἐνερευθές Dsc.3.131; τοῦ αὐχένος εἰς εὐώνυμον ἡ. κεκλιμένου Plu.*Alex.*4; γρυπός Ael.*NA*3.28. ❀ **-ία**, Ion. -ίη, Dor. ἀσ- (?), ἡ, *rest, quiet*, Od.18.22, etc.; personified in Pi.*P.*8.1, Ar. *Av.*1321 (lyr.); ἁ. φιλεῖ συμπόσιον Pi.*N.*9.48: c. gen. obj., ἡ. τῆς πολιορκίης *rest from*.., Hdt.6.135; τῆς ἡδονῆς Pl.*R.*583e; τοῦ λυπεῖσθαι ibid; περί τι ib.c; ἡ ἀπὸ τῆς εἰρήνης ἡ. D.5.25: in pl., αἱ ἡ. σήπουσι Pl. *Tht.*153c. **2.** *silence, stillness*, E.*Alc.*77 (anap.); esp. of the Pythagoreans, Luc.*Vit.Auct.*3. **3.** with Preps., δι' ἡσυχίης εἶναι keep *quiet*, Hdt.1.206; ἐν τῇ ἡσυχίᾳ, opp. ἐν τῷ πολέμῳ, Th.3.12; ἐν ἡ. ἔχειν τι to keep it *quiet*, not speak of it, Hdt.5.92.γ'; ἐν ἡ. ἔχειν σφέας αὐτοὺς ib.93; ἐν ἡ. διατρίβειν Hdn.2.5.2; ἐφ' ἡσυχίας Ar.*V.*1517; μένειν ἐπὶ ἡσυχίᾳ Hdn.1.13.2; κατ' ἡσυχίην πολλήν quite at one's *ease*, Hdt.1.9, cf. 7.208, D.8.12; καθ' ἡσυχίαν at *leisure*, Ar.*Lys.*1224, Th. 3.48, etc.; opp. διὰ σπουδῆς, X.*HG*6.2.28; μετὰ.. ἡσυχίας *quietly*, E. *Hipp.*205 (anap.). **4.** with Verbs, **a.** ἡσυχίαν ἄγειν keep *quiet*, be *at peace* or *at rest*, Hdt.1.66, Pl.*Ap.*38a, Isoc.6.2, D.4.1, etc.; περὶ μὲν τῶν ἄλλων ἡ. ἦγον, ὑπὲρ δὲ.. Isoc.10.49; κινήσεως *from* movements, Pl.*Ti.*89e; keep *silent*, Hdt.5.92, E.*Andr.*143 (lyr.), Ar. *Ra.*321: pl., τὰς ἡ. ἄγειν or ἔχειν, Ath.3.114a, 11.493f. **b.** ἡσυχίαν ἔχειν, = ἡ. ἄγειν, but generally implying less continuance, Hdt.2.45, 7.150, X.*Cyr.*1.4.18, *HG*3.2.27; ἡ. ἔχειν πρός τινα Lys.28.7; keep *silent*, τὰ δεινὰ ἡ. ἑκτέον *about* them, D.58.60. **II.** *solitude, a sequestered place*, *h.Merc.*356, X.*Mem.*2.1.21.

**Ἡσυχίδες**, αἱ, priestesses of the Eumenides, Call.*Fr.*123.

**ἡσῠχ-ικός**, ή, όν, *peaceable*, in Sup., prob. in Plot.3.8.6. **-ιμος**, Dor. ἁσ- (v.l. ἡσ-), ον, = ἥσυχος, ἁμέρα Pi.*O.*2.32. **-ιος**, Dor. ἀσ- (v.l. ἡσ-), ον, = ἥσυχος, *still, quiet, at rest*, ἡσύχιον δ' ἄρα μιν πολέμου ἔκπεμπε Il.21.598; εἰρήνα Pi.*P.*9.22; also in Prose, τρόπου ἡ. of a *quiet* disposition, Hdt.1.107; οὐδ' ἡ. ὁ σώφρων βίος Pl.*Chrm.*160b; αἱ ἡ. πράξεις ib.c; τὸ ἡ. ἦθος Id.*R.*604e; οἱ ἡ. Antipho 3.2.1; τὸ ἡ. τῆς εἰρήνης (v.l. ἥσυχον) Th.1.120: Comp. -ώτερος *more reposeful*, Phld.*Rh.* 2.60S. Adv. -ίως *h.Merc.*438, Pl.*Tht.*179e. **-ιότης**, ητος, ἡ, = ἡσυχία, Id.*Chrm.*159b, d; ἡ. τινός his *quiet disposition*, Lys.26.5. **-όομαι**, Pass., *keep quiet, be at rest*, Aq.*Am.*6.10. **-οποιός**, *silentiarius*, *Gloss.* **-ος**, Dor. ἅσ- (v. fin.), ον, *quiet*, ἡ. ἀνστρέφεται Hes.*Th.* 763; ἥσυχοι ἔργ' ἐνέμοντο Id.*Op.*119; ἡ.. ὁδὸν ἔρχεο go thy way *in peace*, Thgn.331; ἡ. καθεύδειν Anacr.88; ἡ. θακεῖν, θάσσειν, S.*Aj.* 325, E.*Hec.*35; ἥσυχοι ἔστε Hdt.7.13, cf. 1.88; ἔχ' ἥσυχος keep *quiet*, keep *still*, Id.8.65, E.*Med.*550; μέν' ἡ. Ar.*Av.*1199, *Th.*925; γίγνεσθε E.*Cyc.*94, cf. *Ba.*1362; κατεθεᾶτο X.*Cyr.*5.3.55; ἡσύχῳ ποδὶ χωρεῖν E.*Or.*[136]; ἡσύχῳ φρενῶν βάσει, i.e. in thought, A.*Ch.*452; ἐν ἡσύχῳ *quietly*, S.*OC*82; ἡ. δορὶ *inactive* with it, E.*Fr.*998; τὸ ἡ. τῆς εἰρήνης, v.l. for ἡσύχιον, Th.1.120; νοῦς ἡ. τῶν πράξεων *at rest from*.., *free from*.., Plot.6.8.5. **2.** *quiet, gentle*, of character, in Comp. -αιτέρα, A.*Eu.*223, cf. E.*Supp.*952, etc.; οἱ δ' ἀφ' ἡσύχου ποδὸς δύσκλειαν ἐκτήσαντο Id.*Med.*217; ὄμματος παρ' ἡ. A.*Supp.*199; γλῶσσα -ωτέρα S.*Ant.*1089; ὀργῇ ὑπόθες ἥσυχον πόδα *moderate* thy wrath, E. *Ba.*647; τὸ ξύνηθες ἡ. their accustomed *quietness*, Th.6.34; ἡσυχαίτερα *less severe*, Id.3.82. **3.** *cautious*, πρόνοια E.*Or.*1407 (lyr.); of persons, Id.*Supp.*509. **4.** of the voice, *gentle*, φωνὴ -αιτέρα X. *Cyr.*1.4.4. **5.** *implicit*, Plot.6.2.20. **II.** Comp. and Sup. -αίτερος,

-αίτατος, A.*Eu.* l.c., Th.3.82, Pl.*Phlb.*24c, X.*Cyr.*1.4.4, 6.2.12; -ώτερος, -ώτατος, S.*Ant.*1089, Pl.*Chrm.*160a (nisi leg. -ιώτατος); -έστατος Sch.Lyc.3. III. Adv. -χως A.*Supp.*724; κάρτ' ἂν εἶχον ἡ. E.*Supp.* 305; ἡ. ναίειν Id.*Heracl.*7; *gently, cautiously*, Id.*Or.*698; *slowly*, πορεύεσθαι X.*Cyr.*5.3.53, etc.: Ion. Comp. ἡσυχέστερον Hp.*Salubr.*3, 5: Sup., ὡς ἡσυχαίτατα Pl.*Chrm.*160a: neut. ἥσυχον, Dor. ἅσυχον, as Adv., v.l. in Theoc.14.27: pl., ἅσυχα Id.2.11, 100, 6.12, *Hymn.Is.*103. (Dor. ἀσ- is dub., ἥσυχος, ἡσυχῇ, ἡσυχία codd. Pi., ἡσύχ-ιμος, -ιος, as v.l.)

**ἠσχυμμένος**, v. αἰσχύνω.

**ἦτα**, τό, *the letter* η, Hp.*VC*1, Pl.*Cra.*418c, *Epigr.Gr.*1095, *AP*9.385 (Steph.Gramm., v.l. ἧ): **ἧτα**, Sch.D.T.p.486 H. (Hebr. *hêth.*)

**ἤτε** or ἤ τε, *or also*, Il.19.148; later simply, *or*, Ascl.*Tact.*2.7. 2. ἤ τε.. ἤ τε *both..and*, Il.9.276; *either..or*, ib.11.410, 17.42. II. *than*, Od.16.216.

**ἦ τε**, *surely, doubtless*; v. ἦ I. 1. **ἦτε, ἤτην**, Att. 2 pl. and 3 dual of εἶμι (*ibo*).

**ἦτοι**: I. = ἦ τοι, Il.18.446, Pi.*O.*2.3, etc. II. = ἤ τοι, v. ἤ (A).

⊛ **ἦτορ**, τό, Ep. and Lyr. word, always in nom. or acc.; exc. dat. ἤτορι Simon.37.6 codd. Ath.:—*heart*, ἐν ἐμοὶ αὐτῇ στήθεσι πάλλεται ἦ. ἀνὰ στόμα *my heart* beats up to my throat, Il.22.452; *the seat of life, life*, φίλον ἦ. ὀλέσσαι 5.250, etc.: λῦτο γούνατα καὶ φίλον ἦ. 21.114, etc.; ἀνέψυχον φίλον ἦ. 13.84; τὰς δ' ἐσσυμένως λίπεν ἦ. Q.S.1.257 (v.l.): most freq., as *the seat of feeling, passion, desire*, etc., ἐγέλασσε δέ οἱ φίλον ἦ. Il.21.389; κατεπλήγη φίλον ἦ. 3.31; ἀχεῖ βεβολημένος ἦ. 9.9; μινύθει δέ μοι ἔνδοθεν ἦ. Od.4.467; ἐν δέ οἱ ἦ. χαίρει A.R.4.169; βρᾷ ⟨μοι⟩ μελέων ἔντοσθεν ἦ. A.*Pers.*991 (lyr.); ποτῆτος ἄσασθαι φίλον ἦ. Il.19.307; ποθέουσα φίλον κατατήκομαι ἦ. Od.19.136; εἰ δ' ἄεθλα γαρύεν ἔλδεαι, φίλον ἦ. Pi.*O.*1.4; Κύκλωπας ὑπέρβιον ἦ. ἔχοντας Hes.*Th.*139; ἦ. ἄλκιμον Pi.*N.*8.24 (so ἐν δέ τέ οἱ κραδίη στένει ἄλκιμον ἦ. Il.20.169); *of the reasoning powers*, ἐν δέ οἱ ἦ. στήθεσσιν.. διάνδιχα μερμήριξεν Il.1.188, cf. 15.252; Ζηνὸς ἦ. λιταῖς ἔπεισε Pi.*O.*2.79. (Cf. OHG. *âdara*, OE. *ǣdre* 'vein', pl. 'kidneys'.)

**ἠτριαῖος**, α, ον, (ἦτρον) *of the stomach*, τεμάχη *Com.Adesp.*863; τὸ ἠ. *stomach, paunch*, Ar.*Fr.*318.6:—also **ἠτριαία**, ἡ, ib.506.5, Luc. *Lex.*6, Ath.1.4c.

⊛ **ἤτριον**, Dor. **ἄτριον**, τό, *warp* (the woof being κρόκη), Pl.*Phdr.* 268a, Theoc.18.33, *AP*6.288 (Leon., pl.): in pl., *a thin, fine cloth*, such that one could see between the threads, ἤτρια πέπλων E.*Ion* 1421; ἤτρια βύβλων *leaves made of strips of* papyrus, prob. cj. in *AP* 9.350 (Leon. Alex.); τὸ διὰ ἠτρίου ἠθημένον Gal.19.98.

**ἦτρον**, τό, *abdomen*, esp. the *lower part of* it, Hp.*Aph.*2.35, Pl.*Phd.* 118a, X.*An.*4.7.15, D.54.11, Arist.*HA*493ᵃ19, Sor.1.24: metaph., *belly* of a pot, Ar.*Th.*509. II. *pith* of a reed, Nic.*Th.*595.

**ἧττα, ἡττάομαι, ἡττάω, ἥττων**, Att. for ἡσσ-.

**ἥττημα**, ατος, τό, *discomfiture*, Lxx *Is.*31.8; *loss*, 1*Ep.Cor.*6.7: **ἥττησις**, εως, ἡ, = foreg., Suid. s. v. ἧττα.

**ἥττων**, v. ἥσσων.

⊛ **ἤτω**, late form for ἔστω, 3 sg. imper. of εἰμί (*sum*), *IG*3.3509, *BGU* 419.13 (iii A.D.), etc.

**ἠΰ**, = ἠΰτε, Anon. *in Rh.*178.4 (s. v. l., cf. Uhlig ad D.T.642.7).

**ἠϋ-γένειος, -γενής, -δενδρος, -κάρηνος, -κομος, -πυργος**, etc., Ep. and Lyr. for εὐ-.

**ηὐξημένως**, Adv. pf. part. Pass., (αὐξάνω) gloss on ζαφελῶς, Eust. 769.23.

**ἠΰς**, neut. ἠΰ, Ep. for ἐΰς (q.v.), *good, brave*: only masc. nom. and acc. ἠΰς, ἠΰν, neut. nom. and acc. ἠΰ (neut. pl. ἠέα prob. in Emp. 128.10); ἠ. τε μέγας τε Il.2.653, etc.; ἠ. θεράπων 16.464, 653; μένος ἠΰ 17.456, etc.

**ἠΰτε**, Ep. Particle, *as, like as*, ἠ. κούρη Il.2.872, etc.; ἠ. νεβρός B. 12.87; freq. in similes, Il.1.359, 2.87, etc.: after a Comp., τῷ δέ τ' ἄνευθεν ἐόντι μελάντερον ἠ. πίσσα φαίνεται [the cloud] appears to him while afar off very black, *even as* pitch, 4.277, v. Sch.; ἔχετο κλαίουσ' ἀδινώτερον, ἠΰτε κούρη with sobs coming quicker and quicker, *like* a girl, A.R.1.269; but it may = *than* in these passages; cf. εὖτε. (ἠ + I.-E. *ute* (cf. Skt. *uta*) 'also', 'even'.)

**ηὐτοματισμένως**, Adv. pf. part. Pass., (αὐτοματίζω) *arbitrarily*, Procl. *in Prm.*p.650 S.

⊛ **Ἡφαιστεῖον** (on the accent v. Hdn.Gr.1.375), τό (sc. ἱερόν), *temple of Hephaestus*, Hdt.2.110, al., D.33.18; at Rome, = Lat. *Volcanal*, D.H.7.17; at Perusia, App.*BC*5.49:—also **Ἡφαιστιεῖον**, *temple of Ptah* at Memphis, *UPZ*109.13 (i B.C.).

**Ἡφαίστια**, τά, *festival of Hephaestus*, *IG*2².1158 (v/iv B.C.), And. 1.132, X.*Ath.*3.4; = Lat. *Volcanalia*, D.C.78.25.

**Ἡφαιστιάς**, άδος, ἡ, name of a *plaster*, Gal.12.234.

**Ἡφαίστιος**, ὁ (sc. μήν), a month (perh. at Lesbos), *CIG*6850.

**Ἡφαιστιών**, ῶνος, ὁ (sc. μήν), a month in Magnesia (Thess.), dub. in *IG*9(2).1118.

**Ἡφαιστῖτις** (sc. λίθος), ἡ, a precious stone, Plin.*HN*37.166.

**Ἡφαιστό-δαπτα**· πυρίκαυτα, Hsch. **-πονος**, ον, *wrought by Hephaestus*, ὅπλα E.*IA*1072 (lyr.).

⊛ **Ἥφαιστος** (Aeol. and Dor. **Ἀφ-** (**Ἄφ-**) Sapph.66, Pi.*O.*7.35, etc.), ὁ, *Hephaestus*, Il.18.391, etc.; ἔργον Ἡφαίστοιο, of a bowl, Od.4.617; κνημῖδας ὀρειχάλκοιο.. Ἡφαίστου κλυτὰ δῶρα Hes.*Sc.*123; φλογὶ Ἡφαίστοιο Il.17.88, cf. Antim.44; μὰ τὸν Ἥ. *Com.Adesp.*17.35 D. 2. = Lat. *Volcanus*, D.H.2.54, Plu.2.276b, App.*BC*5.49, etc. 3. = Egypt. *Ptah*, *OGI*90.2 (Rosetta, ii B.C.). 4. Pythag. name for *nine*, *Theol.Ar.*58. II. meton. for πῦρ, *fire*, Il.2.426, Hom.*Fr.*18, S.*Ant.*123 (lyr.), 1007, cf. Chrysipp.*Stoic.*2.315, al., D.S.5.74, etc.

⊛ **Ἡφαιστό-τευκτος**, ον, *wrought by Hephaestus*, σέλας S.*Ph.*987, cf. Simon.202 A, D.L.1.32:—also **-τευχής**, ές, δέπας A.*Fr.*69 (lyr., leg. Ἡφαιστοτυκές). ⊛ **-χειρος**, sine expl., Choerob.*Orth.* in *AB*1380.

**ἦφι**, Ep. for ᾗ, Il.22.107.

**ἠχάνω**, = πτωχεύω, Suid. (i.e. ἰχάνω): **ἤχανεν**· εἶπεν, Hsch.

**ἠχέεις**, εσσα, εν, poet. for ἠχήεις, restored for ἠχήεντα in Archil. 74.8, cf. Hdn.Gr.2.925.

**ἠχεῖον**, τό, (ἦχος) *drum, gong*, Plu.*Crass.*23, Apollod.ap.Sch. Theoc.2.36, Procop.Gaz.*Ecphr.*p.153 B.; *tambourine*, as head-dress, Herm.Trism. in *Rev.Phil.*32.254; used for stage-thunder, Sch.Ar. *Nu.*292; as sounding-boards in the theatre, Vitr.5.5.2. II. in the lyre, = χάλκωμα, apptly. *a metallic sounding-plate*, Hsch.; so of the palate, Gal.*UP*7.5. 2. Adj. ἠχεῖον ὄργανον *sounding* instrument, Ph.1.588, cj. ib.444, 510.

**ἠχέτης**, ου, ὁ, Ep. **ἠχέτα**, Dor. **ἀχέτας, ἀχέτα**, (ἠχέω) *clear-sounding, musical, shrill*, δόναξ ἀχέτας A.*Pr.*575 (lyr.); κύκνος E.*El.*151 (lyr.); epith. of the cicada, *chirping*, ἠχέτα τέττιξ Hes.*Op.*582, *AP* 7.201 (Pamphil.); ἀχέτα τ. ib.213 (Arch.): abs., ἀχέτας, ὁ, *the chirper*, i.e. *the male cicada*, Anan.5.6, Ar.*Pax* 1159 (lyr.), *Av.*1095 (lyr.), cf. Arist.*HA*532ᵇ16, 556ᵃ20: Orph.*A.*1250 has Ep. acc. ἠχέτα πορθμόν the *sounding* strait.

⊛ **ἠχ-έω**, Aeol. and Dor. **ἀχέω** [ᾱ]: I. intr., *sound, ring, peal*, ἠχεῖ δὲ κάρη.. Ὀλύμπου Hes.*Th.*42; ὅταν ἀχήσῃ πολιὸς βυθὸς Mosch.*Fr.*1.4; ἀχοῦσι προσπόλων χέρες E.*Supp.*72 (lyr.); of metal, ἠχέεσκε ὁ χαλκὸς τῆς ἀσπίδος Hdt.4.200; τὰ χαλκία πληγέντα μακρὸν ἠχεῖ Pl.*Prt.*329a, cf. Men.66.4; of the grasshopper, *chirp*, Alc.39, Theoc.16.96; of the ears, *tingle*, ἠχήσει τὰ ὦτα Lxx 1*Ki.*3.11; διὰ τί ἠχεῖ ἢ διὰ τί ἐμφαίνεται; impers., of *an echo*, Arist.*APo.*98ᵃ27. 2. *suffer from noises in the ears*, Herod.Med.ap.Orib.10.40.3. II. c. acc. cogn., ἀχεῖν (ἰαχεῖν codd.) ὕμνον *to let* it *sound*, A.*Th.*869 (lyr.); κωκυτόν S.*Tr.*866; γόους Id.*Fr.*523; ὕμνους E.*Ion*883 (lyr.); χαλκέον ἄχει *sound* the cymbal! Theoc.2.36; ἐφεξῆς ἠχοῦντα αὐτά (sc. τὰ φωνήεντα) Demetr.*Eloc.*71:—Med., ἀχεῖσθαί τινα *to sound* his praises, dub. in Pi.*Fr.*75.19:—Pass., ἠχεῖται κτύπος a sound *is made*, S.*OC*1500. (Cf. sq.) **-ή**, Dor. **ἀχά**, ἡ, *sound, noise*, ἠ. ἀμφοτέρων (sc. Ἀργείων καὶ Τρώων) ἵκετ' αἰθέρα Il.13.837: freq. in dat., ἠχῇ, ὡς ὅτε κῦμα.. βρέμεται 2.209; of trees, πρὸς ἀλλήλας ἔβαλον τανυήκεας ὄζους ἠχῇ θεσπεσίῃ 16.769; πέτρη .. ἡ δέ τε ἠχῇ ἔρχεται ἐμμεμαυῖα Hes.*Sc.*438; in Trag., *cry* of sorrow, *wail*, E.*Med.*149 (lyr.), *Hipp.*585 (lyr.), cf. Nic.*Al.*304; but also σάλπιγγος ἠ. E.*Ph.*1378; ἐν ἐμοὶ ἡ ἠ. τῶν λόγων βομβεῖ Pl.*Cri.*54d, cf. *Ti.* 37b; of the grasshopper, Longus 1.23: rarely of articulate sounds, E.*Ph.*1148, Opp.*C.*1.23; *rumour, talk*, Plu.*Cat.Ma.*22. (Perh. fr. *swāgh-*, cf. ἰαχέω, OE. *swōgan* 'resound', Engl. *sough.*) **-ήεις**, Dor. **ἀχ-**, εσσα, εν, *sounding, ringing, roaring*, θάλασσα Il.1.157; δώματα ἠχήεντα *high, echoing* rooms or halls, Od.4.72; δόμοι ἠχήεντες Hes.*Th.*767; χαλκός A.R.1.1236; *id* prob. l. in A.*Th.*915 (lyr.); θρόος αὐλῶν Epic.ap.Plu.2.654f; τέττιξ *AP*7.196 (Mel.); of the ears, ἠ. ἀκουή Parm.1.35; cf. ἠχέεις. **-ημα**, Dor. **ἄχ-**, ατος, τό, *sound*, f.l. in Ph.1.444; μελῳδοῖς ἀχήμασι prob. l. for ἰαχ-, E.*IA*1045 (lyr.).

**ἠχῆνες**, οἱ, = πτωχοί, Hsch.; cf. ἀχήν.

**ἠχ-ητής**, οῦ, ὁ, = ἠχέτης, Hsch. **-ητικός**, ή, όν, *sounding, ringing*, Diom.p.497 K., Simp. *in de An.*142.17, al., Eust.918.19; gloss on βύκτης, *EM*216.50. Adv. **-κῶς** Hsch. s. v. καναχηδά.

**ἤχθετο**, impf. of ἄχθομαι. 2. impf. Pass. of ἔχθω.

⊛ **ἠχι** (not ἠχι), Ep. for ᾗ, Adv. *where*, Il.1.607, Call.*Ap.*91, etc.; ἧχί περ, D.P.176, 258; ἧχί τε Id.67.

**ἠχικός**, ή, όν, (ἦχος) = ἠχητικός, of Alcaeus, ἠ. Αἰολίδης, i.e. *singing* in Aeolic, Epigr.ap.Sch.Pi.*O.*p.10 D.

**ἠχοῖ**, Adv., = ἦχι, *IG*7.235.16 (Oropus, iv B.C.).

**ἠχόπους**, ὁ, ἡ, πουν, τό, gen. ποδος, = Lat. *sonipes*, of horses, Eust. 918.20.

**ἦχος**, ὁ, later form of ἠχή, Arist.*Aud.*804ᵃ30, Theoc.27.57, *Ep. Hebr.*12.19, Ael.*Tact.*35.3, etc.; τεττίγων λιγὺν ἦ. Call.*Aet.Oxy.* 2079.29 (ἦχον Pap.); παγᾶς Mosch.*Fr.*1.12; αὐλοῦ Id.2.98; οἱ τῶν πριόνων ἦχοι A.D.*Synt.*290.24; of the *sound* of words, opp. sense, Phld.*Rh.*2.258 S.; ἦχοι καὶ ψόφοι ib.1.150 S.; τῆς φωνῆς ὁ ἦ. ἐν ταῖς ἀκοαῖς παραμένει Luc.*Nigr.*7; γραμμάτων Demetr.*Eloc.*71; ἦ. ἐν ὠσί, or abs., ἦχοι, ἦχος, *ringing in the ears*, Hp.*Coac.*189, 190, *Prorrh.*1.18, Thphr.*Sens.*19; ἦχοι ὤτων Aret.*SA*1.5. 2. *echo*, Arist.*Pr.*899ᵇ 30. 3. Gramm., *breathing*, ἦχοι ὁ μὲν δασύς, ὁ δὲ ψιλός Demetr. *Eloc.*73. 4. *voice*, τὸν ἦ. εὔτονον καὶ λαμπρὸν ἀποτελεῖ Dsc.5.17. (ἦχος, τό, is found in Lxx *Je.*28(51).16, dub. in *Ev.Luc.*21.25.)

**ἠχοῦ**, Adv., = ἦχι, prob. cj. in *h.Merc.*116.

**ἠχώ**, Dor. **ἀχώ**, ἡ, gen. ἠχοῦς, Dor. ἀχῶς Mosch.*Fr.*2.1: acc. ἠχώ, Dor. ἀχώ ib.3:—*echo*, *h.Hom.*19.21, Hes.*Sc.*279, 348, A.*Pers.*391, etc.: personified in Ar.*Th.*1059, Paus.2.35.10, Mosch.*Fr.*2, Orph. *H.*11.9. 2. generally, *ringing sound*, κτύπου γὰρ ἀχὼ χάλυβος διῆξεν ἄντρων μυχόν A.*Pr.*133 (lyr.); ἠχὼ προφωνεῖν to utter loud *cries*, S.*El.*109 (anap.); ἠ. χθόνιος E.*Hipp.*1201; ἠ. βαρεῖα προσπόλων ib.791; ὀρθία σάλπιγγος ἠ. Id.*Tr.*1267; ἅπασαν τὴν Βοιωτίην κατεῖχε ἠ. all Boeotia *rang with the noise* of mourning, Hdt.9.24; voc. Ἀχοῖ *Rumour*, Pi.*O.*14.21.

**ἠχώδης**, ες, *sonorous*, of the hexameter, Demetr.*Eloc.*42. 2. neut. pl. as Subst., *ringing in the ears*, Hp.*Coac.*163. 3. *full of sounds*, τῆς ἡμέρας -εστέρα ἡ νύξ Plu.2.720c; τὸ τῆς νυκτὸς ἠ. Id.*Arat.*22.

**ἠῶα**· ἡ κέδρος, ἐθνικῶς, Hsch. **ἠωήματι**· μιᾷ ἡμέρᾳ, Id. (leg. ἰῷ ἤματι).

**ἠῶθεν**, Dor. **ἀῶθεν**, Adv., (ἠώς) *from morn*, i.e. *at dawn, at break of day*, Il.11.555, 18.136, Od.1.372, etc.; ἠῶθεν μάλ' ἦρι 19.320; ἀῶ-

θεν ἅμα δρόσῳ Theoc.15.132. **2.** *to-morrow morning*, Od.15.506; *in the morning*, A.R.4.1224.

**ἠῶθι**, old Ep. loc. of ἠώς (q. v.).

**ἠώκοιτος** ὕπνος, ὁ, *morning*-sleep, Hsch., Suid.

**ἠών**, όνος, ἡ, contr. from ἠϊών (q. v.).

* **ἠῷος**, ῴα, ῷον, = ἠοῖος, *at break of day*, with Verbs, ἠ. γεγονὼς *h. Merc.*17; [τέττιξ] ἠ. χέει αὐδήν Hes.*Sc.*396, cf. *Op.*548; ἠῷοι ἔμελλον.. θυμὸν ἀμύξειν Call.*Aet.*3.1.10; ἠ. ἀλέκτωρ κηρύσσων *AP*5.2 (Antip. Thess.): without Verbs, ἠ. ὕπνος ib.7.726 (Leon.); ἀστήρ A.R.1.1274. **2.** *eastern*, Πέρσης ἀνὴρ ἐπάγων..τὸν ἠῷον στρατόν Hdt.7.157; εἰς ἅλα..ἠῴην A.R.2.745.

* **ἠώς**, ἡ, gen. ἠοῦς: dat. ἠοῖ: acc. (ἠόα A.D.*Pron.*88.5) ἠῶ, also ἠοῦν Hedyl.ap.Ath.11.473a, *AP*7.472 (Leon.); Ep. loc. ἠῶθι: never used (exc. by Gramm.) in the uncontr. forms, unless Ἀόος be read in Pi.*N.*6.52:—Att. **ἕως**, gen. and acc. ἕω: Dor. **ἀώς**, **ἀβώρ** (qq. v.): Aeol. **αὔως** Sapph.18, gen. αὔως *Epigr.Gr.*992 (Balbilla), acc. αὔων Sapph. *Oxy.*1787 *Fr.*1+2.18: Boeot. **ἆας**· ἐς αὔριον, Hsch.:—*dawn*, ἦμος δ' ἠριγένεια φάνη ῥοδοδάκτυλος Ἠώς Od.2.1; *light of day*, ὅσον τ' ἐπικίδναται ἠ. Il.7.451, etc.; esp. *morning* as a time of day, opp. μέσον ἦμαρ, δείλη, 21.111, etc.: gen. ἠοῦς *at morn, early*, 8.470,525: acc. ἠῶ *the morning long*, Od.2.434; στάντα πρὸς πρώτην ἕω S.*OC*477; ἐξ ἠοῦς μέχρι δείλης ὀψίης Hdt.7.167; ἐξ ἠοῦς εἰς ἠοῦν Hedyl. l. c.; ἠοῦν ἐξ ἠοῦς *AP*l. c.; ἅμα ἠοῖ with, i. e. at, *daybreak*, Hdt.7.219; Att. ἅμα ἕῳ or ἅμα τῇ ἕῳ, Th.2.90, 4.72; πρὸ τῆς ἕω ib.31; Ep. ἠῶθι πρό Il.11.50, Od.5.469, 6.36; ἐπὶ τὴν ἕω Th.2.84; εἰς τὴν ἐπιοῦσαν ἕω X.*An.*1.7.1; ἐς ἀῶ *to-morrow*, Theoc.18.14. **2.** *day*, Il.1.493, al., Od.19.192, Theoc.12.1, Call.*Aet.*1.1.1; ἠ. δέ μοί ἐστιν ἥδε δυωδεκάτη, ὅτε.. Il.21.80; κατήϊεν ἐς δύσιν ἠ. Musae.110; μεσάτη ἠ. Orph.*A.*649. **3.** *life*, Q.S.10.431; φῶς λίπες ἠοῦς *IG*14.1853. **4.** *the East*, πρὸς ἠῶ τ' ἠέλιόν τε Il.12.239 (*South* acc. to Str.10.2.12); ἀπὸ ἠοῦς πρὸς ἑσπέρην Hdt.2.8; τὰ πρὸς τὴν ἠῶ ibid.; τὰ πρὸς ἠῶ τε καὶ ἥλιον ἀνατέλλοντα Id.4.40, cf. Pl.*Lg.*760d, etc.; πρὸς ἕω τῆς πόλεως, τοῦ ποταμοῦ, *to the East* of.., X.*HG*5.4.49, Plu.*Luc.*27; πρὸ ἠοῦς τοῦ βωμοῦ *IG* 7.235.45 (Oropus, iv B. C.). **II.** pr. n., Ἠώς *the goddess of dawn*, Il. 11.1, Hes.*Th.*372,378, etc. (Cf. Skt. *uṣás* 'dawn', Lat. *aurora*, etc.)

# Θ

**Θ θ, θῆτα, τό**, indecl., ninth (later eighth) letter of the Gr. alphabet: as numeral θ' = ἐννέα, ἔνατος, but ͵θ = 9,000: abbreviation for θάνατος (or ἀπέθανε, τέθνηκε, θανατωτέον) found in certain Ptolemaic Mss. of Hp., acc. to Gal.17(1).612, cf. Pers.4.13, Mart.7.37, Wessely *Schrifttaf. zur ält.lat.Paläogr.* No.8 (ii A. D.), *PFay.*105 iii 26 (ii A. D.), Dessau *Inscr. Lat. Sel.* 5140, etc.; v. θῆτα.

**-θα**, insep. affix in adverbial forms, e. g. ἔνθα.

* **θαάσσω**, Ep. form of θάσσω, used only in pres. and impf., *sit*, λιπὼν ἕδος ἔνθα θαάσσεν Il.9.194, cf. 15.124; οὐδὲ ἔοικε..ἐν δαιτὶ θαασσέμεν Od.3.336, cf. *h.Merc.*172; μετ' ἀθανάτοισι θαάσσεις ib.468.

**θαβακόν** (i. e. θάϝακον)· θακὸν ἢ δμορόν (fort. θᾶκον ἢ θρόνον), Hsch.

**θάεο** [ᾱ], imper. of *θάομαι.

**θαέομαι**, Dor. for θηέομαι (Ion. form of θεάομαι), Pi.*P.*8.45: aor. 1 θαήσατο *Lyr.Adesp.*40; imper. θάησαι Epigr.ap.Phan.Hist.12; cf. *θάομαι.

**θαζός**, ή, όν, *seated*, Cyr.: **θάζω**, *to be seated*, Id.

**θάημα** [θᾱ], ατος, τό, Dor. for θέαμα (θῆμα), αἰπολικὸν θάημα Theoc. 1.56, cf. Aus.*Ep.*10.33.

**θαητός**, ή, όν, Dor. for θηητός (q. v.).

**θαιραῖος**, α, ον, *for axles*, ξύλα Poll.1.253.

**θαιροδύτης** [ῠ], ου, ὁ, pl., *rings through which the reins pass*, Hsch.

**θαιρός**, ὁ, *pivot of a door* or *gate*, ῥῆξε δ' ἀπ' ἀμφοτέρους θαιρούς Il. 12.459, cf. Q.S.3.27, Agath.1.10. **II.** *axle* of a chariot, S.*Fr.* 596. (Perh. for θϝᾰρ-yος, cf. θύρα.)

**θαΐς**, ΐδος, ἡ, a kind of *bandage*, Gal.18(1).792.

**θακαθαλπάς**, άδος, ἡ, *sitting hen*, *Lyr.Alex.Adesp.*4.22 (fort. θακοθ–).

**θᾱκ-εῖον**, τό, *seat*, *IG*2².1672.145 (iv B. C.). **-εύω**, = ἀποπατῶ, Plu.*Lyc.*20, Artem.1.2. **-έω**, Ion. and Dor. **θωκέω**, impf. ἐθάκει Cratin.239: Dor. fut. θωκησῶ Epich.99.1:—*sit*, ἐν θρόνῳ θωκέων Hdt. 2.173; θωκεῖτε Sophr.60; ἀνωτέρω θακῶν..Ζεύς A.*Pr.*315; ἥσυχος θακεῖ S.*Aj.*325· κόραι θάκουν (impf.)..ἧνουν τε (Herm. θάκους..ἧνουν, om. τε) E.*Hec.*1153: c. acc. cogn., θακοῦντι παγκρατεῖς ἕδρας *sitting on* imperial throne, A.*Pr.*391; of suppliants, S.*OT*20, *Aj.*1173; βώμιος θακεῖς E.*Heracl.*239. **-ημα**, ατος, τό, *sitting*, esp. as a suppliant, S.*OC*1160,1179. **2.** *seat*, Πανὸς –ήματα E.*Ion*492 (lyr.). **-ησις**, εως, ἡ, *means of sitting*, *seat*, prob. in S.*OC*9.

* **θᾶκος**, Ion. and Ep. **θῶκος**, Ep. also **θόωκος**, ὁ, *seat, chair*, Νυμφέων καλοὶ χοροὶ ἠδὲ θόωκοι Od.12.318; θεῶν δ' ἐξίκετο θώκους Il.8.439; θῶκοι ἀμπαυστήριοι *seats* for resting, Hdt.1.181, cf. 9.94; κραιπνόσυτος θᾶκος, of the winged car of the Oceanids, A.*Pr.*282 (anap.); θᾶκος Διός, of Dodona, ib.831; σεμνοὶ θ., of the palace, Id.*Ag.*519; εἰς παλαιὸν θᾶκον ὀρνιθοσκόπον ἵζων, of Teiresias, S.*Ant.*999; νεκροῖσι γείτονας θάκους ἔχων E.*HF*1097; θάκους θάσσειν Id.*Tr.*138 (anap.); τῶν θ. τοῖς πρεσβυτέροις ὑπανίστασθαι Ar.*Nu.*993; ἐκαθήμεθα ἐπὶ τῶν θ. Aeschin.Socr.2. **2.** *chair of office*, τὸν θᾶκον τὸν ἐμὸν παράδος Σοφοκλεῖ τηρεῖν Ar.*Ra.*1515. **3.** *privy*, Hp.*Epid.*7.47,84 (in form θῶκος), Thphr.*Char.*14.5, Mnesith.ap.Orib.8.38.11. **II.** in Hom., *sitting in council, a council*, like βουλή, οὔτε..ἀγορὴ γένετ' οὔτε θόωκος Od.2.26; ἐς θῶκον πρόμολον δήμοιό τε φῆμιν 15.468; θῶκόνδε καθίζανον 5.3; ἐν θώκῳ κατήμενος sitting in *council*, Hdt.6.63. (Cf. θάβακος, θάσσω.)

**θᾰλᾰμ-αῖος**, ον, *shut up, kept at home*, γυνή Ph.2.297. **-αξ**, ᾶκος, ὁ, = θαλαμίτης, Ar.*Ra.*1074. **-ευμα**, ατος, τό, = θαλάμη, θάλαμος II, Κουρήτων E.*Ba.*120 (lyr.), *Supp.Epigr.*2.461 (pl., i B. C.). **-εντός**, ή, όν, *hidden in a* θάλαμος, θησαυρὸς Μουσᾶν Tim.*Pers.*245. **-εύτρια**, ἡ, = νυμφεύτρια, *bridesmaid*, Poll.3.41. **-εύω**, *lead into the* θάλαμος, i. e. *take to wife*, Hld.4.6:—Pass., of women, *to be shut up, kept at home*, Aristaenet.2.5; *to be taken to wife*, Ph.1.323. * **-η**, ἡ, *lurking-place, den, lair*, πουλύποδος θαλάμης ἐξελκομένοιο Od.5.432, cf. Arist.*HA* 599ᵇ15, Numen.ap.Ath.7.315b; of the σωλήν and polypus, Arist.*HA* 535ᵃ17, 549ᵇ32; of the *nest* of the fish φωλίς, ib.621ᵇ9; of the Theban dragon's *den*, E.*Ph.*931 (pl.); of the *cave* of Trophonius, Id.*Ion* 394 (pl.); of the *grave*, Id.*Supp.*980 (anap., pl.); of the *hive* or *nest* of bees, in pl., *AP*6.239 (Apollonid.), 9.404 (Antiphil.); cj. in E.*Ba.*561 (v. θάλαμος II). **2.** of *cavities* in the body, Hp.*de Arte* 10 (pl.); *ventricle* of the heart, Arist.*Somn.Vig.*458ᵃ17; of the *pores* of sponges, Id.*HA* 548ᵃ 28; *the nostrils*, Poll.2.79; αὕτη τῶν κοιλιῶν ἡ οἷον θ. of the (Galenic) optic *thalamus*, Gal.*UP*16.3; of *recesses* in the cranial bones, ib.11.3; of the eye-*socket*, Steph. *in Hp.*1.93D. **II.** = θάλαμος III, Luc. *Nav.*2. **-ηγός**, όν, (ἄγω) *carrying* θάλαμοι: as Subst., θ., ὁ, *Egyptian house-boat* or *barge*, Str.17.1.15 (also πλοῖον θ. *POxy.*1650.20 (i/ii A. D.); and θαλαμηγός (sc. ναῦς), ἡ, ib.1738.2 (iii A. D.)); *state-barge*, Callix.1, D.S.1.85; θαλαμηγόν, τό, App.*Prooem.*10. **-ηϊάδης**, ου, ὁ, *son of the* θαλάμη or *hole*, comic patron. of the tunny, Matro *Conv.*53. **-ήϊος**, η, ον (-ος, ον, A.R.4.1130), *of* or *belonging to a* θάλαμος, *fit for building one*, δοῦρα Hes.*Op.*807. **II.** *bridal*, εὐνή A.R. l. c.; ὕμνος Epigr.ap.Luc.*Symp.*41.

**θᾰλᾰμηπολ-έω**, *to be a* θαλαμηπόλος, Sch.Lyc.132. **2.** *put to the stud*, of animals, Opp.*C.*1.393. **-ος**, ἡ, (parox.) *attendant in a lady's chamber, waiting-maid*, Od.7.8, 23.293; but, = ταμίη (cf. θάλαμος I. 2 b), A.*Th.*359 (lyr.). **2.** θ., ὁ, in later Gr., *eunuch of the bed-chamber*, Plu.*Alex.*30, Agath.1.7; of the Galli or *eunuch-priests of Cybele*, *AP*6.220 (Diosc.); but also ἡ, *a priestess of Cybele*, Rhian.67.1. **II.** rarely, *bridegroom*, S.*OT*1210 (lyr.). **III.** Adj., *bridal*, ὄρφνη Musae.231; epith. of Aphrodite, *APl.*4.177 (Phil.).

**θᾰλᾰμ-ίας**, ου, ὁ, = θαλαμίτης, App.*BC*5.107, Them.*Or.*15.195b. **-ιός**, ά, όν (oxyt., Arc.40.13), *of* or *belonging to the* θάλαμος: as Subst., **I.** θαλαμιός, ὁ, = θαλαμίτης, Th.4.32 (gen. pl., perh. fr. θαλαμίας), S.*Fr.*1052 (dub.). **II.** θαλαμιά, Ion. -ιή (sc. κώπη), ἡ, *the oar of the* θαλαμίτης, Ar.*Ach.*553 (pl.): pl., *IG*2².1604.55. **2.** (sc. ὀπή) *the hole in the ship's side, through which this oar worked*, διὰ θαλαμιῆς διελεῖν τινα to place a man so that his upper half projected through *this hole*, Hdt.5.33: metaph., Ar.*Pax* 1232. * **-ίς**, ίδος, ἡ, = θαλαμηπόλος, *An.Ox.*2.376. * **-ίτης** [ῑ], ου, ὁ, (θάλαμος III) *one of the rowers on the lowest bench* of a trireme, who had the shortest oars and the least pay, Sch.Ar.*Ra.*1106. **-όνδε**, Adv. *to the bed-chamber*, Od. 21.8, 22.109,161.

**θᾰλᾰμοποιός**, όν, *preparing the bed-chamber*: Θαλαμοποιοί, name of a play of Aeschylus, Poll.7.122.

**θάλᾰμος** [θᾰ], ὁ, *an inner room* or *chamber, surrounded by other buildings*: freq. in Hom., **1.** generally, *women's apartment, inner part of the house*, like μυχός, Il.3.142,174, Od.4.121, etc.: in pl., Il.18.492; ἐκ τῶν ἀνδρεώνων..ἐς τοὺς θ. Hdt.1.34. **2.** *a special chamber in this part of the house*, **a.** *bedroom*, esp. of the lady of the house, Il.3.423, al., Hdt.1.12, 3.78, Plu.*Alc.*23; esp. *bride-chamber*, Il.11.227, Pi.*P.*2.33 (pl.), S.*Tr.*913, E.*Hipp.*540 (lyr., pl.); also, *bedroom of an unmarried son*, Od.1.425, 19.48. **b.** *store-room*, esp. for valuables, Il.24.191, Od.21.8, X.*Oec.*9.3, etc.; ὄλβου διοίγων θάλαμον E.*Fr.*285.8. **c.** generally, *chamber, room*, Od.23.192, *POxy.*1144.2 (i/ii A. D.). **3.** *house, mansion* (not in Hom.), Pi.*O.*5.13 (pl.), 6.1; βασιλικοὶ θ. E.*Ion* 486 (lyr.). **II.** metaph., ὁ παγκοίτας θ., *of the grave*, S.*Ant.*804 (anap.); τυμβήρης θ., of the prison of Danae, ib.947 (lyr.); θάλαμοι ὑπὸ γῆς the *realms* below, A.*Pers.*624; γᾶς θάλαμοι E.*HF*807 (lyr.); θ. Περσεφονείας Id.*Supp.*1022 (lyr.); θ. Ἀμφιτρίτας, of the sea, S.*OT*195 (lyr.); πολυδενδρέσσιν Ὀλύμπου θαλάμοις E.*Ba.*561 (lyr., θαλάμαις cj. Barnes); ἀρνῶν θ. *folds* or *pens*, Id.*Cyc.*57 (lyr.). **III.** *the lowest, darkest part of the ship, the hold*, Timae. 114, Poll.1.87; cf. θαλάμη II. **IV.** used of *certain mystic shrines* or *chapels*, sacred to Apis, Ael.*NA*11.10, cf. Plin.*HN*8.185; *the inner-most shrine*, Luc.*Syr.D.*31.

* **θάλασσα** [θᾰ], Att. **-ττα** *IG*1².57 (but θάλασσα 2².236 (338/7 B. C.)), ἡ: —*sea*, Il.2.294, etc.: freq. of the Mediterranean *sea*, ἥδε ἡ θ. Hdt.1.1, 185, 4.39, etc.; ἡ παρ' ἡμῖν θ. Pl.*Phd.*113a; ἡ θ. ἡ καθ' ἡμᾶς Plb.1.3.9; ἡ ἐντὸς καὶ κ. ἡ. λεγομένη θ. Str.2.5.18; ἡ ἔσω θ. Arist.*Mu.*393ᵇ29; ἡ ἔξω θ., of the Ocean, Id.*Mete.*350ᵃ22; ἡ Ἀτλαντικὴ θ. Id.*Mu.*392ᵇ22; ἡ μεγάλη θ. Plu.*Alex.*73; of a *salt lake*, Arist.*Mete.*351ᵃ9; ἐς θάλασσαν τὴν τοῦ Εὐξείνου πόντου Hdt.2.33; πέλαγος θαλάσσης A.R.2.608; κατὰ θάλασσαν *by sea*, opp. πεζῇ, Hdt.5.63; opp. κατὰ γῆς, Th.7.28 codd.; κατά τε γῆν καὶ κατὰ θ. Pl.*Mx.*241a; χέρσον καὶ θ. ἐκπερῶν A.*Eu.*240; τῆς θ. ἀνθεκτέα ἐστί one must engage in *maritime affairs*, Th.1.93; οἱ περὶ τὴν θ. *sea*-faring men, Arist.*HA* 598ᵇ24, cf. *Pol.*1291ᵇ20; θ. καὶ πῦρ καὶ γυνή—τρίτον κακόν Men.*Mon.*231, cf. 264: metaph., κακῶν θ. *a sea* of troubles, A.*Th.*758 (lyr.); ὁ Κρὴς τὴν θ. (sc. ἀγνοεῖ), of pretended ignorance, Suid. **2.** *sea-water*, ἔστω ἐν χαλκῷ ἡ θ. Hp.*Coac.*427, cf. Diph.Siph.ap.Ath.3.121d, Moschio ib.5.208a, Plb.16.5.4, Dsc.2. 83. **3.** *well of salt water*, said to be produced by a stroke of

Poseidon's trident, in the Acropolis at Athens, Hdt.8.55; θ. Ἐρεχθηΐς Apollod.3.14.1. 4. *channel*, Lxx 3*Ki*.18.32. 5. χαλκῆ θ. *laver*, ib.2*Ki*.8.8. 6. θ. κοίλη wooden *theatre*, Paus.Gr.*Fr*.208 (= *Com.Adesp*.864).—For the Lacon. form σάλασσα, v. θαλασσομέδων.

**θάλασσ-αίγλη**, ἡ, *bhang, Cannabis sativa*, Plin.*HN*24.164. ❋ **-αῖος**, α, ον, = θαλάσσιος, δῖναι Simon.57.4, cf. Pi.*P*.2.50: **θαλάσσειος**, θεά *Trag.* or *Com.Adesp*. in *PLit.Lond*.84.16; dub. in Orib.14.62.1. 2. *dyed purple*, Tryph.345. **-ερός**, ὁ, a kind of *eyesalve*, Gal.12.781, etc. **-εύς**, έως, ὁ, *fisherman*, Hsch. **-εύω**, *to be at sea*, νῆες τοσοῦτον χρόνον ἤδη θαλασσεύουσαι Th.7.12, cf. App.*BC*1.62; τὰ θαλαττεύοντα τῆς νεὼς μέρη the parts *under water*, Plu.*Luc*.3. 2. *use nautical expressions*, Heraclit.*All*.5. **-ία**, ἡ, = ἀνδρόσακες, Ps.-Dsc.3.133.

❋ **θᾰλασσίγονος** [ῐ], ον, *sea-born*, Nonn.*D*.13.458 (v.l. θαλασσο–).

**θᾰλάσσ-ῐδιος**, α, ον, = θαλάσσιος, χῶροι Hdt.4.199. **-ίζω**, *resemble sea-water*, Diph.Siph. ap. Ath.3.92a, Dem.Ophth. ap. Aët.7.53; τὴν γεῦσιν Xenocr.60. 2. *wash in sea-water*, *PHolm*.17.2. ❋ **-ιος**, later Att. **-ττιος**, α, ον, also ος, ον E.*IT*236: (θάλασσα):—*of, in, on*, or *from the sea*, οὔ σφι θ. ἔργα μεμήλει Il.2.614; κορῶναι εἰνάλιαι, τῇσίν τε θ. ἔργα μέμηλεν Od.5.67; θ. βίος Archil.51; χέλυς Alc.51; θ. ἀνέμων ῥιπαί, κλύδων, Pi.*N*.3.59, E.*Med*.28; Χάριτες *Lyr.Adesp*.85.11; ὁ θ. [Ποσειδῶν] Ar.*Pl*.396; of animals, opp. χερσαῖα, Hdt.2.123, cf. Pl.*Euthd*.298d, Arist.*HA*487ᵃ26; πεζοί τε καὶ θ. landsmen and *seamen*, A.*Pers*.558 (lyr.); θ. ἐκρῖψαί τινα to throw one *into the sea*, S.*OT*1411; θ. νεκρός, of one drowned, Thgn.1229; πλοῖον θ. *sea-going* vessel, *POxy*.1288.6 (iv A.D.). 2. *skilled in the sea, nautical*, Hdt.7.144; γεωργοὶ καὶ οὐ θ. Th.1.142. 3. *like the sea*, in colour, τῇ χρόᾳ Plu.2.395b; = ἁλουργής, στρώματα D.S.34/5.2.35. II. θαλάσσιαι, αἱ, name of certain priestesses at Cyzicus, *CIG*3657.4. ❋ **-ίτης** [ῑ] οἶνος, ὁ, wine *sunk in the sea*, to ripen it, Plin.*HN*14.78.

**θᾰλασσο-βᾰφέω**, *dye purple*, Ph.Byz.*Mir*.2.4 (Pass.). ❋ **-βαφής**, ές, gloss on ἁλιπόρφυρος, Sch.Od.6.53. **-βίωτος** [ῐ], ον, *living on* or *by the sea*, App.*Pun*.89:—also **-βῖος**, ον, Sch.Opp.*H*.2.1. **-βρᾰχής**, ές, *soaked in brine*, Antyll.ap.Orib.8.12.3. **-γενής**, ές, (γενέσθαι) *sea-born*, κήρυκες Archestr.*Fr*.56.7. **-γράφος** [γρᾰ], ον, *describing the sea*, Tz.*H*.1.843.

**θᾰλασσ-οδο-μέτρης**, ου, ὁ, *ship's log*, Tz.*H*.12.977.

❋ **θᾰλασσο-ειδής**, ές, *like the sea, sea-green*, Hp.*Vid.Ac*.1, Democr. Eph.1, Str.17.1.35; χρῶμα Hero *Aut*.30.6. **-κλυστος**, ον, *dashed by the sea*, Sch.Barocc.S.*Aj*.696 (= 704 ed. T. Johnson, Oxon. 1705). **-κοπέω**, (κόπτω) *strike the sea with the oar, make a splash*, metaph. in Ar.*Eq*.830, Lib.*Decl*.26.18. **-κράμβη**, ἡ, *sea-kale*, *Gp*.12.1.1, Gal.6.354. **-κρᾰτέω**, *to be master of the sea*, Hdt.3.122, Th.7.48, Plb.1.7.6, Phylarch.1 J.:—Pass., *to be beaten at sea*, Demetr.Com.Vet.2. **-κρᾰτία**, ἡ, *empire of the sea*, ἡ Μίνω θ. Str.1.3.2. **-κράτωρ** [κρᾰ], ορος, ὁ, ἡ, *master of the sea*, Hdt.5.83, Th.8.63, X.*HG*1.6.2. ❋ **-μᾰχέω**, *fight by sea*, Vett.Val.354.26. ❋ **-μάχος** [μᾰ], ον, *fighting by sea*, A.D.*Adv*.188.26, Vett.Val.18.35. **-μέδων**, οντος, ὁ, *lord of the sea*, Nonn.*D*.21.95: Lacon. fem. **σαλασσομέδοισα** Alcm. 84. **-μελι**, ιτος, τό, *drink of brine and honey*, Dsc.5.12. **-μῑγής**, ές, *mixed with sea-water*, Hsch. s.v. ἁλικίαvες. **-μοθος**, ον, *fighting with the sea*, Nonn.*D*.39.370. **-νόμος**, ον, *dwelling in the sea*, Emp. 76.1, Nonn.*D*.37.265. **-παις**, παιδος, ὁ, ἡ, *child of the sea*, Lyc. 892. **-πλαγκτος**, ον, (πλάζω) *made to wander o'er the sea, sea-tost*, of ships, A.*Pr*.467; of a corpse, E.*Hec*.782:—also **-πλάνητος** [πλᾰ], ον, Sch.Opp.*H*.4.582. **-πληκτος**, ον, (πλήσσω) *sea-beaten*, νῆσος A.*Pers*.307. **-πλοος**, ον, contr. **-πλους**, ουν, gloss on ποντοπόρος, Hsch. **-ποιός**, όν, *sea-making*, [δύναμις] Porph.ap.Eus. *PE*3.11. **-πορέω**, *traverse the sea*, Call.*Ep*.59. ❋ **-πόρος**, ον, *sea-faring*, *AP*6.27.7 (Theaet.), 9.376; ὑμέναιοι Musae.2. **-πόρφῠρος**, ον, = ἁλιπόρφυρος, Suid. s.v. ἁλουργά, *AB*379. **-πρᾰσον**, τό, *sea-weed*, Ath.Mech.18.5. **-σημος**, ον, = θαλασσοπόρφυρος, *Tab. Defix.Aud*.41 *A* 1 (Megara, i A.D.). **-τείχιστος**, ον, gloss on ἁλιερκής, Sch.Pi.*O*.8.34. **-τοκος**, ον, *sea-born*, Nonn.*D*.39.341.

**θᾰλασσουργ-έω**, *to be busy with the sea*, Plb.6.52.1, Str.6.1.1, Max. Tyr.22.3, etc. **-ία**, ἡ, *business on the sea, fishing*, etc., Hp.*Vict*. 3.68 (pl.), Them.*Or*.24.305d. ❋ **-ός**, ὁ, *one who works on the sea, a fisherman* or *sailor*, Charon 10, X.*Oec*.16.7, Plb.10.8.5: as Adj., θ. ἔθνος Philostr.*VA*4.32.

**θᾰλασσ-όω**, Att. **-ττόω**, *make* or *change into sea*, ἠπείρους Arist.*Mu*. 400ᵃ27; Νεῖλος θ. τὴν Αἴγυπτον Hld.2.28. 2. *purify with sea-water*, Hsch. (Pass.). II. Pass., ναῦς θαλαττοῦται she *leaks*, Plb.16. 15.2. 2. of wine, *to be mixed with sea-water*, Thphr.*CP*6.7.6; οἶνοι τεθαλασσωμένοι Ath.1.32d, cf. Gal.13.247 (sg.), *POxy*.468 (iii A.D.). III. Med., *to be a sea-faring man*, Luc.*Ner*.1. **-ώδης**, ες, = θαλασσοειδής, λίμνη Hanno *Peripl*.14; gloss on οἰδματόεις, Sch. Opp.*H*.5.273. **-ωσις**, εως, ἡ, *inundation, submergence*, Thphr.*Fr*. 30.3, Ph.2.174.

❋ **θάλαττα, -ττεύω, -ττιος**, etc., Att. for θάλασσα, etc.

❋ **θάλεα** [ᾰ], Lacon. **σάλ-** (v. infr.), τά, *good cheer, happy thoughts*, of the sleeping Astyanax, θαλέων ἐμπλησάμενος κῆρ Il.22.504; ἐν σάλεσσι πολλοῖς ἥμενος Alcm.10; θαλέεσσιν ἀνατρέφειν τινά Call.*Fr*. *anon*.31.—In form and accent pl. of θάλος, in meaning closer to θάλεια, θαλία.

**θᾰλέθω**, poet. for θάλλω (cf. θαλέω), *bloom, thrive*, used by Hom. only in part., θάμνος ἐλαίης.. θαλέθων Od.23.191, cf. Ibyc.1.6, A.R. 2.843; βίου θαλέθοντος Emp.20.3; of men, ἠΐθεοι θαλέθοντες Od.6.63; θαλέθοντα τόκον *IG*14.1363; θαλέθεσκες ἐν εἴαρι *AP*11.374 (Maced.); αἰεὶ θαλέθοντι βίῳ *Lyr.Adesp*.98 (= *Trag.Adesp*.373); σύες θαλέθοντες ἀλοιφῇ *swelling, wantoning* in fat, Il.9.467, cf. 23.32: c. acc., ποίην λειμῶνες θαλέθουσιν Theoc.25.16.

**θάλεια** [θᾰ], ἡ, *rich, plentiful*, : in Ep. always of banquets, θεῶν ἐν δαιτὶ θαλείῃ Od.8.76, Hes.*Op*.742; θεοῦ ἐς δαῖτα θάλειαν Od. 3.420, cf. 8.99, Il.7.475; so later, Pherecr.152; πίνειν ἐν δαιτὶ θ. Hermipp.82.11; θ. ἑορτὴν ἀγάγωμεν Anacr.54; Δαὶς θ., πρεσβίστη θεῶν S.*Fr*.605; μοῖραν θάλειαν *a goodly* portion, Pi.*N*.10.53; θ. ἥβα *bloom of youth*, B.3.89; without δαίς, dub. cj. for θαλάσσης in Alex. Aet.3.15: in form and accent (cf. ἐλάχεια, λίγεια and Eust.742.36) a fem. Adj., as if from θαλύς: masc. θαλείοις στέφεσιν Emp.112. 6. II. as Subst., = θαλία I, in pl., Pl.*R*.573d (nisi hoc legend.). 2. v. θαλλία II. III. as pr. n., Θάλεια, ἡ, one of the Muses, Hes.*Th*.77; later, the Muse of Comedy, Θαλίη *AP*9.505, cf. Plu.2.744f, 746c. 2. one of the Graces, *patroness of festive meetings*, ib.778d; Θαλίη in Hes.*Th*.909. IV. Pythag. name for *six*, *Theol.Ar*.38.

**θᾰλερόμμᾰτος**, ον, *bright-eyed*, αἰθήρ Orph.*H*.80.5.

**θᾰλεροποιός**, όν, *making full of bloom*, Sch.Hes.*Th*.138.

❋ **θᾰλερός**, ά, όν, (θάλλω, θαλεῖν) *stout, sturdy, buxom*, in Hom. of persons, θ. αἰζηοί, πόσις, παρακοίτης, Il.3.26, 8.190, 6.430, cf. Pi.*N*. 1.71; γόνος *h.Ven*.104; τοκεύς Hes.*Th*.138. 2. *blooming, fresh*, θ. γάμος the marriage *of a youthful pair*, Od.6.66, 20.74; Ὀϊκλῆος θ. λέχος εἰσαναβᾶσα Hes.*Cat.Oxy*.2075.25; θαλερὸς ἥβης χρόνος E.*El*. 20; πρωθήβης ἔαρος θαλερώτερος Alex.Aet.3.7; of plants, ἀμάρακος Chaerem.14.16; ἄνθεον *IG*12(7).410.17 (Amorgos). II. of parts of the body, *stout, sturdy*, μηρώ Il.15.113; χαίτη *luxuriant* mane, 17.439; θ. ἀλοιφή *rich* fat, Od.8.476: hence generally, θ. κατὰ δάκρυ χέουσα shedding *big* tears, Il.6.496, cf. 24.9, 794, etc.; θ. δέ οἱ ἔκπεσε δάκρυ 2.266; θαλερώτερα δάκρυα Mosch.4.56 (so θαλερώτερον ἔκλαεν Theoc.14.32); θ. γόος the *thick and frequent* sob, Od.10.457; θ. φωνή *strong* voice, Il.17.696, al.; μῦθοι *impassioned, torrential*, A.R.4. 1072; θαλερώτερον πνεῦμα a *more genial* wind, dub. in A.*Th*.707 (lyr.); θαλερὸν πνεῦμα *thick*, i.e. *laboured* or *rapid*, breathing, v.l. for θολερὸν πν. in Hp.*Prorrh*.1.39, cf. Gal.16.596; θ. ὕπνος *deep* sleep, E.*Ba*. 692. 2. later θ. πρόσωπον, glossed by εὐεκτικὸν καὶ εὔχρουν, Gal. 16.596; τὸ σῶμα τοῦ ζῴου, μέχρι μὲν ἔμπνουν ἐστὶ καὶ θ. Plu.2.955c, cf. E.*Supp*.62 (lyr.).

**θᾰλερῶπις**, ιδος, ἡ, (ὤψ) = θαλερόμματος, Ἠριγένεια *AP*7.204 (Agath.).

**θᾰλέω**, Dor. for θηλέω (q.v.).

**θᾰλέω**, = θαλέθω, Q.S.11.96 codd., Nonn.*D*.16.78; θαλέων Hp *Insomn*.90; θαλέεσκε v.l. for θαλέθεσκε in Mosch.2.67.

**Θαλῆς**, ὁ, gen. Θάλεω, dat. Θαλῇ, acc. Θαλῆν; gen. also Θαλοῦ Str. 1.1.11; and in Poets Θάλητος, acc. Θάλητα, Call.*Fr*.94, 96, Epigr.ap. D.L.1.34, 39:—*Thales* of Miletus, Hdt.1.74, etc.

❋ **θᾰλία**, Ion. **-ίη**, ἡ, (θάλλω) *abundance, good cheer*, τρέφεται θαλίῃ ἔνι πολλῇ Il.9.143, 285: in pl., *festivities*, μετ' ἀθανάτοισι θεοῖσι τέρπεται ἐν θαλίῃς Od.11.603, cf. *h.Merc*.56, Hes.*Op*.115, Archil.9, Xenoph. 1.12 (sg.), Pi.*O*.7.94, *Trag.Adesp*.397 (anap.), Ar.*Nu*.309, *Pax* 780 (both lyr.), *Av*.733 (anap.); εἶναι ἐν θαλίῃσι Hdt.3.27; θ. κισσοφόροι E.*Ba*.384 (lyr.); of a *funeral-feast*, ἀμφ' ὁσίῃ θαλίῃ.. ἄνακτος Orac. ap.Plu.*Arat*.53. II. v. θαλλία II. III. as pr. n., v. θάλεια III.

**θᾰλιάζω**, *enjoy oneself, make merry*, Plu.2.746f, al. (θαλειάζω ib. 357e); ἑορτὴν θ. Polyaen.4.15.

**θάλικτρον**, τό, prob. *Thalictrum minus, meadow-rue*, Dsc.4.97 (sed fort. θαλίητρον: **θαλίκτρον** Gal.11.884).

❋ **θαλιοποιοί**, οἱ, *leather-covered-box-makers*, Hsch. (Cf. σαλία, θολία.)

**θαλλία**, ἡ, = κάππαρις, Dsc.2.173. II. *foliage, leaf-buds* or *twigs*, esp. of the olive, Thphr.*CP*5.1.3 (cod. Urb.), Ath.11.459, Dsc. 5.75 (v.l. in 2.70), Antyll.ap.Orib.10.23.20, Aët.6.29: pl., Thphr. *CP*1.20.3 (θαλλίας cod. Urb., θαλείας vulg. as in 3.5.1 (sg.), Porph. *Antr*.33); in codd. sts. θαλία, as Thphr.*HP*2.2.12, 2.3.3, v.l. in *CP* 5.1.3; βάτου θαλία Sor.2.41.

❋ **θάλλῐνος**, η, ον, (θαλλός) *of* or *for young shoots*, στέφανος *IG*12(1). 162.3 (Rhodes); ἀγγεῖα Sch.Ar.*Av*.799: **θαλλῑνώδης**, ες, *covered with shoots*, of the Wooden Horse, Cyr.

**θαλλίον**, τό, in pl., *presents* (cf. θαλλός III), *POxy*.1481.7 (ii A.D.): pl. written θάλεια, Wilcken *Chr*.323.20 (ii A.D.).

❋ **θαλλός**, ὁ, (θάλλω) *young shoot, young branch*, Od.17.224, S.*El*. 422, Theoc.4.45, etc.: generally, *branch*, *Gp*.11.10.3; esp. of the olive (cf. Tim.*Lex*. s.v. θαλλός), ἐστεφανῶσθαι ἐλαίης θαλλῷ Hdt.7. 19; ἐλαίας θ. E.*IT*1101 (lyr.); and freq. without ἐλαίας, A.*Ch*.1035, S. *OC*474, etc.; ἱκτὴρ θ. E.*Supp*.10, cf. A.*Ch*.1035; θ. χρυσοῦς *IG*1².287. 200; στεφανῶσαι θαλλοῦ στεφάνῳ as a mark of distinction, Aeschin. 3.187, cf. *IG*2².207, 229, Phld.*Ind.Sto*.68, etc.; στέφανος θαλλοῦ χρυσοῦς *IG*2².1388.33; στέφανος τὸ νικητήριον θαλλοῦ Pl.*Lg*.943c; prov., θαλλὸν προσείοντες ἄγουσι they entice, as one does cattle, by holding out *a green bough*, Id.*Phdr*.230d; θαλλῷ προδειχθέντι ἀκολουθεῖν Luc. *Herm*.68, cf. Lib.*Ep*.212.3. II. θαλλοί, οἱ, *palm-leaves*, which were plaited into baskets, *Gp*.10.6.2. III. *gift* (prob. at first a branch, later in other forms) given to a landlord by one whose bid for a lease was accepted, *UPZ*112 iii 15 (ii B.C.); repeated annually, θαλλῶν κατ' ἔτος ἄρτων ἡμιαρταβίου καὶ ἀλέκτορος *PRyl*.167.16 (i A.D.), etc.; esp. at festivals, *PAmh*.2.93.11 (ii A.D.); *gratuity* additional to wages, *PCair.Preis*.31.21 (ii A.D.); any *gift* given annually at a festival, Ps.-Callisth.1.32.

**θαλλο-φᾰγέω**, *eat young olive-shoots*, Ath.11.587a. **-φορέω**, *carry olive-shoots*, Cratin.31, Pherecr.57, Dicaearch.Hist.46. **-φόρος**, ον, *carrying young olive-shoots*, as the old men did at the Pan-

athenaea, Ar.*V*.544 (lyr.), X.*Smp*.4.17; as a name of Heracles, *IG* 14.904.

**θάλλω**, Hes.*Op*.173, *h.Cer*.402, etc.: aor. 1 ἔθηλα (ἀν–) Ael.*NA* 2.25, 9.21: aor. 2 θάλε *h.Hom*.19.33; ἀν-έθαλον Lxx *Wi*.4.4, *Ep.Phil*.4.10: pf. τέθηλα, in Hom. only part. in pres. sense τεθηλώς, Ep. fem. τεθᾰλυῖα, and 3 sg. plpf. τεθήλει Od.5.69; 3 sg. ind. τέθηλε Hes. *Op*.227, Emp.77, S.*Ph*.259; Aeol. and Dor. τέθᾱλα Sapph.*Supp*.25.12, Pi.*Fr*.129.5, B.9.40, *IG*3.171; subj. τεθήλῃ Epigr.ap.Pl.*Phdr*. 264d; inf. τεθηλέναι Id.*Cra*.414a; part. τεθᾱλώς prob. in A.*Supp*. 107 (lyr.):—Pass., fut. θᾰλήσομαι (ἀνα-) *AP*7.281 (Heraclid.): (cf. θηλέω):—*sprout, grow, thrive*, esp. of fruit-trees, ἐρινεὸς..φύλλοισι τεθηλώς Od.12.103; τεθήλει δὲ σταφυλῇσι, of a vine, 5.69; ἄνθεσι γαῖα θάλλει *h.Cer*. l.c.; (δένδρεα) τέθηλε καρπῶν ἀφθονίῃσι Emp.77; ὦ χρυσέᾳ κόμᾳ θάλλων Λοξία Pi.*I*.7(6).49; πώγωνι θάλλων S.*Ichn*.358: abs., καρπὸν τρὶς ἔτεος θάλλοντα Hes.*Op*.173; θάλλει κατ' ἦμαρ αἰεὶ νάρκισσος S.*OC*681 (lyr.), etc.: freq. in pf. part., as Adj., *luxuriant*, τεθαλυῖά τ' ὀπώρη Od.11.192; τεθαλυῖά τ' ἀλωή 6.293: also, c. acc. cogn., οὐ δένδρε' ἔθαλλεν χῶρος the place *grew* no trees, Pi.*O*.3.23, cf. *AP*9.78 (s.v.l., Leon.); ἐν φύλλοισι θαλλούσης βίον ξανθῆς ἐλαίας (Dind. ἴσον) A.*Pers*.616; simply, *bloom*, Thphr.*HP*1.1.2; but of σίκυοι, etc., ἡ ἀπὸ τοῦ ὕδατος ἀτμὶς οἷον θάλλοντας παρέχει Id.*CP*5.6.5. b. of other natural objects, τεθαλυῖά τ' ἐέρση *copious* dew, Od. 13.245; ῥάχιν τεθαλυῖαν ἀλοιφῇ *rich* with fat, Il.9.208, cf. Od.13.410; εἰλαπίνη τεθαλυίῃ at a *sumptuous* feast, 11.415. 2. of persons, states or conditions, *bloom*, θ. ἁπαλὸν χρόα Archil.100; *thrive, flourish*, Εἰρήνη τεθαλυῖα Hes.*Th*.902; θάλλοισα εὐδαιμονία, ἀρετά, Pi.*P*.7.19, *I*.5(4).17; πατρὸς θάλλοντος S.*Ant*.703, cf. *Ph*.420, etc.; ζῶν καὶ θάλλων alive and *prosperous*, Id.*Tr*.235; ζῇ καὶ θάλλει [ἡ παίδευσις] Antipho Soph.60; θάλε πόθος *h.Hom*.19.33; Ἔρως ἐπὶ Χαλκιδέων θάλλει πόλεσιν *Carm.Pop*.44; Ἔρως τότε μὲν θ. τε καὶ ζῇ, ὅταν εὐπορήσῃ, τότε δὲ ἀποθνήσκει Pl.*Smp*.203e; θ. καὶ εὐδαιμονεῖ χώρα καὶ πόλις Id. *Lg*.945d: c. dat. modi, θάλλουσιν δ' ἀγαθοῖσι Hes.*Op*.236; ἀγλαΐῃ τεθαλυῖαι [δμφαί] Id.*Sc*.276; τοῖσι (sc. ἀνδράσι) τέθηλε πόλις Id.*Op*. 227; πόλις ἐλευθερίᾳ τεθαλυῖα Simon.102; θ. ἀρεταῖς Pi.*O*.9.16; ἐλπίδι B.9.40; εὐγενεῖ τέκνων σπορᾷ S.*Ant*.1164; παρρησίᾳ E.*Hipp*. 422; δαίμων ἀφθίτῳ θ. βίῳ Critias 25.17 D.; θ. ἐπὶ γυμνάδος ἔργοις *Epigr.Gr*.233 (Chios). 3. of disease and the like, in bad sense, *to be fresh, active*, ἡ δ' ἐμὴ νόσος ἀεὶ τέθηλε S.*Ph*.259; πήματα..ἀεὶ θάλλοντα μᾶλλον ἢ καταφθίνοντα *waxing*, Id.*El*.260; ἔρις θάλλει E.*Ph*.812 (lyr.): c. dat., ἀφροσύναις θάλλουσ' Ὕβρις B.14.58. b. τοῖσι αὐτοῖσιν ὅ τε σπλὴν θάλλει καὶ τὸ σῶμα φθίνει the spleen *becomes swollen*, Hp. *Loc.Hom*.24; also τεθηλός (in neutral sense) of the liver, Id.*VM*22.

**Θαλλώ**, οῦς, ἡ, one of the Ὧραι, a divinity of increase, Jusj.ap. Lycurg.77, Paus.9.35.2.

**θάλος** [ᾰ], εος, τό, prop. = θαλλός, but only nom. and acc. in metaph. sense of *scion, child*, φίλον θ. Il.22.87; λευσσόντων τοιόνδε θ. Od.6.157; γλυκερόν, νέον θ., *h.Cer*.66, 187; σεμνὸν θ. Ἀλκαΐδᾶν Pi.*O*.6.68, cf. 2.45, E.*El*.15, etc.—For the pl., v. θάλεα, τά.

**θαλπ-εινός**, ή, όν, = θαλπνός, but as gloss on ἰσχνόν, *EM*479.22. **-είω**, Ep. for θάλπω, ib.620.46. **-ιάω**, (θάλπω) *to be or become warm*, εὖ θαλπιόων right *warm and comfortable*, Od.19.319, cf. Arat. 1073. **-νός**, ή, όν, *warming, fostering*, θαλπνότερον ἄστρον Pi.*O*. 1.6. **-ος**, εος, τό, *warmth, heat*, esp. *summer-heat*, opp. χειμών, A.*Ag*.565, 969; ἐν μεσημβρίαις θ. Id.*Supp*.747; θ. θεοῦ the sun's *heat*, S.*Tr*.145, etc.; μεσημβρινοῖσι θάλπεσιν A.*Th*.431, 446; in Prose, θάλπος, opp. ψῦχος, Hp.*Aph*.3.4: pl., ῥίγη καὶ θάλπη, ψύχη καὶ θ., X.*Oec*.7.23, *Cyr*.1.2.10. 2. metaph., *sting, smart*, [τοξευμάτων] S.*Ant*.1086; of love, *AP*6.207 (Arch.). **-τέον**, *one must warm*, Aët.5.68, *Hippiatr*.1. **-τήριον**, *fomentum, fomes, Gloss*. **-τήριος**, ον, *warming*, σάνδαλα..ποδῶν θ. *AP*6.206.1 (Antip. Sid.). **-ω**, fut. -ψω Orph.*Fr*.258, Alciphr.2.4: fut. Med. in pass. sense θάλψομαι Id.3.42:—*heat, soften by heat*, Od.21.179, al.:—Pass., ἐτήκετο κασσίτερος ὡς .. θαλφθεὶς Hes.*Th*.864, cf. S.*Tr*.697: metaph., *to be softened, deceived*, αἴ κε μὴ θαλφθῇ λόγοις Ar.*Eq*.210. II. *heat, warm*, without any notion of *softening*, καῦμ' ἔθαλπε (sc. ἡμᾶς) S. *Ant*.417; θερμὴ ἡμᾶς ἀκτὶς θ. Ar.*Av*.1092; *keep warm*, χλανιδίων ἐρειπίοις θάλπουσα καὶ ψύχουσα *Trag.Adesp*.7: prov., θ. τὸν δίφρον, of an idle life, Herod.1.37; θ. τὰς κοχώνας Id.7.48; τὴν βαίτην θάλπουσαν εὖ ib.129:—Pass., Hp.*Aff*.4; θάλπεσθαι τοῦ θέρους *to be warm* in summer, X.*Cyr*.5.1.11; τῷ πυρὶ θάλψομαι Alciphr.3.42: metaph., ἔτι ἁλίῳ θάλπεσθαι *to be alive*, Pi.*N*.4.14. 2. *warm at the fire, dry*, θάλπεται ῥάκη S.*Ph*.38, cf. E.*Hel*.183 (lyr.). 3. *hatch*, ᾠὰ *Gp*.14.1.4: so abs., *sit*, ib.3; θ. ἐπὶ τῶν νοσσῶν, ἐπὶ τῶν ᾠῶν, Lxx *De*. 22.6. III. metaph., of passion, *heat, inflame*, ἡ Διὸς θάλπει κέαρ ἔρωτι A.*Pr*.590, cf. S.*Fr*.474 (Pass.); ἔθαλψεν ἄτης σπασμός Id.*Tr*. 1082:—Pass., ἱμέρου βέλει τεθάλφθαι πρός τινος A.*Pr*.650; θάλπῃ (2 sg.) ἀνηκέστῳ πυρί S.*El*.888; εἴ σευ θάλπεταί τι τῶν ἔνδον Herod. 2.81. 2. *comfort*, ὕπνος..θάλπει κέαρ B.*Fr*.3.11, cf. *Fr*.16.2, *Com. Adesp*.5.16 D.; *cherish, foster*, ἄλλον θάλπε φίλον Theoc.14.38; ὡς ἐὰν τροφὸς θάλπῃ τὰ ἑαυτῆς τέκνα 1*Ep.Thess*.2.7; τὴν ἑαυτοῦ σάρκα *Ep.Eph*.5.29; τὸ ἀσθενοῦν Alciphr.2.4; θ. καὶ τρέφειν *PMasp*.6*B* 132 (vi A.D.); τὴν πόλιν θ. *tend it with fostering care*, *OGI*194.5 (Egypt, i B.C.). 3. ἐμὲ οὐδὲν θ. ἡ δόξα I *care* nothing for glory, Alciphr.2.2; ἐμὲ οὐδὲν θ. κέρδος Aristaenet.1.24. IV. intr., *to be full of heat, vigorous*, Arist.*Pr*.879ᵃ33; θάλψαι τρεῖς ποίας *to live* three summers, *AP*7.731 (Leon.). **-ωρή**, ἡ, *warming*: metaph., *comfort, consolation*, οὐ γὰρ ἔτ' ἄλλη θαλπωρή Il.6.412, cf. Od.1.167; ἀντὶ δὲ θαλπωρᾶν [θῆκα γονεῦσι γόους] *IG*4.623 (Argos): pl., Tryph.128.—In late Prose, Jul.*Or*.8.243c.

**θᾰλυκρός**, ά, όν, *hot, glowing*, ἁπάντῃ πάντα θ. ἐγώ Call.*Fr.anon*. 69; θ. κέντρον ἐρωμανίης *AP*5.219 (Agath.):—hence **θαλυκρέομαι**, = ψεύδομαι, Hsch.

**θαλ-ύνω**, = θάλλειν ποιῶ, Hsch. **-ύπτω**, = θάλπω, aor. 1 inf. θαλύψαι, Id.; cf. ἀκροθάλυπτος.

**θᾰλύσια** [ῠ], τά, (θάλος) *offerings of first-fruits*, made to Artemis, Il.9.534; later to Demeter, Theoc.7.3; to Demeter and Dionysus, Men.Rh.p.391 S. 2. θαλύσιος [ἄρτος] bread *made from the first-fruits*, Ath.3.114a.

**θᾰλῠσιάς**, άδος, fem.Adj., κούρη θ. a priestess of Demeter (cf. foreg.), Nonn.*D*.12.103; θ. ὁδός a journey *to the* θαλύσια, Theoc.7.31.

**θαλύσσω**, = θάλπω, Hsch. (Pass.):—also **θαλύεσθαι** (dub. l.), Id.

**θάλψις**, εως, ἡ, (θάλπω) *warming, fomenting*, Hp.*Acut*.21, S.E. *M*.7.354, Ruf.*Sat.Gon*.47. 2. opp. ψῦξις, of seasons, Hp.*Aph*. 3.1; *heat, heating property*, Gal.18(1).228. II. *cherishing*, *PLond*. 5.1727.10 (vi A.D.).

**θᾰμά** (oxyt., A.D.*Adv*.153.5, Hdn.Gr.2.141), Adv. *often*, Il.16. 207, Od.16.27, Pi.*O*.1.17, B.12.193, S.*El*.524, Ar.*Eq*.990 (lyr.), *Pl*. 1166, Pl.*Phd*.72e, X.*Mem*.2.1.22; θ. τῆς ἡμέρας *POxy*.1158.4 (iii A.D.). (Orig. 'thickly', cf. θαμέες, θάμνος.)

**θαμάκης**· σύμβιος, Cyr.

**θᾰμάκῐς**, Adv. = θαμά, Pi.*I*.1.28, *N*.10.38.

**θαματροχεῖ**· οὐχ ἡσυχάζει, Hsch.

**θαμβ-αίνω**, = θαμβέω, *to be astonished at*, Pi.*O*.3.32, v.l. for θαυμαίνω in *h.Ven*.84. **-ᾰλέος**, α, ον, *astonished*, Nonn.*D*.1.126. II. = θαυμαστός, φοβερός, Hsch. **-ευτής**, οῦ, ὁ, *terrifying* person, Aq. *Ze*.3.4. **-εύω**, *terrify*, Id.*Ge*.49.4. **-έω**, *to be astounded*, οἱ δὲ ἰδόντες θάμβησαν Il.8.77, cf. B.5.84; οἱ δ' ἀνὰ θυμὸν ἐθάμβεον Od.4.638, etc.; καὐτὸς τεθάμβηκ' S.*Ant*.1246; ἐθάμβησεν δὲ πᾶς..ὅμιλος E.*Ion* 1205. 2. c. acc., *to be astonished at*, θάμβησαν δ' ὄρνιθας Od.2.155, cf. 16.178; τὸν ἐθάμβεον Ἄρτεμίς τε καὶ Ἀθάνα Pi.*N*.3.50; τέρας δ' ἐθάμβουν A.*Supp*.570 (lyr.): in late Prose, Plu.*Aem*.34. II. later also causal, *alarm*, Lxx 2*Ki*.22.5; τοὺς ὀφθαλμούς τινος *PMag.Par*. 1.237:—Pass., *to be astounded*, *Ev.Marc*.1.27, *POxy*.654.7, *PMag. Leid.W*.11.39; τεθαμβημένος astounded, Plu.*Brut*.20; διά τινος Id. *Caes*.[45]. **-ημα**, ατος, τό, *alarm, terror*, Man.4.559. **-ησις**, εως, ἡ, = foreg., Aq.*Ps*.30(31).23, Man.4.365. II. *haste*, Aq.*De*.16.3, *Is*.52.12. **-ήτειρα**, ἡ, *the fearful one*, of the Furies, Orph.*A*.973 (pl.). **-ητός**, ή, όν, *astonishing*, Lyc.552, Maiist.1. **-όομαι**, *to be terrified*, pf. part. τεθαμβωμένος, Aët.16.66 (s.v.l.). **-ος**, εος, τό, also ὁ Simon.237, Lxx *Ec*.12.5 (pl.): (τέθηπα):—*amazement*, θ. δ' ἔχεν εἰσορόωντας Il.4.79; θ. δ' ἕλε πάντας ἰδόντας Od.3.372; θάμβει δυσφόρῳ τερπνῷ τε μιχθεὶς Pi.*N*.1.55; θάμβει ἐκπλαγέντες E.*Rh*.291, cf. Ar.*Av*.781 (lyr.), Th.6.31, Pl.*Phdr*.254c: pl., Onos.41.2. 2. in objective sense, θάμβοι *terrors* in the way, Lxx l.c.; *object of wonder*, *Epigr.Gr*.1068 (Gerasa). **-ός**, ή, όν, *astonished*, Eust.906.53.

**θᾰμ-έες**, οἱ, gen. θαμέω[ν] dub. in Sapph.*Supp*.15.1; dat. θάμέσι, acc. θάμέας (nom.sg. masc. θαμύς A.D.*Adv*.153.4): fem. nom. and acc. θαμειαί, -άς (oxyt., Aristarch.ap.Hdn.Gr.2.22):—poet. Adj. used only in pl., *crowded, close-set*, ὀδόντες..ὑὸς θαμέες ἔχον Il.10.264; ὀδόντες πυκνοὶ καὶ θ. Od.12.92; θαμέες γὰρ ἄκοντες..ἀΐσσουσι Il.11.552, 17. 661; ἴκρια..ἀραρὼν θαμέσι σταμίνεσσι Od.5.252; πυραί, λίθοι θ., Il.1.52, 12.287; *frequent*, λυχμοί Nic.*Th*.434, *Al*.581 (in Comp. θαμειότερος): Comp. θαμύντερος Hsch. Adv. θαμέως, = θαμά, Alc.*Supp*.25.5 (dub.), Hp.*Superf*.25, Max.600. **-ίζω**, (θαμά) *come often*, πάρος γε μὲν οὔ τι θαμίζεις Il.18.386, al.; ἅμα νηῒ πολυκληῗδι θαμίζων *plying*, Od.8.161; θ. εἰς τούσδε τοὺς τόπους Pl.*Hp.Ma*.281b; ἐφ' ἡμᾶς X.*Cyr*.7.3.2; κεῖσε A.R.2.451; ἐν δονάκεσσι θ. *to haunt* them, Nic.*Al*.578; ἐν ταῖς πομπαῖς Corn.*ND*30; τοῖς μαχομένοις Chor. in *Hermes* 17.227; σοφίης ἐπ' ἄκροισι θαμίζειν v.l. for θοάζειν in Emp.4.8. 2. *to be accustomed*: c. part., οὔ τι κομιζόμενός γε θάμιζεν he *was* not *wont* to be so cared for, Od.8.451; οὐ δὲ θαμίζεις ἡμῖν καταβαίνων we do not *often see* you coming down, Pl.*R*.328c; μινύρεται θαμίζουσα μάλιστ' ἀηδών mourns *constantly*, S.*OC*672 (lyr.): abs., διὰ τὸ θαμίζειν by dint of *repetition*, Pl.*Lg*.843b. II. Med., = Act., τῇδε (τῷδε codd.) S.*Fr*.503.

**θᾰμῐνάκις**, Adv. = θαμάκις, θαμά, Hp.*Mul*.2.203.

**θᾰμῐνός** and **θαμῖνός** (*h.Merc*.44, Call.*Aet*.3.1.36, Nic.*Th*.239 (v.l.); **θαμεινός** Choerob. in *An.Ox*.2.180), ή, όν, *crowded, close-set*, Call.*Cer*. 65, *Lyr.Alex.Adesp*.7.14: usu. neut. pl. θαμινά, as Adv. = θαμά, Pi. *O*.1.53, *Pae*.6.16, Ar.*Pl*.292 (lyr.), X.*Mem*.3.11.15, *An*.4.1.16 (v.l. θαμεινά): sg., θαμινόν A.R.3.1266: Sup. -ώτατος Suid. Adv. -νῶς Hsch.: Comp. -ώτερον Parth.*Fr*.29.

**θάμιξ**· ἀλώπηξ, Hsch.

**θάμνα**, ἡ, *wine from pressed grapes*, a local term, *Gp*.6.13.2; so prob. τὴν προκυκλίην θάμνην Herod.6.90.

**θαμν-άς**, άδος, ἡ, (θάμνος) = ῥίζα, *EM*442.23. **-ίσκος**, ὁ, Dim. of θάμνος, Dsc.4.108, Herod.Med.ap.Orib.8.4.6, Gal.2.355.

**θάμνισον**· ἀποκάλυψον, Hsch.

**θαμνῖτις**, ιδος, ἡ, *shrubby*, ῥάμνος Nic.*Th*.883.

**θαμνο-ειδής**, ές, *shrubby*, Thphr.*HP*3.17.3, Crateuas ap.Dsc.2. 127. **-μήκης** ῥάβδος *a long* stick *cut from a bush*, Ion Trag.40.

**θάμνος**, ὁ, also ἡ D.S.2.49: (cf. θαμέες):—*bush, shrub*, καταπτήξας ὑπὸ θάμνῳ Il.22.191; θάμνῳ ὑπ' ἀμφικόμῳ 17.677; θάμνοις ἐν πυκινοῖσι in the thick *copse*, Od.5.471; θ. δρυὸς Pi.*Pae*.4.52; θ. ἐλαίης a *bushy* olive, Od.23.190, cf. Archil.6.1, A.*Ag*.1316, E.*Ba*.722, S.*El*.55, Ar. *Pax* 1298 (hex.), Pl.*R*.432b, etc.; θ. τὸ ἀπὸ ῥίζης πολύκλαδον Thphr. *HP*1.3.1.

**θαμνοφάγος** [ᾰ], ον, *eating shrubs*, S.E.*P*.1.56.

**θαμνώδης**, ες, = θαμνοειδής, Thphr.*HP*3.12.1 (Comp.), *CP*5.12.5.

⊛ **θᾰμῠρίζω**, *assemble*, Hsch.; *take part in a meeting*, θαμυριδδόντων [τῶν δεῖνα] *BCH*50.401 (Thespiae); **θάμῠρις**, ἡ, *assembly*, Hsch.

**Θάμῠρις** [ᾰ], ὁ, dat. Θαμύριδι Paus.10.30.8, Θαμύρι v.l. in Poll.4.75; acc. Θάμυριν Il.2.595, E.*Rh.*925:—*Thamyris*, a Thracian bard, ll. cc., Str.7 *Fr.*35:—Att. **Θαμύρας** (cf. Cyr.) S.*Fr.*245 (lyr.), Pl.*R.*620a, etc.

**θᾰμῠρός**, ά, όν, *frequented*, ὁδός Hsch.

**θαμύς**, v. θαμέες.

**θᾰνάσῐμος** [νᾰ], ον, (θάνατος) *deadly, fatal*, Hp.*Aph.*2.1, Pl.*R.*610e, etc.; τύχαι A.*Ag.*1276; πέσημα S.*Aj.*1033; χείρωμα Id.*OT*560; πέπλος Id.*Tr.*758; φάρμακα E.*Ion*616, Ph.*Bel.*103.31, cf. Metrod.53, etc.; θηρία θ., *of poisonous* reptiles, Plb.1.56.4: θανάσιμα, τά, *poisons*, *Ev.Marc.*16.18, Dsc.4.108, Gal.14.154. Adv. -μως, τύπτειν to strike *with deadly blow*, Antipho 4.3.4: neut. pl. as Adv., ἀσπίδες -μα δάκνουσαι D.S.1.87. 2. *belonging to death*, θ. αἷμα the *life*-blood, A.*Ag.*1019 (lyr.); μέλψασα θ. γόον having sung her *death*-song, ib.1445; θ. ἐκπνοαί E.*Hipp.*1438. II. of persons, *near death*, S.*Ph.*819; θ. ἤδη ὄντα Pl.*R.*408b; *liable to the death-penalty*, *Abh.Berl.Akad.* 1925(5).21 (Cyrene). 2. *dead*, S.*Aj.*517; θ. βεβηκότα Id.*OT*959.

**θᾰνᾰτ-άω**, Desiderat. of θανεῖν, *desire to die*, Pl.*Phd.*64b, *Ax.*366c, Alex.211, J.*BJ*3.7.18, Gal.8.190, Max.Tyr.26.9, Philostr.*VA*7.31. II. *to be moribund*, Ph.2.505, Lyd.*Mag.*3.40, v.l. in 45. **-ηγός**, όν, *death-bringing*, epith. of Hecate, *PMag.Par.*1.2865; f.l. for θάργηλος, Timocl.7. **-ήριος**, ον, v. θανατήσιος. **-ήσιμος**, v. sq. ⊛ **-ήσιος**, ον, = θανάσιμος, rejected by Poll.5.132 (cod. C; -ήσιμος cett.), but found in Afric.*Cest.*14,16,17 (*Math.Vett.*p.294 Thévenot); cf. θανατήσιον, οὐ θανάσιμον λέγουσιν, Phot.; **θανατήριον** ἀξιοῦσιν οὐ θανάσιμον λέγειν *AB*99 (quoting Pl.*R.*Bk.ii, E.*Med.*). **-ηρός**, ά, όν, *poisonous*, βοτάνη Eust.1336.20; γῆ Sch.rec.S.*OT*181.

**θᾰνᾰτηφορ-ία**, ἡ, *a causing of death*, *AP*5.113 (Maec.). **-ος**, ον, *death-bringing*, αἶσα A.*Ch.*369 (lyr.); περίοδος θ. cycle *of mortality*, Pl.*R.*617d; of hurts or accidents, Hp.*Art.*48; of a surgical operation, Antyll.ap.Orib.45.17.6; ῥίζα ἐν Αἰθιοπίᾳ, of arrow-poison, *Acokanthera Schimperi*, Thphr.*HP*9.15.2; ὀδύναι Arist.*PA*672ᵃ36; γενέθλα.. θ. κεῖται *causing death by contagion*, S.*OT*181 (lyr.); πᾶσαι μεταβολαὶ πολιτειῶν θ. X.*HG*2.3.32; ἁμαρτία Lxx *Nu.*18.22; δίκαι *capital* trials, *Not.Arch.*4.19 (Cyrene, Aug.); ἐπιστολή Hdn.4.12.8; περιστάσεις Vett.Val.225.7. Adv. -ρως, νοσεῖν Phld.*Rh.*2.148S.: neut. sg. as Adv., ἐπλήγη οὐχὶ -φόρον Aen.Tact.27.9; but -φόρον ᾄδειν to sing *a death song*, *AP*11.186 (Nicarch.).

⊛ **θᾰνᾰτ-ιάω**, = θανατάω II, Luc.*Peregr.*32, S.E.*M.*9.153. **-ικός**, ή, όν, *deadly*, θ. ἐγκλήματα *capital* charges, D.S.37.5; νόμοι, ζημία, J.*BJ*3.5.7, *AJ*15.11.5; δίκη θ. trial *on a capital charge*, Plu.*Per.*10, *Alex.*42; of planetary influences, Vett.Val.129.4. 2. Medic., *fatal*, συνδρομή Gal.16.545. 3. Adv. -κῶς, λέγεσθαι, as expl. of δυσηλεγής, Eust.321.40. **-όεις**, εσσα, εν, *deadly*, ἁμαρτήματα S.*Ant.*1262 (lyr.); μόρος E.*IA*1288 (lyr.).

**θᾰνᾰτοποιός**, όν, *causing death*, Sch.S.*Tr.*858.

**θάνᾰτος** [θᾰ], ὁ, (θνῄσκω) *death*, whether natural or violent, Hom., etc.; τῶν ὑπαλευάμενος θάνατον *the death threatened* by them, Od.15.275; ὡς θάνον οἰκτίστῳ θανάτῳ 11.412; θάνατόνδε *to death*, Il.16.693, 22.297; θανάτου τέλος, μοῖρα, A.*Th.*906 (lyr.), *Pers.*917 (anap.), etc.; θανάτου πέρι καὶ ζωᾶς for life and *death*, Pi.*N.*9.29; θ. ἢ βίον φέρει S.*Aj.*802; θάνατος μὲν τάδ' ἀκούειν Id.*OC*529; θανάτῳ ἴσον πάθος Id.*Aj.*215; ἐν ἀγχόναις θάνατον λαβεῖν E.*Hel.*201; πόλεώς ἐστι θ., ἀνάστατον γενέσθαι it is its *death*, Lycurg.61; γῆρας ζῶν θ. Secund.*Sent.*12; θάνατον ἀποθνῄσκειν, τελευτᾶν, Plu.*Crass.*25, D.H.4.76. 2. in Law, *death-penalty*, θάνατον καταγνῶναί τινος to pass *sentence of death* on one, Th.3.81; θανάτου δίκη κρίνεσθαι ib.57; θανάτου κρίνειν X.*Cyr.*1.2.14, Plb.6.14.6; περὶ θανάτου διώκειν X.*HG*7.3.6; πρὸς τοὺς ἐχθροὺς ..ἀγωνίσασθαι περὶ θ. D.4.47; θ. τῆς ζημίας ἐπικειμένης the penalty is *death*, Isoc.8.50; ellipt., παιδίον κεκοσμημένον τὴν ἐπὶ θανάτῳ (sc. στολήν) Hdt.1.109; τὴν ἐπὶ θ. προσαγαγεῖν τινα Luc.*Alex.*44; but δῆσαί τινα τὴν ἐπὶ θανάτῳ (sc. δέσιν) Hdt.3.119; τὴν ἐπὶ θανάτῳ ἔξοδον ποιεῖσθαι to go to *execution*, Id.7.223; ἐπὶ θάνατον ἄγεσθαι Id.3.14; τοῖς Ἀθηναίοις ἐπιτρέψαι περὶ σφῶν αὐτῶν πλὴν θανάτου for any penalty short of *death*, Th.4.54; εὐθύνας εἶναι πλὴν φυγῆς καὶ θανάτου καὶ ἀτιμίας *IG*1².39.73; εἰργόμενον θανάτου καὶ τοῦ ἀνάπηρον ποιῆσαι short *of death* or maiming, Aeschin.1.183. 3. pl., θάνατοι *kinds of death*, Od.12.341; *the deaths* of several persons, S.*OT*1200, E.*Heracl.*628 (both lyr.); poet., of one person, A.*Ch.*53, S.*OT*496, *El.*206 (all lyr.); οὐχ ἑνός, οὐδὲ δυοῖν ἄξια θανάτοιν Pl.*Lg.*908e; πολλῶν θ., οὐχ ἑνὸς ἄξιος D.21.21, cf. 19.16, Ar.*Pl.*483, D.H.4.24; δεύτερος θ. *Apoc.*2.11, cf. Plu.2.942f; esp. of *violent death*, θ. αὐθένται A.*Ag.*1572 (lyr.), cf. *Th.*879 (lyr.); εἰς θανάτους ἰέναι Pl.*R.*399b. II. as pr. n., Θάνατος *Death*, Ὕπνῳ..κασιγνήτῳ Θανάτοιο Il.14.231, cf. S.*Aj.*854, *Ph.*797, etc.; μόνος θεῶν γὰρ Θ. οὐ δώρων ἐρᾷ A.*Fr.*161; ὃν [ἰδὼν] τέκετο Θ. S.*Tr.*834; character in E.*Alc.* III. *corpse*, θ. ἀτύμβευτος *AP*9.439 (Crin.).

**θᾰνᾰτούσια** (sc. ἱερά), τά, *a feast of the dead*, Luc.*VH*2.22.

**θᾰνᾰτοφόρος**, ον, = θανατηφόρος, πάθη A.*Ag.*1176 (lyr.).

**θᾰνᾰτ-όω**, fut. -ώσω A.*Pr.*1053 (anap.), etc.: pf. τεθανάτωκα Phld.*Rh.*1.359S.:—Pass., fut. -ωθήσομαι Lxx 1*Ki.*14.45: fut. Med. in pass. sense θανατώσοιτο X.*Cyr.*7.5.31: aor. 1 ἐθανατώθην Id.*An.*2.6.4, Pl.*Lg.*865d: pf. τεθανάτωμαι Plb.23.4.14:—*put to death*, τινα Hdt.1.113, A.*Pr.* l.c.; esp. of the public executioner, Pl.*Lg.*872c, etc.: metaph., τεθανατωκέναι τὰς Ἀθήνας (sc. τοὺς ῥήτορας) Phld. l.c.:—Pass., *to be made dead*, *Ep.Rom.*7.4; ὁ -ωθεὶς the *murdered* man, Pl.*Lg.*865d. 2. Pass., of flesh, *to be mortified*, Hp.*Fract.*26:—metaph. in Act., *mortify*, τὰς πράξεις τοῦ σώματος *Ep.Rom.*8.13. II. *condemn to death by sentence* of law, Antipho 3.3.11, *Ev.Matt.*26.60:—Pass., X.*An.*2.6.4; οἱ τεθανατωμένοι those *condemned to death*, Plb. l.c. III. *to be fatal, cause death*, ὄφεις -οῦντες Lxx *Nu.*21.6; μυῖαι -οῦσαι ib.*Ec.*10.1; νόσος Ph.2.247 (-ῶσαν, -ώσασαν codd.). **-ώδης**, ες, *indicating death*, σημεῖον Hp.*Prog.*2. II. *deadly, fatal*, αὐχμοί Id.*Aph.*3.15; ἦρ ib.9; σπασμοί Ael.*NA*7.5. **-ωσις**, εως, ἡ, *putting to death*, Th.5.9; καταδίκαι καὶ -σεις πολιτῶν Plu.2.291c.

**θᾶξαι**· μεθύσαι, and τεθαγμένοι· μεμεθυσμένοι, and θαχμῆναι (cod., leg. θαχθῆμεν)· θωρηχθῆναι (Dor.), Hsch.; cf. *θώσσω.

⊛ ***θάομαι**, a form needlessly invented to expl. the foll. Dor. forms of θεάομαι (q.v.), in which θα- is contr. fr. θαε(ο)- and θαη-: 1 pl. θάμεθα Sophr.85: 2 pl. θᾶσθε (Megar.) Ar.*Ach.*770; imper. θάεο *APl.*4.306, *AP*6.354 (Nossis); part. θάμενος, ταὶ θάμεναι τὰ Ἴσθμια, title of mime by Sophron, Arg.Theoc.15; θασεῖσθε Call.*Cer.*3: fut. part. θασόμενος Theoc.15.23: aor. imper. θᾶσαι Epich.114, Theoc.1.149, 3.12; inf. θάσασθαι Id.2.72; part. θασάμενος *Tab.Heracl.*1.118. II. Act. only in part., θάοντα· διδάσκοντα, θεωροῦντα, Hsch., and Lacon. 1 pl. impf. ἔσᾱμεν (i.e. ἐθᾶμεν), = ἐθεωροῦμεν, Id.

**θάπος**, τό, dialectic form of τάφος (B), θάμβος, Eust.468.28: **θάπαν**· φόβον, Hsch. **θάπτα**· μυῖα (Cret.), Id.

**θαπτέον**, *one must bury*, τινα S.*Aj.*1140.

**θαπτήριον**, *sepultorium*, *Gloss.*

⊛ **θάπτω**, fut. θάψω Is.8.21:—Pass., fut. τἀφήσομαι E.*Alc.*632, Lys.13.45, also τεθάψομαι S.*Aj.*577, 1141, E.*IT*1464: aor. 1 ἐθάφθην Simon.167 (cj.), Hdt.2.81, 7.228; more freq. aor. 2 ἐτάφην [ᾰ] Id.3.10, 55, and always in Att., as Ar.*Pl.*556; part. ἐν-θαφεὶς *CIG*2839 (Aphrodisias): pf. τέθαμμαι, Ion. 3 pl. τετάφαται v.l. τεθάφαται Hdt.6.103; imper. τεθάφθω Luc.*DMar.*9.1; inf. τεθάφθαι A.*Ch.*366 (lyr., prob. l.), Lycurg.113: plpf. Pass. ἐτέθαπτο Od.11.52, Hdt.1.113:—*honour with funeral rites*, ὅτε μιν θάπτωσιν Ἀχαιοί Il.21.323, cf. Hes.*Sc.*472; esp. by burial, οὐ γάρ πω ἐτέθαπτο ὑπὸ χθονός Od.11.52 (but freq. used later with ref. to cremation, D.S.3.55, App.*Hann.*35, Philostr.*Her.*10.11, etc.; πυρὶ θάπτειν Plu.2.286f, Philostr.*VS*2.20.3); θάπτειν.. γῆς φίλαις κατασκαφαῖς A.*Th.*1013, cf. E.*Supp.*545 (Pass.); θ. ἐς χῶρον Hdt.2.41; οὐ ἐβούλοντο Th.8.84; θ. ἐξ οἰκίας *to carry out to burial* from a house, Is.8.21; καταλείψει μηδὲ ταφῆναι not even his *burial expenses*, Ar.*Pl.*556; τῷ δ' εἶναι μηδὲ ταφῆναι Id.*Ec.*592.

**θᾰρᾰπ-ευτής**, = θεραπ-, *Annuaire des Études Grecques* 7.95 (Aenos). **-εύω**, = θεραπεύω, *IG*3.1296, *Schwyzer* 200 (Crete, ii B.C.). **-ηνα**, ἡ, Boeot., = θεράπαινα, ib.503ᵃ.5 (iii/ii B.C.).

⊛ **Θαργήλια** (sc. ἱερά), ων, τά, a festival of Apollo and Artemis held at Athens in the month Thargelion, Hippon.37, Archil.113, Lex ap.D.21.10, *IG*2².1138, etc.:—also **Ταργ-**, *SIG*57.20 (Milet., v B.C.), *Schwyzer* 721.8 (Theb. ad Mycalen, iv B.C.). ⊛ **Θαργηλιών**, ῶνος, ὁ, name of month at Athens, Antipho 6.42; also at Amorgos, *IG*12(7).62; and Andros, ib.135:—written **Ταργ-** at Delos, *BCH*5.26 (but Θαργ- *IG* 11(2).287*A* 19 (iii B.C.)); Θαργήλιος and Ταργήλιος as pr. n., both in *GDI*5515 (Iasos); Ταργ- in Anacr.40.

**θάργηλος** ἄρτος, ὁ, = θαλύσιος, Crates Gr.ap.Ath.3.114a, dub. in *IG* 1².840; θάργηλος χύτρα prob. for θανατηγὸς χ. in Timocl.7.

**θαρνεύει**· ὀχεύει, σπείρει, φυτεύει, and **θάρνυσθαι**· ὀχεύειν, κυΐσκεσθαι, Hsch. (Cf. θόρνυμαι.)

**θαρρᾰλέος, θαρρέω, θαρρητικός, θάρρος, θαρρύνω**, Att. for θαρσ-.

**θαρσᾰλ-έος**, Att. **θαρρᾰλέος**, α, ον, (θάρσος) *daring*, πολεμιστής Il.21.589, etc.; ἦτορ 19.169; φωνά Pi.*N.*9.49; ἐλπίδες θ. *confident*, A.*Pr.*536 (lyr.): c. inf., ἀπὸ τῶν ἵππων πολεμεῖν θαρρ. Pl.*Prt.*350a; θ. περί τι Arist.*Rh.*1383ᵃ15: Comp. -ώτερος Id.*PA*667ᵃ16, Pl.*Prt.* l.c.; τὸ θαρσαλέον *confidence*, ἐν τῷ θαρσαλέῳ εἶναι Th.2.51, cf. Lys.21.25: so in Adv., θαρραλέως ἔχειν to be *of good courage*, πρὸς θάνατον Pl.*Ap.*34e; πρὸς τοὺς πολεμίους X.*An.*2.6.14: Comp. -ώτερον Isoc.*Ep.*7.3. 2. in bad sense, *overbold, audacious*, θ. καὶ ἀναιδής Od.17.449; θαρσαλέη, κύον ἀδεές 19.91; θ. καὶ θρασεῖς Pl.*Lg.*649c. Adv., ψευδῆ λέγειν θαρραλέως Is.10.1. II. *that which may be ventured on*, τὰ θ., opp. τὰ δεινά, Pl.*Prt.*359c, *La.*195c, al.; τἀληθῆ..λέγειν ἀσφαλὲς καὶ θ. Id.*R.*450e. **-εότης**, Att. **θαρρᾰλ-**, ητος, ἡ, *boldness, confidence*, Andronic.Rhod.p.578 M., Plu.*Aem.*36, 2.443d, Jul.*Or.*3.107b, Them.*Or.*2.30b; opp. θρασύτης, Ph.1.476.

⊛ **θαρσ-έω**, Att. **θαρρέω** (cf. pr. n. Θαρρίας *IG*1².847), Aeol. part. θέρσεισα (v.l. θαρσ-) Theoc.28.3: (θάρσος):—*to be of good courage*, τεθαρσήκασι λαοί Il.9.420, etc.; ἄνευ νοῦ, σὺν νῷ, Pl.*Men.*88b; in bad sense, *to be over-bold*, ὕβρει θ. Th.2.65; μάτην θ. Pl.*Tht.*189d:—Constr.: 1. abs., Il. l.c., etc.; θάρσει *fear not!* 4.184, A.*Supp.*732, etc.; θαρσεῖτε ib.600, 910; θάρσει, θυμέ Sopat.14; θάρρει Ar.*Pl.*328, al.:—in Epitaphs, θάρσει.. οὐδεὶς ἀθάνατος *CIG*5200b (Ptolemais), etc.: part. in an adverb. sense, θαρσήσας μάλα εἰπέ *with good courage*, Il.1.85, cf. A.*Ch.*666; κόμπασον θαρσῶν Id.*Ag.*1671, cf. *Pr.*916, S.*OC* 491; θαρσέοντες πλούτου πέρι ἐρίζετε Hdt.5.49; πῖθι θαρρῶν Alex.232; λέγε τοίνυν θαρρῶν Pl.*Phdr.*243e; θαρρῶν πλείονα ἔθνεν ἢ ὀκνῶν ἡγεῖτο X.*Ages.*11.2; τὸ τεθαρρηκὸς *confidence*, Plu.*Fab.*26; τὸ θαρροῦν τῆς ὄψεως Id.*Cat.Mi.*44: in aor., *pluck up courage*, καὶ τότε δὴ θάρσησε Il.1.92. 2. c. acc., θάρσει τόνδε γ' ἄεθλον *fear not about* this contest, Od.8.197; later, *feel confidence against, have no fear of*, πάντα Hdt.7.50; θ. γέροντος χεῖρα E.*Andr.*993, cf. S.*OC*649; θάνατον Pl.*Phd.*88b; τὸ τοιοῦτον σῶμα.. οἱ μὲν ἐχθροὶ θαρροῦσιν.. Id.*Phdr.*239d; θ. τὸ ἀποκρίνασθαι Id.*Euthd.*275c; οὔτε Φίλιππος ἐθάρρει τούτους οὔτε οὗτοι Φίλιππον D.3.7; χωρίον Philostr.*Her.*1.3: c. acc. cogn., ἠλίθιον θάρρος θ. Pl.*Phd.*95c; αἰσχρὰ θάρρη θ. Id.*Prt.*360b; ταὐτὰ τισι θ. καὶ φοβεῖσθαι X.*HG*2.4.9; *venture*, θ. τὰς μάχας Id.*An.*3.2.20:—Pass., *to be risked*, Philostr.*Im.*1.17. b. c. acc. pers., also, *to have confidence in*, τινα X.*Cyr.*5.5.42, D.C.51.11. c. θ. τινί τι *entrust* to.., Marin.*Procl.*

9. 3. c. dat., *have confidence in*, τεθαρσηκότες τοῖσι ὄρνισι Hdt.3.76; ἑαυτῷ Plu.2.69c (s.v.l.); τοῖς χρήμασι *PGoodsp.Cair.*15.19 (iv A.D.). 4. with Preps., θ. περί.. *to be confident* about.., S.*Aj.*793, Pl.*R.*574b; ὑπὲρ ἑαυτῶν ib.566b; διά τι Isoc.3.55; ἐπί τινι Id.6.60; πρός τι Pl.*Prt.*350b; πρὸς ἐμαυτόν in myself, Ar.*Ec.*1060. 5. c. inf., *believe confidently that...*, S.*Ant.*668; also θ. ὅτι.. Th.1.81, etc.; θ. τὸ ἐξελέγξειν D.19.3. b. c. inf., *make bold, venture*, X.*Cyr.*8.8.6, Plu.*Per.*22, Ant.Lib.19.2. II. trans., *inspire with confidence*, [λόγοι] οἵ με θαρσοῖεν J.*AJ*19.1.9. **–ήεις**, εσσα, εν, = θαρσαλέος, Call.*Hec.*1.1.5, Nonn.*D.*13.562. **–ηρός**, ά, όν, = foreg., *Cat.Cod.Astr.*7.218. **–ησις**, εως, ἡ, *confidence in* a thing, ταῖς ναυσί f.l. in Th.7.49. **–ητέον**, *one must have confidence in*, ἀρετῇ Iamb.*Protr.*2. **–ητικός**, ή, όν, *courageous*, Arist.*Pr.*947b26.

**θαρσοποιός**, όν, *making confident*, Eust.1344.12.

**θάρσος**, Att. **θάρρος**, Aeol. **θέρσος** (q.v.), εος, τό, (θρασύς) *courage*, Il.6.126; θ. τινός *courage to do* a thing, A.*Ch.*91, S.*OC*48: c. gen., *courage against...*, πολεμίων Pl.*Lg.*647b; πρὸς τοὺς πολεμίους X.*Cyr.*4.2.15; θ. ἴσχε take *courage!* S.*Ph.*807; θ. ἔχειν περί τινος Id.*El.*412; φρεσὶ θ. ἀέξειν Hes.*Sc.*96; αἴρειν πρός τι E.*IA*1598; λαβεῖν *Act.Ap.*28.15; but θ. ἔλαβέ τινας Th.2.92; θ. ἐμπνέειν Od.9.381; ἐνὶ φρεσὶ θεῖναι 3.76; τῷ δ' ἐνὶ θυμῷ θῆκε..θ. 1.321; ἐν κραδίῃ βάλλειν Il.21.547; παρασχεῖν, ἐμποιεῖν τινι, Th.6.68, X.*An.*6.5.17; θ. ἐγγίγνεται, ἐμπίπτει τινί, Id.*Cyr.*4.2.15, *HG*7.1.31; ἐμφύσεται Id.*Cyr.*5.2.32; οὔτ' ἐλπίδος γὰρ οὔτε του δόξης ὁρῶ θ. παρ' ἡμῖν ὡς.. E.*Hec.*371: pl., φόβοι καὶ θάρρη Arist.*EN*1107a33, cf. Pl.*Prt.*360b. 2. *that which gives courage*, ὀλολυγμόν.., θάρσος φίλοις A.*Th.*270, cf. 184: pl., θάρση *grounds of confidence*, E.*IT*1281 (lyr.). II. rarely in bad sense, = θράσος, *audacity*, θάρσος ἄητον ἔχουσα Il.21.395; μυίης θάρσος ἐνὶ στήθεσσιν ἐνῆκεν the *reckless persistence* of a fly, 17.570.—On the diff. of θάρσος and θράσος, v. θράσος.

**θαρσούντως**, Att. **θαρρ–**, Adv. from gen. pres. part. of θαρσέω, *boldly*, X.*Smp.*2.11, Phld.*Rh.*1.325 S., Jul.*Or.*2.83a; θ. ἔχειν D.C.53.3.

**θάρσῠνος**, ον, = θαρσαλέος, Il.16.70: c. dat., *relying on* a thing, οἰωνῷ 13.823.

**θαρσύνω** [ῡ], Att. **θαρρύνω**, causal of θαρσέω, *encourage, embolden*, θάρσυνον (aor. imper.) δέ οἱ ἦτορ Il.16.242; θαρσύνεσκε παριστάμενος ἐπέεσσιν 4.233; θ. μύθῳ 10.190; θ. λόγοις, opp. φοβεῖν, A.*Pers.*216 (troch.); ἔργῳ καὶ λόγῳ X.*Cyr.*6.3.27, cf. Hdt.2.141, Th.2.59, etc. II. intr., = θαρσέω, ἀλλ', ὦ φίλη, θάρσυνε S.*El.*916.—Cf. θρασύνω.

**Θαρσώ**, οῦς, ἡ, name of Athena, Sch.Il.5.2.

**θᾶσαι, θᾶσθε**, v. *θάομαι.

⊛ **Θάσιος** [ᾰ], α, ον, *of* or *from Thasos*, Θάσιος (sc. οἶνος) *Thasian wine*, Hermipp.82.3, Ar.*Fr.*317, etc.; Θάσιον οἴνου σταμνίον Id.*Lys.*196, cf. *Ec.*1119; Θάσια κάρυα *almonds*, Chrysipp.Tyan.ap.Ath.14.647f, Aët.12.37; so Θάσια alone, Plu.2.1097d, Dsc.4.188, *Gp.*10.57 tit.: in sg., ib.76.6: ἡ Θασία ἅλμη *pickled sea-fish*, Cratin.6; and without ἅλμη, ἀνακυκᾶν Θασίαν to make *this pickle*, Ar.*Ach.*671. II. Θάσιος, ὁ (sc. μήν), name of month at Temnos, *Wiener Denkschr.*53.96 (prob.). 2. Θάσιον, τό, a measure in Egypt, *PCair.Zen.*12.19 (iii B.C.), al.

**θᾶσσον**, Att. **θᾶττον**, v. ταχύς. **θάσσουσα**· σπεύδουσα, Hsch.

⊛ **θάσσω**, Ep. **θᾰάσσω** (q.v.), *sit, sit idle*, στρατὸς δὲ θάσσει E.*Supp.*391; ἥσυχος θ. Id.*Ba.*622 (troch.); ἀμφὶ βωμόν Id.*Rh.*509; ἐπ' ἀκταῖς Id.*Hec.*36; τρίποδι ἐν χρυσέῳ Id.*IT*1253 (lyr.); πρὸς βάθροις Id.*HF*715: c. acc. sedis, θάσσειν θρόνον S.*OT*161 (lyr.); θ. τρίποδα E.*Ion*91 (anap.); θ. δάπεδον Id.*Andr.*117 (lyr.): c. acc. cogn., θ. δυστήνους ἕδρας *to sit* in wretched posture, Id.*HF*1214, cf. Ar.*Th.*889. (θᾶσσω contr. fr. θαάσσω (θᾰϝᾰκyω, cf. θάβακος): v. θᾶκος, θοάζω.)

**θάσσων**, Att. **θάττων**, v. ταχύς. **θάτας**· θῆτας (θύτας cod.), τοὺς δούλους (Cypr.), Hsch. **θατέρᾳ, θάτερον**, v. ἕτερος.

**θᾱτέρως**, Adv. *in the other way*, Simp.*in Ph.*210.10.

**θᾱτήρ**, ῆρος, ὁ, Dor. for *θᾱητήρ, = *θεατήρ, = θεατής, B.9.23, Hsch. **θᾱτύς**, ύος, ἡ, Dor. for *θαητύς, = *θεατύς, = θεωρία, Id. s.v. ἐς θατύν. **θαυλακίζειν**, = θυλακ–, Id. **θαυλέα**· οὐρά, κέρκος, Id. **θαύλια**, τά, a festival, Id.:—also **θαυλίζειν**, Id.: prob. connected with ⊛**Θαύλιος**, epith. of Zeus at Pharsalus, *Hermes* 46.154, 286. (Possibly = *throttler*, cf. Καν-δαύλης = Κυνάγχης (q.v.).)

⊛ **θαῦμα**, ατος, τό, Ion. **θῶμα** (cf. θαυμάζω): (v. θεάομαι): I. of objects, *wonder, marvel*, in Ep. always in sg., Il.13.99, etc.; θαῦμ' ἐτέτυκτο πελώριον, of Polyphemus, Od.9.190; θαῦμα βροτοῖσι, of a beautiful woman, 11.287; ἄσπετόν τι θ., of Hercules, S.*Tr.*961 (lyr.), etc.: freq. c. inf., θ. ἰδέσθαι *a wonder* to behold, Il.5.725, etc.; θ. ἰδεῖν *h.Ven.*205, Hes.*Sc.*318; θ. ἰδεῖν εὐκοσμίας E.*Ba.*693; θ. ἀκοῦσαι Pi.*P.*1.26; θ. ἀνέλπιστον μαθεῖν S.*Tr.*673, etc.; θαῦμ' ὅτι.. *strange* that.., Theoc.15.2; οὐ θαῦμά [ἐστι] no *wonder*, Pi.*N.*10.50; so καὶ θ. γ' οὐδέν and no *wonder*, Ar.*Pl.*99; τὸ μὴ πείθεσθαι θ. οὐδέν Pl.*R.*498d, etc.; τί τοῦτο θ.; E.*Hipp.*439; ἦ μάλα θ. κύων ὅδε κεῖται Od.17.306; θῶμα ποιεῖσθαί τι Hdt.1.68; τί τινος Id.9.58; τινος Id.7.99; περί τινος Id.3.23: after Hom. in pl., θαύματ' ἐμοὶ κλύειν A.*Ag.*1166 (v.l. θραύματ'); θαύματ' ἀνθρώποις δρᾶν E.*Ion*1142; θαυμάτων κρείσσονα or πέρα things more than *wondrous*, Id.*Ba.*667, *Hec.*714. 2. in pl., also, *puppet-show, toy theatre*, θ. δεικνύναι, ἐπιδεικνύναι, Pl.*R.*514b, *Lg.*658c; ἐν θ. Thphr.*Char.*6.4, cf. 27.7, Ph.1.28; *mountebank-gambols*, X.*Smp.*2.1, cf. 7.3 (sg.); ἐν τοῖς θ. ὑπεκρίνετο μίμους in the *jugglers' booths*, Ath.10.452f; of menageries, Isoc.15.213; of mechanical devices, Arist.*Mech.*848a11: metaph., ἔνιοι θ. ποιοῦσιν ἐν φιλοσοφίᾳ Phld.*Rh.*1.99 S.: sg., *puppet*, Pl.*Lg.*644d; *trick*, τὸ τῆς σοφιστικῆς δυνάμεως θ. Id.*Sph.*233a. II. *wonder, astonishment*, θ. μ' ἔχει ὡς.. Od.10.326, etc.; ἔσχον θ. S.*El.*897; θ. δ' ὄμμασιν πάρα A.*Eu.*407; θ. μ' ὑπέρχεται S.*El.*928; μ' ἐλάμβανε θ. Ar.*Av.*511; θαύματος ἄξιος worthy of *wonder*, E.*Hipp.*906, etc.; ἐν θώματι εἶναι to be *astonished*, Hdt.1.68, cf. Th.8.14; ἐν θώματι ἔχεσθαι, ἐνέχεσθαι, Hdt.8.135, 7.128; ἐν θ. ἐνέχεσθαί τινος *at* a thing, Id.9.37; ἐν θαύματι ποιεῖσθαι Plu.*Pomp.*14; διὰ θαύματος σχεῖν Hdn.2.2.7: pl., θαυμάτων ἐπάξια E.*Ba.*716, cf. Pl.*Lg.*967a.

⊛ **θαυμ-άζω**, Ion. **θωμ–**, Att. fut. θαυμάσομαι A.*Pr.*476, E.*Alc.*157, Pl.*Prm.*129c, Ep. θαυμάσσομαι Il.18.467; also θαυμάσω Hp.*Nat.Puer.*29, Plu.2.823f, etc. (in X.*Cyr.*5.2.12 θαυμάζουσι is restored for –σουσι, θαυμάσετε is v.l. for –σαιτε, Id.*HG*5.1.14): aor. ἐθαύμασα A.*Th.*772 (lyr.), etc., Ep. θαύμασα *h.Merc.*414: pf. τεθαύμακα X.*Mem.*1.4.2, etc.:—**Med.**, Gal.*Med.Phil.*2 (v.l.), Ael.*VH*12.30: aor. 1 ἐθαυμασάμην v.l. in Aesop.92; οὐκ ἂν θαυμασώμεθα (leg. –σαίμεθα) Procl.*in Prm.*p.750 S.; θαυμάσαιτο v.l. in J.*BJ*3.5.1:—**Pass.**, fut. –ασθήσομαι Isoc.6.105, Th.2.41: aor. ἐθαυμάσθην Id.6.12: pf. τεθαύμασμαι Plb.4.82.1. 1. abs., *wonder, marvel*, Il.24.394, Pl.*Hp.Ma.*282e, etc. 2. c. acc., *marvel at*, Il.24.631, etc.; πτόλεμόν τε μάχην τε 13.11; τύχη θαυμάσαι μὲν ἀξία S.*OT*777, cf. *OC*1152, *El.*393:—Pass., ὡς τέρας θ. Hdt.4.28; μὴ παρὼν –άζεται I *wonder* why he is not present, S.*OT*289. b. *honour, admire, worship*, once in Hom. (but cf. θαυμαίνω), οὔτε τι θαυμάζειν..οὔτ' ἀγάασθαι Od.16.203; freq. later, as Hdt.3.80, A.*Th.*772 (lyr.), S.*Aj.*1093, etc.; θ. τύμβον πατρός E.*El.*519; μηδὲ τὸν πλοῦτον μηδὲ τὴν δόξαν τὴν τούτων θαυμάζετε, ἀλλ' ὑμᾶς αὐτούς D.21.210; μηδὲν θ., Lat. *nil admirari*, Plu.2.44b; technically, of the *attendance* of small birds on the owl, Arist.*HA*609a15; θ. πρόσωπον *to show respect to* a person, i.e. *comply with* their request, Lxx *Ge.*19.21; θ. τινά τινος *for* a thing, Th.6.36; θ. τινὰ ἐπὶ σοφίᾳ Pl.*Tht.*161c, X.*Mem.*1.4.2; ἀπὸ τοῦ σώματος τὸν νεανίσκον Plu.*Rom.*7:—Pass., *to be admired*, Hdt.7.204; ὑπό τινος Id.3.82; ἔν τινι Th.2.39; τῶν προγεγενημένων μᾶλλον –θησόμεθα Isoc.6.105; τοὺς ὁμοίως τεθαυμασμένους [ποιητάς] Phld.*Po.*5.31; διά τι Isoc.4.59: c. gen., τῆς ῥώμης Philostr.*VA*7.42; χάρις δ' ἀφ' ἡμῶν ὀλομένων –άζεται A.*Th.*703; τὰ εἰκότα θ. *to receive* proper *marks of respect*, Th.1.38; θ. τινί Id.7.63. c. *say with astonishment*, ἵνα μηδεὶς.. "εἶτα τότ' οὐκ ἔλεγες ταῦτα..;" θαυμάζῃ D.19.25. 3. c. gen., *wonder at, marvel at*, τούτου (cj. for τοῦτο) Lys.7.23: c. part., ὃ δ' ἐθαύμασά σου λέγοντος Pl.*Prt.*329c, cf. *Cri.*50c; θ. τῶν προθέντων αὖθις λέγειν Th.3.38; θ. τί τινος *to wonder* at a thing in a person, E.*Hipp.*1041; ὃ θ. τοῦ ἑταίρου Pl.*Tht.*161b, cf. *R.*376a: c. dupl. gen., θ. τούτου τῆς διανοίας Lys.3.44:—these phrases are used in Att. as a civil mode of expressing dissent. 4. rarely c. dat. rei, *to wonder at*, Th.4.85. 5. folld. by Preps., τὰ –όμενα περί τινος Pl.*Ti.*80c; θ. περί τινος τί τῇ τέχνῃ συμβάλλεται Sosip.1.37; ἐπί σου θαυμάζω, πῶς δύνῃ.. Plb.23.5.12; θαυμάσονται ἐπ' αὐτῇ Lxx *Le.*26.32. 6. freq. folld. by an interrog. sentence, θαυμάζομεν οἷον ἐτύχθη Il.2.320; θ. ὅστις ἔσται ὁ ἀντερῶν Th.3.38; θαυμάζοντες τί ἔσοιτο ἡ πολιτεία X.*HG*2.3.17; θ. ὡς οὔπω πάρεισιν Th.1.90, cf. X.*Cyr.*1.4.20, etc.; θ. ὅτι I *wonder at the fact that...*, Pl.*R.*489a; πολλάκις τεθαύμακα ὅπως.. *Com.Adesp.*22.46 D.; but more commonly, θ. εἰ.. I *wonder if*.., as a more polite way of saying I *wonder that*.., Hdt.1.155, S.*OC*1140, Pl.*Phd.*97a; ἐὰν..λέγω, μηδὲν θαυμάσῃς Id.*Smp.*215a; ὃ καὶ θαυμάζω, εἰ.. D.19.86; θαύμαζον ἀκούων, εἰ σὺ μὴ εἴης.., Lat. *mirum ni*.., Ar.*Pax*1292 (hex.).—This construction is freq. combined with one or other of the foregoing. b. c. acc., θαύμαζ' Ἀχιλῆα, ὅσσος ἔην οἷός τε Il.24.629; Τηλέμαχον θαύμαζον, ὃ θαρσαλέως ἀγόρευε they *marvelled at* Telemachus, that he spake so boldly, Od.1.382; τὸ δὲ θαυμάζεσκον (Ion. impf.), ὡς.. 19.229; θ. σοῦ γλῶσσαν, ὡς θρασύστομος A.*Ag.*1399, etc.: sts. without a connective, ἀλλὰ τὸ θαυμάζω· ἴδον.. Od.4.655; σοῦ..θαυμάσας ἔχω τόδε· χρῆν γὰρ.. S.*Ph.*1362: sts. c. inf., θαυμάζομεν Ἕκτορα δῖον, αἰχμητὴν ἔμεναι Il.5.601. c. c. gen., θ. τινός, ἥντινα γνώμην ἔχων κτλ. Antipho 1.5; θ. τῶν..ἐχόντων ὅπως οὐ λέγουσιν Isoc.3.3; θ. αὐτοῦ τί τολμήσει λέγειν D.24.66; θαυμάζω τινὸς ὅτι.. Isoc.4.1; θ. τῶν δυναστευόντων εἰ ἡγοῦνται I *wonder at* men in power supposing, ib.170; ὑμῶν θ. εἰ μὴ βοηθήσετε X.*HG*2.3.53; also θ. αὐτοῦ..τοῦτο, ὡς.. Pl.*Phd.*89a. 7. c. acc. et inf., πενθεῖν οὔ σε θ. E.*Med.*268, cf. *Alc.*1130: after a gen., θαυμάζω δέ σου..κυρεῖν λέγουσαν A.*Ag.*1199. **–αίνω**, Ep. fut. θαυμᾰνέω, = θαυμάζω 2, *admire, gaze upon*, ἀέθλια θαυμανέοντες Od.8.108; δένδρεα θαύμαινε (v.l. θάμβαινε) Pi.*O.*3.32, cf. Id.(?)*Parth.*ap.Sch.Il.*Oxy.*221 vii 11:—Pass., θαυμαίνονται καὶ φιλέονται Callicrat.ap.Stob.4.28.17, cf. Diotog.ap.eund.4.7.62. 2. abs., *wonder*, οὐδὲν δεῖ θαυμαίνεν (Dor. inf.), εἰ.. Archyt.ap.eund.3.1.114. **–ακτρον**, τό, *money paid to see conjurers' tricks*, Sophr.120. **–ᾰλέος**, α, ον, *wondrous*, Hsch.

**Θαύμας**, αντος, ὁ, the father of Iris, Hes.*Th.*265; allegorized by Pl.*Tht.*155d.

⊛ **θαυμάσι-ος** [ᾰ], α, ον, Ion. **θωμ–**, rarely ος, ον Luc.*Im.*19: (v. θαῦμα):—*wonderful, marvellous*, ὅσσα *h.Merc.*443; χάρις Hes.*Th.*584 (nisi neut. pl.); [ὁδὸς] θωμασιωτέρη Hdt.2.21; θωμάσια *wonders, marvels*, ib.35: Sup. –ώτατα Id.6.47; θαυμάσια ἐργάζεσθαι Pl.*Smp.*220a; ἧττον θαυμαστά, καίπερ ὄντα θαυμάσια less *admired*, though *admirable*, Plu.2.974d: c. inf., τέρας θ. προσιδέσθαι Pi.*P.*1.26; οὐ θ. [ἐστι] c. inf., Ar.*Th.*468; ἔστιν δὲ..τοῦτο..θ., ὅπως.. Id.*Pl.*340; θ. τοῦ κάλλους *marvellous* for beauty, X.*An.*2.3.9; πρὸς τὴν τόλμαν –ώτατε Aeschin.3.152: with interrog., θαυμάσιον ὅσον *exceedingly*, Pl.*Smp.*217a; θαυμάσι' ἡλίκα D.19.24; τὸ –ώτατον what is *most wonderful*, D.S.1.63. 2. Adv. –ίως *wonderfully*, i.e. *exceedingly*, Ar.*Nu.*

1240: freq. with ὡς, θ. ὡς ἄθλιος *marvellously* wretched, Pl.*Grg*.471a; θ. ἂν ὡς ηὐλαβούμην I should be *wonderfully* cautious, D.29.1. 3. *disposed to wonder*, in Adv., ὧν οὐ -ίως γ' ἔχουσι Hp.*Morb.Sacr*. 1. II. *admirable, excellent*, with slight irony, Pl.*Phdr*.242a, D. 19.113: freq. ὦ θαυμάσιε Pl.*R*.435c, al.; ὦ -ώτατε ἄνθρωπε, in scorn, X.*An*.3.1.27. III. θ. καὶ ἄλογον *strange* and absurd, Pl.*Grg*. 496a; θαυμάσια . . ἐργαζομένους behaving *in an extraordinary manner*, Id.*Ap*.35a. ❀ -ότης, ητος, ἡ, *disposition to wonder*, Hp.*Morb.Sacr*.1, Arist.*Top*.126ᵇ15. II. *marvellous nature* or *quality*, ὅσα ἔχει -ότητά τινα Clearch.69. 2. as a title, ἡ σὴ θ. your *Excellency*, *CIG* 3467.10 (Sardes, v A.D.). -ουργέω, v.l. for θαυματουργέω, X. *Smp*.7.2: -ουργία, ἡ, *jugglery*, Philostr.*VA*6.10: metaph., λέξεως θ. *wizardry* of language, Phld.*Rh*.2.94 S.

**θαυμ-ασμός**, ὁ, *marvelling*, Phld.*Rh*.2.57 S., Corn.*ND*2, Dius ap. Stob.4.21.16, S.E.*M*.9.17, Plu.*Aem*.39, etc. **-αστέος**, α, ον, *to be wondered at*, ἐκεῖνο θ., ὡς . . Pl.*Plt*.302a. II. neut. θαυμαστέον *one must wonder*, εἰ . . E.*Hel*.85, cf. 499, Phld.*Rh*.2.27 S., etc. **-αστής**, Ion. **θωμ-**, οῦ, ὁ, *admirer*, Ps.-Hdt.*Vit.Hom*.5 (θωυμ- codd.), Arist. *Rh*.1384ᵇ37, al., Plu.*Cat.Mi*.25, Ph.Byz.*Mir*.4.2; ἑαυτοῦ Phld.*Vit*. p.14 J. **-αστικός**, ή, όν, *inclined to wonder* or *admire*, Arist.*EN* 1125ᵃ2, *Stoic*.2.62, Plu.2.41a; τινος Str.2.3.4. II. *expressing astonishment*, [ἐπιρρήματα] D.T.642.8. Adv. -κῶς, εἰπεῖν Ph.1.648; ἔχειν, διακεῖσθαι, Id.2.95, J.*AJ*8.6.5, cf. Phld.*Mus*.p.36 K. **-αστοποιός**, *mirificus*, *Gloss*. ❀ **-αστός**, Ion. **θωμ-**, ή, όν, *wonderful, marvellous*, first in neut. as Adv., θαυμαστὸν γανόωντα *h.Cer*.10; ἔργα μεγάλα καὶ θ. Hdt.1 *Prooem*.; θ. καρπός Id.9.122; θ. λόχος γυναικῶν, of the Furies, A.*Eu*.46; οὐδὲν τούτων θαυμαστὸν ἐμοί S.*Ph*.191, etc.; ὁ πάντων -ότατον Pl.*Smp*.220a; θ. πλέγμα, Medic., the *rete mirabile*, Gal.5.196: c. acc., θαυμαστὴ τὸ κάλλος Pl.*Phd*.110c; πᾶσαν ἀρετὴν Id.*Lg*.945e: c. gen., τῆς εὐσταθείας Plu.*Publ*.14; τῆς ἐπιεικείας Id. *Per*.39: c. dat., πλήθει Id.*Caes*.6; πλέοσι ἐσόμεθα θωμαστότεροι Hdt. 9.122; πρός τι Plu.2.980d: folld. by an interrog., εἰ, etc., θαυμαστὸν ὅσον . ., Lat. *mirum quantum*. Pl.*Tht*.150d, etc.; θαυμαστὸν ἡλίκον D.24.122; θαυμαστά γ', εἰ . . X.*Smp*.4.3; οὐδὲν θ., εἰ . . , Pl.*Phdr*.279a, *R*.390a; οὐ δὴ θ., εἰ . . D.2.23. Adv. -τῶς Pl.*Lg*.633b; θαυμαστῶς ὡς σφόδρα Id.*R*.331a: neut. pl. as Adv., Id.*Smp*.192b; θαυμαστὰ ὡς S.*Fr*.960, E.*IA*943. II. *admirable, excellent*, πατήρ, υἱός, ὄλβος, Pi.*P*.3.71, 4.241, *N*.9.45; ἀνὴρ γὰρ οὐ στενακτὸς . . , ἀλλ' εἴ τις βροτῶν θ. S.*OC*1665; iron., πράξας μὲν εὖ θ. ἂν γένοιτ' ἀνήρ A.*Pers*.212; *strange, absurd*, θ. καὶ γελοῖα Pl.*Tht*.154b; θαυμαστὰ δρῶντες ib.151a; θαυμαστὰ ἐργάζεται behaves *in an extraordinary way*, Id.*Smp*.213d, cf. θαυμάσιος III; θαυμαστὸν ποιεῖς, ὅς . . X.*Mem*.2.7.13; ὦ θαυμαστέ Pl. *Plt*.265a; ὦ θαυμαστότατοι X.*An*.7.7.10. III. *to be worshipped*, οὐδείς μ' ἀρέσκει νυκτὶ θαυμαστὸς θεῶν E.*Hipp*.106. **-αστόω**, *magnify*, Lxx *Ps*.4.4, al., *EM*443.37:—Pass., *to be regarded as a marvel*, ὑπό τινων Arist.*HA*633ᵃ8, cf. Plu.*Per*.28.

**θαυμᾰτ-ίζομαι**, *marvel much*, Hsch. **-όεις**, εσσα, εν, = θαυμαστός, Man.6.402.

**θαυμᾰτοποι-έω**, *do wonders, play jugglers' tricks*, Luc.*Peregr*.17, 21: metaph., θ. τοῖς ὀνόμασιν Phld.*Po*.5.24, cf. Jul.*Or*.3.127c: c. acc., θ. παραπαίγνιον Porph.*Chr*.27. **-ία**, ἡ, *conjuring, juggling*, Pl.*R*.602d, Iamb.*Myst*.3.29. II. of orators, *a straining after the marvellous*, Isoc.10.7 (pl.). 2. *marvellous achievement*, D.C.57. 21. **-ικός**, ή, όν, *juggling*: ἡ -κή (sc. τέχνη), = foreg., Pl.*Sph*. 224a; τὸ θ. μόριον ib.268d. **-ός**, όν, *wonder-working*, ὄνειροι Luc. *Somn*.14; *acrobatic*, κοῦραι Matro *Conv*.121: as Subst., *conjurer, juggler*, Pl.*Sph*.235b, D.2.19: as fem., *IG*11(2).110.34 (Delos, iii B.C.), etc.; *puppet-showman*, Pl.*R*.514b, Phlp.in *GA*77.16.

**θαυμᾰτός**, ή, όν, poet. for θαυμαστός, Pi.*O*.1.28, *P*.10.30; esp. in Ep. phrase, θ. ἔργα *h.Merc*.80, 440, *h.Bacch*.34, Hes.*Sc*.165. (θαυμᾰτός fr. θαυμαίνω (θαυμη-yω) as ἀκήρατος fr. κηραίνω.)

**θαυμᾰτουργ-έω**, = θαυματοποιέω, X.*Smp*.7.2; *work wonders* or *miracles*, Ph.2.18,185; but τὰ περίγεια θ. 'play tricks with', of Xerxes, Id.1.674; τὰ τεθαυματουργημένα *wonderful phenomena*, Pl.*Ti*. 80c. **-ημα**, ατος, τό, *wonder-work*, Ph.2.93 (pl.), Hld.10.39. **-ία**, ἡ, = θαυματοποιία, Pl.*Lg*.670a, Iamb.*Myst*.3.29; τοῦ θεοῦ Just.*Nov*. 40.1.1 (pl.). **-ός**, όν, = θαυματοποιός, γυναῖκες *acrobats*, Ath.4. 129d. II. *puppet-maker* or *-showman*, Hero *Aut*.1.7 (pl.).

**θαῦνον**· θηρίον, Hsch. ❀ **θαυσήκρι**· θεωρεῖον, prob. f.l. for θατύς· ἰκρίον, θ., Id. **θαχθῆμεν**, v. θάζαι.

**θαψία**, ἡ, *deadly carrot*, *Thapsia garganica*, Arist.*Pr*.864ᵃ5, Thphr. *HP*9.9.1,6, Dsc.4.153, Plin.*HN*13.124.

**θάψῐνος**, η, ον, *yellow-coloured, yellow, sallow*, γυνή Ar.*V*.1413; κρόκη *IG*1².330.17; χρῶμα Plu.*Phoc*.28; χιτών Callix.2.

**θάψος**, ἡ, *fustic*, *Rhus Cotinus*, *used for dyeing yellow*, brought from the island of Thapsos, Theoc.2.88, Nic.*Al*.570: θαψία ῥίζα Thphr. *Fr*.170.

***θάω**, v. θάομαι.

-θε, inseparable suffix, v. -θεν.

❀ **θεά**, ἡ, in later Ep. θεή Call.*Dian*.119, dat. θεῇ A.R.3.549 codd. (Hom. has dat. pl. θεῇς, θεῇσι, Il.3.158, 8.305), Lacon. **σιά** Ar.*Lys*. 1263 (lyr.): fem. of θεός (q.v.) in Ep., Trag. (with imitations in Com., as Antiph.81, Eub.64), Att. in set phrases (v. infr.) and later Prose: —*goddess*, opp. γυνή, Il.14.315: with another Subst., θ. μήτηρ 1.280; θεαὶ νύμφαι 24.615; Παλλὰς θ. S.*Ant*.1184; θεοὶ θεαί τε A.*Th*.87 (lyr.); μὰ θεούς, μὰ θεάς Pl.*Smp*.219c; μὰ τοὺς θεοὺς καὶ τὰς θεάς D.19.67; τοῖς δώδεκα θεοῖς καὶ ταῖς σεμναῖς θεαῖς *IG*2².112.9, cf. Antiph.206.2, Anaxandr.2; τῷ θεῷ καὶ τῇ θεᾷ *IG*1².76.39: in dual, of Demeter and Persephone, μεγάλα θεά S.*OC*683 (in earlier Att. τὼ θεώ, v. θεός); αἱ θεαί *IG*2².661.28 (iii B.C.); αἱ σεμναὶ θ. the Erinyes, S.*OC*458, etc.; δειναί, ἀνώνυμοι θ., E.*El*.1270, *IT*944. II. name of third τόπος, Vett.Val.69.12, Paul.Al.*L*.3, cf. *Cat.Cod.Astr*.8(4).144. [⏑–, but sts. monosyll. in Trag., as E.*Andr*.978.]

❀ **θέᾱ**, Ion. **θέη**, ἡ, (θεάομαι) *seeing, looking at*, θέης ἄξιος, = ἀξιοθέητος, Hdt.1.25, cf. X.*HG*6.2.34; θέαν λαβεῖν to take or get *a view*, S. *Ph*.536, 656; ἐς θέαν [τινὸς] ἔρχεσθαι, ἐπὶ θέαν τἀνδρὸς ἐλθεῖν, *to go to see*, E.*IA*427, Pl.*La*.179e; κατὰ θέαν ἀναβαίνειν τοῦ χωρίου Th. 5.7, cf. 9, 6.31; ἠγριωμένος ἐπὶ τῇ θέᾳ τινός at the *sight* of . ., X. *Cyr*.1.4.24; βαδίζειν ἐπὶ κωμῳδῶν θέαν Id.*Oec*.3.7. b. of the mind, *contemplation*, ἡ τοῦ ὄντος θ. Pl.*R*.582c, cf. Arist.*Ph*.209ᵇ20, etc. 2. *aspect*, διαπρεπὴς τὴν θ. E.*IA*1588; αἰσχρὰν θ. παρέχειν X.*Eq*.7.2; ἀπὸ τῆς θ. εἰκάζειν Luc.*VH*1.11; ὑποδῦσα θέαν ἀνθρώπου having assumed the *appearance* of a human being, Palaeph.48. II. *that which is seen, sight*, Ζηνὶ δυσκλεὴς θ. A.*Pr*.243; μάλ' ἄζηλος θ. S.*El*.1455; ὡς ἴδω πικρὰν θ. E.*Hipp*.809; ἀταρβὴς τῆς θ. without fear *of the sight*, S.*Tr*.23: pl., θέαι ἀμήχανοι τὸ κάλλος Pl.*R*.615a. 2. *spectacle, performance*, in a theatre or elsewhere, Thphr.*Char*.5.7, etc.; ἐν ταῖς θ. καὶ ἐν ταῖς πομπαῖς *CIG*3068*A*22 (Teos), cf. Plu.*Caes*. 55, *Brut*.21, Hdn.1.15.1 (pl.); μεγάλαι θ., = *Ludi Magni*, Plu.*Cam*. 5. III. *place for seeing from, seat in the theatre* (cf. αἴγειρος), θέαν εἰς τὰ Διονύσια κατανεῖμαι τοῖς πρέσβεσι Aeschin.2.55, cf. D.18. 28; θέαν καταλαμβάνειν to occupy one, Id.21.178; προκαταλαμβάνειν Luc.*Herm*.39; ἔχειν ἐν τῷ θεάτρῳ Plu.*Flam*.19, etc. 2. *auditorium*, *IG*2².1176. IV. αἴδεσσαί με θέας ὕπερ revere me *by thy countenance*, dub. in *h.Cer*.64 codd. (prob. θεὰν σύ περ).

**θεαγγελεύς**, έως, ὁ, *one who proclaims a festival*, Hsch.:—fem. **θεάγγελις**, ιδος, name of an intoxicating herb, used by the Magi, Plin. *HN*24.164.

**θεαγενής**· ὅσιος, θεοσεβής, Hsch. **θεάγισσα**, v. θεαγός.

**θέαγον**, = θεῖον (A) (at Salamis in Cyprus), Hsch.

❀ **θεᾱγός**, ὁ, (θεός, ἄγω) *priest who carried images of the gods* in Egypt, *PPetr*.3p.239 (iii B.C.), *PTeb*.61(*b*).59 (ii B.C.), *PRyl*.196.14 (ii A.D.), etc.:—fem. **θεάγισσα**, ἡ, *PSI*9.1039.45 (iii A.D.), al.

**θεᾰγωγ-έω**, *evoke gods*, Iamb.*Myst*.3.6:—hence **-ία**, ἡ, ib.2.10:— Adj. **-ός**, όν, λόγος *PMag.Par*.1.975,985.

**θεάζω**, *to be divine*, Democr.21.

❀ **θέαινᾰ**, ἡ, Ep. for θεά, *goddess*, in Hom. mostly in phrase πάντες τε θεοὶ πᾶσαί τε θέαιναι Il.8.5, cf. Od.8.341, al.; θεῶν τε καὶ θεαινῶν Antiph.81.3: in later Ep., Call.*Dian*.29.

**θεαίτητος**, ον, *obtained from God*, trans. of *Samuel*, J.*AJ*5.10.3: as pr. n. in Plato, etc.

❀ **θέ-ᾱμα**, Ion. **θέημα**, ατος, τό, (θεάομαι) *sight, spectacle*, Semon.7.67, A.*Pr*.306, E.*Supp*.783, Ar.*Av*.1716, etc.; εἴ τις ὀρχοῖτ' εὖ, θέαμ' ἦν Pl.Com.130; opp. μάθημα, Th.2.39; freq. of a sight which gives pleasure, θεάματα καὶ ἀκροάματα ἥδιστα παρέχεις X.*Smp*.2.2, cf. 7.5; ὀρχήσεις καὶ θεάματα Phld.*Mus*.p.26 K.; ἐμπλήσθητε τοῦ καλοῦ θ. Pl. *R*.440a; but also θ. δυσθέατον A.*Pr*.69, cf. S.*Aj*.992; ἑπτὰ θ. the seven *wonders of the world*, Str.14.2.5, Plu.2.983e: sg., of a marvellously engraved ring, Gal.*UP*17.1. **-άμων** [ᾱ], Ion. **θεήμων**, gen. ονος, ὁ, ἡ, *spectator*, *APl*.5.365.

**θεανὴ** νῆσος, f.l. for θεία νόσος (v. θεῖος A), S.*Fr*.650.

**θεανῶσται**· οἱ ξυστῆρες (Thess.), Hsch.

❀ **θεάομαι**, Ep. and Ion. **θηέομαι** (v. infr.), Dor. **θᾱέομαι**, ***θάομαι** (qq. v.), imper. θεῶ Ar.*Ach*.262; opt. θηοῖο (for Att. θεῷο) Il.24.418; part. θηεύμενος Hdt.7.146: Ion. impf. ἐθηεῖτο, ἐθηεῦντο, Id.1.10, 3. 136; Ep. θηεῖτο Od.5.75, etc., θηεῦντο Il.7.444, al., ἐθηεύμεσθα Od.9. 218, ἐθηεῖτο Hp.*Nat.Puer*.13, θηέσκετο Poet.ap.Parth.21.2: fut. θεάσομαι [ᾱ], Ion. -ήσομαι: aor. ἐθεᾱσάμην, Ep. opt. θηήσαιο, θηήσαιτο, Od.17.315, 5.74; 3 pl. ἐθηήσαντο Euph.51.15; Ion. inf. θεήσασθαι (v.l. θεάσ-) Hdt.1.8: Att. pf. τεθέαμαι X.*Cyr*.7.5.7: codd. of Hdt. vary betw. θεη- and θηη-: a rare Ion. contr. of θηη- to θη- is found in θησαίατ' Od.18.191, θησάμενος *IG*1².826:—*gaze at, behold*, mostly with a sense of *wonder*, θηεῦντο μέγα ἔργον Il.7.444, cf. Od.2.13; λαοὶ δ' αὖ θηεῦντό τε θάμβησάν τε Il.23.728, cf. Hdt.1.8,11, etc.; θ. τὰ καλά Democr.194; πάντες ὥσπερ ἄγαλμα ἐθεῶντο αὐτόν Pl.*Chrm*. 154c; θ. ὄμμασι E.*Ion* 232 (lyr.); ζητεῖ τὸ κακὸν τεθεᾶσθαι Ar.*Th*.797 codd.; ἐθεᾶτο . . τὴν θέσιν τῆς πόλεως . . , ὡς ἔχοι *reconnoitred* it, Th.5. 7; θ. κύκλῳ τὴν πόλιν X.*Cyr*.4.5.7: abs., θεᾷ; *do you see?* Men.*Epit*. 564. 2. of the mind, *contemplate*, τὸ ἀληθές Pl.*Phd*.84b, al. b. *see clearly*, ἵν' ἴδητε καὶ θεάσησθε ὅτι . . D.4.3, cf. Pl.*Prt*.352a; with relat. clause, ὅση δεινότης ἦν ἐν τῷ Φιλίππῳ θεάσεσθε D.18.144. 3. *view as spectators*, esp. in the theatre, Isoc.4.44; οἱ θεώμενοι *the spectators*, Ar.*Ra*.2, cf. *Nu*.518, al. (but also, *onlookers, bystanders*, Antipho 3.3.7): metaph., θ. τὸν πόλεμον *to be spectators of* the war, Hdt. 8.116. 4. θ. τὸ στράτευμα *to review* it, X.*Cyr*.5.5.1. II. Act. **θεάω**, late, Baillet *Tombeaux des rois à Thèbes* 1080: elsewh. in imper. θέα Them.*Or*.3.44b, Jul.*Ep*.89b, Hsch.: aor. ἐθεάθην in pass. sense, Ps.-Callisth.2.42, *Ev.Marc*.16.11, Ap.Ty.*Ep*.49, Just.*Nov*.133.3.1: pres. θεῶνται Philostr.*Her*.2.9. (Orig. prob. θᾱϝέομαι and θᾱϝάομαι, cf. θαῦ-μα.)

**θεάρεστος** [ᾰ], ον, *pleasing to God*, Eustr. in *EN*35.34. Adv. -τως Sch.Iamb.*Protr*.13.

**θεάριον** [ᾱ], τό, Dor. for θεώριον (q.v.), *meeting-place of* θεωροί, Pi. *N*.3.70. II. **Θεάριος**, ὁ, Doric epith. of Apollo as god of oracles, *IG*4.748.16 (Troezen, iv B.C.), Paus.2.31.6.

**θεᾱρίς**, ίδος, fem. Adj. *of* or *for the* θεωροί, ὁδός *IGRom*.4.360.23 (Pergam., ii A.D.).

**θεᾱροδόκος**, **-δοκία**, Dor. for θεωρ- (q.v.).

**θεᾱρός**, ὁ, Dor. for θεωρός (q. v.): Θεαροί, οἱ, title of poem by Epich., Ath.9.408d.

**θέασις**, εως, ἡ, *contemplation*, Porph.*Abst.*4.6. II. *insight*, Gal. 1.52.

**θεαστικός**, ή, όν, (θεάζω) = ἐνθουσιαστικός, βῆμα *Mim.Oxy.*413.91.

**θεᾱτ-έον**, *one must see*, Pl.*Phd.*66e, *R.*390d. **-ής**, Ion. **θεητής**, οῦ, ὁ, (θεάομαι) *one who sees* or *goes to see*, τῆς χώρης Hdt.3.139, cf. E. *Ion* 301; in the theatre, *spectator*, Ar.*Nu.*575, al.; θ. σοφιστῶν Th. 3.38; *one who contemplates*, τἀληθοῦς Arist.*EN*1098ᵃ31. **-ικός**, ή, όν, *for seeing*, δύναμις θ. τινῶν Arr.*Epict.*1.6.3. **-ός**, ή, όν, *to be seen*, S.*Aj.*915; θ. σοφοῖς [Ἔρως] Pl.*Smp.*197d, cf. Isoc.2.49; μόνῳ νῷ Pl.*Phdr.*247c; cf. θαητός.

**θεᾱτρ-εῖον**, τό, = θέατρον, Suid. ⊛ **-ια**, ἡ, fem. of θεατής, Com. ap.Poll.2.56. **-ίδιον**, τό, Dim. of θέατρον, Varro *RR*3.5.13. ⊛ **-ίζω**, *to be* or *play on the stage*, Suid. II. Pass., *to be made a show of, held up to shame*, *Ep.Hebr.*10.33. ⊛ **-ικός**, Ion. **θεητρικός**, ή, όν, *of* or *for the theatre, theatrical*, μουσική Arist.*Pol.*1342ᵃ18; ὄψις Plu.*Alex.* 19: -κά, τά, *properties*, etc., *OGI*510.7 (Ephesus, ii A.D.): -κοί, οἱ, *actors*, *BCH*44.88 (Lagina). Adv. -κῶς, εἰπεῖν Plu.2.1076c. 2. *pretentious*, Hp.*Medic.*4; θ. μέν.. ἀνίατρον δέ Antyll.ap.Orib.10.23. 24; τὸ θ. Plu.2.7a, 15e. Adv. -κῶς, πολεμεῖν, στρατηγεῖν, Id.*Luc.* 11, *Lys.*21. 3. πόδες θ. dub. sens. in *IG*11(2).203*B*13 (Delos, iii B.C.), cf. *Inscr.Délos* 291*b*30. **-ισμός**, ὁ, *theatrical exhibition*, Vett.Val.18.1 (pl.), cf. Thom.Mag.p.283 R. **-ιστής**, οῦ, ὁ, *stage-player*, Hsch., Suid. s. v. ἠθολόγος.

**θεᾱτρο-ειδής**, ές, *like a theatre*, πέτρα Str.4.1.4, cf. D.S.19.45. Adv. -δῶς Str.16.2.41; *like the spectators in a theatre*, Crito ap.Gal. 12.458. **-κόπος**, ον, *courting applause*, Ptol.*Tetr.*165: -κοπία, ἡ, *courting of applause*, in pl., Artem.2.70. **-κορασία** (sic), = ὀχλοκορασία (sic), *EM*444.16 (better -κρασία in both words, Suid.; cf. sq.). **-κρᾰτία**, ἡ, *rule exercised by the spectators in a theatre*, Pl.*Lg.*701a. **-κῡνηγέσιον**, τό, in pl., *beast-hunts in the amphitheatre*, *Ausonia* 6.9* (Gortyn), Just.*Nov.*105.1:—also -κῡνήγιον, τό, ibid. **-μᾰνέω**, *to be mad after stage-plays*, Man.4.277, Ph.2. 167. **-μορφος**, ον, = θεατροειδής, *theatre-shaped*, Lyc.600.

⊛ **θέᾱτρον**, Ion. **θέητρον**, τό, (θεάομαι) *place for seeing*, esp. *for dramatic representation, theatre*, Hdt.6.67, *IG*2².1176, al.; as *a place of assembly*, Th.8.93, Lys.13.32, *SIG*976.4 (Samos, ii B.C.), Posidon.36 J., *Act.Ap.*19.20, etc.; θ. κυνηγετικόν, of the Roman *amphitheatre*, D.C. 43.22; εἰς τὸ θ. εἰσφέρειν to bring upon *the stage*, Isoc.12.122; τὸ καλὸν τοῦ θ. a good place in the theatre, Ael.*VH*2.13, cf. Alciphr.3. 20. 2. collective for οἱ θεαταί, *the spectators*, '*the house*', Hdt.6. 21, Ar.*Eq.*233, al., Pl.*Smp.*194b, *Com.Adesp.*3 D.: metaph., ἐκάθηντο θέατρον αὐτῷ Lib.*Ep.*722.4. 3. = θέαμα, *spectacle*, θ. ἐγενήθημεν τῷ κόσμῳ 1*Ep.Cor.*4.9. 4. metaph., of *life*, τουτὶ τὸ θ. ὑπεκρίθημεν Porph.*Marc.*2.

**θεᾱτρο-ποιός**, όν, *making a theatre*, Anaxandr.34.9 (s. v. l.). **-πώλης**, ου, ὁ, *one who sells seats in a theatre*, Ar.*Fr.*562. ⊛ **-τορύνη** [ῡ], ἡ, = τορύνη θεάτρου, *stage-pounder*, epith. of Melissa, who was a clumsy dancer, Ath.4.157a.

**θεατρ-ώδης**, ες, *theatrical*, in a bad sense, of persons, Vett.Val.14. 27. **-ώνης**, ου, ὁ, *lessee of a theatre*, Thphr.*Char.*30.6.

⊛ **θεάφιον**, τό, = θεῖον (A), *sulphur*, Hsch.: **θέαφος**, ὁ, Eust.1935.22.

**θεάω**, v. θεάομαι. **Θεδαίσιος**, v. Θεοδαίσια II.

**θεειδής**, ές, (θεός) = θεοειδής, [ἄνθρωπος] πάντων θηρίων θεειδέστατον Antipho Soph.48 (prob. l.).

**θέεινος**, η, ον, *sulphur-coloured*, *PTeb.*405.13 (iii A.D.).

**θέειον**, **θεειόω**, Ep. for θεῖον (A), θειόω (q.v.):—also **θέειος**, for θεῖος (A): **θεείω**· θαυμάζω, Suid.

**θέη**, ἡ, Ion. for θέα.

**θεη-γενής**, ές, poet. for θεογενής, Orph.*A.*1347, Q.S.6.9. **-γορέω**, *discourse of God*, Olymp.Alch.p.84 B. ⊛ **-γόρος**, ὁ, *one who discourses of God*, Id.p.83 B.; but, *inspired by God*, Hld.2.4; μῦθος *spoken by a goddess*, Orph.*A.*541. ⊛ **-δόχος**, ον, poet. for θεοδόχος, Nonn.*D.* 13.96.

**θεήϊος**, η, ον, Ion. for θέειος, θεῖος (A), *divine*, Bion *Fr.*15.9.

**θεηκολ-έω**, *to be a* θεηκόλος, *IG*2².1364 (i A.D.), prob. in *Inscr. Olymp.*468 (iii A.D.); παῖδας ἀοιδοπόλους Ζηνὶ -έοντας *BCH*50.529 (ii A.D.). **-εών**, ῶνος, ὁ, *dwelling of a* θεηκόλος, Paus.5.15.8. **-ος**, ον, = θεοκόλος, *priest*, ib.10, *IG*3.305, 487, *Inscr.Olymp.*123; *choirboy*, Luc.*Alex.*41 (pl.).

**θεηκόρος**, ὁ, = -κόλος, Ap.Ty.*Ep.*26tit.

**θεηλ-ᾰσία**, ἡ, *visitation of God*, Sch.S.*Tr.*1235 (ἠλασία cod.). **-ᾰτέομαι**, *to be visited by God*, Hld.8.10. II. *complain of God's visitations*, Id.6.8. **-ᾰτος**, ον, (ἐλαύνω) *driven by a god*, θεηλάτου βοὸς δίκην A.*Ag.*1297; θ. δαίμονες Plu.2.830f. II. *sent* or *caused by a god*, of things evil in themselves or in their consequences, φθορή Hdt.7.18; ἔργον, πρᾶγμα, μάντευμα, S.*Ant.*278, *OT*255, 992; νόσους δ' ἀνάγκη τὰς θ. φέρειν Id.*Fr.*680; ἔκ τινος θεηλάτου from some *destiny*, E.*Ion*1392. III. *built for the gods*, ἕδραι ib.1306.

**θέημα**, ατος, τό, Ion. for θέαμα, Semon.7.67.

**θεημάχος** [ᾰ], ον, poet. for θεομ-, *AP.*9.769 (Agath.); φῦλα Γιγάντων Procl.*H.*7.8.

**θεημοσύνη**, ἡ, *contemplation*: *a problem*, *AP*11.352.10 (Agath.).

**θεήμων**, ονος, ὁ, ἡ, Ion. for θεάμων, *APl.*5.365.

**θεηπολέω**, poet. for θεοπ-, Phot., Suid.

**θεητής, θέητρον**, Ion. for θεατής, θέατρον.

**θέθμιον**, τό, = θέσμιον, v. θέσμιος II:—also **θεθμός**, ὁ, Dor., = θεσμός (q. v.): and **θεθτμός**, *Schwyzer*411 (Elis).

**θεία**, ἡ, *one's father's* or *mother's sister, aunt*, *POxy.*274.5 (i A.D.), Ammon.*Diff.*p.130 V., etc. (Late formation fr. θεῖος (B), replacing τηθίς.)

**θει-άζω**, (θεῖος A) *to be inspired, frenzied*, ὁπόσοι αὐτοὺς θειάσαντες ἐπήλπισαν as many as made them hope *by divinations*, Th.8.1; θ. καὶ θεοφορεῖται *is divinely inspired*, Ph.1.479; ὁπόσοι τελεταῖς ἐθείαζον *obtained inspiration* through ritual, Philostr.*Her.*5.3. 2. *prophesy*, ὅτι στρατοπεδεύσοιτο D.C.*Fr.*57.48:—Pass., [λόγος] ἐπὶ τῇ τελευτῇ τοῦ Ἀλεξάνδρου ἐθειάσθη Arr.*An.*7.18.6; λόγιον ὑπὸ τοῦ ὁμίλου θειασθέν D.C.62.18. II. *worship as divine*, Id.59.27; Πυθαγόραν καὶ Πλάτωνα Dam.*Isid.*36:—Pass., Max.Tyr.8.9. ⊛ **-ασμός**, ὁ, *superstition*, ἄγαν θειασμῷ προσκείμενος, of Nicias, Th.7.50. II. *inspiration, frenzy*, θειασμοῖς κάτοχοι γυναῖκες D.H.7.68; θειασμοῦ [ἐπιρρήματα], such as εὐοῖ, D.T.642.17. **-αστής**, οῦ, ὁ, *worshipper*, Tz.*H.*8.347. **-αστικός**, ή, όν, *like one inspired*. Adv. -κῶς Poll.1.16.

**θειάφιον**, τό, *sulphur*, Tz.*H.*12.743.

**Θείβᾱθεν**, Adv., Boeot. for Θήβηθεν, *from Thebes*, Ar.*Ach.*862:— **Θείβᾱθι**, *at Thebes*, ib.868 codd. (Θείβᾱθε *from Thebes*, Elmsl.).

**θείκελος**, dub. l. in Ar.*Lys.*1252 codd. (σιοείκελοι Mein., συείκελοι Wilam.).

**θεϊκός**, ή, όν, late form for θεῖος (A), θρησκεία *Cat.Cod.Astr.*1.116; σοφία *MAMA*1.228 (Laodicea Combusta).

**θειλο-πεδεύω**, *dry in the sun*, σταφυλήν Dsc.5.6 (Pass.). ⊛ **-πεδον**, τό, *sunny spot* in the vineyard where grapes were dried, Od.7.123, *AP*6.169, 9.586 (Comet.), Sch.E.*Or.*1492; θειλοπέδου τρόπον Dsc.1. 32; v. εἰλόπεδον.

**Θειλούθιος**, ὁ (sc. μήν), month in Boeotia, *IG*7.2861, al.: written Θηλούθιος ib.3326, al.

**θεῖμεν**, for θείημεν, 1 pl. aor. 2 opt. Act. of τίθημι.

**θειμωνιαί**· οἱ σωροὶ τῶν δραγμάτων, Hsch. (Boeot. for θημ-).

**θεῖναι**, aor. 2 inf. Act. of τίθημι.

**θεινίον**, v. θινίον.

**θεϊνός**, ή, όν, = θῖνος (q. v.), *GDI*4940.26 (Crete).

**θείνω**, Ep. inf. θεινέμεναι Od.22.443: impf. ἔθεινον A.*Pers.*418, etc.: fut. θενῶ Ar.*Ach.*564: aor. 1 part. θείνας Il.20.481 (ἔθεινε in 21.491 may be impf.); other moods from an aor. 2 ἔθενον (which does not occur in ind.); imper. θένε E.*Rh.*676, Ar.*Av.*54; subj. θένω E.*Rh.*687 (troch.), Ar.*Lys.*821 (lyr.), cj. in Theoc.22.66; inf. θενεῖν E.*Heracl.* 271; part. θενών Id.*Cyc.*7, Ar.*Eq.*640, *V.*1384, *Av.*1613, *Ra.*855 (these forms were freq. incorrectly written θένειν, θένων, as if from a pres. *θένω):—Pass., only in pres. and impf.:—poet. word, *strike*, τινα Od. 18.63; ξίφεσι 22.443; φασγάνῳ αὐχένα θείνας Il.20.481; μάστιγι.. θείνων 17.430; [τόξοισι] ἔθεινε παρ' οὔατα 21.491:—Pass., 1.588; θεινόμεναι βουπλῆγι 6.135; ἄορι 10.484; θεινομένου.. πρὸς οὔδεϊ *dashed* to earth, Od.9.459; later σκάπτῳ θενών τινα Pi.*O.*7.28; ῥαιστῆρι A. *Pr.*56, cf. 76; τινὰ δ' ἀσπίδος E.*Heracl.*738; ἰτέαν εἰς μέσην Id.*Cyc.*7; τῷ σκέλει θένε τὴν πέτραν Ar.*Av.*54; τῷ πρωκτῷ θενὼν τὴν κιγκλίδ' Id. *Eq.*640; ποσσὶ θ. σκέλος, of a wrestler, Theoc.22.66: abs., θείνετε v.l. in E.*Or.*1303 (lyr.); θεῖν', ἀντέρειδε Id.*Supp.*702; θένε, θένε Id. *Rh.*676 (lyr.):—Pass., A.*Pers.*303, *Ch.*388 (lyr.). 2. metaph., θείνει δ' ὀνείδει μάντιν Id.*Th.*382. 3. intr., of corpses, θ. ἐπ' ἀκτᾶς Id.*Pers.*966. II. to the same Verb, but only with the meaning *slay*, belong the foll. forms formerly referred to a pres. *φένω, viz.: aor. 2 ἔπεφνον Il.21.55, Pi.*P.*10.46, B.17.19, S.*OT*1497; Ep. and Lyr. πέφνον Il.13.363, B.8.13; subj. πέφνῃς, ῃ, Od.22.346, Il.20.172; inf. πεφνέμεν 6.180; part. πεφνών 16.827 (parox. acc. to Aristarch., as if from a pres. πέφνω, which is found in late Ep., Opp.*H.*2.133): from the short form φᾰ (for φη) come pf. Pass. 3 sg. πέφαται Il.15. 140, al.; 3 pl. πέφανται 5.531; inf. πεφάσθαι 13.447: fut. Pass. πεφήσεαι ib.829, Od.22.217; ἢ πέφατ' ἢ.. πεφήσεται Il.15.140; later, part. πεφασμένος Lyc.269, 1374, Opp.*H.*5.122; Gramm. also give aor. 1 φάσαι Hsch. s. v. φάσγανον, Phot. s. v. προσφατος, Sch.Pi.*N.* 1.69: aor. 2 part. παφών Hsch.: aor. 2 Med. ἀπ-έφατο, = ἀπέθανεν, Id. Hence also φᾰτός *slain*, Id., found in compds. Ἀρεί-φατος, μυλή-φατος, ὀδυνή-φατος, πυρί-φατος. (I.-E. gʷhen- cf. Skt. *hánti*, pl. *ghnánti*, Hittite *kuenzi*, pl. *kunanzi* 'strike', 'kill'; gʷhon- in Gr. φόνος; gʷhn- in Skt. *ghn-ánti*, Gr. ἔ-πε-φν-ον (redupl.); gʷhn̥- in Skt. *-hata-*, Gr. -φατο-, πέφαται, etc.)

**θειο-γενής**, ές, = θεο-, *Gloss.* **-δάμη** [ᾰ], ἡ, (δαμάω) *she who tames the gods*, Suid.:—Adj. **-δᾰμος**, ἀνάγκαι Orac.ap.Porph.ap.Eus. *PE*5.8. **-δμητος**, ον, = θεό-, *AP*9.157 (v.l. θεοδηλήτου). **-δομος**, ον, *built by gods*, τεῖχος ib.7.138 (Acerat.), cf. 9.104 (Alph.).

**θειόθεν**, Adv., (cf. θεῖος (A) I. 4) *from the Emperor*, Just.*Nov.*82.9.

**θειολόγος**, ὁ, poet. for θεολόγος, *IG*3.770 (i A.D.).

**θείομεν**, Ep. for θέωμεν, θῶμεν, 1 pl. aor. 2 subj. Act. of τίθημι.

⊛ **θεῖον** (A), Ep. **θέειον** (in Od.22.493 **θήϊον**), τό, *brimstone*, used to fumigate and purify, δέπας.. ἐκάθηρε θεείῳ Il.16.228; οἶσε θέειον.., κακῶν ἄκος Od.22.481; δεινὴ δὲ θεείου γίγνεται ὀδμή, from a thunderbolt, Il.14.415; ἐν δὲ θεείου πλῆτο, of a ship struck by lightning, Od. 12.417; ἐμβαλόντες πῦρ ξὺν θ. Th.2.77, cf. 4.100; Κύριος ἔβρεξεν ἐπὶ Σόδομα καὶ Γόμορρα θ. καὶ πῦρ Lxx *Ge.*19.24; as a natural product, Hp.*Aër.*7, Ph.2.21, 143, Ti.Locr.99c; θ. ἄπυρον Gal.12.903; opp. πεπυρωμένον, Dsc.5.107; cf. θεάφιον, θέαφος. (Perh. cogn. with θύω, θυμιάω, Lat. *suffire*.)

**θεῖον** (B), τό, *the Divinity*, v. θεῖος (A) II.

**θειο-πᾰγής**, ές, *god-made*, ἱστός Orac.ap.Phleg.*Mir.*10; cf. θειοφανής. **-πόλος**, ὁ, *ministrant*, Maiist.43. **-πρόπος**, ὁ, poet. for θεοπρόπος, *IG*12(5).893.6 (Tenos, ii/iii A.D.); ἔγγονε θειοπρόπων, = θεοπροπίδης, Orac.ap.Porph.*Abst.*2.9.

⊕ **θεῖος** (A), α, ον: late Ep. **θέειος** Procl.*H.*2.16; **θεήϊος** Bion *Fr.*15.9; late Aeol. **θήϊος** *Epigr.Gr.*989.4 (Balbilla); Lacon. **σεῖος** (v. infr. I.3): Comp. and Sup. θειότερος, -ότατος, freq. in Pl., *Phdr.*279a, *Mx.*244d, al.: (θεός): 1. *of* or *from the gods, divine*, γένος Il.6.180; ὀμφή 2.41; Ὄνειρος ib.22; ἐπιπνοίαις A.*Supp.*577, cf. Pl.*R.*499c; μάστιξ A.*Pr.*682; μανία S.*Aj.*611 (lyr.); νόσος ib.185 (lyr.) (but θ. νόσος, of a dust-storm, Id.*Ant.*421); κίνδυνοι And.1.139; θ. τινὶ μοίρᾳ by *divine* intervention, X.*HG*7.5.10; θ. τύχῃ γεγονώς Hdt.1.126; θ. τύχῃ χρεώμενος Id.3.139; θ. κάπόνῳ τύχῃ, of an easy death, S.*OC*1585; ἐκ θ. τύχης Id.*Ph.*1326; ἔμαθε ὡς θ. εἴη τὸ πρῆγμα Hdt.6.69; ὁ θ. νόμος Th.3.82; φύσις θ. *SIG*1125.8 (Eleusis), cf. 2*Ep.Pet.*1.4; *appointed of God*, βασιλῆες Od.4.691; σκῆπτρον *given by God*, S.*Ph.*139 (lyr.); v. infr. 2. 2. *belonging* or *sacred to a god, holy*, ἀγών, χορός, Il.7.298, Od.8.264; *under divine protection*, πύργος, δόμος, Il.21.526, Od.4.43; of heralds and bards, Il.4.192, Od.4.17, al.; so perh., of kings, ib.691. 3. *more than human*, of heroes, Ὀδυσσεύς Il.2.335, al., Cratin.144.4 (lyr.); θ. ἀνήρ Pi.*P.*6.38, A.*Ag.*1548 (lyr.), Pl.*R.*331e, *Men.*99d (esp. at Sparta (Lacon. σεῖος), Arist.*EN*1145ᵃ29; ὦ θεῖε (in the mouth of a Spartan) Pl.*Lg.*626c); μετὰ σοῦ τῆς θείας κεφαλῆς Id.*Phdr.*234d, cf. Them.*Or.*9.128a, Lib.*Or.*19.66. b. of things, *excellent*, θεῖον ποτόν Od.2.341, 9.205; ἁλὸς θείοιο Il.9.214; θ. πρήγματα *marvellous* things, Hdt.2.66; ἐν τοῖσι θειότατον Id.7.137. 4. = Lat. *divinus* (or *sacer*), *Imperial*, διατάξεις prob. in *BGU*473.5 (200 A.D.), etc.; θησαυροί *PLips.*62 ii 14 (iv A.D.); θ. ὅρκος oath *by the Emperor*, *POxy.*83.6 (iv A.D.), etc.; θειότατος, of living Emperors, *Inscr.Prien.*105.22 (9 B.C.), etc. b. = Lat. *divus*, of deified Emperors, θ. Σεβαστός Edict.Claud. ap.J.*AJ*19.5.3, cf. *Inscr.Perg.*283 (iii A.D.), Lyd.*Mag.*2.3. II. as Subst., θεῖον, τό, *the Divinity*, Hdt.1.32, 3.108, al., A.*Ch.*958 (lyr.); τοῦ θ. χάριν Th.5.70; ἡμαρτηκότα εἰς τὸ θ. Pl.*Phdr.*242c. 2. in an abstract sense, *divinity*, κεκοινώνηκε.. τοῦ θ. ib.246d; ἢ μόνον μετέχει τοῦ θ..., ἢ μάλιστα [ἄνθρωπος] Arist.*PA*656ᵃ8, etc.; κατὰ θεῖον or κατά τι θ., Aen.Gaz.*Thphr.*p.37 B., p.4 B. 3. θεῖα, τά, *the acts of the gods, course of providence*, S.*Ph.*452, etc.; τὰ θ. θνητοὺς ὄντας εὐπετῶς φέρειν S.*Fr.*585; τὰ θ. μὴ φαύλως φέρειν Ar.*Av.*961. b. *matters of religion*, ἔρρει τὰ θ. *religion* is no more, S.*OT*910 (lyr.), cf. *OC*1537, X.*Cyr.*8.8.2, etc. c. *inquiries concerning the divine*, Pl.*Sph.*232c; τὰ φανερὰ τῶν θείων, i.e. the heavenly bodies, Arist.*Metaph.*1026ᵃ18, cf. *GA*731ᵇ24, *Ph.*196ᵃ33 (Sup.), *EN*1141ᵇ1. III. Adv. θείως *by divine providence*, θ. πως X.*Cyr.*4.2.1, etc.; θειοτέρως *by special providence*, Hdt.1.122; μᾶλλόν τι καὶ -ότερον ib.174. 2. *divinely, excellently*, εὖ γε καὶ θ. Pl.*Tht.*154d; θείως εἰρῆσθαι Arist.*Metaph.*1074ᵇ9.

⊕ **θεῖος** (B), ὁ, *one's father's* or *mother's brother, uncle*, E.*IT*930, Ar.*Nu.*124, And.1.18, 117, Pl.*Chrm.*154b, Men.5 D., etc.; ὁ πρὸς μητρὸς θ. Is.5.10; πρὸς πατρός Ph.2.172. (Cf. τήθη.)

⊕ **θειό-σεπτος**, ⊕ **-τελής**, v. θεο-.

⊕ **θειότης**, ητος, ἡ, *divine nature, divinity*, Lxx *Wi.*18.9, *Ep.Rom.*1.20, *SIG*867.31 (Ephesus, ii A.D.), Plu.2.665a, etc. 2. f.l. for ὁσιότης, Isoc.11.26, Plu.2.857a, and so prob. in Id.*Sull.*6. II. as title of Roman Emperors, Orib.1.1.1, *SIG*900.23 (Panamara, iv A.D.), etc.

**θειοφάνής**, ές, *manifested by the gods*, Alex.162.14 (anap., v.l. -παγές).

**θειόχροος**, ον, contr. -χρους, ουν, *brimstone-coloured*, Dsc.5.101.

**θειόω**, Ep. **θεειόω**, (θεῖον A) *fumigate with brimstone*, ὄφρα θεειώσω μέγαρον Od.22.482; θειώσας τὰς ἀλλοτρίας ἐπινοίας, metaph., from the clothes-cleaner, who used sulphur, Lysipp.4:—Med., δῶμα θεειοῦται he *fumigates his* house, Od.23.50. 2. *purify, hallow*, θείου.. θεσμὸν αἰθέρος μυχῶν dub. in E.*Hel.*866. 3. *smear with sulphur*, Gal.1.658 (Pass.); ἔριον τεθειωμένον *sulphurated*, Orib.*Fr.*35, Paul.Aeg.3.33. II. in Alchemy, *sulphurate*, Ps.-Democr.ap. Zos.Alch.p.153 B. III. (θεῖος A) *hallow, consecrate*, Pl.*Lg.*771b, Ph.1.374.

**θείω**, Ep. for θέω, *run*. II. Ep. for θῶ, 1 sg. subj. aor. 2 of τίθημι.

**θειώδης** (A), ες, (θεῖον A) *sulphureous*, of waters, etc., Anon.Lond.24.45, Antyll.ap.Orib.10.2.3, Archig.ap.Aët.3.167, Phlp.*in Mete.*7.5; ὀδμή Str.1.3.18. 2. of colour, *yellow*, θώρακες *Apoc.*9.17.

⊕ **θειώδης** (B), ες, (θεῖος A) *divine*. Adv. -δως *by Imperial decree*, *PMasp.*451.42, 56 (vi A.D.).

**θέκλεον**· θαυμαστόν, Hsch. (fort. θέσκελον).

**θελγεσίμῡθος** [ῐ], ον, *soft-speaking*, *AP*9.525.9.

**θέλγητρον**, τό, (θέλγω) *charm, spell*, in pl., Hld.7.9: more usu. metaph., ὦ φίλον ὕπνου θ. E.*Or.*211; πόθων θέλγητρα Ath.5.220f; of music, Luc.*Im.*14; of a city, Id.*Scyth.*5; cf. θελκτρον.

**Θελγῖνες**, = Τελχῖνες (q.v.), *wizards*, Hsch., Eust.1391.12.

**θέλγμα**, ατος, τό, = θέλγητρον, Sch.Pi.*P.*1.21; glossed by θαῦμα, Hsch.

**θέλγω**, Ion. impf. θέλγεσκεν Od.3.264: fut. θέλξω 16.298, A.*Pr.*865, Dor. -ξῶ Theoc.*Ep.*5.3: aor. ἔθελξα Il. (v. infr.):—**Med.**, Alc.*Supp.*11.7:—**Pass.**, fut. θελχθήσομαι Luc.*Salt.*85: aor. ἐθέλχθην Od.10.326, Ep. 3 pl. -χθεν 18.212:—poet. Verb (used by Pl.*Smp.*197e, and in late Prose, as Phld.*Mus.*p.72 K., Jul.*Or.*4.150c, etc.), *enchant, bewitch*, [Ἑρμῆς] ἀνδρῶν ὄμματα θέλγει Od.5.47, al.; τὸν.. Ποσειδάων ἐδάμασσε θέλξας ὄσσε φαεινά Il.13.435; [Κίρκη] οὐδ' ὧς θέλξαι σε δυνήσεται Od.10.291, cf. 326 (Pass.); [Σειρῆνες] πάντας ἀνθρώπους θέλγουσιν, ὅτις σφέας εἰσαφίκηται 12.40; [θύελλα] θέλγε νόον *spell-bound* their senses, Il.12.255. 2. *cheat, cozen*, Od.16.195, 298, S.*Tr.*710: c. dat. modi, μήτε τί μοι ψεύδεσσι χαρίζεο μήτε τι θέλγε Od.14.387; μαλακοῖσι καὶ αἱμυλίοισι λόγοισι 1.57; ψεύδεσσι, δόλῳ, Il.21.276, 604; ἔπεσσιν Od.3.264. 3. metaph., *charm, beguile*, 17.521; οἱ ἐλπὶς ἔθελγε νόον h.*Cer.*37, cf. Pi.*P.*1.12, D.Chr.45.5; καί μ' οὔτι μελιγλώσσοις πειθοῦς ἐπαοιδαῖσιν θέλξει A.*Pr.*174: σὺ δὲ θέλγοις ἂν ἄθελκτον Id.*Supp.*1055; θέλγει ἔρως E.*Hipp.*1274 (lyr.); ᾠδῆς.., ἣν ᾄδει θέλγων.. νόημα Pl.*Smp.*197e:—Pass., μήθ' ὕπνῳ θελχθῇς E.*IA*142 (lyr.); τὰ δ' οὔτι θέλγεται A.*Ch.*420 (lyr.); ἔρῳ δ' ἄρα θυμὸν ἔθελχθεν Od.18.212; Μούσαισιν.. τὴν φρένα θελγομένη (which may be Med.) *IG*14.1960. 4. c. inf., ἵμερος θέλξει τὸ μὴ κτεῖναι *will persuade* her not to kill, A.*Pr.*865; ἔρως δέ νιν.. θέλξειεν αἰχμάσαι τάδε S.*Tr.*355; ἕπεσθαι θ. Ael.*NA*10.14. 5. *produce by spells*, ἀοιδαὶ θέλξαν νιν (sc. εὐφροσύναν) Pi.*N.*4.3; [Γαλήνη] θ. ἀνηνεμίην *AP*9.544 (Adaeus). (Perh. cf. Lith. *žvelgiù* 'look', 'glance'.)

⊕ **θελεμός**, όν, epith. of πῶμα, A.*Supp.*1027 (lyr.): glossed by οἰκτρόν, ἥσυχον, Hsch.; but, = θελημός, acc. to Hdn.Gr.1.171, cf. *EM*103.48. Adv. -μῶς Hsch.

**θέλ-εος**, ον, *willing*, θ. ἀθέλεος, Lat. *nolens volens*, A.*Supp.*862 (lyr.). **-ημα**, ατος, τό, (θέλω) *will*, Antipho Soph.58 (pl.), Aen.Tact.18.19, Lxx *Es.*1.8, al., *Ev.Matt.*7.21, *POxy.*924.8 (iv A.D.). II. ἔστιν μοι θ. ἔν τινι *pleasure* in.., Lxx *Ec.*12.1, cf. 5.3: —also **-ήμη**, ἡ, Theognost.*Can.*112. **-ηματικός**, ή, όν, *optional, voluntary, superfluous*. Adv. -κῶς Eust.920.19. **-ημάτιον**, τό, Dim. of θέλημα, ἔσχατον θ. last *will and testament*, *PLond.*1.77.12 (vi A.D.). **-ημός**, όν, *willing*, Emp.35.6. 2. *kindly*, ἄλσος B.16.85; glossed by ἥσυχος, Phot. **-ημοσύνη**, ἡ, = θέλησις, *PMag.Par.*1.2921 (pl.). ⊕ **-ήμων**, ον, gen. ονος, *voluntary*, εἰρεσίη A.R.2.557. **-ησις**, εως, ἡ, *a willing, will*, *Stoic.*3.41, Lxx *To.*12.18, al., Phld.*Rh.*2.297 S., *Ep.Hebr.*2.4; condemned by Poll.5.165: in Dor. pl. θελήσιες, *wishes*, Meliss.*Ep.* II. *goodwill, favour*, Lxx *Pr.*8.35. **-ητής**, οῦ, ὁ, *one who wills*, ἐλέους ib.*Mi.*7.18, cf. Hsch. II. *wizard* (by confusion of Hebr. *'ôbh* 'necromancer' with *'ôbheh* 'wishing'), Lxx 4*Ki.*21.6; = ἐγγαστρίμυθος, Cyr. **-ητός**, ή, όν, *wished for, desired*, Lxx 1*Ki.*15.22, *Ma.*3.12.

⊕ **θέλκ-ταρ**, τό, = θέλγητρον, Hsch. (θέρκαλ cod.). **-τήρ**, ῆρος, ὁ, *soother, charmer*, θελκτὴρ ὀδυνάων, of Asclepius, *h.Hom.*16.4; cf. θέλκτωρ. **-τήριον**, τό, *charm, spell*, of the girdle of Aphrodite, ἔνθα τέ οἱ θ. πάντα τέτυκτο Il.14.215; of heroic lays, βροτῶν θελκτήρια Od.1.337; θεῶν θ. 8.509; πόνων θελκτήρια *means of lightening* toil, A.*Ch.*670 (s.v.l.); γλώσσης ἐμῆς μείλιγμα καὶ θ. Id.*Eu.*886; νεκροῖς θελκτήρια, of offerings to the Manes, E.*IT*166 (lyr.); ψυχῆς θ. Men.559. **-τήριος**, ον, *enchanting, soothing*, μῦθοι, λόγοι, A.*Eu.*81, E.*Hipp.*478; ὄμματος θ. τόξευμα the eye's *magic* shaft, A.*Supp.*1004: c. gen., φίλτρα θ. ἔρωτος E.*Hipp.*509; μύθου μῦθος θ. speech *that heals* speech, A.*Supp.*447: in late Prose, θ. ἀγωνίσματα, of poems, Agath.*Praef.* **-τικός**, ή, όν, = foreg., δύναμις Sch.E.*Or.*211. **-τρον**, τό, = θελκτήριον, S.*Tr.*585, prob. in A.R.1.515 (nisi leg. **θελκτύν**). **-τωρ**, = θελκτήρ, A.*Supp.*1040 (lyr., θεάκτ- cod. M), cf. Suid. (θελκτῷ codd.).

**θελξῐ-επής**, ές, *speaking winning words*, γῆρυς B.14.48. **-μβροτος**, ον, *charming men*, Κύπρις Id.5.175; ᾠδή Orph.*L.*320. ⊕ **-μελής**, ές, *charming with music*, [φόρμιγξ] *IG*3.400. **-νοος**, ον, contr. **-νους**, ουν, *charming the heart*, φίλτρα *AP*6.88 (Antiphan.); ἔαρ ib.10.15 (Paul. Sil.); Ἔρωτες Musae.147. **-πικρος**, ον, *sweetly painful*, κνησμοναί *App.Anth.*3.158.

⊕ **θέλξις**, εως, ἡ, *an enchanting*, Ael.*NA*8.24, Plu.2.662a.

**θελξίφρων**, ον, gen. ονος, = θελξίνοος, Ἔρωτες E.*Ba.*404 (lyr.); παλμός *AP*9.505.17; of Apollo, ib.525.9.

⊕ **θελοντής**, οῦ, ὁ, = ἐθελοντής (q.v.), Hierocl.p.56 A., v.l. in Hdt.6.92.

⊕ **θέλυμνα**, ων, τά, = θέμεθλα, *foundations* or *elements of things*, θ. τε καὶ στερεωπά cj. for θελημνά, θελημά, Emp.21.6. (Cf. προθέλυμνος, τετραθέλυμνος.)

⊕ **θέλω**, v. ἐθέλω and add ὅστις ἂν θέλῃ *IG*1².49.12; ἐὰν δέ τις θέλῃ ib.6.106; ἐάν τις μὴ θέλῃ ib.40.27.

⊕ **θέμα**, ατος, τό, (τίθημι) *that which is placed* or *laid down*: 1. *money deposited, deposit*, Ceb.31, *PCair.Zen.*22.11 (iii B.C.), *SIG*742.58 (Ephesus, i B.C.), Plu.2.116a, b; also, of grain, *PRyl.*199.12 (i A.D.); ἐν θέματι ἔχειν παρά τινος *PTeb.*120.125 (i B.C.); *treasure*, Lxx *To.*4.9. 2. *pile*, of loaves, ib.*Le.*24.6, 7; θ. βρωμάτων παρακείμενα ἐπὶ τάφῳ ib.*Si.*30.18. 3. = θήκη, *coffer*, ib.1*Ki.*6.8. 4. *position, situation*, of land, *IG*14.217 (Acrae). 5. Astrol., *nativity*, '*horoscope*' (in mod. sense), Suet.*Aug.*94, Vett.Val.194.20, al., Man.1.278. 6. either *common burial-place* or *common land*, *Michel*995 *B*50 (pl.); *private burial-ground*, ἡ σορὸς καὶ τὸ βαθρικὸν καὶ τὸ ὑποκείμενον θ. Judeich *Altertümer von Hierapolis* 208, cf. 124, al.; θέμα· ἕξις, τόπος, στάσις, μνῆμα, Hsch. II. *something proposed as a prize*, *IG*9(1).12 (Ambryssus), *SIG*867.67 (Ephesus, ii A.D.), *Sammelb.*6222.27 (iii A.D.). III. *case proposed for discussion, theme* of an argument, Quint.4.2.28, D.L.7.78. b. *proposition, premiss*, θ. ὁμολογούμενα Longin.32.8. c. *case*, in Law, Just.*Nov.*2.3 *Intr.*, 4.2 (pl.), dub. in *IG*4.364 (cf. *Supp.Epigr.*1.64). 2. *arbitrary determination*, opp. φύσις, ὁ κατὰ θέμα καλὸς λόγος Phld.*Rh.*1.151 S.; νόμοις καὶ θέμασιν διαφέρειν ib.259 S., cf. *Po.*5.22. 3. in Gramm., *primary* (non-derivative) *element* or *form*, A.D.*Pron.*11.21, al., cf. *Synt.*47.22; of the present tense, τὸ θ., ἀμύσσω· ὁ μέλλων, ἀμύξω *EM*88.13. 4. in Stoic Logic, *mode of reduction* of an irregular syllogism, *Stoic.*2.77, 83, al.

**θεμᾰτ-ίζω**, *deposit*, ἐπὶ τράπεζαν *BGU*1127.30 (i B.C.); πρὸς τοὺς τραπεζίτας *SIG*742.56 (Ephesus, i B.C.). 2. *place in order*, A.D.*Synt.*11.8:—Pass., κατὰ τύχην τεθεματίσθαι ib.1. II. *lay down, posit, assume*, Phld.*Rh.*1.152 S.:—Pass., *to be arbitrarily assumed*,

ib.259S., cf. 124S. 2. Gramm., *assign arbitrarily* a meaning to a word, S.E.*M*.8.202; *determine arbitrarily* a gender, etc., ib.1.149, 152. **-ικός**, ή, όν, *of* or *for a* θέμα: I. *that in which a valuable prize is proposed*, ἀγὼν θ., opp. στεφανίτης and φυλλίτης, Poll.3.153, cf. *IG*3.128.20, *IGRom*.4.1432.20, 1442.8 (Smyrna), *LW*894.17 (Delph.); τρόπος θ. a style *calculated for effect*, Plu.2.1135c; cf. θεματίτης. II. *arbitrarily fixed, traditional*, παρατηρήσεις Phld. *Rh*.1.195S.: -κόν, τό, ib.151S. 2. Gramm., *primary*, not derivative, e.g. ἄμφω, which has no sg., *EM*91.33: θεματικά, τά, *elements*, ib.232.21: Comp., θεματικώτερα (μέρη) τοῦ λόγου ὀνόματά ἐστι καὶ ῥήματα *principal* parts, A.D.*Adv*.121.5; -ώτεραι αἱ πρωτότυποι ἐν τοῖς γένεσιν the personal pronouns *form* their genders *from different* θέματα, Id.*Pron*.110.24. Adv. Comp. -ώτερον, κλιθῆναι *by means of different* θέματα, e.g. ἐγώ, ἐμοῦ, Id.*Synt*.102.4. **-ιον**, τό, Dim. of θέμα I.5, Antig.Nic.ap.Heph.Astr.2.18. **-ισμός**, ὁ, *laying down*: hence, 1. *conventional arrangement*, Vitr.1.2.5. 2. Gramm., *arbitrary determination*, S.E.*M*.1.149. **-ίτης** [ῑ], ου, ὁ, *depositor*, *SIG*742.59 (Ephesus, i B.C.). 2. θ. ἀγών, ὁ, = θεματικὸς ἀγών, *IG*14.1102.33.

❀ **θεμᾰτοποιέω**, *make into a* θέμα III.3, Sch.Od.4.807 (Pass.).

❀ **θέμεθλα**, τά, (τίθημι) *foundations, lowest part*, ὀφθαλμοῖο θ. *roots* of the eye, Il.14.493; στομάχοιο θ. 17.47; Ὠκεανοῖο θ. Hes.*Th*.816; Ἄμμωνος θ. *the place where* Ammon *stands*, i.e. his temple, Pi.*P*.4.16; Παγγαίου θ. *the roots* of Mt. Pangaeus, ib.180; θ. δίκης Sol.4.14; ἐκ θεμέθλων, Lat. *funditus*, Simm.25.4: dub. in sg., Call.*Dian*.248 (leg. θέμειλον).

❀ **θεμείλια**, τά, = θέμεθλα, θεμείλια..τὰ θέσαν μογέοντες Ἀχαιοί Il.12.28; θ. τε προβάλοντο 23.255; διέθηκε θ. *h.Ap*.254; θ. καρτερὰ πήξας *AP*9.808 (Cyrus), cf. Call.*Del*.260, Opp.*H*.5.680: **θέμειλα**, *Epigr.Gr*.1078.3 (Adana): sg. **θέμειλον**, *AP*9.649 (Maced.), 14.115.

**θεμελῐ-ᾰκός**, ή, όν, *of* or *for the foundation*, Sch.Lyc.615. ❀ **-όθεν**, = Lat. *funditus*, Dosith.p.412 K., *Gloss*. ❀ **-ος**, ον, *of* or *for the foundation*, λίθοι Ar.*Av*.1137; οἰκόπεδα D.S.5.66: abs., θεμέλιος (sc. λίθος), ὁ, *foundation-stone*, Arist.*Ph*.237b13, *Metaph*.1013a5: metaph., τῆς τέχνης θ. Machoap.Ath.8.346a; θ. ἀγνοίας Ph.1.266; οἱ θ. ἐκ παντοίων λίθων ὑπόκεινται the *foundations*, Th.1.93; τοὺς θ. ἐκ τῶν λίθων οἰκοδομεῖσθαι Arist.*PA*668a19: metaph., προλιπεῖν τοὺς προγονικοὺς θ. *SIG*888.70 (Scaptopara, iii A.D.): also neut. θεμέλιον Arist.*APo*.95b37 (s.v.l.), *PPetr*.3p.121 (iii B.C.), al.: pl., τὰ θ. Arist.*Ph*.200a4, *PCair.Zen*.176.71 (iii B.C.), al., Paus.8.32.1: metaph., τὰ ὑποβληθέντα θ., of the *foundations* of the world, Epicur.*Ep*.2p.38U.: gender indeterminate, μὴ ὑποκειμένων..θ. X.*Eq*.1.2; ἐκ τῶν θ. from the *foundations*, Th.3.68 (also sg., ἐνέπρησαν [οἰκίαν] ἐκ θεμελίου *BGU* 909.17 (iv A.D.)): metaph., ἐκ θ. ἐσφαλμένοι Plb.5.93.2, etc.; ἄρδην καὶ ἐκ θ. ἀπόλλυσθαι Hdn.8.3.2; also ἀνεκτίσθη τὸ τεῖχος ἐκ θεμελείων (sic) *Supp.Epigr*.2.480 (Kuban, iv A.D.). II. θεμέλια, τά, *building-sites*, Ptol.*Tetr*.174, cf. Vett.Val.82.24, al. III. Subst., *the fourth* τόπος, = ἀντιμεσουράνημα, Herm.Trism. in *Cat.Cod.Astr*.8(3).101, cf. 8(4).241. ❀ **-οῦχος**, ον, (ἔχω) *upholding the foundations*, Ποσειδῶν *Inscr.Délos* 290.116 (iii B.C.), Corn.*ND*22; ὁ θ. (sc. λίθος) Heraclit. *All*.48. **-όω**, *to lay the foundation of, found firmly*, πύργους..φοίνιξι θεμελιώσας X.*Cyr*.7.5.11, cf. *IG*12(2).11.26 (Mytil.), Lxx *Jo*.6.25 (26), *Ep.Hebr*.1.10, etc.:—Pass., *have the foundations laid*, *IG*2².1343.15 (i B.C.); ἐπὶ τὴν πέτραν *Ev.Matt*.7.25: metaph., βασιλεία καλῶς θεμελιωθεῖσα D.S.11.68; ἡγεμονία κάλλιστα τεθεμελιωμένη Id.15.1; ἐν ἀγάπῃ τεθ. *Ep.Eph*.3.18; τῇ πίστει *Ep.Col*.1.23. II. *destroy utterly*, in Pass., -ωθέντα (θεμειλωθ- cod.)· ἐκ ῥιζῶν ἀρθέντα, Hsch. ❀ **-ωσις**, εως, ἡ, *foundation*, Lxx 2*Es*.3.11, Ph.Byz.*Mir*.2.1; *paving*, *SIG*996.30 (Smyrna). **-ωτής**, οῦ, ὁ, *founder*, *Gloss*.

**θέμεν, θέμεναι**, v. τίθημι.

❀ **θέμερος**, α, ον, = βέβαιος, σεμνός, εὐσταθής, Hsch.; θεμερώτερα *IG* 14.1018.3 (iv A.D.).

**θεμερόφρων**, ον, gen. ονος, *of grave and serious mind*, Hsch.

**θεμερύνομαι** (θεμαρ- cod.), = σεμνύνομαι, Hsch. s.v. θέμερον; also, = τρυφῶ, *Com.Adesp*.1017 (v.l.).

**θεμερῶπις**, ιδος, ἡ, *grave and sedate of look*, Ἁρμονίη Emp.122.2; θ. αἰδώς A.*Pr*.134 (lyr.).

**θέμησις**· δικαιοσύνη, παρὰ Πυτίᾳ, Hsch. (Fort. θέμισις, cf. sq.).

**θεμίζω**, (θέμις) *judge, punish*, imper. θεμιζέτω, = μαστιγούτω, νομοθετείτω (Cret.), Hsch.; θεμισσέτω Paus.Gr.*Fr*.202:—Med., aor. part. θεμισσάμενοι ὀργάς *controlling our* wills, Pi.*P*.4.141.

**θεμινήσασα**· πρακτική, ἀνυσίμη, ἀποτελεσίμη, Hsch. (post θεμιστός).

**θεμί-ξενος**, ον, *just to strangers*, ἀρετά Pi.*Pae*.6.131. **-πλεκτος**, ον, (πλέκω) *rightly plaited*, θ. στέφανος a *well-earned* crown (or, as Sch., *twined with due ceremony*), Pi.*N*.9.52.

❀ **θέμις**, ἡ, old Ep. gen. θέμιστος (in Hom. the only declension): acc. θέμιστα Il.5.761, θέμιν A.*Ag*.1431, etc.: gen. pl. θεμιστέων Hes. *Th*.235: pr. n. Θέμις, Θέμιστος Od.2.68, Θέμιστα Il.20.4; dat. Θέμιστι 15.87; but Θέμιτος Pi.*O*.13.8, Θέμιδος A.*Pr*.18, etc., Θέμιος (v.l. -ιδος) Hdt.2.50, Θέμιν Hes.*Th*.16, *IG*2².1611.71: voc. Θέμι Il.15.93, E.*Med*.160 (anap.): I. *that which is laid down* or *established, law* (not as fixed by statute, but) *as established by custom*, θ. ἐστί 'tis *meet and right*, c. dat. pers. et inf., οὔ μοι θ. ἐστὶ ξεῖνον ἀτιμῆσαι Od.14.56; ἅ τε ξείνοις θ. ἐστὶν [παραθεῖναι] Il.11.779; ὅ οἱ Διόθεν θ. ἦεν [ἐκτελέσαι] Hes.*Sc*.22; γυναικὶ οὐ θ. *SIG*1024.9 (Myconos, iii/ii B.C.): without dat., Il.16.796, 23.44; οὐ θ. ἐν μοισοπόλων οἰκίᾳ θρῆνον ἔμμεν' Sapph.136; ὅτι δυνατὸν καὶ θ. αἰνεῖν A.*Ag*.98, cf. S.*Ant*.880 (lyr.), *Ph*.346, E.*Med*.678, Pl.*Phdr*.250b, Isoc.4.92, etc.; ἣ γὰρ θ. for so 'tis *right* [to do], Od.24.286; freq. ἣ θ. ἐστί as *the custom* is, Il.2.73: c. dat. (= loc.), ἣ θ. ἐστίν..ἀγορῇ 9.33: c. gen., ἣ θ. ἀνθρώπων πέλει ib.134; ἣ θ. ἐστὶ γυναικός Od.14.130; also ἣ θ. ἀνθρώποις κατὰ ἤθεα Hes.*Op*.137; θύειν τοὺς γεωργούς..ᾗ (with ι) θέμις *IG*2².1364 (i A.D.); but ᾗ θέμις ἐστί is rejected for Hom. by Hdn.Gr.2.516, cf. A.D.*Adv*.148.28: indecl., πότερα κατ' ἔχθραν ἢ τὸ μὴ θέμις λέγεις; A.*Supp*.336; ὥστε μή..θέμις σέ γ' εἶναι κεῖνον ἀντιδρᾶν κακῶς S.*OC*1191; οὐδὲ..φασὶ θέμις εἶναι Pl. *Grg*.505c, cf. X.*Oec*.11.11, Ael.*NA*1.60. 2. *justice, right*, S.*Tr*.810; ὅσα τείνει πρὸς θέμιν Pl.*Smp*.188d; *penalty*, ἐκτίνειν ὁμοίαν θ. A.*Supp*.436 (lyr.); *sanctity*, ὁρκίων ἐμῶν θ. Id.*Ag*.1431. II. = ἀγὼν θεματίτης, *IGRom*.3.319 (Pisid.); νικήσας θέμιν ἀνδρῶν ib.437 (Termessus). III. pl. **θέμιστες**, *decrees* of the gods, *oracles*, Διὸς θ. Od.16.403; θέμισσιν *by oracles*, Pi.*P*.4.54, cf. *O*.10(11).24. 2. *dooms*, customary *laws, ordinances*, δικασπόλοι, οἵ τε θέμιστας πρὸς Διὸς εἰρύαται Il.1.238, cf. Hes.*Th*.235; τοῖσιν δ' (i.e. the Cyclopes) οὔτ' ἀγοραὶ βουληφόροι οὔτε θέμιστες Od.9.112; οὔτε δίκας εὖ εἰδότα οὔτε θέμιστας neither rights nor *laws*, ib.215: in sg., ὃς οὔ τινα οἶδε θέμιστα Il.5.761; ἵνα σφ' ἀγορή τε θέμις τε 11.807. 3. *judgements, decisions* given by the kings or judges, οἳ..σκολιὰς κρίνωσι θέμιστας 16.387; σκολιῇς δὲ δίκῃς κρίνωσι θ. Hes.*Op*.221; διακρίνοντα θ. ἰθείῃσι δίκῃσιν Id.*Th*.85. 4. *tribute, dues*, λιπαρὰς τελέουσι θέμιστας Il.9.156. IV. pr. n., *Themis*, ἥ τ' ἀνδρῶν ἀγορὰς ἠμὲν λύει ἠδὲ καθίζει 2.68, cf. Il.15.87, 20.4, Hes.*Th*.16, A.*Pr*.18, etc.

**θεμισκόπος**, ον, *seeing to law and justice*, Pi.*N*.7.47.

**θεμισκρέων**, οντος, ὁ, *reigning by right*, Pi.*P*.5.29.

**θέμιστα, θέμιστας**, v. θέμις.

**θεμιστ-εία**, ἡ, *a giving of oracles*, Str.17.1.43. **-εῖος**, α, ον, *of law and right*, θ. σκᾶπτον the sceptre *of righteous judgement*, Pi.*O*.1.12. **-ευτός**, ή, όν, *ordered by law* or *custom*, Hsch. ❀ **-εύω**, *declare law and right*, c. dat., Μίνωα ἴδον..θεμιστεύοντα νέκυσσιν Od.11.569: c. gen., *govern*, θ. δὲ ἕκαστος παίδων ἠδ' ἀλόχων 9.114. II. *give by way of answer* or *oracle*, νημερτέα βουλὴν πᾶσι θ. *h.Ap*.253, cf. Lys.*Fr*.23S.: abs., *deliver oracles*, E.*Ion*371, D.S.5.67, Plu.*Alex*.14; τινα Orac.ap.Ael.*VH*3.43; cf. θεμιτεύω. **-ιος**, ὁ, *patron of right*, of Zeus, Plu.2.1065e. II. name of month in Thessaly, etc., *IG*9(1).689, etc.

❀ **θεμιστοπόλος**, ον, *ministering law and right*, epith. of kings and judges, *h.Cer*.103. II. *oracular*, σηκοί, of Delphi, *Klio*15.48 (Delph., iii B.C.).

❀ **θεμιστ-ός**, ή, όν, = θεμιτός, A.*Th*.694 (lyr.). Adv. -τῶς cj. in Id.*Ch*.645 (lyr.). II. *oracular*, ὕμνοι Pi.*Fr*.192; cf. θέμις III.1. **-οσύνη**, ἡ, in pl., poet. for θέμιστες, Orph.*H*.79.6. **-οῦχος**, ον, (ἔχω) *upholding right*, βασιλῆες A.R.4.347.

**θεμίστωρ**, ορος, ὁ, *knowing right*, Hsch.

❀ **θεμῐτ-εύω**, = θεμιστεύω, ὄργια θεμιτεύων *keeping lawful* orgies, E.*Ba*.79 (lyr., metri gr.). ❀ **-ός**, ή, όν, (θέμις) *allowed by the laws of God and men, righteous*, οὐ θεμιτόν [ἐστι], = οὐ θέμις, c. inf., οὐ θ. οἱ ἔφασκε πίνειν οἶνον *h.Cer*.207, cf. Pi.*P*.9.42, S.*OT*993, *OC*1758 (anap.), E.*Or*.97, Theoc.5.136, etc.: in Prose, Hdt.3.37, 5.72, Pl.*Ap*.30d, *IG*2.1059.16, 14.1390; μηδὲ θεμιτὸν..μηδ' ὅσιον D.21.148: in pl., τὰ μὴ θεμίτ' ἦν [ἰδεῖν] dub. l. in Call.*Lav.Pall*.78. Adv. -τῶς Phot., Suid. **-ώδης**, ες, *oracular*, Orac.ap.Eus.*PE*5.16.

**θεμόω**, only in phrase [νῆα] θέμωσε..χέρσον ἱκέσθαι *drove* the ship *ashore, stranded* her, Od.9.486; but in ib.542, *drove* her landwards, i.e. towards her destination: cf. θεμούς· διαθέσεις, παραινέσεις, Hsch., who also has **θεμῶν**· θελήμων.

**-θεν**, old termin. of the gen., as in ἐμέθεν, Διόθεν, etc.: freq. with Ablatival sense, denoting *motion from* a place, as in Λεσβόθεν, Ἀβυδόθεν, ἄλλοθεν, οἴκοθεν, etc.: so with Preps., ἀπὸ Τροίηθεν Od.9.38; ἐξ οὐρανόθεν Il.8.19, cf. A.D.*Adv*.184.12 sq.: most of the forms in -οθεν were parox., exc. οἴκοθεν, ἄλλοθεν, πάντοθεν (sts. παντόθεν), ἔκτοθεν, ἔνδοθεν, ib.191.27 sq. (other exceptions in Hdn.Gr.1.500).

**θέναρ**, ἄρος, τό, *palm of the hand*, πρυμνὸν ὕπερ θέναρος, i.e. just below the wrist, Il.5.339; χειρὸς τὸ ἐντὸς θέναρ Arist.*HA*493b32, cf. Poll.2.143. b. pl., *the two muscles forming the borders of the palm*, Gal.*UP*2.3. c. *ball of the thumb*, Ruf.*Onom*.87, Gal.18(2).864. 2. *flat* of the foot, Hp.*Mul*.2.116 (pl.), Arat.718. 3. metaph., θ. βωμοῖο *hollow* in the top of the altar, on which the offerings are laid, Pi.*P*.4.206; ἁλὸς θ. *hollow bed* of the sea, Id.*I*.4(3).56. (Cf. OHG. *tenar* 'palm of the hand'.)

**θεναρίζει**· τύπτει, Hsch. **θένιοι**· οἱ προσήκοντες, Id.

**θένω**, v. θείνω. **θέο**, Ep. for θοῦ, v. τίθημι.

**θεοβλάβ-εια** [βλᾶ], ἡ, *infatuation sent by the gods, madness*, Aeschin.3.133, D.H.1.24, D.C.44.8 (-ία codd.). **-έω**, *to be* θεοβλαβής, A.*Pers*.831, Them.*Or*.4.56c. ❀ **-ής**, ές, *stricken of God, infatuated*, Hdt.1.127, 8.137, Ant.Lib.22.4. Adv. -βῶς Poll.1.22.

**θεό-βουλος**, ον, = θεόμητις, Phot., Suid.:—fem. **-βούλη**, of the Sibyl, Lact.*Inst*.1.6.7. **-βρότιον**, τό, = ἀείζων τὸ μικρόν, Ps.-Dsc.4.89. **-γᾰμία**, ἡ, *marriage of gods*, Ph.2.205 (v.l. -μαχία): in pl., title of poem by Pisander, Suid., Zos.5.29. **-γάμια** [γᾰ], τά, name of festival in Sicily, Poll.1.37; at Athens, Plu. *in Hes*.85; at Nysa, *GDI*3661.11, Head *Hist.Num*.²654, al. ❀ **-γέναιος**, ὁ (sc. μήν), name of month in Egypt, *BGU*713.3 (i A.D.). ❀ **-γενής**, ές, *born of God*, Sch.rec.A.*Pr*.351, *Gloss*. **-γεννής**, ές, *begotten of a god*, S.*Ant*.834 (anap.).

**θεό-γλωσσος**, ον, *with the tongue of a god*, γυναῖκες, of poetesses, *AP*9.26 (Antip. Thess.). **-γνωσία**, ἡ, *the knowledge of God*, Hierocl. in *CA*20p.463M., Heph.Astr.1.1. ❀ **-γνωστος**, ον, *known of God*, ibid., *Gloss*.: as a complimentary term, ἡ θ. σου μνήμη *POxy*.237 vi 29 (ii A.D.).

**θεο-γονία**, Ion. **-ίη**, ἡ, *genealogy of the gods*, title of Hesiod's poem; cf. Hdt.1.132, 2.53, Procl.*in Ti*.3.107 D. II. *generation* or *birth of gods*, Pl.*Lg*.886c, Ph.2.205,264, D.L.*Praef*.3. **-γονος**, ον, *born of God, divine*, E.*Or*.346. **-δαίμων**, ονος, ὁ, *inferior divinity*, *BCH*22.350 (Amphipolis).

**Θεοδαίσια**, τά, Cret. name for the Διονύσια, Call.*Aet.Oxy*.2080.88, *GDI*5075.43(Crete), cf. Hsch.; also, at Rhodes, *SIG*1035c. II. ⊛**Θεοδαίσιος**, ὁ, epith. of Dionysus, Hsch.; also, (sc. μήν) name of month found in various forms: Cret. **Θιοδαίσιος** *GDI*5149; in Cos, Rhodes, etc., **Θευδαίσιος** ib.3593, al., etc.; at Mytilene, **Θεδαίσιος** *IG*11(4).1064*a*2 (Delos).

**θεο-δέγμων**, ον, gen. ονος, = θεηδόχος, θῶκος *AP*7.363; *divine*, πηγή Archestr.*Fr*.13.8. ⊛ **-δέκτωρ**, ορος, ὁ, ἡ, = θεηδόχος, Hsch. **-δήλητος**, ον, *by which the gods are injured*, μιαιφονίη v.l. in *AP*9.157. **-δίδακτος** [ῐ], ον, *taught of God*, 1*Ep.Thess*.4.9. **-δμής**, dat. -δμῆτι· θεόφρονι Cyr. (fort. θεόμητι). ⊛ **-δμητος**, Dor. **-δμᾱτος**, ον, also α, ον Pi.*O*.6.59, *Fr*.87.1: (δέμω) :—*god-built*, *founded by the gods*, πύργοι Il.8.519; Δᾶλος Pi. ll. cc.; πύλαι B.*Fr*.7 Bgk. (cf. p.437 Jebb); Ἀθῆναι S.*El*.707; βωμός E.*Hec*.23: metaph., θ. χρέος, ἀρεταί, Pi.*O*.3.7, *I*.6(5).11. **-δόνιον** or **-δώνιον**, τό, = γλυκυσίδη, dub. in Ps.-Dsc.3.140. **-δοσία**, ἡ, *a gift* or *offering to the gods*, Str.17.1.37 (pl.). ⊛ **-δόσιος**, ον, *given by God*, Hsch.; f.l. in Aristeas 229. **-δότια**, τά, name of various eyesalves, Gal. 12.784, Aët.7.118; *collyrium Theodoti*, Cels.6.6.6. **-δοτος**, ον, = θεόσδοτος, ἔργα Pi.*I*.5(4).23; εὐχαί B.7.50. II. θεόδοτον, τό, *remedy for coughs*, Alex.Trall.5.4. **-δρομέω**, *walk in God's ways*, Phot., Suid. **-δυτα**· ἱερόθυτα, Hsch. (leg. θεόθυτα). **-δώρητος**, ον, *given by God*, Iamb.*VP*2.6, 15.67, Asp.*in EN*25.28. II. θ. λίθος, of the ἀλαβαστρίτης λίθος, Zos.Alch.p.114 B. 2. ἡ θ. *a purgative*, Aët.12.112, Alex.Trall.1.15. **-είδεια**, ἡ, *godlike appearance*, φυσική Iamb.*VP*2.10. ⊛ **-ειδής**, ές, *godlike*, in Hom. of form, Πρίαμος Il.24.217, al.; Ἀλέξανδρος, Τηλέμαχος, 3.16, Od.14.173, al.; Οὐρανίη Hes.*Th*.350; θ. πρόσωπον Pl.*Phdr*.251a; οἱ ποιηταὶ τοὺς καλοὺς θεοειδεῖς ὀνομάζουσιν Plu.2.988d, cf. Pl.*R*.501b. II. generally, *godlike*, θεοειδές τί ἐστιν ἡ ψυχή Id.*Phd*.95c, cf. Muson.*Fr*.17 p.91 H.; of things, λίθους, βοτάνας, ζῷα, ἀρώματα Iamb.*Myst*.5.23: Comp. -έστερος Pl.*Epin*.983d: Sup. -έστατος Eus.Mynd.33; κόσμος ἐπῶν Phalar.*Ep*.147.2: also irreg. θεειδ- (q.v.). Adv. -δῶς Herm.*in Phdr*.p.178 A., Suid. **-είκελος**, ον, *godlike*, of Achilles, Il.1.131, al.; of Telemachus, Od.2.416; of Hector and Andromache, Sapph.*Supp*.20c.6: in Prose, Pl.*R*.501b, Them.*Or*.6.79a. **-επής**, ές, (ἔπος) = θεσπέσιος, Hsch. **-εχθρία**, v. θεοισεχθρία.

**θεόθεν**, Adv. *from the gods*, θ. δ' οὐκ ἔστ' ἀλέασθαι (sc. θάνατον) *death at the hands of the gods*, Od.16.447, cf. Pl.Com.173.14 (hex.); εἴ τις ἄλλα θ. ἀνθρώποισι τέρψις *given by God to man*, *IG*3.171. 2. *by the will* or *favour of the gods*, Pi.*O*.12.8, *P*.11.50, A.*Th*.324, *Pers*.101 (both lyr.), etc.; *by the gods*, οἷς ἂν σεισθῇ θ. δόμος S.*Ant*.584.

**θεο-θρέμμων**, ον, gen. ονος, *maintained by God*, σιγή Orac.ap.Procl. *in Alc*.p.56 C. **-θρεπτος**, ον, = foreg., Sch.A.*Pers*.905. **-θῠτος**, ον, (θύω) *offered to the gods*: θεόθυτον, τό, *a victim*, Cratin.417 (pl.), cf. Poll.1.29 (pl.).

**θεοίνια** (sc. ἱερά), τά, an Attic feast of Dionysus, Jusj.ap D.59.78, Lycurg.*Fr*.56: **θεοίνιον**, τό, his temple, Phot.

**θέοινος**, ὁ, *god of wine*, πάτερ θέοινε A.*Fr*.382, cf. Lyc.1247.

**θεοισεχθρία**, ἡ, *hatefulness to the gods, villainy*, D.22.59 (written θεοῖς ἐχθρίαν), prob. in Ar.*V*.418 (required by Cretic metre), in Archipp.35 (where the first two syll. coalesce), and in Luc.*Lex*.11: in the last three places codd. have θεοσεχθρία or θεὸς ἐχθρία (θεοσεχθρα v.l. Archipp. l. c.): θεοεχθρία is found in Sch.Ar.*Ra*.557, v.l. in Luc.*Lex*.l. c.; cf. θεοῖς ἐχθρ's in D.19.95, 24.195.

**θεο-κατάρᾱτος** [ᾰρ], ον, *accursed of God*, Zos.Alch.ap.Olymp.Alch. p.101 B. **-κατασκεύαστος**, ον, *made by God*, ὕμνος Sch.Pi.*O*.3.11; gloss on θεότευκτον, Hsch. **-κέλευστος**, ον, *ordered by God*, gloss on θέσκελα, Id. **-κῆρυξ**, ῡκος, ὁ, *divine herald*: in pl., name of a family at Eleutherae *claiming descent from Talthybius*, Id. **-κίνητος** [ῑ], ον, *roused by the gods*, gloss on θέορτος, Sch.Pi.*O*.2.67. **-κλητέω**, f.l. for -κλῦτέω, Eust.805.26. **-κλητος**, ον, *sung by gods*, Nonn.*D*.5.92. **-κλῠτέω**, *call on the gods*, A.*Pers*.500, Plu.*Sull*.29, Ael.*Fr*.46, Porph.*Abst*.2.26, D.C.74.13: c. acc. pers., θ. Θέμιν E.*Med*.208; Κυρῖνον Plu.*Rom*.28: also, c. acc. rei, *ask in prayer*, Id.*Arist*.18. II. Pass., *to be inspired*, Id.2.592c:—so in Act., Hld.3.17. **-κλύτησις** [ῠ], εως, ἡ, *calling on the gods, invocation*, Plb.23.10.7 (pl.). **-κλῠτος**, ον, *calling on the gods*, θ. λιταί A.*Th*.143 (lyr.). II. Pass., *heard by God*, expl. of *Ishmael*, J.*AJ*1.10.4. **-κμητος**, ον, *wrought by a god*, βέλεμνα, πύργοι, Q.S.3.419, Tryph.40 (v.l. θεοδμ-). ⊛ **-κόλος**, ὁ, = θεηκόλος, *servant of a god, priest*, *SIG*684.1 (Dyme, ii B.C.), 1021.3 (Olympia, i B.C.):—hence **-κολέω**, *serve as a priest*, θ. Ἀσκλαπιῷ *IG*9(1).1066 (Amphissa):—also **-κολεύω**, ib.417 (Aetol.): **-κολία**, ἡ, *SIG*531.32 (pl., Dyme). ⊛ **-κραντος**, ον, *accomplished* or *wrought by the gods*, A.*Ag*.1488. **-κρᾱσία**, ἡ, (κρᾶσις) *mingling with God*, Iamb.*VP*33.240, Dam.*Isid*.2. II. *Divine Mingling*, title of work by Pherecydes of Syros, Suid. **-κρᾰτία**, ἡ, (κράτος) *rule of God, theocracy*, J.*Ap*.2.16. **-κρήπῑς**, ῖδος, ἡ, *founded by a god*, of Athens, Nonn.*D*.24.96. ⊛ **-κρῐτος**, ὁ, *judge of gods*, of Paris, Dosiad.*Ara* 10. **-κτητος**, ον, *acquired by God*, τρίποδες Aristonous 1.9. **-κτιστος**, ον (also -η, Dor. α, -ον *Trag.Adesp*. 85), *created, established*, or *founded by God*, φλόξ l. c., cf. Limen. 36; πόλις *OGI*168.4 (Egypt, ii B.C., v. corrigenda); νομοθεσία Lxx 2*Ma*.6.23. II. name of an eyesalve, Dessau *Inscr.Lat.Sel*. 8738. **-κτῖτος**, ον, = foreg. I, Sol.36.6; γαῖα *Epigr.Gr*.223.5. **-κυνεῖ**· δόξαν θείαν ἔχουσαν, Hsch. (fort. -κυδῆ).

**θεοληπτ-έομαι**, Pass., *to be inspired*, Ph.1.143. **-ικός**, ή, όν, *belonging to one possessed* or *inspired*: ἡ θεοληπτική (sc. μαντεία) = θεοληψία, S.E.*M*.9.132. **-ος**, ον, *possessed, inspired*, Arist.*EE* 1214ᵃ23, S.E.*P*.2.52, *Cat.Cod.Astr*.8(4).148; γνώμη App.*Hann*.42, cf. Sallust.3, etc.; θ. εἰς ἀρετήν Plu.2.1117a. 2. in bad sense, = θεοβλαβής, Man.4.80, Vett.Val.114.12. 3. *superstitious*, Plu.2.855b.

**θεοληψία**, ἡ, *inspiration*, Plu.2.763a. 2. *superstition*, ib.56e. 3. *frenzy, madness*, Vett.Val.210.4 (pl.).

**θεολογ-εῖον**, τό, in the theatre, *a place above the stage where gods appeared*, Poll.4.130. **-έω**, *discourse on the gods and cosmology*, Arist. *Metaph*.983ᵇ29; περί τινων Id.*Mu*.391ᵇ4, cf. Plu.2.614d, etc.; Δία αὐτὸν [τὸν Φαέθοντα] ζωογόνον θεολογοῦσι *call him* Ζεύς ζ. Antig.*Mir*. 1cb:—Pass., τὰ θεολογούμενα *discourses about the gods*, Plu.2.421e (v.l.), S.E.*M*.9.55; title of work by Asclepiades of Mendes, Suet. *Aug*.94; τρεῖς αἱ Μοῖραι θεολογοῦνται *Theol.Ar*.16. 2. *refer to a divine influence*, τοὺς τόκους Sch.Ptol.*Tetr*.103. ⊛ **-ια**, τά, = *dei proverbia*, *Gloss*. **-ία**, ἡ, *science of things divine*, Pl.*R*.379a, Phld. *Piet*.72, Porph.*Marc*.15, Iamb.*Myst*.1.1, etc.; title of an Orphic work, Dam.*Pr*.124: in pl., Arist.*Mete*.353ᵃ35. II. *oration in praise of a god*, *SIG*1109.115. 2. *incantation, invocation of a god*, *PMag.Par*.1.1037. **-ικός**, ή, όν, *theological*, φιλοσοφία θ., i.e. metaphysics, Arist.*Metaph*.1026ᵃ19, cf. 1064ᵇ3; γένος Str.10.3.23; πραγματεία D.H.4.62; [μῦθοι] Sallust.4; τὸ θ. Cleanth.*Stoic*.1.108; οἱ θ. Olymp.*in Mete*.129.19: Comp. -ώτερος Dam.*Pr*.135. Adv. -κῶς, opp. τραγικῶς, ἀποφαίνεσθαι Plu.2.568d, cf. Iamb.*Myst*.1.2. ⊛ **-ος**, ὁ, (λέγω) *one who discourses of the gods*, of poets such as Hesiod and Orpheus, Arist.*Metaph*.1000ᵃ9, S.E.*M*.2.31; of cosmologists (like the Orphics), Arist.*Metaph*.1071ᵇ27, al., Cic.*ND*3.21.53; θεολόγοι καὶ ποιηταί Phld.*Piet*.48; of diviners and prophets, θ. καὶ μάντιες Philol.14; οἱ Δελφῶν θ. Plu.2.417f, cf. Luc.*Alex*.19, *BMus.Inscr*.4.481*.295 (Ephesus, ii A.D.), *IGRom*.4.1431 (Smyrna): fem., *CIG* 3199,3200 (ibid.). 2. *theologian*: ὁ θ., = Moses, Ph.2.152,416.

**θεολωβήτης**, ου, ὁ, *blasphemer*, Man.4.234.

**θεομᾰν-έω**, *to be* θεομανής, Poll.1.19. **-ής**, ές, *maddened by the gods*, A.*Th*.653, E.*Ion*1402; λύσσα θ. *madness caused by the gods*, Id.*Or*.845; πότμος ib.79. **-ία**, ἡ, *madness caused by God, inspiration*, cj. in Ph.1.571 (ἐνθεομανία, ἐνθέῳ μανίᾳ codd.).

**θεομαντ-εία**, ἡ, *spirit of prophecy*, D.C.62.18. **-εῖον**, τό, *spell for evoking a divine revelation*, *PMag.Leid.V*.5.13. **-ις**, εως, ὁ, *one who has a spirit of prophecy, an inspired person*, Pl.*Ap*.22c, *Men*. 99c, Aristid.2.18 J., Gal.15.442.

⊛ **θεομᾰχ-έω**, *fight against God* or *the gods*, E.*Ba*.45, al., *IA*1408; μὴ θεομάχει Men.187, cf. Hp.*Ep*.14, Lxx 2*Ma*.7.19, Plu.2.168c, Arr. *Epict*.3.24.24. **-ία**, ἡ, *battle of the gods*, Pl.*R*.378d (pl.), cf. Il.20. tit. II. *fighting against God*, Arr.*Epict*.3.24.24. **-ος**, ον, *fighting against God*, Γίγαντες Scymn.637, cf. *Act.Ap*.5.39, Luc.*JTr*. 45, Vett.Val.331.12.

**θεο-μηνία**, ἡ, *wrath of God*, Pall.*in Hp*.2.142 D., Steph.*in Hp*.1. 72 D., Eust.891.24. **-μήστωρ**, ορος, ὁ, *like the gods in counsel*, A. *Pers*.655 (lyr.), *IG*14.1868. II. Pass., *devised by God*, θεομήστορος εἰκόνα κόσμου Alex.Eph.ap.Theon.Sm.p.141 H. (-μήτορος codd., em. Meineke); κόσμον Man.4.7 (-μήτορα edd. vett.). **-μητέω**, *to be divinely wise*, Hsch. **-μητις**, ιδος, ἡ, *divinely wise*, δίκη Maiist.54, cf. Suid. **-μήτωρ**, ορος, ἡ, *mother of a god*, of Olympias, mother of Alexander, Anon.Hist.(*FGrH*153) p.826 J. **-μῖμος**, ον, *imitating God*, θ. πρᾶγμα βασιλεία Diotog.ap.Stob.4.7.62. ⊛ **-μισής**, ές, *hated by the gods*, opp. θεοφιλής, Pl.*Euthphr*.7a, *R*.612e, Them.*Or*.16.210a: Sup. -έστατος Pl.*Lg*.917a, Ph.1.653. Adv. -σῶς Poll.1.22. II. Act., *hating God*, Ar.*Av*.1548 (ubi v. Sch.), Ph.2.597, Suid. (θεομίσης v.l. in Ar.l. c.). **-μῖσητία**, ἡ, = θεοισεχθρία, Sch.Ar.*V*.416. **-μίσητος** [ῑ], ον, = θεομισής I, Arist.(?) in *PLit.Lond*.112, Ph.2.202. **-μοιρία**, ἡ, *the god's portion* of a sacrifice, *SIG*1026.20 (Cos). **-μοιρος**, ον, *partaking of the divine nature*, Ecphant.ap.Stob.4.6.22; φύσις Dam.*Isid*.191. **-μόριος**, α, ον, Ep. θευμ-, collat. form of sq., θευμορίη νοῦσος, ἄτη, A.R.3.676,974. II. **θευμορίη**, ἡ, *destiny*, Call.*Ep*.32.4, *AP*7.367 (Antip.). 2. = θεοῦ μοῖρα, but also, *priest's share of the sacrifice*, Hsch.:—hence **θευμοριάζω**, Id. **-μορος**, ον, *destined by the gods, imparted by them*, ἀοιδαί Pi.*O*.3.10; γάμου θεόμορον γέρας Id.*I*.8(7).42. II. *blessed by the gods*, Id.*P*.5.5. **-μορφος**, ον, *of form divine*, *AP*12.196 (Strat.). **-μῡθία**, ἡ, *divine lore, mythology*, Procl.*Theol.Plat*.1.4: in pl., Herm.*in Phdr*. p.73 A., Marin.*Procl*.27. **-μῠσής**, ές, *abominable before the gods*, A.*Eu*.40. **-ξένιος**, ὁ, epith. of Apollo at Pellene, Paus.7.27.4: name of a month at Delphi, *GDI*1709, al. II. **θεοξένια**, τά, *festival in honour of Apollo* at Pellene, Paus. l. c., Sch.Pi.*O*.9.146; at Delphi, *Michel*995 *D*9, Polemo ap.Ath.9.372a, Plu.2.557f; and, *of the Dioscuri* at Agrigentum, Pi.*O*.3.tit.; also at Paros, *IG*12(5).129.61 (ii B.C.); gloss on Θεοδαίσια, Sch.Call.*Aet.Oxy*.2080.88:—hence **θεοξενιασταί**, οἱ, *the persons who celebrated such a festival*, *IG*12(5). 872.114 (ii B.C.). **-παίγμων**, ονος, ὁ, ἡ, *sporting with the gods*, Nonn. *D*.30.210. **-παις**, παιδος, ὁ, ἡ, *child of the gods*, Ἔρως *AP*12.56 (Mel.); Βαβυλών Herodic.ap.Ath.5.222a; λάβραξ Archestr.*Fr*.45.2; Τύρος *AP*7.419 (Mel.). **-παιστος**, ον, *struck by a god*, κιθάρα Hsch. **-παράδοτος**, ον, *delivered by God*, Procl.*in Cra*.p.59 P.; λόγια Marin. *Procl*.26; σοφία Dam.*Pr*.311. ⊛ **-πάτωρ** [ᾰ], ορος, ὁ, *son of God*, title of Parthian kings, *BMus.Cat.Coins Parthia* p.16, al. ⊛ **-πειθής**, ές,

*obedient to God*, ὑπακοή Hierocl.*in CA* 24p.473 M. **-πεμπτος**, ον, *sent by the gods*, Arist.*EN*1099ᵇ15, Plb.32.15.14, D.H.1.14; ὄνειροι Ph.1.620, cf. Artem.1.6; ἀτυχία D.S.15.24; ἀγαθόν D.H.4.62. 2. *superhuman, extraordinary*, Longus 3.18. **-πιστος**, ον, *faithful to God*, *PMasp.*151.196 (vi A.D.). **-πλαστέω**, *make into a god*, Hld.9.9; θ. τὸν χρυσοῦν μόσχον Ph.1.559; *deify*, τὸν Νεῖλον Id.2.164. **-πλάστης**, ου, ὁ, *maker of gods*, i.e. *of their images*, Ar.*Fr.*787. II. *the divine Creator*, Ph.2.490. **-πληγής**, ές, v. -πλήξ. **-πληκτος**, ον, *stricken of God*, Hsch. (in Dor. form -πλακτος). **-πλήξ**, ῆγος, ὁ, ἡ, τό, = θεόπληκτος, θεοπλήγεσσιν ἐοικότας εἰδώλοισιν Maiist.60 (unless -πληγέσσιν from -πληγής, ές). **-πληξία**, ἡ, = θεοβλάβεια, Oenom.ap.Eus.*PE*5.36. ⊕ **-πλοκος**, ον, = πρὸς θεοὺς προσπλεκόμενος, *Cat.Cod.Astr.*8(4).166. **-πνευστος**, ον, *inspired of God*, σοφίη Ps.-Phoc.129; ὄνειροι Plu.2.904f; πᾶσα γραφὴ 2*Ep.Ti.*3.16; δημιούργημα Vett.Val.330.19. ⊕ **-πνοος**, ον, contr. **-ους**, ουν, = foreg., θ. γενόμενος *Corp.Herm.*1.30; θ. ὕδωρ Numen.ap.Porph.*Antr.*10; πρόσωπον, of the Sphinx, *Epigr.Gr.*1016.

**θεοποι-έω**, *make into gods, deify*, τὰ θνητά D.H.2.56, cf. Luc.*Scyth.*1; Πυθαγόραν S.E.*M.*7.94. II. *make divine*, ἄνθρωπον θ. αἱ ἐπιστῆμαι Hierocl.*in CA Praef.*p.417 M. **-ητικός**, ή, όν, *able to make gods*: ἡ -κή (sc. τέχνη) *the art of making statues of gods*, Poll.1.13. **-ητος**, ον, *made by the gods*, or *by God*, Isoc.7.62. **-ία**, ἡ, *making of gods*, Porph.*Abst.*4.9; *of their statues*, Poll.1.13. II. *being made divine*, ἵνα κατὰ ἀφαίρεσιν τοῦ βροτοῦ ἡ θ. ἡμῶν νοῆται Hierocl.*in CA*27p.483 M. ⊕ **-ός**, όν, *making gods*, Ar.*Fr.*786; ἁ θ. τέχνα, = θεοποιητική, *AP*9.774 (Glauc.); οὐ θ. τις ἀλλ' ἀνθρωποποιὸς ὤν Luc.*Philops.*20. II. *making into gods, deifying*, Dam.(?)ap.Suid. s.v. ἀποκλήρωσις; παραγγέλματα Hierocl.*in CA*19p.462 M.

**θεο-πολέω**, *minister in things divine*, Pl.*Lg.*909d. ⊕ **-πόλος**, ὁ, ἡ, *priest*; v. θεηπόλος. **-πομπεῖν**· ἐνθουσιᾶν, Hsch. (Fort. -προπεῖν.) **-πομπος**, ον, = θεόπεμπτος, τιμαί Pi.*P.*4.69; τύχα B.16.132 (– – ⏑); πόμα, as pr. n., Aët.11.11. II. pr. n. Θεόπομπος: hence, Adj. Θεοπόμπειον (sc. μέτρον), τό, Cretic pentameter used by Theopomp.Com., Heph.13.5. **-πόνητος**, ον, *prepared by the gods*, λέχη, of Helen, E.*Tr.*953, *Hel.*584.

**θεοπρέπ-εια**, ἡ, *divine majesty*, τῆς προσόψεως D.S.5.43, cf. 11.89. **-ής**, ές, *meet for a god*, Ἥρας δῶμα Pi.*N.*10.2; πεδίον D.S.11.89; πομπή, μορφή, Plu.*Dio* 28, 2.780a; ὀνόματα Max.Tyr.6.2; *marvellous*, θέαμα Plu.*Alc.*34, etc.; τὸ θ. τῶν διατεταγμένων Ph.2.137: Sup. -έστατος, ἄγαλμα Plu.2.780f. Adv. -πῶς *IG*5(1).1390.3 (Andania, i B.C.), D.S.4.2, Ph.1.154, al., Luc.*Alex.*15, etc. **-τος**, ον, = foreg., v.l. in A.*Pers.*905 (lyr.).

⊕ **θεο-προπέω**, *prophesy*, but only in part. masc., θεοπροπέων ἀγορεύεις Il.1.109, cf. Od.2.184, Pi.*P.*4.190, A.R.2.922. II. *to be a θεοπρόπος* II, in Boeot. form θιοπρ-, *IG*7.3207 (Orchom.). ⊕ **-προπία**, ἡ, *prophecy, oracle*, Il.1.87, Od.1.415, etc. **-πρόπιον**, τό, = foreg., Il.1.85; θεοπροπίων εὖ εἰδώς 6.438: in Prose, ἐκ θεοπροπίου Hdt.1.7, 165, al.; κατὰ τὸ θ. ib.68, cf. Heraclid.Lemb.*Oxy.*1367.39, Ph.1.514 (pl.). ⊕ **-πρόπος**, ον, *prophetic*, οἰωνιστής Il.13.70; ἔπος S.*Tr.*822 (lyr.); ἦτορ Q.S.12.534. 2. Subst., *seer, prophet*, Il.12.228, Od.1.416; of Moses, Ph.1.199. b. θεοπρόπον, τό, = θεοπροπία, Call.*Lav. Pall.*125 (pl.). II. *public messenger sent to inquire of an oracle*, Ion. for θεωρός, Hdt.1.48, al., A.*Pr.*659, *IG*12(5).141.9 (Paros, iii B.C.), *SIG*548.2 (Delph., iii B.C.), Plu.*Cim.*18: pl., as pr. n. of a family ( = Θεοπροπίδαι, cf. D.L.2.125), Porph.*Abst.*2.9. (-προπο- assim. fr. -προκο-, cf. Lat. *procus, precor.*)

**θεο-πρόσπλοκος**, ον, *very religious*, as gloss on ἱεροπρόσπολος, Procl.*Par.Ptol.*224. **-πρόσπολος**, = foreg., Ptol.*Tetr.*71, 155 (where Procl. renders προσπλεκόμενοι πρὸς τὸ θεῖον (πρὸς θεούς)).

**θεόπτ-ης**, ου, ὁ, (ὁράω, ὄψομαι) *seeing God*, of Moses, Ph.1.579 (s.v.l.). **-ία**, ἡ, *divine vision*, Hsch. **-ικός**, ή, όν, *of* or *for a* θεόπτης: ἡ θ. δύναμις the power *of seeing God*, Herm.ap.Stob.1.3.52, 3.11.31; ἡ θ. ψυχή Iamb.*Myst.*8.6.

**θεό-πτυστος**, ον, *detested by the gods*, γένος A.*Th.*604. **-πῦρος**, ον, (πῦρ) *kindled by the gods*, φλόξ E.*El.*732 (lyr.). **-ρακτος**, ον, (ῥάσσω) *struck*, i.e. *maddened, by God*, nickname of Θεόμναστος, Cic. *Verr.*4.66.148.

**θεόργητος**, ον, = θεομανής, Sch.A.*Th.*653. **θεορέω**, v. θεωρέω.

**θεό-ρρητος**, ον, *spoken of God*, μέτρον *AP*9.505; εὐεπίαι Epic.in *BKT*5(1)p.118. II. Θεόρρητον, τό, name of a building at Delos, *IG*11(2).199*A* 103 (iii B.C.), *Inscr.Délos* 312.1; elsewh. τὸν οἶκον τὸν Θ—ου *IG*11(2).163 *Ba*6 (iii B.C.), al. **-ρρῦτος**, ον, *flowing from the gods*, λύθρος Opp.*H.*5.9.

**θέορτος**, ον, (ὄρνυμαι) *sprung from the gods*, ὄλβος Pi.*O.*2.36; θέορτον ἢ βρότειον A.*Pr.*765.

⊕ **θεός**, ὁ, Boeot. **θιός**, Lacon. **σιός** (v. infr.), Cypr., Cret. **θιός** *Inscr.Cypr.*135.27 H., *Leg.Gort.*1.1, Dor. also **θεύς** Call.*Cer.*58; acc. θεῦν v.l. ib.130; voc. (only late) θεός, also θεέ Lxx *De.*3.24, *Ev.Matt.*27.46, *PMag.Lond.*121.529, etc.; but classical in compd. names, Ἀμφίθεε, Τιμόθεε:—*God, the Deity*, in general sense, both sg. and pl. (εἰ καὶ ἐπὶ θεοὺς καὶ ἔτι μᾶλλον ἐπὶ θεὸν ἁρμόζει μεταφέρειν Plot.6.8.1), θ. δὲ τὸ μὲν δώσει τὸ δ' ἐάσει *God will grant..*, Od.14.444; οὐδέ κεν ἄλλως οὐδὲ θ. τεύξειε 8.177, cf. 3.231, Il.13.730 (also θεὸς Ζεύς Od.4.236, 14.327); θ. καὶ ἀγαθὴ τύχη Pl.*Lg.*757e, cf. Timocl.3 D.; σὺν θεῷ Il.9.49, S.*Aj.*765, etc. (less freq. ξὺν τῷ θ. ib.383); σὺν θ. εἰρημένον Hdt.1.86, cf. 3.153; σὺν θ. εἰπεῖν Pl.*Prt.*317b: so in pl., σύν γε θεοῖσιν Il.24.430; οὐ τοι ἄνευ θεοῦ Od.2.372; οὐ θεῶν ἄτερ Pi.*P.*5.76; ἐκ θεόφι Il.17.101; ὑπὲρ θεόν *against his will*, 17.327; ἂν θ. θέλῃ Alex.231; θ. θέλοντος Men.*Mon.*671: in pl., ἂν θεοὶ θέλωσιν Alex.247; θεῶν συνεθελόντων, βουλομένων, X.*Eq.Mag.*9.8, Luc.*Macr.*29; εἰ ὀρθῶς ἢ μή, θ. οἶδε Pl.*Phdr.*266b, cf. *R.*517b, etc.; in oaths, θ. ἴστω S.*OC*522 (lyr.), etc.; πρὸς θεῶν Hdt.5.49, D.1.15, etc.: τοὺς θεούς σοι *bless you! good heavens! for heaven's sake!* M.Ant.7.17, Arr.*Epict.*2.19.15, al.; τὸν θ. σοι ib.3.7.19, al.: qualified by τις, Od.9.142, etc.; οὐκ ἄνευ θεῶν τινος A.*Pers.*164 (troch.), E.*Ba.*764; κατὰ θεόν τινα Id.*IA*411, Pl. *Euthd.*272e; κατὰ θεόν πως εἰρημένα Id.*Lg.*682a: doubled in poets, θεὸν θεόν τις ἀγλαϊζέτω B.3.21, cf. Diagor.1; θεοὶ θεοὶ τῶν ἀδίκων μέλουσι E.*HF*772, cf. Paus.Gr.*Fr.*203; θεοί (Cret. θιοί) as an opening formula in Inscrr. (sc. τύχην ἀγαθὴν διδοῖεν), *Leg.Gort.*1.1, *IG* 1².52, etc.: sg., θ. τύχη ib.5(2).1, etc.: in Prose also with the Art., ὁ θ. πάντων ἂν εἴη αἴτιος Pl.*R.*379c, cf. *Lg.*716c, etc.; τὰ πρὸς τοὺς θ., τὰ παρὰ τῶν θ., X.*Mem.*1.3.1, 2.6.8. b. θεοί, opp. ἄνδρες, πατὴρ ἀνδρῶν τε θεῶν τε Il.1.544; ὃν Ξάνθον καλέουσι θ., ἄνδρες δὲ Σκάμανδρον 20.74: in Comparisons, θεοῖσιν ἶσ' ἔθελε φρονέειν 5.440; θεοῖς ἐναλίγκια μήδεα Od.13.89; also in sg., θεῷ ἐναλίγκιος αὐδήν Il.19.250; θεὸς ὥς 5.78; ὥς τε θεός 3.381: prov., θεὸς πρὸς ἀνθρώπους, of an 'angel's visit', Herod.1.9. c. of special divinities, νέρτεροι θ. A.*Pers.*622, S.*Ant.*602 (lyr.); ἐνέρτεροι θ. Il.15.225; οἱ κάτωθεν θ. S.*Ant.*1070; θ. οὐράνιοι *h.Cer.*55, A.*Ag.*90 (anap.); οἱ δώδεκα θ. Ar.*Eq.*235, X.*Eq.Mag.*3.2, *IG*2².30, etc.; μὰ τοὺς δώδεκα θ. Men.*Sam.*91; in dual, τὼ σιώ (Lacon.), of Castor and Pollux, ναὶ τὼ σ. X.*An.*6.6.34, *HG*4.4.10, Ar.*Lys.*81: so in Boeot., of Amphion and Zethus, νεὶ τὼ σιώ (leg. θιώ) Id.*Ach.*905. d. ὁ θ., of natural phenomena, ὁ θ. ὕει (sc. Ζεύς) Hdt.2.13; ὁ θ. ἐνέσκηψε βέλος Id.4.79; ἔσεισεν ὁ θ. (sc. Ποσειδῶν) X.*HG*4.7.4; of the sun, Hdt.2.24, A.*Pers.*502, E.*Alc.*722; δύνοντος τοῦ θ. App *BC*4.79; *the weather*, τί δοκεῖ τὰ τοῦ θεοῦ; Thphr.*Char.*25.2. e. Astrol., θεοί, = ἀστέρες, Jul. Laod.in *Cat.Cod.Astr.*8(4).252. f. θεός (sc. Ἥλιος), name of the 9th τόπος, Rhetor.ib.163, etc. 2. metaph., of abstract things, τὸ δ' εὐτυχεῖν τόδ' ἐν βροτοῖς θεός τε καὶ θεοῦ πλέον A.*Ch.*60; ἡ φρόνησις ἀγαθὴ θ. μέγας S.*Fr.*922; θ. γὰρ καὶ τὸ γιγνώσκειν φίλους E.*Hel.*560; ὁ πλοῦτος τοῖς σοφοῖς θ. Id.*Cyc.*316; φθόνος κάκιστος θ. Hippothoon 2. 3. as title of rulers, θεῶν ἀδελφῶν (sc. Ptolemy II and Arsinoe), Herod.1.30, etc.; Πτολεμαῖος ὑπάρχων θεὸς ἐκ θεοῦ καὶ θεᾶς *OGI*90.10 (Rosetta, ii B.C.): Ἀντίοχος ὅτῳ θεὸς ἐπώνυμον γίγνεται App.*Syr.*65; θεὸς ἐκ θεοῦ, of Augustus, *OGI*655.2 (Egypt, 24 B.C.); θ. ἡμῶν καὶ δεσπότης *IPE*4.71 (Cherson., ii A.D.). b. = Lat. *Divus*, *Mon.Anc.Gr.*10.4, Str.4.1.1, etc.; οἱ ἐν θεοῖς αὐτοκράτορες, = *divi Imperatores*, *IG*12(1).786 (Rhodes). c. generally of the dead, καὶ ζῶντός σου καὶ εἰς θεοὺς ἀπελθόντος *PPetr.*2p.45 (iii B.C.); θεοῖς χθονίοις, = Lat. *Dis Manibus*, *IG*14.30, al. 4. *one set in authority, judge*, τὸ κριτήριον τοῦ θ., ἐνώπιον τοῦ θ., Lxx *Ex.*21.6, 22.8; θεοὺς οὐ κακολογήσεις ib.22.28(27). II. θεός fem., *goddess*, μήτε θήλεια θεός, μήτε τις ἄρσην Il.8.7, cf. Hdt.2.35, al.; τοῖς θεοῖς εὔχομαι πᾶσι καὶ πάσαις D.18.1, cf. 141, Orac.ib.21.52; esp. at Athens, of Athena, Decr.ap.And.1.77, Pl.*Ti.*21a, etc.; ἁ Διὸς θεός, Ζηνὸς ἡ θ., S.*Aj.*401 (lyr.), 952 (ἡ Διὸς θεά ib.450); of other goddesses, ποντία θεός Pi.*I.*8(7).36; ἡ νερτέρα θ., = Περσεφόνη, S.*OC*1548, etc.; of Thetis, Pl. *Ap.*28c; of Niobe, S.*El.*150 (lyr.), *Ant.*834 (anap.): in dual, of Demeter and Persephone, τὰ τοῖν θεοῖν ψηφίσματα Ar.*V.*378 (lyr.); οὐδ' ἔδεισε τὼ θεώ And.1.125; freq. in oaths, νὴ τὼ θεώ Ar.*Lys.*112; μὰ τὼ θεώ Id.*Ec.*155, 532. III. as Adj. in Comp. θεώτερος, *divine*, θύραι θ., opp. καταιβαταὶ ἀνθρώποισιν, Od.13.111; χορὸς θ. Call.*Ap.*93, cf. *Dian.*249, D.P.257. (Derived by Hdt.2.52 fr. τίθημι (κόσμῳ θέντες τὰ πρήγματα), by Pl.*Cra.*397d fr. θεῖν. Etym. dub.) [In Ep. (twice in Hom.) and Trag. (E.*Ba.*47, 1347, al., not in Com.), as monosyll. by synizesis, θεοί Il.1.18, Thgn.142; θεῶν *h.Cer.*55, 259; θεοῖς Thgn.171; θεοῖσιν Od.14.251; θεούς *h.Cer.*325: even in nom. θεός before a vowel, E.*Or.*399 (cf. Pors. ad loc.), *HF*347; in Pi.*P.*1.56 apptly. a short monosyll.]

⊕ **θεόσ-δοτος**, ον, poet. and later Prose for θεόδοτος, *given by the gods*, Hes.*Op.*320; δύναμις Pi.*P.*5.13; εὐδαιμονία Arist.*EN*1099ᵇ12; ἀρετή Max.Tyr.38.4. **-δωρος**, ον, poet. for θεοδώρητος, a fiction of Tz. ad Lyc.47.

**θεοσέβ-εια**, ἡ, *service* or *fear of God, religiousness*, X.*An.*2.6.26, Pl.*Epin.*985c, 990a, Plu.*in Hes.*46, Iamb.*Protr.*20. **-έω**, *serve God*, Plu.*Fr.inc.*22, D.C.54.30; τὸ θ. *SIG*708.18 (Istropolis, ii B.C.). **-ής**, ές, *fearing God, religious*, Hdt.1.86, 2.37, S.*OC*260 (Sup.), Pl.*Cra.*394d, al.; θ. μέλος Ar.*Av.*897 (lyr.); τὸ θεοσεβές Pl.*Epin.*977e. Adv. -βῶς X.*Cyr.*3.3.58.

**θεόσεπτος**, ον, *feared as divine*, βροντή Ar.*Nu.*292; *holy*, Orac.ap. Jul.*Ep.*89b. II. Act., = θεοσεβής, Man.4.427.

**θεοσέπτωρ**, ορος, ὁ, = θεοσεβής, E.*Hipp.*1364 (anap.).

**θεοσεχθρία**, ἡ, v. θεοισεχθρία; cf. θεοεχθρία.

**θεοσημεία**, ἡ, *a sign from the gods*, Suid.:—also **θεοσημία**, ἡ, Hsch. s.v. εὐαμερία.

**θεοσκνεῖ**· θεοὺς τιμᾷ, Hsch.; cf. θυοσκέω.

**θεοσοφ-έω**, *have knowledge of things divine*, Porph.*Abst.*4.17. **-ία**, ἡ, *knowledge of things divine*, *PMag.Leid.W.*6.17; ἡ ἄγαν θ. Porph.*Abst.*4.9; Ἑλληνική, Χαλδαϊκὴ θ., Procl.*Theol.Plat.*5.35, Dam. *Pr.*350. **-ος**, ον, *wise in the things of God*, Porph.*Abst.*2.35, Iamb.*Myst.*7.1: pl., of the Γυμνοσοφισταί, Porph.*Abst.*4.17.

**θεό-σπορος**, ον, *sown by a god, divine*, κῦμα E.*Fr.*106. **-σσυτος**, v. θεόσυτος.

**θεόστασις**, εως, ἡ, *base* or *pedestal for statues of gods*, *CIL*2.1724 (Gades).

**θεο-στήρικτος**, ον, *supported by God*, σκῆπτρα *AP*15.15 (Const. Rhod.). **-στιβής**, ές, *trodden by God*, δειράς Limen.21; πυλεῶνες

Procl.*H*.7.7. ⊛ **-στῠγής**, ές, *hated of the gods*, E.*Tr*.1213, *Cyc*.602, Poll.1.21; *hated of God*, *Ep.Rom*.1.30 (where some take it Act., *hating God*). **-στύγητος** [ῠ], ον, = foreg. 1, ἄγος A.*Ch*.635 (lyr.). ⊛ **-σύλης** [ῡ], ου, ὁ, (συλάω) *robbing God, sacrilegious*, Ael. *VH*5.16, *Fr*.124, Ph.ap.Eus.*PE*8.14. **-σῡλία**, ἡ, *sacrilege*, Ael. *NA*10.28: in pl., interpol. in Id.*VH*6.8.

**θεοσύνδετος**, ον, *united by God*, Hierocl.*in CA*26 p.478 M.

**θεόσῠτος**, ον, *sent by the gods*, θ. ἢ βρότειος; A.*Pr*.116; νόσος ib. 596 (lyr.):—also **θεόσσυτος** χειμών ib.643.

**θεο-ταρπέ(ε)ς**· θεὸν τέρποντες, Hsch. **-ταυρος**, ὁ, *god-bull*, a name for Zeus, Mosch.2.135. **-τείχης**, ες, *walled by gods*, of Troy, Epigr.ap.Certamen 311. **-τέρᾰτος**, ον, *with divine portents*, πλάναι θ., of Io's wanderings, dithyrambic phrase in Demetr.*Eloc*.91 codd. **-τερπής**, ές, of a dish, *fit for the gods*, Philox.2.9; *pleasing to God*, βιοτή *AP*9.197 (Marin.); cf. θεοταρπέες. **-τευκτος**, ον, *made by God*, πύργοι Simm.25, cf. Doroth.ap.Heph.Astr.1.1.

⊛ **θεότης**, ητος, ἡ, *divinity, divine nature*, *Ep.Col*.2.9, Plu.2.359d, Luc. *Icar*.9, etc.; διὰ θεότητα *for religious reasons*, Heliod.ap.Orib.50.7.1.

**θεο-τίμητος** [ῑ], Dor. **-ᾱτος**, ον, B.8.98:—*honoured by the gods*, θεοτιμήτους βασιλῆας Tyrt.4.3, cf. A.*Ag*.1337 (anap.); πόλις B. l.c. **-τῑμος**, ον, = foreg., ἄστυ Id.10.12 (trisyll.), cf. Pi.*I*.6(5).13, Orph.*H*.27.1. ⊛ **-τόκος**, ἡ, *mother of God*, of the Virgin, *Cod. Just*.1.1.5.1, Just.*Nov*.3.1, *SIG*910 *B* (vi A.D.). **-τρεπτος**, ον, *turned by the gods*, θεότρεπτα τάδ' αὖ φέρομεν these *divine changes of fortune*, A.*Pers*.905 (-πρεπτα cod. M). **-τρεφής**, ές, *feeding the gods*, ἀμβροσίη *AP*9.577 (Ptol.), cf. Nonn.*D*.9.101.

**θεούδεια**, ἡ, *fear of God*, θεουδείῃ τ' ἐκέκαστο A.R.3.586; cf. sq.

⊛ **θεουδής**, ές, *fearing God*, Hom. only in Od., καί σφιν νόος ἐστὶ θεουδής 6.121, 8.576, 9.176; θεουδέα θυμὸν ἔχοντα 19.364; βασιλῆος .. ὅς τε θεουδὴς ... εὐδικίας ἀνέχῃσι 19.109, cf. *MAMA*1.171 (Laodicea Combusta), etc. Adv. **-δῶς** Orph.*Fr*.169. (θεο-δϝής contr. fr. θεο-δϝεής, compd. of θεός and δέος: but taken as if = θεοειδής by late Poets, as Q.S.1.65, 3.775.)

**θεουργ-ία**, ἡ, *divine work*, Jul.*Or*.7.219a. II. *sacramental rite, 'mystery'*, Porph.ap.Aug.*Civ.D*.10.9; ἱερατικὴ θ. Iamb.*Myst*.9.6; οἱ περὶ θεουργίαν δεινοί Procl.*in Alc*.p.92 C. **-ίασμα**, ατος, τό, = foreg. II, Dam.*Isid*.56. **-ικός**, ή, όν, *of* or *for a* θεουργός, τελεταί Porph.ap.Aug.*Civ.D*.10.9; κοινωνία Iamb.*Myst*.1.8; τέχνη ib.2.11. Adv. **-κῶς** Procl.*in Cra*.p.32 P.; opp. τεχνικῶς, Iamb.*Myst*.3.28: Comp. **-ώτερον** ib.2.11. **-ός**, ὁ, *divine worker*, of the δημιουργός, Dam.*Pr*.341. II. *performer of sacramental rites*, Jul.*Or*.5.173a, Procl.*in Alc*.p.150 C., Iamb.*Myst*.3.18. III. as Adj., ἡ θ. ἐνέργεια ib.20.

**θεοφάν-εια**, ἡ, *vision of God*, *Notiz.Arch*.4.236 (Cyrene). ⊛ **-ια** (sc. ἱερά), τά, *festival at Delphi, at which the statues of Apollo and other gods were shown to the people*, Hdt.1.51, cf. Poll.1.34; at Chios, *SIG*1064.3 (Halic., i B.C.): generally, θ. ἄγειν τινί Philostr.*VA*4.31; θ. θύειν Ael.*NA*11.10.

**θεό-φαντος**, ον, *revealed by God* or *revealing God*, ὄργια Metrod. 38. **-φάντωρ**, ορος, ὁ, *a revealer of God, a priest*, Suid. s.v. Διονύσιος ὁ Ἀρεωπαγίτης. **-φᾰτος**, **-φᾰτίζω**, = θέσφατος, θεσφατίζω, Hsch. **-φημος**, ον, *declaring God's will*, ἀστρολόγοι Man.1.293, 4.128. **-φθεγκτος**, ον, *uttered by God*, Eust.1381.2.

**θεοφίλ-εια** [φῐ], ἡ, = θεοφιλία, Marin.*Procl*.32. ⊛ **-ής**, ές, (φιλέω) *dear to the gods, highly favoured*, of persons, Hdt.1.87, Democr.217, Pl.*R*.382e, *Phlb*.39e, etc.; of Moses, Ph.2.218 (Sup.); as honorary epith. in Egypt, *Sammelb*.421 (Sup.), al.; also, of places, etc., πόλις Pi.*I*.6(5).66; Ἄργος B.10.60; πόλιν .. θεοφιλεστάτην Eup.307; χώρα A.*Eu*.869 (Sup.); τύχαι Id.*Fr*.350.3; ἑορτή Ar.*Ra*.446; μοῖρα X. *Ap*.32; ἐπιτήδευμα Isoc.8.35 (Comp.), cf. Pl.*Euthphr*.7a; θεοφιλές [ἐστιν] εἰ .. 'tis *a mark of divine favour, if*.., Plu.2.30f. Adv. **-λῶς**, πράττειν *to act as the gods will*, Pl.*Alc*.1.134d: Comp. **-έστερον**, διαβεβιωκέναι Isoc.9.70. II. Act., *loving God*, Ph.2.415, Luc. *JTr*.47 (Sup.), Agath.3.13, *Cod.Just*.1.1.5.4 (Sup.). Adv. ἡ πόλις οὐ μόνον **-λῶς** ἀλλὰ καὶ φιλανθρώπως ἔσχεν Isoc.4.29, cf. Poll.1. 22. ⊛ **-ητος**, η, ον, *loved by the gods*, Phint.ap.Stob.4.23.61a (hyperdor. **-ᾱτος**). **-ία**, ἡ, *the favour of God*, Oenom.ap.Eus.*PE*5.34, Sch.S.*OT*40. **-ιον**, τό, *eyesalve invented by Theophilus*, Aët.7.115, Alex.Trall.2. ⊛ **-ος**, ον, = θεοφίλητος, epith. of a city, *BGU*924.1 (iii A.D.). **-ότης**, ητος, ἡ, *a being loved by God*, Men.Rh.pp.361, 362 S.

**θεόφιν**, Ep. gen. and dat., sg. and pl., of θεός.

**θεό-φοβος**, ον, *fearing God*, Porph.*Abst*.1.1, Hsch. **-φοιτος**, ον, *driven by divine frenzy*, of Cassandra, Tryph.374.

⊛ **θεοφορ-έω**, *deify*, τὸ πῦρ S.E.*M*.9.32. II. Pass., *to be possessed by a god, inspired*, Longin.13.2, Ph.2.146, al., Luc.*Philops*.38, S.E.*P*. 1.101; Θεοφορουμένη, name of a play of Menander, Ath.11.504a, cf. Arg.Men.*Oxy*.1235.46. **-ησις**, εως, ἡ, *divine possession, ecstasy*, in pl., D.H.2.19, Plu.2.278c. **-ητος**, ον, *possessed by a god, inspired*, A.*Ag*.1140 (lyr.), Str.12.2.3, Sor.1.88, Plu.2.54c; Θ., name of a play by Alexis. Adv. **-τως** Plu.2.45f. II. Act., *carrying a god* or *goddess*, Luc.*Asin*.37. ⊛ **-ία**, ἡ, = θεοφόρησις, Phld.*Mus*.p.25 K., Iamb. *Myst*.3.5, al.: pl., Phld.*Mus*.p.40 K., Str.12.3.32, 16.2.36:—sg. in poet. form **θευφορίη** *AP*6.220.4 (Diosc.). ⊛ **-ος** (**-φόρ-**), ον, (φέρω) *bearing* or *carrying a god*, πόδες A.*Fr*.225. II. θεόφορος, ον, *possessed by a god, inspired*, θ. ὠδῖναι the pains *of inspiration*, Id.*Ag*. 1150 (lyr.), cf. Phld.*D*.1.4. 2. θ. ὀνόματα names *derived from a god*, as Διόδωρος, Ath.10.448e.

**θεοφρᾰδ-ής**, ές, (φράζω) *speaking from God, prophetic*, Μουσαῖος Orph.*Fr*.271. II. Pass., *indicated by God*, κέλευθοι Procl.*H*.6. 8. **-ία**, ἡ, *a divine saying, oracle*, Hsch. **-μων**, ον, gen. ονος, = θεοφραδής I, Ph.1.516, 2.176.

**θεο-φρονέω**, = θεῖα φρονέω, Hld.2.11. ⊛ **-φροσύνη**, ἡ, *godliness*, Hsch. **-φρουρος**, ον, *guarded by* (or perh. *guarding*) *the gods*, *IG*12(5).241 (Paros, i B.C.). **-φρων**, ον, gen. ονος, (φρήν) *godly-minded, holy*, Κάδμος Thebaïs *Fr*.2.3, cf. Pi.*O*.6.41. **-φύλαξ** [ῠ], ακος, ὁ, *guardian of a god*, gloss on θεωρός, Sch.Pi.*N*.3.122. **-χαρις**· *deo gratus*, Gloss. **-χολωσία**, ἡ, *the wrath of God*, Lyd.*Ost*.37, Sch.Od.8.232:—also **-χολωσύνη**, Sch.Luc.*Lex*.10. **-χόλωτος**, ον, *under God's wrath*, Arr.*Epict*.2.8.14, 3.1.37, Vett.Val.67.19. ⊛ **-χρηστος**, ον, *delivered by God*, λόγια θ., of the Mosaic Law, Ph.2.577.

**θεόω**, *make into God, deify*, Oenom.ap.Eus.*PE*5.34:—Pass., ἔννοιαι θεωθεῖσαι Iamb.*VP*23.103. 2. *become divine*, γυῖα θεωθείς Call. *Dian*.159; καθ' ὅσον πάντα τεθέωται Procl.*in Prm*.p.490 S., cf. Jul. *Or*.5.178b. II. = θειόω I, Arar.12.

⊛ **θέπτανος**· ἀπτόμενος, Hsch. (perh. cogn. with Skt. *dáhati*, Lith. *degù* 'burn', Lith. *degtinė* 'brandy').

⊛ **θεράπαιν-α** [ρᾰ], ἡ, fem. of θεράπων, *handmaid* or *female slave*, Hdt.3.134, Pherecyd.Syr.2, And.1.64, X.*Cyr*.6.4.11, Men.141, etc. **-ίδιον**, τό, Dim. of sq., Men.*Sam*.36, Parth.26.2, Plu.*Ant*. 29, Luc.*Pisc*.17, etc. **-ίς**, ίδος, ἡ, = θεράπαινα, Pl.*Lg*.808a, Men. 142, Parth.10.2.

⊛ **θερᾰπ-εία**, Ion. **-ηΐη** (-είη Hp.*Art*.80, al.), ἡ, *service, attendance*: I. of persons, θ. τῶν θεῶν *service paid* to the gods, Pl. *Euthphr*.13d, cf. E.*El*.744 (lyr.); θεῶν καὶ ἡρώων θεραπεῖαι Pl.*R*.427b, etc.; ἡ περὶ τοὺς θεοὺς θ. Isoc.11.24; ἀγυιάτιδες θ. *worship* of Apollo Agyieus, E.*Ion* 187; τὴν θ. ἀποδιδόναι τοῖς θεοῖς Arist.*Pol*.1329a32; θ. τῆς μήνιδος Jul.*Or*.5.159b: abs., πᾶσαν θ. ὡς ἰσόθεος θεραπευόμενος Pl.*Phdr*.255a, cf. Antipho 4.2.4; of parents, γονέων θεραπείας καὶ τιμάς Pl.*Lg*.886c, cf. Gorg.*Fr*.6 D.; of children, *nurture, care*, μικροὺς παῖδας θεραπείας δεομένους Lys.13.45; θ. καὶ ἐσθής X.*Mem*.3.11.4; θ. σώματος, ψυχῆς, Pl.*Grg*.464b, *La*.185e. 2. *service done to gain favour, paying court*, θ. τοῦ κοινοῦ καὶ τῶν αἰεὶ προεστώτων Th.3.11; ἐν θεραπείᾳ ἔχειν πολλῇ Id.1.55; πάσῃ θεραπείᾳ θεραπεύειν τινά X.*HG* 2.3.14; θεραπείαις προσαγαγέσθαι Isoc.3.22; τῇ θ. ψυχαγωγούμενος D.59.55. II. *medical* or *surgical treatment* or *cure*, χειρός, ποδός, Hp.l.c.; αἱ ὑπὸ τῶν ἰατρῶν θ. αἱ διὰ καύσεων γιγνόμεναι *cures* by cautery, Pl.*Prt*.354a; ἡ ἐκ τῶν γραμμάτων θ. *treatment* secundum artem, Arist.*Pol*.1287a40, cf. Gal.1.400, etc.; τῶν καμνόντων Pl.*Prt*. 345a, cf. Th.2.51, Phld.*Ir*.p.21 W.; τοῦ σώματος Id.*Lib*.p.19 O., *Vit. Philonid*.p.9 C.; *healing*, θεραπείας ἐπιτυχών *Sammelb*.1537*b*: in pl., *cures*, ἰατρὸς ποιεῖ -είας *POxy*.1r.13. III. of animals, *care, tendance*, Pl.*Euthphr*.13a, Arist.*HA*578a7 (pl.). 2. of plants, *cultivation*, Pl.*Tht*.149e, Thphr.*HP*2.2.12. 3. *maintenance* or *repairs* of temples, *SIG*1106.49 (Cos, iv/iii B.C.), 1102.8 (ii B.C.). 4. *preparation* of fat for medical use, Dsc.2.76. IV. in collective sense, *body of attendants, retinue*, Hdt.1.199, 5.21, 7.184, LXX *Ge*. 45.16; σὺν ἱππικῇ θ. X.*Cyr*.4.6.1; ὁ ἐπὶ τῆς θ. τεταγμένος Plb.4.87. 5. ⊛ **-ευμα**, ατος, τό, *a service done to another*: I. θ. θεοῦ *divine worship*, Pl.*Def*.415a. 2. *service paid* to a person, ξενικὰ θ. Id.*Lg*.718b, cf. Plu.2.1117c. II. *care* of the body, Pl.*Grg*.524b (pl.); of a child, E.*Hyps.Fr*.3(1)ii 12 (lyr., pl.). 2. *surgical treatment*, Hp.*Mochl*.40 (pl.), Arist.*EN*1181b3 (pl.); Ἀσκλαπιοῦ *IG*4.952. 96 (Epid.), etc. III. concrete, *preparations, drugs*, Hp.*Morb*.4. 34. **-ευσία**, ἡ, rarer form for θεραπεία II, Hsch. **-ευσις**, εως, ἡ, *treatment, attention*, Phld.*Lib*.p.20 O. ⊛ **-ευτέον**, *one must do service to*, τοὺς θεούς X.*Mem*.2.1.28. 2. *one must court, flatter*, τοὺς ἀκούοντας ἐπαίνῳ Arist.*Rh.Al*.1436b32. II. *one must cultivate*, τὴν γῆν X.l.c. 2. *one must treat medically*, Pl.*R*.408b, Dsc.*Eup*.1.101. 3. *one must prepare* fat, Id.2.76. III. Adj. **θεραπευτέος**, α, ον, *to be courted*, Luc.*Merc.Cond*.38. **-ευτήρ**, ῆρος, ὁ, *attendant*, Aristox.*Fr. Hist*.15, Plu.*Lyc*.11, Charito 4.1; ὁ περὶ τὸ σῶμα θ. X.*Cyr*.7.5.65; τοῦ ἄντρου Max.Tyr.14.2 (pl.). ⊛ **-ευτής**, οῦ, ὁ, *one who serves the gods, worshipper*, θ. Ἄρεως, θεῶν, Pl.*Phdr*.252c, *Lg*.740c; ὁσίων τε καὶ ἱερῶν ib.878a; τοῦ καλοῦ Ph.1.261; οἱ θ. worshippers of Sarapis or Isis, *UPZ*8.19 (ii B.C.), *IG*11(4).1226 (Delos, ii B.C.); title of play by Diphilus, ib.2.992 ii 9; name of certain ascetics, Ph.2.471; θ. ὁσιότητος, of the followers of Moses, ib.177. 2. *one who serves* a great man, *courtier*, οἱ ἀμφὶ τὸν πάππον θ. X.*Cyr*.1.3.7. II. *one who attends to anything*, c. gen., σώματος Pl.*Grg*.517e; τῶν περὶ τὸ σῶμα Id.*R*. 369d. 2. *medical attendant*, τῶν καμνόντων ib.341c. ⊛ **-ευτικός**, ή, όν, *inclined to serve*, c. gen., τῶν φίλων X.*Ages*.8.1; εὐσέβεια δύναμις θ. θεῶν Pl.*Def*.412e; θεοῦ Ph.1.202 (but τὸ θ. γένος, = θεραπευταί, Id.2. 473); *inclined to court*, τῶν δυνατῶν, τοῦ πλήθους, Plu.*Lys*.2, *Comp.Lyc. Num*.2; τὸ θ. τῆς ὁμιλίας Id.*Lys*.4. 2. abs., *courteous, obsequious*, in good and bad sense, X.*HG*3.1.28 (Comp.), Plu.*Luc*.16; θ. παρρησία Id.2.74a. Adv. **-κῶς** Id.*Art*.4; θ. ἔχειν τινός Ph.1.186, cf. Str.6.4. 2. II. *inclined to take care of, careful of*, λόγου dub. l. in Men.402. 15. 2. esp. of medical treatment, ἕξις θ. a *valetudinarian* habit of body, Arist.*Pol*.1335b7; ἡ **-κή**, = θεραπεία, Pl.*Plt*.282a; also τὸ **-κόν** *therapeutics*, Dsc.*Ther.Praef*. (but also τὸ περὶ παθῶν θ., title of a work on *moral remedies* by Chrysippus, Phld.*Ir*.p.17 W.); περὶ θ. μεθόδου, title of work by Galen. **-ευτός**, όν, *that may be fostered* or *cultivated*, Pl.*Prt*.325b. 2. *curable*, Paul.Aeg.4.5. **-εύτρια**, ἡ, fem. of θεραπευτής *EM*47.45. **-ευτρίς**, ίδος, ἡ, = foreg., Ph.1.261, 655: pl., as title of certain female ascetics, Id.2.471. ⊛ **-εύω**, later also **θᾰρᾰπεύω** (q.v.), fut. **-εύσω** Th.2.51, etc.:—Med., fut. **-εύσομαι** *h.Ap*.390: aor. ἐθεραπευσάμην Nicostr.ap.Stob.4.23.65

codd., Gal.11.295:—**Pass.**, fut. -ευθήσομαι Id.10.617: fut. Med. in pass. sense, Antipho 4.2.4, Pl.*Alc.*1.135e: aor. ἐθεραπεύθην Id. *Chrm.*157b, etc.:—*to be an attendant, do service*, once in Hom., Od. 13.265:—Med., *h.Ap.*390. II. *do service to* the gods, ἀθανάτους, θεοὺς θ., Hes.*Op.*135, Hdt.2.37, X.*Mem.*1.4.13, etc.; δαίμονα Pi.*P.*3.109; Διόνυσον, Μούσας, E.*Ba.*82 (lyr.), *IT*1105 (lyr.); θ. Φοίβου ναούς *serve* them, Id.*Ion* 111 (anap.): abs., *worship*, Lys.6.51; *do service* or *honour to* one's parents, E.*Ion* 183 (lyr.), Pl.*R.*467a, *Men.*91a; *serve, wait upon* a master, Id.*Euthphr.*13d, cf. Ar.*Eq.*59, 1261, etc.; θ. τὰς θήκας *reverence* men's graves, Pl.*R.*469a. 2. in Prose, *pay court to*, [τινα] Hdt.3.80, etc.; in bad sense, *flatter, wheedle*, Th.3.12; θ. τὸ πλῆθος, τοὺς πολλούς, Id.1.9, Plu.*Per.*34; *conciliate*, τινὰ χρημάτων δόσει Th.1.137, cf. Hdn.2.2.8; τὸ θεραπεῦον, = οἱ θεραπεύοντες, Th.3.39; θ. γυναῖκα *pay* her *attention*, X.*Cyr.*5.1.18; also τὰς θύρας τινὸς θ. *wait at* a man's door, ib.8.1.6; αὐλὰς θ. καὶ στρατὰς Men.897; αὐλὰς βασιλικὰς θ. D.L.9.63. 3. of things, *consult, attend to*, τὸ ξυμφέρον Th.3.56; ἡδονὴν θ. *indulge* one's love of pleasure, X.*Cyr.*5.5.41; θ. τὸ παρὸν *look to, provide for* the present, S.*Ph.*149 (anap.); τὸ ναυτικὸν Th.2.65; τὴν ἄνοιξιν τῶν πυλῶν Id.4.67; θ. τοὺς καιρούς D.18.307: c. inf., *take care that*.., θ. τὸ μὴ θορυβεῖν, μὴ λείπεσθαι, Th.6.61, 7.70; θ. ὅπως πολιτεύσουσι Id.1.19; θ. ὡς.. Longus 4.1. 4. θ. τὸ σῶμα *take care of* one's person, Pl.*Grg.*513d; θ. αὐτούς Plu.*Eum.*9; θ. τὰς τρίχας Longus 4.4; μύροις χαίτην θ. Archestr.*Fr.*62.3; θ. τοὺς πόδας Lxx 2*Ki.*19.24: c. acc. et inf., θ. κόμην φαίνεσθαι λιπαράν Plu.*Lyc.*22. 5. *foster*, τὴν ψυχήν, τὴν διάνοιαν, Pl.*Cra.*440c, *R.*403d; θ. κάδεα *brood over* sorrows, Pi.*I.*8(7).8. 6. θ. ἡμέρην *observe* a day, *keep* it *as a feast*, Hdt.3.79; ἱερὰ -όμενα Th.4.98. 7. *treat medically*, Hp.*VM*9, Th.2.47,51; τοὺς τετρωμένους X.*Cyr.*3.2.12; τραύματα Phld.*Piet.*89; μὴ θεραπεύειν βέλτιον· θεραπευόμενοι γὰρ ἀπόλλυνται ταχέως Hp.*Aph.*6.38; ταύτην τὴν θεραπείαν θεραπεύσεσθαι Antipho 4.2.4; θ. νόσημα Isoc.19.28; σώματα -όμενα Pl.*Lg.*684c; ὀφθαλμούς Arist.*EN*1102$^{a}$19: abs., οἱ θεραπεύοντες Phld.*Ir.*p.29 W.: metaph., ὁ κοινὸς ἰατρός σε θεραπεύσει χρόνος Philippid.32; λύπην.. οἶδε θεραπεύειν λόγος Men.591; τὰ πονοῦντα μέρη τῆς νεὼς D.S.4.41; τὰς ὑποψίας *allayed*, Plu.*Luc.*22; ὑπόνοιαν Phlp. *in de An.*408.3; δυστυχίαν *assuage* it, Luc.*Ind.*6. 8. of animals, *train*, ἵππους Pl.*Grg.*516e. 9. of land, *cultivate*, X.*Oec.*5.12; of trees, *train*, Hdt.1.193; στέλεχος Thphr.*HP*2.7.3. 10. *prepare, dress*, food or drugs, Archestr.*Fr.*13.4, al., Dsc.2.76 (Pass.). 11. *mend* garments, *PGiss.*79 iv 3 (Pass., ii A.D.). **-ητή**, ἡ, Ion. for θεραπεία (q.v.):—also θεραπητίας· βωμολοχίας, Hsch. **-ήϊος**, α, ον, Ion. and poet. for θεραπευτικός, in neut. pl. -ήϊα, νούσων *AP*7.158.8:—fem. **θεραπηΐς**, ΐδος, Orac.ap.Jul.*Ep.*88b. **-ίδιον**, τό, *means of cure*, Sch.Luc.*Alex.*21. **-ιον**, τό, Dim. of θέραψ, Hyp.*Fr.*99. **-ίς**, ίδος, ἡ, *paying court to, favouring*, πόλις τοῦ ἥττονος θ. Pl.*Mx.*244e. ⊛ **-νη**, ἡ, poet., = θεράπαινα, *handmaid*, Ἑκατηβελέταο θ. *h.Ap.*157; Εὐρώπας θ. E.*Hec.*482 (lyr.), cf. A.R.1.786. II. *dwelling, abode*, E.*Tr.* 211 (lyr.), *Ba.*1043 (pl.), *HF*370 (lyr.), Nic.*Th.*486 (unless it be pr. n. in these places). III. as pr. n. **Θεράπνη**, a Laconian city, Pi.*P.* 11.63, Hdt.6.61, etc.; Lacon. **Σεράπνα** Alcm.4: in pl. **Θεράπναι** Isoc. 10.63. **-νιον**, τό, Dim. of foreg. I, Hsch. **-νίς**, ίδος, ἡ, poet., = θεραπαινίς, *AP*9.603 (Antip.). **-όντιον**, τό, Dim. of θεράπων, D.L.4.59. **-οντίς**, ίδος, ἡ, *of a waiting-maid*, θ. φερνή A.*Supp.* 979 (anap.). **-ουσία**, ἡ, = θεραπεία IV, condemned by Poll.3. 75. ⊛ **-ων**, οντος, ὁ, dat. pl. θεραπόντεσσι Pi.*P.*4.41; Aeol. θέρἀπων Sapph.74, gen. θερράπονος Choerob. in *An.Ox.*2.242 (θεράπονος cod., cf. Hdn.Gr.2.302):—*henchman, attendant*, Od.16.253, etc.; *companion in arms, squire*, 4.23, etc.; ἡνίοχος θ. Il.5.580, 8.119; τώ οἱ ἔσαν κήρυκε.. καὶ θεράποντε 1.321; θεράποντε Διὸς Od. 11.255; θεράποντες Ἄρηος Il.2.110, etc.; Μουσάων θεράποντες *h.Hom.* 32.20, cf. Hes.*Th.*100, Thgn.769, Ar.*Av.*909 (lyr.); Ἔρως Ἀφροδίτης θ. Pl.*Smp.*203c, cf. Sapph. l.c.; *worshipper*, Ἀπόλλωνος Pi.*O.* 3.16, cf. Pl.*Phd.*85a; Ἄρεος *BMus.Inscr.*971 (Cypr., v B.C.): c. dat., οἶκος ξένοισι θεράπων *devoted to the service of* its guests, Pi.*O.*13.3; λωτὸς.. Μουσᾶν θ. E.*El.*717 (lyr.): c. gen., *attending upon*, τῶν ἀδίκως δυστυχούντων Gorg.*Fr.*6 D. II. *servant*, Hdt.1.30, 5.105, Ar.*Pl.*3, 5, And.1.12, Lys.7.34, etc.; at Chios, *slave*, Eust. ad D.P. 533.

**θέραψ**, ἄπος, ὁ, poet., = θεράπων, rare in sg., *Epigr.Gr.*415.3 (Alexandria): acc., Βακχικὸν θέραπα (of Anacreon) *APl.*4.306.10 (Leon.), cf. *IGRom.*4.1655 (Notium): usu. in nom. pl., θέραπες E.*Ion* 94 (anap.), *Supp.*762, Ion Eleg.2.2, Maiist.14, *AP*12.229 (Strato): acc. pl. θέραπας in late Prose, Ant.Lib.13.4, 20.5.

**θερεία**, ἡ, *summer*; v. θέρειος.

**θερεί-αυλος**, ον, prob. *living in villeggiatura*, Theognost.*Can.* 96. **-βοτος**, ον, (βόσκω) *serving for a summer-pasture*, Eust.222. 20. ⊛ **-γενής**, ές, *growing in summer*, Nic.*Th.*601. II. *hot*, ὕδατα Nonn.*D.*26.229. **-λεχής**, ές, *for sleeping under in summer*, πλάτανος Nic.*Th.*584. **-νόμος**, ον, *feeding in summer*, θ. πόα *summer*-pasture, D.H.2.2.

⊛ **θέρειος**, α, ον, also ος, ον Ael. (v. infr.): (θέρος) :—*of summer, in summer*, αὐχμὸς θ. *summer*-drought, Emp.111.7; δρέπανον Orph.*H.* 40.11; καρποί ib.18; θέρειος ὥρα Ael.*NA*2.25. II. **θερεία**, Ion. -είη (sc. ὥρα), ἡ, = θέρος, *summer-time, summer*, Hdt.1.189, Arist. *Mir.*841$^{a}$25, Plb.5.1.3, al., *PTeb.*27.60 (ii B.C.), D.S.19.58 (θερίᾳ); θερείης *in summer*, Nic.*Fr.*81; μεσούσης θ. D.H.1.63; ὑπὸ τὴν θερείαν D.S.3.24: pl., θερείαις Pi.*I.*2.41. III. Sup. **θερείτατος**, η, ον, *very hot*, Arat.149, Nic.*Th.*469.—In Prose θερινός is the more common form.

**θερείποτος**, ον, (πίνω) *watered in summer*, γύαι Lyc.847.

**θερείω**, later poet. form of θέρω, in Med., Nic.*Th.*124, *Al.*567.

**θερέσιμον**· θεριστικόν, Hsch.

**θέρετρον**, τό, (θέρος) *summer-abode*, dub. in Hp.*Epid.*1.20, cf. Gal. 17(1).197.

**θερήγᾶνον**, contr. **θέρηγνον**, τό, (θέρος) *wicker body of the harvest-cart*, Hsch., *EM*447.14; perh. to be read in E.*Fr.*781.1.

**θεριακός**, ή, όν, *for summer*, ἱμάτια *POxy.*1901.37 (vi A.D.).

**θερίδιον**, τό, *summer residence*, Jul.*Ep.*4.

**θερίζω**, Boeot. inf. θερίδδειν Ar.*Ach.*947 (lyr.): fut. Att. -ιῶ Arist. *HA*601$^{b}$17: aor. ἐθέρισα S.*Aj.*239 (anap.), syncop. ἔθρισα A.*Ag.*536 (cf. ἀποθρίζω); poet. ἐθέρισσα *AP*9.451; later (subj.) ἐκθερίξω *Anacreont.*9.7:—**Med.** (v. infr.):—**Pass.**, aor. ἐθερίσθην: pf. τεθέρισμαι (v. infr.): (θέρος) :—*do summer-work, mow, reap*, σῖτον, κριθάς, Hdt.4.42, Ar.*Av.*506, etc.: abs., *harvest*, Phld.*Mus.*p.71 K.: freq. metaph., joined with σπείρω, αἰσχρῶς μὲν ἔσπειρας κακῶς δὲ ἐθέρισας Gorg.*Fr.* 16 D., cf. Plu.2.394e; ἡ ῥητορικὴ καρπὸν ὧν ἔσπειρε θερίζει Pl.*Phdr.* 260d; οὐκ ἔστι μὴ σπείραντα θερίσαι κάρπιμα *Epigr.Gr.*1039.15:—Med., καρπὸν Δηοῦς θερίσασθαι Ar.*Pl.*515:—Pass., ἃ [δράγματα] ἔτυχεν.. τεθερισμένα X.*HG*7.2.8. 2. metaph., *mow down*, Ἄρη τὸν.. θερίζοντα βροτούς A.*Supp.*637 (lyr.), cf. *Ag.*536; βίον θ. ὥστε κάρπιμον στάχυν E.*Hyps.Fr.*34(60).94; θ. Ἀσίαν *to plunder* it, Plu.2.182a. 3. *cut off*, κεφαλὴν καὶ γλῶσσαν ἄκραν S.*Aj.*239; κυνέας E.*Supp.*717; γλῶσσαν *AP*9.451: metaph., σελίδος νεαρῆς θ. στάχυν ib.4.2.3 (Phil.):—Pass., ἥτις [πῶλος].. θέρος θερισθῇ ξανθὸν αὐχένων ἄπο who *had her crop* of yellow mane *cut off*, S.*Fr.*659.4. 4. metaph., *reap a good harvest*, Ar.*Ach.*947 (lyr.); of bribes, Lib.*Or.*47.26. 5. ὁ θερίζων (with or without λόγος), a logical fallacy, Chrysipp.*Stoic.*2.94, D.L.7. 25: pl., ib.44. II. intr., *pass the summer*, X.*An.*3.5.15; θ. ἐν τοῖς ψυχροῖς, χειμάζουσι δ' ἐν τοῖς ἀλεεινοῖς Arist.*HA*596$^{b}$26, cf. 598$^{a}$25.

**θερίκλειον**· ποτήριον, κόνδυ, Hsch. (i.e. Θηρίκλειον).

**θερῖνός**, ή, όν, = θέρειος, Pi.*P.*3.50: the usu. form in Prose, ἀνατολή Hp.*Aër.*4, cf. *Aph.*2.25, Plb.3.37.4; θ. δύσεις, ἀνατολαί, Cleom. 1.9; θ. ζῴδια ib.6; μεσημβρία X.*Cyn.*6.26; ἥλιος Pl.*Lg.*915d; θ. τροπαί or τροπή, the summer solstice, ib.767c, Arist.*Mete.*364$^{b}$2; τροπέων τῶν θερινέων Hdt.2.19; θ. κύκλος, Tropic of Cancer, Ph.1.27; θ. τροπικός (sc. κύκλος) Euc.*Phaen.*p.34 M., Cleom.1.7, Gem.5.39, al.; θερινὸν ὑπηχεῖν to echo *summer-like*, Pl.*Phdr.*230c; θερινά the *summer-haunts* of the sun, Id.*Lg.*683c; ὄμβροι θ. Arist.*HA*601$^{b}$24; θ. ἄνεσις καὶ ἀπόλαυσις D.S.4.84; θ. ὥρα Oenopid.ib.1.41; *for summer use*, ἱμάτιον *PCair.Zen.*148 (iii B.C.); νομαί, opp. χειμεριναί, *PLond.*3.842.12 (ii A.D.).

**θερ-ισμός**, ὁ, *mowing, reaping*, X.*Oec.*18.3, *PHib.*1.90.5 (iii B.C.), *PFlor.*101.4 (i A.D.). II. *reaping-time, harvest*, Eup.202, Plb.5. 95.5, *Ev.Matt.*13.30, al. 2. *harvest, crop*, Lxx *Le.*19.9, *Ev.Matt.* 9.37. **-ιστήρ**, ῆρος, ὁ, *mower, reaper*, Lyc.840. **-ιστήριον**, τό, *reaping-hook*, Lxx 1*Ki.*13.20 (v.l. θέριστρον), Max.Tyr.30.6. ⊛ **-ιστής**, οῦ, ὁ, = θεριστήρ, X.*Hier.*6.10, D.18.51, Arist.*HA*580$^{b}$20, *PCair.Zen.* 292.486 (iii B.C.): θερισταί, οἱ, a satyric play of Euripides, Arg.E. *Med.* **-ιστικός**, ή, όν, *of* or *for reaping*, δρέπανον *PMagd.*8.6 (iii B.C.); ὕμνος Suid. s.v. Λιτυέρσης: as Subst. θ., τό, *crop*, Str.17.3. 11. **-ιστός**, ή, όν, τὸ θ. a kind of *balsam*, Dsc.1.19 codd. (εὐθέριστον Wellm.).

**θέριστος** and **θεριστός**, ὁ, v. θέριτος.

**θέριστρα**, τά, *cost of reaping*, *POxy.*277.8 (i B.C.).

**θερίστρια**, ἡ, fem. of θεριστήρ, Ar.*Fr.*788.

⊛ **θερίστριον**, τό, *light summer garment*, Theoc.15.69, Aristaenet. 1.27.

**θέριστρον**, τό, = foreg., Lxx *Ge.*24.65, al., *PPetr.*1 p.37 (iii B.C.), *AP*6.254 (Myrin.), Ph.1.666. II. *sickle*, Lxx 1*Ki.*13.20 (v.l.).

**θέριτος**, ὁ, *harvest*, and **θεριτός**, ὁ, *harvest-time*, Tz. ad Hes.*Op.*571 (θέριστος and θεριστός cj. Spohn ad Niceph.Blemm.p.40).

**θερίτροπος**, ον, *turning in summer*, of the solstice, Tz. ad Hes.*Op.* 596.

**θέρμᾶ, θέρμᾶν**, alternative nom. and acc. sg. forms for θέρμη, θέρμην, Men.*Georg.*51, Ar.*Fr.*690, dub. in Pl.*Tht.*178c (θερμά codd., but Tim.*Lex.* and Phryn. perh. read θέρμη). II. pl. θέρματα, v. θρέμμα.

**θερμάζω**, = sq., Ep. aor. 1 opt. Med. θερμάσσαιο Nic.*Al.*587.

**θερμαίνω**, aor. ἐθέρμηνα Il.14.7, etc., later ἐθέρμᾶνα Arist.*GA*730$^{a}$ 16: pf. τεθέρμαγκα Hsch. s.v. κεχλίαγκα: pf. Pass. τεθέρμασμαι Apollod.*Poliorc.*147.4, Eust.1573.47, (δια-) Hp.*Vict.*2.64: (θερμός):—*warm, heat*, εἰς ὅ κε θερμὰ λοετρὰ.. Ἑκαμήδη θερμήνῃ Il.14.7; ἥλιος θερμαίνων χθόνα E.*Ba.*679, cf. A.*Pers.*505; τὸ χαλκίον θέρμαινε Eup. 108:—Med., *cause to be warmed*, τῇ ἐρωμένῃ χαλκία δύο ὕδατος *PSI* 4.406.37 (iii B.C.):—Pass., *to be heated*, Od.9.376, Pl.*Phd.*63d; τὸ θερμαῖνον ψύχεται ὑπὸ τοῦ θερμαινομένου Arist.*GA*768$^{b}$18; *feel the sensation of heat*, Pl.*Tht.*186d; *to be* or *grow feverish*, Hp.*Epid.*1.26.ιβ'; *to be parched*, of roots, X.*Oec.*19.11. 2. metaph., θ. φιλότατι νόον Pi.*O.*10(11).87; ἕως ἐθέρμην' αὐτὸν φλὸξ οἴνου E.*Alc.*758; σπλάγχν' ἐθέρμαινον ποτῷ Id.*Cyc.*424; σπλάγχνα θ. κότῳ Ar.*Ra.*844; πολλὰ θερμαίνοι φρενὶ is prob. f.l. for π. θ. φρένα, A.*Ch.*990 (1004); οὐ τοῦτο μή σε θερμήνῃ Herod.1.20:—Pass., κεναῖσιν ἐλπίσιν θερμαίνεται *glows* with hope, S.*Aj.*478; χαρᾷ θ. καρδίαν *have* one's heart *warm* with joy, E.*El.*402.

**θέρμαν-σις**, εως, ἡ, *heating*, Arist.*Metaph.*1067$^{b}$12, Gal.1.253, f.l. in Hp.*Liqu.*1. **-τέον**, *one must heat*, Gal.10.104. II. Adj. **-τέος**, α, ον, *to be heated*, Hp.*Art.*11. **-τήρ**, ῆρος, ὁ, *kettle* or *pot for boiling water*, Poll.6.89, 10.66. ⊛ **-τήριος**, α, ον, *promoting warmth*,

φάρμακα Hp.*Loc.Hom.*17. II. χαλκίον θ., = θερμαντήρ, *IG*1.39 (Aegina), 2².1416, Gal.13.663. ⊛ -τικός, ή, όν, *capable of heating, calorific*, τὸ πῦρ θ. Arist.*Int.*22ᵇ38 ; ὁ οἶνος Epicur.*Fr.*58, cf. 60 ; τὸ θ. πρὸς τὸ -τον Arist.*Metaph.*1020ᵇ29, cf. Thphr.*HP*6.3.6 : Sup., Arist.*Cael.*307ᵃ1, Dsc.1.19.4 : c. gen., τὸ τῆς ψυχῆς θ. οἶνος Pl.*Ti.* 60a. -τός, ή, όν, *capable of being heated*, Arist.*Ph.*224ᵃ30.

**θερμᾰσία**, ἡ, *warmth, heat*, Hp.*Aph.*5.63, Arist.*Pr.*860ᵃ19, Epicur. *Ep.*2 p.40 U., Thphr.*HP*8.11.7. Lxx *Je.*28(51).39, D.S.3.34, Paus.2. 34.6 ; *heating*, opp. ψῦξις, Arist.*GA*764ᵇ7 : pl., Plu.2.128f. (The pure Att. words are θερμότης and θέρμη, Thom.Mag.p.179 R., but θερμασία is used by X.*An.*5.8.15.)

**θέρμασμα**, ατος, τό, *warm fomentation*, Hp.*Acut.*16 (pl.), Gal.*UP* 4.8.

**θέρμασσα**, ἡ, = κάμινος, Hdn.Gr.1.267.

**θερμάστιον**, τό, = θερμαστρίς 1, Aen.Tact.18.6, *IG*2².1425.379 (pl.).

⊛ **θέρμαστις**, ιδος, ἡ, perh. = θέρμαστρις, παρυφὴν ἔχει θέρμαστιν, of a garment, *IG*2².1514.29, 1515.21, 1516.8 (iv B.C.).

**θερμάστρα**, ἡ, *oven, furnace*, Call.*Del.*144 (-αυστραι codd.), Euph. 51.8 (pl.), Hsch. (nom. pl. proparox. cod. Hsch., codd. Call. vary in accent) :—Adv. **θερμαστρῆθεν**, *from the furnace*, Hsch. (-στῆθεν cod.).

⊛ **θερμαστρίς** or **θέρμαστρις** (Hsch.), ἡ, *IG*2².1414.42 ; acc. θερμαστριν Roussel *Cultes Égyptiens* 220 (Delos, ii B.C.) ; gen. θερμαστρίδος Arist.*Mech.*854ᵃ24 : acc. pl. θερμάστρεις Lxx 3*Ki.*7.26(40),31(45) : for forms with -αυστρ- v. infr. :—*tongs* used by smiths to take hold of hot metal, Hsch. : generally, *pincers, pliers*, Arist. l.c. 2. metaph., *a violent dance*, in which the legs were crossed *tong-fashion*, Poll.4.102, Ath.14.630a, Hsch. (θερμαυστρίς codd. Poll., θευμαστρεις cod. A Ath., θέρμαστρις Hsch.) ; cf. θερμαυστρίζω. II. *spike, clamp*, Ath.Mech.34.4. III. = θερμαντήρ, τὰς θερμάστρεις Lxx ll. cc. ; θερμαυστρίς and θερμαστρίς Poll.10.66 ; acc. θέρμαυστριν (prob. in this signf.) Eup.228 : in *IG* and Roussel ll. cc. the signf. may be I. 1 or III. (In signf. I prob. fr. θερμός, αὔω (A), cf. ἐξ-αύω : but the origin of signf. III and the form -αστρ- is not clear.)

⊛ **θερμαύστρα**, ἡ, f.l. for θερμάστρα (q.v.).

**θερμαυστρίζω**, *dance the* θερμαυστρίς (v. θερμαστρίς I. 2), Critias *Fr.*36 D., Luc.*Salt.*34.

**θερμαψίς**, *fornax, Gloss.*

⊛ **θέρμη**, also **θέρμα** (q.v.), ἡ, *heat*, Hp.*VM*19, Lxx *Si.*38.28, *Act. Ap.*28.3 ; τῆς θ. *when it is hot*, Olymp.*in Mete.*98.20 ; *feverish heat*, Pherecr.158, Pl.*Tht.*178c (θερμά codd.), Arist.*Pr.*862ᵃ18 : pl., Hp. *Epid.*7.51, Th.2.49, Arr.*An.*2.4.8. II. θέρμαι, αἱ, *hot springs*, *IG*14.455 (Catana), cf. 1055 : name of a town in Sicily, Plb.1.24. 4. 2. *hot baths*, *POxy.*473.5 (ii A.D.), etc.

**θερμ-ηγορέω**, *speak warmly, hotly*, Orac. ap. Luc. *Peregr.* 30. ⊛ -ημερίαι, ὧν, αἱ, *hot season, summer-time*, Hp.*Nat.Hom.*7, Arist. *HA*544ᵇ11, Thphr.*HP*7.1.7.

**θερμηρός**, ά, όν, *for hot liquid*, ποτήριον Hsch. s.v. κελέβη : **θερμηρόν** (and -ητρον), expld. by *miliarium, Gloss.*

**θερμίζω**, *fall ill with fever*, *IG*12(9).1240.15 (Aedepsus).

**θέρμινος**, η, ον, (θέρμος) *of lupines*, ἄλευρα Dsc.2.110 ; πανοπλία Luc.*VH*1.27.

⊛ **θέρμιον**, τό, Dim. of θέρμος, *Stud.Pal.*22.75.11 (iii A.D.), *Gloss.*, condemned by Thom.Mag.p.183 R.

**θερμο-βαφής**, ές, *dyed hot*, opp. ψυχροβαφής, Thphr.*Od.*22. -**βουλος**, ον, *hot-tempered, rash*, σπλάγχνον E.*Fr.*858 ; parodied in Ar.*Ach.* 119 ; ἄνθρωπος Ael.*NA*8.17. -**δότης**, ου, ὁ, *one who brought the hot water at baths, Gloss.* :—fem. ⊛ -**δότις**, ιδος, ἡ, *female bath-attendant*, *AP* 9.183 (Pall.) : ⊛ -**δοσία**, ἡ, Herod.Med.ap.Orib.5.30.19. -**ειδής**, ές, *of warm nature*, *EM*557.23. -**εργός**, ον, f.l. in A.*Eu.*560. -**κοίλιος**, ον, *hot-stomached*, Hp.*Epid.*6.4.19. -**κρᾶσία**, ἡ, *mixing of hot drink*, Aët.9.30. -**κύᾰμος** [ῠ], ἡ, *a leguminous plant*, of a kind between the θέρμος and the κύαμος, Diph.87.

**Θερμολαῖος**, ὁ (sc. μήν), name of month in Crete, *GDI*5075 *B* 3.

**θερμο-λουσία**, ἡ, *hot bathing*, Hp.*Insomn.*93, Aret.*CD*1.3, *Com. Adesp.*56, Thphr.*Sud.*16, Ph.2.548, Agathin.ap.Orib.10.7 tit. -**λουτέω**, *use hot baths*, Hermipp.76, Alex.75, Herod.Med.ap.Orib.10.39.6 (-**λουτρέω** is incorrect in Arist.*Pr.*863ᵃ4). -**λούτης**, ου, ὁ, *one who uses hot baths*, Agathin.ap.Orib.10.7.9. -**λουτία**, ἡ, f.l. for -λουσίη, Hp.*Insomn.*93. ⊛ -**λυχνον**, τό, *lamp-oil*, *IG*2².1368. 151. ⊛ -**μῐγής**, ές, *half-hot*, ἀήρ *Placit.*2.20.13. -**νους**, ουν, *heated in mind*, A.*Ag.*1172 (dub.).

**θερμοπλ-άω**, *have inflammation in the hoof*, of horses, *Hippiatr.* 53 : -**ησις**, εως, ἡ, the disease itself, ibid. : **θερμόπλα** is dub. in Hsch.

⊛ **θερμο-περίπᾰτος**, ὁ, *sunny promenade*, *Rev.Arch.*1907 ii 418 (Nicopolis ad Istrum). -**ποιός**, όν, *producing heat*, Olymp.*in Mete.* 136.1, 244.14. -**ποσία**, ἡ, *drinking of hot liquid*, Sor.1.117. -**πότης**, ου, ὁ, *one who drinks hot drinks*, Ath.8.352b, Gal.10.828 :—fem. **πότις**, ιδος, *cup for such drinks*, Pamphil.ap.Ath.11.475d, cf. Hsch. s.v. σκαμβίς. -**πρωκτος**, ον, *lascivious*, Sch.Ar.*V.*1030. -**πύλαι** [ῠ], ὧν, αἱ, *Thermopylae*, '*gate of hot springs*', Hdt.7.176,201, Str.9.4. 12. -**πώλιον**, τό, *cook-shop*, in Lat. form *thermopolium*, Plaut. *Curc.*292, *Trin.*1013, but **θερμοπωλεῖον** is expld. by *lupinarium, Gloss.*

⊛ **θερμός**, ή, όν (but θερμὸς ἀϋτμή *h.Merc.*110, Hes.*Th.*696) : (θέρω) :—*hot*, θ. λοετρά Il.14.6, cf. Od.8.249 ; θ. λουτρά Pi.*O.*12.19, S.*Tr.*634 (lyr.), Pl.*Lg.*761c, etc. ; δάκρυα Od.19.362 ; of water, ib.388 ; of glowing wood, 9.388 ; θ. καύματα Hdt.3.104 (Sup.) ; ἦν ἄρα πυρὸς ἕτερα -ότερα Ar.*Eq.*382 : freq. in Att., of *hot* meals or drinks, Teleclid.1.8,32, Pherecr.130.8, etc. ; of blood, S.*OC*622, *Aj.*1411 (anap.) ; -οτάταν αἱμάδα Id.*Ph.*696 ; of fever, θ. νόσοι Pi.*P.*3.66 ; θ. σῶμα *feverish*, Th.2.49. II. metaph., *hot-headed, hasty*, freq. of persons, A.*Th.*603, *Eu.*560 (lyr.), Ar.*V.*918, etc. ; θ. καὶ ἀνδρεῖος Antipho 2.4.5 : of actions, πολλὰ καὶ θ. μοχθήσας S.*Tr.*1046 ; θ. ἔργον Ar.*Pl.* 415 ; δρᾶν τι νεανικὸν καὶ θ. Amphis 33.10 ; θ. ἐπὶ ψυχροῖσι καρδίαν ἔχεις S.*Ant.*88 ; θ. πόθος *AP*5.114 (Phld.) ; φάρμακον Alciphr.1.37 (Comp.) : c. inf., θερμότερος ἐπιχειρεῖν Antipho 2.1.7 : Sup., ὦ θερμόταται γυναῖκες Ar.*Th.*735. 2. *still warm, fresh*, ἴχνη *AP*9.371 ; ἀτυχήματα Plu.2.798f ; θ. κακά, opp. ἕωλα, ib.517f ; γάμοι θ. καὶ ἴσως αὔριον Philostr.*VA*4.25. III. τὸ θ., = θερμότης, *heat*, Hdt.1.142, Pl.*Cra.* 413c, etc. 2. θ. (sc. ὕδωρ), τό, *hot water*, θερμῷ λοῦσθαι, βάπτειν, Ar.*Nu.*1044, *Ec.*216 ; θερμῷ κεκραμένος οἶνος Gal.11.56 ; also, *hot drink*, Arr.*Epict.*1.13.2. 3. θερμόν, τό, *grace, favour*, θ. εὑρεῖν ἐν ἐρήμῳ Lxx *Je.*38(31).2. 4. τὰ θ. (sc. χωρία) Hdt.4.29 ; but (sc. λουτρά), *hot springs*, X.*HG*4.5.3 ; τὰ θ. τοῦ Ἡρακλέους Str.9.4.2. IV. Adv. -μῶς Pl.*Euthd.*284e : Comp. -ότερον, ἔχειν Eub.7.1 : neut. pl. as Adv., θερμὰ θερμὰ πηδῶσαι Herod.4.61.

⊛ **θέρμος**, ὁ, *lupine*, *Lupinus albus*, Alex.162.11, 266.2 (pl.), Timocl. 18.4 (pl.), Thphr.*HP*8.11.2, Dsc.2.109, *PFlor.*379.47 (ii A.D.), *AP* 11.413 (Ammian.) ; εἰς τοὺς θ. to the *lupine-market*, Teles p.13 H.

**θερμοσποδιά**, ἡ, *hot ashes*, Dsc.2.170, Erot. s. v. μαρίλην, Archig. ap.Orib.8.2.30, Philum.ap.Aët.5.120.

**θερμότης**, ητος, ἡ, (θερμός) *heat*, Hp.*VM*16, Pl.*R.*335d, etc. : pl., Id.*Cra.*432c, Diocl.*Fr.*112. II. metaph., *heat, passion*, τοῦ Ἀχιλλέως Philostr.*Her.*12ᵇ ; ἐν τῷ λέγειν Ath.1.1b.

**θερμοτρᾰγέω**, *eat lupines*, Luc.*Lex.*5.

**θερμουργ-ία**, ἡ, *hasty act*, App.*Mith.*108. -**ός**, όν, *doing hot and hasty acts, reckless*, X.*Mem.*1.3.9 (Sup.), Luc.*Tim.*2.

⊛ **θέρμουθις**, ἡ, Egyptian pr. n. applied to the *asp*, *PMag.Par.*1. 2387, *PMag.Lond.*121.782, Ael.*NA*10.31.

**θερμο-φόρον**, τό, *saucepan, Gloss.* : -**φόρος**, ὁ, *boiler*, ib., *POxy.* 2145.15 (ii A.D.). -**φρων**, = δαήμων, Hsch. s. v. δαίμων. -**φύλαξ** [ῠ], ακος, ὁ, *kettle, Gloss.* -**χύτης** [ῠ], ου, ὁ, *vessel for hot drinks*, *AP*9.587 tit.

**θερμόω**, = θέρμω, *An.Ox.*2.448 (Pass.) ; τεθερμῶσθαι dub. l. in Ar. *Lys.*1079.

**θέρμυδρον**, τό, *a place with hot springs*, name of a harbour of Rhodes, Tz.*H.*2.385 :—also -**υδρα**, τά, St.Byz. ; -**υδραί**, αἱ, Apollod. 2.5.11.

**θέρμ-ω**, (θέρω) *heat, make hot*, only in pres. or impf. forms, θέρμετε δ' ὕδωρ Od.8.426, Ar.*Ra.*1339 :—Pass., *grow hot*, θέρμετο δ' ὕδωρ Od. 8.437, Il.18.348 ; πνοιῇ.. μετάφρενον εὐρέε τ' ὤμω θέρμετ' 23.381 ; θέρμετο δὲ χθών Call.*Fr.anon.*24 ; μή πού τις ἐνὶ χροΐ θέρμετ' (Ep. for θέρμηται) ἀϋτμή Opp.*H.*3.522. -**ώδης**, ες, *lukewarm*, Aret.*CA* 2.3. -**ωλή**, ἡ, *feverish heat*, Hp.*Loc.Hom.*19, al.

**θερόεις**, εσσα, εν, *of* or *in summer*, Nic.*Al.*570.

**θέρος**, εος, τό, (θέρω) *summer*, χείματος οὐδὲ θέρευς Od.7.118 ; οὔτ' ἐν θέρει οὔτ' ἐν ὀπώρῃ 12.76 ; ἐν θέρει, opp. ἐν ψύχει, S.*Ph.*18 ; θέρει or θέρει, Il.22.151, Hes.*Op.*640 ; τὸ θέρος *during the summer*, Hdt.1.202 ; τοῦ θέρεος *in the course of it*, Id.2.24 ; τοῦ θέρους Ar.*Fr.*463 ; θέρεος or θέρους (without the Art.), Hes.*Op.*462, Pl.*Phdr.*276b, al. ; τοῦ παρεστῶτος θέρους S.*Ph.*1340 ; τοῦ θ. εὐθὺς ἀρχομένου Th.2.47 ; κατὰ θέρους ἀκμήν X.*HG*5.3.19 ; θ. μεσοῦντος *about midsummer*, Luc.*Hist.Conscr.*1 ; esp. in Th., *campaigning-season*, ἅμα ἦρι τοῦ ἐπιγιγνομένου θέρους 4. 117, cf. 2.31, 6.8 ; τοσαῦτα μὲν ἐν τῷ θ. ἐγένετο 2.68. II. *summer-fruits, harvest, crop*, θ. ἀλλότριον ἀμᾶν Ar.*Eq.*392, cf. D.53.21, *AP*11. 365.3 (Agath.) : pl., θέρη *crops*, *PFlor.*150.5 (iii A.D.) ; θέρη σταχύων the *ripe* ears, Plu.*Fab.*2 : metaph., πάγκλαυτον ἐξαμᾷ θέρος A.*Pers.* 822, cf. *Ag.*1655 ; τὸ γηγενὲς δράκοντος.. θ. E.*Ba.*1026 ; of a horse's mane, v. θερίζω I. 3 ; of a youth's beard, Call.*Del.*298, *AP*10.19 (Apollonid.) ; also τέμνεται τὸ ἱερὸν καὶ ἀπόρρητον θ. τοῦ θεοῦ Γάλλου Jul.*Or.*5.168d. III. Astron., τὸ μέγα θ., ὅταν πάντες οἱ πλάνητες ἐν θερινῷ ζῳδίῳ γένωνται Olymp.*in Mete.*111.30. IV. metaph., in an epitaph for a *year* of life, *Supp.Epigr.*2.874.4 (Egypt).

**θερσῐεπής**, ές, (θέρσος) *bold of speech*, B.12.199 :—so **Θερσίτης**, ὁ, as pr. n. in Hom. : pl., Ph.2.472.

⊛ **θέρσος**, Aeol. for θάρσος, Choerob. *in Theod.*1.166, *EM*447.24.

**θερσός**, ὁ, = ταρσός II. 1, *BGU*350.2 (ii A.D.).

**θερτήρια**· ἑορτή τις, Hsch.

**θέρω**, *heat, make hot*, θέρον αὐγαὶ ἠελίου Λιβύην A.R.4.1312 ; θέρων ἕλκος, = θεραπεύων, Nic.*Th.*687 :— elsewh. only in Pass. **θέρομαι**, fut. Med. θέρσομαι Od.19.507 : aor. 2 ἐθέρην (in Ep. subj. θερέω 17.23) : poet. and later Prose, *become hot* or *warm*, νήησαν ξύλα πολλά, φόως ἔμεν ἠδὲ θέρεσθαι 19.64, cf. 507 ; ἐπεί κε πυρὸς θερέω *at* the fire, 17.23 ; θέρου *warm yourself*, Ar.*Pl.*953 ; ὁπόταν.. τις.. ποτὲ ῥιγῶν θέρηται Pl. *Phlb.*46c ; εἶδον [Ἡράκλειτον] θερόμενον πρὸς τῷ ἰπνῷ Arist.*PA*645ᵃ19 : impf. ἐθέροντο Philostr.*VA*2.18, Alciphr.1.23 ; θέρεσθαι πρὸς τὴν εἵλην Luc.*Lex.*2 : metaph., θέρεσθαι πυρί, of love, Call.*Ep.*27, cf. *APl.* 4.167 (Antip. Sid.). 2. of things, *become warm*, τὰ ψυχρὰ θέρεται Heraclit.126, cf. Archel.ap.Plu.2.954f ; μὴ.. ἄστυ πυρὸς δηΐοιο θέρηται *be burnt* by fire, Il.6.331, cf. 11.667 ; *melt*, ἁ πέτρα θρυπτομένα θέρεται *AP*12.61. (*gʷher-*, cf. θερμός, Lat. *formus* and prob. Engl. *warm*.)

⊛ **θέσις**, εως, ἡ, (τίθημι) *setting, placing*, ἐπέων θ. *setting* of words in verse, Pi.*O.*3.8 ; πλίνθων καὶ λίθων Pl.*R.*333b, cf. *IG*7.3073.33 (Lebad.) ; θ. νόμων *lawgiving*, X.*Ath.*3.2, Pl.*Lg.*690d : in pl., νόμων θέσεις D.18.309, Arist.*Pol.*1289ᵃ22 ; θ. ὀνόματος *giving* of a name,

Pl.*Cra.*390d; ἐπί τινος *application* of word to object, Demetr.*Eloc.* 145; θ. ἀγώνων *institution* of games, D.S.4.53; *ordinance, disposition,* S.*Ichn.*277 (only here in Trag.); *setting forth* in legal form, ἀσφαλειῶν *POxy.*1027.12 (i A.D.). II. *laying down,* ὅπλων, opp. ἀναίρεσις, Pl.*Lg.*814a; of diggers, *plunging* of the spade, opp. ἄρσις, *Gp.*2.45.5. 2. *deposit* of money, preparatory to a law-suit, Ar.*Nu.*1191 (pl.): generally, *sum deposited* in a temple, *Inscr.Délos* 365.14 (iii B.C.), *IG*12(3).322 (pl., Thera). 3. *pledging, giving as security,* D.33.12, Lys.8.10. 4. *payment,* τελῶν Pl.*R.*425d (pl.). III. *adoption* of a child, κατὰ θέσιν υἱωνός Plb.18.35.9, cf. Ph.2.36, Philostr. *VA*6.11; Κρινοτέλην Πινδάρου, θέσει δὲ Φιλοξένου *IG*12(3).274 (Anaphe), cf. 12(7).50 (Amorgos); *adoption* as a citizen of a foreign state, Ἀλεξανδρεὺς θέσει, Ἀθηναῖος θ. (opp. φύσει), Suid. s. v. Ἀρίσταρχος, Ἀριστοφάνης Ῥόδιος. IV. *situation,* of a city, Hp.*Aër.*6; πόλις αὐτάρκη θ. κειμένη Th.1.37, cf. 5.7; ἡ θ. τῆς χώρας πρὸς τὰ πνεύματα Thphr.*CP*3.23.5; τόπων θ. Plb.1.41.7: Astron., θ. τῶν ἄστρων Herm. *in Phdr.*p.149 A.; *position, arrangement,* λεγομένων καὶ γραφομένων Pl.*Tht.*206a; τῶν μερῶν θέσεις Id.*Lg.*668e, cf. Epicur.*Ep.*1 p.11 U., *Fr.*30 (pl.). 2. Math., *local position,* Arist.*GC*322$^{b}$33; ἔχειν θ. Id.*APo.*88$^{a}$34; θ. ἔχειν πρὸς ἄλληλα to have a *local* relation, Id. *Cat.*4$^{b}$21, cf. Pl.*R.*586c: τῇ θ. μέσον Arist.*APr.*25$^{b}$36: Geom., θέσει δεδόσθαι or εἶναι, to be given *in position,* Archim.*Sph.Cyl.*2.3, Euc.*Dat.Def.*4, Apollon.Perg.*Con.*2.46, al.; παρὰ θέσει parallel to a straight line *given in position,* [Euc.]*Dat.Def.*15; εἰς δύο θέσεις τὰς AB, AΓ to meet the two *straight lines* AB, AΓ *given in position,* Hero *Metr.*3.10; κατὰ τὴν θ. τὴν πρὸς ἡμᾶς Arist.*Ph.*208$^{b}$23, etc.; οὐ τῇ θ. διαφέροντα μόνον, ἀλλὰ καὶ τῇ δυνάμει ib.22; so in Music, of notes in a scale, κατὰ θέσιν, opp. κατὰ δύναμιν, Ptol.*Harm.*2.5. V. Philos., *thesis, position,* assumed and requiring proof, Pl.*R.*335a, Arist.*Top.*104$^{b}$19, *APo.*72$^{a}$15; θέσιν διαφυλάττειν to maintain *a thesis,* Id.*EN*1096$^{a}$2; κινεῖν to controvert it, Plu.2.687b, cf. 328a, etc. 2. *general question,* opp. ὑπόθεσις (*special case*), Aphth.*Prog.*13, Theon *Prog.*12, cf. Cic.*Top.*21.79, Quint.3.5.5 (but θ. includes ὑπόθεσις and ὁρισμός, Phlp.*in APo.*35.1; opp. ἀξίωμα, ib.34.9). 3. *arbitrary determination,* esp. in dat. θέσει, τὰ ὀνόματα μὴ θ. γενέσθαι Epicur.*Ep.*1 p.27 U.; opp. φύσει, Chrysipp.*Stoic.*3.76, Str.2.3.7, etc.; τὰ θ. δίκαια, νόμιμα, Ph.1.50,112; σημαίνειν θ. S.E.*P.*2.256. 4. *affirmation,* opp. ἄρσις, ib.1.192, cf. 2.244, Plot.5.5.6, etc. VI. *a setting down,* opp. ἄρσις (*lifting*), πᾶσα πορεία ἐξ ἄρσεως καὶ θέσεως συντελεῖται Arist.*Pr.*885$^{b}$6: hence, in rhythm, *downward beat,* opp. the *upward* (ἄρσις), Aristid.Quint.1.13, Bacch.*Harm.*98, etc. VII. in prosody, θέσει μακρὰ συλλαβή long by *position,* opp. φύσει, D.T.632.30, Heph. 1.3: orig. prob. in signf. v. 3, cf. Sch.D.T.p.206 H. 2. θέσεις, αἱ, in punctuation, *stops,* Donat. in *Gramm.Lat.*4.372 K. VIII. part of a horse's hoof, ἡ θ. τοῦ ποδός *Hippiatr.*82.

⊛ **θέσκελος,** *ον,* Ep. Adj. perh. *set in motion by God* (κέλλω), and so *marvellous, wondrous,* always of things, θ. ἔργα deeds or works *of wonder,* Il.3.130, Od.11.610; θέσκελα εἰδώς Call.*Fr.anon.*385: neut. Adv., ἔϊκτο δὲ θέσκελον αὐτῷ it was *wondrous* like him, Il.23.107; prob. taken by later poets as, = *God-inspired* (κελεύω), θ. Ἑρμῆς Coluth.126.

**θέσμιος,** Dor. and Ep. **τέθμιος,** *ον,* or *α, ον,* (θεσμός) *fixed, settled, lawful,* ἑορτὰ τέθμιος Pi.*N.*11.27; τέθμιαι ὧραι Call.*Ap.*87; θέσμια τάδε καὶ πάτρια Lex ap.Arist.*Ath.*16.10; θέσμιον (sc. ἐστί) A.*Ag.*1564 (lyr.); θέσμιόν ἐστι, = θέμις ἐστί, A.R.2.12; *fitting,* θηρευτῆρσι σιγὴ τέθμιός ἐστι Opp.*C.*1.450. II. θέσμιον, Dor. and Ep. τέθμιον, τό, esp. in pl., *laws, customs, rites,* Hdt.1.59, A.*Eu.*491 (lyr.), S.*Aj.*712 (lyr.); θ. ἀναγράψαι Arist.*Ath.*3.4; προγόνων παλαιὰ θ. E.*Fr.*360.45, cf. Call.*Dian.*174: sg. in Pi.*I.*6(5).20, E.*Tr.*267 (anap.):—in form **θέθμιον** *IG*9(1).334.46 (Locr., v B.C.). 2. *agreement,* τῶ τεθμίω ϝίστωρ ib.7.3172.165 (Orchom. Boeot.). III. Θέσμιος, title of Apollo, Paus.5.15.7; of Demeter, Id.8.15.4.

**θεσμο-δότης,** ὁ, *lawgiver,* cj. for -θέτης, Longin.9.9:—fem. **-δότειρα** Orph.Εὐχή 25. **-θεσία,** ἡ, *office of* θεσμοθέτης at Athens, *IG* 2$^{2}$.1368.133. II. *decree* of fate, Plu.2.573f.

**θεσμοθετ-εῖον,** τό, *hall in which the* θεσμοθέται *met,* Arist.*Ath.*3.5, Plu.2.613b (-θέτιον Suid. s. v. Πρυτανεῖον):—also **θεσμοθέσιον,** τό, Plu.2.714c, Sch.Pl.*Prt.*337d, Suid. s. v. ἄρχων. **-έω,** *to be a* θεσμοθέτης, Is.7.34, D.59.65. **-ης,** *ου,* ὁ, (τίθημι) *lawgiver, legislator,* of Moses, Longin.9.9. II. esp. at Athens, θεσμοθέται, οἱ, the *six junior archons,* *IG*1$^{2}$.39.75, al., Ar.*V.*775 (sg.), al., Antipho 6.35, Arist.*Ath.*3.4, al., Aeschin.3.38; also, title of magistrate in Amorgos, *IG*12(7).57.12 (iii B.C.). ⊛ **-ις,** *ιδος,* ἡ, = θεσμοφόρος, title of Demeter, Corn.*ND*28; of Isis, *Hymn.Is.*20.

**θεσμο-ποιέω,** *make laws,* E.*Ph.*1645. ⊛ **-πόλος,** *ον,* (πολέω) = θεμιστοπόλος, *AP*5.292.3 (Paul. Sil.).

⊛ **θεσμός,** Dor. **τεθμός** (v. infr.), **θεθμός** *IG*5(2).159 (Tegea, v B.C.), Isyll.12, Locr. **τετθμός** *Berl.Sitzb.*1927.8 (v B.C.): ὁ: pl. θεσμοί, poet. θεσμά S.*Fr.*92: (τίθημι):—*that which is laid down, law, ordinance,* once in Hom., λέκτροιο παλαιοῦ θεσμὸν ἵκοντο Od.23.296; εἰρήνης θεσμοί *the order* of peace, *h.Hom.*8.16; esp. of divine *laws,* θ. τὸν μοιρόκραντον ἐκ θεῶν A.*Eu.*391; ἵμερος.. τῶν μεγάλων πάρεδρος θ. S.*Ant.*800 (lyr.); οἱ τῶν θεῶν θ. X.*Cyr.*1.6.6; θ. Ἀδραστείας, οἱ τῆς εἱμαρμένης θ., Pl.*Phdr.*248c, Plu.2.111d; παρέβη θ. ἀρχαίους Ar.*Av.*331 (lyr.). 2. of human *law,* οἱ πάτριοι θ. Hdt.3.31; at Athens, esp. of the laws of Draco, *IG*1$^{2}$.115.20, And.1.81, Decr. ib.83, Arist.*Ath.*4.1, etc., cf. Ael.*VH*8.10: used by Solon of his own laws, Sol.36.16, cf. 31.2, Plu.*Sol.*19; ὁ ταῦτα ἀπεργαζόμενος θ. νόμος ἂν ὀρθῶς εἴη κείμενος Pl.*Ep.*355c; ὁ τοῖς ἄλλοις τιθέμενος θεσμοὺς Δημήτριος Duris 10 J.; ὅδ' ὁ τεθμὸς πὲρ τῶν ἐντοφηΐων *GDI*2561 *C*19 (Delph.): in later poetry, θεσμοί, = *law, jurisprudence,* *Epigr.Gr.* 424.4, al.; θεσμῶν ταμίης, πρόμαχος, *IG*3.637,638. 3. generally, *rule, precept, rite,* S.*Tr.*682; θ. πυρός *the law* of the beacon-fire, A.*Ag.*304; τεθμὸς ἀέθλων Pi.*O.*6.69; στεφάνων τ. the *appointed* crowns, ib.13.29; θ. ὅδ' εὔφρων the cheering *strain* (cf. νόμος), A. *Supp.*1034 (lyr.); ὕμνου τεθμὸν Ὀλυμπιονίκαν Pi.*O.*7.88; μακάρων Id.*Pae.*4.47. II. *institution,* as the *tribunal* of the Areopagus, A. *Eu.*615; τεθμὸς Ἡρακλέος, Ποτειδᾶνος τεθμοί, the Olympian, Isthmian games, Pi.*N.*10.33, *O.*13.40. III. = θησαυρός, Anacr.58. IV. θεσμοί· αἱ συνθέσεις τῶν ξύλων, Hsch.

**θεσμοσύνη,** Dor. **-να,** ἡ, *justice,* *AP*7.593 (Agath.).

**θεσμο-φόρια,** *ων,* τά, women's festival at Athens and elsewhere, in honour of Demeter Θεσμοφόρος (q. v.), Hdt.2.171, Ar.*Av.*1519, *Th.* 80, 182, al.; θ. ἑστιᾶν τὰς γυναῖκας to furnish the women's feast *at the Th.,* Is.3.80; at Ephesus, Hdt.6.16. **-φοριάζω,** *keep the Thesmophoria,* X.*HG*5.2.29, *Gloss.Oxy.*1802.35; Θεσμοφοριάζουσαι, name of a play by Aristophanes. **-φόριον,** τό, *temple of Demeter* Θεσμοφόρος, Ar.*Th.*278, 880, *IG*2.1059.12; at Delos, ib.11(2).159*A*17 (iii B.C.):—also **-εῖον** Theon *Prog.*5: **-φόριον** μέτρον, a form of dactylic metre, Mar.Vict.6.145 K.: ⊛ **-φόριος,** ὁ, demoticon at Memphis, Mitteis *Chr.* 29.5 (ii B.C.); at Alexandria, *Supp.Epigr.*2.866. II. (sc. μήν) name of month at Rhodes, *IG*12(1).3.5; in Crete, *GDI*5149.58. ⊛ **-φοριών,** ῶνος, ὁ, name of month at Heraclea ad Latmum, *SIG*633.55 (ii B.C.); in Crete, *Hemerolog.Flor.* ⊛ **-φόρος,** *ον,* *law-giving,* epith. of Demeter, Hdt.6.91,134, *IPE*2.13 (Panticapaeum, iv B.C.), Call.*Aet.Oxy.* 2079.10, D.S.1.14, etc.; σεμνὴ Θ. *AP*5.149 (Asclep.), cf. Luc.*Tim.*17; τὼ Θεσμοφόρω Demeter and Persephone, Ar.*Th.*83, al.; αἱ Θεσμοφόροι App.*BC*2.70, Plu.*Dio*56, etc.; πότνια Θ., of Persephone, Pi.*Fr.*37; also, as a title of Dionysus, Orph.*H.*42.1. ⊛ **-φύλαξ** [ῠ], *ακος,* ὁ, *guardian of the law,* of Moses, Ph.1.171:—usu. in pl. **-φύλακες,** οἱ, a magistracy at Elis, Th.5.47, cf. D.S.5.67; at Alexandria, *PHal.*1.239 (iii B.C.); in Ceos, *IG*12(5).595*B*16 (iii/ii B.C.); at Ptolemais, *PFay.*22.11 (i A.D.); Boeot. **τεθμοφούλαξ** *IG*7.3172.178 (Orchom.):—hence **-φῠλάκιον** [ᾰ], τό, their office, *PHal.*1.234 (iii B.C.): **-φῠλᾰκι⟨κ⟩ός,** ή, όν, νόμος Plu.2.292d.

**θεσμῳδ-έω,** *deliver oracular precepts*: τὰ θεσμῳδούμενα *oracles,* Ph. 1.650. **-ός,** ὁ, *giver of* θεσμοί, Id.ap.Eus.*PE*8.7, *BMus.Inscr.*4.481*.457 (pl.).

**θέσπαλαι·** αἱ Κῷαι, παρὰ Φιλητᾷ, καὶ αἱ φαρμακίδες, Hsch. (prob. Θεσσαλαί).

**θεσπεσιανή,** ἡ, name of an antidote, Orib.*Fr.*82.

⊛ **θεσπέσιος,** *α, ον,* also *ος, ον* E.*Andr.*296 (lyr.), Luc.*Sacr.*13: (perh. for θεσ-σπέσιος, cf. θεός, ἔσπον):—prop. of the voice, *divinely sounding, divinely sweet,* ἀοιδή Il.2.600; Σειρῆνες Od.12.158; ἔπεα Pi.*I.*4(3).39; ἀχέτας Ar.*Av.*1095 (lyr.). 2. *divinely uttered* or *decreed,* dat. sg. fem. θεσπεσίῃ as Adv., Il.2.367. b. *oracular,* γένος Pi.*P.*12.13 (of the Graiae); δάφνα E. l.c.; θ. ὁδός the way *of divination,* of Cassandra, A.*Ag.*1154 (lyr.); εὐχαῖς ὑπὸ θ. with prayers *to the gods,* Pi. *I.*6(5).44. c. = θεῖος, βηλός Il.1.591; ἄντρον Od.13.363. II. *more than human*: hence, *awful,* of natural phenomena, θ. νέφος Il. 15.669; ἀχλύς Od.7.42; λαῖλαψ 9.68; *marvellous,* χάρις 2.12; θ. ἄωτον, χαλκός, 9.434, Il.2.457; θ. ὀδμή a smell *divinely sweet,* Od.9.211; ὀσμὴ θ. Hermipp.82.9; of human affairs, θ. φύζα, φόβος, Il.9.2, 17.118; πλοῦτος 2.670; ἠχή 8.159; βοή Od.24.49; θ. ὅμιλος Theoc. 15.66: also in Prose, τέχνη θ. τις καὶ ὑψηλή Pl.*Euthd.*289e; θ. βίος Id.*R.*365b; θ. καὶ ἡδεῖα ἡ διαγωγή ib.558a; σοφοὶ καὶ θ. ἄνδρες Id. *Tht.*151b, cf. Philostr.*Dial.*1; φύσεις Id.*VS*2.9.2; θ. τὴν γνώμην Luc. *Alex.*4. III. Adv. -ίως, θ. ἐφόβηθεν they trembled *unspeakably,* Il.15.637: neut. θεσπέσιον as Adv., θ. ὑλᾶν Theoc.25.70; also ἀπόζει θ. ὡς ἡδύ Hdt.3.113; ὠδώδει θ. οἷον Plu.*Alex.*20; θεσπεσίηθεν *divinely,* ἀρηρότα Emp.96.4.—Chiefly Ep., once in Hdt., twice in Trag. (lyr.), once in Ar. (lyr.).

**θεσπεσιότης,** *ητος,* ἡ, = θειότης, Eust.240.8.

**θεσπῐ-ᾰοιδός,** όν, (θέσπις) poet. for θεσπιῳδός, Hsch. **-δᾰής,** ές, (δαίω A) *kindled by a god,* θ. πῦρ *portentous* fire, Il.12.177,441, Od. 4.418, etc. (Ep. word.) **-έπεια,** (ἔπος) fem. Adj. *oracular, prophetic,* S.*OT*463 (lyr.).

⊛ **θεσπίζω,** fut. -ίσω, Att. -ῐῶ, Ion. inf. θεσπιέειν v.l. in Hdt.8.135; Dor. aor. ἐθέσπιξα Theoc.15.63: (θέσπις):—*prophesy, foretell,* τι Hdt. 1.47, al.; τινί τι A.*Ag.*1210, E.*Andr.*1161:—Pass., τί δὲ τεθέσπισται; S.*OC*388, cf. Parth.35.2. II. Pass., c. acc., [χρησμοί,] οὓς ἐθεσπίσθη Μωυσῆς Ph.2.38. III. of the Emperors, = Lat. *sancire, decree,* Jul.*Ep.*75b, Wilcken *Chr.*6.8 (v A.D.), *OGI*521.9 (Abydus), *Cod.Just.*1.12.3 *Intr.*

**θεσπῐόμαντις,** Adj. *oracular,* ἕδρα Aristonous 1.3.

**θέσπιος,** *ον,* = θεσπέσιος, Hes.*Fr.*197, Orac.ap.Ar.*Av.*977.

**θεσπιόφημον·** παροιμίαν τινά, Hsch.

**θέσπ-ις,** *ιος,* ὁ, ἡ (acc. θέσπιδα Nonn.*D.*25.452, dat. ιδι ib.45.133): (cf. θεσπέσιος):—*filled with the words of God, inspired,* Hom. only in Od. in acc. θέσπιν; ἀοιδός 17.385; ἀοιδή 1.328, 8.498, E.*Med.*425 (lyr.); also θέσπιν αὐδάν S.*Ichn.*244 (lyr.). 2. generally, *wondrous, awful,* θέσπις ἄελλα *h.Ven.*208. II. θέσπιδες· θυσίαι, θεοσέβειαι, Hsch. **-ισις,** *εως,* ἡ, *oracular utterance,* Sch.Ar.*Pl.* 11. ⊛ **-ισμα,** *ατος,* τό, mostly in pl., *oracles, oracular sayings,* Hdt. 2.29, A.*Fr.*86, S.*OT*971: sg., E.*Ion*405. 2. *Imperial constitution,* Wilcken *Chr.*6.12 (pl., v A.D.), Just.*Nov.*113.1.1. **-ιστής,** οῦ, ὁ, *prophet,* Man.6.378.

**θεσπῐῳδ-έω,** *to be a* θεσπιῳδός, *sing in prophetic strain,* A.*Ag.*1161,

E.*Ph.*959, Ar.*Pl.*9, Pl.*Ax.*367d; χρησμοὶ τὸ κράτος τῆς οἰκουμένης -ῳδοῦσι Posidon.36J. II. *hold office of* θεσπιῳδός, i. e. *versifier of oracles*, *OGI*530.6 (Amisus), *IGRom.*4.1588 (Claros), etc. **-ός,** όν, *singing in prophetic strain*, of persons, S.*Fr.*456, E.*Hel.*145; also ὀμφαλὸς γῆς θ. Id.*Med.*668; μαντικὴ Philostr.*VS*1 *Praef.*: Subst. θεσπιῳδός, ἡ, = Lat. *Carmenta*, D.H.1.31. II. θ. φόβον *caused by prophecy*, A.*Ag.*1134 (lyr., s. v. l.).

**Θεσσάλ-ειος** [ᾰ], v. Θεσσαλός II. **-ία,** ἡ, *Thessaly*, Hdt.3.96, etc. **-ίζω,** Att. Θεττ-, *imitate the Thessalians*, Ael.*VH*4.15, St.Byz. s. v. Θεσσαλία; *speak like them*, Parth.24.2, D.Chr.11.23. **-ῐκέτης,** ου, ὁ, Att. Θεττ-, *serf in Thessaly*, Philocr.Hist.1. **-ικός,** Att. Θεττ-, ή, όν, *Thessalian*: Θ. ἕδος, a sort of *chair* or *couch*, Hp.*Art.*7; ὄρεα Hdt.7.128; δίφρος Eup.58, cf. Poll.7.112; Θ. ἔνθεσις Hermipp. 41; Θ. δεῖπνα Ar.*Fr.*492, cf. Antiph.34.3. Adv. -κῶς Crates Com. 19. 2. *of the Thessalian dialect*, ἔθος A.D.*Synt.*214.6; διαίρεσις ib.50.9. Adv. -κῶς Id.*Pron.*109.1: Comp. -ώτερον Id.*Synt.*159. 9. **-ιῶτις,** ιδος, ἡ, one of the four districts of Thessaly, Hellanic. 52J., Hdt.1.57, Str.9.5.3. **-ός,** Att. Θεττ-, ή, όν, *Thessalian*, Hdt. 5.63, etc.: prov., Θ. σόφισμα *a Thessalian trick*, E.*Ph.*1407; Θ. νόμισμα, i. e. false money, Phot.; Thess. **Πετθαλός** *IG*9(2).258 (Cierium), 517.14 (Larissa); Boeot. **Φετταλός** (as pr. n.) ib.7.2430.8. II. pr. n. of a physician of the Methodic School:—hence Adj. **Θεσσάλειος,** α, ον, Gal.15.763, al. III. fem. **Θεσσαλίς,** ίδος, *Thessalian*, κυνῆ S.*OC*314: as Subst. Θετταλίς, ἡ, a kind of *shoe*, Lysipp.2.

**θέσσασθαι,** poet. aor. *pray for*, c. acc. θεσσάμενος γενεήν Hes.*Fr.* 201; γλυκερὸν νόστον Archil.11; παίδων γένος A.R.1.824, cf. Euph. 136: c. inf., τάν ποτ' εὔανδρον [εἶναι] . . θέσσαντο *prayed that* this land might be . ., Pi.*N.*5.10 (Hsch. also has θέσσεσθαι, θεσσόμενος, θήσω, θησόμενοι, θησάμενοι):—hence Adj. **θεστός,** only in compds. ἀπόθεστος, πολύθεστος (q. v.), Boeot. pr. n. Θεόφειστος, Ion. Ἑρμόθεστος. (Perh. $g^{wh}$edh-, cf. πόθος (fr. φόθος), OIr. -*guidiu*, Welsh *gweddïo* 'pray', Lith. *gedėti* 'mourn'; θήσω, θησόμενοι, θησάμενοι seem to be analogical formations.)

**θεσφᾰτηλόγος,** ον, *prophetic*, A.*Ag.*1441.

**θεσφᾰτ-ίζω,** *prophesy*, Hsch.:—also **-όομαι,** Id. ❋**-ος,** ον, (θεός, φημί) *spoken by God, decreed*, μόρος A.*Ag.*1321; ἥκει θ. βίου τελευτή S.*OC*1472: mostly in phrase θέσφατόν ἐστι, it is *ordained*, ὡς γὰρ θ. ἐστι Il.8.477, cf. E.*IA*1556: c. dat. pers. et inf., σοὶ δ' οὐ θ. ἐστι . . θανέειν Od.4.561, cf. 10.473, Pi.*P.*4.71, Orac. in Ar.*Pax* 1073; so εἴ τι θ. πατρὶ . . ἱκνεῖθ', ὥστε πρὸς παίδων θανεῖν S.*OC*969. 2. Subst. θέσφατα, τά, *divine decrees, oracles*, Od.11.151, 297; παλαίφατα θ. 13. 172, cf. Pi.*I.*8(7).34: sg., E.*IT*121. II. generally, *wonderful, mighty*, ἀήρ Od.7.143.—Cf. θεσπέσιος, θέσκελος.

**θετέος,** α, ον, *to be counted as*, Pl.*Epin.*984a, Arist.*Pol.*1277$^b$38. II. **θετέον,** *one must establish*, ἆθλα Pl.*Lg.*832e; *one must assume*, X. *Mem.*4.2.15; *one must reckon, count*, τοὺς βαναύσους πολίτας Arist. *Pol.*1277$^b$35, cf. Satyr.*Vit.Eur.Fr.*39 x 6, etc.; ἐν ἁμαρτίᾳ Ph.2.171.

**θετήρ,** ῆρος, ὁ, *EM*177.24; = τολμητής, πράκτης, Hsch.: pl., etym. of θεοί, Corn.*ND*1.

**θέτης,** ου, ὁ, (τίθημι) *one who places*, ὀνομάτων θ. name-giver, Pl. *Cra.*389d. II. *mortgagor*, χωρίων Is.10.24. III. *adoptive father of a child*, Did. ap. Harp.

**Θετίδειον** [ῐ], τό, *temple of Thetis*, E.*Andr.*20, Plb.18.20.6, Str.9. 5.6.

❋**θετικός,** ή, όν, *fit for placing*, ὀνομάτων θ. *prompt at giving* names, D.H.*Comp.*16, cf. Ph.2.101. Adv. -κῶς *appositely*, D.H.*Rh.*3. 5. II. *concerning adoption*, νόμοι Arist.*Pol.*1274$^b$4. III. *belonging to a* θέσις, *disputable*, ὑπόθεσις Philostr.*VS*2.6; τὰ θ. τῶν χωρίων ib.29; so τὰ θ. alone, Phld.*Rh.*1.206 S.; θ. κεφάλαιον Theon *Prog.*2; τὴν ζήτησιν θ. ποιεῖσθαι to make the question *a matter of argument*, Str.2.3.7; Lat. *genus instituendi* θετικώτερον, *addressed to reason rather* than feeling, Cic.*QF*3.3.4. Adv. Comp. -κώτερον Aps. p.333 H. IV. *positive, affirmative*, opp. *negative* (ἀρνητικός), Numen. ap. Eus.*PE*14.8. Adv. -κῶς *positively, affirmatively*, D.L.9. 75; οὐ λίαν θ. not very *positively*, Phld.*Rh.*1.371 S. 2. Gramm., *positive*, τὸ θετικόν the *positive degree*, Sch. D Il.4.277. b. *expressing obligation*, of verbals in -τέον, D.T.642.16; θετικῶς· τὸ ὀφειλόμενον γενέσθαι, Hsch. V. *arbitrary*, χρῆσις τῶν ὀνομάτων S.E.*P.*2.256. Adv. -κῶς ib.1.38.

**Θέτις,** voc. Θέτι Il.24.88, acc. Θέτιν, gen. ιδος 4.512, Dor. ιος Pi.*I.* 8(7).30, dat. Θέτι: ἡ:—*Thetis*, Hom., etc.

❋**θετός,** ή, όν, (τίθημι) *placed, set*, E.*IA*251 (lyr.); *having position*, στιγμὴ οὐσία θετός Arist.*APo.*87$^a$36. II. *taken as one's child, adopted*, Pi.*O.*9.62, E.*Fr.*359, etc.; θετὸν παῖδα ποιεῖσθαι Hdt.6.57, cf. Pl.*Lg.*929c; θετὸς γενέσθαι τινί or ὑπό τινος, Plu.*Thes.*13, App.*BC* 1.5; θετός, ὁ, *adopted son*, dub. in Is.3.69; θετή *adopted daughter*, Hsch.; also θ. πατήρ *adoptive* father, D.S.10.11.

**Θεττᾰλός, Θετταλικός,** etc., Att. for Θεσσ-.

**Θεττᾰλότμητον** κρέας a lump of meat *such as you would cut for a hungry Thessalian*, Philetaer.10.

**θεῦ,** Dor. and Ion. for θέο, θοῦ, imper. aor. 2 Med. of τίθημι.

**θευ-,** Dor. and Ion. for θεο-, cf. Θευδαίσιος, θευμορία, θεύμορος:—hence **θευ-εργέσια,** τά, festival of a θεὸς εὐεργέτης, *Inscr.Délos* 363.53 (iii B. C.). **-κολέω,** = θεοκολέω, *IG*9(1).421 (Aetolia). **-ξένια,** = θεοξένια, Hsch. **-προπία,** ἡ, = θεοπροπία, B.9.41. **-φορία,** ἡ, = θεοφορία, *AP*6.220.4 (Diosc.).

**θεύγεσθαι,** Cret., = θέλγ-, Hsch. **θευρός,** v. θεωρός.

**θεῦσις,** εως, ἡ, *running*, coined as etym. of θεός, Corn.*ND*1.

**θεῦτις,** = τευθίς, Hippon.115.

**θέω** (A), Ep. also **θείω,** Il.6.507, 10.437 (in Att. the syllables εο, εου, εω are not contr.); Ep. subj. θέησι 22.23; 3 sg. impf. ἔθει Od.12. 407 and later, ἔθεε Il.1.483, Hdt.1.43 (and in later Prose, D.S.16.94); Ep. θέε Il.20.275, Hes.*Sc.*224; Ion. impf. θέεσκον Il.20.229: fut. θεύσομαι 23.623, Ar.*Eq.*485, *Av.*205, (ὑπο-) Pi.*P.*2.84, (ἀντι-) Hdt. 5.22, (μετα-) X.*Cyn.*6.22; θεύσω Lyc.1119: aor. 1 ἔθευσα (δι-) Vett.Val.345.35, part. θεύσας *IGRom.*4.1740 (Cyme):—the other tenses are supplied by τρέχω and *δρέμω: (θεϝ-, Skt. *dhávate*):—*run*, ποσί, πόδεσσι, Od.8.247, Il.23.623; βῆ δὲ θέειν 17.698; θέησι τιταινόμενος πεδίοιο 22.23; ποῖ θεῖς; Ar.*V.*854; θᾶττον θανάτου θεῖ [ἡ πονηρία] Pl.*Ap.*39b; ὁ βραδέως θέων Id.*Hp.Mi.*373d; of horses, Id.*Cra.* 423a; ἐν Ὀλυμπίᾳ θεόντων ἵππων Id.*Lg.*822b: in part. with another Verb, ἦλθε θέων, ἦλθε θέουσα, came *running*, Il.6.54, 394, etc.; ἷξε θέων, of a person on ship-board, Od.3.288; θέων Αἴαντα κάλεσσον *run and call him*, Il.12.343, etc. 2. περὶ τρίποδος γὰρ ἔμελλον θεύσεσθαι *to run* for a tripod, 11.701: metaph. (cf. τρέχω II. 2), περὶ ψυχῆς θέον Ἕκτορος they *were running* for Hector's life, 22.161; θ. περὶ ὑμέων αὐτῶν Hdt.8.140.α'; θ. 〈τὸν〉 περὶ τοῦ παντὸς δρόμον ib.74; περὶ γυναικῶν καὶ παίδων Paus.6.18.3. 3. metaph., θ. ἐς νόσους Pl.*Lg.*691c; θ. ἐγγύτατα ὀλέθρου Id.*R.*417b; θεῖν παρὰ τὸν ἔσχατον κίνδυνον Plu. *Fab.*26. II. of other kinds of motion, as, 1. of birds, θεύσονται δρόμῳ Ar.*Av.*205. 2. of things, *run*; of ships, ἡ δ' ἔθεεν κατὰ κῦμα Il.1.483, cf. X.*HG*6.2.29; of a potter's wheel, Il.18.601; of a *rolling* stone, 13.141; of a quoit, ῥίμφα θέων ἀπὸ χειρὸς *flying* lightly . ., Od.8.193. 3. metaph., δύναμις θαυμαστὴ ἐκεῖ θεῖ Plot.2.9.8, cf. 6.5.11. III. of things not actually in motion, [φλὲψ] ἀνὰ νῶτα θέουσα διαμπερές Il.13.547; ἄντυξ ἣ πυμάτη θέεν ἀσπίδος 6.118; ἀμφὶ δέ μιν κίβισις θέε Hes.*Sc.*224; γραμμῆς περὶ [σημεῖον] θεούσης Plot.6. 5.11. IV. c. acc. loci, *run over*, τὰ ὄρη X.*Cyn.*4.6, cf. 5.17; μέσσα θέων πελάγευς *AP*7.273 (Leon.), cf. 10.23 (Autom.); πλωτῶν γένος ὑγρὰ θεόντων Opp.*H.*3.183.—The simple Verb is used in Trag. only by E.*Ion* 1217.

❋**θέω** (B), *shine, gleam*, ὀδόντων λευκὰ θεόντων Hes.*Sc.*146 (λευκαθεόντων cj. Wackernagel); ὕλη χλωρὰ θεούσῃ cj. in Theoc.25.158; ποίην . . χλωρὰ θέουσαν *IG*14.1389 ii 24; cf. θοός (B), Λευκαθέα, λευκαθίζω.

**θεῶ,** for θεάου, imper. of θεάομαι, *behold!*

**θεώματα**· περικαθαρτήρια, Hsch. (leg. θειώματα).

**θεωρ-εῖον,** τό, *place for seeing*, Hsch. s. v. θαυσήκρι. **-έω:—Pass.,** fut. -ηθήσομαι S.E.*M.*8.280: fut. Med. in pass. sense, ib.1.70, Ael.*VH* 7.10: (θεωρός):—*to be a* θεωρός I (q. v.), μαντεύεσθαι καὶ θ. Th.5.18; ἐγὼ δὲ τεθεώρηκα πώποτ' οὐδαμοῖ πλὴν ἐς Πάρον Ar.*V.*1188; of the states which sent θεωροί, οἱ Ἀθηναῖοι ἐθεώρουν ἐς τὰ Ἴσθμια Th.8.10. 2. *to be sent to consult an oracle*, Pl.*Ep.*315b. II. of spectators at games, τὰ Ὀλύμπια Hdt.1.59; ἀγῶνα Id.8.26, X.*An.*1.2.10; θ. τινά *to see* him *act*, Thphr.*Char.*11.3: abs., And.4.20, D.18.265; *to go as a spectator*, ἐς τὰ Ἐφέσια Th.3.104; ἐς Ὀλυμπίαν Luc.*Tim.*50; v. sub ὀβολός I. III. *look at, behold*, γῆν πολλήν Hdt.4.76; τύχας τινός A.*Pr.* 304; τὰ περὶ τὸν πόλεμον Pl.*R.*467c; *inspect, review* soldiers, X.*An.* 1.2.16, *HG*4.5.6: abs., *gaze, gape*, ἑστηκὼς θ. Thphr.*Char.*4.5: Astrol., = ἐπιθεωρέω 5, τὴν σελήνην Gal.19.542. 2. of the mind, *contemplate, consider*, αὐτῇ τῇ ψυχῇ αὐτὴν τὴν ψυχὴν θ. Pl.*Grg.*523e; τὰ ὄντα ᾗ ὄντα Arist.*Metaph.*1003$^b$15, cf. D.1.12, Epicur.*Nat.*2.6, etc.: folld. by an interrog., τοῦτο θ., εἰ τἀληθῆ λέγω D.3.3; θ. τινά, ὁπότερου τοῦ βίου ἐστίν Aeschin.3.168; πόσας ἔχουσι διαφορὰς Arist.*GA* 761$^a$11; θ. τίνας λέγομεν τοὺς φρονίμους Id.*EN* 1140$^a$24; θ. τι ἔκ τινος *to judge of* one thing by another, τὴν ἔννοιαν ἐκ τῶν ἔργων Is.1.13, cf. Aeschin.3.160; θ. τι πρός τι *compare* one thing *with* another, D.18.17; πρὸς τοὺς πρὸ ἐμαυτοῦ . . κρίνωμαι καὶ θεωρῶμαι; ib.315; τοὺς πρέσβεις θ. πρὸς τὸν καιρὸν καθ' ὃν ἐπρέσβευον Aeschin.2.80; θ. [τι τεκμηρίοις] D. 21.199. b. *observe*, θ. μᾶλλον τοὺς πέλας δυνάμεθα ἢ ἑαυτούς Arist. *EN* 1169$^b$33, cf. *Pol.*1263$^b$25, al.; ταῦτα ἐμοῦ ἐθεωρήσατε, ὡς . . ποιουμένου Lycurg.28:—Pass., τεθεώρηται τοῦτο μάλιστα ἐπὶ τῶν περιστερῶν Arist.*HA* 562$^a$23, cf. 540$^b$19, al.; λόγῳ θεωρεῖσθαι, of objects not accessible to sense, Phld.*D.*3.10: abs., ὡς καὶ ἐπ' ἄλλων θεωρεῖται ib.1.13. c. *perceive*, c. inf., ἀναγκαῖον ὑπάρχειν D.S.13.88. d. abs., *speculate, theorize*, ἀκριβῶς, φορτικῶς, Arist.*Pol.*1280$^b$28, *Metaph.* 1001$^b$14; λογικῶς, φυσικῶς, Id.*APo.*88$^a$19, *Cael.*304$^a$25; περί τινος Id. *Metaph.*1004$^b$1, 983$^a$33 (Pass.); θ. ἔκ τινος *to conclude by observation* from . ., ib.1029$^a$26; διά τινος Id.*Mete.*353$^b$18:—Pass., ἡ παρὰ τοῖς Ἕλλησι τεθεωρημένη μάθησις Ael.Tact.*Prooem.* (θεωρήσασα is prob. corrupt for ἑωρ- in S.*OC*1084 (lyr.).) ❋**-ημα,** ατος, τό, *sight, spectacle*, λόγοι καὶ θεωρήματα D.18.68; θ. καὶ ἀκροάματα Aristox.*Fr. Hist.*15; θ. καὶ ἀκούσματα D.C.52.30: generally, *festival*, ὅσα Μουσῶν ὠδὶν ἔχεται θεωρήματα Pl.*Lg.*953a. 2. *object of contemplation*, τὸ ἐν ἡμῖν φάντασμα δεῖ ὑπολαβεῖν . . εἶναι θ. Arist.*Mem.*450$^b$25; *vision*, Id.*Div.Somn.*463$^b$19; *intuition*, θ. κοινά Chrysipp.*Stoic.*3.72, al., cf. Phld.*Po.*5.25 (pl.). II. of the mind, *speculation, theory*, Arist. *Metaph.*1083$^b$18, *Top.*104$^b$1; τὰ κατὰ φυσιολογίαν θ. Metrod.*Herc.*831. 8; *speculative proposition*, M.Ant.1.8. b. *datum* or *rule of art*, Cic.*Fat.*6.11 (pl.); τέχνης θ. Phld.*Rh.*2.94 S., al. (pl.), cf. *Stoic.*3.51; ἰατρικῆς θ. Corn.*ND*33 (pl.); *scheme, plan*, Plb.6.26.10: pl., θεωρήματα, τά, *arts and sciences*, Id.10.47.12; αἱ τέχναι ἐκ -ημάτων εἰσίν Gal.1.106. c. Math., *theorem*, Archim.*Sph.Cyl.*1 *Prooem.*, al., Papp.30.6, al., Procl.*in Euc.*p.201 F.; also ἀστρονομικὰ θ. Phlp.*in Mete.*104.19. 2. *subject of investigation*, Plb.1.2.1, D.H.*Comp.* 2. b. *investigation*, Plu.2.1131c. **-ημᾰτικός,** ή, όν, *to be interpreted as seen*, ὄνειροι, opp. ἀλληγορικοί, Artem.4.1. II. *theoretic*, ἀρετή *Stoic.*3.48, cf. Iamb.*Protr.*21.λβ', D.L.3.49; *dogmatic*, epith. of

Metrodorus, Id.2.113; *contemplative*, βίος Jul.*ad Them.*265b; opp. πρακτικός, Id.*Or.*6.190a. **-ημάτιον**, τό, Dim. of θεώρημα, Arr. *Epict.*2.21.17, 3.5.15. **-ήμων**, ονος, ὁ, ἡ, *contemplative*, Choerob. in *An.Ox.*2.220. **-ησις**, εως, ἡ, *viewing*, τραγικαὶ θ. Pl.*Phlb.* 48a. **-ητέον**, *one must consider, investigate*, εἴτε..εἴτε.. Id. *Lg.*815b; τίνι διαφέρει.. Arist.*Ph.*193$^{b}$23, etc. **-ητήριον**, τό, *seat in a theatre*, Plu.*CG*12 (pl.), *CIG*2782.20 (Aphrodisias). **-ητής**, οῦ, ὁ, *spectator*, ἐργάται τῶν καλῶν καὶ θ. Phld.*Oec.*p.63 J., cf. Hsch. s. v. θεωρούς. II. *overseer, director*, Sch.Opp.*H.*3.257. ⊛ **-ητικός**, ή, όν, *able to perceive*, τοῦ περὶ τὰ σώματα κάλλους Arist.*Pol.*1338$^{b}$1; μὴ πάντων θ. ἀλλὰ ἐνίων Phld.*Rh.*2.108 S.; τῆς ἀφροσύνης S.E.*M.*11. 256. 2. of the mind, *contemplative, speculative*, ὁ περὶ τὴν..οὐσίαν θ. Arist.*Metaph.*1005$^{a}$35; ὁ περὶ φύσεως θ. Id.*PA*641$^{a}$29: c. gen., μαντικὴ ἐπιστήμη θ. τοῦ..μέλλοντος Pl.*Def.*414b; ἐπιστήμη θ., διάνοια, opp. πρακτική, ποιητική, Arist. *Metaph.*1064$^{a}$17, 1025$^{b}$25; νοῦς Id.*de An.*415$^{a}$11; θ. βίος *a contemplative* or *speculative* life (opp. ἀπολαυστικός, πολιτικός), Id.*EN*1095$^{b}$19, cf. Plu.*Cic.*3; θ. φιλόσοφος Id. *Per.*16: Comp. -ώτερος Herm.*in Phdr.*p.59 A. Adv. -κῶς Epicur. *Nat.*28.7, Poll.4.8, Iamb.*Comm.Math.*20. II. = θεωρικός, *Cod.Just.* 10.56.1.1. **-ητός**, ή, όν, *that may be seen*, D.S.14.60; ὄψει θ. Ael.*NA*9.4; θ. κατασκεύασμα Secund.*Sent.*1; of certain days in disease, *to be watched* (cf. ἐπίδηλος II. 1), Hp.*Aph.*2.24. 2. of the mind, *to be reached by contemplation*, τοὺς διὰ λόγου θ. χρόνους Epicur. *Ep.*1p.10 U.; θεοὺς λόγῳ θ. Id.*Fr.*355, cf. Phld.*Sign.*37; opp. ἐμφανής, Plu.2.722d; λόγῳ ib.876c. Adv. -τῶς Gal.18(1).363. **-ητρα**, ων, τά, *presents made by the bridegroom* to the bride, *when she first unveiled* herself, Eust.881.31, Harp. ⊛ **-ία**, Ion. **-ίη**, Dor. **θεᾱρία** (v. infr.), Boeot. **θιαωρία** Ἐφ.Ἀρχ.1892.34: ἡ:—*sending of* θεωροί or *state-ambassadors* to the oracles or games, or, collectively, *the* θεωροί *themselves, embassy, mission*, θεωρίαν ἀπάγειν εἰς Δῆλον Pl.*Phd* 58b: pl., opp. στρατεῖαι, Id.*R.*556c; ἄγειν τῷ Διὶ τῷ Νεμείῳ τὴν κοινὴν ὑπὲρ τῆς πόλεως θ. D.21.115, cf. X.*Mem.*4.8.2, Decr.Byz.ap.D.18.91 (θεᾱρία), Plb.28.19.4. 2. *office of* θεωρός, *discharge of that office*, τῆς Ὀλυμπίαζε θ. Th.6.16, cf. Isoc.19.10, etc. II. *being a spectator at the theatre* or *games*, S.*OT*1491; οὔτ' ἐπὶ θεωρίαν πώποτε ἐκ τῆς πόλεως ἐξῆλθες Pl.*Cri.*52b; personified in Ar.*Pax* 523, al. III. *viewing, beholding*, θεωρίης εἵνεκεν ἐκδημεῖν to go abroad *to see the world*, Hdt.1.30; κατὰ θεωρίης πρόφασιν ib.29; ἐκπέμπειν τινὰ κατ' ἐμπορίαν καὶ κατὰ θεωρίαν Isoc.17.4, cf. Arist.*Ath.*11.1, Th.6.24; *pilgrimage*, E.*Ba.*1047. 2. of the mind, *contemplation, consideration*, Pl.*Phlb.*38b: pl., θεῖαι θ. Id.*R.*517d: c. gen., παντὸς μὲν χρόνου πάσης δὲ οὐσίας ib.486a; ἡ τῶν ἀρχῶν, ἡ τῶν ὅλων θ., Epicur.*Ep.*2 p.55 U., Phld.*Rh.*1.288 S.; θ. ποιεῖσθαι περί τινος Arist.*Metaph.*989$^{b}$25; ἡ περὶ φύσεως θ. Epicur.*Ep.*1 p.3 U., etc.: pl., τὰς σαθρὰς αὐτοῦ θ. Demetr.Lac.*Herc.*124.12. b. *theory, speculation*, opp. practice, Plb. 1.5.3; ἡ περὶ τὰ στρατόπεδα θ. Id.6.42.6; αἱ νυκτεριναὶ καὶ ἡμεριναὶ θ. *theoretic reckoning* of night and day, Id.9.14.6; ἡ μαθηματικὴ θ. Plu. *Rom.*12. 3. Pass., *sight, spectacle*, A.*Pr.*802, etc.; esp. *public spectacle at the theatre* or *games*, Ar.*V.*1005, X.*Hier.*1.12; ἡ τοῦ Διονύσου θ. the Dionysia, Pl.*Lg.*650a. 4. Rhet., *explanatory preface* to a μελέτη, Chor. in *Hermes* 17.208, etc.: so in Philos., *continuous exposition*, Olymp. *in Mete.*18.30, al. ⊛ **-ικός**, ή, όν, *of* or *for* θεωρία (signfs. I and II), πεπλώματ' οὐ θεωρικά no *festal* robes, E.*Supp.*97; θ. σκηνή the tent *used by the* θεωροί, Henioch.5.8; θ. ὁδός, = θεωρίς I. 2, Poll.2.55. Adv. -κῶς Hsch. II. θεωρικόν, τό (θεωρικός, ὁ, seems to be an error in Phld.*Rh.*2.208 S.), at Athens, *fund for providing free seats at public spectacles*, οἱ ἐπὶ τὸ θ. Arist.*Ath.*43.1, cf. 47.2, D.18.113, *IG*2$^{2}$.223 *C*5; ἡ ἀρχὴ ἡ ἐπὶ τῷ θ. Aeschin.3.24: pl. (sc. χρήματα), D.3.11, Harp., etc., cf. Plu.*Per.*9: so elsewh. θεωρικά, with or without χρήματα, *fund for festivals*, *POxy.*1333 (ii/iii A. D.), 473.4 (ii A. D.). **-ιος**, v. θεάριος. II. θεώριον, τό, *box* at the amphitheatre, *PSI*8.953.62 (vi A. D.). ⊛ **-ίς**, ίδος, ἡ, 1. (with and without ναῦς) *sacred ship, which carried the* θεωροί to their destination, Hdt.6.87, cf. Call.*Del.*314: metaph., ἄστολος θ., of *Charon's bark*, A.*Th.*858 (lyr.). 2. (sc. ὁδός) *road by which the* θεωροί *went*, Hsch. II. pl., = Βάκχαι, Id., cf. Plb.30.25.12; of attendants of Apollo, Nonn.*D.*9.261.

**θεωροδοκ-έω**, *act as* θεωροδόκος, *SIG*562.50 (Paros, from Magn. Mae.). ⊛ **-ία**, ἡ, *office of* θεωροδόκος, *BCH*49.91 (Delph., iii B. C.), *SIG*608.5,10 (ib., ii B. C.): Dor. **θεᾱροδοκία**, τῶν Δηλίων *CIG*2329 (Delos). **-ος**, Dor. and Arc. **θεᾱροδόκος**, Thess. **θεουρο-** *Inscr. Magn.*26, Corc. **θιᾱρο-** ib.44: ὁ:—*one who receives the* θεωροί, *IG* 4.727 (Hermione, iv B. C.), 5(2).389 (Lusi), *SIG*608.7 (Delph., ii B. C.), etc.

⊛ **θεωρός**, ὁ (v. infr.), *envoy sent to consult an oracle*, S.*OT*114, *OC* 413; *to present an offering*, Orac.ap.D.21.53; *to be present at festivals*, θεωροὺς εἰς τὰ Πύθια πέμψαι D.19.128, cf. D.H.*Lys.*29, etc. 2. generally, *envoy*, sent to kings regarded as divine, Plu.*Demetr.*11, Ath.13.607c. II. title of a *magistrate* at Mantinea, Th.5.47; at Naupactus, *IG*9(1).360 (pl.), cf. ib.12(5).527 (found in Ceos); at Thasos, ib.12(8).267, etc. III. *spectator*, Thgn.805, A.*Pr.*118, *Ch.* 246, *Fr.*289; πολέμου Pl.*R.*467c, etc.; opp. ἀγωνιστής, Achae.3; *one who travels to see* men and things, Pl.*Lg.*951a, 953c; also λαμπάδα θ. εἰκάδων E.*Ion* 1076 (lyr., s. v. l.). (Uncontr. **θεαορός** *Schwyzer* 664.30 (Orchom. Arc., iv B. C.): contr. **θεᾱρός** in Dor. (*SIG*558.24, etc.), Arc. (*IG*5(2).4 (Tegea), etc.): **θεουρός** Thess. (*Inscr.Magn.*26): **θευρός** Thas. (*IG*12(8). l. c.); **θιᾱρός** Corc. (*Inscr.Magn.*44).) (Perh. fr. θεᾱ-hopϝος, cf. θεη-κόλος and θυρωρός (θυρουρός) fr. θυρᾰ-hopϝος.)

⊛ **θεωροσύνη**, ἡ, = θεωρία, Man.4.460.

**θέωσις**, εως, ἡ, (θεόω) *making divine*, Dam.*Pr.*100 (pl.).

**θεώτερος**, v. θεός III.

**Θηβᾱγενής**, ές, *sprung from Thebes, Theban*, Hes.*Th.*530: distd. fr. Θηβαῖος, Ephor.21 J.:—also **Θηβαιγενής**, E.*Supp.*136, D.P.623.

⊛ **Θῆβαι**, ῶν, αἱ, *Thebes*, Θ. Αἰγύπτιαι..αἳ ἑκατόμπυλοί εἰσι Il.9.381: also sg., Θήβης ἑπταπύλοιο (Boeotia) 4.406:—hence **Θήβασδε** *to Thebes*, 23.679; Att. Θήβαζε Sch.Il.3.29, al.; **Θήβησιν** *at Thebes*, Il. 22.479, Arist.*Rh.*1398$^{b}$2, **Θήβησι** Il.14.114: from the sg., **Θήβηθεν** *from Thebes*, Ephipp.15.7; poet. **-θε** *APl.*4.185; Boeot. **Θείβᾱθεν** *from Thebes*, Ar.*Ach.*862, also **-ᾱθε** (**-αθι** codd.) ib.868:—Adj. **Θηβαιεύς**, έως, Ion. έος, ὁ, epith. of Zeus, *Theban*, Hdt.1.182, etc.: ⊛ **Θηβαῖος**, α, ον, *Theban*, Od.10.492, etc.; Θηβαΐας (metri gr.) S.*Ant.* 1135 (lyr.): ⊛ **Θηβαϊκός**, ή, όν, Hdt.2.4, etc.

**Θηβαΐς**, ίδος, ἡ, *Thebais*, i. e. territory of Thebes (in Egypt), Hdt. 2.28; (in Boeotia), Id.9.65, Th.3.58:—hence **Θηβαΐτης** [ῑ], ου, ὁ, *dweller in the Egyptian Thebais*, Str.17.1.40. II. *Thebaid*, a poem on the siege of Thebes, which formed a portion of the Epic cycle, Paus.8.25.8.

**Θηβάνας**, ὁ, a name for *the north-east wind* (καικίας) in Lesbos, Arist.*Vent.*973$^{a}$9:—also **Θήβανις**, ὁ, St.Byz. s. v. Ἄδανα (because it blew from Hypoplacian Thebes), Hdn.Gr.1.95.

**Θηβάρχης**, ου, ὁ, *governor of the Thebaid*, *OGI*139.6 (pl., Philae, ii B. C.), 190.7 (ibid., i B. C.).

**θῆβος** (i. e. θῆϝος)· θαῦμα, and **θήγεια** (i. e. θήϝεια)· θαυμαστά, ψευδῆ, Hsch.

**θηγᾰλέος**, α, ον, (θήγω) *pointed, sharp*, στάλικες *AP*6.109 (Antip.); τρύφος ib.7.542 (Flacc.). II. Act., *sharpening*, c. gen. rei, ib.6. 68 (Jul. Aegypt.):—also **θηγάνεος**, Hsch.

**θηγάν-η** [ᾰ], ἡ, *whetstone*, A.*Ag.*1536 (lyr.), S.*Aj.*820: metaph., αἱματηρὰς θηγάνας *incentives* to bloodshed, A.*Eu.*859; θ. λάλης Luc. *Lex.*14:—also **θήγανον**, τό, Hsch. **-ίτης** [ῑ] λίθος, ὁ, a hard stone, used for *whetstones*, gen. θηγανείτα, *IG*14.317 (Therm. Himer.). **-ω**, = θήγω, restored by Herm. in A.*Ag.*1535 from Hsch., cf. *EM*450.13.

**θήγη**, ἡ, softer form of θήκη, Hsch. (v. διαθιγή).

**θηγός**, ή, όν, *sharp*, Hsch.

**θήγω**, Dor. **θάγω** [ᾱ] Ar.*Lys.*1256: fut. θήξω E.*Cyc.*242: aor. ἔθηξα Pi.*O.*10(11).20, E.*Or.*[51]:—Med., aor. ἐθηξάμην (v. infr.):—Pass., pf. τέθηγμαι (v. infr.):—poet. Verb (used by X. and later, v. infr.), *sharpen, whet*, Hom. (only in Il.), θήγων λευκὸν ὀδόντα 11.416, cf. 13.475, Hes.*Sc.*388; ὀδόντα Ar.*Ra.*815 (hex.); γένυν E.*Ph.*1380; θ. φάσγανον, ξίφος, μαχαίρας, A.*Ag.*1262, E.*Or.*1036, *Cyc.*242; ξίφη Onos.28; ὀϊστούς Jul.*Or.*7.229a:—Med., δόρυ θηξάσθω *let him whet his* spear, Il.2.382, cf. Phanocl.1.8. 2. metaph., *sharpen, excite*, Pi.*O.*10(11).20; ἰάμβων τοὺς ὀδόντας Babr.*Prooem.*2.14; *provoke*, τὰς ψυχὰς εἰς τὰ πολεμικά X.*Cyr.*2.1.20, cf. 1.2.10 (Pass.), *Mem.*3.3.7; τεθηγμένον τοί μ' οὐκ ἀπαμβλυνεῖς λόγῳ A.*Th.*715; λόγοι τεθηγμένοι *sharp, biting* words, Id.*Pr.*313; οὐ γάρ μ' ἀρέσκει γλῶσσά σου τεθηγμένη S.*Aj.*584; λῆμα τεθ. E.*Or.*1625; τῆς διανοίας ὀργῇ τεθ. Alcid. ap.Arist.*Rh.*1406$^{a}$10. II. intr., ὀργὴ γέροντος..ἐν χειρὶ θήγει σὺν τάχει δ' ἀμβλύνεται dub. in S.*Fr.*894.

**θηέομαι**, Ion. form of θεάομαι. **θήης**, v. τίθημι.

**θηητ-ήρ**, ῆρος, ὁ, Ion. for θεατής, *one who gazes at, an admirer*, θ. τόξων Od.21.397; ἀκρασίης Perict.ap.Stob.4.28.19. **-ής**· ἀπατεών (cf. θηπητής), θεωρός, Hsch. ⊛ **-ός**, ή, όν, Ion. for θεατός, Dor. **θᾱητός**, *gazed at, wondrous, admirable*, Hes.*Th.*31, Tyrt.10.29, Call. *Dian.*141; θ. ἀγών, γυῖα, Pi.*O.*3.36, *P.*4.80: in later Ion. Prose **θεητός** Aret.*CD*1.4.

**θήϊον**, τό, Ep. for θεῖον (A), *brimstone*, Od.22.493. **θήϊος**, Ep. for θεῖος (A); cf. θῆος.

⊛ **θηκ-αῖος**, α, ον, *like a chest* or *coffin*, οἴκημα θ. *burial* vault, Hdt.2. 86; perh. to be read in Plu.2.359a. II. Subst. θηκαῖον, τό, = θήκη, *SIG*1120 (pl., Cos). **-άριον**, τό, Dim. of θήκη, Sch.Opp.*H.* 2.356. **-εῖον**, τό, = θηκίον, *IG*5(1).813 (inc. loc.). ⊛ **-η**, ἡ, (τίθημι) *case, chest*, χρυσοῦ θ. a money-*chest*, Hdt.3.130, 9.83, E.*Hec.*1147, cf. X.*Oec.*8.17, etc. 2. *grave, tomb*, A.*Pers.*405, S.*OC*1763 (anap.); νεκρῶν θήκας ἀνοίγειν Hdt.1.187, cf. 67, al.; αἱ θ. τῶν τεθνεώτων Th.1.8, 3.104; εἰς ἀναισχύντους θ. ἐτράποντο *modes of burial*, Id.2.52, cf. Pl.*R.*427b; θήκην ὀρύττειν X.*Cyr.*7.3.5. 3. ξίφους θ. *sword-sheath*, Poll.10.144; τόξου bow-*case*, *EM*333.41. ⊛ **-ίον**, τό, Dim. of θήκη, *PFay.*104.5 (iii A. D.), *IG*12(3).1238 (Melos, iii/iv A. D.), Hsch.

⊛ **θηκο-ποιέω**, *store up*, *BGU*757.15 (i A. D.):—Pass., χόρτος τεθηκοποιημένος *PRyl.*142.16 (i A. D.). **-ποιός**, ὁ, *scabbard-maker*, Lyd. *Mag.*1.46. **-φόρος**, ὁ, = *cistophorus*, ib.3.8.

**θηκτός**, ή, όν, (θήγω) *sharpened, whetted*, A.*Th.*942 (lyr.), E.*Med.* 40, *AP*6.110 (Leon. or Mnasalc.), Pancrat.*Oxy.*1085.23.

**θηλάζω**, Dor. aor. I ἐθήλαξα Theoc.3.16 (v. l. -αζε): (θηλή): I. of the mother or nurse, *suckle*, Phryn.Com.29, Lys.1.9, Arist.*HA*576$^{b}$ 10: abs., *give suck*, οἱ μαστοί, οἳ οὐκ ἐθήλασαν *Ev.Luc.*23.29:—also in Med., ἐπιμελεῖσθαι, ὅπως μέτριον χρόνον θηλάσονται Pl.*R.*460d, cf. Arist.*HA*566$^{b}$17; οὐ συλλαμβάνουσι θηλαζόμεναι Id.*GA*777$^{a}$13, cf. *IG*5(2).514.12 (Lycosura):—Pass., *to be sucked*, ὁ δελφὶς..θηλάζεται ὑπὸ τῶν τέκνων Arist.*HA*504$^{b}$25. II. of the young animal, *suck*, Id.*GA*733$^{b}$29, etc.; ἐλέφαντος ὁ σκύμνος θ. τῷ στόματι Id.*HA*578$^{a}$ 22; θηλάζων χοῖρος a *sucking* pig, Theoc.14.15; seldom of an infant, Orph.*Fr.*49.87. 2. c. acc., λεαίνας μασδὸν ἐθήλαξεν Theoc.3.16; ἐὰν μὴ τύχῃ τεθηλακὼς ὁ ὄνος ἵππον Arist.*HA*577$^{b}$16. (Written θελάσζ- *PSI*4.368.19 (iii B. C.).)

**θηλᾰμινός**, ὁ, *a suckling*, Hsch. (nisi leg. θηλαμόνος).

**θηλᾰμών**, όνος, ἡ, = θηλάστρια, Sophr.43, Thespis4.2, Lyc.31; prob. for θηλονάς, Plu.2.278d.

**θήλ-ασμα**, ατος, τό, *mother's nursing, suckling*, *PMasp.*5.24 (vi A. D.), *PLond.*5.1708.82 (vi A. D.). **-ασμός**, ὁ, *giving suck, suckling*, Plu.*Rom.*4, *Aem.*14. **-άστρια**, ἡ, *one who suckles, wet-nurse*, S.*Fr.*98, Cratin.418, Eup.417.

**θήλεα, θήλεια**, v. θῆλυς. **θηλεογονία**, = θηλυγονία II, *Gloss.*

**θηλέω**, Dor. **θᾱλέω**, Ep. impf. θήλεον Od.5.73: fut. θηλήσω (ἀνα-) Il.1.236: Dor. poet. aor. θάλησα Pi.*N.*4.88; part. θηλήσας *AP*9.363 (Mel.): (τεθηλημένα is f.l. in Hp.*Insomn.*90):—poet. for θάλλω, *to be full of, abound in*, c. gen., λειμῶνες μαλακοὶ ἴου ἠδὲ σελίνου θήλεον Od.l.c.: c. dat., θάλησε σελίνοις Pi.l.c.; νικοφορίαις ἄστυ θάλησε ib. 10.42. 2. abs., *grow luxuriantly, flourish*, A.R.3.221, *AP*l.c.; of a child, *IG*14.1971; prob. for ἐθάλλεον, Epigr.ap.Plu.2.110b. II. causal, *make to bloom*, Alex.Aet.3.9.

⊛ **θηλή**, ἡ, (θῆσαι) *teat, nipple*, E.*Cyc.*56 (lyr.), Hp.*Epid.*5.101, Pl. *Cra.*414a; τῶν μαστῶν ἡ θ., δι' ἧς..τὸ γάλα διηθεῖται Arist.*HA*493$^{a}$13; of animals, ib.500$^{a}$24; θ. πεφιλοτεχνημέναι dumb *teats*, Sor.1. 115. II. *head* of a pole, κοντοὶ σὺν θηλαῖς σιδηραῖς *PLond.*3.1164$^{h}$9 (iii A. D.).

**θηληνός**, ή, όν, *quiet*, Cyr. ⊛ **θηλητήρ**· κυνηγός, Hsch.

**θηλοειδής**, ές, *nipple-shaped*, *Gloss.*

**θηλονή**, v. θηλαμών.

**θηλῠ-γενής**, ές, *of female sex, womanish*, στόλος A.*Supp.*28, cf. E. *Ba.*1156; ὄχλος ib.117: Comp., Pl.*Lg.*802e. Adv. -νῶς Eust.10. 27. **-γλωσσος**, ον, *with woman's tongue*, Νοσσίς *AP*9.26.7 (Antip. Thess.). **-γονέω**, *generate* or *promote the generation of females*, Thphr.*HP*9.18.5, Ph.1.262, Dsc.3.126. **-γονία**, ἡ, *generation of females*, opp. κουρογονίη, Hp.*Genit.*8; opp. ἀρρενογονία, Arist.*HA* 585$^{b}$11, *GA*765$^{a}$30, S.E.*M.*5.7. II. *kin by the mother's side*, Hdn. 1.7.4; = Lat. *cognatio*, Just.*Nov.*115.3.14. **-γόνος**, ον, *generating females*, Hp.*Steril.*230; καὶ γυναῖκες καὶ ἄνδρες..θ. εἰσίν Arist.*HA* 585$^{b}$13; of animals, ib.573$^{b}$32, *GA*766$^{b}$32. II. θηλυγόνον, τό, a plant supposed *to promote the generation of females, dog-mercury*, *Mercurialis perennis*, Thphr.*HP*9.18.5; *a variety of* φύλλον, Dsc.3. 125; = λινόζωστις θήλεια, Ps.-Dsc.4.189.

**θηλυδρί-ας**, ου, Ion. **-ίης**, εω, ὁ, *effeminate person*, Hdt.7.153, Ph. 1.262, Luc.*DDeor.*5.3, S.E.*P.*3.217 (pl.), Lib.*Or.*64.83 (pl.); of animals, Arist.*HA*631$^{b}$17:—hence **θηλυδριάω**, *Gloss.* **-ώδης**, ες, *effeminate*, μέλος Ar.*Th.*131; λόγοι Sch.E.*Andr.*757. Adv. -δῶς Sch.D.T.p.247 H. **-ῶτις**, fem. Adj., = foreg., ῥᾳστώνη Prisc. p.332 D.

**θηλῠκός**, ή, όν, *woman-like*, ἄνδρες Arist.*GA*747$^{a}$1; *like the female*, of male animals, Id.*HA*589$^{b}$30: Comp., Id.*Pr.*961$^{a}$6. b. of women, *womanish, ultra-feminine*, opp. ἀρρενωπός, Id.*GA*728$^{a}$3. 2. Gramm., *feminine*, γένος D.T.634.17, D.H.*Amm.*2.11; μόριον ibid.; ὄνομα Ph. 1.294. Adv. -κῶς Arist.*Fr.*499, Phld.*Piet.*12, Str.6.1.10, A.D.*Synt.* 222.6, Alex.Aphr.*in Sens.*151.1. 3. = θῆλυς, *female*, *PCair.Zen.* 166.2 (iii B. C.), Lxx *Nu.*5.3, *IG*14.872 (Cumae), Sor.1.32. b. θ. κεντήματα bites *of female* vipers, Philum.*Ven.*16.3. c. Astrol., applied to certain planets or figures of the Zodiac, Ptol.*Tetr.*20, 33.

**θηλυ-κράνεια** [κρᾰ], *the female* κράνεια, *dogwood, Cornus sanguinea*, Thphr.*HP*1.8.2, 3.3.1. **-κρᾰτής**, ές, *swaying women*, ἔρως A. *Ch.*599 (lyr.). **-κτόνος**, ον, *slaying by woman's hand*, Ἄρης θ. Id. *Pr.*860.

**θηλῠκώδης**, ες, *of effeminate nature*, Procl.*Par.Ptol.*265.

**θηλύ-λᾰλος** [ῠ], ον, = θηλύγλωσσος, Man.4.322. ⊛ **-μᾰνέω**, *to be mad after women*, Ph.2.20, Man.4.164. **-μᾰνής**, ές, *mad after women*, *AP*5.18 (Rufin.); Πόθοι Id.9.16 (Mel.); of animals, ἵπποι θ. Lxx *Je.*5.8. II. Act., *maddening women*, κροτάλων θ. ὄτοβοι Antim.*Eleg.*17:—hence **-μᾰνία**, ἡ, Sch.Opp.*H.*1.536, *Cat.Cod.Astr.* 2.177. **-μελής**, ές, *singing in soft strain*, Ἀλκμᾶνος ἀηδόνες *AP* 9.184. **-μίτρης**, ου, ὁ, *with a woman's* μίτρα, *in woman's clothes*, Luc.*DDeor.*18.1: acc. -μίτρην prob. cj. for -μητριν, -μιτριν, Id.*Bacch.* 3. **-μορφος**, ον, *woman-shaped*, E.*Ba.*353; *female in type*, Arist. *Phgn.*809$^{b}$37 (Comp.); ἰδέα Ph.2.261; θεότης Dam.*Pr.*204; of the number 4, Nicom.ap.Phot.*Bibl.*p.144 B. **-νοος**, ον, contr. **-νους**, ουν, *of womanish mind*, A.*Pr.*1003.

**θηλύνω**, Plu.2.999a: aor. ἐθήλῡνα E.*Fr.*360.29, Babr.*Prooem.*1.19, (ἐξ-) Str.5.4.13: pf. τεθήλῠκα Arist.ap.Stob.4.279 M.:—Pass., aor. ἐθηλύνθην (v. infr.), (ἐξ-) D.H.14.8: pf. τεθήλυσμαι Hp.*Aër.*15, J.*AJ* 4.8.40, (ἐκ-) Gal.10.354; but -υμμαι (ἐκ-) Plb.36.15.2, Luc.*DDeor.* 5.3; 3 sg. -υνται D.C.50.27; inf. -ύνθαι (ἐκ-) Plb.31.21.3: (θῆλυς):—*make womanish, enervate*, E.l.c.; τὴν ἡδονήν Plu.l.c.; τοὺς ἄνδρας Vett.Val.76.6; *soften*, Ζέφυρος κῦμα θηλύνει *AP*10.4 (Marc. Arg.):—Pass., τῶν σωμάτων -ομένων X.*Oec.*4.2, cf. Porph.*Abst.*1.34; *become soft*, αἱ σάρκες -ονται Hp.*Art.*52; βαφῇ σίδηρος ὥς, ἐθηλύνθην στόμα S. *Aj.*651; οὔπω ἐθηλύνθης *gav'st* not yet *a sign of yielding*, *AP*5.250 (Iren.); θ. οἴκτοις ib.299 (Paul. Sil.); *play the coquette*, Bion 2.18; τᾷ μορφᾷ θηλύνετο Theoc.20.14; *muliebria pati*, Vett.Val.7.26, al.: Astrol., of planets, Ptol.*Tetr.*20.—Rare in Att.

**θηλύ-πᾰθέω** [ῠ], *muliebria pati*, prob. in Phld.*Herc.*312.4. **-παις**, παιδος, ἡ, *having borne a girl*, Lyc.851. **-ποιός**, όν, *making weak*, of the number 8, Nicom.ap.Phot.*Bibl.*p.144 B. **-πους**, ποδος, ὁ, ἡ, θ. βάσις the tread *of female foot*, [E.]*IA*421. ⊛ **-πρεπής**, ές, *befitting a woman*, ποικίλματα Agath.3.28; *womanish*, οἰνοχόοι *AP* 12.175 (Strat.), cf. Chor.*Lyd.*7: metaph., θεότης θ., of Difference, Dam.*Pr.*192. **-πρῖνος**, ἡ, Arc. name for φελλός, Eust.302. 30. **-πρόσωπος**, ον, *with woman's face*, Suid. s. v. Σειρῆνας. **-πτερίς**, ἴδος, ἡ, *bracken, Pteris aquilina*, Thphr.*HP*9.18.8, Dsc.4.185, Plin.*HN*27.78:—also **-πτέριον**, τό, Alex.Trall.*Verm.*p.597 P.

⊛ **θῆλυς**, θήλεια, θῆλυ: Ep. fem. θήλεα, acc. pl. -εας Il.5.269 (Hom. has regul. fem. θήλεια Il.8.7, al., but also θῆλυς as fem., 10.216, al., as in other poets, v. infr.): Ion. fem. θήλεα, θήλεαν, θηλέης, θηλέῃ, pl. θήλεαι, θηλέας, θηλέων, Hdt. and Hp.: gen. θήλυδος S.*Fr.*1054; acc. fem. θηλείην dub. l. in Nic.*Al.*42, neut. pl. θήλεια Arat.1068: Ep. also θηλύτερος indicating opposition rather than comparison (cf. ἀρρέντερος); θηλύτεραι δὲ γυναῖκες Il.8.520; θηλύτεραι δὲ θεαί Od.8. 324; μάτε ἐρσεναιτέραν μάτε θηλυτέραν *Schwyzer*424 (Elis, iv B. C.); in late Prose θηλύτερος, -ύτατος occur as Comp. and Sup. (v. infr. II): (θη- 'suckle', cf. θῆσαι):—*female*, θήλεια θεός a goddess, Il.8.7; Ἥρη θῆλυς ἐοῦσα being *female*, 19.97, cf. A.*Ag.*1231, S.*Tr.*1062, E.*IT*621; θήλειαι ἵπποι mares, Od.4.636, etc.; σύες θήλειαι sows, 14.16; ὄϊς θῆλυς a ewe, Il.10.216; θήλεια μῆλα Arat.1068; θήλεια ἔλαφος a hind, Pi.*O.* 3.29; θήλεα κάμηλος Hdt.3.102; ἡ θ. ἵππος ib.86; θ. ὄρνις S.*Fr.*477; ζῷα θ. Pl.*Criti.*110c; ἄπαις θήλεος γόνου without *female* issue, Hdt.3. 66; θῆλυς σπορά E.*Hec.*659; θήλειαι γυναῖκες Id.*Or.*1205; θ. κόραι Pl.*Lg.*764d: with masc. nouns, ὁ θῆλυς ὀρεύς the *she*-mule, Arist.*HA* 577$^{b}$22; ἄνθρωπος θῆλυς Id.*PA*688$^{b}$31: masc. pl., θήλεις χοροί Critias 1.8 D.; but μὴ εἶναι θεοὺς ἄρρενας μηδὲ θηλείας Phld.*Piet.*12. b. ἡ θήλεα, Att. -εια, *the female*, Hdt.3.109, X.*Mem.*2.1.4; ἀλέκτωρ ὥστε θηλείας πέλας A.*Ag.*1671 (troch.). c. τὸ θ. γένος the *female* sex, *woman*-kind, E.*Hec.*885; τὸ θ. alone, Id.*HF*536, etc.; opp. τὸ ἄρρεν, Pl.*R.*454d, Arist.*Metaph.*988$^{a}$5; [ἡ δεῖνα] τέτοκεν θῆλυ *PTeb.*422.18 (iii A. D.), al. d. of plants and trees, Thphr.*HP*3.9.1; θ. κάλαμος Dsc.1.85; θῆλυς φοῖνιξ Ach.Tat.1.17; θῆλυ βούτομον Thphr.*HP*4.10. 4. 2. *of* or *belonging to women*, κουράων θῆλυς ἀϋτή Od.6.122; θήλεα νοῦσος among the Scythians (cf. Ἐνάρεες), Hdt.1.105; νόμος A. *Ch.*821 (lyr.); φύσις Pl.*R.*453a; χάρις *APl.*4.287 (Leont.); θ. φόνος murder *by women*, E.*Ba.*796. II. metaph., of persons and things, 1. *soft, gentle*, θῆλυς ἐέρση Od.5.467, Hes.*Sc.*395; θ. νύξ (= ὕπομβρος) S.*Fr.*1053. b. ὕδωρ θ. καὶ μαλακόν Thphr.*CP*2.6.3; θηλυτέρα ὀσμή ib.6.15.4; θηλύτατον πεδίον *most fruitful*, Call.*Fr.* 296; θηλύτατον ὕδωρ, of the Nile, Id.*Sos.*vii 5. 2. *tender, delicate*, Φοίβου θήλειαι..παρειαί Id.*Ap.*37; θῆλυς ἀπὸ χροιῆς *delicate* of skin, Theoc.16.49; of temper or character, *soft, yielding, weak*, θῆλυς ηὕρημαι τάλας S.*Tr.*1075; γυνὴ δὲ θῆλυ κἀπὶ δακρύοις ἔφυ E.*Med.*928; θήλεια φρήν Ar.*Lys.*708, cf. E.*Andr.*181; δίαιτα θηλυτέρα ἢ κατ' ἄνδρα Plu.*Mar.*34; θηλύτατος Luc.*Im.*13; παλλακὴ -υτάτη Philostr.*VS*2. 21.2; τὸ θῆλυ τῆς ψυχῆς *effeminacy*, Men.599. 3. in mechanics, those parts were called female *into which others fitted*, as the *female* vertebra, Poll.2.180; γίγγλυμος J.*AJ*3.6.3. 4. Gramm., *feminine*, θήλεα [ὀνόματα] Ar.*Nu.*682; θήλεα Arist.*Po.*1458$^{a}$10. 5. Pythag., of *even* numbers, Plu.2.264a, 288d. 6. Astrol., of planets, Ptol. *Tetr.*19; cf. θηλυκός 3c. III. θήλειαι, αἱ, kind of cheese made in Crete, Seleuc.ap.Ath.14.650d.

**θηλύσπορος**, ον, *of female kind*, γέννα, of the daughters of Danaus, A.*Pr.*855.

**θηλυστολ-έω**, *wear women's clothes*, Str.10.3.8, 11.13.9. **-ία**, ἡ, *women's dress*, Eust.782.47. **-ος**, ον, *clad in women's clothes*: τὸ θ. *effeminacy*, Id.10.24.

**θηλύτεκνος** [ῠ], ον, *producing female children*, γάμοι *TAM*2(1). 174 *Db.*

**θηλύτης**, ητος, ἡ, (θῆλυς) *womanhood, female nature*, Arist.*GA* 775$^{a}$16; *sexual characters* of the female, Gal.4.570. 2. *womanishness, delicacy*, Corn.*ND*20, Plu.*Crass.*32; ἡ θ. τοῦ κάλλους *the womanish nature* of.., ib.24; also, *effeminacy*, ἐσθήτων Id.*Alc.*16 (pl.).

**θηλῠτοκ-έω**, *bear females*, Hp.*Genit.*7, Arist.*HA*574$^{a}$1, *GA*765$^{a}$24. **-ία**, ἡ, *bearing of females*, ib.767$^{a}$35: pl., J.*AJ*3.11.5. **-ος** (parox.), ον, *bearing females*, Arist.*GA*723$^{a}$27, *Pol.*1335$^{a}$13, Theoc. 25.125.

**θηλύ-τροπος**, ον, *of womanish habit*: metaph., of the planet Venus, *Cat.Cod.Astr.*1.136. **-φᾰνής**, ές, *like a woman*, νεανίσκοι Plu.*Thes.*23; πάθος *AP*11.285 (Pall.). **-φθόριον**, τό, = ἀβρότονον, Ps.-Dsc.3.24. **-φόνος**, ον, *killing women*: θηλυφόνον, τό, *leopard's bane, Aconitum Anthora*, Thphr.*HP*9.18.2, Nic.*Al.*41, Plin.*HN*25. 122, Dsc.4.76 (v.l. θηρο-). **-φρων**, ον, gen. ονος, *effeminate*, Ar. *Ec.*110 (= *Trag.Adesp.*51), Vett.Val.104.21. **-φωνος**, ον, *with woman's voice*, Ael.*NA*6.19; εὐγενὴς φιλοσοφία φεύγουσα τὸ θ. Eust. 10.22. **-χειρ**, χειρος, ὁ, ἡ, *with woman's hand*, Id.550.37. **-χίτων** [ῐ], ωνος, ὁ, ἡ, *with woman's frock*, *AP*6.219 (Antip.), Orac.ap.Luc. *Alex.*27. **-χοίρα**, ἡ, = ὕαινα, Sch.Opp.*H.*5.31. **-ψῡχος**, ον, *of woman's spirit*, Ptol.*Tetr.*162.

**θηλώ**, όος, οῦς, ἡ, *wet-nurse*, Hsch.; = Lat. *Rumina*, Plu.2.278d.

**θῆμα**, ατος, τό, (τίθημι) *tomb*, S.*Fr.*541. II. = *prooemium*, *Gloss.*

⊛ **θημολογέω**, *collect in a heap*, shortd. from θημωνολογέω (metri gr.), ψαμμίτην δόρπον *AP*9.551 (Antiphil.).

**θημών**, ῶνος, ὁ, (τίθημι) *heap*, ἠΐων θημῶνα..καρφαλέων Od.5.368; θ. ἀχύρων Arist.*Mete.*344$^{a}$26; θημῶνα νηῆσαι Opp.*H.*4.496, cf. Ph.ap. Eus.*PE*8.7: pl., Ph.2.97.

⊛ **θημωνιά** (not θημωνία), ἡ, = foreg., θ. ἅλωνος Lxx *Jb.*5.26; συνήγαγον αὐτοὺς θημωνιὰς θημωνιάς ib.*Ex.*8.14(10), cf. Eust.1539.16:—also **θειμωνεῖαι** and **θημονιαί**, Hsch.

**θημωνοθετέω** (θημον- codd.), *put in a heap*, Sch.Theoc.10.46.

⊛ **θην**, enclit. Particle (A.D.*Conj.*257.9) chiefly Ep. and Dor., rare in Trag., A.*Pr.*928:—*in truth, I ween*, freq. ironical, λείψετέ θ. νέας Il. 13.620; ὥς θ. καὶ σὸν ἐγὼ λύσω μένος 17.29, cf. 21.568; strengthd., ἦ θ. *in very truth*, 11.365, 13.813; οὐ θ. *surely* not, 2.276, Od.5.211; οὐ

θ. δή 3.352; καὶ γάρ θ. Il.21.568: coupled with γα, Epich.34, Sophr. 24: freq. in Theoc., 1.97, al.; once in Call., *Aet.Oxy.*2079.46.

✻ **θήνιον**· γάλα, Hsch.

**θῆξις**, εως, ἡ, = ῥοπή, στιγμή, τάχος, Hsch.; θήξει, = Lat. *momento*, *Gloss.*; but κατὰ θῆξιν is f.l. for κατὰ θίξιν in Archig.ap.Gal.12.577.

**θηοῖο**, Ep. for θεῷο, 2 sg. pres. opt. οι θηέομαι.

**θῆος**, α, ον, Dor. for θεῖος (A), Callicr.ap.Stob.4.28.17, Euryph.ap. eund.4.39.27.

**θηπαλέος**· βωμολόχος, Hsch. **θηπέω**, *to be astonished*, Id. **θηπητής**, οῦ, ὁ, *deceiver*, Id. **θηπόν**· καταθύμιον, θαυμαστόν, Id. **θήπω**, *deceive*, Hippon.14.1; but also, = θαυμάζω, Hsch.; cf. θηπέω.

✻ **θήρ**, θηρός, Ep. dat. pl. θήρεσσι, ὁ: later also ἡ, Ael.*NA*6.24, etc.: (v. sub fin.):—*beast of prey*, esp. a lion (so used in Cephallenia, Sch. Il.15.324), Il.15.586, etc.; ὁ Νέμειος θ. E.*HF*153: coupled with λέων, ib.465, Epimenid.2: with λέαινα, *AP*14.63.4 (Mesom.); of the wild boar, Ἐρυμάνθιος θ. S.*Tr.*1097; of Cerberus, Id.*OC*1569 (lyr.); ὁ θ., of a hind, Id.*El.*572: pl., generally, *beasts*, opp. birds and fishes, ἠέ που ἐν πόντῳ φάγον ἰχθύες, ἢ ἐπὶ χέρσου θηρσὶ καὶ οἰωνοῖσιν ἕλωρ γένετ' Od.24.291; ἰχθύσι μὲν καὶ θηρσὶ καὶ οἰωνοῖς πετεηνοῖς Hes.*Op.*277; ἐν θηρσίν, ἐν βροτοῖσιν, ἐν θεοῖς ἄνω S.*Fr.*941.12; ἐν ἄγρῃ θηρῶν Hdt. 3.129; ἄφοβοι θῆρες S.*Aj.*366: metaph., θῆρες ξιφήρεις, of Orestes and Pylades, E.*Or.*1272, cf. *Ph.*1296 (lyr.); ἡ σφοδρότης.. θηρός (sc. Ἔρωτος) Alex.245.12: prov., ἔγνω θὴρ θῆρα Arist.*Rh.*1371ᵇ16. 2. of any *living creature*, πλωτοὶ θῆρες, i.e. dolphins, Arion 1.5; of *vermin* killed by birds, Ar.*Av.*1064 (lyr.); of gnats, *AP*5.150 (Mel.); of the *sacred animals* in Egypt, ἀρχιστολιστὴς θηρῶν *Sammelb.*4011. 4. 3. any fabulous *monster*, as the Sphinx, A.*Th.*558 codd.; esp. of a centaur, S.*Tr.*556, 568 (cf. φήρ); of Satyrs, E.*Cyc.*624; οὐ θεῶν τις οὐδ' ἄνθρωπος οὐδὲ θ. A.*Eu.*70.—Less freq. than θηρίον in Prose, but found in Hdt. l. c. (v.l. θηρίων), X.*Cyr.*4.6.4, Pl.*R.*559d, *Sph.* 235a, Ael. l. c., etc.; ἄγριοι θῆρες Arist.*EE*1229ᵃ25. (I.-E. *ghu̯ēr-*, cf. φήρ, Lith. *žvėris* 'wild beast'.)

**Θήρα**, ἡ, the island *Thera*, Pi.*P.*4.20, etc.:—hence **Θήραθε**, *from Thera*, *Abh.Berl.Akad.*1925(5).20: **Θήρανδε**, *to Thera*, ib.21.

✻ **θήρα**, Ion. **θήρη**, ἡ, *hunting of wild beasts, the chase*, βάν δ' ἴμεν ἐς θήρην Od.19.429; αἴμονα θήρης Il.5.49; ἰέναι ἐπὶ τὴν θήρην Hdt.1.37, 4.114, cf. Ar.*Fr.*2 D.; ζῶσι ἀπὸ θ. Hdt.4.22, cf. Arist.*Pol.*1256ᵃ35; ἐποίησε μεγάλην θήραν X.*Cyr.*1.4.14; θ. ποιεῖσθαι Arist.*HA*541ᵃ20; τὰς θ. τῶν ὀρτύγων ἐποιοῦντο D.S.1.60; τοῦ πτηνοῦ γένους θ., = ὀρνιθευτική, Pl.*Sph.*220b; ἡ περὶ θάλατταν θ. *fishing*, Id.*Lg.*823d; κυνηγεσία καὶ ἡ ἄλλη θ. ib.763b: pl., πέρδικες εἰς τὰς θ. ἀγόμεναι, of decoy birds, Arist.*GA*751ᵃ14, cf. Phld.*Ir.*p.42 W., Ant.Lib.41.2. b. in Ptolemaic Egypt, στρατηγὸς ἐπὶ τὴν θ. τῶν ἐλεφάντων *OGI*82, 86 (iii B.C.), cf. Str.16.4.5, 7, Wilcken *Chr.*385.14 (iii B.C.), *PPetr.*3 p.292 (iii B.C.), etc. 2. metaph., *eager pursuit* of anything, θήραν.. ἔχομεν τόξων, = θηρῶμεν τὰ τόξα, S.*Ph.*840; δυσμενῶν θήραν ἔχειν Id. *Aj.*564; θ. ἀνθρώπων Pl.*Sph.*222b, c; τοῦ ἡδέος Id.*Grg.*500d; ἐπιστημῶν Id.*Tht.*198a, etc. II. *prey, game*, αἶψα δ' ἔδωκε θεὸς μενοεικέα θήρην Od.9.158, cf. A.*Ch.*251, E.*Ba.*1144; πρὶν κινεῖσθαι τὴν θ. X. *Cyr.*2.4.25; θήραν καλήν, of a prisoner, S.*Ph.*609: in pl., ὦ πταναὶ θῆραι, of birds, ib.1146 (lyr.); τὴν θ. ἐπὶ τοῦ μέσου τηροῦσα watching its *prey*, of a spider, Arist.*HA*623ᵃ13. III. *hunting-ground, preserve*, Ἀδριανοῦ θῆραι D.C.69.10. IV. in Roman times, *the games of the Circus*, *Epigr.Gr.*351.3 (Nicaea).

✻ **θηραγρ-έτης**, ου, ὁ, *hunter*, E.*Ba.*1020 (lyr., s.v.l.), *AP*6.184 (Zos.). **-ία**, ἡ, *chase of wild beasts*, Poll.5.12. **-ος**, ον, (ἄγρα) *for catching wild beasts* or *game*, πέδη Ion Trag.40: name of a hound, dub. in *AP*7.304 (Pisand.).

✻ **Θηραϊκόν** or **Θήραιον**, τό, a dress worn in the Satyric drama at Athens, *invented in the island Thera*, Thphr.*Fr.*119.

✻ **θήρ-ᾱμα**, ατος, τό, (θηράω) *prey, spoil*, E.*Ba.*869 (lyr., s.v.l.), *Hel.* 192 (lyr.), *AP*6.105 (pl., Apollonid.), Plu.*Luc.*17: metaph., ἀρετὰ.., θ. κάλλιστον βίῳ Arist.*Fr.*675. **-αρχος**, ὁ, *commander of two elephants*, Ascl.*Tact.*9, Ael.*Tact.*23:—hence **-αρχία**, ἡ, *his command*, Ascl.*Tact.*9. **-άσιμος** [ᾱ], ον, *to be hunted down*, θηρεύοντες οὐ θηρασίμους γάμους A.*Pr.*858. **-άτειρα** [ᾱ], fem. of θηρατήρ, *huntress*, Call.*Del.*230. **-ᾱτέος**, α, ον, *to be pursued, sought eagerly*, S.*Ph.*116, X.*Mem.*2.6.8. II. θηρατέον *one must pursue*, Id.*Cyr.*2.4.10. ✻ **-ᾱτήρ**, Ion. **-ητήρ**, ῆρος, ὁ, poet. for θηρατής, Il. 5.51, etc.; ἀνδρὸς θηρητῆρος 21.574; κοῦροι θ. 17.726. **-ᾱτήριος**, α, ον, = θηρατικός, c. gen., ἴυγγα θ. ἔρωτος S.*Fr.*474.1. II. Subst. **-ατήριον**, τό, *hunting implement*, Hsch. s. v. ἄγκιστρον. **-ᾱτής**, οῦ, ὁ, (θηράω) *hunter*, Ael.*NA*13.12, *PSI*3.222.7 (iii A.D.): metaph., θ. λόγων Ar.*Nu.*358; δόξης D.L.8.8; τῶν ἀθλῶν Philostr.Jun.*Im.* 1. **-ᾱτικός**, ή, όν, = θηρευτικός, σκύλακες Ph.1.628 (s.v.l.), cf. Gal.*Protr.*6; ἔργα Ael.*NA*14.5; θ. σημεῖα signals *given by the hunter*, Plu.2.593b; θ. φόρος tax *for game-licence*, dub. in *PSI*3.222 (iii A.D.). 2. *fit for winning*, τὰ θ. τῶν φίλων *the arts for winning* friends, X.*Mem.*2.6.33. 3. *fond of hunting*, Plu.2.960a, 965b. **-ᾱτός**, ή, όν, *to be caught*: metaph., *attainable*, τὴν ἕξιν ἢ τὰ καλὰ θ. γίγνεται τοῖς ἀνθρώποις Plb.10.47.11; οὐδ' ὅλως ἐπιστήμη θ. ὁ καιρός, ἀλλὰ δόξῃ D.H.*Comp.*12; κριτήριον οὐδὲ στοχασμῷ θ. Phld.*Rh.* 1.167 S. ✻ **-ᾱτρον**, τό, *instrument of the chase, net, trap*, etc., X.*Mem.* 2.1.4, 3.11.7, Plu.2.961c (pl.), Ael.*NA*1.21: pl., of spider's *webs*, Max. Tyr.16.5: metaph., prob. in Lib.*Decl.*22.25. **-άτωρ** [ᾱ], Ion. **-ήτωρ**, ορος, ὁ, = θηρατήρ, θηρήτορας ἄνδρας Il.9.544; [κύων] θηράτωρ Nic. Dam.56 J. **-άφιον** [ᾰ], τό, Dim. of θηρίον, of insects, Damocr.ap.Gal. 14.91. ✻ **-άω**, fut. -άσω [ᾱ] S.*Ph.*958, E.*IT*1424, X.*An.*4.5.24, etc.: aor. ἐθήρᾱσα A.*Pers.*233, E.*Ba.*1215, X.*Cyr.*1.4.10: pf. τεθήρᾱκα ib. 2.4.16; Thess. pf. part. πεφειράκοντες *IG*9(2).536:—**Med.**, fut. θηράσομαι (which, acc. to Moer., is the true Att. fut.) E.*Ba.*228, *IT*1324: aor. ἐθηρᾱσάμην S.*Ph.*1007, E.*Hipp.*919:—**Pass.**, fut. -ᾱθήσομαι *Gp.* 12.9.2: aor. ἐθηράθην (v. infr. III): (θήρ, θήρα):—*hunt, chase*, λαγώς, σφῆκας, X.*An.* l. c., *HG*4.2.12, etc.; καί μ' οὓς ἐθήρων πρόσθε θηράσουσι νῦν S.*Ph.*958; of fishermen, *catch*, Arist.*Fr.*76: metaph., *catch* or *capture*, καί σ' εἷλε θηρῶνθ' ἡ τύχη S.*OC*1026, cf. *Ph.*1007, X.*An.*5.1.9: *captivate*, Id.*Mem.*2.6.28, 3.11.7; θ. πόλιν *seek to destroy* it, A.*Pers.* 233. 2. metaph., *hunt after* a thing, *pursue* it *eagerly*, τυραννίδα S.*OT*542; θηρᾶν οὐ πρέπει τἀμήχανα Id.*Ant.*92; μυρίαι κόραι θηρῶσι λέκτρον τοὐμόν E.*IA*960; ἥμαρτον ἢ θηρῶ τι; have I missed or *do I hit the quarry?* A.*Ag.*1194; τί χρῆμα θηρῶν; E.*Supp.*115; *reach, attain to*, τι Pi.*I.*4(3).46 (s. v. l.). 3. c. inf., *seek, endeavour* to do, θηρᾷ γαμεῖν με E.*Hel.*63; cf. II. 3. 4. = ἐκπράσσω III, θηρήτω δὲ ἁ θοιναρμόστρια *IG*5(1).1498 (Messenia, ii B.C.). II. Med. like Act., *hunt for, fish for*, ἐγχέλεις Ar.*Eq.*864: abs., οἱ θηρώμενοι *hunters*, X.*Cyn.*11. 2. 2. more freq. metaph., *seek after*, ἐμέτοισι θηρώμενοι τὴν ὑγιείην Hdt.2.77; μαστοῖς ἔλεον θ. E.*Or.*568; τὴν τῆς σωφροσύνης δόξαν D. 61.21, etc.; θ. πυρὸς πηγὴν *find, discover* it, A.*Pr.*109; *expect to derive*, τι παρά τινων Phld.*Rh.*1.263 S. 3. c. inf., *seek, endeavour*, ὅς με θηρᾶται λαβεῖν E.*Hel.*545; πεῖράν τιν' ἐχθρῶν ἁρπάσαι θηρώμενον S. *Aj.*2. III. Pass., *to be hunted, pursued*, πρὸς ἄτης θηραθεῖσαι A. *Pr.*1072; ὑπ' ἀνδρῶν E.*Ba.*732; Ἀλκιβιάδης διὰ κάλλος ὑπὸ γυναικῶν θηρώμενος X.*Mem.*1.2.24.—Cf. θηρεύω. **-εία**, ἡ, *hunting*, *Gloss.* ✻ **-ειος**, ον, also α, ον v.l. in Pl.*Phdr.*248d, *AP*5.265 (Paul. Sil.): (θήρ):—*of wild beasts*, δέρμα θ. λέοντος Panyas.1, cf. Hanno *Peripl.*9; μέλεα Emp.101; θήρειον γραφὴν the figures *of animals* worked upon the cloak, A.*Ch.*232; θ. δάκος, = θήρ, E.*Cyc.*325; θ. βία, periphr. for ὁ θήρ, *the centaur*, S.*Tr.*1059; θ. κρέα *game*, X.*Cyr.* 1.3.6; so θήρεια, τά, Hp.*Aff.*52; θ. φύσις Pl. l. c.; θ. αὐλός (ἐκ νεβροῦ κώλων εἰργασμένος) Poll.4.75. II. θ. στόματα the entrance *of the Circus*, *IG*4.365 (Corinth).

**θηρ-επῳδός**, όν, *charming wild beasts*, Suid. s. v. σοφός. **-ευμα**, ατος, τό, (θηρεύω) *spoil, prey*, S.*Ichn.*285, E.*IA*1162. II. pl., *hunting*, Pl.*Lg.*823b. **-ευσις**, εως, ἡ, *hunting, the chase*, πεζῶν ib.824a: metaph., ὀνομάτων θηρεύσεις Id.*Tht.*166c. **-ευτέον**, *one must hunt after*, Plb.1.35.8. **-ευτήρ**, ῆρος, ὁ, = sq., Opp.*C.*1.449. **-ευτής**, οῦ, ὁ, *hunter*, used by Hom. (only in Il.) always as Adj., κύνεσσι καὶ ἀνδράσι θηρευτῇσιν hounds and *huntsmen*, Il.12.41; ἐν κυσὶ θηρευτῇσι 11.325; so θ. ἄνδρες Hes.*Sc.*303, 388; κύνες Thgn.1254, X.*Ages.*9.6: as Subst., Hdt.1.123, Satyr.*Vit.Eur.Fr.*39 xxi 14; of *a fisher*, Hdt.2.70; θ. πέρδιξ *a decoy* partridge, Arist.*HA*614ᵃ10; θ. ἰξός *birdlime*, *AP*5.99. 2. metaph., θ. νέων καὶ πλουσίων Pl.*Sph.*231d, cf. Chor.p.67 B.; καλλίστων ὀνομάτων Ath.3.122c. ✻ **-ευτικός**, ή, όν, *of* or *for hunting*, κύνες θ. *hounds*, Ar.*Pl.*157, X.*Lac.*6.3; βίος θ. the life *of hunters*, Arist.*Pol.*1256ᵇ2: ἡ -κή (sc. τέχνη) *hunting, the chase*, Pl.*Plt.*289a, cf. *Sph.*223b. 2. c. gen., *hunting after*, τῆς τροφῆς Arist.*HA*488ᵃ 19: metaph., θ. τέχνη ἀνθρώπων Pl.*Euthd.*290b. **-ευτός**, ή, όν, = θηρατός, Arist.*Pol.*1324ᵇ40. **-εύτρια**, fem. of θηρευτήρ, βοῦς *PCair.Zen.*292.298 (iii B.C.), cf. Hsch. s. v. θηρότις; θ. κύνες Them. *Or.*18.220b. **-εύτωρ**, ορος, ὁ, *hunter*, θ. ἄνδρες, of men engaged in Circus games, *IG*4.365 (Corinth). ✻ **-εύω**, aor. 1 ἐθήρευσα Pl. *Euthd.*290c: pf. τεθήρευκα Id.*Tht.*200a:—**Med.**, fut. -σομαι Id.*Sph.* 222a: aor. ἐθηρευσάμην Ar.*Fr.*51, Pl.*Tht.*197d:—**Pass.**, pf. τεθήρευμαι Lysipp.Com.7: aor. ἐθηρεύθην Hdt.3.102, A.*Ch.*493, Pl.*Sph.* 221a: (cf. θηράω):—*hunt*, θηρεύοντα *while hunting*, Od.19.465, cf. Hdt.4.112; θηρεύειν διὰ κενῆς, of the motions of the hands of dying persons, Hp.*Prog.*4. 2. *decoy*, Arist.*HA*614ᵃ13. II. c. acc., *hunt after, chase, catch*, ἀττελέβους Hdt.4.172; θηρία, ὄρνιθας ἀγρίας, μῦν, X.*An.*1.2.7, Pl.*Tht.*197c, *PCair.Zen.*300.7 (iii B.C.); ἰχθῦς Arist. *HA*603ᵃ7; [ἐλέφαντας] *OGI*54.11 (Adule, iii B.C.); of men, Hdt. 4.183; θ. ἀνθρώπους ἐπὶ θοίνην ἢ θυσίαν Arist.*Pol.*1324ᵇ39, cf. X.*An.* 1.2.13; Τιτυὸν βέλος θήρευσε it *hit, struck* him, Pi.*P.*4.90:—Med., Ar.*Fr.*51, Pl.*Grg.*464d, *Euthd.*290b:—Pass., *to be hunted*, Hdt.3. 102; *to be preyed upon*, ib.111; *to be caught*, πέδαις A.*Ch.*493: metaph., *to be captivated*, Lysipp.Com.7. 2. metaph., *hunt, seek after*, κερδέων μέτρον Pi.*N.*11.47; γάμους A.*Pr.*858; ἀρετάν E.*IA*568 (lyr.); θ. νέους πλουσίους ὀρφανούς Aeschin.1.170; ἡδονάς, ἐπιστήμην, Isoc.1.16, Pl.*Tht.*200a, al.; [εὐδαιμονίαν] Arist.*Pol.*1328ᵇ1; ὀνόματα, ῥήματα, Pl.*Grg.*489b, And.1.9, cf. Antipho 6.18; τὰς ἀρχὰς τῶν συλλογισμῶν Arist.*APr.*46ᵃ11; θ. τὸν πλησίον, of an orator, Phld.*Rh.* 2.5 S., al.—Trag. preferred θηράω, exc. where metre demanded θηρεύω.

**θηρεφόνος**, ον, = θηροφόνος, Hdn.Gr.2.260.

**θήρημα**, **θηρητήρ**, **-ήτειρα**, **-ήτωρ**, Ion. for θήρᾱμα, etc.

**θηρῑ-άζομαι**, Pass., *pass into a beast*, of the soul, *Corp.Herm.*10. 20. **-ακός**, ή, όν, (θηρίον) *concerning venomous beasts*, λόγος Dsc. *Ther.Praef.*; Φιλῖνος (ὁ) θ., the writer on this subject, Philum.*Ven.*6.1: ἡ -κή (sc. ἀντίδοτος) an antidote *against a poisonous bite*, Androm. ap.Gal.14.32, etc.; θ. φάρμακα Id.17(2).337; θηριακά, title of Nicander's poem on such antidotes; of other works, Gal.14.7; θ. ἄμπελος *Gp.*4.8.1, cf. Plin.*HN*14.117; θ. [οἶνος] Dsc.5.53. **-άλωσις** [ᾰ], εως, ἡ, *capture of wild beasts*, Sm.*Ge.*49.9. **-άλωτος** [ᾰ], ον, *caught by wild beasts*, Lxx *Le.*5.2, Ph.2.355.

**θηρίαμβος**, coined as etym. of θρίαμβος, Suid.

**θηριάνθρωπος**, ον, *beast-man*, ἔθνος Hdn.*Epim.*76.

✻ **θηρίδιον**, τό, Dim. of θηρίον, in pl., *animalculae*, Thphr.*HP*2.8.3, Arr.*Epict.*2.9.6, Gal.16.162, *Gp.*5.53.6.

⊛ **Θηρίκλειος**, α, ον, or ος, ον, *made by Thericles*, a famous Corinthian potter (Eub.31, 43), Θ. κύλιξ Alex.96, Thphr.*HP*5.3.2 (pl.), Cleanth. *Stoic.*1.133; κρατήρ Alex.119, cf. *IG*11(2).124.43, al. (Delos, iii B.C.); ποτήρια Phalar.*Ep.*70; freq. Θηρικλεία (or -ος) alone, Alex.5, Men. 226, 324; Θ. ἡ μεγάλη Diox.4; τῶν Θηρικλείων εὐκύκλωτον ἀσπίδα Aristopho 14; ὅσα δ' ἐστὶν εἴδη Θηρικλείων τῶν καλῶν Dionys.Com.5.1.

**θηριό-βρωτος**, ον, = θηρόβορος, D.S.18.36. ⊛ **-δεῖκται**, οἱ, *exhibitors of wild beasts*, Antioch.Astr. in *Cod.Astr.*7.118, 8(4).212. **-δηγμα**, ατος, τό, *bite of a serpent*, Dsc.2.79. ⊛ **-δήκτης**, *marsus*, *Gloss.* **-δηκτος**, ον, *bitten by a wild beast*, esp. *by a serpent*, Damocr. ap.Gal.14.122, Dsc.1.103, 4.24. **-ειδής**, ές, *like a wild beast*, Adam. 1.4. **-κόμος**, ὁ, *keeper of wild beasts*, Procop.*Arc.*9. **-κτόνος**, ον, = θηροκτόνος, φάρμακον Eust.1416.14. **-μᾰχέω**, *fight with wild beasts*, D.S.3.43, 1*Ep.Cor.*15.32, Vett.Val.129.33, Ptol.*Tetr.*200, Artem.2.54. **-μάχης** [ᾰ], ου, ὁ, *one who fights with beasts*, D.S. 36.10. **-μᾰχία**, ἡ, *fighting with wild beasts*, in pl., = Lat. *venationes*, Str.2.5.33, Ph.1.602. **-μάχος** [ᾰ], ον, *fighting with wild beasts*, M.Ant.10.8, Luc.*Lex.*19. **-μῐγής**, ές, *half man half beast*, as Scylla, Tz. ad Lyc.45. **-μορφος**, ον, (μορφή) *in the form of a beast*, κώδων Eust.1139.57, cf. Procl.*Par.Ptol.*278.

⊛ **θηρίον**, τό (in form Dim. of θήρ), *wild animal*, esp. of such as are hunted, μάλα γὰρ μέγα θηρίον ἦεν, of a stag, Od.10.171, 180 (never in Il.); in Trag. only in Satyric drama, S.*Ichn.*147 (dub. in A.*Fr.*26): used in Prose for θήρ, X.*An.*1.2.7, Isoc.12.163, etc.; of the spider's *prey*, Arist.*HA*623$^{a}$27; freq. of elephants, Plb.11.1.12, al.: pl., *beasts*, opp. men, birds, and fishes, *h.Ven.*4, Hdt.3.108. **2.** generally, *animal*, Id.1.119; νενόμισται πῦρ θ. εἶναι ἔμψυχον Id.3.16; of men, ἄνθρωπος πάντων θ. θεειδέστατον Antipho Soph.48; εἰς θηρίου βίον ἀφικνεῖσθαι Pl.*Phdr.*249b; also θ. ὕειον Id.*R.*535e; of the dog, Theoc.25.79; of fishes, Arist.*HA*598$^{b}$1; of eels, Antiph.147.7; of leeches, *IG*4.951.101 (Epid.); of other small creatures, Arist.*HA* 552$^{b}$11, 625$^{b}$32, Hp.ap.Gal.19.103, Theoc.19.6; οὐκ ἔστιν οὐδὲν θ. τῶν ἰχθύων ἀτυχέστερον Antiph.161.1; opp. plants, Pl.*Smp.*188b: prov., ἢ θηρίον ἢ θεός, either above or below the nature of man, Arist. *Pol.*1253$^{a}$29, cf. *EN*1145$^{a}$25. **3.** *beast*, esp. as hostile and odious to man, θηρία τε καὶ βοτά *carnivora* and graminivora, Pl.*Mx.*237d; *monster*, *creature*, of sharks, etc., Hdt.6.44; of Typhon, etc., Pl. *Phdr.*230a, *R.*588e; of the Satyrs, S.*Ichn.* l. c.; ταυτὶ ποδαπὰ τὰ θ.; Ar.*Nu.*184, cf. *Av.*93. **b.** *poisonous animal*, Dsc.1.75, *Act.Ap.* 28.4. **II.** Medic., = θηρίωμα, Hp.*Coac.*459, *Loc.Hom.*29, cf. Gal. l.c. **III.** as a term of reproach, *beast*, *creature*, ὦ δειλότατον σὺ θηρίον Ar.*Pl.*439, cf. *Eq.*273; κόλακι, δεινῷ θηρίῳ Pl.*Phdr.*240b; Κρῆτες, κακὰ θ. Epimenid.1; δυσνουθέτητον θ., of poverty, Men. *Georg.*78; ἡ μουσικὴ ἀεί τι καινὸν θηρίον τίκτει Anaxil.27, cf. Eup.132; τί δέ, εἰ αὐτοῦ τοῦ θηρίου ἠκούσατε; said by Aeschines of Demosthenes, Plin.*Ep.*2.3.10; θ. συνεστιώμενον, of woman, Secund. *Sent.*8. **IV.** Astron., the constellation *Lupus*, Eudox.ap.Hipparch.1.2.20, Vett.Val.6.13.

**θηριο-νάρκη**, ἡ, a plant *that benumbs serpents*, *Nerium Oleander*, Plin.*HN*24.163, 25.113. **-πληκτος**, ον, *struck by a poisonous animal*, *Cat.Cod.Astr.*8(4).150. **-ποιέω**, *make into wild beasts*, Tz. ad Lyc.815.

**θηριότης**, ητος, ἡ, *brutality*, Arist.*EN*1145$^{a}$17, Metop.ap.Stob.3. 1.115.

**θηριοτροφ-εῖον**, τό, *park where wild beasts are kept*, Hortens. in Varro *RR*3.13.2 (*thero-* codd.). **-έω**, *train as a wild beast*, Alciphr. *Fr.*5 (Pass.). ⊛ **-ος**, ον, (parox.) *abounding in wild beasts*, of a country, Str.2.5.33; *keeping wild beasts*, Procl.*Par.Ptol.*250. **II.** proparox., θηριότροφος, ον, Pass., *fed on reptiles*, Gal.11.143.

**θηριόω**, *make into a wild beast*, τοὺς πρὸς αὐτὴν ἀφικνουμένους ἡ Κίρκη θηριοῖ Phld.*Piet.*144:—Pass., *IG*14.1291. **II.** Pass., *come to the full size of a beast*, πρὶν θηριοῦσθαι τὸν γόνον Eub.107.14. **2.** *become brutal*, θηριούμενος Pl.*Lg.*935a; πρός τινας Phld.*Lib.*p.25 O.; πρὸς ἀγριότητα Ph.2.53. **3.** of seeds, *to be infested with worms*, Thphr. *CP*5.18.1. **b.** of places, *to be infested with reptiles*, Paul.Aeg. 5.1. **4.** Medic., *become malignant*, ἕλκη ἐᾶσαι θηριωθῆναι Thphr. *Char.*19.3; τεθηριωμένον ἕλκος Dsc.3.9.

**Θηρίτας**, α, ὁ, Lacon. name of Ares, Paus.3.19.8, Hsch. (Lacon. for Θερσίτης).

⊛ **θηρῐ-ώδης**, ες, *full of wild beasts*, *infested by them*, of countries, ἡ θ. Λιβύη Hdt.4.181; ὄρεα -έστατα Id.1.110; ἐν τῇ θ. [χώρῃ] Id.4.174, cf. 2.32; -εστάτης ἐούσης τῆς θαλάσσης ταύτης *full of ravenous fishes*, Id.6.44. **II.** of beasts, *savage*, Arist.*PA*663$^{a}$13; ἐπὶ τὸ -έστερον Id.*HA*502$^{b}$4; τὸ θ., of a colt, E.*Tr.*671. **2.** of men and manners, *brutal*, δίαιτα Hp.*VM*3; [βίοτος] E.*Supp.*202, cf. *SIG*704*E*11 (Delph., ii B.C.); ἡδονή Pl.*R.*591c; βρίμωσις Phld.*Ir.*p.58 W.; κατάστασις *OGI*424.3 (Palestine, i A.D.); ὁ θ. ἐν τοῖς ἀνθρώποις σπάνιος Arist.*EN* 1145$^{a}$30; οἱ Λάκωνες..θηριώδεις ἀπεργάζονται [τοὺς παῖδας] Id.*Pol.* 1338$^{b}$12; ἡ θ. ἕξις Id.*EN*1145$^{a}$24: Comp. -έστερος, ἄνθρωπος Plb.30. 12.3; τὸ θ. *brutality*, Pl.*Cra.*394e, al. Adv. -ωδῶς, διακεῖσθαι πρὸς ἀλλήλους Isoc.11.25, cf. Plb.15.20.3. **3.** ζῴδια θ., = θηριόμορφα, Ptol.*Tetr.*200. **III.** Medic., *malignant*, of ulcers, Phld.*Ir.*p.44 W., Dsc.2.108, Plu.2.165e, Aret.*SA*2.8; also of intestinal worms, Hp. *Epid.*6.1.11, 6.2.11. **-ωδία**, ἡ, = θηριότης, v.l. in Arist.*EN*1145$^{a}$ 24, cf. Sch.E.*Or.*518 (written **-ώδεια** Asp. in *EN*130.7). **-ωμα**, ατος, τό, *malignant ulcer* (cf. θηρίον II), Cels.5.28.3, Dsc.2.109, Erot. s.v. τὸ θηριῶδες, Gal.17(1).948. ⊛ **-ώνῠμος**, ον, *named after a wild beast*, Eust. ad D.P.976. **-ωσις**, εως, ἡ, *turning into a beast*, Luc. *Salt.*48.

**θηρο-βολέω**, *slay wild beasts*, S.*Ph.*165 (anap.), v.l. in *AP*6.186 (Diocl.). **-βορος**, ον, *eaten* or *torn by wild beasts*, κρέας Ps.-Phoc.147; θ. θάνατος death *by wild beasts*, Man.4.614. ⊛ **-βοτος**, ον, *where wild beasts feed*, ἐρημοσύνη *AP*9.4 (Cyllen.), cf. Phalar.*Ep.* 34. **-βρομος**, ον, *heralded by the roar of wild beasts*, epith. of Hecate, Orph.*H.*1.6. **-βρωτος**, ον, = θηρόβοτος, Str.6.1.12 (v.l. θηριοβρ-). **-δηκτος**, ον, *stung by a serpent*, Sch.S.*Ph.*696. **-δῐδασκᾰλία**, ἡ, *taming*, *training of wild beasts*, Man.4.245. **-δίωξ** [ῐ], ωκος, ὁ, *hunter*, Choerob. in *Theod.*1.296, *EM*451.23. **-ειδής**, ές, *having the forms of wild beasts*, Hsch. **-ζῠγοκαμψῐμέτωπος**, ον, = ὁ θῆρας ζυγῶν καὶ κάμπτων τὰ μέτωπα, a word formed as part of a verse containing all the letters, *AP*9.538. **-θήρας**, ου or α, ὁ, *hunter*, Hsch. **-θῡμος**, ον, *with brutal mind*, *brutal*, *APl.*3.25 (Phil.). ⊛ **-κόμος**, ον, *keeping wild beasts* or *camels*, Hld.10. 27. ⊛ **-κτόνος**, ον, *killing wild beasts*, epith. of Heracles, *IG*5(2).91 (Tegea); of Artemis, E.*IA*1570, Corn.*ND*3, Porph.*Abst.*1.22; ἐν φοναῖς θ. in the chase, E.*Hel.*154. **-λέξης**, ου, ὁ, *word-chaser*, Hsch.

**θηρ-ολετέω**, *destroy wild beasts*, Eust.561.3, Dosith.p.432 K. **-ολέτης**, ου, ὁ, *slayer of beasts*, Hsch.; ὄζος ὁ θ., of the club of Heracles, *APl.*4.104 (Phil.):—fem. **-ολέτις**, ιδος, cj. for θηρότις, Hsch.

⊛ **θηρο-μᾰχία**, ἡ, = Lat. *venatio*, *Mon.Anc.Gr.*19.7, *OGI*533.48 (Ancyra), *IGRom.*3.631 (Xanthus). **-μῐγής**, ές, *half-beast*, φῦλα θ., of centaurs, Opp.*C.*2.6; θ. τις ὠρυγή a cry *as of beasts*, Plu.*Mar.* 20. **-μικτος**, ον, = foreg., δαίμων Lyc.963. **-νόμος**, ον, *feeding* or *tending wild beasts*, of a mountain, *AP*6.111 (Antip.); of Pan, Castorio 2. **2.** *guiding them*, μάστιξ Nonn.*D.*11.122. ⊛ **-πεπλος**, ον, *clad in the skins of beasts*, Orph.*H.*69.7; θ. μανία the mad fancy *of wearing skins*, Cerc.10, Stratonic.ap.Timae.80. **-πλαστέω**, *to make beasts*, Tz. ad Lyc.673. **-πλαστος**, ον, *changing into beasts*, of Circe, Lyc.673. **-σκόπος**, ον, *looking out for wild beasts*, epith. of Artemis, *h.Hom.*27.11, B.10.107, *AP*6.240 (Phil.).

**θηροσύνη**, Dor. **-να**, ἡ, *the chase*, Opp.*C.*4.43 (pl.), *AP*6.167 (Agath.).

**θηρότις**· θηρεύτρια, Hsch.

**θηρο-τόκος**, ον, *producing beasts*, ἄγκεα *AP*6.186 (Diocl.). **-τροφέω**, = θηριοτροφέω, Aristaenet.2.20. **-τρόφος**, ον, *feeding wild beasts*, ἀνήρ *IGRom.*4.826 (Hierapolis); of places, E.*Ba.*556 (lyr.), A.R.4.1561, Longus 1.1; of Tethys, Orph.*H.*22.6. **II.** proparox., θηρότροφος, Pass., *feeding on beasts*, δράκων E.*Ph.*820 (hex.). **-τῠπος**, ον, *in the form of a beast*, Orph.*H.*24.5, 39.8. **-φᾰνής**, ές, *appearing like a beast*, Procl. ad Hes.*Op.*151. **-φονεύς**, έως, ὁ, *slayer of beasts*, Opp.*C.*1.538. **-φονέω**, *slay beasts*, ib.4.24. **-φόνος**, ον, also η, ον Thgn.11, prob. in Ar.*Th.*320:—*killing wild beasts*, epith. of Artemis, Thgn. l. c., Ar. l. c.; θεά E.*HF*378 (lyr.); of Apollo, *AP*9.525.9; θεός, i. e. Hadrian, Pancrat.*Oxy.*1085.31; κύνες E.*Hipp.*216 (anap.). **II.** θ., τό, v.l. for θηλυφόνον, Dsc.4. 76. **-φόρος**, ον, *producing game*, prob. l. *AP*14.24. **-φύλαξ** [ῠ], ᾰκος, ὁ, *huntsman*, *PPetr.*3 p.321 (iii B.C.), *Sammelb.*286. 3. **-χλαινος**, ον, *clad in the skins of beasts*, Lyc.871.

⊛ **θής**, θητός, ὁ, *serf*, *bondsman*, θῆτές τε δμῶές τε Od.4.644; later, *hired labourer*, θῆτά τ' ἄοικον ποιεῖσθαι Hes.*Op.*602; μισθωτοὺς καὶ θῆτας Pl.*Plt.*290a; βάναυσοι καὶ θ. (opp. δοῦλοι) Arist.*Pol.*1278$^{a}$ 13. **2.** at Athens, members of the fourth class in the constitution of Solon, *IG*1$^{2}$.45, Arist.*Ath.*7.3, Th.6.43, Poll.3.82. **3.** v. θάτας. **II.** fem. **θῆσσα**, later Att. **θῆττα**, ἡ, *hired servant-girl*, opp. ἐπίκληρος, Posidipp.35; θ. γυνή A.R.1.193, cf. Ant.Lib.25.3. **2.** as Adj., = θητική, θῆσσα τράπεζα *menial* fare, E.*Alc.*2; θ. ἑστία Id.*El.*205 (lyr.).

**θῆσαι**, aor. 1 inf. Act., *suckle*, Hsch.; elsewh. Med., *suck*; Hom. has pres. inf., ἀλλ' αἰεὶ παρέχουσιν ἐπηετανὸν γάλα θῆσθαι they give milk *to suck* the year round, Od.4.89: aor. 1, θήσατο μαζόν he *sucked* the breast, Il.24.58, cf. Call.*Jov.*48; part., θησάμενος *having sucked*, *h.Cer.*236; γάλα Call.*Sos.*vii.4; but, **II.** *suckle*, Ἀπόλλωνα θήσατο μήτηρ *h.Ap.*123. (I.-E. *dhē-* 'suck', cf. θηλή, θῆλυς, Lett. *dēt* 'suck', Skt. *dháyati*, Goth. *daddjan* 'suckle', Lat. *fēlare*, *filius.*)

**θησαυρ-ίζω**, *store*, *treasure up*, ἐν ἀσφαλείῃ τὰ χρήματα θ. Hdt.2. 121.α'; θ. τὸν νεκρὸν ἐν οἰκήματι *to lay* it *by*, ib.86; φάρμακα, σῖτα θ. παρ' αὑτῷ, X.*Cyr.*8.2.24, etc.; of fruits, *lay up in store*, *preserve*, *pickle*, [καυλοὺς] ἐν ἅλμῃ Thphr.*HP*6.4.10; τὸ ἔλαιον θ. [τὰς ὀσμάς] *preserves* its smell, Id.*CP*6.19.3:—Pass., ῥὰξ εὖ τεθησαυρισμένη S.*Fr.* 398.2; [ἡ ἐβένη] τὴν χρόαν οὐ -ομένη λαμβάνει τὴν εὔχρουν ἀλλ' εὐθὺς τῇ φύσει Thphr.*HP*4.4.6, cf. 3.12.5; ἡ τεθησαυρισμένη τῶν ἀρωμάτων ἀπόλαυσις Agatharch.97; τὸ θησαυρισθέν *IG*14.423 ii 37 (Tauromenium). **b.** abs., *hoard*, *lay up treasure*, Phld.*Oec.*p.71 J., *Ep.Jac.* 5.3; ἑαυτῷ *Ev.Luc.*12.21. **2.** metaph., θ. σεαυτῷ ὀργήν *Ep.Rom.* 2.5; θ. θησαυροὺς ἐν οὐρανῷ *Ev.Matt.*6.20; θ. εὐτυχίαν *lay up a store of*.., App.*Samn.*4.3:—Med., *store up for oneself*, ἑαυτῷ ὑπομνήματα Pl.*Phdr.*276d, cf. Isoc.15.229:—Pass., τεθησαυρισμένος κατά τινος φθόνος D.S.20.36; χάριτας -ισθησομένας Id.1.90; *to be reserved*, πυρί 2*Ep.Pet.*3.7. **-ικός**, ή, όν, *of the public granary*, μέτρον *PLips.*97 v 7 (iv A.D.). **2.** θησαυρικόν, τό, *charge for use of granary*, *PRyl.*213.3 (ii A.D.), al. **3.** v. θησαυριστικός. **-ισμα**, ατος, τό, *store*, *treasure*, S.*Ph.*37, E.*El.*497, *Ion* 1394, Vett.Val.352.5: metaph., θ. κακῶν Democr.149. **-ισμός**, ὁ, *laying up in store*, χρημάτων Arist.*Pol.*1256$^{b}$ 28, cf. Phld.*Oec.*p.71 J.; *preservation*, *keeping*, ὀσμῶν Thphr.*Od.*14, cf. *HP*8.11.1; θ. φαντασιῶν, definition of memory, Zeno *Stoic.*1. 19. **-ιστέον**, *one must store up*, τὸ πλεονάζον τοῦ καρποῦ Ph.2. 57. **-ιστής**, οῦ, ὁ, *one who lays up in store*, Poll.3.115. **-ιστικός**, ή, όν, *accustomed to lay up in store*, [ζῷα] τροφῆς θησαυριστικά Arist. *HA*488$^{a}$20; prob. l. for θησαυρικός (= *miserly*), Ptol.*Tetr.*158.

**θησαυρο-ποιέω**, *make stores*, Poll.3.116. **-ποιός**, *όν*, *laying up in store*, Pl.*R*.554a.

❀ **θησαυρός**, *ὁ*, *store*, *treasure*, Ar.*Av*.599, etc.; *θ. χθονός*, of the silver-mines of Laureion, A.*Pers*.238 (troch.); *θ. εὑρεῖν* Arist.*Pol*.1303$^{b}$35; *ἄνθρακες ὁ θ.*, prov., 'apples of Sodom', freq. in Luc.*Zeux*.2, al.; *σποδὸς οἱ θ. γενήσονται* Alciphr.2.3.13: metaph., *θ. γλώσσης φειδωλῆς* Hes.*Op*.719; *θ. ὕμνων* Pi.*P*.6.8; *κακῶν* E.*Ion* 923, cf. Hp.*Lex*; *κόμας.., ἱκτήριον θ.* S.*Aj*.1175; *Διὸς θ.*, of a tomb marking the fall of a thunderbolt, E.*Supp*.1010; *οἰωνοῖς γλυκὺν θ.*, of a dead body, S.*Ant*.30; of learning, *θ., οὓς κατέλιπον ἐν βιβλίοις* X.*Mem*.1.6.14; *σοφίας θ.* Pl.*Phlb*.15e, *Ep.Col*.2.3; *χρημάτων καὶ τιμῶν* Pl.*Mx*.247b; *καλὸς θ. παρ' ἀνδρὶ σπουδαίῳ χάρις* Isoc.1.29; *ἐκ τοῦ ἀγαθοῦ θ. τῆς καρδίας Ev.Luc*.6.45. II. *strong-room*, *magazine*, Hdt.2.150, *SIG*419.17 (Delph., iii B.C.), Lxx *De*.32.34, etc.; esp. of the *treasuries* built at Delphi by Greek cities, *SIG*8 (vi B.C.), Hdt.1.14, al., X.*An*.5.3.5, Str.4.1.13, etc.; *vaults* of a bank, *PLips*.62 ii 14 (iv A.D.). 2. *granary*, *PCair.Zen*.232.4 (iii B.C.), Wilcken *Chr*.385.27 (iii B.C.), 192 (i A.D.), etc.; *οἱ δημόσιοι θ. PRyl*.90.9 (iii A.D.), cf. *POxy*.2119.3 (iii A.D.). 3. *receptacle* for valuables, *safe*, *casket*, Hdt.7.190, 9.106, *Ev.Matt*.2.11; *θ. βελέεσσιν*, of a quiver, A.*Pers*.1022 (lyr.). 4. *offertory-box* (for its form, v. *IG*9(2).590), *IG*7.235.23 (Oropus, iv B.C.), 12(3).443 (Thera, iii B.C.), *Jahrb*.16.162 note 13 (Rhodes, iii B.C.), *Schwyzer* 89 (Argos, iii B.C.), *SIG*1015.30 (Halic.), *PTeb*.6.27 (ii B.C.), *IG*5(1).1390.89 (Andania, i B.C.); *σπονδεῖον ἢ θ. coin-in-the-slot machine* which sold holy water, Hero *Spir*.1.21. 5. *cavern*, S.*Ichn*.276; *subterranean dungeon*, Plu.*Phil*.19.

**θησαυρο-φῠλᾰκέω**, *lay by*, *store up*, *ἀργύριον* Ph.2.215; *μνήμας* Id.1.237:—Pass., ib.338. II. *to be a treasurer*, D.S.19.15. **-φῠλᾰκικόν** or **-φῠλᾰκῑτικόν**, *τό*, *tax levied for the protection of granaries*, *PTeb*.68.89, 61(*b*).317 (ii B.C.). **-φῠλάκιον** [ᾰ], *τό*, *treasury*, Artem.1.74, Them.*Or*.7.91d. ❀ **-φύλαξ** [ῠ], *ἄκος*, *ὁ*, *treasurer*, Lxx *Es*.5.14, D.S.18.58, Polyaen.4.9.4, Arr.*Ind*.12.7 (pl.), Vett.Val.85.23. II. *guard of the state-granaries*, *PCair.Zen*.292.155 (iii B.C.), *PTeb*.90.40 (i B.C.), *POxy*.522.9 (ii A.D.).

**θησαυρώδης**, *ες*, *filled with treasure*, *τάφοι* Philostr.*VA*7.23.1.

**Θησεῖδαι**, *οἱ*, *sons of Theseus*, i.e. *Athenians*, S.*OC*1066 (lyr.).

**θησειομύζων**, sine expl., Ar.*Fr*.459 (*Et.Gen*.).

**Θησεῖον**, *τό*, *temple of Theseus*, a sanctuary (*ἄσυλον*) for criminals and slaves, Ar.*Eq*.1312, *Fr*.567:—also **Θησέον**, Pherecr.49 (cf. *Et.Gen*.). II. **Θησεῖα**, *τά*, *festival of Theseus*, Ar.*Pl*.627:—also **Θησέα**, *SIG*1029.78 (iv B.C.). III. **θησεῖον**, *τό*, *holewort*, *Corydalis densiflora*, Thphr.*HP*7.12.3, Plin.*HN*21.107.

**Θησειότριψ**, *ῐβος*, *ὁ*, (*τρίβω*) *one who is always in the Theseum*, i.e. *a runaway slave*, Ar.*Fr*.458.

**θησεύμεθα**, Dor. fut. Med. of *τίθημι*.

❀ **Θησεύς**, *ὁ*, gen. *Θησέως* [trisyll., S.*Ph*.562, *OC*1593, 1657, but disyll., ib.1003, 1103]:—*Theseus*, Il.1.265, etc.: pl. *Θησέες* Pl.*Tht*.169b; *Θησεῖς* Alciphr.2.4.

**Θησηΐς**, *ῐδος*, contr. **Θησῄς**, *ῇδος*, fem. of **Θήσειος*, *of Theseus*, *χθών* A.*Eu*.1026. II. Subst., *Theseid*, a poem on Theseus, Arist.*Po*.1451$^{a}$20, D.L.2.59. 2. name of a mode of hair-cutting, used by Theseus, Plu.*Thes*.5.

**θῆσθαι**, v. *θῆσαι*.

**θησομύζειν**, f.l. for *θησειομύζων*, *EM*451.52.

**θῆσσα**, fem. of *θής* (q.v.). II. = Lat. *tensa*, *sacred car*, Plu.*Cor*.25.

**θήσω**· *ἤσω*, *αἰτήσω* (Boeot.), Hsch.; *θησόμενοι*· *αἰτούμενοι*, Id.; *θησάμενοι*· *αἰτησάμενοι* (Cret.), Id. (Prob. forms of *θέσσασθαι*, q.v.)

**θῆτα**, *τό*, indecl., *the letter* Θ (Hebr. *ṭêth*), Ar.*Ec*.685, etc.: gen. *θήτατος* Democr.20: nom. pl. *θήτατες* (*tetates*) Wessely *Schrifttaf. zur ält. lat. Paläogr*. No.8 (ii A.D.); nickname of Aesop (who was a *θής*), Ptol.Heph.ap.Phot.*Bibl*.p.151 B.

**θηταλά**· *θαυμαστά*, *ψεύδεσιν ὅμοια*, Hsch.

**θητ-εία**, *ἡ*, (*θητεύω*) *hired service*, *service*, S.*OT*1029, Isoc.14.48: in pl., ib.11.38, D.H.2.19. 2. *servility*, *sycophancy*, c. gen., *θ. ὄχλων ἢ δυναστῶν* Epicur.*Sent.Vat*.67. **-εῖον**, *τό*, = *μίσθωμα*, *Μυστάκου θ.*, title of play by Sopatros, Ath.4.175c, al. (*θητίον* codd.). **-εύω**, *to be a serf* or *labourer*, *Λαομέδοντι..θητεύσαμεν εἰς ἐνιαυτόν* Il.21.444, cf. Od.18.357; *θητευέμεν ἄλλῳ, ἀνδρὶ παρ' ἀκλήρῳ* 11.489, cf. E.*Alc*.6, *Cyc*.77 (lyr.), Pl.*Euthphr*.4c, *R*.359d, Phld.*Piet*.63; *θ. ἐπὶ μισθῷ παρά τινι* Hdt.8.137; *θ. εἰς τὸ τεῖχος labour* at it, Philostr.*Her*.12$^{a}$.3; *θ. Παλλάδι καὶ Παφίῃ serve*, *AP*5.292.12 (Paul. Sil.). **-ικός**, *ή*, *όν*, *of* or *for a hireling*, *menial*, *ἔργον* Arist.*Rh*.1367$^{a}$31; *βάναυσος ἢ θ. βίος* Id.*Pol*.1278$^{a}$21; *-ωτέρα ἐργασία* ib.1341$^{b}$14; *θ. καὶ δουλικὸν πράττειν* ib.1337$^{b}$21. 2. *τὸ θ.*, = *οἱ θῆτες*, *the class of θῆτες*, ib.1274$^{a}$21, al.; *θ. τελεῖν* pay *on the assessment of a θής* at Athens, Id.*Ath*.7.4, Lex ap.D.43.54; *θ. τέλος* Epigr.ap.Arist.*Ath*.7.4; *τὸ θ.* in an army, *servants*, *camp-followers*, etc., Arr.*Tact*.2.1. 3. *like a θής*, *servile*, *πάντες οἱ κόλακες θ.* Arist.*EN*1125$^{a}$2, cf. Luc.*Fug*.12.

**θητόν**· *βωμόν*, Hsch. **θῆττα**, *ἡ*, v. *θῆσσα*.

**θητώνιον**, *τό*, (*θής*, *ὦνος*) *hire*, *wages*, Suid.:—hence **θητωνέω**, *receive wages*, prob. in *IG*2$^{2}$.1013.54.

**-θῐ**, termin. of the locative case, *Ἰλιόθι πρό* Il.8.561; *ἠῶθι πρό* 11.50. II. termin. of several locative Advs. formed from Substs., Adjs., and Prons., *ἀγρόθι*, *οἴκοθι*, *ἄλλοθι*, etc., cf. A.D.*Adv*.205.35, al.

**θιαγών**, *όνος*, *ὁ*, an Aetol. sacrificial cake, Nic.*Fr*.136, Hsch.

**θιακχά**· *ἄνθη ἐν Σικυῶνι*, Hsch. **θιάλλαι**· *θῆμνες*, Id. **θιάρατος** (i.e. **θεάρατος*)· *εὐκτός*, Id. **θιᾱρός**, v. *θεωρός*. **θιάσαι**· *χορεῦσαι*, Id.

**θῐᾰσ-αρχέω**, *to be leader of a θίασος*, *OGI*529.5 (Sebastopolis, ii A.D.). **-άρχης**, *ου*, *ὁ*, *leader of a θίασος*, Luc.*Peregr*.11. **-εία**, *ἡ*, *Bacchic revel*, Procl.*H*.1.21. **-εύω**, *initiate into the θίασος*, *Epic.Alex.Adesp*.9 i 2; *ὅς με..κόραις ἐθιάσευσ'* E.*Ion* 552; *θ. χοροῖς* Id.*Ba*.379 (lyr.):—Pass., *-εύεται ψυχάν* ib.75. II. *celebrate Bacchic rites*, Str.12.4.3. **-ίτης** [σῑ], *ου*, *ὁ*, = *θιασώτης*, *IG*12(5).872.60 (Tenos), *SIG*1108 (Callatis), etc.:—fem. **-ῖτις**, *ιδος*, *ἡ*, Kastriotis *Κατάλ. περιγραφικός, Γλυπτὰ τοῦ Ἐθνικοῦ Μουσ*. (1908) No.1485 (pl., Nicaea, iii/iv A.D.). ❀ **-ῑτικός**, *ή*, *όν*, *belonging to a θίασος*, *χρήματα SIG*1108.9 (Callatis). ❀ **-ος** (proparox.), *ὁ*, *Bacchic revel*, *rout*, Hdt.4.79, E.*Ba*.680, Ar.*Ra*.156, etc.; *θ. ἄγειν* E.*Ba*.115 (lyr.); *τοὺς..θ. ἄγων διὰ τῶν ὁδῶν τοὺς ἐστεφανωμένους τῷ μαράθῳ καὶ τῇ λεύκῃ* D.18.260, cf. Ath.5.185c, 8.362e. 2. *religious guild*, *confraternity*, *IG*2.986, 1663, 2$^{2}$.1177, *SIG*1044.45 (Halic.), etc. II. generally, *company*, *troop*, used by Trag. in lyr., *Κενταύρων* E.*IA*1059; *ἡλίκων* Id.*IT*1146; *Μουσῶν* Ar.*Th*.41; *ἐνόπλιος θ.*, of warriors, E.*Ph*.796; *Κενταυρικὸς καὶ Σατυρικός* Pl.*Plt*.303d; *τοῦ σοῦ θ.* of your *company*, X.*Mem*.2.1.31; *Ἀσιανῶν ἀκροαμάτων θ.* Plu.*Ant*.24. III. *feast*, *banquet*, Id.2.301f, *Cleom*.34. **-ώδης**, *ες*, *festive*, *ἀμφίπολοι Βρομίου* Nonn.*D*.45.270. **-ών**, *ῶνος*, *ὁ*, *meeting-place of a θίασος*, Hsch. **-ώτης**, *ου*, *ὁ*, *member of a θίασος*, Ar.*Ra*.327 (lyr.), Is.9.30, *IG*2$^{2}$.1237.95; *θ. καὶ ἐρανισταί* Arist.*EN*1160$^{a}$19. 2. c. gen., *θιασῶται τοῦ θεοῦ τούτου* (sc. *Ἔρωτος*) *worshippers* of Love, X.*Smp*.8.1; *Ἀφροδίτης οἱ θ. IG*2$^{2}$.1261.23; *ὁ ἐμὸς θ.* my *fellow-reveller*, E.*Ba*.548 (lyr.); *οἱ ἑαυτοῦ θ. fellow-members* of his *θ.*, *IG*2$^{2}$.1237.73. 3. of Bacchus, *leader of θίασοι*, *AP*9.524.9. 4. generally, *follower*, *disciple*, Luc.*Fug*.4; *Πλάτωνος* Them.*Or*.2.33c. **-ωτικός**, *ή*, *όν*, *belonging to a θίασος*, Arist.*Oec*.1346$^{b}$15, *BCH*50.233 (Thasos). **-ῶτις**, *ιδος*, *ἡ*, fem. of *θιασώτης*, Opp.*C*.4.298.

**θίβεις**· *γυναῖκές τινες*, Hsch.

**θῖβις** or **θίβις**, *εως*, *ἡ*, *basket* plaited from papyrus, *PPetr*.3 p.145 (iii B.C.), *PCair.Zen*.69 (iii B.C.), *PGrenf*.1.14.10 (ii B.C.), Lxx *Ex*.2.3,6, Suid.: the form **θίβη** given by Hsch., Phot., v.l. in Suid., is false: **θῆβις** (sic) *τῶν ἄρτων*, correction of *πρόθεσις τ. ἄ.*, *UPZ*149.21 (iii B.C.):—Hsch. also gives **θίβωνος** (extra ordinem)· *κιβωτός* (Cypr.), and **θίγωνος**· *κιβωτοῦ*. (Hebr. *tēbhāh*, from Egypt. *ḏbꜣt* 'box'.)

❀ **θιβρός** or **θιμβρός** (v.l. in Nic.*Th*.35), *ά*, *όν*, *hot*, *ὠεὰ θ. χελύνης* (*ἑψηθέντα ἐπ' ἀνθράκων* Sch., cf. Hsch.), Nic.*Al*.555, cf. *Th*.35. II. *delicate*, *dainty*, *luxurious*, *Κύπρις* Call.*Fr*.267; *θ. Σεμίραμις* Euph.81.—Only in Alex. poets. [ῐ in the Spartan pr.n. *Θίβρων*, Philosteph.Com.1.]

❀ **θιγάνα**, *ἡ*, *cover*, *lid*, dub. in *Schwyzer* 323 *C* 39 (Delph.).

❀ **θιγγάνω**, fut. *προσ-θίξῃ* prob. for *-εις* E.*Heracl*.652: 2 fut. *τεθίξομαι* Id.*Hipp*.1086: aor. 2 *ἔθῐγον* Archil.71, E.*Ba*.304, etc.; Lacon. inf. *σιγῆν* Ar.*Lys*.1004:—Pass., aor. *θιχθῆναι* S.E.*M*.9.258:—*touch*, *handle*: abs., *μὴ θίγγανε IG*12(3).451 (Thera), etc.: usu. c. gen., *οἴακος* A.*Ag*.663, etc.; *χερσὶ* or *χερὶ θ. τινός*, Id.*Th*.44, E.*Ba*.1318; *δι' ὁσίων χειρῶν* S.*OC*470: c. acc., *χεῖρα* (s.v.l.) *Νεοβούλης θιγεῖν* Archil. l.c.; *χερσὶ γλαυκᾶς ἐλαίας θιγοῦ[σ' ὄζον]* Limen.6 (dub. l.):—Pass., *to be touched*, Arist.*HA*495$^{a}$6. 2. *take hold of*, *τινος* S.*Aj*.1410 (anap.), etc.; *θ. ὠλέναισιν τέκνου embrace*, E.*Ph*.300 (lyr.); *θ. γυναικός have intercourse with..*, Id.*Hipp*.1044; *θ. εὐνῆς* ib.885, cf. S.*OC*329: abs., E.*El*.51; *γλίχεται θιγεῖν καὶ συνεῖναι*, of man's aspiration after God, Phld.*D*.3.1. 3. *touch*, *attempt*, *παντὸς..λόγου κακοῦ γλώσσῃ θ.* S.*Ph*.408; *μή μοι λεπτῶν θίγγανε μύθων* E.*Fr*.924; *θ. πονηρίας* Isyll.5; in hostile sense, *attack*, *θηρός* E.*Ba*.1183 (lyr.); *σώματος τοῦ σοῦ* Id.*IA*1351 (troch.). II. metaph., of the feelings, *touch*, *θιγγάνει σέθεν τόδε;* Id.*Hipp*.310; *ψυχᾶς*, *φρενῶν*, Id.*Alc*.108; *πολλὰ θ. πρὸς ἧπαρ reach* to the heart, A.*Ag*.432 (lyr.). 2. *touch upon*, in speaking or discussion, Arist.*Metaph*.988$^{a}$23, al., *Pol*.1323$^{b}$38; also of the mind, *apprehend*, *νοῦς..θιγγάνων καὶ νοῶν* Id.*Metaph*.1072$^{b}$21, al. 3. *reach*, *win*, *ἀγώνων* Pi.*I*.1.18, etc.: also c. dat., *θ. ἡσυχίᾳ*, *ἀρεταῖς*, *ψεύδει*, Id.*P*.4.296, 8.24, 9.42; *reach*, *hit*, *διαβολὴ θ. τινός* Plu.*Alex*.10.—Not found in pure Att. Prose (*ἅπτομαι* being used), but used by X.*Cyr*.1.3.5, al.: aor. 1 inf. *θίξαι* v.l. for *ψαῦσαι* in Suid. s.v. *θιγεῖν*, *θῖξαι* v.l. for *δεῖξαι* in Arist.*EN*1111$^{a}$14.

**θίγ-ημα** [ῐ], *ατος*, *τό*, *touch*, prob. for *φιλήματα* in *AP*12.209 (Strat.). **-μα**, *ατος*, *τό*, = foreg., *IGRom*.4.503.11 (Pergam.). II. = *μίασμα*, Hsch. **-ωνος**, v. *θῖβις*.

**θιδρακίνη**, *ἡ*, = *θριδακίνη*, Hsch.

**θίδραξ**, v. *θρίδαξ*.

**θιήϊον** (*θίκ-* cod.)· *θεῖον τὸ ὀρυκτόν* (Cret.), Hsch. **θίημι**· *ποιῶ*, and **θιῆσαι**· *ποιῆσαι*, *φιλῆσαι*, Id. ❀ **θικέλιον**· *τὴν γογγυλίδα* (Lacon.), Id. **θίλα**· *ὁ θημών*, Id.

**θιμβρός**, *ά*, *όν*, v. *θιβρός*.

**θινίον** [θῐ], *τό*, Dim. of *θίς* I.2, dub. in Phld.*D*.3.7. II. coined as etym. of *ἀκροθίνιον*, *AB*367.

**θῖνος**, Cret. for *θεῖνος*, *sacred*, *Leg.Gort*.10.42, *SIG*526.29 (iii B.C.), al.

**θῑνώδης**, *ες*, *like a sandy beach*, *sandy*, Str.8.3.14; *θ. ἄγκιστρον* an anchor *on the sand*, *Trag.Adesp*.379.

**θίξις**, *εως*, *ἡ*, *touching*, Hp.*Mul*.1.40, Arist.*GA*751$^{a}$19, *Ph*.202$^{a}$7, Gal.15.45, S.E.*P*.3.56, al.; *ἄχρι τῆς Ἐρυθρᾶς θαλάσσης κατὰ θίξιν* as far as the Red Sea, *which it touches*, Vett.Val.12.20, cf. 13.19; *ὁ κατὰ θίξιν περισκυθισμός* a scalp operation in which the edges of the wound were made to touch, *Arch.Pap*.4.270 (iii A.D.), cf. Archig.ap.Gal.12.577 (where *θῆξιν*). II. metaph., *apprehension* of the mind, Plot.5.3.10: pl., Procl. *in Prm*.p.628 S.

**θῑπόβρωτος**, v. *θριπόβρωτος*.

❀ **θίς** [ῑ], *θῑνός*: *ὁ* Il.23.693, Od.12.45, Ar.*V*.696, Phld. (v. infr.); *ἡ* S.*Ant*.591, *Ph*.1124, Arist.*HA*548$^{b}$6, Call.*Fr*.126, D.H.3.44:—*heap*,

πολὺς ὀστεόφιν θίς Od.12.45; θῖνες νεκρῶν A.*Pers.*818: metaph., θὶς πημάτων Lyc.812; esp. of *sand-banks*, θῖνες ψάμμου Hdt.3.26; ἄμμου, γῆς, Plu.*Fab.*6, *Art.*18; τοὺς ἐν ἄμμῳ θῖνας Phld.*Piet.*20; ἐν ταῖς θ. Arist.*HA* $548^{b}6$, cf. $537^{a}25$; θῖνας καὶ ψάμμους Porph.*Abst.*4.21; of the *sandy deserts* of Libya, A.R.4.1384; Νασαμώνων αὔλια καὶ δολιχὰς θ. Call.*Fr.*126. **2.** usu. in Hom., etc., *beach, shore*, freq. in oblique cases, παρὰ θῖνα.. θαλάσσης Il.1.34, cf. Od.6.236, etc.; παρὰ θῖν' ἁλὸς ἀτρυγέτοιο Il.1.316, cf. 350, etc.; alone, ἐπὶ θινί Od.7.290; παρὰ θῖνα 9.46; later θῖν' ἁλός Ar.*V.*1521 (parod.); πόντου S.*Ph.*1124 (lyr.); θαλάσσας E.*Andr.*109 (eleg.); θαλαττία D.H.3.44. **b.** *sand-bank, bar* at the mouth of a river, Plb.4.41.6: pl., *banks* of a stream, D.S. 1.30. **3.** *sand* or *mud* at the bottom of the sea, οἶδμα.. κυλίνδει βυσσόθεν κελαινὰν θῖνα S.*Ant.*591: metaph., ὥς μου τὸν θῖνα ταράττεις, i.e. trouble *the very bottom* of my heart, Ar.*V.*696, v. Sch. **4.** *shore-weed*, θίν' ἐν φυκιόεντι Il.23.693, cf. Arist.*HA* $598^{a}5$; θινὸς ὄζειν ib. $620^{a}15$. **II.** ἄκρης [πόλιος] θίς *the temple that crowns* the Acropolis, dub. in Call.*Fr.anon.*332.

**θίσβη·** σορός, Suid. **θισπῶσαι·** εἰκάσαι, Hsch.

**θιώτης** (sc. ἄρτος?), ὁ, a kind of food (loaf?), *PFay.*117.10 (ii A.D.).

**θλᾰδί-ας,** ου, ὁ, *eunuch*, Lxx *Le.*22.24, Ph.2.261. **-άω,** *make* one *an eunuch*, Hsch. s.v. φλαδιᾶν.

**θλάσις** [ᾰ], εως, ἡ, (θλάω) *crushing, bruising*, Arist.*Mete.* $386^{a}18$, *Pr.* $890^{a}2$, Thphr.*Lass.*18, Dsc.2.170 (pl.), S.E.*M.*6.40.

**θλάσμα,** ατος, τό, *bruise*, Arist.*Mir.* $841^{b}11$, Lxx *Am.*6.12(11), Ph. 2.488, Dsc.2.170; = κοίλωμα ἄνευ ῥήξεως, *dint*, Sor.*Fract.*9.

**θλάσπις,** εως, Ion. ιος, ἡ, (θλάω) *shepherd's purse, Capsella bursa-pastoris*, Hp.*Mul.*1.78, al.:—also **θλάσπι,** τό, Dsc.2.156, Plin.*HN* 27.140:—Dim. **θλασπίδιον,** τό, Ps.-Dsc.2.156.

**θλάστ-ης,** ου, ὁ, = ἐμβρυοθλάστης, Hp.ap.Gal.19.104. **-ικός,** ή, όν, *able to crush, crushing*, Arist.*Pr.* $884^{b}35$. **-ός,** ή, όν, *crushed, bruised*, ἐλάα Ar.*Fr.*391, Diph.14.5, cf. *PSI* 5.535.52. **2.** *capable of being crushed* or *compressed*, opp. θραυστός (q.v.), Arist.*HA* $523^{b}7$, cf. *Mete.* $386^{a}25$.

**θλάττω,** late form of sq., f.l. in Gal.*UP* 10.6, cf. Paul.Aeg.6.91 (Pass.).

**θλάω,** imper. θλῆ Herod. (v. infr.); inf. θλᾶν Gal.*UP* 13.8; part. θλῶσα ib.13.3: 3 sg. impf. ἔθλα (συγκατ-) Macho ap.Ath.8.348f: fut. θλάσω [ᾰ] (ἐν-) Hp.*Int.*44: aor. ἔθλᾰσα, Ep. θλάσσα (v. infr.):—**Pass.,** fut. θλασθήσομαι Gal.*UP* 12.15: aor. ἐθλάσθην Hp.*Ulc.*6: pf. τέθλασμαι (συν-) Alex.270, Ph.1.609, Theoc.22.45:—*crush, bruise*, θλάσσε δέ οἱ κοτύλην Il.5.307; ὀστέα δ' εἴσω ἔθλασεν Od.18.97; οὔτ' ἔρρηξε βαλὼν οὔτ' ἔθλασε Hes.*Sc.*140; [φωνὴν] ὥσπερ θλῶσαν [τὴν ἀκοήν] S.E.*M.*6.40: sens. obsc., αὐτὸς τὰ σαυτοῦ θλῆ Herod.2.83:—Pass., Arist.*Pr.* $890^{a}3$, Herod.3.44; τεθλασμένος οὔατα πυγμαῖς Theoc. l.c.; ῥάβδος -μένη Lxx 4*Ki.*18.21. **2.** *overload* (?), τὰς ἅλως *PFay.*112.20 (i A.D.). **3.** metaph., *oppress*, Lxx *Jd.*10.8, al. (Cf. φλάω.)

**θλῐβ-ερός,** ά, όν, (θλίβω) *chafing, rubbing*, Paul.Aeg.6.106. **II.** *oppressive*, Just.*Nov.*135.1. **-ή,** ἡ, *a rubbing*, Gal.18(2).923. **-ίας,** ου, ὁ, = θλαδίας, Str.13.4.1. ⊛ **-ω** [ῑ], Ar.*Pax* 1239, etc.: fut. θλίψω (ἀπο-) E.*Cyc.*237: aor. ἔθλιψα Pl.*Ti.*60c, Call.*Del.*35: pf. τέθλῐφα Crobyl.4 (cj.), Plb.18.24.3:—**Med.,** fut. θλίψομαι (v. infr.):—**Pass.,** fut. θλῐβήσομαι v.l. in Sor.1.33: aor. 1 ἐθλίφθην Pl.*Ti.*91a, Arist.*Pr.* $925^{b}20$: aor. 2 part. θλῐβείς ib.13, v.l. in Dsc.3.7 (cf. subj. ἐκφλῐβῇ Hp. *Loc.Hom.*9): pf. τέθλιμμαι Arist.*Pr.* $925^{b}14$, *AP* 7.472.5 (Leon.):—*squeeze, chafe*, θλίβει τὸν ὄρρον [ὁ θώραξ] Ar.*Pax* 1239, cf. *Lys.*314; τοὺς ὄφεις θλίβων D.18.260; ὅπου με θλίβει where [the shoe] *pinches*, Plu.2.141a: metaph., δούλης ὦτα νωθρίη θλίβει Herod.4.53: abs., *exercise pressure*, Plot.3.6.6:—Pass., of a person heavy-laden, ὡς θλίβομαι! Ar.*Ra.*5, cf. *V.*1289:—Med., πολλῇς φλιῇσι παραστὰς θλίψεται (v.l. φλίψεται) ὤμους he *will rub his* shoulders against many doorposts, of a beggar, Od.17.221: χείλεα θλίβειν, of kissing, Theoc.20.4. **II.** *compress, straiten*, Pl.*Ti.*60c; *reduce, compress*, εἰς τὸ μὴ ὂν τὰ ὄντα θλίβοντες Epicur.*Ep.*1 p.16 U.:—Pass., *to be compressed*, Pl.*Ti.*91a; ὥστε ἐξωθεῖσθαι τὸ ἧσσον θλιβόμενον ὑπὸ τοῦ μᾶλλον θλιβομένου Archim.*Fluit.*1 *Prooem.*; θλιβομένα καλύβα *a small, close* hut, Theoc. 21.18; ὁδὸς τεθλιμμένη, opp. εὐρύχωρος, *Ev.Matt.*7.14; βίος τεθλ. a *scanty* subsistence, D.H.8.73, cf. *AP* 7.472.5 (Leon.). **2.** metaph., *oppress, afflict, distress*, ἀνάγκη ἔθλιψέ τινα Call.*Del.*35; θ. καὶ λυμαίνεσθαι τὸ μακάριον Arist.*EN* $1100^{b}28$; θ. τὰς πόλεις τοῖς ὀψωνίοις *SIG* 700.25 (Macedonia, ii B.C.); *press hard* in battle, Plb.18.24.3:—Pass., θ. διὰ τὸν πόλεμον Arist.*Pol.* $1307^{a}1$; ὑπό τινων *SIG* 685.39 (ii B.C.); ὑπὸ τῆς ἀδοξίας Phld.*Lib.*p.61 O.—Once in Hom., never in Trag. **-ώδης,** ες, *oppressive*, Aq.*Ge.*32.7(8).

**θλιμμός,** ὁ, = θλῖψις, Lxx *Ex.*3.9.

**θλιπτικός,** ή, όν, *due to pressure*, πάθημα Gal.8.949. Adv. -κῶς *by pressure*, S.E.*M.*10.83.

⊛ **θλῖψις,** εως, ἡ, *pressure*, Arist.*Mete.* $382^{a}13$, *Pr.* $890^{a}2$; τῶν νεφῶν Epicur.*Ep.*2 p.49 U.; ἀντέρεισις καὶ θ. Str.1.3.6; of the pulse, Ruf. ap.Orib.8.24.61, cf. Gal.7.306; θ. στομάχου Orib.*Fr.*42; ὑστερικαὶ θ. Sor.1.42. **2.** *crushing, castration*, πώλων *Hippiatr.*20. **3.** metaph., *oppression, affliction*, Lxx *Ge.*35.3, al., *BGU* 1139.4 (i B.C.), *Act.Ap.*14.22 (pl.), al., Vett.Val.71.16 (pl.), *POxy.*939.13 (iv A.D.).

**θνᾴσκω, θνᾱτός,** Dor. for θνήσκω, θνητός.

**θνησ-είδιον,** τό, *carcase of an animal*, ἐσθίειν κενέβρειόν τε καὶ θ. Ael. *NA* 6.2 (θν. preferred to κ. by Phryn.*PS* p.75 B.); ἐσθῆτα ἀπὸ θνησειδίων φορεῖν Philostr.*VA* 8.7.4; ἅψασθαι θνησειδίων Porph.*Abst.*4. 16, cf. D.L.8.33:—Aeol. **θνᾱσίδιον** *Schwyzer* 633.14 (Eresus, ii/i B.C.). **-ῐμαῖος,** α, ον, neut. as Subst. **-αῖον,** τό, = foreg., Lxx 3*Ki.*13.25, al.; τῶν θ. οὐχ ἅψεσθε ib.*Le.*11.8, cf. Hierocl. *in CA* 26 p.480 M.

⊛ **θνῆσις,** εως, ἡ, *mortality*, in a plague, Ruf.*Fr.*69; πολλὴ θ. γέγονε *Stud.Pal.*22.338 (i A.D.); νηπίων *Cat.Cod.Astr.*7.126.

**θνῄσκω** (with ι *IG* 2.2477.7,10,2494, Ἀρχ.Ἐφ.1910.73; θνείσκ- *IG* 2.4040b; [ἀποθν]ήισκειν Pl.*Phdr.* in *PPetr.*1 p.18 (iii B.C.), but θνήσκω Did.ap.*EM* 452.29, freq. in codd.), Aeol. **θναίσκω** Hdn.Gr.2.79, Dor. **θνᾴσκω** *Sammelb.*6754.22 (iii B.C.): fut. θᾰνοῦμαι Simon.85.9, S.*Ant.* 462, etc.; Ep. inf. -έεσθαι Il.4.12; later θνήξομαι *AP* 9.354 (Leon.), Polyaen.5.2.22 codd.: aor. 2 ἔθᾰνον, Ep. θάνον Od.11.412, al.; inf. Ep. and Ion. θανέειν, as always in Hom., exc. Il.7.52, θανέμεν Pi.*P.*4.72: pf. τέθνηκα Il.18.12, etc.; subj. τεθνήκω Th.8.74: plpf. ἐτεθνήκειν Antipho 5.70, Lys.19.48; 3 pl. -ήκεσαν And.1.52: short forms of pf., 3 dual τέθνᾰτον X.*An.*4.1.19, 1 pl. τέθνᾰμεν Pl.*Grg.*493a, 3 pl. τεθνᾶσι Il.22.52, etc.; 3 pl. plpf. ἐτέθνᾰσαν Antipho 5.70, And.1.59, X.*HG* 6.4.16; imper. τέθνᾰθι Il.22.365, τεθνάτω 15.496, *IG* $1^{2}$.10, Pl. *Lg.*933e, etc.; opt. τεθναίην Il.18.98, etc.; inf. τεθνάναι [ᾰ] Semon. 3, Hdt.1.31, Ar.*Ra.*1012, Pl.Com.68, Th.8.92, etc., τεθνᾶναι dub. l. in Mimn.2.10, A.*Ag.*539; Ep. τεθνάμεναι, -άμεν, Il.24.225, 15.497, etc.; Aeol. τεθνάκην Sapph.2.15; part. τεθνεώς Hdt.9.120, Ar.*Av.* 476, etc., fem. τεθνεῶσα Lys.31.22, D.40.27 (τεθνηκυῖα Hippon.29, E. *Or.*109), neut. τεθνεός Hdt.1.112, Hp.*Nat.Mul.*32 (τεθνηκός Pl.*Phd.* 71d, pl. τεθνεῶτα 72c); gen. τεθνεῶτος, etc., Hdt.5.68, etc. (once in Hom., dat. τεθνεῶτι Od.19.331); poet. τεθνεότος Archel.ap.Antig. *Mir.*89, Q.S.7.65; Dor. τεθνᾰότα Pi.*N.*10.74; Ep. τεθνηώς (v.l. -ειώς) Il.17.161, -ηυῖα Od.4.734, (κατα-) 11.141; gen. τεθνηῶτος Il.9. 633, etc.; also τεθνηότος 17.435, Od.15.23, al. [τεθνεῶτι is trisyll. Od.19.331, τεθνεώτων E.*Supp.*272 (hex.): disyll. forms are written in later Gr., nom. τεθνώς *BCH* 18.438 (Argilus); gen. sg. τεθνῶτος *SIG* 799.13 (Cyzicus, i A.D.); dat. sg. τεθνῶτι *Papers of the Amer. School* 3.334 (Pisid.); fem. τεθνώσῃ (and gen. pl. τεθνήτων) *Ath.Mitt.* 50.134 (Macedonia); acc. pl. fem. τεθνώσας Babr.45.9]: from τέθνηκα arose fut. τεθνήξω Ar.*Ach.*325, A.*Ag.*1279 (censured as archaic by Luc.*Sol.*7), later τεθνήξομαι Diogenian.Epicur.1.28, 3.52, Luc.*Pisc.* 10, Ael.*NA* 2.46; part. τεθνηξόμενος Lib.*Ep.*438.7.—The simple Verb is regularly used in early Prose in pf. and plpf.; for pres., fut., and aor. the compd. ἀποθνῄσκω is substituted: θνῄσκει v.l. in Hp. *Mul.*1.9, σάρκες θνῄσκουσι *Art.*69, ἔθνησκον Th.2.47, al., θνησκόντων ib.53, θνῄσκοι Pl.*Phd.*72d, θνῄσκομεν Epicur.*Ep.*1 p.20 U.: aor. part. θανών, subj. θάνῃ, *IG* 12(5).593.2,20,23 (Iulis, v B.C.), *Berl.Sitzb.*1927. 166 (Cyrene), Phld.*Herc.*1649.4: aor. inf. θανεῖν ib.1418.13:—in pres. and impf., *die*, as well of natural as of violent death; in aor. and pf., *to be dead* (cf. τί τοὺς θανόντας οὐκ ἐᾷς τεθνηκέναι; Eup.12.3 D.; τέθνηκ' ἔγωγε πρὶν θανεῖν κακῶν ὕπο E.*Hec.*431), θανεῖν καὶ πότμον ἐπισπεῖν Il.7.52, etc.; ζωὸς ἠὲ θανών alive or *dead*, Od.4.553, cf. 15.350; ἢ ἤδη τέθνηκε 4.834; ὡς ἄμεινον εἴη τεθνάναι μᾶλλον ἢ ζώειν Hdt.1.31, cf. 7.46; τεθνάναι κρεῖττον ἤ.. D.9.65, cf. 10.25; ἄξιος τεθνάναι Ar.*Ra.* 1012, etc.; τεθνάτω *let* him *be put to death*, *IG* $1^{2}$.10.29; ἄτιμος τεθ. Lex ap.D.9.44: freq. in part., νέκυος πέρι τεθνηῶτος Il.18.173; νεκρὸν.. τεθνηῶτα a *dead* corpse, Od.12.10; οἱ τεθνηκότες, οἱ θανόντες, *the dead*, E.*Hec.*278, Eup. l.c., etc.; οὔτε τεθνεῶτα οὔτε ζῶντα Hdt.4.14; οἴχεται θανών (v. οἴχομαι); θανὼν φροῦδος (v. φροῦδος); θανόντι συνθανεῖν S.*Tr.*798, *Fr.*953, cf. E.*Supp.*1007 (lyr.); ὁ θανών, opp. ὁ κτανών, S. *Ph.*336: pres. with pf. sense, θνῄσκουσι γάρ, for τεθνήκασι, Id.*OT* 118, cf. E.*Hec.*695 (lyr.), *Ba.*1041 (lyr.), etc. **2.** used like a pass. Verb, χερσὶν ὑπ' Αἴαντος θανέειν *to fall* by his hand, Il.15.289; θ. ὑπό τινος Pl.*Ep.*329c, Arist.*HA* $625^{a}16$; ἔκ τινος Pi.*P.*4.72, S.*OT* 1454; πρός τινος ib.292, E.*Hec.*773; θεοῖς τέθνηκε S.*Aj.*970: freq. c. dat. instrumenti, θ. χερί, δορί, Id.*OC* 1388, A.*Th.*959 (lyr.); φαρμάκοισι E. *Fr.*464; also ἐν βρόχῳ A.*Ch.*558; τεθνάναι τῷ δέει, τ. τῷ φόβῳ, c. acc., *to be in mortal fear of*, D.4.45, 19.81, cf. Arr.*An.*7.9.4; προοίμιον σκοτεινὸν καὶ τεθνηκὸς δειλίᾳ Aeschin.2.34; θ. ἐπί τινι *to die* leaving one as heir, Luc.*DMort.*7.1. **II.** metaph., of things, *perish*, θνᾴσκει σιγαθὲν καλὸν ἔργον Pi.*Fr.*121; ἐσλῶν ὑπὸ χαρμάτων πῆμα θνᾴσκει.. δαμασθέν Id.*O.*2.19; λόγοι θνῄσκοντες μάτην A.*Ch.*846; θ. πίστις S. *OC* 611; τὸ τρύβλιον τέθνηκέ μοι Ar.*Ra.*986 (lyr.): in Prose, τέθνηκε τὸ τοὺς ἀδικοῦντας μισεῖν D.19.289; τεθνηκός τι φθέγξασθαι D.C.40.54; τεθνηκὸς δρᾶν Callistr.*Stat.*14; τὸ τεθνηκὸς ὁ λίθος ὑπεδύετο ib.2.

**θνητάδιος,** sine expl., Hdn.Gr.2.924: **θνητίδια,** = νεκριμαῖα, Hsch. (θνιτ- cod.).

⊛ **θνητο-γᾰμία,** ἡ, *marriage with a mortal*, Eust.20.17. **-γενής,** Dor. **θνᾱτ-,** ές, *of mortal race*, S.*Ant.*835 (anap.), E.*HF* 799 (lyr.). **-ειδής,** ές, *of mortal nature*, Pl.*Phd.*86a, Plu.2.1002c, Jul.*Or.*6.184a, etc.

⊛ **θνητός,** ή, όν, also ός, όν E.*Ion* 973, *IA* 901, 1396: Dor. **θνᾱτός** (v. infr.): Aeol. **θνᾶτος** Sapph.*Supp.*13.7: (θνῄσκω):—*liable to death, mortal*, opp. ἀθάνατος, freq. in Hom., Od.5.213, al.; θ. ἄνδρες Hes. *Th.*967; οὐδὲν.. θνητὸν ἐόν Hdt.8.98; ζῷα πάντα θ. καὶ φυτά Pl.*Sph.* 265c: as Subst., θνητοί *mortals*, Od.19.593, etc.; θνηταί *mortal women*, 5.213; πάντων τῶν θ. of all *mortal creatures*, Hdt.1.216, 2.68; εἴ τις φθόγγος (φθόγγον cod., but θ. is only used of living persons) εἰσακούεται θνητῶν παρ' Ἅιδῃ E.*HF* 491: Comp., ἐν θνητῷ ὄντες, ἔτι θνητοτέρους ἑαυτοὺς ποιοῦντες Porph.*Abst.*4.20: Sup., θνητότατος πάντων Plot.5.1.1. **2.** of things, *befitting mortals, human*, ἔργματα E.*Ba.* 1069; θνατὰ θνατοῖσι πρέπει Pi.*I.*5(4).16; θνατὰ χρὴ τὸν θνατὸν.. φρονεῖν Epich.[263], cf. S.*Tr.*473; τὸ δαιμόνιον μεταξύ ἐστι θεοῦ τε καὶ θνητοῦ Pl.*Smp.*202e.

**θνητότης,** ητος, ἡ, *mortality*, Diog.Oen.36, Phlp. *in APo.*400.28.

**θνητόψῡχος,** ον, *maintaining the mortality of the soul*, Tz.*H.*8.222.

**θοάζω** (A), (θοός (A)) trans., *move quickly, ply rapidly*, πτέρυγας E.

*IT* 1142 (lyr.); τίς ὅδ' ἀγών..θοάζων σε; what task is thus *hurrying* thee *on?* Id.*Or.*335; θοάζω Βρομίῳ πόνον ἡδύν *urge* it *on*, Id.*Ba.*65; θ. σῖτα γέννυσι *dispatch* it *quickly*, Id.*HF*382 (lyr.). 2. intr., *move quickly, rush, dart*, θοάζων αἰθέρος ἄνω καπνός Id.*Or.*1542; ἐν δὲ δασκίοις ὄρεσι θ. Id.*Ba.*219; θ. δρόμῳ Id.*Tr.*307; κῆτος θοάζον ἐξ Ἀτλαντικῆς ἁλός Id.*Fr.*145. (Cf. θέω, θοός (A).)

**θοάζω** (B), = θάασσω, *sit*, σοφίης ἐπ' ἄκροισι Emp.4.8; ὑπ' ἀρχᾶς οὔτινος θοάζων [Ζεὺς] κρατύνει A.*Supp.*595; τίνας ποθ' ἕδρας τάσδε μοι θοάζετε; why *are ye in* this *suppliant posture?* S.*OT*2, cf. Plu.2.22e. (Cf. ἐπιθοάζω, θόωκος, θῶκος; v. θάσσω.)

⊛ **θοάζω** (C), v. θῳάζω.

**θόαξος**· Ἀπόλλων, Hsch.

**θοάς**, ἄδος, ἡ, fem. Adj. *fleet, swift*, prob. in Pi.*Fr.*107.7.

**θόασμα**, ατος, τό, *a place for dancing*, etc., Orph.*H.*49.6.

**θοδράκιον**, v. θρόδαξ.

**θοηρός**· τεταραγμένος (i.e. θολερός), Hsch., *EM*453.20. **θοιά**, ἡ, *pair of mules*, Hsch., Theognost.*Can.*20. **θοίηβος**, ὁ, = θαῦμα, Cyr.; cf. θῆβος.

**θοιν-άζω**, rare form for θοινάω, X.*Ages.*8.7, Ael.*Fr.*267. **-ᾱμα**, ατος, τό, *meal, feast*, E.*Or.*814, *Ion* 1495 (both lyr.), Posidon.12 J. ⊛ **-αρμόστρια**, ἡ, *mistress of the banquet*, cult-title, esp. in the worship of Demeter and Kore, in Laconia and Messenia, *IG*5(1).584, 1498, etc.: spelt θυν- ib.583, σειναρμόστρηα ib.229. **-ᾱτήρ**, ῆρος, ὁ, *one who gives a feast*, χαλεπὸς θ. *lord of a* horrid *feast*, A.*Ag.*1502 (anap.). **-ᾱτήριον**, τό, = θοίνη, E.*Rh.*515. **-ᾱτικός**, ή, όν, *of* or *for a feast*, X.*Oec.*9.7 (v.l. -ητικός). **-άτωρ** [ᾱ], ορος, ὁ, *feaster*, E.*Ion* 1206, 1217. **-άω**, *feast on, eat*, δελφῖνες ἐθοίνων ἰχθῦς dub. l. in Hes.*Sc.*212. 2. Pass., *to be feasted upon*, i.e. *sacrificed*, ὗς τέλεος θοινῆται *IG*12(1).905 (Rhodes). II. *feast, entertain*, φίλους E.*Ion* 982; τὸ δεῖπνον, τό μιν ἐκεῖνος σαρξὶ τοῦ παιδὸς ἐθοίνησε (v.l. -ισε) the feast, which he *gave* him *upon* his son's flesh, Hdt.1.129. 2. more freq. in Med. and Pass., fut. -άσομαι E.*El.*836, *Cyc.*550, -ήσομαι (ἐκ-) A.*Pr.*1025 codd.: aor. 1 ἐθοινήθην (v. infr.): aor. 1 Med. -ησάμην Nonn.*D.*5.331, *AP*9.244 (Apollonid.): pf. τεθοίνᾱμαι E.*Cyc.*377 (prob.). a. abs., *to be feasted, feast, banquet*, once in Hom., ἐς δ' αὐτοὺς προτέρω ἄγε θοινηθῆναι lead them in *to feast*, Od.4.36; παρὰ κλαίουσι θοινᾶσθαι E.*Alc.*542: θ. καλῶς Cratin.164. b. c. acc., *feast on*, μῶν τεθοίναται ἑταίρους; E.*Cyc.*377; σὲ ὕστερον θοινάσομαι ib.550; θ. τὰ ζῷα Porph.*Abst.*2.2: c. acc. cogn., θ. παστήρια E.*El.*836: c. gen., ἅλις λεόντων ἐστί μοι θοινωμένῳ Id.*Cyc.*248; θοινήσατο θήρης *AP*9.244 (Apollonid.); of an *eating* sore, σάρκα θοινᾶται ποδός E.*Fr.*792, cf. Arist.*Po.*$1458^{b}24$: **-η**, Dor. **θοίνα** (later **θοῖνα** Lxx *Wi.*12.6, perh. to be read in Epich.148.1), ἡ, *meal, feast*, Hes.*Sc.*114, Hdt.1.119, 9.82, A.*Fr.*350.7, etc.: in pl., Id.*Pr.*530 (lyr.), B.*Fr.*18; τὰς θ. κὰτ τὰν ὥραν ἀπάγεσθαι *Michel*995 *D*50; θοίνης δὲ καὶ εἰλαπίνῃσι Thgn.239; ἐκ θοίνας after *dinner*, Epich.148.2; εἰς θ. καλεῖν τινα E.*Ion* 1140; ἐπὶ θοίνην ἰέναι Pl.*Phdr.*247a; παρακαλεῖν ἐπὶ τὴν θ. Arist.*Fr.*549; σκευαζομένης θ. Pl.*Tht.*178d, cf. Arist.*Pol.*$1282^{a}22$; τραπέζας ἱερὰς πρεπούσης θ. γεμίζων *OGI*383.146 (Commagene, i B.C.); ἐν θ. λέγειν τινά to count as a guest, and generally to take into account, Pl.*Lg.*649a: metaph., Id.*Sph.*251b, *Phdr.*236e, X.*Cyr.*4.2.39. II. *food*, πτανοῖς E.*Ion* 504, cf. Tim.*Pers.*150; θ. παντοδαπή Parth.12.2. 2. *feeding upon*, c. gen., τῶν σαρκῶν Porph.*Abst.*2.47. (Cf. θῶσθαι.) **-ήτωρ**, ορος, ὁ, = θοινάτωρ, *AP*7.241 (Antip. Sid.). **-ίζω**, v.l. for θοινάω (q.v.).

**θοινοδοτέω**, *entertain at a banquet*, *Supp.Epigr.*3.774 (Crete, i B.C./i A.D.).

**θοῖτο**, for θεῖτο, 3 opt. aor. 2 Med. of τίθημι.

**θολερεῖν**· ταραχίζεσθαι, Hsch.

⊛ **θολερ-ός**, ά, όν, (θολός) *muddy, foul, turbid*, opp. καθαρός or λαμπρός, prop. of troubled water, Hdt.4.53, Hp.*Aër.*8, Th.2.102; θ. καὶ πηλώδης Pl.*Phd.*113b: metaph., λαμπρὸν δὲ θολερῷ δῶμα συμμείξας E.*Supp.*222; θ. οὖρα Hp.*Epid.*1.7; ἀήρ Pl.*Ti.*58d (Sup. -ώτατος); αἷμα Arist.*Somn.Vig.*$458^{a}14$ (Sup.); χυμοί Thphr.*CP*6.3.4 (Comp.); νεφέλαι *AP*9.277 (Antiphil.): χρώς Ael.*NA*14.9; πλίνθος Theoc.16.62; δύσμορφον ἡ ὗς καὶ θολερόν Plu.2.670a. 2. θ. πνεῦμα dub. l. in Hp.*Prorrh.*1.39 (v. θαλερός). II. metaph., *troubled by passion* or *madness*, θολεροὶ λόγοι *troubled* words of passion (compared to a torrent), A.*Pr.*885 (anap.); θολερῷ χειμῶνι νοσήσας with *turbid* storm of madness, S.*Aj.*206 (anap.); θολερῷ κυνόδοντι with *passionate* tooth, Nic.*Th.*130 codd. (θαλερῷ cj. Schneider). Adv. -ρῶς dub. in *Com.Adesp.*865. **-ότης**, ητος, ἡ, *turbidity*, Hp.*Epid.*2.3.11.

**θολερόφρον**· μέγα, Hsch.

**θολερώδης**, ες, dub. l. for θολώδης, Thphr.*Ign.*24.

**θολία** (Lacon. **σαλία** Hsch.), ἡ, (θόλος) *conical hat with broad brim*, or perh. *parasol*, Theoc.15.39. II. *chest with conical lid*, Poll.10.138; cf. θαλιοποιοί.

**θολικός**, ή, όν, *with a dome*, στοά Suid. s. v. Δαμιανός.

**θολο-ειδής**, ές, *like a* θόλος, Callix.1, Str.4.4.3; of the Roman Pantheon, D.C.53.27. Adv. -δῶς, κοιλανθεῖσα Dsc.4.153, cf. D.L.2.9. 2. *like a* θολία, cj. Scal. for θηλοειδῆ in Thphr.*HP*3.9.6 (fort. θολιοειδής). **-μῐγής**, ές, *mixed with dirt*, Onat.ap.Stob.1.1.39.

⊛ **θόλος**, ἡ, *round building with conical roof, rotunda*, Od.22.442, al., cf. Hsch. 2. at Athens, *the Rotunda*, in which the Prytaneis, etc., dined, Pl.*Ap.*32c, And.1.45, D.19.249, Arist.*Ath.*43.3, Alexand. Com.9, Paus.1.5.1; a similar building at Epidaurus, Id.2.27.3; at Magnesia on Maeander, *SIG*589.43 (ii B.C.). II. θόλος, ὁ, in public baths, *vaulted vapour-bath*, *PMagd.*33.3 (iii B.C.), Asclep.Myrl. ap.Ath.11.501d, Alciphr.1.23, *POxy.*2145.6 (ii A.D.), *PMag.Osl.*1.75. 2. *bandage* for the head, invented by Diocles, Heliod.ap. Orib.48.25 tit.

**θολ-ός** (A), ὁ, *mud, dirt*, esp. in water, Arist.*Fr.*311. 2. *menses*, Orph.*L.*490. II. *ink of the cuttle-fish*, Hp.*Morb.*2.73, Arist.*HA*$524^{a}13$, al. (v.l. θορόν in $544^{a}4$). 2. *the vessel in which this ink is retained*, Id.*PA*$679^{a}1$, $681^{b}26$.—On the accent, v. Hdn.Gr.1.154. **-ός** (B), ή, όν, = θολερός, Ath.10.420d, Olymp.*in Mete.*127.13, cf. Hsch. **-όω**, *make turbid*, prop. of water, θ. ἅπαντα, of the cuttle-fish, Antiph.26.2; of fishermen, Arist.*Fr.*311:—Pass., τεθολωμένα ὕδατα Hp.*Aër.*7; τεθ. ἀήρ Philyll.20. 2. metaph., θολοῖ δὲ καρδίαν E.*Alc.*1067; τεθολωμένος *confounded* by joy, Pherecr.115; θολοῦσθαί τι τῶν σπλάγχνων Philostr.*VA*8.7; γένος..τεθολωμένον γειτόνημα Procop.*Goth.*4.19. II. *soak*, σπόγγοις διὰ ψυχροῦ ὕδατος..τεθολωμένοις Orib.8.6.36. **-ώδης**, ες, *muddy, turbid*, of water, Hp.*Aër.*8 (Sup. -έστατος); ἐν τοῖς ἀμμώδεσι ἢ θολώδεσι Arist.*HA*$620^{b}16$; also θ. καπνός Vett.Val.345.21; πῦρ Iamb.*Myst.*2.4. **-ωσις**, εως, ἡ, *making turbid, troubling*, esp. of water, Arist.*PA*$679^{a}7$; also ἀέρος Gal.16.609.

**θολωτός**, ή, όν, *built like a* θόλος, τεῖχος Procop.*Aed.*4.11.

**θονανία**· ὀξεῖα, Hsch. (fort. θοὴ ἀνία).

⊛ **θοός** (A), ή, όν, (θέω) poet. Adj. *quick, nimble*, epith. of Ares and warriors, Il.5.430, 571, 16.422, 494, etc.: c. inf., θ. μάχεσθαι 5.536; of things, χείρ 12.306; βέλος Od.22.83; ἅρμα Il.17.458; μάστιξ ib.430; νῆες 14.410, etc.; νηυσὶ θοῇσι..πεποιθότες ὠκείῃσι Od.7.34; νύξ *swift* night, Il.10.394, Od.12.284, Hes.*Th.*481; θοὴν ἀλεγύνετε δαῖτα partake of a *hasty* meal, i.e. *in haste*, Od.8.38; later, of animals, Pi.*P.*4.17, E.*Ba.*977 (lyr.); also μάχαι Pi.*P.*8.26; γλῶσσα Id.*N.*7.72; θοὰ βάξις A.*Ag.*476 (lyr.); θ. εἰρεσίας ζυγόν S.*Aj.*249 (lyr.), cf. Orph.*A.*1037; πτέρυξ E.*Ion* 123 (lyr.), cf. A.*Pr.*129 (lyr.); σάκος A.R.1.743; ἀσπίδας..θοὸν ἔχμα βολάων Id.4.201; πνοαί, αὖραι, E.*Andr.*479 (lyr.), *Tr.*454 (troch.): used adverbially with Verbs of motion, ἐκπρολιποῦσα θοὸν δόμον *quickly, in haste*, Antim.71 (expld. by *An.Ox.* from τίθημι); θοὰν νύμφαν ἄγαγες S.*Tr.*857 (lyr.). Adv. -ῶς *quickly, in haste*, Il.3.325, B.14.59, A.*Pr.*1060 (anap.), *Pers.*398, Hp.*Mul.*2.132; θοώτερον A.R.3.1406; *soon*, Od.15.216.

⊛ **θοός** (B), ή, όν, *pointed, sharp*, νῆσοι, name of certain of the Echinades (acc. to Str.8.3.26), Od.15.299; so later θ. γόμφοι, ὀδόντες, πελέκεις, A.R.2.79, 3.1281, 4.1683; ξίφος *AP*9.157; cf. sq.

⊛ **θοόω**, (θοός B) *make sharp* or *pointed*, Od.9.327; τεθοωμένος Nic.*Th.*228. II. metaph., in Pass., ἐν πυρὶ φωνὴν τεθοωμένος Hermesian.7.11; λύσσῃ τεθοωμένος Opp.*H.*1.557, 2.525.

**θοραῖος**, α, ον, (θορός) *containing the semen*, πηρίν Nic.*Th.*586; ὁ θοραῖος, epith. of Apollo as *god of growth and increase*, Lyc.352.

⊛ **θοράνας**· τὸ ἔξω (Paph.), Hsch.

**Θοράτης**, ὁ, title of Apollo in Laconia, Hsch. (-τις cod.).

**θόρε, θορεῖν**, v. θρῴσκω.

⊛ **θορή**, ἡ, = θορός, Hdt.3.101, Alcmaeon *Fr.*3 D.

**Θορῐκόνδε**, Adv. *to Thoricus*, *h.Cer.*126.

**θορικός**, ή, όν, *of* or *for the semen*, πόροι θ. *ductus seminales*, Arist.*GA*$720^{b}13$, al.; [τὰ] θορικά *partes seminales*, ib.$755^{b}20$; τροφὴ θ. Ruf.*Sat.Gon.*12.

**θορινεῦσαι**· ὁ ξιφίας ἰχθύς, Hsch.

**θορίσκομαι**, Pass., *receive semen*, διὰ τῶν ὤτων Ant.Lib.29.3.

**θόρισμα**, ατος, τό, *bait* for fish, Hsch. **θόρναξ**· ὑποπόδιον (Cypr.), Id. (metath. of *θρόναξ).

⊛ **θόρνυμαι**, = θρῴσκω II, [S.]*Fr.*1127.9, Nic.*Th.*130: 3 pl. subj., ἐπεὰν θορνύωνται Hdt.3.109.

**θορό-εις**, εσσα, εν, *in embryo*, βρέφος θ. Opp.*C.*3.522. **-ποιός**, όν, gloss on θοῦρις, *EM*453.51 (v.l. φθορο-, θυρο-).

**θορός**, ὁ, *semen genitale*, Hdt.2.93, Hp.*Morb.*2.51, Arist.*HA*$509^{b}20$, Plu.2.637f, Porph.*Abst.*4.9. II. θορός· ἀφροδισιαστής, Hsch.

**θόρραξ**, v. θώραξ.

**θορῠβ-άζομαι**, Pass., *to be troubled*, *Ev.Luc.*10.41 (v.l. τυρβάζῃ): Act. in Gramm., Dosith.p.432 K., *EM*633.34. ⊛ **-έω**, *make a noise, uproar* or *disturbance*, esp. of crowds, assemblies, etc., Hp.*Ep.*12, Ar.*Eq.*666, *V.*622, etc.; βλέπων εἰς τὸν ἀεὶ θορυβοῦντα τόπον τῆς ἐκκλησίας D.21.194. 2. *shout in token of approbation* or *the contrary*: a. *cheer, applaud*, Isoc.12.264, Pl.*Euthd.*303b:—Pass., λόγος τεθορυβημένος a *loudly cheered* speech, Isoc.12.233, cf. Arist.*Rh.*$1356^{b}23$. b. more freq. *raise clamour*, καί μοι μὴ θορυβήσητε pray *do* not *interrupt*, Pl.*Ap.*20e, cf. D.5.15; θ. ἐφ' οἷς ἂν λέγω Pl.*Ap.*30c; ὁ θορυβῶν, opp. ὁ θέλων λέγειν καὶ ἀκούειν, And.4.7:—Pass., *have clamours raised against one*, ὑπὸ τοιούτων ἀνδρῶν θορυβῇ S.*Aj.*164 (anap.). II. trans., *confuse by noise* or *tumult, bewilder*, Pl.*Phdr.*245b, *Prt.*319c, al.; *throw* [troops] *into confusion*, in battle, Th.3.78; θ. πρός τινας *cause excitement* amongst.., Id.6.61:—Pass., *to be thrown into disorder, confused*, Hdt.3.78, 4.130, Th.4.129, 8.50, Pl.*Ep.*348e, etc.; ὑπὸ τῶν λεγομένων Id.*Ly.*210e; τινι at a thing, D.18.35; ἐπί τινι Bato 7.2; περί τι Th.6.61; πρός τι Plu.*Cam.*29. **-ηθρον**, τό, = λεοντοπέταλον, Ps.-Dsc.3.96. **-ητικός**, ή, όν, *uproarious, turbulent*, Ar.*Eq.*1380.

**θορῠβοποι-έω**, *make an uproar*, Cic.*Fam.*16.23.2, D.S.13.111, App.*BC*2.74. **-ός**, όν, *making an uproar, turbulent*, πλῆθος Plu.*Mar.*28.

**θόρῠβ-ος**, ὁ, *noise*, esp. *the confused noise of a crowded assembly, uproar, clamour*, Pi.*O.*10(11).72, Th.8.92, etc.; θόρυβος βοῆς a confused clamour, S.*Ph.*1263; θ. στρατιωτῶν Ar.*Ach.*546; θ. Πυκνίτης *Com.Adesp.*45 D.; θ. παρέχειν ἐν ταῖς βουλαῖς καὶ ἐν ταῖς ἐκκλησίαις *OGI*48.9 (Ptolemais, iii B.C.); less freq. of an individual, E.*Or.*905;

of animals, θόρυβον δ' οὐκ ἐφίλησαν ὄνων Call.*Aet.Oxy.*2079.30. 2. esp. in token of approbation or the contrary, Pl.*R.*492b,c: a. *applause*, θ. Ληναΐτης Ar.*Eq.*547; θ. καὶ ἔπαινος Pl.*Prt.*339d, D.19. 195; θόρυβον καὶ κρότον ἐποιήσατε Id.21.14. b. *groans, murmurs*, And.2.15; μεγάλοι θόρυβοι κατέχουσ' ἡμᾶς great *murmurs* are abroad among us, S.*Aj.*142 (anap.). II. *tumult, confusion*, θ. παρασχεῖν τινι Hdt.7.181; ἐς θ. ἀπικέσθαι, καταστῆναι, Id.8.56, Th.4.104; ἐγένετο ὁ θ. μέγας, in a battle, ib.14; κραυγὴ καὶ θ. Phld.*Hom.*p.22 O.: pl., θ. ὀχλώδεις καὶ παροινίαι Men.*Mon.*239. 2. *confusion* of mind, θορύβους ἐνθυμηματικοὺς καὶ ἀποφθεγματικοὺς παρασκευάζειν Epicur. *Nat.*14.9; ὁ παρὰ κακὰς δόξας θ. Phld.*Rh.*2.31 S., cf. 40 S. III. c. inf., ἐς θόρυβον ἦλυθον.. λευσθῆναι I ran a *risk* of being stoned, E. *IA* 1349 (troch.). (Perh. cogn. with τονθορύζω.) **-ώδης**, ες, *uproarious, turbulent*, Pl.*Lg.*671a; *clamorous*, -ῶδες φθέγγεσθαι Arist. *HA* 632ᵇ18; θορυβώδεα ἐνυπνιάζεσθαι Hp.*VM* 10. Adv. -δῶς Poll. 5.123, Iamb.*Myst.*3.25 (prob.): Comp. -έστερον, διατίθενται Plu.2. 656f. II. *causing alarm*, τῷ ἵππῳ θ. μηδὲν προσφέρειν X.*Eq.*9. 15. 2. *confusing*, δόξαι Demetr.Lac.*Herc.*1696.4.

**θορώδης**, ες, = θοραῖος, Gal.4.556, al.

**θοῦ**, aor. 2 imper. Med. of τίθημι.

**θουρ-αῖος**, α, ον, = θοῦρος, *violent, lustful*, Hsch.:—fem. **θουράς**, άδος, Nic.*Th.*131, Lyc.612. ❀ **-άω**, *rush* or *leap upon*, c. acc., Id. 85:—also **θουριῶν**· ἐνεργῶν, Hsch. **-ήεις**, εσσα, εν, = θουραῖος, Id. **-ης**, ου, ὁ, *male*, of animals, Id. (s. v. l.). **-ηταῖς**· αἱ τῶν ζῴων μίξεις, Id. **-ητρα**· ὀχεῖα, Id.

**Θουριό-μαντις**, εως, ὁ, *a Thurian prophet*, of the *seer* Lampon, Ar. *Nu.*332 (pl.); v. Sch. ad loc. **-πέρσαι**, οἱ, title of play by Metagenes, Ath.6.270a.

❀ **θούριος**, α, ον, in Trag. (Com. in lyr.), = θοῦρος, λοχαγέται ἄρχων, A.*Th.*42, *Pers.*73 (lyr.); ὄρνις, τόξα, Id.*Ag.*112 (lyr.), *Eu.*627; Αἴας S.*Aj.*212 (anap.); λῆμα Ar.*Eq.*757 (lyr.).

**θοῦρις**, ιδος, ἡ, fem. of sq. (q. v.): in pl. **θούριδες**· νύμφαι, Μοῦσαι (Maced.), Hsch.

**θοῦρος**, ον, (θρῴσκω) *rushing, impetuous, furious*, Hom. (only in Il.), as epith. of Ares, 15.127, al. (of the planet Mars, Doroth.ap. Heph.Astr.1.1); Τυφῶν A.*Pr.*356, cf. *Fr.*199; δόρυ E.*Rh.*492; ἀνὴρ Γαλάτης *Eleg.Alex.Adesp.*2.14:—fem. **θοῦρις**, ιδος, ἡ, epith. of ἀλκή, Od.4.527, Il.7.164, al.; θ. ἀσπίς, prob. the shield *with which one rushes to the fight*, 11.32; αἰγίς 15.308.

**θούσχοινοι** ἢ **θόσχοινοι**· ἅρπαγες, πλανῆτες, Hsch.

**θόωκος**, ὁ, Ep. form of θῶκος; v. θᾶκος.

**θόωσα**, ἡ, (θοός A) *speedy, swift*, as pr. n., Od.1.71, Emp.122.3.

❀ **θραγμός**, ὁ, *crackling*, κυάμων ἐρεικομένων S.E.*P.*1.58; cf. θραύω.

**θράζω**, aor. 1 ἔθρᾶσα, = θραύω, Tz.*H.*9.34.

**θραίειν**· λοιδορεῖν (Lacon.), Hsch.

**Θρᾴκ-η**, ἡ, *Thrace*, Ar.*Ach.*136, Th.1.59, etc.: Ion. **Θρηΐκη** Hdt. 2.134, al.; Ep. and Trag. contr. **Θρῄκη** Il.13.301, A.*Pers.*509, etc.:—**Θρῄκηθεν**, *from Thrace*, Il.9.5,72: **Θρῄκηνδε**, *to Thrace*, Od.8. 361. **-ίας** (sc. ἄνεμος), ὁ, = Θρασκίας (q. v.). 2. (sc. λίθος) stone said to take fire in water, Dsc.5.129, cf. Plin.*HN* 33.94. **-ίζω**, *speak Thracian dialect*, A.D.*Adv.*162.4, St.Byz. s. v. Θρᾴκη. **-ικός**, ή, όν, = sq., Luc.*JTr.*21. ❀ **-ιος**, α, ον, *Thracian*, Th.5.10, etc.: Ion. **Θρηΐκιος**, η, ον, Il.10.559, Hdt.1.168 codd.:—contr. **Θρῄκιος**, α, ον (-ος, ον E.*Fr.*369.4 (lyr.)), A.*Ag.*654, E.*Hec.*36:—Σάμος Θρηϊκίη, = Σαμοθράκη, Il.13.13. [Θρηῑκιος Hom.; Θρηῐκιος Phanocl.1.1, A.R.4. 905.] **-ιστί**, Adv. *in Thracian fashion*, κέκαρμαι Theoc.14. 46. II. *in the Thracian dialect*, Str.7.6.1, H.D.*Adv.*162.4.

**Θρᾳκοφοίτης**, ου, ὁ, *one who keeps going to Thrace*, formed like 'Αιδοφοίτης, Ar.*Fr.*149.7.

**θρακτικόν**· πορευτόν, and **θραξεῖται**· πορεύσεται, Hsch.: dial. forms for θρεκτ-, θρεξ-. **θραμβόν**· καπυρόν, Id. **θράμις**· κριός, Id.

**θρᾰνεύομαι**, Pass. with fut. Med. -εύσομαι, (θρᾶνος) *to be stretched on the tanner's board, tanned*, Ar.*Eq.*369; also, *to be crushed*, Hsch., Phot.

**θρᾰνίας**, ου, ὁ, a kind of fish, ξιφίαι θρανίαι τε Marcell.Sid.29 (cf. θρανίς):—also **θρανίαι**· θρόμβοι, Hsch.

❀ **θρᾰν-ίδιον**, τό, Dim. of θρᾶνος, Ar.*Fr.*309. **-ίον**, τό, = foreg., Id.*Ra.*121, Ael.*NA* 16.33; *the rower's bench*, Poll.1.94 (pl., with v. l. θρανεῖα). 2. *close-stool*, Hsch. 3. = θρᾶνος II. 1, 2, Id.

❀ **θρᾰνίς**, ίδος, ἡ, *sword-fish*, = ξιφίας, Xenocr.17; cf. θρανίας.

❀ **θρᾰν-ίτης** [ῑ], ου, ὁ, (θρᾶνος) *rower on the topmost of the three benches* in a trireme, Th.6.31, Ar.*Ach.*162, cf. Sch.Ar.*Ra.*1106. II. Adj. *of the topmost bench*, σκαλμὸς θ. the *topmost* bench, Plb.16.3.4: fem. **θρᾰνῖτις** κώπη the oar *of a* θρανίτης, *IG* 2².1604.52 (pl.), *EM* 454. 12 (pl.). **-ῑτικός**, ή, όν, *of a* θρανίτης, κώπη Callix.1.

**θραννομένη**· προορῶσα, Hsch.

❀ **θρᾰνογράφος** [γρᾰ], ὁ, = τοιχογράφος, Plb.15.25.32, Hsch.

❀ **θρᾶνος**, ὁ, (θράομαι) *bench, form*, Ar.*Pl.*545 (gen. θράνους codd., θράνου Poll.). 2. *close-stool*, Hp.ap.Gal.19.104. II. Archit., 1. *wooden beam*, ὅσα κατέρρωγεν τοῦ τείχους ἐνδήσει θράνοις *IG* 2².463.75; θράνους ἐπιθήσει διανεκεῖς, of *beams* supporting floors, ib.1668.81, cf. 1672.208. 2. ὁ θ. τοῦ νεώ the *top course* of masonry in a temple, ib.11(2).161 *A* 49 (Delos, iii B. C.); θ. ποικίλος *PCair.Zen.*445.5 (iii B. C.).

**θρᾶνυξ**, v. θρῆνυξ.

**θρᾰνύσσω**, *break in pieces*, Lyc.664. (Cf. συνθρανόω, prob. cogn. with θραύω.)

❀ **Θρᾷξ**, Θρᾳκός, ὁ, *Thracian*: Ep. and Ion. **Θρήϊξ**, ϊκος [ῐ, but ῑ in Nic.*Th.*49, Call.*Aet.Oxy.*2079.13, A.R.1.24,632, etc.], Il.4.533, Hdt.1.28, etc.: Ep. and Trag. contr. **Θρῇξ**, Θρῃκός, Il.24.234, etc., to be read for Θρᾷξ in E.*Hec.*428, *Fr.*360.48; Ion. dat. pl. Θρήϊξιν [⏑ – ⏑] Archil.*Supp.*4.48:—fem. **Θρᾷσσα** (q. v.).

**θρᾶξαι, θρᾶξον**, v. θράσσω.

**θράομαι** (cf. θρᾶνος), *to be seated*, in Ion. aor. 1 Med. θρήσασθαι, πλατάνῳ γ(ρ)αίῃ ὕπο Philet.14.

**θράσις**, εως, ἡ, = θραῦσις, Hsch. **θράσκειν**· ἀναμιμνήσκειν, Id.

**Θρασκίας**, ου, ὁ, *the wind from NNW.*, Arist.*Mete.*363ᵇ29, *Mu.* 394ᵇ30, Thphr.*Vent.*42, Agathem.2.7, Lyd.*Mag.*3.32:—written **Θρακίας**, Arist.*Vent.*973ᵇ17, Thphr.*Sign.*35; **Θρᾳκίας** *IG* 14.1308: —hence **θρασκικός**, ή, όν, *facing NNW.*, of windows, Zos.Alch. p.141 B.

**θράσος** [ᾰ], εος, τό, (θρασύς) = θάρσος (q. v.), *courage*, Il.14.416, A. *Pers.*394, E.*Med.*469, Ar.*Lys.*545 (lyr.); θ. πολέμων *courage* in war, Pi.*P.*2.63; θράσει *boldly*, B.16.63; but more freq. ἰσχύος θ. *confidence* in strength, S.*Ph.*104. II. in bad sense, *over-boldness, rashness, insolence*, ἐς τοῦτο θράσεος (v. l. θάρσεος) ἀνήκει Hdt.7.9.γ', cf. A.*Pr.*42, D.21.194, etc.; παμμάχῳ θράσει βρύων A.*Ag.*169 (lyr.), cf. *Pers.*831; προβᾶσ' ἐπ' ἔσχατον θράσους S.*Ant.*853 (lyr.); τόλμαις καὶ φρενῶν θράσει Id.*Aj.*46; πεπύργωσαι θράσει E.*Or.*1568; πανουργίᾳ τε καὶ θράσει Ar. *Eq.*331, cf. 637; θράσει ἀπίστῳ ἐπαιρόμενος Th.1.120; τοῦ θράσους ἐπισχεῖν τινα Pl.*Hp.Ma.*298a; τὸ τὴν τοῦ βελτίονος δόξαν μὴ φοβεῖσθαι διὰ θράσος Id.*Lg.*701b; ἀναίδεια καὶ θ. Aeschin.1.189; opp. αἰδώς, Arist.*Cael.*291ᵇ26; θράσος μὲν γάρ ἐστιν ἄλογος ὁρμή, θάρσος δὲ ἔλλογος ὁρμή Ammon.*Diff.*p.71 V.; οἷον πέπονθε τὸ θάρσος πρὸς τὸ θράσος Arist.*EE* 1234ᵇ12, cf. Eus.Mynd.56, Luc.*Musc.Enc.*5.—This distn. holds good in Att. Prose: θάρσος is not found in Com.; θαρσύνω and θρασύνω are used indifferently; θρασέω and θαρσύς are not found; cf. θρασύς fin., θρασύτης.

**Θρᾷσσα**, ἡ, Att. **Θρᾷττα**, Trag. **Θρῇσσα**, fem. of Θρᾷξ, S.*Ant.*589, E.*Alc.*967 (both lyr.): **Θρηΐσσα** λᾶας, = Θρᾳκίας λίθος, Nic.*Th.*45:—esp. as Subst., *Thracian slave-girl*, Ar.*Ach.*273, Pl.*Tht.*174a, etc.: **Θραΐσσα** [ᾰ] Theoc.*Ep.*20.1; Ion. **Θρέϊσσα** Herod.1.79.

**θράσσω**, Att. **θράττω**, pres. part. neut. θρᾶττον Pl.*Phd.*86e: aor. 1 inf. θρᾶξαι A.*Pr.*628, E.*Fr.*600:—*trouble, disquiet*, Pi.*I.*7(6).39, A. l. c., Cratin.363, Pherecr.39, S.*Fr.*177, Hp.*Mul.*1.70, E.*Rh.*863, Pl. l. c., *Phdr.* 242c, etc.:—Pass., ὑπὸ ἐδωδῆς θράττεσθαι Jul.*Or.*6.192a: aor. 1 ἐθράχθη S.*Fr.*1055. 2. *disturb, destroy*, *APl.*4.255. 3. for pf. τέτρηχα, v. ταράσσω II.

**θρασύ-βουλος** [ῠ], ον, *bold in counsel*, Arist.*Rh.*1400ᵇ19. **-γλωσσής**, ές, *bold of tongue*, Man.4.184. **-γλωττία**, ἡ, *boldness of tongue*, Poll.2.108. **-γυιος**, ον, *strong of limb*, Κλειτομάχοιο νίκα θ. Pi.*P.*8.37. **-δειλος**, ὁ, ἡ, *impudent coward, braggart, poltroon*, Arist.*EN* 1115ᵇ32, Vett.Val.40.14. II. name of a gem, Ps.-Plu. *Fluv.*17.2. **-εργός**, όν, *bold of deed*, Nonn.*D.*35.365. **-θῡμος**, ον, *bold-hearted*, Man.4.529; cf. θρασύμυθος. **-κάρδιος**, ον, *bold of heart*, Il.10.41, 13.343, Hes.*Sc.*448, Anacr.1.5, B.19.5. **-λογέω**, *speak boldly*, Sch.rec.S.*Aj.*1258. **-λόγος**, ον, *bold of speech*, *EM* 133.42. **-μᾰχος**, ον, *bold in battle*, Arist.*Rh.*1400ᵇ20: as pr. n., *Thrasymachus*:—hence Adj. **-μάχειος**, α, ον, ἑρμηνεία style *of T.*, D.H.*Dem.*3. **-μέμνων**, ον, gen. ονος, (θρασύς, Skt. *mánma*, OIr. *menma* 'spirit', cf. 'Αγαμέμνων) *brave-spirited*, epith. of Heracles, Il. 5.639, Od.11.267; of Meleager, B.5.69. **-μήδης**, ες, *bold of thought* or *plan, daring, resolute*, Pi.*P.*4.143, *N.*9.13, B.15.15:—in Hom. only as pr. n. **-μητις**, ιδος, ὁ, ἡ, = foreg., *AP* 6.324 (Leon. Alex.). ❀ **-μήχᾰνος**, Dor. **-μάχᾰνος** [μᾱ], ον, *bold in contriving, daring in design*, 'Ηρακλέης Pi.*O.*6.67; λέοντες Id.*N.*4.62. **-μῦθος**, ον, *bold of tongue, saucy*, Id.*O.*13.10 (v. l. -θυμος).

**θρᾰσῦνος** [ᾰ], = θρασύς, *EM* 204.17.

**θρᾰσύνω**, (θρασύς) = θαρσύνω, *embolden, encourage*, A.*Ag.*222 (lyr.); πλήθει τὴν ἀμαθίαν θρασύνοντες *lending courage to* their ignorance by number, Th.1.142. 2. c. acc., *boast of*, τὴν ἰσηγορίαν Plb.4. 31.4. II. Pass. and Med., aor. 1 inf. θρασυνθῆναι A.*Supp.*772; ἐθρασυνάμην Isoc.4.12, Ph.2.557:—*to be bold, confident, take courage*, A.*Ag.*1188, etc.; οὐ.. ἀλόγως θρασυνόμεθα Th.5.104; πρὶν ὅρμῳ ναῦν θρασυνθῆναι before the ship *had got confidence in* her moorings, A. *Supp.* l. c.; ἐπί τι *make a bold bid* for.., Philostr.*VS* 2.33.2; θ. τι πρός τινα *carry out a coup de main* against, Aen.Tact.9.1; more freq., 2. in bad sense, *to be over-bold, over-confident*, S.*Ph.*1387, E.*Hec.*1183, Ar.*Ra.*846, D.18.136; ἀλόγως Polystr.p.30 W.; ἐπί τινι Ar.*Ach.* 330; ᾐσχύνοντο ἐφ' οἷς ἐθρασύναντο Isoc.5.23; πρός τι Plu.2.794d, Luc.*Apol.*6; ἔκ τινων Polystr.p.22 W.: c. dat., λαιμαργία ἀθεότητι θρασυνομένη Plu.2.1125a.

**θρᾰσυ-ξενία**, ἡ, *the boldness of a stranger*, Pl.*Lg.*879e. **-πονος**, ον, *bold* or *ready for toil*, ἀκμαὶ ἰσχύος Pi.*O.*1.96. ❀ **-πτόλεμος**, ον, *bold in war*, *IG* 9(1).871 (Corc.).

❀ **θρᾰσύς**, εῖα, ύ, fem. θρασέα, metri gr., Philem.20 (s. v. l.):—*bold*, chiefly of persons, Il.8.89, etc.; also θ. πόλεμος 6.254, 10.28, Od.4. 146; θρασειάων ἀπὸ χειρῶν 5.434, Il.17.662, al.; θ. καρδία Pi.*P.*10.44; πούς Ar.*Ra.*330 (lyr.); ἐν τῷ ἔργῳ θρασύς Hdt.7.49; ἡ ἐλπὶς θρασεῖα τοῦ μέλλοντος *full of confidence*, Th.7.77; θρασὺς τὸ ἦθος Arist.*Pol.*1315ᵃ 11. 2. more freq. in bad sense, *over-bold, rash*, σὺν δ' ὁ θ. εἴπετ' 'Οδυσσεύς Od.10.436 (Sch. προπετής); Γοργόνες Pi.*P.*12.7; *audacious, arrogant, insolent*, A.*Pr.*180 (lyr.), Ar.*Nu.*445 (anap.), etc.; Ἄρης.. πρὸς ἀλλήλους θ., of civil war, A.*Eu.*863; γλώσσῃ θ. S.*Aj.*1142; ἐν τοῖς λόγοις Id.*Ph.*1307; ἐπὶ τῶν λόγων D.*Prooem.*32; ἀνομίᾳ θ. E.*IT* 275; πονηρὸς εἶ καὶ θ. Ar.*Eq.*181; θρασεῖς καὶ ἄδικοι καὶ ὑβρισταί Pl.*Lg.* 630b; ἀλαζὼν ὁ θ. καὶ προσποιητικὸς ἀνδρείας Arist.*EN* 1115ᵇ29; [ὅμοιόν τι ἔχει] ὁ θ. τῷ θαρραλέῳ ib.1151ᵇ7; τὸ μὴ θ. modesty, A.*Supp.*197:

Comp. -ύτερος Pl.*La.*184b, Phld.*Lib.*p.61 O.: Sup. -ύτατος Isoc.12.133, etc. II. of things, *to be ventured*, c. inf., θρασύ μοι τόδ' εἰπεῖν this I am *bold* to say, Pi.*N.*7.50; οὐκ ἆρ' ἐκείνῳ γ' οὐδὲ προσμεῖξαι θρασύ; S.*Ph.*106. III. Adv. -έως Ar.*V.*1031, etc.: Aeol. **θρο-σέως** Jo.Gramm.*Comp.*2.1: Comp. θρασύτερον *too boldly*, Th.8.103; -τέρως Phalar.*Ep.*34: Sup. θρασύτατα Th.8.84 and (with v.l. -άτως) D.S.17.44: neut. as Adv., ἀναιδὲς καὶ θρασὺ βλέπειν Cratin.24 D. (I.-E. *dhers-* in θέρσος (older than θάρσος and θράσος), *dhr̥s-* in θρασύς, Skt. *dhr̥ṣú-*, *dhr̥ṣṇú-* 'bold', cf. Engl. *dare*, *durst*.)

**θρᾰσύσπλαγχνος**, ον, *bold-hearted*, E.*Hipp.*424. Adv. -ως A.*Pr.*730.

**θρᾰσυστομ-έω**, *to be over-bold of tongue*, A.*Supp.*203, S.*Ph.*380, E.*Hec.*1286. -ία, ἡ, *insolence*, *AP*12.141 (Mel.). -ος, ον, *over-bold of tongue*, *insolent*, A.*Th.*612, *Ag.*1399, E.*Fr.*3.

**θρᾰσύτης**, ητος, ἡ, *over-boldness*, Hp.*Lex*4, Th.2.61, Lys.3.45; θ., = τὸ σφόδρα θαρρεῖν, Arist.*Rh.*1390ᵃ31, cf. *EN*1108ᵇ31: pl., Isoc.4.77; ἀνδρεῖαι καὶ θ. D.*Prooem.*45.

**θρᾰσύ-τολμος** [ῠ], ον, *bold*, *Cat.Cod.Astr.*8(4).212. -φρων, ον, gen. ονος, *bold of mind*, Opp.*H.*1.112. -φωνία, ἡ, = θρασυστομία, Poll.2.112. ⊛ -φωνος, ον, = θρασύστομος, ibid. -χάρμης, ου, ὁ, *bold in fight*, Q.S.4.502. -χειρ, χειρος, ὁ, ἡ, *bold of hand*, *AP*7.234 (Phil.); θ. μ[άχ]α, of boxing, B.2.4; in bad sense, θ. καὶ μιαίφονος Id.*Scol.Oxy.*1361 *Fr.*5.10, = *Scol.Oxy.*2081(*e*)10. -χειρία, ἡ, *boldness of hand*, Poll.2.148.

**Θρᾰσώ**, όος, contr. οῦς, ἡ, *Bold*, name of Athena, Lyc.936.

**Θράσων**, ωνος, ὁ, a name of a *braggart* soldier in New Com.

**Θρᾶττα**, ης, ἡ, Att. for Θρῇσσα.

⊛ **θρᾷττα**, ἡ, *a small sea-fish*, Arist.*GA*785ᵇ23, Antiph.211, Mnesim.4.41:—Dim. **θραττίδιον**, τό, Anaxandr.27.

**θράττης**· ὁ λίθος, ὑπὸ Θρᾳκῶν, Hsch.; cf. Θρακίας. **θράττον**· ὕπερον, κόλουρον, Id. **θράττω**, Att. for θράσσω. **θραῦλος**, η, ον, *frangible*, *brittle*, Anon.ap.Suid. (Comp.):—also **θραῦρος**, Hsch.

**θραῦμα**, ατος, τό, (θραύω) *fragment*, A.*Pers.*425, *IG*7.3498.23 (Oropus, iii/ii B.C.), D.S.3.12. II. *breakage*, Jul.*Or.*2.60a. III. *destruction*, ἐχθρῶν Lxx *Ju.*13.5. IV. metaph., θραύματ' ἐμοὶ κλύειν A.*Ag.*1166 (lyr.). (Cf. θραῦσμα.)

**θραύπαλος**, ὁ, *joint fir*, *Ephedra campulopoda*, Thphr.*HP*3.6.4; ἡ, ib.4.1.3.

**θραυπίς**, ίδος, ἡ, *a small bird*, Arist.*HA*592ᵇ30 (v.l. θλυπίς).

**θραυσάντυξ**, ῠγος, ὁ, ἡ, (θραύω) *breaking chariot-rails*, τύχαι Ar.*Nu.*1264.

**θραῦσις**, εως, ἡ, (θραύω) *comminution*, opp. κάταξις, Arist.*Mete.*386ᵃ13, 390ᵇ7, *Placit.*3.3.7, Sor.*Fract.*12. II. *slaughter*, Lxx 2*Ki.*17.9; *destruction* by plague, ib.24.15, *Nu.*16.48. III. *falling off of hair in patches*, Gal.19.430. IV. = ὀργή, πληγή, σφῦρα ἢ τοὺς βώλους θραύουσα, Hsch.

⊛ **θραῦσ-μα**, ατος, τό, = θραῦμα I, Agatharch.25, Arist.*Mu.*394ᵇ4, Luc.*Hist.Conscr.*25. II. in leprosy, *scab*, Lxx *Le.*13.30. III. the best kind of ἀμμωνιακόν, Dsc.3.84. IV. *fracture*, *Hippiatr.*74 (pl.). -μός, ὁ, *breaking*, καρδίας Lxx *Na.*2.10(11). -τήριος, α, ον, *capable of dissolving*, λίθων Aët.2.19. -της, ου, ὁ, *one who breaks* or *crushes*, *POxy.*868.2 (nisi sub θραυστός ponendum). -τός, ή, όν, *frangible*, *brittle*, Ti.Locr.99c, Thphr.*HP*5.3.6; *capable of being broken down*, πύργος D.C.36.18, Asclep.ap.Gal.14.698, S.E.*P.*3.33. 2. *broken*, *crushed*, Epigr. in *PTeb.*3.4: θραυστόν, τό, = θραῦσμα III, Plin.*HN*12.107.

⊛ **θραύω**, Ep. impf. θραύεσκον Orph.*L.*140: fut. -σω Ar.*Av.*466: aor. 1 ἔθραυσα S.*El.*745, E.*HF*779 (lyr.):—Pass., fut. θραυσθήσομαι Gal.10.624: aor. ἐθραύσθην (v. infr.), (κατ-) Pl.*Ti.*56e: pf. τέθραυσμαι Thphr.*Sens.*11, (συν-) X.*Ages.*2.14, (παρα-) Pl.*Lg.*757e (v.l. -τεθραυμένον):—*break in pieces*, *shatter*, Simon.57, A.*Pers.*196, 416, Tim.*Pers.*99, etc.; θ. σάρκας E.*Hipp.*1239:—Pass., θραυομένης τῆς πέτρης *flying into pieces*, Hdt.1.174; σίδηρον θραυσθέντα καὶ ῥαγέντα S.*Ant.*476; πτερὰ θραύονται *have their* wings *broken*, Pl.*Phdr.*248b. II. metaph., *break down*, *enfeeble*, μὴ θραύσαι (-σοι codd.) χρόνος ὄλβον Pi.*O.*6.97, cf. E.*HF*779 (lyr.); διάτορον σφραγῖδα θ. στόματος Tim.*Pers.*160; ἔπος.., ὅ τι τὴν τούτων θραύσει ψυχὴν Ar.*Av.*466; θ. τὴν δύναμιν Plu.*Alc.*23; ἐλπίδα, etc., Hdn.3.2.2, etc.; θ. τι τῶν ἐκ χρόνου φυλασσομένων δικαίων *Supp.Epigr.*1.329.45 (Istrus, i A.D.), cf. Onos.32.10:—Pass., πόθος θραυσθεὶς Asp.ap.Ath.5.219e; θραυόμενος τὸν λογισμόν, Lat. *animo fractus*, Plu.*Ant.*17; θραυσθῆναι ἐπί τινα *to be grieved* for.., Lxx 1*Ki.*20.34.—Rare in Att. Prose.

**Θρεῖσσα**, ἡ, Ion. for Θρᾷσσα (q.v.).

**θρεκ-τικός**, ή, όν, (τρέχω) *able to run*, Att. for τροχαστικός, acc. to Moer.p.187 P.: Sup. -ώτατος Hsch. -τός, ή, όν, = τροχαῖος, θρεκτοῖσι νόμοις, f.l. for κρεκτ-, S.*Fr.*463:—also **θρεκτός**· δρόμος, Phot.

⊛ **θρέμμ-α**, ατος, τό, (τρέφω) *nursling*, *creature*, θ. Νηρεΐδων, of dolphins, Arion 1.9; mostly of tame animals, esp. sheep and goats, X.*Ages.*9.6, *Oec.*20.23, Plb.2.26.5, *Ev.Jo.*4.12, etc.; τὰ ἐν ταῖς ἀγέλαις θ. Pl.*Plt.*261d; τὰ ἀγελαῖα θ. ib.264a; ἡνὰ θ. Id.*Lg.*819d; of game-cocks and quails, ὀρνίθων θ. ib.789b: generally, *animals*, τοῖς ἡμέροις καὶ ἀγρίοις..θ. Id.*Criti.*118b, al. 2. of men, S.*OT*1143, *Ph.*243; Χαρίτων θ. Ar.*Ec.*973; δύσκολον τὸ θ. ἄνθρωπος Pl.*Lg.*777b, cf. *Tht.*174b; esp. of *domestic slaves*, = Lat. *verna*, τὸ Χρυσίππου θ. *GDI*2321.14 (Delph.), cf. *CIG*3113 (Teos). 3. generally, *creature*, ἄπλατον θ. κἀπροσήγορον, of a lion, S.*Tr.*1093 (cf. Pl.*Chrm.*155e); of Cerberus, S.*Tr.*1099; κακὰ θ., of *a swarm* of gnats, *AP*5.150 (Mel.); θ. Σελινοῦντος, of a fish, Archestr.*Fr.*12; Καρύστου θ., comic for a cup made at Carystus, Antiph.182.3; as a term of reproach, θρέμματ' οὐκ ἀνασχετά A.*Th.*182; ὦ θρέμμ' ἀναιδές S.*El.*622, cf. Ar.*Lys.*369; in periphr., ὕδρας θ., for ὕδρα, S.*Tr.*574; νεογενῆ παίδων θρέμματα Pl.*Lg.*790d; θρέμματα παλλακῶν *kept* mistresses, Plu.*Sol.*7. (Written θέρματα *BGU*478.15 (ii A.D.)). -ατικός, ή, όν, *of* or *for cattle-dealing*, ἐργασία Judeich *Altertümer von Hierapolis* 227 *b* 7. -άτιον, τό, Dim. of θρέμμα 2, *CIG*2733 (Stratonicea), *SIG*1211 (Calymna), pl., Keil-Premerstein *Dritter Bericht* 151 (ii/iii A.D.). -ᾰτοτροφέω, *keep cattle*, D.S.2.54, Str.15.1.41.

**θρέξασκον, θρέξομαι**, v. τρέχω.

⊛ **θρέομαι**, only in pres., *cry aloud*, *shriek*, always of women, θρέομαι φοβερὰ μεγάλ' ἄχη A.*Th.*78; elsewh. only in part., μινυρὰ θρεομένας Id.*Ag.*1165; πάθεα μέλεα θρεομένα Id.*Supp.*112, cf. E.*Hipp.*363; αὐτὴ θρεομένη σαυτῇ κακά Id.*Med.*51 (trim., elsewh. lyr.).—Act. only in Hsch. (I.-E. *dhreu-*, cf. θρο-έω, θρῦ-λος.)

**θρέπτα**, v. θρέπτρα, τά.

⊛ **θρεπ-τάριον**, τό, = θρεμμάτιον, *CIG*(add.)4303*h*6 (Lycia), *PPar.* p.422 (ii A.D.). -τειρα, ἡ, fem. of θρεπτήρ, E.*Tr.*195 (lyr.), *AP*5.105 (Diotim.), 6.51: metaph., Δίκη θ. πολήων Opp.*H.*2.680. -τέος, α, ον, (τρέφω) *to be fed*, *nurtured*, metaph., γυμναστικῇ Pl.*R.*403c. II. θρεπτέον *one must feed*, *keep*, Id.*Ti.*19a, X.*Lac.*9.5. 2. (from Pass.) ἢ ἐργαστέον ἢ ἀπὸ τῶν εἰργασμένων θρεπτέον *one must live* on what has been earned, Id.*Eq.Mag.*8.8. -τήρ, ῆρος, ὁ, *feeder*, *rearer*, of a parent or foster-parent, *IG*3.1401, *JRS*2.91 (Antioch in Pisidia), *AP*12.137 (Mel.): pl., *IG*14.1722: as Adj., θ. ἀγοστός Nonn.*D.*3.387. ⊛ -τήριος, ον, *feeding*, *nourishing*, μαστός A.*Ch.*545. II. πλόκαμος Ἰνάχῳ θ. hair *dedicated as a thank-offering* to Inachus, ib.6. III. Subst. θρεπτήριον, τό, = θρεπτάριον, *PLond.*5.1708.248 (vi A.D.). 2. pl., θρεπτήρια, τά, *reward for rearing*, made to nurses by parents, *h.Cer.*168, 223; also, *return made by children for their rearing* (Att. τροφεῖα), Hes.*Op.*188, Ael.*VH*2.7. b. *nourishment*, τὰ ..νηδύος θ. S.*OC*1263. -τήτωρ, ορος, ὁ, *nourisher*, *feeder*, πενήτων *PMasp.*20.11 (pl., vi A.D.). -τικός, ή, όν, *able to feed* or *rear*, τινος Pl.*Plt.*267b, cf. 276b, c; *nourishing*, -ώτερα μῆλα Diph.Siph.ap. Ath.2.82f; -ώτατος οἶνος Mnesith.ib.1.32d. II. *of* or *promoting growth*, ἡ δύναμις τῆς ψυχῆς θ. καὶ γεννητική Arist.*deAn.*416ᵃ19; ἡ θ. ψυχή ib.415ᵃ23; τὸ θ. *the principle of growth*, Id.*EN*1102ᵇ11; ἡ θ. καὶ αὐξητικὴ ζωή ib.1098ᵃ1; opp. φθαρτικός, Polystr.p.23 W. Adv. -κῶς Porph.*Gaur.*1.1. III. *causing to heal up*, ἑλκῶν Dsc.1.43. ⊛ -τός, ή, όν, as Subst., θρεπτός, θρεπτή, *slave bred in the house*, Lys.*Fr.*215 S., Pherecr.125, Lxx *Es.*2.7, *IPE*1².709 (Olbia, ii B.C.), *POxy.*298.46 (i A.D.), etc.; οἱ θ. καὶ αἱ θ. *Inscr.Cos* 131; also of *adopted foundlings*, τὴν ἰδίαν θ. *SIG*1210 (Calymna), Plin.*Ep. ad Traj.*65, etc. II. *pupil*, Vett.Val.157.29. -τρα (A), τά, = θρεπτήρια III. 2, οὐδὲ τοκεῦσι θ. φίλοις ἀπέδωκε Il.4.478, 17.302; θρέπτα is dub. in *Epigr.Gr.*442.4 (ii A.D.), Q.S.11.89, Hsch. -τρα (B), ἡ, = θρέπτειρα, *a nurse*, *CIG*(add.)4300*d* (Antiphellos).

⊛ **θρεσκός**, v. θρῆσκος.

**θρεττᾰνελό**, *sound imitative of the cithara*, Ar.*Pl.*290.

**θρέττε**, τό, = τὸ θρασύ, οὐκ ἔνι μοι τὸ θ., barbarism in Ar.*Eq.*17.

**θρεψίππας**, ου, ὁ, = ἱπποτρόφος, as pr. n. in Apollod.2.7.8.

**θρέψις**, εως, ἡ, *nourishing*, σωμάτων S.E.*M.*11.97, cf. Alex.Aphr.*Pr.*2.66, Gal.1.655, etc.

**θρηϊκή**· ὑποδημάτων εἶδος Περσικῶν, Hsch.

**Θρηϊκίη, Θρηΐκιος**, η, ον, Ep. and Ion. for Θρᾴκιος (q.v.). **Θρῆϊξ**, ϊκος, ὁ, Ep. and Ion. for Θρᾷξ (q.v.). **Θρήϊσσα**, ἡ, poet. for Θρᾷσσα (q.v.). **Θρήκη**, ἡ, **Θρήκηθεν, Θρήκηνδε**, v. Θρᾴκη. **Θρήκιος**, v. Θρᾴκιος.

**θρήν-ερως**, ωτος, ὁ, ἡ, *a querulous lover*, Poll.6.189. -εύω, = θρηνέω, *Epigr.Gr.*406.9 (Iconium). -έω, fut. -ήσω A.*Ag.*1541 (anap.), S.*Aj.*632 (lyr.): aor. 1 -ησα E.*Tr.*[111]:—Med. (v. infr. 2): impers. in pf. Pass. (v. infr.): (θρῆνος):—*sing a dirge*, *wail*, Μοῦσαι δ' ἐννέα πᾶσαι ἀμειβόμεναι ὀπὶ καλῇ θρήνεον Od.24.61; τίς ὁ θρηνήσων; A.*Ag.* l.c.; τίς..ἔσθ' ὁ θρηνῶν; Ar.*Nu.*1260; θ. πρὸς τύμβον A.*Ch.*926; θ. καὶ ὀδύρεσθαι Pl.*Ap.*38d; πρὸς σφᾶς αὐτοὺς Isoc.8.128: c. acc. cogn., στονόεσσαν ἀοιδὴν..ἐθρήνεον *were singing* a doleful dirge, Il.24.722; γόον θ. A.*Fr.*291; ὀξυτόνους ᾠδὰς S.*Aj.* l.c.; ἐπῳδάς ib.582; ὕμνους, of the nightingale, Ar.*Av.*211 (lyr.); φθόγγους ἀλύρους Alex.162.7:—Pass., ἅλις μοι τεθρήνηται γόοις S.*Ph.*1401; ἱκανῶς τεθρήνηται Luc.*Cat.*20. 2. c. acc., *bewail*, θ. πόνους A.*Pr.*615; τὸν θάνατον Pl.*Phd.*85a; ὅσα τὸν..ἐμὸν θρηνῶ πατέρα S.*El.*94 (anap.), cf. 530, *Ev.Luc.*23.27, etc.; τὸν φύντα E.*Fr.*449:—so also Med., ἄκος γὰρ οὐδὲν τόνδε θρηνεῖσθαι A.*Pr.*43:—Pass., *to be lamented*, S.*Aj.*852, *Fr.*653. -ημα, ατος, τό, *lament*, *dirge*, E.*Or.*132, *Hel.*174 (lyr.), etc. -ήσιμος, *flebilis*, *Gloss.* -ητέον, *one must lament*, Apollon.ap.Stob.4.56.35, Jul.*Or.*8.246b. -ητήρ, ῆρος, ὁ, *mourner*, *wailer*, A.*Pers.*938 (lyr.). -ητήριος, ον, = θρηνητικός, ᾠδαὶ θ. Eust.1372.26. -ητής, οῦ, ὁ, = θρηνητήρ, A.*Ag.*1075, *BGU*34 iv 4 (iii A.D.). -ητικός, ή, όν, *inclined to lament*, *querulous*, Arist.*EN*1171ᵇ10. 2. *of* or *for a dirge*, αὔλημα, μόναυλος, Poll.4.73, 75; τὸ θ. *matter for lament*, Plu.2.623a. Adv. -κῶς Poll.6.202. ⊛ -ήτρια, ἡ, fem. of θρηνητήρ, Sch.E.*Ph.*1489. -ήτωρ, ορος, ὁ, = θρηνητήρ, Man.4.190.

**θρηνο-λάλος** [ᾰ], ον, *uttering laments*, Σειρῆνες *IG*12(8).445.5 (Thasos). -λογέω, *bewail*, τινα *IPE*2.197 (Panticapaeum). -ποιός, *luctificus*, *Gloss.*

**θρῆνος**, ὁ, (θρέομαι) *dirge*, *lament*, Il.24.721, Sapph.136, Pi.*I.*8(7).64, Hdt.2.79, 85, etc.; θ. οὑμὸς for me, A.*Pr.*390; εἰπεῖν..θ. θέλω ἐμὸν τὸν αὐτῆς Id.*Ag.*1322. 2. *complaint*, *sad strain*, *h.Pan.*18; Γοργόνων οὔλιον θ. Pi.*P.*12.8; θρῆνοι καὶ ὀδυρμοί Pl.*R.*398d, etc.: pl.,

*lamentations*, θρήνων ᾠδάς S.*El.*88 (lyr.), etc.; title of poems by Pindar, Stob.4.39.6, etc. (Distd. fr. ἐπικήδειον by Trypho ap.Ammon. *Diff.*p.54 V. (cf. Ptol.Asc.p.404 H.), ἐπικήδειον τὸ ἐπὶ τῷ κήδει, θ. δὲ ἐν ᾡδήποτε χρόνῳ.)

**θρῆνυξ**, υκος, ὁ, = sq., Euph.39; Boeot. **θρᾶνυξ** Corinn.38.

⊛ **θρῆνυς**, υος, ὁ, (θράομαι) *footstool*, ὑπὸ δὲ θρῆνυν ποσὶν ἥσει Il.14.240, cf. Od.19.57. II. θ. ἑπταπόδης the seven-foot *bench*, perh. *helmsman's bench* or *bridge*, Il.15.729.

**θρηνῳδ-έω**, *sing a dirge over*, τινα E.*IA*1176. **–ημα**, ατος, τό, *dirge, lament*, Sch.S.*El.*92 (ed. T. Johnson, Oxon. 1705). **–ης**, ες, *like a dirge, fit for a dirge*, ἁρμονίαι Pl.*R.*398e, 411a; ὀδυρμός Tim. *Pers.*113; φθόγγος, μέλος, Plu.*Sull.*7, Hdn.4.2.5; τὸ θ. τῆς ψυχῆς *mournful mood*, Plu.2.822c. 2. = θρηνητικός, of persons, Pl.*Lg.* 792b; τὸ θ. Id.*R.*606b. **–ία**, ἡ, *lamentation*, ib.604d, Plu.2. 657a. **–ικός**, ή, όν, *appropriate to a dirge*, ἁρμονία ib.1136e. **–ός**, ὁ, ἡ, *one who sings a dirge, mourner*, Alciphr.1.36, Ptol.*Tetr.*180, Anon.*Oxy.*864, cf. Poll.6.202.

**θρήνωμα**, ατος, τό, = θρῆνος, εἰς τὸν Ὄσιριν *PTeb.*140 (pl., i B.C.).

**Θρῆξ**, ηκός, ὁ, Ion. for Θρᾷξ (q.v.); fem. **Θρῇσσα**, ἡ (q.v.).

**θρήσασθαι**, v. θράομαι.

⊛ **θρησκ-εία**, Ion. **–είη**, ἡ, (θρησκεύω) *religious worship, cult, ritual*, ἡ περὶ τὰ ἱρὰ θ. Hdt.2.18, *IG*12(5).141.5 (Paros, iii B.C.), J.*AJ*17.9.3, etc.; τοῦ Ἀπόλλωνος *SIG*801 *D* (Delph., i A.D.); ἡ περί τινος θ. ib. 867.48 (Ephesus, ii A.D.): pl., *rites*, Hdt.2.37, D.H.2.63, *PGnom.* 185 (ii A.D.), Wilcken *Chr.*72 (iii A.D.). 2. *religion, service of God*, Lxx *Wi.*14.18, *Act.Ap.*26.5, *Ep.Jac.*1.26; θ. τοῦ θεοῦ μία ἐστί, μὴ εἶναι κακόν *Corp.Herm.*12 fin.; ἑκατέρα θ., i.e. Christianity and Paganism, Them.*Or.*5.69c; θ. τῶν ἀγγέλων *worshipping* of angels, *Ep.Col.*2. 18. 3. in bad sense, *religious formalism*, ἀντὶ ὁσιότητος Ph.1.195; θ. βιωτική vulgar *superstition*, Sor.1.4. **–ευμα**, ατος, τό, *religious worship*, *IG*2².1099.29 (Plotina), Just.*Nov.*103.2 (pl.). **–ευσις**, εως, ἡ, = foreg., Phint.ap.Stob.4.23.61ᵃ (pl.). **–ευτήριον**, τό, *place of worship*, Sch.Pi.*O.*7.33. **–ευτής**, οῦ, ὁ, *worshipper*, *BCH* 37.94 (Thessalonica), Ptol.*Tetr.*159, Sch.Pi.*O.*3.28. **–εύω**, *perform religious observances*, Hdt.2.64, *Sammelb.*991 (iii A.D.). II. c. acc., *worship*, θεούς D.H.2.23, *IG*5(2).268.42 (Mantinea), Porph. *Abst.*4.9, Hdn.1.11.1:—Pass., Dinon 17, Lxx *Wi.*14.16, Porph.ap. Eus.*PE*3.11: impers., εἴ τι ἄλλο –εύεσθαι νόμιμον ἦν D.H.1.76. III. *to be a devotee*, Plu.*Alex.*2. **–ια**, τά, *religious observances*, *OGI* 210.9 (Nubia, iii A.D.). **–ος**, ον, *religious*, *Ep.Jac.*1.26; in bad sense, *superstitious*, Hsch. (Hsch. has also **θρεσκός**.) ⊛ **–ώδης**, ες, = foreg., Vett.Val.104.14.

**Θρῇσσα**, ἡ, Ion. for Θρᾷσσα.

**θρήττανον**· τῆς ἁμάξης ἐφ' ᾧ τὰ ἀγόμενα ἐπιτίθεται, Hsch.

**Θρία**, ἡ, *Thria*, name of an Attic deme, St.Byz., etc.: **Θρίᾳ** *at Thria*, *IG*1².329, but **Θριᾶσι** X.*HG*5.4.21, Is.11.42: **Θριῶζε** *to Thria*, Th.1.114, *BCH*50.529 (ii A.D.): **Θριῶθεν** *from Thria*, *IG*2². 1672.109:—Adj. **Θριάσιος**, α, ον, πεδίον Hdt.8.65, etc.; πύλαι Plu. *Per.*30.

**θρῐάζω**, (θριαί) *to be rapt, possessed*, S.*Fr.*466, E.*Fr.*478; also glossed by φυλλολογεῖν (as if from θρῖον), Hsch., *EM*455.45:—also **θριάομαι**, = μαντεύομαι, *AB*265; cf. sq.

⊛ **θρῐαί**, ῶν, αἱ, *pebbles used in divination*, Philoch.196, Call.*Ap.*45, cf. Sch. ad loc., *EM*455.34. II. personified as nymphs of Parnassus, Philoch. l.c., Sch.Call. l.c., dub. cj. in *h.Merc.*552.

**θρῐαμβ-ευτής**, οῦ, ὁ, *one who enjoys a triumph*, Suid. **–ευτικός**, ή, όν, v.l. for θριαμβικός, Plu.*Cat.Ma.*24. **–εύω**, pf. τεθριάμβευκα Id.*Ant.*34: (θρίαμβος):—*triumph*, Plb.6.53.7, Posidon.1 J., Plu. *Pomp.*45, etc.; ἀπό τινος *triumph over*, Id.*Rom.*25, App.*Celt.*1; κατὰ τῆς πατρίδος Plu.*Cor.*35, cf. App.*BC*1.80; ἐπί τινι ib.4.31; also θ. ἐπὶ νίκῃ Hdn.3.9.1; ἀπὸ μάχης Plu.*Publ.*9: c. acc. cogn., θ. νίκην ἄδακρυν Id.2.318b; δεύτερον θρίαμβον Id.*Fab.*23. II. *lead in triumph*, of conquered enemies, τινα Id.*Comp.Thes.Rom.*4, *Ep. Col.*2.15:—Pass., –εύεσθαι ὑπό τινος Plu.*Cor.*35; μηδ' ἐν ἐμοὶ περιίδῃς –ευόμενον σεαυτόν Id.*Ant.*84. 2. *lead in triumph*, as a general does his army, metaph., ἡμᾶς ἐν Χριστῷ 2*Ep.Cor.*2.14. III. *divulge, noise abroad*, Phot., cf. Suid. s.v. ἐξεφοίτα. **–ικός**, ή, όν, *triumphal*, ἐσθής D.H.5.35, J.*BJ*7.5.4; κόσμος Str.5.2.2; πομπή, τιμαί, Plu.*Aem.* 30, *Sert.*18; κηδεύματα connexions *with triumphal families*, Id.*Cat. Ma.*24 (v.l. –ευτικῶν); ἄνδρες θ., Lat. *viri triumphales*, Id.*Cam.*21, cf. *Crass.*1. Adv. **–κῶς**, ἠμφιεσμένος App.*BC*2.106. **–ίς**, ίδος, pecul. fem. of θριαμβικός, στολή Anon.ap.Suid.

**θρῐαμβοδιθύραμβος** [ῠ], ον, epith. of Bacchus, Pratin.*Lyr.*1.16.

⊛ **θρίαμβος** [ῐ], ὁ, *hymn to Dionysus*, sung in festal processions to his honour, Cratin.36. 2. epith. of Dionysus, *Trag.Adesp.*140, D.S. 4.5, Ath.1.30b, Plu.*Marc.*22, Arr.*An.*6.28.2. 3. metaph., *scandal*, δεδιὼς τὸν ἐκ λόγων θ. Conon 31.1. II. = Lat. *triumphus* (which is borrowed fr. θ. through Etruscan), Plb.6.15.8, D.S.12.64, *Mon. Anc.Gr.*2.20, *SIG*804.9 (Cos, i A.D.), Plu.*Publ.*20, etc.; ὁ μέγας θ. the *triumph*, opp. ὁ ἐλάττων θ. *ovatio*, Id.*Marc.*22, cf. D.H.8.67; ὁ πεζὸς θ., = *ovatio*, Id.9.36. (For the termination perh. cf. ἴαμβος, διθύραμβος, but the origin of θρι- is unknown.)

**θρίᾰσις** [θρῐ], εως, ἡ, (θριάζω) *poetic rapture*, Suid. s.v. θρίαμβος.

**θρῐαστής**, οῦ, ὁ, (θρῖον) *planter of fig-trees*, Poll.7.140.

**θριάτιον**· ἁπαλωτέρα τροφή, Hsch.

**θριγγίον**, **-γός**, **–γόω**, later forms for θριγκίον, etc.

**θριγκ-ίον**, τό, Dim. of sq., Luc.*Gall.*22, App.*Mith.*71, Just.*Nov.* 133.1. ⊛ **–ός**, ὁ, *topmost course of stones in a wall, cornice, coping*, mostly in pl., Od.17.267, S.*Fr.*506, Arist.*Ph.*246ᵃ18, *IG*7.3073.68 (Lebad.); of the row of slabs behind the frieze, *SIG*244 ii 61 (Delph., iv B.C.); δῶμα περιφερὲς θριγκοῖς E.*Hel.*430: sg., Id.*IT*47. b. *frieze*, θ. κυάνοιο Od.7.87; χρυσοῦς D.S.18.26. 2. metaph., *coping-stone*, *last finish*, θ. ἀθλίων κακῶν E.*Tr.*489; δοκεῖ ὥσπερ θ. τοῖς μαθήμασιν ἡ διαλεκτικὴ .. ἐπάνω κεῖσθαι Pl.*R.*534e. II. *wall, fence* of any sort, E.*Ion* 1321, Ar.*Th.*58 (anap.), Paus.1.42.7, Plu.2.85f. 2. *row*, ὀδόντων Hp.*Ep.*23.—Later forms are **θριγγός** v.l. in Plu. l.c.; **θριγχός** v.l. in Dsc.4.85; **τριγχός**, Sch.Il.11.774, Eust.1570.17, *SIG* 1231.6 (Nicomedia, iii/iv A.D.). **–όω**, *surround with a* θριγκός, [αὐλὴν] ἐθρίγκωσεν ἀχέρδῳ *fenced* it with thorn-bushes, Od.14.10, dub. in *IG*1².111. II. *build even to the coping-stone*: metaph., *complete, make an end of*, ἄτας τάσδε θριγκώσων φίλοις A.*Ag.*1283; δῶμα –ῶσαι κακοῖς *to bring* the house *to the height* of misery, E.*HF* 1280; θριγκουμένη .. οἰκία Arist.*Ph.*246ᵃ19. **–ώδης**, ες, *like a coping*, Hsch. s.v. αἱμασιαί. ⊛ **–ωμα**, ατος, τό, *coping, cornice*, cj. for τριχώμασιν, J.*AJ*15.11.3: metaph., θ. τῆς τροφῆς, of salt, Plu.2.685b.

⊛ **θρῐδᾰκ-ηΐς**, ΐδος, fem. Adj., *of the lettuce*, χαίτη Nic.*Th.*838. **–ίας**, ου, ὁ, = μανδραγόρας θῆλυς, Dsc.4.75. **–ίνη** [κῖ], ἡ, Att. form of Ion. and Dor. θρίδαξ (Ath.2.68f):—*lettuce*, Cratin.330, Hp.*Mul.*2. 136, Amphis 20, Eub.14, Thphr.*HP*1.12.2; θ. ἥμερος ib.7.6.2. 2. *wild lettuce, Lactuca Scariola*, Id. l.c.; ἡ πικρὰ θ. ib.9.11.10; in this signf., opp. θρίδαξ, Gal.13.387, Hellad.ap.Phot.*Bibl.*p.532 B. 3. *sea-lettuce*, a kind of sea-weed, Aët.12.42 (pl.). II. fem. Adj. (sc. μᾶζα), a kind of *cake*, Luc.*Lex.*3, Ath.3.114f, Hellad. l.c. **–ινίς**, ίδος, ἡ, = foreg., Stratt.66.6 (lyr.). **–ιον**, τό, Dim. of θρίδαξ, Plu.2. 349a (pl.). **–ίσκα**, ᾶ, Lacon. for θριδακίνη, Alcm.20. **–ώδης**, ες, *lettuce-like*, Dsc.2.132 (Comp.).

⊛ **θρίδαξ** (Cypr. **θρόδαξ**, q.v.), ἄκος, ἡ, Ion. and Dor. for θριδακίνη, *lettuce*, Epich.158, Hdt.3.32, Hp.*Mul.*1.78, Thphr.*HP*7.2.4, *BGU* 1118.13 (i B.C.), *IG*4.955.8 (Epid.), etc.:—also **θρύδαξ**, *POxy.*1212 (ii A.D.); **θίδραξ**, Hsch. s.v. θιδρακίνη. [ῐ, Epich. l.c., *AP*9.412 (Phld.), 11.295 (Lucill.), 413 (Ammian.), cf. θριδακηΐς, -ίνη, -ινίς: the accentuation θρίδαξ lacks authority.]

⊛ **θρίζω**, poet. syncop. for θερίζω, A.*Ag.*536.

**θριήλοοι**· ἱερεῖς, Hsch.

**θριῆσαι**· καπρίσαι, Hsch.

**θριληδεῖν**· θρυλλεῖν, Id. (prob. θρυλίδδην).

**θριμμός**· γογγυσμός, Id.

⊛ **θρῑνάκη**, = θρῖναξ, Call.*Fr.*46 P. (nisi leg. θρίνακ' ἦν).

**Θρῑνᾰκίη**, ἡ, (θρῖναξ) a legendary island, Od.11.107, etc.: afterwards identified with Sicily and written Τρινακρία (from τρεῖς, ἄκραι) (q.v.); cf. Τριναχία:—also **Θρῑνακίς**, ίδος, ἡ, Str.6.2.1:—Adj. ⊛ **Θρινάκιος**, α, ον, *Sicilian*, ῥίζα Nic.*Th.*529.

**θρῖναξ**, ἄκος, ἡ, *trident, three-pronged fork*, used to stir grain, etc., Ar.*Pax* 567, Nic.*Th.*114, *PFay.*120.3 (i/ii A.D.); as a signet, *Tab. Heracl.*1.5. [ῑ: later ῐ, *AP*6.95 codd. (Antiphil.).]

**θρινία**· ἄμπελος ἐν Κρήτῃ, Hsch.

⊛ **θρίξ**, ἡ, gen. τρῐχός, dat. pl. θριξί (τρίχεσιν J.*AJ*16.7.3 is f.l. for τρύχ–):—*hair*, Hom. only in pl., ὀρθαὶ τρίχες ἔσταν ἐνὶ .. μέλεσσι Il. 24.359; mostly, *hair of the head*, 22.77, Od.13.431; αἱ ἐν τῇ κεφαλῇ τρίχες Th.1.6; *sheep's wool*, Il.3.273, Hes.*Op.*517; pig's *bristles*, Il.19.254, Od.10.239; τρίχες ἄκραι οὐραῖαι, of a horse's tail, Il.23. 519; ἀνάστασις τῶν τριχῶν, of a lark's *crest*, Gal.12.361. II. later in sg. collectively, A.*Th.*535, *Ag.*562, S.*El.*451; τριχὸς πλόκαμος, βόστρυχος, A.*Th.*564 (lyr.), *Ch.*229; γενείου θρίξ Id.*Pers.*1056; κόμη θρίξ Lxx *Nu.*6.6; Ἐπαφροδίτου .. τὴν παιδικὴν τρίχα Ὑγίᾳ (sc. ἀνέθηκεν) *IG*12(5).173 (Paros, i A.D.); of a horse's *mane*, S.*Fr.*475; of dogs, X.*Cyn.*4.8 (sg. and pl.). 2. *a single hair*, οὐδὲ τρίχ[α] Alc. *Supp.*14.10: prov., θρὶξ ἀνὰ μέσσον *only a hair's breadth* wanting, Theoc.14.9, cf. X.*Smp.*6.2; ἄξιον τριχός, i.e. good for nothing, Ar. *Ra.*614; οὐδ' ἂν τριχὸς πριαίμην Eup.7.18 D.; ἐκ τριχὸς κρέμασθαι to hang by *a hair*, Aristaenet.2.1, Zen.3.47; ἀπὸ τ. ἠρτῆσθαι *AP*5.229 (Paul. Sil.); ἐπὶ τριχὸς ἦν ἡ σωτηρία Procop.*Aed.*6.6; εἰς ἱερὴν τρίχα ἐλθεῖν, i.e. to come to life's end, v.l. in *AP*7.164 (Antip. Sid.), but cf. *Epigr.Gr.*248.13; μόνον οὐχὶ τῶν τ., φασί, λαμβάνεται 'saute aux yeux', S.E.*M.*7.257. III. Medic., *vein* on the right lobe of the liver, Hp.*Mul.*1.43 (v.l. ἡ σῦριγξ), Gal.19.104.

**Θριξάλλιος**, ὁ (sc. μήν), name of month at Lamia, *IG*9(2).74.

**θρῐοβόλος**, ὁ, (θριαί) *one who throws pebbles into the divining-urn, soothsayer*, Epic.ap.St.Byz. s.v. Θρῖα, Suid.

**θρῖον**, τό, *fig-leaf*, Ar.*Ec.*707, Sotad.Com.1.27: generally, *leaf*, Nic.*Al.*55; *petal*, ib.407. 2. prov., θρίου ψόφος, of empty threats, Ar.*V.*436. II. *mixture of eggs, milk, lard, flour, honey, cheese*, etc., wrapped in fig-leaves, θ. ταρίχους, δημοῦ, Id.*Ach.*1101, 1102; δημοῦ βοείου θρῖον Id.*Eq.*954; ἐγκεφάλου θρίω δύο (a pun on the fig-leaf-like hemispheres of the brain) Id.*Ra.*134, cf. Sch. ll.cc. [ῑ, Ar. *Eq.*954, al., Men.518.11; θρία, θρῖον are ff. ll. for θρύα, θρύον in Theoc. 13.40, *AP*9.723 (Antip. Sid.); cf. λεπτόθριος.]

**θρῑπήδεστος**, ον, (θρίψ, ἐδήδεσμαι) *worm-eaten*, ῥίζαι Thphr.*HP* 9.14.3, cf. *IG*2².1628.163, al., 1672.306; κεραῖαι θριπήδεσται ib.1628. 205, but –οι 1629.328. 2. σφραγίδια θ. seals *made of worm-eaten wood*, Ar.*Th.*427, cf. Sch. 3. metaph., = διεφθαρμένη, Hyp.*Fr.* 82. (Freq. corrupted to –έστατος, as in Ar.*Th.* l.c. (ap.Suid.), Hyp. l.c. (v.l.), Luc.*Lex.*13 (v.l.), cf. Paus.Gr.*Fr.*205, but a Sup. is never necessary exc. in Thphr.*HP*3.8.5 (v. θριπώδης).)

**θρῑπό-βρωτος**, ον, (βιβρώσκω) = foreg., Philosteph.ap.Hsch., Lyc. 508:—a form **θιπόβρωτος** (dissim.) is condemned by Hsch. **–φάγος** [φᾰ], ον, *eating wood-worms*, Arist.*HA*616ᵇ29.

**θρῑπώδης**, ες, *full of wood-worms*, in Sup. –έστατον, ξύλον Thphr. *HP*3.8.5 vulg.; θριπηδέστατον cod. Urb. (v. θριπήδεστος).

**θρίσκειν**· τὸν θροῦν, Hsch.

**θρίσσα**, Att. **θρίττα**, ἡ, *a fish*, = τριχίας, Anaxandr.41.52, Ephipp. 12.5, Arist.*HA*621$^{b}$16, *PCair.Zen.*40 (iii B.C.), al., *Gp.*20.7.1: **θρείσσα**, *BGU*816.20 (iii A.D.): **θρίσσος**, ὁ, is v.l. in *AP*6.304 (Phan.).

**θρισσ-έμπορος**, ὁ, *dealer in* θρίσσαι, *PCair.Zen.*261 (iii B.C.). **-ίον**, τό, Dim. of θρίσσα, *POxy.*1923.9 (v/vi A.D.).

**θρίσσω**, = τὸ κατὰ ψυχὴν ἐξίστασθαι, Ar.Byz.(?) ap.Erot.; Ion. acc. to Greg.Cor.p.571 S.

**θρίττε**, = θρέττε, Hsch.

❀ **θρίψ**, gen. θρῑπός, ὁ (not ἡ, v.l. in Men.540.5), *wood-worm*, Thphr. *HP*5.4.4, *AP*12.190 (Strat.); ὁ θ. τὸ ξύλον (sc. λυμαίνεται) Men. l.c. II. metaph., *skinflint, miser*, Hsch. (Perh. connected with τρίβω.)

**Θριώ**· λίπος· ἑορτὴ Ἀπόλλωνος, καὶ ἡ σύντροφος αὐτοῦ, Hsch. **θρόδαξ**, Cypr. for θρίδαξ, Id.:—Dim. **θοδράκιον**, τό, Choerob. in *An.Ox.* 2.218 (sic cod.).

❀ **θροέω**, aor. ἐθρόησα, poet. θρο- B.3.9, S.*Aj.*947, (δι-) Th.6.46:—Med. and Pass. (v. infr.): (θρόος):—*cry aloud*, B. l. c., S.*El.*1410; παρὰ νοῦν θ. Id.*Ph.*1195 (lyr.); πᾶσιν to all, Id.*Aj.*67, cf. *Tr.*531; *speak, say*, A.*Pr.*608 (lyr.); θρόει, τίς..; E.*Or.*187 (lyr.): c. acc. cogn., θ. αὐδάν A.*Ch.*829 (lyr.), E.*Or.*1248 (lyr.); λόγον S.*Ant.*1287 (lyr.); πολλά Id.*Aj.*592; εὔφημα, ψευδῆ, E.*IA*143 (lyr.), 1345 (troch.):—Med., τοῦτ' ἔπος -ούμενος A.*Eu.*510 (lyr.). 2. c. acc., *tell out, utter aloud*, τοὐμὸν πάθος Id.*Ag.*1137 (lyr.); νόμον ἄνομον ib. 1141 (lyr.), cf. 104; πᾶς τοῦτό γ' Ἑλλήνων θροεῖ S.*OC*597; θάνατόν τινι θ. ib.1425.—Rare exc. in Trag.; in late Prose, J.*AJ*18.6.10, 19.1.16. II. causal, *scare, terrify*, Sch.E.*Hec.*180, al.:—Pass., *to be stirred, moved*, of joy, ἡ κοιλία μου ἐθροήθη ἐπ' αὐτόν Lxx *Ca.*5.4; of fear, μὴ θροεῖσθε *Ev.Matt.*24.6, cf. 2*Ep.Thess.*2.2.

**θρομβ-εῖον**, Ion. **-ήϊον**, τό, Dim. of θρόμβος, Nic.*Al.*295:—also **-ίον**, τό, Dsc.*Alex.*25.

**θρομβο-ειδής**, ές, *full of clots* or *lumps*, Hp.*Mul.*1.11, 38. **-ομαι**, Pass., *to become clotted, curdled*, of blood, Nic.*Al.*315, Gal.18(1).33; of honey, Id.14.22. 2. *contain clots*, ἢν θρομβωθέωσιν αἱ μῆτραι Hp.*Mul.*2.165; of the breasts, Dsc.*Eup.*1.128:—Act., *cause to coagulate*, only as v.l. in Sch.Nic.*Th.*709.

**θρόμβ-ος**, ὁ, (τρέφω, τέτροφα) *lump*, Hdt.1.179; *clot* of blood, A.*Ch.*533, al., Pl.*Criti.*120a, etc.; χολῆς Hp.*Morb.*2.75; of milk, *curd*, αἰγῶν ἀπόρρους θ. Antiph.52.8; θρόμβοι ἁλῶν *coarse* salt, Suid. b. *drop*, θρόμβοι αἵματος καταβαίνοντες.. *Ev.Luc.*22.44. 2. *nipple*, *PLond.*1821.42. II. θ.· ὑψηλὸς τόπος, Hsch. **-ώδης**, ες, = θρομβοειδής, οὖρα Hp.*Aph.*4.69; ἀφροί S.*Tr.*702; σπέρματα Arist.*HA*582$^{a}$31. ❀ **-ωσις**, εως, ἡ, *becoming curdled*, αἵματος καὶ γάλακτος Dsc.5.13; αἵματος Antyll.ap.Orib.7.7.9, cf. Gal.8.408, Lyd.*Mens.*4.116. 2. *blocked vein, thrombosis*, Cael.Aur.*TP*4.40.

**θρον-ίζομαι**, Pass., *to be enthroned*, Lxx *Es.*1.2. II. *to be initiated, consecrated*, τισι *PMag Lond.*121.747. **-ιον**, τό, Dim. of θρόνος, *EM*456.28. II. part of the constellation Cassiopea, Ptol. *Alm.*8.2. **-ίς**, ίδος, ἡ, = foreg. 1, Them.*Or.*31.353d. ❀ **-ισμός**, ὁ, *enthronement*, D.Chr.12.33, Man.4.104 (pl.). **-ιστής**, οῦ, ὁ, *enthroner*, *POxy.*1380.251 (ii A.D.). **-ῑτικός**, ή, όν, *throne-shaped*, συνψέλιον *TAM*2(1).210 (Sidyma).

**θρονίτις**· πρώτιστος, Hsch.

**θρόνον**, τό, only in pl. θρόνα, *flowers embroidered on cloth*, ἐν δὲ θρόνα ποικίλ' ἔπασσε Il.22.441, cf. Sch.Theoc.2.59, and v. τρόνα. II. *herbs used as drugs and charms*, Theoc.2.59, Nic.*Th.*493, 936, Lyc. 674, Aglaïas 7; used in sacrificial offering, *UPZ*96.4 (ii B.C.).

**θρονοποιός**, όν, *making thrones* or *seats*, Poll.7.182.

❀ **θρόνος**, ὁ, *seat, chair*, Od.1.145, Ath.5.192e, *PMasp.*6 ii 63 (vi A.D.), etc. 2. *throne, chair of state*, θ. βασιλήϊος Hdt.1.14, cf. X.*HG*1.5.3, etc.; Ζηνὸς ἐπὶ θρόνον Theoc.7.93: metaph., Pl.*R.*553c: pl., ἐν θρόνοις ἥμενοι A.*Ch.*975; ἐκ τυραννίδος θρόνων τ' ἄϊστον ἐκβαλεῖν Id.*Pr.*910; Διὸς θρόνοι S.*Ant.*1041, cf. Ar.*Av.*1732; *king's estate* or *dignity*, σκῆπτρα καὶ θρόνους S.*OC*425, cf. 448; [γῆς] κράτη τε καὶ θρόνους νέμω Id.*OT*237, cf. *Ant.*166, etc.; in the Prytaneum, τῷ [Ἀπόλλωνι] θ. ἐξελεῖν *IG*1$^{2}$.78. 3. *oracular seat* of Apollo, E.*IT*1254, 1282 (both lyr.); μαντικοὶ θ. A.*Eu.*616, etc. 4. *chair of a teacher*, Pl.*Prt.*315c, Philostr.*VS*2.2, Lib.*Ep.*819, *AP*9.174 (Pall.). 5. *judge's bench*, Plu.2.807b, Him.*Ecl.*10.9, 13.16. 6. Astrol., = ὕψωμα, *PMich.* in *Class.Phil.*22.22 (pl.). b. *favourable combination of planetary positions*, Ptol.*Tetr.*51. II. a kind of *bread*, Neanth.1 J. III. name of a lozenge, Paul.Aeg.3.42, 7.12.

❀ **θρόνωσις**, εως, ἡ, = θρονισμός, *enthronement of the newly initiated*, at the mysteries of the Corybantes, Pl.*Euthd.*277d.

**θρόος**, Att. **θροῦς**, ὁ, (θρέομαι) *noise* as of many voices, οὐ γὰρ πάντων ἦεν ὁμὸς θ. Il.4.437; poet. of musical sounds, πολύφατος θ. ὕμνων Pi.*N.*7.81; θ. αὐλῶν Epic.ap.Plu.2.654f. 2. *murmur* of a crowd or assembly, Th.4.66, 8.79, D.H.6.57, etc. II. *report, rumour*, X.*Cyr.*6.1.37, Plu.*Galb.*26, D.C.44.18.

**θροσέως**, v. θρασύς.

**θρῠαλλ-ίδιον**, τό, Dim. of sq., Luc.*Tim.*14. **-ίς**, ίδος, ἡ, *plantain, Plantago crassifolia*, used for making wicks, Thphr.*HP*7.11.2, Nic.*Th.*899, *BGU*1118.15 (i B.C.). II. *wick*, Ar.*Ach.*874, al., Philyll.26. b. κηρίνη θ. wax-*candle*, Archipp.3 D. III. = φλόμος, Ps.-Dsc.4.103, Plin.*HN*25.121.

**θρύαλλον**, τό, *shower of smuts* from a distant bonfire, Vett.Val. 345.22.

❀ **θρυαρίς**· ψιασθής, Hsch. **θρυασμός**· φωνή, Id. (fort. θρυλισμός).

**θρύβω**, late form, = θρύπτω, Mich. *in PN*14.16.

**θρῡγονάω**, *tap at*, τὴν θύραν Ar.*Ec.*34 (v.l. τρυγον-, τρυγαν-); perh. to be read in Pherecr.10. cf. **θρυγανᾷ**· κνᾶται, ξύει, Hsch., **θρυγονᾶν** τὸ ξύειν Theognost.*Can.*20.

❀ **θρύ-ϊνος** [ῠ], η, ον, (θρύον) *rushy*, Anon.ap.Suid., dub. in *PFlor.* 383.28 (iii A.D.). **-ῖτις**, ιδος, ἡ, *planted with rush*, γῆ *PFlor.*64.22 (iv A.D.), etc.

**θρῡλ-έω**, (θρῦλος) *make a confused noise, chatter, babble*, τὴν νύκτα θρυλῶν καὶ λαλῶν Ar.*Eq.*348; θρυλέοιμι trisyll., Theoc.2.142. II. c. acc., *repeat over and over*, θρυλοῦσ' ἅ γ' εἰπεῖν ἤθελον E.*El.*910; τὰ τοιαῦτα οἱ ποιηταὶ ἡμῖν ἀεὶ -οῦσιν, ὅτι.. Pl.*Phd.*65b; τὰ μυθώδη.., ἃ πάντες -οῦσιν Isoc.12.237; ὃ πάντες ἐθρύλουν τέως, δεῖν.. D.1.7, cf. 19.156; [τὴν τριήρη] θρυλήσει *will keep talking of* it, Id.21.160: abs., καθάπερ πάλαι θρυλῶ Epicur.*Nat.*109 G.; περὶ ἀγαθοῦ θ. Id.*Fr.*423: c. inf., *PSI*5.452.20 (iv A.D.):—Pass., *to be common talk*, τὸ -ούμενον, τὸ.. πανταχοῦ θ. E.*Fr.*285.1, cf. Isoc.*Ep.*6.7, Theopomp.Com.35, Antiph.246.2; τὸ θ. ποτε ἀπόρρητον D.2.6; ἡ ὑπὸ πάντων θρυλουμένη εἰρήνη Id.19.273; τὰ μὲν παλαιὰ καὶ θ. Anaxipp.1.4; περὶ τεθρυλημένου πολλοῖς Arist.*Rh.*1415$^{a}$3; αἱ τεθρ. καὶ κοιναὶ γνῶμαι ib.1395$^{a}$10; τὰ θ. περὶ τὸν βάτραχον Id.*HA*620$^{b}$11; τινῶν λόγων ὑπὸ τῆς μητρός μου θρυλησθέντων (sic) *UPZ*144.45 (ii B.C.). **-ημα**, ατος, τό, *common talk, by-word*, Lxx *Jb.*17.6. **-ητής**, οῦ, ὁ, *babbler*, Gloss. **-ητός**, ή, όν, *generally talked of*, Tz.*H.*12.36.

**θρύλ-ιγμα** [ῡ], ατος, τό, *fragment*, Lyc.880. **-ιγμός** or **-ισμός**, ὁ, *unmusical sound, false note*, D.H.*Comp.*11; ὅταν αὐλητὴς μὴ πιέσας τὸ στόμα θρυλισμὸν ἢ ἐκμελές τι αὐλήσῃ Porph. *in Harm.* p.204 W. **-ίζω**, *make a false note*, *h.Merc.*488 (θρυαλ- codd.).

**θρῡλίσσω**, *crush, shiver, smash*, θρυλίξας Lyc.487:—Pass., θρυλίχθη δὲ μέτωπον Il.23.396.

**θρῦλος**, ὁ, *noise as of many voices, murmur*, Batr.135, Orph.*Fr.* 286 (pl., = *Cat.Cod.Astr.*2.199), Demetr.Lac.*Herc.*1786.1 F., Anon. ap.Suid.—This word and its cognates are written with one λ in Papyri and best codd. (cf. Eust.1307.42), with λλ (as Batr. l. c.) in inferior codd., also in *PLips.*40 ii 10 (iv A.D.).

**θρυμίς**· ἰχθύς ποιός, Hsch.

❀ **θρύμμα**, ατος, τό, (θρύπτω) *that which is broken off, bit*, Hp.*Mul.* 1.75, Ar.*Fr.*160, Aglaïas 20, Gal.6.343; ῥοιῆς θρύμματα *AP*6.232 (Crin.).

❀ **θρυμμᾰτίς**, ίδος, ἡ, *a sort of cake*, Antiph.183.4, Philox.2.18, Luc. *Lex.*6.

**θρυμνεύεται** (θρημν- cod.)· ὑπερηφανεύεται, Hsch.; cf. θρύπτω II. 2.

**θρῠό-εις**, εσσα, εν, *rushy*, Nic.*Th.*200. **-κάλᾰμος** [κᾰ], ὁ, = θρύον 1, *BGU*890 i 20. **-κοπέω**, *cut rushes*, *PLond.*1.131.80 (i A.D.), *POxy.*910.40 (ii A.D., Pass.). **-κοπία**, ἡ, *cutting of rushes*, *PLond.* 3.1171.58 (i B.C.), *POxy.*1628.18 (i B.C.).

**θρύον** [ῠ], τό, *reed, rush*, Il.21.351, Hp.*Steril.*246, Thphr.*HP*4.11.12, Arist.*Mir.*844$^{a}$27: in sg. collectively, ἔπλεκεν Call.*Aet.*3.1.24, cf. D.S.3.10, Theoc.13.40 (pl.), *AP*9.723 (Antip. Sid.); [γῆν] καθαρὰν ἀπὸ θρύου (Pap. θροΐου) *PTeb.*105.26 (ii B.C.), *POxy.*910.41 (ii A.D.): pl. written θροΐα *UPZ*98.12 (ii B.C.). II. = στρύχνον μανικόν, *thorn-apple, Datura Stramonium*, Orph.*A.*916, Thphr.*HP*9.11.6 (θρύορον, βρύορον codd.), Dsc.4.73.

**θρῠο-πώλης**, ου, ὁ, *rush-seller*, *PLond.*1.125.39 (iv A.D.). **-πώλιον**, τό, *rush-seller's shop*, *UPZ*12.13 (ii B.C.). **-τίλλω**, *pluck rushes*, *PLond.*1.131.80 (i A.D., an incorrect formation).

**θρύπτακον**· κλάσμα ἄρτου (Cret.), Hsch.

**θρυπτέον**, *one must crumble*, Aët.9.12 (s.v.l.).

**θρυπτικός**, ή, όν, *able to break* or *crush*, λίθων Dsc.1.121, cf. Gal.8. 409. II. Pass., *easily broken*: metaph., *delicate, effeminate*, X.*Cyr.*8.8.15 (Comp.), *Mem.*1.2.5; σώματα cj. in Max.Tyr.10.2; θ. τι προσφθέγγεσθαι D.C.51.12. Adv. -κῶς Ael.*NA*2.11, Poll.6.185. 2. *saucy*, πρὸς τοὺς ἐραστάς Ael.*VH*3.12.

❀ **θρύπτω**, aor. 1 ἔθρυψα (ἐν-) Hp.*Mul.*1.75:—**Pass.** and **Med.**, fut. θρυφθήσομαι Arr.*An.*4.19.2; θρύψομαι Ar. (v. infr. II. 2c), Luc.*Symp.* 4: aor. 1 ἐθρύφθην Arist. *de An.*419$^{b}$26, (ὑπ-) dub. in *AP*5.293.15 (Agath.): aor. 2 ἐτρύφην [ῠ] (δι-) Il.3.363, ἐθρύβην Dsc.5.123: pf. τέθρυμμαι Hp.*Vict.*2.48: (akin to θραύω):—*break in pieces, break small*, Pl.*Cra.*426e, A.*Ag.*1595; Νεῖλος βώλακα θ. Theoc.17.80:—Pass., *to be broken small*, θρύπτεσθαι κερματιζόμενον ἀνάγκη πᾶν τὸ ὄν Pl.*Prm.*165b, cf. *AP*12.61; χιόνος τὰ μάλιστα θρυφθησόμενα Arr. l.c.; of dried leguminous seeds, *split*, Thphr.*HP*8.11.3, cf. *Sens.*51; of air, *to be dispersed*, Arist. *de An.* l.c., Theo Sm.p.50 H.: the literal sense is more common in compds. ἀπο-, διαθρύπτω, etc. II. metaph. in moral sense, *enfeeble*, esp. by debauchery and luxury, θ. τὰν ψυχάν Ti.Locr.103b; *corrupt*, [τινα] Pl.*Lg.*778a, Phld.*Mus.*p.79 K.; θ. τὰς ψυχὰς καὶ τὰ σώματα Jul.*Or.*1.10c; [οἱ κόλακες] ἀποκναίουσι τῶν κολακευομένων τὰ ὦτα θρύπτοντες Ph.1.453; θ. ἑαυτόν, = θρύπτεσθαι (v. infr.), Ael.*Ep.*9. 2. more freq. in Pass., with fut. Med., *to be enervated, unmanned*, μαλακίᾳ θρύπτεσθαι X.*Smp.*8.8; ἁπαλός τε καὶ τεθρυμμένος Luc.*Charid.*4; θρύπτεται ἡ ὄψις *is enfeebled*, Plu.2.936f; οἱ τεθρυμμένοι τὰς ὄψεις *weak*-sighted people, A.D.*Synt.*199.5. b. *wanton, riot*, ὅλην ἐκείνην εὐφρόνην ἐθρύπτετο f.l. in [S.]*Fr.*1127.9, cf. Luc.*Pisc.*31, *Anach.*29: *display moral weakness*, *POxy.*471.80 (ii A.D.); ἡδοναῖς ἀνάνδροις θ. Plu.2.751b; ἐπὶ τῷ κάλλει Phld.*Hom.*p.55 O.; ὄμμα θρυπτόμενον a *languishing* eye, *AP*5.286.8 (Agath.). c. *to be coy and prudish, bridle up*, esp. when asked a favour, θρύψομαι Ar.*Eq.*1163; ὡραϊζομένη καὶ θρυπτομένη Eup.358; ἁβρὰ καὶ θ. Charito 5.3; ἐθρύπτετο ὡς οὐκ ἐπιθυμῶν λέγειν Pl.*Phdr.*228c, cf. 236c, X.*Smp.*8.4; or when one *pretends to decline* an offer, Plu.*Mar.*14, *Ant.*12; θρύπτεσθαι πρός τινα *give oneself airs* toward him, Id.*Flam.*

18, Luc.*DMeretr.*12.1. d. *grow conceited*, τινι *in* or *of* a thing, *AP* 7.218.2 (Antip. Sid.); ἐσθῆτι πολυτελεῖ Ael.*VH*1.19, etc.; *brag*, Hld. 2.10.

**θρυσέλινον,** τό, an umbelliferous plant, Plin.*HN*25.141.

**θρύσιος,** ὁ, = θρύον, *EM*456.31:—written **θρύσις,** Sch.DIl.21.351. ⊛ **θρύσκα,** τά, glossed by ἄγρια λάχανα, Hsch.

**θρύψις,** εως, ἡ, *breaking in small pieces*, οὔτε..εἴη ἂν ἄπειρος ἡ θ. Arist.*GC*316$^{b}$30; *dispersion*, ἡ θ. τοῦ ἀέρος Id.*de An.*419$^{b}$23; coupled with διάλυσις, Chrysipp.*Stoic.*2.173. II. *softness, weakness*, σώματος Plu.*Dem.*4: esp. metaph., *debauchery*, X.*Cyr.*8.8.16, Plu.*Lyc.* 14: pl., Id.2.732e. 2. *daintiness*, κόμης ib.693b; θ. (cj. for τρίψις) ἐπικρατίδων Hp.*Praec.*10.

⊛ **θρύψιχος,** = θρυπτικός, Theognost.*Can.*20, Hsch.

**θρυψίχρως,** ωτος, ὁ, ἡ, *of delicate skin*, Hsch.

**θρῠώδης,** ες, (θρύον) *full of rushes, rushy*, Str.8.3.24, Sch.Il.11.155.

**θρῶναξ,** ακος, ὁ, Lacon. for κηφήν, Hsch. **θρώπτει·** σκώπτει, Id.

**θρῶσις,** εως, ἡ, *cord, line*, Theognost.*Can.*20, Hsch.

**θρῴσκω** (so in Alc.*Supp.*12.9, but θρώσκω Did.ap.Hdn.Gr.2.522), Il.13.589, A.*Ch.*846, *Eu.*660: Ep. impf. θρῷσκον Il.15.314: fut. θοροῦμαι, Ion. 3 pl. θορέονται (ὑπερ-) 8.179, cf. A.*Supp.*873 (lyr.): aor. ἔθορον (ἐκ-) Il.7.182, etc., Ep. θόρον Il. (v. infr. 2), Hes.*Sc.*321, subj. θόρω Od. 22.303; inf. θορεῖν (ἀνα-) X.*Lac.*2.3, Ion. θορέειν (ὑπερ-) Il.12.53; later ἔθρωξα (ἀν-) Opp *H.*3.293: pf. part. fem. τεθορυίης prob. in Antim.65: (cf. θορός: for the form cf. βλώσκω):—poet. Verb, *leap, spring*, χαμᾶζε θορών Il.10.528; ἐκ δίφροιο 8.320; ἀπὸ λέκτροιο Od.23.32; ἰχθὺς θρῴσκων κατὰ κῦμα Il.21.126; of arrows, ἀπὸ νευρῆφι δ' ὀϊστοὶ θρῷσκον 15.314, cf. 470, 16.773; of beans *tossed* from the winnowing shovel, ἀπὸ πτυόφιν θρῴσκωσιν κύαμοι 13.589; of the oar, S.*OC*718 (lyr.). 2. folld. by Prep., *leap upon, assault*, ἐπὶ Τρώεσσι θόρον Il.8.252, cf. 15. 380; εἴς τινα A.R.1.1296; πλησίον τινός E.*Or.*257 (in this sense Hom. always uses aor.); of a recurring illness, *attack*, S.*Tr.*1028 (lyr.). 3. *rush, dart*, Pi.*P.*9.119; πεδίον *over* the plain, E.*Ba.*873 (lyr.); δόμους *to* the house, S.*Tr.*58: metaph., λόγοι πεδάρσιοι θρῴσκουσι *leap up* into air, i.e. *melt* away, A.*Ch.*846. II. trans., = θόρνυμαι, *mount, impregnate*, κνώδαλα Id.*Fr.*15; ὁ θρῴσκων *the sire*, Id.*Eu.*660; cf. θορός, θορή.

**θρωσμός** (**θρῳσμός** Apollon.ap.Hdn.Gr.2.522), ὁ, *springing*; of *ground rising* from the plain, ἐπὶ θρωσμῷ πεδίοιο Il.10.160, 11.56; ποταμοῖο A.R.2.823 (pl.).

⊛ **θρώσσει·** γεννᾷ, φοβεῖται, Hsch.

**θύα,** ἡ, = θύον I, Thphr.*HP*5.3.7.

**θυάκτας,** α, ὁ, *sacrificing priest*, *IG*4.757*B* (Troezen, ii B.C.).

**θυάλημα,** v. θυήλημα. ⊛ **θυαλόν·** τὸ θυτοῖς διαλαβεῖν, θυμιᾶσαι, Hsch. **θυάματα·** τὸ θύμον, καὶ θυμιάματα, Id.

**θυανία,** ἡ, prob. f.l. for ὑανία, Dor. for ὑην-, Epich.148.

**θύανον·** τὴν **θυώνην** (q.v.), ἐστὶ δὲ πέμμα ἀντὶ βοός, Hsch.

**θύαρος,** ὁ, = αἶρα II, Ps.-Dsc.2.100.

**θῠά⟨ρ⟩παξ,** ἄγος, ὁ, ἡ, = ἱερόσυλος, Hsch.

**θυάς,** άδος, ἡ, (θύω) = θυιάς (q.v.). II. *attack*, πλευρωνίας Mich. *in PN*30.20. III. θύας· πηδήσας, Hsch.; cf. θύασσε· ἐπήδησε, Cyr.

**θῠαφόρος,** ὁ, *thurifer*, *SIG*1025.52 (Cos, iv/iii B.C.).

⊛ **θυάω,** *rut*, of swine, Arist.*HA*546$^{a}$27, 573$^{b}$7.

**Θυβριάς,** άδος, ἡ, = Θυμβριάς, *IG*14.1389i1.

**θῠγᾰτερεῖς,** ίδος, ἡ, = θυγατριδῆ, *Inscr.Magn.*196.9.

⊛ **θῠγάτηρ** [ᾰ], ἡ, gen. θυγᾰτέρος contr. θυγατρός; dat. θυγᾰτέρι, θυγατρί; acc. θυγᾰτέρα Ep. θύγατρα Il.1.13; voc. θύγᾰτερ: nom. pl. θυγατέρες, Ep. and lyr. θύγατρες 9.144, Sapph.*Supp.*20a.16: gen. pl. -τέρων *IG*2$^{2}$.832.19, Pl.*R.*461c, poet. -τρῶν: dat. pl. -τράσι Ep. -τέρεσσι Il.15.197; both sets of forms are found in poetry, θυγατρός, -τρί, -τράσι are used in Prose:—*daughter*, Il.9.148, 290, Od.4.4, etc.; θύγατρες ἵππων, of mules, Simon.7; θ. ταύρων, of bees, Philo Tars.ap.Gal.13.269: metaph., Μοισᾶν θυγατέρες, of Odes, Pi.*N.*4.3; πλάστιγξ ἡ χαλκοῦ θ. Critias 1.9 D.; θ. Σειληνοῦ, of the vine, Jul. *Caes.*25; ψήφου συμβολικῆς θ., of a λάγυνος, *AP*6.248 (Marc. Arg.); of villages dependent on a city, Lxx *Jd.*1.27, 1*Ma.*5.8. II. later, *maidservant, slave*, Phalar.*Ep.*142.3. [ῡ in Ep. in the longer forms, metri gr.] (Cf. Skt. *duhitár-*, Engl. *daughter*, etc.)

**θῠγατρ-ῐδῆ,** ἡ, *daughter's daughter, granddaughter*, And.1.128, Lys.32.2, D.H.*Lys.*21: uncontr. nom. pl. **-δέαι** Euph.94.2. ⊛ **-ῐδοῦς,** οῦ, ὁ, *daughter's son, grandson*, Is.8.17, Arist.*Fr.*473, Ph.2.82, 425, *OGI*520.23 (Sebastopolis): acc. -δῆ, as though from nom. **-δεύς,** ib. 377.5 (Smyrna, i A.D.):—Ion. **-ιδέος** Hdt.5.67, 69. **-ίζω,** *call one daughter*, Araros 7. **-ιον,** τό, Dim. of θυγάτηρ, *little daughter* or *girl*, Stratt.63, Men.428, *PPetr.*3p.155 (iii B.C.), Macho ap.Ath.13. 581c, *Com.Adesp.*14.19 D., *SIG*364.55 (Ephesus, iii B.C.), Plu.*Ant.* 33, Jul.*Or.*7.226b.

**θῠγατρό-γᾰμος,** ον, *married to one's own daughter*, Nonn.*D.* 12.73. **-γόνος,** ον, *begetting* or *bearing daughters*, ib.7.212, al. **-θετέω,** *adopt as daughter*, Tz. ad Lyc.183 (Pass.). **-μιξία,** ἡ, *incest with a daughter*, *POxy.*237 vii 26 (ii A.D.). ⊛ **-ποιία,** ἡ, *adoption of a daughter*, *GDI*3706 vi 61 (Cos):—written **-ποία,** *IG* 12(1).818 (Rhodes). **-ποιός,** όν, *begetting daughters*, of Lot, Ph.1.382. **-τεκνον,** τό, *a daughter's child*, Tz.*H.*1.595.

**θῠεία,** Ion. **-είη** Nic.*Th.*91: ἡ:—*mortar*, Ar.*Nu.*676, *Ra.*124, al., Lys.*Fr.*62a. 2. *cup* of the cottabus, Pl.Com.46.3.—Later **θυία, θυΐα,** Ph.*Bel.*88.49, Dsc.2.76.3 and 4; in the sense of *oil-press*, *PFay.*42(*a*) i 10 (ii A.D.): **θυίη** [ῐ], Androm.ap.Gal.14.41: ⊛ **θυεῖον,** τό, *PLond.*2.193.23 (ii A.D.). II. **θύεια,** v. θυία I.

**θῠείδιον,** τό, Dim. of θυεία, Ar.*Pl.*710; wrongly written θυΐδιον in cod. Rav., as in Damocr.ap.Gal.14.118.

**θύελλ-α** [ῠ], ἡ, (θύω, cf. ἄελλα from ἄημι) *hurricane, squall* (cf. Arist.*Mu.*395$^{a}$6), κακὴ ἀνέμοιο Il.6.346, al.; μισγομένων ἀνέμων..θ. Od.5.317; πυρός τ' ὀλοοῖο θύελλαι, prob. *thunderstorms*, 12.68; κούρας ἀνέλοντο θ. 20.66; τοὺς δ' αἶψ' ἁρπάξασα φέρεν πόντονδε θ. 10.48, cf. S.*El.*1151; ποντία θ. Id.*OC*1660; in similes, φλογὶ ἶσοι ἠὲ θυέλλῃ Il. 13.39; ἴκελοι πυρὶ ἠὲ θ. Hes.*Sc.*345: metaph., ἄτης θύελλαι (nisi leg. θυηλαί, q.v.) A.*Ag.*819; ὀχλικὴ θ. Phld.*Rh.*1.184S. **-ειος,** α, ον, = sq., στροφάλιγγες Orac.ap.Suid. s.v. Ἰουλιανός. **-ήεις,** εσσα, εν, *stormy*, Nonn.*D.*1.22, 2.532. **-ίζω,** pf. part. Pass. -ισμένον (-θυλλιαμένον cod.)· τεταραγμένον, Hsch.

**θῠελλό-πους,** ὁ, ἡ, gen. ποδος, *storm-footed, storm-swift*, Nonn.*D.* 37.441. **-τόκος,** ον, *producing storms*, ib.28.277. **-φορέομαι,** Pass., *to be carried by a storm*, D.S.16.80.

**θῠελλώδης,** ες, *stormy*, Sch.S.*Ant.*418.

**Θῠέστειος,** α, ον, *of Thyestes*, ῥάκη Ar.*Ach.*433; **δεῖπνον** Porph.*Chr.* 69.

**θῠέστης,** ου, ὁ, *pestle*, Dionys.Trag.12.

**θύ-εστον,** τό, *drink made from bruised spices*, Hsch.: **-ευτός·** ὁ ἐξ ὄμβρων ποταμός, dub. l. in Theognost.*Can.*20.

**θῠ-ήεις,** εσσα, εν, (θύος) *smoking with incense, fragrant*, Ep. epith. of βωμός, Il.8.48, Od.8.363, Hes.*Th.*557; σπάργανα *h.Merc.*237. ⊛ **-ηκόος,** ὁ, = θυοσκόος, Hsch.; cf. θυηχόος. **-ηλέομαι,** = θυλέομαι, prob. in Poll.1.27. **-ηλή,** ἡ, (θύω) *part of a victim offered in burnt-sacrifice*, usu. in pl., ὁ δ' ἐν πυρὶ βάλλε θυηλάς Il.9.220, cf. Philoch.172, Nic.*Fr.*62, Ath.13.566a: generally, *sacrifice*, ἄνευ θυηλῶν Ar.*Av.*1520; θυηλαὶ ἀναίμακτοι *AP*6.324.3 (Leon. Alex.); θυσίαι καὶ θ. D.S.3.62, Porph.*Abst.*2.59: metaph., θυηλὴ Ἄρεος *an offering* to Ares, i.e. the blood of the slain, S.*El.*1423; ἄτης θυηλαί cj. Herm. for θύελλαι, A. *Ag.*819; cf. θυάλημα, θύλημα. **-ήλημα,** ατος, τό, *sacrificial offering*, Thphr.*Char.*10.13:—Ion. **θυαλήματα** *SIG*57.38 (Milet., v B.C.); cf. θύλημα. **-ημα,** ατος, τό, (θύω) = foreg., in pl., Tim.*Lex.*: = ἀρώματα, Hp.ap.Erot.

**θῠηπολ-έω,** *perform sacrifices*, A.*Ag.*262, E.*Tr.*330 (lyr.), Pl.*R.* 364e, Polystr.p.9 W.; θεοῖς E.*El.*665. 2. trans., *sacrifice*, γέρας βρότειον τῷ Κρόνῳ θ. S.*Fr.*126, cf. 522, Maiist.13:—Pass., θυηπολεῖται δ' ἄστυ μάντεων ὕπο *is filled with sacrifices* by them, E.*Heracl.* 401. ⊛ **-ία,** Ion. **-ίη,** ἡ, *sacrificing*, A.R.1.1124, *AP*5.16 (Gaet.), D.H.1.21, Hld.3.2, prob. in Puchstein *Epigr.Gr.*36 (pl., Nubia): generally, *mystic rites*, Orph.*A.*470. ⊛ **-ικός,** ή, όν, *sacrificial*, πῦρ, μέρος, Iamb.*Myst.*5.11, 18; θεσμός Zos.4.59. **-ιον,** τό, *altar*, Dorieus ap.Ath.10.413a:—also **-εῖον,** τό, *Rev.Ét.Gr.*19.234 (Aphrodisias).

**θῠηπόλος,** ον, also η, ον Suid., (τελέω, τέλλω) *performing sacrifices, sacrificial*, χείρ A.*Pers.*202: Subst., *diviner, soothsayer*, E.*IA*746, Ar.*Pax*1124; *priest*, Εὐμόλποιο *IG*3.1337.9, cf. Phld.*D.*1.4; **αἱ θ. παρθένοι**, of the Vestal Virgins, D.H.2.64, al.

**θύ[η]σις** [ῠ], εως, ἡ, *sacrifice*, *IG*5(2).514 (Lycosura, nisi leg. θύ[ω]σις).

**θυητά** [ῠ], τά, *fumigations*, Aret.*CD*1.4, *CA*2.10.

**θῠη-φάγος** [ᾰ], ον, *devouring offerings*, φλόξ A.*Ag.*597. **-χόος,** contr. **-χοῦς,** ὁ, = θυηκόος, *IG*1$^{2}$.372.203, 3.244, Eust.1601.3.

**θυία,** ἡ, *odorous cedar, Juniperus foetidissima*, Thphr.*HP*1.9.3, 4.1. 3; or **θύεια,** ib.3.4.2, 6. II. = θύον I (q.v.), Dsc.1.26. III. v. θυεία.

**Θυῖα,** τά, (θύω) festival of Dionysus at Elis, Paus.6.26.1.

**Θυῖαι,** αἱ, = Θυιάδες, Str.10.3.10, prob. l. for Θυιάσιν, S.*Ant.*1151 (lyr.).

⊛ **θυιάς,** άδος, ἡ:—written **θυάς** Tim.*Fr.*3, A.*Th.*498 cod. Med.: (θύω):—*inspired, possessed woman*, esp. *Bacchante*, ll. cc., cf. A.*Th.* 836, *Supp.*564 (both lyr.), Plu.2.293f, etc.; cf. foreg. II. fem. Adj., *frantic, mad for love*, Lyc.143.

**θυΐδιον,** v. θυείδιον.

**θύϊνος** [ῠ], η, ον, *of the tree* θύον (q.v.), **δένδρα, ξύλον,** Str.4.6.2, v.l. in Dsc.1.22; *made of this wood*, Callix.1, *Apoc.*18.12.

**θυϊόεν·** πλῆρες, and **θυϊόεντες·** ἀνθοῦντες, Hsch.

**θυῖον,** τό, *resin*, Thphr.*HP*5.2.1.

**Θυῖος,** ὁ (sc. μήν), name of a month in Thessaly and Boeotia, *IG* 9(2).109*b*57 (Halus), 7.341, etc.; in Naupactus, ib.9(1).357:—also **Θῦος,** ib.9(2).515.3 (Larissa), al.:—Boeot. **Θούιος** or **Θιούιος,** ib.7. 517, 3172.116.

**θυιόω,** aor. part. Pass. θυιωθείς· μανείς, ὁρμήσας, Hsch.

**θῠΐς,** ῖδος (-ΐδος codd.), ἡ, = θυεία, Damocr.ap.Gal.14.130.

**θῠΐσκη,** ἡ, *censer*, Lxx 1*Ma.*1.22, al., J.*AJ*3.6.8, 3.8.10:—**θῠΐσκος,** ὁ, v.l., ib.3.6.8:—also **θύσκη,** *POxy.*1657.13 (iii A.D.), Suid., *EM* 458.53: **θύσκος,** ib.52 (θύκος cod.).

**θῠΐτης** [ῑ] (sc. λίθος), ου, ὁ, *an Ethiopian stone*, Dsc.5.136, Gal. 12.198.

⊛ **θυίω,** = θύω, *to be inspired*, subj. θυίωσι *h.Merc.*560. II. = θύω (B), Hes.*Th.*131 (Pap.), v.l. in A.R.3.755, Nic.*Th.*129.

**θῡλάκ-η** [ᾰ], ἡ, = *scrotum*, *Hippiatr.*50. **-ίζω,** *collect* scraps *in a wallet*: hence, at Tarentum, *beg*, Hsch. ⊛ **-ιον,** τό, Dim. of θύλακος, Hdt.3.105, Ar.*V.*314, *Ra.*1203 codd., *PLille* 10 ii 14 (iii B.C.), *PCair. Zen.*69.6 (iii B.C.). II. *seed-capsule*, Sch.Nic.*Th.*852. ⊛ **-ίς,** ίδος, ἡ, Dim. of θύλακος, = θυλάκιον II, Ael.*NA*6.43, Nic.*Th.*852. **-ίσκος,** ὁ, = θυλάκιον I, *bread-basket*, Ar.*Fr.*545, Crates Com.14. II. = θυλάκιον II, Dsc.2.106. **-ίτης** [ῑ], ου, ὁ, = sq., only fem. θυλακῖτις μήκων the *common* poppy (cf. θυλακίς), Dsc.4.64; θ. νάρδος, = ὀρεινὴ ν., Id.1.9.

**θῡλᾰκό-βολον**, *verrutum*, *Gloss.* **-ειδής**, *ές*, *like a bag*, Arist. *HA*543$^{b}$13. **-εις**, *εσσα*, *εν*, = foreg., Nic.*Al.*403. **-ομαι**, Pass., *become a bag*, Sch.Ar.*Pax* 198.

**θύλᾰκος** [ῡ], ὁ, *sack*, esp. to carry meal in, Hdt.3.46; ἄλφιτ' οὐκ ἔνεστιν ἐν τῷ θυλάκῳ Ar.*Pl.*763; θ. δορκαδέων ἀστραγάλων *PCair.Zen.* 69.18 (iii B.C.); δερῶ σε θύλακον I'll make *a bag* of your skin, Ar.*Eq.* 370; contemptuous word for a garment, ὁ Τηλαύγους θ. prob. in Aeschin.Socr.42: metaph., of a person, θ. τις λόγων 'wind-bag', Pl.*Tht.*161a; τῇ χειρὶ δεῖν σπείρειν, ἀλλὰ μὴ ὅλῳ τῷ θ. Corinn.ap.Plu. 2.348a. 2. *sack in which the eggs of the tunny are enveloped*, Arist. *HA*571$^{a}$14, cf. 552$^{b}$19. II. in pl., slang term for the *loose trousers* of Persians and other Orientals, E.*Cyc.*182, Ar.*V.*1087. III. *ball* used for physical exercise, Antyll.ap.Orib.6.32.12.

**θῡλᾰκο-τρώξ**, ῶγος, ὁ, ἡ, *gnawing sacks*, Hsch., Hdn.Gr.2.37. **-φορέω**, *carry a sack* or *pouch*, Ar.*Fr.*789. **-φόρος**, ον, *carrying a bag*, name for prospectors, Hsch., Phot.

**θῡλᾰκώδης**, ες, = θυλακοειδής, Thphr.*HP*3.7.3, Dsc.1.90, Mnesith. Cyz.ap.Orib.*inc.*15.8.

**θῦλαξ**, ᾰκος, ὁ, = θύλακος, Arcesil.Com.1 D., Aesop.15; = προσκεφάλαιον, Hsch.; cited fr. Hom. by Poll.10.172; cj. in Sor.1.57.

**θῡλάς**, άδος, ἡ, = foreg., v. οὐλάς.

**θῡλ-έομαι**, *offer in sacrifice*, ἀλφίτων ὀλίγας δράκας Porph.*Abst.*2. 17; θυηλήσασθαι shd. be read in Poll.1.27. **-ημα**, ατος, τό, *that which is offered*: mostly in pl., θυλήματα, *cakes, incense*, etc., Ar.*Pax* 1040, Thphr.*Fr.*97.3, Pherecr.23.6, Telecl.33, Porph.*Abst.*2.6,29; cf. θυάλημα, θυήλημα. (Cf. θύος, θύω (A), Lett. *dūlēt* 'smoke (bees)', Lat. *fuligo.*) [ῡ, Pherecr. l. c.]

**θύλλα**· κλάδους ἢ φύλλα, ἡ ἑορτὴ Ἀφροδίτης, Hsch.:—hence **Θυλλοφόρος**, title of Dionysus at Cos, *SIG*1012.7 (ii/i B.C.).

**θυλλίς**, ίδος, ἡ, = θύλακος, Hdn.Gr.1.89, Hsch. **θύλον**· ὀλέθριον (leg. οὖλον), Id.

**θῦμα**, ατος, τό, (θύω A) *victim, sacrifice*, *SIG*56.31 (Argos, v B.C.), A. *Ag.*1310, S.*Ph.*8, Ar.*Av.*901, Wilcken *Chr.*1 iii 3 (iii B.C.), etc.; τὸ θ. τοῦ Ἀπόλλωνος Th.5.53; θ. θύειν, θύσασθαι, Pl.*Plt.*290e, *R.*378a, etc.; usu. of animals, but πάγκαρπα θ. *offerings* of all fruits, S.*El.*634; ⟨ἁγνὰ⟩ θ., opp. ἱερεῖα, expld. by Sch. as *cakes in the form of animals*, Th.1.126, cf. Pl.*Lg.*782c, Poll.1.26: prov., θ. Δελφόν 'Barmecide's feast', Call.*Iamb.*1.98. 2. pl., of *animals slaughtered* for food, Lxx *Ge.*43.16. 3. metaph., of persons, θ. λεύσιμον, prob. of Clytemnestra, A.*Ag.*1118 (lyr.); πρόκεισθε θύματα τῆς ἡμετέρας ἐξουσίας Hdn.2.13.5. II. *act of sacrifice*, ὧδ' ἣν τὰ κείνης θ. S.*El.*573. [θῦμα only *Supp.Epigr.*2.518 (Rome, iv A.D.), cf. Hdn.Gr.2.15.]

**θῡμάγροικος**, ον, *of clownish spirit*, Ar.*Fr.*790.

**θυμαδέων**, Dor. for -ηδέων, = ἀθυμῶν (scr. εὐθ-), Hsch.

**θῡμ-αίνω**, Ep. impf. θυμαίνεσκον A.R.3.1326: (θυμός):—*to be wroth, angry*, Hes.*Sc.*262, Ar.*Nu.*610; τινι *at* one, ib.1478, Eup.191. **-αλγής**, ές, (ἀλγέω) *heart-grieving*, χόλος Il.4.513; λώβη 9.387, Od.20. 285; μῦθος, ἔπος, 8.272, 16.69, Hdt.1.129; μέρμηραι *IG*14.1942. 11. II. Pass., *inly grieving*, [καρδία] A.*Ag.*1031 (lyr.).

**θῡμαλίς**, v.l. for τιθύμαλλος in Nic.*Th.*617.

**θύμαλλος**, ὁ, an unknown *fish*, Ael.*NA*14.22.

**θῡμάλωψ** [ᾰ], ωπος, ὁ, *piece of burning wood* or *charcoal*, Ar.*Ach.*321, *Th.*729, Stratt.55, Luc.*Lex.*24. (τύφω: for the termin., cf. αἰμάλωψ.)

**θυμαμοργάς**· ἡ νόσος (Eretr.), Hsch. **θῡμαντικός**, ή, όν, = *animosus*, *Gloss.*: **-άντρια**, ἡ, dub. sens., φασγάνων θ. *PMag.Par.*1.2267.

**θυμάρεστος**, gloss on θυμαρής, Apollon.*Lex.*

**θῡμᾰρ-έω**, *to be well-pleased*, Theoc.26.9. **-ής**, ές, (θυμός, ἀραρίσκω) *suiting the heart*, i. e. *well-pleasing, delightful*, ἄλοχον θυμαρέα Il. 9.336, Od.23.232; σκῆπτρον θ. ἔδωκεν 17.199: irreg. acc. θυμάρην ὄλβον *IG*14.433 (Tauromenium):—also **θυμήρης**, ες (on the accent v. Hdn.Gr.2.65, al.), Hom. only in neut. as Adv., θυμῆρες κεράσασα Od.10.362: as Adj., ἔπος A.R.1.705; ἑταῖραι Mosch.2.29: also in later Prose, Luc.*Am.*43, Hdn.8.5.9: Comp., Lxx *Wi.*3.14: Sup., Ph.2.36, Sch.Nic.*Al.*577, and in form **θυμερέστατος** (sic) *BCH*27. 330 (Bithynia). Adv. -ήρως Heph.Astr.3.11.

**θῡμάρμενος**, ον, = foreg., τέρας B.16.71, cf. Nic.*Al.*577, Call.*Dian.* 167.

**θύμαρνον**, τό, = ἱππομάραθον, Ps.-Dsc.3.71.

**θῡμάτιον**, τό, Dim. of θῦμα, *Gloss.*

**θυματῖτις**, ιδος, ἡ, = πεντάφυλλον, v.l. in Ps.-Dsc.4.42.

**θύμβρα**, ἡ, (perh. from τύφω) *savory*, *Satureia Thymbra*, Eup.14.5, Thphr.*CP*3.1.4, Dsc.3.37, Plin.*HN*19.165:—also **θυμβραία**, ἡ, Hp. ap.Gal.19.104 (but θύμβρη or -ην *Nat.Mul.*32 codd.).

**θυμβρεπίδειπνος**, ον, *supping on bitter herbs*, i. e. *living poorly*, Ar. *Nu.*421.

**Θύμβρις**, ιδος, ἡ, name of several rivers, esp. *the Tiber*, *AP*9.352 (Leon. Alex.), D.P.352 sq.; cf. Θυβριάς.

**θυμβρίτης** [ῑ] οἶνος, ὁ, wine *flavoured with savory*, Dsc.5.50.

**θύμβρον**, τό, = θύμβρα, Thphr.*HP*7.1.2, Sch.Ar.*Ach.*253.

**θυμβροφάγος** [ᾰ], ον, *eating savory*, θυμβροφάγον βλέπειν to look *as if one had eaten savory*, 'make a *verjuice face*', Ar.*Ach.*254.

**θυμβρώδης**, ες, *like savory*, Thphr.*HP*6.7.5.

**θῠμελαία**, ἡ, prob. *spurge-flax*, *Daphne Cnidium*, Dsc.4.172, Plin. *HN*13.114:—hence **-αΐτης** [ῑ] οἶνος, ὁ, wine *flavoured with* θυμελαία, Dsc.5.68.

**θῠμέλ-η**, ἡ, (θύω A) prop. *place of burning, hearth*, θυμέλαι οἴκων E.*Rh.* 234 (lyr.), cf. A.*Supp.*669 (lyr.); Κυκλώπων θυμέλαι E.*IA*152 (anap.); but usu. of *sacrificial hearths* or *altars*, δεξίπυροι θεῶν θ. Id.*Supp.*64 (lyr.); ἁ Φοίβου θ. Id.*Ion* 114 (lyr.), cf. 46, al.; Ἑστία, δίδου.. ἀμφὶ σὰν θ. χορεύειν Aristonous 2.17; also of *braziers*, θυμέλαι ἐπίτναντο χρυσήλατοι E.*El.*713 (lyr.); ἡ θ. τοῦ βωμοῦ the surface on which fire was kindled, *IG*11(2).161 *A* 95 (Delos, iii B.C.). II. esp. of the *altar* of Dionysus which stood in the orchestra of the theatre, Διονυσιὰς θ. Pratin.Lyr.1. 2, cf. *EM*743.37, etc.: hence in later writers, b. the *orchestra*, Phryn. 142, Sch.Aristid.p.536 D.: hence of the chorus, opp. actors, θυμέλῃσι καὶ ἐν σκηνῇσι τεθηλώς, of Sophocles, *AP*7.21 (Simm.); cf. sq. c. the *stage*, Phryn.*PS* p.74 B., *EM*653.8, etc. (hence generally, *platform, stage*, Plu.*Alex.*67); so ὁ ἀπὸ τῆς θ., of a dramatic poet, Id. *Demetr.*12, etc.; ὥσπερ ἐκ θ., i. e. theatrical, Id.2.405d; actuarii thymelae equorumque currulium, *Cod.Theod.*8.7.21. d. αἱ ἐτήσιοι θ. annual *stage-performances*, Alciphr.2.3, cf. *POxy.*1143.3 (i A.D.), *IG* 14.2342. III. of the θόλος at Epidaurus (containing a *hearth* or *altar*), ib.4.1485 *B* 162. IV. = θυλήματα, Pherecr.214. **-ικός**, ή, όν, *of* or *belonging to the thymele, theatrical*, θέαι, ἄνθρωποι, Plu.*Fab.*4, *Sull.*36; θ. ἔρις *Com.Adesp.*57; τὸ θ. *theatrical, vulgar* style, Plu.2. 853b; of performances of music, dancing, etc., *in the orchestra* (cf. foreg. II. b); θ. ἀγών *SIG*457.1 (Thespiae, iii B.C.), cf. D.S.4.5, *CIG* 3493.11 (Thyatira), etc.; θ. ἀκροάματα Corn.*ND*30; οἱ θ. *the musicians*, opp. οἱ σκηνικοί, the actors, Plu.*Cat.Mi.*46; opp. ὑποκριταί, Ptol. *Tetr.*180 (but later of *actors*, Jul.*Ep.*89b, *Cod.Just.*1.4.14); ἡ θ. σύνοδος the company of θ., *IG*2$^{2}$.1350, *OGI*713, etc.

**θῠμελο-ποιοί**, οἱ, *board of curators of the* θυμέλη III at Epidaurus, *IG*4.1485 *B* 142: also dat. pl. -ποίαις (from **-ποίης**) ib.134,139.

**θῡμ-ηγερέων**, (θυμός, ἀγείρω) *gathering breath, collecting oneself*, Od. 7.283. **-ηδέω**, Dor. -ᾱδέω (q.v.), *to be glad-hearted*, Semon.7. 103; ἐπί τινι Hld.10.3. **-ηδής**, ές, (ἦδος) *well-pleasing, dear*, χρήματα Od.16.389; νόστοιο τέλος A.R.1.249; τὰ λῷστα καὶ τὰ -έστατα A.*Supp.*962; παῖδας *Epigr.Gr.*403.7 (Sebastopolis); θ. ἀναθυμιάσεις cj. for θυμώδεις in Herod.Med.ap.Orib.10.40.1. **-ηδία**, Ion. -ίη, ἡ, *gladness of heart, rejoicing*, Eup.161, Call.*Fr.*2 P., Plu.2.713d, Aret. *SD*1.5, Chor. in *Rev.Phil.*1.225: pl., Ph.2.548, Luc.*Abd.*5, D.C.47. 1. **-ήρης**, v. θυμαρής.

**θῡμία**, Ion. -ίη, ἡ, = θυμίαμα, -ίῃσι κακώδεσι Aret.*SD*2.11.

**θῡμι-άζω**, = -ιάω, *Gp.*12.8.8. **-αίνω**, = -ιάω, *Gloss.* **-ᾱμα**, Ion. -ημα, ατος, τό, *incense*, Hdt.1.198, Amphis 27, *PTeb.*112.22 (ii B.C.), Phld.*Vit.*p.37 J.; name of a particular kind (perh. = ἀμμωνιακόν), *Edict.Diocl.* in Ἀθηνᾶ 18.6 (Tegea): usu. in pl., *fragrant stuffs* for burning, Hdt.2.130, 7.54, S.*OT*4, Ar.*Av.*1716, Pl.*R.*373c, *IG*5(2). 514 (Lycosura), *Apoc.*5.8; -ιάματα ἑρπετῶν *fumigations*, Philum.*Ven.* 6 tit. 2. *stuff for embalming*, Hdt.2.86, 4.71. **-ᾱσις**, εως, ἡ, *fumigating*, Dsc.1.98, Antyll.ap.Orib.10.19.1. II. *passing off in fumes*, Arist.*Mete.*387$^{a}$30; τῶν ἀπὸ γῆς Porph.*Abst.*2.5. **-ατέον**, *one must fumigate*, *Gp.*6.10, Paul.Aeg.6.75. **-ᾱτεύω**, *fumigate*, τὴν ἐκκλησίαν Sch.Aeschin.1.23. **-ᾱτήριον**, Ion. θυμιητ-, τό, *censer*, Hdt. 4.162, Th.6.46, And.4.29, *POxy.*521.19 (ii A.D.), etc. 2. *vessel for fumigation*, Aët.9.41. II. name of the constellation *Ara*, Eudox. ap.Hipparch.1.11.6, Ptol.*Tetr.*28, etc. **-ᾱτίζω**, = θυμιάω, *Gp.*6. 13.3:—Med., ib.6.12.1. **-ᾱτικός**, ή, όν, *good for burning as incense*, σώματα Pl.*Ti.*61c. **-ᾱτός**, Ion. -ητός, ή, όν, *to be burnt as incense*, Hp.*Mul.*2.114; πᾶν τὸ θ. Thphr.*Od.*12; *capable of giving off fumes*, Arist.*Mete.*387$^{b}$7: pl., θυμιητά, = θυμιάματα, Aret.*SD*2. 11. **-ᾱτρίς**, ίδος, ἡ, = θυμιατήριον, Dam.*Isid.*188. **-ᾱτρον**, τό, = foreg., *SIG*577.31 (Milet., iii/ii B.C.). **-άω**, Ion. aor. ἐθυμίησα Hippon.92, Hdt.6.97:—**Med.**, Ion. fut. -ήσομαι Hp.*Mul.*2.126: aor. ἐθυμιησάμην ib.146, *Nat.Mul.*7 (but -ασάμην *Morb.*2.27):—Pass., fut. -ᾱθήσομαι Dsc.1.68.6: aor. ἐθυμιάθην ib.5:—*burn so as to produce smoke*, θ. τὴν στύρακα Hdt.3.107; λιβανωτοῦ τριηκόσια τάλαντα Id. 6.97; θυμιήματα Id.8.99; λιβάνου δάκρυα Pi.*Fr.*122.4: abs., *burn incense*, Hermipp.8, Men.*Sam.*264, Lxx 4*Ki.*22.17, al., *OGI*352.37 (ii B.C.), etc.; τινι in honour of any one, Ath.7.289f:—Med., Ael. *VH*12.51:—Pass., *to be burnt*, [τὸ σπέρμα τῆς καννάβιος] θυμιᾶται (v.l. -ῆται) Hdt.4.75; λίθος.. τεθυμιαμένος Ar.*Fr.*635; *pass off in fumes*, Arist.*Mete.*362$^{a}$11; θυμιωμένων τινῶν Pl.*Ti.*66d. 2. *smoke, fumigate*, τί τινι *PMag.Par.*1.2970:—Med., Hp. ll. cc.:—Pass., θυμιώμεναι μέλισσαι Arist.*HA*623$^{b}$20. II. intr., *smoke*, ἄνθρακες θυμιῶντες Thphr.*Ign.*75.

**θῡμίδιον**, τό, Dim. of θυμός, Ar.*V.*878.

**θῡμίζω**, *taste of thyme*, Archig.ap.Orib.8.1.32:—Pass., *to be embittered*, θυμιχθείς· πικρανθείς, Hsch.

**θῡμικός**, ή, όν, (θυμός) *high-spirited*, of the dog, Arist.*HA*488$^{b}$21: τὸ ἄρρεν -ώτερον Id.*PA*661$^{b}$33: Sup., D.C.49.36. 2. = θυμοειδής 3, Pl.*Def.*415e, Arist.*de An.*432$^{a}$25, Phld.*Oec.*p.33 J., Hierocl. *in CA*26 p.480 M. 3. *irascible*, Ath.2.38b; θ. καὶ ὀξύθυμοι οἱ νέοι Arist.*Rh.* 1389$^{a}$9. 4. Adv. -κῶς Plb.18.37.12: Comp. -ώτερον Id.7.13.3, Cic.*Att.*10.11.5.

**θύμινον** [ῠ], τό (sc. μέλι), *honey made from thyme*, Colum.6.33, *Gloss.*, Apul.*Herb.*p.294 H.-S.

**θύμιον**, τό, = σμῖλαξ, Dsc.*Alex.*12. II. *large wart*, Hp.*Ulc.*14, Dsc.5.1, Plin.*HN*32.128.

**θῠμίτης** [ῑ], ου, ὁ, (θύμον) *flavoured with thyme*, ἅλες Ar.*Ach.*1099; οἶνος Dsc.5.49.

**θῡμο-βᾰρής**, ές, *heavy at heart*, *AP*7.146 (Antip. Sid.):—fem. **-βάρεια** *EM*458.24. **-βορέω**, *gnaw, vex the heart*, Hes.*Op.* 799. **-βόρος**, ον, (βιβρώσκω, βορά) *eating the heart*, θυμοβόρῳ ἔριδι Il.19.58, al.; λύα Alc.*Supp.*23.10; Κῆρες A.R.4.1666; τῆς θυμοβόρου φρένα λύπης cj. for θυμοφθόρον in A.*Ag.*103 (anap.). **-δᾰκής**, ές, *biting the heart*, θ. γὰρ μῦθος Od.8.185; ζάλου κέντρον *AP*9.77 (Antip. Thess.): in late Prose, μῦθοι Aret.*CA*1.1, cf. Jul.*Or.*2.

96a. ❀ -ειδής, ές, *high-spirited*, τὸ θ. Hp.*Aër*.12; opp. ἄθυμος, Pl. *R*.456a; opp. ὀργίλος, ib.411c. 2. *passionate, hot-tempered*, opp. πραΰς, ib.375c. b. of horses, *mettled*, X.*Mem*.4.1.3; opp. εὐπειθέστατος, Id.*Smp*.2.10: Comp., opp. βλακωδέστερος, Id.*Eq*.9.1. 3. Philos., τὸ θ. *spirit, passion*, opp. τὸ λογιστικόν, τὸ ἐπιθυμητικόν, Pl. *R*.440e, al., cf. D.L.3.67. Adv. -δῶς Hdn.4.3.3.

❀ **θῠμόεις**, εσσα, εν, *thymy*, Choeril.8.

**θῡμο-κατοχέω**, *nurse anger*, cj. for θυμω κατοχουντα in Epicur. *Sent.Vat*.62 (*Rh.Mus*.61.421). **-κάτοχος**, ον, *restraining anger*: neut as Subst., *spell for this purpose*, *PMag.Lond*.121.941, *PMag. Osl*.1.35, *PMag.Par*.1.467,831; θ. πρὸς βασιλέας *PMag.Leid.W*.6.38. **-λέαινα**, ἡ, fem. of θυμολέων, *AP*5.299 (Paul. Sil.). **-λεοντοφθόρος**, ον, *bold enough to slay a lion*, *PMasp*.2 iii 22 (vi A. D.). **-λέων**, οντος, ὁ, *lion-hearted*, of Achilles, Il.7.228, Hes.*Th*.1007; of Ulysses, πόσιν ἀπώλεσα θ. Od.4.724; of Hercules, 11.267, cf. Ar.*Ra*.1041 (anap.). **-λῑπής**, ές, (λείπω) = λιπόθυμος, Call.*Fr*.1.55 P., Nonn.*D*.37.540. **-μαντις**, εως, ὁ, ἡ, *prophesying from one's own soul*, A.*Pers*.224 (troch.); cf. θυμόσοφος. **-μᾰχέω**, *to be angry*, Plb.9.40.4; ἐπί τινι Id.27.8.4; πρός τινας Plu.*Demetr*.22; τισι *Act.Ap*.12.20. II. *fight desperately*, D.S.17.33; *contend obstinately*, τινι D.H.5.11. **-μᾰχία**, ἡ, *desperate fight*, Polyaen.2.1.19.

❀ **θύμον** [ῡ], τό, Arist.*HA*626ᵇ21, *Pr*.925ᵃ9, Thphr.*HP*6.2.3: dual θύμω Pherecr.167: pl., θύμα Eup.14.5, Antiph.179.4: gen. θύμων Ar.*Pl*.283; θυμέων *AP*9.226.2 (Zonas):—also **θύμος**, ὁ, Dsc.3.36:—*Cretan thyme, Thymbra capitata*, ll. cc., Hp.*Vict*.2.54, al.; τὸ μύρον φάσκειν οὐδὲν τοῦ θ. ἥδιον ὄζειν Thphr.*Char*.4.1. b. a marine plant, Id. *HP*4.7.2. 2. *mixture of thyme with honey and vinegar*, eaten by the poor of Attica, Ar.*Pl*.253, cf. 283, Antiph.226.7, Luc.*Fug*.14, Hsch.

**θῡμ-οξ-άλμη**, ἡ, *drink of thyme, vinegar, and brine*, Dsc.5.16.

**θῡμο-πληθής**, ές, *wrathful*, A.*Th*.686 (lyr.). **-ποιέω**, *hearten, encourage*, τὸ πλῆθος Satyr.*Vit.Eur.Fr*.39 iv 31. **-ραϊστής**, οῦ, ὁ, (ῥαίω) *life-destroying*, θάνατος Il.13.544, 16.414; δηΐων ὕπο θυμοραϊστέων ib.591. (-**ρραίστης** Glauc.ap.Sch.B Il.16.414.)

**θύμος** (A), ὁ, v. θύμον.

**θύμος** [perh. ῠ] (B), ὁ, *warty excrescence*, Hp.*Alim*.17, Dsc.2.28, Paul.Aeg.6.71; esp. in the anal or genital regions, Gal.7.731. II. *the thymus gland in the neck or breast* of young animals, Ruf.*Onom*.168, Gal.*UP*6.4.

❀ **θῡμός**, ὁ, *soul, spirit*, as *the principle of life, feeling and thought*, esp. *of strong feeling and passion* (rightly derived from θύω (B) by Pl.*Cra*.419e ἀπὸ τῆς θύσεως καὶ ζέσεως τῆς ψυχῆς): I. in physical sense, *breath, life*, θ. ἀπηύρα, ἀφελέσθαι, ἐξαίνυσθαι, ὀλέσαι, freq. in Hom., Il.6.17, 5.852, 155, 1.205: c. dupl. acc., ἄμφω θ. ἀπηύρα 6.17; ἐπεί κε..ῥεθέων ἐκ θ. ἕληται 22.68; λίπε δ' ὀστέα θ. 12.386; ἀπὸ δ' ἔπτατο θ. Od.10.163; ὀλίγος δ' ἔτι θ. ἐνῆεν Il.1.593; μόγις δ' ἐσαγείρετο θυμόν 21.417; ἄψορρόν οἱ θ. ἐνὶ στήθεσσιν ἀγέρθη 4.152; θυμοῦ καὶ ψυχῆς κεκαδών 11.334; of animals, 3.294, 12.150, etc.: less freq. in Trag., A. *Ag*.1388, E.*Ba*.620 (troch.). 2. *spirit, strength*, τείρετο δ' ἀνδρῶν θ. ὑπ' εἰρεσίης Od.10.78; ἐν δέ τε θ. τείρεθ' ὁμοῦ καμάτῳ τε καὶ ἱδρῷ Il.17.744. 3. πάτασσε δὲ θ. ἑκάστου each man's *heart* beat high, 23.370, cf. 7.216. II. *soul*, as shown by the feelings and passions; and so, 1. *desire* or *inclination*, esp. desire for meat and drink, *appetite*, πιέειν ὅτε θ. ἀνώγοι Il.4.263; πλησάμενος..θυμὸν ἐδητύος ἠδὲ ποτῆτος Od.17.603: generally, τά με θ. ἐνὶ στήθεσσι κελεύει Il.7.68; βαλέειν δέ ἑ ἵετο θ. 8.301; αἲ γάρ με μένος καὶ θ. ἀνείη 22.346; θ. ἐποτρύνῃ [τινά] Od.9.139; θ. ἐπέσσυταί τινι, ἐφορμᾶται, Il.1.173, 13.73; ἤθελε θυμῷ he wished *in his heart* or *with all his heart*, 16.255, 21.65; ἵετο θυμῷ 2.589; so later θυμῷ βουλόμενοι wishing *with all their heart*, Hdt.5.49; [ὄσσα ϝ]οι θ. κε θέλῃ γένεσθαι Sapph.*Supp*.1.3; θυμὸς ὦρμα Pi.*O*.3.25, cf. 38; θυμὸς ἡδονὴν φέρει S.*El*.286; ὧν ἐρᾷ θυμός Herod.7.61; τῶν σφι θ. ἦν μάλιστα Hdt.1.1; ἄλλως σφι θ. ἐγένετο θεήσασθαι τὸν πόλεμον Id.8.116, etc.: with Verb omitted, σὲ γὰρ μοι θύμος ὔμμην Alc. 5, ἄρχ' αὐτὸς ὥς σοι θ. S.*El*.1319; ὅπου ὑμῖν θ. X.*Cyr*.3.1.37; βῆξαι θυμός ἐγγίνεται Hp.*Prog*.8. 2. *mind, temper, will*, θ. πρόφρων, ἵλαος, Il.8.39, 9.639; θ. ὑπερφίαλος καὶ ἀπηνής, νηλέα θ. ἔχοντας, σιδήρεος θ., 15.94, 19.229, Od.5.191; ἕνα θ. ἔχειν to be of one *mind*, Il.15.710, etc.; οὐδὲ λύκοι τε καὶ ἄρνες ὁμόφρονα θ. ἔχουσιν 22.263; ἕτερος δέ με θ. ἔρυκε Od.9.302; ἐμὸν θ. ἔπειθεν ib.33; θωπείας κολακικάς, αἳ..τοὺς θ. ποιοῦσιν κηρίνους Pl.*Lg*.633d. 3. *spirit, courage*, μένος καὶ θ. Il.20.174; θ. ἐνὶ στήθεσσι λαβεῖν Od.10.461; πᾶσιν δὲ παραὶ ποσὶ κάππεσε θ. Il.15.280; ψῦχρος ἔγεντο θ., of doves, Sapph.16; θ. ἔχειν ἀγαθόν Hdt.1.120; θ. οὐκ ἀπώλεσεν S.*El*.26; ὁ θυμὸς εὐθὺς ἦν 'Αμυνίας Ar.*Eq*.570; ἴωμεν ῥώμῃ καὶ θυμῷ ἐπί.. X.*Cyr*.4.2.21; φρονήματός τε καὶ θυμοῦ ἐμπίπλασθαι Pl.*R*.411c: so in Philos., opp. λόγος, ἐπιθυμία, ib.440b, al., cf. Arist.*Pol*.1328ᵃ7, 1327ᵇ24, Phld.*Mus*.p.26 K., etc.; personified, *Passion, Emotion*, opp. Λογισμός, Cleanth.*Stoic*.1.129. 4. *the seat of anger*, χωόμενον κατὰ θυμόν Il.1.429; νεμεσιζέσθω ἐνὶ θυμῷ 17.254; θυμὸν ἐχώσατο 16.616, etc.: hence, *anger, wrath*, δάμασον θυμόν 9.496; εἴξας ᾧ θυμῷ ib.598; θυμὸς μέγας ἐστὶ..βασιλῆος 2.196; θ. ὀξὺς S.*OC* 1193; θ. κρείσσων τῶν ἐμῶν βουλευμάτων E.*Med*.1079, etc.; θυμῷ f.l. for θυμοῦ in S.*Ant*.718; οἱ τῷ θ. πραχθέντες φόνοι Pl.*Lg*.867b; opp. λογισμός, Th.2.11, etc.; ἐπανάγειν τὸν θ. Hdt.7.160; ἐκτείνειν And.3.31; καταθέσθαι Ar.*V*.567; δακεῖν Id.*Nu*.1369; θυμῷ χρᾶσθαι Hdt.1.137, al.; ὀργῆς καὶ θυμοῦ μεστοί Isoc.12.81 (so τὴν ὀργὴν καὶ τὸν θ., i.e. the outward manifestation of ὀ., Phld.*Ir*.p.90 W.); of horses, X.*Eq*.9.2: pl. (not earlier than Pl., f.l. in S.*Aj*.718 (lyr.)), *fits of anger, passions*, περὶ φόβων τε καὶ θυμῶν Pl.*Phlb*.40e; οἵ τε θ. καὶ αἱ κολάσεις Id.*Prt*.323e, cf. Arist.*Rh*.1390ᵃ11. 5. *the heart*, as the seat of the emotions, esp. joy or grief, χαῖρε, γήθησε δὲ θυμῷ, Il.14.156, 7.189; θ. ἐνὶ στήθεσσι γεγήθει 13.494; μιν ἄχος κραδίην καὶ θ. ἵκανεν 2.171; ἄχνυτο θ. 14.39, etc.; δόκησε δ' ἄρα σφίσι θ. ὣς ἔμεν ὡς εἰ.. they felt as glad at *heart* as if.., Od.10.415; μηδ' ὀνίαισι δάμνα..θ. Sapph.1.4; of fear, δέος ἔμπεσε θυμῷ Il.17.625, cf. 8.138; of love, τὴν ἐκ θυμοῦ φίλεον 9.343; ἐκ θυμοῦ στέργοισα Theoc.17.130; ἐμῷ κεχαρισμένε θυμῷ my *heart's* beloved, Il.5.243; reversely, ἀπὸ θ. μᾶλλον ἐμοὶ ἔσεαι wilt be alien from my *heart*, 1.562; ἐκ θ. πεσέειν, i.e. to lose thy favour, 23.595; ἔρωτι θυμὸν ἐκπλαγεῖσα E.*Med*.8; ἐκ θ. κλαῦσαι Philet.11. 6. *mind, soul, as the seat of thought*, ταῦθ' ὥρμαινε κατὰ φρένα καὶ κατὰ θ. Il.1.193, etc.; ᾔδεε γὰρ κατὰ θ. 2.409, cf. 4.163, etc.; φράζετο θυμῷ 16.646; ἐν θ. ἐβάλοντο ἔπος 15.566; τοὺς λόγους θυμῷ βάλε A.*Pr*.706; εἰς θ. βαλεῖν τι S.*OT*975, οὐκ ἐς θ. φέρω I bring him not into my *mind* or *thoughts*, Id.*El*.1347.

**θῡμο-σοφικός**, ή, όν, *clever*, Ar.*V*.1280 (Sup.). **-σοφος**, ον, *wise from one's own soul*, i.e. *naturally clever*, Id.*Nu*.877, Plu.*Art*.17; of animals, Arr.*Ind*.14.4, Ael.*NA*16.15; ὄρνεον -ώτερον ib.3; τὸ θ. Plu.2.970e. **-φθορέω**, *to be tormented in soul*, S.*Tr*.142. ❀ **-φθόρος**, ον, *destroying the soul, life-destroying*, φάρμακα Od.2.329 (so, metaph. γράψας ἐν πίνακι θυμοφθόρα πολλά Il.6.169); ἰός Nic.*Th*.140 (v.l. γυιοφθ-). 2. *heart-breaking*, τὴν δ' ἄχος ἀμφεχύθη θ. Od.4.716; κάματος 10.363; πενίη Hes.*Op*.717; of persons, *troublesome, annoying*, Od.19.323; cf. θυμοβόρος.

**θῡμοφονέω**, *to be in the death-agony*, gloss on βεβρυχότες, Hsch.

**θῡμοφόρος**, ον, *bearing thyme*, Eust.ad D.P.791; θ ἡ 'Αττική Sch. Ar.*Pl*.283.

**θυμοχεύων**, = θυμὸν ἀχεύων (v. ἀχεύω), *Et.Gud*.267.34.

**θῡμόω**, *make angry, provoke*, Lxx *Ho*.12.14(15): once in Trag., ὥστε θυμῶσαι φρένας E.*Supp*.581. II. Med. and Pass., 2 sg. θυμοῖ Ar.*Ra*.584: fut. -ώσομαι A.*Ag*.1069, -ωθήσομαι Lxx *Jb*.21.4, Phld.*Ir*. p.89 W.: aor. ἐθυμωσάμην E.*Hel*.1343 (lyr.), more freq. ἐθυμώθην Hdt.3.1, al.; part. -θείς E.*Ph*.461, Pl.*Lg*.931b: pf. inf. τεθυμῶσθαι Hdt.3.52, A.*Fr*.478, Pl.*Ep*.346a:—*to be wroth* or *angry*, abs., Hdt.3.1, A.*Ag*.l.c., Sor.1.88, etc.; θυμοῦ δι' ὀργῆς ἥτις ἀγριωτάτη S.*OT* 344; εἰς ἔριν θ. Id.*Aj*.1018; of animals, *to be wild, restive*, Id.*Ant*.477, X.*Eq*.1.10; θυμοῦσθαι εἰς κέρας *vent fury* with the horns, Virgil's *irasci in cornua*, E.*Ba*.743; cf. ἀοιδὸς ἐς κέρας τεθύμωται Call.*Iamb*.1.321; τὸ θυμούμενον *passion*, Antipho 2.3.3, Th.7.68; θυμοῦσθαί τινι *to be angry with* one, A.*Eu*.733, S.*Tr*.543, 1230, Pl.*Prt*.324a; ἔς τινα Hdt.3.52; περί τινος A.*Ag*.1368 (prob. for μυθοῦσθαι); βοῦς πρὸς τὸν ἐλαύνοντα -ωθείς Plu.*Dio*38; σοι θυγατέρος -ούμενος E.*Or* 751 (troch.): c. dat. rei, τῇ ξυντυχίᾳ Ar.*Ra*.1006.

**θῡμώδης**, ες, = θυμοειδής 2, Arist.*Rh*.1389ᵃ26, *EN*1149ᵇ14, Plu.2.462a; of animals, *fierce*, Arist.*HA*488ᵇ14; θ. τὸ ἦθος Id.*PA*650ᵇ34; = ἀνδρεῖοι, opp. ὀξύθυμοι and ὀργίλοι, Gal.17(1).188: Sup. -έστατος Ael.*NA*3.2. Adv. -δῶς, f.l. for μυθ-, Aristeas 168.

**θῠμώδης**, ες, *like thyme*, Thphr.*HP*6.7.2.

**θύμ-ωμα** [ῡ], ατος, τό, *wrath, passion*, A.*Eu*.860 (pl.); θ. τὸ πόντου *Epigr.Gr*.339.6 (Cyzicus). **-ωσις**, εως, ἡ, *ebullition of anger*, Cic.*Tusc*.4.9.21.

**θῠναρμόστρια**, = θοιν- (q. v.).

**θυνάσαι**· ἀπολαῦσαι, ἐνθουσιάσαι, Hsch.

**θῡνέω**, = θύνω, only impf., *dart along*, δελφῖνες τῇ καὶ τῇ ἐθύνεον Hes.*Sc*.[210]; ἐν δ' Ἶρις, ἐν δὲ Κυδοιμὸς ἐθ. ib.156, cf. 257; νῶθ' ἵππων ἐπιβάντες ἐθύνεον ib.286, cf. eund.*Cat.Oxy*.1358 *Fr*.2.20. (Cf. Skt. *dhūnoti* 'shake', past part. *dhūtás*.)

❀ **θύνν-α**, ης, ἡ, *female tunny*, θύνναν f.l. in Hippon.35.2: θύννης Antiph.129.4, Archestr.*Fr*.37.1. **-άζω**, *spear a tunny-fish, strike with a harpoon*, metaph., ἐς τοὺς θυλάκους Ar.*V*.1087. **-αῖος**, α, ον, = θύννειος, τὸ θ. *an offering of the first tunny-fish caught*, Antig. Car.ap.Ath.7.297e. **-αξ**, ἄκος, ὁ, Dim. of θύννος, Eriph.3. ❀ **-άς**, άδος, ἡ, Dim. of θύννα, Antiph.181. **-ειος**, α, ον, *of the tunny-fish*, ταρίχη θ. pickled *tunny*, Hices.ap.Ath.3.116e; τὸ θ. (sc. κρέας) Clearch.65; τὰ θ. (sc. κρέα) Ar.*Eq*.354. II. **θυννεῖον**, τό, *tunny-fishery*, *IG*4.752.7 (Troezen, pl.). **-ευτικός**, ή, όν, *for tunny-fishing*, σαγήνη Luc.*Sat*.24. **-ίζω**, = θυννάζω, Suid. ❀ **-ίς**, ίδος, ἡ, *young female tunny*, prob. l. in Hippon.35.2, Epich.74, Cratin.161, Stratt.12, Archestr.*Fr*.37.1, Arist.*HA*543ᵃ9, al. **-ίτης** [ῑ], ου, ὁ, *tunny-fisher*, *Rev.Arch*.28(1928).393 (Varna, θυννεῖται lapis).

**θυννο-θήρας**, ου, ὁ, *tunny-fisher*, title of Mime by Sophron, Ath.7.303c, 306d, Ael.*NA*15.6. **-κέφᾰλος**, ὁ, *with the head of a tunny-fish*, Luc.*VH*1.35. **-λογέω**, *speak of the tunny-fish*, Eust.994.47.

❀ **θύννος**, ὁ, *tunny-fish*, Orac.ap.Hdt.1.62, A.*Pers*.424, Arist.*HA* 571ᵃ12, al., Ath.7.301e sqq.; θηρεύειν θύννον Phld.*Rh*.1.251 S. (The connexion with θύνω, suggested by the line θύννοι μὲν θύνοντες, ἐν ἰχθύσιν ἔξοχοι ὁρμήν Opp.*H*.1.181, is dub.)

**θυννοσκοπ-εῖον**, τό, *look out to watch for shoals of tunnies*, Str.5.2.6. **-έω**, *watch for tunnies*, metaph., τοὺς φόρους θ. Ar.*Eq*.313. **-ία**, ἡ, *watch for tunnies*, Str.17.3.16 (s.v.l.). **-ος**, ον, *watcher for tunnies*, Arist.*HA*537ᵃ19, Plu.2.98ca.

❀ **θυννώδης**, ες, *like a tunny-fish*, i.e. *stupid*, Luc.*JTr*.25.

**θῦνος**· πόλεμος, ὁρμή, δρόμος, Hsch.: θυνός acc. to Hdn.Gr.2.938.

**θύνω** [ῡ], only pres. and impf., = θυνέω, *rush, dart along*, θῦνε διὰ προμάχων Il.5.250, etc.; πάντῃ θῦνε σὺν ἔγχεϊ 20.493; ἀν' ὕλην ἐν ὠκὺς ἔθυνεν ὄρος *AP*6.217.8 ([Simon.]): c. part., βασιλῆες θῦνον κρίνοντες they *flitted* to and fro ordering the ranks, Il.2.446; μνηστῆρας ὀρίνων θῦνε κατὰ μέγαρον Od.24.449: c. acc. cogn., θ. ἀτραπὸν ἰθεῖαν Nic.*Th*.264: metaph., ἐπ' ἄλλοτ' ἄλλον ὥτε μέλισσα θύνει λόγον *flits* from one tale to another, Pi.*P*.10.54 (θύνων· ὁρμῶν, Erot. is not in our text of Hp.). II. = θύω (B), Τρώων καὶ 'Αχαιῶν θῦνε μεσηγὺ ἱστάμενος

*raged*, Il.11.570; οἱ δὲ λύκοι ὣς θῦνον ib.73; θῦνε γὰρ ἂμ πεδίον ποταμῷ πλήθοντι ἐοικὼς 5.87.

**θυο-δόκος**, ον, (θύος) *receiving incense, full thereof*, of the Delphic temple, E.*Ion*511, 1549; ἀνακτόρων Id.*Andr.*1157, cf. Hsch. **-εις**, εσσα, εν, (θύος) *laden with incense, fragrant*, νέφος Il.15.153; epith. of Eleusis, *h.Cer.*97, 318; ἄστεος ὀμφαλός, of an altar, Pi.*Fr.*75.3; βωμός Id.*Pae.*3.8, E.*Tr.*1061 (lyr.); Ἀστερίη Call.*Del.*300; ἀνάκτορον *AP*6.277 (Damag.).

**θυοκόχθεις**· μάντεις, Hsch.

**θύον** [ῠ], τό, (θύω A) *thyine-wood, citron-wood, Callitris quadrivalvis*, Od.5.60, Thphr.*HP*5.3.7, *BCH*6.26 (Delos, ii B.C.), Moschio ap. Ath. 5.207e, Plin.*HN*13.100, Ael.*VH*5.6; cf. θυία, θύα. II. = θύος, in pl. θύα, τά, *burnt-offerings* or *incense*, Sapph.*Supp.*8.2, prob. in *IG*5(1). p.vii (Delos, v B.C.), Pi.*Fr.*129.7 (θύματα codd. Plu.), *BCH*37.195 (Chios, iv B.C.), *SIG*1003.10 (Priene, ii B.C.), D.P.936. *EM*457.6.

❋ **θύος** [ῠ], εος, τό, (θύω A) *burnt sacrifice*, A.*Ag.*1409; θύος ὅττι πάχιστον Call.*Aet.Oxy.*2079.23: but usu. in pl., σὺν θυέεσσι Il.6.270, cf. 9.499; σπονδῇσι θύεσσί τε ἱλάσκεσθαι Hes.*Op.*338, cf. Maiist.11; λίσσομ' ὑπὲρ θυέων Od.15.261; θύη πρὸ παίδων A.*Eu.*835, cf. *IG*12(5). 593.17 (Iulis, v B.C.), *Berl.Sitzb.*1927.170 (Cyrene); νιν ἐκ θυέων καταδήσομαι Theoc.2.10, cf. Euph.129. 2. later in pl., = θυμιάματα, Hp.ap.Gal.19.104. II. *a cake*, θύη πέττειν Eup.108.

**θυοσκέω**, *make burnt-offerings*, Hsch.; περίπεμπτα θυοσκεῖς prob. in A.*Ag.*87 (θυοσκινεῖς codd.). (For θυο-σκοέω, cf. sq.)

**θυο-σκόος**, ου, ὁ, *sacrificing priest*, Od.21.145, 22.318, 321, E.*Rh.*68; μάντιες θ. distd. from ἱερῆες, Il.24.221: fem., Μαινάδες θ. E.*Ba.*224: neut., θ. ἱρά *sacrificial* implements, *IG*14.1389i2. 2. pl., = Lat. *haruspices*, D.H.1.30. (θύος, σ-κοϝ-, cf. κοέω, *caveo*: the initial *s*- is found in OE. *scéawian*, OHG. *scauwôn* 'look at'.) **-σκοπία**, ἡ, = *haruspicina*, used as etym. of Θοῦσκος, Lyd.*Mag.Prooem.* **-σκόπος**, ου, ὁ, *inspecting the entrails*, Hsch., Phot., v.l. in E.*Rh.*68.

**θυόω**, (θύος) *fill with sweet smells*: pf. part. Pass. ἔλαιον τεθυωμένον *fragrant* oil, Il.14.172; εἵματα τεθ. Cypria *Fr.*4, cj. in *h.Ap.*184; τεθ. ἄλσος Call.*Lav.Pall.*63: aor. part. θυωθέν Hedyl.ap.Ath.11.486b.— Ep. word.

**θύπτης**· ὀτυρός, Hsch.; cf. χθύπτης.

❋ **θύρα** [ῠ], Ion. θύρη, ἡ, Ion. gen. pl. θυρέων Archil.127, Hdt.1.9:— *door*, Il.24.317, etc.: freq. in pl. of *double* or *folding doors*, θ. δικλίδες Od.17.267; θ. φαεινάί 6.19, al.; θυρῶν ζεῦγος καινῶν *IG*1².313.123, cf. 4.1488.25 (Epid.); ἡ δεξιὰ θ. the right *valve*, ib.2².1457.16; θ. μονόθυρος ib.1627.418; θύραι λίθιναι (including the framework) ib. 1².372.195; θύραι αὔλειαι, v. αὔλειος; ἡ θ. ἡ εἰς τὸν κῆπον φέρουσα D. 47.53, cf. κηπαῖος II; rarely for πύλαι, *gates*, Plu.*Cat.Mi.*65; of the *carceres* in the Roman circus, *barriers*, *Tab.Defix.Aud.*187.59. —Phrases: προσθεῖναι τὰς θ., προστιθέναι τὴν θ., Hdt.3.78, Lys.1. 13; ἐπισπάσαι X.*HG*5.4.36; κλείειν Aristopho 7, Pl.*Prt.*314d; ἐφέλκεσθαι Luc.*Am.*16; τὴν θ. βαλανοῦν, μοχλοῦν, bar *the door*, Ar. *Fr.*251, 369; θύραν κόπτειν, πατάσσειν, κρούειν, knock, rap at *the door*, Id.*Nu.*132, *Ra.*38, Pl.*Prt.*310b; ἀράττειν, ἐπαράξαι, Ar.*Ec.* 977, Pl.*Prt.*314d; τὴν θ. ἀνοιγνύναι open it, v. ἀνοίγνυμι; ὦσαι push *it* open, Lys.1.24; μικρὸν ἐνδοῦναι open *it* a little, Plu.2.597d; δόμου ἐν πρώτῃσι θύρῃσι στῆναι Od.1.255; ἷζε δ' ἐπὶ.. οὐδοῦ ἔντοσθε θυράων 17.339; θυρῶν ἔνδον S.*El.*78; πρὸ θυρῶν ib.109 (anap.); ἐπὶ or παρὰ Πριάμοιο θύρῃσι at Priam's *door*, i.e. before his dwelling, Il.2.788, 7.346: metaph., ἐπὶ ταῖς θύραις τῆς Ἑλλάδος εἶναι X. *An.*6.5.23, cf. D.10.34; τῆς πατρίδος Plu.*Sull.*29, *Arat.*37; ἐπὶ θύραις τῆς Πίσης Philostr.*VA*8.15; πυρετοῦ περὶ θύρας ὄντος being *at the door*, Plu.2.128f (but χειμῶνος ἐπὶ θύραις ὄντος Phlp. *in Mete.*130. 25). 2. esp. of kings and potentates, οἱ τῶν ἀρίστων Περσῶν παῖδες ἐπὶ ταῖς βασιλέως θύραις παιδεύονται are educated at *court*, X.*An.*1.9.3; γυνὴ φοιτῶσα ἐπὶ τὰς θύρας τοῦ βασιλέος, of a petitioner, Hdt.3.119, cf. X.*An.*2.1.8; αἱ ἐπὶ τὰς θ. φοιτήσεις dangling after *the court*, Id.*HG*1.6.7; ἐπὶ ταῖς τῶν πλουσίων θ. διατρίβειν Arist. *Rh.*1391ᵃ12; περὶ θύρας διατρίβειν Id.*Pol.*1313ᵇ7, Theopomp.Hist. 121; applied also to lovers, clients, disciples, etc., ἐπὶ τὴν θύραν (or τὰς θύρας) τινὸς βαδίζειν, ἰέναι, etc., Ar.*Pl.*1007, Pl.*R.*364b, cf. *Phdr.* 233e, etc.; ἐπὶ ταῖσι θύραις ἀεὶ καθῆσθαι Ar.*Nu.*467: metaph., Μουσῶν ἐπὶ ποιητικὰς θ. ἀφικέσθαι Pl.*Phdr.*245a. 3. prov., γλώσσῃ θύραι οὐκ ἐπίκεινται Thgn.421; οὐδέποτ' ἴσχει θ., of admirers of the Demos, Eup.265; ἐπὶ θύραις τὴν ὑδρίαν to break the pitcher *at the* very *door*, 'there's many a slip 'twixt cup and lip', Arist.*Rh.* 1363ᵃ7; τίς ἂν θύρας ἁμάρτοι; Id.*Metaph.*993ᵇ5; λόγος δικαστηρίου ἢ ἀγορᾶς οὐδὲ θύρας ἰδών D.H.*Dem.*23; τὸ κατὰ θύραν τερπνόν *vulgar* pleasures, Eun.*VS*p.496B.; παρὰ θύραν πλανᾶσθαι S.E.*M.*1.43; ἐκ θυρῶν εὐθέως τῆς.. ἀκροάσεως at the very *beginning*, Olymp.*in Mete.* 2.1. 4. *shutter* of a window, τὰς θ. τὰς ἐπὶ τῶν θυρίδων *IG*12(5). 872.37 (Tenos), cf. 2².1668.60. 5. pl., *door* of a chariot, X.*Cyr.* 6.4.9. 6. pl., *axle-trees*, Poll.1.146 (v.l. εὐραί). 7. θύρη καταπακτή trap *door*, Hdt.5.16. 8. *frame of planks, raft*, Id.2.96; φραξάμενοι τὴν ἀκρόπολιν θύρῃσί τε καὶ ξύλοισι with *hurdles* and logs, Id.8.51, cf. Th.6.101. 9. in war, *fenced works* to obstruct landing-parties, in pl., Ph.*Bel.*94.37, 100.7. II. generally, *entrance*, as to a grotto, in pl., Od.9.243, al. 2. *sluice-gate*, *PPetr.*3p.134: pl., ib.2p.41 (iii B.C.). III. metaph., senses, as *the entrances to the soul*, τὸ σῶμα πολλαῖς θυρίσι καὶ θύραις ἀνοίγοντες Seren.ap.Stob.3. 6.17; ἐγγὺς τοῦ στόματος ἡ καρδία, ἡ δὲ ψυχὴ τῶν θ. Aristaenet.2.7. (I.-E. *dhur*-, cf. Lat. *foras, fores*, OE. *duru* 'door', etc.)

**θυραβάθρα**, ἡ, *companion-ladder* in a ship, *PLond.*3.1164ʰ9 (iii A.D.).

**θυράγματα**, τά, (θυράζω) = ἀφοδεύματα, Hsch.

**θύρ-αζε** [ῠ], Adv., for θύρασδε, *to the door*, and so, *out of doors*, ἐκ δὲ θ. ἔδραμον Il.18.29, cf. 416, Od.15.62; δόμων ἐξῆγε θ. ib.465. 2. generally, *out*, Il.5.694, Od.15.451, etc.; ἔκβασις.. ἁλὸς πολιοῖο θ. a way of getting *out of* the sea, 5.410; ἰχθῦν ἐκ πόντοιο θ. [ἕλκειν] Il. 16.408, cf. 21.237; ἐπὶ πρύμνῃσιν ἐείλεον οὐδὲ θ. εἴων ἐξιέναι 18.447; ἐξενεγκὼν θ. Ar.*Ach.*359; ἐξέλκειν τινὰ θ. Id.*Eq.*365; θ. ἐξιέναι Id.*V.* 70; ἐκχεῖν θ. empty *outside*, Id.*Fr.*306; καρδίαν θ. ἔχειν E.*Fr.*1063. 12; τὰ θ. *outside*, opp. τὰ ἔνδον, Id.*Or.*604; θ. ζῳοτοκεῖν or ᾠοτοκεῖν, Arist.*GA*718ᵇ32, 719ᵇ19; ῥεῖ διὰ τῶ σώματος ἔξω θ. τὰ πνεύματα Ti. Locr.102a. 3. c. gen., θ. τῶν νόμων *without* the law, E.*Ba.*331; θ. Ἀττικῶς, ἔξω Ἑλληνικῶς Moer.p.185 P. **-άζω**, aor. inf. θυράξαι, *thrust out of doors*, Hsch. **-āθεν**, Adv. *from outside the door*: and generally, *from without*, αἱ θ. εἴσοδοι E.*Andr.*952; θ. εἰκάσαι Id.*HF* 713; θ. ἐπεισιέναι Arist.*GA*736ᵇ28. 2. *outside the door, outside*, ἡ θ. ἡδονή E.*Fr.*1063.4; ὁ ἀὴρ ὁ θ. Arist.*Resp.*480ᵃ30, cf. *PA*642ᵇ1, οἱ θ. *foreigners, the enemy*, A.*Th.*68, 193. 3. metaph., opp. ἔνδοθεν (q.v.), S.*Tr.*1021 (hex.). **-āθι**, Adv. *at the door*, *EM*25.17:—Ep. θύρηθι, *outside*, μάλα δ' ὦκα θύρηθ' ἔα I was soon *out* (of the sea), Od.14. 352. ❋ **-αῖος**, α, ον, also ος, ον S.*El.*313, E.*Alc.*805, Plu. (ll. cc. infr.): Aeol. θύραος *IG*12(2).14 (Mytil.): (θύρα):—*at the door* or *just outside the door*, A.*Ag.*1055, S.*Aj.*793; θ. οἰχνεῖν to go *to the door*, go *out*, Id.*El.*313; τόνδε βλέπω θ. ἤδη Id.*Tr.*595; θ. στίβος, opp. ἔναυλος, Id. *Ph.*158 (lyr.); θ. ἔστω πόλεμος A.*Eu.*864: metaph., θ. ἀμφὶ μηρόν round the *exposed, naked* thigh, S.*Fr.*872 (lyr.); θ. δόξα Plu.*Cat.Ma.* 18; θ. ὑποψίαι Id.2.38c. 2. *absent, abroad*, A.*Ag.*1608, *Ch.*115; θ. ἐλθεῖν to come *from abroad*, E.*Ion*702 (lyr.); τοὺς δ' ἐν θυραίοις in *the public eye*, opp. τοὺς μὲν ὀμμάτων ἄπο, Id.*Med.*217. 3. *from out of doors, from abroad*, ἄνδρες θ. *strangers*, Id.*Hipp.*409; θυραῖα φρονήματ' ἀνδρῶν the thoughts *of strangers*, ib.395. 4. = ἀλλότριος, ὄλβος θ. the luck *of others*, A.*Ag.*837; πῆμα E.*Alc.*778; χείρ Id.*Ph.*848; παῖδες, i.e. *adoptive*, Id.*Fr.*491. II. *containing a door*, θ. τοῖχος *entrance*-wall, *IG*11(2).165.6 (Delos, iii B.C.), 12 l.c. (pl.), *Milet.*7.56 (Didyma). III. **θυραία**, ἡ, *doorway, opening*, Men.389, *IG*2². 1668.61 (pl.).

**θυρāμάχος** [μᾰ], ον, *assaulting doors*, κῶμοι prob. l. in Pratin.Lyr. 1.8.

**θυρᾰνοίκτης**, ου, ὁ, *door-opener*, A.D.*Synt.*324.8.

**θύρāξ**· πύργος, χιτών, Hsch. (cf. θώραξ).

**θύρᾱσι**, -σιν [ῠ], Adv., (θύρα) *at the door, without*, Ar.*V.*891, *Pax* 942, 1023, al. 2. *abroad* (written θύραισι in codd.), E.*El.*1074, S. *OC*401.

**θυραυλ-έω**, (αὐλή) *live in the open air, camp out*, Pl.*Plt.*272a, *Lg.* 695a, X.*Oec.*7.30, Isoc.6.76, etc.; esp. in war, *keep the field*, Arist.*Pol.* 1319ᵃ24, D.H.9.15, Plu.*Caes.*17, etc. II. *wait at another's door*, of visitors, *POxy.*471.72 (ii A.D.); freq. of lovers waiting on their mistresses, Plu.2.759b, Ph.1.306, etc.; ὁ θυραυλῶν Ἔρως Plot.6.5. 10. **-ία**, ἡ, *living out of doors, camping out*, Ti.Locr.103b (pl.), etc.; of soldiers, Plu.2.498c; of wild animals, Arist.*GA*783ᵃ 19. II. *waiting at the door*, of lovers, in pl., Ph.1.155, Philostr. *Ep.*29: sg., Luc.*Merc.Cond.*10. **-ος** (proparox.), ον, *living out of doors*, of shepherds, Hsch.

**θυρᾱωρός**, όν, *warder of the gate*, v.l. for πυλαωρός, Il.22.69 (pl.); cf. θυρωρός.

**θυργανᾶν**· κρίνειν (fort. θρυγανᾶν· κρούειν), Hsch.

**θύρδα**, Arc. for θύραζε, = ἔξω, Hsch.

**θυρεᾱμᾰχία**, ἡ, *contest in which shields were borne*, *SIG*1061.12 (Samos, ii B.C.).

**θυρέασπις**, ιδος, ἡ, *large shield*, *AP*6.131 (Leon.).

**θυρεᾱτικοὶ** στέφανοι wreaths *worn to commemorate the victory at Thyrea*, Sosib.5.

**θυρεᾱφόρος**, ον, = θυρεοφόρος, *Supp.Epigr.*3.351 (Thisbe, iii B.C.), Plb.5.53.8, Plu.*Aem.*19, Arr.*Tact.*4.4.

❋ **θύρεθρα**· θύραι, Hsch.

**θυρεο-ειδής**, ές, *shield-shaped*: χόνδρος θυρεοειδής (male θυροειδής) the *thyroid* cartilage (in the larynx), Gal.2.839, *UP*7.11, al.; νῆσος θ. Str.17.2.2; θ. τόπος prob. for θυρο- in *Hippiatr.*40. **-κολλίτης** [ῑ], ου, ὁ, *soldier armed with hollow* θυρεός, *IPE*1².687 (Olbia).

❋ **θυρεός**, ὁ, (θύρα) *stone put against a door to keep it shut*, Od.9.240, 313. II. *oblong shield* (*shaped like a door*), *PSI*4.428.36 (iii B.C.), Inscr.ap.Plu.*Pyrrh.*26, Callix.2; hence, of the Roman *scutum* (opp. ἀσπίς, = *clipeus*), Plb.2.30.3, 6.23.2, D.H.4.16, cf. *Ep.Eph.*6.16, Apollod.*Poliorc.*163.2, Arr.*Tact.*3.2, etc. III. *disk* forming part of καθετήρ, *IG*11(2).287*B*68 (Delos, iii B.C.). IV. Math., *oval*, Procl.*in Euc.*1 *Deff.*3,8.

**θυρεοφορ-έω**, *to be armed with the oblong shield*, Plb.10.13.2. **-ος**, ον, *armed with such a shield*, LXX 1*Ch.*12.24, Plb.10.29.6, Ascl.*Tact.* 1.3, Plu.*Crass.*25; cf. θυρεαφόρος.

**θυρεόω**, *cover with a shield*, Aq.*Is.*31.5.

**θυρεπᾰνοίκτης**, ου, ὁ, *door-opener*, of the philosopher Crates, *for whom all doors were open*, Plu.2.632e; or, *who forced all doors*, D.L. 6.86: pl., *burglars*, Vett.Val.202.6; cf. θυρανοίκτης.

**θύρετρ-α** [ῠ], τά, = θύρα, *door*, in pl., Il.2.415, Od.18.385, 21.49, Pi.*I.*7(6).6, E.*Ba.*448, *Or.*1474 (lyr.), Call.*Ap.*3, etc.; prop. the *door-casing, frame*, *IG*11(2).161*A*66 (Delos, iii B.C.); θύραις ἁρμοζούσαις τοῖς θυρέτροισι ib.12(2).14.7; θ. μαρμάρινα ib.6: so in sg., ib.4. 1484.30 (Epid.), *BCH*6.24 (Delos, ii B.C.), Plb.30.18.5. *AP*5.293.7 (Agath.), Ps.-Luc.*Philopatr.*4:—hence **-εας**· φλιᾶς, Hsch. **-ικός**, ή, όν, *belonging to a door-frame*, πῆγμα *BCH*1.82 (Chios).

**θυρευτής**, οῦ, ὁ, *door-keeper*, *Gloss.* (dub.).

**θύρη, θύρηθι,** Ion. and Ep. for θύρα, θύραθι.

**θῡρη-βόλιον·** τὴν ἐπ' ἀγρῷ οἴκησιν, Hsch.; = ἔπαυλις, *EM*459.13: **-βόλος·** τέκτων, Suid.

**θύρηφι** [ῠ], Ep. dat. of θύρα, used as Adv., *outside*, Od.9.238, Hp. *Superf.*2, etc.; τὰ θ., opp. τὰ ἔνδοθι, Od.22.220; τὸ or τὰ θ., Hes.*Op.* 365, Naumach.ap.Stob.4.23.7.

**θῠρῐδεύς,** έως, ὁ, *window-frame*, *Inscr.Délos*290.212 (iii B.C.).

⊛ **θυρίδιον,** τό, Dim. of θύρα, *Gp.*15.6.2.

**θυρῐδ-όω,** *make a window*, *PTheb.Bank*11.10 (ii B.C.):—Pass., οἰκία τεθυριδωμένη *furnished with windows*, *BGU*1116.15 (i B.C.). ⊛ **-ωτός,** ή, όν, *having apertures*, κιβωτός Demioprat.ap. Poll.10.137; καταπάλτης *IG*2[2].1487.89.

**θῠριοβόλος,** ὁ, dub. sens. in *Cat.Cod.Astr.*8(4).126.

⊛ **θύριον** [ῠ] (not θυρίον, Eust.268.9), τό, Dim. of θύρα, *little door, wicket*, Ar.*Nu.*92, *Th.*26, *IG*11(2).154*A*26 (Delos, iii B.C.), Plu. *Cleom.*8, Alciphr.3.30: metaph., τὸ τοῦ λόγου θ. παραβαλοῦ close *the door* of discourse, Plu.2.940f, cf. 965b. 2. *small sluice*, *PLond.* 3.1177.243 (ii A.D.).

⊛ **θυρίς,** ίδος, ἡ, Dim. of θύρα, *window*, Praxill.5, Ar.*V.*379, *Th.*797, Pl.*R.*359d, Arist.*deAn.*404[a]4, *Ath.*50.2, *IG*11(2).161*D*101 (Delos, iii B.C.), *BGU*1116.23 (i B.C.), Plu.2.273b; *window-frame*, ἐναρμόσαι εἰς ἑκάστην τὴν θ. (*opening*) χαλκᾶς θ. (*frames*) *IG*2[2].1668.37. b. *audience-window* of the king or high officials in Egypt, *UPZ*15.7, 16.20, 53.5 (ii B.C.), Heraclid.Cum.4. 2. *opening* at each end of a bee's cell, Arist.*HA*624[a]7. 3. *valve* of a bivalve fish, ib.529[b]7. 4. in pl., *embrasures* in battlements, *IG*2[2].463.55, al.; for artillery, D.S.20.91, D.C.74.10. II. in pl., *planks, boards*, Heraclid.Pont.ap.Ath.12.521f; *tablets*, Hsch. 2. *cell* of wasps, Arist. *HA*628[a]20, 629[a]30.

**θυριώτης,** ου, ὁ, *one found at the door*, Suid.

⊛ **θυρξεύς,** έως, ὁ, title of Apollo in Achaea, Paus.7.21.13.

**θῠροειδής,** ές, *like a door*, τόπος dub. in *Hippiatr.*40 (v. θυρεοειδής); τὸ θ. τρῆμα *the opening in the os pubis*, Gal.2.414.

**θῠροιγός,** ὁ, (οἴγνυμι) *door-keeper*, Hsch.

**θῠροκιγκλίδες,** ίδων, αἱ, *latticed doors*, *IG*2[2].1672.168.

**θῠροκοπ-έω,** *knock at the door, break it open*, esp. as a drunken feat, ἀπὸ γὰρ οἴνου γίγνεται καὶ θυροκοπῆσαι κτλ. Ar.*V.*1254; θυροκοπῶν ὦφλεν δίκην Antiph.239, cf. Chor.in *Hermes*17.232. 2. metaph., *knock as at a door*, θ. τῇ χειρὶ τὴν πλευράν [τινος] Plu.2.503a; ὁ λιμὸς τὴν γαστέρα θ. Alciphr.3.70. **-ία,** ἡ, *knocking at the door*, Diph. 128, Lib.*Or.*11.47. **-ικός,** ή, όν, *of* or *like* θυροκοπία: θυροκοπικόν, τό, *tune played on the flute* (= κρουσίθυρον), Trypho ap.Ath.14.618c:—also **-ιστικόν,** τό, Hsch. **-ος** (parox.), ον, *knocking at the door, begging*, ψευδόμαντις A.*Ag.*1195.

**θῠροκρουστία,** ἡ, *knocking at a door*, dub. in *Sammelb.*4425 ii 24 (ii A.D.).

**θυρουρός,** ὁ, v. θυρωρός.

**θῠρο-πηγία,** ἡ, *making of doors*, Thphr.*HP*5.7.6. **-ποιός,** ὁ, *door-maker*, Poll.7.111; nickname of the Comic poet Aristomenes, Hsch., Suid.

**θυρουλλεῖν,** written for θυραυλεῖν, Hsch.

**θῠροφύλαξ** [φῠ], ᾰκος, ὁ, *door-keeper*, Sch.Il.22.69, prob. in Fronto *Ep.Gr.*5.1.

**θῠρόω,** (θύρα) *furnish with doors*, ἱερόν *IG*1[2].24.7; πρόπυλον ib.2[2]. 1046.16; νεὼς.. θυρῶσαι χρυσαῖσι θύραις Ar.*Av.*614 (anap.): metaph., βλεφάροις θυρῶσαι τὴν ὄψιν X.*Mem.*1.4.6:—Pass., στεγόμενα καὶ τεθυρωμένα roofed and *furnished with doors*, *Tab.Heracl.*1.142, cf. *IG* 11(2).287*A*172 (Delos, iii B.C.), *PAmh.*2.51.14, 24 (i B.C.); *furnished with apertures*, πίναξ *JHS*41.195 (Delos, ii B.C.); πολλαῖς ἐξόδοις τεθυρῶσθαι *to be furnished* with many outlets, Luc.*Hipp.*8.

**θυρσ-άζω,** *bear* or *brandish the thyrsus*, θυρσαδδωᾶν Lacon. part. gen. pl. fem. for θυρσαζουσῶν, Ar.*Lys.*1313. **-άριον,** τό, Dim. of θύρσος, Plu.2.614a:—of vegetables, *head*, Orib.*Fr.*55. **-εχθής,** ές, of Bacchus, prob. f.l. for **-εγχής,** *with thyrsus-spear*, Orph.*H.*45.5 (Ruhnk.). **-ίαμβος** [ῐ], ὁ, coined as etym. of θρίαμβος, Lyd. *Mens.*1.2. **-ίνη,** = ὀροβάγχη, Dsc.2.142 (nisi leg. θυρσῖτιν, cf. θυρσίτης). **-ιον,** τό, = θύμον, Ps.-Dsc.3.36; also, = κατανάγκη, ib.4.131; symbolic of Aquarius, Herm.Trism. in *Rev.Phil.*32. 274. II. θυρσίον, Dim. of θύρσος, Hero *Spir.*2.9. ⊛ **-ίτης** [ῑ], ου, ὁ, = ὠκιμοειδές, Ps.-Dsc.4.28 (with v.l. -ῖτις).

**θυρσίων,** ωνος, ὁ, part of a fish, Ath.7.310e; Lat. *tursio* (v.l. *thurs-*), = a dolphin-like fish, Plin.*HN*9.34.

**θυρσο-ειδής,** ές, *thyrsus-like*, Dsc.3.17. ⊛ **-κόμος,** ὁ, *thyrsus-keeper*, a play of Lysippus, Suid. **-λογχος,** ὁ, *thyrsus-lance*, Callix. 2. II. as Adj., θ. ὅπλα *thyrsus-like* arms, Str.1.2.8. **-μανής,** ές, *he who raves with the thyrsus*, epith. of Bacchus, E.*Ph.*792 (lyr.), Orph.*H.*50.8. **-πλήξ,** ῆγος, ὁ, ἡ, *thyrsus-stricken, frantic*, [ἑσμὸς] τεχνιτῶν Limen.19, cf. Hsch.

**θύρσος,** ὁ, in late Poets with heterocl. pl. θύρσα *AP*6.158 (Sabin.): —*wand wreathed in ivy and vine-leaves with a pine-cone at the top*, carried by the devotees of Dionysus, E.*Ba.*80 (lyr.), *SIG*1109.138, Hero *Spir.*2.9, etc.; also of the *devotees* themselves, Sch.E.*Hec.* 261. II. = κλάδος, ῥάβδος, Hsch. (Prob. a loan-word.)

**θυρσο-τῑνάκτης,** ου, ὁ, *thyrsus-shaker*, of Bacchus, Orph.*H.*52.4. **-φορέω,** *bear the thyrsus*, D.S.4.3. II. θ. θιάσους *assemble* or *lead* companies *with the thyrsus*, E.*Ba.*557 (lyr.). **-φορία,** ἡ, *bearing of the thyrsus*, Plu.2.671e. **-φόρος,** ον, *thyrsus-bearing*, Βάκχαι E.*Cyc.*64 (lyr.), cf. *AP*9.524.9. **-χαρής,** ές, *delighting in the thyrsus*, *Inscr.Magn.*215a.23, *AP*3.1 (Inscr. Cyzic.).

**θυρσόω,** *make into thyrsi*, λόγχαι τεθυρσωμέναι D.S.4.4.

**θύρ-ωμα** [ῠ], ατος, τό, *doorway* (including posts, sill, and lintel), *IG*1[2].372.78, 11(2).287*A*77 (Delos, iii B.C.), Thphr.*HP*3.14.1, Callix. 2, Hsch. s.v. θύρετρα; τὸ μέγα θ. *OGI*193.10 (Branchidae); τὸ πρόπυλον καὶ τὸ θ. ib.734 (Egypt, ii B.C.); διξὰ θ. Hdt.2.169: pl., also in Th.3.68, Lys.19.31, Pl.*Plt.*280d, D.21.167; τὰ θ. ἀποσπάσας Id. 29.3. II. *panel, tablet*, Diotog.ap.Stob.4.1.96; τὸν νόμον οὐκ ἐν οἰκήμασι καὶ θυρώμασι ἐνῆμεν δεῖ, ἀλλ' ἐν τοῖς ἤθεσι Archyt.ap.eund. 4.1.138. 2. in pl., *planks, boards*, D.S.20.86. III. *window*, Lxx 3*Ki.*7.42(5) (pl.). ⊛ **-ών,** ῶνος, ὁ, *hall, antechamber*, S.*El.*328, *OT*1242, *Fr.*649.23, *IG*11(2).158*A*57 (Delos, iii B.C.), Plu.*Pyrrh.* 34, etc.

**θυρωρ-εῖον,** τό, *porter's lodge*, Vitr.6.7.1 (dub.). **-έω,** *to be a door-keeper*, Plu.2.83cb. ⊛ **-ός,** Cypr. θυραϝωρός dub. in *Inscr.Cypr.* 215 H., Ep. **θυραωρός** (q.v.), ὁ, ἡ:—*door-keeper, porter*, Sapph.98, Hdt.1.120, A.*Ch.*565, Pl.*Phlb.*62c, *Ev.Marc.*13.34, *BGU*1061.10 (i A.D.), Luc.*Vit.Auct.*7, etc.:—also **θυρουρός** *PCair.Zen.*292.76 (iii B.C.), *PRyl.*136.6 (i A.D.), *IG*3.1137 (ii A.D.), *PFlor.*71.380 (iv A.D.). (From θυρα-hορϝος, cf. οὖρος, ἐρύω (B): connected with ὠρέω by Corn. *ND*1.)

**θύρ-ωσις** [ῠ], εως, ἡ, *furnishing with a door*, τοῦ ἐργαστηρίου *IG*4. 1484.38 (Epid.). **-ωτός,** όν, *with a door* or *aperture*, στήθη Babr.59. 11: neut. as Subst., **-ωτόν,** τό, *doorway*, *IG*4.1484.304 (Epid., dual).

**θῦσαι,** ῶν, αἱ, like θυιάδες, *Bacchantes*, Lyc.106; v.l. θύστησιν, cf. θυστάς, θύστης.

**θῠσᾰνηδόν,** Adv. *fringe-like*, Ael.*NA*16.11.

**θῠσᾰνο-ειδής,** ές, *fringed*: τὸ τῶν στρωμάτων θ. Eun.*Hist.*p.239 D. **-εις,** Ep. **θυσσανόεις,** εσσα, εν, *tasseled, fringed*, Hom. (only in Il.), αἰγίδα θυσσανόεσσαν 15.229, 17.593, al.; ἀσπίδα (v.l. αἰγίδα) θ. 21.400.

**θύσᾰνος** [ῠ], ὁ, *tassel*: mostly in pl., *tassels, fringe*, Hom. (only in Il.), of the *tassels of the αἰγίς*, 2.448; ζώνη ἑκατὸν θυσάνοις ἀραρυῖη 14.181, cf. Hes.*Sc.*225, Hdt.4.189; οἱ τῆς ὀθόνης θ. Ach.Tat.5.24; πέπλος ἄχρι τῶν θ. πεποικιλμένος Them.*Or.*18.222c; of the *tufts* of the golden fleece, Pi.*P.*4.231; of the *long arms* of the cuttle fish, Opp.*H.*3.178; δικτυωτὸς θ. D.S.18.26. (Possibly connected with θύσσομαι, θύω.)

**θῠσάν-ουρος** [ᾰ], ον, (οὐρά) *with a ragged tail*, Hsch. **-ώδης,** ες, = θυσανόεις, *tassel-like, bunched*, ῥίζα Thphr.*HP*1.6.4. **-ωτός,** ή, όν, = θυσανόεις, κιθών, αἰγέη, Hdt.2.81, 4.189; ἔνδυμα J.*BJ*5.5.7.

**θῡσείω,** Desiderat. of θύω, Hdn.*Epim.*249.

**θύσθεν,** Adv. for θύρθεν, = θύραθεν, *outside*, τᾶς κελεύθω *IG*5(2).3.23 (Tegea, iv B.C.).

**θύσθλα,** ων, τά, (θύω) *sacred implements of Bacchic orgies*, Il.6.134; θύσθλοις παιομένους Jul.*Or.*7.209d. II. *the Bacchic festival itself*, Opp.*C.*1.26: also in sg., Plu.2.501f. III. generally, *sacrifice*, θ. καταίθειν Lyc.459, cf. 720, 929, Orph.*A.*904, etc.

⊛ **θῠσί-α,** Ion. -ίη, ἡ, (θύω) prop. *burnt-offering, sacrifice*, mostly in pl., v.l. in Batr.176, cf. Emp.128.6, etc.; ἐν θυσίῃσι εἶναι Hdt.8.99; θυσίαισι δέκεσθαί τινα Pi.*P.*5.86, cf. *I.*5(4).30; θυσίῃσι ἱλάσκεσθαι τὸν θεόν Hdt.1.50, cf. 6.105; θυσίας ἔρδειν, ἐπιτελέειν, ἀνάγειν, Id.1.131, 2.63, 60: also in sg., θυσίαν ποιεῖσθαι, θύειν, Pl.*Smp.*174c, *R.*362c; ἄγειν Id.*Alc.*2.148e; θ. σωτηρίου, αἰνέσεως, τῆς τελειώσεως, Lxx *Le.*3. 1, 7.2, *Ex.*29.34; of the gods, θυσίαν δέχεσθαι A.*Th.*701 (lyr.). 2. *mode of sacrifice*, θ. ἡ αὐτὴ πᾶσι κατέστηκε Hdt.4.60, cf. 2.39. 3. *festival, at which sacrifices were offered*, Pl.*Phd.*61b, *Ti.*26e, al.; θ. καὶ διαγωγαὶ τοῦ συζῆν Arist.*Pol.*1280[b]37, cf. *EN*1160[a]20; περὶ τῶν ἐν Ῥόδῳ θ., title of work by Theognis Hist. b. generally, *rite, ceremony*, Plu.2.693f, *Thes.*20. II. *victim, offering*, Plu.2.184f, Luc. *Sacr.*12. **-άζω,** *sacrifice*, μῆλα Strato Com.1.21; θυσίαν, θυσίασμα, Lxx 2*Ch.*7.5, 2*Es.*6.3; ὑπέρ τινος dub. l. in Lys.6.4; ὑπὲρ τοῦ δήμου *OGI*339.36 (Sestos, ii B.C.); τῷ Διὶ ὑπὲρ τῶν πλοϊζομένων ib.199.36 (Adule); θ. τῷ θεῷ καὶ βακχεύειν D.S.4.3: abs., Lxx 1*Ch.*21.28, al., *IG*3.74.16, etc.: θυσιάζουσαι, αἱ, title of mime by Herodas. **-άς,** άδος, *frenzied*, φωνή Hsch.: pl. as Subst., = θυιάδες, Id. **-ασμα,** ατος, τό, = θυσία II, Lxx *Ex.*29.18 (v.l. θυμίαμα), 2*Es.*6.3. ⊛ **-αστήριον,** τό, *altar*, ib.*Ex.*27.1, al., *Ev.Matt.*23.18, J.*AJ*8.4.1, *Cod.Just.*1.12. 3.2. **-αστήριος,** α, ον, *sacrificial*, [ὕμνος] Timae.154. ⊛ **-αστής,** οῦ, ὁ, *a sacrificer*, Sch.E.*Hec.*224.

**θύσῐμος** [ῠ], ον, (θύω A) *fit for sacrifice*, κτήνεα Hdt.1.50, cf. Ar. *Ach.*784; τὸ θ. Plu.2.437a, cf. Porph.*Abst.*2.14.

**θῠσῐουργός,** ὁ, *sacrificer, slaughterer*, Ptol.*Tetr.*179.

**θύσις** or **θῦσις,** εως, ἡ, (θύω B) *raging*, ἀπὸ τῆς θ. καὶ ζέσεως τῆς ψυχῆς Pl.*Cra.*419e.

**θύσκα·** κύρια, Hsch. **θυσκάριον,** τό, Dim. of sq., *EM*458.53 (cod. Voss.). **θύσκη, θύσκος,** v. θυΐσκη.

**θυσμικός,** ή, όν, *sacrificial*, ἔτος *IG*12(5).141 (Paros), 903 (Tenos).

**θυσπολίαι·** θυηπολίαι, Hsch.

**θυσσᾰνόεις,** Ep. for θυσαν-.

**θυσσάς,** άδος, ὁ, = θυιάς, epith. of Bacchus, *IG*12(5).972 (Tenos).

⊛ **θύσσομαι,** = τινάσσομαι, Hsch.

**θυστάς,** άδος, ἡ, (θύω A) *sacrificial*, θ. βοή the cry *uttered in sacrificing*, A.*Th.*269; θ. λιταί the prayers *accompanying a sacrifice*, S. *Ant.*1019. II. as Subst., = θυτήρ, Sch.Opp.*H.*5.417; = θυιάς, Hsch. 2. *sacrificial robe*, E.*Fr.*1101.

**θυστήριον·** ὁρμητήριον, Suid.; but θυστηρίοις· θυμιατηρίοις, Hsch.

**θυστήριος,** ὁ, epith. of Dionysus, *EM*455.31. **θύστης,** ου, Dor. **-τας,** α, ὁ, *sacrificing priest* (Cret.), Hsch. **θύστινον·** τρίχινον, οἱ δὲ μεσοτριβῆ, Id. **θύστρα,** τά, = θύματα, *SIG*1026.24 (Cos).

**θῦτ-εῖον**, τό, (θύω A) *place for sacrificing*, Aeschin.3.122. **-έον**, *one must sacrifice*, Ar.*Av*.1237, Pl.*R*.365e, Porph.*Abst*.2.13; τῇ ἀληθείᾳ Luc.*Hist.Conscr*.39. **-ήρ**, ῆρος, ὁ, *sacrificer, slayer*, A.*Ag*. 224,240 (both lyr.), S.*Tr*.613, al.: coupled with μάντις, Call.*Iamb*.1. 221. **-ήριον**, τό, = θῦμα, E.*IT*243. II. = θυσιαστήριον, as name of the constellation *Ara*, Arat.403, Q.S.4.554. III. = θυμιατήριον, Phot. **-ης**, ου, ὁ, *sacrificer* or *diviner*, *SIG*589.18 (Magn. Mae., ii B.C.), D.S.17.17, Onos.10.25, Arr.*Epict*.1.17.18, *IG*14.617.6 (Rhegium), App.*Hisp*.85, Hdn.4.12.3: Thess. **θύτας** *IG*9(2).1234 (Phalanna). **-ικός**, ή, όν, *of* or *for sacrifice*, μαχαιρίδιον Luc.*Pisc*.45: ἡ -κή (sc. τέχνη), the *art of the diviner*, Ph.2.221, Onos.10.28, Ath.14. 659d, Hdn.8.3.7, Porph.*Abst*.2.53; τὸ θ. *Placit*.5.1.3; θ. μαντεία Sch. rec.A.*Pr*.496. II. *given to sacrificing*, Str.3.3.6. **-ις**, ιδος, fem. of θύτης, Hsch. s.v. ἱρήτειρα: **-ρια**, fem. of θυτήρ, Suid. s.v. ἱέρεια.

**θῦψαι, θύψω**, v. τύφω.

**θῦψις**, εως, ἡ, (τύφω) *burning*, Suid. s.v. θυμάλωπες (= Sch.Ar.*Ach*. 320).

**θύω** (A), impf. ἔθυον, Ep. θῦον Od.15.222, Ion. θύεσκον Hippon.37: fut. θύσω [ῡ] E.*El*.1141, Pl.*Lg*.909d, Henioch.5.10, Dor. θυσῶ Theoc. 2.33; 3 pl. θυσέοντι *IG*12(3).452 (Thera): aor. ἔθῡσα Od.9.231, etc., Ep. θῦσα 14.446: pf. τέθῠκα Ar.*Lys*.1062, Pl.*R*.328c:—Med., fut. θύσομαι E.*Heracl*.340 (as Pass., Hdt.7.197): aor. ἐθυσάμην Th.4. 92, (ἐκ-) Hdt.6.91, etc.:—Pass., fut. τυθήσομαι D.S.16.91, Luc. *DDeor*.4.2: aor. ἐτύθην [ῠ] Hdt.1.216, A.*Ch*.242, Philem.155.2 (part. written θυθέν Men.*Sam*.185, cf. τὴν βοῦν τὴν θυθεῖσαν *IG*12(7).241 (Amorgos, iii B.C.), etc.): pf. τέθυμαι A.*Eu*.341 (lyr.), Ar.*Av*.1034, X. *HG*3.5.5 (in med. sense, 5.1.18, *An*.7.8.21): plpf. ἐτέθυτο Id.*HG*3. 1.23. [ῡ in fut. and aor., ῠ in pf. Act. and Pass., and aor. Pass.; ῡ generally in pres. and impf., exc. in trisyll. cases of part., θῡ́οντα Od.15.260, θύοντες *h.Ap*.491, but θύεσκε Hippon.37; ἔθῠε, θύων, Pi. *O*.10(11).57, 13.69; θύειν, at the end of a line, E.*El*.1141 (s.v.l., fort. θύη), *Cyc*.334, Ar.*Ach*.792 (spoken by a Megarian); θύεις, θύω, Strato Com.1.19,20; θύωντι 3 pl. pres. subj., Theoc.4.21.] I. Act., *offer by burning* meat or drink to the gods (ἔστι θύειν δωρεῖσθαί ἐστι τοῖς θεοῖς Pl.*Euthphr*.14c), θεοῖσι δὲ θῦσαι ἀνώγει Πάτροκλον.., ὁ δ' ἐν πυρὶ βάλλε θυηλάς Il.9.219, cf. Aristarch.ap.Sch.ad loc., *Com.Adesp*.7D. (ap. Phryn.*PS*p.74B.); ἦ ῥα καὶ ἄργματα θῦσε θεοῖς, of a drink-offering, Od.14.446, cf. 15.260; so ἔνθα δὲ πῦρ κήαντες ἐθύσαμεν (sc. τῶν τυρῶν) *made an offering* of cheese, 9.231; θ. ἀκρόθινα Pi.*O*.10(11).57; πέλανον, δεῖπνα, A.*Pers*.204, *Eu*.109; πυρούς, ναστούς, Ar.*Av*.565, 567: c. dat. rei, θ. τούτῳ ὅ τι ἔχοι ἕκαστος (with v.l. τοῦτο) Hdt.1. 50. 2. *sacrifice, slay* a victim, [τῷ ἡλίῳ] θ. ἵππους (v.l. ἵπποισι) ib. 216; ταῦρον Pi.*O*.13.69; αὑτοῦ παῖδα A.*Ag*.1417, cf. S.*El*.532, etc.; ἱρά Hdt.1.59; ἱερεῖα Th.1.126, etc.; θ. θῦμα, θυσίαν, Pl.*Plt*.290e, *R*. 362c, etc.; θ. διαβατήρια, ἐπινίκια, etc., Plu.*Luc*.24, Pl.*Smp*.173a, etc.:—Pass., τὰ τεθυμένα *the flesh of the victim*, X.*HG*4.3.14, etc.; τὰ τεθ. ἱερά ib.3.5.5; τὰ θυόμενα Id.*Lac*.15.3. b. simply, *slaughter*, Hdt.1.126, Ar.*Lys*.1062, Lxx *Is*.22.13. 3. abs., *offer sacrifice*, Hdt.1.31, al., A.*Ag*.594, *Fr*.161.2, S.*OC*1159; τοῖσι θεοῖσι θ. Pherecr. 23, cf. Hdt.4.60, 8.138; θεῶν ἕνεκα Men.129.1. 4. *celebrate* with offerings or sacrifices, σῶστρα θ. Hdt.1.118; γενέθλια Pl.*Alc*.1.121c; Λύκαια, Ἡράκλεια, X.*An*.1.2.10, D.19.86; ἐλευθέρια Henioch.5.10; γάμους Plu.*Pomp*.55. 5. c. dupl. acc., εὐαγγέλια θ. ἑκατὸν βοῦς *sacrifice* a hundred oxen *for* the good news, Ar.*Eq*.656. 6. Ἑστίᾳ θύειν, prov. of niggards, because sacrifices to Hestia admitted no one to share the offering, Theopomp.Com.28. II. Med., *cause* a victim *to be offered*, τῶν θυμάτων ὧν δεῖ θύεσθαι καὶ παρίστασθαι *IG*5(1). 1390.65 (Andania, i B.C.), etc.: hence freq. abs., *consult the gods*, Hdt.7.189, E.*Heracl*.340; ἐπὶ Κρότωνα, ἐπὶ τῷ Πέρσῃ, i.e. on marching *against*.., Hdt.5.44, 9.10, cf. X.*An*.7.8.21; θύεσθαι ἐπ' ἐξόδῳ ib. 6.4.9; ὑπὲρ τῆς μονῆς ib.5.6.27: c. inf., θ. ἰέναι *offer sacrifice* [to learn] whether to go or not, ib.2.2.3; also ἐθυόμην εἰ βέλτιον εἴη ib.6.1.31 (so in Act., ἔθυε (v.l. ἐθύετο) τῷ Διί.. πότερά οἱ λῷον καὶ ἄμεινον εἴη.. ib.7.6.44); διαβατήρια θύεσθαι, as in Act., Th.5.54. 2. metaph., *tear in pieces*, of wild beasts, A.*Ag*.137 (lyr.). (Hence θυμός, cf. Skt. *dhūmás*, Lat. *fumus* 'smoke', θυμιάω, θύος, θυήλημα, τύφω, perh. θεῖον (A), Lat. *suffire*; cf. sq.)

**θύω** (B) [ῡ], aor. ἔθῡσα Call.*Fr*.82:—*rage, seethe*, ἄνεμος μὲν ἐπαύσατο λαίλαπι θύων Od.12.400; Ζέφυρος μεγάλῃ σὺν λαίλαπι θύων ib. 408, cf. Hes.*Op*.621, *Th*.874; of a swollen river, ὁ δ' ἐπέσσυτο οἴδματι θύων *seething*, Il.21.234; ὑψόσε θύων ib.324; of a wind-swept sea, ὁ δ' ἔστενεν οἴδματι θύων 23.230, cf. Hes.*Th*.109,131; of the wake of a ship, κῦμα δ' ὄπισθε πορφύρεον μέγα θῦε Od.13.85; δάπεδον δ' ἅπαν αἵματι θῦεν the ground *seethed* with blood, 11.420, 22.309; of persons, *storm, rage*, ἦ γὰρ ὅ γ' ὀλοιῇσι φρεσὶ θύει Il.1.342; ἔγχεϊ θῦεν 11. 180; κασιγνήτα μένει θύοισα Pi.*P*.3.33; θύουσαν Ἅιδου μητέρα A.*Ag*. 1235; πυκνὰ δέ οἱ κραδίη ἔντοσθεν ἔθυεν A.R.3.755 (v.l. ἔθυιεν): c. inf., *desire eagerly*, ἐνισπεῖν ib.685; of a horse, Call.*Fr*.82; of a serpent, Nic.*Th*.129 (v.l. θυίησι). [ῡ always: for θύμενος [ῠ] is f.l. for σύμενος in Pratin.Lyr.1.4.] θυίω (q.v.) should perh. be preferred in later Ep., and is cj. in Pi.l.c. (Cf. Lett. *dusmas* (pl.) 'anger', *dusět* 'puff', 'pant', Lat. *fūro* (fr. *dhūs*–), θύελλα, θυίω, θυιάς (orig. *madwoman*); prob. cogn. with foreg.)

**θυ-ώδης**, ες, (θύος, ὄζ-ωδα, cf. εὐώδης, δυσώδης) *smelling of incense, fragrant*, εἵματα.. θυώδεα Od.5.264; θαλάμοιο θυώδεος 4.121; βωμός *h.Ap*.87; νηός *h.Ven*.59; ναοί Theoc.17.123; Οὔλυμπος *h.Merc*.322; λίβανος Emp.128.6; καπνός E.*Andr*.1026 (lyr.): Comp. -έστερος, τέρμινθος Thphr.*HP*3.15.3. II. (θύον I) *belonging to the tree* θύον, ib. 5.4.2. **-όεις**, εσσα, εν, = θυόεις, Hsch. **-ωμα**, ατος, τό, *that which is burnt as incense*: pl., *spices*, Heraclit.67, Semon.16, Hdt.2.40,86, Luc.*Syr.D*.20.

**Θυώνη**, ἡ, (θύω B) epith. of Semele, *h.Hom*.1.21, Sapph.*Supp*. 6.10, Pi.*P*.3.99, D.S.3.62, etc.:—Adj. **Θυωναῖος** Διόνυσος Opp.*C*. 1.27. II. **θυώνη**, Dor. -ᾱ, ἡ, *portion of sacrifice*, acc. pl. -ας *Abh. Berl.Akad*.1928(6).12 (Cos); cf. Hsch. s.v. θύανον.

**θυωρ-εῖσθαι**· θυωθεῖσθαι, εὐωχεῖσθαι, Hsch. **-ίς** (sc. τράπεζα), ίδος, ἡ, *a table for offerings*, Poll.4.123; cf. θυωρός. **-ίτης**· τραπεζίτης, Hsch.: metaph., θ. κάλλους *an examiner* of beauty, of Paris, Lyc.93; expld. by ἀργυρογνώμων, *EM*457.50. **-ός**, όν, (θύος) *taking care of offerings*: as Subst. (sc. τράπεζα), = θυωρίς, Call.*Dian*.134, *BCH* 11.161 (Lagina); οἱ θεοὶ τὴν τράπεζαν θυωρὸν καλοῦσιν Pherecyd.Syr. 12. II. (θύος) *perfumer*, Nic.*Th*.103.

**θώ**, ὁ, apocop. for θώραξ, *AP*6.85 (Pall.).

**θωάζω**, Elean **θωάδδω**, (θωή) *pay the penalty*, βοῖ *Schwyzer*412.1 (Elis): **θωάω**, *penalize, fine*, *IG*1².4.7,12:—Delph. **θωέω** *Michel*995 *D*19:—Cret. **θωαίω** *GDI*4977 (Gortyn):—Pass., διπλείῳ θωιήστω (imper.), *IG*9(1).333.9 (Locr., v B.C.).

**θωή**, ἡ, *penalty*, θωὴν ἐπιθήσομεν Od.2.192; θωὴν ἀλέεινεν Ἀχαιῶν a *penalty* imposed by them, Il.13.669:—Att. **θωά**, ἡ, *IG*1².114.42:—Ion. also **θωϊή** Archil.109, *BCH*50.214 (Thasos, v B.C.), prob. l. in Democr.262: **θωιιή**, *SIG*58.12 (Milet., v B.C.): Att. gen. pl. θῳῶν with ι acc. to Choerob.*in Theod*.1.405, but v. supr. and cf. θωάω. (I.-E. *dhō*–, in OE. *dóm* 'doom', cf. *dhē*– in τίθημι.)

**θωίασις**, εως, ἡ, *infliction of penalty*, *Michel*995*D*23 (Delph.).

**θωκέω**, Ion. and Dor. for θακέω. **θωκίζω**, *establish, settle*, Hsch. **θῶκος**, Ion. for θᾶκος. **θῶμα, θωμάζω, θωμάσιος**, Ion. for θαυμ–, Hdt. **θῶμαι**, v. θῶσθαι.

**θωμεύω**, (θωμός) *heap up*, Hsch.

**θῶμιγξ**, ιγγος, ἡ, *cord, string*, Hdt.1.199, *AP*9.343 (Arch.), Polyaen.6.50, Ael.*VH*3.26; *bow-string*, A.*Pers*.461, *Eu*.182, *Trag. Adesp*.215; *a fishing-line*, Opp.*H*.3.76, etc. (Perh. cognate with Lat. *fūnis*.)

**θωμίζω** (also -ίσσω, Hsch.), *whip, scourge*, νῶτον μάστιγι θωμιχθείς Anacr.21.10, cf. *EM*459.54:—also, *bind*, Hsch., Suid.

**θώμισσον**· τὸν μισθόν, Hsch. (leg. θὤμισσον· τὸ ἥμισσον).

**θωμός**, ὁ, *heap*, A.*Ag*.295, Ar.*Lys*.973, Thphr.*HP*8.11.4, *AP*6.299 (Phan.): metaph., θ. ψηφισμάτων Ar.*Fr*.217. (Like θημών, fr. I.-E. *dhē*–, τί-θημι.)

**θωός**, ὁ, a kind of *bird*, Hsch.

**θωπ-εία**, ἡ, *flattery*, E.*Or*.670, Jul.*Or*.3.102c, etc.: pl., Ar.*Eq*. 890; θωπεῖαι λόγων Pl.*Lg*.906b; θ. κολακικαί ib.633d. **-ευμα**, ατος, τό, *piece of flattery*, Ar.*V*.563: in pl., *endearments*, E.*Supp*.1103; *flatteries*, Pl.*R*.590c, Plu.2.823c:—Dim. **-ευμάτια**, τά, *bits of flattery*, Ar.*Eq*.788. **-ευτικός**, ή, όν, *disposed to flatter, fawning*, of dogs, Arist.*HA*488ᵇ21; τὰ θωπευτικά *flattery*, Pl.*Lg*.634a. Adv. -κῶς D.C.69.6, Gal.14.600. **-εύω**, (θώψ) *flatter, wheedle*, τινα S.*OC* 1003, 1336, E.*Heracl*.983, Ar.*Ach*.657, *Eq*.48; σὺ ταῦτα θώπευ' *be it* thine to *flatter* thus, S.*El*.397; θ. τὸν δεσπότην λόγῳ Pl.*Tht*.173a; τὸν δῆμον Aeschin.3.226; τὰς πόλεις Phld.*Rh*.2.170S.; καιρὸν θ. *to be a time-server*, Ps.-Phoc.93; ἵνα μὴ ἄλλους θωπεύωμεν σοῦ ὑγιαίνοντος *serve* others (in good sense), *PSI*5.525.16 (iii B.C.); of dogs, *fawn*, Arist.*Phgn*.811ᵇ38; *caress, pat* a horse, X.*Eq*.10.13, *Cyn*.6. 21; of disease, *soothe*, τὴν χολήν Sever.*Clyst*.p.37 D.:—Pass., Ar. *Eq*.1116. **-ικός**, ή, όν, (θώψ) = θωπευτικός, Id.*Lys*.1037, Max.Tyr. 9.7. Adv. -κῶς Suid. **-τω**, = θωπεύω, c. acc., θῶπτε τὸν κρατοῦντ' ἀεί A.*Pr*.937: fut. θώψεις Id.*Fr*.234.

**θωρᾱκ-εῖον**, τό, = θωράκιον II, *breastwork, parapet*, or *dwarf-wall* of an enclosure, A.*Th*.32, *IG*2².463.86, *IGRom*.4.293ᵃi39 (Pergam., ii B.C.), 1465, 1474 (Smyrna), D.S.17.44 (v.l. -ίοις); the *breast-high part* of a wall-surface, ἵνα γραφῇ.. θ. ὀροβοειδές *PCair.Zen*.445 (iii B.C.). 2. *gunwale* of a trireme, *IG*2².1604.31. II. *cuirass*, *PCair. Zen*.14.12 (iii B.C.). **-ίζω**, prose form of θωρήσσω, *arm with a breastplate* or *corslet*, θωρακίσας αὐτοὺς καὶ ἵππους X.*Cyr*.8.8.22:—Med., *put on one's breastplate*, Id.*An*.2.2.14:—Pass., θωρακισθείς ib.3.4.35; τεθωρακισμένοι *cuirassiers*, Th.2.100, X.*An*.2.5.35; ἄγαλμα τεθ. *OGI*332. 7 (Elaea, ii B.C.). II. generally, *cover with defensive armour*, τοὺς ἡνιόχους ἐθωράκισε πλὴν τῶν ὀφθαλμῶν X.*Cyr*.6.1.29; ὄγκῳ.. χλανίδος εὖ τεθωρακισμένος Ephipp.14.10: metaph., θ. ἑαυτούς, of wild boars, *to sheathe* themselves *in mud*, preparatory to fighting, Arist. *HA*571ᵇ16; of the ichneumon, θωρακισθεὶς πηλῷ Str.17.1.39. **-ικός**, ή, όν, *suffering in the chest*, Aët.8.63. II. -ικά, τά, with or without μόρια, *region of the thorax*, Pall. *in Hp*.2.97,102 D. **-ιον**, τό, Dim. of θώραξ, Luc.*Par*.49. II. *breastwork, parapet*, Plb.8.4.4, D.S.17.44 (v.l. for -είοις), J.*BJ*5.7.4, Ph.2.324; *shield* for those who worked the battering-ram, Ath.Mech.18.11; or for those who attempted to burn the enemy's engines, D.S.14.51; λόγου θ. Menodot. 1; also, *the tower on the back of elephants*, or rather *the upper part thereof*, [Plb.]*Fr*.162ᵇ, D.S.2.17, Ael.*NA*13.9; *a crow's-nest at the masthead*, in which javelin-men were stationed, Asclep.Myrl.ap.Ath.11. 475a. III. δυστυχὲς θ. dub. sens. in *Com.Adesp*.15.29 D. **-ίς**, = θώραξ, *Gloss*. **-ισμός**, ὁ, *arming with breastplates*, Lxx 2*Ma*.5. 3. **-ίτης** [ῑ], ου, ὁ, *soldier with breast-armour only*, Plb.10.29. 6, al.:—fem. **-ῖτις**, as Adj., ζώνη *cuirass*-belt, prob. in *PPetr*.3 p.12 (iii B.C.).

**θωρᾱκο-ειδής**, ές, *breastplate-shaped*, ὕφασμα Ph.2.226. **-ζώνη**, ἡ, *cuirass-belt*, Sch.Il.11.234. **-ποιός**, ὁ, *maker of breastplates*, X. *Mem*.3.10.9, *IG*2².1261.3, *PTeb*.278.18 (i A.D.). **-πώλης**, ου, ὁ, *dealer in breastplates*, Ar.*Pax* in Ind. personarum. **-φόρος**, Ion.

**θωρηκ-**, ον, *wearing a breastplate, cuirassier*, Hdt.7.89,92, 8.113, X. *Cyr.*5.3.36, Jul.*Or.*2.63c; τὸ θ. D.C.47.43.

* **θώραξ**, ᾱκος, Ep. and Ion. **θώρηξ**, ηκος, Aeol. **θόρραξ** Alc.15 (codd. Ath.), ὁ:—*corslet*, θ. χάλκεος Il.23.560; παναίολος 11.374; πολυδαίδαλος 4.136, cf. 11.19, etc.; δεκάμνουν θώρηκος κύτος Ar.*Pax*1224; ἔξαιρε παῖ θώρακα..τὸν χοᾶ Id.*Ach.*1133; θ...γυάλοισιν ἀρηρώς Il.15.529 (γύαλα expld. as front- and back-piece fastened with περόναι, Paus.10.26.5); θώρηκος γύαλον Il.5.99; ὅθι διπλόος ἤντετο θ. 4.133; κατὰ ζώνην θώρηκος ἔνερθε 11.234; linen *jerkin* (not worn by Homeric Greeks acc. to Sch.Il.2.529, but cf. λινοθώρηξ), θόρρακες νέω λίνω Alc. l. c., cf. Hdt.2.182, 3.47, *Chron.Lind.*C.36, Paus.6.19.7. 2. *coat of mail, scale armour*, θ. χρύσεος λεπιδωτός Hdt.9.22, cf. 74; φολιδωτός Posidipp.26.7, cf. Paus.1.21.6; of chain mail, v. ἁλυσιδωτός. b. *slough* of a serpent, καθάπερ ὄφις παλαιὸν ἀποδύεται θ. Porph.*Chr.*88. II. *part covered by the θώραξ* I, *trunk*, Hp.*de Arte*10, E.*HF*1095, Arist.*HA*493ᵃ5; κεφαλῆς καὶ θώρακος καὶ τῆς κάτω κοιλίας Id.*Pr.*962ᵃ34; sts. taken as extending below the midriff, Pl.*Ti.*69e; ἀπ' αὐχένος μέχρι αἰδοίων Arist.*HA*491ᵃ30, cf. *PA*686ᵇ5, ἐν τῷ κάτω θώρακος χωρίῳ, of the abdominal cavity, Gal.16.448; but also of the *chest, thorax*, Arist.*HA*493ᵃ17:—there is a play on signfs. I and II in Ar.*V.*1194 sq. b. *thorax* of crustaceans, Arist. *HA*601ᵃ13, al. 2. *bandage for the chest*, Heliod.ap.Orib.48.48 tit., Sor.*Fasc.*33, cf. Gal.18(1).817. III. = θωράκιον II, Hdt.1.181, D.C.74.10.

**θωρηκοφόρος**, ον, Ion. for θωρακοφόρος.

**θωρηκτής**, οῦ, ὁ, (θωρήσσω) *armed with θώραξ*, Ἀργείοισι θωρηκτῇσι Il.21.429; Λυκίων, Τρώων πύκα θωρηκτάων *armed with* stout *cuirass*, 12.317, 15.689.

**θώρηξ**, ηκος, ὁ, Ion. and Ep. for θώραξ.

* **θώρηξις**, εως, ἡ, *drinking to intoxication*, Hp.*Aph.*2.21, 7.48, Gal. 17(2).498, 18(1).154, Aret.*SD*2.6: pl., Hp.*Morb.*2.66.

**θωρήσσω**, Ep. aor. θώρηξα, subj. θωρήξομεν (for -ωμεν) Il.2.72:—*arm with a θώραξ*: generally, *arm*, θωρῆξαί ἑ κέλευε..Ἀχαιούς Il. 2.11; Μυρμιδόνας..θώρηξεν Ἀχιλλεύς 16.155:—more freq. in Med. and Pass., θωρήσσομαι, fut. -ξομαι: aor. ἐθωρήχθην:—*arm oneself, put one's harness on*, αὐτίκα θωρήσσοντο Il.19.352; σὺν τεύχεσι θωρηχθέντες 8.530, etc.; ἐς πόλεμον ἅμα λαῷ θωρηχθῆναι 1.226; τεύχε' ἐνείκω θωρηχθῆναι I will bring you arms *to arm yourselves withal*, Od.22.139; ἐθωρήσσοντο δὲ χαλκῷ 23.369; ἐν τῷδε (sc. θώρακι) πρὸς τοὺς πολεμίους θωρήξομαι Ar.*Ach.*1134; to which Dicaeopolis replies, ἐν τῷδε (sc. χοΐ) πρὸς τοὺς συμπότας θ., with reference to signf. II. II. *fortify with drink*, Hp.*Epid.*2.5.10; ποτῷ φρένα θωρηχθέντες Nic.*Al.* 32; τεθωρηγμένος Ruf.ap.Orib.6.38.23; *make drunk, intoxicate*, Thgn.842:—Med. and Pass., *get drunk*, οἴνῳ Id.470: abs., Id.413, Pi.*Fr.*72; θωρηχθεὶς ὑπὸ οἴνου Hp.*Morb.*4.56, cf. Duris 27 J. III. Med. in causal sense, τὸν μὲν..νέκταρι θωρήξαιο Nic.*Al.*225.

**θώς**, θωός, ὁ, also ἡ, prob. *jackal, Canis aureus*, Τρῶες ἕποντ' ὡς εἴ τε δαφοινοὶ θῶες..ἀμφ' ἔλαφον Il.11.474, cf. Arist.*HA*610ᵃ14, 630ᵃ9; θώων παρδαλίων τε λύκων τ' ἤϊα Il.13.103; θ. καὶ πάνθηρες Hdt.4.192; ἔχει ὁ θ. πάντα τὰ ἐντὸς ὅμοια λύκῳ Arist.*HA*507ᵇ17; a large kind in India, Arr.*Ind.*15.3: pl., θώαντες *IG*14.1302 (mosaic at Praeneste). 2. *hunting dog, Lycaon pictus*, Opp.*C.*3.338, al. 3. *panther*, Cyr.

* **θῶσθαι**, = δαίνυσθαι, εὐωχεῖσθαι (Dor.), A.*Fr.*49, *EM*461.1; cf. θῶται· εὐθηνεῖται, θοινᾶται, and θῶνται· θοινῶνται κτλ., Hsch.: fut. θωσούμεθα Epich.139: aor. 1 inf. θώσασθαι· εὐωχηθῆναι, Hsch.:—Pass., θωθῆναι· φαγεῖν, γεύσασθαι, Id.

***θώσσω**, = θωρήσσω II, aor. 1 θῶξαι, Dor. θᾶξαι Hsch.: aor. Pass. part. θωχθεὶς S.*Fr.*173, Dor. inf. θωχθῆμεν Hsch.

**θωστήριον**, τό, = εὐωχητήριον, ἑορτή, Alcm.23.81, Hsch. (pl.).

**θωτάζω**, = τωθάζω, Hsch.

**θωῠκτήρ**, ῆρος, ὁ, *barker, roarer*, *APl.*4.91.

**θωῦμα, θωυμάζω**, etc., less correct forms for θῶμα, θωμάζω, v. θαυμ-.

**θωῡσσω**, of a dog, *bark, bay*, Hom.*Fr.*25; of a gnat, *buzz*, A.*Ag.* 893: generally, *cry aloud, shout*, S.*Aj.*308, E.*Tr.*153 (anap.), *Or.* 168 (lyr.): c. acc. cogn., τόνδ' ἐθώϋξας λόγον A.*Pr.*395; τάσδ' ἀγγελίας ἐθώϋξεν ib.1041 (anap.); τήνδε θωΰσσει βοήν S.*Aj.*335. 2. c. acc. pers., *call on, call*, φθέγμα..τινὸς θωΰξεν αὐτόν Id.*OC*1624: c. dat., θ. κυσί *shout* to dogs, E.*Hipp.*219 (anap.), cf. *Ba.*871 (lyr.). b. *lament, bewail*, dub. in *IG*12(3).9 (Syme).

**θώψ**, gen. θωπός, ὁ, *flatterer, false friend*, Hdt.3.80; θ. πλούτου Antipho Soph.65, cf. Them.*Or.*20.237d. II. as Adj., θῶπες λόγοι *fawning* speeches, *Trag.Adesp.*24, Pl.*Tht.*175e, Ph.2.52 (cf. τέ-θηπα, θάμβος).

# I

**I ι, ἰῶτα**, τό, indecl., tenth (later ninth) letter of the Gr. alphabet: as numeral ι' = 10, but ͵ι = 10,000.

The ι 'subscript' of modern texts was said προσγράφεσθαι, cf. D.T.639.14, A.D.*Pron.*87.10, Ael.Dion.*Fr.*192 (also τὸ λῃστής (disyll.)..ἔχει προσκείμενον τὸ ῑ Hdn.Gr.2.946), and this mode of writing is found in Papyri, Inscrr., and some medieval Mss. (e.g. cod. A of Plato, saec. ix, which has τῶι = τῷ, etc.); the present mode is found as early as the tenth century, and came into use in the thirteenth. This ι was prob. always pronounced up to ca. 150 B.C., but thereafter dropped in pronunciation, cf. D.T. l.c.; hence called ι ἀνεκφώνητον Choerob. *in Theod.*1.143 and freq. omitted in Pap. and Inscrr. (cf. Epigr.ap.Str.14.1.41, = *SIG*766), later freq. restored in writing, sts. in the wrong place (v. ῥάθυμος). From ca. 150 B.C. (at Argos from ca. 450 B.C., v. *SIG*56.13) ει was pronounced ι and the sound is written indifferently ει or ι.

-ί, *iota demonstrativum*, in familiar Att. (not in Trag.), is attached to demonstr. Prons., to strengthen their force, and as it were point out the individual, as οὑτοσί, αὑτηΐ, τουτί, ἐκεινοσί, ὁδί, ταδί, τοσουτονί, τοσονδί, τυννουτοσί, etc.; also with the Particles γε δέ μέν inserted, as τουτογί, τουτοδί, ταυτηνδί, τηδεδί, τουτομενί, for τουτί γε, ταυτηνὶ δέ, etc.: also to demonstr. Advs., as οὑτωσί, ὡδί, ἐνθαδί, δευρί, νυνί, and νυνδί for νυνὶ δέ.—Of these forms, such as end in σί are sts. written in codd. with ν ἐφελκυστικόν before a vowel, as οὑτοσίν, ἐκεινοσίν, οὑτωσίν, etc.: such forms are recognized by A.D.*Pron.*59.24, 82.11, but are not found in best codd., e.g. of Pl. and D. [ῑ with the acute accent; a long vowel or diphthong before it is short d., as αὑτηΐ, οὑτοΐ.]

**ῑ**, nom. of the reflex. Pron. οὗ, *sui* (q.v.), S.*Fr.*471, cj. Wackernagel in Il.24.608, Bekk. in Pl.*Smp.*175c, 223d: dat. ἶν αὐτῷ, *sibi ipsi*, Hes.*Fr.*11; ἰν (enclit.) prob. in Pi.*P.*4.36; ϝὶν αὐτῷ *Leg.Gort.* 2.40. [ῑ S. l. c., ἶν Pi. l. c.]

**ῑ**, Argive, = εἰ, *SIG*56.29 (v B.C.), *Schwyzer*90.12, al., 91.31 (iii B.C.).

* **ῐ**, Cypr. for ἤ, *or*, before a vowel, *Inscr.Cypr.*135.24 H.

**ἰά** [ῐ], Ion. **ἰή**, ἡ, = ἰωή, *voice, cry*, Orac.ap.Hdt.1.85, A.*Pers.*937 (lyr.); σύριγγος ἰά E.*Rh.*553 (lyr.).

**ἴᾰ**, ἰῆς, ἰῇ, ἴαν, Ep. fem., = *one*, v. εἷς.

**ἰά** [ῐ], τά, heterocl. pl. of ἰός, *arrow*, Il.20.68.

**ἴα** [ῑ], τά, pl. of ἴον, *violet*, *h.Cer.*6.

**ἰάζω** (A), (Ἰάς) = ἰωνίζω, Dicaearch.3.2, A.D.*Adv.*134.31, Hermog. *Id.*2.4.

**ἰάζω** (B), (ἰά) *cry aloud*, Theognost.*Can.*18.

**ἰάζω** (C), (ἴον) *to be of a violet colour*, Hld.2.30. II. (ἰός C) *to be green*, of bile, Gal.18(2).141.

**ἰαθενεῖ**· διαπορεῖ ἐπὶ κακῷ (Coan), Hsch.:—also **ἰηθενέουσα**· ἐκπεπληγμένη καὶ ἀποροῦσα, Id. **ἰαθμός**, v. ἰαυθμός. **ἴαθος**· πρόθυμος, Id.

**ἰαί**, 1. barbarous exclam. of sorrow, S.*Fr.*631. 2. of triumph, Ar.*Lys.*1292; ἰαὶ ἰαί Id.*Ec.*1180.

**ἰαιβοῖ** [ῐ], Comic exclam. for αἰβοῖ, Ar.*V.*1338.

* **ἰαίνω**, Ion. impf. -εσκον Q.S.7.340: aor. ἴηνα Od.8.426, Dor. ἴᾱνα Pi.*O.*7.43:—Pass., aor. ἰάνθην Il.23.598, etc. [ῐ, exc. in augm. tenses, in Hom.; but at the beginning of a verse ῑ without augm., Od.22.59: ῑ freq. in later Poets, *AP*12.95 (Mel.), Q.S. l.c., 4.402, 10.327, Orph.*L.*268, etc.]:—*heat*, ἀμφὶ δέ οἱ πυρὶ χαλκὸν ἴηνατε Od. 8.426:—Pass., ἰαίνετο δ' ὕδωρ 10.359. 2. *melt*, ἰαίνετο κηρός 12. 175: metaph., θυμὸν ἰαίνειν *melt* the heart, Il.24.119. b. *relax by warmth*, Hp.*Mul.*1.69 (Pass.). 3. more freq. (cf. Plu.2.947d) *warm, cheer*, κραδίην καὶ θυμὸν ἰαίνειν *h.Cer.*435; θυμὸν ἰαίνειν τινί Od.15.379, Pi.*O.* l. c., cf. Theoc.7.29; καρδίαν Alcm.36, Pi.*P.*1.11; νόον ib.2.90:—more freq. in Pass., ἵνα..σὺ φρεσὶ σῇσιν ἰανθῇς Il.19. 174; θυμὸς ἐνὶ στήθεσσιν ἰάνθη Od.4.549; εἰς ὅ κε σὸν κῆρ ἰανθῇ 22. 59; ἦτορ ἰανθέν *Anacreont.*48.2: c. dat., σοὶ..μετὰ φρεσὶ θυμὸς ἰάνθη Il.23.600, cf. 24.321, etc.; θυμὸν ἰάνθης Od.23.47; χοροῖσι φρένα ἰανθείς B.16.131; μέτωπον ἰάνθη her brow *unfolded*, Il.15. 103: c. dat. rei, *take delight in*, σφιν ἰαίνομαι εἰσορόωσα Od.19.537; σφισι θυμὸς αἰὲν εὐφροσύνῃσιν ἰαίνεται 6.156; καρδίην ἰαίνεται Archil. 36; ἰανθεὶς ἀοιδαῖς Pi.*O.*2.13; cf. εὐφροσύνη: later ἰαίνειν τινά τινι Man.3.184. II. later, = ἰάομαι, *heal, save*, τινὰ ὀδυνάων Q.S.10. 327; ὑπὲκ κακοῦ ἰαίνονται Id.4.402.—Ep. and Lyr. word; Trag. only Phryn.Trag.1, ἰαίνεται· χολοῦται, πικραίνεται, παρὰ τὸν ἰόν (cf. Hsch.).

**Ἰᾰκός**, ή, όν, (Ἰάς) *Ionic*, ἀσωτία Plb.32.11.10; τὸ Ἰακόν *the Ionic form*, Ath.9.400c; ἡ Ἰ. ἔγκλισις A.D.*Pron.*98.8. Adv. -κῶς ib.4.21.

**Ἰακυνθοτρόφος**, ἡ, epith. of Artemis, *Schwyzer*265 (Cnidus); cf. Ὑακινθοτρόφια.

**ἴακχα**, ης, ἡ, Sicyonic name of *a perfumed garland*, Philet.ap.Ath. 15.678a, Timach.ibid., Hsch.

**Ἰακχ-αγωγός** [ῐ], όν, *bearing the image of Bacchus* on his festivals, *IG*2².1092*B*31 (written Ἰαχχ-), *IG*3.162, 262, Poll.1.35. * **-άζω**, *shout* Ἴακχος, Longus 3.11 (cj. for ἰακχεύσαντες): c. acc. cogn., ἰακχάζειν φωνήν Hdt.8.65. II. generally, = ἰαχέω, of birds, ἰακχ. ἀοιδήν Orph.*L.*46. * **-αῖος**, α, ον, *Bacchanalian*, στέφανος Philet. 27. **-εῖον**, τό, *temple of Bacchus*, Plu.*Arist.*27, Alciphr.3.59.

**ἰακχέω, ἰακχή**, v. ἰαχ-.

**Ἰακχιαστής**, οῦ, ὁ, *worshipper of* Ἴακχος, Benndorf-Niemann *Reisen in Lykien* No.134b.

* **Ἴακχος**, ὁ, *Iacchos*, mystic name of Dionysus, S.*Fr.*959, *Trag. Adesp.*140 (lyr.), Ar.*Ra.*398, Paus.1.2.4, etc.; ἡ Ἐλευσῖνι τοῦ Ἰαάκχου (sic) ὑποδοχὴ *IG*2².847.21; τὸν Ἴακχον ἐξελαύνειν lead forth a Bacchic procession, Plu.*Alc.*34; τὸν Ἴ. προπέμψαι *IG*2².1028.10. 2. *song* in his honour, ὁ μυστικὸς ἴ. Hdt.8.65, cf. Athenio ap.Posidon.36 J., Anon.ap.Suid.; ᾄδειν τὸν Ἴ. Hsch. s. v. Διαγόρας: as Adj., ἴακχος ᾠδά E.*Cyc.*69 (lyr.). 2. in pl., *Epigr.Gr.*985 (Philae): generally, *chorus*, νεκρῶν ἴ. E.*Tr.*1230; τυμπάνων ἴ. dub. in Id.*Fr.*586.4 (lyr.). II. used by the tyrant Dionysius for χοῖρος, Athanis 1 (= Dionys.Trag.12).

**ἰᾱλεμ-έω** [ῐ], = sq., Hdn.Gr.2.236. **-ίζω**, Ion. ἰηλ-, (ἰάλεμος) *bewail*, Call.*Fr.*176. **-ίστρια**, Ion. ἰηλ-, ἡ, *wailing woman*, A.*Ch.*424 (lyr., Herm., from Hsch.). * **-ος**, Ion. ἰήλ-, ὁ, *lament, dirge*, used by Trag. in lyr., A.*Supp.*115, E.*Rh.*895, *Tr.*1304, *Ph.*1033, etc.; τὸν ἰ. ἀρίστευσε Theoc.15.98: rare in Prose, Metrod.*Herc.*831.17 (s. v. l.);

prov., ἰαλέμου ψυχρότερος, of something tedious and dull, Zen.4.39. II. as Adj., *melancholy*, γόοι E.*HF*109 (lyr., s. v. l.); but usu., 2. *tedious, dull, stupid*, ποιηταί Luc.*Pseudol.*24; ἰατροί Gal.14.617: as Subst., *dullard, oaf*, Men.236, Hermog.*Id.*2.6; title of play by Amphis, Ath.2.69b. (Perh. from the cry ἰή.) **-ώδης**, ες, *like an* ἰάλεμος, *wretched*, Phot., Suid.

**ἰαλία**, ἡ, Cret. for φωνή, Hsch. **ἰάλιον**· ἐρέβινθον ἢ τὴν θάλασσαν (Cret.), Id.

**ἰάλλω**, Att. **ἰάλλω** acc. to Hdn.Gr.1.539, cf. ἐφιάλλω: fut. ἰᾰλῶ (ἐπ-) Ar.*Nu.*1299 aor. ἴηλα Il.15.19, Dor. **ἴᾱλα** Sophr.14. [ῐ, unless augmented; Hom. never uses the augm.]:—*send forth*, ὀϊστὸν ἀπὸ νευρῆφιν ἴαλλεν Il.8.300,309, cf. *AP*5.187 (Leon.): used by Hom. mostly in phrase, ἐπ' ὀνείατα χεῖρας ἴαλλον *they put forth* their hands to the dishes, Od.1.149, al.; ἐπὶ σίτῳ χ. ἴ. 10.376; ἑτάροις ἐπὶ χεῖρας ἴ. *laid* hands upon his comrades, 9.288; περὶ χερσὶ δὲ δεσμὸν ἴηλα *threw* chains around thy arms, Il.15.19; ἐπὶ δεσμὸν ἴηλε Od.8.447; so later ὑλακὴν *give* tongue, *AP*7.69 (Jul. Aegypt.); ἴχνος *set down, plant* the foot, Nic.*Al.*242. 2. c. acc. obj., ἄριστον ἀτιμίῃσιν ἰάλλειν *assail* him with insults, Od.13.142. 3. later, *send, dispatch*, ἄγγελον Thgn.573, cf. A.*Ch.*45 (lyr.); ἐπὶ Δωδώνης..θεοπρόπους ἴαλλεν Id.*Pr.*659; Δίκην ἴαλλε σύμμαχον Id.*Ch.*497; ἄρτον τοῖς παιδίοις Sophr. l. c.; τινὰ παρά τινα Id.61; Φθίᾳ ἐλεύθερον ἦμαρ ἴ. *AP*7.529 (Theodorid.). 4. = εὑρίσκω, Hsch. s. vv. ἴαλαι, ἴλλει. II. intr. (sc. ἑαυτόν) *send oneself on*, i. e. *flee, run*, Hes.*Th.*269. (Cf. Skt. *i-yarti* 'set in motion'.)

**ἰαλτός** [ῐ], ἡ, όν, *sent forth*, ἐκ δόμων A.*Ch.*22 (lyr.).

**Ἰᾱλυσός**, Ion. **Ἰηλυσός**, ἡ, one of the three Dorian cities of Rhodes, Il.2.656, Hdt.1.144, Pi.*O.*7.74, Timocr.1.7, Str.14.2.12: **Ἰαλυσία**, ἡ, its territory, D.S.5.57:—Adj. **Ἰηλύσιος**, α, ον, D.P. 505. [ῡ in Hom., ῠ in D.P., doubtful in Pi.; ῐ exc. in Timocr. l. c. and Ἰαλυσοῖο (– ⏑ ⏑ – ⏑) *AP*7.716 (Dionys.).]

**ἴᾱμα**, Ion. **ἴημα**, ατος, τό, (ἰάομαι) *remedy, medicine*, Hdt.3.130, Hp.*Acut.*6, Th.2.51, Pl.*Lg.*771c, etc., στεναγμοί, τῶν πόνων ἰάματα v. l. in A.*Fr.*385. II. = ἴασις, ἰάματα τοῦ Ἀπόλλωνος καὶ τοῦ Ἀσκλαπιοῦ *IG*4.951.2 (Epid.), cf. 1*Ep.Cor.*12.9 (pl.). 2. *soothing, pacification*, Lxx *Ec.*10.4.

**ἰαμβαυλεῖν**· τὸ δι' αὐλοῦ παριαμβίζειν τῇ κιθάρᾳ καὶ ᾠδῇ, Hsch. (emended).

**ἰαμβειογράφος**, v. ἰαμβειοφάγος.

**ἰαμβεῖος** [ῐ], ον, (ἴαμβος) *iambic*, μέτρον Arist.*Po.*1448b31. II. as Subst. ἰαμβεῖον, τό, *iambic verse*, Ar.*Ra.*1133, 1204, Pl.*R.*602b, Arist.*Po.*1458b19, *Sammelb.*6308 (iii B. C.), etc.: in pl., *iambic poem*, Luc.*Salt.*27: generally, *verse, line*, Ath.8.355a (of anapaests). 2. *iambic metre*, Arist.*Rh.*1404a31.

**ἰαμβειοφάγος** [ῐ, φᾰ], ὁ, *glutton at iambics*, or perh. *mouther, murderer of them*, applied to Aeschines by D.18.139 (v. l. -γράφος):—also **ἰαμβο-φάγος**, ὁ, *AB*190.

**ἰαμβ-έλεγος** [ῐ], ὁ, an asynartete verse, formed by substituting an iambic penthemimer for the former half of a pentameter, Heph. 15.11. **-ιάζω**, = sq., *AP*7.405 (Phil.). **-ίζω**, *assail in iambics, lampoon*, τινα Gorg.ap.Ath.11.505d, Arist.*Po.*1448b32, D.H.7.72. II. abs., *talk in iambic verse*, Luc.*JTr.*33 (s. v. l.). 2. etym. of θρίαμβος, Corn.*ND*30. **-ικός**, ή, όν, *of invective*, ἰδέα Arist.*Po.*1449b8; in metric, *iambic*, D.H.*Comp.*18, Heph.5, etc.: ἡ -κή (sc. ὄρχησις) Ath.15.629d. Adv. -κῶς Phld.*Po.*2.29. **-ίς**, ίδος, ἡ, cited without interpr. from A.(*Fr.*81) by Hsch. **-ιστής**, οῦ, ὁ, *one who writes iambics, libeller*, Ath.5.181c.

**ἰαμβο-γράφος** [ῐ, γρᾰ], ὁ, *writer of iambics*, Suid. s. v. Σωτάδης, v.l. in *EM*424.23. **-ειδής**, ές, *like an iambus*, Aristid.Quint.1.17. **-ποιέω**, *parody*, Arist.*Po.*1458b9. **-ποιός**, ὁ, *writer of lampoons*, ib.1451b14; *of iambics*, Phld.*Po.*2.20, Ath.8.359e.

**ἴαμβος** [ῐ], ὁ, *iambus*, the metrical foot ⏑ –, Pl.*R.*400b, etc.; ὁ ἴ. αὐτὴ..ἡ λέξις ἡ τῶν πολλῶν Arist.*Rh.*1408b33; δάκτυλος ὁ κατὰ ἴαμβον, = ⏑ – ⏑ –, Anon.Rhythm.*Oxy.*2.3, Aristid.Quint.1.17. II. *iambic verse*, Archil.22 (pl.), Pl.*Ion*534c, etc.; ἴαμβος τρίμετρος Hdt. 1.12; ἴ. Ἱππώνακτος Ar.*Ra.*661, cf. Arist.*Rh.*1418b29, *Po.*1448b33. III. *iambic poem*, such as those of Callimachus, Str.8.3.30; esp. *lampoon*, mostly in pl., Pl.*Lg.*935e, Arist.*Pol.*1336b20; ἐφ' ὑβριστῆρας ἰάμβους *AP*7.352 Mel.(?)): also in Prose, οἱ καταλογάδην ἴ. Ath.10.445b. b. of the persons lampooned, Luc.*Pseudol.* 2. 2. *a kind of extempore play* got up by αὐτοκάβδαλοι, who themselves had the same name, Semus 20. (For the termination perh. cf. διθύραμβος, θρίαμβος.)

**ἰαμβύκη** [ῡ], ἡ, *musical instrument*, distinct from the σαμβύκη, acc. to Hsch., Eup.139, Phillis ap.Ath.14.636b.

**ἰαμβύλος** [ῐ, ῠ], ὁ, *libeller*, Hdn.Gr.1.164, Hsch. (-βηλος cod.).

**ἰαμβώδης** [ῐ], ες, *iambic, scurrilous*, ἐπίδειξις Philostr.*VA*6.11.

**ἰᾰμεναί**, late form of εἰαμεναί, Hsch.

**ἴαμνοι**, ων, οἱ, = foreg., Nic.*Th.*30, al.; glossed by θάμνοι, κοῖται, νομοί, Hsch. (ἴαμβοι cod.).

**Ἰάν**, ὁ, in pl. **Ἴᾶνες**, contr. for Ἰάων, Ἰάονες, *Ionian*, A.*Pers.*950, al.

**ἴανα** (ἴαννα cod.)· τὰ βαλλόμενα, ἀπὸ τοῦ ἱέναι, Hsch.

**ἰάνθῐνος**, η, ον, (ἴον, ἄνθος) *violet-coloured*, ἱμάτιον Str.15.3.19, cf. Plin.*HN*21.27, Aq., Sm.*Ex.*25.5:—Subst. **ἴανθος**, ὁ, or **ἴανθον**, τό, = ἴον, Hsch., Theognost.*Can.*18.

**ἰᾰνο-γλέφᾰρος** [ῐ], ον, = μαλακο-βλέφαρος, prob. l. in Alcm.23.69: **-κροκα**· λεπτά, Hsch.: but **ἰανο-κρήδεμνος** (sic), ον, is expld. by ἰοῖς ὅμοιον τὸ ἐπικράνισμα, Id.; ὁ στέμμα ἐξ ἴων φορῶν, Suid. (Prob. compds. of a dialectic form of ἑανός, wh. (viz. ἑανός) is glossed μαλακός, λεπτός, λαμπρός in Sch.Il.18.613.) **ἰανόφρυς**, prob. f. l. for κυαν-, *PMich.*11.13.

**ἰάομαι**, imper. ἰῶ (v. infr.), Ion. inf. ἰᾶσθαι Hp.*Loc.Hom.*24 (ἰῆσθαι v. l. in Id.*Morb.Sacr.*13), Cypr. ἰjᾶσθαι *Inscr.Cypr.*135.3 H.: fut. ἰάσομαι E.*HF*1107, Aeschin.3.69; Ion. and Ep. ἰήσομαι Od.9.525, Archil. 13, (ἐξ-) Hp.*Morb.*1.6: aor. ἰασάμην E.*Fr.*1072, Pl.*Phd.*89a; Ion. ἰησάμην Il.5.899, Hp.*Int.*2:—Pass. (v. infr.). [ῑ- in Hom., etc.; also ῐ. E.*Hipp.*597]:—*heal, cure*, in pres. and impf., *attempt to cure, treat*, of persons or bodies, etc., τινα Il.12.2, Hdt.3.134, etc.; τοὺς κάμνοντας Pl.*Plt.*299a, cf. 293b; ὀφθαλμόν Od.9.525; τὸ σῶμα S.*Tr.*1210: abs., Od.9.520, Il.5.899: prov., ὁ τρώσας ἰάσεται *Mantiss.Prov.*2.28. 2. *cure, treat*, of diseases, νόσους Pi.*P.*3.46, cf. E.*Hipp.*597, Pl.*Prt.*340e, *Chrm.*156b, etc.; σμύρνῃσι ἰ. τὰ ἕλκεα Hdt.7.181: metaph., *remedy*, δυσγνοιαν, ἀδικίαν ἰᾶσθαι, E.*HF*1107, *Or.*650; ἀτυχίας Isoc.6.101; δωροδόκημα Aeschin.3.69; ἀσάφειαν Arr.*Tact.*1.3: prov., μὴ τῷ κακῷ τὸ κακὸν ἰῶ, i. e. do not make bad worse, Hdt.3.53, cf. Th.5.65; μὴ κακοῖς ἰῶ κακά A.*Fr.*349; κακοῖς ὅταν θέλωσιν ἰᾶσθαι κακά S.*Fr.*77: abs., οὔτε τι γὰρ κλαίων ἰήσομαι Archil.13. 3. *cure the effects of, counteract*, ἄκρατος ἰ. τὸ κώνειον Plu.2.653a. 4. *repair*, τὸ βλαβέν Pl.*Lg.*933e; τὴν φύσιν τὴν ἀνθρωπίνην Id.*Smp.*191d; θυσιαστήριον Lxx 3*Ki.*18.32; δίκελλαν Lib.*Decl.*27.3. II. Act. only aor. 1 ἰάσαμεν Gal.10.453; part. ἰάσαντες Sch.E.*Hec.*1236: aor. ἰάθην is always Pass., *be healed, recover*, And.2.9, *AP*6.330 (Aeschin.), *IG*4.951.113 (Epid.), etc.; ἀπὸ τῶν νόσων *Ev.Luc.*6.17; Ion. ἰήθην Hp.*Mul.*1.3, *Int.*1: fut. ἰαθήσομαι Luc.*Asin.*14, *Gp.*12.25.3, Gal.10.377; ἰάσομαι Aristid.2.317 J.: pf. ἴαμαι *Ev.Marc.*5.29.

**Ἰᾰοναῦ** [ῐ], barbarism for Ἰάον (voc.), *O Ionian*, Ar.*Ach.*104.

**Ἰάονες** [ῐᾱ], οἱ, = Ἴωνες, *Ionians*, Il.13.685, *h.Ap.*147, etc.; in the mouth of a Persian = Ἕλληνες, A.*Pers.*178, 563 (lyr.): sg., Ἰάων rare, Theoc.16.57:—fem. **Ἰαονίς**, ίδος, Νύμφαισιν Ἰαονίδεσσιν Nic.*Fr.*74.8: **Ἰαονίηθε**, *from Ionia*, ib.2: **Ἰαόνιος**, α, ον, *Greek*, A.*Supp.*69 (lyr.), *Pers.*899 (lyr., Herm. for Ἰόνιον); *Athenian*, Orac.ap.Plu.*Sol.* 10.

**ἰαόντυς**, Boeot., = Att. ἐῶσιν (dat. pl.), *Schwyzer* 462 *A* 5 (Tanagra, iii B. C.).

**ἰαππᾰπαιάξ** [ῐ], exclamation of astonishment, Ar.*Th.*945.

**ἰάπτω** (A) [ῐ], *hurt, spoil* (= βλάπτω, Hsch.), ὡς ἂν μὴ κλαίουσα κατὰ χρόα καλὸν ἰάπτῃ *mar* her beauty, Od.2.376, cf. 4.749; ναυτιλίην A.R.2.875; of a spear, *wound, pierce*, τοῦ δ' οὐ χρόα καλὸν ἴαψεν Q.S.6. 546; Ἔρως..ὅς με κατασμύχων καὶ ἐς ὀστέον ἄχρις ἰάπτει Theoc.3.17; βροτῶν, οὓς αὐτίκα γῆρας ἰάπτει *AP*11.389 (Lucill.); ἃ δειλὸς χαλεποῖς ἐνὶ πένθεσι γῆρας ἰάψει Q.S.3.455; ἐπεὶ ἦ νύ με κῆδος ἰάπτει λευγαλέον ib.481:—Pass., ὃς δὲ..μελλόντων χάριν ἐὸν ἰάπτεται κέαρ B.*Fr.*7.5; ἰάπτομαι ἄλγεσιν ἦτορ Mosch.4.39; ὥς μοι περὶ θυμὸς ἰάφθη Theoc.2. 82. (Perh. cf. ἴπτομαι.)

**ἰάπτω** (B) [ῐ], fut. -ψω A.*Th.*525 (lyr.): aor. ἴαψα S.*Aj.*700 (lyr.): —*send, drive on*, of missiles, *send forth, shoot*, τόξοις βέλη εἴς τινα A. *Ag.*510; χερμάδα ἐπί τινι Id.*Th.*299 (lyr.); πρόσθε πυλᾶν κεφαλὰν ἰ. to *throw* his head before the gates, i. e. lose it, ib.525 (lyr.): metaph., ἐπιτύμβιον αἶνον ἐπ' ἀνδρὶ θείῳ..ἰάπτω Id.*Ag.*1548 (lyr.); μακάρεσσιν ἔπι ψόγον αἶνον ἰ. Rhian.1.4; ἰ. ὀρχήματα *begin* the dance, S. l. c.:—Pass., ἐπί τινι ἰάπτεται βέλη A.*Th.*544. 2. c. acc. objecti, λόγοις ἰάπτειν τινά *assail* one with words, S.*Aj.*501. II. intr. (sc. ἑαυτόν), *rush, hurry*, A.*Supp.*547 (lyr.). (Perh. cf. Lat. *jacio.*)

**Ἰᾶπυξ**, Ion. **Ἴηπυξ**, ῠγος, ὁ, *the NW.* (or rather *WNW.*) *wind*, = ἀργέστης, Arist.*Vent.*973b14, *Mu.*394b26. II. **Ἰάπῠγες**, Ion. **Ἰήπῠγες**, οἱ, a people of Southern Italy, Hdt.7.170: ἡ **Ἰᾱπῠγία**, Ion. **Ἰηπῠγίη**, their *country*, ibid.:—Adj. **Ἰᾱπύγιος**, α, ον, *Iapygian*, ἄκρα Th.6.30.

**ἴαρ**· αἷμα, and **ἰαροπότης**· αἱμοπότης, Hsch.; cf. ἔαρ, εἶαρ.

**ἴαραξ**, Dor. for ἱέραξ, Hsch., perh. to be read in Epich.68.

**ἰαράρχας** and other words beginning with ἰαρ- = ἱερ-, v. ἱερ-.

**ἰαριγμόν**· χαράν, καὶ θροῦν, Hsch. **ἰαροχρείαν**· τὴν δοφῦν (Ital.), Id.:—also **ἰαροχρής**· καθαρός, θύσιμος, Id. (For ἱερο-.) **ἰαρπάλαμος**· ἀκρόχειρος, Id. **ἰάρωμα**· κοσμάριον παιδικόν, Id.

**Ἰάς**, άδος, ἡ, Adj. fem. *Ionic*, στρατιή, ἐσθής, Hdt.5.33,87; [γυνή] Id.1.92; τῇ Ἰάδι συγγενείᾳ Th.4.61; διάλεκτος A.D.*Adv.*189.5, Str. 8.1.2; γλῶττα ibid.: as Subst., Luc.*Hist Conscr.*16. 2. *the Ionian flower*, = ἴον, Nic.*Fr.*74.2. [ῐ, but ῑ in arsi, *App.Anth.*2.21.]

**ἴᾱσι** [ῐ], 3 pl. pres. of εἶμι (*ibo*). **ἱᾶσι** [ῑ], for ἱέασι, 3 pl. pres. of ἵημι.

**ἰάσιμος** [ῑᾱ], Ion. **ἰήσιμος**, ον, (ἰάομαι) *curable*, of persons, φαρμάκοις A.*Pr.*475, cf. Hp.*Morb.Sacr.*11; opp. ἀνίατος, Pl.*Lg.*941d, etc.; διαφθείρεσθαι ἰάσιμος ὤν Antipho 4.2.4: metaph., *appeasable*, θεός E. *Or.*399. 2. of wounds, τραῦμα ἰ. Pl.*Lg.*878c: metaph., ἰ. ἁμάρτημα Id.*Grg.*525b; κακά Id.*Lg.*731d; ἰ. τὸ πάθος Alex.124.4.

**ἴᾱσις** [ῑ], Ion. **ἴησις**, εως, ἡ, (ἰάομαι) *healing, mode of healing, remedy*, Hp.*Aph.*2.17, S.*OT*68, Pl.*Smp.*188c; οἷς [πήμασιν] ἴ. οὐκ ἔνεστ' ἰδεῖν S.*El.*876; [ἀδίκημα] οὗ μὴ ἔστιν ἴ. Arist.*Rh.*1374b31, cf. Antipho 5.94, Arr.*An.*7.29.2; ἔλεγχος ἰ. τοῦ λόγου Arist.*Metaph.* 1009a21: pl., *cures*, ἰάσεις ἀποτελῶ *Ev.Luc.*13.32. 2. *mending, repairs*, ζυγάστρου *SIG*244 I 53 (Delph., iv B. C.). 3. Alch., *cupellation, refining*, *PLeid.X.*21.

**ἰασιώνη**, ἡ, *bindweed, Convolvulus sepium*, Thphr.*HP*1.13.2, cf. Plin.*HN*21.105.

**ἰάσκειν**· ἄγειν, Hsch.: **ἰασσεῖν**· θυμοῦσθαι, δάκνειν, Id. (Prob. connected with ἰάπτω.)

**ἴασμη**, ἡ, *jessamine, Jasminum officinale*, Aët.ap.Ps.-Dsc.1.63 (fr. Pers. *yāsam*): **ἰάσμῐνον**, τό, *oil of jasmine*, ibid.:—also **ἰασμέ-**

**λαιον**, τό, Aët.1.119 (who states that ἰάσμη = ἰάσμινον = ἰασμέλαιον was prepared ἐκ τῶν ἀνθῶν τῶν λευκῶν τοῦ ἴου, καὶ ἐλαίου σησαμίνου).

**ἰασπ-ἄχάτης** [ῐ, χᾱ], ου, ὁ, *jasper-like agate*, Aët.2.37, Plin.*HN* 37.139. **-ίζω**, *to be like a jasper*, Dsc.5.136. ⊛ **-ῐς**, ιδος (but acc. ἴασπιν Orph.*L*.267,613), ἡ, *jasper*, Pl.*Phd*.110d, *IG*2[2].1388.88, 7.2420 (Thebes, iii B.C.), Thphr.*Lap*.23, *AP*9.746 (Polemo). II. = χρυσόγονον, Dsc.4.56. (Cf. Hebr. *yāšpheh*.) **-όνυξ**, ὔχος, ὁ, *jasper-like onyx*, Plin.*HN*37.118.

**Ἰαστί** [ῐ, τῐ], Adv., (Ἰάς) *in the Ionic mode* (of music), Pratin.Lyr. 5, Pl.*R*.398e; κρούων Ἰ. *Com.Adesp*.415; ἡ Ἰ. ἁρμονία Heraclid. Pont.ap.Ath.14.524f: metaph., opp. Δωριστί, Pl.*La*.188d. 2. *in the Ionic dialect*, Call.*Iamb*.1.354, Str.13.4.8, A.D.*Adv*.134.31, Luc. *Herod*.2. 3. = Ἑλληνιστί, Hsch.

**Ἰαστιαιόλιος**, ον, *Ionic-Aeolic*, of a scale, Ptol.*Harm*.2.1.

**Ἰάστιος**, α, ον, *Ionic*, in Music, Max.Tyr.7.1.

**Ἰᾱσώ**, Ion. **Ἰησώ**, όος, contr. οῦς, ἡ, voc. Ἰασοῖ, (ἰάομαι) *Iaso, the goddess of healing and health*, Ar.*Pl*.701, *Fr*.21, Herod.4.6, Paus.1. 34.3.

**ἰά-τειρα** [ῑᾰ], Ion. **ἰητ-**, ἡ, *healing*, φύσις Marc.Sid.1. **-τέον**, *one must heal*, Hp.*Flat*.1, Gal.10.220. ⊛ **-τήρ** [ῑ], Cypr. acc. sg. ἰjατῆραν *Inscr.Cypr*.135.3 H., Ep. **ἰητήρ**, ῆρος, ὁ, poet. for ἰατρός, in Hom. mostly, *surgeon*, Il.2.732, Od.17.384, cf. Pi.*P*.3.65, etc.: generally, *healer*, νόσων Theoc.*Ep*.8: metaph., ἰ. κακῶν S.*Tr*.1209; πένθεος *AP*7.466.8 (Leon.): abs., *deliverer*, Pi.*P*.4.270. **-τήριον**, Ion. **ἰητήριον**, τό, *mode of cure, cure*, Hp.*Epid*.2.3.7 (cf. 6.2.4), Aret. *CA*1.4; ἰητήρια νούσων Q.S.7.61. ⊛ **-τής**, οῦ, ὁ, = ἰατήρ, Lxx *Jb*. 13.4, *PCair.Preis*.20.26 (iv A.D.). ⊛ **-τικός**, ή, όν, *healing*, Ἀπόλλων Str.14.1.6; ἰκτέρου Dsc.3.75, cf. 5.123, Gal.18(2).394, Max.Tyr. 28.7. **-τορία**, Ion. **ἰητορίη**, ἡ, *art of healing* or *of medicine*, B.1. 39; χειροτέχνης ἰατορίας, of a surgeon, S.*Tr*.1001 (lyr.), cf. *IGRom*. 4.507 *a* 18, *b* 7 (Pergam.).

**ἰᾶτον** [ῐ], τό, *drink prepared from honey, wine and violets*, [Orib.] 5.33.6, Alex.Trall.1.16; ἔλαιον ἰ. Aët.1.118.

**ἰᾱτός** [ῑ], ή, όν, *curable*, Pi.*I*.8(7).15, Pl.*Lg*.862c, al.

**ἴατρ-α** [ῑ], Ion. **ἴητρα**, τά, *doctor's fee*, ἴητρα νούσων ἐποιεύμεσθα Herod.4.16, cf. Hsch. II. *thank-offering for cure*, *IG*4.951.45 (Epid.), al.; Ὑγιείᾳ, τῷ Τελεσφόρῳ ἴ., ib.1321, 1334; ἰάτρων ἀντί ib. 5(1).1119 (Geronthrae). **-ᾰλείπτης**, ου, ὁ, (ἀλείφω) *surgeon who practises by anointing, friction, and the like*, Plin.*Ep*.10.5(4), Cels.1.1, Gal.13.104, Paul.Aeg.3.47:—hence **-ᾰλειπτική** (sc. τέχνη), *practice of an* ἰατραλείπτης, Plin.*HN*29.4. **-εία**, Ion. **ἰητρείη**, ἡ, (ἰατρεύω) *healing, medical treatment*, Hp.*Fract*.34, al., Plu.*Pyrrh*.3, *Epigr.Gr*. 305.1 (Smyrna), *Sammelb*.1934 (Serapeum). 2. metaph., *curing, correcting*, ἐπιθυμίας Arist.*Pol*.1267a7; τῆς ἁμαρτίας ib.1272b2, cf. 1284b 19, Plu.2.510c; ἰατρείας ἕνεκεν Arist.*EN*1152b32: pl., ib.1104b17, al. ⊛ **-εῖον**, Ion. **ἰητρεῖον**, τό, *surgery*, Hp.*Off*.2, Pl.*R*.405a, Aeschin.1.40, *BGU*647.3 (ii A.D.); κατ' ἰητρεῖον ἀνόσως διάγειν not to be so ill *as to need medical advice*, Hp.*Epid*.1.1: metaph., ψυχῆς ἰ. D.S. 1.49. 2. *remedy*, Androm.ap.Gal.13.832. II. pl., = ἴατρα I, *doctor's fee, expense of a cure*, Lxx *Ex*.21.10, Poll.4.177, 6.186. 2. = ἴατρα II, -εῖα θεοῖς ἐπηκόοις Roussel *Cultes Égyptiens* 94, al. (Delos, ii/i B.C.). **-ευμα**, ατος, τό, = ἴαμα, παθῶν Dam.*Isid*.189 (pl.): Rhet. in pl., '*specifics*' for allaying prejudice, etc., Arist.*Rh*.1415a25. **-ευσις**, εως, ἡ, = ἰατρεία, Pl.*R*.357c, Arist.*Ph*.193b14, al. **-ευτέον**, *one must treat*, Gal.10.209, Alex.Trall.*Febr*.3. **-ευτικός**, ή, όν, = ἰατικός, φάρμακα Sch.Ar.*Ach*.1211. **-εύω**, Ion. pf. ἰήτρευκα Hp.*Art*.46: (ἰατρός):—*treat medically, cure*, ἕκαστα Id.*Acut*.2; οὐδὲν ἰ. τῆς λύπης Phld.*Mus*.p.69 K.; τινα Hp.*Art*. l.c., Pl.*Lg*.857d, al.:—Pass., *to be under medical care*, Id.*R*.357c, *Grg*.478b sq., al.; *to be cured*, *IG*14.2283 (Bononia). 2. abs., *practise medicine*, Hp.*Art*. 72; τίς ὀρθῶς ἰάτρευκεν; Arist.*Pol*.1281b40. II. metaph., *remedy, correct*, Id.*PA*665a8. **-ια**, ἡ, fem. of ἰατήρ, Alex.318. **-ικός**, Ion. **ἰητρ-**, ή, όν, *of* or *for an* ἰατρός, καρκίνος *IG*2[2].47.16 (iv B.C.): -ικόν (sc. τέλος), τό, tax *for maintenance of doctor*, *SIG*437 (Delph., iii B.C.), *PSI*4.371, 388 (iii B.C.); so perh. τὰ ἰατρικά *PCair.Zen*.36.4, 13 (iii B.C.); but -ικόν, τό, Milit., *medical corps*, Arr.*Tact*.2.1: ἡ -κή (sc. τέχνη), *surgery, medicine*, Hdt.2.84, 3.129, Hp.*VM*1, Pl.*Grg*.478b, Epicur.*Fr*.221, etc. Adv. -κῶς *in medical terms*, ἐκφέρεσθαι Phld. *Po*.5.29, etc. II. *skilled in the medical art*, Pl.*R*.455e, etc.; ἰ. ἐκ τῶν συγγραμμάτων γίνεσθαι by rule, Arist.*EN*1181b2, etc.: Comp. -ώτερος ib.1097a10; -ώτερον τῶν ἰατρικῶν Phld.*Mus*.p.6 K.: Sup. -ώτατος Pl.*Smp*.186d, Gal.*Protr*.10. Adv. -κῶς Alex.124.13, etc. 2. metaph., ἰ. περὶ τὴν ψυχήν Pl.*Prt*.313e. 3. of drugs, *efficacious*, φάρμακα Hp.*Ep*.16 (Sup.). III. ἰατρικός (sc. δάκτυλος), ὁ, *forefinger*, *PLond*.1821.300. ⊛ **-ίνη** [ῑν], ἡ, *midwife*, *IG*3.134, al., J.*Vit*. 37, Gal.8.414, Alex.Aphr.*Pr*.2.64, *POxy*.1586.12 (iii A.D.).

**ἰατρο-κλύστης**, ου, ὁ, *physician who uses douches*, *UPZ*148.7 (ii B.C.). **-λογέω**, *lecture on medicine*, D.L.8.78. **-λογία**, ἡ, *study of medicine*, Ph.1.302. **-μᾰθημᾰτικοί**, οἱ, *those who practised medicine in conjunction with astrology*, esp. in Egypt, Ptol.*Tetr*. 16, Heph.Astr.*Praef*., *Cat.Cod.Astr*.1.126. ⊛ **-μαια**, ἡ, *midwife*, Dessau *Inscr.Lat.Sel*.7806, *CIL*6.9478. **-μαντις**, εως, ὁ, *physician and seer*, of Apollo and Aesculapius, A.*Supp*.263, cf. *Eu*.62: metaph., φρενῶν ἰ. A.*Ag*.1623. **-νίκης** [νῑ], ου, ὁ, *conqueror of physicians*, Inscr. in Plin.*HN*29.9 (epitaph of Thessalus).

⊛ **ἰᾱτρός**, Ion. **ἰητρός**, ὁ, (ἰάομαι) like ἰατήρ, *one who heals, physician* or *surgeon*, Il.16.28, al., Hdt.3.130 sq.; ἰητρὸς ἀνήρ Il.11.514; φὼς ἰ. A.*Supp*.261; ἥρως ἰ., worshipped at Athens and elsewhere, D. 19.249, *IG*2[2].840, *AB*263, etc.; οὐ πρὸς ἰατροῦ σοφοῦ θρηνεῖν ἐπῳδὰς πρὸς τομῶντι πήματι S.*Aj*.581; ἰατρῶν παῖδες, for ἰατροί, Luc.*Hist. Conscr*.7; as a name of Apollo, Ar.*Av*.584 (anap.), Lyc.1207, *IPE*2.6 (Panticapaeum); ἰ. ὀφθαλμῶν, κεφαλῆς, ὀδόντων Hdt.2.84: as fem., of Artemis, Diog Trag.1.5; of Aphrodite, Plu.2.143d: pl., of certain Nymphs in Elis, Hsch.; *midwife*, Hellad.ap.Phot.*Bibl*.p.531 B., Hsch. s.v. μαῖα. II. metaph., εὐφροσύνα πόνων ἰ. Pi.*N*.4.2; ὦ θάνατε, . . τῶν ἀνηκέστων κακῶν ἰ. A.*Fr*.255; ὁ θάνατος λοῖσθος ἰ. νόσων S.*Fr*.698; ὀργῆς νοσούσης εἰσὶν ἰατροὶ λόγοι A.*Pr*.380, cf. *Ch*.699; [ἀτυχίας] Antipho 2.2.13; τῆς πόλεως ⟨κακῶς⟩ βουλευσαμένης Th.6. 14; λύπης ἰ. χρόνος Diph.117; τῆς ὕβρεως Ath.14.627e: Comically, βουλιμίας, of a table, Timocl.13.3; γῆς ἰ., of a farmer, Secund.*Sent*. 16. [ῑᾱ Trag., also Antiph.259, Diph.88, Men.497, etc.: ῐᾱ in [Emp.]157, E.*Fr*.1072, Ar.*Ec*.363, *Pl*.406, Philem.11, Men.282, etc.: ῑα monosyll., *TAM*2(1).369.]

⊛ **ἰᾱτρο-σοφιστής**, οῦ, ὁ, *professor of medicine*, Dam.ap.Suid. s.v. Γέσιος. **-τέχνης**, ου, ὁ, *practiser of medicine*, Ar.*Nu*.332 (anap.). **-τομεύς**, έως, ὁ, *doctor who uses the knife, surgeon*, *Princeton Exp.Inscr*.787 (Syria). **-φῐλόσοφος**, ὁ, *scientific doctor*, Baillet *Inscr. des tombeaux des rois* 1298.

**ἴαττα**, Cret. pres. part. fem. of εἰμί (q.v.).

**ἰαττᾰταῖ, ἰαττᾰταιάξ**, exclamations of astonishment, Ar.*Eq*.1.

**ἰᾱτύς**, ύος, ἡ, *medical attendance*, Hsch. (prob.).

**ἰάτωρ** [ῑᾰ], Ion. **ἰήτωρ**, ορος, ὁ, = ἰατρός, Alcm.23.89, *IG*9(2).317 (Tricca), Hsch.

**ἰαῦ**, a shout in answer to one calling, *ho! holla!* Ar.*Ra*.272.

**ἰαυθμός**, ὁ, (ἰαύω) *sleeping-place*, esp. of wild beasts, *den, lair*, Lyc. 606 (pl.). II. *sleep*, Hsch.

**ἰαυοῖ**, exclamation of sorrow, Ar.*Ra*.1029.

**ἴαυος**· κοίτη, Hsch.; cf. ἰαύω. **ϝιαυτοῦ**, v. ἑαυτοῦ. **ἴαυχεν**, v. ἰάχω.

⊛ **ἰαύω** [ῐ], poet. Verb, mostly used in pres. and impf. (Trag. only in lyr.): Ep. impf. ἰαύεσκον Od.9.184, Perdrizet-Lefebvre *Graffites Grecs du Memnonion d'Abydos* 528: fut. ἰαύσω Lyc.101, 430: aor. 1 ἴαυσα Od.11.261, Call.*Aet*.3.1.2:—*sleep, pass the night*, Ζηνὸς . . ἐν ἀγκοίνῃσιν ἰαύεις Il.14.213, cf. Od.11.261; ἀΰπνους νύκτας ἴαυον Il.9. 325, Od.19.340; of beasts, ἔνθα δὲ πολλὰ μῆλ' . . ἰαύεσκον 9.184; ἄρσενες ἐκτὸς ἴαυον 14.16; δεμνίοις δύστανος ἰαύων E.*Ph*.1537 (lyr.): c. acc. cogn., ἐννυχίαν τέρψιν ἰαύειν *enjoy* the night's sleep, S.*Aj*.1204 (lyr.); ὑπασπίδιον κοῖτον ἰαύειν, of a soldier *sleeping* under arms, E. *Rh*.740 (anap.); ὕπνον Theoc.3.49, Call. l.c. II. c. acc. et gen., Lyc.101. (Prob. redupl. form of αὔω (C), cf. ἄω (A) II, αὐλή.)

**ἰᾰφέτης** [ῐ], ου, ὁ, (ἰός, ἀφίημι) *archer*, of Apollo, *AP*9.525.10.

**ἰᾰχ-έω**, aor. 1 ἰάχησα *h.Cer*.20, *AP*7.745 (Antip. Sid.):— = ἰάχω, *cry, shout*, used by Trag. in lyr., E.*Heracl*.752, *El*.1150, *Or*.826, 965, etc.: c. acc. cogn., ἰαχεῖν μέλος, αἴλινον, Id.*Tr*.515, *HF*349; [ἀοιδάν] Ar.*Ra*.217; χρησμόν *IG*7.4240*b*2. 2. rarely c. acc. obj., *bewail*, νέκυν ὀλόμενον E.*Ph*.1295, cf. [1523]:—Pass., κᾆτ' ἰαχήθης . . ἄδικος *thou wert proclaimed* . ., Id.*Hel*.1147 (prob. for καὶ ἰαχὴ σή . .). II. of things, *sound*, γαῖα σμερδαλέον ἰάχησεν *h.Hom*.28.11; τρίποδες ἰαχεῦσι Call.*Del*.146, cf. Orph.*A*.997, etc.; ὀλολύγματα ἰαχεῖ E.*Heracl*. 783. [ᾰ in Ep.: ᾱ in Trag. (it is unnecessary to write ἰακχ- when α is long): ᾱ in *IG* l.c.: ϝῐ, cf. sq.] **-ή**, ἡ, *cry, shout*, both of victor and vanquished, Il.15.396, etc.; *wail, shriek*, Od.11.43; also, *a joyous sound*, ἰαχὰ ὑμεναίων Pi.*P*.3.17, cf. E.*Tr*.337 (lyr., pl.); κροτάλων τυπάνων τε *h.Hom*.14.3; αὐλῶν *Lyr.Adesp*.96; συρίγγων E.*IA* 1039 (lyr.): in pl., generally, *shouts of joy*, Thgn.779, E.*Ba*.149 (lyr.); but πολύδακρυς ἰ. A.*Pers*.940, cf. E.*El*.142, *Ph*.1302 (all lyr.). (ϝι-, cf. Il.4.456: a vowel is not elided before it in Ep. exc. in *h.Hom*. 14.3, Hes.*Th*.708, *Sc*.404: Trag. only in lyr.; for the quantity cf. foreg.) **-ημα**, ατος, τό, *cry, shout*: *hissing* of a serpent, E.*HF*884 (lyr., pl.); *sound* of an instrument, ῥόπτρων *AP*6.165 (Phalaec.).

**ἰαχρός** [ῐ], όν, *melted, softened*: metaph., *at ease, tranquil*, Hsch.

⊛ **ἰάχω** [ῐ, ᾰ, v. sub fin.], Ion. impf. ἰάχεσκε Hes.*Sc*.232; Aeol. ἴαυχεν, = ἴαχεν, Aristarch.ap.Eust.1654.28:—*cry, shout*, ἰάχοντες ἐπεσσύμεθ' Od.4.454, etc.; of battle-shouts, Ἀργεῖοι δὲ μέγα ἴαχον Il.17. 317; σμερδαλέα ἰάχων 19.41, Od.22.81; *shriek* in alarm or pain, πρὸς κόλπον . . τιθήνης ἐκλίνθη ἰάχων Il.6.468, cf. 5.343, Od.10.323; δμῳαὶ . . θυμὸν ἀκηχέμεναι μεγάλ' ἴαχον Il.18.29; γοηρὸν ἴαχεν *Epigr.Gr*. 790.7 (Dyme, iii B.C.): sts. of articulate speech, of a herald, E.*El*. 707 (lyr.); of the ship Argo, A.R.4.581, 592, cf. *AP*5.298.10 (Agath.). 2. of things, *ring, resound*, of an echo, περὶ δ' ἴαχε πέτρη Od.9.395, cf. Il.21.10, Limen.15; of waves, ἀμφὶ δὲ κῦμα στείρῃ . . μεγάλ' ἴαχε Il.1.482, Od.2.428, cf. Il.2.394; of fire, *roar*, 23.216; of a bowstring, *twang*, 4.125; of hot iron in water, *hiss*, Od.9.392; of a struck shield, Hes.*Sc*.232; also μέλαθρον ὑπὸ μολπᾶς ἴαχεν *AP*7.194 (Mnasalc.). 3. c. acc. cogn., ἰ. μέλος *sound forth* a strain, Call.*Cer*.40; ἄνδρες ἐπήρατον ἴαχον ὄρθιον Sapph.*Supp*. 20c.4; [λογίων ὁδόν] τινι *proclaim* it to him, Ar.*Eq*.1016: c. acc. pers., *sound* one's *praises*, ἴαχον Ἀπόλλω *were sounding* his *praises*, Id. *Av*.772; με Νεμέα ἴαχεν ἀθλοφόρον *Epigr.Gr*.932*a*.—Ep. only 3 sg. and pl. impf. and part.: pres. ἰάχει E.*El*.707: pf. only in part. of the compd. ἀμφιαχυῖα (q.v.): ἰαχέω (q.v.) is commoner in Att. Poets. (ϝιϝάχω, cf. Od.4.454, al.; when ϝ is observed ι is short and the sense pres. or impf.; when a preceding vowel is elided ι is long and the sense aor., as in μεγάλ' ἴαχε Il.1.482, al.: hence in the latter places μεγάλα ϝϝάχε etc. (καὶ εὔαχε (ἔϝϝαχε) in 20.62, ἐν πρώτοισι ϝαχών in 19.424) is prob. cj.: -ᾰ-, exc. in impf. ἴᾱχον (v.l. ἴακχον) Ar.*Av*. l.c.: *wăĝh-* perh. cogn. with *swăĝh-* in ἠχέω, ἀχέω B.)

**Ἰάων**, ονος, ὁ, v. Ἰάονες. **ἴβα**· σιώπα, Hsch.

**ἰβανατρίς**, ίδος, ἡ, *rope of a draw-well*: **ἰβανέω**, *draw water* (nisi leg. ἰβανᾷ): **ἰβάνη**, ἡ, **ἴβανον**, τό, *water-bucket*, all in Hsch. **ἰβάρβιον**· χαλεπόν, ἀνυπόστατον, Id.

**ἴβδης**, ου, ὁ, *cock* or *plug in a ship's bottom*, Eust.525.34, 858.38.

**ἴβη**, ἡ, = σορός, Hsch. **ἴβηνα**, Cret. word for *wine*, Id. **ἴβηνος**, ὁ, = σορός, Id.:—also **ἴβηνος**· πλησμονή, Id.: **ἴβηρ**, name of an animal, etym. of Ἴβηρες, Id.

**ἰβηρίς**, ίδος, ἡ, *pepperwort, Lepidium graminifolium*, Damocr.ap. Gal.13.350; = λεπίδιον, Aët.ap.Ps.-Dsc.2.174. (Prob. from its place of growth.)

**ἰβίβυος**· παιανισμός, Hsch. **ἴβινος**· ἀετός, Id.

**ἰβῐο-βοσκός** [ῑβ], ὁ, *keeper of the sacred ibis*, PCair.Zen.270.7(iii B.C.), Sammelb.1178a,b(iii B.C.), PTeb.72.410(ii B.C.), al. **-πρόσωπος**, ον, *ibis-faced*, PMag.Leid.V.5.6. **-στολιστής**, οῦ, ὁ, *maker of shrouds for the sacred ibis*, PFay.246 (i/ii A.D.). **-τᾰφεῖον**, τό, *tomb of the sacred ibis*, Sammelb.3937(iii B.C.), PTeb.88.53 (ii B.C.). ❋ **-τάφος** [ᾰ], ὁ, *ibis-burier*, PGrenf.2.15(2).7(ii B.C.).

❋ **ἶβις** [ῑβ, Timocl.1], ἡ, gen. ἴβιος Hdt.2.76, etc., ἴβεως Ael.NA10.29, Porph.Abst.4.9, Gp.13.8.5, ἴβιδος Suid.; acc. ἶβιν Hdt.2.75: pl. ἴβιες Arist.(v. infr.), Ion. acc. ἴβῖς Hdt.2.67,75; gen. pl. ἰβίων PTeb.5.70 (ii B.C.); dat. pl. ἴβεσι Ph.2.570, Paus.8.22.5:—*ibis*, an Egyptian bird, of which there were two species, *white ibis, I. religiosa*, and *black ibis, Plegadis falcinellus*, Hdt.2.75, Ar.Av.1296, Arist.HA617$^{b}$27, etc.; ἰβίων τροφή PPetr.3p.229 (iii B.C.).

**ἰβίσκος**, ὁ, Lat. *hibiscus*, = ἀλθαία, v.l. in Ps.-Dsc.3.146, Erot. s. v. ῥίζη ἀλθαίης; also written ἐβίσκος, q. v.

**ἰβιών** [ῑβ], ῶνος, ὁ, *chapel of the sacred ibis*, PTeb.62.23 (ii B.C.), BGU1216 (ii B.C.).

**ἰβρίκαλοι**· χοῖροι, Hsch.; cf. ὀβρ-.

**ἰβύ**, *loudly*, Phot.: hence aor. 1 inf. **ἰβυκινῆσαι**, *shout*, Teleclid.58 (**ἰβυκηνίσαι** EM464.44): but Subst. **ἰβυκανητής**, οῦ, ὁ, = βυκανητής, *trumpeter*, read by Suid. in Plb.2.29.6 (βυκανητῶν, βυκανιτῶν codd.). Ion. words, acc. to Hsch.: derived from the poet Ibycus, Suid.

**Ἰβύκειον** σχῆμα, τό, use of the termination -σι in 3 sg. of Subj., Hdn.Fig.p.101 S. (From the poet Ibycus.)

**Ἰβύκινον**, τό, *musical instrument named after the poet Ibycus*, Suid.

**ἰβυκτήρ**, ῆρος, ὁ, in Cretan, *one who begins a war-song*, Hsch. (-βηκ- cod.). **ἰβύκχα**· σεμνότης, ἢ σωρὸς κρεῶν, Id. (-υηχ- cod.). **ἴβυξ**, υκος, = ἶβις, Id. **ἴβυς**, υος, ὁ, = εὐφημία, στιγμή, Id. **ἰβύω**, *shout*: *strike*, Id.; cf. **ἰβῶν**· εὐφημῶν, στάζων, Id. ❋ **ἴγα**, in Cretan, = σίγα, Id. **ἴγγι** τινί· ἐπιθυμίᾳ τινὶ ἑλκομένη, Id. (leg. ἴυγγι). **ἴγγια**· εἷς (Cypr.), Id. **ἴγδην** and **ἴγνην**· ἄρσην, Id.

**ἰγδίον**, τό, Dim. of sq., Gp.12.19.5, Paul.Aeg.3.59.

**ἴγδις**, εως, ἡ, *mortar*, Sol.39, Damocr.ap.Gal.14.130, Dsc.5.89, AP 9.642 (Agath.): cited as obsol. for θυεία by S.E.M.1.234:—the form **ἴγδη** in Hdn.Gr.2.523, Hp.Mul.1.103, Gal. l. c., Ps.-Democr.Alch. p.55 B. is prob. incorrect. II. = sq., Antiph.127, Com.Adesp.140. (Cf. Lat. *ico*.)

**ἴγδισμα**, ατος, τό, (from ἰγδίζω, which is not found) *pounding*: hence, *a dance, in which the loins were moved like a pestle*, EM464.51, Suid.

**ἰγδοκόπᾰνον**, τό, *a pestle*, Sch.Il.11.147 (ap.Valck.Animadv.ad Ammon.p.140, ὀγδ- cod.). **ἰγδόλης**· ὁ ἐπὶ μέρει γεωργῶν, Hsch. **ἴγκρος**, ὁ, = ἐγκέφαλος, Hdn.Gr.1.204, Hsch. **ἶγμαι**, **ἰγμένος**, pf. of ἱκνέομαι. **ἰγμαλέος**, α, ον, = ἰκμ-, Hdn.Gr.2.523. **ἰγμή**· βοή, Hsch. (for ἰυγμή or ἰυγή). **ἴγνην**, v. ἴγδην.

**ἴγνητες**, ων, οἱ, = αὐθιγενεῖς, Rhodian word, A.D.Pron.56.4 (who derives it, as ἴγνητες, from the Pron. ἵ), Choerob.in Theod.1.161, Hsch.; as pr. n., coupled with Τελχῖνες, Simm.11: sg., EM465.1.

**ἰγνύα**, Ion. **ἰγνύη**, ἡ, *the part behind the thigh and knee, ham*, κατ' ἰγνύην βεβλημένος Il.13.212; παρ' ἰγνύῃσιν ἕλιξε κέρκον Theoc.25.242, cf. 26.17, AP12.176 (Strat.), APl.4.253: also in Prose, Hp.Fract.13, Ruf.Onom.121; τὸ μόριον τὸ τῆς ἄλσεως κύριον (καλεῖται δὲ τοῦτο ἰγνύα) Arist.HA515$^{b}$8: acc. sg. ἰγνύαν Phld.Acad.Ind.p.50 M.; περὶ τὴν ἰγνύαν Plu.Art.11: dat. pl. ἰγνύαις Lxx 3Ki.18.21, Luc.VH1.23. —From a nom. **ἰγνύς**, ύος, ἡ, we find dat. pl. ἰγνύσι h.Merc.152, v.l. in Luc. l. c.: acc. ἰγνύν Arist.HA494$^{a}$8 (v.l. -ύην), Agatharch.53; dat. ἰγνύϊ Gal.10.902: gen. pl. ἰγνύων Arist.HA512$^{b}$22, Herod.1.14: acc. pl. ἰγνύας is indeterminate, Plu.Galb.26. [ῡ in ἰγνύη, v. ll. cc.; but ῠ in ἰγνύων, ἰγνύσι.]

**ἴγνυς**, v. ἴκνυς. **ἰγχηρέω**, v. ἐγχειρέω.

**Ἰδαῖος**, α, ον, *of Ida*, v. Ἴδη.

❋ **ἰδάλιμος** [ῐ], ον, (ἶδος) *causing sweat*, καῦμα Hes.Op.415.

❋ **ἰδαλίς**, ἡ, a bird, Hsch. **ἰδάλτα**· ἴδιά τινα (leg. ἴδ' ἅττα), Id.

**ἰδᾰνικός** [ῐ], ή, όν, (ἰδεῖν, ἰδέα) *existing in idea*, κόσμος Ti.Locr.97d.

❋ **ἰδᾰνός** [ῐ], όν, (ἰδεῖν) *fair, comely*, χάριτες Call.Fr.535.

**ἰδᾰνόχροος** [ῐ], ον, *with lovely colour*, ἄνθη Epic.Alex.Adesp.9 iii 10.

**ἴδδιος**, v. ἴδιος.

❋ **ἰδέ** [ῐ], Ep. Conj., = ἠδέ, *and*, Il.4.147, al., Emp.20.7, etc., prob. l. in S.Ant.969 (lyr.). II. Cypr., *then, in that case*, Inscr.Cypr.135.12 H. (Prob. fr. the demonstrative stem *i-* (cf. Lat. *is*) and δέ.)

**ἴδε** (A) (Att. **ἰδέ** Hdn.Gr.1.431), aor. 2 imper. of εἶδον, *behold*, Il. 17.179, etc.: folld. by ὅτι.., Pl.Phd.72a; used by Trag. in lyr., A.Supp.350, S.Tr.222, E.Or.1541.

**ἴδε** (B), Ep. 3 sg. of aor. 2 εἶδον, *he saw*, Hom.

**ἰδέα** [ῐ], Ion. **ἰδέη**, ἡ, (ἰδεῖν) *form*, ἰδέᾳ καλός Pi.O.10(11).103, cf. Theoc.29.6; τὴν ἰ. πάνυ καλός Pl.Prt.315e; τὴν ἰ. μοχθηρός And.1.100, cf. Ar.Av.1000; ἰδέην δρέων Hdt.1.80; opp. χρῶμα, Id. 4.109; opp. μέγεθος, Pl.Phd.109b (pl.); ἡ ἰ. αὐτοῦ ἦν ὡς ἀστραπή Ev.Matt.28.3, etc.; of the elementary *shapes*, ἄτομοι ἰδέαι Democr. ap.Plu.2.1111a codd., cf. Fr.141 D.; of the four *elements*, Philistion ap.Anon.Lond.20.25. 2. *semblance*, opp. reality, γνώμην ἐξαπατῶσ' ἰδέαι *outward appearances* cheat the mind, Thgn.128. 3. *kind, sort*, φύλλα τοιῆσδε ἰδέης Hdt.1.203; φύσιν παρέχονται ἰδέης τοιῆνδε [οἱ ποτάμιοι ἵπποι] Id.2.71; ἐφρόνεον διφασίας ἰ. they conceived two *modes* of acting, Id.6.100, cf. 119; τὰ ὄργι' ἐστὶ τίν' ἰ. ἔχοντά σοι; what is their *nature* or *fashion*? E.Ba.471; ἑτέραν ὕμνων ἰ. Ar.Ra.384; καινὰς ἰ. εἰσφέρειν new *forms* of comedy, Id.Nu. 547; τίς ἰ. βουλεύματος; Id.Av.993; πᾶσα ἰ. θανάτου every *form* of death, or death in every *form*, Th.3.81, cf. 83, 2.51; πολλαὶ ἰ. πολέμων Id.1.109; ἡ ὑπάρχουσα ἰ. τῆς παρασκευῆς Id.4.55; πᾶσαν ἰδέαν πειράσαντες having tried every *way*, Id.2.19; τῇ αὐτῇ ἰ. Id.3. 62, 6.76; οὐκ ἐν ταῖς αὐταῖς ἰ. not in the same *relations*, Isoc.3.44: εἰς μίαν τινὰ ἰ. into one *kind of existence*, Pl.Tht.184d; ἄλλη ἰ. πολιτείας Id.R.544c, etc.; ἀγοραίας.. ἰδέας τοῦ βίου Epicur.Fr.196. 4. esp. in Rhet., etc., of literary *form*, ἀμφοτέραις ταῖς ἰδέαις κατεχρήσαντο πρὸς τὴν ποίησιν Isoc.2.48, cf. 15.47,183; ἡ ἰαμβικὴ ἰ. Arist. Po.1449$^{b}$8, cf. 1450$^{b}$34, Rh.Al.1425$^{a}$9, etc.; ἡ ἐν τῷ λέγειν ἰ. Phld. Rh.2.258 S. b. *style*, Πλατωνική, Δημοσθενικὴ ἰ., Syrian.in Hermog. 1.112 R. c. *a quality of style* (e.g. σαφήνεια, γοργότης, etc.), Hermog.Id.tit., etc. II. in Logic, = εἶδος, *class, kind*: hence, *principle of classification*, ἔφησθα.. μιᾷ ἰδέᾳ τά τε ἀνόσια ἀνόσια εἶναι καὶ τὰ ὅσια ὅσια Pl.Euthphr.6d, cf. Phdr.265d, Sph.253d, etc. 2. pl. in Platonic Philosophy, *ideal forms, archetypes*, τὰς.. ἰ. νοεῖσθαι μέν, ὁρᾶσθαι δ' οὔ Id.R.507b, cf. 596b, al., Arist.Metaph.990$^{a}$34, al., EN1096$^{a}$17: also in sg., ἡ τοῦ ἀγαθοῦ ἰ. Pl.R.508e, al., cf. εἶδος. 3. *notion, idea*, προάγειν τὸν ἀποκρινόμενον ἐπὶ τὴν ἰ. ἀγνοουμένου πράγματος Nausiph.2. (Written εἰδέα in later Greek, as PGen.16.17 (iii A.D.), v.l. in Ev.Matt.28.3.)

❋ **ἰδέατος**· ἰδήρατος (Sicel), Hsch.

**ἴδεδρος** [ῐ], ον, = ἰδίων τὴν ἕδραν, Did.in D.11.22.

**ἰδεῖν**, Ep. **ἰδέειν**, Dor. **ἰδέμεν**, aor. 2 inf. of ὁράω, v. εἴδω.

**ἰδέν**, dub. sens. in PStrassb.24.16, al. (ii A.D.).

**ἰδέρως** [ῐ], ωτος, ὁ, ἡ, *one who loves at first sight*, Hsch., Suid.

**ἴδεσκον**, ες, ε, Ion. for εἶδον, Il.3.217. **ἰδέω**, v.l. for εἰδέω, Ep. for εἰδῶ, subj. of οἶδα, *know*, 14.235, Od.16.236.

❋ **ἴδη** [ῑ], Dor. **ἴδα**, ἡ, *timber-tree*, in pl., χώρη ὑψηλή τε καὶ ἴδῃσι συνηρεφής Hdt.1.110; ὄρεα.. ἴδῃσι παντοίῃσι συνηρεφέα Id.7.111, cf. 4.109,175: in sg., *wood*, ἐν τῇ ἴδῃ τῇ πλείστῃ in the thick of *the wood*, Id.4.109; ἴδαν ἐς πολύδενδρον Theoc.17.9; ἴδη ναυπηγήσιμος *timber* for.., Hdt.5.23: never in Att.: also in late Prose, Philostr. Dial.2, VA3.4 (s. v. l.). II. pr. n., **Ἴδη**, *Ida*, i. e. *the wooded hill*, 1. in the Troad, Il.2.821, etc.: **Ἴδηθεν**, *from Ida*, 4.475; Ἴ. μεδέων ruling *from I.*, 3.276:—Adj. **Ἰδαῖος**, α, ον (Aeol. **Ἴδαος** as pr. n., Sapph.Supp.20a.3), Ζεύς Il.16.605; ὄρεα 8.170, etc.; Ἰ. ῥίζα, a plant, *Ruscus Hypoglossum*, Dsc.4.44: also Ἰδαία alone, = δάφνη Ἀλεξάνδρεια, ib.145; Ἰ. Δάκτυλοι, prop. 'dwarfs *of the forest*', Hes.Fr.176, Pherecyd.47 J., Hellanic.89 J., etc.; but Ἰ. δάκτυλος is a name for one of the fingers, PMag.Lond.46.455. 2. in Crete, D.P.502, Paus.5.7.6.

**ἴδη**, ἡ, *sheen of metal*, etc., v.l. for σίδη in Philostr.Im.1.28, 2.32.

**ἴδηαι**, 2 sg. aor. 2 subj. Med. of εἰδόμην, Ep. for ἴδῃ. **ἴδημα**, ατος, τό, = ὅραμα, Hsch.: **ἰδήμων**, = εἰδ-, Id. ❋ **ἰδήρατος**, ον, *beautiful*, Id. **ἰδησῶ**, Dor. fut. of εἶδον, *I shall see*, Theoc.3.37. **ἰδίᾳ**, v. ἴδιος VI. 2.

**ἰδῐ-αζόντως** [ῐδ], Adv. *in a special* or *peculiar way*, Stoic.3.94, D.S.19.99, S.E.P.1.182, Cod.Just.1.3.35.3, etc.; *separately*, opp. κοινῇ, Sammelb.7033.53 (v A.D.). **-άζω**, (ἴδιος) *to be alone*, Hdn. 4.12.7, 7.6.7, D.C.66.9; ἰδιάζουσαι Herod.6 tit.; δωμάτιον ἰδιάζον *secluded*, Hld.7.12; ἰ. πρός τινα *to be alone* with.., ib.25; ἰ. θεῷ *to be alone with* God, Ph.1.95; ἰ. πράγματι *devote oneself* to a thing, Com. Adesp.414:—so in Med., of members of a chorus, *sing independently*, Arist.Pr.922$^{a}$35. II. *to be peculiar*, ἰδιάζοντα γένη λίθων Phld. Sign.28, cf. Jul.Gal.143a; ἰ. τῇ φύσει D.S.2.58; ἰδιάζουσα φύσις Id.3. 46, Hld.2.28; ἰδιάζον συμπόσιον Ath.1.12a; αἱ ἰδιάζουσαι ἀρχαί *special* principles, Dam.Pr.134; of drugs, ἰδιάζων *special, superior*, Dsc.1.14; ἃ ἂν ἰδιάσωμεν, ψευδόμεθα S.E.M.7.133; ἰ. τινί *to be peculiarly adapted* to.., Ael.NA6.19; βωμὸς τῷ Διονύσῳ ἰδιάζων *appropriated to* D., Hld.10.6: c. gen., *to be the property of*, J.AJ16.7.3. b. ἡ -άζουσα θερμασία its *proper* heat, Herod.Med.ap.Orib.5.30.12. 2. Gramm., *to be peculiar to an individual*, τὰ κτητικὰ -άζει κατὰ τὸν κτήτορα A.D. Pron.105.4, cf. Synt.128.13, al.:—so in Med., [ὁ βασιλεὺς] μᾶλλον -άζεται τοῦ Πτολεμαίου ib.84.20. **-αίτερος**, **-ατος**, Comp. and Sup. of ἴδιος (q. v.). **-ασμός**, ὁ, *peculiarity*, Iamb.VP35.255. 2. *particularity*, ὁ τοῦ ἑνὸς ἀπεστενωμένος ἰ. Dam.Pr.28 bis. **-αστής**, οῦ, ὁ, *recluse*, D.L.1.25.

**ἰδικός** [ῐδ], ή, όν, (εἶδος) late form of εἰδικός (q. v.), *special*, Stob.2. 7.11$^{a}$, Ath.9.373b, Gal.1.333 (Sup.), Wilcken Chr.6.14 (v A.D.), etc.; τὰ ἰ. τῶν γενῶν Ascl.Tact.12.11, etc. 2. [ῐδ] (ἴδιος) *proper, one's own*, AP5.105 (Diotim.), Man.5.122. Adv. -κῶς Herm.in Phdr. p.185 A.; opp. κοινῶς, Simp.in Ph.848.21: Comp. -ώτερον Ath.7. 299d.

**ἰδῐο-βουλέω** [ῐδ], *follow one's own counsel, take one's own way*, Hdt.7.8.δ' (v.l. -εύειν), D.C.43.27. **-γενής**, ές, *mating only with its kind*, opp. κοινογενής, Pl.Plt.265e. 2. *peculiar in kind*, Herm. ap.Stob.1.49.44, Dsc.2.66. **-γλωσσος**, ον, *of distinct, peculiar tongue*, πόλις Str.5.2.9. **-γνωμονέω**, *hold one's own opinion, be*

*self-opinionated*, Phld.*Vit*.p.30 J., cf. D.C.45.42, 53.21: **-γνωμέω** is f.l. in Id.43.27. **-γνώμων**, ον, gen. ονος, *holding one's own opinion*, Hp.*Aër*.24, Phryn.Com.18, Arist.*EN*1151ᵇ12. **-γονία**, ἡ, *breeding only with one's own kind*, opp. κοινογονία, Pl.*Plt*.265d. **-γρᾰφία**, ἡ, *autograph*, dub. in *BGU*1135.10 (i B.C.). **-γρᾰφος**, ον, *written with one's own hand, autograph*, liber Vergilii, Gell.9.14.7, cf. *POxy*.250.13 (i A.D.), etc.:—Subst. -γραφον, τό, *autograph*, *PFlor*. 27.13 (iv A.D.), etc. 2. *specially* or *separately written*, ψαλμὸς ἰ. εἰς Δαυίδ Lxx *Ps*.151 tit. **-θάνᾰτος** [θᾰ], ον, *dying a natural death* (cf. ἴδιος 1.6b), Vett.Val.19.2. **-θᾰνέω**, *die a natural death*, Procl.*Par.Ptol*.277. **-θηρευτικός**, ή, όν, *hunting by* or *for oneself*: ἡ -κή (sc. τέχνη) *private hunting*, Pl.*Sph*.222d: **-θηρία**, ἡ, ib. 223b. **-θρονέω**, Astrol., of a planet, *enjoy its proper dignity*, Ptol.*Tetr*.51, Paul.Al.*S*.4. **-κρᾶσία**, ἡ, *peculiar temperament*, Procl.*Par.Ptol*.13 (nisi leg. -συγκρασίαν). **-κρῖτος**, ον (-κοιτον cod.), = ἰδιόρρυθμος, Hsch. **-κτήμων**, gen. ονος, ὁ, *private owner*, *PTeb*.124.32 (ii B.C.), Heph.Astr.1.1. ⊛ **-κτητος**, ον, *held as private property*, Hp.*Ep*.26 (dub. l.); γῆ *BGU*1216.83 (ii B.C.), Str.14.6.5, *PFay*.342 (ii A.D.), *Cod.Just*.10.3.7; ἡ ἰ. (sc. γῆ) *PTeb*.5.111 (ii B.C.); ἰ. πανευτυχίη *won all by himself*, *Epigr.Gr*.443 (Namara); ἀρετή Onos. 1.25. **-λογέω**, *develop one's own ideas*, prob. in Phld.*Acad.Ind*. p.4 M.:—Med., *converse in private with*, ἄττα σοι Pl.*Thg*.121a; θεῷ Ph.1.197; πρός τινα Charito 6.7. **-λογία**, ἡ, *subjective theorizing*, dub. cj. in Epicur.*Ep*.2 p.36 U. (ἰδιαλογίας, ἤδη ἀλογίας codd.). II. *private conversation*, Charito 4.6. **-μήκης**, ες, *of their own length*, i.e. *of the same length each way*, of square numbers, Nicom.*Ar*.2. 18. **-μορφος**, ον, *of peculiar form*, Thphr.*HP*9.13.6, Str.4.6.10, Plu.*Mar*.25.

**ἴδιον**, τό, v. ἴδιος.

**ἰδῐο-ξενία** [ἰδ], ἡ, *private friendship*, Anon.ap.Suid. ⊛ **-ξενοδόκος**, ὁ, *private* (opp. official) *guarantor of an alien*, *Rev.Epigr*.2.227 (Doliche). **-ξενος**, ον, *private friend* in a foreign state (opp. πρόξενος), D.S.13.5, Luc.*Phal*.2.1, etc.: as Adj., ἰ. ἄνδρες D.H.1.84: Locr. ϝιδιόξενος (nisi leg. ϝιδίῶ ξένῶ) *IG*9(1).333.12 (v B.C.).

**ἰδῐόομαι** [ἰδ], (ἴδιος) Med., *make one's own, appropriate*, Pl.*R*.547c, *Lg*.742b; of literary plagiarism, Phld.*D*.1.9. 2. *make one's friend*, τινα D.C.39.29. II. Pass., *to be specifically constituted*, Dam.*Pr*.34.

**ἰδῐο-πάθεια** [ἰδ, πᾰ], ἡ, Medic., *affection having a local origin*, Gal. 8.31, al., Alex.Aphr.*Pr*.2.35. **-πᾰθέω**, *suffer from a local affection*, Gal.8.31. **-περιόριστος**, ον, *specially defined* or *limited*, φύσις Suid. s.v. Θεόδωρος. **-πλαστος**, ον, *self-formed*, ἀγαθόν Secund.*Sent*. 3, 14. **-ποιέω**, *make separately*, ἐπίδειξίν τινι Gal.2.672. 2. prob. f.l. for εἰδοπ-, τὴν γραφήν Str.15.1.14. II. *appropriate, plagiarize*, Vett.Val.96.26 (Act., s.v.l.):—elsewh. Med., *appropriate to oneself*, Phld.*Herc*.1788.1, D.S.5.13, etc.; *win over*, Id.15.29, Lxx 2*Ki*.15.6. III. Pass., *to be invested with a specific character*, Dam. *Pr*.75. **-ποίημα**, ατος, τό, *act of appropriation*, Gloss. ⊛ **-ποιός**, όν, *creating particularity*, Dam.*Pr*.36; ἰ. ἐπιστροφή ib.76. ⊛ **-πρᾱγέω**, *act independently*, Plb.8.26.9, Phld.*Ind.Sto*.60; *pursue one's own interest*, D.S.18.39, 64, Str.12.3.28; εἰερεὺς ὢν ἰδιοπραέων (if written for ἰδιοπραγέων) *MAMA*1.237 (Laodicea Combusta); ἰδιοπραγεῖ· τὰ ἴδια πράσσει, ἡσυχάζει, Hsch. **-πρᾱγία**, ἡ, *pursuit of private interests*, πλεονεξία καὶ ἰ. Pl.*Lg*.875b; πρὸς -πραγίαν ὡρμημένος on a *private venture*, D.S.18.52. **-πραγμονέω**, = ἰδιοπραγέω, Sch.Th.1.32, Sch.E.*Med*.217. **-πράγμων**, ον, gen. ονος, *minding one's own business*, opp. πολυπράγμων, D.L.9.112, Ptol.*Tetr*.161; βίος Vett. Val.185.6. **-προσωπέω**, Astrol., of a planet, *possess its proper aspect* (i.e. that of its 'house') with respect to sun and moon, Ptol. *Tetr*.114:—hence **-προσωπία**, ἡ, ib.155: **-πρόσωπος**, ον, ib. 50. **-ρρυθμία**, ἡ, = ἰδία τάξις, Cyr. **-ρρυθμος**, ον, = ἰδιότακτος, Hsch.: gloss on αὐθέκαστος, Thom.Mag.p.25 R.

⊛ **ἴδιος** [ἰδ], α, ον, Att. also ος, ον Pl.*Prt*.349b, Arist.*HA*532ᵇ32 (v. sub fin.): I. *one's own, pertaining to oneself*: hence, 1. *private, personal* (opp. κοινός): twice in Hom., πρῆξις δ' ἥδ' ἰδίη οὐ δήμιος this business is *private*, not public, Od.3.82; δήμιον ἦ ἴδιον; 4.314; ἴδιος ἐν κοινῷ σταλείς embarking as *a private man* in a public cause, Pi.*O*. 13.49; ἰ. στόλῳ χρᾶσθαι, opp. δημοσίῳ, Hdt.5.63; γῆς.. νοσούσης ἰ. κινοῦντες κακά S.*OT*636; κοινὸν ἐξ ἰδίας ἀνοίας κακόν E.*Hec*.641 (lyr.), cf. *Or*.766 (troch.); ἴδια πράσσων ἢ στρατοῦ ταχθεὶς ὕπο; Id.*IA*1363 (troch.); ἰ. κέρδεα Hdt.6.100; συμφορά Antipho 2.1.11; πρόσοδος And.4.11; τὰ ἰ. διάφορα Th.2.37; πλοῦτος ἰ. καὶ δημόσιος Id.1.80, cf. Pl.*R*.521a; ἰ. οὐ κοινὸς πόνος ib.535b, cf. 543b; ξυμβόλαια ib.443e; ἰ. ἢ πολιτικὴ πρᾶξις Id.*Grg*.484d; πόλεις καὶ ἰ. οἶκοι Id.*Lg*.890b, cf. 796d, etc.; τὰ ἱρά, opp. τὰ ἰ., temples, opp. *private buildings*, Hdt. 6.9, 8.109; τὸ ἐν ἰδίοις discussion among *private persons*, Pl.*Sph*. 225b. 2. *one's own*, opp. ἀλλότριος, ἐπικώμια Pi.*N*.6.32; ἡ ἰ. ἐλευθερίη Hdt.7.147; Ζεὺς ἰδίοις νόμοις κρατύνων A.*Pr*.404 (lyr.); ἰδίᾳ γνώμᾳ ib.543 (lyr.); οὔτοι τὰ χρήματ' ἰ. κέκτηνται βροτοί E.*Ph*. 555; φίλων οὐδὲν ἰ., = κοινὰ τὰ τῶν φίλων, Id.*Andr*.376: with Pron., χωρίον ἡμέτερον ἴδιον D.55.8. 3. τὰ ἰ. *private interests*, opp. public, Th.1.82, 2.61, etc.; *one's own property*, Id.1.141, etc.; τὰ ἰ. πράττειν mind *one's own business*, in later Gr., Phryn.405, cf. 1*Ep. Thess*.4.11; μένειν ἐπὶ τῶν ἰ. Plb.2.57.5; εἰς τὸ ἰ. καταθέσθαι for *self*, X.*An*.1.3.3, etc.: with Pron., τοὐμὸν ἰ. εἰπεῖν my *personal* opinion, Isoc.6.8; τὰ ἐμὰ ἰ. D.50.66; τὰ αὑτοῦ ἰ. Thgn.440 (dub.l.), cf. Antipho 5.61, Isoc.8.127; τὰ ὑμέτερα ἰ. D.19.307; τὰ ἰ. σφῶν αὐτῶν, τὰ ἰ. τὰ σφέτερα αὐτῶν, And.2.2, 3.36; ἔγωγε τοὐμὸν ἰ. *I for my own part*, Luc.*Merc.Cond*.9. 4. of persons, *personally attached* to one, ἴδιοι Σελεύκου Plb.21.6.4, cf. Arist.*Pol*.1315ᵃ36, *UPZ*146.38 (ii B.C.), 109.18 (i B.C.); ἄνθρωπος ἴδιος τῇ εὐνοίᾳ τῇ πρὸς.. *PCair.Zen*.32 (iii B.C.); ταῖς εὐνοίαις ἴδιοι D.S.11.26; ἴδιοι, οἱ, *members of one's family, relatives*, *BGU*665 ii 1 (i A.D.), Vett.Val.70.5, etc. 5. ἡ ἰ. (sts. with κώμη added, *BGU*15.13 (ii A.D.)), one's *place of origin*, *PTeb*. 327.28 (ii A.D.), etc.: pl., καταπορεύεσθαι εἰς τὰς ἰ. ib.5.7 (ii B.C.). 6. in later Gr., almost as a possessive Pron., = ἑαυτοῦ, ἑαυτῶν, ἡ ἰ. φιλαγαθία *IG*2².1011.71 (ii B.C.), etc.; χρῶνται ὡς ἰδίοις *UPZ*11.14 (ii B.C.); περὶ τῶν ἰ. βιβλίων, title of work by Galen. b. ἰ. θάνατος *one's own*, i.e. a *natural* death, Ramsay *Cities and Bishoprics* No. 133; ἰδίοις τελευτῶσι θανάτοις Ptol.*Tetr*.199; also ἰδία μοίρῃ Ramsay op.cit. No.187. II. *separate, distinct*, ἔθνος ἰ. καὶ οὐδαμῶς Σκυθικόν Hdt.4.18, cf. 22; ἴδιοί τινές σοι [θεοί]; Ar.*Ra*.890; ἑκάστῳ τῶν ὀνομάτων ὑπόκειταί τις ἴδιος οὐσία Pl.*Prt*.349b; πόλεις.. βαρβάρους καὶ ἰδίας Decr.ap.D.18.183; ὁ βάτραχος ἰδίαν ἔχει τὴν γλῶτταν, τὴν ἰ. ἀφίησι φωνήν, a *peculiar* kind of tongue, ..its *peculiar* note, Arist. *HA*536ᵃ8, 11: folld. by ἤ, ἴδιον ἔπασχεν πάθος ἢ οἱ ἄλλοι *unique and different* from others, Pl.*Grg*.481c; so ἴδιον παρὰ τὰ ἄλλα Thphr.*HP* 6.4.10. b. ἰ. λόγος, in Ptolemaic and Roman Egypt, *private account*, δεδώκαμεν Πύρωνι τὸν ἔσχατόν σου ἰ. λόγον *PCair.Zen*.253 (iii B.C.), cf. *PGrenf*.1.16 (ii B.C.), etc.; later, *special account*, a branch of the fiscal administration, Wilcken *Chr*.162 (ii B.C.), *PAmh*.2.31 (ii B.C.), *PGnom.Prooem*. (ii A.D.), etc.; ὁ γνώμων τοῦ ἰ. λόγου *OGI*669.44 (i A.D.); also as the title of the Controller, Str. 17.1.12 codd., *OGI*408 (ii A.D.), Mitteis *Chr*.372 vi 1 (ii A.D.). 2. *strange, unusual*, ἰδίοισιν ὑμεναίοισι κοὐχὶ σώφροσιν E.*Or*.558; *peculiar, exceptional*, περιττὸν καὶ ἰ. γένος Arist.*GA*760ᵃ5; τὰ περιττὰ καὶ ἰ. τῶν δένδρων Thphr.*CP*2.7.1; παράδοξον εἰπεῖν τι καὶ περιττὸν καὶ ἰ. Plu.2.1068b; *eccentric*, of persons, ib.57e; ἰ. τις ἐν πᾶσι βουλόμενος εἶναι Id.*Them*.18. 3. *peculiar, appropriate*, ἴδια ὀνόματα *proper, specific* words, opp. περιέχοντα, class-names, Arist. *Rh*.1407ᵃ31; ὄνομα ἰ. τινος Pl.*R*.580e; τὸ ἰ. τοῦ ἐπαίνου Luc.*Pr.Im*. 19. III. ἰ. λόγοι *ordinary private* conversation, opp. ποίησις, Pl. *R*.366e, cf. *Euthd*.305d; v. infr. VI.2b. IV. τὸ ἰ. *characteristic property* of a species, Arist.*Top*.102ᵃ18, 103ᵇ11, Chrysipp.*Stoic*.2.75, Plot.5.5.13; but also, *distinguishing feature* in a relative sense, ἰ. πρός τι Arist.*Top*.128ᵇ25. V. regul. Comp. ἰδιώτερος Isoc.12.73, Thphr.*HP*3.1.6: Sup. -ώτατος D.23.65, Thphr.*HP*1.14.2; also ἰδιαίτερος, -αίτατος, Arist.*PA*656ᵃ26, 658ᵇ33; -αίτατος but not -αίτερος acc. to Thom.Mag.p.189 R. VI. Adv. **ἰδίως**, *peculiarly*, Isoc.5.108; *severally*, Pl.*Lg*.807b: Comp. ἰδιωτέρως Thphr.*HP*1.13. 4; ὡς -ώτερον εἰπεῖν Phld.*Oec*.p.68 J.; ἰδιαίτερον Hdn.7.6.7: Sup. ἰδιώτατα (v.l. -αίτατα) D.S.19.1; ἰδίως καλεῖσθαι to be called *specifically*, Arist.*Mu*.394ᵇ28; -αίτατα λέγεσθαι Id.*Mete*.382ᵃ3; ἰδίως, opp. κοινῶς, λέγεσθαι Demetr.Lac.*Herc*.1014.41 F. (but in Gramm., to be used *as a proper name*, D.T.634.13); *in a peculiar sense* or *usage*, Sch. Ar.*Pl*.115; ἰ. Αἰσχύλος τὸν Ἀγαμέμνονα ἐπὶ σκηνῆς ἀναιρεῖσθαι ποιεῖ A. *Ag*.Arg., cf. Sch.E.*Ph*.1116; also, = *extra versum*, τὸ "φεῦ" ἰδίως Sch. Ar.*Nu*.41 (v.l. ἰδίᾳ). 2. **ἰδίᾳ**, Ion. -ίῃ, as Adv., *by oneself, privately, on one's own account*, θύοντι ἰδίῃ μούνῳ Hdt.1.132, cf. 192, Ar.*Eq*.467; οὔτε ἰδίᾳ οὔτε ἐν κοινῷ Th.1.141; καὶ ἰ. καὶ δημοσίᾳ Id.3.45, Pl.*Ap*.30b; καὶ ἰ. καὶ κοινῇ Arist.*Ath*.40.3; ἰδίᾳ ἕκαστος Th.8.1, cf. Pl.*Lg*.946d, etc.: c. gen., ἰ. τῆς φρενὸς *apart from*.., Ar.*Ra*.102. b. *in ordinary talk*, opp. ὑπὸ ποιητῶν, Pl.*R*.363e, cf. 606c; v. supr. III. 3. κατ' ἰδίαν *in private*, Philem.169; κατ' ἰδίαν εἰπεῖν τινι D.S.1.21; κατ' ἰ. λαβεῖν τινα to take him *aside*, Plb.4.84.8; also, *separately, apart*, Plu.2.120d; οἱ κατ' ἰ. βίοι Plb.1.71.1. (ϝίδιος *Tab.Heracl*.1.13, al., *Schwyzer*324.4 (Delph., iv B.C.), *IG*9(1).333.12 (Locr., v B.C.), etc.; with spiritus asper, ἐκ τοῦ hιδίου *Jahresh*.14 *Beibl*.141 (Argos, v B.C.); καθ' ἰδίαν *IG*2².891.6, 5(1).6 (Lacon.), 9(2).66 (Lamia), Aët.3.159, etc.; καθ' ἰδδίαν prob. in *IG*9(2).461.26 (Thess.).)

**ἰδιό-σημος** [ἰδ], ον, *peculiar in signification*, ὀνόματα Sch.Hermog. in Rh.7.195 W. ⊛ **-σπορέομαι**, Pass., of land, *to be sown by one's own labour*, *PFlor*.64.34 (iv A.D.). **-σπορία**, ἡ, *sowing carried out by one's own labour*, *PRyl*.142.18 (i A.D.), *PAmh*.2.131.10 (ii A.D.). **-σπορος**, ἡ (sc. γῆ), *land sown by the landlord's own employees*, *PCair.Zen*.292.508: so -σπορα, τά, ib.60, al. (iii B.C.). **-στολος**, ον, *equipped at one's own expense*, τριήρης Plu.*Alc*.1; *hired for one's own use*, πλοῖον Ath.12.521a, cf. Philostr.*VA*5.20; ἰ. πλεῦσαι sail *in one's own ship*, Plu.*Thes*.26. **-συγκρᾶσία**, ἡ, (κρᾶσις) *peculiar temperament* or *habit of body, idiosyncrasy*, Ptol.*Tetr*.12, Gal.10.169, al.:—also **-σύγκρᾶσις**, εως, ἡ, Ptol.*Tetr*.142:—also **-συγκρῐσία**, ἡ, Sor.2.56 (cj.), Herod.Med.ap.Orib.6.20.24, S.E.*P*.1.79 (pl.): **-σύγκρῐσις**, εως, ἡ, Dsc.*Alex.Praef*. (pl.). **-σύγκρῐτος**, ον, *peculiarly composed*, Herm.ap.Stob.1.49.44. **-συστᾰσία**, ἡ, *peculiar constitution*, prob. in Sor.2.56. **-τακτος**, ον, gloss on ἰδιόρρυθμος, Hsch.

**ἰδιότης** [ἰδ], ητος, ἡ, (ἴδιος) *peculiar nature, property, specific character*, Damox.2.41, Epicur.*Ep*.1 p.17 U.; ἡ ἰ. τῆς ἡδονῆς X.*An*.2.3. 16; τῶν πράξεων Pl.*Plt*.305d; τοῦ πολιτεύματος Plb.1.13.13, etc.; εἰκὼν τῆς ἰδίας ἰ. Lxx *Wi*.2.23; of a mountain, Agatharch.81: pl., *peculiarities*, Plb.9.22.7, Demetr.Lac.*Herc*.1012.41 F.; ἰ. ἐθνικαί, of language, Phld.*Rh*.1.154 S.; ῥυθμῶν Id.*Mus*.p.49 K. 2. Gramm., ἰδιότητός τινων μετέχειν D.T.639.31, cf. A.D.*Synt*.16.14, al.; εἰς ἰδιότητα *as a proper name*, St.Byz. s.v. Θεσσαλία, Sch.Il.18.319. 3. *particular existence*, Chrysipp.*Stoic*.2.126; *individuality*, ἀεὶ πρότερα τὰ ὀλίγης ἰδιότητος Dam.*Pr*.280. 4. *relationship*, *POxy*.1644.21 (i B.C.).

**ἰδῐο-τοπέω** [ἰδ], Astrol., *occupy a congenial position in the zodiac*,

Vett.Val.71.7: -τοπία, ἡ, ib.276.17. -τοπος, ον, *of their own district*, βασιλεῖς cj. in *Peripl.M.Rubr.*47. -τροπία, ἡ, *peculiar quality*, Cleom.2.4, Ptol.*Tetr.*1, Heph.Astr.1.20, etc. 2. *specific form* or *manner*, Simp.*in Ph.*1073.19; *peculiarity*, Dam.*Pr.*90; *idiosyncrasy*, ib.388. -τροπος, ον, *peculiar, distinctive*, ἑνότης, ἡδονή, Epicur.*Ep.*1 p.13 U., *Fr.*186; φύσις, νόσοι, D.S.3.35, 5.10; *of a peculiar species*, ὁ νυκτικόραξ Str.17.2.4. Adv. -πως D.S.3.19, Dam.*Pr.*40: Comp., Marcellin.*Puls.*506. -τρόφος, ον, *feeding individuals*, Pl.*Plt.*261d. II. ἰδιότροφος, ον, *feeding on a peculiar diet*, opp. παμφάγος, Arist.*HA*488$^{a}$15. -τῦπος, ον, *of a peculiar form*, Herm.ap.Stob.1.49.44. -φεγγής, ές, *self-shining*, of the moon, v.l. in *Placit.*2.28.4. ✱-φυής, ές, *of peculiar nature*, ib.1.7.20; σάλπιγγες D.S.5.30; τὰ ἰ., title of work by Archelaus, D.L.2.17. -φῦτον, τό, = κῆμος, Ps.-Dsc.4.133. ✱-χειρος, ον, *autographed*, ἀπογραφή Just.*Nov.*48.1 *Intr.*: Subst. -χειρον, τό, ib.49.2.1. -χρεος, ον, *carrying a personal obligation*, σύμβολα *Sammelb.*4638.15 (ii B.C.). -χροιος, ον, *of peculiar colour*, Ptol.*Tetr.*103 (v.l. -χρονος):—also -χρωμος, ον, *of natural colour, not dyed*, Artem.2.3, *BGU*327.6 (ii A.D.), *PHolm.*24.32, etc.

ἰδιόω, v. ἰδιόομαι.

ἴδισις [ῐδ], εως, ἡ, *sweating, perspiring*, Arist.*Pr.*965$^{a}$2.

ἰδίω [ῐδ], aor. 1 ἴδισα Arist.*HA*521$^{a}$14, Thphr.*Sud.*28: (ἶδος):—*sweat*, of the cold sweat of terror, ἴδιον, ὡς ἐνόησα Od.20.204; πρὶν ἂν ἰδίῃς καὶ διαλύσῃς ἄρθρων ἶνας Ar.*Pax*85, cf. *Ra.*237, Eub.53, Hp.*Mul.*1.38, Diocl.*Fr.*142; ἴδισαν αἱματώδη ἱδρῶτα Arist. l.c., cf. Thphr.*HP*5.9.8; ἱδρόω is more common in Prose. [Second ι in pres. and impf. short in Ep., long in Att., in aor. always long.] (Perh. cogn. with Skt. *svidyati*, Lat. *sudo*, Engl. *sweat*.)

ἰδί-ωμα [ῐδῐ], ατος, τό, (ἰδιόω) *peculiarity, specific property, unique feature*, Epicur.*Ep.*1 p.25 U., *Stoic.*2.25, etc.; τὰ τῶν χρωμάτων ἰ. Epicur.*Ep.*2 p.51 U.; τῆς πολιτείας Plb.2.38.10; τοῦ νόμου *BGU*12.18 (ii A.D.); τὸ καθ' αὑτὸν ἰ. τηρεῖν Plb.2.59.2; τὰ περὶ τὴν χώραν, περὶ αὐτοὺς ἰ., Id.2.14.3, 6.3.3; τὸ ἐξαίρετόν τινος ἰ. A.D.*Synt.*15.19; ἀγαθότητος ἰ. Procl.*Inst.*133; ὕλης Id.*Theol.Pl.*5.35; *property*, φαρμάκου Heras ap.Gal.13.785, cf. Dsc.1.71; of the properties of numbers, *Theol.Ar.*5, al.; τὸ ἰ. τοῦ ἑνός Dam.*Pr.*5: *special subject*, τῆς πραγματείας Sor.1.126. II. *peculiarity of style*, D.H.*Amm.*2 tit., al. 2. *idiom*, ἰ. Ὁμηρικόν A.D.*Synt.*157.9. 3. *style*, παιανικὸν ἰ. Ath.15.696e. -ωνῠμος, ον, *appropriate*, προσηγορία Dam.*Pr.*40. -ωσις, εως, ἡ, *isolation*, opp. κοινωνία, Pl.*R.*462b; *appropriation*, Plu.2.644d.

ἰδιωτ-εία [ῐδ], ἡ, *private station*, opp. τυραννίς, X.*Hier.*8.1; opp. βασιλεία, Pl.*Lg.*696a: pl., opp. ἀρχαί, Id.*R.*618d; ἐν ἰ., opp. ἐν φιλοσοφίᾳ, Phld.*Rh.*2.277 S. II. *uncouthness, want of education*, Luc.*Hist.Conscr.*27, *Abd.*7. III. *defenceless condition*, τῆς ἰ. ἡμῶν καταφρονοῦντες *SIG*888.65 (Scaptopara, iii A.D.). -εύω, *occupy a private station*, opp. δημοσιεύω, Pl.*Ap.*32a, *R.*579c; opp. ἄρχω, X.*Hier.*8.5; opp. τυραννεύω, Isoc.2.4; opp. πολιτεύεσθαι, Aeschin.1.195; of a country, *to be of no consideration*, X.*Cyr.*8.7.7. II. *practise privately*, of a physician, opp. ὁ δημοσιεύων, Pl.*Plt.*259a, cf. *Grg.*514e sq. III. c. gen. rei, τῆς ἀρετῆς ἰ. *to be unpractised, unskilled in*.., Id.*Prt.*327a. IV. in Lit. Crit., *to be vulgar*, of expressions, Longin.31.2. ✱-ης, ου, ὁ, (ἴδιος) *private person, individual*, opp. the State, ξυμφέροντα καὶ πόλεσι καὶ ἰδιώταις Th.1.124, cf. 3.10, *SIG*37.3 (Teos, v B.C.), Pl.*Smp.*185b, X.*Vect.*4.18, etc.; opp. γένος, *SIG*1013.6 (Chios, iv B.C.); opp. φατρία, ib.987.28 (ibid., iv B.C.). II. *one in a private station*, opp. to one holding public office, or taking part in public affairs, Hdt.1.59, 123, al., cf. Decr. ap.And.1.84, Th.4.2, etc.; opp. βασιλεύς, Hdt.7.3; opp. ἄρχων, Lys.5.3, Pl.*Plt.*259b, *SIG*305.71 (iv B.C.); opp. δικαστής, Antipho 6.24; opp. πολιτευόμενος, D.10.70; opp. ῥήτωρ, Hyp.*Eux.*27; *private soldier*, opp. στρατηγός, X.*An.*1.3.11, cf. *PHib.*1.30.21 (iii B.C.); *layman*, opp. priest, *OGI*90.52 (Rosetta, ii B.C.), *PGnom.*200 (ii A.D.), 1*Ep.Cor.*14.16: as Adj., ἰ. ἄνδρες Hdt.1.32, 70, Th.1.115; ἰ. θεοί *homely* (with play on ἴδιος), Ar.*Ra.*891. 2. *common man, plebeian*, οἱ ἰ. καὶ πένητες Plu.*Thes.*24; ἰ. καὶ εὐτελής, opp. βασιλεύς, Hdn.4.10.2. 3. as Adj., ἰ. βίος *private* station, Pl.*R.*578c; ἰ. λόγος *everyday* speech, D.H.*Dem.*2, cf. Longin.31.2. III. *one who has no professional knowledge, layman*, καὶ ἰατρὸς καὶ ἰ. Th.2.48, cf. Hp.*VM*4, Pl.*Tht.*178c, *Lg.*933d; ἰ. ἤ τινα τέχνην ἔχων Id.*Sph.*221c; of prose-writers, ἐν μέτρῳ ὡς ποιητής, ἢ ἄνευ μέτρου ὡς ἰ. Id.*Phdr.*258d, cf. *Smp.*178b; ἰ. καὶ μηδὲν αὐλήσεως ἐπαΐων Id.*Prt.*327c; opp. to a professed orator, Isoc.4.11; to a trained soldier, X.*Eq.Mag.*8.1; ἰδιώτας, ὡς εἰπεῖν, χειροτέχναις (-νας codd.) ἀνταγωνισαμένους Th.6.72; opp. ἀσκητής, X.*Mem.*3.7.7, cf. 12.1; opp. ἀθλητής, Arist.*EN*1116$^{b}$13; opp. a professed philosopher, Id.*Pol.*1266$^{a}$31, Phld.*Lib.*p.5 O., *D.*1.25; in Music, Id.*Mus.*p.42 K.; opp. δημιουργός, Pl.*Prt.*312a, *Thg.*124c: as Adj., ὁ ἰ. ὄχλος, opp. artificers, Plu.*Per.*12. 2. c. gen. rei, *unpractised, unskilled in* a thing, ἰατρικῆς Pl.*Prt.*345a, cf. *Ti.*20a; ἔργου X.*Oec.*3.9; ἰ. κατὰ τοὺς πόνους, κατὰ τὸν ὕπνον, Id.*Cyr.*1.5.11; ἰ. τὰ ἄλλα Hdn.4.12.1; ἰ. ὡς πρὸς ἡμᾶς ἀγωνίζεσθαι X.*Cyr.* l.c., cf. Luc.*Herm.*81. 3. generally, *raw hand, ignoramus*, ἄν τε δεινοὶ λάχωσιν ἄν τε ἰδιῶται.. D.4.35; παιδάρια καὶ ἰ., of slaves, S.E.*M.*1.234 (cf. ἰ. οἰκέται Luc.*Alex.*30); ἀμαθὴς καὶ ἰ., opp. τεχνίτης, Id.*Ind.*29; voc. ἰδιῶτα, as a term of abuse, Men.*Sam.*71. 4. '*average man*', opp. a person of distinction, Plu.2.1104a. IV. ἰδιῶται, οἱ, *one's own countrymen*, opp. ξένοι, Ar.*Ra.*459. -ίζω, *pronounce in the local manner*, Eust.145.10 (Pass.). -ικός, ή, όν, *of* or *for a private person, private*, σῖτος καὶ ἑωυτοῦ καὶ ἰ. Hdt.1.21; πύργος Id.4.164; opp. δημόσιος, ἱερά *SIG*1015.9 (Halic.); opp. κοινός, οἰκίαι ib.987.5 (Chios, iv B.C.); opp. βασιλικός, Pl.*Criti.*117b, cf. Isoc.9.72; ἰ. σύγγραμμα, opp. πολιτικόν, Pl.*Phdr.*258d; ἰ. τριήρεις, opp. the Paralos, D.21.174; οἰωνὸς οὐκ ἰ., i.e. indicating royalty, X.*An.*6.1.23; ἰ. τράπεζα *private* bank, *PLond.*3.1168.21 (i A.D.); δάνεια, opp. δημόσια, ib.932.8 (iii A.D.); συμβόλαια D.H.10.57; ἰ. λόγοι speeches *in private suits*, Id.*Dem.*56; καθαρὸς ἀπὸ δημοσίου ἢ ἰ. free from public or *private* encumbrance, *BGU*446.15 (ii A.D.); ἰ. κανών impost *on private land*, *POxy.*2124.10 (iv A.D.). II. *not done by rules of art, unprofessional, amateurish*, Pl.*Euthd.*282d; φαῦλον καὶ ἰ. Id.*Hp.Ma.*287a, *Ion* 532e; λέξις S.E.*M.*1.234; λήμματα Gal.5.213; of language, *commonplace, everyday*, τὸ ἰ. Arist.*Po.*1458$^{a}$21, 32, cf. D.L.10.13 (Sup.); but also, *vulgar*, Phld.*Po.*2.71, Longin.43.1. Adv., μὴ φαύλως μηδὲ -κῶς Pl.*Lg.*966e; ἰ. καὶ γελοίως Id.*Euthd.*278d; ἰ. ἔχειν Id.*Cra.*394a; ἰ. τὸ σῶμα ἔχειν, i.e. to neglect gymnastic exercises, Id.*Lg.*839e, X.*Mem.*3.12.1; also, *in a special way*, Phld.*D.*3.8. III. of persons, *unprofessional*, Apollon.Cit.3. IV. ἄρτοι ἰ. *common* bread, *UPZ*94.17 (ii B.C.). V. ἰ. βίος *cloistered* life, Marcellin.*Puls.*138. -ις, ιδος (nom. pl. -ώτιες *IG* 5(1).1390.17 (Andania, i B.C.)), ἡ, fem. of ἰδιώτης, J.*AJ*8.11.1; opp. φιλόσοφος, Muson.*Fr.*3 p.11 H.; ἰδιώτιες, opp. ἱεραί, *IG* l.c.; ἰ. πόλις, opp. ἡγεμονίς, App.*BC*4.16, 95. II. *unskilled, uninstructed*, Luc.*Im.*13, Alciphro 2.4; ἰ. ἀκοαί *unlearned* ears, Dam.*Pr.*5. -ισμός, ὁ, *way* or *fashion of a common person*, Epict.*Ench.*33.6, S.E.*M.*1.67, Dam.*Isid.*223; in language, *homely, vulgar phrase*, Phld *Po.*2.71, Longin.31.1, D.L.7.59. 2. Rhet., *argumentum ad hominem*, usu. in the form of a hypothetical question, Rufin.*Fig.*10.

ἰδιωφελής [ῐδ], ές, *of private benefit*, opp. κοινωφελής, νόμος Archyt. ap.Stob.4.1.138, cf. Alex.Aphr.*in Top.*234.16, Sch.Arr.*Epict.*4.10.12.

ἰδμάν, ᾶνος, ὁ, *one who knows*, Hdn.Gr.1.13: ἰδμή, ἡ, = ἰδμοσύνη, Hsch.

ἴδμεν, Ion., Aeol., Dor. for ἴσμεν: ἴδμεν, ἴδμεναι, Ep. for εἰδέναι; v. οἶδα.

ἰδμοσύνη, ἡ, *knowledge, skill*, *APl.*4.273 (Crin.): in pl., Hes.*Th.*377.

✱ ἴδμων, ον, gen. ονος, (ἴδμεν, = εἰδέναι) *having knowledge of* a thing, εὐνομίης ἴ. πόλις *AP*7.575 (Leont.).

✱ ἰδνόομαι, Pass., *bend oneself, double oneself up*, esp. for pain, ἰδνώθη Il.2.266; ἰδνώθη δὲ πεσών 13.618; ἰδνωθεὶς ὀπίσω, of a snake in the clutches of an eagle, 12.205; also, of one throwing up a ball perpendicularly, Od.8.375, cf. *APl.*4.97; of the womb, ἢν.. ἰδνωθῇ Hp.*Mul.*1.2; ἰδνοῦται ib.10:—Act., ἰδνῶ only in Hdn.Gr.1.451.

Ἰδογενής [ῑ], ές, *born on Ida*, Orac.ap.Paus.10.12.3.

ἶδοι· ὀφθαλμοί, Hsch.

ἰδομαλιάδαι, = οἱ τὰς ὄψεις κοσμούμενοι, Alc.150 (ap.Hsch.); v. εἰδομαλίδας.

✱ ἶδος, εος, τό, *sweat*: pl., *sweats*, Hp.*Coac.*105 (s.v.l.). 2. *warmth*, Emp.62.5, prob. in Id.21.4; *violent heat*, Hes.*Sc.*397, Call.*Fr.*124 (prob.), D.P.966; cf. ἰδίω.

ἰδός· ὁδός, σῶμα, Hsch.

✱ ἰδοῦ (ἴδου Hdn.Gr.ap.Choerob.*in Theod.*2.140), aor. 2 imper. Med. of ὁράω; but, II. ἰδού (on the accent v. Hdn.Gr.1.417, al.), as Adv., *lo! behold!* (even with words of hearing, ἰδοὺ δοῦπον αὖ κλύω τινά S.*Aj.*870 (lyr.), cf. *El.*1410): 1. with Nouns and Prons., ἰ. χελιδών Klein *Meistersign.*133 (Attic vase, vi B.C.), etc.; ἰ. ἐγώ *here am* I, Lxx *Ge.*27.1, al.; ἰ. ἡ μνᾶ σου *Ev.Luc.*19.20; οὐκ ἰ. Ἀαρών; Lxx *Ex.*4.14. 2. with Verbs, a. in the imper., ἰ. θεᾶσθε S.*Tr.*1079, Ar.*Ach.*366; esp. in offering a thing, *take it!* ἰ. δέχου παῖ S.*Ph.*776. b. in ind. of all tenses, ἰ. πείθομαι E.*Or.*143 (lyr.): freq. in Lxx and *NT* with past tenses, *Ge.*24.15, al., *Ev.Matt.*27.51, al.; in the middle of a sentence, *Ev.Luc.*13.16. 3. with questions, ἰ., τί ἔστιν; Ar.*Nu.*825, *Eq.*157. 4. in repeating another's words quizzingly, as ἰδού γ' ἄκρατον wine, *quotha!* ib.87; ἰ. λέγειν ib.344; ἰδού γε κλέπτειν Id.*Th.*206, cf. *Ec.*136.

ἰδρεία, Ion. -είη, ἡ, (ἴδρις) *knowledge, skill*, ἰδρείῃ πολέμοιο Il.16.359; οὐδέ τι ἰδρείῃ (Aristarch. for vulg. οὐδέ τ' ἀϊδρείῃ) 7.198, cf. A.R.2.72, Q.S.4.226, Theoc.22.85.

✱ ἴδρ-ις, gen. ἴδριος, Att. ἴδρεως, ὁ, ἡ, neut. ἴδρι: voc. ἴδρι *AP*9.559 (Crin.), prob. in ib.6.182 (Alex. Magnes.): pl. ἴδριες; also ἴδριδα S.*Fr.*1056, ἴδριδες Phryn.Com.90 (= Phryn.Trag.22), cf. πολυ-ίδριδι Sapph.166 (but these forms are censured by Hdn.Gr.2.40): (οἶδα):—poet. Adj. *experienced, knowing, skilful*, ἀνὴρ ἴδρις Od.6.233: c. inf., ἴδριες.. νῆα θοὴν ἐνὶ πόντῳ ἐλαυνέμεν 7.108: c. gen. rei, πόνου καὶ ὀϊζύος Hes.*Sc.*351; καλῶν Pi.*O.*1.104; ἔργων Archil.39, cf. A.*Ag.*446 (lyr.), S.*El.*608, *Ichn.*124, Call.*Jov.*74, etc.: in late Prose, ἴ. τῶν οὐρανίων Vett.Val.4.19: with Preps., κατὰ γνώμαν ἴδρις S.*OT* 1087 (lyr.); οὐδὲν ἴδρις Id.*OC*525 (lyr.); ἐν πολέμοισι D.P.857. 2. as Subst., *the provident one*, i.e. *the ant*, Hes.*Op.*778. -ίτας, ου, ὁ, = ἴδρις, dub.l. in *AP*6.182 (Alex. Magnes.).

✱ ἱδροσύνη, ἡ, *sweating, toil*, σώματος *IGRom.*4.607 (pl., Phrygia).

ἱδρόω [ῐ by nature, cf. ἀφίδρωσον *Com.Adesp.*3 D.], v. sub fin.: fut. -ώσω Il.2.388: aor. ἵδρωσα 4.27, X.*Cyr.*8.1.38: pf. ἵδρωκα Luc.*Merc.Cond.*26:—Pass., pf. ἵδρωται Id.*Herm.*2: (ἶδος):—*sweat, perspire*, esp. from toil, τὸν δ' ἱδρώοντα Il.18.372; ἵππους λῦσαν.. ἱδρώοντας Od.4.39; of a hunted deer, ἤϊξε.. σπεύδουσ' ἱδρώουσα Il.11.119; ἱδρώσει.. τελαμὼν ἀμφὶ στήθεσφιν *it shall reek with sweat*, 2.388: c. acc. cogn., ἱδρῶ θ' ὃν ἴδρωσα μόγῳ 4.27; διὰ τί τὸ πρόσωπον μάλιστα ἱδροῦσιν; Arist.*Pr.*867$^{b}$34, cf. 866$^{b}$28.—The contr. forms (really from ἱδρό-ω) have ω, ῳ for ου, οι (cf. ῥιγόω), fem. part. ἱδρῶσαι Il.11.598; 3 pl. ἱδρῶσι Thphr.*Sud.*36; opt. ἱδρῴη Hp.*Aër.*8: codd. of X.

vary between ἱδροῦντι and ἱδρῶντι, *HG*4.5.7, *Cyr.*1.4.28, but ἱδροῦντι *An.*1.8.1, ἱδροῦσι Arist. ll. cc.; ὡς ἂν ἱδρῶντες, corrupted to ὡσανεὶ δρῶντες, Ph.1.490: pres. ἱδρώω in Luc.*Syr.D.*10,17; Ep. part. ἱδρώουσα, -οντα (v. supr.), -οντας Ar.*Pax*1283 (hex.).

* ἵδρ-ῠμα, ατος, τό, *establishment, foundation*, Ἰάσονος ἵ. Str.6.1.1, cf. Plu.*Marc.*20; Ποιήσσαν Χαρίτων ἵ. Call.*Aet.*3.1.73. 2. *temple, shrine*, θεῶν Hdt.8.144, A.*Ag.*339, cf. *Ch.*1036, E.*Ba.*951, Pl.*Lg.*717b, etc.; *statue*, δαιμόνων ἵ. A.*Pers.*811, cf. Arr.*Epict.*2.22.17. 3. τὸ σὸν ἵ. πόλεως the *stay, support* of thy city, of chieftains, E.*Supp.*631 (lyr.). [ἵδρῡμα Call. l. c. (s. v.l.); ῐ by nature, Lyc.1032.] -ῠσις, εως, ἡ, *founding, foundation*, esp. of temples, ἱερῶν -σεις Pl.*R.*427b, cf. *IG*2².337 (iv B. C.): abs., Pl.*Lg.*909e; ἵ. ξοάνων *setting up* of statues, D.H.2.18; πόλεως ἵδρυσιν λαμβανούσης Plu.*Rom.*9. 2. Ἑρμέω ἱδρύσιες *statues* of Hermes, *AP*6.253 (Crin.). II. *settlement, abode*, Str.8.7.1, Plu.2.408a: metaph., οὐκ ἔχειν ἵ. ib.651d, etc. [ῡ only in later Poets, *AP* l. c.] -ῠτέον, *one must set up*, of a statue, Ar. *Pax*923, Max.Tyr.8tit. II. intr., οὐχ ἱ. *one must* not *sit idle*, S.*Aj.* 809. * -ύω, fut. -ύσω (καθ-) E.*Ba.*1339: aor. ἵδρῡσα Il.15.142, E. *Ba.*1070: pf. ἵδρῠκα (καθ-) Arist.*PA*665ᵇ20:—Med., fut. -ύσομαι E. *Heracl.*397, Ar.*Pl.*1198: aor. ἱδρῡσάμην Hdt.6.105, Anacr.104, Ar. *Pl.*1153:—Pass., fut. ἱδρυθήσομαι D.H.*Comp.*6: aor. ἱδρύθην Ar.*Fr.* 245, etc.; freq. written ἱδρύνθην in codd., as Il.3.78, Hp.*Coac.*309, A.R.3.1269: pf. ἵδρῡμαι, used both in pass. and med. sense (v. sub fin.). [ῐ by nature, E.*Ba.*1070, Ar.*Fr.*26 D., etc., but freq. lengthd. by position, E.*Hipp.*639, Ar.*Pl.*1153, etc.: ῠ by nature, even in ἱδρύεται E.*Heracl.*786; but ἵδρῠε Il.2.191; καθίδρῠε Od.20.257: ῡ in fut. and aor. 1. exc. in late Poets, as *AP*7.109 (ἐν–, ⟨D. L.⟩), Man.3. 80 (dub.), *Arch.Pap.*2.570, Nonn.*D.*4.22: pf. Pass. ἵδρῡμαι A.*Supp.* 413, E.*Heracl.*19, *Hel.*820, Theoc.17.21, etc.:—*make to sit down, seat*, αὐτός τε κάθησο καὶ ἄλλους ἵδρυε λαούς Il.2.191; ἵδρυσε θρόνῳ ἔνι θοῦρον Ἄρηα 15.142, cf. Od.3.37; ἱ. τινὰ εἰς θρόνους E.*Ion*1573; ὄζων ἔπι Id. *Ba.*1070; ἵδρυσε τὴν στρατιὴν ἐπὶ ποταμῷ *encamped* the army, Hdt. 4.124, cf. Th.4.104:—Pass., *to be seated, sit still*, τοὶ δ' ἱδρύνθησαν ἅπαντες Il.3.78; κατ' οἶκον ἵδρυται γυνή E.*Hipp.*639; of an army, *lie encamped*, Hdt.4.203, al., Th.7.77, al.; Πελοπόννησος ἀσφαλέως ἱδρυμένη *secure*, Hdt.6.86.α'; ἐν θεῶν ἕδραισιν ὧδ' ἱδρυμένας A.*Supp.*413; ἡ στρατιὰ βεβαίως ἔδοξεν ἱδρῦσθαι seemed *to have got a* firm *footing*, Th. 8.40; ἱ. ἐπὶ τῶν ἵππων Ael.*Tact.*2.4. 2. *settle* persons in a place, εἰς τόνδε δόμον E.*Alc.*841; ἐν τοῖς ἀστοῖσιν Ἄρη ἐμφύλιον ἱ. *to give a footing to*, i.e. *excite*, intestine war, A.*Eu.*862; ἱ. πολλοὺς ἐν πόλει Plu.*Pomp.* 28:—Pass., *to be settled*, Hdt.8.73; ποῦ κλύεις νιν ἱδρῦσθαι χθονός; S. *Tr.*68; ἐς Κολωνὰς ἱδρυθείς Th.1.131; μεταξὺ φρενῶν ὀμφαλοῦ τε ἱδρῦσθαι Pl.*Ti.*77b; of local diseases, πόνος ἐς στῆθος ἱδρυνθείς Hp.*Coac.* 309; τὸ ἐν κεφαλῇ.. ἱδρυθὲν κακόν Th.2.49. 3. Med., *establish*, τινὰ ἄνακτα γῆς E.*Ph.*1008; τινὰ ἐς οἶκόν τινος Id.*Hel.*46; ἱδρύσασθαι τοὺς βίους *to choose settled* modes of life, D.H.1.68; ἱ. οἴκησιν Pl. *Smp.*195e. 4. pf. Pass. ἵδρυμαι, of places, *to be situated, lie*, of a city, Hdt.2.59. cf. A.*Pers.*231, Pl.*Lg.*745b. 5. Pass., *settle down, become quiet*, Hp.*Epid.*3.17.ιε'. II. *set up, found*, esp. in Med., *dedicate* temples, statues, etc., Anacr.104, Simon.140, etc.; Πανὸς ἱρόν Hdt.6.105, cf. 1.105, al.; βρέτας E.*IT*1453; βωμούς Pl.*Prt.*322a, al.; ἱδρύσασθαι [Ἑρμῆν] *set up a statue of* H., Ar.*Pl.*1153; Εἰρήνην Id. *Pax*1091: also c. dat., τὴν δαίμον' ἣν ἀνήγαγον ἐς τὴν ἀγορὰν ἄγων ἱδρύσωμαι βοΐ Id.*Fr.*26 D.:—Pass., ἐξ οὗ τὸ ἱρὸν ἵδρυται Hdt.2.44, cf. 1.172; βωμὸς -ύθη Ar.*Fr.*245; [Πλοῦτος] -υμένος Id.*Pl.*1192; at Athens, ἥρωες κατὰ πόλιν ἱδρυμένοι the heroes *who had statues erected to them*, Lycurg.1: pf. Pass. in med. sense, Hdt.2.42, Men.202.

ἵδρωα or **ἱδρῷα**, τά, (ἱδρώς) *heat-spots, pustules*, Hp.*Aph.*3.21, cf. Gal. ad loc. II. v. ἱδρῷον.

**ἱδρ-ώδης**, ες, *accompanied by perspiration*, Hp.*Epid.*5.73, 7.51. -ώεις, εσσα, εν, *causing sweat*, πόνος B.12.57. * -ῷον or -ῷον, τό, *cloth for wiping perspiration*, as a piece of harness, *PLond. ined.*2383 *B* (iii B. C.), *PSI*5.527 (iii B. C.), dub. in *PTeb.*116.34 (ii B. C.). -ώς (v. fin.), ῶτος, ὁ, and Aeol. ἡ, Sapph.2.13: dat. ἱδρῶτι, acc. ἱδρῶτα; Hom. has dat. ἱδρῷ (not ἱδρῷ as Choerob. *in Theod.*1.248) Il.17.385,745; acc. ἱδρῶ 11.621, 22.2, cf. A.R.2.87, 4.656: (ἴδος):—*sweat*, Hom. (v. infr.), etc.; μετὰ ἱδρώτων Pl.*R.*350d; κατὰ δ' ἱ. ἔρρεεν ἐκ μελέων Od.11.599; ἱ. ἀνῄει χρωτί S.*Tr.*767; στάζειν ἱδρῶτι (v. στάζω); ῥέεσθαι ἱδρῶτι Plu.*Cor.*3; of *sweat* as the sign of toil, τῆς ἀρετῆς ἱδρῶτα θεοὶ προπάροιθεν ἔθηκαν Hes.*Op.*289; ἱδρῶτα παρέχειν X.*Cyr.*2.1.29: pl., Hp.*Aph.*4.36, Arist.*Pr.*867ᵃ13, etc.; ἱδρῶτες ξηροί, opp. the effect of baths, Pl.*Phdr.*239c. 2. *exudation* of trees, *gum, resin*, σμύρνης E.*Ion*1175; δρυός Ion Trag.40; Βρομιάδος ἱδρῶτα πηγῆς, of wine, Antiph.52.12. II. metaph., *anything earned by the sweat of one's brow*, οὐ γὰρ τὸν ἐμὸν ἱδρῶτα.. ἐκβαλῶ Ar.*Ec.*750, cf. Chor.p.270 B. (pl.). [ῑ in Ep. and Lyr.: ῐ in E. l. c.] (Cf. ἰδίω.) -ωσις, εως, ἡ, *sweating*, Philostr.Jun.*Im.*11 (s. v. l.), Olymp. *in Mete.*103.5. -ώσσω, Att. -ττω, = ἱδρόω, Gal.16.778, Sch.Ar.*Ra.*238. -ωτάρια, τά, = ἵδρωα, Orib.*Fr.*117. -ωτήριον, τό, *sudatorium*, *Gloss.*: pl., *sudorifics*, Paul.Aeg.3.74. -ωτίδες, αἱ, = ἵδρωα, Steph. *in Hp.*2. 370 D. -ωτικός, ή, όν, *sudorific*, Hp.*Vict.*3.72, Orib.2.58.78; δύναμις Gal.11.711. II. *apt to perspire*, Thphr.*Sud.*36, Gal.14.290 (Comp.). Adv. Comp. -κωτέρως, διακεῖσθαι Arist.*Pr.*870ᵇ7. * -ώτιον, τό, Dim. of ἱδρώς, Hp.*Epid.*7.5. -ωτοειδῶς, Adv. *after the manner of sweat*, κενοῦσθαι Steph. *in Hp.*1.112 D.

**ἱδρωτοποι-έω**, *induce perspiration*, Orib.*Fr.*128:—Pass., *to be made to perspire*, Arist.*Pr.*870ᵇ31: hence -ποιΐα, ἡ, ib.38 (pl.), Philum.*Ven.*4.9, Paul.Aeg.5.3. -ός, όν, *sudorific*, Dsc.3.68, Philum.ap.Aët.9.12.

**ἰδύβολαι**· προφαίνεται, Hsch.

**ἰδυῖα** [ῐ], ἡ, Ep. for εἰδυῖα, part. fem. of οἶδα; v. εἴδω.

**ἴδυιοι**, Att. **ἴδυοι**, = συνίστορες, μάρτυρες, Lex Solon.ap.Ar.*Fr.*222, Paus.Gr.*Fr.*151; = οἱ τὰς φονικὰς δίκας κρίνοντες, Hsch.; cf. βιδιαῖοι.

**ἰδύλευμα**· μάθημα, Hsch. **ἰδυλιτρίχες**, sine expl., Id. **ἰδυναγής**· μάντις, Id. **ἶδυξ**, υκος, ὁ, = ἴκτις, Alex.Mynd.ap.Hdn.Gr. 1.44.

**ἰέ**, shortd. form of ἰή, in Paeans, Aristonous 1.4, al., Isyll.37, al., cf. Ephor.31(*b*) J.

**ἴε, ἴεν**, Ep. 3 sg. impf. of εἶμι (*ibo*); also as imper., Hsch. **ἵει**, Ion. and Att. 3 sg. impf. of ἵημι. **ἱείας**· τὰς κυρίας, οἰκογενεῖς, Hsch. **ἰείη**, Ep. for ἴοι, 3 sg. pres. opt. of εἶμι (*ibo*). **ἴελος**, = ἴλεος (i.e. εἰλ–), Id. **ἴεμεν, ἰέμεναι**, Ep. pres. inf. of ἵημι: **ἱέμενος**, pres. part. Pass.:—hence Adv. **ἱεμένως**, *eagerly*, Sch.A.R.3. 890. **ἴεν**, Ep. 3 pl. impf. of ἵημι.

**ἱερά**, ἡ, a kind of *serpent*, v.l. for ἱερόν, Arist.*HA*607ᵃ31. II. a name for many medicines in the Greek pharmacopoeia, Gal.13. 126, al.; of a plaster, ib.778; esp. of aloes, Id.6.354; ἱερὰ πικρά Id. 13.129. III. v. ἱερός.

**ἱερ-άγγελος**, ὁ, *one who proclaims a festival*, Hsch. * -āγέω, *carry offerings*, *Sammelb.*6753a (iii B. C.). -αγωγός, όν, *carrying offerings*, μύσται Hedyl.ap.Ath.11.497d; ναῦς Plb.31.12.11; ἄνδρες D.H.16.3: as Subst., *Inscr.Délos* 291ᵇ8 (iii B. C.), *IG*12(1).1035 (Carpathos), 12(8).190.45 (Samothrace). * -άζω, *serve as priest*, τοῖς Διοσκόροις ib.12(5).129.56 (Paros); τῷ Ἀσκληπιῷ *SIG*²588.43 (Delos, ii B. C.): also c. gen., τοῦ Ἀσκλ. ib.45: abs., *IG*12(7).237. 27 (Amorgos):—Boeot. **ἱαρειάδδω** ib.7.3169 (Orchom.): aor. part. ἱαρειάξασα ib.1816.2 (Leuctra, iv/iii B. C.), 2876.3 (Coronea, ii B. C.), *BCH*50.409, al. (Thespiae); ἱερεάξασα ib.26.292 (ibid.).

* **ἱερᾱκ-άριος** [ἰε], ὁ, = ἱερακοτρόφος, *Cat.Cod.Astr.*8(4).217. -εῖον, τό, *shrine of the hawk*, *PTeb.*5.70 (ii B. C.). -ειος, α, ον, *of a hawk*, πρόσωπον Porph.ap.Eus.*PE*3.12. -ία βοτάνη, = ἱεράκιον 1, Horap.1.6. -ιάς, άδος, ἡ, = foreg., Alex.Trall.2. -ιδεύς, έως, ὁ, *young hawk, eyass*, Eust.753.56. * -ίδιον, τό, *statuette of a hawk*, Roussel *Cultes Égyptiens* 219 (Delos, ii B. C.). -ίζω, *behave like a hawk*, Thphr.*Sign.*16, Arist.*Fr.*253. -ιον, τό, *hawk-weed*: ἱ. τὸ μέγα, = *Urospermum picroides*, ἱ. τὸ μικρόν, = *Hymenonema graecum*, Ps.-Dsc.3.64. II. *a compound eyesalve*, Gal.12.783. -ίσκος, ὁ, Dim. of ἱέραξ, Ar.*Av.*1112. -ιστί, Adv. *in hawks' language*, *PMag.Leid.W.*2.42. -ίτης [ῑτ], ου, ὁ, *stone of the colour of a hawk's neck*, Plin.*HN*37.167, Gal.12.207, *PMag.Par.*2.221. II. = ἱεράκιον 1, ib.1.901.

**ἱερᾱκο-βοσκός**, ὁ, *hawk-feeder, falconer*, *PPetr.*3 p.239 (iii B. C.), Ael.*NA*7.9. -κτόνος, ον, *hawk-killing*, Hsch. s.v. φαβοκτόνος. * -μορφος, ον, *hawk-shaped*, of the Egyptian god Phrê (the Sun), represented with a hawk's head, Ph.Bybl.ap.Eus.*PE*1.10, Horap.1.6, S.E.*P.*3.219, *PMag.Leid.W.*9.43. -πόδιον, τό, = λυχνὶς ἀγρία, Ps.-Dsc.3.101. -πρόσωπος, ον, *hawk-faced*, *PMag. Leid.W.*1.39, Porph.ap.Eus.*PE*3.12. -τάφος [ᾰ], ὁ, *one who buries sacred hawks*, *PStrassb.*91.5 (i B. C.), etc. -τρόφος, ον, = ἱερακοβοσκός, *Cat.Cod.Astr.*7.118, al. II. *pupil of Hierax*, Eun.*Hist.* p.268 D.

**ἱερακώδης**, ες, *hawk-like*, Eun.*Hist.*p.206 D.

**ἱεράμοιβοι**· προφῆται θεῶν, Hsch.

* **ἱερανθεσία**, ἡ, only Dor. ἱαρ–, *dedication*, i.e. *manumission*, *IG*9 (1).193.31, al.

* **ἱερᾱνομέω**, *hold office as commissioner of sacred rites*, *Mon.Ant.*23. 179 (Iotape).

* **ἱέραξ** [ῐ], ᾱκος, ὁ, Ion. and Ep. **ἴρηξ** [ῑ], ηκος (the longer form first in Alcm.28, E.*Andr.*1141, Ps.-Orac.ap.Ar.*Eq.*1052):—*hawk, falcon*, ἴρηξ ὠκύπτερος Il.13.62, cf. 819, Od.13.86, Hes.*Op.*212, Hdt.2.65, Arist.*HA*620ᵃ17; sacred to Apollo, Ar.*Av.*516. II. a kind of *fish*, Epich.68 (in Dor. form ἱάραξ), Epaenet.ap.Ath.7.329a. III. name for a grade of initiates in Mithras-worship, Porph.*Abst.*4. 16. IV. name of a *bandage*, Sor.*Fasc.*12.

**ἱεραοιδός**, ὁ, *sacred bard*, Hsch.

**ἱεράομαι**, Ion. ἱρ–, fut. -άσομαι [ᾱ] J.*AJ*4.2.3; Ion. -ήσομαι *SIG* 1003 (Priene, ii B. C.): aor. -ησάμην ib.708.34 (Istropolis, ii B. C.); pf. part. ἱερημένος ib.5:—Pass., aor. 1 part. ἱεραθεῖσα *Philol.*71.41 (Delph.):—*to be a priest* or *priestess*, θεοῦ Hdt.2.35, cf. *SIG*1037.4 (Milet., iv/iii B. C.), al.; θεᾶς D.H.2.19; θεῷ Paus.6.11.2, cf. *Philol.* l. c.: abs., Th.2.2, Ph.2.157, al.; c. acc. cogn., ἱερωσύνην ἱεράσασθαι Aeschin.1.19 (v. l. ἱερώσασθαι): freq. in Inscrr., ἱερασάμενος τῇ πατρίδι *CIG*4069 (Ancyra), etc.; cf. ἱερόω.

**ἱερᾱ-πολέω**, *to be a* ἱεραπόλος, *IG*4.1444, 1536; of a woman, Ἀρχ. Δελτ.2.app.49 (Palaerus). * -πόλος, ὁ, (τέλλω) *chief priest*, Pi. *Parth.*1.6, *IG*14.256 (Gela), 5(1).29 (Sparta): **ἱερηπόλος** *TAM*2(1). 174 *E*9 (Sidyma).

**ἱεράρχης**, ου, ὁ, *president of sacred rites, high-priest*, *IG*7.303 (Oropus), 9(1).32 (Stiris): Boeot. **ἱἀράρχᾱς** *Schwyzer*515.4, al.:—hence Boeot. **ἱαραρχίω**, *to be high-priest*, ib.544.4.

**ἱερᾱτ-εία**, ἡ, *priesthood*, Arist.*Pol.*1328ᵇ13, *OGI*90.52 (Rosetta, ii B. C.), Lxx *Ex.*29.9, *Ev.Luc.*1.9, *IG*5(2).516 (Lycosura, i A. D.), etc.: Ion. **ἱρητηίη** *Schwyzer*692 (Chios, v B. C.); later **ἱερητείη** and -α *GDI* iv pp.885-6 (Erythrae, iv B. C), *SIG*1014.14 (ibid., iii B. C.), 1015.5 (Halic.). -εῖον, τό, *a sanctuary*, Procop.*Aed.*1.4. -ευμα, ατος, τό, *priesthood*, Lxx *Ex.*19.6, 1*Ep.Pet.*2.9. 2. *body of priests*, ib. 5. * -εύω, Ion. ἱερητ– *GDI*5394 (later also in Northern Greece, Boeot., *IG*7.3097 (perh. i B. C.); Phoc., ib.9(1).32.40 (Stiris, ii B. C.),

al.; Thess., ib.9(2).333 (i A.D.), cf. *SIG*²588.110 (Delos, ii B.C.); Lesb. **ἰρητεύω** *IG*12(2).527.45):—*to be priest* or *priestess*, θεῶν *OGI* 90.51 (Rosetta, ii B.C.); Καίσαρος prob. ib.767.4 (Cyrene); τοῦ Διὸς τοῦ Σωτῆρος *IG*7.2727 (Acraeph., i B.C.); τᾷ Ἀθανᾷ ib.9(1).65 (Daulis), cf. Hdn.5.6.3: abs., *SIG*1044.19 (Halic., iv/iii B.C.), al., Lxx *Ex.* 28.1, *Ev.Luc.*1.8:—also **-εύομαι**, *IGRom.*4.539 (Cotiaeum). II. Pass., *to be made holy*, Zos.Alch.p.108 B. * **-ικός**, ή, όν, *priestly, sacerdotal*, θυσίαι Arist.*Pol.*1285ᵇ10; ὑπομνήματα Plu.*Marc.*5; στέφανος, ἁγιστεῖαι, Id.2.34e, 729a; ὀνόματα Luc.*Philops.*12; λόγος Ptol.*Tetr.* 87 (-ατητικός codd.); βίος Jul.*Ep.*89b; ἡ ἱ. (sc. τέχνη), = ἱερατεία, Pl.*Plt.*290d; οἱ ἱ. *the priestly caste*, Hld.7.11, cf. Dam.*Pr.*399. Adv. -κῶς *in a sacerdotal sense*, ib.256; ἱ. ζῆν *as a priest should*, Jul. l.c.; σεμνῶς καὶ ἱ. κρίνειν δίκας Just.*Nov.*79.1. 2. ἱ. βύβλος, χάρτης, name of a kind of papyrus, Str.17.1.15, *PMag.Par.*1.2105; κόλλημα, πιττάκιον, made of this material, ib.2068, 3142. II. *devoted to sacred purposes*, τὰ ἱ. *the sacred fund*, *IGRom.*3.1137 (Syria, iii A.D.). III. -ικόν, τό, name of a *plaster*, Gal.13.183.

* **ἱεραύλης**, ου, ὁ, *flute-player at sacrifices*, *IG*3.1041.19, 1048.14, al.

**ἱερᾱφορία**, ἡ, *bearing of holy vessels*, D.H.16.3.

* **ἱερᾱφόρος**, ὁ, *bearer of holy vessels*, Plu.2.352b, *SIG*²754 (Pergam.): **ἱεροφόρος**, *IG*9(1).486.16 (ii/i B.C.), Ptol.*Tetr.*181.

* **ἱέρεια**, ἡ, Ion. **ἱρείη**, as v.l. in Hdt.5.72, 8.104: scanned -εῐα in Trag., S.*Fr.*456, E.*Or.*261 (with v.l. ἱερίαι), *Ba.*1114, and perh. to be written **ἱερέα**, as in *IG*1².4.13, 843*a*3, etc., and prob. in Pi.*P.*4.5: Ep. **ἱερέη** Call.*Ep.*41: **ἱερῆ**, *Schwyzer* 725 (Milet., vi B.C.), *GDI*5562 (Panticapaeum), 5584 (Priene), al.: **ἱαρέα** or **ἱάρεα** (pl. ἱαρεαι) ib. 4847: **ἱάρεια** dub. in *IG*7.2465 (Thebes):—fem. of ἱερεύς, *a priestess*, τὴν.. ἔθηκαν Ἀθηναίης ἱέρειαν Il.6.300, al., cf. Ar.*Th.*758, Th.4.133, Pl.*Phdr.*244b, al., *BCH*6.24 (Delos, ii B.C.), etc.

* **ἱερεία**, ἡ, (ἱερεύω) *sacrifice, festival*, Lxx 4*Ki.*10.20. II. = ἱερατεία, *CIG*3491.23 (Thyatira). III. Cypr. **ἰερηϝίjα**, *sanctuary*, τᾶς Ἀθάνας *Inscr.Cypr.*135.20 H. (v B.C.).

**ἱερειάζω**, v. ἱεράζω.

* **ἱερεῖον**, τό, Ion. **ἱερήϊον** or **ἱρήϊον** (the former in Hom. (pl. written ἱερήια *SIG*57.14 (Milet., v B.C.)), the latter in Hdt.), Dor. **ἱᾰρήϊον** *Berl.Sitzb.*1927.159 (Cyrene), prob. in *Leg.Gort.*10.38:—*victim, animal for sacrifice*, ἱρεύειν ἱερήϊον Od.14.94; ἱερήϊα πολλὰ παρεῖχον ib.250; ἐπεὶ οὐχ ἱ. οὐδὲ βοείην ἀρνύσθην Il.22.159 (prov. for 'no trifling stake', Cic.*Att.*1.1.4), cf. Hdt.1.132, 6.57, Ar.*Lys.*84, *Pax* 1091, And.1.126; opp. (ἁγνὰ) θύματα, Th.1.126; ἱερεῖον καὶ ἱερά *Test.Epict.*5.35; freq. of sheep, *OGI*214.62 (Didyma, iii B.C.), *IPE*1².76 (Olbia, perh. iv B.C.); of pigs, *PCair.Zen.*161 (iii B.C.). 2. in Od.11.23 (pl.), *offering for the dead*, for which, acc. to Sch., τόμιον or ἔντομον was more correct. II. *cattle slaughtered for food*, Hp.*Aff.*52, Mnesith.ap.Orib. 2.68.6: in pl., X.*Cyr.*1.4.17; of sucking-pigs, Gal.1.578, 10.489.

* **ἱερειτεύω**, later spelling of ἱεριτεύω. II. Thess. spelling of ἱερητεύω, *Schwyzer* 616ᵃ (Phalanna).

**ἱερεῖτις**, v. ἱερῖτις. **ἱερεύομαι**, v. ἱερόω.

* **ἱερ-εύς** [ῐ], έως, Ion. -ῆος, Cypr. -ῆϝος *Inscr.Cypr.*59 H., ὁ, Att. pl. ἱερῆς: gen. sg. and pl. written ἱερείως, ἱερείων, *PStrassb.*83.2,9 (ii B.C.):—Ion. nom. **ἱρεύς** Il.5.10, 16.604, Od.9.198: Dor. **ἱᾰρεύς** *IG* 4.1182, al. (gen. ἱαρέος ib.1580); acc. pl. τὸς ἱαρές *Schwyzer* 236 (Cyrene); nom. pl. οἱ ἱαρές ibid.; nom. sg. ἱαρές *GDI*4846 (Cyrene):—also **ἱέρεως** (Att. and proparox. acc. to Choerob. *in Theod.*1.253) *SIG*1037.4 (Milet., iv/iii B.C.); gen. ἱέρεω *IPE*1².32 *A* 23, al. (Olbia, iii B.C.); dat. ἵρεῳ *Schwyzer* 692 (Chios, v B.C.); acc. ἱέρεω *Milet.* 1(7).203*b*3 (ii B.C.): **ἱερῆς** *IG*5(2).115.1 (Tegea, iv/iii B.C.), cf. *Inscr. Cypr.*100 H.:—Arc. **ἱαρῆς** *IG*5(2).13.10 (iii B.C.): acc. ἱερῆν ib.3.1 (Tegea, iv B.C.): (ἱερός):—*priest, sacrificer, diviner*, Il.1.62, 16.604, Pi.*P.*2.17, Hdt.2.2, And.1.124, etc.; ἐφ' ἱερέως, as a date, *SIG*332.1 (Potidaea, iv/iii B.C.), etc. (freq. unaspirated, ἐπ' ἰερέως *IG*12(1). 890, etc. (Rhodes)); of the Jewish High Priest, D.S.34/5.1; ἱ. ὁ μέγας Lxx *Le.*21.10, Ph.2.591; ἱ. ὁ χριστός Lxx *Le.*4.5; at Rome, = *pontifex*, *Mon.Anc.Gr.*6.9; ἱ. ὁ μέγιστος, = *pont. maximus*, D.S.27. 2. 2. metaph., ἱ. τις ἄτας *a minister* of woe, A.*Ag.*735 (lyr.); comically, λεπτοτάτων λήρων ἱερεῦ Ar.*Nu.*359; ἱ. Διονύσου, of a wine-bibber, Eup.19; ἱ. φιλοσοφίας Lib.*Or.*52.42. **-εύσιμος**, ον, *fit for sacrifice*, Plu.2.729d. **-ευσις**, εως, ἡ, *slaying, sacrificing*, Sch.E.*Hec.* 224. **-ευτικός**, ή, όν, *belonging to a* ἱερόν, [γῆ] *PTeb.*5.236 (ii B.C.): -κά, τά, ib.257. * **-εύω**, Ion. **ἱρεύω** Od.14.94, al.; Ion. impf. ἱρεύεσκον 20.3: 3 sg. plpf. Pass. ἱέρευτο Il.24.125: (ἱερός):—*sacrifice*, βοῦς.. ἧνις ἠκέστας ἱερευσέμεν 6.94; ταύρους [ποταμῷ] 21.131; τοῖσι δὲ βοῦν ἱέρευσε.. Ζηνί Od.13.24, etc.: abs., *offer sacrifice*, τῇ θεῷ Ant. Lib.20.2. 2. *slaughter* for a feast, βοῦς ἱερεύοντες.. εἰλαπινάζουσιν Od.2.56; ἄξεθ' ὑῶν τὸν ἄριστον, ἵνα ξείνῳ ἱερεύσω 14.414, cf. 8.59; also δεῖπνον δ' αἶψα συῶν ἱερεύσατε ὅς τις ἄριστος 24.215:—Med., βοῦς ἱρεύσασθαι oxen *to slaughter for themselves*, 19.198; μῆλα A.R.2. 302. 3. *consecrate, devote* to a god, ἱερευομένη παρθένος Paus.3.18. 4. 4. *sacrifice*, i.e. *slay*, Ph.2.34, Procop.*Goth.*2.25.

**ἱερεωσύνη**, v. ἱερωσύνη.

**ἱερή**, ἡ, = ἱέρεια, *AP*7.733 (Diotim., nisi leg. ἱερῆ): Att. **ἱερά** Pl. ap.*AB*100.

**ἱερήϊον**, τό, Ion. for ἱερεῖον, Hom.

**ἱερηΐς**, ΐδος, ἡ, poet. for ἱέρεια, *IG*7.113 (Megara).

**ἱερής**, v. ἱερεύς. **ἱερητεία, ἱερητεύω**, Ion. for ἱερᾱτ-. **ἱερία**, Ion. -ίη, v. ἱέρεια.

**ἱερ-ίζω**, *consecrate, purify*, Hsch. s. v. ἁγνίτης. **-ίς**, ίδος, ἡ, = ἱέρεια, *priestess*, dub. in Plu.2.435b. **-ισμός**, ὁ, *sacred service*, εἰς -ισμόν *Inscr.Délos* 338 *Aa* 19 (iii B.C.), *BCH*6.23 (Delos, ii B.C.). * **-ισσα**, ἡ, = ἱέρεια, *PStrassb.*84.14 (ii B.C.), *BGU*994 ii 8, *PLond.*3.880.7 (ii B.C.), *CIG*4009*b* (Iconium). **-ιστής**, οῦ, ὁ, *one who presides at* σπονδαί, *IG*11(2).145 (iv B.C.), 161 *A* 88 (iii B.C.), cf. Hsch. s. v. ἀγνίτης (prob.). **-ῑτεύω**, *serve as priest*, τᾷ Δάματρι *IG* 5(2).266 (Mantinea, i B.C.): Dor. **ἱᾰριτεύω** *GDI*5117 (Crete, iv/iii B.C.), 4841 (Cyrene): pf. part. ἱαριτευωκότες *Abh.Berl.Akad.*1925 (5).7 (ibid.): later **ἱερειτεύω** *GDI*4842 (ibid.). **-ῖτις**, ιδος, ἡ, = ἱκέτις, A.*Fr.*93 ap.Hsch. (-είτην cod., cf. Theognost.*Can.*45).

**ἱερο-βόαι**, οἱ, dub. l. in Hsch. s. v. ἄφετοι. **-βοτάνη** [ᾰ], ἡ, = ἱερὰ βοτάνη (cf. βοτάνη), Isid.*Etym.*17.9.55.

**ἱερογλῠφ-έω**, *represent hieroglyphically*, ζῴδια Eust.632.52; ὀρίγανον Horap.2.34. **-ικός**, ή, όν, *hieroglyphic*: ἱερογλυφικά, with or without γράμματα, τά, D.S.3.4, Plu.2.354f, Ps.-Luc.*Philopatr.*21, Dam.*Isid.*98, etc. Adv. -κῶς *PMag.Leid.V.*8.29: -ιστί, *in hieroglyphic characters*, *PMag.Leid.W.*2.37, al. **-ος**, ὁ, *carver of hieroglyphics*, *UPZ*81 iv 2 (ii B.C.), *POxy.*1029 (ii A.D.), *Sammelb.*3570 (Fayûm), Ptol.*Tetr.*180.

**ἱερο-γλωσσόκομον**, Dor. **ἱᾰρο-**, τό, *sacred deed-box*, *Hermes* 64.64 (Epid., ii A.D.). **-γλωσσος**, ον, *of prophetic tongue*, Epigr.ap.Paus.6. 17.6: -γλωσσον, τό, *sacred formula*, *PMag.Berol.*2.69. **-γραμμᾰτεύς**, έως, ὁ, *sacred scribe*, a lower order of the Egyptian priesthood, Eudox. *Ars* 3.21, *OGI*56.4 (Canopus, iii B.C.), 90.7 (Rosetta, ii B.C.), Luc. *Macr.*4, J.*Ap.*1.32, al., Herasap.Gal.13.776, Aët.15.13, etc. **-γρᾰφικός**, ή, όν, γράμματα *sacred* signs, Man.Hist.p.512 M. **-δακρυς**, υ, gen. υος, epith. of λίβανος, *with hallowed tears* or *gum*, Melanipp. 1. **-δῐδάσκᾰλος**, ὁ, *teacher of holy things* at Rome, = *pontifex*, D.H. 2.73 (pl.). **-δόκος**, ον, *receiving sacrifices*, or **ἱερόδοκος**, *received in temples*, A.*Supp.*363 (lyr., dub. l.). **-δουλεία**, ἡ, *company of* ἱερόδουλοι, *IG*14.914 (Ostia):—also **-δουλία**, ib.1024 (Rome). **-δουλος**, ὁ, ἡ, *temple-slave*, *PCair.Zen.*451 (iii B.C.), *PHib.*1.35.3 (iii B.C.), *UPZ*34.13 (ii B.C.), *PTeb.*6.25 (ii B.C.), *SIG*996.29 (Smyrna), *BMus. Inscr.*986.4 (Cyprus), *OGI*383.174 (Nemrud Dagh, i B.C.), etc.; νεωκόροι καὶ ἱ. Ph.2.420; of the Nethinim, Lxx 1*Es.*1.2, al.; esp. of *temple-courtesans* at Corinth and elsewhere, Str.8.6.20, 6.2.6; also of men, Id.11.4.7, al. **-δρομος**, ον, *flowing in a sacred stream*, ὕδωρ *Epigr. Gr.*835ᵇ4 (Berytus): poet. **ἱρό-**, *running in sacred races*, Philox. 15. **-εργός**, όν, v. ἱερουργός. * **-θαλλής**, ές, *blooming holily*, Orph. *H.*40.17 (Herm. -θηλής). **-θέσιον**, τό, *monument, mausoleum*, *OGI*383.36 (Nemrud Dagh), 403.1 (Kara Kush, i B.C.). **-θετέω**, *ordain sacred rites*, f.l. in *EM*468.57. **-θήκη**, ἡ, *depository for holy things, sanctuary*, *Gloss.* **-θρησκεία**, ἡ, *divine worship*, Edict. Maximini ap.Eus.*HE*9.7. **-θροος**, contr. -θρους, ουν, *of mystic sound*, *Mim.Oxy.*413.90. **-θύσιον** [ῠ], τό, *place of sacrifice*, Paus.4. 32.1. **-θῠτεῖον**, τό, = foreg., *IG*12(1).847 (Rhodes), 1033 (Carpathos). **-θῠτέω**, *sacrifice*, βοῦς Heraclit.*Incred.*39, cf. Ἀρχ.Ἐφ. 1911.59, *IG*14.290 (Segesta), 12(1).67 (Rhodes): Arc. pres. part. nom. sg. masc. ἱεροθυτές ib.5(2).3.7 (Tegea, iv B.C.). * **-θύτης** [ῠ], ου, Dor., etc. **-τᾱς**, α, ὁ, *sacrificing priest*, *IG*5(2).3.5 (Tegea, iv B.C.), *SIG*492.5 (Euboea, iii B.C.), Paus.8.42.12, cj. in Theopomp. Hist.76: as title of magistrate, *IG*14.952 (Agrigentum): pl., ib. 12(3).1270 (Syme). * **-θῠτος**, ον, *devoted, offered to a god*, καπνός smoke *from the sacrifices*, Ar.*Av.*1265; θάνατος death *as a sacrifice for one's country* or *any holy cause*, Pi.*Fr.*78; ὑποδήματα δερμάτινα ἱ. *IG*5(1).1390.23 (Andania, i B.C.); οἷς ἱ. *SIG*624.43 (ii B.C.): **-θυτα**, τά, *sacrifices*, Theopomp.Hist.76 (s.v.l.), Arist.*Oec.*1349ᵇ13, Plu.2. 729c; of meats *offered to idols*, 1*Ep.Cor.*10.28. **-καυτέω**, *sacrifice as a burnt-offering*, Phryn.*PS*p.88 B.:—Pass., *to be burnt as a sacrifice*, D.S.20.65. * **-κηρῡκεύω**, *to be a* ἱεροκῆρυξ, Aristeas 184, *SIG*444.6 (Delph., iii B.C.): **-κηρῡκέω**, *IGRom.*3.711 (Lycia, iii A.D.). * **-κῆρυξ**, ῡκος, ὁ, *herald* or *attendant at a sacrifice*, D.59.78, Herm.Hist.2, prob. in *IG*1².6.89, cf. *Supp.Epigr.*2.258.23 (Delph., iii B.C.), *SIG*577.33 (Milet., iii/ii B.C.), *OGI*332.43 (Elaea, ii B.C.), etc.: Dor. **-κᾶρυξ** *IG*12(1).155.31 (Rhodes, ii B.C.). **-κόμος**, ὁ, *one who takes charge of a temple*, ib.14.621 (Rhegium). **-κορᾰκικά**, τά, *symbols of the* κόρακες, in the cult of Mithras (cf. κόραξ), *CIL*6.751*b* (iv A.D.). **-κτίστης**, ου, ὁ, *founder of a sanctuary*, *Cat. Cod.Astr.*8(4).165. **-κτίστος**, ον, *established as a sanctuary*, πέτρα, of Delphi, Aristonous 1.1.

**ἱερόλας**, ὁ, = ἱερεύς, S.*Fr.*57 (dub.; for the termination cf. μαινόλης).

**ἱερό-ληπτος**, ον, *inspired*, Man.4.227. **-λογέω**, Ion. **ἱρολ-**, *recount a* ἱερὸς λόγος, Luc.*Syr.D.*26; *prophesy*, *EM*468.14. **-λογία**, Ion. **ἱρολογίη**, ἡ, *mystical language*, Luc.*Astr.*10. **-λόγοι**, οἱ, *authors of* ἱεροὶ λόγοι, Dam.*Pr.*38. * **-μαντις**, εως, ὁ, *holy seer*, *Cat.Cod.Astr.*8(4).148. **-μας**· τῶν ἱερῶν ἐπιμελούμενος, Hsch.; uncontr. **ἱαρόμαορ** *Schwyzer* 414, cf. 411 (Elis). **-μηνία**, ἡ, (μήν) *sacred month*, during which the great festivals were held and hostilities suspended, ἱ. Νεμεάς, of the Nemean games, Pi.*N.*3.2; ἱ. ἁ Πυθιάς *IG*2².1126.44 (Amphict.); ἐν σπονδαῖς καὶ προσέτι ἱερομηνίᾳ Th.3. 56; ἐν σπονδαῖς καὶ ἱερομηνίαις ib.65 (s.v.l.); ἱ. ἄγειν D.24.29: in pl., *sacrifices offered during the sacred month*, *IG*11(2).154.11 (Delos, iii B.C.); = Lat. *supplicatio*, App.*BC*5.130: pl., D.C.39.53 (-μήνια, τά, of the Κάρνεια (q.v.), is prob. f.l. in Th.5.54). **-μηνιακός**, ή, όν, *of the* ἱ., ἡμέραι *Inscr.Mus.Alex.*47 (i A.D.).

* **ἱερο-μνημονέω**, Dor. **-μνᾱμονέω**, *to be* ἱερομνήμων, Ar.*Nu.*624, Plb. 4.52.4, *SIG*545.2 (Delph., iii B.C.), etc. **-μνημονικός**, Dor. **-μνᾱμ-**, ή, όν, *of a* ἱ., ψᾶφος ib.554.21 (Thermon, iii B.C.). **-μνημοσύνη**, Dor. **-μνᾱμοσύνα**, ἡ, *right to appoint a* ἱερομνήμων, *Klio* 16.162, 163 (ii B.C.). * **-μνήμων**, Dor., Arc. **-μνάμων** [ᾱ], ονος, ὁ, *mindful of sacred*

*things*, ὅρκων Alciphr.2.4. **II.** as Subst., **1.** *representative sent by each Amphictyonic state* to the Delphic Council, D.18.148, Jusj.ap. eund.24.150, *IG*2$^2$.1126.10, 1299.80, etc.; also at the Amphictyony of Calauria, ib.4.842 (ii B.C.). **2.** *magistrate who had charge of temples* or *religious matters*, ib.4.823 (Troezen, iv B.C.), 5(2).3.22,26 (Tegea), 14.423.3 (Tauromenium), Decr.Byz.ap.D.18.90, etc. **b.** at Rome, = *pontifex*, D.H.8.55, 10.57, Str.5.3.2. **3.** generally, *recorder, registrar*, Arist.*Pol.*1321$^b$38. ✱**-μοσχοσφρᾱγιστής**, οῦ, ὁ, *sealer of sacred calves* for sacrifice, *PGen.*32.4 (ii A.D.). **-μυρτος**, ἡ, = μυρσίνη ἀγρία, Ps.-Dsc.4.144. **-μύστης**, ου, ὁ, *one who initiates in sacred things*, Phot., Suid.

**ἱερόν**, τό, v. ἱερός III. 2.

✱**ἱερο-νίκης** [νῑ], ου, ὁ, *conqueror in the games*, *OGI*332.34 (Elaea, ii B.C.), *SIG*1073.4 (Olymp., ii A.D., in form -νείκης), Phld.*Mus.* p.105 K., Luc.*Hist.Conscr.*30, etc.: Dor. **-νίκας** *IG*5(1).668 (Laconia). **-νομέω**, *to be a* ἱερονόμος, *SIG*982.2 (Pergam.), 1219.1 (Gambreum, iii B.C.). ✱**-νόμοι**, οἱ, *temple-wardens*, ib.982.23, *IGRom.*4.461 (Pergam., sg.), *OGI*219.20 (Sigeum, iii B.C.); of the *pontifices* at Rome, D.H.2.73. **-νουμηνία**, ἡ, *feast of the new moon*, coined by Sch.Pi.*N.*3.1. **-όστεον**, τό, = ἱερὸν ὀστοῦν, prob. in *PMag. Lond.*121.212. **-παρέκτης**, ου, ὁ, (παρέχω) *priest's attendant*, *IG*14.617,621 (Rhegium). **-πλοκος**, ον, *religious*, *Cat.Cod.Astr.*8(4).212 (s.v.l.).

**ἱεροποι-έω**, *serve as* ἱεροποιός, -ποιῶν καὶ θύων ὑπὲρ τῆς δημοκρατίας Antipho 6.45, cf. Pl.*Ly.*207d, *IG*11(2).144*A* (Delos, iv B.C.); τῇ Ἀθηνᾷ ib.2$^2$.1257 (iv B.C.); τῷ Ἀπόλλωνι *SIG*1037.6 (Milet., iv/iii B.C.), etc.: c. acc., ἱ. εἰσιτητήρια ὑπὲρ τῆς βουλῆς D.21.114; οἱ τὰ μυστήρια -ποιήσαντες *IG*2.872; ἱ. τὰ Ἀπολλώνια *BCH*36.413 (Delos, ii B.C.). **II.** *deify*, Aristid.1.191 J. **-ημα**, ατος, τό, *sacrifice*, *Jahresh.*23 *Beibl.* 27, 28 (Maeonia, iii A.D.). **-ία**, ἡ, *sacred service, festival*, Aen. Tact.17.1 (pl.), *BSA*24.154 (Halimus, iv B.C., pl.); αἱ εἰς τὸν θεὸν ἱ. Decr.Halic.ap.J.*AJ*14.10.23, cf. Arist.*Rh.Al.*1423$^b$13 (pl.), Str.5.2.9, Porph.*Abst.*2.18; ἱερεὺς πεντεκαιδέκανδρος ἐπὶ τῶν -ποιῶν, = *XVvir sacris faciundis*, *IGRom.*3.172 (Ancyra). **-ον** (for -ποίιον), τό, *office of* ἱεροποιοί, *IG*11(2).144*A* 104 (Delos, iv B.C.); **-ποίϊον** *Inscr. Délos* 316.69 (iii B.C.). **-ός**, ὁ, (ποιέω) *overseer of temples and sacred rites*, title of magistrates at Athens and elsewhere, *IG*1$^2$.5, al., D.4.26, Arist.*Pol.*1322$^b$24, *Ath.*54.6, Decr.ib.30.2, *IG*12(8).264 (Thasos, iv B.C.), *SIG*410 (Erythrae, iii B.C.), *Inscr.Prien.*14.25 (iii B.C.), etc.; ἱεροποιοὶ τῶν σεμνῶν θεῶν were different, D.21.115, Din.*Fr.*8.1. **II.** *sacrificer*, D.H.1.40. **2.** as Adj., ἱ. νεανίσκος, παρθένοι, ib.80, 9.40.

**ἱερό-πολις**, εως, ἡ, *holy city*, Ph.2.146; of the cities of refuge, ib. 308,321. **-πομπός**, ὁ, *one who conveys the sacred tribute*, ib.224, 578. **-πρακτος**, ὁ, = ἱεροποιός, *Cat.Cod.Astr.*8(4).138 (s.v.l., fort. **-πράκτωρ**). ✱**-πρεπής**, ές, *beseeming a sacred place, person* or *matter*, ὄνομα Pl.*Thg.*122e; τέχνη, of cookery, Men.130; κνῖσα Luc. *Sacr.*13; of persons, -έστατος τῶν προγεγενημένων X.*Smp.*8.40, cf. D.C.56.46, Lxx 4*Ma.*9.25, *Ep.Tit.*2.3. Adv. -πῶς *Michel* 163.21 (Delos, ii B.C.), *Inscr.Prien.*109.216 (ii B.C.), Str.12.5.3, Beros.ap.J. *Ap.*1.19. ✱**-πρόσπολος**, ὁ, *sacred attendant, priest*, Ptol.*Tetr.*159.

✱**ἱερόπτης**, ου, ὁ, = Lat. *haruspex*, D.C.52.36, 64.5.

✱**ἱερός** (v. sub fin.), ά, όν, also ός, όν in the phrase ἱερὸς ἀκτή Hes. *Op.*597, 805, Orac.ap.Hdt.8.77: Ion. and poet. **ἱρός**, ή, όν (v. sub fin.): Dor. and N. Greek **ἱᾰρός** *IG*2$^2$.1126.20, etc.: Aeol. **ἶρος** Sapph.*Supp.*23.25, Alc.*Supp.*8.4, but **ἴαρος** (corr. from ἴερ-) Sapph. *Supp.*20a.6: Sup. ἱερώτατος Ar.*Eq.*582 (lyr.), Pl.*Lg.*755e. **I.** *filled with* or *manifesting divine power, supernatural*, ἱ. ἲς Τηλεμάχοιο Od.2.409, al.; ἱ. μένος Ἀλκινόοιο 8.421, etc.; ἄλφιτον, ἀλωαί, Il.11.631, 5.499; Δημήτερος ἱερὸς ἀκτή Hes.*Op.* ll.cc.; of natural objects or phenomena, rivers, Od.10.351, Il.11.726, E.*Med.*410 (lyr.); λιβάς, of the Spercheus, S.*Ph.*1215 (lyr.); ἱεραὶ βῆσσαι Κίρκης 'faery', Od.10.275; ἱ. ἦμαρ, κνέφας, Il.8.66, 11.194; φάος Hes.*Op.* 339; ἱερὸς δίφρος (where δ. perh. = ἵπποι) Il.17.464; after Hom., ἱ. χεῦμα θαλάσσης A.*Fr.*192 (anap.); ἱ. κῦμα E.*Hipp.*1206, cf. *Cyc.* 265; ὄμβρος S.*OT*1428; δρόσοι E.*Ion*117 (lyr.); ὕπνος, of death, Call.*Ep.*11; ἔστι μὲν οὐδὲν ἱ. no *great* matter, Theoc.5.22. **II.** of divine things, *holy*, ἱεροῖς ἐν δώμασι Κίρκης Od.10.426; ἱ. γένος ἀθανάτων Hes *Th.*21; λέχος, of Zeus, ib.57; δόσις the gift *of God*, ib. 93; πόλεμος *holy* war, '*crusade*', Ar.*Av.*556, etc. **2.** of earthly things, *hallowed, consecrated*, βωμοί Il.2.305; ἱ. δόμος, of the temple of Athena, 6.89; ἱ. ἑκατόμβη 1.99, 431, etc.; ἐλαίη Od.13.372; χοαί S.*OC*469, etc.; ἱρὰ γράμματα *hieroglyphics*, Hdt.2.36; but ἱ. γράμματα of the *Holy* Scriptures, 2*Ep.Tim.*3.15; ἱ. βύβλοι *OGI*56.70 (Canopus, iii B.C.); ἱ. ἄγαλμα, τρίπους, S.*OT*1379, E.*Ion*512, etc.; χρήματα Pl.*R.*568d, etc.; ἱ. τὸ σῶμα τῷ θεῷ δίδωμ' ἔχειν E.*Ion* 1285; ἱ. σώματα, of ἱερόδουλοι, Str.6.2.6; χῆνες Plu.2.325c; of animals regarded as 'taboo', [κριοί] εἰσί σφι ἱ. διὰ τοῦτο Hdt.2.42; so perh. ἱ. ἰχθύς Il.16.407; of the Roman Tribunes, = Lat. *sacrosanctus*, ἱ. καὶ ἄσυλος Plu.*TG*15, etc.; of Augustus, *Mon.Anc.Gr.* 5.17; ἱ. νόμος law *of sacrifice*, D.21.35, cf. *SIG*685.81 (ii B.C.); ἱ. λόγος *legend*, Hdt.2.81, etc.; οἱ παλαιοὶ καὶ ἱ. λόγοι Pl.*Ep.*335a; ἱ. γάμος *mystical* marriage, a religious ceremony, Men.320, Phot. s.v.; opp. βέβηλος, as *sacred* to *profane*, D.H.7.8, *AB*223; but more freq. ἱ. καὶ ὅσιος Th.2.52, X.*Vect.*5.4, etc.; cf. ὅσιος. **3.** *under divine protection*, freq. of places, Ἴλιος Il.5.648, Alc.*Supp.*8.4; Πύλος Od. 21.108; Θήβη Sapph.*Supp.*20a.6; Τροίης ἱερὸν πτολίεθρον, Τροίης ἱερὰ κρήδεμνα, Od.1.2, Il.16.100; Ἀθῆναι Od.11.323, cf. Pi.*Fr.*75, S. *Aj.*1221 (lyr.), Ps.-Orac.ap.Ar.*Eq.*1037; Σούνιον ἱρόν Od.3.278; ἱ. κύκλος the judge's seat *under the protection of Zeus*, Il.18.504: with gen. of the divinity, ἄλσος ἱρὸν Ἀθηναίης, ἄντρον ἱρὸν νυμφάων, Od.6. 322, 13.104, cf. Hdt.1.80, 2.41, Ar.*Pl.*937, X.*An.*5.3.13, etc.; γῆ καὶ ἑστία ἱερὰ πᾶσι πάντων θεῶν Pl.*Lg.*955e; χωρίον ὡς -ώτατον ib.755e, cf. *Ti.*45a; with gen. of a human being, Γναθίου . . ἱ. εἰμι *IG*1$^2$.920. **b.** of persons, φυλάκων ἱ. τέλος Il.10.56; ἱ. πυλαωροί 24.681; στρατός Od.24.81; βασιλέες Pi.*P.*5.97; ἱ. εὐσεβής τε, of Oedipus, S.*OC*287; ἄνθρωπος ἱ. *initiated*, Ar.*Ra.*652; c. gen. of a divinity, *devoted, dedicated*, E.*Alc.*75, Pl.*Phd.*85b. **c.** under the Roman Empire, = *sacer, Imperial*, ἐκ τῶν ἱερῶν τοῦ Καίσαρος γραμμάτων *IGRom.*4.571 (Aezani, ii A.D.); ὁ -ώτατος φίσκος, τὸ -ώτατον ταμιεῖον, ib.3.727 (Lycia), *SIG*888.10 (Scaptopara, iii A.D.), etc.; τὸ -ώτατον βῆμα (of the *praefectus Aegypti*), *PHamb.*4.8 (i A.D.): generally, *worshipful*, ἱ. σύνοδος *OGI*713.9 (Egypt, iii A.D.), etc. **III.** as Subst., **1.** **ἱερά**, Ion. **ἱρά**, τά, *offerings, victims*, ἱερὰ ῥέξας Il.1.147, etc.; ἔρδειν Hes.*Op.*336; διδόναι Od.16.184; ἀλλ' ὅ γε δέκτο μὲν ἱρά Il.2.420, cf. 23.207: less freq. in sg., ὄφρ' ἱρὸν ἑτοιμασσαίατ' Ἀθήνῃ 10.571; θῦσαι ἱρά Hdt.1.59, 8.54, etc.; θυσίας καὶ ἱρὰ ποιέειν Id.2.63; αἴθειν S. *Ph.*1033; ἱ. πατρῷα A.*Th.*1015; ἱ. ἐπιχώρια Democr.259. **b.** after Hom., *omens afforded by sacrifice*, τὰ ἱρὰ οὐ προεχώρεε χρηστά Hdt. 5.44; τὰ ἱερὰ καλὰ [ἦν] X.*An.*1.8.15; simply οὐκ ἐγίγνετο τὰ ἱ. ib. 2.2.3. **c.** generally, *sacred objects* or *rites*, Hdt.1.172, 4.33; τῶν ὑμετέρων ἱ. καὶ κοινῶν μετεῖχον D.57.3; of *cult-images*, *IGRom.*3.800 (Syllium). **2.** after Hom., **ἱερόν**, Ion. **ἱρόν**, τό, *holy place*, Hdt.5. 119, al.; opp. νηός, Id.2.170, cf. Th.4.90, 5.18; freq. of a *temple*, ἔστι δὲ ἐν τῷ τεμένεϊ . . ἱρόν κτλ. Hdt.2.112; of the Jewish temple, Lxx 1*Ch.*29.4, Plb.16.39.4, Str.16.2.34, *Ev.Matt.*24.1. **3.** ἱερὸν τῆς δίκης *a sacred principle* of right, E.*Hel.*1002. **4.** **ἱερός**, ὁ (sc. μήν), name of month at Delos, *IG*1$^2$.377.22, 11(2).203*A* 31 (iii B.C.). **5.** **ἱεροί**, οἱ, members of a religious college or guild, ib.5(1).1390.1, al. (Andania, i B.C.), prob. in *SIG*1010.7 (Chalcedon), etc.; also of women, **ἱεραί**, αἱ, *IG*5(1). l.c., cf. 1511 (Sparta). **b.** = ἱερόδουλος, ib. 1356 (Messenia, v B.C.), *Inscr.Perg.*572, *GDI*5702.39 (Samos). **IV.** special phrases, post-Hom., **1.** prov., ἱ. ἄγκυρα *one's last hope*, Plu. 2.815d, Luc.*JTr.*51, *Fug.*13, Poll.1.93, Gal.11.182. **2.** ἱ. βόλος, name of a throw at dice, Eub.57.1. **3.** ἱ. βοτάνη, v. βοτάνη. **4.** ἱ. (sc. γραμμή) (cf. γραμμή III. 1), *last line* of draught-board, κινήσαις τὸν ἀπ' ἴρας . . λίθον Alc.82, cf. Epich.225, Sophr.127; τὴν ἀφ' ἱερᾶς (v.l. τὴν ἱεράν) Plu.*Cor.*32. **5.** ἱ. ἰχθύς, = ἀνθίας, Arist.*HA* 620$^b$35, cf. Ath.7.282e, Plu.2.981d. **6.** ἱ. λόχος, v. λόχος. **7.** ἱερά (sc. νίκη), ἡ, *drawn contest, dead heat* (because the prize was assigned to the god), *SIG*1073.48 (Olymp.); ποιῆσαι ἱεράν, of the competitor, Wood *Ephesus*, *App.* vi p.70; so ἱ. ἀθλήματα *Inscr. Olymp.*56; ἱερὸς ὁ στέφανος ἐκρίθη *IG*9(2).525 (Larissa); τὸ παγκράτιον ἱ. ἐγένετο ib.527 (ibid.); ἱερός (sc. ἀγών) ib.7.2727.19, 24 (Acraeph.): metaph., ἱερὸν ποιῆσαι τὸν στέφανον 'divide the honours', Plb.1.58.5, 29.8.9. **8.** ἱ. νόσος *epilepsy*, Hdt.3.33, Hp.*Morb. Sacr.* tit., Thphr.*HP*9.11.3, etc., cf. Call.*Aet.*3.1.14: metaph., τὴν οἴησιν ἱ. νόσον ἔλεγε Heraclit.46 (= Epicur.*Fr.*224). **9.** ἡ ἱ. ὁδός *the sacred* road to Delphi, Hdt.6.34; also, from Athens to Eleusis, Cratin. 61, Paus.1.36.3, Harp. s.v.; and that from Elis to Olympia, Paus. 5.25.7. **10.** ἱ. ὀστέον, *os sacrum*, the last bone of the spine, Hp. *Art.*45, Plu.2.981d, Gal.*UP*5.8, etc. **11.** ἱ. συμβουλή *sacred duty of an adviser*, Pl.*Ep.*321c, X.*An.*5.6.4, cf. Pl.*Thg.*122b, Luc.*Rh.Pr.* 1. **12.** ἱ. σῦριγξ *spinal canal*, Poll.2.180. **13.** ἱερὰ τριήρης, of the Delian ship, or one of the state-ships (Salaminia or Paralos), D.4. 34. **14.** freq. in geographical names, e.g. ἱ. ἄκρα, in Lycia, Str. 14.3.8; ἱ. ἀκρωτήριον, in Spain, *Cape St. Vincent*, Id.2.4.3; ἱ. κώμη, in Lydia, Plb.16.1.8; ἱ. νῆσος, one of the Liparean group, Th.3.88; one of the *insulae Aegates*, Plb.1.60.3. **V.** Adv. -ρῶς *holily*, ἀποθανεῖν v.l. in Plu.*Lyc.*27. [ῐ by nature, but sts. ῑ in Ep., esp. in endings of hexameters, ἱ. ἰχθύς, ἱ. ἦμαρ, ἱερὰ ῥέξας, ἀλφίτου ἱεροῦ ἀκτή, Il.16.407, 8.66, 1.147, 11.631; ῑερόν in the first foot of a hex., Theoc.5.22; also in compds. ἱεραγωγός, ἱεροθαλλής, ἱερόφωνος: ῑ always in contr. form ἱρός wh. is used in Ep., Hdt., and some Ion. Inscrr., as *IG*12(8).265.9 (Thasos), cf. Semon.7.56, Herod.4.79, al., but is rarely found in codd. of Hp. (never in Heraclit. or Democr.); also in Trag., A.*Th.*268, etc., but never required by metre in lyr. of Com.]

✱**ἱερο-σαλπικτής**, οῦ, ὁ, *trumpeter at a sacrifice*, Poll.4.87 (v.l. **-ιγκτής**), *CIG*1969 (Thessalonica), 2983 (Ephesus): **-ιστής** *IG*14. 617 (Rhegium). **-σέβαστος** (sc. μήν), ὁ, name of month in Ionian calendar, *Hemerolog.Flor.* ✱**-σκοπέομαι**, *inspect victims, divine therefrom*, Plb.34.2.6; ἱ. μόσχῳ *divine by* the entrails of a calf, D.S. 1.70. **-σκοπία**, ἡ, *divination by inspection of victims*, ib.73, Iamb. *VP*19.93: Ion. **-ίη** Hp.*Acut.*8, Dio ap.Orph.*Fr.*219. ✱**-σκόπος**, ον, *inspecting victims*, Θέμις ἱ. ἀνδρῶν Orph.Εὐχή 23, cf. Porph.*Abst.* 2.50. **II.** = Lat. *haruspex*, D.H.2.22, D.S.32.12. **III.** dub.l. in *Cat.Cod.Astr.*8(4).145 (fort. -σκώπτης). **-στάτης** [ᾰ], ου, ὁ, *governor of the temple*, Lxx 1*Es.*7.2.

**ἱερο-στολικά**, τά, *title of poem on sacred vestments*, Suid. s.v. Ὀρφεύς. **-στολιστής**, οῦ, ὁ, = sq., Chaerem.ap.Porph.*Abst.*4.8, *Sammelb.*5553. **-στολος**, ὁ, an Egyptian priest *who had charge of the sacred vestments*, = στολιστής, Plu.2.352b.

**ἱεροσῡλ-έω**, pf. ἱεροσύληκα *SIG*417.8 (Delph., iii B.C.):—*rob a temple, commit sacrilege*, Ar.*V.*845, Antipho 5.10, Pl.*R.*575b. **II.** c. acc., ἱ. τὰ ὅπλα *steal the sacred* arms, D.57.64, cf. Lycurg.136; ἱ. τὰ ἱερά *rob* or *plunder* the temples, Plb.30.26.9; θεούς Phalar.*Ep.* 84.1. **-ημα**, ατος, τό, *sacrilegious plunder*, Lxx 2*Ma.*4.39; *sacrilege*, Hsch. **-ησις**, εως, ἡ, *temple-robbery, sacrilege*, f.l. in D.S.

16.14. ⊛-ία, ἡ, = foreg., X.*Ap.*25, *SIG*1017.18 (Sinope, iii B.C.), etc.: pl., Pl.*R.*443a. ⊛ -ος, ὁ, (proparox.) *temple-robber*, or generally, *sacrilegious person*, Ar.*Pl.*30, Lys.30.21, Pl.*R.*344b, Men.*Epit.* 560, etc.: fem., ib.504; ἱερόσυλε γραῦ ib.524: neut. as Adj., ἱ. θηρία Id.*Pk.*176. II. of things, *got by sacrilege*. παροψίδες Eub.7.4.

**ἱερο-τᾰμίας**, ου, ὁ, *temple-treasurer*, *IG*9(1).32.25 (Stiris), 12 (1).890 (Rhodes): pl., *Chron.Lind.*A.8, *Supp.Epigr.*2.828 (Damascus). ⊛ **-τᾰμιεύω**, *to be temple-treasurer*, *SIG*804.16 (Cos, i A.D.). **-τέκτων**, ονος, ὁ, *temple-carpenter*, *POxy.*579 (ii A.D.), *Sammelb.*789 (iii A.D.), *Cat.Cod.Astr.*8(4).165. **-τελεστία**, ἡ, *solemnization of sacred rites*, interpol. in Suid. s. v. ἁγίασμα. **-τεύκτης**, ου, ὁ, *temple-builder*, Vett.Val.4.11. **-τροχος**, ον, ἅρμα ἱ. *sacred* car, Orph.*H.*14.2. **-υλίζω**, of wine, τὸν παλαιὸν καὶ ἱερουλίζοντα dub. sens. in Alex.Trall.10.

⊛**ἱερουργ-έω**, *perform sacred rites*, *IG*1².4.4,8, Ph.2.94, etc. II. c. acc., ἱ. τὴν κλίνην, Lat. *lectisternium facere*, *CIG*(add.)4528 (Lebanon); ἱ. ζῷα *sacrifice* them, gloss on σφάξαι, Ammon.*Diff.*p.127 V.; ἱ. τὸ εὐαγγέλιον *minister* the gospel, *Ep.Rom.*15.16; τὸν νόμον v.l. in Lxx 4*Ma.*7.8:—Med., ἱερουργίας ἱερουργεῖσθαι Plu.*Alex.*31:—Pass., τὰ ἱερουργηθέντα *victims offered*, Hdn.5.5.9, cf. Palaeph.51; -ούμεναι τελεταί *celebrated*, Iamb.*VP*3.14; ἱερουργούμενοι βωμοί *consecrated*, Porph.*Marc.*18. **-ημα**, ατος, τό, *sacrifice, offering*, J.*AJ*8.4.5(pl.), Iamb.*VP*28.147 (pl.). **-ία**, ἡ, *religious service, sacrifice*, Hdt.5.83 (in Ion. form ἱρεργίαι, with vv.ll.), Pl.*Lg.*775a, *PTeb.*293.20 (pl., ii A.D.), etc. **-ικός**, ή, όν, *ceremonial*, Iamb.*Myst.*5.14; μάχαιρα Sch.E.*Or.*194. ⊛ **-ός**, ὁ, *sacrificing priest*, Call.*Fr.*450 (in Ep. form ἱεροεργός), Ammon.*Diff.*p.90 V.; ἱερουργοὶ τῆς Ἀθηνᾶς, members of a religious college, *IG*12(7).241.3 (Amorgos, iii B.C.): Dor. ἱερω[ργός] prob. in *Schwyzer*288.91 (Rhodes, iii/ii B.C.).

**ἱεροφαντ-έω**, *to be a* ἱεροφάντης, Luc.*Alex.*39, *SIG*869.19 (Eleusis, ii A.D.). 2. *initiate, instruct in mysteries*, Ph.2.403, al.: c. dat., Id.1.146:—Pass., -ουμένη ψυχή Id.2.187. II. trans., *expound as a hierophant*, τελετάς Heraclit.*All.*64:—Pass., τοὺς ἱεροφαντηθέντας λογισμοὺς θεοῦ *inspired*, Ph.1.194. ⊛ **-ης**, Ion. ἱρ-, ου, ὁ, (φαίνω) *hierophant, one who teaches rites of sacrifice and worship*, ἱ. τῶν χθονίων θεῶν Hdt.7.153; of the *initiating priest* at Eleusis, *IG*1².76.24, al., Lys.6.1, Is.7.9, Plu.*Alc.*33; at Rome, = *pontifex*, D.H.2.73, 3.36; of the *pontifex maximus*, Plu.*Num.*9; of the Jewish High Priest, Ph.2.322; of Moses, Id.1.117; later, *mystical expounder*, ἱ. τῆς τετρακτύος Hierocl.*in CA*20p.466 M. **-ία**, ἡ, *office of hierophant*, Plu.*Alc.*34, Luc.*Alex.*38 (pl.), Theo Sm.p.15 H. ⊛ **-ικός**, ή, όν, *of a hierophant*, στέμμα Luc.*Alex.*60; βίβλοι ἱ., = Lat. *libri pontificales*, Plu.*Num.*22. Adv. -κῶς Luc.*Alex.*39. **-ις** (parox.), ιδος, fem. of -φάντης, *IG*2².1092*B*35, Plu.*Sull.*13, *Cat.Cod.Astr.*1.115, Jul. *Or.*7.221c. ⊛ **-ρια**, ἡ, fem. of ἱεροφάντης, *hierophantria deae Hecatae*, *CIL*6.1780, cf. 1779. **-ωρ**, ορος, ὁ, = ἱεροφάντης, Suid. s.v. Ἰουλιανός.

**ἱερο-φοιτάω**, *visit temples*, Ptol.*Tetr.*158 (-οῦντας codd.). **-φόρος**, v. ἱεραφ-. **-φῠλάκιον** [ᾰ], τό, *treasury for sacred vessels*, D.H.2.70. ⊛**-φύλαξ** [ῠ], poet. ἱρ-, ακος, ὁ, *guardian of a temple*, E.*IT*1027 (cj. Markl.), *IG*14.291 (Segesta). 2. = Lat. *pontifex*, D.H.2.73. ⊛ **-φωνος**, ον, *with sacred voice*: as Subst., prob. *utterer of oracles*, *CIG*4684 (Egypt), *IG*14.914 (Ostia); prob. read for ἠεροφώνων in Il.18.505 by Suid., Phot. (expld. by μεγαλοφώνων); f.l. for ἱμερο- in Alcm.26.1. **-φορέω**, = ἱεροσυλέω, *SIG*530.5 (Achaia, iii B.C.). **-χθων**, poet. ἱρ-, ὁ, ἡ, gen. ονος, *of hallowed soil*, βῶλος *IG*14.1389 ii 27. **-ψάλτης**, ου, ὁ, *singer in the temple*, Lxx 1*Es.*1.15, al., *OGI*737.16 (Egypt, ii B.C.), Antioch.ap.J.*AJ*12.3.3. **-ψῡχος**, ον, *of holy, pious soul*. Lxx 4*Ma.*17.4.

⊛**ἱερ-όω**, Dor. **ἱᾰρ-**, (ἱερός) *consecrate, dedicate*, Pl.*Lg.*771b; [τὰν γᾶν] ἂν Ἀμφικτίονες ἱάρωσαν *IG*2².1126.16 (Amphict.); ἱιαρόντο (= ἱερούντων) Ἀπόλλωνος Ἐχέτο ἄγαλμα *Berl.Sitzb.*1927.8 (Locr., v B.C.); Thess. part. ἱερούντος *Schwyzer*553: pf. Pass. ἱερῶσθαι Th.5.1, *SIG* 1006.4 (Cos, iii B.C.), etc.; ἱερωσύνην ἱερῶσασθαι (v.l. ἱεράσασθαι) *to be consecrated* to a priesthood, Aeschin.1.19:—also **ἱερεόομαι**, τὴν ἱερωσύνην ἀξίως ἱερεώσατο τοῦ θεοῦ *IG*2².1271.13 (iii B.C.); τῷ θεῷ οὗ ἂν ᾖ ἱερειωμένος ib.1183.32 (iv B.C.); Δωρίδος ἱερεωμένης (perh. pres. part. of ἱεράομαι = ἱερωμένης) *IG*2².1561 (iv B.C.). ⊛ **-ωμα**, ατος, τό, *consecrated object, offering*, ἱαρώματα *Supp.Epigr.*1.414.7 (Crete, v/iv B.C., nisi leg. ἀρώματα); ἱαρ[ώ]ματα *IG*4.917 (Epid., iv B.C.), cf. Lxx 2*Ma.*12.40, J.*AJ*1.19.10, Dam.*Isid.*71. II. = σκόλλυς (Lacon.), Hsch. ⊛ **-ωνία**, ἡ, dub. sens. in *PTeb.*119.32 (ii B.C.). **-ώνῠμος**, ον, (ὄνομα) *of hallowed name*, Luc.*Lex.*10. **-ωσις**, εως, ἡ, *consecration*, cj. for ἵδρυσις in D.C.*Fr.*13.3. **-ωστί**, Ion. **ἱρωστί**, Adv. *in holy sort, piously*, Anacr.149. ⊛ **-ωσύνη**, in Att. Inscrr. **ἱερεωσύνη** *IG*2².1235.8, al., also *SIG*²554.22 (Magn. Mae.), *SIG*³1068.22 (Patmos. iii/ii B.C.), *Milet.*7.28, etc.: ἡ:—*priesthood*, Hdt.3.142, etc.; ἱερωσύνης μετασχεῖν D.59.92: in pl., *priestly services, sacrifices*, Sch.Ar.*Pax*923. **-ωσύνιον**, *sacerdotium, sacrimonium*, *Gloss.* **-ώσυνος**, η, ον, in Att. Inscrr. both **ἱερώσ-** *IG*2².1358.15, al. and **ἱερεώσ-** ib.1356, 1361; **ἱερειώσ-** ib.1359:—*priestly*: ἱερώσυνα, τά, *the parts of a victim which were the priest's perquisites*, *IG* ll. cc., cf. *SIG*1038.12 (Eleusis, iv/iii B.C.), Amips.7, Phryn.*PS*p.77 B. **-ωτεία**, **-ωτεύω**, = ἱερατ-, *SIG*1009.12, 1010.3 (Chalcedon), *BCH*44.251 (Boeotia, i B.C.). **-ωτός**, ή, όν, Thess. **ἱαρωτός**, **ἱαρουτός**, *consecrated*, Ἀρχ.Ἐφ.1919.52 (Pharsalus, v/iv B.C.), *IG* 9(2).461 (Crannon).

**ἴεσις**, εως, ἡ, (εἶμι) *going*, coined by Pl.*Cra.*426c (v.l. ἵεσις; fort. ἔσις).

**ἵεσις**, εως, ἡ, (ἵημι) *throwing*, *EM*469.54.

**ἴεσσα**· βαδίζουσα, Hsch. **ἴετταs**· πατέρας, ἢ τοὺς ἀγρίους τράγους (Cret.), Id.

**ἰεῦ**, an ironical exclamation, *whew!* Ar.*V.*1335.

**ἱζαίνω**, = sq., *lodge, settle*, v.l. in Aret.*SD*1.15.

**ἱζάνω**, (ἵζω): I. causal, *make to sit*, ἵζανεν εὐρὺν ἀγῶνα Il.23.258. II. intr., *sit*, ἐν τῷ [κλισίῳ]..ἵζανον Od.24.209, cf. Sapph. 2.3; *settle*, οὔ μοι ἐπ' ὄμμασι νήδυμος ὕπνος ἱζάνει Il.10.92; ἡ δρόσος ἱ. ἐπὶ δόνακας Philostr.*Her.*19.19. 2. of soil, *settle down, subside*, ἐπὶ τὸ κενούμενον Th.2.76.

**ἰζέλα**· ἀγαθῇ τύχῃ (Maced.), Hsch.: **ἰζέλος**· ὁ θαλάττιος σκορπίος, Id.

**ἵζημα**, ατος, τό, *subsidence, sinking*, ἰσθμὸς ἵ. λαμβάνει Str.1.3.17, cf. 2.3.6, Plu.2.434c (pl.): metaph., of language, ὕψη ἱζήματα μηδαμοῦ λαμβάνοντα Longin.9.13.

**ἱζημᾰτίας** (sc. σεισμός), ου, ὁ, earthquake *which causes subsidence*, Lyd.*Ost.*53; v.l. for χασματίαι in Arist.*Mu.*396ᵃ4.

**ἰζίνες**· οἰωνοί, ὄρνιθες, προχόοι, λέβητες, τρίποδες, Hsch. **ἰζοῦνα**· βοόστασις, Id.

⊛ **ἵζω**, imper. ἵζε (not ἷζε) Od.24.394, E.*Hec.*145 (anap.): impf. ἷζον Il.20.15, E.*Alc.*946, Ion. ἵζεσκον Od.3.409: aor. εἷσα Il.23.359, Hdt. 3.61, *IG*3.701, *Hymn.Is.*5, etc.; imper. εἷσον Od.7.163 codd.; part. ἕσας 10.361, Cyren. acc. ἕσσαντα (v. infr.); inf. ἕσσαι Pi.*P.*4.273 (the only tenses in Hom.): aor. ἵζησα D.C.50.2, 58.5, etc.: pf. ἵζηκα (ἐν-) Gal.2.691, 15.452, (συν-) Philostr.*Im.*2.20:—**Med.**, v. infr. I and III, and cf. ἕζομαι.—Mostly in Poets and late Prose, the Att. Prose form being καθίζω: (Redupl. *si-sd-ō*, aor. (augmented) *e-sed-s-*, cf. ἕζομαι, ἕδος): I. causal, *make to sit, seat, place, set*, μή μ' ἐς θρόνον ἵζε Il.24.553, cf. Hdt.3.61; βουλὴν ἷζε Il.2.53; ἵζει μάντιν ἐν θρόνοις A.*Eu.*18; ὅς μ' ἐπὶ βουσὶν εἷσ' *set* me over the oxen, Od.20.210; σκοπὸν εἷσε *set* as a spy, Il.23.359; λόχον εἷσαν *laid* an ambush, 4.392; εἷσεν δὲ (v.l. δ' ἐν) Σχερίῃ *settled* [them] in Scheria, Od.6.8, cf. Il.2.549; ἐπὶ χώρας ἕσσαι Pi.*P.* l. c.; ἐπὶ τὸ δεῖπνον ἵζειν τοὺς βασιλέας Hdt.6.57; ἕσσαντα ἐπὶ τῷ ὠδῷ *having caused* (the suppliant) *to sit* on the threshold, *Berl.Sitzb.*1927.170 (Cyrene): rare in Trag., σύ γάρ νιν εἰς τόδ' εἷσας αὔχημ' for *thou didst throne* her in this pride, S.*OC*713 (lyr.). 2. later in aor. I Med. εἱσάμην, 3 sg. εἵσατο *IG*12(5).615 (Iulis, v B.C., written εσατο), 2.1298.4 (ii B.C.), 1336.1 (ii B.C.):—*set up and dedicate* temples, statues, etc. in honour of gods, Thgn.12, Hdt.1.66; τέμενος ἕσσατο Pi.*P.*4.204; ἕσσατο βωμόν Id.*Oxy.*408.37: Dor. 3 sg. hίσατο *IG*9(1).704 (Corc., vi B.C.), ἵσσατο ib.4.569 (Argos); 3 pl. [ἥ]σσαντο *BCH*33.171 (ibid., iii B.C.); part. ἑσσάμενος *IG*4.840.7, 841.23 (Calauria, iii B.C.): Att. part. prob. ἑσάμενος, θυσίας τὰς πατρίους τῶν ἑσαμένων (ἑσσ-, ἑσσ-, εἱσ- codd.).. ἀφαιρήσεσθε Th.3.58; later εἱσάμενος *IG*2².1364 (i A.D.), Plu.*Them.* 22, *Thes.*17, *Pyrrh.*1, Luc.*Syr.D.*1, also Hdt.1.66 codd.: late fut. εἵσομαι ἱερόν A.R.2.807. II. intr., *sit, sit down*, Il.2.96, 792, etc.; ἷζε ἐν μέσσοισι he *sat* in the midst, 20.15; ἵζειν ἐς θρόνον Od.8.469, Hdt.5.25; ἐς θᾶκον S.*Ant.*1000; ἐπὶ θρόνου Il.18.422, cf. Od.17.339; ἐπὶ [λίθοισιν] 3.409; ἐπ' ἄκρίας ἠνεμοέσσας 16.365; ἐπὶ κώπην, of rowers, Ar.*Ra.*199; ἐπὶ κώπᾳ πηδαλίῳ τε E.*Alc.*441 (lyr.); ἐπὶ τοὺς νεώς Epicr.3.12; νέφεσσι..Ὀλύμποιο..ἵζων Ζεύς Pi.*Pae.*6.93: c. acc. loci, ἵζειν θρόνον A.*Ag.*982 (lyr.); βωμὸν E.*Ion*1314: c. acc. cogn., ἵ. κλωπικὰς ἕδρας Id.*Rh.*512. 2. *sit still, be quiet*, *h.Merc.*457 (dub.). 3. metaph., *sink*, εἰς ὀχετὸν ἄτας ἵζοισαν πόλιν *sink* into.., Pi.*O.*10(11).38; εἰς ἑτέραν ἵζει ἕδραν Pl.*Ti.*53a. III. Med. in signf. II, *sit*, πάροιθ'..ἵζετ' ἐπεῖο Il.3.162; Διὸς..ποτὶ βωμὸν ἑρκείου ἵζοιτο Od.22.335; ἱσσάμενος ἐπὶ τῷ δαμοσίῳ ἱαρῷ *Berl.Sitzb.*1927.169 (Cyrene); late fut. εἵσεται Phylarch.44 J.: Dor. pres. imper. ἵσδευ *Papers of Amer.Sch.at Athens* 3 No.437 (Pisidia); *lie in ambush*, ἔνθ' ἄρα τοί γ' ἵζοντ' Il.18.522; freq. of an army, *take up a position*, ἵζεσθαι ἀντίοι τινί Hdt.9.26; ἵζεσθαι ἐν τῷ Τηϋγέτῳ, ἐς τὸ Τηΰγετον, Id.4.145, 146; ἐν τῷ Ἰσθμῷ, ἐς τὸν Ἰσθμόν, Id.8.71; of a fleet, Id.6.5: generally ἐς ἱρὸν Ἀφροδίτης Id.1.199; ἐς τὰ πρόθυρα Id.3.140; in Trag., ἐν ἁγνῷ ἵζεσθε A.*Supp.*224; ἐς θρόνους E.*Ion*1618: c. acc., ἵζεσθαι κρήνας Id. *IA*141 (lyr.). 2. of things, *settle down, subside*, ἡ νῆσος ἱζομένη Pl.*Ti.*25c.

**ἰή** [ῐ], exclam. of joy or enthusiasm, ἰή, ἰή, ἰή, Ar.*Pax*195; esp. used in the cult of Apollo, ἰὴ παιών ib.453, al.; ἰὴ παιῆον Call.*Ap.*21, 103, *Hec.*1.1.10; ἀλαλαὶ ἰὴ παιήων Ar.*Lys.*1291; cf. ἰέ. 2. of grief, A.*Pers.*1004, *Supp.*114, *Ag.*1485 (all lyr.). (ἵη v.l. in Call.*Ap.* ll. cc., where it is associated with ἵει, imper. of ἵημι.)

**ἰή**, ἡ, v. ἰά, ἡ.

**ἰηγορεῖν**· ἐγρηγορέναι (Lacon.), Hsch. **ἰηδών**, όνος, ἡ, (ἰαίνω) *joy*, formed like ἀλγηδών, Id. (pl.); cf. ἰαίνω. **ἰηθενέουσα**, v. ἰαθενεῖ.

**ἰήϊος**, α, ον, also ος, ον (v. infr. II), epith. of Apollo, the god *invoked with the cry* ἰή or ἰὴ παιών (v. ἰή), ἰήιε παιάν Pi.*Pae.*2.35, cf. A.*Ag.*146, S.*OT*154 (both lyr.), 1096, Ar.*V.*874, A.R.2.702, Duris 79 J. II. *mournful. grievous*, ἰήιοι κάματοι S.*OT*174 (lyr.); ἰήιος βοά, γόος, a cry *of mourning*, E.*Ph.*1036, *El.*1211 (both lyr.). (From the cry ἰή, as Εὔιος from εὐοῖ; but also associated with ἰάομαι, Hsch. (hence applied to Asclepius, *IG*3.171); and, as ἱήϊος, with ἵημι, Hsch., Macr.*Sat.*1.17.16.)

**ἶηλα**, v. ἰάλλω. **ἰήλεμος, ἰηλεμίζω, ἰηλεμίστρια, Ἰηλυσός**, Ion. for ἰαλ-. **ἰηλενές**· πορφυροῦν, μέλαν, Hsch.

**ἴημα**, Ion. for ἴαμα; but found in *IG*2².1121.15 (iv A.D.).

⊛ **ἵημι**, ἵης (v.l. ἵεις S.*El.*596, Castorio 2), ἵησι, 3 pl. ἱᾶσι, Ion. and Ep. ἱεῖσι; imper. ἵει Il.21.338, E.*El.*593 (lyr.); subj. ἱῶ; opt. ἱείην (also ἀφ-ίοιμι, X.*HG*6.4.3); inf. ἱέναι; part. ἱείς:—thematic forms of the pres. (as if from ἱέω) are also found, esp. in compds., cf.

μεθίημι, σύνιημι: also, as if from ἰέω, 3 sg. pres. ἰεῖ A.R.4.634, imper. ξύν-ιε Thgn.1240b codd.: impf. 3 sg. ἵει Il.1.479, Dor. ἀν-ίη *SIG*1 (Abu Simbel, vi B.C.); 3 pl. ἵεσαν E.*Ba.*1099, ἵεν Il.12.33, ξύν-ιεν (v.l. -ιον) 1.273; also 2 sg. ἵεις Ar.*V.*355; Ion. impf. ἵεσκε (ἀν-) Hes.*Th.*157: fut. ἥσω Il.17.515, etc.: aor. 1 ind. ἧκα Il.5.125, etc., Ep. ἕηκα 1.48 (mostly in compds.); 3 sg. subj. ἧσι 15.359; 3 sg. opt. εἵη 3.221; inf. εἶναι Ar.*Ra.*133, Ep. ἐξ-έμεναι Od.11.531: pf. εἷκα, only in compds. (ἀφ-, καθ-, παρ-, συν-), also ἕωκα (ἀφ-) *PCair. Zen.*502.4 (iii B.C.), Hdn.Gr.2.236:—**Med.**, pres. ἵεμαι Od.2.327, etc.; also 3 pl. προ-ίονται *PCair.Zen.*151.4 (iii B.C.): impf. ἱέμην Ar.*Eq.*625, etc.: fut. ἥσομαι (μετ-) Hdt.5.35, (προ-) D.1.12, (ἐξαν-) E.*Andr.*718: aor. 1 ἡκάμην (only in compds. προσ-, προ-): aor. 2 εἵμην, Ep. and Ion. ἕμην, of which we find εἷτο (ἐφ-) S.*Ph.*619, (ἀφ-) X.*Hier.*7.11, ἕτο (συν-) Od.4.76, ἕντο (ἐξ-) Il.9.92, etc.; imper. ἕο (ἐξ-) Hdt.5.39, οὗ (ἀφ-) S.*OT*1521; subj. ὧμαι (συν-) Il.13.381; opt. εἵμην (ἀφ-) Ar.*Av.*628, or οἵμην (προ-) Pl.*Grg.*520c; inf. ἕσθαι (προσ-) Ar.*V.*742; part. ἕμενος (προ-) Th.6.78, Isoc.4.164, etc.:—**Pass.**, fut. ἑθήσομαι (ἀν-) Th.8.63: aor. εἵθην (only in compds. ἀφ-, καθ-, παρ-): pf. εἷμαι (only in compds.); also ἕωμαι in compds. ἀν-, ἀφ-, ἐφ- (q.v.): plpf. εἵμην (only in compds.).—Of the Pass. and Med. Hom. has only pres., impf., and 3 pl. aor. 2 Med. ἕντο.—For varieties peculiar to special compds., v. ἀν-, ἀφ-, ὑφ-ίημι. (Perh. cogn. with Lat. *ja-c-io* or with Lat. *sēmen*:—Med. ἵεμαι prob. from ϝῑ-, cf. εἴσομαι II, Skt. *véti* (pl. *vyánti*) 'press forward, desire', Lat. *vīs* (2 sg.), *invitus*.) [ῑ generally in Hom. and Ep., ῐ in Att.; sts. ῐ in Hom., ἵει Il.16.152, etc.; ἱεῖσαι Od.12.192; also in inf. ἱέμεν, ἱέμεναι, part. ἱέμενος, etc., ξυν-ίετε Archil.50: ῑ sts. in Trag., ἵησι A.*Th.*309 (lyr.), ἵεντα ib.493, ἱείς, ἱεῖσα, E.*IT*298, *IA*1101, *Hec.*338; ἱεῖσαν Id. *Supp.*281; in Com., συνίημι Ar.*Av.*946 (s.v.l.), Strato Com.1.3: with variation of quantity, πλεῖστον οὖλον ἵει [ῑ], ἴουλον ἵει [ῐ] *Carm.Pop.* 1.]:—*release, let go*, ἧκα .. πόδας καὶ χεῖρε φέρεσθαι Od.12.442; ἧκε φέρεσθαι *let* him *float off*, Il.21.120; *let fall*, κὰδ δὲ κάρητος ἧκε κόμας *made* his locks *flow* down from his head, Od.6.231; [ἐθείρας] ἵει λόφον ἀμφί Il.19.383; ἐκ δὲ ποδοῖιν ἄκμονας ἧκα δύω I *let* two anvils *hang* from his two legs, 15.19; ἐκ δ' ἄρα χειρὸς φάσγανον ἧκε χαμᾶζε Od.22. 84, cf. Il.12.205; ἵεις σαυτὸν κατὰ τοῦ τείχους Ar.*V.*355; ἧκαν ἑαυτοὺς *let* themselves *go*, X.*An.*4.5.18; ἵεσαν φυγῇ πόδα E.*Rh.*798. 2. of sounds, *utter*, ὄπα Il.3.152, Od.12.192; ἔπεα Il.3.221; γλῶσσαν Hdt. 1.57; Ἑλλάδα γλῶσσαν ἱ. *to speak* Greek, Id.9.16; Δωρίδα, Ἀττικὴν γλῶσσαν, Th.3.112, Sol.36.10; φωνὴν Παρνησίδα A.*Ch.*563; δύσθροα βάγματα Id.*Pers.*636 (lyr.); ἐκ στηθέων ἄλγος Id.*Th.*865 (lyr.); μέγαν κωκυτόν S.*Aj.*851, etc.; but πᾶσαν γλῶσσαν ἱ. *to let loose* every kind of speech, Id.*El.*596; πᾶσαν (τὸ λεγόμενον) φωνὴν ἱέντα Pl.*Lg.* 890d; τὸ τᾶς εὐφάμου στόμα φροντίδος ἱέντες, i.e. speaking not in words, but in silent thought, S.*OC*133 (lyr.); ἧκε abs. (sc. φωνήν), Plu.2.973e; of instruments, ἄλλα μέλη τῶν χορδῶν ἱεισῶν Pl.*Lg.* 812d. 3. *throw, hurl*, λᾶαν, βέλος, δόρυ, Od.9.538, Il.4.498, E.*Rh.* 63; ἱέναι (sc. τινά) πέτρας ἄπο E.*HF*320, cf. S.*Tr.*273: c. gen. pers., *to throw* or *shoot at* one, ὀϊστὸν τινος Il.13.650; ἐπ' ἀλλήλοις ἵεσαν βέλεα Hes.*Th.*684: metaph., ἐκ μαλθακᾶς φρενὸς ὀϊστοὺς ἱέντες Pi.*O.*2. 90. b. abs., *throw, shoot*, τόσσον γὰρ ἵησιν Od.9.499, cf.8.203, Il.17. 515, Pl.*Tht.*194a, etc.; ἄνω ἱέντες X.*An.*3.4.17; δίσκοισιν τέρποντο .. ἱέντες Il.2.774, al.: c. gen. objecti, τῶν μεγάλων ψυχῶν ἱεὶς *shooting* at great spirits, S.*Aj.*154; ἐπὶ στόχον (στοίχων codd.) at a mark, X. *Ages.*1.25: c. dat. instr., ἵησι τῇ ἀξίνῃ Id.*An.*1.5.12. 4. of water, *let flow, spout forth*, ῥόον Il.12.25; [Ἀξιὸς] ὕδωρ ἐπὶ γαῖαν ἵησι 21.158; ῥέος A.*Pr.*812: abs., [ποταμὸς] ἐπὶ γαῖαν ἵησιν the river *pours* over the land, Od.11.239; [κρήνη] ἵησι 7.130; of tears, δάκρυον ἧκε χαμᾶζε 16. 191; of fire or smoke, ἵει νᾶμα παμφάγου πυρός E.*Med.*1187; λιγνύν A.*Th.*493. 5. *send*, of living beings, τίς γάρ σε θεῶν ἐμοὶ ἄγγελον ἧκε; Il.18.182; Αἰνείαν .. ἐξ ἀδύτοιο ἧκε 5.513; of omens or portents, τοῖσι δὲ δεξιὸν ἧκεν ἐρῳδιόν 10.274; ἔλαφον .. εἰς ὁδὸν αὐτὴν ἧκεν Od. 10.159; τέρας 21.415; generally of things, ἱκμενον οὖρόν τινι Il.1. 479, etc. II. Med., *speed oneself, hasten*, freq. in part. with Advs., πρόσω ἵεσθε Il.12.274; ἐνθένδ' ἱέμην Ar.*Eq.*625; ἱ. Τροίηνδε, Ἐρεβόσδε, Od.19.187, 20.356: with Preps., ἵεσθαι κατὰ τὴν φωνὴν Hdt. 2.70; πρός τινα Id.9.78; δρόμῳ ἵεσθαι ἐς τοὺς βαρβάρους Id.6.112; ἵετ' εὐθὺ πρὸς τὰ νυμφικὰ λέχη S.*OT*1242; ἐς ὄρεα E.*Ba.*140 (lyr.); εἰς Κολωνόν Pherecr.134; ἱ. ἐπί τινα *spring* upon, of the lion, Arist.*HA* 629$^{b}$24: abs., ἰδόντες ἱέμεσθα S.*Ant.*432; ἱέμενος ῥεῖ *rushing*, Pl.*Cra.* 420a, etc. 2. metaph., *to be eager, desire to do* a thing, c. inf., ἵετο γὰρ βαλέειν Il.16.383; βαλέειν δέ ἑ ἵετο θυμός 8.301; ἵετο θυμῷ τείσασθαι.. 2.589: c. gen., *to be set upon, long for* a thing, in part., ἱέμενοι πόλιος, νίκης, 11.168, 23.371; νόστοιο Od.15.69; λεχέων S.*Tr.*514 (lyr.); ἱέμενος ποταμοῖο ῥοάων *setting thyself toward*, Od.10.529: abs. in part., ἱέμενός περ *eager* though *he was*, 1.6, etc.

**ἵηνα**, aor. 1 Act. of ἰαίνω.

**Ἰηπαι-ήων**, ονος, ὁ, epith. of Apollo, from the cry ἰὴ παιῆον, *h.Ap.* 272. II. *hymn* sung to him, ib.500, 517. **-ωνίζω**, *cry* ἰὴ παιών! Ar.*Eq.*408.

* **ἰήρια**, τά, = ἰατήρια, dub. in *Supp.Epigr.*1.414.4 (Crete, v/iv B.C.).

**ἴησι**, Ep. 3 sg. pres. subj. of εἶμι (*ibo*). **ἰήσιμος, ἴησις**, Ion. for ἰασ-.

**Ἰησοῦς**, οῦ, dat. οῖ, *Joshua*, LXX *Jo.*1.1, al., *Act.Ap.*7.45; in *NT*, with dat. -οῦ, JESUS, *Ev.Matt.*9.27, al.

**ἰήτειρα, ἰητέον, ἰητήρ, ἰητόριον, ἰητρός**, etc., Ion. for ἰατ-.

**ἰήτης·** τοξότης, ἰοβόλος, Hsch.

**ἰθᾰγενής** [ῐ], ές, or **ἰθαιγ-**, Od.14.203 (v.l.), Hdt.2.17 (v.l.), A. *Pers.*306 (v.l.), Alex.Aet. (v. infr.):—*born in lawful wedlock*, ἀλλά με ἶσον ἰθαγενέεσσιν (so most codd. and A.D.*Adv.*187.24: v.l. ἰθαιγ-) ἐτίμα honoured me like *his true-born sons*, of a νόθος, Od. l.c., cf. A.R.*Fr.*12.2 (ἰθαγ- cod.), Alex.Aet.3.2 (ἰθαιγ- cod.). 2. of a nation, *from the ancient stock, aboriginal*, opp. ἔπηλυς, ἰ. Αἰγύπτιοι Hdt.6.53, cf. A.*Pers.*306; οὐχ ὑπ' ἰθαγενῶν ἤρχοντο Str.7.7.8, cf. Agath.2.15,25. 3. ἰ. κύημα, opp. an abortion, Hp.*Mul.*1.71; of some mouths of the Nile, *natural, original*, opp. ὀρυκτά, Hdt.2.17; ἰ. νότος, ζέφυρος, *genuine*, Arist.*Mete.*364$^{a}$16,18. (Glossed αὐτόχθων by Hsch., αὐθιγενής by Erot.; *originalis, indigena*, by *Gloss.*; perh. ἰθᾰ-γενής [ᾱ metri gr.], cf. Skt. *ihá*, Avest. *iδa* (fr. **idhá*) 'here'; cf. pr. n. Ἰθαγένης Plu.*Per.*26, Ps.-Hdt.*Vit.Hom.*1, but Ἰθαιγένης *IG* 12(9).192 (iv B.C.).)

* **ἰθαίνω**, = εὐφρονῶ, Hsch.: etym. of ἰθαγενής, A.D.*Adv.*187.25; ἴθαινε θυμόν Anon.ap.*An.Ox.*1.61 (cf. ἰθαινάθυμος Theognost.*Can.* 81). (Cogn. with ἰθαρός.)

**Ἰθάκη** [ῐ, ᾰ], ἡ, *Ithaca*, Od.1.18, etc.: **Ἰθᾰκήσιος**, ὁ, *Ithacan*, Il. 2.184, Od.2.25, B.*Fr.*25, etc.:—**Ἰθάκηνδε**, *to Ithaca*, Od.16.322; **-ηθεν**, *from it*, Q.S.7.187.

**ἴθανα·** σχοινία, Hsch. **ἴθαρ**, = εἶθαρ, Id.

* **ἰθᾰρός** [ῐ], ά, όν, *cheerful, glad*, in Comp. -ώτερος Alc.*Supp.*4. 18. II. *pure*, κρᾶναι Simm.25.6; cf. ἰθαραῖς· ταχείαις, κούφαις, ἱλαραῖς, καλαῖς, καθαραῖς, Hsch.

**ἰθείη**, ἡ, = ἅμαξα (Thess.), Hsch. **ἰθή**, ἡ, = εὐφροσύνη, Id.

* **ἴθῐ**, imperat. of εἶμι (*ibo*), *come, go* (q.v.): used as Adv. of encouragement, *come! well then!* Il.4.362; ἴ. νυν Ar.*Ra.*519, etc.

**ἰθίτας·** ὁ βλεννὸς καὶ μωρός, Hsch.

**ἴθμα**, ατος, τό, (εἶμι *ibo*), always in pl., *step, motion*, πελειάσιν ἴθμαθ' ὁμοῖαι Il.5.778, *h.Ap.*114. II. *feet*, Call.*Cer.*58.

**ἰθμαίνω·** ἀσθμαίνω, Hsch. **ἰθμία·** ἡ τῶν μελισσῶν ἐρυθρὰ κόπρος, Id. **ἰθμίν** (sic)· περιστόμιον, περιτραχήλιον, ἢ στεφανίς, Id. (cf. ἰσθμίον).

**ἴθρῐς**, ὁ, *eunuch*, restored from Hsch. for ἴδρις in *AP*6.219 (Antip.).

**ἰθύ-βῐος** [ἰθῠ], ον, *straightforward, honest*, *IG*5(2).474 (Megalopolis, ii/iii A.D.; ειθ- lapis). **-βόλος**, ον, *straight-hitting*, ἀκόντιον Apollod.3.15.1: Sup. -ώτατος, ἀκοντιστής J.*BJ*1.21.13: metaph., *sagacious*, φύσις Dam.*Isid.*160. **-γραμμος**, ον, *rectilinear*, σχήματα Agath.5.9. **-δίκης** [δῐ], ου, ὁ, *giving right judgement*, Hes. *Op.*230, *APl.*4.35. * **-δῐκος**, ον, *righteous*, *Epigr.Gr.*906 (Gortyn). **-δρομία**, ἡ, *straight course*, διὰ τῶν πόρων Harp.Astr. in *Cat. Cod.Astr.*8(3).148. **-δρόμος**, ον, *straight-running*, πρίων *AP*6.103 (Phil.). **-θριξ**, τρῐχος, ὁ, ἡ, *straight-haired*, opp. οὐλόθριξ (woolly-haired), Hdt.7.70, Hp.*Epid.*1.19. **-κέλευθος**, ον, *straight-going*, Nonn.*D.*15.365. **-κρήδεμνος**, ον, epith. of ships, prob. *with canvas set*, Pamphosap.Paus.7.21.9. **-κτέᾰνον·** τὸ ἰθὺ πεφυκὸς καὶ ὀρθὸν δένδρον, Hsch.; cf. sq. and εὐκτέανος (B). **-κτίων**, v. ἰθυπτίων. **-κῡφος**, η, ον, of parts of the normal spine, *frontally concave*, Hp.*Art.*45 (-κῡφής, ές, *Mochl.*1); opp. **ἰθύ-λορδος**, η, ον (ος, ον *Mochl.* l. c.), *frontally convex*, ll. cc., cf. Gal.18(2).542. **-μᾰχία**, Ion. -ίη, ἡ, *fair, stand-up fight*, ἰ. ποιέεσθαι Hdt.4.120; ἰθυμαχίῃ διώσασθαι στρατόν ib.102. **-μάχος** [ᾰ], ον, *fighting fairly and openly*, Simon.137.

* **ἴθυμβος**, ὁ, *Bacchic dance and song*, Poll.4.104, Hsch., Phot. (For the termination cf. ἴαμβος, διθύραμβος.)

* **ἴθῡνα**, ης, ἡ, = εὔθυνα, *penalty, fine*, *SIG*986.12 (Chios, v/iv B.C.), *GDI*5654 (ibid.).

**ἰθύν-τατα** [ῐ], Adv., Sup. of ἰθύς (A) (q.v.). **-τειρα**, ἡ, fem. of sq., as epith. of Δίκη, Orph.*A.*352. * **-τήρ**, ῆρος, ὁ, *guide, pilot*, A.R. 4.209, 1260, *IG*9(1).390 (Naupactus), Jul.*Or.*1.25c; *shepherd*, Theoc. *Syrinx* 2; ἰ. πυρός, of Hephaestus, v.l. in Coluth.54; *ruler*, Ἑσπερίης χθονός *Epigr.Gr.*905 (Gortyn); προτέρων ὑπέρτερος ἰθυντήρων *Milet.* 1(9).340. **-τήριος**, α, ον, *guiding, directing*, S.*Ichn.*73. II. Subst. -τήριον, τό, *laurel-bough*, used by diviners, Hsch.; = *regimen*, *Gloss.* 2. -τηρία, ἡ, = *canalis*, ib. (prob.). **-τής**, οῦ, ὁ, = ἰθυντήρ, Hsch. s. v. διϊθυντής; = *rector*, *Gloss.*: -τωρ, Orph.*A.*122; ἰθύντορος ἀνθυπάτοιο *IG*4.1603 (Corinth). * **-ω**, Ion. impf. ἰθύνεσκον Q.S.1.273, al., *Hymn.Is.*153: aor. 1 ἴθυνα Od.23.197:—Med. (v. infr. 2), aor. 1 inf. ἰθύνασθαι Q.S.14.500:—Pass., aor. 1 ἰθύνθην Il.16.475: pf. ἴθυμμαι D.P.341, ἀπ-ίθυνται Hp.*Fract.*7: (ἰθύς A). [ἰθῡνω: ῑ- only in *APl.* 74]:—Ion. and Ep. for εὐθύνω (sts. used in Trag., generally with v.l. εὐθυν-; never in Com. or Att. Prose), *make straight, straighten*, ἐπὶ στάθμην ἴθυνεν by the rule, Od.5.245, 23.197, al.:—Pass., ἐκ στάθμης ἰθυμμένος D.P. l. c. 2. *guide in a straight line*, ἵππους τε καὶ ἅρμ' ἰθύνομεν (Ep. for -ωμεν) let us *drive* them *straight*, Il.11.528; νῆα θοὴν ἰθύνει [the pilot] *keeps it straight*, 23.317; τὴν δ' ἄνεμός τε κυβερνήτης τ' ἴθυνε Od.11.10, etc.; τρόπιν *Hymn.Is.* l. c.; ἰ. δρόμον, κῶλον, E.*Hipp.* 1227 (v.l. εὐθ-), *Or.*1016 (lyr.); κέντρα Id.*Ph.*178 (lyr.); βέλος δ' ἴθυνεν Ἀθήνη she *sped* it *straight*, Il.5.290: in late Prose, λεπτοὶ ὕπνοι ἰθύνοντες τὰ σιτία Philostr.*Gym.*48:—Med., *guide* or *steer for oneself*, of missiles, ἐπ' Ἀντινόῳ ἰθύνετο πικρὸν ὀϊστὸν *aimed his arrow straight* at.., Od.22.8; πηδαλίῳ ἰθύνετο (sc. σχεδίην) 5.270; ἡνίοχος ἰθύνετο ἅρμα Hes.*Sc.*324: c. gen., ἀλλήλων ἰθυνομένων.. δοῦρα *as they drove* their spears *straight at* each other, Il.6.3:—Pass., *run straight* or *evenly*, of horses yoked abreast, τὼ δ' ἰθυνθήτην Il.16.475 (but, *to be guided*, οὐ γὰρ ἄτερ μάστιγος ἰθύνεται ἵππος *APl.* l.c.); of a boat, *to be steered*, Hdt.1.194. 3. *guide, direct, rule*, Ζεὺς.. πάντ' ἰθύνει Il.17. 632; ἀμηχανίῃ ἰ. νόον Parm.6.6; ἰ. στρατόν (corr. from ηὐθ- in cod. M) A.*Pers.*773; ἰ. ἑορτάς Orac.ap.D.21.52; ζωὴν *AP*6.68 (Jul. Aegypt.); of a judge, μύθους ἰ. *put straight, rectify* unjust judgements, Hes.*Op.* 263 (dub.), cf. Call.*Jov.*83; ἰ. τὸ πλέον τινί *adjudge* the greater part

to him, Theoc.5.71 :—Pass., ἰθύνεσθαι θανάτῳ *to be visited with the penalty* of death, Hdt.2.177.

**ἰθύπετεῖν** [ῐ] (ἰθυνπ- cod.)· ἐπ' εὐθείας ὁρμῆσαι, Hsch.

**ἰθῦ-πορέω** [ῐ], *go straight on*, Hp.*Oss*.15. ※ **-πόρος**, ον, *going straight on*, γραμμή, γραφίδες, *AP*6.64 (Paul. Sil.), 68 (Jul. Aegypt.). ※ **-πτίων** [πτῐ], ωνος, ὁ, ἡ, only in Il.21.169 μελίην ἰθυπτίωνα Ἀστεροπαίῳ ἐφῆκε, from πέτομαι, *straight-flying* (cf. ἰθύς (A) II) :—Zenod. read **ἰθυκτίωνα**, *straight-fibred* (fort. -κτείωνα, cf. εὐθυκτέανον, κτηδών).

**ἰθύρ**· τὸ σιδήριον τοῦ ἄξονος τὸ τριβόμενον, Hsch.

**ἰθύρροπος** [ῐ], ον, (ῥοπή) *hanging perpendicularly*, Hp.*Art*.44.

※ **ἰθύς** (A) [ῐ], ἰθεῖα, ἰθύ, Ion. fem. ἰθέα Hdt.2.17, Eus.Mynd.63 (but ἰθείης, η, αν are prob. in oblique cases): Comp. ἰθύντερος Hdn.Gr.2. 927: Sup. ἰθύντατος or -ύτατος (v. infr.) :—Ion. and Ep. form of Att. εὐθύς: 1. *straight*, used by Hom. in this sense only in Adv. ἰθύς (infr. II); ἰθείῃ τέχνῃ *straightway, forthwith*, Hdt.9.57; ἰθέα ὁδὸς Id. 2.17; ἰθεῖαν (sc. ὁδὸν) *straight on*, Id.7.193; ἐκ τῆς ἰθείης *outright, openly*, Id.2.161, al.; ἰ. ἀτραπός Nic.*Th*.265, cf. *AP*10.3; ἰθύντατον ἴχνος D.P.651; γραφίδες ἰθύταται *AP*6.63 (Damoch.); ἰθύτατον ὄρος *steepest*, App.*Hisp*.1. 2. in moral sense, *straight-forward, just*, εἰ δ' ἄγ' ἐγὼν αὐτὸς δικάσω, .. ἰθεῖα γὰρ ἔσται [ἡ δίκη] Il.23.580; ἰθείῃσι δίκῃσιν *h.Cer*.152, Hes.*Th*.86, cf. *Op*.36; opp. σκολιαὶ δίκαι, ib.224: in Sup. Adv., δίκην ἰθύντατα εἰπεῖν to give judgement *the most fairly*, Il. 18.508; later οὔποτε δουλείη κεφαλὴ ἰθεῖα πέφυκεν Thgn.535; πρήξιες ἰθύτεραι Id.1026; Δίκα ἰθεῖα B.14.54; ἰθύς τε καὶ δίκαιος Hdt.1.96; λόγος ἰ. ib.118. II. ἰθύς, or less freq. ἰθύ, as Adv., *straight at*, mostly c. gen. objecti, βῆ ῥ' ἰθὺς Διομήδεος Il.5.849, cf. 16.584; ἰθὺς κίεν οἴκου went *straight towards* the dwelling, 24.471, cf. Od.15.511; ἰθὺ βέλος πέτετ' οὐδ' ἀπολήγει Il.20.99; ἔπλεε ἰθὺ τοῦ Ἴστρου Hdt.4.89; ἰθὺ τῆς ἀρχῆς τῆς Τομύριος 1.207, cf. 6.95, al.; ἰθὺ βαδίζειν Semus 20; ἰθὺς πρὸς τεῖχος ἔκιον Il.12.137; ἰθὺς ἐπὶ Θεσσαλίης Hdt.5.64. 2. abs., ἰθὺς φρονέων resolving to go *straight on*, Il.12.124, cf. 13.135; ἰθὺς μεμαώς 11.95, etc.; of a bird's flight, *SIG*1167.7 (Ephesus, vi B.C.); ἰθὺς μαχέσασθαι to fight *face to face*, Il.17.168; μένος χειρῶν ἰθὺς φέρον 5.506; also τέτραπτο πρὸς ἰθύ οἱ (v.l. πρὸς ἰθύν, cf. sq.) he fronted him *face to face*, 14.403; κατ' ἰθὺ γούνασιν *opposite*, i.e. *vertically below*, the knees, Hp.*Off*.3; of Time, *straightway*, Hdt.3. 58. 3. regul. Adv. ἰθέως Id.2.121.β', al.; πλέειν ἰθέως ἐπὶ τὸν Ἑλλήσποντον Id.8.108.

※ **ἰθύς** (B) [ῑθῡ], ἡ, used by Hom. only in acc. ἰθύν: 1. ἀν' ἰθύν, = *against*, πρὸς ῥόον ἀΐσσοντος ἀν' ἰθύν *against* the stream, Il.21.303; ἐπεὶ δὴ σφαίρῃ ἀν' ἰθὺν πειρήσαντο in throwing *straight upwards*, Od. 8.377; πρὸς ἰθύν v.l. in Il.14.403. 2. *enterprise*, οἷσι μάλιστα πεποίθεα πᾶσαν ἐπ' ἰθύν Od.4.434; ἄριστοι πᾶσαν ἐπ' ἰθὺν ἔστε μάχεσθαί τε φρονέειν τε Il.6.79; γυναικῶν γνώομεν ἰθύν their *mood, designs*, Od.16.304; ἐμὴν ἰ. dub. in *h.Ap*.539.

**ἰθυ-σκόλιος** [ῑθ], ον, *curved in one direction, though straight in another*, of the normal spine, Hp.*Art*.45. **-τένεια**, ἡ, *extension in length*, Ptol.*Geog*.1.2.4. ※ **-τενής**, ές, *straight*, ibid.; κανών *AP*6.65 (Paul. Sil.); στάθμη ib.103 (Phil.); γραμμή Simp. *in Cael*.180.11; στοά Chor.p.85 B.; ξύλα Agath.5.21; *upright, perpendicular*, ῥόπαλον *APl*.4.261 (Leon.): metaph., ἰ. κνήμη Aristaenet.1.27.

**ἰθύτης** [ῐ], ητος, ἡ, (ἰθύς A) *straightness*, ὁδοῦ Aret.*CA*2.6.

**ἰθυ-τμής** [ῐ], ῆτος, ὁ, ἡ, *straight-cut*, Nonn.*D*.2.451, 5.282. **-τόνος**, ον, = ἰθυτενής, στάλικες *AP*6.187 (Alph.; v.l. -τενῶν). **-τρητον** (neut. sg.), = ἰθύτρητον, *bored straight*, Democr.128. **-φαλλικός**, ή, όν, *ithyphallic*, of metre, Heph.15.2, Hermog.*Id*.1.6; τὰ ἰ. *poems in such metre*, D.H.*Comp*.4 (ἰθυφάλλια codd.), Poll.4.53. ※ **-φαλλος**, ὁ, *fascinum erectum, the phallos carried in the festivals of Bacchus*, Cratin.14, etc. II. *ode and dance* performed at such festivals, Hyp.*Fr*.50, Duris 13 J. III. *one who danced in such dance*, Hippoloch.ap.Ath.4.129d, Semus 20, Democh.2 J.: metaph., *lewd fellow*, D.54.14. **-φάνεια** [φᾰ], ἡ, *direct incidence of light*, κατ' ἰθυφάνειαν Damian.*Opt*.12 :—Adj. **-φάνής**, ές, in phrase κατ' ἰθυφανές, = κατ' ἰθυφάνειαν, ibid. **-φορικός**, ή, όν, *moving in a straight line*, Phlp. *in Mete*.30.18.

**ἰθύω** [ῐ], aor. ἴθυσα (v. infr.), *go straight, press right on*, rare in pres., ὁ δέ, κρειῶν ἐρατίζων, ἰθύει [ῠ] Il.11.552; ἔνθα καὶ ἔνθ' ἴθυσε μάχη πεδίοιο the tide of war *set straight* over the plain.., 6.2; ἰθύει τὸ ἔμβρυον πρὸς τὸ ἧπαρ Hp.*Mul*.1.32, cf. 2. 145 vulg.: c. gen. objecti, ὡς Ἕκτωρ ἴθυσε νεὸς *dashed straight at* it, Il. 15.693; ἴθυσαν δ' ἐπὶ τεῖχος 12.443; ἴθυσαν πρός.. Hdt.4.122. II. c. inf., *to be eager, strive* to do, τῶν ὁπότ' ἰθύσειε.. ἐπὶ χερσὶ μάσασθαι Od.11.591; ἴθυσέν ῥ' ὀλολύξαι 22.408; ὅκῃ ἰθύσειε στρατεύεσθαι whichever way he *purposed* to march, Hdt.1.204, cf. 3.39; ἰθύοντα στρατεύεσθαι Id.7.8.β'. 2. c. acc., *desire eagerly*, τι μετὰ φρεσίν A.R.2. 950. 3. abs., τί μακρὰν γλῶσσαν ἰθύσας ἐλαύνω ἐκτὸς ὁδοῦ; why *in my zeal* do I drive, etc., B.9.51. (Signf. I never in Od., signf. II never in Il.)

**ἰθυωρίη** [ῑθ], ἡ, Ion. for εὐθυωρία, *direction, straightness*, of a limb, etc., Hp.*Off*.15 (pl.), *Fract*.30, al.

※ **ἰθών**· πυγή, λαγαρός, καὶ πρωκτός, Hsch. (fort. ἴθων).

**ἰίζω**, (ἰός) *to be like rust, ferruginous*, Dsc.5.75, 103.

※ **ἰκάνο-δοσία** [ῐκ], ἡ, = Lat. *satisdatio*, *Cod.Just*.2.12.27.2 (also in pl.), Just.*Nov*.131.15 *Intr*. **-δοτέω**, = Lat. *satisdare*, *POxy*.259.29 (I A.D.). **-δότης**, ου, ὁ, *one who gives security*, *BGU*1189.3. II. *one who requites*, ὁ ἰ. θεός *PMasp*.6 ii 82 (vi A.D.). ※ **-ποιέω**, *make satisfaction*, *Gloss*.

※ **ἰκάν-ός** [ῐ], ή, όν, (ἰκνέομαι) *sufficing, becoming, befitting*; prose Adj., used two or three times by Trag. (v. infr.): I. of persons, *sufficient, competent to do* a thing, c. inf., Hdt.3.45, Antipho 1.15, etc.; ἰ. τεκμηριῶσαι *sufficient* to prove a point, Th.1.9; -ώτατος [εἰπεῖν] καὶ γνῶναι Lys.2.42; τίς σοῦ -ώτερος πεῖσαι; X.*Cyr*.1.4.12; ἰ. ζημιοῦν *with sufficient power* to punish, Id.*Lac*.8.4; ἰ. βοηθεῖν Pl. *Phdr*.277a, cf. *R*.365a; ἰ. ὥστε γνῶναι Id.*Lg*.875a, cf. *Phdr*.258b; ἰ. κατὰ τὴν ἐπιφάνειαν Plb.25.3.6, al.: c. acc. rei, ἀνὴρ γνώμην ἰ. a man of *sufficient* prudence, Hdt.3.4; ἰ. τὴν ἰατρικὴν *sufficiently versed in* medicine, X.*Cyr*.1.6.15: c. dat. rei, ἰ. ἐμπειρίᾳ καὶ ἡλικίᾳ Pl.*R*. 467d; οἱ τοῖς χρήμασιν -ώτατοι X.*Eq*.2.1: c. dat. pers., *a match for, equivalent to*, εἷς ἔχων ἰατρικὴν πολλοῖς ἰ. ἰδιώταις Pl.*Prt*.322c, cf. *Tht*.169a: abs., ἰ. Ἀπόλλων S.*OT*377; οἱ -ώτατοι τῶν πολιτῶν Isoc. 12.132; κριτὴς -ώτερος Id.10.38; ἰ. σοφιστής Pl.*Ly*.204a; αὐληταὶ ἰ. ὡς πρὸς ἰδιώτας *very tolerable* in comparison with.., Id.*Prt*.327c; γυνὴ ἰ. μέν, ἄγροικος δέ Luc.*DDeor*.20.3; ὁ Ἰ. *the Almighty*, LXX *Ru*. 1.21. 2. in bad sense, *capable*, ἰ. εἶ λαλῶν κατακόψαι πάντα Men.*Sam*.69. II. of things, in amount, *sufficient, adequate*, τὰ ἀρκοῦνθ' ἰ. τοῖς γε σώφροσιν E.*Ph*.554; ἰ. τὰ κακὰ καὶ τὰ παρακείμενα Ar.*Lys*.1047; ἱκανὰ τοῖς πολεμίοις ηὐτύχηται they have had successes *enough*, Th.7.77; ἰ. εἴς, ἐπί, πρός τι, X.*Hier*.4.9, Pl.*R*. 371e, *Prt*.322b; [πρόβατα] ἰ. ἐς φορβήν Hdt.4.121; of size, *large enough*, οὐχ ἱκανῆς οὔσης τῆς Ἀττικῆς Th.1.2; οὐδ' ἦν ἱκανά σοι.. μέλαθρα.. ἐγκαθυβρίζειν not *large enough* to riot in, E.*Tr*.996; χώρα ἰ. τρέφειν τοὺς τότε Pl.*R*.373d, al.; of number or magnitude, *considerable*, λῦπαι Antipho 2.2.2; μέρος τῶν ὄντων ib.2.1.6, etc.; of Time, *considerable, long*, ἰ. χρόνον Ar.*Pax* 354 (lyr.); ἰ. χρόνος τινὶ ἐπιλαθέσθαι Lys.3.10; ἱκανόν ἐστί τινι Damox.1.1: with personal constr., ἔφη ἱκανὸς αὐτὸς ἀτυχῶν εἶναι Is.2.7. 2. *sufficient, satisfactory*, ἰ. μαρτυρίαν παρέχεσθαι Pl.*Smp*.179b; ἰ. λόγῳ ἀποδεῖξαι Id.*Hp.Mi*.369c; τὸ ἰ. λαμβάνειν to take *security* or *bail*, *Act.Ap*.17.9, *OGI*629.100 (Palmyra, ii A.D.); τὸ ἰ. ποιεῖν give *security*, Plb.32.3.13, D.L.4. 50, Just.*Nov*.86.4 (but simply, *satisfy*, τῷ ὄχλῳ *Ev.Marc*.15.15); ἰ. δοῦναι *PSI*6.554.23 (iii B.C.), *POxy*.294.23 (I A.D.); ἐφ' ἱκανόν, = ἱκανῶς, Plb.11.25.1, D.S.11.40. III. Adv. **-νῶς** *sufficiently, adequately*, Th.6.92, etc.; λαγόνες λαπαραὶ ἰ. X.*Cyn*.5.30, cf. Arist.*Phgn*. $807^{b}26$; ἰ. εἴρηται περί τινος Id.*EN*$1096^{a}3$, al.; later, *considerably, amply*, Philostr.*VA*3.6, *VS*1.8.3, Ant.Lib.7.7; *fully*, μιᾶς ὥρας ἰ. παρελθούσης Ptol.*Alm*.4.6. b. *excessively*, οὔτε γὰρ ἰ. ὑγρὸν ἐστι not *too* moist, Gal.6.765, cf. 767, 768; ἰ. βλαβερά Id.*Vict.Att*.8; παχὺ ἰ. αἷμα ibid. 2. ἰ. ἔχειν to be *sufficient*, Th.1.91, etc.; ἰ. ἐχέτω let this be *enough*, Pl.*Sph*.245e; ἰ. ἔχει πρός τι Id.*R*.430c, cf. X.*Cyr*.6.3.22; περί τινος Pl.*R*.402a; ἰ. ἔχειν τινί to be *sufficiently* supplied *with*.., Id.*Grg*.493c; ἰ. ἔχειν τοῦ βάθους Id.*Tht*.194d; ἐπιστήμης Id.*Phlb*.62a; ἰ. πεφυκέναι πρὸς τἆλλα Id.*Chrm*.158b; abs., Antipho 2.1.1: Sup. -ωτάτως Hp.*de Arte* 12; -ώτατα Pl.*Phlb*. 67a. **-ότης**, ητος, ἡ, *sufficiency, fitness*, Id.*Ly*.215a. II. *a sufficiency*, παίδων Id.*Lg*.930c. **-όω**, *make sufficient, qualify*, 2*Ep.Cor*.3.6 :—Pass., *to be empowered*, *PTeb*.20.8 (ii B.C.); *to be made complete, brought to perfection*, of the soul, τῷ περιέχοντι Hierocl. p.9 A. II. Pass., *to be satisfied, content*, τινι D.H.2.74: abs., Teles p.39 H., cf. LXX *Ma*.3.10; ἱκανούσθω ὑμῖν, c. inf., *let it suffice* you.., i.e. do it no more, LXX 3*Ki*.12.28, al.: abs., ib.*Nu*.16.7.

**ἵκαντι**, v. ἵκω. **ἰκάντιν**· εἴκοσιν, Hsch. (cf. ϝίκατι).

**ἰκάνω** [ῐκᾰ], impf. ἵκανον [ῑ by the augm.], used only in these tenses, the fut., aor., and pf. being supplied by ἰκνέομαι :—lengthd. form of ἵκω, found in Ep. and Lyr., sts. in Trag., *come*, ἐς Χρύσην, ἐς Σκαιάς.. πύλας, Il.1.431, 9.354; ἐπὶ νῆας 2.17; ἐνθάδε Od.15.492; so οἴκαδε A.*Ag*.1337 (anap.); οἳ ἱκάνομεν S.*El*.8; πρὸς ἐσχατιάν Pi.*O*. 3.43, cf. B.10.96: in Hom. mostly c. acc., *to come to*, ἱκάνω νῆας Ἀχαιῶν Il.24.501; ἱκανέμεν ἡμέτερον δῶ Od.4.139; later ἰ. δόμους A. *Pers*.159 (troch.): abs., ἢ φίλοι ἄνδρες ἱκάνετον Il.9.197; εὖ ἱκάνεις S. *El*.1102. 2. *reach, attain to*, [ἐλάτη] δι' ἠέρος αἰθέρ' ἵκανεν Il.14.288; φωνὴ δέ οἱ αἰθέρ' ἵκανεν 15.686; [ἄνεμος] αἰπὺν ἰ. οὐρανόν Sol.13.21; ἥβης μέτρον ἰ. Od.18.217, 19.532. II. c. acc. pers., esp. of grief, hardship, etc.; με πένθος ἱκάνει Od.6.169; μέγα πένθος Ἀχαιΐδα γαῖαν ἱκάνει Il.1.254; τάφος δέ οἱ ἦτορ ἵ. Od.23.93; ἄλγος, γῆρας, δύη, κάματος, κῆδος, ὀϊζύς, μόρος, ἱκάνει τινά, 2.41, Il.4.321 (v.l.), Od.18. 81, 5.457, Il.15.245, Od.5.289, Il.18.465; ὅτε μιν γλυκὺς ὕπνος ἱκάνοι 1.610; με παλαίφατα θέσφαθ' ἱκάνει they are *fulfilled* upon me, Od.9.507: c. dupl. acc., μιν ἄχος κραδίην καὶ θυμὸν ἰ. Il.2.171: rarely c. dat., σφῶϊν ἐελδομένοισιν ἱκάνω Od.21.209. 2. of a suppliant, σόν τε πόσιν σά τε γούναθ' ἱκάνω 7.147, al. III. Med., in signf. I. 1, οἶκον ἱκάνεται 23.7; in signf. II. 1, χρειὼ γὰρ ἱκάνεται Il.10.118; in signf. II. 2, τὰ σὰ γούναθ' ἱκάνομαι 18.457, Od.3.92, 4.322. (Fr. ἰκ-ἄνϝ-ω, ἰκ-ηϝ-ω (cf. ἰκνέομαι); Aeol. ἴκᾶνε dub. in Alc.*Supp*.34, [ἴκᾶ]νε prob. in Sapph.*Oxy*.2076.16; ἵκᾶνον f.l. in Od.15.101.)

**Ἰκάριος** [ῑκᾰ], α, ον, *Icarian*, πόντος Il.2.145; πέλαγος Hdt.6.96.

※ **ἰκάς** [ῑ], άδος, ἁ, Dor. etc. for εἰκάς, *twentieth* of the month, *SIG* 1025.47 (Cos), *IG*9(2).517.10 (Larissa); ἡικάς ib.12(3).1324 (Thera, vi/v B.C.). (ϝικ- in pr. n. Ϝικάδιος ib.5(2).271.8 (Mantinea).)

**ϝίκατι**, v. εἴκοσι :—hence **ἰκαστός**, = εἰκοστός, *IG*5(2).4.18 (Tegea, iv B.C.): **ϝικατίδειος**, ὁ, *twenty feet broad*, [ἄντομος] *Tab.Heracl*.2.18, al. **ϝικατιϝέτης**, v. εἰκοσαέτης. **ϝικατίπεδος**, ον, v. εἰκοσίπεδος.

※ **ἴκελος** [ῐ], η, ον, poet. and Ion. form of εἴκελος, *like, resembling*, τινι Il.11.467, al., Hes.*Sc*.198, Sapph.*Supp*.20b.1, B.*Fr*.19, Hdt.3. 81, Hp.*Epid*.3.4, Ar.*Av*.575, Theoc.2.51, etc.; ὀργαῖς ἀλωπέκων ἰ. *like* foxes in disposition, Pi.*P*.2.77; ἐπιθυμίη κυνὶ ἰ. Democr.224: c. gen., θέας ἰκέλαν dub. in Sapph.*Supp*.25.4. Adv. **-λως**, c. dat., *in the same way as*, Hp.*Gland*.8, Diotog.ap.Stob.4.1.133.

**ἰκελόω** [ῐ], *make like*, *AP*9.83 (Phil.).

**ἰκενάς·** ὀρχήσεις, Hsch. (cf. σικανοί, σίκιννις).

⊛ **ἰκεσ-ία**, ἡ, (ἰκέτης) (replaced by ἰκετεία in Att., cf. Phryn.3, *PS* p.77 B., but found in *IG*1².434; used later, *SIG*781.11 (Nysa, i B.C.), 888.11 (Scaptopara, iii A.D.), etc.):—*the prayer of a suppliant, supplication*, E.*Or.*1337, Plu.*Sol.*12, J.*AJ*11.8.4, *AP*5.215 (Agath.); πρὸς παντοίαν ἰ. τραπῆναι D.S.20.14: pl., Ph.2.2; ἰκεσίαισι σαῖς at thy *entreaties*, E.*Ph.*91; ἰκεσίας ποιεῖσθαι, on behalf of the state, Aeschin. 3.121; = Lat. *supplicatio*, D.H.8.43. **2.** = ἰκέτευμα, Plu.*Them.*24. [ῐ, but ῑ metri gr. in *AP*l.c., Procl.*H.*1.36.] ⊛ **-ιος**, α, ον, or ος, ον (v. infr.), *of* or *for suppliants*, epith. of Zeus, their protector, A.*Supp.* 616, S.*Ph.*484, E.*Hec.*345, *SIG*929 (Cos); also Ἱκέσιος alone, *IG*12 (3).402 (Thera); πρὸς Ἱκεσίου Luc.*Pisc.*3; ἰκεσία Θέμις Διός A.*Supp.* 360 (lyr.). **2.** *of* or *consisting of suppliants*, παρθένων ἰ. λόχος Id. *Th.*111 (lyr.). **3.** *suppliant*, ἰκεσίους πέμπων λιτάς S.*Ph.*495; ἰκεσίαν.. προστροπάν E.*Heracl.*108 (lyr.); ἰκεσίοις σὺν κλάδοις Id.*Supp.* 102; ἰκεσίᾳ χερί ib.108; ἀνάγκας ἰκεσίους λῦσαι ib.39; of persons, ἰκέσιός σε λίσσομαι S.*Ant.*1230; ἰκεσία τε γίγνομαι E.*Med.*710: ἰκέσιος, ὁ, as Subst., *suppliant*, *Berl.Sitzb.*1927.167 (Cyrene). **II.** ἡ Ἱκέσιος (sc. ἔμπλαστρος), name of a *plaster*, Paul.Aeg.3.62, 7.17; ἡ Ἱκεσίου Id.3.64. [ἰκ-, exc. metri gr. in A.R.2.215.]

**ἰκετᾰδόκος**, ον, *receiving suppliants*, σκοπή A.*Supp.*713.

**ἰκετ-εία** [ῐ], ἡ, more Att. form of ἰκεσία (q.v.), *supplication*, Th.1. 24; ἰκετείαν ποιεῖσθαί τινος to supplicate him, Id.3.67; ἰκετεῖαι θεῶν *addressed to* them, Lys.2.39; ἐφ' ἰκετείαν τραπόμενος Pl.*Ap.*39a; μετὰ δεήσεως καὶ ἰ. *PPetr.*2p.60 (iii B.C.), cf. *SIG*1181.12 (Jewish): pl., -είας ποιεῖσθαι Pl.*Smp.*183a, etc. **-ευμα**, ατος, τό, *mode of supplication*, μέγιστον ἰ. Th.1.137, cf. D.C.68.21. **-ευσις**, εως, ἡ, = ἰκεσία, Suid. ⊛ **-ευτέος**, α, ον, *to be besought* or *entreated*, Luc.*Merc.Cond.*38. **-ευτικός**, ή, όν, *supplicatory*, Sch.S.*OT* 143; = *precarius*, *Gloss.* Adv. -κῶς Hsch. s.v. ἀντήδης. **-εύω**, fut. -σω E.*IA*462 (cj. Markl.), Isoc.7.69: aor. 1 ἰκέτευσα: used by Hom. only in impf. and aor. with ῐ metri gr., but in Trag. ῑ from the augm.:—**Med.** and **Pass.** (v. infr.):—*approach as a suppliant*, ἐπεί σε φυγὼν ἰκέτευσα Od.15.277, al.; ἐς Πηλῆ' ἰκέτευσε Il.16. 574; ἐς Θήβας ἰ. Hes.*Sc.*13; ἰ. σε τῶνδε γουνάτων, πρὸς γονάτων σε, E.*Hec.*752, *Med.*854 (lyr.): abs., Hdt.3.48, Isoc.7.69, Phld.*Piet.* 63. **2.** *supplicate, beseech*, c. acc. pers. et inf., ὁ δέ με μάλα πόλλ' ἰκέτευεν ἱππόθεν ἐξέμεναι Od.11.530, cf. Hdt.1.11, S.*OC*1414, E.*Ion* 468 (lyr.); δέομαι ὑμῶν καὶ ἰ. καὶ ἀντιβολῶ.. βοηθῆσαι D.27. 68; δεόμενον καὶ ἰκετεύοντα σοφίας μεταδιδόναι Pl.*Euthd.*282b; ἰ. τὸν θεόν, ἵνα.. Aristeas 233; ἰκετεύεις ἵνα ἀφεθῇς Arr.*Epict.*3.24.76; ἰ. ὡς.. Luc.*Anach.*1: c. gen. pers. et inf., *beg of* one that.., E.*IA* 1242: c. dat., interpol. in Is.2.8:—Pass., τοῦ θεοῦ ἰκετευθέντος ὑπὸ σοῦ J.*AJ*6.2.2. **3.** c. acc. rei, ὑπὲρ οἴκου.. ἰ. τάδε E.*Or.*673; ὅσα πρὸς ἱεροῖς ἰκέτευσαν Th.2.47; περὶ ὧν ἔδοξεν ἔννομα ἰκετεύειν ἐν τῇ βουλῇ *IG*2².218.8, cf. 337.34:—Pass., τὰ -όμενα Aristeas 192. **4.** in Trag., freq. parenthetic, ἰκετεύω or ἰκετεύω σε, S.*Ph.*932, 1183 (lyr.), E.*Hec.*97 (anap.), cf. Ar.*Nu.*696, al.:—Med., Id.*Ec.*915 (lyr.). ⊛ **-ήριος**, poet. **ἰκτήριος**, α, ον, as Adj. in the latter form only, *of* or *fit for suppliants*, ἰ. θησαυρός, of hair offered to a god, S. *Aj.*1175; κλάδοι Id.*OT*3; ἰκτήριοι, = ἰκέται, ib.327; φωτῶν ἰκτήρια, = φῶτας ἰκτηρίους, Id.*OC*923. **II.** ἰκετηρία, poet. ἰκτηρία, Ion. -ίη (sc. ῥάβδος), ἡ, *olive-branch which the suppliant held in his hand* as a symbol of his condition, λευκοστεφεῖς ἰκτηρίας A.*Supp.*192; ἰκετηρίην λαβεῖν, φέρειν, Hdt.5.51, 7.141; ἰκετηρίαν ἔχειν Ar.*Pl.*383; καταθεῖναι ἐν τῷ Ἐλευσινίῳ And.1.110, cf. *UPZ*1.9 (iv B.C.); esp. of petitions laid before the Athenian people, ἰ. θεῖναι And. l.c., Arist.*Ath.*43.6 (less correctly θέσθαι Poll.8.96, wh. is a later use, cf. *SIG*²666.6 (Samos)); ὑπὲρ θυγατρὸς ἰ. τιθεμένη *PTeb.*326.3 (iii A.D.); ἰ. ἔθηκεν παρ' ὑμῖν, = ἰκέτευσεν ὑμᾶς, D.18.107, cf. 24.12; ὑπὲρ τοῦ μισθοῦ ἰ. θεῖναι εἰς τὴν βουλὴν Aeschin.1.104, cf. 2.15; later ἰ. πέμπειν, προβάλλεσθαι, Plu.*Pomp.*28, Ael.*VH*3.26; ἰκετηρίας προσενέγκας, ἰκετηρίαν προσάγειν, *Ep.Hebr.*5.7, *POxy.*71 i 3 (iv A.D.): metaph., ἰκετηρίαν δὲ γόνασιν ἐξάπτω σέθεν τὸ σῶμα τοὐμόν, where the suppliant represents herself as the olive-branch, E.*IA*1216; νομίζετε τὸν παῖδα τουτονὶ ἰκετηρίαν προκεῖσθαι D.43.83. **2.** = ἰκεσία, v.l. in Isoc.8. 138 (pl.), cf. Plb.3.112.8 (pl.), Jul.*ad Ath.*275c, Hld.7.7. **-ηρίς**, ίδος, ἡ, pecul. fem. of ἰκετήριος, Orph.*H.*3.13, 34.27. ⊛ **-ης**, ου, ὁ, (ἰκνέομαι) *one who comes to seek aid* or *protection, suppliant*; freq. in Hom. of *one who comes to seek for purification after homicide*, ἀνὴρ ἰ. Il. 24.158, cf. Od.9.270, al.: later generally, ἰκέται ἱζόμενοι τοῦ θεοῦ Hdt.2.113, cf. 5.71; ἰ. σέθεν ἔρχομαι Pi.*O.*5.19, cf. S.*OC*634, Th.1. 136; ἰ. πατρῴων τάφων Id.3.59; δέξασθαι ἰκέτην A.*Supp.*27 (anap.); of pilgrims to a healing shrine, ἐγκεκοιμισμένων τῶν ἰκετᾶν *IG*4.951. 90 (Epid.); ὑβρίζειν.. εἰς ἰκέτας Phld.*Ir.*p.35 W.:—wrongly expld. as *protector of suppliants* by some Gramm. in Od.16.422. **-ήσιος**, α, ον, epith. of Zeus, = ἰκέσιος, 13.213. **II.** *suppliant*, Nonn. *D.*36.379. ⊛ **-ικός**, ή, όν, = ἰκετήριος, Ph.2.546, Aq.*Pr.*27.6. Adv. -κῶς Sch.Par.A.R.1.824, Sch.E.*Hec.*147. ⊛ **-ις** (parox.), ιδος, ἡ, fem. of ἰκέτης, Hdt.4.165, 9.76, A.*Supp.*350, 428 (both lyr.), S.*OT* 920, *IG*4.951.4 (Epid.), A.R.4.743, etc.

**ἰκετοδόχος**, ον, = ἰκεταδόκος, Eust.1807.9.

**ἰκετώσυνα** (sc. ἱερά), τά, *purifications*, Hsch.

**ἵκηαι**, Ep. for ἵκῃ, 2 sg. aor. 2 subj. of ἰκνέομαι.

**ἶκκος**, ὁ, = ἵππος, *EM*474.12; cf. ἵππος sub fin.

**ἰκμ-ᾰδώδης**, ες, *moist, wet*, Hsch. s.v. ἴκμενος, dub. in Sch.Arat. 1065: **ἰκματώδης** in Ach.Tat.*Intr.*34. **-άζω**, = sq., Nic.*Fr.*70. 17. **II.** *filter through, ooze*, Alex.Aphr. *in Mete.*87.27. **III.** *evaporate moisture, dry up*, ἰκμασθέντος δὲ τούτου Plu.2.954e codd.; ἰκμάζειν· κατασκελετεύειν, Hsch. ⊛ **-αίνω**, *moisten*, Nic.*Al.*112:—Med., δέμας ἰκμαίνεσθαι *anoint one's* body, A.R.3.847:—Pass., *to be wetted, to be wet*, Nic.*Fr.*70.8, A.R.4.1066. **-αῖος**, ὁ, (ἰκμάς) epith. of Zeus, *god of rain*, Id.2.522, Nonn.*D.*5.270. ⊛ **-ᾰλέος**, α, ον, *damp, wet*, Ath.Med.ap.Orib.*inc.*23.23, Aret.*SD*2.1, Opp.*H.*3.595. **2.** *full of fluid*, of the liver, Hp.*Mul.*1.7.

⊛ **ἴκμαρ**, τό, = sq., Hsch. (Rather ἰκμάρ, if Lacon.) **II.** v.l. ant. for ἴκταρ (B), Erot.

**ἰκμ-άς**, άδος, ἡ, *moisture*, e.g. of oily leather, Il.17.392; ἰκμάδος ἐστὶ ἐν αὐτῇ [τῇ Λιβύῃ] οὐδέν Hdt.4.185; ἀνιεὶς ἐκ τοῦ σώματος ἰκμάδα, of a corpse exposed to the sun, Id.3.125, cf. Hp.*Aër.*8; of *moisture* in the soil, *Ev.Luc.*8.6; also θανόντων ἰσὶν οὐκ ἔνεστ' ἰκμάς no *blood*, A.*Fr.*229 (prob.); of the bodily *humours*, Hp.*Morb.*4.40; of all kinds of *animal juices* or *moist secretions*, τὸ περίττωμα τῆς ὑγρᾶς ἰ. ὃν καλοῦμεν ἱδρῶτα Arist.*PA*668ᵇ4; ἡ τῶν καταμηνίων ἰ. Id.*GA*727ᵇ11, cf. *HA*556ᵇ27, al.: com. metaph., τὴν ἰ. τῆς φροντίδος Ar.*Nu.*233; ἰ. Βάκχου, i.e. wine, *AP*5.133 (Posidipp.); ἰ. δρυός, i.e. gum, ib.6.109 (Antip.). **-ᾰσία**, ἡ, = ἰκμάς, Hsch., *Gloss.*

⊛ **ἰκμάω** (A), = λικμάω, Hsch. (Act. and Pass.):—also **ἰκμάσαι·** ἐφορμῆσαι, Id. (For νικμάω, ν being lost by dissimilation; v. νεικητήρ.)

⊛ **ἰκμάω** (B), in Pass., Cypr. acc. pl. masc. pf. part. ἰκμαμένος *wounded*, *Inscr.Cypr.*135.3 H. (or ἰγμ- as *Schwyzer* 679.3). (Perh. cogn. with Lat. *ico.*)

**ἴκμενος**, only in the phrase ἴκμενος οὖρος, *of a fair* breeze, Il.1.479, Od.2.420, al.; not *moist*, as Hsch. (Perh. not related to ἵκω, ἰκνέομαι.)

**ἴκμη**, ἡ, (ἰκμάς) *a plant growing in moist places, duckweed, Lemna minor*, Thphr.*HP*4.10.1.

**ἴκμιος**, α, ον, *moist*, Nonn.*D.*2.490. **2.** = ἰκμαῖος, as epith. of Aristaeus, Call.*Aet.*3.1.34.

**ἰκμόβωλον**, τό, *wet clod of earth*, Dsc.2.106.

**ἰκμώδης**, ες, *moist, wet*, Sch.rec.A.*Pr.*88.

**ἰκνά·** τροφεῖα, **ἰκνεῖαν·** τροφεῖαν, **ἰκνεῖος·** τροφεύς (Rhodian words), Hsch.

⊛ **ἰκνέομαι**, lengthd. form of ἵκω (q.v.), ἱκάνω, wh. are the Homeric forms of the pres. (exc. ἰκνεύμεναι, ἰκνεύμεσθα, Od.9.128, 24.339), first in Alc.98 (s. v.l.): impf. ἰκνεῖτο S.*OC*970: fut. ἵξομαι Il.6.502, Parm. 3.2, A.*Supp.*159 (lyr.); Dor. ἰξοῦμαι *AP*9.341 (Glauc.): aor. 2 ἱκόμην Il.8.149, etc.; inf. ἵκεσθαι Sapph.*Supp.*1.2 [ῐ, exc. when lengthd. by the augm.]; for part. ἴκμενος v. sub voce: pf. ἷγμαι S.*Tr.*229, part. ἱγμένος Id.*Ph.*494: non-thematic aor. 2 ἷκτο Hes.*Th.*481, [Simon.]179.4, Euph.2: (ἀφικνέομαι is used in early Prose, exc. in signf. III; ἵκοντο is f.l. in Th.5.40, ἵκηται is a poet. reminiscence in Pl.*Phdr.*276d; but ἵκετο is found in Hdt.1.216, ἵκηται Hp.*Loc.Hom.* 47; also in later Prose, Luc.*Salt.*5, *DDeor.*6.4, Procop.*Pers.*1.4, 2.21):—*come*, αἶψα δ' ἵκοντο Il.18.532; ὁππότε Κρήτηθεν ἵκοιτο when he *came to* us.., 3.233; ὑπότροπον οἴκαδ' ἰ. Od.22.35; ἐς χῶρον Il.4. 446; ἐπὶ νῆας 6.69; κατὰ λειμῶνα Od.24.13; πρὸς γούνατα Hes.*Th.* 460; ὑπὸ πτόλιν Il.11.182; εἰς ὁμόν Parm.8.46; πρὸς ὁμοῖον Emp.62. 6; τυἰδ' ἴκεσθαι Sapph. l.c.: freq. in Hom., c. acc., *arrive at*, ἵκετο νῆας Il.8.149; τέλος ἵκεο μύθων 9.56; οἶκον.. καὶ σὴν ἐς πατρίδα γαῖαν Od.23.258; later ἰκέσθαι γαῖαν Pi.*P.*4.118 codd.; βένθος Emp.35.3; ἄλσος A.*Supp.*556 (lyr.); στέγας S.*OT*534, etc. **2.** *reach, attain to*, ποσὶν οὖδας ἰ. Od.8.376; οὐδ' ἵκετο χρόα καλόν, of a spear, Il.11.352; οὐδ' ὀστέον ἵκετο Od.19.451 (v. ὑπερίημι); so of things, ἠχή, καπνὸς αἰθέρ' ἰ., Il.13.837, 18.207; ἔμπης ἐς γαῖάν τε καὶ οὐρανὸν ἵκετ' ἀϋτμή 14. 174; ἐς πόλιν ἵκετ' αὐτή Od.14.265; of Time, ἥβης μέτρον or ἥβην ἰ., Il.11.225, 24.728, etc.; γήραος οὐδόν Od.15.246; so ἐπὶ γῆρας 8.227; ἠῶ ἰ. *live till* morn, 17.497; also ὀλέθρου πεῖραθ' ἰ. Il.6.143; λέκτροιο παλαιοῦ θεσμὸν ἵκοντο Od.23.296, cf. 354; φίλην ἐπὶ γένναν ἰ. Emp. 110.9; ἐς ἄπειρον Xenoph.28; ἐς τὸ τυθῆναι Hdt.1.216; εἰς τὸ λήθης γῆρας Pl.*Phdr.* l.c.:—in various phrases, ἰ. μετὰ κλέος *come* in quest of glory, Il.11.227; ἐς χεῖρας ἰ. *come* into one's power, 10. 448; ὅ τι χεῖρας ἵκοιτο whatever *came* to hand, Od.12.331; ἰ. ἐς γενεάν τινος into his family, Pi.*N.*10.14; ἐς λόγους τοὺς σοὺς ἰ. to speak with thee, S.*El.*315; ἐνθάδ' ἵξομαι *shall come* to this *at last*, Id.*Aj.* 1365; ἥν ποτε δασμὸς ἵκηται if ever a division *come about*, Il.1. 166. **II.** with a person as object, τινα ib.139, etc.; ἔς τινα Od. 6.176; but also, *come to* his *house*, 20.372; Πηλεΐωνάδ' ἰ. *to the hut* of the son of P., Il.24.338; μετὰ Τρῶας ἰ. 3.264: rarely c. dat., ἐπειγομένοισι δ' ἵκοντο *came to* them at need, 12.374; cf. ἱκάνω II. **2.** of suffering, desire, anger, etc., *come upon*, Ἀχιλλῆος ποθὴ ἵξεται υἷας Ἀχαιῶν Il.1.240; τί σε φρένας ἵκετο πένθος; ib.362; ὅν τιν' ἵκηται ἄλη καὶ πῆμα καὶ ἄλγος Od.15.345; ὁππότε μιν κάματός τε καὶ ἱδρὼς γούναθ' ἵκοιτο Il.13.711; ἄδος, σέβας ἵ. τινα θυμόν, 11.88, 18.178; μὲ ἵ. ἄχος κραδίην 23.47. **3.** *approach as suppliant*, τὴν ἱκόμην φεύγων 14.260, cf. 22.123; τὰ σὰ γοῦνα ἱκόμεθ' Od.9.267; θεοὺς προστροπαῖς ἰκνουμένη A.*Pers.*216 (troch.); Ζῆνα.. ἱξόμεσθα σὺν κλάδοις Id.*Supp.*159 (lyr.); [θεὸν] θυέεσσιν ἰκνεῖσθαι *approach* a god with offerings and prayer, Theoc.*Ep.*8.3. **b.** Poet. in pres., *supplicate, beseech*, τάσδε τὰς θεὰς καλῶν ἰκνοῦμαι S.*OC*1011; καί σε πρὸς τοῦ σοῦ τέκνου καὶ θεῶν ἰκνοῦμαι μή.. Id.*Aj.*588, cf. *OC*275, *Ph.*470; ταύτης ἰκνοῦμαί σ' E.*Or.*671: c. inf., πάντες σ' ἰκνοῦνται.. θάψαι νεκρούς Id.*Supp.*130: freq. parenthetic, S.*Ph.*932, *El.*136 (lyr.), Ar.*Ec.*958, Tim.*Pers.*139. **III.** pres. and impf., *it becomes, befits, pertains to*, c. acc. et inf., φαμὲν ἡμέας ἰκνέεσθαι ἡγεμονεύειν Hdt.9.26; τοὺς μάλιστα ἰκνέεται (sc. κεκάρθαι) Id.2.36; ἰκνέεται *it is usual* that.., Hp.*Art.*63; later, not impers., οὐ ἡ ἱερουργία ἰκνεῖτο D.C.*Fr.*25.5; ὅ[σα τὰς δίκας ἰ]κνεῖται *SIG*953.46

(Cnidos, ii B.C.). **b.** *αὐτὸς καὶ ὧν ἱκνεῖται*, of a man and *those to whom he belongs*, i.e. his family, ib.46.25, al. (Halic.). **2.** freq. in part., *τὸ ἱκνεύμενον that which is fitting, proper*, Hdt.6.84; *ὁ ἱ.*, with or without *χρόνος, the fit, proper* time, Hp.*Aer.*7, Hdt.6.86.*α'*; *ἐν ἱκνουμένᾳ ἁμέρᾳ* Orac.ap.D.43.66; *τὸ ἱ. ἀνάλωμα the quota* of expense, Th.1.99; *κατὰ τοὺς ἱ. χρόνους* Arist.*GA*750$^{b}$13 (also of *the latter days*, D.H.1.66); *ἱ. καιροί* Thphr.*CP*1.13.3; *τὰ -ούμενα μεγέθη* Arist.*GA*772$^{a}$8; *ἡ ἱ. ἐπιστήμη* Id.*Pol.*1288$^{b}$16; *τῆς ἱ. ἡλικίας τυχεῖν* ib.1332$^{b}$41; also *ἱκνούμεναι ἀποδείξεις convincing* proofs, Phld.*Piet.*79; *οὐδὲν εἴρηται ἱ.* S.E.*M.*1.205; *λόγος τινὶ ἱκνούμενος favourable*, *SIG*679.77 (Magn. Mae., ii B.C.). Adv. *ἱκνουμένως*, Ion. *-ευμένως, fittingly, aright*, Hdt.6.65, Hp.*Mul.*2.135, M.Ant.5.12.

**ἵκνυς**, *υος, ἡ, dust* or *ashes*, *τὰν ἵκνυν ἀπὸ τῶ βωμῶ..ἀφελὲν ἐς καθαρόν* *Berl.Sitzb.*1927.159 (Cyrene); cf. **ἴκνυον**· *κονίαν, σμῆμα*, Hsch.; *τὴν* **ἴγνυν** *οἴνῳ διατρίψας, δοῦναι πιεῖν* Hp.*Nat.Mul.*88 (v.l. *ἴγδην*).

⊛ **ἴκρια**, *τά* (sg. v. infr. III; for the accent v. Hdn.Gr.1.357), *half-deck* at the stern of a ship, *νηῶν ἴκρι' ἐπῴχετο μακρὰ βιβάσθων* Il.15.676; [*κυβερνήτης*] *κάππεσ' ἀπ' ἰκριόφιν* Od.12.414; *εἰς ἴκρια νηὸς ἔβαινον πρῴρης* (i.e. from the prow) ib.229; *νηὸς ἐπ' ἰκριόφιν καταλέξεται* 3.353; *εὐπάκτων ἐπ' ἰκρίων σταθεὶς ὄρουσε* B.16.83: wrongly expld. by Eust. as = *ἐγκοίλια* in Od.5.252, but perh. so used by Nonn. *D.*40.447,452; expld. as = *κεραία* in A.R.1.566 by Sch., but prob. wrongly, cf. Lyc.751. II. generally, *platform, stage*, *ἴκρια ἐπὶ σταυρῶν ὑψηλῶν..ἕστηκε* Hdt.5.16, cf. Str.12.3.18, Hsch. **2.** *scaffolding*, *IG*1$^{2}$.94.28 (prob. in 374.151), 4.39 (Aegina, v B.C.), *BCH*6.27 (Delos, ii B.C.). **3.** *benches* in a theatre, Cratin.323, Ar.*Th.*395, Ath.4.167f. **4.** dub. sens. in Thphr.*HP*5.6.2. III. sg., = *ἱστός, mast*, Eust.1533.31; *pole*, dub. l. in Nic.*Th.*198; set up on a cenotaph, Marcellin.*Vit. Thuc.*31.

**ἰκριάς**, *ἡ*, = *pergula*, *Gloss.* (dub.).

**ἴκρινον**, *τό*, = *tabulum*, *Gloss.* (dub.).

⊛ **ἰκριο-ποιέω**, = *ἰκριόω* I, *Rev.Phil.*50.69 (Didyma, ii B.C.), *Inscr. Délos* 290.241 (iii B.C.). **-ποίησις**, *εως, ἡ, erection of scaffolding*, ib.240 (prob.). **-ποιός**, *ὁ, maker of scaffolding* or *benches*, Poll.7.125.

**ἰκρι-όω**, *erect scaffolding*, *IG*1$^{2}$.371.22, 374.74 (*ἰκ-*). II. *furnish with benches*, *θέατρον* D.C.43.22:—Pass., ib.59.7. **-ωμα**, *ατος, τό, scaffold*, *IG*1$^{2}$.374.67 (*ἰκ-*), Hsch. s.v. *κατῆλιψ*. II. in pl., = *ἀντηρίδες*, Eust.903.54. **-ωτήρ**, *ῆρος, ὁ, upright* supporting a gallery or loft, *IG*2$^{2}$.1668.78: pl., ib.1$^{2}$.313.110 (*ἰκ-*). II. in pl. *-ῆρες*, *οἱ, flooring of the deck*, ib.2$^{2}$.1629.1156, 1631.339 (or perh. *joists* which support it). **2.** = *ἰκριώματα*, Demioprat.ap.Poll.10.157.

⊛ **ἰκταῖος**, *α, ον*, = *ἱκέσιος*, A.*Supp.*385 [lyr., with penult. short].

**ἴκταρ** (A), Adv. *close together, thickly* ( = *πυκνῶς*, Hsch.), *κεραυνοὶ ἴ. ἅμα βροντῇ τε καὶ ἀστεροπῇ ποτέοντο* Hes.*Th.*691. II. Prep. c. gen., *close to, hard by*, *ἴ. μελάθρων* A.*Ag.*116 (lyr.); *ἴ. ἥμενοι Διός* Id.*Eu.*998 (lyr.): c. dat., Alcm.23.80: abs., *ταῦτα πρὸς τύραννον.. οὐδ' ἴ. βάλλει* do not strike even *near* him, are quite wide of the mark, prov. in Pl.*R.*575c, cf. Ael.*NA*15.29.

**ἴκταρ** (B), *τό*, = *pudendum muliebre*, Hp.*Mul.*2.174 (restored fr. Erot. and Gal.19.105: *ἧπαρ* (*ἦπαρ*) codd. Hp.).

**ἴκταρ** (C), *ὁ*, some kind of *fish*, Call.*Fr.*38:—also **ἰκτάρα**, *ἡ*, Hsch.; = *albula*, *Gloss.*; cf. *κτάρα*.

**ἰκτέα**· *ἀκόντιον*, Hsch.

**ἰκτερ-ίας** *λίθος, ὁ, a yellowish* kind of *stone*, Plin.*HN*37.170. **-ιάω**, (*ἴκτερος*) *to be ill of the jaundice*, v.l. in Dsc.3.1, M.Ant.6.57, Hld.3.8, S.E.*P.*1.44, Gal.18(1).250. **-ικός**, *ή, όν, jaundiced*, Gal.*Nat. Fac.*1.13, *Gp.*12.17.9; *for jaundice*, *φάρμακον* Ruf.ap.Orib.7.26.142. **-ις**, = *aurugo*, *Gloss.* **-ίτης**, = *rosmarinum*, ib.; but **-ῖτις**, Ps.-Dsc.3.75, Apul.*Herb.*80 (v.l. *-es*): **-ιώδης**, *ες*, = *ἰκτερικός*, Hp.*Aph.*5.72, Dsc.3.1; and **-όεις**, *εσσα, εν*, *χλόος* Nic.*Al.*475. **-όομαι**, Pass., *have the jaundice*, Hp.*Prorrh.*1.32, Gal.16.574. ⊛ **-ος**, *ὁ, jaundice*, Hp.*Aph.*4.62 (pl.), *Morb.*2.38, *Int.*35 (pl.), etc. II. *a bird of a yellowish-green colour*, by looking at which a jaundiced person was cured—the bird died! Plin.*HN*30.94 (who identifies it with *galgulus*, the *golden oriole*). **-ώδης**, *ες*, = *ἰκτερικός*, Hp.*Epid.*3.17.*ιγ'*.

**ἴκτευ**· *κρατεῖς* (Lacon.), Hsch. **ἰκτή**, = *ἰκτίν*, Ruf.*Fr.*79.

**ἴκτηρ**, *ερος, ὁ*, = *ἴκτερος*, acc. *ἴκτερα* v.l. in Lxx *Le.*26.16.

**ἱκ-τήρ**, *ῆρος, ὁ*, = *ἱκέτης, a suppliant*, S.*OT*185 (lyr.), E.*Heracl.*764 (lyr.): as Adj., *ἱ. κλάδοι* S.*OT*143; *θαλλός* E.*Supp.*10. II. *Ζεὺς ἱκτήρ the protector of the suppliant*, A.*Supp.*479. **-τήριος**, *α, ον*, v. *ἱκετήριος*. **-της**, *ου, ὁ*, = *ἱκέτης*, Lyc.763, Hsch., Theognost. *Can.*15.

**ἰκτίδεος**, *α, ον*, (*ἰκτίν*) v. *κτίδεος*.

**ἰκτίν**, *ῖνος, ὁ*, = sq., Lyr. in *Philol.*80.336 (*-τειν* Pap.): acc. sg. *ἰκτῖνα* Ar.*Fr.*628, Pl.Com.243, Jul.*Mis.*366a: gen. sg. *ἰκτῖνος* ibid.: nom. pl. *ἰκτῖνες* Paus.5.14.1: dat. pl. *ἰκτῖσι* Ctes.*Fr.*57.11: nom. sg. also **ἰκτίς**, *Gloss.*, prob. in Hsch. (Pamph.).

**ἴκτῖνος** (Sch.Il.*Oxy.*1087.60 (i B.C.), Choerob.*in Theod.*1.267, but **ἰκτῖνος** Hdn.Gr.1.183), *ὁ, kite, Miluus regalis*, Semon.12, Hdt.2.22, S.*Fr.*111, 767, Ar.*Av.*502, al., Pl.*Phd.*82a, Men.926; *ἰκτίνου ἀγχιστρόφου ἦθος* Thgn.1261; *φεύγεις ἰκτίνου σχέτλιον ἦθος ἔχων* Id.1302. II. a kind of *wolf*, Opp.*C.*3.331. (Cf. Arm. *çin* 'kite'.)

⊛ **ἴκτῖς**, *ῖδος* (*ἰκτῖδας* is f.l. in Ar.*Ach.*880), *ἡ, the γαλῆ ἀγρία* or *yellow-breasted marten*, Ar. l.c., Arist.*HA*612$^{b}$10, Nic.*Th.*196, cf. Sch. ad loc., Aret.*SD*1.15. (*ι* is prothetic, cf. *κτίδεος*.)

**ἰκτορεύω**, poet. for *ἱκετεύω*, S.*Fr.*58.

**ἰκτός**, in neut. **ἰκτόν**· *τὸ ἐοικός*, and **ἰκτύς**· *ὁμοίωμα, εἰκών*, Theognost.*Can.*15, 16.

**ἴκτωρ**, *ορος, ὁ*, = *ἱκέτης*, but used of women in A.*Supp.*653 (lyr.).

⊛ **ἵκω** [v. sub fin.], chiefly Ep., Lyr., and Dor., never in Hdt. or Trag. (in A.*Supp.*176 Pors. restored *ἥκετε*); cf. *ἱκάνω, ἱκνέομαι*; Dor., Arc. **ἵκω** *IG*4.329 (Corinth), 952.16 (Epid.), *Schwyzer* 323 *C* 37 (Delph.), *IG*5(2).3.12 (Tegea), written *εἵκω* in Epich.35.13 codd., but *ἵκει* correctly in Ar.*Lys.*87; 3 pl. *ἵκαντι*, = *ἥκουσιν*, Hsch. (cf. *παρίκω*): impf. *ἷκον* Il.1.317: poet. fut. inf. *ἱξέμεν* Pi.*Pae.*6.116; Dor. fut. *ἱξῶ* Megar. in Ar.*Ach.*742: Ep. aor. *ἷξον* (v. infr.); also aor. 1 *ἷξα* Q.S.12.461 (v.l.): for *ἵξομαι, ἷγμαι*, v. *ἱκνέομαι*:—*come*, of persons, *ἐς δόμον ἵκει* Od.18.353; *ἷξεν δ' ἐς Πριάμοιο* Il.24.160, cf. 122; *εἰ δέ κεν οἴκαδ' ἵκωμι φίλην ἐς πατρίδα γαῖαν* 9.414; *ἐς Ῥόδον ἷξεν ἀλώμενος* 2.667; *ἐπὶ Θρῃκῶν..τέλος ἷξον ἰόντες* 10.470; *ἷξε δ' ἐπ' ἐσχατιήν* 20.328; *ποταμοῖο κατὰ στόμα..ἷξε νέων* Od.5.442: in Hom. freq. c. acc., *come to*, *δόμον* Il.18.406, etc.; *Μαλειάων ὄρος* Od.3.288; *εἰ Θεμίστιον ἵκεις ὥστ' ἀείδειν* Pi.*N.*5.50, cf. *O.*5.9; *αἴ κ' αὐτὸς ἵκῃ, ἀνελέσθω* prob. in *IG*5(2).159.2 (*Class.Phil.*20.134). **2.** of things, *Φρυγίην..κτήματα περνάμεν' ἵκει come* or *are brought to..*, Il.18.292; also *ὁπότε χρόνος ἷξε δικασπόλος* Maiist.52. **3.** *attain to, reach*, *κνίση δ' οὐρανὸν ἷκεν* Il.1.317, cf. 2.153, 14.60; *αἴγλη δι' αἰθέρος οὐρανὸν ἷκε* 2.458; *ὀρυμαγδὸς..οὐρανὸν ἷκε δι' αἰθέρος* 17.425; *κλέος οὐρανὸν ἵκει* Od.9.20; *ὕβρις τε βίη τε..οὐρανὸν ἵκει* 15.329; *Ἰθάκης γε καὶ ἐς Τροίην ὄνομ' ἵκει* 13.248; *ἵκῃ τ' ἐς ἄκρον ἀνδρείας* Simon.58.6. **4.** of sufferings, feelings, etc., *ὅτε κέν τινα..χόλος ἵκοι come upon* him, Il.9.525; *τοι πινυτὴ φρένας ἵκει* Od.20.228; *χρειὼ ἵκει τινά* 2.28, 5.189: abs., *χρειὼ τόσον ἵκει* Il.10.142. [In *ἵκω*, *ῑ* always; in *ἱκάνω*, and the unaugmented moods of *ἱκόμην*, *ῐ* always.—*ἵκοντ'* is prob. for *ἵκοντο* [*ῐ*] in Pi.*P.*2.36.] (Prob. cogn. with *ἥκω*.)

**ἴλᾱ** [*ῑ*], *ἡ*, Dor. for *ἴλη*.

**ἰλᾰδόν** [*ῑ*], Adv., (*ἴλη*) *in troops*, Il.2.93, Hdt.1.172 (vv.ll. *ἰλ-*, *εἰλ-*): generally, *in abundance*, *κακότητα καὶ ἰ. ἔστιν ἑλέσθαι* Hes.*Op.*287.

**ἱλάειρᾰ**, *ἡ, mildly-shining*, *φλὸξ ἱλάειρα* [*ῐλᾰ*] Emp.85; *ἱλάειρα* [*ῑλᾱ*] *σελήνη* Id.40: as pr. n., Cypr.*Fr.*8. (Prob. from *ἱλαρός*.)

**ἱλάεις**, *εντος, ὁ*, contr. **ἱλᾶς** (q.v.), Ion. **ἱλῆς** (q.v.), Aeol. **ἰλλάεις**, = *ἵλαος*, *ἰλλάεντι θύμῳ* Alc.*Supp.*4.19: for *ἱλάεος*· *ἱδαρός*, Hsch., read *ἱλάεις*· *ἱλαρός*. [*ᾱ* by nature.]

**ἵλαθι**, v. *ἵλημι*.

**Ἰλαῖος**, *ὁ* (sc. *μήν*), name of month at Delphi, *SIG*$^{2}$847.2, al. (Perh. connected with *ἴλη*.)

**ἵλᾰμαι**, = *ἱλάομαι*, *ἵλαμαι δέ σ' ἀοιδῇ* *h.Hom.*19.48, 21.5; *Ἄρτεμιν ἵλασθαι θέλξαι θ' ὑπερήνορα θῆρα* Orph.*A.*944; cf. *ἵλημι*. [*ῐ* in *h.Hom.*, *ῑ* in Orph.]

⊛ **ἱλάομαι** [*ῑλᾰ*], Ep. pres. for *ἱλάσκομαι*, *ταύροισι καὶ ἀρνειοῖς ἱλάονται* Il.2.550; *ἱλάεσθαι* A.R.2.847:—also **ἱλέομαι**, A.*Supp.*117 (lyr.): **ἱλεόομαι**, Pl.*Lg.*804b and later Prose, as Luc.*Salt.*17, Porph.*Antr.*20, D.C.59.27, Procop.*Aed.*3.6, Ps.-Callisth.1.6:—also **ἱλαόομαι**, *MAMA*1.230 (Laodicea Combusta).

⊛ **ἵλαος** [v. sub fin.], *ον*, Ep. and Lyr. (incl. lyr. of Trag., A.*Eu.*1040, S.*OC*1480, Ar.*Th.*1148): irreg. gen. *ἱλάονος* *UPZ*1.8 (iv B.C.); Att. and later **ἵλεως**, *ων* (also in Herod.4.25, v.l. for *ἵλεον* in Hdt.6.91), dual *ἵλεω* Pl.*Euthd.*273e; nom. pl. *ἵλεῳ* S.*OC*44, X.*Mem.*1.1.9 (later *ἵλεως* indecl. as nom. pl., *SIG*985.47 (Philadelphia, ii or i B.C.), as acc. sg., Lxx *2Ma.*7.37, 10.26, as gen. sg., ib.2.22); neut. *ἵλεα* Pl.*Phd.*95a: **ἵλεος**, *ον*, Hdt.4.94, 6.91 (v. supr.); also Cret., *SIG*527.92 (Dreros, iii B.C.), *GDI*5039.26 (Hierapytna), Hsch.: **ἱληϝος**, dub. in *IG*5(1).1562 (Olymp., vi or v B.C., = Epigr.ap.Paus.5.24.3, where *ἱλάῳ*); Aeol. **ἴλλαος** Hdn.Gr.2.524, cf. *ἱλάεις*:—of gods, *propitious, gracious*, *ἔπειθ' ἵλαος Ὀλύμπιος ἔσσεται ἡμῖν* Il.1.583, cf. Hes.*Op.*340, Thgn.782, Archil.75, Pi.*O.*3.34, Trag. et Ar. ll. cc., Theoc.5.18: in Prose, Pl.*Lg.*712b, Lxx *Ge.*43.23, al., *UPZ*78.24 (*εἵλ-*, ii B.C.), *Ep. Hebr.*8.12, etc.; in deprecation, *ἵλεώς σοι, κύριε* (sc. *ὁ θεός*), i.e. be it far from thee, *Ev.Matt.*16.22; *ἵ. ἡμῖν Πλάτων καὶ ἐνταῦθα* *OGI*721.10 (Egypt, iv A.D.). **2.** of things, *propitious, blameless, atoned for*, *ἵλαον ἦναι*, opp. *ἰνμενφὲς ἦναι*, *IG*5(2).262 (Mantinea, v B.C.). II. of men, *gracious, kindly*, *σὺ δ' ἵλαον ἔνθεο θυμόν* Il.9.639; *σοι.. θυμὸς ἐνὶ φρεσὶν ἵ. ἔστω* 19.178; *ἵλεως κλύειν* S.*El.*655; *δέξασθαι* Id.*Aj.*1009, cf. *Tr.*763; *ἐποίησέ θ' ἱλαρὸν..κἀπέδειξεν ἵλεων* Ephipp.6.7: sts. almost, = *ἱλαρός*, *μειδῆσαι γελάσαι τε καὶ ἵλαον σχεῖν θυμόν* *h.Cer.*204, cf. Pl.*Smp.*206d; *ὁ οἶνος τὸν ἄνθρωπον ποιεῖ ἵλεων* Id.*Lg.*649a. III. Adv. *ἱλάως* and *ἱλέως*, Hsch. [*ῑ* always: *ᾱ* Il.1.583, *h.Cer.*204, Hes. and A. ll. cc., Euph.12, *Pae.Erythr.*19, Theoc.5.18, Epigr.ap.Paus. l.c., *IG*12(2).476, Parth.*Fr.*4; elsewh. *ᾰ*, v. supr., also Id.*Fr.*32, etc.]

**ἱλᾰρ-εία** [*ῐ*], *ἡ, rejoicing*; in pl., = *ἱλάρια, τά*, Sallust.4. **-εύομαι**, *to be joyful, exult*, Sm.*Ca.*1.4, al., Dosith.p.431 K. (prob.). **-ία**, *ἡ*, (*ἱλαρός*) = *ἱλαρότης*, Herod.Med.ap.Orib.5.27.20, Vett.Val.3.27, *PFlor.*391.43 (iii A.D.), dub. in Luc.*Am.*17; *μετὰ πάσης χαρᾶς καὶ ἱλαρίας* *Sammelb.*991 (iii A.D.). II. pet name for a *γαλῆ*, interpol. in Artem.3.28. **-ια** (sc. *ἱερά*), *τά*, = Lat. *hilaria, festival of rejoicing* in various cults, e.g. Isis, *CIL*1$^{2}$.p.334; esp. of Magna Mater, Jul.*Or.*5.168d, Macr.*Sat.*1.21.10, Dam.*Isid.*131.

**ἱλᾰροποιέω** [*ῐ*], *gladden*, *Gloss.*

⊛ **ἱλᾰρός** [*ῐ*], *ά, όν*, (*ἵλαος*) *cheerful, merry*, *φέγγος* Ar.*Ra.*456 (lyr.); *ἱλαροὶ ἀντὶ σκυθρωπῶν* X.*Mem.*2.7.12; *ἱλαρὸς ἴσθι* Thphr.*Char.*17.9, *ἱλαρὸν βλέψαι* *AP*12.159 (Mel.), cf. Phld.*Mus.*p.85 K., Philostr.*Im.*1.16; *ἱ. δότης* 2 *Ep.Cor.*9.7, cf. Lxx *Pr.*22.8: in later Greek, = *ἵλεως, gracious*, *PMag.Leid.W.*14.12, etc.: *τὸ ἱ.*, = *ἱλαρότης*, Plu.*Sull.*34,

Heraclid.Pont.ap.Ath.14.624d; -ωτέρα ἀγγελία *more cheerful* news, *Jahresh*.23*Beibl*.283 (Ephesus). Adv. -ρῶς X.*Ap*.33, Lxx*Jb*.22.26, Phld.*Mus*.l. c., Plu.*Ages*.2. II. of blood, *quick-pulsing*, Philostr. *Gym*.48 (Comp.). III. of imitation gold, *bright*, *PLeid.X*.17 (iii/iv A. D.). Adv. ἱλαρῶς (leg. ἱλαρῷ) ib.87.

**ἱλᾰρότης** [ῐ], ητος, ἡ, *cheerfulness, gaiety*, Lxx*Pr*.18.22, D.S.3.17, *Ep.Rom*.12.8, Plu.*Ages*.2, Alciphr.3.43; ἱ. ἡ πρὸς πάντας *Vit.Philonid*. p.10C.: pl., Phld.*Mus*.p.85 K.

**ἱλᾰροτρᾰγῳδία** [ῐ], ἡ, *burlesque tragedy*, invented by Rhinthon, Suid. s. v. Ῥίνθων.

**ἱλᾰρ-όω** [ῐ], *gladden, brighten*, Lxx*Si*.7.24, al., Aristeas 108; λόγους Phld.*Mus*.p.99 K.:—also -ύνω, Lxx*Ps*.103(104).15:—Pass., fut. -υνθήσομαι, aor. -ύνθην, *PMag.Leid.W*.12.30, 5.20.

⊕ **ἰλ-άρχης** (later written εἰλ-, cf. βειλάρχας), ου, ὁ, (ἴλη) *commander of a troop of horse*, *PPetr*.3 p.8 (iii B. C.), al., Ascl.*Tact*.7.2, Plu.*Tim*. 31 (pl.), Arr.*An*.2.7.3; = Lat. *praefectus turmae*, Plb.6.25.1, 6.35. 8. II. *commander of eight elephants*, Ascl.*Tact*.9, Ael.*Tact*.23:—hence -αρχέω, Boeot. Ϝιλαρχίω, *command cavalry*, *IG*7.3087 (Lebad.), 3206 (Orchom.), 2466 (Thebes). II. at Rome, *to be sevir equitum*, D.C.55.10. -αρχία, ἡ, *contingent of eight elephants*, Ael.*Tact*.23. ⊕ -αρχος, ὁ, = ἰλάρχης I, *IG*4.487.2, al. (Nemea, iii B. C.); = *praefectus turmae*, App.*Hisp*.43.

**ἱλᾰρ-ῳδός** [ῐ], ὁ, (ᾠδή) *singer of joyous* (not 'comic') *songs*, Aristocl.Hist.8:—hence -ῳδέω, Id.7; -ῳδία, Aristox.*Fr.Hist*.58, cf. Ath.14.621c. -ῶπις, ἡ, *of gracious aspect*, prob. in *PMag.Lond*. 121.382.

**ἱλᾶς** [ῑ], ᾶντος, ὁ, = εὐμενής, Hdn.Gr.2.657, cf. 318, al.: pl. ἱλᾶντες (ἱλάντες cod.) Hsch. (contr. fr. ἱλάεις -εντος, q. v.).

**ἱλᾰσ-ία** [ῐ], ἡ, = ἱλασμός, *IGRom*.3.1297 (Arabia). -ιμος, ον, *placable*, πρόνοια M.Ant.12.14. ⊕-κομαι, fut. ἱλάσομαι [ᾰ] Pl. *Phd*.95a, Ep. ἱλάσσομαι Orac.ap.Paus.8.42.6, also ἱλάξομαι A.R. 2.808: aor. I ἱλᾰσάμην, Ep. part. ἱλασσάμενοι Il.1.100, Ep. subj. 2 sg. ἱλάσσεαι 1.147, -ηαι A.R.3.1037; inf. ἱλάσσασθαι Ant.Lib.25.2 codd.; also ἱλάξασθαι A.R.1.1093:—**Pass.** (v. infr. II). [ῑ regularly (written ι, not ει, *SIG*1044.6,9 (Halic., iv/iii B. C.)); ῐ Il.1.100,147]: (ἵλαος):—*appease*, in Hom. always of gods, θεὸν ἱ. ib.386, cf. 100, al., Od.3.419; μολπῇ θεὸν ἱλάσκοντο Il.1.472; σπονδῇσι θύεσσί τε ἱλάσκεσθαι (sc. θεούς) Hes.*Op*.338; ὄφρ' ἡμῖν ἑκάεργον ἱλάσσεαι Il.1. 147; c. part., ἱλάσκομαι πέμπων by presenting, Pi.*O*.7.9; τοῦτον (sc. θεὸν) ἱλάσκου ποῶν μηδὲν ἄτοπον Men.*Epit*.558; of the dead as hero-ized, θυσίῃσί τινα ἱ. Hdt.5.47. 2. of men, *conciliate*, ἱ. τινὰ χρήμασι Id.8.112; πῶς ἱλασόμεθα καὶ τίνι λόγῳ; Pl.*Phd*.l. c.; ἱ. τὴν ὀργήν τινος Plu.*Cat.Mi*.61. 3. *expiate*, τὰς ἁμαρτίας *Ep.Hebr*.2.17. II. Pass. with fut. ἱλάσομαι, also ἱλασθήσομαι v.l. in Lxx4*Ki*.5.18: aor. I ἱλάσθην ib.*Ex*.32.14, al.:—*to be merciful, gracious*, τινι ll. cc.; ἱλάσθητί μοι τῷ ἁμαρτωλῷ *Ev.Luc*.18.13; ταῖς ἁμαρτίαις τινῶν Lxx*Ps*.77(78).38: c. inf., ἱλάσθη κύριος περιποιῆσαι τὸν λαόν ib.*Ex*.32.14. -μα, ατος, τό, *propitiation*, Orac.ap.Phleg.*Macr*.4. -μός [ῐ], ὁ, *a means of appeasing*, in pl., Plu.*Sol*.12, Orph.*A*.39, 554, etc. 2. *atonement, sin-offering*, Lxx*Ez*.44.27, 2*Ma*.3.33, 1*Ep.Jo*.2.2, 4.10, Ph.1.121. ⊕-τήριος, α, ον (ος, ον *PFay*.337 (ii A. D.)), *propitiatory, offered in propitiation*, μνῆμα J.*AJ*16.7.1; θάνατος Lxx4*Ma*.17.22; θυσίαι *PFay*. l. c. II. **ἱλαστήριον** ἐπίθεμα, *the mercy-seat*, covering of the ark in the Holy of Holies, Lxx*Ex*.25.16(17): ἱλαστήριον alone as Subst., ib.*Le*.16.2, al., *Ep.Hebr*.9.5, cf. Ph.2.150. 2. (sc. ἀνάθημα) *propitiatory gift* or *offering*, *Ep.Rom*.3.25; of a monument, *Inscr.Cos* 81, 347. 3. *monastery*, Men.Prot.p.15 D. -τής, οῦ, ὁ, *propitiator*, Aq., Thd.*Ps*.85(86).5, f.l. in Lxx1*Es*.8.53.

**ἱλᾰτ-εύω**, = ἱλήκω, Lxx*Da*.9.18. -ήριον, τό, *expiatory* or *propitiatory offering*, *Chron.Lind*.B.49.

**ἵλεας**, τάς, dub. sens. in *Abh.Berl.Akad*.1928(6).16 (Cos): perh. Coan for τὰς ἴλας (ἴλη) or τὰς ἱλέας (ἵλεως).

**ἱλέομαι, ἱλεόομαι** [ῑ], v. ἱλάομαι. **ἱλεός** [ῐ], ὁ, = εἰλεός I and II, Hsch. **ἵλεος**, = ἵλαος; and **ἵλεως**, ων, Att. for ἵλαος (q. v.).

**ἱλέ-ωσις** [ῑλ], εως, ἡ, *propitiation*, Plu.*inHes*.26. -ωτήριον, τό, = ἱλαστήριον, Phot., Suid.

**ἴλη** [ῐ], Dor. ἴλᾱ (Boeot. Ϝιλ- in Ϝιλαρχίω), ἡ, *band, troop* of men, Hdt.1.73, 202; εὔφρονες ἶλαι merry *companies*, Pi.*N*.5.38; also ἴλα λεόντων E.*Alc*.581 (lyr.). 2. as a military term, *troop of horse*, prop. of sixty-four men, cf. Arr.*Tact*.18.2; but varying in number, Ascl.*Tact*.7.2; = Lat. *turma*, Plb.6.25.1, al., D.H.6.12, al., Plu.*Caes*. 45, al.; later, = Lat. *ala*, *IGRom*.3.272 (Galatia), *BGU*69 (ii A. D.), J. *AJ*17.10.9, etc.; κατὰ ἴλας, = ἰλαδόν, opp. κατὰ τάξεις, X.*An*.1.2.16: generally, *troop* or *company of soldiers*, S.*Aj*.1407 (anap.). 3. at Sparta, subdivision of the ἀγέλα (q. v.), X.*Lac*.2.11; κατ' ἴλην Plu. *Lyc*.16.

**ἰληδόν** [ῐ], Adv., = ἰλαδόν, Q.S.1.7, al.

**ἱλήκω** [ῑ], (ἱλάσκομαι) *to be gracious*, of a god, once in Hom. in subj., εἴ κεν Ἀπόλλων ἡμῖν ἱλήκῃσι Od.21.365; elsewh. in opt., ἱλήκοι Ἀπόλλων *h.Ap*.165; ἱλήκοις, Δέσποινα *AP*5.72 (Rufin.); ἱλήκοις, Πολιοῦχε ib.9.154 (Agath.); θεοὶ μάκαρες, ἱλήκοιτε Alciphr.3.68, cf. Hld. 8.11, 9.25. (Prob. εἰλ-, cf. sq.)

⊕***ἵλημι** [ῑ], = foreg., only in imper. ἵληθι, in prayers, *be gracious!* Od.3.380, 16.184, *h.Hom*.20.8, etc.: Aeol. **ἔλλᾱθι** (q. v.): Dor. **ἵλᾱθι** Theoc.15.143, Luc.*Epigr*.22; both together, ἵλᾰθ', ἄναξ, ἵληθι *AP* 12.158 (Mel.): pl., ἵλᾰτε A.R.4.984, Man.6.754. (Prob. pf. imper. fr. *se-sl-*; Aeol. ἐλλ- points to εἰλ- as the true Ion. spelling; Dor. pf. part. dat. ἱλαότι (leg. εἰλ-) Hsch.: ῑ is genuine in ἵλεως, ἱλάσκομαι [fr. *si-sl-*].)

**ἴληοι·** θηρία διὰ φρυγάνων, κτλ., Hsch. (fort. θηρίδια φ.; cf. εἰλύϊος, ἐλειός III).

**ἰλῆς** [ῐ], Ion. contr. fr. ἰλήεις, = ἰλάεις (q. v.), prob. for εἰλῆς (q. v.).

⊕ **ἴλια·** δῶρα γυναικεῖα, Hsch.

**Ἰλιάδαι** [ῑλ], οἱ, *descendants of Ilos*, i. e. *Trojans*, Sapph.*Supp*. 20a.13, *AP*9.77 (Antip. Thess.): as Adj., Ἰ. βασιλῆες E.*Andr*.1023 (lyr.).

⊕ **Ἰλιᾰκός** [ῑλ], ή, όν, *Ilian, Trojan*, μῦθοι *AP*9.192 (Antiphil.); πόλεμος Str.1.2.9; *concerning the Iliad*, προσῳδία, title of work by Hdn. Gr. II. **ἰλιακά**, τά, word of doubtful meaning in *PTeb*.61(*b*).319, cf. 68.88, al. (ii B. C.).

**Ἰλιάς** [ῑ], άδος, ἡ, pecul. fem. of Ἰλιακός, χώρη Hdt.5.94, cf. A.*Ag*. 453 (lyr.), E.*Hec*.102 (anap.), 923 (lyr.), etc.; epith. of Athena, Hdt. 7.43, *IG*9(1).350 (ii B. C.). II. as Subst., 1. (sc. γῆ) *Troy, the Troad*, Hdt.5.122. 2. (sc. γυνή) *a Trojan woman*, E.*Hel*.1114 (lyr.), *Tr*.245 (lyr.), etc. 3. (sc. ποίησις) *the Iliad* of Homer, Hdt.2.116, Arist.*Po*.1448ᵇ38, al.: prov., κακῶν Ἰλιάς, i. e. *an endless string* of woes, D.19.148, D.S.36.6, etc. III. a kind of *thrush*, perh. *the redwing, Turdus iliacus*, Arist.*HA*617ᵃ21 (s. v. l.); cf. ἰλλάς III.

**ἰλιγγ-ιάω** [ῐ], *become dizzy, lose one's head*, as when one looks down from a height, ἰλιγγιῶν ἀφ' ὑψηλοῦ κρεμασθεὶς Pl.*Tht*.175d; from drunkenness, ψυχὴ ἰ. ὥσπερ μεθύουσα Id.*Phd*.79c; ἰ. κάρα λίθῳ πεπληγμένος Ar.*Ach*.1218; ἰ. καὶ χασμᾶσθαι Phld.*Rh*.2.176 S.; from perplexity, ἐσκοτώθην καὶ ἰλιγγίασα Pl.*Prt*.339e; ἰ. ὑπὸ τῆς τοῦ λόγου ἀπορίας Id.*Ly*.216c; ὑπὸ τοῦ δέους Ar.*Ach*.581; ἐπί τινι Luc.*Tox*.30; πρὸς τὴν θέαν Hld.5.6:—also written εἰλιγγιάω, freq. in codd. of Pl., cf. *AP*7.706 (Diog.), Plu.*Alex*.74; ἰλ- Phld. l. c.; εἰλιγγιάω but ἴλιγγος acc. to Sch.Ar.*Ach*.581, Suid. s. v. εἰλιγγιῶ. ⊕-ος, ὁ, (ἴλλω, εἴλω) *spinning round*; esp. *swimming* in the head, Hp.*Aph*. 3.17 (pl.), Pl.*R*.407c (pl.); σκοτοδινίαν ἴλιγγόν τε ἐμποιεῖν τινι Id.*Lg*. 892e; also, *disturbance of the bowels*, Nic.*Al*.597. 2. in pl., *eddies* or *wreaths* of smoke, A.R.4.142. 3. *whirlpool*, Procop.*Goth*.4.6. 4. *agitation of mind*, Plu.2.1068c:—also written εἴλιγγος, A.R. l. c., Nic. l. c., Plu.*Caes*.60, and codd. Pl. ⊕ -ιώδης (εἰλ- cod.), ες, = *verticulosus*, Gloss.

**ἴλιγξ**, ιγγος, ἡ, *whirling, whirlpool*, D.S.17.97, Alex.Aphr.*Pr*.2. 71. 2. v. l. for ἴλιγγος I, Gal.*UP*7.13. (Written ἶλιξ in Hsch.:—also **ἰλίγγη**, ἡ, Id.)

⊕ **ἴλιον·** τὸ τῆς γυναικὸς ἐφήβαιον δηλοῖ, καὶ κόσμον γυναικεῖον παρὰ Κῴοις, Hsch.

**Ἰλιοπόρος** [ῑλ], ον, *faring to Ilium*, Tim.*Pers*.132.

**Ἰλιορραίστης**, f. l. for Ἰλοραίστης (q. v.).

**Ἴλιος** [ῑλ], ου, ἡ, *Ilios* or *Ilium, the city of Ilus, Troy*, Il.5.210, al., Alc. *Supp*.8.4, E.*Andr*.103 (eleg.): **Ἴλιον**, τό, Hom. only in Il.15.71, but always in Trag. (exc. E. l. c.):—hence Ep. genitives, **Ἰλιόθεν**, *from Troy*, Il.14.251, Od.9.39; **Ἰλιόθι** πρό *before Troy*, 8.581, etc.; **Ἰλιόφι** κλυτὰ τείχεα the walls *of Troy*, Il.21.295. II. as Adj., **Ἴλιος**, α, ον, *Ilian, Trojan*, Ἀθάνα E.*Hec*.1008: -ος, ον is f.l. in Id.*Hel*.1164 (lyr.).

**ἶλις**, = *volumen*, Gloss. (dub.); ἶλις sine expl., Hsch.; cf. ἰλλίς.

**Ἰλισός** [ῑλ], οῦ, ὁ, *the Ilissus*, in Attica, Pl.*Criti*.112a, Hdn.Gr.1. 213, etc.: **Ἰλισός**, *the god I.*, *IG*1².324.89, cf. 310.206: **Ἰλισσός** freq. f.l. in codd., as Hdt.7.189, Str.9.1.24, A.R.1.215, D.P.424: Εἰλισσός f.l. in Paus.1.19.5.

**ἰλίσσαι·** κατωχῆσαι, Hsch. (fort. εἰλῦσαι· καταχῶσαι).

**ἰλλάδεις**, v. ἰλάδεις.

**ἰλλάζω**, *bind up, make into a bundle*, Hsch. **ἶλλαι·** συστροφαί, Id.

**ἰλλαίνω**, *look awry, squint*, Hp.*Epid*.3.1.γ'; of the eyes, *to be distorted*, Id.*Coac*.214, *Epid*.4.12:—so also in Pass., **ἰλλαίνομαι**, Id. *Morb*.3.12. **ἴλλαος**, v. ἵλαος.

**ἰλλάς**, άδος, ἡ, (ἴλλω, εἴλω) *rope, band*, βοῦς, τόν τ' οὔρεσι βουκόλοι ἄνδρες ἰλλάσιν.. δήσαντες ἄγουσιν Il.13.572. II. as Adj., *close-packed, herding together*, of cattle, ἰλλάδες γοναί S.*Fr*.70, E.*Fr*.837. III. = Ἰλιάς III, Ath.2.65a, Eust.947.8.

**ἰλλ-ίζω**, *look askance, leer*, glossed by διανεύω, Suid. -ίς, ίδος, ἡ, fem. of sq., Hsch. -ός, ὁ, (ἴλλω) *squinting* (acc. to Moer., Att. for στραβός), ἰ. γεγενῆσθαι to get a *squint*, Ar.*Th*.846: Comp. ἰλλότερος Sophr.158, cf. Gal.17(1).680. ⊕ -ος, ὁ, Ion. = ὀφθαλμός, Poll. 2.54. -οψ, οπος, ὁ, ἡ, coined as etym. of ἔλλοψ, Ath.7.308b,c, cf. Plu.2.728e.

**Ἰλλυριοί**, οἱ, *Illyrians*, Hdt.1.196, etc. (Ἰλλ- *IG*1².329.24): **Ἰλλυρία**, ἡ, *Illyria*, St.Byz.:—also **Ἰλλυρίς**, ἡ, Ptol.*Geog*.2.16.1, App. *Ill*.6; γονή S.*Fr*.601:—Adj. **Ἰλλυρικός**, ή, όν, *Illyrian*: -κή, (sc. ἱστορία), ἡ, title of work by Appian: -κόν, τό, the *region* or *province of Illyria*, *Ep.Rom*.15.19: **Ἰλλυρίζω**, *speak the Illyrian language*, St. Byz. s. v. Ἰλλυρία:—hence Adv. **Ἰλλυριστί**, ibid.

**ἴλλω**, v. εἴλω: aor. I Med. ἰλλάμην, *plait*, πλοκάμους *IG*5(2).472.11 (Megalopolis, ii/iii A. D.).

**ἰλλ-ώδης**, ες, *squinting, distorted*, ὄμματα Hp.*Mul*.1.41. -ωπέω, -ωπίζω, = ἰλλίζω, *squint*, both in Sch.Ar.*Eq*.292, cf. Suid.: -ώπτω, *Com.Adesp*.1019, Adam.1.23, Hsch. (For the termination cf. γοργώψατο.) -ωσις, εως, ἡ, *distortion*, ὀφθαλμῶν Hp.*Prorrh*.1.69, cf. Aret.*SD*1.7.

⊕ **ἴλμη·** δεσμός, σειρά, Theognost.*Can*.15 (ἰλμηδεσμός cod.).

**Ἰλοραίστης**, Dor. -τᾱς, α, ὁ, (ῥαίω) *destroyer of Ilus*, i. e. *of Troy*, prob. in Dosiad.*Ara* 17.

*Ϝίλσις*, ιος, ἁ, *distress*, *Schwyzer* 686.2 (Pamphylia, iv B. C.).

**ἴλῦμα** [ῐ], ατος, τό, *sediment* deposited in water, Gal.13.45 (sed leg. λύματα).

**ἰλῠόεις** [ῐ], εσσα, εν, (ἰλύς) *muddy*, ποταμός A.R.2.823; ζάλος Nic. *Th.*568: metaph., ἀχλὺς ἰ., of the soul's material envelope, *App. Anth.*3.146 (Theon).

**ἰλῡός** [ῐ], ὁ, = εἰλεός II, εἰλυός, *den, lair*, Call.*Jov.*25.

**ἰλύς** [ῑ], ύος, ἡ, *mud, slime*, τεύχεα.. κείσεθ' ὑπ' ἰλύος κεκαλυμμένα Il.21.318, cf. *IG*1².94.20,23, Zeno *Stoic.*1.29, *Inscr.Délos* 354.19, etc.; of alluvial soil, Hdt.2.7; ἰ. καὶ ψάμμος Hp.*Aër.*9. **2.** *dregs, sediment*, Id.*Mul.*1.66; of wine, Arist.*GA*753ᵃ24, al. **3.** *impurity*, αἵματος Gal.1.603, cf. 616; στέρνων Androm.ap.eund.14.35. [ἰλῦς -ῠν Choerob. *in Theod.*1.331; gen. ἰλῦος *APl.*4.230 (Leon.), A.R. 1.10, but ἰλύος (metri gr. Hdn.Gr.2.117) Il. l. c.] (Cf. Russ. *il*, Polish *ił* 'mud', 'potter's clay'.)

⊛ **ἰλυσπ-άομαι** [ῐ], *crawl*, like a worm, Hp.*Genit.*5, Pl.*Ti.*92a, Meno *Iatr.*37.32, J.*AJ*1.1.4, *BJ*3.7.21, Plu.2.567b, Max.Tyr.26.6, Ael. *NA*8.14, 9.32. (εἰλυσπ- Meno l. c., v.l. in Pl. l. c.) **-ᾱσις**, εως, ἡ, *crawling*, Arist.*IA*709ᵃ28. **-αστικός**, ή, όν, *of* or *for crawling*, Id.*HA*487ᵇ21.

**ἰλύ-ω** [ῑ], (ἰλύς) *cover with slime* or *dirt*, Hsch. **II.** = εἰλύω, Id. ⊛ **-ώδης**, ες, *muddy, slimy*, Hp.*Coac.*512, Max.Tyr.41.3, S.E. *M.*5.75; ὕδωρ Str.4.1.6; πηλός Arr.*Ind.*41.3; περίττωμα Gal.1.616; τὸ -ῶδες Plu.2.935a.

**ἱμ-** in compds., = ἰν, Arc., Cypr., Cret. for ἐν.

**ἷμα**, ατος, τό, = εἷμα, Hsch.

⊛ **ἱμαῖος** [ῑ], α, ον, (ἱμάω) *of* or *for drawing water*, ἱμαῖον (sc. μέλος) *song of the draw-well*, Call.*Hec.*1.4.12, cf. Trypho ap.Ath.14.618d.

**Ἱμάλιος**, ὁ (sc. μήν), v. sq.

**ἱμαλίς**, ίδος, ἡ, Syrac. epith. of Demeter, Polem.Hist.39:—hence **ἱμαλιά**, ἡ, = τὸ ἐπίμετρον τῶν ἀλεύρων, Hsch.: **ἱμάλιος**, α, ον, *abundant*, Id.: as name of a month at Hierapytna, *GDI*5040.4. **II.** Dor. word for ὁ νόστος καὶ τὰ ἐπίμετρα τῶν ἀλεύρων Trypho ap.Ath.14. 618d; = ἐπιμύλιος ᾠδή, Hsch., Poll.4.53.

**ἱμανήθρη** [ῑ], ἡ, = ἱμονιά, Herod.5.11.

**ἱμαντ-άριον** [ῐ], τό, Dim. of ἱμάς, *BCH*29.536 (Delos, ii B.C.), *POxy.*326 (i A.D.). **2.** *halyard*, Hsch. **-ελιγμός**, οῦ, ὁ, *pricking the tape*, '*fast and loose*', a trick practised at fairs, etc., Poll.9.118, Eust.979.28. **-ελικτής**, οῦ, ὁ, (ἑλίσσω) *pricker of tapes* (cf. foreg.): metaph., '*thimble-rigger*', of sophists, Democr.150. **-ηρις** (sic cod., fort. -ῆρες), = *corrigiae, Gloss.* **-ίδιον**, τό, Dim. of ἱμάς, *EM* 671.8. **-ῐνος**, η, ον, *of leathern thongs*, Hdt.4.189, Hp.*Art.* 78. **-ιον**, τό, Dim. of ἱμάς, *strap*, Id.*Mochl.*41. **II.** = ἱμάς II, Aret.*SA*1.8. **-ίσκος**, ὁ, Dim. of ἱμάς, Herod.6.71. **-ισμός**, ὁ, in building, *insertion of bonding courses*, *PTeb.*402.32 (ii A.D.).

**ἱμαντό-δεσμος** [ῐ], ὁ, *leathern band*, Hsch. s. v. ζεύγλας. ⊛ **-δετος**, ον, *bound with thongs*, gloss on τρητοῖσι, Sch.Od.1.440. **-μάχος** [μᾰ], ον, *fighting with the caestus*, Orac. in Tz.*H.*7.422. **-πάροχος**, ὁ, *purveyor of straps*, etc., for the races, *CIG*2758 *D* 6 (Aphrodisias). **-πέδη**, ἡ, *leathern noose*, of a polypus' leg, *AP*9.94 (Isid. Aeg.). ⊛ **-πους**, ποδος, ὁ, (ἱμάς III) *spindle-shanked*; esp., **1.** name of a tribe of Ethiopians, Plin.*HN*5.46, Apollod.ap.Tz.*H.*7. 767. **2.** kind of *water-bird*, Dionys.*Av.*2.9. ⊛ **-σκελής**, ές, = foreg., Tz. l. c. **-τομέω**, *cut straps*, Poll.7.81, 83.

**ἱμαντ-όω** [ῐ], *furnish with straps*, in Pass., Hsch. s. v. πυξ(ίνην). **-ώδης**, ες, *fibrous*, of the hair, Pl.*Ti.*76c; φλοιός, κλῶνες, Dsc.1.84, 3. 15; of asbestos, Id.5.138. **2.** of hair, *ropy*, Gal.1.615; of the uvula when diseased, Id.10.988. **II.** *sinewy, wiry*, of athletes, Philostr. *Gym.*37. **-ωμα**, ατος, τό, *hawser*, Hsch. s.v. σεῖρα. **-ωσις**, εως, ἡ, *binding with thongs*, Id.; of the *straps of a car*, Poll.1. 142. **II.** *piece of timber used instead of a bond-stone*, Lxx *Si.*22.16, Phot., etc.

**ἱμᾰοιδός** [ῐ], ὁ, *one who sings the* ἱμαῖον μέλος, Poll.4.53, Hsch. (ἰλ- cod.).

⊛ **ἱμάς**, ὁ, gen. ἱμάντος (not ἱμᾶς, ἱμᾶντος Hdn.Gr.2.939): Ep. dat. pl. ἱμάντεσσι:—*leathern strap* or *thong*, Il.10.262, etc.; ἱμάντα βοός 3. 375; βοέους ἱμάντας 22.397: mostly in pl., in various senses: **a.** *traces*, 10.475, 499, al. **b.** *reins*, 23.324, etc.; τμητοῖς ἱμᾶσι S.*El.* 747, cf. E.*Hipp.*1222. **c.** *straps* on which the body of the chariot was hung, Il.5.727. **d.** *lash* of a whip, formed by several thongs, 23.363. **e.** *boxing-glove*, consisting of *several straps put round the hand*, ib.684, Pi.*N.*6.35, Pl.*Prt.*342c; ἱ. πυκτικοί Eup.22 D. **2.** in sg., the magic *girdle* of Aphrodite, Il.14.214, 219. **b.** *chin-strap* of the helmet, 3.371. **c.** *thong*, by which the bolt was shot home into the socket, Od.1.442, cf. 4.802, 21.46. **d.** after Hom., *thong* or *latchet* of a sandal, X.*An.*4.5.14, Ephipp.14.9, Men.109.2, *Ev.Marc.*1.7. **e.** *rail-rope*, Aristag.5. **f.** *well-rope*, Poll.10.31, Moer. **g.** *dog-leash*, X.*Cyn.*7.6: prov., ἧσθ' ἱμὰς κύνειος you were tough as a *dog-leash*, Ar.*V.*231; also σὺν τῷ κυνὶ καὶ τὸν ἱμάντα Phot. **h.** *whip, scourge*, ἔξω τις δότω ἱμάντα Antiph.74.8, cf. Men.*Sam.*106; ἡ διὰ τῶν ἱ. αἰκεία *POxy.*1186.2 (iv A.D.), cf. *Act. Ap.*22.25; ἱμάντες παιδαγωγῶν Lib.*Ep.*911.2. **i.** *cord*, Gal.10.1001, cf. 1.616. **II.** *diseased condition of the uvula*, Id.17(1).379. **III.** ἱμάντες, in Archit., *planks* laid on rafters, *IG*1².372.82, 373.236, al., 2². 1668.55, 1672.305; on στρωτῆρες (q.v.), ib.463.66. (Cf. Skt. *sināti* 'bind', Lat. *saeta*.) [⏑ –, usually; but also ῑ in Ep., Il.8.544, etc.: in derivs. and compds. always ῐ.]

⊛ **ἱμάσθλη** [ῐ], ἡ, (ἱμάς) *thong* of a whip, *whip*, Il.23.582, Od.13.82, *Eranos* 13.88 (pl.): metaph., νηὸς ἱ., i. e. ship's *rudder*, *AP*6.28 (Jul.); later, *any thong*, Opp.*C.*4.217.

**ἱμάσκω**, dub. sens., perh. *flog* or *imprison* (ἱμάς), *Schwyzer* 409 (Elis).

**ἱμασσία**, ἡ, perh. = *scaffolding* (cf. ἱμάς), or = αἱμασιά, *IG*4.823.26 (Troezen).

**ἱμάσσω** [ῐ], fut. ἱμάσω [ᾰ]: aor. ἵμᾰσα: (ἱμάς):—*flog* horses, τοὺς ἵμασ' Ἀντίλοχος Il.5.589, cf. 11.531; of men, εἰ.. σε πληγῇσιν ἱμάσσω 15.17, cf. Hes.*Th.*857; ἵμασε χθόνα χειρί *smote* it, *h.Ap.*340; ὅτε.. γαῖαν ἱμάσσῃ when he *smites* it *with lightnings*, Il.2.782:—Pass., ἱμασσόμενος δέμας αὔραις *AP*7.696 (Arch.), cf. Nonn.*D.*42.491.

**ἱμᾰτ-εύομαι** [ῐ], *to be a clothier*, *IGRom.*4.1209 (Thyatira) (nisi leg. πραγματ-). **-ηγός**, όν, *loaded with apparel*, ναῦς Thphr.*Lap.* 68. **-ῐδάριον**, τό, Dim. of ἱμάτιον, Ar.*Fr.*90. **-ίδιον** [ῐδ], τό, Dim. of ἱμάτιον, Id.*Pl.*985, Lys.*Fr.*316 S., *BGU*1103.12 (i B.C.); by crasis with the Art., θαἰματίδια Ar.*Lys.*401. **-ίζω**, fut. -ιῶ, *furnish with clothing*, *UPZ*2.14 (ii B.C.), etc.:—Pass., τοῦ παιδὸς τρεφομένου καὶ -ομένου *POxy.*275.14 (i A.D.); γυνὴ ἱματισμένη ἔχιδνα Secund.*Sent.*8; ἱματισμένος *Ev.Marc.*5.15.

**ἱμᾰτιο-θήκη** [ῐμ], ἡ, *wardrobe*, *IG*2².1672.229, 309, Hsch. s. v. κανδυτάναι. **-κάπηλος** [κᾰ], ὁ, *clothes-seller*, Luc.*Merc.Cond.*38, *Pseudol.*21. **-κλέπτης**, ου, ὁ, *clothes-stealer*, D.L.6.52. **-μίσθης**, ου, ὁ, *one who lets out actor's costumes*, *IG*12(9).207.22 (Eretria, iii B.C.), *SIG*424.85 (Delph., iii B.C.), Poll.7.78, *AB*100. **-μισθωτής**, οῦ, ὁ, = foreg., Poll.7.78.

⊛ **ἱμάτιον** [ῐμᾰ-], τό, in form a Dim. of ἷμα (i. e. εἷμα), *a piece of dress*; in usage always of *an outer garment*, formed by an oblong piece of cloth worn above the χιτών, Ar.*Ec.*333, *IG*2².1524.205, al., D.24. 114, etc.; λαμπρὸν ἱ. ἔχων Epich.[277]; θοἰμάτιον by crasis for τὸ ἱμ-, Ar.*Nu.*179, al.; θοἰμάτιον καθεὶς ἄχρι τῶν σφυρῶν D.19.314; ἱματίων ἑλξεις Pl.*Alc.*1.122c; of the Roman *toga*, Plu.*Brut.*17, *Cor.*14: hence ἐν ἱματίοις, of civilians, = *togati*, Id.*Cam.*10; but ἱ. Ἑλληνικόν, opp. the toga, Luc.*Merc.Cond.*25. **2.** ἱμάτια, τά, generally, *clothes*, Hdt.1.9, Pl.*Plt.*279e, D.27.10; by crasis, θαἰμάτια Hippon.83.1, Ar.*V.*408 (lyr.), *Lys.*1093; of *grave-clothes*, ἐν εἱμ. τρισὶ [θάπτειν] *IG* 12(5).593.2 (Iulis, v/iv B.C.), cf. Plu.*Sol.*21. **3.** metaph., ἱμάτια πόλεως τείχη Eust.1871.50. **II.** generally, *cloth*, Hdt.4.23, D.S. 14.109, Ael.*VH*8.7, Iamb.*VP*21.100. [ἱμ- in Att. Inscrr., *IG*1².427, 386.18, 2².1514.16, etc.; εἱμ- ib.12(5) l. c. (εμ- lap.), 5(1).1390.16, al. (Andania, i B.C.), which is easier to explain, v. εἷμα, εἱματισμός.]

**ἱμᾰτιο-παραλήμπτης** [ῐ], ου, ὁ, *collector of deliveries in kind in the form of clothing*, *BGU*1564.1 (ii A.D.). **-πλύτης** [ῠ], ου, ὁ, = κναφεύς, dub. in ib.118 iii 7 (ii A.D.). **-ποιΐα**, ἡ, *clothes-making*, *Gloss.* ⊛ **-πράτης** [ᾱ], ου, ὁ, = sq., *Stud.Pal.*22.95.2 (iii A.D.). ⊛ **-πώλης**, ου, ὁ, *clothes-dealer*, Critias *Fr.*64 D., *UPZ*8.32 (ii B.C.), *AJP* 38.418 (Egypt), *Ephes.*3 p.146 (εἱμ-), Ptol.*Tetr.*179:—also in form **εἱματοπ.**, *Gloss.*:—fem. **-πωλις**, ιδος, *IG*2.3650, Ath.3.76a; ἡ ἱ. ἀγορά Poll.7.78. ⊛ **-πωλικόν** (sc. τέλος), τό, *tax on clothes-dealers*, *PLeipz.*5.7 (*Ber.Sächs.Ges.d.W.*37.245 (iii A.D.)).

**ἱμᾰτιουργικός** [ῐ], ή, όν, *skilled in making clothes*: ἡ -κή (sc. τέχνη) *the tailor's art*, Pl.*Plt.*280a, Gal.*Thras.*26.

**ἱμᾰτιο-φόριον**, τό, = sq., *Sammelb.*7033.42, 43 (v A.D.). **-φορίς**, ίδος, ἡ, *portmanteau*, *POxy.*116.10 (ii A.D.), Ammon.*Diff.*p.135 V. (cf. Ptol.Ascal.p.406 H.), Ael.Dion.*Fr.*206. **-φῠλᾰκέω**, *take care of clothes*, Luc.*Hipp.*8. **-φῠλάκιον**, τό, *wardrobe*, *Gloss.*:—also in form **εἱματοφ-**, ib. **-φύλαξ** [ῠ], ᾰκος, ὁ, ἡ, *keeper of the wardrobe*, Lxx 4*Ki.*22.14:—in form **εἱματο-**, *Gloss.*

**ἱμᾰτισμός** [ῐ], ὁ, *clothing, apparel*, Thphr.*Char.*23.8, Aen.Tact.31. 15, *SIG*1015.35 (Halic., iii B.C.), *PHib.*1.54 (iii B.C.), *PCair.Zen.*28. 1 (iii B.C.), *BCH*6.24 (Delos, ii B.C.), Plb.11.9.2, *Ev.Luc.*7.25, Plu. *Alex.*39: εἱμ- *PEleph.*1.4 (iv B.C.), *IG*5(1).1390.15 (Andania, i B.C.), etc.

⊛ **ἱμάω**, Att. inf. ἱμῆν Phot.:—*draw up*, esp. water from a well, Ath.8.352a; κάδῳ Orib.*Eup.*1.1.2:—Pass., *to be tapped of, yield*, γάλα Arist.*HA*522ᵇ12, *PA*688ᵇ10. (From ἱμάς 2f, acc. to Ael.Dion. *Fr.*211; ἱμάω has ῑ (v. καθιμάω), like ἱμονιά, ἱμανήθρη, but ἱμαῖος has ῐ.)

⊛ **ϝιμβάναι** (γιμβ- cod.)· ζεύγανα, Hsch. **ἴμβηρις**, = ἔγχελυς, at Methymna, Id. (cf. Lith. *ungurỹs* 'eel').

⊛ **Ἴμβρος**, ὁ, the island of Imbros, Il.13.33, etc.: also, epith. of Pelasgian Hermes, St.Byz. s. v.: hence **Ἴμβριοι**, οἱ, *the Imbrians*, *IG*1². 198.101.

⊛ **ἱμείρω** [ῐ], Aeol. **ἰμέρρω** Sapph.1.27, Alc.*Supp.*26.5, cf. Hdn.Gr. 2.949: (ἵμερος):—*long for, desire*, c. gen., τί κακῶν ἱμείρετε τούτων..; Od.10.431, cf. 555, Hes.*Sc.*31; μεγάλων B.1.62; μάχης A.*Ag.*940; βίου S.*Fr.*952, cf. Ar.*Nu.*435: c. inf., *long* or *wish* to do, Alc. l. c., Sol.13.7, A.*Pers.*233, S.*OT*587, *Ichn.*128; ὄσσα μοι τέλεσσαι θῦμος ἰμέρρει Sapph. l. c.: c. Adj. neut., γνωτὰ κοὐκ ἄγνωτά μοι προσήλθεθ' ἱμείροντες S.*OT*59: abs., Id.*El.*1053; ἀσμένοις.. καὶ ἱμείρουσιν.. τὸ φῶς ἐγίγνετο Pl.*Cra.*418d. **II.** Med. **ἱμείρομαι**, aor. 1 ἱμειράμην Il.14.163:—Pass., aor. 1 ἱμέρθην Hdt.7.44: c. gen., ὁππότ' ἂν ἡβήσῃ τε καὶ ἧς ἱμείρεται αἴης (Ep. aor. subj.) Od.1.41; χρημάτων ἱ. μεγάλως Hdt.3.123: c. inf., εἴ πως ἱμείραιτο παραδραθέειν φιλότητι (cf. ἵμερος) Il.14.163, cf. Od.1.59, Hdt.6.120, S.*OT*386.—Ep., Ion. (Hdt. and Hp.*Morb.*4.39), and Trag. word: never in Att. Prose; introduced as etym. in Pl.*Cra.* l. c.

**ἴμεν, ἴμεναι** [ῐ], Ep. inf. of εἶμι (*ibo*).

**ἱμέρα**, ἡ, old collat. form of ἡμέρα, acc. to Pl.*Cra.*418c, d.

**ἱμεράμπυξ** [ῐ], ῠκος, ἡ, *with lovely diadem*, θεά B.16.9.

**ἱμερό-γυιος** [ῐ], ον, *with lovely limbs*, B.12.137. ⊛ **-εις**, εσσα, εν, (ἵμερος) *exciting desire, lovely, charming*, in Hom. always of things,

ἱμερόεντα..ἔργα γάμοιο Il.5.429, etc.; χροὸς ἱμερόεντος 14.170; ἀοιδή, ἔπεα, Od.1.421, 17.519; γόος (cf. ἵμερος) 10.398; Χαρίτων χορὸν ἱμερόεντα 18.194, cf. Il.18.603; ἱμερόεν κιθάριζε ib.570; so later κισσός D.P.947; ἔρωτες AP5.277 (Agath.); of persons, Pi.Fr.87 (Sup.), Thgn.1365 (Sup.), Theoc.7.118; νύμφη Coluth.295. **-θαλής, ές,** (θάλλω) Dor. for -θηλής, *sweetly blooming*, ἔαρ AP9.564 (Nicias): vulg. ἡμεροθ-. **-νους,** ουν, *lovely of soul*, Orph.H.56.8. **-ομαι,** Pass., of a female, *have sexual intercourse with* τοῦ ἀνδρός, or abs., Hp.Mul.1.12,24. **-πνους,** πνουν, *breathing sweetness*, BMus. Inscr.1084.

❋ **ἵμερος** [ῑ], ὁ, *longing, yearning after*, c. gen. rei, σίτου..περὶ φρένας ἵμερος αἱρεῖ Il.11.89, etc.; γόου ἵμερον ὦρσε raised [in them] *a yearning* after tears, i. e. a desire of the soul to disburden itself in grief, 23.14; ὑφ' ἵμερος ὦρτο γόοιο Od.16.215, etc.: with gen. obj. added, πατρὸς ὑφ' ἵμερον ὦρσε γόοιο *for* his father, 4.113; ἵμερον ἔχειν, = ἱμείρεσθαι, c. inf., Hdt.5.106, 7.43; ἵμερος ἔχει με..ἰδεῖν S.OC1725 (lyr.), cf. Sapph.Supp.24.11; ἵ. ἐπείρεσθαί μοι ἐπῆλθέ Hdt.1.30, cf. 9.3; τῶν (sc. δενδρέων) γλυκὺς ἵ. ἔσχεν..φυτεῦσαι Pi.O.3.33: in pl., πολλοὶ γὰρ εἰς ἓν ξυμπίτνουσιν ἵ. various *impulses* or *emotions*, A.Ch.299, cf. Phld.Ir.p.37 W., Piet.20. 2. abs., *desire, love*, ὥς σεο νῦν ἔραμαι καί με γλυκὺς ἵ. αἱρεῖ Il.3.446; δὸς νῦν μοι φιλότητα καὶ ἵ. 14.198; δαμέντα φρένας ἱμέρῳ Pi.O.1.41, cf. Sapph.Supp.25.16; ἱμέρῳ πεπληγμένος A.Ag.544; ἱμέρου νικώμενος Id.Supp.1005, cf. Pr.649, S.Tr.476, Ar.Ra.59; βλεφάρων ἵ. S.Ant.796 (lyr.). 3. personified, Χάριτές τε καὶ Ἵ. Hes.Th.64; Ἔρως..χαρίτων, ἱμέρου, πόθου πατήρ Pl.Smp.197d, cf. Luc.DDeor.20.15, Nonn.D.1.68, al. II. as Adj., only in neut. as Adv., ἵμερον αὐλήσαντι AP9.266 (Antip.); ἵμερα μελίζεσθαι, δακρῦσαι, ib.7.30 (Antip. Sid.), 364 (Marc. Arg.).—Poet., exc. in Pl. and Ion. and later Prose, as Hdt. ll. cc., Hp.Aër. 22, Phld. ll. cc., Acad.Ind.p.56 M. (Sts. derived fr. *is-mero-*, cf. Skt. *iṣtás* 'desired', *iṣmás* 'god of love', but Aeol. texts have ἴμερος, ἰμέρρω, never ἰμμ-; cf. ἡμερτόν· ἐπέραστον, Hsch. (s.v.l.).)

**ἱμερό-φρων** [ῑ], ονος, ὁ, ἡ, *lovely in spirit*, Doroth.ap.Heph.Astr.3.9. **-φωνος,** ον, *of lovely voice* or *song*, ἀηδών Sapph.39, Alcm.26 (vulg. ἱεροφ-), Theoc.28.7.

**ἰμέρρω** [ῑ], Aeol. for ἱμείρω (q. v.).

❋ **ἱμερτός** [ῑ], ή, όν, (ἱμείρω) *longed for, desired, lovely*, Τιταρήσιος Il.2.751; ὕδατα A.R.2.939; Σαλαμίς Sol.1.1; κίθαρις h.Merc.510; στέφανοι Hes.Th.577; κόμα Sapph.119; λέχος Pi.P.3.99; ἀοιδαί, δόξα, Id.O.6.7, P.9.75; ἱ. ἡλικίη *dear* life, Simon.115; of persons, AP5.297 (Jul.); epith. of Apollo and Dionysus, ib.9.524.10, 525.10.—Poet. and later Prose, as Epicur.Fr.165, Luc.DDeor.20.15: ἱμερτόν, τό, Plu.2.926f; ἐφ' ἱμερτοῖσιν prob. from a poet, ib.394b.

**ἱμερώδης** [ῑ], ες, = ἱμερόεις, Callistr.Stat.11.

**ἰμέσος,** Prep., c. gen., *between*, ἰ. Πελειᾶν Schwyzer664.17 (Orchom. Arc., iv B.C.); also ἰμέσουν τοῖς Διδύμοιυν ib.25; prob. fr. ἰν (= ἐν)-μετ-.

❋ **ἵμεστος·** δίκη (Sicel), Hsch. **ἱμητός** [ῑ], ή, όν, (ἱμάω) *drawn out as from a well*, Id. **ἱμίτραόν·** ὑπόζωσον (-στον cod.) (Cypr.), Id.

**ἰμμεμφής** (ἰνμενφ- lap.), v. ἐμμεμφής.

**ἴμμεναι,** poet. for ἴμεναι, ἰέναι, inf. of εἶμι (*ibo*).

**ἱμονιά** [prob. ῑ, cf. An.Ox.1.217], ἡ, (ἱμάς) *well-rope*, Alex.174.9, Apollod.Gel.1 (pl.), Ph.2.89 (pl.), Luc.Icar.7, JConf.8, Hsch.; ἱμονιάν (abs.) *a rope's length*, i. e. as long as a bucket takes to go down and come up a well, Ar.Ec.351.

**ἱμονιοστρόφος,** ὁ, *water-drawer*, Ar.Ra.1297.

**ἵμοροι·** πόλεμοι, Hsch. **ἵμπασις,** v. ἔμπασις. **ἱμπάταόν·** ἔμβλεψον (Paph.), Id. **ἰμπλατία,** ἡ, Arc. for ἐμπλ-, a sacrificial *cake*, IG5(2).4 (Tegea, iv B.C.). **ἰμπολά,** v. ἐμπολή. **ἰμπόλης·** ληπτής, Hsch. (perh. Arc. for ἐμπολεύς). **ἵμπτω,** v. ἴπτω. **Ἵμψιος,** epith. of Poseidon in Syria, Hsch. **ἵν,** dat. and acc. of the old pers. Pron. ἵ (q. v.). **ἰν,** Arc., Cypr., and Cret. for ἐν (q. v.).

**ἵν** or **εἵν,** gen. εἱνός, τό, an Egyptian and Jewish liquid measure, LxxEx.29.40, al., J.AJ3.9.4, Eust.1282.51 (indecl. in Lxx ll. cc.); cf. ἵνιον.

❋ **ἵνα,** A. Adv., I. of Place, 1. *in that place, there*, once in Hom., ἵ. γάρ σφιν ἐπέφραδον ἡγερέθεσθαι Il.10.127 (acc. to Eust.). 2. elsewh. relat., *in which place, where*, 2.558, Od.9.136, Hdt.2.133, 9.27, 54, Pi.O.1.95, B.10.79, A.Pr.21, al., S.El.22, 855, Ar.Ra.1231, etc.: rarely in Att. Prose, Lys.13.72 (v. infr.), Pl.Ap.17c, Phlb.61b; ἵ. ἡ Νίκη (sc. ἐστίν) IG2².1407.13: rare in later Greek, Arr.An.1.3.2, Luc.Cont.22, Ind.3: with particles, ἵ. τε Il.20.478; ἵ. περ 24.382, Od.13.364, Lys. l. c.; ἵν' ἄν c. subj., *wherever*, S.OC405, E.Ion315; as indirect interrog., Hdt.1.179, 2.150, E.Hec.1008. b. after Hom., like other Advs. of Place, c. gen., ἵ. τῆς χώρης Hdt.1.98; ἔμαθε ἵ. ἦν κακοῦ *in what* a calamity, Id.1.213; οὐδ' ὁρᾶν ἵν' εἶ κακοῦ S.OT367; ἵν' ἕσταμεν χρείας ib.1442; ἵν' ἦμεν ἄτης Id.El.936; ὁρᾷς ἵν' ἐσμὲν αὐτοῦ πέρι τῆς ἀπορίας Pl.Sph.243b. c. with Verbs of motion, *whither*, Od.4.821, al.; ὁρᾷς ἵν' ἥκεις S.OT687, al., Din.2.10; ἵναπερ ὥρμητο Th.4.74. II. of circumstance, γάμος.., ἵ. χρή *at which, when*, Od.6.27; ἵ. μὲν ἐξῆν αὐτοῖς.., ἐνταῦθα.. *when* it was in their power, Antipho6.9. 2. = ἐάν, dub. in Il.7.353 (v.l. ἵν' ἄν, cf. Sch.), Archil.74.7 codd., v.l. in Din.1.1, and Pl.Chrm.176b.

B. Final Conj., *that, in order that*, from Hom. downwards, mostly first word in the clause, but sts. preceded by an emphatic word, Pl.Chrm.169d; ἵ. δὴ Il.7.26, 23.207, Hdt.1.29, Pl.R.420e, 610c: never with ἄν or κε (if found, these particles belong to the Verb, as in Od.12.156, E.IA1579). I. general usage: 1. with subj., a. after primary tenses of ind., also subj. and imper.: pres. ind., Il.3.252, Od.2.111, X.Mem.3.2.3, Cyr.1.2.11, Isoc.3.2: pf. ind., Il.1.203, Isoc.4.129: fut., Od.2.307, 4.591, X.Cyr.1.2.15: subj., S.OT364; imper., Il.19.348, al., A.Pr.61, S.Ph.880, Ar.Ra.297, Pl.R.341b, Men.71d. b. after historical tenses, in similes, where the aor. is gnomic, Od.5.490 (αὔοι codd.); where aor. is treated as equiv. to pf., Il.9.99, Od.8.580, Hdt.5.91, Lys.1.4, D.9.26: when the purpose is regarded from the point of view of the speaker's present, σὲ παῖδα ποιεύμην ἵ. μοι..λοιγὸν ἀμύνῃς Il.9.495, cf. Hdt.1.29, 6.100, Th.1.44, al., Lys.1.11, 12, al. c. after opt. and ἄν, when opt. with οὐκ ἄν is used with sense of imper., Il.24.264, Od.6.58; after βουλοίμην ἄν.., Lys.7.12. d. after impf. with ἄν, D.23.7. 2. with opt., a. after historical tenses, Il.5.3, Od.3.2, A.Th.215, Lys.3.11, Pl.Prt.314c, etc.: after the historical pres., E.Hec.11: sts. both moods, subj. and opt., follow in consecutive clauses, Od.3.77, Hdt.8.76, 9.51, D.23.93, 49.14. b. after opt., Od.18.369, S.Ph.325; βούλοιντ' ἂν ἡμᾶς ἐξολωλέναι, ἵνα..λάβοιεν Ar.Pax413. c. rarely after primary tenses, by a shifting of the point of view, Od.17.250, Ar.Ra.24, Pl.R.410c. 3. with past tenses of ind., a. after unfulfilled wishes, Id.Cri.44d. b. after ind. with ἄν, to express a consequence which has not followed or cannot follow, S.OT1389, Pl.Men.89b, D.29.17: esp. after ἐβουλόμην ἄν.., Ar.V.961, Lys.4.3. c. after such Verbs as ἐχρῆν, ἔδει, E.Hipp.647, Pl.Prt.335c, Smp.181e, Euthd.304e, Isoc.9.5, D.24.48, Men.349.5, etc.: when an unfulfilled obligation is implied, τεθαύμακα ὅτι οὐκ εἶπεν (= ἔδει εἰπεῖν)..ἵ... Pl.Tht.161c; ἀντὶ τοῦ κοσμεῖν (= δέον κοσμεῖν)..ἵ... D.36.47. d. after pres. ind. in general statements (including the past), οὐδὲ γὰρ τὸ εἶναι ἔχει ἡ ὕλη, ἵ. ἀγαθοῦ ταύτῃ μετεῖχεν Plot.1.8.5. 4. ἵ. μή as the neg. of ἵνα, *that not*, Il.19.348, etc. II. special usages: 1. like ὅπως, after Verbs of command and entreaty, is common only in later Gr. (but cf. Od.3.327 with ib.19), ἀξιοῦν ἵ... Decr.ap.D.18.155; δεήσεσθαι ἵ... D.H.1.83; παρακαλεῖν ἵ... Arr.Epict.3.23.27: freq. in NT, ἐκήρυξαν ἵ. μετανοήσωσιν Ev.Marc.6.12, al.; of will, ὅσα ἐὰν θέλητε ἵ. ποιῶσιν.. ib.25: hence ἵ. c. subj. stands for infin., ἐν τούτῳ ἵ. καρπὸν φέρητε (= ἐν τῷ φέρειν) Ev.Jo.15.8, etc.; πρῶτόν ἐστιν ἵ. κοιμηθῶ Arr.Epict.1.10.8, cf. M.Ant.8.29; also for ὥστε, LxxGe.22.14, al., Plu.2.333a, Porph.Abst.2.33, etc. 2. *because*, ἵ. ἀναγνῶ ἐτιμήθην I was honoured *because* I read, Anon.ap.A.D.Synt.266.5, cf. Conj.243.21, Choerob. in Theod.2.257, al.; not found in literature. 3. elliptical usages, a. where the purpose of the utterance is stated, Ζεὺς ἔσθ', ἵν' εἰδῇς 'tis Zeus,—[I tell thee this] *that* thou may'st know it, S.Ph.989; ἵ. μὴ εἴπω ὅτι οὐδεμιᾷ Pl.R.507d; ἵ. συντέμω D.45.5; ἵν' ἐκ τούτων ἄρξωμαι Id.21.43; ἵ. δῶμεν.. *granted that*.., S.E.P.2.34, cf. 1.79. b. in commands, introducing a principal sentence, ἵ. συντάξῃς *order* him.., PCair.Zen.240.12 (iii B.C.); ἵ. λαλήσῃς PSI4.412.1 (iii B.C.); ἵ. ἐλθὼν ἐπιθῇς τὰς χεῖρας αὐτῇ Ev.Marc.5.23, cf. 2Ep.Cor.8.7, Lxx 2Ma.1.9, Arr.Epict.4.1.41, Did.ap.Sch.S.OC156. c. ἵ. τί (sc. γένηται); *to what end?* either abs. or as a question, Ar.Ec.719; or with a Verb following, Id.Pax409, cf. Pl.Ap.26d, etc.; ἵ. δὴ τί; Ar.Nu.1192. d. in indignant exclamations, *to think that*..! Σωκράτης ἵ. πάθῃ ταῦτα Arr.Epict.1.29.16. III. in later Gr. with ind., LxxEx.1.11, al., Ep.Gal.2.4, 4.17, etc.

**ἰναία,** ἡ, *force, strength* of a swell or current at sea, Peripl.M.Rubr.46 (ἰνδίᾳ cod.), Hsch.

**ἰναλίνω,** v. ἐναλίνω.

**ἴναντι** [ῐν], Cret., = ἔναντι, GDI5125a1.

**ἰνάριον** [ῐ], τό, Dim. of ἴς, *strand, fibre*, ἰ. λεπτὸν καὶ μακρόν Phlp. in Mete.61.31.

❋ **ἰνάσσω,** fut. -άσω, = ἰνόω, ἰσχὺν παρέχω, Choerob. in Theod.2.154, EM100.39, Suid.; ὅταν μ' ἰνάσσατο (sic cod.) Call.Fr.anon.126.

**Ἴνᾰχος** [ῐ], ὁ, *Inachus*, a river of Argolis, A.Fr.168, E.El.1. II. son of Oceanus, king of Argos, A.Pr.663, al.:—Adj. **Ἰνάχειος,** α, ον, ib.590.

**-ίνδα,** adverbial termin. of words signifying a game or sport, mostly with παίζειν, Poll.9.110, Theognost.Can.164.

**ἰνδαλίμη,** epith. of the Moon, dub. sens. in PMag.Par.1.2273.

❋ **ἰνδάλλομαι,** almost always used in pres. and impf.: aor. ἰνδάλθην Lyc.597, 961, Max.163:—*appear, seem*, ἄλλοι μοι δοκέουσι παροίτεροι ἔμμεναι ἵπποι, ἄλλος δ' ἡνίοχος ἰνδάλλεται Il.23.460; ἰνδάλλετο δέ σφισι πᾶσι τεύχεσι λαμπόμενος μεγαθύμου Πηλείωνος 17.213 (-θύμῳ -ωνι Aristarch., cf. 2), cf. Od.3.246, h.Ven.178: ὥς μοι ἰνδάλλεται ἦτορ as my memory *seems* to me, or perh., as my heart *pictures him*, Od.19.224; also in Att., ὥστ' ἔμοιγ' ἰνδάλλεται ὁμοιότατος κλητῆρος εἶναι πωλίῳ Ar.V.188; τοῦτο γάρ μοι ἰ. διανοουμένη [ἡ ψυχή], οὐκ ἄλλο τι ἢ διαλέγεσθαι it *seems* to me to be merely engaged in a dialogue, Pl.Tht.189e; τὰ δι' ὀφθαλμῶν ἰνδαλλόμενα ἡμῖν Arist.Mu.397b18, cf. Iamb.Myst.2.3; *flash on one's mind*, ἀμφὶ δὲ..μεληδόνες ἰνδάλλοντο *appeared*, A.R.3.812, cf. 2.545. 2. c. dat., *resemble*, θεοὶ ξένοις -όμενοι Pl.R.381e, cf. Lg.959a; ἀργύρῳ Theoc.22.39; κύκνοις Lyc.597. (Never in Trag.; connected with *vid-*, *εἴδω.)

❋ **ἴνδαλ-μα,** ατος, τό, *form, appearance*, LxxWi.17.3, Ael.NA17.35; ἰ. ψυχῆς, = εἴδωλον, IG3.1403: pl., ἰ. ζωῆς Plot.1.4.3; κρυφίων ἰνδάλματα πυρσῶν AP5.250 (Iren.); *mental image*, ἰ. καὶ δόκησις ψυχῆς Them.Or.26.327d: in pl., *hallucinations*, Luc.Gall.5, Aret.SD1.6. **-ματίζομαι,** = ἰνδάλλομαι, dub. in Lib.Descr.30.1. **-μός,** ὁ, = ἴνδαλμα, in pl., Hp.Ep.18: title of work by Timon, D.L.9.65, 105.

**ἰνδάριον,** τό, name of an *eye-salve*, Aët.7.118.

**ἰνδέα·** μεσημβρία (Maced.), Hsch. **ἰνδικάζω, ἴνδικος,** v. ἐνδ-.

**ἰνδικοπλάστης** (-πλεύστης cod.), *dyer*, *Gloss.*

**Ἰνδικός**, ή, όν, *Indian*: ἡ Ἰ. χώρη Hdt.3.98: Sup. -ώτατος Philostr. *VA*1.10:—fem. Ἰνδίς, ίδος, f.l. in Nonn.*D*.17.377. II. Ἰνδικὸν φάρμακον *a* kind of *pepper*, Hp.*Mul*.1.81; but, *indigo* (cf. infr. 2), *PHolm*.11.2; also called *l*. μέλαν ib.9.8. 2. the plant *indigo*, *Indigofera tinctoria*, Dsc.5.92. 3. name of an *eye-salve*, Gal.12.780, al.

**Ἰνδιστί**, Adv. *in the Indian language*, Ctes.*Fr*.57.4.

**Ἰνδογενής**, ές, *born in India*, Man.1.297.

**Ἰνδολέτης**, ου, ὁ, *Indian-killer*, of Dionysus, *AP*9.524.

**Ἰνδός**, ή, όν, *Indian*, Hdt.3.38, al., cf. A.*Supp*.284; esp. of the drivers of elephants, Phylarch.36 J., Plb.1.40.15, al. 2. **Ἰνδός**, ὁ, the river *Indus*, Hdt.4.44, etc. 3. name of a *fallacy*, Plu.2.133b. II. as Adj., = Ἰνδικός, *Indian*, *AP*9.544.1 (Addaeus). 2. **Ἰνδή**, ἡ, (sc. ἔμπλαστρος) name of a *plaster*, Orib.*Fr*.88.

**Ἰνδοσκυθία**, ἡ, *the country on the banks of the Indus*, Ptol.*Geog*.7.1.

**ἴνδουρος**, ὁ, *mole* (ἀσπάλαξ), Hsch.

**Ἰνδοφόνος**, ὁ, = Ἰνδολέτης Nonn.*D*.17.387.

**Ἰνδῷος**, α, ον, = Ἰνδικός, Nonn.*D*.17.380, St.Byz.

**Ἰνεῖον**, τό, *sanctuary of Ino*, Sch.Euph.*Oxy*.2085 *Fr*.1.15.

**ἰνεύει**· τείνει, Hsch.

**ἰν-έω** or -άω, *carry off by evacuations*, Ion. word, Hsch., Phot.: fut. Med. ἰνήσομαι Hp.*Mul*.1.52, and prob.l. ib.119; in pass. sense, Id.*Loc.Hom*.27:—Pass., ἰνῶνται, -ώμενος, ibid., ib.33.

**ἴνϝοικος**, ὁ, Arc. for ἔνοικος, *IG*5(2).343 (Orchom. Arc., iv B.C.).

**ἴνη** [ῑ], ἡ, = ἴς (A), ταῖς ἀπὸ τῶν καλάμων ἴναις *Peripl.M.Rubr*.65.

**ἰν-ηθμός**, ὁ, *emptying, purging*, Hp.*Loc.Hom*.16, 33. **-ησις**, εως, ἡ, = foreg., ib.20 (νῆσις codd., cf. Erot. s. v. ἰνήσεται), Pherecyd.66 J.

**ἰνίον** [ῐν], τό, (ἴς A) *occipital bone, occiput*, [τοῦ τριχωτοῦ κρανίου] .. τὸ ὀπίσθιον [ἐστὶν] ἰνίον Arist.*HA*491ᵃ33, cf. Gal.*UP*9.17, al.; κεφαλῆς κατὰ ἰνίον Il.5.73; διὰ ἰνίου ἦλθεν [δόρυ] 14.495, cf. Hp.*Aph*.3.26, Pherecyd.66 J., Theoc.25.264, Euph.41, Plu.*Mar*.33. (ἰ- codd., κατ' ἰν- Gal. l. c., but cf. ἐφινίους· τὰς ἐπὶ τοῦ ἰνίου σάρκας, Hsch.)

**ἴνιον**, τό, Dim. of ἶν (q.v.), an Egyptian measure of capacity, *PSI*4.333.6 (iii B.C.), Kalbfleisch *Ind.Lect.Rost*.1902.10 (ii A.D.), *PLond.ined*.186 (ii A.D.), Gal.19.769.

**ἶνις**, ὁ, *son*, A.*Eu*.323, *Supp*.42, prob. in Id.*Ag*.717, cf. E.*Tr*.571, *HF*354, Lyc.570, Isyll.53 (dub.), Call.*Aet*.3.1.63, *IG*12(8).p.vii (Egypt):—fem. ἶνις, ἡ, *daughter*, E.*IA*119.—Trag. only in lyr.; Prose only in Cypr. dialect, *Inscr.Cypr*.101, al.

**ἰνκαπάταόν**· ἐγκατάβλεψον, Hsch.

**ἰνμενφής**, v. ἐμμεμφής.

**ἴννην**· κόρην μικράν, καὶ τὴν ἐν τῷ ὀφθαλμῷ, Hsch.

**ἴννος**, ὁ, = γίννος (q. v.):—also **ἴννους**· παῖδας, Hsch.

**ἰνόω** [ῑ], (ἴς) *make strong and nervous*, Hdn.*Epim*.49:—Pass., ἰνῶνται (also ἰννοῦνται), glossed by ζῶσιν, Hsch.

**ἴντῠβος**, ὁ, (ἴντουβος *Edict.Diocl*.6.3) = ἔντυβος, *endive*, Gal.6.628:—also **ἰντῠβολάχᾰνον**, τό, [Id.]14.321.

**ἰνύεται** (ἰνν- cod.)· κλαίει, ὀδύρεται, Hsch.:—also **ἰνύεσθαι**· κοσμεῖν, ἱδρύνεσθαι, and **ἰνύρετο**· ἐμύρετο, Id. **ἴνυξ**, = ἴυγξ, Id. **ἰνφορβίειν, ἰνφορβισμός**, v. ἐμφ-.

**Ἰνώ** [ῑ], όος contr. οῦς, ἡ, *Ino*, daughter of Cadmus, worshipped as a sea-goddess by the name of Leucothea, Od.5.333, Hes.*Th*.976, Alcm.84, Pi.*O*.2.30, etc.: prov., Ἰνοῦς ἄχη Zen.4.38.

**ἰνώδης** [ῑ], ες, *fibrous*, of parts of animals, X.*Cyn*.4.1, Arist.*HA*497ᵃ21; ἰνωδέστατον αἷμα Id.*PA*651ᵃ3; of vegetables, φλοιός, φύλλον, Thphr.*HP*3.12.1,5, cf. Dsc.4.20; *sinewy*, X.*Cyn*.4.1.

**Ἰνωπός**, ὁ, name of a stream on Delos; also of a building at its source, *IG*11(2).144 *A* 72 (iv B.C.):—hence **Ἰνωποφύλαξ** [ῠ], ἄκος, ὁ, *warden of the I.*, ib.142.52, 144 *C* 10 (iv B.C.).

**ἴξ** (on the accent v. Hdn.Gr.1.396), ἰκός, ἡ, *worm* or *grub that destroys the vine-buds*, Alcm.43. (ῐ, perh. cogn. with ἴψ.)

**ἰξάλῆ** (ἰξάλη in codd., but ἰξαλῆ Ael.Dion.*Fr*.398), ἡ, *goat's skin* (τελείας αἰγὸς δέρμα, Erot.), Hp.*Fract*.29, cf. Gal.19.106; used as a dress for actors in satyric dramas, Poll.4.118. (**ἰξάλη** Hsch., **ἰζάνη** Poll. l. c., **ἰσάλη** Sch.Ar.*Nu*.72; cf. the forms **ἰσσέλα, ἰτθέλα, ἰσθλῆ** Hsch., **ἰσσέλη** Theognost.*Can*.14: cf. sq.)

**ἴξᾰλος**, ον, epith. of the Ibex, = τέλειος acc. to Ar.Byz.ap.Eust.1625.33, or *bounding, springing* (as Sch.Il., Hsch., etc.), or = ταμίας (as Porph.ap.Sch.Il.), ἰξάλου αἰγὸς ἀγρίου Il.4.105, cf. *AP*6.32 (Agath.), 113 (Simm.), 9.99 (Leon.). (Perh. borrowed fr. Asia Minor.)

**ἴξ-ευμα**, ατος, τό, = *aucupium*, *Gloss.* **-ευτήρ**, ῆρος, ὁ, *fowler*, Man.4.339. **-ευτήριος**, α, ον, *like birdlime*, v. ἰξεύτρια. II. ἰξευτήριον, τό, = *aucupium*, *Gloss.* **-ευτής**, οῦ, ὁ, *fowler, bird-catcher*, Lyc.105, Lxx *Am*.8.1, *AP*9.824 (Eryc.), *Cat.Cod.Astr*.1.166, Apollod.*Poliorc*.152.2, Porph.*Abst*.1.53; *l*. κῶρος Bion *Fr*.9. II. as Adj., *catching with birdlime*, *l*. κάλαμοι *AP*5.152 (Agis). **-ευτικός**, ή, όν, *of an* ἰξευτής, Artem.2.19; τὰ Ἰ., title of lost poem by Opp.: ἡ -κή (sc. τέχνη) Poll.7.139. **-εύτρια**, ἡ, fem. of ἰξευτήρ, epith. of Τύχη, Plu.2.322f:—written **ἰξευτηρία**, ib.281e (s. v. l.). **-εύω**, (ἰξός) *catch by birdlime*, Artem.2.19, *EM*471.53:—Med., Poll.7.135.

**ἰξία**, ἡ, = ἰξός I, Thphr.*HP*3.16.1, *CP*2.17.1, prob. in Dsc.3.89. II. = χαμαιλέων λευκός, *pine-thistle*, *Atractylis gummifera*, Dsc.3.8, Plin.*HN*22.45; ἡ *l*. ἡ ἐν Κρήτῃ Thphr.*HP*9.1.3. 2. = sq., Sch.Nic.*Al*.279. III. = κιρσός, *varicocele*, Arist.*HA*518ᵇ25, *Pr*.878ᵇ37, Plu.2.202b.

**ἰξίας**, ου, ὁ, = χαμαιλέων μέλας, *chamaeleon-thistle*, *Cardopatium corymbiferum*, Dsc.3.9, *Alex*.21, Gal.14.140.

**ἰξίνη** [ῑ], ἡ, = ἰξία II, *pine-thistle*, *Atractylis gummifera*, Thphr.*HP*6.4.3; ἄκανθα ἡ *l*. ib.9.1.2, al.: confused with ἐλξίνη by Plin.*HN*21.94, 22.41.

**ἰξιόεις**, εσσα, εν, *made from* ἰξίας, πῶμα Nic.*Al*.279.

**ἰξίον**, τό, *leaf of* χαμαιλέων λευκός (= ἰξία II), Gal.19.106.

**Ἴξιος**, ὁ, epith. of Apollo in Rhodes, from a place **Ἰξίαι**, Artem ap. St.Byz. s. h. v.

**ἴξις**, Ion. **ἶξις**, εως, ἡ, (ἵκω) *coming*, E.*Tr*.396 (prob. l.); οὐ πτύσις ἀλλ' ἀναγωγὴ καλέεται, τῆς ἄνω ἴξιος [τῆς ὁδοῦ] τοὔνομα ἔχουσα Aret.*SA*2.2; οἶνος ὠκὺς ἐς τὴν ἄνω ἴξιν Id.*CA*2.4. 2. *passage through*, οὐδαμῇ .. κατὰ τὴν τοῦ θώρηκος ἴ. Hp.*Acut*.15 (but perh. simply, 'at no point *in* the θ.'); ἴξιν παρέχεσθαι allow *free passage*, dub. in Sch. Epicur.*Ep*.1 p.8 U. (fort. εἶξιν). II. *direction, straight line*, esp. *vertical line*, καθημένῳ πόδες ἐς τὴν ἄνω ἴ. κατ' ἰθὺ γούνασι his feet when he is seated should be *vertically* opposite his knees, Hp.*Off*.3; ἐπιδεῖν δεξιὰ ἐπ' ἀριστερά, ἀριστερὰ ἐπὶ δεξιά, πλὴν κεφαλῆς· ταύτην δὲ κατ' ἴξιν *vertically*, ib.9; βάλλεσθαι χρὴ τὸ ὀθόνιον κατ' αὐτὴν τὴν ἴ. τοῦ ἕλκεος directly *over* the wound, Id.*Fract*.26; τοὺς νάρθηκας .. μὴ κατὰ τὴν ἴ. τοῦ ἕλκεος προστιθέναι ibid.; ὁκόσα κοινωνεῖ τοῖσι τῆς κνήμης ὀστέοισι καὶ αὐτέῃ τῇ ἴξει ib.9 codd. (κατὰ τὴν ἴξιν Gal.18(2).423; κατ' αὐτὴν τὴν ἴ. Ermerins). 2. κατ' ἴξιν c. gen., *corresponding to*, *on the same side as*, ἤλγησεν κατὰ βουβῶνα, σπληνὸς κατ' ἴ., i. e. on the spleen or left side of the body, Hp.*Epid*.1.26.γ', cf. 4.35, 37, *Art*.33, *Fract*.16, 18, *Mul*.1.17; τῶν ὀδόντων τῶν τε ἄνω καὶ τῶν κάτω κατ' ἴ. Id.*Art*.31; = *ex ipsa parte*, Cass.Fel.37; ἐν πυρετοῖσι ἀπὸ σπληνὸς καὶ ἥπατος διὰ ῥινῶν αἱμορραγέουσι, κατ' ἴ. τοῦ σπλάγχνου τοῦ μυκτῆρος ῥέοντος the nostril *corresponding to* the organ in question, Aret.*SA*2.2; ἡ κατ' ἴ. κληΐς the *corresponding* (i.e. liver or right side) collar-bone, ib.2.7, cf. *CA*1.10; κατὰ τὴν ὄπισθεν ἴ. *at the back* of the leg, Hp.*Art*.60. 3. more generally, *in line with*, κατ' ἴ. τοῦ πυγαίου ποιησάμενον τὴν σανίδα ib.75; κατ' ἴ. τῇ ἐντομῇ τῇ ἐς τὸν τοῖχον ib.47.

**Ἰξίων** [ῑ], ονος, ὁ, *Ixion*, Pi.*P*.2.32, etc.: perh. connected with ἱκέτης, cf. A.*Eu*.441: pl., Ἰξίονες *tragedies on the subject of I.*, Arist.*Po*.1456ᵃ1.

**ἰξο-βολέω**, *practise bird-liming*, οὐκ ἰδίην -βολῶν μελέτην *AP*9.273 (Bian.). **-βόλος**, ον, *setting limed twigs*: as Subst., *fowler*, Man.4.243. **-βόρος**, ον, (βορά) *eating mistletoe-berries*, ἡ *l*. (sc. κίχλη) *missel-thrush*, *Turdus viscivorus*, Arist.*HA*617ᵃ18; cf. ἰξοφάγος. **-ειδές**, τό, = *viscidum*, *Gloss.* **-εργός**, ὁ, *one who uses birdlime, fowler*, *AP*9.264.5 (Apollonid. vel Phil.), 273 tit.

**ἶξον**, ες, ε, aor. of ἵκω.

**ἰξόομαι**, Pass., *to be smeared with birdlime*, Thphr.*Ign*.61.

**ἰξοποιέω**, *make viscous* like birdlime, of a plaster, Paul.Aeg.2.43.

**ἰξός**, ὁ, *oak-mistletoe*, *Hozanthus europaeus*, Arist.*GA*715ᵇ30, Dsc.3.89. 2. *mistletoe-berry*, Thphr.*CP*2.17.8. II. *birdlime* prepared from the mistletoe-berry, E.*Cyc*.433; θηρευτὴς *l*. *AP*5.99. b. *oak-gum*, used for the same purpose, Ath.10.451d, cf. Plu.*Cor*.3, Philox.ap.Gal.13.742. c. *any sticky substance*, Hp.*Mul*.1.74, *IG*1².314.42 (ἰ-), 2².1673.63. 2. metaph., *l*. ὀμμάτων of one who causes the eyes to be *fixed* upon him, Tim.Com.2; ἐκφυγὼν τὸν *l*. τὸν ἐν πράγματι Luc.*Hist.Conscr*.57; καθάπερ ἰξῷ τινι προσέχεται τοῖς τοιούτοις ἡ ψυχή Id.*Cat*.14. b. *skinflint, miser*, Ar.*Fr*.718. (Prob. ϝιξός, cf. Lat. *viscum, viscus*.)

**ἰξο-φάγος** [ᾰ], ον, = ἰξο-βόρος, Ath.2.65a. **-φορεύς**, έως, ὁ, *limed*, δόνακες ἰξοφορῆες *AP*9.209. **-φόρος**, ον, *having mistletoe growing thereon*, δρύες S.*Fr*.403: read by Agathocl. in Il.14.398. II. *limed*, δόναξ Opp.*H*.1.32.

**ἰξύα**, ἡ, = ἰξύς, *EM*770.13; ἰξύη ib.636.24.

**ἰξῠόθεν**, Adv. *from the loins*, Arat.144; prob. l. for ἰξυόφιν in Opp.*C*.2.6.

**ἰξύς**, ύος, ἡ, *waist*, of women, περὶ δὲ ζώνην βάλετ' ἰξυῖ (contr. for ἰξύϊ) Od.5.231, cf. Longus 1.4; of a man, Arat.310; of centaurs, Opp.*C*.2.6; of a deer, *APl*.4.96: pl., ἰξύες, αἱ, *loins*, Hp.*Fract*.20, cf. Gal.19.106: sg., = ὀσφύς, [Id.]14.7c6. (Perh. akin to ἰσχύς, cf. ἰσχίον.) [ῡ in nom. and acc. sg., Choerob. *in Theod*.1.331; ῠ in trisyll. cases.]

**ἰξώδης**, ες, *like birdlime, sticky, clammy*, Hp.*Ulc*.12, Luc.*Tim*.29.

**Ἰοβακχ-εια** [ῐ], τά, *festival in honour of Bacchus*, Jusj.ap.D.59.78. **-ιος**, ὁ (sc. μήν), name of month at Astypalaea, *IG*12(3).169.15, 170.14; at Amorgos, ib.12(7).67 *A* 6. **-ος**, ὁ, *Bacchus invoked with the cry of* ἰώ, *APl*.4.289, Max.496, Corn.*ND*30, Hsch. 2. in pl., *worshippers of the God*, name of a guild at Athens, *SIG*1109.35, al. (ii A.D.). 3. *hymn beginning with* ἰὼ Βάκχε, such as were ascribed to Archilochus, Heph.15.9.

**ἰο-βάπτης** [ῐ], ου, ὁ, *violet-dyer*, *Gloss.* **-βαφής**, ές, *violet-coloured*, Democr.Eph.1; of water, Ath.2.42e. **-βλέφᾰρος**, Dor. ἰογλέφ-, ον, *violet-eyed*, Pi.*Fr*.307; Χάριτες, Μοῦσαι, B.18.5, 8.3, cf. Man.5.145, Luc.*Im*.8.

**ἰο-βολέω** [ῐ], *shoot arrows, dart*, A.R.4.1440, *AP*5.187 (Leon.); ἐς ἐμὴν κραδίην ib.5.9 (Alc.). II. *emit poison*, *Gp*.2.47.12. **-βόλος**, ον, (ἰός) *shooting arrows*, τόξον *AP*6.34 (Rhian.). II. *shedding venom, venomous*, of animals, Numen.ap.Ath.7.304f, Hdn.3.9.5: Sup., J.*AJ*17.5.5; ἰοβόλα, τά, *venomous animals*, Arist.*HA*607ᵃ28; περὶ ἰοβόλων ζῴων, title of work by Philumenus; τὰ τῶν *l*. ἄκη Philostr.*VA*3.44. 2. of arrows, *poisoned*, Orph.*H*.12.16; αἷμα *AP*11.237 (Demod.): metaph., *l*. γένυες, of Momus, *APl*.4.266. 2. **-βόρος**, ον, (ἰός B) *poison-eating*, Opp.*C*.3.223; of a serpent, διψάς *IG*4.620 (Argos). II. *eating venomously*, πυθεδόνες Nic.*Th*.467.

**ἰο-βόστρῠχος** [ῐ], ον, *dark-haired*, Μοῦσαι Pi.*I*.7(6).23. **-γληνος**,

η, ον, *dark-eyed*, Hsch. **-δετος**, ον, (δέω) *violet-twined*, στέφανοι Pi.*Fr.*75.6. **-δνεφής**, ές, (δνόφος) *dark as the flower* ἴον (v. ἴον IV), *purple-dark*, εἶρος Od.4.135, 9.426.

**ἰοδόκος** [ῑ], ον, (ἰός A) *holding arrows*, φαρέτρη Il.15.444, Od.21.12, Pittac.Lyr.1: **ἰοδόκη** (sc. φαρέτρα), ἡ, *quiver*, A.R.2.679, 3.156, 279, *AP*6.296 (Leon.), 12.45 (Posidipp.): **ἰοδόχη**, Hsch., Phot. II. *containing poison*, ὀδόντες ἰ. *poison*-fangs, Nic.*Th.*184.

**ἰοειδής** [ῐ], ές, (ἴον) *like the flower* ἴον I, *purple*, in Hom. always of the sea, ἰοειδέα πόντον, whether calm or stormy, Il.11.298, Od.5.56, 11.107, Hes.*Th.*844; κρήνη ib.3. II. (ἰός B) *poisonous*, κέντρον Nic.*Th.*886; λοιγός ib.243. [Nic. makes ῐ short, as conversely he has ῑάσι from ἴον (q.v.).]

**ἰόεις** [ῐ], εσσα, εν, (ἴον) *violet-coloured, dark*, ἰόεντα σίδηρον Il.23.850, cf. Phoronis *Fr.*2, Q.S.6.48; ἰόεντα θάλασσαν Nic.*Al.*171. II. **ἰόεις**, (ἰός B) *poisonous*, ἄκανθαι Androm.ap.Gal.14.38 [who makes ῐ short; cf. foreg. II].

⊛**ἰό-ζωνος** [ῐ], ον, (ζώνη) *with purple girdle*, Hsch., dub. in Call. in *Stud.Ital.*7(1929).9. **-θαλής**, ές, *blooming with violets*, στέφανοι Philox.2.42. ⊛ **-κολπος**, ον, = ἰόζωνος, Alc.63 (Sapphus est), Sapph. *Supp.*17.5. **-κουρος**, ὁ, = βιόκουρος, *Ephes.*3 p.165.

**ἰολόχευτος** [ῑ], ον, (ἰός B) *born of venom*, Procl.*H.*1.41.

**ἴομεν**, Ep. for ἴωμεν, 1 pl. pres. subj. of εἶμι (*ibo*).

**ἰομιγής** [ῑ], ές, (ἰός B) *tainted with poison*, θηλή *AP*9.1 (Polyaen.).

**ἰόμωροι**, οἱ, twice in Hom., Ἀργεῖοι ἰόμωροι, ἐλεγχέες Il.4.242; Ἀργεῖοι ἰόμωροι, ἀπειλάων ἀκόρητοι 14.479. (Expld. by Sch. as *caring for arrows* (cf. μέριμνα), but ῑ is against this: perh. *noisy* (cf. ἰά).)

**ἴον** [ῐ], τό, heterocl. dat. pl. ἰάσι [ῐᾰ] Nic.*Fr.*74.2:—*violet, Viola odorata*, στέφανοι ἴων Sapph.*Supp.*23.12, cf. Pi.*O.*6.55, etc.; καὶ τὸ ἴον μέλαν ἐντί Theoc.10.28, cf. *AP*4.1.21 (Mel.); κυαναυγές ib.5.73 (Rufin.); ἴ. τὸ μέλαν Thphr.*HP*1.13.2, *CP*1.13.12; ἴον alone, Dsc.4.121:—in Od.5.72, λειμῶνες μαλακοὶ ἴου ἠδὲ σελίνου θήλεον, there were vv.ll. σίου (Ptol. Euerg.) and θρύου. II. ἴον τὸ λευκόν (= λευκόϊον, q.v.) *gilliflower, Matthiola incana*, Thphr.*HP*6.6.3; also ἴον alone, ib.6.8.1. III. = κρίνον, Philin.ap.Ath.15.681b. IV. generally, any *flower*, *EM*473.10. V. a precious stone of dark colour, Plin.*HN*37.170. (ϝίον, cf. γία· ἄνθη, Hsch., Lat. *viola*.)

**ἰονθάς**, άδος, ἡ, *shaggy*, epith. of the wild goat, Od.14.50.

**ἴονθος**, ὁ, *root of a hair, young hair*, ἰόνθους ἐκθλιβομένους Phld. *Sign.*13, cf. Eun.*Hist.*p.250 D., Phryn.*PS*p.77 B. II. *eruption on the face, which often accompanies the first growth of the beard*, etc., Hp.*Epid.*1.26.β′, Arist.*HA*556ᵇ29, *Pr.*963ᵇ40, Erot. s.v. ὀλοφλυκτίδες:—hence **ἰονθώδης**, ες, ἐπάρσεις Thphr.*Sud.*16, cf. Gal.12.824.

⊛ **Ἰόνιος** [ῑ], α, ον, (Ἰώ) *of* or *called after Io*, epith. of the sea between Epirus and Italy, at the mouth of the Adriatic sea, across which Io swam, πόντιος μυχὸς . . Ἰόνιος κεκλήσεται, τῆς σῆς πορείας μνῆμα A.*Pr.*840; another expl. in Theopomp.Hist.125; Ἰ. κόλπος Hdt.6.127, Th.1.24; θάλασσα, πόρος, Pi.*P.*3.68, *N.*4.53; also simply ὁ Ἰόνιος Th. 6.30; later Ἰόνιον πέλαγος *AP*6.251 (Phil.).

**ἰόομαι**, Pass., (ἰός C) *become* or *be rusty*, Arist.*Col.*793ᵇ6, Thphr. *Char.*10.14, Dsc.5.78, Antig.*Mir.*151. 2. *become acrid, embittered*, Hsch.:—Act. **ἰόω**, only late, *rust*, ὁ σίδηρος μᾶλλον ἰοῖ Olymp. *in Mete.* 266.26, cf. 270.14; *convert into* ἰός, Zos.Alch.pp.148, 238 B.

**ἰό-πεπλος** [ῐ], ον, *with violet robe*, Hsch. **-πλόκᾰμος**, ον, *with dark locks*, Μοῖσαι Pi.*P.*1.1, cf. Simon.18. **-πλοκος**, ον, = foreg., Alc.55; κόρα, Νηρῆιδες, B.8.72, 16.37; Μοῖσαι *Lyr.Adesp.*53; of Apollo, *AP*9.524.10.

**ἰοποίησις** [ῑ], εως, ἡ, = ἴωσις, Zos.Alch.p.252 B.

**ἰόππα**· μιξόθης, Hsch. **ἴορκος**, ὁ, v. δορκάς.

**ἰός** (A) [ῑ], ὁ, pl. ἰοί, heterocl. ἰά Il.20.68 (Cypr., acc. to *AB*1095):—*arrow*, ἰὸν ἕηκε Il.1.48; βλήμενος ἢ ἰῷ ἢ ἔγχεϊ 8.514, cf. A.*Pers.*461; ἧκεν κομήτην ἰόν S.*Tr.*567. (Cf. Skt. *iṣus* 'arrow'.)

⊛ **ἰός** (B) [ῑ], ὁ, *poison*, as of serpents, A.*Eu.*478, S.*Tr.*771, E.*Ion* 1015, Plu.2.562c, etc.; *venom* of a mad dog, Ruf.*Fr.*118; ἰὸς ἀμεμφὴς μελισσᾶν, of honey with which snakes fed Iamos, Pi.*O.*6.47: metaph., of envy, A.*Ag.*834. (Cf. Skt. *viṣám* 'poison', Lat. *vīrus*.)

⊛ **ἰός** (C) [ῑ], ὁ, *rust* on iron, or *verdigris* on copper and bronze, Sapph.141 (dub.), Thgn.451, Pl.*R.*609a, *Ti.*59c, Theoc.16.17; ἰ. σιδήρου Dsc.5.80; ἰ. χαλκοῦ Hp.*Mul.*1.75, Dsc.5.79, Gal.12.218; *patina* on bronze statues, ὅπως καθαρὸς ἰοῦ ἔσται ὁ ἀνδριάς *SIG*284.15 (Chios, iv B.C.), cf. Plu.2.395b. (Perh. identical with ἰός B.)

**ἰός** [ῐ], ἴᾰ, ἰόν, *one*, commonest in fem. (v. εἷς): neut. ἰῷ κίον ἤματι Il.6.422: masc. dat. ἰῷ, = ἐκείνῳ, *Leg.Gort.*8.8; but, = ἑνί, ib.7.23; acc., τόν γ' ἰὸν ἐνιαυτόν the *same* year, *IG*5(1).1390.126 (Andania, i B.C.); ἰός, = μόνος, acc. to Trypho ap.A.D.*Pron.*56.4.

**ἰός**, Boeot. for ἑός (q.v.).

**ἰο-σάκχαρ** [ῐ], τό, *sugar of violets*, Ruf.*Fr.*80. ⊛ **-στέφᾰνος**, ον, *violet-crowned*, epith. of Aphrodite, *h.Hom.*6.18, Sol.19.4; of the Muses, Thgn.250; esp. of Athens, Pi.*Fr.*76, cf. B.5.3, Ar.*Ach.*637, *Eq.*1323.

**ἰότης** [ῐ], ητος, ἡ, *will, desire*, Ep. and Lyr. almost always in dat., θεῶν ἰότητι *by the will* of the gods, Il.19.9, Od.7.214, al., cf. Alc.13A; μητρὸς ἐμῆς ἰότητι *at* her *will*, Il.18.396; κακῆς ἰ. γυναικός Od.11.384; μνηστήρων ἰ. 18.234; ἀλλήλων ἰ. Il.5.874; ἀναιδήτῳ ἰ. with shameless *will*, A.R.4.360: acc. only in Il.15.41 δι' ἐμὴν ἰ. II. once in Trag., *for the sake of*, ἰότατι γάμων A.*Pr.*558 (lyr.).—Hsch. explains it by βουλήσει, αἰτίᾳ, ὀργῇ, χάριτι.

**ἰο-τόκος** [ῑ], ον, (ἰός B) *poison-bearing, venomous*, Opp.*C.*3.73. **-τῠπής**, ές, (ἰός A) *arrow-stricken*, *AP*5.86 (Rufin.), 9.265 (Apollonid. or Phil.).

⊛ **ἰού** or **ἰοῦ** (v. sub fin.), Interj., a loud cry expressive of sorrow, joy, or surprise, 1. of grief or annoyance, usu. twice repeated, ἰοὺ ἰού D.19.209; ἰ. ἰ. δύστηνος or δύστηνε, S.*Tr.*1143, *OT*1071; ἰ. ἰ. βοᾶν, κεκραγέναι, Ar.*Nu.*543, *Pax* 345: c. gen., ἰ. ἰ. τῶν . . κιγκλίδων Jul. *Caes.*330d: rarely once, φῦ (φεῦ codd.), ἰ. τῆς ἀσβόλου Ar.*Th.*245; or thrice, Id.*Pax* 110: with other Interj., ἰ. ἰ. ὢ ὢ κακά A.*Ag.*1214; ἰ. ἰ. πόπαξ Id.*Eu.*143 (lyr.). 2. of joyful surprise, *hallo!, hurrah!*, Id.*Ag.*25, E.*Cyc.*464, 576, Ar.*Eq.*1096, Pl.*R.*432d, *Grg.*499b, *Smp.* 223a. (Sch.Ar.*Pax* 345, 316 says that ἰοὺ ἰού is of woe, ἰοῦ ἰοῦ of joy: the rule is not observed in codd. In Att. Poets it sts. stands extra versum, A.*Ag.*25, Ar.*Nu.*1.)

**Ἰουδαῖος**, ὁ, *a Jew*: **Ἰουδαία**, *a Jewess*; ἡ Ἰουδαία (sc. γῆ) *Judaea*: —**Ἰουδα-ϊκός**, ή, όν, *Jewish*, Lxx 2*Ma.*8.11, etc. Adv. **-κῶς** J.*BJ*6.1.3, *Ep.Gal.*2.14, *Cod.Just.*1.1.7.4: **-ΐζω**, *side with* or *imitate the Jews*, Lxx *Es.*8.17, *Ep.Gal.* l.c.: **-ϊσμός**, ὁ, *Judaism*, Lxx 2*Ma.*2.21, *Ep. Gal.*1.13: **-ϊστί**, *in the Hebrew tongue*, Lxx 4*Ki.*18.26.

**ἴουκαι**· πεπόρευται, Hsch.

⊛ **Ἰουλαῖος**, ὁ (sc. μήν), name of month in Lesbos (?), *CIG*6850*A*; in Cyprus, *Cat.Cod.Astr.*2.139:—also **Ἰουλίηος**, *CIG*2827, 2836 (Aphrodisias): **Ἰούλιος**, = Lat. *Julius*, *Hemerolog.Flor.*

**ἰουλίζω** [ῑ], *become downy* or *hairy*, Tryph.53, cf. Phot.

⊛ **ἰουλίς** [ῑ], ίδος, ἡ, *rainbow-wrasse, Coris iulis*, Arist.*HA*610ᵇ6, *AP* 7.504.5 (Leon.), Numen.ap.Ath.7.304f, Artem.1.14.

**ἰουλόπεζος** [ῑ], ον, (ἴουλος IV) *footed like the centipede*, i.e. *many-footed, many-oared*, of a ship, Lyc.23.

⊛ **ἴουλος** [ῑ], ὁ, *down, the first growth of the whiskers and beard*, in pl., πρίν σφωϊν ὑπὸ κροτάφοισιν ἰούλους ἀνθῆσαι Od.11.319: later in sg., στείχει δ' ἴ. ἄρτι διὰ παρηΐδων A.*Th.*534; πρᾶτον ἴ. ἀπὸ κροτάφων καταβάλλειν Theoc.15.85; ἔτι χνοάοντας ἰούλους ἀντέλλων A.R.2.43; ὑπὸ κροτάφοισιν ἰούλους κειράμενος *AP*6.198 (Antip. Thess.); ἰούλοις πλησαι παρειάς *IG*14.1601. II. *corn-sheaf*, whence Demeter is said to be named Ἰουλώ, Semus 19, *Carm.Pop.*1. 2. *song in honour of Demeter*, Semus l.c., Apollod.Hist.149 J., Eratosth.*Fr.*10. III. *catkin*, Thphr.*HP*3.5.5, 3.7.3; *tendril*, ib.3.18.11. IV. *creature like the centipede*, prob. the *wood-louse*, Arist.*HA*523ᵇ18, *PA*682ᵇ3, Thphr.*Sign.*19, Arat.959; *earthworm*, Numen.ap.Ath.7.305a. V. = ἰουλίς, Eratosth.*Fr.*12 (pl.). (Perh. cogn. with οὖλος, q.v.)

⊛ **ἰουλοφόρος** [ῑ], ον, *downy*, γένυς Demitsas Μακεδ. No.410 (Thessalonica, ii A.D.).

**Ἰουλώ** [ῑ], οῦς, ἡ, *goddess of sheaves*, epith. of Demeter, Semus 19; cf. ἴουλος II.

⊛ **ἰουλώδης** [ῑ], ες, *scolopendra-like*, Arist.*PA*682ᵃ5.

**ἰόφ**, prob. corrupt in A.*Supp.*828: interj. expressing aversion, acc. to Sch.

**ἰο-φόρος** [ῑ], ον, (ἰός B, φέρω) *poison-bearing*, Opp.*C.*3.433. **-χέαιρα**, ἡ, (ἰός A) *arrow-pourer, shooter of arrows*, epith. of Artemis, Il.5.53, etc.; ἰ. παρθένος Pi.*P.*2.9: as Subst., Ἰοχέαιρα Il.21.480, Od. 11.198, *Schwyzer*758 (vi B.C.), *IG*14.1389 i 53; later ἰ. φαρέτρα *AP* 6.9 (Mnasalc.). II. (ἰός B) *poison-shedding*, of serpents, Nic.*Fr.* 33. (-χέϝαιρα from χέω, not as expld. by Apollon.Lex. etc. from χαίρω.) [ῑ as in ἰός: yet ῐ in Pi. l.c.]

**Ἴοχια**, τά, name of a festival, perh. *Parilia* (*parelia, pardia* codd.), *Gloss.*

**ἴπαμα**· κάμινη, Hsch. **ἶπαρ**, Aeol. for ὕπαρ, Jo.Gramm.*Comp.* 3.15. ⊛ **ἰπνασία**· γαστήρ (Tarent.), Hsch.

⊛ **ἰπνευ-τής**, οῦ, ὁ, = *furnarius*, *Gloss.*; prob. for ἰπνίτης in *AP*6.299 (Phan.). **-ω**, (ἰπνός) *dry* or *bake in the oven*, Hsch., prob. in *IG* 1².4.15 (ἱπν-).

**ἴπνη**, ἡ, *woodpecker*, Ant.Lib.21.6; cf. ἴππα (ἴπτα cod.)· = δρυοκόλαψ, Hsch.: **ἰπνή**· ἐφιππίς (Sicel), Id.

**ἰπν-ίον**, τό, Dim. of ἰπνός, Dieuch.ap.Orib.4.5.2. **-ιος**, α, ον, (ἰπνός I) *of an oven*:—hence **ἴπνια**, τά, *soot*, Hsch., cf. Sch.Ar.*V.* 832. II. (ἰπνός IV) *of a dunghill*, Call.*Fr.*216. ⊛ **-ίτης** [ῑτ], ου, ὁ, *baked in the oven*, οἱ ἰ. ἄρτοι Hp.*Vict.*2.42, Polem.Hist.86, *IG*5 (1).363.18 (Sparta, i A.D.: written -είταν): without ἄρτος, Timocl. 33; ἰ. φθοῖς *AP*6.299 (Phan., sed leg. -ευτής).

**ἰπνο-δόμαν**· τὴν φρυγίαν (Cret.), Hsch. **-κᾰής**, ές, (καίω) *baked in the oven*, Luc.*Lex.*6. **-καύστης**, = *furnarius*, *Gloss.* (also **-καύτης**, ibid.). **-κήιον**· φρύγιον, οἱ δὲ τὴν ὑπόκαυσιν τοῦ ἰπνοῦ, Hsch. **-λέβης**, ητος, ὁ, *boiler, cauldron*, Luc.*Lex.*8, Ath.3.98c. **-λεβήτιον**, τό, Dim. of foreg., Poll.10.66.

**ἴπνον**, τό, *mare's-tail, Hippuris vulgaris*, Thphr.*HP*4.10.1.

**ἰπνοπλάθος** [ᾰ], ὁ, (πλάσσω) *oven-maker, fire-clay moulder, worker in terra-cotta*, much like κοροπλάθος (q.v.), Pl.*Tht.*147a:—later **ἰπνοπλάθης**, Poll.7.163, Tim.*Lex.*, Harp.:—also **-πλάστης**, ου, ὁ, Gal.*Thras.*43: **-ποιός**, όν, Luc.*Prom.Es*2, Them.*Or.*21.256d.

⊛ **ἰπν-ός**, ὁ, *oven, furnace*, Hdt.5.92.η′, Hp.*Morb.*2.47, Antiph.176.4, Diph.Siph.ap.Ath.2.54a, Archestr.*Fr.*46; esp. for heating water for the bath, Ar.*V.*139, *Av.*437 (ἵπν-). II. *the place of the oven*, i.e. *the kitchen*, Semon.7.61, Ar.*V.*837, Lycurg.*Fr.*73. III. *lantern*, Ar.*Pax*841, *Pl.*815, *SIG*1027.13 (Cos, iv/iii B.C.), Ael.*NA*2.8. IV. = κοπρών, *dunghill, privy*, Ar.*Fr.*353, Hsch. (Prob. cogn. with Engl. *oven*.) **-ών**, ῶνος, ὁ, *kitchen*, *IG*11(2).287 *A* 147, al. (Delos, iii B.C.).

**ἰποκτόνος** [ῑ], ον, (ἴψ) *killing the worms in vines*, epith. of Heracles at Erythrae, Str.13.1.64.

⊛ **ἶπ-ος**, ἡ (so in Pi. l.c.) or τό (Eust.844.39), in a mouse-trap, *the piece of wood that falls and catches the mouse*, Ar.*Pl.*(815?) ap.Poll. 10.155, Id.7.41, Eust.16.40, etc. cf. εἶπος. 2. *any weight, fuller's*

*press*, Archil.169; ἶ. ἀνεμόεσσα, of Aetna as the weight which holds Typhoeus down, Pi.*O*.4.8; *press* used in surgery, Hp.*Mochl*.38. (Perh. cf. ἵπτομαι.) **-όω,** *press, squeeze*, Cratin.91; esp. in surgery, Hp.*Art*.47; ἰ. τὴν κεφαλὴν τοῦ βραχίονος Heliod.ap.Orib.49.13.8:—Pass., *to be weighed down*, ἰπούμενος ῥίζαισιν Αἰτναίαις ὕπο A.*Pr*.365; ἰπούμενος ταῖς ἐσφοραῖς Ar.*Eq*.924.

⊛ **ἵππα,** ἡ, v. sub ἵπνη: as pr. n. **Ἵππα,** *Hippa*, nurse of Dionysus, Orph.*H*.48.4.

**ἱππ-αγρέται,** ῶν, οἱ, (ἀγρέω) three officers at Lacedaemon, *who chose* 300, the flower of the ἔφηβοι, *to serve as a body-guard for the kings* (v. ἱππεύς II.1), X.*HG*3.3.9, *Lac*.4.3, Archyt.ap.Stob.4.1.138: sg., Th.4.38 (unless it be pr. n.). **-αγρος,** ὁ, = ἵππος ἄγριος, *wild horse*, Opp.*C*.3.252. **-ᾰγωγός,** όν, *carrying horses*; esp. of ships used as *cavalry transports*, πλοῖα Hdt.6.48; νέες ib.95; ναῦς Th.2.56, 4.42, Arr.*An*.2.19.1; τριήρεις D.4.16, D.S.11.3; ἱππαγωγοί alone, Ar.*Eq*.599, D.4.21: Ἱππαγωγός as pr. n. of a ship, *IG*2$^2$.1623.14. **-άζομαι,** Dor. fut. 3 sg. ἱππασεῖται *Dialex*.6.4:—*drive horses, drive a chariot*, Ἀντίλοχ', ἀφραδέως ἱππάζεαι Il.23.426; later, *ride*, Hdt.4.114, Hp.*Aër*.17, Ar.*Nu*.15, etc.; ἱ. ἐφ' ἵππων Hdt.4.110; ἵππῳ X.*Eq*.10.1: metaph., ἁ ξυσμὰ ἐκ ποδὸς εἰς κεφαλὰν ἱππάζεται Sophr.53:—rare in Act., ἱππάσαι πῶλον ap.Poll.1.182. 2. Pass., of the horse, *to be ridden* or *driven*, Pl.*Ion* 540e; *to be broken in for riding*, X.*Eq*.3.1. II. c. acc. loci, ἱππάζεσθαι χώραν *ride over* a country, Plu.*Cam*.23; τὰς ὁδούς D.S.13.88. **-ᾱΐς,** ΐδος, ἡ, hyperdor. for ἱππηΐς, fem. of ἱππικός I.3, *of a knight*, πόρπα, i.e. *fibula* which fastened the *trabea* of a Roman *eques*, *Epigr.Gr*.985.1 (Philae). **-αιχμία,** ἡ, *cavalry-action*, Sch.Pi.*N*.1.23 (pl.). **-αιχμος,** ον, *fighting on horseback, equestrian*, Pi.*N*.1.17. **-άκη** [ᾰ], ἡ, *mare's-milk cheese*, used by the Scythians, Hp.*Aër*.18, A.*Fr*.198, Theopomp.Hist.48, Thphr.*HP*9.13.2, Dsc.2.71:—also **ἱππάκης,** ου, ὁ, Eust.916.16. 2. *horse's rennet*, Dsc.2.75. II. *a leguminous plant*, Ph.*Bel*.86.25, Plin.*HN*25.83. **-ᾰκοντιστής,** οῦ, ὁ, *mounted javelineer*, Ael.*Tact*.2.13, Arr.*An*.4.4.7, Poll.1.131. **-άκοπον,** τό, (cf. ἄκοπος) *remedy for horses*, *Hippiatr*.130. **-ᾰλεκτρυών,** όνος, ὁ, *horse-cock, gryphon*, a fabulous animal in A.*Fr*.134, cf. Ar.*Ra*.932, *Av*.800. **-ᾰλέος,** α, ον, poet. for ἱππικός, Opp.*C*.1.169, 242, etc. **-ᾰλος,** ὁ, name of the *monsoon* in the Indian Ocean (from the name of the pilot who observed it), prob. in *Peripl.M.Rubr*.57. **-αναβάτης** [βᾰ], ου, ὁ, *mounted man*, *PLond*.1821.80. **-άνθρωπος,** ὁ, *centaur*, Gal.*UP*3.1, Eust.1909.53.

⊛ **ἱππᾰπαῖ,** a cry of the Ἱππεῖς, a parody of the boatmen's cry (ῥυππαπαῖ), Ar.*Eq*.602.

⊛ **ἱππ-άριον,** τό, Dim. of ἵππος, *pony*, *PCair.Zen*.30, al. (iii B.C.), Arr.*Tact*.19.3. 2. *wretched horse*, in contempt, X.*Cyr*.1.4.19, Plu.*Phil*.7, Them.*Or*.24.306d. 3. *statuette of a horse*, *IG*11(2).203*B* 84 (Delos, iii B.C.). **-αρμοστής,** οῦ, ὁ, Laced. for ἵππαρχος, *commander of cavalry*, X.*HG*4.4.10, 5.12; cf. ἵπφαρμος.

**ἱππαρχ-εῖον,** τό, *head-quarters of the* ἵππαρχος, *IG*2$^2$.895 (ii B.C.). **-έω,** *to be* ἵππαρχος, *command cavalry*, c. gen., τῆς ἵππου Hdt.9.20, 69; ἱππαρχηκὼς ἀνδρῶν καλῶν κἀγαθῶν Din.3.12; ἱππέων D.21.164: abs., X.*Ages*.2.4, Lys.26.20, D.21.172; οἱ ἱππαρχηκότες Hyp.*Lyc*.17; of the Roman *magister equitum* and *praefectus equitum*, D.C.43.48, App.*BC*5.8:—Pass., *serve under an* ἵππαρχος, Arist.*Pol*.1277$^b$10. ⊛ **-ης,** Dor. **-άρχας,** Ion. gen. **-άρχεω** *IG*12(8).194.7 (Samothrace), *Michel* 596 (Cyzicus), ὁ, = ἵππαρχος, *OGI*217 (Caria, iii B.C., pl.), Plb.10.22.6 (Achaean), 18.22.2 (Macedonian), cf. Lxx 2*Ki*.1.6, *PTeb*.54.2 (i B.C.), Plu.*Tim*.32; at Sparta, *IG*5(1).32$^A$, al.; = Lat. *magister equitum*, Plb.3.87.9, D.H.5.75, Nic.Dam.130.17 J., etc.; = *praefectus equitum*, App.*BC*2.102; = *praefectus alae*, J.*BJ*2.14.5. **-ία,** ἡ, *office of* ἵππαρχος, X.*Ath*.1.3 (pl.); of the *magister equitum*, D.C.*Fr*.36.26, Lyd.*Mag*.2.13. II. *a squadron of horse such as he commands*, Plb.10.23.4, D.S.17.57, Str.17.1.12, Plu.*Eum*.7, Arr.*An*.1.24.3; consisting of 512 men, Ascl.*Tact*.7.11, etc. **-ικός,** ή, όν, *of* or *for a* ἵππαρχος, ἡγεμονία ἱ., = ἱππαρχία, Suid. s.v. ἵππαρχος; ἱ. ἐστί it is *part of his duty*, X.*Eq.Mag*.5.1: -ικός, ὁ (sc. λόγος), title of treatise by Xenophon. **-ος,** ὁ, *ruling the horse*, epith. of Poseidon, Pi.*P*.4.45. II. *commander of cavalry*, τῆς ἵππου Hdt.7.154; at Athens, *IG*2$^2$.116.15 (iv B.C.), Ar.*Av*.799, Lys.16.8, Pl.*Lg*.755c, 880d, X.*Eq.Mag*.1.7, al.; ἵ. εἰς Λῆμνον χειροτονεῖν Hyp.*Lyc*.17, cf. D.4.26; in other states, Th.4.72, *IG*7.2466 (Thebes, iii B.C.), etc.; in the Achaean league, ib.5(2).344.7 (Orchomenus), etc.; = Lat. *magister equitum*, D.S.12.64, Plu.*Cam*.5, etc.; = *praefectus equitum*, App.*Hisp*.47; cf. ἱππάρχης.

**ἱππ-άς,** άδος, ἡ, pecul. fem. of ἱππικός, ἱ. στολή *a riding-dress*, Hdt.1.80; = Lat. *equester*, ἱ. ἐσθής D.C.38.14. II. as Subst., ἡ ἱ. (sc. τάξις) *the order of knights* (ἱππεῖς) at Athens, Arist.*Pol*.1274$^a$21; θυσίαι, βοῦς ἱππάδες of sacrifices *offered by the knights*, Hsch.; πύλαι ἱ., name of a gate at Athens, Plu.2.849c. 2. *knights' tax*, ἱππάδα τελεῖν Is.7.39, Arist.*Ath*.7.4, Plu.*Sol*.18; θητικοῦ ἀντὶ τέλους ἱππάδ' ἀμειψάμενος Epigr.ap.Arist.*Ath*. l.c. 3. at Rome, = *ordo equester*, D.C.40.57, al.; in full ἡ ἱ. τάξις Hdn.5.1.5. 4. a boy's game, Poll.9.122. 5. = ἵππος, ἡ, *mare*, Opp.*C*.1.162, *Hippiatr*.14, *BGU*21 iii 8 (iv A.D.). ⊛ **-ᾰσία,** ἡ, *riding, horse-exercise*, Ar.*Ach*.1165 (lyr.); ἱ. ποιεῖσθαι, = ἱππάζεσθαι, to take *a ride*, X.*Eq*.8.9, cf. *An*.2.5.33; ἱ. ἱππάσασθαι Id.*Oec*.11.17; *horsemanship*, Id.*An*.2.5.33; as a subject of competition, *IG*7.3087 (Lebad.). 2. *chariot-driving*, Luc.*DDeor*.12.1, etc. II. *cavalry*, Arr.*An*.4.4.7. **-άσιμος** [ᾰ], η, ον, *fit for horses, fit for riding*, Αἴγυπτον τὸ πρὶν ἐοῦσαν ἱππασίμην καὶ ἁμαξευομένην, opp. ἄνιππος, Hdt.2.108, cf. 5.63, 9.13, X.*Cyr*.1.4.14, Aen.Tact.6.6, Plb.10.49.5, Onos.31.1, etc.; τὸ ἱππάσιμον, i.e. τὸ πεδινόν, X.*HG*7.2.12; τὰ ἱ. τῆς χώρας ἄνιππα ποιεῖν Aen.Tact.8.4: metaph., τοῖς κόλαξιν ἑαυτὸν ἀνεικῶς ἱππάσιμον allowing himself *to be ridden* by flatterers, Plu.*Alex*.23. **-άσιον,** τό, Dim. of ἵππος, Theognost.*Can*.125. **-ασμα,** ατος, τό, *a ride*, Ach.Tat.1.13. **-ασμός,** ὁ, *riding*, Sch.E.*Hel*.1355. ⊛ **-αστήρ,** ῆρος, ὁ, = sq., metaph. of the μύωψ, *AP*5.202 (Asclep.); κημός ib.7.424 (Antip. Sid.). **-αστής,** οῦ, ὁ, = ἱππευτής, Luc.*Am*.46. II. as Adj., *fit for riding*, of a horse, X.*Eq*.10.17. **-αστί,** Adv. *like a horseman*, καθίζειν Hsch. **-αστικός,** ή, όν, *fond of riding*, Plu.*Alc*.23. **-αστός,** ή, όν, *that can be ridden*, Arist.*HA*576$^b$17. **-άστριαι** κάμηλοι, αἱ, *dromedaries*, Plu.*Eum*.15. **-άφεσις,** εως, ἡ, *starting-post in a race-course*, Plb.*Fr*.52 (pl.), *Abh.Berl.Akad*.1904(2).9 (Pap., ii B.C.), D.H.3.68 (pl.), Epigr.ap.Paus.6.20.14 (Olymp.), prob. in *SIG*251*H* ii 63, 253*U* (Delph., iv B.C.):—also **ἱππάφια,** τά, *Tab.Defix.Aud*.234.21 (Carthage, i A.D.). **-αφίδες,** *caballi ammissi, carceres*, *Gloss*. (prob. -αφέσεις). **-εία,** ἡ, (ἱππεύω) *riding* or *driving* of horses, *horsemanship, racing*, S.*El*.505 (lyr.): pl., E.*HF*374 (lyr.). II. *cavalry*, X.*An*.5.6.8, *Ages*.1.23. III. *breed of horses*, ἐνδόξου γενομένης ἐνθένδε ἱ. Str.5.1.9. ⊛ **-ειος,** α, ον, (ἵππος) *of a horse* or *horses*, ζυγόν, φάτνη, Il.5.799, 10.568; κάπαι Od.4.40; ἵ. λόφος *horse-hair* crest, Il.15.537; ἔντεα Pi.*N*.9.22; γένος, μάνδραι, S.*Ant*.341 (lyr.), *Fr*.659.3; ἔθειραι Theoc.16.81; τὸ ἵππειον [γάλα] Arist.*HA*522$^a$28, Posidon.ap.Gal.19.712; κάλω ἱππείω δύο *IG*1$^2$.330.19. Adv. -είως Dam.*Pr*.58. 2. ἵππειος, ὁ (sc. μήν), name of month at Thronion, *Klio*16.176 (Delph.). (ἵππιος is the usual form in Trag., ἱππικός in Prose.) **-ελάτειρα** [ᾰ], fem. of sq., Orph.*H*.32.12. **-ελάτης** [ᾰ], ου, ὁ, *driver* or *rider of horses*, Opp.*C*.1.95. ⊛ **-έλᾰφος,** ὁ, lit., *horse-deer*, perh. *nylghau, Portax picta*, Arist.*HA*498$^b$32; ἡ θήλεια ἱ. οὐκ ἔχει κέρατα ib.499$^b$2. **-εραστής,** οῦ, ὁ, *lover of horses*, Ael.*NA*2.28. **-ερος,** ὁ, *horse-fever*, formed after ἴκτερος, ὕδερος, etc., with a pun on ἔρος (= ἔρως), Ar.*Nu*.74. **-ευμα,** ατος, τό, *ride on horseback* or *journey in a chariot*, E.*IT*1428; [Νύξ], μακρὸν ἵ. διώκεις Id.*Fr*.114 (lyr.). ⊛ **-εύς,** gen. έως (-έω dub. in Hsch.), Ep. ῆος, ὁ, (ἵππος) *one who fights from a chariot*, Hom. (only in Il.), opp. πεζός, 2.810; either of *the driver* or of *the hero who fights*, 12.66, 15.270; also of *one who drives in a chariot-race*, 23.262. 2. *horseman, rider, cavalryman*, ἰππήων στρότος Sapph.*Supp*.5.1, cf. Hdt.3.88, 9.49, A.*Pers*.14 (anap.), Arist.*Pol*.1270$^a$29, etc.; τῆς πολιτείας ἱ. a public *courier*, Aristaenet.1.26. 3. *groom*, *Class.Rev*.27.12 (Laodicea Combusta), 24.12, *JHS*18.108 (near Lysias). II. ἱππεῖς, in social and political sense, *knights*, forming an aristocracy in early Greek communities, Arist.*Pol*.1297$^b$18, etc.; at Eretria, ib.1306$^a$35, *Ath*.15.2; at Sparta, a royal bodyguard, Hdt.8.124, cf. 1.67, etc.; esp. at Athens, the Second Class in Solon's constitution, Arist.*Ath*.7.3; later, an aristocratic corps of cavalry, Ar.*Eq*.225, And.3.5, Philoch.100, etc. 2. of the Roman *equites*, D.S.37.8, D.H.4.24, App.*BC*1.22, etc.; ἱππεὺς Ῥωμαίων, = Lat. *eques Romanus*, *Mon.Anc.Gr*.7.17, *IG*3.768*a*, *IGRom*.3.204 (Ancyra), *OGI*547.2 (ibid.), 645.7 (Palmyra), prob. in *IGRom*.4.1213 (Thyatira). III. *nimble* kind of *crab*, Arist.*HA*525$^b$8. IV. kind of *comet*, Plin.*HN*2.90, Lyd.*Ost*.11. V. *girl's ornament*, Hsch., cf. *Ostr*.323 (ii B.C.). VI. a *measure*, πυρῶν, ἀμυγδάλων, ἀλεύρων, *Supp.Epigr*.2.710 (Pednelissus). **-ευσις,** εως, ἡ, *riding*, in pl., Sch.E.*Ph*.791. **-ευτήρ,** ῆρος, ὁ, = sq., πῶλος, ἱ. πεδίων, οὐχ ἁλός *AP*9.295 (Bianor). **-ευτής,** οῦ, ὁ, *rider, horseman*, Pi.*P*.9.123: as Adj., Τρῶες B.12.160; στρατός E.*HF*408 (lyr.). **-εύω,** *to be a horseman* or *rider, ride*, Hdt.1.136, etc.; ἱ. ταῖς κυούσαις ἵπποις Arist.*HA*576$^a$21; ἱ. ἐπ' ὄνου Luc.*Bacch*.2; of a people, ἱππεύει ταῦτα τὰ ἔθνη Hdt.7.84, cf. 87:—also in Med., Id.1.27, 79. 2. metaph., of the wind, ζεφύρου πνοαῖς ἱππεύσαντος E.*Ph*.212 (lyr.); σελάνα ἱππεύουσα δι' ὀρφναίας Id.*Supp*.994 (lyr.); also, *rush*, πρὸς φόνον Id.*HF*1001. II. *serve in the cavalry*, Lys.14.7, X.*HG*3.1.4, Pl.*Lg*.756b, etc. 2. at Rome, *to be an eques*, D.C.49.12; τὸ -εῦον the *ordo equester*, Id.60.7. III. of a horse, as we say 'the horse *rides* (i.e. *carries his rider*) well', X.*Eq*.1.6, 3.4, 10.3. IV. *drive* a team, Ar.*Nu*.1406. **-ηγέτης,** ου, ὁ, *driver of horses*, of Poseidon, Lyc.767. **-ηγός,** όν, (ἄγω) = ἱππαγωγός, νῆες (expressed or understood) Philoch.132, Plb.1.27.9, D.S.20.83; τριήρης Ἱππηγός as pr. n., *IG*2$^2$.1628.423, 1629.944. **-ηδόν,** Adv. *like a horse*, A.*Th*.328 (lyr.), *Supp*.431 (lyr.). II. *like a horseman*, Ar.*Pax*81. **-ηλᾰσία,** ἡ, (ἐλαύνω) *driving* or *riding of horses*, Hld.8.14, Them.*Or*.15.188a, 18.216d:—Adj. **-ηλάσιος,** α, ον, *fit for riding* or *driving*, ἱ. ὁδός *chariot*-road, Il.7.340.

**ἱππηλᾰτ-έω,** *ride* or *drive*, Ar.*Av*.1443. **-ης,** ου, ὁ, *driver of horses, one who fights from a chariot*, Hom. (always in Ep. form ἱππηλάτα, and only in nom.), as an epith. of honour, *Knight*, ἱ. Τυδεύς, γέρων ἱ. Πηλεύς, Φοῖνιξ, Οἰνεύς, Il.4.387, 7.125, 9.432, 581; Νέστωρ Od.3.436: generally ἱππηλάται E.*Rh*.117: as Adj., ἱ. λεώς, opp. πεδοστιβής, A.*Pers*.126 (lyr.). **-ος,** ον, *fit for horsemanship* or *driving*, νῆσος Od.4.607; γαῖα 13.242; ὁδὸς ἱ. *chariot*-road, Luc.*Rh.Pr*.3, Poll.9.37; ἱ. οἶδμα Nonn.*D*.20.157; θάλασσα Agath.4.29, cf. 5.11; ἱ. ἔργον Ἀθήνης, i.e. the Trojan horse, Tryph.2; τὸ δι' ἡδονῆς καθάπερ ἱ. τι χωρίον Porph.*Marc*.6.

**ἱππημολγ-ία,** ἡ, *milking of mares*, Scymn.855 (pl.). **-οί,** οἱ, (ἀμέλγω) *the Mare-milkers*, a Scythian or Tartar tribe, Il.13.5, cf. Str.7.3.2; Σκύθαι ἱ. Hes.*Cat.Oxy*.1358 *Fr*.2.15; ἱ. Κιμμέριοι Call.*Dian*.252.

**Ἱππιάζω,** *ape Hippias*, Philostr.*VS*2.21.3.

⊛ **ἱππιάναξ** [ᾰν], ακτος, ὁ, *king of horsemen*, A.*Pers*.996 (lyr.).

**ἱππίας,** ου, ὁ, = ἱππεύς IV, Apul.ap.Lyd.*Mens*.4.7.

**ἱππιατρ-ός** (on the accent v. Hdn.Gr.1.229), ὁ, *veterinary surgeon*, *farrier*, *IG*9(2).69.5 (ii B.C.), *PGen*.42.35 (iii A.D.), *Hippiatr*.12, etc.; cf. ἱπποϊατρός:—Adj. **-ικός**, ή, όν, *of* or *for farriery*: ἱππιατρικόν, τό, *a work on farriery*, Suid. s. v. Χείρων: -κά, τά, title of extant compilation: also -κόν, τό, *tax on farriers*, *PHib*.1.45.21 (iii B.C.).

**ἱππίδιον**, τό, *a* kind of *fish*, Epich.44.

⊛ **ἱππικός**, ή, όν, (ἵππος) *of a horse* or *horses*, freq. in Trag., ἱ. ἐκ πλευμόνων A.*Th*.61; ἱ. φρυάγματα ib.245, cf. S.*El*.717, 719; ὀχήματα, ἄντυγες, ib.740, *Aj*.1030; φάτναι E.*Ba*.509. **2.** *of horsemen* or *chariots*, ἀγών Hdt.1.167, And.4.26 (pl.); in ἱππικῶν ἀγών S.*El*.698, ἱππικῶν is prob. neut. (v. infr. IV); δρόμος ib.754; ναυάγια ib.730; ἆθλον Pl.*Lg*.949a. **3.** = Lat. *equester*, τάξις, ἀξίωμα, D.H.12.1, Plu.*Pomp*.23; of persons, *of equestrian rank*, ἱ. ἄνδρες Str.3.4.20, cf. *IGRom*.3.474 (Lycia, iii A.D.), etc. **II.** *of riding* or *horsemanship*, *equestrian*, X.*HG*5.3.20; ἱ. ἄσκησις training *in horsemanship*, *IG*2$^2$.1042.21, al.; ἱ. ἡγήτωρ leader *of the knights*, ib.3.693; *skilled in riding*, opp. ἄφιππος, Pl.*Prt*.350a, al.: Comp., Satyr.1, Phld.*Mus*.p.6 K.: Sup., Arr.*Tact*.16.9. **2.** ἡ -κή (sc. τέχνη), *horsemanship*, *riding*, Ar.*Nu*.27, etc.; περὶ -κῆς, title of treatise by Xenophon: ἱ. ἐπιστήμη Pl.*La*.193b; ἱ. λόγοι X.*HG*5.3.20; τὰ ἱ. [πράγματα] Pl.*Alc*.1.124e, cf. *Thg*.126a; ἡ ἐμὴ ἱ. this *riding* of mine, Lys.24.10. **III.** *fit for riding*, Sup. -ώτατον, χρῆμα γυνή Ar.*Lys*.677. **IV.** τὸ ἱ. the *horse*, *cavalry*, Hdt.7.87, E.*Supp*.682, X.*An*.6.5.29, etc.; τὰ ἱ. Plb.3.114.5. **2.** *course* or *space of four stadia*, Plu.*Sol*.23. b. the *circus* at Rome, *Tab.Defix.Aud*.187.59. **V.** Adv. **-κῶς** *like a horseman*: Sup. -κώτατα *with best horsemanship*, X.*Oec*.21.7.

⊛ **ἵππιος**, α, ον, (ἵππος) poet. form of ἵππειος (q. v.), *of a horse* or *horses*, λόφοι crests *of horsehair*, Alc.15.2; σθένος ἵ. Pi.*P*.2.12; Ἄργος ἵ. (cf. ἱππόβοτος) Id.*I*.7(6).11, B.18.15; δρομεύς, prob. l. in E.*El*.825; ἄνασσα ἵ. *Queen of the Amazons*, Id.*Hipp*.307; epith. of Poseidon as creator of the horse, B.16.99, A.*Th*.130 (lyr.), Ar.*Eq*.551, *Nu*.83, *IG* 1$^2$.310.142, etc.; hence, of Colonos as sacred to him, Arg.S.*OC*, Paus.1.30.4 (but cf. Pherecr.134); also of Athena, Pi.*O*.13.82, S.*OC* 1070 (lyr.), Harp.; of Hera, at Olympia, Paus.5.15.5; of Ares, Id.5.15.6, cf. Tryph.105. **II.** *of horsemen* or *the horse-race*, ἵ. νόμος Pi.*O*.1.101; ἱππίαν ἔσοδον Id.*P*.6.50; ἄεθλα *AP*6.312 (Anyte); sc. ἀγών *SIG*1064.8 (Halic., i B.C.). **III.** Ἵππιος, ὁ (sc. μήν), month at Rhegium, *IG*14.612.

⊛ **ἱππιο-χαίτης**, ου, ὁ, *shaggy with horsehair*, λόφος Il.6.469. **-χάρμης**, ου, ὁ, *one who fights from a chariot*, 24.257, Od.11.259, Hes.*Fr*.7; later, *horseman*, *rider*, A.*Pers*.29 (anap.). **II.** as Adj., ἱ. κλόνοι the tumult *of the horse-fight*, ib.105; cf. ἱπποχάρμης.

**ἱππ-ίσκος**, ὁ, Dim. of ἵππος, name of a play by Alexis, Ath.3.120b. **2.** *small statue of a horse*, *Michel*832.41 (Samos, iv B.C.). **II.** *an ornament for the head* (cf. ἱππεύς v), Cratin.Jun.5, Hsch. **-ιστί**, Adv., = ἱππηδόν, *astride*, Ἀφροδίτη ἱ. καθημένη ἐπὶ Ψυχῆς *PMag.Par*.1.1724. **-ίτας**· ἱπποφορβός, Hsch. **-ιών**, ῶνος, ὁ (sc. μήν), month at Eretria, *IG*11(4).1066*b*21 (found in Delos).

**ἱππο-βάμων** [ᾰ], ον, gen. ονος, (βαίνω) *going on horseback*, *equestrian*, Ἀριμασπὸν ἱπποβάμονα στρατόν A.*Pr*.805; στρατὸς ἱ., of centaurs, S.*Tr*.1095. **2.** *trotting like a horse*, or *used for riding*, κάμηλοι A.*Supp*.284 (cj. Turneb.). **3.** metaph., ῥήματα ἱ. *high-paced* words, *bombast*, *fustian*, Ar.*Ra*.821. **-βάτης** [ᾰ], ου, ὁ, *horseman*, A.*Pers*.26 (anap.). **II.** ἱ. ἵππος or ὄνος, *stallion*, Str.8.8.1, *Hippiatr*.14; cf. ἱπποβότης.

**Ἱππόβῑνος**, ὁ, (βινέω) comic distortion of the pr. n. Ἱππόνικος, = ἱππόπορνος, Ar.*Ra*.433.

**ἱππο-βόσιον**, τό, *horses' keep*, Theognost.*Can*.125. **-βοσκός**, όν, (βόσκω) *feeding horses*, Ael.*NA*6.10, Suid., *Gloss*. **-βότης**, ου, ὁ, (βόσκω) *feeder of horses*, Ἀτρεύς E.*Or*.1000 (lyr., but prob. -βῶτα), *IA*1059 (but prob. -βάτας). **II.** ἱπποβόται, οἱ, at Chalcis in Euboea a social class (cf. ἱππεύς II), *Knights*, Hdt.5.77, 6.100; ἡ ἱπποβοτῶν πολιτεία Arist.*Fr*.603. **-βοτος**, ον, (βόσκω) *grazed by horses*, Od.4.606, E.*Andr*.1229 (anap.), *IG*1$^2$.1034, Just.*Nov*.25.1; ἡ ἱ., at Chalcis, Ael.*VH*6.1 (cf. foreg.); esp. of the plain of Argos, from the rich pastures of Lerna, Il.2.287, al., B.10.80, E.*Supp*.365 (lyr.). **-βουκόλος**, ὁ, *horse-herd*, *horse-keeper*, S.*Fr*.1057, E.*Ph*.28. **-βροτοι** ὠδῖνες pangs that gave birth *to a horse and man* (Pegasus and Chrysaor), Lyc.842. **-γέρᾰνοι**, οἱ, *crane-cavalry*, Luc.*VH*1.13. **-γνώμων**, ον, gen. ονος, *judging well of horses*: hence generally, *quick in judging*, τινος A.*Fr*.243, cf. Hsch. **-γῡποι**, οἱ, *vulture-cavalry*, Luc.*VH*1.13. **-δᾰμαστής**, οῦ, ὁ, = ἱππόδαμος, Poll.1.181, Hsch. **-δάμνοις**· ἐφίππων, Id. ⊛ **-δᾰμος**, ον, (δαμάω) *tamer of horses*, Hom., epith. of heroes, Il.2.23, Od.3.17; Τρῶες Il.4.352, etc.; Γερηνοί Hes.*Fr*.15; ἥρωες Pi.*N*.4.29:—fem. **Ἱππο-δάμεια**, as pr. n., *Hippodamia*, Il.2.742, etc. **-δάσεια** [ᾰ], ἡ, fem. Adj., Ep. epith. of κόρυς and κυνέη, *bushy with horsehair*, 3.369, Od.22.111, etc. **-δεσμα**, ων, τά, *horse-bands*, *reins*, E.*Hipp*.1225: Adj. δακτύλιοι **ἱππόδεσμοι**, *snaffle-rings*, *IG*2$^2$.1542.25. **-δέτης**, ου, ὁ, *binding horses*, ῥυτήρ S.*Aj*.241 (anap.); epith. of Heracles at Thebes and Onchestos, Paus.9.26.1. ⊛ **-δίνητος** [ῑ], ον, *whirled in chariots*, Συρακόσιοι, B.5.2. ⊛ **-διώκτης**, ου, ὁ, Dor. **-τας**, = ἱππηλάτης, *driver* or *rider of steeds*, Theoc.14.12, Hsch.; a kind of gladiator, *IGRom*.4.1455 (Smyrna). **-δρομία**, ἡ, *horse-race* or *chariot-race*, Pi.*P*.4.67, *I*.3.13, X.*Smp*.1.2, Pl.*Ion* 537a, Arist.*Ath*.60.1, *IG*2$^2$.784 (iii B.C.), *SIG*730.30 (Olbia, i B.C.); ἱ. ἄγειν Ar.*Pax*900; ποιεῖν Th.3.104; ἱ. παιδική, ἣν καλοῦσι Τροίαν, = Lat. *ludus Troiae*, Plu.*Cat.Mi*.3. **-δρομικός**, ή, όν, *of horse-racing*, ἀγών Sch.Il.23.757. ⊛ **-δρόμιος**, ον, *of the horse-race*: -δρόμιος, ὁ (sc. μήν), name of month in Boeotia, *IG*7.531, al. (Tanagra), cf. Plu.*Cam*.19; at Delphi, *GDI*1987, al.; at Naupactus, *IG*9(1).359. **II.** epith. of Poseidon (cf. ἵππιος), Pi.*I*.1.54. ⊛ **-δρομος**, ὁ, *chariot-road*, λεῖος δ' ἱ. ἀμφίς Il.23.330. **2.** *race-course* for chariots, Pl.*Criti*.117c, D.47.53; at Olympia, Paus.6.20.15; at Delphi, *SIG*636.24 (ii B.C.); at Andania, *IG*5(1).1390.31; at Rome, the *circus*, D.H.1.79; ὁ μέγας ἱ., = *circus maximus*, Id.5.36, *Mon.Anc.Gr*.10.8: comic metaph., ἱ. οὗτός ἐστί σου μαγειρικῆς Posidipp.26.23. **II.** **ἱπποδρόμος**, ὁ, *light horseman*, ἱ. ψιλοί Hdt.7.158. **-ζώνη**, ἡ, acc. -ζώνην, f.l. for ὑπὸ ζώνην, *Hippiatr*.26; the gloss in Hsch. is missing.

⊛ **ἱππόθεν**, Adv., (ἵππος) *forth from the horse*, of the heroes descending from the Trojan horse, Od.8.515, 11.531. **-θήλεια**, ἡ, = *equa*, *Gloss*.

**ἱππο-θήλης**, ου, ὁ, *ass which has been suckled by a mare*, such being kept for the stud, acc. to Arist.*HA*577$^b$17. **-θοος**, ον, *swift-riding*, Hsch.: in Il. only as pr. n. ⊛ **-θόρος**, ὁ, (θόρνυμι) *covering mares*, esp. of a he-ass kept for breeding mules, Hsch. **II.** as Adj., ἱ. νόμος a tune *played to a mare*, *while she was being covered*, Plu.2.138b, 704f. **-θοώντειον**, τό, *sanctuary of Hippothoon*, Hsch. **-θῠτέω**, *sacrifice horses*, τῷ Ἡλίῳ Str.11.8.6. **-ίατρος**, = ἱππιατρός, *Hippiatr*.27, *CIG*1953 (Maced.), *POxy*.92 (iv A.D.). **-κάμπιον**, τό, Dim. of ἱππόκαμπος, Epich.115. **II.** a kind of *ear-ring*, Poll.5.97. **-καμπος**, ὁ, *monster with horse's body and fish's tail*, on which the sea-gods rode, Men.831; ἑστήκει Ποσειδῶν χάλκεος, ἔχων ἱ. ἐν τῇ χειρί Str.8.7.2, cf. Philostr.*Im*.1.8. **2.** a small fish, *the sea-horse*, Dsc.2.3, Ael.*NA*14.20, Gal.12.362. **-καμπτος**· στρουθίον τι, Hsch. **-κάνθᾰρος**, ὁ, *horse-beetle*, Com. word in Ar.*Pax*181. **-κέλευθος**, ον, *travelling by means of horses*: *driver of horses*, epith. of Patroclus, Il.16.126, 584, 839; *rider*, *AP*9.210. **-κενταύρειος**, α, ον, *of a centaur*, S.E.*M*.9.125. **-κένταυρος**, ὁ, *horse-centaur*, *half-horse half-man*, Pl.*Phdr*.229d, X.*Cyr*.4.3.17: also as fem., θήλειαν ἱ. ἐποίησεν Luc.*Zeux*.3. **-κέντωρ**, ορος, *stinging horses*, Tz.*H*.9 No.290 tit. **-κλείδης**, ου, ὁ, (κλείω) *pudenda muliebria*, Ar.*Fr*.703. ⊛ **-κοινάριον**, τό, *stable*, *Raccolta Lumbroso* 374. **-κομέω**, *groom horses*, ἱ. κάνθαρον *groom* his beetle, Ar.*Pax*74. **-κόμος**, ὁ, (κομέω) *groom*, *esquire*, *who attended the* ἱππεύς *in war*, Hdt.3.85, 88, X.*HG*2.4.6: generally, *groom*, Pl.*Plt*.261d, *PSI*4.371.13 (iii B.C.), Plb.13.8.3, etc.; ἱ. τῶν καμήλων Philostr.*VA*2.1. **II.** Adj. **ἱππό-κομος**, ον, (κόμη) *decked with horsehair*, epith. of a helmet (not in Od.), κόρυς Il.13.132, cf. S.*Ant*.116 (anap.); πήληξ Il.16.797; τρυφάλεια 13.339. **-κόρῡθος**, ον, coined as compd. of ἵππος and κόρυς, Porph. ad Il.2.1 (v. l. **-κόρυθες** as nom. pl.). **-κορυστής**, οῦ, ὁ, *marshaller*, *arranger of chariots*, ἀνέρες ἱπποκορυσταί Il.2.1, 24.677; epith. of the Paeonians, 16.287, 21.205. **-κόσμια**, τά, *horse-trappings*, Hsch. s.v. φάλαρα, Charis.p.549 K., *Gloss*. **-κούριος**, ὁ, *tender of horses*, epith. of Poseidon at Sparta, Paus.3.14.2. **-κράτειος**, α, ον, *Hippocratic*, διδασκαλία Gal.6.753, cf. 15.147; ἀπολίνωσις Paul.Aeg.6.78. Adv. -ως Gal.*UP*8.3. **-κρᾰτέω**, *to be superior in horse*, D.19.148, Plb.3.66.2, Onos.31.1:—Pass., *to be inferior in horse*, Th.6.71. **-κρᾰτία**, ἡ, *victory in a cavalry action*, X.*Cyr*.1.4.24. **-κράτωρ** [ᾰ], ορος, ὁ, the constellation *Centaurus*, Teucer in Boll *Sphaera* 20. **-κρημνος**, ον, *tremendously steep*, ἱ. ῥῆμα *a neck-breaking* word, Ar.*Ra*.929. **-κρήνη**, ἡ, = Ἵππου κρήνη, the spring of Pegasus on Helicon, v.l. in Str.9.2.25. **-κροτος**, ον, *sounding with the tramp of horses*, ὁδός Pi.*P*.5.92; γυμνάσια E.*Hipp*.229 (anap.); ἱ. δάπεδα γυμνάσιά τε Id.*Hel*.207 (lyr.), cf. *AP*12.131 (Posidipp.): in late Prose, Chor.*Lyd*.17. ⊛ **-κύων** [ῠ], -κῠνος, ἡ, *half-mare half-bitch*, epith. of the moon-goddess, *PMag.Par*.1.2614. **-λάπᾰθον** [λᾰ], τό, *Rumex aquaticus*, *dock-sorrel*, Dsc.2.115, Gal.12.56. **-λειχήν**, ῆνος, ὁ, *a* sort of *moss* used in farriery, Sch.Nic.*Th*.945.

**ἱππολέτας**, ου, ὁ, (ὄλλυμι) *destroyer of horses*, Hdn.*Epim*.211.

**ἱππο-λεχής**, ές, *having given birth to a horse*, Δηώ Orac.ap.Paus.8.42.6. **-λήπτρας**· τὰς τριχίνους σειρὰς Πάρθοι οὕτω καλοῦσιν, Hsch. (-ληµπρα cod., fort. -λήμπτρας). **-λούστρας**· ἔνθα τοὺς ἵππους ἀπένιζον, Id. **-λοφία**, ἡ, *horse's mane*, Iamb. post Polem.p.50 Hinck. ⊛ **-λοφος**, ον, *with horsehair crest*, κόρυς *IG*12(2).129 (Mytilene); ἱ. λόγοι, by comic metaph., Ar.*Ra*.818. **-λῡτος**, ον, *letting horses loose*, dub. l. in *APl*.4.44 (fort. ἱππελάτης). **-μᾰνέω**, *to be a-horsing*, of mares, Arist.*HA*572$^a$10. ⊛ **-μᾰνής**, ές, *abounding in*, *swarming with horses* (cf. καρπο-, ὑλο-, φυλλο-μανής), λειμών S.*Aj*.143 (anap.); variously expld. by Sch. **II.** as Subst., ἱππομανές, έος, τό, an Arcadian plant, *thorn-apple*, *Datura stramonium*, *of which horses are madly fond*, or *which makes them mad*, Theoc.2.48; f.l. for -φαές in Thphr.*HP*9.15.6. b. = κάππαρις, Dsc.2.173; = ἀπόκυνον, Ps.-Dsc.4.80. **2.** *small black fleshy substance on the forehead of a new-born foal*, which, if procured before it was eaten off by the dam, was held to be a powerful φίλτρον, Arist.*HA*577$^a$9, 605$^a$2, Thphr.*Fr*.175, Ael.*NA*3.17, 14.18. **3.** *mucous humour that runs from mares a-horsing*, used for like purposes, Arist.*HA*572$^a$21, Paus.5.27.3. **-μᾰνία**, ἡ, *mad love for horses*, Luc.*Nigr*.29. **-μάρᾰθον** [μᾰ], τό, *horse-fennel*, *Prangos ferulacea*, Diocl.*Fr*.155, Thphr.*HP*6.1.4, Dsc.3.71, Zopyr.ap.Orib.14.64.1, etc.: sts. misspelt -μάραθρον in codd.

**ἱππομᾰχ-έω**, *fight on horseback*, Th.4.124, X.*Cyr*.6.4.18; ἱ. πρὸς ὁπλίτας *to fight*, *cavalry* against infantry, Id.*Ages*.2.3. **-ία**, ἡ, *horse-fight*, *action of cavalry*, Th.2.22, 4.72, Pl.*La*.193b, etc. **-ικός**, ή, όν, *of a horse-fight*, νίκη St.Byz. s. v. Ἀλάβανδα. **-ος**, ον (parox.,

Hdn.Gr.1.230), *fighting on horseback, trooper*, Il.10.431 (v.l. -δαμοι), Simon.107.8 (= *IG*7.53), Luc.*Macr.*17, *IG*9(1).871 (Corc., iii/ii B.C.).

**Ἱππο-μέδων**, οντος, ὁ, *horse-ruler*, as a pr. n., A., etc. [In *Th.*488, with the 2nd syll. long, metri gr.] **-μητις**, ὁ, ἡ, *skilled in horses* or *in riding*, Pi.*I.*7(6).12. **-μῑγής**, ές, *partly a horse, half-horse half-man*, Ael.*VH*9.16. **-μολγία, -μολγός**, ff. ll. for ἱππη-. **-μορφος**, ον, *horse-shaped, horse-like*, Pl.*Phdr.*253c. **-μύρμηξ**, ηκος, ὁ, *horse-ant*, dub. in Arist.*HA*606ᵃ5. II. pl., *ant-cavalry*, Luc.*VH* 1.12. **-νῑκος**, ον, *victorious in the chariot-race*, *Gloss.*, prob. l. in B.13.22: freq. as pr. n. **-νομεύς**, έως, ὁ, *horse-keeper*, *Gloss.* **-νόμος**, ον, *keeping horses*, Poll.1.181. II. **ἱππόνομα**, τά, prob. *horse-hire*, Hsch. **-νώμας**, ου, ὁ, *guiding* or *keeping horses*, S.*Aj.*232 (lyr., Pors. for ἱππονόμους), E.*Hipp.*1399, Ar.*Nu.*571 (lyr.).

**ἱππόομαι**, Pass., *have the concept* or *idea of a horse*, opp. its real existence, Plu.2.1120d, 1121a; cf. ἀνθρωπόομαι.

**⊛ἱππο-πάρηος** [ᾰ], ον, *with large cheeks*, Apollon.*Lex.* s.v. ἱππόβοτον. **-πέδη**, ἡ, *horse-fetter*, *Hippiatr.*106. II. a name given by Eudoxus to a *figure-of-eight curve described by a planet*, Simp. *in Cael.*497.3, Procl.*in Euc.*pp.127,128 F. **-πῆραι**, ῶν, αἱ, *saddle-bags*, Sen.*Ep.*87.7. **-ποδες**, οἱ, *horse-hoofed men*, name of a fabulous tribe in Sarmatia, D.P.310. **-πόλος**, ον, *herding horses*, of the Thracians, Il.13.4, 14.227. (Cf. αἰ-πόλος, βου-κόλος.)

**ἵπποπορ**, prob. corrupt for ἵππορ, Lacon. for ἵππος, Hsch.: **ἱππόπορι**· κοιλάς, αὐλή, δῶμα, Id.

**ἱππό-πορνος**, ὁ, ἡ, *excessive prostitute*, Ath.13.565c, Alciphr.1.38, al.; cf. ἵππος VII; also, *one on horseback*, Diog.ap. Eust.1909.63. **⊛-πότᾰμος**, ὁ, *hippopotamus*, Dsc.2.23, Gal.14.241, Dam. *Isid.*98:—also **-ποτάμις** (for -ποτάμιος), ὁ, *POxy.*1220.21 (iii A.D.). **-πρόσωπος**, ον, *horse-faced*, epith. of the Moon-goddess, *PMag.Par.*1.2549; of a fabulous tribe, *Peripl.M.Rubr.*62.

**⊛ἵππος**, ὁ, *horse*, ἡ, *mare*, most freq. fem. in Poets; in full θήλεες ἵπποι Il.5.269; ἵπποι θήλειαι 11.680, Od.4.635; ἄρσενες ἵπποι 13.81, cf. Hdt.3.86, Pl.*Hp.Ma.*288b: pl., ἵπποι *team of chariot-horses*, Il.16.370, al.: freq. in dual, 5.237, 8.41, al.: hence, of *the chariot* itself, ἀφ' ἵπποιιν, ἀφ' ἵππων, *from the chariot*, Il.5.13,19, al.; καθ' ἵππων ἅλτο, ἐξ ἵππων βῆσε, ib.111,163; ἵππων ἐπιβησόμενος intending to mount *his chariot*, ib.46; opp. πεζοί, πλῆτο δὲ πᾶν πεδίον πεζῶν τε καὶ ἵππων Od.14.267, cf. 9.49; ἵπποι τε καὶ ἀνέρες Il.2.554; λαός τε καὶ ἵπποι 18.153; of riders, νῶθ' ἵππων ἐπιβάντες ἐθύνεον Hes.*Sc.*286; freq. of race-horses, ἵ. ἀκαμαντόποδες Pi.*O.*3.4; ἀελλόποδες Simon.7; ἀθληταί Lys.19.63: metaph., ἁλὸς ἵ., of ships, Od.4.708, cf. Secund. *Sent.*17. 2. the constellation *Pegasus*, Eudox.ap.Hipparch.1.2.12, Ptol.*Tetr.*27, Vett.Val.12.11. 3. title of Hecate in the Mithraic cult, Porph.*Abst.*4.16. 4. perh. an instrument of torture, Lat. *eculeus*, Plu.*Luc.*20 (pl.). II. as Collective Noun, ἵππος, ἡ, *horse, cavalry*, ἡ τῶν Θεσσαλῶν ἵ. Hdt.5.64, etc.: always in sg., even with numerals, ἵ. χιλίη a thousand *horse*, Id.7.41; μυρίη ibid.; μυρία, τρισμυρία, A.*Pers.*302,315; ἡ διακοσία ἵ. Th.1.62; ἵππον ἔχω εἰς χιλίαν X.*Cyr.*4.6.2. III. *a sea-fish*, Antim. et Numen.ap.Ath.7.304e; but ὁ ἵ. ὁ ποτάμιος *the hippopotamus*, Hdt.2.71, Arist.*HA* 502ᵃ9; ὁ ἵ. τοῦ Νείλου Ach.Tat.4.2. IV. *lewd woman*, Ael.*NA* 4.11. b. *pudenda muliebria et virilia*, Hsch. V. *a complaint of the eyes*, such that they are always winking, Gal.16.611, al. (also in Hp., acc. to [Gal.]19.436). VI. title of ministrants ('chuckers-out') in certain religious ceremonies, *IG*2².1368.144 (Athens, ii A.D.), 3.1280a. VII. in compds., to express *anything large* or *coarse*, as in our *horse-chestnut, horse-laugh*, v. ἱππό-κρημνος, -λάπαθον, -μάραθον, -πορνος, -σέλινον, -τυφία, and cf. βου-. (From ἵκϝος, v. ἴκκος; cf. Skt. *áśvas*, Lat. *equus*: the ἵ- (in place of ἐ-) and the aspirate are unexplained; the latter acc. to Gell.2.3.2 was confined to Attic; cf. Λεύκ-ιππος, Γλαύκ-ιππος.)

**⊛ἱππο-σείρης**, ου, ὁ, *one who leads a horse by the rein*, Anacr.75.6. **-σέλῑνον**, τό, *Alexanders, Smyrnium olus-atrum*, Thphr. *HP*2.2.1, Arist.*Pr.*923ᵃ34, Dsc.3.67: metaph., γελᾶν ἱπποσέλινα Pherecr.131.4. **-σκελής**, ές, *with horse's legs*, ἄνθρωπος Gal. *UP*3.1. **-σκόπος**, ὁ, *inspector of horses*, *PPetr.*3 pp.157,158 (iii B.C.). **-σόας**, ου, ὁ, (σεύω) *driving horses*, ἄνδρες Pi.*P.*2.65; Ἰόλαος Id.*I.*5(4).32:—fem. **ἱπποσόα**, epith. of Artemis, Id.*O.*3.26 (as Subst., *Pae.*9.7):—also **ἱπποσσόος**, ον, Nonn.*D.*37.320. **⊛-στάσιον** [ᾰ], τό, = sq., Lys.*Fr.*56 S.: pl., App.*Pun.*95, *Mith.*84:—also **⊛-στᾰσία**, ἡ, *Hippiatr.*29. **⊛-στᾰσις**, εως, ἡ, *stable*, Plb.13.8.3, Ph.2.307 (pl.), Poll.1.184, Anon.*Oxy.*1368.46: metaph., Ἀελίου κνεφαία ἱππόστασις the dark *stable* of the Sun, i.e. the West, E.*Alc.*594 (lyr.); but Ἕω φαεννὰς Ἡλίου θ' ἱπποστάσεις, of the East, Id.*Fr.*771.5.

**⊛ἱπποσύνη**, ἡ, (ἵππος) *the art of driving the war-chariot*: generally, *driving, horsemanship*, ἱπποσύνῃ . . πεποιθώς Il.4.303, cf. 11.503; ἔξοχοι ἱπποσύνᾳ Simon.108 (= *IG*1².946): in pl., λελασμένος ἱπποσυνάων Il.16.776, Od.24.40; ἱπποσύνας ἐδίδαξαν Il.23.307. II. = ἵππος II, *horse, cavalry*, Orac.ap.Hdt.7.141.

**ἱππόσῡνος**, η, ον, = ἱππικός, Δαρδανία E.*Or.*1392 (lyr.); unless ἱπποσύνα is Dor. gen. from nom. ἱπποσύνης, ὁ, cf. Sch., or ἱπποσυνᾳ be read.

**ἱππότᾰ**, ὁ, Ep. form of ἱππότης.

**ἱππο-τακτικά**· ἵππων τάξεις μισθοφόρων, Hsch. **-ταυρος**, ὁ, *horse-bull*, Hld.10.29. **⊛-τέκτων**, ονος, ὁ, *maker of the Trojan horse*, Lyc.930.

**⊛ἱππότης** (A), ου, ὁ, *driver* or *rider of horses, horseman, knight*, Hdt.7.55, 9.49,69; in Hom. always in Ep. nom. ἱππότᾰ, as Γερήνιος ἱππότα Νέστωρ Il.2.336, etc.; ἱππότης Κολωνός S.*OC*59; ἱππότης *on horseback*, Luc.*Tox.*47; τοὶ ἱππότη, Boeot. for οἱ ἱππεῖς, *IG*7.3087 (Lebad.), cf. Ascl.*Tact.*10.2. II. Adj., ἱππόται λαοί Pi.*P.*4.153; ἱ. λεώς *the horse*, A.*Th.*80 (lyr.); λεὼν ἄνιππον ἱ. τε S.*OC*899; ἱ. ὄχλος E.*Supp.*660; στρατός Plu.*Aem.*9.—Never used in correct Att. Prose.

**ἱππότης** (B), ητος, ἡ, *horse-nature, the concept of horse*, Antisth. et Pl.ap.Simp. *in Cat.*208.30,32, Sch.Aristid.p.167 F.

**⊛ἱππό-τιγρις**, ιδος, ὁ, *a large* kind of *tiger*, D.C.77.6; cf. ἵππος VII. **-τῖλος**, ὁ, (τιλάω) *diarrhoea of horses*, *Hippiatr.*56.

**⊛ἱππότις**, ιδος, fem. of ἱππότης, Tryph.670, Nonn.*D.*1.172.

**ἱππο-τόκος**, ον, *horse-bearing*, of Medusa, Nonn.*D.*47.693. **-τοξεία**, ἡ, *the art of the* ἱπποτοξότης, Tz.*H.*6.996,998. **-τοξότης**, ου, ὁ, *mounted bowman, horse-archer*, Hdt.9.49, 4.46; employed as police at Athens, Th.2.13, Lys.15.6: Com., ἱέρακας ἱ. Ar.*Av.*1179. **-τρᾰγέλᾰφος**, ὁ, *horse-goat-stag*, a fabulous monster: used of a *cup made to represent it*, Philem.87.

**ἱπποτροφ-εῖον**, τό, *place for horse-breeding, stud-stable*, Str.5.1.4, 16.2.10 (-τρόφιον). **⊛-έω**, aor. -τρόφησα Paus.3.8.1: pf. -τρόφηκα D.L.8.51, (καθ-) Is.5.43; but ἱπποτετρόφηκα Lycurg.139 codd.:—*breed* or *keep horses*, Lycurg. l. c., Isoc.16.33, Hyp.*Lyc.*16, Satyr.1; ἱπποτροφοῦσα πόλις Aen.Tact.26.4; *feed horses*, ποῖ χλωρᾷ Dsc.4.15 (v.l. πόαν χλωράν). **-ία**, ἡ, *breeding* or *keeping of horses*, esp. for racing, ἱ. γὰρ οὐ Ζακύνθῳ . . ὁπαδεῖ Simon.15: freq. in pl., ἱπποτροφίας νομίζειν Pi.*I.*2.38, cf. X.*Oec.*2.6, Pl.*Lys.*205c, Arist.*Pol.*1289ᵇ35, Anon.*Oxy.*664.27: sg., Th.6.12, Plu.*Ages.*20. 2. as a liturgy, ἀτελὴς ἔσται . . -ίας *SIG*1003.26 (Priene, ii B.C.). **⊛-ικός**, ή, όν, *of* or *for horse-keeping*: **-κόν**, τό, *allowance made to* ἱπποτρόφοι, *PTheb.Bank*6.8 (ii B.C.). **⊛-ος**, ον, (parox.) *horse-feeding, abounding in horses*, of Thrace, Hes.*Op.*507; of Argos, Pi.*N.*10.41; πόλις B.10.114. II. of persons, *breeding and keeping race-horses*, Pi.*I.* 4(3).32, etc.; μέγας καὶ λαμπρὸς ἱ. D.18.320, cf. Plu.*Them.*5, Paus. 6.2.1. 2. generally, *horsebreeder*, *POxy.*2110.6 (iv A.D.), *Hippiatr.* 34.

**ἱπποτῡφία**, ἡ, (τῦφος) *horse-pride*, i.e. *excessive pride* or *conceit*, Luc.*Hist.Conscr.*45, Pl.ap.D.L.3.39.

**ἱππούρ-αιον**, τό, = ἵππουρος, *horse-tail*, Arat.438. **-εύς**, έως, ὁ, = ἵππουρος, Hices.ap.Ath.7.304c. **-ις**, ιδος, ἡ, (οὐρά) as fem. Adj., *horse-tailed, decked with a horse-tail*, freq. in Hom. (esp. Il.), in nom. and acc. ἵππουρις, -ιν, κόρυς Il.6.495; τρυφάλεια 19.382; κυνέη Od. 22.124. II. as Subst., *horse-tail*, Ael.*NA*16.21; *Satyr's tail*, Phryn.*PS*p.77 B. 2. a water-plant, *horse-tail, Equisetum silvaticum*, Dsc.4.46, Ps.-Democr. in *Gp.*2.6.27; also, = *Equisetum maximum*, Dsc.4.47. 3. *a complaint in the groin*, caused by constant riding, dub. in Hp.*Epid.*7.122. **⊛-ος**, ον, (οὐρά) *horse-tailed*: as Subst., 1. a sea-fish, *Coryphaena hippurus*, Epich.51, Arist.*HA* 543ᵃ23, Numen.ap.Ath.7.304d, Opp.*H.*1.184. 2. *a kind of insect*, Ael.*NA*15.1. 3. = ἵππουρις II. 2, *Hippiatr.*27.

**ἱπποφάγοι** [ᾰ], οἱ, *horse-eaters*, name of a Scythian tribe, Ptol. *Geog.*5.9.

**ἱπποφαές**, έος, τό, a kind of *spurge, Euphorbia spinosa*, used for carding cloth, Asclep.ap.Gal.*Nat.Fac.*1.13, Dsc.4.159 (also **ἱππόφαος** ibid., **ἱπποφανής** Ps.-Dsc.ibid.). 2. = sq., Ps.-Dsc.4.160; = ἱππόφεως, Gal.19.106; as a drug, Thphr.*HP*9.15.6.

**ἱππόφαιστον**, τό, a plant, *Centaurea spinosa*, Dsc.4.160, Plin.*HN* 27.92, Ruf.ap.Orib.7.26.37.

**ἱππό-φεως**, εω, ὁ, *spurge, Euphorbia acanthothamnos*, gen. -φεω (v.l. -φαέως, -φέως) Hp.*Int.*13,25,26; nom. -φεως Thphr.*HP*6.5.2. 2. = ἐπίθυμον, Plin.*HN*26.55, *Gloss.* **-φλομος**, ὁ, *giant* φλόμος, i.e. *belladonna, Atropa belladonna*, Plin.*HN*25.148. **-φοβάς**, άδος, ἡ, *horse-fear*, a fabulous plant, Ps.-Democr.ap.Plin.*HN*24.161.

**ἱπποφορβ-εύς**, έως, ὁ, = ἱπποφορβός, Poll.7.185:—fem. **-άς**, άδος, Sch.Luc.*Ind.*5: **-έω**, = *keep horses*, Choerob. *in Theod.*2 lxxxv. **-ία**, ἡ, *horse-keeping*, Pl.*Plt.*299d. **⊛-ιον**, τό, *herd of horses*, Hdt.4.110, X.*HG*4.6.6, Arist.*HA*576ᵃ20. II. = ἱπποτροφεῖον, E.*El.*623, Arist.*HA*576ᵃ25, Ph.2.307. **⊛-ός**, όν, (φέρβω) *horse-keeper*, Pl.*Plt.* 261d, Arist.*HA*577ᵃ15, Jul.*Or.*7.227c: as Adj., ἱ. γῆ D.H.1.37. 2. αὐλὸς ἱ. a flute *used by* ἱπποφορβοί, made of laurel bark, Poll.4.74.

**ἱππο-χάρμης**, ου, ὁ, = ἱππιοχάρμης, Pi.*O.*1.23, *Pae.*2.104. **-χθων**, ονος, dub. sens., *Tab.Defix.Aud.*38.29 (Alexandria, iii A.D.).

**ἱππ-ώδης**, ες, *horse-like*, X.*Eq.*1.11 (Comp.), Poll.1.192; κεφαλή *Hippiatr.*14. **-ώκης**, ες, *riding in a swift chariot*, ἀέλιος B.10.101. **-ών**, ῶνος, ὁ, *place for horses*: 1. *stable*, *IG*1².336 (pl.), X.*Eq.*4.2, Moschio ap.Ath.5.207f, *PCair.Zen.*193.5 (iii B.C.). 2. *posting-house, station*, X.*Cyr.*8.6.17, *Supp.Epigr.*2.481 (Scythia, iii A.D.).

**ἱππ-ωνέω**, (ὠνέομαι) *buy horses*, X.*Eq.Mag.*1.14, *Eq.*11.13. **-ωνία**, Ion. -ίη, ἡ, *buying of horses*, Id.*Eq.Mag.*1.12 (with v.l. ἱππωνεία, which is found in codd. of *Eq.*1.1, 3.1), Poll.1.182. II. *tax on sale of horses*, *SIG*4 (Cyzicus, vi B.C.).

**⊛ἵπταμαι**, = πέτομαι, Mosch.3.43, Babr.65.4, Jul.*Or.*2.72a, etc.; censured by Luc.*Sol.*7, *Lex.*25.

***ἴπτομαι**, fut. ἴψομαι: aor. 1 ἰψάμην:—*press hard, oppress*, μέγα δ' ἴψαο λαὸν Ἀχαιῶν Il.1.454, 16.237; τάχα δ' ἴψεται υἷας Ἀχαιῶν 2.193: generally, *hurt, harm*, σὺ τόνδε μηρὸν ἴψῳ; Theoc.*Adon.*19, cf. Str. 8.6.7:—Act., **ἴπτω**, = βλάπτω, only in *EM*481.3; **ἴψαι, ἴψας**, Hsch. (Perh. related to ἰάπτω (B) or to ἶπος.)

**ἰπύα**, ἡ, = σιπύα, Hsch. (prob. ἰπύα).

**ἴφαρμος**· ἀρχή τις, Hsch. (prob. = ἱππαρμοστής).

**ἴπ-ωσις** [ῑ], εως, ἡ, (ἰπόω) *pressing hard, squeezing*, esp. in reducing

dislocations, Hp.*Art.*47, Heliod.ap.Orib.49.27.5 and 32.7. **-ωτήριον**, τό, *olive-* or *wine-press*, *l.* ληνοῦ, *Gloss.*; ὅλμοι καὶ *l.* *PRev.Laws* 49.13, cf. 51.2 (iii B.C.). II. in surgery, *bougie*, Heliod.ap.Orib. 50.9.7, Antyll.ap.eund.44.23.61, Meges ap.eund.44.24.9. 2. name of a plaster, Heracl.Tarent.ap.Gal.13.725, Orib.*Fr.*52. **-ωτρίς**, ίδος, ἡ, *for pressing in* dislocated joints, σπάθη Heliod.ap.Orib.49.32.4 and 17.9.

**ἶραι**, ῶν, αἱ, v.l. for εἶραι, Il.18.531; v. εἴρη.

**ἰράνα**, v. εἰρήνη. **ἰράνθεμον**, τό, = ἠράνθεμον, *Hippiatr.*44.

**ἱράομαι**, Ion. for ἱεράομαι. ❀**ἱρέα**, **ἱρέη**, **ἱρεία**, **ἱρηΐη**, v. ἱέρεια. **ἵρερος**, v.l. for εἴρερος. **ἱρεύς**, **ἱρεύω**, **ἱρήϊον**, Ion. and Ep. for ἱερ-.

**ἰρήν**, ένος, ὁ, Ion. for εἰρήν, prob. in Hdt.9.85.

**ἴρηξ**, ηκος, ὁ, Ion. and Ep. for ἱέραξ.

**ἱρήτειρα**, ἡ, (ἱεράομαι) *priestess*, Hsch.

**ἰρίζω** [ῑ], *to be iridescent*, *PHolm.*7.6.

**ἰρικάν**· ἵππος οἰνωπὸς χρώματι, Hsch.

**ἰρίνεος** [ῑρῐν], α, ον, = ἴρινος, Nic.*Al.*203, 241.

**ἰρῑνόμικτος** [ῐ], ον, *mixed with iris-oil*, Philox.2.40.

**ἴρῐνος** [ῑ], η, ον, *made from the iris*, μύρον Pl.Com.69.7, Cephisod. 3.2, Alex.62.8, Thphr.*HP*9.9.2, Plb.30.26.2.

**ἰριοειδής** [ῐρ], ές, *rainbow-like*, Luc.*Hist.Conscr.*19, Olymp.*in Mete.*230.21, al.

**Ἶρις**, ιδος, ἡ, acc. Ἶριν, voc. Ἶρι:—*Iris*, the messenger of the gods among themselves, Il.8.398 (never in Od.), Hes.*Th.*780, etc. (Perh. fr. *Ϝῖρις, cf. ὠκέα Ἶρις Il.2.786, al., Hes. l.c.; ὦκα δὲ Ἶρις Il.23.198 (Pap.); possibly also fr. *ἘϜῖρις: Εἶρις is the name of a ship, *IG*2[2]. 1611c137 (iv B.C.), but ἶρις is written in *Michel*832 (Samos, iv B.C.): allegorized as προφορικὸς λόγος and derived from εἴρω by *Stoic.*2. 43.) II. as Appellat., **ἶρις**, ἡ, gen. ἴριδος Thphr.*CP*6.11.13, also εως Androm.ap.Gal.14.43, *POxy.*1088.34 (i A.D.), *Gp.*6.8.1; acc. ἶριν *Michel* l.c., Plu.2.664e, ἴριδα Nic.*Al.*406; Ep. dat. pl. ἴρισσιν (v. infr.):—*rainbow*, δράκοντες.. ἴρισσιν ἐοικότες, ἅς τε Κρονίων ἐν νέφεϊ στήριξε, τέρας μερόπων ἀνθρώπων Il.11.27, cf. Arist.*Mete.*375[a]1, Epicur. *Ep.*2p.51U. 2. any *bright-coloured circle* surrounding another body, as *the* lunar *rainbow*, Arist.*Mete.*375[a]18; *halo* of candle, Thphr.*Sign.*13; round the eyes of a peacock's tail, Luc.*Dom.*11; *the iris* of the eye, Ruf.*Onom.*24, [Gal.]14.702; also, *section through the ciliary region*, Gal.*UP*10.2. 3. *iridescent garment*, *Michel* l.c. 4. various species of the botanical genus *iris*, e.g. *the purple Iris*, *I. germanica* or *pallida*, εὐάνθεμον ἶριν *AP*4.1.9 (Mel.); τὸ ἄνθος πολλὰς ἔχει ἐν αὑτῷ ποικιλίας Arist.*Col.*796[b]26, cf. Plin.*HN*21.40; also, *the white variety of it*, *I. florentina*, from the rhizome of which *the orris-root* of commerce is made, Thphr.*HP*1.7.2, *CP*6.11.13, etc.; ἶρις Ἰλλυρική Dsc.1.1, cf. Plin.*HN*13.14: in this sense some wrote it oxyt. ἰρίς, ίδος, Eust.391.33, Sch.Nic. l.c. 5. a precious stone, Plin.*HN* 37.136.

**ἰριώδης**, ες, *like the rainbow*, Arist.*Mete.*374[a]28.

❀ **ἰρμοφόρος**, ὁ, perh. *sack-bearer*, *Schwyzer* 230 (vi B.C.).

**ἱρο-**, Ion. and Ep. contr. for ἱερο-.

**ἱροδρόμος**, ὁ, poet. for ἱεροδρ- (q.v.).

**ἱρόν**, τό, Ion. for ἱερόν: **ἱρουργίη**, v. ἱερουργία.

**ἱροπόλος**, ὁ, ἡ, *priest* or *priestess*, *IG*3.736, 5(2).461 (Megalop.).

**ἱρός**, Ion. and Ep. for ἱερός, but also in Att. Poets, v. ἱερός sub fin.: **ἶρος**, Aeol. for ἱερός.

**Ἶρος**, ὁ, *Irus*, a name given by the suitors to the Ithacan beggar Arnaeus because he carried messages (cf. Ἶρις), Od.18.5 sq.: hence, later as Appellat., *an Irus*, i.e. *a beggar*, Lib.*Or.*18.140: pl., Ἶροι Luc.*Nav.*24.

**ἱρο-φάντης**, ὁ, Ion. for ἱεροφ-. **-χθων**, ὁ, ἡ, gen. ονος, *of sacred earth*, βῶλος *IG*14.1389ii27.

❀ **ἰρών**, ῶνος, ὁ, perh. = *region*, dub. word in *Inscr.Cypr.*135.8,31 H. (where *toironi* may be τοῖ οἰρῶνι; v. οἰρών).

❀ **ἰρωστί**, Ion. for ἱερωστί, *in sacred fashion*, Anacr.149.

**ἱρωσύνη**, ἡ, Ion. for ἱερωσύνη, *priesthood*, v.l. in Hdt.4.161.

**ἴς** (A) [ῑ], ἡ, gen. ἰνός, acc. ἶνα, nom. pl. ἶνες, dat. ἴνεσι Il.23.191, also ἰσίν Sor. (v. infr.), Suid. s.v. ἶνες, cj. Nauck for εἰσίν in A.*Fr.*229:—*sinew*, *tendon*, sg. once in Hom., ὡς δ' ὅτ' ἂν.. ἀνὴρ.. ἶνα τάμῃ διὰ πᾶσαν Il.17.522: usu. in pl., *sinews*, οὐ γὰρ ἔτι σάρκας τε καὶ ὀστέα ἶνες ἔχουσιν Od.11.219, cf. Il.23.191; ἶνες ἄρθρων Ar.*Pax*86, cf. Archil.138; ἶνες αὐτὸ μόνον καὶ λεπτὴ δορά, of a person wasted by disease, Ph.2.432; δοράς, σάρκας, ἶνας ib.527: metaph., Τρωίας ἶνας ἐκταμὼν δορί Pi.*I.*8(7).57. 2. later, *the fibrous vessels in the muscles*, Pl.*Ti.*84a, Arist.*HA*515[b]27, al.; in blood, *fibrine*, Id.*PA*650[b]14, cf. Pl.*Ti.*82c, Meno *Iatr.*17.34: metaph., of metals, Plu.2.434b. 3. *rib* in the leaves of plants, Thphr.*HP*3.12.7 (sg.). 4. *strip* of papyrus, ταῖς τῶν χαρτῶν ἰσίν Sor.1.13: sg., Gal.10.1000. b. λεπτὴ ἴς a small *fibre* of papyrus, Id.17(1).795.

❀ **ἴς** (B) [ῑ], ἡ, three times in acc. sg. ἶνα (elided ἶν') Il.5.245, 7.269, Od.9.538, freq. in instr. ἶφι (q.v.), elsewh. only nom. sg.:—*strength*, *force*, of persons, ἀλλ' ἄρα καὶ ἴς ἐσθλή Il.12.320; ἐπέρεισε δὲ ἶν' ἀπέλεθρον 7.269; ἤ μοι ἔτ' ἐστὶν ἴς, οἵη πάρος.. Od.21.283, cf. 11.393, 18.3: freq. in periphr., ἱερὴ ἴς Τηλεμάχοιο the *strong* Telemachus, 2.409; κρατερὴ ἴς Ὀδυσῆος Il.23.720; ἴς Ἡρακλῆος Hes.*Th.*951; and in twofold periphr., ἴς βίης Ἡρακληείης ib.332; also of things, ἴς ἀνέμου or ἀνέμοιο, Il.15.383, 17.739, Od.9.71; ἴς ποταμοῖο Il.21.356; κρᾶται' ἴς was read by Ptol.Asc. in Od.11.597; v. κρατύς. (Ϝι-, cf. γίς· ἰσχύς, Hsch., pr. n. Ϝιφιάδας *IG*7.3172.70, Lat. *vis*, *vim*; prob. cogn. with ἵεμαι but not with ἴς (A).)

**ἰσ-άγγελος**, ον, *like an angel*, *Ev.Luc.*20.36, Hierocl. *in CA*4p.425 M. **-άδελφος** [ᾰ], ον, *like a brother*, of Pylades, E.*Or.*1015 (anap.); εὔνοια *IPE*1[2].359. ❀ **-άζω**:—Pass., fut. ἰσασθήσομαι Arist.*EE* 1243[b]31: aor. 1 ἰσάσθην Id.*EN*1133[a]14: pf. ἴσασμαι ib.[b]5: (ἴσος):—*make equal*, *balance*, of a person holding scales, σταθμὸν.. καὶ εἴριον.. ἀνέλκει ἰσάζουσ' Il.12.435; *l.* τὰς κτήσεις *to equalize* them, Arist.*Pol.* 1265[a]38; *l.* τὸ ἄνισον Id.*EN*1132[a]7; τὴν φιλίαν ib.1163[b]33:—Med., *make oneself equal to another*, οὕνεκ' ἄρα Λητοῖ ἰσάσκετο (sc. Νιόβη) Il. 24.607:—Pass., *to be made* or *to be equal*, θεοῖς Pl.*Ti.*41c: abs., Arist. *EN*1133[a]14, al.; μήκει ποδὸς ἴχνος ἰσάζεται Nic.*Th.*286; δίστιχα ψήφοισιν ἰσάζεται *AP*9.356 (Leon.). II. intr. in Act., *to be equal*, Pl.*Lg.*773a, Arist.*EN*1154[b]24; ἀλλήλοις Id.*Pol.*1304[a]39. 2. *to be even*, *normal*, Hp.*Morb.*4.49. [ῑ in Hom.; ῐ in Nic.*Th.*286, 886.] **-αθάνατος** [ᾰθᾰ], ον, *equal to the Immortals*, καρπός Arist. *Fr.*675.7 as quoted by Did. in D.(6.37). **-αίομαι**, poet. for ἰσάζομαι, *resemble*, Nic.*Al.*399, *Fr.*74.56; *to be made equal*, Arat.235, 513:—Act., ἰσαίω is implied in ἰσῄι (Boeot. for ἰσαίει)· ἰσοῖ, ἰσάζει, Hsch. **-αῖος** [ῐ], α, ον, late poet. form of ἴσος, Nic.*Th.*360:—ἡ ἰσαία (sc. μοῖρα), *equality*, ἐπ' ἰσαίῃ Call.*Jov.*63, cf. Philostr.Jun.*Im.* 3; τὰ ἰσαῖα (ἴσεα lapis) *an equal share*, *SIG*57.10 (Milet., v B.C.).

**ἰσαίτερος**, **ἰσαίτατος**, v. ἴσος.

**ἰσάκῐς** [ῐσᾰ], Adv. from ἴσος, *the same number of times*, *as many times*, Str.3.5.8; *l.* πολλαπλάσιος c. gen., *the same* multiple of.., Euc.7*Def.*21, al.; *l.* πολλαπλάσια *equimultiples*, Id.5*Def.*5, al.; *l.* ἴσος, of a number, *equal multiplied by equal*, i.e. *square*, Pl.*R.*546c, *Tht.* 147e, 148a, Euc.7*Def.*19, Ph.1.11, etc.; *l.* ἴσος *l.* *equal multiplied by equal multiplied by equal*, i.e. *cube number*, Euc.7*Def.*20, etc.

**ἰσάκτιος**, ον, *ranking with the Actian games*, *CIG*4472.11 (Laodicea ad Mare).

**ἰσᾱμέριος**, ου, Dor. for ἰσημέριος, *lasting an equal time*, φύλλοις αἰγείρου S.*Fr.*593.2.

❀ **ἴσᾱμι**, v. *εἴδω (B), and add: ἴσαμι Theoc.5.119; ἴσαις (2 sg.) Id. 14.34; ἴσατι Id.15.146; ἴσατε Periand.ap.D.L.1.99; ἴσαντι Theoc. 15.64; inf. γισάμεναι (i.e. Ϝισ-)· εἰδέναι, Hsch.; Arc. ἰσάμεν (ισμεν lapis), *IG*5(2).357.12; 3 pl. subj. ἴσαντι *Schwyzer* 190 (Cretan).

**ἰσ-άμιλλος** [ᾰ], ον, *equal in the race*: neut. pl. as Adv., ἰσάμιλλα δραμεῖν τινι *AP*9.311 (Phil.). **-άμμορος**· δύσμορος, Hsch. (leg. κάμμορος).

**ἴσαν**, *they went*, 3 pl. impf. Ep. of εἶμι (*ibo*), Hom. II. *they knew*, 3 pl. plpf. Ep. of οἶδα, Il.18.405, Od.4.772.

**ἰσάναν**· ἰσάνιον, ῥητίνην, Hsch.

**ἰσ-ανάτολος**, ον, *taking the same time to rise*, ζῴδια Vett.Val.142. 27:—also **-ανάφορος**, ον, ibid., cf. Paul.Al.*E.*4, *S.*2. **-ανδρος**, ον, (ἀνήρ) *like a man*, Hsch. **-άνεμος** [ᾰ], ον, *swift as the wind*, E.*IA* 206 (lyr.). **-άξιος**, ον, *of equal worth*, Porph.*Abst.*2.55; τῷ Διί Procl.*in Cra.*p.50 P.; τοῖς θεοῖς Iamb.*Myst.*3.21; *adequate*, πρός τι Dam.*Pr.*43, cf. 28. Adv. -ίως Iamb.*Myst.*9.7. **-άργῠρος**, ον, *worth its weight in silver*, πορφυρᾶς *l.* κηκῖδα A.*Ag.*959, cf. Achae.5, Ephipp.21.4. ❀ **-αριθμέω**, *to be equal in number*, τινι Tz.*H.*1. 939. **-αρίθμιος**, ον, = sq., c. gen., Μουσῶν *IG*14.1747. **-άριθμος** [ᾰ], ον, *equal in number with*, ψυχαὶ *l.* τοῖς ἄστροις Pl.*Ti.*41d, cf. *Lg.*845a, Arist.*EN*1156[a]7, al., Call.*Del.*175, Puchstein *Epigr.Gr.*p.9; εἰσαριθμοις ἔπεσι, = ἰσοψήφοις, *IG*5(1).257 (Laconia): poet. ἰσήριθμος, *AP*6.84 (Paul. Sil.), 328 (Leon.), Lyc.1258. Adv. ἰσαρίθμως Gal.19.469, Them.*Or.*33.367b. II. Gramm., *of the same grammatical number*, A.D.*Synt.*170.13. Adv. -μως ib.143.9. **-άρχαιος**, ον, *equally ancient*, Choerob. *in Theod.*2.55. **-άρχων**, οντος, ὁ, *equitable ruler*, *POxy.*41.12,28 (iii/iv A.D.).

**ἰσάσκετο** [ῑ], Ep. 3 sg. impf. Med. of ἰσάζω, Il.24.607.

**ἰσασμός** [ῐ], ὁ, *equalization*, Epicur.*Nat.*15.21 (pl.).

**ἰσάστερος**, ον, *like a star*, *bright as a star*, Lxx 4*Ma.*17.5.

**ἰσαστικός**, ή, όν, *equalizing*, *handicapped*, στάθμη, in a race, Eust. 1023.5.

**ἰσάτις**, ιδος, Hp.*Ulc.*11, *Michel*832 (Samos, iv B.C.) (but -ιος Hp. *Aff.*38, -εως *POxy.*101.12): ἡ:—a plant producing a dark blue dye, *woad*, Lat. *Isatis tinctoria*, Hp. ll.cc., Thphr.*Sens.*77, Dsc.2.184, Plin.*HN*20.59.

**ἰσατώδης**, ες, *like woad*, Hp.*Epid.*4.45, 2.3.1; χολή Aret.*CD*1.15.

**ἰσαύδης** [ῐ], ες, (αὐδή) *of the same name*, Theoc.*Syrinx* 9.

**ἰσᾰχῶς** [ῐ], Adv., (ἴσος) *in the same number of ways*, Arist.*Metaph.* 1013[a]16, al.; παρακολουθεῖν *l.* τινί ib.1054[a]14; τἀγαθὸν *l.* λέγεται τῷ ὄντι *in as many ways as*, Id.*EN*1096[a]23.

**ἰσγίνη**, **ἰσγένη**, v. ὕσγινον.

**Ἰσεία**, τά, and **Ἴσεῖον**, τό, v. Ἰσιεῖα, Ἰσιεῖον.

**ἰσεννύω**, *to be of an intermediate age*, ἰσεννύουσαι Hp.*Mul.*2.111 (so Gal.19.106; ἴσαι νῦν ἐοῦσαι Hp. codd.; ἴσενοι ἐοῦσαι cj. Schneider (cf. ἔνος)).

**ἰσήβας** [ῑ], ου, ὁ, (ἥβη) = ἰσῆλιξ, Tim.*Pers.*226.

**ἰσηγορ-έομαι**, *speak as an equal*, v.l. in Lxx *Si.*13.11:—Act. **-έω**, Sch.D Il.1.187, Hsch., Phot. **-ία**, Ion. -ίη, ἡ, *equal right of speech*, and generally, *political equality*, Hdt.5.78, Eup.291, X.*Cyr.*1.3.10, Zeno *Stoic.*1.54, Phld.*Hom.*p.20 O., etc.; *l.* καὶ ἐλευθερία D.21.124; *l.* καὶ παρρησία Jul.*Or.*1.17b. **-ος**, ον, *enjoying equal right of speech*, *freedom of speech*, Poll.6.174.

**ἰσ-ήλῐκος**, η, ον, *equal in magnitude*, τάφρος Ph.*Bel.*91.21; *equal in age*, Procl.*in Prm.*p.944 S., al., Dam.*Pr.*316. **-ῆλιξ**, ῐκος, ὁ, ἡ, *of the same age with*, τινι X.*Smp.*8.1, *Com.Adesp.*874: c. gen., *l.* χρόνος κόσμου Ph.1.6: abs., Id.2.303. **-ημερία**, ἡ, *equinox*, *l.* ἐαρινή, μετοπωρινή, ὀπωρινή, Arist.*Mete.*364[b]1,2, 371[b]30; φθινοπωρινή

Id.*HA*570ᵇ14, etc.: in pl., Hp.*Aër.*11, Pl.*Ax.*370c, Porph.*Antr.* 24. ※ **-ημερινός**, ή, όν, *equinoctial*, ἀνατολή, δυσμή, Arist.*Mete.*363ᵃ34,ᵇ1, cf. Str.2.1.11; σκιά Hipparch.1.3.6, cf. Str.2.1.20; ζῴδιον Ptol.*Tetr.*31; ὧραι *standard* hours (opp. καιρικός, q.v.), each = 1/24 of the νυχθήμερον, Hipparch.1.1.10, Ptol.*Alm.*2.9, Gal.10.479, etc.; πυρὸς ἰ. wheat *sown at that time*, Thphr.*CP*4.11.4; ὁ ἰ. κύκλος *celestial equator*, Arist.*Mete.*345ᵃ3, Euc.*Phaen.*p.4 M., Plu.2.429f, etc.; ὁ ἰ. (sc. κύκλος), Hipparch.1.10.22, Str.1.1.21, etc.; ἁψίς Jul.*Or.*5.168c; ἰ. χρόνοι time-degrees [each = 4 time-minutes] *of the equator*, Ptol. *Alm.*1.16.

**ἰσημέριον**, τό, = *aequinoctium*, *Gloss.* **ἰσήμερος**, ον, = *aequidialis*, ib. **ἰσήμορτεν**· ἀπέθανεν, Hsch.

**ἰσήρετμος** [ῐ], ον, *with as many oars as*, τινι E.*IA*242 (lyr.).

※ **ἰσήρης**, ες, = ἴσος, ἰ. ψῆφοι E.*IT*1472, cf. Nic.*Th.*643 [ῐσ]: c. dat., ῥαιβοῖσιν ἰσήρεες [ῐσ] ib.788.

**ἰσήριθμος**, ον, poet. for ἰσάριθμος.

**ἴσθι**, *know*, imper. of οἶδα. II. **ἴσθι**, *be*, imper. of εἰμί.

**ἰσθλῆ**, v. ἰξαλῆ.

**ἴσθμα**, = ἄσθμα, and **ἰσθμαίνω**, = ἀσθμαίνω, Hsch. (also **ἰσμ-**, Id.).

**Ἴσθμ-ια**, ων, τά, v. ἴσθμιον IV. ※ **-ιάζω**, *attend the Isthmian games*: prov., *to be unhealthy*, Suid., Hsch. II. (ἰσθμός I) *drink*, Phot. ※ **-ιακός**, ή, όν, = Ἰσθμικός (q.v.): Ἰσθμιακά, τά, a kind of *garlands*, Ar.*Fr.*491. ※ **-ιάς**, άδος, pecul. fem. of foreg., νίκα Pi. *I.*8(7).3; αἱ Ἰ. σπονδαί Th.8.9. II. ἡ Ἰ. (sc. ἑορτή) the *Isthmian festival*, Pl.Com.46.10: pl., αἱ Ἰσθμιάδες, = τὰ Ἴσθμια, Pi.*O.*13.33; *a period of two years*, between each celebration of the games, Apollod.2.7.2. **-ιαστής**, οῦ, ὁ, *spectator of the Isthmian games*: Ἰσθμιασταί, οἱ, title of a play by Aeschylus. ※ **-ικός**, ή, όν, *of the Isthmus*, ἀγών, σπονδαί, Str.8.6.20, Paus.5.2.1.

※ **ἴσθμιον**, τό, (ἰσθμός) *anything belonging to the neck* or *throat*, *necklace*, Od.18.300. 2. ἴσθμια, τά, *pharynx*, *fauces*, Hp.*Dent.*21, Nic. *Al.*191,615, unless = παρίσθμια. II. *neck of a bottle*, ἴσθμιον ἀμφιφορῆος Poet.ap.Suid.; *big-bellied bottle with a long neck*, Cypr. word in Pamphil.ap.Ath.11.472e; v. ἴσφνιον. 2. *curb-stone* of a well, Phot., Moer. 3. part of dagger, perh. the *guard*, Philet.ap.Ath. 15.677c. III. *isthmus*, Hsch. IV. Ἴσθμια (sc. ἱερά), τά, *the Isthmian games*, held on the Isthmus of Corinth, Ar.*Pax*879, etc.; Ἴσθμι' ἐνίκα Simon.153, cf. *IG*1².606; Ἴσθμια.. ἐστεφανώθην Simon. 188; στέφος Ἴσθμι' ἑλών Id.158.

※ **Ἰσθμιονίκης** [νῑ], ου, ὁ, *conqueror in the Isthmian games*, B.9.26 (also **-νῑκος**, ὁ, Id.1.46): Ἰσθμιονῖκαι, οἱ, title of one book of Pindar's odes, A.D.*Synt.*156.11, etc.

**ἴσθμιος**, α, ον, also ος, ον E.*Tr.*1098 (lyr.):—*of* or *belonging to the Isthmus*, *Isthmian*, Ποτειδᾶν Pi.*O.*13.4; χθών S.*OT*940.

**ἰσθμοειδής**, ές, *like an isthmus*, αὐχήν *Peripl.M.Eux.*58.

**Ἰσθμ-όθεν**, Adv. *from the Isthmus*, *AP*9.588 (Alc.). **-όθι**, Adv. *on the Isthmus*, ib.6.259 (Phil.). **-οῖ**, loc. of Ἰσθμός II. 2, Ar.*Fr.* 14 D.:—usu. *on the Isthmus*: *at the Isthmian games*, *IG*1².77, Pi. *O.*13.98, Lys.19.63, Timocr.1.10; also ἐν Ἰσθμοῖ Simon.125 cod. [Ἰσθ- *IG*1².77,829; Ἰθμοῖ *SIG*36 *A* (Delph., iv B.C.), but Ἰσθμοῖ ib. *B* (Olymp., v B.C.); cf. Ἰσθμός.] ※ **-ός**, οῦ, ὁ (ἡ *Inscr.Délos* 353 *A* 29, 34 (iii B.C.), but ὁ 354.29, and v. infr. II), *neck*, *narrow passage*, esp. of the body, *neck*, Emp.100.19; ἰ. καὶ ὅρος τῆς τε κεφαλῆς καὶ τοῦ στήθεος Pl.*Ti.*69e: metaph., βίου βραχὺν ἰσθμόν S.*Fr.*568 (lyr.). 2. *pharynx*, *fauces*, Gal.18(2).961, Aret.*SA*1.6. II. *neck of land* between two seas, *isthmus*, ὁ ἰ. τῆς Χερσονήσου Hdt.6.36; of Athos, Id.7.22; Κιμμερικός A.*Pr.*729; ὁ ἰ. τῆς Παλλήνης Th.1.56; ὁ Λευκαδίων ἰ. Id.3.81. 2. Ἰσθμός (also Ἰθμός *SIG*507 (Delph., iii B.C.), cf. foreg.) ὁ (ἡ in Pi., as *O.*7.81, 8.48), *the Isthmus* of Corinth, Hdt.8.40, etc.; Ἰσθμοῦ δειράς, αὐχὴν Ἰσθμοῦ, Pi.*I.*1.9, B.2.7; dat. Ἰσθμῷ prob. f.l. for Ἰσθμοῖ (q.v.) in Th.5.18, *AP*13.15; but ἐν Ἰσθμῷ correctly in Hdt.9.27,81. 3. *narrow ridge*, of the Caucasus, between Caspian and Euxine, Arist.*Mu.*393ᵇ25, D.P.20. 4. of the sea, *strait*, *narrow channel*, *Inscr.Délos* ll. cc., App.*Hann.*34. (Perh. fr. εἶμι (*ibo*), cf. ἴθμα, εἰσ-ίθμη, and the spellings Ἰθμός (supr.), Ἰθμο-νίκα *IG*4.951.10.) **-ώδης**, ες, = ἰσθμοειδής, Th.7.26: Sup., Scymn.926.

**ἴσι**· γνῶσιν, Hsch.

**Ἰσ-ῐᾰκός** [ῐ], ή, όν, *of* or *for Isis*, σύνοδος *IGRom.*1.1303 (Philae, i B.C.): Subst. **-κός**, ὁ, *priest of Isis*, Dsc.3.23, Plu.2.352b. **-ιασταί**, οἱ, *guild of worshippers of Isis*, at Rhodes, *IG*12(1).157,165 (i B.C.). ※ **-ῑδεῖον**, τό, *temple of Isis*, Roussel *Cultes Égyptiens* 223 (Delos, ii B.C.), *Sammelb.*3926 (Ptolemais Hermiu, i B.C.):—also Ἰσιεῖον, τό, *SIG*588.230 (Delos, ii B.C.); pl. Εἰσιεῖα, τά, *festival of I.*, *PCair.Zen.*154 (iii B.C.):—later ※ Ἰσεῖον, τό, *temple of I.*, Plu.2. 352a, prob. in *AP*11.212 (Lucill., pl.); pl. Ἰσεῖα, τά, *festival of I.*, D.S.1.14,87.

※ **ἰσῑκιάριος** [ῐσ], ὁ, *sausage-maker*, *PStrassb.*46 (vi A.D.).

※ **ἰσῑκιομάγειρος** [ισ], ὁ, = foreg., *Wien.Stud.*24.129 (vi A.D.).

※ **ἰσίκιον** [ῐσῑ], τό, or **ἴσῑκος**, ὁ, *a dish of mince-meat* (formed from Lat. *insicium* acc. to Macr.*Sat.*7.8.1), Ath.9.376b, *POxy.*1730 (iv A.D.):—also **ἴσικος**, ὁ, Alex.Aphr.*Pr.*1.22, Alex.Trall.*Febr.*1: pl., Olymp. *in Grg.*p.36. J.

**ἰσινδίη**· καθίνη, Hsch.

**ἴσιον**, τό, purgative bark, Aët.3.37,104.

**Ἰσιονόμος**, ὁ, *warden of the temple of Isis*, *PCair.Zen.*172.14 (iii B.C.), *BGU*993 (ii B.C.).

※ **Ἶσις**, ἡ, voc. Ἶσιν *UPZ*81 ii 19 (ii B.C.), gen. Ἴσιδος *BGU*993 ii 10 (ii B.C.), Plu.2.353f, etc.; Ion. and later Ἴσιος Hdt.2.41, *PPetr.*3 p.216 (iii B.C.), etc. (written Ἔσιος *Schwyzer* 749 (v B.C.)); dat. Ἴσιδι *OGI*175.4 (ii B.C.), etc., Ἴσι or Ἴσει Hdt.2.59, *OGI*61.4 (iii B.C.); acc. Ἶσιν:—*Isis*, Hdt. ll. cc., Call.*Ep.*58, Apollod.2.1.3, Plu.2.351f, *POxy.*1380 (ii A.D.), etc.; Ἴσιδος τρίχες, name of a *plant*, Plu.2. 939d, cf. Plin.*HN*13.142. II. name of a *plaster*, Gal.11.126, 13. 774. III. Pythag. name for the δυάς, *Theol.Ar.*12.

**ἴσκαι**, ῶν, αἱ, *fungus growing on oaks and walnut-trees*, used as a cautery, Aët.7.91, Paul.Aeg.6.49, Alex.Trall.12.

**ἰσκάνδιον**· σαλπίγγιον, Hsch. **ἰσκανδοτόν**· σαλπιγγωτόν, Id. **ἴσκλος**, ὁ, v. ὕσκλος. **ἰσκός**· κλέπτης, Id.; cf. κίσκος.

**ἴσκω** (A), iterat. pres. of εἶμι, *go*, ἐνς πόλεμον *Schwyzer* 180 (Crete).

※ **ἴσκω** (B), = ἐΐσκω (q.v.), only 3 sg. impf. ἴσκε(ν) in early Ep., *make like*, φωνὴν ἴσκουσ' ἀλόχοισιν *she made* her voice *like* (the voice of) their wives, Od.4.279; *feign*, ἴσκε ψεύδεα πολλὰ λέγων ἐτύμοισιν ὁμοῖα 19.203. II. *think like*, ἐμὲ σοὶ ἴσκοντες *thinking* me *like* (i.e. taking me for) you, Il.16.41; σὲ τῷ ἴσκοντες 11.799 (ἐΐσκ- Aristarch.). 2. *guess*, *imagine*, ἴσκεν ἕκαστος ἀνήρ Od.22.31; *suppose*, c. acc. et inf., Simon.130. III. in Alex. Poets, through a misinterpretation of Hom., *speak*, *say*, A.R.2.240, al.: 1 sg. ἴσκον Theoc.22.167, part. ἴσκων Lyc.574.

**ἴσμα**, ατος, τό, (ἵζω) *foundation*, *seat*, Lyc.731.

※ **ἴσμα**, ἰσμαίνω, v. ἴσθμα.

※ **ἰσμή**, ἡ, (οἶδα, ἴσμεν) *knowledge*, Hsch.

**ἰσο-αχθής**, ές, *equal in weight*, Nic.*Th.*44. **-βᾰθής**, ές, *of equal depth*, Thphr.*CP*3.4.2, Heliod.(?)ap.Orib.46.8.2. **-βᾰρέω**, *to be of equal weight*, τὰ -βαρέοντα τῷ ὑγρῷ Archim.*Fluit.*1.3, cf. Sch.Il.17.742. **-βᾰρής**, ές, *of equal weight*, Arist.*Cael.*273ᵇ 24, 308ᵇ34, Chrysipp.*Stoic.*2.175, Archim.*Fluit.*1.3, Luc.*Vit.Auct.* 27. **-βᾰσῐλεύς**, έως, ὁ, ἡ, *equal to a king*, Plu.*Alex.*39. **-βῐος**, ον, *holding office for life*, γραμματεύς *IGRom.*4.1675 (Belevi). **-βοιος**, ον, (βοῦς) *worth an ox*, Hsch. s.v. ἀντίβοιος. II. ἰσόβοιον, τό, a poppy-like flower, Id.

**ἰσοβόλων**· ἰσοστασίων, Hsch., Phot.

**ἰσό-γαιος**, ον, *of equal height in relation to the land*, θάλασσαι Luc. *Ner.*5: Att. **-γεως**, *even with the ground*, τέμνειν ἰσόγεων Thphr.*CP* 3.7.3:—written **-γειως**, *IG*2².1665 (iv B.C.).

**ἴσογκος** [ῐ], ον, *equal in bulk*, Archim.*Fluit.*1.7, 2.4.

**ἰσο-γλώχῐν**, ῑνος, ὁ, ἡ, *equiangular*, Nonn.*D.*6.23. **-γονία**, ἡ, *equality of birth*, Pl.*Mx.*239a, D.C.52.4. ※ **-γρᾰφος** or **-γράφος**, ον, *writing like*: metaph., ἰ. τέττιξιν *musical* as the cicada, of Plato, Timo 30.2 (s.v.l.): **-γρᾰφή**, ἡ, name of a work by Antisthenes, D.L. 6.15: **-γρᾰφον**, τό, *copy*, Men.Prot.p.24 D. (pl.). **-γώνιος**, ον, *equiangular*, τετράγωνα Arist.*Metaph.*1054ᵇ2, cf. Plu.2.427a, etc.; πεντάγωνον Gal.5.67. **-δαίμων**, ον, gen. ονος, *godlike*, A.*Pers.*634 (lyr.), Ariphron 1.4, Hierocl. *in CA*4p.425 M. II. *equal in fortune* or *happiness*, ἰ. βασιλεῦσι Pi.*N.*4.84. **-δαίτης**, ου, ὁ, (δαίω) *dividing equally*, *giving to all alike*, epith. of Dionysus and Pluto, Plu.2.389a, Luc.*Ep.Sat.*32; of Pluto, Hsch. (ἰσοδέτης cod.). II. Subst., name of a δαίμων, Hyp.*Fr.*177. **-δᾰμιοργός**, ὁ, (ϝισο- lapis) *enjoying the privileges of a* δαμιοργός (cf. δημιουργός), at Elis, *Schwyzer* 415.4 (Olymp.). **-δενδρος**, ον, *equal to that of a tree*, ἰσοδένδρου.. αἰῶνος Pi.*Fr.*165. 2. *as big as a tree*, Thphr.*HP*3.1.1. **-δέξιος**, ον, *ambidextrous*, Philostr.*Gym.*41. **-δίαιτος** [ῐ], ον, *living on an equal footing*, πρός τινα with one, Th.1.6; τινι Luc.*Bis Acc.* 33. **-διάστατος**, ον, *equal in dimension*, of the surfaces of a cube, Nicom.*Ar.*2.16, cf. Iamb. *in Nic.*p.93 P., Eust.ad D.P.2. **-δομος**, ον, of walls, *built in equal courses*, Vitr.2.8.6, Plin.*HN*36.171. **-δοξος**, ον, gloss on ἰσοκλεής, Hsch., Phot., Suid. **-δουλος**, ον, *like a slave*, Sch.A.*Ch.*135. **-δρομέω**, *keep pace with*, τινι Arist.*Pr.* 913ᵃ38; ἰσοδρομεῦσα χελιδοῖ (Ion. part.) Nic.*Fr.*74.33. 2. metaph., *concur with*, τοῖς οὐρανίοις ἔργοις Longin.15.4: abs., *to be concurrent*, Arist.*GA*727ᵇ10. ※ **-δρομος**, ον, *keeping pace with*, τινι Pl.*Ti.*38d, Ti.Locr.96e, Ph.1.469; τινος Arist.*Mu.*399ᵃ8: abs., ἰ. μῆκος a course of equal length, *AP*7.212 (Mnasalc.). II. ἡ ἰσοδρόμη Μήτηρ, i.e. Cybele, Str.9.5.19.

※ **ἰσοδῠνᾰμ-έω**, *have equal power*, τὸ ψεῦδος ἰ. πρὸς τὴν ἀλήθειαν Plb.2.56.2; *to be equivalent to*, τινι *Stoic.*3.9, Ph.2.291, etc.; ἀλλήλοις Arr.*Epict.*1.8.1; esp. in meaning, A.D.*Pron.*41.15, al.: Math., Ptol.*Alm.*2.7: abs., Chrysipp.*Stoic.*2.83, Lxx *Si.Prol.*13; of sounds in speech, Phld.*Po.Herc.*994*Fr.*22; of drugs, etc., *possess the same properties*, Dsc.1.70, 5.75: Astrol., *to be equipollent*, Ptol.*Tetr.*36, Vett.Val.142.27. **-ία**, ἡ, *equal force* or *power*, Ti.Locr.95b. 2. *equivalence in meaning*, A.D.*Conj.*244.17. 3. Astrol., *equipollence*, Ptol.*Tetr.*132, Vett.Val.296.11. **-ος**, ον, *equal in force* or *power*, Alex.Aphr.*Pr.*1.135; of drugs, Paul.Aeg.2.30; *equivalent in meaning*, Men.Prot.p.24 D.: generally, *equivalent*, c. dat., Lxx 4*Ma.*3.15. Adv. **-μως**, ἔχειν Eust.72.33, cf. Gal.18(2).483.

**ἰσο-ελκής**, ές, *equal in weight*, Nic.*Th.*41, v.l. ib.44. **-επίπεδος**, *equal in plane surface*, Iamb. *in Nic.*p.93 P. **-έτηρος**, ον, *equal in years*, Nonn.*D.*21.177 [ῐ]. **-ετής**, ές, = foreg., gloss on οἰέτεας, Apollon.*Lex.*, Sch.Il.*Oxy.*1086 i 21. II. ἰσοετές, τό, = ἀείζωον τὸ μικρόν, Plin.*HN*25.160. **-ευρής**, ές, *equal in breadth*, Phot.

**ἰσοζῠγ-έω**, *make equal in weight*, Nic.*Th.*908. **-ής**, ές, *evenly balanced*: *equal*, *AP*10.16.3 (Theaet.). **-ος**, ον, Gramm., *of the same number and person*, ῥῆμα A.D.*Pron.*69.8. II. gloss on ἀντίζυγα, Hsch.

**ἰσο-θάνᾰτος** [θᾰ], ον, *like death*, S.*Fr.*359; ἀρρωστία *PHaw.*65. 19; κίνδυνος Vett.Val.293.4; censured by Poll.6.174. **-θεος**, ον, *equal to the gods*, *godlike*, of heroes, ἰ. φώς Il.2.565, Od.1.324, A. *Pers.*80 (lyr.); Δαρεῖος ib.857 (lyr.); οἱ ἰ. S.*Ant.*837 (anap.); γένος

E.*IA*626, cf. Pl.*Phdr.*255a, Isoc.2.5, etc.; ἰητρὸς φιλόσοφος ἰ. Hp. *Decent.*5: Com., νομίσαι τ' ἰσόθεον τὴν ἔγχελυν Antiph.147.2. 2. of things, ἰ. τυραννίς E.*Tr.*1169; δόξα Isoc.5.145; εἴσοδος Epicur. *Fr.*165; τιμαί Men.*Mon.*378, Plb.10.10.11, *IG*5(2).432.4 (Megalop.); χάριτες *OGI*666.21 (Egypt, i A.D.); freq. of medicines or remedies, Gal.13.65,279, Aët.7.11: neut. -θεον as Adv., *PMag.Par.*2.220. [ῑσ- in Hom. and Trag. (always lyr.); hyperaeol. ἰσσο- *Schwyzer*647.15 (Cyme, i A.D.).] **-θεόω**, *make equal to the gods*, in Pass., Aesop.160.

**ἰσόθι**, Arc. Adv. *within*, ἰ. πλέθρω *SIG*306.13 (Tegea, iv B.C.).

**ἰσό-θροος**, ον, *sounding like*, Ἠχώ Nonn.*D.*36.473. **-θῡμος**, ον, *equal in spirit*, Sch.Il.7.295. **-καινος**, ον, *as good as new*, Hsch. s. v. ἀντίκαινον. **-κάμπᾰνος**, ον, *equal in weight*, Sch.Od. 4.129; cf. κάμπανος. **-κᾰπῐτώλιος**, ον, *ranking with the* Καπιτώλια, ἀγών *BGU*1074.16 (iii A.D.). **-κατάληκτος**, ον, *ending alike*, Eust.1839.43: -ληκτα, τά, Gell.18.8.1. **-κέλευθος**, ον, *walking alike, keeping up with*, Nonn.*D.*48.316 [ῐ]. ⊛**-κέφᾰλος**, ον, *like-headed*, dub. in Ibyc.16. **-κίνδῡνος**, ον, *facing equal risks*, Th. 6.34; τισί D.C.41.55. **-κιννάμωμος** [ᾰ], ον, *like cinnamon*, of cassia (prob. = ἄχυ, q.v.), Plin.*HN*12.98. **-κλεής**, ές, *equal in glory*, Hsch., Phot. **-κληρονόμος**, ον, *inheriting equally*, Sch. Hermog. in Rh.4.169 W. **-κληρος**, ον, *equal in property*, Plu. *Lyc.*8. **-κλῐνής**, ές, *evenly balanced*, Arist.*Mu.*400ᵇ28. **-κνημος**, ον, *with the legs on a level*, Erot. **-κοιλος**, ον, *with equal cavities*, αὐλός Plu.2.1021a, Theo Sm.p.60 H. (pl.). **-κόρῠφος**, ον, *equally high* or *eminent*, πόλεις D.H.3.9. **-κρᾱής**, ές, *equally mixed*, prob. l. (for -κρατεῖ) Hp.*Morb.*2.42. **-κραιρος**, ον, *with equal horns*, Nonn.*D.*27.24. **-κράς**, ὁ, ἡ, = ἰσοκραής, Hdn.Gr.1. 525. **-κράτεια** [κρᾰ], ἡ, = ἰσοκρατία, *equilibrium, equivalence*, Gal. *Hist.Phil.*126.

**Ἰσοκράτειος** [ᾰ], ον, *of Isocrates*, λόγοι Phld.*Rh.*1.100 S.; ἀγωγή D.H.*Isoc.*20:—also **Ἰσοκρᾰτικός**, ή, όν, Id.*Vett.Cens.*3.3: -κοί, οἱ, *followers of I.*, Phld.*Rh.*1.148 S.

**ἰσοκρᾰτ-έω**, *to be of equal force*, S.E.*M.*10.81. **-ής**, ές, *of equal power, possessing equal rights with others*, ἰσοκρατέες..αἱ γυναῖκες τοῖσι ἀνδράσι Hdt.4.26; ἰ. καὶ ὁμότιμοι Plu.2.827b: generally, *evenly balanced*, ἡ ἰσημερία ἐστὶ χειμὼν καὶ θέρος ἰσοκρατής Arist.*Pr.*942ᵇ37; ἰ. οἶνος *half-and-half*, Hp.*Morb.*2.42 (nisi leg. ἰσοκραής); ἐκ τῆς ἀμφοῖν -οῦς μίξεως Gal.6.528; ἰ. κράσεις *normal* temperaments, Ruf.ap. Orib.8.24.61. Adv. -τῶς, ἀπομάχεσθαι Ph.1.198; *with even balance*, Zeno *Stoic.*1.27, Iamb.*in Nic.*p.79 P. **-ία**, ἡ, *equality of strength* or *power*, Ti.Locr.95c. 2. = ἰσονομία, *equality of rights, republic*, opp. τυραννίς, Hdt.5.92.α' (pl.).

**ἰσό-κρᾱτος**, ον, = ἰσοκραής, Praxag.ap.Ruf.*Onom.*226. **-κρῑθος**, ον, *equal to barley in price*, Plb.2.15.1. **-κτῐτος**, ον, (κτίζω) *made alike*, Hsch., Phot. **-κτῠπος**, ον, *sounding like*, τινι Nonn.*D.*27. 92. **-κυκλος**, ον, *equally round*, Philox.2.10. **-κωλία**, ἡ, *equality of members* or *clauses*, Hermog.*Id.*1.12 (pl.). **-κωλος**, ον, *of equal members* or *clauses*, Arist.*Top.*148ᵇ33; τὸ ἰ. *a sentence consisting of equal members*, Demetr.*Eloc.*25, Plu.2.350e: in pl., D.S. 12.53, Ath.5.187c. 2. *formed of an equal number of strands*, χορδαί Nicom.*Harm.*6. **-λᾰχής**, ές, = ἰσόμοιρος, cj. in Philol. 6. **-λεκτοι** *versus, antithetically composed*, Diom.p.498 K. **-λεχής**, ές, *with the same bed*, Apollon.*Lex.Hom.* **-λογέω**, *speak freely with*, τινι Sch.E.*Hipp.*702. **-λογία**, ἡ, = ἰσηγορία, Plb.30. 31.16; -λογίαν ἔχειν πρός τινα Id.24.10.9. II. in pl., *counterbalancing arguments*, S.E.*M.*1.144. **-λόγχητος**, ον, = ὁ τὰ ἴσα λαχών (cf. λόγχη), dub. in *IG*9(1).309 (Thronium).

**ἰσολύμπιος**, ον, *like those rendered to the Olympians*, τιμαί Ph. 2.181, cf. 567. II. *ranking with the Olympic games*, [ἀγὼν] γυμνικός *SIG*630.13 (Delph., ii B.C.), cf. *IG*12(7).506.7 (Nicuria), etc.

**ἰσό-λῠρος**, ον, *like the lyre*, Sch.S.*Tr.*643. **-μάτωρ** [ᾱ], Dor. for -μήτωρ, ὁ, ἡ, *like one's mother* or *dam*, ἀμνός Theoc.8.14; said to be Cret. by Hsch. **-μᾰχος**, ον, *equal in the fight*, D.H.3.52; ἀρετή, κίνδυνος, D.S.16.12, 17.83: τισι Ant.Lib.14.2. **-μεγέθης**, ες, *equal in size*, X.*Cyn.*5.29, Plb.10.44.2, Phld.*Mort.*3, Herod.Med.ap. Orib.10.8.2: c. dat., κύστις ἰ. ληκύθῳ Aen.Tact.31.10; ἰ. γῇ Jul.*Gal.* 135c. Adv. -θως Aristid.Quint.3.6. **-μέρεια**, ἡ, *equality*, ἐξ -μερίας *Sammelb.*6266.17 (vi A.D.). **-μερής**, ές, *equally divided*, δόσεις *BGU*1122.12 (i B.C.); *of equal length*, ib.393.12 (ii A.D.): generally, *equal*, κέρδος Just.*Nov.*97.1. **-μέτρητος**, ον, *of equal measure* or *weight*, εἰκών Pl.*Phdr.*235d, Plu.*Sol.*25; τινι D.C.59.11, cf. Max.Tyr.31.2. **-μετρία**, ἡ, *equality of measure*, Arist.*Fr.* 47. **-μετρος**, ον, = ἰσομέτρητος, Ephipp.14.9, Palaeph.30; λίθοι, prob. in *IG*2².463.46; σφηνίσκος Sever.ap.Aët.7.92: c. dat., ἰ. τῇ προτέρᾳ δοῦναι προῖκα Just.*Nov.*97.5; *of equal perimeter*, περὶ ἰ. σχημάτων, title of work by Zenodorus; *in the same latitude*, Nech. in *Cat.Cod.Astr.*7.149: Subst., ἰσόμετρον, τό, *life-size statue*, τινος *BCH* 48.484 (Delos, iv B.C.). **-μέτωπος**, ον, *with equal forehead* or *front*, X.*HG*4.5.16. **-μήκης**, ες, *equal in length*, Arist.*HA*506ᵇ 14; τῇ Ἀττικῇ Str.9.2.1; of numbers, *having a common factor*, Pl.*R.* 546c. **-μῑλήσιος**, α, ον, *of Milesian fashion*, ἱμάτιον D.S.12.21.

**ἰσομοιρ-έω**, *have an equal share*, Th.6.39, X.*Cyr.*2.3.17; τινος *of a thing*, D.48.19; τινὸς πρός τινα Th.6.16; πρὸς ἀλλήλους Isoc.5. 39; τινός τινι Is.1.2, D.H.6.66. II. Astrol., *occupy the same degree*, *Cat.Cod.Astr.*5(1).219. **-ία**, Ion. -ίη, ἡ, *equal share*, κακοῖσιν ἐσθλοὺς ἰσομοιρίαν [ῑσ-] ἔχειν Sol.ap.Arist.*Ath.*12.3; τινος in a thing, Th.7.75. 2. = ἰσονομία, Nymphod.21, D.C.52.4. 3. *equability*, of climate, Hp.*Aër.*12; τῶν κράσεων Gal.1.534. 4. Astrol., *equivalence of degree*, Vett.Val.139.16. **-ικός**, ή, όν, *of equivalent positions*, κανονογραφία Id.336.11. ⊛**-ος**, ον, Cret. ϝισϝόLeg.Gort.10.53, *GDI*4974 (Gort.): (μοῖρα) *sharing equally* or *alike*, c. gen. rei, πάντων X.*Cyr.*4.6.12, etc.; τῶν ἄλλων ἰ. ἔστω *SIG*1044. 40 (Halic., iv B.C.); γῆς ἰσόμοιρ' ἀὴρ air that *sharest* earth *equally* [with light], S.*El.*87 (anap.): c. dat., τιμαῖς ἰσόμοιρον ἔθηκεν τὰν ὁμόλεκτρον ἥρωσιν *IG*12(3).1190.3 (Melos); ἰσόμοιρον, τό, *equal portion*, Nic.*Th.*592: abs., ἰσόμοιρα.. ἐν τῷ κόσμῳ φῶς καὶ σκότος D.L.8.26. Adv. -ρως Eust.161.20. 2. *equivalent, corresponding*, c. dat., κίβισιν, βάκτρῳ ἅρπην ἰσόμοιρον *AJA*9.320 (Sinope). 3. Astrol., *occupying the same degree*, αἱ κατ' ἰσόμοιρον στάσεις Vett.Val.70.31, cf. Man.4.194; τὴν Ἀφροδίτην ἰσόμοιρον οὖσαν ἡλίῳ Procl.*Hyp.*1.21. Adv. -ρως *Cat.Cod.Astr.*5(1).219.

**ἰσόμορος**, ον, = ἰσόμοιρος, used by Poseidon of himself in relation to Zeus, Il.15.209: generally, *like*, τινι *AP*6.206 (Antip.Sid.); ἰσόμορον, τό, *equal portion*, Nic.*Th.*105, Androm.ap.Gal.14.41. [ῑσ- Il. cc.]

**ἰσόνειρος**, ον, *dream-like, empty*, A.*Pr.*549 (lyr.) [perh. ῑ].

⊛**ἰσό-νεκυς**, υος, ὁ, ἡ, *dying equally* or *alike*, E.*Or.*200 (lyr.), ubi v. Sch. **-νέμεος**, ον, *ranking with the Nemean games*, ἀγών *SIG*402.10, al. (Delph., iii B.C.), *IG*2².680.17 (prob.):—also⊛**-νέμειος** *Klio* 14. 275 (Delph., iii B.C.).

**ἰσονομ-έομαι**, Pass., *have equal rights*, μετά τινος Th.6.38. **-ία**, Ion. -ίη, ἡ, *equal distribution, equilibrium, balance*, δυνάμεων Alcmaeon 4, cf. Ti.Locr.99b, Epicur.*Fr.*352. II. *equality of political rights*, Hdt.3.80,142; ἰ. ποιεῖν Id.5.37; opp. δυναστεία, Th.4.78; ἰ. πολιτική Id.3.82; ἰ. ἐν γυναιξὶ πρὸς ἄνδρας καὶ ἀνδράσι πρὸς γυναῖκας Pl.*R.*563b. **-ικός**, ή, όν, *devoted to equality*, ἀνήρ ib.561e. **-ος**, ον, *where all have equal rights*, ἰσονόμους τ' Ἀθήνας ἐποιησάτην *Scol.* 12; ὀλιγαρχία ἰ. Th.3.62; δίκαιος καὶ ἰ. πολιτεία Pl.*Ep.*326d; ἐν ἰσονόμῳ πολιτεύειν App.*BC*1.15; ζῷον ἰ. θεῷ M.Ant.8.2; Γαλατία ἰ. *enjoying full citizen rights*, of Gallia Cisalpina, Nic.Dam.130.28 J. II. χαλκὸς ἰ. copper *at par* (24 obols = 1 stater), opp. χαλκὸς οὗ διαλλαγή (copper at a discount), *UPZ*112 v 19 (ii B.C.), *PTeb.*99.4 (ii B.C.), *PPetr.*3 p.193, al. (ii B.C.).

**ἰσονύκτιον**, τό, *equinox*, *Gloss.*:—Adj. **-νύκτιος**, ον, *equinoctial*, Gal.16.407.

**ἴσοξ**, ὁ, a fish, Hsch. (Celtic word, cf. Welsh *ehawc, eog* 'salmon', Lat. *esox.*)

**ἰσό-ξῠλος**, ον, *like wood*, Hsch. s. v. ὄξυλον. **-ογκος**, ον, *of equal bulk* or *volume*, Simp.*in Cael.*691.35, *in Ph.*1016.23. **-παις**, ὁ, ἡ, *like a child, as of a child*, ἰσχύς A.*Ag.*75 (lyr.). **-πάλαιστος** [ᾰ], ον, *a span long*, *AP*6.287 (Antip.). [ῐ..ᾰ] ⊛**-πᾰλής**, ές, *equal in the struggle, well-matched*, μαχομένων..καὶ γενομένων ἰσοπαλέων Hdt. 1.82, cf. 5.49; *evenly balanced*, μάχη Ctes.*Fr.*29.31. 2. generally, *equivalent, equal*, ἰ. πάντη Parm.8.44; ἰ. κίνδυνοι Th.2.39; πλήθει ἰ. τισί Id.4.94; οὔτι ὤριφος ἰ. τοι Theoc.5.30; ἰ. ἤματι νύξ *AP*9.384.18, cf. Orph.*Arg.*1014. Adv. -λῶς Sch.Arat.364. **-πᾰλος**, ον, = foreg., Luc.*Nav.*36, D.C.40.42, Poll.3.149, 5.157, Hsch.; prob. in Ibyc.14, X.*Ages.*2.9. ⊛**-πᾰχής**, ές, *of equal* or *even thickness* or *density*, Arist.*HA*527ᵃ7, Thphr.*HP*3.5.6, Dsc.5.90, Gal.10.431, Nicom.*Harm.*6:—late nom. sg. **-πᾰχυς** Herod.Med.ap.Orib.8.4.3 codd. **-πεδής**, ές, = ἰσόπεδος, *Gloss.* **-πεδον**, τό, *level ground, a flat*, Il.13.142, X.*Cyr.*3.1.5; φυλάττειν ἐπὶ τοῦ ἰσοπέδου ἑαυτήν Luc.*Im.*21. **-πεδος**, ον, *of even surface, level*, ἐξ ἰ. χωρίου Hp.*VC*11, cf. Luc.*Hipp.*4; ἰ. τῷ δέρματι Gal.10.1011; ἰ. χρώματα *flat in appearance*, opp. κοῖλα, Alex.Aphr.*Pr.*1.49. 2. c. dat., *level* or *even with*, χοῦν ποιέων τῇ ἄλλῃ γῇ ἰσόπεδον Hdt.4.201, cf. D.S. 19.94, Plu.*Num.*10. **-πέλεθρος**, ον, *of the same number of* πλέθρα, Hsch. **-πενθής**, ές, *in equal distress*, Sch.A.*Eu.*783. **-πέραστος** or **-πέρατος**, ον, *equally bounded*, Sch.Od.1.98. **-περίμετρος**, ον, *of equal perimeter*, Damian.*Opt.*3, Hero *Def.*82, Procl.*in Ti.*2.71 D., al. **-πετρος**, ον, gloss on ἀντίπετρος, Sch.S.*OC*192. ⊛**-πηχυς**, υ, *of the length of a cubit*, Philostr.*Gym.*12, Opp.*H.*1.213. **-πλαστος**, ον, gloss on ἀντίπλαστος, Hsch. **-πλᾰτής**, ές, *equal in breadth*, Arist.*Oec.*1345ᵃ33, Archimel.ap.Ath.5.209c; ἄρτος ἰ. Hippoloch.ap. Ath.4.128d (-πλατυς codd.): c. dat., ἰ. τῷ τείχει Th.3.21. **-πλάτων**, ωνος, ὁ, *a second Plato*, *AP*11.354. [ῐ..ᾰ] **-πλευρος**, ον, *with equal sides*, πλαίσιον X.*An.*3.4.19, etc.: freq. in Geom., *equilateral*, τρίγωνον Pl.*Ti.*54a,e; ἐπίπεδον ib.55e; τετράγωνον Plb.6.31.10. II. of numbers, *square*, opp. ἑτερομήκης, Pl.*Tht.*148a, Arist.*APo.*73ᵃ40. Adv. -πλεύρως Nicom.*Ar.*2.13. III. Rhet., of periods, Hermog. *Inv.*4.3. **-πληγής**, ές, *struck in the same way*, χορδή Porph. *in Harm.*p.296 W. **-πληθής**, ές, *equal in number* or *quantity*, ἠήρ Hp.*Morb.*2.4; ἱππεῖς X.*Ages.*2.9: Math., *equal in number*, Euc.12. 4, al.; σχήματα τὰς πλευρὰς ἰ. ἔχοντα Papp.332.14: c. dat., τινι to a person or thing, Th.6.37, D.C.50.33; ἰ. θαλάσσῃ ποταμοί Poll.3.103. Adv. -θῶς Euc.12.5. **-πληθόπλευρος**, ον, *having an equal number of sides*, εὐθύγραμμα, σχήματα, Anon.Geom. in Papp.1142.21.

**ἰσοπολῑτ-εία**, ἡ, *equality of civic rights*, Arist.*Fr.*575; granted to individuals, *IG*7.4264 (Oropus, iii B.C.), 5(2).11 (Tegea, iii B.C.), etc.; or to communities, *SIG*472.11 (Phigalea, iii B.C.), Plb.16.26.9, D.S.15.46, etc. 2. esp. *reciprocity of such rights* (guaranteed by treaty between two states), *GDI*5040 (Crete), *OGI*265 (Pergam., iii B.C.), etc.; Λεβαδεῦσίν ἐστιν ἰ. πρὸς Ἀρκάδας Plu.2.300b. **-ης**, ου, ὁ, *enjoying equal political rights*, τινὰς τοῖς Μακεδόσιν ποιήσας ἰ. J. *AJ*12.1.1, cf. Lxx 3 *Ma.*2.30, *GDI*5183.25 (Crete), *Inscr.Magn.*34.28, al., *IPE*1².357. 2. *enjoying reciprocity of rights*, of the citizens of Roman *municipia*, D.H.8.76:—fem.⊛**-πολῖτις**, ιτιδος, of cities *enjoying such rights*, αἱ ἰ. πόλεις, = *municipia*, App.*BC*1.10. 3. *equitable citizen*, *POxy.*41.28 (iii/iv A.D.).

**ἰσο-πραξία**, ἡ, *a faring equally, like condition*, Eust.662.35. **-πρέσβυς**, υ, *like an old man*, A.*Ag*.78 (anap.). **-προικον**, τό, *wedding-gift* of bridegroom to bride, *CPR*30 ii 10 (vi A.D.), etc. 2. *as good as given away*, Hsch. s. v. ἀντίπροικα. **-πρόξενος**, ον, (Ϝισο- lapis) *enjoying the privileges of a* πρόξενος, *Schwyzer*415.3 (Olymp.). **-πτερος**, ον, gloss on ἄπτερος, Sch.A.*Ag*.276 :—also ἰσόπτεροι· ἰσότιμοι, Hsch.

**ἰσο-πτῠχής**, ές, *with similar folds*, χιτώνιον *IG*2$^2$.1518.82, 84. **-πτωτος**, ον, (πτῶσις) *with like cases*, A.D.*Pron*.90.6. ⊛ **-πύθιος** [ῡ], ον, *ranking with the Pythian games*, ἀγών *SIG*402.24 (Delph., iii B.C.), prob. in *IG*2$^2$.680.16 ; στέφανος *SIG*557.29 (Magn. Mae.); ἱερὰ Αὐγουστεῖα Ἰ. *IGRom*.4.1265 (Thyatira). **-πυκνος**, ον, *equally condensed* (by tension), χορδή Porph. *in Harm*. p.296 W. (comment on πυκνοτέρας in Ptol.*Harm*.1.8). **-πυργος**, ον, gloss on ἀντίπυργος, Hsch. **-πῡρον**, τό, *fumitory, Fumaria capreolata*, Dsc. 4.120, Plin.*HN*27.94, Gal.11.891. **-πῡρος**, ον, *reckoned as of equal value with wheat*, λωτός, κρότων. *PLond.ined*.2360. **-ρρεπής**, ές, = ἰσόρροπος, Nic.*Th*.646, Poet. *de Herb*.98.

**ἰσορροπ-έω**, *to be equally balanced, in equipoise*, Pl.*Ti*.52e, *Lg*.733c, 794e ; τινι *with..*, Plb.1.11.1. **-ησις**, εως, ἡ, *equipoise, equilibrium*, Hero *Spir*.1.1. **-ία**, ἡ, *equipoise, equilibrium*, Pl.*Phd*. 109a : metaph., Ἰ. τοῦ χρόνου Agath.4.25. **-ικά**, τά, title of *work on equilibrium* by Archimedes. ⊛ **-ος**, ον, (ῥοπή) *in equipoise*, of the balance, Pl.*Phd*.109a, *Plt*.270a (Sup.), etc.; τάλαντα βρίσας οὐκ ἰσορρόπῳ τύχῃ A.*Pers*.346 ; ἰσορρόπου τοῦ πήχεως (sc. τοῦ ζυγοῦ) γινομένου *IG*2$^2$.1013.34. 2. generally, *well-balanced, well-matched*, Ἰ. αὐτὸς ἑαυτῷ of a man *with his legs of the same length*, Hp.*Fract*.19 ; of a nose, *flattened, but not awry*, Id.*Art*.37 ; of a bone, *cylindrical*, ib. 34 ; δέρμα Ἰ., opp. περιρρεπής, ib.50 ; Ἰ. ἀγών *evenly balanced*, E.*Supp*. 706 ; μάχη Th.1.105 ; δυνάμεις Pl.*Ti*.52e ; βίος Id.*Lg*.733c ; τιμή Arist.*EN*1164$^b$4 : c. dat., τὸ γένος τὸ Ἀττικὸν Ἰ. τῷ ἑωυτῶν ἂν γίνοιτο would become *a match for* their own, Hdt.5.91 ; Ἰ. Ῥωμαίοις Hdn.6. 7.8 ; Ἰ. καταστῆναί τινι *IPE*1$^2$.40.18 (Olbia, ii A.D.) ; Ἰ. ὁ λόγος τῶν ἔργων *in precise equipoise with..*, Th.2.42 ; Ἰ. πρός τι Hdn.6.3.2. 3. *of equal weight*, χρυσίον *Inscr.Delos*313$^a$.45 (iii B.C., -ορο-). II. Adv. -όπως, ἀφιέναι Hp.*Art*.43 ; πορεύεσθαι Pl.*Phdr*.247b ; ἀγωνίσασθαι D.C.41.61 : neut. pl. ἰσόρροπα as Adv., Tim.*Pers*.47.

⊛ **ἰσόρυθμος**, ον, perh. *of like form*, Pi.*Pae*.*Fr*.90.

⊛ **ἴσος**, η, ον, Ep. **ἶσος** and **ἔϊσος** (v. infr.); Cret., Arc. ϝίσϝος *GDI* 4998 ii 2, 4982.2, *Schwyzer*665, cf. γισγόν· ἴσον, Hsch.; later **ἴσος** *Schwyzer*708$^a$(1) (Ephesus, iv B.C.), *Tab.Heracl*.1.175, etc. :—*equal* in size, strength, or number, c. dat., κύματα ἶσα ὄρεσσιν Od.3.290, etc.; freq. of appearance, *like*, ἴσος ἀνάδῳ 10.378 ; ἴσος Ἄρευι Sapph.91 (dub.); ἴσος θεοῖσιν Ead.2.1 : freq. abs., ἴσην.. βίην καὶ κῦδος Il.7.205 ; ἶσον θυμὸν ἔχειν to be of *like* mind, 13.704, 17.720 : neut. as Adv., ἶσον ἐμοὶ φρονέουσα 15.50 ; θεοῖσιν ἶσ' ἔθελε φρονέειν 5.441, cf. 21.315, etc.; ἴσος τινὶ τὸ μέγαθος, ὕψος, Hdt.2.32, 124 ; τὸ μῆκος, τὸ πλάτος, X.*An*. 5.4.32 ; ἀριθμόν E.*Supp*.662 ; ἴσα τὸν ἀ. Pl.*R*.441c ; ποτὴν ἴσον *equal* in flight of song, Alex.Aet.5.5 ; ἴσον, τό, *copy* of a document, *PLond*. 3.1222.5 (ii A.D.), etc. : with dat. pers. in place of an object of comparison, οὐ μὲν σοί ποτε ἶσον ἔχω γέρας (i. e. τῷ σῷ γέραϊ) Il.1.163 ; τοιάσδ' ἴσας ναῦς (i. e. ταῖς τῶνδε) E.*IA*262 (lyr.); ἴσα τοῖς νῦν στρατηγοῖς ἀγάθ' εἰργασμένους D.13.21 : folld. by a relative word, ἐμοὶ ἴσον.., ὅσονπερ ὑμῖν *the same* to me as to you, Ar.*Ec*.173 ; τὰ ἐκεῖ ἴσα, ὥσπερ τὰ ἐνθάδε Lys.19.36 codd. (fort. σὰ); τὰ ἴσα ὅσαπερ.. Lex ap.D.23. 44 ; ἴσον.. ὅπερ Pl.*Erx*.405b. 2. repeated to denote equal relations, ἴσα πρὸς ἴσα *tit for tat*, Hdt.1.2 ; ταχθέντες ἴσοι πρὸς ἴσους S. *Ant*.142 (anap.); ἴσους ἴσοισι.. ἀντιθεὶς E.*Ph*.750 ; ἴσα ἀντὶ ἴσων λαμβάνειν, ἐκδοῦναι Pl.*Lg*.774c ; ἴσος ἴσῳ (sc. οἶνος ὕδατι) Cratin.184, *Com.Adesp*.107, etc.; κύλικος ἴσον ἴσῳ κεκραμένης (where ἴσον is adverbial) Ar.*Pl*.1132 ; διδόναι γάλα καὶ οἶνον πίνειν ἴσον ἴσῳ Hp. *Epid*.2.5.1 : metaph., 'fairly blended', μηδὲν ἴσον ἴσῳ φέρων Ar.*Ach*. 354. 3. of persons, *equal in rights*, βούλεται ἡ πόλις ἐξ ἴσων εἶναι καὶ ὁμοίων Arist.*Pol*.1295$^b$25 ; ἡ πολιτικὴ ἐλευθέρων καὶ ἴσων ἀρχή ib. 1255$^b$20 ; τὸ κατ' ἀξίαν Ἰ. ib.1307$^a$26, al. II. *equally divided* or *distributed*, ἴση μοῖρα Il.9.318 ; ἴση alone, *one's equal share*, μή τίς μοι ἀτεμβόμενος κίοι ἴσης Od.9.42 (ἴσσης cj. Fick, cf. ἰσσασθαι) ; τὴν Ἰ. ἔχων Cratin.250 ; οὐ μὴν Ἰ. ἔτεισεν (sc. τίσιν) S.*OT*810 ; ἄχρι τῆς Ἰ. up to *the point of equality*, D.5.17 : neut., μὴ ἴσον νεῖμαι ἑκατέρῳ Pl.*Prt*.337a; οὐ μόνον ἴσον, ἀλλὰ καὶ πλέον ἔχειν Isoc.17.57 ; οὐκ ἀνέξῃ δωμάτων ἔχων ἴσον καὶ τῷδε νεῖμαι; E.*Ph*.547 ; τὰ ἴσα *fair measure*, τὰ Ἰ. νέμειν Hdt. 6.11 ; μὴ ἴσων ἕκαστον τυγχάνειν ἀλλὰ πλεονεκτεῖν, X.*Cyr*.2.2.20 ; προστυχεῖν τῶν Ἰ. to obtain *fair terms*, S.*Ph*.552 ; κἂν ἴσαι (sc. ψῆφοι) γένωνται *equally divided*, Ar.*Ra*.685. 2. *based on equality of rights*, Ἰ. καὶ ἔννομος πολιτεία Aeschin.1.5 ; τὴν πολιτείαν ἰσαιτέραν καθιστάναι Th.8.89 ; τὰ Ἰ. *equal rights, equality*, freq. joined with τὰ ὅμοια or τὰ δίκαια, ὡς τῆς πολιτείας ἐσομένης ἐν τοῖς Ἰ. καὶ ὁμοίοις X.*HG*7.1.45 ; τῶν Ἰ. καὶ τῶν δικαίων ἕκαστος ἡγεῖται ἑαυτῷ μετεῖναι ἐν τῇ δημοκρατίᾳ D.21.67 ; οὐ μέτεστι τῶν Ἰ. οὐδὲ τῶν ὁμοίων πρὸς τοὺς πλουσίους τοῖς λοιποῖς ib.112 ; τῶν Ἰ. μετεῖχε τοῖς ἄλλοις ib.96 ; also ἡ Ἰ. καὶ ὁμοία (sc. δίκη), τῆς Ἰ. καὶ ὁμοίας μετέχειν Th.4.105 ; ἐπ' Ἰ. τε καὶ ὁμοίῃ on *fair* and equal terms, Hdt.9.7,α', cf. Th.1.145 ; ἐπὶ τῇ Ἰ. καὶ ὁμοίᾳ ib.27, cf. *SIG*312.27 (Samos, iv B.C.), *OGI*229.44 (Smyrna, iii B.C.), etc. : generally, *just, fair*, ἐκ ποίας Ἰ. καὶ δικαίας προφάσεως; D.18.284. 3. of persons, *fair, impartial*, S.*Ph*.684 (lyr.), *OT*677 ; Ἰ. δικαστής Pl.*Lg*. 957c ; Ἰ. καὶ κοινοὶ ἀκροαταί D.29.1, cf. 18.7 ; Ἰ. καὶ κοινὸν δικαστήριον Id.7.36 ; κοινοὺς μὲν.., Ἰ. δὲ μή Pl.*Prt*.337a ; Ἰ. ἴσθι κρίνων Men.*Mon*. 266, cf. 257 ; κριταὶ Ἰ. καὶ δίκαιοι Plb.24.15.3, etc. 4. *adequate*, ἡ Ἰ. φρουρά Th.7.27 (expld. by Sch. as *regular*, τεταγμένη); ἴσος τοῖς παροῦσι Id.1.132. III. of ground, *even, flat*, εἰς τὸ Ἰ. καταβαίνειν, of an army, X.*An*.4.6.18 (but ἐν ἴσῳ προσιέναι to advance *with even step*, ib.1.8.11); λέουσιν εἰς τὸ Ἰ. καθιστάμενοι μάχεσθαι, opp. μετὰ πλεονεξίας ἀγωνίζεσθαι, *on even terms*, Id.*Cyr*.1.6.28 ; Ἰ. τοῖχος, opp. κεκλικώς, *perpendicular*, Phlp. *in APo*.2.27. IV. Adv. ἴσως (v. sub voc.): but also, 1. neut. sg. and pl. from Hom. downwds. (v. sub init.), ἶσον.. ἀπήχθετο κηρὶ μελαίνῃ *even as* Death, Il.3.454 ; ἶσον ἐμοὶ βασίλευε be king *like* me, 9.616 ; ἶσον γάρ σε θεῷ τίσουσιν Ἀχαιοὶ ib. 603 ; ἶσον ἐμῇ κεφαλῇ 18.82 ; τὸν.. ἶσα θεῷ.. εἰσορόωσιν Od.15.520 ; ἶσα φίλοισι τέκεσσι Il.5.71, cf. 13.176, Od.1.432, 11.304, etc.: later abs., *alike*, δείλαιε τοῦ νοῦ τῆς τε συμφορᾶς ἴσον S.*OT*1347 ; τὴν Σάμον καὶ Ἡρακλέας στήλας ἴσον ἀπέχειν Hdt.8.132 : c. dat., ἴσον ναοῖς θεῶν E.*Hel*.801 ; ἴσον ἄπεσμεν τῷ πρὶν *equally* as before, Id.*Hipp*.302 (v. l. τῶν πρὶν); ἴσα τοῖς πάνυ D.C.*Fr*.70.6 ; ἴσα καί.. *like as, as if*, S.*OT* 1187 (lyr.), E.*El*.994 (anap.), Th.3.14 ; ἴσον ὡς.. E.*Ion* 1363 ; ὥσπερ .. S.*El*.532 ; ὥστε.. E.*Or*.882 ; ἅτε.. Id.*HF*667 (lyr.); ὅσονπερ.. D.15.1. 2. with Preps.: ἀπὸ τῆς ἴσης *equally*, Th.1.15 ; ὁ ἀπὸ τῆς Ἰ. ἐχθρός Id.3.40 ; ἀπ' ἴσης εἶναι D.14.6 ; ἀφ' ἴσου *SIG*426.14 (Teos, iii B.C.); δι' ἴσου D.C.43.37 ; at *equal* distance, Pl.*R*.617b : also in Math., *ex aequali*, of proportions, Euc.5 *Def*.17, al.; δι' Ἰ. ἐν τεταραγμένῃ ἀναλογίᾳ *ex aequali* in disturbed proportion, Archim. *Sph.Cyl*.2.4, al., Papp.932.11 ; ἐν ἴσῳ *equally*, Th.2.53, 4.65 ; ἐν ἴσῳ ἐστί it matters not, E.*IA*1199 ; ἐν ἴσῳ [ἐστὶ] καὶ εἰ.. Th.2.60 ; ἐν τῷ ἴσῳ εἶναι Id.4.10 ; ἐξ ἴσης Pl.*Lg*.861a : more freq. ἐξ ἴσου Hdt.7.135, S.*OT*563, etc.; ἐξ Ἰ. τινί Id.*Ant*.516, 644, Antipho 5.1, Pl.*Grg*.517a; *evenly*, εὐθεῖα γραμμή ἐστιν ἥτις ἐξ Ἰ. τοῖς ἐφ' ἑαυτῆς σημείοις κεῖται Euc. 1 *Def*.4 ; ἐξ Ἰ. καί.. S.*OC*254 ; ὡς.. Id.*OT*61 ; οἱ ἐξ Ἰ. persons *of equal station*, Pl.*Lg*.777d, cf. 919d ; ὁ ἐξ Ἰ. κίνδυνος Plb.9.4.4 ; ἐκ τοῦ Ἰ. γίγνεσθαί τινι Th.2.3 ; τοῖς ἐκ τοῦ ἴσου ἡμῖν οὖσι X.*Hier*.8.5 ; ἐξ ἴσου τισὶ τῆς πολιτείας μεταδιδόναι Lys.25.3 ; ἐκ τοῦ Ἰ. μάχεσθαι *to be evenly matched*, X.*HG*2.4.16 ; ἐξ Ἰ. πολεμεῖν D.8.47 ; κατὰ μῆνα τὸ αἱροῦν ἐξ Ἰ. the sum due in *equal* monthly instalments, *PAmh*.2.92.14, etc.; ἐπὶ or ἐπ' ἴσης, ἐπὶ Ἰ. διαφέρειν τὸν πόλεμον Hdt.1.74 ; τοῦτο ἐπ' ἴσης ἔχει Id.7.50, cf. S.*El*.1062 (lyr.), etc.; ἐπ' ἴσου Plb.1.18.10 ; ἐπ' ἴσον Id. 6.38.4, cf. Docum.ap.D.18.106, Phld.*Ir*.p.21 W.; ἐπὶ ἶσα μάχη τέτατο Il.12.436 ; cf. κατὰ ἶσα μάχην ἐτάνυσσε 11.336 ; κατ' ἴσον Dsc.1.68.6, Gal.*UP*1.19 ; μετ' ἴσου *equally*, Demetr.Lac.*Herc*.124.12. V. Comp. ἰσαίτερος E.*Supp*.441, Th.8.89, X.*HG*7.1.14 : Sup. ἰσότατος Timo 68 ; ἰσαίτατος Ph.1.462. Adv. ὡς ἰσαίτατα Pl.*Lg*.744c, but ὡς ἰσότατα *SIG*531.30 (Dyme). [ῑ in early Ep. (exc. Hes.*Op*.752), cf. Sol.24.1 : ῐ first in Thgn.678, Sapph.2.1 (but ἶσος Ead.91 s. v. l.), B. 5.46 (but ἶσον 1.62, *Fr*.2.2), and always in Pi. (exc. in compd. ἰσοδαίμων) and Trag. (A.*Fr*.216 is dub. l.) exc. in compd. ἰσό-θεος (q. v.); dub. in ἰσ-όνειρος. Both quantities are found in later poetry, sts. in same line, ἔχοισαν ἶσον κάτω, ἴσον ἄνωθεν Theoc.8.19 ; πρέσβυν ἶσον κούροις, ἴσον ἀδόντα κόραις *APl*.4.309.]

**ἰσοσθέν-εια**, ἡ, *equipollence*, [τῶν αἰσθήσεων] Epicur.*Fr*.36, cf. Chrysipp.*Stoic*.2.37, S.E.*P*.1.8, D.L.9.74. **-έω**, *possess equal force*, [κινήσεων] κατ' ἴσον ἀμφοῖν -σθενουσῶν Gal.*UP*1.19 ; of arguments, D.L.9.73 ; *to be equal in strength*, of military forces, Ascl. *Tact*.3.2, 4. **-ής**, ές, *equal in force* or *power*, πενίαν Ἰ. πλούτῳ ποιεῖν Democr.284 ; ἀδάμαντος Ἰ. ἄορ Opp.*H*.2.466 ; μύες τὴν ῥώμην Ἰ. Gal.*UP*7.14 ; *evenly balanced*, μάχαι Id.1.364 ; διαφωνία S.E.*P*.1.26 ; τὸ Ἰ. D.L.9.107. Adv. -νῶς Gal.9.81.

**ἰσοσκέλ-εια**, ἡ, *having two sides equal* ; κατ' -ειαν *in trine aspect*, Ptol.*Tetr*.125. **-ής**, ές, *with equal legs*, esp. in Geom., *having two sides equal, isosceles*, τρίγωνον Pl.*Ti*.54a, etc.; τὸ Ἰ. Arist.*APo*.41$^b$ 14. 2. of numbers, *that can be divided into two equal parts, even* (as 6 = 3 + 3), opp. σκαληνός, odd (as 7 = 4 + 3), Pl.*Euthphr*.12d. 3. Rhet., of periods, *containing equal members*, Hermog.*Inv*.4.3. 4. Medic., *having equal tails*, of a bandage, Heliod.ap.Orib.48.62 tit.

**ἰσόσπριος**, ον, *bean-like* ; ὄνος Ἰ. an insect *that rolls itself up like a bean*, the *wood-louse*, S.*Fr*.363.

**ἰσο-στάδην** [ᾰ], Adv., (ἵστημι) = ἰσοστασίως, with marginal gloss ἢ συστάδην, Suid. s. v. ἀνταγωνιστής. **-σταθμέω**, *to be equal in weight*, Id. s. v. ἄγουσαν. **-σταθμος**, ον, *equal in weight*, Dsc.1.44, Orib.*Fr*.106, App.*Sic*.3 ; even, σφυγμός [Gal.] 19.641 ; gloss on σύσταθμος, ib.143 :—also **-σταθμής**, ές, Ptol.*Tetr*.98. ⊛ **-στάσιος** [ᾰ], ον, *equal in weight*, χρυσός, χρυσίον, Str.4.4.5, Plu.*CG*17 ; *equivalent* or *adequate*, τινι Hp.*Ep*.16, Luc.*DMort*.10.5, D.C.44.40, Max.Tyr.6.6 ; τίς σοι Ἰ. νεκρός; Polem.*Call*.46, cf. 31 ; ἆρα οὖν Ἰ. τῷ Κρόνῳ ὁ Ζεύς; Dam.*Pr*.91 : ἰσοστάσιον, τό, prob. name of a ἑταίρα, title of a play by Alexis. 2. *equally poised, in equilibrium*, metaph., Dam.*Pr*.122. Adv. -ίως Poll.8.11 : neut. pl. as Adv., βαίνειν Ph.1.462. **-στᾰτέω**, = ἰσοσταθμέω, Lib.*Decl*.43.2. **-στοιχέω**, = ἀντιστοιχέω, Sch.D.T. p.44 H.; *to be co-ordinate*, Simp. *in Ph*.408.13. **-στοιχος**, ον, *occupying a corresponding place*, of terms in parallel series, Id. *in Cael*. 156.18 ; gloss on ἀντίστοιχος, Sch.E.*Andr*.745. **-στροφή**, ἡ, *correspondence*, Ammon. *in APr*.35.23, Phlp. *in APr*.40.3. **-στροφος**, ον, *equally twisted, even*, χορδαί Nicom.*Harm*.6. II. = ἀντίστροφος, S.E.*M*.7.6, Ammon. *in APr*.35.26 : coupled with ἀντίστρ., Herm. *in Phdr*.p.189 A.; ἀνάγκη πᾶν πρὸς πᾶν ἢ Ἰ. εἶναι ἢ ἕτερον Dam. *Pr*.312. **-σύγκρῐτος**, ον, gloss on ἀμφήριστος, Sch.Opp.*H*.1.90.

**ἰσοσυλλᾰβ-έω**, *have the same number of syllables*, A.D.*Pron*.11. 20, al., *PLit.Lond*.183. **-ία**, ἡ, *equality of syllables*, A.D.*Adv*.174. 16. **-ος**, ον, *having the same number of syllables*, Plu.2.739a, Hermog.*Id*.1.12, A.D.*Pron*.11.8, etc. Adv. -βως St.Byz. s. v. Ἄβαι, *EM*552.34.

**ἰσο-σώμᾰτος** or **-σωμος**, ον, glosses on ἀντίστοιχος, Sch.E.*Andr*.

745. -τᾰγής, ές, *corresponding in order*, Philol.6(v.l.); χῶραι *Theol.Ar.*51. -τάλαντος [τᾰ], ον, gloss on ἀτάλαντος, Hsch. -ταυρος, ον, *like a bull*, cj. in S.*OT*478 (lyr.).

**ἰσοτάχ-εια** [τᾰ], ἡ, *equal velocity*, Simp.*in Ph.*1019.23. -έω, *travel with equal velocity*, Thphr.*Fr.*89.11; τινι Ph.1.463, Hld.8.17. -ής, ές, *possessing equal velocity*, Arist.*Ph.*216ᵃ20, al., Plb.10.44.9, Cleom.2.1, Ph.1.588; ἄτομοι Epicur.*Ep.*1 p.18 U., *Nat.*2.2; πλοῖα Ph.*Bel.*73.21; τινι Arist.*Ph.*240ᵃ8: generally, *equally swift*, νίκης κρίσις *Epigr.Gr.*939.2 (Synnada). Adv. -χῶς Arist.*Mech.*848ᵃ16, Sch.Epicur.*Ep.*1 p.8 U. II. *uniform in rate*, of the pulse, Gal.8.459, Plb.10.44.13, Str.1.2.17. Adv. -χῶς Gal.9.454.

**ἰσοτέλ-εια**, ἡ, *condition of an* ἰσοτελής, *equality in tax and tribute*, X.*HG*2.4.25, *Vect.*4.12, *IG*2².109*b*20, 276.13, al., *GDI*3077 (Mesembria), Ph.1.160, etc.: freq. in Boeot. Inscrr., ϝισοτέλια *IG*7.505, al. (Tanagra). -εστος, ον, (τελέω) *made exactly like, exact*, ἰ. μίμημα Nonn.*D.*18.247. 2. *coming at the last to all alike*, ἐπίκουρος, of Death, S.*OC*1220 (lyr.). -ευτον, τό, *leading to the same result*, Sch.Hermog.in Rh.4.169 W.

**ἰσοτελής**, ές (gen. sg. ἰσοτελοῦ (sic), *Epigr.Gr.*48), (τέλος) *bearing equal burdens*; at Athens and elsewh., of a favoured class of μέτοικοι, subject to the same taxation as the citizens, Lys.*Fr.*225 S., Is.*Fr.*45, D.20.29, Arist.*Ath.*58.2, *IG*2².276.15, al., cf. *SIG*742.44 (Ephesus, i B.C.); of freedmen, *IG*9(1).412 (Aetolia), Hsch. II. metaph., of Hera, [τῷ Διΐ] ἰ. his *consort*, Orph.*Fr.*163.

**ἰσο-τενής**, ές, *level*, [ἵπποι] τὰ νῶτα ἰσοτενεῖς Tim.Gaz.ap.Ar.Byz.*Epit.*147.4. -τετράγωνος [ᾰ], ον, *of four equal rectangles*, συναγωγή Ps.-Hero *Poliorc.*p.238 W. -τεχνος, ον, *equal in art* or *skill*, τινι *Epigr.Gr.*532 (Perinthus); τοῖν ἰ. αὐλητοῖν Plu.*Nob.*9.

⊕ **ἰσότης**, ητος, ἡ, (ἴσος) *equality*, Arist.*Metaph.*1054ᵇ3, etc.: in pl., Pl.*Lg.*733b; ἰ. χρόνου Id.*Prm.*140e: Math., ἰ. γεωμετρική *equality of ratios, proportion*, Id.*Grg.*508a; ἀναλογία ἰ. λόγων Arist.*EN*1131ᵃ31. 2. esp. *political equality* or *justice*, personified in E.*Ph.*536, cf. Pl.*Lg.*757a; ἰ. πολιτική Plb.6.8.4, etc.: in dual, Pl.*Lg.*757b, cf. Arist.*Pol.*1302ᵃ7, Isoc.7.21. II. *fair dealing, impartiality*, Men.*Mon.*259, Plb.2.38.8, *Ep.Col.*4.1. III. *equiformity*, of the earth, Epicur.*Nat.*11.10. (On the accent v. Hdn.Gr.1.83, 2.945; ἰσοτῆς is said to be Hellenistic by Moer.202.)

**ἰσοτίμ-ημα** [τῑ], gloss on ἰσωνία (-ονία cod.), Hsch. -ία, ἡ, *equality of privilege*, opp. πλεονεξία, X.*Hier.*8.10, cf. Str.8.5.4, Ph.1.160; ἐξ ἰσοτιμίας διαλέγεσθαί τινι to converse with him *as his equal*, Luc.*Pisc.*34. -ος, ον, *equal in honour* or *privilege*, Ἀπόλλων (i.e. sharing the honours paid to Zeus) *OGI*234.25 (Delph., iii B.C.), *CRAcad.Inscr.*1906.419 (Alabanda); ὁ θεὸς . . -ον παρέχι τράπεζαν τοῖς ὁποθενοῦν ἀφικνουμένοις *BCH*51.73 (Panamara); πίστις 1*Ep.Pet.*1.1; οἱ πρῶτοι καὶ ἰ. Plu.*Lys.*19, cf. Wilcken *Chr.*13.10 (i A.D.), Luc.*DMort.*24.3, etc.; πόλεις τισί D.Chr.41.2: Comp. -ότεροι, τοῖς κρατοῦσιν Id.39.4; τὸ ἰ., = ἰσοτιμία, Ph.2.246; of a person, *maintaining equality of privilege*, Hdn.2.4.9. Adv. -μως, τινάς τισιν ἄγειν Ath.5.177c; ζῶντα δικαίως καὶ ἰ. *OGI*544.34 (Ancyra, ii A.D.), cf. *CIG*4032.5 (ibid.), *IGRom.*3.195 (ibid.); ἰ. ἔχουσι πρὸς ἀλλήλους οἱ ὅροι Phlp.*in APr.*167.14, cf. Alex.Aphr.*in Metaph.*241.11. 2. generally, *equal in value*: hence, *equal*, ἁμάρτημα ἀκούσιον ἰ. ἑκουσίῳ Ph.2.248; τὸ ἰ. δυσέφικτον ἐν ταῖς ἀμοιβαῖς Hdn.2.3.6; ἰ. μάχη *evenly balanced*, Ael.*NA*10.1. 3. as title of rank at the Ptolemaic court, τῶν ἰσοτίμων τοῖς πρώτοις φίλοις *PRyl.*66 intr., 253 (ii B.C.), *Arch.Pap.*6.372.

**ἰσό-τοιχος**, ον, *with equal walls* or *sides*, of ships, gloss on ἐΐσας, Hsch. -τονία, ἡ, in Music, *uniformity of pitch, level pitch*, Ptol.*Harm.*1.4 (pl.), Porph.*in Harm.*p.287 W. -τονος, ον, *pulling evenly*, βρόχος Gal.18(1).351, Paul.Aeg.6.102. II. *bearing the same accent*, Hermog.*Id.*1.12. 2. in Music, *of level* (*unvarying*) *pitch*, Ptol.*Harm.*1.4; but, *in unison*, ib.7, 2.1. III. generally, *equal, even*, ἰ. τῇ συγκρίσει τοῦ χρώματος Dsc.5.123. Adv. -νως *equally*, θυμιᾶσθαι Id.68.6. -τράπεζος [ᾰ], ον, *equal to the table*, i.e. *large enough to fill it*, κάκκαβος Antiph.182.2, cf. Philox.2.15. -τρῐβής, ές, in A.*Ag.*1443, σελμάτων ἰσοτριβής (cj. Pauw. pro ἰστοτρ-) *pressing* the benches *like others*. ⊕ -τῠπος, ον, *shaped alike*, Nonn.*D.*1.448. II. *executed in duplicate*, ὁμολογία *PLond.*1.113 i 65 (vi A.D.), cf. *PMasp.*32.79 (vi A.D.); misspelt σοιτυπος *POxy.*2134.29 (ii A.D.): Subst., ἰσότυπον, τό, *copy, counterpart* of a legal instrument, Just.*Nov.*7.12 *Ep.* -τύραννος [ῠ], ον, *despotic, absolute*, ἀρχή Arist.*Pol.*1270ᵇ14, D.H.5.70.

⊕ **ἰσ-ουράνιος** [ᾰ], α, ον, *high as heaven*, δόξα *Arch.Pap.*1.220 (Ptol.). -ουργός, όν, (ἔργον) *doing like things*, Phot.

**ἰσο-ϋψής**, ές, *of equal height*, Euc.11.34, al.; τείχει, νεῴ, Plb.8.4.4, Str.17.1.28:—also -ϋψος, ον, Gal.18(1).757. -φᾰνής, ές, *appearing like*, Nonn.*D.*9.233.

**ἰσοφᾰρίζω** [ῑ], = ἀντιφερίζω, *match oneself with, vie with*, οὐδέ τίς οἱ δύναται μένος ἰσοφαρίζειν Il.6.101; ἔργα δ' Ἀθηναίῃ . . ἰσοφαρίζοι 9.390; μνήμην οὔτινά φημι Σιμωνίδῃ -φαρίζειν Simon.146, cf. Theoc.7.30: generally, *to be equal to*, τινι Il.21.194, Hes.*Op.*490. II. trans., *make equal*, Nic.*Th.*572.

**ἰσό-φθογγος**, ον, *sounding equally*, Nonn.*D.*6.202. -φονος, ον, gloss on ἀντίφονος, Sch.A.*Th.*895. -φορία, ἡ, *equal* or *regular movement*, ὀρχηστοῦ Poll.4.97. ⊕ -φόριος, ον, dub. sens. in *POxy.*1684.4 (iv A.D.). -φόρος, ον, *bearing* or *drawing equal weights, equal in strength*, βόες . . ἥλικες, ἰσοφόροι Od.18.373; τὰ σκέλη τοῖς ὤμοις -φορα ἔχειν X.*Smp.*2.20. II. proparox., *moving regularly*, Poll.4.97.

**ἰσοφρυς**, ὁ, name of a *plant*, Herm.Trism. in *Rev.Phil.*32.252.

**ἰσό-φρων**, ονος, ὁ, ἡ, *fair-minded*, εὐθυντήρ *IG*9(1).877 (Corc., i B.C.). -φυής, ές, *of equal growth*, i.e. *symmetrical*, coined as etym. of ὀσφύς, Arist.*HA*493ᵃ23. 2. *like in character*, Thphr.*HP*3.7.4. -φυτον, τό, name of an *eyesalve*, Aët.7.112 (109 Lat. vers.). -χειλής, ές, *level with the brim*, κριθαὶ ἰσοχειλεῖς grains of malt *floating level with the brims* of the vessels, i.e. on the surface of the liquor, X.*An.*4.5.26; ζωρὸν κεράσας ἰσοχειλέα *AP*6.105 (Apollonid.); ἰ. τὴν κάτω σιαγόνα ποιήσας [ὁ βάτραχος] *level with the surface of the water*, Arist.*HA*536ᵃ16: c. dat., Εὐφράτης ἰ. τῇ γῇ Arr.*An.*7.7.5; *equally full*, Max.Tyr.31.2. -χειλος, ον, = foreg., τῇ γῇ *Gp.*2.19.4, cf. 13.15.8. -χειρ, χειρος, ὁ, ἡ, *ambidextrous*, Philostr.*Gym.*41. -χνοος, ον, *equally woolly with*, τινι *AP*6.252 (Antiphil.). -χοιρον, Achaean for βούθουτον (i.e. βούθυτον), Hsch. s.h.v. -χοος, ον, *of the same number of* χόες, ὄξος ἰ. ὕδατι Hp.*Morb.*2.26. -χορδος, ον, *with like strings*, Hsch. s.v. ἀντίχορδα.

**ἰσοχρον-έω**, *to be as old as*, τινι Luc.*Syr.D.*3; *to have the same period* of maturity, τὸ μὴ -χρονεῖν τὰ σπέρματα καθάπερ καὶ τὰ ζῷα Thphr.*CP*4.11.9. II. Gramm., *have the same number of time-units*, of syllables, A.D.*Synt.*257.16; of feet, -χρονοῦντες πόδες Aristid.Quint.1.23. ⊕ -ιος, ον, = sq., Thphr.*CP*4.11.2, Euc.*Phaen.*p.4 M., al., Hero *Dioptr.*38; στροφή Cleom.2.4; διαστήματα Ptol.*Tetr.*36: c. dat., τὸ -χρόνιον εἶναι τὸ παρὰ φύσιν τῷ κατὰ φύσιν Simp.*in Cael.*430.6. Adv. -ίως Ptol.*Alm.*13.2, Heph.Astr.1.10; τῷ ἡλίῳ Theo Sm.p.171 H. -ος, ον, *equal in period of revolution*, οἱ ἀπλανεῖς ἀστέρες ἰσόχρονοί εἰσιν ἀλλήλων Eudox.*Ars* 16.15; *equal in period* of maturity, cj. in Thphr.*CP*1.18.3 (περισσόχρονος codd., παρισό- Schneid., alternatively). 2. *contemporary*, *Gloss.*; τινος *Vit.Theoc.* 3. *even, regular*, σφυγμός Gal.8.830. 4. Adv. -νως Eudox.*Ars* 5.8, Gem.6.27, S.E.*M.*5.83, Ruf.*Syn.Puls.*3. II. Gramm., *consisting of the same number of time-units*, A.D.*Synt.*272.23, Hermog.*Id.*1.12, Aristid.Quint.1.23.

**ἰσό-χροος**, ον, *of uniform colour*, Dsc.2.146. -χρῡσος, ον, *like gold, worth its weight in gold*, Archipp.49, Archestr.*Fr.*15.3. II. ἰσόχρυσον, τό, name of an *eyesalve*, *CIL*13.10021.85, Gal.12.785. -ψηφία, ἡ, *equality of votes*, D.H.7.64. II. *equal right to vote*, Plu.*CG*9. -ψηφιστής, οῦ, ὁ, *valuer*, cj. for -ψίστης in *Gloss.* -ψηφος, ον, *with* or *by an equal number of votes*, ἦν ἰ. κριθῇ A.*Eu.*741; ἰ. δίκη ib.795. II. *having an equal vote with* others, ξύμμαχοι Th.1.141, cf. 3.11; of a commander, ib.79; ποιεῖν [δύναμιν] ἰσόψηφόν τινι Pl.*Lg.*692a; of communities, *possessing an equal franchise*, ἐλευθερώσας τήνδ' ἰ. πόλιν E.*Supp.*353. 2. *voting alike*, D.H.4.20. III. *equal in numerical value*, of words *in which the values of letters added together make up the same sum*, "Δαμαγόραν" καὶ "λοιμὸν" ἰσόψηφόν τις ἀκούσας (both words make up 270), *AP*11.334; ἰσόψηφος δυσὶ τούτοις "Γαΐος" ὡς "ἅγιος", ὡς "ἀγαθὸς" προλέγω *IGRom.*4.743 (Eumenia), cf. Gell.14.6.4, Artem.3.34, 4.24; for examples cf. the epigrams of Leonidas, *AP*6.321 sqq. 2. ἰ. ἑστία, name of a plaster, containing a number of drachms *equal to the numerical value* of its name, Nech.ap.Aët.15.13. -ψιστος and -ψίστης, = *aestimator*, *Gloss.* (dub.). ⊕ -ψῡχος, ον, *of equal spirit*, κράτος ἰ. A.*Ag.*1470 (lyr.). Adv. -χως, μάχεσθαι Eust.831.52. 2. *of like soul* or *mind*, *Ep.Phil.*2.20.

**ἰσόω** [ῑ, exc. in Od. l. c.], *make equal*, τινί τι S.*El.*686, Ar.*V.*565 (dub. l.), Hp.*Morb.*4.39:—Med., ὄνυχας χεῖράς τε ἰσώσαντο *they made their* nails and hands *alike*, i.e. used them in like manner, Hes.*Sc.*263:—Pass. (with aor. 1 Med.), *to be made like* or *equal to*, τοῖσίν κεν ἐν ἄλγεσιν ἰσωσαίμην Od.7.212; θεοῖσι μέν νυν οὐκ ἰσούμενόν σ' . . κρίνοντες S.*OT*31, cf. 581, Hp.l.c.: abs., ἰσούμενος, opp. κρείττων, Pl.*Phdr.*239a; *to be made level*, of a bank, *POxy.*1674.7 (iii A.D.).

**Ἱσπᾱνία**, ἡ, *Spain*, *Mon.Anc.Gr.*16.1, Str.3.4.19, Agathem.7; ἀπὸ τῆς Ἰβηρίας ἢ Ἱσπανίας ἢ ὅπως ἄν τις ὀνομάζειν ἐθέλῃ Gal.12.388; τὴν Ἰβηρίαν τε καὶ **Σπανίαν** (v.l. Ἱσπανίαν) ὀνομαζομένην Id.6.613, cf. 12.428, D.S.5.37.

⊕ **Ἱσπᾱνός**, ή, όν, *Spanish*, μάχαιραι Ph.*Bel.*71.14, etc.: **Ἱσπανόν**, τό, a kind of oil, in form **Σπᾶνον** or **Σπανόν**, Gal.10.551, 790, 822, 12.513, *POxy.*2052 (vi A.D.), *Gp.*9.26; ἡ Σπάνη [λιθάργυρος] Dsc.5.87.

**ἴσσα**, exclam. of malicious triumph over another's distress, Pl.Com.66, Men.36; ἰσσᾷ Herod.3.94. (Onomatop.; cf. σίττα.)

**ἴσσασθαι**· κληροῦσθαι, Λέσβιοι, Hsch.

**ἰσσέλα, ἰτθέλα**, v. ἰξαλῆ.

**ἰσσόθεος**, v. ἰσόθεος fin.

**ἴσσυπος**, = ὕσσωπος, *PGoodsp.Cair.*30.42 (ii A.D.).

**ἱστάνω**, later collat. form of ἵστημι, first in inf. **ἱστάνειν**, (ἀνθ-) *PPetr.*2 p.120 (iii B.C.), (καθ-) *Michel*1006.22 (Teos, ii B.C.), (συν-) Plb.3.108.4, (ἀποκαθ-) Ascl.*Tact.*10.9, cf. Dsc.4.43, etc.; cf. ἱστάναι Ἀττικοί, ἱστάνειν Ἕλληνες Moer.200; part. (ἐφ)ιστάνοντες Plb.11.2.5; τὸ ἱστάνον Simp.*in Ph.*1257.34: ind. ἱστάνει Philistio ap.Ath.3.115e, ἱστάνομεν *Ep.Rom.*3.31, (παρ)ιστάνουσι Phld.*Rh.*1.266 S., etc.: impf. (συν)ἵστανον Plb.4.5.6, (δι-) App.*Hisp.*36, etc.:—**Pass.**, ἱστανόμενος *IG*2².1343.26 (i B.C.):—introduced by the copyists into Lys.25.3, Is.2.29, etc.

**ἱστάριον**, τό, Dim. of ἱστός, Men.142, *PLond.*5.1728.13 (vi A.D.), Choerob. in *Theod.*1.332.

**ἱστάρχης**, ου, ὁ, = ἱστωνάρχης, *Ostr.*1155.

**ἱστάω**, collat. form of ἵστημι, 3 sg. pres. ἱστᾷ Hdt.2.143, 4.103: impf. ἵστα Id.2.106 (v.l. ἵστη): freq. in later Gr., (καθ-) *UPZ*18.11 (ii B.C.), Aristeas 228, (συν-) Str.9.5.16, cf. Dsc.1.129 (v.l. in 4.43), Aesop.340, Them.*Or.*23.292c, etc.

**ἰστεῖον**, τό, = ἰστεών, *PCair.Zen.*176.323 (iii B.C.): gen. pl. written ἱστέων *BGU*1359, al., *PTeb.ined.*703.90.

**ἰστέον**, (*εἴδω, οἶδα) *one must see*, ἰστέον δή Pl.*Tht.*202e; *l.* ἤδη τί ἐστι τὸ πρᾶγμα Id.*Smp.*217c. II. *one must know*, Gal.5.480, Sch. Nic.*Th.*11.

**ἱστεών**, ῶνος, ὁ, *weaving-shed*, Men.*Sam.*19: censured by Phryn. 144.

***ἵστημι** (cf. ἱστάω, ἱστάνω), I. causal, *make to stand*, imper. ἵστη Il.21.313, E.*Supp.*1230, καθ-ίστα Il.9.202: impf. ἵστην, Ep. ἵστασκε Od.19.574; 3 pl. ἵσταν B.10.112: fut. στήσω, Dor. στᾱσῶ Theoc.5.54: aor. 1 ἔστησα, Ep. 3 pl. ἔστᾰσαν for ἔστησαν dub. in Od.18.307, 3.182, 8.435, al. (v. ἔστᾰσαν): hence, in late Poets, ἔστᾰσας, ἔστᾰσε, *AP*9.714, 708 (Phil.): aor. 1 Med. ἐστησάμην (never intr.), v. infr. A. III. 2, 3: pf. ἕστᾰκα Cerc.3, (καθ-) Hyp.*Eux.*28, *UPZ* 112.5 (ii B.C.), (περι-) Pl.*Ax.*370d, (ἀφ-) Lxx *Je.*16.5, (παρ-) Phld.*Rh.* 1.9 S., al., (συν-) S.E.*M.*7.109; also ἕστηκα (v. infr.) in trans. sense, (δι-) Arist.*Vent.*973ᵃ18, (ἀφ-) v.l. in Lxx l.c.; ἑστακεῖα trans. in *Test. Epict.*1.25. II. intr., *stand*, 1. Act., aor. 2 ἔστην, Ep. στάσκον Il.3.217; 3 pl. ἔστησαν, more freq. in Hom. ἔσταν, στάν [ᾰ]; imper. στῆθι, Dor. στᾶθι Sapph.29, Theoc. 23.38; subj. στῶ, Ep. 2 and 3 sg. στήῃς, στήῃ (for στῇς, στῇ), Il.17.30, 5.598; 1 pl. στέωμεν (as disyll.) 22.231, στείομεν 15.297; opt. σταίεν, Ep. 3 pl. σταίησαν 17.733; inf. στῆναι, Ep. στήμεναι 17.167, Od.5.414, Dor. στᾶμεν Pi.*P.*4.2; part. στάς: pf. ἕστηκα: plpf. ἑστήκειν, sts. with strengthd. augm. εἱστήκειν, as E.*HF*925, Ar.*Av.*513, Th.1.89, etc.; Ion. 3 sg. ἑστήκεε Hdt. 7.152:—from Hom. downwds. the shorter dual and pl. forms of the pf. are preferred, ἕστᾰτον, ἕστᾰμεν, ἕστᾰτε, ἑστᾶσι (*IG*12(8).356 (Thasos, vi B.C.), etc.), in Hdt. ἑστέᾱσι; imper. ἕστᾰθι Aristomen. 5; subj. ἑστῶ; opt. ἑσταίην; inf. ἑστάναι, Ep. ἑστάμεν, ἑστάμεναι (ἑστηκέναι only late, as Ael.*VH*3.18); part. ἑστώς (ἑστηκώς rare in early Gr., Hdt.2.126, Pl.*Men.*93d, *Lg.*802c, Arist. (infr. B. II. 2), Alex.126.16, εἱστηκότα *IG*1².374.179), fem. ἑστῶσα (not ἑστυῖα; but συνεστηκυιῶν prob. in Hp.*Aër.*10), neut. ἑστός Pl.*Ti.*40b, *Tht.* 183e, *SIG*1234 (Lycia), etc., (καθ-) *POxy.*68.32 (ii A.D.), (ἐν-) *PRyl.* 98(a).10 (ii A.D.), (παρ-) Ar.*Eq.*564 (-ώς freq. v.l. as in Pl. and Ar. ll.cc., preferred by Choerob. *in Theod.*2.313); gen. ἑστῶτος; Ion. ἑστεῶς, ἑστεός, ῶτος; Ep. ἑστηῶς Hes.*Th.*747; dat. pl. ἑστηῶσι cj. in Antim.16.5, cf. Call.*Dian.*134; Hom. does not use the nom., but has gen. ἑστᾰότος, acc. ἑστᾰότα, nom. pl. ἑστᾰότες, as if from ἑσταώς: so also plpf. ἑστάτην, ἕστᾰμεν, ἕστᾰτε, ἕστᾰσαν: late pres. ἑστήκω, formed from pf., Posidipp.ap.Ath.10.412e: hence, fut. ἑστήξω Hom. *Epigr.*15.14, X.*Cyr.*6.2.17, Hegesipp.1.25, ἑστήξομαι X.*Cyn.*10.9 codd. 2. Pass., ἵσταμαι: imper. ἵστασο Hes.*Sc.*449, ἵστω S.*Ph.* 893, Ar.*Ec.*737: impf. ἱστάμην: fut. στᾰθήσομαι And.3.34, Aeschin. 3.103: more freq. στήσομαι Il.20.90, etc.: aor. ἐστάθην Od.17.463, etc.; rarely ἔστην, Dor. 3 sg. ἔσστα *SIG*56.43 (Argos, v B.C.): pf. ἕσταμαι (δι-) v.l. in Pl.*Ti.*81d, κατεστέαται v.l. in Hdt.1.196. (From I.-E. *sthā-*, cf. Skt. *sthā-* (aor. *á-sthā-t*), Lat. *stare*, etc.; Gr. redupl. pres. and pf. fr. *si-sthā-*, *se-sthā-*.)

A. Causal, *make to stand, set up*, πελέκεας ἑξείης Od.19.574; ἔγχος μέν ῥ' ἔστησε φέρων πρὸς κίονα *he set* it against the pillar, 1.127, cf. Il. 15.126; *l.* ἱστόν *set up* the loom, or *raise* the mast (v. ἱστός I and II); κρητῆρας στήσασθαι *to have* bowls *set up*, Od.2.431; θεοῖς.. κρητῆρα στήσασθαι in honour of the gods, Il.6.528; στῆσαί τινα ὀρθόν, στ. ὀρθὰν καρδίαν, Pi.*P.*3.53, 96; ὀρθῷ στ. ἐπὶ σφυρῷ Id.*I.*7(6).13; ἐς ὀρθὸν *l.* τινά E.*Supp.*1230; ὁ Ξανθίας τὸν φαλλὸν ὀρθὸν στησάτω Ar.*Ach.*243; ὀρθὸν οὖς ἵστησιν S.*El.*27; στῆσαι λόγχας, for battle, Id.*Ant.*145 (lyr.); esp. *raise* buildings, statues, trophies, etc., *l.* ἀνδριάντα Hdt.2.110; τροπαῖα S.*Tr.*1102; τροπαῖον *l.* τῶν πολεμίων Isoc.4.150, cf. *IG*2².1457.26; τροπαῖον στησάμενοι X.*HG*2.4.7; τροπαῖον ἂν στήσαιτο τῶν ταύτης τρόπων Ar.*Pl.*453; τὰ μακρὰ στῆσαι τείχη Th.1.69; *l.* τινὰ χαλκοῦν *set* him *up* in brass, *raise* a brazen statue to him, D.13.21, 19.261 (so in pf., *stand*, οὗτος ἕστηκε λίθινος Hdt.2.141:—Pass., σφυρήλατος ἐν Ὀλυμπίᾳ σταθητι Pl.*Phdr.*236b; σταθῆναι χαλκοῦς Arist.*Rh.*1410ᵃ33). II. *set, place*, of things or persons, τρίποδ' ἔστασαν ἐν πυρί Od.8.435, etc.; ὥς σ' ἄγχι γῆς στήσωσι Καδμείας S.*OC*399, etc.; *fix*, τοὺς ὀφθαλμοὺς εἰς τὴν γῆν Philostr.*VA*1.10; esp. *set* men *in order* or *array*, πεζοὺς δ' ἐξόπιθε στῆσεν Il.4.298, cf. 2.525, etc.; στῆσαί τινας τελευταίους X. *Cyr.*6.3.25, etc. III. *bring to a standstill, stay, check*, λαὸν δὲ στῆσον Il.6.433; νέας, ἵππους, ἡμιόνους στῆσαι, Od.3.182, Il.5.755, 24. 350; μύλην στῆσαι *to stop* the mill, Od.20.111; στῆσεν ἄρ' (sc. ἡμιόνους) 7.4; στῆσε δ' ἐν Ἀυλισῷ (sc. νῆα) 19.188; βᾶριν Iamb.*Myst.*6. 5; στῆσαι τὴν φάλαγγα *halt* it, X.*Cyr.*7.1.5; ἵστησι ῥοῦν Pl.*Cra.*437b, etc.; *l.* τὴν ψυχὴν ἐπὶ τοῖς πράγμασιν ib.437a; στ. τὰ ὄμματα *fix* them, of a dying man, Id.*Phd.*118; στ. τὸ πρόσωπον *compose* the countenance, X.*Cyr.*1.3.9; στήσαντες ἐπὶ τούτων τὴν διήγησιν Plb. 3.2.6: esp. in Medic., *l.* κοιλίαν Dsc.1.20; τὰς κοιλίας Philotim.ap. Orib.4.10.1; αἱμορραγίας Dsc.1.129: abs., Arist.*HA*605ᵃ29:—Med., ἱστάμενος τῷ νοσήματι Hp.*Ep.*19 (*Hermes* 53.65). 2. *set on foot, stir up*, κονίης.. ἱστᾶσιν ὁμίχλην Il.13.336; ἵστη δὲ μέγα κῦμα 21. 313; νεφέλην ἔστησε Κρονίων Od.12.405, cf. Il.5.523; of battle, etc., φυλόπιδα στήσειν *stir up* strife, Od.11.314; ἔριν στήσαντες 16.292 (so intr. φύλοπις ἕστηκε the fray *is on foot*, Il.18.172):—also in Med., στησάμενοι δ' ἐμάχοντο ib.533, Od.9.54; πολέμους ἵστασθαι Hdt.7. 9.β', 175, 236; so ἱστάναι βοήν A.*Ch.*885; κραυγὴν E.*Or.*1529 (Pass., θόρυβος ἵσταται βοῆς *arises*, S.*Ph.*1263); also of passions and states of mind, μῆνιν, ἐλπίδα στῆσαι, Id.*OT*699, E.*IA*788 (lyr.). 3. *set up, appoint*, τινὰ βασιλέα Hdt.1.97; τύραννον S.*OT*940, cf. *OC*1041, *Ant.*666:—Med., ἐστάσαντο τύραννον Alc.37A; φύλακας στησόμεθα Pl.*R.*484d:—Pass., ὁ ὑπὸ Δαρείου σταθεὶς ὕπαρχος Hdt.7.105, cf. *IG* 9(1).32.23 (Stiris, ii B.C.). 4. *establish, institute*, χορούς, παννυχίδα, Hdt.3.48, 4.76 (so στήσασθαι ἤθεά τε καὶ νόμους Id.2.35; ἀγῶνα *h.Ap.*150); στῆσαι χορόν, Ὀλυμπιάδα, ἑορτάν, Pi.*P.*9.114, *O.*2.3, 10(11).58; κτερίσματα S.*El.*433; χορούς B.10.112, D.21.51; οὐχ ὑγιῶς ἱστάμενος λόγον *setting up* a bad argument, Anon.Lond.26. 34:—Pass., ἀγορὴ ἵσταταί τινι Hdt.6.58. 5. = Lat. *statuere, determine*, γνῶναι καὶ στῆσαι D.H.8.68; διαγεινώσκειν καὶ ἱστάναι *Not. Arch.*4.21 (Aug.):—Pass., τὰ ὑπό τινος σταθέντα *OGI*665.27 (Egypt, i A.D.); τὰ ἑσταμένα Wilcken *Chr.*167.27 (ii B.C.). 6. *fix by agreement*, ὁ σταθεὶς τόκος *PGrenf.*1.31.1 (i B.C.), cf. *PFlor.*14.11 (iv A.D.); τὸ ἑσταμένον ἐνοίκιον *BGU*253.15 (iii A.D.). 7. *bring about, cause*, ἀμπνοάν Pi.*P.*4.199; στῆσαι δύσκηλον χθόνα *make* its case desperate, A.*Eu.*825. IV. *place in the balance, weigh*, Il.19.247, 22.350, 24.232, Ar.*V.*40; [ἐκπώματα] Thphr.*Char.*18.7; ἀριθμοῦντες καὶ μετροῦντες καὶ ἱστάντες X.*Cyr.*8.2.21, etc.; ἱστάναι τι πρὸς ἀργύριον *weigh* a thing against silver, Hdt.2.65; ἀγαθὸς ἱστάναι good *at weighing*, Pl.*Prt.*356b; τὸ ἐγγὺς καὶ τὸ πόρρω στήσας ἐν τῷ ζυγῷ ibid., cf. Lys.10.18; ἐπὶ τὸ ἱστάναι ἐλθεῖν have recourse to *the scales*, Pl.*Euthphr.*7c:—Pass., ἵστασθαι ἐπὶ ζυγοῦ Arr.*Epict.*1. 29.15; σταθεὶς *weighed*, *IG*11(2).161*B*113 (Delos, iii B.C.). 2. *weigh out, pay*, Lxx 3*Ki.*21.39, cf. *Za.*11.12, *Ev.Matt.*26.15.

B. Pass. and intr. tenses of Act., *to be set* or *placed, stand*, Hom. etc., ἀγχοῦ, ἄσσον, Il.2.172, 23.97; ἄντα τινός 17.30; ἐς μέσσον Od.17. 447; σταθεὶς ἐς μέσον Hdt.3.130; ἀντίοι ἔσταν, ἐναντίοι ἔστησαν, Il.1. 535, Od.10.391: prov. of critical circumstances, ἐπὶ ξυροῦ ἵσταται ἀκμῆς Il.10.173: freq. merely a stronger form of εἶναι, *to be* in a certain place or state, ἀργύρεοι σταθμοὶ ἐν χαλκέῳ ἔστασαν οὐδῷ Od.7. 89, etc.; ἑστάτω for ἔστω, S.*Aj.*1084; τὰ νῦν ἑστῶτα, = τὰ νῦν, Id. *Tr.*1271 (anap.); ἐμοὶ δ' ἄχος ἕστᾰκεν Id.*Aj.*200 (lyr.): with Adv., ξυμφορᾶς ἵν' ἕσταμεν, ἵν' ἕστ. χρείας, in what case or need *we are*, Id. *Tr.*1145, *OT*1442; ποῦ τύχης ἕστηκεν; Id.*Aj.*102; later also ἀδίκως, ὀρθῶς, εὐλαβῶς ἵστασθαι, *behave* wrongly, etc., Plb.18.3.2, 33.6.3, 18.33. 4. 2. *take up an* intellectual *attitude*, ὡς ἵστασθαι δεῖ περὶ χρημάτων κτήσεως Phld.*Oec.*p.38 J.; οὐκ ὀρθῶς *l.* Id.*Rh.*1.53 S. 3. in pregnant sense, στῆναι ἐς.. Hdt.9.21; στ. ἐς δίκην E.*IT*962; στ. παρά τινα Il.24. 169 (but οἱ μὴ στάντες παρὰ τὰ δεινά those who did not *face* the danger, D.H.9.28): c. acc. loci, τί τοῦτ' αἰθερίαν ἕστηκε πέτραν; E.*Supp.*987 (lyr.); στῆτε τόνδε τρίβον Id.*Or.*1251: c. acc. cogn., ποίαν μ' ἀνάστασιν δοκεῖς.. στῆναι; S.*Ph.*277. II. *stand still, halt*, ἀλλ' ἄγε δὴ στέωμεν Il.11.348, cf. Od.6.211, 10.97; opp. φεύγω, 6.199, etc.; *stand idle*, Il.4.243, al.; ἑστάναι *to be stationary*, opp. κινεῖσθαι, Pl.*R.*436c, etc.; κατὰ χώρην ἑστάναι Hdt.4.97; οὐ μὴν ἐνταῦθ' ἕστηκε τὸ πρᾶγμα *does* not *rest* here, D.21.102, cf. 10.36; ἐὰν ἡ κοιλία στῇ if the bowels *are constipated*, Arist.*HA*588ᵃ8: c. part., οὐ στήσεται ἀδικῶν D.10.10; *come to a stop, rest satisfied*, ἄν τις ὀρθῶς ἐπιβάλῃ, ἔπειτα σταθῇ Epicur. *Fr.*423; οὐχ ἱστάμενοι Plot.3.1.2: impers., ἵσταται *there is a stop, one comes to a stop*, Arist.*APr.*43ᵃ37, al.; οὐκ ἔστη ἐνταῦθα κακοῖς γενομένοις ἀποθανεῖν Plot.3.2.8; also ἵστασθαι μέχρι τοῦ γένους Them.*in APo.* 55.8, al. 2. metaph., *stand firm*, X.*HG*5.2.23; τῇ διανοίᾳ Plb.21. 11.3; of arguments or propositions, *hold good*, Phld.*Rh.*1.83, 2.192 S.: part., ἑστηκὼς *fixed, stable*, Arist.*GA*776ᵃ35, *EN*1104ᵃ4, *Metaph.* 1047ᵃ15; δεῖ τὸ κρίμα ἑστηκὸς καὶ κύριον εἶναι *SIG*826 ii 29 (Delph., ii B.C.); λογισμὸς ἑστὼς καὶ νουνεχής Plb.3.105.9; τέχναι οὐκ ἔχουσαι τὸ ἑστηκός, ἀλλὰ τὸ στοχαστικόν Phld.*Rh.*1.71 S. (so Adv. ἑστηκότως, opp. στοχαστικῶς, ib.70 S.), cf. Iamb.*Protr.*21.κ'; χρεία ἑστηκυῖα καὶ τεταγμένη Plb.6.25.10; ἑστηκότα θεωρήματα, ἑστηκότες σκοποί, Phld.*Rh.*1.2 S., *Po.*5.22; of age, ἑστηκυῖα ἡλικία Pl.*Lg.*802c; τιμαὶ ἑστηκυῖαι *fixed* prices, *PTeb.ined.*703.177. III. *to be set up* or *upright, stand up, rise up*, κρημνοὶ ἔστασαν Il.12.55; ὀρθαὶ τρίχες ἔσταν 24.359, cf. A.*Th.*564 (lyr.), Pl.*Ion* 535c, etc.; κονίη ἵστατο Il.2.151; ἵστατο Il.21.240; of a horse, ἵστασθαι ὀρθὸς *to rear*, Hdt.5.111; ἵστασθαι βάθρων *from* the steps, S.*OT*143. 2. *to be set up, erected*, or *built*, στήλη, ἥ τ' ἐπὶ τύμβῳ ἑστήκῃ Il.17.435; ἔστακε τροπαῖον A. *Th.*954 (lyr.); μνημεῖον Ar.*Eq.*268, etc.; v. supr. A. II. 3. generally, *arise, begin*, ἵστατο νεῖκος Il.13.333; cf. A. III. 2. 4. in marking Time, ἔαρος νέον ἱσταμένοιο when spring is not long *begun*, Od.19.519; ἕβδομος ἑστήκει μείς the seventh month *was begun*, Il. 19.117; τοῦ μὲν φθίνοντος μηνός, τοῦ δ' ἱσταμένοιο as one month ends and the next *begins*, Od.14.162, cf. Hes.*Op.*780; later μὴν ἱστάμενος, μεσῶν, φθίνων, first in Hdt.6.57, 106, cf. And.1.121, Aeschin.3.67; σχεδὸν ἤδη μεσημβρία ἵσταται Pl.*Phdr.*242a. 5. *to be appointed*, στῆναι ἐς ἀρχήν Hdt.3.80; v. supr. A. III. 3.

**ἱστία, ἰστία, ἱστίη, Ἱστίη, Ἱστιαία**, v. ἑστία. ***Ἱστιαϊκός**, ή, όν, *Histiaean*, of currency, *BCH*2.579, 6.51, 35.260 (Delos). **ἱστίασις**, εως, ἡ, = ἑστίασις, *POxy.*471.53 (ii A.D.). **ἱστιατορία**, ἡ, = ἑστ., *feast*, *PTeb.*584 (ii A.D.). **ἱστιάτωρ**, v. ἑστιάτωρ. **ἱστιητόριον**, and **-ατόριον**, v. ἑστιατόριον.

**ἱστιο-δρομέω**, *run under full sail*, Hp.*Ep.*17, Plb.1.60.9, D.S.3. 28. **-κωπος** (sc. ναῦς), ἡ, *with oars and sails*, a type of boat, Gell. 10.25.5.

**ἱστίον**, τό (Dim. of ἱστός in form only), *web, cloth, sheet*: hence in pl., *hangings*, Lxx *Ex.*27.9, 15; as a measure, *piece*, *PRyl.*70.25 (ii B.C.); but, II. from Hom. downwds., *sail*, mostly in pl. ἱστία, ἕλκον δ' ἱστία λευκὰ.. βοεῦσιν they hauled *them* up with ox-hide ropes, Od.2.426; τέταθ' ἱστία *the sails* were spread, 11.11, cf. Pi. *N.*5.51; ἱστία στέλλεσθαι, μηρύεσθαι, καθελεῖν, to lower or furl *sail* (v. sub vocc.): λύειν Od.15.496; ἱστίοισι χρᾶσθαι Hdt.4.110; ἄκροισι χρώμενος τοῖς ἱστίοις Ar.*Ra.*1000: prov., πλήρεσιν *l.* under full *sail*,

with all one's might, Philostr.*VS*1.25.5, cf. Suid.: rarely in sg., ἐν δ' ἄνεμος πρῆσεν μέσον ἱστίον Il.1.481; ἐξίει ἱ. ἀνεμόεν Pi.*P.*1.92; ἱστίῳ καταπετάσαι τινά Pl.*Prm.*131b, cf. *PMagd.*11.7 (iii B.C.).

**ἱστιο-πετής**, *velivolus, Gloss.* **-ποιέομαι**, Pass., *to be furnished with sails*, of ships, Str.15.1.15. ❀**-ρράφος** [ᾰ], ὁ, (ῥάπτω) *sail-patcher, CIG*9175, Poll.7.160. **2.** metaph., *tricky, cheating fellow*, Ar.*Th.*935:—also **ἱστιαρράφος**, Gramm. in Reitzenstein *Ind.Lect. Rost.*1892/3 p.4.

❀**ἱστο-βοεύς**, έως, Ion. ῆος, ὁ, *plough-tree* or *pole*, Hes.*Op.*435, cf. A.R.3.1318: prov., ἱστοβοῆι γέροντι νέην ποτίβαλλε κορώνην put a new tip on the old *plough*, of an old man marrying a young wife, Orac.ap.Paus.9.37.4.—Acc. ἱστοβόην, prob. f.l. for ἱστοβοῆ, *AP*6.104 (Phil.). **-δόκη**, ἡ, *mast-holder*, a piece of wood standing up from the stern, on which the mast rested when let down, Il.1.434; glossed by **-θήκη**, Sch.D ad loc., *EM*478.30. **-κεραία**, ἡ, *sail-yard*, Orph.*A.*696, Artem.1.35. **-πέδη**, Dor. **-πέδα**, ἡ, *a piece of wood* set in the keel *to which the mast was bound*, or, *a hole* in the keel *for stepping the mast*, Od.12.51,162, Alc.18.6. **-ποδες**, οἱ, = κελέοντες, *the long beams of the loom*, between which the web was stretched, *AP*7.424 (Antip. Sid.): sg., Eub.145, *POxy.*264.5 (i A.D.). **-ποιία**, ἡ, *loom-making*, Sch.Nic.*Th.*11. ❀**-πόνος**, ον, *working at the loom, AP*6.48, Man.4.423; Παλλάς *AP*6.247 (Phil.); κερκίδες ib.9.778 (Id.); v.l. for ἱστότονος, Ar.*Ra.*1315.

**ἱστορ-έω**, (ἵστωρ) *inquire into* or *about* a thing, τι Hdt.2.113, A.*Pr.*632, etc.; περί τινος Plb.3.48.12; also, *inquire about* a person, τινα S.*OT*1150, 1156; ὅδ' εἰμ' Ὀρέστης.. ὃν ἱστορεῖς E.*Or.*380, cf. *Tr.*261: folld. by relat. clause, Αἴγισθον ἔνθ' ᾤκηκεν ἱστορῶ S.*El.*1101. **2.** *examine, observe*, χώραν, πόλιν, Plu.*Thes.*30, *Pomp.*40, cf. J.*AJ*1.11.4; τὴν τοῦ Μέμνονος [σύριγγα] *OGI*694.7; τὴν σύνεσίν τινος Plu.*Cic.*2, etc.; τινὰς ἀπολουμένους Gal.11.109: hence, *to be informed about, know*, κακῶς τὸ μέλλον ἱστορῶν A.*Pers.*454; πατέρα ἱστορεῖς καλῶς Id.*Eu.*455, cf. Hp.*Praec.*12: metaph., εἴ τις ἀκτὶς ἡλίου νιν ἱστορεῖ βλέποντα *has news of* him, A.*Ag.*676: folld. by relat., τὴν πορείαν ἱστορῶν, ὡς δυσδίοδος ὑπάρχει Plb.3.61.3; *read in history*, Id.1.63.7. **2.** c. acc. pers., *inquire of, ask*, ἱστορέων αὐτοὺς ἥντινα δύναμιν ἔχει ὁ Νεῖλος Hdt.2.19, cf. 3.77; *inquire of an oracle*, E.*Ion* 1547; *visit* a person for the purpose of inquiry, Κηφᾶν *Ep.Gal.*1.18:—Pass., *to be questioned*, κληθέντας ἱστορέεσθαι εἰ.. Hdt.1.24; ἱστορούμενος S.*Tr.*415, E.*Hel.*1371. **b.** c. dupl. acc., *inquire of* one *about* a thing, τί μ' ἱστορεῖς τόδε Id.*Ph.*621, cf. Lyc.1. **4.** abs., *inquire*, ἀκοῇ ἱ. Hdt.2.29, etc.; esp. in part., ἱστορέων εὕρισκε Id.1.56, etc.; οὔθ' ὁρῶν οὔθ' ἱστορῶν S.*OT*1484; folld. by a relat. word, ἱστορέον τε ὅτεῳ τρόπῳ περιγένοιτο Hdt.1.122. **II.** *give an account of what one has learnt, record*, τοὺς βίους τῶν χερσαίων Thphr.*HP*4.13.1, cf. Luc.*Hist.Conscr.*7, etc.; ἱστοροῦσί τινες.. *it is stated that*.., Dsc.4.75, etc.:—freq. in Pass., ὁ καρπὸς.. ἐπιληπτικοὺς ἱστορεῖται ὠφελεῖν Id.1.83; περί τινος ἱστορεῖται διότι Phld.*Mus.*p.18 K.; ἱστορεῖται περὶ Γοργοῦς τοιοῦτον Plu.2.227e, cf. Id.*Cic.*1, Ael.*Tact.*34.3, etc.; Ἀπολλόδωρος εἴρηκεν ἀπελθόντας Ὕαντας ἱστορεῖσθαι *are represented* as having gone, Str.10.3.4; τῶν ἱστορουμένων οὐδενὸς ἧττον πολυπράγμων the most industrious person *on record*, Phld.*Mus.*p.108 K. **-ημα**, ατος, τό, *narrative, tale*, φευκτὸν ἱ. *Anacreont.*4.9; μυθικὰ ἱ. D.H.2.61, cf. Plu *Per.*1: pl., μαθήματα καὶ ἱ. Aristid.*Or.*46(3).28. **-ητέον**, *one must relate*, λόγον Plu.2.882b. **-ία**, Ion. **-ίη**, ἡ, *inquiry*, ἱστορίῃσι εἰδέναι τι παρά τινος Hdt.2.118, cf. 119; ἡ περὶ φύσεως ἱ. Pl.*Phd.*96a; αἱ περὶ τῶν ζῴων ἱ. Arist.*Resp.*477$^{a}$7, al.; ἡ ἱ. ἡ περὶ τὰ ζῷα Id.*PA*674$^{b}$16; ἡ ζωικὴ ἱ. ib.668$^{b}$30; περὶ φυτῶν ἱ., title of work by Theophrastus; *systematic* or *scientific observation*, Epicur.*Ep.*1 p.29 U.: abs., of *science* generally, ὄλβιος ὅστις τῆς ἱ. ἔσχε μάθησιν E.*Fr.*910 (anap.); of *geometry*, Pythag.ap.Iamb.*VP*18.89: in empirical medicine, *body of recorded cases*, Gal.1.144; *mythology*, Ἡσίοδον πάσης ἤρανον ἱστορίης Hermesian.7.22. **2.** *knowledge so obtained, information*, Hdt.1 *Praef.*, Hp.*VM*20; ὄψις ἐμὴ καὶ γνώμη καὶ ἱ. Hdt.2.99; πρὸς ἱστορίαν τῶν κοινῶν for *the knowledge of*.., D.18.144; ἡ τῆς ψυχῆς ἱ. Arist.*de An.*402$^{a}$4. **II.** *written account of one's inquiries, narrative, history*, prob. in this sense in Hdt.7.96; αἱ τῶν περὶ τὰς πράξεις γραφόντων ἱ. Arist.*Rh.*1360$^{a}$37, *Po.*1451$^{b}$3, Plb.1.57.5, al.; ἐκ τῶν ἱστοριῶν καὶ ἐκ τῶν ἄλλων μαρτυριῶν *OGI*13.12 (iii B.C.); αἱ Μαιανδρίου ἱ. *Inscr.Prien.*37.105; κοινὴ ἱ. general *history*, D.H.1.2; ἱ. Ἑλληνική, Ῥωμαϊκή, Plu.2.119d; restricted by some to contemporary history, Lat. *rerum cognitio praesentium*, Verr.Flacc.ap.Gell.5.18: generally, *story, account*, Call.*Aet.*3.1.7.

**ἱστοριαγράφος**, v. ἱστοριογράφος.

**ἱστορικός**, ή, όν, *exact, precise, scientific*, μίμησις Pl.*Sph.*267e; τῶν παρὰ τοῖς ἄλλοις εὑρημένων ἱ. *well-informed respecting*.. or *able to recount*.., Arist.*Rh.*1359$^{b}$32; ἀποδείξεις ἱστορικῶν Phld.*D.*1.23. Adv. **-κῶς** *scientifically, accurately*, Arist.*GA*757$^{b}$35; *by personal observation*, καταμαθεῖν τι Gal.14.275. **II.** *belonging to history, historical*, πραγματεῖαι D.H.1.1; τύπος (opp. λογικός) Id.*Dem.*24; ἀναγραφή Id.1.4; γράμματα Plu.*Them.*13: Subst., *historian*, Arist.*Po.*1451$^{b}$1, Aristeas 31, Phld.*Rh.*1.200 S., D.H.4.6, D.S.1.6, etc.; **-ώτατος** βασιλέων Plu.*Sert.*9. Adv. **-κῶς**, ἱ. καὶ διδασκαλικῶς Str.1.1.10; ἱ. καὶ ἐξηγητικῶς, opp. ἀποδεικτικῶς, Phld.*Mus.*p.12 K.; but ἐξηγητικώτερον ἢ **-ώτερον**, of Aristotle's method in *HA*, Antig.*Mir.*60.

**ἱστοριογρᾰφ-έω**, *write history*, D.H.*Th.*42. **-ία**, ἡ, *history-writing*, interpol. in J.*Ap.*1.19. **-ικός**, ή, όν, = ἱστορικός II, Sch.D.T.p.167 H. **-ος**, ὁ, *writer of history, historian, Inscr.Prien.*37.107 (ii B.C.), Plb.2.62.2, Phld.*Rh.*1.359 S., D.S.1.9, Ath.Mech.7.2, etc.: *chronicler*, as distd. from συγγραφεύς (writer of contemporary history), Sch.D.T.p.168 H.; Ἔφορος ὁ ἱ., opp. Ἡρόδοτος ὁ συγγρ., *Placit.*4.1.6:—Dor. **ἱστοριαγράφος**, οἱ ἱ. οἱ συγγεγραφότες τὰς Μαγνήτων πράξεις *SIG*560.13, cf. 702.3 (Delph., ii B.C.), 685.93 (Crete).

**ἱστόρ-ιον**, τό, (ἵστωρ) *fact* or *illustration in proof*, Hp.*Nat.Puer.*31, *Morb.*4.54, *Ep.*19 (*Hermes* 53.66). **-ισμα**, ατος, τό, *clinical history*, Gal.17(1).648 (pl.). **-ιώδης**, ες, *like history*, Tz.*H.*8 No.231 tit.

❀**ἱστός**, ὁ, (ἵστημι) *anything set upright*: **I.** *mast*, ἱστὸν.. στῆσαν ἀείραντες they stepped *the mast*, Od.15.289, cf. Il.23.852, etc.; ἱστοὺς στησάμενοι Od.9.77, cf. Il.1.480; ἱστὸν αἴρεσθαι X.*HG*6.2.29; opp. καθαιρεῖν, κὰδ δ' ἕλον ἱστόν took *it* down, unstepped *it*, Od.15.496; κεραία καὶ ἱ. *IG*2$^{2}$.657.14: generally, *rod, pole*, ἱστὸς χάλκεος Hdt.8.122; *beam, IG*2$^{2}$.1672.306 (pl.). **II.** *beam* of a loom, which stood upright, instead of lying horizontal as in our looms; πόσσω κατέβα τοι ἀφ' ἱστῶ; (sc. τὸ ἐμπερόναμα) Theoc.15.35; later ἱ. ὄρθιος (opp. the horizontal loom), Artem.3.36: generally, *loom*, ἱστόν τ' ἠλακάτην τε Il.6.491, *Schwyzer*180 (Crete), etc.; ἱ. στήσασθαι to set up *the beam* and so begin a web, Hes.*Op.*779; ἱ. ἐποίχεσθαι to traverse *the loom*, because the weaver was obliged to walk to and fro, Il.1.31, Od.5.62. **2.** *warp fixed to the beam*: hence, *the web* itself, ἱστὸν ὕφαινε Il.3.125, etc.; ἠματίη μὲν ὑφαίνεσκεν μέγαν ἱ., νύκτας δ' ἀλλύεσκεν Od.2.104; ἱ. μεταχειρίζεσθαι Pl.*Phd.*84a; ὁ ἐκτετμημένος ἱ. *the web* cut from the loom and finished, opp. ὁ πρὸς ἐκτομήν, Artem. l.c.: *web of a certain size, piece, PHib.*1.67.12 (iii B.C.), etc.; ὀθονίων ἱ. τρισχίλιοι Plb.5.89.2; τρεῖς ἱ. καθελεῖν Str.8.6.20. **3.** ἱ. ἀραχνᾶν spiders' *webs*, B.3.7. **4.** *comb* of bees, Arist.*HA*624$^{a}$5. **III.** *shin-bone, leg*, Opp.*C.*1.408. **IV.** a constellation, Aët.3.164.

**ἱστό-τονος**, ον, *stretched on the loom*, πηνίσματα v.l. in the codd. other than Rav. for ἱστόπονα, Ar.*Ra.*1315; κερκίς E.*Hyps.Fr.*1 ii 10 (lyr.). **-τρῐβής**, v. ἱσοτριβής.

**ἱστουργ-εῖον**, τό, = ἱστών, *Gloss.* **-έω**, *work at the loom*, S.*OC*340, Trypho ap.Ath.14.618d (Epit.), Orph.*Fr.*192. **-ία**, ἡ, *weaving*, Pl.*Smp.*197b, Alciphr.3.41. **-ικός**, ή, όν, *of* or *for weaving*, Poll.7.35, 10.126; ἡ ἱ. (sc. τέχνη), = foreg., Phld.*Mus.*p.24 K. Adv. **-κῶς** Poll.7.35. **-ός**, ὁ or ἡ, *worker at the loom, weaver, PSI*4.371.8 (iii B.C.), J.*BJ*1.24.3.

❀**ἱστοφόρος**, ον, *bearing a mast*, Hsch.

**ἵστραξ**, a kind of *bird*, Hsch. (fort. τέτραξ).

**Ἴστρος**, ὁ, *Ister, Danube*, Hes.*Th.*339, etc.; **Ἴστρος**, ἡ, *Milesian colony at its mouth*, St.Byz.; also called **Ἰστρία**, ἡ, Arr.ap.eund., Ion. **-ίη**, Hdt.2.33:—Adj. ❀**Ἰστριᾱνός**, Ion. **-ηνός**, ή, όν, *of* or *from Istria*, Hdt.4.78, St.Byz., etc.; Ἰστριανὰ πρόσωπα *tattooed* masks, like the faces of Scythian slaves, Ar.*Fr.*88; Ἰστριαναὶ ζειραί *Scythian* tunics, prob. for ἰσπνιᾶται σειραί (glossed ἰστρηνίδες), Theognost.*Can.*14; ἰστριανά, τά, covers for the baskets carried by κανηφόροι, Poll.10.191:—fem. **Ἰστριᾱνίδες**, of these garments and covers, Hsch.; but also Ἰστριανίδων ὕφη S.*Fr.*210.67.

**ἱστρίδες**, αἱ, a kind of *garment* (perh. f.l. for foreg. (or for ϝεστρ-)), Hsch. **ἱστυάζει**· ὀργίζεται, Id.; cf. οἶστρος. **ἱστυλόν**· τὸ στυχηδόν (leg. στοιχηδόν), Id. **ἴστω**, 3 sg. imper. of οἶδα; cf. ἴττω.

❀**ἱστών**, ῶνος, ὁ, = ἱστεών (q.v.), *weaving-shed*, Varro *RR*1.2.21.

**ἱστων-άρχης**, ου, ὁ, *controller of weaving, PGiss.*12, *Ostr.*1154, al. **-αρχία**, ἡ, *his office, PRyl.*98.5 (ii A.D.), *BGU*753 iv 4 (iii A.D.).

❀**ἵστωρ** or **ἴστωρ**, Boeot. ϝίστωρ *Schwyzer*491, etc., ορος, ὁ, ἡ:—*one who knows law and right, judge*, ἐπὶ ἵστορι πεῖραρ ἑλέσθαι Il.18.501; ἵστορα δ' Ἀτρεΐδην Ἀγαμέμνονα θείομεν ἄμφω 23.486; ϝίστορες *witnesses, IG*7.1779 (Thespiae); τῶ τεθμίω ϝίστωρ *Schwyzer*523.64 (Orchom. Boeot.); θεοὺς πάντας ἵστορας ποιεύμενος Hp.*Jusj.*init., cf. Poll.8.106. **II.** Adj. *knowing, learned*, Hes.*Op.*792; ἴ. τινός *knowing* a thing, *skilled in* it, ᾠδῆς *h.Hom.*32.2; ἐγχέων B.8.44; κἀγὼ τοῦδ' ἴ. ὑπερίστωρ S.*El.*850 (lyr), cf. E.*IT*1431, Pl.*Cra.*406b. (From ϝιδ-τωρ, cf. *εἴδω, οἶδα: ἴστωρ acc. to Hdn.Gr.2.108, etc.)

❀**ἰσφαίνειν**· μεριμνᾶν, Hsch.

**ἴσφνιον**, τό, prob. f.l. for ἴσθμιον, *neck of a jar*, E.*Fr.*656: prov., χαλεπὸς βίος ἴσφνι' ἄγοντος, expld. of a potter's life, cod.Par.ap. Nauck l.c., nisi leg. Ἴσθμι' (cf. ἰσθμιάζω).

**ἴσφωρες**· λησταί, κλέπται (Lacon.), Hsch.

❀**ἰσχάδιον** [ᾰ], τό, Dim. of ἰσχάς, Ar.*Pl.*798.

❀**ἰσχᾰδο-κάρῠον** [κᾰ], τό, *mixture of figs and almonds*, Arr.*Epict.*4.7.23: pl., ib.3.9.22, 4.7.22. **-πώλης**, ου, ὁ, *dealer in figs*, Pherecr.4, Nicoph.19:—fem. **-πωλις**, ιδος, Ar.*Lys.*564. **-φάγος** [φᾰ], ον, *eating figs*, Hsch. s.v. κραδοφάγος.

**ἰσχᾰδώνης**, ου, ὁ, *buyer of figs*, Pherecr.4.

**ἴσχαιμος**, ον, (ἴσχω, αἷμα) *staunching blood*, Thphr.*HP*9.13.1, Dsc.4.43; *styptic*, Luc.*Tim.*46, Aret.*CA*2.6 (dat. pl. -αίμασι codd.), *POxy.*1088.19. **2.** ἴσχαιμος, ἡ, *plant used as a styptic, Andropogon ischaemum*, Thphr.*HP*9.15.3, Sch.Il.11.846.

**ἰσχαίνω**, f.l. for ἰσχάνω or ἰσχναίνω (qq.v.).

❀**ἰσχᾰλέος**, α, ον, poet. for ἰσχνός, *dried*, κρομύοιο λοπὸς ἰσχαλέοιο Od.19.233; *thin, paltry*, περόναι Man.6.434:—later **ἰσχνᾰλέος**, Eust.1863.60.

**ἰσχαλεῦσαι**· θηλάσαι, Hsch. (Cf. ἀνίσχαλος.) **ἰσχαλωμέναι**· δεδερματωμέναι, Id. (cf. ἴξαλος).

**ἰσχᾰνάω**, Ep. lengthd. form of ἰσχάνω (cf. sq.): Ion. impf. ἰσχανάασκον Il.15.723:—*hold back, stay*, 5.89; νῦν δ' ἐπεὶ ἰσχανάᾳς (sc. με) Od.15.346:—Pass., *hold back, wait*, νηυσὶν ἔπι.. ἐελμένοι ἰσχανόωντο Il.12.38; σὸν μῦθον ποτιδέγμενοι ἰσχανόωνται Od.7.161, cf. Il.19.234; *to be stayed*, A.R.2.864. **II.** intr., c. gen., *cling to*, and so, *long after, desire eagerly*, μέγα δρόμου ἰσχανόωσαν Il.23.300; ἰσχα-

νόων φιλότητος Od.8.288: c. inf., [μυῖα]..ἰσχανάᾳ δακέειν Il.17.572; ἰσχανόωσιν ἰδεῖν Procl.*h.Ven.*2.6. (ἰχαν– is v.l. in Il.23.300, Od.8.288, and shd. prob. be preferred; cf. ἰχανάω.)

**ἰσχάνω** [ᾰ], Ep. lengthd. form of ἴσχω (v. foreg.), *hold in check, hinder*, δέος ἰσχάνει ἄνδρας Il.14.387; Αἴαντ' ἰσχανέτην ὥς τε πρὼν ἰσχάνει ὕδωρ 17.747; τὸν δ' οὐκ ἴσχανε δεσμά *h.Bacch.*13: c. gen., *keep back from*, κρύος ἀνέρα ἔργων ἰσχάνει Hes.*Op.*495; so in Prose, ὁ ἥλιος..ἰσχάνει [τὸν σῖτον] *checks* its growth, Thphr.*CP*4.13.6 (v.l. ἰσχαίνει, fort. ἰσχναίνει). II. *get, obtain, have*, ἀπεμνημόνευεν ἢ ἀνάλογον τῇ ἀπομνημονεύσει πάθος ἴσχα[νε] *had* an experience.., Epicur.*Nat.*27 G., cf. 51 G.; περὶ..δάκτυλον (δακτύλων codd.) πάθος ἰσχάνουσιν Vett.Val.65.13; μᾶλλον ἐκ τῶν πραγμάτων ἢ ἐκ τῶν λόγων τὰς λαβὰς ἰσχάνουσι Phld.*Herc.*873.6; ἐμέθεν πέρι θυμὸν ἀρείω ἴσχανε A.R.1.902.

**ἰσχάριον**, τό, Dim. of ἰσχίον, *hip*, Hero *Aut.*29.

❀ **ἰσχάς**, άδος, ἡ, (ἰσχνός) *dried fig*, Ar.*Eq.*755, Hermipp.63.16, Alex. 162.15, Arist.*HA*577$^{a}$10, *IG*2$^{2}$.1013.24, *PCair.Zen.*110 (iii B.C.), Theoc.1.147, etc.; ἰσχάδος ἐγκώμιον *POxy.*2084; also, of *over-ripe olives*, Eust.1963.55. 2. *spurge, Euphorbia Apios*, Thphr.*HP*9.9.6, Dsc.4.175, Plin.*HN*26.72. II. (ἴσχω) *that which holds, anchor*, S.*Fr.*761, Luc.*Lex.*15.

**ἴσχαυδαι**· ἰσχ[ν]όφωνοι, Hsch.

**ἰσχέ-γᾱον**, τό, (ἴσχω, γῆ) *retaining wall*, *SIG*241 *A*7, 247 *I*$^{2}$14 (Delph., iv B.C.). **–θῡρον**, τό, perh. *frame of a window*, *IG*11(2). 165.10, al. (Delos, iii B.C.). ❀ **–πλινθα**, τά, *uprights* (perh. *door-jambs*), *SIG*247 *I*$^{2}$15 (Delph., iv B.C.).

**ἰσχερῶ**· ἑξῆς, Hsch. (Cf. σχερός.)

**ἰσχητήριος**, α, ον, (ἴσχω) *astringent*, Hp.*Loc.Hom.*20, cf. Erot.

**ἰσχῐ-ᾰδικός**, ή, όν, (ἰσχίον) *of the hips*, φθίσις Hp.*Coac.*140. II. of persons, *subject to sciatica*, Dsc.1.30.6, Gal.13.986. III. *good for sciatica*, ἐπίπλασμα Dsc.2.174 (as v.l.), cf. Gal. l.c. **–άζω**, *move the hips*, of a rider, Procop.*Goth.*4.31; of a woman, Id.*Arc.*9; in walking, Suid., Phot. II. Pass., καὶ ἰσχιασθέντα, of a bandage, prob. f.l. for καὶ σχισθέντα, Gal.18(1).786. **–ᾰκός**, ή, όν, = ἰσχιαδικός, Thphr.*Fr.*87, *Cat.Cod.Astr.*7.241. **–άς** (sc. νόσος), άδος, ἡ, *hip-disease*, Hp.*Aph.*6.59,60. 2. *sciatica*, ib.3.22 (pl.), Id.*Aër.* 22 (pl.), Thphr.*HP*9.13.6 (pl.); ἰ. χρονία Dsc.1.10. II. = λευκάκανθα, Id.3.19, cf. Gal.12.58. **–ᾰσις**, εως, ἡ, *hip-disease*, Pall.*in Hp.*2.13 D. **–οίδης** (οἰδέω)· ὁ μεγάλα ἰσχία ἔχων, *Com.Adesp.* 1022. **–ον** (parox.), τό, *hip-joint*, in which the thigh turns, κατ' ἰσχίον, ἔνθα τε μηρὸς ἰσχίῳ ἐνστρέφεται, κοτύλην δέ τέ μιν καλέουσιν Il. 5.305, cf. 11.339, Od.17.234, etc.; later τὸ κατ' ἰσχίον ἄρθρον Gal. *UP*15.8; also, the intra-capsular ligament of the hip-joint, Poll.2. 186; = κεφαλὴ τοῦ μηροῦ, Hp.*Art.*53,58, Cael.Aur.*TP*4.38. 2. in pl. (dual, Autocr.1.6), *fleshy parts round the hip-joint, haunches*, of a boar, ἰσχία τε γλουτούς τε Il.8.340; of a lion, πλευράς τε καὶ ἰσχία 20.170; of a horse, Pl.*Phdr.*254c, cf. e; freq. of men, ἐκ τῶν μηρῶν ἔς τε τὰ ἰ. καὶ τὰς λαπάρας Hdt.6.75, cf. X.*Eq.*7.7; ἰσχίων φύσιν.. πρὸς τὰς ἀναπαύσεις χρήσιμον Arist.*PA*689$^{b}$15; τὰ ἰ. σαρκώδη ἐποίησεν [ἡ φύσις] ib.$^{b}$14: hence, other animals are said to have no ἰ., ib. $^{b}$6,33. II. later, *the projecting part of the os innominatum*, upon which man rests when sitting, Gal.2.772.

**ἰσχιορρωγικός**, ή, όν, (ῥώξ) *with broken hips, limping*, μέτρον ἰ. an iambic trimeter ending in five long syllables ascribed to Ananius, Gramm. Harl. in Studemund *Ind. Lect. Vratisl.* 1887/8 p.16:—also **ἰσχιορρώξ** (sc. στίχος), ῶγος, ὁ, Tz. in *An.Ox.*3.310.

❀ **ἰσχν-αίνω**, fut. –ᾰνῶ (συν–) E.*IA*694 codd.: aor. ἴσχνᾱνα A.*Eu.* 267, Ar.*Ra.*941; Ion. –ηνα Hdt.3.24, Hp.*Off.*13:—Med. (v. κατισχναίνω):—Pass., aor. ἰσχνάνθην Id.*Coac.*369,407: (ἰσχνός):—*make dry, wither*, ἐπεὰν τὸν νεκρὸν ἰσχνήνωσι, of a mummy, Hdt.3.24, cf. Hp.*Aph.*5.22, A.*Eu.*267, Pl.*Grg.*522a, etc.; ἰ. τὸ σῶμα Hp.*Art.* 33, cf. Pl.*Plt.*293b, Arist.*Metaph.*1048$^{b}$27; ἔπινε βρῦτον ἰσχναίνων χρόα A.*Fr.*124. 2. *reduce* a swelling, Hp.*Liqu.*6, *Aph.*5.25: metaph., σφυδῶντα θυμὸν ἰ. *to bring down* a proud stomach, A.*Pr.* 382; τὸ δεινὸν καὶ διαφθαρὲν φρενῶν ἴσχναινε E.*Or.*298; τὴν τέχνην οἰδοῦσαν ἴσχνανα I *reduced* the swollen art (Tragedy), Ar.*Ra.*941.—In the metaph. sense, ἰσχαίνω is a constant v.l. (as in the compds. κατισχναίνω, συνισχναίνω); cf. ἰσχάνω fin. **–ᾰλέος**, v. ἰσχαλέος. **–ανσις**, εως, ἡ, *emaciation*, Paul.Aeg.3.69, Aët.16.80(75), Mich.*in PN*46.6. **–αντικός**, ή, όν, *fit for reducing*, Arist.*Pr.*885$^{a}$ 28, Dsc.1.24. **–ᾰσία**, Ion. –ίη, ἡ, *thinness, leanness*, Hp.*Aff.*12, Arist.*Metaph.*1013$^{b}$1, 1048$^{b}$29. **–ασμός**, ὁ, *reducing treatment*, τοῦ σώματος Hp.*Fract.*14.

**ἰσχνεῦσαι**· ὑφεῖναι, θηλάσαι, Hsch. (Cf. ἰσχαλεῦσαι.) **ἰσχνίδες**· ἄγκυραι, ἰσχάδες· καὶ φιλήματος εἶδος, Id.

**ἰσχνο-κᾰλᾰμώδης**, ες, *with slender reed*, Eust.1165.12. **–κωλος**, ον, *with thin limbs*, Antyll.ap.Orib.7.16.15. **–μῡθέω**, = λεπτολογέω, and **–μῡθία**, ἡ, *subtle dispute*, Hsch. **–πους**, ποδος, ὁ, ἡ, gloss on ταναύποδα, Sch.Od.9.464.

❀ **ἰσχνός**, ή, όν, *dry, withered*, φυλλεῖα Ar.*Ach.*469; ἰ. τυρός, opp. χλωρός, Poll.6.48, *POxy.*1338 (v A.D.). 2. of persons, *thin, lean*, Hp.*Aph.*2.44, Theoc.10.27, etc.; ἰσχνοὶ καὶ σφηκώδεις Ar.*Pl.*561; ἰσχνοὶ καὶ ἄσιτοι Pl.*Lg.*665e; ἰ. ἕξεις a *spare* habit of body, Plu.*Lyc.* 17; of roots, –ότεραι Dsc.1.9,10; of the voice, ἰσχνὸν φθέγγεσθαι to speak *thin* or *small*, Luc.*Nigr.*11. 3. *weak, feeble*, σφυγμός Gal. 8.506. 4. *reduced*, of a swelling, οὕτω ἂν τάχιστα ἰσχνὸν τὸ οἴδημα γένοιτο Hp.*Fract.*21, cf. *Epid.*4.26. Adv. –νῶς, ἑστηκώς *without external swelling*, Id.*Coac.*481. 5. *light, thin*, of clothing materials, *POxy.*1535 *B*9 (ii/iii A.D.), etc.: metaph., of style, *spare, plain, unadorned*, ἰ. χαρακτήρ D.H.*Pomp.*2, cf. Demetr.*Eloc.*190, Quint. 12.10.58, Plu.2.42d. Adv. –νῶς, εἰπεῖν to speak *plainly*, Plb.1.2.6; –νῶς ἰδεῖν τὴν ἀρετήν dub.l. in Lycurg.80. (Perh. cogn. with Lat. *vescus*: a connexion with ἴσχω was imagined by the Greeks; cf. ἰσχνόφωνος II.)

**ἰσχνοσκελής**, ές, *lean-shanked*, D.L.5.1, Gal.6.322.

**ἰσχνότης**, ητος, ἡ, *thinness, leanness*, σαρκός Hp.*Aër.*21; σώματος Arist.*HA*581$^{b}$26; φύσιος Aret.*SA*1.7. 2. of style, *spareness*, i.e. *plainness*, ἰ. φράσεως, of Lysias, D.H.*Vett.Cens.*5.1; cf. Phld.*Rh.*1. 165 S., Demetr.*Eloc.*14. 3. *thinness, weakness* of pronunciation, opp. πλατειασμός, Quint.1.5.32.

**ἰσχνουργής**, ές, *finely wrought*, gloss on εὐϋφής, Sch.S.*Tr.*602.

**ἰσχνο-φωνία**, Ion. –ίη, ἡ, *hesitancy of speech*, Hp.*Epid.*2.5.1, Arist. *Pr.*895$^{a}$16, 902$^{b}$25. ❀ **–φωνος**, ον, *thin-voiced, weak-voiced*, Phld. *Po.*2.25, Gal.17(1).186; of Isocrates, Plu.2.837a; of partridges, Antig.*Mir.*6; but, II. *having an impediment in one's speech* (connected by the Greeks with ἴσχω), οἱ ἰ...ἴσχονται τοῦ φωνεῖν Arist.*Pr.*903$^{a}$38, cf. 895$^{a}$15, 905$^{a}$21, *AB*100; ἰ. καὶ τραυλός Hdt.4. 155, cf. Hp.*Epid.*1.19; ἰ. καὶ βραδύγλωσσος LXX *Ex.*4.10, cf. Ezek. *Exag.*114; also of metals, etc., χρυσὸς καὶ λίθος ὑπὸ πληρότητος ἰ. καὶ δυσηχῆ Plu.2.721c: metaph., ἡ φιλία ἰ. γέγονεν ἐν τῷ παρρησιάζεσθαι ib.89b. Adv. –φώνως Zos.Alch.p.108 B.

**ἰσχν-όω**, = ἰσχναίνω, *make dry*, Arist.*Pr.*885$^{a}$19; *put on low diet*, Orib.*Syn.*9.37.4. **–ωσις**, εως, ἡ, *drying up*, μαστῶν Sor.1.59; of the body, Id.2.36. **–ωτικός**, ή, όν, *of* or *for drying up* or *reducing*, δύναμις Dsc.5.109 (interpol.).

**ἰσχομένως**, Adv., (ἴσχω) *with checks* or *hindrances*, Pl.*Cra.*415c.

**ἰσχουρ-έω**, *suffer from retention of urine*, Aret.*SD*2.4, Herod.Med. ap.Orib.10.37.2. **–ία**, ἡ, *retention of urine*, Sor.2.6, Gal.8.403, Herod.Med.ap.Orib.10.37.16.

**ἰσχῡρ-ιείω**, Desiderat. from sq., *venture to affirm*, Hp.*Art.*1, cf. Gal.18(1).309. ❀ **–ίζομαι**, fut. –ῐοῦμαι Lys.6.35, Isoc.17.24: aor. ἰσχῡρῐσάμην Th.5.26, Pl.*Grg.*489c:—*make oneself strong, be strong*, ἰσχυριζόμενος ὑφ' ἵππων σίδηρος *gaining force* from the impetus of the horses, X.*Cyr.*6.4.18. II. *use one's strength*, τῷ σώματι Pl. l.c.; esp. in overcoming resistance, πρὸς τὸ πολὺ ἧττον Arist.*Pr.*951$^{a}$13; εἰς τοὺς ἀσθενεῖς Id.*EN*1124$^{b}$23; *contend stoutly*, ὑπὲρ ἄθλων Ael.*NA* 15.15; *persist* or *continue obstinately in* doing.., c. part., Th.7.49: abs., ibid.; esp. by word of mouth, *maintain stiffly, obstinately*, c. acc. et inf., Id.3.44, Is.11.1; ταῦτα Pl.*Grg.*495b; ὅτι.., ὡς.. Th. 4.23, 6.55, Pl.*Tht.*172b; περί τινος Id.*Sph.*249c. 2. *put firm trust in* a thing, *rely on* it, τῷ ξυνῷ πάντων Heraclit.114; λόγῳ Lys.6.35; διαθήκαις Is.1.3; τῷ νόμῳ Hyp.*Eux.*4, D.33.27; παρασκευῇ Id.44.3, cf. Isoc.17.24; *feel confidence*, Antipho 5.76. **–ικός**, ή, όν, *stubborn*, Pl.*Tht.*169b (Comp.), prob. l. in Alex.194, cf. Phot. **–ιστέον**, *one must maintain stoutly*, Pl.*R.*533a. **–ιστικῶς** ἔχω, *to be inclined* to *affirm*, gloss on ἰσχυριείω, Gal.18(1).309.

**ἰσχῡρο-γνωμοσύνη**, ἡ, *obstinacy*, Ph.1.653, J.*Ap.*1.22. **–γνώμων**, ον, gen. ονος, *stiff in opinion*, Arist.*EN*1151$^{b}$5, D.L.2.24: Sup., Ph.*Fr.*23 H.: metaph., λογισμός Id.2.413. **–δετος**, ον, *fast-bound*, Sch.A.*Pr.*148. **–θώραξ**, ᾱκος, ὁ, ἡ, gloss on χαλκοχιτώνων, Hsch. **–κάρδιος**, ον, gloss on τλήθυμος, Id. **–πᾰθέω**, = δεινοπαθέω, Sch.Arat.71. ❀ **–παίκτης**, ου, ὁ, *one who plays valiantly*, *IG*14.1535, *Delph.*3(1).216, Vett.Val.4.17. **–πλήκτης**, ου, ὁ, *wounding severely*, gloss on διοπλήκταν, Hsch. **–ποιέω**, *strengthen*, τὴν δύναμιν D.S.17.65; τὰς ἐπικρατείας τινός Plb.28.20. 7; τόπον J.*AJ*15.8.5; στόμαχον [Gal.]14.752; *establish*, τὰς διατριβὰς τῶν ῥητορικῶν Phld.*Rh.*1.192 S.:—Med., Onos.21.2:—Pass., ἰσχυροποιεῖται τὰ μέσα Ascl.*Tact.*10.16; τῆς δυναστείας –ουμένης D.S.14.9, cf. Arr.*Epict.*2.18.7; of assertions, Vett.Val.333.7; *to be valid*, ἡ ἀναλογία οὐκ –εῖται S.E.*M.*1.201. **–ποίησις**, εως, ἡ, *strengthening*, τῶν ἀσθενούντων μορίων Aët.12.21. II. *confirmation, corroboration*, *Gloss.* **–ποιός**, όν, *strengthening*, *EM* 480.12, Sch.A.*Ch.*415, etc. **–πότης**, ου, ὁ, gloss on ζαπότης, Hsch. **–πους**, ποδος, ὁ, ἡ, *strong-footed*, gloss on χαλκόποδας, Id. **–πράγμων**, ον, gen. ονος, *doing mighty deeds*, Paul.Al.*O.*1; gloss on ὀβριμοεργός, Sch.D Il.5.403. **–ρριζος**, ον, (ῥίζα) *with strong root*, Thphr.*CP*2.12.3, etc.

❀ **ἰσχῡρός**, ά, όν, (ἰσχύς) *strong*, esp. of personal strength, S.*Ph.*945, E.*Fr.*290, etc.; of things, ἰ. βέλος Alc.15.4; ῥεύματα Hdt.8.12; ἰ. χθών *hard*, A.*Pers.*310; of food, *indigestible*, Hp.*Art.*50; of taste, *strong*, Thphr.*HP*7.6.1; of armies, ἰσχυροτέρα φάλαγξ X.*Cyr.*7.1.30; of places, Th.4.9, X.*An.*4.6.11, etc.; τῆς χώρης τὸ –ότατον Hdt.1.76; τὸ ἑαυτοῦ ἰ., opp. τὰ τοῖς πολεμίοις ἰ., X.*Eq.Mag.*8.24: τὰ ἰσχυρότατα your *strongest points*, Th.5.111; τὰ τῆς πόλεως ἰ. *that in which the strength* of the state *lies*, Aeschin.3.66; δρῶντες οὐδὲν ἰ. ἀπὸ τῶν Λεσβίων no *show of strength*, Th.3.6; ἰ. τι πρὸς τὸ πρᾶγμ' ἔχειν a *strong* point, Men.*Epit.*130; –ότατον τεκμήριον *SIG*685.84 (Crete, ii B.C.). 2. *powerful*, ἄλοχος Διός A.*Supp.*302; πόλις E.*Supp.*447; θεός Ar.*Pl.*946; ἰ. τὸ πολλόν Hdt.1.136; οἱ ἰ. ἐν ταῖς πόλεσιν X.*Ath.* 1.14: Comp. –ότερος, ἐς πειθώ Democr.51; ὁ ὀπίσω μου ἐρχόμενος –ότερός μου ἐστίν *Ev.Matt.*3.11. 3. *forcible, violent, severe*, σιτοδείη, ψύχη, Hdt.1.94, 4.29; λιμός *Ev.Luc.*15.14; ἀναγκαίη Hdt.1.74; αἱ λίαν ἰ. τιμωρίαι *violent, excessive*, Id.4.205; ὅρκος –ότατος, ἀνάγκαι –όταται, Antipho 5.11, 6.25; νόσημα Hp.*Acut.*(*Sp.*)4; βήξ Th.2.49; γέλως, ἐπιθυμίαι, etc., Pl.*R.*388e, 560b, etc.; νόμος ἰ. *severe*, Hdt.7. 102, Lys.15.9; ἔχθρα Pl.*Phdr.*233c; γνώμη –οτέρη *more positive*, Hdt.9.41; τρόπῳ ᾧ ἂν δύνωνται –οτάτῳ Foed.ap.Th.5.23; κατὰ τὸ ἰσχυρόν *by main force*, opp. δόλῳ, Hdt.4.201, cf. 9.2. 4. of literary

style, *vigorous*, D.H.*Comp.*22; also of syllables, *strong*, ib.16; στάσεις λαμβάνειν ἰ. ib.22. II. Adv. -ρῶς *strongly, with all force*, ἐγκεῖσθαι Th.1.69, etc.; φυλάττειν τινάς X.*An.*6.3.11. 2. *very much, exceedingly*, with Adjs., Hdt.4.108; ἔθνος μέγα ἰ. ib.183; διώρυγες ἰ. βαθεῖαι X.*An.*[1.7.15], etc.; ἰ. χλωρόν Hp.*Progn.*11; κίνησις ν· θὴς ἰ. Arist.*HA*503ᵇ9; ἰ. φιλοπλάτων Phld.*Ind.Sto.*61: with Verbs, ἰ. ἥδεσθαι, ἀνιᾶσθαι, X.*Cyr.*8.3.44; ἀπήγγειλεν ὅτι πάντα δοκοίη ἰ. τῷ εὐνούχῳ ib.5.3.15: Comp. -οτέρως Heraclit.114, Hdt.3.129; -ότερον X.*Cyr.*4.5.12, etc.: Sup., in answers, ἰσχυρότατά γε *most certainly*, Id.*Oec.*1.15.

**ἰσχῡροσώματος**, ον, gloss on ὀβριμοεργός, Sch.Opp.*H.*1.360.

**ἰσχῡρότης**, ητος, ἡ, *strength*, Ph.1.128; v.l. for ἐχ-, D.H.3.65, for ὀχ-, Ph.1.644.

**ἰσχῡρό-φρων**, ονος, ὁ, ἡ, *strong-minded*, D.C.*Fr.*43.25. **-φωνος**, ον, *strong-voiced*, Antyll.ap.Orib.6.10.10. **-χρως**, ωτος, ὁ, ἡ, gloss on ταλαύρινος, Sch.Il.5.289. **-ψῡχος**, ον, *strong-souled*, Hsch. s. v. λάσιον κῆρ.

**ἰσχῡρόω**, *strengthen*, Lxx *Is.*41.7.

❀ **ἰσχ-ύς** [v. sub fin.], ύος, ἡ, *strength* of body, Hes.*Th.*146, 823, etc.; ἀκμαὶ ἰσχύος Pi.*O.*1.96; δεινὸν ἰσχύος θράσος S.*Ph.*104; τὴν ἰ. δεινὰ καὶ τὴν ῥώμην Pl.*Smp.*190b; πρὸς ἰσχὺν ὀφθαλμοὶ ἄριστα πεφυκότες X.*Smp.*5.5: pl., ἰσχύες καὶ ἀσθένειαι Pl.*R.*618d; κατὰ σωμάτων ἰσχὺς καὶ εὐμορφίας Id.*Lg.*744c; of places, ἰσχὺς γῆς S.*OC*610; of a fortified place, Th.4.35. 2. *might, power*, θεοῦ, θεῶν, A.*Th.*226 (lyr.), S.*Aj.*118; ἰ. βασιλεία A.*Pers.*590 (lyr.), cf. 12 (anap.); ὅπου γὰρ ἰ. συζυγοῦσι καὶ δίκη *might* and right, Id.*Fr.*381; φύσεως ἰ., of Themistocles, Th.1.138; ἐπὶ μέγα ἐλθεῖν ἰσχύος to a great height *of power*, Id.2.97, cf. 1.85, etc.; παρὰ ἰσχὺν τῆς δυνάμεως Id.7.66; ἰ. μάχης fighting *power*, Id.2.97; ἰ. τῆς ἐλπίδος Id.4.65, cf. 2.62; ἡ τῶν νόμων ἰ. *POxy.*67.14 (iv A.D.); *validity*, *PGrenf.*2.71 ii 11 (iii A.D.), etc. 3. *brute force*, κατ' ἰσχύν *perforce*, opp. δόλῳ, A.*Pr.*214; πρὸς ἰσχύος κράτος S.*Ph.*594; πρὸς ἰσχύος χάριν E.*Med.*538; ὑπὸ τῆς ἰσχύος Epicr.3.10; κατέχοντες ἰσχύϊ τὸ πλῆθος Th.3.62; εἴ τι ἰσχύϊ πράττεται, ἰσχυρῶς πράττεται Pl.*Prt.*332b. 4. *motive force*, Arist.*Ph.*250ᵃ6; ἡ κινοῦσα ἰ. Id.*Cael.*275ᵇ20, al. 5. in Lit. Crit., *vigour* of style, D.H.*Pomp.*3, *Comp.*2, al. II. in Tactics, the *main body* of troops, οὔπω ἡ ἰ. πάρεστιν X.*Cyr.*1.4.19. [ῠ in gen., etc.: in nom. and acc. sg. ῠ in Pi.*N.*11.31 (acc.): ῡ in Trag. and Com., A.*Th.*1080 (anap.), *Ch.*721 (anap.), S.*Aj.*118, Men.449.] (Perh. ϝισχύς, cf. βίσχυν, γισχύν.) **-ῡσις**, εως, ἡ, mistranslation of Hebr., Lxx *Ca.*2.7, 3.5 prob. for diff. root; prob. f.l. for χύσις (cj. Wendl.) in Ph.1.354. ❀ **-ύω** (ἰσχύς), Batr.279: impf. ἴσχυον Ar.*V.*357, X.*HG*6.4.18: fut. ἰσχύσω Ar.*Av.*1607, etc.: aor. ἴσχῡσα S.*Aj.*502, etc.: pf. ἴσχῡκα Aeschin.1.165, Cerc.17.34:—Pass., aor. κατ-ισχύθην D.S.15.87: (ἰσχύς):—*to be strong* in body, S.*Tr.*234; ὅπως ὑγιαίνοιεν καὶ ἰσχύοιεν X.*Cyr.*6.1.24; ὃς μέγιστον ἴσχυσε στρατοῦ S.*Aj.*502; ἰ. τοῖς σώμασιν X.*Mem.*2.7.7; τοῦ σώματος ἰσχύοντος Antipho 5.93; ἴσχυόν τ' αὐτὸς ἐμαυτοῦ, i.e. I *had* all my *strength*, Ar.*V.*357; ἰ. ἐκ νόσου *to be recovering*, X.*HG*6.4.18. 2. *to be powerful, prevail*, μηδὲν μεῖον ἰ. Διός A.*Pr.*510, etc.; πλέον, μεῖζον ἰ., E.*Hec.*1188, Ar.*Av.*1607; later ἰ. πρός τινα *prevail* against, Lxx *Ps.*12(13).4; ἐπί τινας ib.1*Ma.*10.49; ἰ. τινί *to be strong in* a thing, σοφίᾳ ἀνὴρ ὑπὲρ ἀνδρὸς ἰσχύει Pi.*Fr.*61; θράσει E.*Or.*903; ἐν τῇ ποιητικῇ Phld.*Po.*5.9; ἰ. τινὶ πρὸς τοὺς πολεμίους Th.3.46; ἰ. ἐκ πονηρίας D.2.9; ὅθεν ἰσχύομεν, ἧπερ ἰσχύουσι, Th.1.143, 2.13; ἰ. παρά τινι *have power* or *influence* with one, Id.8.47, Aeschin.2.2, D.38.20, etc. b. of things, *prevail*, ὅρκος οὔτι Ζηνὸς ἰ. πλέον A.*Eu.*621; τἀληθὲς γὰρ ἰσχῦον τρέφω S.*OT*356; τὸ δίκαιον ἐν πᾶσιν ἰ. D.37.59; *have force*, ἃ ὡρίσω σὺ δίκαια, ταῦτά.. καὶ κατὰ σοῦ προσήκει τοῖς ἄλλοις ἰσχύειν D.19.241, cf. 25.71; ὁ λόγος δόξειεν ἂν ἰσχύειν Arist.*Pol.*1280ᵃ28; νομὴ ἄδικος οὐδὲν ἰ. *is of* no *force*, *PTeb.*286.7 (ii A.D.); ἰσχῦόν τι something *permanent*, prob. in Epicur.*Ep.*1 p.7 U.: c. inf., ὁ καιρὸς ἰσχύει.. πράττειν D.17.9, cf. Lxx 2*Ch.*2.6(5), al., Plu.*Pomp.*58; οὐκ ἰ. ἀρτιστομεῖν Str.14.2.28, cf. *Ev.Marc.*5.4, D.Chr.33.22, etc. 3. *to be worth* or *equivalent to*, ἡ μνᾶ ἰσχύει λίτρας δύο καὶ ἥμισυ J.*AJ*14.7.1, cf. *PGnom.*106, Ptol.*Tetr.*134; αἱ ψῆφοι τάλαντον ἰσχύουσιν (prob. for ἴσχουσιν) Plb.5.26.13. 4. Act., *condense*, νεφέλας Lxx *Si.*43.15. b. ἄρτον πᾶσαν ἡδονὴν ἰσχύοντα *making strong*.., ib.*Wi.*16.20 (*in se habentem*, Vulg.). 5. -ύοντες ἀστέρες those *in dominating positions*, Serapion in *Cat.Cod.Astr.*8(4).226. [ῡ in Batr. l.c., Trag. and Com., S.*Aj.*1409, *OT*356, Ar.*V.*357, *Av.*488, 1606; later, ῠ sts. in pres. and impf., *AP*5.166 (Asclep.), 211 (Mel.).]

❀ **ἴσχω**, redupl. form of ἔχω (only found in pres., and impf. Act. and Pass., Ep. inf. ἰσχέμεναι, ἰσχέμεν, Od.20.330, Il.17.501), but in Hom. and Hes. almost always with a limited sense, *keep back, restrain* (v. infr. II), δέος ἴσχει τινά Il.5.812, 817, etc.; ἴ. τινὰ ἀνάγκη Od.4.558; θυμὸν ἴ. ἐν στήθεσσι Il.9.256; Ζεὺς ἴσχεν ἑὸν μένος Hes.*Th.*687; οὐδ' ἔτι σηκοὶ ἴσχουσι (the calves) Od.10.413; [πρὼν] ἴσχει ῥέεθρα Il.17.750; ἵππους ἴ. 15.456, etc.; ἴσχον βουλομένους τοὺς ἑπτὰ ἐς τὸ πρόσω παριέναι Hdt.3.77; μηδὲν ἡμᾶς ἰσχέτω Ar.*V.*1264; οὐδέποτέ γ' ἴσχει θύρα, prov. of those who keep open house, Eup.265; ἴσχε στόμα E.*HF*1244; ἴσχε δακὼν στόμα σόν S.*Tr.*976 (anap.); τὸ ἴσχον τὴν πορείαν X.*An.*6.5.13; χείμαρρον.. ἔρκεα ἴσχει ἀλωάων *keep it back*, Il.5.90: c. gen., ξίφος ἴ. τινός *to keep* it *from* him, E.*Hel.*1656; ἴ. τῆς βοῆς, τοῦ ἱέναι, Pl.*Cra.*416b, 420e: folld. by inf., ἴ. τινὰ μὴ πράσσειν E.*IA*661:—Pass., *to be checked*, Gal.*UP*15.3: also impers., ἐν τούτῳ ἴσχετο here *the matter stopped*, X.*An.*6.3.9. 2. abs., ἴσχε *hold, stay, stop!* A.*Ch.*1052, S.*Ichn.*95; of ships, *put in*, v.l. in Th.2.91; πρὸς ταῖς πόλεσι Id.7.35, cf. A.R.2.390; of rivers, *stop*, Arr.*An.*5.9.4:—in this sense Hom. uses Med. or Pass., ἴσχεσθ' Ἀργεῖοι, μὴ φεύγετε Od.24.54, cf. Il.3.82; ἴσχεο *check thyself, be calm*, 1.214, 2.247, Od.22.356, etc.; *keep quiet*, 11.251: c. gen., ἴσχεσθαί τινος *desist from* a thing, 18.347, 24.323. II. *hold fast, hold*, once in Hom., [κανόνα] ἀγχόθι στήθεος Il.23.762, cf. S.*Aj.*575, *Ph.*1111 (lyr.): metaph., *keep, maintain*, εὐφημίαν Id.*Tr.*178; ἐλπίσιν ἴ. τι ib.138; γνώμαν Id.*Ph.*853 (lyr.); ἐπιστήμην λαβόντα ἴσχειν Pl.*Tht.*198a; of outward matters, ὀδύνη ἴ. τὴν γαστέρα *affects* it, Hp.*Nat.Mul.*14; τὸν αἰσ' ἄπλατος ἴσχει S.*Aj.*256 (lyr.); αἱ ἄτομοι τὸν παλμὸν ἴσχουσι *keep up*, Epicur.*Ep.*1 p.8 U.:—Pass., φθόῃ ἴσχεσθαι Isoc.19.11 (s. v.l., σχόμενον Blass); also τὸ ἰσχόμενον κατὰ διαφοράν that which *is permanent* in distinction, Chrysipp.*Stoic.*2.128. III. after Hom., *hold* or *have in possession*, v.l. in Hdt.3.39, Th.3.58; *have a wife*, Hdt.5.92.β'; of women, ἴ. ἐν γαστρί or simply ἴ. *to be pregnant*, Hp.*Epid.*2.2.18, etc.; μετὰ τοῦτον ἴ. Κλεόμβροτον *conceives* Cl., Hdt.5.41: generally, like ἔχω, ἴσχε κάμοῦ μνῆστιν S.*Aj.*520; λῆστιν ἴ. to be forgetful, Id.*OC*584; ἄλγος ἴ. Id.*OT*1031; γνώμαν ἴ., = γνῶναι, Id.*El.*214 (lyr.); ἴ. δοῦλον βίον Id.*Tr.*302; νοῦν Pl.*Smp.*181d; ἐπωνυμίαν Id.*Prm.*130e; χρώματα Hp.*Prog.*12; κακώσιας Id.*Art.*61; *receive*, [πεμπάδα] *SIG*57.35 (Milet., v B.C.); ἰσχέτω δίκην καὶ ὑπεχέτω ib.286.15 (iv B.C.), cf. *IG*5(2).357.23 (Stymphalus, iii B.C.): c. dupl. acc., ἴ. τινὰ ξύνευνον S.*Aj.*1301; θεὸν οὐ λήξω προστάταν ἴσχων Id.*OT*882 (lyr.). 2. *have in it, involve*, ὄλβος ἴ. φθόνον Pi.*P.*11.29; μετάστασιν ἴ. *to be susceptible, capable of* cure, Hp.*Aph.*5.7; ἀνάληψιν μετ' εὐπετείας Pl.*Ti.*83e; *to be worth*, dub. l. in Plb.5.26.13; v. ἰσχύω 3. 3. intr., *to be*, like ἔχω, ἀπολέμως ἴσχοντες Pl.*Plt.*307e; εὖ ἴ. τὸ σῶμα Id.*R.*411c; ὧδε Id.*Phil.*38c; τοῖς πᾶσι χαλεπώτερον Th.7.59.

❀ **ἰσωνία**, ἡ, (ὠνή) *the same price, cost price*, τῆς ἰ. Ar.*Pax*1227; τὰς ἰ. ἀπολυσάτω he shall release him at *the original price*, *Milet.*3 No.140.55 (Crete).

**ἰσωνῠμ-ία**, ἡ, rejected as a name for a *pronoun* by A.D.*Pron.*9.7. **-ος**, ον, (ὄνομα) *bearing the same name as*, c. gen., καλεῖν τινα ἰσώνυμον ἔμμεν μάτρωος Pi.*O.*9.64; ἠελίοιο τροπαῖς ἰσώνυμον [ῑ] ἔρνος, i.e. ἡλιοτρόπιον, Nic.*Th.*678.

❀ **ἴσως**, Lacon. ϝίῳρ (v. βίωρ), Adv. of ἴσος, *equally, in like manner*, Sapph.*Supp.*25.11, S.*Ph.*758, Pl.*Lg.*805a, etc.; ὡς ἰσαίτατα ib.744c; *evenly*, Hp.*Off.*3. II. *equally, with reference to equality*, τὸ ὀρθὸν ληπτέον ἴσως Arist.*Pol.*1283ᵇ40; *fairly, equitably*, ἴ. καὶ κοινῶς Aen.Tact.22.24; οὐκ ἴ. οὐδὲ πολιτικῶς D.10.74; μηδὲν ἴ. καὶ δικαίως φρονοῦντας D.H.10.40; οὐκ ἴσως χρήσασθαί τινι Plb.23.2.7. III. *probably, perhaps*, Alc.*Supp.*33, Hdt.6.124, A.*Pr.*319, S.*Ph.*144, Pl.*Grg.*473b, etc.; ἴ. που E.*El.*518; οὔτε συμφόρως οὔτ' ἴ. καλῶς D.5.10; οὐκ ἴσως, ἀλλ' ὄντως Pl.*Lg.*965c: ironical, σμικρά γε ἴ. προσθήκη Id.*R.*339b: freq. joined with ἄν or τάχ' ἄν, e.g. S.*Aj.*691, 1009, Pl.*Ap.*31a; ἀμφισβητοῦντες προστιθέασιν ἀεὶ τὸ ἴσως καὶ τάχα Arist.*Rh.*1389ᵇ18; ἴσως without ἄν c. opt. is f.l. in A.*Supp.*727, E.*IT*1055; ἴ. μέν.., ἴ. δέ.. *perhaps* so or so, X.*Cyr.*4.3.2: repeated ἴ., ἴ. Ar.*Nu.*1320, D.3.33: used to soften or qualify a positive assertion, S.*OC*661, Ar.*Ra.*224, Pl.*Phd.*61c, *Phdr.*233e, Arist.*Metaph.*987ᵃ26, etc. IV. with numerals, *about*, Ar.*Pl.*1058, Damox.3.2.

**ἴσωσις**, εως, ἡ, (ἰσόω) *making equal, comparison*, *Gloss.*

**ἴταλα**· ἰστία εἰς ἃ τοὺς ἱστοὺς διατείνουσιν, Hsch. (Cf. ἰτλαί.)

**Ἰτᾰλ-ία**, Ion. -ίη, ἡ, *Italy*, Hdt.1.24, etc. [Ῑτ-, S.*Ant.*1119 (lyr.), Call.*Dian.*58.] **-ιάζω**, Dor. fut -ιάξω, *live in Italy*, Hsch., Phot. ❀ **-ίδης**, ου, ὁ, poet. for Ἰταλιώτης, *AP*9.344 (Leon.), Call.*Fr.*448. **-ικός**, ή, όν, *Italian*, Pl.*Lg.*659b, etc.; αἵρεσις *Placit.*1.3.9; σπεῖρα, = *Cohors Italica*, *Act.Ap.*10.1; Ἰταλικοί, οἱ, *Italians* resident at Delos, *SIG*726.4 (i B.C.), etc.:—pecul. fem. ❀ **-ίς**, ίδος [ῑ], *AP*7.373 (Thall.); ἡ Ἰταλίς (sc. γῆ), = Ἰταλία, D.C.54.22 codd. **-ιώτης**, ου, ὁ, *Greek inhabitant of Italy*, Hdt.4.15, Th.6.44, etc.; cf. Σικελιώτης:—fem. **-ιῶτις**, ιδος, Adj. *Italian*, νῆες, πόλεις, Th.8.91, Str.5.4.4: Adj. **-ιωτικός**, ή, όν, Pl.*Ep.*326b, Luc.*Hist. Conscr.*15. ❀ **-ός**, ὁ, *Italian*, Parth.7.1, Str.5.1.1: as Adj., Ἰ. αἰχμητής [ῑ] *AP*7.741 (Crin.), etc.

**ἰτᾰλός**, ὁ, = ταῦρος, D.C.*Fr.*4.2, Hsch.; whence Italy is said to be called, Timae.12, cf. Fest. s. v. Ἰταλία. (ϝιταλός, cf. Lat. *vitulus*, Osc. *Viteliú* (*Italia*).)

**ἰτᾰμ-εύομαι** [ῐ], *to be* ἰταμός, interpol. in Jul.*Or.*7.210c. **-ία**, ἡ, = ἰταμότης, Lxx *Je.*29.17(49.16). **-ός**, ή, όν, (εἶμι *ibo*, ἴτης) *headlong, hasty, eager*, κύνες A.*Fr.*282, Alex.234; ἰ. πρόσωπον Nicol.Com.1.28; *bold, reckless*, ἰταμὸν καὶ τολμηρὸν ἡ πονηρία D.25.24; ἀναιδὴς καὶ ἰ. Men.*Epit.*311; ἰ. πρὸς τὸ πράττειν Arist.*Pr.*953ᵇ4; πρὸς τὰ δεινά Plu.*Galb.*25; πρὸς λόγους ἰταμώτερος Id.2.1041a: Sup. -ώτατος Phld.*Rh.*1.341 S., Luc.*Icar.*30; τὸ ἰ., = ἰταμότης, Plu.*Fab.*19, etc.; *vigour* of style, Diog.Oen.12; τὸ ἰ. τῆς ψυχῆς Plu.*Rom.*7; ἰ. τι δεδορκώς Luc.*Fug.*19; ἰ. ἀντιβλέπειν Ael.*NA*17.12. Adv. -μῶς Alex.105, Euphro 1.25, Men.*Pk.*306, Plu.2.93b, Gal.11.232; οἱ ἰ. πολιτευόμενοι D.8.68: Comp. -ώτερον Pl.*Lg.*773b; -ώτερον τῷ βίῳ χρῆσθαι D.19.233. ❀ **-ότης**, ητος, ἡ, *initiative, vigour*, Pl.*Plt.*311a; *effrontery*, Plu.2.715e, Jul.*Or.*7.225c; συγγραφέως Plb.12.9.4.

**ἶτας**· ὅρκος, καὶ ὁ ᾅδης, Hsch.

**ἰτέα** [ῐ], Ep. and Ion. ἰτέη, also ἰτείη (A.R.4.1428): ἡ:—*willow*, Il.21.350, Hecat.292(a) J., Hdt.1.194, *PTeb.ined.*703.195, etc.; ἰ. λευκή, = *Salix alba*, ἰ. μέλαινα, = *Salix amplexicaulis*, Thphr.*HP*3.13.7. II. *wicker shield, target*, E.*Heracl.*376 (lyr.), *Supp.*695, *Tr.*1193, *Cyc.*7, Ar.*Fr.*65. III. ἰ. δένδρος, = ἵππουρις, Ps.-Dsc.4.46. (Εἰτέα, the Attic deme-name, is a different word; cf. ἰτεΐνος, ἰτεόφυλλος; prob. cogn. with Lat. *viēre*, *vīmen*, Lith. *výti* 'twist', 'wind', *vytis* 'willow-twig', OE. *wiþig* 'willow'.)

⊛ **ἰτέϊνος** [ῑτ], η, ον, *of willow*, ἰ. ῥάβδος Hdt.4.67, cf. Thphr.*HP*5.3.4, *PCair.Zen.*353.5 (iii B.C.); τὰ ἰ. *Sammelb.*5807.3. II. *made of withy rods, wicker*, ἰ. σάκεα Theoc.16.79.

**ἰτέον** [ῐ], (εἶμι *ibo*) *one must go*, Hp.*Acut.*38, Pl.*R.*394d, *Lg.*803e, etc.

⊛ **ἰτεόφυλλος** [ῑ], ον, *decorated with a pattern of willow-leaves*, φιάλη *Annuario* 4/5.463 (Halic., iii B.C.).

⊛ **ἰτεών** [ῑ], ῶνος, ὁ, *willow-ground*, *Gp.*3.6.6.

⊛ **ἴτηλος**, η, ον, expld. by Hsch. as ἔμμονος, οὐκ ἐξίτηλος, A.*Fr.*42.

**ἰτ-ήριος** [ῐ], coined as etym. of ἐξιτήριος, *EM*348.45. **-ης**, ου, ὁ, = ἰταμός, Ar.*Nu.*445, Pl.*Smp.*203d; ἴτας γε ἐφ' ἃ οἱ πολλοὶ φοβοῦνται ἰέναι Id.*Prt.*349e, cf. 359c; ἴ. καὶ πολυπράγμων D.C.55.18. **-ητέον**, = ἰτέον, Ar.*Nu.*131, Diph.31. **-ητικός**, ή, όν, = ἰταμός, Max.Tyr. 41.5: Comp., ib.21.2: Sup. -ώτατον ὁ θυμὸς πρὸς τοὺς κινδύνους *most ready to encounter* dangers, Arist.*EN*1116$^{b}$26.

**ἶτθαι**· ἧσθαι, Hsch. **ἰτθέλαν**· διφθέραν, Id. (cf. ἰξαλῆ). **ἰτλαί**· οἳ ⟨ἐν⟩τείνουσι τὰς ᾤας τοῦ ὑφαινομένου μυγελεῖς (fort. Πυγελεῖς)· οἱ δὲ τοὺς μίτους, Id.

**ἴτον**, τό, Thracian name for a kind of *mushroom*, Thphr.*Fr.*167, Plin.*HN*19.36; prob. fr. ϝίτον, cf. οἰτόν, οὐιτόν.

**ἰτός**, ή, όν, (εἶμι *ibo*) *passable*, ὁδός *AP*7.480 (Leon.).

⊛ **ἴτριον** (on the accent v. Hdn.Gr.1.357, al.), τό, a kind of *cake* (πεμμάτιον λεπτὸν διὰ σησάμου καὶ μέλιτος γινόμενον Ath.14.646d, but cf. πλακοῦντες, σησαμοῦντες, ἴτρια Ar.*Ach.*1092, μελιτώμασι καὶ ἰτρίοις Dsc.4.63), Anacr.17, Hp.*Acut.*(*Sp.*)72, Anon.Lond.*Fr.*2.3, *POxy.*736.50: freq. in pl., Sol.38, S.*Fr.*199, Archipp.9, prob. in Herod.3.44; ἴτρια, τραγήμαθ' ἧκε, πυραμοῦς, ἄμης Ephipp.8.3; later, of any cake, ἴτρια καρποῦ πεποιημένα πυρίνου D.H.1.55; of the Roman *libum*, πλακοῦς ἐκ γάλακτος ἰτρίων καὶ μέλιτος Ath.3.125f.

**ἰτρίνεος** [ῐν], α, ον, *like* ἴτρια, *AP*6.232 (Crin.).

⊛ **ἰτριοπώλης**, ου, ὁ, *dealer in* ἴτρια, prob. in Poll.7.30.

⊛ **ἴττα**, dialect word for δρυοκόλαψ, Hsch. **ἰττέλα**, v. ἰξαλῆ. ⊛ **ἴττιον**· οὐσία (Elean), Id. **ἴττον**· ἕν (Cret.), Id. **ἴττυγα**· ἐκπληκτικά A.*Fr.*427 (ap. Hsch.).

**ἴττω**, Boeot. for ἴστω, 3 sg. imper. of οἶδα, esp. in phrase ἴττω Ζεύς Zeus *be witness!* says Cebes the Theban in Pl.*Phd.*62a; Θήβαθεν ἴττω Δεύς, and ἴττω Ἡρακλῆς, says the Boeotian in Ar.*Ach.*911, 860, cf. Pl.*Ep.*345a.

⊛ **Ἴτῠλος** [ῐ], ὁ, *Itylus*, son of Zethus and Aëdon, Od.19.522, Pherecyd.124 J.: expld. as, = μόνος, ὀρφανός, νέος, ἁπαλός by Hsch.

**ἴτυξ**, a bird, Phot., Suid.; cf. ἴδυξ.

⊛ **ἴτῠς** [ῐ], υος, ἡ, in Hom. (only in Il.) always of the *felloe* of a wheel, ὄφρα ἴτυν κάμψῃ Il.4.486 (made of poplar), cf. 5.724, *PMasp.*303.14 (vi A.D.); *outer edge* or *rim* of a shield, Hes.*Sc.*314, Hdt.7.89: hence, *the round shield* itself, Tyrt.15.3, E.*Ion* 210 (lyr.), *Tr.*1197, X.*An.*4.7.12; ἴ. βλεφάρων *arch* of the eyebrows, *Anacreont.*15.17; ἀγκίστρων ἴ. *AP*6.28 (Jul.), cf. Opp.*H.*5.138; ἴ. τῆς πλευρᾶς *border* of rib, Gal.2.681; *rim* of joint-socket, Id.*UP*2.17; *guard* of trepan, Id.10.448. (Aeol. ϝίτυς Ter.Maur.658.)

**Ἴτυς**, υος, ὁ, *Itys*, son of Tereus and Procne, A.*Ag.*1144 (lyr.), Ar.*Av.*212, etc. [ῐτῠ-, but ἃ Ἴτῠν αἰὲν Ἴτῡν ὀλοφύρεται S.*El.*148 (lyr.), cf. Ar. l. c.]

**ἴτω** [ῐ], 3 sg. imper. from εἶμι (*ibo*); in Trag. almost an exclam., *go to!* S.*Ph.*120; *well, well!* E.*Med.*798.

**Ἴτων** [ῐ], ὁ, St.Byz., and **Ἴτωνος**, ὁ, Str.9.5.8, a town in Thessaly:—hence ⊛ **Ἰτωνία**, ἡ, title of Athena who was worshipped there, Hecat. 2 J., Paus.1.13.3, 10.1.10; χρυσαιγίδος Ἰτωνίας ναός B.*Fr.*11.2; also at Coronea, Plb.4.25.2, 25.3.2, Str.9.2.29, Paus.9.33.1; at Athens, *IG* I$^{2}$.310.217; at Amorgos, ib.12(7).33 (ii B.C.):—also **Ἰτωνιάς**, ἡ, Call.*Cer.*75, *AP*9.743 (Theodorid.): **Ἰτωνίς**, ἡ, A.R.1.551, *AP*6.130 (⟨Leon.⟩).

**Ἰτώνιος**, ὁ (sc. μήν), name of month in Thessaly, *IG*9(2).259.5, al.: **Ἰτώνια**, τά, festival of Athena Itonia, ib.12(7).22, al. (Amorgos), cf. Polyaen.2.54.

**ἰῦ**, exclam. of surprise, Hdn.Gr.1.506.

**Ἰυγγίης**, ὁ, epith. of Dionysus, Hsch.

**ἰυγγικός**, ή, όν, (ἴυγξ) *of the* ἴυγγες (cf. ἴυγξ 3), φύσις Dam.*Pr.*112, 119.

⊛ **Ἰύγγιος**, ὁ (sc. μήν), name of month in Thessaly, *IG*9(2).258.5 (cf. p.xii); cf. Ἰυγγίης.

**ἰυγγοδρομέω**, = βοηδρομέω, βοηθέω, (Boeot.) Hsch. (leg. ἰυγο-).

**ἰυγή**, ἡ, = ἰυγμός, *howling, shrieking*, as of men in pain, Orac.ap. Hdt.9.43, S.*Ph.*752; = γυναικῶν οἰμωγαί *AB*267; but also of the *shout* of heralds, Tim.*Pers.*233; the *hissing* of snakes, Nic.*Th.*400, Opp.*H.*1.565. [ῑῠ- Orac.ap.Hdt. l. c., Nic.; ῐῠ- in S. l. c.]

**ἰυγμός**, ὁ, (ἰύζω) *shout of joy*, Il.18.572; also, *a cry of pain, shriek*, A.*Ch.*26 (lyr.), E.*Heracl.*126. [ῑ in Il.; ῐ in Trag.]

**ἴυγξ**, ἴυγγος, ἡ, (ἰύζω, cf. Dam.*Pr.*213), *wryneck, Iynx torquilla*, Arist.*HA*504$^{a}$12, *PA*695$^{a}$23, Ael.*NA*6.19; used as a charm to recover unfaithful lovers, being bound to a revolving wheel, ἴ. τετράκναμος Pi.*P.*4.214, cf. *AP*5.204; ἕλκειν ἴυγγα ἐπί τινι X.*Mem.*3.11.18; ἴ. ἕλκε τὺ τῆνον ἐμὸν ποτὶ δῶμα Theoc.2.17: metaph., ἕλκομαι ἴυγγι ἦτορ *as by the magic wheel*, Pi.*N.*4.35; ὥσπερ ἀπὸ ἴυγγος τῷ κάλλει ἑλκόμενος Luc.*Dom.*13. 2. metaph., *spell, charm*, τῇ σῇ ληφθέντες ἴυγγι Ar.*Lys.*1110, cf. S.*Fr.*474 (prob. cj.), Lyc.310, D.L.6.76, Plu.2.1093d (prob. cj. in 568a), Philostr.*VA*8.7 (pl.), Hld.8.5; *passionate yearning for*, ἀγαθῶν ἑτάρων A.*Pers.*989. 3. in pl., name of certain 'Chaldaic' divinities, Procl.*in R.*2.213 K., *in Cra.*p.33 P., Dam.*Pr.*111, al.: in sg., ἡ πρώτη ἴ. ib.217, cf. 213. 4. = σῦριγξ μονοκάλαμος, *EM*480.1. [ῑ Ep. and Pi.; ῐ Att.]

**ἰύζω**, aor. ἴυξα Pi.*P.*4.237:—*shout, yell*, in order to scare beasts, πολλὰ μάλ' ἰύζουσιν Il.17.66; οἱ δ' ἰύζοντες ἕποντο Od.15.162; later, *yell* from grief or pain, *cry out*, ἴυξεν ἀφωνήτῳ ἄχει Pi. l. c.; used by A. in lyr., only in imper., ἴυζ' ἄποτμον βοάν *Pers.*281, cf. 1042, *Supp.*808, 872; part., ἰύζων S.*Tr.*787; ἰύζων ἀν' ὄρος Call.*Fr.*512 (perh. here = *piping*, cf. sq.); of bees, *buzz*, Q.S.1.440. (From the Interjection ἰῦ, q. v. (from ἰού acc. to *EM*480.6): ϝι-, cf. ἀβίυκτος, ἐκβιούζει.) [ῑ Ep. and Pi.; ῐ in S.*Tr.*787, and prob. in A.]

**ἰυκτής** [ῑ], οῦ, ὁ, (ἰύζω) *one who shouts* or *yells*: *singer, piper*, Theoc.8.30, in poet. form ἰυκτά [ᾰ].

**ἴυρκες**· αἶγες ἀγρίαι, ὑστριχίδες, Hsch. **ἰυχμός**, ὁ, = ἰυγμός, Id. **ιφειομαχω**, = *ario*, *Gloss.* (dub., fort. κριομαχῶ, = *arieto*).

**Ἰφθῖμις**, ὁ, Egyptian deity (prob. Nefertem) identified with Prometheus, *PHib.*1.27.86 (iii B.C.).

⊛ **ἴφθῑμος**, η, ον, also ος, ον (v. infr.), *stout, strong*, of bodily strength, ὤμοις ἰ. Il.18.204; κρατὶ ἐπ' ἰ. 3.336; ἰ. ποταμῶν 17.749; βοῶν ἴ. κάρηνα 23.260; of heroes, ἴ. ψυχαί, κεφαλαί, 1.3, 11.55; of Hades, Od.10.534; also, of women, *comely, stately*, ἰ. βασίλεια 16.332; ἄλοχος Il.5.415, Theoc.17.128; παράκοιτις Od.23.92, etc.; θυγάτηρ 15.364; Πηρώ 11.287: later, generally, *strong, powerful*, ἰφθίμης φιλότητος D.P.655:—Hom. uses ἰφθίμη of women; but ἴφθιμοι ψυχαί, κεφαλαί, speaking of men. (No ϝ-; prob. not cogn. with ἴς, ἶφι.)

⊛ **ἶφι** (A) (instrum. of ἴς, q. v.), Ep. Adv. *by force* or *might*, freq. in Hom., but only with four Verbs, ἶ. ἀνάσσειν Il.1.38, etc.; ἶ. μάχεσθαι 1.151; ἶ. δαμῆναι 19.417, Od.18.156; βοὸς ἶ. κταμένοιο Il.3.375; later ἶ. βιησάμενος Euph.90, etc.—Freq. in prop. names, e. g. Ἰφιάνασσα, Ἰφιγένεια, Ἰφιγόνη, Ἰφιδάμας, Ἴφικλος, ϝιφιάδας, etc.

**ἶφι** (B), an Egyptian measure, prob. = $\frac{1}{4}$ and $\frac{1}{5}$ artaba, *PMasp.*138, 139, al. (vi A.D.), *PLond.*5.1687.11 (vi A.D.):—hence **ἴφιον** μέτρον *PMasp.*308.3 (vi A.D.): written οἶφιν Hsch.

**ἰφῐ-γένειᾰ** [ῑφ], ἡ, *strong-born, mighty*, epith. of Artemis, Paus.2.35.1, Hsch. II. pr. n., *Iphigeneia*, Agamemnon's daughter, the Homeric Ἰφιάνασσα (but distd. by S.*El.*158), Stesich.27, etc.; also called Ἰφιγόνη, E.*El.*1023; Ἶφις Lyc.324. [-ειᾱ A.*Ag.*1526 (lyr.).] **-γένητος**, ον, *produced by might*, πῦρ Orph.*Fr.*247.28.

**ἴφικλος**· δυσχερής, Hsch.: as pr. n., Il.2.705, al.:—hence Adj., Ἰφίκλειος, α, ον, σφυρόν Call.*Aet.*3.1.46.

**Ἰφικρᾰτίδες**, αἱ, a kind of *shoes*, called from the Athen. general Iphicrates, D.S.15.44, Alciphr.3.57, Dam.*Isid.*89.

**ἰφίν**· καλήν, Hsch. **ἰφιντάν**· κρύφα λαλοῦσαν, αἰνιγματωδῶς, Id.

**ἴφιος** [ῑφ], α, ον, Ep. Adj., freq. in Hom., but only in phrase ἴ. μῆλα *fat, goodly* sheep, Il.5.556, al., cf. D.P.753, etc.

**ἶφις**· ταχύς, Hsch. **ἰφίτην**· ἁγνίτην, Id. **ἴφλημα**· τραῦμα, Id. (i.e. ἴφλ-, cf. σίφλωμα).

⊛ **ἶφυον** [ῑ], τό, *spike-lavender, Lavandula Spica*, Ar.*Th.*910 (pl.), *Fr.*560 (pl.), Epich.161, Thphr.*HP*6.6.11, 6.8.3.

⊛ **ἰχαίνω** [ῑ], = sq., ὅσσα δ' ἐμεῖο σέθεν παρὰ θυμὸς ἀκοῦσαι ἰχαίνει Call.*Aet.*1.1.22, cf. *EM*568.7.

**ἰχᾰνάω** [ῑ], *crave, yearn*, v.l. for ἰσχ- in Il.23.300, Od 8.288; τυροῦ ἀλώπηξ ἰχανῶσα Babr.77.2:—Med., ἰχανᾶσθ' ἐπαυρέσθαι Herod.7.26, cf. Hsch., *EM*478.44. (Cf. sq.; **Ἴχανα**, name of a town in Sicily, is derived from the root by St.Byz.: prob. cogn. with ἀχήν, ἠχήν; Avest. *āzi-* 'craving', Skt. *īhate* 'crave'.)

**ἶχαρ** (**ἴχαρ** codd.), τό, *vehement desire*, dub. l. in A.*Supp.*850 (lyr.), cf. Sch.

**ἴχθον**· ἄστρον, ἐγχειράδιον, ξυλοφάνιον, Hsch.

⊛ **ἰχθύ-α** [ῠ], Ion. -ύη, ἡ, (ἰχθῦς) *dried skin of the fish* ῥίνη, like our *shagreen*, Hp.*Foet.Exsect.*1, Archig.ap.Gal.12.406; of *fish-skin* in general, Ruf.ap.Orib.4.2.16. II. *pot*, perh. for pickled fish, *CIG* 8345c (Nola, vase). III. *fishing, fishery*, *BGU*1123.9 (i A.D.), *PSI*3.160.8 (ii A.D.). IV. ταριχηρὰ ἰ. pickled *fish*, *PLond.*3.856.20 (i A.D.). **-ᾰγωγός**, v. ἰχθυόνερ. **-άζομαι**, = ἰχθυάω, *AP*7.693 (Apollonid.). ⊛ **-ᾰκός**, ή, όν, = ἰχθυϊκός, ζῴδια, *Cat.Cod.Astr.*1.160. II. **-ᾰκὴ** πύλη, ἡ, *fish*-gate, Aq., Sm., Thd.*Ze.*1.10: cf. ἰχθυϊκός. **-άω**, *fish, angle*, mostly in Ep. pres. and impf., ἰχθυάασκον γναμπτοῖς ἀγκίστροισιν Od.4.368: c. acc., *fish for*, αὐτοῦ δ' ἰχθυάᾳ.. δελφῖνας 12.95, cf. Opp.*H.*1.426:—Med., Lyc.46. II. *sport* (like fish), δελφῖνες.. ἐθύνεον ἰχθυάοντες Hes.*Sc.*210. III. Pass., *to be made of fish*, ἰχθυώμενος ἄρτος (vulg. ἄργος) Horap.1.14.

**ἰχθῠβολ-εύς**, έως, ὁ, = ἰχθυβόλος 2, Nic.*Th.*793, Call.*Del.*15, *AP*7.504 (Leon.), 10.9, cf. Ps.-Hes.ap.Ath.3.116a. ⊛ **-έω**, *strike, harpoon fish*, *AP*7.381 (Etrusc.), 635 (Antiphil.). ⊛ **-ος**, ον, (parox.) *striking fish, catching fish*, ἰ. μηχανή of the trident, A.*Th.*132 (lyr.); αἴθυιαι *AP*6.23. 2. Subst., *fisher, angler*, ib.7.295 (Leon.), 9.227 (Bianor). II. Pass., (proparox.) ἰ. θήρα a spoil *of speared fish*, ib.6.24; ἰ. δεῖπνα Opp.*H.*3.18.

**ἰχθῠ-βόρος**, ον, *fish-eating*, λαρίδες *AP*7.652 (Leon.). ⊛ **-βοτος**, ον, *fed on by fish*, Opp.*H.*2.1, Epic.*Oxy.*213$^{v}$.15. **-γόνος**, ον, *producing fish*, Nonn.*D.*26.275.

⊛ **ἰχθύδιον**, τό, Dim. of ἰχθύς, *little fish*, freq. in Com. (v. infr.), Chrysipp.*Stoic.*2.208, *PFlor.*119.7 (iii A.D.), Jul.*Mis.*350b, etc. [ῡ, Ar.*Fr.*387.8, Theopomp.Com.62.3, Anaxil.19, Cratin.Jun.13, *POxy.*784 (i B.C.), etc.; but ῠ in dact., *AP*11.405 (Lucill.), Archestr.*Fr.*45.18.]

**ἰχθῠ-δόκος**, ον, (δέχομαι) *holding fish*, σπυρίδες *AP*6.4 (Leon.). **-εῖον**, τό, *fish-market*, dub. in *IG*12(2).646$^{a}$.49 (Nesos). **-η**, ἡ,

Ion. for ἰχθύα. -ήματα, τά, (ἰχθύα) *fish-scales*: hence, *scrapings, shavings*, λωτοῦ Hp.*Ulc.*13, al.: sg. only, ib.21. -ηρός, ά, όν, (ἰχθῦς) *fishy, scaly*, i. e. *foul, dirty*, πινακίσκοι Ar.*Pl.*814, *Fr.*532; ἔλαιον Ph. *Bel.*90.19; ζωμός Luc.*Lex.*5; οὐκ ἔστιν ἰχθυηρόν nothing *of the fish kind*, Diph.32.21; ἡ πύλη ἡ ἰ. the *fish-gate*, Lxx *Ne.*3.3:—Subst., **ἰχθυηρά**, ἡ, *tax on fish*, *UPZ*110.98 (ii B. C.), *PFay.*42(a)ᵛ2 (ii A. D.). -ία, ἡ, *fishing*, Procl.*Vit.Hom.*p.25 W. -ικός, ή, όν, = ἰχθυηρός, πύλη Lxx 2*Ch.*33.14; ζῴδια Ptol.*Tetr.*152:—Subst., -ική, ἡ, *fishery toll*, *Inscr.Magn.*116.42, *OGI*496.9 (Ephesus): -ικά, τά, *Ostr.*343 (iii B. C.):—also -ινος, η, ον, Ael.*NA*17.32. -κεντρον, τό, *trident*, Poll.10.133, Paus.Gr.*Fr.*216: **ἰχθυόκεντρον**, Hsch., Suid. -μέδων, οντος, ὁ, *king of fish*, Marc.Sid.54. -νόμος, ον, *ruling fish*, Opp.*H.*1.643.

**ἰχθυο-βολεύς**, -βόλος, = ἰχθυβ-, Phot., Eust.191.33. -βρωτος, ον, *eaten by fish*, Plu.2.668a, *SIG*997.7 (Smyrna). -ειδής, ές, *fish-like*, λεπίς Hdt.7.61. -εις, εσσα, εν, *full of fish, fishy*, πόντος, Ἑλλήσποντος, Il.9.4, 360; ἰ. κέλευθα, i. e. the sea, Od.3.177; μυχὸς ἰ., of the Bosporus, Ar.*Th.*324; *fish-like*, δέμας Opp.*H.*3.548. II. *consisting of fish*, θήρη ib.1.666; βόλος *AP*6.223 (Antip.). -θήρα, = κυκλάμινος, Ps.-Dsc.2.164. -θήρας, ου, ὁ, *fisherman*, Sch.Lyc.1200: also -θηρευτής, οῦ, ὁ, Man.4.243: -θηρητήρ, ῆρος, ὁ, *AP*7.702 (Apollonid.). -θηρία, ἡ, *fishing*, Eust.1165.3: ἡ ἰχθυοθηρική (sc. τέχνη) Poll.1.97. -κένταυρος, ὁ, ἡ, *half-man and half-fish*, of Triton, Tz. ad Lyc.34. -κολλα, ἡ, *fish-glue*, i. e. *isinglass*, Dsc.3.88, Gal.13.662, cf. Plin.*HN*32.84:—also -κολλον, τό, *Gloss.* -λογέω, *discourse of fish*, Ath.7.308d, 8.360d. -λύμης [λῡ], ου, ὁ, *plague of fish*, Com. epith. of a fish-eater, Ar.*Pax* 814. -μαντις, εως, ὁ, *one who prophesies by means of fish*, Ath.8.333d. -μετάβολος, ὁ, *fishmonger*, *PRyl.*196.7 (ii A. D.).

**ἰχθυόνερ**· ἰχθυαγωγοί, Hsch.

**ἰχθυοπράτης** [ᾰ], οῦ, ὁ, = -πώλης, *PLond.*1.113.5ᵇ4 (vi A. D.), etc.

**ἰχθυοπτρίς** (v.l. -οπτίς), ίδος, fem. Adj. *for broiling fish*, ἐσχάρα Poll.6.88, 10.95.

**ἰχθυο-πώλαινα**, irreg. fem. of -πώλης, Pherecr.64. -πωλέω, *sell fish*, Poll.7.26. -πώλης, ου, ὁ, *fishmonger*, freq. in Com., Ar. *Fr.*387.10, Antiph.68.7, Alex.56.1; also in Pap., *BGU*330.10, etc.: —fem. -πωλις ἀγορά *fish*-market, Plu.2.849e, Maiuri *Nuova Silloge* 440 (Cos). -πωλία, ἡ, *fishmongering*, Ath.7.276f, Plu.2.668a (nisi leg. τὰ ἰχθυοπώλια). -πώλιον, τό, *fish-market*, *IPE*1².32 *B*4 (Olbia), *PFlor.*119.9 (iii A. D.), Sch.Ar.*Ra.*1068: -πωλεῖον, Hsch. -ρροος, ον, contr. -ρους, ουν, (ῥέω) *swarming with fish*, ποταμός Timocl.15.1. -τροφεῖον, τό, *fish-pond*, Moschio ap.Ath.5.208a, D.S.11.25: -τρόφιον, τό, *SIG*997.13 (Smyrna). -τροφικός, ή, όν, *of* or *for keeping fish*, *Gp.*20.1 tit. -τρόφος, ον, *feeding fish*: *full of fish*, διαδρομαί Plu.*Luc.*39.

**ἰχθυουλκός**, ὁ, (ἕλκω) *angler*, Phot., Suid.:—written -ολκός in Hsch.

**ἰχθυοφᾰγ-έω**, *feed on fish*, Arist.*HA*616ᵃ32, Str.11.8.7. -ία, ἡ, *fish diet*, *PMag.Berol.*1.290, Eust.135.19. -ος, ον, *eating fish*, Clearch.74; ἔθνη Porph.*Abst.*1.13; οἱ Ἰ. ἄνδρες the *Fish-eaters*, a tribe on the Arabian Gulf, Hdt.3.19, cf. Str.16.4.4, Paus.1.33.4; another on the Persian Gulf, Str.15.2.1.

**ἰχθυοφορ-έω**, *convey fish*, εἰς Ἀρκαδίαν, Ἀρχ.Ἐφ.1918.168 (Epid.). II. *produce fish*, *EM*117.26. -ος, ον, *producing fish*, κρηνῖδες Ctes.*Fr.*57.10. 2. *carrying fish*, πλοῖα Sm.*Jb.*40.26(31): Subst. -φόρος, ὁ, Ἀρχ.Ἐφ.1918.168 (Epid.).

**ἰχθυ-πᾰγής**, ές, *piercing fish*, ἀγκίστρων στόματα *AP*6.27 (Theaet.). -πόρος, ὁ, (πείρω) *harpoon*, *Inscr.Delos* 354.60 (iii B. C.).

**ἰχθῦς** (so Hdn.Gr.2.936, -ῦς and -ύς freq. in codd.), ύος, ὁ, acc. ἰχθύν Pi.*Fr.*306, cf. Hdn.Gr.1.416, Choerob. *in Theod.*1.383, in late Poets also ἰχθύα *AP*9.227 (Bianor), Theoc.21.45: voc. ἰχθύ Erinn. 1, Crates Com.14: pl. ἰχθύες Pl.*Phd.*109e, etc., ἰχθῦς Alex.261.9, acc. ἰχθύας, contr. ἰχθῦς Od.5.53, both forms being used in Com., -ῦς Ar.*Ra.*1068, Archipp.29, -ύας Antiph.68.12, Ephipp.21; codd. vary in Arist.*HA*564ᵇ19, *PA*644ᵃ21, D.S.5.3, Str.8.3.19, etc.; -ῦς *SIG*997.1 (Smyrna, perh. i B. C.); -ύας *BGU*1123.9 (Aug.), etc.: dual ἰχθύ Antiph.194.15:—*fish*, ὠμηστής Il.24.82, cf. 21.122, al., cf. Hes.*Op.*277, Hdt.2.93, S.*Aj.*1297, etc.: prov., ἀφωνότερος τῶν ἰχθύων Luc.*Gall.*1, cf. S.E.*M.*2.18: metaph., of *a stupid fellow*, Plu.2.975b. II. in pl., οἱ ἰχθύες *the fish-market* at Athens, παρὰ τοὺς ἰχθῦς Ar.*Ra.*1068; ἐν τοῖς ἰχθύσι Id.*V.*789, Antiph.125.1. III. pl., the constellation *Pisces*, Eudox.ap.Hipparch.1.2.3; ἰ. Διός Porph. *Antr.*22. (ἰχθύς Att. acc. to Gell.2.3.2.) [ῡ in disyll. cases, nom. -ῦς Il.21.127, Damox.2.20, Archestr.*Fr.*52 (ἰχθῦς οὖσα shd. be read for ἰχθὺς ἐοῦσα in Matro *Conv.*35), acc. -ῦν Pherecr.120, Antiph.166.7, Archestr.*Fr.*28, but -ῠν Theoc.21.49, and apptly. Pi. l. c.: ῠ in trisyll. cases and in all compds.] (Cf. Lith. *žuvìs*, Arm. *jukn*, 'fish'.)

**ἰχθυσιληϊστήρ**, ῆρος, ὁ, *a stealer of fish*, *AP*7.295 (Leon.).

**ἰχθυ-στεφής**, ές, *fish crowned*, κόλποι Ἀμφιτρίτας Tim.*Pers.*38. -φάγος [ῠ, ᾰ], ον, = ἰχθυοφάγος, *AP*9.83 (Phil.). -φόνος, ον, *killing fish*, Opp.*C.*2.444. -ώδης, ες, = ἰχθυοειδής, Arist.*PA*697ᵇ5, al. Adv. -δῶς Id.*HA*536ᵃ9. 2. *full of fish*, λίμνη Hdt.7.109, Arr. *Ind.*41.1. II. (ὄδ-ωδα) *fishy, smelling* or *tasting of fish*, ἐρυγή Aret.*SD*1.5, Gal.7.76; πρόβατα Philostr.*VA*3.55, cf. Arr.*Ind.*26.7.

**ἰχλα**· κίχλα, Hsch. **ἰχματα**· ἴχνια, Id. (Perh. for ἴθματα.)

**Ἰχν-αῖος**, α, ον, *of Ichnae in Thessaly*, of Themis, h.*Ap.*94; of Nemesis, *AP*9.405 (Diod.), Lyc.129: Ἴχναι (in Thessaly), ὅπου ἡ Θέμις Ἰ. τιμᾶται Str.9.5.14. -άομαι, = ἰχνεύω, Hsch., Suid. -εία, ἡ, *casting about for the scent*, of hounds, X.*Cyn.*3.7 (pl.). -ελάτης, v. ἰχνηλάτης. -ευμα, ατος, τό, *track*, Poll. 5.11. -εύμων, ονος, ὁ, *tracker*: hence, 1. an Egyptian animal of the weasel-kind, *which hunts out* crocodile's eggs (asp's eggs, Ael.*NA*6.38), *Herpestes ichneumon*, Arist.*HA*612ᵃ16, Eub.107.12, Nic.*Th.*190, Plu.2.966d, *PLond.*3.904 (ii A. D.); cf. ἰχνευτής II. 2. a small kind of wasp, *that hunts* spiders, *Pelopaeus spirifex*, Arist.*HA*552ᵇ26, 609ᵃ5, cf. Plin.*HN*10.204. 3. a bird, Ant.Lib. 14. -ευσις, εως, ἡ, *tracking*, X.*Cyn.*3.4, 10.5, Poll.5.11. II. *method of investigation*, cj. in Epicur.*Ep.*2 p.42 U. -εύτειρα, ἡ, fem. of ἰχνευτήρ, τέχνα *IG*9(1).880.9 (Corc.). -ευτέος, α, ον, *to be searched out*, δικαιοσύνη Philostr.*VA*6.21. -ευτήρ, ῆρος, ὁ, = sq., Opp.*C.*1.76, 450, 468; as Adj., ἰ. ταρσός Nonn.*D.*46.115. -ευτής, οῦ, ὁ, *tracker, hunter*, Poll.5.10; of dogs which hunt by scent, ib.17: metaph., Κύπριδος ἰχνευτὰς ἀργυρέους σκύλακας, of money given to a ἑταίρα, *AP*5.15 (Marc. Arg.): Ἰχνευταί, οἱ, title of a satyric play by Sophocles (cf. v. 298). 2. *detective* who *traces* missing persons, *PRyl.*188.22 (ii A. D.). II. = ἰχνεύμων 1, Hdt.2.67, Nic.*Th.*195. -ευτικός, ή, όν, *good at tracking*, κύων Ael.*NA*6.59, Arr. *Epict.*1.2.34, Ph.2.38. -εύω, *track out, hunt after*, S.*Aj.*20, *OT* 221, 476 (lyr.); ἰ. θῆρας κυσίν E.*Cyc.*130; κύνες ἰχνεύουσαι *hunting by scent*, Pl.*Lg.*654e: metaph., κατὰ σοῦ τὴν ψῆφον ἰ. *seeking for* a vote of condemnation, Ar.*Eq.*808; ἰ. τὰ λεχθέντα Pl.*Prm.*128c; τὴν τοῦ καλοῦ φύσιν Id.*R.*401c; [σοφίαν] Lxx *Si.*51.15; ἰχνεύεις.. τίς εἰμ' ἐγώ..; *Epigr.Gr.*227 (Teos); *follow on the track of, emulate*, ματραδελφεούς Pi.*P.*8.35. 2. ἰ. ὄρη *to hunt* the mountains, X.*Cyn.*4.9.

**ἰχνηλ-ᾰσία**, ἡ, (ἐλαύνω) *tracking out, search*, Them.*Or.*13.165d. -ατέω, *track out*, τἀληθὲς λόγῳ Ph.1.12, cf. 2.475, al. -άτης [ᾰ], ου, ὁ, *tracker*, [ἀληθείας] Plu.2.762b:—poet. **ἰχνελάτης** *AP*6.183 (Zos.), *APl.*4.289. -ατία or -εία, ἡ, = ff. ll. for -ηλασία in Poll. 5.11. -ατικός, ή, όν, = ἰχνευτικός, Sch.S.*Aj.*8.

**ἴχνιον**, τό (Dim. of ἴχνος only in form, cf. Hdn.Gr.2.903, but written ἰχνίον by Eust.233.44), *track, footprint*, ἴχνι' ἐρευνῶντες κύνες ἤισαν Od.19.436; μετ' ἴχνια βαῖνε θεοῖο followed on her *track*, 5.193; μετ' ἀνέρος ἴχνι' ἐρευνῶν Il.18.321; κατ' ἴχνιά τινος ἐφέπεσθαι A.R.1.575; ἴχνια ἵππων X.*An.*1.6.1 (v.l. ἴχνη): less freq. in sg., τὸ ἴ. μοῦνον λέλειπται τῶν ποδῶν Democr.228; ἴ. ὀξέος ἵππου Call.*Aet.*3.1.86; ἕπεσθαί τινι κατ' ἴχνιον Q.S.8.361; ἴ. ἑδράσασθαι to plant one's *step*, *AP*6.70 (Maced.). 2. metaph., *trace, remnant*, προτέρης ἀγλαΐης ib.58 (Isid.).

**ἰχνιπτος**· ὅπου οἱ λίθοι τρίβονται, ἀκόνη, Hsch.

**ἰχνο-βάτης** [ᾰ], ου, ὁ, *going on the track*, name of a hound, Ov.*Met.* 3.207. -βλᾰβής, ές, *hurt in the foot*, Man.4.500. -γρᾰφία, ἡ, *tracing out*: *ground-plan*, Vitr.1.2.2. -πέδη, ἡ, a kind of *fetter* or *trap*, *AP*6.109 (Antip.), 7.626. -ποιέω, *track out*, ταῖς ῥισὶν ἰ. τὰ θηρία *EM*395.39.

**ἴχνος**, εος, τό, *track, footstep*, Od.17.317, Hes.*Op.*680, Hdt.4.82; of the *spoor* of game, X.*Cyn.*6.15, etc.: metaph., *track, trace*, κατ' ἴχνος πλατᾶν ἄφαντον A.*Ag.*695 (lyr.); ἐς ταὐτὸν ἐλθὼν.. λόγων ἴ. Id.*Pr.*845; ἴ. κακῶν ῥινηλατούσῃ Id.*Ag.*1184; ἴ. παλαιᾶς δυστέκμαρτον αἰτίας S. *OT*109; ἴ. τειχέων E.*Hel.*108; ἴχνη τῶν πληγῶν Pl.*Grg.*524c; τὰ τῶν κονδύλων ἴ. Aeschin.3.212: with neg., not *a trace*, μαζῶν οὐδὲ ἴχνη Aret.*SD*1.8; ἴ. ποδὸς θεῖναι, Lat. *vestigia ponere*, E.*IT*752, cf. *Or.*234; θέσθαι *AP*7.464 (Antip.); λεπτὸν ἴ. ἀρβύλης τίθετε step softly, E.*Or.*140 (lyr.); ἴ. ἐπαντέλλειν ποδός Id.*Ph.*105 (lyr.); ἴ. ἐρείδειν *AP*5.300 (Paul. Sil.); ἐν ἴχνεσί τινος πόδα νέμειν (metaph.) Pi.*N.*6.15; ἰχνῶν τινος ἔχεσθαι Lib.*Or.*64.4; τοῖς στοιχοῦσι τοῖς ἴχνεσι τῆς πίστεως *Ep.Rom.*4.12; κατ' ἴχνος ᾄσσειν, κατ' ἴχνη διώκειν, S.*Aj.*32, Pl.*R.*410b, cf. E.*Hec.*1059 (lyr.); εἰς ἴχνος τινὸς ἰέναι Pl.*Ep.*330e; ἴ. μετιέναι, μετελθεῖν, Id.*Phdr.*276d, *Tht.*187e; ἴχνους προσάπτεσθαι hit upon a *trail*, Id.*Plt.*290d; τοῖς ἀρχαίοις ἴ. ἐς τὰ θεμέλια χρωμένους Jul.*Or.*2.66b; ἴχνη ὑποψίας εἴς τινα φέρει Antipho 2.3.10; μήτ' ἴ. μήτ' αἴθυγμα.. παραδιδόντων Phld.*Sign.*29, cf. *Rh.*1.91 S. 2. poet., *foot*, E.*Ba.*1134, Herod.7.20. 3. *hard sole of the foot*, Lxx *De.*11.24, al., Gal.10.876, Orib.47.9.7; *sole of a shoe*, Hp.*Art.*62, Arr.*Ind.*16.5; *sandal*, *POxy.*1449.51 (pl., iii A. D.). 4. τὰ ἴ. τῶν χειρῶν the *palms* of the hands, Lxx 1*Ki.*5.4. 5. ἴ. ἀνθρώπινον, as a measure of length, Ruf.*Anat.*31. 6. *track, route* in the desert, *PRyl.*197.8 (ii A. D.). 7. pl., *representations of footprints* as votive offerings indicating the presence of a God, ἀνέθηκαν.. κατὰ τὴν τοῦ θεοῦ ἐνέργιαν ἴχνη αὐτοῦ χρύσεα τέσσερα *BCH*51.106 (Panamara), etc.

**ἰχνοσκοπ-έω**, *look at the track* or *traces*, ἐν στίβοισι τοῖς ἐμοῖς A.*Ch.*227, cf. S.*Ichn.*7; ἰ. καὶ στιβεύειν τὸ μέλλον Plu.2.399a. -ία, ἡ, *looking at the tracks*, Plu.2.917f.

**ἰχώρ** [ῑ], ῶρος, ὁ, *ichor, the juice*, not blood, that flows in the veins of gods, Il.5.340, etc.: Ep. acc. ἰχῶ ib.416: in pl., of the Giants, Str. 6.3.5; later simply, *blood*, A.*Ag.*1480 (anap.). II. *the watery part* of animal juices, *serum* (cf. Gal.15.345), of the blood, Hp.*Cord.*11, Pl.*Ti.*83c, Arist.*HA*521ᵇ2 (also in pl., v.l. in 521ᵃ18), *PA*651ᵃ18; of gall, χολώδεας ἰχῶρας Hp.*Acut.*(*Sp.*)1; of milk, *whey*, Arist. *HA*521ᵇ27; *gravy* of underdone meat, Archestr.*Fr.*57.6; *juice* of burning logs, Dsc.1.119, *Eup.*1.120. 2. *serous* or *sero-purulent discharge*, Hp.*VC*19, Arist.*HA*630ᵃ6 (pl.), Gal.10.184, etc.; ἰχῶρες ὑδαρεῖς ὕπωχροι, from women in childbirth, Arist.*HA*586ᵇ32; of the *putrefied blood* of a viper, Id.*Mir.*845ᵃ8; of *naphtha* (prob.), regarded in legend as due to the putrefaction of Giants' corpses, ib.838ᵃ29.

**ἰχωρο-ειδής** [ῐ], ές, *serous*, αἷμα Hp.*Nat.Hom.*12, Arist.*HA*521ᵃ13, Alex.Trall.12. -ρροέω, (ῥέω) *run with serous matter*, Hp.

Coac.501, Erot. s.v. δακρυῶδες ἕλκος :—later **ἰχωρροέω**, ὦτα ἰχωρροοῦντα Dsc.3.23, cf. Archig.ap.Orib.46.26.2.

**ἰχωρώδης** [ῑ], ες, = ἰχωροειδής, Hp.*Morb.*3.16, v.l. in Arist.*HA*586ᵃ 29.

**ἴψ** (on the accent v. Hdn.Gr.1.404), ὁ, gen. ἰπός [ῐ], nom. pl. ἶπες : (ἴπτομαι):—*wood-worm,* Od.21.395, Thphr.*HP*8.10.5; found in vines, Id.*CP*3.22.5, *Lap.*49, Str.13.1.64. (Cf. ἴξ.)

**ἴψαο**, v. ἴπτομαι.

**ἴψ-ηλος**, α, ον, Aeol. for ὑψηλός, *Lyr.Adesp.*60. **-οθεν**, Aeol. for ὑψόθεν, Jo.Gramm.*Comp.*3.15. **-οι**, Aeol. for ὑψοῦ, Sapph.91.

**ἴψον** (ἴπτομαι)· τὸ δεσμωτήριον, Hsch.

**ἴψος** (A) or **ἰψός**, ὁ, *cork-oak, Quercus Suber* (?), Thphr.*HP*3. 4.2. 2. at Thurii, = κισσός, Hsch.

**ἴψος** (B), τό, Aeol. for ὕψος, Hdn.Gr.2.928; cf. ἴψοι.

**ἴω**, subj. of εἶμι (*ibo*). **ἰῶ**, contr. for ἰάου, imper. of ἰάομαι.

**ἰώ**, an exclam., chiefly in dramatic poetry (lyr.); freq. repeated twice, rarely three times, as A.*Supp.*125; esp. in invoking aid, ἰ. μάκαρες, ἰ. θεοί, Id.*Th.*96, S.*Ph.*736; ἰ. ἰ. Παιάν Id.*Tr.*222; ἰ. Βάκχαι E.*Ba.*578. 2. freq. also of grief or suffering, *oh!* ἰ. δύστανος S. *Ant.*850; ἰ. μοί μοι Id.*OC*199, etc.; ἰ. κακοπάρθενε Μοῖρα *AP*7.468 (Mel.); ἰ. Σπάρτα ib.434 (Diosc.): c. gen., ἰ., πάτερ, σοῦ τῶν τε.. τέκνων A.*Ag.*1305; ἰ. μοι πόνων E.*Ph.*1290; ἰ. ἰ. τραυμάτων Ar.*Ach.* 1205. 3. rarely in Prose, ἰ., φασί τινες, of an objector, Gal.*Thras.* 32. II. with other Interj., ἰ. ὢ ὤ S.*OC*224; ἒ ἒ ἰ. Id.*El.*840. [ῐ: yet sts. ῑ, in anap., A.*Ag.*1455, S.*El.*149, E.*Alc.*741.]

**Ἰώ** [ῑ], Ἰοῦς, ἡ, acc. Ἰοῦν Hdt.1.1; voc. Ἰοῖ A.*Pr.*635, etc.:—*Io,* daughter of Inachus. II. name of *the moon* at Argos, Eust.ad D.P.92.

**ἰωά** (A), = ἰώ, A.*Pers.*1070 (lyr.). **ἰωά** (B), ἡ, *smoke,* prob. in Call.*Fr.*1.40P.

**ἰώγα**, v. ἐγώ.

**ἰωγή**, ἡ, Ep. word, *shelter,* Βορέω ὑπ' ἰωγῇ under *shelter* from the north wind, Od.14.533.

**ἰώδης** [ῑ], ες, (ἰός) *like verdigris, green,* Hp.*Prog.*11, Dsc.5.79, Gal. 10.871; of bile, Id.18(1).107; κακόνοια.. τουτὶ τὸ ἰῶδες.. ἀφίησιν Plu.2.565c. 2. *rust-coloured, ferruginous,* Thphr.*Lap.*37, Call. Hist.4, Dsc.5.152. 3. *poisonous,* ὕδωρ Ath.2.42a, cf. Gal.11.327; ὀδόντες, of serpents, Philostr.Jun.*Im.*5: metaph., of persons, *virulent,* Ptol.*Tetr.*158. II. (ὄδ-ωδα) *acrid,* ὀξύτητες Hp.*VM*19; ἄσθμα Philum.*Ven.*36.3, etc.

**ἰωεῖ**· βέλει, Hsch.

**ἰωή**, ἡ, *any loud sound*: *shout,* or *cry* of men or women, περὶ φρένας ἤλυθ' ἰωή Il.10.139; ὦρτο δ' ἰ. λεπταλέη ὀδυρομένων A.R.3.708; ἰ. δενδρώδης (of Daphne) Nonn.*D.*15.300; *sound* of the lyre, περὶ δέ σφεας ἤλυθ' ἰωὴ φόρμιγγος Od.17.261; of the wind, ὑπὸ Ζεφύροιο ἰωῆς by *the roaring blast* of Zephyrus, Il.4.276, cf. 11.308; of fire, πυρὸς δηΐοιο ἰωήν 16.127; of footsteps, ποδῶν αἰπεῖα ἰ. Hes.*Th.*682; *clang* of arms, Coluth.56.—Ep. word, once in Trag., βοᾷ τηλωπὸν ἰωάν S.*Ph.*216 (lyr.).

**ἰωκή**, ἡ (for διωκή acc. to A.D.*Conj.*256.27, v. sq.), *rout, pursuit,* οὔτε βίας.. ὑπεδείδισαν οὔτε ἰωκάς Il.5.521: personified, with Ἔρις and Ἀλκή, 5.740:—metaplast. acc., πόνον αἰπὺν ἰῶκά τε δακρυόεσσαν 11.601.

**ϝιώκω**, = διώκω, *GDI*3153 (Corinthian vase).

**ἰωλία**, ἡ, (ἰά) = φήμη, δειλή, Hsch. **ἰῶλκα**, = αὔλακα, Id., Cyr.; cf. ὦλκα. **ἴωλον**· μέλαν, Hsch. **ἰών, ἰώνγα, ἰώνει**, Boeot. for ἐγώ, ἔγωγε, ἐγώνη, v. ἐγώ.

**Ἴων**, ωνος, ὁ, *Ion,* Hdt.7.94, 8.44, E.*Ion* 74, etc.: **Ἴωνες**, οἱ, *the Ionians,* v. Ἰάονες; of those who spoke the Ionic dialect, A.D.*Pron.* 4.22, al.: **Ἰωνία**, ἡ, *their country,* A.*Pers.*771.

**ἰωνᾶς**· περιστερά, Hsch.

**ἰωνιά**, ᾶς, ἡ, (ἴον) *violet-bed,* Ar.*Pax* 577; ἰ. λευκή *gilliflower, Matthiola incana,* Thphr.*HP*6.8.5; ἰ. μέλαινα *violet, Viola odorata,* ib. 6.6.2. II. *ground-pine, Ajuga Chamaepitys,* Apollod.ap.Ath.15. 681d, Dsc.3.158; ἰ. ἀγρία Sch.Nic.*Al.*55. III. ἐς ἰωνιάν· ἐς κοπρῶνα, Hsch.

**Ἰωνίζω**, *speak Ionic,* A.D.*Adv.*162.7.

**Ἰωνικολόγος**, ὁ, *reciter of* Ἰωνικά, Ath.14.620e.

**Ἰωνικός**, ή, όν, *Ionic, Ionian*: -κοί, οἱ, = Ἴωνες, Philostr.*VS*1.21.5: -κόν (sc. ὑπόδημα), τό, a kind of *shoe,* Herod.7.59; esp. with the connotation, *effeminate,* Ar.*Pax* 46, Pl.Com.69.14, etc. Adv. -κῶς *in the Ionic fashion,* i.e. *softly, effeminately,* Ar.*Th.*163. 2. Ἰ. μέτρον, συζυγία, *Ionic,* defined in Heph.11, cf. D.H.*Comp.*4, etc.; πούς Heph.1.9, cf. Aristid.Quint.1.15: -κά, τά, poem in this style, Ath.14.620e. Adv. -κῶς, prob. in D.H.*Dem.*43. 3. Ἰ. ἔθος, of the *Ionic dialect,* A.D.*Pron.*74.9. Adv. -κῶς Sch.Porph.*Abst.*2.36: Comp. -ώτερον A.D.*Adv.*135.1.

**Ἰώνιος**, α, ον, = foreg., τρόπος, of the *Ionic* dialect, Philostr.*VA*7. 35:—fem. **Ἰωνίς**, ίδος, *Ionian,* Paus.6.22.7, etc.: as Subst., Call.*Ep.* 27, Plu.*Luc.*18: **Ἰωνιάς**, άδος, Nic.*Fr.*74.4, Str.8.3.32.

**ἰωνίς**, ίδος, ἡ, *a water bird,* Ar.Byz.*Epit.*5.5.

**ἰωνίσκος**, ὁ, Ephes. name for the fish χρύσοφρυς, Archestr.*Fr.* 12.

**Ἰωνιστί**, Adv. *in Ionic dialect,* A.D.*Adv.*162.8.

**Ἰωνο-κάμπτης**, ου, ὁ, *one who sings with soft Ionic modulations,* Tim.*Fr.*27. **-κῦσος**, ὁ, *debauchee,* Cratin.419.

**ἰωνός**, ὁ, a kind of *fish,* Hsch. **ἴωξις**, εως, ἡ, = ἰωκή (q.v.), Id., *EM*481.30, Suid. **ἰωπάτερ**· τὰ ἐν τοῖς ἱματίοις σημεῖα (Lacon.), Hsch. **ἴωπι**· δεῦρο (Lydian), Id.

**ἰωρός**, ὁ, Att. for ὁ αὐτῆς τῆς πόλεως φύλαξ acc. to A.D.*Pron.*55. 26 (pl., derived from ἴ), cf. Hdn.Gr.1.200, Hsch., Phot.; but ἐντὸς (ἐν τοῖς) and ἐκτὸς ἰωροῦ, of the *ban* placed on manslayers, Prov.ap. Suid., *App.Prov.*4.39.

**ἴωσις** [ῐ], εως, ἡ, (ἰόω) *refinement* (because freq. due to oxidization of impure substances), χρυσοῦ *PMag.Leid.V.*6.18, cf. Olymp. Alch.p.94 B., Zos.Alch.p.145 B., al. 2. *making of a tincture,* ib. p.219 B.

**ἰῶτα** [ῑ], τό, indecl., (Hebr. *yōd*) *the letter* ι, Pl.*Cra.*418b, Aen. Tact.31.18, Call.Gramm.ap.Ath.10.453d, etc. 2. *line, stroke,* on a sundial, *Bull.Soc.Alex.*4.83 (iii B.C.). 3. prov., of anything very small, *smallest letter, jot, Ev.Matt.*5.18.

**ἰωτᾰκισμός**, οῦ, ὁ, doubling of *i*, as in *Troiia, Maiia,* Quint.1.5.32, Isid.*Etym.*1.32.7. II. *repetition of i,* as *Iunio Iuno Iovis iure irascitur,* Mart.Cap.§ 514.

**ἰωτογρᾰφέω**, *write with iota,* Sch.Ar.*V.*926 (Pass.), etc.

**ἰωχμός** [ῑ], ὁ, = ἰωκή, ἦλθον ἀν' ἰωχμόν through *the rout,* Il.8.89, 158; ἰωὴ ἀσπέτου ἰωχμοῖο Hes.*Th.*683, cf. Theoc.25.279.

**ἴωψ** [ῑ], ωπος, ὁ, *a small fish,* Dorio ap.Ath.7.300f, Nic.*Fr.*18, Call. *Fr.*38, Ael.*NA*1.58, Hdn.Gr.1.247.

# K

**K κ, κάππα**, τό, indecl., eleventh (later tenth) letter in Gr. alphabet: as numeral κʹ = 20, but ͵κ = 20,000. The numeral καʹ (21) is perh. used as one syll. in a metrical (?) Inscr., *IG*12(7).296 (Minoa), like ζήσασα ἔτη εʹ, at the end of a hexam. (?), *CIG*3025 (Lydia).

**κᾱ**, Dor. for Ep., Aeol. κε(ν), = Att., Arc. ἄν, *SIG*9 (Olympia, vi B.C.), Epich.35, al., *Leg.Gort.*1.9, *Foed.Delph.Pell.*2 A 9, Ar.*Ach.* 737, 799, *Lys.*117, Th.5.77, Theoc.1.4. [Although long, the α is elided in Epich.170.12, al., *SIG*56.8 (Argos, v B.C.), *Leg.Gort.*1.1, etc.]

**κᾰ**, shortd. form of κατά used before the article, κα τὸν νόμον *IG*5 (2).16 (Arcadia); κα τῶννυ ib.262; κα τοὺς νόμους *SIG*²860.9 (Delph., ii B.C.), etc.; κα τὰ τῆς συγκλήτου δόγματα *SIG*705.12 (ibid.) κα τὰ δόξαντα.. τῇ βουλῇ *Inscr.Magn.*179.33 (ii A.D.): also in compds., cf. καβαίνων, etc. II. Cypr., = κάς, *Inscr.Cypr.*135.5 H., *Schwyzer* 683.8.

**κἀ**, crasis for καὶ ἐ, i.e. καὶ ἐμ (= ἐν), Herod.2.62 (κἠμ corr. m.rec.).

**κααρτίας**· βάτραχος, Hsch. **κάαυκα**· περιδέραια, πλόκια, Id. (leg. κάλυκας).

**καβάδης**, ὁ, *military garment named after the Persian king* Καβάδης, Tz.*H.*12.792.

**καβαθα** (accent dub.), ἡ, prob. = Lat. *gabata, dish, Edict.Diocl.* 15.51: also as neut. pl., καβαθα βʹ *UPZ*149.40 (iii B.C.); [γ]αβαθα τρία Cumont *Fouilles de Doura-Europos* p.372 No.13; cf. γαβαθόν, ζάβατος II.

**κᾰβαίνων**, Dor. for καταβ–, Alcm.38.

**κάβαισος** [ᾰ], ὁ, *gluttonous fellow,* Cratin.103. (Derived by Gramm. fr. κάβος and αἶσα and said to be a pr. n.; cf. Κάβαισος *IG* 5(2).271.9 (Mantinea, iv B.C.).)

**κᾰβάλλειον**, τό, = sq., κ. καὶ ἐργάτας δεκαπέντε *Rev.Arch.*1925.63 (Callatis): **καβάλλιον**, Hsch.

**κᾰβάλλης**, ου, ὁ, *nag,* Lat. *caballus,* Plu.2.828e; = ἐργάτης ἵππος, Hsch.:—hence **καβαλλαρικός**, ή, όν, *of* or *for a horse,* μύλος *Edict. Diocl.*15.52; τάπης 19.22: **καβαλλάτιον**, τό, = κυνόγλωσσον, Ps.-Dsc.4.127.

**κάβαξ**, = πανοῦργος, Phot., *EM*482.26, Suid.

**Κάβαρνος**, ὁ, *priest of Demeter* at Paros, *IG*12(5).292 (iii A.D.): pl., Hsch. (From Κάβαρνις, a poetical name of Paros, St.Byz.)

**κάβασα** and **καβάσας**, both perh. nom. sg., name of an unknown object in temple inventories, *Inscr.Délos* 298 A 111, 300 B 16, *IG*11 (2).287 B 89 (Delos, iii B.C.). (Perh. fr. Κάβασα in Egypt.)

**κάβᾱσι** [κᾰ], Lacon. for κατάβηθι, Hsch.

**καβάτας**, = καταιβάτης (q.v.), title of Zeus in Laconia, *IG*5(1). 1316 (Thalamae).

**καββᾰλικός**, ή, όν, Lacon. for καταβλητικός, *good at throwing,* of wrestlers: in Comp. καββαλικώτερος Plu.2.236e, Gal.*Thras.*45: metaph., *more ready to trip up* one's neighbour, M.Ant.7.52: καββαλική (sc. τέχνη), ἡ, *art of wrestling,* Gal. l.c.

**καββάλλω**, Aeol. for καταβάλλω, Alc.343; **κάββαλε**, Ep. for κατέβαλε, aor. 2 of καταβάλλω:—also **κάβαλεν**· κατέβαλεν, Hsch. **καββάς**, v. καταβαίνω. **καββασία**, v. καταβασία. **καββιόρνους**· κατεσθίων, Id. **κάββλημα**· περίστρωμα (Lacon.), Id.

**Κάβειροι** [ᾰ], οἱ, *the Cabeiri,* divinities worshipped especially in Lemnos, Samothrace, and Boeotia, Pi.*Fr.*74ᵇ Schr., Hdt.2.51, 3.37, Str.10.3.15, etc.; at Miletus, Nic.Dam.52 J., *Milet.*(v. infr.), *BCH*1. 288; title of play by Aeschylus, Ath.10.428f, Sch.Pi.*P.*4.303: sg., Κάβειρος Pi. l.c.; freq. in Boeotian Inscrr. (written -βιρ-), *IG*7.2457, al., cf. *AP*6.245 (Diod.), Q.S.1.267: **Καβειρίδες** Νύμφαι, and **Καβειρώ**, ἡ, *the sisters* and *mother of the Cabeiri,* Acus.20 J., Pherecyd. 48 J.:—Adj. **Καβειρικός**, ή, όν, fem. **Καβειριάς**, άδος, *Cabeiric,* St. Byz.:—also **Καβειραῖος**, α, ον, Id., Paus.9.25.8: **Καβειρία**, ἡ, epith. of Demeter at Κάβειροι, Id.9.25.5 codd.: **Καβείριον**, τό, *sanctuary of the C.,* Id.9.26.2; more correctly **Καβείρ[ε]ιον** *IG*11(2).144 A 90

(Delos, iv B.C.): **Καβείρια**, τά, *their mysteries*, *Inscr.Perg.*252, Hsch. :—hence **Καβειριάζομαι**, *celebrate these mysteries*, St.Byz.: **Καβῑριάρχας**, ὁ, *IG*7.2428 (Boeot.): **-αρχίω** (= -έω), ib.2420. (The spelling -**βειρ**- is correct, ib.11(2).l.c., Hdn.Gr.2.411: the form -**βιρ**- is Boeot. (v. supr.) and late Gr., *Milet.*6.26 (i A.D.), Alexio and Philox.ap.*Et.Gud.*289.30.) (The connexion with the Semitic root *KBR* '*great*' (cf. the title Μεγάλοι Θεοί) is not certain; nor is that with Skt. *Kúbera*- (name of a divinity), fr. **Kabera*-, cf. Patron. *Kāberaká*-.)

**κάβειος**· νέος (Paph.), Hsch. **κάβηλος**· ὁ ἀπεσκολυμμένος τὸ αἰδοῖον, ἢ ὄνος, Id.

⊛ **καβιδάριος**, ὁ, *gem-engraver*, Lat. *cabidarius*, *Gloss.*, Rhetor. in *Cat.Cod.Astr.*8(4).216.

**καβιτᾶς**, ὁ, dub. sens. (apptly. a nomen agentis), *PLond.*1821.368.

**καβλέει**· καταπίνει, Hsch. ⊛ **καβλής**· μάνδαλος τῶν θυρῶν (Paph.), Id.

**καβολά**, ἁ, = Dor. καταβολή, *Schwyzer*110[8] (Argos).

**κάβος**, ὁ, (Hebr. *ḳab*) *corn-measure*, = 4 ξέσται, Lxx 4*Ki.*6.25; f.l. in *Gp.*7.20.1.

⊛ **κάγ**, poet. form for κατά before γ, κὰγ γόνυ for κατὰ γόνυ, Il.20.458; κὰγ γόνων Sapph.44; κὰγ γᾶν dub. in *SIG*179.9 (Boeot., iv B.C.).

⊛ **καγκαίνω**, *parch, dry*, Hsch. :—also **κάγκω**, metaph. in Pass., καγκομένης· ξηρᾶς τῷ φόβῳ (cf. αὖος), Id. (Cf. κέγκω.)

⊛ **κάγκαμον**, τό, *Bissa Bol*, *Balsamodendron Katuf*, an Arabian gum, Dsc.1.24, Plin.*HN*12.98:—also **κάγκαλον**, τό, Hsch.

⊛ **κάγκανον**, τό, = κακκαλία (q.v.), Gal.12.8, Paul.Aeg.7.3.

**κάγκᾰνος**, ον, (καγκαίνω) *dry*, ξύλα κ. Il.21.364, Od.18.308, Theoc. 24.89; κάγκανα κᾶλα *h.Merc.*112; κ. κῆλα Epich. in *Arch.Pap.*7 p.7; σταχύς Lyc.1430: **καγκαλέα**· κατακεκαυμένα, Hsch.: **καγκάνεος**, Man.4.324.

**κάγκελλον** μέτρον, a system of measures of capacity, μέτρῳ τῷ κ. ἀρτάβας ἕνδεκα τέταρτον *POxy.*1447 (i A.D.), cf. 133.15 (vi A.D.), etc.

⊛ **κάγκελος**, ὁ, = Lat. *cancelli*, *barrier*, *starting-gate*, in races, Sch. Theoc.8.57, Hsch. :—also **κάγκελλοι**, οἱ, *IG*7.1681 (Plataea), *POxy.* 2146.12 (iii A.D.) :—whence ⊛**καγκελλάριος**, ὁ, orig. *usher* at the (lattice-work) bar of a court, then = λογοθέτης, Lyd.*Mag.*3.36,37, *PMasp.*5.19, al. (vi A.D.): **κάγκελον**, τό, *bar*, τοῦ δικαστηρίου Sch. Ar.*Eq.*641,675: ⊛**κάγγελλον**, *railing*, *balustrade*, *PRyl.*233.4 (ii A.D.): —hence ⊛**καγκελο-ειδῶς**, Adv. *like a grating*, *criss-cross*, *Hippiatr.*117 (v.l. -λλ-): **-θυρίς**, ίδος, ἡ, = κιγκλίς, *EM*513.4 :—also ⊛**καγκελωτὴ** θύρα Sch.Ar.*V.*124, Poll.8.124; διαβάθρα **καγγελλωτή** *furnished with a railing*, *PRyl.*233.3 (ii A.D.).

**καγκές**· πτύελος, Hsch.

**καγκύλη**, ἡ, Aeol. for κηκίς, Hsch. **καγρᾶ⟨ς⟩**· καταφαγᾶς (Salam.), Id. (prob. l.).

**καγχάζω**, later form for καχάζω (q.v.).

**καγχᾰλάω**, *rejoice*, *exult*, καγχαλόωσι..'Αχαιοί, κτλ. *rejoice* because a Trojan champion has been chosen for his looks, Il.3.43; καγχαλόων 6.514, 10.565; καγχαλόωσα Od.23.1,59; καγχαλάασκε A.R.4.996; ἐπακτὴρ καγχαλῶν ἀγρεύματι Lyc.109; καγχαλάασκον ἐτώσια μητιόωντι Q.S.8.12; ἐνὶ φρεσὶ -όωντες κρύβδ' Ἥρης Id.3.136, cf. 200, al., Opp.*C.*4.377, *H.*5.234; of hounds, deer, Id.*C.*1.523, 2.237; of pards, οἴνῳ μέγα -όωσι ib.3.80; of a polypus, Id.*H.*4.281.

**καγχαλίζομαι**, **καγχάομαι**, = foreg., Hsch. **κάγχαμος**, ὁ, in Crotoniate dialect, = κισσός, Id. **κάγχαρμον**· τὸ τὴν λόγχην ἄνω ἔχειν (Maced.), Hsch.

**καγχ-ασμός**, ὁ, *loud laughter*, Poll.6.199; v. καχασμός. **-αστής**, οῦ, ὁ, *loud laugher*, Phryn.*PS* p.78 B., Poll.6.29.

**καγχλάζω**, = καγχάζω, Ath.10.438f, Aq.*Jb.*41.23, Hsch.

**καγχρύδιον**, **κάγχρυς**, etc., v. καχρύδιον, κάχρυς, etc.

**κἀγώ** [ᾱ], Att. crasis for καὶ ἐγώ.

**κάδ**, Ep. for κατά before δ, κὰδ δώματα Od.4.72; κ. δύναμιν Hes. *Op.*336; before δέ, Il.2.160, etc.; κ. δ' ἔβαλε by tmesis for κατέβαλε δέ, Od.4.344.

**καδᾰλέομαι**, Dor. for καταδηλέομαι (q.v.). **καδαλίων**, ὁ, *one who walks on stilts*; and **κάδαλοι**, οἱ, *stilts*, Hsch. **κάδαμος**· τυφλός (Salam.), Id. **καδαρόν**· θολερόν, Id.

**καδδαιμονέστερος**, = κακοδ-, Epich. 1 Demiańczuk.

**κάδδιον**, v. κάδιον.

⊛ **κάδδῐχος**, ὁ, (κάδος) *jar*, κάδδιχος καλεῖται τὸ ἀγγεῖον εἰς ὃ τὰς ἀπομαγδαλίας ἐμβάλλουσι Plu.*Lyc.*12: hence, *voting-urn*, whence **κεκαδδίχθαι**, *to be rejected on a vote*, ibid.; also, a *measure*, = ἡμίεκτον, Hsch., cf. *Tab.Heracl.*1.52, *IG*5(1).1447.10 (Messene, iii/ii B.C.):— Lacon. **καδίκορ**, Hsch. s.v. ἐνδεκαδίκορ.

**κάδδος**, = κάδος (q.v.). **καδδρᾱθέτην**, v. καταδαρθάνω. **καδδῦσαι**, Ep. nom. pl. fem. aor. 2 part. Act. of καταδύω. ⊛ **κᾱδεστής**, Dor. for κηδεστής. **κάδης**· ἁγιασμός, Hsch.

**καδικεύω**, perh. *hold a priesthood*, dub. in *Rev.Phil.*35.302 (Pharsalus).

**κάδ-ιον** [ᾰ], τό, Dim. of κάδος, *IG*11(2).287 *A* 64 (Delos, iii B.C.), Lxx 1*Ki.*17.40; = ὑδρία (Salam.), Hsch. (pl.): **κάδδιον** Sch.D.T. p.195 H. :—also **κάδιν**, ἔλαιον καὶ κάδιν *Abh.Berl.Akad.*1925(5).31 (Cyrene, ii/iii A.D.). **-ίσκιον**, τό, Dim. of sq., *part of a spice-box*, Nicoch.2. **-ίσκος**, ὁ, Dim. of κάδος, Cratin.193, Stratt.22, *BCH* 35.286 (ii B.C.), Ph.2.89, Gal.11.555. II. *voting-urn* used in law-courts, ὁ δὲ κ... ὁ μὲν ἀπολύων οὗτος, ὁ δ' ἀπολλὺς ὁδί Phryn.Com.32, cf. Ar.*V.*853, Lys.13.37, Lycurg.149; καδίσκων τεττάρων τεθέντων κατὰ τὸν νόμον (in a civil cause), D.43.10, cf. Is.11.21.

**καδμεία** (in codd. **καδμία**) (sc. γῆ), ἡ, *cadmia*, *calamine*, Dsc.5.74, Gal.1.413, al., *PTeb.*273.14 (ii/iii A.D.):—written **καδμήα**, *POxy.* 1088.4 (i A.D.).

**Καδμει-ῶνες**, οἱ, = Καδμεῖοι, Il.4.385, etc. **-ώνη**, ἡ, *daughter of Cadmus*, i.e. Semele, *IG*14.1389 i 59.

⊛ **Καδμῖλος** (on the accent v. Hdn.Gr.1.162), ὁ, name of one of the Cabiri in Samothrace, St.Byz. s.v. Καβειρία, Hdn.Gr.2.446 :— also **Κασμ**-, Dionysodor.ap.Sch.A.R.1.917, cf. *IG*12(8).74 (Imbros, ii A.D.), Call.*Fr.*409; identified with Hermes, ibid., Hdn.Gr.1.162, Sch.Lyc.162: with Lat. *camillus* (*casm*-), Varr.*LL*7.3, cf. Plu.*Num.* 7; Καδμῖλοι is prob. for Κάδωλοι, title of ministrants in the cult of the Curetes and Μεγάλοι Θεοί, D.H.2.22.

**Καδμογενής**, ές, *Cadmus-born*, A.*Th.*302, S.*Tr.*116, E.*Ph.*808 (all lyr.).

**Κάδμος**, ὁ, *Cadmus*, Od.5.333, Hes.*Th.*937, etc.:—Adj. **Καδμεῖος**, α, ον, Ion. **Καδμήιος**, η, ον, *Cadmean*, Hes.*Th.*940, etc. :—fem. **Καδμηΐς**, ΐδος, ἡ, *h.Bacch.*57, Hes.*Op.*162, Th.1.12, prob. in *Trag. Adesp.*177 :—poet. **Καδμέϊος**, Pi.*I.*3(4).71, S.*Ant.*1115 (lyr.): Καδμεῖοι, οἱ, *the Cadmeans* or *ancient inhabitants of Thebes*, Il.4.388, Hes. *Th.*326, Hdt.5.57, etc.: Καδμεία, ἡ, *the citadel of Thebes*, X.*HG*6.3.11; also, Pythag. name for *eight*, *Theol.Ar.*54: prov., K. νίκη a victory involving one's own ruin (from the story of the Σπαρτοί, or that of Polynices and Eteocles), Hdt.1.166, cf. Pl.*Lg.*641c, Plu.2.488a, Suid. (but = a *great* victory, Arr.*Fr.*21 J.); so K. κράτος *AP*5.178 (Mel.): metaph., K. παιδεία Pl. l.c.; K. γράμματα the alphabet, supposed to have been brought by K. from Phoenicia, Hdt.5.59. (The spelling Κάσσμος is found on a vase of Rhegium, Roscher *Lex.d.Gr.u.Röm.Myth.*2(1).842.)

**κάδμος**· δόρυ, λόφος, ἀσπίς (Cret.), Hsch.

**κᾰδοποιός**, όν, *making pails* or *vessels*, Sch.Ar.*Pax*1202.

⊛ **κάδος** [ᾰ], ὁ, *jar* or *vessel for water* or *wine*, Anacr.17, Archil.4, Hdt.3.20, S.*Fr.*534.3 (anap.), Ar.*Ach.*549, etc.; κ. ἀντλητικός *CPR* 232.12 (ii A.D.); said to be Ion. for κεράμιον, Clitarch.Gloss.ap.Ath. 11.473b. 2. a liquid measure, = ἀμφορεύς, Philoch.155a; ἐλαίου Lxx 2*Ch.*2.10(9) (cod. A), cj. in Simon.155.4 (*Hermes*64.274); πίνει τετραχόοισι κάδοις Hedyl.ap.Ath. l.c.; later, *half an* ἀμφ., *Script. Metrol.*1.257, 2.144 Hultsch. II. = καδίσκος II, Ar.*Av.*1032. III. *funerary urn*, *Jahresh.*8.154.—The metre usu. requires κάδος, never κάδδος which is written in Them. in *Ph.*268.2, al.; cf. κάδδιχος.

**κᾶδος**, Dor. for κῆδος. **κάδουσα**· εἶδος σταφυλῆς, Hsch. **καδρανές** (perh. for καπρανές, i.e. κατα-πρηνές)· κατωφερές, Id. **κάδυρος**· κάπρος ἔνορχις, Id.

**καδύτας**, ου, ὁ, a parasitic plant, *dodder*, *Cassyta filiformis* (Arabic *kašūth*), Thphr.*CP*2.17.3.

**Κάδωλοι**, v. Καδμῖλος.

**Κάειρα** [ᾰ], ἡ, fem. from Κάρ, *Carian woman*, Il.4.142, Hdt.1.92, al. II. Adj. fem., = Καρική, ἐσθής Hdt.5.88.

**κᾱείς**, **κᾱήμεναι**, v. καίω. **κάζελε**, Arc. for κατέβαλε, Hsch. **κάηνα**· τὰ εὖ καιόμενα ξύλα, Id.

⊛ **καθά** [θᾰ], Adv. for καθ' ἅ, *according as*, *just as*, *IG*1².90.43, 116.27, Men.*Mon.*551, *PCair.Zen.*188.8 (iii B.C.), Plb.3.107.10, Lxx *Ge.*7.9, etc.; ὁ κ. παρατεταγμένος σφυγμός the (*so to speak*) 'regular' pulse (a military metaphor), Archig.ap.Gal.8.626. II. also **καθάπερ**, Ion. **κατάπερ**, Philol.14, Democr.164, Hdt.1.182, al., Ar.*Eq.*8, *Ec.* 61, *IG*1².39.42, al., D.37.16, etc.: freq. in legal instruments, ἡ πρᾶξις ἔστω κ. ἐκ δίκης *PEleph.*1.12 (iv B.C.), etc.: with a part., like ὡς, ἅτε, D.C.37.54 (nisi leg. καίπερ):—strengthd., **καθάπερ εἰ** (Ion. κατάπερ εἰ, Hdt.1.170), *like as if*, *exactly as*, Pl.*Phlb.*22e, 59e, al.; **καθάπερ ἄν** (for ἐάν) D.23.41; **καθάπερ ἂν εἰ** Pl.*Lg.*684c, Arist.*Ph.*240[b]10, Plb. 3.32.2, etc.:—μάχαιραν κ. *like* a knife, Porph.*Chr.*31. Cf. καθό, καθώς.

**καθᾰγ-ιάζω**, = sq., Lxx *Le.*27.26, 2*Ma.*1.26; ὁ σοφὸς -άζει ψυχὴν Ph.1.115:—Pass., Iamb.*Myst.*5.24. **-ίζω**, Att. fut. -ιῶ: Ion. fut. inf. κατ-αγιεῖν Hdt.1.86:—*devote*, *dedicate*, ἀκροθίνια θεῶν ὅτεῳ δή l.c.; νήττη πυρούς Ar.*Av.*566, cf. *Lys.*238, Pl.*Criti.*120a, Men. 319.13, etc.; esp. of a burnt offering, θυμιήματα κ. Hdt.2.130; κ. πυρὶ ib.47; κ. ἐπὶ πύρης Id.7.167; ἐπὶ τοῦ βωμοῦ Id.1.183; ἀρκεύθου ξύλοις Paus.2.10.5; abs., Hdt.2.40, etc.; *make offerings* to the dead, Luc. *Luct.*9:—Pass., cj. in Ph.1.190 (καταγιζ- Pap., καθαγνιζ- codd.), 558 (καθαγνιζ- codd.). II. generally, *burn*, καταγιζομένου τοῦ καρποῦ τοῦ ἐπιβαλλομένου [ἐπὶ τὸ πῦρ] Hdt.1.202; esp. *burn* a dead body, τὸ σῶμα τοῦ Καίσαρος ἐν ἀγορᾷ κ. Plu.*Ant.*14, cf. *Brut.*20; so (as cj. for καθήγνισαν) ὅσων σπαράγματ' ἢ κύνες καθήγισαν whose mangled bodies dogs *have buried*, i.e. *devoured*, S.*Ant.*1081 (= μετὰ ἄγους ἐκόμισαν, Sch.). **-ισμός**, ὁ, *funeral rites*, Luc.*Luct.*19. **-νίζω**, Att. fut. -ιῶ, *purify*, *hallow*, τὸν τόπον θείῳ καὶ δᾳδὶ Id.*Philops.*12; μήτηρ πυρὶ καθήγνισται δέμας, i.e. has been burnt on the funeral-pyre, E.*Or.* 40. II. *offer as an expiatory sacrifice*, πέλανον ἐπὶ πυρὶ καθαγνίσας Id.*Ion*707 (lyr.).—On S.*Ant.*1081, Ph.1.190,558, v. καθαγίζω.

**καθαιμ-ακτός**, όν, *bloodstained*, φόνος E.*Or.*1358 (lyr.). **-άσσω**, *make bloody*, *sprinkle* or *stain with blood*, τινα A.*Eu.*450; χρόα, δέρην, E.*Hec.*1126, *Or.*1527; σκήπτρῳ κ. κάρα Id.*Andr.*588; τὴν γλῶτταν Pl.*Phdr.*254e. **-ᾰτόω**, = foreg., E.*Hel.*1599, *HF*234, 256, *Ph.* 1161, Ar.*Th.*695:—Pass., Luc.*Ind.*9. **-ος**, ον, *bloody*, τραύματα, σῖτα, E.*IT*1374, prob. in *HF*383 (lyr.).

⊛ **καθαίρ-εσις**, εως, ἡ, *pulling down*, *demolition*, Th.5.42, Isoc.7.66, X.*HG*2.2.15, *IG*2².1672.75 (iv B.C.), *PMagd.*9.6 (iii B.C.), etc.: metaph., τινῶν, opp. οἰκοδομή, 2*Ep.Cor.*10.8; ἀναστήσωμεν τὴν κ. τοῦ

λαοῦ ἡμῶν Lxx 1*Ma.*3.43: in concrete sense, *αἱ καθαιρέσεις the débris*, Ph.*Bel.*92.31. 2. generally, *overthrow, subjugation*, Jul.*Caes.* 320d; τῆς ἀνέτου ἐξουσίας Hdn.2.4.4; Ἰουλιανοῦ Id.3.1.1; *killing*, Plu.*Ant.*82. 3. *reduction, diminution*, opp. πρόσθεσις, Arist.*Ph.* 207ᵃ23: Medic., *bringing down superfluous flesh, lowering, reducing*, Hp.*Epid.*6.3.1, cf. Gal.17(2).368; τῶν σωμάτων Arist.*GA*738ᵃ31; τῶν ὄγκων Pl.*Ti.*58e. 4. *eclipse* of sun or moon (with reference to the magical process of *drawing down* those bodies), Sch.A.R.3.533 (pl.). **-ετέος**, α, ον, *to be put down*, Th.1.118. II. καθαιρετέον *one must put down, overthrow*, κ. καὶ καταγωνιστέον τινάς Aristid. 1.445 J.; κ. ἐξ ἀκροπόλεως τὴν τυραννίδα Them.*Or.*21.256a. **-έτης**, ου, ὁ, *overthrower*, πολεμίων Th.4.83; Καίσαρος D.C.44.1. II. *house-breaker*(?), *BGU*14v12 (iii A.D.). ⊕ **-ετικός**, ή, όν, *destructive*, c. gen., Corn.*ND*30, Ph.2.548. 2. *reducing, catheretic*, φάρμακα, of mild caustics, Gal.11.756; σπληνὸς καθαιρετικόν Dsc.2.112; *putting a stop to*, παλμῶν Gal.7.600: generally, ὑγίεια κ. παθῶν Ph.*Fr.* 103 H. **-ετός**, ή, όν, *able to be achieved*, ὃ ἐκεῖνοι ἐπιστήμῃ προύχουσι, καθαιρετὸν ἡμῖν ἐστι μελέτῃ Th.1.121 (v.l. καθαιρετέον, but cf. D.C.*Fr.*43.11). ⊕ **-έω**, Ion. κατ-, Aeol. **κατάγρημι**, q.v.: fut. -ήσω Il.11.453, etc.: fut. 2 καθελῶ *APl.*4.334 (Antiphil.): aor. 2 καθεῖλον, inf. καθελεῖν: aor. 1 καθεῖλα Lxx 3*Ki.*19.14: Ion. pf. part. Pass. καταραιρημένος Hdt.2.172:—*take down*, καθείλομεν ἱστία Od. 9.149; κὰδ δ' ἀπὸ πασσαλόφι ζυγὸν ᾕρεον Il.24.268; κ. ἄχθος *take it down*, i.e. off one's shoulders, Ar.*Ra.*10; κ. τὸ σημεῖον And.1.36; κ. τῶν ἐκ τῆς στοᾶς ὅπλων some of them, X.*HG*5.4.8; κ. εἰκόνα ἐξ ἀκροπόλεως Lycurg.117; κ. τινά, from the cross, Plb.1.86.6, Ph.2. 529:—Med., κατελέσθαι τὰ τόξα *take down one's* bow, Hdt.3.78; τοὺς ἱστούς Plb.1.61.1. 2. *put down, close* the eyes of the dead, ὅσσε καθαιρήσουσι θανόντι περ Il.11.453; ὀφθαλμοὺς καθελοῦσα Od.24.296; χερσὶ κατ' ὀφθαλμοὺς ἑλέειν 11.426. 3. of sorcerers, *bring down* from the sky, σελήνην Ar.*Nu.*750, Pl.*Grg.*513a. 4. κατά με πέδον γᾶς ἕλοι may earth *swallow* me! E.*Supp.*829 (lyr.). II. *put down by force, destroy*, ὅτε κέν μιν μοῖρ' ὀλοὴ καθέλῃσι Od.2.100, 19.145, cf. 3. 238, etc.; μὴ καθέλοι μιν αἰών Pi.*O.*9.60; φῶτ' ἄδικον καθαιρεῖ A.*Ag.* 398 (lyr.); μοῖρα τὸν φύσαντα καθεῖλε S.*Aj.*517, cf. E.*El.*878 (lyr.), etc.; *kill, slay*, ταῦρον ib.1143, cf. Stesich.23, S.*Tr.*1063, *Fr.*205; ἐάν τις ἀποκτείνῃ.. ἐν ὁδῷ καθελών Lex ap.D.23.53:—Pass., of criminals, *to be executed*, Plu.*Them.*22. 2. *put down, reduce*, κ. Κῦρον καὶ τὴν Περσέων δύναμιν Hdt.1.71, etc.; καθαιρεθῆναι, opp. ἀρθῆναι, D.2.8; esp. *depose, dethrone*, Hdt.1.124, etc.; κ. τὸ λῃστικὸν ἐκ τῆς θαλάσσης *remove* it *utterly* from.., Th.1.4, cf. *POxy.*1408.23 (iii A.D.); κ. ὕβριν τινός Hdt.9.27, Lxx *Za.*9.6; ὄλβον S.*Fr.*646.4; ὑπερηφάνους Aristeas 263:—Pass., καθῃρημένος τὴν αἴσθησιν *bereft* of sense, Plu.*Per.*38; καθαιρεῖσθαι τῆς μεγαλειότητος [Ἀρτέμιδος] *Act.Ap.*19.27. 3. *raze to the ground, demolish*, πόλεις Th.1.58, al., Lxx *Is.*14.17; τείχη Pl. *Mx.*244c; τῶν τειχῶν a part of the walls, X.*HG*4.4.13:—Pass., Th. 5.39, etc.; καθῃρέθη.. Οἰχαλία δορί S.*Tr.*478. 4. *cancel, rescind*, τὸ Μεγαρέων ψήφισμα Th.1.140, cf. 139, Plu.*Per.*29; ἔργον κ. λόγῳ Philem.140. 5. as law-term, *condemn*, ἡ καθαιροῦσα ψῆφος a verdict of *guilty*, Lys.13.37: c. inf., ἐμὲ πάλος καθαιρεῖ.. λαβεῖν S. *Ant.*275; so prob. κατά με.. Ἀΐδας ἕλοι πατρὶ ξυνθανεῖν Id.*OC*1689 (lyr.), cf. E.*Or.*862; simply, *decide*, ὅ τι ἂν αἱ πλείους ψῆφοι καθαιρῶσι D.H.7.36,39; in book-keeping, ἃν καθαιρῶσιν αἱ ψῆφοι whatever the counters (or accounts) *prove*, prob. in D.18.227. 6. *reduce*, τῶν αὐξανομένων καὶ καθαιρουμένων γραμμῶν Arist.*Ph.*237ᵇ9; τοῦ ἀποστήματος πεφυκότος ἐπὶ πολὺ καθαιρεῖν τὰ μεγέθη Phld.*Sign.*9; of mild caustics, τὰ ὑπερσαρκέοντα καθαιρεῖ (prob. for καθαίρει) Hp.*Ulc.*14, cf. Gal.11.756; τὸ σῶμα κ. διαίταις Plu.*Ant.*53: Rhet., *minimize*, Arist.*Rh.*1376ᵃ34. III. *overpower, seize*, κὰδ δέ μιν ὕπνος ᾕρει Od. 9.372; κ. τινά *overtake*, X.*Cyr.*4.3.16; κ. τινὰ ἐν ἀφροσύνῃ *catch* in the act of folly, S.*Ant.*383 (anap.): c. gen. partis, κ. τῶν ὤτων *seize by*.., Theoc.5.133:—Pass., κ. ὑπό τινος Hdt.6.29. IV. *fetch down as a reward* or *prize*, καθαιρεῖν ἀγῶνας Plu.*Pomp.*8: metaph., *achieve*, ἀγώνιον.. εὖχος ἔργῳ καθελών Pi.*O.*10(11).63: fut. inf. καθαρεῖν, παστόν, μίτραν, Epigr. in *Berl.Sitzb.*1894.908 (Asia Minor):—Med., φόνῳ καθαιρεῖσθ', οὐ λόγῳ, τὰ πράγματα E.*Supp.*749:—Pass., Hdt.7. 50. V. less freq. like the simple αἱρεῖν, *take and carry off*, Id.6. 41, cf. 5.36 (Pass.). Cf. καθαίρω.

⊕ **κᾰθαίρω**, fut. κᾰθᾰρῶ X.*Oec.*18.6, prob. in Pl.*Lg.*735b, etc.: aor. 1 ἐκάθηρα Od.20.152, Th.3.104, Hp.*Mul.*1.47, *IG*2².1672.47 (ἀνα-), Theoc.5.119, etc.; ἐκάθᾱρα is found in codd. of Antipho 6.37, X.*An.* 5.7.35, Hp.*Acut.*(*Sp.*)11, and commonly in later Gr., Thphr.*Char.* 16.7, *BCH*6.23 (Delos, ii B.C.), (ἀνα-) *PPetr.*3p.141 (iii B.C.), (συναναι-) *IG*11(2).163*A*56 (Delos, iii B.C.), cf. διακαθαίρω, ἐκκαθαίρω, etc., and Phryn.16; v. infr. Med.: pf. κεκάθαρκα (ἐκ-) Sch.Ar.*Pax*752:—Med., fut. καθαροῦμαι Pl.*Cra.*396e, Hp.*Morb.*2.38 (in pass. sense, ib. 2.13, *Nat.Mul.*13, *Mul.*2.160): aor. ἐκαθηράμην A.*Fr.*354, Hp.*Epid.* 5.43, Pl.*Lg.*868a, *IG*11(2).146*A*78 (Delos, iv B.C.), 153.9, 154*A*37 (ibid., iii B.C.); later ἐκαθᾱράμην ib.146*A*80 (iv B.C.), *Inscr.Délos* 290. 79, al. (iii B.C.), etc., (ἀνα-) *IG*2².1668.8 (iv B.C.): Pass., fut. καθαρθήσομαι Ruf.ap.Orib.7.26.64, Gal.7.222: aor. ἐκαθάρθην Hdt.1.43, Th. 3.104, Hp.*Epid.*5.2, etc. (aor. 2 ἀποκαθαρῇ is f.l. in Arr.*Cyn.*27.1): pf. κεκάθαρμαι Hp.*Nat.Mul.*8, Pl.*Phd.*69c, etc.: (καθαρός): I. *cleanse*, of things, καθήρατε δὲ κρητῆρας Od.20.152; τραπέζας ὕδατι.. καθαίρειν 22.439; καθήραντες χρόα καλὸν ὕδατι 24.44; κ. οἰκίαν Antipho l.c., Thphr. l.c.; of wounds, Hp.*Ulc.*6, al. (cf. καθαιρέω II. 6): c. gen., ἵππον αὐχμηρᾶς τριχός S.*Fr.*475; κ. σῖτον X.*Oec.*18.6; γῆν *clear* of weeds, ib.20.11, cf. *PLille* 5.24 (iii B.C.), etc.; χρυσόν *purify, refine*, Pl.*Plt.*303d: metaph., *purge, clear* a land of monsters and robbers, S.*Tr.*1012 (hex.), 1061, Plu.*Thes.*7; κ. λῃστηρίων τὴν ἐπαρχίαν Id.*Mar.*6: c. acc. cogn., καθαρμὸν κ. Pl.*Lg.*735b:—Pass., τὴν νηδὺν ἀνασχισθεῖσαν καὶ καθαρθεῖσαν Hdt.4.71. 2. in religious sense, *purify*, [δέπας] ἐκάθηρε θεείῳ by fumigating with sulphur, Il.16.228; κ. τινὰ φόνου *purify* him *from* blood, Hdt.1.44, cf. *Berl.Sitzb.*1927. 160 (Cyrene); Δῆλον κ. Hdt.1.64, cf. Th.1.8; στόλον κ., Lat. *classem lustrare*, App.*BC*5.96: abs., *IG*5(1).1390.68 (Andania, i B.C.):—Med., *purify oneself, get purified*, Hdt.4.73; οἱ φιλοσοφίᾳ καθηράμενοι Pl.*Phd.*114c, cf. *Phdr.*243a, *Cra.*396e; καθαίρεσθαι καθαρμούς Id.*Lg.* 868e; καθήρασθαι στόμα *keep one's* tongue *pure*, A.*Fr.*354:—Pass., κεκαθαρμένος καὶ τετελεσμένος Pl.*Phd.*69c. 3. Medic., *purge, evacuate*, either by purgatives or emetics, κ. κάτω ἢ ἄνω Hp.*Mul.*1.64 (Pass.), cf. Thphr.*HP*9.11.11, etc.:—Med., κατὰ κύστιν ἐκαθήρατο Hp.*Epid.* 1.15:—Pass., ib.5.2, etc.; also of menstruation, Id.*Superf.*33; of the after-birth, τὰ λοχεῖα κ. Id.*Mul.*1.78; καθαίρων, ὁ, name for ἶρις, Ps.-Dsc.1.1. 4. *prune* a tree, i.e. *clear* it of superfluous wood, *Ev.Jo.* 15.2. 5. *sift, winnow* grain, *PTeb.*373.10 (ii A.D.). 6. metaph., = μαστιγόω, Theoc.5.119. II. of the thing removed by purification, *purge away, wash off*, λύματα πάντα κάθηρεν Il.14.171; ἐπεὶ πλῦνάν τε κάθηράν τε ῥύπα πάντα Od.6.93; *clear away*, τὰ λῃστικά D.C.37. 52: metaph., φόνον κ. A.*Ch.*74 (lyr.); also perh., *clear up, explain* an action, τὴν σύστασιν Epicur.*Nat.*66 G., cf. 73 G. III. c. dupl. acc., αἷμα κάθηρον.. Σαρπηδόνα *cleanse* him *of* blood, *wash* the blood *off* him, Il.16.667:—Pass., καθαίρομαι γῆρας I *am purged of* old age, A. *Fr.*45; ὁ καθαρθεὶς τὸν φόνον Hdt.1.43.

**κάθακα**, τά, apptly., = καθήκοντα, πάντα τὰ κ. ποιήσασα *BSA*18.148 (Beroea).

**καθάλλομαι**, fut. -ᾰλοῦμαι: aor. part. -αλόμενος or -αλάμενος (both readings in X.*HG*4.5.7):—*leap down*, ἀπὸ τοῦ ἵππου, ἀπ' ὄχθων, Id. l.c., *Eq.*3.7; ἐντὸς τοῦ τείχους Luc.*DMort.*14.5: abs., App.*Hisp.*22: metaph., of a storm, *rush down*, καθαλλομένη ἰοειδέα πόντον ὀρίνει Il. 11.298; of convulsions, Anon.ap.Gal.7.624.

**καθαλμ-άω**, (ἅλμη) *become crusted with salt*, κέραμον τὸν καθηλμηκότα *IG*11(2).287*A*112 (Delos, iii B.C.). **-ής**, ές, *salt, saltish*, Nic. *Al.*514.

**κάθᾰλος**, ον, (ἅλς A) *full of salt, over-salted*, Diph.17.13: comically, of the cook, Posidipp.1.7.

**καθᾰμαξεύω**, *wear with wheels*: metaph., ἕτεροι κατημάξευσαν (sic) τάσδε τὰς τρίβους Nech.ap.Vett.Val.354.2; *crush*, καθημάξευσε ταῖς συμφοραῖς Eun.*Hist.*p.240 D.: elsewh. in pf. part. Pass., καθημαξευμένος, η, ον, metaph., γύναιον κ. ὑπὸ παντὸς τοῦ προσιόντος, of a *common* prostitute, Ael.*Fr.*123: but almost always written κατημ-, *hackneyed, stale, trite*, ἀντιλογίαι D.H.10.41, cf. *Th.*11.2; ἔθη κ. Ph. 1.513; πρόχειρον καὶ κ. ib.426; τὰ κοινὰ καὶ κ. Ath.15.677a, cf. Artem.1.31 (in marg.), Simp.*in Cat.*424.13, Sch.Pi.*N.*6.91 (ind., [ὁ λόγος] κατημάξευται Conon 46). Adv. καθημαξευμένως *in a trite way*, Ael.Dion.*Fr.*218.

**κάθαμμα**, ατος, τό, (καθάπτω) *knot*: metaph., κ. λύειν λόγου (dub. l.) to solve a *knotty point*, E.*Hipp.*671 (lyr.); κ. λύειν, proverb from the Gordian knot, to overcome a difficulty, Zen.4.46, Suid.

**καθαμματίζω** (κατ- cod.), *innodo*, *Gloss.*

**καθαμμίζω**, *cover with sand*, ἑαυτά Arist.*HA*620ᵇ29, prob. in Antig.*Mir.*48.

**καθᾰνύω**, Att. for κατανύω, acc. to Hdn.Gr.1.541; καθήνυσαν cited by Phryn.*PS*p.23 B.; καθανύσαι· συντελέσαι, Hsch.: but codd. of Att. writers have only κατανύω, q.v. (καθήνυσαν is cj. in S.*El.*1451 (Dobree), καθανύσαι, -σας, -σειν, in X.*HG*7.1.15, 5.4.49, 20 (Cobet)).

**καθάπαν** [ᾰπ], Adv. *on the whole*; better divisim καθ' ἅπαν, cf. Lxx 2*Ma.*15.30.

⊕ **καθάπαξ** [ᾰπ], Adv. *once for all*, Od.21.349, D.18.231, Phld.*D.*3 *Fr.*23, Jul.*Or.*2.70c; *out-and-out, absolutely*, οἱ κ. ἐχθροί D.18.197; κ. ἄτιμος γέγονεν Id.21.87, cf. 25.30; κ. σπουδαῖος, opp. κατά τι, Phld. *Po.*5.16, cf. Ph.2.6; opp. πρός τι, Archig.ap.Gal.8.626; οἱ κ. μὴ συναπτόμενοι not *at all*, Ocell.4.4; οὕτω κ. πέπρακεν ἑαυτόν D.19. 118; οὐδὲ κ. not even *once*, Plb.1.2.6, 1.20.12, etc.; οὐδὲ τὸ κ. S.E.*M.* 11.97; πάντως δ', οὐ κ. not merely *in a single case*, Demetr.Lac.*Herc.* 1055.22; *singly*, Plb.3.90.2. II. *each time*, = ἑκάστοτε, *PMag. Par.*1.326.

**καθάπερ, καθαπερεί, καθαπερανεί**, v. καθά.

**καθαπλόω**, *spread over*, τοῦ αὐχένος, of the hair, Aristaenet.2.4.

⊕ **καθαπτής**, οῦ, ὁ, or -ή, ή, a kind of vase, in pl., γάστρας καὶ καθαπτάς *PSI*4.420.26 (iii B.C.).

⊕ **καθαπτός**, ή, όν, *bound with, equipped with*, θύρσοισι καὶ νεβρῶν δοραῖς E.*Fr.*752. II. κ. ὄργανον *percussion* instrument, e.g. cymbal or drum, Aristocles ap.Ath.4.174c.

**καθάπτω**, Ion. κατ-, *fasten* or *fix on, put upon*, καθῆψεν ὤμοις.. ἀμφίβληστρον S.*Tr.*1051; κ. τι ἀμφί τινι E.*Ion*1006; τι ἐπί τι X.*Cyn.* 6.9; τι εἴς τι Plb.8.6.3; τι ἔκ τινος Plu.2.647e; ἄγκυραν καθάψας *having made* it *fast*, Philem.213.10; τὰ ὀστέα καθάπτει τὰ νεῦρα Arist. *Spir.*483ᵇ31:—Med., κισσὸν ἐπὶ κρατὶ καθάπτεσθαι Theoc.*Ep.*3.4:—Pass., βρόχῳ καθημμένος S.*Ant.*1222, cf. Theoc.*Adon.*11. 2. *equip* by fastening or hanging on, in Med., σκευῇ σῶμ' ἐμὸν καθάψομαι E.*Rh.*202, cf. *AP*9.19 (Arch.):—Pass., νεβρίνῃ καθημμένος δορᾷ *with* a fawn-skin *slung round him*, S.*Ichn.*219; καθημμένοι νεβρίδας Str.15.1.71. 3. intr., *attach itself*, εἴς τι, πρός τι, Arist.*HA*514ᵇ 30, 515ᵃ3; later = II. 5, *fasten upon*, τῆς χειρός τινος *Act.Ap.*28.3, cf. Poll.1.164. II. used by Hom. only in Med., καθάπτεσθαί τινα ἐπέεσσι, in good or bad sense, as, σὺ τόν γ' ἐπέεσσι καθάπτεσθαι μαλακοῖσι *do* thou *accost* him.., Il.1.582; μαλακοῖσι καθαπτόμενος

ἐπέεσσιν Od.10.70; μειλιχίοις ἐπέεσσι κ. 24.393; but also ἀντιβίοις ἐπέεσσι καθαπτόμενος *assailing*.., 18.415, 20.323; χαλεποῖσι κ. ἐπέεσσι Hes.*Op.*332: without a qualifying Adj., *accost, assail*, ἐπέεσσι καθάπτετο θοῦρον Ἄρηα Il.15.127, cf. Od.2.240; without ἐπέεσσι, γέροντα καθαπτόμενος προσέειπεν 2.39, cf. 20.22, Il.16.421. 2. after Hom., c. gen., *upbraid*, Hdt.6.69, Th.6.16, Pl.*Cri.*52a, X.*HG* 1.7.4: abs., Th.6.82. 3. in military sense, *attack*, καθαψάμενοι τῆς οὐραγίας Plb.1.19.14. 4. *appeal* to, θεῶν..καταπτόμενος *appealing* to them, Hdt.6.68; Δημαρήτου καὶ ἄλλων μαρτύρων Id.8.65. 5. *lay hold of*, τυραννίδος Sol.32.3; βρέφεος χείρεσσι Theoc.17.65; τῆς θαλάσσης *take to* the sea, Philostr.*VA*3.23: Act., καθάπτων τοῦ τραχήλου Arr.*Epict.*3.20.10 (cf. 1.3). 6. *to be sensitive in respect of*, ψόφου Hp.*Prorrh.*1.16.

**καθάρβυλος**, v. κατάρβυλος.

⊛ **κᾰθάρ-ειος**, later **καθάριος** [θᾰ], ον, (καθαρός) of persons, *cleanly, neat, tidy*, τοὺς καθαρείους περὶ ὄψιν, περὶ ἀμπεχόνην, περὶ ὅλον τὸν βίον Arist.*Rh.*1381$^{b}$1: -ιώτατόν (v.l. -ειότατόν) ἐστι τὸ ζῷον (i.e. the bee) Id.*HA*626$^{a}$24; καθάρειοι ταῖς διαίταις D.S.5.33 (καθάριοι codd.); οἱ καθαρειότεροι *decent, respectable* men, Phld.*Rh.*2.150S., Hierocl. p.63A. (-ριώτ-, -ρώτ- codd., em. Meineke); of things, ἐὰν ἡ σκευασία καθάρ⟨ε⟩ιος ᾖ Men.*Phasm.Fr.*2; καθαριώτερα (or -ειότερα) ὅπλα Plb. 11.9.5; τὸ κ., *daintiness*, of food, Plu.2.663c; κ. ἄρτος *white* bread, *Sammelb.*5730 (iv/v A.D., sg.), *PMag.Lond.*46.230 (pl.); βίος, δίαιτα καθάρειος, *refined*, Ath.3.74d, *Carm.Aur.*35; εἰς τὰ καθάρεια λιμὸς εἰσοικίζεται Men.841 (καθαρά codd.). Adv. -είως *cleanly, tidily*, ἐγχέουσιν X.*Cyr.*1.3.8, cf. Posidon.15J., Dsc.1.44; *neatly*, κ. εἰργασμένος Ph.*Bel.*76.27; *clearly*, ὑποδεῖξαι Plb.15.5.5; also, *frugally*, μὴ πολυτελῶς, ἀλλὰ καθαρείως Eub.110.1, Ephipp.15.3, Nicostr.6.2; ἔχειν καθαρ⟨ε⟩ίως ἐγχελύδιον Amphis 35; μονοτροφοῦντες καθαρίως καὶ λιτῶς Str.3.3.6; *irreproachably*, ἀναστραφεὶς ἀνδρήως καὶ καθαρήως (sic) *AJA*17.31 (Sardes, i B.C.). II. Gramm. of language, *pure, correct*, ὄνομα Sch.Ar.*Ach.*244; οἱ κ. *purists*, Archig.ap.Gal.8.578. [-ειος is written in Phld.*Rh.* l.c. (Comp.), *PSI*3.158.50 (Comp., iii A.D.), Phld.*D.*3.8, *PMag.Lond.* l.c., and required by metre in Eub., Nicostr., *Carm.Aur.*, ll. cc.: -ιος never.] ⊛ **-ειότης**, later **καθᾰριότης**, ητος, ἡ, *cleanliness, neatness*, Hdt.2.37, X.*Mem.*2.1.22; *purity*, διαφέρει ἡ ὄψις ἁφῆς καθαρειότητι Arist.*EN*1176$^{a}$1, cf. 1177$^{a}$26; τοῦ ἀέρος Thphr.*Sens.*48; *purity* of language, Plu.*Lyc.*21, S.E. *M.*1.176. 2. *scrupulousness, moral integrity*, *IG*4.1 (Aegina, ii B.C.), *OGI*339.14 (Sestos, ii B.C.). 3. *elegance, refinement*, τῇ κ. Κυπρίους..[ὑπερέβαλε] Duris 10J.; opp. περιεργία, Plu.2.693b, cf. 142a, *Crass.*3; opp. λιτότης, Hierocl.*in CA*17p.457M.; also, *simplicity, frugality*, τῆς διαίτης Plu.2.644c; *economy of movement* in a surgeon's hand, ib.67e. ⊛ **-εσις**, εως, ἡ, perh. Dor. for καθάρισις, στέγας *IG*4.1484.293 (Epid.). **-ευσις**, εως, ἡ, gloss on ἁγιασμός, Hsch., cf. *EM*10.38. **-ευτέον**, *one must keep oneself clean*, τινος *from* a thing, Luc.*Hist.Conscr.*6; περὶ ἀφροδίσια Epict.*Ench.* 33.8. **-εύω**, (καθαρός) *to be clean* or *pure*, Pl.*Phd.*58b, *Lg.*759c, Phld.*Lib.*p.9O., Porph.*Abst.*4.6; of *sifted* grain, *PPetr.*2p.2 (iii B.C.): c. gen., *to be clean* or *free from*, φόνου Pl.*Ep.*357a; [κακιῶν] Phld.*Rh.*1.218S.; ἁμαρτημάτων Plu.*Cat.Mi.*24; ὀνείδους Luc.*Am.* 22; κ. πυρετοῦ *to be free from* fever, Gal.7.503: hence ἡμέραι -εύουσαι ibid.; κ. ἀπ' αὐτοῦ (sc. τοῦ σώματος) Pl.*Phd.*67a; κ. γνώμῃ *to be pure* or *clean* in mind, Ar.*Ra.*355; περί τι Plb.6.56.15. 2. Rhet., of a writer, *to be pure, correct* in language, κ. τὴν διάλεκτον D.H. *Lys.*2; οἱ καθαρεύοντες *purists*, Hdn.Gr.2.224. 3. Gramm., *to be preceded by a vowel, to be 'pure'* (cf. καθαρός I. 5b), A.D.*Pron.*99.24, Theodos.*Can.*p.70H.; *contain a 'pure' syllable*, Hdn.Gr.2.923, Id. ap.Eust.1859.13. **-ιεύω**, *to be* καθάριος, in Med., Alex.Aphr. *Pr.*2.53. II. = καθαρεύω 3, Hdn.Gr.ap.Choerob.*in Theod.*1.232, Theognost.*Can.*28, etc. ⊛ **-ίζω**, fut. -ιῶ *Ep.Hebr.*9.14:—*cleanse*, θυσιαστήριον Lxx*Ex.*29.36, cf. *Ev.Matt.*23.25, *Act.Ap.*10.15; *sift* grain, *PStrassb.*2.11 (iii A.D.); *prune away*, περισσὰ βλαστήματα *PLond.*1.131$^{r}$192 (i A.D.); *clear* ground of weeds, etc., *PLips.*111. 12 (iv A.D.); *keep* a precinct *clear*, ἀπό τινων *IG*5(1).1390.37 (Andania, i B.C.):—in Med., fut. -ιοῦμαι, of the menses, Hp.*Superf.* 43. II. of persons, *purify*, ἀπὸ ἁμαρτίας Lxx*Si.*38.10; ἀπὸ παντὸς μολυσμοῦ 2*Ep.Cor.*7.1; τὴν συνείδησιν ἀπὸ νεκρῶν ἔργων *Ep. Hebr.*9.14; *cleanse* from leprosy, *Ev.Matt.*8.2 (and in Pass., of the disease, ib.3):—Pass., -ιζέστω ἀπὸ γυναικός κτλ. *IG*2$^{2}$.1366.4, cf. 1365. **-ιος**, v. καθάρειος. II. καθάριον, τό, *purgative medicine*, *POxy.*116.15 (ii A.D.). **-ιόω**, *purify*, in Pass., Lxx*La.*4.7, prob. in *PTeb.ined.*703. **-ῐσις**, εως, ἡ, = κάθαρσις, *PHeid.*1.6.18 (iv A.D.), v.l. in Lxx*Le.*12.4,6, Aq.ibid.; cf. καθάρεσις. ⊛ **-ισμός**, ὁ, later form for καθαρμός, Lxx*Ex.*29.36, *Ev.Luc.*2.22, *Ev.Jo.*2.6, Luc. *Asin.*22, *PLond.*2.168.11 (ii A.D.). **-ιστήριον**, τό, *place for purifying, sifting*, Harp. s.v. Κεγχρεών. **-ιστής**, οῦ, ὁ, *tree-pruner*, *Gloss.*

⊛ **κάθαρμα** [κᾰ], ατος, τό, (καθαίρω) *that which is thrown away in cleansing*: in pl., *offscourings, refuse of a sacrifice*, A.*Ch.*98; *residuum* of ore after smelting, *slag*, Str.3.2.8: sg., = κάθαρσις II, Hp.*Epid.* 5.2. 2. = φαρμακός, Sch.Ar.*Pl.*454, Sch.Id.*Eq.*1133: hence metaph., of persons, *outcast*, Ar.*Pl.*454; αἱρούμενοι καθάρματα στρατηγούς Eup.117.8; τοὺς μὲν καθάρματα, τοὺς δὲ πτωχούς, τοὺς δ' οὐδ' ἀνθρώπους ὑπολαμβάνων εἶναι D.21.185, cf. 199, 18.128, Aeschin.3. 211, etc. II. in pl., = κάθαρσις, *purification*, E.*IT*1316; ποντίων καθαρμάτων..ἀμοιβάς in return *for clearing* the sea (of pirates), Id. *HF*225. III. ἐντὸς τοῦ καθάρματος within *the purified ground* where the assembly was held, Ar.*Ach.*44.

**κᾰθαρματώδης**, ες, *connected with* καθαρμοί, ὄνομα *EM*512.7.

**καθαρμόζω**, *join* or *fit to*, βρόχον δείρᾳ E.*Hipp.*771 (lyr.); [πλόκαμον] ὑπὸ μίτρᾳ Id.*Ba.*929; βάσιν χερσὶ προσθίαν καθαρμόσας *fitting* its forefeet to my hands, Id.*Rh.*210; *fit clamps* into their places, *IG*7. 3073.72 (Lebad.):—Med., Ph.1.342.

**κᾰθαρμός**, ὁ, (καθαίρω) *cleansing, purification*, from guilt, νίψαι καθαρμῷ τήνδε τὴν στέγην S.*OT*1228: hence, *purificatory offering, atonement, expiation*, καθαρμὸν τῆς χώρης ποιέεσθαί τινα Hdt.7.197: freq. in pl., μύσος ἐλαύνειν καθαρμοῖς A.*Ch.*968 (lyr., dub. l.), cf. *Th.* 738, *Eu.*277, 283, *Berl.Sitzb.*1927.156 (Cyrene): sg., S.*OT*99; θοῦ νῦν καθαρμὸν δαιμόνων make *an offering to avert* their wrath, Id.*OC*466; καθαρμὸν θύειν E.*IT*1332; λύσεις τε καὶ καθαρμοὶ ἀδικημάτων Pl.*R.* 364e; ὁ περὶ τὴν διάνοιαν κ. Id.*Sph.*227c; κ. ποιεῖσθαι τῆς δυνάμεως, Lat. *lustrare exercitum*, Plb.21.41.9, Plu.*Caes.*43; of the Roman *lustrum*, D.H.4.22; κ. ὅπλων, σάλπιγγος, = Lat. *armilustrium, tubilustrium*, Lyd.*Mens.*4.34,60. 2. *purificatory rite* of initiation into mysteries, Pl.*Phd.*69c, *Phdr.*244e; ἀνιστὰς ἀπὸ τοῦ καθαρμοῦ D.18. 259, cf. Plu.2.47a: hence in pl., as title of poem by Empedocles, Ath.14.620d; by Epimenides, Suid. s.h.v. 3. *purgation* by ordeal, *PMag.Lond.*46.180,196. II. *purging, evacuation, discharge*, Arist.*HA*587$^{b}$1, Plu.2.134d. 2. metaph., *purge, clearance* of unhealthy animals, Pl.*Lg.*735b. III. = κάθαρμα I. 2, Plu. 2.518b.

**καθάρμοσις**, εως, ἡ, *precise adaptation*, *Theol.Ar.*54.

**κᾰθᾰρο-λογέω**, *to be precise* or *accurate in language*, Eust.352. 35. ⊛ **-ποιέω**, *cleanse*, ἕλκη Gal.11.683. 2. *sift, winnow*, gloss on πτίσσειν, Sch.Ar.*Ach.*506. II. *clear* property from debts and encumbrances, *PMasp.*97.32 (vi A.D.):—hence ⊛ **-ποίησις**, εως, ἡ, ib. 151.122 (vi A.D.).

⊛ **κᾰθᾰρ-ός**, ά, όν, Dor. **κοθαρός** *Tab.Heracl.*1.103, Orph.*Fr.*32c.1, Aeol. **κόθ-** Alc.*Supp.*7.3; cf. ἀνακαθαίρω, κάθαρσις: 1. *physically clean, spotless* (not in Il.), εἵματα Od.6.61, Archil.12, cf. E.*Cyc.*35, 562, etc.; of persons, *cleanly*, κ. περὶ ἐσθῆτα Arist.*VV*1250$^{b}$28, cf. *Rh.*1416$^{a}$ 23 (nisi leg. καθάριος). 2. *clear of admixture, clear, pure*, esp. of water, Βορυσθένης ῥέει καθαρὸς παρὰ θολεροῖσι Hdt.4.53; κ. ὕδατα E. *Hipp.*209 (anap.); ὕδωρ κ. ζῶν Lxx*Nu.*5.17; δρόσοι E.*Ion*96 (anap.); κ. καὶ διαφανῆ ὑδάτια Pl.*Phdr.*229b; οὖρον Hp.*Epid.*1.3; διαχώρημα Id.*Coac.*640; κ. φάος, φέγγος, Pi.*P.*6.14, 9.90; πνεῦμα κ. οὐρανοῦ E.*Hel.*867; κ. ἄρτος Hdt.2.40; of *white* bread, Wilcken *Chr.*30i17 (iii/ii B.C.), Lxx*Ju.*10.5, Gal.6.482, 19.137; ἄλευρον κ. Diocl.*Fr.*139; χρυσίον, ἀργύριον -ώτατον, Hdt.4.166, cf. Theoc.15.36, Ph.1.190, etc.; σῖτος X.*Oec.*18.8; σῖτος κ. ἀπὸ πάντων *PHib.*1.84(*a*).6 (iv/iii B.C.): freq. of grain, *winnowed*, πυρὸς κ. ἄδολος *POxy.*1124.11 (i A.D.), cf. *PTeb.*93.36 (ii B.C.), etc.; of metals, etc., σίδηρος *Sammelb.*4481.13 (v A.D.), etc.; ἀρωμάτων, καθαρῶν, λαχάνων, dub. sens. in *PLond.*2.429. 6 (iv A.D.); ἄκρατος καὶ κ. νοῦς X.*Cyr.*8.7.30; χρόαι Arist.*Sens.*440$^{a}$5; φωναί Id.*Aud.*801$^{b}$28; of feelings, *unmixed*, μῖσος τῆς ἀλλοτρίας φύσεως Pl.*Mx.*245d, cf. Thgn.89; *serene*, φρήν E.*Hipp.*1120 (lyr.). 3. *clear of objects, free*, ἐν καθαρῷ (sc. τόπῳ) in an *open* space, ἐν κ., ὅθι δὴ νεκύων διεφαίνετο χῶρος Il.8.491; ἐν κ., ὅθι κύματ' ἐπ' ἠιόνος κλύζεσκον 23.61, cf. Ph.2.535 (Sup.); πάξαις Ἄλτιν ἐν κ. in *a clearing*, Pi.*O.*10 (11).45; ἐν κ. βῆναι to leave the way *clear*, S.*OC*1575 (lyr.); ἐν τῷ κ. οἰκεῖν live in *the clear sunshine*, Pl.*R.*520d; διὰ καθαροῦ ῥέειν, of a river whose course is *clear and open*, Hdt.1.202: with Subst., κελεύθῳ ἐν κ. Pi.*O.*6.23; χῶρος κ. Hdt.1.132; ἐν κ. λειμῶνι Theoc.26.5; ἐν ἡλίῳ κ. in the *open* sun, opp. σκιά, Pl.*Phdr.*239c; ὥς σφι τὸ ἐμποδὼν ἐγεγόνεε κ. was *cleared away*, Hdt.7.183; κ. ποιεῖσθαι τὰς ἀρκυστασίας set up the nets *in open ground*, X.*Cyn.*6.6; freq. of land, *free* from weeds, etc., παραδώσω τὸν κλῆρον κ. ἀπὸ θρύου καλάμου ἀγρώστεως κτλ. *PTeb.*105.59 (ii B.C.); παραδώσω τὰς ἀρούρας κ. ὡς ἔλαβον *BGU*1018.25 (iii A.D.): c. gen., γλῶσσα καθαρὴ τῶν σημηΐων *clear* of the marks, Hdt.2.38; καθαρὸν τῶν προβόλων, of a fort, Arr.*An.*2.21.7; of documents, *free from mistakes*, *POxy.*1277.13 (iii A.D.); χειρόγραφον κ. ἀπὸ ἐπιγραφῆς καὶ ἀλείφαδος *free* from interlineation and erasure, *PLond.*2.178.13 (ii A.D.). b. metaph., *free, clear* of debt, liability, etc., κ. ἀπὸ δημοσίων καὶ παντὸς εἴδους *BGU*197.14 (i A.D.); κ. ἀπό τε ὀφειλῆς καὶ ὑποθήκης καὶ παντὸς διεγγυήματος ib.112.11 (i A.D.); γῆ κ. ἀπὸ γεωργίας βασιλικῆς *POxy.*633 (ii A.D.); καθαρὰ ποιῆσαι to give a *discharge*, *PAvrom.*1 *A* 22; in moral sense, *free from pollution*, καθαρῷ θανάτῳ an *honourable* death, Od.22.462; θάνατον οὐ κ., τὸν δι' ἀγχόνης Ph.2.491; ψυχαὶ ἀρηΐφατοι καθαρώτεραι ἢ ἐνὶ νούσοις Heraclit.136; freq. *free from guilt* or *defilement, pure*, χεῖρες A.*Eu.* 313 (anap.); καθαρὸς χεῖρας Hdt.1.35, Antipho 5.11, And.1.95; κ. παρέχειν τινὰ κατὰ τὸ σῶμα καὶ κατὰ τὴν ψυχήν Pl.*Cra.*405b; ἔρχομαι ἐκ κοθαρῶν κοθαρά Orph.*Fr.*32c.1, al.; of ceremonial *purity*, καθαρὰ καὶ ἁγνή εἰμι ἀπό τε τῶν ἄλλων τῶν οὐ καθαρευόντων καὶ ἀπ' ἀνδρὸς συνουσίας Jusj.ap.D.59.78, cf. *UPZ*78.28 (ii B.C.), Lxx*Nu.*8.7, al.; ἀπὸ τάφου καὶ ἐκφορᾶς καθαροί *SIG*982.9 (ii B.C.); esp. of persons *purified* after pollution, ἱκέτης προσῆλθες κ. A.*Eu.*474, cf. S.*OC*548, etc.; also of things, βωμοί, θύματα, δόμος, μέλαθρα, A.*Supp.*654 (lyr.), E. *IT*1163, 1231 (troch.), 693: c. gen., *clear of* or *from*.., κ. ἐγκλημάτων Antipho 2.4.11; ἀδικίας, κακῶν, Pl.*R.*496d, *Cra.*404a; ὁ τῶν κακῶν κ. τόπος Id.*Tht.*177a; κ. τὰς χεῖρας φόνου Id.*Lg.*864e; Κόρινθον..ἀποδεῖξαι τῶν μιαιφόνων καθαράν X.*HG*4.4.6; κ. εἰμι ἀπὸ τοῦ αἵματος πάντων *Act.Ap.*20.26, cf. D.C.37.24; κ. ἀπὸ ὅρκου Lxx*Ge.*24.8; *ceremonially pure*, of food, ὄσπριον Hdt.2.37; of victims, Lxx*Ge.*7.2, al., *PGen.*32.9 (ii A.D.), etc.; κ. ἡμέραι, opp. ἀποφράδες, Pl.*Lg.*800d. c. in act. sense, *purifying, cleansing*, λέβης Pi.*O.*1.26; θέειον Theoc. 24.96. 4. of birth, *pure, genuine*, σπέρμα θεοῦ Pi.*P.*3.15; πόλις

E.*Ion*673; τῶν Ἀθηναίων ὅπερ ἐστράτευε καθαρὸν ἐξῆλθε, i.e. were *citizens of pure blood*, Th.5.8; οἱ τῷ γένει μὴ κ. Arist.*Ath.*13.5; κ. ἀστοί Sch.Ar.*Ach.*506; καθαρόν a *real, genuine* saying, Ar.*V.*1015; κ. Τίμων a Timon *pure and simple*, Id.*Av.*1549; κ. δοῦλος Antiph.9 (glossed by ἀπηκριβωμένος, *AB*105); ζημία κ., of a person, Alciphro 3.21. 5. of language, *pure*, ὀνόματα, λέξις, D.H.*Comp.*1,3; διάλεκτος Id.*Dem.*5; so of writers, [Λυσίας] κ. τὴν ἑρμηνείαν Id.*Lys.*2; [Ξενοφῶν] κ. τοῖς ὀνόμασι Id.*Pomp.*4; also, *clear, simple*, σεμνὸς καὶ κ. Jul.*Or.*2.77a. b. Gramm., *preceded by a vowel, pure*, D.T. 635.10, 639.5, Hdn.Gr.2.930, al.; *containing a 'pure' syllable*, ib. 928. 6. *without blemish, sound*, ὁ κ. στρατός, τὸ κ. τοῦ στρατοῦ, the *sound portion* of the army, Hdt.1.211, 4.135; v. supr. 4. 7. *clear, exact*, ἂν κ. ὦσιν αἱ ψῆφοι if the accounts are *exactly balanced*, D.18.227 (sed cf. καθαιρέω II.5). II. Adv. *purely*, ἁγνῶς καὶ καθαρῶς *h.Ap.*121, Hes.*Op.*337: Comp. -ωτέρως Porph.*Abst.*2.44. 2. of birth, κ. γεγονέναι Hdt.1.147; αἱ κ. Ἑλληνίδες Sor.1.112, cf. Luc.*Rh. Pr.*24. 3. *with clean hands, honestly*, σὺν δίκῃ..καὶ κ. Thgn.198; δικαίως καὶ κ. D.9.62; κ. τε καὶ μετρίως τὸν βίον διεξελθεῖν Pl.*Phd.* 108c. 4. *clearly, plainly*, λέγειν Ar.*V.*631, cf. E.*Rh.*35 (anap.); λέξις κ. καὶ ἀκριβῶς ἔχουσα Isoc.5.4; κ. γνῶναι Ar.*V.*1045, Pl.*Phd.*66e; εἴσεσθαι ibid.; καθαρώτατα ἀποδεῖξαι Id.*Cra.*426b. 5. of language, *purely, correctly*, -ώτερον διαλέγεσθαι Plu.2.1116e, cf. Luc.*Im.*15. 6. *entirely*, Ar.*Av.*591; κ. τις ὢν ἀόργητος Phld.*Ir.*p.71 W.; κ. ἐς ἐφήβους τελεῖν D.C.36.25, cf. *Cod.Just.*1.4.34.9: Sup. -ώτατα *in its purest form*, Phld.*Piet.*66. ❋ -ότης, ητος, ἡ, *purity* of αἰθήρ as compared with ἀήρ, Pl.*Phd.*111b: metaph., [ἡ σοφία] χωρεῖ διὰ πάντων διὰ τὴν κ. Lxx *Wi.*7.24; ἡ τῶν εἰδῶν κ. Dam.*Pr.*308; ἄμικτος καὶ ἀσύγχυτος κ. ibid. 2. *cleanliness*, of a town, Pl.*Lg.*778c. 3. *clearness*, ὀφθαλμῶν Hp.*Coac.*213. 4. moral *purity*, ψυχῆς Aristeas 234. 5. *honesty*, ἡ περὶ τὰ χρήματα κ. Plb.31.25.9; ἐπιείκεια καὶ κ. *POxy.*67.6 (iv A.D.); πίστις καὶ κ. *Michel* 545.18 (Phrygia, ii B.C.). 6. *purity, lucidity*, of literary style, Sch.Hermog.in Rh.7.81 W. 7. as a title, *Rectitude, Holiness*, *POxy.*2110.16 (iv A.D.).

❋ **κᾰθᾰρουργ-(ε)ῖον**, τό, *bakery for fine bread*, *CPR*207.12 (ii A.D.). -ία, ἡ, *artistic work* (the exact sense is dub.), *CIG*4558 (Syria). II. *baking of fine bread*, *POxy.*2128.10 (ii A.D.). ❋ -ικός, ή, όν, *sifted, fine*, γῦρις *Gp.*20.35. ❋ -ός, ὁ, *baker of fine bread*, *Sammelb.*984.5 (pl., i A.D.), *PLond.*2.454a (iv A.D.).

**καθαρο-φόνος** and -**φόντης**, glosses on Ἀργειφόντης, Hsch.

**καθαρπ-ᾰγή** (κατ- cod.), ἡ, *direptio*, *Gloss.* -**άζω**, *snatch down*, ἐκ δεξιᾶς ξίφη, τεύχη πασσάλων, E.*Andr.*813, 1122; *seize, appropriate*, τὰ ἀλλότρια Str.16.2.37:—Pass., Ph.2.7, *PThead.*23.14 (iv A.D.).

❋ **κᾰθάρ-σιος**, ον, (καθαίρω) *cleansing* from guilt or defilement, *purifying*, Ζεύς Hdt.1.44, cf. Arist.*Mu.*401a23, etc.; of Dionysus, μολεῖν καθαρσίῳ ποδί S.*Ant.*1144 (lyr.); of sacrifice, αἷμα A.*Eu.*449, *Th.*680; πῦρ E.*HF*937, *IA*1112, J.*AJ*20.8.5, al.; φλόξ E.*Hel.*869; προχύται Id.*IA*1471: c. gen., [Λοξίας] δωμάτων κ. A.*Eu.*63; ἱερὰ κ. οἴκων E. *HF*923; also κ. φόνου *cleansing from*.., A.*Eu.*578. II. as Subst., 1. καθάρσιον (sc. ἱερόν), τό, *purificatory offering*, Aeschin. 1.23, cf. Phot.: pl., *BMus.Inscr.*481*.280: hence, *expiation*, καθαρσίου ἐδέετο κυρῆσαι Hdt.1.35, cf. Jul.*Or.*2.58d. 2. (sc. φάρμακον) *purge*, Alex.Trall.1.15, *POxy.*1384.1 (v A.D.), Phlp. *in Ph.*318. 12. III. καθάρσια, τά, = Lat. *illuvies*, *Gloss.* (nisi leg. ἀκαθαρσία). ❋ -**σις**, εως, ἡ, Elean **κόθαρσις** *Schwyzer*412, *cleansing* from guilt or defilement, *purification*, Hdt.1.35, Pl.*Cra.*405a, etc.; κάθαρσις..τὸ χωρίζειν ὅτι μάλιστα ἀπὸ τοῦ σώματος τὴν ψυχήν Id.*Phd.*67c, cf. *Sph.*227c (pl.); *cleansing* of the universe by fire, Zeno and Chrysipp.*Stoic.*2.184; *cleansing* of food by or before cooking, Diocl. *Fr.*138. 2. *clarification*, φυσικῶν προβλημάτων Epicur.*Ep.*2p.36 U.; καθάρσεως δεῖται needs *explanation*, Phld.*Lib.*p.22 O. II. Medic., *clearing off of morbid humours*, etc., *evacuation*, whether natural or by the use of medicines (cf. Gal.17(2).358), Hp.*Aph.* 5.36, cf. *Acut.(Sp.)*31, etc.; ἰατρικὴ κ. Pl.*Lg.*628d; καθάρσεις, the menses in women, Hp.*Aph.*5.60; καθάρσεις καταμηνίων Arist. *HA*572b29; so κάθαρσις alone, Id.*GA*775b5; κ. μετὰ τόκον Hp.*Aër.* 7; ἡ ἐν τοῖς τόκοις κ. Arist.*HA*574b4; κ. αἵματος αὐτομάτη μοι.. συνέβη D.54.12. b. τραγῳδία... δι' ἐλέου καὶ φόβου περαίνουσα τὴν τῶν τοιούτων παθημάτων κ. Arist.*Po.*1449b28, cf. *Pol.*1341b 38. III. *pruning* of trees, Thphr.*CP*3.7.12. IV. *winnowing* of grain, in pl., *PTeb.*92.10 (ii B.C.); κ. πυροῦ *PRyl.*71.9 (i B.C.); τοῦ καρποῦ Ph.2.57 (sg.). V. *clearing* of land, *PSI*6.577.13 (iii B.C.), *PPetr.*3p.122 (iii B.C.), etc. -**τέος**, α, ον, *to be purged*, Gal. 10.971. II. -**τέον**, *one must purge*, Hp.*Loc.Hom.*23. 2. *one must prune*, δένδρον *Gp.*10.77.2. -**τήρ**, ῆρος, ὁ, = καθαρτής, Man. 4.251; a name given to ὄροβος at Tralles, Plu.2.302b. -**τήριος**, ον, *purificatory*, θυσίαι D.H.9.40; τὰ κ. Poll.1.32. II. -**τήριον** (sc. φάρμακον), τό, *drug which effects* κάθαρσις, λοχείων, ἐπιμηνίων, Hp.*Mul.*1.78; *purgative*, Aret.*CA*1.4, Gal.11.354; κ. κατωτερικόν Aet.16.52. -**τής**, οῦ, ὁ, *cleanser, purifier*, μάγοι καὶ κ. Hp.*Morb. Sacr.*1, cf. D.Chr.4.89 (pl.); σοῦ γὰρ ἔρχομαι..κ. S.*El.*70; στρατοῦ κ. Id.*Fr.*34; τῆς χώρας Ar.*V.*1043; ποταμῶν Plu.*Luc.*26; θηρίων, of Heracles, Max.Tyr.21.6: metaph., δοξῶν... περὶ ψυχὴν κ. εἶναι Pl.*Sph.* 231e; as occupational name, *IG*5(1).209.25 (i B.C.). -**τικός**, ή, όν, *of, fit for cleansing* or *purifying*, ἐλαίου καὶ γῆς Pl.*Ti.*60d; τὰ μέλη τὰ κ. (v. κάθαρσις II) Arist.*Pol.*1342a15; τὰ κ. *purgatives*, Phld.*Sign.* 25; κ. ἀρεταί Hierocl.*in CA*2p.422 M.: ἡ -κή (sc. τέχνη) Pl.*Sph.* 231b. Adv. -κῶς Marin.*Procl.*19. II. Medic., *promoting* κάθαρσις, πρόσθετον Hp.*Mul.*1.74; usu. *purgative*, δύναμις Gal.11.768 (metaph., Cebes 14); φάρμακον Plu.2.999f, cf. Gal.5.128; οἶνος Dsc.5.66 (Comp.); κ. alone, Hp.*Fract.*24, S.E.*M.*8.480. -**τρια**, ἡ, fem. of καθαρτής, Sch.Pi.*P.*3.139. -**υλλος**, ον, Com. Dim. of καθαρός, *dainty*, ἄρτοι Pl.Com.86. Adv. -λλως Cratin.27. -**ώδης**, ες, *clear*, ὄμμα v.l. for καρώδης, Hp.*Epid.*5.99.

**καθαναίνω**, v. καταναίνω.

**κάθαψις**, εως, ἡ, *good reaction*, produced by friction after the bath, ἄχρι πολλῆς κ. Agathin.ap.Orib.10.7.18.

**κάθε·** ἐπίδος, Hsch.

❋ **καθέδρ-α**, ἡ, *seat*, κ. τοῦ λαγῶ a hare's *seat* or *form*, X.*Cyn.*4.4; *chair*, Herod.Med.ap.Orib.6.25.1, *CPR*22.8 (ii A.D.), Hdn.2.3.7; opp. κλίνη, Plu.2.714e; of rowers' *seats*, Plb.1.21.2; κ. λοιμῶν, πρεσβυτέρων, Lxx *Ps.*1.1, 106(107).32. 2. *sitting part, posteriors*, Hp.*Int.*47, Poll.2.184, *PRyl.*63.10 (iii A.D.). 3. *base* of a column, Str.17.1.46. II. *sitting posture*, Arist.*Cat.*6b11, *PA*689b21, Thphr.*Lass.*5,7, Plu.2.45c, etc. 2. *sitting idle, inaction*, ἐν τῇ καθέδρᾳ Th.2.18; κ. καὶ σχολή Plu.*Cam.*28. 3. *session*, Luc. *JTr.*11. III. *chair* of a teacher, ἐπὶ τῆς Μωυσέως κ. ἐκάθισαν *Ev. Matt.*23.2; *professorial chair*, ἐπὶ τῆς κ. σοφιστής *SIG*845 (Eleusis, iii A.D.). IV. imperial *throne*, τὸν ἐπὶ τῇ κ. τοῦ Αὐτοκράτορος, the Emperor's representative, *BSA*27.234 (Sparta, ii A.D.). -**άριον**, τό, Dim. of foreg., *POxy.*963 (ii/iii A.D.). -**ιος**, ον, *of* or *for sitting*, σχῆμα Antyll.ap.Orib.9.14.6, Aët.15.5; καθέδριόν τινα σχηματίζειν ib.7; -ιος σχηματιζέσθω Id.8.51. 2. *sedentary*, βίος Sor. 1.27. II. Subst. -**ιον**, τό, *small chair*, ib.106; gloss on διέδριον, Zonar. -**ωτός**, όν, *provided with seats*, καρρίον *Gloss.*

❋ **καθέζομαι** (v. infr.), impf. ἐκαθεζόμην in Prose, X.*An.*1.5.9, *Cyr.*5.3. 25 (but freq. as aor. 2, And.1.44, Th.4.110, Pl.*Euthd.*272e); in Poets, καθεζόμην Od.9.417, A.*Eu.*6, Ar.*Lys.*1139: fut. καθεδοῦμαι Id.*Ra.*200, *Av.*727 (anap.), And.1.111, Pl.*Tht.*146a, D.5.15; later καθεδήσομαι D.L.2.72, καθεσθήσομαι Lxx *Le.*12.5: aor. καθεσθείς *AP*9.644.5 (Agath.), Paus.9.3.4, Charito 3.2, but v. Luc.*Sol.*11 (καθίζομαι, Pass. of καθίζω, which supplies the trans. sense, is more common in pres. and impf., but we have κατ' ἄρ' ἕζεαι Od.10.378, καθεζόμεσθα E.*Heracl.* 33, καθέζονται Lys.13.37, etc.):—*sit down, take one's seat*, ἀγορήνδε καθεζώμεσθα κιόντες Od.1.372; εἰνὶ θύρῃσι καθέζετο 9.417, cf. Il.24. 126, etc.; κατ' ἄρ' ἕζευ ἐπὶ θρόνου ib.522; κατ' ἄρ' ἕζετ' ἐπὶ..λίθοισιν Od.3.406; καθεζομένη πρόχνυ (v. πρόχνυ); so κ. ἐν..εὐνατηρίοις S. *Tr.*918; ἐπὶ ζυγοῖς ἀρχῆς E.*Ph.*75; ἐς θρόνον A.*Pr.*231; *preside*, Lys. l.c., Aeschin.3.73; ἐνθαδί Ar.*Ra.*200; οὐ λαχόντες προεδρεύειν, ἀλλ' ἐκ παρασκευῆς καθεζόμενοι *taking their seats*, Aeschin.3.3: Medic., Hp.*Epid.*7.3. 2. *sit down in, occupy*, a country, *encamp*, Th.2. 18, 7.77; *settle*, εἰς χώραν *OGI*201.13 (Nubia, vi A.D.). II. *remain seated*, in various senses: 1. *sit still*, with collat. notion of inaction, τίφθ' οὕτως κατ' ἄρ' ἕζεαι ἶσος ἀναύδῳ; Od.10.378, cf.6.295. 2. *sit* as suppliants, ἱκέται καθεζόμεσθα βώμιοι E.*Heracl.* l.c.; πρὸς τὰ ἱερὰ ἱκετῶν καθεζομένων Th.3.70, cf. Ar.*Lys.*1139, D.18.107. 3. *sit* for one's portrait, Porph.*Plot.*1. 4. of a teacher, πρὸς ὑμᾶς ἐκαθεζόμην διδάσκων *Ev.Matt.*26.55.

**καθείατο**, Ep. for ἐκάθηντο, 3 pl. impf. of κάθημαι.

**καθείμαρται**, pf. Pass., used impers., *it is ordained by fate*, esp. to one's ruin, Ps.-Luc.*Philopatr.*14; τινι c. inf., ib.16, Arr.*Epict.*2.6.10: plpf., καθείμαρτο Chrysipp.*Stoic.*2.292; also pers., βραχὺς χρόνος ὁ τοῦ ζῆν ἑκάστῳ καθείμαρται Luc.*Am.*19; part., πάλαι καθειμαρμένων τούτων *having been ordained by fate*, Plu.*Alex.*52.

❋ **καθειργνῡμι**, and in Luc.*Am.*39 **καθείργω** (= **κατείργω**, q.v.): aor. 1 καθεῖρξα E.*Ba.*618 (troch.), etc.:—*shut in, confine*, usu. of animals or persons, κατὰ συφεοῖσιν ἐέργνυ Od.10.238; οὗ καθεῖρξ' ἡμᾶς E.*Ba.* l.c.; τὸν πατέρα..ἔνδον καθεῖρξας Ar.*V.*70, cf. Cratin.72, Lys. *Fr.*75.4, Pl.*Tht.*197e; κηρίνοις πλάσμασι κ. ib.200c; ἐν τῷ σταυρώματι X.*HG*3.2.3; ἐν οἰκίσκῳ D.18.97. 2. rarely of things, καθεῖρξαι χρυσὸν ἐν δόμοις Anan.3; τὴν σελήνην..ἐς λοφεῖον Ar.*Nu.*751; τὴν μακρολογίαν κ. *confine* it *within bounds*, Pl.*Grg.*461d.

**κάθειρξις**, εως, ἡ, Att. for κάτειρξις, *shutting in, confining*, Plu.2. 366d, Ael.*NA*15.27, Aristid.*Or.*48(24).58.

❋ **καθείς**, for καθ' εἷς, *one by one, one after another*, Lxx 3*Ma.*5.34; εἷς καθεῖς *Ev.Marc.*14.19, etc.: formed backwards from the neut. ἓν καθέν, noted by Luc.*Sol.*9.

**καθεῖσα**, v. καθίζω:—but καθεῖσαν 3 pl. aor. 2 of καθίημι.

**καθειστόν·** εἶδος φιλήματος, Hsch.

**καθεκ-τέον**, (κατέχω) *one must keep back, restrain*, Plu.*Cat.Mi.*63, etc. -**της**, ου, ὁ, *trap-door*, *Gp.*14.6.6. -**τικός**, ή, όν, *capable of holding* or *retaining*, ἡ μνήμη ἕξις κ. ὑπολήψεως Arist.*Top.*125b18; κ. δύναμις Gal.1.654, Alex.Aphr.*Pr.*2.60; τὸ κ. καὶ ἰξῶδες Artem.2.14: c. gen., κ. τοῦ πνεύματος, opp. προετικός, Arist.*Pr.*963a21 (Comp.). Adv. -κῶς, ἔχειν τῶν μαθημάτων Marin.*Procl.*5. -**τός**, ή, όν, (κατέχω) *to be held back, checked*, θρασὺς καὶ βδελυρὸς καὶ οὐδὲ κ. ἔτι D. 21.2, cf. Plu.*Fab.*10, *Pomp.*66; τῶν πραγμάτων οὐκέτι πολλοῖς ὄντων καθεκτῶν since power *could* not *be retained in the hands of* many, Id. *Brut.*47; ἐν τῷ κ. εἶναι to *contain* oneself, Philostr.*Im.*2.6. Adv. οὐ -τῶς so as not *to be restrained*, μάχεσθαι Id.*Her.*10.5. II. *in the grip of*, λούπησι χαλεπῇσιν Corinn.*Supp.*1.28.

❋ **καθελίσσω**, Ion. **κατειλίσσω**, Att. aor. part. **κατειλίξας** (v. infr.), *wrap with bandages*, κατειλίσσουσι πᾶν τὸ σῶμα σινδόνος..τελαμῶσι, of mummies, Hdt.2.86; of wounds, Id.7.181; σώματα σπαργάνοις καθειλίξαντες Max.Tyr.36.2 (v.l. κατ-); καττίτερον..κατειλίξας ἐρίοις *IG*2².204.32 (iv B.C.); καθελίξας, v.l. κατελλ-, κατελ-, Hp.*Nat.Mul.* 32:—Pass., τὰς κνήμας ῥάκεσι..κατειλίχατο (3 pl. plpf.) Hdt.7.76; κατειλίχθαι ταινίῃ Hp.*Art.*5; ἐρίοις..καθείλικτο Gal.*UP*4.9; ὅταν

κατελιχθῇ Ath.Mech.24.8. II. of a serpent, *drag down in its coils*, συνέσφιγγεν ἅπαντα, καθελίττων ἐς τὴν ἑαυτοῦ χειάν Eun.*Hist*.p.257 D.

**καθελκόομαι**, Pass., *break out into ulcers*, χείλεα καθηλκωμένα Hp. *Epid*.7.11; but καθελκωθεὶς *covered with wounds*, Arist.*HA*621a20.

**καθελκυσμός**, ὁ, *launching*, Moschio ap.Ath.5.207a. II. *collapse*, Marcellin.*Puls*.293.

⊛ **καθέλκω**, fut. καθέλξω Ar.*Ra*.1398, καθελκύσω Luc.*DDeor*.21.1: aor. part. καθελκύσαντες Th.6.34: pf. καθείλκυκα D.5.12:—Pass., aor. and pf. (v. infr.): 1. of ships, *draw to the sea, launch*, E.*Hel*. 1531, Ar.*Ach*.544, *Eq*.1315, Isoc.4.118; καθεῖλκον ναῦς ἐς τὸν Πειραιᾶ Th.2.94: abs., Phld.*Mus*.p.15 K., al.:—Pass., τῶν νεῶν κατελκυσθεισέων ἐς θάλασσαν Hdt.7.100; εἴ τι ναυτικόν ἐστι καθειλκυσμένον Th.6.50. 2. *draw down, depress* the scale, Ar.*Ra*.1398: metaph., *outweigh*, καθέλκει δρῦν πολὺ τὴν μακρὴν ὄμπνια Θεσμοφόρος Call.*Aet*. *Oxy*.2079.9; [ἡ τροφὴ] τοῖς λοιποῖς.. ἰσοσθενεῖ καὶ κ. τὰ πάντα Gal. 19.190. 3. in building, *carry down*, τὰ σκέλη καθείλκυσται the long walls *have been carried down to the sea*, Str.8.6.22. II. metaph., *drag down*, τὸ χεῖρον.. καθελκυσθὲν συνεφελκύσασθαι τὸ μέσον Plot.2.9.2, cf. Luc.*Apol*.11. 2. *constrain, compel*, *BGU*648.12 (ii A.D.), *POxy*.899.25 (iii A.D.); τινὰ εἰς φιλανθρωπίαν Lib.*Or*.15.29 (Pass.).

⊛ **κάθεμα**, ατος, τό, (καθίημι) *necklace, collar*, Lxx *Is*.3.19:—written **κάθημα** in Antiph.319.

**κάθεμεν**, Ep. 1 pl. aor. 2 of καθίημι. **καθέν**, for καθ' ἕν, v. κατά B.II.3.

**καθέννῡμι**, *clothe*, v. καταέννυμι. **καθένς**, v. κατατίθημι.

**καθεξῆς**, Adv., = the more usu. ἐφεξῆς, *Ev.Luc*.1.3, Plu.2.615c, Ael.*VH*8.7, *IGRom*.4.1432.9 (Smyrna); poet. κατὰ θ' ἑξείης Opp. *C*.3.59.

**κάθεξις**, εως, ἡ, (κατέχω) *holding, retention*, τῆς ἀρχῆς Th.3.47; ἐν μνήμῃ καὶ καθέξει Plu.2.968c; *possession*, Plot.6.1.23. 2. *holding in, restraining*, τοῦ πνεύματος Arist.*Somn*.456b16; [θυμοῦ] Id.*EE* 1223b20. 3. *retentive power*, of the bladder, Aret.*CA*1.4.

**καθέξω**, fut. of κατέχω.

**κάθερμα**, ατος, τό, in pl., = ἕρματα (v. ἕρμα II), Anacr.21.12.

**καθέρπω**, aor. 1 καθείρπῡσα Ar.*Ra*.485:—*creep, steal down*, ἀπ' ὀρθίων πάγων καθεῖρπεν ἔλαφος S.*Fr*.89; καθέρπυσόν νυν ἐς Κεραμεικόν Ar.*Ra*.129, cf. 485: metaph., παρὰ τὰ ὦτα ἄρτι ἴουλος καθέρπει X. *Smp*.4.23. II. *return* from exile, *SIG*306.54 (Delph., from Tegea, iv B.C.): in this signf. the aor. part. is κατενθών ib.4; pf. part. κατηνθηκώς ib.39.

**κάθες**, aor. 2 imper. of καθίημι. **καθέσαι**, aor. 1 inf. of καθίζω.

**καθέσιμον** (sc. ἀργύριον), τό, (καθίζω) *fee for attendance* at the βουλή, *IG*2².956.14, al.

⊛ **κάθεσις**, εως, ἡ, (καθίημι) *letting down*, τῆς κόμης D.L.1.109; of a diving-bell, Arist.*Pr*.960b33. 2. *production* of a play, Sch.Ar. *V*.1317, prob. in Sch.*Ra*.1060, Sch.*Lys*.1096. 3. *insertion*, τοῦ αὐλίσκου Ruf.*Ren.Ves*.7; of a finger, Antyll.ap.Orib.44.23.1; of a lancet, Orib.7.5.12. II. (from Pass.) *descent*, Arist.*Mete*.356a11; κ. νέφους εἰς τοὺς κάτω τόπους Epicur.*Ep*.2 p.47 U.

**κάθεσσαν, καθέσσαντο**, aor. 1 of καθίζω.

**καθεστέον**, (καθέζομαι) *one must sit down*, Pherecr.215.

**καθεστηκότως**, Adv. pf. part. Act. of καθίστημι, *fixedly, steadily*, κ. ἔχειν πρός τι Arist.*Pol*.1340b3.

**καθεστήξω**, fut. 3 of καθίστημι, with intr. sense.

**καθεστήριον**, τό, *guest-room* of a monastery, *PMasp*.110.36 (vi A.D.).

**καθεστιάω**, v. καθιστιάω.

**καθεστῶτα**, ων, τά, neut. pl. pf. part. of καθίστημι.

**καθεστώτως**, Adv. = καθεστηκότως, *steadily*, πορεύεσθαι prob. in D.Chr.31.162.

**καθέσω**, v. καθίζω.

**καθετ-ήρ**, ῆρος, ὁ, (καθίημι) *anything let down into, inserted*: 1. *plug of lint, pessary*, Hp.*Mul*.2.157 ap.Gal.19.107 (καθετηρίῳ codd. Hp.). 2. *surgical instrument* for emptying the bladder, Gal.1. 125, al., Sor.2.59; κ. ἀρρενικός Ruf.*Oss*.12. 3. *fishing-line*, Artem. 2.14. 4. = κάθεμα, Nicostr.Com.33, *IG*11(2).287 *B*68 (Delos, iii B.C.). **-ηρίδιον**, τό, Dim. of foreg. 4, *BCH*35.286 (ib., ii B.C.). **-ηρίζω**, *treat with the* καθετήρ 2, Orib.*Fr*.64. **-ήριον** (sc. ὄργανον), τό, = καθετήρ 1, f.l. in Hp.*Mul*.2.157; τὸ ὄργανον τὸ κ. Aret.*CA*2.9. **-ηρισμός**, ὁ, *insertion of the* καθετήρ, Ruf.ap.Aët. 11.27, Paul.Aeg.6.59. **-ηριστέον**, *one must treat with the* κ., Ruf. ap.Aët.11.21. **-ης**, ου, ὁ, prob. *portcullis* (v. πτερόν III.9), Sch. E.*Ph*.114. II. *plummet*, Aen.Tact.32.6 cod., *Gloss*. **-ικός**, ή, όν, *perpendicular*, Sch.Arat.881. ⊛ **-ος**, ον, (καθίημι) *let down, perpendicular*, πρὸς τὴν γῆν Arist.*Mech*.857b28; καθέταν is f.l. in Alc. 39: usu. Subst., 1. κάθετος (sc. γραμμή), ἡ, *perpendicular*, Arist.*Mete*. 373a11, Ti.Locr.98b, etc., al.; *plumb-line*, Aen.Tact.32.6; πρὸς τὴν κ. δ' ἐμετρήθη Epigr.ap.Plu.*Aem*.15; κατὰ κάθετον *vertically, perpendicularly*, Ph.*Bel*.69.22, Heliod.ap.Orib.49.13.1, *Placit*.2.24.1, Apollod.*Poliorc*.155.9; κατὰ κ. τοῦ ὀμφαλοῦ *vertically below*, Paul.Aeg.6. 50; πρὸς κ. Plu.2.938a; *perpendicular height*, τριῶν ἥμισυ σταδίων ἔχειν τὴν κ. Str.8.6.21. 2. (sc. ὁρμιά), ἡ, *fishing-line*, Opp.*H*.3. 77,138, *AP*7.637 (Antip., v.l. καθέτης). 3. (sc. ἀμνός or βοῦς), ὁ, *an animal let down into the sea* as an offering to Poseidon, Lys. *Fr*.227 S., cf. Phot., Suid.

**καθευδητέον**, *one must sleep*, Pl.*Phdr*.259d.

⊛ **καθεύδω**, so also in Ion., Hdt.2.95 codd.: impf. καθεῦδον (καθηῦδον) Il.1.611, Ar.*Av*.495, Pl.*Smp*.217d, al.; ἐκάθευδον Lys.1.13,23, X.*Oec*.7.11: fut. καθευδήσω Ar.*Ec*.419, X.*Cyr*.6.2.30, etc.: aor. ἐκαθεύδησα (not in Att.), Luc.*Asin*.6; inf. καθευδῆσαι Hp *Int*.12:—*lie down to sleep, sleep*, Il.1.611, Od.3.402, etc.; opp. ἀγρυπνέω, ἐγρήγορα, Thgn.471, Pl.*Phd*.71c, etc.; καλὸς νέκυς, οἷα καθεύδων Bion 1.71; κ. μάτην A.*Ch*.881; νυκτὸς κ. *to sleep* by night, Pl.*Phdr*. 251e; κ. τὰς νύκτας *to sleep* all one's nights, Bato 4; μαλακῶς, σκληρῶς κ., Antiph.187.6, Timocl.16.2; of male and female, ἵνα τώ γε καθεύδετον ἐν φιλότητι Od.8.313; κ. μετά τινος Pl.*Smp*.219d: generally, *pass the night*, τὴν βουλὴν εἰς ἀκρόπολιν ἰέναι κἀκεῖ κ. And.1.45; κ. ἐπὶ ξύλου *roost*, of a fowl, Ar.*Nu*.1431; ἐκ τοῦ καθεύδοντος from *a sleeping state*, Pl.*Phd*.72b. II. metaph., *lie asleep, lie idle*, χερὶ A. *Ag*.1357, cf. X.*HG*5.1.20, *An*.1.3.11, D.19.303; κ. τὸν βίον *to be asleep* all one's life, *sleep away* one's life, Pl.*R*.404a; opp. ἐνεργεῖν, Arist.*EN*1157b8; opp. προσέχειν τοῖς πράγμασι, Plu.*Pomp*.15. 2. of things, *lie still, be at rest*, ἐλπίδες οὔπω κ. E.*Ph*.634; καθεύδειν ἐᾶν ἐν τῇ γῇ κατακείμενα τείχη Pl.*Lg*.778d: τοὺς νόμους ἐᾶν κ. Plu.*Ages*. 30. 3. of the *sleep* of death, καθεύδοντες ἐν τάφῳ Lxx *Ps*.87(88).6, cf. *Da*.12.2, 1*Ep.Thess*.5.10.

**καθεύρεμα**, ατος, τό, *invention*, Lxx *Si*.32(35).10(12) (but prob. καθ' εὕρεμα).

**καθευρεσῐλογέω**, *invent reasons*, Plb.12.25k.9.

**καθευρίσκω**, *discover*, Luc.*Ocyp*.68:—Pass., καθευρέθη κοσμοῦσα *she was found* in the act of adorning.., S.*Ant*.395 (prob. f.l. for καθῃρέθη *she was caught*).

**καθεφθ-έος**, α, ον, = sq., prob. cj. in Nic.*Al*.573 (κατεφθέος, καθεψίοιο, καθεψέος codd.). **-ός**, όν, *boiled down*, Hp.*Mul*.2.110, Achae. 7, Diocl.*Fr*.139 (κάτ- codd.), Mnesith.ap.Orib.*Inc*.15.18, Dieuch. ap.Orib.4.7.31, Diph.Siph.ap.Ath.2.59b.

**καθέψησις**, εως, ἡ, *a boiling down*, Hp.*Vict*.2.42, D.S.1.40.

**καθεψιάομαι**, *mock at*, c. gen., ὥς σέθεν αἱ κύνες αἵδε καθεψιόωνται Od.19.372.

**καθέψω**, fut. -εψήσω, *boil down*, in Pass., Dsc.*Alex*.6, Plu.2.555b; of plants, *to be dried up* by the sun, cj. in Thphr.*HP*7.5.2; of a person, ἡλίῳ -ψεῖσθαι (sic) *to be broiled, swelter*, Luc.*Asin*.25; of a river, to be *softened* (sweetened) by boiling, D.S.1.40: Act., -ψοντες ἑαυτούς, by hot baths, Gal.6.185. II. metaph., *soften, temper*, joined with πραΰνειν, X.*Eq*.9.6. 2. *digest*, ἀργύριον Ar.*V*.795 codd. (prob. καταπέψεις).

**καθῆ**, Att. for κάθησαι, 2 sg. pres. of κάθημαι.

**καθηγεμ-ονία**, ἡ, *headship* of a philosophical school, *IG*2².1099.35 (Plotina): generally, *primacy, leadership*, Phld.*Piet*.76. ⊛ **-ών**, Ion. κατηγ-, Dor. καθᾱγ-, όνος, ὁ, ἡ, *leader, guide*, τῆς ὁδοῦ Hdt.7. 128, cf. Plb.3.48.11; *pilot*, Id.4.40.8; of a statesman, Ἀράτῳ καθηγεμόνι χρησάμενος περὶ τῶν ὅλων Id.7.14.4; of the founders of the Epicurean school, Phld.*Rh*.1.49 S., *Ir*.p.89 W., al.; of Crates, Jul. *Or*.6.202d; κ. τῆς ἀρετῆς *in* or *to* virtue, Plu.*Dio* 1; as a title of gods, Διόνυσος κ. *CIG*3068 (Teos); τᾷ εὐεργέτιδι καὶ καθαγεμόνι τᾶς πόλιος *SIG*559.36 (Arc., from Magn. Mae., iii B.C.); Ἀφροδίτην κ. ποιεῖσθαι Plu.*Thes*.18; of divinities, τῷ Διί, καθηγεμόνι τούτῳ τῆς τῶν ὄντων διοικήσεως ὄντι *Stoic*.1.43; καθηγεμόνες εὐτυχοῦς ἀρχῆς *OGI* 383.86 (Nemrud Dagh, i B.C.): metaph., κ. ταττόμενοι τὸν θυμόν Lxx 2*Ma*.10.28.

⊛ **καθηγ-έομαι**, Ion. κατηγ-, *act as guide, lead the way*, abs., Hdt. 9.40,66, 6.135, Th.6.4; οἱ κατηγεόμενοι the *guides*, Hdt.7.130; σὺ καθηγοῦ, ἕψομαι δ' ἐγώ Pl.*Ep*.312b; κατ. τινὶ ἐς χώρους Hdt.4.125, cf. 6.102; ἐπὶ Φωκέας Id.7.215; also κατ. τινὶ ὁδόν Id.9.104. 2. c. acc. rei, *show, explain, indicate*, τὸ ἕρμα κατ. τινί Id.7.183, cf. X. *An*.7.8.10; ὁ τὸν ποταμὸν κ. *he who was explaining* it, i.e. showing where it was fordable, Pl.*Tht*.200e. 3. c. gen., κ. τοῦ λόγου *to begin* the discourse, Id.*Smp*.199c; ὧν καθηγήσαιτ' ἂν τοῦτο of which this *would be the beginning*, Id.*La*.182c. b. *lead, command, exercise authority over*, κ. τῆς στρατείας, τοῦ πολιτεύματος, Plu.*Cam*.15, *Thes*.35. 4. *to be the first to do, establish, institute*, Hdt.2.49,56: c. part., οὐ κατηγήσομαι νόμον τόνδε τιθεὶς I *will not begin* establishing this law, Id.7.8.α'. 5. *instruct, teach*, abs., Phld.*Lib*.p.21 O., al.; κ. γραμματιστοῦ τρόπον Diog.Oen.11; ὁ καθηγησάμενος the *teacher*, Plu.2.120a: c. gen. pers., *to be teacher of*.., Str.14.5.14, D.H.*Is*.1, *Amm*.5. 6. in Logic, *to be antecedent*, *Stoic*.2.72. **-ησις**, εως, ἡ, *rule, principle*, αἱ τοῦ τακτικοῦ κ. Ascl. *Tact*.12.11, cf. Ael.*Tact*.42.2; also f.l. in Antig.*Mir*.171. **-ητής**, οῦ, ὁ, *guide*, Numen.ap.Ath.7.313d. 2. *teacher, professor*, Phld.*Ir*. p.43 W., al., D.H.*Th*.3, *Ev.Matt*.23.10, Plu.2.70e, Philum.*Ven*.5.6, *OGI*408 (Theb. Aegypt., ii A.D.), *POxy*.930.6 (ii/iii A.D.), etc.:—also **-ητήρ**, ῆρος, ὁ, Man.2.300, Dor. καθᾱγ-, κελεύθου *IG*12(1).44 (Rhodes):—fem. **-ήτειρα** Call.*Fr*.33 P., Orph.*H*.76.6. **-ητικός**, ή, όν, *able to guide, guiding*, c. gen., Gal.*Phil.Hist*.16,19.

**καθηδύνω** [ῡ], *sweeten*, αἱ μέλιτται κ. τὸ πόμα Max.Tyr.27.6; ζωμὸς καθηδυσμένος περιττῶς Ath.4.140a. 2. *gratify*, τινα Eun.*VS* p.458 B.

**καθηδῠπᾰθέω**, *squander in luxury* or *revelling*, τοὺς δαρεικοὺς X. *An*.1.3.3; τὰς εὐπορίας D.H.20.8; τὸν χρόνον κ. καὶ ἀναλίσκειν Plu. *Ant*.28; τοὺς τοῦ πολέμου καιροὺς κ. Luc.*DMort*.12.6: abs., Ph.2. 106,357, Alciphr.1.21.

**καθηκόντως**, v. sq. II.4.

**καθήκω**, Ion. κατήκω, (v. ἥκω) *come* or *go down*, esp. to fight, A. *Ch*.455 (lyr.). 2. *come down to, reach to*, ἐς θάλασσαν Hdt.7.22, 130; ἐπὶ θάλ. Id.2.32, 5.49, Th.2.27; πρὸς τὸν Μηλιακὸν κόλπον Id.3. 96; κέρκος.. εἰς λεπτὸν καθήκουσα *tapering* away, Arist.*HA*503a20: metaph., of descent, ὁ [γένος] εἰς αὐτὸν κ. Arr.*An*.1.11.8. 3. *come*

*in due course* to any one, καθῆκεν ἐς ἡμᾶς ὁ λόγος the turn of speaking *came* to us, Aeschin.2.25; παρὰ τετάρτην ἡμέραν ἑκάστῃ σημαίᾳ καθήκειν τὴν λειτουργίαν Plb.6.33.9, cf. *PCair.Zen.*218.24 (iii B.C.); τῆς βολῆς καθηκούσης ἐς αὐτόν Plu.*Alc.*2; ἐν τῷ ξυμποσίῳ.. ἐπὶ τὸν Θεσμόπολιν καθῆκε τὸ σκῶμμα Luc.*Merc.Cond.*34. 4. of Time, ὁπότε καθήκοι ὁ χρόνος X.*HG*4.7.2; ὅταν οἱ χρόνοι καθήκωσι Arist. *HA*591ᵃ8; πρότερον ἢ τὴν ὥραν καθήκειν *PRev.Laws*41.14 (iii B.C.); in part., τοῦ καθήκοντος χρόνου the *normal* time, S.*OT*75, D.4.35, cf. Aeschin.3.126; αἱ κ. ἡμέραι the *regular, proper* days, D.59.80; ἐν τῇ κ. ὥρᾳ Arist.*HA*568ᵃ17; ἐν τοῖς κ. καιροῖς ib.573ᵃ30; of events, ἑορτῆς εἰς τὰς ἡμέρας ἐκείνας καθηκούσης as the festival *fell* on those days, Plu.*Fab.*18, cf. Plb.4.7.1; ἐκκλησίαν ποιῆσαι, ὅταν ἐκ τῶν νόμων καθήκῃ when it *is* legally *due*, D.19.185; ἡ κ. σύνοδος or ἐκκλησία, Plb.4.14.1, 1.15.8, etc. II. *to be meet, fit, proper*, τοῖς κ. [νομίμοις] Arist.*Pol.*1325ᵃ13; τὰς ἐσθῆτας τὰς κ. ἀεὶ ταῖς περιθεταῖς *suiting* them, Plb.3.78.3; ὁ καθήκων ἐκ τῶν νομίμων ἀριθμός *a quorum*, D.C.39.30; also καθῆκόν ἐστιν αὐτὸν ἐπαινεῖσθαι *Inscr.Prien.*114.32 (i B.C.). 2. impers., καθήκει μοι *it belongs* to me, *is my duty*, c. inf., οἷς καθήκει ἀθροίζεσθαι X.*An.*1.9.7, cf. *Cyr.*8.1.4, etc.: in later writers, impf. καθῆκε in pres. sense, *it is meet, proper*, οὐδ' ἅψασθαι καθῆκέ τινων Aristeas 149; οὐ κ. αὐτὸν ζῆν *Act.Ap.*22.22: freq. in part., τὰ καθήκοντα *one's due* or *duty*, X.*Cyr.*1.2.5; τὰ κατήκοντα Σπαρτιήτῃσι Hdt.7.104; ποιεῖν τὸ κ. Men.575: esp. in Stoic philos. (from signf. I. 3 acc. to D.L.7.108, cf. κατά B. I. 3), περὶ τοῦ κ., title of work by Zeno, cf. *Stoic.*1.55, etc.: freq. in pl., ib.3.30, etc.; μὴ κ. unbecoming, *Ep.Rom.*1.28. 3. τὰ κατήκοντα the *present crisis*, Hdt. 1.97, 5.49; τὰ κ. πρήγματα Id.8.19,40,102. b. τὰ καθήκοντα the *payments due*, *UPZ*42.15 (ii B.C.); τὴν -ουσαν ἡμῖν δίδοσθαι σύνταξιν τῶν δεόντων ib.6. 4. Adv. pres. part. καθηκόντως *fittingly, properly*, Epicur.*Ep.*2 p.53 U., *OGI*90.28 (Rosetta, ii B.C.), Plb.5.9.6, v.l. in D.S.1.93; πρός τι Porph.*Abst.*1.43; *consistently with duty*, *Stoic.*3.188, Plu.2.448e; *appropriately*, c. dat., τῷ τόπῳ Aristeas 81; κ. ἔχειν πρός τι Id.87. III. τὸ καθῆκον the *precise proportion*, Thphr.*Lap.*46.

**καθηλιάζω**, *bring the sun upon, illuminate*, νύκτα Luc.*Epigr.*19.

**καθῆλιξ**, λῖκος, ὁ, ἡ, *contemporary*, *Inscr.Prien.*117.56 (i B.C.).

**καθηλ-όω** or **κατηλόω** (cf. ἧλος), *nail on*, παραβλήματα κατηλῶσαι *IG*2².1604.31 (iv B.C.); τι πρός τι Plu.*Alex.*24; περί τι Apollod.1.9.1, cf. *IG*2².463.79, 1668.57; οἷον κ. τὴν ψυχὴν πρὸς τὴν ἀπόλαυσιν Porph. *Abst.*1.38:—Pass., κλῖμαξ σανίσι καθηλωμένη with boards *nailed thereto*, Plb.1.22.5, cf. Apollod.*Poliorc.*189.5; καθηλωθήσεται σύριγξι καμαρικαῖς Ath.Mech.36.5; λεπίδες καθηλωμέναι *nailed on*, D.S.20.91, cf. Orib.49.4.51; χάλκωμα συμμαχίας.. ἐν Καπετωλίῳ κατηλωθῆναι *IG* 12(3).173.7 (Astypalaea, ii B.C.). II. by confusion of Hebr. *sāmar* 'bristled' with *sāmar*, imper. *sĕmōr* 'nail thou', καθήλωσον ἐκ τοῦ φόβου σου τὰς σάρκας μου Lxx *Ps.*118(119).120. -ωμα, ατος, τό, *that which is nailed on, revetment*, ib.3*Ki.*6.20. -ωσις, εως, ἡ, *nailing on*, ἀσθενὴς [τῶν ἥλων] γίνεται ἡ κ. Hero *Bel.*95.6, cf. Sm., Thd.*Ez.*7.23, *PLond.*3.1177.239 (ii A.D.). -ωτής, οῦ, ὁ, *one who nails on*, *Gloss.*

**κάθημα**, v. κάθεμα.

❀ **κάθημαι**, Ion. **κάτ-**, 2 sg. κάθησαι (Ion. κάτ- Hdt.3.134) X.*Cyr.*3.1.6, prob. in Call.*Sos.* vi 4, κάθῃ Hyp.*Fr.*115, *Act.Ap.*23.3, dub. l. in *Com. Adesp.*1203, (προ-) Them.*Or.*13.171a codd.; 3 sg. κάθηται Ar.*Lys.* 597, Pl.*Ap.*35c, D.9.70, *SIG*987.26 (Chios, iv B.C.); Ion. 3 pl. κατέαται Hdt.2.86; imper. κάθησο Il.2.191, E.*IA*627; κάθου Ar.*Fr.*620, Anaxandr.13, Men.1017, Alex.224; κάθουσο Sch.Theoc.11.42; 3 sg. καθήσθω A.*Pr.*916; 3 pl. καθήσθωσαν *IG*9(2).1109.38 (Thess.); subj. καθῶμαι, κάθῃ Cratin.277, καθῆται Ar.*Eq.*754; opt. καθοίμην Id.*Ra.*919, prob. in Id.*Lys.*149; inf. καθῆσθαι; part. καθήμενος: impf. ἐκαθήμην Ar. *Ec.*152, D.48.31, etc., ἐκάθητο *h.Bacch.*14, Ar.*Av.*510, Th.5.6, ἐκάθησθε Ar.*Ach.*638, ἐκάθηντο, Ion. ἐκατέατο v.l. in Hdt.3.144, 8.73; also without syll. augm. καθῆστο Il.1.569, E.*Ba.*1102, *Ph.*1467, Pl.*R.*328c, Is.6.19, καθῆτο D.18.169,217; Ion. κατῆστο Hdt.1.46, καθῆσθε D. 25.21 (with vv. ll.), καθῆντο Ar.*Ec.*302, v.l. in Th.5.58; Ep. καθήατο Il.11.76; Ion. κατέατο Hdt.3.144, 8.73, 9.90 (v.l. καθ-): the later fut. καθήσομαι Lxx *Le.*8.35, *Ev.Luc.*22.30 is corrupt in E.*Fr.*960:—*to be seated, sit*, αὐτός τε κάθησο καὶ ἄλλους ἵδρυε λαούς Il.2.191; κάθησ' ἕδραία E.*Andr.*266: freq. in part., πέτρῃ ἔπι προβλῆτι καθήμενος Il.16.407; ἐπ' ἀκτῆς κλαῖε κ. Od.5.82; κ. οἷος ἐν Ἴδῃ Il.8.207; ἐν ἀγῶνι κ. 23.448; κλαῖον δ' ἐν λεχέεσσι κ. Od.10.497; θύρῃσι κ. 17.530; ἐπὶ ταῖσι θύραις Ar.*Nu.*466; αὐτόθεν ἐκ δίφροιο κ. even from his seat *as he sat there*, Od.21.420; καθήμεθ' ἄκρων ἐκ πάγων S.*Ant.*411; ἐκ μέσου κατῆστο *sate* aloof, remained neutral, Hdt.3.83, cf. 4.118, 8.73; ἐν θρόνῳ κ. Id.2.149; θρόνῳ κ. E.*El.*315; κ. πρὸς τάφῳ Id.*Hel.*1084; πρὸς τὸ πῦρ Ar.*V.*773; ἐπὶ δίφρου Pl.*R.*328c; ἐπὶ τῶν ἵππων X.*Cyr.*4. 5.54; ἐπὶ τοῦ ἅρματος *Act.Ap.*8.28; ἐς τοὐργαστήριον Alciphr.3.27: c. acc. cogn., ἕδραν κ. E.*Heracl.*55: c. acc. loci, *sit on*, ὀφρύην ib. 394. 2. esp. of courts, councils, assemblies, etc., *sit*: οἱ καθήμενοι *the judges, the court*, And.1.139, D.6.3, etc.; δικαστὰς οὐχ ὁρῶ καθημένους Ar.*Nu.*208; ὑμεῖς οἱ καθήμενοι you *who sit as judges*, Th. 5.85; οὐκ ἐπὶ τούτῳ κ. ὁ δικαστής Pl.*Ap.*35c; κ. ὑπὲρ τῶν νόμων D.58. 25; of the βουλή, And.1.43; βουλῆς περὶ τούτων καθημένης D.21.116; of an assembly, X.*An.*5.10.5; οἱ κ. *the spectators in a theatre*, Hegesipp.1.29. 3. *sit still, sit quiet*, ὕψι περ ἐν νεφέεσσι καθήμενω Od. 16.264; σφοῖσιν ἐνὶ μεγάροισι καθήατο (for ἐκάθηντο) Il.11.76; ἐν πένθεϊ μεγάλῳ κατῆστο Hdt.1.46; μετὰ κόπον κ. *rest* after labour, S.*Fr.* 479.3: and, in bad sense, *sit doing nothing, lie idle*, Il.24.403, Hdt. 3.134; of an army, Id.9.56, Th.4.124; of a boat's crew, *PCair.Zen.* 107.6 (iii B.C.); οὐδὲν ποιοῦντες ἐνθάδε καθήμεθα, μέλλοντες ἀεί D.11. 17, cf. 2.23, S.*Fr.*142.20, etc.; also, of an army, *to have its quarters, be encamped*, περὶ τὰς Ἀχαρνάς Th.2.20, cf. 101; ἐχθρῶν ὑπ' αὐτοῖς τείχεσιν καθημένων E.*Ph.*752. 4. *reside* in a place, Lxx *Ne.*11.6; λαὸς καθήμενος ἐν σκοτίᾳ *Ev.Matt.*4.16; *settle*, εἰς Σινώπην Muson.*Fr.* 9 p.43 H. 5. *lead a sedentary, obscure life*, ἐν σκότῳ καθήμενος Pi. *O.*1.83; ἔσω καθημένη A.*Ch.*919; αἱ βαναυσικαὶ [τέχναι] ἀναγκάζουσι καθῆσθαι X.*Oec.*4.2; *to be engaged* or *employed*, esp. in a sedentary business, ἐπ' αὐτῷ τούτῳ Hdt.2.86; κ. ἐπὶ τῇ τραπέζῃ, of bankers, D.49.42, cf. 45.33; ἐπ' ἐργαστηρίου Id.59.67; ἐπὶ τοῦ.. ἰατρείου Aeschin.1.40; καθῆσθαι ἐν πόλει, opp. ζῆν ἐν χωρίῳ, Muson.*Fr.*11 p.59 H. 6. *sit as a suppliant*, ἐν Δελφοῖσι Hdt.5.63, cf. Orac.ib. 7.140. 7. of districts and countries, *lie*, χωρία ὁμοίως καθήμενα Thphr.*HP*8.8.7. b. *to be low-lying*, τὰ λεῖα καὶ καθήμενα Ael.*VH* 3.1, cf. *NA*16.12; πεδίον κ. Him.*Or.*14.17; πόπανον.. κ. δωδεκόμφαλον prob. *flat* in the middle, *IG*2².1367. 8. of a statue, *to be placed*, Pl.*Smp.*215b, Arist.*Pol.*1315ᵇ21. 9. of things, *to be set* or *placed*, λαγῴοις ἐπ' ἀμύλῳ καθημένοις Telecl.32, cf. Pherecr.108.17; τὸ πηδάλιον κ. πλάγιον Arist.*Mech.*851ᵃ4, cf. ib.13.

**καθημαξευμένως**, Adv. pf. part. Pass. of καθαμαξεύω (q. v.).

**καθημερ-εία**, ἡ, *daily business*, Plb.6.33.4 (pl.). -ιος, Dor. **καθᾱμ-**, α, ον, *day by day, daily* (καθ' ἡμέραν), neut. as Adv., E.*Ph.* 229 (lyr.); μοῖρα κ. S.*El.*1414 (dub., lyr.):—later also **καθημερινός**, ή, όν, δίαιτα Lxx *Ju.*12.15, cf. Plu.2.141b, al.; διακονία *Act.Ap.*6.1; γυμνασία Ael.*Tact.*3.1, Plu.*Lyc.*10, Ath.1.10c; of fevers, *quotidian*, later word for ἀμφημερινός (q.v.), esp. of *non-remittent quotidians*, Gal.7.354, 17(1).221; ῥῖγος *PTeb.*275.21 (iii A.D.); φρίξ *POxy.*924. 3 (iv A.D.). -ίσια, τά, *daily wages*, *IG*1².373.245.

**καθημεροθύτης** [ῠ], ου, ὁ, *priest who offers daily sacrifice*, *SIG*1021. 22 (Olymp.).

**καθημερόω**, *soften, tranquillize*, τὴν ψυχήν Porph.*VP*32:—Med., *smooth down*, κύματα v.l. in Ps.-Callisth.1.1:—Pass., καθημερούμενα ζῷα Hierocl.p.59 A.

**κᾰθῆραι, καθήρας**, aor. 1 inf. and part. of καθαίρω.

**καθησῠχάζω**, strengthd. for ἡσυχάζω, Plb.9.32.2, Ph.2.71, *BGU* 36.14 (Trajan):—Med., fut. καθησυχάσομαι *Lyr.Alex.Adesp.*4.24.

❀ **καθθηρᾱτόριον**, τό, Lacon. (for *καταθηρατόριον), *contest in hunting* at Sparta, *IG*5(1).278, etc.; cf. κασσηρατόριν.

❀ **καθιγνῦσαι**· νεκροῖς θῦσαι, Phot. (Apptly. corrupt for καθαγνίσαι.)

**κάθιδοι**· ὑδρίαι (Arc.), Hsch.

**κάθιδρος**, ον, *sweating violently*, Lxx *Je.*8.6, Hsch., Phot.

**καθίδρ-ῦμα**, ατος, τό, = ἵδρυμα, *Gloss.* -ῦσις, εως, ἡ, = ἵδρυσις, ἑαυτῆς, of Artemis, D.S.4.51; ἀγαλμάτων Iamb.*Myst.*5.23 (pl.), cf. Poll.1.11, *Cat.Cod.Astr.*8(4).252; ἀνδριάντων *Cod.Just.*1.4.26.6 (pl.); *foundation-festival*, *BGU*1.28 (ii/iii A.D.). -ύω, causal of καθέζομαι, *make to sit down*, Ὀδυσῆα καθίδρυε Od.20.257; μακάρων ἐς αἶαν σὸν καθιδρύσει βίον *will carry* thee to the land of the Blest that thou mayst live there, E.*Ba.*1339:—Pass., *sit down, settle*, Ar. *Av.*45; ἐν πόλει, ἐν τῷ ὄρει, Pl.*Sph.*224d, Th.4.46; κ. ἐς Ἀργώ *take one's seat in*.., Theoc.13.28; *to be quartered*, of troops, *PLond.*3. 1313.11 (vi A.D.). 2. *establish, place*, ἐν τοῖς τιμιωτέροις τὸ τιμιώτερον (sc. τὴν καρδίαν) καθίδρυκεν ἡ φύσις Arist.*PA*665ᵇ20; ἐφ' ἑνὸς τόπου κ. τὴν ἱστορίαν *to limit* it, D.H.*Th.*6:—Pass., κ. ἐς τὴν ἑωυτῶν χώρην *to be restored, replaced*, Hp.*Fract.*31, cf. *Prorrh.*2.19; ἐν αἷς [ἱστορίαις] καθιδρῦσθαι τὴν ἀλήθειαν ὑπολαμβάνομεν D.H.1.1. 3. *consecrate, dedicate*, aor. 1 Med. καθιδρῡσάμην E.*IT*1481; -ῡσάμην *IG*14.882 (Capua): pf. Pass. in act. sense, E.*Cyc.*318:—Pass., Ποσειδῶνος τοῦ κατιδρυθέντος ὑπὸ.. *SIG*1020.5 (Halic., i B.C.); τεμένη -ύετο τῷ θεῷ Luc.*Cal.*17. 4. *found*, γυμνάσιον Lxx 2*Ma.* 4.12.

**καθιέρ-ευσις**, εως, ἡ, *consecration, deification*, ζῴων Plu.2.380d (pl.). -εύω, *sacrifice, offer*, αὐτούς Pl.*Phdr.*252c; τὴν μητέρα Arist. *EN*1148ᵇ26; τὸν ἱκέτην D.H.8.1: cf. κατιαραίω. -ουργέω, = foreg., D.S.20.14 (Pass.). ❀ -όω, Ion. **κατιρόω**, *dedicate, devote*, Hdt.1.92, 164; τῇ μὲν γὰρ Ἀθηναίᾳ καθιέρωσεν εἰς ἀναθήματα.. πεντακισχιλίους στατῆρας Lys.19.39; τὸ λαχὸν μέρος ἑκάστῳ τῷ θεῷ Pl.*Lg.*745d; χώραν Aeschin.3.109; ἑαυτοὺς ὑπὲρ τῆς πατρίδος τῷ δαίμονι κ. Plu.*Cam.*21; τὸ θέατρον D.C.39.38, cf. *SIG*791 *B* 5 (Delph., i A.D.), etc.:—Pass., ἐμοὶ τραφείς τε καὶ καθιερωμένος [ῐ] A.*Eu.*304; ἡ Κιρραία χώρα καθιερώθη *was consecrated*, D.18.149; καθιερωμένα ἀναθήματα Plb.7.14.3, cf. 3.22.1; οἱ καθιερούμενοι τῷ Διί his priests, S.E.*P.*3.224. 2. *set up, establish as sacred*, τὴν φήμην Pl.*Lg.*838d:—Pass., νόμιμον καθιερωθέν ib.839c; δίκαια ἐν στήλῃ καθιερωμένα Plb.9.36.9.—Prose word, used once by A. -ωσις, εως, ἡ, *dedication*, Aeschin.3.46, D.H. 6.1, J.*AJ*19.7.5, Ph.2.234, Plu.*Publ.*15, *BMus.Inscr.*481*.21 (pl.), etc.: Dor. **καθιάρωσις** *Schwyzer* 203.9 (Crete, from Teos, iii/ii B.C.). -ωτέος, α, ον, *to be dedicated*, Pl.*Lg.*809b. -ωτικός, ή, όν, *dedicatory*, λόγος Sopat. in Rh.5.14 W.

**καθιέψεν**· ἐξέθετο, Hsch.

**καθιζάνω**, Aeol. **κατισδάνω** Sapph.*Supp.*19.5, irreg. impf. ἐκαθίζανον (παρ-) *IG*2².1011.22 (ii B.C.):—*sit down*, θῶκόνδε καθίζανον *they went* to the council *and took their seats*, Od.5.3; μάντις ἐς θρόνους κ. A.*Eu.*29; παρά τινα Polyaen.8.64: abs., σὺ δὲ καθίζανε Pherecr.172; of bees, birds, etc., *settle, perch*, μέλιτταν ἐφ' ἅπαντα βλαστήματα καθιζάνουσαν Isoc.1.52, cf. Arist.*HA*601ᵃ7; ἐπὶ δονάκων, πέτραις, ib. 593ᵇ10, 619ᵇ8.

❀ **καθίζω**, Ion. **κατ-**, impf. κάθιζον Il.3.426, al.; in Prose ἐκάθιζον X.*HG*5.4.6, Din.2.13: fut. καθέσω Eup.12.11 D.; καθίσω (intr.) Apollod.Com.5; Ion. κατίσω (trans.) Hdt.4.190; Att. also καθιῶ X.*An.*2.

1.4, D.24.25, 39.11, *IG*2$^2$.778.13 (iii B.C.); Dor. καθιξῶ Bion *Fr.*10.16: aor. 1 καθεῖσα Il.18.389, al., subj. καθέσω *h.Ap.*ap.Th.3.104; inf. καθέσαι *IG*2$^2$.46*a B** 21, 25 (v/iv B.C.); poet. κάθεσσα Pi.*P.*5.42 codd.; this aor. καθεῖσα has Ms. authority in E.*Hipp.*31 (ἐγκαθ–, Med.), *Ph.* 1188, Hdt.1.88, 4.79, Th.7.82, but we also find Ep. κάθῖσα, Ion. κάτ– (for which κάθεσα, κάτεσον, etc., shd. perh. be restored), Il.19.280 (v.l. κάθεσαν), al., Hdt.1.89, 2.126, καθῖσα Ar.*Ra.*911, Th.6.66 (leg. καθεῖσα), later ἐκάθῖσα X.*Cyr.*6.1.23, Men.544, etc., cf. Poll.3.89; also Ep. part. καθίσσας Il.9.488; Dor. καθίξας Theoc.1.12, subj. καθίξῃ ib.51; late part. καθιζήσας, subj. -ζήσῃ, D.C.54.30, 37.27: pf. κεκάθῖκα D.S.17.115, *Ep.Hebr.*12.2, A.D.*Synt.*323.23:—**Med.**, impf. ἐκαθιζόμην Ar.*V.*824, κὰδ..ἵζ– Il.19.50: fut. καθιζήσομαι Pl.*Phdr.*229a, *Euthd.*278b, (προσ–) Aeschin.3.167, later καθίσομαι *Ev.Matt.*19.28, Plu.2.583f, -ιοῦμαι Lxx *Ma.*3.3, al.: aor. 1 καθεσσάμην Anacr.111; also ἐκαθισάμην *SIG*975.6 (Delos, iii B.C.), Hsch., (ἐπ–, παρ–) Th.4.130 codd., D.33.14; Ep. ἐκαθισσάμην Call.*Dian.*233, καθισσάμην A.R.4.278, 1219:—**Pass.**, aor. 1 part. καθιζηθείς D.C.63.5: **I.** causal, *make to sit down, seat*, ἄλλους μὲν κάθισον Τρῶας Il.3.68; μή με κάθιζ' 6.360; σ' ἐπ' ἐμοῖσιν ἐγὼ γούνεσσι καθίσσας 9.488; κὰδ δ' εἷσ' ἐν θαλάμῳ 3.382; τὴν μὲν..καθεῖσεν ἐπὶ θρόνου 18.389; κατίσαι τινὰ ἐπ' οἰκήματος Hdt.2.121.έ; καθιεῖν τινα εἰς τὸν θρόνον, i.e. to make him king, X.*An.*2.1.4; ἐπὶ θρόνον Phld.*Vit.*p.22 J. **2.** *set, place*, τὸν μὲν..καθεῖσεν ἐπ' ἠϊόεντι Σκαμάνδρῳ Il.5.36; κὰδ δ' ἐν Ἀθήνης εἷσεν 2.549; Κρόνον..Ζεὺς γαίης νέρθε καθεῖσε 14.204; καθίζειν τινὰ εἰς δόμον E.*Ion* 1541; κ. στρατόν *encamp* it, Id.*Heracl.*664, cf. Th.4.90; κ. τὸ στράτευμα ἐς χωρίον ἐπιτήδειον Id.6.66; σύλλογον εἰς χωρίον κ., χωρὶς μὲν τοὺς ὁπλίτας, χωρὶς δὲ τοὺς ἱππέας Pl.*Lg.*755e. **b.** *post* watchers, guards, etc., σκοπὸς ὅν ῥα καθεῖσεν Αἴγισθος Od.4.524; κατίσαι φυλάκους *set* guards, Hdt.1.89, cf. X.*Cyr.*2.2.14; ἄλλους κάτισον ἀγαγὼν κατὰ τὰς..πύλας Hdt.3.155; κ. ἐνέδραν Plu.*Publ.*19: rarely of things, τι ἐπὶ τηγάνοις Pherecr.127. **3.** *set up*, ἀνδριάντα κάθεσσαν Pi.*P.*5.42 codd.:—Med., καθέσσασθαι Anacr.111, A.R.4.1219. **4.** *cause* an assembly, court, etc., *to take their seats, convene*, ἀγορὰς ἠμὲν λύει ἠδὲ καθίζει Od.2.69; ὅταν καθέσωσιν ἀγῶνα *h.Ap.*ap.Th.3.104; κ. τὸ δικαστήριον Ar.*V.*305, cf. D.39.11, *IG*2$^2$.778.13; νομοθέτας D.24.25, prob. in Id.3.10; but κ. τινὶ δικαστήν *appoint* a judge to try a person, Pl.*Lg.*874a; ἐάν τε χιλίους ἐάν θ' ὁποσουσοῦν ἡ πόλις καθίσῃ D.21.223; *constitute, establish*, δικαστήρια Pl.*Plt.*298e; βουλὴν ἐπίσκοπον πάντων Plu.*Sol.*19. **5.** *put into a certain condition*, esp. in the phrase κλαίοντά τινα κ. *set* him a-weeping, κλάοντα καθέσω σ' Eup. l.c., cf. Pl.*Ion* 535e, X.*Cyr.*2.2.15; but ib.14 κλαίειν τινὰ κ. *to make* him weep: for Theoc.1.51, v. ἀκράτιστος. **6.** *marry*, γυναῖκας ἀλλοτρίας Lxx *Ne.*13.27, cf. 23. **II.** intr., *take one's seat, sit*, abs., Il.3.394, etc.; μετ' ἀθανάτοισι, ἐν θρόνοισι καθίζειν, 15.50, Od.8.422; ἐν [θώκοισι] Hdt.1.181; ἐπὶ τοῖς ἐργαστηρίοις or τῶν -ίων, Isoc.18.9, 7.15; ἐπὶ σκίμποδα Ar.*Nu.*254; ἐπὶ δένδρου Arist.*HA*614$^a$34 (but κ. ἐπὶ κώπην, of rowers, Ar.*Ra.*197); of suppliants, κ. ἐπὶ τὸν βωμόν Th.1.126, Lys.13.24; εἰς γόνυ D.S.17.115: in Poets also c. acc., κ. τρίποδα E.*Ion* 366, *El.*980; βωμόν, ὀμφαλόν, ἱερά, Id.*HF*48, *Ion* 6, 1317. **2.** *sit, recline at meals*, X.*Cyr.*8.4.2. **3.** *sit as judge*, Hdt.1.97, 5.25, Pl.*Lg.*659b, Ph.1.382; *hold a session*, of the πρόεδροι, D.24.89, cf. *Hermes* 17.5 (Delos). **4.** *reside*, μετά τινος Lxx *Ru.*2.23 (3.1); ἐν πόλει ib.*Ne.*11.1. **5.** *settle, sink down*, ἐπὶ τὰ ἰσχία καθίσαι τὼ ἵππω Pl.*Phdr.*254c; καθίσας ὁ φελλὸς ἀνοίξει τὸν κρουνόν Hero *Spir.*1.20. **6.** of ships, *run aground, be stranded*, Plb.1.39.3, Str.2.3.4. **III.** Med. in intr. sense, Il.19.50 (in tmesi), Theoc.15.3, etc.; εἰς τὸν αὐτὸν θᾶκον Pl.*R.*516e; ἐὰν δὲ καθίζεσθαι κελεύσῃ if he order them *to take their seats* (among the spectators in the theatre), D.21.56 (nisi leg. καθέζεσθαι, as also ib.162, both readings are found ib.119); καθίζεσθαι ἢ κατακλινῆναι Pl.*Phdr.*228e. **2.** of birds, *settle, alight*, Arist.*HA*614$^b$23. **3.** *leave goods purchased* in a market, *SIG*975.6 (Delos, iii B.C.).—Att. in this signf. acc. to Hsch.

⊛**καθίημι**, Ion. **κατ–**, fut. καθήσω A.*Eu.*555 (lyr.): aor. 1 καθῆκα, Ep. καθέηκα Il.24.642: 2 dual aor. 2 κάθετον *h.Ap.*487: pf. καθεῖκα Lysipp.1, D.29.46: (v. ἵημι):—*let fall, drop, send down*, κὰδ δὲ [κεραυνὸν]..ἧκε χαμᾶζε Il.8.134; κατὰ δ' ὑψόθεν ἧκεν ἐέρσας 11.53; οἶνον λαυκανίης καθέηκα I *have sent* the wine *down* my throat, 24.642; καθίετε ἵππους ἐν δίνῃσι *sink* them in the stream, as an offering to the river-god, 21.132; [ἱστία] ἐς νῆας κάθεμεν we *let* them *down, lowered* them, Od.9.72; λαῖφος καθήσειν A.*Eu.* l.c.; σχοίνῳ σπυρίδα κ. *let* it *down* by a cord, Hdt.5.16; σῶμα πύργων κ. E.*Tr.*1011; κοντὸν ἐς [τὴν λίμνην] κ. Hdt.4.195; ἐμαυτὸν εἰς ἅλα E.*Hel.*1614; ὅπλα εἰς ἅλα ib.1375; καθεῖσαν δέλεάρ μοι φρενῶν Id.*IT* 1181 (so metaph. τοῦτον τὸν λόγον καθεῖκε D.29.46); κ. τι ἐς πῶμα E.*Ion* 1034; νάρθηκ' ἐς πέδον Id.*Ba.*706; κ. σπονδάς *pour* them, Id.*IA* 60; τὸν κλῆρον ἐς μέσον καθείς, of putting lots into a helmet or urn, S.*Aj.*1285; ἄγκυραν Hdt.7.36; τὰ δίκτυα Arist.*HA*533$^b$18; κατιεμένην καταπειρητηρίην, of a sounding-line, Hdt.2.28: abs., καθιέναι *reach by sounding, sound*, οὐδεὶς καθεὶς ἐδυνήθη πέρας εὑρεῖν Arist.*Mete.*351$^a$13: Medic., [αὐλίσκον] *pass* a catheter, Ruf.*Ren.Ves.*7.11; οἵαν πρόφασιν καθῆκε (παρὰ προσδοκίαν for οἷον ἄγκιστρον) Ar.*V.*174; λόγους συμβατηρίους κ. *make* offers of peace, D.C.41.47; κ. πεῖραν *make* an attempt, Ael.*VH*2.13, *NA*1.57; εἰς ὤμους κ. κόμας *let* one's hair *flow loose*, E.*Ba.*695, cf. *IT*52; κ. πώγωνα *let* one's beard *grow long*, Ar.*Ec.*100, cf. *Th.*841, Arr.*Epict.*2.23.21 (Pass., τὰς τρίχας καθειμέναι Crates Com.27; πώγωνα καθειμένος Plu.*Phoc.*10; τὸ γένειον αὐτῷ καθεῖτο Ael.*VH*11.10); [αἱ ὄϊες] μείζω τὰ οὔθατα καθιᾶσιν Arist.*HA*596$^a$24 (Pass., of a mare's udder, Hdt.4.2); also τείχη καθεῖναι ἐς θάλασσαν *carry* them *down* to the sea, Th.5.52 (Pass., καθεῖτο τείχη 4.103); καθῆκε τὰ σκέλη *let down* his legs, of one who had been lying, Pl.*Phd.*61c; κατ' ἀμφοῖν ἄμφω (sc. τὰ σκέλη) καθέντος, of a wrestler, Gal.6.143; κ. δόρατα *let down* one's pike, *bring* it *to the rest*, X.*An.*6.5.25; κ. τὰς κώπας *let down* the oars, so as to stop the ship's way, Th.2.91; rarely of striking, δι' ὀμφαλοῦ καθῆκεν ἔγχος E.*Ph.*1413; καθῆκε ξύλον παιδὸς ἐς κάρα Id.*HF*993; κ. πρὸς γαῖαν γόνυ to kneel down, Id.*Hec.*561; ἐς δὲ γῆν γόνυ καμάτῳ καθεῖσαν Id.*IT*333; κ. τινὰ ἐς ὕπνον *let* him *fall* asleep, Id.*HF*1006; εἰς κίνδυνον ἐμαυτόν D.H.5.27; [πώλους] ἐς λειμώνων χλόην E.*IA*423; of a general, κ. στρατόπεδα εἰς.. *let* them *march* into.., Plb.3.70.11; εἰς τὸ πεδίον τὴν δύναμιν Id.3.92.7; κ. ἐπί τινας τόπους ἐνέδρας *lay* an ambush, Id.4.63.9:—Pass., *stretch down seawards*, ὄρεα μέχρι πρὸς τὴν θάλατταν καθειμένα Pl.*Criti.*118a; ἕως γῆς τοῦ πρηστῆρος καθιεμένου Epicur.*Ep.*2 p.47 U., cf. p.51 U.; τὸ καθειμένον τῆς φωνῆς *low tone* of voice, Hdn.5.2.3. **2.** *send down into the arena, enter for racing*, ἅρματα, ζεύγη, Th.6.16, Isoc.16.34; of plays, *produce*, Eratosth.ap.Sch.Ar.*Nu.*552 (Pass.); διδασκαλίαν Plu.*Cim.*8; so ἔδοξε τοῖς πρυτάνεσι..γνώμας καθεῖναι (Com. for προθεῖναι) Ar.*Ec.*397; κατὰ τὴν ἀγορὰν λογοποιοὺς κ. D.24.15: freq. in later Greek in a general sense, *set in motion, employ*, Luc.*DMeretr.*7.4; κ. ἔς τινας ὑποψίας Philostr.*VA*6.38; φίλους καὶ ῥήτορας κ. *employ* them, Plu.*Per.*7, cf. Philostr.*VA*4.42:—Pass., *to be put in motion*, ἡ στρατηλασίη κατίετο ἐς πᾶσαν τὴν Ἑλλάδα Hdt.7.138. **3.** *allow to return* from exile, φυγάδας X.*HG*2.2.20. **II.** intr., *swoop down* like a wind, λαμπρὸς καὶ μέγας καθιείς Ar.*Eq.*430; of rivers, *run down*, ἑκατέρωσε μέχρι τοῦ μέσου Pl.*Phd.*112e; κ. εἰς γόνυ *sink* on the knee, Plu.*Ant.*45; κ. εἰς ἀγῶνα, Lat. *descendere in arenam*, Id.2.616d, Luc.*Alex.*6; κ. ἐς Ῥόδον *arrive* there, v.l. for κατῆγεν, Polyaen.5.17.2.

**καθῑκετεύω**, Ion. **κατ–**, strengthd. for ἱκετεύω, *entreat earnestly*, κατικ. τινί Hdt.6.68; πολλὰ κ. τινά Hld.6.14; τινα c. inf., Plu.*Cat.Mi.*32, cf. Parth.5.2, Ph.2.384:—also in Med., E.*Or.*324 (lyr.).

**καθικμαίνω**, = κατικμαίνω (q.v.).

**καθικνέομαι**, fut. -ίξομαι Plb.5.93.5, etc., dub. in *IG*5(2).4.13 (Tegea, iv B.C.): aor. -ῑκόμην (v. infr.): pf. part. καθιγμένον Hsch.:—*come down to*: in Hom. only metaph., *reach, touch*, με μάλιστα καθίκετο πένθος ἄλαστον Od.1.342, μάλα πώς με καθίκεο θυμὸν ἐνιπῇ thou *hast touched* me *nearly*, Il.14.104; later, of any down-stroke, κάρα..κέντροισί μου καθίκετο *came down upon* my head, S.*OT*809; εἰς ὄλμους κ. ὑπέροις Paus.5.18.2: abs., ἐπανατεινάμενος τὸ ξίφος καθικνεῖται Parth.8.9: generally, *take effect*, Phld.*Mus.*p.85 K.; *attack, affect*, τῆς ὀπτήσεως καθικνουμένης καὶ ἐξατμιζούσης τὸ τροφῶδες Ath.Med.ap.Orib.1.9.1: freq. in Prose, c. gen., κ. τῆς πηγῆς Paus.7.21.12; κ. τῆς ψυχῆς *reach* or *touch* it, Pl.*Ax.*369e; ἡμῶν ὁ λόγος καθίκετο Luc.*Nigr.*35; ἡ ὕβρις οὐ μετρίως μου καθίκετο Id.*Tox.*46; κ. τινὸς πικρότατα Ael.*VH*14.3; κ. τινὸς σκύτεσι, κονδύλῳ, *strike* one with a strap, etc., Plu.*Ant.*12, *Alc.*7. **2.** κ. τῆς ἐπιβολῆς *attain* one's purpose, Plb.2.38.8, cf. 4.50.10; ποιεῖν [πόλιν] τηλικαύτην ἡλίκην καὶ τειχίζειν ἐπιβαλλόμενοι καθίξονται *they will succeed*, Id.5.93.5. **3.** κατικόμενον, τό, *that which comes to one*, one's share of an inheritance, *IG*9(1).334.30 (Locr., v B.C.).

**καθῑλᾰρ-εύομαι**, c. gen., and **-ύνω**, c. dat., sine expl., Suid.

**καθιλύσας**· ἀθροίσας, Hsch. (fort. καθειλήσας = κατ–).

**καθῑμ-άω**, *let down by a rope*, αὐτόν Ar.*V.*379, 396; κάδον Arist.*Mech.*857$^b$4; τὸν τράχηλον..καθιμήσας, of the heron, Babr.94.3:—Pass., ἐς τὸ Καπιτώλιον ἐκ τοῦ οὐρανοῦ καθιμῆσθαι D.C.45.2. **-ησις**, εως, ἡ, *a letting down by a rope*, Plu.2.264f. **-ονεύω**, = καθιμάω, Hsch.

**καθίννυμαι**, by-form of καθίζομαι, Hp.*Fract.*3, 8; *take a hip-bath*, ἐν ὕδατι θερμῷ Id.*Mul.*1.84, cf. 2.154, al.; cf. ἰνύεσθαι.

**κάθιξις**, εως, ἡ, *arrival* at a point, τῆς συναφῆς Vett.Val.244.35.

**καθιξῶ** and **καθίξω**, Dor. fut. and aor. 1 subj. of καθίζω.

**καθιππ-άζομαι**, Ion. **κατ–**: **I.** trans., *ride down, overrun with horse*, χώρην Hdt.9.14. **2.** metaph., *trample under foot*, δαίμονας A.*Eu.*150 (lyr.); νόμους ib.779 (lyr.), cf. 731: later c. gen., κ. φιλοσοφίας D.L.4.47. **II.** Pass., pf. καθιππάσθαι Macho ap.Ath.13.581d (sens. obsc.). **III.** intr., *ride*, Polyaen.1.3.5. **-ευσις**, εως, ἡ, *charging down*, of cavalry, D.H.9.9 (pl.). ⊛**-εύω**, *ride over, overrun with horse*, τὰ πεδία Id.3.26, cf. Hdn.6.2.5; *ride upon*, οἶδμα *Hymn.Is.*154; of fish, κῦμα κ. Opp.*H.*2.515:—Pass., of frozen rivers, *to be ridden over*, Arist.*Mir.*846$^b$32, Hdn.6.7.6. **2.** *ride down, trample under foot*, Ἀργείων στρατόν E.*Ph.*732. **3.** *conquer by means of a horse* (i.e. the δούρειος ἵππος), Tryph.174.

**καθιππο-κρᾰτέω**, *conquer with horse*, Poll.1.164, 9.141. **-μᾰχέω**, = foreg., ibid. **-τροφέω**, *squander* a fortune *in keeping horses*, Is.5.43.

**καθίπταμαι**, v. καταπέτομαι.

**καθίππαξις** (leg. καθίππαξις), εως, ἡ, *cavalcade* (Lacon.), Hsch.

⊛**κάθῐσις**, εως, ἡ, *sitting*, καθίσεις ἄμορφοι Plu.2.609c, cf. Gal.*UP*3.9 (pl.). **II.** *causing to sit down*, Plu.2.158b.

**κάθισμα**, ατος, τό, *part on which one sits*: in pl., *buttocks*, Sch.Aeschin.1.126. **2.** *seat*, Simp.*in Ph.*347.9, Pall.*in Hp.Fract.*12.278 C. **3.** *base* of a still, Zos.Alch.p.224 B. **II.** *sinking, settling down*, of a wall, Apollod.*Poliorc.*150.1. **2.** *sediment*, Sch.Nic.*Al.*95.

⊛**καθιστάνω**, = καθίστημι, inf., Is.2.29, Lys.26.15, 28.7, *CIG*3065.22 (Teos), etc.: impf., D.S.15.33, etc.:—also **καθιστάω**, *SIG*531.32 (Dyme, iii B.C.); inf. -ιστᾶν D.S.19.15; part. -ιστῶν Lxx *De.*17.15, -ιστῶντες (v.l. -ιστάνοντες) *Act.Ap.*17.15.

⊛**καθίστημι**, **A.** in causal sense:—**Act., in pres., impf., fut.,**

and pf. καθέστᾰκα Hyp.*Eux*.28, Lxx *Je*.1.10, D.H.*Dem*.54, D.S.32.11, etc.; once καθέστηκα *PHib*.1.82 i 14 (iii B.C.): plpf. -εστάκει Demetr. Sceps.ap.Ath.15.697d:—also in **Med.**, fut. (Paus.3.5.1), aor. 1, more rarely pres. (infr. A.II.2):—*set down*, κρητῆρα καθίστα Il.9.202; νῆα κατάστησον *bring* it *to land*, Od.12.185; κ. δίφρους *place, station* them, before starting for the race, S.*El*.710; ποῖ [δεῖ] καθιστάναι πόδα; E.*Ba*.184; κ. τινὰ εἰς τὸ φανερόν X.*An*.7.7.22; *set up, erect*, of stones, *Inscr.Cypr*.94, 95 H.:—Med., [λαῖφος] κατεστήσαντο βοεῦσι *steadied* it, *h.Ap*.407. **2.** *bring down* to a place, τούς μ' ἐκέλευσα Πύλονδε καταστῆσαι Od.13.274: generally, *bring*, κ. τινὰ ἐς Νάξον Hdt.1.64, cf. Th.4.78; esp. *bring back*, πάλιν αὐτὸν κ. ἐς τὸ τεῖχος σῶν καὶ ὑγιᾶ Id.3.34; κ. τοὺς Ἕλληνας εἰς Ἰωνίαν πάλιν X.*An*.1.4.13; without πάλιν, *replace, restore*, ἐς φῶς σὸν κ. βίον E.*Alc*.362; ἃς (sc. τὰς κόρας) οὐδ' ὁ Μελάμπους.. καταστήσειεν ἂν *cure* their squint, Alex.112.5; ἰκτεριῶντας κ. Dsc.4.1; τὸ σῶμα *restore* the general health, Hp.*Mul*.2.133:—Med., κατεστήσαντο (v.l. for κατεκτήσαντο) εὐδαιμονίαν Isoc.4.62:—Pass., οὐκ ἂν ἀντὶ πόνων χάρις καθίσταιτο *would be returned*, Th.4.86. **3.** *bring before* a ruler or magistrate, Hdt.1.209, *PRyl*.65.10 (i B.C.), etc.; τινὰ ἐπί τινα *PCair.Zen*.202.6 (iii B.C.), *POxy*.281.24 (i A.D.). **II.** *set in order, array*, of soldiers, X.*An*.1.10.10; *set* as guards, προφυλακάς ib.3.2.1, etc. **2.** *ordain, appoint*, κατέστησε τύραννον εἶναι παῖδα τὸν ἑωυτοῦ Hdt.5.94, cf. 25: usu. without the inf., κ. τινὰ ὕπαρχον Id.7.105; ἄλλον [ἄρχοντα] ἀντὶ αὐτοῦ X.*Cyr*.3.1.12, etc.; βασιλέα ἐπί τινας Lxx 1*Ki*.8.5, al.; τινὰ ἐς μοναρχίαν E.*Supp*.352; ἐπὶ τὰς ἀρχάς Isoc.12.132; τινὰ τύραννον Ar.*Av*.1672; κ. ἐγγυητάς Hdt.1.196, Ar.*Ec*.1064; δικαστάς, ἐπιμελητάς, νομοθέτας, Id.*Pl*.917, X.*Cyr*.8.1.9, D.3.10 (sed leg. καθίσατε, cf. καθίζω I.4); of games, etc., γυμνικοὺς ἀγῶνας κ. Isoc.4.1: rarely c. inf., οἱ καθιστάντες μουσικῇ.. παιδεύειν Pl.*R*.410b:—so in Pass., κυβερνᾶν καταστα θείς X. *Mem*.1.7.3: aor. Med., *appoint for oneself*, τύραννον καταστησάμενοι παρὰ σφίσι αὐτοῖσι Hdt.5.92.α'; ἄρχοντας X.*An*.3.1.39, etc. **b.** esp. of laws, constitutions, ceremonies, etc., *establish*, νόμους, τελετάς, E.*Or*.892, *Ba*.21, etc.; πολιτείαν, δημοκρατίαν, Arist.*Ath*.7.1, Decr.ib.29.3; ὀλιγαρχίαν Lys.12.42; also, *set in order, arrange*, πολιτείαν Pl. *R*.590e:—also in Med., τοῦτο βουλευτήριον φρούρημα γῆς καθίσταμαι A.*Eu*.706; τὴν Ἱππίου καθίσταμαι τυραννίδα Ar.*V*.502; καθίστατο τὰ περὶ τὴν Μυτιλήνην ᾗ αὐτῷ ἐδόκει Th.3.35; πόλεις ἐπὶ τὸ ὠφέλιμον Id.1.76; [Εὔβοιαν] ὁμολογίᾳ ib.114; πρὸς ἐμὲ τὸ πρᾶγμα καταστήσασθαι *settle* it with me, D.21.90. **3.** *bring into a certain state*, τινὰ ἐς ἀπόνοιαν Th.1.82; ἐς ἀπορίαν Id.7.75; εἰς ἀνάγκην Lys.3.3; εἰς αἰσχύνην Pl.*Sph*.230d; εἰς ἐρημίαν φίλων Id.*Phdr*.232d; εἰς ἀγῶνα Id.*Ap*.24c; τινὰ εἰς ἀσφάλειαν Isoc.5.123; τίνας εἰς ἀγῶνα καθέστακα; Hyp.*Eux*.28, cf. Lycurg.2; κ. τινὰ ἐν ἀγῶνι καὶ κινδύνῳ Antipho 5.61; τὴν πόλιν ἐν πολέμῳ Pl.*Mx*.242a; τοὺς φίλους ἐν ἀκινδύνῳ X.*Cyr*.4.5.28; κ. ἑαυτὸν ἐς κρίσιν *present* himself for trial, Th.1.131, cf. Lycurg.6; κ. τινὰ εἰς τοὺς ἀρχικοὺς *reckon* him as one of.., X.*Mem*.2.1.9. **4.** c. dupl. acc., *make, render so and so*, ψευδῆ γ' ἐμαυτὸν S.*Ant*.657; ἡ ἐπιθυμία κ. τινὰ ἀμνήμονα Antipho 2.1.7; τὸ πιστὸν ὑμᾶς ἀπιστοτέρους κ. Th.1.68; κ. τι φανερόν, σαφές, Id.2.42, 1.32; τινὸς ἐπίπονον τὸν βίον κ. Isoc.10.17: c. part., κλαίοντα καθιστάναι τινά *bring* one to tears, E.*Andr*.635: rarely c. inf., κ. τινὰ φεύγειν *make* him fly, Th.2.84, cf. E.*Alc*.283, Luc.*Charid*.8:—Pass., ἀνάγκη τὴν ναυμαχίαν πεζομαχίαν καθίστασθαι Th.2.89. **5.** Med., *get for oneself*, τὴν ζόην καταστήσασθαι ἀπ' ἔργων ἀνοσιωτάτων Hdt.8.105. **6.** *make*, in periphrases, πάννυχοι.. διάπλοον καθίστασαν A.*Pers*.382:—Med., κρυφαῖον ἔκπλουν οὐδαμῇ καθίστατο ib.385.

**B.** intr. in aor. 2, pf. καθέστηκα, and plpf. of Act. (also fut. καθεστήξω Th.3.37, 102), and all tenses of Med. (exc. aor. 1) and Pass.: pf. καθέσταμαι in later Greek, *IG*2².1006.24 (ii B.C.), Lxx *Nu*.3.32, etc.:—*to be set, set oneself down, settle*, ἐς [Αἴγιναν] Hdt.3.131, cf. Th.4.75; [ὀδύναι] καθίσταντο ἐς ὑπογάστριον Hp.*Epid*.7.97; of joints, ἐξίσταται ἀνωδύνως καὶ κ. goes out of joint and *in again*, Id. *Art*.8; κ. ἐς Ῥήγιον *to make* R. *a base* of operations, Th.3.86; simply, *to be come to* a place, ὅποι καθέσταμεν S.*OC*23. **b.** *come before* another, *stand in* his *presence*, Pi.*P*.4.135; λέξον καταστάς A.*Pers*.295 (unless it be taken in signf. 4), cf. Hdt.1.152; κ. ἐς ὄψιν τινός Id.7.29; καταστάντες ἐπὶ τοὺς ἄρχοντας ἔλεγον Id.3.46, cf. 156; καταστὰς ἐπὶ τὸ πλῆθος ἔλεγε Th.4.84. **2.** *to be set* as guard, ὑπό τινος Hdt.7.59, cf. S.*OC*356, X.*An*.4.5.19, etc.; *to be appointed*, δεσπότης.. καθέστηκα E.*HF*142; στρατηλάτης νέος καταστάς Id.*Supp*.1216; κ. χορηγὸς εἰς Θαργήλια, στρατηγός, etc., Antipho 6.11, Isoc.4.35, etc.; οἱ πρόβουλοι καθεστᾶσιν ἐπὶ τοῖς βουλευταῖς Arist.*Pol*.1299ᵇ37; δικτάτωρ.. καθε[στάμενος τὸ τέταρτον], = Lat. *dictator designatus quartum*, of Caesar, *IG*12(2).35b7 (Mytil.). **3.** *deposit a sediment*, Hp. *Epid*.1.2, 7. **4.** also, *stand* or *become quiet* or *calm*, of water, ὅταν ἡ λίμνη καταστῇ Ar.*Eq*.865, cf. *PHolm*.16.3; θάλασσα γαληνὴ καὶ κ. Plb.21.31.10; πνεῦμα λεῖον καὶ καθεστηκός calm and *settled*, Ar.*Ra*.1003; ὁ θόρυβος κατέστη *subsided*, Hdt.3.80; of laughter, Philostr. *VA*3.4; of a swelling, Hp.*Prog*.7; ἕως τὰ πράγματα κατασταίη Lys.13.25; also of persons, καταστάς *composedly*, A.*Pers*.295 (but v. supr. 1 b); [ἡ ψυχὴ] καθίσταται καὶ ἠρεμίζεται Arist.*Ph*.248ᵃ2; δρώμεν [τοὺς ἐνθουσιαστικοὺς].. καθισταμένους Id.*Pol*.1342ᵃ10; καθεστηκυίας τῆς διανοίας Ocell.4.13; καθεστῶτι προσώπῳ with *composed, calm* countenance, Plu.*Fab*.17; μαίνεσθαι καὶ ἔξω τοῦ καθεστηκότος εἶναι Luc.*Philops*.5; τίς ἂν καθεστηκὼς φήσαιε; what person *of mature judgement* would say..? Phld.*Po*.5.15; ἡ καθεστηκυῖα ἡλικία *middle* age, Th.2.36; ἡλικία μέση καὶ κ. Pl.*Ep*.316c; οἱ καθεστηκότες *those of middle age*, Hp.*Aph*.1.13: also, with metaphor from wine, *mellow*, of persons, Alex.45.8. **5.** *come into a certain state, become*, and in pf. and plpf., *to have become, be*, ἀντὶ φίλου πολέμιόν τινι κ. Hdt.1.87; οἱ μὲν ὀφθαλμῶν ἰητροὶ κατεστέασι, οἱ δὲ κεφαλῆς Id.2.84; ἔμφρων καθίσταται S.*Aj*.306; τῶν ἄνωθεν ὑπόπτων καθεστώτων Epicur. *Sent*.13; ἐς μάχην Hdt.3.45; ἐς πόλεμον ὑμῖν καὶ μάχην κ. E.*HF*1168; ἐς πάλην καθίσταται δορὸς τὸ πρᾶγμα Id.*Heracl*.159; ἐς τὴν ἴησιν Hp.*Prorrh*.2.12; ἐς τὸ αὐτό they *recover*, Id.*Coac*.160 (later abs., καταστῆναι καὶ μηδενὸς ἔτι φαρμάκου δεηθῆναι Gal.*Vict.Att*.1); ἐς τοὺς κινδύνους Antipho 2.3.1; ἐς φόβον Hdt.8.12, Th.2.81; ἐς δέος, λύπην, Id.4.108, 7.75; ἐς φυγήν Id.2.81; ἐς ἔχθραν τινί Isoc.9.67; εἰς ὁμόνοιαν, εἰς πολλὴν ἀθυμίαν, Lys.18.18, 12.3; καταστῆναι ἐς συνήθειάν τινος τὴν πόλιν ποιεῖν make the city *become* accustomed to it, Aeschin.1.165; ἀντιστασιώτης κατεστήκεε *had been*, Hdt.1.92, cf. 9.37; ἐν δείματι μεγάλῳ κατέστασαν Id.7.138; καταστάντων σφι εὖ τῶν πρηγμάτων ib.132; τίνι τρόπῳ καθέστατε; in what case *are ye*? S.*OT*10; φονέα με φησὶ.. καθεστάναι ib.703; ἄπαρνος δ' οὐδενὸς καθίστατο Id.*Ant*.435; κρυπτὸς καταστὰς E.*Andr*.1064; οἱ ἐν τούτῳ τῆς ἡλικίας καθεστῶτες ἐν ᾧ.. Antipho 2.1.1; ἐν οἵῳ τρόπῳ [ἡ τῶν Ἀθηναίων ἀρχὴ] κατέστη how it *came into being*, Th.1.97, cf. 96; ἀρξάμενος εὐθὺς καθισταμένου (sc. τοῦ πολέμου) from its first *commencement*, Id.1.1. **6.** *to be established* or *instituted, prevail*, καί σφι μαντήϊον Διὸς κατέστηκε Hdt.2.29; ἄγραι.. πολλαὶ κατεστᾶσι ib.70, cf. 1.200; ὅδε σφι νόμος κατεστήκεε ib.197; βροτοῖσιν ὃς καθέστηκεν νόμος E. *Hipp*.91: c. inf., θεὸν Ἀμφιάραον πρώτοις Ὠρωπίοις κατέστη νομίζειν Paus.1.34.2: pf. part., *existing, established, prevailing*, τὸν νῦν κατεστεῶτα κόσμον Hdt 1.65; ἦν κατεστηκὸς οὐδὲν φόρου πέρι Id.3.89; τοὺς κατεστεῶτας τριηκοσίους the *regular* 300, Id.7.205; οἱ καθεστῶτες νόμοι S.*Ant*.1113, Ar.*Nu*.1400; τὰ καθεστῶτα the *present state of life*, S.*Ant*.1160; also, *existing laws, usages*, τὰ τότε κ., τά ποτε κ., Pl.*Lg*.798b, Isoc 7.56; ἐπὶ τοῖσι κατεστεῶσι ἔνεμε τὴν πόλιν Hdt.1.59. **7.** of purchases, *cost*, πλέον ἢ ὅσου ἐμοὶ κατέστησαν more than *they stood* me *in*, And.2.11, cf. Plu.2.349a. **8.** *stand against, oppose*, πρός τινα dub. l. in Plb.23.18.5:—Pass., Τιτήνεσσι κατέσταθεν Hes. *Th*.674.

**C.** aor. 1 Med. and sts. pres. Med. are used in trans. sense, v. supr. A.II.2 sq.

**καθιστήριον**, τό, *seat*, Sch.Ar.*Ec*.729, Hsch. s.v. δίφρον.

**καθιστ-ιᾰσις**, εως, ἡ, *expenditure on feasts*, *IG*7.2710 (Acraeph.). **-ιάω**, *spend on feasts*, τόκον ib.12(7).237.25, cf. 56 (Amorgos).

**καθιστορέω**, *observe*, Gp.15.2.31.

**καθίστρα**, ἡ, = καθέδρα (?), *Supp.Epigr*.2.727 (Pednelissus).

**✱καθό**, Adv. for καθ' ὅ (which shd. perh. be written), *in so far as, according as*, Lys.34.5, Arist.*Metaph*.1022ᵃ14, D.S.31.16, 2*Ep.Cor*.8.12, etc.; κ. μεγέθει καὶ κ. ποιότητι *in respect of*.., Phld.*Ir*.p.91 W. **II.** *wherefore*, Pl.*Sph*.267d, Plu.2.51b.

**καθοδηγ-έω**, *guide*, Lxx *Jb*.12.23, Plu.*Cat.Ma*.13: c. acc., Id.2.558d. **-ησις**, εως, ἡ, *guidance*, Th.*Is*.38.15. **-ία**, ἡ, = foreg., Str.2.3.4. **-ός**, ὁ, *guide*, Hellanic.51 J., Str.15.2.6, Orph.*H*.8.8, Apollod.3.4.1; τῆς Ἴσιδος *PMag.Osl*.1.338.

**καθόδιον**, τό, *expenses of return journey*, *Milet*.3 No.152.106 (Eresus, ii B.C.).

**καθοδοιπορέω**, strengthd. for ὁδοιπορέω, Erot.*Fr*.36.

**✱κάθοδος**, Ion. κάτοδος, ἡ, *descent*, esp. of Demeter, Plu.2.378e; represented in mysteries, Herod.1.56; and so of a *procession*, ἥρωος κ. Call.*Aet*.1.1.26: generally, *going down*, τῶν ἐδεστῶν ἐν τῇ κ. ἡ ἡδονή Arist.*PA*690ᵇ30, cf. Luc.*Nec*.2; *way down*, Id.*DMort*.27.1; of planets, *declination*, Simp.*in Cael*.510.29. **2.** ἡ κ. ἡ ἐπὶ θάλασσαν, = κατάβασις, Arr.*An*.1.2.4. **3.** *journey down* the Nile, *POxy*.1119.27 (iii A.D.), etc. **II.** *coming back, return*, E.*HF*19, Th.3.114; esp. of an exile to his country, Hdt.1.60, 61, al., Th.3.85, 5.16, etc.; κ. καὶ ἄδεια Id.8.81. **III.** *cycle, recurrence*, χιλίων ἐτῶν κ. a thousand years *twice told*, in pl., Lxx *Ec*.6.6, cf. Phot.; also τρεῖς καθόδους three *times*, Lxx 3*Ki*.9.25, cf. Aq.*Ex*.34.24, al.; ἄχρι δύο καθόδων *twice over*, Alex.Trall.1.17.

**✱καθολικός**, ή, όν, (καθόλου) *general*, ὕδερος Hp.*Int*.26; καθολικόν, τό, *generic description*, *Stoic*.2.74; καθολικά, τά, title of work by Zeno, ib.1.14; ἔμφασις (v. sub voc.) Plb.6.5.3, cf. 1.57.4; κ. καὶ κοινὴ ἱστορία Id.8.2.11; κ. περίληψις D.H.*Comp*.12; κ. παραδόσεις Phld. *Rh*.1.126 S.; κ. θεώρημα Cic.*Att*.14.20.3; κ. *praecepta*, Quint.2.13.14; -ώτεροι λόγοι *general*, opp. εἰδικοί, S.E.*P*.2.84, cf. Hermog.*Meth*.5; κ. προσῳδία, title of work by Hdn.Gr. on accents; νόμος -ώτερος Ph.2.172; κ. ἐπιστολή an epistle *general*, 1*Ep.Pet*.tit.; *of general interest*, *BGU*1915 (ii A.D.); *universal*, κ. τίς ἐστιν καὶ θεία ἡ ταυτότης καὶ ἡ ἑτερότης Dam.*Pr*.310. Adv. -κῶς *generally*, ἀποφήνασθαι Plb.4.1.8; εἰπεῖν *in general terms*, Str.17.3.10, cf. Phld.*Rh*.1.161 S.; κ. εὑρίσκεταί τι Hermog.*Inv*.3.11; κ., opp. πληθικῶς ('in the majority of cases'), *OGI*669.49 (Egypt, i A.D.); *universally*, Porph.*Sent*.22: Comp. -ώτερον Plb.3.37.6, Gal.18(1).15; -ωτέρως Tz.ad Lyc.16. **II.** as Subst., καθολικός, ὁ, *supervisor of accounts* (οἱ καθόλου λόγοι), = Lat. *procurator a rationibus*, Εὐφράτης ὁ κ. Gal.14.4, cf. *Jahresh*.23 *Beibl*.269 (Ephes., ii A.D.); in Egypt, = Lat. *rationalis*, *PLond*.3.1157 (iii A.D.), *IGRom*.1.1211 (Diocletian), *POxy*.2106.25 (iv A.D.), etc.; also, = *consularis*, *Gloss.*; in cent. iv, also, = *rationalis summarum*, Γεωργίῳ κ. Jul.*Ep*.188, 189 tit.

**καθολκ-εύς**, έως, ὁ, (καθέλκω) *a kind of bandage*, Gal.18(1).785. **-ή**, ἡ, *drawing down* of ships to sea, opp. ἀνολκή, Aen.Tact.10.12, cf. *IG*2².1028.37 (pl.), Callix.1, Hero *Aut*.22.3. **-ός**, ὁ, = καθολκεύς, Gal.18(1).786.

**καθόλου**, Adv. *on the whole, in general*, = καθ' ὅλου (as it shd. perh. be written), Epist.Philipp.ap.D.18.77; κ. γράφειν, opp. κατὰ μέρος,

Plb.3.32.8; κ. εἰπεῖν Arist.*Top.*156$^{a}$13, Plu.2.397c, etc.; οἱ κ. λόγοι *general* statements, opp. οἱ ἐπὶ μέρους, Arist.*EN*1107$^{a}$30 (but in Roman times, accounts *kept by the central government*, = Lat. *summae rationes*, *OGI*715.3 (Alexandria), D.C.79.21, etc.); τοῦτο γάρ ἐστι κ. μᾶλλον too *general*, Arist.*Pol.*1265$^{a}$31, cf. *GA*748$^{a}$8; ἡ τῶν κ. πραγμάτων σύνταξις *general* history, Plb.1.4.2; τὸ κ. D.S.1.77, Plu.2.569f; τὸ κ. τῆς μοχθηρίας, opp. τὸ πρὸς ἡμᾶς, ib.468e; οὐδ' οὗτος ἀποφαίνει κ. τὸ καταλειφθέν the *whole* amount left, D.27.43; ἐν τῷ κ. *in general, speaking generally*, Ath.1.30e, Arr.*Epict.*1.8.8, al. 2. in the Logic of Arist., of terms, τὸ κ. *general*, opp. τὸ καθ' ἕκαστον (singular), λέγω δὲ κ. μὲν ὃ ἐπὶ πλειόνων πέφυκε κατηγορεῖσθαι, καθ' ἕκαστον δὲ ὃ μή *Int.*17$^{a}$39, cf. *Metaph.*1023$^{b}$29; opp. τὸ κατὰ μέρος, *Rh.*1357$^{b}$1, al.; hence, τὰ κ. *universal* truths, ἡ ποίησις μᾶλλον τὰ κ., ἡ δ' ἱστορία τὰ καθ' ἕ. λέγει *Po.*1451$^{b}$7; = γνῶμαι, ib.1450$^{b}$12; esp. *commensurate* predicate, ὃ ἂν κατὰ παντός τε ὑπάρχῃ καὶ καθ' αὑτὸ καὶ ᾗ αὐτό *APo.*73$^{b}$26; as Adj., of propositions, λόγος κ. a *universal* statement, opp. ἐν μέρει, κατὰ μέρος (particular), ἀδιόριστος (infinite), *APr.*24$^{a}$17 sq.; of inference, ἡ κ. ἀπόδειξις *universal* proof, opp. κατὰ μέρος, *APo.*85$^{a}$13; hence, as predicate, κ. εἰσὶν [αἱ ἀρχαί] *Metaph.*1003$^{a}$7; as Adv., κ. ἀποφαίνεσθαι ἐπὶ τοῦ κ. *Int.*17$^{b}$5, al. 3. *completely, entirely*, Plb.1.20.2; οὐδὲ κ. μακρὸν πλοῖον no warships *at all*, ib.13, cf. Lxx*Da.*3.50, al.; μηδὲ τέχνην εἶναι τὸ κ. τοῦ πείθειν Phld.*Rh.*1.327S. (Written κατὰ ὅλου Pl.*Men.*77a.)

**κάθομα**, f.l. for καθ' ὁμά, Call.*Fr.*293, = Id.*Oxy.*2079.26.

**καθομηρ-εύω**, *express in Homeric language*, Hsch. s.v. καθωμηρευμένα. **-ίζω**, *describe Homerically*, Aristaenet.1.3,12. II. intr., *speak in the style of Homer*, Eustr.*in EN*268.33.

**καθομῑλέω**, *conciliate by daily intercourse, win the favour of*, τοὺς γνωρίμους Arist.*Pol.*1315$^{b}$4, cf. Plu.2.52e, *Caes.*15, App.*BC*5.63: c. dat., κ. τῷ πλήθει (nisi leg. τὰ πλήθη) D.S.14.70; κ. τοὺς καιρούς Ath.12.513b, v.l. in Sch.Ar.*Ra.*1001, v.l. in Suid. s.v. ἀγχίστροφοι (nisi leg. τοῖς καιροῖς, as in Sch.Ar.*Ra.*47,546):—Pass., ὑπὸ Δημάδου καθομιληθεὶς D.S.16.87. II. Pass., *to be used in daily intercourse, to be current*, esp. in pf. part. Pass., ἡ καθωμιλημένη δόξα Plb.10.5.9; κ. φράσεις Phld.*Rh.*1.161S.; κ. ὄνομα Alex.Aphr.*in Mete.*7.9, cf. Antig.*Mir.*8; also Σαρδόνιος γέλως καθωμίληται *has become a proverb*, Dsc.*Alex.*14: c. dat., νόμοι οὐ -μένοι τῷ τῶν πολλῶν ἔθει which *have* nothing *to do* with.., Max.Tyr.23.2.

**καθομοιόω**, *assimilate*, Simp.*in Cat.*328.30.

**καθομολογ-έω**, *confess, allow*, esp. to one's detriment, Pl.*Cri.*49d, *Grg.*499b. 2. *consent*, abs., And.1.42. b. *consent to accept in payment*, τόκους D.56.14. II. *promise, engage, vow*:—Pass., ἀνάθημα τῷ θεῷ Luc.*Phal.*2.1, cf. Philostr.*VA*5.30. 2. *betroth*, τινὰ τῷ υἱῷ Lxx*Ex.*21.9 (Med.); Κλαυδίαν ἀνδρί Plu.*TG*4:—pf. Pass. in med. sense, τὴν ἀδελφὴν.. γυναῖκά τινι καθωμολογημένος Id.*Crass.*33; but in pass. sense, Id.*Pomp.*47: plpf. καθωμολόγητο Parth.13.2. 3. *pledge, mortgage*, ὑποθήκην κ. τί τινι Alciphr.3.3. III. Med. in sense of Act. II. 1, c. fut. inf., Parth.9.4. **-ία**, ἡ, *engagement, agreement*, *Foed.Delph.Pell.*2 A 3.

**κάθομον**, f.l. for καθ' οἶμον, Hsch.

**καθόπερ**, = καθ' ὅπερ: Ion. **κατόπερ**, *just as*, *SIG*45.43 (Halic., v B.C.), 57.11 (Milet., v B.C.).

⊛ **καθοπλ-ίζω**, *equip, arm fully*, τῇ πανοπλίᾳ Aeschin.3.154, cf. Decr. ap.D.18.116, Aristeas 14:—Med., *arm oneself fully*, Batr.122,160, Plb.3.62.7, Plu.*Phil.*9, etc.; πανοπλίας κ. *arm oneself in*.., Lxx 4*Ma.*3.12:—Pass., *to be so armed*, X.*Cyr.*2.1.11; καθωπλισμένοι εἰς τὰ Μακεδονικά D.S.19.27; θυμιατηρίῳ καθωπλισμένος *furnished with*.., Lxx 4*Ma.*7.11: metaph., καλοκἀγαθίᾳ ib.11.22. II. *array, set in order*: metaph., τὸ μὴ καλὸν καθοπλίσασα δύο φέρειν so *ordering* that which is not well as to.., S.*El.*1087 (lyr., Sch. καταπολεμήσασα τὸ αἰσχρὸν καὶ νικήσασα). **-ισις**, εως, ἡ, *arming, making of arms*, Philoch.ap.Anon.*Oxy.*1241 v6; *mode of arming, armour*, Plb.6.23.14, Ael.*Tact.*2.7:—so **-ισμός**, ὁ, Plb.11.32.7, Ael.*Tact.*2.9, *SIG*569.33 (Halasarna, iii B.C.); οἱ ἐν τοῖς βαρέσι κ. Plb.3.113.7; κοῦφοι κ. D.S.5.34.

**καθοπτεύει**· καθορᾷ, Hsch.; cf. κατοπτεύω.

**καθορ-ᾱτικός**, ή, όν, *able to see into*: *keen-sighted*, Poll.9.151. **-άω**, Ion. κατ-, impf. καθεώρων X.*Cyr.*3.2.10, Ion. 3 sg. κατώρα Hdt.7.208: pf. καθεώρακα Pl.*Lg.*905b: fut. κατόψομαι Hdt.3.17: 3 sg. pf. κατῶπται Pl.*R.*432b: aor. 1 κατώφθην Id.*Phlb.*46b: for aor. Act., v. κατεῖδον:—*look down*, ἐξ Ἴδης καθορῶν Il.11.337; ἐπί τινος Hdt.7.44:—Med., ἐπὶ Θρῃκῶν καθορώμενος αἶαν Il.13.4. II. trans., *look down upon*, ὅσους θνητοὺς ἠέλιος καθορᾷ Sol.14, cf. Thgn.168,616, X.*Cyr.*3.2.10; ὑψόθεν τὸν τῶν κάτω βίον Pl.*Sph.*216c, etc.: metaph., φρένα Δίαν κ., ὄψιν ἄβυσσον A.*Supp.*1058 (lyr.):—Med., Τροίην κατὰ πᾶσαν ὁρᾶται Il.24.291. 2. *have within view, see distinctly, descry*, Hdt. 7.208, 9.59, Ar.*Nu.*326, Pl.*R.*516a, etc.:—Pass., Th.3.20,112, Pl.*Phlb.*38d, etc. 3. *behold, observe, perceive*, Pi.*P.*9.49, E.*Fr.*910.5 (anap.); καθορᾶν τι ἔν τινι *to observe* something therein, Pl.*Lg.*905b, cf. *Grg.*457c; τι ἐν τῇ ζητήσει Id.*R.*368e; ἵν' ἃ πανουργεῖς μὴ καθορᾷ σου that he *may* not *observe* thy knavish tricks, Ar.*Eq.*803; also κ. τὰς τρίχας εἰ.. *to look and see* whether.., Hdt.2.38. 4. *explore*, τὰ ἄλλα Id.3.17, cf. 123. 5. *regard, reverence*, τὸ τοῦ θεοῦ κράτος Lxx 3*Ma.*3.11.

**καθορ-ίζω**, *determine*, τὰς αἰτίας τινός Phld.*D.*1.14; *bound, define*, Hsch.:—Med., *lay claim to*, τόπους *Sammelb.*5240.9 (i A.D.). **-ιστικῶς**, Adv. *definitely*, οὐδὲν κ. δογματίζειν Anon.*in Tht.*61.12.

⊛ **καθορμ-ίζω**, *bring* a ship *into harbour, bring to anchor*, καθώρμισαν πρός τι πολισμάτιον Plb.1.53.10 codd. (dub.); τὸν στόλον εἰς τὸ νεώριον Plu.*Cat.Mi.*39:—Pass., with aor. Med., *come into harbour, put in*, ἐς τὴν Ἔφεσον Th.3.32, cf. 6.97, etc.: aor. 1 Pass., Anon.Hist. (*FGr.H*160) ii 20 (iii B.C.), Plb.1.21.5, Plu.*Sull.*26; ὑπ' Ἀκραγαντίνων (Cobet ὑπ' ἄκραν τινὰ) καθωρμίσθησαν Polyaen.6.16.4. 2. metaph., ἐς τάσδε σαυτὸν πημονὰς καθώρμισας *hast brought* thyself to such miseries, A.*Pr.*965; κ. ἑαυτὸν εἰς ἡσυχίαν Plu.2.455c:—Pass., καθώρμισται ἡ κύστις ἐκ τῶν νεφρῶν *is suspended* from them, Arist. *PA*671$^{b}$25: metaph., γένος ἐν μεταιχμίῳ ἀρετῆς καὶ κακίας -ισμένον Max.Tyr.30.3; of logical dependence, τὰ αἴτια τὰ νοητά, εἰς ἃ διὰ νοῦ -ίζεται ἡ ἐπιστήμη Simp.*in de An.*124.23. ⊛ **-ιον**, τό, = ὅρμος, *necklace*, *PMagd.*42.5 (iii B.C.), Lxx*Ho.*2.13(15), Phot., Suid.; κάθορμον Hsch. **-ισις**, εως, ἡ, *bringing to land*, Dion.Byz.40.

**καθόσι-ος**, ον, in Sup. -ώτατος *devotissimus*, *Gloss.* **-ότης**, ητος, ἡ, *defunctio*, *Gloss.* ⊛ **-όω**, *dedicate*, ἄγαλμα Poll.1.11, cf. *OGI* 383.109, al. (Commagene, i B.C.), *SIG*799.6 (Cyzicus, i A.D.):—Med., ὃν τοῖσδε βωμοῖς θεὰ καθωσιώσατο E.*IT*1320:—Pass., ἐπεὶ δὲ βωμῷ πόπανα καὶ προθύματα καθωσιώθη Ar.*Pl.*661, cf. D.H.2.23; καθωσιωμένος τινὶ *devoted*, of a person, Hdn.7.6.4; -ωμένοι νόμοι Ph.2.581; στρατιῶται Just.*Edict.*13.9. 2. *betroth*, J.*BJ*1.24.5. 3. κ. πόλιν καθαρμοῖς *purify*, Plu.*Sol.*12. **-ωσις**, εως, ἡ, *dedication*, [ἀγαλμάτων] Poll.1.11. 2. *devotion, fidelity*, *POxy.*2106.9 (iv A.D., written κατοσ-), Just.*Nov.App.*4.1; as a title, ἡ ἐμὴ κ., *SIG*905.11 (Chalcis, iv A.D.), cf. *Arch.Pap.*1.298 (iv A.D.). II. *crimen laesae majestatis*, Just.*Nov.*95.1.1, cf. Suid. s.v. εὐνοῦχος. **-ωτέον**, *one must dedicate oneself*, c. dat., *Theol.Ar.*50.

⊛ **καθότι**, Ion. κατ-, for καθ' ὅ τι (which shd. perh. be written) *in what manner*, *IG*1$^{2}$.24.8, al., Hdt.7.2, Th.1.82, etc.; κ. γέγραπται *as* is written, *SIG*577.18 (Milet., iii/ii B.C.), etc.; *so far as, inasmuch as*, Plb.4.25.3, al.

**καθοῦ**, aor. 2 imper. Med. of καθίημι. **κάθου**, imper. of κάθημαι.

**καθουφήν**· ἀλώπεκα, Hsch.; cf. κοθοῦριν.

**καθυβρίζω**, Ion. κατ-, *treat despitefully, insult*, c. acc., S.*El.*522; σῶμ' ἐμόν E.*El.*698, cf. *PHal.*1.210 (iii B.C.), Ph.2.574, etc.; κ. ταῦτα αὐτόν E.*Ba.*616 (troch.); τὸν δῆμον Ar.*Ach.*631, cf. *PLit.Lond.*52.2: c. acc. cogn., πολλὰ κ. Plu.*Crass.*29: also c. gen., S.*OC*960, *Ph.*1364: abs., Id.*OC*1535:—Pass., Phld.*Vit.*p.12 J.; καθυβρίζεται τοιαῦτα τῶν χειρωνακτέων ὑπὸ τῶν ἀνθρώπων such *are occasions of* the practitioners *being mocked*, Hp.*Acut.*44. 2. c. dat., Hdt.1.212, Paus.4.27.3; also κ. εἰς θυγατέρας dub. l. in D.H.11.2.

**καθυγρ-αίνω**, *moisten well*, Arist.*Pr.*863$^{b}$23, Thphr.*CP*6.18.10, Plu.*Luc.*32:—Pass., Thphr.*CP*1.13.6; of the bowels, *to be relaxed*, Hp.*Aph.*4.27, etc. II. *liquefy*, in Pass., Plu.2.953e. **-ασμός**, ὁ, *moistening*, Sor.1.120, Aët.5.118. **-ος**, ον, *very wet*, Hp.*Aph.*5.62; χώρα, γῆ, *Gp.*2.13.1, Porph.*Antr.*28; of plants which grow in wet places, Thphr.*HP*1.4.2; χωρίον v.l. in Plb.5.24.4; Γαλάται ταῖς σαρξὶ κ. with *flowing* muscles, D.S.5.28. 2. *connected with water* or *the sea*, πράγματα Vett.Val.82.32; ζῴδια Ptol.*Tetr.*181.

**κάθυδρος** [ῠ], ον, *very watery, full of water*, κ. κρατήρ S.*OC*158 (lyr.); χωρίον v.l. in Plb.5.24.4.

**καθῠλακτέω**, *bark at* one, Plu.2.969d:—also **καθυλάσσω** (written κατ-), *Gloss.*

**καθῡλίζω**, *strain, filter*, τὸν οἶνον Ath.10.420d; of a drug, *clarify*, τὸ αἷμα κ. Archig.ap.Aët.3.114, cf. 9.31.

⊛ **καθῡλομᾰνέω**, *run all to wood*, Hp.*Ep.*13.

**καθυμνέω**, *sing of much* or *constantly, descant upon*, Cleanth.1.6, Phld.*Rh.*1.221S., D.S.11.11, J.*BJ*1.31.3, Plu.2.1117a; *make a hymn of*, τὸν αὐτῶν βίον Epicur.*Fr.*605.

**καθύομαι** [ῡ], Pass., *to be rained upon*, σφοδροῖς ὄμβροις St.Byz. s.v. Ὑητός.

**καθυπ-ᾰκούω**, *consent*, σῖτον ἀποδόσθαι τῆς καλῶς ἐχούσης τιμῆς *IG* 7.4262.4 (Oropus, iii/ii B.C.). **-άρχω**, strengthd. for ὑπάρχω, Plu.*Cic.*23. **-είκω**, strengthd. for ὑπείκω, Nicom.*Harm.*3.

**καθυπερ-ᾰκοντίζω**, *overshoot completely*, ἵν' οἱ θεοὶ τοὺς Γηγενεῖς.. καθυπερηκόντισαν Ar.*Av.*825. **-βάλλω**, v.l. for ὑπερβάλλω, Ruf. ap.Orib.7.26.35. **-έχω**, *to be much superior*, -έχων, opp. ἥττων, Aristeas 257: c. gen., ἀλόγων ζῴων κ. τῷ ἀρετᾶς ἐπίμοιρος ἦμεν Euryph. ap.Stob.4.39.27; τινι *in* or *by* a thing, Plb.2.25.9; γένει Callicrat. ap.Stob.4.28.18: rarely c. acc., ἐξουσίαν κ. Theano *Ep.*5.4: c. acc. pers. et dat. rei, τὼς ἄλλως ἀρετᾷ Diotog.ap.Stob.4.7.62:—Pass., Ps.-Philol.ap.Stob.1.20.2. **-ηφᾰνέω**, strengthd. for ὑπερηφανέω, Arg. Ar.*Ach.*: c. gen., *treat with disdain*, τῶν φιλοσόφων Phld.*Vit.*p.7 J.:—also **-ηφᾰνεύομαι**, Hsch. s.v. κατεπλατύνετο, Eust.561.1:—hence Subst. **-ηφᾰνία**, ἡ, Phld.*Vit.*p.28 J.

⊛ **καθύπερθε** [ῠ], poet. before a vowel -θεν (also v.l. in Th.5.59, S.*El.*1090 (lyr.)); Ion. κατύπερθε: Adv.:—*from above, down from above*, δεινὸν δὲ λόφος κ. ἔνευεν Il.3.337, cf. 22.196, Od.12.442, etc.; κ. μελαθρόφιν 8.279; ἐκ μὲν τοῦ πεδίου.., κ. δέ.. Th.5.59, cf. *IG*1$^{2}$.398: c. gen., πυρός Nic.*Th.*691. 2. *atop, above*, opp. ὑπένερθε, Od.10.353; κ. ἐπιρρέει floats *atop*, Il.2.754; κ. τῶν ὅπλων τοῦ τόνου Hdt.7.36; of geographical position, Λέσβος ἄνω.., καὶ Φρυγίη καθύπερθε Il.24.545: c. gen., καθύπερθε Χίοιο *above*, i.e. *north of*, Chios, Od.3.170: in Prose, Κέρκιος κατύπερθε *SIG*1.3 (Abu Simbel, vi B.C.); ἡ χώρη ἡ κ. Hdt.4.8; ἡ κ. ὁδός Id.1.104, etc.; τὰ κ. *the upper country*, i.e. farther inland, τὰ κ. τῆς λίμνης Id.2.5; τὰ κ. τῆς θηριώδεος ib.32; τοῖσι κ. Ἀσσυρίων οἰκημένοισι Id.1.194. 3. *above, having the upper hand of*, κ. γενέσθαι τινός, prop., of a wrestler *who falls atop of* his opponent, ib.67, 8.60.γ'; κ. χερὶ πλούτῳ τε τῶν ἐχθρῶν S.*El.* l.c. (lyr.); also, of affairs, ἐλογίζετο.. κ. οἱ τὰ πρήγματα ἔσεσθαι τῶν Ἑλληνικῶν Hdt.8.136; κακοὶ δ' ἀγαθῶν καθύπερθεν Thgn.679; μόχθου κ. *superior*

*to* misery, unconquered by it, Pi.*P.*9.31; also κ. ἤ.. Hdt.8.75. II. of Time, *before*, c. gen., Id.5.28.

**καθυπερτερ-έω**, Astrol., of planetary influences, *prevail*, Heph. Astr.1.16, Porph.*in Ptol.*188: c. gen., Ptol.*Tetr.*119: c. acc., *overcome*, Vett.Val.102.14, al.:—Pass., Ptol.*Tetr.*88 (but expld. by ἐπαναφερομένου *PSI*3.158.22): generally, c. gen., *prevail over*, ἐχθρῶν Vett. Val.11.8, cf. M.Ant.8.8, Man.6.687 (s.v.l.): abs., Herm.ap.Stob.1.42.7 (prob.). **-ησις**, εως, ἡ, Astrol., *prepollence*, Antioch.Astr. in *Cat. Cod.Astr.*8(3).106, Ptol.*Tetr.*193, Vett.Val.5.15, al.: generally, *prevalence*, prob. in Herm.ap.Stob.1.42.7. **-ητικός**, ή, όν, *prevalent, prepollent*, δύναμις Vett.Val.102.14. **-ία**, ἡ, = καθυπερτέρησις, *Cat. Cod.Astr.*4.6. **-ος**, α, ον, Ion. **κατ-**, η, ον, Comp. Adj.: (καθύπερθε):—*above*, Σεληναίης Man.6.604. II. commonly metaph., *having the upper hand, superior*, κ. γίνεσθαι τῷ πολέμῳ Hdt.1.67: abs., Th.5.14; κ. τῶν Περσέων γινόμενα τὰ πρήγματα Hdt.7.233, cf. Th.7.56; θεοῦ δ' ἔτ' ἰσχὺς κ. A.*Th.*226 (lyr.); κ. Ζεύς Theoc.24.99: c. gen., πόλις κ. τῶν ἀντιπάλων X.*Mem.*4.6.14, cf. Theoc.24.100, etc.: neut. καθυπέρτερον as Adv., = καθύπερθε, Id.2.60 (s. v. l.):—Sup. **καθυπέρτατος**, η, ον, *highest*, ἐν τῇ κατυπερτάτῃ τῆς γῆς Hdt. 4.199. 2. Astrol., *prevalent, prepollent*, ἀστέρες Vett.Val.98.27.

**καθυπερτίθεμαι**, *communicate*, [τί] τινι Nic.Dam.66 J.

**καθυπηρετέομαι**, *assist*, τῇ ἀποκρίσει Sor.1.25; τῷ τάχει.. καθυπηρετούμενας χεῖρας *keeping up with*.., Sch.Pl.*Phdr.*244b.

**καθυπισχνέομαι**, strengthd. for ὑπισχ-, Luc.*Herm.*6, *Rh.Pr.*25, Hsch.

**καθυπν-ής**, ές, = κάθυπνος, Nic.*Al.*434. **-ιος**, ον, *happening in sleep*, Oenom.ap.Eus.*PE*5.25. **-ος**, ον, *fast asleep*, Parmeno 1, Arist.*Pr.*876ᵃ21. **-όω**, Ion. **κατ-**, *fall fast asleep*, Hdt.4.8, 7.12, al., X.*Mem.*2.1.30, Aen.Tact.18.17, Phld.*Hom.*p.25 O., *IG*4.952.51 (Epid.): Ep. part. καθυπνώοντι dub. in Maiist.16:—Pass., κατυπνωμένος *asleep*, Hdt.3.69, 7.14, 17. **-ωσις**, εως, ἡ, *falling asleep*, Arist. *Pr.*900ᵇ37.

**καθυπο-βαίνω**, pf. -βέβηκα, *occupy a lower place than*, τῶν ἐπάνω Ach.Tat.*Intr.Arat.*18. **-βάλλω**, *subject*, Heliod. *in EN*109.20, Eust.1406.41; τινὰς τῇ τοῦ τετραπλασίου ἀποδόσει Just.*Nov.*161.1.3:—Pass., ποιναῖς ib.134.7. II. *place underneath*, τοὺς δακτύλους τῇ ἕδρᾳ Aët.16.110 (= 100). **-γράφω**, *describe*, Eust.974.13; *append signature* to a document or edict, *Sammelb.*5251.4 (ii B.C.), *PFlor.*36.22 (iv A.D.), *Cod.Just.*1.1.7.11, etc. **-δύομαι**, strengthd. for ὑποδ-, Eustr.*in EN*372.27. **-κειμαι**, strengthd. for ὑπόκ-, *to be 'in being', 'in evidence'*, Artem.1.1. **-κρίνομαι** [ῑ], *subdue by histrionic arts*, D.19.337; κ. καὶ διαφθείρουσι τὰς βουλήσεις τῶν ποιημάτων destroying *by bad acting*, D.H.*Dem.*53. II. c. inf., κ. εἶναι.. *pretend* to be some one else, Luc.*DMar.*13.2; κ. μειδιᾶν Ph. 2.280: c. acc., *counterfeit*, φιλίαν ib.520; τὴν σεμνότητα Him.*Ecl.*3.2. **-νοέω**, *suspect*, c. acc. et inf., *PRyl.*127.15 (i A.D.); *harbour suspicions*, εἴς τινα *POxy.*1465.7 (i B.C.): c. acc., Iamb.*Myst.*5.10: abs., Procl.*in Prm.*p.586 S. II. *form a vague conception of*, τῷ γνωστῷ τὸ ἄγνωστον κ. Dam.*Pr.*29: c. acc. et inf., *suppose*, Sor.2.64; *perceive, understand*, πρὸς τίνος ἂν μάλιστα σῴζοιντο Phld.*Rh.*2.18 S.

**καθυποπτεύω**, *suspect*, f.l. in Arist.*Rh.Al.*1426ᵇ28 (Pass.) (ὑπ- *PHib.*1.26.302).

**καθυπο-στιβίζω**, *paint underneath with* στίβι (v. στίμμι), in Pass., -ισμένος τὼ ὀφθαλμώ Nic.Dam.4 J. **-τάσσω**, Att. **-ττω**, *subject*, Phleg.*Fr.*17 J., *PMag.Lond.*123.4. II. = καθυπογράφω, *PFlor.* 377.7 (vi A.D.). **-τοπέομαι**, *place a sinister construction upon*, *EM*762.15 (nisi leg. καχ-).

**καθυπουργέω**, *render service*, Eustr.*in EN*387.8.

**καθυστερ-έω**, *fall behind*, κ. πολὺ τῇ διώξει Plu.*Crass.*29: metaph., *fall short*, τῇ φύσει Plb.23.7.5. 2. of Time, κ. τῆς ἑορτῆς *come too late for*.., *PSI*6.607.7 (iii B.C.); κ. τῆς καταστάσεως τῶν ὑπάτων Plb. 11.33.8; πάντων Id.5.17.7; τῆς ἐκτάξεως Id.10.39.5, cf. D.S.5.53, Str.14.2.5: c. acc., ἀπαρχὰς ἅλωνος οὐ -ήσεις *shall* not *be slow to offer*, Lxx *Ex.*22.29 (28): abs., ξενίας ἀεὶ φρόντιζε, μὴ καθυστέρει Men.*Mon.* 396; *delay*, Plb.5.16.5; of growing plants, *to be later*, Thphr.*CP*1.17.2. 3. *fare badly*, ἐν αἷς (sc. πρεσβείαις) ἐν οὐδενὶ καθυστέρησεν ὁ δῆμος *OGI*339.22 (Sestos, ii B.C.): c. gen., *come short of*, πάσης τροφῆς Lxx *Si.*37.20; *lack*, ἀγαθοῦ νοῦ Phld.*Rh.*2.61 S.; δικαίου μηθενὸς κ. *SIG*568.13 (Halasarna, iii B.C.); *fail in*, πράξεων Ph.*Bel.*103.11. 4. c. dupl. gen., *fail* a person *in*, ἐλιπάρεον [τὸν Ἀσκληπιὸν] μὴ -έειν μου τῆς θεραπείης Hp.*Ep.*15. 5. *to be kept waiting for* a thing, c. gen., ἐντονίων Ph.*Bel.*58.3; θανάτου Ps.-Luc.*Philopatr.* 16. **-ίζω**, = foreg. 2, περὶ τὴν σποράν *Gp.*2.13.2. **-ικῶς**, Adv. *behind* their *time*, Ptol.*Phas.*p.11 H.

**καθυφαίνω**, *interweave, weave in*, Lxx *Ex.*28.17:—Med., aor. 1 part. καθυφηνάμενος *Lyr.Alex.Adesp.*10.15:—Pass., *to be inwoven*, Lxx *Ju.*10.21.

❄**καθύφ-εσις**, εως, ἡ, *collusion*, Poll.8.143; *praevaricatio*, *Gloss.* **-έτης**, ου, ὁ, *praevaricator*, ib. ❄**-ίημι**, *give up, surrender treacherously*, [καιρὸν] ἐάν τις ἑκὼν καθυφῇ τοῖς ἐναντίοις καὶ προδῷ D.19.6, cf. 16.18, al.; τὰ τῆς πόλεως Id.58.6, cf. Luc.*Prom.*5; esp. in a lawsuit, κ. τὸν ἀγῶνα *conduct it collusively, compromise* it, D.21.151; οὐ μόνον τῷ μὴ καθυφεῖναι ταῦτα σεμνύνομαι Id.18.107: abs., καθυφέντων τῶν κατηγόρων *when* they *let the action drop*, Id.23.96. II. Med., καθυφίεσθαί τινι *give way, yield*, c. dat. pers., X.*HG*2.4.23; ἔν τινι *slacken*, ἐν μάχαις Polyaen.8.24.1: abs., Luc.*Abd.*7. 2. Med., with pf. Pass., used trans. like the Act., εἰ καθυφείμεθά τι τῶν πραγμάτων D. 3.8; καθυφεῖντο ἑαυτούς Plb.3.60.4; ἐπ' ἀργυρίῳ τὸ τίμημα καθυφειμένος Plu.*Cic.*8; οὐδὲν.. καθυφηκάμην J.*BJ*2.16.4; -ίενται τὴν τοῦ ἑνὸς τιμήν Ph.2.220. ❄**-ίσταμαι**, pf. inf. καθυφεστάναι *to be really existent*, Jul.*Or.*4.163d.

**κάθω**, barbarism for καθίζω, Tim.*Pers.*168.

**καθωπλισμένως**, Adv. pf. part. Pass. (καθοπλίζω), *like armed warriors*, Sch.Ar.*Pl.*325.

**καθωραΐζομαι**, = ὡραΐζομαι, Phot. (ubi κατωρ-), Suid.

**καθώς**, Adv. = καθά, Hdt.9.82 codd., Arist.*Pr.*891ᵇ34, *IG*5(2).344.20 (Arc., iii B.C.), Wilcken *Chr.*11 *A* 53 (ii B.C.), *IG*2².1030.22 (i B.C.), al.; *even as*, *Ev.Jo.*15.12. 2. *how*, ὑπομιμνήσκειν κ... Aristeas 263, cf. *Act.Ap.*15.12. II. of Time, *as, when*, ib.7.17, Lxx *2Ma.*1.31, Aristeas 310. (Condemned by Phryn.397, Moer.212.)

❄**καθώσπερ**, Adv. = foreg., Him.*Or.*1.20.

❄**καί**, Conj., copulative, joining words and sentences, *and*; also Adv., *even, also, just*, freq. expressing emphatic assertion or assent, corresponding as positive to the negative οὐ (μή) or οὐδέ (μηδέ).

A. copulative, *and*, I. joining words or sentences to those preceding, ἦ, καὶ κυανέῃσιν ἐπ' ὀφρύσι νεῦσε Κρονίων Il.1.528, etc.: repeated with two or more Nouns, αἱ δὲ ἔλαφοι κ. δορκάδες κ. οἱ ἄγριοι οἶες κ. οἱ ὄνοι οἱ ἄγριοι X.*Cyr.*1.4.7; joining only the last pair, Cleom.2.1 (p.168.5 Z.), Phlp.*in APr.*239.30, etc., v.l. in Arist.*Po.*1451ᵃ20; ὁ ὄχλος πλείων κ. πλείων ἐπέρρει more *and* more, X.*Cyr.*7.5.39; to add epithets after πολύς, πολλὰ κ. ἐσθλά Il.9.330; πολλὰ κ. μεγάλα D.28.1, etc. 2. to add a limiting or defining expression, πρὸς μακρὸν ὄρος κ. Κύνθιον ὄχθον to the mountain *and specially* to.., *h.Ap.*17, cf. A.*Ag.* 63 (anap.), S.*Tr.*1277 (anap.) (sts. in reverse order, πρὸς δῶμα Διὸς κ. μακρὸν Ὄλυμπον Il.5.398); to add by way of climax, θεῶν.. κ. Ποσειδῶνος all the gods, *and above all*.., A.*Pers.*750, etc.; ἐχθροὶ κ. ἔχθιστοι Th.7.68; τινὲς κ. συχνοί Pl.*Grg.*455c; freq. ἄλλοι τε καί.., ἄλλως τε καί.., v. ἄλλος II. 6, ἄλλως I. 3; ὀλίγου τινὸς ἄξια κ. οὐδενός little *or* nothing, Id.*Ap.*23a: joined with the demonstr. Pron. οὗτος (q. v.), εἶναι.. δούλοισι, κ. τούτοισι ὡς δρηπέτῃσι Hdt.6.11, cf. 1.147; κ. ταῦτα *and* this *too*.., γελᾶν ἀναπείθειν, κ. ταῦθ' οὕτω πολέμιον ὄντα τῷ γέλωτι X.*Cyr.*2.2.16, etc. II. at the beginning of a sentence, 1. in appeals or requests, καί μοι δὸς τὴν χεῖρα Il.23.75; καί μοι λέγε.., καί μοι ἀπόκριναι.., Pl.*Euthphr.*3a, *Grg.*462b; freq. in Oratt., καί μοι λέγε.. τὸ ψήφισμα, καί μοι ἀνάγνωθι.., D.18.105, Lys.14.8, etc. 2. in questions, to introduce an objection or express surprise, κ. τίς τόδ' ἐξίκοιτ' ἂν ἀγγέλων τάχος; A.*Ag.*280; κ. πῶς..; *pray* how..? E. *Ph.*1348; κ. δὴ τί..; *but* then what..? Id.*Hel.*101; κ. ποῖον..; S.*Aj.* 462; κ. τίς εἶδε πώποτε βοῦς κριβανίτας; Ar.*Ach.*86; κᾆπειτ' ἔκανες; E.*Med.*1398 (anap.); κ. τίς πώποτε χαριζόμενος ἑτέρῳ τοῦτο εἰργάσατο; Antipho 5.57, cf. Is.1.20, Isoc.12.23, Pl.*Tht.*163d, al. 3. = καίτοι, *and yet*, Ar.*Eq.*1245, E.*HF*509. 4. at the beginning of a speech, Lys.*Fr.*36a. III. after words implying sameness or likeness, *as*, γνώμῃσι ἐχρέωντο ὁμοίῃσι κ. σύ they had the same opinion *as* you, Hdt.7.50, cf. 84; ἴσον or ἴσα κ..., S.*OT*611, E.*El.*994; ἐν ἴσῳ (sc. ἐστὶ) κ. εἰ.. Th.2.60, etc. 2. after words implying comparison or opposition, αἱ δαπάναι οὐχ ὁμοίως κ. πρίν Id.7.28; πᾶν τοὐναντίον ἔχει νῦν τε κ. ὅτε.. Pl.*Lg.*967a. 3. to express simultaneity, ἦν ἦμαρ δεύτερον.., κἀγὼ κατηγόμην S.*Ph.*355, cf. Th.1.50; παρέρχονταί τε μέσαι νύκτες κ. ψύχεται [τὸ ὕδωρ] Hdt.4.181, cf. 3.108; [οἱ Λακεδαιμόνιοι] οὐκ ἔφθασαν τὴν ἀρχὴν κατασχόντες κ. Θηβαίοις εὐθὺς ἐπεβούλευσαν Isoc.8.98. IV. joining an affirm. clause with a neg., ἀλλ' ὥς τι δράσων εἶπε κοὐ θανούμενος S.*Tr.*160, etc. V. καί.., καί.. correlative, *not only*.., *but also*.., κ. ἀεὶ κ. νῦν, κ. τότε κ. νῦν, Pl.*Grg.*523a, *Phlb.*60b; κ. κατὰ γῆν κ. κατὰ θάλατταν X.*An.*1.1.7. VI. by anacoluthon, ὡς φαμένη κ. κερδοσύνῃ ἡγήσατ' Ἀθήνη, for ὡς ἔφη κ..., Il.22.247; ἔρχεται δὲ αὐτῇ τε.. κ. τὸν υἱὸν ἔχουσα, for κ. ὁ υἱός, X.*Cyr.*1.3.1; ἄλλας τε κατηγεόμενοί σφι ὁδούς, κ. τέλος ἐγίνοντο Hdt.9.104; τοιοῦτος ὤν, κᾆτ' ἀνὴρ ἔδοξεν εἶναι Ar.*Eq.*392, cf. *Nu.*624.

B. *even, also, just*, 1. τάχα κεν κ. ἀναίτιον αἰτιόῳτο *even* the innocent, Il.11.654, cf. 4.161, etc.; δόμεναι κ. μεῖζον ἄεθλον an *even* greater prize, 23.551, cf. 10.556, 5.362: with numerals, κ. πέντε *full* five, 23.833; γενομένης κ. δὶς ἐκκλησίας Th.1.44, cf. Hdt.2.44, 60, 68, al. (but ἐτῶν δύο κ. τριῶν two *or* three, Th.1.82, cf. X.*Eq.*4.4). 2. *also*, κ. ἐγώ I *also*, Il.4.40; κ. αὐτοί they *also*, X.*An.*3.4.44, etc.; Ἄγις καὶ Σωκράτης κ. τούτω ἀπεθανέτην *likewise* died, ib. 2.6.30; in adding surnames, etc., Ὦχος ὁ κ. Δαρειαῖος Ctes.*Fr.*29.49 (sed Photii est): Ptol. Papyri have nom. ὃς κ., gen. τοῦ κ. etc., Πανίσκος ὃς κ. Πετεμῖνις *PLond.*2.219(*b*)2 (ii B.C.); dat. τῷ κ. ib.(*a*)ᵛ2, *PRein.*26.5 (ii B.C.); nom. ὁ κ. first in *PTeb.*110.1 (i B.C.), freq. later, *BGU*22.25 (ii A.D.), etc.; Ἰούδας ὁ κ. Μακκαβαῖος J.*AJ*12.6.4; Σαῦλος ὁ κ. Παῦλος *Act.Ap.*13.9: with ἄλλος, λαβέτω δὲ κ. ἄλλος Od.21.152; εἴπερ τι κ. ἄλλο, ὥς τις κ. ἄλλος, X.*Mem.*3.6.2, *An.*1.3.15, cf. Pl. *Phd.*59a, Ar.*Nu.*356: freq. in antithetic phrases, οὐ μόνον.., ἀλλὰ καί.., not only.., but *also*.., v. μόνος; οὐδὲν μᾶλλον.. ἢ οὐ καί.. Hdt.5.94, al. b. freq. used both in the anteced. and relat. clause, where we put *also* in the anteced. only, εἰ μὲν κ. σὺ εἶ τῶν ἀνθρώπων ὧνπερ κ. ἐγώ Pl.*Grg.*458a, cf. Il.6.476, X.*An.*2.1.21. 3. freq. in apodosi, after temporal Conjs., ἀλλ' ὅτε δὴ ῥα.., κ. τότε δή.. Il.1.494, cf. 8.69, Od.14.112; also after εἰ, Il.5.897: in Prose, ὡς δὲ ἔδοξεν, κ. ἐχώρουν Th.2.93: as a Hebraism, κ. ἐγένετο.. κ... Lxx *Ge.*24.30, al., *Ev.Luc.*1.59, etc. 4. with Advs., to give emphasis, κ. κάρτα Hdt.6.125; κ. λίην *full* surely, Il.19.408, Od.1.46; κ. μᾶλλον Il.8.470, cf. E.*Heracl.*386; κ. πάλαι, κ. πάνυ, S.*OC*1252, Pl. *Chrm.*154e; κ. μάλα, κ. σφόδρα, in answers, Ar.*Nu.*1326, Pl.*La.* 191e. 5. with words expressing a minimum, *even so much as, were it but, just*, ἱέμενος κ. καπνὸν ἀποθρῴσκοντα νοῆσαι Od.1.58; οἷς

ἡδὺ κ. λέγειν Ar.*Nu.*528; τίς δὲ κ. προσβλέψεται; who will *so much as* look at you? E.*IA*1192, cf. Ar.*Ra.*614, Pl.*Ap.*28b, 35b. **6.** *just*, τοῦτ' αὐτὸ κ. νοσοῦμεν 'tis *just* that that ails me, E.*Andr.*906, cf. *Ba.*616, S.*Tr.*490, Ar.*Pax*892, *Ra.*73, Pl.*Grg.*456a, *Tht.*166d: freq. with a relat., τὸ κ. κλαίουσα τέτηκα Il.3.176; διὸ δὴ καὶ.. Th.1.128, etc.: also in interrogations (usu. to be rendered by emphasis in intonation), ποίου χρόνου δὲ καὶ πεπόρθηται πόλις; and *how long ago* was the city sacked? A.*Ag.*278; ποῦ καὶ σφε θάπτει; *where* is he burying her? E.*Alc.*834, cf. S.*Aj.*1290, al., X.*An.*5.8.2, Ar.*Pax*1289, Pl. *Euthphr.*6b, D.4.46, etc. **7.** *even, just*, implying assent, ἔπειτά με κ. λίποι αἰών thereafter let life *e'en* leave me, Il.5.685, cf. 17.647, 21.274, Od.7.224. **8.** κ. εἰ *even if*, of a whole condition represented as an extreme case, opp. εἰ κ. *although, notwithstanding that*, of a condition represented as immaterial even if fulfilled, cf. Il.4.347, 5.351, Od.13.292, 16.98 with Il.5.410, Od.6.312, 8.139, etc.; εἰ κ. ἠπιστάμην if I *had* been able, Pl.*Phd.*108d, cf. *Lg.*663d. (This remark does not apply to cases where εἰ and καί each exert their force separately, as εἴ περ ἀδεής τ' ἐστί, καὶ εἰ.. *and if*.. Il.7.117, cf. Hdt.5.78, etc.) **9.** before a Participle, to represent either καὶ εἰ.., or εἰ καί.., *although, albeit*, Ἕκτορα κ. μεμαῶτα μάχης σχήσεσθαι ὀΐω, for ἢν κ. μεμάῃ, *how much soever* he rage, *although* he rage, Il.9.655; τί σὺ ταῦτα, κ. ἐσθλὸς ἐών, ἀγορεύεις; (for εἰ κ. ἐσθλὸς εἶ) 16.627, cf. 13.787, Od.2.343, etc.: κ. τύραννος ὢν ὅμως S.*OC*851.

**C.** Position: καί *and*, is by Poets sts. put after another word, ἔγνωκα, τοῖσδε κοὐδὲν ἀντειπεῖν ἔχω, for καὶ τοῖσδε οὐδὲν A.*Pr.*51, cf. Euph.51.7, etc. **2.** καί *also*, sts. goes between a Prep. and its case, ἐν κ. θαλάσσᾳ Pi.*O.*2.28. **3.** very seldom at the end of a verse, S.*Ph.*312, Ar.*V.*1193.

**D.** crasis: with ᾰ, as κἄν, κἀγαθοί, etc.; with ε, as κἀγώ, κἄπειτα, etc., Dor. κἠγώ, κἤπειτα, etc.; with η, as χἡ, χἠμέρη, χἠμεῖς, etc.; with ῐ in χἰκετεύετε, χἰλαρή; with ο, as χὠ, χὤστις, etc.; with υ in χὐμεῖς, χὐποχείριον, etc.; with ω in the pron. ᾧ, χᾦ; with αι, as κᾀσχρῶν; with αυ, as καὐτός; with ει, as κεἰ, κεἰς (but also κἀς), κᾆτα; with εὐ-, as κεὐγένεια, κεὐσταλής; with οι in χοἰ (χῳ *EM*816.34); with ου in χοὖτος, κοὐ, κοὐδέ, and the like.

**καιάδας**, ου, Dor. α, ὁ, *a pit* or *underground cavern* at Sparta, into which state-prisoners or their corpses were thrown, Th.1.134, Paus. 4.18.4:—the forms **καιάτας** and **καιέτας** are found in Eust.1478.45: —also **καιετός**, ὁ, *fissure produced by earthquake*, Str.8.5.7: hence Λακεδαίμονα καιετάεσσαν *full of hollows* or *abysses*, read by Zenod. for κητώεσσαν in Od.4.1: but Εὐρώτας καιετάεις Call.*Fr.*224, is expld. by καλαμινθώδης in Str.l.c.; cf. **καιέτα**· καλαμίνθη (Boeot.), Hsch.; **καιέτας** in Apollon.*Lex.* s.v. κητώεσσαν; gen. pl. **καιατῶν** Anon. Lond.36.57.

**καὶ γάρ**, *for also, for in fact*, combining καί (in various senses) with γάρ, Il.3.188, Od.18.261, Hdt.3.15, etc.; also, *for else*, Arist.*Pol.* 1280ᵃ36: with strengthening Particles, κ. γ. δή *for of a surety*, Il. 16.810; in Ep., κ. γ. ῥα 1.113; in Att., κ. γ. καί, κ. γ. οὖν, Pl.*Prt.* 317c, X.*An.*1.9.8, etc.

**καὶ..γε**, v. γε II. 1. **καὶ δέ**, v. δέ II. 2b. **καὶ δή, καὶ δὴ καί**, v. δή IV. 4. **καὶ εἰ**, by crasis **κεἰ**, v. καί B. 8, D.

**καιετάεις, καιέτας, καιετός**, v. sub καιάδας.

**καΐκα**, by crasis for καὶ αἴκα (v. αἰ), Theoc.3.27.

**καικίας**, ου, ὁ, *north-east wind*, Arist.*Mete.*363ᵇ17, *Pr.*940ᵃ18, *Mu.* 394ᵇ22, *IG*14.1308, Plu.*Sert.*17, *Gp.*1.11.2; καικίας καὶ συκοφαντίας πνεῖ Ar.*Eq.*437. (Derived from the river Κάϊκος by Ach.Tat.*Intr. Arat.*33.)

**καιλοῖα**, v. κελοῖα. **καὶ μήν**, v. μήν II. 2.

⊛ **καίμιον**, τό, *fowl*, *POxy.*1656.14 (iv/v A.D.). (Coptic *gaime*.)

⊛ **καινέω**, prob. misspelling for καινίζω in aor. 1 part. καινήσασα, *PThead.*19.11 (iv A.D.).

**καινία**· νίκη, Hsch.

**καινίζω**, (καινός) prop. *make new* or *strange*, but usu. in deriv. senses, καί τι καινίζει στέγη the house *has* something *new, strange* about it, S.*Tr.*867; κ. εὐχάς *offer new, strange* prayers, E.*Tr.*889; ἀμφίβληστρον ὡς ἐκαίνισαν (corr. Blomf. for ᾧ σ' ἐκαίνισαν) how they *devised a new, strange* net, A.*Ch.*492; ὅστις τόνδ' ἐκαίνισεν λόγον E. *Fr.*598 (= Critias 21 D.); so later, *innovate*, καθολικόν τι καινίζειν *OGI*669.47:—Pass., ib.62 (Egypt, i A.D.), Just.*Nov.*7.12 *Ep.*; πολλὰ τῷ βίῳ κ. Vett.Val.270.27; in Poets, esp. *use for the first time, handsel*, καίνισον ζυγόν *try on* thy *new* yoke, A.*Ag.*1071; πρῶτος τὸν ταῦρον ἐκαίνισεν first *handseled* the bull [of Perilaus], Call.*Fr.*119; κ. δόρυ *first to feel* the spear, Lyc.530.

**καινίς**, ίδος, ἡ, *knife*, v.l. for κοπίς, Luc.*Asin.*40, cf. Hdn.*Epim.*63.

**καίν-ισις**, εως, ἡ, *renovation*, ἡ τῶν πατρίων κ. καὶ μεταβολή J.*AJ* 18.1.1; v.l. for -ωσις in Ph.2.45. **-ισμός**, ὁ, *renewal*, *PLond.* 2.354.16 (ii B.C.). **2.** *innovation*, Vett.Val.192.15, Just.*Nov.*20.4, 118.6. **-ιστής**, οῦ, ὁ, = *innovator*, Gloss.

**καινίτα**· ἀδελφή, and **καινίτας**· ἀδελφοὺς καὶ ἀδελφάς, Hsch. (For καίνιτα, -ιτας, i.e. κασιγνήτα, -ήτας.)

**καινό-γρᾰφος**, ον, *written in a new style*, σύνθεσις prob. for -γραφής in Philic.ap.Heph.9.4. **II.** parox., καινογράφος, ὁ, *composer in a new style*, prob. in Anon.Metr.*Oxy.*220 vi 3. ⊛ **-κουφον**, τό, *new cask*, *POxy.*1911.181 (vi A.D.). **-λεκτος**, ον, *new-fangled*, Hdn. *Epim.*3. **-λογέω**, *tell new* or *strange tales*, cj. for κενο- in J.*Ap.* 1.24; *say something new*, Anon.Lond.34.7. **-λογία**, ἡ, *strange language* or *phraseology*, Plb.38.9.2, D.H.*Lys.*3; *telling of strange tales*, κ. τίς ἐστιν ὁ μῦθος Str.1.2.8. ⊛ **-λόγος**, ον, *using new phrases*, ποιητής Eust.1801.27.

**καινόν**, τό, v. καινός.

**καινο-πᾰγής**, ές, v. καινοπαθής. ⊛ **-πᾰθέω**, *suffer things unheard of*, Plu.2.1106a. **-πᾰθής**, ές, *new-suffered*: *unheard of*, πήματα S.*Tr.*1277 (anap., v.l. -παγῆ). **-πηγής**, ές, *newly put together, new-made*, A.*Th.*642. **-πήμων**, ονος, ὁ, ἡ, *new to misery*, δμωΐδες ib. 363 (lyr.). **-ποιέω**, pf. κεκαινοποίηκα Plb.4.2.4:—*make new, renew*, τὴν θεραπείαν Id.15.25.17; κ. ἐλπίδας *gives new life to* hopes, Id.3. 70.11; κ. τά τινος ἁμαρτήματα *renew the memory of*.., Id.30.4.17:— Pass., ἐκαινοποιήθη τὰ τῆς ὀργῆς Id.21.31.3, cf. 11.4.5, 31.28.9; of a plaster, Philum.*Ven.*7.9. **II.** *make changes, innovate*, πολλὰ κ. [ἡ τύχη] Plb.1.4.5, etc.: abs., Luc.*Prom.Es* 3, etc.:—Pass., τί καινοποιηθὲν λέγεις; what *new-fangled, strange* words are these? S.*Tr.*873, cf. Plb.9.2.4; τὰ καινοποιηθέντα *innovations*, *OGI*669.44 (Egypt, i A.D.), cf. *POxy.*237 viii 42 (ii A.D.). **-ποιητής**, οῦ, ὁ, *inventor of new pleasures*, X.*Cyr.*8.8.16. **-ποιΐα**, ἡ, *complete change*, περί τι Plb.4.2. 10: c. gen., Vett.Val.48.10 (pl.), al. **-ποιός**, *novator*, Gloss. **-πρᾱγέω**, Gramm., *coin new forms* or *phrases*, in Pass., Eust.36.16. **-πρᾱγία**, ἡ, *innovation*, f.l. for κοινοπραγία in D.S.15.8. **-πρέπεια**, ἡ, *novelty*, τοῦ σχήματος Eust.93.31. **-πρεπής**, ές, *novel*, σχήματα Hermog.*Id.*1.12; of innovations in law, κ. πρὸς τὸ πρότερον Just. *Nov.*105.1. Adv. **-πῶς** *in a new-fangled manner*: Comp. **-πεστέρως**, λέγειν Arist.*Metaph.*989ᵇ6: Sup. **-πέστατα** D.C.79.11.

⊛ **καινός**, ή, όν, *new, fresh*, ἔργα οὔτ' ἂν κ. οὔτε παλαιά Hdt.9.26; κ. ὁμιλία A.*Eu.*406; κ. λόγους φέρειν to bring *news*, Id.*Ch.*659; τί δ' ἐστὶ κ.; S.*OC*722, cf. *Ph.*52; τὰ κ. τοῖς πάλαι τεκμαίρεται Id.*OT*916; θυτῆρα καινῷ καινὸν ἐν πεπλώματι Id.*Tr.*613; ἢ βούλεσθε περιιόντες πυνθάνεσθαι, "λέγεταί τι κ.;" D.4.10; γένοιτ' ἄν τι -ότερον ἤ.. ibid.; ἐκ καινῆς (sc. ἀρχῆς) *anew, afresh*, Th.3.92, Thphr.*CP*5.1.11, *Jahresh.*23 *Beibl.*91 (Pamphyl., i A.D.), etc. (also ἐκ καινοῦ *CPR*244.14 (iii A.D.)); esp. of *new* dramas, τραγῳδῶν γιγνομένων καινῶν Aeschin.3.34; briefly τραγῳδοῖς κ. at the representation of the *new* tragedies, Docum.ap.D. 18.54; τραγῳδῶν τῇ κ. [ἐπιδείξει] ib.55; καινῇ κωμῳδῶν, τραγῳδῶν, *CIG*2759 iii (Aphrodisias); but κ. κωμῳδία, τραγῳδία, of a *new style* of drama, *IG*7.1773 (Thebes, ii A.D.). **2.** *newly-made*, κύλικες, τριήρης, ὀθόνια, οἶνος, *SIG*1026.26 (Cos, iv/iii B.C.), *IG*2².1623.289, *PLond.*2.402ᵛ12 (ii B.C.), *Ostr.*1142.4 (iii A.D.). **3.** Adv. **-νῶς** *newly, afresh*, Alex.240.4. **II.** *newly-invented, novel*, καινότεραι τέχναι Batr.116; κ. προσφέρειν σοφά E.*Med.*298; ἔνθα τι κ. ἐλέχθη Philox.3.23; οὐκ ἀείδω τὰ παλαιά, καινὰ γὰρ ἀμὰ κρείσσω Tim.*Fr.*21; κ. θεοί *strange* gods, Pl.*Euthphr.*3b; κ. δαιμόνια Id.*Ap.*24c; κ. τινες σοφισταί Id.*Euthd.*271b; κ. καὶ ἄτοπα ὀνόματα Id.*R.*405d; καινὰ ἐπιμηχανᾶσθαι *innovations*, X.*Cyr.*8.8.16; οὐδὲν -ότερον εἰσέφερε τῶν ἄλλων he introduced *as little of anything new as* others, Id.*Mem.*1.1.3, cf. Pl.*Phd.*115b; πεπόνθαμεν -ότατον D.35.26; τὸ κ. τοῦ πολέμου prob. f.l. for κενόν (v. κενός), Th.3.30; οὐ καινόν nothing *to be surprised at*, Hp.*Int.*17; τὸ -ότατον *what is strangest*, parenthetically, Luc.*Nigr.*22, al.; εἰ χρὴ -ότατα μᾶλλον ἢ κακουργότατα εἰπεῖν Antipho 2.4.2. Adv., μὴ σύ -νῶς μοι λάλει *in new, strange style*, Alex.144, cf. Pl.*Phdr.*267b: Comp. -οτέρως, νοῆσαι περί τινος Arist.*Cael.*308ᵇ 31; *without precedent*, -νῶς κατακριθῆναι *OGI*669.46,49 (Egypt, i A.D.). **III.** κ. ἄνθρωπος, = Lat. *novus homo*, Plu.*Cat.Ma.*1; πράγματα κ., = *res novae*, Id.*Cic.*14, cf. 2.212c.

**καινό-σπουδος**, ον, *fond of novelty*, τὸ περὶ τὰς νοήσεις κ. Longin.5. 1. **-σχημάτιστος**, ον, *newly* or *strangely formed*, Eust.141. 32. **-σχήμων**, ον, gen. ονος, foreg., Id.1479.57, Sch.rec.S.*Aj.* 1398. **-τάφια**· νεκροτάφια, Hsch. (leg. κενο-). **-τάφον** σχῆμα, for καινὸν σχῆμα τάφου, *AP*7.686 (Pall.).

**καινότης**, ητος, ἡ, *newness, freshness*, Plu.*Per.*13; αἱ τῶν δερμάτων -τητες Philostr.*Ep.*18. **2.** *novelty*, λόγου Th.3.38; τῶν εὑρημένων Isoc.10.2; χρὴ γὰρ εἰς ὄχλον φέρειν.. ὅσ' ἂν τις καινότητ' ἔχειν δοκῇ Anaxandr.54.6; ἡ ἐν τοῖς σχηματισμοῖς κ. D.H.*Amm.*2.3: pl., καινότητες *novelties*, Isoc.2.41; αἱ κ. καὶ αἱ ὑπερβολαὶ τῶν τιμῶν D.C. 44.3.

**καινο-τομέω**, *cut fresh into*, in mining, *open a new vein*, X.*Vect.*4.27 sq., Phot.; in road-making, metaph., ἀτραπὸν ἄλλην Ph.2.445, cf. J. *BJ*5.9.4, Luc.*Rh.Pr.*10 (Pass.). **II.** mostly metaph., *begin something new, institute anew*, τελετήν τινι Ar.*V.*876 (anap.): abs., *make changes* or *innovations* in the state, Id.*Ec.*584 (anap.), Arist.*Pol.* 1305ᵇ41, 1316ᵇ19, Plb.15.30.1, *PLips.*35.19 (iv A.D.), etc.: generally, μὴ καινοτομεῖν Phld.*Mus.*p.9 K.; κ. τι νέον Pl.*Lg.*797c, cf. 709a; κ. περὶ τὰ θεῖα Id.*Euthphr.*3b, 16a; περὶ τῶν θείων ib.5a; τὰ θεῖα Jul.*Or.* 5.159b; κ. τὴν περὶ τὰ τέκνα κοινότητα Arist.*Pol.*1266ᵃ35; οὐθὲν κ. εἰς [τὰ γινόμενα περὶ θεῶν σεβασμούς] D.H.7.70, cf. *Comp.*25:—Pass., Pl.*Lg.*797b, D.59.75. **-τόμημα**, ατος, τό, *innovation, new form*, ἐγκλημάτων Procop.*Arc.*21 (pl.). **-τομητέον**, *one must be an innovator*, Ath.Mech.8.2. **-τομία**, ἡ, *opening of new mines*, Hyp. *Eux.*36 (pl.), *IG*2².1587.5 (prob.), Poll.3.87, 7.98 (pl.). **II.** mostly metaph., *making anew, inventing*, ὀνομάτων Pl.*Lg.*715d; *innovation*, κ. περὶ τοὺς λόγους Plu.*Cic.*2: in Music, Satyr.*Vit.Eur.Fr.*39 xxii 5; μηδεμίαν κ. γίγνεσθαι Mitteis *Chr.*96 ii 19 (iv A.D.): pl., *innovations* in the state, Lat. *res novae*, Pl.*Lg.*950a; κ. τῆς πολιτείας Plb.13.1.2: in Law, *interference* with another's right or easement, Just.*Nov.*7.5.1: pl., ib.63 tit. **2.** = καινότης, *novelty, strangeness*, ἡ κ. τοῦ συμβαίνοντος Plb.1.23.10: pl., Plu.*Alex.*72. **-τόμος**, ον, (τέμνω) *innovating*, ἔχουσι.. οἱ τοῦ Σωκράτους λόγοι.. τὸ κομψὸν καὶ τὸ κ. are marked by cleverness and *novelty*, Arist.*Pol.*1265ᵃ12; of persons, Hermog.*Inv.*3.5: metaph., -τόμον πρᾶγμα ὁ πόλεμος ibid. **-τροπία**, ἡ, *strangeness*, Eust.1200.56. **-τροπος**, ον, *new-fashioned, unusual*, μῦθος [E.]*Fr.*1132.49 (lyr.); χειμών App.*BC*5.90.

**καινουργ-έω**, *make new*, Alciphr.3.3; *re-create*, τινα Zos.Alch. p.108 B. 2. *begin something new*, τι Hp.*VM*21; τί καινουργεῖς; *what new plan art thou meditating?* E.*IA*2 (anap.); κ. λόγον *speak new, strange* words, ib.838; *coin*, ὄνομα Dam.*Pr*.439: abs., ἐπὶ τὸ κ. φέρου Antiph.29: usu. in bad sense, *make innovations*, περί τι X.*HG*6.2.16, cf. D.H.11.21:—Pass., τὰ καινουργούμενα *all attempts at alteration*, Arist.*Mu*.398ᵃ35. **-ής**, ές, *newly made*, τρίποδες Sch.Il.9. 122. **-ησις**, εως, ἡ, *new manufacture*, Suid. s.v. καταβολή. **-ία**, ἡ, *making new*: *innovation* in the state, ταραχὴ καὶ κ. Isoc.6.50; of Christianity, prob. in *OGI*569.18 (Arycanda, iv A.D.); *renewal, re-creation*, τοῦ ὅλου Max.Tyr.41.4; of *manufacture*, J.*AJ*12.2.9, cf. D.H.*Isoc*.9, Hierocl.p.52 A. **-ιος**, α, ον, *newly made*, *Sammelb.* 7033.44 (v A.D.), *Gloss.*; χύτρα Aët.8.6. **-ισμός**, ὁ, = καινουργία, Suid. (v.l. -ησμός). **-ός**, όν, (ἔργον) *producing changes*, πόλεμος Hld.9.5; κ. βασάνων *inventing new* tortures, Lxx 4*Ma*.11.23. II. Pass., τὸ κ. *novelty*, Luc.*Prom.Es* 3; τῶν κολάσεων τὸ πρὸς ὠμότητα κ. Id.*Cat*.26.

**καινο-φᾰνής**, ές, *appearing new*, λέξεις Eust.39.16. **-φῐλος**, ον, *often changing one's friends*, Phot., Suid. **-φωνέω**, *use new words*, Eust.67.6. **-φωνία**, ἡ, *vocum novitas*, *Gloss.*, cf. Phlp. *in APo.* 11.7. **-φωνος**, ον, *new-sounding*, λέξεις Eust.1761.23, etc. **-χωρισμός**, ὁ, *renewed execution*, συναλλάξεως *POxy*.1644.19 (i B.C.).

**καινόω**, (καινός) *make new, change*, τὰ ἐπιβουλεύματα D.C.47.4; of language, D.H.*Th*.21: Pass., of political changes, Th.1.71; καινοῦσθαι τὰς διανοίας in *inventing new* devices, Id.3.82, cf. Ph.1.326, 2.156. II. = καινίζω, *use for the first time, handsel*, Hdt.2. 100. III. *renew*, φόβον Ph.2.78.

**καί νύ** (κε), *and now*, κ. νύ κεν .. ἄσπετον ἤρατο κῦδος, εἰ μή .. Il. 3.373, cf. 8.90, Od.24.50; so κ. νύ κε δή Il.17.530: also folld. by εἰ without μή, Od.11.317; by ἀλλά, ib.630: with no protasis, κ. νύ κεν ἐς δεκάτην γενεὴν ἕτερόν γ' ἔτι βόσκοι 14.325.

❀ **καίνῡμι**, *overcome*, Act. only in imper. καινύτω, μή σ' ἀπάτη φρένα κ. Emp.23.9:—elsewh. **καίνυμαι**, *surpass, excel*, in impf., c. acc. pers. et inf. modi, ἐκαίνυτο φῦλ' ἀνθρώπων νῆα κυβερνῆσαι he *surpassed* mankind in steering, Od.3.282: c. dat. rei, ἣ ῥα γυναικῶν φῦλον ἐκαίνυτο .. εἴδεΐ τε μεγέθει τε Hes.*Sc*.4: more freq. in pf. and plpf. κέκασμαι, ἐκεκάσμην, Dor. κέκαδμαι, *excel* one in a thing, c. acc. pers. et dat. rei, ἐγχείῃ δ' ἐκέκαστο Πανέλληνας Il.2.530; ὃς ἡλικίην ἐκέκαστο ἔγχεΐ θ' ἱπποσύνῃ τε 16.808; ὃς ἀνθρώπους ἐκέκαστο κλεπτοσύνῃ θ' ὅρκῳ τε Od.19.395: c. inf. pro dat. rei, ὁμηλικίην ἐκέκαστο γνῶναι *surpassed* them all in knowledge, 2.158; ἐκέκαστο ἰθύνειν A.R.2.867: c. dat. rei only, δόλοισι κεκασμένε *excellent* in wiles, Il.4.339; παντοίῃς ἀρετῇσι κεκασμένον ἐν Δαναοῖσιν Od.4.725; μαντοσύνῃ 9.509, cf. Il.5. 54; [ἀγλαΐῃ] μετὰ δμῳῇσι κέκασσαι Od.19.82; ἐκ πάντων τέχνῃσι κεκασμένος Οὐρανιώνων Hes.*Th*.929: c. gen., τῶν σε .. πλούτῳ τε καὶ υἱάσι φασὶ κεκάσθαι *above* all these (as if ἐκ τούτων), Il.24.546. II. later, *to be adorned, equipped*, ἐλέφαντι ὦμον κεκαδμένον Pi.*O*.1.27; φρουραῖς κέκασται *is well furnished* with.., E.*El*.616; πανουργίαις μείζοσι κεκασμένον Ar.*Eq*.685; μῦθος ἀληθείῃ κέκασται *AP*3.18.1 (Inscr. Cyzic.): abs., εὖ κεκασμένον δόρυ a *well-armed* band, A.*Eu*. 766.—Poet. word (Pl.*R*.334b is borrowed from Od.19.395; κεκασμένος etym. of κεστός Corn.*ND*24.)

**καὶ νῦν**, *so now*, Hom., mostly to confirm a general statement by an example, e.g. Il.1.109; ὣς κ. ν. Od.1.35; κ. ν. ἦ τοι 4.151.

❀ **καίνω**, A.*Ag*.1562, *Ch*.886: fut. κᾰνῶ E.*HF*1074 (lyr.): aor. 2 ἔκᾰνον A.*Ch*.930; inf. κανεῖν, Dor. κανῆν Theoc.24.92: pf. κέκονα S. *Fr*.1058:—Pass., A.*Th*.347 (lyr.), E.*IT*27:—*kill, slay*, A.*Th*.630 (lyr.), S.l.c., Timocr.1.9, Theoc.l.c.: once in X., *Cyr*.4.2.24 (nisi leg. κατακ–, q.v.).

**καίνωσις**, εως, ἡ, *renewal*, ὧν ὑπέμεινε Ph.2.45 (v.l. -ισις); τῶν λόγων *news*, J.*AJ*18.6.10.

**καίπερ**, in Hom. always with a word between (exc. καί περ πολλὰ παθόντα Od.7.224); but one word in Pi. and Prose, and usu. in Trag. I. *even*, καὶ αὐτοί περ πονεώμεθα Il.10.70. II. *although, albeit*, usu. c. part., καὶ αὐτῇ περ νοεούσῃ 1.577; καὶ ἀχνύμενός περ ἑταίρου 8.125; καὶ πρίν περ θυμῷ μεμαὼς 5.135; καὶ κήδεά περ πεπαθυίῃ Od.17.555: so in later Poets, κ. ἀχνύμενος Pi.*I*.8(7).4, cf. *N*.6.6; καὶ θοῦρός περ ὢν A.*Fr*.199.2; κ. αὐθάδη φρονῶν Id.*Pr*.907; κ. οὐ στέργων ὅμως Id.*Th*.712; κ. οὐ δύσοργος ὢν S.*Ph*.377: preceded by ὅμως, Pl. *R*.495d: the part. must freq. be supplied, καὶ θεός περ [ὤν] A.*Ag*. 1203; γιγνώσκω σαφῶς, κ. σκοτεινὸς [ὤν], τήν γε σὴν αὐδὴν ὅμως S.*OT* 1326; also εἰ μέμονάς γε, καὶ ὀψέ περ [ἐρυόμενος], .. ἐρύεσθαι Il.9.247; ἐπιμνησαίμεθα χάρμης, καὶ πρὸς δαίμονά περ [μαχούμενοι] 17.104; λέγεις ἀληθῆ, κ. ἐκ μακροῦ χρόνου [λέγων] S.*OT*1141; ἀλλ' ἔστιν ὧν δεῖ, κ. οὐ πολλῶν ἄπο, = καίπερ οὐ πολλῶν ὄντων, Id.*Ph*.647: with finite Verbs only as dub. l., κ. ἔχει (leg. καίπερ) Pi.*N*.4.36; κ. (leg. καίτοι) ἐκεῖνό γε φημὶ ἔν τι εἶναι Pl.*Smp*.219c.

**καίπετος**· ἀξίνη, Hsch.

**καί ῥα**, Ep., to make a transition, *and so*, Il.1.360,569, etc.

**καίραμα**· μέρος νεὸς, ἢ ἀμφίεσμα, Hsch.

**καιρία**, ἡ, *tape* or *cord* used for ligatures, etc., Archig.ap.Orib.47. 13.7, Heraclas ib.48.1.1. (From κείρεσθαι or καῖρος acc. to Sch. Orib.4 p.537 D.; cf. κειρία.)

❀ **καιρ-ικός**, ή, όν, *timely*, ἀπαγγελίαι *IG*3.769. 2. *appropriate to certain times* or *seasons, seasonable*, ἄνθη *PMag.Leid.W*.24.1. b. Astrol., *belonging to the* καιρός or *chronocratory*, κ. χρόνοι Ἀφροδίτης Nech.ap.Vett.Val.289.37. c. Astron., ὧραι κ. hours of the kind *that vary in length with the season*, opp. ἰσημεριναί, Ptol.*Alm*.4.11, 7.3, *Tetr*.76. 3. Gramm., *temporal*, Eust.17.3. 4. καιρικαὶ βαφαί, dub. sens. in Zos.Alch.p.246 B., cf. p.228, 239, al. **-ῐμος**, η, ον, = καίριος, dub. in Macho ap.Ath.13.581b, cf. Al.*Le*.16.21; -ώτερος οἶνος *PFlor*.143.2 (iii A.D.).

**καιριολεκτέω**, (λέγω) *use a word appropriately*, Eust.909.17 (Pass.).

**καίριος**, α, ον, also ος, ον Thgn.341, A.*Ch*.1064, S.*Ph*.637, Luc.*Nigr*. 35: I. (καιρός II) in Hom. always of Place, *in* or *at the right place*, hence of parts of the body, καίριον *a vital part*, Il.8.84,326; ἐν καιρίῳ 4.185; ὁ αὐχὴν ἐστὶ τῶν καιρίων X.*Eq*.12.2, cf. 8 (Sup.); of wounds, *mortal*, καιρίῃ (sc. πληγῇ) τετύφθαι Hdt.3.64; πέπληγμαι καιρίαν πληγὴν A.*Ag*.1343; καιρίας πληγῆς τυχεῖν ib.1292, cf. X.*Cyr*.5.4.5; καιρίας (v.l. -ίους) σφαγάς E.*Ph*.1431; ἔχειν τὴν καταφορὰν κ. Plb.2.33.3; but also, *grave, serious*, νουσήματα, τρώματα, Hp.*Morb*.1.5: generally, καιριωτάτης τετευχέναι χώρας *Theol.Ar*.44. II. of Time, *in season, timely*, εὑρίσκε ταῦτα καιριώτατα εἶναι Hdt.1.125, cf. Emp.111.6; χρὴ λέγειν τὰ κ. A.*Th*.1, cf. *Ch*.582; καίριοι συμφοραί ib.1064; εἴ τι κ. λέγει S.*Ant*.724; δρᾶν, φρονεῖν τὰ κ., Id.*Aj*.120, *El*.228 (lyr.); καίριος σπουδή Id.*Ph*.637; -ωτέρα βουλή E.*Heracl*.471; κ. ἐνθύμημα X. *HG*4.5.4; τὸ ἀεὶ κ. Id.*Cyr*.4.2.12, etc.; πρὸς τὸ κ., = καιρίως, S.*Ph*. 525; *critical*, αὐτὰ τὰ κ. ἔχων ἐκκαίδεκα (sc. ἔτη) *AP*12.22 (Scyth.); agreeing with the subject, καιρίαν δ' ἡμῖν ὁρῶ στείχουσαν Ἰοκάστην coming *at the right time*, S.*OT*631; καίριος ἤλυθες E.*El*.598; καιρία (Dind. for καὶ δορία) πτώσιμος falling *at the exact* or *fatal moment*, A. *Ag*.1122 (lyr.); τὰ κ. *timely circumstances, opportunities*, Th.4.10; *emergencies*, D.C.*Fr*.70.8. 2. *lasting but for a season*, *AP*12.224 (Strato). III. *chief, principal*, τὰ καιριώτατα τῶν κλημάτων Thphr. *CP*3.15.4, cf. 6.4.2. IV. Adv. -ίως *in season, seasonably*, κ. εἰρημένον A.*Ag*.1372; σκοπεῖν E.*Rh*.339: Comp. -ωτέρως X.*Cyr*.4.5. 49. 2. *mortally*, οὐτασμένος A.*Ag*.1344, cf. Plb.2.69.2.

**καιροδᾰπιστής**, οῦ, ὁ, (καιρός, δάπις) *carpet-weaver*, Judeich *Altertümer von Hierapolis* 342 (pl.).

**καιρόεις**, v. καιροσέων.

**καιρομᾰνέω**, prob. f.l. for **καιρονομέω**, *guide in season*, εἰς τέχνην ὄρνιν ἐκαιρονόμει (–μάνεις cod.) *AP*9.272 (Bianor).

**καιροπτία** or **–εία**, ἡ, as if from *καιρόπτης, διὰ καιροπτείας by *watching their opportunity*, J.*Ap*.2.11.

❀ **καιρός**, ὁ, *due measure, proportion, fitness* (not in Hom.), καιρὸς δ' ἐπὶ πᾶσιν ἄριστος (which became a prov.) Hes.*Op*.694, Thgn. 401; κ. παντὸς ἔχει κορυφάν Pi.*P*.9.78; κ. χάριτος A.*Ag*.787 (anap.) (cf. ὑποκάμπτω II); εἰ δ κ. ἦν σαφής the *distinction*, the *point*, E.*Hipp*. 386; ἡ ἀπορία ἔχει τινὰ κ. has some *point* or *importance*, Arist. *Metaph*.1043ᵇ25; καιροῦ πέρα beyond *measure, unduly*, A.*Pr*.507; μείζων τοῦ κ. γαστήρ X.*Smp*.2.19; καιροῦ μεῖζον E.*Fr*.626 codd.; προσωτέρω or πορρωτέρω τοῦ κ., X.*An*.4.3.34, *HG*7.5.13; ὀξύτερα τοῦ κ. Pl.*Plt*.307b; νωθεστέρα τοῦ κ. ib.310e; ὑπερβάλλων τῇ φιλοτιμίᾳ τὸν κ. Plu.*Ages*.8, cf. Hp.*Loc.Hom*.44. II. of Place, *vital part* of the body (cf. καίριος I), ἐς καιρὸν τυπεὶς E.*Andr*.1120. III. more freq. of Time, *exact* or *critical time, season, opportunity*, χρόνου κ. S.*El*. 1292: usu. alone, κ. [ἐστιν] ἐν ᾧ χρόνος οὐ πολὺς κτλ. Hp. *Praec*.1, cf. Chrysipp. et Archig.ap.Daremberg *Notices et extr. des MSS. médicaux* 1 p.200; κ. ὀξὺς Hp.*Aph*.1.1; κ. πρὸς ἀνθρώπων βραχὺ μέτρον ἔχει 'time and tide wait for no man', Pi.*P*.4.286; κ. ὄλβου, = καίριος ὄλβος, Id.*N*.7.58; δηλοῦν, ὅ τι περ δύναται κ. Ar.*Ec*.576 codd. (sed leg. δύνασαι); τίνα κ. τοῦ παρόντος βελτίω ζητεῖτε; D.3.16; κ. δόσιος *for* giving, Hp.*Acut*.20; κ. τοῦ ποτισμοῦ, τῆς τρύγης, *BGU*1003.12 (iii B.C.), *PStrassb*.1.8 (v A.D.); τὰ ἐκ τοῦ κ. προγινόμενα Plb.6.32.3; καιρὸν παριέναι to let *the time* go by, Th.4.27 (so in pl., τοὺς κ. παριέναι Pl.*R*.374c; τοὺς κ. ὑφαιρεῖσθαι Aeschin.3.66); κ. τῶν πραγμάτων τοῖς ἐναντίοις καθυφιέναι καὶ προδοῦναι D.19.6; καιροῦ (τοῦ κ.) τυχεῖν E.*Hec*. 593, Pl.*Lg*.687a, Men.*Mon*.281; καιρὸν εἰληφέναι Lys.13.6 (but καιρὸς ἐλάμβανε Th.2.34; cf. καιροῦ διδόντος Lib.*Or*.45.7); καιρὸν λαβέσθαι Luc.*Tim*.13; καιρὸν ἁρπάσαι Plu.*Phil*.15; κ. τηρεῖν Arist.*Rh*. 1382ᵇ11; καιρῷ χρήσασθαι Plu.*Pyrrh*.7; καιρῷ χειμῶνος ξυλλαβέσθαι co-operate with the *occurrence* of a storm, Pl.*Lg*.709c; ἔχει κ. τι it happens *in season*, Th.1.42, etc.; κ. ἔχειν τοῦ εὖ οἰκεῖν to be *the chief cause* of.., Pl.*R*.421a; ὑμέας καιρός ἐστι προβοηθῆσαι Hdt.8.144, cf. A.*Pr*.523, etc.; νῦν κ. ἔρδειν S.*El*.1368: sts. c. Art., ἀλλ' ἔσθ' ὁ κ... ξένους .. τυγχάνειν τὰ πρόσφορα A.*Ch*.710; ὁ κ. ἐστι μὴ μέλλειν ἔτι Ar. *Th*.661, cf. *Pl*.255. b. adverbial phrases, ἐς καιρόν *in season*, Hdt. 7.144, E.*Tr*.744, etc.; ἐς κ. ἐπείγεσθαι Hdt.4.139; ἐς αὐτὸν κ. S.*Aj*. 1168; εἰς δέοντα κ. Men.*Sam*.294; ἐν καιρῷ A.*Pr*.381, Th.4.59, etc.; ἐν κ. τινὶ Pl.*Cri*.44a; ἐπὶ καιροῦ D.19.258, 20.90, etc.; κατὰ καιρόν Pi.*I*.2.22; ὥς οἱ κατὰ κ. ἦν Hdt.1.30 (but also οἱ κατὰ κ. ἡγεμόνες in office at *the time*, *BGU*15.10 (ii A.D.), etc.); παρὰ τῷ ἐντυχόντι αἰεὶ καὶ λόγου καὶ ἔργου κ. Th.2.43; πρὸς καιρὸν S.*Aj*.38, *Tr*.59, etc.; σὺν καιρῷ Plb.2.38.7: without Preps., καιρῷ S.*OT*1516; καιρόν, abs., S.*Aj*.34, E.*Fr*.495.9 (in Comp. form καιριώτερον, Achae.49); κ. γὰρ οὐδὲν ἦλθες E.*Hel*.479; opp. ἀπὸ καιροῦ *out of season*, Pl.*Tht*.187e; ἄνευ καιροῦ Id.*Ep*.339d; παρὰ καιρόν Pi.*O*.8.24, E.*IA*800 (lyr.), Pl. *Plt*.277a; πρὸ καιροῦ *prematurely*, A.*Ag*.365 (anap.); ἐπὶ καιροῦ also means *on the spur of the moment*, ἐπὶ κ. λέγειν Plu.*Dem*.8, cf. *Art*.5; ἐξενεγκεῖν πόλεμον Id.*Ant*.6. 2. *season*, πᾶσιν καιροῖς at all *seasons* of the year, *IG*14.1018, cf. Lxx *Ge*.1.14, Ph.1.13, Porph.ap. Eus.*PE*3.11; κ. ἔτους, later Gr. for Att. ὥρα ἔτους, acc. to Moer.424; *time of day*, Philostr.*VA*6.14. b. *critical times, periodic states*, καιροὶ σωμάτων Arist.*Pol*.1335ᵃ41. 3. generally, *time, period*, κατὰ τὸν κ. τοῦτον Plb.27.1.7; κατ' ἐκεῖνο καιροῦ Conon 3, al.: more freq. in pl., κατὰ τούτους τοὺς κ. Arist.*Ath*.23.2, al., cf. Plb.2.39.1; τὰ κατὰ καιροὺς *chronological sequence* of events, Id.5.33.5; ἐν τοῖς πάλαι,

ἐν τοῖς μεταξὺ κ., Phld.*Rh.*1.28,363 S. 4. in pl., οἱ καιροί *the times*, i.e. *the state of affairs*, freq. in bad sense, ἐν τοῖς μεγίστοις κ. at the most *critical times*, X.*HG*6.5.33, cf. D.20.44; περιστάντων τῇ πόλει κ. δυσκόλων *IG*2².682.33, etc.: also in sg., X.*An*.3.1.44, D.17.9; ὁ ἔσχατος κ. extreme *danger*, Plb.29.27.12, etc.; καιρῷ δουλεύειν *AP*9.441 (Pall.). IV. *advantage, profit*, τινος *of* or *from* a thing, Pi.*O*.2.54, *P*.1.57; εἴ τοι ἐς κ. ἔσται ταῦτα τελεόμενα to his *advantage*, Hdt.1.206; ἐπὶ σῷ κ. S.*Ph*.151 (lyr.); τίνα κ. με διδάσκεις; A.*Supp*.1060 (lyr.); τί σοι καιρὸς.. καταλείβειν; what *avails* it..? E.*Andr*.131 (lyr.); τίνος εἵνεκα καιροῦ; D.23.182; οὗ κ. εἴη where it was *convenient* or *advantageous*, Th.4.54; ᾗ κ. ἦν ib.90; χωρίον μετὰ μεγίστων κ. οἰκειοῦταί τε καὶ πολεμοῦται with the greatest *odds*, the most *critical results*, Id.1.36. V. Pythag. name for *seven*, *Theol.Ar.* 44.

**καῖρος**, ὁ (on the accent v. Eust.907.13), *row of thrums* in the loom, to which the threads of the warp are attached, *ravel*, Ael. Dion.*Fr*.400, Phot.:— hence **καιρ-όω**, *make fast these threads*: **-ωσις**, εως, ἡ, *act of fastening* them, Poll.7.33, Hsch.: **-ωμα**, ατος, τό, = καῖρος, Ael.Dion.l.c.; of the *web so fastened*, Call.*Fr*.295: **-ωστρίς** or **-ωστίς**, ίδος, ἡ, *woman-weaver*, ib.356, Hsch.

**καιροσέων**, (καῖρος) *close-woven*, only in gen. pl. fem., καιροσέων ὀθονέων ἀπολείβεται ὑγρὸν ἔλαιον Od.7.107. (Archaic spelling of καιρουσσέων (trisyll.), Ion. gen. pl. of καιρόεις, like Τειχιόσης for Τειχιούσσης in *SIG*3*d* (Milet., vi B.C.).)

**καιρο-σκοπέω**, gloss on καιροφυλακέω, Hdn.*Epim*.63; prob. (for καιρῷ σκόπει) in Men.*Mon*.307. **-σπάθητος** [ᾰ], ον, (καῖρος) *close-woven*, ὕφασμα Hermipp.5. **-τηρέω** τὰς μεταβολάς *observe the seasons* of change, D.S.19.16, cf. 13.22: generally, *lie in wait for*, τινὰς ἀσχολουμένους *PAmh*.2.35.8 (ii B.C.), cf. *UPZ*19.26 (ii B.C.):— also in Med., -τηρησάμενός με ἐξερχόμενον *BGU*909.6 (iv A.D.): **-τηρησία**, ἡ, Aristeas 270. **-φῐλος**, ὁ, *lover* or *observer of times*, epith. of an astrologer, Vett.Val.271.25. **-φυλᾰκέω**, *watch for the right time*, c. acc., τὴν πόλιν D.23.173, Hyp.*Phil*.8; τὴν χρῆσιν Arist.*Pol*.1337ᵇ41; ἔχθραν παλαιάν Olymp.Hist.p.460 D.: abs., App. *Pun*.88, *Mith*.70; also, *attend on*, Luc.*Abd*.16:—Pass., καιροφυλακεῖται Metrod.*Fr*.60.

**καιρόω, καίρωμα, καίρωσις, καιρωστίς** or **-τρίς**, v. καῖρος.

**Καῖσαρ**, ᾰρος, ὁ, (said to be Punic, = *elephant*, Lyd.*Mens*.4.102) *Caesar*, a *cognomen* of the Gens Julia; esp. of Julius Caesar, D.S. 5.22, Str.4.5.3, etc.; Κ. ὁ θεός prob. in *OGI*767.5; also of Augustus, ib.458.9 (9 B.C.), Nic.Dam.*Vit.Caes.* tit., etc.; ὁ νέος Κ., opp. ὁ πρεσβύτερος Κ., ib.6; in general, *the Emperor*, *OGI*473.8, etc.; Καίσαρος ἀπελεύθερος ib.629.90, etc.; Πρίμος Καίσαρος, i.e. P. *the Emperor's slave*, Wilcken *Chr*.112.4; ἀπόδοτε τὰ Καίσαρος Καίσαρι *Ev.Luc*.20.25: pl., οἱ Καίσαρες *OGI*516.21: as title of the designated successor, Καίσαρα ἀποδεικνύει Hdn.2.15.3, etc.; name of month in the province of Asia, *OGI*458.54, etc.:—hence **Καισάρειος**, ον, *of, belonging to Caesar*, οἱ Κ. *his household* or *officials*, *POxy*.477.5 (ii A.D.), D.C. 52.24, al.; οἶκος Κ., hall in Herod the Great's palace, J.*BJ*1.21.1; τὸ Κ. *temple of Julius Caesar* at Alexandria, Str.17.1.9: **Καισάρεια** (-ηα), τά, *games in honour of Gaius Caesar* at Cos, *SIG*1065.9 (Cos); at Corinth and elsewhere, *IG*7.1856 (Thespiae), etc.: **Καισάρειος**, or **-ιος**, ὁ (sc. μήν), name of month in Egypt and elsewhere, *POxy*.45.17 (i A.D.), *Hemerolog.Flor.*, etc.:—also **Καισαρεών**, ῶνος, ὁ, *Rev.Ét. Gr.*19.268 (Κεσ-, Aphrodisias): **-εύω**, *play the Caesar*, D.C.66.8: **Καισαριανοί**, οἱ, *the Caesarian party*, App.*BC*3.91:—also, = Καισάρειοι, *PGnom*.241 (ii A.D.): **Καισαριασταί**, οἱ, *worshippers of Caesar*, *IGRom*.4.1348 (Mostene).

**καισάραι**· περικεφαλαῖαι, Hsch. **καισεκπρώπιον**· δρέπανον, ξηροκόπιον, Id.

**καιτάεις**, f.l. for καιετάεις in Sch.Od.4.1.

**καί τοι**, *and indeed, and further*, freq. in Hom. with one or more words between, Il.1.426, al.; καὶ σύ τοι E.*Med*.344; καὶ τἄλλά τοι X.*Cyr*.7.3.10: once in Hom. as one word, Il.13.267. II. after Hom. usu., *and yet*, to mark an objection introduced by the speaker himself, freq. in Rhetorical questions, καίτοι τί φημι; A.*Pr*.101; κ. τί φωνῶ; S.*OC*1132, cf. Isoc.4.99, etc.: without a question, κ. φύγοιμ' ἂν E.*Cyc*.480; κ. καὶ τοῦτο.. D.4.12, 18.122: strengthd., καίτοι γ' Ar.*Ach*.611, E.*Fr*.953.10, X.*Mem*.1.2.3, Ph.1.274, etc.: mostly separated, καίτοι..γε E.*Or*.77, Ar.*Ra*.45, X.*Mem*.3.12.7, etc. (καίτοι is f.l. in A.*Eu*.849); so καίτοι περ v.l. in Hdt.8.53. III. with a participle, much like καίπερ, Simon.5.9, Ar.*Ec*.159, Pl.*R*.511d, Plb.22.8.13, Phld.*Ir*.p.22 W., Luc.*Alex*.3: once in the Att. Oratt., Lys.31.34; also καίτοι γε διαχλευάζων Pl.*Ax*.364b.

**καίτρεαι**· ὅπλα Ἰβηρικά· οἱ δὲ κυρτίας, Hsch. (Cf. Lat. *caetra.*)

**καιφος** (corrected to **κεφος**), = *sparrow*, *PLond*.1821.162 (fort. κέπφος).

**καίω**, Att. **κάω** [ᾱ], impf. ἔκαιον Od.9.553, Att. ἔκᾱον, Ep. καῖον Il. 21.343: fut. καύσω X.*Cyr*.5.4.21, (ἐπι-) Pl.Com.186.4, (κατα-) Ar. *Lys*.1218; also καύσομαι Id.*Pl*.1054: aor. 1 ἔκαυσα Id.*Pax*1088, Th. 7.80 (bis), Pl.*Grg*.456b, etc.; Ep. ἔκηα (certain Act. and Med. forms have κει- in codd. of Hom., v. infr.), ἔκηα Il.1.40, al.; 3 sg. ἔκηε(ν) 22.170, 24.34, al.; unaugm. κῆεν 21.349; 3 pl. ἔκηαν (v.l. ἔκειαν) Od.22.336; imper. κεῖον 21.176 codd.; 1 pl. subj. κείομεν Il.7.333 (κατα-), 377,396 (better attested than κήομεν); opt. κήαι, κήαιεν, 21.336, 24.38; inf. κῆαι Od.15.97 (v.l. κεῖαι), κατα-κῆαι 10.533, 11.46, κακκῆαι ib.74 (v.l. κακκεῖαι); part. κείαντες 9.231, 13.26, Att. κέαντες A.*Ag*.849, S.*El*.757, (ἐκ-) E.*Rh*.97, ἐκκέας Ar.*Pax*1133 (lyr.), ἐγκέαντι *IG*1².374.96,261: pf. κέκαυκα (κατα-, προσ-) X.*HG*6.5.37, Alex.124.3:—**Med.**, aor. 1 ἐκαυσάμην (ἀν-) Hdt.1.202, 8.19; Ep. κείαντο, κειάμενοι, Il.9.88,234; κειάμενος Od.16.2, 23.51:—**Pass.**, fut. καυθήσομαι Hp.*Nat.Mul*.107, (κατα-, ἐκ-) Ar.*Nu*.1505, Pl.*R*.362a; late κἀήσομαι 1*Ep.Cor*.3.15: aor. 1 ἐκαύθην Hp.*Epid*.4.4, *Int*.28, (κατ-) Hdt.1.19, Th.3.74; Ep. and Ion. aor. 2 ἐκάην [ᾰ] Il.9.212 (κατ-), Od.12.13, (δι-) Hp.*Loc.Hom*.40, (κατ-) Hdt.2.180; inf. καήμεναι Il.23.210, καῆναι Parth.9.8: pf. κέκαυμαι E.*Cyc*.457, Th.4.34, etc., κέκαυσμαι Hp.*Int*.28; inf. κεκαῦσθαι Arist.*Mete*.343ᵃ9. (From κᾰϝ-yω.) I. *kindle*, πυρὰ πολλά Il.9.77; πῦρ κείαντες Od.9.231; πῦρ κῆαι 15.97, etc.:—Med., πῦρ κείαντο *they lighted them* a fire, Il.9.88, cf. 234, Od.16.2:—Pass., *to be lighted, burn*, πυραὶ νεκύων καίοντο Il.1.52; θεείου καιομένοιο 8.135; καιομένοιο πυρός 19.376, cf. Hdt.1.86, Ar.*V*.1372, etc.; φῶς πυρὸς καόμενον Pl.*R*.514b; αἱ φλόγες αἱ καιόμεναι..περὶ τὸν οὐρανόν the meteors *which blaze*, Arist.*Mete*.341ᵇ2; of ore, *to be smelted*, Id.*HA*552ᵇ10. II. *set on fire, burn*, μηρία, ὀστέα, Od.9.553, Hes.*Th*.557; νεκρούς Il.21.343; δένδρεα ib.338:—Pass., νηυσὶν καιομένῃσιν 9.602. 2. *make hot*, of the sun, ἀνθρώπους Hdt.3.104: abs., ibid., Pl.*Cra*.413b; [χείμαρρος] ἡελίῳ κεκαυμένος *smelted*, *AP*9.277 (Antiphil.). 3. of extreme cold, ἡ χιὼν καίει τῶν κυνῶν τὰς ῥῖνας X.*Cyn*.8.2, cf. 6.26 (Pass.); κάειν λέγεται..τὸ ψυχρόν, οὐχ ὡς τὸ θερμόν Arist.*Mete*.382ᵇ8. 4. Pass., of fever heat, τὰ ἐντὸς ἐκάετο Th.2.49: metaph., of passion, esp. of love, *to be on fire*, ἐν φρασὶ καιομένα Pi.*P*.4.219; κάομαι τὴν καρδίαν Ar.*Lys*.9; ἔρως..ὕβρει καόμενος Pl.*Lg*.783a; καίεσθαί τινος (sc. ἔρωτι) Hermesian.7.37, Charito 4.6, cf. Parth.14.2; also καομένη Ἑλλάς Greece *being in a fever* of excitement, Lys.33.7. 5. *suffer from inflammation*, ἐκαύθη ἔσω Hp.*Epid*.4.20, cf. 4. III. *burn and destroy* (in war), τέμνειν καὶ κ., κ. καὶ πορθεῖν, *waste with fire* and sword, X.*HG*4.2.15, 6.5.27. IV. of surgeons, *cauterize*, ὤμους Hp.*Art*.11:—in Pass., Id.*Aph*.6.60: abs., τέμνειν καὶ κάειν *to use* knife and *cautery*, Pl.*Grg*.480c, 521e, X.*An*.5.8.18, etc.: rarely reversed, κέαντες ἢ τεμόντες A.*Ag*.849. V. *burn* or *bake* pottery, κανθάρους dub. in Phryn.Com.15.

**κάκ** (A), name of the letter κ, κάμηλος θήλεια κεχαραγμένη κὰκ λὰλ ἄλφα *PLond*.3.909*a*7 (ii A.D.), cf. *BGU*153.17 (ii A.D.).

**κάκ** (B), apocop. for κατά before κ, in Hom. mostly κὰκ κεφαλῆς, κὰκ κεφαλήν, Il.18.24, 16.412, al.; also κὰκ κόρυθα 11.351; κὰκ κορυφήν 8.83; cf. κάγ, κάδ.

**κάκ**, crasis for καὶ ἐκ. **κάκα**· κακία ἢ ὄρνεον, Hsch. **κακάβη**, ἡ, **κάκαβος**, ἡ, **κακάβιον**, τό, v. κακκ-.

**κᾰκαγγελ-έω**, *bring evil tidings*, *Trag.Adesp*.122. **-ία**, ἡ, *evil tidings*, Antig.*Mir*.12, prob. in Man.4.556, cf. Hp.ap.Gal.19.107. **-ος**, ον, *bringing ill tidings*, γλῶσσα A.*Ag*.636, cf. Plu.2.241b, Ant.Lib.15.4. **-τος**, ον, *caused by ill tidings*, κ. ἄχη the sorrow *of ill tidings*, S.*Ant*.1286 (lyr.).

**κακᾱγόρος, κακᾱγορία**, Dor. for κακηγ-, Pi.*O*.1.53, *P*.2.53.

**κακαλία**, v.l. for κακκαλία II (q.v.) in Dsc.4.122; cf. **κακαλίς**· νάρκισσος, Hsch.

**κάκαλον**, τό, = τεῖχος, A.*Fr*.166. (Perh. connected with ποδοκάκκη.)

**κᾰκανδρία**, ἡ, *unmanliness*, S.*Aj*.1014, E.*Rh*.814.

**κακάνειν**, v. κακκανῆν.

**κᾰκ-ανθήεις**, εσσα, εν, *with noxious blossom*, Nic.*Al*.420. **-ανθέω**, *bear such blossom*, Sch. ad loc.

**κᾰκάω**, cf. κακκάω. **κἀκεῖ, κἀκεῖθεν, κἀκεῖνος**, Att. crases for καὶ ἐκ-.

**κάκεις** or **κακεῖς**, οἱ, a kind of *Egyptian loaves*, Str.17.2.5.

**κᾰκ-ελκής**, ές, *suffering from malignant ulcer*, Hp.*Aff*.20; cf. κακοελκής. **-ελπιστέω**, *have ill hopes*, Arr.*Epict*.4.5.27. **-έμφᾰτος**, ον, *ill-sounding*, κακέμφατόν ἐστι τὸ "ὑπεξαίρεσις" Demetr.Lac.*Herc*.1012.23; esp. of words *used in a vulgar* or *equivocal sense*, Quint.8.3.44, Sch.Luc.*Lex*.21; τὸ κ. Sch.Ar.*Ach*.258, al. Adv. -τως Sch.Ar. *Ra*.48,426, etc. II. = ἄδοξος, Hsch. **-εντρέχεια**, ἡ, *activity in mischief*, Plb.4.87.4. **-εντρεχής**, ές, *active in mischief*, Epich. [259], Plb.22.19.3, Str.7.3.7; κ. τῇ διανοίᾳ Vett.Val.17.5. **-επίθυμος** οἴνου *fatally fond* of wine, Hsch. s.v. οἰνόφλυξ. **-εργᾰσία**, ἡ, *bad effect*, prob. f.l. for κατ-, Thphr.*Sud*.10. **-εργέτης**, ου, ὁ, *evil-doer*, nickname of Ptolemy Euergetes II, Ath.4.184c: **-εργέτις**, ιδος, ἡ, Herm. *in Phdr*.p.75 A. (written κακοεργ- Porph.*Antr*.30, s.v.l.): —also **-γάτις** [ᾰ], Them.*Or*.2.33d. **-έρως**, ωτος, ὁ, ἡ, *fatally in love*, Hdn.*Epim*.206. **-εστώ**, οῦς, ἡ, *ill-being*, opp. εὐεστώ, Hsch., cj. in Democr.182.

**κάκη** [ᾰ], ἡ, (κακός) *wickedness, vice*, E.*Hipp*.1335, Ar.*Av*.541, etc.; of a horse, Pl.*Phdr*.247b. 2. *baseness of spirit, cowardice, sloth*, ἄψυχον κάκην A.*Th*.192; λήματος κάκῃ ib.616; δειλίαν καὶ κ. E.*IT*676, cf. *Med*.1051; εἴκοντας κάκῃ Pl.*Mx*.246b; διὰ κάκην Id.*R*.468a.

**κᾰκηγορ-έω**, *speak ill of, abuse, slander*, τινα Pl.*Smp*.173d, *R*.395e, al.; τινὰ πρός τινα (v.l. παρά τινι) Ps.-Phoc.226: abs., ἀπεχόμενος..τοῦ κακηγορεῖν *from evil-speaking*, Pl.*Lg*.934e, cf. Arist.*EN*1129ᵇ23, Hyp.*Fr*.246:—Pass., *to be abused*, Pl.*R*.368b. **-ία**, ἡ, *evil-speaking, abuse, slander*, Pi.*P*.2.53 (pl.), Arist.*EN*1131ᵃ9, Phld. *Ir*.p.52 W. (pl.); κ. τινός *abuse* of one, Pl.*Phdr*.243a,b; κακηγορίας δίκη action *for abusive language*, D.21.32, cf. 81; κακηγορίας δικάζεσθαι Lys.10.2, etc.; ἔνοχος κακηγορίᾳ D.57.30. **-ίου δίκη**, = foreg., Test.ap.D.21.93. **-ος**, ον, Dor. **κᾰκᾱγόρος**, (ἀγορεύω) *evil-speaking, abusive, slanderous*, Pi.*O*.1.53; γλῶττα Pl.*Phdr*.254e; κ. τινος *abusive of* one, Ath.5.220a: Comp. κακηγορίστερος Pherecr.96: Sup. -ίστατος Ecphant.5. Adv. -ρως Poll.8.81.

**κᾰκήθης,** ες, = κακοήθης, Hp.*Mul.*2.141, Nic.*Th.*152.

**κᾰκηλόγος,** ον, *evil-speaking*, Men.*Mon.*117.

**κᾰκηπελ-έων,** *in evil plight*, Ep. part., formed after Homer's ὀλιγηπελέων (q. v.), Nic.*Th.*878, *Al.*93. **-ία,** Ep. -ίη, ἡ, *evil plight*, opp. εὐηπελία, Id.*Th.*319, Doroth.ap.Heph.Astr.3.36.

**κάκησις** [ᾰ], εως, ἡ, *taedium*, *Gloss.*

**κᾰκία,** ἡ, (κακός) *badness* in quality, opp. ἀρετή (excellence), Thgn. 322, S.*OT*512 (lyr.), Pl.*Smp.*181e, *R.*348c, etc.; κακίᾳ ἡνιόχων by their *incapacity*, Id.*Phdr.*248b: pl., κακίαι *defects*, Luc.*Hist.Conscr.* 6. 2. *cowardice, faint-heartedness*, Th.2.87, Pl.*R.*556d; κ. καὶ ἀνανδρία Id.*Cri.*46a. 3. *moral badness, vice*, μετ' ἀρετῆς ἀλλ' οὐ μετὰ κακίας And.1.56; ἡ ἀρετή, ὡσαύτως δὲ..καὶ ἡ κ. Pl.*Men.*72a, etc.; personified in the Fable of Prodicus, X.*Mem.*2.1.26: pl., περὶ κακιῶν, title of treatise by Philodemus. 4. Philos., *Evil*, ὕλη κακίας αἰτία Plot.1.8.14. II. *ill-repute, dishonour*, κ. ἀντιλαβεῖν Th.3.58. 2. *hurt, damage* done or suffered, Lxx 1*Ki.*6.9, 1*Ma.* 7.23, *Ev.Matt.*6.34.

**κᾰκιζότεχνος,** ον, *finding fault with one's craftsmanship, meticulous*, of the sculptor Callimachus, v.l. in Paus.1.26.7; cf. κατατηξίτεχνος.

**κᾰκίζω,** (κακός) *abuse, reproach*, τινα Hdt.3.145, D.34.2; κ. τινὰ ὅτι οὐκ.. Th.2.21; νουθετεῖν τε καὶ κ. Pl.*R.*560a; τὴν τύχην κ. D.18. 306, cf. 21.73: abs., Epicur.*Nat.*28.12,72 G.:—Pass., *to be reproached*, ὑπό τινος Th.1.105. II. *make cowardly*, E.*IA*1435:—Pass., *play the coward*, οὔ ἑ κακιζόμενόν γε κατέκτα Il.24.214; καὶ μὴ κακισθῇς E. *Med.*1246, cf. *El.*982, Pl.*Mx.*247c; κακιζόμενοι τύχῃ *worsted* by fortune alone, Th.5.75.

***κακιθά·** λιμηρά, Hsch. ***κακιθής·** ἄτροφος ἄμπελος, and **κακιθές·** χαλεπόν, λιμηρές, Id. **κακίμην·** τὴν ἀτυχῆ, Id. **κακῑότερος,** v. κακός.

**κάκ-ισις** [ᾰ], εως, ἡ, *blame*, ἐν τοῖς διαπραττομένοις Vett.Val.182.20 (pl.). **-ισμός,** ὁ, = foreg., Phld.*Vit.*p.10 J., Str.9.3.10. **-ιστέον,** *one must bring reproach on*, c. acc., E.*IT*105.

**κάκιστος, κᾰκίων,** v. κακός. **κακίω,** v. κηκίω.

**κακκάβη** [ᾰ] (A), ἡ, *three-legged pot* (= χύτρα, Ath.4.169c), Ar.*Fr.* 215, Antiph.217.3, Dorio ap.Ath.8.338a: **κάκκᾰβος,** ὁ, Nicoch.14, Antiph.182.4, 249: **κάκαβος,** ἡ, Alex.Trall.3.7: **κακάβη,** ἡ, Gal.14. 309.

**κακκάβη** [ᾰ] (B), *partridge*, so called from its cry, Ath.9.390a.

**κακκᾰβίζω,** *cackle*, of partridges, Arist.*HA*536$^b$14, Thphr.*Fr.*181; of doves and partridges coupled, Chrysipp.*Stoic.*3.180; of owls, *hoot*, Ar.*Lys.*761 (v.l. **-άζω**):—also **κακκάζω,** Hsch. Cf. κικκαβαῦ.

***κακκάβ-ιον,** τό, Dim. of κακκάβη (A), Eub.38, Orib.5.33.3 (**-βιν**), *PLond.*5.1657.6 (iv A.D.): also **κακάβιν** Aët.1.130. **-ίς,** ίδος, ἡ, collat. form of κακκάβη (B), Alcm.25. **-ος,** v. κακκάβη (A).

**κακκαλία,** ἡ, = στρύχνον ὑπνωτικόν, Dsc.4.72. II. *Mercurialis tomentosa*, ib.122, Plin.*HN*25.135; v. κακαλία.

**κακκανῆν,** Lacon. inf., perh. *stir up, incite*, νέων ψυχάς dub. in Leonidas ap.Plu.*Cleom.*2, cf. 2.235f (κακάνειν codd.), 959b (κακύνειν codd.).

**κακκάω,** *cacare*, Ar.*Nu.*1384, 1390.

**κακκεῖαι,** v. κατακαίω. **κακκεῖναι·** κατακόψαι (Cypr.), Hsch.

**κακκείοντες,** Ep. for κατακείοντες, part. of κατακείω.

**κάκκη,** ἡ, *human ordure*, Ar.*Pax*162. **κακκῆαι,** v. κατακαίω.

**κακκόρ·** ὁ μικρὸς δάκτυλος, Hsch. (Lacon. for κασκός, q. v.)

**κακκρύπτω,** Ep. for κατακρ-, Nic.*Fr.*78.

**κακκώνιον·** σκαφίον, Hsch.

**κᾰκο-ανάστροφος,** ον, *of bad conversation*, Procl.*Par.Ptol.*233. **-ανδρος,** ον, = ἄνανδρος, Sch.E.*Med.*436. **-αυλος,** ον, = ἄναυλος, Sch.E.*Ph.*790. **-βάκχευτος,** ον, = ἀβάκχευτος, Sch.E.*Or.*316, 319. **-βας·** ἐπὶ κακῷ ἥκων, Hsch. **-βῐος,** ον, *living poorly, living a hard life*, Hdt.4.95, X.*Cyr.*7.5.67 (Sup.), Arist.*HA*616$^b$31, Str.17.2. 1. **-βίωτος** [ῐ], ον, = ἀβίωτος, Sch.Ar.*Pl.*970. **-βλαστέω,** *sprout ill* or *with difficulty*, Thphr.*CP*4.7.3. **-βλαστής,** ές, *sprouting ill* or *with difficulty*, ib.1.20.6, 4.7.2: Comp. κακοβλαστότερος Id.*HP*4.14. 1. **-βλητος,** ον, *ill-thrown, missed*, Suid. s. v. ἀβλῆτα βέλη. **-βολέω,** *have unlucky throws* (with dice), Sch.Ar.*Ra.*1001 (prob.), Suid. s. v. Θηραμένης. **-βόρος,** ον, *eating bad food*, Ael.*NA*10.29 (Sup.).

**κᾰκοβουλ-εύομαι,** Pass., *to be ill-advised*, ψυχὴ κακοβουλευθεῖσα E. *Ion*877 (anap.); but the form is incorrect and corrupt. **-ία,** ἡ, *ill-advisedness*, J.*BJ*2.11.3, D.L.7.93, Quint.*Ps.*138(139).20, prob. in *POxy.*1101.7 (iv A.D.). ***-ος,** ον, *ill-advised, foolish*, φροντίς S. *Fr.*592 (lyr.); φῶτες E.*Ba.*401 (lyr.), cf. Ar.*Eq.*1055 (hex.), Ph.2.280 (Sup.), D.Chr.31.50, Vett.Val.66.3: Comp., Sch.Th.1.120. II. Act., *giving bad advice*, opp. εὔβουλος, Pl.*Sis.*391c.

**κᾰκό-γαμβρος** γόος distress *for her wretched brother-in-law*, E. *Rh.*260 (lyr.). **-γᾰμία,** ἡ, *bad marriage*, *Cat.Cod.Astr.*8(4). 159. **-γᾰμίου** δίκη, action *for forming an unlawful* or *improper marriage* at Sparta, Plu.*Lys.*30; ζημία punishment for that offence, Aristo *Stoic.*1.89. **-γᾰμος,** ον, *marrying unlawfully*, μνηστῆρες Eust.1415.47; κ. γάμος an *ill-starred* marriage, Sch.Triclin.S.*OT* 1214, cf. Paul.Al.*O.*2. **-γείτων,** ον, gen. ονος, *a bad neighbour*, Call.*Cer.*118. 2. οὐδέ τιν' ἐγχώρων κακογείτονα *neighbour to* his *misery*, S.*Ph.*692 (lyr.). **-γένειος,** ον, *with a poor beard*, Suid. s. v. εἰς Τροιζῆνα. **-γενής,** ές, *base-born*, τὸ κ. D.C.44.37. **-γηρως,** αος, ὁ, ἡ, *unlucky in old age*, Hdn.*Epim.*205. **-γλωσσία,** ἡ, *slanderousness*, Sch.Pi.*P.*4.504. **-γλωσσος,** ον, *ill-tongued*, βοὴ κ. a cry *of misery*, E.*Hec.*661. II. *bringing evil* [on oneself] *by one's tongue*, of Niobe, Call.*Del.*96. **-γνωμονέω,** *to be ill-disposed*, Quint.*Ps.*30(31).14. **-γνωμοσύνη,** ἡ, = κακοβουλία, Aesop.417b, Thd.*Ps.*25(26).10: pl., Sch.E.*Ph.*1727. **-γνώμων,** ον, gen. ονος, *ill-judging, wanting in judgement*, Sm.1*Ki.*25.3, D.C.77.11. **-γονία,** ἡ, *evil birth*, Iamb.*in Nic.*p.82 P. **-γονος,** ον, *born to ill*, Sch.S.*OT* 26. **-γρᾰφος,** ον, *badly written*, γραμματεῖον Phlp.*in de An.*533. 30. **-γύναιος** [ῠ], ον, *bringing ills to women*, Procl.*Par.Ptol.*228.

**κᾰκοδαιμον-άω,** *to be tormented by an evil genius, possessed by an evil spirit*, Ar.*Pl.*372, X.*Mem.*2.1.5, D.8.16 (-οῦσι codd.), Din.1.91, v. l. for sq. in M.Ant.2.8. **-έω,** *to be unfortunate, unhappy*, X. *Hier.*2.4, Epicur.*Fr.*485, Phld.*Vit.*p.34 J., J.*BJ*1.22.1, Plu.2.76a, Arr.*Epict.*1.25.13. II. Astrol., *occupy the region of* κακὸς δαίμων, Doroth ap.Heph.Astr.3.9, Ptol.*Tetr.*195, *Cat.Cod.Astr.*8(4). 130. **-ημα,** ατος, τό, Astrol., *occupation of the region of* κακὸς δαίμων, Vett.Val.74.6, *Cat.Cod.Astr.*8(2).119, 8(4).126, al. **-ία,** Ion. **-ίη,** ἡ, *unhappiness, misfortune*, opp. εὐδαιμονία, Hdt.1.87, Antipho 5.79, X.*Mem.*1.6.3, Arist.*Po.*1450$^a$17, Phld.*Rh.*1.220 S., etc. II. *possession by an evil spirit*, Ar.*Pl.*501, X.*Mem.*2.3.19, D.2.20. **-ίζω,** *deem unhappy*, Phld.*Mort.*33, Str.11.11.8, Ph.1.219. **-ικός,** ή, όν, *bringing unhappiness* or *misfortune*, πικρία Phld.*Ir.*p.56 W., cf. D.L. 7.104, S.E.*M.*9.176. **-ιστής,** οῦ, ὁ, *worshipper of the* κακὸς δαίμων, *member of a 'Satanist' club*, Lys.*Fr.*53.2.

**κᾰκοδαιμ-οσύνη,** ἡ, = κακοδαιμονία II, Hippod.ap.Stob.4.1.95, Ael. *Fr.*110. **-ων,** ον, gen. ονος, *possessed by an evil genius*, Antipho 5.43; ὁ κ. Σωκράτης Ar.*Nu.*104; *ill-starred*, E.*Hipp.*1362 (anap.), Max.Tyr.36.4: freq. in Com., ὦ κακόδαιμον *poor devil!* Ar.*Pl.*386; οἴμοι κακοδαίμων Pherecr.117, etc.; -ονος ἔπαρμα Phld.*Mort.*31: Comp. -έστερος Luc.*Lex.*25: Sup., Id.*Deor.Conc.*7. Adv. -μόνως Id. *Vit.Auct.*7. II. *evil genius*, τοῦ δαίμονος δέδοιχ' ὅπως μὴ τεύξομαι κακοδαίμονος Ar.*Eq.*112, cf. Arr.*Epict.*4.4.38.

**κᾰκο-δάκρῡτος,** ον, *producing inferior gum*, of trees, Hsch. s. v. δύσ⟨σ⟩τακτον. **-δεκτεύω,** = κακῶς δέχομαι, Id. **-δερκής,** v. κακο-λ⟨α⟩ῆ. **-δερμος,** ον, *with a bad skin*, Sch.Theoc.4.63. **-δήνης,** ες, *ill-counselling*, Epic.in *Arch.Pap.*7 p.5.

**κᾰκοδία,** ἡ, opp. εὐοδία, = κακὴ ὁδός, *Et.Gud.App.*672.5.

**κᾰκο-δῐαιτησία,** ἡ, *bad habit of life*, Sor.1.92. **-διάκονος** [ᾱ] (-διάβολος cod.)· κακοικονόμος (Lacon.), Hsch. **-δῐδασκᾰλέω,** *instruct in evil*, τοὺς πολλούς S.E.*M.*2.42, cf. *Tab.Defix.* in *IG*12(7).p.1 (Amorgos). **-δῐκία,** ἡ, *corruption of justice*, Pl.*Lg.*938b.

**κάκοδμος** [ᾰ], ον, (ὀδμή) Ion. for κάκοσμος, Hp.*Prog.*11.

**κᾰκοδοξ-έω,** *to be in ill repute*, X.*Mem.*1.7.2, Muson.*Fr.*9 p.47 H., Sch.E.*Andr.*777. ***-ία,** ἡ, *bad repute*, X.*Ap.*31, Pl.*R.*361c. II. *heretical opinion*, Just.*Nov.*109 *Praef.* **-ος,** ον, *in ill repute, of low reputation*, Thgn.195, X.*Ages.*4.1: Comp. -ότερος Pl.*Min.*321a; of things, *inglorious*, νίκα E.*Andr.*778 (lyr.).

**κᾰκο-δουλία,** ἡ, *badness of slaves*, D.Chr.38.15. ***-δουλος,** ὁ, *ill-treating one's slaves*, Cratin.81. II. *bad slave*, Ps.-Luc.*Philopatr.*7. ***-δρομία,** poet. -ίη, ἡ, *bad passage* (by sea), *AP*7. 699. ***-δωρος,** ον, gloss on ἄδωρος, Suid. **-ειδής,** ές, *ill-featured*, D.C.78.9 (Sup.). **-ειμονία,** ἡ, *bad clothing*, Sch.A.R. 1.308. **-είμων,** ον, gen. ονος, *ill-clad*, πτωχοί Od.18.41, cf. Ps.-Luc.*Philopatr.*21, Hsch. s. v. λιναγερτουμένη. **-ελκής,** ές, *badly festering*, Man.1.54.

**κᾰκο-εξία,** ἡ, (ἔχω) = καχεξία, ἐπὶ κ. f.l. for καρδίᾳ in Lxx *Si.*19. 5. **-έπεια,** ἡ, *bad language, blasphemy*, Suid., (in form -πία) Phot. **-εργᾰσία,** ἡ, = κακεργασία, Lesb.Rh.3.7. **-έργετα** (neut. pl.), = sq., πήματα, prob. for -είργετα, Antioch.Astr. in *Cat.Cod.Astr.* 1.109. **-εργέτις,** ιδος, ἡ, *evil-doing*, ψυχή Porph.*Antr.*30; cf. κακεργέτις. **-εργής,** ές, poet., = κακοεργός, *IG*12(5).229.15 (Paros), Man. 1.249. **-εργία, -εργός,** = κακουργία, -γος, v. sub vocc. **-ζηλία,** ἡ, *unhappy imitation* or *rivalry*, v.l. for -ζηλωσία, Plb.10.22.10 (ap. Suid. s. v. Φιλοποίμην). II. Rhet., of style, *affectation*, Luc.*Salt.* 82, Demetr.*Eloc.*189. ***-ζηλος,** ον, *having bad taste*: hence in Rhet., *using a bad, affected style* (cf. ζῆλος), ῥήτωρ D.L.1.38; τὸ κ. = κακοζηλία, Longin.3.4, cf. Demetr.*Eloc.*186, Hermog.*Inv.*4.12. Adv. κακοζήλως, εἰπεῖν Gal.18(1).180. **-ζηλωσία,** v. κακοζηλία. **-ζωΐα,** ἡ, *evil life*, Procl.*in Alc.*p.58 C., Herm.*in Phdr.*pp.90, 179 A.: poet. **κακοζοΐα,** *miserable life*, Sapph.120.

**κᾰκοήθ-εια,** Ion. **-ίη,** ἡ, *bad disposition, malignity*, Pl.*R.*348d, 401a, Hyp.*Eux.*32 (-ηθία), *Ep.Rom.*1.29; κ. τὸ ἐπὶ τὸ χεῖρον ὑπολαμβάνειν ἅπαντα Arist.*Rh.*1389$^b$20: pl., κ. ὑπὲρ τοῦ πράγματος λεγόμεναι Aeschin.1.166, cf. Isoc.15.284, D.C.*Fr.*96.2. II. *bad manners* or *habits*, X.*Cyn.*13.16. III. Medic., *malignant character*, τῆς νόσου Epicur.*Fr.*471: in pl., *malignant diseases* or *growths*, Dsc.3. 92 (v. l. for τὰ -ήθη). **-ευμα,** ατος, τό, *malicious deed*, Plu.*Pomp.* 37. **-εύομαι,** *act maliciously, play a scurvy trick*, Men.*Epit.*334; πρὸς τὸν δῆμον Sch.Ar.*Lys.*313. II. Medic., *to be malignant*, Gal.18(2).464. **-ης,** ες, (ἦθος) *ill-disposed, malicious*, opp. εὐήθης, Ar.*Pax*822 (Comp., 823), D.18.11, Pl.*Ep.*360c, Ph.1.529, etc.; of animals, κ. ὄρνεον καὶ πανοῦργον Arist.*HA*613$^b$23; esp. *thinking evil, prone to put the worst construction on everything*, Id.*Rh.*1389$^b$20; τὸ κακόηθες *malice, wickedness*, Pl.*R.*401b, Men.653, Ph.1.684, etc. Adv., πανούργως καὶ -ήθως Men.*Epit.*318; κ. πολιτεύεσθαι Philipp.ap. D.18.78, cf. J.*AJ*13.11.1: Comp. -εστέρως Poll.4.148. II. of things, *infamous, abominable*, κλειδία κρυπτὰ -έστατα Ar.*Th.*422. 2. Medic., of sores, fevers, etc., *malignant*, Hp.*Aph.*6.4, *Prog.*20 (Sup.); ἐξάνθημα Phld.*Ind.Sto.*26. Adv. -θως Hp.*Art.*41 codd. **-ίζομαι,** = κακοηθεύομαι, Arr.*Epict.*3.16.4, etc. II. *put a bad construction on* things, κ. τὴν φιλοσοφίαν (sed leg. κ. ⟨εἰς⟩ τὴν φ.) Stob.2.7.2. **-ίη,** ἡ, v. κακοήθεια. **-ιστέον,** *one must put a bad construction*, ἐπὶ τὸ χεῖρον ἐκλαμβάνοντι Arist.*Rh.*1416$^b$10.

**κᾰκο-ηχής**, ές, *ill-sounding, dissonant*, Phld.*Po*.2.42: Comp. ἠχὴ -εστέρα Adam.2.42:—also ⊛**-ηχος**, ον, Suid. s. v. ἐκμελές. **-θαλπής**, ές, (θάλπω) *warming badly*, Hsch. s. v. δυσθαλπέος. **-θᾰνᾰσία**, ἡ, *miserable death*, Paul.Al.*M*.4, Vett.Val.126.10, al. **-θάνᾰτος** [θᾰ], ον, *dying miserably*, Plu.2.22c (as expl. of ῥιγεδανός), cf. Vett.Val. 128.19, Sch.E.*Hipp*.1143. **-θέλεια**, ἡ, *malevolence*, *Gloss*. **-θελής**, ές, *malevolent*, Adam.2.19. **-θέλω** (incorrect form), *to be ill-disposed*, *PMasp*.151.177 (vi A.D.). **-θεος**, ον, *having bad gods*, Thphr.ap.Porph.*Abst*.2.7. **-θερᾰπεία**, Ion. -είη, ἡ, *bad treatment*, Hp.*Aff*.20, 22. **-θέρειος**, ον, *with a bad summer*, Tz.*Proll.Hes*. p.12. **-θερής**, ές, *unfitted to endure summer heat*, φύσεις Sor.1. 41. **-θημοσύνη**, ἡ, *disorderliness*, Hes.*Op*.472. **-θηνέω**, *to be in a bad state, to be weakly*, of sheep, Arist.*HA*574$^{a}$15. **-θῐγία**, ἡ, (θιγγάνω) *aimlessness*, γνώμης Democr.223. **-θροος**, ον, contr. **-θρους**, ουν, *evil-speaking, slanderous*, S.*Aj*.138 (anap.). **-θῡμία**, ἡ, *malevolence*, πρὸς ἀλλήλους Plu.*Lyc*.4. **-θῡμος**, ον, *ill-disposed*, Man.4.564, Adam.2.24. **-θυρσος**, ον, gloss on ἄθυρσος, Sch.E. *Or*.1492. **-θῦτος**, ον, *offering bad sacrifices*, Thphr.ap.Porph. *Abst*.2.7. **-ῐδρῡτος**, ον, gloss on ἀΐδρυτος, Hsch.

**κᾰκοικονόμος**, ὁ, *bad manager*, Ph.2.269.

**Κᾰκοΐλιος** [ῑλ], ἡ, *unhappy Ilios*, Κακοΐλιον οὐκ ὀνομαστήν Od.19. 260, al.

**κᾰκο-καρπία**, ἡ, *bearing bad* or *imperfect fruit*, Thphr.*HP*1.4.1, al. **-κέλᾰδος**, ον, gloss on δυσκέλαδος, Procl. ad Hes.*Op*. 196. **-κέρδεια**, ἡ, *base love of gain*, Thgn.225 (pl.). **-κλεής**, ές, (κλέος) *ill-famed*, Tryph.127. **-κνημος**, Dor. **-κνᾱμος**, ον, (κνήμη) *weak-legged, thin-legged*, Theoc.4.63, Call.*Fr*.472. **-κοίμητος**, ον, gloss on δυσηλεγής, Hsch. **-κρᾱτος**, ον, *badly tempered*, τὸ κ. (sc. τοῦ αἵματος) Gal.17(1).565. **-κρῐσία**, ἡ, *bad judgement*, *AP*7.236 (Antip. Thess.); ἀπειρία καὶ κ. Plb.12.24. 6. **-κρῐτος**, ον, = δύσκριτος, Gal.17(2).575, al. **-κτερής**, ές (-οτερής cod.)· κακῶς θάπτων (κακοθ- cod.), Hsch. **-κτέριστος**, ον, gloss on ἀκτέριστος, Sch.S.*Ant*.1207. **-λ⟨α⟩ῆ**· κακοδερκῆ, Hsch. **-λεκτρος**, ον, = κακόγαμος, Opp.*C*.1.261. **-λῐμένιστος**, ον, gloss on ἄνορμος, Sch.rec.S.*OT*423.

**κᾰκολογ-έω**, *revile, abuse*, τινα Lys.8.5, Isoc.6.98, Hyp.*Fr*.25, Lxx *Ex*.21.16(17), *Ev.Matt*.15.4, al.: abs., D.36.61:—Pass., Gorg. *Hel*.7, *PFay*.12.15 (ii B.C.). **-ία**, ἡ, *coarse expression, bad style*, Pl.*R*.401a: but usu. *abuse, reviling*, Hdt.7.237, X.*Cyr*.1.2.6, Hyp. *Fr*.247, Thphr.*Char*.28, etc. **-ικός**, ή, όν, *vituperative*, τὸ κ. Arist.*Rh.Al*.1440$^{b}$5. **-ος** (parox.), ον, *evil-speaking, slanderous*, Pi.*P*.11.28, Men.256, Arist.*Rh*.1381$^{b}$7; τινος *of* one, Id.*EN* 1125$^{a}$8.

**κᾰκό-λῡρος**, ον, gloss on ἄλυρος, Sch.E.*Ph*.1028. **-μᾰθής**, ές, *bad at learning*, Anaxandr.8. **-μᾰνέω**, *to be exceeding mad*, Ph.2.501. **-μαντις**, εως, ὁ, ἡ, *prophet of evil*, Ἐρινύς A.*Th*.722 (lyr.); θυμός Id.*Pers*.10 (anap.). **II.** abs., *sorry prophet*, A.R.3. 936. **-μᾰχέω**, *fight unfairly*, Plu.2.32b, Luc.*Demon*.49. **2.** *fight against odds, use desperate expedients*, Phlp.*in GC*16.28. **-μέλετος**, ον, (μελέτη) *busied with evil, full of evil augury*, κ. ἰά A.*Pers*. 937 (lyr.).

**κᾰκομετρ-έω**, *give bad measure*, Luc.*Herm*.59. **-ητος**, ον, *ill-measured*: τὸ κ., = sq., Eust.1644.32. **-ία**, ἡ, *short measure*, *POxy*. 1447.6 (i A.D.). **II.** *false metre*, Sch.Heph.p.106C. (pl.), Eust. ad D.P.739. **-ος**, ον, *in bad metre, unmetrical*, Plu.2.747f, etc.; τὸ κ. Phld.*Po.Herc*.1676.8.

**κᾰκο-μηδής**, ές, (μῆδος) *contriving ill, deceitful*, *h.Merc*.389. **-μήτης**, ου, ὁ, = foreg., pl. -μῆται Orph.*Fr*.119. **-μητίη** [ῐ], ἡ, *cunning*, Man.2.308. **-μητῐς**, ὁ, = -μήτης, E.*Or*.1403 (lyr., -μήτας codd.); pl. -μήτιες, Astrol., = κακοποιοί, ἀστέρες Doroth.ap.Heph. Astr.3.30. **-μήτωρ**, ορος, ἡ, *mother of ill*, gloss on ἀμήτωρ, Hsch.:—but prob. **-μήστωρ** (= κακόμητις) shd. be read in Man. 4.307.

**κᾰκομηχᾰν-έω**, *practise base arts*, περί τινα Plb.13.3.2. **-ία**, ἡ, *practising of base arts, mischief*, Luc.*Phal*.1.12, Adam.1.5. **-ος**, Dor. **-μάχᾰνος** [μᾱ], ον, *mischief-plotting*, Il.6.344, Od.16.418; λῃσταί B.17.8; κῶρος Mosch.*Fr*.3.7; of things, *mischievous, baneful*, ἔρις Il.9.257. Adv. -νως Phot.*Bibl*.p.292 B.

⊛**κᾰκομῑλία**, ἡ, *bad intercourse* or *society*, D.S.12.12 (nisi leg. καχομιλία, q.v.).

**κᾰκό-μισθος**, ον, *ill-rewarded*, Sch.A.*Ch*.733. **-μοιρία**, ἡ, *ill fate*, Sch.S.*Tr*.850, Sch.E.*Ph*.156. **-μοιρος**, ον, *ill-fated*, ὠδῖνες *AP*7.375 (Antiphil.), cf. Maiuri *Nuova Silloge*630. **-μορος**, ον, = foreg., Hsch. s. v. ἄμμορον, Suid. s. v. ἄμμορος. Adv. -ως *Cat.Cod. Astr*.8(4).129, 142. **-μορφία**, ἡ, *ill shape, ugliness*, *Gloss*.; gloss on δυσχλαινία, Sch.E.*Hec*.240. **-μορφος**, ον, *misshapen*, Sor. 1.39, 47, *AP*5.88 (Marc. Arg.). ⊛**-μουσία**, ἡ, *corruption of music*, Plu.2.748c. **-μουσος**, ον, *unmusical*, χορεία Sch.E.*Ph*.786 (Sup.). **-μοχθος**, ον, *working ill* or *perversely*, Lxx *Wi*.15.8.

**κάκονες**· κακὸς ὄλεθρος, Hsch.

⊛ **κᾰκο-νοέω**, *to be ill-disposed, bear malice*, Lys.29.10. **-νόητος**, ον, = κακόνοος, Polem.*Phgn*.10. **-νοια**, ἡ, *ill-will, malice*, opp. εὔνοια, Lys.22.16, X.*An*.7.7.45, *Cyr*.3.1.38, D.21.204, Ph.2.120, al.

**κᾰκονομ-έομαι**, Pass., *to be badly governed*, Ocell.4.8. **-ία**, ἡ, *bad system of laws and government*, opp. εὐνομία, X.*Ath*.1.8. **-ος**, ον, *with bad laws, ill-governed*, opp. εὔνομος, in Sup., Hdt.1.65, Ph. 2.268.

**κᾰκό-νοος**, ον, contr. **-νους**, ουν: Att. pl. κακόνοι:—*ill-disposed, disaffected*, opp. εὔνους, Antipho Soph.109, Ar.*Pax*496 (lyr.), 671; εὐνοεῖν τοῖς κακόνοις X.*Cyr*.8.2.1; τινι Id.*An*.2.5.16; τῇ πόλει Th.6. 24; τῷ πλήθει Lys.25.7; τῷ δήμῳ κακόνους ἔσομαι, oligarchical oath in Arist.*Pol*.1310$^{a}$9; εἰς τὰ ὑμέτερα πράγματα Lys.20.20: Sup. κακονούστατος Id.7.28, D.23.6. Adv. κακονόως Sch.E.*Or*.108; κακόνως Poll.5.115: Sup. -νούστατα ib.116.

**κᾰκονύμφ-ευτος**, ον, gloss on ἀνύμφευτος, Sch.rec.S.*Ant*.980. **-ιον** ἔργον the work *of an evil bride*, Nonn.*D*.3.308. **-ος**, ον, *ill-married*, κακονυμφοτάτα ὄνασις *most unprofitable wedlock*, E.*Hipp*.756 (lyr.). **II.** Subst., *unhappy bridegroom*, Id.*Med*.206, 990 (both lyr.).

**κᾰκό-νωτος**, ον, *with foul back*, of fish, Antiph.129.7. **-ξενία**, ἡ, *inhospitality*, Charond.ap.Stob.4.2.24, Plu.*Cat.Mi*.12. **-ξενος**, Ion. **-ξεινος**, ον, *unfortunate in guests*, in Ep. Comp., οὔ τις σεῖο κακοξεινώτερος ἄλλος Od.20.376. **II.** *unfriendly to strangers, inhospitable*, E.*Alc*.558 (v.l. for ἐχθρόξ-), *AP*7.699, Lyc.1286: Comp., Σκυθῶν -ώτεροι Jul.*Ep*.89b. **-ξύνετος**, ον, *wise for evil*, οὐκ ἀξυνετωτέρου, κακοξυνετωτέρου δέ not less wise, but *more wise for evil*, Th. 6.76. **-οινία**, ἡ, *bad quality of wine*, opp. καλλιοινία, *Gp*.5.43 tit.

**κᾰκοπάθ-εια** [πᾰ], ἡ, *distress, misery*, Hp.*VM*10, Antipho 3.2.11, Isoc.6.55, Arist.*Pol*.1278$^{b}$28; σώματος Antipho 5.18; of plants or trees, Thphr.*CP*3.7.8; *strain, stress*, on the parts of a machine, Hero *Bel*.93.1: pl., Hp. l. c.; ταῖς παρὰ τὴν ἀξίαν νῦν κακοπαθείαις your present unmerited *sufferings*, Th.7.77:—later, usu. written **-παθία**, *IG*2$^{2}$.900.16 (ii B.C.), *SIG*685.30 (Magnesia, ii B.C.), *BGU* 1209.7 (i B.C.), *Ep.Jac*.5.10: pl., *IG*12(7).386.24 (Amorgos, iii B.C.), Phld.*Piet*.86, etc.; *laborious toil, perseverance*, *BGU* l. c. (i B.C.). ⊛ **-έω**, fut. -παθήσομαι *PLond*.1.98$^{r}$73 (i/ii A.D.): pf. κεκακοπάθηκα Aen.Tact.26.7:—*to be in ill plight, be in distress*, Th.1.78, X.*Mem*.2.1.17, And.2.26, Lys.6.28, D.18.146; πολλὰ κ. *PCair.Zen*. 93.17 (iii B.C.); τινι *by* or *from* a thing, τοῦ χωρίου τῇ ἀπορίᾳ Th.4.29; ὑπό τινος Id.2.41; πρός τι Phld.*Oec*.p.53 J.; of sickness, Hp.*VM*19; κ. σώματι *suffer in* body, Antipho 5.2, 18, Isoc.2.46; τῇ ψυχῇ Democr. 191; of plants or trees, Thphr.*CP*3.4.4, al. **-ής**, ές, (πάθος) *miserable, in evil plight*, Vett.Val.2.5. Adv. -θῶς *in patient wretchedness*, Arist.*Pol*.1269$^{b}$10; διάγειν Vett.Val.121.34. **II.** *troublesome, difficult*, Hero *Aut*.5.1. **-ητικός**, ή, όν, *miserable*, Arist.*EE* 1221$^{a}$31. **-ος**, ον, = κακοπαθής, *miserable*, βίος D.H.8.83. **2.** *troublesome, laborious*, κατασκευή Ph.*Bel*.56.46; μεταλλεῖαι Posidon. 48 J. (cod. Ath.), cf. A.D.*Synt*.187.24. **3.** of persons, *laborious, persevering*, γυνή Muson.*Fr*.3 p.11 H.

**κᾰκο-παρθενεύτως**, gloss on ἀπαρθένευτα, Sch.E.*Ph*.1740. ⊛ **-πάρθενος**, ἡ, *accursed maiden*, Sch.E.*Hec*.612. **II.** Adj. *unbecoming a maid*, Μοῖρα *AP*7.468 (Mel.). **-παστος**, ον, dub. in A.D.*Synt*.187. 23. **-πατρίδης**, ου, Aeol. **-ας**, α, ὁ, *base-born* (cf. εὐπατρίδης), prob. in Alc.*Supp*.28.11; cf. sq. **-πατρις**, ιδος, ἡ, *base-born*, Thgn.193; masc. in Alc.37 A. codd. (leg. -ίδαν). **-περίπᾰτος**, ον, *walking ill*, of horses, *Hippiatr*.115. **-πέτης**, ες, (πέτομαι) *flying badly*, Arist. *HA*616$^{b}$11. **-πηρος**, ον, *with a bad wallet* or *scrip*, *EM*670. 56. **-πῑνής**, ές, *filthy, loathsome*, κακοπινέστατόν τ' ἄλημα S.*Aj*. 381 (lyr.); οὐ μόνον τοῖς ἤθεσιν ἀλλὰ καὶ ἕξει Ath.13.565e. Adv. -νῶς, διακείμενος Archig.(?) ap.Aët.3.114. **-πιστοτέρως**, Adv. Comp. *with misplaced confidence*, Phld.*D*.3 *Fr*.75. **-πλαστος**, ον, *ill-conceived*, Hermog.*Stat*.1.1. Adv. -τως Tz. ad Lyc.805. **-πλοέω**, *sail badly*, Str.15.1.15. **-πλοος**, ον, contr. **-πλους**, ουν, *ill for sailing*, θάλασσα Sch.Philostr.*Her*.p.478 B. **-πνευστος**, ον, gloss on δυσαής, Sch.D Od.13.99. **-πνοια**, ἡ, *difficulty of breathing*, Gal. 17(1).757. **-πνοος**, ον, Att. **-πνους**, ουν, (πνοή) *breathing with difficulty*, Poll.1.197.

**κᾰκοποι-έω**, *do ill, play the knave*, A.*Fr*.111, Ar.*Pax*731; *manage one's affairs ill*, X.*Oec*.3.11. **II.** trans., *do mischief to, injure*, πολλὰ μὲν τὴν βασιλέως χώραν κ. Id.*Mem*.3.5.26, cf. Plb.4.6.10; τὰς νῆας Id.13.4.1:—Pass., Id.27.7.6. **-ησις**, εως, ἡ, = κακοποιΐα, Lxx 3 *Ma*.3.2, 2 *Es*.4.22. **-ητικός**, ή, όν, *prone to do evil*, τρόπος Aristeas 163, cf. Andronic.Rhod.p.572 M., Hierocl.p.49 A.: Astrol., *maleficent*, ἰδιοτροπία Ptol.*Tetr*.210. **-ῐα**, ἡ, *evil-doing*, Arist. *Rh.Al*.1432$^{a}$9, Chrysipp.*Stoic*.2.249: pl., *injuries*, Isoc.12.122; opp. εὐεργεσίαι, Id.1.26. **-ός**, όν, *doing ill, mischievous*, ὄνειδος Pi.*N*. 8.33; σκεῦος, of a man, Plb.15.25.1; κακοποιοί *evil-doers*, Arist.*EN* 1125$^{a}$18; esp. of poisoners and sorcerers, 1 *Ep.Pet*.4.15; of things, *noxious*, χυλός Thphr.*CP*2.6.4, etc.; φάρμακα *PSI*1.64.21 (i B.C.); τὸ κ. [τῆς ὕλης] Arist.*Ph*.192$^{a}$15: Astrol., *maleficent*, Ptol.*Tetr*.19, Artem.4.59, etc.

**κᾰκο-πολῑτεία**, ἡ, *bad government*, Plb.15.21.3, Plu.*Pomp*.75: pl., Id.*Lyc*.7, Ph.1.41, 601. **-πονητικός**, ή, όν, *unfit for toil*, ἕξις Arist.*Pol*.1335$^{b}$7. **-ποτμος**, ον, *ill-fated, ill-starred*, B.5.138; τύχαι A.*Ag*.1136 (lyr.); ἐμὲ κ. E.*Hel*.694 (lyr.); κ. ὄρνις ἡ κρέξ Arist. *HA*616$^{b}$21. **-πους**, ὁ, ἡ, πουν, τό, gen. ποδος, *with bad feet*, ἵππος X.*Mem*.3.3.4, *Eq*.1.2; εὔπτερα μέν, κακόποδα δέ Arist.*HA*487$^{b}$26.

**κᾰκοπρᾱγ-έω**, *fare ill, fail in an enterprise*, Th.4.55; *to be in ill plight*, Id.2.43; κ. ἀναξίως Arist.*Rh*.1386$^{b}$26, cf. Aphth.*Prog*.1, al.: in physical sense, ἥπατος ἢ γαστρὸς κακοπραγούντων Gal.10.789, al. **-ής**, ές, *evil-doing*, Hsch. **-ία**, ἡ, *misadventure, failure*, αἱ κατ' οἶκον κ. Th.2.60; ἡ ἐκ τῆς Σικελίας κ. Id.8.2; κ. γίγνεται Arist. *Pol*.1296$^{a}$17; ἡ τοῦ πέλας κ. Corn.*Rh*.p.393 H.: pl., κ. ἀνάξιαι Arist. *Rh*.1386$^{b}$10, cf. Plb.8.12.8, Phld.*Herc*.1251.11, Artem.4.56, etc. **b.** *bad physical condition*, Gal.10.255. **II.** *ill-doing*, Lxx *Wi*.5.24, J.*AJ*2.4.4: pl., *misdeeds*, Isoc.15.300. **-μονέω**, *do ill*, Plb.3.2.8, al. **-μοσύνη**, ἡ, *evil-doing*, Democr.297, D.25.101, Plb.4.23.8, al., Phld.*Acad.Ind*.p.54 M. **-μων**, ον, gen. ονος, *doing evil, mis-*

*chievous*, X.*HG*5.2.36, Isoc.15.225,236, Arist.*Ath*.35.3: Sup. -έστατος, περί τι Plb.8.9.3. Adv. -μόνως *Klio* 16.163 (Delph.).

**κᾰκο-πρόσωπος**, ον, *ugly-faced*, Posidipp.43, Plu.2.1058a; τὸ κακοπρόσωπον Xenocr.ap.Stob.4.40.24. **-πτερος**, ον, *with bad wings, weak in the wing*, opp. εὔπτερος, Arist.*HA*617b4, al.; of the Sphinx, as a *bird of ill omen*, Epigr.ap.Sch.E.*Ph*.50. **-πώγων**, ωνος, ὁ, *with a thin beard*, *PPetr*.3 p.23 (iii B.C.).

**κακόρας·** κατακόψας, Euclus ap.Hsch. (Perh. for κα-κορά(α)ς, cf. κοραίω.) **κακόρδαξε·** ἀπεχώρει, Hsch.

**κᾰκορέκτης**, ου, ὁ, (ὀρέγω) *with evil yearnings*, ἀνήρ Adam.2.39.

**κᾰκο-ρρᾰφεύς**, έως, ὁ, = κακοποιός, Hsch. **-ρρᾰφία**, ἡ, *contrivance of ill, mischievousness*, κακορραφίης ἀλεγεινῆς Il.15.16; κακορραφίῃσι νόοιο Od.2.236; μή τι κακορραφίῃ ἀλεγεινῇ .. ἀλγήσετε 12.26. **-ρρέκτης**, ου, ὁ, (ῥέζω) *evil-doer*, A.R.3.595. **-ρρημοσύνη**, ἡ, *evil-speaking*, Plb.8.10.3; *slander*, Poll.8.80. **-ρρήμων**, ον, gen. ονος, (ῥῆμα) *telling of ill, ill-omened*, A.*Ag*.1155 (lyr.). 2. *a poor speaker*, D.C.77.11. II. τὸ κ., = foreg., Suid. s. v. Ἀρχίλοχος. Adv. -όνως Poll.8.81. **-ρροθέω**, = κακολογέω: c. acc., *abuse, revile*, E.*Hipp*.340, *Alc*.707, Ar.*Ach*.577, *Th*.896. **-ρροος**, ον, contr. **-ρρους**, ουν, *bringing a grievous flux*, of disease, dub. in Ἀρχ.Ἐφ. 1920.80 (Crete, vi B.C.). **-ρρυγχος**, ον, *with ugly muzzles*, παιδία Arr.*Epict*.3.22.77. **-ρρυθμος**, ον, *in bad rhythm* (κακόρυθμ-), Phld.*Rh*.1.162 S.; τὸ κ. Id.*Po.Herc*.1676.8; of the pulse, Gal.19.409. **-ρρῠπος**, ον, *filthy*, Aesop.73 (= Babr.10.1).

® **κᾰκός**, ή, όν, *bad*: I. of persons, 1. of appearance, *ugly*, εἶδος μὲν ἔην κακός Il.10.316, cf. Paus.8.49.3. 2. of birth, *ill-born, mean*, γένος ἐστὲ διοτρεφέων βασιλήων.., ἐπεὶ οὔ κε κακοὶ τοιούσδε τέκοιεν Od.4.64; Ζεὺς δ' αὐτὸς νέμει ὄλβον.. ἐσθλοῖς ἠδὲ κακοῖσι 6.189; οὐ κακὸν οὐδὲ μὲν ἐσθλόν 22.415; οὐδ' ἐὰν .. φανῶ τρίδουλος, ἐκφανῇ κακή S.*OT*1063; κακός τ' ὢν κἀκ κακῶν ib.1397. 3. of courage, *craven, base*, Il.2.365, 6.489; κακοῦ τρέπεται χρὼς ἄλλυδις ἄλλῃ (called δειλὸς ἀνήρ in the line above) 13.279; Ἕκτωρ σε κ. καὶ ἀνάλκιδα φήσει 8.153, cf. Od.3.375; κ. καὶ ἀνήνορα 10.301; οἵτινες .. ἐγένοντο ἄνδρες κ. ἢ ἀγαθοὶ ἐν τῇ ναυμαχίῃ Hdt.6.14; κ. καὶ ἄθυμος Id.7.11; οὐδαμῶν κακίονες ib.104; κακοὺς πρὸς αἰχμήν S.*Ph*.1306; κακὴ τ' ἐς ἀλκὴν καὶ σίδηρον εἰσορᾶν E.*Med*.264; οὐδενὶ ἐπιτρέψοντας κακῷ εἶναι X.*An*.3.2.31. 4. *bad* of his kind, i.e. *worthless, sorry, unskilled*, ἡνίοχοι Il.17.487; [τοξότης] ἢ κ. ἢ ἀγαθός ib.632; νομῆες Od.17.246; κ. ἀλήτης a *bad beggar*, ib.578; ἰατρός A.*Pr*.473; κυβερνήτης, ναύτης, E.*Supp*.880, *Andr*.457; μάγειρος Pl.*Phdr*.265e: c. acc. modi, πάντα γὰρ οὐ κακός εἰμι I am not *bad* in all things, Od.8.214; κ. γνώμην S.*Ph*.910: also c. dat., κακοὶ γνώμαισι Id.*Aj*.964: c. inf., κ. μανθάνειν Id.*OT*545; [νῆσος] φυτεύεσθαι κακή *Trag.Adesp*.393; cf. II. 5. in moral sense, *base, evil*, Od.11.384, Hes.*Op*.240; opp. χρηστός, S.*Ant*.520; ὦ κακῶν κάκιστε Id.*OT*334, *Ph*.984; πλεῖστον κάκιστος Id.*OC*744; κ. πρός τινας Th.1.86; εἰς φίλους E.*Or*.424 codd.; περὶ τὰ χρήματα Pl.*Clit*. 407c. 6. *wretched*, Herod.3.42. II. of things, *evil, pernicious*, freq. in Hom., etc., as δαίμων, θάνατος, μοῖρα, αἶσα, κῆρες, νοῦσος, ἕλκος, φάρμακα, ὀδύναι, Od.10.64, Il.3.173, 13.602, 1.418, Od.2.316, Il.1.10, 2.723, 22.94, 5.766; χόλος, ἔρις, Il.16.206, Od.3.161; πόλεμος, ἔπος, ἔργα, Il.4.82, 24.767, Od.2.67, al.; ἦμαρ, ἄνεμος, Il.9.251, Od.5.109; of omens and the like, *unlucky*, ὄρνις, ὄναρ, σῆμα, Il.24.219, 10.496, 22.30: also in Trag., κ. τύχη, δαίμων, μόρος, S.*Tr*.328, A.*Pers*.354, 369, etc.; of words, *abusive, foul*, κ. λόγοι S.*Ant*.259, cf. *Tr*.461; κ. ποιμήν, i.e. the storm, A.*Ag*.657: Astrol., *unlucky*, τόποι Heph.Astr.1.12; κ. τύχη, name for the sixth region, Paul.Al.*M*.1.

B. κακόν, τό, and κακά, τά, as Subst., *evil, ill*, δίδου δ' ἀγαθόν τε κακόν τε Od.8.63; ἀθάνατον κακόν 12.118; ἐκ μεγάλων κακῶν πεφευγέναι Hdt.1.65; so κ. ἄμαχον, ἄπρηκτα, Pi.*P*.2.76, *I*.8(7).8; ἔκπαγλον, ἄφερτον, ἀμήχανον, etc., A.*Ag*.862, 1102, E.*Med*.447, etc.; κακὸν ἥκει τινί there's *trouble* in store for some one, Ar.*Ra*.552; δυοῖν ἀποκρίνας κακοῖν the least of two *evils*, S.*OT*640, cf. *OC*496; κακῶν Ἰλιάς, v. Ἰλιάς; κακόν τι ῥέξαι τινά to do *harm* or *ill* to any one, Il.2.195, etc.; πολλὰ κάκ' ἀνθρώποισιν ἐώργει Od.14.289; κακὰ φέρειν, τεύχειν τινί, Il.2.304, Hes.*Op*.265; κακόν τι (or κακὰ) ποιεῖν τινα (v. δράω, ποιέω, ἐργάζομαι); κακὸν πάσχειν ὑπό τινος to suffer *evil* from one, Th.8.48, etc.: in Trag. freq. repeated, κακὰ κακῶν, = τὰ κάκιστα, S.*OC*1238 (lyr.); εἴ τι πρεσβύτερον ἔτι κακοῦ κακόν Id.*OT*1365 (lyr.); δεινὰ πρὸς κακοῖς κακά Id.*OC*595, cf. *Ant*.1281; δόσιν κακὰν κακῶν κακοῖς A.*Pers*.1041 (lyr.). 2. κακά, τά, *evil words, reproaches*, πολλά τε καὶ κακὰ λέγειν Hdt.8.61, cf. A.*Th*.571, S.*Aj*.1244, *Ph*.382, etc. 3. Philos., κακόν, τό, *Evil*, *Stoic*.3.18, al., Plot.1.8.1, al. 4. of a person, *pest, nuisance*, τουτὶ παρέξει τὸ κ. ἡμῖν πράγματα Ar.*Av*.931; also, comically, ὅσον συνείλεκται κακὸν ὀρνέων what a *devil* of a lot of birds, ib.294.

C. degrees of Comparison: 1. regul. Comp. in Ep., κακώτερος Od.6.275, 15.343, Theoc.27.22, A.R.3.421, etc.: also in late Prose, Alciphr.3.62: irreg. κακίων, ον [with ῑ], Od.2.277, Thgn.262, etc., with ῐ in Trag., exc. E.*Fr*.546 (anap.); κακιότερος *AP*12.7 (Strato). 2. Sup. κάκιστος Hom., etc.—Cf. also χείρων, χείριστος, and ἥσσων, ἥκιστος.

D. Adv. κακῶς *ill*, ἢ εὖ ἠὲ κακῶς Il.2.253, etc.; κακῶς ποιεῖν τινα to treat one *ill*; κακῶς ποιεῖν τι to hurt, damage a thing; κακῶς ποιεῖν τινά τι to do one any evil or harm; κ. πράσσειν to fare *ill*, A.*Pr*.266, etc.; κάκιον ἢ πρότερον πράττειν And.4.11; κ. ἔχειν Ar.*Ra*.58, etc.; of illness, *Ev.Matt*.4.24; rarely κακῶς πάσχειν A.*Pr*.759, 1041 (anap.); χρῆν Κανδαύλῃ γενέσθαι κ. Hdt.1.8; κ. ὄλοισθε S.*Ph*.1035, etc.; with play on two senses, ὡς κ. ἔχει ἅπας ἰατρός, ἂν κ. μηδεὶς ἔχῃ Philem.Jun.2; κ. ἐρεῖν τινά, λέγειν τὴν πόλιν, Mimn.7.4, Ar.*Ach*.503; κ. εἰδότες, = ἀγνοοῦντες, X.*Cyr*.2.3.13, Isoc.8.32, cf. Hyp.*Eux*.33; κακῶς ἐκπέφευγα I have *barely* escaped, D.21.126: Comp. κάκιον Hdt.1.109, S.*OT*428, And. l. c., Pl.*Mx*.236a, etc.: Sup. κάκιστα Ar.*Ra*.1456, *Pax* 2, Pl.*R*.420b, etc. 2. Adv. and Adj. freq. coupled in Trag., Att., etc., κακὸν κακῶς νιν .. ἐκτρῖψαι βίον S.*OT*248; κακὸς κακῶς ταφήσῃ E.*Tr*.446 (troch.); ἀπό σ' ὀλῶ κακὸν κακῶς Ar.*Pl*.65, cf. *Eq*.189, 190, D.32.6, Procop.*Pers*.1.24; κακοὺς κακῶς ἀπολέσει αὐτούς *Ev.Matt*.21.41; κακοὺς κάκιστα S.*Aj*.839; in reversed order, ὥσπερ ἀξία κακῶς κακὴ θανεῖται E.*Tr*.1055; with intervening words, κακῶς .. ἀπόλλυσθαι κακούς S.*Ph*.1369, cf. E.*Cyc*.268, Ar.*Eq*.2. (Perh. cogn. with Avest. *kasu-*, Comp. *kasyah-*, Sup. *kasišta-* 'small', Lith. *nukašėti* 'grow feeble, thin', Germ. *hager*.)

**κᾰκό-σημος**, ον, gloss on ἄσημος, Sch.rec.S.*Ant*.1013. **-σῖνος**, ον, *very harmful*, in Sup. -ώτατος (v.l. -ώτερος) Hp.*Fract*.46. **-σῑτία**, Ion. -ίη, ἡ, *lack of appetite*, Archig.ap.Orib.8.23.3, Poll.6.36; κ. στομάχου Aret.*SD*1.6. ® **-σῖτος**, ον, *eating badly*, i.e. *having a poor appetite, fastidious*, Hp.*Steril*.215, Eub.17; ὁ περὶ τὰ σιτία δυσχερής Pl.*R*.475c, Ael.*NA*3.45, cf. Arr.*Cyn*.8.2. 2. metaph., *fastidious*, πρὸς Κύπριν οὐ κ. (of Priapus), Ἀρχ.Δελτ.2 *App*.47 (Thyrrheum). **-σκελής**, ές, *with bad legs*, ἵππος X.*Mem*.3.3.4. **-σκήνης**, ες, *of a bad, mean body*, *AP*7.401 (Crin.).

**κᾰκοσμ-ία**, ἡ, *a bad smell*, Poll.2.75. **-ος**, ον, *ill-smelling*, A.*Fr*.180.2, S.*Fr*.565, Ar.*Pax* 38.

**κᾰκό-σπερμος**, ον, *with bad seed*, Thphr.*HP*7.4.4. **-σπλαγχνος**, ον, *faint-hearted*, A.*Th*.237. **-σπορία**, poet. -ίη, ἡ, *impious sowing*, *AP*7.175 (Antiphil.). **-στᾰθέω**, *to be in bad case*, Nic.*Th*.431; of the wind, *to be contrary*, ib.269. **-στένακτος**, ον, *sighing lamentably*, Sch.Ar.*Th*.1068, Sch.rec.A.*Th*.856. **-στέφᾰνος**, ον, gloss on ἀστέφανος, Sch.E.*Andr*.1020. **-στόμᾰτος**, ον, *foul-mouthed*, sens. obsc., = Lat. *fellator*, *AP*11.155 (Lucill.).

**κᾰκοστομᾰχ-έω**, *have a sensitive stomach*, S.E.*M*.11.212. **-ία**, ἡ, *bad state of the stomach*, Gal.14.735. **-ος**, ον, *having a sensitive stomach*, Cic.*Fam*.16.4.1, Aët.8.45; f.l. in *AP*11.155; cf. κακοστόματος. II. Act., *bad for the stomach, unwholesome*, Heraclid. Tarent.ap.Ath.3.120c, Philistion Locr.ap.eund.3.115d, Dsc.1.127, al., Sor.1.94, Gal.6.641: Comp. -ώτερος Diph.Siph.ap Ath.2.56b.

**κᾰκοστομ-έω**, *revile*, τινα S.*El*.597. **-ία**, ἡ, *faulty pronunciation*, Str.14.2.28. **-ος**, ον, *foul-mouthed*, λέσχαι E.*IA* 1001. 2. *lacking in eloquence*, Ptol.*Tetr*.166. II. *bad to pronounce, ill-sounding*, Longin.43.1.

**κᾰκό-στρωτος**, ον, *ill-spread*, i.e. *rugged*, A.*Ag*.556. **-συμβίβαστος** [ῐ], ον, *hard to reconcile*, Eust.1946.13. **-σύμβουλος**, = *malesuadus*, Gloss. **-συνάντητος**, ον, gloss on δυσαντής, Sch. Opp.*H*.1.370. **-σύνετος**, ον, *of bad understanding*, Eustr.*in EN* 368.31; cf. -ξύνετος. ® **-συνθεσία**, ἡ, gloss on κακορραφία, Hsch.:—also -σύνθεσις, εως, ἡ, Phot., Suid. **-σύνθετος**, ον, *ill-composed*, in Rhet., Quint.8.3.59; ἔπη Luc.*Cal*.14; λόγος Sch.E.*Or*.674; *ill put together*, κ. τὸ σῶμα Sch.Ar.*V*.818. Adv. -τως Sch.E.*Hec*.801, al. **-συνταξία**, ἡ, *bad grammar*, Eust.210.29, al. **-σφαιρος**, ον, *ill-rounded*, Tz.*H*.11.492. **-σφυκτος**, ον, *with a bad pulse*, Gal.9.831. **-σφυξία**, Ion. -ίη, ἡ, *bad pulse*, Aret.*SA*2.8, Gal.6.238. **-σχημος**, ον, *badly formed*, of a period, Sch.E.*Or*.307, cf. Hdn.*Epim*.177. **-σχήμων**, ον, gen. ονος, *unseemly*, only in Adv. -νως Lib.*Or*.25.15; Sup. -ονέστατα Pl.*Lg*.728b.

**κᾰκοσχολ-εύομαι**, *play mischievous tricks*, Porph.*Ep.Aneb*.26; in mal. part., Hsch. s. v. ὀρχιπεδίζειν. **-έω**, of children, *to be mischievous*, Chrysipp.*Stoic*.3.77; πρὸς ἡδονὴν Theano *Ep*.4.3. **-ία**, ἡ, *mischief, malpractice*, *Delph*.3(1).362 i 32 (ii B.C.), Plu.2.274d. **-ος**, ον, (σχολή) *mischievous, frivolous*, Arr.*Epict*.2.19.15; κακόσχολε *naughty!* *AP*5.103 (Marc. Arg.). Adv. -λως, οἰκονομεῖν act *with frivolous delay*, Ptol.Philad.ap.Aristeam 24; *frivolously*, προσφιλονεικεῖν, ἐγκαλεῖν, Simp.*in Cat*.67.15, *in Ph*.433.7; τὰ καλῶς λεγόμενα -λως ἐκδεχόμενον ἀδόκιμα δεικνύναι Id.*in Cat*.7.27; also, = κακεμφάτως, Tryph.*Trop*.p.193 S., *EM*634.6, Sch.Ar.*Ach*.397, Eust.1638.17. II. Act., κ. πνοαί winds *that enforce harmful idleness*, A.*Ag*.193 (lyr.).

**κᾰκό-τακτος**, ον, gloss on δύστακτος, Hsch. **-τᾰφος**, ον, gloss on ἀτύμβευτος, Sch.Opp.*H*.5.346. **-τεκνία**, ἡ, *having bad children*, Phryn.*PS* p.80 B. **-τελεύτητος**, ον, *ending ill*, Sch.A.*Pers*.910. **-τέρμων**, ον, gen. ονος, *ending ill* or *with difficulty*, ψυγμός Poet.*de Herb*.94.

® **κᾰκοτεχν-έω**, *use base arts, deal fraudulently*, ἔς τινα Hdt.6.74, *PEleph*.1.9 (iv B.C.); περὶ τὰς δίκας D.46.25: abs., Antipho 1.22, D.29.11, 35.56. 2. Rhet., *use false artifices* of style, Demetr.*Eloc*.28, 250. II. trans., *misuse*, τινὰ περὶ τὸ σῶμα Arr.*Epict*.4.6.4; *mislead*, τοὺς νέους Aristaenet.2.18. 2. *falsify*, οὐ κακοτεχνησῶ οὐδὲν τῶν .. γεγραμμένων *GDI*5039.19 (Hierapytna); *counterfeit, imitate*, [αἱματίτης] κεκακοτεχνημένος Dsc.5.126. **-ημα**, ατος, τό, *base art*, Oenom.ap.Eus.*PE*5.24. **-ής**, ές, = κακότεχνος, Luc.*Cal*.10 (Comp.). **-ία**, ἡ, *base artifice, malpractice*, Heraclit.[129], *PRein*.16.26 (ii B.C.), *OGI*669.55 (Egypt, i A.D.), *CIG*2712.15 (Mylasa), Ph.1.636, Iamb.*Myst*.10.2 (pl.): freq. in pl., as law-term, *fraudulent* or *malicious conspiracy*, κακοτεχνιῶν διαδικάζεσθαι Pl.*Lg*.936d; esp. *subornation of perjury*, D.47.1, 49.56; δόλοι καὶ ἐπιορκίαι καὶ κ. Luc.*Alex*.4. II. *bad art*, applied to forensic oratory by Epicur.*Fr*.51: generally, Plu.2.228b: esp. in Rhet., *false artifice*, Demetr.*Eloc*.27, 247, Luc.*Par*.27, Ath.14.631f: pl., ἡδονὰς καὶ κ. εἰσάγων Str.7.3.7. **-ίζω**, = κακοτεχνέω, Alc.Com.7. **-ίου** (sc. δίκη), = κακοτεχνιῶν, Lys.*Fr*.116. **-ος**, ον, (τέχνη) *using evil practices, artful*, δόλος Il.15.14: esp. in mal. part., *lascivious*, *AP*5.

128 (Autom.): Sup., ib.131 (Phld., v.l. κατατ-); of songs, Plu.2.706d. Adv. -νως *with bad art*, Ph.1.195.

**κᾰκότης**, ητος, ἡ, (κακός) *badness*: I. of moral character, *baseness, cowardice*, Il.2.368, 13.108, Od.24.455; ἀτιμίη καὶ κ. Tyrt.10.10; κ. καὶ δειλία Th.5.100; οὐδεμιῇ κ. λειφθῆναι τῆς ναυμαχίης not through *cowardice*, Hdt.7.168. 2. *wickedness, vice*, τείσασθαι Ἀλέξ-ανδρον κακότητος Il.3.366, cf. Hes.*Op.*287, Democr.178; κακότητος ἄπειροι Emp.112.3; κακότητ' ἀσκεῖν A.*Pr.*1066 (anap.); ἄνευ κακότητος [συμφορά] Antipho 6.1: pl., Emp.145. II. of condition, *evil case, distress, misery*, ἐκφυγέειν κακότητα Od.5.414, cf. 290, 379, 397, Pi.*P.*2.35, Hdt.2.128, 6.67, S.*El.*236 (lyr.); esp. in war, Τρῶες ἀνέπνευσαν κακότητος Il.11.382, cf. 12.332, Hdt.8.109, etc.: pl., *distresses, miseries*, Alc.59, E.*Fr.*303 codd. (lyr.); αἱ ἐντὸς κ. Pl.*Ax.*366a. III. of quality, *badness*, τῶν οὔρων Hp.*Epid.*3.10: pl., *bad qualities*, Id.*Acut.*57.

**κᾰκοτράχηλος** [τρᾰ], ον, gloss on ἀτράχηλος, Apollon.*Lex.* s.v. ἀ.

**κᾰκοτροπ-εύομαι**, *deal perversely*, πρός τινα Plb.5.2.9, cf. *AB* 354. -έω, *become malignant*, of ulcers, Hp.*Mul.*1.38. -ία, ἡ, *badness of habits, mischievousness*, Th.3.83, D.C.54.21, Artem.4.63; in argument, *malice, unfairness*, Simp.*in Cael.*156.27. ⊛ -ος, ον, *malignant*, D.C.52.2, Vett.Val.74.12, *PMasp.*97 ii 20 (vi A.D.): Comp., D.C.*Fr.*85.1: Sup., Zen.5.41. Adv. -πως D.C.47.4. 2. of animals, *mischievous*, κτήνη *Hippiatr.*129. II. Medic., *malignant*, Antyll.ap.Orib.9.23.13.

**κᾰκοτροφ-έω**, *have poor nourishment*, κακοτροφήσας Thphr.*HP* 5.2.2:—also in Pass., κακοτροφηθείς ibid. II. Pass., *to be ill cared for*, of vines, Theano *Ep.*4.4. -ία, ἡ, *poor nourishment*, Thphr.*HP*5.2.3; *malnutrition*, Gal.7.73.

**κᾰκοτῠχ-έω**, *to be unfortunate*, Th.2.60, D.C.*Fr.*36.15. II. Astrol., *occupy the region named κακὴ τύχη*, Vett.Val.66.7. -ής, ές, *unfortunate*, used by E. in lyr., *Med.*1274, *Hipp.*669: Sup., ib. 679; τὸ κ., = sq., Id.*HF*133; κ. καὶ ἄθλιον γένος Sch.rec.A.*Pers.* 1013, cf. *Cat.Cod.Astr.*8(4).142. -ία, ἡ, *misfortune*, Eust.1422.44.

**κακουβαι**, gloss on *uniones* (*onions*), *Gloss.* (dub. l.).

**κάκουλοι**· κακοί, σκληροί, κύαμοι, Hsch.

**κακόϋπνος**, ον, gloss on ἄϋπνος, Hsch.

**κᾰκοϋπονόητος**, ον, (ὑπονοέω) gloss on δυστόπαστος, Suid.

⊛ **κᾰκουργ-έω**, *do evil, work wickedness*, E.*Or.*823 (lyr.), etc.; κ. τι Antipho 2.3.2; μηδὲν κ. Pl.*Prt.*326a; περί τινας Id.*R.*416d; ἵππος ἢν κακουργῇ *be vicious*, X.*Oec.*3.11; ἀδικεῖν καὶ κ. Ar.*Nu.*1175; κ. καὶ ἐξαμαρτάνειν Pl.*Hp.Mi.*375d:—Pass., εὑρέν τι -ηθέν found that *a fraud had been committed*, *POxy.*1468.19 (iii A.D.). 2. of discussion, κ. ἐν τοῖς λόγοις *use captious* or *unfair arguments*, Pl.*Grg.* 489b, cf. 483a, Arist.*Rh.*1404$^b$39. 3. of things, ὁ . . ἱδρὼς κακουργεῖ X.*Mem.*1.4.6. II. c. acc. pers., *maltreat, injure*, A.*Fr.*266, E.*Supp.*537; κ. ἀλλήλους καὶ ἀδικεῖν Pl.*Lg.*679e. 2. c. acc. rei, *ravage* a country, τὴν Εὔβοιαν Th.2.32, cf. 3.1; κ. τὴν χώραν καὶ τὰ κτήματα Pl.*Lg.*760e, etc.; κ. τὸν λόγον *spoil* the argument, Id.*R.* 338d. 3. *corrupt, falsify*, τοὺς νόμους D.24.65:—Pass., τὰ ἀληθῆ καὶ μὴ κακουργούμενα τῶν πραγμάτων Id.31.8. 4. c. dat., κ. τοῖς προβάτοις, of dogs, Pl.*R.*416a. -ημα, ατος, τό, *knavish trick, fraud*, Id.*Lg.*933e, D.18.31, 24.86, etc.; τὰ ἐν τοῖς συμβολαίοις κ. Pl.*R.*426e; *crime*, Antipho 5.10, etc. -ία [ῐ], Ep. κακοεργίη [ῑ metri gr.], ἡ, *wickedness, villainy, malice*, ὡς κακοεργίης εὐεργεσίη μέγ' ἀμείνων Od.22.374, cf. Th.1.37, etc.; of a horse, *vice*, X.*Eq.Mag.* 1.15: in pl., *malpractices*, τὰ κιβδηλεύματά τε καὶ κ. τῶν πωλούντων Pl.*Lg.*917e: κ. καὶ ἀπάται καὶ δολώσεις X.*Cyr.*1.6.28, etc. II. *bad workmanship*, only in form κακοεργία Pl.*R.*422a. III. *injury*, τῆς ἑαυτοῦ πόλεως ib.434c: pl., *ill effects*, ἀποκρούειν τὰς τῶν φαρμάκων κ. Dsc.1.90. -ικός, ή, όν, *malicious*, ἀδικήματα Arist. *Rh.*1391$^a$18. -ος, Ep. κακοεργός (also late Prose, Porph.*Abst.* 2.38; δαιμόνια κακοεργά Aen.Gaz.*Thphr.*p.60 B.), ον, (ἔργον) *doing ill, mischievous, knavish*, once in Hom., ἀλλά με γαστὴρ ὀτρύνει κακοεργὸς *importunate*, Od.18.54; freq. later, κλῶπες κακοῦργοι Hdt. 1.41; κ. ἀνήρ S.*Aj.*1043; also κακουργότατος λόγος D.20.125; κ. μάχαιρα *AP*11.136 (Lucill.); -ότατα εἰπεῖν Antipho 2.4.2. Adv. -γως Poll.3.132. 2. as Subst., *malefactor, criminal* in the eye of the law, Ps.-Phoc.133, Th.1.134, *PLille* 1.7.20 (iii B.C.), *Ev.Luc.* 23.32, etc.; οὐδεὶς κακοεργός Theoc.15.47; at Athens, technically, *thief, robber*, ὁ τῶν κακούργων νόμος Antipho 5.9, cf. 16, Lys.13.78, D.22.28, 24.102. II. c. gen., *doing harm to*, κ. μὲν τῶν ἄλλων, ἑαυτοῦ δὲ πολὺ -ότερος, X.*Mem.*1.5.3, cf. Pl.*R.*421b: abs., *harmful*, κ. ἐπιθυμίαι ib.554c; καρτερία Id.*La.*192d; ἄγνοια -οτάτη καὶ αἰσχίστη Id.*Alc.*1.118a.

**κᾰκουχ-έω**, (ἔχω) *wrong, injure*, αὐτόν Teles p.34 H.; *maltreat*, esp. a wife, Mitteis *Chr.*284.6 (ii B.C.), *POxy.*281.17 (i A.D.), etc.:—Pass., *to be afflicted* or *injured*, Lxx 3*Ki.*2.26; ὑπὸ τοῦ δηγμοῦ D.S.3. 23; κακουχουμένους τελευτῆσαι τὸν βίον Plu.2.114e. ⊛ -ία, ἡ, *maltreatment*, Pl.*R.*615b; of a wife, *BGU*1105.18 (Aug.); '*mobbing*', Plb.5.15.6 (dub. l.); ἐν χθονὸς κ. *devastation*, A.*Th.*668. II. = καχεξία, *bad condition*, Alex.80; *misery, distress*, Plb.3.64.8, Vett. Val.127.13: pl., of ascetic practices, μάτην ἑαυτοὺς καταικισάμενοι ταῖς κ. Plu.2.117f.

**κᾰκό-φᾰτις**, ιδος, ἡ, *ill-sounding, ill-omened*, βοά A.*Pers.*936 (lyr.). -φημία, ἡ, *evil report*, ἡ ἐκ τῶν πολλῶν κ. Ael.*VH*3. 7. -φημίζω, = *inclamo*, *Gloss.* -φημος, ον, *ill-sounding, ominous*, Sch.S.*Aj.*214; τὸ κ. *evil* or *ominous words*, J.*BJ*6.5.3; of persons, *foul-mouthed*, Ptol.*Tetr.*166. Adv. -μως *with evil words, abusively*, Man.5.323. -φθαρτος, ον, *wasted away*, Hsch. s.v. κακόκνημος. -φθόρος, ον, *destructive, deadly*, Nic.*Th.* 795, *Al.*168: heterocl. gen. κακοφθορέος (as if from -φθορεύς) ib. 465. -φῐλος, ὁ, *bad friend*, Phld.*Lib.*p.24 O., *Cat.Cod.Astr.*8(4). 146. -φλοιος, ον, *with bad rind*, v.l. for κακό-χλοος (q.v.), Nic. *Al.*331. -φονος, ον, gloss on ἀπόφονος, Sch.E.*Or.*163. -φορεσία, ἡ, gloss on δυσχλαινία, Sch.E.*Hec.*240.

**κᾰκοφρᾰδ-ής**, ές, (φράζομαι) poet. word, *bad in counsel, foolish*, Αἶαν, νεῖκος ἄριστε, κακοφραδές Il.23.483, cf. A.R.3.936: neut., κακοφραδές, as Adv., *foolishly*, Euph.98.2. -ία, Ion. -ίη, ἡ, *folly*, κακοφραδίῃσι τιθήνης *h.Cer.*227: sg., Nic.*Th.*348, Q.S.12.554. -μοσύνη, ἡ, = foreg., Democr.273, Orph.*Fr.*285.41 (pl.).

**κᾰκοφράσμων**, ον, gen. ονος, = κακοφραδής, prob. in Theoc.4.22; v. -χράσμων.

**κᾰκό-φραστος**, ον, *ill-conceived*, Sch.E.*Or.*674. -φρονέω, *bear ill-will* or *malice*, A.*Ag.*1174 (lyr.). II. *to be foolish*, Sch.E.*Or.* 821. -φρονίζω, *stultify*, Aq.2*Ki.*15.31. -φροσύνη, ἡ, *folly*, Lxx *Pr.*16.18, Opp.*H.*3.363 (pl.). -φρων, ον, gen. ονος, (φρήν) *ill-minded, malignant*, πραπίδων καρπός Pi.*Fr.*211, cf. E.*Heracl.*372 (lyr.), *Supp.*744; κ. [μέριμνα] A.*Ag.*100 (anap.): in late Prose, Porph. *Abst.*2.7. II. *imprudent, heedless*, S.*Ant.*1104, E.*Or.*824 (lyr.).

**κᾰκοφῠ-ής**, ές, (φυή) *of bad natural qualities*, κατὰ τὴν ψυχήν Pl. *R.*410a. II. (φύομαι) *growing ill*, Thphr.*HP*8.11.8; σπόρος *PTeb.* 61(*b*).370 (ii B.C.). -ΐα, ἡ, *bad natural qualities*, Pl.*Def.*416.

**κᾰκοφων-έω**, *speak ill*, opp. καλλιφωνέω, prob. in Phld.*Rh.*1.176 S. -ία, ἡ, *ill-sound*, of a name, Str.13.2.4; *cacophony*, Demetr. *Eloc.*255, A.D.*Conj.*228.20; opp. εὐφωνία, Phld.*Po.Herc.*994.23: dist. fr. δυσφωνία, Gal.7.59. -ος, ον, *ill-sounding, not producing agreeable sounds*, τὰ ξηρὰ κ. Arist.*Aud.*802$^b$23; *with a bad voice*, τραγῳδός D.T.631.21, Phlp. *in de An.*533.32; opp. εὔφωνος, Phld.*Po. Herc.*994 *Fr.*11; of words, *cacophonous*, D.H.*Comp.*12, cf. 16 (Sup.), D.T.631.20; τὸ κ., = κακοφωνία, Sch.Ar.*Eq.*248.

**κᾰκό-χαρτος**, ον, *rejoicing in evil*, Ἔρις, ζῆλος, Hes.*Op.*28, 196, cf. Hsch. -χείμερος, ον, *unfitted to endure winter*, Sor.1.41. -χλοος, ον, *with poor foliage*, Nic.*Al.*331 (-χλοίοιο metri gr., Schneid.). -χορος, ον, gloss on ἄχορος, Hsch. -χρήσμων, Dor. -χράσμων, ον, gen. ονος, (χράομαι) *difficult to live with*, v.l. for -φράσμων, Theoc.4. 22, cf. Sch. ad loc. -χρηστος, ον, *ill-used*, Sch.Philostr.*Her.* p.412 B. -χροέω, *to be of a bad complexion*, Dsc.1.128. -χροια, ἡ, *bad complexion*, Ruf.ap.Orib.45.30.48, Gal.17(2).215; of a corpse, Phld.*Mort.*30: pl., *blotches*, Dsc.3.1, Gal.6.814. -χροος, ον, contr. -χρους, ουν, *of bad complexion*, Hp.*Prorrh.*2.42, *Aff.*20; *of bad coloration*, Arist.*HA*616$^b$31; *of bad colour*, κύμη Nic.*Fr.*85.5; ὀφθαλμοί Gal.17(2).214; of urine, Id.19.598. -χῡλος, ον, *with bad juice* or *flavour*, μῆλα Diph.Siph.ap.Ath.2.54a: Comp., ib.68f, 3.80c, Diocl. *Fr.*138; of meat, Sor.1.94. -χῡμία, ἡ, *unhealthy state of the humours*, Gal.6.553, 10.891: pl., Dsc.2.87. 2. *unwholesomeness*, τροφῶν Gal.6.749. -χῡμος, *with unhealthy juices*, Arist.*Pr.*954$^a$ 10, Ath.1.24f (Sup.), Hices.ib.7.309b, Dsc.2.88; τὸ κ. Alex.Aphr. *Pr.*2.10. 2. *unwholesome*, of foods, Gal.6.641. 3. *having an unpleasant taste*, S.E.*P.*1.52.

**κάκοψις** [ᾰ], ιδος, ἡ, *short-sighted*, *PLips.*1.9 (ii B.C.), *PGrenf.*2.28 (ii B.C.); *sinister*, Vett.Val.14.23.

⊛ **κᾰκό-ψογος**, ον, *malignantly blaming, censorious*, πόλις Thgn.287, cf. Ptol.*Tetr.*166. -ψῡχία, ἡ, = κακοφυΐα, *bad natural qualities*, opp. εὐψυχία, Pl.*Lg.*791c.

⊛ **κᾰκόω**, *maltreat, distress*, in Hom. always of persons, κεκακωμένοι ἐν Πύλῳ ἦμεν, ἐλθὼν γάρ ῥ' ἐκάκωσε βίη Ἡρακληείη Il.11.689; μηδὲ . . κάκου κεκακωμένον *afflict* not *the afflicted*, Od.4.754; ἦμὲν κυδῆναι . . βροτὸν ἠδὲ κακῶσαι 16.212, cf. 20.99; ὅσοι παθόντες εὖ κακοῦσί μ' ἐκδίκως A.*Pr.*976; κ. [θεὸς] δῶμα Id.*Fr.*156; κ. τοὺς ἀναιτίους E.*HF* 1162; τοὺς Ἀθηναίους Th.8.32; τὸν δῆμον Lys.13.91; ἑαυτούς Pl. *Mx.*248c:—in Pass., *to be in ill plight, be distressed*, κεκακωμένος ἅλμῃ *befouled* with brine, Od.6.137 (v. supr.): generally, Hdt.1.170, al., A.*Pers.*728 (troch.), S.*OC*261, And.2.16, Th.4.25; πρὸς θεῶν κακοῦται E.*Hel.*268; ἐκάκωτο ὑπὸ τῆς πορείας X.*An.*4.5.35; ἐκ πυρετοῖο *AP*11. 382.1 (Agath.). 2. of things, *spoil, ruin*, τὰ κοινά Hdt.3.82; τὸ ναυτικόν Th.8.78; of the air, *injure* a plant, Thphr.*CP*2.11.2; τὰ κακούμενα τῆς χώρας Aen.Tact.15.1: Astrol., *render unpropitious*, Vett. Val.70.22 (Pass.): physically, *injure, paralyse*, τὰς ἀρχὰς τῶν νεύρων Gal.2.690:—Pass., κακοῦται πᾶν τὸ σκέλος *deteriorates*, Hp.*Art.*58.

**κακτάμεναι, κάκτανε, κάκτεινε**, v. κατακτείνω.

**κάκτος**, ἡ, *cardoon*, *Cynara Cardunculus*, Thphr.*HP*6.4.10, Philet. 16, Theoc.10.4, Antig.*Mir.*8, Dsc.*Alex.*33. 2. κάκτος, ὁ, *the fruit*, μακωνίδες, μάραθα, τραχέες τε κάκτοι Epich.159; also the edible leaf, Thphr. l.c.

**κάκυνσις** [ᾰ], εως, ἡ, *corrupting*, Sch.E.*Hec.*251.

**κακύνω**, *damage*, in prev., κ. τὸν πηλόν· τὸν ἄξιον ὕβρεως ὑβρίζειν, Suid.; τὰς τύχας Antioch.Astr. in *Cat.Cod.Astr.*8(3).105:—Pass., *turn bad*, Thphr.*Od.*56. 2. in moral sense, *corrupt*, *Com.Adesp.* 138:—usu. in Pass., *to be corrupted*, D.C.60.2: esp. *become bad*, E. *Hec.*251, Pl.*Ti.*42c; of soldiers, *show cowardice*, v.l. for μαλακύνω, X.*Cyr.*6.3.27. 3. Pass. also, *to be reproached*, E.*Hipp.*686.

**κακχαδίαι**· ἰσχνόφωνοι, Hsch. **κακχάζω**, = καχάζω, Id. **κάκχαρτος**· κατάχαρτος, Id.

**κακχεῦαι**, Ep. for καταχεῦαι, aor. 1 inf. of καταχέω. **κακχύδην**, poet. for καταχύδην (q.v.).

**κᾰκώδ-ης**, ες, (ὄδωδα) *ill-smelling*, Hp.*Mul.*2.204, Arist.*Pr.*867$^b$10 (Comp.), Thphr.*Od.*2. -ία, ἡ, *stench*, ibid., *Sud.*5, 9, al.

**κᾰκώλεθρος**, ον, *very destructive*, Sch.rec.S.*El.*492.

**κἄκωνῦμ-ία,** ἡ, *bad name, ill report,* Sm.*Ex.*32.25. **-ος,** ον, (ὄνομα) gloss on δυσώνυμος, Suid., cf. Paul.Al.*N.*3.

**κάκ-ωσις** [ἄ], εως, ἡ, (κἄκόω) *ill-treatment,* τοῦ ἡγεμόνος X.*An.*4.6.3, cf. *Stud.Pal.*1.8.10 (v A.D.); *oppression,* τοῦ λαοῦ Lxx *Ex.*3.7. 2. esp. in Law, *ill-usage,* of persons by their natural protectors, ὁ τῆς κ. νόμος Lys.13.91, cf. Is.8.32, D.10.40, etc.; γραφὴ κακώσεως Id.58.32, Men.328; κ. γονέων, ὀρφανῶν, ἐπικλήρου, οἴκου ὀρφανικοῦ, Arist.*Ath.*56.6; τοκέων κ. Lycurg.147; also κ. ἐπαρχίας *misgovernment,* of the Rom. *actio repetundarum,* Plu.*Caes.*4. II. *suffering, distress,* Th.2.43; πληρωμάτων Id.7.4; αἰκίαι σωμάτων καὶ κακώσεις Arist.*Rh.*1386$^{a}$8, cf. 1385$^{a}$24; of the effects of disease, Hp.*VM*17: pl., Id.*Aër.*19; αἱ τᾶς σαρκὸς τακομένας κακώσιες Ti.Locr.102c, cf. Phld.*Mort.*21, Sor.1.31. **-ωτής,** οῦ, ὁ, *one who ill-treats, oppressor,* Ph.1.544, Ptol.*Tetr.*159; γυναικῶν Vett.Val.49.4. **-ωτικός,** ή, όν, *hurtful, noxious,* Ph.2.557, Herm.ap.Stob.1.41.6; τινος Dsc.1.94, cf. Gal.6.260, Sch.D Il.1.10; κ. τι παθεῖν Chor.p.221 B.; κ. αἰτία, ἀκτίς, Vett.Val.49.11, 151.6. Adv. -κῶς, διάγειν Id.165.34, cf. Sch.Epict.*Ench.*42.

**καλαβάς·** καλαβώτης, Hsch. **Καλαβίδια, Καλαβίς,** v. Καλλαβίς. **καλαβοίδια** (i.e. καλαϝοίδια), τά, hymns in honour of Artemis, Id. (καλαβοῦτοι cod.); cf. Καλαοίδια. **κἄλαβρίζω, κἄλαβρισμός,** v. κολαβρ-. **καλαβρός·** βάρβαρος, Id. **καλαβύστας·** τοὺς κωλώτας (Argive), Id.

**κἄλἄβώτης,** ου, ὁ, = ἀσκαλαβώτης, Lxx *Le.*11.30, *PMag.Lond.*121.186.

**καλαδία·** ῥυκάνη, Hsch. **καλάζει** (fort. καλα⟨μά⟩ζει)· ὀγκοῦται (Achaean), Id. **κάλαθα·** λάλαβοι, οἱ δὲ ἄνθη, Id. **καλάθαρβα·** παροινία, Id.

⊛ **κἄλἄθηφόρος,** ον, *basket-carrying,* Hsch.: Καλαθηφόροι, title of play by Eubulus.

**κἄλάθ-ιον** [λἄ], τό, Dim. of κάλαθος, Poll.10.125, Sch.Call.*Cer.*1; part of a surgical machine, in the shape of a κάλαθος, Orib.49.4.41:—also **-ίς,** ίδος, ἡ, Hsch. s.v. πλαγγών. **-ίσκιον,** τό, = foreg., Anon. *in Rh.*108.30: also **-ίσκον,** τό, Roussel *Cultes Égyptiens* 232 (Delos, ii B.C.). ⊛ **-ίσκος,** = foreg., ὁ, Ar.*Th.*822, *Lys.*535, 579, *Jahresh.*16 *Beibl.*51 (iv B.C.), Theoc.21.9. 2. Archit., = κόφινος, of the *coffers, panels* of a ceiled roof, Chor.p.118 B. II. a kind of *dance,* Apolloph.1, Men.1018, Poll.4.105; prob. l. for **-ισμός,** Ath.14.629f.

**κἄλἄθο-ειδής,** ές, *basket-shaped, narrow at the base,* Cleom.2.2, Gal.18(1).822, Theo Sm.p.196 H., Simp.*in Cael.*546.31. Adv. **-δῶς** Heraclit.*All.*46. **-πλόκος,** ὁ, *basket-weaver,* P.cit. ad *PFlor.*13.9. **-ποιός,** όν, *making baskets,* A.D.*Adv.*189.7.

⊛ **κάλἄθος** [κἄ], ὁ, *basket narrow at the base,* Ar.*Av.*1325 (lyr.); esp. for wool, Hsch.; for fruit, Arist.*Rh.*1413$^{a}$21; carried in procession in honour of Demeter, Call.*Cer.*1, cf. *Gloss.Oxy.*1802 *Fr.*3.30. 2. Archit., *capital of a column,* in this form, Callix.1, cf. Vitr.4.1.9. II. *wine-cooler,* = ψυκτήρ, Hsch. III. *mould for casting iron,* Id. IV. *reservoir* of an oil-lamp, Hero *Spir.*2.22.

**κἄλάθωσις** [λἄ], εως, ἡ, *coffering* of a ceiled roof, *Gloss.*; cf. καλαθίσκος I.2.

⊛ **κἄλάϊνος** or **καλλάϊνος,** η, ον, *like the* κάλαϊς, *shifting between blue and green,* κ. πτέρυξ, of the cock, *AP*7.428.2 (Mel.); χρῶμα κ., of jasper, Dsc.5.142; = *venetus,* Lyd.*Mens.*4.30, *Tab.Defix.Aud.*15.5, 16.13 (Syria, iii A.D., written καλλαεινου and καλαεινου); κ. λίθος, = sq., *Peripl.M.Rubr.*39 (καλλεανός cod.); πλινθίς *AP*6.295.6 (Phan.). II. κ. κέραμος *glazed* pottery made at Alexandria, *EM*486.51, Suid.; κ. ὄστρακον Gal.12.866; τὰ καλάϊνα *PSI*4.396.9 (iii B.C.).

⊛ **κάλαϊς** or (in Plin. l.c.) **κάλλαϊς,** ιδος, ἡ, *precious stone of a greenish blue, turquoise,* Plin.*HN*37.151. II. *cock, IG*4.914.3 (Epid., v B.C.). III. = ἱστίον, Hsch.

**καλακάνθη,** ἡ, = χαλκάνθη, *Gp.*13.11.1.

**κάλαμα·** ὄγκος, ἰχθύς, Hsch.

**κἄλἄμ-άγρωστις,** εως, ἡ, *Dactyloctenium aegyptiacum,* Dsc.4.30. ⊛ **-αῖος,** α, ον, *of* or *in the cornstalks* (καλάμαι): **κἄλἄμαία,** ἡ, a kind of *grasshopper,* μάντις ἁ κ. Theoc.10.18, cf. Sch., Hsch.: **κἄλἄμαῖον,** τό, a small τέττιξ, Paus.Gr.*Frr.*87, 401, Hsch. s.v. κερκώπη. II. **Καλαμαῖα,** τά, festival of Demeter and Persephone at Eleusis, *IG*2$^{2}$.949.9 (ii B.C.).

**Κἄλἄμαιών,** ῶνος, ὁ (sc. μήν, cf. foreg. II), name of month at Miletus, *SIG*683.42 (ii B.C.); at Olbia, *IPE*1$^{2}$.49; at Cyzicus, *CIG*3663$^{A}$.

**καλαμανθήλη,** ἡ, = ἀνθήλη, *Edict.Diocl.*18.6.

**κἄλἄμ-άομαι,** (καλάμη) *gather cornstalks, glean,* Cratin.420; κ. τὰ ὀπίσω Lxx *De.*24.20: metaph., [Alexander] ἐθέριζε τὴν Ἀσίαν, ἐγὼ δὲ [Antigonus] καλαμῶμαι Plu.2.182a; *gather up* the stragglers of an army, Lxx *Jd.*20.45; οἱ πράκτορες καλαμῶνται ὑμᾶς ib.*Is.*3.12. **-άριον,** τό, (κάλαμος) *reed-case, pen-case,* Lyd.*Mag.*2.14, *PLond.*3.1007.5 (vi A.D.). II. = τευθίς, Sch.Opp.*H.*3.166. ⊛ **-αύλης,** ου, ὁ, *one who plays on a reed-pipe,* Ath.4.176d. **-αυλητής,** οῦ, ὁ, = foreg., Hedyl.ap.Ath.ibid. **-αυλος,** ὁ, = foreg., *Cat.Cod.Astr.*8(4).217. **-εία,** ἡ, *reeds,* in a collective sense, *PTeb.*5.199 (ii B.C.); *crop of reeds* (in form **-μία**), *PLond.*2.163.22 (i A.D.). 2. (sc. γῆ) *reed-land, PTeb.*457 (ii A.D.). **-ειφὔή,** ἡ, *growth of reeds, POxy.*1141.4 (iii A.D.). **-εύς,** έως, ὁ, *angler,* Pancrat. ap.Ath.7.305c. ⊛ **-ευτής,** οῦ, ὁ (as if from *καλαμεύω), *reaper, mower,* Theoc.5.111. II. = καλαμεύς, *AP*6.167 (Agath.), 10.8 (Arch.). **-εών,** ῶνος, ὁ, = καλαμών, condemned by Phryn.144. ⊛ **-η,** ἡ, (v. κάλαμος) *stalk,* esp. *the stalk* or *straw of corn,* metaph. in Hom., αἶψά τε φυλόπιδος πέλεται κόρος ἀνθρώποισιν, ἧς τε πλείστην μὲν καλάμην χθονὶ χαλκὸς ἔχευεν, ἄμητος δ' ὀλίγιστος, i.e. when there is much *straw* and little harvest, much *slaughter* and little profit, Il.19.222; κ. πυρῶν wheat-*straw,* Hdt.4.33; σῖτος σὺν τῇ καλάμῃ ἀποκείμενος X.*An.*5.4.27; καλάμαν τε καὶ ἱερὰ δράγματα.. ἀσταχύων Call.*Cer.*20; prov. of a greedy farmer, πυροὺς ἐπὶ καλάμῃ ἀροῦν to exhaust ground by one corn-crop after another, Lys.*Fr.*77: pl., σῖτος ἐπὶ ταῖς κ. D.H.5.13. 2. *stubble,* Arist.*Mete.*341$^{b}$27, *PSI*4.380.6 (iii B.C.), 1 *Ep.Cor.*3.12, etc.: metaph., of an old man, καλάμην γέ σ' ὀΐομαι εἰσορόωντα γιγνώσκειν thou mayst still, I ween, perceive *the stubble* (i.e. *the residue*) of former strength, Od.14.214; τὸ γῆρας καλάμη Arist.*Rh.*1410$^{b}$14; τὴν κ. δωρῇ, δοὺς ἑτέροις τὸ θέρος *AP*11.36 (Phil.); Ῥήσου κ. *the remains* of Rhesus, i.e. his *corpse,* Orac.ap.Polyaen.6.53; ἀπὸ τῆς κ. τεκμαίρεσθαι to judge from *the remains,* Luc.*Alex.*5. 3. κολχὶς κ., = λίνον, Call.*Fr.*265. II. = κάλαμος, Hld.8.9. **-ηδόν,** Adv. *like a broken reed,* of a kind of fracture, Sor.*Fract.*10, Paul.Aeg.6.89. **-ημα,** ατος, τό, *gleanings,* Thd.*Ob.*5.

**κἄλἄμη-τομία,** Ep. -ίη, ἡ, *cutting of stalks, reaping, AP*6.36 (Phil.). **-τόμος,** ον, *cutting stalks, reaping,* ἅρπη A.R.4.987. **-τρια,** ἡ, *gatherer of stalks, gleaner,* Plu.2.784a (nisi leg. -τρίδας). **-τρίς,** ίδος, ἡ, = foreg., Hsch. **-φάγος** [φἄ], ον, *devouring reeds,* i.e. *cutting* or *trimming pens,* χάλυψ *AP*6.65.3 (Paul.Sil.). **-φορέω,** *bring a corn-token* in order to receive a ration of corn (cf. κάλαμος VI), Them.*Or.*23.292a. **-φόρος,** ον, *carrying reeds,* X.*HG*2.1.2 (v.l. καλαμοφ-).

**κἄλἄμία,** v. καλαμεία.

⊛ **κἄλἄμ-ίζω,** (κάλαμος) *pipe on a reed,* Ath.15.697c (**καλαβίζω** cj. Lobeck, cf. Καλλαβίς). **-ικός,** ή, όν, *made of reeds,* σφυρίδιον *PTeb.*120.77 (i B.C.).

**κἄλἄμίνδαρ·** πλάτανος ἡδονιεῖς (sic), Hsch.

⊛ **κἄλἄμίνθη** (so Hsch., but -μίνθα Philum.*Ven.*7.9, 14.6, Phot.), ἡ, = καλάμινθος, Ar.*Ec.*648 (gen. sg.), Thphr.*CP*2.16.4 (pl.).

**κἄλἄμινθίνη,** ἡ, = foreg., Zopyr.ap.Orib.14.62.1 codd.

**Κἄλἄμίνθιος,** ὁ, *Minty,* comic name of a frog, Batr.224.

**κἄλἄμινθ-ίτης** [ῑ] οἶνος, ὁ, wine *flavoured with mint,* Dsc.5.52. **-ος,** ἡ, (μίνθα) *catmint, mint,* Nic.*Th.*60. **-ώδης,** ες, *full of mint,* Str.8.5.7, Apollon.*Lex.* s.v. κητώεσσαν.

⊛ **κἄλάμ-ῐνος** [λἄ], η, ον, *of reed,* οἰκίαι Hdt.5.101; ὀϊστοί, τόξα, Id.7.61, 65; χάραξ *PSI*4.393.6 (iii B.C.); σῦριγξ, αὐλός, Ar.*Fr.*719, Ath.4.182d; κ. πλέγμα cheese-*crate,* Poll.7.173: σκελετός, ἄπυγος, καλάμινα σκέλη φορῶν with legs *like reeds,* Pl.Com.184.3. II. *of cane, bamboo,* πλοῖα κ. Hdt.3.98. **-ιον,** τό, Dim. of καλάμη, Hsch. (pl.). II. of κάλαμος: 1. = sq. I, *POxy.*1631.14 (iii A.D.): without diminutive sense, κ. μεγάλα ib.1742.4 (iv A.D.). 2. = κάλαμος II.8, Eust.1181.53. 3. καλάμια τῶν ὑποδέσεων, = ἀναγωγεῖς, Id.995.30: sg., Sch.Ar.*Pl.*784. 4. *splint,* Paul.Aeg.6.8. **-ίς,** ίδος, ἡ, (κάλαμος) *limed twig,* acc. -ῖδα (perh. metri gr.) *AP*10.11 (Satyr.). 2. *case for a writing-reed, pen-case,* Poll.10.59, Hsch.; *pen* (?), Phld.*Po.*2.41. 3. *toothpick* or *toothbrush,* Dsc.1.70; = κάλαμος II.7, Id.*Eup.*1.60, Paul.Aeg.6.24; also of *quills* used as *splints* for broken noses, ib.91. 4. = κάλαμος II.8, Poll.5.96, Hsch. 5. pl., καλαμίδες (sic *AB*269), αἱ, *reeds put in layers* to strengthen buildings, *IG*11(2).144 *A* 61, 62 (Delos, iv B.C.), *Inscr.Délos* 366 *A* 36 (iii B.C.), *IG*2$^{2}$.1672.64, cf. *AB* l.c.; also, *bundles,* ibid. 6. at Cerynea, = καλαμαία, Hsch. **-ίσκος,** ὁ, Dim. of κάλαμος, used as a tube or phial, Ar.*Ach.*1034, *Gp.*20.24.1; in Surgery, Antyll.ap. Orib.44.23.39, Gal.2.873, Paul.Aeg.6.88. 2. *branch of a candlestick,* Lxx *Ex.*25.30(31). **-ιστρος,** ὁ, *stipula, Gloss.* ⊛ **-ίτης** [ῑ], ου, ὁ, = καλάμινος, *reed-like,* στύραξ Alex.Trall.5.4, al., Aët.1.133. II. ὁ κ. ἥρως, perh. the hero *of the probe* or, *of the splints,* nickname of Aristomachus, a surgeon who had a statue at Athens, called ὁ ἥρως ὁ ἰατρός, D.18.129, cf. 19.249. ⊛ **-ῖτις,** ιδος, ἡ, = καλαμαία, *AP*7.198 (Leon.).

**κἄλἄμο-βόας,** α, ὁ, *noisy with the pen,* nickname of Antipater, who dared not argue *viva voce* with Carneades, Plu.2.514d. **-γλῠφέω,** *cut reeds, make pens,* Hdn.Gr.1.468. **-γλύφος** [ῠ], ον, *making pens, EM*485.35. **-γρᾰφία,** Ep. -ίη, ἡ, *writing with a reed* or *pen,* Man.4.72. **-δύτης** [ῠ], ου, ὁ, (δύω) a kind of bird, perh. *the reed-warbler,* Ael.*NA*6.46. **-ειδής,** ές, *reed-like,* Dsc.3.142. **-εις,** εσσα, εν, *of reed,* συρίγγων καλαμοεσσᾶν E.*IA*1038 (lyr.). **-θήκη,** ἡ, *reed-case, Gloss.* **-θήρας,** ου, ὁ, *angler,* Procl. *in Cra.*p.40 P. **-κεντρῖτις** (sc. γῆ), ιδος, ἡ, land *overgrown with prickly rush, POxy.*1911.101 (vi A.D.). **-κόπιον,** τό, *reed-bed for cutting, Gp.*2.6.31. **-κόπος,** ὁ, *reed-cutter, BGU*1529.2 (iii B.C.). **-κρῖνον,** τό, prob. = κάλαμος ἀρωματικός, Aët.1.132. **-πώλης,** ου, ὁ, *reed-seller, PCair.Zen.*398.5 (iii B.C.).

⊛ **κάλἄμος** [κἄ], ὁ, *reed,* used for thatching or wattling, Hdt.5.101, al., Th.2.76; for wreaths, κ. λευκός Ar.*Nu.*1006 (anap.); for bedding, Plu.*Lyc.*16; for fuel, *PCair.Zen.*85 (iii B.C.); various species, κ. εὐώδης, ἀρωματικός, *sweet flag, Acorus Calamus,* Thphr.*HP*4.8.4, 9.7.1, *Od.*33, Dsc.1.18; κ. αὐλητικός *pole-reed, Arundo Donax,* Thphr.*HP*4.11.1, 9; κ. εἰλετίας *marram, Ammophila arundinacea,* ib.13; κ. ἐπίγειος *bush-grass, Calamagrostis epigeios,* ibid.; κ. Ἰνδικός *bamboo, Bambusa arundinacea,* ibid., Dsc.5.92, *PLond.*2.191.11 (ii A.D.), *Gp.*2.6.23, cf. Hdt.3.98; κ. Ἰνδικὸς ὁ ἄρρην *male bamboo, Dendrocalamus strictus,* Thphr.*HP*4.11.13; κ. κύπριος, = δόναξ, Asclep.ap.Gal.12.414; κ. πλόκιμος *spear-grass, Phragmites communis,* Thphr.*HP*4.11.1; κ. χαρακίας, *Arundo Donax,* ibid. II. applied to various uses, 1. *reed-pipe, flute,* Pi.*O.*10(11).84, *N.*5.38, E.*El.*702 (lyr.), *IT*1126 (lyr.). 2. *fishing-rod,* Pl.Com.11, Theoc.21.43, Luc.*DMort.*27.9; κ. ἁλιευτικός Arist.*PA*693$^{a}$23. 3. *limed*

*twig* used by fowlers, Bion *Fr.*10.5, Aesop.171, 296. **4.** *shaft* of an arrow, Ptol.*Alm.*7.5; made of κ. τοξικός or Κρητικός, Thphr.*HP*4.11.11. **5.** *reed-pen*, Lxx *Ps.*44(45).1, 3*Ep.Jo.*13, Plu.*Dem.*29, Luc. *Hist.Conscr.*38; κάλαμοι γραφικοί *PGrenf.*2.38.7 (i B.C.); κ. γραφεῖς Poll.10.61. **6.** *measuring-rod*, *Apoc.*11.1, al.: hence, a definite measure, *IG*9(1).61.50 (Daulis, ii A.D.); = 5 πήχεις, Hero *Geom.*4.11; = 6⅔ πήχεις, ib.23.13. **7.** Medic., *tube* for insufflation, Aret. *CA*1.9, Asclep.ap.Gal.12.985; for fumigation, Dsc.*Eup.*1.56; for extraction, Cels.7.5.2; also, *splint*, Pall. *in Hp.Fract.*12.282 C. **8.** ornament of female dress, *AP*6.292 (Hedyl.). **9.** *stake* to which vines were tied, *PFlor.*369.4 (ii A.D.), Jul.*Or.*3.125b, etc. **III.** collectively, **1.** *reed*, i.e. *reeds*, Arist.*Mete.*359b1, *POxy.*742.2 (i B.C.), etc.: in pl., *reed-beds*, Plb.3.71.4. **2.** of plants, which are neither shrub nor bush (ὕλη), nor tree (δένδρον), X.*An.*1.5.1. **3.** *mat of reeds*, Pl.*R.*372b; *roof of reeds* (Coan), Hsch. **IV.** = καλάμη, *stalk* of wheat, X.*Oec.*18.2. **V.** ὁ κ. τοῦ σκέλους the *shinbone*, Sch.Luc.*VH*1.23. **VI.** *ticket* for obtaining corn-rations, = *tessera frumentaria*, *Gloss.* (Cf. Lat. *culmus*, OHG. *halm*, etc.)

**κᾰλᾰμο-στᾰσία**, ἡ, *fixing of vine-poles*, *PGiss.*56.12 (vi A.D.). ⊛**-στεφής**, ές, *covered with reed*, βύρσαι Batr.127. **-σφάκτης**, ου, ὁ, *one who kills with a pen*, Ph.2.536. **-τομος**, ον, *furnished with reeds cut for vine-poles*, κτῆμα *BGU*863.16 (ii A.D.). **-τύπορ** [ῠ], ὁ, *one who catches birds with limed twigs* (Lacon.), Hsch. (-ον cod.).

**κᾰλᾰμουργ-έω**, *set up poles for vines*, *PTeb.*120.141 (i B.C.), *PSI* 4.317.6 (i A.D.):—hence ⊛**-ία**, ἡ, *PLond.*2.163.24 (i A.D.).

**κᾰλᾰμό-φθογγος**, ον, *played on a reed*, of tunes, Ar.*Ra.*230 (lyr.). **-φόρος**, ον, cf. καλαμηφ-. **-φυλλος**, ον, *with leaves like those of reeds*, Thphr.*HP*1.10.5. **II.** Subst. -φυλλα, τά, = καλάμου φύλλα, *Gp.*10.44, *Hippiatr.*129.

**κᾰλᾰμόχνοος**, contr. **-χνους**, ὁ, = ἀδάρκη, Plin.*HN*32.140.

**κᾰλᾰμ-όω**, *bind* a fractured bone *with a splint of reed*, Gal.14.561. **II.** Pass., *grow into stalk*, Thphr.*HP*8.2.4. **-ώδης**, ες, *rushy*, *full of reeds*, τὰ κ. Arist.*HA*550b7, 568a21; κ. λίμνη *AP*7.365 (Zonas); κ. τόπος D.C.63.28; *of a reedy character*, Thphr.*HP*1.6.7, al. ⊛**-ών**, ῶνος, ὁ, *reed-bed*, Posidipp.(?) in *PLit.Lond.*60.21, *Gp.* 3.6.6, Paus.Dam.p.160 D., Sch.Il.18.576. **-ωτή**, ἡ, *fence* or *edging of reed*, Eust.1533.51; cf. καλαμῶται· εἶδος ἐσχάρας, Hsch.

**κᾰλάνδαι**, ῶν, αἱ, = Lat. *Calendae*, D.H.6.49, Plu.*Cic.*2, etc.:—hence **καλανδικά**, τά, *new year's allowances*, *POxy.*1869 (vi A.D.), Just.*Edict.*13.3.

**κάλανδρος**, ὁ, a kind of *lark*, Dionys.*Av.*3.15.

**καλάνι**, for καλή, barbarism in Ar.*Av.*1678.

**καλαντίων**, dub. sens. in *PCornell*33 (iii A.D.).

**Καλαοίδια**, τά, festival of Artemis in Laconia, Hsch.; cf. καλαβοίδια.

**κᾱλάπους**, ποδος, ὁ, (κᾶλον) *shoemaker's last*, Pl.*Smp.*191a, Poll. 10.141:—also **κᾱλόπους**, v.l. in Pl.l.c., cf. Poll.2.195, Gal.*Thras.* 43, *Edict.Diocl.*9.1a, *EM*486.6. **II.** a kind of *servant*, Suid. s.v. ὄνον ὄρνιν, οἰωνοί (= Sch.Ar.*Av.*722).

**κᾱλαπόδιον**, τό, Dim. of foreg. 1, Gal.6.364 (v.l. καλοπόδιον, q.v.).

**καλαρῖνες**· ὀχετοί (Lacon.), Hsch.

**κάλαρις**, ὁ, a small *bird*, preyed on by the αἰγώλιος and birds of prey generally, Arist.*HA*609a27.

**καλαρρυγαί**· τάφροι, Amerias ap.Hsch.:—Ambraciot word, acc. to Sch.Gen.Il.21.259 (in form **καλαρύα**).

⊛**κᾰλάσῑρις** [λᾰ], ιος, ἡ, *a long Egyptian garment*, with tassels or fringe at bottom, Hdt.2.81, Cratin.30; also, *a Persian garment* of like kind, Democr.Eph.1; used in the Mysteries of Andania, *IG*5(1). 1390.17 (in form **καλάσηρις**):—title of a Comedy of Alexis. Cf. τρυφοκαλάσιρις. **II.** as pr. n., Καλασίριες, οἱ, a branch of the military caste in Egypt, Hdt.2.164, etc.

**καλασίριτα**· τὰ λοχία ἃ καλοῦσιν ᾠά, Hsch.

**καλαυνεῖ**· τρυφᾷ, ἐμπίπλαται, and **καλαυρεῖ**· τρυφᾷ, Hsch.

**Κᾰλαύρεια**, ἡ, *Calauria*, an island off Troezen, A.R.3.1243, *IG*4. 752.18 (Troezen, ii B.C.), etc.; later **Καλαυρία**, Str.8.6.3, etc.: **Κᾰλαυρῖα**, ἡ, D.P.499:—hence **Κᾰλαυρεάτης**, ου, Dor. **-τᾱς**, α, ὁ, *citizen of C.*, *IG*4.839 (Calauria, iv B.C.); **Καλαυρῖτις** λιθάργυρος, f.l. for σκαλαυθρῖτις, Dsc.5.87.

**κᾰλαυρόπιον**, τό, Dim. of καλαῦροψ, Artem.4.72.

**καλαυρόφις**· βακτηριοφόρος, Hsch.

⊛**κᾰλαῦροψ**, οπος, ἡ, *shepherd's staff* or *crook*, which was thrown so as to drive back the cattle to the herd, Il.23.845, Antim.61, A.R. 2.33, *AP*6.106 (Zonas), *APl.*4.74, D.H.1.39, Longus 1.8, *BSA*16.107 (Pamphylia, ii/iii A.D.). (Prob. καλά-ϝροψ, from *ϝρέπω, v. ῥέπω: but the first part of the word is uncertain.)

**κάλαφος**, ὁ, = ἀσκάλαφος (Magnesia), Hsch.

**καλβάτεινος**, = καρβάτινος, Ephor.(?) in *PLit.Lond.*114.

**καλέας** or **καλλέας**, ὁ, = δορύκνιον, Crateuas ap.Dsc.4.74.

**καλειάς**, v. καλιάς.

**κᾰλεσάνδρα**, ἡ, *summoner of men*, epith. of ἄρκτος, *PMag.Lond.* 121.696 (καδ- Pap.).

**κάλεσις**, εως, ἡ, v. κλῆσις III.

**κᾰλεσίχορος** [ῐ], ον, only in Ep. form **καλεσσ-**: *calling forth the dance*, *calling to the dance*, Βρόμιος Orph.*L.*718.

**κᾰλεστής**, οῦ, ὁ, gloss on κλητήρ, Sch.rec.A.*Th.*574: **κᾰλεστός**, ή, όν, = κλητός, *Gloss.*

**καλεύειν**· λιθοβολεῖν, Hsch. (κα- for κατα-). ⊛**καλέχες**· κατάκεισο (Paph.), Id. (cf. foreg. and λέχομαι). **κάληβος**, = κάβηλος, Id. **καλημνεῖ**· καλεῖ σαφῶς, Id.

⊛**κᾰλέω**, Aeol. **κάλημι** (q.v.), Ep. inf. καλήμεναι Il.10.125: Ion. impf. καλέεσκον 6.402; 3sg. κάλεσκε A.R.4.1514: fut., Ion. καλέω Il.3.383, Att. καλῶ Pl.*Smp.*175a, X.*Smp.*1.15, etc.; later καλέσω Lxx *Ge.*16.11, al., Ph.1.69, (παρα-) D.8.14 codd., *SIG*656.40 (Teos, ii B.C.), (ἐγ-) v.l. in D.19.133, cf. 23.123 codd. (καλέσω in S.*Ph.*1452 (anap.), Ar.*Pl.* 964, etc., is aor. 1 subj.): aor. 1 ἐκάλεσα, Ep. ἐκάλεσσα, κάλεσσα, Od. 17.379, Il.16.693 (late Ep. ἔκλησα Nic.*Fr.*86, late Prose ἐκάλησα Ps.-Callisth.3.35): pf. κέκληκα Ar.*Pl.*260, etc.:—**Med.**, Att. fut. καλοῦμαι Id.*Nu.*1221, *Ec.*864; in pass. sense, S.*El.*971, E.*Or.*1140, etc.; later καλέσομαι (ἐκ-, ἐπι-) dub. l. in Aeschin.1.174, Lycurg.17: aor. 1 ἐκαλεσάμην Hdt.7.189, Pl.*Lg.*937a; Ep. καλεσσάμην Il.1.54, 3 pl. καλέσαντο ib.270:—**Pass.**, fut. κεκλήσομαι Il.3.138, A.*Th.*698 (lyr.), *Pr.* 840, etc.; κληθήσομαι Pl.*Lg.*681d, Lxx *Ge.*48.6, v.l. in E.*Tr.*13: aor. ἐκλήθην Archil.78, S.*OT*1359, Ar.*Th.*862, etc.: pf. κέκλημαι, Ep. 3 pl. κεκλήαται A.R.1.1128, Ion. κεκλέαται Hdt.2.164; Ep. 3 pl. plpf. κεκλήατο Il.10.195; opt. κεκλῄμην, κεκλῇο S.*Ph.*119, κεκλῄμεθα Ar.*Lys.* 253: late pf. κεκάλεσμαι Suid. s.v. κλητή. **I.** *call*, *summon*, εἰς ἀγορὴν καλέσαντα Od.1.90; ἐς Ὄλυμπον Il.1.402; ἀγορήνδε, θάλαμόνδε, θάνατόνδε, Il.20.4, Od.2.348, Il.16.693: c. acc. only, κεκλήατο (for -ηντο) βουλήν *they had been summoned* to the council, 10.195: folld. by inf., αὐτοὶ γὰρ κάλεον συμμητιάασθαι ib.197; καιρὸς καλεῖ.. S.*Ph.* 466; κἀμ' ὑπηρετεῖν καλεῖς Id.*El.*996; κ. τινὰ εἰς ἕ, ἐπὶ οἷ, Il.23.203, Od.17.330, etc.; εἰς μαρτυρίαν κληθείς Pl.*Lg.*937a; ἐμὲ νῦν ἤδη καλεῖ ἡ εἱμαρμένη Id.*Phd.*115a; *demand*, *require*, ἡ ἡμέρα 'κείνη εὔνουν καὶ πλούσιον ἄνδρα ἐκάλει D.18.172: aor. Med., καλέσασθαί τινα *call to oneself*, freq. in Ep., Il.1.270, Od.8.43, etc.; φωνῇ Il.3.161; ἀγορήνδε λαόν 1.54; *call* a witness, Pl.*Lg.* l.c. **2.** *call to one's house* or *to a repast*, *invite* (not in Il.), Od.10.231, 17.382, al., 1*Ep.Cor.*10.27; later usu. with a word added, κ. ἐπὶ δεῖπνον Hdt.9.16 (Pass.), X.*Cyr.*2.1.30, etc.; ἐς ἔρανον Pi.*O.*1.37; ἐς θοίνην E.*Ion*1140; ὑπὸ σοῦ κεκλημένος Pl.*Smp.*174d, etc.; κληθέντες πρός τινα *invited* to his house, D.19.196; ὁ κεκλημένος the *guest*, Damox.2.26. **3.** *invoke*, Δία Hdt.1.44, cf. Pi.*O.*6.58, A.*Th.*223; at sacrifices, Sch.Ar.*Ra.*482; μάρτυρας κ. θεούς S.*Tr.*1248, cf. D.18.141:—Med., τοὺς θεοὺς καλούμεθα A.*Ch.* 201, cf. 216; ἀλλὰ μαρτύριά τε καὶ τεκμήρια καλεῖσθε Id.*Eu.*486; but ἀράς, ἅς σοι καλοῦμαι which I *call down* on thee, S.*OC*1385:—Pass., of the god, *to be invoked*, A.*Eu.*417. **4.** as law-term, *summon*, of the judge, καλεῖν τινας εἰς τὸ δικαστήριον *cite* or *summon* before the court, D.19.211, etc.; simply καλεῖν ib.212, Ar.*V.*851, etc.; ἐὰν μὲν καλέσῃ D.21.56; also ὁ ἄρχων τὴν δίκην καλεῖ *calls on* the case, Ar. *V.*1441:—Pass., ἡ πατροκτόνος δίκη κεκλῆτ' ἂν αὐτῷ S.*Fr.*696; πρὶν τὴν ἐμὴν [δίκην] καλεῖσθαι before it *is called on*, Ar.*Nu.*780; καλουμένης τῆς γραφῆς D.58.43; but, **b.** of the plaintiff in Med., καλεῖσθαί τινα *to sue* at law, *bring before the court*, Ar.*Nu.*1221, al., D.23.63; κ. τινὰ ὕβρεως Ar.*Av.*1046; κ. τινὰ πρὸς τὴν ἀρχήν Pl. *Lg.*914c; ὁ καλεσάμενος the *plaintiff*, *PHal.*1.224 (iii B.C.). **5.** with an abstract subject, *demand*, *require*, καλεῖ ἡ τάξις c. inf., *CP Herm.*25 ii 7 (iii A.D.). **6.** metaph. in Pass., καλουμένης τῆς δυνάμεως πρὸς τὴν συναναλῆψίαν *called forth*, *summoned*, Sor.1.29. **II.** *call by name*, *name*, ὃν Βριάρεων καλέουσι θεοί Il.1.403, cf. Od.5.273, etc.; κοτύλην δέ τέ μιν καλέουσι Il.5.306; ὥς σφας καλοῦμεν Εὐμενίδας S.*OC*486, cf. A.*Pr.*86, etc.; ὄνομα καλεῖν τινα *call* him by a name, εἴπ' ὄνομ' ὅττι σε κεῖθι κάλεον Od.8.550, cf. E.*Ion*259, Pl.*Cra.*383b, etc. (in Pass., οὔνομα καλέεσθαι Hdt.1.173, cf. Pi.*O.*6.56): without ὄνομα, τί νιν καλοῦσα τύχοιμ' ἄν; A.*Ag.*1232; τοῦτο αὐτὴν κάλεον Call. *Fr.*66b; τούτοις τὸ ὄνομα "ἱμάτια" ἐκαλέσαμεν Pl.*Plt.*279e (Pass., τύμβῳ δ' ὄνομα σῷ κεκλήσεται *shall be given* to thy tomb, E.*Hec.*1271); κ. ὄνομα ἐπί τινι *give* a name *to* something, Pl.*Prm.*147d; but *call* (a man) a name *because of* some function, Id.*Sph.*218c; κ. τινὰ ἐπὶ τῷ ὀνόματι τοῦ πατρὸς *Ev.Luc.*1.59; ἐπ' ὀνόματος καλεῖν τινα Plb.35. 4.11:—Pass., *to be named* or *called*, Μυρμιδόνες δὲ καλεῦντο Il.2.684; εἰ τόδ' αὐτῷ φίλον κεκλημένῳ A.*Ag.*161 (lyr.); ὁ καλούμενος the *so-called*, ἐν τῇ Θεράπνῃ καλεομένῃ Hdt.6.61; ὁ κ. θάνατος Pl.*Phd.*86d; οἱ "τῶν ὁμοτίμων" κ. X.*Cyr.*2.1.9; κεκλημένος τινός *called from* or *after* him, Pi.*P.*3.67; καλεῖσθαι ἐπί τινι Lxx *Ge.*48.6; κέκληνται δέ σφιν ἕδραι Pi.*O.*7.76. **2.** Pass., *to be called*, almost = εἰμί, esp. with words expressing kinship or status, ἐμὸς γαμβρὸς καλέεσθαι Od.7.313, cf. A.*Pers.*2 (anap.); ἀφνειοὶ καλέονται Od.15.433; esp. in pf. Pass. κέκλημαι, οὕνεκα σὴ παράκοιτις κέκλημαι because I *am* thy wife, Il.4.61; φίλη κεκλήσῃ ἄκοιτις 3.138; αἲ γὰρ ἐμοὶ τοιόσδε πόσις κεκλημένος εἴη Od.6.244; ἠγάγετ' ἐς μέγα δῶμα φίλην κεκλῆσθαι ἄκοιτιν Hes.*Th.*410; σὴ κεκλημένη..ἦα *h.Ap.*324; μηδ' ἔτι Τηλεμάχοιο πατὴρ κεκλημένος εἴην Il.2.260; οὗτινος δοῦλοι κέκληνται A.*Pers.*242, cf. S.*El.*366, etc. **3.** special constructions, **a.** Ἀλησίου ἔνθα κολώνη κέκληται where *is* the hill *called* the hill of Alesios, Il.11.758; ἵνα κριοῦ καλέονται εὐναί A.R.4.115; ἔνθα ἡ Τριπυργία καλεῖται X.*HG*5.1.10, etc.:—so in Act., ἔνθα Ῥέας πόρον ἄνθρωποι καλέοισιν where *is* the ford men *call* the ford of Rhea, Pi. *N.*9.41, cf. κικλήσκω, κλῄζω, κλέω. **b.** folld. by a dependent clause, ἐκάλεσσέ νιν ἰσώνυμον ἔμμεν *said that* his *name* should be the same, Id.*O.*9.63; καλεῖ με πλαστὸς ὡς εἴην πατρί, i.e. καλεῖ με πλαστόν S. *OT*780; καλοῦμέν γε παραδιδόντα μὲν διδάσκειν *we say* that one who delivers teaches, Pl.*Tht.*198b, cf. *Smp.*205d; τὰς ἀμπέλους τραγᾶν καλοῦσιν Arist.*HA*546a3.

**κάλη**, **καλήτης**, v. κήλη, κηλήτης.

**καλήγιον**, v. καλίγιον.

**καλήζω**, Cypr., = καλέω, Hdn.Gr.1.444.

⊛**κᾰλήμερος**, ον, *bringing a fair day* (opp. κακήμερος), *AP*9.508 (Pall.); καλήμερε, χαῖρε *Mim.Oxy.*413.67.

**κάλημι** [ᾰ], Aeol. for καλέω, Sapph.1.16 (v.l. -ημμι), *Supp.*21.4: 3 sg. impf. ἐκάλη Alc.*Supp.*10.5.

**κᾰλήτωρ**, ορος, ὁ, (καλέω) *crier*, κήρυκα καλήτορα τοῖο γέροντος Il.24.577: pr. n. in 15.419.

⊕ **κᾰλιά**, Ion. -ιή, ἡ, *wooden dwelling, hut*, Hes.*Op.*374, 503, Call.*Fr.*131; esp. *barn, granary*, Hes.*Op.*301, 307; bird's *nest*, Theoc. 29.12, Ps.-Phoc.84, A.R.1.170, 4.1095, Luc.*Syr.D.*29, *Anacreont.* 25.7; *lair*, ὕστριχος Call.*Dian.*96; *shrine* or *grotto*, containing the image of a god, *AP*6.253 (Crin.), *IG*12(2).484.15 (Mytil.). Cf. καλιός. [ῐ in Hes., etc.; ῑ in Theoc. and Ps.-Phoc.]

**κᾰλῑάδιον**, τό, Dim. of sq., *model of a hut*, κ. ἐλεφάντινον *JHS*41.196 (Delos, ii B.C.).

**κᾰλῑάς**, άδος, ἡ, = καλιά, *hut*, *AP*11.44 (Phld.), Plu.2.418a; *chapel, shrine*, *IG*2².1533.5 (iv B.C.), D.H.3.70, Plu.*Num.*8, etc.; *nest*, in form καλειάς, Max.Tyr.16.5 (pl.).

⊕ **κᾰλίγιον** [ῐγ], τό, Dim. of Lat. *caliga*, *boot*, *PSI*8.886 (iv A.D.), Anon. *in Rh.*123.21; written **καλήγιον** Aët.7.101.

**κᾰλίδιον** [ῐδ], τό, Dim. of καλιά, Eup.42, prob. in *Com.Adesp.* 1335:—also **καλίδια**· ἔντερα (Cypr.), Hsch.

**κᾰλῑδόω**, v. κηλιδόω.

⊕ **κᾰλίζομαι**, (καλιά) *live in huts*, in Lacon. aor. 1 ἐκαλίξαντο, Hsch.

**κάλιθος**· οἶνος, Ameriasap.Hsch.

⊕ **κάλικα**, ἡ, only in gen. pl. καλικῶν, = Lat. *caliga*, *boot*, *Edict. Diocl.*9.5, al.:—hence **κᾰλῐκαρικός**, ή, όν, *belonging to boots*, φόρμαι ibid.

**καλίκιοι**, οἱ, = Lat. *calcei*, Plb.30.18.3.

**κάλικον**· βόθρον, Hsch.

**κᾰλινδ-έομαι**, only in pres. and impf., = κυλινδέομαι (q.v.), *roll about, wallow*, ἀποθνήσκοντες ἐν ταῖς ὁδοῖς ἐκαλινδοῦντο, of plague-stricken persons, Th.2.52; of birds, κ. ἐν τῇ γῇ, κ. τοῖς πτεροῖς πρὸς τὴν κόνιν, Arist.*HA*612ᵃ20, ᵇ24; ⟨ἐν⟩ ῥεύμασι Plu.*Tim.*28; ἐπὶ ἐλαίου, as a form of exercise, Gal.6.220, cf. 324; *roam*, κατὰ τὰς νάπας X.*An.*5.2.31; ἐν τῇσι στοιῇσι Hdt.3.52: metaph., ἐν θιάσοις καὶ μεθύουσιν ἀνθρώποις κ. D.19.199: hence, to *be continually busy with, pass one's time in* a thing, ἐν τῷ πειρᾶσθαι X.*Cyr.*1.4.5 (v.l. κυλινδ-); περὶ τὰς ἔριδας, περὶ τὰ δικαστήρια, Isoc.13.20, 15.30; κ. ἐπὶ τοῦ βήματος Id. 5.81 (v.l. κυλ-); ἐν ἀγοραῖς S.E.*M.*2.27. **-ήθρα**, ἡ, = ἀλινδήθρα, *place for horses to roll after exercise*, Ael.*NA*3.2. **-ησις**, εως, ἡ, = κυλίνδησις, *a throw of the dice*, Alciphr.3.42 (pl.).

**κάλῐνος** [ᾰ], η, ον, (κᾶλον) *wooden*, Lyc.1418, Epich.100a, A.R.2.381a; κολοσσός *Berl.Sitzb.*1927.167 (Cyrene).

**κάλιον**, τό, Dim. of κᾶλον, Hsch.

⊕ **κᾰλιός**, ὁ, *cabin, hovel*, Epich.39. **2.** *fowl-coop*, Cratin.72. **3.** *prison*, Hsch.

**καλιότερος**, irreg. Comp., = καλλίων, *BGU*948.8.

**καλίς**· σκέπαρνον, Hsch.

**κᾰλίστρα**, ἡ, = κυλίστρα, f.l. in X.*Eq.*5.3.

**κᾰλιστρέω**, = καλέω, D.47.60 (restored fr. Harp. s. v. ἐκαλίστρουν), Call.*Dian.*67, *Cer.*98.

**καλιῶσαι**· πρᾶξαι (fort. ἀρᾶξαι), πατάξαι, Hsch.

**κάλκιος**, = κάλτιος, *PGen.*80.9 (iv A.D.).

**κάλλα ἢ κάννα**· κάλαμος, Hsch.

**καλλά**, Adv., Dor. for καλά, Alcm.98, cf. A.D.*Adv.*155.10.

**Καλλᾰβίς**, ίδος, ἡ, *a wanton dance*, Καλλαβίδας βαίνειν Eup.163 (lyr.), cf. Phot.:—written **Καλαβίς** in Hsch.

⊕ **καλλαινιοποιοῖς** (dat. pl.), prob. *makers of blue dye*, *PBodl.ined.* c.88 (P.).

**καλλάϊνος**, v. καλάϊνος.

**κάλλαιον**, τό, *cock's comb*, Arist.*HA*631ᵇ10, 28: pl., κάλλαια, τά, *wattles*, Ar.*Eq.*497, Ael.*NA*5.5, 15.2, Paus.9.23.4. **2.** *cock's tail-feathers*, Ael.Dion.*Fr.*219.

**κάλλαϊς**, v. κάλα-.

**καλλαμβάνω**, aor. part. Pass. καλλάφθεις, Aeol. for καταληφ-, *IG* 12(2).526.20 (Eresus).

⊕ **καλλᾰρίας**, ου, ὁ, a kind of *cod-fish*, Archestr.*Fr.*14, Opp.*H.*1.105, Hsch. s. v. λαζίνης.

**καλλαροί**· βάρβαροι, Hsch. **καλλέας**, v. καλέας. **καλλείπω**, Ep. for καταλείπω. **κάλλειψιν**· κατάλειψιν, Id. **κάλλης**· καρπίμου, Id.

**καλλῐ-**, in compds., *beautiful*: καλο- is later and less common. **2.** like a mere Adj. with its Subst., as καλλίπαις, = καλὴ παῖς.

**καλλῐ-άζω**, *to be a member of the* κάλλιον (q.v.) at Cyzicus, *IGRom.*4.153, 157:—also **-αρχέω**, *to be president of the* κάλλιον (q.v.) at Cyzicus, *CIG*3661.

**καλλῐᾰρία**, ἡ, Dor. for *καλλιερία, *auspicious sacrifice* (cf. καλλιερέω), *Abh.Berl.Akad.*1928(6).16 (Cos).

⊕ **καλλίας**, ου (Lacon. **καλλίαρ** Hsch.), ὁ, = πίθηκος, *tame ape*, Din. *Fr.*6.2; Ion. **καλλίης** Herod.3.41: a euphemism, cf. Gal.18(2).236, 611.

**καλλῐαστράγᾰλος** [ᾰγ], ον, *with fine ankle*, Arist.*HA*499ᵇ22.

**καλλιβάντες**· ὅμοια σμιλίοις καὶ ψαλίσιν, ἐν αἷς τὰς ὀφρῦς κοσμοῦσιν αἱ γυναῖκες, Hsch.

**καλλι-βλέφᾰρος**, ον, *with beautiful eyelids*: *beautiful-eyed*, E.*Ion* 189 (lyr.). **II.** as Subst., κ. (sc. φάρμακον), τό, *paint for the eyelids and eyelashes*, Dsc.1.69, 1*Enoch*8.1, Gal.12.211: as Adj., κ. δυνάμεις ib.62. **-βόας**, α, ὁ, *beautiful-sounding*, αὐλός Simon.46.3, S.*Tr.*640 (lyr.), Ar.*Av.*682 (lyr.). **-βολος**, ὁ, name of a *throw at dice*, Poll. 7.204. **-βοτος**, ον, *with fine pastures*, Nonn.*D.*35.59. **-βοτρυς**, υ, *beautiful-clustering*, νάρκισσος S.*OC*682 (lyr.). **-βωλος**, ον, *with rich soil*, Ἴδας ὄρος E.*Or.*1382 (lyr.). **-γάληνος**, Dor. **-γάλᾱνος** [γᾰ], ον, *beautiful in its calm*, πρόσωπα Id.*Tr.*837 (lyr.). **-γᾰμος**, ον, *of happy marriage*, λέκτρα *AP*9.765 (Paul. Sil.). **-γένεθλος**, ον, *beautifully formed*, καρπός prob. in Poet. *de herb.*104. **II.** Act., *having a fair offspring*, Corinn.23, Procl.*H.*6.1. **-γένεια**, ἡ, *bearer of a fair offspring*, name by which Demeter was invoked in the Thesmophoria, Ar.*Th.*299, Alciphr.2.4, cf. *IG*14.205 (Acrae); or her nurse, Ar.ap.Phot.; epith. of the Moon, *Hymn.Mag.*5.31; of the Earth, Apollod.ap.Phot.:—neut. pl., **Καλλιγένεια** θύειν offer *sacrifice to Demeter K.*, Alciphr.3.39 (nisi leg. τῇ Κ.). **-γέφῡρος**, ον, *with beautiful bridges*, ποταμός E.*Rh.*349 (lyr.). **-γλουτος**, ον, = καλλίπυγος, Nic.*Fr.*23. ⊕ **-γονος**, ον, *of noble race*, Porph.ap.Eus. *PE*3.11 (v.l. καλλιγόνης); τέκνων καλλιγόνους σταχύας *IG*12(3).1188 (Melos):—fem. **Καλλιγόνη**, ἡ, epith. of Demeter at Pergamon, *Ath. Mitt.*37.288.

**καλλιγρᾰφ-έω**, *write beautifully*, in point of style, metaph. in Med., κ. τὴν ἀπομίμησιν τοῖς τῆς ἀρετῆς στοιχείοις Arist.*Rh.Al.*1420ᵇ17: pf. Pass. in act. sense, Longin.33.5; in pass. sense, κεκαλλιγραφημένοι λόγοι J.*Ap.*2.31, cf. D.L.7.18: later use for Att. εἰς κάλλος γράφειν, Phryn.99. **II.** *paint beautifully*, τὸ πρόσωπον Poll.5.102. **-ία**, ἡ, *beautiful writing*, whether of the characters or the style, cf. Plu. 2.397c with 145f; as a subject of competition in schools, *good handwriting*, *CIG*3088 (Teos): in pl., *elegances* of style, D.L.3.66. **-ικός**, ή, όν, *suited for fine penmanship*, ἐργαλεῖον Suid. s. v. κανονίς; but σφάλμα κ. *copyist's* error, Steph. *in Hp.*2.407 D. **-ος** (parox.), *penman, copyist*, *Edict.Diocl.* in *IG*5(1).1406 (Asine), Hdn. post Moer. p.477 P., *An.Ox.*2.397, Pall. *in Hp.*2.102 D.

**καλλῐ-γύναιξ** [ῠ], ὁ, ἡ, gen. αικος, *with beautiful women*, poet. word, only in obl. cases, Ἑλλάδα καλλιγύναικα, Ἀχαιΐδα κ., Σπάρτην κ., Il.2.683, 3.75, Od.13.412: gen., Sapph.[26]: dat., Pi.*P.*9.74. **-δενδρος**, ον, *with fine trees*, of places, Plb.5.19.2 (Sup.), Sch. Pi.*O.*9.27. **-δίνης** [δῑ], ου, Dor. **-ᾱς**, α, ὁ, *with beautiful eddies*, Πηνειός E.*HF*368 (lyr.). **-διφρος**, ον, *with beautiful chariot*, πῶλοι Id.*Hec.*467 (lyr.). **-δόναξ**, ὁ, ἡ, gen. ἄκος, *with beautiful reeds*, Εὐρώτας Id.*Hel.*493. **-δώρα**· καλλιονύμφη, Hsch. **-έθειρος**, ὁ, ἡ, *with beautiful hair*, Orph.*H.*50.7: pecul. fem. καλλιέθειρα Nonn. *D.*27.248. ⊕ **-έλαιος**, ἡ, *garden olive*, opp. ἀγριέλαιος, *Ep.Rom.* 11.24:—fem. **-ελαία**, ἡ, *Arch.Pap.*2.218 (iii/iv A.D.): as Adj., κ. ἐλαία *PCair.Zen.*125.3 (iii B.C.), *Gp.*9.8; φυτόν ib.9.10.6.

**καλλιέπ-εια**, ἡ, *beautiful language*, Herm. *in Phdr.*p.68 A., Hsch. **-έομαι**, *say in fine phrases*, κ. ὡς . . εἰκότως ἄρχομεν Th.6.83; εἰ δοῦλος καλλιεποῖτο *use fine language*, Arist.*Rh.*1404ᵇ16; ῥημάτων ὧν οἱ δεξιοὶ περὶ τὰς δίκας -εποῦνται Pl.*Hipparch.*225c:—Pass., λόγοι κεκαλλιεπημένοι ῥήμασί τε καὶ ὀνόμασι Id.*Ap.*17b:—later in Act. ⊕ **καλλιεπέω**, Them.*Or.*20 p.285 D. **-ής**, ές, *elegant in diction*, Ar. *Th.*49 (of Agathon), 60, D.H.*Comp.*18; etym. of Καλλιόπη, Corn. *ND*14.

⊕ **καλλιεργ-έω**, in Pass., *to be worked beautifully*, Phlp. *in Ph.*327.1; of land, *to be well-cultivated*, *Sammelb.*5168.27 (ii A.D.). **-ία**, ἡ, *good work*, of improvements made by a tenant, Just.*Nov.*64.1: generally, *good cultivation*, *Sammelb.*4481.16 (v A.D.), etc. ⊕ **-ος**, ον, f.l. for καλεῖ ἔργον (cj. Bernays) in Ph.2.490.

**καλλῐερ-έω**, pf. κεκαλλιέρηκα Ph.1.319: plpf. ἐκεκαλλιερήκειν X. *Cyr.*6.4.12: (ἱερόν):—*have favourable signs in a sacrifice, obtain good omens*, of the person, κἂν καλλιερήσῃ τε Pl.Com.51, cf. X. l. c., *IG*1².45.5, etc.:—also in Med., Hdt.6.82, Isoc.14.60, X.*An.*5.4.22, etc.; ἐς τὸν (sc. ποταμὸν) . . ἐκαλλιερέοντο σφάζοντες ἵππους (where ἐς τόν is constructed with σφάζοντες) Hdt.7.113. **2.** c. acc., *sacrifice with good omens*, ταῖς Νύμφαις τὰν ἀμνόν Theoc.5.148; καλλιερεῖν βοῦν prob. l. in Orac.ap.D.21.53; ἑαυτὸν τῷ πατρίῳ νόμῳ Plu.*Alex.*69: abs., κ. τοῖς θεοῖς X.*Eq.Mag.*3.1, cf. Pl.*Lg.*791a:—Med., Ar.*Pl.*1181:—Pass., ἐὰν καὶ καλλιερηθῇ τοῖς θεοῖς Men.319.8; τοὺς ξένους τῇ Ἀρτέμιδι καλλιερεῖσθαι S.E.*P.*1.149. **II.** of the offering, *give favourable omens*, καλλιερησάντων [τῶν ἱρῶν] Hdt.9.19; καλλιερῆσαι θυομένοισι οὐκ ἐδύνατο (sc. τὰ ἱρά) Id.7.134: c. inf., οὐκ ἐκαλλιέρεε ὥστε μάχεσθαι Πέρσῃσι Id.9.38; οὐκ ἐκαλλιέρεε οὐδαμῶς διαβαίνειν μιν Id. 6.76:—Med., ὡς οὐδὲ ταῦτα ἐκαλλιερεῖτο X.*HG*3.1.17. **-ημα**, ατος, τό, *auspicious sacrifice*, Hsch., *EM*487.14. **-ησις**, εως, ἡ, = foreg., *IG*1².98.23, Onos.10.26. **-ία**, v. καλλιαρία.

**καλλι-ζῠγής**, ές, *beautifully yoked*, ἅρμα E.*Andr.*278 (lyr.). **-ζωνος**, ὁ, ἡ, *with beautiful girdles*, γυναῖκες Il.7.139, 24.698, Od.23.147; Ἥρα B.5.89: in late Prose, κόραι Hld.3.2. **-θέμεθλος**, ον, *with beautiful foundations*, νηός Musae.71. **-θριξ**, τρῐχος, ὁ, ἡ, *with beautiful manes*, καλλίτριχας ἵππους Il.5.323, Od.3.475, etc.; of sheep, *with fine wool*, καλλίτριχα μῆλα νομεύων 9.336, cf. 469: in late Prose, *with beautiful hair*, Herm.ap.Stob.1.49.45. **II.** Subst., **καλλίθριξ**, *waterwort*, *Asplenium trichomanes*, Plin.*HN*25.132. **-θῠτέω**, *offer in auspicious sacrifice*, κάπρον *AP*6.240 (Phil.). **-θῦτος**, ον, *offered auspiciously*, αἶγες *Epigr.Gr.*872 (Patmos).

**καλλῐκαρπ-έω**, *bear fine fruit*, Thphr.*HP*3.15.2, *Gp.*3.3.6. **-ία**, ἡ, *beauty of fruit*, Thphr.*HP*1.4.1, *Gp.*10.1.4. ⊕ **-ος**, ον, *rich in fine fruit*, of places, Σικελία A.*Pr.*371, cf. E.*HF*464, Str.17.3.21: Comp. -ότερος Thphr.*HP*3.8.1: Sup. -ότατος, τόπος Plb.5.19.2. **2.** of trees, *bearing fine fruit*, μίλαξ E.*Ba.*108 (lyr.), cf. Thphr.*CP*1.17.10 (Comp.). **II.** Διόνυσος κ., identified with Domitian, *Jahresh.*18 *Beibl.*55 (Anazarba).

**καλλῐκέλᾰδος**, ον, *beautiful-sounding*, Suid.

⊕ **καλλῐ-κέρας**, -κέρα, *with beautiful horns*, δάμαλις B.18.24. **-κε-**

**ρως**, = foreg., ταῦρος, ἔλαφος, *AP*7.744 (D.L.), 9.603 (Antip.). II. = τῆλις, Gal.12.426.

**καλλίκλιον**, τό, *inkstand*, Lyd.*Mag*.2.14. (Lat. *caliculus*, late Lat. *callicula*.)

**καλλί-κοκκος** [ῐ], ον, *with beautiful seeds*, ῥόα Thphr.*CP*1.9.2. **-κολώνη**, ἡ, *Fair-hill*, a hill near Troy, on the Simois, Il.20.53, 151:—also **Καλλικόλωνος**, ὁ, Demetr.Sceps.ap.Sch.Il.20.53. **-κόμας**, ὁ, = sq., πλόκαμος E.*IA*1080 (lyr.). **-κομος**, ὁ, ἡ, *beautiful-haired*, of women, Il.9.449, Od.15.58, Pi.*P*.9.106; Ὧραι Hes.*Op*.75, cf. *Th*.915; Ἀφροδίτη Epimenid.19; Μοῖσαι Sapph.60; Χάριτες Ar.*Pax* 798 (lyr.), *IG*1².821; also of trees, *with beautiful foliage*, *IG*2.3412. **-κοττᾰβέω**, = καλῶς κοτταβίζω, S.*Fr*.537.2. **-κρεας**, gen. κρέως, τό, = πάγκρεας, Gal.2.781. **-κρήδεμνος**, ὁ, ἡ, *with beautiful head-band*, ἄλοχοι Od.4.623; θεά B.*Scol.Fr*.5i22. **-κρηνος**, Dor. **-κρᾶνος**, ον, *with beautiful spring*, Pi.*Fr*.198. **-κριτα**· χελώνην, οἱ δὲ φώκην, Hsch. **-κτῐτος**, ον, *beautifully built*, Nonn.*D*.26.85. **-λαμπέτης**, ου, ὁ, *beautifully shining*, Ἥλιος Anacr.27. **-λεκτέω**, *use elegant diction*, S.E.*M*.2.55, D.L.5.66. **-λεξία**, ἡ, *beauty of language*, Herm.*in Phdr*.p.191 A., Simp.*in Epict*.p.129 M. **-λογέω**, *express in elegant diction*, *embellish*, D.H.8.32, *Comp*.3 (Pass.):—Med., *use specious phrases*, Luc.*Tox*.35. **-λογία**, ἡ, *elegance of language*, D.H.*Comp*.16; ἡ Προδίκου κ. Max.Tyr.23.1. **-μάρτυς**, ὁ, *one who gives good evidence*, Hdn.*Epim*.186. **-μᾰχος**, ον, *fighting nobly*, Lib.*Or*.18.280 (sed fort. pr. n.). **-μηρος**, ον, *with beautiful thighs*, Herm.ap.Stob.1.49.45. **-μορφος**, ον, *beautifully formed*, δέμας E.*Andr*.1155; χορὸς τέκνων Id.*HF*925; ταῶς Antiph.175.5.

✱**κάλλῐμος**, ον, poet. for καλός, *beautiful*, δῶρα Od.4.130, 8.439; οὖρος 11.640; χρόα, ὄπα κάλλιμον, 11.529, 12.192.

**καλλί-νάος** [ῑ], ον, *beautifully flowing*, Κηφισός E.*Med*.835 (lyr.), cf. *Alc*.589 (lyr.); κρήνη A.R.1.1228: Sup., Hsch. (καλλινοτάτη cod.). ✱**-νῑκος**, ον, (νίκη) *gloriously triumphant*, τήνελλα ὦ καλλίνικε χαῖρ' ἄναξ Ἡράκλεες Archil.119, cf. *IG*12(5).234 (Paros); κῦδος κ. the glory *of noble victory*, Pi.*I*.1.12; χάρμα κ. ib.5(4).54; καλλίνικος ἅρμασι Id.*P*.1.32: c. gen., τῶν ἐχθρῶν *triumphant over* one's enemies, E.*Med*.765; ἐραστῶν Pl.*Alc*.2.151c; epith. of Helios, *IG* 12(2).127 (Mytil.); of kings, as Seleucus II, Plb.2.71.4, Str.16.2.4, etc.; of martyrs, *Cod.Just*.1.3.35.3 (Zeno). II. *adorning* or *ennobling victory*, μέλος, ὕμνος, Pi.*P*.5.106, *N*.4.16 codd.; ᾠδά, μοῦσα, E.*El*.865 (lyr.), *Ph*.1728 (lyr.); στέφανος, στέφη, Id.*IT*12, *Alex*.in *Gött. Nachr*.1922.10; κ. ἠλαίη Call.*Iamb*.1.283; τὸ κ. *the glory of victory*, Pi.*N*.3.18; so καλλίνικος (sc. ὕμνος) Id.*O*.9.2; καλλίνικον οἴσεται E.*Med*.45; τὸν καλλίνικον μετὰ θεῶν ἐκώμασε Id.*HF*180; also τὰν Ἡρακλέους κ. (sc. ᾠδὰν) ἀείδω ib.681 (lyr.). III. τὸ κ. *an air for the flute*, Trypho ap.Ath.14.618c. **-οινία**, ἡ, *goodness of wine*, *Gp*.6.3.10, 5.2.19.

**κάλλιον** (A), neut. of καλλίων, used as Adv., v. sub καλός c.

**κάλλιον** (B), τό, precinct used as a Court at Athens, *AB*269, cf. Androt.ap.Poll.8.121 (**Κάλλειον**, fr. Καλλίας, Phot.); at Cyzicus, apptly. a *board* or *bench of magistrates*, ἄρχων τοῦ κ. *IGRom*.4.153 (ii A.D.); cf. καλλιάζω, καλλιαρχέω.

**Καλλῐόπη**, ἡ, (ὄψ) *Calliope, the beautiful-voiced*, name of the Epic Muse, Hes.*Th*.79, *h.Hom*.31.2, Sapph.82, etc.; ἡμετέρη Κ. my *Muse*, Call.*Aet*.3.1.77:—also **Καλλιόπεια**, *AP*4.3b.61 (Agath.): as Adj., κούρα καλλιόπα, of Echo, Theoc.*Syrinx*19.

**καλλῐοπλία**, ἡ, *possession of fine armour*, subject of competition at Priene, *Inscr.Prien*.112.109 (i B.C.).

**καλλίουλος** [ῐ], ὁ, a song to Demeter, Semus 19; cf. ἴουλος.

**καλλῐ-ουργέω**, *work artistically*, in Pass., Them.*Or*.20.237d: **-ούργημα**, ατος, τό, *work of art*, Jul.*Ep*.205 (pl.).

**καλλιόω**, *make more beautiful*, Lxx *Ca*.4.10 (Pass.).

**καλλί-παις** [ῐ], παιδος, ὁ, ἡ, *with beautiful children*, *blessed with fair children*, Λητώ *Trag.Adesp*.178; κ. πότμος A.*Ag*.762 (lyr.); κ. στέφανος E.*HF*839: also in Prose, Pl.*Phdr*.261a, Arist.ap.Ael.*VH*1.14, Aristid.*Or*.17(15).20. II. *beautiful child*, Περσέφασσα κ. θεά E.*Or*.964 (lyr.). ✱**-πάρηος** (so, not -ῃος, in most codd., cf. εὐπάρᾳος) [πᾰ], ον, *beautiful-cheeked*, Χρυσηΐς, Ἑλένη, Il.1.143, Od.15.123; Λητώ Il.24.607, al., cf. B.19.4 (prob. l.), *AP*9.96 (Antip. Thess.):—written **-πάρειος** Poll.2.87. **-πάρθενος**, ον, *with beautiful nymphs*, Νείλου . . κ. ῥοαί E.*Hel*.1; δέρη κ. neck *of a beauteous maiden*, Id.*IA*1574:—later **-παρθένιος**, ον, πηγή *Inscr.Magn*.252.

**κάλλῐπε**, Ep. for κατέλιπε, inf. **καλλιπέειν**, v. καταλείπω.

**καλλῐ-πέδῑλος**, ὁ, ἡ, *with beautiful sandals*, *h.Merc*.57. **-πεπλος**, ὁ, ἡ, *with beautiful robe*, *beautifully clad*, of women, Pi.*P*.3.25, E.*Tr*.338 (lyr.). **-πέτᾰλον**, τό, = πεντέφυλλον, Dsc.4.42. **-πέτηλος**, ον, *with beautiful leaves*, *AP*9.64 (Asclep. or Arch.), 10.16 (Theaet.). **-πηχυς**, υ, gen. εως, *beautiful* arm, κ. βραχίων E.*Tr*.1194; *with beautiful arms*, παρθένος Alciphr.3.67. **-πλόκᾰμος**, ὁ, ἡ, *with beautiful locks*, Δημήτηρ, Θέτις, Il.14.326, 18.407; Ἑλένα Pi.*O*.3.1; Πιερίδες E.*IA*1040 (lyr.); χρυσέαν ἄρνα κ. Id.*El*.705 (lyr.). **-πλουτος**, ον, *adorned with riches*, πόλιες Pi.*O*.13.111. **-πνοος**, ον, contr. **-πνους**, ουν, *beautifully breathing*, αὐλός Telest.2.1; also of smell, κ. ἄνθη Hsch. s. v. κρίνα, prob. in Porph. *in Ptol*.182. **-πολις**, εως, ἡ, *fair city*, Pl.*R*.527c: freq. as pr. n.:—hence **Καλλιπολῖται**, οἱ, Hdt.7.154, etc.

**κάλλῐπον**, Ep. for κατέλιπον, v. καταλείπω.

**καλλῐ-πότᾰμος**, ον, *of beautiful rivers*, νοτίς E.*Ph*.645 (lyr.). **-πους**, ποδος, ὁ, ἡ, *with beautiful feet*, Hsch. s. v. ἀργυρόπεζα. **-πρόβᾰτος**, ον, *with beautiful sheep*, Suid. s. v. εὔρηνος, *EM*395.54. ✱**-πρόσωπος**, ον, *with beautiful face*, Γαλάτεια Philox.8. **-πρῳρος**, ον, (πρῷρα) *with beautiful prow*, of ships, E.*Med*.1335: metaph., of men, *with beautiful face*, *beautiful*, βλάστημα A.*Th*.533; στόμα κ. Id.*Ag*.235 (lyr.). **-πῡγος**, ὁ, ἡ, *with beautiful* πυγή, Cerc.14; epith. of Aphrodite, Ath.12.554c: Comp., ibid. **-πῠλος**, ον, *with beautiful gates*, Θήβη *Epigr.Gr*.993. **-πυργος**, ον, *with beautiful towers*, ἄστυ E.*Ba*.1202; τὰ κ. πεδία, of Thebes, Id.*Supp*.618 (lyr.); κ. σοφία *high-towering*, Ar.*Nu*.1024. **-πύργωτος**, ον, = foreg., E.*Ba*.19. **-πῡρος**, ον, dub. sens. in *Epic.Alex.Adesp*.9 ii 22. **-πωλος**, ον, *with beautiful steeds*, Pi.*O*.14.1. **-ρέεθρος**, ον, *beautifully flowing*, κρήνη Od.10.107; Ἴστρος Hes.*Th*.339; Δίρκα E.*HF*784 (lyr.).

**καλλί-ροος**, ον, poet. for καλλίρροος (q. v.):—also **καλλῐρόας**, B.10.26, 96, *Inscr.Prien*.376. **-ρραβδος**, ὁ, ἡ, *with beautiful wand*, Hsch. s. v. ἀκαλαυρόπις. **-ρρημονέω**, *speak beautifully*, Eust.829.50. **-ρρημοσύνη**, ἡ, *elegance of language*, D.H.*Th*.23, Luc.*JTr*.27. II. *braggart language*, Id.*DDeor*.21.2. **-ρρήμων**, ον, gen. ονος, *elegant*, λέξις D.H.*Comp*.3; λέξεως μόρια ib.16. ✱**-ρροος**, ον, poet. also **καλλίροος** [ῐ] (contr. **καλλίρους** S.*Fr*.649.39), *beautiful-flowing*, ὕδωρ, κρουνώ, Il.2.752, 22.147; ποταμοῖο κατὰ στόμα καλλιρόοιο Od.5.441; κρήνην καλλίροον 17.206; πηγή A.*Pers*.201; Ὠκεανός Orph.*Fr*.15: metaph., of the voice, καλλιρόοισι πνοαῖς Pi.*O*.6.83:—fem., Καλλιρόη, one of the Oceanids, *h.Cer*.419, Hes.*Th*.288, etc. II. pr. n., Καλλιρρόη, a famous spring at Athens, later Ἐννεάκρουνος, Th.2.15, Pl.*Ax*.364a. **-στάδιος** [στᾰ], ον, *with a fine race-course*, Ἀχιλλῆος δρόμοι E.*IT*437 (lyr.). **-στάφῠλος** [στᾰ], ον, *with fine grapes*, gloss on ἐριστάφυλος, Hsch.

✱**καλλιστεῖον**, τό, (καλλιστεύω) *offering of what is fairest*, E.*IT*23: pl., name of a festival and *beauty-contest* at Lesbos, Sch.Il.9.129: in pl. also, *the fairest prize*, τὰ πρῶτα κ. ἀριστεύσας στρατοῦ S.*Aj*.435 (cf. Sch.); τῶν φαλύρων τὰ κ. *SIG*56.9 (Argos, v B.C.); so in sg., *IG* 12(9).189.36 (Eretria, iv B.C.), 207.19 (ibid., iii B.C.). II. *beauty-prize*, of the apple of Paris, Luc.*DDeor*.20.1.

**καλλίστερνος**, ὁ, ἡ, *beautiful-breasted*, Nonn.*D*.5.553.

**καλλίστ-ευμα**, ατος, τό, *offering of what is most beautiful*, E.*Ph*.215 (lyr., pl.); *the fairest prize*, Id.*Or*.1639. II. τὰ δευτερεῖα καλλιστευμάτων second *prize for beauty*, Lyc.1011. **-εύω**, (κάλλιστος) *to be the finest* or *most beautiful*, Hdt.1.196, al., E.*Tr*.226 (lyr.); of animals, Hdt.4.72, 163: c. gen., καλλιστεύσει πασέων τῶν γυναικῶν Id.6.61, cf. 7.180:—Med., δῶρ' ἃ καλλιστεύεται νῦν ἐν ἀνθρώποισι E.*Med*.947, cf. *Ba*.409 (lyr.), *Hipp*.1009: pf. part. Pass., ἀγώνων τῶν κεκαλλιστευμένων E.*Oen*.p.39 A.; κεκ. θέαμα Procop.*Aed*.1.1.

✱**καλλιστέφᾰνος**, ον, *beautiful-crowned*, of Demeter, *h.Cer*.251, 295; of Hera, Tyrt.2; εὐφροσύναι E.*Ba*.376 (lyr.); Λιβύη Orac.ap. D.S.8.29. II. κ. ἐλαία the wild olive tree at Olympia, *from which the crowns of victory were taken*, Arist.*Mir*.834ᵃ12, Paus.5.15.3.

**κάλλιστος**, η, ον, Sup. of καλός B.

**καλλιστρᾰτεύω**, *win glory in war*, *Cat.Cod.Astr*.7.227.

**καλλιστρούθια**, τά, name of a kind of *fig*, Ath.3.75e: *callistruthis* in Colum.10.416.

✱**καλλίσφῠρος**, ὁ, ἡ (fem. -σφύρα Sch.B.*Scol.Fr*.5i24), *beautiful-ankled*, of women, καλλισφύρου εἵνεκα νύμφης Il.9.560, cf. 14.319, Od.5.333; Νίκη Hes.*Th*.384; Ἥβη Poet.ap.Luc.*DMort*.16.1.

**καλλῐτεκν-έω**, *have beautiful children*, *OGI*308.9 (Hierapolis, ii B.C.). **-ία**, ἡ, *possession of beautiful children*, *IG*12(7).397 (Amorgos), Parth.33.1. **-ος**, ον, *with beautiful children*, Arist.*Eleg*.2, *IG*12(7).477 (Amorgos), *Inscr.Prien*.225 (Aug.): Comp., Luc.*DDeor*.16.1: Sup., Plu.*Aem*.5:—also **καλλίτεξ**, ἡ, Hdn.*Epim*.186.

✱**καλλῐτέχν-ης**, ου, ὁ, *beautiful artist*, *Anacreont*.4.1: pl., -τέχνεις *Epigr.Gr*.796. **-ία**, ἡ, *beauty of workmanship*, Plu.*Per*.13, Ath.5.191b. ✱**-ος**, ὁ, ἡ, *making beautiful works of art*, Str.1.2.33, 16.2.24, Them.*Or*.4.56b.

**καλλῐ-τόκεια**, ἡ, pecul. poet. fem. of sq., Opp.*C*.1.6. **-τοκος**, ον, = καλλίτεκνος, Hsch. **-τοξος**, ὁ, ἡ, *with beautiful bow*, E.*Ph*.1162. **-τράπεζος** [ᾰ], ον, *with beautiful*, i.e. *well-spread*, *table*, Call.Com.5, Amips.19. **-τρῐχον**, τό, = ἀδίαντον, Ps.-Dsc.4.134, Ael.*NA*1.35, Archig.(?)ap.Gal.14.321. **-τρῐχος**, ον, later form for καλλίθριξ, Opp.*C*.1.321. II. *producing luxuriant hair*, Dsc.1.125. **-φεγγής**, ές, *beautiful-shining*, ἡλίου σέλας, Ἕως, E.*Tr*.860, *Hipp*.455, cf. Theodect.10.1. **-φθογγος**, ον, *beautiful-sounding*, ᾠδαί E.*Ion*169 (lyr.); ἱστοί Id.*IT*222 (lyr.). **-φλοξ**, ὁ, ἡ, gen. φλογος, *auspiciously burning*, πέλανος Id.*Ion*706 (lyr.). **-φυής**, ές, *of beautiful growth* or *shape*, Nonn.*D*.15.171. **-φυλλον**, τό, = ἀδίαντον, Hp.*Epid*.7.59 (-φυτον Gal.19.107). **-φυλλος**, ον, *with beautiful petals*, ῥόδον *Anacreont*.42.3. **-φῠτος**, ον, *bringing beauty to birth*, ὧραι Orph.*Fr*.183; καλλιφύτων κοίρανον ἡμερίδων lord of the *beautiful* vine, Nonn.*D*.47.38.

**καλλῐφων-έω**, *speak beautifully*, opp. κακοφωνέω, Phld.*Rh*.1.176 S.; *pronounce euphoniously*, ὁ τὴν τετράπεζαν -φωνήσας εἰς τράπεζαν Eust.664.41. **-ία**, ἡ, *beauty of sound* or *pronunciation*, D.H.*Rh*.1.5, 4.1, Luc.*Pisc*.22. 2. Gramm., *euphony*, D.T.(*Suppl*.)675.14. **-ος**, ὁ, ἡ, *with a fine voice*, ὑποκριταί Pl.*Lg*.817c; expl. of Καλλιόπη, Corn.*ND*14.

**καλλίφως**, *shining gloriously*, epith. of a divinity, *PMag.Par*.1.594.

**καλλί-χειρ** [ῐ], χειρος, ὁ, ἡ, *with beautiful hands*, ὠλέναι Chaerem.14.7. **-χέλωνος**, ον, *with a beautiful tortoise on it*, ὀβολός Eup.141.

**κάλλιχθυς**, υος, ὁ, *beauty-fish*, = ἀνθίας, Arist.*Fr*.316, cf. Hedyl.

ap.Ath.8.344f, Numen.ap.eund.7.295b; but distd. from it by Dorion ib.282e, cf. Opp.*H*.3.335.

❋ **καλλί-χοιρος** [ῐ], ον, *with fine pigs*, ὗς Arist.*HA*573$^{b}$12. **-χορος**, ον, *with fair dancing-grounds*, epith. of cities, Od.11.581, *h.Hom*.15.2, Pi.*P*.12.26, E.*Heracl*.359 (lyr.); of Olympia, B.10.32; ἀγορή Simon. 164.2. II. *of* or *for beautiful dances*, στέφανοι, ἀοιδαί, E.*Ph*.786 (lyr.), *Fr*.453.7 (lyr.); τρόπον τὸν καλλιχορώτατον παίζοντες Ar.*Ra*.452 (lyr.); ὁ Κ., a sacred spring near Eleusis, *the fount of goodly dances*, *h.Cer*.272, cf. E.*Ion* 1075 (lyr.), *Supp*.392, 619 (lyr.). 2. *beautiful in the dance*, of Apollo, Id.*HF*690 (lyr.); κ. δελφῖνες Id.*Hel*.1454 (lyr.). **-χροος**, ον, *beautiful-coloured*, νάρκισσος prob. l. in Cypr. *Fr*.4.6.

**καλλίων**, ον, gen. ονος, Comp. of καλός; v. καλός B.

❋ **καλλιώνῠμος**, ον, *with beautiful name*: as Subst., a kind of fish, *Uranoscopus scaber*, Hp.*Vict*.2.48, Arist.*HA*598$^{a}$11, Men.31, Anaxipp.2.2: sens. obsc., *Com.Adesp*.1023.

**καλλονάριον**, τό, *broom, besom*, *Gloss.*

**καλλονή**, ἡ, *beauty*, rarer form of κάλλος, Hdt.3.106, 7.36, E.*Tr*. 977, *Ba*.459, *IA*1308 (lyr.), Pl.*Smp*.206d, Herod.1.35, *Lyr.Alex. Adesp*.4 *B* 4, etc.; [κιόνων] *IG*5(2).268.51 (Mantinea, i B.C./i A.D.): metaph., κ. βίου Hp.*Decent*.1; *fine quality*, of pitch, Thphr.*HP*9.2.4; οἴνου *PFlor*.65.12 (vi A.D.).

**καλλοποιός**, όν, *producing beauty*, ἄνθος κάλλους κ. Plot.6.7.32, cf. Procl.*in Ti*.1.269 D., *in Prm*.p.543 S.; cf. καλοποιός.

❋ **κάλλος**, εος, Att. ους, τό, (καλός) *beauty*, esp. of body, Il.9.130, 20. 235, etc.; κάλλεΐ τε στίλβων καὶ εἵμασιν 3.392; κάλλεϊ καὶ χάρισι στίλβων Od.6.237; περί τ' ἀμφί τε κ. ἄητο *h.Cer*.276: in a concrete sense, as though external to the body, κάλλεϊ μέν οἱ πρῶτα προσώπατα καλὰ κάθηρεν ἀμβροσίῳ, οἵῳ Κυθέρεια χρίεται Od.18.192: freq. in Trag. and Prose, γυναικε..κάλλει ἀμώμω A.*Pers*.185; κ. σώματος Democr.105; opp. αἶσχος, Pl.*Smp*.201a: in a general sense, τῶν ἔργων τῷ μεγέθει καὶ τῷ κάλλει χαλεπὸν ἐξισῶσαι τοὺς ἐπαίνους Isoc.12.36; χώρη κάλλεϊ καὶ ἀρετῇ μέγα ὑπερφέρουσα Hdt.8.144, cf. Pl.*Chrm*.157e, D.S.1.30; of ships, Th.[3.17]; ἀρετὴ ἂν εἴη κ. ψυχῆς Pl.*R*.444d; τὸ τῶν μαθημάτων κ. Id.*Grg*.475a; ἐς κάλλος *with an eye to beauty*, so as to set off her *beauty*, E.*El*.1073; οὐ γὰρ ἐς κ. τύχας δαίμων δίδωσιν so as to regard *beauty* or *show*, Id.*Tr*.1201; ὁ εἰς κ. βίος, opp. αἰσχρουργία, X. *Ages*.9.1; ἐς κ. ζῆν Id.*Cyr*.8.1.33; but ἐς κ. κυνηγετεῖν hunt for *pleasure*, Arr.*Cyn*.25.9: in pl., σωμάτων κάλλη, opp. ψυχῶν ἀρετή, Pl. *Criti*.112e. 2. concrete, of persons, κ. κακῶν ὕπουλον S.*OT*1396; of a bird, Clitarch.21 J. codd.; mostly of women, *a beauty*, τὴν θυγατέρα, δεινόν τι κάλλος καὶ μέγεθος X.*Cyr*.5.2.7; Γαλάτεια, κάλλος Ἐρώτων Philox.8 (nisi leg. θάλος); Ἑλένη καὶ Λήδα καὶ ὅλως τὰ ἀρχαῖα κάλλη Luc.*DMort*.18.1, cf. *Im*.2. 3. in pl., *beautiful things*, as garments and stuffs, ἐν ποικίλοις..κάλλεσιν βαίνειν A.*Ag*.923; βάπτειν τὰ κ. Eup.333, cf. Pl.*Phd*.110a, Poll.7.63, Hsch. s. v.; κυπαρίττων ὕψη καὶ κάλλη Pl.*Lg*.625c; μεγέθεσιν κάλλεσίν τε ἔργων Id. *Criti*.115d, etc.; τὰ κ. τῆς ἑρμηνείας *beauties* of style, Longin.5.1 (also in sg., τὸ κ. τῆς ἑρμ. D.H.*Comp*.3); κάλλεα κηροῦ *beautiful works* of wax, i.e. honeycombs, *AP*9.363.15 (Mel.); κάλλη τοιαῦτα καὶ τοσαῦτα ἱερῶν D.3.25; κ. οἰκοδομημάτων, = καλὰ οἰκοδομήματα, Plu.2. 409a, cf. 935a, D.C.65.15. 4. Pythag. name for *six*, Iamb.*in Nic*. p.34 P.

**καλλοσύνη**, Dor. **-σύνα**, ἡ, poet. for κάλλος, in lyr., E.*Or*.1386, *Hel*.383; also eleg., *Supp.Epigr*.1.570; κ. ἐπέων, title of work by Democr.

❋ **κάλλυν-θρον**, τό, *sweeper, duster* made of palm-leaves, κ. φοινίκων Lxx *Le*.23.40, *BGU*1120.17 (i B.C.). **-τήριος**, ον, *of* or *for beautifying*: hence τὰ Κ., a festival on the 19th Thargelion, *when the statue of Athena Polias was fresh adorned*, Phot., *EM*487.13. **-τής**, οῦ, ὁ, *sweeper, cleaner*, esp. in temples, οἱ ἐκ τοῦ ἱεροῦ κ. *UPZ*8.6 (ii B.C.). II. = κουρεύς, Hsch. **-τρον**, τό, *broom, brush*, Cleanth.*Stoic*.1.130, Plu.*Dio* 55; ἀντὶ τοῦ δόρατος κ. φέρων Anon.ap. Suid. II. an unknown shrub, Arist.*HA*553$^{a}$20. **-ω**, (καλός) *beautify*, νέα πρόσωπα S.*Fr*.871.6:—Pass., Plot.6.1.20; λίθῳ Λακαίνῃ Them.*Or*.18.223a. 2. metaph., *gloss over*, ὅταν ἐν κακοῖσί τις ἁλοὺς ἔπειτα τοῦτο καλλύνειν θέλῃ S.*Ant*.496; εὐδιάβολον κακὸν κ. Pl. *Lg*.944b. 3. Med., *pride oneself in* a thing, Id.*Ap*.20c; ἐπί τινι Ael.*VH*3.19. II. *sweep clean*, Arist.*Pr*.936$^{b}$27, *UPZ*79.17 (ii B.C.); ὡς ῥαίνηται καὶ καλλύνηται [ἡ πλατεῖα] Plb.6.33.4.

**κάλλυσμα**, ατος, τό, *sweeping*, in pl., *IG*12(5).593 *A* 22 (Ceos), prob. in Thphr.*Char*.10.6, cf. Hsch. s. v. σάρματα.

❋ **καλλωπ-ίζω**, (ὤψ) prop. *beautify the face*: hence, *give a fair appearance to* a thing, *embellish*, κ. ὄνομα Pl.*Cra*.408b, cf. 409c (Pass.), Phld. *Hom*.p.58 O.; τὴν πόλιν, ὥσπερ γυναῖκα Plu.*Per*.12; τὸ λογικόν Arr. *Epict*.3.1.26:—Pass., οἰκία..δαπάνῃ κεκαλλωπισμένη X.*Hier*.11.2, cf. *Oec*.9.4; κεκ. τὸ χρῶμα, i.e. painted, Id.*Mem*.2.1.22: metaph., λόγος κεκ., opp. καθαρός, Hermog.*Id*.1.3; λέξις κεκ. S.E.*M*.2. 55. II. Med., *adorn oneself, make oneself fine* or *smart*, Pl.*Smp*. 174a. 2. metaph., *pride oneself in* or *on* a thing, τινι Id.*Phdr*. 252a, X.*Ages*.11.11; ἐπί τινι Pl.*R*.405b: also κ. ὅτι.. Id.*Prt*.317c; ὡς.. c. part., Id.*Cri*.52c, *Tht*.195d: abs., *make a display, show off*, Arist.*Rh.Al*.1421$^{a}$4; of a horse, X.*Eq*.10.5: c. acc. cogn., πολλὰ πρὸς αὐτούς Phld.*Rh*.1.238 S.; ταῦτα -ίζεται *makes a fair show*, Iamb. *Protr*.20. 3. *to be coy* or *mock-modest*, τινι or πρός τινα towards another, Pl.*Prt*.333d, *Phdr*.236d: c. inf., κ. παραιτεῖσθαι *affecting* to deprecate, Plu.*Caes*.28, cf. Phalar.*Ep*.92. **-ισμα**, ατος, τό, *ornament*, χρυσᾶ, ἀργυρᾶ κ., Plu.*Lyc*.9; τραπέζης Porph.*Abst*.3.19; *source of pride*, Luc.*Merc.Cond*.36. 2. *ornament of speech*, D.H.*Th*. 46. 3. metaph., *fair show, pretence*, Pl.*Grg*.492c (pl.). ❋ **-ισμός**, ὁ, *adorning oneself, making a display*, Id.*R*.572c; *showing off*, ὁ πρὸς ἵππους κ. X.*Eq*.10.16, cf. Jul.*Mis*.349c. II. *ornamentation*, κ. φορτικός Hp.*Medic*.2; εἰς κ. for *ornament*, X.*An*.1.9.23; καλλωπισμοί οἱ περὶ τὸ σῶμα Pl.*Phd*.64d. 2. *making euphonious*, of words, Id.*Cra*.414c, 426d. b. Rhet., *embellishment*, φράσεως Steph.*in Hp*.2.419 D. **-ιστεία**, ἡ, *beauty of style*, *poetica* κ. Serv. ad Verg.*Aen*.1.223. **-ιστής**, οῦ, ὁ, *one who adorns himself, dandy*, opp. φιλόκαλος, Isoc.1.27, cf. Arist.*Rh*.1401$^{b}$24, Phld.*Vit.Herc*.1457. 9. **-ιστικός**, ή, όν, = καλλυντήριος, c. gen., Arr.*Epict*.2.23.14: ἡ -κή (sc. τέχνη) *the art of embellishment*, Gal.14.766. ❋ **-ίστρια**, ἡ, fem. of καλλωπιστής, Muson.*Fr*.3 p.10 H., Plu.2.140c.

**καλλωσόν**, τό, (Lat. *callosum*) *rind of pork, crackling*, Orib.3.5.2, 3.16.7; = κόλλοψ, *Gp*.19.6.3.

**κᾰλοᾰγόραστος**, ον, *well-bought, cheap*, Zonar.

**κᾰλο-βάμων** [βᾰ], ονος, ὁ, (κάλως) *tight-rope walker*, Man.4.287. **-βᾰτέω**, *walk on the tight-rope*, Porph.*Abst*.3.15. **-βάτης** [βᾰ], ου, ὁ, *tight-rope walker*, *SIG*847.5 (Delph.), Man.5.146; = *funambulus*, *Gloss.*

**κᾰλό-βῐος**, ον, *living decorously*, Paul.Al.*N*.4. **-βουλία**, ἡ, = εὐβουλία, *Gloss.* **-γένειος**, ον, gloss on ἠϋγένειος, Hsch. **-γηρος**, ον, *venerable*; esp. of monks, *EM*230.48. **-γηρυς**, υος, ὁ, ἡ, *with a fine voice*, as etym. of κρήγυον, Suid. s. h. v. **-γνώμων**, ον, gen. ονος, *noble-minded*, Ptol.*Tetr*.158. **-δῐδάσκᾰλος**, ὁ, *teacher of virtue*, *Ep.Tit*.2.3. **-ειδής**, ές, *of beautiful form*, στροφαί Sopat. in Rh.8.56 W. **-έργαστος**, ον, *well-wrought*, gloss on εὐεργής, Zonar. **-εργέτις**, ιδος, ἡ, *doing good*, ψυχή Porph.*Antr*.30. **-εργός**, όν, *well-doing, good*, Man.1.256. **-ετής**, unexplained Adj. in *EM* 435.42. **-ήθης**, ες, *well-disposed*, M.Ant.1.1, Procl.*Par.Ptol*.232, Procop.*Arc*.22. **-θέλεια**, ἡ, *goodwill*, *Gloss.* **-θελής**, ές, *benevolent*, ib. Adv. -λῶς *PLond*.5.1674.68 (vi A.D.). **-θριξ**, τριχος, ὁ, ἡ, = καλλίθριξ, Suid. s. v. εὐχαίτης ἵππος.

**καλόϊς**· βασιλεύς, Hsch. (Perh. Lydian.)

**κᾰλοιώνιστος**, ον, *of good omen*, gloss on Augustus, Lyd.*Mag*.1. 23; name of certain θεράποντες, Sch.Ar.*Av*.722.

**κᾰλοκᾰγᾰθ-έω**, *practise noble arts*, καλοκαγαθεῖν ἀσκοῦντας dub. cj. in Ar.*Fr*.198.8. ❋ **-ία**, ἡ, *the character and conduct of a* καλὸς κἀγαθός (v. καλοκἀγαθός), *nobleness, goodness*, X.*Mem*.1.6.14, Arist.*EN* 1124$^{a}$4, al., Poll.4.10; freq. in Inscrr., ἁ ποτὶ τοὺς Ἕλλανας κ. *SIG* 558.15 (Ithaca, found at Magn. Mae.); ἀρετᾶς ἕνεκεν καὶ κ. τᾶς εἴς τινας ib.649 (Olymp.); τῆς πόλεως κ., opp. ἡ Φιλίππου κακία, D.18.93, cf. Isoc.1.6, D.25.24; opp. ῥᾳδιουργία, X.*Ages*.11.6: pl., ἀρεταὶ καὶ κ. Phld.*Rh*.2.33 S. **-ικός**, ή, όν, *beseeming a* καλὸς κἀγαθός, *honourable*, προαίρεσις Plb.7.11.9. Adv. -κῶς *BMus.Inscr*.925 *b* 8 (Branchidae), Plu.*Phoc*.32. 2. *inclined to* καλοκἀγαθία, Id.*Them*.3, 2.225f: Comp., Muson.*Fr*.14 p.76 H. **-ος**, ον, an adject. form, perh. only in Poll.4.11 (in all early writers written divisim καλὸς κἀγαθός); καλὸς κἀγαθός orig. denotes a *perfect gentleman*, Hdt.1.30, Ar.*Eq*.185, 735, al., Th.4.40, 8.48, X.*HG*5.3.9, Arist.*Pol*.1293$^{b}$39, etc.; καλώ τε κἀγαθώ X.*An*.4.1.19; but later in a moral sense, a *perfect character*, Arist.*MM*1207$^{b}$25; also applied to qualities, actions, etc., οὐδὲν καλὸν κἀγαθὸν εἰδέναι Pl.*Ap*.21d; τῶν καλῶν τε κἀγαθῶν ἔργων X. *Mem*.2.1.20; καρτερία κ. κ. Pl.*La*.192c; καρδία κ. καὶ ἀ. *Ev.Luc*.8. 15; πάντα ἔμοιγε δοκεῖ τὰ καλὰ καὶ τἀγαθὰ ἀσκητὰ εἶναι X.*Mem*.1.2. 23, cf. *Cyr*.2.1.17; of things, *admirable, splendid*, ib.3.3.6; πᾶν ὅ τι κ. καὶ ἀ. ἐστιν ἐν Σάρδεσιν ib.7.2.12; μαντεῖαι πολλαὶ καὶ καλαὶ κἀγ. καὶ ἀληθεῖς D.*Ep*.1.16: Sup., ὅ τι κάλλιστον καὶ ἄριστον ἔχετε X.*An*. 2.1.9, cf. 5.6.28: rarely with words between, ἦν καὶ κ., ὦ δέσποτα, καὶ ἀ. v.l. in Id.*Cyr*.4.6.3; ἅμα μὲν κ., ἅμα δὲ ἀ. Pl.*Ti*.88c; κ. μὲν γὰρ ἦν καὶ ἀ. ὁ Βρασίδας Plu.*Lyc*.25.

**κᾰλοκαιρ-ία**, ἡ, = εὐετηρία, Melamp.p.30 D., Hsch. **-ιᾰνός**, ὁ, name of an eye-salve, Orib.*Fr*.102. **-ῐνός**, ὁ, name of an ἐγχυματισμός, *Hippiatr*.129.8. ❋ **-ος**, ὁ, = *bonum tempus*, *Gloss.*

**κᾰλο-κάρφωτος**, ον, gloss on εὐγόμφωτος, Sch.Opp.*H*.1.58. **-κέραστος**, ον, *well-mixed*, gloss on εὔζωρον, Zonar.

**κᾰλοκοπέω**, *cut wood*, Hsch.

**κᾰλολάϊγξ** [λᾱ], ῐγγος, ἡ, *beautiful pebble*, Tz.*H*.7.254.

**κᾰλολογέω**, = εὐλογέω, Sch.E.*Ph*.967.

**κᾶλον**, τό, *wood*, κᾶλον ἐν ἱαρῷ πεφυκὸς *Berl.Sitzb*.1927.157 (Cyrene); elsewh. only in pl. κᾶλα, = ξύλα, *logs*, for burning, κάγκανα κ. *h.Merc*.112; παλαίθετα κ. Call.*Fr*.66c; τὰ κ. καὶ τοὺς ἄνθρακας Ion Trag.29; also, *timber* for joiner's work, ἐπικαμπύλα κ. Hes.*Op*.427; esp. of ships, ποττὰ κᾶλα (κάλα cod.) Ar.*Lys*.1253; ἔρρει τὰ κᾶλα the *ships* are lost (καλά codd.), X.*HG*1.1.23, Plu.*Alc*.28. (κᾶλον and κῆλον (q. v.) perh. fr. *κάϝελος, cf. καίω.)

**καλόνης**· εἴρων (Rhodian), Hsch.

**κᾰλοπαίκτης**, ου, ὁ, (κάλως) *trapeze-artist*, *PSI*8.953 (vi A.D.), prob. cj. for *calopettas* in *GGM*ii 519 (*Arch.Lat.Lex*.13.552).

❋ **κᾰλοπέδῐλα**, τά, (κᾶλον) *wooden shoes*, prob. *a hobble tied to a cow's legs* to keep her still while milking, Theoc.25.103.

**κᾰλοπλόκος**, ὁ, *one who plaits* or *weaves*, *Gloss.*

**κᾰλοπόδιον**, τό, = καλάπους, Gal.6.364 (v.l.), Suid.:—hence **κᾰλοποδάριαι** φόρμαι *lasts*, *Edict.Diocl*.9.1.

**κᾰλοποι-έω**, *do good*, 2*Ep.Thess*.3.13, Ph.1.698, *Gp*.2.22.3. **-ός**, όν, *making beautiful*, c. gen., τὸ δίκαιον κ. τῆς ψυχῆς Procl.*in Alc*. p.327 C.; *creating beauty*, Dam.*Pr*.33, *Cat.Cod.Astr*.7.101, *PMag. Leid.V*.9.3; cf. καλλοποιός.

**κᾰλόπους**, ὁ, v. καλάπους.

**κᾰλό-πους**, ὁ, ἡ, πουν, τό, gen. ποδος, *with beautiful feet*, Suid.: but

**καλοπούς** (leg. καλωπούς)· εὐοφθάλμους, Hsch. **–πρᾱγέω**, = καλῶς πράσσω, Sch.E.*Hec*.951, 984. **–πρᾱγία**, ἡ, = καλοποιΐα, Sch.A.R.3.68. **–πρόσωπος**, ον, *with fair face*, Sch.D Il.1.310. **–ρρημοσύνη**, ἡ, = καλλιρρημοσύνη, Hsch. s.v. εὐηγορία.

**κάλος**, ὁ, v. κάλως.

⊛ **καλός**, ή, όν, Aeol. **κάλος** (v. infr.), α, ον, Boeot. **καλϝός** *Schwyzer* 538 (vi B.C.):—*beautiful*, of outward form, freq. of persons, κάλλιστος ἀνὴρ ὑπὸ Ἴλιον ἦλθεν Il.2.673: in Hom. usu. in the phrase κ. τε μέγας τε Il.21.108, al.; μέγας καὶ κ. Od.9.513; καλή τε μεγάλη τε 13.289, 15.418; καλὸς δέμας *beautiful* of form, 17.307; κ. ἰδέᾳ Pi.*O*.10(11).103; εἶδος κάλλιστος X.*Cyr*.1.2.1; κ. τὸ σῶμα Id.*Mem*.2.6.30; τὰς ὄψεις Theopomp.Hist.195; χορῷ καλή *beauteous* in the dance, Il.16.180: c. inf., καλλίονες καὶ μείζονες εἰσοράασθαι Od.10.396; ἐσορᾶν κ. Pi.*O*.8.19: freq. of parts of the body, *fair, shapely*, κ. πρόσωπα, ὄμματα, παρῄα, σφυρά, Il.19.285, 23.66, Od.19.208, Il.4.147; χρώς 5.354, al.; of clothes, εἵματα, φάρεα, χιτών, χλαῖνα, πέδιλα, Od.6.111, 24.277, Il.2.43, Od.10.365, 1.96; πέπλος κάλλιστος ποικίλμασιν ἠδὲ μέγιστος Il.6.294; of arms and armour, κνημῖδες, ἀσπίς, σάκος, κόρυς, φάσγανα, ἔντεα, 3.331, 11.33, 22.314, 18.612, 15.713, Od.19.18; of buildings, manufactured articles, etc., αὐλὴ κ. τε μεγάλη τε 14.7; κ. δώματα, τεῖχος, πόλιες, 3.387, Il.21.447, 18.491; ἅμαξα, τράπεζα, θρόνος, 24.267, 11.629, Od.1.131; also τέμενος, ἀγρός, Il.12.314, Od.24.206; so after Hom., Λύδιον κ. ἔργον Sapph.19, etc.; ἐέρσα κ. ead.*Supp*.25.12. 2. in Att. added to a name in token of love or admiration, as Ἀρίσημος κ. *IG*1².921, etc.; ἐν τοῖσι τοίχοις ἔγραφ' "Ἀθηναῖοι καλοί" Ar.*Ach*.144, cf. *V*.98; Ἀλκιβιάδης ὁ καλός, Σαπφὼ ἡ καλή, Pl.*Alc*.1.113b, *Phdr*.235c. b. ἡ Καλή or Καλλίστη, as epith., A.*Ag*.140 (lyr.), Paus.1.29.2, *CIG*4445 (Beroea). c. Καλοί, οἱ, divinities worshipped in childbirth, *IG*5(1).1445 (Messene, ii B.C.). 3. τὸ καλόν *beauty*, Sapph.79, E.*IA*21 (anap.), etc.; τὰ καλά *the proprieties* or *elegancies* of life, Hdt.1.8, 207; ἁπάντων καλῶν ἄμμορος Pi.*O*.1.84; αἱ τέχναι ἃς πηγάς φασι τῶν κ. εἶναι X.*Cyr*.7.2.13. II. with ref. to use, *good, of fine quality*, κ. λιμήν Od.6.263; Βορέῃ ἀνέμῳ.. καλῷ *fair*, 14.253, 299; κ. ἀργύριον, opp. κίβδηλον, *genuine* silver, X.*Mem*.3.1.9; opp. ἀποτετριμμένον, *good* silver currency, *PCair.Zen*.21.33 (iii B.C.); ἐλαῖαι *PHib*.1.49.12 (iii B.C.); γῆ *Ev.Luc*.8.15; κ. οἶνος *PFay*.133.8 (iv A.D.); στρατόπεδον κάλλιστον Th.5.60; ἀνταπεδώκατε πονηρὰ ἀντὶ καλῶν Lxx *Ge*.44.4; κ. ἐς στρατιάν X.*Cyr*.3.3.6; πρός τι Pl.*Hp.Ma*.295c, *Grg*.474d, etc.: c. inf., λόφος κάλλιστος τρέχειν X.*An*.4.8.26; ἐν καλῷ [τόπῳ] in a *good* place, καθίζεσθαι, ὁρμεῖν, Ar.*Th*.292, X.*HG*2.1.25; ἐν καλῷ μὲν τοῦ κόλπου καὶ τῶν πόλεων, ἐν κ. δὲ τοῦ τὴν χώραν βλάπτειν, ib.6.2.9; ἐν καλῷ under *favourable circumstances*, Th.5.59, 60; ἐν κ. (sc. χρόνῳ) in *good time*, in *season*, E.*IA*1106; ἐν οὐ κ. Id.*Or*.579; ἐν καλῷ [ἐστι] c. inf., S.*El*.384 (so καλόν ἐστι c. inf., Id.*Ph*.1155 (lyr.), Ar.*Pax* 278, Th.8.2); ἐς καλόν S.*OT*78, Pl.*Men*.89e, *Smp*.174e; τί γὰρ ἐμοὶ ζῆν καλόν; what is the *good* of life to me? Ph.2.594; καλῇ πίστει, = Lat. *bona fide*, *PTeb*.418.14 (iii A.D.). 2. of sacrifices, *auspicious*, σφάγια A.*Th*.379; οἰωνοί E.*Ion* 1333; ἱερά Th.4.92; τὸ τέλος κ. τῆς ἐξόδου X.*An*.5.2.9; κ. τὰ ἱερὰ ἦν αὐτῷ Id.*Cyr*.3.2.3: c. inf., ἰέναι.. κ. ἡμῖν τὰ ἱερὰ ἦν Id.*An*.2.2.3: Com., τὰ τῆς πυγῆς κ. (for τοῦ θεοῦ) Ar.*Pax* 868. III. in a moral sense, *beautiful, noble, honourable*, in Hom. only in neut., οὐ καλὸν ἔειπες Od.8.166, cf. 17.381; μεῖζον κλέος.. καὶ κάλλιον 18.255; freq. καλόν [ἐστι] c. inf., κ. τοι σὺν ἐμοὶ τὸν κήδειν ὅς κ' ἐμὲ κήδῃ Il.9.615; οὐ γὰρ ἔμοιγε κ. (sc. ἄρχειν) 21.440; οὐ κ. ἀτέμβειν οὐδὲ δίκαιον Od.20.294; so in Trag., καλόν μοι τοῦτο ποιούσῃ θανεῖν S.*Ant*.72, etc.; μάθετε καλὸν ποιεῖν Lxx *Is*.1.17: Comp., οὐ μέν τοι τόδε κάλλιον οὐδὲ ἔοικε Od.7.159, cf. Il.24.52; after Hom. freq. of actions, etc., κάλων κἄσλων Sapph.*Supp*.2.4 (unless of persons here); κ. ἔργματα *noble* deeds, Pi.*I*.4(3).42, cf. S.*Fr*.839, etc.; ἀναστροφή κ. 1*Ep.Pet*.2.12: in pl., *excellences*, πλῆθος καλῶν Pi.*O*.13.45; πολλῶν καλῶν δεῖ τῷ καλόν τι μωμένῳ S.*Fr*.938; τὰ τοῦ παιδὸς κ. X.*Smp*.8.17. 2. τὸ κ. *moral beauty, virtue, honour*, opp. τὸ αἰσχρόν, Id.*Mem*.1.1.16, cf. Pl.*Smp*.183d, etc.; ὅττι καλόν, φίλον ἐστί, τὸ δ' οὐ καλὸν οὐ φίλον ἐστίν Thgn.17, cf. E.*Ba*.881 (lyr.), Pl.*Ly*.216c; οὐ ταὐτὸν ἡγῇ σύ, ὡς ἔοικας, κ. τε καὶ ἀγαθὸν καὶ κακὸν καὶ αἰσχρόν Id.*Grg*.474d, cf. *Smp*.201e; τοὐμὸν κ. E.*Supp*.300. 3. of persons, in early writers coupled with ἀγαθός, v. καλοκἀγαθός; later κ. ποιμήν *Ev.Jo*.10.11; κ. στρατιώτης 2*Ep.Tim*.2.3. IV. in Att. and Trag. freq. ironically, *fine, specious*, γέρας κ. A.*Eu*.209; κ. γὰρ οὑμὸς βίοτος ὥστε θαυμάσαι S.*El*.393, cf. E.*Ba*.652; κ. χάρις D.9.65; κ. ὕβριν ὑβρισμένοι Id.23.121; καί σοι.. θωπεῦσαι καλὸν S.*OC* 1003; μετ' ὀνομάτων καλῶν Th.5.89.

B. Degrees of Comp.: Comp. καλλίων, ον, Il.24.52, Od.10.396, etc.: neut. κάλιον [ᾰ] Alc.134: Sup. κάλλιστος, η, ον, Il.20.233, etc.; late καλλιώτερος or -ότερος, *POxy*.1672.6 (i A.D.), Sch.E.*Tr*.966; also καλώτερος Hdn.*Epim*.69.

C. Adv.:—Poets freq. use neut. καλόν as Adv., κ. ἀείδειν Il.18.570, Od.1.155; καλά Il.6.326; later τὸ κ. Theoc.3.3, 18, Call.*Ep*.53, Herod.1.54. II. regul. Adv. **καλῶς** (Dor. **καλώς** Sophr.22), *well, rightly*, οὐδ' ἔτι κ. οἶκος ἐμὸς διόλωλε Od.2.64; κ. ζῆν, τεθνηκέναι, etc., S.*Aj*.479, etc.; κ. φρονεῖν to be in one's *right* mind, Id.*Fr*.836; οὐ κ. ταρβεῖς Id.*Tr*.457; κ. ἀγωνιεῖσθαι *fairly, on the merits of the case*, Lys.13.88; χρήματα δατῆθθαι κ. *Leg.Gort*.4.39; κ. εἰρημένα S.*Fr*.576.6; κάλλιον λέγεις Pl.*Tht*.161b; κάλλιστ' ἂν εἴποι S.*OT*1172: freq. in phrase καλῶς καὶ εὖ, καλῶς τε καὶ εὖ, Pl.*Prt*.319e, *Prm*.128b, etc. 2. of good fortune, *well, happily*, κ. πράσσειν, = εὖ π., A.*Pr*.979, S.*Ant*.271; κ. καὶ εὖ πράττειν Pl.*Chrm*.172a; κ. ἔχειν to be *well*, A.*Th*.799, etc.; κ. ἔχει σοι Ar.*Ach*.946, cf. S.*El*.816; κ. ἔχει c. inf., 'tis *well* to.., X.*Mem*.3.11.1: c. gen., κ. ἔχειν τινός to be *well off in respect to* a thing, Hp.*Superf*.29; κ. παράπλου κεῖσθαι Th.1.36; εἰ κ. σφίσιν ἔχοι Id.4.117; οὔτε τοῖς θεοῖς ἔφη κ. ἔχειν, εἰ.. X.*Mem*.1.3.3; καλλιόνως ἔχει Pl.*Tht*.169e, etc.; κάλλιστα ἕξει Id.*Hp.Ma*.295b. 3. καλῶς, = πάνυ, *thoroughly, altogether*, τὸν κ. εὐδαίμονα A.*Fr*.317, = S.*Fr*.934; κ. ἔξοιδα Id.*OC*269, cf. *OT*1008; κ. ὑπὸ τοῦ πυρὸς διεφθάρθαι D.S.13.108: Comp., κάλλιον εἰδέναι Pl.*Hp.Ma*.300d; κάλλιον ἐοικέναι to be *just* like, Hp.*Genit*.8. 4. κ. ἀκούειν to be *well* spoken of, Men.*Mon*.285, Plu.2.177e. 5. κ. ποιῶν *rightly, deservedly*, κ. ποιῶν ἀπόλλυται Ar.*Pl*.863, cf. D.1.28, al., Aeschin.3.232; in requests, κ. ποιήσεις πριάμενος, etc., *PPetr*.3 p.143 (iii B.C.), etc.; also c. inf., κ. π. γράψαι *BGU*1203.7 (i B.C.), etc. 6. in answers, to approve the words of the former speaker, *well said!* E.*Or*.1216, D.39.15; also, to decline an offer courteously, *no, thank you!* Ar.*Ra*.888; κ. ἔχει Antiph.165, Men.*Pk*.266; πάνυ κ. Ar.*Ra*.512; ἀμέλει κ. ib.532: Sup., κάλλιστ', ἐπαινῶ ib.508; ἔχει κάλλιστα Theoc.15.3. 7. ironically, *finely*, καλῶς ἐρήμης γ' ἂν σὺ γῆς ἄρχοις μόνος S.*Ant*.739, cf. E.*Med*.588, Ar.*Eq*.344, Din.1.69. 8. κ. ὁ ἱερεύς *hurrah for the priest!* *SIG*1109.14 (Athens, ii A.D.). 9. repeated with the Adj., καλὴ καλῶς Ar.*Ach*.253, *Pax* 1330, *Ec*.730; καλὸς κάλλιστά τε ῥέξαις Pi.*O*.9.94. 10. Comp. καλλιόνως Pl.*Tht*. l.c., *Lg*.660d: Sup. καλλίστως *PMag.Par*.1.2443, 2465, Sch.E.*Hec*.310.

D. for compds., v. καλλι-, καλο-.

E. Quantity: ᾱ in Ep. and early Iamb. Poets (exc. *h.Ven*.29, Hes.*Op*.63, *Th*.585): ᾰ in Lyr. (exc. κᾱλῶς B.12.206) and Trag. (A.*Fr*.314, S.*Ph*.1381 are corrupt).—In Eleg., Epigr., and Bucol. Poets ᾱ or ᾰ (the latter usu. in thesi); τὰ μὴ κᾱλὰ κᾰλὰ πέφανται Theoc.6.19, cf. Herod.7.115, Call.*Jov*.55.—In Comp., ῐ in Hom., ῑ in Trag. and later.

**κᾰλο-σύμβουλος**, ον, *giving good counsel*, Ptol.*Tetr*.163. **–σύντῠχος**, ον, *sociable*, Zonar. s.v. εὐθεῖος. **–σχηματίζομαι**, Pass., Astrol., *to be grouped in propitious lineation*, *Cat.Cod.Astr*.6.61. **–τεχνία**, ἡ, = καλλιτεχνία, Sopat. in Rh.4.51 W.

**καλότης**, ητος, ἡ, = κάλλος, *beauty*, a word formed by Chrysipp. *Stoic*.3.60.

**κᾰλο-τίθηνος** [ῐ], ον, *well-reared*, Hsch. **τράχηλος** [τρᾰ], ον, *with beautiful neck*, *Cat.Cod.Astr*.8(4).181. **–τροπος**, ον, *well-mannered*, *Gloss*. **–τροφος**, ον, gloss on καλοτίθηνος, Hsch.

**κᾰλοτύπος** [ῠ], ὁ, (κᾶλον) *woodpecker*, Hsch.

**κᾰλο-ύφαντος** [ῠ], ον, *beautifully woven*, Sch.rec.S.*Tr*.602. **–φῐλος**, ον, gloss on εὔξεινος, Sch.Opp.*H*.1.627.

**κᾰλοφόρος**, ον, (κᾶλον) *wood-carrier*, one of a soldier's attendants, Dosiad.Hist.1.

**κᾰλό-φρων**, ον, gen. ονος, gloss on εὔφρων, Hsch. **–φυλλος**, ον, *with beautiful leaves*, Thphr.*HP*5.3.2. **–ψῡχος**, ον, = εὔψυχος, Hsch. s.v. εὔθυμος.

**καλπ-άζω**, (κάλπη A) *trot*, of a horse, A.*Fr*.145 A, Aq.*Je*.8.6, Suid. **–ασμός**, ὁ, *trotting*, ὁ ἐν ἀναβολῇ κ. Philum.ap.Orib.45.29.36.

⊛ **κάλπᾰσος**, ἡ, = κάρπασος, *PMag.Par*.1.2046, al.

**κάλπη** (A), ἡ, *trot*: κάλπης δρόμος the *trotting*-race in the Olympic games, Paus.5.9.1; ὁ τῆς κ. ἀγών Plu.2.675c, cf. *Hippiatr*.34. (Perh. cogn. with OHG. *hlaufan*, Germ. *laufen*.)

**κάλπη** (B), ἡ, = κάλπις, Hsch.; κάλπην v.l. for κάλπιν in Aristaenet.2.4, Plu.*Marc*.30, Hdn.3.15.7:—of a *pitcher*, Aristaenet. l.c.; of a *cinerary urn*, Plu., Hdn. ll.cc. II. Astron., name of a group of stars in Aquarius, Vett.Val.12.29, v.l. in Gem.3.6.

**κάλπιον**, τό, Dim. of foreg. (B), Pamphil.ap.Ath.11.475c.

⊛ **κάλπις**, ιδος, ἡ, acc. κάλπιν Od.7.20, κάλπιδα Pi.*O*.6.40:—*pitcher* (Thess. word for ὑδρία, acc. to *AB*1095), Od. and Pi. ll.cc., *h.Cer*.107, E.*Hipp*.123 (lyr.), Ar.*Ra*.1339 (lyr.), *Lys*.358, etc.; a kind of *cup*, Philem.Gr.ap.Ath.11.468f; *box* for unguent, Antiph.106.2, Plb.30.25.17; *urn for drawing lots* or *collecting votes*, Luc.*Herm*.40, 57; *cinerary urn*, Plu.*Demetr*.53: with play on the original sense, *AP* 12.74 (Mel.), 7.384 (Marc. Arg.); *Panathenaic vase*, Call.*Fr*.122; = κάλπη (B) II, Gem.3.6, S.E.*M*.5.92:—in Hsch. also **κάλπη**, ἡ (q.v.), and **κάλπος**, ὁ.

**κάλτιος**, ὁ, Sicil. form of Lat. *calceus, shoe*, Rhinth.5, Plu.*Aem*.5, 2.813e, *Edict.Diocl*.9.7:—**κάλτοι**· ὑποδήματα κοῖλα, ἐν οἷς ἱππεύουσι, Hsch.:—**καλίκιοι**, Plb.30.18.3 codd.:—**κάλσιοι**, *Gloss*.

**κᾰλῠβ-εύς**, έως, ὁ, *cottager*, *Gloss*. **–η**, ἡ, *hut, cabin*, Hdt.5.16, Th.1.133, 2.52, Theoc.21.7, 18, Agatharch.47, etc.; σχοινῖτις κ. *AP*7.295.7 (Leon.); ἡ ἱερὰ κ. *CIG*4591 (Palestine). 2. *bridal bower*, A.R.1.775. 3. *sleeping-tent* on roof of house, *PFlor*.335.2 (iii A.D.). II. *cover, screen*, Theopomp.Hist.195. **–ιον**, τό, Dim. of foreg., Phld.*Acad.Ind*.p.54 M., D.H.10.19, Plu.*Pomp*.73, Alciphr.1.1, D.L.4.19. **–ίτης** [ῑ], ου, ὁ, *living in a hut*, Str.7.5.12.

**κᾰλῠβο-ποιέομαι**, Med., *make oneself a cabin*, Str.4.5.2. **–ποιΐα**, ἡ, *making of cabins*, Id.15.2.13.

⊛ **κᾰλῠβός**, ὁ, = καλύβη, *chamber*, *Epigr.Gr*.260 (Cyrene), Hsch.

**κάλυγες**· τὰ ἔμβρυα, Hsch. **καλυδίλα**· γέφυρα, Id.

⊛ **κᾰλύδριον**, τό, Dim. of κάλως, *small cable*, *BCH*29.543 (Delos, ii B.C.).

**κᾰλῠκ-άνθεμον**, τό, = κλύμενον, Ps.-Dsc.4.13; = περικλύμενον, ib.14. **–ειος λίθος**, ὁ, stone found in the head of the fish σάλπης, Hsch. **–η**, ἡ, name of a song, Aristox.*Fr.Hist*.72. **–ίζειν**· ἀνθεῖν, Hsch. **–ιον**, τό, Dim. of κάλυξ, Dsc.ap.Orib.11.1.50, Hsch.

**κᾰλῠκοστέφᾰνος**, ον, *crowned with flower-buds*, B.5.98, 10.108, *AP* 6.55 (Barbuc.); ὧραι Emp.(?)154.2.

⊛ **κᾰλῠκ-ώδης**, ες, *cup-shaped*, ἄνθος Thphr.*HP*3.5.6, 3.10.4. II. dub. sens., ἐνθάδε Κλειτόριος κεῖται ὄριλον καλυκῶδες κτλ. *Raccolta*

*Lumbroso* 257 (iii B. C.). **-ῶπις**, ιδος, ἡ, (ὤψ) *like a budding flower in face*, i. e. *blushing, roseate*, *h.Cer.*8,420, *Ven.*284, B.*Scol.Oxy.Fr.*5 i 11, Orph.*Fr.*49 ii 23, *H.*79.2.

⊛ **κάλυμμα** [ᾰ], ατος, τό, (κᾰλύπτω) *head-covering, hood, veil*, κ. κυάνεον dark *veil* worn in mourning, Il.24.93, *h.Cer.*42; χρύσεον κ. B. 16.38; ὁ χρησμὸς οὐκέτ' ἐκ καλυμμάτων ἔσται δεδορκὼς νεογάμου νύμφης δίκην A.*Ag.*1178 (but metaph., δείξω τάδ' ἐκ καλυμμάτων 'I will lift the *veil*', S.*Tr.*1078); λεπτῶν ὄμμα διὰ καλυμμάτων ἔχουσ' E.*IT* 372, cf. Ar.*Lys.*532, *Fr.*320.5, Dicaearch.1.18; κάρα καλύμμασι κρυψάμενον S.*Aj.*245 (lyr.); χαλᾶτε πᾶν κάλυμμ' ἀπ' ὀφθαλμῶν Id.*El.*1468; Μωυσῆς ἐτίθει κ. ἐπὶ τὸ πρόσωπον 2*Ep.Cor.*3.13. 2. *fishing-net* shaped like a sack, Opp.*H.*3.82; βουλευτοῖσιν ἐν καλύμμασιν, of the garment thrown by Clytaemnestra over her husband, A.*Ch.* 494. 3. *skull* (as the brain's covering), Nic.*Th.*906. 4. *grave*, *AP*7.227 (Diotim.). 5. in animals, *the covering* of the gills of fishes, Arist.*HA*505ᵃ2; *operculum* of testaceans, ib.547ᵇ5; *eyelid*, Poll.2.66. 6. *covering of honeycomb*, Arist.*HA*624ᵇ31. 7. *shell* of fruit, Nic.*Al.*269. 8. *shutter*, D.S.20.91. 9. *sheathing-planks* for a roof, *IG*2².1668.57; but, *slabs* for closing coffers, ib.4. 1484.57 (Epid., iv B. C.), 11(2).144 *A* 42 (Delos, iv B. C.). 10. perh. *paving-slab*, *Milet.*7.60.53.

⊛ **κᾰλυμμάτιον**, τό, Dim. of κάλυμμα 9, Ar.*Fr.*73.

⊛ **κάλυξ** [ᾰ], ῠκος, ἡ, also ὁ v.l. in Dsc.2.143: (perh. cogn. with καλύπτω):—*covering*, used only of flowers and fruits: 1. *seed-vessel, husk, shell* or *pod*, of the water-lily, Hdt.2.92; of rice, Id.3.100; of wheat, πρὶν ἂν ἐν τῇ κάλυκι γένηται [ἡ στάχυς] Thphr.*HP*8.2.4, cf. 8.4.3; κάλυκος ἐν λοχεύμασι, i.e. when the fruit is setting, A.*Ag.* 1392, cf. S.*OT*25, Ar.*Av.*1065 (lyr.). 2. *cup* or *calyx of a flower*, ἀνεμωνῶν κάλυξι..ἠριναῖς Cratin.98; κισσοῖο καλύκεσσι Theoc.3.23; ὅσα ἐν κάλυκι ἀνθεῖ Arist.*HA*554ᵃ12; [φύλλοις] τοῖς τῶν ῥόδων ὅταν ἐν κάλυξιν ὦσι Thphr.*HP*4.10.3; ῥόδου κ. ibid.; so in Poets, *rose-bud*, *h.Cer.*427, *AP*12.8 (Strato), etc.: metaph., σταθερὰ..κ. νεαρᾶς ἥβης Ar.*Fr.*467. II. in pl., *women's ornaments*, perh. *ear-rings shaped like flower cups*, Il.18.401 (other expl. in Sch.), cf. *h.Ven.* 87. III. = ἄγχουσα, Dsc.4.23.

⊛ **κάλυξις** [ᾰ], εως, ἡ, = foreg. I. 1, Hsch.; also, = foreg. II, Id.

**κᾰλύπτ-ειρα**, ἡ, fem. of sq., = καλύπτρα, *veil*, *AP*6.206 (Antip. Sid.). **-ήρ**, ῆρος, ὁ, *covering, sheath*, Hp.*Haem.*4; νάρθηκας ἢ κ. Arist.*Pr.*923ᵇ25, cf. Thphr.*CP*5.6.4. 2. *cover*, Lxx *Nu.*4.13; *lid*, D.S.18.26: metaph., γῆ ᾅδου κ. Secund.*Sent.*15. 3. pl., *tiles*, *IG*2².463.71, D.H.6.92; κ. ἀνθεμωτοί *IG*2².1627.306 (sg.), *BCH*35. 76 (Delos, ii B. C.), *IG*7.3498.61 (Oropus, ii B. C.), Demioprat.ap. Poll.10.157. 4. metaph., οἱ τῆς πόλιος κ. 'pillars of society', Herod.2.31. **-ηρίζω**, *cover with tiles*, Att. fut. -ιῶ, *IG*2².463.71: **-ηριάζω**, *Gloss.* **-ήριον**, τό, *covering*, ib. **-ης**, ου, ὁ, *tile*, ib. II. *one who hides* or *conceals*, τῶν φανερῶν *PMag.Leid.V.*7.9 (pl.). **-ός**, ή, όν, *covered*, S.*Fr.*534.4 (anap.), Ar.*Th.*890, Arist. *Fr.*308; τεύτλῳ περὶ σῶμα κ. Eub.35. II. (from καλύπτω II) *put round so as to cover*, καλυπτῆς ἐξέκειντο πιμελῆς from the *enfolding* fat, S.*Ant.*1011. **-ρα**, Ion. **-ρη**, ἡ, *veil* or *head-dress*, ἀπὸ δὲ λιπαρὴν ἔρριψε καλύπτρην Il.22.406, cf. Od.5.232, Parm.1.10, A.*Pers.*537 (anap.), *Supp.*122; κ. πλοκάμων Archil.18; esp. *bride's veil*, Euph.107.4: metaph., δνοφερὰ κ. the dark *veil* of night, A.*Ch.* 811 (lyr.). 2. land given to queens as *veil-money* (cf. ζώνη I. 3), Pl.*Alc.*1.123c, Aristid.*Or.*19(41).4. II. *cover, lid*, φαρετρέων Hdt. 4.64 (pl.); θυμιατηρίου *IG*2².1396.31 (iv B. C.). 2. *seed-capsule*, *Gp.*11.11.2. **-ω**, Ep. impf. κάλυπτον Il.24.20: fut. -ψω A.*Th.* 1045: aor. ἐκάλυψα, Ep. κάλ- Il.23.693:—**Med.**, fut. καλύψομαι (ἐγ-) Ael.*NA*7.12, (συγ-) Aristid.2.59 J.: Ep. aor. καλυψάμην Il.3.141, al.:—**Pass.**, fut. καλυφθήσομαι Paus.8.11.11, Aristid.1.130 J., Gal. *UP*9.3, (δια-) D.11.13: aor. ἐκαλύφθην Od.4.402, E.*Supp.*531: aor. 2 part. καλῠφείς *CPR*239.5 (iii A. D.): pf. κεκάλυμμαι Il.16.360, X.*Cyr.* 5.1.4, Aen.Tact.26.3: plpf. κεκάλυπτο Il.21.549.—Rare in Prose, exc. in compds. (Cf. κέλυφος, καλύβη, Lat. oc-*culo*, *celo*.) I. *cover*, freq. c. dat. instr., παρδαλέῃ..μετάφρενον εὐρὺ κάλυψε Il.10.29; σάωσε δὲ νυκτὶ καλύψας 5.23 (but in 13.425, ἐρεβεννῇ νυκτὶ καλύψαι is *to kill*); simply, *cover*, μέλαν δὲ ἑ κῦμα κάλυψεν 23.693; ἐπισκύνιον κάτω ἕλκεται ὄσσε καλύπτων 17.136; [πέτρον] περὶ χεὶρ ἐκάλυψεν his hand *covered*, *grasped* a stone, 16.735; of death, τὼ..τέλος θανάτοιο κάλυψεν 5.553; τὸν δὲ σκότος ὄσσε κάλυψεν 4.461,503, etc.; τὸν δὲ κατ' ὀφθαλμῶν ἐρεβεννὴ νὺξ ἐκάλυψεν 13.580; τῷ δέ οἱ ὄσσε νὺξ ἐκάλυψε μέλαινα 14.439; so τὸν δ' ἄχεος νεφέλη ἐκάλυψε 17.591; ἑ πένθος ὀφθαλμοὺς ἐκάλυψε 11.250: freq. in Lyr. and Trag., ὅταν θανάτοιο κυάνεον νέφος καλύψῃ B.12.64; κ. χθονὶ γυῖα, i. e. *to be buried*, Pi.*N.*8.38; but χθονί, τάφῳ κ., *bury*, A.*Pr.*582 (lyr.), S.*Ant.*28; γῇ, χέρσῳ, E.*Ph.*1633, *Hel.*1066: abs., καὐτὴ καλύψω A.*Th.*1045: rare in Prose, μὴ καλύπτειν τὰ δολοσχερέα τοῖς εἱματίοις *SIG*1218.7 (Ceos, v B. C.); of armour, *protect*, X. *Eq.*12.5:—Med., *cover* or *veil oneself*, ἀργεννῇσι καλυψαμένη ὀθόνῃσιν Il.3.141; κρηδέμνῳ δ' ἐφύπερθε καλύψατο 14.184; λευκοῖσιν φαρέεσσι καλυψαμένω (fem. dual) χρόα καλόν Hes.*Op.*198: abs., καλυψάμενος δ' ἐνὶ νηὶ κείμην Od.10.53:—Pass., ἀσπίδι ταυρείῃ κεκαλυμμένος..ὤμους Il.16.360; ἐν χλαίνῃ κεκ. 24.163; χαλκῷ, ἠέρι, 13.192, 21.549; οἰὸς ἀώτῳ Od.1.443; φρικὶ καλυφθείς, of the sea, 4.402: in Prose, τὸν νεκρὸν κεκαλυμμένον φερέτω σιγᾷ *Michel* 995 *C* 32 (Delph., v/iv B. C.); [βράγχια] καλυπτόμενα καλύμματι Arist.*HA*505ᵃ6; κεκαλυμμένος *veiled* *IG*5(2).514.10 (Lycosura). 2. *hide, conceal*, κεκαλυμμένοι ἵππῳ *concealed* in it, Od.8.503:—Act., Hippon.52, etc.: ἔξω μέ που καλύψατε S.*OT*1411, cf. *Ev.Luc.*23.30; κρυφῇ κ. καρδίᾳ τι S.*Ant.* 1254; σιγῇ κ. E.*Hipp.*712: metaph., ἐκάλυψας τὰς ἁμαρτίας αὐτῶν Lxx *Ps.*84(85).2, cf. *Ep.Jac.*5.20. 3. *cover with dishonour, throw a cloud over*, σὺ μὴ κάλυπτε τὰς εὐδαίμονας ἔργοις 'Αθήνας ἀνοσίοις S. *OC*282. II. *put over as a covering*, πρόσθε δέ οἱ πέπλοιο πτύγμ' ἐκάλυψεν Il.5.315; τόσσην οἱ ἄσιν καθύπερθε καλύψω I *will put* mud *over* him, 21.321; ἀμφὶ Μενοιτιάδῃ σάκος εὐρὺ καλύψας 17.132; πρόσθεν δὲ σάκος στέρνοιο κάλυψε 22.313.

**κᾰλῠφή**, ἡ, (καλύπτω) *submerged land*, *CPR*32.5 (iii A. D.), *BGU* 640.7 (iii A. D.). II. etym. of καλύβη, *EM*486.22.

**κᾰλύφιον** (Dim. of κᾶλον)· ξυλήφιον, Hsch. (-ύριον cod.).

⊛ **κάλυψ** [ᾰ], ῠβος, ὁ, = καλύβη, S.*Fr.*574.6.

⊛ **κάλυψις** [ᾰ], εως, ἡ, *covering*, Sch.Ar.*Pl.*22 (pl.), Hsch. s. v. στρέφωσις.

**Κᾰλυψώ**, όος, contr. οῦς, ἡ (prob. from καλύπτω, 'she that conceals'), *Calypso*, Od.1.14, Hes.*Th.*359, etc.

**καλχαίνω**, (κάλχη) prop. *make purple*:—Pass., *to be purple*, Nic. *Th.*641. II. metaph. (cf. πορφύρω), *make dark and troublous* like a stormy sea, *ponder deeply*, κ. ἔπος S.*Ant.*20; ἀμφὶ τέκνοις E.*Heracl.* 40: c. inf., *long, desire*, Lyc.1457; cf. sq.

**Κάλχας**, αντος, ὁ, voc. Κάλχαν or Κάλχα Il.1.86:—*Calchas*, the Greek Seer at Troy, ib.69, al.: prob. connected with foreg. II.

⊛ **κάλχη**, ἡ, (perh. a loan-word) *murex, purple limpet*, = πορφύρα, Nic.*Al.*393. 2. *purple dye*, Str.11.14.9. II. *rosette* on the capitals of columns, *IG*1².372.90, 4.1484.83 (Epid., iv B. C.), 11(2). 161 *A* 73 (Delos, iii B. C.), Hsch.:—written **χάλκη** *IG*1².374.317, al., **χάλχη** ib.374.103. III. *purple flower, Chrysanthemum coronarium*, Alcm.39, Nic.Dam.76 J.:—written **χάλκη** in Nic.*Fr.*74.60, cf. Ps.-Dsc.4.58.

**κάλχιον**, τό, *purple dye*, Sch.Nic.*Al.*393.

⊛ **κᾰλῴδιον** (ῳ *IG*2².1632.3, 1648.13, *EM*486.15), τό, Dim. of κάλως, *small cord*, Eup.313, Ar.*V.*379, Th.4.26, Apollod.*Poliorc.*171.8.

**κᾰλωνῠμ-έομαι**, *to be in good repute, bear a good name*, Heph.Astr. 2.32. ⊛ **-ος**, ον, *bearing a fair name*, εὐσέβεια *IG*5(1).1331 (Laconia), cf. *EM*143.22.

**κᾰλωπός**, ή, όν, (ὤψ) *with beautiful eyes*, prob. in Hsch.

**κᾰλῶς**, Adv. from καλός (q. v.).

⊛ **κάλως** [ᾰ], ὁ, gen. κάλω, acc. κάλων: Ep. and Ion. **κάλος**, ου, ὁ, Od.5.260, Hdt.2.36, also Aen.Tact.11.6; Att. Inscrr. have nom. dual κάλω *IG*1².330.19, nom. (and acc.?) pl. κάλως ib.2².1610.13, 1611.57, 1612.68: as nom. sg. (?) ib.1673.18; late Ep. nom. pl. κάλωες A.R.2.725; acc. κάλωας Orph.*A.*255, Opp.*H.*2.223; dat. κάλωσι Orph.*A.*239:—*reefing rope, reef*, Od. l. c.; τῶν ἱστίων τοὺς κάλους Hdt.2.36, cf. Aen.Tact. l. c.; κάλως ἐξιέναι let out *the reefs*, i. e. *set sail*, ὅταν στράτευμ' 'Αργεῖον ἐξίῃ κάλως E.*Tr.*94; ἐχθροὶ γὰρ ἐξιᾶσι πάντα δὴ κάλων are letting out every *reef*, i. e. using every effort, Id. *Med.*278, cf. Ar.*Eq.*756 (and Sch. ad loc.); τοὺς κάλως ἔκλυε καὶ χάλα πόδα Epicr.10.5; πάντας ἔσεισε κάλους *AP*9.545 (Crin.); φόνιον ἐξίει κάλων let murder *loose*, E.*HF*837; πάντα κάλων ἐκτείναντα Pl.*Prt.* 338a; ἐφέντες Id.*Sis.*389c; κινεῖν Luc.*Scyth.*11; γαστρὶ πάντας ἐπιτρωπῶσι κάλωας Opp.*H.*2.223; κάλων τείνας οὔριον εὐφροσυνᾶν *IG*14. 793.8 (Naples). II. generally, *rope, line*, κάλον (v.l. -ων) κατεῖναι let down *a sounding-line*, Hdt.2.28; ἀπὸ κάλω παραπλεῖν to be towed along shore, Th.4.25; *cable*, Hdt.2.96; πρυμνήτης κ. E.*Med.* 770; οἱ ἐπὶ τῶν κ. βαίνοντες tight-*rope* walkers, Luc.*Rh.Pr.*9.

**κᾰλωστρόφος**, ὁ, *rope-twister, rope-maker*, Plu.*Per.*12.

**κάμ**, Ep. and Lyr. shortd. form for κατά before μ, Il.11.172, etc.

**κᾰμᾰκ-ίας** σῖτος, ὁ, corn *which makes too much straw*, Thphr.*HP* 8.7.4. **-ῖνος**, ον, *made of reed* or *cane*, δόρυ κ., opp. κρανέϊνον, X. *Eq.*12.12. **-ιον**, τό, Dim. of κάμαξ, Sch.E.*Ph.*188.

**καμάν**· τὸν ἀγρόν (Cret.), Hsch. (i. e. χαμάν, cf. χαμαί).

⊛ **κάμαξ** [κᾰ], ᾰκος, ἡ (ὁ in A.*Fr.*171, *AP*6.165, cf. infr. 3), *vine-pole, vine-prop*, Il.18.563, Hes.*Sc.*299. 2. *any pole* or *shaft*, κ. πεύκης A.*Fr.*171; θύρσου χλοερὸν κ. *AP*l. c. (Phal.); in an engine of war, Apollod.*Poliorc.*171.8, al. 3. *shaft of a spear*, A.*Ag.*66 (anap.), E. *Hec.*1155, *El.*852, Ar.*Fr.*404; χαλκέαι κάμακες, with rings at the top, J.*AJ*3.6.2 (masc. in this sense, acc. to *EM*487.38). 4. *tiller*, Luc. *Nav.*6. 5. = κερκίς I, *AP*6.247 (Phil.). 6. in pl., *steering-paddles*, Alc.*Supp.*4.16. 7. *tent-pole*, Gal.2.218. 8. *perch* for fowls, *Gp.*14.7.2, 14.24.5.

⊛ **κᾰμάρ-α**, Ion. **-η** [μᾰ], ἡ, *anything with an arched cover, covered carriage*, Hdt.1.199, D.C.36.49; *covered boat* or *barge*, Str.11.2.12, cf. Gell.10.25; *vaulted chamber*, Agatharch.62, *PStrassb.*91.5 (i B. C.), D.S.18.26, *BGU*731 (ii A. D.); *vault* of a tomb, *CIG*2241 (Chios), 3007 (Ephesus), 3104 (Teos), *IG*7.2725.4 (Acraeph.); *vault* of heaven, Lxx *Is.*40.22; *vaulted ceiling*, τοῦ ἑπτακλίνου *PCair.Zen.*445.9 (iii B. C.); *tester-bed*, Arr.*An.*7.25.4; *vaulted sewer*, as gloss on ψαλίς, Sch.Pl.*Lg.* 947d, Hsch. II. Medic., *hollow near the auditory meatus*, Poll. 2.86. III. pl., = ζῶναι στρατιωτικαί, Hsch. (Cf. Avest. *kamarā* 'girdle', Lat. *camurus*, unless Carian, cf. καμαρός II.) **-εύω**· σωρεύω, φιλοπονῶ, πορίζω, κακοπαθῶ, συνάγω, and **καμαρεύουσα**· φιλοπονοῦσα, πορίζουσα, Hsch. **-ικός**, ή, όν, = καμαρωτός, Ath.Mech. 36.5: **-ικά**, τά, *treatise on vaulting*, title of work by Hero, Eutoc. *in Archim.Sph.Cyl.*3.84 H. **-ινῶς λέγει**· παροιμιακῶς λέγει, ἀποτόμως, ἀνδρείως, Hsch. **-ιον**, τό, Dim. of καμάρα, *Papers of Amer. Sch. at Athens* 1 No.71 (Assus). 2. Medic., *fornix* of the brain, Gal.*UP*8.11. **-ίς**, ἡ, woman's ornament, Hsch.

**κᾰμᾰροειδής**, ές, *like a vault, vaulted* or *arched*, Dsc.5.79, Erot. s. v. κοτυληδόνας, Ruf.*Oss.*25.

**κάμαρος**, ὁ, v. κάμμαρος. II. **καμαρός**, ά, όν, Carian word, = ἀσφαλής, κάμαρα (sic codd.) λέγεσθαι τὰ ἀσφαλῆ Apollon.ap.Sch.

Orib.46.21.7. III. **κάμαροι**· στῆλαι ἐν αἷς ἀναγέγραπται ὁ περιορισμὸς τῆς Ἀσίας, Hsch.

**κᾰμᾰρόω**, *furnish with a vault*, *BGU*1545.8 (iii B. C.):—Pass., *to be vaulted*, *PGrenf.*1.21.9 (ii B.C.), *IG*4.203.25 (Corinth.).

**κᾰμάρ-ωμα** [μᾰρ], ατος, τό, *vault, arch*, Str.16.1.5, Gal.10.449. ⊛**-ωσις**, εως, ἡ, *building of a vault* or *cellar*, *PPetr.*3p.143 (iii B. C.). II. Medic., *arched fracture* (opp. depressed fracture), Sor.*Fract.* 4. **-ωτικός**, ή, όν, *used in vaulting*, πήχεις *POxy.*921 (iii A. D.); ὠλέναι *BGU*1545.5 (iii B. C.). **-ωτός**, ή, όν (-ός, όν Erot. s. v. καμμάρῳ), *vaulted, arched*, Str.16.1.5; στέγη Callix.2; ἅρματα Ath.4.139f.

**κᾰμᾰσῆνες**, ων, οἱ, *fish*, Emp.72,74; a special kind of fish, *AP*11.20 (Antip. Thess.): sg., Hdn.Gr.2.923.

⊛ **καμάσιον**, τό, *shirt*(?), κ. Δαμάσκινον ἓν *Sammelb.*7033.41 (V A. D.); sine expl., *Gloss.*

**καμασός**· βάραθρον, Hsch. II. **κάμασος**, = ἀμφίμαλλος, *Gloss.* (Cf. late Lat. *camasus.*) **καμάσσυται**· πτερύσσεται, Hsch.

**κᾰμάσσω**, *shake* (from κάμαξ 3), Hsch.: καμάσαι is prob. f. l. for καμάξαι, cf. ἐκάμαξεν, διεκάμαξεν, Id.

**καμαστίς**· μέτρον τι, Amerias ap. Hsch.

**κᾰμᾰτ-άω** (κάματος), = κοπιάω, Hsch. **-εύω**, aor. ἐκαμάτευσε· μετὰ κακοπαθείας εἰργάσατο, καὶ ἔφυγεν, Id. **-ηδόν**, Adv. *laboriously*, Man.4.622. ⊛ **-ηρός**, ά, όν, *toilsome, wearisome*, γῆρας *h.Ven.*246; κόπος Ar.*Lys.*542; καματηρὸν ἀϋτμένα φυσιόωντε A.R.2.87; καματηρὸν τὸ ἄρχειν Arist.*Mu.*400$^{b}$9. 2. *tiring, exhausting*, σφοδρὰ καὶ κ. πηδήματα Luc.*Salt.*34. II. Pass., *bowed down with toil, broken down, worn out*, Hdt.4.135; κ. σώματα D.H.10.53, cf. Arr.*An.*5.16.1, *Cat.Cod.Astr.*2.166. 2. *hard-working, toiling*, βόες Porph.*Chr.* 29. **-ος**, ὁ, (κάμνω) *toil, trouble*, ἄτερ καμάτοιο Od.7.325; ἄνευ καμάτου Pi.*P.*12.28; κ. ἵππων A.*Fr.*192.6 (anap.); οὐδέποτ' ἐκ καμάτων ἀποπαύσομαι S.*El.* 231, cf. 130 (both lyr.); of the pangs of childbirth, Id.*OT*174 (lyr.); εὐκάματος E.*Ba.*67 (lyr.): pl., καμάτων ἅλις *AP*9.359 (Posidipp. or Pl.Com.): rare in early Prose, κ. ἐστι τοῖς αὐτοῖς μοχθεῖν Heraclit.84, cf. 111; of the *pains* of disease, Hp. *de Arte* 3 (pl.); κ. ὁ πολύς Luc.*Herm.*71; freq. later, Arist.*Mu.*397$^{b}$23, *OGI* 717.8 (pl., iii A. D.), *POxy.*913.15 (pl., V A. D.). 2. *the effect of toil, weariness*, ὁππότε κέν μιν γυῖα λάβῃ κ. Il.4.230, cf. 13.85,711, etc.; κ. πολυάϊξ γυῖα δέδυκεν 5.811; αἴθρῳ καὶ κ. δεδμημένον Od.14.318; ὕπνῳ καὶ κ. ἀρημένος 6.2; κ. τε καὶ ἄλγεσι θυμὸν ἔδοντες 9.75, cf. Sapph. *Supp.*19.4, etc.: in Prose, Aen.Tact.26.8, Parth.1.1, Jul.*Or.*2. 87b. 3. *illness*, Simon.85.10 (= Semon.29 Diehl): pl., D.H.10.53. II. *the product of toil*, ἡμέτερος κ., viz. the pigs we have reared, Od.14.417; ἀλλότριον κ. σφετέρην ἐς γαστέρ' ἀμῶνται Hes. *Th.*599, cf. Thgn.925; τόρνου κ. *a thing wrought* by the lathe, A. *Fr.*57.3 (anap.), cf. *AP*6.206 (Antip. Sid.); κ. μελίσσης, of honey, Nic.*Al.*71 (pl.), cf. 144. **-ώδης**, ες, *toilsome, wearisome*, θέρεος καματώδεος ὥρη Hes.*Op.*584; πλαγαί, μέριμναι, Pi.*N.*3.17, *Fr.*218.1; καματωδέστερος Thphr.*Lass.*13.

**καμβατηθείς**· καταπονηθείς, Hsch. **κάμβει**· παύεται, Id.

**καμβολίαι**· κακολογίαι, λοιδορίαι, Hsch.

**κάμε**, Ep. aor. 2 of κάμνω; but, 2. **κἀμέ**, crasis for καὶ ἐμέ.

**κάμηλα** [κᾰ], ἡ, = Lat. *camella*, *Edict.Diocl.*15.51.

⊛ **κᾰμηλ-άριος**, ὁ, *camel-driver*, *PLond.*5.1796.15 (vi A. D.). **-ᾰσία** (for *καμηλελασία), ἡ, *camel-driving*, *Dig.*50.4.1.2. **-άσιον**, τό, *wages of camel-driver*, *PLond.*5.1904.7 (v/vi A. D.). **-άτης** (for *καμηλελάτης), ου, ὁ, *camel-driver*, *PBasel* 2.2 (ii A. D.), *BGU*14 vi 12 (iii A. D.). **-ειος**, α, ον, *of a camel*: καμήλεια (sc. κρέα) *camel's flesh*, Porph.*Abst.*1.14 fin., cf. Gal.8.183; κ. οὖρον *PHolm.* 15.18. **-έμπορος**, ὁ, *one who carries his wares on a camel*, of merchants travelling in caravans, Str.17.1.45. **-ίζω**, *to be like a camel*, Hld.10.27. **-ικός**, ή, όν, *of* or *for a camel*, γόμοι *OGI* 629.16 (Palmyra, ii A. D.); *transportable by camels* (cf. ὀνικός), λίθοι *POxy.*498.8 (ii A. D.). **-ιον**, τό, Dim. of κάμηλος, *PHamb.*1.54.7 (ii/iii A. D.), etc. **-ίτης** [ῑ], ου, ὁ, *camel-driver*, Arist.*HA*630$^{b}$35, *POxy.*710.4 (ii B.C.), etc.; *camel-rider*, Hld.10.5, Hdn.4.15.2. 2. also, = καμηλέμπορος, Str.1.2.32, 16.1.27. II. κ. βοῦς, prob. *buffalo*, Suid.

**κᾰμηλο-βοσκός**, ὁ, *camel-herd*, Str.16.4.2. **-κόμος**, ον, *keeping camels*, Eust. ad D.P.954. **-πάρδᾰλις**, εως (or ιδος), ἡ, *camelopard, giraffe*, Agatharch.72, Lxx *De.*14.5, Callix.2, D.C.43.23, Hld. 10.27. **-πόδιον**, τό, = πράσιον, Ps.-Dsc.3.105.

⊛ **κάμηλος** [ᾰ], ὁ and ἡ (as in Ar.*Av.*1563), *camel, Camelus bactrianus* and *C. dromedarius* (cf. Arist.*HA*499$^{a}$13), A.*Supp.*285, etc.; τοὺς ἔρσενας τῶν κ. Hdt.3.105; κ. ἀμνός *a camel*-lamb, i.e. young camel, Ar.*Av.*1559 (lyr.); κ. δρομάς Plu.*Alex.*31: prov., κάμηλον καταπίνειν *Ev.Matt.*23.24; cf. κάμιλος. 2. ἡ κ. *camelry*, Hdt.1.80. (Semitic word, cf. Hebr. *gāmāl.*)

**κᾰμηλο-τροφέω**, *feed, keep camels*, D.S.3.45. **-τρόφος**, ὁ, *camel-keeper*, *BGU*607.12 (ii A. D.), etc.

**κᾰμηλ-ώδης**, ες, *camel-like*, Gal.6.664. **-ών**, ῶνος, ὁ, *stable for camels*, *POxy.*507.26 (ii A. D.), *BGU*393.15, etc.

⊛ **κάμῑλος**, ὁ, *rope*, Sch.Ar.*V.*1030, Suid. (Perh. coined as an emendation of the phrase εὐκοπώτερόν ἐστι κάμηλον διὰ τρυπήματος ῥαφίδος διελθεῖν ἢ πλούσιον εἰς τὴν βασιλείαν τοῦ θεοῦ εἰσελθεῖν *Ev.Matt.*19.24: but cf. Arab. *jummal* 'ship's cable'.)

**κᾰμῑν-αία**, ἡ, *furnace*, Lxx *Ex.*9.10. **-αῖος**, α, ον, *of* or *from a furnace*, τέφρα Ezek.*Exag.*136. **-εία**, ἡ, *furnace-work*, Thphr. *HP*5.9.6 (-ίας codd.), Gal.12.220. **-εύς**, έως, ὁ, *furnace-worker, smith* or *potter*, D.S.20.63. **-ευτήρ**, ῆρος, ὁ, = foreg.; αὐλὸς κ. the pipe *of a smith's bellows*, *AP*6.92 (Phil.):—fem. **-εύτρια** Aristarch. ap.Eust.1835.41, Hsch. s.v. καμινοῖ. **-ευτής**, οῦ, ὁ, = καμινεύς, *PPetr.*3p.173 (dub., iii B. C.), Luc.*Sacr.*6. II. title of priests at Ostia, *IG*14.914. **-ευτικός**, ή, όν, *of* or *for a furnace*, Suid. s. v. κοδομῆϊον. **-εύω**, *heat in a furnace*, Arist.*Mir.*833$^{b}$25, Thphr. *Lap.*69, etc.; σίδηρος καμινευόμενος Str.5.2.6. **-η**, ἡ, = κάμινος, *PLond.*3.994.11 (vi A. D.). ⊛**-ιον**, τό, Dim. of κάμινος, *Gp.*2.3.9, Olymp.Alch.p.76 B. **-ιος**, α, ον, *of* or *for a furnace*, Thphr.*HP* 5.9.6. **-ίτης** [ῑ], ὁ, *baked in an oven*, ἄρτος Philistion ap.Ath.3. 115e. **-ίων**, ωνος, ὁ, *furnace-attendant*, *IG*5(2).50.82 (ii A. D.).

**κᾰμῑνο-γρᾰφία**, ἡ, *treatise on furnaces*, i. e. *alchemy*, title of work by Maria, Olymp.Alch.p.90 B. **-θεν**, Adv. *from a furnace*, Nic. *Th.*707, Call.*Dian.*60. ⊛ **-καύστης**, ου, ὁ, *one who heats a furnace* or *oven*, *Gloss.* (fem. **-καύστρια** Sch.Od.18.27). II. κ. γύψου *one who burns* gypsum *in a kiln*, *BGU*952.8 (ii/iii A. D.).

⊛ **κάμῑν-ος** [ᾰ], ἡ, *oven, furnace*, or *kiln*, for smelting, baking, burning earthenware and bricks, Hom.*Epigr.*14, Hdt.1.179, 4.164, A.*Fr.* 281, Critias 2.13 D., *PPetr.*3p.141 (iii B. C.), etc.: pl., of Hephaestus' forge, *Anacreont.*27A2; *flue* for warming a room, Gal.6.332, cf. 10. 843; *alcove*, Lxx *Nu.*25.8: prov. of one who ate hot dishes, κάμινος οὐκ ἄνθρωπος Crobyl.8; κάμινον ἔχων ἐν τῷ πνεύμονι, of a drunkard, *Com.Adesp.*633. (Perh. cogn. with καμάρα, q. v.) **-ώ**, οῦς, ἡ: γρηῢς κ. an old *furnace*-woman, i. e. an old woman *who worked at a furnace*, Od.18.27. **-ώδης**, ες, *like an oven* or *furnace*, ἀναπνοαί Str.5.4.6.

⊛ **καμίσιον**, τό, *shirt*, *Stud.Pal.*20.245.10 (vi A. D.), etc.:—also **κάμισον**, τό, *PGen.*80.1 (*Arch.Pap.*3.404, iv A. D.). [ῑ inferred from Romance languages; κάμασος and καμάσιον are perh. different.]

**κάμμα**, ατος, τό, (κάπτω) *that which is supped up*, in pl., = ψαιστά, Nicocl.2; cf. καμματίδες.

**κάμμᾰρος**, ὁ, a kind of *lobster*, Epich.60, Sophr.26, Rhinth.18:—also **καμμαρίς**, ίδος, ἡ, Gal.6.735. II. a kind of *aconite*, used as a cooling medicine, Hp.*Loc.Hom.*27, Stratt.21, Dsc.4.76, Nic.*Al.*41; also, = δελφίνιον, Ps.-Dsc.3.73; = μανδραγόρα ἄρρεν, Id.4.75. (Meaning and spelling are dub. in Hp., cf. Erot. s. v.: **κάμαρος** and **κάμμορον** were variants, the latter is v.l. in Dsc. l. c., cf. Sch.Nic. l. c.)

**κάμμαρψις**· μέτρον σιτικόν, τὸ ἡμιμέδιμνον (Aeol.), Hsch.

**καμματίδες**, ων, αἱ, (κάπτω) *laurel leaves* used for supping up κάμματα, Nicocl.2.

**κάμμει**· καθέζει, Hsch.

**καμμονίη**, ἡ, Ep. for καταμονή, *steadfastness, endurance* (ἡ ἐκ καταμονῆς νίκη Sch., cf. Plu.2.22c), *steady courage*, αἴ κεν ἐμοὶ Ζεὺς δώῃ καμμονίην Il.22.257, cf. 23.661, *APl.*4.221.4 (Theaet.).

**κάμμορον**, τό, variant for κάμμαρος II (q. v.): expld. as, = κακόμορον, Erot. s. v. καμμάρῳ, cf. Sch.Nic.*Al.*41; but, = κώνειον, Zeno Herophileus ap.Gal.19.108.

**κάμμορος**, ον, Ep. for κατάμορος, *subject to destiny*, i. e. *ill-fated* (not in Il.), περὶ πάντων κάμμορε φωτῶν Od.11.216, cf. 2.351, 5.160, A.R. 4.1318. (Cf. κάσμορος, ἤμορος.)

**κάμμυσις**, εως, ἡ, = κάταμυσις, *Corp.Herm.*1.30; cf. sq.

**καμμύω**, Ep. for καταμύω, v.l. in Batr.191: also in later Gr., τοὺς ὀφθαλμοὺς ἐκάμμυσαν Lxx *Is.*6.10, al., cf. Ph.1.645, Hero *Aut.*22.1, *PMag.Lond.*121.855 (iii A. D.), Paul.Aeg.3.22.29: pf. κεκάμμυκα A.D.*Synt.*323.22: cited from Alex.319 by Phryn., but censured as un-Attic.

⊛ **κάμνω**, fut. κᾰμοῦμαι, καμῇ, A.*Eu.*881, S.*Tr.*1215; καμεῖται Il.2.389, Pl.*Lg.*921e; Ep. inf. -έεσθαι A.R.3.580: aor. 2 ἔκᾰμον, Ep. κάμον Il.4.187, al.; inf. καμεῖν, Ep. subj. redupl. κεκάμω, κεκάμῃσι, κεκάμωσιν, Il.1.168, 17.658, 7.5 (but Aristarch. read κε κάμω, etc., prob. rightly): pf. κέκμηκα Il.6.262, etc.: plpf. ἐκεκμήκεσαν Th.3.98; Ep. part. κεκμηώς, κεκμηῶτι, κεκμηῶτα, Il.23.232, 6.261, Od.10.31; κεκμηότας Il.11.802; κεκμηῶτας is v.l. for κεκμηκότας in Th.3.59:—Med., aor. 2 ἐκᾰμόμην Od.9.130, Ep. καμ- Il.18.341. I. trans., *work*, μίτρη, τὴν χαλκῆες κάμον ἄνδρες *wrought* it, 4.187, 216; ἐπεὶ πάνθ' ὅπλα κάμε 18.614; σκῆπτρον.., τὸ μὲν Ἥφαιστος κάμε τεύχων 2.101, cf. 8.195; κ. νῆας Od.9.126; πέπλον Il.5.338, cf. Od.15.105; ἵππον 11.523; λέχος 23.189; ἄστυ *build*, A.R.1.1322: also in aor. Med., ἱρόν Il.2.718. 2. aor. Med., *win by toil*, τὰς (sc. γυναῖκας) αὐτοὶ καμόμεσθα βίηφί τε δουρί τε μακρῷ Il.18.341. 3. aor. Med., *labour, till*, οἵ κέ σφιν καὶ νῆσον.. ἐκάμοντο Od.9.130; οἴκους Philet.8. II. intr., *toil, labour*, τινι *for* one, Od.14.65; ὑπὲρ τῆς πόλεως Th.2.41: then, from the effect of continued work, *to be weary*, ἀνδρὶ δὲ κεκμηῶτι μένος μέγα οἶνος ἀέξει Il.6.261, cf. 11.802: with acc. of the part, οὐδέ τι γυῖα.. κάμνει nor *is* he *weary in* limb, 19.170, etc.; περὶ δ' ἔγχεϊ χεῖρα καμεῖται 2.389; ὁ δ' ἀριστερὸν ὦμον ἔκαμνεν 16.106: freq. c. part., κ. πολεμίζων, ἐλαύνοντες, ἐρεθίζων, *is weary* of fighting, rowing, etc., 1.168, 7.5, 17.658, etc.; οὐ μέν θην κάμετον.. ὀλλῦσαι Τρῶας 8.448; ἔκαμον δέ μοι ὅσσε πάντῃ παπταίνοντι Od.12.232; but οὐδέ τι τόξον δὴν ἔκαμον τανύων I *did* not long *strain over* stringing the bow, i. e. did it without *effort*, 21.426, cf. Il.8.22: later freq. with neg., οὔτοι καμοῦμαι.. λέγουσα I *shall* never *be tired* of saying, A.*Eu.*881; μὴ κάμῃς λέγων E.*IA*1143; οὐκ ἂν κάμοιμι τὰς κακὰς κτείνων Id.*Or.*1590; οὔποτε κάμοιμ' ἂν ὀρχουμένη Ar.*Lys.*541 (lyr.); κ. εὐεργετῶν, ἐπαινῶν, Pl.*Grg.*470c, *Lg.*921e: c. dat., κ. δαπάναις *to grow tired* in spending, spare expense, Pi.*P.*1.90. 2. *to be hard-pressed, worsted*, in battle or contest, ib.1.78, 80; τὸ κάμνον στρατοῦ E.*Supp.* 709. 3. *to be sick* or *suffering*, τί πάσχεις; τί κάμνεις; Ar.*Nu.*708; οἱ κάμνοντες *the sick*, Hdt.1.197, cf. S.*Ph.*282, And.1.64, Pl.*R.*407c, *Ep.Jac.*5.15, etc.; of a doctor's *patients*, Hp.*Acut.*1, D.18.243, *SIG*943.10 (Cos); καμοῦσα ἀπέθανε *having fallen sick*, And.1.120: c. acc. cogn., κάμνειν νόσον E.*Heracl.*990, Pl.*R.*408e; [τὴν ποδάγραν]

v.l. in Arist.*HA*604a23; τοὺς ὀφθαλμοὺς Hdt.2.111; τὰ σώματα *to be ill* or *distempered* in body, Pl.*Grg*.478a; ὡσίν τε κάμμασιν Herod.3.32; πάθᾳ Pi.*P*.8.48; νοσήμασι Arist.*HA*603a30; ἀπὸ τοῦ τραύματος Luc.*Tox*.60; ὑπὸ νόσου Hdn.3.14.2. 4. generally, *to be distressed, meet with disaster*, στρατοῦ καμόντος A.*Ag*.670; τῷ πεποιημένῳ κ. μεγάλως Hdt.1.118, cf. A.*Ag*.482 (lyr.), E.*Med*.1138, *HF*293; οὐ καμῇ τοὐμὸν μέρος *wilt* not *have to complain..*, S.*Tr*. 1215; κ. ἔν τινι E.*Hec*.306, *IA*966; of a ship, νεὼς καμούσης ποντίῳ πρὸς κύματι A.*Th*.210: c. acc. cogn., οὐκ ἴσον καμὼν ἐμοὶ λύπης not *having borne* an equal share of grief, S.*El*.532. 5. in aor. part., of the dead, i.e. either *outworn*, or *those whose work is done*, or *those who have met with disaster*, οἳ ὑπένερθε καμόντας ἀνθρώπους τίνυσθον Il.3.278, cf. Theoc.17.49; βροτῶν εἴδωλα καμόντων Od.11.476; εἴδωλα κ. 24.14, Il.23.72, cf. A.*Supp*.231, etc.: also in pf. part. in Trag. and Prose, κεκμηκότες S.*Fr*.284, E.*Supp*.756, Th.3.59, Pl.*Lg*.718a, 927b, Arist.*EN*1101a35; ἱερὰ τῶν κ. E.*Tr*.96; also in the finite Verb, ὅπῃ ἄνθρωπος ἔκαμε *Berl.Sitzb*.1927.158 (Cyrene).—The pf. is always intr. (Cf. Skt. *śamnīte* 'work hard', 'serve zealously', *śamitár-* 'sacrificing priest', Gr. εἰρο-κόμος, κομέω, κομίζω.)

**κάμορος**· κλῆθρα τὸ δένδρον, Hsch.

⊛ **καμπαγών**, ῶνος, ὁ, a kind of *boot*, *IG*2[2].1120 (*Edict.Diocl.*).

**καμπᾰλέος**, α, ον, (καμπή) = καμπτός, Hsch.

**καμπανίζω**, *weigh*, *PLond*.5.1708.130 (vi A.D.).

**κάμπανος**, ὁ, *weighing-machine, steelyard*, *PMasp*.325 iv*A* 37 (vi A.D.), *Gloss*. (Lat. *campana*).

**καμπεσί-γουνος** [ῐ], ον, *bending the knees*, Ἐρινύς Hsch. ⊛ **-γυιος**, ον, *bending the limbs*, παίγνια κ. *puppets*, Orph.*Fr*.34.

**καμπή**, ἡ, (κάμπτω) *winding*, of a river, Hdt.1.185; Εὐβοΐδα κ., of the Euripus, A.*Fr*.30; τὰς κ. τῶν χωρίων Aen.Tact.15.6; τόπους καμπὰς ἔχοντας Ael.*Tact*.35.4. 2. *flexion, bending*, τὰ ἄποδα δυσὶ χρώμενα προέρχεται καμπαῖς Arist.*IA*707b9, cf. *HA*490a31. 3. *curved part*, Hero *Spir*.2.16, Sor.2.62. II. *turning-post in a race-course*, περὶ ταῖσι καμπαῖς ἡνίοχοι πεπτωκότες Ar.*Pax*905; καμπαῖσι δρόμων E.*IA*224 (lyr.); εὐλαβηθῆναι περὶ τὴν κ. Pl.*Ion*537a: metaph., μῦθον ἐς καμπὴν ἄγε bring a speech to *its goal* (cf. καμπτήρ II), E.*El*. 659; καμπὴν ποιεῖσθαι Pl.*Phd*.72b. III. in Music, *turn, sudden change*, εἴ τις κάμψειέν τινα καμπὴν Ar.*Nu*.969; ἐξαρμονίους κ. Pherecr. 145.9, cf. ib.28; καμπαὶ ᾀσμάτων Philostr.*VS*2.28. 2. Rhet., *rounding off* of a period, Cic.*Att*.1.14.4 (pl.), Demetr.*Eloc*.10, 17. IV. *bend* or *flexure* of a limb, τῶν ὤμων, τῶν ἰσχίων, τῶν δακτύλων, etc., Arist.*HA*498a25 sqq., cf. Pl.*Ti*.74e; of the skull, οὐκ ἔχουσα καμπάς ib.75c; οὐλὴ καμπῇ (= -ῇ) χιρὸς δεξιᾶς *Sammelb*.7031.5 (i A.D.).

⊛ **κάμπη**, ἡ, *caterpillar*, Hp.*Superf*.28, Aristopho 10.4, Lxx*Am*.4.9, etc.; of the *silk-worm*, Arist.*HA*551b11, Thphr.*HP*4.14.9. 2. *ornament* of this shape, dub. in *IG*12(5).134.13 (Paros). II. *a fabulous Indian monster*, D.S.3.72, Nonn.*D*.18.237; cf. κάμπος.

**κάμπῐμος**, η, ον, (καμπή) *bent, turning*, δρόμος E.*IT*81:—also **κάμπιος**, Ptol.*Tetr*.150: **κάμπειος**, Hsch.

**κάμπος**, εος, τό, *a sea-monster*, Lyc.414. II. = ἱπποδρόμος (Sicel), Hsch. **καμπουλίρ**· ἐλαίας εἶδος (Lacon.), Id. (-ούληρ cod.).

⊛ **καμπ-τήρ**, ῆρος, ὁ, *bend, angle*, X.*Cyr*.7.1.6, Str.14.2.14. II. *turning-point in the* δίαυλος, which was *the goal* in the single race (cf. καμπή II), Arist.*Rh*.1409a32, *BCH*23.567 (Delph., iii B.C.), Babr.29. 4: pl., as works of art, Plin.*HN*36.25: metaph., κ. βίου *the 'last lap'* of life, Herod.10.3; κ. πύματος, of the colophon which marks the last page, *AP*12.257.1 (Mel.). **-τηρία**, ἡ, = foreg. II, Tz.*H*.8.27:—also **-τήριος** (sc. νύσσα), Sch.Opp.*H*.1.205. **-τικός**, ή, όν, *bending, flexible*, δακτύλου τὸ κ. *the joint*, Arist.*HA*493b28; κίνησις ἡ κ. Id.*Spir*.484b13; φωνάριον Poll.4.64. **-τός**, ή, όν, *flexible*, Pl. *Ti*.44e, Arist.*Mete*.385a13, al. II. masc. as Subst., = καμπτήρ II, Aq.*Pr*.2.9, Sch.Ar.*Nu*.28, v.l. in *EM*609.29 and Choerob.*in Theod*. 2.151. 2. *flank*, Hippiatr.32. ⊛ **-τρα**, ἡ, *case, chest* (cf. κάμψα), *IG*5(1).1390.11 (Andania, i B.C.), *BGU*781.12 (i A.D.), *Gloss*.:—Dim. **-τρίον**, τό, *Gp*.10.21.10, *Gloss*.; cf. καπτρίον. **-τρον**, τό, *turning-point* in the race-course, ib. s.v. *intermetium*. II. = κάμπτρα, ib.; cf. κάπτρον.

**καμπτρο-ποιός**, ὁ, *basket-maker*, *Gloss*. **-φόρος**, ὁ, = *capsarius*, ib.

⊛ **κάμπτω**, fut. κάμψω Il.7.118, S.*OC*91: aor. 1 ἔκαμψα Od.5.453, Pi.*P*.2.51, etc.:—Pass., fut. καμφθήσομαι D.Chr.77.33, Gal.*UP*2.15: aor. ἐκάμφθην A.*Pr*.513, Th.3.58: pf. inf. κεκάμφθαι Hp.*Art*.67, part. κεκαμμένος Arist.*Metaph*.1016a12, (ἐπι-, συγ-) Hp.*Prog*.3, X. *Eq*.7.2. (Cogn. with Lith. *kam̃p-as* 'corner', *kum̃p-as* 'curved', and prob. Lat. *campus*):—*bend, curve*, ὄφρα ἴτυν κάμψῃ that he *may bend* it into a chariot-rail, Il.4.486 (so metaph., κ. νέας ἁψῖδας ἐπῶν Ar.*Th*.53): freq. in phrase, γόνυ κ. *bend* the knee so as to sit down and rest, φημί μιν ἀσπασίως γόνυ κάμψειν Il.7.118, cf. 19.72; ὁ δ' ἄρ' ἄμφω γούνατ' ἔκαμψε χεῖράς τε στιβαράς Od.5.453; οὐ κάμπτων γόνυ, i.e. never resting, A.*Pr*.32; ἀσμενὸς τἂν..κάμψειεν γόνυ ib. 398; ἵζω..κάμψας γόνυ E.*Hec*.1150; so κ. κῶλα S.*OC*19; then κάμπτειν alone, *sit down, rest*, ib.85, E.*Hec*.1080 (lyr.); also γόνυ κ. *bend* the knee in worship, Lxx*Is*.45.23, etc.:—Pass., *bend oneself*, opp. ἐκτείνεσθαι, Pl.*Ti*.74b; ὥσπερ ξύλον καμπτόμενον εὐθύνουσιν Id.*Prt*. 325d; ἡ κεκαμμένη (sc. γραμμή) a *bent* line, Arist.*Metaph*.l.c. II. *turn* or *guide* a horse or chariot *round* the turning-post (cf. καμπτήρ II), κάμψαι διαύλου θάτερον κῶλον πάλιν *to double* the post and return along the second half of the δίαυλος, A.*Ag*.344; κ. δρόμον B. 9.26; κάμπτοντος ἵππου as the horse *was turning*, S.*El*.744; κ. περὶ νύσσαν Theoc.24.120: metaph., κ. βίον *to make the last turn in the course* of life, S.*OC*91; κ. βίου τέλος E.*Hipp*.87, *El*.956; ὅταν κάμψῃς καὶ τελευτήσῃς βίον Id.*Hel*.1666; ἑξηκοστὸν ἥλιον κ. Herod.10.1; διὰ λόγου κάμψαι κακά *to end* evils by reasoning, E.*Supp*.748. 2. of seamen, *double* a headland, Ἡρακλέας στήλας Hdt.4.42; τὸ ἀκρωτήριον, τὴν ἄκρην, Id.4.43, 7.122; ὡς δὲ τὴν ἄκραν κάμπτοντας ἡμᾶς εἶδον Men. 15, cf. Aeschrio 8.3; Μαλέαν κ. Poet.ap.Str.8.6.20, D.S.13.64, etc.; κ. περὶ ἄκραν Ar.*Ach*.96; κ. κόλπον *wind round* the bay, Hdt.7.58. 3. abs., πάλιν κ. *turn* back, E.*Ba*.1225, *Rh*.234 (lyr.); ἐγγὺς τῶν ἐμῶν κάμπτεις φρενῶν (κάμπτῃ codd.) thou *comest* near my meaning, Id.*IT* 815. III. in Music, κάμπτων με καὶ στρέφων ὅλην διέφθορεν (sc. Phrynis) with his *turns* and twists, Pherecr.145.15; κ. καμπήν Ar.*Nu*. 969; κ. ᾠδάς Philostr.*VA*4.39. IV. metaph., κάμπτειν τινά *bow down, humble*, Pi.*P*.2.51; ὁ χρόνος μ' ἔκαμψε Crates Theb.17:—Pass., *to be bent* or *bowed down*, πημοναῖσι A.*Pr*.239, 308, cf. 513; κάμπτομαι I *submit*, Pl.*Prt*.320b, etc.; κάμπτεσθαι καὶ ἕλκεσθαι πρὸς φιλοσοφίαν Id.*R*.494e; πολλὰ κάμπτονται καὶ συγκλῶνται are *warped*, Id.*Tht*. 173b: abs., *to be moved to pity*, Th.3.58 (in full κ. εἰς ἔλεον Lib.*Or*. 59.85).

**καμπ-ύλη** [ῠ] (sc. βακτηρία), ἡ, *crooked staff*, Ar.*Fr*.128, Plu.2. 790b, Alciphr.3.3. **-ῠλιάζω**, = sq., Phot., Suid. **-ύλλω**, Ion. for κάμπτω, *bend, crook*, Hp.*Art*.60 (Pass.):—Med., ib.46: **-υλεύομαι**, Pass., Erot., Aret.*SA*1.6.

**καμπῠλο-ειδής**, ές, *appearing crooked*, φαντασία Plu.2.1121c. **-εις**, εσσα, εν, poet. for καμπύλος, ἴτυς *AP*6.28 (Jul. Aegypt.). **-ομαι**, Pass., *become curved*, Antyll.ap.Aët.7.74. ⊛ **-πρυμνος**, ον, *with rounded stern*, Sch.D Il.2.392, Hsch. s.v. κορωνίς. **-ρρῖν**, ῖνος, ὁ, ἡ, *hook-nosed*, *EM*395.36, Hsch. s.v. γρυπός.

**καμπύλος** [ῠ], η, ον, (κάμπτω) *bent, curved*, opp. εὐθύς, of a bow, κ. τόξα Il.3.17, etc.; ἅρμα 5.231; κ. κύκλα, of wheels, ib.722; ἄροτρα *h.Cer*.308, Sol.13.48; δίφρος Pi.*I*.4(3).29; ὄχημα A.*Supp*.183; σελίς *IG*1[2].374.57; κῦμα *BMus.Inscr*.1012 (Chalcedon); κ. ἐς τὸ ἔξω Hp. *Art*.1; καμπύλα τε καὶ εὐθέα Pl.*R*.602c: metaph., κ. μέλος an ode *of varied metre*, Simon.29; cf. καμπύλη.

**καμπῠλοσαλπιστής**, οῦ, ὁ, *horn-blower*, = Lat. *cornicen*, *Gloss*.

**καμπῠλότης**, ητος, ἡ, *crookedness, curvature*, Hp.*Coac*.214, Arist. *Cat*.10a13, *PA*643a33, Gal.4.796.

⊛ **καμπύλοχος** [ῠ], ον, *with curved carriage*, κερκίδες, i.e. ploughs, Orph.*Fr*.33.

⊛ **κάμψα**, ης, ἡ, *basket, case*, Hsch.:—also **κάψα** (cf. Lat. *capsa*), Phot., Suid.:—Dim. ⊛ **καμψίον**, τό, *PMasp*.6 ii 90 (vi A.D.), Hsch.:—also **καμψάκης** or **καψάκης**, ου, ὁ, *cruse, flask*, ἐλαίου Lxx *Ju*.10.5, cf. *3Ki*.17.12, 16; μέλιτος καψάκαι *PSI*4.428.64 (iii B.C.), cf. *PCair. Zen*.12.107, al. (iii B.C.); ⊛ **καμψάκιον**, τό, *BGU*387 ii 19 (ii A.D.), Cumont *Fouilles de Doura-Europos* 372; **καψάκιον**, Hsch.

**καμψάνεμα**, gender and declension unknown, = λιβανωτίς, Dsc. 3.74.

⊛ **καμψάριος**, ὁ, = Lat. *capsarius*, *Edict.Diocl*.7.75.

**κάμψη**, ἡ, = *ebulus*, *Gloss*.

**καμψῐδίαυλος** [δῐ], ον, *turning the post* (καμπτήρ II) *so as to run the whole* δίαυλος: metaph., of a harp-player, *running quickly up and down* the strings, χεὶρ κ. Telest.4.

**καμψικίζω**, = βαρβαρίζω, Hsch. ⊛ **καμψίον**, τό, v. κάμψα.

⊛ **καμψί-ουρος** [ῐ], ον, *bending the tail*, v. σκίουρος. **-πους**, ὁ, ἡ, πουν, τό, gen. ποδος, *bending the foot*, in running, i.e. *swift-running*, Ἐρινύς A.*Th*.791 (lyr.).

**κάμψις**, εως, ἡ, (κάμπτω) *bending*, Pl.*Ti*.74a, Gal.*UP*12.4; κάμψιν ἔχειν εἰς τὸ πλάγιον to have a *bend*, of joints, Arist.*HA*498a18; κ. δέχεσθαι Thphr.*HP*4.11.11.

**καμψός**, ή, όν, (κάμπτω) *crooked, bent*, Hsch.

**κάμων** [ᾰ], ωνος, = σκαμμωνία, Nic.*Al*.484.

**κάν**, poet. for κατά before ν, κὰν νόμον Pi.*O*.8.78, prob. in Alc. *Supp*.19. **κἀν**, crasis for καὶ ἐν.

**κἄν** (not κᾂν), by crasis, I. for καὶ ἄν.., v.l. in Hes.*Op*.357, freq. in Att.: not often when καί is simply copul., Pl.*Phd*.79a, *Grg*. 514d; but freq. when καί is intens., ὅ γε κ. μέγα δοίη *even* a great thing, Hes. l.c.; κακὸν δὲ κ. ἐν ἡμέρᾳ γνοίης μιᾷ S.*OT*615, cf. 591, *Aj*.45, Ar.*Nu*.1130, Th.7.61, etc.; sts. repeated after or before a Verb with ἄν, ἐπεὶ κ. σὺ.., εἴ τίς σε διδάξειεν.., βελτίων ἂν γένοιο Pl. *Prt*.318b, cf. *R*.515e; freq. in the phrase κ. εἰ, where καί properly belongs to εἰ, *even if*, and ἄν to the Verb that follows in apodosi, νῦν δέ μοι δοκεῖ, κ. ἀσέβειαν εἰ καταγιγνώσκοι, τὰ προσήκοντα ποιεῖν (for καὶ εἰ καταγιγνώσκοι, ποιεῖν ἄν) D.21.51: hence, 2. even when the Verb in apodosi was of a tense that could not be joined with ἄν, κ. εἰ πολλαὶ [αἱ ἀρεταί].. εἰσιν, ἕν γέ τι εἶδος ταὐτὸν ἅπασαι ἔχουσι Pl.*Men*. 72c; κ. εἰ μή τῳ δοκεῖ Id.*R*.473a, 579d, cf. 408b, *Phd*.71b, *Sph*.247e, Arist.*Top*.136a31, al. 3. in later Gr. without εἰ, simply as a stronger form of καί, *even*, εἰσελθὲ κ. νῦν Men.342; κ. νεκρῷ χάρισαι τὰ σὰ χείλεα Theoc.23.41, cf. 35 (v.l.) (and so with εἷς, μία, ἕν, κ. μίαν ἡμέραν δόντες αὐτοῖς v.l. in X.*HG*1.7.19; εἰ κ. ἕν τι φαίνοιτο S.E. *P*.2.195, cf. Ph.2.29); ἐὰν ἅψωμαι κ. τῶν ἱματίων *Ev.Marc*.5.28; κἂν νῦν now *at any rate*, *POxy*.2151.7 (iii A.D.); κἂν ὡς *even so, nevertheless*, ib.123.7 (iii/iv A.D.); οἷς οὐδὲ κ. ὄνος ὑπῆρξε πώποτε Luc.*Tim*.20 codd., cf. *DDeor*.5.2, etc. II. for καὶ ἄν (= ἐάν), *even if*, with the same moods as ἐάν, S.*Aj*.15, Pl.*Prt*.319c, etc.: freq. used ellipt., ἄνδρα χρὴ δοκεῖν πεσεῖν ἂν κ. (sc. πέσῃ) ἀπὸ σμικροῦ κακοῦ S.*Aj*.1078, cf. Ar.*V*.92, *Ach*.1021, and so prob. in S.*El*.1483: later folld. by ind., κἂν γὰρ οὕτω φαμὲν A.D.*Synt*.70.22. 2. κἄν.., κἄν.., *whether* .., *or*.., κἂν μεγάλην πόλιν οἰκῶσι κἂν μικράν D.25.15.

**κανάβευμα**, v. κιν-.

**κανάβῐνος**, η, ον, *of* or *for a block-figure*, κηρός Hsch.; σῶμα κ. a body *so lean as to be a mere skeleton*, *AP*11.107 (Lucill.): κανάβιον codd. in ll. cc.; κᾰ- in *APl*. c. (nisi leg. καννυ-).

⊛ **κανᾰβιουργός**, ὁ, *maker of* κάναβοι, *Tab.Defix*.87$^a$7 (iv B.C.).

⊛ **κάνᾰβος** or **κάννᾰβος**, ὁ, *wooden framework* round which artists moulded wax or clay, *block-figure*, Hsch., Poll.7.164, 10.189. 2. *mannikin* or *rough drawing of the human frame*, Arist.*HA*515$^a$35, *GA*743$^a$2 (wrongly expld. as *cistern* by Phlp. *in GA*109.27). 3. metaph., *lean person*, '*skeleton*', Stratt.20, Hsch. (Spelling and quantity undetermined: cf. κίναβος.)

**κάναδοι**· σιαγόνες, γνάθοι, Hsch. **καναδόκα**· χείλη ὀϊστοῦ (Lacon.), Id.; cf. κανδόχα.

⊛ **κάναθρον** or better **κάνναθρον**, τό, (κάννα) *cane* or *wicker carriage*, X.*Ages*.8.7, cf. Hsch., Eust.1344.44.

**κάνακις**· ξίφος, Hsch.

**κάνασθον**, τό, = κάναστρον, *Schwyzer* 748.3 (Naucratis).

**κᾰνάσσω**, only in aor. inf. and part. κανάξαι, -άξας, *pour with a gurgling sound*, Hsch.; τὸ ἐκκενῶσαι ἢ ἐκπιεῖν κανάξαι λέγουσι Poll. 10.85: elsewh. only in compds. δια-, ἐγ-, ἐκ-κανάσσω; cf. καναχέω.

⊛ **καναστραῖα**· κοῖλά τινα ἀγγεῖα, Suid.

⊛ **κάναστρον** [κᾰ], τό, = κάνεον, *wicker basket*, *GDI*5087.9 (Crete), dub. in *Supp.Epigr*.1.414 (Crete), cf. Hsch.: **καναῦστρον**, *IG*1$^2$.330. 11 (cited as **κάναστρον** and **κάνυστρον** by Poll.10.86), cf. *Carm.Pop*. 41.9; **κάνιστρον** (?), *PLond*.5.1657.9 (iv/v A.D.). II. *earthen vessel, dish*, = τρύβλιον, Hom.*Epigr*.14.3, Nicopho 24.

**καναφόρος**· μεσόδμη, Hsch.

⊛ **κᾰνᾰχ-έω**, a Verb expressing various sounds, κανάχησε δὲ χαλκός *rang, clashed*, Od.19.469; καναχοῦσι πηγαί *plash*, Cratin.186; καναχῶν ὀλόφωνος ἀλέκτωρ *crowing*, Id.259: c. acc. cogn., κ. μέλος *to let a song ring loud*, A.R.4.907. -ή, Dor. -χά, ἡ, (κανάσσω) *sharp sound*; esp. *ring* or *clang* of metal, δεινὴν .. πήληξ βαλλομένη καναχὴν ἔχε Il.16.105, cf. 794; κ. δ' ἦν ἡμιόνοιιν *loud* rang their *tramp*, Od.6.82; ὀδόντων μὲν κ. πέλε *gnashing* of teeth, Il.19.365, Hes.*Sc*.164: pl., ib. 160; κ. [χαλκ]όκτυπος B.13.15; χρυσοῦ κ. S.*Ant*.130 (lyr.); κ. αὐλῶν *sound* of flutes, Pi.*P*.10.39 (pl.), B.2.12, cf. S.*Tr*.642 (lyr.); of the lyre, *h.Ap*.185. -ηδά, Adv. *with a loud noise*, ποταμοὶ καναχηδὰ ῥέοντες Hes.*Th*.367, cf. A.R.3.71, Call.*Del*.45; of flutes, v. μίτρα. -ηδής, ές, *resounding*, ἀνθερεών Jo.Gaz.2.162 (s. v. l.). -ηδόν, Adv., = καναχηδά, D.P.145, Aret.*SD*1.3. -ήπους, ποδος, ὁ, ἡ, *with sounding feet*, of the horse, Certamen 100, Opp.*C*.2.431; Dor. acc. sg. masc. -άποδα [ᾱ] Alcm.23.48. -ής, ές, of water, *plashing*, κ. δάκρυ A.*Ch*.152 (lyr.). -ίζω, = καναχέω, κανάχιζε δὲ δούρατα Il. 12.36; δῶμα σμερδαλέον κανάχιζε v.l. in Od.10.399; κανάχιζε πόδ' εὐρεῖα χθών Hes.*Sc*.373. -ός, ή, όν, *noisy*, κ. βάτραχοι Nic.*Th*.620.

**κανδαλιστής**, οῦ, ὁ, *acrobat*, *Delph*.3(1).226 (sed leg. σκανδ-).

**κάνδαλοι**· κοιλώματα, βάθρα, κωλοβάθραι, Hsch. **κάνδαρος**, ὁ, = ἄνθραξ, Id. (Cf. *candeo*.)

**Κανδαύλης**, ὁ, Lydian name for Hermes, expld. as *dog-throttler*, Hippon.1; name of a Lydian king, Hdt.1.7, al.

**κάνδαυλος**, ὁ, a *Lydian dish*, of which there were several varieties, Nicostr.Com.17, Alex.172.1, Philem.60, Men.462.11:—also **κάνδῠλος**, Id.518.6, Euang.1.8, [Cerc.]18 ii 15, Plu.2.664a, *PGiss*. 93.12 (ii A.D.), Sch.Ar.*Pax* 122 (v. l.), Hsch.; **κάνδυτος** f.l. (cod. Phot.) in Ar.*Fr*.791.

⊛ **κανδήλη**, ἡ, Lat. *candela, candle, torch*, Ath.15.701b:—hence **κανδηλο-σβέστης**, ου, ὁ, fem. -**σβέστρια**, ἡ, *moth*, Sch.Nic.*Th*.763, Sch.Opp.*H*.1.404.

**κανδοφόρους**· μελανειμοῦντας, Hsch. **κανδόχα**· κήλη (Lacon.), Id.; cf. καναδόκα. ⊛ **κανδύλη**, v. κανδύταλις. **κάνδυλος**, v. κάνδαυλος.

**κάνδυς**, υος, ὁ, *Median double* or *upper garment with sleeves*, X.*Cyr*. 1.3.2, *An*.1.5.8, Luc.*DMort*.14.4, Them.*Or*.2.36c; κ. ποικίλος *IG*2$^2$. 1514.19.

⊛ **κανδύτᾰλις** [ῠ], ὁ, *clothes-press*, Maced. word in Diph.40, Men.82: **κανδύλη** or **κανδυτάνη**, Hsch.: pl. **κανδύτανες** prob. in Ael.*NA*17. 17, cf. Poll.7.79, Phot. (who also explains it as a kind of *fish*, or = αἰδοῖον).

**κάνδυτος**, v. κάνδαυλος.

**κάνειον**, τό, Ep. for sq. II. *lid of a vessel*, Hp.*Mul*.1.11, 2.133.

⊛ **κάνεον** [ᾰ], τό, Ep. also **κάνειον**, Att. contr. **κανοῦν** *IG*1$^2$.313.136, 2$^2$.1414.20, al.; dual κανώ ib.1$^2$.280.10; pl. κανᾶ ib.2$^2$.1414.38:—*basket of reed* or *cane*, esp. *bread-basket*, καλοῖς ἐν κανέοισιν Il.9.217; περικαλλέος ἐκ κανέοιο Od.17.343, cf. Hdt.1.119, etc.; χάλκειον κάνεον Il.11.630; χρύσεια κάνεια Od.10.355; esp. used for the sacred barley at sacrifices, ἔχεν οὐλὰς ἐν κανέῳ 3.442; κανοῦν ἐνῆρκται E.*El*. 1142, cf. *HF*926, Aeschin.3.120, Men.*Sam*.7; τὸ κανοῦν ὀλὰς ἔχον Ar.*Pax* 948, cf. *Ach*.244, al., Pherecr.137, etc.; carried in procession, Men.*Epit*.222; as a votive offering (perh. a vessel of basket-shape), *IG*11(2).161*B*34, al. (Delos, iii B.C.), 7.2424 (Thebes), *CIG* 2855.21 (Branchidae).

**κανῆν**, Dor. aor. 2 inf. of καίνω (q. v.).

⊛ **κάνης** [ᾰ], ητος, ὁ, a *mat of reeds* such as the Athen. women took with them when they went out, Lex Solonis ap.Plu.*Sol*.21: generally, *mat*, D.H.2.23 (pl.): prov., ὁ κ. τῆς κοίτης ὑπερέχει, of those who make a show abroad with poverty at home, Crates Com.12, cf. Phot. s. v. II. = λίκνον, Poll.6.86.

**κᾰνήτιον**, τό, = κανίσκιον, Poll.6.86.

**κᾰνητοποιός**, ὁ, *maker of reed-mats*, prob. in Hippon.116, cf. Poll. 10.184 (καννηνο- cod.).

**κᾰνηφορ-έω**, *carry a basket*, Ph.2.55, al.; esp. *carry the sacred basket in procession*, Ar.*Lys*.646, al., *IG*2.1204, al., 3.921; κ. Παναθηναίοις Arist.*Ath*.18.2; also κ. Δήλια καὶ Ἀπολλώνια Durrbach *Choix d'Inscriptions de Délos* 115 (ii B.C.); τῷ Διὶ τῷ βασιλεῖ Plu.2.772a; Ἴσιδι *CIG*2298 (Delos), cf. 3602 (Ilium). -ία, ἡ, *office of* κανηφόρος, Pl.*Hipparch*.229c. -ικός, ή, όν, *of the* Κανηφόροι, κόσμος *IG* 2$^2$.333c10. -ος (parox.), ον, *carrying a basket*: Κανηφόροι, αἱ, at Athens, title of maidens who carried baskets in procession at festivals, Ar.*Ach*.242 (sg.), al. (cf. Sch. ad loc.), Hermipp.26, *IG*2$^2$.896.9 (sg.); represented in works of art, Cic.*Verr*.4.3.5, Plin.*HN*36.25; elsewh., as title of priestess, κ. θεᾶς Ἀρτέμιδος *CIG*4362 (Pisid.); κ. Ἀρσινόης Φιλαδέλφου *PCair.Zen*.3 (iii B.C.), *PTeb*.176 (iii/ii B.C.), cf. *PStrassb*.83.10 (ii B.C.), etc.

**κανθάρ-εως** or -**εος** [θᾰ], ὁ, name of a kind of *vine*, Thphr.*CP*2.15.5: -**ιος** Hsch. -**ιον**, τό, Dim. of κάνθαρος II, *IG*2$^2$.1517.10, 101, Plu.2.461e. ⊛ -**ίς**, ίδος, ἡ, a kind of *beetle*, prob. *blister-beetle*, *Cantharis vesicatoria*, Arist.*HA*531$^b$25, 542$^a$9; used in medicine, Hp.*Nat.Mul*.32, Plu.2.22a: pl., *POxy*.1088.14 (i A.D.); *beetle hurtful to corn*, Pl.Com.37, Thphr.*HP*8.10.1, Nic.*Al*.115; also to fruits, etc., Arist.*HA*552$^b$1; so prob. in Gal.12.363. II. a kind of *fish*, Numen.ap.Ath.7.326f. -**ίτης** [ῑ] οἶνος, ὁ, *wine from the vine* κανθάρεως, Plin.*HN*14.75.

**κανθᾰροποιός**, ὁ, *maker of* κάνθαροι II, *IG*12(9).292 (Eretria).

⊛ **κάνθᾰρος**, ὁ, *dung-beetle*, *Scarabaeus pilularius*, Arist.*HA*490$^a$ 15, al., Ael.*NA*10.15, Ar.*Lys*.695, Crates Theb.10.6, Theoc.5.114, Aesop.7, etc.; Αἰτναῖος κ., a specially large kind, A.*Fr*.233, S.*Ichn*. 300, cf. Epich.76: prov., κανθάρου σκιαί, of some paltry fear, Hsch., Diogenian.5.88; so ἀθυμῶν ὅτι αὐτοῦ καταθέουσι δύο κανθάρω Lib.*Ep*. 91.4. II. a sort of *drinking-cup* with large handles, Phryn.Com. 15, Amips.2, Axionic.7. III. a kind of *Naxian boat*, Ar.*Pax* 143, Sosicr.2, Nicostr.Com.10. IV. *black sea-bream*, *Cantharus lineatus*, Arist.*HA*598$^a$10. V. in Egypt, *mark* or *knot* on the tongue of the Apis-bull, Hdt.3.28. VI. *woman's ornament*, prob. a gem in scarab-form, Antiph.61.

**κανθᾰρ-ώδης**, ες, *like a beetle*, ζῷον Sch.Ar.*Ach*.920. -**ώλεθρος**, ὁ, *death-to-beetles*, name of a district in Thrace, Arist.*Mir*.842$^a$6, Str. 7*Fr*.30, Plu.2.473f.

**κανθήλη**, ἡ, = καλαμανθήλη, *rush used for candle-wicks*, *Edict. Diocl*.18.6.

⊛ **κανθήλ-ια**, ων, τά, *panniers* at the sides of a pack-saddle, Ar.*V*. 170: hence, *any large baskets*, for carrying grapes at the vintage, Artem.4.5, *Gp*.6.11.1, Hsch.: generally, *pack-saddle*, κ. καμηλικά prob. in *PGoodsp.Cair*.30 xxxiv 18 (ii A.D.). II. *wooden frame that rises in a curve at a ship's stern*, Hsch. III. sg., **κανθήλιον**, τό, in Archit., *rafter*, *IG*2$^2$.463.73. (Lat. *cantherius*, Vitr.4.2.3.) -**ικός**, ή, όν, *belonging to a pack-saddle*, σαγή prob. in *PGoodsp.Cair*.30 xxxviii 16 (ii A.D.).

**κανθήλιος**, ὁ, *pack-ass*, Ar.*Lys*.290 (lyr.), Luc.*Pseudol*.3, *POxy*. 1733.4 (iii A.D.); ὄνος κ. Hermipp.9, X.*Cyr*.7.5.11, Pl.*Smp*.221e, etc.: metaph., *ass*, *blockhead*, Lysipp.7, Luc.*JTr*.31.

**κανθίαι**· σπυρίδες, Hsch. **κανθίς**, ίδος, ἡ, *ass's dung*, Id.

⊛ **κανθός**, ὁ, *corner of the eye*, Arist.*HA*491$^b$23, *PA*657$^b$18, Nic.*Th*. 673, *CPR*29.10 (ii A.D.). 2. poet., *eye*, Call.*Fr*.150, Cerc.7.2, *IG*12(9).954.8 (Chalcis), *Supp.Epigr*.3.543 (Philippopolis, iii(?) B.C.), *AP*6.62 (Phil.), 5.218 (Paul. Sil.), Moschio Trag.9.9, Opp.*C*. 4.118, etc. II. *tyre of a wheel*, *Edict.Diocl*.15.36, *EM*364.29, Sch. Il.5.725. III. *chimney*, Hsch. IV. *pot, pan*, Id. (Lat. *cantus* (in signf. II) is said to be African or Spanish by Quint.1.5.8.)

**κανθύλη**, ἡ, *swelling, tumour*, A.*Fr*.220.

**κανθώδης**, ες, *curved*, prob. in Call.*Fr*.204.

**κάνθων**, ωνος, ὁ, = κανθήλιος, *pack-ass*, Ar.*V*.179, *AP*11.383 (Pall.), 399 (Apollinar.), Apion ap.J.*Ap*.2.9; of Trygaeus' beetle (with play on κάνθαρος), Ar.*Pax* 82 (anap.).

**κᾰνίας**, ου, ὁ, = κάλαθος, dub. in Hsch. **κᾰνίδιον**, τό, *little basket* (unless = κνίδιον), *PPar.Wess*.p.245, *Sammelb*.7243.12 (iv A.D.).

**κᾶνις**, crasis for καὶ ἄνις, = ἄνευ, Megar.ap.Ar.*Ach*.834.

**κᾰνίσκιον**, τό, Dim. of κάνεον, Ar.*Fr*.160, *IG*2$^2$.1472.41, Ptol. Euerg.7 J., Babr.108.20:—also **κανίσκος**, ὁ, *Gloss*.: **κανισκώδης**, ες, *basket-like*, πλέγμα Sch.Ar.*V*.672.

**κάνιστρον**, τό, v. κάναστρον:—also **κάνιτρον**, = κανίσκιον, Hsch., Phot.

**κάννα** or **κάννη**, ης, ἡ, *pole-reed*, *Arundo Donax*, Plb.14.1.15; κάννας τιμά (prob. for making pens) *SIG*241.103 (Delph., iv B.C.). 2. *reed-mat*, Cratin.197, Eup.228, dub. in *IG*1$^2$.330.12: in pl., *reed-fence*, Ar.*V*.394, Pherecr.63. (Cf. Bab. *ḳanû*, Hebr. *ḳāneh* 'reed'.)

⊛ **κανναβάριος**, ὁ, (Lat. *canabae*) *booth-keeper, stall-holder*, *Jahresh*. 24 *Beibl*.31 (Ephesus). II. = *stupparius*, *Gloss*.

**καννάβ-ῐνος** [ᾰβ], η, ον, *like hemp*, κράμβη *AP*11.325 (Autom.); *hempen*, Apollod.*Poliorc*.159.5; σφήκωμα *Hippiatr*.24. -**ιον**, τό, = sq., Ps.-Dsc.3.148, *Gp*.13.11.9. -**ις**, ἡ, gen. ιος Hdt.4.74, εως Sor.2.46, Gal.6.549; acc. κάνναβιν Moschio ap.Ath.5.206f, κανναβίδα (sic codd.) Hdt. l. c., Paus.6.26.6:—*hemp*, *Cannabis sativa*, S.*Fr*.243, Hdt. l. c., Dsc.3.148, etc. (but κ. ἀγρία *hemp-mallow*, *Althaea cannabina*, ib.149): in pl., -ίδες *hemp-seed*, Ephipp.13.6; burnt and used to medicate vapour baths. Hdt.4.75:—hence **κανναβισθῆναι** *take a vapour-bath*, Hsch. (Cf. OE. *hænep* 'hemp', Skt. *śaṇás* 'a kind of hemp', etc.; borrowed perh. fr. Ugro-Finnish, cf. Čeremissian *kene*, *kińe* 'hemp' and Syrianian *piš* 'hemp'.) -**ίσκα**, τά, *hempen shoes*, Herod.7.58. -**ος**, ἡ, = κάνναβις, Poll.10.176. II. v. κάναβος.

**κάνναθρον,** τό, = κάναθρον.  **καννεύσας,** Ep. for κατανεύσας, Od.15.464.  **κάννεώσασθαι,** poet. for καὶ ἀνανεώσασθαι.  **κάννη,** v. κάννα.  **κάννηκες·** πλέγματα ταρσῶν, Hsch.

**καννοχερσαία,** ἡ, = ἑλξίνη, Ps.-Dsc.4.39.

**Κάννωκος,** ὁ, title of Zeus Panamaros, *BCH*12.261.

**κᾰνον-ίας,** ου, ὁ, *one as straight as a* κανών, Hp.*Aër*.24.  **-ίζω,** (κανών) *measure* or *judge by rule*, Longin.16.4; *measure, regulate*, τὰς πράξεις ἡδονῇ καὶ λύπῃ Arist.*EN*1105$^{a}$3, cf. S.E.*M*.7.158; τῇ πείρᾳ τὴν ἐνέργειάν τινος Dsc.*Praef*.2; τὴν ψυχήν Procl.*Par.Ptol.* 16:—Pass., πάντα κεκανόνισται πρὸς δικαιοσύνην Aristeas 168; ἡδονῇ κανονιζόμενον Phld.*Po*.5.25; τοῖσιν [τοῖς πλάνησι] κανονίζεται αἰών *App.Anth*.3.147 (Theon or Hermes).  2. *prescribe rules for*, c. acc., Simp.*in Ph*.980.23.  II. *assess* for taxation, *PLond*.5.1674.34 (Pass., vi A.D.).  III. Gramm., κανονίζεται *the rule is..*, A.D.*Pron*.21.20: generally, Heliod.ap.Orib.46.9.4.  2. Act., *conjugate, give the paradigm* of a verb, Sch.E.*Hec*.1293:—Pass., Sch.Opp.*H*.1.259, etc.; *to be parsed as..*, εἰς ἀόριστον Sch.E.*Ph*.1188.

⊛**κᾰνονικάριος,** ὁ, *collector of an Imperial tax*, *Cod.Just*.10.19.9, Just.*Nov*.30.7.1.

**κᾰνον-ικός,** ή, όν, (κανών) *of* or *belonging to a rule*, ἀρχή A.D.*Adv*.141.29; *regular, according to rule*, διαφοραί Gal.7.417; ἀναλογία Eust.113.40, etc.  Adv -κῶς Artem.1.1a.  2. *connected with assessment* (cf. κανών II. 6), *PMasp*.131.13 (vi A.D.).  II. ἡ -κή (sc. τέχνη) *the mathematical theory of music* (Pythag., cf. Ptolemais ap. Porph.*in Harm*.p.207), based on the division of the monochord (cf. κανών I. 10), Gell.16.18; κ. θεωρία, τέχνη, Ph.1.22, Procl.*in Euc*.p.40F.  2. *belonging to an astronomical table*, Vett.Val.141.14; κανονικοί, οἱ, *constructors of such tables*, Cleom.2.6.  3. κανονικόν, τό, the equivalent of Logic in Epicurean philosophy, D.L.10.30: pl., τὰ κ. S.E.*M*.7.22; title of work by Antiochus, ib.201; ὁ κ. λόγος dub. in Phld.*Ir*.p.65 W.  ⊛**-ιον,** τό, *small bar* or *rod*, Ph.*Bel*.74.11, Hero *Spir*.1.5, al., Apollod.*Poliorc*.182.6, Hero *Bel*.77.1.  II. *compass*, S.E.*M*.10.149,153.  III. = σταμίς, Poll.1.92.  IV. *tabulation, table*, Ptol.*Harm*.2.15, Gaud.*Harm*.22, Vett.Val.321 sq.  V. *correct list*, *PLond*.2.259.126 (i A.D.).  VI. Dim. of κανών I. 10, Ptol.*Harm*.1.15 (pl.), 2.13.  ⊛**-ίς,** ίδος, ἡ, acc. to Suid., = ἐργαλεῖον καλλιγραφικόν, *ruler*, dub. in *AP*6.62 (Phil.), dub. in *IG*2$^{2}$.1678.4.  II. *frame with parallel cross-ledges*, Arist.*Ath*.64.2; *door-frame*, *IG*2$^{2}$.1672.155 (pl.).  2. in pl., *cross bars* for strengthening an engine, Ph.*Bel*.57.11.  III. pl., *profile-stones* running along the top of a wall, *IG*2$^{2}$.1666*A*16: sg., *row of such stones*, ib.1672.186. [ῐ *AP*l.c., s.v.l.]  **-ισμα,** ατος, τό, *ruler*, *AP*6.295 (Phan.).  II. *grammatical rule*, Eust.439.26.  ⊛**-ισμός,** ὁ, perh. *the frieze* of a building, in pl., Man.1.299, 4.151.  **-ιστέον,** *one must regulate*, κἂν ἡδονῇ κ. ἢ τὰ ἀρεστά Muson.*Fr*.24p.119 H., cf. Luc.*Hist.Conscr*.9.  **-ιστικός,** ή, όν, *regulative*, οἱ κανόνες τῶν ὑγιῶν, οὐ τῶν πεπονθότων εἰσὶ -κοί Choerob.*in Heph*.p.226C.

**κᾰνονο-γρᾰφία,** ἡ, *construction of astronomical tables*, Ptol.*Alm*.2.9, Vett.Val.336.12:—also **-ποιΐα,** ἡ, Ptol.*Alm*.3.1, Theon *in Ptol.Alm*.p.109 H., Vett.Val.353.14.

⊛**κᾰνονωτός,** ή, όν, *furnished with cross-bars*, θυρίδες *PSI*5.547.4 (iii B.C.); ἀγγεῖον, ζωγρεῖον κ., a *cage* for pigs, Sch.Ar.*V*.840 ed. Ald. (v.l. κανωτόν).  2. *made straight* or *even*, ῥάβδοι Eust.707.59.

**κάντορες·** οἱ κρατοῦντες, Hsch. (Fort. κράντορες.)

**κανυσῖνος,** ὁ, *dress of Canusian wool*, Ath.3.97e; cf. **κανύσια** ἔρια *PHolm*.22.26.

**κάνυστρον,** τό, v. κάναστρον.

⊛**Κάνωβος** [ᾰ], ὁ (**Κάνωπος** St.Byz., cf. Scyl.106, Luc.*Nav*.15, Ath.7.326a), *Canopus* in lower Egypt, A.*Pr*.846, Hdt.2.15, D.C.50.27; name of the star *Canopus*, Hipparch.1.11.7 (Κάνωπος), Ptol.*Alm*.8.1 (Κάνωβος), etc.:—hence **Κανωπίτης** [ῑ], *of Canopus*, αἰγιαλός Call. in *PSI*9.1092.58; also epith. of Sarapis, who had a temple there, Id.*Ep*.56.1; or **Κανωβεύς,** Orac.ap.Paus.10.13.8:—Adj. **Κανωβικός,** ή, όν, στόμα, i.e. the westernmost mouth of the Nile, Hdt.2.17,113; ἡ πύλη ἡ Κανωβική Str.17.1.10 and 16; Κανωπικά, τά, a kind of *cake*, Chrysipp.Tyan.ap.Ath.14.647c: **Κανωβισμός,** *luxurious living*, Str.17.1.16.

⊛**κᾰνών,** όνος, ὁ, *straight rod, bar*, esp. to keep a thing straight: 1. in pl., *staves* which preserved the shape of the shield, [ἀσπίδα] δύω κανόνεσσ' ἀραρυῖαν Il.13.407, cf. 8.193, Them.*Or*.21.257a.  2. *weaver's rod*, to which alternate threads of the warp were attached, Il.23.761, Ar.*Th*.822 (anap.), Plu.2.156b, Nonn.*D*.37.631.  3. *ruddled line* used by masons or carpenters, πύργους..ὀρθοῖσιν ἔθεμεν κανόσιν E.*Tr*.6; βάθρα φοίνικι κανόνι..ἡρμοσμένα Id.*HF*945; also κ. λίθινος *rule, straight-edge*, *IG*1$^{2}$.313.113, 373.217, al., cf. Pl.*Phlb*.56b, X.*Ages*.10.2, *AP*11.120 (Callicter); ὥστε τέκτονος παρὰ στάθμην ἰόντος ὀρθοῦται κ. S.*Fr*.474.5; κανόνα προσφέρειν Aeschin.3.199; ποιῶν ὀρθὰ πάντα πρὸς κανόνα *IG*7.3073.108 (Lebad., ii B.C.); κανόνεσσι..μετρήσασθαι A.R.1.724, cf. Ar.*Av*.1004; μολίβδινος κ., i.e. a flexible *rule* that cannot be depended on for straight measurement, Arist.*EN*1137$^{b}$31 (unless = κῦμα); κανόνα ποιῆσαι στρεβλόν Id.*Rh*.1354$^{a}$26.  b. *ruler*, *AP*6.63.2 (Damoch.).  c. metaph., κανόνες καὶ πήχεις ἐπῶν Ar.*Ra*.799; λαμπρὰ μὲν ἀκτὶς ἡλίου, κ. σαφής E.*Supp*.650.  4. *beam* or *tongue of the balance*, στῆσαι ἐκ κανόνος *AP*11.334, cf. Sch.Ar.*Ra*.811.  5. *curtain-rod*, Chares *Fr*.4 J.  6. in pl., *reeds* of a wind-organ, *AP*9.365 (Jul. Imp.).  7. *bed-post*, Lxx *Ju*.13.6.  8. in pl., *poles* from which the *ancilia* were suspended when carried, D.H.2.71.  9. pl., *bars* of a window, *PSI*5.547.9 (iii B.C.).  10. in Music, *monochord*, κατατομὴ κανόνος, title of work by Euc., cf. Phld.*Mus*.p.100 K., Ptol.*Harm*.1.8, 2.12; ὀκτάχορδος, πεντεκαιδεκάχορδος κ., ib.2.2, 3.1 tit.  11. *cross-bar of* κιθάρα, Porph.*in Harm*.p.207.  II. metaph., *rule, standard*, κανόνι τοῦ καλοῦ μαθών E.*Hec*.602; γνώμης πονηροῖς κανόσιν ἀναμετρούμενος τὸ σῶφρον Id.*El*.52; κανόνα προσάγειν Luc.*Hist.Conscr*.5; of the law, Lycurg.9; ὁ σπουδαῖος..ὥσπερ κ. καὶ μέτρον αὐτῶν (sc. καλῶν καὶ ἡδέων) ὤν Arist.*EN*1113$^{a}$33, cf. Arr.*Epict*.3.4.5; τὴν ἐλευθερίαν καὶ τὸ μηδέν' ἔχειν δεσπότην αὑτῶν, ἃ τοῖς προτέροις Ἕλλησιν ὅροι τῶν ἀγαθῶν ἦσαν καὶ κανόνες D.18.296; ὡς κανόνι τῷ πάθει πᾶν ἀγαθὸν κρίνοντες Epicur.*Ep*.3 p.63 U.; ὁ Ἐπικούρου κ. his treatise on Logic, Id.*Fr*.34, Damox.2.15; ὁ τῆς φιλοσοφίας κ. Lxx 4*Ma*.7.21: Κανόνες, οἱ, title of treatise by Democritus; of a philosophic *principle*, Dam.*Pr*.312.  2. in Art, *model, standard*, ὁ κ., a statue by Polyclitus which furnished a model of proportions, Plin.*HN*34.55; also his treatise on the same, Chrysipp.*Stoic*.3.122 (adnot.); also in Literature, Ἡρόδοτος τῆς Ἰάδος ἄριστος κ., Θουκυδίδης δὲ τῆς Ἀτθίδος D.H.*Pomp*.3.  c. of a person, *severe critic*, κ. *scriptorum*, Cic.*Fam*.16.17.1.  3. Gramm., *general rule*, *AB*1180, Choerob.*in Theod*.2 p.xxi; *paradigm*, οἱ κ. τῶν ὀνομάτων A.D.*Adv*.141.25.  b. metrical *scheme* showing all possible forms of a verse, Heph.14.1, al.  4. in Astronomy and Chronology, *table* of dates, κανόνες χρονικοί Plu.*Sol*.27; sg., κανών, ὁ, *system of chronology*, D.H.1.74.  b. astrological *table*, κανόνων καὶ εἰσόδων πήξεις Vett.Val.108.19.  5. *limit, boundary*, expl. as τὸ μέτρον τοῦ πηδήματος, Poll.3.151.  b. '*province*', *sphere of action*, 2*Ep.Cor*.10.15.  6. *assessment* for taxation, *PLond*.1.99.5 (iv A.D.), etc.; οἱ δεσποτικοὶ κ. the Imperial *taxes*, ib.234.9 (iv A.D.); ἰδιωτικὸς κ. *POxy*.2124.10 (iv A.D.).  7. *tariff*, *Stud.Pal*.20.143.5 (v/vi A.D.).

**Κανωπικόν,** τό, = πιτύουσα, Dsc.4.165.  II. a kind of *cake*, *POxy*.1774.15 (iv A.D.); cf. Κανωβικός.

**κάνωπον,** τό, *elder-flower*, Paul.Aeg.7.3; *elder-bark*, Alex.Trall.12.

**Κάνωπος,** ὁ, v. Κάνωβος.

**κάος** [ᾰ], εος, τό, (καίω) *that which burns*, etym of χάος, Corn.*ND*17.

**κάπ,** Ep. for κατά before π, φ, κὰπ πεδίον Il.6.201; κὰπ φάλαρα 16.106; also Thess., *IG*9(2).517.20 (Larissa).

**κᾰπαῖος,** α, ον, *of the crib* or *manger*, epith. of Zeus, Antiph.111.

**καπαλευτής,** οῦ, ὁ, = ὀνηλάτης, Hsch.:—also **καπαλαί·** κάπηλοι, φάτναι, and **καπαλίζω,** = ζευγηλατέω, Id.

**κᾰπάνη** [πᾱ], ἡ, *chariot*, Thess. for ἀπήνη, Xenarch.11. (Prop. *the cross-piece in a chariot seat*, *the side-pieces* being **καπάνᾰκες,** Poll.1.142.)  II. = κάπη, Hsch.; also, *a felt helmet*, Id.

**καπανῆται,** sine gl., Suid.  **καπάνια·** ἁρπεδόνες, Hsch.

**κᾰπᾱνικός,** ή, όν, (καπάνη) dub. in τὰ Θετταλικὰ (sc. δεῖπνα) μὲν πολὺ καπᾱνικώτερα Ar.*Fr*.492: expld. by Ath.9.418d as, = ἁμαξιαῖα, *enormous*, by Hsch. as χορταστικώτερα, *more foodful, more plenteous* (from καπάνη = κάπη).

**καπανοι·** ἀλφίτων εἶδος, Phot. (sine accentu).

**καπαρδεῦσαι·** μαντεύσασθαι, Hsch.; cf. σκαπαρδεύω.

**καπάριον, κάπαρις,** written for καππ- (q.v.).

**κὰπατᾶ** (sic)· κατακόψεις (Paph.), Hsch.  **κάπατας·** καθορῶν, Euclus ap.Hsch. (leg. καπατάς, cf. ἰμπάταδν, ἰνκαπάταδν).

**καπέτις,** ιος, ἡ, a Persian measure, $\frac{1}{48}$ *of the* ἀρτάβη, Polyaen.4.3.32; = χοῖνιξ, Hsch.; cf. καπίθη.

**κάπετον,** Dor. for κατέπεσον, Pi.*O*.8.38.

**κάπετος** [ᾰ], ἡ, (for σκάπετος, from **σκάπτω**) *ditch, trench*, ὄχθας καπέτοιο βαθείης Il.15.356, cf. 18.564; *hole, grave*, ἐς κοίλην κάπετον θέσαν [ὀστέα] 24.797, cf. S.*Aj*.1165, 1403 (both anap.); *groove* for lever, Hp.*Art*.72, 74.  II. *shovel, spade* (?), *GDI*4992*a* ii 6 (Gortyn).

⊛**Κᾰπετώλιον,** τό, = Lat. *Capitolium*, D.H.1.34 (v.l.), etc.:—hence **Κᾰπετώλιος,** ὁ, = *Capitolinus*, epith. of Zeus = Jupiter, Paus.2.4.5, *SIG*694.24 (Elaea, ii B.C.), etc.: **Κᾰπετωλιονίκης** [νῑ], ὁ, *victor in the Ludi Capitolini*, *Sammelb*.5725: **Κᾰπετώλιος,** ὁ (sc. μήν), name of month of *December*, *Gloss*., cf. *Cat.Cod.Astr*.2.140: ⊛**Κᾰπετώλια,** τά, = *Ludi Capitolini*, *IG*3.129.

**κάπη** [ᾰ], ἡ, (κάπτω) *crib, manger*, [ἵππους] κατέδησαν ἐπ' ἀμβροσίῃσι κάπῃσιν Il.8.434; ἐφ' ἱππείῃσι κάπῃσι Od.4.40; βουστάθμου κάπης S.*Ichn*.8; ἀντὶ κάπης Lyc.95: **κάπηθεν** as Adv., Suid.

⊛**κᾰπηλ-εία,** ἡ, *retail trade*, esp. *provision-dealing, tavern-keeping*, Pl.*Lg*.849d, 918d, Arist.*Pol*.1256$^{a}$41: in pl., *petty trades*, ib.1291$^{a}$6; κ. ἀσκεῖν προσώπῳ, of women who paint, Poll.5.102.  **-εῖον,** τό, *shop of a* κάπηλος, freq. of a *tavern*, *Com.Adesp*.493 (in a parody of Sophocles), Ar.*Lys*.427, *Ec*.154, Lys.1.24, Eub.80, Isoc.7.49, cf. Theopomp.Hist.65, *Tab.Defix*.87 (iv B.C.), Ἀρχ.Ἐφ.1923.39 (pl., Orop., iv B.C.), *PTeb*.43.18 (ii B.C.), *POxy*.2109.11 (iii A.D.): pl., καπηλεῖα, τά (prob. l. for κάπηλα), the *meat-market* at Tarentum, Hsch.  **-ευτικός,** ή, όν, = καπηλικός, Pl.*Lg*.842d.  **-εύω,** *to be a retail-dealer, drive a petty trade*, Hdt.1.155, 2.35, Isoc.2.1, Nymphod.21, *IG*11(2).161*A*16 (Delos, iii B.C.), *BGU*1024 vii 23 (iv A.D.); δι' ἀψύχου βορᾶς σίτοις καπήλευ' *drive a trade, chaffer* with your vegetable food, E.*Hipp*.953.  II. c. acc., *sell by retail*, τὸν ἕρπιν Hippon.51.  2. metaph., κ. τὰ πρήγματα, of Darius, Hdt.3.89; κ. τὰ μαθήματα *sell* learning *by retail*, *hawk* it *about*, Pl.*Prt*.313d; κ. τὸν λόγον τοῦ θεοῦ 2*Ep.Cor*.2.17; so ἔοικεν οὐ καπηλεύσειν μάχην will not *peddle in* war, i.e. fight half-heartedly, A.*Th*.545; κ. τῇ χάριτι τὴν ἀμοιβήν Epicur.*Sent.Vat*.39; κ. τὴν πολιτείαν *traffic in* grants of citizenship, D.C.60.17; κ. τῆς ὥρας ἄνθος or τὴν ὥραν, of prostitutes, Ph.2.394, 576; εἰρήνην πρὸς Ῥωμαίους χρυσίου κ. Hdn.6.7.9; τύχη καπηλεύουσα..τὸν βίον *playing tricks with* life,

*corrupting* it, *AP*9.180 (Pall.). **-η**, ἡ, *steersman's seat, hold*, or *belaying-pin*, Hsch. ***-ικός**, ή, όν, *of* or *for a* κάπηλος, ζυγόν Dinol. 2 (fort. καπανικόν); ἀργύρωμα *IG*11(2).110 (Delos, iii B.C.), cf. 111; *mercenary*, ἦθος M.Ant.4.28; σοφιστής Poll.4.48; ἡ -ική (sc. τέχνη), = καπηλεία, Pl.*Sph.*223d, Arist.*Pol.*1257ᵃ18: καπηλικόν, τό, *camp-followers, sutlers* of an army, Arr.*Tact.*2.1; but also, *tax on retail-traders*, *BGU*1237 (iii/ii B.C.). 2. *like a petty trader, knavish, cozening*, κ. μέτρα φιλεῦσα *AP*9.229 (Marc. Arg.); ὕθλος Porph.*Chr.* 49. Adv. -κῶς, ἔχειν to be *vamped up for sale*, Ar.*Pl.*1063; τὰ πράγματα κ. διανέμων Plu.2.369c; *in a mercenary spirit*, Gal.14.216: Comp. -ώτερον Numen.ap.Eus.*PE*14.8. **-ιον**, τό, = καπηλεῖον, *Tab.Defix.Aud.*70 (iii B.C.). **-ίς**, ίδος, ἡ, fem. of κάπηλος, Ar.*Th.* 347, *Pl.*435, 1120, *Com.Adesp.*567, Aeschin.Socr.4, *PFay.*12.23 (ii B.C.): Καπηλίδες, αἱ, title of play by Theopomp. Com.:—accented κάπηλις, acc. to Hdn.Gr.1.91, cf. Oenom.ap.Eus.*PE*6.7:—late **καπήλισσα**, ἡ, Sch.Ar.*Pl.*426.

**κᾰπηλο-γείτων**, ονος, ὁ, = *attubernalis*, *Gloss.* **-δύτης** [ῠ], ου, ὁ, (δύω) *tavern-haunter*, *Cat.Cod.Astr.*7.242, Hsch.

**κάπηλος** [ᾰ], ὁ (also ἡ, *AP*9.180 (Pall.)), *retail-dealer, huckster*, Hdt. 1.94, 2.141, Sophr.1, etc.; opp. ἔμπορος, Lys.22.21, X.*Cyr.*4.5.42, Pl.*R.*371d, *Prt.*314a; also opp. the producer (αὐτοπώλης), Id.*Sph.* 231d, *Plt.*260c; applied to Darius, Hdt.3.89; κ. ἀσπίδων, ὅπλων, *a dealer in..*, Ar.*Pax* 447, 1209. 2. esp. *tavern-keeper*, Ar.*Th.*347, Lys.*Fr.*1, *PMagd.*26.2 (iii B.C.), *PTeb.*612 (i/ii A.D.), Luc.*Herm.*58, etc. 3. metaph., κ. πονηρίας *dealer in petty roguery*, D.25.46. II. as Adj., ος, ον, = καπηλικός, βίος D.H.9.25; esp. *cheating, knavish*, κ. προσφέρων τεχνήματα A.*Fr.*322; κ. φρόνημα *Com.Adesp.*867.

**καπήλτια**· γυναικεῖα ἱμάτια, Hsch. (leg. καππάτια). **κάπηξ**, *projecting piece at a ship's stern*, Id. ***κάπητόν**, τό, (κάπη) *fodder*, Id. II. in pl., = *wicker baskets*, Lyd.*Mag.*1.46.

**κάπια**, τά, *onions* (at Cerynea), Hsch.

**καπίθη**, ἡ, *a Persian measure containing two* χοίνικες, X.*An.*1.5.6; = *two Attic* κοτύλαι, Hsch.

**καπίστριον**, τό, *halter*, Hsch.

**καπν-αύγης**, ου, ὁ, *smoke-observer, diviner*, *IG*14.617 (Rhegium): pl. -αῦγαι ib.618 (ibid.). **-ειος** (sc. ἄμπελος), ἡ, vine *with smoke-coloured grapes*, Thphr.*HP*2.3.2, *PCair.Zen.*33.14 (iii B.C.):—written **κάπνεος** in Arist.*GA*770ᵇ20; **καπνέως** in Thphr.*CP*5.3.1 (cod. Urb., v.l. **κάπνεος**); **καπνία** in Suid., Sch.Ar.*V.*151; **καπνός** in cod. Hsch. s.v. καπνίας; **κάπνιος** in *App.Prov.*3.43. **-είω**, poet. for καπνίζω, *turn into smoke*, Nic.*Th.*36. **-έλαιον**, τό, *oily resin* from trees, Gal.13.626, Alex.Trall.3.2. II. = καπνιστὸν ἔλαιον, *Edict.Diocl.Delph.* **-εος, -έως**, v. κάπνειος. **-η**, ἡ, = καπνοδόκη, Eup.88, Ar.*V.*143, Alex.173.13. II. = καπνιαῖος λίθος, *PHolm.* 5.11. **-ηλός**, όν, *smoky*, ὀδμή Nic.*Th.*54. ***-ία**, ἡ, = κάπνη I, Moer.292, *Gloss.* **-ιαῖος** λίθος *smoky* quartz, *PHolm.*10.9, cf. 4.6. **-ίας**, ου, ὁ, (καπνός) *smoky*, nickname of the Comic poet Ecphantides, Sch.Ar.*V.*151. II. as Subst., 1. κ. οἶνος, ὁ, expl. by Hsch., Phot. as wine *that had a smoky taste* from having been long hung up in smoke, Pherecr.130.6, Anaxandr.41.71 (anap.), Pl.Com. 244: perh. rather to be expld. as *made from the vine* κάπνειος. 2. κ. (sc. λίθος), ὁ, a kind of *jasper*, Dsc.5.142, Plin.*HN*37.118. **-ιάω**, *smoke* a bee-hive, A.R.2.131. ***-ίζω**, *make smoke*, i.e. *make a fire*, Ep. aor. 1 κάπνισσαν Il.2.399; *use as a fumigation*, τροχίσκον Paul.Aeg.3.28. II. *smoke, blacken with smoke*, D.54.4, Sopat.6.9, *PMasp.*141 ii a25 (vi A.D.):—Pass., *to be smoked*, ὁ ἠπίολος φεύγει -όμενος Arist.*HA*605ᵇ16; of the eyes, *suffer from smoke*, Id.*Pr.*957ᵇ 33, cf. 896ᵇ8; of cookery, καπνιζομένη τυραννίς empire *of the smoke*, Demetr.Com.Nov.1.4; κλίβανος -όμενος *smoking* furnace, Lxx *Ge.*15. 17. 2. intr. in Act., *to be black with smoke*, pf. κεκάπνικα Ar.*Pax* 892; τὸ ὄρος τὸ καπνίζον Lxx *Ex.*20.18; κρύσταλλος ἡ -ίζουσα *smoky* quartz, *PHolm.*6.38: metaph., [θυμὸν] καπνίζοντα (v.l. -ιῶντα) καὶ διακαιόμενον Plu.2.454e. **-ιος** (sc. ἄμπελος), ἡ, v. κάπνειος. II. κάπνιος, ἡ, = καπνός II, Gal.12.8. **-ισις**, εως, ἡ, *exposure to smoke*, Arist.*Pr.* 896ᵇ9. **-ισμα**, ατος, τό, *offering of smoke*, i.e. *incense*, *AP*9.174.5 (Pall.). **-ιστέον**, *one must smoke*, 'gas', τοὺς ἐν τοῖς μετάλλοις ὄντας Ph.*Bel.*99.18. **-ιστήριον**, τό, perh. *vapour-bath*, *Inscr.Prien.*112. 98 (i B.C.). **-ιστός**, ή, όν, *smoked*, κρέα Posidon.1 J.; but τροχίσκος κ. *for use as a fumigation*, Paul.Aeg.3.28; κ. ἔλαιον *fragrant* oil, Aët. 1.138; κ. μύρον Id.16.66(67). **-ίτης** [ῑ] λίθος *smoky* quartz, Alex. Trall.1.15. II. fem. **-ῖτις** (v.l. -ίτης), = καπνός II, Ps.-Dsc.4.109.

***καπνο-βάτης** [βᾰ], ου, ὁ, epith. of a pastoral people, dub. in Posidon.104 J. **-γόργιον**, τό, = καπνός II, Ps.-Dsc.4.109. **-δόκη**, ἡ, prop. *smoke-receiver*, i.e. *hole in the roof for the smoke to pass through*, Hdt.4.103, 8.137, Pherecr.141, Eup.133:—later **-δόχη** Lxx *Ho.*13.3 codd. AQ, Luc.*Icar.*13, Gal.2.727. **-δοχεῖον**, τό, = foreg., *Gloss.* **-δόχος**, ον, *receiving smoke*, ib. **-ειδής**, ές, *smoke-coloured*, Ael.*NA*6.20. **-κορτῠάζομαι**, *leap, frisk*, Epich. 195. **-μαντις**, εως, ὁ, *smoke-diviner*, Lact. ad Stat. *Theb.*4. 411. ***-ομαι**, Pass., *to be turned into smoke, burnt to ashes*, Pi.*P.* 5.84, E.*Supp.*497, *Tr.*8.

**καπνοόν**· τὰ πνέοντα, Hsch.

**καπνοποιός**, όν, *making smoke, smoky*, Sch.Ar.*V.*145.

**καπνός**, ὁ, *smoke*, Il.1.317, etc.; κνισάεντι καπνῷ Pi.*I.*4(3).66; καπνῷ πυρός A.*Ag.*497; *spray*, καπνοῦ καὶ κύματος ἐκτὸς ἔεργε νῆα Od. 12.219 (hence metaph., Porph.*Abst.*1.47): prov., καπνοῦ σκιά, of things worth nothing, A.*Fr.*399, S.*Ph.*946; τἄλλ' ἐγὼ καπνοῦ σκιᾶς οὐκ ἂν πριαίμην Id.*Ant.*1170; also περὶ καπνοῦ στενολεσχεῖν Ar.*Nu.* 320; κ. καὶ φλυαρία Pl.*R.*581d: and in pl., γραμμάτων καπνοί learned *trifles*, E.*Hipp.*954; καπνοὺς ..καὶ σκιάς Eup.51; nickname of a man, Id.122: metaph. also of envy, ὕδωρ καπνῷ φέρειν to throw water *on the smoking embers*, Pi.*N.*1.24: prov., ἐς αὐτὸ τὸ πῦρ ἐκ τοῦ καπνοῦ βιαζόμενος 'out of the frying-pan into the fire', Luc.*Nec.*4, al. II. *fumitory, Fumaria officinalis*, Anon.Lond.36.58, Dsc.4.109.

**καπν-οσφράντης**, ου, ὁ, *smoke-sniffer*, of a miser or a parasite, *Com.Adesp.*1025: as pr. n., Alciphr.3.49. **-οῦχος**, ὁ, *chimney*, *Gloss.* ***-ώδης**, ες, *smoky*, opp. ἀτμιδώδης, Arist.*Mete.*360ᵃ10, al.; [φλόξ] Thphr.*Ign.*76; κ. καὶ συννεφὴς ἀήρ Plb.9.16.3. Adv. -δῶς Gal. 4.507. 2. of colour, *dark, dusky*, Thphr.*CP*5.3.2, Luc.*Philops.* 16; φύλλον δριμὺ καὶ κ. D.Chr.66.5. **-ωτήριον**, τό, *altar*, *Gloss.*

**κᾶπος**, Dor. for κῆπος.

***κάπος**, ὁ, *breath*, Eust.1280.34, Hsch.:—also **κάπυς**, Id.; **κάφος**, Eust. l.c. ***κάπουπλος**· βάρυγξ, Hsch.

**κάππα**, τό, v. sub K κ.

**Καππαδόκαι**, ῶν, οἱ, *Cappadocians*, Hdt.5.49, etc.:—also **Καππάδοκες**, ων, Str.6.4.2, etc.:—fem. **Καππαδόκισσα** Id.14.2.17:—hence **Καππαδοκία**, Ion. **-ίη**, ἡ, *Cappadocia*, Hdt.1.71, etc.; **Καππαδοκίζω**, *favour the Cappadocians*, App.*Mith.*53:—Pass., *to be Cappadocianized* (with pun on Joannes Cappadox), [Demod.]5.

***καππάριον**, τό, Dim. of sq., *Gloss*; πρὸς καππάριον ζῆν prov. in *Com.Adesp.*459: **καπάριον**, *PGen.*62.17 (iv A.D.).

**κάππᾰρις**, εως, Ion. ιος, ἡ, *caper-plant, Capparis spinosa*, or its fruit, *caper*, Hp.*Fist.*10 (v.l. καπαρ-), Arist.*Pr.*924ᵃ1, Antiph.62, Timocl. 23, Alex.127.6, Thphr.*HP*6.5.2, *PCair.Zen.*488 (iii B.C.), Lxx *Ec.* 12.5, Dsc.2.173, etc.; ὁ Ζήνων ὤμνυε τὴν κ. Empedus ap.Ath.9.370c.

**κάππαρος**, ὁ, a kind of *fish*, *PCair.Zen.*83 (iii B.C.).

**κάππαστον** (i.e. κατάπαστον)· ποικίλον, Hsch. **καππύτια**· γυναικεῖα ἱμάτια, Id.

**κάππεσον**, Ep. aor. 2 Act. of καταπίπτω.

**καππῠρίζω**, for καταπυρίζω, *catch fire*, aor. 1 part. καππυρίσασα dub. in Theoc.2.24.

**Καππώτας**, α, ὁ, Ζεὺς Κ., Doric name given to a large unworked stone at Gythium on which Orestes was said to have sat down and recovered his sanity (παύσασθαι τῆς μανίας), Paus.3.22.1.

**κάπρα**· αἴξ, Τυρρηνοί, Hsch.; but **κάπρας**· ἀκολασίας, Id.

**κάπρ-αινα**, ἡ, fem. of κάπρος, *wild sow*: metaph., *lewd woman*, Phryn.Com.33, Hermipp.10: dub. sens. in Lyr. in *Philol.* 80. 334. **-άω**, of sows, *want the boar*, Arist.*HA*572ᵇ24: metaph., *to be lecherous*, καπρῶσα γραῦς Ar.*Pl.*1024, cf. Men.917. **-ειος**, α, ον, *of the wild boar*, ὀδόντες Nonn.*D.*18.245. **-ία**, ἡ, *the ovary of sows*, cut out to prevent their breeding, Arist.*HA*632ᵃ21. II. *virus in sows*, like ἱππομανές in mares, ib.572ᵃ21, 573ᵇ2. III. *dance in armour*, Hsch. IV. = κάππαρις, Dsc.2.173. **-ιάω**, = καπράω, used of mares, Ar.Byz.*Epit.*145.12. **-ίδιον**, τό, Dim. of κάπρος, Ar.*Fr.*506.2. **-ίζω**, = καπράω, Arist.*HA*572ᵃ16. **-ίολος**, *furcilla*, *Gloss.* **-ιος**, ὁ, poet. for κάπρος, *wild boar*, Il.11.414, 12. 42, A.R.1.126; σῦς κάπριος Il.11.293, 17.282. II. Adj. κάπριος, ον, = κάπρειος, *like a wild boar*, καπρίους ἔχειν τὰς πρῴρας Hdt.3. 59. **-ίσκος**, ὁ, Dim. of κάπρος, Crobyl.7, Diph.Siph.ap.Ath.5.355f.

**καπροβόλ(ι)ον**, τό, gloss on συβίνη, Hsch.

***κάπρος** [ᾰ by nature], ὁ, *boar*, esp. *wild boar*, Il.17.725, Pl.*La.* 196e, etc.; also σῦς κ. Il.5.783, 17.21, cf. Ar.*Lys.*202 (ubi v. Sch.); ἧπαρ κάπρου Id.*Fr.*318.5: in fem. sense, *sow*, ὀχευομένους τοὺς κάπρους Anaxandr.47. II. a *sea-fish*, *Capros aper*, Philem.79. 21, Arist.*HA*505ᵃ13; a species found in the Achelous, ib.535ᵇ18. (Cogn. with Lat. *caper*, ONorse *hafr* 'he-goat', but not with Lat. *aper*.)

**καπροσύρη**· περικάθαρσις, Hsch.

**καπρο-φάγος** [φᾰ], ον, *eating boar's flesh*, epith. of Artemis at Samos, Hsch. **-φόνος**, ον, *killing wild boars*, κύων *AP*9.83 (Phil.).

**καπρ-ῴζομαι**, *rut*, of the boar, Sciras 1. **-ών**, ῶνος, ὁ, *pig-sty*, *IG*11(2).154*A* 41 (Delos, iii B.C.).

**καπτρ-ίον**, τό, = καμπτρίον, Anon.*in Rh.*74.11, *Gloss.* **-ον**, = κάμπτρον II, ib.

**κάπτω**, fut. κάψω (v. infr.), *gulp down*, ἐμπίδας Ar.*Av.*245 (lyr.), cf. Sophr.64; [ἄλφιτα] Nicocl.2; of liquids, Xenarch.9 codd. Ath., Arist.*HA*593ᵃ21; ἀφρόν ib.620ᵃ13; κ. αὔρας Eub.10: c. gen. partit., κ. τῶν θυλημάτων Telecl.33: abs., ἄχρις ἑσπέρης κ. Herod.7.41; expressing greater greediness than φαγεῖν, Ar.*Ec.*687; ἡ ἄρκτος οὐδὲ σπάσει οὐδὲ λάψει ἀλλὰ κάψει Arist.*HA*595ᵃ10: metaph., σευ τὸ ὥριον τέφρη κάψει Herod.1.38. (Cogn. with Lat. *capio*, Germ. *haben*, *Heft.*)

**καπυκτά**· πνέοντα, Hsch. **καπύνιοι**· ἀκόλουθοι, Id.

**κᾰπῠρ-ίδια**, ων, τά, a kind of *cakes*, Chrysipp.Tyan.ap.Ath.3.113d codd.:—perh. ***καπύρια** (καπήρια Suid.), cf. *POxy.*1655.3 (iii A.D.); **καπύριον**, *crustulum*, *Gloss.* **-ίζω**, *live riotously, revel* (cf. καπυρός II), Str.17.1.16. **-ις**, *Persian gown with sleeves*, Poll.7. 58. **-ιστής**, οῦ, ὁ, *debauchee*, Str.14.2.26. ***-όομαι**, Pass., *become dry* or *parched*, Id.4.4.1; *become crackly*, Orib.*Fr.*74. **-ός**, ά, όν, *dried by the air*, κάρυα Epich.150; χοιρίων σκέλη Antiph.185; ἄλφιτον κ. Arist.*Pr.*927ᵃ24, cf. Dieuch.ap.Orib.4.7.3; τυρός *Test. Epict.*5.36; χαῖται (of thistle-down) Theoc.6.16. b. *brittle*, ὀστέον Hp.*VC*19 (v.l. εὔπριστον); cj. in Thphr.*HP*3.13.4 and 7 (*Comp.*); *crisp, crackly*, Diocl.*Fr.*147. 2. Act., *drying, parching*, κ. νόσος, of love, Theoc.2.85. II. of sound, *crackly*, καπυρὸν ψοφεῖν Gal.6.434: metaph., κ. γελάσας laughing *loud*, *AP*7.414 (Nossis), cf. Longus 2.5; κ. γέλως Alciphr.3.48; κ. στόμα *clear-sounding*, of Poets, Theoc.7.37; κ. συρίζειν to play *clearly* on the syrinx, Luc.*DDeor.*

22.3; καπυρώτεραι ᾠδαί *rude* songs, opp. ἐσπουδασμέναι, Ath.15.697b. **-ώδης**, ες, *dry*, Hsch. s. v. ἴτρια, *EM*479.39.

**κάπυς**, v. κάπος.

⊕ **κᾰπύω**, *breathe forth*, Ep. aor. 1 κάπυσσεν Q.S.6.523; cf. κεκαφηώς.

**κάπων**, ωνος, ὁ, *capon*, *Gloss.*

**κάρ**, for κατά before ῥ, κὰρ ῥόον Il.12.33; κάρ ῥα 20.421.

***κάρ** (A), a word of uncertain gender, nom. form, and meaning, typifying what is worthless, τίω δέ μιν ἐν καρὸς αἴσῃ I value him at *a* ..*'s worth*, Il.9.378: καρός is variously expld. by Ar.Byz. etc. ap. Sch., e.g. as = κηρός or as pr.n. Καρός. II. = κάρα, ἐπὶ κάρ *head*-long (nisi junctim scrib.), Il.16.392; ἀνὰ κάρ *upwards*, Hp.ap.Gal.19.79.

**κᾶρ** (B), τό, Aeol. for κῆρ (q.v.).

**Κάρ**, ὁ, gen. Κᾱρός, pl. Κᾶρες (contr. fr. Κάερ-), *Carian*, Il.2.867, etc.:—fem. **Κάειρα** [ᾰ] (q.v.): employed as mercenaries, καὶ δὴ 'πίκουρος ὥστε Κὰρ κεκλήσομαι Archil.24, cf. Ephor.12 J.: hence prov., ἐν τῷ Καρὶ κινδυνεύειν (cf. *experimentum facere in corpore vili*), E.*Cyc.*654, cf. Sch.Pl.*La.*187b, *Euthd.*285c; ἐν Καρὶ τὸν κίνδυνον.. πειρᾶσθαι Cratin.16, cf. Philem.18; δεῖ ἐν Καρὶ τὴν πεῖραν, οὐκ ἐν τῷ στρατηγῷ γίνεσθαι Plb.10.32.11; ἐν τῷ Καρὶ καὶ οὐκ ἐν τοῖς ἑαυτῶν σώμασι τὰς πείρας ποιούμενοι Aristid.1.163 J. II. v. Κήρ.

⊕ **κάρᾱ** (A), Ep. and Ion. **κάρη** [ᾰ], τό, poet. for κεφαλή, Luc.*Lex.*5:—*head*, of men or animals, πολιόν τε κάρη πολιόν τε γένειον Il.22.74; ὑψοῦ κάρη ἔχει [ἵππος] 6.509; περὶ πόδα περὶ κάρα from *head* to foot, A.*Eu.*165 (lyr.): metaph., ἐν δ' ἐμῷ κάρᾳ θεὸς μ' ἔπαισεν S.*Ant.*1272, cf. *OC*564; of *the face*, γέλωτι φαιδρὸν κ. Id.*El.*1310; μου κ. τὸ δυσπρόσοπτον Id.*OC*285. 2. *peak, top*, κάρη νιφόεντος Ὀλύμπου Hes.*Th.*42; of a tree, S.*Fr.*23; *edge, brim* of a cup, Eub.56.6. 3. in Trag., as periphr. for *a person*, Οἰδίπου κάρα, i.e. Οἰδίπους, S.*OT*40, 1207 (lyr.); αὐτάδελφον Ἰσμήνης κ. Id.*Ant.*1; ὦ κασίγνητον κ., for ὦ κασίγνητε, Id.*El.*1164; ὦ φίλον κ. Id.*OC*1631; φίλον κ. A.*Ag.*905.—Hom. uses nom. acc. κάρη, gen. dat. κάρητος, κάρητι, Od.6.230, Il.15.75; also καρήατος, καρήατι, 23.44, 19.405, nom. pl. καρήατα 11.309 (whence was formed nom. sg. κάρηαρ, Antim.76); acc. pl. κάρη Il.10.259 (but perh. sg.), nom. acc. pl. κάρᾱ Sannyr.3, perh. S.*Ant.*291; κάρᾱ ἐξεπεφύκει *h.Cer.*12; dat. pl. κάρησι f.l. in Tryph.602:—post-Homeric Poets inflected κάρη as if it were of decl. 1, gen. κάρης Mosch.4.74, Call.*Fr.*125; dat. κάρῃ Thgn.1024, Nic.*Th.*249; acc. κάρην D.P.562, Nic.*Th.*131; Trag. dat. κάρᾳ with neut. Prons., A.*Ch.*230, etc.; late acc. κάραν *Anacreont.*50.9. (Cf. Skt. *śiras* (neut.) 'head', gen. *śīrṣṇás*, abl. *śīrṣatás*: κάρηνα (fr. κᾰρᾰσ-ν-α) and κράατα (perh. fr. κρᾱσ-ṇ-τα) are forms of this word, v. κάρηνον, κράς, κρανίον: cogn. with Lat. *cerebrum* (fr. *ceres-ro-*), ONorse *hjarne* 'brain', and prob. κέρας, κόρση.)

⊕**κάρα** (B), ἡ, *tame goat* (Cret.), Hsch.; also, *fig*, Id. **καραβαία**· δίκρουν ξύλον, Id.

**κᾱράβιον** [ρᾰ], τό, Dim. of κάραβος III, Hsch. s. v. ἐφόλκια, Sch.E.*Hec.*631.

**κᾱρᾰβίς**, ίδος, ἡ, = κάραβος I (Methymn.), Hsch. II. = κάραβος II, Sch.Opp.*H.*1.261; but distd. by Gal.19.686.

**κᾱρᾰβο-ειδής**, ές, *of the* κάραβος *kind*, Arist.*HA*526ᵇ26, *PA*679ᵃ31. **-πρόσωπος**, ον, *with the face of a* κάραβος, Luc.*VH*1.35.

**κάρᾰβ-ος** [κᾱ], ὁ, *horned* or *cerambycid beetle*, Arist.*HA*531ᵇ25, 551ᵇ17 (with vv.ll. καράβιοι, καράμβιοι). II. a prickly crustacean, *crayfish*, Epich.57, Ar.*Fr.*318.7, Gal.12.313, etc.: distd. from καρκίνος, Arist.*PA*684ᵃ1, cf. *HA*525ᵇ32, 590ᵇ20; μαλακόστρακος ib.490ᵇ11, cf. Speus.ap.Ath.3.105b; an Eastern species, Nearch.ap.Arr.*Ind.*29.14. III. a *light ship*, *EM*490.31. VI. Maced., *gate*, Hsch. **-ώδης**, ες, = καραβοειδής, Arist.*HA*607ᵇ4, *GA*758ᵃ12.

**κάραγος**· ὁ τραχὺς ψόφος, οἷον πρι(όντ)ων, Hsch. **καραδάλη**· ἁρμενοθήκη, Id.

**κᾱρᾱδοκ-έω**, *wait for the outcome of*, κ. τὴν μάχην, τὸν πόλεμον τῇ πεσέεται, *wait to see* how the battle will end, Hdt.7.163,168; τὸν πόλεμον κῇ ἀποβήσεται Id.8.67; τἀκεῖθεν οἷ προβήσεται E.*Med.*1117; ἀδήλους ἐλπίδας *Trag.Adesp.*16; τἀνθένδε E.*Heracl.*279; ἀγῶνας Id.*Hel.*739; κ. ὅταν στράτευμα.. ἐξίῃ κάλως Id.*Tr.*93: simply, *wait for*, αὔραν ἱστίοις κ. ib.456 (troch.); παρουσίαν τινὸς Id.*IA*1432; τἀπιόντα τραύματα Id.*IT*313, etc.; τὰ προσταχθησόμενα X.*Mem.*3.5.6: freq. in later Prose, κ. τὸν καιρόν Plb.1.33.11, al.; τὸ μέλλον Cic.*Att.*9.10.8; τινα Zos.3.15, *PMasp.*2.2 (vi A.D.); also κ. εἴς τινα *look expectantly* at one, Ar.*Eq.*663. **-ητής**, οῦ, ὁ, gloss on ὕποπτος, Sch.E.*Hec.*1135. **-ία**, ἡ, *eager expectation*, Aq.*Ps.*38(39).8, *Pr.*10.28.

**καραιβαράω**, v. καρηβαρέω.

⊕ **Κᾰραιός**, ὁ, (κάρα A) name of Zeus in Boeotia, *IG*7.3208 (Orchom.), Hsch., cj. Mein. in Cratin.111; cf. Κάριος.

**κᾰράκαλλον** [ρᾰ], τό, *hood*, *AP*11.345, *Edict.Diocl.*26.120:—Dim. ⊕**-κάλλιον**, τό, *Sammelb.*7033.37 (v A.D.), *PMasp.*6 ii 64 (vi A.D.), *Gloss.*

**καράμβας**· ῥάβδον ποιμενικήν, Hsch.

**καράμβιος**, ὁ, = κάραβος I, prob. in Ar.Byz.*Epit.*9.11, v.l. in Arist. *HA*551ᵇ17.

⊕ **κᾱρᾱν-ιστήρ**, ῆρος, ὁ, ἡ, *beheading, touching the head*, κ. δίκαι A.*Eu.*186:—also **-ιστής** μόρος E.*Rh.*817.

**κάραννος**· κεκρύφαλος, κρήδεμνον, ἢ ἔριφος (cf. κάρνος), ἢ ζημία (cf. κάρνη, αὐτόκαρνος), Hsch.

**κάρᾱνον**, τό, v. κάρηνον.

**κάρᾱνος** [ᾰ], ὁ, (κάρα A) *a chief*, X.*HG*1.4.3, cj. in *Anacreont.*15.3.

**κᾱρᾱνόω**, like κεφαλαιόω, *achieve*, A.*Ch.*528 (Pass.), 705.

**καρανώ**, ἡ, *goat* (Cret.), Hsch. **κάραξι**· στρώσω, Id. **καραρύες**, Scythian *travelling-wagons*, Id. **καράς**· ὁ ἀποσπερματισμός, Id. **καραταί**· κεφαλαί, Id.

**κᾱρᾱτομ-έω**, *behead*, E.*Rh.*586, J.*BJ*1.17.8, al.:—Pass., Lyc.313, Agath.1.12. **-ος** (proparox.), ον, (τέμνω) *beheaded*, Γοργών E.*Alc.*1118 (dub. l.); κ. ἐρημία νεανίδων, i.e. their slaughter, Id.*Tr.*564 (lyr.); so Ἕκτορος.. κ. σφαγαί Id.*Rh.*606. 2. *cut off from the head*, κ. χλιδαί one's *shorn* locks, S.*El.*52. II. parox., Act., *beheading*, c. gen., Ἑλλάδος Lyc.187.

**καρβάζω** and **καρβᾱνίζω**, = βαρβαρίζω, Hsch.

⊕ **κάρβᾱνος**, ον, = βάρβαρος, *outlandish, foreign*, A.*Supp.*914; χεὶρ Id.*Ag.*1061, cf. Lyc.1387: also **καρβάν**, Hsch. s. v. ἐκαρβάνιζεν; acc. καρβᾶνα, αὐδάν A.*Supp.*129 (lyr.).

**καρβάρεοι**· κάραβοι, Hsch.

**Κάρβας**, name in Cyrene for the wind Εὖρος, Arist.*Vent.*973ᵇ4 (ἀπὸ τῶν Καρβανῶν τῶν κατὰ Φοινίκην): Phoenician word, acc. to Thphr.*Vent.*62.

⊕ **καρβάτινος** [βᾰ], η, ον, *made of hide*, οἰκίαι Ph.*Bel.*101.31:—esp. **καρβάτιναι**, αἱ, *shoes of undressed leather, brogues*, X.*An.*4.5.14, Arist.*HA*499ᵃ30, Luc.*Alex.*39:—also **καρπάτινον**, τό, Hsch.

**καρβᾰτιών**, ῶνος, ὁ, *engine* of war, βάλλοντες λίθοις ἀπὸ τῶν κ. Ph.*Bel.*92.28 codd. (fort. καρβατίνων (sc. οἰκιῶν)).

**κάρβις**· μαστροπός, Hsch.

**κάρβων**, ωνος, ὁ, Lat. *carbo, coal*, *PMasp.*58 viii 14 (vi A.D.): pl., Anon. *in EN*428.13.

⊕ **κάρδακες**, οἱ, Persian name for *foreign mercenaries*, Theopomp. (Hist. or Com.) ap.Paus.Gr.*Fr.*222, Plb.5.79.11 and 82.11: derived by Str.15.3.18 from Pers. κάρδα, = τὸ ἀνδρῶδες καὶ πολεμικόν.

**καρδᾰμ-άλη**, ἡ, Persian *loaf* or *cake made of* κάρδαμον, Trypho ap. Ath.3.114f, Hsch., Phot.:—also **καρδάμη** Poll.6.76; **παρδαμάλη** Phot. **-ίζω**, *to be like cress*, τί καρδαμίζεις; why *chatter so much about cresses*, i.e. about nothing? Ar.*Th.*617. **-ίνη**, ἡ, = σισύμβριον, Dsc.2.128. 2. = ἰβηρίς, Aët.12.1. 3. = κάρδαμον, Ps.-Dsc.2.155. **-ίς**, ίδος, ἡ, = κάρδαμον, Nic.*Al.*533, Plu.2.466d. ⊕ **-ον**, τό, *nose-smart*, *Lepidium sativum*, of which the seed was eaten like mustard, X.*Cyr.*1.2.8, *POxy.*1429.5, Ael.*VH*3.39: pl., Ar.*Nu.*234; κάρδαμ' ἐσκευασμένα Eub.36: metaph., βλέπειν κάρδαμα look *sharp and stinging*, Ar.*V.*455: prov. of worthless things, ὅσῳ διαφέρει σῦκα καρδάμων Henioch.4.2.

**καρδᾰμύσσω**, = σκαρδαμύσσω, Hsch., *EM*490.53.

**καρδάμωμον** [ᾰ], τό, *cardamum*, *Elettaria Cardamomum*, Thphr.*HP*9.7.2, Dsc.1.6, etc. II. = γεράνιον, Ps.-Dsc.3.116. (For καρδαμάμωμον.)

**καρδάνη**, = κάρδαμον, *Gloss.*

⊕ **καρδί-α**, ἡ, Ion. **καρδίη**, Ep. **κρᾰδίη** (καρδίη in Hom. only in καρδίῃ ἄλληκτον πολεμίζειν ἠδὲ μάχεσθαι Il.2.452, al., καρδία always in Trag., exc. in some dact. and anap. verses, A.*Pr.*881, *Th.*781, E.*Med.*99, *Hipp.*1274); Aeol. **κάρζα** *EM*407.21 (but **καρδία** Sapph.2.6); Cypr. **κορζία** (Paph.), Hsch. (fort. κόρζα):—*heart*, ἐν δέ τέ οἱ κραδίη μεγάλα στέρνοισι πατάσσει Il.13.282; κραδίη δέ μοι ἔξω στηθέων ἐκθρῴσκει, of one panic-stricken, 10.94; πηδᾷ ἡ κ. Pl.*Smp.*215e, cf. Ar.*Nu.*1391 (lyr.): esp. as the seat of feeling and passion, as rage or anger, οἰδάνεται κραδίη χόλῳ Il.9.646; τέτλαθι δή, κραδίη Od.20.18, cf. E.*Alc.*837; καρδίης πλέως full of *heart*, Archil.58.4; of fear or courage, κυνὸς ὄμματ' ἔχων, κραδίην δ' ἐλάφοιο Il.1.225; [σφηκῶν] κραδίην καὶ θυμὸν ἔχοντες 16.266; ἐν μέν οἱ κραδίῃ θάρσος βάλε 21.547, etc.; ὀρχεῖται καρδία φόβῳ A.*Ch.*166; θερμὴν ἐπὶ ψυχροῖσι κ. ἔχεις S.*Ant.*88; τὸν νέον τίνα οἴει κ. ἴσχειν; what do you think are his *feelings?* Pl.*R.*492c; of sorrow or joy, ἐν κραδίῃ μέγα πένθος ἄεξε Od.17.489; κ. καὶ θυμὸς ἰάνθη 4.548; ἄχος κραδίην καὶ θυμὸν ἵκανεν Il.2.171, cf. 10.10, B.10.85, etc.; καρδίην ἀλγέων ἰαίνεται Archil.36; κελαινόχρως.. πάλλεταί μου κ. A.*Supp.*785; ὦ τάλαινα κ. ψυχή τ' ἐμή E.*Or.*466; of love, Sapph. l. c., etc.; ἐκ τῆς κ. φιλεῖν Ar.*Nu.*86; φιλέειν ἀπὸ κ. Theoc.29.4 (but ἐρεῖν τἀπὸ κ. to speak *freely*, E.*IA*475); λαλῆσαι ἐπὶ καρδίαν τινός speak *kindly* to.., Lxx *Jd.*19.3. 2. *inclination, desire, purpose*, ἔμ' ὀτρύνει κραδίη καὶ θυμὸς Il.10.220; πρόφρων κ. ἐν πάντεσσι πόνοισι ib.244; καρδίας δ' ἐξίσταμαι S.*Ant.*1105. 3. *mind*, ὡς ἄνοον κραδίην ἔχες Il.21.441; κραδίη πόρφυρε Od.4.572; κραδίη προτιόσσετ' ὄλεθρον 5.389; εἰ θεάσῃ τοῖς τῆς καρδίας ὀφθαλμοῖς *Corp.Herm.*4.11, cf. 7.2; διαλογισμοὶ ἀναβαίνουσι ἐν τῇ κ. *Ev.Luc.*24.38. II. *cardiac orifice of the stomach*, Th.2.49, Hp.*Prorrh.*1.72, Gal.8.338, al. III. *heart in wood, pith*, Thphr.*HP*3.14.1; = ἐντεριώνη, ib.1.2.6; ἀρτεμισίας μονοκλώνου καρδίας ζ' *PMag.Berol.*1.245, cf. *PMag.Leid.V.*13.24; λαβὼν βάϊν χλωρὰν καὶ τῆς κ. κρατήσας σχίσον εἰς δύο *PMag.Leid.W.*6.51. IV. metaph., κ. θαλάσσης *depths* of the sea, Lxx *Ez.*27.4. V. Κ. Λέοντος, name of the star *Regulus*, Gem.3.5. (I.-E. *kṛd-*, cf. Lat. *cor(d)-*, Lith. *širdìs* 'heart', etc.) ⊕ **-ακός**, ή, όν, *of* or *belonging to the heart*, πῦρ Rhet.ap.Eust.801.36: in Medic. sense, κ. πάθος Diog.Oen.66; συγκοπαί Gal.8.302; νόσος Alex. Aphr. *de An.*98.23. Adv. **-κῶς** Gal.8.368; κ. κινδυνεύειν S.E.*P.*1.84. II. of persons, *suffering from heart disease*, Archig.ap.Gal.9.19; but prob. = καρδιαλγής, Dsc.1.112, Ath.1.10d.

**καρδῐαλγ-έω**, *suffer from heartburn*, Hp.*Epid.*2.2.1. **-ής**, ές, *suffering from heartburn*, Id.*Acut.*30, Gal.6.604. **-ία**, ἡ, *heartburn*, Id.8.343, al., Ruf.ap.Orib.7.26.8. **-ικός**, ή, όν, *afflicted with heartburn*, Hp.*Epid.*3.17.ι'.

**καρδιᾶτις**, ιδος, ἡ, Pythag. name for *five*, *Theol.Ar.*32.

**καρδιάω**, = καρδιαλγέω, in Ep. part. καρδιόωντα, Nic.*Al.*581.

**καρδῐηβολέω**, *lay to heart*, Herod.4.52 (s. v.l.).

**καρδῐκός**, ή, όν, *heart-shaped* (?), *PMag.Berol.*2.68.

**καρδῐο-βολέομαι**, Pass., *to be stricken in heart, grieved*, Hsch. **-βόλος**, ον, *affecting the cardia* (v. καρδία II) *injuriously*, βρώματα

Aret.*SA*2.3; φάρμακον Ruf.ap.Orib.7.26.86. **-γνώστης**, ου, ὁ, *knower of hearts*, *Act.Ap.*1.24, 15.8. **-δαιτος**, ον, *feasting on* men's *hearts*, *PMag.Par.*1.2865. **-δηκτος**, ον, *gnawing the heart*, κ. ἐκ γυναικῶν κράτος (prob. for καρδίᾳ δηκτόν) A.*Ag.*1471 (lyr.). ⊛ **-ειδής**, ές, *heart-shaped*, σχῆμα Herm. *in Phdr.*p.199A.

**κάρδιον**, τό, Dim. of καρδία, *heart-shaped ornament*, *IG*11(2).161*B* 116 (pl., Delos, iii B.C.).

**καρδῐό-πληκτος**, ον, gloss on ἐμβρόντητος, Sch.X.*An.*3.4.12 (ed. L. Dindorf). **-της**, *praecordia*, *Gloss.* **-τρωτος**, ον, *wounded in the heart*, Gal.1.112.

**καρδῐ-ουλκέω**, (ἕλκω) *draw the heart of the victim* at a sacrifice, Luc. *Sacr.*13. II. κ. φοινίκινα perh. *extract the pith* (cf. καρδία III), *Sammelb.*7188.43 (ii B.C.). **-ουλκία**, ἡ, *drawing out the heart*, Hsch. (pl.). ⊛ **-ουργέω**, = καρδιουλκέω, Id. s. v. καρδιοῦσθαι.

**καρδῐοφύλαξ** [ῠ], ἄκος, ὁ, *breastplate*, Plb.6.23.14.

**καρδῐ-όω**, *hearten*, Lxx *Ca.*4.9. II. in Med., = καρδιουργέω, Hsch., *EM*492.12. **-ωγμός**, ὁ, = καρδιαλγία, Hp.*Prog.*24, *Aph.* 4.17 (pl.), Dsc.1.7, Alex.Aphr.*Pr.*2.35, etc. **-ώσσω**, Att. -ττω, = καρδιαλγέω, *have heartburn* or *stomach-ache*, Hp.*Prog.*24, *Mul.* 1.9, Arist.*Pr.*$873^{b}29$, Ael.*NA*9.11, Aret.*SA*2.3, prob. l. in Ar.*Fr.* 362. II. in Sicil. Greek, = βουλιμιάω, Epich.202.

**καρδοπεῖον**, τό, *cover of a kneading-trough*, Hsch. II. = παυσικάπη, *muzzle*, Ar.*Fr.*301.

**καρδοπογλύφος** [ῠ], ον, *scooping out kneading-troughs* or other *wooden utensils*, Crates Com.6.

⊛ **κάρδοπος**, ἡ, *kneading-trough*, Eup.228 (pl.), Ar.*Ra.*1159; κ. πλατεῖα Pl.*Phd.*99b: generally, *wooden vessel*, Hom.*Epigr.*15.6; *mortar*, Nic.*Th.*527: Com. fem. **καρδόπη**, ἡ, coined by Ar.*Nu.*678.

**κάρδος**, ἡ, = κάκτος, Ath.2.70e.

**κᾰρέα**, ἡ, = καρύα, Phlp. *in GA*23.7, al.

**κάρειον** [ᾰ], τό, poet. for κάρα (A), Nic.*Fr.*74.51 (fort. καρήνοις).

⊛ **Κάρειος**, ὁ (sc. μήν), name of month in Western Locris, *IG*9(1). 331, *BCH*22.10.

**κάρζα**, Aeol. for καρδία (q. v.). **κάρη, κάρηαρ**, v. κάρα (A).

**κᾰρηβᾰρ-έω**, *to be heavy in the head, drowsy*, τὴν κεφαλὴν κ. Arist. *PA*$653^{a}14$; [ἰχθύδια] κ. ὑπὸ τοῦ ψόφου *bewildered*, Id.*HA*$534^{a}4$; *stagger* as one drunken, Ph.2.123; τῷ σώματι κ. καὶ σφάλλεσθαι Plu.*Art.* 11, cf. *Ant.*85, Q.S.6.266; *to be top-heavy*, of a spindle charged with yarn, *AP*6.160 (Antip. Sid.); μῆλα -έοντα κορύμβοις ib.5.257 (Paul. Sil.); *have a headache*, ναυτιῶντα καὶ -οῦντα ὑπὸ τοῦ σάλου Luc.*Herm.* 28:—also **-άω** Pherecr.218 (καραι- codd. Eust.), Thphr.*Od.*46 (but -βαρεῖν *HP*9.8.6), v.l. in Luc.*Lex.*13; and **-ιάω** v.l. in Ar.*Fr.*792, prob. l. in Telecl.44, cf. Sch.Opp.*H.*3.368:—the form **κᾰρηβοάω**, = ἰλιγγιάω is quoted by Ael.Dion.*Fr.*221, and καρηβορᾶν, καρυβοᾶν are vv.ll. in Ar. l. c. **-ής**, ές, *drowsy, comatose*, prob. l. in Hp. *Epid.*3.6, cf. Gal.16.579. II. *producing drowsiness*, νότος Sch. Arat.786. **-ησις**, εως, ἡ, *heaviness in the head* or *headache*, Polem. Hist.83. **-ία**, Ion. -ίη, ἡ, = foreg., Hp.*Acut.*49, *Aph.*5.22, Arist. *Somn.*$456^{b}29$, Porph.*Abst.*1.28, Agath.2.38; κ. βάκτρου, paraphrase for a 'knobby' stick, *AP*9.249 (Maec.). **-ικός**, ή, όν, *subject to headache*, Hp.*Epid.*3.17.ς′; τὸ -κόν, = καρηβαρία, Telecl. 47. II. *causing headache*, οἶνος Hp.*Acut.*50, Arist.*Fr.*106; νότος Hp.*Aph.*3.5:—so **-ίτης** [ῑ], ου, ὁ, οἶνος Sch.Ar.*Pl.*808.

**κᾰρηκομόωντες**, οἱ, (κομάω) *with hair on the head, long-haired*, epith. of the Achaians, Il.2.11, al. (sed divisim scrib.): Com. metaph., ἐχῖνοι κ. ἀκάνθαις Matro *Conv.*18:—hence Verb **καρηκομόω**, coined by Diog.*Ep.*19.

**κᾰρῆναι**, aor. 2 inf. Pass. of κείρω.

**κάρηνον** [ᾰ], τό, Dor. **κάρᾱνον** A.*Ch.*396 (lyr.), Mosch.1.12 (Ion. κάρηνον 2.87); in derivs. the ᾱ prevails: (v. κάρα A):—*head*, mostly in pl. (as always in Hom.), ἀνδρῶν κάρηνα, periphr. for ἄνδρες, Il.11.500; νεκύων ἀμενηνὰ κ. Od.10.521, etc.; βοῶν ἴφθιμα κ. Il.23.260; ἵππων ξανθὰ κ. 9.407: metaph., of mountain *peaks*, Οὐλύμποιο κ. 1.44, etc.; of towns, πολλάων πολίων κατέλυσε κάρηνα 2.117, 9.24; Μυκάλης αἰπεινὰ κ. 2.869: in pl., of a single person, κάρηνα.. Μελανίππου σπάσας E.*Fr.*537: sg. in *h.Hom.*8.12, 28.8, Mosch. ll. cc., Coluth.264, *Anacreont.*1.11.

**κάρητος, κάρητι**, v. κάρα (A).

**καρθμός**, ὁ, = κίνησις (i.e. = σκαρθμός), Hsch.

**κάρθρα**, τά, *wages for clipping* or *shearing*, *Edict.Diocl.*7.20; cf. κάρτρα.

**κάρι**, τό, dub. sens. in Hdn.Gr.1.354; ἀπὸ κάρεως ἀναθυμίασις perh. *caraway*, Gal.17(1).563; cf. κάρον, καρώ.

**κᾱρῑδάριον**, τό, Dim. of καρίς, Anaxandr.27 (anap.):—also **κᾱρίδιον**, τό, Arist.*HA*$547^{b}17$.

**κᾱριδόω**, (καρίς) *wriggle, twist about like a shrimp*, Anaxandr.37. [ῑ prob.]

**καρίεντο**, barbarism in Ar.*Th.*1210, for χαρίεν.

**Κᾱρίζω**, *act like a Carian*, Diogenian.7.65. II. *speak like a Carian*, i.e. *barbarously*, Str.14.2.28.

**Κᾱρικοεργής**, ές, *of Carian work*, ὄχανον Anacr.91.

⊛ **Κᾱρικός**, ή, όν, *Carian*, λόφος Alc.22, cf. Hdt.1.171, al.; used for εὐτελής, *worthless*, κ. τράγοι S.*Fr.*540. II. Κ. ἔλαιον a kind of *salve*, Ophel.5; Κ. φάρμακον Hp.*Ulc.*16. III. Καρικὴ μοῦσα *funeral song, dirge*, Pl.*Lg.*800e; Κ. αὐλήματα Ar.*Ra.*1302; Κ. μέλος Pl.Com.69.12 (dub. l.). IV. Καρική (καρίκη cod.)· ἀσύνθετος (leg. ἀσύνετος), καὶ ἄμπελος, Hsch. V. Καρικόν, τό, *Carian quarter* in Memphis, *PSI*4.409.21 (iii B.C.).

**καριμοίρους**· τοὺς ἐν μηδεμιᾷ μοίρᾳ, ἢ μισθοφόρους, Hsch.; cf. *κάρ.

**Κᾱρίνη** [ῑ], ἡ, *Carian woman*, Phan.Hist.6; Κ. παρθένος Plu.2. 246e; Κ. κύνες Poll.5.37. 2. esp. *woman hired to sing Carian dirges*; title of plays by Antiphanes and Menander.

**Καρινός**, ὁ (sc. μήν), a month at Byzantium, = November, dub. in *Philol.*2.248.

**καριόθρεπτος**, ον, dub. sens. in *PRyl.*1.35 (iii A.D.).

**Κάριος** [ᾱ], α, ον, = Καρικός, Hdt.8.135; esp. as epith. of Zeus, Id.1.171, 5.66, Str.14.2.23: worshipped in Thessaly and Boeotia, Phot. (Possibly from κάρα (A), cf. Καραιός.)

**καριόω**, aor. ἐκαρίωσα, *kill*, Hsch.

**κᾱρίς** (v. sub fin.), ἡ, prob. a general term for small crustaceans, incl. *shrimp* (*Crangon*) and *prawn* (*Palaemon*), Anan.5, Arist.*HA* $525^{a}33$, Luc.*Merc.Cond.*3; Dor. **κουρίς** Epich.31, Sophr.26, cf. Hsch., or **κωρίς** Epich.89. [ῐ in Anan. l. c., Ar.*V.*1522 (lyr.), Cratin.283, Eup.7, 107: later ῑ, gen. ῖδος, Arar.8, Anaxandr.22, Eub.78, Archestr. *Fr.*25, Numen.ap.Ath.7.287c.]

**κάρισο**, barbarism in Ar.*Th.*1195, for χαρίσω.

**Κᾱριστί**, Adv. *in Carian language, barbarously*, Str.14.2.28.

**Κᾱρίων**, ωνος, ὁ, prop. Dim. of Κάρ, common name of slaves in Comedy, as in Ar.*Pl.*

**καρκάδων**, ονος, gender unknown, *the fee paid to Charon by the dead*, Phot., Suid.:—expld. by some Gramm. as name of a plant.

**καρκαίρω**, *quake*, of the earth, κάρκαιρε δὲ γαῖα πόδεσσιν ὀρνυμένων Il.20.157. II. ἐκάρκαιρεν· ἐπλήθυεν, and ἐκάρκαιρον· ψόφον τινὰ ἀπετέλουν, Hsch.

**κάρκαρα**, τά, = πίτυρα (ἐπιτυρά cod.), Semon.33.

**καρκαρίς**, ἡ, *load of timber*, Hsch. **κάρκαροι**· τραχεῖς, Id.

⊛ **κάρκᾰρον**, τό, *prison*, Sophr.147:—also **κάρκᾰρος**, ὁ, D.S.31.9: indeterm. in Vett.Val.68.26: pl. κάρκαροι, = δεσμοί, and κάρκαρα, = μάνδραι, Hsch.

⊛ **καρκῐν-άς**, άδος, ἡ, Dim. of καρκίνος I, Gal.6.717, Ael.*NA*7.31, Artem.2.14, Opp.*C.*2.286, *H.*1.320. **-ευτής**, οῦ, ὁ, *crab-catcher*, Artem.2.14. ⊛ **-ηθρον**, τό, = *Polygonum*, *Gloss.*; f.l. for -ωθρον, Dsc.4.4. **-ίας**, ου, ὁ, *crab-coloured gem*, Plin.*HN*37.187. **-ιον**, τό, Dim. of καρκίνος, *hermit-crab*, *Pagurus*, Arist.*HA*$529^{b}20$; a smaller species, ib.$547^{b}17$. II. = καρκίνος III, Hp.*Morb.*2.37. III. a kind of *slipper*, in pl., Herod.7.128.

**καρκῐνο-βάτης**, ου, ὁ, *walking like a crab*, Aristonym.2 (sed leg. -βήτης). **-ειδής**, ές, *of the crab kind*, τὰ κ. Arist.*PA*$684^{a}14$, cf. Ael.*NA*6.20. II. *like a still*, Zos.Alch.p.140B. (cf. *intr.* p.149B.). **-πους**, πουν, gen. ποδος, *crab-footed*, i.e. *lame*, *IG*3. 171*a*.

⊛ **καρκίνος** [ῐ], ὁ, heterocl. pl. καρκίνα (v. sub fin.: on the accent v. Hdn.Gr.2.926):—*crab*, Epich.53, Hellanic.103 J., S.*Ichn.*298, Ar. *Eq.*608, Pl.*Euthd.*297c, Batr.299; κ. ποδήνεμοι Crates Com.29.3: various species distinguished, Arist.*HA*$525^{a}34$, cf. $601^{a}17$, al.: prov., οὔποτε ποιήσεις τὸν καρκίνον ὀρθὰ βαδίζειν Ar.*Pax*1083; εἶς μ' ὀρεῦσα καρκίνου μέζον 'with saucer-eyes', Herod.4.44. II. *Cancer*, as a sign in the zodiac, Eudox.ap.Hipparch.1.2.18, Euc. *Phaen.*p.10 M., Arat.147, etc. III. *eating sore* or *ulcer, cancer*, = καρκίνωμα, Hp.*Aph.*6.38, D.25.95, Gal.10.83. IV. from likeness of shape to crab's claws, 1. *pair of pincers*, Aen.Tact.20.3, 32.5, *IG*11(2).165.11 (Delos, iii B.C.), *AP*6.92 (Phil.), Ath.10.456d; κ. σιδηροῦς *POxy.*521.14 (ii A.D.); used as an instrument of torture, D.S.20.71: in Surgery, *forceps*, κ. ἰατρικός *IG*$2^{2}$.47.16: metaph., λήψεται τὸν τράχηλον ἐντόνως ὁ κ. E.*Cyc.*609. 2. = ζυγώματα, bones of the temples, Poll.2.85. 3. a kind of *shoe*, Pherecr.178. 4. a kind of *bandage*, Heliod.ap.Orib.48.54 tit., Gal.18(1).777. 5. *pair of compasses*, Ph.*Bel.*55.25, Ph.2.192, Gal.*Opt.Doctr.*3, S.E.*M.* 10.54: heterocl. pl., καρκίνα σπειροῦχα *AP*6.295.5 (Phan.). 6. *still*, implied in καρκινοειδής II (q. v.). V. pr. n. of Attic tragedian, hence prov., Καρκίνου ποιήματα, = τὰ αἰνιγματώδη, Men.525; Megarian pr. n. **Κερκίνος** *SIG*201.12 (iv B.C.). (Cf. Lat. *cancer*, Skt. *karkaṭas* 'crab'.)

**καρκῐνόχειρες**, ων, *with crab's claws for hands*, Luc.*VH*1.35.

**καρκῐν-όω**, *make crab-like*, κ. τοὺς δακτύλους *crook* one's fingers *like crab's claws*, Antiph.55.15:—Pass., of roots, *spread crab-wise*, Thphr.*HP*1.6.3, *CP*3.21.5:—also in Act., *cause to spread*, ὁ χειμὼν πιλώσας καὶ καρκινώσας τὰς ῥίζας ib.3.23.5. II. in Pass., also, *suffer from cancer*, Hp.*Nat.Mul.*31; *become cancerous*, ἐκινδύνευσεν καρκινωθῆναι τὰ ἕλκεα Id.*Mul.*1.40. ⊛ **-ώδης**, ες, = καρκινοειδής, Arist.*PA*$683^{b}31$, Plu.2.980b. II. *cancerous*, Dsc.*Eup.*2.72, Ruf. ap.Orib.45.11.1; ὄγκος Gal.18(1).80, Alex.Aphr.*Pr.*1.92. ⊛ **-ωθρον**, τό, = ψίλωθρον, Sch.Nic.*Th.*902; = πολύγονον ἄρρεν, prob. in Dsc. 4.4. **-ωμα**, ατος, τό, = καρκίνος III, Hp.*Epid.*5.101, 7.111, Xenophon Med.ap.Ruf.ap.Orib.45.11.2, Dsc.2.10, Plu.2.65d. **-ωσις**, εως, ἡ, *formation of a cancerous growth*, Aët.16.41 (pl.).

**Καρκώ**· Λαμία, Hsch.

⊛ **κάρμα**, ατος, τό, (κείρω) *wool shorn off*, Hsch.; *cream skimmed off*, Id.

**κάρμορον**· τὸν κηριγμεμορημένον, Hsch.

**καρναβάδιον**, τό, *caraway*, *Carum Carvi*, *Gp.*9.28.2.

**Καρνεᾶται**, οἱ (cf. sq.), unmarried ministrants of Apollo, Hsch.

**Καρνειάσιον**, τό, (sc. ἄλσος) *grove sacred to Apollo Carneus*, *IG* 5(1).1390.54, al. (Andania, i B.C.): written **Καρνάσιον** in Paus.4.33. 5, al.

⊛ **Κάρνειος**, ὁ, (κάρνος) title of Apollo in Peloponnesus, Pi.*P.*5.80, Call.*Ap.*71, etc.:—hence **Κάρνεια**, τά, (Κάρνεα metri gr., Theoc.5. 83) *festival held in his honour* by Dorians, esp. by the Spartans, Hdt.

7.206, Th.5.75, *SIG*735.25 (Argos, i B.C.), etc.; τὰ Κ. νικᾶν Ath.14.635e; πανηγυρίζειν Plu.2.873e:—**Κάρνειος** or **Καρνήϊος**, ὁ (sc. μήν), name of month in which the festival was held, E.*Alc.*449 (lyr.), Th.5.54, cf. *IG*4.1485 (Epid.), *GDI*5009 (Crete), etc.; Κάρνειαι θυσίαι at Argos, *IG*4.620.

**κάρνειος** Δωρικός dub. l. in Thphr.*HP*3.16.4.

**Καρνεονίκης** [ῑ], ου, Dor. **-ας**, α, ὁ, *victor in the Carnean games*, *IG* 5(1).82,209 (Sparta): in pl., Κ., οἱ, title of work by Hellanicus.

**κάρνη**· ζημία, Hsch.

⊛**κάρνον**, τό, *Gallic horn*, Hsch. II. *cart*, *PFlor.*140.2, al. (iii A.D.):—hence **καρνάριος**, ὁ, *carter*, ib.207.5, al.

**κάρνος**, ὁ, (cf. κέρας) expld. by Hsch. as βόσκημα, πρόβατον, i.e. *ram*:—hence **καρνοστάσιον**, τό, *pen, fold*, Id. II. = φθεῖρ, Id.

⊛**κάρνυξ**, ὁ, = κάρνον I, Celtic word in Sch.T Il.18.219, Eust.1139.57.

**κάροινον**, τό, *sweet wine boiled down*, καροίνου Μεονίου *Edict.Diocl.*2.13 (v.l. καρυηνου), cf. *Hippiatr.*2, *Gloss.*; οἶνος **Καρΰϊνος** produced in Maeonia, Gal.15.632, 6.801, al. II. ἀβόλλης, χιτὼν καρόϊνος perh. = καρΰϊνος, *nut-brown*, *Stud.Pal.*20.46.13 (iii A.D.), cf. *POxy.*929.9 (ii/iii A.D.), unless a geographical name, cf. I.

**καρόκερκος**, ὁ, name of constellation, *Head and Tail* of Dragon (Οὐροβόρος), *Cat.Cod.Astr.*7.123.

**κάρον** [ᾰ], τό, = καρώ, *Theb.Ostr.*135 (i A.D.); also v.l. for καρώ, Dsc.3.57. II. = μεγάλη ἀκρίς, Hsch.

**κάροπερ**· ἔπακμος παῖς, Hsch. **καρορύς**· ὕδρα (Cret.), Id.

**κάρος** [ᾰ], ὁ, *heavy sleep, torpor*, κ. καὶ κραιπάλη Arist.*Pr.*873b14, cf. A.R.2.203, Phld.*D.*1.18, Str.16.4.19, Max.Tyr.16.1, Gal.8.231; κάρῳ προσφερὴς κατάληψις Iamb.*Myst.*3.2: pl., μελαγχολίαι καὶ κάροι καὶ λήθαργοι *Stoic.*3.57; *drowsiness*, Luc.*Am.*39.

**καρός**· κωφός, οἱ δὲ σκοτόδινος, Hsch. **κάρουα**, Lacon., = κάρυα, Id.

**καροῦχα**, ἡ, Lat. *carruca, carriage*, Sm.*Is.*66.20, Sch.E.*Ph.*847:—also **-οῦχον**, τό, *Edict.Diocl.*15.37:—Dim. **-ούχιον**, τό, *PFlor.*335.8 (iii A.D.), *Gloss.*:—also⊛**-ουχάριος**, *cisiarius, mulio*, ib.

**καροῦχος**· εὐχερής, εὔκολος, Hsch.

**κᾰροφόρος**, ον, *soporiferous*, *Gloss.*

⊛**κᾰρόω**, *plunge into deep sleep* or *torpor, stun, stupefy*, πληγαὶ καροῦσαι Hp.*Art.*30; of wine, Antipho Soph.34, Anaxandr.3, cf. Ath.1.33a; ὀδμὴ καροῦσα a *stupefying* smell, Id.15.675d:—Pass., *to be stupefied*, ὑπὸ βροντῆς, of certain fish, Arist.*HA*602b23; ὑπὸ μύρου, of bees, Id.*Mir.*832a3; ὑπὸ τῶν εὐωδιῶν Str.16.4.19; θανάτῳ κεκαρωμένα..πέλωρα Theoc.24.59; τραύμασι D.H.3.19, cf. Plu.*Art.*11; τὴν διάνοιαν D.H.*Th.*34; of drunken *sleep*, Lxx *Je.*28(51).39.

**καρπαία**, ἡ, *mimic dance* of the Thessalians, in which a peasant scuffles with a cattle-stealer, τὴν καρπαίαν..ἐν τοῖς ὅπλοις ὀρχεῖσθαι X.*An.*6.1.7, cf. Ath.1.15f:—also **κάρπεα**, ἡ, Maced., acc. to Hsch.

**καρπάλῐμος** [πᾰ], ον, (κάλπη A) Ep. Adj. *swift*, πόδες Il.16.342,809, A.R.3.280, cf. Ar.*Th.*957 (lyr.): more freq. in Adv. **-μως** *swiftly*, Il.1.359, etc. 2. *eager, ravenous*, γέννες Pi.*P.*12.20.

**καρπαλίον**· κάρπημα, Hsch.

**καρπάσινος** [πᾰ], η, ον, *made of* κάρπασος, Lxx*Es.*1.6, Str.7.2.3, D.H.2.68.

**καρπάσιον**, τό, *flax*, *CPR*61.13 (iii A.D.):—but λίνον **Καρπάσιον**, *asbestos* (*from Carpasia* in Cyprus), Paus.1.26.7.

**κάρπᾰσος**, ἡ, with heterocl. pl. κάρπασα, *AP*9.415.6 (Antiphil., with play on the meanings 'sails' and 'clothes'); also **κάλπᾰσος** (q.v.):—*flax, Linum usitatissimum* (or perh. *L. angustifolium*), D.H.2.68, Sch.Ar.*Lys.*736. 2. *cotton*, *Peripl.M.Rubr.*41 (cf. Skt. *karpāsas*). II. **κάρπασον**, τό, *white hellebore, Veratrum album*, Orph.*A.*922; ὀπὸς καρπάσου Archig.ap.Gal.12.445, Dsc.*Alex.*13; *sucus carpathi*, Plin.*HN*32.58; cf. ὀποκάρπασον, καρπησία.

**καρπαστῖναι**· σκορπισθῆναι, Hsch.

**καρπάτινον**, v. καρβάτινος.

**καρπ-εία**, ἡ, *usufruct, enjoyment*, Plb.31.21.8, *Test.Epict.*3.5, v.l. in Ph.2.380; τῶν κρεῶν *IG*12(5).721 (Andros): in pl., *profits* or *emoluments* of an office, *PEleph.*14.13 (iii B.C.), *PTeb.*6.34 (ii B.C.), etc. **-εῖον**, τό, = καρπός (A), Nic.*Al.*277: pl., Ar.*Fr.*177; = καρπεία, Πρακτικὰ τῆς Ἀκαδ. Ἀθηνῶν 1928.109 (Epid., iii/ii B.C.). **-ευμα**, ατος, τό, *fruit*, in pl., dub. in Sosith.2.17. ⊛**-εύω**, *enjoy the fruits of*, χώραν Hyp.*Fr.*107, *IG*9(1).693.3 (Corc.), cf. Plb.10.28.3: generally, *profit by*, Gal.9.790: abs., *SIG*1044.18 (Halic., iv/iii B.C.):—Med., *Supp.Epigr.*3.378 *B* 30 (Delph., ii/i B.C.).

**καρπέω**, inf. καρπεῖν· πληώττειν, Hsch. **κάρπη**· τὰ σπέρματα· καὶ τήγανα ὀβελίσκους ἔχοντα, Id. **κάρπημα**, ατος, τό, gloss on καρπαλίον, Id.

**καρπήσιον**, τό, *an aromatic plant, Valeriana Dioscoridis*, chiefly brought from Asia, Gal.12.15, Alex.Trall.9.1:—but **καρπησία**, ἡ, = κάρπασος II, Paul.Aeg.5.44.

**καρπ-ίζω** (A), (καρπός A) *enjoy the fruits of*, *IG*12(5).243 (Paros):—elsewh. always in Med., κ. γῆν Theopomp.Hist.217b; κλῆρον *PFrankf.*7.7 (iii B.C.), cf. Hyp.*Fr.*119, Lxx*Jo.*5.12, *IG*5(2).419.14 (Phigalea, iii B.C.), ib.7.413.28, al. (Oropus, i B.C.), etc.; χρόνον Epicur.*Ep.*3 p.61 U.; but also, *exhaust* the soil, καρπίζεται τὴν γῆν μάλιστα πυρός Thphr.*HP*8.9.1, cf. *CP*4.8.1: metaph., δόξαν ἐσθλήν E.*Hipp.*432; κῦδος ἐκαρπίσατο *Epigr.Gr.*516.4 (Aegae), cf. *Supp.Epigr.*3.781 (Gortyn); *exploit*, *BGU*1571 (i A.D.); βέλτιον ἐμὲ (sc. τὴν σοφίαν) καρπίζεσθαι ὑπὲρ χρυσίον Lxx*Pr.*8.19. II. *make fruitful, fertilize*, E.*Ba.*408 (lyr.), *Hel.*1328 (lyr.). **-ίζω** (B), (κάρφος II) *enfranchise a slave by touching him with the rod*, καρπίζομαι ἐπὶ ἐλευθερίᾳ, = Lat. *adseror*, *Gloss.* **-ιμος**, ον, *fruit-bearing, fruitful*, θέρος A.*Pr.*455; στάχυς, πέδον, E.*Supp.*31, *Or.*1086; καρπίμους ἐτῶν κύκλους Id.*Hel.*112; μυρρίναι Ar.*Pax*1154; κισσοῦ κλάδοι Alex.119.5; ξύλον Lxx*Ge.*1.11; κάρπιμα πρῷα early *crops*, Ar.*V.*264; θερίσαι κάρπιμα to reap *the fruits*, *CIG*4310.15 (Limyra), cf. *PSI*4.292.13 (iii A.D.); κ. [ἀγαθά] property *that yields a produce*, opp. ἀπολαυστικά, Arist.*Rh.*1361a17; opp. ἄκαρπα, Id.*EN*1125a12: metaph., ἀμέλγεις τῶν ξένων τοὺς κ. *from whom money can be wrung*, Ar.*Eq.*326.

⊛**καρπίον**, τό, Dim. of καρπός (A), Thphr.*Od.*32, *BGU*1120.50 (i B.C.). II. vulgar name for ἐλλέβορος, *Hippiatr.*11. III. καρπία· κλονία (fort. κλωνία), Hsch.

**κάρπιον**, τό, *screw-pine, Pandanus odoratissimus*, Ctes.*Fr.*57.28.

⊛ **Κάρπιος**, ὁ, variant for Ἐπικάρπιος, title of Zeus in Arist.*Mu.*401a19 (ap.Stob.1.1.36).

**καρπ-ισμός** (A), ὁ, (καρπίζω A) *exhaustion*, τῆς γῆς Thphr.*CP*4.8.2. II. *profit*, Arist.*Pr.*952b6. **-ισμός** (B), ὁ, (καρπίζω B), **-ιστεία** and **-ιστία**, ἡ, = Lat. *vindiciae*, *Gloss.* ⊛**-ιστής**, οῦ, ὁ, *emancipator*, Arr.*Epict.*3.24.76, 4.1.113. **-ιστικός**, ή, όν, *connected with emancipation*, *Gloss.*; of a suit, = *liberale judicium*, ib.

**καρπο-βάλσᾰμον**, τό, *the fruit of the balsam*, Gal.14.166, v.l. in Dsc.1.58. **-βόλον**· τὸ σιτοβόλον ἀγγεῖον, Hsch. **-βρωτος**, ον, *with edible fruit*, ξύλον Lxx*De.*20.20. **-γένεθλος**, ον, = καρπογόνος, epith. of Apollo, *AP*9.525.11.

**καρπογον-έω**, *to be productive, bear fruit*, Thphr.*HP*9.1.1, *CP*3.9.2, Porph.*Abst.*4.20. **-ία**, ἡ, *productiveness*, X.*Smp.*2.25, Thphr.*CP* 1.5.5, Sor.1.42 (pl.), Lib.*Or.*25.67, Aen.Gaz.*Thphr.*p.54B. ⊛ **-ος** (parox.), ον, *bearing fruit*, Dsc.5.141, prob. in Lyr. in *Philol.*80.338.

⊛**καρπο-δαιστάς**, ᾱ, ὁ, Cret., *distributor of produce*, *GDI*4993 (Gortyn). **-δεσμα**, ων, τά, *chains for the arms, armlets*, Luc.*Lex.*10: **-δεσμος**, ὁ, *bandage for wrist*, Sor.*Fasc.*50, Cass.Fel.24. **-δέσμιος**, ον, *wearing a knee-halter*, Horap.2.78. II. Subst. **-δέσμιον**, τό, *armlet*, *POxy.*1153.13 (i A.D.). **-δότειρα**, ἡ, *giver of fruit*, Orph.*H.*43.9. **-δόχος**, ον, v. καρπολόχος.

⊛ **καρπολογ-έω**, *gather fruit*, *SIG*1000.29 (Cos):—in Pass., of trees, Thphr.*CP*1.15.1. **-ία**, ἡ, *gathering of fruit*, *Gp.*10.78.1. ⊛**-ος** (parox.), ον, *gathering fruit*, Polyaen.3.10.9. II. title of magistrates at Thasos, *BCH*45.147 (iv B.C.).

**καρπο-λόχος**, ον, *bearing fruit*, of Demeter, cj. for καρποδόχος in *AP*12.225 (Strat.). **-μᾰνής**, ές, *running to fruit, luxuriant*, S.*Fr.*652. **-ποιός**, όν, *making fruit*, of Demeter, E.*Rh.*964:—later **-ποιητικός** Phlp. *in GA*193.21.

⊛ **καρπός** (A), ὁ, *fruit*, in Hom. and Hes. (only in sg.), usu. of *the fruits of the earth, corn*, ἀρούρης κ. Il.6.142; κ. δ' ἔφερε ζείδωρος ἄρουρα Hes.*Op.*117; κ. Δήμητρος Hdt.1.193, etc.; Δηοῦς Ar.*Pl.*515; κ. ἀρούρης, also of wine, Il.3.246; ἀμπέλινος κ. Hdt.1.212; so κ. alone, Ar.*Nu.*1119 (codd. and Sch.); but of corn, opp. Βάκχιον νᾶμα, Id.*Ec.*14; καρποῦ ξυγκομιδὴ *harvest*, Th.3.15; κ. λωτοῖο, κρανείης, Od.9.94, 10.242; μελιηδέα κ., of grapes, Il.18.568; κ. ἐλαίας Pi.*N.*10.35; τὸν ἐπέτειον κ. the *crops* of the year, Pl.*R.*470b: generally, *produce*, κ. ὑγρός, of honey, Porph.*Abst.*2.20; also κ. εὐανθὴς μήλων, of wool, Opp.*H.*2.22: pl., καρπῶν ἐστερήθητε διξῶν robbed of two years' *produce*, Hdt.8.142; καρπῶν ἀτελεῖς Id.6.46; κ. ὑγροὶ καὶ ξηροὶ *produce* of trees and fields, X.*Oec.*5.20; ξύλινοι, σιτικοὶ κ., Str.5.4.2; of *fruits* offered in sacrifice, *BMus.Inscr.*975.7 (Amathus), cf. κάρπωσις II; also of *taxes paid in kind*, opp. χρυσικά, *PHib.*1.47.5 (iii B.C.), al. 2. *seed*, X.*Oec.*16.12; defined as *seed with seed-vessel*, Thphr.*HP*1.2.1. 3. of children, Δῖοι κ. *offspring* of Zeus, E.*Ion*922 (lyr.). II. *returns, profits*, οἱ κ. οἱ ἐκ τῶν ἀγελῶν γενόμενοι X.*Cyr.*1.1.2; τῶν ἀνηλωμένων..τοὺς κ. Is.5.29. III. of actions, *fruit, profit*, εἰ κ. ἔσται θεσφάτοισι Λοξίου if his oracles shall bear *fruit*, i.e. be fulfilled, A.*Th.*618; γλώσσης ματαίας κ., i.e. curses, Id.*Eu.*831 codd.; ὁμιλίας κακῆς κάκιον οὐδέν, κ. οὐ κομιστέος Id.*Th.*600; οὐκ ἐξάγουσι καρπὸν οἱ ψευδεῖς λόγοι S.*Fr.*834, cf. Pl.*Phdr.*260d: freq. in Pi., κ. ἐπέων οὐ κατέφθινε, i.e. poesy, *I.*8(7).50; κ. φρενῶν wisdom, *P.*2.74; κ. φρενός, of his own ode, *O.*7.8; ἥβας κ., of the *bloom* of youth, ib.6.58, *P.*9.109; later, *reward, profit*, ἐπιτηδευμάτων Epicur.*Sent.Vat.*27; ὅπου ὁ κίνδυνος μέγας, καὶ ὁ κ. Diog.Oen.27; κ. νίκης Hdn.8.3.6: freq. in *NT*, κ. εἰρηνικὸς δικαιοσύνης *Ep.Hebr.*12.11, etc. (Cf. Lat. *carpo*, Engl. *harvest*.)

⊛ **καρπός** (B), ὁ, *wrist*, Il.24.671, Od.24.398, Hp.*Fract.*3, Arist.*HA*494a2, etc.; ἐπὶ καρπῷ χερός E.*Ion* 1009; καρποὶ χειρῶν ib.891, cf. X.*Cyr.*6.4.2. (Perh. cf. ONorse *huerfa* 'turn round'.)

**καρπο-σπόρος**, ον, *sowing fruit*, Man.4.256. **-τελής**, ές, *bringing fruit to perfection, fruitful*, A.*Supp.*688.

**καρποτόκ-εια**, ἡ, poet. fem. of καρποτόκος, Nonn.*D.*21.26. **-έω**, *bear fruit*, Thphr.*CP*5.2.3, Ph.1.444. **-ία**, ἡ, *bearing of fruit*, Thphr.*HP*1.2.1, *CP*2.1.2 (pl.). **-ος** (parox.), ον, *bearing fruit*, epith. of Demeter, v.l. in *AP*12.225 (Strat.), of Isis, *APl.*4.264: metaph., Ph.1.53.

⊛**καρπο-τρόφος**, ον, *rearing* or *ripening fruit*, δρῦς Lyc.1423: metaph., ἧβαι E.*Ion*475 (lyr.); epith. of Demeter, *Milet.*7.64; of the clouds, Orph.*H.*21.1. **-φᾰγέω**, *live on fruit*, Arist.*HA*593a15; κ. πρώτης δρυός Porph.*Abst.*2.5. **-φάγος** [φᾰ], ον, *living on fruit*, opp. σαρκοφάγος, παμφάγος, ζῷα Arist.*HA*488a15, cf. *Pol.*1256a25, Max.Tyr.35.7. **-φθόρος**, ον, *spoiling fruit*, δένδρων *AP*9.256 (Antiphan.), cf. Orph.*Fr.*285.55.

**καρποφορ-έω**, *bear fruit*, X.*Vect.*1.3, Arist.*GA*755b10, Ph.1.602, al., Orph.*Fr.*255: metaph., of virtue, Ph.1.154; τῷ θεῷ *Ep.Rom.*7.4; also τῷ θανάτῳ ib.5:—Med., *Ep.Col.*1.6, *BMus.Inscr.*918

(Halic.):—Pass., Ptol. *Tetr.*80. **-ημα**, ατος, τό, *fruit borne*, Eust. 1572.33. **-ία**, ἡ, *fruit-bearing*, Ocell.4.9 (pl.). Ph.1.105, *Cod.Just.* 1.3.38.2 (pl.). ※ **-ος** (parox.), ον, *fruit-bearing, fruitful*, of trees, Hdt. 1.193, 2.156, X.*Cyr.*6.2.22, etc.; of lands, Λιβύα, πεδία, Pi.*P.*4.6, E. *Hel.*1485 (lyr.); τῇ κ. γαίῃ *Sammelb.*6598 (iii A.D.), al.; of Demeter, τὴν κ. βασίλειαν Ar.*Ra.*384 (lyr.), cf. Paus.8.53.7, *CIG*4082 (Pessinus), *IG*12(5).226 (Paros), *SIG*820.5 (Ephesus, i A.D.): hence of Agrippina, *IG*12(2).212 (Mytilene), *IGRom.*4.1300 (Aeolis, in fem. -φόρα); κ. καιροί *Act.Ap.*14.17.

**καρπο-φύλαξ** [ῠ], ἄκος, ὁ, *watcher of fruit*, *AP*6.22 (Zonas). **-φυλλον**, τό, = δάφνη Ἀλεξανδρεία, Plin.*HN*15.131.

**καρπόχειρ**, late word for μετακάρπιον, Eust.1572.38.

※ **καρπόω**, *bear fruit* or *bear as fruit*, metaph., ὕβρις γὰρ ἐξανθοῦσ' ἐκάρπωσε στάχυν ἄτης A.*Pers.*821:—Pass., τὰ πλεῖστα τῶν ῥιζοφύτων καρπωθέντα Ocell.1.13. 2. *offer* by way of sacrifice, Lxx *Le.*2.11; ἐπὶ τοῦ βωμοῦ, of burnt-offerings, *SIG*1025.33 (Cos, iv/iii B.C.):—so in Pass., ib.997.9 (Smyrna), cf. Hsch. II. *take as fruit* or *produce*, Lxx *De.*26.14:—elsewh. in Med., καρπόομαι *get fruit for oneself*, i.e., 1. *reap crops from*, c. acc. rei, [ἀρούρας] Hdt.2.168; χθόνα A.*Pr.*851, *Supp.*253; δὶς τοῦ ἐνιαυτοῦ τὴν γῆν καρποῦσθαι *to crop* the land twice a year, Pl.*Criti.*118e: metaph., βαθεῖαν ἄλοκα διὰ φρενὸς καρπούμενος A.*Th.*593: hence, *exhaust, drain, exploit*, καρπουμένῳ τὴν Ἑλλάδα Ar.*V.*520, cf. Isoc.4.133, 166; οὐσίας D.19.249. 2. *enjoy the usufruct* or *interest* of money, ἔδωκεν ἑβδομήκοντα μνᾶς καρπώσασθαι Id.27.5; τοὺς λιμένας καὶ τὰς ἀγορὰς καρποῦσθαι *to derive profits from*.., Id.1.22; ἔθνη X.*HG*6.1.12; ἰδίᾳ κ. τὰς τῆς πόλεως συμφορὰς Lys.25.25; [πλεονεξίαν] D.23.126: in pf. Pass., τὸ ἐργαστήριον κεκαρπωμένος *having enjoyed the profits of* the shop, Id.27.47: abs., *make profit*, Ar.*Ach.*837. 3. *enjoy the free use of*, τὰ αὑτοῦ ἀγαθὰ γιγνόμενα Th.2.38; τὴν τῶν πολεμίων [χώραν], τὰς τῶν θεῶν τιμάς, X. *Ages.*1.34; τὴν οἰκείαν ἀδεῶς κ. D.1.25, cf. 28. 4. simply, *enjoy*, ἄελπτον ὄμμα.. φήμης S.*Tr.*204; τἀμὰ.. λέχη E.*Andr.*935; ἐλευθερίαν Th.7.68; τὴν σοφίαν Pl.*Euthd.*305e; ἡδονὴν ταύτην Id.*Phdr.* 252a, cf. 240a, etc.; ἀσφάλειαν καὶ εὔκλειαν X.*Cyr.*8.2.22; τὴν δόξαν τινός D.20.69; τὴν ἡλικίαν Id.59.19; δωρεάς Plu.*Them.*31: in bad sense, ἰδίας καρποῦσθαι λύπας Hp.*Flat.*1; φρενῶν τὴν ἁμαρτίαν A.*Ag.* 502; τὰ ψευδῆ καλά ib.621; πένθη E.*Hipp.*1427; ἄπαιδα κ. βίον Id. *Fr.*571.3; τὰ μέγιστα ὀνείδη Pl.*Smp.*183a; λοιδορίας Phld.*Vit.* p.34 J.

**καρπύλη**, ἡ, an *Indian plant*, Clitopho ap.Stob.4.36.22.

**καρπυραί**· ξύλων ξηρῶν κοῖται, Hsch.; cf. καρφηρός.

**καρπ-ώδης**, ες, *fruitful*, ἔλαιον Orac.ap.Phleg.*Fr.*1 J., cf. *Gloss.* ※**-ωμα**, ατος, τό, *fruit*, A.*Supp.*1001; *profit*, Hsch. II. *offering of fruits*, Lxx *Nu.*18.9; cf. κάρπωσις II. **-ώνης**, ου, ὁ, *buyer of fruit*, $IG2^2$.1100 (ii A.D.), *PFay.*133.12 (iv A.D.). ※**-ωνία**, ἡ, *fruit-buying*, *PLond.ined.*2338 (iii B.C.), *BGU*830.8 (i A.D.). **-ώσιμος**, ον, *yielding fruit, profitable*, Hermipp.Hist.81. ※ **-ωσις**, εως, ἡ, *use, profit*, X.*Cyr.*4.5.16. II. *offering of fruits*, Lxx *Le.*4.10, al., *IG* 3.77 (pl., ii A.D.); *sacrifice* to Aphrodite at Amathus, Hsch. **-ωτός**, όν, (καρπός B) *reaching to the wrist*, κ. χιτών a coat *with sleeves down to the wrist*, Lxx 2*Ki.*13.18,19.

**καρρέζουσα**, Ep. for καταρρέζουσα, Il.5.424.

**καρρ-ικός**, ή, όν, *sufficient to fill a wagon*, γόμος *OGI*629.16 (Palmyra, ii A.D.). **-ιον** καθεδρωτόν, *covinnus*, *Gloss.*

**κάρρον**, τό, *car, cart*, Lxx 1*Es.*5.55 (cod. A), *PGoodsp.Cair.*30 xxix 21 (ii A.D.), *Edict.Diocl.*15.38a: **κάρρος**, ὁ, ib.39:—hence **καρροπηγός**, ὁ, and **-ποιός**, ὁ, *coach-builder*, *Gloss.*

**κάρρων**, ον, gen. ονος, *stronger, better*, Dor. for κρείσσων, Alcm.89, Epich.165, Sophr.59, Ti.Locr.94c, *AP*7.413.7 (Antip.), Plu.*Lyc.*25; κάρρον ἐστίν c. inf., it is *better to*.., Cerc.5.13:—hence **καρρόθεν**, Adv. *from something better*, Dam.ap.Suid. s. v. κάρρων.

**κάρσιος**, α, ον, *crosswise*, Hsch. Adv. **-ίως** Suid.; cf. ἐγκάρσιος.

**κάρτᾰ** (cf. κράτος), Adv., freq. in Ion. and Trag., rare in Com. and Att. Prose (v. infr.):—with Adjs. and Advbs., *very, extremely*; with Verbs, *very much*; κ. κακῶς ῥιγῶ Hippon.16; ἐσθλοὺς κ. μαχητάς Aristeas Epic.*Fr.*3; κ. ἀπὸ θερμέων χωρέων *very* hot, Hdt.2.27; κ. θεραπεύειν τινά, opp. μετρίως, Id.3.80; κ. δεόμενος Id.8.59; κ. ὀξὺ Hp. *Acut.*58; κ. πρευμενεῖς A.*Ag.*840; κ. ἰδεῖν ὀμόπτερος Id.*Ch.*174; εἰ καὶ μακρὰ κ. ἐστίν S.*Tr.*1218; ὥς σου κ. νῦν μνείαν ἔχω E.*Med.*328, cf. 222, etc.; once in Pl., πηλοῦ κ. βραχέος *Ti.*25d; ληρεῖς ἔχων κ. Ar. *Av.*342 (troch.). 2. *surely, in very deed*, κ. δ' ἔστ' ἐγχώριος A.*Th.* 413; κ. δ' ὢν ἐπώνυμος *true* to thy name, Id.*Eu.*90, cf. *Th.*658; κ. δ' εἰμὶ τοῦ πατρός *all* on the father's side, Id.*Eu.*738; κ. δ' εἰσ' ὅμαιμοι Id.*Th.*939 (lyr.); ἦ κ. Id.*Ag.*592, 1252, S.*El.*312, 1278, etc.; σὺ δὲ κ. φείδῃ Amips.22. 3. καὶ κ., used to increase the force of a previous statement, τὰ ἀνέκαθεν λαμπροί, ἀπὸ δὲ Ἀλκμέωνος.. καὶ κ. λαμπροί Hdt.6.125; esp. in dialogue, *yes, verily*, ἦ γάρ τινες ναίουσι..; Answ. καὶ κ.... S.*OC*65; ἆρ' ἄν τί μου δέξαιο..; Answ. καὶ κάρτα γ' E.*Hipp.* 90; once in Ar., καὶ κ. μέντἂν.. καθείλκετε *Ach.*544; in Hdt. also, τὸ κ. 1.71, 4.181; esp. with a slightly iron. sense, *with a vengeance*, ἐς ὃ δὴ καὶ τὸ κ. ἐπύθοντο 1.191, cf. 3.104, 6.52.

**καρτάζω** (in Pass.) and **καρταίνω**, = καρτύνω, Hsch.

**καρτάζωνος**, ὁ, = μονόκερως, Ael.*NA*16.20.

**καρταίπους**, ὁ, ἡ, πουν, τό, gen. ποδος, = κραταίπους (q.v.), Pi.*O.* 13.81: neut. pl., **καρταίποδα**, τά, *larger cattle, beasts*, *Leg.Gort.*4. 36, al.: sg., **καρταῖπος**, τό, *GDI*4998 I 7 (Gortyn), al.

**καρτάλαμον**, τό, = περίζωμα, Lyd.*Mag.*2.13:—Dim. **-άμιον**, τό, = *fiscella*, *Gloss.*

**κάρταλλος**, ὁ, *basket with pointed bottom*, Lxx 4*Ki.*10.7, al., *Sammelb.*6801.4 (iii B.C.). Ph.1.694, Hsch.; also, of a *feast*, Ph.2.298 (κάρταλος cod.):—Dim. **καρτάλλιον**, τό, *Sammelb.*6801.26 (iii B.C.), *Gloss.*; cf. κερτύλλιον.

**καρτέον**, (κείρω) *one must shear*, Muson.*Fr.*21 p.115 H.

**καρτερ-αίχμης, -αύχην**, v. κρατερ-.

※ **καρτερ-έω**, *to be steadfast, patient*, S.*Ph.*1274, Men.*Sam.*112, etc.; ῥᾷον παραινεῖν ἢ παθόντα καρτερεῖν E.*Alc.*1078, cf. Th.7.64; κ. μάχῃ E.*Heracl.*837; κ. ἐλπίδι τινός Th.2.44: freq. with a Prep., κ. πρός τι *to hold up* against a thing, e.g. πρὸς ἡδονάς τε καὶ λύπας Pl.*R.*556c; πρὸς λιμὸν καὶ ῥῖγος X.*Cyr.*2.3.13; ἐπὶ τοῖς παροῦσι Isoc.6.48, cf. Pl. *La.*194a; κ. ἐν ταῖς ἡδοναῖς *to be patient* or *temperate* in.., Id.*Lg.* 635c; ἐν πολέμῳ Id.*La.*193a; κ. ἀπὸ τοῦ ὕπνου *refrain* therefrom, Ael.*NA*13.13: c. part., *persevere* in doing, οἱ δ' ἐκαρτέρουν πρὸς κῦμα λακτίζοντες E.*IT*1395; κ. ἀναλίσκων ἀργύριον φρονίμως Pl.*La.*192e; ἀκούων Aeschin.3.241; κ. ἐν ἐπιτηδεύμασιν Isoc.2.32; also τὰ δείν' ἐκαρτέρουν *was* strangely *obdurate* or *obstinate*, S.*Aj.*650: in later Prose meaning little more than *wait*, καρτέρει καὶ θεώρει *wait* and see, Lxx 2*Ma.*7.17; οὐ κ. μέχρι θαλάμων ἐλθεῖν S.E.*M.*1.291. II. c. acc. rei, *bear patiently, endure*, τὰ δ' ἀδύναθ' ἡμῖν καρτερεῖν οὐ ῥᾴδιον E.*IA*1370; κ. θεοῦ δόσιν Id.*Alc.*1071; τῷ σώματι τὰ συντυγχάνοντα X.*Mem.*1.6.7; τὸν τῶν ὑπεροπτικῶν ὄγκον Isoc.1.30; πολλὴν κακοπάθειαν Arist.*Pol.*$1278^b27$:—Pass., κεκαρτέρηται τἀμά my *time for patience is over*, E.*Hipp.*1457.—In Hsch., οὐ καρτεριάδδει· οὐ φρόνιμος εἶ, should prob. be οὐ καρτερίδδει (Lacon. for καρτερίζει). **-ημα**, ατος, τό, *act of endurance*, Pl.*Men.*88c (pl.). **-ησις**, εως, ἡ, *bearing patiently, patience*, Id.*La.*193d: in pl., Id.*Lg.*637b. 2. c. gen., *patient endurance of* a thing, αἱ τοῦ χειμῶνος κ. Id.*Smp.*220a; αἱ κ. τῶν ἀλγηδόνων Id.*Lg.*633b. **-ία**, ἡ, *patient endurance, perseverance*, opp. μαλακία, X.*Cyr.*8.8.15, cf. Pl.*La.*192b, al.; κ. ἡ περὶ τοὺς πόνους D.H.2.28; distd. from ἐγκράτεια (self-control), Arist.*EN*$1150^b1$: pl., εἴ πού τινες.. κ. πρὸς ἅπαντα.. λέγονται Pl.*R.*390d. **-ιάζω, -ίζω**, v. καρτερέω (sub fin.). **-ικός**, ή, όν, *capable of endurance, patient*, Amips.9, Isoc.8.109, etc.; πρὸς χειμῶνα X.*Mem.*1.2.1 (Sup.); ῥώμη κ. πρὸς ἀρετήν Pl.*Def.*412a: Sup., Luc.*Anach.*38; opp. μαλακός and distd. from ἐγκρατής (cf. καρτερία), Arist.*EN*$1150^a33$. Adv. **-κῶς** ib. $1179^b33$, Marin.*Procl.*12.

**καρτερο-βρόντης**, ου, ὁ, *thundering mightily*, Pi.*Fr.*155. **-εις**, εσσα, εν, = καρτερός, *Epic.Alex.Adesp.*9 iv 7. **-θῡμος**, ον, *stronghearted*, of heroes, Od.21.25, Il.13.350; Μυσοί 14.512; [Ζεύς], Ἔρις, Hes.*Th.*476, 225: generally, *strong, mighty*, ἄνεμοι ib.378. **-πληγής**, ές, *striking fiercely*, D.S.5.34 (v.l. -πλῆγες, nom. pl.). **-πονος**, ον, *bearing labours stoutly*, Sch.Opp.*H.*1.35.

※ **καρτερός**, ά, όν, (κάρτος) = κρατερός (q.v.), *strong, staunch*, φάλαγγες Il.5.592; καὶ εἰ μάλα κ. ἐστιν [Hector] 13.316; Ἡρακλῆς ὁ κ. Ar.*Ra.*464: c. inf., κ. ἐστι μάχῃ ἔνι φῶτας ἐναίρειν Il.13.483; πολέμῳ ἔνι κ. ἔσσι 9.53; Ζεὺς Τυφῶ -ώτερος μάχῃ A.*Th.*517; τὰ καρτερώτατα *the strongest*, S.*Aj.*669. 2. c. gen., *possessed of, in control of, master of*, Ἀσίης Archil.26; οὐκέτι τῆς αὑτοῦ γλώσσης κ. οὔτε νόου Thgn.480; ἁμῶν Theoc.15.94; παθῶν D.H.5.8; γῆς καὶ οἰκίων *SIG*45. 28 (Halic., v B.C.); Θηβαίων Arr.*Fr.*91 J. 3. = καρτερικός, *steadfast, patient*, πρὸς πάντα X.*Cyr.*1.6.25; *obstinate*, -ώτατος ἀνθρώπων πρὸς τὸ ἀπιστεῖν Pl.*Phd.*77a; κ. πρὸς τὸ λέγειν *mighty* in disputation, Id. *Tht.*169b. 4. of things, *mighty, potent*, ὅρκος Il.19.108; κ. ἔργα deeds *of might*, 5.872; κ. ἕλκος *severe*, 16.517; κ. μάχη *strongly contested, sharp, severe*, Hdt.1.76, Th.4.43; ναυμαχίη Hdt.8.12; ἀγών Plb.1.27.11; ἀλαλά, μέριμναι, Pi.*I.*7(6).10, 8(7).13; λίθος Id.*O.*1.58, E.*Fr.*1044; κτύπος A.*Pr.*923; -ώτατον βέλος Pi.*O.*1.112; τὸ κ. *force, violence*, A.*Supp.*612; but τόλμης εἶμι πρὸς τὸ κ. *the utmost verge of*.., E.*Med.*394; κατὰ τὸ κ. in Adv. sense, Hdt.1.212, 3.65, Ar.*Ach.*622, etc.; πρὸς τὸ κ. A.*Pr.*214: abs., τὸ κ. Theoc.1.41. 5. of place, *strong*, Hdt.9.9, Th.4.3; τὸ -ώτατον τοῦ χωρίου Id.5.10; λόφος κ. Id.4.131. 6. = κύριος, *fixed, determined*, τοῦτο κ. εἶναι *SIG*45.22 (Halic., v B.C.). II. Adv. **-ρῶς** *strongly, violently*, Lxx 4*Ma.*15. 31, Arr.*An.*2.23.7, Luc.*Somn.*6; κ. ὑπνοῦσθαι to sleep *sound*, Hdt. 3.69. 2. *resolutely*, Ach.Tat.8.17; κ. ὑπόμενε Luc.*Prom.*21.

**καρτερούντως**, Adv. of καρτερέω, *strongly, stoutly*, Pl.*R.*399b, Iamb.*VP*32.220.

**καρτερό-φρων**, ονος, ὁ, ἡ, *stout-hearted*, *EM*745.8. **-χειρ**, χειρος, ὁ, ἡ, *strong-handed*, Ἄρης *h.Hom.*8.3; βασιλεύς *AP*9.210. 4. **-ψῡχία**, ἡ, *strength of spirit*, Lxx 4*Ma.*9.26.

**καρτερόω**, *strengthen*, ὄνυξι καὶ ὁπλαῖς Herm.ap.Stob.1.49.69, cf. Aq.*Ps.*30(31).25, al.

**καρτερώνυξ, καρτερώνῠχος**, v. κρατερ-.

**κάρτη**, η, a kind of *garment*, Juba Hist.85.

**κάρτιστος**, η, ον, Ep. for κράτιστος. **καρτομιστής**, ὁ, = κερτ-, Hsch.

**καρτός**, ή, όν, (κείρω) *shorn smooth*, opp. rough, of cloths, $IG2^2$. 1514.40. II. *chopped, sliced*, esp. of the leaves of the leek, πράσον κ. Dsc.2.149, *Eup.*2.123; also κ. κρόμμυα Gal.10.815; τὸ κ. abs., *Gp.*2.6.32. (On the accent v. Hdn.Gr.1.216.)

**κάρτος**, εος, τό, Ep. and Dor. for κράτος (for which it is v.l. in Hdt.8.2), *strength, vigour*, κάρτεϊ καὶ σθένεϊ σφετέρῳ Il.17.322; κάρτος τε βίη τε Od.6.197; *violence, force*, κάρτεϊ νικήσας πατέρα Hes.*Th.* 73; κάρτεϊ, = βίᾳ, *Leg.Gort.*2.3, al.

**κάρτρα**, τά, = κάρθρα, *PLond.*1.131[r] 111 (i A.D.).

**καρτύνω**, Ep. for κρατύνω (q.v.).

**κάρτων**, Dor. for κρείττων, *Leg.Gort.*1.15.

**κάρῠα** [ῠ], ἡ, *nut-bearing tree* of various kinds, S.*Fr.*759 (pl.), Lxx *Ca.*6.10(11), Plu.2.647b, etc.; esp. *hazel*, *Corylus Avellana*, Thphr.

*HP*1.12.1, 3.2.3; κ. Περσική *walnut, Juglans regia*, ib.3.6.2, 3.14.4; κ. Εὐβοϊκή *sweet chestnut, Castanea vesca*, ib.5.4.2; κ. Ἡρακλεωτική *filbert*, variety of *Corylus Avellana*, ib.1.3.3; -ῶτις ib.3.3.8; cf. κάρυον.

**Κᾰρύαι** [ῠ], ῶν, αἱ, *Caryae*, a place in Laconia with a famous temple of Artemis, Th.5.55, etc.:—hence **Κᾰρῠᾶτις**, ιδος, ἡ, μέλισσα (prob. priestess of Artemis) St.Byz.; as Subst. esp. **1.** *Artemis*, Paus.3.10.7. **2.** *dance in honour of Artemis*, Poll.4.104; cf. καρυατίζω 2. **II.** **Κᾰρῠᾶτίδες**, ων, αἱ, *priestesses of Artemis at Caryae*, Pratin.Lyr.4. **2.** Archit., *female figures used as bearing-shafts*, Lync.ap.Ath.6.241e, Vitr.1.1.5. **3.** a kind of *ear-rings*, Poll.5.97.

**Κᾰρῠάτεια** [ᾱτ], τά, festival of Artemis Καρυᾶτις, Phot.

**κᾰρῠατίζω**, *play with nuts*, Ph.1.11. **2.** dance the Καρυᾶτις, Luc.*Salt.*10.

⊛ **κᾰρύδιον** [ῠ], τό, Dim. of κάρυον, *small nut*, Philyll.19.

**κάρυδοι**· κορυδαλλοί (καρύδαλοι cod.), Hsch.

**καρυδόω**, *castrate* a horse, and **καρύδωσις**, εως, ἡ, *castration*, *Hippiatr.*99.

**κᾰρῠ-ερία** (sc. κυβεία), ἡ, *dicing for nuts*, dub. l. in Max.Tyr.6.6. **-ηδόν**, *like a* κάρυον: κ. κάταγμα fracture *like a broken nut*, i.e. *comminuted fracture*, Sor.*Fract.*10, Gal.14.792, Paul.Aeg.6.89. **-ήματα**, τά, *nuts* (Lacon.), Hsch.

**καρυηνόν**, τό, or **Καρυηνός**, ἡ, όν, v. κάροινον.

**κᾰρῠ-ηρός**, ά, όν, *nut-like*, σπέρματα Thphr.*HP*1.11.3, cf. 3.11.4. **-ῖνος**, η, ον, *of nuts*, ἔλαιον Gal.11.871; κ. χρῶμα *nut-brown*, Thphr.*Sens.*78; cf. καρόϊνος. **II.** *made of walnut-wood*, σανίδες *IG*11(2).203*B*100 (Delos, iii B.C.); ῥάβδος Lxx *Ge.*30.37, cf. *Je.*1.11. **III.** καρυίνη, ἡ, *narrow jar*, *Gp.*13.7.2. **IV.** Καρύϊνος οἶνος, v. κάροινον. **-ίσκος**, ὁ, Dim. of κάρυον, Lxx *Ex.*25.32, al. (pl.). **-ίτης** [ῑ], ου, ὁ, *like a nut*, τιθύμαλλος κ., *Euphorbia Myrsinites*, Dsc.4.164.

**κᾰρῠκ-άζω**· ταράττω, Hsch.; cf. sq. 2. **-εία**, ἡ, *cooking with* καρύκη: hence, *rich cookery*, Ath.14.646e (pl.), Luc.*Symp.*11, *Lex.*6, Ael.*NA*4.40; ἄνευ γάρου καὶ τῆς ἄλλης κ. Gal.6.298. **2.** metaph., *meddling*, Hsch. (pl.). **-ευμα**, ατος, τό, *savoury dish*, Poll.6.56 (pl.), Phlp.*in de An.*601.16, Sch.Ar.*Eq.*342, Hsch. **-εύω**, *dress with rich sauce*, ἱερεῖα Ath.4.173d:—more freq. in Pass., ὄψα κεκαρυκευμένα Alex.163.6, cf. Men.462.7, Sor.1.51, Alciphr.3.53; ἐς ταὐτὸν κ. *make up* into one *sauce*, Men.518.7: metaph., κ. λόγον *season* a story *well*, Plu.2.55a; [ἡ ἱστορία] κ. τὰς ἀπαγγελίας τῇ ποικιλίᾳ τῶν παραδειγμάτων Agath.*Praef.* **2.** metaph., *embroil*, Erot. s.v. καρυκοειδέα, Hsch. **-η**, ἡ, *rich sauce*, invented by the Lydians, *composed of blood and spices*, Pherecr.181, Ath.12.516c, Gal.8.568, Max.Tyr.3.9, Luc.*Tim.*54: in pl., Ath.4.160b, Plu.2.664a. (Freq. written καρύκκη in codd. (as also in derivs.), and this spelling is preferred by Hdn.Gr.1.317.) ⊛ **-ινος**, η, ον, *of the colour of* καρύκη, *dark-red*, X.*Cyr.*8.3.3.

**κᾰρῠκο-ειδής**, ές, *like* καρύκη, *of the consistency and appearance of* κ., Hp.*Epid.*4.25. ⊛ **-ποιέω**, *make a* καρύκη, Ar.*Eq.*343. **-ποιός**, ὁ, *maker of a* καρύκη, Achae.12.

**καρυμνόν**· μέλαν, Hsch. **κάρυννος**, ὁ, a throw of the dice, Phot. **κᾶρυξ**, Dor. for κῆρυξ.

**κᾰρῠο-βᾰφής**, ές, *stained with walnut-juice*, *EM*492.55, cf. Hsch. s.v. καρυχρ(οῦς). **-δενδρον**, τό, *walnut-tree*, *Gloss.* **-κατάκτης**, ου, ὁ, *nut-cracker*, Pamphil.ap.Ath.2.53b, Hsch. s.v. μουκηροβαγός.

**κάρυον** [ᾰ], τό, any kind of *nut*, Ar.*V.*58, *Pl.*1056, Theoc.9.21; κάρυα, = ἀκρόδρυα, Ath.2.52a (but τὰ κ. ἢ...τὰ ἀκρόδρυα Thphr.*Char.*11.4); κ. πλατέα, i.e. *filberts*, X.*An.*5.4.29; esp. of *walnuts*, Batr.31, Epich.150, Philyll.25, Gal.6.609; but this is prop. κ. βασιλικόν, Thphr.*CP*4.2.1, Agatharch.96, *PCair.Zen.*13.6 (iii B.C.), Dsc.1.125; or Περσικόν ibid.; κ. Εὐβοϊκόν *sweet chestnut*, Thphr.*HP*1.11.3, 4.5.4; also καστανaϊκόν ib.4.8.11, Agatharch.43; κ. Ἡρακλεωτικόν *filbert*, Thphr.*CP*4.2.1, *IG*2[2].1013.19; also κ. Ποντικόν *PCair.Zen.*12.48 (iii B.C.), Dsc.1.125, Ruf.ap.Orib.8.47.20; κ. πικρά *almonds*, Archig. ap.Gal.12.409, Erot. s.v. νίωπον; so κ. alone, Lxx *Nu.*17.8, Ph.2.162. **2.** *nut-shaped boss* as ornament, *OGI*214.49 (Branchidae, iii B.C.). **II.** *stone, kernel*, Thphr.*HP*3.9.5; κ. κοκκυμήλου ib.4.2.5. **2.** *seed* of conifers, Id.*CP*1.19.1; κ. πιτύϊνα pine-*kernels*, Diocl.*Fr.*127. **III.** = ἠρύγγη, Dsc.3.21.

**κᾰρῠο-ναύτης**, ου, ὁ, *one who sails in a nut*, Luc.*VH*2.38. **-πώλης**, ου, ὁ, *nut-seller*, *Jahresh.*16 *Beibl.*51, prob. rest. in *IG*2[2].10. **-τομία**, ἡ, dub. sens. in *Gloss.* ⊛ **-φυλλον**, τό, *dried flower-bud of the clove-tree*, *Eugenia caryophyllata*, Alex.Trall.1.17, *Febr.*7, Paul.Aeg.7.3.

**κᾱρύσσω**, Dor. for κηρύσσω. **καρυστεῖναι**· κεκραγέναι (Lacon.), Hsch. **καρυτίζομαι**, = εὐφραίνομαι, Id.

**κᾰρυ-χρ∴** (sic cod.)· καρυοβαροῦς, Hsch. (fort. καρυκοχροῦς (gen. of *κᾰρῡκοχρής)· καρυοβαφοῦς). **-ώδης**, ες, *like a walnut*, σπέρμα Thphr.*CP*1.19.1; τὰ κ. Str.12.3.15. **-ῶτις**, ιδος, ἡ, *date*, Dsc.1.109. ⊛ **-ωτός** [φοῖνιξ], ὁ, *date-palm, date, Phoenix dactylifera*, Str.17.1.15, Dsc.*Eup.*2.31, Gal.6.607. **II.** φιάλη καρυωτή cup *adorned with a nut-shaped boss*, *IG*11(2).161*B*30, al. (Delos, iii B.C.), *OGI*214.31 (Branchidae, iii B.C.), Semus 16; also κ. λαμπάδια Lxx *Ex.*38.16(37.19).

**καρφ-ᾰλέος**, α, ον, (κάρφω) *dry, parched*, ὡς ἄνεμος ἠϊῶν θημῶνα τινάξῃ καρφαλέων Od.5.369; δέρμα Hp.*Aph.*5.71, *Prog.*2, Gal.10.674; ἀστάχυες, ἄρουρα, *AP*9.384.14, Orph.*L.*269; κ. δίψει *AP*9.272 (Bianor), 7.536 (Alc.); of sound, καρφαλέον δέ οἱ ἀσπὶς..ἄϋσεν the shield rang *dry*, i.e. *sharply*, Il.13.409. **II.** Act., *drying, parching*, πῦρ v.l. for καρχ- (q.v.), Nic.*Th.*691. **-ᾱμάτιον** (fort. -ατρον), τό, (ἀμάω) prob. *rake for collecting fallen ears of corn*, Hsch. **-εῖα**, τά, *ripe fruit* or (as Sch.) *chips*, κέδρου Nic.*Al.*118. ⊛ **-η**, ἡ, *hay*, X.*An.*1.5.10, Arr.*An.*1.3.6. **-ηρός**, ά, όν, (κάρφος) *of dry straw*, εὐναῖαι καρφηραί *nests*, E.*Ion* 172:—misquoted as **καρφυραί**, Hsch.; cf. καρπυραί.

**κάρφινος**, = Lat. *carpineus*, Apollod.*Poliorc.*176.5.

⊛ **καρφ-ίον**, τό, Dim. of κάρφος, Dsc.4.102, Ruf.ap.Orib.8.47.20. **2.** in pl., *suckers* of a polypus, Sch.Opp.*H.*2.312. **-ισμός**, ὁ, *gleaning*, *CIG*2700e (Mylasa). **-ίτης** [ῑ], ου, ὁ, *built of* κάρφη (pl.): θάλαμος κ., of a swallow's nest, *AP*10.4 (Marc. Arg.).

**καρφο-ειδής**, ές, *like dry sticks*, κλῶνες, κλωνία, Dsc.4.42, *Gp.*2.6.29. **-λογέω**, prop. *gather dry twigs*: hence, *pick bits of hair*, etc., off a person's coat, Thphr.*Char.*2.3, Gal.8.227, 18(2).74:—hence **-λογία**, ἡ, Id.14.733.

⊛ **κάρφος**, εος, τό, *any small dry body*, esp. *dry stalk*, as of the *dry sticks* of cinnamon, Hdt.3.111; of *rice-straw*, Polyaen.4.3.32, cf. Luc. *Herm.*33: generally, in pl., *dry twigs, chips, straws, bits of wool*, such as birds make their nests of, Ar.*Av.*643, Sophr.32, Arist.*HA*612[b]23, *AP*10.14 (Agath.): collectively in sg., A.*Fr.*24, Arist.*HA*560[b]8, Ath.5.187c: in sg., *chip* of wood, Ar.*V.*249; *toothpick*, Alciphr.1.22: prov., κινοῦσα μηδὲ κ. 'not stirring an inch', Ar.*Lys.*474, cf. Herod. 3.67; οὐδὲ κ. ἐβλάβη *Epigr.Gr.*980.9 (Philae); ἀπὸ τῆς κύλικος κάρφος τῷ μικρῷ δακτύλῳ ἀφαιρετεῖν Ion Hist.1. **II.** = Lat. *festuca*, Plu.2.550b. **III.** *a small piece of wood* on which the watchword was written, Plb.6.36.3. **IV.** in pl., *ripe fruit*, Nic.*Al.*230, 491, *Th.*893, 941. **V.** = τῆλις, Dsc.2.102. (σκάρφος is v.l. (perh. right) in A.l.c., Plb.l.c.: perh. cogn. with Engl. *sharp*.)

**καρφόω**, = κάρφω, *AP*7.385 (Phil., Pass.). **II.** *nail*, Sch.Ar.*Ra.*844 (Pass.).

**καρφυκτοί**· φρύγιοι (leg. φρυκτοί) (Rhod.), Hsch. **καρφύνω**, = καρφόω, Id. **κάρφυροι**· νεοσσοί, Id.; cf. καρφηρός.

**κάρφ-ω**, poet. Verb, *dry up, wither*, κάρψω μὲν χρόα καλόν *will wither* the fair skin, *wrinkle* it, Od.13.398, cf. 430; ἠέλιος χρόα κάρφει Hes. *Op.*575:—and in Pass., [χρὼς] κάρφεται ἤδη Archil.100; πυρὶ καρφόμενα Euph.50; περὶ χροΐ καρφομένη θρίξ Nic.*Th.*328. **2.** metaph., ἀγήνορα κάρφει Ζεύς Zeus *withers* the proud of heart, Hes.*Op.*7; κάματοι κάρφοντες γυῖα Nic.*Al.*383:—Pass., οἴτῳ κάρφεσθαι A.R.4.1094; v. κάρφος. **-ώδης**, ες, *full of* κάρφη, of *uncleansed* wool, *Gloss.*

**κάρχαι**· καρκίνοι, καὶ ⟨κ⟩όχλοι (Sicel), Hsch.

**καρχᾰλέος**, α, ον, *rough*, δίψῃ καρχαλέοι *rough in the throat* with thirst, Il.21.541 (v.l. καρφαλέοι), cf. A.R.4.1442, Nonn.*D.*14.426. **II.** *rough, fierce*, κύνες A.R.3.1058; λύκοι Tryph.615 (v.l. καρχαρέος); of sounds, χρεμετισμός, ἱμάσθλη, Nonn.*D.*29.199, 48.307; of fire, *fierce*, Nic.*Th.*691 (v.l. καρφ-, q.v.). (Redupl. of *khar-*, cf. Skt. *khára-* 'rough, sharp'.)

**καρχᾰρ-έος**, α, ον, = κάρχαρος, κύνες *EM*493.1; cf. foreg. II. ⊛ **-ίας**, ου, ὁ, a kind of *shark*, so called from its saw-like teeth, Pl.Com.173.13, Mnesim.4.36 (anap.), Thphr.*HP*4.7.2, Numen.ap.Ath.7.327a: metaph., ἁ γαστὴρ ὑμέων κ. Sophr.46. ⊛ **-όδους**, ὁ, ἡ (neut. -όδουν Plot.6.7.9), gen. -όδοντος, *with saw-like teeth*, καρχαρόδοντε δύω κύνε Il.10.360; κυνῶν ὕπο κ. 13.198; ἅρπην κ. Hes.*Th.*180; applied to Cleon, Ar.*Eq.*1017, *V.*1031; καρχαρόδοντα..ὅσα ἐπαλλάττει τοὺς ὀδόντας τοὺς ὀξεῖς Arist.*HA*501[a]18; opp. χαυλιόδους, Id.*PA*661[b]19; of the lobster's claws, Id.*HA*526[a]19. ⊛ **-όδων**, οντος, ὁ, ἡ, = foreg., λύκος Theoc.24.87. **-ος**, ον, and α, ον Alcm.140:—*saw-like, jagged*, so *with saw-like jagged teeth*, κύων Lyc.34, Luc.*Luct.*4, cf. Ael.*NA*16.18; στόμα Opp.*C.*3.142; ἕρκος Id.*H.*1.506; ὀδόντες Philostr.*Im.*2.18; δῆγμα Luc.*Trag.*302; κάρχαρον μειδήσας, of the wolf, Babr.94.6. **2.** metaph., *harsh*, of sounds or language, καρχάραισι φωναῖς Alcm.l.c., cf. Luc.*Hist.Conscr.*43; ῥήτωρ Id.*Merc.Cond.*35; nickname of Thrason, Bato Sinop.3; *rough, rude*, [ἤθη] κ. καὶ σκολιά Plu. 2.468c.

**Καρχηδονίζω**, *side with the Carthaginians*, Plu.*Marc.*20.

**Καρχηδών**, όνος, ἡ, *Carthage*, Hdt.3.19, S.*Fr.*602:—Adj. **Καρχηδόνιος**, α, ον, *Carthaginian*, Hdt.l.c., etc.; **Καρχηδονιακός**, ή, όν, κόλπος Str.17.3.13.

**καρχήματα**· θέλγητρα, Hsch.

⊛ **καρχήσιον**, Dor. -άσιον [χᾱ], τό, *drinking-cup* narrower in the middle than at the top and bottom, Sapph.51.3, Pherecyd.13 J., Cratin.38, Herodor.16 J., S.*Fr.*660, Callix.3, *IG*1[2].265, al., 2[2].47, 12(8).51.25 (Imbros, ii B.C.). **II.** *mast-head of a ship*, through which the halyards worked, ζυγὸν καρχασίου *sailyard*, Pi.*N.*5.51, cf. Hp.*Art.*43, Luc.*Merc.Cond.*1 (interpol.), Asclep. Myrl. ap. Ath.11.474f: in pl., E.*Hec.*1261, Plu.*Them.*12; cf. sq.—In Epicr.10 there is a play on the double meaning (I and II). **III.** *triangular instrument used in carpentry*, Hsch. **IV.** *cage* or *chamber* in a torsion-engine, Ph.*Bel.*74.15, Hero *Bel.*88.5 (χαλκ- codd.), Ath.Mech.35.4. **V.** *crane* for unloading ships, Vitr.10.2.10, 10.16.3.

**καρχήσιος**, ὁ, in pl., *halyards of a ship*, Gal.19.109. **2.** *cords* used in surgical operations, Id.18(1).351, 522.

**καρώ**, ἡ, *caraway*, Dsc.3.57, Orib.3.2.3: perh. to be read in Ath. 9.371e.

**κᾰρώδης**, ες, *drowsy, heavy*, ὄμματα Hp.*Epid.*7.30; τὸ καρῶδες, = κάρωσις, Id.*Prorrh.*1.63; τὰ καρώδεα *fits of stupor*, ib.103, cf. *Coac.*523. **II.** *causing stupor*, Id.*Art.*31; *soporific*, Aret.*CA*2.1. Adv. -δῶς Gal.14.4, Alex.Trall.*Febr.*7.

**Καρώνιος**, ὁ (sc. μήν), name of month at Cnossus, prob. in *SIG* 712.21 (ii B.C.).

**κάρωσις** [ᾰ], εως, ἡ, (κᾰρόω) *heaviness in the head, drowsiness*, νωθρὴ κ. Hp.*Art.*31, cf. Philonid.ap.Ath.15.675b, Aët.9.31.

**κᾰρωτίδες**, ων, αἱ, *carotid arteries*, Aret.*SA*2.11, Gal.*UP*16.12: derived fr. καρόω by Ruf.*Onom.*210: sg., τὴν καρωτὶν (sic) ἀρτηρίαν Antyll.(?)ap.Orib.45.17.6.

**κᾰρωτικός**, ή, όν, *stupefying, soporific*, κ. ὁ κρίθινος Arist.*Fr.*106, cf. Dsc.4.64; κ. φάρμακα Gal.10.817; δυνάμεις, ἐπιβροχαί, Id.11.711, 14.733, cf. Porph.*Abst.*1.27.

**κᾰρωτόν**, τό, *carrot*, dub. in Diph.Siph.ap.Ath.9.371e; but, = *gleanings of grapes*, *PLond.*1821.202.

⊕**κάς**, *skin*, Hsch. II. Cyprian for καί, Id., cf. *Inscr.Cypr.*135.1 H. (Idalion); also Arc., *IG*5(2).261, 262 (Mantinea, v B.C.).

**κἀς**, crasis for καὶ εἰς or καὶ ἐς, Ar.*Ach.*184, etc.

**κάσα**, ἡ, prob. = Lat. *casa, cot*, dub. in Ath.Mech.25.7, cf. Hsch.

**κᾰσαλβ-άζω**, *behave like a strumpet*, Hermipp.Com.71. 2. c. acc., κ. τοὺς στρατηγούς *abuse* them *in strumpet fashion*, Ar.*Eq.* 355. **-άς**, άδος, ἡ, *strumpet*, Id.*Ec.*1106, *Fr.*478; cf. κασαύρα, κασωρίς. **-ιον**, τό, v.l. for κασώριον in Id.*Eq.*1285 (ap.Sch.).

**κάσαμον**, τό, = κυκλάμινος, Aët.16.146(136).

⊕**κασάνδρα**, gloss on ἐπάγων, Hsch. **κασᾶς**, v. κασῆς. **κασαύρα** and **κασαυράς**, ἡ, = κασαλβάς, Id.

**κασαυρεῖον**, τό, *brothel*, Hsch. (pl.), prob. for κασαυρίοισι in Ar. *Eq.*1285; cf. κασώριον.

**κάσεν** (indecl.?), Lacon. for κάσις or κάσιος (v. κάσιοι), denotes relationship of a Spartan boy to the βουαγός (ἀγελάρχης) of his class (ἀγέλη): usu. c. dat., *IG*5(1).60, al., but c. gen., ib.298.

**κασέρηνον**· κάθελε (Lacon.), Hsch. (fort. κασαίρηνον).

**κασῆς**, ὁ (on the accent v. Hdn.Gr.1.63), *skin* used as a *saddle* or *horse-cloth*, acc. sg. κασᾶν X.*Cyr.*8.3.8; acc. dual κασᾶ ib.8.3.7; acc. pl. κασᾶς ib.8.3.6 (καλέσας codd.), Agatharch.20; nom. sg. κασῆς *PTeb.*38.22 (ii B.C.); abbreviated in *PLond.*2.402ᵛ5 (ii B.C.): written κασσ- by Poll.7.68; cf. κάσσος, κασσοποιός. (Ethiopian word, Agatharch. l.c.; cf. Hebr. *kāsāh* 'covered'.)

**κάσης**· ἡλικιώτης, Hsch.

⊕**κᾰσία**, Ion. -ίη, ἡ, *cassia, Cinnamomum iners*, Sapph.*Supp.*20c.2, Hdt.2.86, 3.110, Thphr.*HP*9.4.2, *Od.*30, *OGI*214.59 (Branchidae, iii B.C.), etc.; λίβανον εὐώδεις τε φοίνικας κασίαν τε.., τέρενα Συρίας σπέρματα Melanipp.1, cf. Mnesim.4.58. (Cf. Hebr. *qeṣīʿāh*, Assyr. *kasia*: sts. written κασσία, as in Dsc.1.13, Str.16.4.25, cf. κασσίζω.)

⊕**κᾰσιγνήτ-η**, ἡ, fem. of κασίγνητος, *sister*, Il.4.441, etc.; dual -τα A.*Pers.*185: metaph., συκῆ ἀμπέλου κ. Hippon.34, cf. 70ᴬ; λάγυνε, ..κ. νεκταρέης κύλικος *AP*6.248 (Marc. Arg.):—Cypr. **κασινήτα** *Gött.Nachr.*1914.95, and **καίνιτα** (q.v.): Aeol. **κασιγνήτα** Sapph. *Supp.*1.9 (prob.). **-ικός**, ή, όν, *brotherly* or *sisterly*, Eust.775. 2. ⊕**-ος**, ὁ, (κάσις, γενέσθαι, cf. γνήσιος) *brother*, Od.8.585, *IG*9(1). 867.6 (Corc., prob. vi B.C.), etc.; esp. of those *born from the same mother*, κ. καὶ ὄπατρον Il.11.257: later as fem., *sister*, τώδε τὼ κασιγνήτω these two *sisters*, S.*El.*977, cf. Ps.-Luc.*Philopatr.*11: in more general sense, *cousin*, κ. τε ἔται τε Il.16.456, cf. 15.545: Astrol., *Gemini*, Doroth.ap.Heph.Astr.3.36. II. as Adj., κασίγνητος, η, ον, *brotherly, sisterly*, κασίγνητον κάρα S.*Ant.*899, 915, *El.*1164, dub. l. in E.*Or.*294; κασιγνήτοιο φόνοιο a *brother's* murder, Il.9.567. (Mostly poet.; also Aeol., Sapph.*Supp.*1.2 (prob.), *IG*12(2).526*d* 19 (Eresus), and Cypr., *Inscr.Cypr.*135.3 H. (Idalion): Thess. **κατίγνειτος** *IG*9(2).894 (Larissa).)

**κασίδιον**, τό, Dim. of Lat. *cassis, helmet*, *Sammelb.*7247.25, al. (iii/iv A.D.).

**κᾰσιοβόρος**, ον, *eating cassia*, of a worm, Hsch.

⊕**κάσιοι** [ᾰ], οἱ, *brothers* or *cousins belonging to the same* ἀγέλη (q.v.) at Sparta, Hsch.

**κᾰσιόπνους**, ουν, *breathing of cassia*, Antiph.52.14.

⊕**κάσις** [ᾰ], ὁ, gen. κάσιος first in Orph.*A.*1229; dat. pl. κασίεσσι Nic.*Th.*345:—*brother*, A.*Th.*674, etc.; voc. κάσι S.*OC*1440: ἡ, *sister*, E.*Hec.*361, Call.*Aet.*3.1.23: metaph., λιγνύν, αἰόλην πυρὸς κ. A.*Th.*494; κ. πηλοῦ..κόνις Id.*Ag.*495.

**Κασιωτικόν** (sc. πλοῖον), τό, kind of *boat used by the inhabitants of Kasion*, *PCair.Zen.*289.7, al. (iii B.C.).

**κασκαλίζεται**· γαγγαλίζεται, Hsch. **κάσκανα**, τά, (κάς 1) = κασσύματα, Id. **κασκάνδιξ**· ἡ γηθυλλίς, Id. (Redupl. and dissim. from σκάνδιξ.) **κασκός**, ὁ, *little finger*, Id. (cf. κακκόρ). **κάσμορος**· δύστηνος, Id.; cf. κάμμορος.

**κασοποιός**, ὁ, (κασῆς, κάσσος) *maker of thick garments*, *PPetr.*2 p.108 (iii B.C.), *Ostr.*1616, al. (ii B.C.):—also **κασσοποιός** (q.v.).

**κασπολέω**, Aeol. fut. = καταστελῶ, or perh. aor. subj. Pass. = κατασταλῶ, Sapph.81; cf. **κασπέλη**· στορνύει, Hsch. (leg. κασπέλλει).

**κάσσα**, ἡ, = κασαλβάς, Lyc.131: **κασσαβάς**, *EM*493.28.

**κάσσει**· νεοσσειᾷ, Hsch. **κασσία**, ἡ, v. κασία.

⊕**Κασσιέπεια**, ἡ, the constellation *Cassiopea*, Eudox.ap.Hipparch. 1.2.13.

**κασσίζω**, *look, taste*, or *smell like cassia*, Dsc.1.14.

**κασσιτερᾶς**, ᾶτος, ὁ, *tinker*, *BGU*9iv22, 1087iv9 (iii A.D.).

**Κασσῐτερίδες**, ων, αἱ, *the Cassiterides* or *tin-islands*, prob. the Scilly Islands, Hdt.3.115, cf. Str.2.5.15 and 30, etc.

⊕**κασσῐτέρινος**, Att. **κοττ-**, η, ον, *made of tin*, ἐνῴδια *IG*2².1388.78, cf. Arist.*SE*164ᵇ24, Plu.2.1075c.

⊕**κασσῐτεροποιός**, ὁ, = κασσιτερουργός, Ptol.*Tetr.*180.

**κασσίτερος** [ῐ], Att. **καττ-**, ὁ, *tin* (never in Od.), Il.11.25, 23.503, *SIG*247 I 3 (Delph., iv B.C.), etc.; ἐτήκετο κασσίτερος ὣς τέχνῃ ὕπ' αἰζηῶν Hes.*Th.*862, cf. Il.18.474; χεῦμα κασσιτέροιο a plating of *tin*, 23.561; κ. πάνεφθος Hes.*Sc.*208; κνημῖδας ἑανοῦ κ. Il.18.613; δύο καττιτέρω two *plates of tin*, *IG*2².204.23, cf. Hdt.3.115. (Elamite word, cf. Bab. *kassi-tira*: hence Skt. *kastīram*.)

⊕**κασσῐτερ-ουργός**, ὁ, *tinker*, Gloss. **-όω**, *plate with tin*, λέβης κεκασσιτερωμένος Dsc.1.30.5.

**κασσοποιός**, ὁ, = κασοποιός, *Ostr.*1081, al. (ii B.C.).

⊕**κάσσος**, ὁ (cf. κασῆς), *thick garment*, Hdn.Gr.1.208, Hsch.

**κάσσ-ῡμα**, Att. **κάττ-**, ατος, τό (cf. sq.), *anything stitched of leather*, esp. *sole of a shoe* or *sandal*, Hp.*Epid.*5.45, Ar.*Ach.*301 (ubi v. Sch.), *Eq.*315, 869, Crates Com.29.4; of cork soles, Dsc.*Eup.*2. 30; ὑποδήσασθαι ἐχθρῶν παρ' ἀνδρῶν καττύματα to put on *shoes* made by an enemy, Ar.*V.*1160. II. metaph., in pl., *patchings, botchings*, of bad music, Plu.2.1138b. ⊕**-ύω** [ῡ], Att. **κατт-**, (καττύς) *stitch, sew together like a shoemaker*, Pl.*Euthd.*294b; πέδιλα Nic.*Fr.*85.6:—Med. (nisi leg. καττύομεν), Pherecr.178. II. metaph., *stitch up* a plot, οἶδ' ἐγὼ τὸ πρᾶγμα τοὖθ' ὅθεν πάλαι καττύεται (says Cleon the tanner), I know the shop that this piece of leather comes from, Ar.*Eq.*314; καττύειν διαβολάς Alciphr.3.58.

**Κασταλία**, Ion. -ίη, ἡ, the spring of the Muses on Mt. Parnassus, Hdt.8.39, Pi.*P.*1.39, etc.

**κάστᾰνα**, ων, τά, *sweet chestnuts*, Mnesith.ap.Ath.2.54b, v.l. in Gal.6.621, v.l. in Dsc.1.106:—also **κάστανοι**, αἱ, Gal.*Vict.Att.*10; **καστανίαι** (οἱ or αἱ?) Dsc. l.c.; **καστάναια**, τά, *IG*2².1013.19; **καστάνεια**, τά, Heracleon ap.Ath.2.52b (καστάν⟨ε⟩ιος as Adj., φλοιός v.l. in Dsc.*Eup.*2.49); βάλανοι **καστανικαί** Gal.6.777, 791; **καστηνοῦ** (gen. sg.) Nic.*Al.*269. **καστανέα**, ἡ, *chestnut-tree*, *Gp.*2.8. 4:—also **κάστανος**, ἡ, Hsch. s.v. καρύαι; **κάστανον**, τό, *Gp.*10.63.1; derived by the ancients from **Καστανέα**, a place in Asia Minor (πόλις Μαγνησίας), *EM*493.26 (cf. **Καστανὶς αἶα** Nic.*Al.*271); but cf. Armen. *kask*: for κάρυον **κασταναϊκόν**, v. κάρυον. **καστᾰνεών**, ῶνος, ὁ, *chestnut-grove*, *Gp.*3.15.7.

**καστεία**, ἡ, (Lat. *castus*) in pl., *ascetic practices*, Marin.*Procl.*19.

**κάστον**· ξύλον (Athaman.), Hsch.

⊕**Καστόρειος**, α, ον, *of* or *belonging to Castor*: τὸ Κ. μέλος a martial song, set to the flute, used in celebrating victories in the horse or chariot races, Pi.*P.*2.69; ὁ Κ. ὕμνος Id.*I.*1.16; also, of a battle-march, Plu.*Lyc.*22, cf. 2.1140c, Phld.*Vit.*p.25 J. II. **καστόρειος** or **-όριος**, α, ον, *of the beaver*, ὄρχεις Hsch. s.v. κάστωρ; αἷμα Dsc.2. 24:—esp. **καστόρειον** or **-όριον**, τό, *castor*, secretion found in the body of the beaver, used in medicine, Anon.Lond.37.51, *POxy.* 1088.27 (i A.D.), Plu.2.55a, Sor.2.29, Phlp.*in GC*65.29, etc.

⊕**καστορ-ίδες**, αἱ, a famous Laconian breed of *hounds*, said to be first reared by Castor, *AP*6.167 (Agath.), cf. Poll.5.39:—also **καστόριαι** κύνες X.*Cyn.*3.1. II. *sea-calves, seals*, Opp.*H.*1.398, Ael. *NA*9.50. **-ίζω**, *to be like castor*, τῇ ὀσμῇ Dsc.2.8, 3.84; τῇ χρόᾳ Vett.Val.2.23. **-ιον**, τό, v. καστόρειος. **-ιος**, v. καστόρειος, καστορίδες.

**καστορνῦσα**, Ep. for καταστορνῦσα, v. καταστόρνυμι.

⊕**Κάστωρ**, ορος, ὁ, *Castor*, Il.3.237, etc.

**κάστωρ**, ορος, ὁ, *beaver, Castor fiber*, Hdt.4.109, Arist.*HA*594ᵇ31, Hierocl.p.17 A., Ael.*NA*6.34. II. = καστόρειον, Hp.*Mul.*2.157, Aret.*CA*2.10. III. = κρόκος, Ps.-Dsc.1.26.

**κασύας**· ὄρκυνος (Perg.), Hsch. **κασύτας**, ου, ὁ, prob. = καδύτας (q.v.), Id. **κασφυράσσεται**· κατασπείρει, Id. **κάσχεθε**, Ep. for κατέσχεθε, κατέσχε, v. κατέχω.

**κασωρ-εύω**, *fornicate*, Lyc.772. **-ικὸς** δόμος *brothel*, cj. in Hippon.74:—also **-ιον**, τό, Ar.*Eq.*1285 ap.St.Byz. s.v. Κασώριον (κασωρεῖον Hsch.); cf. κασαυρεῖον. **-ίς**, ίδος, ἡ, = κασαλβάς, Lyc. 1385, St.Byz. **-ίτης** [ῑ], ου, ὁ, *fornicator*, Id. **-ῖτις**, ιδος, ἡ, = κασωρίς, Hippon.117, Antiph.320.

**κασωτός**, ή, όν, (κασῆς) *thick*, ἐσθῆτες, opp. στρεπταί, Diog.Oen.10.

⊕**κάτ**, for κατά before τ, v. καττά.

⊕**κατά** [κᾰτᾰ], poet. καταί acc. to A.D.*Synt.*309.28, found in Compds., as καταιβάτης: Prep. with gen. or acc.:—*downwards*.

A. WITH GEN., I. denoting motion from above, *down from*, βῆ δὲ κατ' Οὐλύμποιο καρήνων, κατ' Ἰδαίων ὀρέων, βαλέειν κ. πέτρης, Il. 22.187, 16.677, Od.14.399; κατ' οὐρανοῦ εἰλήλουθας Il.6.128; καθ' ἵππων ἀϊξαντε ib.232; δάκρυα..κ. βλεφάρων χαμάδις ῥέε 17.438; ἵεις σαυτὸν κ. τοῦ τείχους Ar.*V.*355; ἁλόμενοι κ. τῆς πέτρας X.*An.*4.2.17; κ. τῶν πετρῶν ὦσαι Pl.*Phdr.*229c; κ. κρημνῶν ῥιφέντες Id.*Lg.*944a:—for κατ' ἄκρης v. ἄκρα: Μοῖσα κ. στόματος χέε νέκταρ Theoc.7.82 (but perh. in sense II. 1). II. denoting *downward motion*, 1. *down upon* or *over*, κ. χθονὸς ὄμματα πήξας Il.3.217; of the dying, κατὰ..ὀφθαλμῶν κέχυτ' ἀχλύς a cloud settled *upon* the eyes, 5.696, cf. 20.321; τὸν δὲ κατ' ὀφθαλμῶν..νὺξ ἐκάλυψεν 13.580; φᾶρος κὰκ κεφαλῆς εἴρυσσε *down over*.., Od.8.85; [κόπρος] κ. σπείους κέχυτο.. πολλή 9.330; ὕδωρ κ. χειρός, v. χείρ; μύρον κ. τῆς κεφαλῆς καταχέαντες Pl.*R.*398a; νάρκη μου κ. τῆς χειρὸς καταχεῖται Ar.*V.*713; κ. τῆς τραπέζης καταπάσας τέφραν Id.*Nu.*177; ξαίνειν κ. τοῦ νώτου πολλὰς [πληγάς] D.19.197; ἐσκεδασμένοι κ. τῆς χώρας Plb.1.17.10; οἱ κ. νώτου πονοῦντες Id.3.19.7; ῥόπαλον ἧλασα κὰκ κεφαλῆς Theoc.25. 256; κ. κόρρης παίειν, = ἐπὶ κόρρης, Luc.*Cat.*12, al. b. Geom., *along, upon*, πίπτειν κατ' [εὐθείας] Archim.*Sph.Cyl.*1 *Def.*2; αἱ γωνίαι κ. κύκλων περιφερειῶν ἐνεχθήσονται will move *on*.., ib.1.23, al., cf. Aristarch.Sam.1. 2. *down into*, νέκταρ στάξε κ. ῥινῶν Il.19.39; of a dart, κ. γαίης ᾤχετο 13.504, etc.; ἔθηκε κατ' ὄχθης μείλινον ἔγχος 21. 172; ψυχὴ κ. χθονὸς ᾤχετο 23.100; κ. γᾶς *under*ground, Pi.*O.*2.59; κατ' ὕδατος *under* water, Hdt.2.149; [ποταμὸς] δὺς κ. τῆς γῆς Pl.*Phd.*

113c, cf. *Ti.*25d; κ. γῆς σύμεναι A.*Eu.*1007 (anap.); κ. χθονὸς κρύψαι to bury, S.*Ant.*24; ὁ κ. γῆς one dead and buried, X.*Cyr.*4.6.5; οἱ κ. χθονὸς θεοὶ A.*Pers.*689, etc.; θεοὶ ⟨οἱ⟩ κ. γᾶς Id.*Ch.*475 (lyr.), etc.; so κ. θαλάσσης ἀφανίζεσθαι, καταδεδυκέναι, Hdt.7.6,235; also βᾶτε κατ' ἀντιθύρων go *down by* or *through*.., S.*El.*1433. 3. later, *towards* a point, τοξεύειν κ. σκοποῦ to shoot *at*, Hdn.6.7.8; κατ' ἰχνῶν τινος ὁδεύειν Luc.*Rh.Pr.*9. 4. of vows or oaths, *by*, καθ' ἡμῶν ὀμνύναι D.29.26, cf. 54.38; ἐπιορκήσασα κ. τῶν παίδων Lys.32.13; esp. of the victims, etc., *over* which the oath is taken, ὀμνύντων τὸν ἐπιχώριον ὅρκον καθ' ἱερῶν τελείων Foed.ap.Th.5.47, cf. Arist.*Ath.*29.5, *Foed.Delph.Pell.*1 *A* 9, etc.; κ. τῶν νικητηρίων εὐξάμενοι D.*Ep.*1.16; also κατ' ἐξωλείας ὀμνύναι to imprecate destruction on oneself, Id.21.119; κατ' ἐξ. ἐπιορκεῖν Id.57.22. b. to make a vow *towards*, i.e. make a vow of offering.., κ. χιλίων εὐχὴν ποιήσασθαι χιμάρων Ar.*Eq.*660. 5. in hostile sense, *against*, A.*Ch.*221, S.*Aj.*304, etc.; κ. πάντων φύεσθαι D.18.19; esp. of judges giving sentence *against* a person, A.*Th.*198, S.*Aj.*449, etc.; ψεύδεσθαι κατά τινος Lys.22.7; λέγειν κατά τινος κακά S.*Ph.*65, cf. X.*HG*1.5.2, etc.; of speeches, [λόγος] κ. Μειδίου, etc. (opp. πρὸς Λεπτίνην, in reply to L.); δῶρα εἰληφέναι κατά τινος Din.3.6, cf. 18. 6. of Time, *for*, μισθοῦν κ. εἴκοσι ἐτῶν *IG*1².94.37; κ. βίου *for* life, *Tab.Heracl.*1.50; κὰπ παντὸς χρόνοι *IG*9(2).517.20 (Larissa) (but κ. παντὸς τοῦ χρόνου σκέψασθε D.22.72 falls under 7); κ. παντὸς τοῦ αἰῶνος ἀείμνηστον Lycurg.7. 7. *in respect of, concerning*, μὴ κατ' ἀνθρώπων σκόπει μόνον τοῦτο Pl.*Phd.*70d; κ. τῶν ἄλλων τεχνῶν τοιαῦτα εὑρήσομεν Id.*Sph.*253b; οἱ κ. Δημοσθένους ἔπαινοι praises *bestowed on* D., Aeschin.3.50; ἐρεῖν or λέγειν κατά τινος to say *of* one, Pl.*Ap.*37b, *Prt.*323b, etc.; εἰ κ. θηλείας φαίης A.D.*Synt.*198.10; εἴπερ ἕν γέ τι ζητεῖς κ. πάντων Pl.*Men.*73d, cf. 74b; ὅπερ εἴρηται καθόλου κ. πασῶν τῶν πολιτειῶν Arist.*Pol.*1307ᵇ2; freq. in the Logic of Arist., κατά τινος λέγεσθαι or κατηγορεῖσθαι to be predicated *of*.., *Int.*16ᵇ10, *Cat.*1ᵇ10, etc.; καταφῆσαί (or ἀποφῆσαί) τι κατά τινος to affirm (or deny) *of*.., *Metaph.*1007ᵇ21; so κ. τινὸς ὑπάρχειν *Int.*16ᵇ13: and in Adv. καθόλου (q.v.).

B. WITH ACC., I. of motion *downwards*, κ. ῥόον *down* stream, Od.14.254, Il.12.33; opp. ἀνὰ τὸν ποταμόν, Hdt.2.96; κ. τὸν ποταμόν, κ. τὸ ὑδάτιον, Id.1.194, Pl.*Phdr.*229a; κατ' οὖρον ἰέναι, ῥεῖν, *down* (i.e. *with*) the wind, A.*Th.*690, S.*Tr.*468; κ. πνεῦμα, κατ' ἄνεμον ἵστασθαι *to leeward*, Arist.*HA* 535ᵃ19, 560ᵇ13, Dsc.4.153. 2. with or without signf. of motion, *on, over, throughout* a space, freq. in Hom., καθ' Ἑλλάδα καὶ μέσον Ἄργος Od.1.344; κατ' Ἀχαιΐδα, κ. Τροίην, Il.11.770, 9.329; κατ' ἠερόεντα κέλευθα Od.20.64; κ. πόντον, κῦμα, ὕλην, Il.4.276, 6.136, 3.151; κ. πτόλιν Od.2.383; κ. ἄστυ, οἶκον, Il.18.286, 6.56; κ. ὅμιλον, στρατόν, 3.36, 1.229; κ. κλισίας τε νέας τε ib.487; πόλεμον κάτα δακρυόεντα 17.512; κ. ὑσμίνην, μόθον, κλόνον, 5.84, 18.159, 16.331; τὸ ὕδωρ κ. τοὺς ταφροὺς ἐχώρει X.*Cyr.*7.5.16, etc. (in later Gr. of motion *to* a place, κ. τὴν Ἰταλίαν Zos.3.1); καθ' Ἑλλάδα A.*Ag.*578; κ. πτόλιν Id.*Th.*6; αἱ σκηναὶ αἱ κ. τὴν ἀγοράν D.18.169; τὰ κατ' ἀγροὺς Διονύσια Aeschin.1.157, etc.; κ. τὸ προάστιον Hdt.3.54; τύμβον κατ' αὐτόν A.*Th.*528, cf. *Supp.*869 (lyr.): Geom., *at* a point, Euc.1.1, al.; τέμνειν [σφαῖραν] κ. κύκλον *in* a circle, Archim.*Aren.*1.17; also, *in the region of*, οἱ κ. τὸν ἥλιον γινόμενοι ἀστέρες Gem.12.7: freq. in Hom. in describing the place of a wound, βαλεῖν κ. στῆθος, γαστέρα, etc., Il.11.108, 16.465, al.; νύξε κ. δεξιὸν ὦμον 5.46; οὔτασε κατ' ἰσχίον 11.339; so βαλεῖν κατ' ἀσπίδα, κ. ζωστῆρα, 5.537, 615; βέλος κ. καίριον ἦλθεν struck *upon* a vital part, v.l. in 11.439: metaph., ἄχος κ. φρένα τύψε 19.125: generally, κ. φρένα καὶ κατὰ θυμόν *in* heart and soul, 4.163, al. 3. *opposite, over against*, κ. Σινώπην πόλιν Hdt.1.76, cf. 2.148, Th.2.30, etc.; ἀνὴρ κατ' ἄνδρα A.*Th.*505; μολὼν..μοι κ. στόμα Id.*Ch.*573; κατ' ὀφθαλμούς τινος LXX *2Ki.*12.11; οἱ μὲν Ἀθηναῖοι κ. Λακεδαιμονίους ἐγένοντο X.*HG*4.2.18; κατ' Ἀχαιοὺς ἀντετάχθησαν ibid.; ἐν συμποσίῳ.., περίμενε, μέχρις ἂν γένηται κατὰ σέ Epict.*Ench.*15, cf. D.L.7.108. II. *distributively*, of a whole divided into parts, κρῖν' ἄνδρας κ. φῦλα, κ. φρήτρας *by* tribes, *by* clans, Il.2.362; κ. σφέας μαχέονται *by* themselves, *separately*, ib.366, cf. Th.4.64; ἐσκήνουν κ. τάξεις X.*Cyr.*2.1.25; αὐτὴ καθ' αὑτήν A.*Pr.*1013; κ. κώμας κατοικημένοι *in separate* villages, Hdt.1.96; κατ' ἑωυτοὺς ἕκαστοι ἐτράποντο each *to his own* home, Id.5.15; κ. πόλεις ἀποπλεῦσαι, διαλυθῆναι, Th.1.89, 3.1: στρατιὰ κ. ἕνδεκα μέρη κεκοσμημένη Pl.*Phdr.*247a; later οἱ κατ' ἄνδρα λόγοι *PLond.*2.259.72 (i A.D.), cf. D.Chr.32.6, etc.; ἡ κατ' οἰκίαν ἀπογραφή *PLond.*3.904.20 (ii A.D.), etc.; κατ' ἔπος word *by* word, Ar.*Ra.*802; κατ' ὄνομα *individually*, 3*Ep.Jo.*15, etc.; παῖδα κ. κρήνην *at each* fount a boy, *Lyr.Alex.Adesp.*37.13, cf. *POxy* 2108.9 (iii A.D.). 2. of Time, καθ' ἡμέραν, κατ' ἦμαρ, day *by* day, daily, v. ἡμέρα III; καθ' ἐνιαυτόν, κατ' ἔτος, *Test.Epict.*6.24, *Ev.Luc.*2.41, etc.; κ. μῆνα *POxy.*275.18 (i A.D.). 3. of Numbers, *by* so many *at a time*, καθ' ἕνα one *at a time, individually*, Hdt.7.104 (later τὸ καθ' ἓν *detailed list*, *PTeb.*47.34 (ii B.C.), etc.); κ. μίαν τε καὶ δύο *by* ones and twos, Hdt.4.113; δύο μνέαι τεταγμέναι κατ' ἄνδρα αἰχμάλωτον ἕκαστον Id.6.79; ἐκ τῶν συμμάχων ἐξελέγετο κατ' ὀλίγους Id.8.113; κ. τὰς πέντε καὶ εἴκοσι μνᾶς πεντακοσίας δραχμὰς εἰσφέρειν to pay 500 drachmae *on every* 25 minae, D.27.7; κ. διακοσίας καὶ τριακοσίας δμοῦ τι τάλαντον διακεχρημένον *in separate sums of* 200 and 300 drachmae, Id.27.11; of ships, κ. μίαν (sc. ναῦν) *in column*, Th.2.90; κ. μίαν ναῦν ἐπιτάττειν Plb.1.26.12, cf. Th.2.84: Geom., μετρεῖν, μετρεῖσθαι κατά.., measure, be measured a certain number of times, Euc.7 *Def.*8,9, al.; μετρεῖν κ. τὰς ἐν τῷ Β μονάδας *as many times as* there are units in B, Id.7.16. III. of direction *towards* an object or purpose, πλεῖν κ. πρῆξιν *on* a business, *for* or *after* a matter, Od.3.72, 9.253; πλάζεσθαι κ. ληΐδα to rove *in search of* booty, 3.106; κ. ληΐην ἐκπλῶσαι Hdt.2.152; ἔβη κ. δαῖτα Il.1.424; ἐπιδημεῖν κατ' ἐμπορίαν *IG*2².141.32, cf. Arist.*Ath.*11.1; κ. χρέος τινὸς ἐλθεῖν come to seek his help, consult him, Od.11.479, etc.; ἵεται κ. τὴν φωνήν Hdt.2.70; κ. θέαν ἥκειν to have come *for the purpose of* seeing, Th.6.31; κ. πλοῦν ἤδη ὤν Id.7.31; καθ' ἁρπαγὴν ἐσκεδασμένοι X.*An.*3.5.2; κ. τί; *for* what purpose? why? Ar.*Nu.*239. 2. of pursuit, κ. πόδας τινὸς ἐλαύνειν Hdt.9.89; simply κ. τινά *after* him, Id.1.84; ἰέναι κ. τοὺς ἄλλους Id.9.53; κατ' ἴχνος *on* the track, S.*Aj.*32, A.*Ag.*695 (lyr.); ὥσπερ κατ' ἴχνη κ. τὰ νῦν εἰρημένα ζῆν Pl.*Phd.*115b. 3. Geom., in adverbial phrases, κ. κάθετον *in the same* vertical line, Archim.*Quadr.*6; κατ' εὐθεῖάν τινι *in the same* straight line with.., Papp.58.7. IV. of fitness or conformity, *in accordance with*, κ. θυμόν Il.1.136; καθ' ἡμέτερον νόον *after* our liking, 9.108; κ. νόον πρήξωμεν Hdt.4.97; κ. μοῖραν *as is* meet and right, Il.1.286; κατ' αἶσαν, κ. κόσμον, 10.445, 472; κ. νόμον Hes.*Th.*417; κὰν νόμον Pi.*O.*8.78; κ. τοὺς νόμους *IG*2².1227.15; αἰτίαν καθ' ἥντινα *for* what cause, A.*Pr.*228; κατ' ἔχθραν, κ. φθόνον, *for* (i.e. *because of*) hatred, envy, Id.*Supp.*336, *Eu.*686; καθ' ἡδονήν τι δρᾶν, ποιεῖν, do *as* one pleases, Th.2.37, 53; κ. τὸ ἔχθος τὸ Θεσσαλῶν Hdt.8.30, cf. 9.38; κ. φιλίαν, κατ' ἔχθος, Th.1.60, 103, etc.; κατ' ἄλλο μὲν οὐδέν, ὅτι δέ.. *for* no other *reason* but that.., Pl.*Phdr.*229d: κ. δύναμιν *to the best of* one's power, Hdt.3.142, etc. (κὰδ δ. Hes.*Op.*336); κ. τρόπον διοικεῖν arrange *suitably*, Isoc.2.6, al.; κατ' εὐνοίην *with* goodwill, Hdt.6.108; κ. τὰ παρηγγελμένα X.*An.*2.2.8, etc.; in quotations, *according to*, κατ' Αἰσχύλον Ar.*Th.*134; κ. Πίνδαρον Pl.*Phdr.*227b, etc. 2. *in relation to, concerning*, τὰ κατ' ἀνθρώπους = τὰ ἀνθρώπινα, A.*Eu.*930, 310; τὰ κ. τὸν Τέλλον Hdt.1.31; τὰ κ. τὴν Κύρου τελευτήν ib.214; τὰ κ. πόλεμον *military* matters, Aeschin.1.181; αἱ κ. τὴν πόλιν οἰκονομίαι (opp. αἱ πολεμικαὶ πράξεις) the management of *public* affairs, Din.1.97; τὰ κ. τὰς θυσίας *SIG*506.7 (Delph., iii B.C.); so τὸ κατ' ὑμέας *as far as concerns* you, Hdt.7.158; τὸ κατ' ἐμέ *as far as* I *am concerned*, D.18.247; κ. τοῦτο *in* this *respect*, Hdt.5.3, etc.; κ. ταὐτά *in* the same *way*, Id.2.20; καθ' ὅτι *so far as*, Th.1.82, etc. 3. in Comparisons, *corresponding with, after the fashion of*, κρομύοιο λοπὸν κ. *like* the coat of an onion, dub. in Od.19.233; μέλος κ. Φοίνισσαν ἐμπολὰν πέμπεται Pi.*P.*2.67; κ. Μιθραδάτην *answering to the description of* him, Hdt.1.121; τὴν ἰδέαν κ. πνιγέα *like* an oven in appearance, Ar.*Av.*1001; κηδεῦσαι καθ' ἑαυτόν to marry *in* one's own *rank* of life, A.*Pr.*890; οὐ κατ' ἄνθρωπον φρονεῖν Id.*Th.*425; λέγω κατ' ἄνδρα, μὴ θεόν, σέβειν ἐμέ Id.*Ag.*925; οὐ κατὰ σέ none *of* your *sort*, Chionid.1 (but ἵνα προσείπω σε κατὰ σέ to address you *in* your own *style*, Pl.*Grg.*467c); τὸ κατ' ἐμὲ καὶ οὐ κατ' ἐμέ Arr.*Epict.*1.28.5; οὐ κ. τὰς Μειδίου λῃτουργίας D.21.169; ἡ βασιλεία κ. τὴν ἀριστοκρατίαν ἐστί Arist.*Pol.*1310ᵇ3: freq. after a Comp., μέζων ἢ κατ' ἀνθρώπων φύσιν Hdt.8.38, cf. Pl.*Ap.*20e, etc.; μείζω ἢ κ. δάκρυα too great for tears, Th.7.75; ἤθεα βαθύτερα ἢ κ. Θρήϊκας more refined than *was common among* the Thracians, Hdt.4.95. V. *by the favour of* a god, etc., κ. δαίμονα Pi.*O.*9.28, cf. *P.*8.68; κ. θεῖον Ar.*Eq.*147 codd. (κ. θεὸν Cobet); κ. τύχην τινά D.48.24. VI. of round numbers (v. infr. VII. 2), *nearly, about*, κ. χίλια ἑξακόσια ἔτεα 1600 years *more or less*, Hdt.2.145, cf. 6.44, al.; κατ' οὐδέν *next to* nothing, Pl.*Plt.*302b. VII. of Time, *during* or *in the course of* a period, κ. τὸν πόλεμον Hdt 7.137; καθ' ἡμέραν, κατ' ἦμαρ, *by* day, A.*Ch.*818, *Ag.*668; κατ' εὐφρόνην Id.*Pers.*221; κ. χειμῶνα, κ. θερείαν, *PLille* 1ʳ14 (iii B.C.), *PTeb.*27.60 (ii B.C.). 2. *about*, κ. τὸν αὐτὸν τοῦτον χρόνον Hdt.3.131, etc.; κ. τοὺς θανάτους τῶν βασιλέων Id.6.58; esp. with names of persons, κ. Ἄμασιν βασιλεύοντα *about the time of* Amasis, Id.2.134; κ. τὸν κ. Κροῖσον χρόνον Id.1.67; οἱ κατ' ἐκεῖνον (sc. τὸν Ἀλκιβιάδην) ὑμέτεροι πρόγονοι D.21.146 (v.l. κατ' ἐκ. τὸν χρόνον); κ. τοὺς Ἡρακλείδας X.*Lac.*10.8; οἱ καθ' ἑαυτοὺς ἄνθρωποι their contemporaries, Id.*Mem.*3.5.10. 3. κ. ἔτος *this* year, *SIG* 284.24 (Erythrae, iv B.C.), *OGI*458.64 (i B.C./i A.D.), *CIG*3641 *b* 5,38 (Lampsacus). VIII. periphrastically with abstract Subst., κατ' ἡσυχίην, κ. τάχος, = ἡσύχως, ταχέως, Hdt.1.9, 7.178; κ. κράτος *by* force, X.*HG*2.1.19, etc.; κ. μέρος *partially*, Arist.*Po.*1456ᵃ16; *individually, severally*, Pl.*Tht.*157b, *Lg.*835a; κ. φύσιν *naturally*, Hdt.2.38, Pl.*R.*428e; κ. τὴν τέχνην *skilfully*, Luc.*DDeor.*20.7; οὔτ' ἐμοὶ λέγειν καθ' ἡδονὴν [ἐστί] it is not *pleasant* for me to tell you, A.*Pr.*263.

C. POSITION: κατά may follow both its cases, and is then written with anastr. κάτα, as Il.20.221, etc.; so also in tmesi, when it follows its Verb, 17.91.

D. abs. as ADV. in all the above senses, esp. like κάτω, *downwards, from above, down*, freq. in Hom.

E. κατά in COMPOS., I. *downwards, down*, as in καταβαίνω, καταβάλλω, κατάκειμαι, καταπέμπω, καταπίπτω, καταπλέω I. II. *in answer to, in accordance with*, as in κατᾴδω (*occino*), καταινέω, καταθύμιος. III. *against*, in hostile sense (cf. A. II. 5), as in καταγιγνώσκω, κατακρίνω, καταψηφίζομαι: more rarely with a Subst., as καταδίκη. IV. *back, back again*, as in κάτειμι, καταπορεύομαι, καταπλέω II. V. freq. only to strengthen the notion of the simple word, as in κατακόπτω, κατακτείνω, καταφαγεῖν, etc.; also with Substs. and Adjs., as in κατάδηλος, κάτοξος. VI. sts. to give a trans. force to an intr. Verb, our *be-*, as in καταθρηνέω *bewail*. VII. implying *waste* or *consumption*, as in καταλειτουργέω, καθιπποτροφέω, καταζευγοτροφέω: and generally in a *disparaging* sense, as in καταγιγνώσκω I.

F. κατά as a Prep. was shortd. in some dialects, esp. in Ep., into κάγ, κάδ, κάκ, κάμ, κάν, κάπ, κάρ, κάτ, before γ, δ, κ, μ, ν, π (or φ), ρ, τ (or θ), respectively; see these forms in their own places. Mss. and the older Edd. join the Prep. with the following word, as καγγόνυ, καδδέ, κακκεφαλῆς, καππεδίον, καπφάλαρα, καρρόον, καττάδε,

καττόν, etc. In compd. Verbs, κατά sts. changes into καβ, καλ, καρ, κατ, before β, λ, ρ, θ, respectively, as κάββαλε, κάλλιπε, καρρέζουσα, κάτθανε; and before στ, σχ, the second syll. sts. disappears, as in καστορνῦσα, κάσχεθε, as also in the Dor. forms καβαίνων, κάπετον.

**κατά**, = κατὰ τά, *IG*2².334.15; cf. κά. **κᾆτα**, Att. crasis for καὶ εἶτα, v. εἶτα sub fin. **κατάβα**, for κατάβηθι, aor. 2 imper. of καταβαίνω.

**καταβάδην** [βᾰ], Adv. *with one's feet down* (coined as opp. to ἀναβάδην, q. v.), Ar.*Ach.*411.

**καταβαθμός**, ὁ, *descent*, a name of the *steep slope* which separates Egypt and Nubia, and causes the Cataracts, A.*Pr.*811 (in Att. form **Καταβασμός**), Plb.31.18.9, Str.17.1.5, *Abh.Berl.Akad.*1925(5).6 (Cyrene).

***καταβαίνω**, Dor. κᾱβαίνω Alcm.38: fut. -βήσομαι Hes.*Th.*750, etc.: pf. -βέβηκα; Boeot. part. καταβεβάων *IG*7.3055: aor. κατέβην Il.10.541, Pi.*O.*9.43, etc.; poet. 3 pl. κατέβαν Il.24.329, κατέβησαν Lxx 2*Ki.*23.13; imper. κατάβηθι Od.23.20, Ar.*Lys.*873, Lacon. κάβασι Hsch., κατάβᾱ Ar.*V.*979, *Ra.*35; Ep. 1 pl. subj. καταβήομεν (v.l. -βείομεν) Il.10.97; late 3 sg. opt. κατάβοι Lxx 2*Ki.*1.21 (cod. B), Conon 45.2 J.; poet. part. καββάς Pi.*N.*6.51; Ep. inf. καταβήμεναι Il.14.19:—Med., Ep. aor. 1 κατεβήσετο 6.288, 13.17, Od.2.337, al. (with v.l. κατεβήσατο); imper. καταβήσεο Il.5.109:—*go* or *come down from*.., c. gen., πόλιος κ. 24.329; οὐρανόθεν κ. 11.184; Παρνασοῦ Pi.*O.*9.43, etc.: also with Preps., ἐξ ὄρεος Il.13.17; ἐς πεδίον 3.252, etc.: also c. acc. loci, θάλαμον κατεβήσετο Od.2.337; κ. Ἀΐδαν, Ἀΐδα δόμον, S.*Ant.*822 (anap.), E.*Heracl.*913 (lyr.); but κατέβην δόμον Ἄϊδος εἴσω Od.23.252 (later abs., *die*, Lib.*Or.*38.16); ἔσω κ. Hes.*Th.*750: also c. acc. in quite different senses, κατέβαιν' ὑπερώϊα she *came down from* the upper floor, Od.18.206, 23.85; κλίμακα κατεβήσετο *came down* the ladder, 1.330 (κ. κατὰ τῆς κλίμακος Lys.1.9); ξεστὸν ἐφόλκαιον καταβάς *having got down by* the lading-plank, Od.14.350: abs., καταβαίνειν δ' οὐ σχολή *come downstairs*, Ar.*Ach.*409; esp. 1. *dismount from* a chariot or from horseback, δίφρου Il.5.109; ἐκ τῆς ἁρμαμάξης Hdt.9.76; ἀφ' ἁρμάτων Pi.*N.*6.51; ἀπὸ τοῦ ἵππου X.*Cyr.*5.5.6; but κ. ἀπὸ τῶν ἵππων *give up* riding, D.42.24, cf. Arist.*Ath.*49.1:—hence in Pass., ἵππος καταβαίνεται the horse *is dismounted from*, X.*Eq.*11.7. 2. *go down from the inland parts to the sea*, esp. from central Asia (cf. ἀναβαίνω II.3), Hdt.1.94, etc.; also from Athens, κ. ἐς Πειραιᾶ, ἐς λιμένα, Pl.*R.*327a, *Tht.*142a. 3. *go down into the scene of contest*, γυμνὸν ἐπὶ στάδιον κ. Pi.*P.*11.49; κ. ἐπ' αὐτὸ τοῦτο (sc. τὸ ἀεθλεύειν) Hdt.5.22: abs., = Lat. *in certamen descendere*, Pi.*N.*3.42, S.*Tr.*504 (lyr.), X.*An.*4.8.27; cf. καταβατέον; μέτρῳ καταβαίνειν 'seek no more contests' (μέτρῳ by litotes for μή), Pi.*P.*8.78; μεθ' ὅπλων κ. Pl.*Lg.*834c. 4. of an orator, *come down from the tribune*, Lys.12.92, D.19.23, etc.; rarely in full, κ. ἀπὸ τοῦ βήματος ib.113; so κατάβα.—καταβήσομαι Ar.*V.*979; later, also κ. ἀπὸ τοῦ λόγου, ἀπὸ τῶν ἰαμβείων, *to cease* from.., Luc.*Tox.*35, *Nec.*1. 5. less freq. of things, πρὶν.. καταβήμεναι ἐκ Διὸς οὖρον Il.14.19; of tears, E.*Andr.*111 (eleg.); of streams, Pl.*Criti.*118d; of the womb, Arist.*HA*582ᵇ24; πόσσω κατέβα τοι ἀφ' ἱστῶ; at what price did [the robe] *come down* from the loom? Theoc.15.35; of the heavenly bodies, *set*, Vett.Val.31.3. II. metaph., 1. *attain*, πόμπιμον κατέβαινε νόστου τέλος Pi.*N.*3.25; κ. ἐπὶ τελευτήν Pl.*R.*511b: abs., *attain one's end*, ἐν φάει κ. Pi.*N.*4.38; simply, *come to*, *arrive* at in course of speaking, κατέβαινε ἐς λιτάς he *ended* with prayer, Hdt.1.116: usu. c. part., κατέβαινε αὖτις παραιτεόμενος ib.90, cf. 118, 9.94; καταβάς, of a writer, Eun.*VS* p.454 B. 2. κ. εἰς.. *conform to*, εἰς τοὺς χρόνους κ. τούτους Arist.*Pol.*1335ᵃ11. 3. *condescend*, Timocl.1.2 D. 4. *fall in value*, *POxy.*1223.33 (iv A.D.), cf. Poll.1.51. 5. λέγεται μηδὲν αὐτοῖς τούτων καταβαίνειν, of abusive language, does not *affect* them or *get home*, Chrysipp.*Stoic.*2.242.

**καταβακχιόομαι**, Pass., *to be full of Bacchic frenzy*, καταβακχιοῦσθε δρυὸς.. κλάδοισι in oak-wreaths *rave with Bacchic rage*, E.*Ba.*109 (lyr.).

***καταβάλλω**, fut. -βᾰλῶ: aor. κατέβᾰλον; Ep. 3 sg. κάββαλε Od.6.172, Hes.*Th.*189, etc.; imper. καββαλόντων *Foed.Delph.Pell.*1 B 14:—*throw down*, *overthrow*, κατὰ πρηνὲς βαλέειν Πριάμοιο μέλαθρον Il.2.414; ἐς μέσσον κ. τι 15.357; ἐνὶ πόντῳ Hes.*Th.*189; ἐπ' ἀκτῆς Il.23.125 (tm.); ἐπὶ χθονί Hes.*Sc.*462, etc.; κ. [τινὰ] ἐνθάδε Od.6.172; κ. τὰ οἰκήματα, τὰ ἀγάλματα, Hdt.1.17, 8.109; τεῖχος Th.7.24; κ. τινὰ ἀπὸ τοῦ ἵππου X.*HG*5.2.41; ἀπ' ἐλπίδος Pl.*Euthphr.*15e; κ. ἐς τὸ μηδέν *to bring down* to nothing, opp. ἐξᾶραι ὑψοῦ, Hdt.9.79; κάββαλλε τὸν χείμωνα *confound*, *defy* the storm, Alc.34.3. 2. κ. ἑαυτόν *throw* oneself *down* to sleep, Plu.*Caes.*38. 3. *strike down* with a weapon, *slay*, Il.2.692 (tm.), Hdt.4.64, etc.; by a blow, κ. πατάξας Lys.13.71; esp. of slaying victims, E.*Or.*1603, Isoc.2.20; κ. θῦμα δαίμοσιν E.*Ba.*1246. b. Pass., *to be stricken*, νόσῳ *POxy.*1121.9 (iii A.D.). 4. *throw* into prison, κ. τινὰ ἐς ἑρκτήν Hdt.4.146: generally, *throw*, *bring* into a certain state, κ. [τινὰ] ἐς ξυμφορὰς E.*IT*606, Antipho Soph.58; εἰς ἀπορίαν, εἰς ἀπιστίαν, Pl.*Phlb.*15e, *Phd.*88c, etc. 5. *overthrow*, *refute*, οἱ -βάλλοντες (sc. λόγοι), title of work by Protagoras: κ. τινά Democr.125; δόξαν Gal.*UP*6.20. 6. *abuse*, *bully*, Phld.*Rh.*2.164 S. 7. *cast down* or *away*, *cast off*, *reject*, Isoc.12.24: metaph., *forget*, Ael.*Fr.*111; κ. εἴς τι *throw away* upon a thing, Pl.*Lg.*960e:—Pass., οἱ καταβεβλημένοι *despicable fellows*, Isoc.12.8; cf. καταβεβλημένως. II. *let fall*, *drop*, ἀπὸ ἕο κάββαλεν υἱόν Il.5.343; κάββαλε νεβρόν, of an eagle, 8.249; of a fawning dog, οὔατα κάββαλεν ἄμφω Od.17.302; ἴουλον ἀπὸ κροτάφων κ. Theoc.15.85; of sails, καθ' ἱστία λευκὰ βαλόντες Thgn.671; τἀκάτια Epicr.10; κατ' ὀφθαλμοὺς βαλεῖ A.*Ch.*574; τὰς ὀφρῦς κ. E.*Cyc.*167; κ. τὰ κέρατα *droop* their feelers, Arist.*HA*590ᵇ26: in Politics, *abandon* a measure, καταβάλλοντ' ἐὰν ἐν ὑπωμοσίᾳ D.18.103. 2. *lay down*, *set down*, κρεῖον μέγα κάββαλεν ἐν πυρὸς αὐγῇ Il.9.206, cf. Ar.*Ach.*165, *V.*727, etc. 3. *lay down*, *lay in* stores, κ. σιτία Hdt.7.25:—Pass., κὰτ ἄσπιδες βεβλήμεναι *stored up*, Alc.15.5. 4. *pay down*, *yield*, *bring in*, ἡ λίμνη καταβάλλει ἐπ' ἡμέρην ἑκάστην τάλαντον ἐκ τῶν ἰχθύων Hdt.2.149; τὰς ἐπικαρπίας τῇ πόλει And.1.92, cf. Lex ib.93. b. *pay*, τἀργύριον Th.1.27; τριώβολον Amips.13; ἀρραβῶνα Men.743, cf. *PRev.Laws* 48.10 (iii B.C.), etc.; τιμήν τινι ὑπέρ τινος Pl.*Lg.*932d, Luc.*Vit.Auct.*25; τέλη *GDI*5018ᵃ17 (Gortyn), *PHib.*29.6 (iii B.C.); λύτρα *GDI*5151.8 (Cret., found at Delphi); καταβαλών σοι δραχμὴν τῶν βοτρύων for them, Philostr.*Her.Praef.*1; κ. ζημίαν *pay up*, *discharge* a fine, D.24.83, cf. 59.27:—later in Med., μισθὸν καταβαλέσθαι Alciphr.1.12. 5. *put in*, *deposit*, in Pass., εἰ ἡ μαρτυρία κατεβάλλετο ἐνταῦθα D.34.46:—but usu. in Med., *deposit*, γράμματα εἰς κιβωτόν *BCH*25.100 (Tlos), cf. *IG*12(1).3.15 (Rhodes); ψευδεῖς γραφὰς εἰς τὰ δημόσια γράμματα Docum.ap.D.18.55; λόγους *IG*7.2850 (Haliartus); δόγμα *GDI*5182.10 (Cret., found at Teos). 6. *throw down* seed, *sow*, Men.*Georg.*37, cf. καταβλητέον; κ. τὸ σπέρμα, of the male, Epicur.*Nat.*908.1:—Pass., *Placit.*5.7.4, Sor.1.33, Ocell.4.14: metaph., σπέρμα κ. τοιούτων πραγμάτων D.24.154; κ. φάτιν ὡς.. *spread abroad* a rumour, Hdt.1.122, cf. E.*HF*758 (lyr.). 7. *lay down as a foundation*, mostly in Med., τὴν τῆς ναυπηγίας ἀρχὴν καταβαλλόμενος Pl.*Lg.*803a: esp. metaph., -βαλλομένα μέγαν οἶκτον *beginning* a lament (cf. infr. 8), E.*Hel.*164 (lyr.); Ἀρίστιππος τὴν Κυρηναϊκὴν φιλοσοφίαν κατεβάλετο Str.17.3.22; καταβαλέσθαι τοὔπτάνιον Sosip.1.39; ἐξ ἀρχῆς καινὴν νομοθεσίαν D.S.12.20; τὴν Στωϊκῶν αἵρεσιν Plu.2.329a: hence generally, *to be the author of*, *commit to writing*, ἱστορικὰς καταβαλόμενοι πραγματείας D.H.1.1; λόγον Darius ap.D.L.9.13; φλυαρίας Gal.7.476:—Pass., ὅταν δὲ κρηπὶς μὴ καταβληθῇ.. ὀρθῶς E.*HF*1261: freq. metaph., δεδημοσιωμένα που καταβέβληται Pl.*Sph.*232d; πολλοὶ λόγοι πρὸς αὐτὰ -βέβληνται Arist.*EN*1096ᵃ10; καταβεβλημέναι μαθήσεις *fundamental*, *established*, Arist.*Pol.*1337ᵇ21; τὰ κ. παιδεύματα ib.1338ᵃ36, cf. Phld.*Rh.*1.27 S. 8. c. inf., γάμον καταβάλλομ' ἀείδειν I *begin* my song of, Call.*Fr.*196. III. Pass., *lie down*, εἰς εὐνάν Theoc.18.11. 2. like καταβαίνω II.1, *arrive* at in a course of lectures, εἰς Γοργίαν Dam.*Isid.*54. B. intr., *fall*, εἰς φθόνον καὶ ἀπορίαν Pl.*Ep.*344c.

**καταβαπτ-έον**, *one must dip*, εἰς ἔλαιον Sor.2.16. **-ίζω**, *dip*, *drown*, of wine, κ. τὴν ζωτικὴν δύναμιν Alex.Aphr.*Pr.*1.17; τὴν ψυχήν Ach.Tat.1.3:—Pass., *to be submerged*, *overwhelmed*, ὑπὸ τῆς ὑγρότητος Steph. *in Gal.*1.278 D.; καταβαπτισθήσεταί μοι τὸ ζῆν Alciphr.2.3. **-ω**, *dip*, εἰς ζεστὸν ὕδωρ Sor.1.50; εἰς γλεῦκος *Gp.*8.23.1; *soak*, ὄξει βαφικῷ *PHolm.*1.3. II. *dye*, *colour*, πρόσωπον ἐρυθήματι Eun.*Hist.*p.267 D.; χρυσόν *produce it by dyeing*, Ps.-Democr.Alch.p.45 B.:—in Pass., Luc.*Im.*16: Medic., οὖρον καταβεβαμμένον *deep-coloured*, Pall.*Febr.*15; ἀπὸ αἵματος -ομένου τοῦ οὔρου Gal.19.604.

**καταβαρβαρόω**, *make quite barbarous*, τὴν τέχνην Tz.*H.*12.230.

**καταβᾰρ-έω**, *weigh down*, *overload*, v.l. for καταπονέω in Luc.*DDeor.*21.1: metaph., *impose a burden on*, τινας 2*Ep.Cor.*12.16; κ. τὴν Ἰταλίαν ἐσφοραῖς App.*BC*5.67; ἀθληταὶ -βαροῦσι τοὺς τεχνίτας Plu.*Cleom.*27; τῶν -βαρούντων τὸ σῶμα καμάτων Ps.-Plu.*Vit.Hom.*207:—Pass., *to be overborne*, *crushed*, καταβαρεῖσθαι τῇ μάχῃ Plb.11.33.3; τοῖς ὅλοις Id.18.21.8; ὑπὸ τοῦ πάθους D.S.19.24; ἐν ταῖς λειτουργίαις *POxy.*487.10 (ii A.D.); also, *to be outweighed*, ὑπὸ τοῦ συμφέροντος Arr.*Epict.*2.22.18. **-ής**, ές, *heavy-laden*, πλάστιγγες Poll.4.172; νῆες, πλοῖα, D.C.39.42, 74.13. **-ησις**, εως, ἡ, *weighing down*, *oppression*, Demoph. in *Cat.Cod.Astr.*5(1).189 (pl.), *Gloss.* 2. ὀχλικὴ κ. mob *violence*, *Rev.Ét.Gr.*19.234 (Aphrodisias). **-ύνω**, = καταβαρέω, Thphr.*Vert.*9:—in Pass., Lxx 2*Ki.*13.25, al.; of sleep, *Ev.Marc.*14.40: metaph., κ. τὸν βίον Antip.ap.Stob.4.22.25, cf. *Corp.Herm.*2.9 (Pass.).

**καταβᾰσᾰνίζω**, strengthd. for βασανίζω, *examine thoroughly*, Hp.*Prorrh.*2.3.

**κατα-βᾰσία**, v. καταιβασίη. **-βάσιον** [βᾰ], τό, = κατάβασις, *a way down*, esp. to the nether world, Dam.*Isid.*131; εἰς Ἅιδου Suid. s.v. πορθμήϊον. **-βάσιος** [βᾰ], ον, = καταιβάσιος, πῦρ Lxx *Wi.*10.6. **-βᾰσις**, εως, ἡ, opp. ἀνάβασις, *way down*, *descent*, Hdt.1.186 (pl.), 7.223, etc.; ἡ εἰς Ἅιδου κ. Isoc.10.20, Str.8.6.12, cf. Hdt.2.122; title of work by Dicaearchus, Cic.*Att.*13.31.2; cf. καταίβασις. 2. *descent from* central Asia, X.*An.*5.5.4; ἡ ἐπὶ θάλατταν κ. D.S.14.25. 3. metaph., *descent* of an idea into the mind, Chrysipp.*Stoic.*2.242. 4. *steep ground*, *declivity*, Demetr.*Eloc.*248 (pl.). 5. ἔργον καταβάσεως *hanging* work, Lxx 3*Ki.*7.16(29).

**καταβασκαίνω**, strengthd. for βασκαίνω, Plu.2.680c, 682b, Hld.3.8; τῇ θέᾳ τινά Id.4.5.

**καταβασμός**, v. καταβαθμός.

**καταβᾰτ-έον**, (καταβαίνω) *one must descend*, Ar.*Lys.*884, Pl.*R.*520c. **-εύω**, *tread* or *walk upon*, Sch.S.*OC*467. **-ης**, ου, ὁ, *one who dismounts* and fights on foot, Pl.*Criti.*119b. * **-ικός**, ή, όν, *affording a means of descent*, Porph.*Antr.*22. Adv. -κῶς *by a descending* or *deductive process*, ψυχὴ -κῶς νοοῦσα τὰ πράγματα, opp. ἀθρόως, Olymp. *in Alc.*p.78 C. * **-ός**, ή, όν, *descending*, *steep*, ὁδός Sch.A.R.2.353, cf. Porph.*Antr.*23; v. καταιβατός. II. καταβατόν, τό, = σελίς, Hdn.*Epim.*2, 122, cf. Hsch. s. v. σελίς.

**καταβαΰζω**, *bark at*, prob. in Heraclit.97; τινος *AP*7.408 (Leon., καταβαΰξας metri gr.).

**καταβαυκᾰλ-άω**, *lull to sleep*, Ael.*NA*14.20, Poll.9.127. **-ησις**,

εως, ἡ, *lullaby*, Ath.14.618e (pl.). -ίζω, = καταβαυκαλάω, *Com. Adesp.*1030. II. (βαύκαλις) *gulp down*, Sopat.25.

**κατα-βᾰφή**, ἡ, *tincture*, in alchemy, Zos.Alch.p.228 B. **-βᾰφής**, ές, *soaked*, δρώπακι Paul.Aeg.1.30.

**καταβεβαι-όομαι**, *affirm strongly*, Plu.*Caes.*47. **-ωσις**, εως, ἡ, *strong asseveration*, in pl., D.S.9*Fr.*10.5, Plu.2.1120d.

**καταβεβλημένως**, Adv. pf. part. Pass. of καταβάλλω, *contemptibly*, Isoc.15.305.

**καταβελής**, ές, *stricken by many arrows*, D.H.2.42, 5.24.

**καταβῐάζω**, *subdue by force*, Anon.Hist.(*FGrH*160)*Fr.*1 i 2 (iii B.C.); τὴν ψυχήν Ph.1.685 :—more freq. in Med., *constrain*, καταβιάσασθαι παρὰ γνώμην τοὺς πολλούς Th.4.123; τὴν πόλιν App.*BC*2. 28, cf. Eun.*Hist.*p.259 D.; χάρισι τὴν δόξαν Plu.2.385e; τὰ πράγματα πρὸς τὰς ὑποθέσεις ὁμολογεῖν μὴ πεφυκότα κ. ib.75f. 2. *contend, strive to show*, ὢν εὐνοῦχος ἀνὴρ εἶναι κατεβιάζετο Eun.*Hist.*p.256 D. II. Pass., *to be forced*, Plu.*Thes.*11, Id.2.639f; [νούσημα] ἤδη ὑπὸ χρόνου πολλοῦ καταβεβιασμένον, of a *chronic* disease, Hp.*Morb. Sacr.*2.

**καταβῐβ-άζω**, causal of καταβαίνω, *make to go down, bring down*, τινὰ ἀπὸ τῆς πυρῆς Hdt.1.87, cf. 86; τοὺς ἐκ τοῦ καταστρώματος ἐς κοίλην νέα Id.8.119; στρατιώτας..εἰς τὴν χώραν τῶν Φρυγῶν *Hell.Oxy.* 16.3; τὴν πόλιν πρὸς τὴν θάλασσαν Plu.*Them.*4; *bring from town to country*, Id.*Cam.*10; down into a mine, Th.7.86, Plu.2.262d: metaph., *bring down, lower*, κ. σεαυτὸν ἀπὸ αὐχημάτων εἰς τὸ δημοτικώτερον D.H.7.45 :—Pass., κωμῳδία -βιβασθεῖσα εἰς τὸ λογοειδὲς Str.1. 2.6. 2. *force to come down*, εἰς τὸ ὁμαλὸν τὸ στρατόπεδον X.*HG*4. 6.7, cf. Th.5.65; *drive away*, Hp.*Prorrh.*1.143. II. *bring down*, τὴν διήγησιν ἐπὶ τὴν ἀρχὴν τοῦ πρώτου Φοινικικοῦ πολέμου D.H.1.8; τὸν λόγον ἐπὶ τὰ νῦν καθεστῶτα Luc.*Rh.Pr.*20. III. *bring down* the accent, i.e. *throw* it *forward*, A.D.*Synt.*213.16, *EM*774.34. IV. Astron., ὁ -βιβάζων (sc. σύνδεσμος) the *descending node*, Vett.Val.30. 6, Procl.*Hyp.*5.101. -άσκω, frequentat. of καταβαίνω, *trespass*, *Schwyzer* 126a (Corinth, v B.C.). -ασμός, ὁ, *decrease*, = ὑπόβασις, Procl.*Par.Ptol.*67. II. *throwing* of the accent *forward*, Sch.Od.5.248, Eust.1361.39 :—also **καταβίβᾰσις**, εως, ἡ, *EM*610. 24. -αστέος, α, ον, *to be brought down*, Pl.*R.*539e.

⊕**καταβιβρώσκω** (pres. not found, v. ἐσθίω), aor. κατέβρων *h.Ap.* 127: pf. Pass. καταβέβρωμαι: aor. κατεβρώθην (v. infr.):—*eat up, devour*, *h.Ap.* l.c.; καταβεβρωκὼς σιτία ἴσως ἐλεφάντων τεττάρων Antiph.82: metaph., καταβεβρώκασι..τὰς οὐσίας Hegesipp.Com.1. 30; τὰ ὄντα Hyp.*Fr.*249 :—Pass., ὑπὸ εὐλέων κατεβρώθη Hdt.3.16; κατεβρώθη ὑπὸ τῶν ἰδίων κυνῶν Palaeph.6; καταβέβρωται Hdt.4.199; ὑπ' ἰχθύων prob. in Phld.*Mort.*32; *to be corroded*, Pl.*Phd.*110a.

**καταβῑνέω**, = βινέω; 3 sg. καταβηνῆσι, barbarism in Ar.*Th.*1215.

**καταβῐ-όω**, aor. κατεβίων Pl.*Prt.*355a, later κατεβίωσα Plb.12.28. 6, Plu.*Dem.*24:—*pass one's life*, τὸ ἡδέως καταβιῶναι τὸν βίον Pl. l.c., cf. *R.*578c, Ph.1.627: c. part., κ. ξενιτεύων, σοφιστεύων, Plb. l.c., Plu. l.c.; κ. διώξαντες ἕτερον ἢ καὶ φυγόντες ὑφ' ἑτέρου Phld.*Rh.*2. 166 S.; κ. γεωργοῦντες Str.13.4.10. 2. *bring one's life to an end, die*, λέγεται ἄρτιος καταβιῶναι καὶ τὰς αἰσθήσεις ἡβῶν Philostr.*VS*1. 9.3. ⊕-ωσις, εως, ἡ, *decline of life*, Cic.*Att.*13.1.2. 2. *residence*, D.S.18.52, App.*BC*4.16.

**καταβλᾰβεύς**, έως, ὁ, *damager*, prob. in *IG*14.432.9 (Tauromenium), = *Supp.Epigr.*4.58.

**καταβλᾰκεύω**, *treat carelessly, mismanage*, Hp.*Art.*52 (sed leg. καταμβλ-), X.*An.*7.6.22 :—in Pass., καταβλακευόμενοι ἄνθρωποι *negligent, slothful*, Just.*Nov.*95.1.2.

⊕**καταβλάπτω**, *hurt greatly, damage*, *h.Merc.*93, Pl.*Lg.*877b, Lex ap.D.23.28, etc.; βλάβην κ. τινά *inflict* damage upon him, Pl.*Lg.* 864e; κατεβλαφότες τὰς προσόδους *IG*7.303.51 (Oropus); ὅ κα καταβλάψῃ for whatever *damage* he *may have done*, ib.9(1).694.102 (Corc.):—Pass., πολλὰ καταβλαβῆναι μέρη Str.1.3.20.

**καταβλέθει**· καταπίνει, Hsch.

**καταβλέπω**, *look down at*, Lxx *Ge.*18.16; ἄνωθεν εἰς.. Plu.*Arat.* 32; *view*, Id.2.680d. b. metaph., *despise*, *BGU*15 ii 5 (ii A.D.). 2. *examine, contemplate*, Call.*Del.*303; τὸ σεαυτοῦ κακόν Plu.2.469b.

**καταβλεφᾰρίζω**, gloss on κατιλλώπτω, Hsch.

⊕**κατά-βλημα**, ατος, τό, *overthrow*, in argument, πτῶμά τοι τὸ κ. Democr.125. II. *anything let down*: hence, 1. in ships, *tarpaulin* for keeping off missiles, *IG*2².1629.409, 1631.262, al. 2. *curtain, drop-scene* of a theatre, in pl., Poll.4.127,131. 3. *skirt, fringe*, Duris 14 J. 4. *outer wrapper*, Hp.*Art.*33. III. *payment*, dub. in *IG*1².354. -βλής, ῆτος, ὁ, = ἐπιβλής, *bolt*, Hsch. -βλητέον, (καταβάλλω) *one must sow*, εἰς ποίαν γῆν ποῖον σπέρμα κ. Pl.*Tht.*149e. 2. *one must pay*, χρέος (metaph. of life), Plu.2.107a. -βλητικός, ή, όν, *fit for throwing off horseback*, X. *Eq.*8.11; *of throwing* in wrestling, τέχνη Gal.*Thras.*45: c. gen., κ. τοῦ μεγέθους τῆς Ἑλλάδος D.H.*Th.*19: metaph., *fond of confuting*, τῶν πέλας Gal.9.217; *abusive*, Phld.*Lib.*p.18 O.

**καταβληχάομαι**, strengthd. for βληχάομαι, Theoc.5.42.

**καταβλώσκω**, poet. for κατέρχομαι, *go down* or *through*, ἄστυ καταβλώσκοντα Od.16.466; πτόληος νόσφι A.R.1.322; of seamen, Lyc.1068 (in irreg. fut. -βλώξω); of a stream, A.R.4.227.

**καταβο-άω**, fut. -βοήσομαι Ar.*Eq.*286; Ion. -βώσομαι Hdt.6.85: strengthd. for βοάω :—*bawl*, οὐ μόνον βοᾶν, ἀλλ' ἤδη καὶ καταβοᾶν Ph. 1.475: but usu. 2. c. gen., *cry out, inveigh against*, τινὸς περί τινος Hdt. l.c.; κ. τινῶν ὅτι σπονδὰς λελυκότες εἶεν Th.1.67, cf. 115, 5.45 :—Pass., *have clamour raised against one*, ὑπό τινων App.*BC*5. 13. II. c. acc., *shout down*, Ar.*Ach.*711, *Eq.*286. III. c. acc. cogn., κατά μοι βόασον..ὅπα τοῖς Ἀτρείδαις *carry down* my voice.., S.*El.*1067 (lyr.). IV. *call for help*, τινὶ περί τινος *PSI*6.551.2 (iii B.C.), *PMagd.*42.5 (iii B.C.): c. gen. et inf., *demand clamorously from*.., κ. τινὸς κολάζειν τὸν στρατιώτην J.*BJ*2.12.1. 2. Pass., *to be loudly entreated*, Nic.Dam.4 J. -ή, ῆς, ἡ, *outcry against* any one, c. gen. pers., Th.1.73, 8.85; κ. ἡ ἐς Λακεδαίμονα ib.87, cf. *UPZ*1.6 (iv B.C.); κ. ποιήσασθαι J.*AJ*15.10.3, cf. Men.Prot.p.29 D. -ησις, εως, ἡ, = foreg., αἰτίαι καὶ κ. Plu.*Pomp.*67, cf. 2.420f, *IG*12(3).325.34 (Thera, ii A.D., pl.). II. *shouting*, Ph.2.537 (pl.); *loud cry*, κ. ἀγαθαί, κακαί, Artem.1.24. III. *divulgation*, τῶν ἔξωθεν Philostr.*Ep.*7.

**καταβολ-άδας**· κλάδους, Hsch. ⊕-αῖον, τό, *storehouse*, *PFay.*110. 6, 30 (i A.D.). -εύς, έως, ὁ, *founder*, Sch.Pi.*O.*3.1. II. *one who pays*, *Gloss.* III. in pl., officers *who collect payments* due to the state, *IG*5(2).357.9 (Stymphalus, iii B.C.). ⊕-ή, ἡ, *throwing down*: hence, *sowing*, *Corp.Herm.*9.6; esp. of *begetting*, κ. σπέρματος, σπερμάτων, Philol.13, Luc.*Am.*19, cf. *Ep.Hebr.*11.11, Arr.*Epict.*1.13.3; ἡ Ῥωμύλου σπορὰ καὶ κ. Plu.2.320b. b. *congenital defect*, ἀπὸ ξυγγενικῆς αἰτίας καὶ κ. Plu.*Tim.*37. c. Astrol., *nativity*, ἡ ἐξ ἀρχῆς κ. Vett.Val.220.29, al. 2. *paying down*, esp. by instalments, καταβάλλειν τὰς κ. D.59.27; τὸ ἀργύριον ἔφερε καταβολὴν τῇ πόλει paid money as *a deposit* (by way of caution), Docum.ib.37.22, cf. *IG*12(7). 515.26 (Amorgos, ii B.C.), *UPZ*112 v 12 (pl., ii B.C.), etc.; ἔχειν τῆς γῆς..καταβολὴν *liability for rent*, *PEleph.*23.17 (iii B.C.): pl., *instalments*, *PLips.*12.17 (iii A.D.), etc. II. *laying of a foundation*: hence, *building, structure*, Lxx 2*Ma.*2.29; τῆς ἀρχιτεκτονίας Bito 49.2; ἔργου *J.AJ*12.2.9: but usu. metaph., 1. *foundation, beginning*, ἱερῶν ἀγώνων Pi.*N.*2.4; τῆς περιόδου Arist.*Mete.*352ᵇ15; κ. ἐποιεῖτο καὶ θεμέλιον ὑπεβάλλετο τυραννίδος Plb.13.6.2; κ. κόσμου *Ev. Matt.*13.35, *Ep.Eph.*1.4; κ. κοσμική *Cat.Cod.Astr.*8(3).138 (Thessal.); ἡ πρώτη κ. τῆς φιλοσόφου θεωρίας Procl. *in Alc.Praef.*p.8 C.; ἐκ καταβολῆς from *the foundations*: hence, *anew*, σκάφη ἐκ κ. ἐναυπηγοῦντο, of *fresh* construction, Plb.1.36.8; ἐκ κ. πλάττων, of *pure* invention, Id.15.25.35: hence, *of set purpose, deliberately*, Id.1.47.7, 24.8.9. 2. = θυσία, τελετή, Hsch., cf. κατηβολή. III. *periodical attack* of illness, *fit*, τῆς ἀσθενείας Pl.*Grg.*519a, cf. κατηβολή; πυρετοῦ D.9.29, Ph.1.399, 2.563, cf. Aristid.*Or.*50(26).59, Id.2.166 J.; *trance*, Poll.1. 16; cf. Lat. *catabolicus*. IV. *detraction, abuse*, Phld.*Rh.*2.56 S.: pl., Ph.2.571 codd. V. perh. *outer wrapper* (cf. κατάβλημα II. 4) of a bandage, Hp.*Off.*9.

**καταβόλ-ια**, *conjectores* (sic), *Gloss.* ⊕-ος (proparox.), ὁ, *stewpond, oyster-bank*, Xenocr.ap.Orib.2.58.96. II. *naval station*, = ἐπίνειον, Sch.Th.1.30; *entrepôt*, = ἐμπόριον, *EM*336.21.

**καταβομβέω**, in Pass., *to be deafened*, τῇ σάλπιγγι τὸ Ἐνυάλιον ἐπηχούσῃ Agath.2.1.

**καταβορβόρωσις**, εως, ἡ, *wallowing in mud*, Plu.2.166a (pl.).

**καταβόρειος**, ον, (Βορέας) = sq., Thphr.*HP*2.8.1.

**κατάβορρος**, ον, *sheltered from the north*, i.e. *facing the south*, ἀπὸ τῶν ἄρκτων κ. Pl.*Criti.*118b, cf. Thphr.*CP*2.9.7; [οἰκία] κ. Arist.*Oec.* 1345ᵃ33.

**καταβόσκησις**, εως, ἡ, *feeding down* or *off*, Sm.*Is.*6.13.

**καταβόσκω**, *feed flocks upon* or *in* a place, ἀγρόν Lxx *Ex.*22.5(4); χὼ τὰν Σαμίαν καταβόσκων the *shepherd* of Samos, Theoc.15.126, cf. *PSI*4.346.5 (iii B.C.):—Med., with aor. 1 Med. and Pass., fut. Pass., of the flock, *feed upon*, Longus 2.16; καταβοσκηθήσονται βοτάνην *Gp.* 2.39.2; *devour, consume*, of disease or pestilence, Call.*Dian.*125; δέμας καταβόσκεται ἄτῃ Nic.*Th.*244; ἡσυχίῃ δὲ πόλιν κ. *reigns throughout*.., Tryph.503.

**καταβόστρῠχος**, ον, *with flowing locks*, νεανίας E.*Ph.*146 (lyr.), cf. Aristaenet.2.19, Iild.7.10.

**καταβουκολέω**, *lead astray, beguile*, Them.*Or.*26.330a (Pass.).

**καταβρᾰβεύω**, *give judgement against* one as βραβεύς, and so, *deprive* one *of the prize, deprive* one *of one's right*, c. acc., *Ep.Col.*2.18, Sch.Il.1.399:—Pass., ὑπὸ Μειδίου καταβραβευθέντα *being cast in his suit* by means of Meidias, Test.ap.D.21.93, cf. *Sammelb.*4512 B 58 (ii B.C.). 2. c. gen., *rule over*, ἡ γῆ κ. τῶν λοιπῶν Vett.Val.344. 29.

**καταβρᾰδύνω**, *retard*, Asclep.ap.Gal.12.413.

**καταβράζει**· καταβοᾷ, Hsch. (sed leg. -κράζει).

**κατα-βρεκτέον**, *one must drench*, τὸν στόμαχον οἴνῳ Alex.Trall. 9.3. -βρεξις, εως, ἡ, *soaking*, *Gloss.* -βρέχω:—Med., fut. -βρέξομαι v.l. in Hp.*Mul.*2.133:—Pass., aor. 1 κατεβρέχθην Ar.*Nu.* 267: aor. 2 κατεβράχην [ᾰ] Thphr.*CP*6.17.2:—*drench, soak, steep*, μὴ καταβρεχθῶ Ar. l.c.; δρῦς ἐν τῷ ὕδατι -βρεχομένη Thphr.*HP*5.4.3; σμύρνα -βραχεῖσα μελικράτῳ Id.*CP* l.c.; Ἀσκληπιὸς κατέβρεξεν [τὴν Θασίαν ἄμπελον?] *watered* the Thasian vine, i.e. gave it its healing property, Antid.4.4: metaph., κ. τινὰ κάδοις Χίου Hedyl.ap.Ath.10. 473a; μέλιτι πόλιν κ. Pi.*O.*10(11).99; καύχημα κ. σιγᾷ *steep* boasting in silence, i.e. be silent instead of boasting, Id.*I.*5(4).51. *inundate*, *PPetr.*3 p.108 (iii B.C.).

**καταβρίζω**, *fall asleep*, Hsch.

**καταβρίθω** [ῑ], intr., *to be heavily laden, weighed down* by a thing, ὄϊες μαλλοῖς καταβεβρίθασι Hes.*Op.*234; ὄρπακες βραβύλοισι καταβρίθοντες ἔραζε Theoc.7.146. II. trans., *weigh down, outweigh*, ὄλβῳ μὲν πάντας κε καταβρίθοι βασιλῆας Id.17.95.

**καταβρῑμάομαι**, strengthd. for βριμάομαι, Corinna 18 (s.v.l.).

**καταβροντάω**, fut. -ήσομαι, *to thunder down*, τοὺς ῥήτορας Longin. 34.4; καταστράψουσι καὶ -ήσονται Them.*Or.*27.337d; κατέσεισεν ἅπαντα καὶ κατεβρόντησεν Eun.*Hist.*p.256 D.

**καταβρόξειε,** v. *βρόχω 2. **καταβροτόω,** *soil with gore,* Hsch.

**καταβροχή,** ἡ, *soaking, steeping,* Dsc.1.54 (pl.), Thd.*Pr.*3.8, Orib.10.15.2.

**καταβροχθίζω,** *gulp down,* Hp.*Coac.*62, Ar.*Eq.*357, 826; ὀβολόν Id.*Av.*503, cf. Antiph.190.6; τὴν Πελοπόννησον ἅπασαν Hermipp.45: metaph., λόγους κ. Ath.6.270b.

**καταβροχίζω** (-βρογχ- codd.), *tie up, ligature,* Orib.*Fr.*38.

**κατάβροχος,** ον, *inundated, PMagd.*3.5 (iii B.C.), etc.

**καταβρύκω** [ῡ], aor. 1 κατέβρυξα Nic.*Th.*675:—*bite in pieces, eat up,* Hippon.36, *AP*6.263 (Leon.), Nic. l.c.

**καταβρύω,** *to be overgrown,* κισσῷ καταβρύουσαν, of a cup with ivy ornament, Eub.56.6 (s. v.l.).

**κατάβρωμα,** ατος, τό, *that which is eaten, food,* Lxx *Nu.*14.9, al., *EM*453.53.

**καταβρώξειε,** v. *βρόχω 2.

**κατάβρωσις,** εως, ἡ, *eating up, devouring,* Lxx *Ge.*31.15.

**καταβρώσομαι,** fut. of καταβιβρώσκω.

⊕**καταβῡθ-ίζω,** *cause to sink,* Hp.*Ep.*17, Thphr.*HP*5.4.7 (Pass.); ναῦν D.S.15.34: metaph., κ. αὐτάνδρους τοὺς βίους Longin.44.6:—Pass., πολέμοις-βυθισθεῖσαν πόλιν *IPE*1².34.7 (Olbia, i B.C.). **-ισμός,** ὁ, *sinking, Gloss.*

**καταβυρσόω,** *cover with hides,* ναῦς Th.7.65. 2. *sew up in a skin,* Plu.*Cleom.*38.

**καταβυσσόω,** *bury,* in Pass., εἴδωλα καταβυσσούμενα ἐν τῷ ὀφθαλμῷ Alex.Aphr.*in de An.*135.19.

**καταγαΐδιοι** θεοί gods *of the underworld,* = Lat. *di manes, IG*14.581 (Centuripa).

**κατάγαιος,** ον, Ion. for κατάγειος.

**κατ-ᾰγᾰπάω,** strengthd. for ἀγαπάω, *to be content with, accept,* Epicur.*Ep.*2 p.55 U.: pf. part. κατηγαπηκώς ib.p.41 U.

**κατάγαστρον,** τό, *stomach-band, Gloss.*

**κατάγαστρος,** ον, *gluttonous, Cat.Cod.Astr.*7.212.

**κατ-αγγειόομαι,** *to be furnished with blood-vessels,* Ruf.*Anat.*13, Heliod.ap.Orib.50.47.3 (-γι- codd.); cf. κατηγγειωμένως.

**καταγγελ-εύς,** έως, ὁ, *one who proclaims, herald,* ἀγώνων *IG*12(2).58ᵃ10 (Mytilene, i B.C.), cf. *BSA*26.163 (Sparta, ii A.D.); ξένων δαιμονίων *Act.Ap.*17.18. **-ία,** ἡ, *proclamation,* πολέμου Luc.*Par.*42; esp. of games or festivals, ἐκ καταγγελίας ἐπιτελεῖν ἀγῶνα Plu.*Rom.*14; τὴν κ. ἐποιήσαντο πρεπόντως *OGI*319.13 (Magn. Mae., ii B.C.), cf. *CIG*3656.6 (Cyzicus, ii B.C.); τὰν κ. ἀποδέχεται ib.12. II. *denunciation,* J.*AJ*10.7.4 (pl.).

**κατ-αγγέλλω,** *announce, proclaim, declare,* πόλεμον κατηγγέλκασι Lys.25.30, cf. D.S.14.68, Plu.*Pyrrh.*26; κ. ῥυσιά τινι Plb.4.53.2; δεῖπνον Plu.2.727b: freq. in *NT,* κ. τὸ εὐαγγέλιον, Χριστόν, 1*Ep.Cor.*9.14, *Ep.Phil.*1.17: c. inf., κ. ἱκέσθαι *report* one's arrival, *Berl.Sitzb.*1927.170 (Cyrene). 2. *recite, recount,* ἀγῶνα Luc.*Par.*39. 3. *denounce,* τινὸς τὴν ἐπιβουλήν X.*An.*2.5.38; δοῦλοι ὅσοι δεσπότας κ. Hdn.5.2.2; *lay an information,* πρός τινα *CIG*3641b.32 (Lampsacus): metaph., κ. ἀπειρίαν τοῦ ποιητοῦ A.D.*Pron.*78.20. 4. of symptoms, *threaten,* σπασμόν Antyll.ap.Orib.10.2.6.

**κατάγγελ-ος,** ὁ, = μυρσίνη ἀγρία, Ps.-Dsc.4.144 (nisi leg. κακ-). **-σις,** εως, ἡ, *giving of information, Gloss.* **-της,** ου, ὁ, *informer,* ib. **-τικός,** ή, όν, *announcing,* c. gen. rei, Hld.3.1. **-τος,** ον, *denounced, betrayed,* κ. γίγνεσθαί τινι Th.7.48, cf. D.C.*Fr.*11.14.

⊕**καταγγ-ίζω,** *put into a vessel, bottle,* Dsc.5.6.7, *POxy.*2153.6 (iii A.D., Pass.):⊕**-ισμός,** ὁ, *packing,* λάρδου *PLond.ined.*2147 (iv A.D.); ἀνθρακος *PBaden*29.8 (v A.D.).

⊕**κατάγειος,** Ion. κατάγαιος, ον, *under the earth, subterranean,* θησαυρός Hdt.2.150; οἰκήματα Id.3.97, etc.; οἰκίαι X.*An.*4.5.25; οἴκησις Pl.*R.*514a, *Prt.*320e; ἐκ τοῦ κ. from *below ground,* Id.*R.*532b; οἰκίσκος κ. v.l. in Paul.Aeg.6.21. II. *on the ground,* τὰ κ. *ground-floor* rooms, opp. ὑπερῷα, D.H.10.32; στρουθοὶ κ. ostriches, Hdt.4.175, 192; cf. κατώγειος. 2. Subst., κατάγειον or κατάγαιον, τό, *cellar, POxy.*75.19 (ii A.D.), etc.

**Καταγέλα,** ἡ, Comic name of a town, with a play on the Sicil. *Gela,* Γέλα καὶ Καταγέλα Ar.*Ach.*606, cf. Ath.7.314f.

**καταγελάσ-ιμος,** ον, *ridiculous,* with play on the name Γελάσιμος, Plaut.*Stich.*631. **-τής,** οῦ, ὁ, *mocker, Gloss.* **-τικός,** ή, όν, *satirical,* ὕμνοι Men.Rh.p.337 S. (Comp.). Adv. **-κῶς** *scoffingly,* Poll.5.128. **-τος,** ον, *ridiculous, absurd,* κ. εἶ Ar.*Nu.*849; ὦ καταγέλαστ' Id.*Ra.*480; κ. δῆτ' ἔσει.. ἔχων Id.*Th.*226; Πέρσας ποιῆσαι κ. γενέσθαι Ἕλλησι *ridiculous* in their eyes, Hdt.8.100, cf. Pl.*Ap.*35b; of things, κ. τὸ χρῆμα γίγνεται Id.*Grg.*485a; φοβοῦμαι οὔ τι μὴ γελοῖα εἴπω ἀλλὰ μὴ καταγέλαστα Id.*Smp.*189b, cf. Epicur.*Nat.*28.5, etc.: c. gen., τῆς ἀλλαγῆς because of.., Max.Tyr.2.3: Comp., Pl.*Ep.*314a: Sup., Isoc.10.9, 15.56, Pl.*Plt.*296d. Adv. **-τως** X.*Mem.*1.7.2, Pl.*Lg.*781c, Aeschin.1.31, D.H.*Comp.*18, etc.: Sup. **-τότατα** Pl.*Sph.*252b.

**καταγελάω,** fut. -άσομαι Lys.3.9, late -γελάσω Hsch. s. v. κατακριδεύσει:—Pass., fut. -γελασθήσομαι Epict.*Ench.*22: pf. -γεγέλασμαι Luc.*DMort.*1.1: plpf. κατεγεγέλαστο Id.*Icar.*19:—*laugh, jeer at,* c. gen., Hdt.5.68, Ar.*Ach.*1081, And.4.29, Pl.*Grg.*482d: also c. dat., Hdt.3.37, 4.79, al.: abs., *laugh scornfully, mock,* E.*IA*372 (troch.), Ar.*Eq.*161, X.*An.*1.9.13, Pl.*Prt.*319c, D.21.151; ἅπαντες καταγελῶσιν, ὅταν τις.. Epicur.*Nat.*28.9; ἐπί τινι Them.*Or.*22.272b. 2. c. acc., *laugh down, deride,* E.*Ba.*286, Lxx *Si.*7.11:—Pass., *to be derided,* ὑπό τινος A.*Ag.*1271, Ar.*Ach.*680; καταγελάμενος (Dor. pres. part. Pass.) ὑπὸ τῶν ἄλλων *IG*4.951.123 (Epid.); τὸ εὔηθες καταγελασθὲν ἠφανίσθη Th.3.83; τὸ καταγελᾶσθαι γὰρ πολὺ αἴσχιόν ἐστι Men.*Epit.Fr.*7, cf. Pl.*Euthphr.*3c, al.

**κατ-άγελος** [ᾰ], ον, (ἀγέλη) *rich in herds,* Hdn.*Epim.*206.

**κατάγελως,** ωτος, ὁ, *derision,* τί δῆτ' ἐμαυτῆς καταγέλωτ' ἔχω τάδε; these ornaments *which bring ridicule* upon me? A.*Ag.*1264, cf. Ar.*Ach.*76; -γέλωτος ἄξιος X.*Oec.*13.5; κ. πλατύς sheer *mockery,* Ar.*Ach.*1126; κατάγελων.. φίλοις παρασχεθεῖν Id.*Eq.*319; διπλοῦν προσλήψῃ -γέλωτα Epict.*Ench.*22; κ. τῆς πράξεως *the crowning absurdity* of the matter, Pl.*Cri.*45e; κατάγελων ἡγούμην πάντα Philostr.*VA*7.23. 2. of persons, *laughing-stock,* οὗτος κ. νομίζεται Men.160.4.

**καταγεμίζω,** *load heavily,* σκάφη D.C.74.13.

**καταγέμω,** only pres. and impf., *to be full of,* c. gen., -γέμοντος τοῦ στρατοπέδου τῆς λείας Plb.14.10.2, cf. D.S.5.43, J.*BJ*6.5.1, Luc.*Somn.*6: c. dat., J.*BJ*4.3.10.

**καταγενής,** ές, in Comp. -έστερος, prob. f.l. for μεταγ- (q. v.), Procl.*in Prm.*p.850 S.

**καταγεύομαι,** *taste,* οἴστρου Orac.ap.Phleg.37 J. 2. Medic., *examine, probe,* τοῦ βάθους Heliod.ap.Orib.46.11.13. II. also as Pass., *to be conquered in taste,* Phot., Suid.

**καταγεύστριον,** τό, dub. sens. in *PLond.*3.1164h17 (iii A.D.).

**καταγεωμετρέω,** *geometrize, turn into geometry,* τὴν φύσιν Simp.*in Ph.*1341.20.

**καταγεωργέω,** *bring into tillage,* Str.9.3.4.

**καταγεώτης,** ου, ὁ, *grave-digger,* Hsch.

**καταγηρ-άσκω,** Od.19.360 (= Hes.*Op.*93), E.*Med.*124 (anap.), Hyp.*Lyc.*12, Arist.*HA*622ᵃ26, etc.:—also **-άω,** Pl.*Criti.*112c, Is.2.22 (-γηράνω Dobree): fut. -γηράσομαι [ᾱ] Ar.*Eq.*1308, etc., -άσω Pl.*Lg.*949c (aor. subj. in *Smp.*216a): aor. -εγήρασα Hdt.2.146, Pl.*Tht.*202d, Ath.14.633b:—from *-γήραμι (cf. γηράσκω) come inf. -γηράναι or -γηρᾶναι (Att., acc. to Moer.p.115 P., v. supr.) Ath.5.190e, and prob. -εγήρα Od.9.510, Hdt.6.72: pf. καταγεγήρακα Isoc.10.1:—*grow old,* ll. cc.; αἶψα.. ἐν κακότητι βροτοὶ καταγηράσκουσιν Od.19.360; μαντευόμενος κατεγήρα Κυκλώπεσσιν 9.510, cf. Hdt.6.72. **-ασμός,** ὁ, *old age, Hippiatr.*13.

**καταγῑγαρτίζω,** *take out the kernel*: metaph., *deflower,* Ar.*Ach.*275 (lyr.).

**καταγίγνομαι,** Ion. and later **-γίνομαι** [ῑ], *abide, dwell,* ἐν [χρυσοχοείῳ] Test.ap.D.21.22, cf. Teles p.27 H., *PMagd.*9.3 (iii B.C.), Lxx *Ex.*10.23, *OGI*666.14 (Egypt, i A.D.), etc. 2. *busy oneself* about, *be concerned* with a thing, ἔν τινι Plb.31.29.6; ἐν ἀριθμοῖς καὶ προσώποις A.D.*Synt.*226.28 (but κ. ἐν δοτικῇ *to be constructed* with the dative case, 298.10); ὑφ' ὧν καὶ δι' ὧν καὶ περὶ ὧν τὸ χειρουργικὸν μέρος τῆς τέχνης καταγίνεται Gal.18(2).667; περί τι Phld.*Mus.*p.40 K., Arr.*Epict.*3.2.6; περὶ τὸ ποιὸν μᾶλλον ἢ τὸ ποσόν Ptol.*Geog.*1.1.4, cf. S.E.*M.*4.1; τὴν γεωμετρίαν οὐ περὶ μεγέθη ἀλλὰ περὶ ποιότητα κ. Plot.6.3.14; εἴς τι A.D.*Synt.*298.21; πρός τι ib.280.15; πρὸς τὸ οἴκοι ἐνδιατρίβειν Agatharch.101. 3. = διάγω II. 2, οὕτω, ἐν τρυφῇ, Id.40, 101.

**καταγιγνώσκω,** Ion. and later **-γῑνώσκω,** fut. -γνώσομαι Pl.*Euthphr.*2b:—*remark, observe,* esp. something *to one's prejudice,* c. gen. pers.: I. generally, καταγνοὺς τοῦ γέροντος τοὺς τρόπους *having observed* his foibles, Ar.*Eq.*46; πολλήν γέ μου δυστυχίαν κατέγνωκας I have been very unfortunate *by your way of it,* Pl.*Ap.*25a; πολλὴν ἡμῶν ἐρημίαν Is.1.2; οὐκ ἐπιτήδεα κατά τινος κ. *having formed* unfavourable *prejudices* against one, Hdt.6.97: c. inf., of an unfavourable judgement, κ. ἑαυτοῦ μὴ περιέσεσθαι Th.3.45, cf. 7.51; αὐτὸς ἐμαυτοῦ κατέγνων μὴ ἂν καρτερῆσαι X.*Cyr.*6.1.36, cf. Pl.*Ti.*19d: folld. by ὅτι, ὡς, ἐμοῦ κατέγνωκας ὅτι εἰμὶ ἥττων τῶν καλῶν Pl.*Men.*76c; οὐκ ἂν καταγνοίην ὑμῶν οὐδενὸς ὡς.. ἀμελήσετε D.21.4 (but κατεγνωκότες ὅτι.. ἐφθείρομεν *despising* us because.. Th.6.34, cf. *PMagd.*42.4 (iii B.C.), Jul.*Or.*3.108b): c. part., κ. τινὰ πράττοντα X.*Oec.*2.18, cf. *Cyr.*8.4.9; τὸ χωρίον νοσερὸν ⟨ὂν⟩ καταγνόντες D.L.2.109:—Pass., *to be judged unfavourably, lightly esteemed,* παρολιγωρεῖσθαι καὶ καταγινώσκεσθαι Plb.5.27.6; κατεγνωσμένος *despised,* Philostr.*VS*2.29. II. c. acc. criminis, *lay as a charge against* a person, κ. ἑωυτῶν ἀνανδρείην Hp.*Aër.*22; κ. τινὸς μηδὲν ἀνόσιον Antipho 2.2.12; δειλίαν, δωροδοκίαν κ. τινός, Lys.14.16, 21.21; οὐδὲν ἀγεννὲς ὑμῶν καταγιγνώσκω D.21.152; ἑαυτῶν ἀδικίαν And.1.3; πολλὴν μανίαν, μωρίαν, Isoc.4.133, 5.21; σκληρότητα ἡμῶν καὶ ἀγροικίαν Pl.*R.*607b; τοσαύτην ὑμῶν εὐήθειαν D.30.38: with gen. understood, οὐ γὰρ ἐκεῖνό γε (sc. σοῦ) καταγνώσομαι, ὡς.. Pl.*Euthphr.*2b; later κ. κατά τινος τὸν φόνον Porph.*Abst.*2.30:—Pass., καταγνωσθεὶς δειλίαν *being convicted* of cowardice, D.H.11.22; κ. ἐπὶ λογοκλοπίᾳ D.L.8.54; κατεγνωσμένος *self-condemned, Ep.Gal.*2.11. 2. c. gen. criminis, παρανόμων κ. τινός D.25.67; παρανοίας ὑμῶν αὐτῶν Id.*Prooem.*35: c. acc. pers., κ. τινὰ φόνου *pronounce a verdict* of murder *against..,* Lex ap. Lys.1.30; μὴ καταγιγνώσκωμεν τὸ (fort. τοῦ) μηδὲν εἰρηκέναι τὸν ἀποφηνάμενον Pl.*Tht.*206e. 3. c. inf., κ. σφῶν αὐτῶν, ἑαυτοῦ ἀδικεῖν, *charge* oneself *with..,* Lys.20.6, Aeschin.2.6, cf. D.21.175, 206; κ. ὡς.. Isoc.9.78:—so in Pass., καταγνωσθεὶς νεώτερα πρήσσειν *being suspected* of doing, Hdt.6.2; κ. αὐθέντης (sc. εἶναι) Antipho 3.3.11; *to be detected,* ἔν τινι *PFlor.*175.16 (iii A.D.); also κατέγνωσται μελίκρητον ὑπὸ τῶν ἀνθρώπων ὡς καταγυιοῖ τοὺς πίνοντας Hp.*Acut.*56. 4. c. gen. pers. only, *condemn,* τοῦ ἀνθρώπου Pl.*Demod.*382e. III. c. acc. poenae, *give judgement* or *sentence against* a person, κ. τινὸς θάνατον *pass sentence* of death on one, Th.6.60; Μηδισμοῦ κ. τινὸς θάνατον *for* Medism, Isoc.4.157; κ. τινὸς φυγήν And.1.106; φυγὴν αὐτοῦ καταγνοὺς Lys.14.38: c. inf., κ. αὐτοῦ ἀποτεῖσαι τὰ χρήματα D.56.18; later θάνατον, φυγὴν κ. κατά τινος, D.S.18.62, 19.51:—Pass., θάνατός τινος κατέγνωστο Antipho 5.70, cf. Lys.13.39, Jusj.ap.D.24.149;

later καταγνωσθεὶς θανάτῳ Ael.*VH*12.49: abs., κατεγνώσθησαν *they were condemned*, Th.4.74, cf. And.4.8; τὸ ἀδίκημα κεκριμένον ἐστὶ καὶ κατεγνωσμένον Lycurg.52. 2. *decide* a suit, δίκην Ar.*Eq.*1360:—Pass., A.*Eu.*573 codd.; δίκη μὴ ὀρθῶς -γνωσθεῖσα Antipho 6.3.

**κατ-ᾰγίζω**, Ion. for καθαγίζω, Hdt.1.86, al.

**κατ-ᾰγῑνέω**, Ion. for κατάγω, *bring down*, Od.10.104. II. *bring back, recall*, Hdt.6.75.

**κατ-αγλᾰΐζω**, *glorify*, *AP*11.64.8 (Agath.); ναὸν λίθοις J.*AJ*8.5.2:—Pass., κατηγλαϊσμένοι *splendidly attired*, *Com.Adesp.*1275.

**καταγλισχραίνω**, strengthd. for γλισχραίνω, Hp.*Acut.*53:—Pass., ib.16.

**κατάγλισχρος**, ον, *viscous*, Alex.Trall.8.2.

**καταγλῠκαίνω**, *sweeten*, Gal.14.753:—metaph. in Med., ἐν ἐννέ' ἂν χορδαῖς κατεγλυκάνατο Chionid.4.

**κατά-γλυμμα**, ατος, τό, *sculptured ornament*, *IG*4.1485.94 (pl., Epid.). **-γλυπτόν·** εἶδος φιλήματος, Hsch. **-γλῠφή**, ἡ, (γλύφω) *incision, groove*, Hp.*Art.*72, *Mochl.*38 (-γλῦφος, ἡ, ibid., is doubtful). 2. *carving*, λίθων *IG*4.1485.117 (pl., Epid.); γάστρων, σχοινίδος, *Milet.*7.59.4 and 17. **-γλῦφος**, ον, *carved*, σοροί Judeich *Altertümer von Hierapolis* 323. **-γλύφω** [ῠ], *scoop out, groove*, pf. part. Pass. -γεγλυμμένος Hp.*Mochl.*38. 2. *carve*, κυμάτια *IG* 11(2).199*A*76 (Delos, iii B.C.); σπεῖραν *Milet.*7.59.14.

**καταγλωττ-ίζω**, *bill, kiss wantonly by joining mouths and tongues*, *Com.Adesp.*882: hence, μέλος κατεγλωττισμένον *wanton, lascivious* song, Ar.*Th.*131. II. *use the tongue against* another, ψευδῆ κ. τινός Id.*Ach.*380. III. κ. τινά *talk* one *down*, hence in Pass., πόλιν ὑπὸ σοῦ κατεγλωττισμένην σιωπᾶν Id.*Eq.*352. IV. (γλῶσσα II. 2) in pf. part. Pass., *composed of far-fetched words*, λέξις Philostr.*VA* 1.17, Eun.*VS* p.496.25 D. **-ισμα**, ατος, τό, *lascivious kiss*, Ar.*Nu.*51. **-ισμός**, ὁ, = foreg., *Com.Adesp.*1027. **-ος**, ον, *glib, fluent*, ἐν τῇ σχολῇ γοργοὶ καὶ κ. Arr.*Epict.*2.16.20; *babbling, garrulous*, Gell.1.15.17. II. *written in rare* or *far-fetched language*, ποιήματα *AP*11.218 (Crates), prob. l. in Luc.*Lex.*25; τὸ κ. τῆς λέξεως D.H.*Th.*53.

**κάταγμα** (A), ατος, τό, (κατάγω) *wool drawn* or *spun out, worsted*, Pl.*Plt.*282e; *flock of wool*, S.*Tr.*695, Ar.*Lys.*583, Philyll.22, Chor. p.92 B. [τᾰ by nature, Ammon.*Diff.*p.78 V.]

**κάταγμα** (B), ατος, τό, Ion. **κάτηγμα**, later **κατέαγμα** (cf. κατάγνυμι), *fragment*, *BCH*35.286 (Delos, ii B.C.); later μικρὰ κατεάγματα λίθου *BGU*647.13 (ii A.D.); πλίνθων κατάγματα dub. cj. in Alc. 153. II. *breakage*, *PAmh.*2.93.19 (ii A.D., in form -αίαγμα = -έαγμα); esp. 2. Medic., *fracture*, Hp.*Aph.*5.22, Thphr.*HP*4.8.6, Sor.*Fract.*1, al., Gal.10.423; μελῶν Vett.Val.110.5. [τᾰ by nature, Ammon.*Diff.*p.78 V.]:—hence **-αγματικός**, ή, όν, *liable to fracture*, Vett.Val.110.23; but usu. 2. *of* or *for fracture*, ἔμπλαστρος Asclep.ap.Gal.13.536; ἀγωγή Pall.*in Hp.Fract.*12.279 C.; ἐπίδεσις Gal.18(2).441. Adv. -κῶς ib.536.

**καταγνάμπτω**, *bend down*, *AP*4.3[b].5 (Agath.).

**καταγνάφω** [γνᾰ], *lacerate*, v.l. for καταγράφω, Hdt.3.108.

**κατ-αγνοέω**, strengthd. for ἀγνοέω, Phld.*Lib.*p.16 O.

**κατ-άγνῡμι**, inf. -ύναι [ῠ] Th.4.11, Pl.*Phdr.*265e; **καταγνύω** Eub. 107.14, X.*Oec.*6.5; late pres. **κατάσσω, κατεάσσω** (qq. v.): fut. κατάξω Eup.323: aor. κατέαξα Hom., etc. (v. infr.); Ion. κατῆξα Hp.*Epid.*5.26; 3 sg. subj. κατάξει *SIG*38.37 (Teos, v B.C.); part. κατάξας (Dobree for κατεάξας) Lys.3.42, Plu.2.526b (v.l. κατεάξας, κατάγξας); Ep. opt. κανάξαις = καϝϝάξαις for κατ-ϝάξαις, Hes.*Op.* 666, 693:—**Pass.**, κατάγνῠμαι Hp.*Fract.*45, *Art.*67, Ar.*Pax*703: impf. κατεάγνυτο Epicur.*Nat.*113 G.: aor. 2 κατεάγην [prob. ᾰ] Ar. *V.*1428, subj. κατ-αγῶ (contr. fr. κατᾰ ϝάγ-) Id.*Fr.*604, prob. in Id. *Ach.*928, opt. καταγείην ib.944; part. καταγείς [prob. ᾰ] *IG*2².1673.33, 39, al., later κατᾰγέντος *APl.*4.187: fut. καταγήσομαι *Cat.Cod. Astr.*8(4).129: pf. κατέᾱγα, Ion. κατέηγα Hp.*Art.*67 (in pass. sense); part. κατεαγώς, written κατειαγώς *IG*2².1673.55, contr. κατηγώς Phoenix 5.1: pf. Pass. κατέαγμαι Luc.*Tim.*10, Paus.8.46.5, Artem. 5.32: aor. 1 κατεάχθην Lxx *Je.*31(48).25; inf. καταχθῆναι Arist.*PA* 640[a]22; part. καταχθείς Anon.Lond.26.52, D.Chr.11.82.—The forms κατέαξα, κατεάγην led the copyists to insert the ε in unaugmented forms, as κατεάξας Lys. l. c., κατεαγῇ Hp.*Art.*50, κατεαγῆναι Pl.*Grg.*469d, and such forms were in use in later Gr., as κατεάξει *Ev. Matt.*12.20, κατεαγῶσιν *Ev.Jo.*19.31, κατέαξαν *BGU*908.25 (ii A.D.): —*break in pieces, shatter*, κατὰ θ' ἅρματα ἄξω Il.8.403; ἄξονα Hes.*Op.* 693; τὸ (sc. ἔγχος) γὰρ κατεάξαμεν Il.13.257; νέα μέν μοι κατέαξε Ποσειδάων Od.9.283, cf. Hes.*Op.*666; εἴ τινες μαχεσάμενοι ἔτυχον ἀλλήλων κατάξαντες τὰς κεφαλάς Lys.3.42; κατάξειέ τις αὐτοῦ μεθύων τὴν κεφαλήν Ar.*Ach.*1166 cod. R (v.l. τῆς κεφαλῆς, cf. οὐ γὰρ κατάξει τῆς κεφαλῆς τὰ ῥήματα Eup.323, κατῆξε τῶν πλευρέων Hp.*Epid.* 5.26, v. sub fin.); κατάξω τὴν κεφαλήν, ἄνθρωπε, σου Men.*Sam.*173; γυνὴ κατέαξ' ἐχῖνον Ar.*V.*1436; Ναξίαν ἀμυγδάλην καταξαι Phryn. Com.68; τὰς ἀμυγδαλᾶς.. κάταξον τῇ κεφαλῇ σαυτοῦ λίθῳ Ar.*Fr.*590: metaph., *break up* into species, μὴ κ. μηδὲ κερματίζειν τὴν ἀρετήν Pl.*Men.*79a. 2. *weaken, enervate*, πατρίδα θ', ἣν αὔξειν χρεὼν καὶ μὴ καταξαι E.*Supp.*508; τὰς ψυχὰς καταγνύουσι X.*Oec.*6.5: abs. in pf. part. κατεαγώς *effeminate*, D.H.*Comp.*18, Ath.12.524f; αὐλητὴς τῶν κ. Plu.*Dem.*4; κ. μουσική S.E.*M.*6.14. II. Pass. with pf. Act., *to be broken*, δόρατα κατεηγότα Hdt.7.224; ὀστέα Hp. *Fract.*8; κληῖς Id.*Art.*14; περὶ δ' ἐμῷ κάρᾳ κατάγνυται τὸ τεῦχος S. *Fr.*565.3; κατέαγεν ἡ χύτρα Ar.*Th.*403; esp. καταγῆναι τὴν κεφαλήν *have* one's head *broken*, And.1.61, Lys.3.14; τὴν κεφαλὴν κατεαγέναι D.54.35: Com., στάμνου κεφαλὴν κατεαγότος Ar.*Pl.*545; τὸ κρανίον E.*Cyc.*684; τὸ σκάφιον Ar.*Fr.*604; κατεαγέναι or κατάγνυσθαι τὰ ὦτα, of pugilists, Pl.*Grg.*515e, *Prt.*342b; τὴν κλεῖν κατεαγώς D.18.67: also c. gen. partit. (οὐ πᾶσαν τὴν κεφαλὴν ἀλλὰ μέρος τι αὐτῆς Hdn.*Philet.* p.448 P.), τῆς κεφαλῆς κατέαγε περὶ λίθῳ πεσών Ar.*Ach.*1180; κατεάγη τῆς κ. Id.*V.*1428; τῆς κ. καταγῆναι (-εαγῆναι, -εαγέναι codd.) δεῖν Pl.*Grg.*469d; κατέαγα τοῦ κρανίου Luc.*Tim.*48: metaph., *to be shattered*, of an argument, Epicur. l. c.

**καταγνῡπόομαι**, Pass., *to be weak*, in pf. Pass. κατεγνυπῶσθαι, Hsch., *EM*236.40; κατεγνυπωμένον cj. in Plu.2.753c. Adv. κατεγνυπωμένως *lazily*, Men.1020; cf. γνύπετος.

**κατά-γνωσις**, εως, ἡ, *thinking ill of, low* or *contemptuous opinion of*.., κ. ἀσθενείας τινός Th.3.16; *moral condemnation, blame, censure*, Ephor.1 J., Plb.6.6.8, Phld.*Vit.Herc.*1457.9. II. *judgement given against* one, *condemnation*, Th.3.82, Arist.*Ath.*45.1 (pl.), D.21.175; τοῦ θανάτου *to* death, X.*Mem.*4.8.1. III. *dereliction of duty*, *PFlor.* 313.5 (v A.D.), *POxy.*140.17 (vi A.D.). **-γνωσμα**, ατος, τό, = foreg. II, *PTeb.*5.4 (ii B.C.), 124.24 (ii B.C.). **-γνωστέον**, *one must condemn*, τι Ph.1.698; τινος Luc.*Salt.*80; τινων Gal.13.793; κ. τῶν ἀξιούντων τι ὅτι.. *one must reject* the view of.., on the ground that.., Phld.*Po.*5.35. **-γνωστικός**, ή, όν, *damnatory*, Gal.8.656.

**καταγογγύζω**, *murmur against*, τινος Lxx 1 *Ma.*11.39.

**καταγοητεύω**, *bewitch*: hence, *cheat* or *blind by trickery*, τινα X. *Cyr.*8.1.40; ἡδονὴ τὸ σῶμα -γεγοήτευκεν Plu.2.986e:—Pass., v.l. in X.*An.*5.7.9, M.Ant.10.13; κρέως καρυκείᾳ καταγοητευθέντος meat *disguised* by sauce, Ael.*NA*4.40.

**κατάγομος**, ον, *deep-laden, heavy-laden*, πλοῖα Plb.9.43.6, D.S.5.35; ἅμαξαι Id.3.34: c. gen., *laden with, full of*, στρατοῦ λαφύρων καταγόμου App.*Syr.*21; ψευσμάτων J.*Ap.*2.9: also c. dat., ἀπῄεσαν κ. ταῖς ὠφελείαις D.S.31.45.

**καταγομφόω**, strengthd. for γομφόω I, Sch.Od.5.248.

**κατᾰγορ-άζω**, Dor. aor. inf. -αγοράξαι, σῖτον *IG*5(1).1379.21 (Thuria, ii/i B.C.):—**Pass.**, aor. 1 subj. -αγορασθῇ ib.13:—*buy up, purchase*, φορτία D.34.7, cf. Ephipp.21 (sed leg. κἆτ' ἀγ-); ἐκ τῶν ἰδίων ταῦρον *Milet.*1(9).368. **-αξις**, εως, ἡ, *buying up, purchase*, *IG*5(1).1379.22 (Thuria, ii/i B.C.). **-ασμός**, ὁ, = foreg., *Milet.*7.28 (ii B.C.); σῖτου *IG*12(9).900*c*2 (Chalcis, ii B.C.), D.S.16.13. **-ευσις**, εως, ἡ, *declaration*, Plu.2.428f. 2. *denunciation*, J.*AJ*17.3.2. **-ευτικός**, ή, όν, *declaratory, definitive*, D.L.7.70; περὶ τῶν κ., title of work by Chrysippus, ib.190. **-εύω** (aor. in use κατεῖπον, hence καταγορεύῃ shd. be restored for -εύσῃ in Ar.*Pax*107), *tell, announce*, τί τινι Ar. l. c.; cf. κατερῶ. 2. more freq. *denounce*, Th.4.68, 6.54; τι πρός τινα X.*HG*3.3.4. II. *accuse*, τινος Arist. *Pol.*1314[a]22, Ael.*NA*7.15. III. Pass., *to be predicated*, αἱ κατηγορίαι ὠνομάσθησαν ἀπὸ τοῦ -εύεσθαι Dexipp.*in Cat.*6.27.

**κατα-γραπτέον**, *one must describe, draw*, of a figure, Ph.*Bel.*52.33; ἐν πίνακι ἐπιπέδῳ κ. Str.2.5.10. **-γραπτος**, ον, *striped, variegated*, Περσικά, σῦκα, ἀμύγδαλα, *Gp.*10.14 tit., 47 tit., 60 tit., cf. Eust.852.11.

**καταγρᾰφ-εύς**, έως, ὁ, *cataloguer*, τῶν ἐθνικῶν Eust.335.41. **-ή**, ἡ, *drawing, delineation*, τῆς σφαίρας D.S.3.60; *drawing of maps*, Ptol.*Geog.*1.2.5; ποιεῖσθαι τὴν τῆς οἰκουμένης κ. ib.1.4; of the celestial globe, Gem.5.45; *diagram, figure*, Ael.*Tact.*18.1, Simp.*in Cael.* 652.10. 2. *delineation in profile*, in bas-relief, οἱ ἐν ταῖς στήλαις καταγραφὴν ἐκτετυπωμένοι Pl.*Smp.*193a. 3. *marking out*, τῆς χώρας D.H.8.69. 4. *engraving* of an inscription, *Abh.Berl.Akad.* 1925(5).21 (Cyrene, iv B.C.). II. *list, register*, ὀνομάτων Plu.2. 492b (pl.); esp. *roll of soldiers*, in pl., Plb.2.24.10, D.H.4.19; ἡ τῶν συνέδρων κ. the *roll* of the Senate, D.S.20.36. III. *conveyance* of land or houses, *BGU*1131.21 (Aug.), *POxy.*306 (i A.D.), *Annuario*4/5.469 (Halic.), etc.; also of slaves, etc., *BGU*1114, Charito 1.14. **-ος**, ον, = κατάγραπτος, Alex.Mynd.ap.Ath.9.387f, Dsc.3.156, Luc.*Alex.*12, *Hippiatr.*14. II. *drawn in profile*, Hipparch. 1.4.5; κατάγραφα, τά, = Lat. *obliquae imagines*, Plin.*HN*35.56. **-ω**, *scratch, lacerate*, Hdt.3.108 (v.l. καταγνάφω), Ael.*VH*10.3; ἰὸς δένδρεα κ. *marks* them, Nonn.*D.*21.329; κατέγραφεν ἠέρα ταρσῷ *grazed* it, ib.4.407, cf. Tryph.669:—Pass., καταγεγράφθαι ταῖς ῥυτίσι *EM*239.31. 2. *engrave, inscribe*, εἰς τοὺς τοίχους στίχον Plb.5.9.4:—Pass., νόμοι κατεγράφησαν (for Att. ἀνεγρ-) εἰς ἄξονας Plu.*Sol.*25. 3. *draw in outline, delineate*, Paus.1.28.2. 4. *describe*, Ptol.*Geog.*1.2.2, D.P. 707, Aret.*CA*1.5 (Pass.): in Geom., ἑξάγωνον κ. Simp.*in Cael.*653.7. 5. *paint over*, τοίχων ἀμορφίαν βαφαῖς Luc.*Am.*34. II. *fill with writing*, [σανίδας] E.*Alc.*969 (lyr.):—Pass., Luc.*VH*1.7. 2. *register, record*, μνήμας εἰς τὸν ἔπειτα χρόνον -γεγραμμένας Pl.*Lg.*741c; ὠνάς *BGU*1213.9 (iii B.C.); κατεγράφησαν ἄνδρες οὓς ἔδει θνῄσκειν Plu. *Cic.*46; esp. *enroll*, ναύτας Plb.1.49.2; δυνάμεις D.S.11.1; τινὰς εἰς φυλὰς καὶ φρατρίας D.H.2.35:—Pass., τμηθέντων τῶν ὁρκίων.. καὶ καταγραφέντων, ..τοὺς δημόυς.. τοὺς.. καταγραφέντας, Plb.29.3.6; σύγκλητος ὑπὸ τῶν τιμητῶν καταγραφεῖσα D.S.20.36; Σαπφὼ ἐν Μούσαις δεκάτη καταγράφεται *AP*9.571. 3. *summon by a written order*, [χορηγοὺς] κ. τινάς Arist.*Oec.*1352[a]7; κοινοβούλιον Plb.28.19.1. b. *prescribe, ordain*, c. acc. et inf., Luc.*Am.*19. 4. *convey, transfer by deed*, Plu.2.482c; οἰκίαν εἴς τινα *PPetr.*2 p.70 (iii B.C.), cf. *BGU*50.8 (Pass., ii A.D.), *POxy.*1703 (iii A.D.), etc. (also in Med. of the purchaser, *have conveyed* to one, *Annuario*4/5.469 (Halic.):—Pass., ὁ καταγραφείς the person *to whom* property *is conveyed*, *POxy.*472.19 (ii A.D.)): generally, *assign*, ἑαυτῷ λύτρα Ael.*Fr.*71: c. inf., *reckon* that.., Id.*NA*7.11. 5. *devote* to the infernal gods, *curse*, *IG*9(1).977 (Corc.), *Tab.Defix.*p.vii; so prob. in Plu.*Cic.*32.

**κατ-άγρημι**, Aeol. = καθαιρέω, Sapph.43, Alc.*Supp.*16.9; imper.

κατάγρεντον *IG*12(2).6.15 (Mytilene): irreg. Pass. part. καταγρόμενος Theoc.*Ep*.3.6 (dub. l.).

⊛**καταγρῡπόω**, *curl the nose*: αὐστηρὸν καὶ κατεγρυπωμένον *scornful*, Plu.2.753c codd. (κατεγνυπωμένον Schneid.).

⊛**κατ-αγυιόω**, *enfeeble*, Hp.*Acut*.56.

**καταγυμν-άζω**, *train, discipline*, τὰ σώματα Luc.*Anach*.24; πολλὰ κ. τινά Id.*Merc.Cond*.42: c. inf., τοὺς νέους ἀντέχειν καταγυμνάζωσιν Id.*Nigr*.27. II. Med., *squander in gymnastic exercises and games*, Hsch. **-ἄσία**, ἡ, = γυμνασία, Orib.*Fr*.59.

**καταγυμνόω**, *strip naked*, Aristaenet.1.7 (Pass., s. v.l.).

**καταγύναιος** [ῠ], ον, = sq., *Gloss*.

**κατάγῡνος**, ον, *much given to women*, Arist.*Mir*.837ᵃ34.

**καταγυψόω**, *plaster with gypsum*, κεράμια Gal.17(2).164.

**κατ-άγχουσα**, ἡ, = ἄγχουσα, Ps.-Dsc.4.23.

⊛**κατ-άγχω**, *strangle*, Thd.*Jd*.11.35. II. κατάγξας f.l. for κατάξας in Plu.2.526b.

⊛**κατ-άγω** [ᾰγ], fut. -ξω Th.1.26, etc.: aor. κατήγᾰγον Od.11.164, Epig.7: rarely aor. 1 κατῆξα v.l. in X.*HG*2.2.20, *PGrenf*.2.44 (ii A.D.), Philum.*Ven*.10.4: Ep. aor. inf. -αξέμεν Il.6.53: pf. καταγήοχα Decr.ap.D.18.73:—*lead down*, esp. *into the nether world*, ψυχὰς μνηστήρων κατάγων Od.24.100; εἰς Ἀΐδαο 11.164, cf. Pi.*O*.9.34, Paus. 3.6.2: generally, *bring down* to a place, Od.20.163; τὴν ἐκ τῶν ὀρῶν ὕλην εἰς τὸ ἄστυ Pl.*Criti*.118d, etc.; *bring down* a river or canal, *PGrenf*. l. c.:—Pass., *POxy*.708.3 (ii A.D.). 2. *draw down*, κατῆγεν ἦγεν ἦγεν ἐς μέλαν πέδον E.*Ba*.1065; esp. by magic arts, κ. τὸν Δία Plu.*Num*.15; ἀετόν ib.8, dub. sens. in Thphr.*CP*2.9.4. 3. *bring down to the sea-coast*, κατάγειν κοίλας ἐπὶ νῆας Il.5.26, cf. 6.53; ἐπὶ θάλατταν τὸ στράτευμα X.*Ages*.1.18. b. *launch*, σκάφος εἰς τὴν θάλασσαν Callix.1. 4. *bring down from the high seas to land*, τὸν Κρήτηνδε κατήγαγε ἲς ἀνέμοιο Od.19.186: abs., *put in to shore*, 3.10 Aristarch. (κατάγοντο codd.); esp. for purposes of exacting toll or plundering, X.*HG*4.8.33, *An*.5.1.11, D.5.25, al.; κ. ναῦς ἐς τοὺς ἑαυτῶν συμμάχους X.*HG*5.1.28; also κ. τοὺς ἐμπόρους Plb.5.95. 4, cf. D.S.20.82; κ. σαγήνην *draw* it *to land*, Plu.*Sol*.4; τοῦ πνεύματος κλύδωνα κατάγοντος πολὺν *bringing in* a heavy swell *from the sea*, Id.*Mar*.36; ὥρα πνεῦμα λαμπρὸν ἐκ πελάγους κατάγουσα Id. *Them*.14:—Pass., *come to land, land*, opp. ἀνάγεσθαι, of seamen as well as ships, Od.3.178; ἐπ' ἀκτῆς νηὶ κατηγαγόμεσθα 10.140, cf. Hdt.4.43; Σίγειον οὐρίῳ πλάτῃ κατηγόμην S.*Ph*.356; κατάγεσθαι ἐς τὸν Μαραθῶνα Hdt.6.107, cf. 8.4, Pl.*Mx*.240c; εἰς τὸν λιμένα X.*HG*6.2.36. b. κατάγεσθαι παρά τινι *turn in and lodge* in a person's house, Eup.344, X.*Smp*.8.39, *PFlor*.248.11 (iii A.D.); ὥς τινα D.52.22; εἰς οἰκίαν Id.49.22; εἰς πανδοκεῖον Plu.2.773e. 5. *draw down* or *out, spin*, Pherecr.46, Epig.7, Pl.*Sph*.226b; κατάγουσα, ἡ, *spinning-girl*, statue by Praxiteles, Plin.*HN*34.69: metaph., κ. λόγον Pl.*Men*.80e. 6. *reduce* to a state, ἐς κίνδυνον φανερὸν κ. τὴν πόλιν Th.4.68; ὁ οἶνος εἰς ὕπνον κ. Ael.*VH*13.6. 7. *bring home, gain*, θρίαμβον καὶ νίκην τῇ πατρίδι Plb.11.33.7; ἐκ πολέμων Plu.*Fab*. 24; *escort*, ἐπὶ τιμητείαν Id.*Aem*.38, etc. 8. κ. γένος *derive* a pedigree, ἀπό τινος Id.2.843e, Nic.Dam.61 J.:—Pass., τὰ στέμματα κατάγεται εἴς τινα *are traced down* to.., Plu.*Num*.1; φᾶμαι κατάγοντο Call.*Fr*.1.39 P.; of persons, *to be descended*, ἀπό τινος Olymp. *Vit.Pl*.p.1 W. 9. *derive* a word, S.E.*M*.1.242 (Pass.): generally, *derive*, ὅθεν δεῖ κατῆχθαι καὶ πῶς ἀποδεικνύειν Phld.*Rh*.1.203 S.; κ. [βοάν] *lower* the voice, E.*Or*.149 (lyr.): metaph., *bring down, lower*, πρὸς αὐτόν to one's own standard, D.Chr.40.11. 10. Medic., *couch* a cataract, Gal.18(2).680. 11. *wind up* a torsion-engine, Ph.*Bel*.76.13:—Pass., Hero *Bel*.79.6; ὁ κατάγων τὴν χεῖρα Ph.*Bel*.75. 9. 12. καταγόμενος *current*, ἐνιαυτός Vett.Val.27.16. II. *bring back*, κατὰ δὲ φρόνιν ἤγαγε πολλὴν *brought back* much news [of Troy], Od.4.258; esp. from banishment, *recall*, Hdt.1.60, Th.1.26, A.*Th*. 647, 660, etc.; κ. οἴκαδε X.*An*.1.2.2: generally, *restore*, τυραννίδας ἐς τὰς πόλις Hdt.5.92.α'; εἰς τὰς πατρίδας.. εἰρήνην Plb.5.105.2; ἐκ ταλαιπωρίας Jul.*Or*.2.58c:—Pass., *return*, ἐπὶ τὸ στρατόπεδον X.*An*. 3.4.36.

⊛**κατάγωγ-εύς**, έως, ὁ, *cattle-drover*, *BGU*92 (ii A.D.). ⊛**-ή**, ἡ, *bringing down from* the high sea, *landing*, Th.6.42 (pl.); ποιεῖσθαι τὴν κ. Str.8.3.26. 2. *bringing down* a river, *PMagd*.11.10 (iii B.C.), *PCair.Zen*.518 (iii B.C.), etc. 3. *bringing down* from a height, ὑδάτων J.*BJ*2.9.4. 4. concrete, *halting-place, inn*, like καταγώγιον, Hdt.1.181, al.; *place of rest*, καλὴ ἡ κ. Pl.*Phdr*.230b; *lodging, residence*, *IGRom*.4.1209 (Thyatira); τῶν ἀρχόντων Lib.*Or*.51.4; *shelter* for cattle, *PFlor*.103.12 (iv A.D.). 5. metaph., κ. τοῦ γένους *genealogy, pedigree*, Plu.2.843e. II. *bringing back* from banishment, *restoration*, Plb.32.12.1, D.S.5.4. 2. *winding up* of a torsion-engine, Ph.*Bel*.58.8 (pl.), Hero *Bel*.84.1; *stringing* of a stomach-bow, ib.79.2. 3. Medic., *couching* for cataract, Paul.Aeg.6. 21. III. *anything reaching downwards*, of the nose, Thom.Mag. p.323 R. **-ιμον**, τό, = καταγώγιον II, *PTeb*.35.5 (ii B.C.). ⊛**-ιον**, τό, *lodging, inn, resting-place*, Th.3.68, Pl.*Phdr*.259a, X.*Vect*.3.12; Μουσῶν κ. Plu.*Luc*.42; κ. ἀσωτίας Id.*Eum*.13; *official residence* of a magistrate, Procop.*Arc*.29, al.; τὸ τῶν δαιμόνων κ. *OGI*610.1 (Zorava, vi A.D.):—the form -γεῖον is required by metre in Antiph.53.5, Macho ap.Ath.8.337d. II. *extra payment for transport*, *PEleph*.14.11 (iii B.C.), *PTeb*.35.18 (ii B.C.). III. in pl., τὰ καταγώγια *festival of the return*, opp. ἀναγώγια, Ath.9.395a, *SIG*1109.114 (ii A.D.). **-ιος**, ὁ, *returned*, epith. of Dionysus, ib.1003.5 (Priene, ii B.C.). ⊛**-ίς**, ίδος, ἡ, *winding-mechanism* of a torsion-engine, Ph.*Bel*.75.46. 2. *curved end* of a stomach-bow (used for stringing it), Hero *Bel*.78.3. II. *woman's dress*, Sapph.*Supp*.14.5, cf. Poll.7.49, Hsch. **-ός**, όν, *seductive*, Σειρήνων μέλος *AP*15.12 (Leo Phil.). 2. *lowering*, ψυχῆς, opp. ἀναγωγός, Iamb.*Myst*.3.25; τὸ κ. ἔθνος τῶν δαιμόνων Procl. *in Alc*.p.45 C.; *debasing*, παθήματα Iamb.*VP*32.228, cf. Hierocl. *in CA* 24p.472 M. 3. = κατωφερής, Iamb.*Myst*.5.11. II. *fit for ships to put in at*, of a harbour, Sch.Il.2.494.

⊛**κατᾰγων-ίζομαι**, *prevail against*, τινας Plb.2.42.3, al., *OGI*553.7 (Xanthus); τὰ αἰσχρὰ τῶν παθῶν Metrod.*Herc*.831.19; κ. Ὀδυσσέα περὶ στεφάνου Luc.*VH*2.22; ἕλκη διαίτῃ Dam.*Isid*.122:—Pass., καταγωνισθῆναι τὰ ὅλα Plb.3.4.12; ὑπό τινος Luc.*Symp*.19. 2. *contend against*, τὴν ἀλήθειαν Plb.13.5.5, cf. 12.25ᵈ.6. II. *win by a struggle*, βασιλείας *Ep.Hebr*.11.33. **-ισις**, εως, ἡ, *conquest*, *Gloss*., Hsch. (κατάγωσις cod.). **-ισμός**, ὁ, = foreg., Poll.9.142. **-ιστής**, οῦ, ὁ, *conqueror*, Iamb.*VP*14.63. **-ιστικός**, ή, όν, *arguing for victory, polemical*, Procl. *in Prm*.p.706 S.

**καταδαίνυμαι**, only in aor. 1 κατεδαισάμην, *devour, consume*, νιν φλὸξ κατεδαίσατο Phryn.Trag.6, cf. Is.*Fr*.152, Theoc.4.34, Ael.*NA* 12.6, Ath.9.399a.

**κατάδαιτον**, corrupt word in Orac.ap.Phleg.*Fr*.36.10 J.

**καταδαίω**, *burn up*, in aor. 2 Pass. κατεδάη, Hsch.

⊛**καταδάκνω**, *bite*, v.l. in Batr.45; κέντρα Ael.*NA*1.32:—Pass., κατὰ χρόα πάντ' ὀνύχεσσι δακνόμενος Theoc.7.110.

**καταδακρύω**, *bewail*, τὴν ἑαυτοῦ τύχην X.*Cyr*.5.4.31; τινας Id.*HG* 2.4.22; τινος *for* one, Suid.: abs., *weep bitterly*, E.*Hel*.673 (lyr.), Tim. *Pers*.151, Plu.*Caes*.41, etc. II. causal, *make weep, move to tears*, App.*Pun*.70, *BC*4.114.

⊛**καταδακτῠλ-ίζω**, *feel with the finger*, sens. obsc., Phryn.*PS*p.83 B., Sch.Ar.*Pax*548. **-ικός**, ή, όν, *inclined thereto*, Ar.*Eq*.1381.

**καταδᾰμάζω**, *subdue*, aor. 1 Act. κατεδάμασα Lxx *Jd*.14.18: aor. inf. Med. καταδαμάσασθαι Th.7.81: aor. Pass., D.C.50.10, 78.39.

**καταδάμναμαι**, = foreg., *h.Merc*.137.

**καταδάνειος** [δᾰ], ον, *burdened with mortgages*, D.S.17.109.

**καταδᾰπᾰν-άω**, *squander*, τὴν οὐσίαν Arist.*Pol*.1316ᵇ23; τὸ στρωμάτων βάρος κ. εἰς τἀπιτήδεια X.*Cyr*.6.2.30:—Pass., [τὰ χρήματα] κατεδεδαπάνητό σφι Hdt.5.34:—Med., *to be prodigal*, Pyrrho ap.Ath. 10.419e. II. *consume*, of an army, X.*An*.2.2.11; τὸν Ὅμηρον λιμὸς κατεδαπάνησεν Sotad.15.16:—Pass., καταδαπανᾶσθαι ἐν τῇ κακίᾳ Lxx *Wi*.5.13; κατεδαπανῶντο ταῖς μάστιξι τὰ σώματα Eun.*Hist*. p.269 D. 2. *absorb, do away with*, Aët.7.91. **-ησις**, ἡ, *absorption, drying up*, τῆς ὑγρᾶς τροφῆς Alex.Aphr.*Pr*.2.75. **-ητικός**, ή, όν, *tending to consume*, *EM*110.2.

**καταδάπτω**, *devour*, μή με ἔα.. κύνας καταδάψαι Ἀχαιῶν Il.22.339; κύνες τε καὶ οἰωνοὶ κατέδαψαν Od.3.259; of fire, *consume*, Q.S.1.2, *Rev.Phil*.46.129 (Isaura): metaph., καταδάπτετ' ἀκούοντος φίλον ἦτορ, like δαίεται ἦτορ, Od.16.92.

**καταδαρδάπτω**, = foreg., Hsch.

⊛**καταδαρθάνω**, aor. κατέδαρθον (Att. inf. -δάρθειν acc. to Sch.Ar. *Nu*.38), Ep. κατέδρᾰθον, subj. καταδράθω Od.5.471; part. -δαρθόντα Ar.*Pl*.300 (-δαρθέντα codd.): aor. 1 Pass. κατεδάρθην is found in later writers, as Philostr.*VA*2.36, and 3 pl. κατέδαρθεν A.R.2.1227: pf. καταδεδάρθηκα Pl.*Smp*.219c:—*fall asleep*, mostly in aor., *to be asleep*, ἐν θάμνοισι κατέδραθον Od.7.285, cf. 23.18; τὼ δ' ἐς δέμνια βάντε κατέδραθον 8.296; καδδραθέτην, for κατεδραθέτην, 15.494; εἰ δέ κεν.. καταδράθω 5.471; ἔασον.. καταδαρθεῖν τί με Ar.*Nu*.38; ὁ μακαρίτης οἴχεται, κατέδαρθεν Ar.*Fr*.488.11, cf. Hp.*Epid*.5.37, X.*Ages*. 9.3: in pres., *to be falling asleep*, opp. ἀνεγείρεσθαι (to be waking), Pl.*Phd*.71d, 72b. 2. *pass the night*, κατέδαρθον ἐν Θησείῳ ἐν ὅπλοις Th.6.61: so in pf., Pl.*Smp*. l. c.

**καταδᾰτέομαι**, fut. -δάσομαι (v. infr.):—Med., *divide among themselves, tear and devour*, κύνες τε κατὰ πάντα δάσονται Il.22.354:—Pass., ὑπ' ἰχθύων καταδασθῆναι (nisi leg. κατεδεσθῆναι) Luc.*Demon*. 35; καταδέδασται· καταβέβρωται, καταμεμέρισται, Hsch. II. τὰν γᾶν κατεδασσάμεθα *divided, allotted* it, *Tab.Heracl*.2.28.

**καταδειδίττομαι**, = καταφοβέομαι, Hsch.

⊛**καταδεής** (A), ές, (καταδέω B) *wanting in, lacking*, c. gen., χρημάτων κ. ἀγγήϊα Hdt.2.121.β'; abs., of persons, *needy*, v.l. for ἐπιδεής, D.10. 36; κ. τάφος a *sorry, shabby* burial, Pl.*Lg*.719e; κ. τὴν ἡλικίαν *under* age, *POxy*.54.2 (iii A.D.). 2. more freq. in Comp., καταδεέστερος *weaker, inferior*, Isoc.2.7, D.27.2, Phld.*Piet*.7, etc.; καταδεέστερός τινος τῷ τάχει, πρὸς τὸ φρονεῖν, Isoc.3.5, 5.18, cf. Thphr. *Char.Prooem*.3. II. Adv. -δεῶς, mostly in Comp., καταδεέστερον Isoc.5.84, 6.67; -τέρως Id.12.37; -τέρως ἔχειν περί τι to be *very ill off* in a thing, D.48.55; τῶν ἀντιδίκων -τέρως ἔχειν πρὸς τὸ λέγειν Arist. *Rh.Al*.1442ᵃ16.

**καταδεής** (B), ές, (καταδείδω) *timid*, ἵππος Poll.1.197, cf. 3.136. Adv. -δεῶς ib.137.

**καταδεῖ**, impers., *there is wanting*, v. καταδέω (B).

**καταδείδω**, only in aor. -δεῖσαι, and (in Phalar. infr. cit.) fut. -δείσειν:—*fear greatly*, τι Ar.*Pax*759 (anap.), And.4.1, Th.2.93; τὸν Ἀχιλλέα Jul.*Or*.2.53b; περί τινος Ph.2.102; μή.. ib.590. II. *put into great fear, scare*, Phalar.*Ep*.91.

⊛**καταδείκνῡμι**, Ion. aor. κατέδεξα, *discover and make known*, τὸν Ταρτησσὸν οὗτοί εἰσι οἱ καταδέξαντες Hdt.1.163; Νεκῶ.. πρώτου καταδέξαντος (sc. τὴν Λιβύην περίρρυτον ἐοῦσαν) Id.4.42: folld. by a Conj., κατέδειξεν ἐναργῶς, ὡς.. Arist.*Fr*.673:—Pass., c. part., κατεδέδεκτο ἐοῦσα οὐδὲν χρηστή *had been proved* to be.., Hdt.7.215. 2. *invent and teach, introduce*, προαγωγούς Ar.*Ra*.1079 (anap.); τέχνην Antiph. 123.1, cf. Diod.Com.2.4; ἰατρικήν Pl.*R*.407d, cf. 406c; τελετάς D.25. 11; τὸν οἶνον τοὺς θεοὺς θνητοῖς καταδεῖξαι *Com.Adesp*.106.2: c. inf.,

*show how* to do, ἐπὶ τὰ κράνεα λόφους ἐπιδέεσθαι Κᾶρές εἰσι οἱ καταδέξαντες Hdt.1.171; οἱ πατέρες ἡμῶν ἐν ταῖς φονικαῖς δίκαις κατέδειξαν τέμνοντας τὰ τόμια ἐξορκίζεσθαι Aeschin.2.87; κ. τοῖς λαοῖς θεοὺς σέβεσθαι D.S.1.45: both constr. joined, τελετάς θ' ἡμῖν κατέδειξε φόνων τ' ἀπέχεσθαι Ar.*Ra.*1032, cf. 1062.

**καταδειλιάω,** *show cowardice,* D.61.28; *spoil by cowardice,* οὐδέν X.*An.*7.6.22.

**καταδειμαίνω,** *fear,* τὸ μέγεθος τῆς φύσεως Eun.*VS* p.487 B.

**καταδειπν-έω,** *eat at a meal,* τὸν Ἆπιν Plu.2.355c; ταῦρον Ael.*VH* 1.24. **-ον,** τό, = δεῖπνον, οἰωνῶν Man.4.200 (pl.).

**καταδεκ-τέον,** *one must accept,* Ps.-Gem. in Iriarte *Cat.Cod.Matr.* 389. **-τικός,** ή, όν, *receptive,* Simp. *in Cat.*247.34.

⊛**κατάδενδρος,** ον, *thickly wooded,* Nymphod.12, D.S.17.68, Ael. *Tact.*35.4; τὰ κ. [τῶν ὀρέων] *Gp.*2.6.1.

**καταδέομαι,** *entreat earnestly,* c. gen. pers., Pl.*Ap.*33e, Lxx *Ge.* 42.21, al.

⊛**καταδέρκομαι,** aor. 1 κατεδέρχθην S.*Tr.*999 (anap.): aor. 2 κατέδρᾰκον Opp.*H.*1.10 (tm.):—poet. for καθοράω, *look down upon,* αὐτοὺς Ἠέλιος..καταδέρκεται ἀκτίνεσσιν Od.11.16; μανίας ἄνθος καταδερχθῆναι S.l.c., cf. *Lyr.Adesp.*87; ἐπὶ χθόνα κ. ἀκτίνεσσι *h.Cer.*70.

**καταδερμᾰτόω,** in Pass., *to be covered with hide,* Hsch. s.v. κατερρινωμένον.

**καταδέρω,** *flay*: hence, in Pass., *to be subject to extortion,* aor. 2 inf. καταδᾰρῆναι Anon. *in Rh.*117.35.

⊛**κατάδεσις,** εως, ἡ, *binding fast,* Plu.2.771a. II. *binding by magic knots*: hence, *spells, enchantments,* in pl., Pl.*Lg.*933a.

**κατάδεσμα,** ατος, τό, = κατάδεσμος II, *PMag.Lond.*121.299 (pl., abbrev.):—but pl. **κατάδεσμα,** τά, = κατάδεσμος I, *IG*1².314.43.

**καταδεσμ-εύω,** *bind up,* τραύματα Lxx *Si.*30.7. 2. *bind on,* *Gp.* 12.21 (Pass.). II. *inhibit by means of a spell,* τινα *PMag.Lond.* 46.321; τὸν νοῦν τινος ib.326. III. *bind fast, retain,* κ. δὶς *repeat,* Lxx *Si.*7.8. **-έω,** = foreg., *Gloss.* ⊛**-ος,** ὁ, *tie, band,* κ. ἥβης *bathing-drawers,* Theopomp.Com.37. II. = κατάδεσις II, -δέσμοις τοὺς θεοὺς πείθοντες Pl.*R.*364c, cf. Plot.4.4.40 (pl.), *PMag.Par.*1. 2176 (pl.); κ. καὶ φαρμακεῖαι Artem.1.77.

**καταδέτης,** ου, ὁ, *cross-beam, tie,* Apollod.*Poliorc.*141.10.

**καταδεύω,** *wet through,* κατέδευσας ἐπὶ στήθεσσι χιτῶνα οἴνου ἀποβλύζων Il.9.490; μήποτέ σ'..νέφος ἀμφικαλύψῃ..κατὰ θ' εἵματα δεύσῃ Hes.*Op.*556; ἵν' οὔατα μὴ καταδεύῃ that [the rain] *may* not *wet* your ears, ib.546; of a river, *water,* πεδίον E.*Ph.*827 (anap.). II. metaph., ὁ -όμενος τῇ καρδίᾳ he whose heart *is easily melted,* Lxx *Ex.* 35.5.

⊛**καταδέχομαι,** Arc. κατυ- *SIG*306.58 (iv B.C.):—*receive, admit,* τι εἰς τὴν ψυχήν Pl.*R.*401e; [τὸν θεὸν] τῇ σκηνῇ J.*AJ*3.8.1; πάσαις ταῖς πύλαις τὴν ἡδονήν Luc.*Nigr.*16; esp. of food, τοὺς φακοὺς Eup. 350; πόμα Hp.*Epid.*7.41; τροφήν Pl.*Ti.*84b, cf. Arist.*Resp.*476ª29:—Pass., -δεχθῆναι ἐπὶ γάμον Luc.*Tox.*44. 2. *receive back, take home again,* esp. from banishment, And.3.3, Lys.6.13, D.26.6, etc.: aor. Pass. καταδεχθῆναι in pass. sense, Luc.*Bis Acc.*31, D.C.78.39: fut. καταδεχθήσεσθαι ib.40.40. 3. *accept, admit the truth of,* τὸ γενεθλιαλογεῖν Str.16.1.6. 4. *allow, permit of,* ἀναβολήν Suid. s.v. εἰσαγγελία; τὴν μῖξιν Phlp. *in GC*189.6.

⊛**καταδέω** (A), fut. -δήσω, *bind on* or *to, bind fast,* πρυμνήσια, ἱστόν, Il.1.436 (tm.), Od.2.425 (tm.); ἵππους μὲν κατέδησαν..ἱμᾶσι φάτνῃ ἐφ' ἱππείῃ Il.10.567; ἐπ' ἀμβροσίῃσι κάπῃσιν 8.434; ἐμὲ μὲν κατέδησαν ..ἐνὶ νηΐ Od.14.345; κ. λάρνακας Hdt.3.123:—Pass., καταδεδεμένος τοὺς ὀφθαλμοὺς Hdt.2.122; ἐν φόβῳ καταδεθεῖσα E.*Ion* 1498 (lyr.) (so μανίῃ καταδεῖ τινα Hermesian.7.85); καταδεῖται ψυχὴ ὑπὸ σώματος Pl. *Phd.*83d; γλῶττα -δεδεμένη Arist.*HA*492ᵇ32:—Med., *bind to oneself,* ἀγχόνιον βρόχον κατεδήσατο E.*Hel.*687 (lyr.); σπόγγους περὶ τὰ ὦτα Arist.*Pr.*960ᵇ15: metaph., ἀριθμῷ καταδήσασθαι *tie up for oneself* in lots, D.H.*Rh.*11.3; καταδησαμένη τινὰ ὁρκίοις Parth.12.3. b. κ. τι ἀπό or ἔκ τινος, metaph., *establish securely,* τὴν διὰ πάντων διήκουσαν ὠφέλειαν ἀπὸ [τοῦ συλλογισμοῦ] Procl. *in Alc.*p.252 C., cf. Simp. *in de An.*15.34. 2. *bind up,* θραῦμα, τραύματα, Lxx *Si.*27.21, *Ev. Luc.*10.34. 3. *put in bonds, imprison,* Hdt.3.143, Th.8.15, Pl.*Ti.* 70e, etc.; κ. τὴν ἐπὶ θανάτῳ (sc. δέσιν) Hdt.5.72. 4. *convict of* a crime, opp. ἀπολύω, c. inf., κ. τινὰ φῶρα εἶναι Hdt.2.174, cf. 4.68. II. *tie down, stop, check,* ἀνέμων κατέδησε κελεύθους or κέλευθα, Od.5.383, 10.20; ὅς μοι ἐφορμήσας ἀνέμους κατέδησε κελεύθου 7.272, cf. 4.380; τοῦ γε θεοὶ κατὰ νόστον ἔδησαν 14.61. III. *bind by spells, enchant* (with fut. -δήσομαι Theoc.2.3), Din.*Fr.*6.7 (Pass.), *SIG*1175.2 (iv/iii B.C.), etc.; κ. τὸ ἐργαστήριόν τινος *Tab.Defix.*71.2 (iii B.C.); κ. τινὰ γλῶτταν καὶ ψυχὴν καὶ λόγον *Tab.Defix.Aud.*49.1 (iv/iii B.C.); γοητεῦσαι καὶ κ., of Cleopatra, D.C.50.5:—Pass., *Tab.Defix.*107ª2, Clearch.38, Plu.2.378f; cf. καταδηνύω, καταδίδημι.

**καταδέω** (B), *lack, need,* c. gen., esp. of numbers, ἡ [ὁδὸς] καταδέει πεντεκαίδεκα σταδίων [ὡς] μὴ εἶναι πεντακοσίων Hdt.2.7; πυραμίδα.. εἴκοσι ποδῶν καταδέουσαν τριῶν πλέθρων *wanting* 20 feet of 3 plethra, ib.134; ἕνδεκα μυριάδες ἦσαν, μιῆς χιλιάδος..καταδέουσαι Id.9.30, cf. 70; [τὸ ναυτικὸν] δύο νεῶν κατέδεε ἐς τὸν ἀριθμόν *there was a lack* of two ships, 8.82 (unless κατέδεε be impersonal). 2. *come after, be behind,* Θῆβαι ἀνδρὸς ἰδιώτου καταδέουσιν εἰς εὐδαιμονίαν Paus.8.33.2.

**καταδηϊόω,** contr. -δηόω, *ravage, waste,* in Pass., D.H.11.42 (interpol.).

**καταδηλέομαι,** *injure, violate,* Men.Prot.p.108 D.: Elean forms καδαλέοιτο, καδαλήμενοι, *Schwyzer* 413.8,6; καζαλήμενον ib.418.19.

**κατάδηλος,** ον, *manifest, visible,* τούτοις οὐ κ. ἦν ἡ μάχη ὑπὸ τοῦ.. ὄρους Th.4.44; κ. γενέσθαι *to be discovered,* Hdt.1.5, 3.68; κ. μᾶλλον ..τὰ τῶν Χίων ἐφάνη Th.8.10; κατάδηλον ποιῆσαι make *known, discover,* Hdt.3.88, cf. Phld.*Vit.Herc.*1457.10: c. part., φυλάσσων κ. ἔσται S.*OC*1214 (lyr.); κ. γίγνονται προσποιούμενοι Pl.*Ap.*23d, etc.; κ. ὦσιν ὅτι.., κ. ἔσται ὡς.., Id.*Prt.*342b, 355b, cf. Arist.*Top.*109ᵇ2, *Ep.Hebr.*7.15, etc. Adv. -λως Poll.6.207.

**κατάδημα,** ατος, τό, *band, fastening,* Arist.*Pr.*938ª14.

**καταδημᾰγωγέω,** *conquer by the arts of a demagogue,* τινα Plu.2. 482d, cf. Arr.*Fr.*150 J.:—Pass., Plu.*Per.*9; *to be won by such arts,* Id. *Cleom.*13, etc.

**καταδημο-βορέω,** *consume,* λαοῖσι δότω -δημοβορῆσαι Il.18.301. **-κοπέω,** *overcome by courting popularity,* τοὺς πολεμίους App.*Mith.*19.

**καταδηνύω,** = καταδέω (A) III, *Tab.Defix.*75ª1 (iii B.C.).

**καταδήω,** = foreg., *Tab.Defix.Aud.*73.1.

**καταδιαίρ-εσις,** εως, ἡ, *division,* τοῦ κανόνος Phld.*Mus.*p.100 K.; τοῦ κλήρου *PTeb.*376.27 (ii A.D.). ⊛ **-έω,** *divide,* τὴν Ἐρυθρὰν θάλασσαν Lxx *Ps.*135(136).13; τὸν κύκλον εἰς δώδεκα μοίρας S.E.*M.*5.23:—Pass., κ. ἐς τὰ μέρη Asclep.*Tact.*10.22. 2. *distribute,* τὸ πλῆθος εἰς λόχους D.H.4.19, cf. *CPR*22.25 (ii A.D.):—Med., *distribute among themselves,* Lxx *Jo.*3(4).2, Plb.2.45.1, D.S.3.29. 3. *analyse,* τὰς συνδρομάς Gal.1.158.

**καταδῐαιτάω,** *decide as arbitrator against* one, *give judgement against,* opp. ἀποδ-, ὁ διαιτητὴς οὐ κατεδιῄτα, ἀλλ' ἀπιὼν ᾤχετο ἀποδιαιτήσας τούτου τὴν δίαιταν D.49.19, cf. 21.84; οἷός τ' ἦν πείθειν αὐτόν, ἣν κατεδεδιῃτήκει, ταύτην ἀποδεδιῃτημένην ἀποφαίνειν ib.85; ἔρημον κ. τινὸς [δίκην] *give judgement* in default *against* one, Id.21. 92, cf. 40.17, Luc.*Pr.Im.*15: metaph., *condemn,* c. gen., Alciphr.1. 31:—Med., καταδιαιτᾶσθαι δίαιτάν τινος *to be the cause of an arbitration being given against* one, Lys.25.16.

**καταδιαλλάσσω,** *reconcile again,* aor. 2 Pass. -διηλλάγην Ar.*V.* 1284.

**καταδια-σπλεκόω,** strengthd. for σπλεκόω, v.l. in Sch.Ar.*Pl.* 1082. **-φθείρω,** *squander,* τὰ πατρῷα Eup.44. 2. in Pass., *to be consumed,* ἐν πυρὶ Luc.*Tim.*44 (s.v.l.). **-χέω,** *diffuse completely,* Arist.*Spir.*483ᵇ21 (Pass.).

⊛**καταδίδημι,** = καταδέω (A) III, *Tab.Defix.*42.1 (iii B.C.), al.: Dor. καδδίδημι ib.74.1.

⊛**καταδίδωμι,** *assign,* τὰ ἀριστεῖα τῆς ἐν λόγοις δεινότητός τινι D.H. *Comp.*18. II. intr., of a channel, *open into,* ἡ Προποντὶς καταδιδοῖ ἐς τὸν Ἑλλήσποντον Hdt.4.85, cf. Plu.*Fab.*6.

**καταδιήγησις,** εως, ἡ, *pure narrative,* Fortunat.*Rh.*2.19.

**καταδιΐστημι,** strengthd. for διΐστημι, Hsch., Phot.

⊛**καταδῐκ-άζω,** *give judgement* or *sentence against* a person, *condemn,* opp. ἀποδικάζω:—Constr.: c. gen. pers. et acc. rei, κ. τινὸς θάνατον Hdt.1.45; τὴν διπλασίαν (sc. ζημίαν) Lexap.D.24.105; πολλὴν μοχθηρίαν J.*Ap.*1.24; πολλὴν τὴν ἀπόγνωσιν Luc.*Merc.Cond.*11: c. gen. pers. et inf., κ. σεαυτοῦ τὰ ἔσχατα παθεῖν X.*Cyr.*3.1.9, cf. *An.* 6.6.15: c. gen. pers. only, Luc.*DMort.*29.2: abs., Pl.*Lg.*958c; τᾶν ψάφων ταὶ -δικάζουσαι *SIG*953.83 (Calymna, ii B.C.):—Med., *get sentence given against* a person, δίκην καταδικάσασθαί τινος Th.5.49, D.21. 176; κ. τινός, without acc., Lys.23.14, D.47.18; κ. τινὸς χρημάτων *get* a person *condemned* [to a payment] of money, Paus.6.3.7: abs., Pl. *Lg.*857a, *PHal.*1.65 (iii B.C.), etc.:—Pass., καταδικασθεὶς *condemned,* Pl.*Lg.*958c; ὑπὸ ἐχθρῶν Phld.*Ir.*p.51 W.; ἐπὶ φόνῳ *for* murder, D.S. 4.76; ἐπὶ κακουργίᾳ Id.3.12; later καταδικασθῆναι θανάτῳ *to be condemned* to death, Id.13.101, etc.; θάνατον D.C.68.1; τὴν ἐπὶ θανάτῳ Artem.4.60; φυγήν App.*Ital.*3; εἰς ἀλαβαστρῶνα *Sammelb.*4639. 2 (iii A.D.); εἰς δοῦλον, εἰς νῆσον, Artem.4.65, 5.21: c. inf., καταδικάζεται ἀποθανεῖν Luc.*VH*1.29; of the sentence, ἀντέλεγον μὴ δικαίως σφῶν καταδεδικάσθαι *that judgement had been given against* them unjustly, Th.5.49; later -δικασθείσης αὐτοῦ δίκης *PHal.*1.44 (iii B.C.), cf. *PLille* 29.6 (iii B.C.); of fines imposed, τὰ -θέντα ἐκπραξέω *IG*2². 1126.5 (Amphict. Delph.). II. Med., *have judgement given in one's favour,* Is.4.9, 10.24. III. *declare by express judgement,* ὅτι.. X.*An.*5.8.21. IV. Pass., *to be bound by* a law, Men.Prot.p.39 D. **-αστής,** οῦ, ὁ, *one who condemns,* τοῦ πατρὸς Iamb.*VP*25. 113. **-αστικός,** ή, όν, *condemnatory,* Sch.Ar.*V.*167. ⊛ **-η,** ἡ, *judgement given against* one, *sentence,* Epich.148.5, Plb.25.3.1 (pl.), Lxx *Wi.*12.27, Phld.*Rh.*1.12 S., *Act.Ap.*25.15, Plu.*Cor.*29, *PGnom.*208 (ii A.D.); κ. εἰς μονομάχους Artem.4.65. 2. *damages* or *fine,* Th.5. 49, 50, D.47.52, *PHal.*1.52 (iii B.C.); μετεῖναι αὐτῷ τὸ ἥμισυ τῆς κ. *IG* 12(8).267.16 (Thasos, iii B.C.), cf. *Tab.Heracl.*1.156 (pl.). **-ος,** ον, (δίκη) *having judgement given against* one, *found guilty, condemned,* *SIG*484.1 (Delph., iii B.C.): c. gen., φυγῆς *to* banishment, D.S.13.63; θανάτου Id.27.1; *mulcted in,* μυρίων στατήρων *GDI*2516.7 (Delph.): abs., J.*AJ*5.1.14, Arr.*Epict.*4.11.24, App.*BC*1.2, *CIG*2759b (Aphrodisias).

**καταδιφθερόω,** *cover over with skins,* Plu.2.664c.

**καταδιφρεύω,** *throw down from a chariot,* Eust.183.38.

**καταδίχιον,** τό, = *καδδίχιον, Dim. of κάδδιχος, *IG*14.427 i 15, al. (Tauromenium).

⊛ **καταδίψιον·** εἶδος καύματος, Hsch. (fort. κατὰ δ. ἴδος· ⟨ὥρᾳ⟩ κ.).

**καταδῐωκτικός,** ή, όν, *pursuing,* τινος Horap.2.90.

**καταδιώκω,** *follow hard upon, pursue closely,* Th.1.49, 2.84, Lxx *Ps.*17(18).38, *PCair.Zen.*439 (Pass., iii B.C.), Phld.*Ir.*p.29 W., etc.: metaph., *try to gain,* Plb.6.42.1. 2. *search for,* τινα *Ev.Marc.*1. 36. 3. *overdrive* cattle, Lxx *Ge.*33.13.

**καταδοκέω,** prop. *think* or *suppose* a thing *to* any one's *prejudice,* c. inf., κ. τινὰ ποιέειν τι *suspect* one *of..,* Hdt.3.27; σφέας κ. εἶναι κλῶπας Id.6.16: with inf. understood, Id.1.22, 3.69: c. dat. pers., τοῖσι

κατεδόκεον νεοχμὸν ἄν τι ποιέειν Id.9.99: c. acc. neut., τάδε καταδόξας ..σφέας ἐθελοκακέειν Id.8.69:—Pass., *to be suspected*, ὑφ' ὑμῶν Antipho 2.2.3: also c. inf., καταδοχθεὶς φονεὺς εἶναι Id.2.2.2; later in good sense, καταδόξαντα [ὑπέρμεγαν] εἶναι τοῖς τότε ἀνθρώποις *who was recognized* to be great by his contemporaries, Numen.ap.Eus.*PE*14.8. 2. generally, *guess*, οὐ γὰρ ἄν κοτε κατέδοξα ἔνθεν ἦν *should* never *have guessed* whose son he was, Hdt.1.111.

**κατ-ᾱδολεσχέω**, *chatter at, weary by chattering*, καταδολεσχήσει ἐπ' ἐμὲ ἡ ψυχή μου Lxx *La*.3.20; τινος Plu.2.22a; ταῦτα ἴσως -ηδολέσχησά σου Jul.*Ep*.32: pf. -ηδολέσχηκα Plu.2.503b: abs., *PSI*5.495.3:—Pass., pf. part. κατηδολεσχημένος Suid. s. v. διατεθρυλημένος τὰ ὦτα.

**καταδοξάζω**, = καταδοκέω, X.*An*.7.7.30, D.S.32.10:—Pass., ibid. 2. *form a wrong opinion*, Epicur.*Nat*.2.9, *Herc*.1413.4; ὑπέρ τινος D.H.6.10.

**κατάδοσις**, εως, ἡ, *instalment* of a payment, *POxy*.1632.21 (iv A. D.).

**καταδουλ-εύομαι**, *reduce to slavery*, Sm.*Le*.27.17, f. l. in Eus. Mynd.*Fr*.10 (v. καταδουλόω I. 2). -ίζω, = foreg., *IG*9(1).119 (Elatea):—but usu. Med., -ίζομαι *GDI*1701.7, al. (Delph.): aor. καταδουλίξασθαι *IG*9(1).42 (Stiris). -ισμός, ὁ, *enslavement*, ἅπτεσθαι or ἐφάπτεσθαί τινος ἐπὶ καταδουλισμῷ, *GDI*1685.5, 1686.8, al. (Delph.). -ος, ὁ, *slave*, κ. παῖς *PStrassb*.40.24 (vi A. D.). -όω, *reduce to slavery, enslave*, Ἀθήνας Hdt.6.109; τὴν Ἑλλάδα Id.8.144; Ἀθηναίοις κ. Κέρκυραν Th.3.70; νῆσον βασιλεῖ Isoc.9.20:—Pass., κατεδεδούλωντο Hdt.5.116; κατεδουλώθησαν Id.6.32; καταδεδουλωμένος ὑπό τινος Pl.*Smp*.219e: abs., Lys.18.5. 2. more freq. in Med., *make a slave to oneself, enslave*, τὴν μητρόπολιν Hdt.7.51, cf. Pl.*R*.351b; τινας X.*Mem*.2.1.13, cf. *GDI*4982 (Gortyn), *PEleph*.3.3 (iii B. C.), etc.; ἡ τύχη τὸ σῶμα κατεδουλώσατο Philem.95.8; τὸ κρέσσον τῷ χείρονι -εύμενοι (Ion. for -ούμενοι) Eus.Mynd.*Fr*.10; κ. τὸν Ἰσραὴλ δουλείαν Lxx 1*Ma*.8.18; ἔργα ὧν κατεδουλοῦντο αὐτούς ib.*Ex*.1.14. II. metaph., *enslave in mind*, παιδισκάριόν με καταδεδούλωκ' εὐτελές Men.338, cf. 2*Ep.Cor*.11.20; κ. τὴν ψυχήν *PMag.Lond*.123.4 (iv/v A. D.); *break in spirit*, καταδουλοῖ τὴν τόλμαν ἡ ἀνάγκη App.*Pun*.81. 2. more freq. in Med., ἡ ἀνάγκη καταδουλοῦται τὴν γνώμην Hp.*Fract*.15; οἴει τι μᾶλλον καταδουλοῦσθαι ἀνθρώπους τοῦ ἰσχυροῦ φόβου; X.*Cyr*.3.1.23, cf. E.*IA*1269; κ. τὰς ψυχάς Isoc.12.178; τὸ λογιστικόν Pl.*R*.553d; τὰς ἐπιθυμίας Aristox.*Fr.Hist*.15. -ωσις, εως, ἡ, *enslavement*, Th.3.10, 7.66, Pl.*Lg*.776d, *GDI* 1869.7 (Delph.), *Mémoires de la mission arch. de Perse* 20.85 (Susa, ii B. C.).

**καταδουπέω**, *fall with a loud heavy sound, crash*, aor. 2, τυπεὶς κατέδουπε κεραυνῷ *AP*7.637 (Antip.).

**Κατάδουποι**, ων, οἱ, *the first Cataract* of the Nile, Hdt.2.17 (in gen. -δούπων), Thphr.*Lap*.34, Philostr.*VA*6.23, Plin.*HN*5.54; *Catadupa*, neut. pl., Cic.*Somn.Scip*.5.

**καταδοχή**, ἡ, *receiving back, restoration* of exiles, Pl.*Lg*.867e; *reception* of soul by body, Porph.*Sent*.35; τοῦ θεοῦ Id.*Marc*.19. II. *receptacle*, Gal.14.713.

**καταδράθω**, v. καταδαρθάνω.

**καταδράσσομαι**, *lay hold of*, τῆς φθοροποιοῦ δυνάμεως -δραξαμένης τῶν σωμάτων Dsc.*Ther.Praef.*; *grasp, apprehend*, τῆς ἀληθείας Procl. *in Prm*.p.534 S.; τῆς λέξεως τοῦ Πλάτωνος Id.*in Ti*.3.107 D.; [τοῦ ὅλως ἀγαθοῦ] Id. *in Alc*.p.153 C., cf. Olymp.*in Alc*.p.194 C.

❀ **καταδρέπω**, *strip off*, τῶν δενδρέων τὰ φύλλα Hdt.8.115.

❀ **καταδρομή**, ἡ, *inroad, raid*, Th.1.142; ἐνέδραι καὶ κ. Id.5.56; καταδρομὰς ποιεῖσθαι Id.7.27, etc.; κ. γενομένης Lys.20.28; ὥσπερ κ. ἐποιήσω ἐπὶ τὸν λόγον μου Pl.*R*.472a; *charge*, of troops in battle, Lxx 2*Ma*.5.3; *assault*, *PRein*.18.19 (pl., ii B. C.). 2. metaph., *attack, invective*, κ. μέλλει περὶ ἐμοῦ ποιεῖσθαι Aeschin.1.135, cf. D.H.*Th*.3; κατά τινος Plb.12.23.1; ἐν καταδρομῆς μέρει λέγεται περί τινος S.E.*M*.2.43. II. *recourse*, κ. γίγνεται ἐπί.. A.D.*Pron*.25.15. III. *lurking-place, lair, den*, δακέτου Ael.*NA*2.9, cf. 5.49 (pl.); ὕπαντροι ἢ λοχμώδεις κ. ib.9.1. 2. perh. = *cryptoporticus*, *IGRom*.4.159.23 (Cyzicus).

**κατάδρομος**, ον, *overrun, wasted*, μέλαθρα πυρὶ κ. E.*Tr*.1300 (lyr.). II. Subst., *course* or *lists for exercising in*, Suet.*Ner*.11.

**καταδροσίζω**, *drench*, v. l. in Sch.Pi.*O*.6.88 (Pass.).

**κατάδρυμμα**, ατος, τό, (καταδρύπτω) *tearing, rending*, σαρκῶν.. καταδρύμματα χειρῶν *of* flesh *with* hands, E.*Supp*.51.

**κατάδρυμος**, ον, *thickly wooded*, Str.4.5.2.

**καταδρύπτω**, *tear in pieces, rend*, τὸ πρόσωπον *AP*5.42 (Rufin., v. l. for -τρίψεις); παρειάς ib.7.487 (Pers.), cf. M.Ant.6.20:—Med., κατὰ δ' ἐδρύπτοντο παρειάς Hes.*Sc*.243.

**καταδρῠφάσσω**, *hedge* or *fence in*, Lyc.239.

**καταδῠναστ-εία**, ἡ, *oppression*, Lxx *Ex*.6.7, al., Aristeas 23. -εύω, *oppress*, τινα Lxx *Ex*.1.13, al.; τοὺς πτωχοὺς ἀπὸ τῆς γῆς ib.*Am*.8.4: metaph., δέδοικα μὴ πλοῦτός με -εύσῃ X.*Smp*.5.8; τινος D.S.13.73, *Ep.Jac*.2.6: abs., Str.16.1.26, Ph.1.421, Plu.2.367d:—Pass., *to be oppressed*, *PPetr*.3 p.74 (iii B. C.), Lxx *Ne*.5.5, D.S.37.8; ὑπό τινος Str.6.2.4; ὑπὸ τοῦ διαβόλου *Act.Ap*.10.38; ταῦτα-εύετο ἕκαστα these districts *were under their* several *rulers*, Str.7.7.8. 2. *get control*, abs., of mutineers, Ps.-Ptol.*Centil*.56.

**καταδύνω**, v. καταδύω.

**κατά-δῠσις**, εως, ἡ, *dipping*: hence, *setting*, of stars, in pl., Hipparch.2.6.1, Ptol.*Tetr*.140: metaph., κ. εὐλογιστίας, opp. ἀνατολὴ ἀφροσύνης, Ph.1.415. 2. of a river, *descent into* an underground course, Str.8.8.4. 3. generally, *going down into, descent*, Luc. *VH*1.33. II. *hiding-place, hole*, Id.*Am*.34, Ph.1.315, Ath.11.477d, Gal.11.167 (pl.). 2. *depth*, Sm.*Ps*.68(69).3. 3. = θαλάμη, Erot. s. v. ὑποφρον. III. *present world* (as subject to *decline*), Aq.*Ps*.16(17).14, Id., Sm.*Ps*.48(49).2; so of *human life*, Aq.*Ps*.38 (39).6. IV. rendering of Hebr. *miphleseth* 'a thing to shudder at', Lxx 3*Ki*.15.13. V. (καταδύω II. 2) *ducking* of the head in a bath, Orib.*Fr*.48. -δυστής, οῦ, ὁ, *one who dips under*, Hsch. s. v. καταυστής.

**καταδῠσωπέω**, strengthd. for δυσωπέω, *put to the blush* by earnest intreaty, τινα Luc.*Sacr*.3.

**κατάδῦτος**, ἡ, = κατάδυσις II. 2, Quint.*Ps*.87(88).7. 2. = κατάδυσις III, Al.ib.48(49).2.

**καταδύω** or -δύνω: I. intr., in Act. pres. καταδύνω and Med. καταδύομαι: fut. -δύσομαι: aor. -εδυσάμην, Ep. 2 and 3 sg. -δύσεο, -δύσετο:—Act., aor. 2 κατέδυν: pf. καταδέδῦκα:—*go down, sink, set*, esp. of the sun (as Hom. always in aor. 2 Act.), ἠέλιος κατέδυ Il.1.475, etc.; ἅμα..ἠελίῳ καταδύντι ib.592; ἐς ἠέλιον καταδύντα Od.10.183; ἠελίοιο -δυομένοιο *h.Merc*.197; καταδεδυκέναι τὴν [νῆσον] κατὰ θαλάσσης Hdt.7.235; also of ships, *to be sunk* or *disabled*, Id.8.90, Th.2.92, 7.34, X.*HG*1.6.35, etc.; also οἱ ἱππεῖς καταδύνοντες ἐν τέλμασιν Plb. 5.47.2; κ. ὑφ' ὕδατι *duck* under water, Batr.89; καταδεδυκώς *having popped down*, Ar.*V*.140. 2. *go down, plunge into*, c. acc., καταδῦναι ὅμιλον Il.10.231, etc.; κατεδύσετο πουλὺν ὅμιλον ib.517; καταδύσεο μῶλον Ἄρηος 18.134; so μάχην, δόμον, πόλιν καταδύμεναι, 3.241, 8.375, Od.4.246: folld. by Prep., μυῖαι καδδῦσαι (Ep. for καταδ-) κατὰ..ὠτειλάς Il.19.25; σπάργαν' ἔσω κατέδυνε *h.Merc*.237; καταδυσόμεθ'.. εἰς Ἀΐδαο δόμους we *shall go down* into.., Od.10.174; so καταδύνειν ἐς ὕλην Hdt.9.37, cf. 4.76; εἰς φάραγγας, of hares, X.*Cyn*.5.16; εἰς ἅπασαν [τὴν πόλιν] Pl.*R*.576e; κατὰ τῆς γῆς Hdt.4.132; κατὰ τέφρας πολλῆς Plu.*Cam*.32; of souls, εἰς βυθὸν κ. Plu.2.943d: c. dat., *sink into*, ταῖς ὁμοιοπαθείαις Metrod.*Fr*.38: freq. with a notion of secrecy, *insinuate oneself, steal into*, καταδύεται εἰς τὸ ἐντὸς τῆς ψυχῆς ὅ τε ῥυθμὸς καὶ ἁρμονία Pl.*R*.401d; ἡ ἀναρχία εἰς τὰς ἰδίας οἰκίας κ. ib. 562e; κ. ἡ ψῦξις ἕως πλείστου the cold *penetrates* most, Gal.15.90, cf. 6.178. 3. *slink away and lie hid*, καταδύεσθαι ὑπὸ τῆς αἰσχύνης X.*Cyr*.6.1.35, cf. D.21.199 (so abs., *to be overcome with shame*, ἐπὶ τῇ ἀγνοίᾳ Zos.5.40); καταδεδυκὼς ἐν τῇ οἰκίᾳ Pl.*R*.579b; εἰς ἄπορον ὁ σοφιστὴς τόπον καταδέδυκεν Id.*Sph*.239c, etc. 4. *get into, put on*, κατέδυ κλυτὰ τεύχεα Il.6.504, cf. Od.12.228; κατεδύσετο τεύχεα καλά Il.7.103; εἵματα Mosch.4.102. II. causal, *make to sink*, rare in pres., ἐμπίπτων καὶ καταδύων Pherecr.12; ἐμὲ καταδύουσι τῷ ἄχει X.*Cyr*.6.1.37: mostly in aor. 1, γαύλους καταδύσας Hdt.6.17; in naval warfare, καταδῦσαι ναῦν *cut* it *down to the water's edge, disable* it, Id.8.87, al., Ar.*Ra*.49, Th.1.50; ἥλιον ἐν λέσχῃ κατεδύσαμεν we *let* the sun *go down* in talk, Call.*Ep*.2, cf. Aristaenet.1.24. 2. *duck*, τὴν κεφαλήν, in a bath, Herod.Med.ap.Orib.10.37.13.

**κατ-ᾴδω**, uncontr. -αείδω, *sing to*: hence, I. trans., *charm, appease by singing*, τινα D.H.4.29, Plu.2.745e, Luc.*JTr*.39, *Philops*. 31: c. dat., *sing a spell* or *incantation* (ἐπῳδή) to.., καταείδοντες.. τῷ ἀνέμῳ Hdt.7.191:—Pass., *to be induced by charms* to do a thing, c. inf., Ael.*NA*5.25 (dub. l.). b. κ. δεῖπνον *enliven* a repast *by song*, Id.*VH*7.2. 2. *sing in mockery*, Luc.*DMort*.2.2:—Pass., *to have* another *sing before one*, Id.*Bis Acc*.16. 3. *fill with song*, τὰς λόχμας Longus 1.9: c. gen., ἀηδὼν κ. τῶν ἐρημαίων χωρίων Ael.*NA* 1.43. II. c. acc. cogn., *sing by way of incantation*, κατῇδε βάρβαρα μέλη μαγεύουσ' E.*IT*1337. III. intr., *sing from above* or *sing throughout* a place, of birds or insects, Ael.*VH*3.1, *NA*1.20.

**καταδωροδοκέω**, *betray in return for bribes*, Ar.*V*.1036, Lys.27.3:—Med., Ar.*Ra*.361, Arist.*Pol*.1271$^a$3.

**καταείδω**, v. κατᾴδω. **καταειδώς**, v. κάτοιδα.

**καταειμένος**, η, ον, pf. part. Pass., 1. of καταέννυμι, Od.13.351. 2. of καθίημι, *hanging down over*, A.R.1.939, 3.830.

**καταείσατο**, 3 sg. aor. Med. (cf. εἴσομαι II, ἐπιείσομαι), ὅθι οἱ κ. γαίης where it *had sped* to earth, Il.11.358: also expld. as fr. εἴδω (εἴδομαι), where it *was visible* to him (he *descried* it) on the ground, Sch. l. c.

**καταέννῡμι** or -ειννύω, Ep. Verb, not found in the form καθέννυμι because of the digamma, only in impf., aor. Act., and pf. Pass.:—*clothe, cover*, θριξὶ δὲ πάντα νέκυν καταείνυσαν (aor., v. l. -είνυον) Il.23.135; νηοὺς αἵματι καπνῷ τε..κατείνυον Opp.*H*.2.673:—Pass., ὄρος καταειμένον ὕλῃ Od.13.351, 19.431, *h.Merc*.228, *h.Ven*.285; ἕδος κ. ὕλῃ *h.Ap*.225.

❀ **καταέρρω**, Aeol. for καταίρω, Alc.41 (tm.).

**καταϝελμένος**, v. κατειλέω. **καταϝέργω**, v. κατείργω. **καταϝοικίδδω**, v. κατοικίζω.

**κατ-αζαίνω**, *make dry, parch up*, καταζήνασκε δὲ δαίμων (Ion. aor. 1) Od.11.587.

**καταζάω**, v. καταζῶ.

❀ **κατάζευγ-μα**, ατος, τό, *cross-beams*, ὀροφῆς *IG*11(2).161 *A* 113 (Delos, iii B. C., pl.). -νῡμι and -νύω, *yoke together*, ἐν ἅρματα κ. σθένος ἵππιον Pi.*P*.2.11:—Pass., δύο πλοῖα κατεζευγμένα (v. l. χελώνας -μένας) D.S.20.85: metaph., *to be united*, ταῖς πρώτον οὕτω καταζευγνυμέναις πόλεσιν Pl.*Lg*.753e; of marriage, Ael.*VH*4.1. 2. in Pass., *to be straitened, confined*, ὑπ' ἀναγκαίης κατέζευχθε Hdt.8.22; ἐν τυμβήρει θαλάμῳ κατεζεύχθη S.*Ant*.947. 3. Pass., of a right angle, *to be made acute*, κἂν μικρῷ τινι μᾶλλον κατεζευγμένη ᾖ ἡ εὐθεῖα γωνία Asp.*in EN*19.32. II. intr., *fix one's quarters, halt, encamp*, ταῖς δυνάμεσι Plb.3.95.3, cf. Plu.*Sull*.25, etc.

**καταζευγοτροφέω**, *squander money on teams of horses*, Is.5.43.

**κατάζευξις**, εως, ἡ, *yoking*, τοῦ ζυγοῦ *Hippiatr*.103; βοῶν Porph.

*Abst.*3.18: metaph., of marriage, Plu.2.750c. II. opp. ἀνάζευξις, *encamping*, Id.*Sull.*28, etc.

**καταζηλόω**, *create prejudice against*, τινας Epicur.*Nat.*14.6.

**καταζήνασκε**, v. καταζαίνω.

**καταζητέω**, *search out*, Iamb.*VP*29.158 (Pass.); *hold inquiry into*, τι Just.*Nov.*123.18.1, cf. *Cod.Just.*1.3.41.26 (Pass.).

**καταζοφόω**, in Pass., *to be darkened*, Sch.E.*Hec.*912.

**καταζῠγίς**, ίδος, ἡ, iron *connecting-rod* in a torsion-engine, Ph. *Bel.*60.5 (s.v.l.), 64.31. II. as Adj., λίθοι κ. *connecting* stones, *PCair.Zen.*499.21 (iii B.C.).

**κατάζῡμος**, ον, *fermented*, ἄρτος Dieuch.ap.Orib.4.7.10.

**καταζῶ**, *live one's life out, live on*, ἐν ἀνακτόροις θεοῦ καταζῇ δεῦρ' ἀεὶ σεμνὸν βίον E.*Ion* 56, cf. Pl.*Smp.*192b, Arist.*EN*1100$^{b}$16, Plu.2.194a; ἐν ἡσυχίᾳ Phld.*Rh.*2.162 S., Plu.*Cic.*4.

**καταζωμεύω**, *sup up*, Hsch.

**κατα-ζώννῡμι**, *gird fast*:—Med., *gird for oneself*, δορὰς ὄφεσι κατεζώσαντο E.*Ba.*698; ἐν ἱματίοις κ. τοὺς χιτωνίσκους Plu.*Pyrrh.*27:—Pass., χιτῶνας μίτραις κατεζωσμένοι D.H.2.70. **-ζωσμα**, ατος, τό, gloss on ἔλατρον, Hsch. II. *body of initiates wearing a special girdle* (cf. καταζωστικός), prob. to be read in Buresch *Aus Lydien* p.12. **-ζώστης**, ου, ὁ, *girth, strap*, Hsch. ⊛**-ζωστικός**, ή, όν, *of* or *for girding*: τὸ κ. *work on the girding of sacred robes*, Suid. s.v. Ὀρφεύς.

⊛**κατ-άημι**, Ep. aor. part. καταέσσας, = κατακοιμηθείς (cf. ἄεσα), Hsch.: fut. καταήσεται· καταπνεύσει, Id.

**καταθᾰλαττόω**, *throw into the sea*, Tz. ad Lyc.712.

**καταθάλπω**, strengthd. for θάλπω, Plu.2.367d, D.L.7.152, Alciphr. 3.41.

**καταθαμβέομαι**, Pass., *to be astonished at*, c. acc., Plu.*Num.*15, *Fab.*26.

**καταθάπτω**, Ep. aor. inf. κατθάψαι Il.24.611:—*bury*, 19.228, A. *Ag.*1553 (lyr.), Lys.6.47, Isoc.19.22, Luc.*Philops.*24.

**καταθαρσ-έω**, later Att. **-θαρρέω**, *to be confident*, in pf. part., Plb. 1.40.3; κ. τοῖς ὅλοις *looking forward confidently to* a complete victory, Id.3.86.8; κατεθάρσησεν ὁ λαὸς ἐπὶ τοῖς λόγοις Lxx 2*Ch.*32.8: c. inf., *make bold to*.., παρεπιδείκνυσθαι δημοσίᾳ τὸ ἀνοσιούργημα Ph.2.220; τοῖς ὕδασι παραδοῦναι σφᾶς αὐτούς Agath.3.20. 2. c. gen., *behave boldly against*, τῆς τῶν Σπαρτιατῶν δυνάμεως D.S.15.34; χώρας Str. 12.8.6. 3. Pass., *to be confirmed*, *Cod.Just.*9.4.6.5. **-ύνω**, *embolden, encourage against*, τινὰ πρὸς τὸ μέλλον Plu.*Luc.*29:—Pass., in form **καταθρασύνομαι**, = foreg., Ph.1.41, Luc.*DMort.*21.2, D.L.2. 127: c. gen., πρὸς τοὺς ἀλόγως -ομένους τῶν ἐν τοῖς πολλοῖς δοξαζομένων, title of work by Polystr., cf. Them.*Or.*34 p.464 D.

**καταθε-άομαι**, *look down upon, watch from above*, τὰ γιγνόμενα κ. ἀπὸ λόφου X.*An.*6.5.30; κ. εἰς τοὺς πολεμίους ib.1.8.14: abs., Id. *Cyr.*3.2.1: generally, *contemplate*, φορὰς ἄστρων Plu.2.426d: metaph., with the mind, X.*Cyr.*8.2.18. **-ᾱτέον**, *one must observe*, τὴν τάξιν Procl. *in Prm.*p.537 S.

**καταθείω, καταθείομαι, καταθείομεν**, v. κατατίθημι.

**καταθέλγω**, *subdue by spells* or *enchantments*, τοὺς αὐτὴ κατέθελξεν (sc. Circe) Od.10.213, cf. Luc.*Ind.*12, etc.

**κατάθελξις**, εως, ἡ, *enchantment*, Luc.*Philops.*9.

**κατάθεμα**, ατος, τό, = ἀνάθεμα, *accursed thing*, *Apoc.*22.3. II. *curse*, *Tab.Defix.Aud.*22.23 (Curium, iii A.D.).

**καταθεματίζω**, = ἀναθεματίζω, *Ev.Matt.*26.74.

**καταθεμελιόω**, in Pass., *to be founded, based*, εἰς τὴν Γῆν Lyd.*Mens.* 4.51.

**κατάθεος**, ον, *godly*, ὑφηγήσεις Ph.2.298, cf. Poll.1.20; *superstitious*, Phot. s.v. ὄλολυν.

**κατα-θερμαίνω**, strengthd. for θερμαίνω, dub. l. in Philagr.ap.Orib. 5.21.1. **-θερμος**, ον, strengthd. for θερμός, Aët.9.1, Sch.Pi.*O.*3.42.

⊛**κατά-θεσις**, εως, ἡ, *layering* of branches for propagation, κ. κλάδων D.S.2.53; φυτῶν ἐν τῇ γῇ *Gp.*9.5.1: generally, *planting*, χορτασμάτων *PStrassb.*10.10 (iii A.D.). 2. *paying down, payment*, Ph.2.224, Poll.4.47, 5.103, dub. in *CIG*2826.17 (Aphrodisias). 3. *laying down* or *affirming, positive statement*, δύο στερήσεις κ. ποιοῦσιν *EM* 97.38. 4. *laying aside, giving up*, τοῦ πολέμου Anon.ap.Suid. s.vv. καταθέσει, κτηματίτην. 5. in Surgery, *position*, '*putting up*' of a limb, Erot. s.v. κατατεῖναι, Pall. *in Hp.Fract.*12.273 C. 6. in Law, *promise, covenant*, Just.*Nov.*85.3.1, 94.2; also, *disposition*, *POxy.*243.11 (i A.D.), *Sammelb.*5679.18 (iv A.D.). 7. *burial*, *POxy.*475.31 (ii A.D.). **-θετέον**, *one must lay down*, Them.*Or.* 16.199c. 2. *one must layer*, *Gp.*4.12.15.

**καταθέω**, *run down*, ἀπὸ λόφων Th.3.97, cf. X.*Cyr.*3.2.1; of ships, *run into port*, εἰς Πειραιᾶ Id.*HG*1.1.35. II. *make inroads*, εἰς πόλεις ib.5.2.43: c. acc., κ. χώραν *overrun, ravage*, Th.7.27, X.*Cyr.* 5.4.15; κ. θάλατταν Polyaen.1.23.1. 2. metaph., *attack, persecute*, Parth.13.3 cod.; τοὺς τετελευτηκότας Lib.*Or.*63.42; esp. *in argument*, '*run down*', Pl.*Tht.*171c; cf. κατατρέχω: c. gen., *treat insultingly*, τῆς τοῦ αὐτοκράτορος ἡλικίας Procop.*Pers.*1.2.

**καταθεωρ-έω**, *observe, contemplate*, in Pass., ἡ ἰατρικὴ ὑπὸ ψυχῆς κ. Pl.*Grg.*465d. **-ησις**, εως, ἡ, *observation*, Apollod.*Poliorc.*139.2.

**καταθήγω**, *sharpen, whet*, ἐν βύβλοισι καταθήξετ' ὀδόντα (sc. μύες) *AP*6.303 (Aristo); = παροξύνω, Hsch.: Dor. aor. inf. κατθᾶξαι, = παρακονῆσαι, μεθύσαι, Id.

**καταθήκη**, ἡ, *deposit*, prob. f.l. for παρακαταθ- in Lys.*Fr.*70 tit., Isoc.17.27.

**καταθηλύνω**, *make womanish*, Luc.*Peregr.*19, *DMeretr.*5.3; καρποὶ κατατεθηλυσμένοι *softened*, f.l. in Hp.*Aër.*15.

***καταθήπω**, v. κατατέθηπα.

**καταθηρατόριον**, v. καθθηρ-.

**καταθλάττειν**, gloss on φλᾶν, Cyr.

**καταθλάω**, aor. 1 -έθλασα, *crush in pieces*, ὀστᾶ Lxx *Ps.*41(42).11: metaph., τινὰς ὡς γῆν ib.*Is.*63.3.

⊛**κατ-αθλέω**, *wrestle down, overcome*, τινα Plu.*Cleom.*27: metaph., τὴν ἀμαθίαν Id.2.47f; ἀσκήσει τὸ ἄλογον ib.459b. 2. *master by practice*, τοῦτον τὸν τόπον Arr.*Epict.*2.17.31. 3. *train, exercise*, τινὰς ἐν ἀκοντισμοῖς Plu.2.8d:—Pass., -ηθλημένοι ἐν πολέμοις D.H. 13.12. II. intr., *exercise oneself, train*, Plu.2.2e; -ηθληκότες *well-trained*, of soldiers, Id.*Mar.*26.

**κατα-θλίβω** [ῑ], *press down*, τοὺς δαλούς Thphr.*Ign.*23; [τοὺς μαστούς] Sor.1.76; τὸ πνεῦμα Plu.2.133d; καταθλῐβεῖσα ἀναθυμίασις Id. *Aem.*14. **-θλιψις**, εως, ἡ, *pressing down*, *Gloss.*

**καταθνήσκω**, Aeol. **κατθναίσκω** Sapph.62 (καταθνάσκ- codd.): fut. -θανοῦμαι: aor. κατέθᾰνον, Ep. κάτθᾰνον; late poet. aor. 1 κάθθανα Maiuri *Nuova Silloge* 48: pf. -τέθνηκα (v. infr.):—poet. Verb, *die away, be dying*, τὸν δὲ καταθνήσκων προσέφη Il.22.355; κάτθανε καὶ Πάτροκλος *died*, 21.107: in pf., *to be dead*, κατατεθνήκασι, opp. ζώουσι, 15.664: freq. in pf. part., ἀνδρὸς..κατατεθνηῶτος 7.89, 22. 164; νέκυι κατατεθνηῶτι 16.565; νεκροὺς κατατεθνηῶτας 18.540, etc.: used by Trag. only in sync. fut. κατθανοῦμαι, E.*Med.*1386, *Alc.*150, etc.; and in inf. and part. of sync. aor. κατθανεῖν, κατθανών, A.*Ag.* 1290, 873, etc.: once in ind., κάτθανε ib.1553 (anap.). 2. metaph., *perish*, μέλι..κάτθανε ἐν κηρῷ λυπεύμενον Mosch.3.34; κάτθανε δ' ἁ μορφὰ σὺν Ἀδώνιδι Bion 1.31.

⊛**καταθνητός**, ή, όν, *mortal*, Il.5.402, *h.Ap.*464, etc.: fem., *h.Ven.* 39, 50.

**καταθοινάω**, *feast upon*, Hsch.:—aor. Med., Aesop.14, Diogenian. 7.52:—aor. Pass. in med. sense, Pancrat.ap.Ath.7.283b.

**καταθορεῖν**, v. καταθρῴσκω.

**καταθορῠβέω**, *shout down*, ἕως ἂν ἀποστῇ ὁ ἐπιχειρῶν λέγειν καταθορυβηθείς Pl.*Prt.*319c:—Act. in Numen. ap. Eus. *PE*14.6: also c. acc. cogn., τὴν ἀπὸ ἁμάξης πομπείαν πᾶσαν κ. ibid.

**καταθρᾰσύνομαι**, v. καταθαρσύνω.

**κατά-θραυσις**, εως, ἡ, *breaking up*, τοῦ φλέγματος Steph. *in Hp.*1. 176 D. **-θραυστος**, ον, *broken in pieces*, f.l. in Dsc.5.87. **-θραύω**, *break in pieces, shatter*, Pl.*Plt.*265d, *Ti.*56e (Pass.), Plu.2.949c; εἰς λεπτά Gal.18(1).471.

**κατ-αθρέω**, *look down on from above*, Man.4.421. 2. *examine*, Alex.Aphr. *in SE*176.11. 3. = καθοράω, κατανοέω, Anon.ap.Hsch.

**καταθρηνέω**, *bewail*, E.*El.*1326 (anap.), prob. in Phld.*Mort.*24: c. acc., τὴν Ἀλεξάνδρου τελευτήν D.S.17.118; ἀποθνήσκοντας Plu.2. 1103a; ἑαυτούς App.*Pun.*81.

**καταθροέω**, = καταθορυβέω, Poll.8.154.

**καταθρύβω**, = καταθρύπτω, λάγανον Bilabel Ὀψαρτ. p.11.

**καταθρῡλέω**, = καταθορυβέω, Poll.8.154.

**κατάθρυπτος**, ον, (cf. θρύπτω II. 2c) *mincing, affected*, Eub.108.

**καταθρύπτω**, *break in pieces*, γυῖα Nic.*Al.*61; λάγανον Artem.ap. Ath.14.663e; κ. ἄρτους εἰς γάλα D.S.1.83, cf. Dieuch.ap.Orib.*Syn.* 5.33 (Pass.).

**καταθρῴσκω**, aor. 2 κατέθορον, *leap down*, κὰδ δ' ἔθορ' ἐς μέσσον Il. 4.79: c. acc., κ. τὴν αἱμασιήν *leap down* the wall, Hdt.6.134; καταθορόντες ἀπὸ τῶν ἵππων Id.3.86: c. gen., Nonn.*D.*23.220.

**καταθῡμέω**, *to be cast down, lose heart*, X.*HG*3.2.7.

⊛**καταθύμιος** [ῡ], α, ον, also ος, ον Eumel.13:—*in the mind* or *thoughts*, ὄφρα ἔπος εἴπωμι τό μοι καταθύμιόν ἐστιν Od.22.392; μηδέ τί τοι θάνατος κ. ἔστω let not death sit *heavy on thy heart*, Il.10.383, cf. 17.201. II. *according to one's mind*, τῷ Ἰθωμάτᾳ κ. ἔπλετο Μοῖσα Eumel. l.c.; οὔτι μάλ' ἀνθρώποις κ. πάντα τελεῖται Thgn.617, cf. 1086; Μαρδονίῳ τὰ σφάγια οὐ δύναται κ. γενέσθαι Hdt.9.45; ἐούσης ταύτης [γυναικός] οἱ καταθυμίης Id.5.39; τί γὰρ ἥδιον ἀνθρώπῳ γυναικὸς καταθυμίας; Antipho Soph.49, cf. Muson.*Fr.*14 p.74 H.; παῖς κ. Democr.277; ὄρνις *Lyr.Alex.Adesp.*4*B*16; ποιοῦντες τὰ κ. αὐτῶν Lxx *Is.*44.9, cf. *Mi.*7.3, D.C.37.56.

**καταθῡμοβορέω**, strengthd. for θυμοβορέω, [ζωὴν] κ. Pythag.ap. Ps.-Plu.*Vit.Hom.*154 (= ap.Stob.4.56.24).

**καταθύω**, *sacrifice*, πρόβατα Hdt.8.19, cf. X.*An.*4.5.35, *Milet.*1(9). 368, D.C.65.13, etc.; [τοῖς θεοῖς] πάντα Anon.*Oxy.*2159; of incense, *burn as an offering*, λιβανωτοῦ χίλια τάλαντα Jul.*Or.*2.79b. 2. *offer, dedicate*, τὴν δεκάτην Inscr.ap.X.*An.*5.3.13, D.S.4.21. 3. simply, *kill*, αἶγα Aret.*CD*2.12. II. Med., φίλτροις καταθύσομαι *will compel by* magic *sacrifices*, Theoc.2.3 (-δήσομαι Sch.).

**καταθωπεύω**, strengthd. for θωπεύω, δώροις τοὺς πολεμίους Agath. 5.14, cf. Sch.Theoc.6.30.

**καταθωρᾱκίζομαι**, Pass., *wear protective armour*, ἵπποι -ισμένοι X. *Cyr.*6.2.17.

⊛**καταί**, rare poet. form for κατά, A.D.*Synt.*309.28.

**καται-βᾰσία**, Ep. -ίη, ἡ, poet. for κατάβασις, Q.S.6.484 (pl.). II. καταιβασίαι *thunderbolts*, Plu.2.555a. **-βάσιος** [βᾰ], ον, *descending*, epith. of the thunderbolt, κ. Διὸς ἔγχος Orac.ap.Porph.ap.Eus. *PE*6.3; cf. καταβάσιος. II. of Apollo, as *invoked by those who prayed for a return* (κατάβασις) to their country, Sch.E.*Ph.*1408, Zen.4.29. **-βᾰσις**, εως, ἡ, poet. for κατάβασις, *AP*11.23 (Antip.). ⊛**-βάτης** [ᾰ], ου, ὁ, a name of Zeus as *descending in thunder and lightning*, Ar.*Pax* 42, Clearch.9, Lyc.1370, *IG*2.1659*b*, 12(3). 1360 (Thera), 1093 (Melos), *BCH*50.245 (Thasos), Ἀρχ.Ἐφ.1924. 146 (Thess.), Paus.5.14.10, Corn.*ND*9: applied by Athenian flattery to Demetrius, Plu.*Demetr.*10; also κ. κεραυνός, σκηπτός, A.*Pr.*361,

Lyc.382. 2. of Hermes, *who led souls down* to the nether world, Sch.Ar.*Pax*649. 3. of Ἀχέρων, *that to which one descends, downward*, E.*Ba*.1360. 4. of a person, *descending underground*, Dam. *Isid*.131. 5. καταιβάται, οἱ, members of a thiasos of worshippers of Dionysus, *Inscr.Magn*.215*a*36.—In these senses the form καταβάτης never occurs; cf. καταιβάσιος, καταιβάτις, etc. ❋**-βάτις** [ᾰ], ιδος, ἡ, fem. of foreg., ζῶσ' ἐς Ἅιδην ἵξεται κ. Lyc.497. 2. κ. κέλευθος *steep, downward* path, A.R.2.353, 3.160; τρίβος Lyc.91. II. Act., *that brings down*, κόρη σελήνης κ. *that brings down* the moon by spells, Sosiph.1. ❋**-βᾰτός**, ή, όν, poet. for καταβατός, θύραι.. καταιβαταὶ ἀνθρώποισιν gates *by which* men *descend*, Od.13.110.

**κατ-ᾱΐγδην**, Adv. *coming violently down*, A.R.1.64, Opp.*H*.3.574, Orph.*L*.508, etc.

**καταιγ-ῐδώδης**, ες, *tempestuous*, πνοαί, ἄνεμοι, Sch.A.R.1.1016, Eust.1414.38. **-ίζω**, *rush down like a storm*, πρὶν καταιγίσαι πνοὰς Ἄρεως A.*Th*.63, cf. Str.16.4.5, J.*AJ*3.5.2, Hld.1.22; στρόμβος καταιγίζων *a rushing roaring* sound, A.*Fr*.195; ἐκνεφίας καταιγίσας ἐς τὴν ἀγοράν Alex.46.5; εἰς τοὔψον Id.247.3; of the sea, *AP*10.16.9 (Theaet.): metaph., of pain and sickness, Hp.*Morb*.3.7,16; of love, *AP*12.88; of rumour, Ach.Tat.6.10; of drunken frenzy, τὴν καταιγίζουσαν ἐκ μέθης ζάλην *Com.Adesp*.1227. 2. Pass., *to be visited by storms*, of places, τοῖς βορέαις Str.7.4.3, cf. 9.3.15: metaph., ὁλκὰς θορύβοις -ομένη Hld.5.24; also, of the sea, ὅταν ὑπ' ἀνέμου -ίζηται ὁ πόντος Gal.6.709. **-ίς**, ίδος, ἡ, (αἰγίς II) *squall descending from above, hurricane*, Democr.14, Arist.*Mu*.$395^{a}5$, *AP*7.273 (Leon.), Corn.*ND*9, Erot. s. v. πόνος, Gal.18(2).178, D.C.74.12, Lib.*Or*.59.138: metaph., of *gusts* of passion (cf. sq.), Phld.*Herc*.1251.6; of battles, Tz.*H*.1.984 (pl.). **-ισμός**, ὁ, = foreg., in pl., *gusts* of physical passion, Epicur.*Fr*.413.

**καταιδέομαι**, fut. -έσομαι: aor. Pass. -ηδέσθην in act. sense:—*feel shame* or *reverence before* another, *stand in awe of* him, c. acc., Hdt.3.72,77, S.*OT*654, E.*Or*.682; δαίμονα καταιδεσθεῖσα Id.*Hipp*.772 (lyr.); καταιδέσθητι πατρῷον Δία Ar.*Nu*.1468 (paratrag.): c. inf., *to be ashamed to do* a thing, E.*Heracl*.1027: abs., Id.*Hel*.805, D.C.38.3. II. later in Act., **καταιδέω**, *put to shame*, Hld.4.18, Them.*Or*.15.191b, f.l. in Plu.2.801f, cf. Hsch., Phot.

**καταιέτια** γεῖσα *raking* cornices *of a pediment* (cf. ἀετός IV), *IG*$2^2$.1668.39.

**καταιθᾰλόω**, *burn to ashes*, δόμους..καταιθαλώσω A.*Fr*.160; ὃν Ζεὺς κεραυνῷ πυρπόλῳ καταιθαλοῖ E.*Supp*.640; Μίμαντα πυρί Id.*Ion* 215 (lyr.); σῶμα καὶ δόμων περιπτυχὰς κ. Ar.*Av*.1242, cf. 1248; γαῖαν Lyc.1376: metaph., of love, καταιθαλώσεις τῶν νεωτέρων τινά Ar.*Av*.1261:—Pass., [Τροίας] πυρὶ κατηθαλωμένης E.*Tr*.60; ὑπ' ἀσβόλου κατηθαλωμένος *all burnt* and sooty, Luc.*DDeor*.5.4, cf. Artem.2.10; ἱερῶν -ουμένων Hp.*Ep*.27.

**καταιθύσσω**, *wave* or *float down*, πλόκαμοι..νῶτον καταίθυσσον Pi.*P*.4.83; εὐδίαν ὃς καταιθύσσει ἑστίαν *sheds* fair weather *down upon* the hearth, ib.5.11:—hence **καταῖθυξ** ὄμβρος, *Trag.Adesp*.216.

**καταίθω**, *burn down, burn to ashes*, καταίθουσα..δαλόν (Canter for κ' αἴθουσα) A.*Ch*.607 (lyr.); σὺ δ' οὖν κάταιθε E.*Andr*.258; ὕφαπτε καὶ κάταιθε Ar.*Th*.730; πυρὶ καταίθεται τέραμνα E.*Tr*.1296 (lyr.). 2. metaph., *kindle, rouse*, Lyc.249; ἔρως με καταίθει Theoc.7.56:—Pass., καταίθεσθαι ἐπί τινι Id.2.40:—A.*Fr*.359 is corrupt.

**καταικίζω**, *maltreat*, τεύχεα..κατῄκισται the arms *have been disfigured* [by smoke and soot], Od.16.290:—Med., σῶμα σὸν καταικιῇ (fut. Att.) E.*Andr*.828 (lyr.), cf. D.S.18.47:—Pass., βασάνοις -αικισθέντες D.H.3.73: metaph., μουσικὴ -ῃκισμένη τὸ σῶμα Plu.2.1141d.

**καταίν-εσις**, εως, ἡ, *betrothal*, Plu.*TG*4. ❋**-έω**, poet. aor. 1 -ησα Pi. (v. infr.):—*agree to* a thing, *approve of* it, opp. ἀναίνομαι, c. acc. rei, Hdt.4.80, 6.62; κ. [τι] ἐπί τινι to *agree* to it on conditions, Id.3.53: c. dat. rei, Th.4.122: abs., οὐ καταινέσαμεν ἀλλὰ ἀπειπάμεθα Hdt.9.7.α'. 2. *agree, promise to* do, c. aor. inf., γάμον μεῖξαι Pi.*P*.4.222: c. fut. inf., καταίνεσον μή ποτε προδώσειν S.*OC* 1633, cf. 1637; also τοῦτον κ. βασιλέα σφίσι εἶναι *agree that* he should be king, Hdt.1.98; κ. τινὰ ταγόν (sc. εἶναι) *AP*9.98 (Stat. Flacc.). 3. *grant, promise*, τοῦτ' ἐμοὶ πόλις τὸ δῶρον..κατῄνεσεν S.*OC*432, cf. *Ichn*.158; esp. *promise in marriage, betroth*, παῖδά τινι E.*IA*695, cf. Plu.*Pomp*.47; κ. πρὸς γάμον Nic.Dam.10 J.

❋**κατ-άϊξ** [τᾱ], ῑκος, ἡ, = καταιγίς, Eumel.9 (pl.), A.R.1.1203, Call.*Dian*.114.

**καταιον-άω**, *pour upon* or *over, foment*, of ailing parts, Hp.*Mul*.1.68, Plu.2.74d: metaph., κ. τινὰ σοφίᾳ D.C.38.19:—Pass., Luc.*Lex*.5. **-ημα**, ατος, τό, *fomentation*, Ael.*NA*8.22, Alex.Trall.1.13. **-ησις**, εως, ἡ, = foreg., D.Chr.17.6, M.Ant.5.9, Poll.4.180, Gal.12.675; αἱ κατὰ κεφαλῆς κ. Ath.1.24d.

**καταίρεσις, -αιρέω**, Ion. for καθαίρεσις, -αιρέω.

❋**καταίρω**, *take down*, only in Aeol. form **κατ-αέρρω** for κατ-αείρω (q. v.): elsewh. II. intr., *come down, swoop*, of birds, ἐς τὰ βιβλία Ar.*Av*.1288; ἐς Δελφούς Paus.10.15.5; ἀφ' ἑτέρας τινὸς γῆς ἐνταῦθα Plu.*Rom*.9; of bees, ἐπὶ τὸν θύμον κ. Id.2.41f; of persons, κ. ἀπ' ὄχθων X.*Eq.Mag*.6.5; ἐκεῖσε E.*Ba*.1294; εἰς τὰς Ἀθήνας Pl.*Hp.Ma*.281a; εἰς τὰς τῶν πολεμίων χεῖρας Plu.*Phil*.14. 2. of ships, *put into port, put in*, ἐς Καῦνον Th.8.39; εἰς τὴν χώραν *Hell.Oxy*.16.1; ἐπὶ νῆσον, πρὸς τὴν Πανορμῖτιν, Plb.1.60.3, 1.56.3; ἀπὸ τῆς Συρίας δευρί Alciphr.1.38.

**καταισθάνομαι**, *perceive*, τι S.*OT*422.

**καταίσιμ-ος**, ον, = αἴσιμος, Hsch. **-όω**, *consume utterly*, Eub.15.6 (Pass.); κ. πῶμα *to drink* it *off*, Epin.1.10.

**καταίσιος**, ον, = αἴσιος, *righteous*, ἔργον οὐ κ. A.*Ag*.1598, cf. Cerc.18.36, Hsch.

**κατ-ᾱΐσσω**, fut. -ΐξω, *rush down from*, ἔκποθεν ὀλέθρου A.R.2.224; opp. ἀναΐσσω, Herm.ap.Stob.1.49.68:—Med., *rush in from above*, αἰθὴρ καταΐσσεται Emp.100.7. II. c. acc., *rush, dart through*, φρὴν..κόσμον..καταΐσσουσα Id.134.5.

**καταϊσχαλέος**, α, ον, = ἰσχαλέος, dub. l. in Od.19.233.

**καταισχόφιλος**, v. κατασκάφιλος.

**καταισχρεύομαι**, *speak* or *act foully*, Tz.*H*.6.32.

**καταισχυμμός**, ὁ, *shaming, disgrace*, Sm.*Mi*.2.6.

**καταισχυν-τήρ**, ῆρος, ὁ, *dishonourer*, δόμων A.*Ag*.1363. **-ω**, fut. -αισχῠνῶ Id.*Th*.546:—*dishonour, put to shame*, μή τι καταισχύνειν πατέρων γένος Od.24.508; καταισχύνητέ τε δαῖτα 16.293; τὰ πρόσθε ἐργασμένα Hdt.7.53, cf. A.*Supp*.996, D.18.101, etc.; τὴν σὴν οὐ κ. φύσιν I *put* not thy nature *to shame*, i.e. show myself not unworthy of thee, S.*El*.609; κ. τὸ Τρωϊκὸν κλέος E.*Hel*.845; τὸ γένος οὐ καταισχυνῶ Ar.*Av*.1451; κ. τὴν πατρίδα Id.*Nu*.1220; τοὺς προγόνους Pl.*La*.187a; ὑποσχέσεις Id.*Smp*.183e; τὰς εὐγενείας ταῖς αὑτῶν..κακίαις Isoc.7.76, etc. 2. *dishonour* a woman, ἀλλοτρίας γυναῖκας Lys.1.49; also of a male, D.45.79. 3. ὁ μέλλων χρόνος ἐμὸν καταίσχυνε..χρέος *covered* me *with dishonour* in that my debt remained unpaid, Pi.*O*.10(11).8. 4. = καταχέζειν, χαίτην Babr.82.8. II. Med., *feel shame before*, θεούς S.*Ph*.1382, cf. *OT*1424:—aor. Pass., καταισχυνθέντες τὴν ἀρετὴν αὐτῶν Isoc.4.97: c. inf., *to be ashamed* to.., ἰητρεύειν Hp.*Art*.42; καταισχυνθῆναι..ὅπως μὴ δόξει..*to be ashamed* of being thought.., Th.6.13.

**καταΐσχω**, Ep. for κατίσχω, κατέχω, Od.9.122 (Pass.).

**καταιτι-άομαι**, *accuse, arraign*, ἀλλήλους Hdt.6.14; τί σαυτὸν ἀδικῶν τὴν τύχην καταιτιᾷ; Men.618; τινὰ περί τινος D.57.27; τινὰς ἀσεβείας D.C.68.1, cf. J.*AJ*8.13.3; τινα c. inf., χρήματα εἰληφέναι D.C.*Fr*.104.3; τινος X.*Cyr*.6.1.4 (v.l.): abs. in med. sense, *accuse one another*, Hdt.5.92.γ':—Pass., *PTeb*.64(*a*).84 (ii B.C.). 2. c. acc. rei, *lay* something *to one's charge, impute*, ἀμαθίαν Th.3.42; καταιτιώμενος ταῦτα D.21.118. II. aor. 1 part. Pass. καταιτιαθείς in pass. sense, *accused person, defendant*, οἱ κ. Th.6.60, Plb.30.32.11; οἱ ἐκ τοῦ Περσικοῦ πολέμου κ. Id.3.5.4: c. inf., καταιτιαθεὶς ταῦτα πρᾶξαι X.*HG*1.1.32; so also οἱ κατῃτιαμένοι Plb.32.3.14; κατῃτιᾶσθαι τὴν κλοπήν D.S.4.31. **-ᾱσις**, εως, ἡ, *accusation*, Plu.2.546f (pl.), M.Ant.1.16. **-ασμός**, ὁ, = foreg., Vett.Val.2.8 (pl.), al., *Cat.Cod.Astr*.2.161 (pl.).

**καταῖτυξ**, ῠγος, ἡ, *leathern helmet*, without φάλος or λόφος, Il.10.258.

**καταίφλεξ**, *burning with heat*, Hsch. s. v. καταῖθυξ.

**καταιχμάζω**, *strike down*, c. gen., Nonn.*D*.21.6, al.

**καταιωρέομαι**, Pass., *hang down*, θύσανοι κατῃωρεῦντο Hes.*Sc*.225.

**κατακαγχάζω**, *laugh aloud at*, τινος *AP*5.215.6 (Agath.), cf. Anon. ap.Suid. s. v. ἀνατεινάμενος.

**κατακαῆμεν, κατακαιέμεν**, v. κατακαίω.

**κατακαίνυμαι**, pf. -κέκασμαι, *to be adorned*, κεφαλῇ κατὰ γυῖα κέκασται Emp.134.1.

❋**κατακαίνω**, = κατακτείνω, *kill*, in early writers in aor. 2 κατέκανον, X.*Cyr*.4.6.5 (v.l. -καίνων), *An*.3.2.12; 3 sg. subj. κατακάνῃ Anon. in *PSI*9.1091.4; κατέκανον (for -έκτανον) is required by the metre in S.*Ant*.1340: pf. part. -κεκονότες (cf. καίνω) shd. be read in X.*An*.7.6.36: pres. in later Prose, Parth.7.2, Arr.*Ind*.11.10, App.*Pun*.1, Eun.*Hist*.p.212 D.; Hsch. has κατακαινιῶ· ἀποκτενῶ (fort. leg. κατακενίω, Dor. fut.).

**κατακαίριος**, ον, = καίριος, Il.11.439, *AP*9.227 (Bianor).

**κατακαίω**, Att. **-κάω** [ᾱ], Ep. inf. κατακαιέμεν Il.7.408: fut. -καύσω Ar.*Lys*.1218: aor. κατέκαυσα Th.7.25; Ep. 3 sg. κατέκηε Il.6.418; 1 pl. subj. κατακήομεν (v.l. -κείομεν) Il.7.333; inf. κατακῆαι Od.11.46, κακκῆαι ib.74 (v.l. -κεῖαι): pf. -κέκαυκα X.*HG*6.5.37, Phld.*Acad.Ind*.p.69 M.:—**Pass.**, fut. -καυθήσομαι Ar.*Nu*.1505, -καήσομαι 1*Ep.Cor*.3.15: aor. κατεκαύθην (the Att. form) Hdt.4.69, 6.101, κατεκάην Id.1.51, 2.107; Lacon. inf. -καῆμεν Plu.*Lyc*.20; -εκαύσθην *Chron.Lind*.D.41: pf. -κέκαυμαι And.1.108:—*burn completely*, in Hom. of sacrifices and dead bodies, κατακήομεν αὐτούς Il.7.333; μιν κατέκηε σὺν ἔντεσι 6.418; κ. τοὺς μάντιας *burn* them *alive*, Hdt.4.69; ζῶντα κατακαυθῆναι Id.1.86, cf. 2.107; of cities and houses, etc., κατὰ μὲν ἔκαυσαν..πόλιν Id.8.33; κατεκαίετο ὁ ἐν Δελφοῖσι νηός Id.1.50; [οἰκίη] κατεκάη Id.4.79; κατακαυθέντων ἱρῶν Id.6.101; τείχη -κεκαυμένα And. l. c.; γῆ κατακεκαυμένη *burnt* earth, Arist.*Mete*.$358^{a}14$; Κατακεκαυμένη, name of the upper valley of the Hermus, in Lydia, Str.13.4.11, cf. κατακεκαυμενίτης; of the fingers, *to be burnt* with hot food, Porph.*Abst*.4.15; also κ. τὴν κοιλίαν *PMagd*.33.4 (iii B.C.). 2. of hot winds, *parch*, τὰ ἐκ τῆς γῆς *PHib*.1.27.73 (iii B.C.), al. 3. metaph., ὁ ἔρως ἐμέ..κατακέκαυκεν *Lyr.Alex.Adesp*.8(*c*):—Pass., τὰ στόματα -κάεται ἐπὶ τέχνην Anaxandr.33.6; -καίομαι καταλελειμμένη *Lyr.Alex.Adesp*.1.24. II. Pass., of fire, κατὰ πῦρ ἐκάη *had burnt down, burnt out*, Il.9.212.

❋**κατακᾰλέω**, *call down*, Plu.*Oth*.18; but usu. *summon*, ἐκ τῆς μητροπόλεως κατακληθείς Th.1.24; δοῦλοι -κεκλημένοι ἐπ' ἐλευθερίᾳ Str.14.1.38:—Med., κ. Ἀθήναζε Plu.*Sol*.24; *call upon* for performance, *BGU*1185.25 (i B.C.). II. *call upon, invoke*, τοὺς θεούς App.*Pun*.81; κατακαλέσασθαι v.l. Isoc.10.61, cf. Plu.*Them*.13. 2. *appeal to*, τοὺς ἐπιδώσοντας *SIG*591.3 (Lampsacus, ii B.C.). III. *call back, recall*, εἰς τὴν Μακεδονίαν Plb.25.3.1, cf. Oenom.ap.Eus.*PE*5.34.

**κατακαλλύνω**, *clear away*, κόπρον *IG*11(2).287*A*62 (Delos, iii B.C.).

**κατακάλυμμα** [κᾰλ], ατος, τό, *covering, veil*, Lxx *Ex.*26.14, J.*BJ*5.12.3 (dub. l.).

**κατακᾰλύπτω**, *cover up*, κατά τε κνίσῃ ἐκάλυψαν (sc. μηρούς) Il.1.460, cf. Hdt.2.47 (tm.); με τεθνηῶτα..κατὰ γαῖα καλύπτοι Il.6.464; κατὰ δὲ σκότος ὄσσε κάλυψεν 16.325; Ἴδην δὲ κατὰ νεφέεσσι κ. 17.594; κἀμὲ θανάτου κατὰ μοῖρα καλύψαι A.*Pers.*917 (anap.), cf. Hes.*Op.*121, E.*Tr.*1315 (lyr.), etc.:—Med., **κατὰ κρᾶτα καλυψάμενος γοάασκεν** *having covered his* head, Od.8.92; so -**καλυψάμενος** alone, Hdt.6.67; **κἂν κατακεκαλυμμένος τις γνοίη** even one *veiled* would perceive, Pl.*Men.*76b; λογισμῷ κατακαλυψάμενος Id.*Ep.*340a.

**κατακάλυψις** [κᾰλ], εως, ἡ, *covering, concealment*, Longin.17.3; **τὰ** ἐν -καλύψει ἀποστήματα Scrib.Larg.ap.Gal.13.99, Cass.Fel.21.

**κατακᾰμᾰρόω**, *cover with a vault*, Hsch.

**κατακάμπτω**, *bend down*, so as to be concave, ἐξ ὀρθοῦ **κ.** Pl.*Ti.*71c; εἰς ἓν κύκλῳ ib.36b; **κ.** τὰς στροφάς, v. στροφή 1.3:—Pass., opp. ἀνακάμπτομαι, Arist.*Mete.*$386^{a}1$; φλὲψ ἐπὶ τὴν ῥάχιν -ομένη Gal.15.530: pf. part. Pass. -κεκαμμένος *bending over*, cj. in Thphr.*HP*3.18.8. II. *cover with a vault*, λίθῳ κατακαμφθέντες Str.5.3.8. III. metaph., κ. ἐλπίδας *bend down, overthrow* hopes, E.*Tr.*1252 (Burges, -γναψε codd., anap.):—Pass., *to be bent* (by entreaty), Aeschin.1.187.

**κατάκαμψις**, εως, ἡ, *bending down*, κλάδων Str.3.5.10; *bending into a concave form*, opp. ἀνάκαμψις, Arist.*Mete.*$386^{a}5$.

**κατακάρδιος**, ον, *in* or *to the heart*, πληγαί Hdn.7.11.3.

**κατακάρπ-ιον**, τό, = περικάρπιον, Thphr.*HP*4.10.3 codd. (dub. l.). **-ος**, ον, *fruitful*, Aristodem.ap.Ath.11.495f, Lxx *Ho.*14.7. Adv. -πως *abundantly*, κ. κατοικηθήσεται Ἰερουσαλήμ ib.*Za.*2.4(8). **-όω**, *offer burnt-sacrifices*, esp. *of fruits*, Suid. **-ωσις**, εως, ἡ, *ashes of a burnt-sacrifice*, Lxx *Le.*6.10(3), 11(4).

⊛ **κατακαρφής**, ές, *dried*, φλοιός (of a turnip) Nic.*Fr.*70.9.

**κατακάρφω**, fut. -κάρψω, *parch up*, Hsch.:—Pass., *wither, fall into the sere*, A.*Ag.*80 (anap.).

**κατάκασσα** or **-κᾶσα**, ἡ, = κάσσα, Call.*Fr.*184 (κατακάσαι Hsch.).

**κατά-καυμα**, ατος, τό, *anything burnt*: pl., *burnt parts*, Paul.Aeg.4.13. 2. *fiery inflammation*, Hp.*Coac.*154, Lxx *Le.*13.24,25; *burns*, in pl., Thphr.*Ign.*57, Dsc.5.123, Crito ap.Gal.13.800, *Gp.*12.17.11. II. *burning*, Lxx *Ex.*21.25, Luc.*Asin.*6. **-καύσιμος**, ον, *combustible*, ξύλα Hsch. s.v. ἄθινα. **-καυσις**, εως, ἡ, *burning*, Gal.19.542, Porph.*Abst.*4.15. **-καύτης**, ου, ὁ, *one who burns* (a corpse), Plu.2.296b.

**κατακαυχάομαι**, *boast against* one, *exult over* him, τινος *Ep.Rom.*11.18, Eust. ad D.P.*Prooem.*p.67 B.; κατά τινος *Ep.Jac.*3.14: metaph., -καυχᾶται ἔλεος κρίσεως ib.2.13; κ. ἔν τινι *to glory* in it, Lxx *Za.*10.12.

**κατακαχρύω**, fut. -ύσω Hsch., Phot.: aor. inf. -ῦσαι Paus.Gr.*Fr.*227:—prop. *grind roasted corn*: metaph., *grind, crush*, ll. cc.

**κατακεῖαι, -κείομεν**, v. κατακαίω.

⊛ **κατάκειμαι**, Ep. 3 pl. κατακείαται Il.24.527: Ion. plpf. κατεκέατο Hdt.7.229; subj. -κέωμαι Pl.*Smp.*213b:—**Pass.**, only in pres. and impf. with fut. Med. -κείσομαι:—*lie down*, μῆλα τὰ δὴ κατάκειτ' ἐσφαγμένα Od.10.532; ἐπὶ πλευρὰς κ. Il.24.10; νέκυς κ. Tyrt.11.19; ἐφ' ἁρμαμαξῶν μαλθακῶς κατακείμενοι Ar.*Ach.*70. 2. *lie hid*, ἐν λόχμῃ..κατέκειτο μέγας σῦς Od.19.439; θάμνῳ ὑπ' ἀμφικόμῳ κατακείμενος Il.17.677. 3. *lie stored up*, δοιοὶ γάρ τε πίθοι κατακείαται ἐν Διὸς οὔδει Il.24.527; τό γ' ἐν οἴκῳ κατακείμενον ἀνέρα κήδει Hes.*Op.*364: metaph., ἄλγεα..ἐν θυμῷ κ. Il.24.523. b. *to be deposited*, of deeds in a registry, *POxy.*1040.32 (iii A.D.), etc. 4. *lie sick, keep one's bed*, Hdt.7.229, *Ev.Marc.*1.30, etc.; *lie in bed*, Ar.*Ec.*313; ἐφ' ὃ κατέκειτο *Ev.Luc.*5.25. 5. *lodge, reside*, Hp.*Epid.*1.26.ε', 3.1.γ', al. 6. *to be idle*, X.*An.*3.1.14; of things, *lie neglected*, καθεύδειν ἐᾶν ἐν τῇ γῇ κατακείμενα τὰ τείχη Pl.*Lg.*778d. 7. *recline at meals*, πῖνε, κατάκεισο Ar.*Ach.*985, cf. Hdt.3.121, Pl.*Smp.*185d, *Ev.Marc.*14.3. 8. of land, *lie sloping to the sea*, πρῶνες ἔξοχοι -κεινται Pi.*N.*4.52. 9. ἀρετᾷ κατάκειται πᾶσαν ὀργάν *is expended* in every impulse *on*.., Id.*I.*1.41.

**κατακείρω**, fut. -κερῶ (v. infr.), *shear, clip close*, τὸν πώγωνα Plu.2.52c (Pass.): Com., ὁ κουρεὺς..ὑπὸ τῆς ὑπήνης κατακερεῖ τὴν εἰσφοράν Eup.278:—Med., κ. τὰς κεφαλὰς *crop their* heads *close*, Hdt.1.82. II. in Hom. only metaph., *cut away, waste*, βίοτον κατακείρετε πολλόν Od.4.686; ὅτι μοι κατεκείρετε οἶκον 22.36; μῆλα δ' ἅ μοι μνηστῆρες..κατέκειραν 23.356.

**κατακείω**, = κατάκειμαι, used in imperat. and as fut., δαισάμενοι κατακείετε οἴκαδ' ἰόντες Od.7.188, 18.408; σπείσαντες κατακείομεν οἴκαδ' ἰόντες ib.419; κακκείοντες, Ep. part., in phrases οἱ μὲν κακκείοντες ἔβαν οἶκόνδε, κλισίηνδε ἕκαστος, Il.1.606, 23.58.

**Κατακεκαυμένη**, ἡ, v. κατακαίω:—hence **κατακεκαυμενίτης** οἶνος, wine from that district, Str.13.4.11.

**κατακεκλεισμένως**, Adv. pf. part. Pass. (κατακλείω), κ. ἔχειν Hsch. s.v. κατεκλάζετο.

**κατακελευ-σμός**, ὁ, *calling to one, encouraging*, name of a part of the Πυθικὸς νόμος, Str.9.3.10, Poll.4.84. **-ω**, *command silence*, Ar.*Av.*1273: generally, *command*, c. inf., Plu.*Oth.*18 (s.v.l.). 2. of the boatswain, *give the time in rowing*, Ar.*Ra.*207.

**κατακενόω**, strengthd. for κενόω, σάκκους Lxx *Ge.*42.35; φάρμακον εἰς τὸ πῦρ J.*BJ*1.30.6, cf. Androm.ap.Gal.13.886.

**κατακεντ-έω**, *pierce through*, Pl.*Ti.*76b; *prick*, Gal.12.323 (Act. and Pass.); *stab severely*, D.S.3.37; *cut down, stab*, δόρασι καὶ ξίφεσι Zos.4.49, cf. 5.23:—Pass., Ctes.*Fr.*29.54. 2. *shoot down*, Zos.5.21. 3. metaph., πάθη κ. τινάς Ph.1.299:—Pass., ὑπὸ ἀπιστίας κατακεντούμενοι ib.287:—later form **κατακεντάννυμι** Palaeph.1, Ps.-Luc.*Philopatr.*4 (Pass.). **-ημα**, ατος, τό, *puncture*, Pl.*Ti.*76b. **-ίζω**, *slay with a spear*, Ael.*NA*7.2. **-ρόομαι**, Pass., *to be furnished with spikes*, D.S.18.71.

**κατακέραμα**, *sarta tecta*, *Gloss.*

**κατα-κεράννῡμι**, *mix, temper*, in Pass., Arist.*Pr.*$949^{a}38$, Sor.1.53, Plu.2.132d:—Act., *dilute, weaken*, δριμύτητα Dsc.5.11; cf. κατακίρνημι:—also -ύω, Poll.10.149. **-κέρᾰσις**, εως, ἡ, *process of mixing*, κατακεράσει αὐξάνεται Arist.*GA*$723^{a}18$. **-κεραστέον**, *one must mix, temper*, Aët.4.6. **-κεραστικός**, ή, όν, *demulcent, restoring normal* κρᾶσις, Gal.8.41, 10.486; τροφή Herod.Med.ap.Aët.5.129: c. gen., οὔρων δριμέων *Gp.*12.19.8.

**κατακεραυνόω**, *strike down by thunder*, Ps.-Luc.*Philopatr.*4.

**κατακερδαίνω**, *make gain of* a thing *wrongly*, X.*Oec.*4.7.

**κατακερκίζω**, *divide into* κερκίδες, στάδιον -ίζων τοῖχος *LW*141 (Ephesus), cf. *Jahresh.*15 *Beibl.*181 (ibid.).

**κατακερματ-ίζω**, (κέρμα) *chop up, cut into pieces*, freq. metaph., κ. αὐτὴν (sc. ἀρετὴν) κατὰ μόρια Pl.*Men.*79c; τὴν μίαν τέχνην εἰς πολλὰς Gal.*Thras.*24; κ. τὴν τέχνην εἰς μικρά *fritter* it *away*, Demetr.*Eloc.*76; τὴν μουσικήν Plu.2.1142b; τοὺς ἀγῶνας Str.4.4.2; τὸν λόγον Gal.1.246:—Pass., *to be cut up*, φαίνεται εἰς σμικρότερα κατακεκερματίσθαι ἡ τοῦ ἀνθρώπου φύσις Pl.*R.*395b; κατακεκερμάτισται..ὡς οἷόν τε σμικρότατα Id.*Prm.*144b; κατακεκ. ἐρωτήσεσι πρὸς ἀποκρίσεις *cut up* into questions and answers, Id.*Sph.*225b, cf. 257c, 258e, Plot.3.9.2; διήγησις εἰς μικρὰς κ. τομάς D.H.*Th.*9; σύνθεσις κατακεκομμένη καὶ -ισμένη Demetr.*Eloc.*4; ἄντικρυς μικρὰ καὶ -ισμένα Longin.42; τοῦ πυρετοῦ..κατακερματιζομένου *gradually becoming slighter*, Hp.*Acut.*(*Sp.*)13: seldom in lit. sense, Porph.*Marc.*10 (Pass.); also, *change into smaller coin*, *POxy.*1411.12 (iii A.D.). **-ισμός**, ὁ, *dividing into small parts*, Porph.*Sent.*35.

**κατακερτομέω**, *rail violently*, Hdt.1.129; τινα *at* a person, Id.2.135, Ph.2.440; τινος Nic.Dam.3 J., Polyaen.1.34.2, Longus 2.20.

**κατακερχνόομαι**, strengthd. for κερχνόομαι, Hsch.

**κατακεύθομαι**, *to be hidden*, εἰς δνοφερὸν τύμβον *AP*15.29 (Ignat.).

⊛ **κατακέφᾰλα**, Adv., for κατὰ κεφαλῆς, *head downwards*, Teucer in Boll *Sphaera* p.17, *Gp.*10.30; *from head to foot*, λούσασθαι *IG*$2^{2}$.1365, 1366.

**κατακεφάλαιον** [φᾰ], τό, *poll-tax*, dub. in *PTeb.*119.6 (ii B.C.).

**κατακηλ-έω**, *charm, cast a spell over*, τήνδ' ἄτην S.*Tr.*1002 (anap.):—Pass., Pl.*Cra.*403e, Plu.*Num.*20, Ath.4.174b, Dam.*Isid.*48. **-ητικός**, ή, όν, *fit for enchanting*, τινος Ael.*NA*17.19.

⊛ **κατακηλῑδόω**, strengthd. for κηλιδόω, v.l. in D.C.*Fr.*39.7.

**κατακήομεν**, v. κατακαίω.

**κατακηρόω**, *cover with wax*, Hdt.1.140, v.l. in X.*Eq.*10.7 (ap.Poll.1.207):—Pass., κατακεκηρωμένον τὸ σῶμα Hdt.4.71.

**κατακηρύσσω**, Att. **-ττω**, *proclaim* or *command by public crier*, σιωπήν *IG*12(7).237.36 (Amorgos); σιγήν v.l. in X.*An.*2.2.20:—Pass., *to be promulgated*, Plb.22.4.6. 2. Pass. also, *to be summoned by crier*, Poll.8.61. II. at auction, κ. τι εἴς τινα *order* it *to be knocked down* to one, Plu.*Comp.Lys.Sull.*3.

**κατακίκκας**, v. κατακόκκας. **κατακικλάσκω**, = κατακλάω, Phot. s.v. κατεκίκλασκε.

**κατακῑνέω**, strengthd. for κινέω, in Pass., f.l. in Sch.Theoc.5.116.

**κατακίρνημι**, = κατακεράννυμι, in Pass., Longin.15.9, *AP*9.362.12, Iamb. *in Nic.*p.119 P.:—also **-κιρνάω**, Id.*Protr.*21.ιϛ'.

**κατακισηρίζω**, *rub smooth with pumice-stone*, pf. part. Pass., of an effeminate youth, Ctes.*Fr.*20.

**κατακισσᾶν** (-κίσσαν cod.)· προσποιεῖσθαι, Hsch.

**κατάκισσος**, ον, *ivy-wreathed*, *Anacreont.*41.5.

**κατακλᾰδαίνω**, aor. 1 -εκλάδᾱνα, = ἀναιρέω, Hsch.; cf. κλαδάω.

**κατάκλῠδος**, ον, gloss on κατάπρεμνος, Hsch.

**κατακλᾴζω**, v. κατακλείω.

**κατακλαίω**, Att. **-κλάω** [ᾱ], *bewail loudly, lament*, τινα Ar.*V.*386:—Med., E.*El.*156 (lyr.), *IT*149 (lyr.). 2. abs., *wail aloud*, Id.*El.*113 (lyr.). II. c. gen. pers., *lament before* or *to* another, Herod.1.59, Arr.*Epict.*1.23.4, etc.; κ. αὐτὸς ἑαυτοῦ ib.3.13.4.

**κατάκλᾰσις**, εως, ἡ, *forced position*, τῶν ἄρθρων Hp.*Epid.*6.1.15 (pl.). 2. κ. ὄμματος *drooping* of the eyelid, Id.*Prorrh.*1.84 (vv. ll. -κλισις, -κλεισις), cf. *Epid.*6.1.15, Gal.16.675. II. *refraction* of light or sound, opp. ἀνάκλασις (reflexion), Arist.*Pr.*$901^{b}20$, $904^{b}30$, Cleom.2.6.

**κατάκλαυσις**, εως, ἡ, (κατακλαίω) *bewailing*, *Gloss.*

**κατακλάω** (A) [ᾱ], Att. for κατακλαίω (q.v.).

**κατακλάω** (B) [ᾰ], impf. κατέκλων Il.20.227, Hdt.9.62: aor. 1 -έκλᾰσα Pl.*Phd.*117d:—**Pass.**, pf. and aor. (v. infr.):—*break short, snap off*, ἐπ' ἀνθερίκων καρπὸν θέον οὐδὲ κατέκλων Il. l.c.; κατεκλάσθη δ' ἐνὶ καυλῷ ἔγχος 13.608; τὰ δόρατα κατέκλων Hdt. l.c., cf. Pi.*P.*5.34; φυτευτήρια ἐλαῶν D.53.15; κατὰ δ' αὐχένα νέρθ' ἐπὶ γαίης κλάσσε *bowed* it *down*, Theoc.25.146; κ. τὸν ὀφθαλμόν *ogle*, Phryn.*PS*p.79 B.; but ὄμματα κατακεκλασμένα eyes *with drooping lids*, Arist.*Phgn.*$808^{a}8$; τὸ σῶμα..-κέκλασται *has been crushed*, *PMasp.*77.12 (vi A.D.). II. metaph., *break down*, οὐδένα ὅντινα οὐ κατέκλασε he *broke* us all *down*, Pl.*Phd.* l.c.; πάθος, εἴτ' οἶκτος εἴτ' αἰδώς, κατέκλασε τὴν διάνοιαν Plu.*Tim.*7; [Ἔρως] κατακλάσας τὸ σοβαρόν Id.2.767f:—more freq. in Pass., ἐμοί γε κατεκλάσθη φίλον ἦτορ, κλαῖον δ' ἐν ψαμάθοισι καθήμενος Od.4.538; of fear, ἡμῖν δ' αὖτε κατεκλάσθη φίλον ἦτορ δεισάντων 9.256, cf. 10.198; τὸ θράσος κατεκέκλαστο Plu.*Fab.*11; of passion, ἐρώτων..νόσῳ φρένας..κατεκλάσθη E.*Hipp.*766 (lyr.); of pity, οὐδὲ κατεκλάσθης Call.*Del.*107; of persuasion, D.L.7.114. 2. Pass., κατακεκλασμένος *reduced by fever*, Hp.*Coac.*510:

metaph., of character, *to become enfeebled, degenerate*, Aristeas 149: in pf. part. Pass., *enervated, effeminate*, of men, *Com.Adesp.*339.2; γραφαὶ κ. D.H.*Comp.*18:—Act., κ. ἑαυτόν, of an effeminate dancer, Luc.*Symp.*18, *Salt.*27. III. Pass., of light, *to be refracted*, opp. ἀνακλᾶσθαι (to be reflected), ὄψεως -κλωμένης *Placit.*3.18.1; of sound, αἱ κατακλώμεναι φωναὶ μετὰ φαρμακείην *broken, feeble* voice, Hp. *Coac.*246.

**κατα-κλείδιον**, τό, Dim. of κατακλείς I. 3, Bito 65.11. **-κλειμμα**, ατος, τό, f.l. for κατάλημμα (q.v.). **-κλείς**, εῖδος, or **κατάκλεις**, ειδος, Ion. and Ep. **-κληΐς**, ῖδος, ἡ, *instrument for shutting* or *fastening doors*, distd. from the bolt (μοχλός) and bolt-pin (βάλανος), Ar.*V.*154, *IG*11(2).158*A* 65 (Delos, iii B.C., pl.); αἱ κ. τῶν ἀξόνων *linch-pins*, prob.l. in D.S.17.53. 2. *pawl, check-hook*, Ph.*Bel.*68.5, Hero *Bel.*79.13. 3. κατακληῖς βελέμνων *case* for arrows, quiver, Call.*Dian.*82; *cap* or *case* fitted to an engine, Bito 59.3; also, *socket* for the arrow in the γαστραφέτης, Id.62.9. 4. pl., *locks* on a canal, *PPetr.*2 p.43 (iii B.C.). 5. *sheath for a pin*, in pl., Sch.Od.18.294, Aristeas 65, cf. Hsch. s.v. κληῖδα. II. = ἀκρώμιον, Heliod.ap.Orib.48.48.1, Sor.2.62, Gal.2.766. 2. *first rib*, Id.18(2).956. 3. *clavicular region*, Id.14.703, Hdn.4.13.5. III. *final remark, conclusion*, Cic.*Att.* 9.18.3, prob. l. in ib.2.3.3. 2. *close of a verse* or *set of verses*, Heph.5.1, 6.6, Aristid.Quint.1.27, Sch.Ar.*Ach.*659. **-κλεισις**, εως, ἡ, *shutting up, closing*, Gal.19.445. II. *completion*, Nicom.ap. *Theol.Ar.*43. III. *beam* resting on the pillars of the χελώνη, Ath. Mech.18.9 (pl.). **-κλειστος**, ον, *shut up*, of women, Call.*Fr.*118, cf. Lxx 2*Ma.*3.19, Luc.*Tim.*15, Hsch.; οἴκοι κατάκλειστος ἦν D.L.6.94; κ. εἶχεν τὰ βιβλία Str.13.1.54; *precious*, τίμιον ἢ κ. S.E.*P.*1.143. **-κλείω**, old Att. -κλῄω Th. (v. infr.): a rare fut. κατακλιῶ dub. in Eup.287, cf. Hero *Bel.*107.13:—Med., aor. -εκλεισάμην X. *Cyr.*7.2.5:—Pass., aor. -εκλῄσθην, -εκλείσθην (v. infr.); Ion. -εκληΐσθην Hdt.2.128; Dor. -εκλᾴσθην Theoc.7.84: pf. -κέκλημαι Ar.*Pl.* 206. I. c. acc. pers., *shut in, enclose*, e.g. a mummy in its case, Hdt.2.86: freq. of blockading, τοὺς Ἕλληνας ἐς τὴν νῆσον κ. Th.1.109; κ. ἑαυτοὺς εἰς ἔρυμα X.*Cyr.*4.1.18; κατακλείειν τοὺς γυμνῆτας εἴσω τῶν ὅπλων Id.*An.*3.4.26; κ. εἰς πολιορκίαν, εἰς δυσχωρίας, D.H. 6.74, 11.26; κ. τινὰ ἐν φυλακῇ *Ev.Luc.*3.20, cf. *OGI*669.17 (Egypt, i A.D.): metaph., κ. ἑαυτὸν εἰς πολιτείαν, i.e. not to be a cosmopolite, X.*Mem.*2.1.13:—Pass., ἐς τὸ τεῖχος κατακλῄεσθαι Th.4.57; ναυσὶ κατεκλῄσθησαν Id.1.117, cf. X.*An.*3.3.7; ὅταν ἐς [νεφέλας] ἄνεμος κατακλῃσθῇ Ar.*Nu.*404; εἰς μικρὸν τόπον -κεκλῃμένοι Isoc.4.34; διὰ τοῦ ζῆν..κ. ἐν Ἀπόλλωνος ἢ Ἀθηνᾶς Phld.*D.*1.17:—Med., *shut oneself up*, ἐν τοῖς βασιλείοις X.*Cyr.*7.2.5; also κατεκλᾴζετο *shut up* the bride *with oneself* [in the bridal-chamber], Theoc.18.5:—Pass., κατεκλᾴσθης Id.7.84. 2. metaph., νόμῳ κ. *shut up*, i.e. *compel, oblige*, ἂν..πᾶσαν τὴν δύναμιν νόμῳ κατακλείσητε ἐπὶ τῷ πολέμῳ μένειν D.4.33, cf. And.3.7, Antiph.190.15. 3. metaph., τῆς πόλεως εἰς κίνδυνον μέγιστον κατακεκλειμένης *being reduced*, D.26.11; εἰς σπάνιν κατακλεισθῆναι D.S.20.74: generally, *confine*, ἐν τῷ κατὰ φύσιν πέρατι -κέκλειται τἀγαθόν Metrod.*Herc.*831.8; πᾶσαι αἱ ἐπιχειρήσεις εἰς μίαν ἀπόδειξιν -κλείονται Phld.*Rh.*2.283 S.; κατακλείειν τὸ πᾶν τῆς τέχνης εἰς.. *confine* the whole business of art to.., Hld.3.4. II. c. acc. rei, *shut up, close*, τὰς πυλίδας Hdt.1.191; τὰ ἱρὰ Id.2.124, cf. 128 (Pass.); τὸ ἐργαστήριον Id.4.14; τὸν δίφρον X.*Cyr.*6.4.10; εὑρὼν ἅπαντα κατακεκλῃμένα Ar.*Pl.*206:—in Pass., of humours in the body, Hp.*Loc.Hom.* 27. 2. *clamp down, make fast*, of stones in masonry, *IG*7.3073.158 (Lebad.); also κ. [τὴν δεξιάν] Luc.*Prom.*2. 3. *close* a speech, *conclude*, D.L.10.138; εἰς ἀπειλὴν κ. τὸν λόγον with a threat, D.H. 7.14, cf. A.D.*Synt.*234.17; οὐ κ. διάνοιαν *give* no *complete* sense, Id. *Adv.*119.6 (δ. shd. be supplied, Id.*Synt.*179.13); *conclude* an argument or inference, Phld.*Sign.*15, 33.

**κατακλῇθρον**, τό, = κατακλείς I. 1, *IG*11(2).144*A* 41 (Delos, iv B.C., pl.).

**κατακληΐς**, ῖδος, ἡ, Ion. for κατακλείς.

**κατακληρο-δοτέω**, *seize and parcel out*, τὴν γῆν αὐτῶν v.l. in Lxx 1*Ma.*3.36, *De.*1.38, *Act.Ap.*13.19. **-νομέω**, I. c. acc. rei, 1. *obtain as one's assured possession*, Lxx *Si.*4.16. 2. *leave as an inheritance*, τοῖς υἱοῖς τὰ ὑπάρχοντα ib.*De.*21.16. 3. *assign as a possession*, ib.3.28, 12.10, *Act.Ap.*13.19. II. c. acc. pers., *make one's heir*, Lxx 2*Ki.*7.1.

**κατακληρ-ουχέω**, *receive as one's portion*, esp. of a conquered country, *divide among themselves, portion out*, τὴν χώραν Plb.2.21.7; τὰς οὐσίας Id.7.10.1; τὴν Σικελίαν D.S.13.30; τὴν νῆσον Str.8.6.16; τὴν γῆν εἰς κλήρους Ael.*VH*6.1. 2. *assign as a portion*, τισὶ τὴν ἀρίστην τῆς χώρας D.S.1.54, cf. *PLond.*2.383.2 (Pass., iii A.D.); *portion out to colonists*, πᾶσαν ὀλίγου δεῖν τὴν Ἰταλίαν Plu.*Ant.* 55. **-όω**, = foreg. 2, D.S.13.2 codd., *PSI*4.344 (iii B.C.):—Med., *receive as one's portion*, Plu.*Pomp.*41; *draw the lot*, Lxx 1*Ki.*14.42; but also ὃν ἂν κατακληρώσηται κύριος, ἀποθανέτω ibid.

**κατα-κλησία**, ἡ, = sq. 2, Poll.8.116, Hsch. **-κλησις**, εως, ἡ, *summoning by name*, Ph.2.388. 2. *summoning of the whole body of citizens, incl. rural population*, πρὸς ἐπίσκεψιν μείζονα τῶν πραγμάτων, opp. ἐκκλησία, Ammon.*Diff.*p.47 V. 3. *invocation* of the gods, Ph.2.342, Arr.*An.*5.2.7, Poll.1.29. II. *recalling*, D.S. 13 Arg. (nisi leg. μετάκλησις); ἡ [τῆς θεοῦ] κ. *CIG*6850ᴬ. **-κλητικός**, ή, όν, *for invoking*: -κλητικόν, τό, *invocatory spell*, *PMag.Par.* 1.2373. **-κλητος**, ον, *specially summoned*, ἐν κ. ἁλίᾳ *Tab.Heracl.* 1.11, 2.10.

**κατα-κλινής**, ές, *bed-ridden*, Hp.*Epid.*3.17.β', *PRyl.*124.26 (i A.D.), dub.l. in Plb.31.13.7. II. *sloping*, ἀταρπός Leonid.ap.Stob.4.52.28; γεώλοφος D.H.5.38. 2. *hanging down*, Thphr.*CP*2.9.11. **-κλινοβάτης**, ές, *making one lie abed*, ποδάγρα Luc.*Trag.*198 (in voc. -βατές, prob. f.l. for -βάτις). **-κλίνω** [ῑ], *lay down*, [δόρυ] κατακλίνας ἐπὶ γαίῃ Od.10.165; κ. τοὺς Πέρσας ἐς λειμῶνα *having made* them *recline* (for dinner) in a meadow, Hdt.1.126, cf. Pl.*R.*363c, 420e, *Ev.Luc.*9.14, *Milet.*1(9).368; κ. παιδίον *put it to bed*, Ar.*Lys.*19, cf. Plu.*Lyc.*3; κ. τινὰ ἐν ἁρμαμάξῃ X.*Cyr.*6.4.11; also, *cause one to take to his bed*, i.e. *strike with disease*, *PMag.Par.*1.2075; of animals, X. *Cyn.*9.3; κ. τινὰ εἰς Ἀσκληπιοῦ *lay* a sick person in the temple of Asclepios, Ar.*Pl.*411, *V.*123; ταύταν ὀβολῷ κ. (sens. obsc.) Cerc.5.31:—Pass. (with aor. 2 Att. -εκλίνην, aor. 1 -εκλίθην Att. and in other dialects), *lie at table*, κατακλιθέντας πίνειν Hdt.2.121.δ'; κατακλινήσομαι Ar.*Eq.*98, cf. *V.*1208; generally, *lie down*, κατακλινεὶς δευρί Id.*Nu.*694; κατακλίνεσθαι παρά τινα *lie* at table *next* him, Pl. *Smp.*175a; but, παρά τινι *lie with* him sexually, ib.203c; κατακλίνηθι μετ' ἐμοῦ Ar.*Lys.*904; κ. ἐπὶ ταῖς κοίταις, ἐπὶ στιβάδος, Ar.*V.*1040, X.*Cyr.*5.2.15; of a sick man, *take to one's bed*, Hp.*Epid.*1.2; simply, *lie in bed*, Id.*Prog.*3, Diocl.*Fr.*141; κατακλιθέντα ἐς τὸ ἱερόν Hyp.*Eux.* 18; κατεκλίθη ὕπτιος Pl.*Phd.*117e codd.; κατακεκλιμένος, of a corpse, Plb.6.53.1. II. *cause to incline, bend downwards*, ἕως ἂν κατακλίνῃ [ὁ ἐλέφας τοὺς φοίνικας] Arist.*HA*610ᵃ23: metaph., *lay prostrate, overthrow*, τύραννον Thgn.1181. III. Pass., of ground, *slope*, ἤπειρόνδε A.R.2.734. 2. of the sun, *set*, Poll.4.157. 3. of crabs' eyes, *turn sideways*, Arist.*HA*529ᵇ28. 4. *kneel*, ὅταν κατακλιθῇ εἰς γόνατα [κάμηλος] ib.499ᵃ17. 5. c. dat., *to be set under, made subject to*, ὅταν κατακλιθῇ τὸ θητικὸν τῷ προπολεμοῦντι Herm.*in Phdr.*p.157 A. **-κλισις**, εως, ἡ, *making* one *to lie down, seating* him *at table*, opp. ὑπανάστασις, Pl.*R.*425b, Arist.*EN*1165ᵃ28; ἡ κ. τοῦ γάμου the *celebration* of the marriage *feast*, Hdt.6.129. II. (from Pass.) *lying at table, sitting at meat*, Arist.*Pol.*1336ᵇ9, 21; παρά τινι Pl.*Smp.*175e; τὸ σχῆμα τῆς κ. Plu.2.679f, cf. Porph.*Abst.*2.61. 2. *way of lying in bed*, τὴν κ. ποιείσθω ἐπὶ τὴν ὑγιᾶ γνάθον Hp.*Art.*33, cf. *Prog.*3 (pl.). b. *taking to one's bed*, of a sick person, Id.*Epid.*4.31, J.*AJ*4.8.33, etc. c. *causing* one *to take to his bed*, i.e. *striking with disease*, *PMag.Par.*1.2496. d. Astrol., *horoscope cast at the hour when a patient takes to his bed*, Gal.19.529, *Cat.Cod.Astr.*1.20, 8(4).57. **-κλιτέον**, *one must cause to lie down, put to bed*, Sor.1.78, Herod.Med.ap.Orib.6.20.5. **-κλιτον**, τό, *couch, chaise-longue*, Suid., Phot. **-κλιτος**, ον, perh. *flowing down*, of light summer garments, θέριστρα κ. Lxx *Is.*3.23; cf. κατάκλιτος· τελευταία, Hsch.

*κατα-κλύζω, fut. -κλύσω [ῠ], poet. -κλύσσω Pi.*O.*10(11).10: pf. κατακέκλυκα *PMagd.*28.10 (iii B.C.):—*deluge, inundate*, τὴν γῆν Hdt. 2.13 (of the Nile), cf. 99 (Pass.), Pi.*O.*9.50, Th.3.89, Pl.*Ti.*22d, *OGI* 90.24 (Rosetta, ii B.C.):—Pass., *PPetr.*2 p.15 [= 3 p.xv] (iii B.C.), etc.; ὑπ' ὄμβρων -κλυζόμενος Isoc.11.12; κόσμος ὕδατι -κλυσθεὶς 2*Ep.Pet.* 3.6. 2. metaph., *deluge, overwhelm*, τοίους γὰρ κατὰ κῦμα..ἔκλυσεν Archil.9.3; τὴν Φρυγῶν πόλιν..ἤλπισας κατακλύσειν δαπάναισιν E.*Tr.* 995; ἅπαντα..κατακλύσει ποιήμασιν Cratin.186; κ. ἀφθονίᾳ δίαιταν *make* life *overflow* with plenty, X.*Oec.*2.8; κατακλύσαι δεινῶν πόνων *deluge* with sufferings, E.*Or.*343 (lyr.); εἰ καὶ μέλλει γέλωτι..ὥσπερ κῦμα..κατακλύσειν Pl.*R.*473c:—Pass., ἀλλοδαπῶν κύματι φωτῶν -κλυσθῆναι, of a city, A.*Th.*1084 (anap.); -κλυσθεὶς ὑπὸ τοῦ τοιούτου ψόγου ἢ ἐπαίνου Pl.*R.*492c; χρυσίῳ -κεκλυσμένος Plu.*Dem.*14; -κλυσθέντα πλήθει κακῶν Lib.*Ep.*5.1. II. *wash down* or *away*, κῦμα κ. ψᾶφον ἑλισσομέναν Pi.*O.*10(11).10, cf. Thphr.*CP*3.22.3. 2. *wash out*, τὰ ἴχνη τοῦ λαγῶ X.*Cyn.*5.4. III. *fill full of water*, τὴν πύελον Ar. *Pax*843. IV. *clean out* a bath, Gal.15.198. **-κλυσις**, εως, ἡ, *douche*, Hp.*Hum.*1, cf. Gal.16.162. **-κλυσμα**, ατος, τό, *purge* or *clyster*, Hp.*Salubr.*5. **-κλυσμός**, ὁ, *flood*, Pl.*Lg.*679d, Arist. *Ph.*222ᵃ23, *Stoic.*2.337, *Marm.Par.*6, etc.; *inundation*, *PMagd.*28ᵛ. 4 (iii B.C.): pl., Pl.*Ti.*25c, *Lg.*677a. 2. metaph., κ. τῶν πραγμάτων political *deluge*, D.18.214. II. Medic., *affusion, douche*, Cael. Aur.*TP*4.1.1. **-κλυστρον**, τό, = Lat. *compluvium*, *Gloss.*

**κατακλύω** [ῠ], *hear of*, θαῦμα S.*Ichn.*224 (v.l. κατήλυθεν Theon ap. Sch.).

**κατακλῶθες**, αἱ, *the Spinners*, v. κλῶθες.

**κατακλώθω**, *spin one's fate*, *CIG*6870:—Med., Lyc.145.

**κατακναίω**, = sq., metaph., *wear out*, ἑαυτόν Them.*Or.*32.362b.

***κατακνάω**, *scrape away*, ἀπόκριναι.., εἰ μὴ κατέκνησας τοῖς στρατιώταις ἄλαβες whether you did not *scrape away, make away with*.., Ar. *V.*965; -κνήσας (-κνίσας codd.) [τοῦ κηροῦ] τὸ λευκόν Dsc.2.83:—Pass., κατακνησθείην Ar.*Eq.*771; κηρὸς -κεκνησμένος wax *scrapings*, Asclep.ap.Gal.13.1022. 2. v. κατακνίζω II. 3.

**κατακνήθω**, = foreg., Nic.*Th.*944.

**κατάκνημος**, ον, *thin-legged*, *UPZ*121.20 (ii B.C.).

**κατακνῆστις**, ιδος, ἡ, = τυροκνῆστις, Hsch.

**κατακνιδεύω**, (κνίδη) = καταξύω, Hsch. (prob. f.l. for Lacon. κατέκνιδδεν, cf. sq.).

**κατακνίζω**, *chop up, mince*, τι εἰς λεπτά Ath.9.376d. 2. metaph., *pick to pieces*, λόγους Isoc.12.17; τὰ τοῦ Ὁμήρου κ. λεπτά Luc. *Hes.*5. II. *scratch, irritate, stimulate* the scalp, Asclep.ap.Gal. 12.420:—Pass., v.l. in Dsc.2.123; *to be prurient*, ἐγὼ δὲ κατακεκνισμαι Ar.*Pl.*973. 2. *cut grooves in, score*, ξύλα καὶ λίθους τραχύνουσι -ζοντες Diocl.*Fr.*26. 3. *scarify, let blood from*, -κνίσω (prob. for -κνήσω) σου τὸν πόδα Luc.*Ocyp.*91:—Pass., -κνισθεὶς τὸ σκέλος Orib.7.20.8 (= Gal.19.524, where -κνήσας).

**κατακνισμός**, ὁ, = κνισμός, Sch.Ar.*Pl.*975.

**κατακνώσσω**, *fall asleep*, A.R.3.690, Orph.*L.*321.

**κατακοιμ-άω** (on the Hom. usage v. infr. II. 2): I. intr., *sleep*,

*pass the night*, ξεῖνόν τινα χρήμασι πείσας κατεκοίμησε (v.l. -ισε) ἐς Ἀμφιάρεω he *went to sleep* there, Hdt.8.134: freq. v.l. for -κοιμίζω II (q.v.). II. causal, *put to sleep*, οὐδὲ..λάθα κατακοιμάσῃ (sc. τοὺς νόμους) S.*OT*871 (lyr.); κατεκοίμησα τοὐμὸν ὄμμα ib.1222 (lyr.); v.l. for -κοιμίσαντ' in Pl.*Smp.*223d:—Pass., -κοιμηθεὶς ὑπὸ μέθης Them. *Or.*26.326b; θυμὸς κ. ὑπὸ λογισμοῦ ib.8.110c. 2. used by Hom. only in aor. Pass., *sleep*, κατακοιμηθῆναι Il.2.355, Hdt.2.121.δ'; κατακοιμηθήτω Il.9.427; κατακοιμηθέντες ἐν τῷ ἱρῷ Hdt.1.31; ὃς ἂν ὑπαίθριος κατακοιμηθῇ Id.4.7, cf. Plb.3.67.2 (v.l.); imper. pres. κατακοιμάσθω Ar.*Th.*46 (anap.). -ησις, εως, ἡ, *sleeping, lodging*, τῆς πενίας παρὰ τῷ πόρῳ Them.*Or.*13.162b. -ητικός, ή, όν, *of* or *for lulling to sleep*, Arg.Theoc.18. -ίζω, = κατακοιμάω II (for which it is a constant v.l.), *lull to sleep*, τὴν φυλακήν Hecat.33 J.; τὰ δυσυπνοῦντα τῶν παιδίων Pl.*Lg.*790d, cf. *Smp.*223d (v.l. -κοιμήσαντ'), Luc.*VH*2.34, *Asin.*6: metaph., κ. τὸν λύχνον Phryn.Com.24; ὀργάς *Com.Adesp.*521; τοὺς πολεμίους Plu.2.346c:—Pass., *go to sleep*, Plb.3.67.2; of troublesome questions, ἵνα..ἀεὶ ἂν κατακοιμισθῶσιν *IG*2².1121.26. II. *sleep through*, τὴν φυλακήν *sleep out* one's watch, Hdt.9.93, Ael. *NA*1.15, al.; τῆς ἡμέρας τὸ χρησιμώτατον -κοιμίζουσα X.*Mem.*2.1.30. -ισμός, ὁ, *putting to sleep*, τῶν βρεφῶν Phld.*Po.*2.47 (pl.). -ιστής, οῦ, ὁ, *one who puts to bed, chamberlain*, D.S.11.69, Ph.2.571, Plu.2.173e, Jul. *ad Ath.*272d, prob. in Ephor.191.131 J.

**κατακοινωνέω**, *make one a partaker, give one a share*, τισι D.32.25; κ. τὰ τῆς πόλεως *share* the public property *among themselves*, Aeschin. 3.66 (v.l. κατακοινώσαντες).

**κατακοιρᾰνέω**, *govern*, Hsch., cf. Sch.Il.5.332.

**κατάκοιτος**, ον, *in bed*: *at rest, quiet*, Ibyc.1.7.

**κατακόκκας** ἢ **κατακίκκας**· κατάπλασμα, Hsch.

**κατακολλάω**, *glue* or *fasten upon, inlay*, θύρας χρυσῷ J.*AJ*8.3.3:—Pass., ὀθονίῳ..κατακεκολλήσθω..τὸ ξύλον Hp.*Art.*7; θύραι κατεκεκόλληντο σανίσιν Callix.1. 2. *glue together*, Arist.*Pr.*889ᵇ14.

**κατάκολλος**, ον, *mixed with glue*, μέλαν Aen.Tact.31.10.

**κατακολλῠβίζω**, = κατακερματίζω, *AB*104.

❀ **κατ-ᾰκολουθ-έω**, *follow after*, ὀπίσω τινός Lxx *Je.*17.16, cf. Longus 3.15 codd.: c. gen., Dioxipp.2 (s. v.l.); *comply with*, εἰ ταῖς τῶν ἀνθρώπων εὐχαῖς ὁ θεὸς κατηκολούθει Epicur.*Fr.*388; *obey*, νόμῳ, προστάγμασιν, Lxx *Da.*9.10, 1*Ma.*6.23; λόγῳ Plu.*Lys.*25; *follow* a historical or philosophical authority, Phld.*Rh.*2.146S.; Ἀράτῳ, Δημοκρίτῳ, Plb. 2.56.2, Plu.2.1108f; in fortification, κ. ταῖς ὀχυρότησι τῶν τόπων Plb.6.42.2; *emulate, imitate*, ἀδυνάτοις ἐπιβολαῖς Hegetorap.Apollon.Cit.3; κ. τοῖς ἱεροῖς, mistranslation of *prosecuisset*, as though *prosecutus esset*, Plu.*Cam.*5: abs., *obey instructions*, *PAmh.*2.31.12 (ii B.C.). -ητέον, *one must follow*, κριτηρίῳ, τέχνῃ, S.E.*M.*1.186, 11.175. -ία, ἡ, *compliance* with instructions, *CPHerm.*97.8ᵃ (iii A.D.). -ος, ον, *following*, of persons, c. dat., Vett.Val.220.4; of things, Id.125.31.

**κατακολούω**, *cut short*, Poll.8.154.

**κατακολπ-ίζω**, *run into a bay*, κ. ἐς Αἴγιναν Th.8.92, cf. Str.8. 3.33. -ισις, εως, ἡ, *putting into a bay*, Anon.ap.Suid. s. v. ἐπιβάθρα.

**κατακολυμβ-άω**, *dive down*, Th.7.25, Arist.*HA*620ᵇ34, Luc.*JTr.*48. -ητής, οῦ, ὁ, *diver*, Arist.*HA*631ᵃ31, Ath.7.296e.

**κατακομάω**, *wear the hair long*, Procop.*Arc.*7: metaph., of a ship, κ. τοῖς ἀναθήμασι Id.*Aed.*1.4.

**κατακομ-ῐδή**, ἡ, *bringing down to the sea-shore for exportation*, opp. ἀντίληψις (importation), Th.1.120. 2. *bringing home*, σώματος D.S. 18.3. -ίζω, *bring down*, esp. *from the inland to the coast*, σῖτον τῷ στρατεύματι Th.6.88; ⟨ὕλην⟩ ποταμοῖς κ. Str.11.2.17, cf. *OGI*132.10 (Egypt, ii B.C.), Hdn.8.2.3 (Pass.), etc.:—Med., *cause to be brought down*, ὡραῖα πλοίοις Pl.*Criti.*118e. 2. *bring into harbour*, ναῦν D. 50.55; ναῦν Ἀθήναζε Id.56.27; εἰς τὸν Πειραιᾶ ib.20; *bring home*, τριήρεις Aeschin.2.71. 3. *bring into a place of refuge*, κ. τὰ ἐλεύθερα σώματα καὶ τοὺς καρποὺς ἐν τῇ πόλει Aen.Tact.10.3; κ. γυναῖκας ἐκ τῶν ἀγρῶν D.19.125; κ. τὰ ἐκ τῶν ἀγρῶν Decr.ap.eund.18.38; παῖδας καὶ γυναῖκας ἐκ τῶν ἀγρῶν εἰς τὰ τείχη Lycurg.16, cf. D.S.12.39. 4. *import*, κεράμου πανταχόθεν -ομένου Ath.11.784c. 5. *bury*, prob. in *Berl.Sitzb.*1927.161 (Cyrene).

❀ **κατάκομος**, ον, *with falling hair* or *beard*, E.*Ba.*1187 (lyr.); πρόσωπον ἐχίδναις κ. Luc.*DDeor.*19.1, cf. Poll.4.140.

**κατακομπολᾰκῡθέω**, *boast loudly*, Tz.*H.*10.278.

**κατακομψεύομαι**, *speak elegantly* or *boastfully*, Sch.Luc.*Apol.*6.

**κατᾰκονά**, ἡ, (κατακαίνω) *destruction*, κατακονὰ ἄβιοτος βίου E.*Hipp.* 821 (lyr.).—The v.l., supported by Sch. (cf. *EM*50.25, Eust.381.22), κατακονᾷ..βίος, implies a Verb **κατ-ᾰκονάω**, *wear away*, as is done in whetting steel.

**κατακονδῠλ-ίζω**, strengthd. for κονδυλίζω, Aeschin.3.212 (Pass.), Lxx *Am.*5.11; ὄχλος -ισμένος τὴν ψυχήν Ph.1.387. -ιστος, ον, *well cuffed*, Hsch. s. v. ἐπικόρριστον. -όω, = κατακονδυλίζω, Id. s. v. κρομβότατον (Pass.).

**κατ-ᾰκοντίζω**, Att. fut. -ιῶ, used also by Hdt.9.17:—*shoot down*, Id. l. c., Th.8.108, D.18.151, Lxx *Ju.*1.15: pf. inf. Pass. κατηκοντίσθαι Phld.*Piet.*34; θηρία -όμενα Luc.*Tox.*59.

❀ **κατάκοος**, v. κατήκοος.

**κατα-κοπή**, ἡ, *cutting back, pruning*, δένδρων Thphr.*CP*2.12.6 (pl.); *cutting in pieces*, πρὸς κατακοπὴν ἱερεία Theopomp.Hist.283a; τραύματα καὶ κ. Artem.1.50. -κοπος, ον, *very weary*, κ. τῷ σώματι Lxx *Jb.*3.17, al.; ἐξ ὁδοῦ μακρᾶς D.H.6.29; ὑπὸ τῆς μάχης D.S.13.18, cf. Plu.*Arat.*8. II. *wearisome, tedious*, Phld.*Rh.*1.173S. -κόπτης, ου, ὁ, *cutter up*, σπλάγχνων Sch.Lyc.35 (ed. Bachm.). -κοπτικός, ή, όν, dub. sens. in *PMag.Lond.*121.430. -κόπτω, *cut down, fell*, of trees, in Pass., Thphr.*HP*3.15.1, *CP*2.15.4, etc. 2. *cut in pieces, cut up*, Hdt.1.48,73, 2.42, Ar.*Av.*1688 (Pass.), etc.; κρέα Pl.*Euthd.*301c; κατακοπεὶς *cut in pieces*, Hdt.8.92. 3. *cut down, massacre, butcher*, Id.6.75, Th.7.29:—Pass., ὥσπερ βόες κατεκόπησαν Phld.*Rh.*1.235S. 4. in a military sense, *cut in pieces*, '*cut up*', τὴν μόραν D.13.22:—Pass., κατακοπῆναι X.*An.*1.2. 25; κατακεκόψεσθαι ib.1.5.16. 5. κ. πληγαῖς τινα *PLips.*37.20 (iv A.D.), etc. 6. generally, *break in pieces, destroy*, στεφάνους D. 22.70; κέραμον Plb.5.25.3; ἔρια ὑπὸ τῶν σέων κατακοπτόμενα *fretted in pieces*, Ar.*Lys.*730, cf. Luc.*Ind.*1: metaph., κ. τὴν ἀρχήν Plu. *Demetr.*30; κατακέκοπταί οἱ τὸ τῆς ψυχῆς γαῦρον Id.2.762f; κατεκόπημεν ἄν we *should have been made mince-meat of*, Pl.Com.35. 7. *weary, bore*, Anaxipp.1.23, Men.*Sam.*70,77. 8. Rhet., λέξις -κεκομμένη '*staccato*', *jerky* composition, Demetr.*Eloc.*4. 9. in Med., μαστοὺς κατεκόψατο, in vehement grief, *Epigr.Gr.*316 (Smyrna). II. *strike with a die, coin* bullion *into money*, Hdt.3.96; τὸν θρόνον ὄντα ἀργυροῦν X.*HG*1.5.3; τὰς χρυσᾶς πλίνθους εἰς νόμισμα D.S.16.56, cf. Demetr.*Eloc.*281, Lib.*Or.*14.45.

**κατακόπωσις**, εως, ἡ, *wearying*, Gloss.

❀ **κατακορᾰκόω**, *fasten up, close* a sarcophagus, *BSA*17.225 (Pamphyl.), *Jahresh.*23 *Beibl.*101 (ib., ii A.D.).

**κατακορέω**, = ἐκλύω, Hp.ap.Gal.19.109 (s. v.l.).

**κατακορής**, ές, *satiated, glutted*, οἴνῳ Phryn.*PS*p.83B.; σιτίοις Procop.*Arc.*13. 2. of solutions, *saturated, strong*, φάρμακον Hp. *Epid.*5.15, cf. Gal.19.108; ἅλμη Id.5.111. 3. of colours, *deep*, μέλαν κατακορές Pl.*Ti.*68c, cf. Arist.*Col.*795ᵃ3; χρῶμα ὅμοιον ῥόδῳ κ. Thphr. *HP*4.8.7, cf. S.E.*P.*1.105; διαχώρημα Hp.*Coac.*596, cf. *Epid.*4.20; τὰ κ. πονηρά Id.*Coac.*601; ἐρύθημα Id.*Epid.*7.7; στήθεα κ. dub. sens. ib.2.6.14, cf. Gal.19.108. 4. of harmony, *complete*, τῆς κοσμικῆς συμφωνίας κ. τι καὶ παναρμόνιον φθεγγομένης Nicom.*Harm.*3; -κορεστάτη συμφωνία ἡ διὰ πασῶν ib.5; -κορέστερον μέλος, of the spheres, Iamb.*VP*15.65. II. metaph., *intense, violent*, δίψα, φύσις, Hp. *Epid.*7.11, *Medic.*6; βήξ Id.*Epid.*7.16; *profound*, ὕπνος ib.7.2. b. metaph., βαθὺ καὶ κ. αἴνιγμα a *profound* problem, Ph.1.659; ἀμετάβλητος καὶ κ. γνώμη a *deep* resolve, Id.1.78. 2. *immoderate, wearisome*, παρρησία, συνουσία, Pl.*Phdr.*240e, *Lg.*776a; ἂν ᾖ κατακορὴ [τὰ ἐπίθετα] Arist.*Rh.*1406ᵃ13, cf. Demetr.*Eloc.*303; κατακορὴς ἀπειλεῖ Tim.*Pers.*79; τοῦ τῶν γυναικῶν γένους λάλου καὶ κ. ὄντος Plb. 31.26.10, cf. 32.2.5; ὁ Δημοσθένης..ἐν τῷ γένει τούτῳ -έστατος Longin.22.3; -εστέραις κέχρηται ταῖς αὐστηραῖς ἁρμονίαις D.H.*Dem.* 45. III. Adv. -κορῶς, Ion. -ρέως, *deeply, intensely*, κ. δίαιμον *deeply* tinged with blood, Aret.*SA*1.10. 2. *to excess*, διαχωρήματα μᾶλλον τοῦ καιροῦ -έως χολώδεα Hp.*Acut.*54; cf. κατάκορος.

**κατακορμ-ίζω**, *cut wood into logs* or *pieces*, Paus.Gr.*Fr.*224:—also -άζω, Hsch.

❀ **κατάκορος**, ον, = κατακορής, Poll.5.151, Thom.Mag.p.105 R.; κ. χρῆσις ἀφροδισίων Steph. *in Gal.*1.239 D.:—in Adv., of colours, *deeply*, κ. μέλας *Gp.*16.2.1. II. metaph., *immoderate*, κ. καὶ περίεργοι ἱερουργίαι Plu.*Alex.*2. Adv. -ρως, *to excess*, ᾧ -κόρως χρῶνται οἱ λογογράφοι Arist.*Rh.*1408ᵃ33; τῇ τύχῃ κ. χρώμενος Decr.ap.D.18.182, cf. Plu.*Cic.*5; κ. χρώμενοι τῇ κραυγῇ Plb.4.12.9, cf. Phld.*Rh.*1.157, 366S., Dsc.2.52, Iamb.*Protr.*21.κ'.

**κατακοσμ-έω**, *set in order, arrange*, ἐπὴν..δόμον κατακοσμήσησθε Od.22.440; ἐπὶ νευρῇ κατεκόσμει πικρὸν ὀϊστόν *was fitting* it on the string, Il.4.118; πόλιν καὶ ἰδιώτας κ. v.l. in Pl.*R.*540b; εἰς τάξιν κ. τινὰ πρὸς ἄλληλα Id.*Ti.*88e:—Med., κ. εἰς τὴν γνώμην τινός Plu. *Comp.Per.Fab.*3:—Pass., Pl.*R.*560a, *Lg.*685d; ὅπως πεπαινόμενον τὸ ἦθος δύναιτο -κοσμεῖσθαι Diotog.ap.Stob.4.1.96, cf. 133. 2. *fit out, equip*, ὅπλοις κατακεκοσμημένος X.*Hier.*11.3; σεμνοτέροις πράγμασι Ar.*V.*1473 (lyr.); κ. τινὰ οἷον ἄγαλμα *adorn*, Pl.*Phdr.*252d. II. *reduce to order, regulate*, Plu.*Num.*14; ἑαυτούς Id.*Rom.*23:—Pass., Pl.*Plt.*273a. -ησις, εως, ἡ, *arrangement*, ib.271e; *order*, Id. *Ti.*47d. 2. *adornment*, ναῶν Andronic.Rhod.p.572 M. 3. metaph., πλάσις καὶ κ., of an *assumed demeanour*, Plu.2.712d. -ητέος, α, ον, *to be adorned*, ἱερόν Porph.*Marc.*11. -ος, ον, *adorned*, θρόνοι App.*Mith.*115.

**κατακοττᾰβίζω**, *squirt* or *throw wine over* any one, τινος Ar.*Fr.* 152.

**κατακούρην**· τοῦ ξυροῦ τὴν τομήν, Gal.19.109.

**κατ-άκουσις** [ᾰκ], εως, ἡ, *hearing*, Arr.*An.*5.7.5. -ᾰκουστής, οῦ, ὁ, *listener*, *Gloss.* -ᾰκούω, *hear and obey, be subject*, Ἀράβιοι οὐδαμὰ κατήκουσαν ἐπὶ δουλοσύνῃ Πέρσῃσι Hdt.3.88, cf. App.*Syr.* 55; τινος D.1.23, Arr.*Fr.*7 J., App.*Mith.*57, Hierocl. *in CA*19 p.461 M. 2. *give ear, listen* to one, D.6.35; of eavesdroppers, Str.14. 1.32. 3. *hear plainly*, τι E.*Rh.*553 (lyr.), Th.2.84, Pl.*R.*531a; τίνος Ar.*Ra.*312, cf. Pl.*Prt.*330e; ὁ θυρωρὸς..κατήκουεν ἡμῶν *overheard* us, ib.314c; κ. αὐλοῦντος Arist.*EN*1175ᵇ4: abs., Th.3.22.

❀ **κατακράζω**, fut. -κεκράξομαι, *cry down, outdo in crying*, Ar.*Eq.*287.

**κατακραιπᾰλάω**, strengthd. for κραιπαλάω, Procop.*Goth.*4.19.

**κατακρανία**, ἡ, *an affection of the head*, *Hippiatr.*103.

**κατάκρας**, Ion. -άκρης, v. ἄκρα.

**κατάκρᾱσις**, εως, ἡ, = κατακέρασις, Plu.2.688c, Gal.1.212. II. Arith., *multiplication*, opp. παράθεσις (addition), *Theol.Ar.*10,12; ἄρσενος καὶ θήλεος κ., i. e. *multiplication* of two by three, Iamb. *in Nic.* p.34 P.

❀ **κατακρᾰτ-έω**, *prevail over*, c. gen. pers., κατακρατεῖν ἀνδρὸς εἴωθεν γυνή Men.646, cf. Thphr.*CP*2.14.4; τῶν πολεμίων Plb.16.30.5: metaph., of pleasure, κ. τοῦ οἴκου *Stoic.*3.98; also c. acc., τοὺς ἀλ-

λους ἀρετῇ κ. D.C.54.29; ὁ ἵππος πρεσβύτερος ἤδη ὢν οὐ κ. τὰς θηλείας PCair.Zen.225.8 (iii B.C.):—Pass., *to be overcome*, ὑπὸ νόμου βελτίονος Zaleuc.ap.Stob.4.2.19. 2. abs., *prevail, gain the mastery, gain the victory*, κατὰ μοῖρ' ἐκράτησεν A.Pers.101 (lyr.), cf. Hdt.7.168, Th. 6.55, Pl.Lg.840e; ὁ Πηνειὸς τῷ οὐνόματι κατακρατέων ἀνωνύμους τοὺς ἄλλους [ποταμοὺς] εἶναι ποιέει Hdt.7.129; of an opinion, D.C.57.15; of planetary influence, *predominate*, Procl.Par.Ptol.18, al. II. c. acc. rei, *gain the mastery over*, ἀμάχους ῥώμας, εὔνοιαν, Ph.2.117, 438; *win*, στέφανον D.Chr.9.13: c. gen. rei, τῆς προθέσεως *become master of* one's purpose, Plb.5.38.9; τοῦ γενέσθαι τι Id.28.13.13; τῶν ὅλων Id.3.81.10; *retain possession of*, τῆς πόλεως Id.1.8.1; *master*, τῆς Ἑλληνικῆς διαλέκτου Id.39.1.4, cf. Cleom.1.10; ἰδιότητος Porph.Sent.33. 2. *digest, concoct*, τὰς τῶν σίτων τροφάς Pl. Lg.789d, cf. Arist.Pr.930b31:—Pass., τῇ εὐχυλίᾳ Sor.1.53 (fort. -κραθῇ). **-ησις**, εως, ἡ, *subduing*, Poll.9.142.

**κατακρᾱτικός**, ή, όν, *fit for tempering*, Philagr.ap.Orib.5.21.10 (Comp.); v.l. for κατακεραστικός in Archig.ap.Aët.9.35 (9.56 cod. Laud.Gr.60).

**κατακραυγάζω**, = κατακράζω, τινος Arr.Epict.4.4.28.

***κατακρέμ-ᾰμαι**, Pass., *hang down, be suspended*, Hdt.4.72, Cratin. 164; τινος *from* a thing, Plu.2.672a. ***-άννυμι**, *hang up*, κὰδ δ' ἐκ πασσαλόφι κρέμασεν φόρμιγγα Od.8.67; τὸν νέκυν κατὰ τοῦ τείχεος κ. Hdt.2.121.γ'; δίκτυα Aen.Tact.11.6: in med. sense, κατακρεμάσασα..τόξα *having hung* the bow *on herself*, h.Hom.27.16: Ep. Subj., ὄφρα -κρεμάσῃσιν Nic.Fr.74.42:—Pass., *hang down, be suspended*, Hp.Fract.21; κατακεκρέμαστο στέμμα D.S.18.26. **-ασμός**, ὁ, *hanging down*: κ. τῆς κιονίδος *relaxation* of the uvula, Apollon.ap. Gal.12.981. **-αστος**, ον, *hanging, pendent*, βότρυες Thphr.HP 3.18.12.

**κατακρεουργέω**, Ion. -οργέω, *hew in pieces, as a butcher does* meat, Hdt.7.181 (Pass.), Xanth.12.

**κατάκρεως**, unexplained word in Hdn.Epim.206.

**κατακρῆθεν**, Adv., better written divisim κατὰ κρῆθεν, v. κράς II.

**κατακρήμνᾰμαι**, Pass., = κατακρέμαμαι, Hp.Morb.2.10, Ar.Nu. 377: impf. κατεκρημνῶντο (from -κρημνάομαι) h.Bacch.39, prob. in Dsc.4.46, J.AJ3.7.5.

***κατακρημν-ίζω**, fut. -ιῶ Carm.Pop.46.33: (κρημνός):—*throw down a precipice*, ἑαυτούς Phld.Ir.p.56 W., cf. Plu.Mar.45, 2.825b, Ev.Luc. 4.29: with a word added, ἀπὸ τοῦ ἄκρου τοῦ κρημνοῦ Lxx 2Ch.25. 12:—Pass., D.19.327, Plu.Sull.1, etc.: pf. part., *having fallen over a precipice*, X.Cyr.8.3.41. 2. generally, *throw headlong down*, ἐκ τριηρέων X.HG2.1.31; ἀπὸ τῶν ἵππων Plb.3.116.12; ἀπὸ τοῦ πύργου D.S.4.31:—Pass., X.Cyr.1.4.7. **-ισμός**, ὁ, *throwing headlong*, Ath.Mech.37.6. **-ιστής**, οῦ, ὁ, *one who throws headlong down*, Gloss. **-ος**, ον, *steep and rugged*, χῶρος Batr.154, cf. Gp.18. 18.2.

**κατάκρης**, Adv., Ion. for κατάκρας (q. v.).

**κατ-ακρῑβόω**, strengthd. for ἀκριβόω: pf. part. Pass. -ωμένος *careful, precise*, Men.Prot.p.40 D.

**κατ-ακρῐδεύω**, *chatter like a swarm of locusts*, Hsch., Phot.

***κατά-κρῐμα**, ατος, τό, *condemnation, judgement*, D.H.6.61. 2. *punishment, fine, damage*, CPR1.16 (i A.D.), PAmh.2.114.8 (ii A.D.), Ep.Rom.5.16, 8.1. ***-κρίνω**, Arc. κακρίνω (v. infr.) [ῑ], *give as sentence against*, τὸ τελευτῆσαι πάντων ἡ πεπρωμένη κατέκρινε Isoc.1.43:—Pass., τοῖσι κατεκέκρῐτο θάνατος *sentence* of death *had been passed upon* them, Hdt.7.146; κατακεκριμένων οἱ τούτων *when* this *sentence has been given against* him, Id.2.133; φυγὴν κατακριθείς Suid. s. v. Ἱεροκλῆς: impers., ἂν κατακρῐθῇ μοι if *sentence be given against* me, X.Apol.7: Arc., c. dat. pers. et gen. rei, ὁσέοι ἂν χρηστήριον κακρίνη ἡ γνωσίαι κακριθῆ τῶν χρημάτων anyone whom the oracle *has condemned* or who by judicial process *has been condemned* to forfeit his property, IG5(2).262.14, 15 (Mantinea, v B.C., = Class.Phil.20.137). 2. c. acc. pers., *condemn*, v.l. in Antipho 4. 4.2: c. acc. et inf., κατέκρινάν μιν ἔκδοτον ἄγεσθαι Hdt.6.85, cf. 9.93, Theoc.23.23 (ubi sc. βαδίζειν); κ. τινὰ θανάτῳ Ev.Matt.20.18, cf. J. BJ5.13.1; εἴκοσι δραχμαῖς IG5(1).1390.161 (Andania, i B.C.): c. acc. rei, *deem guilty of* a thing, κ. πολλὴν ἄνοιάν τινων Arist.Rh.Al.1423b 29; ψευδολογίαν τινός J.AJ3.14.4:—Pass., *to be condemned*, X.HG 2.3.54; ψήφῳ θανάτου E.Andr.496 codd. (anap.), cf. Phld.Herc.1251. 18; ἀποθνῄσκειν X.Hier.7.10; also of the crime, τὰ ὁμολογούμενα τῶν πραγμάτων ὑπὸ τοῦ νόμου -κέκριται Antipho 3.1.1; -κεκρίσθαι τὰ ὑπὸ ἰδιωτῶν πραχθέντα OGI669.27 (Egypt, i A.D.). II. Pass., simply, *to be judged, deemed*, κατεκρίθη θνατοῖς ἀγανώτατος ἔμμεν Pi. Fr.149. **-κρίσιμος** [κρῐ], ον, *condemned*: κατακρίσιμοι *convicts*, Peripl.M.Rubr.59. II. of a case, *ready to be judged*, Sammelb. 5230.18 (i A.D.). **-κρῐσις**, εως, ἡ, *condemnation*, 2Ep.Cor.3.9, 7.3, Vett.Val.108.4, 117.35 (pl.). 2. *judgement*, κ. ψευδὴς a *false estimate*, Gal.5.76. ***-κρῐτος**, ον, *condemned, sentenced*, κ. γενόμενος ἐπί τινι D.S.33.2, cf. Plu.2.188b; θανάτου to death, Luc.Am. 52, cf. 23, 36; ἡ κ. γενεά Ph.2.411.

**κατ-ακροάομαι**, *listen attentively to*, μου τὰ μουσοδονήματα Eup. 245; τινος J.BJ4.1.5, Anon. in Gött.Nachr.1922.33.

**κάτ-ακρος**, ον, strengthd. for ἄκρος, Sch.D Il.15.536. Adv. -ως Anon.Prog. in Rh.1.627 W.

**κατακροτᾰλίζω**, *make a loud rattling noise*, πόδεσσιν Call.Dian. 247.

**κατακροτέω**, *applaud excessively*, Hsch., Phot.

**κατάκροτος**, ον, *noisy*, Hld.1.30.

**κατακρουν-ίζω**, *pour down over*, Archestr.Fr.13.8; of a douche or shower-bath, Philum.Ven.5.3, Gal.10.935:—Pass., *to have water poured over one*, D.L.6.41. **-ισμός**, ὁ, *douche*, Sor.2.15, al.

**κατά-κρουσις**, εως, ἡ, *downward pressure*, Arist.Pr.874b12, 963b 9. II. *shock*, λαμβάνειν κ. ἐκ πληγῆς Ph.Bel.80.6. **-κρουστικός**, ή, όν, *exercising downward pressure*, οἶνος Arist.Pr.873b26. ***-κρούω**, *knock*, τι ἐς τρύπημα Gp.10.61. 2. *make narrow incisions* or '*stabbings*', Hp.Ulc.24, 25, Medic.7. 3. *beat copper pans*, etc., in order to entice bees, Pl.Lg.843e. 4. in Archit. perh., = διακρούω, IG 7.4255.14.

**κατα-κρύβδην**, Adv. *in private, in secret*, opp. ἀναφανδόν, Ptol. Tetr.64. **-κρύπτω**, Ep. aor. part. κακκρύψας Nic.Fr.78.5: aor. 2 κατέκρῠβον Plu.Crass.23:—Pass., aor. 2 κατεκρύβην [ῠ] Id.2.310e, Alciphr.3.47:—*hide, conceal*, μή τι κατακρύψειν Il.22.120; τοὺς δ' ἄρ' Ἀθήνη νυκτὶ κατακρύψασα..ἐξῆγε Od.23.372; κατακρύψας ὑπὸ κόπρῳ 9.329; ὑπὸ κόλπῳ 15.469; σπέρμα -κρύπτων Hes.Op.471; ὑπὸ τὴν θύρην Hdt.1.12; ἐς κυψέλην Id.5.92.δ'; εἰς τὴν γῆν X.Cyr.3.3.3; ἐν μεγάρῳ πλοῦτον κ. Pi.N.1.31; ἐν ἀδήλῳ *put away* (euphem.) Pl.R. 460c: metaph., κόνις οὐ κ. χάριν Pi.O.8.79; ἄστυ..πένθει δνοφερῷ κ. A.Pers.536 (anap.). II. abs., *use concealment, conceal oneself* or *one's true nature*, οὔ τι κατακρύπτουσιν, of the gods, Od.7.205; ἄλλῳ δ' αὐτὸν φωτὶ κατακρύπτων ἤϊσκε 4.247. **-κρῠφή**, ἡ, *means of concealment*, οὐ γὰρ ἔχω κ. S.OC218 (lyr.). **-κρύφω** [ῠ], = κατακρύπτω, Q.S.2.478, Nonn.D.25.476.

**κατακρώζω**, *croak at, croak down*, like jackdaws, μίσει σφε κ. κολοιοί Ar.Eq.1020.

**κατακτάμεν** and **-κτάμεναι**, v. κατακτείνω.

**κατακτάομαι**, fut. -κτήσομαι Lxx 2Ch.28.10:—*get for oneself, win*, κράτος, νοῦν, S.Aj.768, 1256; ἐγκλήματα, πλούτους, Th.4.86, Isoc.4. 182: metaph., *win over, gain completely*, τὸ θέατρον Ael.VH3.8: aor. 2 Act. κατέκτην (as if from κατάκτημι) dub. in IG14.1934. II. Pass., τοῖς ἰδιώταις -κτώμενα *possessed* by.., Phld.Vit.Herc.1457.10: aor., D.S.16.56.

**κατακτάς, κατακτάμενος**, v. κατακτείνω.

**κατακτεᾰτίζομαι**, Ep. fut. -ίσσομαι, Med., = κατακτάομαι, A.R. 3.136.

***κατακτείνω**, Ep. fut. -κτενέω, in 3 sg. -κτενεῖ Il.23.412; -κτᾰνέω 6.409: aor. 1 κατέκτεινα Hom. (in all moods but ind.), SIG58.7, al. (Miletus, v B.C.): aor. 2 κατέκτᾰνον Il.6.204, etc., Ep. imper. κάκτανε ib.164: poet. aor. 2 κατέκτᾰν, ας, α, Il.4.319, al., A.Eu.460, Fr.181, 221; Ep. inf. κακτάμεναι Hes.Sc.453, κατακτάμεν Il.15.557; part. κατακτάς ib.335, Od.15.224, A.Th.965 (lyr.), E.IT715: pf. κατέκτονα A.Eu.587:—Pass., fut. Med. in pass. sense κατακτανέεσθε Il.14.481 codd. (-κτενέεσθε Cobet): aor. κατεκτάθην [ᾰ], 3 pl. -θεν 5.558, etc.; part. Med. κατακτάμενος (in pass. sense) Od.16.106; but καθανεῖν is freq. used as Pass. to this Verb:—*kill, slay*, freq. in Ep. and Trag., ll. cc.; rare in Prose, Heraclit.56, Hdt.2.75, SIG l. c., X.Hier.6.14, 7.12, etc.

***κατακτεν-ίζω**, *comb, dress carefully*, κατεκτενισμένοι τὰς κόμας Duris 60 J. **-ισμός**, ὁ, *careful combing*, Herod.Med.ap.Orib. 10.17.1. **-ος**, ον, *carefully combed* or *dressed*, Hsch.

**κατάκτης**, ὁ, (κατάγω I.4b) *visitor, guest* at an inn, Poll.7.16.

**κατάκτησις**, εως, ἡ, *acquisition*, πραγμάτων, χώρας, γῆς, Plb.4.77.2, Str.8.3.33, Plu.Caes.22; αὐτονομίας D.S.17.74; δυνάμεως ῥητορικῆς Phld.Rh.2.261 S.

**κατακτός**, ή, όν, (κατάγνυμι) *capable of being broken*, Arist.Mete. 385a14; θραυστὸν καὶ κ., ἀλλ' οὐ θλαστόν Id.HA523b10. II. (κατάγω) *to be sunk* or *let down*, of a kind of κότταβος, Pherecr.66, Ar.Pax 1244, cf. Ath.15.667e.

**κατάκτρια**, ἡ, *spinning woman* (κατάγω I. 5), Hsch.

**κατακτῠπ-έω**, *make a loud noise, roar against*, κατεκτύπουν ἡμῶν οἱ ἄνεμοι Alciphr.1.23. **-ησις**, εως, ἡ, *making a noise at*, Eust.1602. 18. **-ος**, ον, gloss on κατάδουπος, Zonar.

**κατακῠβεύω**, pf. -κεκύβευκα D.C.45.28:—*gamble away*, τὰ ὄντα Lys.14.27:—Pass., Aeschin.1.95. II. Pass., also, *to be beaten in play*, Eust.1397.45.

**κατακῠβιστάω**, *turn a somersault*, Ael.NA5.54.

**κατακῠκάω**, *beat up*, as white of egg in water, Hp.Morb.3.17.

**κατακυκλόω**, *encompass, encircle*, in Pass., J.BJ3.8.6 (v.l. κυκλωθέντα), Gal.18(1).787.

**κατακῠλίνδω** or **-κυλίω** (J.BJ6.1.6:—Med., v. infr.), *roll down*, D.H.11.26, Lxx Je.28(51).25:—Med., λίθους κατακυλιομένους Arr. Tact.11.6:—Pass., *to be rolled down* or *thrown off*, Hdt.1.84, 5.16; κατακεκυλισμένοι ἀπὸ τῶν ἵππων X.Cyr.5.3.1:—pres. **κατακῠλινδέω** J.BJ4.1.10; impf. κατεκυλίνδουν D.C.56.14.

**κατακύλλωμα**, ατος, τό, *a particular case of lameness* (κύλλωμα), Eust.1599.13. II. metaph., *turning-point*: hence, *extreme point*, = τὸ πέρας τῶν κακῶν, Phot., Suid. (post τοκάς), cf. EM761.38.

**κατακῠματάκης**, ές, *melting the waves*, αὖραι Tim.Pers.144.

**κατακυνῶν ἢ κατακύων**· ὅταν τὸ σχοινίον ἑλίγκας (fort. ἑλίξας) τῶν ἄκρων προσκατακλείσῃς, Hsch.

***κατακύπτω**, *bend down, stoop*, πρόσσω γὰρ κατέκυψε Il.16.611, cf. Aristeas 91, Ev.Jo.8.8; *to be bowed down* by shame, AP12.8 (Strato). 2. *look down* from a window, Lxx 4Ki.9.32; *stoop down and look*, εἰς τὸν βυθόν Arr.Epict.2.16.22; κ. εἴσω τοῦ χάσματος Luc.DMort.21.1; κ. ἐς τὸ ἄστυ Id.Pisc.39, cf. Icar.15.

**κατακῡριεύω**, *gain* or *exercise complete dominion*, Lxx Ps.71(72). 8. 2. κ. τινός *gain dominion over, gain possession of*, ib.Ps.9.26 (10.5), 1Ep.Pet.5.3; [πλοίου] D.S.14.64.

***κατάκυψις**, εως, ἡ, *stooping*, Ruf.ap.Orib.inc.20.7 (pl.).

**κατακῡρόω,** *confirm, ratify,* Arist.*Ath.*47.2; κ. τὴν ὠνήν *confirm* a contract with a tax-farmer, J.*AJ*12.4.4:—Pass., *to be ratified,* Thphr.*Fr.*97.1; *to be fulfilled,* S.*Ant.*936 (anap.); ψήφῳ θανάτου κατακυρωθείς *condemned* to death, E.*Or.*1013 (anap.).

**κατακωκύω,** *wail, shriek loudly,* Hsch., Phot.

**κατακωλύω,** *hinder from doing,* c. acc. et inf., Simon.41, cf. Ar.*Ach.*1088; *detain, keep back,* τινα X.*Oec.*12.1, D.53.5; κ. ἔξω τινάς X.*An.*5.2.16; ἄχθεται.. τῷ κατακωλύοντι Pherecr.153.7:—Pass., c. gen. rei, κατεκωλύθη τοῦ ἐς Σικελίαν πλοῦ D.33.13.

**κατακωμάζω,** *burst riotously in upon,* τὸ δαιμόνιον κατεκώμασε δώμασιν E.*Ph.*352.

**κατακωμῳδέω,** *attack in comedy,* Tz.*H.*6.869, Sch.Ar.*V.*61 (Pass.).

**κατακωχή, κατακώχιμος,** incorrect forms for κατοκωχή, -χιμος.

**καταλᾰβ-εύς,** έως, ὁ, *holder, nail,* in pl., Hsch., Phot. **-ή,** ἡ, *grasping, comprehension,* Pl.*Def.*412c.

**κατάλαβρος,** ον, strengthd. for λάβρος, Eup.293.

**καταλαγνεύομαι,** Pass., *to be very lewd,* καταλαγνευθείς Hsch.

**καταλαγχάνω,** *hold possession of,* χῶρον dub. l. in Ael.*NA*9.35.

**κατ-ᾰλαζονεύομαι,** *boast, brag largely,* πρός τινα D.21.169; ὡς.. Plu.*Luc.*22. **2.** *exaggerate invidiously,* Isoc.15.5,31. **3.** also, *depreciate invidiously,* Thphr.ap.D.L.5.40. **II.** κ. τινός *to boast against* one, Ph.1.339, 2.85, Sm.*Ps.*136(137).3, Suid. s.v. Ἀδράστεια.

**καταλαθισταί·** ἐξηγηταί, ἢ ἐνδεικνύοντες τὰ δημόσια, Hsch.

**καταλακτίζω,** *inculco, Gloss.*

**κατ-ᾰλᾰλάζω,** *shout, exult,* Aq.*Ps.*146.7.

**καταλᾰλ-έω,** pf. -λελάληκα A.D.*Synt.*323.7:—*talk, babble loudly,* τοῖς θύραζε ταῦτα κ. Ar.*Ra.*752; τινος *before* another, Luc.*Asin.*12. **II.** *talk down, rail at,* ἡμᾶς *IG*9(2).338.6 (Thess.); τινὰ πρὸς πάντας Plb.3.90.6; τὸ δόγμα Id.18.45.1; τινος D.S.11.44; ὑμῶν ὡς κακοποιῶν 1*Ep.Pet.*2.12; τινὸς ψευδῆ Lxx*Ho.*7.13; κατά τινος ib.*Ps.*49(50).20:—Pass., ἐπί τινι Plb.27.13.2; *to be outdone in speech,* ὑπ' ἰδιωτῶν Phld.*Rh.*1.343S. **2.** *weary by talking,* gloss on καταγλωττίζειν, Phryn.*PS*p.79B. **3.** simply, *interview, address* a person, *PHib.*1.151 (iii B.C.). **-ητέον,** *one must talk against,* cj. in Thom.Mag.p.224R. (who censures it). **-ιά,** ἡ, *evil report, slander,* Lxx*Wi.*1.11, 1*Ep.Pet.*2.1 (pl.). **-ος,** ὁ, *slanderer, Ep.Rom.*1.30, *POxy.*1828r.3.

⊛ **καταλαμβάνω,** fut. -λήψομαι Pl.*Prt.*311a (in pass. sense, A.D.*Synt.*48.9), Ion. -λάμψομαι Hdt.6.39, Aeol. -λᾶμψομαι dub. in Alc.*Supp.*5.9 (v. λαμβάνω): pf. -είληφα Pl.*Phdr.*250d, etc. (καθ- *SIG*129.18 (Carpathos, iv B.C.)), -λελάβηκα Pherecyd.Syr.ap.D.L.1.122, Hdt.3.42 (v.l. -λελαβήκεε):—Pass., Ion. aor. -ελάμφθην Id.5.21; -ελάφθην *SIG*279.7 (Zelea, iv B.C.): pf. in med. sense, D.S.17.85:—*seize, lay hold of,* c. acc., τοῦ κατὰ νῶτα λαβών Od.9.433, cf. Ar.*Lys.*624, etc.; κατέλαβε τὴν ἀκρόπολιν Th.1.126, cf. Hdt.5.71, Ar.*Lys.*263 (lyr., tm.), Isoc.4.153, etc. (metaph., τὴν τοῦ νέου τῆς ψυχῆς ἀκρόπολιν κ. Pl.*R.*560b); πάντα φυλακαῖς κ. Plu.*Per.*33; κ. ἕδρας Ar.*Ec.*21, 86; φάσκων Ποσειδῶ πρότερον Ἀθηνᾶς καταλαβεῖν αὐτήν (sc. τὴν πόλιν) Isoc.12.193; later, simply, *arrive at* a place, *POxy.*1829 (vi A.D.), etc.:—Med., *seize for oneself,* τὰ πρήγματα Hdt.6.39; τὰ ἄλλοι οὐ κατελάβοντο matters which others *had* not *preoccupied,* ib.55: freq. in Plb., κ. λόφον 1.19.5, al.:—Pass., of a person, ὑπὸ τοῦ θεοῦ καταληφθείς *possessed,* Plot.5.8.11. **2.** of death, fatigue, disaster, etc., τὸν δὲ κατ' ὄσσε ἔλλαβε.. θάνατος Il.5.82; Ἄργον.. κατὰ μοῖρ' ἔλαβεν.. θανάτοιο Od.17.326: c. dupl. acc., εὖτ' ἄν μιν κάματος κατὰ γυῖα λάβησιν 1.192; Δίκη καταλήψεται ψευδῶν τέκτονας Heraclit.28; *befall, overtake,* συμφορὰ κ. πόλεις E.*Hipp.*1161: freq. in Hdt., θεῖα πρήγματα καταλαμβάνει τοὺς αἰελούρους 2.66; πένθεα μεγάλα τοὺς Αἰγυπτίους κ. ibid., cf. 3.42; ὅσα φεύγοντας ἐκ τῆς πατρίδος κακὰ ἐπίδοξα καταλαμβάνειν may be expected *to befall* them, 4.11; ἤν τι καταλαμβάνῃ νεώτερον τὸν πεζόν 8.21: folld. by inf., νοῦσός τινα κ. νοσῆσαι 3.149, cf. 3.75; πρίν τι ἀνήκεστον ἡμᾶς κ. Th.4.20; κίνδυνος κ. τινά D.18.99; rarely of good fortune, τοῦτον κατέλαβε εὐτυχίη τις Hdt.3.139. **3.** *seize with the mind, comprehend,* Pl.*Ax.*370a, Chrysipp.*Stoic.*2.39, Plb.8.2.6, *Ev.Jo.*1.5 (perh. *overcome*); κάλλος διὰ τῆς [ὄψεως] Pl.*Phdr.*250d; ἐκ τοῦ φάσματος ὅτι.. D.H.5.46, cf. Arr.*Epict.*1.5.6:—so in Med., D.H.2.66, S.E.*M.*7.288; ὅτι.. *Act.Ap.*4.13; τί τὸ πλάτος *Ep.Eph.*3.18:—Pass., Phld.*Sign.*22, *Mus.*p.62K., Numen.ap.Eus.*PE*14.8. **4.** *accept,* παρὰ τοῦ βασιλέως.. δωροδοκήματα dub. l. in Pl.Com.119.1 (κᾆτ' ἔλαβον Mein.). **II.** *catch, overtake, come up with,* τοὺς φεύγοντας Hdt.1.63, cf. 2.30, etc.:—Pass., Id.7.211, Plb.1.47.8. **2.** *find on arrival,* c. part., τινὰ ζῶντα Hdt.3.10; τὰ πλεῖστα.. προειργασμένα Th.8.65; πάντα ἔξω Id.2.18; ἀνεῳγμένην τὴν θύραν Pl.*Smp.*174d; τοὺς ἄρχοντας ἐξιόντας D.21.85; τινὰ ἔνδον Pl.*Prt.*311a; τῶν φορτίων πολλὴν ἀπρασίαν D.34.8; τι ὑπάρχον Arist.*Top.*131a29; *detect,* ἐπ' αὐτοφώρῳ ἐμαυτόν Pl.*Ap.*22b:—Pass., κατελήφθη σοῦ λάθρᾳ πωλῶν τὰ σά E.*Cyc.*260, cf. *Ev.Jo.*8.3, etc.; κατείληπτο σοφιζόμενος D.21.164; *to be taken by surprise,* Plu.*Publ.*20. **III.** impers., καταλαμβάνει τινά c. inf., *it happens to* one, *it is* one's *fortune* to.., καταλαμβάνει μιν φεύγειν Hdt.2.152, cf. 3.118; καταλελάβηκέ με.. τοῦτο.. ἐκφῆναι Id.3.65, cf. 4.105, 6.38. **IV.** abs., πρὸς τὴν καταλαβοῦσαν συμφορήν *that had befallen,* Id.4.161; τὰ καταλαβόντα, = τὰ συμβάντα, *what had happened, the circumstances,* Id.9.49; ἢν πόλεμος καταλάβῃ Th.2.54, cf. 18; εἰ -λαμβάνοι ἀναχώρησις Id.4.31; τῆς νυκτὸς -λαμβανούσης as night *was coming on,* D.S.20.86; χειμῶνος ἤδη -λαμβάνοντος Hdn.7.2.9. **V.** *hold down, cover,* τῇ χειρὶ τὸν ὀφθαλμόν Pl.*Tht.*165b; τὰς χεῖρας Plu.*Sert.*26; *fasten down,* κ. πῶμα γόμφοις Id.2.356c, cf. Gal.13.358 (so in Med., D.S.3.37):—Pass., *to be compressed,* opp. διαλύεσθαι, Arist.*Pr.*870b11; τὰς φλέβας -λαμβανόμενοι Id.*Somn.*455b7. **2.** *keep under, repress, check,* κ. τινῶν αὐξανομένην τὴν δύναμιν Hdt.1.46; κ. τὸ πῦρ *get* it *under,* ib.87; ἴσχε καὶ κ. σεωυτόν Id.3.36; κ. τὰς διαφοράς *put an end to* them, Id.7.9.β'; κ. ἐρίζοντας *stop* their quarrelling, Id.3.128: folld. by inf., κ. τοὺς Αἰγυπτίους ταῦτα μὴ ποιέειν Id.2.162; ὁ τῶν Περσέων θάνατος καταλαμφθεὶς ἐσιγήθη *inquiries about* their death *being checked..,* Id.5.21. **b.** κ. τὸ πνεῦμα *hold* the breath, Gal.6.176, al. **3.** *bind,* κ. πίστι καὶ ὁρκίοισι Hdt.9.106; ὅρκοις Th.4.86, etc.:—Pass., εἴ τινι -λέλαμμαι ὅρκῳ *SIG*360.41 (Chersonesus); νόμοις, ἔθεσι κατειλημμένα *enforced,* Arist.*Pol.*1324b22; ζημίαις Pl.*Lg.*823a; [τὰς σπονδὰς] ηὗρε κατειλημμένας he found the treaty *concluded,* Th.5.21 codd. **4.** *compel, constrain* one *to do,* c. inf., ἀναγκαίῃ μιν κ. φαίνειν *forces* him to bring out the truth, Hdt.3.75:—Pass., ἀναγκαίῃ καταλαμβανόμενος *being constrained,* Id.2.65, cf. Th.7.57. **5.** *convict, condemn,* Antipho 2.4.11; opp. ἀπολύειν, Id.4.4.9; ἐὰν καταληφθεὶς ἀποθάνω Id.2.2.9, cf. *IG*12(2).526A20 (Eresus, iv B.C.); of the prosecutor, *secure a conviction, Rev.Phil.*1928.192 (Erythrae, v B.C.); ὁ -λαβών *SIG*578.58 (Teos, ii B.C.), etc.

**κατάλαμπρος,** ον, *very bright,* Gal.19.576, *EM*790.29.

⊛ **καταλαμπρύνω,** *make splendid,* νεὼν κάλλει τε καὶ μεγέθει Procop.*Aed.*1.6.

**καταλαμπτέος,** α, ον, Ion. for καταληπτέος, *to be arrested,* θανάτῳ by death, Hdt.3.127.

⊛ **καταλάμπω,** *shine upon* or *over,* c. gen., ὧν ὁ ἥλιος κ. Pl.*R.*508d: also c. acc., κ. τοὺς στενωπούς *to light them,* Plu.*Cic.*22; ἡμέρα κατέλαμψεν αὐτόν Id.*Ages.*24, cf. Luc.*Prom.*19:—Pass., ὑπὸ τοῦ ἡλίου καταλαμπόμενοι X.*Mem.*4.7.7, cf. E.*Tr.*1070 (lyr.), *Ion* 87 (anap.). **II.** abs., *shine,* of the sun, Hp.*Aër.*5, E.*El.*464 (lyr.), v.l. in *h.Merc.*141.

**κατάλαμψις,** εως, ἡ, *bright reflection,* κ. ἀντίρροπος v.l. in Iamb.*VP* 15.67; *illumination,* Ptol.*Alm.*13.7 (pl.).

**καταλαπριώσει·** ἀποκτενεῖ, καταδέξεται, κατατρυπήσει ἢ καταπερήσει, Hsch.

**καταλγ-έω,** *feel sore pain,* S.*Ph.*368, Plb.3.80.4. **-ύνω,** *grieve very much,* in Pass., Hsch.

**καταλεαίνω,** fut. -λεᾰνῶ Lxx*Da.*7.23:—*grind down,* Plu.2.802b:—Pass., -ομένη τροφή Anon.Lond.24.23. **II.** *smooth down, placate,* Just.*Nov.*129 *Praef.*

**κατάλεγμα,** ατος, τό, *dirge,* Sm.*Ez.*2.10, Al.*Is.*16.9.

**καταλέγω** (A), *lay down;* v. καταλέχομαι.

⊛ **καταλέγω** (B), *recount, tell at length and in order,* Hom., always in fut. or aor. 1, ταῦτα μάλ' ἀτρεκέως καταλέξω Il.10.413, al.; τόδε εἰπὲ καὶ ἀτρεκέως κατάλεξον ib.384, al.; πᾶσαν ἀληθείην κατάλεξον 24.407: freq. in Hdt., as 4.83, 114; ἑξῆς κ. Ath.13.610b; κ. τὰς προσηγορίας ib.c:—Pass., τούτων ὧν τῶν καταλεχθέντων of those *which have been recounted,* Hdt.4.50, cf. 23, al.:—Med., Ps.-Hdt.*Vit.Hom.*21: folld. by interrog. Adv., κατάλεξον ὅπως ἤντησας Od.17.44, 3.97; κεῖνον ὀϊζυρὸν κατάλεξον, ἤ που ἔτι ζώει.. *tell* me *the tale of* that unhappy man, 4.832. **b.** *repeat, recite,* τῶν χρησμῶν Hdt.7.6; τετράμετρα πρὸς τὸν αὐλόν X.*Smp.*6.3; τὰς πατρίους εὐχάς Herm.Hist.2; καταλέγεσθαι· ὀδύρεσθαι τὸν τεθνεῶτα, Hsch.; cf. κατάλεγμα, καταλογή III. **2.** *reckon up, tell in full tale,* μνηστῆρας ἀριθμήσας κατάλεξον Od.16.235; of a line of kings or ancestors, κατέλεγον οἱ ἱρέες ἐκ βύβλου.. βασιλέων τ' καὶ λ' οὐνόματα Hdt.2.100; τοὺς αἰεὶ πατέρας Id.6.53; κ. ἑωυτὸν μητρόθεν *reckoned up* his pedigree, Id.1.173; κ. τοὺς ἄρχοντας Pl.*Hp.Ma.*285e, cf. *Ep.*327e, X.*Mem.*2.4.4:—later in Med., Ph.1.187, 2.593, Ath.11.504f. **b.** *reckon, count as,* οὓς οἱ πολλοὶ πλουσίους κ. Pl.*Lg.*742e, cf. X.*An.*2.6.27: so perh. in Pass., χήρα -έσθω 1*Ep.Ti.*5.9. **c.** *conclude by enumeration,* ὡς.. Arist.*Rh.Al.*1429b35. **3.** with pf. κατείλοχα Paus.10.24.1:—Pass., aor. (v. infr.): pf. κατείλεγμαι; 3 pl. plpf. κατειλέχατο J.*AJ*19.1.15:—*enumerate, draw up a list,* hence, *enrol, enlist,* ἄνδρας οἳ δορυφόροι μὲν οὐκ ἐγένοντο Πεισιστράτου, κορυνηφόροι δέ Hdt.1.59; στρατιώτας, ὁπλίτας, Ar.*Ach.*1065, *Lys.*394, etc.; ἱππέας Arist.*Ath.*49.2; κ. εἰς ὁπλίτας Lys.15.7; εἰς τὸν κατάλογον Ἀθηναίων Id.25.16; ἐς τὰς ναῦς Th.3.75: generally, τοὺς πεντακισχιλίους Arist.*Ath.*29.5; κ. τὸν Ἡρακλέα εἰς τοὺς δώδεκα θεούς D.S.4.39: c. dat., κ. τινὰ τοῖς δημοσίᾳ ἱππεύουσιν Philostr.*VS*1.22.3, cf. 1.25.3 (nisi leg. ἐγκατ-): c. inf., τοὺς πλουσιωτάτους ἱπποτροφεῖν κ. X.*HG*3.4.15:—in Med., *enrol for oneself,* δορυφόρους, ὁπλίτας, Hdt.1.98, Th.7.31:—Pass. (aor. 2 κατελέγην more common in Att. than aor. 1, cf. *IG*2[2].896.9, Pl.*Lg.*762e, 943a), *to be enlisted* or *enrolled,* Hdt.7.1; τῶν τρισχιλίων κ. *to be enrolled* of their number, Lys.30.8; κ. στρατιώτης Id.9.4; κατειλεγμένος ἱππεύειν Id.16.13; καταλεγεὶς τῶν τριηράρχων Is.7.5; ὁ κατειλεγμένος D.39.8; εἰς τὴν σύγκλητον κ. Plu.*Pomp.*13; ἀγορανόμον -λεγέντα, = Lat. *adlectum inter aedilicios, Ann.Épigr.*1905.120. **4.** later, *select,* τοῖς παισὶ τοὺς διδασκάλους *AB*105:—Med., τὸν πλωτικὸν [βίον] Pl.*Ax.*368b. **II.** = μηνύειν, τῷ βασιλεῖ τὴν ἐπιβουλήν J.*AJ*15.3.2: c. gen., *inform against,* ib.19.6.3; *accuse,* μάρτυς ἄδικος -λέγων αὐτοῦ ἀσέβειαν Lxx*De.*19.16.

**καταλείβω,** *pour down:* hence, *cause to waste away,* δέμας E.*Andr.*131 (lyr.):—Pass., *drop down,* γλυκίων μέλιτος καταλειβομένοιο Il.18.109; [ὕδωρ] ἐκ πέτρης καταλείβεται Hes.*Th.*786; δάκρυά τ' ἐκ δακρύων καταλείβεται E.*Tr.*605 (lyr.); *melt away* (in tears), καταλειβομένης ἄλγεσι πολλοῖς Id.*Supp.*1119 (anap.); also καταλείβεσθαί νιν καὶ καταρρεῖν ὥσπερ τοὺς κολοσσούς, in an imprecation, *Abh.Berl.Akad.*1925(5).21 (Cyrene).

**κατάλειμμα,** ατος, τό, *remnant,* Lxx*Ge.*45.7, al. **2.** v. κατάλημμα.

**καταλειπτέον**, *one must leave behind*, Ph.*Bel.*100.37, Antyll.ap. Orib.45.2.9.

**κατ-άλειπτος** [ᾰλ], ον, *anointed*, σμύρνῃ Ar.*Eq.*1332; μύρῳ Id.*Pax* 862.

⊛**καταλείπω**, later **καταλιμπάνω** (q.v.), Ep. also **καλλείπω** Il.10. 238: fut. καλλείψω 14.89: aor. κάλλῐπον 12.92: aor. 1 subj. καλλείψῃς Q.S.10.299; part. καλλείψας Nonn.*D.*32.130; καταλείψας Luc. *DMeretr.*7.3; Ion. iterat. καταλίπεσκε (κατελίπεσκε, καταλειπέεσκε codd.) Hdt.4.78: pf. -λέλοιπα Ar.*Lys.*736:—**Med.**, fut. καταλείψομαι (in pass. sense) X.*An.*5.6.12: aor. 2 -ελιπόμην Hdt.3.34, Pl. *Smp.*209d (in pass. sense, *Berl.Sitzb.*1927.161 (Cyrene)):—**Pass.**, fut. καταλειφθήσομαι Isoc.15.7, 17.1:—*leave behind*, πὰρ δ' ἄρ' ὄχεσφιν ἄλλον.. κάλλιπεν Il.12.92; esp. of persons dying or going into a far country, κὰδ δέ με χήρην λείπεις ἐν μεγάροισι 24.725; οὖρον.. κατέλειπον ἐπὶ κτεάτεσσιν Od.15.89; οἷόν μιν Τροίηνδε κιὼν κατέλειπεν Ὀδυσσεύς 17.314; so later, τὴν στρατιὴν καταλίπεσκε ἐν τῷ προαστίῳ Hdt.4.78; φύλακον κ. τινά Id.1.113, cf. 2.103:—Med., καταλείπεσθαι παῖδας *leave behind one*, Pl.*Smp.* l. c., cf. Hdt.3.34, etc.:—Pass., *to be left, remain behind*, κατελέλειπτο ἐν Πέρσῃσι Hdt.1.209, cf. 7.170, X.*An.*5.6.12: c. gen., [στρατὸς] καταλελειμμένος τοῦ ἄλλου στρατοῦ a force *left behind* the rest, Hdt.9.96. 2. *bequeath*, [τόξον] παιδὶ κάλλιπ' ἀποθνήσκων Od.21.33: metaph., ἐμοὶ δ' ὀδύνας τε γόους τε κάλλιπεν 1.243, cf. 11.279; δόκησιν ἰσχύος καὶ ξυνέσεως ἐς τὸ ἔπειτα Th.4.18; τοῖς θρέψασι λύπας Lys.2.70; παισὶν αἰδῶ οὐ χρυσὸν κ. Pl.*Lg.*729b: c. inf., εἰ καταλείψει μηδὲ ταφῆναι not enough to be buried with, Ar.*Pl.*556:—Pass., [χρήματα] καταλειφθέντα Is.1. 45. b. κ. διαθήκας *leave* a will (when going on service), Id.9. 14. 3. Med., *leave* in a certain state, κόλπον βαθὺν καταλιπόμενος τοῦ κιθῶνος Hdt.6.125. II. *forsake, abandon*, οὕτω δὴ μέμονας Τρώων πόλιν.. καλλείψειν; Il.14.89, cf. 22.383; πολλοὺς καταλείψομεν we *shall leave* many *upon the field*, 12.226; ὤ μοι, εἰ μέν κε λίπω κάτα τεύχεα 17.91; κὰδ δέ κεν εὐχωλὴν Πριάμῳ καὶ Τρωσὶ λίποιεν Ἀργείην Ἑλένην 2.160: c. inf., κάλλιπεν οἰωνοῖσιν ἕλωρ καὶ κύρμα γενέσθαι Od.3.271; σχεδίην ἀνέμοισι φέρεσθαι κ. 5.344; μέλη.. θηρσὶν βοράν E.*Supp.*46 (lyr.); μή ποτ' ἐμὸν κατ' αἰῶνα λίποι θεῶν πανάγυρις A. *Th.*219; μή με καταλίπῃς μόνον S.*Ph.*809; οἰκίας τε καὶ ἱερά Th. 2.16; πατέρας καὶ ξυγγενεῖς ἀτίμους κ. Id.3.58; κ. τὴν δίαιταν *not to appear at* the trial, Test.ap.D.21.93. 2. *let drop, give up*, τὰ αὑτῶν ἔργα X.*Cyn.*3.10, cf. 10.15; εἰ ἐνταῦθα -λίποιμι τὸν λόγον Isoc. 9.33. III. *leave remaining*, ὀκτὼ μόνον X.*An.*6.3.5 codd.; κ. ἄφοδον *leave* an exit, ib.4.2.11:—Med., κ. στενὴν διέξοδον Pl.*Ti.*73e; -λείπεσθαι ἑαυτῷ *reserve* for oneself, X.*Mem.*1.1.8; ὑπερβολὴν οὐ κ. χαρᾶς Plb.16.23.4, cf. 16.25.6:—Pass., *to be left, remain*, τίς ἔτι ἡδονὴ -λείπεται; Lys.2.71, cf. *Ep.Hebr.*4.1, etc.; of the *remainder* in calculations, *PPetr.*3 p.326, al. (iii B.C.), Nicom.*Ar.*1.13.13, etc.: impers. καταλείπεται c. inf., *it remains that*.., τὸν κόσμον κ. ἀθάνατον εἶμεν Aristaeus ap.Stob.1.20.6, cf. D.Chr.37.16, etc.; -λείπεται μάχη *yet remains to be fought*, X.*Cyr.*2.3.11. 2. *leave alone*, opp. περιαιρέω, Id.*Mem.*3.2.4, cf. Arist.*Pol.*1342ᵃ34. b. *leave undisputed*, τὰς παραλλαγάς Phld.*Sign.*24: hence, *admit, allow the truth of* a doctrine, Id.*Po.*5.34, Demetr.Lac.*Herc.*1055.13:—Pass., Phld.*Piet.* 80. c. *omit*, c. inf., Alex.Aphr.*in SE*118.10.

**καταλειτουργέω**, Att. -ληιτουργέω, *spend one's substance in bearing the public burdens*, D.36.39:—Pass., prob. in Is.*Fr.*130 S. (= 29 T.); τὰ ἴδια πατρίδι χρήματα *BCH*44.91 (Lagina).

**κατ-ᾰλείφω**, *besmear*, τὸ κηρίον Arist.*HA*627ᵃ10; πηλῷ φράγματα Aen.Tact.37.9; κατήλειψε τὸν χηραμὸν τῷ πηλῷ Ael.*NA*3.26: abs., *apply an ointment*, Hp.*Liqu.*6:—Med., dub. l. in Arist.*HA*555ᵃ 14:—Pass., καταλήλειπταί τινι ib.551ᵇ5; ὅταν καταλειφθῇ ib.554ᵃ 30, cf. Poll.9.112, Gal.1.657. 2. *plaster*, τέγη *IG*12(7).62.26 (Amorgos, iv B.C.); ὀροφὴν *Inscr.Délos* 290.97 (iii B.C.).

**καταλείψᾰνον**, τό, *remnant*, *PMag.Par.*1.1405a.

**κατάλειψις**, εως (poet. **κάλλειψις** only in Hsch.), ἡ, *leaving behind*, συγγραμμάτων Pl.*Phdr.*257e, cf. Arist.*Fr.*151; ἐκ χρημάτων καταλείψεως by a *legacy*, *CIG*4369 (Sagalassus), cf. *POxy.*75.12 (ii A.D.), *IG Rom.*4.671 (Prymnessus, ii A.D.), Vett.Val.177.22, al. II. *posterity*, Lxx *Ge.*45.7.

**καταλεκτέον** or -έα, *one must reckon*, τοῦτον ἐς τοὺς κόλλοπας Eub. 11. II. **καταλεκτέος**, α, ον, *to be drawn up*, κ. ἂν εἴη κατάλογος Pl. *Lg.*968c. 2. *to be reckoned*, ἐν τῷ αὐτῷ ἀριθμῷ Plu.*Nob.*7.

**κατάλεκτος**, *catalectum, Gloss.*

⊛**καταλέκτρια**, ἡ, perh. = θαλαμηπόλος, Βύνης -ιαι αὐδηέσσης Call. (*Fr.anon.*82) ap.*EM*217.5, Tz.ad Lyc.107.

**κατάλεξις**, εως, ἡ, *levying*, = Lat. *dilectus*, App.*Hisp.*49.

**καταλεπτολογέω**, *refine away by talk, 'pulverize'*, πνευμόνων πολὺν πόνον Ar.*Ra.*828 (lyr.).

**κατάλεπτον**, τό, and **κατάλεπτα**, τά, *'petty cash', minor expenses*, *PTeb.*120.85 (i B.C.), *POxy.*1729.6, 13 (iv A.D.).

**καταλεπτύνω**, *make very thin*, in Pass., τὸ πρόσωπον -λελεπτύνσθαι Hp.*Aër.*7; οἱ μάλιστα -λελεπτυσμένοι Arist.*PA*668ᵃ22, cf. Gal.18(2). 18, 25.

**καταλευγαλέα**· κάθυγρος, Hsch.

**καταλευκόω**, *whiten*, [πινάκιον] Aen.Tact.31.15.

**κατα-λεύσιμος**, ον, *worthy to be stoned*, Din.*Fr.*8.3. **-λεύω**, *stone to death*, Hdt.1.167, al., Ar.*Ach.*285, Th.1.106, etc.:—Pass., Aeschin.1.163, Ph.2.165, Luc.*Anach.*39. II. *condemn to work in mines*, Hsch. (Pass.).

**κατ-αλεύω**, strengthd. for ἀλεύω, in aor. inf. καταλεῦσαι, Hsch.

⊛**καταλέχομαι**, pres. only in Cypr. imper. **καλέχες** (fort. καλέχεο), = κατάκεισο, Hsch. (cf. λέγω A); Ep. only in Med. and Pass. fut. and aor.:—*lie down, go to bed*: aor. 1 κατελέξατο Il.9.690, Od.10. 555: non-thematic aor. (or impf.) Pass. κατέλεκτο Il.9.662, etc.; part. καταλέγμενος Od.22.196; inf. καταλέχθαι 15.394: fut. καταλέξομαι Hes.*Op.*523.

**κατ-ᾰλέω**, aor. 1 κατ-άλεσα, *grind*, κατὰ πυρὸν ἄλεσσαν Od.20.109; κριθὰς ἐς τὸ πῶμα Hecat.323 J., cf. Hdt.4.172, Hp.*VM*3, Ph.*Bel.*88. 46, Str.6.1.8; κ. [μόσχον] λεπτόν Lxx *Ex.*32.20:—Pass., καταλεσθείς Ph.1.257.

⊛**καταλήγω**, *leave off, stop*, πρὶν καταλῆξαι.. ἄχος A.*Ag.*1479 (anap.): ποῖ καταλήξει μένος ἄτης; at what point *will it cease?* Id.*Ch.*1075 (anap.); κ. ἐν.. *to end* at or with.., Plu.2.791c; ἐπί τι D.S.14.2, Arr.*Epict.*6.20.21, M.Ant.4.20; [ἡδοναί] περὶ τὸ σῶμα κ. Plu.2.705a; πρός τι Arist.*Mete.*340ᵇ9; εἴς τι D.S.20.2, Hierocl.*in CA*19 p.462 M., Porph.*Sent.*37: abs., Thphr.*Ign.*50; τὰ καταλήγοντα *limits* of a district, Plu.*Fab.*6, *Arist.*11; πόλεως J.*BJ*3.7.34: in sg., τὸ κ. τοῦ πελάγους *extremity*, Plb.5.59.5, cf. Poll.2.71, 177. 2. esp. in Metric and Rhetoric, of feet, verses, or periods, κρητικοῦ εἰς σύμφωνον -λήγοντος A.D.*Pron.*50.17; εἰς τὸ αὐτὸ ὄνομα Demetr.*Eloc.* 154, cf. 4, Hermog.*Id.*1.6. II. trans., *close, finish*, ναυμαχίᾳ εἰς ἣν Θουκυδίδης κατέληξε τὴν πραγματείαν D.S.14.84.

**καταλήθομαι**, *forget utterly*, τινος Il.22.389.

**καταληΐζομαι**, *plunder*, τοὺς ὑπηκόους Procop.*Arc.*21, cf. Hsch., Phot.

**καταληκτ-έον**, *one must end*, ἢ ἐπ' ἄπειρον [ἰτέον] ἢ εἴς τινας ἑνάδας κ. Procl.*in Prm.*p.948 S. ⊛ **-ικός**, ή, όν, *leaving off*; esp. in Metric, of verses *having the last foot incomplete*, Heph.4.2, Anon.Metr.*Oxy.* 220 ix 19, etc.; τὸ κ. Heph. l. c.; of feet, κ. [εἶδος παίωνος] Demetr. *Eloc.*38. II. Adv. **-κῶς** *disinterestedly*, διδόναι τι M.Ant.9.42, cf. 7.13 (-ληπτ- codd.), Arr.*Epict.*2.23.46.

**κατάλημμα**, ατος, τό, *comprehension*, D.L.7.45. 2. *outer bandage*, Orib.48.19.24 (prob.), Heliod.ap.eund.48.20.4; written κατάλειμμα in Gal.18(2).740; κατάκλειμμα Id.18(1).836.

**κατάληξις**, εως, ἡ, *ending, termination*, S.E.*M.*10.61, Nicom.*Ar.* 1.13.13; ἡ εἰς ὃ κ. A.D.*Pron.*29.17. 2. *cadence* or *close* of a period, Longin.41.2, Demetr.*Eloc.*19; *final syllable*, D.H.*Comp.*18.

**καταληπ-τέος**, α, ον, (καταλαμβάνω) *to be seized* or *occupied*, Plu. *Caes.*32; *to be comprehended*, Vett.Val.272.30; Ion. καταλαμπτέος (q.v.). 2. **-τέον**, *one must cover* with a plaster, Philum.ap.Orib. *Syn.*8.3, Philum.*Ven.*3.5. **-τήρ**, ῆρος, ὁ, *strap for holding fast*, Hsch. s.v. μαχαιροδέτης. 2. *clamp*, *BCH*29.468 (Delos). 3. Archit., *top course of stylobate*, *IG*2².1682.11; *coping laid on ὀρθοστάται*, ib.11(2).287 *A*120 (Delos, iii B.C.). **-τικός**, ή, όν, *able to check*, τοῦ θορυβητικοῦ Ar.*Eq.*1380. 2. *conveying direct apprehension* of an object, κ. φαντασία *Stoic.*2.26, etc.; κ. λόγος Phld.*Rh.* 2.120 S.; τὸ -κόν M.Ant.4.22. Adv. **-κῶς** *by direct apprehension*, *Stoic.*2.27; *manifestly*, φαίνεσθαι Cleom.1.8. **-τός**, ή, όν, *seized*, D.S.24.1; *capable of being seized*, Procop.*Goth.*3.24; *liable*, θανάτῳ Id.*Vand.*1.4. 2. *to be achieved*, ὅσον.. τὰ πράγματα ἐφαίνετο κ. Th.3.11; ὅ τι ἂν ἔσω δέκα ἡμερέων ἐμβάλλῃς, πᾶν κ. whatever joint you set within ten days, is *manageable*, i.e. *curable*, Hp.*Art.*67; σοφίᾳ κ. ἅπαντα Philostr.*Her.*10.4. 3. *capable of being apprehended* or *grasped*, κ. τὸ ἦθος ἐξ εἴδους Cleanth.*Stoic.*1.137, al.; λόγῳ, αἰσθήσει κ., Phld.*Po.*5.20, Diog.Oen.4(-ληπτ-). 4. *certain*, opp. εὔλογος, Herod.Med.ap.Aët.9.37. II. Act., πένθος θεόθεν κ. grief *that falls on us* from the gods, E.*Hipp.*1346 (anap.).

**καταληρέω**, *lose by idle talking*, τὴν ἐξωμίδα Eub.53. II. *overpower with talk*, τινος Jul.*Ep.*32: abs., Ach.Tat.7.11.

**καταλήψιμος**, ον, *to be seized and condemned*, opp. ἀπολύσιμος, Antipho 4.4.9.

⊛**κατάληψις**, εως, ἡ, *seizing*, οὐκέτι ἐν καταλήψει ἐφαίνετο to be within one's *grasp*, Th.3.33. 2. *seizing, assaulting*, Ar.*Nu.*318. 3. *taking possession, occupation*, τῆς βασιλείας Isoc.9.69; χωρίων Pl. *Grg.*455c, *R.*526d (pl.); ἱεροῦ D.19.21; καταλήψεις πολέμου prob. f.l. for πολέων, App.*BC*4.14. 4. Philos., *direct apprehension* of an object by the mind, Zeno *Stoic.*1.20, Luc.*Par.*4, al.; τῶν μετεώρων Philostr.*Her.*10.9; ἀκριβὴς κ. *certainty*, Herod.Med.ap.Aët.9. 37: pl., *perceptions*, *Stoic.*2.30, Luc.*Herm.*81, etc.; introduced into Latin by Cicero, Plu.*Cic.*40. II. *holding, grip*, with the fingers, bandages, or instruments, Hp.*Off.*9; τὰς -λήψιας ποιεῖσθαι ibid., cf. *Art.*11 (in pl. also = *ligatures*, *Medic.*8); ὁ ὕπνος τοῦ.. αἰσθητηρίου κ. *compression*, Arist.*Somn.*458ᵃ29. 2. *stoppage*, οὔρων Gal.17 (1).423; σπέρματος Ruf.ap.Orib.6.38.4; *holding*, πνεύματος Gal.6. 152. 3. in Music, *stopping* of the strings of an instrument, Sch. Ar.*Nu.*317. III. later, *catalepsy*, Gal.8.485, al.

**καταλῐθάζω**, = καταλιθόω, *Ev.Luc.*20.6.

**καταλῐθοβολέω**, *throw stones at, stone*, Lxx *Ex.*17.4.

**καταλῐθ-ος**, ον, *set with precious stones*, ὕφασμα Lxx *Ex.*28.17. **-όω**, *stone to death*, D.18.204, Paus.6.9.7 (Pass.), Philostr.*VA*1.16, al. II. gloss on καταχρυσόω, Hsch.

⊛**καταλιμπάνω**, = καταλείπω, Hp.*Mul.*1.78, Th.8.17, Antiph.35, *PPetr.*3 pp.4, 12 (iii B.C.), Lxx *Ge.*39.16, Ocell.4.13, etc.

**κατ-αλῖναι**· κατ-αλεῖψαι (-μῖξαι cod.), Hsch., cf. Phot.

**καταλῐπαίνω**, *make very fat*, Hsch.

⊛**καταλῐπᾰρέω**, *entreat earnestly*, Luc.*DDeor.*25.2, *Cat.*4.

**καταλίπᾰρος** [ῐ], ον, *very greasy*, [κηροῦ] τὸ κ. Dsc.2.83. II. v. κατάλυπρος.

**κατ-ᾰλῐφή**, ἡ, *plastering, whitewashing*, *IG*2².1664.12 (iv B.C.), *OGI*737.10 (Memphis, ii B.C.).

**καταλιχμ-άζομαι**, *lick all over*, Opp.*C.*2.389 (tm.). **-άομαι**, *lick up*, *eat*, S.E.*P.*1.57.

**καταλλ-άγδην**, Adv. *reciprocally*, Hsch. **-αγή**, ἡ, *exchange*, esp. of money, Arist.*Oec.*1346ᵇ24, *PHib.*1.100.4 (iii B.C.). 2. *money-changer's profit*, *agio*, D.50.30, Diph.66.14, Euphro 3.4. 3. *freight*, *merchandise*, metaph., [ἀραὶ] βαρεῖαι κ. A.*Th.*767 (lyr.). 4. *change*, *difference*, Phld.*Mus.*p.74 K. II. *change from enmity to friendship*, *reconciliation*, καταλλαγὰς ποιεῖσθαι πρός τινας D.1.4; κ. πολέμου Ar.*Av.*1588. 2. *reconciliation* of sinners *with God*, 2*Ep. Cor.*5.18; κόσμου *Ep.Rom.*11.15. ❀ **-αγμα**, ατος, τό, = foreg. II, Hsch. s. v. καταλλαγὴν δορός. **-ακτήριος**, ον, *reconciliatory*, συμβάσεις Ph. 1.673; fem. -ία as epith. of Aphrodite, *Milet.*7.19. **-άκτης**, ου, ὁ, *money-changer*, *EM*137.24. II. *reconciler*, *mediator*, J.*AJ*3.15.2, D.C.*Fr.*72.1 (pl.). **-ακτικός**, ή, όν, *easy to reconcile*, *placable*, Arist. *EE*1222ᵇ2, *Rh.*1367ᵇ17 (Comp.): c. dat., κ. τοῖς ὑπηκόοις prob. in Muson.*Fr.*33 p.122 H. **-αξις**, εως, ἡ, *varied exercise*, νεύρων Antyll. ap.Orib.6.35.1. ❀ **-άσσω**, Att. **-ττω**, *change* money, Plu.*Arat.* 18, etc. (also in Med., D.19.114:—Pass., Matreas ap.Ath.1.19b, with a play on signf. II); *change* or *give away*, τὴν χάριν τῶν νόμων for the laws, Din.3.21 (s. v. l.); καταλλάσσειν τὸν βίον *to leave* life, Ael.*VH*5.2. b. abs., *transgress*, *contravene* regulations, *IG*5(2). 3.2 (Tegea). 2. Med., *exchange* one thing *for* another, ἡδονὰς πρὸς ἡδονάς Pl.*Phd.*69a; ἀντί τινος πάντα ibid., cf. Phld.*Vit.Herc.*1457. 10; βίον πρὸς μικρὰ κέρδη Arist.*EN*1117ᵇ20; τι ἐπ' ἀργυρίῳ Hdn. 2.13.6: abs., *exchange prisoners*, D.C.*Fr.*57.36. II. *change* a person *from enmity to friendship*, *reconcile*, σφέας Hdt.5.29, cf. 95, 6.108; κ. τινὰς πρὸς ἀλλήλους Arist.*Oec.*1348ᵇ9; θεὸς κόσμον κ. ἑαυτῷ 2*Ep.Cor.*5.19:—Med., καταλλάσσεσθαι τὴν ἔχθρην τινί *to make up one's* enmity with any one, Hdt.1.61, cf. 7.145:—Pass., esp. in aor. κατηλλάχθην or κατηλλάγην (former preferred by Trag., latter in Prose), *to become reconciled*, τινι E.*IA*1157, X.*An.*1.6.1, etc.; πρὸς ἀλλήλους Th.4.59; θεοῖσιν ὡς καταλλαχθῇ χόλου that *he may be reconciled* to them after his anger, S.*Aj.*744; κ. πρός τινα ἐκ διαφορᾶς Ael.*VH*2.21. 2. Pass., of an offence, *to be atoned for*, φόνον ἐπιγαμίαις μὴ καταλλάσσεσθαι μηδὲ χρήμασιν *OGI*218.105 (Ilium, iii B.C.).

**καταλληλ-ία**, ἡ, *systematic construction*, τῆς τεχνολογίας Nicom. *Ar.*1.20.2. ❀ **-ος**, ον, *set over against one another*, *correspondent*, πόροι Arist.*Pr.*905ᵇ8, cf. Thphr.*CP*6.9.2; φύσει ἅμα κατάλληλα τελειοῦται· διὸ καὶ ἀκούει τε ἅμα καὶ φωνεῖ [τὰ παιδία] Arist.*Pr.*902ᵃ 11; γλῶσσα κ. τῷ στόματι Artem.1.32, cf. Str.2.1.29; κ. κεῖσθαι to be *parallel*, of lines, S.E.*M.*3.100; τὰ κ. the *corresponding states*, Id. *P.*1.238; κ. λόγος D.H.*Th.*37; τὸ κ. τῆς διανοίας ib.31; φαντασίαι δόγμασι κ. M.Ant.7.2; τοῖς στρατιωτικοῖς ἔργοις καταλληλότερος D.C. 71.1. 2. *appropriate*, κ. καὶ κατὰ φύσιν Arr.*Epict.*1.9.9, cf. Zos.4. 53; πρὸς ὑγίειαν M.Ant.5.8. Adv. -λως, κ. λέγεσθαι prob. f.l. for κατ' ἀλλήλων, Arist.*Metaph.*1041ᵃ33, cf. *Stoic.*3.42; κ. τῇ φύσει Arr. *Epict.*1.22.9. 3. Gramm., *rightly constructed*, *congruent*, A.D. *Synt.*4.3, al.; also, *well-arranged*, *in good order*, of the text of Aristotle, Alex.Aphr.*in Metaph.*172.13 (Comp.). Adv. Comp. -ότερον ib. 37.20. II. *one after another*, *in succession*, neut. pl. κατάλληλα, as Adv., Plb.3.5.6, 5.31.5; *in a row*, ἑπτὰ κεφαλὰς κ. J.*AJ*3.6.7; ληφθέντα κατάλληλα taken *in corresponding order*, Euc.5.4. **-ότης**, ητος, ἡ, Gramm., *correct construction*, A.D.*Synt.*3.5, al.

**κατ-ᾰλοάω**, *crush in pieces*, *make an end of*, c. acc., X.*Cyr.*7.1.31, Aeschin.2.140:—Pass., κατηλόηται Eub.15.5; τὴν ὀφρὺν κατηλοημένος Luc.*Icar.*15; cf. καταλοιάω.

**καταλοβεύς**, έως, ὁ, *cornice over a door*, *IG*4.1485.94 (Epid.). II. *course* laid on ὀρθοστάται, *GDI*5045 (Hierapytna).

**καταλογάδην**, Adv. *by way of conversation*, *in prose*, κ. συγγράφειν, διηγεῖσθαι, Pl.*Smp.*177b, *Ly.*204d; τὰ κ. συγγράμματα, opp. τὰ μετὰ μέτρου ποιήματα, Isoc.2.7; οἱ κ. ἴαμβοι Ath.10.445b, cf. Ph.1.694, Plu.2.316d, *IG*7.418 (Oropus), Jul.*Or.*1.3a. 2. *in detail*, *long-windedly*, Steph. *in Hp.*2.238 D.

❀ **καταλογεῖον**, τό, *record office*, *POxy.*73.34 (i A.D.), 2134.2 (ii A.D.).

**καταλογεύς**, έως, ὁ, (καταλέγω (B) I. 3) *officer who enrols* citizens, Lys.20.13, Arist.*Ath.*49.2.

**κατ-ᾰλογέω**, v. κατηλογέω.

❀ **καταλογ-ή**, ἡ, (καταλέγω (B) I. 3) *enrolment*, *enlistment*, στρατιωτῶν D.Chr.43.10. II. (καταλέγω (B) I. 2 b) *regard*, *respect*, Plb.22.12. 10 codd. (-δοχῇ Reiske), cf. *SIG*739.9 (Delph., i B.C.); καταλογῆς [ἕνεκα], *honoris causa*, with gen., *IG*7.413.37 (Oropus); καταλογή σοι εἴη 'saving your reverence', prob. for καταλογισθείη, Hsch.; εἰς τὴν ἐμὴν κ. on my *recommendation*, used in letters of introduction, *PStrassb.*117.5 (i A.D.), *POxy.*787 (i A.D.), etc.; ὅπως..κ. αὐτῶν γένηται *IG*14.951.9; condemned by Phryn.403. III. (καταλέγω (B) I. 1 b) *recitation*, opp. music, *IG*9(2).531.12 (Larissa, i B.C./i A.D.), Hsch. **-ίζομαι**, *count up*, *reckon*, X.*An.*5.6.16, *HG*3.2.18; κ. εὐεργέτημα πρός τινα *put it down to* his *account*, D.7.6; μηδ' ἐν ἀρετῇ τοῦθ' ὑμῶν μηδεὶς -λογιζέσθω *let* no one *impute* it as a virtue, Aeschin.3.202: c. inf., κατελογίσατο τῇ βουλῇ τὴν Ἰταλίαν ἡμερῶσαι App.*Ill.*16. II. *count*, *reckon among*, τοὺς ἀχαρίστους ἐν τοῖς ἀδίκοις X.*Mem.*2.2.1:—Pass., ἔν τισι -λογισθῆναι Lxx *Is.*14.10, *Wi.* 5.5. III. *recount in order*, τισὶ τὰ ἔργα τὰ ἑαυτοῦ App.*Syr.*61, cf. *Mac.*19. ❀ **-ος**, ὁ, *enrolment*, *register*, *catalogue*, Pl.*Tht.*175a, *Lg.*968c; ὀσπρίων Diocl.*Fr.*117; κ. νεῶν *the catalogue* of ships in Il. 2, Plu.*Sol.*10: prov., of a long story, νεῶν δὲ κατάλογον δόξεις μ' ἐρεῖν Apollod.Com.13.17. 2. at Athens, *register of citizens* liable for service, ὁπλίτης ἐντεθεὶς ἐν κ. Ar.*Eq.*1369; [ὁπλῖται] ἐκ καταλόγου those on *the list for service*, Th.6.43, al.; ἐκ κ. στρατευόμενος κατατέτριμμαι X.*Mem.*3.4.1; οἱ ἐν τῷ κ. Id.*HG*2.4.9; οἱ ὑπὲρ τὸν κ. the *superannuated*, opp. οἱ ἐν ἡλικίᾳ, D.13.4; of trierarchs, Id.18. 105; καταλόγους ποιεῖσθαι make up *the lists for service*, Th.6.26, D. 50.6; εἰς τὸν κ. καταλέξαι Lys.25.16; καταλόγοις χρηστοῖς ἐκκριθέν, of picked troops, Th.6.31; προγράφειν στρατιᾶς κ. Plu.*Cam.*39; τὸν κ. ἀποδιδράσκειν Luc.*Nav.*33; κ. ἀνδρῶν χιλίων *authority to conscript* 1000 recruits, Polyaen.3.3. b. *list of the* βουλή, ἐκ τοῦ κ. ἐξαλείφειν X.*HG*2.3.51. c. κατάλογοι βουλᾶς, οἱ, committee of the βουλή at Epidaurus, *IG*4.925, al.

**κατ-ᾰλοιάω**, = καταλοάω, Phot.

**καταλοιδορέω**, *rail violently against*, τινα App.*Mith.*59.

❀ **κατάλοιπος**, ον, *left remaining*, τὸ κ. ἀπεργάζεσθαι Pl.*Ti.*39e; ἐκ τοῦ κ. Arist.*HA*548ᵇ18, cf. *Michel*829.23 (i B.C.), etc.; τὰ κ. τῆς διεξόδου Phld.*Rh.*1.120 S.; τοῦτο..κατάλοιπόν [ἐστι] c. inf., Strato Com. 1.10; ἡ κ. εἰσβολή Plb.3.91.9; ἡ κ. the *other* of two, Gal.7.314.

❀ **κατ-ᾰλοκίζω**, *cut into furrows*, κατὰ μὲν ὄνυξιν ἠλοκισμεθ' E.*Supp.* 826 (lyr.).

❀ **κατα-λούομαι**, Med., *spend in bathing*, καταλόει [prob. cj. for -λούει] μου τὸν βίον Ar.*Nu.*838. ❀ **-λουστικοί**, οἱ, *members of a guild which performed ceremonial ablutions*, Keil-Premerstein *Zweiter Bericht* 183 (Lydia, ii A.D.).

**καταλοφάδεια** [ᾰδ], Adv., (λόφος) = κατὰ τὸν λόφον, *on the neck*, βῆν δὲ καταλοφάδεια φέρων (sc. τὸν ἔλαφον) Od.10.169: by metrical lengthening for καταλοφάδια (cf. κατωμάδιος), v. Eust. ad loc.—Perh. to be read divisim, cf. λοφάδεια.

❀ **καταλοχ-ία**, ἡ, = καταλοχισμός, v.l. in Lxx 2*Ch.*31.18. ❀ **-ίζω**, *form into* λόχοι, τὴν φάλαγγα Ascl.*Tact.*2.1. 2. *distribute into* λόχοι, Ael.*Tact.*2.4, Arr.*Tact.*5.2: generally, *distribute*, εἰς τάξεις D.S.18.70; εἰς ἀγέλας Plu.*Lyc.*16; εἰς τοὺς ὁπλίτας Id.*Sull.*18; εἰς τοὺς..ποιητάς Lib.*Ep.*36.1 (-ελόχησας codd.):—Pass., Plu.*Cic.* 15. ❀ **-ισμός**, ὁ, *register*, *enrolment*, Lxx 1*Ch.*4.33, Plu.*Cic.*15, Ael.*Tact.*15.1, Luc.*Hist.Conscr.*29: in pl., *muster-rolls*, *OGI*229.45, 47 (Smyrna, iii B.C.), *POxy.*2129.6, al. (iii A.D.). 2. *register of grants of land to military settlers*, φυλακιτῶν καὶ ἐφόδων τῶν ἐν κ. *PPetr.*3 p.230 (iii B.C.), cf. *POxy.*45 (i A.D.), etc.

**κατ-ᾰλσής**, ές, (ἄλσος) *woody*, Str.5.3.11:—later **-αλσος**, ον, Eust. ad D.P.321.

**καταλῠγίζω**, = λυγίζω, Hsch. (Pass.).

**καταλῠκουργίζω**, *press the laws of Lycurgus against*, τῆς ἀνθρωποπαθείας Alciphr.2.1.

**κατάλῠμα**, ατος, τό, *lodging*, Plb.2.36.1 (pl.), *UPZ*120.5 (ii B.C.), Lxx *Ex.*4.24, Aristeas 181 (pl.), *Ev.Marc.*14.14, Iamb.*Bab.*13; δημόσιον κ. D.S.14.93; *billet* for troops, *PSI*4.341.8 (iii B.C.): in pl., *provision of quarters*, *IG*5(2).515 (Lycosura, i B.C./i A.D.):—Dim. -λῠμάτιον, τό, *PCair.Zen.*205 (iii B.C.).

❀ **καταλῠμαίνομαι**, Dep., *ruin utterly*, *destroy*, τὸν οἶκον, τὰ σώματα, X.*Oec.*2.13, 6.5; τὰς ὀροφάς Plb.5.9.3.

**καταλῠμάκόομαι**, (λύμαξ) Pass., *to be silted up*, *Tab.Heracl.*1.56.

**καταλύμανσις** [ῡ], εως, ἡ, *ravaging*, *Gloss.*

**κατάλυπρος**, ον, *sad*, ὄμμα κ., στίλβον, dub. in Herod.Med. in *Rh. Mus.*58.96 (v. l. ὄμματα καταλίπαρα).

**κατα-λύσιμος** [ῠ], ον, *to be dissolved* or *done away*, κακόν S.*El.*1247 (lyr.). ❀ **-λῠσις**, εως, ἡ, *dissolution*, *putting down*, esp. of governments, ἡ τῶν τυράννων κ. ἐκ τῆς Ἑλλάδος Th.1.18; τοῦ δήμου And.1. 36, Lys.13.20; τῆς παρούσης πολιτείας Pl.*Lg.*864d; τῆς ἀρχῆς X.*Cyr.* 8.1.47, cf. Arist.*Pol.*1305ᵇ3, al.; Κρόνου Phld.*Piet.*94: generally, τὴν τῶν πονηρῶν ὁμιλίαν κ. εἶναι ἀρετῆς X.*Mem.*1.2.20; κ. χρείας Gal.9. 44. 2. *dismissal*, *disbanding* of a body of men, στρατιᾶς X.*Cyr.* 6.1.13; κ. τριήρους *breaking up* of a ship's crew, D.50.11; εἰς κατάλυσιν till *dismissal*, of soldiers at a review, X.*Eq.Mag.*3.12. 3. κ. πολέμου *pacification*, Th.8.18, X.*Mem.*2.8.1, Isoc.6.51. 4. generally, *end*, *termination*, συμποσίου X.*Smp.*9.7; βίου Id.*Ap.*30, *PMagd.* 8.10 (iii B.C.). 5. *settlement* of disputes, *IG*5(2).357.21 (Stymphalus, iii B.C.). 6. *feebleness*, *impotence*, χειρῶν καὶ σκελέων Hp. *Epid.*4.53. II. *resting*, *lodging*, δεξώμεθ' οἴκων καταλύσεις E. *El.*393; κ. ποιεῖσθαι to *rest*, Plb.2.15.5. 2. = κατάλυμα, *resting-place*, *guest-chamber*, *quarters*, *lodging*, σταθμοὶ καὶ καταλύσιες (Ion.) κάλλισται Hdt.5.52; ξένοις κ. ποιεῖν Pl.*Prt.*315d, cf. *Lg.*919a (pl.), Antiph.15, Alex.2.2, Dicaearch.1.6 (pl.), *IG*4.203 (Corinth); κ. βασιλική *PPetr.*3 p.137 (iii B.C.). 3. pl., *billets* for troops, *PHal.* 1.168 (iii B.C.). **-λῠτέος**, α, ον, *to be put down*, τύραννος κ. ἐστίν Chio *Ep.*15.2. II. neut., *one must put down*, κ. ἐστὶ τύραννον D.S.14.65. 2. *one must rest*, Suid. s. v. διασκηνητέον. **-λῠτήρ**, ῆρος, ὁ, *arbitrator*, *IG*5(2).357.36 (Stymphalus, iii B.C.). ❀ **-λῠτήριον**, τό, = κατάλυμα, Poll.1.73. ❀ **-λύτης** [ῠ], ου, ὁ, *lodger*, *stranger*, Plb.2. 15.6, Plu.*Sull.*25. II. *arbitrator*, *IG*5(2).357.15. **-λῠτικός**, ή, όν, *able to dissolve* or *put an end to*, ὑδέρων Antyll.ap.Orib.6.28.1; ποιότητες κ. τῶν δυνάμεων Gal.11.97. ❀ **-λύω**, fut. -λύσω Od.4.28: 3 pl. plpf. -λελύκεσαν Hdn.8.4.2:—**Pass.**, fut. -λυθήσομαι Pl.*Lg.*714c, D. 38.22 (fut. Med. in pass. sense, v. infr. I. 2 a): pf. -λέλυμαι Th.6.36:—*put down*, *destroy*, πολλάων πολίων κατέλυσε κάρηνα Il.2.117, 9.24; τείχη, [πτόλιν], E.*Tr.*819, 1080 (both lyr.); γέφυραν *break* it *up*, Hdn. l.c. 2. of political or other systems, *dissolve*, *break up*, *put down*, κ. ἀρχήν, βασιληΐην, ἰσοκρατίας, Hdt.1.53, 54, 5.92.α'; τοῦ Διὸς τὴν δύναμιν Ar.*Pl.*142; τὸ κράτος τῆς βουλῆς Plu.*Per.*7; τὰς προσόδους τὰς Μιλησίων *SIG*633.40 (Milet., ii B.C.): freq. in Att., κ. τὸν δῆμον Ar.*Ec.* 453, Th.3.81; τὴν δημοκρατίαν Ar.*Pl.*948; τὰς πολιτείας Decr.ap.D. 18.182:—Pass., καταλελυμένης τῆς δημοκρατίας Lex ap.And.1.96, cf.

95, Lys.13.4, Arist.*Pol.*1292ᵃ29: fut. Med. as Pass., καταλύσεται..ἡ ἀρχή (Cobet καταλελύσεται) X.*Cyr.*1.6.9. b. c. acc. pers., *put down, depose*, κ. τύραννον Th.1.18, etc.; κ. τινὰ τῆς ἀρχῆς X.*Cyr.*8.5.24:—Pass., τῶν ἄλλων καταλελυμένων στρατηγῶν *having been dismissed*, Hdt.6.43; καταλυθῆναι τῆς ἀρχῆς Id.1.104, cf. 6.9. c. *dissolve, dismiss, disband* a body, καταλύειν τὴν βουλήν, τὸν στόλον, Id.5.72, 7.16.β´; τῶν πόλεων τά τε βουλευτήρια καὶ τὰς ἀρχάς Th.2.15; τὸ ναυτικόν D.18.102 (Pass.). d. *abolish* or *annul* laws, customs, etc., δίκην Gorg.*Pal.*17; νόμους Isoc.6.66 (Pass.), Plb.3.8.2, cf. *Ev.Matt.*5.17; ψήφισμα *Michel* 725.20 (ii B.C.); also κ. τὸν ἱππέα *render* him *useless*, X.*Eq.*12.5. e. τὴν φυλακὴν κ. *neglect* the watch, Ar.*V.*2, cf. Arist.*Pol.*1308ᵃ29; τὴν φρουράν Pl.*Lg.*762c; τὴν κοινὴν φυλακὴν καταλυθῆναι βούλεται Din.1.112. f. κ. τὴν τριηραρχίαν *lay* it *down*, Isoc.18.59; τὴν ἄσκησιν, v. infr. 3a. 3. *bring to an end*, τὸν βίον X.*Ap.*7; ἐς Ἅιδαν καταλύσουσ᾽ ἔμμοχθον βίοτον E.*Supp.*1004 (lyr.); μόμου ἀδικίαν καὶ δόξης ἀμαθίαν Gorg.*Hel.*21; ἐλπίδα Th.2.89; δόξα, ἣν αἰσχρόν ἐστιν ἐν σοὶ -λῦσαι D.10.73; κ. τὸ πλεῖν, τὴν ἄροσιν, Id.33.4, Ael.*NA*13.1; κ. τὰς θυσίας Lys.30.17, Isoc.6.68; τὰ γυμνάσια And.4.39; τὸν λόγον Aeschin.2.126, Isoc.12.176; τοὺς λόγους περὶ τὰ μέγιστα κ. ib.199: abs., *make an end*, ὥρᾳ κ. *die* in good time, Diocl.Com.14, cf. Philostr.*VA*8.28; πύκτης ὢν κατέλυσε *retired* from the ring, *AP*11.79 (Lucill.), cf. 161 (Id.) (in full -λῦσαι τὴν ἄσκησιν Gal.*Protr.*14); καθάπερ ἐν τοῖς χοροῖς ἐν τῷ καταλύειν in the *ending*, Arist.*Pr.*921ᵃ20: also pf. part. Pass. καταλελυμένος *disused, obsolete*, Phld.*Mus.*p.68 K. b. κ. τὴν ὑπάρχουσαν εἰρήνην *break* the peace, Aeschin.3.55; but, c. more commonly, κ. τὸν πόλεμον *end* the war, make peace, Ar.*Lys.*112, Th.7.31, X.*An.*5.7.27, etc.; δίκας *settle* disputes, *IG*5(2).357.15 (Stymphalus, iii B.C.): abs. (sc. τὸν πόλεμον), Foed.ap.Th.5.23; πρός τινα Foed.ib.8.58:—more freq. in Med., καταλύσασθαι τὰς ἔχθρας, *componere inimicitias*, Hdt.7.146; τὸν πόλεμον And.3.17, Th.6.36; στάσιν Ar.*Ra.*359: abs., *make peace*, Hdt.8.140.α´, Th.1.81, X.*HG*6.8.6, etc.; καταλύεσθαί τινι *come to terms with* one, Hdt.9.11, etc. 4. Pass., ἤδη καταλελυμένης τῆς ἡλικίας in the *decay* of life, Arist.*Pol.*1335ᵃ34. II. *unloose, unyoke*, καταλύσομεν ἵππους Od.4.28; τὸ σῶμα τοῦ ἀδελφεοῦ κ. *take* it *down* from the wall where it was hung up, Hdt.2.121.γ´:—Pass., *to be taken down* from hanging, Hp.*Aph.*2.43. 2. intr., *take up one's quarters, lodge*, παρ᾽ ἐμοὶ καταλύει he *is* my *guest*, Pl.*Grg.*447b, cf. *Prt.*311a, D.18.82: abs., Pl.*Prt.*315d: c. acc., κ. παρά τινα *turn off* the road to a person's house, *go and lodge* with him, Th.1.136; κ. εἰς πανδοκεῖον Aeschin.2.97; Μεγαροῖ Pl.*Tht.*142c; ἐν τῷ ἱαρῷ *SIG*978.8 (Cnidos, iii B.C.):—Med., θανάτῳ καταλυσαίμαν *may I take my rest* in the grave, E.*Med.*146 (anap.).

**καταλωβάω**, *mutilate*, Plb.15.33.9.

**καταλωφάω**, Ion. -έω, *rest from* a thing, κὰδ δέ κ᾽ ἐμὸν κῆρ λωφήσειε κακῶν Od.9.459. II. trans., *give rest from*, κούρην δ᾽ ἐξ ἀχέων ..καταλώφεεν ὕπνος A.R.3.616.

**καταμαγγανεύω**, *subdue by sorceries*, gloss on καταγοητεύω, Hsch. (prob.).

**καταμᾰγεῖον**, τό, (μάσσω) *cloth for wiping*, Artem.1.64.

**καταμᾰγεύω**, *bewitch*, Luc.*Nec.*7.

**καταμᾰθημᾰτικεύω**, *reduce to mathematical terms*, in Med., -εύσατο τὴν φύσιν Phlp.*in de An.*481.34.

**καταμάθ-ησις** [μᾰ], εως, ἡ, *thorough knowledge*, Hermog.*Id.*2.7, Plot.3.8.6. -ητέον, *one must learn thoroughly, observe closely*, Hp.*Aph.*6.5. -ητικός, ή, όν, *apt at learning*, Poll.9.152.

**καταμαίνομαι**, aor. Pass. -εμάνην [ᾰ], *do mad acts against*, τῶν Ἰουδαίων Ph.2.542, cf. J.*BJ*7.8.1.

**καταμάκτης**, ου, ὁ, (μάσσω) *one who wipes off, Gloss.*

⊕**καταμακτος**, ον, *cast, moulded*, of votive offerings, σῶμα, οὖς, *IG*2².1534.45,48.

**καταμᾰλᾰκίζω**, in Pass., *to be* or *become soft* or *effeminate*, X.*Oec.*11.12, Arist.*MM*1202ᵇ37, 1203ᵇ7.

**καταμᾰλάσσω**, Att. -ττω, *soften*, σώματα ἐλαίῳ Luc.*Anach.*24: metaph., *appease*, Id.*JTr.*24, Ach.Tat.6.19; τοῦ θυμοῦ τὸ φλεγμαῖνον Hld.7.21.

**καταμαλθᾰκίζομαι**, Pass., *to be enervated*, Pl.*Ep.*329b.

**καταμαλθάσσω**, = καταμαλάσσω, Hsch.

**καταμανθάνω**, pf. μεμάθηκα Hp.*Art.*8, X.*Cyr.*1.1.1:—*observe well, examine closely*, τὴν στρατιήν Hdt.7.146; τὸν Οἰνέα Timocl.6.16, cf. 10; τὸ τραῦμα Plu.*Dio* 34; *look to, inspect*, τὸν ἐλαιῶνα *PFay.*114.11 (100 A.D.); κ. ἦν που.. X.*Oec.*12.3. 2. *learn, acquire knowledge of*, Pl.*Tht.*198d, etc.; ὑπακούειν how to obey, v.l. in X.*Oec.*13.7. 3. *perceive with the senses, observe*, Arist.*Pr.*960ᵃ7: more commonly with the mind, *understand, perceive, observe*, οὐκ ὀρθῶς κ. Pl.*Prm.*128a; εἰ ἄρα μου καταμανθάνετε ὃ λέγω Id.*Lg.*689c; ἐκ τῶν νόμων κ. τοὺς λόγους εἰ ὀρθῶς.. Antipho 5.14; κ. ὁπόσα θνητῇ φύσει δυνατά Pl.*Epin.*986c; κ. ὅτι.. Hp. l. c.; ῥᾴδιον τοῦτο κ., ὅτι.. Arist.*Pol.*1285ᵃ1: pf., *to be aware*, Λυκοῦργον -μεμάθηκας ὅτι... X.*Mem.*4.4.15: c. acc. et part., κ. πολλοὺς ἔχοντάς τι Id.*Cyr.*1.1.1; καταμαθόντες μιν ἀγοράζοντα Hdt.4.164; κ. τινὰ θύοντα X.*Mem.*1.4.2; καταμαθὼν δὲ.. καταστασιαζόμενος that a party was being formed against him, Id.*HG*1.6.4: καταμαθεῖν τοῦ Κύρου δοκοῦμεν, ὡς.. Id.*Cyr.*8.1.40. 4. *consider*, τι Id.*An.*3.1.44; ὅτι.. Id.*Cyr.*7.5.80, etc.

**καταμαντ-εία**, ἡ, *divination*, Jul.Laod. in *Cat.Cod.Astr.*5(1).190 (pl.). ⊕-**εύομαι**, *foretell against* or *about* one, τι τῶν ἐχθρῶν J.*BJ* 4.4.6; ⟨αὐτὸς⟩ αὐτοῦ σιωπὴν κ. Ath.15.686c; τοῦτο τῇ πόλει, c. fut. inf., App.*Pun.*77. 2. *divine, surmise*, ἐκ τῶν προγεγονότων τὰ μέλλοντα -μαντευόμενοι κρίνομεν Arist.*Rh.*1368ᵃ31; κ. τὸ μέλλον Plb.2.22.7, etc.: c. gen., ἰητροῦ ἐστι -μαντεύσασθαι τῶν τοιούτων Hp.*Art.*9; κ. τῆς τῶν ποιημάτων διανοίας Ath.14.634d; τοῦ εἰκότως συμβαίνοντος Hierocl. in *CA*10 p.437 M.; κ. περὶ τῶν γυναικῶν, ὁποῖαι.. Nicostr. ap.Stob.4.22.102, cf. Gal.15.907; ὑπέρ τινος Onos.36.2.

**κατ-ᾰμαξεύω**, v. καθαμαξεύω.

**καταμᾰραίνω**, aor. -εμάρᾱνα Ph.1.266:—*cause to wither*, Thphr. *Ign.*10, Ph. l. c.; *make lean*, Luc.*Tim.*17:—Pass., *die away*, of dropsical swellings, Hp.*Prorrh.*2.6; τὸ πῦρ κ. Arist.*Resp.*479ᵃ14, cf. Thphr.*HP*5.9.3, etc.; τὸ πάθος (sc. τοῦ σεισμοῦ) κ. Arist.*Mete.*368ᵃ7; of persons, πρὶν ἀνθῆσαι..κ. Plu.2.804e.

**καταμαργάω**, Ion. -έω, *to be stark mad, rave*, φθόνῳ Hdt.8.125.

**καταμάρπτω**, *catch*, ὥς κεν ἔμ᾽ ἔντοσθεν πόλιος καταμάρψῃ ἐόντα Il.6.364; esp. *catch, overtake* one running away, ὅτε δὴ κατέμαρπτε διώκων 5.65, cf. 16.598, Pi.*N.*3.35; κατὰ γαῖ᾽ αὐτόν τέ νιν καὶ..ἵππους ἔμαρψεν Id.*O.*6.14; ἐπεὶ κατὰ γῆρας ἔμαρψεν Od.24.390; ἄλλον δ᾽ οὐ -έμαρψε δίκη Thgn.207; κρέσσον ἔσφαλε τέχνα -μάρψαισ᾽ Pi.*I.*4(3).35; κατὰ μητέρα πότμος ἔμαρψε *IG*14.1389i17.

**καταμαρτῠρέω**, *bear witness against*, τινος Antipho 2.4.10, D.19.120, 29.9, Mitteis *Chr.*31 v33 (ii B.C.), etc.; κατά τινος D.28.3, etc.: c. acc. rei, ψευδῆ κ. τινός Id.45.46 (Docum.), 29.2, Is.5.12, cf. *Ev.Matt.*26.62: abs., αὐτὸ τὸ ψήφισμα τῆς βουλῆς—μαρτυρήσει Lys.13.28:—Pass., *have evidence given against* one, μὴ πιστῶς καταμαρτυρηθεὶς Antipho 2.4.7; κ. ὑπὸ τοῦ βίου τοῦ ἑαυτοῦ *to be convicted*, Aeschin.1.90. 2. Pass., of evidence, *to be given against* one, ἃ καταμαρτυρεῖται αὐτοῦ Is.5.25, cf. 6.15: abs., D.29.55. II. *assert concerning*, οὐδὲν κ. τῶν οὐ παρόντων Plot.5.5.13. III. Astrol., *exercise malign influence over*, '*aspect*', Vett.Val.104.2.

**καταμαρτύρομαι** [ῡ], *bear witness against*, *IG*2.4322.34.

**καταμᾰσάομαι**, *chew, bite*, γλῶσσαν Hp.*Epid.*5.53 (=7.74): metaph., ἅπαντα κ. Alex.105.

**καταμάσσω**, *wipe off*, Hld.1.2, Palaeph. in Westermann Μυθογράφοι p.310; *wipe*, τὰς χεῖρας *EM*587.48, cf. *PMag.Osl.*1.212:—Med., Luc.*Asin.*10. 2. *rub, shampoo* after a bath, *Edict.Diocl.*7.75 (Pass.).

**καταμαστῑγόω**, *scourge*, v.l. in Lib.*Decl.*26.20 (Pass.).

**καταμαστίζω**, *reverbero, Gloss.*

**κατάμαστρος**, ον, (μαστροί) = ὑπεύθυνος, *liable to condemnation*, ἱερῶν χρημάτων φωρᾶς *GDI*2642.21 (Delph.).

**καταματτεύομαι**, Pass., *to be tickled*, πτερῷ (as an emetic) Hp.*Int.*6, 27 (v.l. -ματευόμενος):—also -ματέομαι Gal.19.109; -μάττομαι Hp.*Int.*12 (v.l. -ματτεόμενος).

**καταμάχ-ησις** [μᾰ], εως, ἡ, *subduing, conquest, Gloss.* -ομαι, pf. -μεμάχημαι Plu.*Flam.*3:—*subdue by fighting, conquer*, τινα l. c.; πύκτην Paus.6.11.2: metaph., *overcome*, τὴν ὑπερβολὴν τῆς εὐωδίας D.S.3.47.

⊕**κατ-ᾰμάω**, once in Hom. in Med., *scrape up, heap up*, τήν ῥα (sc. τὴν κόπρον) κυλινδόμενος καταμήσατο χερσὶν ἑῇσι Il.24.165; τὸν χοῦν καταμήσονται (Mein. for κατακοιμήσονται) Pherecr.121: c. gen., *heap upon*, καταμώμενοι τῆς κεφαλῆς κόνιν J.*BJ*2.15.4, v.l. ib.2.21.3. II. κατ᾽ αὖ νιν..νερτέρων ἀμᾷ κοπίς (Jortin for κόνις) *cuts* it *down, reaps* it *like corn*, S.*Ant.*601 (lyr.); if κόνις is retained, καταμᾷ must be rendered *covers over*.

**καταμβλᾰκεύω**, = καταβλ-, Aret.*CD*1.1, Apollon.Cit.3.

**καταμβλ-ύνω**, *blunt, dull*, κατημβλύνθη κέντρον *AP*5.219 (Agath.): metaph., παρεὶς καὶ καταμβλύνων κέαρ S.*OT*688. -νόω, = foreg., τὸ κατημβλυωμένον Diph.18.7.

**καταμεγᾰλ-αυχέομαι**, strengthd. for μεγαλαυχέομαι, in aor., Hsch. -ύνομαι, *exalt oneself against*, τινος Aq., Thd., Sm.*Ps.*40(41).10.

**καταμεθύσκω**, aor. -εμέθῠσα, causal, *make drunk*, Hdt.1.106, 2.121.ε´, Pl.*Grg.*471b, etc.; εὐτυχία -ύσκουσα τοῖς ἀγαθοῖς τὰν διάνοιαν Archyt.ap.Stob.3.1.114:—Pass., *to be made quite drunk*, ὑπό τινος D.S.4.84: abs., *get drunk*, Plb.5.39.2.

**καταμεθύω**, *rave in drunken style against*, τινος Ph.1.361.

**κατ-ᾰμείβω**, in Pass., *to be divided between*, -μειφθεὶς δύο τισίν f.l. in *EM*358.44 (fort. -μερισθείς).

**καταμείγνῡμι** or -ύω, *mix in, combine*, καταμειγνύντας τούς τε μετοίκους κτλ. Ar.*Lys.*580; τὴν φροντίδα καταμείξας..εἰς τὸν ὅμοιον ἀέρα Id.*Nu.*230; τὴν προῖκα εἰς τὴν οὐσίαν D.30.10; τινὰ εἰς ὑμᾶς αὐτούς Id.25.63; συμπόταις ἑαυτόν Plu.2.148a; δένδρα τοῖς φυτοῖς ib.648c; τοῖς ἀναγκαίοις ἀρετῆς τινα ζῆλον Id.*Lyc.*27:—Pass., [ὕδωρ] καταμεμειγμένον ἐς τὸν ἠέρα Hp.*Aër.*8; τούτοις καταμεμεῖχθαι τοιαύτην δύναμιν Arist.*Spir.*485ᵇ10; οἱ στρατιῶται εἰς τὰς πόλεις κατεμείγνυντο, i.e. *were mingled* with the citizens, X.*An.*7.2.3; εἰς γένος Plu.*Cat.Ma.*20.

**καταμειδιάω**, *smile at, despise*, θανάτου J.*BJ*3.7.33.

**καταμεικτέον**, *one must mix*, Paul.Aeg.3.14.

**καταμειλίσσομαι**, Att. -ττομαι, *appease*, τὸν θυμόν τινος J.*AJ*6.13.7.

**κατάμειξις**, εως, ἡ, *admixture*, Arist.*Pr.*868ᵇ4, Anon.Rhythm. *Oxy.*4.12, Dsc.*Alex.Praef.* (pl.); ἡ πρὸς τὸ σῶμα κ. τοῦ οἴνου Plu.2.1110a (-μειξ- Anon.Rhythm. l. c., -μιξ- freq. in codd.).

**καταμελαίνω**, *make black, darken*, in Pass., ὁ ἀὴρ -εμελαίνετο Agath.5.3.

**καταμελεϊστί**, Adv. *limb by limb*, Arat.624 [κατᾱ-, metri gr.].

**καταμελετάω**, *train fully, exercise*, τινα Pl.*Phlb.*55e:—Pass., ib.57a; τὴν ἀνδρείαν ἐν τοῖς φόβοις δεῖ -μελετᾶσθαι Id.*Lg.*649c. 2. *study carefully*, for the purpose of composing, τὸν ἔπαινον περί τινος Id.*Clit.*410b; ῥητορικήν Phld.*Rh.*1.236 S.; λόγον Them.*Or.*26.312b.

**κατ-ᾰμελέω**, *give no heed to*, c. gen., ὁδοιπορίης, ἐδωδῆς, Hp.*Art.*14, cf. X.*Oec.*4.7, J.*AJ*18.6.9 (Med.); *neglect*, τῶν προσηκόντων ἔργων

*BGU*195.19 (ii A.D.): folld. by relat. clause, ὁπόθεν δὲ καταφαγεῖν ἔχοι, τούτου κατημέληκεν Eup.352: abs., *pay no heed*, S.*Aj.*45, 912 (lyr.), Pl.*Ti.*44c, D.S.29.3 (nisi leg. -μέλλ-), etc.: c. acc., *ruin by neglect*, μηδὲν κ. X.*HG*6.2.39; τὰ πράγματα Antipho Soph.76 :—Pass., *to be neglected*, Hp.*Art.*60: pf. part. κατημελημένος Isoc.12.8.

**καταμελῐτόω**, *spread with honey*: metaph., of the nightingale's voice, κατεμελίτωσε τὴν λόχμην ὅλην Ar.*Av.*224.

**καταμέλλω**, *procrastinate*, Plb.4.30.2, al., Phld.*Herc.*1251.8.

**κατάμεμπτος**, ον, *blamed by all, abhorred*, γῆρας S.*OC*1235 (lyr.): neut. pl. as Adv., οὔ τοι κατάμεμπτ' ἔβητον ye have fared not *so as to have cause to find fault*, ib.1696 (lyr.).

*__καταμέμφομαι__, fut. -μέμψομαι Phld.*Oec.*p.74 J.: aor. Pass. -εμέμφθην in act. sense, Pi.*N.*11.30; also in pass. sense, *Sammelb.*5357.11 (v A.D.):—*find fault with*; esp. with a sense of *distrust in oneself*, ἰσχύν Pi. l. c.; τὴν δύναμιν τὴν σφετέραν αὐτῶν Isoc.15.61, cf. 5.110; σφᾶς αὐτούς Th.8.106, cf. D.22.27; ἐμαυτόν, ὡς.. Pl.*Men.*71b; τὴν ἐμαυτοῦ ἡλικίαν D.29.1: more generally, *blame, censure*, τὴν τυραννίδα ἔν τινι X.*Hier.*8.6; τὴν ἱστορίαν D.S.20.43; ὑμᾶς αὐτοὺς ταῖς ξυμφοραῖς *blame for*.., Th.7.77; ἐπί τινι Plb.5.87.4; τινος Plu.*Dio* 8, Sch.Arat.147 (v. l.), Nicom.*Exc.*4 (v. l.); ὅτι.. D.S.15.6: c. dat. rei, *AP*11.57 (Agath.), Anon.ap.Suid., Longus 2.21, Ps.-Luc.*Philopatr.* 27; *disparage*, Σωκράτην Phld.*Piet.*77.

**κατάμεμψις**, εως, ἡ, *blaming, finding fault with*, κ. σφῶν αὐτῶν πολλὴ ἦν Th.7.75, cf. Plu.*Mar.*39; οὐκ ἔχει τινὶ κατάμεμψιν it leaves him no *ground for censure*, Th.2.41, cf. J.*AJ*6.6.3.

**καταμένω**, fut. -μενῶ Men.*Epit.*197:—*stay*, Thgn.1373, Hdt.2.103, 121.δ', etc.; ἐνθάδ' αὐτοῦ κ. Ar.*Pl.*1187; ἐνταῦθα X.*Cyr.*1.4.17; κ. ἐν τοῖς δήμοις Lys.31.18; παρά τινι Eub.21; *reside*, *PHal.*1.183 (iii B.C.), *Act.Ap.*1.13; ἐν ἐποικίῳ *PFay.*24 (ii A.D.), etc. 2. *remain fixed, continue* in a state, ἐν τοῖς ὑπηρετικοῖς ὅπλοις X.*Cyr.*2.1.18; ἐπὶ τῶν αὐτῶν Gal.6.328; ἔν τινι Id.2.27; ἐπὶ τοῖς ὑπάρχουσι Nymphod.21: abs., τῆς εἰωθυίας ἀρχῆς καταμενούσης X.*Cyr.*3.1.30.

**κατ-ᾰμέργω**, strengthd. for ἀμέργω, Poll.1.225.

**καταμερ-ίζω**, *cut in pieces*, [τὸν Πλοῦτον] εἰς πολλά Luc.*Tim.*12; λίθους εἰς μεγέθη D.S.5.13: metaph., εἰς πολλὰς ταλαιπωρίας τὸν θάνατον Id.3.40:—Pass., of flavours, *to be resolved* into components, Thphr.*Od.*65. 2. *distribute*, τὰ βοεικὰ ζεύγη τοῖς λοχαγοῖς κατεμερίσθη X.*An.*7.5.4; κ. εἰς λόχους, = καταλοχίζω, Ascl.*Tact.*2.1:—Med., ἕκαστόν τι εἰς τὴν ἑαυτοῦ φύσιν Thphr.*CP*5.2.5. -ῐσις, εως, ἡ, *division into parts*, Epicur.*Ep.*2 p.48 U.; *distribution*, τῶν μερῶν Metrod.*Herc.*831.10. -ισμός, ὁ, = foreg., Lxx *Jo.*13.14.

**καταμέστ-ιος**, ον, poet. for sq., *quite full*, Nic.*Al.*45. -ος, ον, strengthd. for μεστός, gloss on κατάπαστος, Sch.Ar.*Eq.*500. -όω, *fill quite full of* a thing, τινος Pherecr.145.28.

*__καταμετρ-έω__, *measure out*, [σῖτον] τοῖσι ἐπικούροισι Hdt.3.91; of a garden, X.*Oec.*4.21; μεγέθη, πέρατα, Epicur.*Ep.*1 p.17 U., *Sent.*19; ὑμῖν αὐτοῖς τὰ ὅρια Lxx *Nu.*34.10:—Med., ἐν τῷ -μετρεῖσθαι ὑμᾶς τὴν γῆν ib.*Ez.*45.1; of castrametation, Plb.6.41.4; *assign* land held by military tenure, τῶν -μεμετρημένων [κλήρων] *PPetr.*2 intr.p.22 (iii B.C.), cf. *PCair.Zen.*215.2 (iii B.C.), al.; also of the grantees, τοὺς -μεμετρημένους ἱππεῖς *PHal.*15.5 (iii B.C.), cf. *PLille* 14.3 (iii B.C.). 2. *measure exactly, be the measure of*, μόριον ὃ -μετρήσει τὴν ὅλην Arist. *Ph.*$237^{b}28$ (for wh. ἀναμ- is used $238^{a}22$); τὰ -μετροῦντά τινων *aliquot parts*, Id.*Metaph.*$1023^{b}15$:—Pass., ὁ λόγος -μετρεῖται συλλαβῇ Id.*Cat.*$4^{b}33$: esp. in Metric, of feet or rhythms, D.H.*Comp.*17, cf. *Dem.*39. -ημα, ατος, τό, *unit of measurement*, Epicur.*Ep.*1 p.17 U. -ησις, εως, ἡ, *measuring out*, Plb.6.41.5, S.E.*M.*1.46; τῆς τοῦ σώματος ἰδέας Iamb.*Myst.*10.5. -ητέον, *one must measure*, S.E.*M.*6.65. -ητικός, ή, όν, *of* or *for measuring*, ἡμερῶν καὶ νυκτῶν Epicur.*Herc.*1413.10; πλάτους S.E.*M.*3.73, 9.427.

**καταμηγγές**· παρακμὴ σώματος, Hsch. (Corruption of Od.14.214.)

**καταμηκύνω**, *lengthen out*, Gal.1.246; ἀκτῖνας Ptol.*Tetr.*100.

**καταμηλόω**, *put in the probe*, so as to sound wounds, Suid., Phot., etc.; or to produce vomiting, ἐμεῖ καταμηλῶν Phryn.Com.62: metaph., κημὸν κ. *use* the funnel of the ballot-jar *as a probe*, i. e. *make* a peculator *disgorge* what he has stolen, Ar.*Eq.*1150 (lyr.). 2. κ. τὰ ἔρια *plunge* them into dyestuff, Poll.7.169.

**καταμηνι-αῖα**, τά, (μήν) = sq. II. 2, *Gloss.* *-ος, ον, *monthly*, of wages, *IG*$1^{2}$.339.30, al.; καθάρσεις Pl.1.45; αἷμα Gal.*UP*14.3. 2. *hired by the month*, *BGU*1521 (iii B.C.), *POxy.*2155.8 (iv A.D.). II. Subst. καταμηνίη, ἡ (sc. κάθαρσις), = καταμήνια, τά, prob. in *IG*12(5).646 (Ceos). 2. τὰ κ. *menses of women*, Hp.*Aph.*3.28, Arist.*GA* $727^{a}18$, al., Plot.2.9.12, etc.: sg. -μήνιον, τό, Arist.*HA*$573^{a}16$, Gal.8.423, Speus.ap.Alex.Aphr.*in Metaph.*699.31. -ώδης, ες, *subject to menstruation*, Arist.*GA*$748^{a}20$. 2. *menstruous*, περίττωμα ib.$751^{a}3$.

**καταμήν-ῦσις**, εως, ἡ, *information*, Him.*Ecl.*4.18; as law-term, Just.*Nov.*115.3.7. -ῡτής, οῦ, ὁ, *informer*, *Cod.Just.*10.11.8 *Intr.* -ύω, *point out, make known*, κ. διὰ γραμμάτων τοὺς οὔρους Hdt.7.30; τόδ' ἐγὼ καταμηνύσω A.*Pr.*176 (anap.), cf. Plu.*Them.*23, etc.; κ. ἑωυτὸν ὡς εἴη Ἱστιαῖος Hdt.6.29; τὸν Ὅμηρον ὅτι.. Phld. *Hom.*p.54 O.:—Pass., Jul.*ad Ath.*273d. 2. *inform against*, τινος Lys.13.49, cf. D.24.60; also τινὰς πρός τινα D.H.4.43:—Pass., ὑπό τινος -μηνυθείς ib.62, cf. *Cod.Just.*10.11.8.4. 3. of a god, *give a sign*, X.*HG*3.3.2.

**καταμηρίζω**, = διαμηρίζω, Suid. s. v. καταγιγαρτίσαι.

**καταμήσας**· καθάπαξ, Hsch.

**καταμηχᾰνάομαι**, *plan and execute*, Plot.4.4.31.

**καταμῐαίνω**, *defile*, ψεύδεσιν -μιάναις γέννα Pi.*P.*4.100; [τὰ καλὰ] Pl.*Lg.*937d; τὸ φῶς Luc.*Cat.*27:—Pass., *wear squalid garments* as a sign of grief, Hdt.6.58.

**καταμῐαιφονέομαι**, *defile oneself with bloodshed*, Heraclit.*Ep.*7.6.

**καταμίγας**, f. l. for κατὰ μόνας, Gal.18(2).774.

**καταμίγνυμι**, later spelling of καταμείγνυμι.

*__καταμιεῖ__· καταπίνει, κατεσθίει· μιεῖν γὰρ τὸ ἐσθίειν, Hsch.

**καταμῑμέομαι**, *burlesque*, c. acc., D.H.7.72.

*__καταμιμνήσκομαι__, = μιμνήσκομαι, Lxx 4*Ma.*13.12.

**κατάμιξις**, v. κατάμειξις.

*__καταμίσγω__, = καταμείγνυμι, Str.1.2.9:—Med., Nic.*Al.*353:—Pass., *h.Pan.*26.

**καταμισθο-δοτέω**, *corrupt by high pay*, D.H.4.31. -φορέω, *spend in paying* δικασταί, ἐκκλησιασταί, etc., Ar.*Eq.*1352, v. Sch.; κ. τὰ ὑπάρχοντα *in paying mercenaries*, Aeschin.2.131; κ. προσόδους Theopomp. Hist.90; πλοῦτον εἰς τοὺς πολεμίους D.H.*Dem.*20: c. dat., ξενικοῖς στρατεύμασι Id.4.23.

**κατάμῑτον**, Adv. *in a series, one after another*, παντὸς ὀργάνου κ. ἧπται Protagorid.2. (Perh. rather κατὰ μίτον, cf. μίτος, μίττος.)

**κατάμιττα** or **κατὰ μίττα**, perh. = εὐτενῆ, of dressing stones, *IG* $2^{2}$.1670.18; cf. foreg. and μίτος, μίττος.

*__καταμνημονεύω__, *call to mind*, Plu.2.748f, 974e, Gal.17(1).515.

**καταμνίω**, = κατεσθίω, Phot.; cf. καταμιεῖ.

**καταμοιχ-εύω**, *seduce*, *PMasp.*4.17 (vi A.D.). -ος, ὁ, *adulterer*, Vett.Val.117.9.

**καταμολύνω**, *defile utterly*, in Pass., Sch.E.*Hec.*912.

**κατάμομφος**, ον, *liable to blame, inauspicious*, A.*Ag.*145 (lyr.).

**καταμόνᾱς**, Adv. *alone, apart*, better divisim κατὰ μόνας, v. μόνος B. III.

**καταμονή**, ἡ, *a remaining*, Plb.3.79.12, Ael.*NA*9.46, A.D.*Synt.*310.19, Artem.5.70.

**καταμονίη**, ἡ, = foreg., only found in poet. form καμμονίη (q. v.).

**καταμονομᾰχέω**, *conquer in single combat*, Plu.*Thes.*11, Ael.*VH* 10.22.

**κατάμονος**, ον, *permanent*, *SIG*141.8 (Corc. Nigr., iv B.C.); τιμαί Plb.39.3.9, *IG*5(1).1432.16 (Messene, i B.C.); ψαφίσματα *SIG*563.8 (Aetol., from Teos, iii B.C.). 2. ἐψηφίσατο τὸν πόλεμον κ. εἶναι should *continue*, Plb.18.12.1, cf. 21.2.6, al.

**καταμόσχ-ευσις**, εως, ἡ, *propagation by suckers*, *Gloss.* *-εύω, *propagate by suckers*, ib.

**καταμουσίζω**, *charm with song*, Men.Rh.p.408 S.

**καταμουσον**· κατάκρυψον, Hsch. (i. e. -μυσον).

**καταμουσόω**, *embellish*, Jul.*Ep.*10.

**κατ-άμπελος**, ον, *wine-growing*, χώρα Str.4.1.5.

**κατ-αμπέχω** and -ίσχω, *encompass*, εὔψυχον ἄνδρα κούφῃ καταμπίσχουσιν ἐν τύμβῳ χθονί, i. e. bury him, E.*Hel.*853; μηκάδων μέλη, χλόην καταμπέχοντα *full of* green herbs, i. e. either *fed on grass* or *stuffed with herbs*, Antiph.1; *cover*, τὰ κράνη -αμπέχοντες Plu.*Crass.* 11.

*__κατ-αμπῠκόω__, *cover with a fillet*, κρᾶτα S.*Fr.*402.

**καταμῡθολογέω**, *amuse with fables*, τινα Philostr.*Her.*1.1.

**καταμυκτηρίζω**, *mock with upturned nose*, gloss on κατιλλώπτειν, Paus.Gr.*Fr.*209:—Pass., Hsch. s. v. κατιλλάνθη.

**κατ-ᾰμύνω** [ῡ], *ward off*, βίαν prob. in *PCair.Preis.*4.17 (iv A.D.):—Med., *avenge oneself*, dub. in Ael.*NA*5.11.

**κατάμῠσις**, εως, ἡ, *closing of the eyes*, Plu.*Cam.*6 (pl.): κ. ὀφθαλμῶν A.D.*Synt.*291.16. 2. *winking*, γέλωτι καὶ λαλιῇ καὶ κ. Aret. *SD*1.7.

**κατ-ᾰμύσσω**, *tear, scratch*, κατὰ δὲ χρόα καλὸν ἀ. Theoc.6.14; καλὸν ἄμυξε κάτα ῥέθος *AP*7.218 (Antip. Sid.): c. acc. cogn., μεγάλας ἀμυχὰς κ. Phryn.Com.3.6 (anap.):—Med., καταμύξατο χεῖρα ἀραιήν she *scratched her* hand, Il.5.425; μέτωπον καὶ ῥῖνα καταμύσσονται Hdt.4.71; κὰδ δέ σ' ἀμυξάμεναι *AP*7.491 (Mnasalc.):—Pass., καταμυχθεὶς τὴν κνήμην ὑπὸ κυνοσβάτου Did.ap.Ath.2.70d.

**καταμυττωτεύω**, *make mincemeat of*, in pf. Pass., Ar.*Pax*247.

**καταμύω**, Ep. aor. inf. καμμῦσαι v. l. in Batr.191; καμμύειν, aor. ἐκάμμυσα, etc., also in later Gr., v. καμμύω:—*close the eyes*, κ. τὰ βλέφαρα X.*Cyn.*5.11; τὰ ὄμματα Hp.*Epid.*7.83; τοὺς ὀφθαλμούς Lxx (v. καμμύω); τὸ τῆς ψυχῆς ὄμμα Ph.1.645, cf. 2.414; κ. τῷ νοερῷ ὄμματι M.Ant.4.29: more freq. alone, *close the eyes*, Str.6.1.14; κ. ὑπ' ἐκπλήξεως Philostr.*VA*6.11: hence, *drop asleep, doze*, Batr. l. c., Ar.*V.*92: euphem. for καθευδήσκειν, Luc.*DMer.*7.2, D.L.4.49. [ῡ in pres., Hedyl.ap.Ath.8.345a: in aor., Batr. l. c.; v. μύω.]

**καταμφι-έννῡμι**, *clothe completely, cover all round*, τοίχους πριστῷ [λίθῳ] J.*AJ*8.5.2. -κᾰλύπτω, strengthd. for ἀμφικαλ-, *put all round*, κεφαλῇ δὲ κατὰ ῥάκος ἀμφικαλύψας Od.14.349.

**καταμωκ-άομαι**, *mock at*, c. gen., Plu.*Demetr.*13, Epict.*Ench.*22: c. acc., Anon.ap.Suid.: abs., Lxx 2*Ch.*30.10, Hld.7.25, Sch.A.R.3.791. -ημα, ατος, τό, = sq., Hsch. s. v. χήνημα. -ησις, εως, ἡ, *mockery*, Plb.12.26$^{c}$.1, Ath.2.55d.

**καταμωλύνομαι**, Pass., = καταμαραίνομαι, of ulcers, Hp.*Prorrh.*1.170, f. l. in Id.*Epid.*2.2.6.

**καταμωλωπίζω**, *cover with weals* or *stripes*, Suid.

**καταμωραίνω**, *waste through folly*, τὰ πατρῷα Antiph.239.

**καταμώσας**· καθεὶς ἕνεκα τοῦ ζητῆσαι, κτλ., dub. l. in Gal.19.109.

**κατανά**· κατὰ νοῦν, Hsch.; cf. ἐγκατάνα.

**καταναγιγνώσκω**, *read through*, πᾶσαν τὴν ἱστορίαν Ath.13.610d.

**κατᾰναγκ-άζω**, *force back*, esp. of dislocated or fractured limbs, *force* them *into their place*, Hp.*Fract.*8, al. II. *overpower by force, constrain*, δεσμοῖς ἦν κατηναγκασμένος E.*Ba.*643; κ. τὸ σῶμα *torture*,

Luc.*Nec.*4. 2. *coerce*, τινὰ ἐς ξυμμαχίαν Th.4.77; τινά τι Luc.*Laps.* 8; τινὰ ποιεῖν τι Is.7.38, cf. *PGen.*49.24 (iv A.D.): Pass., ὅσα -άζεται πρὸς μικρότητα καὶ μέγεθος Thphr.*CP*1.16.11; κινήσεις τινὲς ὑπὸ φαρμάκων -άζονται Gal.6.150; κατηναγκασμένος *necessary, inevitable*, ὁμολογούμενον καὶ κ. ἅπασι Plb.3.4.3, cf. A.D.*Synt.*43.1, al.; αἱ -ασμέναι ὑπηρεσίαι τοῦ βίου Ph.*Fr.*101 H. **-ἄσις,** εως, ἡ, *reduction* of dislocated limbs, Hp.*Art.*48, al. **-αστικός,** ή, όν, *conclusive, cogent*, λόγος *EM*239.43. **-η,** ἡ, *means of constraint*: *spell*, βιαιότεραι κ. cj. in Hld.6.14. II. kind of *vetch, Ornithopus compressus*, used in making philtres, Dsc.4.131, Plin.*HN*27.57, *PMag.Osl.*1.370. 2. = κῆμος, Ps.-Dsc.4.133.

**κατανα-γρᾰφέω,** *ordain duly*, καθά κα ἁ βουλὰ καταναγραφήσῃ *IG* 14.256.29 (Phintias). **-θεμα,** ατος, τό, *curse*, *Apoc.*22.3; and **-θεμᾰτίζω,** *curse*, *Ev.Matt.*26.74, both vv. ll. for καταθ-.

**κατ-αναιδεύομαι,** *behave impudently to*, τινος Eust.69.22.

**κατ-αναισῑμόω,** *use quite up*, in Pass., Hp.*Art.*11, *Gland.*3.

**καταναίω,** *make to dwell, settle*:—Act. only in poet. aor., κατένασσε πατὴρ ἐς πείρατα γαίης Hes.*Op.*168; κ. ὑπὸ χθονός Id.*Th.*620; γουνοῖσιν Νεμείης ib.329, cf. B.3.60:—aor. Med., δυσαρέστους δαίμονας αὐτοῦ καταναssαμένη A.*Eu.*929 (anap.):—Pass., only in aor., *take up one's abode, dwell*, ὑπὸ δειράσι Παρνασοῦ κατενάσθη E.*Ph.*207 (lyr.); ἐν τῇ χώρᾳ κατένασθεν (3 pl.) Ar.*V.*662: so in aor. Med., ἐν Κέῳ κατενάσσατο A.R.2.520. 2. *establish*, βωμόν B.10.41.

⊛**καταναλ-ίσκω,** impf. -ανάλισκον Isoc.1.18: plpf. -ανηλώκει (intr.) Pl.*Ti.*36b: but aor. -ηνάλωσα Isoc.9.60:—**Pass.,** aor. -αναλωθῆναι Pl.*Phd.*72d; subj. -αναλωθῇ Hp.*Epid.*2.4.1; indic. -ηναλώθησαν ib. 2: pf. -ανήλωμαι Isoc.3.31 codd.; inf. κατηναλῶσθαι Plu.2.112a:—*use up, spend, lavish*, χρήματα X.*Mem.*1.2.22; εἴς τι *upon a thing*, εἰς τὴν στρατείαν τάλαντα μύρια Isoc.9.60; τὴν σχολὴν εἰς φιληκοΐαν Id.1.18; τὰς δυνάμεις εἰς τὰ ἄλογα Pl.*Prt.*321c; τέσσαρας μνᾶς εἰς ὀψοφαγίαν Ister ap.Ath.8.345d; of space in a treatise, Phld.*Herc.*1508.10; also κ. πολλὰ ἡδοναῖς D.S.17.108; τὸ πλεῖστον τοῦ βίου ἐν ὁμιλίᾳ Ael.*VH*3.13:—Pass., with plpf. Act., *to be lavished*, Pl.*Ti.* l. c.; εἴς τι Id.*Phd.* l. c.; πάσας [τιμὰς] κατηναλῶσθαι ἄλλοις Plu. l. c. 2. *consume*, τὴν τροφήν Arist.*GA*763$^{a}$13, Plu.2.160b; *devour* fuel, of fire, Arist.*Juv.*469$^{b}$29; later, *eat*, [ἰχθύν] Agatharch.109; [ῥοιᾶς κόκκον] Apollod.1.5.3:—Pass., ἡ τροφὴ κ. εἰς τὴν αὔξησιν, εἰς τὸ σῶμα, Arist.*GA*771$^{a}$28, 725$^{b}$31, cf. Hp.*VM*11; ἐπιστήμη οὐ κ. ὑπὸ πόνων Andronic.Rhod.p.578 M. **-ωσις,** εως, ἡ, *waste, consumption*, Plu.2.678f. **-ωτέον,** *one must expend*, τὴν σπουδὴν εἰς τὰ μηδενὸς ἄξια Arist.*Rh.Al.*1420$^{b}$22.

**καταναρκάομαι,** Ion. **-έομαι,** Pass., *grow quite numb*, Hp.*Art.*48; *to be reduced to a torpid condition*, Phld.*Lib.*p.52 O. II. Act., καταναρκᾶν τινος *to be slothful towards, press heavily upon..*, 2*Ep.Cor.*11.9, 12.13.

**κατανάσσω,** *stamp, beat down firmly*, κατανάξαντες τὴν γῆν Hdt. 7.36:—Pass., -νενασμένος σφυγμός *firm* pulse, Archig.ap.Gal.8.662.

⊛**καταναυμᾰχέω,** *conquer in a sea-fight, beat at sea*, βασιλέα And.3.5, cf. D.20.68, X.*HG*7.1.10, Din.1.75, *TAM*2(1).265 (Xanthos):—Pass., ὑπὸ τῆς βασιλέως δυνάμεως Isoc.12.105, cf. Luc.*Hist.Conscr.*38.

**κατ-ανδρᾰποδίζω,** *enslave*: metaph., in Pass., ἐννοίαις Just.*Nov.* 42 *Praef.*

**κατ-ανδρᾰφύσσω,** *slay*, in aor. κατηνδράφυξα, Hsch.

**κατ-ανδρίζομαι,** *fight manfully against*, expld. by καταπαλαῖσαι, Hsch.

**κατανδρίζω,** (κατ' ἄνδρα) *place on a list*, *BGU*1095.14 (i A.D.).

**κατανεᾱνιεύομαι,** *prevail over by youthful vigour*, or *exult over*, Hsch.

**κατανείφω,** fut. -νείψω (v. infr.), *snow all over, cover with snow*, κατένειψε χιόνι τὴν Θρᾴκην [ὁ θεός], i.e. *snow fell over all* Thrace, Ar. *Ach.*138:—Pass., Plu.*Luc.*24: metaph., *sprinkle as with snow*, Luc. *VH*2.14; κατανείψων ἀπὸ γλώσσης ἅπαντας Id.*Lex.*15. II. abs., κατανείφει *it snows*, κεἰ κριμνώδη κατανείφοι even *were it to snow* thick as meal, Ar.*Nu.*965.

**κατανεκρόω,** *kill*, prob. in *Tab.Defix.Aud.*16 *Fr.*x 13. 2. *deaden*, τὴν ζῳογόνον φύσιν ἐν τῷ χειμῶνι -ωθεῖσαν Lyd.*Mens.*4.67.

**κατανέμησις,** εως, ἡ, *pasturage*, διὰ τῶν προβάτων *PRyl.*141.16 (i A.D.), cf. Sch.Pi.*O.*7.61.

**κατ-άνεμος,** ον, f.l. for κατήνεμος, Poll.1.101.

**κατανέμω,** *distribute, allot*, freq. of pasture land, κ. χώρην τισί Hdt. 2.109, cf. Isoc.3.28; τὴν ὀργάδα D.H.1.79, etc.; θέαν τινί D.18. 28. 2. *distribute, divide into portions*, δέκα⟨χα⟩ δὲ καὶ τοὺς δήμους κατένειμε ἐς τὰς φυλάς *distributed* or *apportioned* them in ten groups among the tribes, Hdt.5.69, cf. Decr.ap.D.59.104: without Prep., τὸ στράτευμα κατένειμε δώδεκα μέρη X.*Cyr.*7.5.13; τὴν νῆσον δέκα μέρη κ. Pl.*Criti.*113e; of a single person, κ. τινὰ εἰς τὴν τάξιν *assign* him to his post, Aeschin.1.155:—Pass., δεῖ τὸ πλῆθος ἐν συσσιτίοις κατανενεμῆσθαι Arist.*Pol.*1331$^{a}$20. 3. *graze*, τὰ πρόβατα τὰ -νενεμηκότα τὰ ἐκεῖ *BGU*885.6 (ii A.D.); *occupy grazing land*, *PHib.*1.52.3 (iii B.C.); of shepherds, *pasture*, [πρόβατα] Eust.212.39. II. Med., *divide among themselves*, Th.2.17, Pl.*R.*547b. 2. with aor. and pf. Pass., *occupy, overrun*, esp. with cattle, *feed* or *graze land*, τὴν χώραν ἡμῶν -νενέμηνται Isoc.14.7, cf. ib.20 (also in Act., βοσκήμασι κ. [τὴν χώραν] Decr.ap.D.18.154); γέρανοι -ενέμοντο χώρην Babr. 26.1: hence, *plunder, ravage*, πᾶσαν τὴν Λιβύην Ath.15.677e. 3. metaph., of a plague, ἡ λοιμώδης φθορὰ -ενεμήθη τὴν ἀκμάζουσαν ἡλικίαν Plu.*Per.*34; ἀλφὸς κ. τὸ σῶμα *spreads over*, Plu.*Art.*23; so of fire, *spread*, εἰς τὰς πρώτας σκηνάς Plb.14.4.6.

**κατανέναι·** κατανεῦσαι, Hsch.

**κατάνευρος,** ον, *full of nerves* or *sinews*, μέρη, τόπος, *Hippiatr.*57, 96.

**κατάνευσις,** εως, ἡ, *assent*, J.*AJ*17.9.5; αἰτήσεων ibid. (pl.).

**κατανεύω,** fut. -νεύσομαι Il.1.524, Pl.*R.*350e: aor. κατένευσα Il.1. 558, etc.; Ep. part. καννεύσας Od.15.464:—*nod assent*, κεφαλῇ κατανεύσομαι Il.1.524; χαίταις Pi.*N.*1.14; κατανεύσομαι καὶ ἀνανεύσομαι Pl.*R.* l. c., cf. *Euthd.*277c, Ar.*Ec.*72: abs., of granting a request, ὑπέστην καὶ κατένευσα Il.4.267, cf. Hdt.9.111, Ar.*Th.*1020: c. acc. rei, *grant, promise*, ὅτι μοι κατένευσε Κρονίων νίκην καὶ μέγα κῦδος Il.8.175: later c. dat., *consent to*, *BGU*1119.24 (i B.C.): c. fut. inf., δωσέμεναι κατένευσε Il.10.393; ὑπέσχετο καὶ κατένευσεν Ἴλιον ἐκπέρσαντ' εὐτείχεον ἀπονέεσθαι 2.112: later c. aor. inf., Bion *Fr.*5.8: generally, *make a sign by nodding the head*, ὁ δὲ τῇ -ένευσε σιωπῇ Od.15.463. II. *bow down*, εἰς γῆν v.l. in Ach.Tat.7.14; ἐπειδὰν -νεύσῃ τὸ ἀγγεῖον *Gp.* 2.4.2; κ. τὴν κεφαλήν Poll.1.205: pf. part. -νενευκώς *downcast*, Vett. Val.2.4. III. Astron., *tilt downward*, of the pole, Eudox.*Ars* 6.31. [κατᾱνεύων Od.9.490.]

**κατανεφόω,** *overcloud*, Plu.*Tim.*27.

**κατανέω** (A), aor. -ένησα, *heap, pile up*, Hdt.6.97.

**κατανέω** (B), *spin out*, in pf. Pass., Hsch. s. v. λίνοιο.

**κατάνη,** ἡ, = τυρόκνηστις, Sicil. word in Plu.*Dio* 58.

**κατανήχομαι,** *swim down stream*, Sch.A.R.4.937.

**κατ-ανθίζομαι,** Pass., *to be decked with bright colours*, χρώμασι παντοδαποῖς κατηνθισμένος D.S.18.26; πέδιλον κατήνθιστο χρυσῷ Callistr.*Stat.*7; οἰκία πολυτελέσι λίθοις κατηνθισμένη Hierocl. *in CA* 17 p.458 M. (Act. perh. to be read in Plu.2.789c.)

**κατανθρᾰκ-ίζω,** = sq.: metaph., of love, *AP*12.99. **-όω,** fut. -ώσομαι, *burn to cinders*, στέγην πυρώσω καὶ κατανθρακώσομαι A.*Fr.*281.4. II. elsewh. only in Pass., δέμας φλογιστὸν ἤδη καὶ κατηνθρακωμένον S.*El.*58; ἅπαν κατηνθρακώθη θῦμ' ἐν.. φλογί E. *IA*1602; κατηνθρακώμεθ' ὀφθαλμοῦ σέλας I *have* it *burnt out*, Id.*Cyc.* 663.

**κατανθρωπ-ίζω,** *treat in a friendly manner*, *BGU*1141.5 (i A.D.). **-ισμός,** ὁ, *hospitality, entertainment*, τινος *POxy.*736.11, al. (i A.D.).

**κατ-ᾰνιάω,** strengthd. for ἀνιάω, Hsch. s. v. κατήφησας:—also **κατανιάζω,** Id. s. v. κατηφήσας (Pass.).

**κατανίζω** (pres. **-νίπτω** Ph.2.45), *wash well*, ὄξει πάντα κ. Hp.*Ulc.* 27, cf. 24; τὸν κηρόν Gal.13.743; γάλακι κατανενιμμένος Pherecr.108. 18. II. *wash out, purge*, αἱ διάρροιαι.. -νιφθεῖσαι πεπαύσονται Hp. *Prorrh.*2.23; κατανίζεται τὸ σῶμα τοῖς οἴνοις Mnesith.ap.Ath.11. 484a.

**κατανῑκάνδρα,** ἡ, *she that subdues men*, epith. of Ἄρκτος, *PMag. Lond.*121.762.

**κατανῑκάω,** strengthd. for νικάω, ὅταν οἵ γ' ἀγαθοὶ πρὸς τῶν ἀγενῶν -νικῶνται S.*Fr.*84, cf. J.*AJ*3.2.2, *PFlor.*338.11 (iii A.D.); ὑπὸ τῆς φθοροποιοῦ δυνάμεως Philum.*Ven.*4.3.

**κατάνιμμα,** ατος, τό, *water for washing in*, Ath.1.19a (pl.).

**κατανίπτης,** ου, ὁ, *washer*: at Athens, *he who washed the peplos of Athena Polias*, *AB*269, *EM*494.25.

**κατανίσσομαι,** *go* or *come down from*, ἐξ ὀρέων A.R.2.976. II. *go through*, c. acc., Hermesian.7.65.

**κατ-ανίσταμαι,** aor. κατανέστην: pf. κατανέστηκα:—*rise up against*, τῶν πολεμίων, τῶν ἀρχόντων, Plb.1.46.10, 38.12.7: abs., Id. 38.13.1; ἐπὶ τὴν συναγωγήν Lxx *Nu.*16.3.

**κατανίφω,** late spelling of κατανείφω q. v.).

**κατανο-έω,** *observe well, understand, apprehend*. ὡς ἐμὲ κατανοέειν Hdt.2.28, cf. 93; οὐ χαλεπὸν τῷ βουλομένῳ κ. Lys.25.34; οὐ.. κατανοῶ τὸ νῦν ἐρωτώμενον Pl.*Sph.*233a; κ. ὅ τι λέγω Id.*Grg.*455b; οὐ πάνυ κατανοῶ Id.*Phlb.*48a; κ. ὅτι.. Id.*Sph.*264b; κατανοεῖς τίς ποτ' ἐστίν..; Antiph.33.1; ἐκεῖνο, ὅτι.. Epicur.*Ep.*1 p.30 U.; ἐκ τίνων.. καὶ πότε.. καὶ πῶς.. Plb.1.12.9:—Pass., of a doctrine, *to be grasped and* hence *accepted*, μᾶλλον μᾶλλον κ. Epicur.*Nat.*138 G.; εἰς καρδίαν -εῖται *is understood* of.., Heph.Astr.1.1. 2. *perceive*, τῷ κατανοουμένῳ τὸ κατανοοῦν ἐξομοιῶσαι *the percipient to the perceived*, Pl.*Ti.*90d, etc.: c. part., κ. οὐ πολλοὺς ὄντας Th.2.3. 3. *learn*, τῆς Περσίδος γλώσσης ὅσα ἐδύνατο κατενόησε Id.1.138. 4. *consider*, περί τινος X.*Cyr.*1.6.20. 5. *look at, view*, τὴν οἰκίαν Ath. 5.179a. II. *to be in one's right mind, in one's senses*, Hp.*Epid.*1. 26.γ', 5.39. **-ημα,** ατος, τό, *purpose, contrivance*, τὸ τῶν θεῶν τοῦ κόσμου κ. Pl.*Epin.*987d; κ. χρηματιστικόν Arist.*Pol.*1259$^{a}$7. **-ησις,** εως, ἡ, *observation, consideration*, Pl.*Ti.*82c, *Criti.*107d, Lxx *Si.*41. 21; ἡ αὑτοῦ κ. *introspection*, Plot.5.3.1; ἑαυτῆς (sc. ψυχῆς) Id.4.7. 10; of sense perception, ἡ δι' αἰσθήσεως κ. Id.6.2.4. 2. *means of observing*, πολλὴν ἑαυτοῦ παρέχειν κ. Plu.*Rom.*6. **-ητέον,** *one must observe, learn*, Pl.*Plt.*305c, Porph.*Marc.*27; *one must consider*, πάλιν περί τινος Ph.1.83. **-ητικός,** ή, όν, *observant, intelligent*, Poll.9.151.

**κατ-ανοίγνυμι,** strengthd. for ἀνοίγω, Lxx *Ps.*4.4, Philostr.*Dial.*2.

**κατ-άνομαι** [ᾱ], Pass., (ἄνω) *to be used up* or *wasted*, πολλὰ κατάνεται Od.2.58; μέτρα κατανομένων ἐνιαυτῶν *completed*, Arat.464.

**κατανομή,** ἡ, *pasture*, προβάτων *PIand.*26.33 (i A.D.), cf. Sch.Ar. *Av.*769, Sch.S.*Tr.*13 (pl.).

**κατανομ-ίζω,** *recognize*, *PGrenf.*1.11 ii 2 (ii B.C.). **-ιστεύω,** *melt down into coin*, J.*BJ*1.18.4.

⊛**κατανομοθετέω,** *legislate*, Pl.*Lg.*861c.

**κατανοστέω,** *return from banishment*, Plb.4.17.10.

**κατανοσφίζομαι,** Med., *embezzle*, τὰ δημόσια D.H.4.11.

**κατανοτιαῖος,** α, ον, *with south aspect*, ἐξέδριον *CIG*2554.124 (Cret., dub.).

**κατανοτίζω**, *bedew*. κατὰ δὲ γόος ἅμα χαρᾷ τὸ σὸν νοτίζει βλέφαρον E.*IT*833 (lyr.).

**κάταντ-α**, Adv. *downhill*, πολλὰ δ' ἄναντα κ. πάραντά τε δόχμιά τ' ἦλθον Il.23.116, cf. Luc.*Merc.Cond.*26: c. gen., *below*, prob. in *PFlor.*370.7 (ii A. D.). **-άω**, *come down to, arrive*, εἰς τὰ βασίλεια, ἐπὶ κοίτην, D.S.4.52, 3.27, cf. *PTeb.*59.3 (i B. C.), etc.: metaph., ἐπὶ τὴν φυσικὴν ὁδὸν Vett.Val.259.3, cf. 185.16, 251.30. 2. in a speech or narrative, *come to, arrive at* a point, εἰς τὴν ἔκπτωσιν Plb. 4.1.8; ἐπί τινας λογισμούς Id.10.37.3; κ. ἐπὶ τὸν ὅρκον D.S.1.79, cf. J.*AJ*3.10.4, etc.; *have recourse to*, ἐπὶ [τὴν ἡδονήν] Epicur.*Ep.*3 p.63 U.; ἐπὶ τὰ δάκρυα Phld.*Lib.*p.62 O. 3. of persons, κ. εἰς ἑαυτοὺς *attack, commence hostilities against* each other, Plb.30.11.3. 4. of events, *come upon*, πᾶς δ' ἀγὼν ἐπ' ἐμὲ κατήντα Alex.261.13; κ. εἴς τινα *affect* him, Phld.*Ir.*p.83 W.; of blood-guiltiness, *fall*, ἐπὶ κεφαλήν τινος Lxx 2*Ki.*3.29. b. *turn out, result*, ποῦ καταντήσει πάλιν Plb.6.4.12; τὸ πρᾶγμα κ. εἰς ὑπόνοιαν D.S.1.37; εἰς τὸ μηδέν Plb.4.34.2; so of numbers, *to be reduced*, εἰς μόνους ἄνδρας δέκα *BGU*903.14 (ii A. D.), etc. 5. of an inheritance, κ. εἴς τινα *fall* to one's share, 1*Ep.Cor.*10.11, *POxy.*75 (ii A. D.), etc. II. trans., *make to come back, bring back*, τινα Palaeph.2; εἰς ἑαυτὸν τὴν ἀρχιερωσύνην Lxx 2*Ma.*4.24 (so intr. in pf., *return*, εἰς τὸν αὐτὸν κατηντηκέναι βίον *BGU* 1101.5 (i B. C.)). ✱**-ημα**, ατος, τό, *end, goal*, Lxx *Ps.*18(19).7, Sch. Ar.*Ra.*1026; κ. σκέψεως Sch.E.*Hec.*744; *result*, *PSI*6.698.5 (iv A. D.). **-ην**, Adv., = κάταντα, Them.*Or.*13.168b. ✱**-ης**, ες, (ἄντα) *downhill, steep*, opp. ἀνάντης, κ. ἀτραπός Ar.*Ra.*127; ἐς τὰ κατάντεα *downwards*, Hp.*Off.*9; ἐπὶ κάταντες, = κάταντα, Pl.*Ti.*77d; εἰς τὸ κάταντες X.*Eq.*8.8; ἐν τῷ κατάντει Id.*HG*4.8.37; ἀπὸ τοῦ κατάντους ib.3.5.20; ἐν τοῖς κατάντεσι Diocl.*Fr.*142: neut. as Adv., κάταντες κινεῖσθαι Arist.*Ph.*218ᵃ22; τὰ κατάντη ἁμιλλώμενοι X.*Eq.* 8.6; τὰ κ. ἐλαύνεσθαι Id.*Eq.Mag.*8.3; θεῖν Id.*Cyn.*5.17; φέρεσθαι Arist.*HA*567ᵃ7; καταβαίνειν Thphr.*Lass.*11. II. metaph., *prone, inclined*, πρός τι E.*Rh.*318, Epicur.*Nat.*908.4, Plu.2.53e. **-ησις**, εως, ἡ, *recourse*, ἐπὶ τὴν ἀρετήν Phld.*Rh.*1.265 S. II. Astrol., *encounter*, of planetary influences, Vett.Val.247.26 (pl.). **-ητέον**, *one must have recourse*, ἐπὶ φλεβοτομίαν Aët.5.115. **-ία**, ἡ, *hanging downwards*, Hp.*Off.*3. II. καταντία, v. καταντίον.

**κατ-αντιβολέω**, *entreat earnestly*, τινα Ar.*Fr.*625: c. inf., J.*BJ* 1.6.4, al.

**κατ-αντικρύ**, Prep. c. gen., *straight down from*, καταντικρὺ τέγεος πέσε Od.10.559, cf. 11.64. 2. in Att., = Homeric ἀντικρύ, *over against, right opposite*, πρυτάνεων καταντικρύ Ar.*Ec.*87; τὰ κ. Κυθήρων the parts *opposite* Cythera, Th.7.26, cf. X.*HG*4.8.5; κ. ᾗ.. ἐξέπεσεν *exactly opposite* to the point at which.., dub. l. in Pl. *Phd.*112d: c. dat., κ. τῇ θέσει Arist.*Mete.*356ᵃ10; τῷ ἡλίῳ D.C.60.26. II. Adv. of Place, *right opposite*, ἡ ἤπειρος ἡ κ. Th.1.136; ἐν τῷ κ. προσστῆναί τινι Pl.*Euthd.*274c, cf. *Prt.*315c; τὸ κ. αὐτῶν τοῦ σπηλαίου Id.*R.*515a; ἐκ τοῦ κ. from the *opposite* side, ib.b; κ. ὁρᾶν look *right in the face*, Id.*Chrm.*169c; ἐπὶ τὸ κ. in the *opposite* direction, Arist.*HA*528ᵇ10 (but εἰς τὸ κ. towards the *opposite* end, Pl.*Phd.* 72b); πρὸς τὸ κ. κείμενος Plb.4.39.6. b. *in opposition, to the contrary*, κατὰ τὴν κ. ἢ ὡς Γλαύκων λέγει Arist.*Po.*1461ᵃ35. 2. *straight forward*, Id.*HA*591ᵇ24; opp. πλάγια, Pl.*Tht.*194b. 3. *outright, downright*, Th.7.57 (nisi leg. καὶ ἄντικρυς); παραβάλλειν.. μὴ κ. Arist.*Rh.*1419ᵇ36. [On the quantity v. ἀντικρύ: the form **καταντροκύ** is found in Att. Inscrr., *IG*2².1668.88.]

**κατ-αντίον**, Adv. *over against, right opposite*, c. gen., Hdt.6.103, 118, 8.52: c. dat., Id.7.33: abs., χὼ κ. θανὼν *facing him*, S.*Ant.*512, cf. *APl.*4.95 (Damag.): **καταντία**, πόντου κ. κυμαίνοντος Agesianax ap.Plu.2.921b, cf. Opp.*H.*2.555.

**κατ-αντιπέρας**, = καταντικρύ II, c. gen., X.*An.*1.1.9; **κατ' ἀντιπέραν** is found ib.4.8.3, Luc.*JTr.*42; **καταντίπερα** Man.4.188:— also **-πέρην** Id.2.22, al.

✱**καταντλ-έω**, *pour* water or liquid *down* one's throat, Alex.85; *pour over*, εἰς τὰ λοιπὰ μέρη τοῦ σώματος κατήντλουσαν (3 pl. impf.) *PSI* 3.168 (ii A. D.): metaph., *pour a flood of words over*, ταῦτά τινος Ar. *V.*483; κ. λόγον κατὰ τῶν ὤτων Pl.*R.*344d; φιλοσοφίας γέλωτα κ. ib. 536b; τὰ ποιήματα ἡμῶν κ. Id.*Ly.*204d:—Pass., metaph., **-ούμενος** ταῖς τῶν βασάνων τρικυμίαις Lxx 4*Ma.*7.2. 2. *bathe*, κ. τι ἐλαίῳ Gal.8.366; τὴν ὁδὸν αἵματι J.*AJ*8.4.1:—Pass., μύροις Id.*BJ*4.9.10. **-ημα**, ατος, τό, *douche*, Dsc.1.104. **-ησις**, εως, ἡ, = foreg., Hp.*Medic.*3, Antyll.ap.Orib.9.23.1, Gal.10.237. **-ητέον**, *one must douche*, Antyll.ap.Orib.9.23.4, Archig.ap.Aët.3.191, *Gp.* 16.7.1. **-ητικός**, ή, όν, *of* or *for douching*, Herod.Med. in *Rh. Mus.*58.113. **-ος**, ον, = ὑπέραντλος, Poll.1.113.

**καταντροκύ**, v. καταντικρύ.

**κατα-νυκτικός**, ή, όν, *pricking at heart*, Suid. s. v. γοερόν. **-νυξις**, εως, ἡ, *stupefaction, bewilderment*, ἐπότισας ἡμᾶς οἶνον -νύξεως Lxx *Ps.* 59(60).3, cf. *Is.*29.10. 2. *contrition*, Just.*Nov.*137.6 *Intr.* ✱**-νύσσω**, *stab, gouge*, τοὺς ὀφθαλμούς τινος Phleg.36.4 J.:—elsewh. in Pass., with fut. -νυγήσομαι Lxx *Si.*20.21: aor. -ενύγην [ῠ] (v. infr.); *to be sorely pricked*, metaph., κατενύγησαν τὴν καρδίαν *Act.Ap.*2.37, cf. Lxx *Ge.* 34.7: hence, *to be bewildered, stunned*, κάθισον -νενυγμένη Lxx *Is.*47.5, cf. *Ps.*4.5, al.; *keep silence*, ib.*Le.*10.3.

**κατανυστάζω**, aor. κατενύσταξα Poll.2.67:—*doze, fall asleep*, Alex. 286. II. trans., *lull asleep*, dub. in Ael.*NA*14.20.

**κατ-ανύω**, Att. καθ- (q. v.) (-ύτω [ῠ] X.*Cyr.*8.6.17):—Pass. (v. infr. II):—*bring to an end*; esp. 1. *accomplish, cover* a certain distance, τὸν προκείμενον δρόμον Hdt.8.98; νηῦς -ανύει ἐν μακρημερίῃ ὀργυιὰς ἑπτακισμυρίας Id.4.86; δυοῖν ἡμέραιν ὁδὸν ἐν μιᾷ X.*HG*5.4.49, etc.; then, 2. intr., *arrive at* a place, νηῒ κατανύσας ἐς Λῆμνον Hdt.6.140, cf. X.*HG*5.4.20: c. gen., φίλης γὰρ προξένου (sc. ἐς οἶκον) κατηνύσαν they *have come to* a kind hostess's, S.*El.*1451: metaph., πρὶν σᾶν.. κατανύσαι φρενῶν before thou *arrivest at* thy purpose, E. *Hipp.*365 (s. v. l., lyr.). II. *accomplish, perpetrate*, τάδε Id.*El.*1163 (lyr.); αἷμα γενέθλιον κ. Id.*Or.*89:—Med., πολλὰ τῇ πατρίδι κ. *IPE* 1².40.10 (Olbia, ii/iii A. D.):—Pass., *to be fulfilled*, τὸ τέρας αὐτῷ εἰς τὴν ὑπατικὴν ἀρχὴν κατηνύσθη Dam.*Isid.*64. III. *procure*, ὑποζυγίοις χόρτον Plb.9.4.3. IV. *slay*, Sch.E.*Ph.*1062.

**κατανωτ-ίδιος** (v. l. **-ιαῖος**), ον, *on the back*, Poll.1.148. **-ίζομαι**, *carry on one's back*, Plu.2.924d, Luc.*Lex.*5, Longus 1.20. II. *turn one's back upon*: hence, *ignore, disdain, reject*, *BGU*1296.9 (iii B. C.), *PFay.*11.21 (ii B. C.), Phld.*Mort.*35; of critics, Simp. *in Ph.*1036.17, al., Dam.*Isid.*150. **-ιστής**, οῦ, ὁ, *one who despises*, παντὸς δικαίου Dicaearch.1.14.

✱**καταξαίνω**, fut. -ξᾰνῶ Lxx *Jd.*8.7:—*card, comb well*, καταξῆναι Pl. Com.245:—Pass., εἴρια κατεξασμένα Hp.*Ulc.*24; πέτρα κατεξαμμένη *hollowed out*, D.S.17.71 (hence καταξάνωσι cj. Dind. Id.1.98). 2. *tear in pieces, rend in shreds*, πλόκους κόμης E.*Ion* 1267; πολλοὺς αἱ σαὶ καταξανοῦσι.. χέρες Lyc.300; σάρκας Lxx l. c.; κεφαλήν Plu.*Agis* 2; so κ. τινὰ εἰς φοινικίδα *pound* him (by stoning) to red rags, Ar. *Ach.*320:—Pass., πέτροισι.. καταξανθεὶς θανεῖν *crushed to atoms*, S. *Aj.*728; πρὶν κατεξάνθαι βολαῖς E.*Ph.*1145; πέτραις καταξανθέντες ὀστέων ῥαφάς Id.*Supp.*503; πυρὶ καταξανθέντας Id.*HF*285; λύγου ξηρᾶς πληγαῖς -εξασμένης Longus 2.1. 3. *wear, waste away*, πνοαὶ.. τρίβῳ κατέξαινον ἄνθος Ἀργείων A.*Ag.*197 (lyr.); τὴν σάρκα Epicur. *Sent.Vat.*51; νόσοι κ. ὅλα δι' ὅλων Ph.2.432:—Pass., κατεξάνθην πόνοις E.*Med.*1030; δακρύοις Id.*Tr.*509; κατέξανται δέμας Id.*Hipp.* 274; ὅπλα κατεξάνθαι *were worn out by use*, D.S.17.94; ἐν τοῖς ὀρύγμασι καταξαινόμενοι τὰ σώματα Id.5.38.

**καταξενόομαι**, Pass., *to be received as a guest, hospitably treated*, κατεξενωμένος A.*Ch.*706.

✱**κατα-ξέσματα**, τά, *chips, filings*, Suid. s. v. μύγματα. **-ξεστικῶς**, Adv., gloss on ἀμύξ, Sch.Nic.*Th.*131. **-ξέω**, *polish smooth*, τοὺς ὀρθοστάτας -ξοῦντι *IG*1².374.221, cf. 12(2).10.22 (Mytil.); λίθον *Milet.*7.59:—Pass., κατεξέσθη τὸ ὑπέρθυρον Haussoullier *Milet* p.163, cf. Plu.2.953b: metaph., of style, τῇ λέξει -εξεσμένον Ps.-Plu.*Vit. Hom.*72. II. *carve*, in Pass., Arist.*Mir.*838ᵇ15.

**καταξηρ-αίνω**, *dry up*, Arist.*GA*772ᵃ12; θάλατταν Lxx *Jo.*2.10:— Pass., Pl.*Ti.*76a, Arist.*Mete.*340ᵇ1. **-ος**, ον, *very dry, parched*, γλῶσσαι Hp.*Prorrh.*1.3, cf. Arist.*de An.*422ᵇ5, Thphr.*CP*6.18.3, etc.; τὸ κ. τῆς βώλου Alciphr.3.35: metaph., ψυχὴ κ. Lxx *Nu.*11.6; τὸ κ. τῆς ἐπιθυμίας Alciphr.1.22; of persons, κ. γινομένους πρός τι ἀπαγορεύειν *stale*, Plu.2.8c. Adv. **-ρως**, πυρέσσειν Antyll.ap.Orib.9.23.6.

**κατ-αξιοπιστέομαι** (-εύομαι Suid.), *demand implicit belief to the prejudice of*, τινος Plb.12.17.1.

✱**κατάξι-ος**, ον (fem. -αξία *Inscr.Prien.*109.220 (ii B. C.), al.), strengthd. for ἄξιος, *quite worthy*, c. gen., S.*Ph.*1009: abs., E.*El.*46; κρίσις Lxx *Es.*16.18; χάριτας τὰς κ. ἀποδιδόναι *IG*12(1).155.11 (Rhodes), cf. *GDI* 3585.22 (Iasos); τὰς κ. τιμάς τισι ἀπονέμειν *OGI*763.24 (Milet., ii B. C.): neut. pl. as Adv., *AP*3.14 (Inscr. Cyzic.). Regul. Adv. -ίως S.*OC*911, *El.*800, *SIG*577.87 (Milet., 200 B. C.), Plb.1.88.5, etc. ✱**-όω**, *deem worthy*, c. acc. et inf., D.59.111; *hold in honour*, Plb.4.86.8: c. gen. rei, *deem worthy of* a thing, τάξεως τὸν κίνδυνον Id.1.23.3; τινὰ μεγάλης ἀποδοχῆς D.S.2.60:—Med., οὔτε νιν.. Δίκη προσεῖδε καὶ κατηξιώσατο did not regard and *hold in high esteem*, A.*Th.*667:—Pass., *to be held worthy*, πρεσβείας Plb.12.10.8, cf. Iamb.*VP*36.265; ἔργον ἐπιφανὲς καὶ κατηξιωμένον Plb.5.83.4. II. *command, bid*, πολλὰ χαίρειν ξυμφοραῖς καταξιῶ A.*Ag.*572; σύ τοι κατηξίωσας thou *didst decree it so*, S.*Ph.*1095 (lyr.). III. *deign, vouchsafe*, c. inf., Luc. *Ind.*3, Jul.*Ep.*204, *PLond.*2.232.14 (iv A. D.), *POxy.*1214 (v A. D.), etc. IV. in bad sense, τῶν ἐν μέρους εἴδει πεφυκότων μηδενὶ καταξιώσωμεν *let us* not *degrade it by likening it to..*, Pl.*Ti.*30c. V. in argument, *claim, maintain*, Phld.*Sign.*30, al.:—Med., c. inf., Id. *Rh.*1.32 S.

**κάτ-αξις**, εως, Ion. **-ηξις**, ιος, ἡ, *fracture*, including all forms of skull injury, Hp.*VC*9, al.; *breaking into large fragments*, distd. from θραῦσις, Arist.*Mete.*386ᵃ12, Thphr.*Lass.*18.

**κατ-αξίωσις**, εως, ἡ, *high esteem, reputation*, Plb.1.78.1.

**κατα-ξοή**, Dor. **-ξοά**, ἡ, *polishing, smoothing*, *IG*4.1484.56, al. (Epid.), *Rev.Phil.*50.70 (Didyma, ii B. C.). **-ξύή**, ἡ, = foreg., πλίνθου ib.67 (ibid., ii B. C.).

**κατάξυλ-ος**, ον, gloss on ἄξυλος, Sch.D*Il.*11.155. **-ωσις**, εως, ἡ, = δόκωσις, *IG*4.1485.130 (Epid.); κ. ἐπὶ στέγης, *tignatio*, *Gloss.*

**καταξυράω**, *shave close*, κατεξυρημένος τὸν πώγωνα Ctes.*Fr.*20 M.: abs., Nic.Dam.4 J.

**κατάξυροι θυρίδες**, (ξυρόν) *embrasures*, Ph.*Bel.*81.12.

**κατά-ξυσις**, εως, ἡ, *scraping*, Apollon.*Lex.* s. v. γραπτῦς (pl.). **-ξυσμα**, ατος, τό, *scraping, filing*, Sch.E.*Andr.*826, *Gloss.* **-ξυσμή**, ἡ, gloss on δρυφή, Hsch. **-ξυσμός**, ὁ, *scarification*, Sor.ap.Gal. 12.415. **-ξυστικῶς**, v. l. for -ξεστικῶς (q. v.). ✱**-ξύω**, *scrape down*, Hp.*VC*19, Sor.2.12, Gal.10.132. 2. *scratch, mark*, Luc. *Nigr.*27; γραφίδεσσι κ. *inscribe*, *Hymn.Is.*11. II. *polish, smooth, plane down*, Thphr.*HP*3.15.2, D.S.2.13:—Pass., σανὶς -εξυσμένη εἰς εὐθεῖαν τομήν Agatharch.27; γλῶσσα -εξυσμένη ὑπὸ τέκτονος Lxx *Ep.Je.*8. III. Pass., of land, *to be eroded*, *PTeb.*74.52 (ii B. C.), etc. IV. Pass., *to be worried*, πράγματι *POxy.*525.4 (ii A. D.); καταξύομαι μὴ ὁρῶν σε ib.1676.24 (iii A. D.).

**κατάορος** [ᾰ], ον, Dor. for κατήορος, E.*Tr.*1090 (lyr., s. v. l.); cf. καταορᾷ· καταντεῖ, Hsch.

**καταπάγιος** [πᾰ], ον, *solidly built*, of persons, Sor.1.34; *fixed*, cf. καταπάγιον (-πάτιον cod.)· ἀσαλές, ἢ ἀθροῦν, Hsch.: **-πάγιον**, τό, *fixed payment*, *IG*12(5).572 (Ceos). Adv. -ίως *constantly*, πόλιν κ. οἰκεῖν Isoc.15.156.

**καταπαγκρᾰτιάζω**, *conquer in the* παγκράτιον, Ph.1.681; τινα Id. 2.348.

**καταπαιγμός**, ὁ, *mockery*, Apollon.*Lex.* s.v. μωμήσονται.

**καταπαιδεραστέω**, *waste in* παιδεραστία, οἶκον Is.10.25.

**καταπαιδεύω**, *chastise*, Sm.*La.*1.13.

**καταπαίζω**, fut. -παίξομαι (v. infr.), *jest, mock at*, c. gen., καταπαίζεις ἡμῶν Ar.*Fr.*166, cf. Lxx 4*Ki.*2.23, *AP*5.39 (Nicarch.); τῶν δογματικῶν S.E.*P.*1.62: c. acc., D.L.2.136. 2. *deceive*, ἕκαστος κατὰ τοῦ φίλου -παίξεται Lxx *Je.*9.5(4). II. Med. in sense of Act., ἐπί τινι πράξει τινῶν κ. Hdn.*Fig.*p.92 S.

**κατάπαις**, *puerarius*, *Gloss.*

**καταπαίω**, *strike hard*, Hsch.

**καταπακτός**, ή, όν, (καταπήγνυμι) only in the phrase καταπακτὴ θύρα, a door *shutting downwards*, *trap*-door, Hdt.5.16. [Cf. πακτός, πακτόω (ἐμ-, ἐπι-), with ᾰ by nature.]

**καταπᾰλαιόομαι**, Pass., *grow very old*, Gal.18(2).475.

✱**καταπᾰλαίω**, *throw in wrestling*, Εὐάθλους δέκα Ar.*Ach.*710: metaph., *overthrow*, λόγοι -παλαίουσιν λόγους E.*IA*1013; τὰ ῥηθέντα Pl. *R.*362d; κ. πάθος λόγῳ S.E.*M.*8.475:—Pass., καταπαλαισθεὶς ὑπὸ τοῦ Θανάτου Luc.*Cont.*8.

**καταπαλλᾰκεύω**, *make a concubine of*, Nic.Dam.51 J.

✱**καταπάλλομαι**, Pass., *dart down*, ἅρπη ἐϊκυῖα . . οὐρανοῦ ἐκ κατέπαλτο (Ep. aor. 2) Il.19.351 (but this form shd. perh. be referred to κατεφάλλομαι, q. v.); Νὺξ φυγὰς οὐρανόθεν καταπάλλεται *PMag.Berol.* 2.95: aor. 1, ἑοῦ κατεπήλατο δίφρου *leapt down from*, Nonn.*D.*18. 13.

**καταπάλμενος**· καταπηδήσας, Hsch.; of a waterfall, *AP*9.326 cod. (Leon.): nisi leg. κατεπ-, v. κατεφάλλομαι.

**καταπαλτ-αφεσία**, ἡ, *discharging of catapults, artillery practice*, *IG* 2².1006.65, 12(5).647.25 (Ceos). **-αφέτης**, ου, ὁ, *artilleryman*, ib.30, 2².665.27, al., (-πελτ-) Ph.*Bel.*82.13. **-ης**, ου, ὁ, (πάλλω) *engine of war for hurling bolts, catapult*, *IG*2².120.37, 554.15, 12(5). 647.36 (Ceos):—freq. written **-πέλτης** in literary texts, Mnesim.7. 10, Timocl.12.5, Onos.42.3, etc.; καταπάλτην ἀφιέναι Arist.*Ath.*42. 3, *EN*1111ᵃ11, cf. *Aud.*800ᵇ13, Ath.Mech.8.7, Ael.*VH*6.12; used as an instrument of torture, D.S.20.71, Charito 3.4, Lxx 4*Ma.*8.13. 2. *bolt, shot*, (-πέλτης) Hp.*Epid.*5.95, 7.121, (-πάλτης) Hsch.:—hence **-ικός**, ή, όν (in literary texts -πελτ-), *of* or *belonging to catapults*, βέλη *IG*2².1487.102; ὄργανα καὶ βέλη Plb.11.11.3, cf. Str.17.3.15, Bito 62.4; τὰ κ., = καταπάλται, Plb.9.41.5; τὸ κ. *artillery*, D.S.14. 42.

**καταπαλτός**, ή, όν, *hurled down*, ἐξ αἰθέρος ὕδωρ A.ap.Aristid.*Or.* 36(48).53.

**καταπαννῠχίζω**, *pass the night in revelry*, Alciphr.1.39.

**καταπᾰνουργ-εύομαι**, *devise villainously*, ἐπὶ τὸν λαὸν κ. γνώμην Lxx *Ps.*82(83).3. **-εύω**, *act villainously*, Suid.

✱**κατ-άπαξ**, = καθάπαξ, *Ath.Mitt.*49.3 (Attica, iv B. C.).

**καταπάομαι**, *gain possession of*, in aor. 1 -επάσατο, Hsch.

**καταπαραλλήλως**, Adv. *along a parallel of latitude*, κινεῖσθαι *Vit. Pyth.*ap.Phot.*Bibl.*p.440 B.

**κατα-παρμός**, ὁ, (καταπείρω) *piercing, boring*, Sor.2.62. **-παρσις**, εως, ἡ, = foreg., ib.61, Aët.16.23, Paul.Aeg.6.64. **-παρτέον**, *one must pierce*, ib.74.

**κατά-πασμα**, ατος, τό, *powder*, Antyll.ap.Orib.10.31.1, Paul.Aeg. 7.13. **-πασμός**, ὁ, prob. f. l. for κατασπασμός, Cael.Aur.*TP*1. 166.

**καταπασσᾰλεύω**, Att. -πεττ-, *nail down*: hence, *bewitch*, *SIG* 1261.17 (Attica, iv/iii B. C.).

✱**κατα-πάσσω**, Att. -ττω, fut. -άσω [ᾰ] (v. infr.): aor. 1 -έπᾰσα Men. 708:—*besprinkle, bespatter with*, πάντα καταπάσω βουλευματίων Ar. *Eq.*99: usu. c. dat. rei, ἀψινθίῳ κ. μέλι Men. l. c.; γῇ τὰς κεφαλὰς κ. Lxx 2*Ma.*10.25: also abs., *pour out*, κ. χύδην Pherecr.168:—Pass., καταπαττόμενος Ar.*Nu.*262:—Med., κ. τὰς κεφαλὰς πηλῷ *their own* heads, v. l. in D.S.1.72, 91. II. c. acc. rei, *sprinkle, strew over*, ἄνθος χαλκοῦ Hp.*Fist.*3; ἄλευρα Arist.*HA*627ᵇ20; κατὰ τῆς τραπέζης κ. τέφραν Ar.*Nu.*177:—Med., καταπασάμενος τῆς κεφαλῆς κόνιν *on his own* head, J.*BJ*2.21.3 (v. l. καταμησάμενος); γῆν ἐπὶ τῆς κεφαλῆς v. l. in Lxx *Jb.*1.20; τῶν στρωμάτων ῥόδα πολλὰ κατεπέπαστο Luc.*Asin.*7. **-παστέον**, *one must sprinkle*, Orib.*Fr.* 38. **-παστος**, ον, *besprinkled, bespattered with*, στεφάνοις Ar.*Eq.* 502; ἡδυσματίοις Telecl.1.11; σαργὸν τυρῷ κ. Archestr.*Fr.*36.3. 2. *suitable for use as a powder*, Asclep.ap.Gal.13.159, etc. 3. *embroidered*, ἁλουργίς Ar.*Eq.*968; χιτὼν χρυσῷ κ. D.C.72.17; χρυσαῖς ἀκτῖσι Hld.3.4, cf. 10.9, Aristid.*Or.*17(15).10.

**καταπᾰτάκτην**, v. l. καταπατηκτην, prob. ff. ll. for καταπακτήν or καταπηκτήν (sc. θύραν) *trap-door*, i. e. *dungeon*, Aq.*Je.*29(36).26.

**καταπᾰτ-έω**, *trample under foot*, Th.7.84, etc.; ὑσὶ τὸ σπέρμα κ. *trample down* the seed (i. e. *have it trampled down*) by swine, Hdt. 2.14:—Pass., Id.7.173, 223, Th.5.72, D.34.37; τὸν ἐγκέφαλον ἐν ταῖς πτέρναις -πεπατημένον φορεῖν Id.7.45. 2. metaph., κατὰ δ' ὅρκια πιστὰ πάτησαν Il.4.157; κ. τοὺς νόμους Pl.*Lg.*714a; τὰ γράμματα Id.*Grg.*484a; τὸν υἱὸν τοῦ θεοῦ *Ep.Hebr.*10.29; ὅρκον Lib.*Ep.*14. 1. **-ημα**, ατος, τό, *that which is trampled under foot*, Lxx *La.*2.8, al. ✱**-ησις**, εως, ἡ, *trampling on*, ib.4*Ki.*13.7. 2. *perambulation, inspection*, χωρίων καὶ παραδείσων *CPHerm.*7 ii 6 (ii A. D.). **-ητέος**, α, ον, *to be trampled down*, *Gp.*6.13.1. **-ητής**, οῦ, ὁ, gloss on κατάσκοπος, Sch.E.*Hec.*239.

**καταπάτιον**, v. καταπάγιον.

**κατά-παυμα**, ατος, τό, *means of stopping*, δειλοῖσι γόου κ. γενοίμην Il.17.38. II. *rest*, Lxx *Si.*36.15(18). **-παυσις**, εως, ἡ, *stopping*: metaph., *putting down, deposing*, τυράννων Hdt.5.38; τῆς βασιλητ̂ης *deposition* from . ., Id.6.67; Κολλατίνου D.C.46.49. II. *rest, calm*, Lxx *Is.*66.1, al.; *place of rest*, ib.*Ps.*94(95).11, al.; αἱ κ. τῶν πνευμάτων Thphr.*Vent.*18: metaph., *allaying*, στάσεως Phld. *Mus.*p.86 K. **-παυστέον**, *one must stop, staunch*, τὴν φορὰν [τοῦ αἵματος] Antyll.(?)ap.Orib.50.3.7. **-παυστήριον**, τό, *means of putting to rest*, gloss on κηλητήριον, Sch.S.*Tr.*575. **-παυστικός**, ή, όν, *causing to cease*, ταραχῶν Phld.*Mus.*p.20 K.; κακοῦ Eust.138. 2. **-παύω**, poet. καππαύω Pi.*N.*9.15, B.*Scol.Oxy.Fr.*1.2:—*put an end to, stop*, κατέπαυσα θεῶν χόλον Od.4.583; μηνιθμὸν καταπαυσέμεν (Ep. fut. inf.) Il.16.62; πόλεμον καταπαυσέμεν ἀνδρῶν 7.36; νεῖκος κ. Hes.*Th.*87; τὴν ναυπηγίην Hdt.1.27; νόσους A.*Supp.*586 (lyr.); λιγυρὰν γᾶρυν B. l. c.; αἱμορραγίαν Gal.16.777; *bring to a close*, τὸν λόγον Plb.2.8.8; τὸ σύγγραμμα Phld.*Po.*5.26; κ. τὸν πρῶτον λόγον εἰς . . *conclude* the first section *and proceed* to . ., Olymp.*in Mete.*78.9:—Med., πόνους -παυόμενοι E.*Hel.*1154 (lyr.):—Pass., -παύεται τὰ ἀρρωστήματα τοῖς τῶν ἰατρῶν εὑρήμασι D.26.26. II. c. acc. pers., *put an end to*, i. e. *kill*, τάχα κέν σε . . ἔγχος ἐμὸν κατέπαυσε Il.16.618; σοῦ κ. τὰς πνοάς Ar.*Av.*1397. 2. *make one stop from* a thing, *hinder, check*, μιν καταπαύσειν ἀγηνορίης ἀλεγεινῆς Il.22.457; παῖδας καταπαυέμεν ἀφροσυνάων Od.24.457; so κ. τινὰ δρόμου Pl.*Plt.*294e: c. part., κ. ταύτην λαλοῦσαν Men.66.5: c. acc. only, *keep in check*, τινα Od.2.244 (cf. 168), Il.15.105. 3. *depose from* power, κ. τινὰ τῆς ἀρχῆς, τῆς βασιλητ̂ης, Hdt.4.1, 6.64; τοὺς τυράννους Id.5.38, cf. 2.144, 7.105; Μούσας *depose* them *from their honours, cease to worship* them, E. *HF*685 (lyr.):—Pass., τῆς βασιλητ̂ης κατεπαύσθη Hdt.1.130, cf. 6. 71. b. *put down*, τὴν ἑωυτοῦ ἀρχήν Id.1.86; τὴν Κύρου δύναμιν ib. 90; δῆμον Th.1.107; τοὺς τετρακοσίους Id.8.97; τιμὰς ἐνέρων E.*Alc.* 31 (anap.). III. Pass. and Med. (fut. -πᾱήσομαι *PMag.Lond.* 121.916), *leave off, cease*, Ar.*Eq.*1265; λόγος κ. ἐν . . Pl.*Phlb.*66c: c. part., οὐ -παήσεται ἐρχομένη *PMag.* l. c. IV. Act. used intr. like Med., μολπᾶν δ' ἄπο . . καταπαύσας πόσις . . ἔκειτο E.*Hec.*918 (lyr., s. v. l.); εὐημερῶν κατάπαυσον *rest* while you are well off, *Com.Adesp.* 110.8, cf. Lxx *Ge.*8.22, al.; κ. τοῦ πορευθῆναι ib.3*Ki.*12.24.

**καταπεδάω**, *fetter, hamper*, κατὰ δ' οὖν ἕτερόν γε πέδησε Il.19.94; θεοῦ κατὰ μοῖρ' ἐπέδησεν Od.11.292 (μοῖρα πέδησεν Aristarch.), cf. Mosch.2.4 (tm.).

**καταπεζεύω**, *dismount*, ἐξ ἵππων Eust.866.14.

**καταπεζομᾰχέω**, *conquer by land*, Poll.9.141.

**καταπειθ-ής**, ές, *obedient*, τινι Ph.2.118, J.*AJ*2.4.2, al., Plu.2. 5c. **-ησις**, εως, ἡ, *persuasion*, Sch.E.*Hec.*816. **-ω**, *persuade*, Lxx 2*Ki.*17.16, Luc.*Charid.*16:—Pass., Sch.Ar.*Pl.*507.

**κατ-ᾰπειλέω**, strengthd. for ἀπειλέω, κ. ἔπη *use threatening* words, S.*OC*659; ἀκραιφνεῖς τῶν κατηπειλημένων *by the threats uttered*, ib. 1147.

**κατάπειρ-α**, ἡ, *attack*, of disease, πάθους, νόσου, Philum.*Ven.*1.4, Orib.*Fr.*76, Paul.Aeg.3.78, 5.3. **-άζω**, fut. -πειράσω Lys.30.34:—*make an attempt on*, τὴν τινος ψῆφον Lys. l. c.; τοὺς τόπους Lxx 2*Ma.* 13.18; τοὺς στρατηγούς *Inscr.Prien.*111.135 (i B. C.). 2. c. gen., *make trial of*, τῶν πολεμίων, τῆς πόλεως, Plb.4.11.6, 4.13.5, cf. *PAmh.*2. 134.3 (ii A. D.):—also in Med., Herod.Med.ap.Orib.10.40.5. **-άομαι**, Pass., *to be much tried*, -αθεὶς ὑπ' ἀρρωστίας D.S.17.107. II. Med., v. l. for κατασπείρασαι in Ph.2.567. **-ασμός**, ὁ, *attack*, of disease, τοῦ συμπτώματος Dsc.*Ther.*3, cf. Philum.*Ven.*4.11: in pl., *skirmishes*, Anon.ap.Suid. s. v. χειραψίαι. **-ᾱτηρία**, Ion. -πειρητηρίη, ἡ, *sounding-line*, Hdt.2.5, 28; *catapirātes* in Lucil.*Fr.*1191 Marx; *anchor-cable*, prob. in *CIL*8.27790 (Althiburos).

**καταπείρω**, *insert*, ἐμβρυουλκὸν εἰς τόπον Sor.2.62; τοῖς κατὰ τοὺς βουβῶνας τὰ σκέλη Hld.10.32:—Pass., -πεπαρμένον ἐν ποδὶ σκόλοπα Gal.*Nat.Fac.*1.14; -παρεῖσαι (aor. 2 part.) τῇ φάρυγγι ἄκανθαι Paul. Aeg.6.32; of persons, -παρέντες εἰς τὴν Ἱμεραίων θηρόβοτον ἄχρι τῶν στηθῶν Phalar.*Ep.*147.4. (καταπείραντες (-ροντες cod.)· καταδύσαντες (-δήσ- cod.), dub. in Hsch.)

**κατάπεισις**, εως, ἡ, *persuasion*, Hdn.*Epim.*110, Sch.E.*Or.*705.

**καταπελεκάω**, *hew with an axe*, in Pass., Sch.Il.16.642.

**καταπελεμίζω**, strengthd. for πελεμίζω, A.R.2.91 (tm.).

**καταπελμᾰτόομαι**, Pass., *to be cobbled, clouted*, of shoes, Lxx *Jo.* 9.5.

**καταπελτάζω** (cf. πελταστής), *overrun with light-armed troops*, καταπελτάσονται τὴν Βοιωτίαν ὅλην Ar.*Ach.*160.

**κατα-πελταφεσία, -πελταφέτης, -πέλτης, -πελτικός**, v. καταπαλτ-.

**κατάπεμνοι**· καθαπτόμενοι, Hsch. **καταπεμπάμενα**· καθημένηα, Id. (fort. καταπεπταμένα· καθημμένα).

**καταπεμπ-τέος**, α, ον, *to be sent down*, Luc.*DDeor.*5.4. **-τος**, ον, *sent down*, ἀνὴρ κ. ἐκ θεῶν Attic.ap.Eus.*PE*11.2. **-ω**, *send down*, εἰς ἔρεβος Hes.*Th.*515; esp. from the inland to the sea-coast, X.*HG*5.1.30, *An.*1.9.7 (Pass.); in Egypt, *down* the Nile, *PEleph.* 10.7 (iii B. C.), etc. II. *send from head-quarters, dispatch*, ληστάς D.12.13; στρατηγὸν κ. τινά as general, Plu.*Flam.*15; ἐς ἐπισκοπήν τινος Luc.*DDeor.*20.6; γράμματα Hdn.2.12.3.

**καταπενθέω**, *bewail*, *AP*7.618, Lxx *Ex.*33.4.

**καταπεπαίνω**, *ripen*, καρποὶ -πεπανθέντες Ph.2.429; cj. in Thphr. *HP*3.13.6.

**καταπεπλᾰνημένως**, *erroneously*, f.l. for sq., in Poll.4.51. **καταπεπλασμένως**, *affectedly*, ibid.

**καταπεπτηυῖα**, Ep. fem. pf. part. of καταπτήσσω.

**καταπέπτω**, late form of καταπέσσω, πάθος Iamb.*VP*31.196.

**καταπεπῠκασμένως**, (πυκάζω) *covertly, slily*, f.l. in Poll.4.51.

**κατάπερ**, Ion. for καθάπερ (q.v.).

**καταπεραι-όω**, *conclude, close*, εἰς πόδα ἀμφίμακρον Eust.13.14, cf. 81.3. **-ωσις**, εως, ἡ, *conclusion, close*, τῆς λέξεως εἰς τέλειον ib.5.

**καταπέρδομαι**, only in aor. 2 Act. κατέπαρδον:—*break wind at*, τινος, in sign of contempt, Epicr.11.28 (anap.), Ar.*Pax*547; τοῦ σοῦ δίνου Id.*V*.618; τῆς Πενίας Id.*Pl*.618 (anap.).

**καταπερί-ειμι**, *surpass, have the advantage of*, τινος Plb.5.67. 2. **-ῑστημι**, intr. in aor. 2, *surround*, *Sammelb*.4638.18 (ii B.C.). **-ξῠσις**, εως, ἡ, v.l. for κατάξυσις, *scarification*, Sch.Od. 24.229 (pl.).

**καταπερονάω**, *rivet*, λαβίσι Plb.6.23.11.

**καταπερπερεύομαι**, = περπερεύομαι, *Com.Adesp*.1031.

**καταπέσημα**, ατος, τό, *downfall*, *Com.Adesp*.621 (dub. l.).

**καταπέσσω**, Att. -ττω Thphr.*CP*2.11.10, later -πτω (q.v.), *digest* food, Diocl.*Fr*.141:—esp. in Pass., Arist.*GA*756ᵇ11; ἕως ἂν καταπεφθῇ [ἡ τροφή] Id.*Somn*.457ᵇ19, cf. *Hippiatr*.46. 2. metaph., *digest, keep from rising*, χόλον Il.1.81; -πέψαι μέγαν ὄλβον, i.e. *bear* great fortune *meekly*, Pi.*O*.1.55.

**καταπετάννῡμι**, *spread out over*, κατὰ λῖτα πετάσσας Il.8.441, cf. E.*Hel*.1459 (lyr., tm.); δέρρεις πρό τινος κ. Ph.*Bel*.91.13, cf. D.S. 20.9. II. *spread* or *cover with*, τὴν αὐλὴν δικτύοις Ar.*V*.132; τὴν κεφαλὴν φοινικίδι Id.*Pl*.731; ἱστίῳ ἀνθρώπους Pl.*Prm*.131b; ἵπποι ἱματίοις καταπεπταμένοι X.*Cyr*.8.3.16.

**καταπέτασμα**, ατος, τό, *curtain, veil*, Hld.10.28, *PGrenf*.2.111.7 (v/vi A.D.); esp. *the veil of the Temple*, Lxx*Ex*.26.31, Aristeas 86, *Ev.Matt*.27.51, etc.; prop. *the inner veil*, the outer being τὸ κάλυμμα, cf. Ph.2.148: metaph., κ. δόξης Id.1.270. 2. κ. τραπέζης *table-cover*, *Michel*832.25 (Samos, iv B.C.).

**καταπέτομαι**, *fly down*: fut. καταπτήσομαι Luc.*Prom*.2: aor. κατέπτᾰτο Ar.*Av*.789, al. codd.; part. καταπτάμενος Hdt.3.111 (v.l. -πετομένας, -πετευμένας), Ar.*V*.16, *Av*.1624 codd.; subj. and opt. κατάπτωμαι, -πτοῖο, Luc.*Icar*.13, *Bis Acc*.8: aor. 2 Act. κατέπτην, part. καταπτάς Arist.*HA*614ᵇ21, Ph.2.318, Luc.*Charid*.7, Porph. *Abst*.1.25: pf. κατέπτηκα Men.*Kol*.39: aor. 1 Pass. κατεπετάσθην Lxx*Pr*.27.8, D.S.2.20.

**καταπετροκοπέω**, *dash against rocks*, D.S.16.60.

**καταπετρόω**, *stone to death*, X.*An*.1.3.2 (Pass.). II. *throw down from a rock*, Str.3.3.7.

**καταπεφνών**, v. κατέπεφνον.

**καταπεφρονηκότως**, Adv. pf. part. Act. of καταφρονέω, *contemptuously*, D.17.29, D.S.14.17, etc. II. Adv. pf. part. Pass. **-πεφρονημένως**, *despisedly*, v.l. for -μένος in Sch.Luc.*Ind*.10.

**καταπηγάζω**, (πηγή) *form a spring*, *Stoic*.2.197.

**καταπήγνῡμι** and -ύω (Arist.*Pol*.1324ᵇ20), *stick fast* in something, *plant firmly*, ἔγχος μὲν κατέπηξεν ἐπὶ χθονί Il.6.213; ἐν δὲ σκόλοπας κ. 7.441, cf. Hdt.4.72, Ar.*Av*.360, *PPetr*.3 p.121 (iii B.C.), etc.; εἰς τὴν γῆν κ. τὸν καυλόν Arist.*HA*555ᵇ20; τὸ κέντρον ἐπὶ δένδρον Philum.*Ven*.37.1:—Pass., -πᾰγέντος σκόλοπος S.E.*P*.1.238, cf. Thphr.*HP*3.1.1. 2. metaph., *fix, crystallize*, τὴν χύσιν τῆς ἀπειρίας τῷ περατοειδεῖ δεσμῷ Dam.*Pr*.57. II. Pass., with pf. and plpf. Act., *stand fast* or *firm in*, ἰὸς ἐν γαίῃ κατέπηκτο Il.11.378; ἱστὸς -πεπηγώς Hp.*Art*.43; στήλη -πεπηγυῖα Hdt.7.30. 2. *become congealed, freeze*, Plb.3.55.5; of fish, ὑπὸ τοῦ ψύχους κ. Arist. *HA*601ᵇ31.

**καταπηδάω**, *leap down*, ἀπὸ τοῦ ἵππου X.*Cyr*.7.1.38, cf. Lxx*Ge*.24.64, *BGU*1201.12 (i A.D.), Plu.*Caes*.49; ἐκ τοῦ ἵππου Charito 5.3; ἀφ' ὑψηλῶν Aen.Tact.22.19.

**καταπημαίνω**, *hurt, damage*, in aor. 1 opt. καταπημήνειε, Hsch., Phot.

**κατάπηξ**, πηγος, ὁ, ἡ, *fixed in the ground*, *EM*194.24. II. as Subst. **καταπήξ**, ῆγος, ὁ, *pivot* of door-post, J.*BJ*6.5.3; *post*, *PPetr*. 3 p.121 (iii B.C.), Apollod.*Poliorc*.189.9, Sm.*Jb*.38.6. 2. *graft*, *Gp*.10.65.2.

**κατάπηρος**, ον, *maimed, mutilated*, Hp.ap.Erot. s.v.

**καταπήττω**, = καταπήγνυμι, Str.4.3.5, D.H.3.22, Apollod.*Poliorc*. 166.16 (Pass., -πησσ-).

**καταπῐαίνω**, *fatten*, in Pass., -πεπιασμένον ζῷον Pl.*Lg*.807a, cf. Ael.*VH*9.13, *PFlor*.130.1 (iii A.D.).

**κατα-πιέζω**, *compress*, Thphr.*Ign*.23. **-πίεσις** [ῐ], εως, ἡ, *compression*, τοῦ ψύχους Id.*CP*2.1.4.

**καταπῐθᾰνεύομαι**, *use probable arguments*, S.E.*M*.8.324.

**κατάπικρος**, ον, *very bitter*, τῇ ψυχῇ Lxx 2*Ki*.17.8, cf. Sm.*Jb*.6.3; χολή *PLeid.X*.62.

**καταπῑλέω**, lit. *wrap up in felt*:—Pass., *wrap oneself close*, πόκοις Alciphr.2.2.

**καταπῑμελ-ής**, ές, = sq., Xenocr.ap.Orib.2.58.148 (Sup.). **-ος**, ον, *very fat* or *rich*, of persons or lands, Dsc.1.24, Antyll.ap.Orib.7. 16.4, Gal.19.451; στέαρ Dsc.2.76.

**καταπίμπλημι**, *fill quite full*, dub. l. in Lync.1.16. II. c. acc. et gen., *fill full of*, κ. [τινὰ] φρονήματος Plu.2.715a; βίον πολέμων Ph. 1.411, cf. 2.558:—Pass., καταπιμπλάμενοι ἀνομίας Pl.*R*.496d: also c. dat., ἡδύσμασιν.. καταπεπλησμέν' Antiph.183.4:—Med., πηλοῦ κατεπίμπλαντο τὰς σκηνὰς *their own* tents, Plu.*Brut*.47.

**καταπίμπρημι**, fut. -πρήσω D.C.39.9: pf. -πέπρηκα Id.59.16:—*burn to ashes*, *AP*11.131 (Lucill.), Ph.1.516, Plu.*Cam*.22, Polyaen.8. 65, Hdn.8.1.4, Jul.*Or*.2.62d:—Pass., κατεπρήσθησαν Plb.14.4.10; καταπρησθέντας Luc.*Par*.57 (nisi leg. -πτισθέντας).

**καταπίνω** [ῑ], fut. -πίομαι Ar.*Eq*.693, later -πιοῦμαι Plu.*Alc*.15: aor. κατέπιον *IG*4.951.102 (Epid.); poet. κάππιον Hes.*Th*.p.45 R.: pf. -πέπωκα Ar.*Av*.1137:—*gulp, swallow down*, both of liquids and solids (οὐδ' ἐν τῷ καταπίνειν ἦν πάντως τὸ πίνειν Ph.1.478), τοὺς μὲν κατέπινε Κρόνος (sc. υἱούς) Hes.*Th*.459, cf. 467, E.*Cyc*.219; ὁ τροχίλος.. καταπίνει τὰς βδέλλας Hdt.2.68, cf. 70; τεμάχη Ar.*Nu*.338; λίθους Id.*Av*. l.c.; [κίχλας] Pherecr.108.24; [μάζας] Telecl.1.5; of the sea, μὴ ναῦν κατὰ κῦμα πίῃ Thgn.680, cf. Arist.*Pr*.931ᵇ39 (Pass.); τὸ στόμα [τῆς γῆς] -πίεται αὐτούς Lxx*Nu*.16.30:—Pass., τὸ -ποθὲν ὕδωρ (sc. by the earth) Pl.*Criti*.111d; of rivers *that disappear underground*, Arist.*Mete*.351ᵃ1; ὑφ' ἄμμου D.S.1.32; of cities *swallowed* by an earthquake, Str.1.3.17; πόλις καταποθεῖσα ὑπὸ τῆς θαλάττης Plb.2.41.7. 2. abs., *swallow*, μόλις καταπίνειν δύνηται Hp.*Aph*. 4.35, cf. Gal.*Nat.Fac*.3.6. II. metaph., τὸν ἡμίοπον ὁ μέγας [αὐλὸς] κ. A.*Fr*.91; καταπιοῦνται ὑμᾶς οἱ Ἀθηναῖοι Plu.*Alc*.15:—Pass., *to be absorbed*, of knots in wood, Thphr.*HP*5.2.2; τῆς -πεπομένης ὑπ' αὐτοῦ φύσεως Dam.*Pr*.10. b. κ. Εὐριπίδην *drink in* Euripides, i.e. *imbibe* his spirit, Ar.*Ach*.484, Luc.*JTr*.1:—Pass., τὸ τεχνίον ἀεὶ τοῦτό μοι κατεπίνετο Antid.2.4. c. *swallow, absorb*, τὰς τέχνας Chrysipp.*Stoic*.2.257 (Pass.); but, *swallow* one's anger, ib.242. 2. *swallow up, consume*, [the robe] ἐρίων τάλαντον καταπέπωκε ῥᾳδίως Ar.*V*.1147; ὁ δικαστὴς αὐτὰ [the revenue] καταπίνει μόνος Id.*Ra*.1466; τὸν ναύκληρον αὐτῷ σκάφει κ. Anaxil.22.19; τι Men. *Epit*.151. 3. *spend, waste in tippling*, [τὴν οὐσίαν] οὐ μόνον κατέφαγεν, ἀλλὰ.. καὶ κατέπιεν Aeschin.1.96, cf. D.C.45.28.

**καταπιπράσκω**, *sell outright*, καταπρᾱθείς Luc.*Sat*.16.

**καταπίπτω**, fut. -πεσοῦμαι: aor. κατέπεσον, poet. κάππεσον (the only tense used by Hom.), Dor. κάπετον (q.v.), also κατέπετον *IG* 4.951.80 (Epid.); late 3 sg. opt. -πέσειεν Apollod.*Poliorc*.168.5 (v.l. -οιεν): pf. -πέπτωκα:—*fall, drop*, καππεσέτην Il.5.560; κάππεσον ἐν Λήμνῳ 1.593; κάππεσον ἐν κονίῃσι 12.23; πρηνὴς ἐπὶ γαίῃ κάππεσε 16.311,414; πρηνὴς ἁλὶ κάππεσε Od.5.374; ἀφ' ὑψηλοῦ πύργου Il. 12.386; ἀπὸ τῶν ἡμιπλινθίων Hdt.1.50; ἀπὸ τῆς κλίμακος Ar.*Av*. 840; ἀπ' ὄνου Id.*Nu*.1273; ἀφ' ἵππου X.*Oec*.1.8; ἐς μέσους τοὺς ἄνθρακας E.*Cyc*.671; ἐπὶ τῆς γῆς X.*Cyr*.4.5.54; πληγεὶς κ. Lys.1.27; οἰκίαι καταπεπτωκυῖαι And.1.108, *BGU*282.7 (ii A.D.), etc.: used as Pass. of καταβάλλω, πρὸς ἡμῶν κάππεσε, = κατεβλήθη, A.*Ag*.1553 (lyr.). 2. metaph., παραὶ ποσὶ κάππεσε θυμός their spirit *fell*, Il. 15.280; μήτε καταπεσὼν ὀδύρεο Archil.66.5; πρὸς τὴν φήμην τῆς ἐφόδου -πεσόντες J.*BJ*7.4.2, cf. Paus.10.20.1; κ. τὴν ψυχήν v.l. in J. *AJ*6.14.2: freq. in pf. part. καταπεπτωκώς, *base, contemptible*, λόγος Aristeas 144; γένος ἄτιμον καὶ κ. Plu.*Phoc*.4; ἀγεννεῖς καὶ καταπεπτωκότες Lib.*Decl*.30.45; ταῖς ψυχαῖς καὶ τοῖς σώμασι Them.*Or*.10. 136b. b. κ. εἰς ἀπιστίαν Pl.*Phd*.88d; εἰς ἀπορίαν Id.*Men*.84c; πρὸς τὸ χεῖρον J.*AJ*2.16.1. 3. τὰ -πίπτοντα *the accidents* of fortune, Vett.Val.40.15. 4. τὰς νυνὶ -πεπτωκυίας [ἐμβολάς] which *have just been rejected*, Hegetor ap.Apollon.Cit.3. 5. ἄλλα, ἃ -πέπτωκε τούτοις which *fall under the same head*, Gal.5.723. II. *have the falling sickness*, Luc.*Tox*.24, *Philops*.16.

**καταπισσόω**, Att. -ττόω, *cover with pitch*, as was done to wine-jars, etc., Cratin.189 (Pass.), Ar.*Ec*.1109, Gal.17(2).164: metaph., *paint black*, opp. καταχρυσόω (in v. 826), κατεπίττου πᾶς ἀνὴρ Εὐριπίδην Ar.*Ec*.829. II. *tar and burn* (as a punishment), Heraclid. Pont.ap.Ath.12.524a:—Pass., Pl.*Grg*.473c.

**καταπιστ-ευτέον**, *one must trust*, Sor.1.33. **-εύω**, *trust*, ταῖς ἰδίαις δυνάμεσι Plb.2.3.3; τινι Hld.4.13: c. pres. or fut. inf., Id.6.7, 1.23; ἐν φίλοις Lxx*Mi*.7.5: abs., *feel confidence*, Plu.*Lys*.8, Gal.12. 692. II. *entrust*, τινὶ τὴν ἄμυναν, τὴν διοίκησιν, Zos.1.36, 3.2; ἑνὸς ἀνδρὸς ἐξουσίᾳ τοσαύτης ἀρχῆς κίνδυνον Id.1.5; τινι c. inf., *Sammelb*. 5273.4 (v A.D.):—Pass., *to be entrusted*, *POxy*.136.8 (vi A.D.): also in pf. part., *devoted*, ἀνὴρ ταῖς Μούσαις -πεπιστευμένος Phalar.*Ep*.93. 1. **-όομαι**, Med., *become security*, ὑπέρ τινος πρός τινα for one to another, Plu.*Cleom*.21. **-ωσις**, εως, ἡ, *assurance, pledge of faith*, καταπιστώσεις ποιεῖσθαι, of lovers, Arist.*Fr*.97, cf. Plu.2. 258b.

**καταπιττόω**, Att. for καταπισσόω.

**καταπλᾱγής**, ές, *panic-struck, scared*, κ. γενέσθαι τὴν ἔφοδον Plb. 1.7.6; κ. μή.. Id.2.69.6.

**καταπλᾰκών**, aor. 2 part. (v. ἀμπλακεῖν); the gloss of Hsch. (καταπλακών· καταπλήξας, διαμαρτών) shd. be corrected thus: καταπλακών· διαμαρτών·—καταπτακών· καταπτήξας.

**καταπλᾰνάω**, strengthd. for πλανάω, *deceive, mislead*, *App.Prov*. 1.50 (cod. C).

**κατά-πλᾰσις**, εως, ἡ, *plastering* or *poulticing*, Hp.*VC*13, cj. in Sor.1.73. **-πλασμα**, ατος, τό, *plaster, poultice*, Hp.*Art*.40 (pl.), Ar.*Fr*.320.12, Arist.*Pr*.863ᵃ6, Thphr.*HP*9.11.4, *Od*.59, *PLit.Lond*. 170 (pl., i A.D.), etc. **-πλασμάτιον**, τό, Dim. of foreg., Sor.1. 50. **-πλασμός**, ὁ, = κατάπλασμα, Anon.Lond.36.58. **-πλάσσω**, Att. -ττω, fut. -πλάσω [ᾰ], *plaster over*, πηλῷ κατ' ὧν ἔπλασε τοὺς ὀφθαλμούς Hdt.2.70, cf. Arist.*HA*612ᵃ18; ὄξει τὰ βλέφαρα Ar.*Pl*. 721; τὰ ὦτα κηρῷ Plu.2.15d:—Pass., καταπεπλασμένη ψιμυθίῳ Ar. *Ec*.878; κηρῷ Arist.*HA*624ᵃ13:—Med., τὴν κεφαλὴν κατ' ὧν ἐπλάσατο *plastered her own* head, Hdt.2.85, cf. D.S.1.72,91; τοῦτο κατα-

πλάσσονται πᾶν τὸ σῶμα this they *plaster over their* whole body, Hdt.4.75:—Pass., καταπλαττομένων ἢ ἐπιπλαττομένων Phld.*Mus.* p.52K. 2. Medic., *plaster* or *poultice*, Hp.*VC*13,al.; also, *apply as a plaster* or *poultice*, in Pass., Dsc.4.87,88: metaph., c. gen., θεὸς κ. τῶν ψυχῆς τραυμάτων Ph.1.455. 3. metaph., καταπεπλασμένος, = καταπλαστός II, Aristid.*Or.*28(49).101; τὸ κ. the *artificial sound* produced by stopping the higher notes in a flute, Quint.1.11.6. **-πλαστέον**, *one must plaster*, Antyll.ap.Orib.7.16.4, Archig.ap.Aët.3.191. **-πλάστης**, ου, ὁ, *one who plasters*, Ph. 2.478. ***-πλαστός**, όν, *plastered over*, φάρμακον καταπλαστόν, = κατάπλασμα, *plaster*, Ar.*Pl.*717; opp. χριστά and ποτά, v. Sch. ad loc. II. metaph., *affected*, ἀπαμφιεῖ τὸ κ. σου ἡ μέθη your *false assumptions*, Men.339; κ. βαρύτης Plu.2.44a. **-πλαστύς**, ύος, ἡ, Ion. for κατάπλασμα, Hdt.4.75.

**καταπλᾰτύνω**, strengthd. for πλατύνω, Gal.2.298: **-πλᾰτύς**, εῖα, ύ, for πλατύς, Tz.*H.*11.855.

***καταπλέκω**, *entwine, plait*, [φλοῦν] φορμοῦ τρόπον κ. Hdt.3.98. b. in Anatomy, Pass., perh. *inosculate, anastomose*, in aor. -επλάκην [ᾰ], Hp.*Oss.*18 (aor. part. Pass. -πλεκεῖσι Hsch.); also, *to be entwined, matted*, Sor.1.88. c. *twine round*, τὰ εὐώνυμα μέρη Meno *Iatr.*16.16; *compose*, τὸν ὄχεον Paul.Aeg.6.63. 2. metaph., *implicate*, κ. τινὰ προδοσίῃ Hdt.8.128 (as v.l.):—Pass., πόλεμος.. καταπεπλεγμένος τῇ ποικιλίᾳ in the variety of its events, *complicated*, Arist. *Po.*1459ᵃ34; *to be involved*, ἐν τούτῳ ψεῦδος κατεπέπλεκτο S.E.*M.* 2.71. 3. c. dat. pers., *entangle, involve in contradictions*, *POxy.* 1673.20 (ii A.D.), 903.35 (iv A.D.). II. *finish twining*: hence metaph., *bring to an end*, τὴν ζόην, τὴν ῥῆσιν, Hdt.4.205, 8.83.

**καταπλεονεκτέω**, *to have mastered*, & -εῖ νῦν ἡ ἰητρικὴ Hp.*Decent.*6.

**κατάπλεος**, ον, Att. -πλεως, ων, gen. ω, *quite full*, τινος of a thing, Ph.2.568, Plu.2.498f: *fouled, stained with*, γῆς τε κατάπλεων τὸ γένειον καὶ αἵματος X.*Cyr.*8.3.30, cf. *IG*4.952.44 (Epid.); [πηλῷ] D.H.1. 79: c. dat., *filled with*, λύχνος ὥσπερ κέγχροις πολλοῖς κ. Thphr.*Sign.* 42; χωρίον ὀχετοῖς κατάπλεων App.*Pun.*117.

**καταπλέω**, Ion. -πλώω Hdt.2.93 codd.: aor. -έπλωσα Id.1.2, al.:— *sail down*; i.e., 1. *sail from the high sea to land, put in*, ἔνθα κατεπλέομεν Od.9.142: abs., Hdt.6.97, 7.137, Lys.28.5, etc.; ἐς Αἶαν Hdt.1.2, cf. 8.132; ἐπὶ Ἑλλησπόντου ib.109, 9.98; ἐπ' Ἀρτεμίσιον Id.7.195; τὰς ἐκ Πόντου ναῦς Ἀθήναζε κ. X.*HG*5.1.28; ἕως ἂν δεῦρο -πλεύσωμεν Test.ap.D.21.168; ἐνταῦθα κ. Id.32.14; *sail home*, Lys. 21.3, Phoenicid.2.3; νεωστὶ καταπεπλευκώς having lately *come ashore*, Pl.*Euthd.*297c; of things, *to be brought by sea*, πυρὸς Ἀθήναζε -πλέων Thphr.*CP*4.9.5; ἡ -πλέουσα ἀγορά App.*Pun.*100. 2. *sail down stream*, [ἐς] τὸν Εὐφρήτην Hdt.1.185; in Egypt, *down the Nile*, κ. εἰς τὴν πόλιν (sc. Alexandria) *PMagd.*22.4 (iii B.C.), cf. *PTeb.*58.44 (ii B.C.), etc.; of fish, *swim down stream*, κ. ἐς θάλασσαν Hdt.2.93, cf. Arist.*HA*598ᵇ16. II. *sail back*, Hdt.1.165, 3.45, And.2.13, Phld.*Acad.Ind.*p.102M., etc.

**κατάπλεως**, ων, gen. ω, Att. for κατάπλεος.

**κατα-πληγία**, ἡ, *panic fear*, Poll.3.137. **-πληγμός**, ὁ, = κατάπληξις, Lxx *Si.*21.4. **-πλήγνυμι**, = καταπλήσσω, Dam.*Isid.* 284. **-πληκτέον**, οὐ κ. *one must* not *be terrified*, Din.1. 108. ***-πληκτικός**, ή, όν, *striking, astonishing*, εὐπρόσωπος καὶ κ. Macho ap.Ath.13.578c; εὐπρέπεια κ. Phld.*Hom.*p.58O.; *terrible*, προσβολαί Plb.3.13.6; πρόσοψις, διήγησις, κραυγή, Id.3.114.4, 4.28.6, 11.16.2; τὰ εἰς πόλεμον κ. D.S.2.16; but expressly opp. φοβερός in Muson.*Fr.*33p.122H. (nisi leg. καταλλακτικός). Adv. -κῶς Plb.3.41. 3, D.S.3.35, etc. **-πληκτος**, ον, *astonishing*, f.l. for foreg., Id.31. 8. ***-πλήξ**, ῆγος, ὁ, ἡ, *stricken, struck*, ὑπὸ τῶν γυναικῶν Theopomp.Com.59: usu. metaph., *stricken with amazement, astounded*, ὑπὸ τῶν τούτου ἁμαρτημάτων Lys.6.50; ἄτολμος καὶ κ. Plu 2.7b; κ. καὶ περιδεής ib.814f; μὴ ὦσιν οἱ ἵπποι καταπλῆγες Ael.*NA*16.25. 2. *shy, bashful*, opp. ἀναίσχυντος, Arist.*EN*1108ᵃ34, *EE*1233ᵇ28, Jul. *Or.*7.233b. 3. c. gen., *nervous, apprehensive of*, πολλῶν Plu. *Fab.*14 codd. 4. Medic., *fixed*, ὀφθαλμός (in paralysis) Hp.*Epid.* 5.50. ***-πληξις**, εως, ἡ, *amazement, consternation*, Th.7.42, 8.66, *BGU*1209.16 (i B.C.), etc.; κ. ὀμμάτων *fixation*, Hp.*Epid.*7.56. 2. *extreme shyness*, Arist.*MM*1193ᵃ1. **-πλήσσω**, Att. -ττω, fut. -ξω D.21.194:—*strike down*, τινὸς εἰς τὴν κατακλεῖδα [ξίφος] *PMag.Par.* 1.300: usu. metaph., *strike with amazement, astound, terrify*, κατέπλησσεν ἐπὶ τὸ φοβεῖσθαι Th.2.65; ὁ φόβος κ. τὰς ψυχάς X.*Cyr.*3.1.25; καταπλήξειν ᾤετο τὸν δῆμον D.l.c.; κ. τοὺς ἀκροατάς, of orators, Arist.*Rh.*1408ᵃ25; -πλῆξαί τινα τῇ προδοσίῃ *tax* him with his treachery, Hdt.8.128 (v.l. -πλέξαι); *browbeat, bully*, *POxy.*237 viii 10 (ii A.D.):—Med., -πλήξασθαι τοὺς ὑπεναντίους Plb.3.89.1, cf. D.S. 11.77, Jul.*Or.*6.191a, etc.—Pass., *to be panic-stricken, astounded*, most freq. in aor.2 and pf. (pres., Eup.159.10), κατεπλήγη φίλον ἦτορ Il.3.31; -πλαγῆναι τῷ πολέμῳ Th.1.81; τῷ πλήθει Id.4.10; μὴ -πέπληχθε ἄγαν Id.7.77: c. acc., πάνυ τοῦτ' ἐπαινῶ καὶ -πλήττομαι Eup. l.c.; τὴν ἀπειρίαν τὴν αὐτοῦ -πεπλῆχθαι Isoc.*Ep.*4.11; μηδὲν -πλαγέντες τὸν Φίλιππον Decr.ap.D.18.185; -πεπλῆχθαι τὸν βίον Id.37. 43 codd.; -πεπληγμένοι τὸν στόλον Plb.1.20.6; *to be amazed at*, τὴν ἀπαθίαν τινῶν Phld.*Sto.Herc.*339.7: later intr. in pf. -πέπληγα, plpf. -πεπλήγη App.*Mith.*19, Paus.10.22.2, Luc.*DMeretr.*13.2: esp. in part., -πεπληγότες τὸ τῶν Ῥωμαίων τάχος D.H.6.25, etc.; τὸ περιδεὲς καὶ -πεπληγός *abject terror*, Plu.*Comp.Pel.Marc.*1.

***καταπλίσσομαι**, Pass., *to be tripped up*, ἡμῶν ἴσως σὺ καταπλῐγήσει (fut. 2) τῷ χορῷ *will be tripped up, beaten* by our chorus, dub. in Ar. *Fr.*198.3, cf. Hsch. s. v. καταπλιγήσει.

***καταπλοκή**, ἡ, *entwining, interlacing*, τοῦ νεύρου καὶ τοῦ δέρματος Pl.*Ti.*76d; *complication*, τῶν πραγμάτων Artem.2.5. II. in Music, *descending progression*, opp. ἀναπλοκή, Ptol.*Harm.*2.12.

**κατάπλοος**, contr. -πλους, ὁ, *sailing down, bearing down*, Th.4. 10; *sailing to land, putting ashore*, ib.26; ὁ Σικελικὸς κ. the *arrival* of the corn-fleet from Sicily, D.56.9. 2. *sailing down stream*, esp. *down the Nile*, ὁ κατ' ἐνιαυτὸν εἰς Ἀλεξάνδρειαν κ. *OGI*90.17 (Rosetta, ii B.C.), cf. *PTeb.*27.103 (ii B.C.). II. *sailing back, return*, ὁ οἴκαδε κ. X.*HG*1.4.11; παρῆν τις ἐκ κ. one *who had just returned*, Plb.15.23.3.

**καταπλουτίζω**, *enrich greatly*, τινα Hdt.6.132, X.*Oec.*4.7; τινὰ εὐεργεσίαις Ph.2.588.

**καταπλουτομᾰχέω**, *conquer by money*, D.S.5.38.

**κατα-πλυντηρίζω**, *drench with foul abuse*, *Com.Adesp.*715. **-πλύνω** [ῡ], *drench*, ὕδατι τὴν κεφαλήν X.*Eq.*5.6. II. *wash out, remove by washing*, [ἅλμυρόν τι] Arist.*Mete.*357ᵇ5:—Pass., καταπλυθείσης τῆς ἅλμης Thphr.*CP*3.24.3: metaph., καταπέπλῠται τὸ πρᾶγμα the affair *is washed out, has become worthless*, Aeschin.3.178, cf. Poll.7. 38. **-πλῠσις**, εως, ἡ, *bathing in water*, τῶν σκελῶν X.*Eq.*5.9.

**κατά-πλωσις**, εως, ἡ, Ion. for κατάπλους, *home-coming by sea*, Herod.1.68: **-πλώω**, Ion. for καταπλέω.

***καταπνέω**, Ep. -πνείω, *blow* or *breathe upon* or *over*, τί τινος, χώρας (Reisk. for χώραν) καταπνεῦσαι ἡδυπνόους αὔρας E.*Med.*839 (lyr.); Ἔρως ἵμερον κ. ἡμῶν κατὰ τῶν κόλπων Ar.*Lys.*552: with gen. understood, Arist.*HA*541ᵃ29, 594ᵇ27: also c. acc., κ. τόπον εὐωδίᾳ *fill* the place with fragrance, Hld.3.2: c. acc. cogn., ἡδὺ κ. *h.Cer.* 238:—Pass., σπινθὴρ -πνευσθεὶς Ph.1.455; -πνευσθέντες ὑπὸ ἀνέμων ψυχρῶν *blown upon* by.., Gal.12.599; στρατόπεδον οὐ -πνεόμενον ἐκ τῆς θαλάσσης App.*Pun.*99: abs., ὅταν Βορρᾶς -πνεύσῃ Cratin. 207. 2. *inspire*, θεόθεν καταπνείει πειθὼ.. ξύμφυτος αἰών A.*Ag.* 105 (s.v.l., lyr.); θεοῦ ὁμόνοιαν, ὀργὴν δικαίαν -πνέοντος, Ael.*NA*12. 2,7: c. acc. pers., θεὸς καταπνεῖ σε E.*Rh.*387:—Pass., -πνευσθείς Ph.1.411. 3. *blow upon*, c. dat., τοῖς πρὸς ἄρκτον οἰκοῦσι.. κ. ὁ νότος Arist.*Pr.*945ᵃ36: metaph., μή σοι νέμεσις θεόθεν καταπνεύσῃ Pl. Com.173.14. II. Pass., *to be blown up*, φλόξ Plu.2.474d.

**κατα-πνίγω** [ῑ], *choke, smother*, γόγγρον ἐν ἅλμῃ Sotad.Com.1.21; ὁ ὕπνος κ. τὸ θερμόν Arist.*Fr.*233; ταῦτα κ. τὰ δένδρα Thphr.*CP*2. 18.3; τὴν αὔξησιν Plu.2.806c; πνεῦμα Nic.*Al.*286; λύγγας Arist. *Pr.*962ᵃ7:—Pass., *to be choked up*, of the secretions, ib.967ᵃ6; of a fire, opp. ἐγκρύπτω 2, Id.*Juv.*470ᵃ16; καταπεπνιγμένοι τόποι *choked up, close*, opp. εὐπνούστεροι, Id.*Pr.*869ᵃ35; φωναὶ καταπεπν. *stifled* utterances, Id.*Aud.*800ᵃ15, cf. Poll.4.114. 2. κ. τὰς φύσας *close* the bellows, Arist.*Resp.*474ᵃ15. **-πνιξις**, εως, ἡ, *choking, smothering*, opp. εὔπνοια, ib.966ᵇ36, cf. Thphr.*HP*5.9.4, *Sud.*9.

**κατα-πνοή**, ἡ, *blowing*, ἀνέμων Pi.*P.*5.121 codd. **-πνοος**, ον, contr. -πνους, ουν, *blown upon*, Poll.1.240.

**καταποδίζω**, *obstruct, hamper*, Phld.*Lib.*p.15O.

**καταπόθρα**, ἡ, *gullet, pharyngeal region*, Paul.Aeg.6.32, *Hippiatr.* 16.

**καταποιέω**, *depress*, Hp.*Mochl.*2 (v.l. κακοποιεῖ).

**καταποικίλλω**, *deck with various colours* or *in divers modes, mottle*, τὸ σῶμα Pl.*Ti.*85a; θάλαμος, ὃν αἱ Χάριτες κατεποίκιλαν Men.Rh. p.407S.; διττὰ ὑφάσματα Ph.2.226:—Pass., ὑπὸ τῶν γραφέων τὰ ἱερὰ ἡμῖν καταπεποίκιλται Pl.*Euthphr.*6c; ὀροφὴ ἀστέρας καταπεποικιλμένη D.S.1.47. 2. metaph., of style, κ. τὸν λόγον Isoc.13.16, Phld. *Rh.*1.167S.; also κ. τὰ γεγενημένα, of historians, Agath.*Praef.* p.136D.

**καταπολεμ-έω**, *war down*, i.e. *exhaust by war, reduce*, τὴν Πελοπόννησον Th.2.7, cf. 4.1, And.3.15, X.*HG*7.1.10: pres., *attempt to subdue*, ἐγκλήμασι Th.4.86:—Pass., ἐλπίζοντες αὐτὴν [τὴν πόλιν] καταπεπολεμῆσθαι Id.6.16, cf. Pl.*Mx.*243c,d. II. simply, *make war against*, τινα Phld.*Piet.*54: abs., *carry on warfare*, τοῖς ὅλοις Plu. *Caes.*26. **-ησις**, εως, ἡ, *subduing*, condemned by Poll.9.142.

**καταπολεύω**, *revolve*, ὁ ἰσημερινὸς τῷ βορείῳ κύκλῳ -εύοντι βραδυτέρω(ς).. ὁμοχρόνως κινεῖται Sch.Arat.147; of the constellation Ἄρκτος, *move downwards in an orbit*, opp. ἀναπολεύω, *PMag.Par.*1.702.

**καταπολιός**, όν, *white-haired*, Gloss.

**καταπολῑτεύομαι**, *subdue* or *reduce by policy*, τινα D.19.315, Plu. *Pomp.*51, *Galb.*20, etc.

**κατάπομα**, ατος, τό, *drink*, Aq., Sm.*Je.*51(28).44.

**καταπομπ-εύω**, *scoff at*, τινος Luc.*Am.*37. **-ή**, ἡ, *delivery, rendering* of goods or returns, *POxy.*1415.7, *BGU*362 viii 15 (both iii A.D.). II. *sending back*, Afric.ap.Eus.*DE*8.2. **-ός**, ὁ, *one who conveys* or *delivers*, c. gen., *POxy.*1415.5 (iii A.D.), etc.

***καταπον-έω**, *subdue*, τῇ ἐνδείᾳ τῆς τροφῆς τὴν ἀλκὴν τοῦ θηρίου D.S.3.37, cf. Heraclit.*Incred.*11: in fut. Med., τὰς ὀλίγας ναῦς ταῖς πολλαπλασίαις D.S.11.15; *worst* in a lawsuit, *POxy.*1101.9 (iv A.D.):—Pass., *to be subdued, reduced, worn out*, δῆμος -πεπονημένος Aeschin.2.36, cf. Plb.29.27.11, D.S.11.6; πάντα ταῖς ἐνδελεχείαις -πονεῖται πράγματα Men.744; *to be exhausted*, τῷ θάλπει Gal.10. 715. 2. *handle roughly, crush, damage*, τὰ -πονούμενα καὶ συμπατούμενα Thphr.*HP*8.7.5; *maltreat, oppress*, esp. in Pass., ὑπὸ τῶν τυράννων, ὑπὸ τῶν τελωνῶν, Arist.*Fr.*575, *BGU*1188.17 (Aug.), cf. *Act.Ap.*7.24, Diog.Oen.1. 3. *digest* food, Sor.2.32 (Pass.). II. intr. in pf. part. -πεπονηκὼς *ruinous*, Procop.*Aed.*1.4,8. **-ησις**, εως, ἡ, *affliction*, Sm.*Ex.*3.7. **-ος**, ον, *tired, wearied*, ἀθλητής Plu. *Sull.*29; *worn out, exhausted*, of cattle, *PLond.*3.1170ᵛ462 (iii A.D.); ὑπ' ἀλλήλων Plu.*Alc.*25. II. *laboured*, of poetry or works of art, Id.*Tim.*36; *wearisome*, λατρεία Lxx 3*Ma.*4.14; κ. βάρος Phld.*D.* 3.13.

**καταποντ-ίζω**, *throw into the sea, plunge* or *drown therein*, τινα Lys. 14.27, D.23.169, Plu.2.403c, etc.: metaph., Axiop.6 (Pass.); κ. τὰς βουλάς Lib.*Or.*49.10:—Pass., v.l. in Plb.2.60.8; καταποντισθεὶς ὑπὸ τῆς θαλάσσης D.S.18.20; ἐν τῷ πελάγει *Ev.Matt.*18.6; εἰς τὸ πέλαγος Plu.*Tim.*13; *sink*, *Ev.Matt.*14.30; of a ship, *PPetr.*2 p.135 (iii B.C.). ❀ **-ισμός**, ὁ, *drowning*, Isoc.12.122 (pl.), Lxx *Ps.*51(52).4(6); ὁ κ. τῶν χρημάτων App.*Mac.*16. **-ιστής**, οῦ, ὁ, *one who throws into the sea*, of pirates, λῃσταὶ καὶ κ. Isoc.12.226, D.23.166,167, cf. Jul. *Or.*6.201b: metaph., καταποντισταὶ τῆς Ἑλλάδος Paus.8.52.3, cf. Lib.*Or.*63.17. **-όω**, = καταποντίζω, Hdt.1.165, 4.154, Xenarch.2. 5, etc.; κ. ἐς τὴν θάλασσαν Hdt.3.30; εἰς ποταμόν Polem.Hist.54; τὴν οὐσίαν Philostr.*VA*1.13:—Pass., Antipho 5.28, Pl.*Grg.*511e, Ph.1. 264,394, Plu.*Cat.Mi.*11.

**καταπορεύομαι**, *come back* from banishment, Plb.4.17.8, *OGI*90.19 (Rosetta, ii B.C.). 2. *return home*, Lxx 2*Ma.*11.30, 3*Ma.*4.11. 3. κ. εἰς τάξιν, = Lat. *regredi in ordinem*, *IG*7.2225.42 (Thisbe).

**κατ-απορέω**, *fail in treating*:—hence in Pass., κατηπορήθη ὀστέα ἐμπεσεῖν *there was a failure in* reducing the fracture, Hp.*Fract.*33; οἷσι ἂν ὦμος κ. ἐμβληθῆναι Id.*Art.*12, cf. 61.

**καταπορθέω**, *ravage utterly*, Gloss.

**καταπορθμίας**, ὁ, *an East wind, blowing down the Straits* of Messina, Arist.*Vent.*973ᵃ25.

**καταπορίζω**, = *remeo*, Gloss.

**καταπόρν-ευσις**, εως, ἡ, *prostitution*, θυγατέρων παρθένων Plu.*Tim.* 13 (pl.). **-εύω**, *prostitute*, τὰ θήλεα τέκνα Hdt.1.94,196:—Pass., Str.11.14.16. II. *violate, treat as prostitutes*, Plu.2.821d, Ael.*VH* 9.8:—Pass., prob. in *POxy.*1241 iii 11. III. *squander on courtesans*, D.C.45.28.

**καταπορνοκοπέω**, = foreg. III, Poll.3.117.

**καταπόρφῠρος**, ον, *all-purple*, Lyd.*Mag.*2.13.

**καταπόσια**, τά, = *ludi Florales*, Gloss.

**κατάποσις**, εως, ἡ, *gulping down, swallowing*, Pl.*Ti.*80a, Arist. *PA*690ᵇ28, Gal.10.506; τῆς τροφῆς Aret.*CA*1.4; τοῦ Κρόνου τῶν παίδων Sallust.4 (pl.); [τέχνης] Chrysipp.*Stoic.*2.257. II. *gullet*, Muson.*Fr.*18ᴬ p.97 H., Epict.*Gnom.*22, Dsc.3.80, Sor.1.86, Xenocr. ap.Orib.2.58.93, Aret.*SD*1.7.

**κατ-αποστέλλω**, *send down* (to Alexandria), *UPZ*110.137 (ii B.C.).

**καταποτάομαι**, *fly down*, v.l. in Lib.*Or.*11.86.

**κατα-πότης**, ου, ὁ, = λάρυγξ, Hsch. s.v. βρόγχος, Suid. **-ποτον**, τό, *pill, bolus*, v.l. for καταπότια in Hp.*Acut.*(*Sp.*)70, *Mul.*2.133, cj. for κατὰ ποτόν in Thphr.*HP*9.20.2: in pl., *things swallowed*, Aret. *CA*2.2:—Dim. **-πότιον**, *little pill*, Hp. ll. cc., Thphr.*HP*9.8.3, Ruf. ap.Orib.7.26.125, Archig.ib.8.2.30, *POxy.*2144.4 (iii A.D.), etc.

**κατ-αποφαίνομαι**, *pronounce dogmatically*, Diog.Oen.8.

**κατ-αποχή**, ἡ, *receipt*, *Arch.Pap.*3.418 (vi A.D.).

**καταπραγμᾰτεύω**, Act. and Med., c. gen., sine expl., Suid.

**καταπραιδεύω**, (Lat. *praeda*) *ravage*, Suid. s.v. καταδηοῦν.

**καταπρακτικός**, ή, όν, *fitted for accomplishing*, τῶν νοηθέντων Muson.*Fr.*8 p.39 H. II. Subst. -κόν, τό, *spell for achieving* success, *PMag.Par.*1.2373.

**καταπρᾱνής**, ές, Att. for καταπρηνής, πρόσχωσις J.*AJ*4.8.5, cf. Hsch.

**κατάπραξις**, εως, ἡ, *execution*, τῶν βεβουλευμένων J.*AJ*19.1.4.

**καταπράσσω**, Att. -ττω, *accomplish, execute*, τινί τι X.*An.*7.7.46; τι τῶν ἐπειγόντων Plu.*Per.*5; κ. ὥστε τι γίγνεσθαι X.*HG*7.4.11. b. *construct, build*, ἡρῷον *IG*12(7).478.2 (Amorgos). 2. *achieve, gain*, ἀρχήν X.*Cyr.*7.5.76:—Med., *achieve for oneself*, dub. in Id.*An.*7.7. 27, cf. Zos.1.44; ὅπως καταπράξεται τὸν γάμον Men.242; ἰδίαν ἀσφάλειαν D.H.6.68:—Pass., τὰ κατεπεπραγμένα X.*Cyr.*7.5.35; τὴν ἡγεμονίαν -πραχθῆναι Id.*Vect.*5.5.

**καταπρᾱτικόν**, τό, (πιπράσκω) *tax on sales*, *Inscr.Magn.*116.42.

❀ **καταπρᾱΰν-σις**, εως, ἡ, *placation*, Gloss. **-ω**, fut. -πραΰνῶ Hsch.: Ep. and Ion. **-πρηΰνω**:—*soften*, opp. τραχύνω, Pl.*Ti.*67a: usu. metaph., *soften down, appease*, Pl.*Euthd.*288b, A.R.1.265, Q.S.14. 328; κ. τοὺς ἀκροατάς, of an orator, Isoc.4.13, cf. Arist.*Rh.*1380ᵇ30; κ. τὴν ταραχήν Plb.5.52.14; κ. τινὰ τῆς ὀργῆς Plu.*Them.*31:—Pass., *to be pacified*, of animals, Phld.*Mus.*p.20 K.; *to be allayed*, of emotions, Id.*Rh.*1.370 S.

**κατάπρεμνος**, ον, *with many branches*, Hsch.

**καταπρεσβεύω**, *undertake an embassy against*, τινος Str.17.1.11: abs., Plb.22.11.8.

**καταπρην-ής**, ές, *down-turned*, opp. ὕπτιος, in Hom. always of the hand as used in striking or grasping, πλῆξεν . . χειρὶ καταπρηνεῖ *with the flat of* his hand, Il.16.792, cf. Od.13.164; πεπλήγετο μηρὼ χερσὶ καταπρηνέσσι Il.15.114; χέρεσσι κ. λαβοῦσα Od.19.467; ἐς τὸ κ. ῥέποντα Hp.*Fract.*40. (Ion. for καταπρανής, q.v.) ❀ **-ίζω**, *throw headlong down*, ἁλιῆας . . κατεπρήνιξεν ἐπάκτρου εἰς ἅλα Nic.*Th.*824, cf. Nonn.*D.*4.395. **-όω**, = foreg., τινὰ πόντῳ καταπρηνώσασθαι *AP* 7.652 (Leon.).

**κατά-πριστος**, ον, *sawn*, ἐλέφας prob. in Hermipp.63.15. **-πρίω** [ῑ], *saw up*, κορμοὺς ξύλων Hdt.7.36; *saw asunder*, Lxx *Su.*59. 2. *cut* or *bite into pieces*, κύμινον Theoc.10.55; γλῶσσαν κυνόδοντι Nic. *Al.*283.

**καταπρο-βάλλω**, *prostrate*, prob. f.l. for προκατα-, Gal.19.622. **-δίδωμι**, *betray utterly, leave in the lurch*, Hdt.7.157, 8.94, Ar.*V.*1044, Th.1.86, 7.48, etc.; τὰς Ἀφίδνας τινί Hdt.9.73; τὰ πράγματα Lys.20. 6:—Pass., Hdt.9.7.α΄, Th.3.111. **-θῡμέομαι**, strengthd. for προθυμέομαι, c. acc., Suid. **-ἵεμαι**, Med., *throw away, abandon*, τοὺς καιρούς Plb.1.77.3, etc.; τοὺς ἰδίους βίους Id.3.81.4, cf. *PRev.Laws* 27.11 (iii B.C.), *PTeb.*27.61 (ii B.C.); τὸ ζῆν Phld.*Mort.*5; πολλὰ τῶν κοινῶν τοῖς κλέπτουσιν Plu.*Arist.*4; ἀλλήλω Procop.*Arc.*1 (ἀλλήλων codd.): aor. καταπροηκάμην Poll.8.143.

**καταπροΐξομαι**, Att. **-προίξομαι**, in early writers only fut., later also aor. 1 (v. infr.): used with neg., and usu. c. part., οὐ γὰρ δή ἐμέ γε ὧδε λωβησάμενος καταπροΐξεται he *shall* not *escape unpunished for* thus insulting me, Hdt.3.156; οὐ καταπροΐξονται ἀποστάντες Id.5.105, cf. 7.17; οὔτοι καταπροίξει τάλαντα πολλὰ κλέψας Ar.*Eq.*435; οὔτοι καταπροίξει τοῦτο δρῶν you *shall* not *escape unpunished for* doing this, Id.*V.*1366; οὔτοι . . καταπροίξει λέγουσα ταυτί Id.*Th.*566: abs., ἐκείνους οὐ καταπροΐξεσθαι ἔφη *should* not *get off scot-free*, Hdt.3.36: without a neg., Them.*Or.*2.25b: in aor. 1, οὐ μὴν ἐκεῖνός γε παντελῶς κατεπροίξατο Plu.2.10c (-πράξ- codd.), cf. Hsch. 2. c. gen. pers., ἐμεῦ δ' ἐκεῖνος οὐ καταπροΐξεται he *shall* not *escape* me *unpunished*, Archil.92; οὔτοι ἐμοῦ . . καταπροίξει Ar.*Nu.*1240; οὔτοι . . καταπροίξει Μυρτίας Id.*V.*1396. 3. both constructions combined, οὐ καταπροίξῃ αὐτὸς μεθύων νηφούσης γυναικός Hdn.1.17.5.—Ion. word, used in colloquial Att. of Com. (Glossed προῖκα ἐκφύγοι in Suid., δωρεὰν καταγνώσεται in *EM*495.34, and connected by both with προΐσσομαι, προΐκτης; but perh. rather from κατα-προ-ἱκνέομαι.)

❀ **καταπρολείπω**, *forsake utterly*, A.R.3.1164.

**καταπρονομεύω**, *carry off as booty*, Lxx *Nu.*21.1, *Jd.*2.14.

**κατάπροσθεν**, = ἔμπροσθεν, *IG*11(2).161 *A* 45, 165.22 (Delos, iii B.C.); **κατάπροσθε** ib.163.51.

**καταπροτείνομαι**, *hold out as a pretence*, Gal.5.92.

**καταπροτερέω**, *get the better of*, τινος D.S.17.33; κ. τὸν καιρόν *seize a favourable* opportunity, Men.Prot.p.102 D.:—Pass., *to be beaten, yield*, τοῖς ἐπιβατικοῖς, ταῖς εὐχειρίαις, Plb.1.47.9, 16.19.1.

**καταπροχέω**, *pour down over*, δάκρυα παρειῶν A.R.3.1118.

**κατάπρωκτος**, ον, = καταπύγων, dub. l. in Ar.*Ec.*364.

**κατάπτερ-ος**, ον, *winged*, A.*Pr.*798, E.*Or.*176 (lyr.). **-όω**, *furnish with wings*, ἱππείᾳ τριχί E.*Melanipp.Sap.Prol.*15, cf. Apollod. 1.6.3 (Pass.).

**καταπτήσομαι**, fut. of καταπέτομαι.

**καταπτήσσω**, fut. -πτήξω (v. infr.): 3 dual Ep. aor. 2 καταπτήτην Il.8.136: poet. aor. part. καταπτᾰκών A.*Eu.*252 (cf. καταπλακών): pf. κατέπτηκα Lxx *Jo.*2.24 (v.l. -έπτηχε), Did. *in D.*11.25, Them.*Or.*24. 309b, or κατέπτηχα D.4.8, Plu.*Per.*25, Gal.5.510; Ep. part. καταπεπτηώς (v. infr.):—*crouch, cower*, esp. from fear, καταπτήτην ὑπ' ὄχεσφι Il.8.136; καταπτήξας ὑπὸ θάμνῳ 22.191; κατὰ δ' ἔπτηξαν ποτὶ γαίῃ Od.8.190; λιμῷ καταπεπτηυῖα Hes.*Sc.*265: also in Prose, κατέπτηχε μέντοι ταῦτα πάντα νῦν D. l. c., cf. D.H.7.50; ταπεινοὶ -πτήξετε πρὸς τὸ μέλλον Plu.*Aem.*27; διὰ τὸ μέγεθος Id.*Sull.*7. 2. c. acc., *cower beneath*, ἐξουσίαν D.H.11.18; τὸ θεοῦ κράτος Ph.1.677, cf. 322, 2.600; of a breach in a wall, ἀπειλουμένην ὅσον οὔπω κατεπτηχέναι τὴν ἐπίκλυσιν Hld.9.5.

**καταπτίσσω**, *grind to powder*, Plu.2.449e, Nic.Dam.118 J.

**καταπτοέω**, *frighten*, Ps.-Luc.*Philopatr.*29.

**καταπτύρομαι**, *to be terrified*, Aq.*Ge.*41.8.

**κατάπτυσμα**, = *putacilla*, Gloss.

**κατάπτυστος**, ον, also η, ον Anacr.152; *to be spat upon, abominable*, Anacr. l. c., A.*Ch.*632 (lyr.), *Eu.*68; ὦ κ. κάρα E.*Tr.*1024: also in Com. and Prose, Anaxil.22.6, D.18.33, etc.

**καταπτῠχής**, ές, *with ample folds*, ἐμπερόναμα Theoc.15.34.

❀ **καταπτύω**, *spit upon* or *at*, esp. as a mark of abhorrence or contempt, c. gen., τίς οὐχὶ κατέπτυσεν ἂν σοῦ; D.18.200, cf. Aeschin.3. 73, Luc.*Cat.*12, etc.; κ. δωροδοκίας Aeschin.2.23; πλούτου Luc.*Icar.* 30: abs., Ar.*Ra.*1179. [On the quantity, v. πτύω.]

**κατά-πτωμα**, ατος, τό, *downfall*, Lxx *Ps.*143(144).14. 2. τὸ κ. τοῦ ὄντος μὴ ὄν the Not-Being which forms the *lower limit* of Being, Porph.*Sent.*26. II. *debility, collapse*, Alex.Trall.9.2. **-πτωσις**, εως, ἡ, *fall*, Hp.*Art.*42; ἐξ ὀχήματος Gal.7.560; λίθου Simp. *in Ph.*261.17. 2. Medic., *collapse*, ἡ συγκοπή ἐστι κ. δυνάμεως Gal. 10.837; of epileptic *seizures*, Alex.Aphr.*Pr.*2.64, cf. Vett.Val.38.13 (pl.): hence of a spell which induces a *trance*, *PMag.Par.*1.850. 3. *downfall, calamity*, Lxx 3*Ma.*2.14.

**καταπτώσσω**, = καταπτήσσω, τίπτε καταπτώσσοντες ἀφέστατε; Il. 4.340, al.; of dogs, *Gp.*19.2.11.

**καταπτωτικός**, ή, όν, *liable to fits*, Vett.Val.112.34.

**καταπτωχεύω**, *reduce to beggary, beggar*, Plu.*Cat.Mi.*25:—Pass., *to be* or *become beggared*, Id.*Cic.*10; τύχαι κατεπτωχευμέναι *beggared* fortunes, D.H.9.51.

**καταπῡγίζω**, *to be* or *act like a* καταπύγων, Phot.

**καταπυγμομαχέω**, *conquer in boxing*, Sch.*AP*11.80 (Lucill.).

**κατάπῡγ-ος**, ον, = καταπύγων (q.v.), Hsch., Phot., prob. in Gerhard *Phoinix* p.7 (cf. p.153): Comp. -ότερος Sophr.63: Sup. -ότατος *Epigr.Gr.*1131. **-οσύνη**, ἡ, *unnatural lust*, Cratin.53, Ar.*Nu.*1023 (anap.), *Fr.*130, Luc.*Gall.*32. ❀ **-ων**, ονος, ὁ, ἡ, neut. κατάπυγον Ar. *V.*687: (πυγή):—*given to unnatural lust*: generally, *lecherous, lewd*, Id.*Ach.*79, al., Luc.*Tim.*22, Alciphr.3.45, etc.; ὦ κατάπυγον Ar.*Th.* 200.—The oblique cases are sts. wrongly written -πύγωνος, cf. Hdn. Gr.2.725: irreg. Comp. -πυγωνέστερος (metri gr.) Ar.*Lys.*776. II. in Att., *the middle finger* (used in an obscene gesture), Poll.2.184.

**καταπύει**· ἐνέπλησε, κατ. γνόει, Hsch.

**καταπύθω** [ῡ], *putrefy*, τὴν . . κατέπυσ' ἱερὸν μένος Ἠελίοιο *h.Ap.* 371:—Pass. (with pf. -πέπυθα Hsch. (-οιθα cod.)), *become putrefied*, ξύλον . . τὸ μὲν οὐ καταπύθεται ὄμβρῳ Il.23.328.

**καταπῠκάζω**, *cover over*, Hsch. s.v. κατερρινωμένον (Pass.): metaph., μύθοις τὴν ἱστορίαν Eust.1379.12.

**κατάπυκν-ος**, ον, strengthd. for πυκνός, *thick, tufted*, ἔρπυλλος Theoc.*Ep*.1.1. 2. Milit., ἐν κ. στάσει in *close* formation, Ascl. *Tact*.5.1. II. Medic., *very costive*, κοιλίη Hp.*Acut*.(*Sp*.)56. III. κ. εἰς σχηματισμόν *often using* a formation, A.D.*Adv*.186.2 ; ἡ διάλεκτος κ. ἐπὶ τὴν χρῆσιν Id.*Synt*.50.18. **-όω**, *stud thickly*, τρήμασι τὸ τεῖχος Plb.8.5.6 ; θύρας ἥλοις D.S.18.71 ; τοῖς ἀφώνοις τὰς συλλαβάς D.H.*Comp*.16 ; παραδειγμάτων πλήθει τὴν πόλιν Plu.*Lyc*.27 ; τοῖς ὑπερβατοῖς Phld.*Rh*.1.160S. :—Pass., of the sky, καταπεπυκνῶσθαι..πλήθει ἀστέρων Arist.*Mete*.346ᵃ29 ; of a country, ἐλαίαις καταπεπυκνῶσθαι *to be thickly planted with*.. (v.l. for -πεφυτεῦσθαι), D.S.3.44 : metaph., βίος ἐν θαλίαις -πεπυκνωμένος Porph.*Plot*.23. II. *force into a small compass, compress, condense*, Ἐπίκουρος οὕτω κατεπύκνου τὴν ἡδονήν Damox.2.62 ; τάλαντ' ἐγώ σοι κατεπύκνωσα τέτταρα *spent* four talents *in a lump*, ib.4 ; to illustrate this is cited the dogma of Epicur., *Sent*.9, εἰ κατεπυκνοῦτο πᾶσα ἡδονὴ κτλ., cf. καταπύκνωσις ; ὁ Λυκοῦργος τοὺς πολίτας τῇ σιωπῇ πιέζων συνῆγε καὶ κατεπύκνου Plu.2.510f :—Pass., -πεπύκνωται ἡ πραγματεία Porph.*Plot*.14 ; also εἰ μὴ -πυκνοῦταί σοι τὸ ἀπὸ δογμάτων ὀρθῶν ἕκαστα πράσσειν that your *habit* of acting..*is not consolidated*, M.Ant.5.9. 2. in Music, κ. τὸ διάγραμμα *fill up* the intervals in a scale (with smaller intervals), Aristox.*Harm*.p.7 M. :—Pass., Theo Sm.p.91 H., Nicom.*Exc*.7. III. Pass., *to be condensed*, of complex forms of inference (cf. πυκνόω v), Arist.*APo*.79ᵃ30. **-ωσις**, εως, ἡ, *condensation* (v. καταπυκνόω II), τοῦ ἡδομένου *densification, solidification* of pleasure by filling in unoccupied gaps in time and completing the penetration of the organism, Epicur.*Fr*.432 : pl., Dam.*Pr*.354. 2. in Music, *close packing* of the intervals in a scale, Aristox.*Harm*.p.7 M., Nicom.*Harm*.11. **-ωτέον**, *one must fill up*, of intervals in music, Theo Sm.p.91 H. ; cf. καταπυκνόω II.2.

**καταπυκτεύω**, *conquer in boxing*, Sch.A.R.2.98 (Pass.), cj. in Pl. Com.124.

**καταπῡρίζω**, v. καππυρίζω.

**καταπῡρόω**, *dry*, ἕως ἂν..-ωθῇ [τὸ ἔριον] *PHolm*.20.24 (fort. καπυρωθῇ).

**καταπυρπολέω**, *waste with fire*, Ar.*Th*.243 (Pass.), Plb.5.19.8, Palaeph.52 (Pass.), Phalar.*Ep*.104.

**κατάπυρρος**, ον, *very red, deep red*, Dsc.5.77 ; f.l. for καπυρός, Id.2.154.

**καταπώγων**, ον, gen. ωνος, *with a long beard*, D.S.3.63, Str.16.4.10.

**καταπωλέω**, *sell*, *BGU*8 iii 13 (iii A. D.), *PThead*.16.18 (iv A. D.).

**καταπωμάζω**, *close up*, ὀπήν Hero *Aut*.28.5.

**κατ-άρα** [ἄρ], Ion. -άρη, ἡ, *curse*, κατάρας ποιέεσθαί τινι to lay *curses* upon one, Hdt.1.165 ; ἐποιήσαντο νόμον τε καὶ κατάρην μὴ..θρέψειν κόμην..μηδένα ib.82 ; ἐκ κατάρης τευ in consequence of.., Id.4.30 ; διδόναι τινὰ κατάρᾳ E.*Hec*.945 (lyr.), cf. *El*.1324 (pl., anap.), A.*Th*.725 (pl., lyr.) ; opp. εὐχή, Pl.*Alc*.2.143b (pl.), cf. *SIG*1241 (Lyttus, iii A. D.), etc. ; opp. εὐλογία, *Ep.Jac*.3.10 ; κατάραι γίγνονται κατά τινος Plb.23.10.7 ; τὴν κ. ἀναγράψαι, στηλιτεῦσαι, D.S.1.45, Plu.2.354b ; *cursing*, κ. καὶ λοιδορία Phld.*Lib*.p.11 O.

**κατ-ᾰραιρημένος**, Ion. pf. part. Pass. of καθαιρέω, q. v.

**κατ-άρακτοι** θυρίδες, *shutters*, *IG*2².463.76 ; cf. καταρράκτης.

**κατάρ-ᾱμα** [ἄρ], ατος, τό, *curse*, Sch.E.*Ph*.1355. **-άομαι** [ᾱρ Ep., ᾰρ Att.], *call down curses upon*, τῷ δὲ καταρῶνται πάντες βροτοὶ ἄλγε' ὀπίσσω Od.19.330 ; πολλὰ κατηρᾶτο he *called down* many *curses*, Il.9.454 ; κεφαλῇ πολλὰ κ. Hdt.2.39 ; κ. ὁ κῆρυξ "εἴ τις ἐξαπατᾷ" λέγων D.23.97 ; κ. τὴν Ἶσίν τινι *AP*11.115 (Nicarch.) : c. inf., καταρῶνται δ' ἀπολέσθαι they *pray* that he may perish, Thgn.277 ; κ. μήτε πλοῖα στεγανὰ γενέσθαι Arist.*Fr*.554, cf. 148 : c. dat., *curse, execrate*, τῷ ἡλίῳ Hdt.4.184, cf. Ar.*Nu*.871, *Ra*.746, D.19.292 codd., etc. : c. acc., Lxx *Ge*.12.3, al., *Ev.Marc*.11.21, Plu.*Cat.Mi*.32 codd., Luc. *Asin*.27 : abs., Ar.*V*.614, D.18.283 :—Pass., aor. κατηράθην [ᾱ] Lxx *Jb*.3.5 : pf. part. κατηραμένος *accursed*, ib.4*Ki*.9.34, *Ev.Matt*.25.41, Plu.*Luc*.18 : also pf. κεκατήραμαι with double redupl., Lxx *Nu*.22.6 ; part. κεκατηραμένος ib.*Si*.3.18, al. **-άσιμος** [ᾰσ], ον, *accursed*, Suid. s. v. ἀρίσιμος. **-ᾱσις**, εως, ἡ, *cursing*, Lxx *Jd*.5.23.

**κατ-ᾰράσσω**, Att. -ττω, *dash down, break in pieces*, ὁ παῖς ἐμπεσὼν κατήραξε (sc. τὴν κύλικα) Hippon.38 :—Pass., ἡ θύρη κατήρακται Herod.2.63 : metaph., διασείειν καὶ κ. τὰ βουλεύματα cj. for ταράττειν in Luc.*Dem.Enc*.38 ; esp. of a broken and routed army, τοὺς λοιποὺς κατήραξεν ἐς τὸν Κιθαιρῶνα Hdt.9.69 ; κ. εἰς τὴν θάλασσαν ἅπαντας D.23.165 ; τὸ στράτευμα κατηράχθη εἰς τὰ τειχίσματα Th.7.6, cf. D.H.9.58, Arr.*An*.5.17.2 : fut. Med. in pass. sense, Plu.*Caes*.44. II. of sea-birds, κ. αὑτοὺς εἰς τὰς κεφαλὰς αὐτῶν *dash down* head foremost, Arist.*Mir*.836ᵃ13 : but more freq. 2. intr., *fall down, fall headlong*, Clearch.44 ; of rain, Arist.*Mu*.392ᵇ10 ; of rivers, εἰς τὸ χάσμα κ. D.S.17.75, cf. Plb.10.48.7, Str.14.4.1 : c. gen., τοῦ ἀγγείου, of a stream of water, Gal.10.554. (Freq. written καταρρ-, augm. κατερρ-, in part perh. correctly, if fr. κατα-ρράσσω, cf. ῥάσσω, ἐπιρράσσω.)

⊕**κατ-άρᾱτος** [ᾰρ], ον, Ion. κατ-ήρητος Herod.5.44, but κατάρητος *Schwyzer*702.11 (Erythrae, iv B. C.) :—*accursed, abominable*, E.*Med*.112 (anap.) : freq. in Com., ὡς σεμνὸς ὁ κ. Ar.*Ra*.178, cf. *Pax*33 ; ὦ κατάρατε Id.*Lys*.530, etc. : Comp. καταρατότερος D.18.212 : Sup. -ότατος S.*OT*1345 (lyr.).

**καταρᾰχίζω**, *make a rough surface* on masonry, dub. in *IG*2².1665.12 (iv B. C.).

**καταραψῳδῆσαι**· φλυαρῆσαι, Hsch.

**κατ-άρβῠλος**, ον, (ἀρβύλη) *reaching down to the shoes*, χλαῖναι S.*Fr*.622 :—also **καθάρβυλος**, χλανίς Hsch.

⊕**καταργ-έω**, *leave unemployed* or *idle*, χέρα E.*Ph*.753 ; κατηργηκέναι τοὺς καιροὺς *to have missed* the opportunities, Plb.*Fr*.176 ; κ. τὴν γῆν *make* the ground *useless, cumber* it, *Ev.Luc*.13.7. 2. *cause to be idle, hinder* in one's work, Lxx 2*Es*.4.21, *POxy*.38.17 (i A. D.) :—Pass., Lxx 2*Es*.6.8 ; *to be rendered* or *lie idle*, *PFlor*.176.7 (iii A. D.), etc. II. *make of no effect*, *Ep.Rom*.3.3, 31, al. :—Pass., *to be abolished, cease*, ib.6.6, 1*Ep.Cor*.2.6, etc. ; κ. ἀπὸ τοῦ νόμου *to be set free* from.., *Ep.Rom*.7.2 ; *to be parted*, ἀπὸ Χριστοῦ *Ep.Gal*.5.4. **-ησις**, εως, ἡ, *making null, abolishing*, cj. in Sm.*Ps*.45.9, *La*.1.7. **-ητέον**, *one must abolish, cancel*, τὰ πάθη Iamb.*Protr*.5. **-ία**, ἡ, *reduction to inactivity, inhibition*, τῶν αἰσθήσεων *Corp.Herm*.10.5.

**κάτ-αργμα**, ατος, τό, only pl. κατάργματα, *first offerings* (cf. κατάρχω II. 2), χέρνιβάς τε καὶ κατάργματα E.*IT*244, cf. Plu.*Thes*.22.

**κατάργῠρ-ος**, ον, *covered with silver, silvered*, Callix.2, Socr. Rhod.1, J.*BJ*5.5.3, Plu.2.828e. **-όω**, *cover with silver, silver over*, Philoch.138 :—Pass., καταργυρωμένους (Ion. for κατηργ-) ἔχων τοὺς προμαχεῶνας Hdt.1.98, cf. D.S.1.57. II. *buy* or *bribe with silver*, ἄθρησον εἰ κατηργυρωμένος λέγω S.*Ant*.1077.

**κατάρδ-ευτος**, = *irriguus*, *Gloss*. **-εύω**, = sq., Sch.A.*Pr*.813. ⊕**-ω**, *water*. Θρῄκην (-ης codd. Ath.) Antiph.105, cf. D.H.2.2. 2. *besprinkle*, πολυτελείᾳ τῶν ἀλειμμάτων J.*AJ*11.6.2 (Pass.) : metaph., *besprinkle with praise*, Ar.*Ach*.658 ; also, *to be swept along*, χειμάρρῳ οἷα -αρδόμενα, of the poetry of Aeschylus, *AP*7.411 (Diosc.).

**καταρέζω**, poet. for καταρρέζω.

**κάταρϝος**, ον, (ἀρά) *accursed*, *IG*5(2).3.4 (Tegea, iv B. C.).

⊕**καταρής** ἄνεμος, ὁ, a wind *rushing from above*, Alc.135, Sapph. 160 (v. l. κατώρης).

**καταρθεία** and -θία, v. καταρτεία.

⊕**καταρῑγηλός**, ή, όν, *making* one *shudder, horrible*, λυγρά, τά τ' ἄλλοισίν γε καταριγηλὰ πέλονται [κατᾰρ-] Od.14.226.

**κατᾰριθμ-έω**, *count* or *reckon among*, μετά τινων E.*Tr*.872 (Pass.) ; ἔν τισι Pl.*Plt*.266a, cf. D.S.4.85, Plu.*Sol*.12 ; εἰς εὐδαιμονίαν κ. *reckon* as.., Ath.1.9d : c. dupl. acc., Pl.*Sph*.266e :—Pass., Arist.*Pol*.1329ᵃ27 ; μετά τινων ib.1293ᵇ26 ; ἔν τισι *Act.Ap*.1.17, Phld.*Rh*.1.239 S. 2. *recount in detail*, τὴν ἀτοπίαν σου Pl.*Smp*.215a :—Med., *recount, enumerate*, Id.*Phlb*.27b, *Grg*.451e, Isoc.1.11 ; τι πρός τινα Aeschin.3.54 : pf. Pass. in med. sense, τὰς τῶν πολλῶν κατηριθμημένοι δόξας *having summed up*.., Arist.*Top*.101ᵃ31 :—Pass., Phld. *Ir*.p.78 W. ; τὰ συμβεβηκότα -ρίθμηται S.E.*M*.7.281. 3. Med., *count* or *reckon* so and so, εὐδαιμονέστατον κ. τινά Pl.*Phlb*.47b ; ἐν ἀδικήματι κ. τὴν πρᾶξιν Plb.5.67.5. II. abs., *count, reckon*, διὰ τί πάντες ἄνθρωποι εἰς τὰ δέκα κ. ; Arist.*Pr*.910ᵇ24. **-ησις**, εως, ἡ, *computation*, χρόνων J.*Ap*.1.21 ; *enumeration, list*, Herod.Med.ap. Orib.5.30.29, M.Ant.4.45, Gal.6.95. **-ητέον**, *one must count*, Ph.2.488.

**καταρῑνάω** or -έω, v. καταρρ-.

**καταρίπτω**, = καταρρίπτω, Man.3.55.

**κατ-ᾰριστάω**, *squander in breakfasts* : generally, *squander*, Antipho Soph.73 :—Pass., *Com.Adesp*.1032.

**καταριστήν**, = τὴν χάλαζαν, dub. in Call.*Fr*.357.

**καταρκ-έω**, *to be fully sufficient*, χώρη οὐδεμία καταρκέει πάντα ἑωυτῇ παρέχουσα Hdt.1.32 ; ἐμοὶ δὲ φῶς ἐν ἡλίου καταρκέσει E.*Rh*.447 ; πρὸς τὰς παρασκευάς Jul.*Or*.1.29c : impers., *it is enough*, καταρκεῖ τοῦδε κεκλῆσθαι πατρός S.*Fr*.86. **-ής**, ές, *fully sufficient*, Hsch. (-χής cod.).

**κατ-αρκτικός**, ή, όν, *forming the beginning*, ἡ δυὰς ἑτερότητος κ. Nicom.*Ar*.2.17 ; ἡ Δημήτηρ πόλεως -κή, οἱονεὶ ἡ γῆ Lyd.*Mens*.4.63, cf. Eust.432.3.

**καταρμόζω**, Ion. for καθαρμόζω.

⊕**καταρν-έομαι**, *deny strongly, persist in denying*, φῄς, ἢ καταρνῇ μὴ δεδρακέναι τάδε ; S.*Ant*.442, cf. *PFlor*.181.5 (iii A. D.). **-ητικός**, ή, όν, *prone to deny* or *raise objections*, Sch.Ptol.*Tetr*.18 (Comp.).

⊕**κάτ-αρξις**, εως, ἡ, *beginning*. τοῦ πάθους Archig.ap.Aët.12.1.

**κατ-ᾰρόω**, *plough up*, τὴν γῆν Ar.*Av*.582 : fut. -αρόσω Jusj.ap. Poll.8.106 : 2 sg. aor. κατήροσας Hsch.

**καταρραγή**, ἡ, *collapse, falling in*, τοῦ σώματος Hp.*Mul*.1.1. 2. *rending*, καταρραγαὶ πέπλων Lyc.256.

**καταρρᾱθῡμέω**, *to be remiss* or *idle*, X.*Mem*.3.5.13, D.24.210, *PHib*.1.44.4 (iii B. C.), Porph.*Abst*.2.46, etc. :—also in Med., Ammon.*in Cat*.7.12. II. trans., *neglect*, τι *Cod.Just*.1.2.24.16 : also c. gen., Just.*Nov*.22.45.3. 2. *lose through negligence*, μηδὲν κ. X.*HG*6.2.39 :—Pass., τὰ κατερραθυμημένα πάλιν ἀναλήψεσθε will recover *ground lost through negligence*, D.4.7. 3. *make languid*. -θυμοῦντος τὴν χεῖρα τοῦ ὕπνου Philostr.*Im*.1.2 :—Pass., Philostr.Jun.*Im*.2.

**καταρραίνω**, *besprinkle*, οἴνῳ καὶ ἐλαίῳ Hp.*Art*.63 ; βίβλους ζωμῷ D.S.34.1 : without dat., Ath.10.45 a :—Pass. (pf. part. καταρεράσμένος), Apollon.ap.Gal.12.504 ; of a spotted snake, κατέρρανται στιγμαῖς Philum.*Ven*.23.1. II. *sprinkle*, ὕδωρ *Gp*.2.32.1 (Pass.) :—Pass., S.E.*P*.1.55.

⊕**καταρρᾰκόω**, *tear into shreds* : pf. part. Pass. κατερρακωμένος *in rags*, S.*Tr*.1103.

**καταρρακ-τήρ**, ῆρος, ὁ, *down-swooping*, κίρκος Lyc.169, cf. 539. ⊕**-της**, ου (from καταρράσσω), or **κατ-ᾰράκτης** (from καταράσσω, cf. Eust.1053.5) ; ὦ κατάρακται *Epigr.Gr*.979.7 (Philae). I. as Adj., *down-rushing*, ὄμβρος Str.14.1.21. 2. *sheer, abrupt*, τὸν καταρράκτην ὀδὸν S.*OC*1590 (cf. Sch. ; καταφράκτην Suid. s. v. ὀδός). II. as Subst., *waterfall, cataract*, esp. of the Nile, D.S.1.32, 17.97, Str.17.1.2 and 49, *Epigr.Gr*. l. c. :—Ion. **Καταρρήκτης**, name of a river in Phrygia, Hdt.7.26. 2. *portcullis*, Plu.*Ant*.76, *Arat*.26, D.H.8.67. 3. *trap-door*, οἱ κ. τοῦ οὐρανοῦ ἠνεῴχθησαν Lxx *Ge*.7.11, cf. 4*Ki*.7.2. 4.

*movable bridge*, for boarding ships, App.*BC*5.82; for attacking elephants, D.H.20.1. 5. *sluice*, Hld.9.8. 6. a sea-bird, prob. so called from *swooping down* upon its prey, Ar.*Av.*887, Arist.*HA*509ᵃ4, 615ᵃ28, Juba 68a, Dionys.*Av.*2.2, 3.22; *cormorant*, Hebr. *shālākh*, Lxx *De.*14.16(17), al.; of an eagle, S.*Fr.*377; of the Harpies, ib. 714. **-τικῶς**, Adv. *rushing down, swooping*, Eust.688.52.

**καταρραντέον**, *one must besprinkle*, Gp.6.10.

**καταρραντίζω**, = καταρραίνω, Philum.*Ven.*14.2 (Pass.).

**καταρρᾰπιστέον**, *one must strike*, Eust.512.20.

**καταρραπτέον**, *one must stitch up*, Antyll.(?)ap.Orib.45.3.8.

**καταρραπτίτης** [ῑ] (sc. ἀγών), ου, ὁ, contest at Rhodes, Gorgon 2.

**καταρράπτω**, *stitch on* or *over*, θύρη κατερραμμένη ῥιπὶ καλάμων a frame *lashed to* a crate, Hdt.2.96. II. *stitch tight*, τι ἔς τι Hp.*Acut.*21; *sew up*, Thphr.*HP*9.5.3; λίθον εἰς τὴν ζώνην κ. Plu.*Ant.*81; in Surgery, Gal.14.783:—Pass., Aen.Tact.31.4; καταρρᾰφῆναι ἐν μηρῷ Agatharch.7; τοῖς δέρμασι Sor.1.68. 2. metaph., *devise, compass*, Πενθεῖ καταρράψας μόρον A.*Eu.*26.

**καταρράσσω**, Att. -ττω, v.l. for καταράσσω (q.v.) Ph.2.98, etc.; ἐκτραχηλίζειν καὶ καταρράττειν Id.1.676; ἐπάρας κατέρραξάς με Lxx *Ps.*101(102).10; cf. καταρρήσσω (B). II. = καταρρήγνυμι II.4, Ael. *NA*3.18 (s.v.l.).

**καταρρᾳστωνεύω**, strengthd. for ῥᾳστωνεύω, Sch.Luc.*Par.*41 (Pass.).

**καταρρᾰφή**, ἡ, *stitching*, of an operation on the eyelid, Leonid.ap. Aët.7.72. II. *hem*, Lyd.*Mag.*2.13.

**κατάρρᾰφος**, ον, *sewn together, patched*, Luc.*Ep.Sat.*28.

**καταρρᾰχίζω**, strengthd. for ῥαχίζω, Anon. in Rh.3.577 W.

**καταρρέζω**, Ep. impf. καταρρέζεσκε Opp.*H.*5.481:—*pat, stroke, caress*, χειρί τέ μιν κατέρεξεν (Ep. for κατέρρ-) Il.1.361, al., cf. A.R.4.687: abs., καρρέζουσα (Ep. for καταρρ-) Il.5.424, cf. Call.*Dian.*29.

**κατάρρειθρον**, = *endoriguum*, Gloss.

**καταρρεμβεύω**, *lead astray*, Lxx *Nu.*32.13 codd. AF.

❋ **καταρρεπής**, ές, = ἑτερορρεπής, Hsch.

**καταρρέπω**, *sink down* or *to one side, hang down*, Hp.*Art.*43; opp. ἰσορροπέω, Plb.6.10.7: metaph., *incline, fall back upon*, ἐπὶ τὸν μοναχὸν τρόπον Epicur.*Ep.*2 p.41 U.; ἐπὶ τὴν αὐτὴν γνώμην *OGI*315.51 (Pessinus, ii B.C.). II. trans., *cause to incline, make to fall*, τύχη γὰρ ὀρθοῖ καὶ τύχη καταρρέπει τὸν εὐτυχοῦντα τόν τε δυστυχοῦντ' ἀεί S.*Ant.*1158.

❋ **καταρρέω**, pf. -ερρύηκα: aor. -ερρύην (v. infr.):—*flow down*, αἷμα καταρρέον ἐξ ὠτειλῆς Il.4.149, 5.870; κατὰ δὲ νότιος ῥέεν ἱδρὼς ὤμων καὶ κεφαλῆς 11.811; κατὰ δ' αἷμα.. ἔρρεε χειρός 13.539; ποταμοὶ κατ' ὄρεσφι ῥ. 4.452; καταρρέον φλέγμα ἐκ τῆς κεφαλῆς Hdt.4.187; of rivers, παρὰ τὴν Ἄλτιν κ. X.*HG*7.4.29; τὸ καταρρέον ὕδωρ D.55.10. 2. of men, *stream, rush down*, ἀθρόοι καταρρέοντες Ar.*Ach.*26; οἱ δὲ ἐμπαλασσόμενοι κατέρρεον, i.e. into the river, Th.7.84; μὴ σφαλεὶς καταρρυῇς Ar.*Pax*146, cf. 71; *sink down*, κ. ἀπὸ τῆς κλίνης ἐπὶ τοὺς πόδας Hp.*Prog.*3; εἰς τοὺς ὁμαλοὺς τόπους Plb.8.14.6; διὰ τοῦ τέγους κ. Luc.*Tim.*41: c. acc., τὴν ἀτραπὸν κατερρύην Ar.*Fr.*47. 3. of fruit, leaves, etc., *fall, drop off*, X.*Cyr.*1.5.10, Thphr.*CP*4.13.3, etc. 4. *fall in ruins*, τὰ τοιαῦτα.. περὶ αὐτὰ καταρρεῖ D.2.10: metaph., κατερρύη τὸ τῆς πόλεως ἀνδρεῖον Arist.*Fr.*557; σιγᾷ κατερρύη μέλος dub. in Pi. *Fr.*177; of a crater, *fall in*, Plb.34.11.12; of a roof, Paus.1.44.3, etc.; νεκροῦ κατερρυηκότος τὰς σάρκας *having collapsed*, Id.10.2.6; καταλείβεσθαί νιν καὶ κ. ὥσπερ τοὺς κολοσσούς *Abh. Berl. Akad.*1925(5).21 (Cyrene). 5. κ. ἔς τινα *come to, fall to the lot of*, Theoc.1.5, Bion 1.55. 6. *burrow*, εἰς τὴν γῆν Arist.*HA*556ᵇ5. 7. metaph., *fall into*, ἐπὶ τὸν μῦθον Epicur.*Ep.*2 p.36 U. II. *run down, drip with*, φόνῳ E.*Tr.*16:—and in Pass., αἵματι, ἱδρῶτι καταρρεῖσθαι, Plu.*Galb.*27, Luc.*Nigr.*35.

**κατα-ρρήγνῡμι** and -ύω, fut. -ρήξω E.*HF*864: late pf. κατέρρηχα *Arch.Pap.*2.125ᵇ10 (ii A.D.):—*break down*, τὴν γέφυραν Hdt.4.201; μέλαθρα E. l.c. 2. *tear in pieces, rend*, κατερρήγνυε.. τὰ ἱμάτια D.21.63; τὸ διάδημα D.S.19.34; τὴν ἐσθῆτα Luc.*Pisc.*36:—Med., κατερρήξαντο τοὺς κιθῶνας they *rent their* coats, Hdt.8.99, cf. X.*Cyr.*3.1.13, etc. 3. metaph., τροπὰς καταρρήγνυσι [ἡ ἀναρχία] *breaks up* armies *and turns them to* flight, S.*Ant.*675. 4. κ. τινῶν γέλωτας *make* them *burst out* laughing, Ath.4.130c; cf. II. 2. II. Pass., esp. in aor. κατερράγην [ᾰ], with pf. Act. κατέρρωγα:—*to be broken down*, κρημνοὶ καταρρηγνύμενοι Hdt.7.23; καταρρήγνυσθαι ἐπὶ γῆν *to be thrown down and broken*, Id.3.111; τὸ οἴκημα κατερράγη Th.4.115; ἄκρας κατερρωγυίας εἰς τὴν θάλασσαν Str.5.2.6. 2. *fall, rush down*, of storms, waterfalls, etc., Hp.*Aër.*8; *break* or *burst out*, χειμὼν κατερράγη Hdt.1.87; ὄμβροι καταρραγέντες Arist.*Mu.*400ᵃ26; of tears, ἐξ ὀμμάτων πηγαὶ κατερρώγασι E.*Alc.*1068: c. gen., τοῦ ῥεύματος -ρηγνυμένου τῶν ὀρῶν Philostr.*VA*6.23 (also intr. in Act., of a river, -ρηγνὺς ἐς τὴν θάλατταν 3.52); of wind, Plu.*Fab.*16: metaph., ὁ πόλεμος κατερράγη Ar.*Eq.*644, cf. *Ach.*528; γέλως Ph.2.598; κρότος Plb.18.46.9 (but κατερρήγνυτο πᾶς ὁ τόπος ὑπὸ τοῦ κρότου 15.32.9); βροντή Luc.*VH*2.35. 3. *to be broken in pieces*, Αἴγυπτος μελάγγαιός τε καὶ καταρρηγνυμένη *with comminuted, crumbling soil*, Hdt.2.12; γῆ κατερρωγυῖα Arist.*HA*556ᵃ5; *to be ruinous*, ὅσα κατέρρωγεν τοῦ τείχους *IG*2².463.75. 4. Medic., *have a violent discharge, suffer from diarrhoea*, καταρρήγνυται ἡ κοιλίη Hp.*VM*10, cf. καταρράσσω II; of persons, κατερρήγνυντο τὰς γαστέρας App.*Hisp.*54; ἢν μὴ φῦσαι -ραγέωσιν Hp.*Aph.*4.73. b. of menstruation, τοῖς θήλεσιν.. τὰ καταμήνια κ. Arist.*HA*581ᵇ1. 5. of tumours, *break, burst*, Hp.*Coac.*613, *Epid.*6.8.18, al. 6. of parts of the body, *fall in, collapse*, οἵ τε μαζοὶ καὶ τὰ ἄλλα μέλεα κ. Id.*Nat.Puer.*30, cf. *Mul.*1.1; κατερρωγότα τὰ στέρνα [ἔχων] *flat*-chested, Jul.*Or.*6.198a; of the lips or tongue, *to be fissured*, Antyll.ap.Orib.10.27.13, Aët.5.118. **-ρρηκτικός**, ή, όν, Medic., *promoting discharge*, φυσέων Hp.*Acut.*23 (Comp.); οὔρων Aret.*CA*1.2: abs., *purgative*, Hp.*Acut.*51. **-ρρηξις**, εως, ἡ, Medic., κ. κοιλίης *violent diarrhoea*, Id.*Coac.*235: abs., Id.*Epid.*4.26. 2. *rupture* of membranes, Id.*Nat.Puer.*30.

**κατάρρησις**, εως, ἡ, *accusation*, Jul.*Or.*2.85d, *PLond.*5.1680.9 (vi A.D.), Hsch.; *condemnation*, Suid.

**καταρρήσσω** (A), Att. -ρρήττω, = καταρρήγνυμι, in Med., τὰς ἐσθῆτας D.S.1.72.

**καταρρήσσω** (B), Ion. for καταρράσσω, Hsch.

**καταρρητορεύω**, *overcome by rhetoric*:—Pass., *to be so overcome*, Hyp.*Dem.Fr.*7, Plu.2.801f, Luc.*Anach.*19, Agath.5.7. II. = Lat. *peroro*, Gloss.

**καταρρῑγέω**, *shudder greatly*, ἰδέσθαι A.R.3.1132.

**κατάρριζ-ος**, ον, *having roots below*, Thphr.*HP*1.6.8. **-όω**, *make rooted, plant firmly*, τὸ θνητὸν γένος Pl.*Ti.*73b; ἑαυτὸν εἰς τὴν πολιτείαν Plu.2.805f; λᾶα *AP*9.708 (Phil.):—Pass., *take root*, Pl.*Ti.*76c, 77c, etc.; σύριγγος -ερριζωμένης *planted, terminated*, Antyll.ap.Orib. 44.22.10.

**καταρρικνόομαι**, *to be shrivelled*, in pf. part. Pass., S.*Ichn.*295; also glossed by συνεστραμμένον, καμπύλον γενόμενον, Suid.

**κατάρρῑν**, ῑνος, ὁ, ἡ, *hook-nosed*, *PPetr.*1 p.51 (iii B.C.).

**καταρρῑνάω** or -έω, (ῥίνη) *file down, make thin*, ἰσχναίνων καὶ καταρινῶν τὰ συγκρίματα Antyll.ap.Stob.4.37.16: metaph., κατερρινημένον τι λέγειν *polished, elegant*, Ar.*Ra.*901; of men, βραχίον' εὖ κατερρινημένους, i.e. *having had all superfluous flesh worked off*, A.*Supp.*747 (κατερρινωμένους *covered with shields*, Wellauer; cf. **κατερρινωμένον**· καταπεπυκασμένον, καταδεδερματωμένον, Hsch.).

**καταρρῑπισμός**, ὁ, *treatment by a blast of air*, Sor.2.41.

**καταρριπτ-άζω**, in Pass., *to be blown away, scattered*, Hsch. **-ω** (later -ριπτέω Man.4.288:—Pass., καταρειπτούμενα *IG*12(3).325.41 (Thera, ii A.D.), also pf. part. κατηρειμμένος ib.326.20), *throw down, overthrow*, εἴ τε δημόθρουν ἀναρχία βουλὴν καταρρίψειεν A.*Ag.*884; τὰ βασίλεια Plu.*Luc.*34, cf. Luc.*Salt.*9; κ. τοὺς πολεμίους, opp. ἐπαίρω, Id.*Hist.Conscr.*7. 2. *bring into disrepute*, μάθησιν Vett.Val. 238.31; ἑαυτούς Id.2.2. 3. *despise*, δόξαν, ἔπαινον, D.S.13.15, 22.

**καταρροή**, ἡ, *flowing down, defluxion*, Aesop.145 Chambry.

**κατάρροια**, ἡ, = foreg., Aq.*Ps.*77(78).44. II. = κατάρροος II, Arr.*Epict.*1.26.16, Plu.2.128a, prob. in Cass.Fel.34.

**καταρροιβδέω**, *swallow up*, Hsch. (-ρυβδήσας cod., fort. recte, v. ἀναρροιβδέω).

**καταρροιζέω**, *rush hurtling against*, τινος Nonn.*D.*1.217, 6.116.

**καταρρο-ῑζομαι**, *have a catarrh*, Dsc.1.40 (as v.l.), Gal.6.548. **-ϊκός**, ή, όν, *of a catarrh, catarrhal*, Hp.*Aph.*5.24; κ. νοσήματα Pl.*Ti.*85b. II. *subject to catarrh*, Arist.*Pr.*967ᵇ20. **-ϊστικός**, ή, όν, = foreg. II, cj. ib.929ᵇ27 (-ιτικοί, -ητικοί codd.). **-ος**, ον, contr. **-ρους**, ουν, *down-flowing*, Νεῖλος Philostr.*VA*6.23. 2. *full of streams*, νῆσος Id.*Im.*2.17. II. Subst., *running from the head, catarrh*, Hp.*Aph.*3.12 (pl.), Pl.*R.*405d (pl.), *Cra.*440c, etc.: distd. from κόρυζα etc. by Gal.7.263: metaph., Pl.*Cra.*440d.

**καταρροπ-ή** (v.l. -ροπίη), ἡ, *weight of a hanging body*, opp. ἀναρροπίη, Hp.*Art.*43. **-ος**, ον, *inclining downwards*, κ. ποιεῖν τι ib. 69; ἐπὶ τὸ κ. ῥέπειν ibid.; *pendent*, φύματα Id.*Epid.*6.1.10, cf. Gal. 7.567, 15.330. 2. *sloping*, κλίνη Antyll.ap.Orib.9.14.6. 3. *tending to descend*, νοῦσος Hp.*Hum.*5, 7.

**καταρροφ-άνω**, *gulp* or *swallow down*, Hp.*Morb.*2.54, 59. ❋ **-έω**, = foreg., Id.*Loc.Hom.*17, X.*Cyr.*1.3.9, Arist.*Pr.*876ᵃ27, Herm.Iamb. 4; τινος some of.., Orib.8.6.16:—Pass., Ruf.*Sat.Gon.*18:—later **-ροφάω**, Alex.Trall.11.2, Sm.*Jb.*39.30. **-ησις**, εως, ἡ, *swallowing*, Sor.2.41, Dsc.*Eup.*2.5.

**καταρροώδης**, ες, *subject to catarrh*, Hp.*Vict.*1.32.

**καταρρυής**, ές, *slipping away*: hence, *dripping with fat*, μηροί S.*Ant.*1010.

❋ **καταρρυθμ-ίζω**, *bring into rhythm*, Hld.3.3; τὰ κατερρυθμισμένα passages *over-rhythmical*, Longin.41.2: metaph., κ. τινὰ (neut.) ἐς τὴν τοῦ δικαίου δόξαν Philostr.*VA*7.18:—Pass., γέροντα εἰς βίον ἥμερον Ath.5.179a. ❋ **-ος**, ον, *very rhythmical*, Longin.41.1. II. κατάρυθμος, prob. f. l. for κακόρρυθμος in Paul.Aeg.2.11.

**καταρρῠπ-αίνω**, fut. -ρυπᾰνῶ Isoc.12.63:—*defile, sully*, ταῖς κατηγορίαις τὰς εὐεργεσίας l.c., cf. Pl.*Lg.*919e, 937d; ἑαυτόν Arist.*Ath.*6.3, cf. Lib.*Or.*64.41; ἀκόλαστα ῥήματα τοὺς λέγοντας κ. Plu.2.456c; βραχεία κηλῖδι τοὺς πόνους κ. Chor.*Milt.*64. **-όω**, = foreg., David *Proll.*40.20: metaph., δικαστήριον Lyd.*Mag.*3.66:—Pass., *to be soiled and dirty*, of a dress, *SIG*1219.6 (Gambreum, iii B.C.). 2. κατερρυπωμένος, = *destitutus*, Gloss.

**κατάρρῠσις**, εως, ἡ, *flowing down*, of soap into the eyes, Philum. ap.Orib.45.29.60; of phlegm, Mich. *in PN*78.17. 2. *sinking down*, Gal.18(2).702.

**καταρρῠσόομαι**, Pass., *become wrinkled*, *EM*737.1.

**κατάρρῠτος**, ον, *irrigated, watered*, κῆπος E.*El.*777; νάπη χιόνι κατάρυτα Id.*Tr.*1067 (lyr.), cf. *Andr.*215; γῆ ἔνδροσός τε καὶ κ. Ael. *NA*10.37; λίμνη κ. αἵματι Lxx 2*Ma.*12.16; ὅρος κ. *channelled by streams*, *OGI*199.12 (Adule). 2. *flowing*, ὕδωρ Olymp. *in Mete.*128.32. II. *carried down by water, alluvial*, of the Delta, Hdt.2.15. III. *with a steep slope*, of a testudo, Plb.28.11.2.

**κατ-αρρωδέω**, Ion. for καταρρωδέω, *fear, dread*, τι Hdt.1.34, 80, al.; τινας Id.9.8; ὑπέρ τινος Id.7.178: abs., Id.8.75, 103; κ. μή.. Id.9.45.

**καταρρώξ**, ῶγος, ὁ, ἡ, *jagged, broken*, πέτραι S.*Ph.*937; of earth, *friable*, prob. l. in Hsch. (-ρύγεα cod.).

**κάταρσις**, εως, ἡ, (καταίρω) *landing, bringing to land*, opp. ἄπαρσις, Poll.1.102; but usu. *landing-place*, Th.4.26, Plu.*Pomp.*65, D.C. 60.11, Ael.*VH*9.16.

**κάταρσον**· κατάκλεισον, Hsch.

**καταρτ-άω**, *hang up, suspend*, Plu.*Rom.*16; τι ἔκ τινος Id.*Marc.* 8:—Pass., *to be suspended*, Arist.*Pr.*874ᵃ18; κατήρτηντο βότρυσιν *were hung thick with* grapes, Luc.*Am.*12. II. *fasten, adjust*, χρῆμα κατηρτημένον a *well-adjusted* or *convenient* thing, Hdt.3.80; κατήρτητο *became normal, recovered sense*, Hp.*Epid.*1.26.η'; οὐδὲν -ημένον λέγειν to talk no *connected sense*, Id.*Acut.*(*Sp.*)16:—later in Act., τῇ θεῷ κατάρτησον σαυτήν Herod.1.62. -εία or -ία, ἡ, = ἐξαρτία, *PSI*9. 1030.6 (ii A.D.). *POxy.*1208.14 (iii A.D.); written **καταρθία** and -εία *PLond.*3.1164(*h*)17,25 (iii A.D.), *PSI*9.1072.10 (iii A.D.). II. v.l. for -άρτιος, Artem.2.53. ⊛-ίζω, *adjust, put in order, restore*, πάντα ἐς τὠυτό Hdt.5.106; Μίλητος νοσήσασα στάσι, μέχρι οὗ μιν Πάριοι κατήρτισαν ib.28, cf. 30; τὸν δῆμον Plu.*Marc.*10; ἵνα καταρτισθῇ [ἡ πόλις] D.H.3.10; κ. δίκτυα *mend*, *Ev.Matt.*4.21; *set* a dislocated limb, in Pass., Apollon.Cit.2, Heliod.ap.Orib.49.1.3 (Act. and Pass.); but κ. τὴν ὀσφὺν καὶ τοὺς ὤμους *form* them by exercise, Arr.*Epict.*3.20.10: metaph., *restore to a right mind*, *Ep.Gal.* 6.1; κ. τινὰ εἰς τὸ συμφέρον Plu.*Cat.Mi.*65; *reconcile*, φίλους διαφερομένους Eus.Mynd.1; *make good*, τὰ ὑστερήματα τῆς πίστεως 1*Ep. Thess.*3.10:—Med., ἠσθένησε, σὺ δὲ κατηρτίσω αὐτήν Lxx *Ps.*67(68). 10. II. *furnish, equip*, τετρήρη πληρώματι Plb.1.47.6, al., cf. *PTeb.*6.7 (ii B.C., Pass.), D.S.13.70, etc.:—Pass., πλοῖα ταῖς εἰρεσίαις κατηρτισμένα Plb.5.2.11; κατηρτισμένος abs., *in battle array*, Hdt. 9.66; *instructed*, *Ev.Luc.*6.40; *prepare, make ready*, σφενδόνην Ph.*Bel.*78.24:—Med., Lxx *Ex.*15.17, al.: σῶμα κατηρτίσω μοι *Ep. Hebr.*10.5; ὁ τὸν κόσμον καταρτισάμενος *PMag.Par.*1.1147: c. inf., κατηρτίσατο δίδοσθαι *OGI*177.10 (Egypt, i B.C.):—so in Pass., ib.179. 8 (ibid., i B.C.): abs. in imper., καταρτίζεσθε 2*Ep.Cor.*13.11. 2. *compound, prepare* dishes, medicines, etc., Dsc.*Alex.Praef.* codd. (v. καταρτύω):—Med., Nic.*Th.*954. -ιον, τό, *mast*, *EM*478. 23:—also ⊛-ιος, ἡ, but distd. from ἱστός, Artem.2.12,53, *EM* l.c., *Gloss.* 2. *part of the loom*, Artem.3.36. -ισις, εως, ἡ, *restoration*, 2*Ep.Cor.*13.9. II. *training, discipline*, Plu.*Alex.*7. III. = καταρτισμός II, Paul.Aeg.6.99. -ισμα, ατος, τό, *finished product*, *Gloss.* (pl.). ⊛-ισμός, ὁ, *restoration, reconciliation*, Sm.*Is.*38.12. II. *setting* of a limb, Heliod.ap.Orib.49.1.1 (pl.), Sor.1.73 (pl.). III. *furnishing, preparation*, αὐλῆς *PTeb.*33.12 (ii B.C.); ἱματίου *PRyl.* 127.28 (i A.D.). IV. *training, discipline*, τῶν ἁγίων *Ep.Eph.*4. 12. -ιστήρ, ῆρος, ὁ, *one who restores order, mediator*, Hdt.4.161, 5.28, Them.*Or.*4.61c. ⊛-ύσις, εως, ἡ, *training, discipline*, παιδεία καὶ κ. Plu.*Them.*2; ψυχῶν Iamb.*VP*16.68, cf. 20.95. 2. = *confectio*, *Gloss.* -ύω, *prepare, dress*, of food, Luc.*Hist.Conscr.*44; τὴν ξεινίην Hp.*Ep.*12:—Pass., τὰ -τυμένα τῶν ἐδεσμάτων restored in Dsc. *Alex.Praef.* fr. Paul.Aeg.5.28. 2. *train, discipline*, τὴν φύσιν Plu. 2.38d: c. inf., καρτύσων μολεῖν *to procure* his coming, S.*OC*71:—Pass., καταρτύεται νόος ἀνδρός Sol.27.11; σμικρῷ χαλινῷ δ' οἶδα.. ἵππους καταρτυθέντας S.*Ant.*478; παῖς ἔχει πηγὴν τοῦ φρονεῖν μήπω κατηρτυμένην Pl.*Lg.*808d; μανθανόμενα καὶ καταρτυόμενα Id.*Men.* 88b; τὸ πρεσβύτερον καὶ κατηρτ. Junc.ap.Stob.4.50.9. 3. *equip*, λέμβος.. ἐρέταις κατηρτυμένος Alciphr.1.8. II. intr. in pf. part., κατηρτυκώς *thoroughly furnished, full-grown*, used of horses which have lost their foal's-teeth, Hsch., cf. E.*Fr.*41, *AB*105 (so in pres. οἱ καταρτύοντες τῶν ἵππων Philostr.*VA*7.23); κάμηλος τῷ σώματι κατηρτυκώς *BGU*13.5 (iii A.D.); also of men, τὸ κατηρτυκεναι Philostr.*VA* 5.33: metaph., κατηρτυκὼς.. ἱκέτης προσῆλθες a *perfected* suppliant, one *who has done all that is required*, or one *that is broken in* like a horse *tamed*, A.*Eu.*473: c. gen., ἀμβλὺς εἰμὶ καὶ κατηρτυκὼς κακῶν *tamed, broken in spirit* by them, E.*Fr.*821.5. [ῡ, exc. in Sol. l. c.]

**καταρυβδήσας**, v. καταρροιβδέω. **κατάρυτος**, ον, = κατάρρυτος (q.v.).

**κατ-αρχαιρεσιάζω**, *beat in an election*, esp. by unfair means, τινα Plu.*CG*11:—metaph. in Pass., *to be corrupted as by office*, Longin.44.9.

**καταρχ-ή**, ἡ, *beginning*, πράγματος *BGU*1209.11 (i B.C.), cf. Callicr. ap.Stob.4.28.16, Plb.2.12.8; κ. διαφορᾶς Id.22.4.14, al.; ἀνέμου *Mim. Oxy.*413.213. II. Astrol., *forecast of an undertaking, voyage*, etc., Serapio in *Cat.Cod.Astr.*1.99, Vett.Val.187.15 (pl.); περὶ καταρχῶν, title of poems by Maximus and Heph. Astr. III. *part of victim first offered*, *IG*2².1359. IV. *primacy, sovereignty*, τοῦ ἀθρόου Epicur.*Fr.*314; *starting-point, basis*, Chrysipp.*Stoic.*2.246; τὰς Χάριτας [εἶναι] τὰς ἡμετέρας κ. Phld.*Piet.*14. -ης, voc. -άρχα, ὁ, *founder, creator*, γῆς *PMag.Par.*1.713. -ικός, ή, όν, *pertaining to* καταρχαί II, *Cat.Cod.Astr.*2.41. ⊛-ω, *make beginning of* a thing, c. gen., τίνες κατῆρξαν.. μάχης; A.*Pers.*351; ὁδοῦ κατάρχειν *lead* the way, S.*OC*1019; δεινοῦ λόγου Id.*Tr.*1135; λόγων χρησίμων Ar.*Lys.*638, cf. Pl.*Prt.*351e, etc.; τραυμάτων Ascl.*Tact.*7.1; τὸ κατάρχον αἰσθήσεως, τῆς κινήσεως, the *source* of perception, of motion, Gal. 5.588: rarely c. acc., *begin* a thing, θαυμαστόν τινα λόγον Pl.*Euthd.* 283b: c. part., *begin* doing, X.*Cyr.*1.4.4, 4.5.58: abs., Pl.*Smp.*177e, Arist.*Mu.*399ᵃ15. 2. θανόντα δεσπόταν γόοις κατάρξω I *will lead* the dirge over.., E.*Andr.*1199 (lyr., with reference to the religious sense, infr. II. 2). II. Med., *begin*, like Act., c. gen., ἐχθρᾶς ἡμέρας κατάρχεται Id.*Ph.*540; τοῖς κατηργμένοις τῆς πορείας Pl.*Phdr.*256d; κ. τῆς προσβολῆς Plb.2.67.1; τοῦ λόγου Plu.2.151e: c. acc., κ. νόμον, στεναγμόν, E.*Hec.*685 (s.v.l.), *Or.*960 (both lyr.): abs., κατάρχεται μέλος *is beginning*, Id.*HF*750 (lyr.), cf. 891 (lyr.); τὸ -άρξασθαι Ael. *Tact.*17. 2. in religious sense, *begin the sacrificial ceremonies*, once in Hom., Νέστωρ χέρνιβά τ' οὐλοχύτας τε κατήρχετο Nestor *began* [*the sacrifice*] *with* the washing of hands and sprinkling the barley on the victim's head, Od.3.445: abs., Hdt.4.60,103, And.1.126; κατάρχομαι μέν, σφάγια δ' ἄλλοισιν μέλει I *begin the rite*, but leave the slaughter of the victim to others, E.*IT*40; ἐπὶ τῶν θυσιῶν κριθαῖς κ. D.H.2.25: c. gen., κατάρχεσθαι τοῦ τράγου *make a beginning of* the victim, i.e. *consecrate* him *for sacrifice* by cutting off the hair of his forehead, Ar.*Av.*959; ἐπεὶ δὲ αὐτοῦ (sc. Ἡρακλέος) πρὸς τῷ βωμῷ κατάρχοντο Hdt.2.45; πῶς δ' αὖ κατάρξῃ θυμάτων; E.*Ph.*573, cf. *IT*56,1154; κατάρξασθαι τῶν ἱερῶν D.21.114: metaph., σκυτάλην λαβών μου κατήρξατο Luc.*Somn.*3, cf. Plu.*Caes.*66:—so later in Act., Hld.2.34, al. b. *sacrifice, slay*, ξίφει, φασγάνῳ κ., E.*Alc.*74, *El.*1222 (lyr.):—Pass., ᾗ (sc. τῇ θεᾷ) σὸν κατῆρκται σῶμα *hath been devoted*, Id.*Heracl.* 601. III. Act., *rule, govern*, c. gen., Alciphr.3.44 (s.v.l.). IV. κατάρξω ὑμᾶς ἐν σκορπίοις *will chastise* you.., Lxx 3*Ki.*12.24r.

**κατ-ασαμινθεύω**, *throw into a bath*, ἐσθῆτας *PMasp.*9 ii 29 (vi A.D.).

**κατάσαρκ-ος**, ον, *fleshy, plump*, Agatharch.*Fr.Hist.*7 J., Sor.2.57, Antyll.ap.Orib.7.12.8, Alciphr.*Fr.*5.3; gloss on σωμασκίας, Hdn. *Epim.*130. -ωσις, εως, ἡ, *plumpness*, Eust.1656.42.

**κατασάττω**, *stamp down*, τὴν γῆν Thphr.*CP*5.6.2: pf. part. Pass. κατασεσασμένα, glossed by κατασεσεισμένα, Hsch.

**κατα-σβέννυμι** or -ύω, Ion. aor. inf. -σβῶσαι Herod.5.39:—*put out, quench*, κατέσβεσε θεσπιδαὲς πῦρ Il.21.381, cf. 16.293 (tm.), E. *Or.*697, etc.: metaph., ἔστιν θάλασσα, τίς δέ νιν κατασβέσει; who *shall dry it up?* A.*Ag.*958, cf. *Th.*584; κ. βοήν, ἔριν, *quell* noise, strife, S.*Aj.*1149, *OC*422; ἀνομίαν Critias 25.40 D.; τὰς ἡδονὰς Pl. *Lg.*838b; τὴν δυσχέρειαν Id.*Prt.*334c; τὴν ταραχὴν X.*Cyr.*5.3.55; χολὴν Herod. l. c.; κ. τὰ τραύματα *heal* them, Luc.*DMar.*11.1. II. Pass., fut. -σβήσομαι (v. infr.), with aor. 2 and pf. Act., *go out, be quenched*, καιόμενον τὸν χρυσὸν κατασβῆναι (aor. 2) Hdt.4.5; κατασβεσθῆναι τὴν πυρήν Id.1.87; ὁ κάνθαρος (i.e. the Sun) -σβήσεται *PMag.Leid.V.*2.18: metaph., κλαυμάτων πηγαὶ.. κατεσβήκασι A.*Ag.* 888; of tumours, κατέσβη Hp.*Epid.*1.1; κατασβεννύμενος, of passion, Pl.*R.*411c; κατασβεσθεὶς ταῖς ἐλπίσιν Plu.2.168f; of the wind, Id. *Tim.*19. -σβεσις, εως, ἡ, *putting out*, D.C.54.2. -σβεστέον, *one must quench*, Plu.2.787f.

**κατά-σεισις**, εως, ἡ, *shaking*, Hp.*Art.*43; τῆς κεφαλῆς Gal.10. 1019. -σεισμός, ὁ, = foreg., Sor.1.60 (pl.), Archig.ap.Gal.12. 657, Aët.6.87. -σειστέον, *one must shake*, Sor.1.65. -σείω, fut. -σείσω Hp.*Art.*43: pf. -σέσεικα Philem.84:—*shake down, throw down*, οἰκοδομήματος ἐπὶ μέγα Th.2.76; τεῖχος, τοῦ τείχους ἐπὶ μέγα, Arr.*An.*1.19.2, 2.23.1; σεισμὸς κ. τὴν πόλιν Ael.*VH*6.7:—Pass., *fall down*, Ph.2.512; of a lion's mane, αὐχένος ἐκ λασίοιο χαίτη -εσείετο Pancrat.*Oxy.*1085.21: metaph., κ. ἀκροατοῦ ὦτα Philostr.*VS*2.29; νόμους Procop.*Arc.*27.33; κατέσεισεν ἅπαντα καὶ κατεβρόντησε Eun. *Hist.*p.256 D.; ἕως κατέσεισε until he *laid* him *on the floor* (with drinking), Men.8, cf. Philem. l. c., Ath.10.431c. 2. *impel, drive headlong*, νεανίσκον εἰς τὸν μανιώδη καὶ σφαλερὸν τῆς βασιλείας ἔρωτα Eun.*Hist.*p.235 D., cf. p.267 D.:—Pass., πρὸς τὸ λέγειν κ. ib. p.223 D. 3. in Surgery, *treat by shaking*, Hp.*Art.*42:—Pass., ib. 43. 4. κατασείσας τὴν χεῖρα *with a motion of* the hand, *Act.Ap.* 19.33; κ. ἱκετηρίας J.*BJ*2.21.8; κ. τὰ ἱμάτια, by way of signal, Plu. *Pomp.*73: more freq. c. dat., κ. τῇ χειρί *beckon* with the hand, Plb. 1.78.3, Hld.10.7; κ. τῇ χειρὶ σιγᾶν *Act.Ap.*12.17; κ. τῷ λύχνῳ ἅμα λέγων τὸν λόγον *PMag.Lond.*46.453; κ. ὀθόναις Hld.9.6: abs., κ. τινί *beckon* to another, as a sign for him to be silent, X.*Cyr.*5.4.4; κ. τισὶν ἐπεξιέναι J.*AJ*17.10.2; but also, *shake the head* in token of contempt, Phld.*Vit.*p.37 J.

⊛**κατ-ασελγαίνω**, *to be libidinous*, Suid. s.v. καταπυγῶν.

**κατασεύομαι**, Pass., *rush down along*, c. acc., κῦμα κατέσσυτο καλὰ ῥέεθρα Il.21.382: abs., *rush down*, κατεσσύμενος Q.S.4.270. 2. *rush against*, κατεσσεύεσθε λεόντων Nonn.*D.*5.353.

**κατασήθω**, aor. -έσησα, *strain through a sieve*, Hp.*Mul.*2.133:—Pass., aor. part. -σησθεῖσα *Gp.*12.17.1. 2. *strew*, ναόν [τέφρᾳ] Thd.*Bel.*14.

⊛**κατασημ-αίνομαι**, Med., *cause to be sealed up*, ὄφεις.. ἐν κίστῃ που κατασήμηναι Ar.*Fr.*28; [ἐχίνους] Arist.*Ath.*53.2; χρυσίον Pl.*Men.* 89b; ὑδρίαν *IG*2².204.39:—Pass., ib.41; τὰς ἐπισκήψεις φυλάττειν -σεσημασμένας ὑπ' ἀμφοῖν Pl.*Lg.*937b. II. *cause to be noted down*, ib.756c:—Pass., τὰ κατασημανθέντα ὀνόματα ib.756e, cf. Arist.*Ath.* 49.2. -αντικός, ή, όν, *marking distinctly*, Longin.32.5. -ειόομαι, Pass., = κατασημαίνομαι I. *Klio* 17.187 (Delph., i A.D.), cf. Hsch.

⊛**κατασήπω**, *cause* or *allow to rot*, X.*Cyr.*8.2.21:—Pass., *rot away*, ib.8.2.22; μή.. κατὰ χρόα πάντα σαπῇ Il.19.27; ἕως ἂν κατασαπῇ Pl. *Phd.*86d; -σαπέντων τῶν καρπῶν *CPHerm.*6.16 (iii A.D.): so in pf. -σέσηπα Ar.*Pl.*1035, Philetaer.9. 2. metaph., *cause* or *allow to linger*, τοὺς ἀνθρώπους ἐν τοῖς πάθεσι Gal.10.264:—Pass., *pine away*, -σήπεσθαι ἐπὶ τῆς κλίνης ib.263; πρὸς ταῖς ἀλλοτρίαις θύραις -σαπῆναι Arr.*Epict.*4.10.20.

**κατ-ασθενέω**, *to be* or *grow weak*, οἱ κατησθενηκότες Aët.9.42, cf. Sor.2.11, Erot. s.v. κατηπέδανον. 2. later causal, *weaken*, κνησμονάς *App.Anth.*3.158.

**κατ-ασθμαίνω**, *pant, struggle against*, c. gen., ἵππος χαλινῶν ὣς κατασθμαίνων μένει A.*Th.*393.

**κατασῑγ-άζω**, *put to silence*, Arist.*HA*614ᵃ20, Ael.*VH*14.9; τὸν δῆμον Hdn.1.9.3; σάλπιγγα Ael.*NA*16.23:—Pass., Posidon.36 J.; τὰ Πινδάρου ἤδη κατασεσιγασμένα *not now perused*, Ath.1.3a (cf. Eup.

366). **-αίνω**, *silence, calm*, Hsch. s. v. πραΰνει. **-αστικός**, ή, όν, *of* or *for silencing*, Eust.197.48. **-άω**, *remain silent*, Pl.*Phd.* 107a. II. = κατασιγάζω, *CPHerm.*25 ii 2, Luc.*JTr.*13 (v. l. -σιώπησον).

**κατασῐδηρόω**, *plate with iron*, κριοὶ κατασεσιδηρωμένοι D.S.13.54, cf. Bito 53.7, Str.15.3.11.

**κατασῐκελίζω** τυρόν, *Sicilize* the cheese (in allusion to the *peculations* of Laches in Sicily), Ar.*V.*911, cf. Sch. ad loc.

**κατασιλλαίνω**, *mock at*, Hp.*Praec.*8.

**κατάσῐμος**, ον, = σιμός, *Gloss.*

**κατασίνομαι** [ῑ], *injure, damage*, Hsch.: aor. 1 part., κατασινάμενος τὰ κάλλιστα τῆς χώρας prob. l. in Malch.p.407 D.

**κατασῑτέομαι**, *eat up, feed on*, c. acc., Hdt.1.216, 3.38, Str.15.2.14, D.S.3.36.

**κατασῐωπ-άω**, *keep silence*, Isoc.8.38, Arist.*Rh.*1413$^b$7, J.*Ap.*2.33, etc.; εἰδότες κ. Arist.*Ath.*14.2; πρός τι D.41.23. 2. c. acc. rei, *keep silent, pass over*, τὸ γεγονὸς D.S.32.10:—Pass., Isoc.4.27. 3. *condemn by silence*, πόλιν D.Chr.32.98. II. causal, *make silent, silence*, τὴν γυναῖκα X.*HG*5.4.7, cf. Luc.*Bis Acc.*17, *Anach.*19, *Dom.* 16:—Med., *cause silence*, X.*HG*2.4.20; κατασιωπήσασθαι διὰ τοῦ σαλπιγκτοῦ τὸν θόρυβον Plb.18.46.9. **-ητέον**, *one must keep silence*, Isoc.12.96.

**κατασκαίρω**, *bound up and down*, Opp.*H.*4.322.

**κατασκάπτω**, pf. -έσκᾰφα Isoc.14.35:—*dig down*, ἐπὶ θάτερα τῆς ἀμπέλου Thphr.*HP*4.13.5; but usu., II. *destroy utterly, raze to the ground*, τὸ ἄστυ Hdt.7.156; Τροίαν κ. βίᾳ S.*Ph.*998, cf. A.*Ag.* 525; πάτραν S.*OC*1421; δόμους E.*HF*566; πόλιν *SIG*344.7 (Teos, iv B.C.), cf. D.18.71; τὸ τέγος Ar.*Nu.*1488; τὰ τείχη ἐς ἔδαφος Th. 4.109, cf. Lys.12.40, Isoc. l. c., Arist.*Ath.*37.1; τὸν λιμένα Aeschin. 3.123; τὰ θυσιαστήρια Lxx 3*Ki.*19.10; τὴν οἰκίαν εἰς ἔδαφος Plu.*Publ.* 10, etc.:—Pass., ϝοικία κατασκαπτέσθω *Berl.Sitzb.*1927.8 (Locr., v B.C.); τὰ οἰκία οἱ κατεσκάφη Hdt.6.72; πατρῷα ἑστία κατεσκάφη E. *Hec.*22; τὰ κατεσκαμμένα ἀναστήσω Lxx *Am.*9.11.

**κατασκᾰρῑφάω**, *peck at*, Ath.11.507c.

***κατασκᾰφ-ή**, ἡ, *razing to the ground, destruction*, S.*OC*1318, Th. 5.63; τειχῶν Lys.13.8; ἀκροπόλεως *SIG*285.9 (Erythrae, iv B.C.): more freq. in pl., Ἰλίου κ. E.*Hel.*196 (lyr.); ἰὼ κ. δόμων A.*Ch.*50 (lyr.); πόλει κατασκαφὰς θέντες Id.*Th.*46; πύργων κ. E.*Ph.*1196; τειχῶν Aeschin.3.157. II. *that which is dug*, esp. *grave*, in pl., θάπτειν.. γῆς.. κατασκαφαῖς A.*Th.*1013, cf. 1042; ἐς θανόντων.. κατασκαφὰς S.*Ant.*920. **-ής**, ές, *dug down*, κ. οἴκησις the *deep-dug* dwelling, i. e. the grave, ib.891.

**κατασκάφιλος**· καταισχύνων τοὺς φίλους, Hsch. (leg. καταισχόφιλος).

**κατασκεδ-άζω**, = sq., Suid.:—Pass., Sch.E.*Hec.*916. **-άννῡμι** and **-ύω** (D.54.4 codd.), Att. fut. -σκεδῶ Antiph.25:—*scatter, pour upon* or *over*, κατάχυσμα.. κατεσκέδασαν θερμὸν τοῦτο καθ' ὑμῶν Ar.*Av.* 536, cf. *PMagd.*33.4 (iii B.C.); τὰς ἀμίδας D. l. c.: usu. c. acc. et gen., τὴν μεγίστην ἀρύταιναν ὑμῶν Antiph. l. c., etc.; ὥσπερ ἑωλοκρασίαν τινά μου τῆς πονηρίας -σκεδάσας D.18.50: κ. ὕβριν τινός *pour* abuse *upon* one, Plu.2.10c; λῆρον κ. τινός Luc.*Salt.*6; ὅλας ἁμάξας βλασφημιῶν κ. τινός Id.*Eun.*2, etc. 2. κ. φήμην *spread* a report *against* one, Pl.*Ap.*18c:—Pass., ἡ φήμη κατεσκέδασται τοῦ Μίνω Id.*Min.*320d; ὁ λόγος ἐν τῇ πόλει κατεσκέδαστο (prob. l. for -σκεύασται) Lys.10. 23; τοῦ πόνου πλείονος -ασμένου τῆς σαρκός Hp.*Medic.*7. 3. Med., *pour, sprinkle about*, X.*An.*7.3.32 (Suid., Phot.: συγκατ- codd.). 4. *overthrow, destroy*, *IG*12(9).1179.9 (Euboea).

***κατασκελετ-εύω**, *reduce to a skeleton*, ἑαυτούς Plu.2.7d; τὸ σῶμα Sch.Ar.*Ra.*153:—Pass., *to be wasted away*, '*desiccated*', μὴ περιιδεῖν τὴν φύσιν -ευθεῖσαν Isoc.15.268, cf. Ph.1.198, al., Onos.1.5 (Act.), D.L.8.41: metaph., τὰ φυσικὰ ἔργα ταῖς τεχνολογίαις -ευόμενα Longin.2.1. **-όω**, = foreg., Phot. (Pass.).

***κατασκελής**, ές, *meagre*, of style, D.H.*Isoc.*2; τὸ τῶν παρ' ἡμῖν ἐπιτεχνημάτων κ. the *meagreness* or *inadequacy* of human contrivances, Ptol.*Alm.*13.2. II. *hard, difficult*, μέθοδος Id.*Harm.*2. 13, cf. 2.2.

**κατασκέλλομαι**, Pass., *become a skeleton, wither away*, φαρμάκων χρείᾳ κατεσκέλλοντο A.*Pr.*481: mostly in pf. Act. κατέσκληκα, Thphr. *CP*6.14.11, Luc.*Gall.*29, Gal.*UP*8.7, etc.; ὑπὸ τῶν πόνων Alciphr.3. 19, cf. Luc.*Bis Acc.*34: plpf., λιμῷ κατεσκλήκει Babr.46.8; *to be hard* or *frozen*, Thphr. l. c.: metaph., -εσκληκώς *austere*, Philostr.*VS*1.18.1.

***κατασκένω**, Cret., = κατακτείνω, *GDI*4998 i 14.

**κατασκεπ-άζω**, *cover entirely*, Aen.Tact.37.3, Thphr.*HP*9.3.2, J. *AJ*8.4.1: pf. inf. Pass. κατεσκεπάσθαι Artem.2.32. 2. metaph., μοχθηρὰ ἤθη λόγοις ἐπιεικέσιν κ. Ph.2.341. **-ασμα**, ατος, τό, *covering*, Al.*Ex.*26.36. **-αστέον**, *one must cover*, Herod.Med. in *Rh.Mus.*58.85. **-αστός**, όν, *covered*, Aq.*Nu.*7.3.

**κατάσκεπος**, ον, v. κατάσκοπος II.

**κατασκέπτομαι**, later pres., = κατασκοπέω (q. v.), Just.*Nov.*22 *Praef.*: impf., Plb.3.94.7.

**κατασκέπω**, = κατασκεπάζω, *AP*5.59 (Rufin.), Muson.*Fr.*19 p.106 H.

***κατασκευ-άζω**, fut. -σκευάσω, Att. -σκευῶ *SIG*1097.9 (Athens, iv B.C.), *IPE*1².32*B*53 (Olbia, iii B.C.): Dor. aor. -εσκεύαξα Ti. Locr.94d, *Test.Epict.*1.14, also κατεσκέαξα *Africa Italiana* 1.330 (Cyrene): Boeot. aor. inf. -σκευάττη *SIG*1185.13 (Tanagra, iii B.C.): pf. -εσκεύᾰκα D.42.30: fut. Med. 3 sg. -ᾶται *SIG*1015.28 (Halic.): Dor. aor. Med. -εσκευαξάμην *Test.Epict.*1.9:—*equip, furnish fully with..*, [πᾶσι] κ. τὸ πλοῖον *with* all appliances, D.18.194:—Med., τοὺς ἵππους χαλκοῖς.. προβλήμασι κ. X.*Cyr.*6.1.51:—freq. in Pass., ἱρὸν θησαυροῖσί τε καὶ ἀναθήμασι κατεσκευασμένον Hdt.8.33, cf. 2.44; κατασκευῇ χρυσῷ τε καὶ ἀργύρῳ κατεσκ. Id.9.82; οἷς ἡ χώρα κατεσκεύασται Th.6.91. 2. without dat., *furnish, equip fully*, τὴν χώραν X.*An.*1.9.19; κ. τινὰ ἐπὶ στρατιάν Id.*Cyr.*3.3.3; [ἐλέφαντας] κ. πρὸς τὴν πολεμικὴν χρείαν *OGI*54.12 (Adule, iii B.C.):—Med., κ. τοὺς ὄνους *having got his* asses *ready*, Hdt.2.121.δ', etc.:—Pass., τῆς Ἀντάνδρου μελλούσης -σκευάζεσθαι Th.4.75, cf. 8.24; ἔργα -ασμένα *cultivated* farms, Anaxag.4; of persons, *to be under treatment*, Phld. *Lib.*p.3 O., al. 3. *construct, build*, γέφυραν Hdt.1.186 (Pass.); διδασκαλεῖον Antipho 6.11; πόλιν Pl.*R.*557d; γυμνάσια Id.*Lg.*761c; ἱερὰ θυσίας τε αὐτοῖς κ. Id.*Criti.*113c; ἐπιτείχισμ' ἐπὶ τὴν Ἀττικὴν D. 18.71: generally, *prepare, arrange, establish*, κ. δημοκρατίαν X.*HG* 2.3.36; δύναμιν τῇ πόλει And.3.39; συμπόσιον Pl.*R.*363c; ἰσότητα τῆς οὐσίας Id.*Lg.*684d, cf. Arist.*Pol.*1265$^a$39; ὀλιγαρχίαν Id.*Ath.* 37.1; ναύτας D.50.36; κ. τινὰς μελέτῃ *train* them, X.*Cyr.*8.1. 43, etc.; *turn out*, πολιτικούς Phld.*Rh.*2.264 S., al.:—Med., κατασκευάζεσθαι ναυμαχίαν *prepare* it, *make ready for* it, v.l. for παρασκ- in Th.2.85; *make for oneself*, esp. *build* a house *and furnish* it, opp. ἀνασκευάζομαι Id.1.93, 2.17; *unpack*, opp. ἀνασκ., X.*Cyr.*8.5.2; κ. ἐρημίαν αὑτῷ Pl.*Lg.*730c, etc.; κ. τράπεζαν *set up* a bank, Is.*Fr.*66; κατασκευάζομαι τέχνην μυρεψικήν I *am setting up* as a perfumer, Lys.*Fr.* 1.2; τοὺς ἐγγυτάτω τῆς ἀγορᾶς κατεσκευασμένους Id.24.20; [πρόσοδον] οὐ μικρὰν κατεσκευάσαντο *made themselves* a good [income], D.27.61, cf. And.4.11. 4. of fraudulent transactions, *fabricate, trump up*, πρόφασιν X.*Cyr.*2.4.17; τὸ ἀπόρρητον κατασκευάσαι D.2.6; λιποταξίου γραφὴν κατεσκεύασεν Id.21.103, cf. 92; χρέα ψευδῆ Id.42.30, cf. 45. 22 (Pass.); of persons, *suborn*, λογοποιούς Din.1.35; *set up*, ἤ.. ἐπιτίθενται αὐτοὶ ἢ κατασκευάζουσιν ἕτερον Arist.*Pol.*1306$^a$1; οἱ κατεσκευασμένοι τῶν Θετταλῶν men *prepared for the purpose*, D.18.151; κατεσκ. δανεισταί Id.42.28: c. inf., τὸν ἀνεψιὸν.. κατεσκεύασεν ἀμφισβητεῖν Id.55.1. 5. c. dupl. acc., *make, render*, [φρούρια] κ. ὡς ἐχυρώτατα X.*Cyr.*2.4.17; ἀριστερὰ δεξιῶν ἀσθενέστερα κ. Pl.*Lg.*795a; φοβερὸν κ. τὸ αὐτόχειρα γενέσθαι D.20.158; ἀνομοθέτητον ἑαυτῷ τὸν βίον Duris 10 J.; κ. τινὰ τοιοῦτον.. Arist.*Rh.*1380$^a$2 (also with Adv., πρὸς ἑαυτὸν κ. εὖ τὸν ἀκροατὴν *render* the audience favourably disposed towards oneself, 1419$^b$11). 6. *represent as* so and so, κ. τινὰς παροίνους, ὑβριστάς, ἀγνώμονας, D.54.14, cf. 45.82; εἰ μὴ Γοργίαν Νέστορά τινα κατασκευάζεις unless you *make out* a Gorgias *to be* Nestor, Pl.*Phdr.* 261c. 7. in argument, *maintain, prove*, τῶν ἐν Εὐβοίᾳ πραγμάτων.. ὡς ἐγὼ αἴτιός εἰμι, κατεσκεύαζε *tried to make out* that.., D.21.110; κ. ὅτι.. Arr.*Epict.*3.15.14, S.E.*P.*1.32; κ. τῷ λόγῳ *establish* a proposition by reasoning, Damian.*Opt.*5; διὰ λόγου -σκευασθήσεται Phld. *Sign.*6. 8. in Logic, *construct* a positive argument, opp. ἀναιρέω, ἀνασκευάζω (of negative arguments), Arist.*Rh.*1401$^b$3, cf. Plu.2.1036b, etc.: Philos., κ. τὴν ἀριθμῶν ἰδέαν *construct, postulate*, Arist.*EN*1096$^a$ 19, cf. *Metaph.*984$^b$25, al. 9. Geom., *construct*, Euc.5.7 (Pass.), Archim.*Sph.Cyl.*2.6 (Pass.); *solve by a construction*, πρόβλημα Papp. 54.25. 10. Rhet., *frame*, ὀνόματα D.H.*Comp.*16; *elaborate*, κατεσκεύασται τὸ δοκοῦν εἶναι ἀφελές Id.*Is.*7; λόγος κατεσκευασμένος Str. 1.2.6. 11. abs. in Med., *prepare oneself* or *make ready for* doing, ὡς πολεμήσοντες Th.2.7; ὡς οἰκήσων X.*An.*3.2.24; ὡς εἰς μάχην Paus. 5.21.14. 12. Pass., of disease, *to become established*, -σκευαζομένου τοῦ πάθους Gal.8.332. **-ᾰσία**, ἡ, *preparation* of drugs, Suid. s. v. κῦφι. ***-ασμα**, ατος, τό, *that which is prepared* or *made, work of art*, τὰ Κορίνθια κ. Hippoloch.ap.Ath.4.128d, cf. Plb.4.18.8, Aristeas 52, J.*BJ*7.5.5, Arr.*Epict.*2.19.26; surgical *apparatus*, Orib.49. 24.2; esp. *building, structure*, D.23.207, *SIG*330.39 (pl., Ilium, iv B.C.), Plb.10.27.9, D.H.3.27, D.S.1.50; οἰκητήριον κ. Cleanth.*Stoic.*1. 132; θεωρητὸν κ., of the world, Secund.*Sent.*1: in pl., *engines of war*, Plb.1.48.5; *furniture*, ἱεροῦ *SIG*330.4 (Ilium, iv B.C.). II. *arrangement, contrivance*, D.23.13; τὸ κ. τῶν συσσιτίων Arist.*Pol.*1271$^a$ 33; τὰ [τυραννικὰ] κ. ib.1319$^b$27; σοφιστοῦ Phld.*Rh.*1.183 S.; ἐκ κατασκευάσματος, Lat. *ex composito*, D.C.52.7. **-ασμάτιον**, τό, Dim. of foreg., Hero *Spir.*1.7. **-ασμός**, ὁ, *contrivance*, D.24.16; ἐκ κατασκευασμοῦ, Lat. *ex composito*, D.C.38.9, al. **-αστέος**, α, ον, *to be prepared* or *made*, X.*Ages.*1.23, Gal.14.262. II. neut., *one must prepare, make*, etc., Pl.*Lg.*964d, X.*HG*3.4.15, etc.; κ. ἔθος πρὸς τὸν ἔμετον Philum.ap.Aët.9.23. 2. *one must construct a proof* or *argument*, Aphth.*Prog.*6, Theon *Prog.*3. **-αστής**, οῦ, ὁ, *contriver*, Hsch. and Suid. s. v. μηχανορράφος. 2. *one who makes provision, commissariat officer, quartermaster*, Just.*Nov.*30.7.1. **-αστικός**, ή, όν, *fitted for providing*, τινος Arist.*VV*1250$^b$29; *fitted for bringing about*, τοῦ μὴ πλανᾶν Phld.*Rh.*1.347 S. 2. in Logic, *constructive, positive*, opp. destructive (λυτικός, ἀνασκευαστικός), Arist.*Rh.*1403$^a$25, Theon *Prog.*12, etc.: c. gen., λόγος κ. ζητήματος Corn.*Rh.*p.377 H., cf. Nicol. *Prog.*p.29 F. Adv. -κῶς, opp. ἀνασκευαστικῶς, Arist.*APr.*52$^a$31. 3. (κατασκευή VIII) *systematic*, γυμνάσια Gal.6.177. **-αστός**, ή, όν, *artificial*, opp. αὐτοφυής, τὸ κ. D.H.*Is.*11; ἡ κατασκευαστὴ δόξα, opp. ἡ σιωπωμένη ἀλήθεια, Id.1.76; εἰκὼν κ. Plu.2.210d. Adv. -τῶς *under artificial conditions*, Theon *Intr.* ad Euc.*Opt.*p.146 H. 2. *suborned*, ἄνδρες Arist.*Oec.*1348$^a$7. **-άστρια**, ἡ, fem. of κατασκευαστής, *she who prepares*, Sch.Lyc.578 (ed. Bachm.). ***-ή**, ἡ, *preparation*, ὄντων ἐν κατασκευῇ τοῦ πολέμου being engaged in *preparing for* it, Th. 8.5; *construction*, λιμένων ἢ νεωρίων Pl.*Grg.*455b; *fitting out*, πλοίων Plb.1.21.1, etc. 2. *unpacking*, X.*Cyr.*8.5.5. 3. *training*, *Stoic.* 3.89. II. *permanent* or *fixed assets*, opp. what is movable or temporary (παρασκευή), *fixtures, plant*, etc., Th.1.10; ἀνειληφότες τὰς κ. having repaired their *estates*, Id.2.16; ἡ περὶ τὸν κλῆρον κ. Pl.

*Lg.*923d; τῆς ἄλλης κ., ἐν ᾗ κατοικοῦμεν καὶ μεθ' ἧς πολιτευόμεθα καὶ δι' ἣν ζῆν δυνάμεθα the aggregate of our possessions, Isoc.4.26; αἱ κ. αἱ ἐπὶ τῶν ἀγρῶν ἢ αἱ ἐντὸς τείχους Id.7.52; but also, like παρασκευή, any *furniture* or *fittings*, τὴν Μαρδονίου κ., i.e. his *tent and its furniture*, Hdt.9.82; κ. πολυτελέσι χρησαμένων Th.6.31; φιάλας τε.. καὶ θυμιατήρια καὶ ἄλλην κ. ib.46; ἡ κ. τῆς οἰκίας D.47.54; τῇ τῶν θεῶν κ. χρῆσθαι *whatever* the gods *provided*, X.*Ages.*9.5. III. *state, condition, constitution* of a thing, θεοῦ κ. βίῳ δόντος τοιαύτην E.*Supp.*214; αἱ.. κ. τῆς ψυχῆς Pl.*R.*544e; ἡ τοῦ βίου κ. Id.*Lg.*842c; ἡ τῶν νόμων κ. ib.739a; ἐν πάσῃ κ. πολιτικῇ ib.736b; ἐν χρημάτων κ. in *the constitution* of a man's fortune, Id.*Grg.*477b; ἐν σώματος κ. ibid.; κ. τις παρὰ φύσιν, definition of νόσος, Gal.6.837. IV. *device, trick*, τέχναι καὶ κ. Aeschin.2.1, v.l. in Din.1.34; ἄνευ κατασκευῆς ᾄδειν *artlessly*, Ael.*NA*5.38. V. in Logic, *constructive reasoning*, opp. ἀνασκευή, D.H.*Lys.*24, Hermog.*Prog.*5, etc.: in pl., Cic.*Att.*1.14.4, Longin.11.2, Quint.2.4.18. VI. Rhet., *artistic treatment*, κ. ποιητική Str.1.2.6, D.H.*Comp.*1; *manipulation*, συλλαβῶν, γραμμάτων, ib.15, 16; *elaboration*, Id.*Pomp.*2, etc.; *correct style*, opp. ἰδιωτισμός, Diocl.*Stoic.*3.214; *technical resources*, πλάσμα καὶ ἡ ἄλλη κ. δημηγόρου Phld.*Rh.*1.199S. VII. Geom., *construction*, Archim.*Sph.Cyl.* 2.4, cf. Procl.*in Euc.*p.203F.: κ. ὀργανική *solution by* mechanical *construction*, Papp.174.17. VIII. *system of gymnastic exercise*, as t.t., Gal.6.169. -ος, ον, *furnished*, οἶκος dub. l. in *IG*12(3).185 (Astypalaea). ※-όω, Dor. = κατασκευάζω, aor. κατεσσκέωσα *IG* 14.241 (Neëtum): pf. κατεσκεύωκα *Test.Epict.*4.13:—Med., εἴ τι κα -σκευώσωνται *GDI*1874.26 (Delph.).

**κατάσκεψις**, εως, ἡ, *careful examination*, χωρίων Str.6.1.12.

**κατ-ασκέω**, *practise*: pf. part. Pass. κατησκημένος *regular, ascetic*, δίαιτα Plu.*Ages.*33.

**κατασκην-άω**, = sq., aor. -εσκήνησα X.*An.*3.4.32, *HG*4.5.2, etc.: —Med., κατασκηνᾶσθαι Pl.*R.*614e. -όω, *take up one's quarters, encamp*, εἰς.. X.*Cyr.*4.5.39, *Hell.Oxy.*16.2, etc.; ἐν.. Lxx 1*Ch.*23.25; ἔνθα κατεσκηνώκατε X.*Cyr.*6.2.2: generally, *rest*, ἐπ' ἐλπίδι Lxx *Ps.*15(16).9; *settle*, of birds, ἐν κλάδοις *Ev.Matt.*13.32: metaph., οὐ ψυχῇ ἐν μόνῳ ἀνθρώπῳ κ. Porph.*Abst.*4.9. ※-ωμα, ατος, τό, *covering, veil*, A.*Ch.*985. 2. gloss on αὔλιον, Sch.Opp.*H.*2.524, cf. 3.5. -ωσις, εως, ἡ, *encamping, taking up one's quarters*, Lxx 1*Ch.*28.2, al.; καλεῖν τινα πρὸς κατασκήνωσιν Plb.11.26.5; διδόναι εἰς κ. to give them as *quarters*, *OGI*229.57 (Smyrna, iii B.C.); ἐν κ. in *camp*, Onos.11.6: pl. -σκηνώσεις βασιλέων *Gp.*11.2.9. 2. of birds, *resting-place, nest*, *Ev.Matt.*8.20 (pl.).

**κατα-σκήπτω**, fut. -ψω E.*Hipp.*1418:—*rush down* or *fall upon*, Arist.*Mu.*395ᵃ25, D.S.16.80, etc.; of the rainbow, Arist.*HA*553ᵇ30; of divine visitations, τοῖσι Λακεδαιμονίοισι μῆνις κατέσκηψε Ταλθυβίου Hdt.7.134; ἐς ἀγγέλους ib.137; ἣν κατασκήψῃ ἐς τὴν Πελοπόννησον, of an omen, Id.8.65; ὀργαὶ κ. ἐς τὸ σὸν δέμας E. l. c.; τίς κατέσκηψεν τύχη; A.*Supp.*327; ἐς Οἰδίπου παῖδε Ἄρης κ. Ar.*Fr.*558; of Nemesis, D.H.3.23; esp. of sickness, *attack*, [ἡ νόσος] κατέσκηπτε ἐς ἄκρας χεῖρας καὶ πόδας Th.2.49, cf. Hp.*Epid.*3.8; εἰς γυναῖκας D.H.9.40; ῥεῦμα κ. τινὶ ἐς τὰ νεῦρα Paus.6.3.10, cf. Gal.1.286; ἡ ξανθὴ [χολὴ] ὀδόντι Alex.Aphr.*Pr.*1.40, etc. 2. c. acc., *fall upon*, τινα dub. l. in E.*Med.*94 (fort. τινι):—Pass., κατασκηφθέντα χωρία *struck by lightning*, Hsch. s. v. ἐνηλύσια. II. causal, εἰς ὅ τι -σκήψει τέλος ὁ δαίμων νέμεσιν Plu.*Aem.*27. III. κ. λιταῖς *storm* or *importune* with prayers, c. inf., S.*OC*1011. IV. abs., *break out, go forth*, of a report, App.*BC*3.25; κ. εἰς τέλος *come* to an issue, of a war, D.H.3.54. -σκηψις, εως, ἡ, *attack*, τῶν παθῶν Dsc.*Ther.Praef.*

※**κατασκῐ-άζω**, fut. -σκιάσω, Att. -σκιῶ S.*OC*406:—*overshadow, cover over*, κατὰ δ' ἐσκίασαν βελέεσσι Τιτῆνας Hes.*Th.*716; ἡ δέ οἱ κόμη ὤμους κ. Archil.29; σαρξὶν πάντα κατεσκίασεν ἄνωθεν Pl.*Ti.*74d; *spread awnings*, E.*Ion* 1142; κόνει *bury* one, S. l. c.; θανόντα.. γαῖα κατεσκίασε *IG*7.580 (Tanagra). -άω, poet. for foreg., Od.12.436:—Pass., Opp.*H.*3.467.

**κατασκίδναμαι**, Pass. of κατασκεδάννυμι, Plu.2.776f.

**κατάσκῐος**, ον, *shaded* or *covered with*, λάχνῃ δέρμα κ. Hes.*Op.*513, cf. Hdt.2.138, A.*Ag.*493, S.*El.*422; *shaded*, νῶτον Pi.*Pae.*6.139: later c. gen., αἰγείροιο *AP*9.333 (Mnasalc., v.l. αἰγείροισι): metaph. in Astrol., ἀργὸς καὶ κ. τόπος, of a region, Vett.Val.77.25; name of second τόπος, Id.179.13; of third, *Cat.Cod.Astr.*8(4).144. II. trans., *overshadowing*, λόφοι A.*Th.*384, Ar.*Ach.*965 codd., cf. E.*Ph.* 654 (lyr.).

**κατασκῑρόομαι**, Pass., *become hard* or *dry* through age, κατεσκιρωμένης (-σκηρ- cod.)· πεπαλαιωμένης, Hsch., cf. eund. s. v. κατεσκληκότα (ubi -σκληρ- cod.). II. pf. inf. κατεσκιρῶσθαι (sic cod. Patm., -σκειρῶ- cod. Phot.), = λελευκάνθαι, Apollod.Hist.*Fr.*107(*c*) J. (nisi leg. κατεσκυρῶσθαι eodem sensu).

**κατασκιρτάω**, *leap upon*, τοῦ βήματος Plu.2.790c. 2. *leap about*, Ael.*NA*5.6. II. metaph., *show contempt for*, τινος ib.2.6, Polyaen. 8.23.7, etc.

**κατασκλῆναι**, v. κατασκέλλομαι.

**κατασκληρ-αίνω**, *harden*, Hsch. s. v. καταμαλάσσοντα (dub.). -όομαι, pf. part. Pass. κατεσκληρωμένα, gloss on κατεσκληκότα, Id. (fort. κατεσκιρωμένα). -ος, *very hard*, Ph.*Bel.*71.30, *Hippiatr.* 96. -ύνομαι [ῠ], Pass., *become hard*, Thphr.*CP*4.12.9, Gal.11.531.

**κατασκόπ-ευσις**, εως, ἡ, *reconnoitring*, Eust.69.37. -εύω, = sq., Lxx *Ex.*2.4, al., *PTeb.*230 (ii B.C.). ※-έω, fut. -σκέψομαι: aor. -εσκεψάμην:—*view closely, spy out, reconnoitre*, κ. ὅποι.. E.*Hel.*1607; τὰ ἀγγελλόμενα *reconnoitre*, Aen.Tact.23.10; εἴ πῃ.. X.*Cyr.*7.1.39, cf. Th.6.50, al.; τῶν πολεμίων Plu.*Sol.*9; *keep a look-out*, of ships, Plb. 3.95.6:—Med., -σκοπεῖσθαι ἑαυτήν X.*Mem.*2.1.22; αὐτὸς ἑαυτὸν κ. Arist.*MM*1213ᵃ5; *inspect*, τὰς πανοπλίας Plb.10.20.2; γραφήν *POxy.* 1414.4 (iii A.D.); of a medical examination, Gal.1.293. -ή, ἡ, *viewing closely, spying*, πέμπειν τινὰ εἰς κατασκοπήν S.*Ph.*45; μολεῖν εἰς κ. E.*Ba.*838; ἐπὶ κατασκοπήν X.*Cyr.*6.2.9, cf. *HG*1.4.11, Arist.*Ath.* *Fr.*4, Plb.3.95.8; ἐπὶ -σκοπῇ τῶν πραγμάτων Aeschin.2.28; κατασκοπῆς ἕνεκα X.*An.*7.4.13; ἔχειν κ. Plu.*Fab.*12; κατασκοπαῖς χρωμένους Th.6.34; ἐς τὴν κ. τῶν χρημάτων *to inspect* the money, ib.46. -ησις, εως, ἡ, = foreg., *Gloss.* -ία, ἡ, fem. of κατάσκοπος, epith. of Aphrodite at Troezen, Paus.2.32.3. -ικός, ἡ, όν, *for scouting*: -κά, τά (sc. πλοῖα), Plu.*Cat.Mi.*54. -ιον, τό, *look-out ship*, Gell.10.25 (sed leg. -σκοπικόν). -ίς (sc. ναῦς), ἴδος, ἡ, = foreg., *Gloss.* -ίσκος, ὁ, = foreg., *CIL*8.27790 (Althiburos). -ος, ὁ, *one who reconnoitres, scout, spy*, Hdt.1.100, 112, al.; κατάσκοπον πολεμίων πέμπειν E.*Rh.*125; πεμφθεὶς Ἰλίου κ. ib.505, cf. *Hec.*239, Th.6.63; τριήρεις πέμψαι κ. Plu.*Lys.*10; τῶν λόγων κ. Ar.*Th.*588, cf. X.*Cyr.*6.1.31; πραγμάτων Men.*Pk.*105. 2. *examiner, inspector*, Th.4.27, cf. 8.41; τῆς προσόδου ἐκ σίτου *Fouilles de l'Institut Français d'Arch. Orientale du Caire* 4(2).p.74: metaph., κ. βίου Secund.*Sent.*7. II. κατάσκοπος, ον, *closely covered*, Sch.Opp.*H.*3.636 (sed leg. -σκεπος).

**κατασκορπίζω**, *scatter abroad*, D.S.24.1.

**κατασκοτίζω**, *veil in darkness*, Gal.*UP*10.3.

**κατασκυθρωπ-άζω**, *look gloomy*, J.*AJ*11.5.6. -άω or -έω, = foreg., c. gen., Suid.

**κατασκώπτω**, *make jokes upon*, τινα Hdt.2.173; mostly in bad sense, *jeer, mock*, Id.3.37, 151.

**κατασμῑκρ-ίζω**, *disparage, depreciate*, Arist.*EN*1163ᵃ14, Phld.*Vit.* p.37 J. -ολογέω, *speak disparagingly of, accuse as niggardly*, τὴν φύσιν Hp.*Ep.*17. ※-ύνω, *lessen, abridge*, τὴν τοῦ λόγου σεμνότητα Demetr.*Eloc.*44, cf. Luc.*Gall.*14, Porph.*Sent.*40:—Pass., *to be made small*, Lxx 2*Ki.*7.19; *become less*, Marcellin.*Puls.*310: metaph., M.Ant.8.36. II. = κατασμικρίζω, *belittle*, -σμικρῦναι καὶ διαφαυλίσαι Hierocl.p.59A., cf. Max.Tyr.22.2, Ath.8.359a, Simp. *in Epict.* p.102D. III. = κατακερματίζω, εἰς λεπτὰ καὶ ἀγεννῆ μόρια Max. Tyr.34.1 (Pass.).

**κατάσμυρνος**, ον, *smelling of myrrh*, Dsc.1.27.

**κατασμύχω** [ῡ], *burn with a slow fire, burn up*, κατά τε σμῦξαι πυρὶ νῆας Il.9.653: metaph., ὅς με κατασμύχων, of love, Theoc.3.17:—in Pass., of a disappointed rival, *waste away*, Id.8.90, cf. Phalar.*Ep.* 144.4; σεσηρός τι καὶ κατεσμυγμένον ὑποβλέπειν Hld.7.21.

**κατασμώχομαι**, Med., *rub in pieces, bruise*, Nic.*Th.*860, *Al.*332.

**κατασοβᾰρεύομαι**, *regard haughtily*, τινος J.*BJ*3.1.1, D.L.1.81, Men.Prot.p.32D.

**κατασοβέω**, *frighten away, scare*, τοὺς ὄρνιθας Arist.*Mir.*841ᵇ22; *drive down*, εἰς βαθὺ φρέαρ Parth.14.3.

**κατασοφ-ίζομαι**, *outwit by sophisms* or *fallacies*, c. acc. pers., Lxx *Ex.*1.10, Luc.*DDeor.*1.1, etc.; ταῖς εὑρησιλογίαις κ. τὴν δύναμιν τῆς πεπρωμένης D.S.17.116; τὸν νόμον διὰ τῆς ἑαυτοῦ κακουργίας κ. Just. *Nov.*72.5: c. gen., Ael. in Ar.Byz.*Epit.*58.6:—also as Pass., *to be outwitted*, Plu.2.80c, Alex.Aphr.*in SE* 43.22, Luc.*DDeor.*16.2, Longin.17.1. 2. κ. τι περί τινων *evade by quibbling*, *CIG*(add.)4224*d* 10 (Anticragus). 3. *falsify*, J.*AJ*8.15.5. -ισμός, ὁ, *outwitting, trickery*, Alex.Aphr.*in SE*48.10, Eust.1695.36, Sch.Hermog. in Rh. 4.215 W. -ιστεύω, = κατασοφίζομαι, c. gen., Suid.

**κατ-ασπάζομαι**, *embrace, kiss*, τινα Plu.*Cor.*9; σορόν Id.*Ant.*85; *treat lovingly*, φιλήμασι, θρήνοις, Hld.5.11, 7.7. 2. *do homage to* a king, J.*AJ*7.10.5.

**κατασπαθάω**, v.l. for σπαθάω, Alciphr.3.50.

**κατασπᾰράσσω**, Att. -ττω, *tear in pieces*, Ar.*Eq.*729; βυβλίον Plb.23.14.8, D.S.29.21; κατεσπαραγμένη τὴν ἐσθῆτα Luc.*Asin.*22.

**κατασπαργᾰνόω**, *wrap in swaddling-clothes*, βρέφη Ph.2.495.

**κατά-σπᾰσις**, εως, ἡ, *drawing down*, Arist.*Mete.*369ᵇ20; ἐντέρων dub. in Herod.Med. in *Rh.Mus.*58.108. -σπασμα, ατος, τό, in pl., *vibrations* of the reed-tongue of a pipe, Thphr.*HP*4.11.5. II. *part, fragment*, τῆς στρατιᾶς J.*BJ*5.12.1 (dub. l.), cf. Hsch. and Suid. s. v. κάταγμα. -σπασμικός, ή, όν, of a drug, *curing* κατασπασμός, *POxy.* 1088.68 (i A.D.). ※-σπασμός, ὁ, = κατάσπασις, ὑγρῶν Plu.2.650c; ὑποχονδρίων Sor.2.36; *pulling down, demolition* of buildings, Nech. in *Cat.Cod.Astr.*7.136 (pl.), *PRyl.*125.6 (i A.D.). 2. *plucking, gathering* of fruit-crops, ib.97.6 (ii A.D.), etc. 3. *stroking* or *rubbing down*, cj. for -πασμός in Cael.Aur.*TP*1.166. II. metaph., *depression of spirits*, Plu.2.78a (pl.). III. *lowering* of the voice, Antyll.ap.Orib.6.8.5. -σπαστικός, ή, όν, *fitted for drawing down*, γάλακτος Dsc.2.136, cf. Antyll.ap.Orib.6.31.6 (v.l. -παυστικός); κ. δύναμις Philum.*Ven.*10.4.

**κατασπᾰτᾰλάω**, *live wantonly, wanton*, Lxx *Pr.*29.21, *Am.*6.4, Luc. *Epigr.*50.

※**κατασπάω**, fut. -άσω [ᾰ]: pf. -έσπᾰκα Ar.*Eq.*718:—*draw, pull down*, μολυβδὶς ὥστε δίκτυον κατέσπασεν S.*Fr.*840; κατασπάσαι τινὰ τῶν τριχῶν *drag* one *down by* the hair, Ar.*Lys.*725; τινὰ τοῦ σκέλους Antiph.86.3; κ. τὰς πεντηκοντέρους *haul* them *down to the sea, set* them *afloat*, Hdt.1.164, cf. 7.193; τὰ σημεῖα κατεσπάσθη (in token of defeat), Th.1.63; κ. τινὰ ἀπὸ τοῦ ἵππου X.*An.*1.9.6; κατεσπακὼς τὰς ὀφρῦς, of one frowning, Alciphr.3.3:—Pass., *to be drawn down*, τὰ κατασπώμενα.. κἀνασπώμενα, of the limbs of puppets, X.*Mem.*3.10.7; κατεσπασμέναι ὀφρύες, of one frowning, Arist.*HA*491ᵇ17; κατασπᾶσθαι ἐς ὕπνον, ἐς δάκρυα, Luc.*DMar.*2.2, *Anach.*23. b. *gather* fruit from, τὸν ἐλαιωνοπαράδεισον, prob. in *PSI*1.33.26 (iii A.D.). 2. Pass., *to be displaced downwards*, of a dislocated bone, Hp.*Mochl.*

4, 5; *to be convulsed, suffer a spasm*, Id.*Epid*.3.17.β′ (or perh. *to be drawn*, as in facial paralysis); *fall into a trance*, *PMag.Lond*.121. 549. II. *draw down* or *forth*, τὰ γυναικεῖα Hp.*Epid*.6.8.32, cf. Arist.*GA*750b35; γάλα Dsc.3.58; *draw off*, τὸ τὴν νοῦσον παρέχον Hp.*Loc.Hom*.30 (Pass.); χυμοὺς κ. [τὸ λουτρόν] *App.Anth*.3. 158. III. *quaff, swallow down*, Ar.*Eq*.718, *Ra*.576, Antiph.204. 13. IV. *pull down*, οἶκον, ἄλση, Lxx 2*Ch*.24.7, 34.7; τὰ ὑψηλά ib. 31.1, cf. *PTeb*.5.134 (ii B.C., Pass.); τὴν Σμύρναν Str.14.1.37, cf. 16.2. 30 (Pass.); κ. τὰς τάξεις *break* the ranks, Plb.1.40.13: metaph., Phld. *D*.1.17. V. *lower*, τὴν φωνήν Antyll.ap.Orib.6.9.5. VI. *precipitate*, Zos.Alch.p.195 B. (Pass.). VII. v. κατασπεύδω.

**κατασπειράω**, in pf. part. Pass., τοῦ ἀπὸ τῶν ἄστρων κατεσπειραμένου φωτός dub.l. in Epicur.*Ep*.2 p.45 U.; fort. κατεσπαρμένου (*scattered, given out*).

⊛**κατασπείρω**, fut. -σπερῶ Lxx (v. infr.):—*sow, plant*, εἰς μήτραν ζῴα Pl.*Ti*.91d: metaph., ἀνίας μοι κατασπείρας S.*Aj*.1005:—Pass., ὁ κατεσπαρμένος σπόρος *PMagd*.7.8 (iii B.C.). 2. *beget*, τινα E.*HF* 469, Phint.ap.Stob.4.23.61a; τὸν κατασπείραντα *him that begat* me, Diph.93. II. *spread as in sowing*, τοῦ χάρακος κ. [πυροβόλα] *scatter* them *over*.., Plu.*Cam*.34; αὐτοῖς αὔραν τινὰ κ. ἡ χώρα νότιον Id.*Dio* 25:—Pass., *to be spread abroad, dispersed*, εἰ μὴ κατεσπαρμένοι ἦσαν οἱ τοιοῦτοι λόγοι ἐν τοῖς πᾶσιν Pl.*Lg*.891b. III. *plant*, ἀμπελῶνα Lxx *De*.22.9; γῆν *PMagd*.28.3 (iii B.C.), Ph.2.262: metaph., [νόσοι] χωρία καὶ πελάγη κατασπείρασαι τῶν ἀβουλήτων Id.2.567; πλούτῳ Ἑλλάδα κ. D.H.*Dem*.29. IV. *besprinkle*, ἤδη καὶ λευκαί με κατασπείρουσιν ἔθειραι *AP*11.41 (Phld.).

⊛**κατάσπεισις**, εως, ἡ, *besprinkling with holy water*, Plu.2.438a (pl.). II. *self-devotion*, of Spanish retainers, Id.*Sert*.14; cf. κατασπένδω II. 3.

⊛**κατασπένδω**, fut. -σπείσω E.*Or*.1187:—*pour as a drink-offering*, c. acc. cogn., χοὰς ὑπὲρ μητρὸς τάφῳ E. l. c.; κ. κατὰ τῆς κεφαλῆς ἀρυβάλλῳ ἀμβροσίαν κατὰ σοῦ Ar.*Eq*.1094: abs., *pour drink-offerings*, Hdt.2.151; τοῖς θεοῖς Plb.3.11.6:—Pass., -σπένδεται (-τε lapis) ἀκρήτῳ *SIG*57.26 (Milet., v B.C.). II. c. acc., *wet*, λιβάσι κ. παρηΐδα *Trag.Adesp*.548. 2. c. acc. pers., κ. τινὰ δακρύοις *honour with offerings* of tears, E.*Or*.1239; simply, κ. τινὰ *lament with tears*, *AP* 7.260 (Carph.). 3. c. acc. pers., *offer up, devote, consecrate*, τινα D.S.5.31; κατασπένδειν ἑαυτοὺς *devote* themselves, of Spanish retainers, Str.3.4.18; cf. κατάσπεισις II:—Pass., ἄνθρωπος κατεσπεισμένος Id.4.4.5; πρόβατα κ. Plu.*Alex*.50; Μούσαισι.. κατεσπείσθη πᾶς ὁ τεὸς βίοτος *AP*7.27 (Antip. Sid.), cf. Longus 2.6; of a priest, *to be consecrated*, ἐπὶ τὰ ἱερά prob. in *OGI*331.20 (Pergam., ii B.C.).

**κατασπέρχω**, *urge on*, λῃστὰς δορί with a spear, Ar.*Ach*.1188; ἐλάτῃσι νῆα Opp.*H*.4.91; ὁ ἄνεμος ἰσχυρῶς -έσπερχε *drove* [them] *on*, D.C.41.46; κατασπέρχον, of circumstances, *urgent, pressing*, Th.4. 126:—Pass., *to be driven on*, J.*BJ*4.2.4.

**κατασπερχωτήν**· ἐπὶ τὴν οἰκίαν, ἢ ἐπὶ τὴν ἑστίαν κεκαυμένη, Hsch.

⊛**κατα-σπεύδω**, *urge, hasten on*, πρᾶγμα Aeschin.3.67, cf. Lxx *Ex*. 5.13:—Pass., of words, *to be urgent* or *rapid*, κατεσπεῦσθαι τὴν φράσιν D.H.*Comp*.20 (Upton for κατεσπάσθαι); κατεσπεῦσθαι (v.l. -εσπάσθαι) τὴν λέξιν Gal.16.548; τὰ κατεσπευσμένα Longin.19.2; ἡ ἁρμονία οὐ κ. Id.40.4. 2. *agitate, dismay*, τινα Lxx *Da*.4.16(19). II. intr., *make haste, hasten*, ib.*De*.33.2. **-σπευσις**, εως, ἡ, *haste*, Thd.*Pr*.1.27.

**κατασπῐλ-άζω**, (σπιλάς B) *spot, stain*, Hsch. 2. = κατακρύπτω, Anon.ap.*EM*495.42. II. (σπιλάς C) *swoop down upon*, as a sudden storm, Ph.*Fr*.28 H., Suid. s. v. κατεσπίλασεν. **-ος**, ον, *blemished*, βοῦς Porph.*Abst*.4.7.

**κατασπλεκόω**, = σπλεκόω, Hsch.

**κατασποδέω**, *throw down in the dust, make to bite the dust*, τὸν ἄνδρα τῷ πελέκει κατεσπόδησεν Ar.*Th*.560; κατεσποδημένω A.*Th*.809.

**κατασπορ-ά**, ἡ, *sowing*, *PTeb*.341.5 (ii A.D.), *POxy*.2121.42 (iii A.D.), Sch.Pl.*Lg*.853d, Phot. s. v. κερασβόλα. ⊛**-εύς**, έως, ὁ, *sower*, *PFay*.118.11 (ii A.D.), *PLond*.1821.217. **-εύω**, = κατασπείρω, dub. in *BGU*12.10 (ii A.D.).

**κατασπουδ-άζομαι** (with aor. and pf. Pass.), *to be earnest, serious*, Hdt.2.173; οὐδαμῶς κατεσπουδασμένος ἀνήρ ib.174; κατεσπουδασμέναι δεήσεις D.H.11.61, cf. 4.67:—later in Act., ἐὰν αὐτός τις.. φαίνηται -εσπουδακώς Phld.*Mort*.31: also c. dat., *take a serious interest in*, βλαβεροῖς κ. Id.*Mus*.p.56 K.: abs., Apollon.*Lex*. s. v. ἐπείγετον. II. as Pass., *to be troubled*, Lxx *Jb*.23.15, Aq.2*Ki*.4.1, al. 2. *to be oppressed*, ὑπὸ μειζόνων Vett.Val.254.16. **-αζόντως**, Adv. *eagerly*, Hsch. s. v. ἠπειγμένως (ἐπηγ- cod.). **-αίως**, Adv. = foreg., *BGU* 1206.7, 1207.10 (i B.C.). **-ασμός**, ὁ, *trouble, amazement*, Aq.*Ze*.1.18.

**κατάσσῠτος**, ον, *rushing down*, ἰχώρ, πῦρ, Nonn.*D*.4.388, 45.338.

**κατάσσω**, later for κατάγνυμι, impf. κατέασσε Aesop.7:—Pass., Apollod.*Poliorc*.189.6, App.*Pun*.129, Artem.1.66, *PHolm*.6.40. [ᾱ by nature, Hdn.Gr.2.109.]

**κατασταγμός**, ὁ, *running at the nose*, Cels.4.5.2, Orib.*Fr*.27; κ. ἀρτηρίας *tracheitis*, Gal.13.92.

**καταστάζω**, *shed, drip*, I. of persons, 1. c. acc. rei, *let fall in drops upon, shed over*, κ. δάκρυ τινός E.*Hec*.760; ἀφρὸν κατέσταζ' εὐτρίχου γενειάδος Id.*HF*934; also of a garment, νώτου καταστάζοντα βύσσινον φάρος S.*Fr*.373.3: c. acc. only, *let fall in drops* (sc. αἷμα), A. *Fr*.327. 2. c. dat. rei, *run down with* a thing, νόσῳ κ. πόδα *to have* one's foot *running* with a sore, S.*Ph*.7. II. of the liquid, 1. intr., *drip, trickle down*, βωμοῦ from the altar, E.*IT*72; τάφου Id. *Hel*.985; δάκρυα κ. τὰ μὲν κατὰ τῶν πέπλων, τὰ δὲ ἐπὶ τοὺς πόδας (v.l. for στάζω) X.*Cyr*.5.1.5; αἷμα κ. εἰς τὴν γῆν Luc.*VH*1.17; ὁ ἄκρατος κ. πρὸς ἡμᾶς Id.*Luct*.19. 2. trans., *bedew, wet*, ἱδρώς γέ τοί νιν πᾶν καταστάζει δέμας S.*Ph*.823, cf. E.*Hec*.241; ἀφρῷ Id.*Supp*.587.

**κατασταθμ-εύω**, *put into a stable* or *stall*, Str.4.5.2:—Pass., *to be oppressed by having soldiers quartered upon* one, ὑπό τινος Id.16.1. 16. **-ησις**, εως, ἡ, *accurate measurement*, Epicur.*Nat*.11. 5. **-ισμός**, ὁ, *weighing out*, Dsc.1.59.

**κατασταλάω**, = καταστάζω I, Nonn.*D*.38.434.

**κατασταλτικός**, ή, όν, *fitted for checking*, opp. ἐγερτικός, c. gen., S.E.*M*.6.19; ὑπερσαρκωμάτων Dsc.2.4, cf. Antyll.ap.Orib.6.23.2; κ. φάρμακα Gal.14.763. II. *sedate*, τὸ θηλύτερον -σταλτικώτερον Ptol. *Tetr*.172. III. -κή, ἡ, *the plant* βατράχιον, Apul.*Herb*.8.

**κατασταμνίζω**, *draw off wine into a smaller vessel* (στάμνος), *rack off, bottle*, οἶνος κατεσταμνισμένος wine *in bottle*, Thphr.*CP*2.18.4; λάγυνοι κατεσταμνισμένοι bottles of wine, Nicostr.Com.11:—Act., Com.ap.Poll.7.162.

**κατάσταξις**, εως, ἡ, *dropping down, dripping*, Gal.19.140.

⊛ **καταστᾰσι-άζω**, *overpower by forming a counter-party*, τινα Theopomp.Hist.233, D.S.19.36, etc.; ἐν τῷ δήμῳ κατεστασίασε τὴν βουλήν Plu.*Per*.9:—Pass., *to be factiously opposed* or *overpowered*, ὑπό τινος X.*HG*1.6.4; ὑπὸ παρατάξεως D.44.3; κατὰ γάμους ἢ δίκας Arist.*Pol*. 1306a33. 2. = στασιάζω, Lxx *Ex*.38.22(1), J.*BJ Prooem*.7, *BGU* 836.5 (vi A.D.). **-αστικός**, ή, όν, *factious*, Hld.7.19.

⊛ **κατά-στᾰσις**, εως, ἡ, I. trans., *settlement, establishment, institution*, χορῶν A.*Ag*.23, cf. Ar.*Th*.958; πραγμάτων ἀρχὴ καὶ κ. πρώτη D.18.188; αὕτη ἡ κ. τῆς δημοκρατίας *mode of establishing* democracy, Pl.*R*.557a; ἐπιτροπῆς κ. *constitution* of a wardship, Arist.*Ath*.56.6: also c. gen. agentis, δαιμόνων κ. their *ordinance, decree*, E.*Ph*.1266. 2. *appointment* of magistrates, ἀρχόντων, δικαστῶν, etc., Pl.*R*.414a, 425d; τῶν τετρακοσίων Arist.*Ath*.41.2, etc.; αἱ περὶ τὰς ἀρχὰς κ. Pl. *Lg*.768d. b. at Athens, *payment on enrolment* in the cavalry, Eup. 268, Pl.Com.165, Lys.16.6 (pl.). 3. *bringing* of ambassadors *before* the senate or assembly, *introduction, presentation*, Hdt.3.46, 8.141, 9.9. 4. κ. ἐγγυητῶν *bringing* one's bail *forward*, D.24.83, 84; ἐμφανῶν *production* of goods, etc., in dispute, Id.53.14, Arist.*Ath*.56.6, Is.6.31. 5. *pleading* of a case, τὰ πρὸς τὴν κ. δικαιώματα *PPetr*.3 p.55 (iii B.C.), cf. *PAmh*.2.33.7 (ii B.C.), etc.; opp. ἀφήγησις, Aps.p.251 H.; opp. διήγησις, Corn.*Rh*.p.371 H., cf. Syrian. *in Hermog*.2.64 R.; αἱ κ. τῶν δημηγοριῶν Arist.*Rh.Al*.1438a2; f.l. for προκατάστασις, Hermog.*Inv*.2 tit. 6. *settling, quieting, calming*, εἰς ἠρεμίαν καὶ κ. ἐλθεῖν Arist.*Ph*.247b27; ἔστω πράϋνσις κ. καὶ ἠρέμισις (-ησις codd.) ὀργῆς Id.*Rh*.1380a8; πραότης κ. κινήσεως τῆς ὑπ' ὀργῆς Pl.*Def*.412d; κατάστασιν ὥσπερ ἐκ μανίας ὁ πότος ἐλάμβανεν Plu.2.704e; opp. μανία, S.E.*M*.7.404: hence, of disease, opp. παροξυσμός, Hp.*Aph*.1.12 (pl.), *Epid*.1.25 (pl.). 7. *restoration*, opp. διαφθορά, Pl.*Phlb*.46c; εἰς δέ γε τὴν αὑτῶν φύσιν ὅταν καθιστῆται, ταύτην αὖ τὴν κ. ἡδονὴν ἀπεδεξάμεθα ib.42d; [ἡ ἡδονὴ] κ. εἰς τὴν ὑπάρχουσαν φύσιν Arist.*Rh*.1369b34. 8. rarely, *setting* of fractures, Hp.*Fract*.31, cf. Gal.18(2).590. II. intr., *standing firm, settled condition, fixedness*, κ. γένοιτ' ἂν οὐδενὸς νόμου S.*Aj*.1247. 2. *state, condition*, οὕτω δὴ ἀνθρώπου κ. so is *the condition* of man, Hdt.2.173; ἐν ἀνθρώπου φύσι καὶ καταστάσι Id.8.83; ἡ αὐτὴ κ. ἐστι τῇ πρὸ τῆς γενέσεως ἡ μετὰ τὴν τελευτήν Epicur.*Fr*.495; of climatic and seasonal conditions, Hp.*Epid*.1.3, 20; αἱ κ. τοῦ ἐνιαυτοῦ Id.*Aph*.3.15; ἀέρος Thphr.*HP*8.8.7; λοιμικὴ κ. Plb.1.19.1, Dsc. 4.115 (pl.); νηνεμία καὶ κ. *settled weather*, Plu.2.281b; θαυμαστή τις εὐδίας κ. Luc.*Halc*.4; κ. τοῦ χρώματος καὶ σώματος Hp.*Prorrh*.2.4; κ. ὀμμάτων, προσώπου, E.*Med*.1197, Plu.2.260c; κ. κακῶν E.*Hipp*.1296; νυκτὸς ἐν κ. in the *stillness* of night, Id.*Rh*.111; ἐν τοιαύτῃ κ. τῆς ἡλικίας at such a mature age, Hyp.*Fr*.205; τὰς ψυχὰς ἐπὶ τὴν ἀρχαίαν κ. ἄγειν Pl.*R*.547b; οὐ τὴν αὐτὴν ἔχει κ. Arist.*HA*601b7; equiv. to διάθεσις, Id.*Rh*.1370a2; *state of affairs*, Isoc.4.115, D.18.62, Plb.2. 71.2; also τὴν προσήκουσαν ἔχειν κ. the proper *attitude*, Carneisc. *Herc*.1027.10. 3. *settled order* or *method, system*, ἀπὸ φύσιος καὶ κ. ἀρχαίης Democr.278; esp. of political constitutions, ἐχρᾶτο καταστάσι πρηγμάτων τοιῇδε Hdt.2.173; Κορινθίοισι ἦν πόλιος κ. τοιήδε Id.5.92.β′; ἡ κ. τῆς πόλεως Pl.*R*.426c; κ. πολιτείας Id.*Lg*.832d, Arist.*Ath*.42.1; λέγεις δὲ.. τὴν ποίαν κ. ὀλιγαρχίαν; Pl.*R*.550c; ἡ παροῦσα κ. Isoc.3.55, cf. 26, Arist.*Pol*.1292a35; τῆς περὶ τοὺς ἀγῶνας κ. *CIG*2741 (Aphrodisias); ἡ πρώτη κ. τῶν περὶ τὴν μουσικὴν ἐν τῇ Σπάρτῃ Plu.2.1134b. 4. *position* of troops in battle, Plb.2.68. 9. 5. Gramm., *construction*, ἡ δέουσα κ. A.D.*Synt*.132.3 (but τῆς κ. οὕτως ἐχούσης the *state of the case* being as follows, Id.*Adv*.157. 1). **-στᾰτέον**, *one must appoint*, ἄρχοντα, ταξιάρχους, Pl.*R*.414a, X.*Cyr*.8.1.10. 2. *one must lay down, define*, A.D.*Synt*.238.26; κ. πῶς.. Id.*Adv*.135.21. 3. Gramm., *one must construct*, Did. *in D*.7.2. **-στατήρια**, τά, = ἀποπεμπτήρια, καταπαυστήρια, Hsch. ⊛ **-στάτης** [ᾰ], ου, ὁ, *establisher, restorer*, δόμων S.*El*.72. 2. in dual, καταστάτω (Elean), as official title, *Schwyzer*418.13 (Olympia). **-στᾰτικός**, ή, όν, *fitted for calming*, ἔννοιαι Eust.1041.20; τὸ κ. *power to calm*, of music, Plu.*Lyc*.4; cf. καταστηματικός II. 2. = ἀποκαταστατικός I, μοῖρα τοῦ Ἡλίου Rhetor. in *Cat.Cod.Astr*.8(1). 247. 3. -κόν, τό, perh. banker's *charge for weighing*, *PPetr*.3 p.191 (iii B.C.). Adv. -κῶς, = ἀνηπλωμένως καὶ ἀφηγηματικῶς, Aps. p.243 H., al.: Comp. -ώτερον, διηγεῖσθαι Sch.E.*Hipp*.392; διαβάλλειν ib.616. **-στᾰτόν**, τό, *kind of cake*, gloss on ἄμυλον, Sch.rec. Theoc.9.21 (Mod.Gr. καταστατός = *starch*).

⊛ **καταστεγ-άζω**, *cover over*, ῥιψὶ [τὸν νεκρόν] Hdt.4.71, cf. Pl.*Criti*. 115e; κ. τάφρον χόρτῳ Arist.*HA*603a5; *roof over*, *IG*2².463.52:—Pass., *Gp*.13.14.7. **-ασμα**, ατος, τό, *covering*, τῆς ὀροφῆς Hdt.2. 155. **-νόομαι**, Pass., *to be closely covered*, Moschio ap.Ath.5.207d,

v.l. in *Gp.*13.14.7. **-νος**, ον, *close-covered*, Myia *Ep.*4. **-ος**, ον, (στέγη) *covered in, roofed*, αὐλαὶ κατάστεγοι Hdt.2.148; ἐν τῷ κ. δρόμῳ Pl.*Euthd.*273a; [νεοττιαὶ ἀλκυόνος] Arist.*HA*616ᵃ25, cf. Men. *Sam.*76, Ph.*Bel.*80.32, Plb.9.41.9; ὁδοί Lib.*Or.*9.8.

**καταστείβω**, *tread down*, τὰν ὑάκινθον πόσσι Sapph.94. II. *tread*, κατέστειψας πέδον S.*OC*467 (vv. ll. κατέστεψας, κατάστεψον).

**κατάστειρος**, ον, *barren*, Vett.Val.14.26.

**καταστείχω**, aor. 2 -έστῐχον, = κατέρχομαι, *AP*9.298 (Antiphil.); *return from exile*, *IG*2².1113.12.

***καταστέλλω**, fut. -στελῶ E.*Ba.*933 (for Aeol. forms v. καστολέω):—*put in order, arrange*, [πλόκαμον] E. l. c.; *equip, clothe, dress*, κ. τινὰ τὰ περὶ τὼ σκέλει Ar.*Th.*256, cf. Plu.2.69c. II. *let down, lower*, τὰς ῥάβδους D.H.8.44; κ. τὰ βράγχια *shut* them, Plu.2.979c; *press down*, τὴν γλῶσσαν Gal.15.792. 2. *repress, restrain*, οἶκτον E.*IA*934; τὸν ὄχλον *Act.Ap.*19.35, cf. Wilcken *Chr.*10 (ii B.C., prob.); κ. τὰς ἐπιθυμίας Phld.*Rh.*2.284 S., cf. Arr.*Epict.*3.19.5; τοὺς νέους Plu.2.207e, cf. 547b, etc.:—Pass., ἅπαντα λήξει καὶ καταστα-λήσεται Apollod.Com.18; of persons, *to be placed under restraint, reduced to order*, *PTeb.*41.21 (ii B.C.), *BGU*1192.5 (i B.C.); also κατεσταλμένοι τοῖς ἤθεσι *of calm, sedate character*, opp. τολμηρός, D.S.1. 76, cf. Arr.*Epict.*4.4.10; κατεσταλμένον ἦθος D.S.10.3; κατέσταλται πρὸς τὸ κόσμιον Plu.*Comp.Lyc.Num.*3, cf. Ael.*NA*4.29, Arr. *Epict.*3.23.16. 3. Medic., *reduce*, τὰ ὑπερσαρκοῦντα Dsc.2.1.

**κατάστελμα**, ατος, τό, *grain dropped* in transport, *PMasp.*2iii11 (vi A.D.).

**καταστέλξαι**· καταγαγεῖν τὸν βοῦν, Hsch.

**κατάστεμα**, τό, late form of κατάστημα (q.v.).

***καταστεν-άζω**, *sigh, mourn*, Lxx *Ex.*2.23, al.:—Pass., δυστυχεῖς καὶ κατεστεναγμέναι τῶν ἐραστῶν χάριτες Alciphr.1.36. **-αχέω**, *mourn for*, θυγατρα *Epigr.Gr.*205 (Halic., ii B.C.).

**καταστενοχωρέω**, *drive into a narrow space*, Zos.5.16 (Pass., sed leg. κατὰ στ.).

**καταστένω**, *sigh over, lament*, c. acc., S.*OC*1440, E.*Tr.*317 (lyr.), *HF*1141; κατὰ σὲ δακρύοις στένω ib.1045 (lyr.); ὑπέρ τινος Id.*IA*470; ὧν κατέστενες κακῶν (gen. by attraction) S.*El.*874.

**καταστερεόω**, strengthd. for στερεόω, Steph.*in Hp.*1.174 D. (Pass.).

**κατ-αστερ-έω**, = sq., in Pass., Nech.ap.Vett.Val.50.28. **-ίζω**, *place among the stars*, [στέφανον] Pherecyd.148 J.; τὸν ἐν οὐρανῷ στέφανον κ. D.S.4.61, cf. Plu.2.308a, Heph.Astr.1.1:—Pass., D.H.1.61, Theo Sm.p.130 H. 2. *mark out* a constellation, τὴν Πλειάδα δι' ἑπτὰ ἀστέρων -ίζομεν Ps.-Alex.Aphr.*in Metaph.*832.34. II. pf. part. Pass., *adorned with stars*, κατηστερισμένα ζῴδια Hipparch.1.1.9, Gem.1.4; κ. σφαῖραι Id.5.65; ποτήριον Asclep.Myrl.ap.Ath.11. 489e. **-ῐσις**, εως, ἡ, = sq., *Gloss.* **-ισμός**, ὁ, *placing among the stars*: Καταστερισμοί, οἱ, title of treatise on constellations by Hipparchus, Suid.; also of an extant work wrongly attributed to Eratosthenes; cf. Plin.*Epp.*5.17.1, Ps.-Alex.Aphr.*in Metaph.*833. 2. **-όω**, f.l. for καταστερίζω I, Palaeph.51:—Pass., οἱ κατηστερωμένοι ἄνδρες prob. in Phld.*D.*3.9, cf. Sch.E.*Or.*1631.

**καταστεφᾰν-όω**, *crown*, τινὰ ῥόδοις *AP*12.189 (Strat.):—Pass., D.S.12.9. **-ωσις**, εως, ἡ, *crowning*, of a cult-statue, *IG*12(5).946. 11 (Tenos).

**κατα-στεφής**, ές, *crowned*, S.*Tr.*178, A.R.3.220, etc. **-στέφω**, *deck with garlands, crown, wreath*, κ. βωμόν (with branches wreathed in wool) E.*Heracl.*124; κ. νεκρόν (with libations) Id.*Ph.*1632; πλόκαμος ὅδε καταστέφειν here are my tresses for you *to crown*, Id.*IA*1478 (lyr.); ἄντομαί σε καὶ κ. χεροῖν *encircle* thee, Id.*Heracl.*226; κατέστεψας πέδον and κατάστεψον π. are vv.ll. in S.*OC*467, cf. καταστείβω; κ. τὰς πρῴρας D.C.51.5; οὔρεα Epic. in *Arch.Pap.*7 p.7:—Pass., κατεστέφθαι Aeschin.3.164; δάφνῃ κατεστεμμένος τὰς κόμας D.H.2. 34; κλάδος ἐρίῳ κατεστ. Plu.*Thes.*18: metaph., πεδία λῃίοις κατεστεμμένα Men.Rh.p.345 S.; ὁ πόλος ἀστέρας κατέστεπται Hp.*Ep.* 12. **-στεψις**, εως, ἡ, *crowning*, Theo Sm.p.15 H.

**καταστηλῑτεύω**, *post up, publish* a name, etc., Luc.*DMeretr.*4.2, cf. Hsch. s. v. κατεστήριξεν:—Pass., δόγματα κατεστηλιτευμένα Ph. *Fr.*54 H., cf. Poll.8.73.

**καταστηλόω**, *mark with pillars*, ὁδὸς κατεστηλωμένη Plb.34.12.2ᵃ ap.Str.7.7.4 (-στηλοθετημένη in Str.*Chr.*).

***κατάστημα**, ατος, τό, later **κατάστεμα** Lxx 3*Ma.*5.45:—*condition, state*, not necessarily permanent: 1. bodily or mental *condition*, τὸ εὐσταθὲς σαρκὸς κ. Epicur.*Fr.*68, Metrod.*Fr.*5, cf. Diog.Oen.29, Asp. *in EN*143.22; τὸ κατὰ φύσιν καὶ οἰκεῖον κ. Dsc.*Alex.Praef.*, cf. Sor. 1.36; τῆς ψυχῆς ib.39; τὸ κατὰ μέθην κ. Ath.2.38e; κ. μανιῶδες Lxx l.c. 2. *weather*, Diocl.*Fr.*30, Ptol.*Alm.*3.1; τὸ θερινὸν κ. Ps.-Plu. *Fluv.*12; κ. χειμέριον Polyaen.5.12.3; αἰθρίου ὄντος τοῦ κ. Dsc.*Praef.* 6, cf. Cleom.2.1, Sabin.ap.Orib.9.15.1; *direction of wind*, νοτίου τοῦ κ. ὄντος Alex.Aphr.*in Mete.*47.2; *time, season*, κ. νυκτερινόν A.D.*Synt.* 198.27; τὰ ἐνιαύσια κ. Ptol.*Tetr.*93. 3. *demeanour, behaviour*, *Ep. Tit.*2.3, Porph.*Abst.*4.6; τὸ σύνηθες κ. Plu.*Marc.*23; ἀτρεμαῖον κ. J. *AJ*15.7.5; τὸ τῆς εὐσεβείας, τῆς ἀρετῆς κ., Aristeas 210, 278; τὸ μέσον κ. Id.122. 4. *political condition, constitution*, τὸ Λακωνικὸν κ. Plb.6. 50.2, cf. *OGI*669.3 (Egypt, i A.D.). 5. generally, *state of the case, state of affairs*, A.D.*Pron.*25.18. 6. Astrol., *position* of the heavens, Vett.Val.71.23. 7. *physical constitution*, τὸ κοσμικὸν κ., i.e. the four elements and four winds, Id.175.10; ἐν στερεῷ τινι καὶ οὐσιώδει κ. Dam.*Pr.*124; of the Intelligible World, ib.119; ὑποστάσεως κατάστημα Simp.*in Ph.*232.1.

**καταστηματικός**, ή, όν, *pertaining to a state or condition* (cf. foreg. I), opp. κατὰ κίνησιν, ἡδοναί Epicur.*Fr.*2, cf. Metrod.*Fr.*29. II. (cf. καθίστημι B. 4) *sedate*, of persons, Plu.*TG*2; διάθεσις τῆς ψυχῆς Simp.*in Epict.*p.114 D.; of musical instruments, *calming*, v.l. for -στατικά in Procl.*in Alc.*p.198 C.

**κατάστημον**, τό, = στημνίον, Hsch. s. h. v.

**καταστηρίζω**, *establish*, Nonn.*D.*38.424; *prove*, Lyd.*Mens.*1.14:—Pass., *to be propped* or *stayed*, ἐπί τινι E.*Fr.*382.9; *to be firmly fixed* or *established*, Lxx *Jb.*20.7; κατεστηριγμένος, opp. ἀβέβαιος, Arist. *Mu.*395ᵇ16. II. intr., κ. εἰς .. *settle* in a spot, of disease, Hp. *Aff.*15, cf. 11.

**κατά-στιγμα**, ατος, τό, *point, spot*, Sch.D.P.443 (*GGM* ii p.415). **-στίζω**, *cover with marks*, βιβλία Hdn.Gr.1.10; *brand*, τινὰς χαρακτῆρσι D.S.34/5.2.27: freq. in pf. Pass., *to be marked* or *spotted*, ᾠὰ κατεστιγμένα *spotted*, Arist.*HA*559ᵃ24, cf. Dsc.5.143; κυανέαις σταγόσι κατέστικται Ael.*NA*12.24; τὴν χρόαν κατέστ. D.C.43.23; χρυσοειδῆ ἰνδάλματα ἐπ' αὐτῶν κατέστ. *are marked* upon them, Ael.*NA*10.13: metaph., *to be spotted and stained*, Philostr.*VA*1. 11. **-στικτος**, ον, *spotted, speckled, brindled*, κύων S.*Fr.*11; δορά E.*Ba.*697; ὁ κνιπολόγος Arist.*HA*593ᵃ13; of garments, *IG*2².1514. 11, al.; ἐσθὴς Arr.*Ind.*5, cf. Men.1019; *tattooed*, Str.7.5.4: metaph., *dotted*, χώρα κ. οἰκήσεσι Id.2.5.33; κατοικίαις μικραῖς Id.17.3.1; *studded*, κ. ἄστροις τιάραν Jul.*Or.*5.171a.

**καταστίλβω**, *send beaming forth*, σέλας *h.Mart.*10. 2. *irradiate*, πάντα *AP*12.254 (Strat.).

**κατάστιξις**, εως, ἡ, *dotting*, of Argus' eyes, Sch.E.*Ph.*1115.

**καταστοιβάζω**, in pf. part. Pass. -ασμένος *packed, compressed*, of the style of Thucydides, Anon.*in Rhet.*p.212 H.

**καταστοιχ-ειόομαι**, Pass., *to be reduced to its elements*, τύπος κατεστοιχειωμένος Epicur.*Ep.*1 p.3 U. **-ίζω**, *instruct in the rudiments*, Chrysipp.*Stoic.*2.39.

**καταστολ-ή**, ἡ, *equipment, dress*, 1*Ep.Ti.*2.9, J.*BJ*2.8.4: metaph., κ. δόξης Lxx *Is.*61.3. II. *putting down, checking*, D.S.15.94; *reduction, subjugation*, Θηβαΐδος Wilcken *Chr.*12.15 (i B.C.). 2. *modesty, reserve*, Hp.*Decent.*5,8; *moderation*, κ. περιβολῆς in dress, Plu.*Per.*5: abs., *dignity, restraint*, κ. καὶ εὐσχημοσύνη *Inscr.Prien.* 109.186 (ii B.C.), cf. Aristeas 284; τὴν βίου σώφρων κ. *IGRom.* 4.1756.66 (Sardes, i B.C.), cf. Arr.*Epict.*2.10.15, 21.11, Porph.*Abst.* 4.6. 3. *conclusion*, '*finale*', *Mim.Oxy.*413.95; δράματος Sch.Ar. *Pax*1203; *remission*, τῆς ὀδύνης Orib.*Fr.*74. **-ίζω**, *clothe, dress*, Plu.2.65d (Pass.), Eun.*Hist.*p.248 D.

**καταστομ-ίζω**, v.l. for ἐπι-, *put to silence*, Plu.*Arist.*4. **-ιον**, τό, *mouth* of a pipe or tube, Hero *Spir.*1.25. **-ίς**, ίδος, ἡ, *mouthpiece of a flute*, Hsch.

**καταστοναχέω**, *bewail*, c. acc., *AP*7.574 (Agath.).

**κατάστοργος**, ον, *of love*, γόμφοι Emp.87.

**κατα-στορέννῡμι**, part. καστορνῦσα (as if from καταστόρνυμι) (v. infr.): fut. -στορέσω: aor. Pass. κατεστορέσθην Hp.*VM*19: pf. κατεστόρεσται Them.*Or.*15.194d:—*spread, cover with* a thing, [κάπετον] λάεσσι κατεστόρεσαν μεγάλοισι Il.24.798. II. *spread upon*, κώεα καστορνῦσα θρόνοις ἔνι δαιδαλέοισι Od.17.32, cf. 13.73. III. *throw down, lay low*, κατεστόρεσαν αὐτῶν ἑξακοσίους Hdt.9.69; κ. κύματα *smooth* the waves, *AP*7.668 (Leon.): metaph., of morbid humours, Hp. l. c. (Pass.); κ. τὴν ἀνωμαλίαν Plu.*Comp.Lyc.Num.*2; τὴν φιλοτιμίαν, τὰ πάθη, Id.*Luc.*5, 2.101c; τὸν θυμόν Ael.*Fr.*103. IV. *layer*, κλῆμα *Gp.*4.3.2, cf. 4.1.7. **-στόρεσις**, εως, ἡ, *layering*, ἀμπέλων ib.3.3.8.

**καταστοχ-άζομαι**, *aim at*, τὸ συμφέρον Alex.Trall.*Febr.*6: hence, *hit, guess, infer*, τι Plb.12.13.4; τὸ μέλλον D.S.19.39; τινος Ath.9. 391b, Procl.*in Alc.*p.46 C., Phlp.*in Ph.*640.3: abs., Heph.Astr.3. 4:—Act. is f.l. in Suid. s. v. προφητεία, and dub. cj. for καταστοχέω (q.v.):—Pass., τὸ -ασμένον εἰκότως Phld.*Rh.*1.362 S.; κατεστοχάσθαι, gloss on ἐσκευωρῆσθαι, *EM*385.15. **-ᾰσις**, εως, ἡ, = sq., τῆς ἀνατολῆς τῶν ἄστρων Phlp.*in APo.*385.23. **-ασμός**, ὁ, *conjecture*, D.S.1.37. **-αστέον**, *one must guess*, c. acc., Ptol.*Tetr.* 176, Heph.Astr.3.37. **-αστής**, οῦ, ὁ, *one who guesses*, cj. for -στοχάσαι in Suid. s. v. προφητεία. **-αστικός**, ή, όν, *of conjecture*, δύναμις Phld.*Rh.*2.12 S. **-έω**, *hit the mark*, τινος, i.e. succeed in bribing him, *PTeb.*58.35 (ii B.C.).

**καταστραγγίζω**, fut. -ιῶ, *squeeze out*, τὸ λοιπὸν τοῦ αἵματος -ιεῖ Lxx *Le.*5.9.

**κατ-αστράπτω**, *hurl down lightning, flash lightning*, κατ' Οἰταῖον νάπος S.*Tr.*437: abs., καταστράπτει *it lightens*, Plu.*Galb.*23. II. trans., *strike with lightning, dazzle*, τὰς ὄψεις Id.*Tim.*28; τινα Them. *Or.*27.337d; τινὰ τῷ κάλλει Hld.1.21; ὅπλοις κ. τὸ πεδίον *make* it *gleam* with arms, Id.9.14.

**καταστρᾰτεύω**, *take the field against, make war upon*, τινος Suid. II. Med., *overrun in war*, τὸν Πόντον Chio *Ep.*2.

**καταστρᾰτηγ-έω**, *overcome by generalship* or *stratagem*, τινα Plb. 3.71.1 (dub. l.), D.S.11.21, D.H.3.26, Str.4.4.2, etc.; τινος Sopat. in Rh.8.201 W.: metaph., *out-general, outwit*, D.S.16.11, D.H.4.10; τοὺς δικαστάς Id.*Is.*3, cf. Ph.2.203:—Pass., D.S.4.9, Onos.11.5; ὑπὸ τῆς τύχης Charito 2.8. II. *counteract by stratagem*, διαμαρτίαν Zos.3.24. **-ία**, ἡ, *conquest by stratagem*, Tz.*H.*9.70 (pl.).

**καταστρᾰτοπεδ-εία**, ἡ, *pitching a camp*: *living in camps*, Phylarch. 41 J. (pl.), Ael.*VH*9.3 (pl.). ***-εύω**, *encamp*, τοὺς ἑαυτοῦ X.*Cyr.*7.2.8, cf. Onos.6.12; *station*, τὸ ναυτικόν X.*HG*6.2.7. II. intr., *take up quarters*, εἰς [πόλιν], ἐν μέρεσι τῆς πόλεως, πρὸ τῆς πόλεως, Plb.1.30.15, 1.18.2, 3.77.1: abs., Ph.*Bel.*103.48:—Med., X.*An.*3.4.18, Arr.*An.* 5.9.1. III. *march*, εἰς Φοινίκην Lxx 2*Ma.*4.22.

**καταστρεβλόω**, *put to torture*, Plu.*Art.*19, 2.105b (Pass.).

**καταστρεπτικῶς**, Adv. *so as to end*, ἐπ' αὐτά, opp. ἀνεκτικῶς (fort. κατενεκτικῶς) ἐφ' ἕτερα, *Stoic.*3.34 ap.Sch.Luc.*Bis Acc.*22 (v.l. καταστρεπτικῶς).

**καταστρέφω**, pf. κατέστραφα (trans.) Plb.23.11.2:—**Pass.**, fut. -στρᾰφήσομαι D.C.42.42: pf. imper. κατεστρέφθω Epicur. (v. infr.): plpf. 3 sg. -έστραπτο Hdn. (v. infr.); 3 pl. -εστράφατο D.C.39.5:— *turn down, trample on*, ποσσί *h.Ap.*73; *turn the soil*, X.*Oec.*17.10; κάνθαρον κ. *turn* it *upside down*, so as to drain it, Alex.115, cf. Sotad. Com.1.33, Lxx 4*Ki.*21.13; κατεστραμμένῳ τῷ ὀστράκῳ Arist.*HA* 622ᵇ8. **II.** *upset, overturn*, τὴν πόλιν κ. Ar.*Eq.*274; τὰς εἰκόνας D.L.5.82; *ruin, undo*, βίον καὶ τέκνα καὶ πόλεις Plb.23.11.2; τινα *AP* 11.163 (Lucill.):—Pass., τὰ προάστεια κατέστραπτο Hdn.8.4.8. **2.** Med., *subject to oneself, subdue*, πολέμῳ Hdt.1.64, cf. 71, al., Th.3.13, D.18.244, etc.; νόσον E.*Hipp.*477; τοὺς μὲν κατεστρέψατο ἐς φόρου ἀπαγωγὴν *subdued and made* them tributary, Hdt.1.6: c. inf., Ἰωνίην κατεστρέψατο δασμοφόρον εἶναι Id.7.51. **3.** Pass., in aor. and pf., *to be subdued*, Id.1.130, 68: plpf., Th.5.29: c. inf., ἀκούειν σοῦ κατέστραμμαι *am constrained* to hear, A.*Ag.*956: pf. Pass. also in sense of Med., Hdt.1.171; πάντα κατέστραπται καὶ ἔχει D.4.6, cf. X.*HG*5.2.38, Isoc.5.21. **III.** of a floating solid, *right itself*, Archim.*Fluit.* 2.9 (Pass.). **b.** intr., *return*, εἰς ταὐτόν Arist.*Pr.*921ᵃ26, cf. *Mech.* 856ᵇ17. **IV.** *turn round, direct*, [καταπάλτην] *train* it on the enemy, Ph.*Bel.*82.14; esp. towards an end, ποῖ καταστρέφεις λόγων τελευτήν; A.*Pers.*787; οὕτω κατέστρεψεν ἡ τύχη ταῦτα, ὥστ' ἐναντία γενέσθαι τοῖς προσδοκωμένοις Din.1.32; κατέστρεψεν εἰς φιλανθρωπίαν τοὺς λόγους *guided* the conversations *to* a friendly *end*, Aeschin.2.39: hence, *bring to an end*, κ. τὴν βίβλον, τὸν λόγον, Plb.3.118.10, 22.9.4 (Pass., ταῦτα μὲν αὐτοῦ κατεστρέφθω Epicur.*Nat.*14.6); esp. κ. τὸν βίον Cebes 10, Ael.*NA*13.21, Plu.*Thes.*19, etc.; ὑπὸ τῶν πολεμίων Id.*Comp.Sol.Publ.*1: abs., *come to an end, close*, Plb.4.2.1; τοῦ ἐνιαυτοῦ -στρέφοντος Plu.*Caes.*51; esp. *end life, die*, Epicur.*Ep.*3 p.61 U., Plu.*Them.*31, Arr.*An.*7.3.1, Hdn.5.8.10; κ. εἰς ἀπώλειαν *end* in.., Alciphr.3.70; τοὺς λόγους ἐπὶ τὰ πράγματα -στρέφειν οἰόμενος Plu. *Phil.*4; ἡ ἡμέρα κ. εἰς ὥραν δεκάτην *inclines* towards.., Id.*Sull.* 29. **2.** Rhet., metaph., λέξις κατεστραμμένη *periodic* style, opp. εἰρομένη, Arist.*Rh.*1409ᵃ26, cf. Demetr.*Eloc.*12, 21. **V.** *screw* or *stretch tight*, αἱ κατεστραμμέναι χορδαί Arist.*Aud.*803ᵃ28.

**καταστρηνιάω**, *behave wantonly towards*, τοῦ Χριστοῦ 1*Ep.Ti.* 5.11.

**καταστροφ-εύς**, έως, ὁ, *one who ruins* or *spoils* his work, *bungler*, *Mim.Oxy.*413.102; = *eversor, tergiversator*, *Gloss.* **2.** *subverter*, τοῦ πολιτεύματος Lyd.*Mag.*3.69. **-ή**, ἡ, *overturning*, θεσμίων A.*Eu.*490 (lyr., pl.). **2.** *subjugation, reduction*, Hdt.1.6, 92, etc.: καταστροφὴν ποιήσασθαί τινος Id.6.27; ἐπὶ Λιβύων καταστροφῇ πέμπεσθαι Id. 4.167; ἐπ' ἄλλων καταστροφῇ ἐξιέναι Th.1.15: pl., καταστροφαὶ ἐθνῶν Phld.*Rh.*1.255 S. **3.** *return* of vibrating string to axial position, Arist.*Pr.*921ᵃ17 (pl.). **II.** *end, close, conclusion*, ἄνευ δὲ λύπης οὐδαμοῦ καταστροφή A.*Supp.*442; κ. βίου, i.e. death, S.*OC*103, cf. Plb.5. 54.4, etc.; κ. τοῦ ζῆν Men.*Pk.*12: without βίου, Th.2.42, Epicur.*Sent.* 35; ποία κ. εὐδαιμονεστέρα; Arr.*Epict.*4.10.17; τὸ τέλος αὐτῶν τῆς κ. the event of their *life's end*, Plb.6.8.6; κ. καὶ συντέλεια τῶν γεγονότων Id.3.1.9; κ. λαμβάνειν Id.3.47.8; τὴν κ. τῆς βίβλου ποιεῖσθαι εἰς.. Id.1.13.5; in the drama, *dénouement, ending*, Antiph.191.19, Hero *Aut.*22.6, Luc.*Alex.*60, al., Euanth. et Donat. in *CGF* pp.67, 69 K.: pl., αἱ κ. τῶν δραμάτων Plb.3.48.8. **III.** *ruin, undoing*, κ. γῆς (of a person) Men.548.8. **IV.** *crane*, *Stud.Pal.*10.259. 13 (pl., vi A.D.). **-ικῶς**, Adv. *by way of conclusion*, Ath.10. 453c.

**κατά-στρωμα**, ατος, τό, *that which is spread upon* or *over*: in a ship, *deck*, Hdt.8.118, 119, Th.1.49, X.*HG*1.4.18, Pl.*La.*184a, Thphr.*Char.* 22.5, etc.; καταστρώματα διὰ πάσης [τῆς νεώς] Th.1.14; οἱ ἀπὸ τῶν κ., i.e. the fighting men, opp. the rowers, Id.7.40. **II.** part of the constellation Argo, Hipparch.1.8.1, Ptol.*Alm.*8.1. **III.** πλίνθινα κ. a tile *roof*, *AB*269, cf. *LW*3.141 (Ephesus). **IV.** *floor, pavement*, Ath.Mech.13.4, *Gp.*6.2.10. **-στρώννῡμι**, also -ύω Lxx *Jb.*12.23, Mitteis *Chr.*31 viii 18 (ii B.C.): fut. -στρώσω:—Pass., fut. -στρωθήσομαι Lxx *Ju.*7.14: aor. -εστρώθην (v. infr.):—*spread out*, κλίνην Hierocl.p.63 A. **II.** *spread over, cover*, οἶκον.. ῥόδοις Ael.*VH*9.8:—Pass., πεδίον νεκρῶν κατεστρώθη *was strewed with*.., D.S.14.114; σκορπίων κανθήλιον -εστρωμένον Str.14.2.26. **III.** *lay low*, δάμαρτα καὶ παῖδ' ἑνὶ κατέστρωσεν βέλει E.*HF*1000, cf. X. *Cyr.*3.3.64:—Pass., ὡς δὲ Ἕλλησι κατέστρωντο οἱ βάρβαροι Hdt.9. 76, cf. 8.53, 1*Ep.Cor.*10.5. **IV.** *layer*, in Pass. of vines, *Gp.*5. 17.11. **2.** βοτάνιον κατὰ τοῦ ἐδάφους -εστρωμένον *prostrate*, Dsc. 2.130. **-στρωσις**, εως, ἡ, *spreading, laying*, τρικλίνου Aristeas 319. **-στρωτέον**, *one must pave*, ἔδαφος πλίνθοις *Gp.*6.2. 10. **-στρωτήρ**, ῆρος, ὁ, *pavement-slab*, *IG*7.3073.91, al. (Lebad.). **-στρώτης**, ου, ὁ, = *scansor*, *Gloss.*

**καταστῠγ-έω**, aor. κατέστῠγον Il.17.694:—*to be horror-struck*, κατέστυγε μῦθον ἀκούσας l.c.: c. acc., *abhor, abominate*, κατὰ δ' ἔστυγον αὐτήν Od.10.113; δόρπα Nic.*Al.*476: later aor. κατεστύγησα Eun. *VS*p.471 D., Apollon.*Lex.* s.v. κατέστυγε. **II.** causal in aor. 1 κατέστυξα, *make abominable*, *EM*731.26 (but in Hsch. = μισῆσαι): pf. part. Pass. κατεστυγημένος Phot., Suid.; f. l. -μένως in Hsch. **-νάζω**, pf. -εστύγνᾰκα, *to be of sad countenance*, Apollon. *Lex.* s.v. κατέστυγε; ὄμμα -νακὸς Sch.E.*Or.*1317:—Pass., pf. part., Sch.E.*Med.*1009. **-νόομαι**, Pass., = καταστυγνάζω, Hsch. s.v. ἔστυγμαι. **-νος**, ον, *of sad countenance*, Ath.13.585d, Vett.Val. 2.5, Sch.E.*Alc.*800.

**κατα-στύφελος** [ῠ], ον, *very hard* or *rugged*, πέτρη, χῶρος, *h.Merc.* 124, Hes.*Th.*806. **-στυφλος**, ον, = foreg., Hsch.

**καταστύφω** [ῡ], *astringe*: metaph. in Pass., of a person, αὐστηρὸς καὶ κατεστυμμένος Men.Rh.p.389 S.; τὸ κατεστ. *sourness, harshness*, Plu.*Cat.Mi.*46.

**καταστωμύλλομαι**, *chatter*, οἷα κατεστωμύλατο οὐκ ἄκαιρα (Dind. κἀστωμύλατο) Ar.*Th.*461: pf. part. κατεστωμυλμένος *a chattering fellow*, Id.*Ra.*1160, Numen.ap.Eus.*PE*14.5. **II.** in pass. sense, τὰ κατεστ. *things blabbed out*, *EM*524.31.

**κατασῡβωτέω**, *fatten like a pig*, τὴν ψυχὴν ἡδοναῖς Plu.2.1096d.

**κατασυγκρίνω**, *reduce* the pores *to a proper state*, Steph. *in Gal.*1. 337 D.

**κατασῡκοφαντέω**, *criticize captiously*, τὸν Εὐριπίδην Sch.E.*Andr.* 733.

**κατασυλλογίζομαι**, Pass., *have a conclusion drawn against one*, Arist.*APr.*66ᵃ25.

**κατασυμβαίνω**, dub. l. in Iamb. *in Nic.*p.12 P.

**κατασυν-ηγορῆσαι**, f. l. for κατηγορῆσαι in Sch.B D Il.21.79 (v. Sch.Gen. l.c. ii p.190). **-ήθεια**, ἡ, *customary gift*, *PMasp.*136.3 (vi A.D.).

**κατασῡρίζω**, in Pass., of the monochord, *to be subdued by an accompaniment of the syrinx*, Ptol.*Harm.*2.12.

**κατασύρω** [ῡ], aor. 1 κατέσῡρα (v. infr.):—**Med.**, aor. 1 κατεσῡράμην Pherecyd.158 J.:—**Pass.**, aor. 2 κατεσύρην [ῠ] (v. infr.):—*draw, pull down*, Philum.ap.Aët.9.12 (Pass.): usu. with a notion of violence, τὰ [ἀεροπόρα] ἐκ τοῦ οὐρανοῦ D.C.*Fr.*30.4: metaph., ἐπιθυμία κ. τὸν ἡνίοχον λογισμὸν Ph.1.58, cf. 1.627 (Pass.): esp. *lay waste, ravage*, τὰς [πόλιας] ὅσας πρότερον οὐ κατέσυραν Hdt.6.33; κατὰ μὲν ἔσυραν Φάληρον, κατὰ δὲ.. πολλοὺς δήμους Id.5.81; ὡς πλείστην τῆς χώρας Aen.Tact.16.8, cf. Plb.1.56.3, al. **2.** *drag, carry off*, λείαν Pherecyd. l.c.; γυναῖκας Parth.19; τινὰ πρὸς τὸν κριτήν *Ev.Luc.*12.58: metaph., τινὰ εἰς ἐκμελῆ πολιτεύματα Phalar.*Ep.*93.1. **3.** *sweep away*, πελάγη κ. πόλεις Ph.2.142:—Pass., metaph., σκολιὰ ῥεῖθρα ὑφ' ὧν οἱ πολλοὶ -σύρονται, ὡς τὰ λόγιά φησιν *Orac.Chald.*ap.Procl. *in Ti.* 3.326 D.; εἰς τὸ πλῆθος ὑπὸ τοῦ μερισμοῦ καὶ τῆς διαστάσεως τῶν ὄντων Id. *in Prm.*p.551 S., cf. Hierocl. *in CA*19 p.461 M. **b.** Pass., *rush down*, of rivers, etc., D.P.296, Alciphr.3.13, *Gp.*5.2.17. **4.** *drag out*, οὐρανὸς.. δρόμον ἀΐδιον -σύρων *Orac.Chald.*ap.Dam.*Pr.*284. **5.** Pass., *to be reduced*, σωμάτων λοιμῷ -συρέντων Lib.*Or.*61.19 (v.l. συρέντων). **II.** *draw down, launch*, τὸ σκαφίδιον Alciphr.1.1; τοὺς φελλοὺς κ. ὑφάλους, of a net, ibid.

**κατασυστάδην**, Adv., = συστάδην, ἡ κ. χειρονομία Hld.9.16.

❋**κατασφᾰγή**, ἡ, *slaughtering*, Nech. in *Cat.Cod.Astr.*7.143 (pl.).

**κατασφάζω**, later **-σφάττω** Luc.*Sacr.*12 (Pass. -σφάττεσθαι Jul. *Or.*5.174a): fut. -ξω Lxx *Ez.*16.40:—*slaughter, murder*, Hdt.6.23, 8.127, Lxx l.c., al., *Ev.Luc.*19.27, D.C.40.48: freq. in aor. Pass. κατεσφάγην [ᾰ] A.*Eu.*102, S.*OT*730, X.*An.*4.1.17, etc.

**κατ-ασφᾰλίζομαι**, *fortify*, Men.Prot.p.15 D. **2.** *confirm*, τοὺς πραττομένους Lyd.*Mag.*3.12; ὅρκοις πρᾶγμα Just.*Nov.*102 *Praef.*; *assure oneself of*, τι Steph. *in Hp.*1.76 D. **3.** abs., *take refuge*, εἰς τὸ ἐνδότερον Aesop.196. **II.** Pass., *to be made fast*, Lxx 3*Ma.*4.9, Aesop.376; δεῖ κατησφαλίσθαι τὸν νοῦν εἰς.. S.E.*M.*7.23.

**κατασφηκόω**, *nail fast, fasten*, in Pass., ἑλίκεσσι χελώνης Tryph. 88, cf. Hsch.

**κατασφηνόομαι**, Pass., *to be wedged, bound tight*, Hp.*Nat.Puer.*24.

**κατασφίγγω**, *bind tightly*, Plu.2.983d:—Pass., J.*AJ*3.7.2.

❋**κατασφρᾱγίζω**, Ion. and Ep. **-σφρηγίζω**, *seal up*, Lxx *Jb.*9.7, 37. 7: mostly pf. part. Pass. κατεσφρηγισμένος *sealed up, made fast, secured*, ὅρκοις Emp.115.2, cf. A.*Supp.*947, E.*Fr.*762, Pl.*Erx.*400a, etc.: impf. Pass. κατεσφρηγίζετο Tryph.68: fut. -σφραγισθήσομαι *Hermes* 64.64 (Epid., ii A.D.): aor. κατεσφραγίσθην Lxx *Wi.*2.5, Hsch.:—Med., κ. τὰς θύρας Arist.*Mir.*842ᵃ29, cf. *UPZ*6.21 (ii B.C.): Ep. aor. 1 -ίσσατο Nonn.*D.*45.188.

**κατα-σχάζω**, *slit, cut open*, στελέχη Thphr.*HP*2.7.6; συκῆ κατασχασθεῖσα Id.*CP*1.17.10, al.; κ. φλέβα *open* a vein, let blood, Gal. 19.139:—also **-σχάω**, *scarify*, Hp.*Int.*22, Heliod.ap.Orib.46.29. 2. **-σχᾰσις**, εως, ἡ, *scarification*, Archig.ap.Orib.44.26. 6. **-σχασμα**, ατος, τό, *incision* of a poisoned wound, Dsc.*Ther. Praef.* **-σχασμός**, ὁ, = κατάσχασις, Gal.11.321, Antyll.ap.Orib. 7.16.15, Orib.7.18 tit. **-σχαστέον**, *one must scarify*, Archig.ap. Orib.44.26.8, Dsc.*Ther.*2; cf. κατασχιστέον. **-σχαστήρ**, ῆρος, ὁ, = σχαστήρ, prob. in *IG*11(2).165.11 (Delos, iii B.C.).

**κατασχεδιάζω**, *affirm rashly of*, τῆς οἰκουμένης Plb.12.26ᵈ.3; θεοῦ J.*BJ*3.8.9.

**κατα-σχεθεῖν**, inf. of κατέσχεθον, poet. aor. 2 of κατέχω (v. *σχέθω): —*hold back*, κατὰ δ' ἔσχεθε λαὸν ἅπαντα Od.24.530; κάσχεθε (Ep. for κατέσχεθε) Il.11.702; χειρὶ παιωνίᾳ κατασχεθών A.*Supp.*1066 (lyr.); κατασχεθόντες ἱππικὸν δρόμον S.*El.*754; also ὀργάς, θυμὸν κατασχεθεῖν, Id.*Ant.*1200, E.*HF*1210 (lyr.). **II.** νηῒ θοῇ Θορικόνδε κατέσχεθον *put in at* Th., *h.Cer.*126. ❋**-σχεσις**, εως, ἡ, *holding back, restraining, retention*, πνεύματος Hp.*Vict.*2.64. **II.** *possession*, Lxx *Le.*25.25, *Za.*11.14, al., *Act.Ap.*7.5. **III.** *relation, attitude*, κ. φιλικὴ πρὸς τῶν πέλας *Stoic.*3.24. **-σχετέος**, α, ον, *to be held fast*, Sch.Ar.*Ach.* 258. **2.** **-σχετέον**, abs., *one must hold back, delay*, Sch.E.*Ph.* 1279.

**κατασχετλιάζω**, *complain indignantly*, J.*BJ*1.32.4.

**κατάσχετος**, ον, poet. for κάτοχος, *held back, kept back*, κατάσχετόν τι καλύπτειν S.*Ant.*1253. **II.** *held fast, possessed*, κακίαις Phld. *Lib.*p.27 O.; κ. δαιμονίῳ πνεύματι D.H.1.31; θείᾳ μέθῃ Ph.1.103;

[ταῖς θεαῖς] Phalar.*Ep.*93.1; οἴστρῳ *AP*5.225 (Paul. Sil.); λύσσῃ Paus.8.19.3; ἐκ Νυμφῶν Id.10.12.11: abs., *inspired*, Str.11.4.7.

**κατασχημᾰτίζω**, *dress up* or *invest with* a certain form or appearance, σφᾶς αὐτοὺς οὕτως Isoc.11.24; κ. ἑαυτὸν σχήματί τινι Plu.*Rom.* 26:—Pass., *to be conformed, modelled*, Id.*Lyc.*27.

**κατ-ασχημονέω**, *act indecently*, Phot. s. v. σινωπῆσαι; *act indecently towards*, τινος App.*Sam.*7, Sch.Ar.*Ra.*153.

***κατα-σχίζω**, fut. -σχίσω X.*An.*7.1.16:—*cleave asunder, split, slit*, Ar.*V.*239, cj. in Hp.*Mochl.*36 (Pass.); κ. τὰς πύλας, τὰς θύρας, *burst them open*, X. l. c., D.21.79; *tear*, τοὺς χιτωνίσκους Phld.*Ir.*p.39 W.: —Med., κατεσχίσω τὸ ῥάκος Ar.*Ra.*405 (lyr.):—Pass., of nerves or veins, *branch*, Gal.2.390, 8.65; of leaves, Dsc.2.130. **-σχίσις**, εως, ἡ, *splitting up*, Gal.2.851, Dsc.3.60. **-σχιστέον**, *one must slit*, κύκλῳ Archig.ap.Aët.9.28 (melius -σχαστέον cod. Laud.Gr.60).

**κατασχολάζω**, *pass the time in idleness, loiter*, χρόνου τι κ. *tarry* somewhat too long, S.*Ph.*127; κ. ἐν ἀγρῷ Plu.*Tim.*36. II. κατεσχόλαζε τῆς Γναθαινίου λέγων, for ἐσχόλαζε λέγων κατὰ τῆς Γν., Macho ap.Ath.13.581d.

***κατ-ασχολέομαι**, *to be engaged*, περὶ τῶν ἐόντων, of sciences, Perict. ap.Stob.3.1.121; τὸ κατησχολημένον περὶ τὸν ἀνθρώπινον βίον *Placit.*1 *Prooem.*, cf. Archyt.ap.Iamb.*Comm.Math.*8, Apollon.*Mir.*7, *Theol. Ar.*18; *to be concerned, worried* about, περί τι *PRein.*18.18 (ii B.C.), Phld.*Rh.*2.139 S.

**κατασχόμενος**, aor. part. Med. used in pass. sense, v. κατέχω C. II.

**κατασῴζω**, *restore*, κατεσῴσαμες *Tab.Heracl.*1.51; -εσῴξαμες ib. 2.30.

**κατασωρεύω**, *heap up*, πλῆθος ὅπλων Plu.*Mar.*22, cf. *Cat.Ma.*20 (Pass.).

**κατ-ασωτεύομαι**, *squander on profligate living*, τὰς οὐσίας J.*BJ* 4.4.3.

**κατασώχω**, *rub in pieces, pound*, κ. περὶ λίθον τρηχὺν τῆς κυπαρίσσου pieces of cypress-wood, Hdt.4.75.

**καταταγή**, ἡ, (κατατάσσω) *replacing* of dislocated bones, Heliod. (?)ap.Orib.49.30.8. II. *placing* in position of names on a map, Ptol.*Geog.*1.18.5.

**καταταινιόω**, *bind with a* ταινία, Anon.ap.Suid. s. v. ἐταινίωσε (s. v. l.).

**κατατάκερος** [τᾰκ], ον, *softened much*, Gal.6.669.

**κατατακ-τέον**, *one must place, class*, τινὰ ἔν τισι Artem.2.34. **-τικῶς**, Adv., = *ordinate, Gloss.*

**κατατάκω** [ᾱ], Dor. for κατατήκω.

**κατατᾰνύω**, = κατατείνω, *h.Bacch.*34 (in Ep. aor. 1 καττάνυσαν), Hp. *Fract.*14, 44.

**κατάταξις**, εως, ἡ, *ordering, arranging*, Arr.*Epict.*4.1.53, Porph. ap.Iamb.*Myst.*1.8; κ. ἀστεροειδής Hierocl. *in CA*27 p.488 M.; *classification*, Crinis *Stoic.*3.268. 2. *ordinance, regulation*, *Milet.*3 No. 152.102 (Eresus, ii B.C.). II. Medic., *reduction* of dislocations, Heliod.(?) ap.Orib.49.29.5; of rupture, Heliod.ib.50.47.7.

***καταταρᾰ́σσω**, f. l. for καταράσσω, *Gloss.*

**καταταρτᾰρ-όω**, *hurl down to Tartarus*, Orph.*Fr.*57, Corn.*ND*7, S.E.*P.*3.210; οἱ μυθικοὶ τὸν Κρόνον -οῦσιν Lyd.*Mens.*4.159:—Pass., Apollod.1.1.3, Sch.E.*Med.*1296:—hence **-ωσις**, εως, ἡ, Procl. *in Ti.* 1.188 D., Lyd. l. c.

**κατάτᾰσις**, εως, ἡ, *stretching*, κ. τῶν χορδῶν (κατάστασις codd.) Arist.*Aud.*803$^a$37. 2. esp. for the purpose of setting broken or dislocated bones, Hp.*Fract.*13 (pl.), *Mochl.*38. 3. *torture, torment*, D.H.7.68, Ael.*Fr.*276; κατατάσεις τῆς ψυχῆς Ph.2.599. 4. *violent exertion*, μετὰ φιλονικίας καὶ κ., cj. for -στάσεως in Pl.*Lg.* 796a. II. *extension* in space, *spreading*, Id.*Ti.*58e (-στασιν cod.). 2. = ὁλκὴ εἰς τοὺς κάτω τόπους, Gal.19.461.

***κατατάσσω**, Att. -ττω, pf. -τέταχα Plb.8.9.5, al.:—*draw up in order, arrange*, τὴν στρατιάν X.*Cyr.*3.3.11, cf. *Oec.*9.13; esp. *place in, refer to* a class, εἰς φυλήν Lys.13.79; τινὰ εἰς τοὺς δικαστάς Plu.2.178f; τινὰ μετά τινος Ath.8.335b:—Pass., εἰς τοὺς ἀσεβεῖς -ταχθείς D.S. 4.74; ἐς τοὺς ἱππεύοντας -ταγείς Hdn.6.8.1: Geog., *insert* in a map, Ptol.*Geog.*1.18.4: in Surgery, *replace*, τὸν δίδυμον Heliod.ap.Orib. 50.47.6: pf. part. Pass. -τεταγμένος *in an ordered series*, opp. ἀόριστος, μονάδες Procl. *in Prm.*p.561 S.; opp. ἐξῃρημένος, μονάδες ib.p.573 S. 2. *appoint*, ἐπί τι to do a thing, D.25.13; κ. τινὰ εἰς τάξιν ἡντινοῦν Pl.*Lg.*945a; εἰς λειτουργίαν *POxy.*1415.18 (iii A. D., Pass.); κ. τινὰ εἰς.. *appoint* one to go to a place, Plb.3.33.12. 3. *pay* into a treasury, εἰς τὸ βασιλικόν *PSI*5.510.13 (iii B.C.):—Pass., *to be allocated* to a fund, *SIG*459.6 (Beroea, iii B.C.). II. *set down in order, narrate* or *describe fully*, ἐν τοῖς ὑπομνήμασι Plb.2.47.11, cf. Phld.*Ir.* p.74 W., etc.; κ. εἰς τὴν ἀπόκρισιν διότι.. Plb.24.10.7, etc. III. κατατάξασθαι τοῖς φυλέταις ὑπέρ τινος *make arrangements* with.., D. 58.17. IV. *assimilate* food, in Pass., Sor.1.37; of things inhaled, Anon.Lond.23.31, al.

**καταταχέω**, *accelerate*, *PTeb.*19.13 (ii B.C.):—Pass., ib.24.29 (ii B.C.). II. *outstrip, overtake*, τινὰ τῇ παρασκευῇ Plb.8.3.3; *escape by superior speed*, Id.1.47.8; κ. τινά c. part., *anticipate* in doing, Id. 3.16.5, 4.68.5:—Pass., κ. ὑπὸ τῆς ὀξύτητος τοῦ καιροῦ D.S.14.72. 2. abs., *to be first, arrive first*, πρὸς τὴν πύλην Plb.9.17.4, cf. 1.86.8; *come in time*, Id.3.86.3, 9.18.3: c. part. only, do *quickly* or *in good time*, Id.2.18.6, 3.16.4, etc.

**κατατέγγω**, *wet thoroughly*, σπόγγον Hp.*Mul.*2.113:—Pass., Phld. *Mort.*29.

**κατατεθαρρηκότως**, Adv. pf. part. Act. of καταθαρρέω, *boldly, confidently*, Plb.1.86.5, Plu.*Ant.*27.

**κατατέθηπα**, pf. with pres. sense, *to be astonished at*, Hsch. (with inf. -τεθήπειν), Suid.

**κατατεθνεώς**, and (in Hom.) -ηώς, pf. part. of καταθνήσκω.

***κατατείνω**, fut. -τενῶ E.*IA*336: aor. -έτεινα (v. infr.):—*stretch, draw tight*, κατὰ δ' ἡνία τεῖνεν ὀπίσσω Il.3.261, 311; κ. χαλινούς Hdt.4. 72; κ. τὰ ὅπλα *draw* the cables *taut*, Id.7.36; τὰ νεῦρα εἰς τὸ ἐξόπισθεν κ. Pl.*Ti.*84e. 2. *stretch for the purpose of setting* a bone, Hp.*Fract.* 15:—also Med., ib.5:—Pass., μῦς κατατεταμένος ib.8. 3. *rack, torture*, κατατεινόμενος ὑπὸ τῆς βασάνου προσωμολόγησε D.48.18, cf. Ael. *Fr.*176; κατατείνειν ταῖς κολάσεσι Id.*Fr.*279: metaph., κ. τὴν ψυχήν Id.*Fr.*60; κατέτεινέ με διηγούμενος Lib.*Decl.*33.25; κατατείνεσθαι ὑπὸ ποδάγρας Phylarch.40 J., cf. *AP*11.128 (Poll.). 4. *stretch out* or *draw in a straight line*, κατέτεινε σχοινοτενέας ὑποδέξας διώρυχας, i. e. he marked out the ditches by drawing straight lines, Hdt.1.189; δόλιχον κ. τοῦ λόγου *make a very long* speech, Pl.*Prt.*329b; μακρὸν λόγον, πολλοὺς καὶ μακροὺς ἐλέγχους, Phlp. *in APr.*262.10, *in APo.*243.19; φεύγουσι κατατείναντες τὴν κέρκον Arist.*HA*629$^b$35:—Pass., *extend throughout*, Id.*PA*650$^a$29. 5. Pass., *to be tightly bound*, ὑπὸ δεσμοῦ Plu.*Luc.*24. 6. *stretch on the ground, lay at full length*, [ὁ ἐλέφας] τοὺς φοίνικας κ. ἐπὶ τῆς γῆς Arist.*HA*610$^a$24; κ. τινὰς ἐπὶ τοὔδαφος Plu. *Publ.*6:—Pass., *to be extended over* a space, ἐπὶ γῆν Pl.*Ti.*58e; πρὸς γῆν πᾶν τὸ σῶμα ib.92a; σκέλη ἐπὶ τῇ γῇ -τεταμένα Arist.*IA*713$^a$19. 7. metaph., *strain, exert*, κ. τὴν ῥώμην ὅλην Plb.21.34.7 (s. v. l.):—Pass., *to be strained*, μᾶλλον, ἧττον -τείνεσθαι, Pl.*Ti.*63c; λόγοι κατατεινόμενοι words *of hot contention*, E.*Hec.*130 (anap.); δρόμημα συνεχῶς -τεταμένον Arist.*HA*629$^b$19; κ. τῷ προσώπῳ *strain* with the muscles of *one's* face, Plu.*Ant.*77; cf. infr. II. 2. b. *overwork*, τοὺς γεωργούς *PTeb.* 61$^b$197 (ii B.C.). II. intr., *extend* or *run straight towards*, τάφρον -τείνουσαν ἐκ τῶν Ταυρικῶν ὀρέων ἐς τὴν Μαιῆτιν λίμνην Hdt.4.3, cf. 9.15; γῆ κ. πρὸς ἑσπέρην ἐπὶ ποταμὸν Ἀγγίτην it *stretches* westward up to.., Id.7.113, cf. 4.19, X.*HG*4.4.7: abs., *extend*, ταύτῃ κ. Hdt.8. 31. b. *extend downwards*, Plu.2.566d. c. metaph., *tend*, εἴς τι Metrod.*Fr.*6. 2. *strive earnestly, be vehement*, E.*IA*336; ἰσχυρῶς κ. X.*An.*2.5.30; opp. χαλάω, Pl.*R.*329c; κ. ἡ ὀδύνη v. l. for κατακτείνει in Hp.*Fract.*42, cf. Gal.6.311: freq. in aor. part. with adverb. sense, *with all one's force* or *might*, κατατείνας ἐρῶ Pl.*R.*358d, cf. 367b; ὁ λέων τρέχει κ. Arist.*HA*629$^b$18; ᾠχόμην κ. Luc.*Lex.*3; ὄρνεις κατατείνασαι ἐκπτήσονται Id.*Sat.*35.

**κατατειχίζω**, *fortify*, Sch.D Il.19.99 (Pass.).

**κατατειχογρᾰφέω**, f. l. for κατατοιχ- (q. v.).

**κατατελευτάω**, *terminate*, εἰς τοὺς νεφρούς Arist.*PA*671$^b$13.

**κατατελέω**, *contribute*, φόρον dub. in *IG*1$^2$.231.

**κατατέμνω**, Ion. -τάμνω, fut. -τεμῶ Ar.*Ach.*301: aor. κατέτεμον (v. infr.); Ion. and Dor. κατέταμον Hdt.4.26, *Tab.Heracl.*1.14:—*cut in pieces, cut up*, κρέα Hdt. l. c., cf. Ar.*Pax*1059; ἑαυτόν X.*Mem.*1.2.55; τὴν κεφαλήν Aeschin.3.212; γέρρα X.*An.*4.7.26:—Med., κ. δέραν ὄνυχι *lacerate*, E.*El.*146 (lyr., tm.):—Pass., τελαμῶσι κατατετμημένοις with regularly *cut* bandages, Hdt.2.86; σπλάγχνα κατατετμημένα Ar.*Av.* 1524; χώρη ἐς διώρυχας -τέτμηται *is cut up* into ditches or canals, Hdt. 1.193, cf. 2.8; κατετέτμηντο ἐξ αὐτῶν (sc. τῶν διωρύχων) τάφροι ἐπὶ τὴν χώραν X.*An.*2.4.13. b. metaph., τι ἐν τοῖς λόγοις κ. Pl.*Hp.Ma.* 301b. 2. c. dupl. acc., κ. τινὰ καττύματα *cut* him up into strips, Ar.*Ach.*301; σῶμα κατατεμὼν κύβους *having cut* it *up* into cubes, Alex.187.4; τὴν βατίδα τεμάχη κατατεμών Ephipp.22; ὅτι σμικρότατα τὸ σῶμα Pl.*R.*610b; κ. (sc. τὰν γᾶν) μερίδας τέτορας *Tab.Heracl.* l. c.: —Pass., κατατμηθείην λέπαδνα *may I be cut up* into straps, Ar.*Eq.* 768. 3. κ. τὸν Πειραιᾶ *lay* it *out* in streets, Arist.*Pol.*1267$^b$23:—Pass., τὸ ἄστυ κατατέτμηται τὰς ὁδοὺς ἰθέας *has its* streets *cut* straight, Hdt.1.180. 4. *cut into* the ground, κ. τοῦ χωρίου βάθος τρεῖς πόδας *IG*2$^2$.1668.7; τὰ κατατετμημένα *places where mines have already been worked*, opp. τὰ ἄτμητα, X.*Vect.*4.27. 5. *cut down, pare*, [τὸ δέρμα] ὁμαλῶς Hp.*Fract.*11. 6. *abuse, revile*, Pl.*R.*488b, Hyp.*Ath.*12.

**κατατέρπω**, *delight greatly*, in Pass., Lxx *Ze.*3.14.

**κατατεταγμένως**, Adv. pf. part. Pass., (κατατάσσω) *in order*, D.S. 9.10 (sed leg. -τεταμένως (κατατείνω), *eagerly*).

**κατατετραίνω**, found as pres. only in the form -τιτράω Gal.11. 402: aor. 1 -έτρησα Plu.2.689c:—*bore through, perforate*, ll. cc.: usu. in pf. Pass., σήραγγας κατατετρημένας cavities *bored through* it, Pl.*Ti.*70c, cf. Str.15.1.36; ὁ πλεύμων πόροις κατατέτρηται Plu.2.699a.

**κατατεύχω**, *make, construct*, ἰδίην σορόν *Epigr.Gr.*460 (Trachonitis); [ἐγκώμιον] Phld.*Rh.*1.215 S. (Pass.). II. *make, render*, αὐτοὺς θαρσαλέους Q.S.7.676.

**κατατεφρόω**, *cover with ashes*, τὴν Λιπαραίων πόλιν, of the volcano, Arist.*Mete.*367$^a$7:—Pass., Str.5.4.8.

**κατατεχνέω**, *frame artificially*, Ph.1.608 codd. (κακο- Wendl.).

***κατάτεχνος**, ον, *artificial*, κίνημα (v. l. κακο-) *AP*5.131 (Phld., Sup.); τὸ κ. Plu.2.79b; epith. of Callimachus the sculptor, Vitr.4.1.10 codd. (sed leg. κατατηξίτεχνος); cf. κακιζότεχνος.

**κατατήκω**, Dor. -τάκω [ᾱ], *melt* or *thaw away*, and in Pass., *to be melted* or *thawed*, ὡς δὲ χιὼν κατατήκετ'.. ἥν τ' Εὖρος κατέτηξεν Od.19. 205; κ. ὦπας δάκρυσι Theoc.*Ep.*6; ψυχὴν λύπαις D.L.8.18; κατατήκεσθαι τὸ θυμοειδές Phld.*Mus.*p.103 K. 2. *dissolve*, λίτρον κ. τὰς σάρκας Hdt.2.87, cf. *POxy.*40.8 (ii/iii A. D.); ἀέρα κ. πῦρ, i. e. rarifies it, Pl.*Ti.*61a; κ. ὁ χρόνος Arist.*Ph.*221$^a$31; τὸ αἷμα *dilute* it, Gal.6. 262. 3. metaph., κ. τέχνην εἴς τι *waste* art and skill upon a thing, D.H.*Dem.*51. II. Pass., with pf. Act. κατατέτηκα, *melt away*, κατατήκομαι ἦτορ Od.19.136; τὰ σπλάγχνα κατατετηκότα ἐξάγειν *dissolved*, Hdt.2.87; κατατάκομαι S.*El.*187 (lyr.), cf. *Ant.*977 (lyr., tm.), ὑπὸ τοῦ.. ἄλγους κατατέτηκα Ar.*Pl.*1034; ἔρωτι κατατήκεσθαι X.*Smp.*

8.3, Eub.104: so with gen. added, τούτω κατετάκετο.. ἔρωτα Theoc. 14.26; κ. ἐν ψήφοις *wear oneself away* in.., Luc.*Epigr.*12.

**κατατηξίτεχνος** [ῐ], ον, *enfeebling his art*, epith. of the artist Callimachus, Paus.1.26.7 (v.l. κακιζότεχνον), prob. in Plin.*HN*34.92 (*calat*–, *catot*–, codd.), and in Vitr.4.1.10 (*catalechnos*, *catathecnos*, codd.).

❋**κατατίθημι**, fut. -θήσω: Hom. freq. uses the Ep. aor. forms, Act. κάτθεμεν, κάτθετε, κάτθεσαν, inf. καθθέμεν (Dor. καθθέμειν prob. in Epich.71, Aeol. κά(θ)θηκε *Schwyzer*647[a] (Naucratis, vi B.C.)), Med. κατθέμεθα, κατθέσθην, κατθέμενοι (sg. κάτθετο A.R.3.867); also καταθείομεν, aor. subj. for καταθῶμεν, Od.21.264; καταθείομαι, aor. subj. Med. for καταθῶμαι, Il.22.111, Od.19.17:—*place, put, lay down*, folld. by various Preps., κ. ἄρνας ἐπὶ χθονός Il.3.293; κόρυθ' ἐπὶ χθονὶ 6.473; κ. τινὰ ἐν Λυκίης δήμῳ or εἰς Ἰθάκην, *set* him *down in*.., 16.683, Od.16.230; τινὰ ἐν λεχέεσσι Il.18.233; τεύχε' ἐς θάλαμον Od.24.166; ἐς μέγαρον ἐπὶ θρόνου 20.96; κλισίην τινὶ παρὰ πυρί 19.55; τι ὑπὸ ζυγά 13.20; τι ἐκ καπνοῦ *take down* out of the smoke, 16.288, 19.7. **2.** *put down, offer as a prize*, ἄπυρον κατέθηκε λέβητα Il.23.267, cf. 885 (tm.); κ. ἄεθλα Od.24.91; but κ. ἄεθλον *ordain* a contest, 19.572; εἰς τὴν ἀγορὰν γράμματα κ. *set up* as a public notice, Pl.*Lg.*946d; so also κ. τι ἐς μέσον *put* it *down* in the midst, i.e. for common use, E.*Cyc.*547, cf. Ar.*Ec.*602; οὐσίαν, χρήματα κ., ib.855, 871; τὰ ὅπλα εἰς τὸ μέσον X.*Cyr.*2.1.14; but ἐς μέσον Πέρσῃσι κ. τὰ πρήγματα *communicate* power to them, *give* them *a common share of* it, Hdt.3.80; ἐς μέσον Κῴοισι κ. τὴν ἀρχήν Id.7.164; τὸ αὐτῶν ἔργον ἅπασι κοινὸν κ. Pl.*R.*369e; κ. εἰς τὸ μέσον or εἰς τὸ κοινόν, *propose* for common discussion, Id.*Phlb.*14b, *Cra.*384c. **3.** *put down as payment, pay down*, Hdt.9.120, Ar.*Ra.*176, *Nu.*246, Th.1.27, Pl.*Prt.*314b, *Lg.*921d, etc.; τέλη Antipho5.77; μετοίκιον Lys.31.9; τὸ ὄφλημα D.21.99, cf. 151; τὰς συμβολάς Antiph.26.8; *put down as paid* (in accounts), X.*Oec.*9.8; τί..τουτονὶ καταθῶ σοι..; *what shall I pay* you for these? Ar.*Pax*1214: generally, *pay, perform* what one has promised, νικῶντί γε χάριν κ. Pi.*N.*7.76; ἃ δ' ὑπέσχεο ποῖ καταθήσεις; S.*OC*227(anap.):—also in Med., v. infr. II.7. **b.** *dedicate*, *Schwyzer*647[a] (Naucratis, vi B.C.), 682(2) (Cypr.), al. **4.** *deposit*, παρακαταθήκην ἐς.. Hdt.5.92.η'; ἐνέχυρα *IG*5(2).344.18 (Orchom. Arc., iii B.C.):—in this sense usu. in Med., cf. II.4. **b.** *mortgage*, *Leg.Gort.*6.19, *Test.Epict.*2.13, etc. **5.** *deposit* in the tomb, *bury*, v.l. in *Ev.Marc.*15.46. **6.** *sow* seed, *POxy.*1031.17 (iii A.D.). **7.** κ. ὁδόν *lay down*, *make* a road, Pi.*P.*5.90. **8.** *dish up, serve*, Epich.71. **9.** in late form κατατίθω, *consign*, ἀγγέλοις καταχθονίοις *Tab.Defix.Aud.*75.1. **II.** Med., *lay down from oneself, put off, lay aside*, esp. of arms, τεύχεα.. τὰ μὲν κατέθεντ' ἐπὶ γαίῃ Il.3.114, cf. Od.22.141 (hence, comically, θυμὸν κατάθου παρὰ τὴν ὀργὴν ὥσπερ ὁπλίτης Ar.*Av.*401); χλαίνας μὲν κατέθεντο κατὰ κλισμούς Od.17.86; ζώναν καταθηκαμένα, of a maiden, Pi.*O.*6.39; θοἰμάτιον, etc., Ar.*Pl.*926, etc.; τὴν χλαμύδα (of the ἔφηβος) prob. in Philem.34; τὴν μοναρχίαν *lay down*, Plu.*Fab.*9. **2.** metaph., *put an end to, settle*, τὸν πόλεμον Th.1.121, Lys.33.6, D.19.264:—Pass., ξυμφορὰς μετρίως κατατιθεμένης *being arranged* on tolerable terms, Th.4.20. **b.** *put aside, leave out of the question*, τοὺς ποιητάς Pl.*Prt.*348a, cf. *Ti.*59c, Democr.3; κ. ἐν ἀμελείᾳ *treat* negligently, X.*Mem.*1.4.15. **3.** *lay down* in a place; of the dead, *bury*, Od.24.190; κ. πηδάλιον ὑπὲρ καπνοῦ Hes.*Op.*45; τὰς μαχαίρας ἐνθάδι Ar.*Eq.*489; [τὰ στρώματα] Id.*Ra.*166; ὤμοισι κατ' ἄμβροτα θήκατο τεύχη on one's shoulders, Q.S.12.303; *put on shore, disembark*, Luc.*Alex.*57; ποῖ δὴ ἡμᾶς ὁ ἀνὴρ -θήσεται; Plu.*Caes.*37: metaph., πολλὰ αἱ μακραὶ ἁμέραι κατέθεντο λύπας ἐγγυτέρω *have brought* them *nearer*.., S.*OC*1216(lyr.). **4.** *deposit for oneself, lay by, lay up in store* (v. supr. I.4), [γαστέρας] ἐπὶ δόρπῳ for supper, Od.18.45; ἔντεα ἐς θάλαμον 19.17; ὅπλα εἰς τὰς ἄκρας X.*Cyr.*7.5.34; βίον Hes.*Op.*601; σμικρὸν ἐπὶ σμικρῷ ib.361; καρποὺς ἐς φορβήν Hdt.1.202; παραθήκην Id.6.73; χρήματα Antipho Soph.54; θησαυρὸν παισί Thgn.409; θησαυροὺς ἐν οἴκῳ X.*Cyr.*8.2.15; μυρίους δαρεικοὺς εἰς τὸ ἴδιον ἐμοί Id.*An.*1.3.3; [σῖτον] *hoard it up* in hope of high prices, Lys.22.9. **b.** metaph., κλέος *lay up store of* glory, Hdt.7.220, 9.78, Pl.*Smp.*208c; ἀΐδιον δόξαν κ. Th.4.87; κ. ἀποστροφήν τινι X.*An.*7.6.34: freq. χάριτα or χάριν καταθέσθαι τινι or πρός τινα, *lay up a store of* gratitude or favour, Hdt.6.41, 7.178, Antipho5.61, Th.1.33, D.59.21, etc.; εὐεργεσίαν κ. ἐς Βασιλέα Th.1.128 (so in Pass., μεγάλων μοι κατατεθεισῶν ἐς αὐτὸν εὐεργεσιῶν Hdn.3.6.2, cf. 1.4.3); also ἔχθραν καταθέσθαι πρὸς ἐκείνους ὑπὲρ αὐτῶν Lys.2.22; κατέθετο μῖσος διπλάσιον τῆς οὐσίας Men.646: but κ. ὀργήν εἴς τινας *vent* one's fury upon.., X.*Cyn.*10.8. **5.** *deposit in a place of safety*, τοὺς πρέσβεις κατέθεντο εἰς Αἴγιναν Th.3.72; τὴν λείαν ἐς τοὺς Βιθυνούς X.*HG*1.3.2; κ. εἰς τὸ οἴκημα D.56.4; οἴκαδε Pl.*Prt.*314a; διαθήκην παρά τινι Is.6.27; φιλίαν παρὰ θεοῖς X.*An.*2.5.8; [Διόνυσον] ἐν Δρακάνῳ Theoc.26.34:—Pass., of prisoners, ἐν τῷ δεσμωτηρίῳ κατατεθῶσιν Lex ap.D.24.63, cf. D.C.58.1. **6.** *lay up in memory* or *as a memorial*, χρὴ..γνώμην ταύτην (ταύτῃ Bgk.) καταθέσθαι Thgn.717; μνημεῖον παρά τινι Pl.*Tht.*209c; κ. εἰς μνήμην *record, register*, Id.*Lg.*858d; κ. τι ἐς βιβλίον D.61.2; γνώμην -θέσθαι εἰς μέσον D.H.*Rh.*9.4. **7.** *pay* (cf. I.3), ἐκφόριον *BGU*1059.22 (i B.C.), cf. *PTeb.*329.7 (ii A.D.), etc. **b.** *employ, spend*, τὴν ἀκμὴν ..πρὸς τί κατατιθέμενος on what he is *employing* the prime of life, Apollod.Com.13.4; τὸν βίον ἔς τι Phld.*Rh.*1.244S.; κ. τὴν σχολὴν εἴς καλόν τι *employ one's* leisure in.., Plu.2.135d; τὴν τοῦ λέγειν δύναμιν εἰς τὴν τῶν ἀδικουμένων βοήθειαν D.S.9.13; σπουδὴν -τιθέμενοι Polystr.p.19 W. **8.** *impose*, ὄνομα Parm.19.3, cf. 8.39; but μορφὰς κατέθεντο δύο γνώμας ὀνομάζειν *recorded their decision, decided* to name, ib.53. **9.** in Law, *depose, aver*, ἐν ὑπομνήμασι *PLips.*35.16 (iv A.D.), cf. *Cod.Just.*1.5.16.1, etc. **b.** = συγκατατίθεμαι, Eust.1261.19. **c.** *make* a testamentary *disposition*, κ. διαθηκιμαίαν βούλησιν *PMasp.*151.43, al. (vi A.D.).—Freq. in Hom. and familiar Att.; rare in Trag.

**κατατῑλάω**, *make dirt over*, τῆς στήλης, τῶν Ἑκαταίων, Ar.*Av.*1054, *Ra.*366:—Pass., τοῖς ὄρνισι κατατιλώμενοι Id.*Av.*1117; κατὰ τῆς κεφαλῆς κατατετιλῆσθαι Artem.2.26.

**κατατίλλω**, aor. 1 -έτῑλα, *pull to pieces*, ῥάκος Hp.*Nat.Mul.*32: metaph., κ. ἑαυτὸν ἐπὶ θρήνου Hsch. s.v. δρύπτεται.

**κατατῑμωρέω**, *punish*, *Tab.Defix.Aud.*76.7 (Attica).

**κατατιτρ-άω**, v. κατατετραίνω. **-ησις**, εως, ἡ, = κατάτρησις, Crito ap.Gal.13.883.

**κατατιτρώσκω**, *wound*, X.*An.*3.4.26; λίθοις καὶ τοξεύμασι ib.4.1.10; ἑαυτόν D.L.1.60, cf. Plb.33.9.6, Plu.*Sol.*30, etc.:—Pass., Id.*Caes.*66: metaph., πάθη κ. τινάς Ph.1.299; κατατετρωμένοι τὰς ψυχὰς ἐκ νοσημάτων Id.1.156. **2.** *open an abscess*, ἔμπλαστρος -σκουσα Aët.15.17.

**κατατῐτύσκομαι**, *aim at*, ἀλλήλων Eust.1331.14.

**κατατλάω**, strengthd. for *τλάω, in med. form κατετλᾶτο, Hsch. **κατατοιόντα**· κατασκευάζοντα, Id. (fort. καταρτύοντα).

**κατατοιχογρᾰφέω**, *write upon a wall*, κ. τί τινος *write up libels against* a person, Str.14.5.14; v.l. κατατειχ-.

**κατατοκίζω**, *beggar by usurious interest*, τινας Anon.*Vit.Thuc.*:—Pass., *to be thus beggared*, Arist.*Pol.*1316[b]16.

**κατατολμάω**, *behave boldly towards*, τῶν πολεμίων Plb.3.103.5; *make an insolent attack upon*, τῆς πόλεως Id.12.8.2; κ. τῆς κοινῆς πίστεως S.E.*M.*7.27; ὁ πρῶτος -ήσας θαλάττης Philostr.*Ep.*38; ἐρωμένης ib.16; ἀλλοτρίων ἔργων Jul.*Or.*1.3c; κ. τοῦ καλῶς ἔχοντος *presume beyond* propriety, Plb.39.1.9: also c. gen., *make a bold bid for*, τῆς τῶν ὅλων ἀρχῆς Id.15.25.28. **II.** strengthd. for τολμάω: abs., Id.1.47.10, *UPZ*42.20 (ii B.C.); κατατετολμηκότες *desperate, reckless persons*, Phld.*Sto.Herc.*339.12: c. inf., Plb.2.13.5, Lxx 2*Ma.*3.24, Gal.14.644: c. acc., κ. ἔφοδον Hld.7.24.

❋**κατατομή**, ἡ, *incision, notch, groove*, Thphr.*HP*4.8.10, Sm.*Je.*31(48).37; ἄνευ -τομῆς *uncarved, smooth*, *IG*1[2].372.134, cf. 373.231: pl., Artem.1.67. **II.** *part of a theatre*, Hyp.*Dem.Fr.*3: variously expld. as = ὀρχήστρα or διάζωμα, *AB*270, cf. Phot. **2.** *face* of rock, ἐπέγραψεν ἐπὶ τὴν κ. τῆς πέτρας Philoch.138; μέταλλον καὶ κ. perh. a mine and a *quarry-face*, *IG*2[2].1582.70. **III.** = καταγραφή, *profile*, Hsch. (s.h.v.). **IV.** *mutilation*, opp. true *circumcision*, a παρονομασία in *Ep.Phil.*3.2.

**κατάτονος**, ον, *stretching down*: *depressed*, i.e. less high than broad, opp. ἀνάτονος, Vitr.10.10.6.

**κατατόξ-ευσις**, εως, ἡ, gloss on βολή, Sch.Opp.*H.*4.559 (pl.). **-εύω**, *strike down with arrows, shoot dead*, τινα Hdt.3.36, Th.3.34, etc.; ῥηματίοισιν καινοῖς αὐτὸν καὶ διανοίαις κ. Ar.*Nu.*944:—Pass., X.*HG*4.7.6, Phld.*Piet.*34: metaph., κ. τινὰ τὸ περιττὸν τῆς τρυφῆς Eun.*Hist.*p.263 D.

**κατατορνεύω**, *turn*, in Pass., κ. τὴν ἐντὸς ἐπιφάνειαν πρὸς ἐμβολέα Hero *Spir.*1.28.

**κατατρᾰγεῖν**, aor. 2 inf. Act. of κατατρώγω.

**κατατρᾰγῳδέω**, *describe tragically, exaggerate*, κάλλος Ach.Tat.6.4: also c. gen., ὅσα κατετραγῴδησέ μου *uttered in tragic phrase against*, Id.8.9.

**κατατραυματίζω**, Ion -τρωματίζω, *wound*, ἑαυτόν Arist.*Ath.*14.1, D.S.13.95; opp. ἀποκτείνειν, Plb.3.67.3:—Pass., Hdt.7.212, Th.7.80, etc. **II.** of ships, *disable, cripple*, ib.41, 8.10.

**κατατρεπτικῶς**, v. καταστρεπτικῶς.

**κατατρέπω**, *put to flight*, *PMasp.*4.13 (vi A.D.).

❋**κατατρέχω**, aor. 1 inf. καταθρέξαι only in Hsch.: aor. 2 κατέδρᾰμον Ar.*Ec.*961, etc.: pf. -δεδράμηκα ἅμ] X.*HG*4.7.6:—Pass., aor. inf. καταδρᾰμηθῆναι Heph.Astr.1.21:—*run down*, Ar. l.c.; ἀπὸ τῶν ἄκρων Hdt.7.192; κάτω Id.3.156; ἐπὶ θάλατταν X.*An.*7.1.20; ἐπί τινας *Act.Ap.*21.32. **2.** of seamen or passengers by sea, *run to land, disembark*, X.*HG*5.1.12; εἰς ἐμπόρια Plb.3.91.2: metaph., κ. ξένιον ἄστυ *come to a haven in*.., f.l. in Pi.*N.*4.23. **II.** trans., *run down, inveigh against*, τὴν Σπάρτην Pl.*Lg.*806c, cf. Diog.Oen.12, D.C.50.2, etc.: more freq. c. gen., Phld.*Vit.*p.42 J., etc.; κ. τῶν μαντέων D.L.2.135; τῶν συνόντων τοῖς δυνάσταις D.C.61.10; τῆς μέθης Ath.1.11e; Ἀλκιβιάδου ὡς οἰνόφλυγος Id.5.220c, cf. A.D.*Synt.*100.19; κατὰ τῆς βουλῆς, κατὰ τῆς μοναρχίας, D.C.36.44, 66.13. **2.** *overrun, ravage, lay waste*, τῆς Σαλαμῖνος τὰ πολλά Th.2.94, cf. 8.92, Dionys.Com.3.5, D.S.2.44, Luc.*Alex.*2, etc., *oppress*, τοὺς γεωργούς *PTeb.*41.30 (ii B.C.). **3.** *run over*, c. gen., κὰδ δ' ἄρα οἱ βλεφάρων βαρὺς ἔδραμεν ὕπνος Theoc.22.204. **4.** *pursue*, Lxx *Le.*26.37. **5.** *hurry*, Plu.2.512e. **6.** *slip down*, of a bandage, Gal.18(1).829.

**κατάτρησις**, εως, ἡ, *aperture*, mostly pl., Epicur.ap.*Placit.*2.20.14, Dsc.5.102, Gal.7.728, al., Erot. s.v. σπόγγοι.

**κατατρῐᾱκοντουτίζω**, Com. word in Ar.*Eq.*1391, alluding to the σπονδαὶ τριακοντούτιδες, personified upon the stage as courtesans, with an obscene pun upon ἀκοντίζω (i.e. περαίνω).

**κατα-τρῐβή**, ἡ, *wasting, squandering*, τὴν Πλάτωνος διατριβὴν κ. [ἔλεγε ὁ Διογένης] D.L.6.24. **-τρίβω** [ῑ], fut. -ψω X.*Cyr.*8.4.36: pf. -τέτρῐφα Isoc. (v. infr.):—Pass., fut. -τρῐβήσομαι X.*HG*5.4.60:—*rub down* or *away*: hence, **1.** of clothes, *wear out*, ἀμφὶ πλευρῇσι δορὰς Thgn.55, cf. Ar.*Fr.*345, Pl.*Phd.*87c, Metrod.*Fr.*55: hence metaph., πολλὰ σώματα κατατρίψασα ἡ ψυχή Pl.*Phd.*91d, cf. 87d; οἱ τὰ βήματα κατατετριφότες, i.e. *constant frequenters* of the tribune, Isoc.*Ep.*8.7; ὁ σταλαγμὸς κ. Arist.*Ph.*253[b]15: metaph., κ. τὸ τῆς

ἀρετῆς ὄνομα *to have* it *always on one's tongue*, Luc.*Par*.43. b. *press downwards*, –ομένης πάτῳ τῆς ῥίζης Thphr.*HP*6.6.10. c. *rub* or *roll* thread, περὶ γούνατι νῆμα χειρί Theoc.24.77. 2. of persons, *wear out, exhaust*, αὐτοὺς περὶ ἑαυτοὺς τοὺς Ἕλληνας κ. Th.8.46 :—Pass., *to be quite worn out*, c. part., κατατετρίμμεθα πλανώμενοι Ar.*Pax*355, cf. X.*Mem*.1.2.37; –τριβήσοιντο ὑπὸ πολέμου Id.*HG*5.4.60; ἐν τοῖς στρατοπέδοις Isoc.15.115; περὶ τὸν πόλεμον Plu.*Fab*.19. 3. of Time, *spend, consume*, κατέτριψε τὴν ἡμέραν δημηγορῶν D.57.9, cf. Aeschin. 2.14, Men.*Epit*.54, Plu.*Caes*.13; τὰς ἡμέρας περὶ τῶν τυχόντων Arist. *EN*1117ᵇ35, cf. Plb.5.62.6, etc.; κ. τὸν βίον *employ* it *fully*, X.*Mem*. 4.7.5, Nicol.Com.1.23, cf. Phld.*Rh*.1.38 S.:—so in Med., τὸ πολὺ τοῦ βίου ἐν δικαστηρίοις φεύγων τε καὶ διώκων κ. *waste* the greater part of one's life in.., Pl.*R*.405b: in pf. Pass. (later in aor. 2 -τρῐβέντες *Cod.Just*.1.5.16.5), *wear away one's life, pass one's whole time*, c. part., αὐλοῖς καὶ λύραισι κατατέτριμμαι χρώμενος Ar.*Fr*.221; κ. στρατευόμενος X.*Mem*.3.4.1; ἐπί τινι Them.*Or*.26.312c. 4. of property, etc., *squander*, ἅπαντα X.*Cyr*.8.4.36; τὸν λόγον περί τι D.H.*Comp*. 11.

✻**κατατρῐδομέω**, perh. *lay three layers of stones*, *IG*12(2).11.18 (Mytil.).

**κατατρίζω**, strengthd. for τρίζω, Batr.88.

**κατατρίχιος** [τρῐ], ον, *fine as a hair*, Hsch.

**κατάτριψις**, εως, ἡ, *a being worn out*, τῶν ὀργάνων Hp.*Epid*.6.3.1.

**κατα-τροπά**, ᾶ, Dor. name of a part of the νόμος κιθαρῳδικός, Poll. 4.66. **-τροπος**, ον, = κατάντης, *steep*, prob. in Hsch. **-τροπόω**, *put to flight*, Aesop.291ᵇ:—also in Med., Id.21.

✻**κατατροχ-άζω**, *cause to run smoothly*: hence, *promote*, τὴν εὐανδρίαν *OGI*339.84 (Sestos, ii B.C.). II. = κατατρέχω II.2, Nech. in *Cat.Cod.Astr*.7.141 (Pass.). **-ίζω**, *upset* from a chariot, Sch. A.R.1.752; *break on the wheel*, condemned by Phryn.*PS*p.114 B. (Pass.).

**κατατρύζω**, *chatter against*, τινος *AP*11.321 (Phil.).

**κατατρῡπάω**, *bore through*, *Gloss*.

**κατατρῠφάω**, *make merry, be insolent*, Luc.*JTr*.53; = κατασπαταλάω, Hsch. II. c. gen., *delight in*, τοῦ Κυρίου Lxx*Ps*.36(37).4; ἐπὶ πλήθει εἰρήνης ib.11.

**κατατρύχω** [ῡ], *wear out, exhaust*, δώροισι κατατρύχω καὶ ἐδωδῇ λαούς Il.17.225; ἵνα μή σε κ. καὶ ἑταίρους Od.15.309, cf. 16.84; τίς τυ κατατρύχει; Theoc.1.78, cf. *AP*7.630 (Antiphil.), Luc.*Herm*.77, *Dips*.4, *PLond*.5.1677.50 (vi A.D.):—Pass., μελέτῃ κατατρυχόμενοι E.*Med*.1100 (anap.).

**κατατρύω**, = foreg., in Med., κατατρύσαιο δὲ γυῖα Nic.*Al*.593:—Pass., pf. inf. –τετρῦσθαι prob. l. in X.*Cyr*.5.4.6.

**κατατρώγω**, fut. -τρώξομαι Cratin.143: aor. 2 κατέτρᾰγον Ar.*Ach*. 809:—*eat up*, esp. fruits and vegetables, ll.cc., Thphr.*HP*9.11.9, Lxx*Pr*.24.23(29.27), Theoc.5.115, Luc.*Apol*.5: c. gen., Plu.*Art*.3, etc.: aor. 1 part. κατατρώξαντες Timo 66.6:—Pass., Arist.*Pr*.925ᵃ31.

**κατατρωματίζω**, Ion. for κατατραυμ-.

**κατατυγχάνω**, *hit one's mark, reach the object of*.., [τῆς ἐλπίδος] Demad.6, cf. Diocl.*Fr*.138: τῆς στρατείας D.S.13.3; τῆς σπουδῆς Ael. *NA*3.25. 2. abs., *to be lucky* or *successful*, opp. ἐξαμαρτάνω, D.18. 178; τὴν θέσιν εὔχεσθαι δεῖ κατατυγχάνειν as to the situation of the city, one must hope *to be successful*, Arist.*Pol*.1330ᵃ37. 3. c. dat., *fall to the lot of*, Procop.*Arc*.4. 4. Pass., in abs. sense, τὸ κ. Euryph.ap.Stob.4.39.27. II. *to be in office at the time*, ὁ κ. ἀρτυτήρ *Test.Epict*.4.37, cf. *IG*12(3).249.36 (Anaphe).

✻**κατατυμβοχοέω**, *heap a funeral mound over*, Call.*Fr.anon*.262 (dub.).

**κατατύπτω**, *pound, crush*, Sch.E.*Hipp*.977:—Med., *beat one's breast*, καττύπτεσθε, κόραι Sapph.62: c. acc., *beat one's breast for*, Εὔκλειτον.. κατετύψατο μήτηρ *Supp.Epigr*.4.190 (Halic., iv B.C.).

**κατατῠραννέω**, *to be tyrant over*, c. gen., Sm.*Nu*.16.13.

**κατάτῡρος**, ον, *covered with cheese*, Archestr.*Fr*.57.8.

**κατατωθάζω**, *jeer, scoff at*, τινος Hld.6.2, cf. Lib.*Descr*.5.6.

**κατ-αυαίνω**, fut. -αυᾰνῶ Archil.61:—*wither up*, l.c.:—later **καθαυαίνω** Lyc.397, Luc.*Am*.12.

✻**καταυγ-άζω**, *shine upon, illuminate*, c. acc., Lxx *Wi*.17.5, Str.2.5. 42, Corn.*ND*32, S.E.*M*.9.247, Hld.1.1:—Pass., Id.7.7, Ph.1.150; ὑπὸ μεταρτίου φωτός Heraclid.Pont.ap.*Placit*.3.2.5. 2. *outshine, occult*, of the Sun or Moon, Theo Sm.p.193 H. (Act. and Pass.), Jul.*Or*.3.109c (Pass.): metaph., ἡ ἀγαθοεργία σου κ. πάντας Them. *Or*.15.192a. II. intr., *shine brightly*, Hld.5.31. III. Med., *gaze at, see*, A.R.4.1248, *AP*9.58 (Antip.). **-ασμα**, ατος, τό, *radiance*, *PMag.Par*.1.1130. **-ασμός**, ὁ, *shining brightly*, Plu.*Nic*. 23 (pl.). **-άστειρα**, ἡ, as if fem. of *καταυγαστήρ, *illuminator*, of the Moon, Orph.*H*.9.6. **-εια**, ἡ, *illumination, brightness*, Aristeas 307. **-έω**, in Pass., ὑπὸ τοῦ ἡλίου, *to be occulted*, of planets near the Sun, Gem.12.7, al.

**καταυδ-άω**, *speak out, speak plainly*, S.*Ant*.86. **-ησις**, εως, ἡ, *loud speaking, shouting*, Hp.*Praec*.14.

**κατ-αυθᾰδίζω**, *act* or *speak obstinately against*, τινος Suid.:—Med., Men.Prot.p.102 D.:—also **-ιάζομαι**, *defy*, τῶν νόμων Just.*Nov*.12.1.

**κατ-αῦθι**, Adv. *again, once more*, A.R.1.1079, 2.528; in Od.10.567, 21.55 κατ' belongs to the Verb.

✻**κατ-αυλέω**, *charm by flute-playing*, τινος Pl.*Lg*.790e, cf. *R*.411a; τινα Alciphr.2.1: metaph., σε..-ήσω φόβῳ I will *flute to* you on a ghastly flute, E.*HF*871 (troch.):—Pass., of persons, μεθύων καὶ καταυλούμενος drinking wine *to the strains of the flute*, Pl.*R*.561c; κ. πρὸς χελωνίδος ψόφον *to be played to on the flute* with lyre accompaniment, Posidon.10 J., cf. Call.*Fr*.10.3 P., Phld.*Mus*.p.49 K. 2. c. gen. loci, *make a place sound with flute-playing*, Thphr.*Fr*.87:—Pass., *resound with flute-playing*, νῆσος κατηυλεῖτο Plu.*Ant*.56. II. in Pass., [τὸν μονόχορδον κανόνα] παρέχειν ταῖς αἰσθήσεσι..καταυλούμενον *subdued by a flute accompaniment*, Ptol.*Harm*.2.12: metaph., *to be piped down, ridiculed*, γελώμενοι καὶ -ούμενοι Anon.ap.Suid., cf. Porph.*Chr*.34. III c. acc. rei, *play on the flute*, τὰ μητρῷα Duris 16 J.:—Pass., *to have played to one as an accompaniment on the flute*, -ούμενοι πρὸς τῶν ἑπομένων τὰ μητρῷα μέλη D.H.2.19.

**κατ-αύλημα**, ατος, τό, *residence*, Lyd.*Mag*.2.21 (nisi leg. -ίσματα).

**κατ-αύλησις**, εως, ἡ, *flute-playing*, Thphr.*HP*4.11.5, Apollon.*Mir*. 49; *treatment by music*, Sor.2.29.

**κατ-αυλίζομαι**, aor. κατηυλίσθην Hippon.63 (dub. l.), S.*Ph*.30, E. *Rh*.518, X.*An*.7.5.15; later κατηυλισάμην Plu.*Pyrrh*.27, etc.:—*to be under shelter of a hall, house, tent*, ll.cc.

**κάταυλον**· καταυλημένον (sic), ἀναπεπταμένον, Hsch.

**κατ-αύστηρος**, ον, *very harsh* or *morose*, Arr.*Epict*.1.25.15.

**καταυστής**· καταδυστής, Hsch.; cf. καταύω.

**κατ-αυτόθι**, Adv. *on the spot*, A.R.2.16,776, etc.; but in Hom. κατ' αὐτόθι shd. be read, for κατά belongs to the Verb, v. Hdn.Gr.(2.71) ad Il.10.273 on the accent.

**κατ-αυτοί**, *by themselves*, αὐτοὶ καταυτοί *PCair.Zen*.294.2 (iii B.C.).

**κατ-αυχένιος**, ον, *on* or *over the neck*, πλόκαμοι *AP*5.72 (Rufin.).

**κατ-αυχέω**, *exult in*, πλήθει καταυχήσας νεῶν A.*Pers*.352.

**κατ-αύω**, = καθαιρέω, *destroy*, τὰν Μῶσαν καταύσεις Alcm.95; cf. καθαῦσαι· ἀφανίσαι, κεταῖσαι· καταυλῆσαι (καταντλῆσαι Lobeck), καταδῦσαι, Hsch.; cf. αὔω (A), ἐν-(A), ἐξ-(B), προσ-αύω.

**καταφᾰγᾶς**, ᾶ, ὁ, v. κατωφαγᾶς.

**καταφᾰγεῖν**, serving as aor. 2 to κατεσθίω (q.v.); Dor. inf. -ῆμεν Epich.42.4: later fut. καταφάγομαι Lxx 3*Ki*.12.24m, *Pland*.26.23,34 (i A.D.), *Gloss*.:—*devour, eat up*, αὐτὰρ ἐπεὶ κατὰ τέκν' ἔφαγε Il.2.317, cf. Hdt.2.141 (tm.), 3.25, Eup.352, Luc.*Merc.Cond*.17. 2. *spend in eating, waste*, μή τοι κατὰ πάντα φάγωσι κτήματα Od.3.315, 15.12; τὴν πατρῴαν οὐσίαν Aeschin.1.96; πατρῴαν γῆν Men.349.4.

**καταφαίνω**, Dor. aor. 1 ἐφᾶνα, *declare, make known*, τοῦτον λόγον Pi.*N*.10.11. II. Pass., fut. -φᾰνήσομαι dub. in E.*Fr*.781.65 (lyr.):—*become visible, appear*, *h.Ap*.431, Hdt.7.51, Th.5.6, E.l.c., Plu.*Luc*. 27:—also intr. in Act., Orph.*A*.370,762. 2. *to be clear, plain*, τῷ Ὀτάνῃ μᾶλλον κατεφαίνετο τὸ πρῆγμα Hdt.3.69, cf. Plu.2.40c,682a; *seem, appear*, ὥς γε κ. ἐμοί Pl.*Phlb*.16c; ὅτι μοι ἄτοπ' ἄττα κ. περὶ σωφροσύνης Id.*Chrm*.172c, cf. Plu.2.802f, etc.: also c. inf., ὡς ἐμοὶ καταφαίνεται εἶναι Hdt.1.58, cf. 6.13; κατεφάνη τῷ Δαρείῳ τεχνάζειν, i.e. Darius *well knew* that he was evading, Id.3.130; ταὐτόν σοι πάθος -φαίνομαι πεπονθέναι Pl.*Lg*.712e; πάντων μοι μετριώτατοί γε εἶναι κατεφάνησαν ib.811d: c. part., ὀρθῶς ἔτι μοι κατεφάνης λέγων ib. 631a, cf. *Sph*.232b; δαιμονία..τις ἔμοιγε κ. τὸ μέγεθος Id.*Grg*.456a, cf. *Sph*.217e; τοιαύτη ἡ ἕξις τοῦ σώματος κ. X.*Oec*.7.2; οἱ ἀντιλέγοντες ὄχλος καὶ βασκανία κατεφαίνετο D.19.24.

**καταφάν-εια** [ᾰν], ἡ, *clearness*, κ. καὶ γαλήνη Plu.2.914f. II. *manifestness*, κ. ποιεῖν ἐν τοῖς λόγοις ib.715f. **-ής**, ές, *clearly seen, in sight*, οὔπω κ. ἦσαν οἱ πολέμιοι X.*An*.1.8.8, cf. *Eq.Mag*.7.8; ἐν κ. στρατοπεδεύεσθαι *in an open place*, Id.*Cyr*.3.3.28. 2. *manifest, evident*, κ. ποιέειν τι Hdt.2.120, cf. Isoc.11.4, Pl.*Grg*.453c, X.*Cyr*.1.6.14, etc.; κ. ἐστί τι, γίγνεταί τι Hp.*Off*.3: Comp., Pl.*Lg*.812a: Sup., Id. *Tht*.186e, etc.: freq. c. part., καταφανέες εἰσὶ ἁμαρτάνοντες Hp.*VM* 1; κ. ἦν τῇ βουλῇ αὐτὸς θεὶς τὴν ἱκετηρίαν And.1.116, cf. Aeschin.2.39, Isoc.2.1; κ. ἐγένοντο οὐχ ὅσιοι ὄντες Antipho 5.82, cf. Plb.7.12.8; καταφανέστερος εἶναι κακουργῶν Th.5.16; κ. ἐστί τις, ὅτι.. Pl.*Plt*. 265d, *R*.506b; κ. γίγνονται, ὅτι.. X.*Oec*.1.20; κ. ποιεῖν τινα Antiph. 235.6. Adv. -νῶς *evidently, plainly*, Ar.*Eq*.943, D.35.27; καταφανέστερον ἢ ὥστε λανθάνειν *too manifestly* to escape detection, Th.8.46.

**κατ-αφᾰνίζω**, strengthd. for ἀφανίζω, Hsch. s.v. καταδηώσαντες, Sch.E.*Hec*.1142.

**καταφαντ-άζομαι**, *to be like*, τινι Herm.ap.Stob.1.49.44 codd. **-ικός**, ή, όν, v.l. for -φατικός, Numen.ap.Eus.*PE*14.8. **-ός**, ή, όν, *to be affirmed*, opp. ἀποφαντός, D.L.7.65, Suid. s.v. ἀξίωμα.

**κατάφαρκτος**, ον, = κατάφρακτος (q.v.).

**καταφαρμᾰκεύω**, *dose with drugs*, Alex.Trall.9.3, *Febr*.7. II. *anoint with drugs* or *charms*, τὰ πρόσωπα φαρμάκοις Luc.*Am*.39: hence, 2. *enchant, bewitch*, Pl.*Phdr*.242e (Pass.), Plu.2. 141b. III. *poison*, Id.*Dio* 3.

**καταφαρμάσσω**, *bewitch with drugs*, κατά με ἐφάρμαξας Hdt.2.181: metaph., τῷ Πλάτωνος λόγῳ Διονύσιον κ. Plu.*Dio* 14.

**κατάφᾰσις**, εως, ἡ, *affirmation, affirmative proposition*, opp. ἀπόφασις, Pl.*Def*.413c, Arist.*Int*.17ᵃ25, al., *EN*1139ᵃ21. 2. *affirmative particle*, A.D.*Adv*.124.9, *Synt*.245.22.

**καταφάσκω**, = κατάφημι, Phld.*Piet*.123, Ph.1.104; περί τινος Gal. 10.37, al.; *answer in the affirmative*, ἐρώτησιν Id.7.526:—Pass., A.D. *Synt*.245.12.

**καταφᾰτίζω**, *declare*, Arist.*Ath*.7.1, Plu.*Sol*.25.

**καταφᾰτικός**, ή, όν, *affirmative*, opp. ἀποφατικός, λόγος Arist.*APr*. 24ᵃ16; προτάσεις ib.25ᵃ3; ἀξίωμα *Stoic*.2.56, al.; τὸ κ. Plu.2.1047d, A.D.*Adv*.122.13. Adv. -κῶς Arist.*APr*.64ᵃ15, Gal.16.328, Eust.92. 22. 2. *emphatic*, A.D.*Pron*.49.11 (Comp.).

**καταφαυλίζω**, *depreciate*, Plu.*Alex*.28.

**καταφέγγω**, *illuminate*, in Pass., Max.Tyr.19.6. 2. *dazzle, overpower* by oratorical brilliance, Longin.34.4 (prob. l.).

**καταφέρ-εια**, ἡ, *proneness*, ἡδονῆς to pleasure, Ath.7.352c: abs., *lechery*, Eust.827.31. **-ής**, ές, *going down*, εὖτ' ἂν κ. γίνηται ὁ

ἥλιος when the sun is *near setting*, Hdt.2.63; of ground, *sloping*, X. *Cyn.*10.9, *PLille* 1 v 1 (iii B.C.); κ. ἐπί τι *inclined* towards.., Hp.*Art.* 57; πρός τι, opp. εὐθεῖα, ib.75; κ. φυγή *downhill*, Plb.2.68.7; κ. κοιλία, of *diarrhoea*, Dieuch.ap.Orib.4.7.21: metaph., *headlong, rapid*, ῥύσις τῆς λέξεως D.H.*Dem.*40. II. *inclined, prone*, esp. to sensual pleasures, εἰς λίθων βολάς prob. in Phld.*Ir.*p.31 W.; πρὸς οἶνον, πρὸς τἀφροδίσια, Plu.*Alex.*23, Ath.13.589d: abs., *lecherous*, D.L.4.40, Sor.1.38 (Comp.), Phot. s. v. μύραινα: freq. written κατωφερής (q. v.).

***καταφέρω**, fut. κατοίσω Plu.*Per.*28, -οίσομαι Il.22.425: aor. 1 κατήνεγκα Lxx *Ge.*37.2, inf. -ενεγκεῖν Plb.1.62.9; Dor. κατέφειρα *GDI* 2317.8 (Delph.):—*bring down*, once in Hom., οὗ μ' ἄχος ὀξὺ κατοίσεται Ἄϊδος εἴσω *will bring* me *down* to the grave, Il. l. c.; βαρυπεσῆ καταφέρω ποδὸς ἀκμάν A.*Eu.*370 (lyr.); of rivers, κ. χρυσίον, γῆν, Arist.*Mir.*833$^b$17, *Pr.*935$^a$16: Com., ὁ Κρᾶθις ἡμῖν κ. μάζας Metag. 6.1; esp. of cutting instruments, κ. τὴν σμινύην Ael.*NA* 11.32; τὴν δίκελλαν, τὴν σφῦραν, Luc.*Tim.*7, *Prom.*2: c. dat. obj., κ. τὸ ξίφος τῷ πολεμίῳ *let it fall upon* him, Plu.2.236e: c. gen., τὴν ἅρπην τῆς ἰξύος Ach.Tat.1.3; τῶν γνάθων τὸ ξυρόν Alciphr.3.66: metaph., ψόγον τινός Lxx *Ge.*37.2: abs., *hew downwards, deal a blow*, Luc.*DDeor.* 8, *Somn.*3; κ. πληγήν Id.*Tim.*40, cf. D.S.11.69 (but also κατήνεγκε πληγαῖς τὴν κεφαλήν *PTeb.*138 (ii B.C.)). b. *pull down, demolish*, πύργους Plb.4.64.11; ἥλους (warts) Philum.*Ven.*10.4. c. *pay down, discharge*, Arist.*Oec.*1348$^a$2, Plb.1.62.9, 33.13.6, *GDI* 1754 (Delph.), Plu.*Per.*28. d. *pass, evacuate*, τὰ σπλάγχνα μετὰ τῶν σιτίων J.*BJ* 5.9.4. e. *refer* a thing, ἀπό τινος ἐφ' ἕτερον, v.l. for μεταφέρειν, Lex ap.D.21.94. f. *carry down*, in reckoning, etc., πλῆθος ἀμήχανον ἐτῶν Plu.*Num.*18; τὸ τῆς εὐδαιμονίας εἰς τὰ ζῷα Plot. 1.4.1. 2. Pass., *to be brought down* by a river, of gold dust, Hdt. 1.93; from an upper story, D.47.63; *to move downwards with violence, to be discharged*, of humours, Hp.*Epid.*6.8.18; *to be couched*, of a cataract, -ενεχθέντος τοῦ ὑποχύματος Gal.7.89. b. *descend, sink*, Arist.*HA* 590$^b$8; κ. ὁ ἥλιος, ἡ σελήνη, ἡ ἡμέρα, ib.552$^b$21, Plu.*Nic.*21, *Tim.*12; κ. ὁ λύχνος *is near going out*, Id.*Caes.*69; κ. [ἡ ἄμπελος] *is perishing*, Thphr.*HP* 4.13.5; of dancers, κ. ἐπὶ γῆν Critias 36 D., cf. Democr.228; of a sick person, κ. καθάπερ νεκρόν Gal.7.591; but ἐπὶ πόδας, of a patient in bed, Id.18(2).60. c. *fall, flow down*, of rain or rivers, *Gp.*5.2.16, Hsch. s. v. Πεντέλεια. d. *tumble down*, αἱ οἰκίαι κ. ἐπί τινα.. Plu.*Dio* 44; ἀφ' ὕψους -ενεχθεῖσα γυνή Sor.2.84. e. *to be weighed down*, ἐν τοῖσιν ὕπνοισι v.l. in Hp.*Epid.*4.45, cf. 5.50; κ. καὶ νυστάζειν Arist.*Somn.Vig.*456$^b$31; ἐς ὕπνον Luc.*DMeretr.*2.4; ὕπνῳ βαθεῖ *Act.Ap.*20.9, cf. Philostr.*Gym.*54; ὑπὸ μέθης Ath.11.461c: abs., *drop asleep*, opp. ἐγείρεσθαι, Arist.*GA* 779$^a$9, *Insomn.*462$^a$10; *to be semi-comatose*, ἀγρυπνεῖν τε ἅμα καὶ -εσθαι Gal.16.497. II. *carry back, carry home*, Ar.*Ach.*955. 2. of a storm, *drive to land*, ὁ χειμὼν κατήνεγκε τὰς ναῦς ἐς τὴν Πύλον Th.4.3, cf. Plb.3.24.11:— Pass., καταφέρεται χειμῶνι ἐς τὸ Ἀθηναίων στρατόπεδον Th.1.137, cf. 3.69: generally, in Pass., *to be landed, discharged*, of cargoes, *PFlor.* 278 ii 13 (iii A.D.), etc. III. Pass., metaph., *to be brought* to a point, ἐπὶ γνώμην, ἐλπίδα, etc., Plb.30.19.13, 6.9.3, Plot.2.6.1; ἐπὶ τὰς αὐτὰς διανοίας D.H.*Lys.*17, cf. Phld.*Mort.*29, al.: abs. (cf. καταφορά II. 3), ib.30:—also Act., *have recourse*, ἐπ' οὐθὲν ψεῦδος Id.*Rh.*1.159 S. 2. *tend*, ἡ [σύνταξις] ἐπὶ τὸ προστακτικὸν φύσει κ. A.D.*Synt.*232.8; τῶν ῥημάτων -φερομένων εἰς τὴν ἐπὶ τέλους βαρεῖαν ib.134.25. 3. *enter the lists*, like Lat. *descendere in arenam*, Lib.*Or.*59.67. IV. *bring against*, τὴν διαβολήν κ. τινός Arist.*Rh.Al.*1437$^a$19. V. intr. in Act., *to be prone, inclined*, κ. εἰς τὰς γυναῖκας *POxy.*465.146.

**κατα-φεύγω**, fut. -φεύξομαι D.8.41:—*flee for refuge*, ἐς τὸ [ἱρόν] Hdt. 2.113, cf. 1.145; ἐπὶ Διὸς βωμόν Id.5.46: c. acc., οὐκ ἔχω βωμὸν κ. E.*IA* 911 (troch.); -πεφευγέναι ἐν τόπῳ *flee and take refuge* in.., Pl.*Sph.* 260c, cf. X.*HG* 4.5.5; ἐκεῖ, ἐνθάδε κ., Th.3.71, Isoc.14.28; ὅποι.. X. *Mem.*3.8.10; κ. ἐς τινα *flee for protection* to him, ὃς ἂν φεύγων καταφύγῃ ἐς τούτους Hdt.4.23; εἰς ὑμᾶς κ. καὶ ἀντιβολῶ And.1.149; ἐπί τινα D 18.19, etc.; πρὸς ὑμᾶς Id.8.41; παρ' ἡμῖν Isoc.12.194. 2. ἐκ τῆς μάχης κ. *escape* from.., Hdt.6.75: abs., ἄνω μάλ' εἶσι καταφυγών (sc. ὁ ἀτμός) Alex.124.17. 3. *have recourse*, εἰς ἔλεον Antipho 3.2.2; εἰς σωτηρίαν Id.2.4.1; εἰς τοὺς λόγους Pl.*Phd.*99e, cf. 76e; εἰς ὅρκον Arist.*Rh.Al.*1432$^a$38; ἐπὶ τὰς μηχανάς Pl.*Cra.*425d; ἐπὶ τὸν δικαστήν Arist.*EN* 1132$^a$20; ἐπὶ τὸν λόγον ib.1105$^b$13; ἐπὶ Καρχηδονίους Plb.1. 10.1, cf. Plu.*Cam.*7; πρὸς θεῶν εὐχάς Pl.*Phdr.*244e; ὥς τινας Plb.24. 10.11: c. dat., τῇ μητρί Ctes.*Fr.*29.57. 4. εἰς τὴν τοῦ βίου μετριότητα κ. *fall back* upon, *appeal to*.., D.25.76; ἐπὶ τὸ φάσκειν.. Phld. *D.*3.8. **-φευκτέον**, *one must fall back upon, have recourse to*, ἐπὶ τὰς ἀτυχίας Arist.*Rh.Al.*1429$^a$14; ἐπί τινα Luc.*Pisc.*3. **-φευξις**, εως, ἡ, *flight for refuge*, κ. ποιεῖσθαι ἐς τὸν ὅρμον Th.7.41. II. *place of refuge*, ib.38.

**κατάφημι**, *assent*, S.*OT* 506 (lyr., μεμφομένων is gen. abs.); opp. ἀπόφημι, in aor. 1 inf. -φῆσαι, Arist.*Metaph.*1007$^b$21; οἷον -φάσαι ἢ ἀποφάσαι [ἡ ψυχὴ] διώκει ἢ φεύγει Id.*de An.* 431$^a$9:—Pass., aor. inf. -φαθῆναι Id.*Int.*18$^b$39. II. *promulgate*, νόμοι οὓς κατέφησεν θεὸς Ἰουδαίοις f.l. in J.*BJ* 3.8.4 (v. κατηφέω).

**καταφημ-ίζω**, aor. -εφήμισα, Dor. -εφάμιξα Pi.*O.*6.56:—Pass., pf. -πεφήμισμαι (v. infr.):—*spread abroad, announce*, κατεφάμιξεν καλεῖσθαί νιν Pi. l. c.; λίμνη Μαιῶτις, ἣν μητέρα..τοῦ Πόντου κ. *made it known as*.., Dion.Byz.2:—Pass., καταπεφήμισται *it is rumoured*, Plb.16.12.3; of persons, *become notorious* or *infamous*, Vett.Val.118. 5. II. *assign* or *dedicate* to a god, τὰ τοῖς θεοῖς καταπεφημισμένα Plb.5.10.8; θρόνος Ἀλεξάνδρῳ -ισμένος Plu.*Eum.*13, cf. Jul.*Or.*4. 156c. **-ος**, ον, *infamous*, Gloss.

**καταφθάνω** [φθᾱ], *fall upon unawares*, ἐπί τινα Lxx *Jd.*20.42. II. c. inf., κ. τεκεῖν bring forth a child *first*, *BGU* 665 ii 14 (i A.D.): also c. acc., *pay in advance*, κατέφθακα ἀρτάβας ιβ *POxy.*1482.10 (ii A.D.).

**καταφθᾰτόομαι**, (φθάνω) *take first possession of*, γῆν καταφθατουμένη A.*Eu.*398; cf. καταφ(θ)ατουμένη· κατακτωμένη, Hsch.

**καταφθέγγω**, *sound loudly*, βροντήν, ἧς οὐδὲν -ει μεῖζον Horap. 1.29.

***καταφθείρω**, fut. -φθερῶ Plu.2.240d:—*destroy, bring to naught*, στρατόν, πόλιν, ἔθνη, A.*Pers.*345, S.*OT* 331, Pl.*Lg.*697d, cf. Democr. 159; ἔργα νομήων Theoc.25.122; κατέφθαρται ὄλβος A.*Pers.*251; ἐπεὶ δέ χ' εἴκω οἴκαδις καταφθερεὶς *in sorry plight*, Epich.35.13; -φθαρεὶς τὸν βίον Men.*Epit.*429, cf. *Raccolta Lumbroso* 17 (iii B.C.); δένδρα -εφθαρμένα *IG* 9(2).1109.74 (Coropa, ii B.C.), cf. *PMagd.*11.9 (iii B.C.), etc. 2. *corrupt*, τινα Plu. l. c.

**καταφθινύθω** [ῠ], = καταφθίω, *h.Cer.*353, Emp.111.4; cf. sq.

**καταφθίνω** ῐ, sed v. infr.], *waste away, decay*, Pi.*I.*8(7).51, Hdt. 2.123; κ. νόσῳ, γήρᾳ, S.*Ph.*266, E.*Alc.*622: in later Att. Prose, Thphr.*HP* 9.16.5: aor. part. καταφθινήσας Plu.2.117c: pf. part. κατεφθινηκώς ib.621f, Arr.*Epict.*4.11.25: καταφθίνουσι trans. is f.l. in Theoc.25.122.

**καταφθίω** (pres. only in the simple φθίω): I. causal in fut. καταφθίσω [ῑ] Od. (v. infr.), aor. 1 κατέφθῐσα Trag. (v. infr.):—*ruin, destroy*, οὐ μὲν δή σε καταφθίσει Od.5.341; παλαιὰς διανομὰς -φθίσας A.*Eu.*727; κατὰ μὲν φθίσας τὰν γαμψώνυχα παρθένον S.*OT* 1198 (lyr.). II. Pass., aor. κατεφθίμην, part. καταφθίμενος, inf. καταφθίσθαι; poet. καπφθίμενος restored in anapaestic and choriambic verses of E., *Rh.*378, *Supp.*984, *El.*1299:—*waste away, perish*, κεν ἤϊα πάντα κατέφθιτο καὶ μένε' ἀνδρῶν *would all have been consumed, spent*, Od.4.363; ὡς καὶ σὺ καταφθίσθαι σὺν ἐκείνῳ ὤφελες 2.183; σεῖο καταφθιμένοιο *if* thou *shouldst die*, Il.22.288; νεκύεσσι καταφθιμένοισιν ἀνάσσειν Od.11.491, cf. *h.Cer.*347; νόμοι περὶ τῶν -φθιμένων *IG* 12(5).593 *A* 1 (Ceos); ἐκεῖ κατέφθιτο there he *died*, A.*Pers.*319, cf. S. *Ph.*346; τῷμῷ πόθῳ κ. Id.*OT* 970; φέγγος ἡλίου κατέφθιτο the sun's light *died away*, A.*Pers.*377.

**καταφθορά**, ἡ, *destruction, death, ruin*, λεύσιμοι καταφθοραί E.*Ion* 1237 (lyr.); κ. τῶν ἀνδρῶν, τῆς Ἑλλάδος, Plb.1.49.4, 11.5.1; χώρας Id. 4.67.1, cf. 1.48.9; τῶν ἰδίων *OGI* 339.5 (Sestos, ii B.C.), cf. *UPZ* 11. 126 (ii B.C.). 2. metaph., *confusion, perturbation*, φρενῶν A.*Ch.* 211.

**κατ-αφίημι**, *let slip down*, κατηφίει (impf.) τὸ δόρυ διὰ χειρός f.l. in Pl.*La.*184a; λέβητα (sc. εἰς θάλασσαν) Arist.*Pr.*960$^b$32.

**καταφῐλ-έω**, *kiss, caress*, δίφρον X.*Cyr.*6.4.10; χεῖρας καὶ πόδας τινός ib.7.5.32, cf. Men.*Epit.*56, Arr.*Epict.*4.10.20, τοὺς μὲν καλοὺς φιλήσοντος, τοὺς δ' ἀγαθοὺς καταφ. X.*Mem.*2.6.33, cf. Arist.*Fr.*553, Lxx *Ru.*1.9, *Ev.Matt.*26.49; dist. from φιλεῖν, Ph.1.478; esp. of an amorous kiss, Luc.*Am.*13. **-ημα**, ατος, τό, *kiss*, f.l. for φίλημα in Ph.1.480.

**καταφῐλονεικέω**, sine expl., Suid.

**καταφῐλοσοφέω**, *overcome in philosophizing*, τινος Ael.*NA* 6.56; but -σοφήσαντες· διὰ τῆς σιγῆς νικήσαντες, Hsch., cf. Phot., Suid. II. *prove philosophically*, κ. ὅτι.. Arr.*Epict.*4.1.167.

**καταφῑμόω**, *conticisco*, Gloss.

**καταφλάω**, *press, crush*, Hsch.:—Pass., dub. l. in Str.4.1.7.

**κατάφλεβος**, ον, *full of veins, vascular*, Ruf.*Onom.*153.

**κατα-φλέγω**, fut. -φλέξω Il.22.512: aor. -έφλεξα Hes.*Sc.*18:— *burn up, consume*, πυρί ll. cc., cf. Arist.*Mu.*400$^a$31 (v.l. προσ-), Plu. *Caes.*68, Diog.Oen.38, etc.; of a caustic drug, Paul.Aeg.6.31: metaph., of love, θεὸς ἄνδρα κ. *AP* 5.9 (Alc.):—Pass., *to be burnt*, aor. 1 -εφλέχθην Th.4.133, D.S.8 *Fr.*11, Philostr.*VA* 8.15: aor. 2 -εφλέγην J.*AJ* 13.4.4, D.Chr.46.1. **-φλεκτος**, ον, *burnt*, Hld. 1.1. **-φλεξίπολις** [ῐ], ὁ, ἡ, *inflamer of cities*, of a courtesan, *AP* 5.1. **-φλεξις**, εως, ἡ, *burning*, Luc.*Salt.*39, Ptol.*Tetr.*86.

**καταφλογίζω**, *set on fire*, Lxx *Ps.*17(18).8.

**καταφλῠαρέω**, *keep on chattering*, τι Ps.-Luc.*Philopatr.*20, 25: c. gen., ὀνόματα ἅπερ Ἑλλάνικος καὶ Ἡρόδοτος -εφλυάρησαν ἡμῶν Str. 12.3.21, cf. D.L.5.20, *Corp.Herm.*1.29.

**καταφοβ-έω**, *strike with fear*, Th.7.21, Luc.*DMeretr.*13.5, D.C.39. 36:—Pass., c. fut. Med., *to be greatly afraid of*, τι Ar.*Ra.*1109 (lyr.): abs., καταφοβηθεὶς Th.6.33. **-ος**, ον, *fearful, afraid of*, κ. ἦν, = κατεφοβεῖτο, c. acc., ἐλέφαντας Plb.1.39.12; τὸ μέλλον Id.3.107.15; κ. ἦν μή.. Id.10.7.7: abs., κ. γίγνεσθαι Lxx *Pr.*29.16, cf. Ath.Med.ap. Orib.*Inc.*21.3; κ. βίος Plu.*Dio* 4. II. Act., *terrifying*, μήνυσις *PSI* 6.684.17 (iv/v A.D.).

**καταφοινίσσω**, *dye red*, Hsch., Phot., Suid.

**καταφοιτάω**, Ion. -έω, *come down constantly* or *regularly*, as wild beasts from the mountains to prey, Hdt.7.125 (-τωντες, -τέωντες, -τέοντες codd.).

**καταφονεύω**, *slaughter*, Hdt.1.106, 165, al., E.*Ba.*1178 (lyr.):— Pass., Id.*Or.*536.

**καταφορ-ά**, ἡ, (καταφέρω) *conveyance*, of materials to the sea, *IG* 2$^2$. 1672.125. 2. *bringing down*, esp. of a sword, *downward stroke*, Plb. 2.33.3, etc.; ἐκ καταφορᾶς *cutting*, opp. *thrusting*, Id.3.114.3; τραῦμα ἐκ κ. γεγενημένον a *sword* wound, Plu.*Dio* 34. 3. metaph., *attack, tirade*, Phld.*Lib.*p.48 O. (pl.), cf. Hermog.*Inv.*4.5: c. gen., against.., Anon.*in Rh.*53.9. 4. *payment*, *SIG* 230 *C* 26, 252.70 (Delph., iv B.C.). II. (from Pass.) *downward motion*, Epicur.*Nat.*15.26, 27; *descent, fall*, καταφοραὶ ὄμβρων Pl.*Ax.*370c; χαλάζης J.*AJ* 6.5.6; αἱ κ. πέντε, ὑετοῦ, χιόνος, δρόσου, χαλάζης, πάχνης *Theol.Ar.*31; *sinking*, κ. ἡλίου *sunset*, Thphr.*Vent.*12, Anon.Hist.(*FGr.Hist.*160)p.887 J.;

ἡ ἰσημερινὴ κ. Plb.3.37.5, etc.; *setting* of a zodiacal sign, Ptol.*Tetr.* 134: pl., Longus 2.24. 2. Medic., κ. κοιλίης *diarrhoea*, Hp.*Aph.* (*Sp.*)7.86, cf. Ath.2.53d (pl.). b. *lethargic attack*, Hp.*Epid.*3.6, cf. Plu.*Aem.*37 (pl.); κ. πρὸς ὕπνον Gal.9.476; κ. πόνους παρέχουσα *PHerc.* 1041.2. 3. in reasoning, *deduction*, τὴν κ. ἐκ τῶν φαινομένων μεθοδεύειν Hp.*Praec.*1. 4. *sloping surface*, *IG*2$^2$.463.66, 1668.51, 7.4255.16 (Oropus, iv B.C.). **-έω**, = καταφέρω, of a river, *carry down*, ψῆγμα χρυσοῦ κ. ἐκ τοῦ Τμώλου Hdt.5.101, cf. 3.106 (Pass.): metaph., ἀμήχανον.. λογισμὸν καταπεφόρηκας τῆς διαφορότητος.. you *have poured forth* a wonderful *stream* of calculation of the difference.., Pl.*R.* 587e; πολλὰ.. κατεφόρει τῆς προνοίας he *went on inveighing* much against.., Plu.2.548c. **-ικός**, ή, όν, *violent, vehement*, σφοδρὸς καὶ κ. λόγος Hermog.*Id.*1.1. Adv. -κῶς Olymp. *in Grg.*p.370 J.; opp. εὐλαβῶς, Simp. *in Cat.*1.21. II. *lethargic, somnolent*, Hp.*Dent.*8; *causing lethargy*, ψύξεις, νοσήματα, Gal.8.161,162. III. Adv. -κῶς *by evacuation*, prob. in Hsch. **-ος**, ον, *rushing down, tempestuous*, τὸ κ. τῆς θαλάσσης, opp. τὸ γαληνίζον, Arist.*Pr.*936$^a$6 (dub. l.). b. *having a downward tendency*, τὸ ψυχρὸν ἀεὶ κ. Olymp. *in Mete.*85.5. 2. *inclined, tending* to.., ἐπὶ τὸ παροξύνεσθαι A.D.*Adv.*189.28, cf. *Synt.* 134.1. II. *bearing down, lethargic*, ὕπνος prob. in Hsch. III. of a burial-ground, *accessible*, Judeich *Altertümer von Hierapolis* 336. 21 (fort. κατάφωρα; καταφωορα lapis).

**καταφορτ-ίζω**, *load heavily*, ὄνους τοῖς ἐπιτηδείοις J.*AJ*7.9.3 (Pass.): metaph., *weigh down*, τὰν ψυχὰν κακοῖς Hipparch.ap.Stob.4.44.81; *weary, burden*, τινὰς τοῖς Πλάτωνος λόγοις Jul.*Or.*2.69b; of financial burdens, κ. τὸ δημόσιον χρέεσι Just.*Nov.*148 *Praef.* (Pass.). ❀**-ος**, ον, *laden with*, τινος J.*Vit.*26.

❀**καταφράζω**, *declare*, τὸ σαφανὲς Pi.*O.*10(11).55:—Med., with aor. Pass. and Med., *consider, think upon, weigh*, καταφράζεσθε καὶ αὐτοὶ τήνδε δίκην Hes.*Op.*248; καταφρασθεὶς αὐτὸν ταῦτα ποιεῦντα *having observed*.., Hdt.4.76; κατεφράσατο Sol.13.38; εἰ τήνδε -φράσσαιο κέλευθον D.P.884.

**κατα-φράκτης**, ου, ὁ, *coat of mail*: a kind of *bandage*, so called from its likeness, Gal.18(1).816. **-φρακτος**, ον, *covered, shut up*, ἐν δεσμῷ S.*Ant.*958 (lyr., in old Att. form **κατάφαρκτος**); πλοῖα κ. *decked* vessels, Th.1.10 codd., cf. Plb.1.20.13; ἔν τε ταῖς ἀφράκτοις καὶ ταῖς κ. ναυσί *IG*12(1).41 (Rhodes, i B.C.); ἡ κ. ἵππος cavalry *clad in full armour, mailed*, Plb.30.25.9, cf. Arr.*Tact.*4.1, 19.4; ἱππεῖς Plu. *Crass.*21; τὰ κ. *coat of mail*, *PMagd.*13.6 (iii B.C.): metaph., *encased* in ignorance of the future, ψυχαί Ion Trag.6. **-φραξις**, εως, ἡ, *stopping up*, τῆς χοινικίδος *Hippiatr.*96. **-φράσσω**, *fortify, protect*, in Pass., -φρασσόμενοι ἐν ταῖς φάλαγξιν Lxx 1*Ma.*6.38; πύργος σιδήρῳ -πεφραγμένος J.*BJ*7.8.5; τόπους ὅπλοις -πεφραγμένους καὶ ἵπποις Plu. *Alex.*16; ἵπποι κ. χαλκοῖς καὶ σιδηροῖς σκεπάσμασιν Id.*Crass.*24: metaph., πολλοῖς ἱππεῦσι καταπεφραγμένος Id.*Alex.*33.

**καταφρίσσω**, pf. -πέφρικα, strengthd. for φρίσσω, Hsch.

**καταφρον-έω**, *look down upon, think slightly of*, τινος Hdt.4.134, Th.7.63, etc.; τῶν παρόντων καταφρονῶν, τῶν ἀπόντων ἐπιθυμῶν Lys. 12.78; κ. τοῦ κινδύνου Pl.*Ap.*28c; τῆς τέχνης Id.*Grg.*512c, al.; καύματος καὶ ψύχους Ephor.149 J.; κυνηγεσίων X.*Cyn.*1.18; θεῶν E.*Ba.* 199, Antiph.262; τῶν πτωχῶν Men.301.10; οὐ δεῖ διαβολῆς κ. Id.88. 1. 2. c. acc., *regard slightly, despise*, E.*Ba.*503; τοὺς ἐπιόντας Th.6.34:—Pass., *to be despised*, ὑπό τινων Pl.*R.*556d; εἰς τὰ πολεμικὰ καταφρονούμενοι X.*HG*7.4.30: fut. -φρονηθήσομαι Isoc.6.95, Aeschin. 1.176: also in med. form -φρονήσομαι Pl.*Hp.Ma.*281c: aor. -εφρονήθην Isoc.6.108, Pl.*Euthd.*273d. 3. abs., *to be disdainful, deal contemptuously*, Th.2.11, Amphis 1.3, Arist.*Rh.*1378$^b$15; τὸ -φρονοῦν *contempt*, D.H.5.44. 4. c. inf., *think contemptuously that.., presume*, καταφρονήσαντες Ἀρκάδων κρέσσονες εἶναι Hdt.1.66; καταφρονοῦντες κἂν προαισθέσθαι Th.3.83: also c. acc., -φρονήσαντες ταῦτα Hdt.8.10. 5. c. acc. et gen., like καταγιγνώσκω, κ. τῶν Ἀθηναίων ἀδυνασίαν Th.8.8. II. c. acc. rei, *fix one's thoughts upon, aim at*, τὴν τυραννίδα Hdt.1.59; τοὺς βύστακας μὴ καταφρόνει do not *think of* your moustache, *do not aim at having* one (because the Spartans had to shave the upper lip, cf. μύσταξ), Antiph.44. III. *come to one's senses*, Hp.*Morb.Sacr.*15, *Nat.Mul.*3 (prob. l.), Plu.2.165f. **-ημα**, ατος, τό, *contempt*, μὴ φρονήματι μόνον, ἀλλὰ κ. not only spirit, but *a spirit of disdain*, Th.2.62, cf. J.*AJ*19.1.16, al., D.C.51.9. **-ησις**, εως, ἡ, *contempt, disdain*, Th.1.122, Pl.*R.*558b, Arist.*Rh.*1378$^b$14, D.S.1.93, etc.; *disregard, neglect*, *PMasp.*94.13 (vi A.D.), etc.; εἰς κ. ἄγειν τοὺς λόγους D.H.*Orat.Vett.*2; περὶ ἀλόγου κ., title of work by Polystratus: also without any bad sense, opp. αὔχημα, Th.2. 62. **-ητέον**, *one must despise*, τινος Ath.14.625d: also in pl., -φρονητέα, τοῦ τυράννου Philostr.*VA*6.22. **-ητής**, οῦ, ὁ, *despiser*, νόμων Arr.*Epict.*4.7.33; θανάτου Plu.*Brut.*12; πλούτου J.*BJ*2.8.3: abs., Lxx *Hb.*1.5, *Ze.*3.4, Vett.Val.47.33. **-ητικός**, ή, όν, *contemptuous, disdainful*, Arist.*EN*1124$^b$29, *Rh.*1379$^b$31, 1388$^b$25, Plu. 2.40f: c. gen., Phld.*Herc.*1457.10, Porph.*Abst.*3.27. Adv. -κῶς Pl. *Tht.*161c, X.*HG*4.1.17, 5.3.1, D.43.72 (καταφρονικός Gal.17(1).188, and Adv. -κῶς v.l. in App.*BC*2.45, are incorrectly written). ❀**-ητος**, ον, *despicable*, Phld.*Rh.*2.175 S.

**καταφροντίζω**, used in a Com. phrase, [θοἰμάτιον] οὐκ ἀπολώλεκ', ἀλλὰ καταπεφρόντικα I have not lost it, but I've *thought* it *away, spent* it *in the schools*, Ar.*Nu.*857. II. *attend to*, τι Plb.28.13.10 (dub. l.).

❀**καταφρυάττομαι**, *snort at*, prop. of a horse: metaph., *behave insolently*, M.Ant.7.3; τινι Id.9.41; τινος Suid.

**καταφρύγω** [ῡ], *burn away, burn to ashes*, of lightning, Ar.*Nu.* 396:—Pass., of love, v.l. in Theoc.14.26 (Pap. ined.). 2. *parch*, *consume*, of disease, Alex.Trall.*Febr.*4:—Pass., *to be dried up*, γλῶσσαι καταπεφρυγμέναι Ruf.ap.Aët.5.95: fut. -φρυγήσομαι Hsch.:—also -φρύσ(σ)ω, -φρύττω, Id., Olymp. *in Mete.*299.11.

**κατα-φῠγᾶς**, ᾶ, ὁ, *runaway*, Hdn.Gr.2.657 cod. (-φαγᾶς Lentz). **-φυγγάνω**, = καταφεύγω, Hdt.6.16, Aeschin.3.208, *PCair.Zen.*495.10 (iii B.C.). ❀**-φυγή**, ἡ, *place of refuge*, Hdt.7.46; ἔχει γὰρ καταφυγὴν θὴρ μὲν πέτραν, δοῦλος δὲ βωμοὺς E.*Supp.*267; κ. σωτηρίας a safe *retreat*, Id.*Or.*724; μηδεμίαν ἔχειν κ. Isoc.14.55; μόνην οἴονται κ. εἶναι τοὺς φίλους Arist.*EN*1155$^a$12; κύριος κ. μου Lxx *Ex.*17.15; ἐπί τινα κ. πεποιῆσθαι *Sammelb.*4638.29 (ii B.C.), etc. 2. c. gen. obj., κ. κακῶν *refuge from*.., E.*Or.*448 (pl.); τῶν ἀκουσίων ἁμαρτημάτων κ. εἶναι τοὺς βωμοὺς Th.4.98; κ. ποιεῖσθαι εἰς τέκνα E.*Or.*567 (pl.), cf. Antipho 1.4; ηὕρισκον κ. αὐτοῖς εἰς θεούς Pl.*Lg.*699b, etc.; ἡ εἰς τοὺς νόμους κ. Hyp.*Eux.*10; ἐμοὶ πόλις ἐστὶ καὶ κ. καὶ νόμος ὁ δεσπότης Men. 581. II. *way of escape, excuse*, μεγάλων ἀδικημάτων D.46.9, cf. 54.21 (pl.). ❀**-φύγιον** [ῠ], τό, Dim. of foreg., Democr.180, Sch. Hermog. in Rh.4.172 W.

**καταφῡλᾰδόν**, Adv. *in tribes, by clans*, Il.2.668, Opp.*H.*3.644.

**καταφυλάσσω**, *watch, guard well*, Ar.*Ec.*482.

**καταφυλλοροέω**, *shed the leaves*: metaph., *lose its splendour*, τιμὰ κατεφυλλορόησε Pi.*O.*12.15.

**κατάφυλλος**, ον, *leafy*, κ. ἀνὰ κῆπους Stratt.66.1.

**καταφύξει**· καταςβέσει, Hsch.

**καταφύξιμος**, ον, *to which one can fly for refuge*, Plu.2.290c.

**καταφῡσάω**, *spray, besprinkle*, σμῆνος οἴνῳ Arist.*HA*627$^b$15; [ἰσχίον] οἴνῳ καὶ ἐλαίῳ *Hippiatr.*30. 2. *discharge*, κ. τὸν θορόν (sc. τῇ θηλείᾳ) Arist.*HA*544$^a$4 (v.l. θολόν).

**κατάφῠσις**, εως, ἡ, *insertion* of tendons, Gal.*UP*1.17, al. II. = ψύλλιον, Ps.-Dsc.4.69.

**καταφῠτ-εία**, ἡ, *planting*, *BGU*1120.20 (ii B.C.). **-ευσις**, εως, ἡ, = foreg., Lxx *Je.*38(31).22. ❀**-εύω**, *plant*, ib.*Ex.*15.17, al.; ἀγορὰν πλατάνοις Plu.*Cim.*13, cf. Luc.*VH*2.42; λαὸν εἰς τόπον Lxx 2*Ma.*1.29. II. *transplant, acclimatize*, τοὺς πέραν Εὐφράτου καρποὺς ἐπὶ τὰ κάτω τῆς Ἀσίας μέρη *SIG*22.13 (Epist. Darei), cf. Posidon. 68 J., Str.15.3.11. **-ος**, ον, *full of plants* or *trees*, τόποι Plb.18. 20.1: c. dat., *planted* with.., κηπεύμασι καὶ καρποῖς D.S.2.37; δένδροις Str.12.2.1; ἀσφοδέλῳ Luc.*Nec.*11.

**καταφύω**, aor. 1 -έφῡσα, *implant, insert*, [ἡ φύσις νεῦρα] εἰς τὰς σάρκας κατέφυσε Gal.*UP*1.18, cf. 4.11:—Pass., aor. 2 κατέφυν Hsch. (also in part. -φυέν Id.): pf. -πέφυκα Plu.2.442c:—*to be inserted*, of muscles, nerves, etc., Gal.5.563, 7.185, *UP*13.12 (pres. Act. in same sense, Id.2.240); *penetrate*, εἰς τὴν πεπονθυῖαν σάρκα Id.18(2).599: generally, *to be produced*, περὶ τὸ σῶμα Plu. l. c. II. Med., *overrun* a country, Suid., Phot.

**καταφωνεῖ**· ταράσσει, Hsch.

**καταφωρ-άω**, *catch in a theft*: generally, *detect*, Th.8.87, Luc.*Gall.* 28; κ. τινὰς ἐπιβουλεύοντας Th.1.82; [ψυχὴν] ὡς οὖσαν κ. *discover* its existence, X.*Cyr.*8.7.17: aor. Pass., καταφωραθῆναι τῆς κακοηθείας J.*AJ*16.10.1. **-ος**, ον, *detected*, Onos.39.2, J.*AJ*20.11.1, Plu.2.301b, App.*BC*1.25, Chariton 1.1, Ach.Tat.2.17, *POxy.*71.11 (iv A.D.). II. *evident, manifest*, D.H.*Rh.*9.5; κ. τῆς γνώμης γεγονέναι Plu.*Cat.Mi.* 54. III. v. κατάφορος III.

**καταφωτ-ίζω**, *illuminate, light up*, *AP*9.178 (Antiphil.), Sch.E. *Hec.*367. **-ισμός**, ὁ, *illumination*, Hero *Deff.*135.12.

**καταχαίρω**, fut. -χᾰροῦμαι Lxx *Pr.*1.26:—*exult over*, ἐόντι αἰχμαλώτῳ.. Hdt.1.129; εἴτε εὐνοίῃ.., εἴτε καὶ καταχαίρων *with malicious joy*, Id.7.239. II. *rejoice much*, Alciphr.2.4, *IG*14.2410.11, *Supp. Epigr.*2.844 (Syria).

**καταχᾰλαζάω**, *shower down like hail upon*, λίθους τινός Luc.*Gall.* 22.

**καταχᾰλάω**, *let down*, τινὰς διὰ θυρίδος Lxx *Jo.*2.15.

**καταχαλκ-εύω**, *work* or *mould in bronze*, ἀνδριὰς καταχαλκευόμενος Plu.2.559d; ὅπως μὴ καταχαλκεύοιτο that [the coin] *might* not *be worked up*, Id.*Lys.*17. ❀**-ος**, ον, *overlaid with bronze* or *copper*, ἰτέα E.*Heracl.*376 (lyr.); κ. ἅπαν πεδίον ἀστράπτει flashes *with gleaming armour*, Id.*Ph.*110 (lyr.); δράκων κ. a serpent *lapt in mail*, i.e. scales, Id.*IT*1246 (lyr.); κ. πανοπλίαι Onos.1.20. 2. *alloyed with bronze*, χρυσός Thphr.*Lap.*46. **-όω**, *cover* or *point with bronze*, τὰ κέρεα Hdt.6.50:—Pass., θυρώματα κεχαλκωμένα χαλκῷ Lxx 2*Ch.*4.9. II. κ. τόπον θυρίσι *block up with bronze* doors, Heraclid.ap.Ath.12.521f; στοὰς ὅπλοις D.S.12.70.

**καταχᾰράσσω**, *scratch all over*, τὰ πρόσωπα ταῖς μαχαίραις Men. Prot.p.89 D.:—Pass., ἵνα μὴ -χαράσσωνται τὰ βιβλία Sch.D.T.p. 139 H.

❀**καταχᾰρίζομαι**, *corruptly make* one *a present of* a thing, τινὶ λάφυρα, λείαν, D.H.6.30, 7.63. 2. *surrender* a thing *corruptly*, τι Lys. 27.14; τὸν ἀγῶνα Aeschin.3.53; κ. τὰ δίκαια *give* judgement *by private interest*, Pl.*Ap.*35c, cf. Din.1.105, J.*AJ*4.8.14; κ. καὶ προέσθαι D.26.20; καταδωροδοκεῖσθαι καὶ κ. πολλὰ τῶν κοινῶν Arist.*Pol.*1271$^a$3; κ. τἀληθὲς τοῖς πολίταις Ael.*VH*14.5, cf. 11.9; κ. ταῖς γυναιξὶ τοὺς προδότας Plu.*Publ.*7. 3. *show favour*, c. dat. pers., κ. Ἀνδοκίδῃ Lys.6.3; ταῖς ὑμετέραις γνώμαις Isoc.8.10: abs., μὴ καταχαριζόμενον, ἀλλὰ διαμαχόμενον Pl.*Grg.*513d, cf. Phld.*Lib.*p.53 O.; πάντα ταῦτα κ. D.41.12; [ἡ δόξα] τὰ μὲν κ., τὰ δὲ ψεύδεται Ael.*VH*1.23.

**κατάχαρμα**, ατος, τό, *mockery*, ἐχθροῖς Thgn.1107.

**καταχάσκω**, aor. 1 -έχηνα, *gape, jeer at*, Hsch.

**καταχασμ-άομαι**, = foreg., Hsch. s.v. ἐγχαλεῖν. II. Pass., *split, burst open*, Thphr.*CP*4.12.11. **-ησις**, εως, ἡ, gloss on καταχήνη, Hsch., Phot.

**καταχέζω**, fut. -χέσομαι Ar.*Fr.*152: aor. κατέχεσα Id.*Nu.*174, κατέχεσον Alc.Com.4:—*befoul*, τινος ll. cc.

**καταχειρ-ίζομαι**, *make away with*, D.C.77.6. II. *take in hand*, Ptol.*Tetr.*206 (Pass.). **-ιος**, ον, *fitting the hand*, ἐρετμός A.R.1.1189. **-όομαι**, *subject to oneself, conquer*, Hsch.

**καταχειροτον-έω**, *vote by show of hands against, vote in condemnation of* or *so as to commit for trial*, τινος D.21.2, Din.2.20, etc.: c. inf., ἀδικεῖν Εὐάνδρου κατεχειροτόνησεν ὁ δῆμος D.21.175, cf. 51.8; καταχειροτονηθὲν αὐτοῦ καὶ ταῦτ' ἀσεβεῖν *a vote of condemnation having been passed against* him, and that for sacrilege, Id.21.199; κ. θάνατόν τινος *vote* the death-penalty *against* him, Lys.29.2, D.19.31, Pl.*Ax.* 368e; καταχειροτονίαν κ. τινός Aeschin.3.52:—Pass., *to be condemned*, πανδήμῳ φωνῇ D.S.18.67, cf. Plu.*Tim.*23. **-ία**, ἡ, *condemnation*, esp. *by show of hands*, καταχειροτονίαν ὁ δῆμος ἐποιήσατο D.21.6, cf. Aeschin.3.52, Arist.*Ath.*59.2 (pl.), Harp., *EM*481.46.

**καταχεύω**, Ep. for sq.:—Med., τέττιξ καταχεύετ' ἀοιδήν Hes.*Op.* 583.

⊛ **καταχέω**, Il.6.496 (tm.), al.: aor. 1 κατέχεα, Ep. and Lyr. κατέχευα (v. infr.):—Med., Ep. aor. 1 κατεχεύατο Call.*Hec.*1.1.11; inf. -χέασθαι Hdt.1.50:—Pass., pf. κατακέχυμαι Orac.ap.Hdt.7.140 (tm.): aor. -εχύθην E.*Hipp.*854 (lyr.): Ep. aor. Pass. (freq. in tm.) κατέχυτο, κατέχυντο, Il.20.282, Od.12.411, *h.Ven.*228:—*pour down upon, pour over*, c. dat., κὰδ δέ οἱ ὕδωρ χεῦαν Il.14.435; so ᾗ ῥά οἱ ἀχλὺν θεσπεσίην κατέχευε Od.7.42; ὕρεος κορυφῇσι Νότος κατέχευεν ὀμίχλην Il.3.10; τῷ γε χάριν κατέχευεν Ἀθήνη Od.2.12, etc.; σφιν.. πλοῦτον κατέχευε Κρονίων Il.2.670; μὴ σφῶϊν ἐλεγχείην καταχεύῃ 23.408, cf. Od.14.38; οἷ.. κατ' αἶσχος ἔχευε 11.433; ἐμῇ κεφαλῇ κατ' ὀνείδεα χεῦαν 22.463; νεφέλαν κρατὶ κατέχευας Pi.*P.*1.8; ἀντιπάλοις φόνον Epigr.ap.Plu. *Marc.*30:—Pass., κὰδ δ' ἄχος οἱ χύτο ὀφθαλμοῖσι Il.20.282; κατὰ.. ὀρόφοισιν αἷμα.. κέχυται Orac.ap.Hdt. l. c.; δάκρυσι βλέφαρα -χυθέντα E. l. c.; οἱ -χυθέντες J.*BJ*3.7.29:—also Act. c. gen., rarely in Hom., ὃς σφῶϊν.. ἔλαιον χαιτάων κατέχευε Il.23.282, cf. 765: freq. later, καταχέουσι αἷμα τοῦ ἀκινάκεος Hdt.4.62; κατάχει σὺ τῆς χορδῆς τὸ μέλι Ar.*Ach.*1040; ἔτνος τοὐλατῆρος ib.246; τοῦ δήμου καταχεῖν.. πλουθυγίειαν Id.*Eq.*1091; Ἵππερόν μου κατέχεεν τῶν χρημάτων Id.*Nu.*74, cf. *Pl.*790; βλασφημίαν τῶν ἱερῶν κ. Pl.*Lg.*800d; also κὰδ δὲ χευάτω μύρον.. κὰτ τῶ στήθεος Alc.36, cf. Pl.*R.*398a:—Med., κατὰ τῶν ἱματίων καταχεόμενοι [ἄκρατον] *letting* it *be poured over*.., Id.*Lg.*637e:—Pass., κατὰ τοῖν κόραιν ὕπνου τι καταχεῖται γλυκύ Ar.*V.*7. 2. simply, *pour, shower down*, χιόνα, νιφάδας ἐπὶ χθονί, Od.19.206, Il.12.158; ψιάδας κ. ἔραζε 16.459; so κατὰ δ' ἠέρα πουλὺν ἔχευεν 8.50; κατὰ δ' ὕπνον ἔχευεν Od.11.245:—Med., νότος.. χύσιν κατεχεύατο φύλλων Call. l. c.:—Pass., ἴδρως κακχέεται Sapph.2.13. b. *throw, cast down*, θύσθλα χαμαὶ κατέχευαν Il.6.134; κατὰ δ' ἡνία χεῦεν ἔραζε 17.619; ὅπλα τε πάντα εἰς ἄντλον κατέχυνθ' Od.12.411; πέπλον μὲν.. κατέχευεν ἐπ' οὔδει *let* the robe *fall upon* the floor, Il.5.734; τεῖχος.. εἰς ἅλα πᾶν κ. 7.461:—Med., Pl.*Ti.*41d; χαίταν *let fall*, Call.*Cer.* 5. c. metaph., κοινολογίας.. ἡδονὴν -χεούσης Phld.*D.*3.14. 3. Pass., *to be poured over* the ground, *be there in heaps*, ὁ χῶρος, ἐν ᾧ αἱ ἄκανθαι [τῶν ὀφίων] κατακεχύαται Hdt.2.75; of persons, *to be spread, dispersed*, Eun.*Hist.*p.239 D. II. *cause to flow, run*, [χρυσὸν] ἐς πίθους τήξας κ. Hdt.3.96:—Med., χρυσὸν καταχέασθαι *to have* it *melted down*, Id.1.50.

**καταχήνη**, ἡ, *flouting, mockery*, Ar.*V.*575, *Ec.*631; Καταχῆναι, αἱ, title of play, *IG*14.1097.8. II. *amulet in the shape of a locust* offered in the Acropolis of Athens, Hsch.

**καταχηρεύω**, *pass in widowhood*, τὸν βίον D.29.26.

**καταχής**, ές, Dor. for κατηχής, *sounding*, ὕδωρ Theoc.1.7.

**καταχθ-έω**, *weigh down, afflict*, J.*AJ*18.6.7: pf. part. Pass. -ηχθημένος, = βεβαρημένος, Phot. (-ισμένος Hsch.). **-ής**, ές, (ἄχθος) *loaded with*, καρποῖο Arat.1044; *laden, surcharged*, γαστήρ Nic.*Al.* 322. II. *heavy*, λᾶαν Nonn.*D.*40.517.

**κατ-αχθίζομαι**, *to be hateful*, Hsch.

⊛ **καταχθον-ίζω**, *devote to the infernal gods*, *Tab.Defix.*ap.Herwerden *Lex.Suppletorium*s. h. v. ⊛ **-ιος**, ον, also η, ον A.R.4.1413:—*subterranean*, Ζεὺς καταχθόνιος, i. e. Pluto, Il.9.457 (but Ζεὺς κ., = *Veiovis*, D.H.2.10); of Pluto, Demeter, Persephone, and the Erinyes, *IG*3.1423; δαίμονες κ. Hierocl.*in CA*1 p.419 M.; = Lat. *Di Manes*, *AP*7.333; κ. θεοί, = Lat. *Di Manes*, freq. in sepulchral Inscrr., *IG*14.1660, al. **-ος**· ὁ λιπαρός, ὁ τρόφιμος, Hsch.

**καταχιονίζω**, *cover with snow*, in Pass., Hsch. s. v. κατανίφεται.

**καταχλαινόω**, *clothe with a* χλαῖνα, Anon.ap.Suid.

**καταχλευ-άζω**, *scoff, jeer*, D.H.*Comp.*25, Poll.6.199: c. gen., τῆς παρακλήσεως J.*BJ*2.18.7:—Pass., f. l. in Ph.2.598. **-αστικός**, ή, όν, *derisive*, Poll.6.200. Adv. -κῶς v. l. ibid.

**καταχλιαστέον**, (χλιαίνω) *one must warm thoroughly*, Sor.1.69.

**καταχλιδάω**, Ion. -έω, *to be effeminate*, Hp.*Praec.*7 (v.l. -χλιδευσιν): c. gen., *display pomp* or *luxury by way of insult over*, τινος Posidon.36 J.

**καταχλοάζομαι**, *to be covered with green weed*, of rocks, Sch.Opp. *H.*1.131.

**κατ-αχλύομαι**, *to be dimmed*, Cerc.4.21.

**κατάχολος**, ον, *very bilious*, ὑποχωρήματα Hp.*Epid.*7.14, cf. Aët.8.74.

**καταχορδ-εύω**, *mince up as for a sausage*, κ. [τὴν γαστέρα] Hdt.6.75; κ. τινὰ ἐν βασάνοις Them.*Or.*21.261d. **-έω**, = foreg., Ael. *Fr.*280.

**καταχόρ-ειον**, τό, = sq., μέρος τὸ λεγόμενον -ριον (sic) Demetr.Lac. *Herc.*1014.53 F. **-ευσις**, εως, ἡ, *song*, finale of the Πυθικὸς νόμος, representing Apollo's *dance of triumph*, Poll.4.84. ⊛ **-εύω**, *dance in triumph over*, τινος Ael.*NA*1.30: metaph., *insult*, τῶν Ῥωμαϊκῶν συμφορῶν Anon.ap.Suid.

**καταχορηγέω**, *lavish as* χορηγός, ὑπέρ τινος πεντακισχιλίας δραχμάς Lys.19.42: generally, *spend* or *contribute lavishly*, οὐσίας τισί D.H.3.72; τὰ οἰκεῖα Plu.*Lys.*9; *squander upon*, τι εἰς δεῖπνα Id.*Eum.* 13; εἰς τὸ θέατρον Id.2.348f; κ. τοῖς στρατεύμασιν ἀφειδῶς τῶν χρημάτων Id.*Cat.Ma.*3.

**καταχόρηον**, v. καταχόρειον.

**καταχραίνω**, *befoul*, οὔπω νιν ὑπὸ προτέρων ἵππων κατέχρᾶνεν κόνις B.5.44, cf. Eustr.*in EN*316.34:—also in Med., *sprinkle*, γάλακτι with milk, *AP*7.657 (Leon.).

⊛ **καταχράομαι**, Delph. -χρέομαι *SIG*672.32 (ii B.C.), al.: fut. -χρήσομαι Pl.*Mx.*247b: pf. -κέχρημαι both in act. and pass. senses (v. infr.): aor. -εχρήσθην (v. infr. II. 4):—*make full use of, apply*, τινὶ εἰς.., ἐπί.., πρός τι, Pl.*Lg.*700c, *R.*520a, *Cra.*426e; μάρτυσι κ. πρὸς τὸ.. Id.*Phlb.* 51a; κ. ἡ φύσις ἐν παρέργῳ τῇ.. ἀναπνοῇ πρὸς τὴν ὄσφρησιν Arist.*Resp.* 473[a]23, cf. *Sens.*444[a]25; λόγους.. οἷσπερ νυνὶ κατακέχρηται (in act. sense) D.35.44; ἐν καιρῷ [πράξεσι] κ. Isoc.4.9; κενῇ προφάσει ταύτῃ κατεχρῶ D.18.150: c. acc., τὴν.. ὑπερβολὴν ἐπὶ βοήθειαν κ. ἡ φύσις Arist.*PA*663[b]33; σχολὴν ἐς ἀκρόασιν Luc.*Prom.*4; τι εἴς τι *IG*2[2].1672.307 (iv B.C.), cf. J.*BJ*5.9.1: abs. in pf. part. in pass. sense, ἐξεύρημα.. Ἀθήνησιν.. κατακεχρημένον ἐν συμποσίοις ἰδίᾳ 'στί is *fashionable* at private banquets there, Amphis 14.4. II. *do what one likes with* a person or thing, καταχρήσασθέ μοι, εἰ δοκῶ τοιοῦτος εἶναι Aeschin.1.122. 2. *use up, consume*, of money, etc., c. acc., Lys. 19.22 (bis); στέαρ *PRev.Laws* 50.14 (iii B.C.); τὰ κρέα ἐν τὰν δαμοθοινίαν *SIG*671 *A*7 (Delph., ii B.C.); *lay out, apply* money, εἴς τι D.49.4, *IG*9(1).694.34 (Corc., ii B.C.), 12(1).155.86 (Rhodes); ἐνταῦθα on this, D.47.50: pf. in act. sense, ὅσα κατακέχρημαι Ἀθήνησι D.L.5.69:—Pass., *to be spent, consumed*, Isoc.4.74; πλίνθου τῆς -χρησθείσης εἰς τοὺς τοίχους *PPetr.*3 p.139 (iii B.C.). 3. *misuse, abuse*, D.19.277: c. dat., τῇ τῶν προγόνων δόξῃ μὴ -χρησόμενοι Pl.*Mx.* l. c.; κ. ὀνόματι *use* it *in a wrong sense, misapply* it, Arist.*Cael.*270[b]24, Phld. *Rh.*1.43 S., cf. Str.5.1.2 (also abs., Phld.*Rh.*1.59 S.; *fall into an error*, Olymp.*in Mete.*279.11): c. acc., κ. τὴν σχολὴν εἰς τοῦτο Dionys. Com.4; τοῦ ἀρχαίου τι κ. *misappropriate*, *Test.Epict.*8.8. 4. of persons, in bad sense, *make away with, destroy, kill*, c. acc., Hdt. 1.82,117, 4.146, al., Plb.1.85.1:—Pass., aor. -χρησθῆναι, ἐδέοντό μιν κ. requested that he might *be put to death*, Hdt.9.120. III. *pretend, allege*, ὡς.. D.43.39; ὅτι.. Id.48.44.

B. Act. **καταχράω** only Ion., used only in 3 sg., ἀντὶ λόφου ἡ λοφιὴ κατέχρα the mane *sufficed them* for a crest, Hdt.7.70; elsewh. impers., *it suffices*, οὐδέ οἱ καταχρήσει.. ὑμέων ἀπέχεσθαι nor *will he be satisfied* to keep his hands off you, Id.4.118; ὥς οἱ καταχρᾷ εἰ βούλονται that *it is sufficient* for him, if.., Id.1.164; καταχρήσει *it will suffice*, Phoen.2.21.

**κατ-αχρειόομαι**, Pass., *to be ill-treated*, κατηχρειωμένη *AP*9.203 (Phot. or Leo).

**καταχρέμπτομαι**, *spit upon*, τινος Ar.*Pax* 815.

⊛ **κατάχρεος**, ον, also -χρεως, of persons, *involved in debt*, Plb.13.1.1, Agatharch.*Fr.Hist.*16 J., D.S.19.9, App.*Mith.*48, etc.; -χρεως δανείοις S.E.*M.*5.101: metaph., -χρεος ἁμαρτίας *involved in*.., Lxx *Wi.* 1.4. II. of things, τὰ κ. *that which is owing, debts*, *IG*14.759.20 (Naples); τὸ κ. κεφάλαιον dub. in Philem.88.9.

**καταχρηματ-ίζω**, *deal with*, *SIG*1023.73 (Cos, iii/ii B.C.), *GDI* 3624[a]32 (ibid.): *dispose of* property, *POxy.*506.42 (ii A.D.), etc. **-ισμός**, ὁ, *deed, instrument* dealing with property, ib.237 iv 7 (ii A.D.), *PFlor.*381.11 (ii A.D.).

**κατά-χρησις**, εως, ἡ, *excessive use* or *consumption*, *PTeb.*61(*b*).305 (ii B.C.), Gal.19.679. II. *analogical application* of a word (e.g. γόνυ καλάμου, ὀφθαλμὸς ἀμπέλου), Arist.ap.Cic.*Orat.*27.94, Demetr.Lac. *Herc.*1014.49, D.H.*Comp.*3 (pl.), Quint.8.6.34, Sch.D.T.p.459 H., etc.: pl., Suid. s. v. Γοργίας; ἐκ -χρήσεως Gal.6.136. **-χρηστέον**, *one must use*, τινὶ εἴς τι Luc.*Am.*17. **-χρηστικός**, ή, όν, *misused, misapplied*, of words and phrases, ὑπάκουσις Phld.*Rh.*1.89 S., cf. S.E. *M.*8.129. Adv. -κῶς *by a misuse of language*, Str.7.7.11, S.E.*P.*1.191, etc.; opp. κυρίως, D.T.632.24, Phld.*Po.*5.15, Ph.1.68: Comp. -ώτερον A.D.*Synt.*4.26, S.E.*M.*6.2. 2. *serviceable*, τὰ κ. καὶ συνεργατικὰ πρός τι Ptol.*Tetr.*80.

**κατά-χρισις**, εως, ἡ, *smearing on*, Alex.Aphr.*Pr.*2.59, Hld.6.11. **-χρισμα**, ατος, τό, *salve, ointment*, Antyll.ap.Orib.10.27.1. **-χριστέον**, *one must anoint*, Gp.16.18.2, Aët.7.24. ⊛ **-χριστος**, ον, *for use as ointments*, τροχίσκοι Antyll.ap.Orib.10.24.10, cf. Dsc.5.106; φάρμακον *Tab.Defix.Aud.*8. **-χρίω** [ῑ], *anoint, smear, coat*, Arist.*HA*625[b]31; τέγη *IG*11(2).203 *A*54 (Delos, iii B.C.); τὰ τείχη τῆς σκηνῆς ib.199 *A*102 (ibid.); θῖβιν ἀσφαλτοπίσσῃ Lxx *Ex.*2.3; πηλῷ πρόσωπον Luc.*Anach.*9; θρόνους ἀσβόλῳ Ael.*VH*2.15:—Med., -κεχρῖσθαι τὸ πρόσωπον Artem.4.41:—Pass., Dsc.2.70; βολβίτῳ -κεχρισμένος M.Ant.3.3; ἐλαίῳ κ. Ph.2.158; κατακεχριμένα, = *oblita*, Gloss.

**κατάχρους**, ουν, = εὔχρους, ἔριφος *IG*12(1).892 (Netteia, dub., cf. *Arch.f.Relig.*19.285).

⊛ **κατάχρυσ-ος**, ον, *overlaid with gold-leaf, gilded*, *IG*1[2].280.78, 2[2].1388.75, *SIG*1106.125 (Cos, iv/iii B.C.), Onos.1.20, Plu.2.753f, Luc. *Alex.*13; κόμη κ. τῇ χρόᾳ Ach.Tat.5.13. 2. metaph., of persons, *gilded*, Diph.60.1. 3. *rich in gold*, ψάμμος Poll.7.97. 4. metaph., *spurious*, Phld.*Po.*5.15. Adv. -σως *speciously*, Id.*Piet.*17. **-όω**, *cover with gold-leaf, gild*, Hdt.2.129, 3.56, 4.26:—Pass., Id.1.98, 2.63, *IG*2[2].1388.77. II. metaph., *make golden* (i.e. *splendid*), τὴν πόλιν

Plu.*Per.*12; κατεχρύσου πᾶς ἀνὴρ Εὐριπίδην *plastered* him *with gold* (opp. κατεπίττου), Ar.*Ec.*826.

**κατα-χρώννῡμι**, Poll.7.169, Suid.: impf. **κατέχρωζεν** Anon.ap. Suid. (s.h.v.):—*colour*, -χρῶσαι τὴν κόμην Poll.2.35, cf. Alex.Aphr. *in SE*9.3:—Pass., metaph., κατὰ δὲ κηλῖδα..κέχρωσαι E.*Hec.*911 (lyr.). **-χρωσις**, εως, ἡ, *colouring*, Poll.7.169.

**κατα-χύδην** [ῠ], Adv. *pouring down, profusely*, πίνειν Anacr.90. 3. **-χῦμα**, ατος, τό, *bath-water*, Ammon.*Diff.*p.78 V.; κ., = *perfusio* and κ. ζωμοῦ, = *tucca*, *Gloss.*: but in pl., = καταχύσματα, Them.*Or.* 23.293c. **-χύννω**, late form of καταχέω, *Gloss.* **-χῠσις**, εως, ἡ, *pouring on* or *over*, πολλοῦ ψυχροῦ Hp.*Aph.*5.21; *affusion, besprinkling*, Id.*Art.*27; ἡ τοῦ θερμοῦ κ. *Gp.*13.14.11. II. *vase for pouring*, later Gr. for Att. πρόχους, Moer.p.296 P., cf. Hsch. s.v. προχοΐδια. III. mistransl. of Hebr. *mûṣaq* 'straitness', as if *mûṣāq* 'smelting', Lxx *Jb.*36.16. IV. = ἀήρ, Hsch. ❋**-χυσμα**, ατος, τό, *that which is poured over, sauce*, Ar.*Av.*535 (anap.), 1637; βολβοὺς.. καταχύσματι δεύσας Pl.Com.173.9; τὰ κ. ὄξος οὐκ ἔχει Philonid.9. 2. καταχύσματα, τά, *handfuls* of nuts, figs, etc., *showered over* a bride, τὰ κ. κατάχει τοῦ νυμφίου Theopomp.Com.14; also on a new slave, by way of welcome, Ar.*Pl.*768 (cf. Sch. adloc.), D.45.74; cf. κατάχυμα. **-χυσμάτιον**, τό, Dim. of foreg., *sauce for pouring over* a dish, Pherecr.108.11, Poll.6.68. **-χῠτήρια**, τά, festival in Egypt at the inundation of the Nile, *PCair.Zen.*176.39 (iii B.C.), Eudox.*Ars* 3.24. **-χυτλον**, τό, *watering-pot, portable shower-bath*, κατάχυτλον τὴν ῥῖν' ἔχεις Eup.283; ἐν καταχύτλοις λεκάναισι Pherecr.108.19.

**καταχυτρίζω**, = ἐγχυτρίζω, Ar.*Fr.*793.

**κατάχωλος**, ον, *dead lame*, Alc.Com.2.

**καταχών-ευσις**, εως, ἡ, *melting down*, *BCH*35.243 (Delos, ii B.C.). **-εύω**, *melt down*, D.22.76, Din.1.69, Str.9.1.20, etc.; [ἀνδριάντας] εἰς ἀμίδας Plu.2.820f; τοῦ στόματος κατεχώνευσε χρυσίον *poured molten* gold down his throat, App.*Mith.*21.

**καταχώννῡμι** (-ύω *Gp.*2.42.5, *Hippiatr.*34), fut. -χώσω Pl.*Tht.* 177c:—*cover with a heap, overwhelm, bury*, ὁ νότος κατέχωσέ σφεας *buried* them in sand, Hdt.4.173; κ. τινὰ λίθοις Ar.*Ach.*295 (tm.); σφέας..κατέχωσαν οἱ βάρβαροι βάλλοντες Hdt.7.225; ἐν λίθοις σφενδόνης Lxx *Za.*9.15; ἐν κοπρίᾳ *Hippiatr.*l.c.:—Pass., Lib.*Or.*61.15. 2. *silt up, dam up*, τὸ στόμιον τοῦ λιμένος D.S.24.1. 3. metaph., ἐπιρρέοντα καταχώσει..τὸν ἐξ ἀρχῆς λόγον with fresh streams they *will choke up the channel of* our original argument, Pl.l.c.; κ. τινὰ λόγοις Id.*Grg.* 512c; τὴν ἐρώτησιν Plu.2.512e:—Pass., *to be buried in obscurity*, τὰ πρῶτα ὀνόματα -κέχωσται ὑπὸ τῶν βουλομένων τραγῳδεῖν αὐτά Pl.*Cra.* 414c; ἐνθυμήσεις μυστικῶς -κεχωσμέναι Vett.Val.301.9. 4. *overwhelm, ruin*, Lib.*Or.*63.19.

❋**καταχωρ-έω**, *yield* or *give up to* a person *in* a thing, τινί τινος D.L. 5.71; τινί τι Plu.2.312b. II. = κάτειμι III, τοὺς τόκους -εῖν..ἐς τὸ θεῖον *Supp.Epigr.*2.481 (Scythia, iii A.D.). ❋**-ίζω**, Att. fut. -ιῶ *OGI* 229.75 (iii B.C.), Apollon.Cit.2:—*place in position*, freq. in X., as *Cyr.* 4.3.3, al.; mostly of soldiers, as *An.*6.5.10, *Cyr.*2.2.8: generally, *place*, κατ' ἀξίαν Plot.3.2.12:—Pass., *take up a position*, ὅπου δέοιτο X.*Cyr.*8.5.2. II. *enter in a register* or *record*, κ. εἰς μνημόσυνον ἐν τῇ βιβλιοθήκῃ Lxx *Es.*2.23; εἰς τὴν τῶν ὑπομνημάτων δέλτον *IG*7.413.31 (i B.C.); ὑπόμνημα *PAmh.*2.35.36 (ii B.C.), etc.:—Pass., *POxy.*515.3 (ii A.D.), etc.; τὰ ἐν τῷ ψηφίσματι -κεχωρισμένα *SIG*618.6 (Heraclea ad Latmum, ii B.C.), cf. *Supp.Epigr.*3.378 *C*13 (Delph., ii/i B.C.); -εχωρίσθη ὁ ἀριθμὸς ἐν βιβλίῳ Lxx 1 *Ch.*27.24; [διαμαρτυρίαν] -κεχωρισμένην ἐν στασίμῳ Satyr.*Vit.Eur.Fr.*39 xvii 27. 2. *assign*, τινὰς εἰς φυλὰς *OGI*l.c.; εἰς τὸ στρατιωτικὸν σύνταγμα Aristeas 36. b. *invest, allocate* funds, etc., μισθὸν εἴς τι D.S.5.17 cod., cf. *PSI*4.372.10 (iii B.C.); of confiscated property, τὰ ὑπάρχοντά τινος κ. εἰς τὸ βασιλικόν *PAmh.*2.33.36 (ii B.C.):—Pass., τὰ εἰς τὸ ναυτικὸν -ισμένα Wilcken *Chr.*385.30 (iii B.C.), cf. *SIG*578.44 (Teos, ii B.C.). 3. *convey by deed*, τινι *PAmh.*2.52 (ii B.C.). III. *set down in a book, place on record*, Phld.*Po.*994 *Fr.*48, al.; εἰς τὴν ποίησιν Str.1.2.3; ἐν τοῖς ποιήμασι D.S.5.5, cf. 1.31, D.H.1.6; Κτησίβιος κατεχώρισεν, ὥστε.. Ath. Mech.29.10; οὕτως -κεχώρικεν (sc. ὁ Ἱπποκράτης) Apollon.Cit.1:—Pass., Id.3; ἐν ἱστορίαις κ. *Inscr.Prien.*37.54 (ii B.C.), cf. Demetr.Lac. *Herc.*1647.27 F.; παρά τισι Phld.*Rh.*1.160 S. **-ισμός**, ὁ, *registration, deposit in a registry*, *PAmh.*2.35.37 (ii B.C.), *POxy.*514.4 (ii A.D.), etc.: *setting in order*, πράξεων Andronic.Rhod.p.576 M. (pl.). **-ιστέον**, *one must assign a place to*, ἐν τάξει Dam.*Pr.*252.

**κατάχωσις**, εως, ἡ, *covering up, burying*, *Gp.*4.3.2.

**καταψαίρουσι**· κινοῦνται, Hsch.

**καταψακάζω**, Att. for καταψεκ- (q.v.).

❋**καταψάλλω**, *play stringed instruments to*, [συμπόσιον] καταυλεῖν καὶ κ. Plu.2.713e:—usu. in Pass., *have music played to one, enjoy music*, ib.785e; of places, *resound with music*, Id.*Ant.*56. 2. Pass., *to be buried to the sound of music*, Procop.*Pers.*2.23. 3. metaph., καταψάλλεται..ὁ δημιουργός *is drummed out*, Porph.*Chr.*34.

**κατάψᾱσις**, v. κατάψησις.

❋**καταψάω**, *stroke, caress*, καταψῶντα τοῦ παιδίου τὴν κεφαλὴν Hdt.6. 61; καταψῶν αὐτὸν [τὸν κάνθαρον] ὥσπερ πωλίον Ar.*Pax*75, cf. X.*Ap.* 28; τὸ φαλακρόν Herod.6.76:—Pass., Asclep.ap.Gal.12.411; *to be stroked the right way*, Sch.Gen.Il.21.474. 2. metaph., *smooth down*, Plb.2.13.6, 10.18.3; *cajole, wheedle*, *BGU*1011.13 (ii B.C.). 3. *scrape down*, τοὺς τοίχους *IG*11(2).199 *A*48 (Delos, iii B.C.); *rub down*, ἅτερος τὸν ἕτερον Luc.*Anach.*1.

**καταψεκ-άζω**, Att. **καταψᾰκ-**, *wet by continual dropping*, δρόσοι κατεψάκαζον A.*Ag.*561; κ. φαρμάκῳ Plu.*Alex.*35:—hence **-αστέον** *Gp.*5.39.2.

**καταψελλίζομαι**, Pass., *to be made to lisp*, κατεψελλισμένοι τὴν φωνὴν ὑπὸ τοῦ οἴνου Philostr.*Im.*1.25.

**κατα-ψεύδομαι**, fut. -ψεύσομαι: pf. -έψευσμαι D.55.8, *Ep.*3.35: also in pass. sense, as also aor. -εψεύσθην, v. infr. II:—*tell lies against, speak falsely of*, τινος Ar.*Pax*533, Lys.16.8, Antipho 2.4.7, Pl.*R.*381d, D.21.134, etc.; κ. τινὸς πρός τινα *accuse falsely* to another, Plu. *Them.*25, *Phoc.*33: abs., Hyp.*Lyc.*8. 2. *allege falsely against*, τί τινος And.1.8, Pl.*Euthd.*283e, *R.*391d; τὰ πλεῖστα κατεψεύσατό μου D.18.9; ἑαυτοῦ μωρίαν D.H.4.68. 3. *say falsely, pretend*, ὡς.. E.*Ba.*334; *feign, invent*, τι D.18.11. 4. c. gen., *make a pretence of*, ὕπνου Luc.*Asin.*7; *give a false account of*, γένους Arist.*Pr.*950ᵇ6; τῶν πραγμάτων J.*BJ Prooem.*1. II. Pass., *to be falsely reported*, Ἑλληνικὸς ὅρκος -ψεύδεται Theon *Prog.*2; τὰ κατεψευσμένα *false allegations*, Antipho 5.19; *to be falsely accused*, προδότης εἶναι κατεψεύσθη Philostr.*Her.*10.7, cf. *VA*5.24. 2. of writings, *to be falsely attributed*, τινος *to* one, Ael.*VH*12.36: abs., *to be spurious*, Ath.15.697a, Plu.2.833c. 3. *to be wrong, in error*, Phld.*Mus.*p.103 K., Str.9.2. 33: c. gen., *about*.., Sor.1.14, 2.4. **-ψευδομαρτῠρέω**, *bear false witness against*, τινος X.*Ap.*24:—Med., D.29.6:—Pass., *to be borne down by false evidence*, Pl.*Grg.*472a, Is.5.9, D.21.136. **-ψευσις**, εως, ἡ, *false account*, τῶν τόπων Str.1.3.18. **-ψευσμα**, ατος, τό, *false accusation*, Metrod.*Fr.*18: generally, *fiction, falsity*, Arr.*Epict.* 2.20.23. **-ψευσμός**, ὁ, *slander, calumny*, Lxx *Si.*26.6. **-ψεύστης**, ου, ὁ, = *commentor*, *Gloss.*

**καταψέφω**, = κατασκοτίζω, Hsch.

**καταψηλαφάω**, = ψηλαφάω, Luc.*Asin.*14.

**κατάψησις**, Dor. -ᾱσις, εως, ἡ, *raking over*, *BCH*23.566 (Delph., iii B.C.).

❋**καταψηφ-ίζομαι**, fut. -ιοῦμαι Lys.12.90:—*vote against* or *in condemnation of*, τινος Antipho 1.12, Lys.10.31, Pl.*Ap.*36a, 41d, X.*Ap.* 32: metaph., τῆς ψυχῆς Democr.159; κ. τινὸς θάνατον *pass a vote* of death *against* him, Lys.12.100; κατεψηφισμένοι αὐτοῦ θάνατον X. *HG*1.5.19; κ. τινὸς δειλίαν, κλοπήν, *find* him *guilty* of cowardice, of theft, Lys.14.11, Pl.*Grg.*516a; ἀδικίαν ὑμῶν αὐτῶν Isoc.15.297: abs., οἱ -ψηφισάμενοι δικασταί Pl.*Lg.*878d: later in pf. Act. κατεψήφικα D.H.4.58, 5.8. 2. Pass. (so always in aor.), *to be condemned*, ἑάλωκεν ἤδη καὶ κατεψήφισται D.21.151; θανάτου ἡ φυγῆς καταψηφισθῆναι *to* death or exile, Pl.*R.*558a, cf. *Plt.*299a. b. of the sentence, *to be pronounced against* a person, δίκη κατεψηφισμένη τινός Th.2.53; κατεψηφισμένος ἦν μου ὁ θάνατος X.*Ap.*27, cf. 23; τὰ ὑφ' ὑμῶν ψηφισθέντα Lys.14.12. 3. Med., *carry measures adverse to* a person, Plu.*Caes.*29. II. *vote in affirmation*, opp. ἀποψηφ-, Arist. *Pol.*1298ᵇ39; generally, *come to a determination*, Id.*Po.*1461ᵇ2:—so in Pass., τὰ κοινῇ τοῖς Ἀχαιοῖς -ψηφισθέντα εἰς τιμήν τινος D.S.29. 18. 2. metaph., ἀείμνηστον ἡμῶν δόξαν Vett.Val.351.28. **-ισις**, εως, ἡ, *voting against, condemnation*, Antipho 1.3, D.C.36.38 (pl.):—also **-ισμός**, ὁ, Poll.8.149. **-ιστέον**, *one must condemn*, τινος X. *HG*2.4.9, cf. Democr.262.

❋**καταψήχω**, *rub down, pound in a mortar*, Nic.*Th.*898. 2. *wear away, consume*, χρόνος πάντα κ. cj. in Simon.176:—Pass., *crumble away*, ῥεῖ πᾶν ἄδηλον καὶ κατέψηκται S.*Tr.*698, cf. Pl.*Ti.*84a. II. *stroke, caress*, ἵππους E.*Hipp.*110; χεῖρα Clearch.25; κόμην Luc.*Am.* 44; ἄκρα γενείου *AP*11.354.12 (Agath.): metaph., ὣς φάτο μειλιχίοισι καταψήχων ὀάροισι A.R.3.1102.

**καταψῐθῠρίζω**, *whisper against*, τινὸς πρός τινα Plu.2.483c. 2. abs., ἡ ἐπιδίφριος καὶ -ψιθυρίζουσα λέξις *in a low, conversational tone*, Hieronym.ap.Phld.*Rh.*1.199 S.

**καταψῑλόω**, *strip bare*, in Pass., D.S.20.96.

**καταψίω**, *crush, grind small*, *EM*818.35.

**καταψοφέω**, *make a loud noise*, θεὸς κ. βρονταῖς J.*AJ*6.2.2.

**κατα-ψυκτικός**, ή, όν, *cooling*, Arist.*Resp.*479ᵃ31. **-ψυξις**, εως, ἡ, *cooling* or *becoming cold, chill*, αἱ μετὰ καταψύξιος δυσφορίαι Hp. *Prorrh.*1.27, cf. *Coac.*337, al.: freq. in Arist., ὁ φόβος κ. δι' ὀλιγαιμότητά ἐστι *PA*692ᵃ23, cf. *Rh.*1389ᵇ32; simply, *cold*, Thphr.*HP*6.8. 4. II. = κώνειον (from its effect), Ps.-Dsc.4.78. **-ψῡχος**, ον, = *opacus*, *Gloss.* **-ψυχραίνω**, gloss on σβέννυμι, Sch.Opp.*H.*2. 76. **-ψυχρος**, ον, *very cold*, Hp.*Art.*67, S.E.*P.*1.125, etc.; τόπος Dsc. 2.76; χειμών *Gp.*1.12.33; of character, Vett.Val.11.32, al. ❋**-ψύχω** [ῡ], *cool, chill*, ὕδωρ κ. τὴν ξηρὰν ἀναθυμίασιν Arist.*Mete.*361ᵃ2, cf. 368ᵇ 34; ὁ φόβος καταψύχει Id.*PA*650ᵇ28, cf. *Pr.*954ᵇ13, al.; αἱ ἄτομοι.. κατέψυξαν [τὸ σῶμα] Epicur.*Fr.*60:—Pass., fut. -ψῠγήσομαι Vett.Val. 73.21: pf. -έψυγμαι: aor. -εψύχθην, also -εψύγην [ῠ] Arist.*Pr.*897ᵃ 22:—*to be chilled, become cold*, Hp.*Aph.*4.40, Arist.*HA*531ᵇ31, etc.; of persons, κατεψυγμένοι, opp. θερμοί, Id.*Rh.*1389ᵇ30. 2. metaph., οὐ -έψυξαν τὴν ὁρμὴν *did* not *allow* their ardour *to cool*, J.*BJ*1.2.7:—Pass., κατέψυκτο τὸ πρακτικόν Plu.*Pomp.*46, cf. Critodem. in *Cat.Cod. Astr.*8(1).259, Vett.Val.l.c. 3. *cool, refresh*, καταψύχει πνοή A. *Fr.*127. II. *dry* land after irrigation, *PCair.Zen.*155 (iii B.C.):—Pass., of a country, χώρα κατεψυγμένη *dried* or *parched up*, D.S.1.7, cf. Plu.*Pomp.*31. III. intr., *cool down*, of persons, Lxx *Ge.*18.4.

**κατέᾱγα, κατεάγην** [ᾰ], **κατέαξα**, v. κατάγνυμι.

**κατ-έαγμα**, ατος, τό, later form of κάταγμα, *BGU*647.12 (ii A.D.), *PAmh.*2.93.19 (ii A.D.), *Gloss.* **-εακτέος**, α, ον, = *perfringendus*, ib. **-έαξις**, εως, ἡ, = *confractio*, ib. **-εάσσω**, later form of κατάγνυμι, *break*, ib.:—Pass., Arist.*Mech.*852ᵇ22 (though καταγνύῃ, καταγνύμενον occur ib.23,28), Aesop.179c; cf. κατάσσω.

**κατεβλᾰκευμένως**, Adv. pf. part. Pass. of καταβλακεύω, *slothfully, tardily*, Ar.*Pl.*325, *AP*4.3a.16 (Agath.).

**κατεγγυ-άω**, aor. κατηγγύησα D.33.10, κατενεγύησα J.*AJ*16.7.6,

etc.:—*pledge, betroth*, τινά τινι E.*Or.*1079, 1675; γάμον θυγατρός τινι J.*AJ*6.10.2:—Med., Parth.5.3. II. as law-term, *make responsible, compel to give security*, τινὰ πρὸς τὸν πολέμαρχον or πρὸς τῷ -χῳ, D.32.29, 59.40, cf. Pl.*Lg.*871e, *PTeb.*490 (i B.C.), etc.; κ. τινὰ πρὸς εἴκοσι τάλαντα *make* him *give security* to the amount of 20 talents, Plb.5.15.9; πρὸς δίκην τινά Plu.*Tim.*37:—Pass., *to be held to bail*, D.59.49; [ἐγγύην] κ. Pl.*Lg.*872b. 2. *sequester, put an embargo upon*, πυρόν *PAmh.*2.35.23 (ii B.C.). 3. *seize as a security*, ὑπὲρ ἀργυρίου τὴν ναῦν καὶ τοὺς παῖδας D.33.11: metaph., *bind, subject*, τὸ ζῆν λύπαις αὐθαιρέτοις κ. Thalesap.Stob.4.22.65:—Pass., πατρίοις ἔθεσιν κατηγγυημένος Apion ap.J.*Ap.*2.2. 4. in Pass., *undertake* to do, c. inf., Plb.3.5.8. -εύω, *give security*, ποτὶ τοὺς ἱερούς *IG*5(1).1390.69 (Andania, i B.C.). -η, ἡ, *giving of security*, D.25.60. -ησις, εως, ἡ, = *taking of pledges, sequestration, PTeb.*148 (ii B.C.), *PRyl.*119.13 (i A.D.). -ητικά, ῶν, τά, *betrothal, Gloss.*

**κάτεγγυς**, Adv. *near*, c. gen., prob. in Hippon.42.

**κατέγ-κειμαι**, v.l. for κάτω ἔγκ., Hp.*Mul.*2.137. -**κλημα**, ατος, τό, *accusation*, Eust.922.46. -**κονέω**, *to be in great haste*, Hsch. -**κρᾰτεύομαι**, strengthd. for ἐγκρατ-, c. acc., Suid.

**κατεγνῡπωμένως**, Adv., v. καταγνυπόομαι.

**κατεγχειρέω**, *treat fully, discuss thoroughly*, Phld.*Mort.*4, *Lib.*p.27 O. II. *plot against* one, abs., Them.*Or.*19.232a.

**κατεγχλῐδάω**, *look haughtily down upon*, τινι Machoap.Ath.13.577e.

**κατεδᾰφίζω**, *dash to earth*, Suid.:—Pass., Sch.E.*Hec.*21.

❋**κατέδω**, Homeric pres., = κατεσθίω, *eat up, devour*, μυίας αἵ ῥά τε φῶτας.. κατέδουσιν Il.19.31; εὐλαὶ.. φῶτας ἀρηϊφάτους κ. 24.415: metaph., οἶκον, βίοτον, κτῆσιν κ., *eat up* house, goods, etc., Od.2.237, 19.159,534; ὃν θυμὸν κατέδων *eating* one's heart for grief, Il.6.202:—later in Pass., ὑπὸ ὄφεως κατέδεσθαι Arist.*Fr.*145.—For fut. κατέδομαι and other tenses, v. κατεσθίω.

**κατεζητημένως**, Adv. pf. part. Pass. from καταζητέω, *in a far-fetched, recondite style*, Vett.Val.301.29.

**κατεηγώς**, Ion. pf. 2 part. of κατάγνυμι, for κατεαγώς.

**κατεθίζω**, aor. -είθισα Plb.4.21.3:—*make customary*, τινί τι l.c.:—Pass., τὰ -ειθισμένα ἱερεῖα D.S.12.30, cf. *EM*752.38. 2. *accustom, habituate*, ῥαθυμίᾳ τινάς Ath.Med.ap.Orib.*inc.*21.1.

❋**κατείβω**, poet. for καταλείβω, *let flow down, shed*, τί νυ δάκρυ κατείβετον Od.21.86:—Med., *flow apace*, θαλερὸν δὲ κατείβετο δάκρυ παρειῶν Il.24.794; τὸ κατειβόμενον Στυγὸς ὕδωρ Styx's *downward flowing* water, Od.5.185: metaph., κατείβετο δὲ γλυκὺς αἰών life *was flowing, passing away*, ib.152: rare in Att., τί δάκρυον κατείβεται; Ar.*Lys.*127 (paratrag.). II. trans., *flood, overflow*, metaph., Ἔρος κατείβων καρδίαν Alcm.36:—Pass., *overflow with*, γλυκερῇ κατείβετο θυμὸν ἀνίῃ, A.R.3.290; κατείβετο θυμὸς ἀκουῇ ib.1131.

**κατεῖδον**, inf. κατῐδεῖν, part. κατῐδών, aor. 2 with no pres. in use, καθοράω being used instead:—*look down*, Περγάμου ἐκ κατιδών Il.4.508 (nisi leg. ἐκκατ-). II. c. acc., *look down upon, view*, τὰς νήσους ἁπάσας ἐν κύκλῳ Ar.*Eq.*170. 2. *see, behold, regard*, Thgn.905, A.*Pers.*1026 (lyr.); *catch sight of*, τὰς νέας Hdt.7.194, cf. E.*Supp.*1044; κατιδεῖν βίον to live, A.*Ag.*474 (lyr.). 3. of mental vision, *perceive, discern*, S.*OT*338, Pl.*Euthphr.*2c. III. Med. in act. sense, aor. 2 κατειδόμην, inf. κατιδέσθαι, τι Hdt.4.179, 7.208, S.*El.*892, etc.; κατιδέσθαι ἔς τι Hdt.5.35.

**κατείδωλος**, ον, *full of idols, given to idolatry*, *Act.Ap.*17.16.

**κατεικάζω**, *liken to*, κατεικάζουσιν ἡμᾶς ἰσχάδι Eup.345:—Pass., *to be* or *become like*, ὦ.. τοῖς ἐν Αἰγύπτῳ νόμοις φύσιν κατεικασθέντε S.*OC*338. II. *guess, surmise*, Hdt.6.112; ἐν ὑπονοίῃ κ. Hp.*Ep.*17; *suspect*, Hdt.9.109.

**κατεικής**, ές, = ἐπιεικής, Hsch.

❋**κατεικονίζω**, *imaginor, Gloss.*

**κατειλάδα**· ἡμέραν χειμερινήν, Hsch.; cf. κατουλάς.

**κατειλ-έω**, *force into a narrow space, coop up*, in Pass., ἐς τὸ τεῖχος Hdt.1.80; ἐς τὸ ἄστυ ib.176; ἐς Διὸς ἱρόν Id.5.119, cf. Onos.42.19, Parth.32.2; εἰς χωρία προσάντη Plu.*Cam.*41; ἐν ὀλίγῳ χώρῳ.. πολλαὶ μυριάδες κατειλημέναι Hdt.9.70, cf. J.*AJ*14.16.2, al.; ἐρευγμὸς εἴσω κατειλούμενος Hp.*Coac.*622, cf. Arist.*Pr.*869a21; τοιαύτην δίνην κατειληθῆναι τοῖς ἄστροις Epicur.*Ep.*2 p.40 U. b. καταϝελμένων τῶν πολιατᾶν *when* the citizens *are assembled*, *Leg.Gort.*10.35, 11.13. 2. *wrap up*, X.*Eq.*10.7, Ael.*NA*5.3, 15.10 (Pass.); ταινίᾳ κατειλημένος τὴν ὀσφύν Diocl.*Fr.*142; κατειλημένος ταινίαις τὴν κεφαλήν Luc.*Symp.*47; τελαμῶνι τὸν μηρὸν -ειλημένον Paus.8.28.6. 3. *roll up*, βιβλίον Luc.*Alex.*20. II. v. κατίλλω. -**ησις**, εως, ἡ, *crowding, compression*, Epicur.*Ep.*2 pp.46, 54 U. 2. *wrapping*, εἰρίων Aret.*CA*2.9, cf. Herod.Med.ap.Orib.10.18.1; -ησία is f.l. in Archig.ap.Gal.13.168. -**ητέον**, *one must wrap*, Antyll.ap.Orib.7.21.8.

**κατείλια** (fort. -είλεα)· τὰ ἐσώτερα οἰκήματα (Erythr.), Hsch.

**κατειλίσσω**, v. καθελίσσω.

**κατειλυσπάομαι**, Pass., *wriggle down*, Ar.*Lys.*722.

**κατειλύω**, *cover up*, κὰδ δέ μιν αὐτὸν εἰλύσω ψαμάθοισιν Il.21.318; ἐν βοείαις A.R.3.206; ὄρος πέτρινον ψάμμῳ κατειλυμένον Hdt.2.8.

**κατειλωτισμένος**, (Εἵλωτες) *reduced to serfdom*, Suid.

❋**κάτειμι**, Dor. 3 sg. [κάτε]ιτι *Berl.Sitzb.*1927.166 (Cyrene), part. fem. κατίασσα ibid.: Ep. impf. κατήϊεν Od.10.159: (εἶμι *ibo*):—*go, come down*, ποταμόνδε Od. l.c.; Ἴδηθεν Il.4.475: in Trag., as fut. to κατέρχομαι, E.*Alc.*73, etc.; esp. *go down* to the grave, κατίμεν δόμον Ἄϊδος εἴσω Il.14.457; Ἀϊδόσδε 20.294; εἰς Ἅιδου δόμους E. l.c.; so κάτειμι alone, S.*Ant.*896; of a ship, *sail down* to land, νῆα.. κατιοῦσαν ἐς λιμέν' ἡμέτερον Od.16.472; of a person, *travel down* the Nile, κ. ἐπὶ or εἰς Ἀλεξάνδρειαν, *PLips.*45.12, 14 (iv A.D.); of a river, ποταμὸς πεδίονδε κάτεισι χειμάρρους Il.11.492; of a wind, *come sweeping down*, Th.2.25, 6.2; ὡς τὸ πνεῦμα κατῄει Id.2.84: metaph., ὀνείδεα κατιόντα ἀνθρώπῳ φιλέει ἐπανάγειν τὸν θυμόν Hdt.7.160; ἅμα ταῖς πολιαῖς κατιούσαις Ar.*Eq.*520. II. *come back, return*, ἀγρόθεν Od.13.267; ἐς ἄστυ 15.505; of exiles, *return home*, Hdt.1.62, 3.45, 5.62, A.*Ag.*1283, And.1.80, etc.; ἐκ τῶν Μήδων Hdt.4.3:—as Pass. of κατάγω, E.*Med.*1015; ὑπὸ τῶν ἑταίρων παρακληθεὶς κάτεισι Th.8.48. III. *come in*, of revenue, *PFay.*20.7 (iii/iv A.D.).

**κατεῖναι**, Ion. for καθεῖναι, aor. 2 inf. of καθίημι.

**κατείνυον**, v. καταέννυμι.

**κατεῖπον**, inf. κατειπεῖν, used as aor. to the pres. καταγορεύω (κατερῶ (v. κατερέω) being the fut.): also in form κατεῖπα Hdt.2.89, Ar.*Pax* 20:—*speak against* or *to the prejudice of, accuse, denounce*, τινος Ar.*Pax* 377, *Th.*340; κ. τινὸς πρός τινα Pl.*Tht.*149a, cf. X.*Mem.*2.6.33: abs., *give information*, Hdt.2.89, πρὸς τοὺς βασιλέας *SIG*986.7 (Chios, v/iv B.C.). II. c. acc., *declare, report*, εἴ σοι γάμον κατεῖπον E.*Med.*589; κ. τοῖς θεαταῖς τὸν λόγον Ar.*V.*54; τὰν Σάμῳ ib.283 (lyr.); πατέρα κ. *make* him *known*, E.*Ion* 1345; κ. τοὺς ποιήσαντας, τὰ γεγενημένα, *denounce* them, And.2.7: c. acc. et part., κ. σῷ κασιγνήτῳ πόσιν ἥκοντα E.*Hel.*898; *enumerate*, φύλλα δένδρων *Anacreont.*13.2. 2. abs., *tell*, κάτειπέ μοι *tell* me, Ar.*Nu.*155, *Pl.*86: folld. by interrog., κ. ὅκως.. Hdt.1.20; πόθεν.. Ar.*Pax* 20; ὅ τι σιωπᾷς, κ. μοι ib.657; πρὸς σὲ κ., ἐφ' οἷς ἐλύπησάν με Isoc.5.17, etc.

**κατεῖρα**· ἀσπίς, πέλτη, Hsch. (fort. καιτρέα).

**κατειργᾰθόμην**, poet. aor. Med. of κατείργω, A.*Eu.*566.

❋**κατείργω**, Ion. -έργω (v. ἔργω), Cypr. aor. 2 κατέϝοργον *Inscr.Cypr.*135.1 H.:—also -έργνυμι (v. infr.), Att. also καθείργω, καθείργνυμι (q.v.): fut. -είρξω, Ion. -έρξω:—*drive into, shut in*, τοὺς περιγενομένους ἐς τὰς νέας κατεῖρξαν Hdt.5.63; κατεργνῦσι [αὐτοὺς] ἐς μέσα τὰ φρύγανα *shut* them *up* into the middle of the fire-wood, Id.4.69: generally, *press hard, reduce to straits*, κατέργοντες πολλὸν τοὺς Ἀθηναίους Id.6.102; *besiege*, πτόλιν *Inscr.Cypr.* l.c.:—Pass., *to be hemmed in, kept down*, ὑπὸ τοῦ δυνατωτέρου Th.1.76; ὑπ' ἀνάγκης D.H.6.2; ὅρκοις -ειργόμενοι ib.45; τὸ πολέμῳ καὶ δεινῷ τινι -ειργόμενον *what is done under stress of*.., Th.4.98. II. *hinder, prevent*, τινα E.*Med.*1258 (lyr.): c. acc. et inf., κατείργοντας νεκροὺς τάφου.. λαχεῖν Id.*Supp.*308: abs., *delay*, Id.*Alc.*256 (lyr.); *limit*, τὴν φιλαρχίαν Plu.*Pomp.*53.

**κατειρωνεύομαι**, *use irony towards, banter*, τινας Plu.2.211d, cf. *Cat.Ma.*11; τινος J.*BJ*7.8.1, al., Jul.*Or.*6.198b; τῆς ἀγνοίας J.*BJ*4.3.1: abs., -όμενος *jestingly*, Parth.7.2, cf. Plu.*Agis* 18. 2. *treat in a spirit of raillery*, τι Id.*Comp.Dem.Cic.*1. II. *feign*, πένθος J.*BJ*2.2.5. 2. *conceal, dissimulate*, τὴν ἐξουσίαν, τὸν χρησμόν, Plu.*Phoc.*29, *Comp.Ages.Pomp.*1; ὑπόσχεσιν Aristaenet.1.4.

**κατεισ-άγω** [ᾰγ], *display to one's own loss*, μωρίαν *AP*10.91 (Pall.). -**ᾰγωγεύς**, έως, ὁ, *magistrate's clerk*, *POxy.*2154.7 (iv A.D.). ❋-**ἀγωγή**, ἡ, *disparagement*, Phld.*Vit.*1457.9 (pl.). -**έρχομαι**, *return*, *Sammelb.*4284.8, etc.

**κατεκλύω**, *cause to relax in* one's *effort*, τὸν Ἀντίοχον Plb.5.63.2.

**κατέκτᾰθεν**, Aeol. and Ep. 3 pl. aor. 1 Pass. of κατακτείνω (q.v.).

**κατεκτός**, Adv. *outside*, c. gen., τοῦ σώματος *Corp.Herm.*2.8.

**κατέλαιος**, ον, *oily*, Archestr.*Fr.*57.9.

**κατελαύνω**, *drive down*, τὰς ἀγέλας Longus 2.10; τὰς ναῦς *bring* them *in*, Plu.*Nic.*14. 2. *push down*, τὴν σπαθίδα [ἐς τὴν λήκυθον] Ar.*Fr.*205. 3. sens. obsc., κ. γυναικός, = Lat. *subagitare*, Id.*Pax* 711, *Ec.*1082; τινα Theoc.5.116. 4. κατελάσαι· καταπῆξαι, Hsch.

❋**κατελέγχω**, *convict of falsehood, belie*, σὲ δὲ μὴ τι νόον κατελεγχέτω εἶδος Hes.*Op.*714, cf. Tyrt.10.9 (tm.); ἔργῳ οὐ κατ' εἶδος ἐλέγχων Pi.*O.*8.19:—Pass., ὑπό τινος *PSI*4.442.20. II. *disgrace*, Pi.*P.*8.36; ἀνδρῶν ἀρετάν Id.*I.*3.14. III. *betray*, ὑλακῇ τινας, of dogs, Poll.5.42.

**κατελεέω**, strengthd. for ἐλεέω, *have compassion* upon, τινα or τι, Pl.*R.*415c, And.2.15, Lys.6.3; τὰς συμφοράς Plb.2.6.2: abs., Arist.*HA*631a19.

**κατελίσσω**, v. καθελίσσω. **κατέλκω**, Ion. for καθέλκω.

**κατελπ-ίζω**, *hope* or *expect confidently*, κ. εὐπετέως τῆς θαλάσσης κρατήσειν Hdt.8.136, cf. Plb.2.31.8; μηδὲν ἄγαν κ. D.S.15.33, cf. Phld.*Oec.*p.73 J.: c. gen., *base* one's *hopes upon*, τῆς αὐτῶν δυνάμεως J.*AJ*5.1.20:—Pass., ἀποβαίνειν οἷα κατηλπίσθη Phld.*Lib.*p.27 O. -**ισμός**, ὁ, *confident hope*, Plb.3.82.8.

**κατεμβλέπω**, strengthd. for ἐμβλέπω, Lxx *Ex.*3.6. II. *look down upon, despise*, c. dat., Phld.*Vit.*p.37 J.

**κατεμέω**, aor. 1 -έμεσα, *vomit, be sick over*, τινος Ar.*Fr.*152, Ael.*NA*4.36, Luc.*Sat.*38.

**κατεμμᾰτέω**, = ἐμματέω, ἐμματεύω, Nic.*Al.*536.

**κατεμπάζω**, = καταλαμβάνω, ὁππότ' ἂν χρειώ σε -εμπάζῃ Nic.*Th.*695.

**κατέμπαρσις**, v. κατέπαρσις.

**κατεμπείρω**, = καταπείρω, τὴν τοῦ ἐμβρυουλκοῦ καμπήν Philum.ap.Aët.16.23 (s.v.l.).

**κατεμπορεύομαι**, sine expl., c. gen., Suid.

**κατεμφορέομαι**, Med., *take one's fill of*, τινος Eun.*Hist.*p.256 D.

**κατεναίρομαι**, *slay, murder*, κατενήρατο χαλκῷ Od.11.519, cf. Nic.*Al.*401: aor. Act. κατήνᾱρον S.*Ant.*871 (lyr.), Call.*Ap.*101, *AP*7.201 (Pamphil.); -ένηρα Orph.*A.*666.

**κατ-έναντα**, Adv. *over against, opposite*, c. gen., Cydias 1, Pancrat.*Oxy.*1085.4, Q.S.1.552, Man.3.176: c. dat., Id.6.277: abs., Id.3.132:—also -έναντι Lxx *Ex.*19.2; πύλη ἡ κ. ib.*Ez.*11.1; κώμη ἡ κ. ὑμῶν *Ev.Marc.*11.2, cf. *UPZ*79.11 (ii B.C.), *Inscr.Prien.*37.170 (ii

B.C.). **-εναντίον**, = foreg., τινι Il.21.567; ἀλλήλοισιν *AP*9.132, Man.1.215, etc.; ἐκείνου (v.l. ἐκείνῳ) Hes.*Sc*.73, cf. A.R.2.360; τῆς ἀκροπόλιος Hdt.3.144: abs., Man.1.285:—also **-εναντία**, νήσου A.R. 2.1116: abs., κ. κεῖνται D.P.114. **-εναντιόω**, pf. part. Pass. -ηναντιωμένος *in opposition to*, τοῖς προειρημένοις Phld.*Po.Herc*.1676.3.

**κατενᾰρίζω**, strengthd. for ἐναρίζω, *kill outright*: aor. Pass. κατηναρίσθης A.*Ch*.347 (lyr.): pf. part. Pass. κατηναρισμένος S.*Aj*.26.

**κατένασσε**, v. καταναίω.

**κατένεξις**, εως, ἡ, (κατενεγκεῖν) = καταφορά, Suid. s. v. καταλύσας, Eust.152.14.

**κατενεχῠρ-άζω**, *pledge, pawn*, Poll.3.84 (v.l. -ιάζω), 8.148. **-ασία**, ἡ, *pledging*, *Jahresh*.18 *Beibl*.287 (Ephesus, i B.C.). **-ασμός**, ὁ, = foreg., Poll.8.148.

**κατενήνοθεν**, 3 sg. and pl. plpf., *covered*, πολλὴ δὲ κόνις κ. ὤμους Hes.*Sc*.269; ξανθαὶ δὲ κόμαι κ. ὤμους *h.Cer*.279; cf. ἐπενήνοθε.

**κατενιαύσιος**, ὁ, title of an *annual* magistrate at Gela, *IG*14.256, 257.

**κατεν ισχύω**, *become firmly established*, ἐπὶ τῆς βασιλείας v.l. in Lxx 1 *Ch*.29.30 (2 *Ch*.1.1). **-τείνομαι**, strengthd. for ἐντείνομαι, M.Ant.4.3. **-τευκτής**, οῦ, ὁ, *accuser*, Lxx *Jb*.7.20. **-τρῠφάω**, c. gen., = ἐντρυφάω κατά τινος, Iamb.*Bab*.11. **-τυγχάνω**, *seek an interview with*, τινι *PGen*.31.4 (ii A. D.). II. *plead against, accuse*, Suid. and Phot. s.v. κατεντευκτήν. III. κ(ατ)εντευχθέντα· κατεντυχηθέντα, Hsch.

**κατένωπα** (cf. Hdn.Gr.2.94, **κατενῶπα** or **κατ' ἐνῶπα** Aristarch. ap.Hdn.Gr. l. c.), *over against, right opposite*, c. gen., Il.15.320, Orph. *L*.132, 464: c. acc., Puchstein *Epigr.Gr*.p.76 (Memphis):—also **ἐνώπιον**, τινος Lxx *Jo*.1.5, *Ep.Eph*.1.4, al., *BGU*954.6 (vi A. D.).

**κατεξᾰγιάζω**, *assay*, *Arch.Anz*.38/39.154 (Pass.).

**κατεξ-ανάστᾰσις**, εως, ἡ, *rebellion against, resistance to*, τινος Longin.7.3; δόξης καὶ πλούτου Iamb.*VP*16.69. **-αναστᾰτικός**, ή, όν, *fit for resisting*, ἀλγηδόνων, ὀχληρῶν, S.E.*M*.11.104, 106; ἀρετὴ κ. δικαιοσύνης M.Ant.8.39. **-ανίσταμαι**, aor. 2 Act. κατεξανέστην, *rise up against, struggle against*, τινος Ph.2.47, Plu.*Alex*.6; τῆς τύχης Eun. *Hist*.p.256 D.; τοῦ πάθους D.S.10.7; κατεξαναστῆναι τοῦ μέλλοντος *to be on one's guard against*.., Plb.*Fr*.172; τοῦ πολέμου Plu.*Demetr*.22; παντὸς δεινοῦ D.S.17.21. 2. *rise*, -ιστάμενα [νέφη] *Cat.Cod.Astr*. 8(1).139. **-εράω**, *vomit upon*, τὸ φλέγμα κ. τινός Arr.*Epict*.3.13.23: metaph., [σχόλιά] τινος ib.3.21.6. **-ετάζω**, *decide, try*, δίκην *Cod. Just*.1.4.29 *Intr*.; *examine carefully*, Agath.5.9 (Pass.). **-ευμᾰρίζω**, strengthd. for ἐξευμαρίζω, Hsch. **-ουσία**, ἡ, *sovereignty, dominion*, τῶν νερτέρων θεῶν *IG*14.1047.5 (= *Tab.Defix.Aud*.188): c. gen., *power over*, τοῦ βιοθανάτου πνεύματος *PMag.Par*.1.1949; also δὸς αὐτῷ τὴν κ. κατὰ τῶν ἐχθρῶν αὐτοῦ *CIG*4710 (Egypt). **-ουσιάζω**, *exercise authority over*, τινος *Ev.Matt*.20.25, *Ev.Marc*.10.42; τῶν ὅλων Jul. *Gal*.100c.

**κατεπ-αγγελία**, ἡ, *promise*, Gloss. **-αγγέλλομαι**, Med. with pf. Pass., *make promises* or *engagements*, τινι with one, D.32.11; τὸ παρὸν λυμαινόμενος, τὸ δὲ μέλλον κ. Aeschin.3.223; *promise*, c. acc., τινὶ τιμήν J.*AJ*8.14.4; κ. τῇ φιλίᾳ τὴν πολιτείαν *devote* it to.., Plu. 2.807b: c. pres. inf., τέχνας -όμενος διδάσκειν Aeschin.1.117, cf. Ph. 2.316: c. fut. inf., κ. πρός τινας λήσειν Aeschin.1.173; προκαταλήψεσθαι τὰς παρόδους D.S.11.4: abs., μέχρι τοῦ -αγγείλασθαι Phld. *Rh*.2.23 S.:—Pass., ἡ -ομένη ζημία J.*AJ*6.5.3. **-άγω** [ᾰγ], *bring down upon*, τιμωρίαν τινί Plu.2.551d (sed leg. -επείγει): κατεπάγων is f.l. for κατ' ἐπ. in Ar.*Eq*.25. ® **-ᾴδω**, *subdue by song* or *enchantment*, τινα Pl.*Grg*.483e, *Men*.80a, Plu.*Dio*14, Lib.*Or*.64.91; τὰς τῶν νέων ψυχάς Max.Tyr.23.3; *overcome by a spell*, Phld.*Lib*.p.29 O.; *soothe*, τινος Ach.Tat.7.10. 2. *sing by way of enchantment*, Id.2. 7. II. *to be always repeating*, Ph.2.304, Anon.ap.Suid., Hld.7. 10, Ach.Tat.2.19. **-αίρομαι**, Pass., *to be arrogant towards*, c. gen., Sm.*Ps*.65(61).3, Just.*Nov*.129 *Praef*. **-άλληλος**, ον, = ἐπάλληλος, κίνησις dub. l. in Sch.A.R.3.1018. **-άλμενος**, **-αλτο**, v. καταπάλλομαι, κατεφάλλομαι. **-ᾰμύνω**, strengthd. for ἐπαμύνω, c. acc., Suid.

**κατέπαρσις**, εως, ἡ, *insertion*, ἀγκίστρων Sor.2.40 cod. (pl., leg. κατέμπ- vel κατάπ-).

® **κατεπ-είγω**, *press down*, χαλεπὸν κατὰ γῆρας ἐπείγει Il.23.623. 2. *press hard*, οἱ χρῆσται κατήπειγον αὐτόν his creditors *were pressing* him *hard*, D.33.6, cf. Th.1.61; κατεπείγει ὕδωρ ῥέον the ebbing water (of the clepsydra) *urges* him *on*, Pl.*Tht*.172e; ἡ φιλοτιμία κατήπειγεν αὐτόν Id.*Ep*.338e: c. acc. et inf., οὐδὲν ἡμᾶς ἐστὶ τὸ κατεπεῖγον τὸ μὴ..σκοπεῖν Id.*Lg*.781e; οὐδὲν ὑμᾶς κ. ἀκοῦσαι D.24.18; τὸ -επεῖγον πράττειν X.*Mem*.2.1.2; τὰ ἀναλώματα τὰ -επείγοντα *PFlor*.161.5 (iii A. D.); τὸ κ. alone, the *urgent symptom*, Gal.17(2). 426; οὔτε τι κωλύει οὔτε -επείγει Hp.*Fract*.14; τὰ μάλιστα -επείγοντα Isoc.8.132, cf. Plb.1.66.6; τῶν ἐν ἐκείνῳ μὲν τῷ χρόνῳ πραχθέντων, ῥηθῆναι δὲ νῦν οὐ -επειγόντων not *urgently requiring* mention, Isoc.12. 192; τῆς ὥρας -επειγούσης Plb.3.99.9; θόρυβος φόβος μετὰ φωνῆς -επείγων *Stoic*.3.98:—Pass., *to be pressed*, Hyp.(?)*Oxy*.1607.43, Phld.*Rh*.1.138 S.; περί τινος *PCair.Zen*.530 (iii B. C.). II. intr., *hasten, make haste*, ἔπου κατεπείγων Ar.*Ec*.293: c. inf., Βοιωτοὶ οὐδέν τι κατήπειγον ξυνάψαι *were in no haste*, X.*HG*4.2.18; οὐδέν κω κατεπείγων αὐτὸς ἥκειν prob. in Hdt.8.126. III. Med., *hasten*, ἐκ Κορίνθου Ἀθήναζε Alciphr.3.51. 2. c. gen., *to be anxious, long for*.., Plb.5.37.10, 30.5.9: also c. dat., *press for*, τῷ ἐφοδίῳ *PSI*6.603. 22 (iii B. C.). **-ειξις**, εως, ἡ, *bustling, hurrying*, *Stoic*.3.98.

**κατεπεμβαίνω**, *overflow to its injury*, θάλασσα κ. τῆς γῆς Sch.Opp. *H*.2.34. II. *plant one's foot firmly upon*, κορυφαιότητι *Corp.Herm*. 18.16.

**κατέπεφνον**, Ep., Lyr., and Trag. (in lyr.) aor. 2 with no pres. in use (v. θείνω), *kill, slay*, καταπέφνῃ Il.3.281; κατέπεφνε 6.183, 24. 759, Od.3.252, 4.534, S.*El*.486; κατέπεφνες Id.*Aj*.901, Pi.*Fr*.171 (tm.); καταπεφνών Il.17.539.

**κατεπι-γάστριος**, ον, *abdominal*, μύες Gal.7.199. **-δείκνῡμαι**, Med., *show off before* another, M.Ant.11.13. **-δέω**, *bandage afresh*, Gal.18(2).387. **-θεσις**, εως, ἡ, = δόλος, Aq.*Ps*.31(32).2, 119(120). 3. **-θῡμέω**, strengthd. for ἐπιθυμέω, Eun.*VS*p.477 B., Phot. and Suid. s. v. λίχνος. **-θύμιος** [ῡ], ον, *desirable*, *Gloss*. ® **-θῡμος**, ον, *very eager*, c. inf., Lxx *Ju*.12.16. **-κειμαι**, Pass., *lie, rest upon*, *IG*14.1888, *CIG*4152*d* (Amastris). **-κύπτω**, *bow down upon*, Lxx *Es*.15.10 (v.l. ἐπέκυψεν). **-ορκέω**, *commit perjury against*, τῶν θεῶν Nicol.*Prog*. in Rh.1.348, 365 W. II. Med., *effect by perjury*, οὐ κατεπιορκησόμενος τὸ πρᾶγμα D.54.40.

**κατεπίσταμαι**, *know fully*, Ael.*Fr*.284.

**κατεπιτηδεύω**, *finish too elaborately*, of style, D.H.*Th*.42.

**κατεπι-φύω**, in Med., = καταφύω II, Hsch. **-χειρέω**, *lay hands upon, attempt*, τοῦ πράγματος *AB*154, cf. Eustr. *in EN*51.21.

**κατεποικοδομέω**, *build over* or *upon*, in Pass., *CIG*3281 (Smyrna).

**κατεπτηχότως**, Adv., (καταπτήσσω) *in abject fear*, Poll.3.137.

**κατεράω**, *pour out, pour off*, Str.17.1.38, Plu.2.968d; εἰς ἀγγεῖον Agatharch.28, Dsc.1.30. II. *pour over*, δυσφημίαν κ. τοῦ δικαστηρίου Demetr.*Eloc*.302; κατὰ τῶν ξηρῶν Gal.13.53.

**κατεργ-άζομαι**, fut. -άσομαι, later 3 sg. -ᾶται *PTeb*.10.2 (ii B. C.): aor. κατειργασάμην, and (in pass. sense) κατειργάσθην (v. infr.): pf. κατείργασμαι both in act. and pass. sense (v. infr.):—*effect by labour, achieve*, πρήγματα μεγάλα Hdt.5.24; πᾶν S.*El*.1022; μόρον.. ἐπαλλήλοιν χεροῖν Id.*Ant*.57; ταῦθ' ἁπινοεῖς Ar.*Ec*.247; τὰ δυνατά Th.4.65; τὰ πρὸς εὐδαιμονίαν Phld.*Rh*.2.31 S.; μεγάλα μὲν ἐπινοεῖτε, ταχὺ δὲ κατεργάζεσθε X.*Hier*.2.2; κ. εἰρήνην τινί And.3.8; ἣν κατεργάσῃ if you *do the job*, Ar.*Eq*.933: pf. κατείργασμαι, μέγιστα ἔργα X.*Mem*. 3.5.11: in pass. sense, *to have been effected* or *achieved*, Hdt.1.123, 141, 4.66, E.*IT*1081, etc.; κατειργασμένη ὠφέλεια Antipho 2.1.4; ἐλθεῖν ἐπὶ κατειργασμένοις Lys.31.9: aor. -ειργάσθην Luc.*Herm*.5. b. *earn, gain by labour, acquire*, τὴν ἡγεμονίην Hdt.3.65; πόλει σωτηρίαν E. *Heracl*.1046; μεγάλα τῇ πόλει Aeschin.3.229; τοῦτο D.45.66; ὁ κατειργασμένος τὴν τυραννίδα Pl.*Grg*.473d: in pass. sense, ἀρετὴ ἀπὸ σοφίης κατεργασμένη Hdt.7.102. c. abs., *achieve one's object, be successful*, αὐτὸς ἑωυτῷ Id.5.78; simply, *work*, ἐν τοῖς ἐργαστηρίοις *PTeb.ined*.703.148. 2. c. acc. pers., *make an end of, finish, kill*, ἑωυτόν Hdt.1.24, cf. E.*Hipp*.888, etc.; λέοντα βίᾳ S.*Tr*. 1094. b. *overpower, subdue, conquer*, Hdt.6.2, Ar.*Eq*.842, Th.4. 85, Isoc.9.59, etc.; τὴν Ἑλλάδα Hdt.8.100; ποσὶ καὶ στόματι κ. [τινά] *attack* him, of a horse, Id.5.111: in pass. sense, of land, μακέλλῃ τῇ κατείργασται πέδον *is subdued, brought under cultivation*, A.*Ag*. 526; κατεργαζομένη ἡ γῆ Thphr.*CP*3.1.3; later trans., *cultivate*, *PTeb*.10.2 (ii B. C.), etc. c. *prevail upon*, κατεργάσατο καὶ ἀνέπεισε Ξέρξην, ὥστε.. Hdt.7.6, cf. X.*Mem*.2.3.16, Parth.13.1, Plu.*Fab*.21; κ. τινὰ πειθοῖ Str.10.4.2:—Pass., οὐκ ἐδύνατο κατεργασθῆναι [ἡ γυνή] could not *be prevailed upon*, Hdt.9.108. d. c. dupl. acc., *do something to one*, καλόν τι τὴν πόλιν And.2.17 (but κ. τὴν πόλιν *carry on business in* the city, *SIG*899 (Mesambria, iii A. D.)). II. *till, cultivate* land, *PSI*6.632.9 (iii B. C.), etc.; *work up for use*, freq. of food, by chewing or digestion, ὀδόντας ἔχει οἷς κ. τὴν τροφήν Arist.*HA*501[b] 30, cf. *Juv*.469[a]31, *Spir*.482[b]16, Gal.11.649 (Pass.); τὸ -αζόμενον ἔχειν εὔρωστον a strong *digestion*, Id.17(2).430; κ. τὰ ἐδέσματα Sch. Ar.*Eq*.714; by grinding (of corn), Longus 3.30, cf. D.H.5.13 (Pass.); by ripening (of fruits), κατειργασμένα ἐπὶ τοῦ δένδρου Gal.11.367; κ. μέλι *make*.., Hdt.4.194; κ. τὴν κόπρον *prepare* it, Arist.*HA*552[a] 24; σίδηρον D.27.10; ξύλα -ειργασμένα Thphr.*CP*5.17.2; στίππυον τὸ κατειργαζόμενον *PCair.Zen*.472.9 (iii B. C.); λίθους D.S.1.98. 2. *turn* bullion *into coin*, *PCair.Zen*.21.6 (iii B. C.). III. *work at, practise*, ἄλλην μελέτην κ. Pl.*Ti*.88c. IV. κ. ὄρη *level* them, J.*AJ* 11.3.4 (fr. Lxx 1 *Es*.4.4). **-ᾰσία**, ἡ, *working up*, freq. of food, by digestion or by chewing, Arist.*PA*675[b]5, *Pr*.931[a]32, etc.; ἡ τοῦ πυρὸς κ. *stewing, boiling*, Mnesith.ap.Ath.2.59b: generally, *production*, χυμῶν (in the body) Hp.*Praec*.9; κοιλωμάτων Epicur.*Ep*.1 p.9 U. (pl.); σίτου Phld.*Oec*.pp.51, 55 J.; *working* or *manufacture*, ἐλαίου Thphr. *CP*1.19.4; *cultivation* of land, ib.1.16.6 (pl.), 3.20.1, *PTeb*.61(*b*).129 (ii B. C.), etc.; καρπῶν D.S.1.14; of mines, Str.3.2.10; ξύλων Bito 52. 2; παραδείγματος Lxx 1 *Ch*.28.19; τυγχάνειν κατεργασίας ἀφ' ἡλίου, of vapour, D.L.7.153; *completion*, κ. λαμβάνειν Thphr.*HP*1.1. 2. **-ασμα**, ατος, τό, *work, achievement*, Aq.*Ps*.45(46).9, *Pr*.8. 22. **-αστέον**, *one must promote digestion*, Xenocr.ap.Orib.2.58.90; *one must combat, counteract*, of poison, Dsc.*Ther.Praef*. **-αστικός**, ή, όν, *of* or *for accomplishing, effective*, δύναμις Thphr.*CP*1.8.4. II. *likely to wear out, consume*, Hp.*Coac*.472; of fire, Vett.Val.345.18 (Comp.).

**κατεργολᾰβέω**, *exact tribute*, Phld.*Rh*.1.224 S.

**κάτεργος**, ον, *worked, cultivated*, χώρα Thphr.*CP*5.14.5. II. κάτεργον, τό, *wages*, *PHib*.1.119 (iii B. C.), *PRev.Laws* 45.8 (iii B. C.), *PCair.Zen*.472.6 (iii B. C.), etc.; *labour-costs*, τὸ εἰς τὴν πλίνθον κ. γεινόμενον *PSI*4.365.4 (iii B. C.), cf. *PLille*1.50 (iii B. C.); εἰς κ. τῆς σκηνῆς for the *service* of the tabernacle, Lxx *Ex*.30.16; εἰς πάντα τὰ κ. αὐτῆς ib.35.21.

**κατέρεαι**· κάθισαι (Paph.), Hsch.

**κατερέθω**, *irritate, provoke*, in Pass., Hsch.

**κατερείδω**, intr., *swoop down*, of a storm, D.Chr.74.7.

**κατερείκω**, *bruise, grind*, κάχρυς κατηριγμέναι Demon 22: metaph.,

θυμὸν κατερεῖξαι *crush, subdue*, Ar.*V.*649:—Med., *rend one's garments*, in token of sorrow, κίθωνας Sapph.62, cf. Hdt.3.66, A.*Pers.* 538 (anap.).

**κατερειπ-όω**, = sq., in pf. part. Pass., D.S.32.14, Hld.9.5, Porph. *Plot.*12, *Gloss.* ⊛**-ω**, *throw* or *cast down*, Ἴλιον κατερεῖψαι Pi.*Pae.* 8.33; κατὰ γάρ μιν ἐρείπει πῦρ Orac.ap.Hdt.7.140; σεισμοὶ κατήρειψαν πολὺ τῆς κατοικίας Str.6.1.6, cf. Max.Tyr.1.3: metaph., κ. τινά *ruin, corrupt* him, Plu.*Sol.*6:—Pass., *fall in ruins*, of Troy, E.*Hec.*477 (lyr.); [τὸ τεῖχος] κατερήρειπτο Hdn.8.2.4 codd.; κατηρειμμένα *IG* 5(1).538.22 (Sparta); κατηριμμένα ib.12(5).1097.11 (Ceos, ii A.D.), 12(3).324.17 (Thera, ii A.D.). II. intr. in aor. 2, *fall down, fall prostrate*, [ὑπὸ ποταμοῦ] ἔργα κατήριπε κάλ' αἰζηῶν Il.5.92; κ. ἐς μέλαν ὕδωρ Theoc.13.49: pf., τεῖχος μὲν γὰρ δὴ κατερήριπεν Il.14.55. **-ωσις**, εως, ἡ, *overthrow*, Suid. (-ριπ- codd.).

**κατερεύγομαι**, aor. 2 -ήρῠγον, *belch over* or *upon*, θερμόν τί τινος Ar.*V.*1151.

**κατερεύθω**, *make all red*, κατὰ δ' αἵματι πόντον ἐρ. Opp.*H.*2.612.

**κατερευνάω**, *lay bare, uncover*, τὸν Ἠσαῦ Lxx *Je.*29(49).10 (-εραυν-, v.l. κατέσυρα); κατερευνᾷ, = *dirimat*, *Gloss.*

**κατερέφω**, *cover over, roof*, τὰς σκηνὰς κλήμασιν Plu.*Caes.*9; ἀλλήλους τοῖς θυρεοῖς Id.*Ant.*49:—Med., *roof over for oneself* or *what is one's own*, κατηρέψασθε κεράμῳ τὸ νῶτον Ar.*V.*1294; ὡς ὅτε τις κεράμῳ κατερέψεται ἑρκίον ἀνὴρ A.R.2.1073.

**κατερέω**, Att. **κατερῶ**, serving as fut. of aor. κατεῖπον: pf. κατείρηκα:—*speak against, accuse*, τινος X.*Cyr.*1.4.8; τινὸς πρός τινα Pl.*R.* 595b; τινὸς ἐναντίον τινός Id.*Thg.*125a. 2. c. acc., *denounce*, τινὰ πρός τινα Hdt.3.71: abs., κατερῶ Ἀθηναίοισι *IG*1$^2$.39.25. II. *declare*, πόθεν.. Pi.*Pae.*6.129; *tell plainly*, κ. ἐν τῷ κεῖται χώρῳ ἡ παρακαταθήκη Hdt.5.92.η'; κατερῶ πρὸς ὑμᾶς ἐλευθέρως τἀληθῆ Ar.*Nu.*518, cf. E.*Med.*1106 (anap.); κ. τοὔνομ' ὅτι ποτ' ἐστί σοι Ar.*Pax* 189:—Pass., κατειρήσεται *shall be declared*, Hdt.6.69.

**κατερημόω**, *strip entirely off*, τὰ πτερά Aesop.6.

**κατερήρῐπε**, v. κατερείπω.

**κατερητύω**, fut. -ύσω [ῡ] S.*Ph.*1416 (anap.):—*hold back, detain*, κατερήτυον ἐν μεγάροισι Il.9.465, Od.9.31; φωνῇ.. κατερήτυε 19.545; κατερητύσων ὁδόν S.l.c.; κ. αὐδήν, θυμόν, Orph.*A.*1170, 1177.

**κατερῑθεύομαι**, *overcome by intrigue*, Plb.*Fr.*173 (dub.).

**κατ-ερικτός** or **-ερεικτός**, ή, όν, *bruised, ground*, of pulse, Ar.*Ra.* 505, cf. Phryn.*PS*p.14B., *EM*387.15.

**κατέρνης**, ες, *with luxuriant branches*, Orph.*A.*918.

⊛**κατερυθρ-αίνομαι**, *turn red*, Dsc.5.79. **-ιάω**, *blush deeply*, Hld. 10.18.

**κατερῠκ-άνω** [ᾰ], lengthd. form of κατερύκω, μή μ' ἐθέλοντ' ἰέναι κατερύκανε Il.24.218. **-τικός**, ή, όν, *restraining, inhibiting*, *PMag. Lond.*121.450. **-ω**, *hold back, detain*, μάλα δή σε καὶ ἐσσύμενον κατερύκω Il.6.518; κ. καὶ ἔσχεθεν ἱεμένω περ Od.4.284, cf. 1.315, 15.73; μηδένα.. ἀέκοντα μένειν κατέρυκε Thgn.467: rare in Att., τῶν ἀγαθῶν οἵων ἀποκλείεις καὶ κατερύκεις Ar.*V.*601:—Pass., κατερύκεται εὐρέϊ πόντῳ Od.1.197, 4.498.

**κατερύω**, Ion. **-ειρύω**, *draw, haul down*, freq. in Od. of ships, τήν γε [σχεδίην] κατείρυσεν εἰς ἅλα δῖαν 5.261:—Pass., νηῦς τε κατείρυσται 8.151, etc.; so κατειρύσαντες ἐς Σαλαμῖνα τὰ ναυήγια Hdt.8.96; also κ. οὔθατα μόσχου *to draw* or *milk* them, Nic.*Th.*552; τόξα κ. *draw* a bow, *AP*9.16 (Mel.):—Med., κὰδ δ' ἄρα λαῖφος ἐρυσσάμενοι *unfurling*, A.R.2.931.

⊛**κατέρχομαι**, fut. κατελεύσομαι Od.1.303, Hdt.5.125, Arr.*An.*6.12.3 (but in good Att. κάτειμι, as also κατῄειν is always used for the impf.): aor. κατήλυθον or κατῆλθον, inf. κατελθεῖν; Dor. subj. κατένθῃ *Berl. Sitzb.*1927.165 (Cyrene); Arc. part. κατενθών, pf. part. κατηνθηκώς, v. καθέρπω II: pf. κατελήλυθα *SIG*975.24 (ii B.C.):—*go down*, Οὐλύμποιο κατήλθομεν Il.20.125, etc.; τιν' ἀθανάτων ἐξ οὐρανοῦ ἀστερόεντος.. κατελθέμεν 6.109; *go down to the grave*, κ. Ἄϊδος εἴσω, Ἄϊδόσδε, ib. 284, 7.330; εἰς Ἅιδου E.*HF*1101, etc.: rarely c. acc., τίς.. σκότου πύλας ἔτλη κατελθεῖν; Ar.*Fr.*149.2 (parod.); from high land to the coast, ἐπὶ νῆα θοὴν κατελεύσομαι Od.1.303; from country to town, 11. 188; *down* the Nile, εἰς Ἀλεξάνδρειαν *PLille* 3.80 (iii B.C.), etc. 2. of things, κατερχομένης ὑπὸ πέτρης by the *descending* rock, Od.9.484, 541; of a river, κατέρχεται ὁ Νεῖλος πληθύων *comes down* in flood, Hdt.2.19; κατελθόντος αἰφνιδίου τοῦ ῥεύματος Th.4.75. 3. κ. εἰς τὸν ἀγῶνα, Lat. *descendere in certamen*, S.E.*M.*7.324. 4. c. acc., *come to* a place, ὑμέτερον δῶ Od.24.115; ἀφθονία κατελήλυθε τὴν πόλιν Lyd.*Mag.*3.76. 5. of property, *pass to*, *PRein.*42.28 (i/ii A.D.), *POxy.*1704.5 (iii A.D.). II. *come back, return*, esp. *come back from exile*, Hdt.4.4, al., A.*Ag.*1647, *Ch.*3, *Eu.*462, S.*OC*601, Ar.*Ra.*1165, 1167, Pl.*Ap.*21a, *OGI*90.20 (Rosetta, ii B.C.), etc.; φυγὰς κατελθών S.*Ant.*200; ὃς ἂν κατέλθῃ τήνδε γῆν E.*IT*39: in pass. sense, ὑπ' ὀλιγαρχίας κατελθεῖν *to be brought back* by.., Th.8.68; cf. κάτειμι II, καθέρπω II.

**κἀτέρωτᾰ**, Aeol. crasis for καὶ ἀτέρωτα (ετερωτα cod. A.D.*Adv.* 194.5), = καὶ ἄλλοτε, Sapph.1.5, Hsch. s.v. κἀτέρωτα.

⊛**κατεσθίω**, poet. and later **-έσθω** *APl.*4.240 (Phil.), *Ev.Marc.*12. 40, *Dialex.*2.14 (Pass., 1.5, *PMag.Lond.*46.279 (iv A.D.)): fut. κατέδομαι Il.22.89, Od.21.363, Ar.*Av.*588: aor. κατέφαγον (v. καταφαγεῖν): pf. κατεδήδοκα Id.*V.*838, *Pax*386, etc.; part. κατα..εδηδώς Il.17.542:—Pass., pf. κατεδήδεσμαι Pl.*Phd.*110e, Antiph.161.3: aor. κατηδέσθην Pl.Com.35:—*eat up, devour*, in Hom. freq. of animals of prey, λέων κατὰ ταῦρον ἐδηδώς Il.17.542; of a serpent, [νεοσσοὺς] κατήσθιε 2.314, cf. Od.12.256; of a dolphin, κατεσθίει ὅν κε λάβῃσιν Il.21.24; also of men, οἳ κατὰ βοῦς.. ἤσθιον Od.1.8; τοὺς γονέας Hdt.3.38, cf. 8.115, E.*Cyc.*341; [τυρὸν] αὐτοῖς τοῖς ταλάροις κ. Ar.*Ra.*560; κατεδηδόκασι τὰ λάχαν' Alex.15.12: c. gen. partit., κ. πολλῶν πουλύπων Amips.6. 2. *eat up, devour* one's substance, τὰ κοινά, τὰ πατρῷα, Ar.*Eq.*258, Antiph.239; τὰ ὄντα D.38.27; πατρῴαν οὐσίαν Anaxipp.1.32. 3. *corrode*, [ῥεύματα] κ. γνάθους Hp.*VM*19; λίθοι κατεδηδεσμένοι ὑπὸ σηπεδόνος Pl.l.c., cf. *Dialex.*1.5 (Pass.); of the wind, κ. τὰ ἄνθη Thphr.*CP*2.7.5:—Pass., *to be gnawed*, ib.5.17. 7. 4. *bite*, τοῦ παλαιστοῦ τὸ οὖς Philostr.*Im.*1.6. 5. κ. ἑαυτόν, metaph., of remorse, Lib.*Or.*29.32, *Ep.*256.

**κατέσκληκα**, v. κατασκέλλομαι.

**κατεσκολιωμένως**, Adv. pf. part. Pass. as if from *κατασκολιόω, *crookedly*, Antyll.ap.Orib.44.23.1.

**κατεσπευσμένως**, Adv., (κατασπεύδω) *hastily*, Dsc.*Ther.Praef.*, Plu.2.522d.

**κατεσπουδασμένως**, Adv., (κατασπουδάζομαι) *earnestly*, Procop. *Pers.*2.21.

**κατεστραμμένως**, Adv., (καταστρέφω) *reversely*, *Placit.*5.14.2.

**κατεστράφατο**, v. καταστρέφω. **κατέσχεθον**, v. κατέχω.

**κάτευγμα**, ατος, τό, always in pl., *vows*, A.*Ch.*218, *Eu.*1021. 2. *imprecations, curses*, Id.*Th.*709, E.*Hipp.*1170. II. *symbols of prayer*, S.*OT*920.

**κατευ-δαιμονίζω**, strengthd. for εὐδαιμ-, J.*BJ*1.33.8. **-δοκέω**, *to be well content with*, τινι Plb.21.33.2. **-δοκῐμέω**, *surpass in reputation*, τινος D.S.33.1.

**κατεύδω**, for καθεύδω, barbarism in Ar.*Th.*1193.

**κατευ-εργετέω**, strengthd. for εὐεργ-, Tz.*H.*10.811 (Pass.). **-ημερέω**, *to be influential*, κατευημερηκὼς παρ' ὑμῖν Aeschin.2.89. **-θικτέω**, *hit exactly*, τῇ πληγῇ Lxx 2 *Ma.*14.43.

**κατευθύ**, Adv. *straight forward*, τὸ κ. δρᾶν X.*Smp.*5.5, cf. Luc. *Jud.Voc.*11; τὴν κ. ἔρχεσθαι Paus.2.11.3: c. gen., κ. τινός Plu.2.3b; *on the same side* (cf. ἰθύς), ὁ κ. δίδυμος Ruf.(?)ap.Paul.Aeg.3.45. (Better written κατ' εὐθύ.)

**κατευθυν-τηρία**, ἡ, *carpenter's line*, Sch.Il.15.410, *EM*740.42. **-ω**, poet. impf. κατευθύνεσκον *IGRom.*4.507*b* (Pergam.):—*make* or *keep straight*, τὴν πτῆσιν Arist.*IA*710$^a$2; ναῦν τῷ πηδαλίῳ D.Chr.13.18; βιοτῆς οἴακα κατευθύνεσκες ἐν οἴκῳ *IGRom.* l.c.:—Pass., αἱ περιφοραὶ κατευθυνόμεναι Pl.*Ti.*44b. 2. *guide, direct*, τὰς φύσεις Id.*Lg.* 809a; τινὰ εἰς τὸν αὑτοῦ δρόμον ib.847a; [τὸν ἐλέφαντα] τῷ δρεπάνῳ Arist.*HA*610$^a$28; [ναῦν] Id.*Fr.*11; κ. τὰς πράξεις ὁ θεός Aristeas 18; τὰ παρόντα πρὸς τὸ τέλος Plu.*Cam.*42; πρὸς τὰ βελτίονα τοὺς νέους Id.2.20d; τὴν ψυχὴν ib.780b; τὸν λόγον πρός τι Gal.17(2). 362. 3. κ. τινός *demand an account from* one, *condemn*, Pl.*Lg.* 945a, cf. *IG*2$^2$.1183.10 (prob.), Poll.8.22. II. intr., *make straight towards*, κατεύθυναν αἱ βόες ἐν τῇ ὁδῷ εἰς ὁδὸν Βαιθσάμυς Lxx 1 *Ki.*6. 12; κ. τῇ πτήσει ὄρθιον ἐπὶ τοὺς πολεμίους Plu.*Alex.*33. 2. *prosper*, Lxx *Si.*29.18: c. gen., *succeed* in doing.., οὐ κατεύθυνε τοῦ λαλῆσαι οὕτως ib.*Jd.*12.6. 3. οἱ -ευθύνοντες the *righteous*, ib.*Pr.*15.8.

**κατευ-καιρέω**, *find a good opportunity*, Plb.12.4.13. **-κηλέω**, *calm, quiet*, A.R.4.1059.

**κατευκ-τικός**, ή, όν, *entreating*. Adv. -κῶς Sch.S.*Aj.*831 (s.v.l.). **-τός**, ή, όν, *vowed*, Hsch.

**κατευ-λογέω**, strengthd. for εὐλογέω, Plu.2.66a, Lxx *To.*11. 1. **-μᾰρίζω**, strengthd. for εὐμαρίζω, Hsch., Suid., Phot. **-μεγεθέω**, = καταδυναστεύω, Hsch.

**κατευν-άζω**, aor. -ηύνασα (v. infr.), *put to bed, lull to sleep*, Ἅλιον, ὃν αἰόλα νὺξ.. τίκτει κατευνάζει τε S.*Tr.*95 (lyr.); of death, με δαίμων κατευνάζει Id.*Ant.*833 (lyr.); ἐκτὸς αὐτὸν τάξεων κατηύνασεν *assigned* him *quarters* outside the army, E.*Rh.*614: metaph., *quiet, calm*, πόντον A.R.1.1155 (tm.); θηρὸς ἐρωήν Opp.*C.*3.374 (tm.); μόχθων οὐδ' Ἀίδης με κατεύνασεν *gave* me no *rest* from.., *AP*7.278 (Arch. Byz.); [κίνημα] Hierocl.*in CA* 24p.474M.:—Pass., *lie down to sleep*, ἐν τρητοῖσι κατεύνασθεν λεχέεσσιν Il.3.448; *to be quieted*, ἔρως δοκῶν κατευνάσθαι λογισμοῖς Plu.*Ant.*36. **-ασμός**, ὁ, *lulling to sleep*, Id.2.378f (pl.). **-αστήρ**, ῆρος, ὁ, *chamberlain*, Agath.1.19 (pl.). **-αστής**, οῦ, ὁ, = foreg., Plu.*Alex.*40, *Oth.*17, Them.*Or.*10.138a, etc.: metaph., of Hermes, Plu.2.758b. 2. generally, *servant*, ib.945d. **-αστικός**, ή, όν, *lulling to sleep*, βοῆς Eust.1424.6; κ. λόγος, ποίημα, *epithalamium*, Men.Rh.p.405S. **-άστρια**, ἡ, *female chamberlain*, Eust. 1943.58. **-άω**, = κατευνάζω, ἄλλον μέν κεν ἔγωγε θεῶν.. ῥεῖα κατευνήσαιμι Il.14.245, cf. 248: metaph., of stanching blood, αἱμάδα.. ἠπίοισι φύλλοις κατευνάσειεν S.*Ph.*699 (lyr.):—Pass., τὸν μὲν ἐπήν.. κατευνηθέντα ἴδησθε Od.4.414, cf. 421. **-ησις**, εως, ἡ, *putting to rest*, ἀνέμων Iamb.*VP*28.135 (pl.). **-ήτειρα**, ἡ, *she who lulls*, κυδοιμοῦ Nonn.*D.*33.225.

**κατευοδ-όω**, = εὐοδέω, Lxx *Jd.*18.5 cod. A:—also in Pass., ib.*Pr.* 17.23, *Gp.Prooem.*11. 2. *bring prosperity*, ἡμῖν Lxx *Ps.*67(68). 20. **-ωσις**, εως, ἡ, *good success*, *Gloss.*

**κατευ-ορκέω**, *swear right solemnly*, an exaggerated word used by Gorgias, Arist.*Rh.*1406$^a$1. **-πᾰθέω**, *waste in dissipation*, in Pass., Phryn.*PS*p.80B. **-ποιέω**, *do much good to*, τοὺς φίλους Tz.*H.* 3.638. **-πορέω**, *to be sufficiently provided*, τοῖς βοηθήμασι D.S. 17.45.

**κατευρύνω**, *widen*, τοὺς πόρους *EM*482.10:—Pass., Hsch.

**κατευ-στοχέω**, strengthd. for εὐστοχέω, *to be quite successful*, ἐν πᾶσιν D.S.2.5: abs., Plu.*Aem.*19. **-τελίζω**, strengthd. for εὐτελίζω, Id.2.1097c, Sch.E.*Or.*414. **-τονέω**, strengthd. for εὐτονέω, *have the power to..*, c. inf., Hp.*Ep.*17. II. abs., *to be finely tempered*, Ph.*Bel.*71.24. **-τρεπίζω**, *put in order*, Ar.*Ec.*510, X. *Cyr.*8.6.16. **-τῠχέω**, *to be quite successful, prosper*, Arist.*EE*1229$^a$

19 (cj. ib.1247b31), Phld.*Rh.*1.132 S.; τὰ πλεῖστα Plu.*Sert.*18:—also in Pass., τούτων κατευτυχηθέντων D.S.20.46. **-φημέω**, *applaud, extol*, τινα Lxx 3*Ma.*7.13, Plu.*Sert.*4, *Cic.*9, *Epigr.Gr.*430.12 (Egypt): abs., τὸ -φημοῦν Plu.2.487b; περὶ τᾶς ἰδίας πατρίδος πολλὰ κατευφάμηκε *OGI*234.18 (Delph., iii B.C.):—Pass., D.H.3.18:—also **-φημίζω**, Hsch. s.v. Τραυσός. ※**-φραίνω**, strengthd. for εὐφραίνω, τινα Luc.*Am.*1. **-χειρίζω**, gloss on κατευμαρίζω, Phot., Suid.

※**κατ-ευχή**, ἡ, *prayer, vow*, A.*Ch.*477 (anap.), Plu.*Dio* 24 (pl.); κ. καὶ σπονδαί *OGI*309.7 (Teos, ii B.C.), cf. *SIG*589.7 (Magn. Mae., ii B.C.). **-εύχομαι**, fut. -εύξομαι E.*IA* 1186:—*pray earnestly*, c. inf., τοῖσι Πέρσῃσι κατεύχεται εὖ γίνεσθαι Hdt.1.132; τί σοι κατεύξη τἀγαθόν (sc. γενέσθαι); E.l.c. 2. c. acc. et inf., A.*Ch.*139, *Eu.*922 (lyr.), S.*OC* 1575 (lyr.); κ. τινί *pray to* one, A.*Ch.*88, E.*Andr.*1105; κ. τῇ θεῷ ἀπάξειν Ath.13.573e; κ. τινά c. inf., *entreat* a person to.., Theoc.2.71. 3. abs., *make a prayer* or *vow*, Hdt.2.40, 4.172, A.*Ag.*1250, S.*Tr.*764, etc. 4. c. gen., *pray over*, τῶν ἱερῶν *IG*7.235.25 (Oropus, iv B.C.). II. in bad sense, 1. c. gen. pers., *pray against* one, *imprecate* curses *on* one, τινῶν πρὸς τὸν θεόν Pl.*R.*393a: c. acc. rei, οἵας ἀρᾶται καὶ κ. τύχας A.*Th.*633, cf. S.*Aj.*392; πολλὰ καὶ δεινὰ καθ' αὑτῶν Plu.*Num.*12. 2. c. acc. et inf., τὸν δεδρακότα κακῶς.. ἐκτρῖψαι βίον S.*OT*246; κ. τεῖσαι τοὺς Ἀχαιοὺς τὰ ἃ δάκρυα Pl.*R.*394a. 3. abs., μηδὲν κατεύχου E.*IT*536, cf. Pl.*Lg.*934e. III. *boast*, c. fut. inf., Theoc.1.97.

**κατευωχέομαι**, *feast and make merry on*, ἑψήσαντες τὰ κρέα κατευωχέονται Hdt.1.216, cf. 3.99, Str.3.3.7; βοῦν Plu.2.363c. 2. later in Act., *feast, entertain*, τινα J.*AJ* 11.6.1:—Pass., ib.6.1.3, al.

**κατεφ-άλλομαι**, *leap down against*, ἐξ ἵππων κατεπάλμενος ἀντίος ἔστη Il.11.94 (where Sch.A read κατ-απ-άλμενος); *swoop down upon*, κῦμα..νηὸς ὕπερ πάσης κατεπάλμενον A.R.2.583, cf. Opp.*C.*3.120; κατέπαλτο *leapt upon* him, Tryph.478; *leapt down*, οὐρανόθεν Nonn.*D.*48.614; cf. καταπάλλομαι, καταπάλμενος, καταπαλτός.

**κατεφθός**, όν, *boiled*, Philum.ap.Aët.9.12.

**κατεφίσταμαι**, *rise up against*, in aor. Act., κατεπέστησαν τῷ Παύλῳ *Act.Ap.*18.12.

**κατεχθραίνω**, *hate inveterately*, τινα Jul.*Or.*5.171b.

**κατεχμάζω**, *hold fast, keep back*, Hsch.

**κατεχομένιον**, τό, = κώνειον, Ps.-Dsc.4.78.

※**κατέχω**, fut. καθέξω (of duration) Il.18.332, κατασχήσω (of momentary action) Hdt.5.72, Th.4.42: aor. κατέσχον, poet. κατέσχεθον Hes.*Th.*575, S.*El.*754; Ep. 3 sg. κάσχεθε Il.11.702, Aeol. κατέσκ[εθε] Alc.*Supp.*1a.12; imper. κατάσχες E.*Ba.*555 (lyr.), later κατάσχε Philostr.*Ep.*38 (v.l.), *PMag.Lond.*97.404; late aor. κατέσχα *PGen.*54.22 (iv A.D.). I. trans., *hold fast*, καλύπτρην χείρεσσι Hes.*Th.*575. b. *hold back, withhold*, εἴ με βίῃ ἀέκοντα καθέξει Il.15.186, cf. 11.702, Od.15.200; ἐν κολεῷ ξίφος Pi.*N.*10.6: *check, restrain, bridle*, ἑωυτόν Hdt.6.129, cf. Pl.*Chrm.*162c, Men.*Sam.*112; [γυναῖκε] A.*Pers.*190; ἱππικὸν δρόμον S.*El.*754; δάκρυ A.*Ag.*204 (lyr.); ὀργήν, θυμόν, ὕβριν, etc., S.*El.*1011, *OC*874, E.*Ba.*555 (lyr.), etc.; δύναμιν S.*Ant.*605 (lyr.); τὴν διάνοιαν Th.1.130; κ. τὴν ἀγωγὴν *put it off*, Id.6.29; κ. τὸ πλῆθος ἐλευθέρως, ἰσχύϊ, Id.2.65, 3.62; κ. τινὰ πολέμῳ Id.1.103; τὰ δάκρυα Pl.*Phd.*117d, al.; τὸν γέλωτα X.*Cyr.*2.2.5, Pl.*La.*184a, Thphr.*Char.*2.4; οὖρον *hold in*, Gal.8.407 (but -όμενα [οὖρα] as a disease, Hp.*Prorrh.*1.59, cf. Gal.16.639); ἑαυτὸν κατέχει μὴ ἐπιπηδᾶν *restrains* himself *from*.., Pl.*Phdr.*254a:—Pass., *to be held down*, γλῶσσα κατείχετο Hp.*Epid.*5.50; ἐπιθυμίας -ομένας Pl.*R.*554c; *to be bound*, ὁρκίοισι μεγάλοισι Hdt.1.29; ὑποσχέσει *PAmh.*2.97.17 (ii A.D.); τοῖς τινων ὀφειλήμασιν *PRyl.*117.13 (iii A.D.); of a nation, *to be kept under* (by tyrants), Hdt.1.59. c. *detain*, κ. [αὐτοὺς] ἐνιαυτόν Id.6.128, cf. 8.57, Th.8.100; κ. [αὐτοὺς] ὥστε μὴ ἀπιέναι X.*Mem.*2.6.11:—Pass., *to be detained, stay*, Hdt.8.117, S.*Tr.*249; περὶ Κρήτην Th.2.86, etc. d. in imprecations, *inhibit* (cf. καταδέω (A) III), *Tab.Defix.Aud.*50.11 (iv B.C.), *PMag.Par.*1.2077; Μανῆν καταδῶ καὶ κατέχω *Tab.Defix.*109. e. *place under arrest*, *PFlor.*61.60 (i A.D.), etc. f. *keep* an oath, ὅρκον *SIG*526.39 (Itanos, iii B.C.). 2. c. gen., *gain possession of, be master of*, τῶν ἐπιστημῶν μὴ πάνυ κ. Arist.*Cat.*9a6; τῆς ὀργῆς Philem.185 codd. Stob.; τῆς παραποταμίας βίᾳ κατέσχον D.S.12.82, cf. Plb.14.1.9; τῆς Ἀσίας ἐθνῶν App.*Praef.*9; *control*, τινων Lxx 1*Ma.*6.27; ἑαυτῶν Erot. s.v. προπετής; μηκέτι κατέχων ἑαυτοῦ Hdn.1.15.1, cf. 1.7.3; *cling to*, τῶν κεράτων τοῦ θυσιαστηρίου Lxx 3*Ki.*1.51. II. *possess, occupy*, esp. of rulers, A.*Th.*732 (lyr.), E.*Hec.*81 (anap.); σῴζειν ἅπερ ἂν ἅπαξ κατάσχωσι whatever they *have got*, Isoc.12.242; esp. of property, *enjoy possession of*, *PTeb.*5.47 (ii B.C.), etc. (but also, *sequestrate*, *PLille* 3.16 (Pass., iii B.C.), etc.); ὡς μηδὲν ἔχοντες καὶ πάντα κατέχοντες 2*Ep.Cor.*6.10. b. *dwell in, occupy*, Ὀλύμπου αἴγλαν S.*Ant.*609 (lyr.); esp. of tutelary gods, Παρνασίαν ὃς κ. πέτραν, of Dionysus, Ar.*Nu.*603 (lyr.), cf. X.*Cyr.*2.1.1, *SIG*662.10 (Delos, ii B.C.), Luc.*Alex.*10; of a place, μέσον ὀμφαλὸν γᾶς Φοίβου κ. δόμος E.*Ion* 223 (lyr.); of the dead, θῆκας Ἰλιάδος γᾶς..κατέχουσι *occupy*, A.*Ag.*454 (lyr.), cf. S.*Aj.*1167 (anap.). 2. of sound, *fill*, οἱ δ' ἀλαλητῷ πᾶν πεδίον κατέχουσι Il.16.79; κ. στρατόπεδον δυσφημίαις *fill* it with his grievous cries, S.*Ph.*10; οἰμωγὴ..κατεῖχε πελαγίαν ἅλα A.*Pers.*427, cf. E.*Hipp.*1133 (lyr.):—Pass., οἶκος καυθμῷ κατείχετο Hdt.1.111. 3. πανδάκρυτον βιοτὰν κ. *continue to live* a life.., S.*Ph.*690 (lyr.). 4. *to be spread over, cover*, νὺξ..δνοφερὴ κάτεχ' οὐρανόν Od.13.269; ἡμέρα πᾶσαν κατέσχε γαῖαν A.*Pers.*387, cf. Ar.*Nu.*572 (lyr.); τίνες αὖ πόντον κατέχουσ' αὖραι; Cratin.138; ὀσμὴ..κατὰ πᾶν ἔχει δῶ Hermipp.82.9:—Pass., σελήνη..κατείχετο..νεφέεσσιν Od.9.145, cf. Il.17.368, 644:—Med., Ep. aor., κατέσχετο χερσὶ πρόσωπα Od.19.361; κατασχομένη ἑανῷ *having covered her face*, Il.3.419. 5. of the grave, *confine, cover*, τοὺς δ' ἤδη κάτεχεν φυσίζοος αἶα 3.243, cf. Od.11.301, Orac.ap. Hdt.1.67; as a threat, πάρος τινὰ γαῖα καθέξει sooner shall earth *cover* many a one, Il.16.629, cf. Od.13.427, etc. 6. of circumstances, etc., *hold fast, have* one *in their power*, μιν κατὰ γῆρας ἔχει χεῖράς τε πόδας τε Od.11.497; ὃν θάνατος δακρυόεις καθέχει (sic) *IG*1².987; ἐχθρὰ Φάλαριν κ. φάτις Pi.*P.*1.96; τινὰ..λάθα κ. Id.*N.*8.24; [φθορὰ] κ. τὸν σὸν δόμον S.*OC*370; τύχη, πόλεμος κ. τινά, Pl.*Hp.Ma.*304c, *Ep.*317a; κ. κίνδυνος Σικελίαν ib.355d; συνέβη λοιμώδη νόσον κατασχεῖν τὴν Ἰταλίαν Hdn.1.12.1:—Pass., ὑπὸ μεγάλης ἀνάγκης κατεχόμενοι Pl.*Lg.*858a: rarely in good sense, ὁ δ' ὄλβιος, ὃν φᾶμαι κατέχοντ' ἀγαθαί Pi.*O.*7.10; μεγάλαι κ. τύχαι γένος ὀρνίθων Ar.*Av.*1726 (lyr.); εὐμοιρίας -εχούσης τὸν βίον Hdn.2.5.1. b. of circumstances, etc., *prevail, prevail among, engage*, ἄλλα τῶν κατεχόντων πρηγμάτων χαλεπώτερα Hdt.6.40, cf. 1.65; μεγάλοι θόρυβοι κατέχουσ' ἡμᾶς murmurs *are rife among* us, S.*Aj.*142 (anap.); φήμης ἀθρόας -σχούσης τὸ Ἑλληνικόν a sudden rumour *having overspread* Greece, Philostr.*VA* 8.15. 7. *seize, occupy*, in right of *conquest*, τὸ Καδμείων πέδον dub. in S.*OC* 381; esp. in histor. writers, -σχήσειν [τὴν ἀκρόπολιν] Hdt.5.72; τὰ πρήγματα Id.3.143; τὰ ἐχυρὰ X.*Cyr.*3.1.27; τὰ κύκλῳ τῆς Ἀττικῆς ἁρμοσταῖς D.18.96; φρουραῖς τὰς πόλεις Plu.2.177d. 8. *achieve, effect* an object, Isoc.2.25; πρᾶξιν Arist.*Pol.*1312a33. 9. *master, understand*, οὐ κατέχω τί βούλει φράζειν Pl.*Phlb.*26c, cf. *Men.*72d, Ceb.34; περὶ φύσεως κ. πάντας τοὺς λόγους Sosip.1.17, cf. 33; κ. νοῦν στίχων *grasp* the sense of.., Puchstein *Epigr.Gr.*p.9. b. *keep in mind, remember*, χρήσιμον καὶ τοῦτο κατασχεῖν τὸ στοιχεῖον Epicur.*Ep.*1 p.10 U., cf. Thphr.*Char.*26.2, Men.*Epit.*109; κ. τινὰ ὀψοφάγον Chrysipp.Tyan.ap.Ath.1.5e; κ. ὅτι, διότι, *PCair.Zen.*60.10 (iii B.C.), Phld.*Herc.*1251.15:—Pass., Epicur.*Ep.*1 p.31 U. 10. *possess*, of a god, εἰ θεός ἐστιν ὁ σὰς κατέχων φρένας *PLit.Lond.*52.12; τοιοῦτος ἔρως κατεῖχε τὴν ἄνθρωπον she *was so infatuated*, Plu.*Alc.*23; of an actor, κ. τὸ θέατρον *held* the audience *spellbound*, Plu.*Dem.*29 (but, *kept* the audience *waiting*, *Phoc.*19); of poets, μύθοις [τοὺς ἀκούοντας] κ. Luc.*JTr.*39 (v.l. κατηχοῦσι):—mostly in Pass., of persons, *to be possessed, inspired*, Pl.*Ion* 533e; ἐξ Ὁμήρου ib.536b; ἐκ θεῶν X.*Smp.*1.10; κάρῳ Phld.*D.*1.18; τὸ θέατρον κατείχετο the audience *was spellbound*, Eun.*Hist.*p.247 D.; of hydrophobia patients, Philum.*Ven.*4.11; of a lover, τῷ αὐτῷ θεῷ (sc. Ἔρωτι) κατέσχημαι Luc.*DMort.*19.1:—also in aor. Med., Pl.*Phdr.*244e. III. *follow close upon, press hard*, X.*Cyr.*1.4.22 (dub. l.), *Cyn.*6.22:—Pass., ib. 9.20. IV. *bring* a ship *to land*, Hdt.6.101, 7.59, Plu.2.162a.

B. intr., 1. (sc. ἑαυτόν) *control oneself*, S.*OT*782; οὐκέτι καθέξω Men.*Pk.*394; εἶπεν οὖν μὴ κατασχὼν Plu.*Art.*15; οὐ κατέσχεν App.*BC*3.43: c. inf., κ. τὸ μὴ δακρύειν Pl.*Phd.*117c. b. *stop, cease*, of the wind, Ar.*Pax* 944 (lyr.). 2. *come from the high sea to shore, put in* (v. supr. IV), νηῒ Θορικόνδε *h.Cer.*126; τῆς Μαγνησίης χώρης ἐς τὸν αἰγιαλόν Hdt.7.188, cf. 6.101, Plb.1.25.7, Plu.*Thes.*21; τίνες ποτ' ἐς γῆν τήνδε..κατέσχετε; S.*Ph.*221, cf. 270, E.*Heracl.*83 (lyr.), Antipho 5.21, etc.: c. acc. loci, E.*Hel.*1206, *Cyc.*223; of a journey by land, *rest*, προξένων δ' ἔν του κατέσχες; Id.*Ion* 551, cf. Plb.5.71.2: metaph., εὖ κατασχήσει *shall come safe to land*, S.*El.*503 (lyr.). 3. *prevail*, ὁ λόγος κ. the report *prevails*, Th.1.10; κληδὼν ἐν ἁπάσῃ τῇ πόλει κατεῖχεν And.1.130; σεισμῶν -εχόντων Th.3.89; ὁ Βορέας κατεῖχεν Arist.*Mete.*345a1, cf. 360b33, Thphr.*CP*1.5.1. 4. *gain the upper hand*, παρά τινι Thgn.262; *gain one's purpose*, Lys.3.42; ὁ δὲ κατεῖχε τῇ βοῇ Ar.*Ec.*434; νομίζοντες ῥᾳδίως κατασχήσειν Arist.*Pol.*1307b10.

C. Med., *keep back for oneself, embezzle*, [τὰ χρήματα] Hdt.7.164. 2. *cover oneself*, v. supr. A.II.4. 3. *hold, contain*, Plb.9.26a.7. II. aor. Med., = κατέχω B.2, Od.3.284. 2. in pass. sense, τεαῖς ῥιπαῖσι κατασχόμενος *subdued*, Pi.*P.*1.10; καρδίαν κατέσχετο ἔρωτι *was seized with, possessed by*, E.*Hipp.*27; v. supr. A. II.10.

**κατη-βολέω**, *swoon*, Nic.*Al.*194, 458. **-βολή**, ἡ, = τὸ ἐπιβάλλον, E.*Fr.*614, 750. 2. = καταβολή III, Hp.ap.Gal.19.110, Pl.*Hp.Mi.*372e (cf. Sch.), Hsch., Phot. 3. = θυσία, τελετή, τὰ νομιζόμενα, Hsch.

**κατηγάθεος** [ᾰ], ον, strengthd. for ἠγ-, epith. of Zeus, Antioch. Astr. in *Cat.Cod.Astr.*1.109.

**κατηγγειωμένως**, Adv. pf. part. Pass., (καταγγειόομαι) *by means of blood-vessels*, Sor.1.73.

※**κατηγορ-έω**, *speak against*, esp. before judges, *accuse*, opp. ἀπολογέομαι, c. gen., Hdt.2.113, 8.60, Lys.14.21, Ar.*Pl.*1073, etc.; τῆς πόλεως Pl.*Mx.*244e: less freq. κατά τινος X.*HG*1.7.9; κ. τινὸς πρὸς τὴν πόλιν *denounce* him publicly, Pl.*Euthphr.*2c; κατηγόρεις [αὐτῶν] ὡς λέγοιεν you *accused* them of saying, D.21.134, cf. X.*HG*7.1.38; κ. τινὸς ὅτι.. ib.1.7.17; τῶν ἱππέων ἐλθὼν πρὸς ὑμᾶς εἰς τὴν ἐκκλησίαν κατηγόρει D.21.197; τῆς ἐμῆς [τύχης] κατηγορεῖς Id.18.266, cf. Isoc.3.4. 2. κ. τί τινος *bring as a charge against* a person, *accuse* him *of it*, δεῖν' ἔπη μου S.*OT*514, cf. E.*Or.*28, etc.; τῶν ἄλλων μωρίαν X.*Mem.*1.3.4; ὃς ἐμοῦ Φιλιππισμὸν κατηγορεῖ D.18.294; κ. τι κατά τινος Hyp.*Eux.*23; τινὸς περί τινος And.1.110, Th.8.85: c. inf., κ. τινὸς παθεῖν τι Pl.*Grg.*482c: c. dupl. gen., παρανόμων κ. τινός D.21.5. 3. c. acc. rei only, *allege in accusation*, Hdt.2.113; μωρίαν ἐμὴν E.*Heracl.*418; τὴν πονηρίαν τῶν γονέων Pl.*Prt.*346a; τὰ γεγονότα κ. Antipho 1.10, cf. Ar.*V.*932, *Ra.*996 (lyr.), Lys.13.31, D.19.9:—Pass., *to be brought as an accusation against*, κατηγορεῖτο τοὐπίκλημα τοῦτό μου; S.*OT*529; ἀδικία πολλὴ κ. αὐτοῦ Th.1.95; τὰ πρῶτά μου ψευδῆ -ημένα the first false *charges brought against*

me, Pl.*Ap.*18a, cf. Lys.16.9; τὰ -ηθέντα Antipho 5.85, And.1.24; τἀδικήμαθ' ἃ κατηγορεῖται D.21.136: impers., folld. by inf., σφέων.. κατηγόρητο μηδίζειν *a charge had been brought against* them that.., Hdt.7.205; κατηγορεῖτό τινος ὡς βαρβαρίζοι X.*HG*5.2.35; κατηγορουμένου δ' αὐτοῦ, ὅτι.. *a charge being brought against* him, that.., ib.3.5.25. b. rarely in Pass., of the person, *to be accused*, οἱ κατηγορούμενοι And.1.7, cf. Luc.*Tim.*38 (s. v. l.). 4. abs., *to be an accuser, appear as prosecutor*, Ar.*V.*840, 842, *Pl.*917, Pl.*Ap.*18c, etc. II. *signify, indicate, prove*, c. acc. rei, [τὸ νεαρὸν] κ. τὴν ὀλιγοετίαν X.*Cyr.*1.4.3, cf. Plu.2.695d, Adam.1.5, al.; ἀσθένειαν μᾶλλον ἢ δύναμιν Plot.4.6.3; *display*, οἱ πολλὴν -οῦντες ἀπειροκαλίαν Luc.*Nigr.* 21: c. gen. pers., εὖ γὰρ φρονοῦντος ὄμμα σοῦ κατηγορεῖ A.*Ag.*271, cf. E.*Fr.*690, S.*Aj.*907, etc.; ὠκύτητα κ. τοῦ κυνός Philostr.*Im.*2.26. 2. folld. by relat., *declare, assert*, αὐτὸ κατηγορέει τὸ οὔνομα ὡς ἔστι Ἑλληνικόν Hdt.3.115; κ. ὅτι.. Id.4.189, Pl.*Phd.*73b (impers.): abs., *make a definite assertion*, Id.*Tht.*208b. III. in Logic, *predicate of* a person or thing, τί τινος Arist.*Cat.*3ᵃ19, al., Epicur.*Fr.*250; κυρίως, καταχρηστικῶς κ., Phld.*Po.*5.15; ἐναντίως ὑπὲρ τῶν αὐτῶν Id.*Oec.*p.60 J.: —more freq. in Pass., *to be predicated of*.., τινος Arist.*Cat.*2ᵃ21, *APr.* 26ᵇ9, al.; κατά τινος Id.*Cat.*2ᵃ37; κατὰ παντὸς ἢ μηδενὸς Id.*APr.*24ᵃ 15: less freq. ἐπί τινος Id.*Metaph.*998ᵇ16, 999ᵃ15; so later ἐφ' ἑνὸς οἴονται θεοῦ ἑκάτερον τῶν ὀνομάτων -εῖσθαι D.H.2.48; περί τινος Arist. *Top.*140ᵇ37; τὸ κοινῇ -ούμενον ἐπὶ πᾶσιν Id.*SE*179ᵃ8: abs., τὸ κατηγορούμενον *the predicate*, opp. τὸ ὑποκείμενον (the subject), Id.*Cat.*1ᵇ11, cf. *Metaph.*1043ᵃ6, al.; κατηγορεῖν καὶ -εῖσθαι *to be subject* and *predicate*, Id.*APr.*47ᵇ1. 2. *affirm*, opp. ἀπαρνέομαι, ib.41ᵃ10. Adv. κατηγορουμένως *categorically, roundly*, Phld.*Ir.*p.90 W. -ημα, ατος, τό, *accusation, charge*, Gorg.*Pal.*22, Pl.*Lg.*765b, 881e, *PFrankf.*7 *B* 3 (iii B.C.); τὰ τοῦ τρόπου σου κ. D.18.263, cf. Din.1.1, D.H.7.64; τοῦτο φωνῆς κ. this is the *fault* of.., A.D.*Pron.*27.25. II. in Logic, *predicate*, Arist.*Int.*20ᵇ32, *Metaph.*1053ᵇ19, etc.; οὐκ εὔοδον τὸ ἁπλοῦν ἐστι κ. Epicur.*Fr.*18. 2. *head of predicables*, Arist.*Metaph.*1028ᵃ33, *Ph.*201ᵃ 1, Zeno *Stoic.*1.25, etc.; περὶ κατηγορημάτων Sphaer.ib.140. III. *sign, indication*, ὁ ἐπικεκυφὼς τράχηλος μωροῦ ἀνδρὸς κ. Polem.*Phgn.* 36. -ησείω, Desiderat., *to be anxious to accuse*, Agath.4.2. -ησις, εως, ἡ, *predication*, Chrysipp.*Stoic.*2.108 (dub.). -ητέον, *one must accuse, lay the blame on*, τῶν πραγμάτων Isoc.3.2; αὐτοῦ Pl.*Grg.*508b. II. *one must assert*, ὡς.. Id.*Tht.*167a; *one must predicate*, τι κατά τινος Epicur.*Ep.*1 p.25 U.; τοῦ ἐπέκεινα οὐδὲ τοῦτο κ. Plot.3.7.2. -ητής, οῦ, ὁ, *accuser*, J.*AJ*17.5.4. -ητικός, ή, όν, = κατηγορικός 1, Arist. *Rh.Al.*1421ᵇ10 codd. (leg. κατηγορικόν as in 1426ᵇ22, 25 = *PHib.*1. 26.295, 297). -ία, Ion. -ίη, ἡ, *accusation*, Hdt.6.50, etc.; opp. αἰτία (expostulation), Th.1.69; opp. ἔπαινος, ib.84; opp. ἀπολογία, Arist.*Rh.*1358ᵇ11; τὴν κ. ποιεῖσθαι Antipho 6.10, And.1.6; ὡς ὑβρίζοντος κ. ἐποιοῦντο X.*An.*5.8.1; κ. ἐγένοντο πολλαὶ τῶν Ἀθηναίων *charges* were made against.., Id.*HG*2.1.31; κατηγορίαι κατὰ τινος γεγόνασιν Isoc.5.147; εἰ.. ἐπὶ τοῖς πεπραγμένοις κατηγορίας ἔχω I am liable to *accusation*, D.18.240. II. in Logic, *predication*, Arist.*Metaph.*1007ᵃ35, etc.: pl., Id.*APo.*84ᵃ1; esp. *affirmative predication*, opp. στέρησις, Id.*APr.*52ᵃ15; ἄπορον ἐν κ. *Stoic.*2.93. 2. *predicate*, Arist.*Metaph.*1004ᵃ29, 1028ᵃ28, al., Epicur.*Ep.*1 p.23 U.. etc. 3. more freq.. *category, head of predicables*, Arist.*Top.*103ᵇ 20 (ten), *APo.*83ᵇ16, *Ph.*225ᵇ5 (eight), *Metaph.*1068ᵃ8 (seven), cf. *EN* 1096ᵃ29. -ικός, ή, όν, *accusatory*, opp. ἀπολογικός, Id.*Rh.Al.* 1426ᵇ25, cf. Erot.*Prooem.*; οἱ κ. *informers*, = Lat. *delatores*, Plu.*Galb.* 8. Adv. -κῶς, λέγειν πρός τινα J.*BJ Prooem.*4. II. *affirmative*, opp. στερητικός, Arist.*APr.*26ᵃ18, al. Adv. -κῶς ib.26ᵇ22. 2. *categorical*, opp. hypothetical, κατηγορικόν, τό, *statement combining subject and predicate*, *Stoic.*2.66; κ. συλλογισμοί S.E.*P.*2.163, Procl.*in Prm.* p.790 S.; λόγοι S.E.*P.*2.166, Ammon.*in Int.*74.1. Adv. -κῶς, opp. ὑποθετικῶς, Gal.4.609. -ος, ὁ, *accuser*, Hdt.3.71, S.*Tr.*814, And. 4.16, Lys.7.11, Pl.*Ap.*18a (pl.), *Apoc.*12.10, etc.; δημόσιος κ. public *prosecutor*, *PFlor.*6.6 (iii A.D.); *betrayer*, φρονημάτων ἡ γλῶσσ' ἀληθὴς γίγνεται κ. A.*Th.*439; ἀμέλειά ἐστι σαφὴς ψυχῆς κ. κακῆς X.*Oec.*20. 15; πνεῦμα ὧν κατήγορον,.. δρόμοις [ἡ φύσις] ἐκβιᾶται κατηγορέειν what the respiration *reveals*, Hp.*de Arte* 12. -ουμένως, v. κατηγορέω III. 2.

**κατήγωρ**, ὁ, = κατήγορος, *PMag.Lond.*124.25, v.l. in *Apoc.*12.10.

**κατηγώς**, v. κατάγνυμι.

**κατήκοος**, ον, (κατακούω) *hearing*, τῶν εἴ τίς ἐστιν.. κατήκοος if any *has heard tidings of* them, S.*Ichn.*77; *listening to*, κ. λόγων *student* of philosophy, Pl.*Ax.*365b. 2. *spy, eavesdropper*, κατάσκοποι καὶ κ. Hdt.1.100, D.C.42.17. II. *hearkening to, obedient*, Hdt.7.155, S.*Ant.*642; τινος *to* another, Μήδων, Περσέων κ., Hdt.1.72, 143, al.; τὰ παραθαλάσσια.. Περσέων κ. ἐποίεε Id.5.10; κ. τοῦ κοσμητοῦ *IG*2². 1011.20; τὸ ἐπιθυμητικὸν κ. [τοῦ λόγου] Arist.*EN*1102ᵇ31: c. dat., Κροίσῳ κ. Hdt.1.141, cf. 3.88; τῇ πόλει κ. γενέσθαι Pl.*R.*499b. III. *giving ear to*, εὐχωλῇσι *AP*6.199 (Antiphil.).

**κατηκρῑβωμένως**, Adv. pf. part. Pass., (ἀκριβόομαι) *precisely*, Gal. 18(2).861.

**κατήκω**, Ion. for καθήκω.

**κατηλέποντα**· φροντίδας ποιοῦντα, Hsch.

**κατῆλιψ**, ῖφος, ἡ, variously expld. as *ladder, roof-beam, upper story*, etc. in Ar.*Ra.*566, cf. Sch. ad loc., Poll.7.123, Hsch.; also used by Luc.*Lex.*8.

**κατηλογέω**, *make of small account, neglect*, c. acc., Hdt.1.84, 144, 3.121: c. gen., Parth.23.1, J.*AJ*12.4.6.—The form καταλογέω does not occur.

**κάτ-ηλῠς**, ῠδος, ὁ, ἡ, *going downward*, Nonn.*D.*37.24. -ηλῠσία, Ion. -ίη, ἡ, *descent*, λαιψηροῖο -ίῃ Ζεφύροιο A.R.4.886; κατηλυσίη τ' ἄνοδός τε Arat.536. ✱-ήλῠσις, εως, ἡ, *going down, descent*, εἰς Ἀΐδην *AP*10.3; νιφετοῖο κ. *a falling* of snow, Simon.179.1. II. *return*, τῶν Ἡρακλειδῶν D.S.12.75.

**κατημελημένως**, Adv., (ἀμελέω) *negligently*, v.l. in Procop.*Pers.*1.5.

**κατημύω**, *droop*, ἔρνεα κ. ἔραζε A.R.3.1400: metaph., κατήμυσαν ἀχέεσσι θυμόν Id.2.862. (V. ἡμύω.)

**κατηναγκασμένως**, Adv. pf. part. Pass., (καταναγκάζω) *of necessity*, D.S.15.50, Demetr.Lac.*Herc.*1012.45, Diog.Oen.33, Alex.Aphr.*Fat.* 181.23.

**κατήνεμος**, ον, *exposed to the wind*, cj. in Thphr.*Vent.*34, cf. Ael. *NA*4.6, Poll.1.115.

**κάτηξις**, ιος, ἡ, Ion. for κάταξις.

✱**κατήορος**, Dor. -άορος [ᾱ], ον: (ἀείρω):—*hanging down*, τέκνων δὲ πλῆθος.. κατάορα στένει *hanging on their mother's neck*, E.*Tr.*1090 (lyr.); τελαμὼν κ. A.R.2.1041; βόστρυχα *AP*5.259 (Paul. Sil.).

**κατηπέδανον**· κατησθενηκός, Erot.

**κατηπειγμένως**, Adv. pf. part. Pass., (κατεπείγω) *hurriedly*, Hld. 8.1, Sch.E.*Or.*1433.

**κατηπιάω**, *assuage, allay*, ὀδύναι δὲ κατηπιόωντο Il.5.417.

**κατηρεμίζω**, *calm, appease*, X.*An.*7.1.22, Plu.2.384a.

✱**κατηρεφής**, ές, (ἐρέφω) *covered over, vaulted, overhanging*, σπέος εὐρὺ κ. Od.13.349; κλισίας τε κ. Il.18.589; ἐν σμήνεσσι κ. μέλισσαι Hes.*Th.*594; μέγα κῦμα.. κ. Od.5.367: c. dat., σπέος δάφνῃσι κ. *shaded by, embowered in* them, 9.183; δώματα πέτρῃσι κ. Hes.*Th.* 778; so in Trag., κ. πέτρος, of a cave, S.*Ph.*272; ἐν κ. στέγῃ χθονὸς Id.*El.*381; κ. τύμβος Id.*Ant.*885; κ. αὐτῇ τῇ πέτρᾳ Pl.*Criti.*116b; of trees, *thick-leaved*, Theoc.7.9; κ. πόδα τιθέναι keep the foot *covered*, of Pallas seated, when the robe falls over her feet, opp. ὀρθὸν πόδα τ., A.*Eu.*294. 2. c. gen., στέγην, ἧς κατηρεφεῖς δόμοι E.*Hipp.*468; τράπεζαι κ. παντοίων ἀγαθῶν *covered with, full of*, Anacr.121.

**κατήρης**, ες, (ἀραρίσκω) *fitted out, furnished* with, χλανιδίοις E. *Supp.*110; ὀσμῇ Id.*El.*498; δένδρεα.. καρπῶν ἀφθονίῃσι κατήρεα cj. in Emp.78; [ἕρπυλλος] φύλλοισι κ. Nic.*Th.*69; esp. of ships, *furnished with oars*, εἶχε πλοῖον κατῆρες ἑτοῖμον had a *rowing* boat ready, Hdt.8.21; but ταρσὸς κ. *a well-fitted* oar, E.*IT*1346.

**κατήρητος**, v. κατάρατος.

**κατήρυδες** ἄμπελοι, *laden with fruit*, Hsch.

✱**κατῆτος**, = κατὰ ἔτος, *yearly*, *Hymn.Curet.*37.

**κατηφ-εια**, Ion. and Ep. -είη, ἡ, (κατηφής) *dejection* (λύπη κάτω βλέπειν ποιοῦσα Plu.2.528e), δυσμενέσιν μὲν χάρμα κατηφείην δὲ σοὶ αὐτῷ Il.3.51; κ. καὶ ὄνειδος 16.498, 17.556; κ. τέ τις ἅμα καὶ κατάμεμψις σφῶν αὐτῶν πολλὴ ἦν Th.7.75; opp. χαρά, *Ep.Jac.*4.9; δυσθυμία καὶ κ. Plu.*Them.*9; τὴν βουλὴν ἄχος καὶ κ. ἔσχε Id.*Cor.*20, cf. D.H.3.19, Corn.*ND*28, Charito 6.8; κ. καὶ σύννοια Ph.2.204; κ. καὶ οἰζὺς Rhian. 1.8. -έω, *to be downcast, to be mute* with horror or grief, στῆ δὲ κατηφήσας Il.22.293; ἀκάχοντο κατήφησάν τ' ἐνὶ θυμῷ Od.16.342, cf. Call.*Epigr.*22, A.R.2.443, etc.; τί δαὶ κατηφεῖς ὄμμα; E.*Med.*1012; of animals, Arist.*HA*604ᵇ12; καὶ κατηφῆσαι [ἂν] θεὸς and well *might* God *grieve*, J.*BJ*3.8.4 (v.l. οὐ κατέφησεν). -ής, ές, *with downcast eyes, downcast*, κατηφέες ἐσσόμεθ' αἰεί Od.24.432, cf. Cic. *Att.*13.42.1; τὸν μὲν κατηφῆ E.*Or.*881; κ. ὄμμα Id.*Heracl.*633 (but κ. ὀφθαλμοί *sunken* eyes, Hp.*Epid.*7.25); κ. καὶ ὑπεραύστηρος *POxy.* 471.92 (ii A.D.); of animals, αἱ ἵπποι ὅταν ἀποκείρωνται, γίνονται κατηφέστεραι Arist.*HA*572ᵇ9; τὸ κ. Id.*Phgn.*808ᵃ10, cf. 807ᵇ12: metaph., κ. ἄμπελος *drooping* in sorrow, Him.*Or.*9.4. 2. metaph., *dim, obscure*, νύξ *AP*9.658 (Paul. Sil.); χωρίον Poll.5.110; of colour, κ. ὁ λίθος καὶ μέλας Philostr.*VS*2.1.8, cf. Him.*Ecl.*12.7. -ιάω, = κατηφέω, *AP*14.3, Ph.2.519 (nisi leg. -φῶμεν), Plu.2.119c; Ep. part. κατηφιόων A.R.1.461, etc.; Ep. iterat. κατηφιάασκε *MAMA* 1. 319. -ών, όνος, ὁ, *one who causes grief* or *shame*, σπεύσατέ μοι, κακὰ τέκνα, κατηφόνες Il.24.253 (κατηφέες Crates).

**κατηχ-έω**, *sound over* or *through*, ἁρμονία κ. τῆς θαλάττης Philostr. *Im.*1.19, cf. 2.12. 2. *sound amiss*, opp. συνηχέω, Vitr.5.8.1. II. *teach by word of mouth*: hence generally, *instruct*, κ. τινὰ πολλὰ τῶν ἀγνοουμένων Agrippa II ap.J.*Vit.*65, cf. Luc.*Asin.*48, *PStrassb.*41. 37 (iii A.D.):—Pass., *to be informed* or *instructed*, περί τινος *Act. Ap.*21.21; κ. ὅτι.. Ph.2.575; ὥσπερ κατηχήμεθα S.E.*M.*5.5. 2. in *NT*, *instruct in the elements of religion*, 1*Ep.Cor.*14.19:—Pass., περὶ ὧν κατηχήθης λόγων *Ev.Luc.*1.4; ὁ κατηχούμενος τὸν λόγον *Ep. Gal.*6.6; κατηχημένος τὴν ὁδὸν τοῦ Κυρίου *Act.Ap.*18.25, cf. Porph. *Chr.*26. -ής, v. καταχής. -ησις, εως, ἡ, *instruction by word of mouth*: generally, *instruction*, Hp.*Praec.*13, Cic.*Att.*15.12.2, D.H. *Dem.*50, *Din.*7, Ath.Med.ap.Orib.*inc.*21.6, S.E.*M.*1.7; διὰ τὴν κ. τῶν συνόντων by *communication* with companions, in bad sense, Chrysipp. *Stoic.*3.54, cf. 55, Gal.5.463. II. *accompaniment* of the monochord by louder instruments *which drown* its tune, Ptol.*Harm.*2.12 (pl.). -ίζω, = κατηχέω II, Hsch., *Gloss.*

**κάτθᾰνε**, v. καταθνήσκω. **κατθᾶξαι**, v. καταθήγω. **κατθάψαι**, v. καταθάπτω. **κατθέμεν, κάτθεμεν, κάτθετε, κάτθεσαν, κατθέμεθα, κατθέσθην, κατθέμενοι, κάτθεο**, v. κατατίθημι.

**κατιάδιον**, τό, = κατιάς, Aret.*CD*1.2.

**κατῑάπτω**, *harm, hurt*, ὡς ἂν κατὰ χρόα καλὸν ἰάπτῃ Od.2.376, cf. 4.749; τίφθ' ὧδε κατὰ θυμὸν ἰάπτεις; Mosch.4.1.

**κατιάς**, άδος, ἡ, *lancet* or *stylet*, Heliod.ap.Orib.44.14.4 (cf. Sch. ad loc.), Philum.ap.Aët.8.48, Sor.2.59.

**κατῑδίω**, *desudasco*, *Gloss.*

✱**κατιερόω**, ✱**κατιέρωσις**, Ion. for καθ-:—Elean ✱**κατῑαραίω** *Schwyzer* 424.5 (iv B.C.): aor. opt. -ιαραύσειε, [τινος] ib.409.2 (v B.C.).

**κατ-ῑθύνω**, Ion. and Ep. for κατευθύνω, κ. τὸν πλόον Hdt.2.96, cf. Hp.*Art.*71, Luc.*Trag.*56, Aristaenet.1.15; κῦμα Mosch.2.121; χεῖρα τοξότιν *AP*6.188(Leon.); ῥήματος ἁρμονίην *APl.*4.226(Alc.). ※**-ῑθύς**, Adv. *opposite*, c. gen., Babr.95.42, Q.S.7.136:—also **κατῑθύ** Herod. 8.60, Man.1.30; cf. ἰθύς II. 2.

**κατῐκετεύω**, Ion. for καθικετεύω.

**κατικμ-άζω**, *let fall in drops*, σπόρον Nic.*Al.*582. **-αίνω**, *moisten, wet*, τινὰ ῥοαῖς Lyc.1053; χρόα λοετροῖς Nonn.*D.*5.606:—Pass., ib. 11.508:—Med., *bathe*, τινθαλέοισι λοετροῖς Call.*Fr.anon.*60.

**κατιλλαίνω**, *look askance at*, Hsch. (Pass.):—Act. is prob. in Arist.*Phgn.*813ᵃ21.

※**κατίλλω**, = κατειλέω, φωναὶ κακούμεναι καὶ κατίλλουσαι (v.l. κατειλοῦσαι) dub. sens. in Hp.*Epid.*3.5 (cf. Gal.17(1).678, Erot.); = κατείργω, Phot. s.v. κατουλάδα.

※**κατιλλώπτω**, *look askance at, leer at*, τινι Philem.124; θῆλυ κ. *AP* 5.199. 2. *look scornfully*, Poll.2.52, Hsch.

**κατῑλύω**, *fill with mud* or *dirt*, X.*Oec.*17.13.

**κατίμεν** [ῐ], Ep. pres. inf. Act. of κάτειμι, Il.14.457.

**κατῑμονεύω**, *let down*, Hsch.

**κατῑόομαι**, Pass., *become rusty, tarnished*, Lxx*Si.*12.11 (Act. is v.l.), Str.16.2.42, *Ep.Jac.*5.3, Dsc.4.82, Arr.*Epict.*4.6.14: metaph., βασιλεία σιδηρᾶ καὶ -ιωμένη D.C.71.36.

**κάτῑσος**, ον, *equal*, c. dat., Sch.Ar.*Pax*728.

**κατισχάνω**, Ep. form of κατίσχω, κατὰ σὸν νόον ἴσχᾰνε Od.19.42.

**κατισχν-αίνω**, *cause to pine* or *waste away*, A.*Eu.*138:—Pass., ὑδροποτῶν καὶ κατισχναινόμενος Pl.*R.*561c, cf. J.*AJ*7.8.1:—fut. Med. inf. κατισχνᾰνεῖσθαι A.*Pr.*271. II. *reduce* a swelling, Hp.*Prog.* 23; αἱ Μοῦσαι τὸν ἔρωτα κ. Call.*Epigr.*47.3; *weaken*, ὀσμήν Thphr. *Od.*47. **-άω** or **-έω**, = foreg., ἐπιφθέγγεσθαι κατισχνημένον in a *thin* voice, Ps.-Luc.*Philopatr.*20. **-όομαι**, = κατισχναίνομαι, J. *AJ*2.5.5, Gal.*UP*1.21, Aët.4.34:—Act., Hsch., Phot., Sch.Nic.*Al.* 592. ※**-ος**, ον, *very lean, emaciated*, Antyll.ap.Orib.7.7.9, Plu.*Dem.* 4, etc.

**κατισχῡρεύομαι**, *strengthen oneself, be violent*, Aq.*Ps.*85(86).14.

**κατισχύω**, fut. -ύσω *Ev.Matt.*16.18:—*overpower, prevail over*, τινα Men.*Epit.*74, Aristeas 21, Lxx 2*Ch.*8.3, al.; ὅταν ἡ τῆς πείρας ἀκρίβεια -ισχύῃ τὴν τῶν λόγων πιθανότητα D.S.1.39: also c. gen., Lxx*Je.*15. 18, Alex.Aphr.*in Top.*248.19; [τῆς ἐκκλησίας] *Ev.Matt.*l.c.; τινὸς σοφίᾳ Ael.*NA*5.19; Ἄρης κ. τῆς Σελήνης Vett.Val.104.10; γενναίας φύσεως Chor. in *Rev.Phil.*1.57:—Pass., *to be worsted*, ὑπ' ἔρωτος D.S.1.71; τῇ μάχῃ Id.17.45. 2. abs., *have the upper hand, prevail*, Lxx*Ex.*17.11, al.; κ. τῷ πλήθει *to be superior in*.., Plb.11.13.3; κατίσχυον αἱ φωναὶ αὐτῶν *Ev.Luc.*23.23. b. *to be prevalent*, ὁρμαὶ καὶ ζῆλοι παρά τισι κ. Plb.3.4.6; κατισχυούσης τῆς θερμότητος Thphr. *CP*6.11.7; κατίσχυκεν ἡ φήμη παρὰ τοῖς πλείστοις Antig.*Mir.* 152. II. *come to one's full strength*, δέμας in body, S.*OC*346, cf. Phld.*Rh.*1.189S. III. trans., *strengthen, encourage*, c. acc., Lxx *De.*1.38, al.; τὰς χεῖράς τινων ib.1*Es.*7.15; οὐδετέραν τῶν στάσεων D.H.6.65.

※**κατίσχω**, collat. form of κατέχω, *hold back*, οὐδὲ κατίσχει [ἵππους] Il.23.321; τὰς νέας Hdt.2.115; θυμοῦ μένος ὀξὺ κατισχέμεν *h.Hom.* 8.14:—Med., *keep by one*, γυναῖκα νέην.., ἥν τ' αὐτὸς.. κατίσχεαι Il. 2.233. II. *possess, occupy*, οὐ ποίμνῃσιν καταΐσχεται Od.9.122, ἀράχνια κ. ὅλον τὸ σμῆνος *cover* it, Arist.*HA*626ᵇ18. III. = κατέχω A. IV, ἐς πατρίδα γαῖαν νῆα κατισχέμεναι Od.11.456, cf. Hdt.8. 41; ἐνὶ Φάσιδι νῆα *put in* there, A.R.3.57. IV. intr., σέλας κατίσχει ἐξ οὐρανοῦ ἐπὶ τὴν βοῦν the light *comes down* from heaven, Hdt.3.28. 2. of ships, *put in*, Th.7.33.

**κατῑτήρια** (sc. ἱερά), τά, = ἡ ἐπὶ καθόδῳ θυσία, Hsch.

**κάτογκος**, ον, *bulky*, τῷ σώματι Sor.1.117.

**κατοδερικαῖς**, τοῖς, dat. pl. masc., dub. sens. in *BGU*1240.24,26 (ii B.C.).

**κατοδῡνάω**, *afflict grievously*, τὴν ζωήν τινων Lxx*Ex.*1.14:—Pass., ib.*Ez.*9.4.

**κατοδύρομαι** [ῡ], *deplore*, τὸ ζῆν Pl.*Ax.*367d; τὴν ἑαυτοῦ τύχην D.S.13.58; ταυτὶ -όμενος X.Eph.5.1, cf. Parth.26.4:—Pass., *to be mourned*, *Arch.Pap.*1.220 (Ptol.).

**κατόζω**, *spread a stink*, σαυτοῦ, i.e. *tuo foetore fruitus*, Arr.*Epict.* 4.11.16.

**κάτοθεν**, later form for κάτωθεν, *PHib.*1.110.76 (iii B.C.).

**κατοιάδες**, αἱ, (οἶς) *leading the sheep*, αἶγες Paus.9.13.4.

**κάτ-οιδα**, -οισθα, inf. κατειδέναι, part. κατειδώς (Locr. καταειδώς *Schwyzer* 366 *A* 6 (Tolophon, iii B.C.)), pf. (in pres. sense), plpf. κατῄδη (in impf. sense):—*know well, understand*, c. acc. rei, ἄστρων ὁμήγυριν A.*Ag.*4; οὐδὲν κάτοισθα τῶν σαυτοῦ πέρι S.*Ph.*553; θεσφάτων βάξιν κατῄδη Id.*Tr.*87; φύλλον νώδυνον Id.*Ph.*44; κατειδὼς τὴν γυναικείαν φύσιν, ὡς.. ἥδεται Eub.43; μηδὲν κατειδώς, ἀλλὰ προσποιούμενος Men.628; ἵν' εὖ κατειδῇς S.*Ichn.*164. 2. c. acc. pers., *know by sight, recognize*, τὸν βοτῆρα Id.*OT*1048, cf. *Tr.*418, E.*Or.*1183, 1521. 3. abs., esp. in part., οὐ κατειδώς *unwittingly*, Id.*Med.*992 (lyr.), *Supp.* 1033. 4. c. part., *know well that*.., κάτισθι μὴ πολλοὺς ἔτι τρόχους.. τελῶν S.*Ant.*1064. 5. folld. by an interrog., οὐ κάτοιδ' ὅπως λέγεις I *understand* not how... Id.*Aj.*270; οὐ κ. ὅτῳ τρόπῳ.. E.*Hipp.*1245. 6. c. inf., *know how* to, ἢ κάτοισθα δηλῶσαι λόγῳ; S.*OT*1041.

**κατοιδέω**, pf. -ῴδηκα, *to be swollen*, Sor.2.43.

**κατοίησις**, εως, ἡ, *self-conceit*, Plu.2.1119b (pl.).

**κατοικ-άς**, άδος, ἡ, poet. fem. of κατοικίδιος, στρουθός Nic.*Al.* 60, 535. **-εσία**, ἡ, = κατοίκησις, Lxx*Ps.*106(107).36, Eust.106. 44. **-έσια** (sc. ἱερά), τά, *anniversary festival of a colony*, *EM*221. 3. ※**-έω**, *settle in, colonize*, πόλιν Hdt.7.164; γῆν E.*Med.*10; τοῖς κατοικεῖν ἐθέλουσι τὰν πόλιν Decr.Byz.ap.D.18.91: generally, *inhabit*, τόπους S.*Ph.*40; τὴν Ἀσίαν *SIG*557.17 (Magn. Mae., iii B.C.), etc.:—Pass., *to be dwelt in* or *inhabited*, opp. κατοικίζομαι (to be just founded), Arist.*Pol.*1266ᵇ2. 2. abs., *settle, dwell*, ζητοῦσα.. ποῦ κατοικοίης S.*OC*362; ἵνα χρὴ κατοικεῖν Ar.*Av.*153; ἐν δόμοις, ἐν ἄστεσι, E.*Hel.* 1651, Pl.*Lg.*666e, etc.; αὐτόθι Th.3.34; ἐν μοναρχίᾳ Isoc.1.36; ἐπὶ γῆς *Apoc.*3.10; esp. of non-citizens, Ἐφέσιοι καὶ οἱ -οῦντες *SIG*352.4 (Ephesus, iv B.C.), cf. 633.67 (Milet., ii B.C.):—pf. and plpf. Pass., *to have been planted* or *settled*, κατὰ κώμας Hdt.1.96, cf. 2.102; κ. νῆσον, τὴν μεσόγειαν, Id.4.8, Th.1.120. II. *administer, govern*, οἱ τὰς πόλεις -οῦντες Phld.*Rh.*2.225S.:—more freq. in Pass., κατῴκηνται καλῶς, of Athens, S.*OC*1004; ὀρθῶς κ., of Sparta, Pl.*Lg.*683a. III. intr. of cities, *lie, be situated*, ἐν τοῖς πεδίοις ib.677c, cf. 682c: also c. acc. loci, τὰς τὴν Ἀσίαν κατοικούσας *which are situated in*.., Isoc. 5.123. **-ησις**, εως, ἡ, *settling in* a place, διὰ τὴν ταύτῃ κ. Th. 2.15. II. *dwelling, abode*, Pl.*Ti.*71b, *Criti.*115c, Lxx*Ge.*10.30, etc.; τὴν κ. εἶχεν ἐν τοῖς μνήμασι *Ev.Marc.*5.3; *inhabited district*, ἡ κατὰ τὴν Ἰταλίαν κ. Ath.12.523e. **-ητήριον**, τό, *dwelling-place, abode*, Lxx*Ex.*12.20; κ. θεοῦ, δαιμονίων, *Ep.Eph.*2.22, *Apoc.* 18.2. **-ητήριος**, α, ον, = κατοικίδιος, ὄρνεις Sor.1.51. **-ία**, ἡ, *habitation*, βαρβάρων Hecat.119J.; τόπος εὐφυὴς πρὸς κ. Plb.5.78. 5; ὑγιεινὴν ποιεῖν τὴν κ. Str.5.4.8; *farm, village*, Plb.2.32.4, etc.: generally, *dwelling-place*, *Act.Ap.*17.26; *domicile*, Mitteis*Chr.*31 i 23 (ii B.C.). 2. *settlement, colony*, Str.5.4.11; esp. of *military colonies* in Egypt, *PTeb.*61(*b*).227 (ii B.C.), etc.; also, = Lat. *colonia*, Str.6. 2.5, Plu.*Ant.*16, App.*BC*5.19; κατοικίαι πόλεων foundation of *colonies*, Plu.*Pomp.*47. 3. *body of residents* in a foreign *city*, ἡ κ. τῶν ἐν Ἱεραπόλει κατοικούντων Ἰουδαίων *IGRom.*4.834. ※**-ια**, τά, *household goods*, *GDI*2141.22 (Delph.). ※**-ίδιος**, ον, (α, ον only *Gp.*1. 3.8) *living in* or *about a house, domestic*, μῦς Theopomp.Hist.258(*a*); [σκύλαξ] Nic.Dam.56J.; ὄρνεις *Gp.* l.c., 2.35.5; ὄρνις Longus 3.6; οἱ κ. *stay-at-home* historians, Luc.*Hist.Conscr.*37; κ. βίος Ph.2.378, D.S. 3.53; κ. κατατάσιες *domestic* means or methods of extension, Hp. *Art.*78; τὰ κ. τῶν ἔργων *household* duties, Hierocl.p.62A.; κατοικίδιοι (sc. θεοί), οἱ, = Lat. *Penates*, *Gloss.* ※**-ίζω**, Cret. **καταϝοικίδδω** *Schwyzer* 175.2 (Gortyn): Att. fut. -ιῶ A.*Pr.*725:—*settle, establish*, κ. τινὰς ἐς Μέμφιν Hdt.2.154, cf. Ar.*Pax*205, Decr.ap.D.18. 182, etc.; κ. πόλιν εἰς τόπον *place* it.., Pl.*R.*370e; γυναῖκας ἐς φῶς ἡλίου κ. E.*Hipp.*617, cf. Pl.*Ti.*70a, Critias *Fr.*25.38, etc.; κ. ψυχὴν ἐν τάφῳ S.*Ant.*1069; ἐκγόνους ἐν τόπῳ Pl.*Criti.*113c; ἐλπίδας ἔν τινι κ. *plant* them in his mind, A.*Pr.*252; κ. τινὰ χώρᾳ S.*OC*637; τινὰς ἐκ Ῥώμης εἰς τὴν Καμερίαν κ. Plu.*Rom.*24:—Pass., *to be settled*, ἐν Αἰγύπτῳ Hdt.2.154; περὶ τὸ ἧπαρ Pl.*Ti.*71d; τοὺς ἐπὶ τοῦ Πόντου κατῳκισμένους App.*Mith.*15; κ. Λατώσιον *Schwyzer* l.c. II. c. acc. loci, *colonize, people* a place, αἳ Θεμισκυράν ποτε κατοικιοῦσιν A. *Pr.*725; Μέγαρα Hdt.5.76, cf. E.*Andr.*295 (lyr.), Th.6.76, etc.; τὴν Σικελίαν Pl.*Ep.*357a; τὸν Εὔξεινον πόντον κ. πόλεσι λαμπραῖς Ath.12. 523e:—Pass., *to be settled*, ἡ Ἑλλὰς -ῳκίζετο Th.1.12, cf. 2.17; *to be founded, established*, Isoc.9.19; πόλεις κατοικιζόμεναι εὐθύς, opp. ἤδη κατοικούμεναι, Arist.*Pol.*1266ᵇ1. III. Med., *establish oneself, settle*, Th.2.102; ἐν Τροιζῆνι, εἰς Αἴγιναν, Isoc.19.23, 24. IV. *bring home and re-establish there, restore to one's country*, A.*Eu.*756, Pl.*Ep.* 357b. **-ικός**, ή, όν, *assigned to* κάτοικοι, κλῆρος *PTeb.*105.13 (ii B.C.), etc.; γῆ *POxy.*46.22 (100 A.D.); ὑποθήκη ib.2134.14 (ii A.D.). **-ίς**, ίδος, ἡ, v.l. for κατοικάς, Nic.*Th.*558. **-ῐσις**, εως, ἡ, *settlement*, Pl. *R.*453b, *Lg.*969c: pl., Th.6.77, App.*BC*5.19. **-ισμός**, ὁ, = foreg., in pl., Pl.*Lg.*683a, Arist.*Mete.*351ᵇ22; ἐς -οικισμόν for *habitation*, J. *AJ*4.7.4. **-ιστής**, οῦ, ὁ, *founder of a city*, Sm.*Je.*50(27).7, Hsch. s.v. ἀποικιστής.

**κατοικο-δομέω**, *build upon* or *in* a place, τι δημόσιον X.*Ath.*3.4; τὰς ὁδοὺς Arist.*Ath.*50.2:—Pass., of the place, *to be built on*, Lxx *Ge.*36.43, Str.5.4.5. II. *squander in building*, Plu.*Publ.*15 (but simply, *use in building*, πλίνθου τῆς -δομηθείσης *PPetr.*3 p.141 (iii B.C.)). III. *shut up in a house*, Is.8.41 (s.v.l.), cf. Harp. s.v. κατῳκοδόμησε. 2. Pass., *to be built up, blocked up*, σανίσι D.C.66. 25. **-νομέω**, *manage well*, τὴν χρείαν Plu.*Brut.*36:—Med., πάντα *OGI*339.23 (Sestus, ii B.C.).

**κάτοικος**, ὁ, *inhabitant*, Arist.*Oec.*1352ᵃ33, Plb.5.65.10, al.; esp. of *military colonists*, οἱ ἐν Μαγνησίᾳ κ. *OGI*229.71 (Smyrna, iii B.C.); in Egypt, *PTeb.*30.7 (ii B.C.), etc.; κ. is f.l. for κάτοικτος in A.*Ag.* 1286.

**κατοικοφθορέω**, *ruin utterly*, τὴν πόλιν Plu.*Alc.*23.

**κατοικτ-είρω** or **-ίρω**, irreg. aor. -οικτείρησα Lxx 4*Ma.*8.20, 12.2:—*have mercy* or *compassion on*, τινα Hdt.1.45, 4.167, al., S.*OT*13, E. *Heracl.*445, *IG*9(2).255 (Pharsalus); τὸ τῆς μητρὸς γῆρας Lxx 4*Ma.* 8.20. II. intr., *feel, show compassion*, κατοικτείραντα ἐρωτᾶν ask *in compassion*, Arist.*Rh.*1393ᵇ28; -οικτίραι ὡς βραχὺς εἴη ὁ βίος *feel compassion at the thought* that.., Hdt.7.46. **-ίζω**, Att. fut. -ιῶ A.*Supp.*903:—foreg., c. acc. rei, πόνους S.*OC*384, etc.; λακὶς χιτῶνος ἔργον (i.e. χιτῶνα) οὐ κατοικτιεῖ A. l.c.:—Med., *bewail oneself, utter lamentations*, Hdt.2.121.γ', 3.156, A.*Eu.*121 (prob.); τί κατοικτίζει μάτην; Id.*Pr.*36:—aor. Pass. κατῳκτίσθην E.*IA*686: c. acc., as in Act., στρατὸν A.*Pers.*1062 (lyr.). II. causal, *excite pity*, ῥήματα.. κατοικτίσαντά πως S.*OC*1282. **-ῐσις**, εως, ἡ, *compassion*, ἡ πρὸς αὐτὴν κ. X.*Cyr.*6.1.47. **-ος**, ον, *pitiable*, prob. for κάτοικος, A.*Ag.* 1286.

**κατοιμώζω**, *bewail, lament*, E.*Andr.*1159.

**κατοιν-όομαι**, Pass., *to be drunken*, κατῳνωμένος Pl.*Lg.*815c. **-ος**, ον, *drunken with wine*, E.*Ion* 553 (troch.). 2. *addicted to wine*, D.S.5.26. 3. *wine-coloured*, Vett.Val.1.13.

**κατοινύσαι**· κατακρύψαι, Hsch.

**κατοίομαι**, *to be conceited of oneself*, Lxx *Hb.*2.5, Ph.*Fr.*99 H.

**κατοίσεται**, v. καταφέρω.

**κατοιχνέω**, *spread over, fill*, ὀμφὰ κ. τόπου S.*Ichn.*321 (lyr.).

**κατοίχομαι**, *have gone*, οἱ κατοιχόμενοι *the departed, dead*, D.43.67, 60.8, Arist.*VV*1250ᵇ21, *PGnom.*17, Aret.*SA*2.4: sg., Nic.*Fr.*108, *BMus.Inscr.*1032.19 (Teos), 1032*a* (Ephesus).

**κατοιωνίζομαι**, *take as an omen*, Phalar.*Ep.*14².2.

**κατοκλάζω**, = ὀκλάζω, Opp.*C.*3.473:—Med., Str.3.4.15. II. *flag, grow inattentive*, Anon. *in Rh.*233.17.

**κατοκνέω**, *shrink from*, c. inf., ὅπως.. μὴ κατοκνήσεις κτανεῖν Αἴγισθον S.*El.*956; κ. ὀρθοῦσθαι Hp.*Mochl.*20; κ. γῆν περιιδεῖν τμηθεῖσαν Th.2.18; μὴ κατόκνει.. πορεύεσθαι Isoc.1.19: c. acc., τὴν στρατείαν App.*Mith.*110: abs., *shrink back*, A.*Pr.*67, Th.2.94, Isoc.6.75, D.29.1, etc.; *to be sluggish*, εἰ τῇ δυνάμει κ. [ἡ ψυχή] Phld.*Mus.*p.30 K.

**κατοκωχ-ή**, ἡ, = κατοχή, *possession*, τῆς χώρας Anon.ap.Suid.; *mental grasp*, τῶν εἰρημένων Zeno *Stoic.*1.58. II. *being possessed, inspiration*, θείᾳ μοίρᾳ καὶ κατοκωχῇ Pl.*Ion* 536c; ἀπὸ Μουσῶν κ. Id. *Phdr.*245a, cf. Ph.1.174, al., Dam.*Isid.*32:—the forms κατακωχή, -ιμος are late and incorrect; cf. ἀνοκωχή, συνοκωχή. **-ιμος**, η, ον, *held in possession, held as a pledge*, [χωρίον] Is.2.28 (vulg. κατόχιμον); τὸ κ. Hsch. 2. *capable of being possessed* by a feeling or passion, ὑπὸ κινήσεως Arist.*Pol.*1342ᵃ8; ἐκ τῆς ἀρετῆς Id.*EN*1179ᵇ9; τῷ πάθει *possessed*, Id.*HA*572ᵃ32; *inclined*, πρός τι Id.*Pol.*1269ᵇ30: abs., *frantic*, Luc.*JTr.*30 (vulg. κατόχιμος).

**κατολῐγωρέω**, *neglect utterly*, τοῦ δικαίου Lys.9.16; [ἀνδρός] Longin.13.2, cf. Jul.*Or.*1.2a:—Pass., *SIG*888.153 (Scaptopara, iii A.D.). 2. abs., *to be negligent*, ἐν τοῖς ἀλλοτρίοις Diogenian.2.75, cf. *PSI*4.426.3 (iii B.C.); κατολιγωρήσαντες *with contempt*, Arist.*Rh.Al.*1421ᵃ15.

**κατολισθ-άνω**, later -αίνω Gal.7.36, Agath.1.1: Ep. aor. 2 κατόλισθε A.R.1.390: aor. 1 -ωλίσθησα Alciphr.3.64: pf. -ωλίσθηκα Orib.50.42.3:—*slip, sink down*, Str.4.6.6; of hernia, Gal.l.c.; of a building, *collapse*, Agath.1.10: metaph., ἐς πάθος, εἰς ἔρωτα, Luc.*Abd.*28, Alciphr.l.c.; εἰς τὸ βλάσφημον Ael.*Fr.*60; εἰς πλεονεξίαν Agath.1.1. **-ησις**, εως, ἡ, *slipping down*, Sor.1.108, Gal.19.447, Paul.Aeg.6.65.

**κατόλλυμι**, in pf. Act., *perish utterly*, νεολαία.. κατὰ πᾶσ' ὄλωλεν A.*Pers.*670 (lyr.).

**κατολολύζω**, *shriek over*, θύματος A.*Ag.*1118 (lyr.).

**κατολοφύρομαι** [ῡ], aor. 1 -ωλοφυράμην Diog.Oen.1:—*bewail*, c. acc., E.*IT*644 (lyr.), X.*Cyr.*7.3.16; τινῶν τὸν βίον Diog.Oen. l.c.; κ. πολλὰ ἑαυτόν D.H.5.12: abs., E.*Or.*339 (lyr.).

**κατομβρ-έομαι**, Pass., *to be rained on*, Plb.34.1.16, Str.16.1.5: metaph., ὄμματα κατομβρηθέντα γόοισιν *AP*7.389 (Apollonid.). **-ία**, ἡ, *heavy rain*, Lyd.*Ost.*30, al.: pl., ib.58. **-ίζομαι**, Pass., = κατομβρέομαι, *Gp.*2.8.4. **-ιμος**, ον, *rainy*, ἔτος Orph.*Fr.*252. **-ιος**, ον, = foreg., dub. l. in Ph.2.515. **-ισις**, εως, ἡ, = κατομβρία, Lyd. *Ost.*40. **-ος**, ον, *rainy*, νότος Arist.*Vent.*973ᵇ9; ἔαρ *Gp.*1.12.24. II. *wet with rain, drenched*, Thphr.*CP*3.12.1, 3.22.3: metaph., ὄμματ' ἐρώντων *AP*5.144 (Asclep.).

**κατόμνῡμι**, aor. -ώμοσα E.*Hel.*835:—*confirm by oath*, τινί τι Ar.*Av.*444. 2. c. acc., *call to witness, swear by*, τὴν ἐμὴν ψυχὴν E.*Or.*1517 (troch.), etc.; κ. τὼ θεώ Ar.*Ec.*158: c. dupl. acc., ἁγνὸν ὅρκον σὸν κάρα κατώμοσα E.*Hel.* l.c.: c. gen., κ. τῆς κεφαλῆς Anon.ap.Suid. 3. *swear*, c. inf., *IG*12(9).1273.1 (Eretria, vi B.C.). II. Med. = Act., *tender an oath*, Antipho Soph.*Oxy.*1364.140, Arist.*Rh.*1377ᵃ16, *PMagd.*26.13 (iii B.C.): *swear by*, τοὺς θεοὺς Aristaenet.2.20: c. acc. et inf., D.39.4, cf. Paus.6.18.3. 2. c. dat., *take an oath against, accuse on oath*, Hdt.6.65 (gen. as v.l.): abs., ib.69.

**κατομόργνῡμι**, *wipe clean off*, Hsch.

⊛**κατομφάλιος** [φᾰ], ον, *from the navel*, v.l. for παρομφ-, Nic.*Th.*290.

**κατονειδ-ίζω**, = ὀνειδίζω, D.H.11.42. **-ιστήρ**, ῆρος, ὁ, = ὀνειδιστήρ, Man.4.235.

**κατονεύομαι**, v.l. for ὀνεύομαι, Gal.19.126.

**κατονίναμαι**, *enjoy*, in aor. 1, σαυτῆς κατόναιο Ar.*Ec.*917 (lyr.); τέκνων, σπορῶν, καρπῶν, οὐσίας κατόνασθαι *SIG*826 C 15 (Delph., ii B.C.).

**κατονομάζω**, *name*, Str.7.3.2, al.; ἀπό τινος ib.13.1.48 (dub. l.):—Pass., ζωμὸς κατωνόμασται Anaxandr.34.5; *to be named*, Arist.*EE* 1221ᵇ10, Thphr.*Od.*2; *to be expressed in terms*, of numbers, Archim. *Aren.*1.3; τὰ -ωνομασμένα the *aforesaid*, Meno *Iatr.*11.33, Philum. *Ven.*27.3. II. Pass., *to be betrothed*, c. dat., Plb.5.43.1, Hsch. s.v. τᾶλις; *to be devoted* to the gods, D.H.1.16, Phalar.*Ep.*84.1.

⊛**κατόνομαι**, *censure bitterly, depreciate, abuse*, c. acc., Hdt.2.172: aor., μή με κατονοσθῇς πρὸς τὰς.. πυραμίδας ib.136.

**κατονομ-αξία**, ἡ, Dor. for κατονομασία, *expression* of numbers, Archim.*Aren.*1.7 (prob.):—also **-αξις**, εως, ἡ, ib.3.1. **-ασία**, ἡ, *name, denomination*, Str.1.2.34 (pl.). **-αστος**, ον, *named*, Hdn. *Epim.*203.

**κάτοξ-ος**, ον, *drenched with vinegar, over-sour*, Posidipp.1.7. **-ύνω**, *hasten on*, τι Artemon *Fr.*12. **-υς**, εια, υ, strengthd. for ὀξύς, *very sharp, piercing*, βοή Ar.*V.*471; of disease, *acute*, Hp.*Aph.*1.7 (cf. Gal.18(2).254), Aret.*SA*1.7, *CA*1.10; τὸ κ. τῆς ὀρέξεως Hld.1.26.

**κατοπάζω**, *follow hard upon, tread on the heels of*, αἰδὼ δέ τ' ἀναιδείη κατοπάζῃ Hes.*Op.*324.

**κατόπερ**, Ion. for καθόπερ (q.v.).

**κατ-όπιθεν**, Adv., = κατόπισθεν, *POxy.*2146.8 (iii A.D.), *Gloss.* ⊛**-όπιν**, Adv., (v. ὄπις) *behind, after*, Hp.*Mul.*1.12, Th.4.32, X.*Cyr.*1.4.21: c. gen., Ar.*Eq.*625, Pl.*Prt.*316a; κ. ἐπὶ τῷ στόλῳ Plb.1.50.5; ἐκ τῶν κ. Id.2.67.2: metaph., κ. χωρεῖν τῶν εἰργασμένων *fall short of, fail in describing*, Chor.p.23 B. II. of Time, *after, hereafter*, f.l. in Thgn.280; εὐθὺς κ. Thphr.*HP*7.13.7; κ. ἑορτῆς ἥκομεν 'too late for the fair', Pl.*Grg.*447a; ἡ κ. [ἡμέρα] Plb.1.46.7, Phld.*Ind.Sto.*19; ὁ κ. ἐνιαυτός Plu.*Cam.*43; σε μένει καὶ κ. δάκρυα *AP*9.70 (Mnasalc.). ⊛**-όπισθεν**, in Poets also -θε, Adv. of Place, *behind, after*, Il.23.505, Od.22.92: c. gen., 12.148, Pancrat.*Oxy.*1085.14: metaph., of rank, ἃ δ' Ἀρετὰ κ. θνατοῖς ἀμελεῖται E.*IA* 1093 (lyr.). II. of Time, *hereafter, afterwards, henceforth*, Od.22.40, 24.546; ὁ κ. λογισμός Pl.*Ti.*57e, cf. Thgn.280; also κ. λιποίμην Od.21.116, cf. Pl.*R.*363d. **-οπίσω**, Adv., = foreg., Lxx *Jd.*18.22.

**κατοπτάω**, *roast* or *bake thoroughly*, Archestr.*Fr.*13.6, Phld.*D.*1.19, Str.15.2.2, 16.4.13:—Pass., *to be well baked*, Arist.*Aud.*802ᵇ2, 803ᵃ29; *to be overheated*, of the blood, Gal.7.246.

**κατοπτ-εία**, ἡ, *spying, reconnoitring*, J.*AJ*18.9.7. II. = κάτοψις, οὐρανοῦ *Corp.Herm.*3.3 (-οπτία). **-ευσις**, εως, ἡ, *observation*, Procl.*Par.Ptol.*155, *Gloss.*:—also written καθόπτ-, ib. **-ευτήριος**, ον, *fit for looking out*, τὸ κ., = σκοπιά, Sch.E.*Ph.*233. ⊛**-εύω**, *spy out*, ὠτακουστεῖν καὶ κ. v.l. for διοπτ- in X.*Cyr.*8.2.10; *observe closely*, ἅπαντα, φύσιν ἀνθρώπων, Plb.1.4.11, D.H.*Lys.*7; *reconnoitre*, Plb.3.45.3; of a night-policeman, *POxy.*1033.13 (iv A.D.); *visit, explore* a country, Plb.34.1.8, 34.5.9; τὸν οὐράνιον χῶρον Arist.*Mu.*391ᵃ10; ἐπὶ τοῦ Πηγάσου τὸν οὐρανόν Asclep.Myrl.ap.Sch.Il.6.155; κ. ἐς.. *AP* 5.122 (Phld.):—Pass., Plb.3.37.11, Str.2.4.6; *to be observed*, S.*Aj.*829; μὴ κατοπτευθῶ παρών Id.*Ph.*124; ἐκ τῶν φαινομένων κατωπτευμένων Phld.*Sign.*25. II. Astrol., *exert a baleful aspect*, Petos.ap. Vett.Val.112.37. **-ήρ**, ῆρος, ὁ, *spy, scout*, A.*Th.*36 (pl.). II. = ἑδροδιαστολεύς, Hp.*Fist.*3, *Haem.*5 (κάτοπτρον Erot.). **-ήριος**, ον, = κατοπτευτήριος, χῶρος Str.9.3.15; κατοπτήριον, τό, *height which commands a view*, *Delph.*3(2).136. **-ης**, ου, ὁ, = κατοπτήρ I, *h.Merc.*372, Hdt.3.17, 21, etc. 2. *one who visits* or *explores*, κλιμάτων καὶ ἐθνῶν Vett.Val.330.15; *one who contemplates*, οὐρανοῦ Ph. Bybl.ap.Eus.*PE*1.10. II. *overseer*, κατόπτης δ' εἴμ' ἐγὼ τῶν πραγμάτων A.*Th.*41; ὦ Ζεῦ διόπτα καὶ κατόπτα Ar.*Ach.*435. 2. κατόπτας, ὁ, title of an officer in Boeot. towns, *IG*7.303.21 (Oropus), 3172.140 (Orchomenus).

**κατόπτησις**, εως, ἡ, *roasting* or *baking*, Phld.*D.*1.19, Gal.11.694.

**κατοπτικὸς** νόμος law *concerning the* κατόπτης II. 2, *IG*7.3073.88 (Lebad.).

**κατοπτίλλεταί** μοι, = δοκεῖ μοι, Dius ap.Stob.4.21.16; Dor. word, cf. ὀπτίλος.

**κάτοπτος** (A), ον, (ὄψομαι) *visible*, ὥστε μὴ κάτοπτα εἶναι Th.8.104; χωρίον ἄερκτον καὶ πανταχόθεν κ. Lys.7.28. II. c. gen., *looking down over*, πορθμοῦ κάτοπτον πρῶνα (Canter for κάτοπτρον) A.*Ag.*307.

**κάτοπτος** (B), ον, *dried-up*, of a kind of myrrh, Dsc.1.64; ἡ ἐκ τῶν καμίνων κ. γῆ Id.5.158; *over-baked*, ἄρτοι Ath.Med.ap.Orib.1.9.2, cf. *Gloss.*

**κατοπτρ-ίζω**, *show as in a mirror* or *by reflexion*, τοῦ -ίζοντος [τὴν ἶριν] ἀστέρος *Placit.*3.5.11:—Pass., *to be mirrored*, Anon.*Oxy.*1609.19. II. Med., *look into a mirror, behold oneself in it*, Zeno *Stoic.*1.66, S.E.*P.*1.48, Ath.15.687c, etc. 2. *behold as in a mirror*, ἰδέαν Ph.1.107; δόξαν Κυρίου 2*Ep.Cor.*3.18 (but here perh. *reflect*). **-ικός**, ή, όν, *of* or *in a mirror*, φαντασία *Placit.*3.1.2; ἐμφάσεις ib.3.2.1; τὰ κ. *reflected images*, ib.3.5.6; but, *Theory of Reflexion*, title of work by Hero, Damian.*Opt.*14:—also **-κή**, ἡ, Procl. in *Euc.*p.40 F.; **-κόν**, τό, Hero *Deff.*135.12. Adv. -κῶς *by reflexion*, βλέπεσθαι *Placit.*2.24.1. **-ῖτις** λίθος *reflecting* stone found in Cappadocia, Plin.*HN* 37.152.

**κατοπτροειδής**, ές, *like a mirror*, prob. l. in *Placit.*2.25.14, cf. Alex.Aphr. *in Mete.*144.6.

**κάτοπτρον**, τό, *mirror*, κ. εἴδους χαλκός A.*Fr.*393, cf. E.*Hipp.*429, etc.; τίς γὰρ κατόπτρῳ καὶ τυφλῷ κοινωνία; Com.ap.Stob.4.30.6a; κ. ἀνδρομήκη Phld.*Rh.*2.206 S.; ἐν κατόπτρῳ.. κατιδεῖν εἴδωλα παρέχοντι Pl.*Ti.*71b; ὥσπερ ἐν κ. ἑαυτὸν ὁρῶν Id.*Phdr.*255d, etc.; = μηλωτίς, Hp.ap.Erot. (v. κατοπτήρ II): metaph., εὖ γὰρ ἐξεπίσταμαι ὁμιλίας κ. companionship's true *mirror*, A.*Ag.*839; ἡ Ὀδύσσεια καλὸν ἀνθρωπίνου βίου κ. Alcid.ap.Arist.*Rh.*1406ᵇ13; κ. φύσεος, of a wine-cup, Theopomp.Com.32.3:—spelt **κάτροπτον** in Att. Inscrr., *IG*2².1471.47, 1544.58 (iv B.C.), al., and this form shd. be restored in Pl.*Cra.*414c: **κάθοπτρον** shd. perh. be restored in *Annuario* 4/5.463.

**κατοργανίζω**, *sound with music through*, τῆς ἐρημίας *AP*9.264 (Apollonid. or Phil.).

**κατοργάω**, strengthd. for ὀργάω, Hsch., Phot.

**κατοργιάζω**, *initiate in orgies, prepare for them*, Plu.*Sol.*12:—Pass., Id.2.766b, *Fr.*6.2, Luc.*Trag.*125.

**κατοργόω**, pf. Med. κατωργώμεθα *we have quarrelled with each other*, *PMagd.*10.3 (iii B.C.).

**κατορέγομαι**, Med., strengthd. for ὀρέγομαι, Simp. *in Epict.*p.6 D.

**κάτορθ-ος**, ον, *straight*, Mnesith.ap.Orib.8.38.4. **-όω**, *set upright, erect*, δέμας E.*Hipp.*1445, *Andr.*1080; *set straight* a fractured or dislocated bone, Hp.*Fract.*16, al. (Med., *have it set straight*, 8, al.); κ. τὰ κηρία, of bees, Arist.*HA*625ᵇ19. 2. metaph., *keep straight, set right*, πολλά τοι σμικροὶ λόγοι.. κατώρθωσαν βροτοὺς S.*El.*416; κατορθοῦντος φρένα Id.*OC*1487; κ. τοὺς ἀγωνιζομένους *make* them *prosper*, D.18.290. b. *accomplish successfully, bring to a successful issue*, τὸν

ἀγῶνα Lys.18.13; πολλὰ καὶ μεγάλα Pl.*Men.*99c; εἰ γὰρ ἐν ὧν ἐπεβούλευσεν κατώρθωσεν D.21.106; ὁδόν Id.24.7; μηδὲν ἁμαρτεῖν ἐστὶ θεῶν καὶ πάντα κ. Epigr.ib.18.289; τουτὶ κατωρθώκαμεν περὶ ἐπιστήμης Pl.*Tht.*203b, cf. E.*Hel.*1067; τὰς ἐπιβολάς Plb.10.2.5, etc.:—Pass., *succeed, prosper*, Hdt.1.120, E.*Hipp.*680, Arist.*EN*1106b26; ἐπειδὴ δρᾶν κατώρθωσαι φρενί *thou hast rightly purposed*, A.*Ch.*512; κατωρθωμένος, of works of art, *successful*, Str.9.1.17, al.; τὰ μάλισθ' ὑπὸ τῶν τεχνικωτάτων -ούμενα Phld.*Vit.*p.33 J.; ὅσα κατώρθωται αὐτῶν *the most perfect examples*, Plot.5.8.2: Gramm., βαρυνόμενον τὸ "ἔστε" κατώρθωται *is correctly accented*, A.D.*Synt.*263.14. II. intr. as in Pass., *go on prosperously, succeed*, opp. πταίειν, Th.6.12, cf. D.11.11, Men.*Epit.*339; opp. ἡττᾶσθαι, ἔν τινι Isoc.4.124; opp. ἀτυχεῖν, ib.48; opp. ἁμαρτάνειν, Arist.*EN*1106b31, Chrysipp.*Stoic.*2.295; κ. τῷ σώματι Pl.*Lg.*654c; of success in war, X.*Mem.*3.1.3; τῇ μάχῃ, τοῖς ὅλοις, Plb.2.70.6, 3.48.2; περί τινας τῶν πράξεων Isoc.7.11; τὸ κατορθοῦν *success*, D.2.20. III. Med. in sense of Act. I. 2 b, τῇ πόλει κατορθωσάμενος ἀγαθά *IPE*1².34.28 (Olbia, i B.C.). **-ωμα**, ατος, τό, *success*, opp. εὐτύχημα, Arist.*MM*1199a13, cf. Plb.1.19.12, Str.15.1.54, D.S.13.22, Plu.*Mar.*10; of literary style, Longin.33.1, 36.2: pl., opp. ἀποτεύγματα, Phld.*Vit.*p.35 J.; v.l. for διορθ-, *Act.Ap.*24.2 (pl.). 2. *that which is done rightly, virtuous action*, in pl., opp. ἁμαρτήματα, Chrysipp.*Stoic.*2.295, al., cf. *IG*5(2).268.15 (Mantinea, i B.C.), etc.; τῶν καθηκόντων τὰ τέλεια, = τὰ κ., *Stoic.*3.134. 3. *perfection*, τέλος καὶ πέρας καὶ κ. Herm.*in Phdr.*p.173 A., cf. S.E.*M.*9.16. 4. Gramm., *correct use*, opp. βαρβαρισμός, Ph.1.124. **-ωσις**, εως, ἡ, *setting straight*, of a fractured bone, Hp.*Fract.*26 (pl.), *Art.*71. 2. *setting up*, τοῦ θρόνου Lxx *Ps.*96(97).2. II. *successful accomplishment* of a thing, *success*, Arist.*Rh.*1380b4, Plb.9.19.4: in pl., *successes*, Id.39.7.7. 2. *setting right, reform, amendment*, τῆς πολιτείας Id.3.30.2; τῶν πραγμάτων Id.2.53.3. 3. as philos. term, *right action*, = foreg. 2, Chrysipp.*Stoic.*3.21 (pl.), al. **-ωτέον**, *one must correctly estimate*, Ptol.*Tetr.*193. 2. *one must set* dislocated limbs, Paul.Aeg.6.120. **-ωτής**, οῦ, ὁ, *one who successfully accomplishes*, πραγμάτων, ἔργων, Vett.Val.48.3, Max.Tyr.21.6. 2. τριῶν ἀνδρῶν δημοσίων πραγμάτων κ., trans. of Lat. *triumvir reipublicae constituendae*, *Mon.Anc.Gr.*4.2. **-ωτικός**, ή, όν, *likely* or *able to succeed*, opp. ἁμαρτητικός, Arist.*EN*1104b33; *successful*, ἐν ταῖς μάχαις Plu.*Phil.*8; μεγάλων [πραγμάτων] Vett.Val.15.10; *virtuous*, ἔρως Herm.*in Phdr.*p.170 A.

**κατορουβάν**· ἡ ἀγορά, Hsch.

**κατορούω**, *rush downwards*, *h.Cer.*341.

**κάτορρα**· ἡ καταρόα, βωμὸς ἐνόδιος (βώμενος ἐνόδειος cod.), Hsch.

**κατορρωδέω**, Ion. **καταρρ-** (q.v.), *fear, dread*, c. acc., Plb.14.1.5, Luc.*Dem.Enc.*3: abs., *to be afraid*, μή.. Plb.10.3.5, cf. Onos.11.3.

**κατ-ορυκτός**, ή, όν, *deep-buried*, Suid. **-όρυξις**, εως, ἡ, *burying deep*, Thphr.*HP*5.7.7. ✻**-ορύσσω**, Att. **-ττω**, fut. Pass. -ορυχθήσομαι cj. in Antipho 3.2.10, -ορῠχήσομαι cj. in Ar.*Av.*394 (lyr.): pf. Pass. -ορώρυγμαι Antipho 3.3.12, etc., later κατώρυγμαι *LW*1075 (Apollonia ad Rhyndacum), Str.9.3.8, cf. Moer.p.240 P.: aor. 2 inf. Pass. -ορῠγῆναι Arr.*Epict.*4.8.36:—*bury, sink in the earth*, Hdt.2.41, Hp.*Fract.*13; ζώοντας ἐπὶ κεφαλὴν κατώρυξε Hdt.3.35, cf. 7.114; ἐν τῇ κεφαλῇ Ar.*Av.*475; πατέρα ζῶντα κ. X.*Mem.*1.2.55; κ. κατὰ γῆς Hdt.8.36; κατὰ τῆς γῆς Ar.*Pl.*238; τινὰ εἰς πηλόν (of poets' descriptions) Pl.*R.*363d; [τὰ ᾠὰ] εἰς τὴν κόπρον Arist.*HA*559b2:—Pass., ζῶντες κατορωρύγμεθα Antipho 3.3.12, cf. X.*An.*5.8.11, *Com.Adesp.*1224; τὰ -ορυττόμενα κατὰ γῆς Thphr.*HP*5.7.6, cf. Archestr.*Fr.*62.21; of metals, *lie buried*, Pl.*Euthd.*288e; of money, *to be buried*, D.27.53 (metaph., 29.49); ἐν πορφυρίσι -ορωρυγμένος, of Sardanapallus, Max.Tyr.35.1. 2. metaph., *ruin utterly*, Pherecr.145.19. b. *suppress*, κ. τῷ λόγῳ Lib.*Or.*42.14:—Pass., πρᾶγμα καταπεφρονημένον καὶ κατορωρυγμένον ib.62.32. **-ορῠχή**, ἡ, = κατόρυξις: *buried treasure*, Hsch. (pl.).

**κατορφνάομαι**, Med., *darken*, Hsch.

**κατορχέομαι**, *dance in triumph over* one, *treat despitefully*, Hdt.3.151, Lxx *Za.*12.10, Phld.*Piet.*52, Ael.*NA*5.54; τῆς ἀναισθησίας Plu.2.57a. II. *subdue* or *enchant by dancing*, Luc.*Salt.*22. III. intr., *dance vehemently*, Str.17.1.17.

**κατορχίτης** [ῑ] οἶνος, ὁ, = συκίτης, v.l. for τροχίτης in Dsc.5.32.

**κατόσσομαι**, *contemplate, behold*, *AP*12.91 (Polystr.).

**κατοσφραίνομαι**, *smell*, c. gen., Suid.

**κατότι**, Adv., Ion. for καθότι or καθ' ὅ τι.

**κατουδαῖος**, ον, (οὖδας) *under the ground*, οἱ κ. Hes.*Fr.*60; κ. βόθρος *h.Merc.*112; κ. γίγας, of Briareus, Call.*Del.*142; κ. φόβοι Juba Hist.9.

**κατουλάς**, άδος, ἡ, *shrouding*, νύξ S.*Fr.*433; but taken as = ὀλοή, A.R.4.1695. (From κατειλέω, cf. Hsch. s.v. κατειλάδα.)

✻**κατουλέω**, and **κατούλη**, ἡ, dub. sens. in *IG*5(2).357.6 (Stymphalus).

**κάτουλ-ος**, ον, *cicatrized*, *Gloss.* **-όω**, *cause to cicatrize*, D.S.32.10, Dsc.5.74:—Pass., *cicatrize, heal over*, *AP*9.311 (Phil.), Thessal. ap.Gal.10.250. **-ωσις**, εως, ἡ, *cicatrization*, Dsc.*Eup.*1.51, Heliod. ap.Orib.44.8.12. **-ωτικός**, ή, όν, *causing cicatrization*, Heras ap. Gal.13.432.

**κατουρέω**, *make water upon*, τινος Ar.*Ec.*832: abs., *make water*, Arist.*HA*556b15, Luc.*Merc.Cond.*34.

**κατουρ-ίζω**, *bring into port with a fair wind*, metaph., *bring safe to port, bring to fulfilment*, τάδ' ὀρθῶς ἔμπεδα κατουρίζει (sc. the oracle), or (as others) intr., these things *come to fulfilment*, S.*Tr.*827 (lyr.). **-όω**, *sail with a fair wind*, Plb.1.44.3, 1.61.7:—also in Med., Luc.*Lex.*15.

**κατουτάω**, = οὐτάω, Q.S.14.318 (Pass.).

**κατούχιος**, = κάτοχος I. 3, epith. of Hermes, *Tab.Defix.Aud.*72.13.

**κατοφρῡόομαι**, *to be furnished with eyebrows*, in pf. part., Philostr.*VA*3.8: metaph., λόγοι κατωφρυωμένοι *stern, severe* words, Luc.*Am.*53.

**κατοχ-εύς**, έως, ὁ, *holder, support* in machinery, Hero *Bel.*78.2; κ. πυλάων *bolt*, Call.*Ap.*6; *tenon*, Sm.*Ex.*26.17. **-εύω**, *have* a female animal *covered*, Lxx *Le.*19.19, cf. Hsch. II. pf. part. Pass. κατωχευμένος *fertilized*, φοίνικες Mitteis *Chr.*151.26 (iii A.D.). ✻ **-ή**, ἡ, (κατέχω) *holding fast, detention*, τινὸς ἐν Σούσοισι Hdt.5.35; of *detention* by the god in the Sarapeum, *UPZ*5.3, 59.8, al. (ii B.C.), cf. Man.1.239 (pl.); *arrest*, *PAmh.*2.80.9 (iii A.D.), *Cod.Just.*1.4.22.1; ἡ πρὸς τὸ χρέος κ. *PSI*4.282.28 (ii A.D.). 2. *hindrance, delay*, ἀνείρξεις καὶ κ. Plu.2.584e, cf. Vett.Val.43.17. 3. *retention*, τοῦ πνεύματος *holding* the breath, Gal.6.161, Alex.Aphr.*Pr.*1.47; *retention* of waste products, Gal.8.440. 4. *retention* in memory, Corn.*ND*14; μνήμη καὶ κ. Plot.4.3.29: pl., τὰς μνήμας κ. μαθημάτων καὶ αἰσθήσεων εἶναι Id.4.6.1. 5. *sequestration* of property, ἐν κ. *PTeb.*143 (ii B.C.), cf. *PRyl.*174.23 (ii A.D.), etc.; *lien, charge*, καθαρὸς ἀπὸ πάσης κ. *POxy.*483.26 (ii A.D.), etc. II. *possession*, Sm.*Ca.*8.11; ἐν κ. ποιεῖσθαι Men.Prot.p.30 D.; = Lat. *bonorum possessio*, *BGU*140.24 (ii A.D.); *mental grasp*, κοινῶν τινων Phld.*Rh.*1.71 S. 2. *possession by a spirit, inspiration*, κ. καὶ ἐνθουσιασμοί Plu.*Alex.*2; πάντα ἐν τῇ κ. ἀληθεύειν Arr.*An.*4.13.5. 3. *catalepsy*, Gal.9.189, 10.932; κ. τῶν ἄρθρων *stiffness*, Asclep.ap.eund.13.967. **-ῐμος**, later form for κατοκώχιμος (q.v.), *held in possession*, εἰς αἰῶνα Lxx *Le.*25.46; *sequestered*, κλῆρος *PFrankf.*7B9 (iii B.C.), cf. *PTeb.*61(*b*).253 (ii B.C.). 2. *possessed* by a supernatural power, Hsch. s.v. κατοκώχιμον, *Gloss.*; of things, '*eerie*', *uncanny*, κ. πάντα καὶ φρικώδη καὶ μυστικά Luc.*JTr.*30. 3. Alch., of *fixing* agents, *mordants*, Syn.Alch.p.62 B., Zos.Alch.p.216 B., *PHolm.*15.19, *PLeid.X.*92. **-ιον**, τό, ἐμβρύων *preventive of miscarriage*, Aët.2.32. **-ῖτις** [ῑ] λίθος stone *with adhesive properties*, Plin.*HN*37.152.

✻**κατοχμάζω**, strengthd. for ὀχμάζω, Opp.*H.*5.226.

✻**κάτοχος**, ον, (κατέχω) *holding down*, γῆ *Tab.Defix.*101.1 (iv B.C.); κ. λίθοι, of sepulchral stones, Hsch.; κ. alone, *tombstone*, *IG*3.1425a; also, οἰκουμένης κ., of ocean, Secund.*Sent.*2. 2. *holding fast*, μοχλοί Lxx *Jn.*2.7; δεσμοί Plu.2.321d; φάρμακα κ. τῶν ἐμβρύων drugs which prevent miscarriage, Aët.16.21; *retentive*, of memory, Plu.*Cat.Mi.*1; *secure*, κτῆσις κ. καὶ βέβαιος D.H.*Isoc.*9. 3. *possessing, inspiring*, Μοῦσα Asp.ap.Ath.5.219d; in magic, *inhibiting*, Ἑρμῆς *Tab.Defix.*89.2 (iv B.C.), al. II. Pass., *kept down, held fast*, κάτοχ' ἀμαυροῦσθαι σκότῳ A.*Pers.*223 (troch.); *overpowered, overcome*, ὕπνῳ S.*Tr.*978 (anap.); *subject*, Ἄρει E.*Hec.*1090 (lyr.). 2. *possessed, inspired*, δαίμονί τινι Arist.*Mir.*846b24; τῷ Σαβαζίῳ Iamb.*Myst.*3.9; ἐκ θεοῦ Plu.*Rom.*19, etc.; ἐκ τοῦ θείου Arr.*An.*4.13.5; ἐκ Μουσῶν Luc.*Hist.Conscr.*8; ἐξ Ἄρεως Polyaen.1.20; ἐκ πυξίου Luc.*Ind.*15; στροφὴν ὁλοσώματον ὥσπερ οἱ κ. δινεύοντες Hld.4.17, cf. 8.11, 10.9; also perh. of *cloistered worshippers, recluses*, οἱ κ. οὐρανίου Διός *OGI*262.25 (Baetocaece, iii A.D.), cf. *CIG*4475 (ibid., iii A.D.): abs., Cleanth.*Stoic.*1.123; ἐν ἱεροῖς κ. Vett.Val.73.24. 3. *cataleptic*, of disease, Hp.*Prorrh.*1.92, cf. Gal.16.696. b. *suffering from catalepsy*, Id.9.189. III. Subst. κάτοχος, ὁ, *handle* of a τρύπανον, Hsch. s.v. κατωχάνης: pl. κάτοχα, Id. 2. *bandage*, Gal.18(1).785. 3. *inhibitory spell*, *PMag.Par.*1.1052, 2.162, *Tab.Defix.Aud.*187.55. 4. pl., *processes on the second cervical vertebra*, Poll.2.132. IV. Adv. κατόχως *retentively*, of the memory, Hermipp.21. 2. *in fast colours*, βεβάφθαι *AB*237. 3. *as if possessed*, Ael.*VH*3.9, Poll.1.16. 4. *accompanied by catalepsy*, Hp.*Coac.*570, al.

**κατοχῡρόω**, strengthd. for ὀχυρόω, in Pass., Paul.Aeg.6.118.

**κατοχ-ώδης**, ες, *resembling catalepsy*, Aret.*SA*2.11. **-ωτικός**, ή, όν, f.l. in Ph.1.509, 511 (leg. κατοκωχή τε καὶ μανία).

**κατοψέ**, Adv., strengthd. for ὀψέ, *late at night*, Alex.Trall.2.

**κατόψιος**, ον, (ὄψις) *visible*, A.R.2.543. II. *in sight of, opposite*, γῆς τῆσδε E.*Hipp.*30.

**κάτοψις**, εως, ἡ, *sight*, Epicur.*Nat.*11.4, 7.

**κατόψομαι**, fut. of καθοράω (q.v.).

**κατοψοφᾰγ-έω**, *spend* or *waste in eating*, Aeschin.1.95 (Pass.), Lib.*Decl.*33.31 (Act.). 2. *eat greedily*, Ph.2.479, Ath.5.186c. **-ία**, ἡ, *ruinous gluttony* or *luxury*, Poll.6.37.

**κατράγοντες**· οἱ βόαγροι (Lacon.), Hsch.

**κατρεύς**, έως, ὁ, an Indian bird, prob. the *monal pheasant*, Clitarch.20, 21 J., Nonn.*D.*26.212.

**κάτροπον**· κάταντες, Hsch. (Dor. for κατάτροπον, q.v.). **κάτροπτον**, v. κάτοπτρον. **κατρός**· κακός, Id.

**κάττα**, ἡ, *cat*, late word for αἴλουρος, Sch.Ar.*Pl.*693:—also **κάττος**, ὁ, Sch.Call.*Cer.*111.

**καττά**, Dor. for κατὰ τά, **καττάδε** for κατὰ τάδε, **καττάν** for κατὰ τήν, **καττaύταν** for κατὰ ταύτην, etc. **καττάνῠσαν**, v. καταναύω.

**καττίτερος, καττιτέρινος, κάττῡμα**, Att. for κασσ-.

**καττῡματοποιός**, ὁ, *cobbler*, prob. in *Inscr.Délos* 363.64 (iii B.C.).

**καττύς** [ῠ], ύος, ἡ, *piece of leather*, Ar.*Fr.*285 (v. κασσύω).

**καττύω**, v. κασσύω.

**κατύ**, Arc. for κατά, *IG*5(2).6.11, al. (iv B.C.).

**κατυβρίζω, κατύπερθε, κατυπέρτερος, κατυπνόω**, Ion. for καθ-.

✻**κάτω**, Adv., (κατά): I. with Verbs implying Motion, *downwards*, ἐπισκύνιον κ. ἕλκεται Il.17.136; κ. ὁρόων Od.23.91; κατὰ τείχεος κ. ῥίπτειν Hdt.8.53; κατώρυξέν με κατὰ τῆς γῆς κ. Ar.*Pl.*238; χώρει κ. A.*Pr.*74; κ. δάκρυ' εἰβομένη S.*Ant.*527 (anap.), cf. E.*Fr.*384;

esp. of the nether world, A.*Pers.*839, S.*Ant.*197, etc.; κ. βλέπειν, φέρεσθαι, Pl.*R.*500b, 584e; κ. διεχώρει αὐτοῖς they suffered from diarrhoea, X.*An.*4.8.20, cf. Hp.*Epid.*5.20; φάρμακον πῖσαι κ. give a purgative, Id.*Aff.*32, cf. 15; κ. βοηθεῖν go *down* to help, D.32.5; for ἄνω καὶ κάτω, ἄνω κάτω, etc., v. ἄνω (B) A. II. 2. 2. *downwards*, in a chain of causes, ἐπὶ τὸ κ. ἰέναι Arist.*Metaph.*994$^a$19. 3. c. gen., *down from*, πετρῶν ὦσαι κ. E.*Cyc.*448. II. with Verbs implying Rest (so more freq. in Prose), *beneath, below*, opp. ἄνω, Hes.*Th.*301, etc.; ὁ τόπος ὁ κ. καλούμενος Pl.*Phd.*112c. b. *in the world below*, S.*Aj.*660, *OC*1563 (lyr.), etc.; οἱ κ. *the dead*, Id.*Aj.*865, *Ant.*75, etc.; οἱ κ. θεοί Id.*El.*292, cf. E.*Alc.*851. c. geographically *below, southward*, Hdt., v. ἄνω (B) A. II. 1 e; also κ. οἰκεῖν to dwell *on the coast*, Th.1.7; οἱ κ., opp. οἱ τὴν μεσόγειαν κατῳκημένοι, ib.120; ἡ. κ. Γαλατία *lower* Galatia, Plu.*Aem.*9, etc.; βασιλεὺς τῶν τε ἄνω καὶ τῶν κ. χωρῶν *OGI*90.3 (Rosetta, ii B.C.). d. in the race-course, τὰ κ. *the starting-place*, opp. τὰ ἄνω (the goal), Pl.*R.*613b. e. τὰ κ. τῶν μελῶν *the lower* limbs of the body, Id.*Lg.*794d; ἡ κ. κοιλία, opp. ἡ ἄνω, Arist.*Mete.*360$^b$24, *PA*676$^a$5; περὶ τὰ κ. χωρεῖν *miscarry, fail*, Luc.*Ind.*1. f. of Time, *afterwards, later*, Ael.*VH*5.13; οἱ κ. χρόνοι Plu.*Cor.*25; οἱ κ., opp. οἱ πάλαι, Luc.*Hipp.*1; τοῦ χρόνου κ. *later* in time, Ael.*VH*3.17, *NA*2.18; Δαρεῖος ὁ κ. ib.6.48; cf. ἄνω (B) A. II. 1 i. g. in Logic, τὰ κ. *the lower members* in a descending series of genera and species, Arist.*APo.*97$^a$31, *Metaph.*992$^a$18. III. c. gen., *under, below*, κ. χθονός, γῆς, A.*Eu.*1023, S.*OT*968, etc. IV. Comp. κατωτέρω *lower, downwards*, Ar.*Ra.*70, Alex.173.2: c. gen., *lower than, below*, Hdt.8.132. 2. Sup. κατωτάτω *at the lowest part*, τὰ κ. Id.2.125 (but in signf. II. g, Phld.*Sign.*29).

**κατω-βλέπων** or -βλεπον, οντος, ὁ or τό, *down-looker*, name of an African animal, Alex.Mynd.ap.Ath.5.221b, Ael.*NA*7.5, cf. Lat. *catoblepas*:—also ⊛**κατῶβλεψ**, επος, ὁ, Archelaus ap.Ath.9.409c.

**κατώγαιος**, = κατάγειος, οἴκημα Alex.Trall.*Febr.*4: **κατώγειος** τόπος *Gp.*9.22.2: **κατώγεως**, Suid.

**κατώδῠνος**, ον, *in great pain* or *affliction*, Lxx 1 *Ki.*1.10, al.

**κάτωθεν**, rarely -θε Eub.16, Alex.128.3, Theoc.4.44: (κάτω):—Adv. *from below, up from below*, ἐλθεῖν A.*Pers.*697 (troch.); ἀμπέμπων Id.*Ch.*382 (lyr.); ἐπανιέναι Pl.*Ti.*22e; ἐκ τῆς γῆς κάτωθεν ἀνίεται ὁ πλοῦτος Id.*Cra.*403a; ἡ κ. ἄνω πληγὴ ἀναπτωμένη Id.*Sph.*221b; also, *from the low country, from the coast*, Hdt.3.60. II. *below, beneath*, τὰ κ. Pl.*Cra.*408d; τὰ κ. ἰσχυρότατ' εἶναι δεῖ D.2.10; ὁ κ. νόμος the law *below*, Id.23.28, cf. Did.ap.Harp. s. v. ὁ κ. νόμος; τίς οἶδεν εἰ κ. εὐαγῆ τάδε; S.*Ant.*521; οἱ κ. θεοί ib.1070, cf. E.*Alc.*424. 2. of Time, τοὺς εἰς τὸ κ. those *belonging to the next generation*, Pl.*Ti.*18d. 3. in Logic, = κάτω II. g, Arist.*APo.*96$^b$37, *Top.*144$^a$29. III. as Prep. c. gen., *below*, κ. τοῦ ὀμφαλοῦ Hp.*Aff.*15; τῶν ἄκρων Thphr.*Sign.*24.

**κατ-ωθέω**, *push down*, κὰδ δ' ἄρ' ἐπὶ στόμ' ἔωσε Il.16.410; ὅν τε κατὰ στεφάνης ποταμὸς χειμάρροος ὤσῃ 13.138:—Pass., Ph.2.498, Hsch.

⊛**κᾰτωκάρα** [ᾰρ], Adv. *head downwards*, Pi.*Fr.*161, Ar.*Ach.*945 (lyr.), Ph.1.207, Agath.2.2; *heels over head*, Ar.*Pax*153.

⊛**κατωμάδ-ιος** [ᾰδ], α, ον, (ὦμος) *from the shoulder*, δίσκος κ. a quoit *thrown down from the shoulder*, i.e. from the upturned hand held above the shoulder, Il.23.431. II. *worn* or *borne on the shoulder*, Call.*Cer.*45, Mosch.*Fr.*4. -ίς, Adv., = sq., Hdn.Gr.1.512. -όν, Adv., (ὦμος) *from the shoulders*, μάστιγι κ. ἤλασεν ἵππους Il.15.352, cf. 23.500. II. *on* or *hanging from the shoulders*, A.R.2.679; δωρηθεὶς ἐνετῆσι κ. ἠλέκτροιο *BCH*50.529 (ii A.D.).

**κατώμηλ(ος)**, perh. *hanging from the shoulder*, χιλω(τήρ) *PLond.*2.402$^v$9 (ii B.C.).

**κατωμ-ίζω**, *set* a dislocated limb *by putting one's shoulder* under the joint, κ. ἐς ὀρθόν Hp.*Art.*4:—hence -ισμός Gal.18(1).333. -ίς, ίδος, ἡ, v. κατωτίδες. -ιστής, οῦ, ὁ, *throwing the rider over the shoulders*, ἵππος Hsch. -ος, ον, *low in the shoulder* or *forequarter*, *Hippiatr.*14.

**κατ-ωμοσία**, Ion. -ίη, ἡ, *accusation on oath*, Hdt.6.65. -ωμοτικός, ή, όν, *of* or *for an affirmative oath*, opp. ἀπωμοτικός, ἐπίρρημα (i.e. νή, opp. μά) D.T.642.15, Eust.92.19. Adv. -κῶς ib.21, Sch.Ar.*Pl.*202. ⊛-ώμοτος, ον, *sworn in affirmation*, ὅρκος Harp. s. v. ἐπακτός.

**κατωνάκη** [νᾰ], ἡ, *coarse frock with a border of sheepskin* (νάκος), worn by slaves and labourers, Ar.*Lys.*1151, *Ec.*724, Theopomp.Com.99.

**κατωνᾰκοφόρος**, ον, *wearing the κατωνάκη*, name of slaves at Sicyon, Theopomp.Hist.172.

**κατωπιάω**, *cast the eyes down*, of horses, Arist.*HA*604$^b$11, Porph.*Abst.*3.7; Ep. part. -ιόων Q.S.3.133.

**κατωπός**, όν, (ὤψ) *with downcast looks*, *Hippiatr.*29, 66.

**κάτωρ**, ορος, ὁ, dub. l. (δῖε κ., v. l. δι' ἑκάτωρ) *h.Bacch.*55.

**κατωρᾰΐζομαι**, Ion. for καθωραΐζομαι, Hsch.

⊛**κατώρης**, ες, = κάτω ῥέπων, Hsch. (κατωρής cod.).

**κατωρθωμένως**, Adv. pf. part. Pass., (κατορθόω) *successfully*, Phlp. *in Ph.*142.10.

**κατωρίς**, ίδος, ἡ, in dual, *bands* or *ribbands hanging from* the στέφανος, *IG*2$^2$.1388.22.

**κατώρροπος**, ον, = κατάρροπος, Olymp. *in Phd.*p.244 N.

**κατῶρυξ**, ῠχος, ὁ, ἡ, (κατορύσσω) *dug out, quarried*, ἀγορὴ . . λάεσσι κατωρυχέεσσ' ἀραρυῖα (as if from κατωρυχής) Od.6.267, cf. 9.185; λίθοι κ. Poll.7.123; τὴν κατώρυγα (sic) θεμελίωσιν foundation *of quarried stone*, Ph.Byz.*Mir.*6.2. 2. *excavated, hewn out*, ἐκ κατώρυχος στέγης, of a rock tomb, S.*Ant.*1100; οἰκήματα κ. D.C.56.11. II. *underground*, κατώρυχες δ' ἔναιον A.*Pr.*452. 2. *beneath the horizon*, [ἄστρα] Arat.510. III. Subst. κατῶρυξ, ἡ, *cavern*, S.*Ant.*774; χρυσοῦ κατώρυχες treasure *caves*, E.*Hec.*1002, cf. Max.Tyr.6.3. 2. *rooting branch*, Str.15.1.21.

**κατ-ωρύομαι**, *howl much*, Apollod.3.4.4.

**κατώρῠχος**, ὁ, apptly. a nickname, *Inscr.Prien.*313.720. II. κατώρυχος, ον, = κατῶρυξ II. 1, βελοστάσεις interpol. in Ph.*Bel.*82.9.

**κατώτατος**, η, ον, Sup. Adj. from κάτω, *lowest*, X.*Cyr.*6.1.52, Lxx *Ps.*87(88).6, al.: neut. pl. as Adv., Hdt.7.23. Adv. κατωτάτω, v. κάτω.

**κατωτερικός**, ή, όν, of medicines, *purgative*, Hp.*Epid.*5.20, Gal.10.527. II. *used as an enema*, τροχίσκος Archig.ap.Aët.9.42, cf. Cass.Fel.48.

⊛**κατώτερος**, α, ον, Comp. Adj. from κάτω, *lower*, Hp.*Fract.*31, Lxx 3 *Ki.*9.17, etc.; τὰ κ. μέρη τῆς γῆς *Ep.Eph.*4.9; *more southerly*, Vett.Val.34.21. 2. of Time, *later, younger*, Call.*Cer.*131. Adv. κατωτέρω, v. κάτω.

**κατωτέρωθεν**, *from a greater depth*, Thphr.*CP*3.20.8.

**κατωτίδες**, αἱ, (οὖς) *lappets covering the ears*, Hsch. (Fort. κατωμίδες, *capes*.)

**κατώτιον**, τό, *life-boat*, *PLond.*3.1164(*h*)10 (iii A.D.).

**κατωφᾰγᾶς**, οῦ or ᾶ, ὁ, (φαγεῖν) *eating with the head down to the ground, gluttonous*, name of a bird, Ar.*Av.*288; also **καταφαγᾶς** (of human beings) A.*Fr.*428, Myrtil.4, Men.424, which is censured by Phryn.400, Poll.6.40.

**κατωφελής**, ές, (ὄφελος) *very useful*, Thphr.*CP*4.11.4.

**κατωφέρ-εια**, ἡ, *propensity*, πρὸς συνουσίαν Sch.D Il.24.30, cf. Sch.A.*Ch.*600; *downward tendency*, Eustr. *in EN*60.3. -ής, ές, = κάτω φερόμενος, *hanging down*, κεφαλή X.*Cyn.*5.30 (v. l. καταφερής); *steep*, κατάβασις Plb.3.54.5; κ. θέσις *sloping* posture, Sor.2.60; *descending*, χελώνη Orib.49.4.51; *with a downward tendency, heavy*, στοιχεῖα, opp. ἀνωφερής, *Stoic.*2.175, al., cf. Herm.ap.Stob.1.49.68, Simp. *in Ph.*386.23; ὁρμή Eust.603.39. Adv. -ρῶς Vett.Val.153.4; gloss on κατωκάρα, Sch.Ar.*Pax*152. II. metaph., *prone to vice, lewd*, v. l. for καταφερής in Apollod.Ath.ap.Ath.7.281f, cf. Vett.Val.18.3, *EM*451.2; κ. εἰς τὰ ἀφροδίσια Hsch. s. v. Σαλαβακχώ.

**κατώφορος**, ον, *having a downward tendency*, Phlp. *in Mete.*30.19, Simp. *in Ph.*671.32.

**κατωχάνης**, ου, ὁ, *handle* or *holder of a borer*, Hsch.

⊛**κατωχεύει**· πηδᾷ, ἐπικάθηται, Hsch.; cf. κατοχεύω.

**κατωχριάω**, *turn very pale*, Ps.-Luc.*Philopatr.*18:—also **κατωχράω**, aor. part. κατωχρήσασα *AP*10.71 (Maced.).

⊛**καυάζοντα**· ἀποσκάζοντα, Hsch. **καυᾰλέος**, α, ον, *burnt up, parched*, Id.:—also **καυαλής**, ές, Id. **καυαλός**· μωρολόγος, Id. **καύαξ**, ᾶκος, Ion. **καύηξ**, ηκος, ὁ, v. κήξ. **καυάξαις**, v. κατάγνυμι. **καυαρόν**· κακόν, καπυρόν, Id.

**καῦδος** or -ον, ἐπιμελητὴς καύδου dub. sens. in *BSA*26.166 (Sparta, ii A.D.).

***καύεις**, Lydian word, only in acc. sg. καύειν, title of priestess of Artemis at Sardis, *IGRom.*4.1755, etc.: ⊛**καύης**, ὁ, prob. masc. form of the same, Hippon.2.

**καυθμός**, ὁ, *burning, scorching*, esp. a disease in trees, produced by keen winds, Thphr.*HP*4.14.11, *CP*5.12.4. II. *firewood*, *PPetr.*3 p.327 (iii B.C.).

**καυκᾰλίας**, ὁ, kind of *bird*, Hsch.; cf. καυκιάλης.

**καυκάλιον**, τό, v. βαυκάλιον.

**καυκᾰλίς**, ίδος, ἡ, an umbelliferous plant, *Tordylium apulum*, Thphr.*HP*7.7.1, Nic.*Th.*843 (pl.), Dsc.2.139, *Gp.*12.32.1, prob. in Numen.ap.Ath.9.371c; cf. καυσαλίς and καυκιάλης.

**καύκαλον**, τό, part of a military boot, Anon. *in Rh.*123.22.

**Καύκᾰσος**, ὁ, *Mt. Caucasus* between the Euxine and Caspian, Hdt.1.203 sq.: also a gen. Καυκάσιος (as if from Καύκασις) Id.3.97, cf. St.Byz. s. v.: τὸ **Καυκάσιον** ὄρος Hdt.1.104.—The region was **Καυκασία**, ἡ, and the inhabitants **Καυκασῖται, Καυκασιανοί**, St.Byz.

**καυκιάλης**· βοτάνη τις, ὁμοία κορίῳ (κωρίῳ cod.), καὶ ὄρνις, Hsch. (cf. καυκαλίς and καυκαλίας).

**καῦκον**, τό, = καυκαλίς, Ps.-Dsc.2.139.

**καῦκος**, ὁ, a kind of *cup*, *Gloss.*:—Dim. ⊛**καυκίον**, τό, *AP*9.749 (in lemmate), Just.*Nov.*105.2.1; κ. ἀργύρεον *PMasp.*167.10 (vi A.D.).

**καυλ-εῖον**, τό, = καυλίον, Nic.*Th.*75, 535, 882. -έω, *form a stalk*, Suid. ⊛-ηδόν, Adv. *like a stalk*, Opp.*C.*2.511; κ. τέμνειν [εὐθεῖαν] Ascl. *in Metaph.*214.8. II. surgical name of a kind of fracture, Sor.*Fract.*10, Paul.Aeg.6.89. -ίας, ου, ὁ, *extracted from a stalk*, ὀπός Thphr.*HP*6.3.2, 9.1.7. -ίζομαι, Pass., *have a shaft*, of a spear, Ar.*Fr.*404. -ικός, ή, όν, *like a stalk, cauline*, πρόσφυσις Thphr.*HP*7.9.1. -ίνης, ου, ὁ, *a kind of* κωβιός, Diph.Siph.ap.Ath.8.355c. -ινος, η, ον, *made of a stalk* or *stick*, Luc.*VH*1.16. -ίον, τό, Dim. of καυλός, Nic.*Al.*46 (καυλέα codd.), *Gp.*2.6.32, Dsc.2.183, *PGiss.*93.3 (ii A.D.). II. a kind of *sea-weed*, Arist.*HA*591$^b$12. III. *part of a column*, Hsch. -ίσκος, ὁ, Dim. of καυλός I. 1, Dsc.4.114. 2. *branch of a candlestick*, J.*BJ*7.5.5 (pl.). 3. *tube, catheter*, D.S.32.11.

**καυλο-ειδής**, ές, *like a stem*, ἔκφυσις Dsc.3.141. -κῖνάρα, ἡ, *artichoke stem*, *Gp.*20.31. -κλυστήρ, ῆρος, ὁ, (καυλός III) a surgical instrument, *Hermes*38.282. -κοπία, ἡ, *cutting of stalks*, prob. in *PCair.Preis.*38.16 (iv A.D.). -μύκητες, οἱ, *stalk-fungi*, burlesque name in Luc.*VH*1.16. -πώλης, ου, ὁ, *greengrocer*, Critias *Fr.*70 D., Poll.7.197.

**καυλός**, ὁ, *stem* of a plant (opp. στέλεχος, of trees, Thphr.*HP*1.1.9), Epich.158, Ar.*Eq.*824 (anap.); κ. σιλφίου ib.894; ἢ σίλφιον ἢ ὀπὸς

ἡ κ. Hp.*Acut.*37; called ἐκ Κυρήνης κ. Hermipp.63.4; κ. ἐκ Καρχηδόνος Eub.19; κ. Λίβυς Antiph.217.13, cf. 325; κράμβης *BGU*1118.12 (pl., i B.C.), cf. Dsc.2.120, Archig.ap.Gal.13.331. **2.** Hom. (only in Il.), *spear-shaft*, ἐν καυλῷ ἐάγη δολιχὸν δόρυ Il.13.162; κατεκλάσθη δ' ἐνὶ καυλῷ ἔγχος ib.608; once of a *sword-hilt*, ἀμφὶ δὲ καυλὸν φάσγανον ἐρραίσθη 16.338. **3.** of various tubular structures in animals, πτεροῦ καυλός *quill part* of a feather, Pl.*Phdr.*251b, cf. Arist. *HA*504$^{a}$31; *neck* of the bladder, ib.497$^{a}$20; *duct* of the penis, ib. 510$^{a}$26; *cervix uteri*, ib.510$^{b}$11; *ovipositor* of locusts, ib.555$^{b}$21. **4.** *shank* of a fish-hook, Opp.*H.*3.148. **II.** *vegetable of the cabbage kind, cole, kail, cauliflower*, Alex.127.5, Anaxandr.41.58 (pl.), Eub.7.3 (pl.). **III.** *membrum virile*, Hp.*Int.*14, D.S.32.11, Gal.*UP*14.12, Ruf.*Onom.*101, etc. (Cf. Lat. *caulus, caulis*, Lith. *káulas* 'bone'.)

**καυλοφορέω,** *run to stalk*, Gal.6.657.

**καυλ-ώδης,** ες, *running to stem*, Thphr.*CP*3.6.9: Comp., Dsc.2.136. **-ωτός,** ή, όν, *with a stalk* or *stem*, Eudem.ap.Ath.9.371a.

⊛**καῦμα,** ατος, τό, (καίω) *burning heat*, esp. of the sun, καύματος ἔξ after *sun-heat*, Il.5.865, cf. Hes.*Op.*415, 588, Alc.39, S.*Ant.*417, Epinic.1.10, etc.; πρὶν ἂν τὸ κ. παρέλθῃ the *heat of the day*, Pl.*Phdr.* 242a, cf. *Ti.*70d; ἐὰν ᾖ κ. Arist.*Mete.*342$^{b}$10: freq. in pl., ἡλίου τε καύμασιν S.*OC*350, cf. Hdt.3.104, X.*Cyn.*5.9, etc.; [τόποι] ὑπὸ καυμάτων διαφθειρόμενοι Isoc.11.12; καύματα καὶ χειμῶνες Phld.*Piet.*87: in pl., also of frost, Ath.3.98b, Luc.*Lex.*2. **2.** *fever heat*, Th.2.49; of *inflamed* conditions, Hp.*VM*19, *Aph.*7.13: metaph., of love, κ. ἀρσενικόν *AP*12.87. **II.** in pl., *holes burnt by cautery*, Hp.*Art.*11, Arist.*Pr.*863$^{a}$31. **III.** *brand* on cattle, *IG*7.3171.44 (Orchom. Boeot.). **IV.** *embers* of sacrifices, Pl.*Criti.*120d. **V.** *firewood*, *PLond.*3.1166.6, al. (i A.D.).

**καυμᾰτ-ηρός,** ά, όν, *very hot*, Str.16.4.1. **-ίας,** masc. Adj., *burning hot*, of the sun, Thphr.*Sign.*11, 26, al. **-ίζω,** *burn, scorch up*, *Apoc.*16.8:—Pass., *to be burnt up*, *Ev.Matt.*13.6; *become heated, suffer from heat*, Plu.2.100b, 691f, Arr.*Epict.*1.6.26, Sor.1.108, M.Ant.7.64. **-ώδης,** ες, = καυματηρός, *burning, scorching*, θέρος οὐ λίην κ. Hp.*Epid.*1.4; νότος Arist.*Mete.*364$^{b}$23; ὁδός D.S.19.18; ὥρα Longus 1.30. **2.** *feverish*, ῥίγεα Hp.*Prorrh.*1.67, al.: metaph., ἡδονή Ach.Tat.2.37.

**καυμός,** ὁ, *fever*, perh. to be read in Call.*Aet.*3.1.19.

⊛**καυνάκης** [ᾰ], ου, ὁ, *thick cloak*, Ar.*V.*1137; κ. πορφυροῦς Men.972; said to be of Persian or Babylonian make, Arr.*An.*6.29.5, Poll.7.59, cf. Sch.Ar. l. c., Semus 20, *PCair.Zen.*48.3 (iii B.C.), *PHib.*1.121.11 (iii B.C.):—also **καυνάκη,** ἡ, *PSI*6.605 (iii B.C.); cf. γαυνάκη (which is also found in codd. of *Peripl.M.Rubr.*6):—Dim. **καυνάκιον,** τό, Zonar. (Assyr. *gaunakka* 'frilled and flounced mantle'.)

**καυνᾰκο-πλόκος,** ὁ, *weaver of* καυνάκαι, *PMasp.*283 ii 17 (vi A.D.). **-ποιός,** ὁ, = foreg., ib.288 iv 5 (vi A.D.).

**Καυνιακή** (sc. ἔμπλαστρος), name of a *plaster*, Gal.13.532.

**Καυνίας,** ου, ὁ, *a wind blowing from Caunus* (in Caria) to Rhodes, Arist.*Vent.*973$^{a}$4.

⊛**Καύνιος,** α, ον, *of* or *from Caunus* (in Caria), Hdt.1.172, etc.; ἡ Κ. βοῦς, of labour in vain—for this cow overturned the pail after being milked, *App.Prov.*3.6; but Κ. ἔρως, of illicit love, from *Caunus*, brother and lover of Byblis, Arist.*Rh.*1402$^{b}$3.

**καυνός** (on the accent, v. Hdn.Gr.1.178), ὁ, = κλῆρος, Cratin.194, Ar.*Fr.*660.

**καῦρος** (on the accent, v. Hdn.Gr.1.193), α, ον, = κακός, S.*Fr.* 1059.

**καυσᾰλίς,** ίδος, ἡ, prob. glossed by ἡ μέλαινα καὶ ὑπέρυθρος, Hsch. (καύσαλις cod.); perh. to be read for καυκαλίς, of a kind of σμύρνα, Dsc.1.64 (and so in Orib.12 s. v.), and for καυχαλίς (q. v.).

⊛**καυσία,** ἡ, felt hat used by the Macedonians, forming part of the regalia of their kings, Men.331, Duris 14 J., Ephipp.(*FGrH*126)5 J., Nearch.28 J., Plb.4.4.5, *AP*6.335 (Antip. Thess.), Plu.*Ant.*54, Arr. *An.*7.22.2, Hdn.4.8.2.

⊛**καύσῐμος,** ον, *combustible*, ἔκαιον πάντα, ὅσα κ. ἑώρων X.*An.*6.3.19; κ. ξύλα Alex.307, *PStrassb.*117.3 (i A.D.); ὕλη Pl.*Lg.*849d, Str.16.4.19; ἄχυρον *Ostr.Fay.*21 (iv A.D.); τούτοις καυσίμοις χρῶνται *as fuel*, Thphr.*HP*4.3.2.

**καῦσις,** εως, ἡ, *burning*, [τῶν ἱρῶν] Hdt.2.40; λύχνοι τῆς κ. Lxx *Ex.* 39.17(37), cf. *PLond.*3.1177.74 (ii A.D.). **II.** in Surgery, *cautery*, Hp.*Mochl.*3; ἢ καύσει ἢ τομῇ Pl.*R.*406d: in pl., Hp.*Art.*11, Pl.*R.* 426b, *Ti.*65b. **III.** in pl., *burning heat*, ψύξεις τε καὶ κ. Id.*Tht.* 156b. **IV.** *smelting*, χαλκοῦ, ἀργύρου, Str.14.6.5.

**καυσμένης·** ἔνυδρος, Hsch. **καυσμός,** ὁ, = *cautery*, prob. in *Gloss.* (written *casmos*).

**καυσοποιός,** όν, *causing heat*, gloss on αἴθων, Eust. ad D.P.591.

⊛**καῦσος** (A), ὁ, *causus*, i. e. *bilious remittent fever* (the endemic fever of the Levant), Hp.*VM*17 (pl.), *Aph.*3.21 (pl.), Arist.*Pr.*861$^{b}$34, 862$^{a}$2; πυρέττειν καύσῳ Id.*Metaph.*981$^{a}$12; κ. στομάχου *heartburn*, Dsc. 1.43, al.: generally, *fever, heat*, Nic.*Th.*338. **II.** in pl., lands fertilized by burning brushwood, etc., Ath.Med.ap.Orib.1.2.4.

**καῦσος** (B), εος, τό, = καῦμα I, Procl.*Par.Ptol.*41, 81.

**καυσ-όω,** *heat*, Ptol.*Tetr.*18:—Pass., *burn with intense heat*, 2*Ep. Pet.*3.10, 12: generally, *to be burnt*, *PHolm.*25.27. **II.** *suffer from* καῦσος (A) I, Antyll.ap.Orib.9.13.1, Gal.15.720; καυσουμένη ἐπιφάνεια Dsc.2.134. ⊛**-τειρᾰ,** fem. of καυστήρ, *burning hot, raging*, only as Adj. in gen., μάχης καυστείρης Il.4.342, 12.316; καυστείρης.. καμίνου Nic.*Th.*924: accented καυστειρῆς in good codd. of Hom. and Nic.:—later in the form ⊛**καυστηρός,** Opp.*H.*2.509, v. l. in Nic. l. c., cf. *EM*493.44, Hsch. **-τέον,** *one must burn*, Dsc. 5.79. **-τήρ,** ῆρος, ὁ, *cauterizing apparatus*, Hp.*Haem.*6 (cited as καυτήρ by Gal.19.111); in form καυτήρ, *Hippiatr.*26, Gal.14. 782; on the accent, v. Hdn.Gr.2.922. **-τηριάζω, -τήριον,** v. καυτ-. **-τηρός,** v. καύστειρα. **-της,** ου, Dor. **-τας,** ὁ, *one that burns*, τινος Dosiad.*Ara*11; νεκρῶν *Gloss.*; *one that smelts*, Ptol. *Tetr.*179; *stoker*, *BGU*952.5 (ii/iii A.D.). **-τικός,** ή, όν, *capable of burning*, opp. καυστός (*capable of being burnt*), τὸ καυστὸν οὐ καίεται .. ἄνευ τοῦ καυστικοῦ Arist.*de An.*417$^{a}$8, cf. *Ph.*251$^{a}$16; τὸ πῦρ φύσει κ. Phld.*Mus.*p.71 K.: Comp. -ώτερος Arist.*PA*648$^{b}$18: Sup. -ώτατος Id.*Cael.*307$^{a}$1, Corn.*ND*32. **b.** *corrosive, caustic*, δύναμις κ. Dsc. 2.4 (Comp.); φάρμακα κ. Gal.11.754, Zopyr.ap.Orib.14.57.1. **2.** *of* or *by means of burning*, βάσανοι Lxx 4*Ma.*6.27. Adv. -κῶς, βλάπτειν Eust.70.36. **3.** of persons, *feverish*, Hp.*Prorrh.*1.70; also τὰ κ. *inflammatory humours*, Id.*Epid.*4.2.

⊛**καῦστις,** ἡ, = ἀμφίκαυστις I, Hsch.

**καυσ-τός** or **καυτός** (as Inscrr.), ή, όν, *burnt, red-hot*, καυτὸν μοχλόν E.*Cyc.*633 (Scal. for καὶ τὸν): καυστόν, τό, *burnt-offering for the dead*, Phot.; so καυτόν Hsch.; *whole burnt-offering*, ἄγοντι τὸμ βοῦν καὶ τὸγ καυτόν *SIG*1025.31 (Cos); ἀρὴν καυτός ib.1027.9 (ibid.). **2.** *capable of being burnt*, opp. ἄκαυστος, Arist.*Mete.*387$^{a}$17, al.; cf. καυστικός: Comp. -ότερος Thphr.*Ign.*72. ⊛**-τρα,** ἡ, *place where corpses were burnt*, Str.5.3.8, *CIG*2942 (Tralles), *Gloss.*

**Καΰστριος,** α, ον, *of* or *from the river Cayster* (in Lydia), Ar.*Ach.* 68, etc.

⊛**καυσ-ώδης,** ες, *suffering from heat, parched*, [χῶραι] Thphr.*CP*3.14. 3; τόποι *Arch.Pap.*6.101 (ii A.D.). **2.** = καυματώδης 2, πυρετοί Hp. *Aph.*4.54, *Coac.*570; κ. ὕδατα, ταρίχη, *heating*, Id.*Aër.*7, Diph.Siph. ap.Ath.3.120e; κ. ποιεῖν τὸν στόμαχον Heraclid.Tar.ap.eund.3.79f. Adv. -δῶς Archig.ap.Gal.12.543. **3.** Astrol., of signs, *causing fevers*, Heph.Astr.1.1. **-ωμα,** ατος, τό, = πύρωσις, Gal.19.110. **-ων,** ωνος, ὁ, *burning heat, summer heat*, *Ev.Matt.*20.12, Orph.*Fr.*264, Luc. *Philops.*25; καύσωνος ὥρᾳ Diph.Siph.ap.Ath.3.73a; ἄνεμος καύσων *sirocco*, Lxx *Je.*18.17, al.; κ. alone, ib.*Ju.*8.3, *Ep.Jac.*1.11, Ath.Med. ap.Orib.1.2.13, Ptol.*Tetr.*85. **2.** κ. στομάχου *heartburn*, Dsc.1. 22. **3.** κ. πυρετός, = καῦσος (A) I, Alex.Trall.*Febr.*2. **II.** = διψάς II, Ael.*NA*6.51, Philum.*Ven.*20.1.

**καυ-τήρ,** ῆρος, ὁ, *burner*, ταύρῳ χαλκέῳ, of Phalaris, Pi.*P.*1.95. **II.** v. καυστήρ. **III.** = **καυτήριον** II, Luc.*Pisc.*46, Jul.*Caes.*309c. **-τηριάζω,** *brand*, Str.5.1.9:—Pass., *Hippiatr.*1: metaph., κεκαυτηριασμένοι τὴν ἰδίαν συνείδησιν 1*Ep.Ti.*4.2. **-τηρίδιον,** τό, Dim. of sq., Gal.19.111. ⊛**-τήριον,** τό, *branding iron*, E.*Fr.*815 (cj.), Lxx 4*Ma.*15.22, Luc.*Pisc.*52 (vulg. καυστ-), *Apol.*2, *Hippiatr.*26: metaph., ὥσπερ καυτήρια ταῖς ψυχαῖς προσάγειν D.S.20.54. **II.** *burnt mark, brand*, Str.5.1.9, *BGU*469.7 (ii A.D.). **III.** instrument used in encaustic painting, *Dig.*33.7.17. **IV.** (in form καυστ-) *kiln*, *PLond.*2.391.8 (vi A.D.). **-τικός,** ή, όν, *capable of burning*, χυμός Thphr.*CP*6.1.3. **-τός,** ή, όν, v. καυστός.

**καυχᾰλίς·** φλύκταινα (φυλακταίνα cod.), Hsch.; cf. καυσαλίς.

**καυχ-άομαι,** Dor. **καυχέομαι** Theoc.5.77; 2 sg. καυχᾶσαι in late Gr., as *Ep.Rom.*2.17, 23, etc.: fut. -ήσομαι Hdt.7.39, Eup.134, Epicr.6: aor. ἐκαυχησάμην Arist.*Pol.*1311$^{b}$4; Aeol. opt. καυχάσαιτο Sapph.*Supp.*4.2: pf. κεκαύχημαι 2*Ep.Cor.*7.14:—Act., *EM*527.1:—*speak loud, be loud-tongued*, κ. παρὰ καιρόν Pi.*O.*9.38, cf. Eup. l. c., etc.; *boast, vaunt oneself*, ἐπ' αἰζηοῖσι κ. μέγα Cratin.95, cf. Lycurg.*Fr.*78; εἴς τι Arist. l. c.; ἔν τινι *Ep.Rom.* ll. cc.: c. acc. et inf., aor. or pres., *boast that*.., Hdt. l. c., Epicr. l. c., etc.: c. part., *boast of* doing or being, Men.*Mon.*616, D.H.8.30; ὅτι.. Str.13.1.27: c. acc., *boast of*, Philem.141, 2*Ep.Cor.*9.2: c. gen., ὧν Ἱππίας ἐκαυχᾶτο Phld.*Vit.* p.35 J.: c. dat., κάλλει *AP*12.234 (Strat.). **-η,** ἡ, = sq., ἐπέων καύχας, of heroic verse, Pi.*N.*9.7 (nisi leg. καυχᾶσσ', i. e. καυχάεσσα, Dor. fem. of καυχήεις). ⊛**-ημα,** Dor. **-ᾱμα,** ατος, τό, *a boast, vaunt*, Pi.*I.*5(4).51. **2.** *subject of boasting*, Lesb.Rh.3.4 (pl.), *Ep.Rom.* 4.2. **-ημᾰτίας,** ου, ὁ, *boaster, braggart*, Ptol.*Tetr.*159, *EM*121.7; *boastful*, λόγος Sch.Il.13.373. **-ηματικός,** ή, όν, *boastful*, Sch.Il. 8.535 (Comp.). **-ήμων,** ον, gen. ονος, *boastful*, Babr.5.10, Heph. Astr.1.1. **-ησις,** εως, ἡ, *boasting*, Epicur.*Fr.*93, Lxx 1*Ch.*29.13, al., Phld.*Vit.*p.27 J., Ph.1.534, *Ep.Rom.*15.17. **-ητής,** οῦ, ὁ, *boaster*, Sch.Il.7.96:—written **-ηστής,** *EM*121.6. **-ητιάω,** *boast aloud*, ib.206.22, Sch.Ar.*Pl.*572.

⊛**καυχός, καυχοῦς,** v. χαλκός, χαλκοῦς. **κάφα·** λουτήρ (Lacon.), Hsch. (Lacon. form of σκάφη). **καφάζειν·** γελᾶν, Id. **καφάν,** Dor. for κηφήν, Id. **καφίδιος,** v. κηφ-. **κάφος,** = κάπος, *EM* 499.38.

**καφουρά,** ἡ, *camphor*, Arabic *kāfūr*, *Cinnamomum Camphora*, interpol. in Gal.14.761, Aët.12.63, 16.130.

**κάφρυκτοι** (καρφ- cod.)· φρύγιοι (Rhod.), Hsch. (For κατάφρ-).

**καφώρη,** ἡ, *she fox*, Anon.ap.Suid.; cf. σκαφώρη.

**κᾰχ-άζω,** Dor. fut. καχαξῶ Theoc.5.142:—also in nasalized form **καγχάζω,** S.*Aj.*198 (lyr., v. l.), Babr.99.8, *AP*5.229 (Paul. Sil.), 6.74 (Agath.); cf. ἀνακαγχάζω:—*laugh aloud*, S.*Ichn.*348, Ar.*Ec.*849, *Anacreont.*31.29, Luc.*DMeretr.*6.3; ἐπί τινι at one, Eub.8, Luc. *Am.*23; μέγα κατά τινος Theoc. l. c.; *jeer, mock*, ἁπάντων καγχαζόντων γλώσσαις S.*Aj.* l. c. (Prob. onomatopoeic, by dissim. fr. χὰ χά '*ha! ha!*') **-ασμός,** ὁ, *loud laughter*, v. l. for κιχλισμός, Ar. *Nu.*1073 (pl.).

**κᾰχειμονία,** ἡ, gloss on δυσχλαινία, Sch.E.*Hec.*240.

**καχείτης,** ου, ὁ, dub. sens. in *JHS*32.161 (Pisidia).

**κᾰχεκ-τεύομαι,** *to be in a miserable plight*, *BGU*1141.31 (i B.C.). **-τέω,** *to be in a bad habit of body, be unwell*, Plb.29.17.4, Alex.Aphr.

*in SE*9.1; κ. ταῖς ψυχαῖς *to be ill-disposed, disaffected*, Plb.20.7.4; of the condition of a State, ib.4.1. **-της**, ου, ὁ, (κακός, ἕξις) *in a bad habit of body*, Dsc.2.2, Gal.6.213, 12.321. 2. metaph., *disaffected* in a political sense, Plb.1.68.10, 28.17.12, Cic.*Att.*1.14.6, Nech. in *Cat.Cod.Astr.*7.142. **-τικός**, ή, όν, = foreg. 1, Gal.11.307.

**κᾰχεξ-ής**, ές, = foreg., opp. ἀγαθός, dub. in Phld.*Rh.*1.36 S. ⊛ **-ία**, ἡ, *bad habit of body*, opp. εὐεξία, Hp.*Aph.*3.31 (pl.), Pl.*Grg.*450a, Arist.*EN*1129ᵃ20, *PSI*6.632.8 (iii B.C.); distd. from κακοχυμία, Gal. 10.263. 2. of the mind, *bad disposition, disaffection*, Diph.24, Nicol.Com.1.12, Plb.5.87.3, Hierocl.*in CA*7 p.430 M.: play on both meanings in Str.14.5.14. 3. in Lit. Crit., *bad style*, κ. τῆς ἑρμηνείας Phld.*Rh.*1.188 S., al.: pl., ib.189 S.

**κᾰχ-εταιρεία**, poet. -είη, ἡ, *ill company*, Thgn.1169. **-ήμερος**, ον, *passing an unhappy day*, *AP*9.508 (Pall.); v.l. κακ-.

**καχίλα**· ἄνθη (Cypr.), Hsch.

**κάχλα**, ἡ, = βούφθαλμον, Dsc.3.139.

**καχλ-άζω**, also κοχλάζω (q.v.), usu. pres. and impf., *plash* or *bubble*, of the sound of liquids, φιάλαν ἀμπέλου καχλάζοισαν δρόσῳ Pi. *O.*7.2, cf. Philostr.*VA*3.25; of the sea, περὶ πρύμναν A.*Th.*761 (lyr.), cf. 115 (lyr.); ἄσυχα καχλάζοντος αἰγιαλοῖο Theoc.6.12 (imitated by D.P.838), cf. Arr.*An.*5.20.8; of rain, Lyc.80; of boiling water, Zos. Alch.p.109 B. (cf. κοχλ-): c. acc. cogn., [κῦμα] πέριξ ἀφρὸν πολὺν καχλάζον *frothing forth* foam, E.*Hipp.*1211: metaph., of exuberant eloquence, τὸ Πλατωνικὸν νᾶμα.. μεγάλας παρασκευὰς καχλάζον D.H.*Dem.*28:—also **καχλαίνω**, Hsch. [κᾰ- Pi., A., E. ll.cc., κᾱ- by position, Theoc. l.c.] **-ασμα**, only in form κόχλασμα (q.v.). **-ασμός**, ὁ, = foreg., Zos.Alch.p.119 B. (pl.), *Gloss.*

**κάχληξ**, ηκος, ὁ, *pebble* in the beds of rivers, etc., Str.4.1.7 (pl.), Gal.12.292, Sch.Theoc.6.12 (pl.); = *caementum*, *Gloss.*: collectively, *gravel, shingle*, Th.4.26, J.*AJ*5.1.3: also **κόχλαξ**, = *glarea*, *Gloss.* (Onomatopoeic word, cf. καχλάζω.)

**καχνάζει**· κακχάζει, Hsch.

**κᾰχομῑλ-ία**, ἡ, v. κακομιλία. **-ος**, ον, *keeping bad company*, Phld.*Ir.*p.53 W.

**κᾰχορμῑσία**, poet. -ίη, ἡ, *unlucky harbourage*, *AP*7.640 (Antip.).

**κάχρυ**, v. κάχρυς II.

**καχρύδια**, τά, *husks of* κάχρυς, Arist.*Pr.*923ᵇ11: sg., prob. in Thphr.*CP*5.6.3.

**καχρῠδιάζομαι**, *sprout in winter*, ὁ σπόρος -άσεται *Cat.Cod.Astr.* 8(4).251.

**καχρῠδίας**, ου, ὁ, *made of* κάχρυς, ἄρτος Poll.6.33,72. II. κ. πυρός wheat *that resembles* κάχρυς, Thphr.*HP*8.4.3, *CP*3.21.2, Orib. *inc.*13.7. (The words of this group are freq. written καγχρ-.)

**καχρῠό-εις**, εσσα, εν, *bearing* κάχρυ, ῥίζα, = λιβανωτίς, Nic.*Th.* 40. **-φόρος**, ον, *bearing winter-buds*, Thphr.*HP*3.5.6.

⊛ **κάχρῠς**, ῠος (acc. κάχρυδα Dieuch.ap.Orib.4.7.7, gen. υδος ib.20), ἡ, *parched barley*, Cratin.274, Hp.*Mul.*1.97, Ar.*Nu.*1358, *V.*1306, Gal.11.404. 2. *winter-bud*, Thphr.*HP*3.5.5, 5.1.4: acc. pl., τὰς κάχρυς ib.3.14.1. II. neut. **κάχρυ**, τό, *fruit of* λιβανωτίς, ib.9.11. 10, Ph.*Bel.*86.23, Dsc.3.74 (v.l. κάγχρυς); also, *the whole plant*, Ps.-Dsc. l. c.; κάχρυος ῥίζα Hp.*Nat.Mul.*32, Philum.*Ven.*6.1.

**καχρῠφόρος**, ον, *bearing* κάχρυ, Nic.*Th.*850. **καχρύω**, fut. -ύσω· συγχεῶ, ταράξω, Hsch.

**καχρυώδης**, ες, *like a winter-bud*, Thphr.*HP*3.12.8 and 17.3.

**καχυπο-νόητος**, ον, = sq., cited in error by Poll.2.57 from Pl.*Phdr.* 240e; v. καχυπότοπος. **-νοος**, ον, contr. **-νους**, νουν, = καχύποπτος, Phld.*Ir.*pp.60,74 W., Ph.2.570.

**κᾰχ-ύποπτος**, ον, *suspecting evil, suspicious*, Ar.*Fr.*794, Pl.*R.*409c, Arist.*Rh.*1389ᵇ21. **-υπότοπος**, ον, = foreg., Pl.*Phdr.*240e.

**κάψα, καψάκης, καψάκιον**, v. κάμψα, etc.

**καψάμενος**· ἐλάττωμα ἵππου, Hsch.

⊛ **καψάριος**, ὁ, = Lat. *capsarius*, *IG*3.1171.

**καψιδρώτιον**, τό, (κάπτω, ἱδρώς) *napkin* or *shirt*, *Com.Adesp.*325 (-όκιον male Hsch.).

**καψικός**, ή, όν, *like a box*, κάρνον *PFlor.*241.7 (iii A.D.).

**καψῑπήδαλος**, ὁ, = ὁ μετὰ τῶν τὰ ἄλφιτα [ἐχόντων] καὶ μὴ διδόντων ἀλόμενος, Hsch.: καπηδάλους is corrupt in Eratosth.ap.*EM*286. 36; cf. ἐγκαψικίδαλος.

**κάψις**, εως, ἡ, (κάπτω) *gulping*, κάψει πίνειν, of the bear, opp. σπάσει and λάψει, Arist.*HA*595ᵃ10.

⊛ **καψοί**· οἱ τοῖχοι, Hsch.

**κάω**, v. καίω.

**κε**, also **κεν**, Ep., Lesb., Cypr. (*Inscr.Cypr.*135.10 H., al.), Thess. (*IG*9(2).517.13, al. (Larissa)); always enclitic, = ἄν and κᾱ (qq.v.); οὐκ ἄν.. ἀλλά κεν Il.13.290; οὐκ ἄν.. οὐδέ κε 19.272, al.; both coupled, ἄν κεν 11.187, Od.5.361, Parm.8.19, etc.; [ὅσσα] κε θέλῃ Sapph. *Supp.*1.3; τί κεν ποείην; Ead.*Oxy.*1787 *Fr.*1 + 2.16; κεν ἄν dub. in *IGRom.*4.1302.51 (Cyme); εἴ κ' ἄν (more prob. εἰκ ἄν) *IG*5(2).6 (Tegea, iv B.C.); κε repeated, Od.4.733.

**κεάδας**, ὁ, = καιάδας, D.Chr.80.9.

**κεάζω**, Ep. fut. κεάσσω Orph.*A.*849: aor. κέάσα, κέασσα, ἐκέασσα Hom. (v. infr.):—Pass., aor. κεάσθην Il.16.412, but part. κεᾰθείσης *App.Anth.*3.167: pf. part. κεκεασμένος (v. infr.):—*split, cleave* wood, κέασε ξύλα νηλέϊ χαλκῷ Od.14.418; κέασαν ξύλα 20.161; ξύλα ..νέον κεκεασμένα χαλκῷ 18.309, cf. Hp.*Mul.*2.153, Call.*Fr.*289, etc.; of lightning, *shiver*, νῆα..κεραυνῷ Ζεὺς ἔλσας ἐκέασσε Od.5.132; of a spear, κέασσε δ' ἄρ' ὀστέα λευκά Il.16.347; [κεφαλὴ] ἄνδιχα πᾶσα κεάσθη *was cloven* in twain, ib.412; κεκεασμένον εὐρέϊ κύκλῳ οὐρανὸν Arat.474. 2. *pound, rub to pieces*, ἢ σφέλᾳ ἢ ὅλμῳ κεάσας Nic.*Th.* 644. (κεᾰ-ζω fr. κεᾰ- in κεᾰθείσης (v. supr.), εὐ-κέα-τος, κέαρνον, and perh. κείων, v. κείω (B); perh. cf. Skt. *śásati* 'cut', Lat. *castrare.*)

**κέαθοι**· βοηθοί, Hsch.; cf. κηθοί.

**κεάνωνος** or **-ωθος**, ὁ, *corn-thistle, Carduus arvensis*, dub. l. in Thphr. *HP*4.10.6.

**κέᾱρ**, contr. κῆρ (q.v.). **κέαρνον**, τό, (κεάζω) *carpenter's axe*, Hsch. (pl.). **κέαρος**· ὄρτυξ, Id. **κεάσματα**, τά, *chips*, Id. **κέᾰται, κέᾰτο**, Ep. 3 pl. pres. and impf. of κεῖμαι.

**κεβλή** (on the accent, v. Hdn.Gr.1.318), ἡ, Maced. form of κεφαλή, Call.*Fr.*140, cf. *EM*498.41: **κεβαλή**, ib.195.39, Hsch.

**κεβλήγονος**, ον, *with its seed in its head*, of the poppy, Nic.*Al.* 433. II. *born from the head*, Ἀτρυτώνη Euph.108.

**κεβλήνη**· ἡ ὀρίγανος, Hsch.

⊛ **κεβλήπῡρις**, name of a bird, Ar.*Av.*303; nickname of Themistocles, Hermipp.72.

**κέβλος**, ὁ, *dog-faced baboon*, Hsch. **κέγκλος**, ὁ, an unknown *sea-bird*, Suid. **κεγνώειν**· τεθραῦσθαι, τετρύσθαι, Hsch. **κέγχει**· ἐπιδάκνει, Id. **κέγχρα**, ἡ, = κέγχρος, Sch.Ar.*V.*91.

**κεγχρᾰλέτης**, ου, ὁ, (ἀλέω) *grinding millet*, gloss on πασπαλέτης, Gal.19.128.

**κεγχρᾰμῐδώδης**, ες, *like the* κεγχραμίς I, Thphr.*HP*1.11.3.

**κεγχρᾰμίς**, ίδος, ἡ, (κέγχρος) *seed of fig*, Hp.*Nat.Mul.*109, Arist. *HA*549ᵃ29, Thphr.*HP*1.11.6, 2.8.2. 2. *olive-kernel*, Suid. 3. pl., *trachomata* of the eye, Orib.*Eup.*4.27 tit.

**κεγχρανοπώλης**, ου, ὁ, = τραγηματοπώλης, Hsch.

**κεγχρ-είοισι**, poet. lengthd. dat. for κέγχροις, Arat.986. ⊛ **-εών**, ῶνος, ὁ, (κέγχρος) *place where iron is granulated and made malleable*, Docum.ap.D.37.26. **-ηΐς**, ΐδος, ἡ, v. κέρχνη. **-ιαῖος**, α, ον, *of the size of a grain of millet*, μεγέθη Dsc.2.83, cf. Luc.*Icar.*18, Theo Sm. p.125 H. **-ίας**, ου, ὁ, *like grains of millet*: κ. ἕρπης *an eruption on the skin*, Gal.7.722, 10.1009. II. *serpent with millet-like protuberances* on the skin, Philum.*Ven.*22.1:—also -ιδίας, Dsc.*Ther.*32; cf. κέγχρος III: -ίτης, Aët.13.27: -ίνης [ῑ], ὁ, is another species in Philum.*Ven.* 26.1, Nic.*Th.*463, Lyc.912, Paul.Aeg.5.18. III. in Poll.1.248, κεγχριδίας and κεγχρίας are f.ll. for κεγχρυδίας. ⊛ **-ίδιον** (κιχρηδῶν cod.), τό, Dim. of κέγχρος, *grain of seed like millet*, Hsch. **-ίνης**, ὁ, v. κεγχρίας II. II. a bird, Suid. **-ῐνος**, η, ον, *made of millet*, κ. ἄλευρον Dsc.5.3, cf. Gal.6.519; ἡ κεγχρίνη *millet-pottage*, Hsch. **-ίς**, ίδος, ἡ, = κέρχνη (q.v.). b. a small millet-eating bird, *ortolan* or *bunting*, Ael.*NA*13.25. 2. masc., = κεγχρίας II (q.v.), Lucan.9. 712, Plin.*HN*20.245. II. = κέγχρος I, Hp.*Nat.Mul.*32. **-ίτης** [ῑ], ου, ὁ, *like millet*, 1. = κεγχρίας II (q.v.). 2. a kind of *stone*, Plin.*HN*37.188. 3. a bird, Dionys.*Av.*3.23. II. fem. **-ῖτις**, ἡ, ἰσχάς *a dried fig* (from its number of grains), *AP*6.231 (Phil.). 2. a fabulous plant, Ps.-Plu.*Fluv.*19.2.

**κεγχρο-βόλοι**, οἱ, *millet-throwers*, fabulous tribe in Luc.*VH*1. 13. **-ειδής**, ές, *like grains of millet*, ἱδρῶτες interpol. in Hp.*Prog.*6; κ. τραχύσματα *granulated* work on silver cups, Ath.11.475b. Adv. -δῶς Steph.*in Hp.*1.114 D.

⊛ **κέγχρος**, ὁ (also ἡ, Arist.*Ph.*250ᵃ20, Dieuch.ap.Orib.4.7.15, Glauc. ap.*POxy.*1802.42, Dsc.2.97, Gal.6.791, Jul.*Or.*3.112a, Iamb.*VP*24. 106), *millet, Panicum miliaceum*, usu. in pl., Hes.*Sc.*398, Hdt.4.17, Hp.*Acut.*21, X.*An.*1.2.22, etc.: sg., Hecat.154 J., Hdt.1.193, Thphr. *HP*1.11.2, al., *OGI*55.15 (Telmessus, iii B.C.); of a single grain, Hdt.3.100, Plot.6.3.11, prob. in Sapph.*Supp.*1.13:—also **κέρχνος**, Anaxandr.41.27, Gal.18(1).574; cf. κέρχνωμα, κέρχνη. II. *anything in small grains*: 1. *spawn of fish*, Hdt.2.93. 2. *small beads*, Ath.12.525e. 3. *speck, sty* in the eye, Adam.1.11, al. III. = κεγχρίας II (q.v.), Dsc.*Ther.*15. IV. *small* kind of *diamond*, Plin.*HN*37.57.

**κεγχροφόρος**, ον, *bearing millet*, Str.5.1.12.

**κεγχρ-ώδης**, ες, *millet-like*, of eruptions, Hp.*Liqu.*6, *Epid.*2.3.1; of plants, Thphr.*HP*8.3.3,4; σάρξ *granulated* tissue, Archig.ap.Orib. 46.26.1. **-ώματα**, ων, τά, *things of the size of millet-grains*: hence, *eyelet-holes* in the rim of a shield, E.*Ph.*1386. **-ων**, ωνος, ὁ, a local wind on the river Phasis, Hp.*Aër.*15. **-ωτός**, ή, όν, *covered with specks*, εἴδη ὀφθαλμῶν Adam.1.11. II. *with granulated, roughened surface*, of tables, *BGU*781 v 14 (i A.D.).

**κεδαίω**, later Ep. for κεδάννυμι (Act. only διὰ..κεδαίη in tmesi, Nic.*Al.*458), in Pass., Arat.159, 410, A.R.2.626, Nic.*Th.*425; κεδόωνται (from **κεδάομαι**) A.R.4.500; κεδᾶται Hsch.

**κεδάννυμι**, poet. for σκεδάννυμι, late in pres., *AP*5.275 (Agath.); Ep. aor. Act. ἐκέδασσα Hom. (v. infr.), Opp.*H.*1.412, 3 pl. κέδασαν Hsch., Pass. ἐκεδάσθην Hom. (v. infr.), κεδάσθη Orph.*A.*557; plpf. Pass. κεκέδαστο A.R.2.1112:—*break up, scatter*, ἐκέδασσε φάλαγγας Il.17. 285; θεὸς δ' ἐκέδασσεν Ἀχαιούς Od.14.242; so [ποταμὸς] ἐκέδασσε γεφύρας Il.5.88; νεφέλας ἐκέδασσαν ἄελλαι A.R.3.1360:—Pass., κεδασθείσης ὑσμίνης when the battle *was broken up*, i. e. when the combatants were no longer in masses, Il.15.328, 16.306; ἔμειναν ἀθρόοι, οὐδ' ἐκέδασθεν ἀνὰ στρατόν 15.657; [δούρατα] ῥαισθείσης (sc. νηός) κεκέδαστο A.R.2.1112; κῶμα κεδάσθη *was shed*, Orph. l. c.

**κέδματα**, ων, τά, word of doubtful meaning in Hp.*Aër.*22, *Loc. Hom.*10, *Epid.*6.5.15, 7.122, *Morb.*1.3; expld. by Gal.19.111, Erot., Hsch., as *arthritic affections*; applied to *aneurism* of the vena cava by Aret.*SA*2.8: sg., Hp.ap.Erot.*Fr.*54 (s. v.l.).

**κεδμᾰτώδης**, ες, *like* κέδματα, Hp.ap.Erot. s. v. κέδματα (dub. l.).

⊛ **κεδνός**, ή, όν, (cf. κήδ-ομαι) Act., *careful, diligent, trusty*, ἄναξ Od. 14.170, etc.; ἀμφίπολος 1.335; πολῖται Pi.*P.*4.117; οἰακοστρόφος A. *Th.*62, E.*Med.*523; στρατόμαντις A.*Ag.*122 (lyr.); γυνή E.*Alc.*97

(lyr.): generally, *noble*, Φοίνικος κόρα B.16.29; παρθένος Pi.*P*.9.122. 2. Pass., *cared for, cherished, dear*, οἵ οἱ κεδνότατοι (v.l. κήδιστοι) καὶ φίλτατοι ἦσαν Il.9.586; ὅς μοι κήδιστος.., κεδνότατός τε Od.10.225; τοκῆες Il.17.28, cf. Pi.*I*.1.5; μήτηρ Hes.*Th*.169, Pi.*Pae*.6.12,105; ἀδελφεοί B.5.118; [ἄλοχος] Id.3.33; λέχος E.*Fr*.591. II. of things, Hom. only in neut. pl., κεδνὰ ἰδυῖα *true*-hearted, Od.1.428, 19.346, al.; ἤθεα κ. Hes.*Op*.699; πολίων κυβερνάσιες Pi.*P*.10.72; κ. χάρις *valued, prized*, Id.*O*.8.80; φροντίς, βουλεύματα, *wise*, A.*Pers*.142 (lyr.), 172 (troch.); ἐφετμαί Id.*Supp*.206; of news, *good, joyful*, Id.*Ag*.622, cf. 261; οὔπω τι κ. ἔσχον S.*Aj*.663; κεδνὰ πράξειν E.*Alc*.605 (lyr.).

**κεδνοσύνη**, ἡ, *trustiness, goodness*, *IG*3.1370.

**κέδρακε·** ῥιγοῖ, πέφρικεν, Hsch.

**κεδρέα**, ἡ, = κεδρία, *PAmh*.2.125.3 (i A.D.), Gal.12.16, al., Paul.Aeg.7.3, Alex.Trall.1.1.

**Κεδρεᾶτις**, ιδος, ἡ, (κέδρος) title of Artemis at Orchomenus in Arcadia, Paus.8.13.2.

**κεδρ-έλαιον**, τό, *oil of cedar*, extracted from cedar-resin, Aët.1.196. **-ελάτη** [ᾰ], ἡ, *Syrian cedar, Juniperus excelsa*, Plin.*HN*13.53, 24.17. ⊛ **-ία**, Ion. **-ίη**, ἡ, *oil of* κεδρελάτη, Hdt.2.87, D.S.1.91, Dsc.1.77, Erot. s. v. κεδρίνῳ; cf. κεδρέα. **-ίνεος** [ῐ], α, ον, poet. for sq., Nic.*Al*.488. **-ῐνος**, η, ον, (κέδρος) *of cedar*, θάλαμος Il.24.192; δόμοι E.*Alc*.160; ξύλα *IG*11(2).161*D*92 (Delos, iii B.C.); ξυλεία Plb.10.27.10; φατνώματα J.*BJ*5.5.2; τῶν ξύλων τὰ κ. Thphr.*HP*5.9.8. 2. *made from* κεδρελάτη, ἔλαιον Hp.*Mul*.1.78, Arist.*HA*583$^a$23; οἶνος Dsc.5.36. 3. κέδρινον, τό, *orange-coloured dye*, *PHolm*.21.30. **-ίον**, τό, as etym. of κιτρίον, Phan.Hist.35; Lat. *cedrium*, = κεδρία, Vitr.2.9.13, Plin.*HN*16.52; κέδριον, with v.l. κέδρινον, Hp.*Nat.Mul*.32. **-ίς**, ίδος, ἡ, *fruit of* κεδρελάτη, Id.*Mul*.2.192, *Nat.Mul*.32, Dsc.1.77; also, *juniper-berry*, Ar.*Th*.486. II. *juniper, Juniperus communis*, Thphr.*HP*1.9.4, etc. **-ίτης** [ῑ] οἶνος, ὁ, wine *flavoured with* κεδρία, Dsc.5.37.

**κεδρόμηλον**, τό, = κίτριον, Dsc.1.115, *Alex.Praef.*

⊛ **κέδρον**, τό (Att. acc. to Hsch.), = κεδρίς, *juniper-berry*, *EM*498.42, Hsch.:—also ⊛ **κέδρος**, ὁ, *Com.Adesp*.34 (ap.Ammon.*Diff*.p.80 V.). II. representation of a *cedar-cone*, *IPE*1$^2$.327.

**κέδροπα**, τά, = χέδροπα, Erot. s. h. v., Hsch. (nisi oxyt. sunt).

**κεδροπᾰγής**, ές, (πήγνυμι) *made of cedar-wood*, σανίδες *Supp.Epigr*.1.567.6 (Karanis, iii B.C.).

**κέδρος**, ἡ, *cedar-tree*, ὀδμὴ κέδρου..θύου τ' ἀνὰ νῆσον ὀδώδει δαιομένων Od.5.60; τὸ ἀπὸ κ. ἄλειφαρ γινόμενον Hdt.2.87, cf. 4.75; applied to *prickly cedar, Juniperus Oxycedrus*, Od. l. c., Thphr.*HP*3.12.3; *Syrian cedar, J. excelsa*, ib.3.2.6, Dsc.1.77; *Phoenician cedar, J. phoenicea*, Thphr.*HP*9.2.3; *Himalayan cedar, J. macropoda*, Str.15.1.29; κ. μικρά *juniper, J. communis*, Dsc. l. c. 2. *anything made of cedar-wood*: *cedar coffin*, E.*Alc*.365 (pl.), *Tr*.1141; *cedar box*, for a bee-hive, Theoc.7.81. 3. *cedar-oil*, τῇ κ. ἀλείφειν Luc.*Ind*.16. 4. v. κέδρον I.

**κεδροχᾰρής**, ές, (χαίρω) *rejoicing in cedar*, Man.4.191.

**κεδρόω**, *embalm with* κεδρία, Posidon.ap.Str.4.4.5, D.S.5.29.

**κέδρωστις**, εως, ἡ, *bryony*, Dsc.4.182.

**κεδρωτός**, ή, όν, *made of* or *inlaid with cedar-wood*, παστάδων τέραμνα E.*Or*.1371 (lyr.).

**κέεσθαι, κέεται**, v. κεῖμαι.

⊛ **κεῖ**, Adv., = κεῖθι, ἐκεῖθι, Archil.170, Herod.1.26.

**κεῖα·** καθάρματα, Hsch.; cf. κήϊα. **κειάμενος, κείαντες**, v. καίω. **κειανθί·** καίοντες, Id. ⊛ **κεῖθεν**, ⊛ **κεῖθι**, v. ἐκεῖθεν, ἐκεῖθι. **κείθιον**, v. κηθίς.

**κεῖλος**, ὁ, *donkey*, *Sammelb*.5224.29; cf. κίλλος.

⊛ **κεῖμαι**, κεῖσαι Il.19.319, etc. (κατά-κειαι *h.Merc*.254, Arc. κεῖοι *Tab.Defix*. in *Philol*.59.201), κεῖται Il.6.47, Hdt.1.9, 4.62 (v.l. κέεται), *IG*1$^2$.94.25; pl. κεῖνται A.*Supp*.242, Ion. κέᾰται Il.11.659, al., Hdt. (προσ-κέανται is f.l. 1.133, cf. προσ-κέαται, v.l. -κέονται, Hp.*Fract*.6), κείᾰται Mimn.11.6 (κατα- Il.24.567), κέονται Il.22.510, Od.16.232, prob. in Alc.94, συγ-κέονται Aret.*SD*2.4; imper. κεῖσο, κείσθω, Il.18.178, Hdt.2.171; subj. 3 sg. κέηται Pl.*Sph*.257c, Lycurg.113, Ep. κεῖται (fr. κέγ-ε-ται) Il.19.32, Od.2.102, al., δια-κένησθε Isoc.15.259, κείωνται *IG*2$^2$.1176.21; opt. 3 sg. κέοιτο Hdt.1.67, Hp.*Art*.14 (κατα-), Is.6.32, Pl.*R*.477a; inf. κεῖσθαι Il.8.126, Hp.*Prog*.3, Hdt.2.127, al., κέεσθαι v.l. in ib.2, cf. Hp.*Aër*.6, Archim.*Aequil*.1 *Prooem*.; part. κείμενος Il.7.265, etc.: impf. ἐκείμην Od.13.284, etc., Ep. κείμην 9.434; Ep. 3 sg. κέσκετο 21.41, (παρε-) 14.521; Ion. 3 pl. ἐκέατο Hdt.1.167, Ep. κέατο Il.13.763, κείατο 11.162; κεῖντο 21.426, (ἐπέ-) Od.6.19: fut. κείσομαι Il.18.121, A.*Ch*.895, etc., Dor. κεισεῦμαι Theoc.3.53. (Cf. Skt. *śéte* (= κεῖται), also *śáyate* 'lie', Gr. κοίτη, κοιμάομαι, perh. Lat. *cunae*, etc.): *to be laid* (used as Pass. to τίθημι): hence, *lie, lie outstretched*, used by Hom. mostly with Preps., πυρὴν..ἣ ἔνι κεῖται Πάτροκλος Il.23.210; κεῖτο παρὰ μνηστῇ ἀλόχῳ 9.556; ἐπὶ γαίῃ 11.162; ὑπ' αἰθούσῃ Od.21.390; also ἐπί τινος, ὀστέα..κείμεν' ἐπ' ἠπείρου 1.162; τὸ δ' ἥμισυ κεῖτ' ἐπὶ γαίης Il.13.565, cf. 20.345; but ὁ δ' ἐπ' ἐννέα κεῖτο πέλεθρα *lay stretched* over.., Od.11.577, al.; later κεῖσθαι εἰς.., in pregnant sense, εἰς ἀνάγκην κείμεθ' E.*IT*620; εἰς ὀλίγην κ. κόνιν *AP*9.677 (Agath.); also ἐπὶ τὴν ὁδὸν κ. *to be strewn* upon the path, Call.*Iamb*.1.250: Archit., κείμενον σχῆμα, opp. ὠρθωμένον, *plan*, opp. elevation, Apollod.*Poliorc*.163.3: c. acc., τόπον..ὅντινα κεῖται S.*Ph*.145 (anap.). 2. *lie down to rest, repose*, Od.13.281, etc.; πορφυρέᾳ κείμενος ἐν χλανίδι Simon.37.12; *lie, remain*, κεῖτο γὰρ ἐν νήεσσι..'Αχιλλεύς Il.2.688, cf. 7.230, etc.; οὐ χρῆν ἥσυχον κεῖσθαι πόδα S.*Fr*.142.13; *lie still*, λασίην ὑπὸ γαστέρ' ἐλυσθεὶς κείμην, of Odysseus under the ram's belly, Od.9.434: metaph., κακὸν κείμενον a *sleeping* evil, S.*OC*510 (lyr.); τοῦ κύματος κειμένου Ael.*NA*15.5. 3. *lie sick* or *wounded*, ἐν νήσῳ κεῖτο, of Philoctetes, Il.2.721, cf. 15.240; κείσεται οὐτηθείς 8.537, cf. 11.659; γήραϊ λυγρῷ κεῖται ἐνὶ μεγάροις ἀρημένος 18.435; κεῖτ' ὀλιγηπελέων Od.5.457; *lie in misery*, ἐοικότι κεῖται ὀλέθρῳ 1.46; κεῖται ἐν ἄλγεσι θυμός 21.88, cf. S.*Ph*.183 (lyr.); κ. ἐν κακοῖς E.*Ph*.1639, *Hec*.969; κειμένῳ ἐπεμπηδᾶν to kick him *when he's down*, Ar.*Nu*.550. 4. *lie dead*, Il.5.467, 16.541, al., A.*Ag*.1438, 1446, S.*Ph*.359; κεῖται δὲ νεκρὸς περὶ νεκρῷ Id.*Ant*.1240: rare in Prose, χίλιοι..νεκροὶ κείμενοι Hdt.8.25, cf. Hdn.2.1.8. b. freq. also in epitaphs, *lie buried*, τῇδε κείμεθα Simon.92, cf. 97; κεῖσαι ζῶν ἔτι μᾶλλον τῶν ὑπὸ γᾶς Id.60; also κ. ἐν Ταρτάρῳ Pi.*P*.1.15; ἐν τάφῳ, ἐν Ἅιδου, παρ' Ἅιδῃ, A.*Ch*.895, S.*El*.463, *OT*972; also in Prose, τὸν χῶρον ἐν τῷ κέοιτο 'Ορέστης Hdt.1.67, cf. 4.11, 9.105, Th.2.43; κ. ὑπό τινων *to be buried* by.., Plu.2.583c. 5. freq. of a corpse, *lie unburied*, Il.18.338, 19.32; κεῖται..νέκυς ἄκλαυτος ἄθαπτος 22.386; μὴ δή με ἕλωρ Δαναοῖσιν ἐάσῃς κεῖσθαι 5.685; also κεῖτ' ἀπόθεστος..ἐν πολλῇ κόπρῳ *lay uncared for*, of the old hound of Odysseus, Od.17.296; εὐνὴ..κάκ' ἀράχνια κεῖται ἔχουσα 16.35; of places, *lie in ruins*, δόμοι..χαμαιπετεῖς ἔκεισθ' ἀεί A.*Ch*.964 (lyr.), cf. Pl.*R*.425a, Lyc.252. 6. of wrestlers, *have a fall*, A.*Eu*.590; πεσών γε κείσομαι Ar.*Nu*.126. II. of places, *to be situated, lie*, νῆσος ἀπόπροθεν εἰν ἁλὶ κεῖται Od.7.244, cf. 9.25, 10.196, etc.; ἐν τῇ [γῇ] κείμενά ἐστι τὰ Σοῦσα (for κεῖται) Hdt.5.49; Αἴγινα..πρὸς νότου κ. πνοάς A.*Fr*.404; πρὸ Μεγάρων κ. Th.3.51; πόλις αὐτάρκη θέσιν κειμένη Id.1.37; θέσιν κέεσθαι νοσερωτάτην Hp.*Aër*.6, cf. Arist.*HA*496$^a$14; κ. πρὸς τὸν ἥλιον, πρὸς ἄρκτον, Id.*Mete*.360$^b$14, 363$^a$3. 2. of things, *lie* or *be* in a place, ὅθι οἱ φίλα δέμνι' ἔκειτο Od.8.277; ἕλε δίφρον κείμενον *placed there*, 17.331, cf. 410; φόρμιγγα.., ἥ που κεῖται ἐν ἡμετέροισι δόμοισι 8.255: in Prose, δύο τράπεζαι ἐκείσθην Lys.13.37; χύτρας εὐκρινῶς κειμένας X.*Oec*.8.19. 3. *fit*, of shoes, Herod.7.121. 4. κεῖσθαι, *posture, attitude*, as a category, Arist.*Cat*.2$^a$2. III. *to be laid up, in store*, of goods, property, etc., δόμοις ἐν κτήματα κεῖται Il.9.382; πολλὰ δ' ἐν ἀφνειοῦ πατρὸς κειμήλια κ. 6.47; βασιλῆϊ δὲ κεῖται ἄγαλμα *is reserved*.., 4.144; μνῆμα ξείνοιο..κέσκετ' ἐνὶ μεγάροισι *was left lying*.., Od.21.41; of things dedicated to a god, κ. ἐν θησαυρῷ Hdt.1.51, cf. 52, Alc.94; of money, κείμενα *deposits*, Hdt.6.86.α'; κ. σοι εὐεργεσία ἐν τῷ ἡμετέρῳ οἴκῳ Th.1.129, cf. *SIG*22.15 (Epist. Darei), Pl.*R*.345a; πολλὰ χρήματα ἐπὶ τῇ τούτου τραπέζῃ κεῖταί μοι at his bank, Isoc.17.44; παρά τινι Pl.*Ep*.346c; τἀργύριόν σοι κείσεται the caution-money *shall be deposited*, Ar.*Ra*.624; δραχμὴν ὑπόθες.—Answ. κεῖται πάλαι Diph.73.2: metaph., εἰ ταῦτ' ἀνατὶ τῇδε κείσεται κράτη *shall be placed to* her *credit*, S.*Ant*.485, cf. Pi.*I*.5(4).18. IV. *to be placed in position*, τῶν ἐπὶ τοῦ τοίχου..κειμένων κιόνων *IG*1$^2$.372.46. 2. *to be set up, ordained*, ἄεθλα κεῖτ' ἐν ἀγῶνι Il.23.273, cf. Hdt.8.26, 93, Th.2.46; ὅπλων ἔκειτ' ἀγὼν πέρι S.*Aj*.936 (lyr.). 3. of laws, κεῖται νόμος the law *is laid down*, E.*Hec*.292; νόμοι ἐπ' ὠφελίᾳ τῶν ἀδικουμένων κεῖνται Th.2.37; νόμοι κεῖνται περί τινος Antipho 6.2; οἱ νόμοι οἱ κείμενοι the *established* laws, Ar.*Pl*.914, cf. Lys.1.48, etc.; οἱ ὑπὸ τῶν θεῶν κείμενοι νόμοι X.*Mem*.4.4.21; οἱ νόμοι οἱ ὑπὸ τῶν βασιλέων κείμενοι Isoc.1.36, cf. D.24.62; καινὰ κεῖσθαι θέσμι' ἀνθρώποις E.*Med*.494; αἱ κείμεναι ὑπὸ τῶν ὑπατικῶν γνῶμαι the votes *given* by.., D.H.7.47; οὐκέτι κ. ἡ διαθήκη no longer *holds*, Is.6.32; so of philosophical arguments, *hold good*, κατά τινων Phld.*Rh*.1.51 S.; θάνατος ὧν κεῖται πέρι E.*Ion*756; κείμεναι ζημίαι Lys.14.9, cf. Th.3.45. 4. *to be laid down in argument, posited, assumed*, τοῦτο ἡμῖν οὕτω κείσθω Pl.*R*.350d, etc.; ὡμολογημένον ἡμῖν κ. Id.*Plt*.300e; freq. in Arist., κείσθω *let it be assumed*, *APr*.34$^b$23, al.; τὸ ἐξ ἀρχῆς κείμενον the *assumption*, *Metaph*.1008$^b$2, 1047$^b$10 (pl.); τὰ περὶ τὴν διάνοιαν ἐν τοῖς περὶ ῥητορικῆς κ. *Po*.1456$^a$35. 5. of names, οὔνομα κεῖται the name *is given*, Hdt.4.184, 7.200, cf. X.*Cyr*.2.2.12, Pl.*Sph*.257c, etc.; ὑπὸ τοῦ πατρὸς κείμενον [ὄνομα] Is.3.32; κεῖσθαι without ὄνομα, Pl.*Cra*.392d; κείμενα ὀνόματα *established* terms, Arist.*Top*.140$^a$3, Demetr.*Eloc*.96. 6. metaph., πάντα δεινὰ κἀπικινδύνως βροτοῖς κεῖται, παθεῖν μὲν εὖ, παθεῖν δὲ θάτερα danger *is set before* men, that they may.., S.*Ph*.503. V. metaph., of continuing conditions, ἐνὶ φρεσὶ πένθος ἔκειτο *lay heavy*, Od.24.423; εὔστομα κείσθω *remain* unspoken, Hdt.2.171; νεῖκος ἔκειτό τισι there *was* an *enduring* feud, S.*OT*491 (lyr.); 'Ελλήνων κείσομαι ἐν στόματι my name *shall be a household word*, *AP*9.62 (Even.); πολλῶν κείμενος ἐν στόμασιν Thgn.240; εὖ κείμενα A.*Ch*.693; μὴ κινεῖν (sc. κακὸν) εὖ κείμενον 'let sleeping dogs lie', Pl.*Phlb*.15c, cf. Hyp.*Fr*.30, Suid. 2. ταῦτα θεῶν ἐν γούνασι κεῖται, i. e. these things *are* yet *in the power of* the gods, to give or not, Il.17.514, 20.435. 3. κεῖσθαι ἔν τινι *to rest entirely* or *be dependent* on him, ἐν ἀγαθοῖσι κ. πολίων κυβερνάσιες Pi.*P*.10.71; ἐν ὔμμι ὡς θεῷ κείμεθα S.*OC*248 (lyr.); also ἐπί τινι, τὰ δ' οὐκ ἐπ' ἀνδράσι κ. Pi.*P*.8.76: also with simple dat., Λεωφίλῳ πάντα κεῖται Archil.69, prob. in *Com.Adesp*.1325; of things, *depend upon*, τὸ πανηγυρικὸν ἐν μελέτῃ καὶ τριβῇ κ. Phld.*Rh*.1.93 S.; τὰ..γυμνάσια ἐν τῇ κινήσει κ. Antyll.ap.Orib.6.23.1. 4. Medic., *to be left to settle*, of urine, Hp.*Epid*.1.26.β'. b. φάρυγξ οὐ φλεγμαίνουσα, κειμένη δέ, i. e. not swollen, ib.2.2.24. 5. Gramm., of words and phrases, *to be found, occur*, παρὰ τῷ ποιητῇ Str.7.3.6, cf. Ath.2.58b; κεῖται ἐν τῷ Περὶ Πλούτου Phld.*Oec*.p.39 J.; ποῦ κεῖται; Ath.4.165d, cf. Κειτούκειτος; κ. ἀντί τινος *to be used* instead of.., Str.8.6.7; τὸ κείμενον the *received text*, Sch.vulg.Pi.*O*.2.48.

⊛ **κειμηλι-άρχης**, ου, ὁ, *treasurer*, Just.*Nov*.40 *Praef*.1. **-άρχιον**, τό, *treasury*, *Cod.Just*.11.48.20.1, al. ⊛ **-ον**, τό, (κεῖμαι) *anything stored up as valuable, treasure, heirloom*, τῇ νῦν, καὶ σοὶ τοῦτο, γέρον, κ. ἔστω Il.23.618, cf. Xenoph.2.9, etc.; δῶρον..ὅ τοι κ. ἔσται Od.1.312;

ἐν ἀφνειοῦ πατρὸς κ. κεῖται, χαλκός τε χρυσός τε πολύκμητός τε σίδηρος Il.6.47; opp. live chattels (πρόβασις), Od.2.75 (pl.), S.*El.*438, E. *Heracl.*591; of a person, Id.*Rh.*654; of a fish, κ. Ἀμφιτρίτης Theoc. 21.55: metaph., κ. ἐσθλά. of γνῶμαι, E.*Fr.*362.4: rare in Prose, Hdt. 3.41, Luc.*Prom.Es* 4, *PGiss.*35.2 (iii A.D.): metaph., φίλος ἀνυπόστατον κ. Secund.*Sent.*11; in bad sense, κακὸν κ. Hp.*Lex* 4. II. *relic*, ἅγια κ. τῆς ἐκκλησίας *PGrenf.*2.111.1 (v/vi A.D.). –ος, ον, *treasured up*, πατὴρ..ὅτῳ καὶ μήτηρ..ἐν οἰκίᾳ κεῖνται κειμήλιοι Pl.*Lg.* 931a; κειμήλιον θέσθαι [τὸν θησαυρόν] ib.913a.

*κειμηλιοφῠλάκιον [ᾰ], τό, *treasury*, Just.*Nov.*59.6.

**κειμηλιόω**, *treasure up*, Eust.1376.13:—Med., Hdn.*Epim.*66.

**κεῖνος**, η, ο, Ion. and poet. for ἐκεῖνος. Adv. κείνως. **κεινός**, ή, όν, Ion. and poet. for κενός. **κεινόω**, v. κενόω. **Κεῖος**, v. Κέως. **κεῖρα**· γενεά, ἡ ἡλικία, Hsch.

**κειράς**, άδος, ἡ, *shorn*, Lxx *Je.*31(48).31,36; prob. f.l. for κουράς, v.l. κιδάρας.

*κειρία, ἡ, *girth of a bedstead*, Ar.*Av.*816, Lxx *Pr.*7.16, Plu.*Alc.* 16. II. *swathing-band, bandage*, written κηρία, *PMed.Lond.*155 iv 10,28, al., Sor.1.83, 2.59,61, Hsch.(-ρεί-); καιρία (q.v.); κιρία, *PCair.Zen.*69.9,11, *PSI*4.341.7, 387.4 (iii B.C.); *grave-clothes*, in form κειρίαι (v.l. κηρίαι) *Ev.Jo.*11.44. III. κηρίαι, *tapeworms*, Hp.ap.Erot.; κειρίαι Gal.14.755.

**κειριάτης**, *taeniosus*, *Gloss.*

**κειριόω**, *swathe*, in Pass., Herm.Trism. in *Rev.Phil.* 32.254,264.

**κεῖρις**, εως, ἡ, fabulous bird, expld. by ἱέραξ or ἀλκυών, Hsch., cf. Verg.*Ciris* tit. **κειρύλος**, v. κηρύλος.

*κείρω, fut. κερῶ Pl.*R.*471a, Ion. κερέω Il.23.146: aor. ἔκειρα Pi. *P.*9.37, E.*Tr.*1173, etc., Ep. ἔκερσα Il.13.546 (ἀπο–, in tmesi), A. *Supp.*666 (lyr.): pf. κέκαρκα *Sammelb.*6002 (ii B.C.), (περι–) Luc. *Symp.*32:—Med., fut. κεροῦμαι E.*Tr.*1183, (ἀπο–) Pl.*Phd.*89b: aor. ἐκειράμην Lys.2.60, etc., Ep. ἐκερσάμην Call.*Fr.*311, A.*Pers.*953 (lyr.): —Pass., aor. 1 part. κερθείς (v.l. καρθ-) Pi.*P.*4.82: aor. 2 ἐκάρην [ᾰ] *PSI*4.368.45 (iii B.C.), subj. κᾰρῇ Hdt.4.127, inf. κᾰρῆναι, part. καρείς, Luc.*Sol.*6, Plu.*Lys.*1: pf. inf. κεκάρθαι Hdt.2.36: Att. plpf. ἐκεκάρμην Luc.*Lex.*5. (Cf. Skt. *kr̥nāti* 'wound', Lat. *caro*: prob. also OE. *scieran*, Eng. *shear*.):—*cut short, shear, clip*, esp. of hair, σοί τε κόμην κερέειν (sc. Σπερχειῷ) Il.23.146, cf. Paus.1.37.3; κ. ἐν χροΐ [τὰς τρίχας] *crop* it close, Hdt.4.175; ἀλόχων κείραντες ἔθειραν E.*Hel.*1124 (lyr.): —more freq. in Med., *cut off one's* hair or *have it cut off*, as a sign of mourning (cf. κουρά), τοῦτο..γέρας οἶον ὀϊζυροῖσι βροτοῖσι, κείρασθαί τε κόμην βαλέειν τ' ἀπὸ δάκρυ παρειῶν Od.4.198, cf. 24.46, Il.23.46; πολύν σοι βοστρύχων πλόκαμον κεροῦμαι E.*Tr.*1183; κείρομαι κόμαν Id.*Ph.* 322 (lyr.): abs., *cut off one's hair*, κείρασθε, συμπενθήσατ' Id.*HF* 1390; ἐφ' οἷς ἡ πόλις ἐπένθησε καὶ ἐκείρατο Aeschin.3.211, etc.; ἄξιον ἦν ἐπὶ τῷδε τῷ τάφῳ κείρασθαι τῇ Ἑλλάδι Lys. l.c.: Com., πρὸς φθεῖρα κείρασθαι *to have oneself* close *shorn*, Eub.32:—Pass., κουρᾷ..πενθίμῳ κεκαρμένος E.*Or.*458; σύμβολον κ. half-*cropped*, Hermipp.14; τὰ ῥόδα κ. Pherecr.108.29; also, of the hair, *to be cut off*, πλόκαμοι κερθέντες Pi.*P.*4.82; βοστρύχους κεκαρμένους E.*El.*515. 2. *crop* a person, σφέας αὐτοὺς καὶ τοὺς ἵππους, in sign of mourning, Hdt.9.24; κεκάρθαι τὰς κεφαλάς *to have* their heads *shorn*, Id.2.36; Θρακιστὶ κέκαρμαι Theoc.14.46; v. χρώς I. 2, ἐγκυτί; *shear* sheep, μάχαιραι κουρίδες, αἷς κείρομεν τὰ πρόβατα καὶ τοὺς ποιμένας Cratin.37; κείρεσθαί (*tonderi*) μου τὰ πρόβατα, ἀλλ' οὐκ ἀποξύρεσθαι (*deglubi*) βούλομαι Tiber.ap.D.C. 57.10 (cf. infr. 3); τὸ μὲν [καρῆναι] ἐπὶ προβάτων τιθέασι καὶ ἐπὶ ἀτίμου κουρᾶς (cf. Luc.*Sol.*6), κείρασθαι δὲ ἐπὶ ἀνθρώπων Phryn.292; but τῶν Ἀργείων ἐπὶ πένθει καρέντων Plu. l.c.; τῷ σε χρὴ δρεπάνοισι καὶ οὐ ψαλίδεσσι καρῆναι *AP*11.368 (Jul. Antec.). 3. metaph., '*fleece*', *plunder*, τὴν μάμμην Herod.3.39. II. *cut down*, δοῦρ' ἐλάτης κέρσαντες Il. 24.450; ὕλην S.*Tr.*1196; *crop close*, opp. ἐπιτέμνειν, Thphr.*CP*3.23. 3; *pluck*, ἄνθη Philostr.*VA*1.5: metaph., ἐκ λεχέων κ. μελιαδέα ποίαν Pi.*P.*9.37; Ἄρης κέρσειεν ἄωτον A.*Supp.*666 (lyr.). 2. *ravage* a country, esp. *by cutting down* crops and fruit-trees, τὸ πεδίον Hdt.5. 63; τέμενος Id.6.75, cf. *OGI*765.10 (Priene); τὴν γῆν Hdt.6.99, Th. 1.64; χώραν Aen.Tact.15.9; *destroy*, πόλιν Call.*Fr.*1.60P.; also, *clear*, of pioneers, ὄρος Hdt.7.131:—Pass., of a country, *to be ravaged*, καρῆναι Id.4.127, cf. 8.65; κεκαρμένα κτήματα *SIG*364.67 (Ephesus, iii B.C.):—Med., χθὼν πεύκας κειραμένη *having its* pine-trees *cut down*, *AP*9.106 (Leon.); ἄρουραι λήϊα κειράμεναι Ps.-Phoc.166: metaph., Σπάρτη..ἐκείρατο δόξαν *had her* glory *shorn off*, Epigr.ap.Paus. 9.15.6; Ἄρης νυχίαν πλάκα κερσάμενος *having had* the plain *swept clean* (by destroying the men), A.*Pers.*953 (lyr.). 3. ἔκειρε πολύκερων φόνον *slaughtered* many a horned beast *by hewing*, S.*Aj.*55. 4. *hew, carve*, ἐπίβασιν *Inscr.Cypr.*99 H. 5. *cut through transversely*, opp. σχίζειν (slit longitudinally), φλέβα Antyll.ap.Orib.7.11.3. III. generally, *destroy, consume*: 1. *tear, eat greedily*, of beasts, κείρει τ' εἰσελθὼν βαθὺ λήϊον [ὄνος] Il.11.560; of fish, δημὸν..ἐπινεφρίδιον κείροντες 21.204; of vultures, ἧπαρ ἔκειρον Od.11.578, cf. Luc.*DDeor.* 1.1, *DMort.*30.1. 2. metaph., *waste, devour*, ἐκείρετε πολλὰ καὶ ἐσθλὰ κτήματ' ἐμά Od.2.312; ἔκειρον κτήματ' ἐνὶ μεγάρῳ 22.369, etc.: abs., κείρετε (sc. βίοτον) 1.378.

**κεῖσε**, Adv., Ion. and Ep. for ἐκεῖσε. **κεισός**, a plant, Hsch. (Perh. for κισσός.) **κεῖσσα**, Lacon. for κίσσα, Id. **κείστη**, v. κίστη.

**Κειτούκειτος**, ὁ, comic name of a Gramm., who asked respecting every dish—κεῖται ἢ οὐ κεῖται; (cf. κεῖμαι v. 5) Ath.1.1e.

**κείω** (A), once in Hom. κέω (v. infr., cf. A.D.*Adv.*143.11), Ep. Desiderat. of κεῖμαι, βῆ δ' ἴμεναι κείων he went *to lie down*, went *to bed*, Od.14.532, cf. 18.428; ἔνθ' ἴομεν κείοντες Il.14.340; κείω I *will lie*, Od.19.340; κειέμεν οὕτω *that they will lie* thus, 8.315; ὄρσο κέων get thee *to bed*, 7.342. 2. later, simply, *sleep, rest*, Arat. 1009.

**κείω** (B), *cleave*, radic. form of κεάζω, only in pres. part. κείων (perh. for *κεῶν = *κεάων) Od.14.425.

**κειώδης**, = κηώδης, Hsch.

**κεκάδήσω**, **κεκάδοντο**, **κεκαδών**, v. χάζομαι:—but for **κεκαδήσομαι**, v. κήδω:—for *κεκαδδίχθαι, v. κάδδιχος. **κεκαδμένος**, v. καίνυμαι.

**κεκᾰκουργημένως**, Adv. *maliciously*, Sch.Aeschin.3.3.

**κεκάλακας**· καλὴ γέγονας, ἡ ἐκάλεσας, Hsch. **κεκαλμένον**· ἐπὶ γῆς ἐκπεπτωκός, Id. **κέκασμαι, κεκασμένος, κέκαστο**, v. καίνυμαι.

*κεκᾰφηώς, Ep. pf. part. with no pres. in use, Hom. only in phrase κεκαφηότα θυμόν *breathing forth* one's life, Il.5.698, Od.5.468: in later Poets intr., *worn out, fordone*, κεκαφηότα γυῖα Opp.*C.*4.206; κ. γυῖα κεραυνῷ Nonn.*D.*2.539; δέμας κ. λιμῷ ib.26.108; δίψῃ κεκαφηότας ib.29.299; ἄνδρα..κεκαφηότα δηϊοτῆτι ib.46.93; κεκαφηότι θυμῷ Opp.*H.*3.572; κ. ταρσῷ *weary*, *AP*9.653 (Agath.). (Cogn. with καπύω, κάπτω: Hsch. has **κέκηφε**· τέθνηκεν.)

**κεκεῖνα**· κισσός, Hsch. *κεκῆνας· λαγωούς (Cret.), Id.

**κεκηρυγμένως**, Adv., (κηρύσσω) *notoriously*, Poll.6.208.

**κέκιλος**· ἰσχνόφωνος, Hsch.

**κεκλασμένως**, Adv., (κλάω A) *effeminately*, Anon.ap.Suid. s. v. ληκυθισμός.

**κεκλέᾰται, κεκλήατο**, v. καλέω:—**κέκλετο**, v. κέλομαι. **κέκληγα**, part. κεκληγώς, v. κλάζω. **κεκλίᾰται, κεκλῐμένος, κέκλῐτο**, v. κλίνω. **κέκλομαι, κεκλόμενος**, v. κέλομαι. **κέκλῠθι, κέκλῠτε**, v. κλύω.

**κεκμηκότως**, Adv., (κάμνω) *wearily*, Sch.S.*El.*164.

**κεκμηώς**, ότος and ῶτος, Ep. pf. part. Act. of κάμνω. **κέκνακεν**· ὑπὸ κακῶν ἀπειρήκει, Hsch.

**κεκολασμένως**, Adv., (κολάζω) *modestly, regularly*, Ath.6.273d, Ael.*NA*2.11, 6.1.

**κεκορεσμένως**, Adv., (κορέννυμι) *to satiety*, gloss on ἄδην, *EM*16. 42.

**κεκόρημαι, κεκορηώς**, v. κορέννυμι.

**κεκοσμημένως**, Adv., (κοσμέω) *modestly*, Ael.*NA*2.11, Philostr. *VA*7.42, Jul.*Mis.*344d.

**κεκοτηώς**, v. κοτέω. **κεκράανται, κεκράαντο**, v. κραίνω.

**κέκρ-αγμα**, ατος, τό, *scream, cry*, Ar.*Pax*637 (pl.). **-αγμός**, ὁ, = foreg., E.*IA*1357, Plu.2.654f (pl.). **-άκτης**, ου, ὁ, *bawler*, Hp. *Morb.Sacr.*15, Ar.*Eq.*137, Luc.*JTr.*33.

**κεκρᾱμένως**, Adv., (κεράννυμι I. 3) *in a mixed manner*, πρὸ τῶν ἀμίκτων ἐλέγχων κ. παρέχεται τοῖς ἐπαίνοις αὐτούς Procl.*in Alc.*p.102 C. 2. in painting, *with well-blended colours*, Plu.2.335a (fort. leg. κεκριμένως).

**κεκραξῐδάμας** [δᾰ], αντος, ὁ, (κέκραγα, δαμάω) coined by Ar.*V.*596 (by analogy to Ἀλκιδάμας) as epith. of Cleon, *he who conquers all in bawling.*

**κεκρᾰτημένως**, Adv., (κρατέω) *in a masterly manner*, ἀποδεδωκέναι Hipparch.1.8.11, cf. Phld.*Po.*5.26,29. 2. *vigorously*, v.l. in D.H. *Comp.*25. 3. *positively*, S.E.*M.*11.42.

**κέκραχθι**, v. κράζω.

**κεκρῐμένως**, Adv., (κρίνω) *judiciously, discreetly*, μουσικῇ χρῆσθαι Plu.2.1142c; cf. κεκραμένως.

**κεκροτημένως**, Adv., (κροτέω) *elaborately*, of style, D.H.*Comp.*25 (v.l. κεκρατημένως).

**Κέκροψ**, οπος, ὁ, *Cecrops* mythical king of Athens, Hdt.8.44; represented with a serpent's tail, and hence called διφυής, Sch.Ar.*V.* 436; with the tail of a θυννίς, Eup.156: pl., = Κεκροπίδαι, *IG*3.1335. (Κέκροψ a barbarian name acc. to Hecat.119J.) II. Adj. **Κεκρόπιος**, α, ον, *Cecropian, Athenian*, πέτρα Κ. *the Acropolis*, E.*Ion*936 (also simply Κεκροπία, ἡ, used for *Athens* itself, *Supp.*658, *El.*1289); Κ. χθών *Attica*, Id.*Hipp.*34, etc.; Κεκρόπιοι, οἱ, *the Athenians*, *APl.*4. 295. *Κεκροπία, ἡ, village-community in Early Attica, Str.9.1.20; **Κεκρόπιον**, τό, *shrine of Cecrops*, *IG*1².372.63:—also **-ικός**, ib. 374.144. 2. fem. **Κεκροπίς**, ίδος, φυλή Ar.*Av.*1407, *IG*1².302.59, etc.; Κ. αἶα *AP*7.81 (Antip. Sid.). 3. **Κεκροπίδαι**, οἱ, *descendants of Cecrops, Athenians*, Hdt. l. c., etc.: in sg., Ar.*Eq.*1055. 4. Adv. **Κεκροπίᾱθεν**, Ep. -ηθεν, *from Athens*, Call.*Dian.*227, A.R.1.95.

**κεκρυμμένως**, Adv., (κρύπτω) *secretly*, Lxx *Je.*13.17, Arr.*Epict.* 3.7.11.

**κεκρυφάλιον** [ᾰ], τό, Dim. of κεκρύφαλος, Poll.7.179. II. **κεκρυφάλεος**· ἀριστερόν (Aeol.), *AB*1095.

**κεκρυφᾰλοπλόκος**, ον, *netting* κεκρύφαλοι (v. sq.), Critias 69 D.

**κεκρύφᾰλος**, ὁ, *woman's hair-net*, τῆλε δ' ἀπὸ κρατὸς βάλε δέσματα σιγαλόεντα, ἄμπυκα, κεκρύφαλόν τε ἰδὲ πλεκτὴν ἀναδέσμην Il.22. 469, cf. Hp.*Steril.*219, Ar.*Th.*138, D.H.7.9; κ. καὶ μίτρα Ar.*Th.*257; λιθόβλητοι, λιθοκόλλητοι κ., *AP*5.269 (Paul.Sil.), 275 (Agath.). 2. *part of the head-stall of a bridle*, X.*Eq.*6.8; ἱππικὸς κ. *IG*2².1388.74, cf. Poll.1.184, 10.55. II. *second stomach* of ruminating animals, from its net-like structure, Arist.*HA*507b4, *PA*674b14, Ael.*NA*5. 41. III. *pouch* or *belly of a hunting-net*, X.*Cyn.*6.7, Plu.*Alex.* 25. [ῠ in Hom., *AP*; but ῡ in Att., Ar. l.c., Eup.170, Antiph.117, 189.]

**κεκρύφαται** [ῠ], v. κρύπτω. **κέκτικε**· τέτοκεν, Hsch. **κεκύθωσι** [ῠ], v. κεύθω. **κεκύκη**· καμπύλη, Id. **κέκυλτα**· δῶρα τὰ τῇ χειρὶ ἑλκόμενα, Id.

**Κεκυπώσιος**, ὁ (sc. μήν), name of month at Zelea, *SIG*279.17 (iv B.C.).

**κελᾰδ-εινός**, ή, όν, *sounding, noisy*, Ζέφυρος Il.23.208; Ἄρτεμις 16.183 (παρὰ τὸν γιγνόμενον ἐν τοῖς κυνηγίοις κέλαδον Sch. ad loc.); and so κελαδεινή alone, Il.21.511; of Dionysus, *AP*9.524.11; αὐλῶνες *h.Merc.*95; σῦριγξ Opp.*H.*5.455: neut. pl. as Adv., ποταμοὶ κελαδεινὰ ῥέοντες A.R.3.532:—Pi. has Aeol. form **κελαδεννός**, ἔπεα κ. *high-sounding* verses, *P.*3.113; ὀμφά *Pae.*5.46; κ. Χάριτες the *loud-voiced* Charites, *P.*9.89; κ. ὕβρις *noisy* insult, *I.*4(3).8. ⊛**-έω**, Sapph.4, E.*IT*1093 (lyr.); 3 pl. -έοντι Pi.*P.*2.15: fut. -ήσω Terp.5, Pi.*O.*2.2, E.*HF*694 (lyr.), -ήσομαι Pi.*O.*10(11).79: poet. aor. κελάδησα B.15.12, A.*Ch.*609 (lyr.), E.*Hel.*371 (lyr.): (κέλαδος):—Ep. and Lyr. (Trag. and Com. only in lyr. and anap., exc. Theopomp.Com.40: late in Prose, Aq.*Is.*49.13, Philostr.*VA*6.17, Ps.-Luc.*Philopatr.*3) Verb (cf. κελάδω), *sound as flowing water*, ὕδωρ ψῦχρον κ. Sapph.l.c.; κῦμα κελαδοῦν Orac.ap.Aeschin.3.112. 2. of persons, *shout aloud*, ἀτὰρ κελάδησαν Ἀχαιοί, in applause, Il.23.869; ἐμὲ δεῖ κ. Pratin.Lyr.1.3, cf. B.l.c.; κελαδέοντι ἀμφὶ Κινύραν φᾶμαι Pi.*P.*2.15: c. acc. cogn., κ. ὕμνους Terp.5, cf. Pi.*N.*4.16 codd.; νόμον Id.*Pae.*2.101; ἀδυμελῆ κόσμον κ. Id.*O.*11(10).14; [βοάς], παιᾶνας, E.*Ion*93, *HF* l.c. 3. of various *cries*, e.g. of a new-born babe, A.*Ch.*609; of the swallow, Ar.*Pax*801, *Ra.*684; of the grasshopper, Theopomp.Com.l.c.; of the cock, ἐξ εὐνᾶς κ. *crows* from his perch, Theoc.18.57; of bells, *ring, tinkle*, E.*Rh.*384; of the flute, κ. φθόγγον κάλλιστον Id.*El.*716; of the sea, Ar.*Th.*44. II. trans., *sing of, celebrate loudly*, τινα Pi.*O.*1.9, 2.2, 6.88, E.*IT*1093, Ar.*Ra.*1527; τέμενος B.13.21, cf. E.*Tr.*121; τινὰ ἀμφ' ἀρετᾷ Pi.*P.*2.63. **-ημα**, ατος, τό, *rushing sound*, Ζεφύρου E.*Ph.*213 (lyr.); ποταμῶν Ar.*Nu.*283 (anap.); later, of any *loud sound*, κ. σάλπιγγος *AP*6.350 (Crin.). **-ῆτις**, ιδος, ἡ, *loud-sounding*, γλῶσσα Pi.*N.*4.86.

**κελᾰδοδρόμος**, ον, *rushing amid the noise of the chase*, epith. of Artemis, Orph.*A.*902.

**κέλᾰδος**, ὁ, poet. word, *a noise as of rushing waters*: generally, *loud noise, din, clamour*, θῆκε πολὺν κέλαδον καὶ ἀϋτήν, of persons quarrelling, Il.9.547, cf. 18.530, Od.18.402; κ. Εὐίου E.*Ba.*578 (lyr.). 2. of *musical sound*, κ. λύρας Id.*IT*1129 (lyr.), cf. *Cyc.*489 (anap.). II. *loud clear voice*, as of an oracle, Pi.*P.*4.60; *shout, cry*, κ. οὐ παιώνιος A.*Pers.*605, cf. 388, *Ch.*341 (anap.), S.*El.*737, etc. 2. *chirp* of the τέττιξ, Ael.*NA*1.20; of the *twittering* of birds, κ. παντομιγής *Lyr.Alex.Adesp.*7.6.

**κελάδω**, Ep. form of κελαδέω, used in part. only, *sounding*, πὰρ ποταμὸν κελάδοντα Il.18.576, cf. B.8.65, Posidipp.ap.Tz.*H.*7.661; πλῆτο ῥόος κ. Il.21.16, cf. Theoc.17.92; Ζέφυρον κελάδοντ' ἐπὶ οἴνοπα πόντον Od.2.421; πόντον κ. Ar.*Nu.*284 (anap.); Βορέης κ. Q.S.8.243.

**κελαιν-εγχής**, ές, *with black* (i.e. *bloody*) *spear*, Pi.*N.*10.84.

**κελαι-νεφής**, ές, sync. for κελαινο-νεφής, *black with clouds*, Homeric epith. of Zeus, *shrouded in dark clouds, cloud-wrapped*, παρὰ πατρὶ κελαινεφεῖ Il.21.520, cf. Pi.*Pae.*6.55; addressed as κελαινεφές in Il.15.46, Od.13.147. 2. generally, *dark-coloured*, ῥέε δ' αἷμα κ. 11.36, cf. Il.4.140; πεδίον κ. *black, rich* soil, Pi.*P.*4.52; σκότος κ. Id.*Fr.*142.

**κελαινιάω**, *to be black*, in Ep. 3 pl. κελαινιόωσι, Opp.*H.*4.67; part. κελαινιόων Nonn.*D.*38.18.

**κελαινό-βρωτος**, ον, *black and bloody with gnawing*, ἧπαρ A.*Pr.*1025. **-λωτα**· κεράσια, Hsch. (fort. -λωπα *with dark skin*). **-ομαι**, Pass., *grow black* or *dark*, A.*Ch.*413 (lyr.). **-ρρῖνος**, ον, *with black skin* or *hide*, Opp.*H.*5.18, Nonn.*D.*15.158: pl. κελαινόρινες S.*Fr.*29.

⊛**κελαινός**, ή, όν, *black, dark*, freq. in Hom., αἷμα Il.1.303, Od.16.441; νύξ Il.5.310, etc.; κῦμα 9.6; λαῖλαψ 11.747; χθών 16.384; δέρμα 6.117; ἦτορ Hes.*Sc.*429; ὄμβρος Emp.111.6; κ. φῦλον a *swarthy* race, of the Ethiopians, A.*Pr.*808; Ἔπαφος ib.851; ξίφη, λόγχα, S.*Aj.*231, *Tr.*856 (both lyr.), cf. E.*Ba.*628 (troch., prob. from the colour of the metal rather than *black with blood-stains*); of things on which the sun does not shine, esp. of the nether world, *dark, murky*, A.*Pr.*433 (lyr.); Ἐρινύες Id.*Ag.*462 (lyr.); Στύξ Lyc.706; κ. θῖνα, of the bottom of the sea, S.*Ant.*590 (lyr.); λύει κ. βλέφαρα suffers her eyes to close *in darkness*, ib.1302: *great, mighty*, δίψα Lyc.1425. (Cf. Skt. *kalaṅkas* 'spot': κηλίς may be cogn.)

**κελαινο-φαής**, ές, *black-gleaming*, ὄρφνα κ. *murky* twilight, Ar.*Ra.*1331 (lyr.). **-φρων**, ον, gen. ονος, *black-hearted*, μήτηρ A.*Eu.*459. **-χρως**, ωτος, ὁ, ἡ, *black-coloured*, σίλφη *AP*9.251 (Even.), prob. l. in A.*Supp.*785 (lyr.): also **-χροος**, ον, Man.4.261.

**κελαιν-ώπας**, α, ὁ, (ὤψ) *black-faced*: hence, *gloomy*, θυμός S.*Aj.*955 (lyr.):—fem. **-ῶπις** νεφέλα Pi.*P.*1.7:—also **-ωπός**, ή, όν, Hdn.Gr.1.188. **-ώψ**, ῶπος, ὁ, ἡ, *swarthy*, Κόλχοι Pi.*P.*4.212.

**κελᾰρ-ύζω**, fut. -ύσομαι or -ύξομαι prob. in Hsch. (-ύζεται· μετὰ ποιᾶς φωνῆς ἠχήσει cod.): aor. κελάρυξε *Lyr.Adesp.*90.1; Poet. and late Prose (v. infr.):—*babble, murmur*, of running water, κατειβόμενον κελαρύζει Il.21.261, cf. Theoc.7.137, Phld.*Po.Herc.*994.14, Philostr.*VA*1.16, *Im.*1.21; later, of a rushing torrent, c. acc. cogn., ὡς ποταμὸς κ. μέγας..σμερδαλέον μύκημα Opp.*C.*2.145; also, *gush out like water*, ἀπὸ δ' ἕλκεος..αἷμα μέλαν κελάρυζε Il.11.813; [ἅλμη] ἀπὸ κρατὸς κελάρυζεν *ran gushing*, Od.5.323; of milk, *Lyr.Adesp.*l.c. 2. *pour with a gush* or *gurgling sound*, ἀφύσσοντες οἶνον κελαρύζετε IonTrag.10 (lyr.). (Onomatopoeic, acc. to Str.14.2.28, Plu.2.747d.) **-υξις**, εως, ἡ, *rushing sound*, as of water, Hsch. **-υσμα**, ατος, τό, = foreg., Opp.*C.*4.325.

**κέλε**· τέρπε, Hsch.

⊛**κελέβειον**, Ion. **-ήϊον**, τό, Dim. of sq., Antim.17.

**κελέβη**, ἡ (ποτηρίου εἶδος θερμηροῦ καὶ ποιμενικὸν ἀγγεῖον, Hsch.), *cup, jar*, Anacr.42, Theoc.2.2, Euph.8, Call.*Fr.anon.*34 (Aeol., acc. to Clitarch. and Silen.ap.Ath.11.475c).

**κελεβρά**· λεπτὰ καὶ νεκρὰ κτήνη, Hsch. **κελεΐς**· ἀξίνη, Id. **κελένδρυον** (-υνον Id.), τό, *oaken beam*, derived from κελέων, δρῦς by Id., Phot. (who glosses it by κιχήσιππον).

**κελέοντες**, ων, οἱ, = ἱστόποδες, *the vertical beams in the upright loom*, between which the web hung down, Ar.*Fr.*795, Antipho*Fr.*11, Theoc.18.34, Ant.Lib.10.2, cf. Paus.Gr. and Ael.Dion.*Fr.*228: sg., v. foreg.

**κελεός**, ὁ, *green woodpecker, Picus viridis*, Arist.*HA*593ᵃ8, 610ᵃ9.

**κελέτρα**, ἡ, dub. sens. in *IG*9(2).521.26,33 (Larissa, iii B.C.).

**κέλετρον**· ᾧ τοὺς ἰχθύας θηρῶσιν ἐν τοῖς ποταμοῖς, Hsch.

**κελευθ-είοντες**· ὁδεύοντες, Hsch. **-ειος**, α, ον, *belonging to the road*, δαίμονες Id.: κελευθειά, epith. of Athena at Sparta, Paus.3.12.4. **-ήτης**, ου, ὁ, *wayfarer*, *AP*6.120 (Leon.: prob. -ίτης).

**κελευθο-ποιός**, όν, *road-making*, A.*Eu.*13. **-πόρος**, ὁ, *wayfarer*, *AP*7.337.

⊛**κέλευθος**, ἡ, with poet. heterocl. pl. κέλευθα; poet. Noun (also Arc., *IG*5(2).3.23 (Tegea, iv B.C.)), *road, path*, not common in lit. sense, πολλαὶ γὰρ ἀνὰ στρατόν εἰσι κέλευθοι Il.10.66; Ἴσθμία κ. B.17.17; ἐν κελεύθοις in *the streets*, A.*Ch.*349 (lyr.); ἐγγὺς γὰρ νυκτός τε καὶ ἤματός εἰσι κέλευθοι Od.10.86, cf. Parm.1.11; ἀνέμων κέλευθα or κέλευθοι, Il.14.17, Od.5.383, etc.; ὑγρὰ, ἰχθυόεντα κ., of the sea, 3.71,177; ἁλὸς βαθεῖαν (vel -είας) κ. Pi.*P.*5.88; ἄρκτου στροφάδες κ. *paths, orbits*, S.*Tr.*131 (lyr.), cf. E.*Hel.*343 (lyr.); θεῶν δ' ἀπόεικε κελεύθου withdraw from the *path* of the gods, Il.3.406 (v.l. ἀπόειπε κελεύθους): metaph., ἔργων κέλευθον ἂν καθαράν on the open *road* of action, Pi.*I.*5(4).23, cf. *O.*6.23; στείχει δι' εὐρείας κ. μυρία παντᾷ φάτις B.8.47; ἔστι μοι μυρία παντᾷ κ. Pi.*I.*4(3).1, cf. B.5.31: Πειθοῦς, Δίκας κ., Parm.4.4, B.10.26. II. *journey, voyage*, by land or water, ὅς κέν τοι εἴπῃσιν ὁδὸν καὶ μέτρα κελεύθου Od.4.389; οὐκ ἂν πω χάζοντο κελεύθου would not have halted from *their onward way*, Il.11.504, cf. 12.262; πολλὰ κ. a far *journey*, i.e. a great distance, S.*OC*164 (lyr.). 2. *expedition*, A.*Ag.*127 (lyr.), *Pers.*758 (troch.). III. *way of going, walk, gait*, μιμήσομαι λύκου κ. E.*Rh.*212; δι' ἀψόφου βαίνων κ. Id.*Tr.*888. IV. metaph., *way* of life, ἀργαλέας βιότοιο κ. Emp.115.8; κ. ἁπλόαι ζωᾶς Pi.*N.*8.35; τὰν ἀνόστιμον βίου κ. E.*HF*433 (lyr.).

**κελεύθρας**· κελεύσεως, Hsch.

**κέλ-ευμα**, ατος, τό, = κέλευσμα (q.v.). **-ευσις**, εως, ἡ, *command*, Plu.2.32c (pl.), Plot.4.8.2: freq. in Inscrr. and Pap., κατὰ κέλευσιν θεοῦ *OGI*589 (Syria), cf. 455.3 (Aphrodisias, i B.C.), *BGU*286.9 (iv A.D.), etc.; ἐκ κελεύσεώς τινος *IGRom.*4.214 (Ilium, iii/iv A.D.); ἀπὸ κ. *CIG*5187*b*3 (Ptolemais, v/vi A.D.). **-ευσμα** or **-ευμα** (v. infr.), ατος, τό, (κελεύω) *order, command*, A.*Eu.*235, S.*Ant.*1219 (pl.), etc.; *call, summons*, A.*Ch.*751 (pl.): in Prose, *word of command* in battle, Hdt.4.141, 7.16, cf. E.*Hec.*929 (lyr.); ὁ Κύριος ἐν κ. καταβήσεται ἀπ' οὐρανοῦ 1*Ep.Thess.*4.16; also, the *call* of the κελευστής (q.v.), which gave the time to the rowers, ἀπὸ ἑνὸς κελεύσματος all at once, Th.2.92, D.S.3.15; ἐξ ἑνὸς κελεύματος Sophr.25; ἐκ κελεύματος at *the word of command*, A.*Pers.*397, cf. E.*IT*1405; καχάζετε..ἀπὸ κ. Eub.8; στρατεύσονται ἀφ' ἑνὸς κ. Lxx*Pr.*30.27; of the boatswain's *pipe*, κέλευσμα προσαυλεῖν Phld.*Mus.*p.15K.; also, the *call* of the driver to his horses, κελεύματι μόνον καὶ λόγῳ ἡνιοχεῖται Pl.*Phdr.*253d; of the huntsman to his hounds, X.*Cyn.*6.20; κ. κυνηγετῶν S.*Ichn.*225. (κέλευμα is the more ancient form, as in A.*Pers.*397, *Ch.*751, S., Sophr., Pl. (codd. l. c.), X., ll. cc., v.l. in Hdt. ll. cc., Th. l. c.)

**κελευσ-ματικῶς**, Adv. *by way of command*, Eust.1080.63. **-μός**, ὁ, *order, command*, E.*IA*1130, *Cyc.*653 (pl.). **-μοσύνη**, ἡ, Ion. for κελευσμός, κέλευσμα, Hdt.1.157. **-τέον**, *one must order*, Gal.17(2).171. ⊛**-τής**, οῦ, ὁ, *boatswain, who gives the time to the rowers*, E.*Hel.*1576, Ar.*Ach.*554, Th.2.84, X.*HG*5.1.8, Pl.*Alc.*1.125c, Phld.*Rh.*1.361 S., D.S.20.50, Arr.*Fr.*151 J. **-τικός**, ή, όν, *hortatory*: -κή (sc. τέχνη), Pl.*Plt.*260e; τοῦ ψόγου τὸ κ. Plu.2.72d (s.v.l.). **-τός**, ή, όν, *ordered, commanded*, Luc.*Vit.Auct.*8. **-τρα** or **κελεύστα**· ἅμαξα ἡμιονική, Hsch. **-τωρ**, ορος, ὁ, *one who commands*, more general than κελευστής, Phryn.*PS* p.81 B.

**κελευτιάω**, Frequentat. of κελεύω, only in Ep. part., Αἴαντε κελευτιόωντ' ἐπὶ πύργων πάντοσε φοιτήτην *continually urging on* [the men], Il.12.265; -όων γαιήοχος ὦρσεν Ἀχαιοὺς 13.125 (v.l. κελευθιόων, = ὁδηγῶν, Sch. ad loc.; κελευστιόων Hsch.).

⊛**κελεύω**, Ep. impf. κέλευον Il.23.767: fut. -σω, Ep. inf. -σέμεναι Od.4.274: aor. ἐκέλευσα, Ep. κέλ- Il.20.4: pf. κεκέλευκα Lys.1.34, Luc.*Demon.*44:—Med., aor. ἐκελευσάμην Hp.*Nat.Puer.*13: more freq. in compds. δια-, ἐπι-, παρα-κελεύομαι (q.v.):—Pass., fut. -ευσθήσομαι D.C.68.9: aor. ἐκελεύσθην Hdt.7.9.α', S.*OC*738, Th.7.70: pf. κεκέλευσμαι X.*Cyr.*8.3.14, Luc.*Sacr.*11: plpf. ἐκεκέλευστο D.C.78.4 (ἐκελεύθην v.l. in Hdt.7.9.α', and κεκέλευμαι *IG*2².1121.13 (iv A.D.), v.l. in App.*BC*5.141 are later forms). (A lengthd. form of κέλομαι, q.v.):—prop. *urge, drive on*, [ἵππους] ὁ γέρων ἐφέπων μάστιγι κέλευε..κατὰ ἄστυ Il.24.326: hence, *exhort, bid*, 1. c. acc. pers. et inf., *order* one to do, σ' ἔγωγε..κελεύω ἐς πληθὺν ἰέναι 17.30, cf. 2.11, al., Hdt.1.8, 24, etc.; ἐκέλευσε τὸν παῖδα περιμεῖναί ἑ κελεῦσαι he *bade* the lad *bid* us to wait for him, Pl.*R.*327b; ὁ νόμος τὸν ἐπιβουλεύσαντα κελεύει φονέα εἶναι, i.e. *bids that* he be held guilty, Antipho4.2.5; ὁ τὸν νόμον κελεύων ἄρχειν δοκεῖ κελεύειν ἄρχειν τὸν θεὸν καὶ τὸν νοῦν Arist.*Pol.*1287ᵃ29; ἐς τὴν Μίλητον ἔπεμπον κελεύοντες σφίσι τὸν Ἀστύοχον βοηθεῖν Th.8.38; *request*, Lys.16.16; opp. ἐπιτάττειν, *IG*1².76.33. 2. c. acc. pers. et rei, σφῶϊ μὲν οὔ τι κελεύω Il.4.286; τά με θυμὸς..κελεύει (sc. εἰπεῖν) 7.68, etc.: with inf. subjoined,

τί με ταῦτα κελεύεις..μάχεσθαι; 20.87. **3.** c. acc. pers. only, εἰ μή θυμός με κελεύοι (sc. φείδεσθαι) Od.9.278; ὥς με κελεύεις (sc. μυθεῖσθαι) 11.507: in Prose, ἐκέλευσε τοὺς ἕνδεκα ἐπὶ τὸν Θηραμένην *ordered* them [to go] against him, *ordered* them to seize him, X.*HG*2.3.54; κ. τινὰς ἐπὶ τὰ ὅπλα ib.20:—Pass., *receive orders*, Arist.*Pol.*1253ᵇ34. **4.** c. acc. rei only, ὃ μὴ κελεύσαι Ζεύς (Herm. for -σει) A.*Eu.*618; ὁ νόμος τὰ μὲν κελεύων τὰ δ' ἀπαγορεύων Arist.*EN*1129ᵇ24:—Pass., τὸ κελευόμενον *commands, orders*, Hdt.7.16, Antipho Soph. 61, X.*Cyr.*4.1.3: pl., Pl.*R.*340a. **5.** c. dat. pers. folld. by inf., *urge* or *order* one to do, κηρύκεσσι..κέλευσε κηρύσσειν.. Il.2.50, Od. 2.6, etc.; ἀλλήλοισι κέλευον ἅπτεσθαι νηῶν.. Il.2.151; ἑτάροισι.. ἐκέλευσα ἐμβαλέειν Od.9.488: in later Prose, D.S.19.17, Ceb.32.4 codd., Luc.*DMort.*1.1, Phalar.*Ep.*121.1, etc. **6.** rarely c. dat. pers. et acc. rei, τί δ' ἐστὶν ὃ κελεύεις ἐμοί; Men.*Pk.*224, cf. Ael.*NA* 9.1. **7.** c. dat. pers. only, ἵπποισι καὶ Αὐτομέδοντι κελεύσας Il. 16.684; cf. infr. III. **8.** abs., freq. in Hom., ὡς σὺ κελεύεις Il.23. 96, al.; λέξω, κελεύεις γάρ A.*Ch.*107; κελεύων, opp. αὐτοχειρίῃ, Democr.260; κελευούσης τῆς Πυθίης Hdt.6.36; κελεύοντος καὶ δεομένου Lys.5.1. **9.** c. inf. only, σιγᾶν κελεύω I *order* silence, S.*Ph.* 865; οὐκ ἂν κελεύσαιμ' εὐσεβεῖν Id.*Ant.*731; *recommend, propose*, Lys. 12.25, D.4.21, etc.; opp. οὐκ ἐάω, Hdt.6.109, X.*Ath.*2.18. **II.** of inferiors, *urge, entreat*, Il.24.599, Od.10.17, Hdt.1.116. **III.** of the boatswain, *give time* to rowers, c. dat., Pl.*R.*396b: abs., Ath.12. 535d. **2.** *sing a chanty*, S.E.*M.*6.24.

⊛ **κελεφος**, sine expl., *Gloss.*; ποιεῖ κελεφοὺς *lepers*, *Cat.Cod.Astr.* 8(4).189; cf. κελυφοκομῖον.

**κελέων**, ὁ, v. κελέοντες.

**κελημοσύναις**· κελεύσεσιν, Hsch.

**κέληξ**, ὁ, = sq., *IG*5(1).213 (Sparta, v B.C.).

⊛ **κέλης**, ητος, ὁ, (κέλλω) *courser, riding-horse*, Ὀδυσσεὺς ἀμφ' ἑνὶ δούρατι βαῖνε, κέληθ' ὡς ἵππον ἐλαύνων bestrode one plank, as if riding on a *horse*, Od.5.371 (κ. ἵππος also in later Prose, *SIG*314*A*7,36, al. (Arc., iv B.C.), Plu.*Alex.*3, Paus.6.14.4); κ. καὶ ἅρματα Hdt.7.86; ἵππον κέλητ' ἀσκοῦντα Eup.152; κέλης κέλητα παρακελητιεῖ Ar.*Pax* 901; freq. in the titles of Pindar's Odes, as *O.*1; νίκας Πυθοῖ καὶ Ἰσθμοῖ καὶ Νεμέᾳ τεθρίπποις τε καὶ κέλησι Pl.*Ly.*205c, cf. Plin.*HN* 34.19; κ. πωλικός, τέλειος, *IG*2.966. **II.** *fast-sailing yacht* with one bank of oars, Hdt.8.94, Th.4.9, 8.38, X.*HG*1.6.36, Ephipp.5.17 (anap.), Plb.5.94.8, Plin.*HN*7.208, etc. **III.** sens. obsc. (with play on I), Ar.*Lys.*60; so ἥρως Κέλης Pl.Com.174.18. **2.** *pudenda muliebria*, Eust.1539.34.

**κελητ-ιάω**, = sq., Hsch. ⊛ **-ίζω**, (κέλης) *ride*, ἵπποισι κελητίζειν εὖ εἰδώς, of one who leaps from horse to horse, Il.15.679. **II.** sens. obsc., Ar.*V.*501, *Th.*153, Machoap.Ath.13.577d. **-ιον**, τό, Dim. of κέλης II, Th.1.53, 4.120, App.*BC*2.56.

**κέλλ-α**, ἡ, = Lat. *cella, room, chamber*, *POxy.*1128.15 (ii A.D.), etc. **-ārίδιον**, τό, Dim. of κελλάριον, *Sammelb.*4292 (written κελαρίδιν). **-āρικά**, τά, *wine delivered to* a landlord's *cellar*, *PSI*8.953.73 (vi A.D.):—sg. -āρικόν, τό, *store-chamber*, *Stud.Pal.*20.75 ii 9 (iii/iv A.D.). **-άριον** [ᾰ, Hdn.Gr.2.13], τό, *cupboard* for glasses, κ. τριλάγυνον *POxy.*741.12 (ii A.D.), *PLond.*2.191.9 (ii A.D.); *store-chamber*, *POxy.*1851 (vi A.D.). ⊛ **-άριος** [ᾰ], ὁ, *cellarman*, *Wien.Stud.*24.131 (ii A.D.). **-āρίτης** [ῑ], ου, ὁ, = foreg., *Stud.Pal.*20.107.4 (iv A.D.), *PKlein.Form.*40 (vi A.D.).

**κελλάς**· μονόφθαλμος, Hsch.

⊛ **κελλίβας**, ατος, ὁ, prob. = κιλλίβας, *portable table*, *PRyl.*136.10 (i A.D.); cf. Lat. *cilibantum, cilliba*.

⊛ **κελλικάριος** (for *κελλαρικάριος), ὁ, *cellarman, butler*, *PSI*8.955.13 (vi A.D.).

**κέλλικας**· δημότας, Hsch.

**κελλίον**, τό, Dim. of κέλλα, *PAmh.*2.152.16 (v/vi A.D.); *garret*, *AP*11.351 (Pall.).

**κελλίων**· ἡ τῶν ὅλων φύσις, Hsch. **κελλόν**· στρεβλόν, πλάγιον, Id.

⊛ **κέλλω**, poet. (exc. D.H.14.1 as etym. of Κελτική), = Prose ὀκέλλω: fut. κέλσω A.*Supp.*331, E.*Hec.*1057 (lyr.), κελῶ Hsch.: aor. ἔκελσα (v. infr.):—*drive on*, Hom. only in Od., always in phrase νῆα κέλσαι *run* a ship *to land, put* her *to shore*, νῆα μὲν αὐτοῦ κέλσαι Od.10.511; νῆα..ἐκέλσαμεν ἐν ψαμάθοισιν 9.546; *cause to land*, ἀνδρῶν ἡρώων στόλον A.R.2.1090: metaph., Ἄργει κ. πόδα E.*El.*139 (lyr.). **II.** intr., of ships or seamen, *put to shore* or *into harbour*, κελσάσῃσι δὲ νηυσὶ καθείλομεν ἱστία Od.9.149; κέλσαντες Σιμόεντος ἐπ' ἀκτάς A.*Ag.*696 (lyr.), cf. *Eu.*10; ἐς Ἄργος Id.*Supp.*331; πρὸς γῆν S.*Tr.*804: c. acc. loci, κέλσαι..Ἄργους γαῖαν A.*Supp.*15 (anap.); Τροίας ἄστυ E.*Rh.*934: metaph., A.*Pr.*186 (lyr.); κ. ποτὶ τέρμα E.*Hipp.*140 (lyr.); πᾷ κέλσω; where *shall I find a haven?* Id.*Hec.*1057 (lyr.). (Cf. κέλομαι.)

**κελλῶσαι**· πλαγιάσαι, Hsch. **κελμάς**, ἡ, = κεμάς, Id. **Κελμίς**, name of an Idaean Dactyl, also glossed by παῖς ἢ λύκιθον (sic), Id. **κελοί**, οἱ, = τὰ ξύλα, Id. s. v. κελέοντας.

**κελοῖα**, ἡ, also written **καιλοῖα, κελύα, κελέα, κελῆα, κελεῖα**, name of contest for boys and youths at Sparta, *IG*5(1).263, al.: perh. neut. pl., ib.258.

**κέλομαι**, Ep. 2sg. κέλεαι, sts. disyll., Il.24.434, Od.4.812, 10.337: impf. κελόμην Il.1.386, κέλευ Theoc.2.11, κέλετο Il.15.119 (Dor. κέντο Alcm.141, acc. to Eust.756.30), ἐκέλετο *IG*4²(1).122.35 (Epid., iv B.C.): fut. κελήσομαι Od.10.296: aor. 1 ἐκελήσατο, κελήσατο, Epich.71, 99, Pi.*O.*13.80, *I.*6(5).37, *IG*4²(1).121.108 (Epid., iv B.C.): Ep. aor. 2 ἐκέκλετο, κέκλετο, Il.11.285, 16.421, Hes.*Sc.*341: hence was formed by later Poets pres. **κέκλομαι** A.R.1.716, etc.; Dor. opt. κεκλοίμαν A.*Supp.*591 (lyr.); part. κεκλόμενος, v. infr. II. 1; imper. κέκλεο and κέκλου Hsch. (this pres. used in pass. sense by Man.2.251, 3.319): poet. (also in Dor. Prose, *IG*ll. cc., al. (Epid., iv B.C.), cf. infr. II; ὅν κα κέλωνται τοὶ ἱαροποιοί *Abh.Berl.Akad.*1928(6).12 (Cos, iv B.C.)): Act. aor. 1 ἐκέλησεν Hsch.:— = κελεύω, *urge, exhort, command*.—Constr. like κελεύω: **1.** c. acc. pers. et inf., Il.5.810, 16.657, al., Alc.46, Pi. ll. cc., A.*Ag.*1119 (lyr.); of the *commands* of a god, *IG*4²(1).121.50 (Epid., iv B.C.), al.; μεταλλῆσαί τί ἑ θυμὸς..κέλεται, καὶ κήδεά περ πεπαθυῖῃ (instead of -υῖαν) Od.17.555. **2.** c. dat. pers. et inf., φυλασσέμεναί τε κέλονται ἀλλήλοις Il.10.419: more freq. without inf., Ἀργείοισιν ἐκέκλετο μακρὸν ἀΰσας 6.66; ἀμφιπόλοισι κέκλετο ib.287; ἵπποισιν ἐκέκλετο 8.184; ἀλλήλοισι κέλεσθε 12.274. **3.** abs., κέλομαι γὰρ ἔγωγε for [so] I *advise*, 23.894, Od.17.400; κέλεαι γάρ 5.98; ἐγὼ κέλομαι καὶ ἄνωγα 3.317; ἐπὶ δ' Ἕκτορι κέκλετο θυμὸς (sc. ἑ ἰέναι) Il. 16.382; less freq. of things, ἰαίνετο κηρός, ἐπεὶ κέλετο μεγάλη ἲς the wax melted, since mighty force *constrained* it, Od.12.175; ὡς..παρ' ἡμετέρης κέλεται πιστώματα Μούσης Emp.5. **II.** *call to*, κέκλετο δ' Ἥφαιστον Il.18.391; *call upon for aid*, *h.Cer.*21; πρῶτά σε κεκλόμενος, θύγατερ Διός S.*OT*159 (lyr.), cf. A.*Supp.*591 (lyr.); ἂν μὴ κελομένου πρίαται *Milet.*3.140*C*56 (iii B.C.), cf. *Leg.Gort.*6.48, *Schwyzer* 181 v 4,8 (Crete). **2.** *call by name*, νιν ὄρνιχος κέκλετ' ἐπώνυμον Pi. *I.*6(5).53. (κέλομαι, κέλλω, κελεύω may be cogn. with Skt. *kalayati* 'push', Lat. *celer*.)

**Κελτ-ίβηρες** [ῐ], οἱ, *tribes of mixed Celtic and Iberian descent*, Str. 1.2.27. **-ιστί**, Adv. *in the language of the Celts*, Arr.*Tact.*43.2, Luc.*Alex.*51.

**Κελτοί**, οἱ, *Celts*, Hdt.2.33, X.*HG*7.1.20, Plb.1.13.4:—later **Κέλται**, Str.4.1.1, etc.:—hence **Κελτικός**, ή, όν, *Celtic, Gallic*, Id.3.1.3:—poet. **Κελτός**, ή, όν, Call.*Del.*173:—fem. **Κελτίς**, ίδος, *AP*10.21 (Phld.); ἡ Κελτική the *country of the Celts* or *Gauls*, Arist.*HA*606ᵇ4, Str.4.1.1; ἡ Κελτία Foed.ap.Plb.7.9.6.

**Κελτο-λίγυες** [ῐ], οἱ, *tribes of mixed Celtic and Ligurian descent*, Str.4.6.3. **-σκύθαι** [ῠ], οἱ, *tribes of mixed Celtic and Scythian descent*, Id.1.2.27.

**κελύφ-ανον** [ῠ], τό, = κέλυφος, Lyc.89, Luc.*VH*2.38 (dub.). **-ανώδης**, ες, *like a shell* or *husk*, Thphr.*CP*1.7.2. **-ιον**, τό, Dim. of κέλυφος 2d, Arist.*HA*622ᵃ7.

**κελυφοκομῖον** (= -εῖον), τό, *lepers' hospital*, *BMus.Cat.Coptic MSS.* p.453 No.1077; cf. κελεφος.

⊛ **κέλῠφος**, εος, τό, *sheath, case*, **1.** in fruits, *pod, shell*, Arist.*GA* 752ᵃ20, Thphr.*HP*2.4.2, etc. **2.** in animals, *sheath*, Arist.*HA* 510ᵃ28. **b.** τὰ κ. τῶν ᾠῶν egg-*shells*, Id.*GA*743ᵃ17; in fish, *encasing membrane*, Id.*HA*568ᵇ9; τὸ περὶ τὰς γενέσεις κ. ib.600ᵇ17. **c.** *envelope*, of a chrysalis, ib.551ᵃ20, 601ᵃ6,8, *GA*758ᵇ17; of the chrysalis of the stag-beetle, Id.*HA*551ᵇ19. **d.** *shell* of crustaceous fish, ib. 549ᵇ25. **e.** *hollow* of the eye, *AP*9.439 (Crin.). **3.** metaph., of old dicasts, ἀντωμοσιῶν κελύφη mere affidavit-*husks*, Ar.*V.*545 (lyr.); of an old man's *boat*, which served as his *shell* or *coffin*, *AP*9.242 (Antiphil.). [ῡ, exc. Opp.*C.*3.503.] (Prob. cogn. with καλύπτω.)

**κέλωρ**, ωρος, ὁ, *son*, poet. word in E.*Andr.*1033 (lyr.), Lyc.495, al., Puchstein *Epigr.Gr.*p.76, etc. **2.** *eunuch*, Hsch. **II.** = φωνή, βοή Id., *PMasp.*151.249 (vi A.D.).

**κελώριον**, τό, = παιδίον, Hsch. **κελωρύω**, *shout*, Id., Phot.; cf. κέλωρ II.

⊛ **κεμάδειον** (sc. κρέας), τό, *venison*, *Edict.Diocl.*4.45 (prob.).

⊛ **κεμᾰδοσσόος**, ον, *chasing deer*, Nonn.*D.*5.230, 46.147.

⊛ **κεμάς**, άδος, ἡ, *young deer, pricket*, between νεβρός and ἔλαφος (so Ar.Byz.ap.Eust.711.37, cf. Miller *Mélanges de litt.gr.*p.431), Il.10. 361, Call.*Dian.*112, A.R.3.879, Herodic.ap.Ath.5.222a, Ael.*NA*14. 14:—also κεμμάς (q.v.), and in Hsch. κεμφάς. (Cf. Skt. *śáma-* 'hornless', Lith. *šmùlas* 'hornless', OE. *hind*.)

**κεμασῖνας**, = καμασῆνας, Hsch.

**κεμέλει**, τό, *measure of length*, Hero *Geom.*4.13.

**κέμμα**, ατος, τό, prob. f.l. for κέρμα, Emp.101.

**κεμμάς**, άδος, ἡ, poet. for κεμάς, Q.S.1.587, *AP*9.2 (Tiber. Illustr.), etc.

**κέμμερος**· ἀχλύς, ὁμίχλη, Hsch. **κέμμης**· ὄριον, Id. **κέμμορ**· μέγα κῆτος, Id. **κεμφάς**, v. κεμάς. **κέμων**· ἑτερόφθαλμος, Id. **κεν**, = κε (q.v.).

**κεναγγ-ής**, ές, (κενός, ἄγγος) *emptying the vessels of the body*: hence, *breeding famine*, ἄπλοια A.*Ag.*188 (lyr.). **-ία**, Ion. **κενεαγγίη** (q.v.), ἡ, *emptiness of vessels*; esp. *hunger*, Pl.Com.156; κ. ἄγειν to *fast*, Ar.*Fr.*608.

**κενανδρ-ία**, ἡ, *lack of men*, A.*Pers.*730 (troch.). **-ος**, ον, (ἀνήρ) *empty of men*, ἄστυ, πόλις, ib.119 (lyr.), S.*OC*917.

**κεναυχής**, ές, v. κενεαυχής.

**κένδῡλα**, τά, also **κένδῡλα** or **κενδύλη**, ἡ, dub. l. for σχένδυλα (q.v.).

**κενεαγγ-έω**, (κενεός, ἄγγος) *have the vessels of the body empty, undergo lowering* or *evacuant treatment*, Hp.*Art.*69, al. **-ητέον**, *one must fast*, Id.*Acut.*11. **-ίη** (in Mss. mostly -είη), ἡ, Ion. for κεναγγία, *lowering* or *evacuant treatment*, ibid., al., *Aph.*1.2, *Coac.*54; *evacuation by bleeding*, Aret.*CD*2.3. **-ικός**, ή, όν, *exhausted*, κ. σημεῖον Hp.*Acut.*48; of persons, Id.*Liqu.*2.

**κενεᾱγορία**, ἡ, *empty talk*, *Lyr.Adesp.*135 (pl.).

**κενέαρος**· κενός, ἐλαφρός, Hsch.

**κενεαυχής**, ές, (αὐχή) *vain-glorious*, κενεαυχέες ἠγοράασθε Il.8.230; κενεαυχέα πλοῦτον *AP*7.117 (Zenod.), cf. *POxy.*1015.19 (v.l.):—later **κεναυχής**, ές, Plu.2.103e; τὸ κ. κάλλος *AP*12.145.

**κενέβρειος**, ον, = θνησείδιος (cf. Ael.*NA*6.2), esp. of dead cattle:

κενέβρεια, τά, *carrion*, Ar.*Av.*538 (anap.), cf. *Fr.*693. 2. τὰ κ. *the dog's-meat market*, Erot. (sg. as v.l.), Phot.

**κενεγκράνιος** [ᾱ], ον, *brainless*, Sch.Juv.15.23.

**κενέθας**· σπόγγος, Hsch.; **κενέφας**, Cyr.

**κενεμβᾰτ-έω**, *step on emptiness*, Plu.*Flam.*10; *step into a hole*, Gal. 18(2).887, Luc.*Gall.*26. 2. Medic., of a lancet, catheter, etc., *reach a cavity*, Orib.44.11.3, Gal.14.786, Paul.Aeg.6.59. II. metaph., *lack solid foundation*, κενεμβατοῦν καὶ σφαλλόμενον, of Alexander's Empire, Plu.2.336f; κενεμβατοῦμεν ταῦτα λέγοντες Dam.*Pr.*4, cf. Plot.3.9.2. 2. *lead a frivolous life*, Men.Prot. p.2 D. **-ησις**, εως, ἡ, *piercing of a cavity*, Sor.2.62, Paul.Aeg. 6.21. II. *'emptiness'* of the pulse, Gal.8.509,931.

**κενεολογία**, v. κενολογία.

**κενεός**, ή, όν, Ep., Ion., and Dor. for κενός (q.v.).

**κενεότης**, ητος, ἡ, = κενότης, *empty space*, Hp.*Acut.*62.

**κενεο-φροσύνη**, ἡ, *empty-mindedness*, Timo 48.2: κενοφρ-, Plu. *Ages.*37. **-φρων**, ον, gen. ονος, *empty-minded*, δῆμος Thgn.233; μῦθος, αὖχαι, Simon.75, Pi.*N.*11.29:—also **κενόφρων**, βουλεύματα A. *Pr.*762.

**κενέφας**, v. κενέθας.

**κενέωμα**, ατος, τό, = κένωμα, τάφου, = κενοτάφιον, *Epigr.Gr.*234 (Smyrna).

**κενεών**, ῶνος, ὁ, (κενός) *hollow between ribs and hip, flank*, Od.22. 295, Poll.2.166, etc.; νείατον ἐς κενεῶνα, ὅθι ζωννύσκετο μίτρῃ Il.5. 857, cf. Hp.*Prog.*8 (pl.); of horses, X.*Eq.*12.8; of dogs, Id.*Cyn.* 4.1. 2. οἱ κ. τοῦ περιτοναίου the *hollows* of the peritonaeum, Heliod.ap.Orib.50.48.4. II. any *hollow*, hence periphr. οὐράνιοι *AP*9.207; αἰθέριος, χθόνιος κ., Nonn.*D.*13.453,9.82; κενεὼν ἀρούρης ib.41.3; *vacant space* in a crowd, Lxx 2*Ma.*14.44.

**κενέωσις**, εως, ἡ, poet. for κένωσις (q.v.).

**κενήριον**, τό, *empty monument, cenotaph*, Dieuchid.3, Euph.91, Lyc.370, *AP*7.569 (Agath.).

**κενογάμιον** [ᾰ], τό, (γάμος) *empty, unreal marriage*, coined after κενοτάφιον by Ach.Tat.5.14.

**κεν-οδοντίς**, ίδος, ἡ, *toothless*, *AP*6.297 (Phan.).

**κενοδοξ-έω**, *hold a vain opinion*, περί τι Plb.12.26[c].4; περὶ τὸ ἀληθές Lxx 4*Ma.*5.9. 2. *to be vain-glorious*, Hld.9.19; ἐκενοδόξει τὴν ἐξουσίαν, f.l. for ἐκαινοτόμει, J.*AJ*16.11.1. **-ία**, ἡ, *liability to vain imagination*, Epicur.*Sent.*30, Phld.*Rh.*1.332 S. II. *vanity, conceit*, Plb.3.81.9, Lxx *Wi.*14.14, D.S.17.107, Ph.2.47, *Ep.Phil.*2.3, Plu.2.57d, Porph.*Marc.*15; esp. of *false prudery*, Gal.6.415. **-ος**, ον, *vain-glorious, conceited*, Plb.27.7.12, Ph.1.672, *Ep.Gal.*5.26, Arr. *Epict.*3.24.43, Jul.*Or.*6.180d; κληρονομία Vett.Val.271.2.

**κενοδρομ-έω**, Astrol., *to be without attendant planets*, *'void of course'*, Ptol.*Tetr.*114, Man.2.486:—hence **-ία**, ἡ, Antioch.Astr. in *Cat.Cod.Astr.*8(3).107, Porph. *in Ptol.*189.

**κενοκοπέω**, *labour in vain*, Plu.2.1037b.

**κενολογ-έω**, *talk emptily*, Eup.418, Arist.*Rh.*1393[a]17; καταψηφίζεσθαι ὑποθέσεως ὡς -λογούσης Procl. *in Prm.*p.845 S. **-ία**, ἡ, *empty, idle talk*, Plu.2.1069d; *chicanery*, *PMasp.*126.50 (vi A.D.): **κενεολογία**, v.l. for γενεολογία in Max.Tyr.23.1. **-ος**, ον, *talking emptily, prating*, *Gloss.*

**κενοπάθ-εια** [πᾰ], ἡ, *unreal sensation*, S.E.*M.*8.184. **-έω**, *have unreal sensations*, i.e. with no object corresponding to them, ib.213, *P.*2.49. **-ημα**, ατος, τό, *unreal sensation*, Id.*M.*8.354.

**κενο-πονέω**, *toil in vain*, v.l. in Ph.1.658. **-πρησις**, εως, ἡ, *flatulence*, *Hippiatr.*46. **-ρρημοσύνη**, ἡ, (ῥῆμα) = κενολογία, Eust. 1151.8.

**κενός**, ή, όν, Ion. and poet. κεινός Il.3.376, 4.181, 11.160, 15.453, Pi.*O.*2.65, 3.45, Hdt.1.73, al.; Ep. also κενεός, as always in Hom. (exc. in Il. ll. cc., and κενός Od.22.249 (s.v.l., fort. κενέ' εὔγματα or κεῖν' εὔγματα)), also Hp.*Aph.*7.24, Meliss.7, Timo 20.2 (Comp.), and in Dor., *IG*4[2](1).121.73 (Epid., iv B.C.); Aeol. **κέννος**, acc. to Greg. Cor.p.610 S.: Sup. κεννότατος Sch.Tz. in *An.Ox.*3.356.18; but οἱ Αἰολεῖς.. οὐ λέγουσι κέννος Choerob. in *An.Ox.*2.242, cf. Hdn.Gr.2.302, and the true Aeol. is prob. κένος or κένεος, from *κενϝος, κενεϝος, cf. Cypr. κενευϝός *Schwyzer*683.4. I. mostly of things, *empty*, opp. πλέως, Ar.*Eq.*280; opp. πλήρης, Id.*Nu.*1054; opp. μεστός, Diph.12; κενεὰς σὺν χεῖρας ἔχοντες Od.10.42; νοστήσαντας κεινῇσι χερσί Hdt.1.73; κεναῖς χερσίν Pl.*Lg.*796b (v. infr. II. 2); τὸ κ. (sc. τάλαντον) the *empty* one, Ar.*Fr.*488.5; κ. οἴκησις S.*Ph.*31; γῆ Id. *OT*55; εὐνή Id.*Ant.*424; χώματα κεινά, = κενοτάφια, Hdt.9.85; κ. τάφος E.*Hel.*1057; κατέθισαν ἐπὶ κενευϝῶν (sc. τάφων gen. sg.) *Schwyzer* l. c. (Cypr.); κ. χρόνος a *pause* in music, Anon.Bellerm.83; σφυγμὸς κ. Agathin.ap.Gal.8.936; of wool and wine, dub. sens. in Archig.ap.Gal.8.945; τὸ κ. *the void of space*, Democr.9, Meliss. l.c., Emp.13, al., Epicur.*Ep.*1 p.6 U., etc.; τὸ κ., = τόπος ἐστερημένος σώματος, Arist.*Ph.*208[b]26, cf. 213[a]13 sqq., *Cael.*279[a]13; κ. χώρα Pl. *Ti.*58a; ἣν κενεὸν λάβῃ [ἡ διακοπή] if it penetrates the (brain-) *cavity*, Hp.*Aph.* l. c.; esp. Astrol., *not occupied by a planet*, κ. δρόμος Man.2.452, cf. Vett. Val.94.27; cf. κενοδρομέω. 2. *empty, fruitless, void*, κενὰ εὔγματα εἰπών Od.22.249 (v. supr.); ἐλπίς, ἐλπίδες, Simon.5.16, A.*Pers.*804; γνώμα Pi.*N.*4.40, cf. S.*Ant.*753; ἔξοδοι Id.*Aj.*287; φροντίδες Id.*Fr.*949; τέρψις ib.577; φόβοι E.*Supp.*548, cf. X.*An.*2.2.21; φρόνημα Pl.*R.*494d, etc.; κ. πρόφασις καὶ ψευδής D.18.150; λοιδορία κ. Id.2.5; μάταιον καὶ κ. ib.12; κενὸν ἆρα καὶ τὸ φάρμακον πρὸς τὸ κ. prob. in Men.530.19; ἀπόντων κενὴν κατηγορεῖν bring an *idle* charge, Arist.*Resp.*470[b]12; *ineffectual*, λόγῳ Th.2.49; πουλυμαθημοσύνης, τῆς οὐ κενεώτερον ἄλλο Timo l. c.; πολλὰ κ. τοῦ πολέμου Arist.*EN*1116[b]7; κ. δόξαι Epicur. *Sent.*15; ἐπιθυμίαι, opp. φυσικαί, Id.*Ep.*3 p.62 U., Diog.Oen.59; κ. ὀρέξεις Metrod.*Herc.*831.16; freq. in adverbial usages, neut. pl., κενεὰ πνεύσαις Pi.*O.*10(11).93; ἡ διὰ κενῆς ἐπανάσεισις τῶν ὅπλων *empty* flourishing of arms, Th.4.126; διὰ κενῆς ῥίπτειν throw *without a projectile*, Arist.*Pr.*881[a]39; κεκλάγγω διὰ κενῆς ἄλλως *to no purpose*, Ar. *V.*929; μάτην διὰ κ. Pl.Com.174.21; οὐ μαχοῦμαί σοι διὰ κ. Men.*Sam.* 260; ἐν κενοῖς S.*Aj.*971; κατὰ κενῆς Procl. *in Ti.*2.167 D.; εἰς κενόν D.S. 19.9, Hld.10.30; εἰς κ. ἡ δαπάνη *IG*14.1746; εἰς κ. μοχθεῖν Men.*Mon.* 51; κατὰ κενοῦ χανεῖν Suid. s.v. λύκος ἔχανεν; κατὰ κενοῦ φέρειν τὰς χεῖρας Ph.1.153; κατὰ κ. βαίνειν, = κενεμβατεῖν, Plu.2.463c: regul. Adv. κενῶς, διαλεκτικῶς καὶ κ. Arist. *de An.*403[a]2; λογικῶς καὶ κ. Id. *EE*1217[b]21; μὴ κ. πόνει Men.1101, cf. Epicur.*Ep.*3 p.61 U., Polystr. p.7 W., Arr.*Epict.*2.17.6, Plu.2.35e. II. of persons and things, 1. c. gen., *destitute, bereft*, τοῦ νοῦ S.*OC*931; φρενῶν Id.*Ant.*754; δακρύων E.*Hec.*230; συμμάχων κ. δόρυ Id.*Or.*688; πεδίον κ. δένδρων Pl.*R.*621a; κ. φρονήσεως, ἐπιστήμης, Id. *Ti.*75a, *R.*486c; κ. πόνου *without the fruits* of toil, A.*Fr.*241. 2. abs., *empty-handed*, αἰσχρόν τοι δηρόν τε μένειν κενεόν τε νέεσθαι Il.2.298, cf. Od.15.214; ἀπίκατο, οἱ μὲν κεινοί, οἱ δὲ φέροντες κτλ. Hdt.7.131; κενὸς κενὸν καλεῖ A.*Th.*353 (lyr.); ἥκεις οὐ κενή S.*OC*359, cf. *Tr.*495; οὐθ' ὑπεργέμων.. οὔτε κ. Alex.216; of camels, *without burdens, unloaded*, opp. ἔγγομοι, *OGI*629.166 (Palmyra, ii A.D.); κ. ἂν ἴῃ.., κ. ἄπεισιν Pl.*R.*37ce; κ. τινὰ ἐξαποστεῖλαι Lxx *Ge.*31.42; *bereft of* her mate, λέαινα S.*Aj.*986; *orphan*, Ἔρωτες Bion 1.59; ὑπ' ἄσθματος κενοί *exhausted*.., A.*Pers.*484; of places, *without garrison*, χῶραι Aeschin.3.146, cf. Hdt.5.15; of the body, *without flesh*, Plu.2.831c. b. *devoid of wit, vain, pretentious*, κεινὸς εἴην Pi.*O.*3.45; διαπτυχθέντες ὤφθησαν κενοί S.*Ant.*709; ἀνόητον καὶ κ. Ar.*Ra.*530, cf. *Ep.Jac.*2.20. III. Comp. and Sup., κενότερος Stratt.10 D.; -ότατος D.27.25, Phld.*Rh.*1.67 S., al., cf. Choerob. *in Theod.*2.76, *EM*275.50; κενώτερος, -ώτατος, Pl.*Smp.*175d, v.l. in Arist.*EN*1107[a]30 (Comp.); κενεώτερος Timo (v. supr.); κενεώτατος v.l. in Hp.*Acut.*62.

**κενόσαρκος**, ον, *destitute of flesh, meagre*, *EM*779.8.

**κενοσπουδ-έω**, *to be zealous about frivolities*, J.*AJ*16.4.3, Artem. 4.11. **-ία**, ἡ, *zealous pursuit of frivolities*, D.H.6.70, D.L.6.26; πομπῆς κ. M.Ant.7.3. **-ος**, ον, *zealous about frivolities*, Hipparch. 1.3.11, Plu.2.560b, 1061c; κ. τάχος 'more haste, less speed', Heliod. ap.Orib.47.14.3; τὸ κ. D.L.9.67; τὰ κ. *matters of mere curiosity*, Cic. *Att.*9.1.1. Adv. -δως Plu.2.234e.

**κενοτάφ-έω**, *honour with an empty tomb*, κενοταφοῦντ' ἐμὸν δέμας E.*Hel.*1060; ὃν.. ἤδ' ἀπόντα κενοταφεῖ ib.1546: metaph., κ. τὸν βίον Plu.2.1130b. **-ιον**, τό, *empty tomb, cenotaph*, X.*An.*6.4.9, Plu.2. 870e, App.*Mith.*96, *CIG*4340d, e (Attalia); also Adj., κενοτάφιος οἶκος Plu.2.349b (s.v.l.). II. *image*, = Heb. *tĕraphim*, Lxx 1*Ki.*19.13.

**κενότης**, ητος, ἡ, *emptiness*, Pl.*R.*585b, *Ti.*58b, Thphr.*Sens.*54; *vanity*, Phld.*D.*1.17; εἰς κενότητας ἄν μοι ὁ λόγος ἐξέπιπτε D.H.*Is.*20; κ. σφυγμοῦ Agathin.ap.Gal.8.936; cf. κενεότης.

**κενο-φροσύνη** and **-φρων**, v. κενεοφρ-.

**κενοφων-έω**, *speak idly*, Suid. **-ία**, ἡ, *vain talking*, Dsc.*Praef.* 2: in pl., 1*Ep.Ti.*6.20, 2*Ep.Ti.*2.16, Porph.*Chr.*58; ἄγραφοι κ. Just. *Nov.*146.1.2.

**κενόω**, E.*Med.*959, Pl.*Smp.*197d; Ep. **κεινόω** Nic.*Th.*56, *Al.*140: fut. κενώσω E.*Ion*447: aor. ἐκένωσα Id.*Ba.*730: pf. κεκένωκα App.*BC* 5.67:—Pass., fut. κενωθήσομαι Gal.4.709, κενώσομαι Emp.16: aor. ἐκενώθην Th.2.51: pf. κεκένωμαι Hdt.4.123, Hp.*Morb.Sacr.*9: (κενός): —*empty*, πᾶσαν ἠπείρου πλάκα A.*Pers.*718 (troch.); ναούς E.*Ion* l. c.: c. gen., *empty of* a thing, ἀνδρῶν τάνδε πόλιν κενῶσαι A.*Supp.*660, cf. E.*Rh.*914 (lyr.); χέρας [δώρων] Id.*Med.* l. c.; τινὰ τᾶς συοπλουτοσύνας Cerc.4.13; opp. πληροῦν τινά τινος, Pl. l. c., cf. *R.*560d:—Pass., *to be emptied, made* or *left empty*, S.*OT*29; ἐς τὸ κενούμενον into the *space continually left empty*, Th.2.76; οἰκίαι πολλαὶ ἐκενώθησαν ib.51: c. gen., τούτων κενεώσεται.. αἰών *will be left without* them, Emp. l. c.; κεκενωμένου τοῦ τείχεος πάντων *stripped* of all things, Hdt. l. c. 2. *make* a place *empty by leaving* it, *desert* it, βωμοῦ ἐσχάραν E.*Andr.*1138; λόχμην Id.*Ba.* l. c.:—Pass., κενωθεισῶν τῶν νεῶν Th.8.57. 3. Medic., *empty by depletion*, opp. πληροῦν, Hp.*Aph.*2.51, cf. Aret.*CA*1.2, Gal. l. c.; τινα Phld.*Lib.*p.30 O.; *carry off*, αἷμα Luc.*Ocyp.*93; ἐκ τοῦ σώματος χολήν Gal.*Nat.Fac.*1.13:—Pass., τὰ κενούμενα *evacuations*, Id.6.78, Antyll.ap.Stob.4.37.27. 4. *empty out, pour away*, φάρμακον Iamb.*Bab.*7: metaph., πλοῦτον f.l. in Ph.1.119:—Pass., τοῦ λαοῦ κενωθέντος D.S.24.1; *make away with*, θανάτου βάρος Cypr. *Fr.*1.6. 5. *expend*, εἴς με κένωσον πᾶν βέλος *AP*5.57 (Arch.). 6. in Pass., *waste away, shrivel*, Thphr.*HP*7.4.3, 9.14.3. II. metaph., *make empty*, ἑαυτόν *Ep.Phil.*2.7; *make void* or *of no effect*, καύχημα 1*Ep.Cor.*9.15; ὑπάρξεις Vett.Val.90.7:—Pass., *to be* or *become so*, *Ep.Rom.*4.14.

**κένσαι, κένταε**, v. κεντέω.

**κενταύρειον** or **-ιον**, *centaury*, *Centaurea salonitana*, Thphr.*HP* 3.3.6, Diocl.*Fr.*83, al., *POxy.*1088.59; κ. τὸ μέγα Dsc.3.6; but κ. τὸ μικρὸν *feverfew*, *Erythraea Centaurium*, ib.7: **κενταυρίη**, Hp.*Morb.* 2.59.

**Κενταύρ-ειος**, α, ον, *of Centaurs*, γένος E.*IA*706; αἷμα Luc.*Peregr.* 25. **-ίδης**, ου, ὁ, *sprung from Centaurs*, ἵππος K. a *Thessalian* horse, Id.*Ind.*5. **-ικός**, ή, όν, *like a Centaur*, i.e. *savage, brutal*. Adv. -κῶς Ar.*Ra.*38.

**κενταυρίς**, ίδος, ἡ, = κενταύρειον τὸ μικρόν, Thphr.*HP*9.8.7, 9.14. 1. II. a kind of *ear-ring*, *Com.Adesp.*1034 (pl.). III. *female Centaur*, Philostr.*Im.*2.3.

**Κενταυρο-κτόνος**, ον, *Centaur-slaying*, Lyc.670. **-μᾰχία**, ἡ, *battle*

*of Centaurs*, D.S.17.115, Plu.*Thes.*29, *Comp.Thes.Rom.*1. **-πληθής**, ές, *full of Centaurs*, πόλεμος E.*HF*1273.

**Κένταυρος**, ὁ (in Luc.*Zeux.*4 also ἡ), *Centaur*: I. in Ep., a savage race, dwelling between Pelion and Ossa, Il.11.832, Od.21.295 sq. (opp. ἄνδρες, ib.303), Hes.*Sc.*184, *h.Merc.*224 (perh. in signf. II), Batr.171: hence, *brigands*, Hsch. II. later, monsters of double shape, *half-man and half-horse*, Pi.*P.*2.44, etc., cf. Arist. *Insomn.*461$^{b}$20, D.S.4.69: prov., οὐ παρὰ Κενταύροισι 'we don't live in fairyland', Telecl.45. III. the constellation *Centaurus*, Eudox. ap.Hipparch.1.2.20. IV. = παιδεραστής, from the brutal sensuality ascribed to the Centaurs, Hsch. 2. *the pudenda*, Theopomp.Com.89.

**Κενταυροφόνος**, ὁ, *slaying Centaurs*, epith. of Heracles, prob. in Theoc.17.20.

**κεντάω**, late form of sq., Pass. inf. -ᾶσθαι (v.l. -εῖσθαι) Gal.6.192.

⊛ **κεντ-έω**, Pi.*P.*1.28, etc.: fut. -ήσω S.*Aj.*1245: aor. ἐκέντησα Hp.*Epid.*5.45, Dor. κέντᾱσα Theoc.19.1; Ep. inf. κένσαι (as if from *κέντω) Il.23.337:—Pass., fut. -ηθήσομαι (συγ-) Hdt.6.29: aor. ἐκεντήθην Arist.*Spir.*483$^{b}$16, Thphr.*HP*9.15.3: pf. κεκέντημαι Hp.*Anat.*1:—*prick, goad, spur on*, Il.l.c., Ar.*Nu.*1300, etc.: prov., κ. τὸν πῶλον περὶ τὴν νύσσαν, of impetuous haste, Suid. 2. of bees and wasps, *sting*, Ar.*V.*226, al.; Ἔρωτα κακὰ κέντασε μέλισσα Theoc.l.c.; τὠφθαλμὼ κεντούμενος ὥσπερ ὑπ' ἀνθρηνῶν Ar.*Nu.*947; of the porcupine, Ael.*NA*12.26: then, 3. generally, *prick, stab*, Pi.l.c., Theoc.15.130, etc.; μηδ' ὀλωλότα κέντει S.*Ant.*1030; τὴν γλῶσσαν καὶ τὴν ψυχὴν αὐτῶν κέντησον *Tab.Defix.*97.26; ἐκέντει . . (αἰθέρ'), ὡς σφάζων ἐμέ E.*Ba.*631 (troch.), etc.; κ. τὸν ἀέρα Theo Sm.p.61 H., cf. p.72 H.; τύπτειν οὐδὲ κ. Pl.*Grg.*456d:—Pass., κεντηθείσης τῆς φλεβός Thphr.l.c.; παιομένους καὶ κεντουμένους Th.4.47; μαστιγούμενος καὶ κεντούμενος X.*HG*3.3.11, cf. *An.*3.1.29: metaph., σὺν δόλῳ κ. *stab in the dark*, S.*Aj.*1245; λιμῷ κεντούμενος Alciphr.3.4. 4. = βινέω, Mnesim.4.55. **-ημα**, ατος, τό, *point* of a weapon, Plb.2.33.5, etc. 2. *prick, dot* in a cipher, Aen.Tact.31.30 (pl.). 3. *puncture*, Heliod.ap.Orib.46.22.4: pl., Ruf.*Fr.*63. II. *wound inflicted, sting*, κ. γλώσσης A.*Fr.*169; of poisonous bites, Philum.*Ven.*27.2, al.: in pl., *punishment*, Hsch.

⊛ **κεντην-άριος**, ὁ, = Lat. *centenarius*, *official drawing salary of* 100,000 *sesterces*, *Epigr.Gr.*446: **-αρία**, ἡ, *office of such a value*, *IG*14.1480: **-άριον**, τό, *weight of* 100 *lbs.*, *Edict.Diocl.*18.5, Olymp.Hist.p.469 D., Men.Prot.p.100 D.

⊛ **κέντ-ησις**, εως, ἡ, *pricking*, Arist.*Spir.*484$^{a}$34. II. *mosaic*, *IG Rom.*4.1417 (Smyrna). **-ητήριον**, τό, *pricker, awl*, Luc.*Cat.*20; gloss on ῥαφίς, Gal.19.134; gloss on στιγεύς, Suid. **-ητής**, οῦ, ὁ, *mosaic-worker*, *Edict.Diocl.*7.6: generally, *one who pierces*, Tz.*H.*9.466. ⊛ **-ητικός**, ή, όν, *prickly*, Thphr.*HP*3.9.6 (Comp.). **-ητός**, ή, όν, *embroidered*, ὑπόδημα Epict.*Ench.*39; prob. *decorated with mosaic*, *BGU*781 iv 10 (i A.D.). **-ιον**, v. κέντριον.

**κέντο**, Dor. for κέλετο, Alcm.141.

**κεντορίων**, ωνος, ὁ, = Lat. *centurio*, *OGI*196 (Philae):—also **κεντουρίων**, Lyd.*Mag.*1.9; **κεντυρίων**, *Ev.Marc.*15.39.

**κεντόω**, v.l. for κεντρόω I in Hdt.3.16.

**κεντρ-ήεις**, εσσα, εν, *sharp, prickly*, ῥίζεα Nic.*Al.*146. **-ηνεκής**, ές, *spurred* or *goaded on*, ἵπποι Il.5.752, 8.396. **-ιάδαι**, οἱ, *priests* at Athens, *who drove* the ox to the altar *with goads* at the Dipolia, Porph.*Abst.*2.30. **-ίζω**, = κεντέω, X.*Eq.*11.6: metaph., ἔρως κ. εἰς ἔρωτα Id.*Smp.*8.24; ἔπαινος κ. Plu.2.84c; *stimulate*, τὰ σώματα Sor.2.54:—Pass., κεντρίζεσθαι ὑπὸ φιλονικίας X.*Cyr.*8.7.12; ὑπὸ πάθους Ph.2.386. **-ικός**, ή, όν, *of* or *belonging to a cardinal point*, σχῆμα Vett.Val.134.26. II. Adv. -κῶς, metaph., ὁ νοῦς . . ἀδιαιρέτως καὶ κ. οἶδε τὰ διαιρούμενα Phlp.*in de An.*542.29. **-ίνης** [ῑ], ου, ὁ, *spiny shark*, Arist.*Fr.*310, Opp.*H.*1.378. II. kind of ψήν or *fig-insect*, Thphr.*HP*2.8.2, Plin.*HN*17.255. III. = κεντρίς, Ael.*NA*9.11 (-ίτης codd.), Sch.Nic.*Th.*334. **-ιον**, τό, a surgical instrument, called modern spelling of κέντιον, Gal.13.407; = βουκέντριον, Suid., cf. *EM*503.39. **-ίς**, ίδος, ἡ, = διψάς II.1, Ael.*NA*6.51. **-ίσκος**, ὁ, a kind of *fish*, Thphr.*Fr.*171.9; Schneid. κεστρινίσκος. **-ισμός**, ὁ, = *stimulatio*, *Gloss.* **-ιστέον**, *one must stimulate*, Orib.*Fr.*64. ⊛ **-ίτης**, ου, ὁ, v. κεντρίνης III. II. κ. κάλαμος *prickly* reed, *PTeb.*152 (ii B.C.). III. fem. **-ῖτις**, ιδος, ἡ, *place* where a horse is *tapped* for dropsy, *Hippiatr.*38. 2. κ. βοτάνη, magical plant, *PMag.Par.*1.773.

**κεντρο-βᾰρικά**, τά, title of a treatise of Archimedes *on the centre of gravity*: *problems relating to this subject*, Simp.*in Cael.*543.30: ἡ -κή *theory of the subject*, *An.Ox.*3.168. **-δήλητος**, ον, *torturing with goads*, ὀδύναις κεντροδαλήτοις (Dor.) A.*Supp.*563 (lyr., fort. leg. κεντροδαλήτισι). **-ειδής**, ές, *like a centre, centriform*, Plot.6.8.18. **-θεσία**, ἡ, *arrangement of heavenly bodies on cardinal points*, Vett.Val.226.33 (pl.). **-μανής**, ές, *maddened by the spur*, *AP*13.18 (Parmeno; -ραγῆ cod.). II. ἄγκιστρον κ., of love, *maddening by its barbs*, ib.5.246 (Maced.). **-μυρσίνη**, ἡ, = ὀξυμυρσ-, *butchers'-broom*, *Ruscus aculeatus*, Thphr.*HP*3.17.4, *Gp.*10.3.7.

⊛ **κέντρον**, τό, (κεντέω) *any sharp point*: 1. *horse-goad*, [ἵπποι] ἄνευ κέντροιο θέοντες Il.23.387, cf. 430, Ar.*Nu.*1297, X.*Cyr.*7.1.29, etc.; διπλοῖς κέντροισι S.*OT*809; ὄνειδος ἔτυψεν δίκαν διφρηλάτου μεσολαβεῖ κ. A.*Eu.*157 (lyr.): post-Hom., *ox-goad* (Hom. βουπλήξ), used as an instrument of torture, Hdt.3.130; κέντροις καὶ μάστιξιν Pl.*Lg.*777a: prov., πρὸς κέντρα λακτίζειν (v. λακτίζω 2); δεῖ . . κέντρου πολλάκις, οὕτω δὲ καὶ χαλινοῦ Longin.2.2; as a symbol of sovereignty, λαβὼν . . χεροῖν κέντρα κηδεύει πόλιν S.*Fr.*683. b. metaph., *goad, spur, incentive*, Pi.*Fr.*124.4, A.*Pr.*691 (lyr.); τοῦ γὰρ τοσοῦτο κ. ὡς μητροκτονεῖν; Id.*Eu.*427; κέντροις ἔρωτος E.*Hipp.*39, cf. 1303; πόθου κ. Pl.*R.*573a; κέντρα καὶ ὠδῖνες Id.*Phdr.*251e; κ. ἐγερτικὸν θυμοῦ Plu.*Lyc.*21; κέντρα πτολέμοιο, of the Argives, Orac.ap.Sch.Theoc.14.48; κ. ἐμοῦ *desire for* me, S.*Ph.*1039. 2. metaph., in pl., *tortures, pangs*, Id.*Tr.*840 (lyr.): sg., τὸ κ. τοῦ θανάτου ἡ ἁμαρτία 1 *Ep.Cor.*15.56. 3. *point* of a spear, Plb.6.22.4: pl., of the περόναι with which Oedipus pierced his eyes, S.*OT*1318. 4. *peg* of a top, Pl.*R.*436d. 5. of animals, a. *sting* of bees and wasps, Ar.*V.*225, 407 (lyr.), al.; of scorpions, Arist.*PA*683$^{a}$12 (so of the constellation *Scorpio*, Arat.505): hence, metaph., of malicious persons, ἐς τοὺς ἔχοντας κέντρ' ἀφιᾶσιν E.*Supp.*242; πορεύεται, ὥσπερ σκορπίος, ἠρκὼς τὸ κ. D.25.52; of Pericles as an orator, τὸ κ. ἐγκατέλειπε τοῖς ἀκροωμένοις Eup.94.7; of Socrates, ὥσπερ μέλιττα τὸ κ. ἐγκαταλιπών Pl.*Phd.*91c; οἷον ὀφθαλμῷ κ. ἐνθεῖσα Philostr.*Im.*2.1; βλέμματος κ. Onomarch.ap. Philostr.*VS*2.18. b. *spur* of a cock, *Gp.*14.7.17. c. *quill* of the porcupine, Ael.*NA*12.26. d. = πόσθη, Sotad.1. 6. *stationary point of a pair of compasses*, Vitr.3.1.3: generally, *centre* of a circle, Pl.*Ti.*54e, Arist.*APr.*41$^{b}$15, al.; ἡ ἐκ τοῦ κ. (sc. εὐθεῖα) *radius*, Euc.*Opt.*34; ὥσπερ κύκλον κέντρῳ περιέγραψαν τὴν πόλιν Plu.*Rom.*11; τὸ κ. τᾶς σφαίρας Ti.Locr.100e; τὸ κ. τῆς γῆς Ptol.*Tetr.*52; κ. βάρεος *centre* of gravity, Archim.*Aequil.*1 *Def.*4: metaph., κ. καὶ διαστήματι περιγράφειν *circumscribe*, Plu.2.513c, 524f. 7. *pin, rivet*, Paus.10.16.1; *spur, tip*, for fixing a machine in the ground, Apollod.*Poliorc.*144.1. 8. ῥακτηρίοις κέντροισιν, of *oars*, S.*Fr.*802. 9. Astron., *cardinal point* on the ecliptic, Ptol.*Tetr.*74, S.E.*M.*5.12, Vett.Val.50.18, etc. 10. *hard knot* in stone, Thphr.*HP*5.2.3; *flaw* in crystals, Plin.*HN*37.28.

**κεντρο-ποιός**, όν, *making goads*, gloss on sq., Hsch. **-τύπος** [ῠ], ον, Act., *striking with a goad*, Sch.Ar.*Nu.*449. II. proparox., **κεντρότῠπος**, = μαστιγίας, *EM*503.47, cf. Hsch. **-φόρος**, ον, *with a sting*, Id. s.v. τενθρηδών. 2. Subst., -φόρος, ὁ, = κεντρίνης I, Opp.*H.*4.244. II. *containing the centre of the universe*, Porph.ap. Eus.*PE*3.11.

**κεντρ-όω**, *furnish with a sting*:—Pass., *to be so furnished*, Pl.*R.*552d, 555d. 2. *strike with a goad*, Hdt.3.16 (cf. κεντόω): metaph., *spur on*, κεκεντρωμένος εἰς λόγους Aristid.*Or.*50(26).26. II. Pass., Astron., *occupy a cardinal point*, Ptol.*Tetr.*153, Man.1.90. **-ώδης**, ες, *pointed, prickly*, λάπαθον Aët.6.24; ἔδαφος Sch.Pi.*P.*1.54; of the chorus in Ar.*V.*, Sch.ib.224. ⊛ **-ων**, ωνος, ὁ, *one that bears the marks of the* κέντρον, *a rogue that has been put to the torture*, S.*Fr.*329, Ar.*Nu.*450 (anap.). II. *piece of patch-work, rag*, Bito 55.4, Heras ap.Gal.13.1044, Sch.Ar.*Nu.*449; perh. *pen-wiper*, *POxy.*326 (i A.D.): hence, *copy of verses made up of scraps from other authors*, Eust.1099.51, 1308 fin. ⊛ **-ωνάριον**, τό, *case for* κέντρωνες, *POxy.*326 (i A.D.; -νόρ- Pap.). **-ωνορράφος** [ᾰ], = Lat. *centonarius*, *Gloss.* **-ωσις**, εως, ἡ, *goading, piercing*, Sch.Pi.*P.*1.54. II. Astron., *situation at cardinal point*, Ptol.*Tetr.*79, 99. ⊛ **-ωτός**, ή, όν, *'spiky'*, colloquial for θυμικώτεροι, κηφῆνες Arist.*HA*624$^{b}$16; *spiked*, of bucklers, Str.11.5.6; of planks, Plu.2.200b. 2. name of a throw in dicing, Eub.57.1.

**κεντῠρίων**, v. κεντορίων.

**κέντωρ**, ορος, ὁ, *goader, driver*, κέντορες ἵππων Il.4.391, 5.102, cf. *APl.*4.358; κ. παρδαλίων *AP*7.578 (Agath.).

**κέν-ωμα**, ατος, τό, *empty space, vacuum*, Erasistr.ap.Gell.16.3.8 (in Ion. form κείνωμα), Ph.*Bel.*57.17 (pl.), Plb.6.31.9, Phld.*Sign.*36 (pl.), Plu.2.655b (pl.). 2. *vacancy, non-existence*, Anon. *in Prm.* in *Rh.Mus.*47.603. 3. *empty vessel*, *POxy.*1292.4 (i A.D.), *PAmh.*2.48.8 (ii B.C.): pl., ῥοιᾶς κ. *empty shells*, Asclep.ap.Gal.13.302. II. Medic., *evacuation*, Phld.*Lib.*p.30 O., Dsc.5.11, Plu.2.381d. 2. *evacuant*, in pl., Herod.Med. in *Rh.Mus.*58.89, Ruf.*Fr.*116. **-ώσιμος**, η, ον, *purgative*, τὸ κ. τῆς ἰατρείας Anon.ap.Suid. s.v. κενώτερος. **-ωσις**, εως, ἡ, *emptying, depletion*, οὐχὶ πεῖνα καὶ δίψα . . κενώσεις τινές εἰσι . .; Pl.*R.*585b, cf. *Phlb.*35b, *BGU*904.13 (ii A.D.):—poet. κενέωσις, πόντου κ. ἀνὰ πέδον Pi.*Fr.*107.12: metaph., κένωσις βίου Vett.Val.190.30; κ. τοῦ γιγνώσκειν Iamb.*Comm.Math.*11. 2. Medic., *evacuation*, Hp.*Aph.*2.8, interpol. in Dsc.2.50; κ. τῶν οἰκείων, opp. κάθαρσις τῶν ἀλλοτρίων, Gal.18(2).134. b. *depletion, low diet*, opp. πλήρωσις, Hp.*VM*9, cf. *Art.*49; κ. σίτου ib.50. 3. of the moon, *waning*, opp. πλήρωσις, Epicur.*Ep.*2 p.40 U. **-ωτέον**, *one must purge*, Gal.17(2).359, cf. 10.904, Ruf.ap.Orib.7.26.18. **-ωτικός**, ή, όν, *tending to empty*, κύστεως Ael.*NA*14.4; *depletive*, Gal.18(1).118 (Sup.). 2. *purgative*, Id.15.198.

**κέοιτο, κέοντο**, v. κεῖμαι.

**κεπφαττελεβώδης**, ες, *as brainless as a* κέπφος *or an* ἀττέλεβος, cj. Bentl. in Archestr.*Fr.*23.14.

⊛ **κέπφος**, ὁ, perh. *stormy petrel*, *Thalassidroma pelagica*, Arist.*HA*593$^{b}$14, 620$^{a}$13, Thphr.*Sign.*28, Lyc.76, 836, Nic.*Al.*166. 2. metaph., *feather-brained fellow*, Ar.*Pax* 1067, *Pl.*912.

⊛ **κεπφόω**, *ensnare like a* κέπφος:—hence in Pass., *to be easily cajoled*, Lxx *Pr.*7.22; *become feather-brained*, Cic.*Att.*13.40.2.

**κερᾱβάτης**, ου, ὁ, = κεροβάτης, Suid., Zonar.

**κεράδιον**, τό, Dim. of κεραία, *IG*2$^{2}$.1648.22, prob. in *BCH*35.16 (Delos): less prob. κεραΐδιον.

**κεράεις**, f.l. for κερόεις, Nic.*Al.*135.

**κερᾰελκής**, ές, *drawing by the horns*, [βόες] Call.*Dian.*179 (v.l. κερεαλκέες); Ἰώ Nonn.*D.*3.382. II. = κερουλκός II.2, τόξα ib.20.225. III. v. κερατεσσεῖς.

⊛ **κεραία**, poet. -αίη, ἡ, (κέρας) *horn*, Nic.*Th.*36, Opp.*C.*3.476. 2. *antennae* of the crayfish or of insects, Arist.*HA*526$^{a}$6, 532$^{a}$26. II. *anything projecting like a horn*: hence, 1. *yard-arm*, A.*Eu.*557 (lyr.),

Th.7.41, *IG*2$^2$.657, 1604.17, *PMagd.*11.4(iii B.C.), etc.; κ. καθελέσθαι, ὑφιέναι, i.e. lower sail, Plb.14.10.11, Plu.2.169b; opp. ἐντείνασθαι Call. *Fr.anon.*382; ἀπὸ ψιλῆς τῆς κ. 'under bare poles', Luc.*Tox.*19. b. *projecting beam* of a crane, etc., Th.2.76, cf. 4.100, *IG*11(2).161*A*90 (Delos, iii B.C.), Ph.*Bel.*100.18, Plb.8.5.10, Arr.*An.*2.19.2. c. *projecting parts* of the hucklebone, Arist.*HA*499$^b$30. d. *branching stake of wood*, used as a *pale* in a palisade, Plb.18.18.7, App.*BC*4.78. e. *horns of the ancilia*, Plu.*Num.*13. 2. pl., *horns* of the moon, Arat.785, 790. 3. in writing, *apex* of a letter, *IG*2.4321.10 (iv B.C.), A.D.*Synt.*28.27, cf. *Ev.Matt.*5.18, *Ev.Luc.*16.17, Antyll. ap.Orib.45.57.4; ζυγομαχεῖν περὶ συλλαβῶν καὶ κ. Plu.2.1100a; διὰ πάσης κ. διῆκον showing itself in every *word* of a speech, D.H.*Din.*7. 4. *leg* of a pair of compasses, S.E.*M.*10.54. 5. *projecting spur* of a mountain, Plu.*Cat.Ma.*13; of the *horns* of Europe and Africa at the Straits of Gibraltar, *AP*4.3$^b$.40 (Agath.); *arms* of a harbour, Philostr.*VS*1.21.2. 6. = κέρας v. 3, *wing* of an army, Hld.9.20. 7. pl., supposed teat-like *projections* inside the womb, Diocl.*Fr.*27; but the *Fallopian tubes*, Gal.*UP*14.11, Ruf.*Onom.*194. III. *bow made of horn*, *AP*6.75 (Paul. Sil.).

**κεραΐδιον**, v. κεράδιον.

**κεραιέλοντα**· ὁ εἰς κέρατα ἔλαιον ἄγων, Hsch.

**κεραΐζω**, Ep. impf. κεράϊζον Hom. (v. infr.): fut. inf. κεραϊξέμεν Il. 16.830: aor. ἐκεράϊσα Hdt.2.115, -ϊξα Nonn.*D.*23.21: (κείρω):—*ravage, plunder*, σταθμοὺς ἀνθρώπων κεραΐζετον Il.5.557, cf. 16.752; πόλιν κεραϊξέμεν ἀμήν ib.830, cf. Od.8.516, Parth.21.1, etc.; τὸ τῶν Λυδῶν ἄστυ Hdt.1.88; τὰ οἰκία τοῦ ξείνου Id.2.115; οἰκίας J.*BJ*6.8.5; τοὺς σωροὺς τῶν δραγμάτων Ael.*NA*6.41:—Pass., θαλάμους κεραϊζομένους Il.22.63; εὐνὰς θανάτοις κεραϊζομένας E.*Alc.*886 (anap.). 2. of ships, *sink, disable*, Hdt.8.91, cf. 86 (Pass.). 3. of living beings, *slaughter*, Τρῶας κεράϊζε καὶ ἄλλους Il.2.861, cf. 21.129; θῆρας Pi.*P.*9.21; οἱ [λέοντες] τὰς καμήλους ἐκεράϊζον Hdt.7.125. II. *carry off as plunder*, [τὰ χρήματα] Id.2.121.β'; τοὺς ἱκέτας ἐκ τοῦ νηοῦ Id.1.159. III. *exalt, uplift*, opp. ἀμαλδύνω, dub. in Corn.*ND*27.

**κεραίνω**, v. κέραιρε.

❊ **κεραιός** (⏑⏑⏑), = κεραός, *Epigr.Gr.*833.1.

❊ **κεραιοῦχος**, ον, = κεροῦχος II: metaph., *upholding the right*, Hsch.

**κεραιοφόρος**, ον, *furnished with projecting spears*, ἅμαξαι D.H.20.2.

**κέραιρε** (κέραινε and κέραιρε cod.)· κέρασον, Hsch., cf. v.l. in Il.9. 203.

**κεραΐς**, ΐδος, ἡ, *worm that eats horn*, v.l. Od.21.395 (pl.). II. gen. ΐδος, = κεράς (A) (q.v.). III. = ῥάφανος ἀγρία, Thphr.*HP*9.15.5.

**κεραΐς**, ΐδος, ἡ, = κορώνη (Hsch.), used of Medea by Lyc.1317.

**κερᾰ-ϊσμός**, ὁ, *devastation*, D.H.16.1. -ϊστής, οῦ, ὁ, *plunderer*, *h.Merc.*336. II. *baneful comet*, Hsch.

**κεραΐτης** [ῑ], ου, ὁ, = Lat. *cornicularius*, Lyd.*Mag.*3.3.

**κεραΐτις**, ιδος, ἡ, = τῆλις, Ps.-Dsc.2.102.

**κεραίω**, Ep. for κεράω, radic. form of κεράννυμι, ζωρότερον δὲ κέραιε *mix* the wine stronger, Il.9.203; ἀμβροσίην ἐκέραιον Q.S.4.139:—Pass., ᾧ κα κεραίηται *Schwyzer*321.3 (Delph., v B.C.); part. κεραιόμενος Emp.35.8, Nic.*Al.*178,511.

**κερᾰμαῖος**, α, ον, v. κεραμεοῦς.

❊**κεράμβηλον**, τό, *scarecrow* in a garden, Hsch.; also, a kind of *beetle* fixed on fig-trees to drive away gnats, Id.; cf. sq.

**κεράμβυξ**, υκος, ὁ, *longicorn beetle, cerambyx*, which feeds on dead wood, Nic.*Fr.*39, Hsch.

**κερᾰμ-εία**, ἡ, *the potter's craft*, Pl.*Prt.*324e: prov., ἐν πίθῳ τὴν κ. μανθάνειν, of those who undertake the most difficult tasks without learning the elements of the art, Id.*Grg.*514e, cf. *La.*187b, Dicaearch. Hist.51; τῆς αὐτῆς κ., of the same *make*, Eratosth.ap.Ath.11. 482b. -εικός, ή, όν, = κεραμικός (cf. A.D.*Adv.*166.29), τροχός Arist.*Mech.*851$^b$20, cf. X.*Smp.*7.2, Hsch. II. Κεραμεικός, ὁ, *the Potters' Quarter* at Athens, Menecl.3, cf. Sch.Ar.*Av.*395, *Eq.*769, *Ra.*131. -εῖον, τό, *potter's workshop*, Aeschin.3.119, *IG*2$^2$. 1635.143, *PSI*4.445.2 (iii B.C.). II. Ion. -ήϊον, = κεράμιον, Hom. *Epigr.*14.14. -ειος, v. sq. -εοῦς, ᾶ, οῦν, (κέραμος) *of clay* or *earth, earthen*, μάνην εἶχε κεραμεοῦν ἁδρόν Nico1, cf. *IG*2$^2$. 463.51, Thphr.*HP*5.3.2, Phld.*Mort.*39, Dsc.1.71; τὸ χρῶμα κεραμεοῦς Alex.Mynd.ap.Ath.9.398d:—other spellings found in codd. are **κεραμειος**, Plu.*Galb.*12; **κεράμεος**, Pl.*Ly.*219e, Ctes.*Fr.*51 M., Antiph.163.5, Theophil.2, cf. κεράμεα· ὁ παντοδαπὸς κέραμος, Hsch., and κεράμεον, τό, collect., = *tile-work*, *BCH*36.197 (Delos, iii/ii B.C.); **κεραμαῖος**, Plb.10.44.2, v.l. in Ph.2.273; **κεραμιαῖος**, ibid. (v.l.), *Gp.*2.18.14; **κεράμιος**, Str.17.2.3; **κεραμοῦς**, Heraclid.Tar. ap.Gal.13.827. ❊-εύς, έως, ὁ, *potter*, ὡς ὅτε τις τροχὸν.. κεραμεὺς πειρήσεται Il.18.601, cf. Hom.*Epigr.*14.1, etc.; οἱ κ., a guild at Thyatira, *IGRom.*4.1205: prov., καὶ κεραμεὺς κεραμεῖ κοτέει Hes.*Op.*25, cf. Arist.*Rh.*1381$^b$16, *EN*1155$^a$35; κεραμέως πλοῦτος and κεραμεὺς ἄνθρωπος, prov., of anything frail and uncertain, Diogenian.5.97, 98. II. **Κεραμεῖς**, Att. **Κεραμῆς**, οἱ, name of an Attic deme, Ar. *Ra.*1093 (anap.), Pl.*Prt.*315d, etc. -ευτικός, ή, όν, *of* or *for a potter*, ὁ κ. τροχός D.S.4.76, cf. S.E.*M.*10.93; ἀκολασία Luc.*Am.*11, etc.; ἡ -κὴ τέχνη *the potter's art, pottery*, D.S.19.1,2: without τέχνη, Poll. 7.161; τὰ κ. *earthenware*, *PTeb.*342.17 (ii A.D.). ❊-εύω, *to be a potter*, Phryn.Com.15, Pl.*R.*467a, etc. 2. c. acc., κ. κανθάρους *make earthenware* cups, Epig.4; τὰ τρύβλια κακῶς κ., τὴν δὲ πόλιν εὖ καὶ καλῶς he *tinkers* the state, of the demagogue Cephalos, whose father was a potter, Ar.*Ec.*253; κ. τὸν κεραμέα *make a pot of* the potter, Pl.*Euthd.*301d; τὸ Νέστορος ποτήριον πολλοὶ -εύουσι, i.e. *discuss its manufacture*, Ath.11.781d:—Med., ἐκεραμεύσαντο.. ποτήρια *they had* them *made*, Pherecr.143:—Pass., χύτρα κεκεραμευμένη ὑπὸ ἀγαθοῦ κεραμέως Pl.*Hp.Ma.*288d, cf. Nicostr.Com.10. ❊-εών, ῶνος, ὁ, *large wine-jar*, Ar.*Lys.*200. -ήϊος, η, ον, Ep. for κεράμειος, τεῦχος Nic.*Th.*80, cf. κεραμεῖον II:—fem. -ηΐς, Marc.Sid.60. -ίδιον, τό, Dim. of κεραμίς, *IG*12(9).907.26 (Chalcis, iv A.D.), Sch.D.T. p.196 H. -ιδοπλάστης, ου, ὁ, *tile-maker*, *Gloss.* -ιδόω, *make a roof as of shields* to protect the soldiers (the Roman *testudo*), Apollon.*Lex.* s.v. σάκος, Hsch. s.v. σάκε' ὤμοισι κλίναντες:—Pass., *to be roofed* or *coped with tiles*, κεραμιδουμένη.. ἡ οἰκία Arist.*Ph.*246$^a$28 (but κεραμουμένη ib.19 codd.). ❊-ικός, ή, όν, *of* or *for pottery*, γῆ κ. *potter's* earth, Hp.*Int.*7, cf. Sannyr.4; κ. ῥύμη, = Κεραμεικός, Ar. *Ec.*4; κ. κέραμος *IG*4$^2$(1).102.281 (Epid., iv B.C.); ὁ κ. τροχός Str.7. 3.9; κ. μάστιξ, Com. phrase for ostracism, *Com.Adesp.*33; ἐργαστήριον *PFlor.*50.68 (iii A.D.); ἡ -κή (sc. τέχνη) *the potter's art, pottery*, Pl.*Plt.*288a; v. κεραμεικός. -ινος, η, ον, = κεραμεοῦς, Hdt.3.96, 4.70, Anaxil.5, *PFlor.*388.98 (ii A.D.). -ιον, τό, *earthenware vessel, jar*, *IG*2$^2$.1672.13, Men.*Sam.*88 (pl.), etc.; κ. οἰνηρόν Hdt.3.6, cf. Hp.*Art.*78; οἴνου X.*An.*6.1.15; ὀξηρόν Ar.*Fr.*723; κ. ταριχηρόν Arist.*HA*534$^a$21; ταρίχους, as a measure, Test.ap.D.35.34, cf. *PSI* 5.585 (iii B.C.), *OGI*90.31 (Rosetta, ii B.C.), Lxx *Is.*5.10, *SIG*1109. 162 (ii A.D.). 2. *sarcophagus*, D.C.42.26. -ιος, ὁ, = κεραμεύς, *CIG*5021, 5028 (Nubia). II. v. κεραμεοῦς. -ίς, ίδος [ῐ], ἡ, Diph.84, Ion. and later -ῖδος Emp.ap.Arist.*EE*1235$^a$12, *MM*1208$^b$11, cf. Hdn.Gr.2.18: (κέραμος):—*roof-tile*, Ar.*V.*206, Th.3.22, *Inscr. Délos*366.21, al. (iii B.C.), etc.; κ. ἀγελαῖαι common *tiles*, *IG*2$^2$.1672. 209; Κορίνθιαι ib.71; collectively, *tiling*, Arist.*Ph.*246$^a$27, cf. ll. cc.; prop. of clay, but also of marble, *IG*2$^2$.1666*B*21,25; κ. ἀργυραῖ Plb. 10.27.10; κ. μολυβῆ Ath.14.621a, cf. Moschioib.5.207a. 2. = κεράμιον, *PLond.*3.1177.158 (ii A.D.), *PLand.*12.3 (iii/iv A.D.). II. as Adj., γῆ κ. *potter's* earth, clay, Pl.*Criti.*111c, *Lg.*844b; ὦ γαῖα κεραμί Eub.43. -ισμα, ατος, τό, = foreg., *Gloss.* -ίτης, ου, ὁ, v. sq. -ῖτις, ιδος, ἡ, *of* or *for pottery*, κ. γῆ *potter's* earth, Hp. *Morb.*1.17, 3.1, Plu.2.827e, Gal.2.137; κ., ἡ, a gem of the colour of potsherds, Plin.*HN*37.152 (acc. -την, nisi leg. -τιν, *Cat.Cod.Astr.* 8(2).169, cf. 8(1).190).

**κερᾰμο-πλάστης**, ου, ὁ, *potter*, *PLips.*97 xxvi 10 (iv A.D.), *PLond.* 1821.234. -πλαστικὸν κεραμεῖον *pottery*, *PMasp.*110.22 (vi A.D.). -ποιός, ὁ, *potter*, *Gloss.*

**κερᾰμοπωλ-εῖον**, τό, *pottery-market*, Din.*Fr.*89.18. -έω, *sell earthenware*, Alex.320. ❊-ης, ου, ὁ, *seller of pottery*, Din.*Fr.*89.18.

❊**κέρᾰμος**, ὁ, rare pl. κέραμα, τά, *PPetr.*3 p.327 (iii B.C.):—*potter's earth, potter's clay*, Pl.*Ti.*60d, Arist.*Mete.*384$^b$19, etc.; κ. ὠμός, ὀπτώμενος, ib.380$^b$8, 383$^a$21. II. *anything made of this earth*, as 1. *earthen vessel, wine-jar*, ἐκ κεράμων μέθυ πίνετο Il.9.469, cf. Hdt.3.96; in collective sense, *pottery*, Ar.*Ach.*902, Men.*Sam.*75, al.; κ. ἐσάγεται πλήρης οἴνου *jars* full of wine, Hdt.3.6, cf. 5.88, Alex.257.3, etc. b. *jar* of other material, κ. ἀργυροῦς Ptol.Euerg.7 J. 2. *tile*, Ar.*V.*1295 (of a tortoise's shell); collectively, *tiling*, τοῦ τέγους τὸν κέραμον αὐτοῦ χαλάζαις.. ξυντρίψομεν Id.*Nu.*1127, cf. *Fr.*349, Th. 2.4; Κορίνθιοι κ. *IG*2$^2$.1668.58; Λακωνικὸs ib.463.69, 1672.188; *roof*, Pherecr.130.6, Herod.3.44, Gal.8.26, 9.824. 3. *pottery* (i.e. place of manufacture), ὁ κ. ὁ χυτρικός *Tab.Defix.Praef.*p.ii$^b$. III. *dungeon* (said by Sch. to be Cyprian), χαλκέῳ ἐν κεράμῳ δέδετο Il.5.387, cf. Thphr.*Char.*6.6 cod. M; pl., Nonn.*D.*16.162. (Possibly cogn. with Lat. *cremo*.)

**κερᾰμοτήξ**, ῆγος, ὁ, (τήκω) *potter*, Theognost.*Can.*40.

**κερᾰμ-ουργός**, ὁ, = κεραμοποιός, *PPetr.*3 p.173 (iii B.C.), Man.4. 291, *Cat.Cod.Astr.*8(4).213. -όω, *roof with tiles*, *IG*1$^2$.373.246, 2$^2$.1668.58, al., Ἀρχ.Δελτ.8.270:—Pass., ναὸς κεκεραμωμένος *SIG* 996.18 (Smyrna, i A.D.), cf. Simp.*in Ph.*1055.17; ὡς εἰπεῖν -ωθέντες, of soldiers in the Roman *testudo*, Onos.20.1. -ύλλιον, τό, Dim. of κεράμιον, *jar*, *IG*11(2).161*C*101 (Delos, iii B.C.), *PCair.Zen.*12.35 (iii B.C.), *Inscr.Délos*442*B*179 (ii B.C.), Aq.*Is.*63.3. -ών, ῶνος, ὁ, *store for pottery* or *tiles*, Hdn.Gr.1.32,40. -ωσις, εως, ἡ, *roofing with tiles*, *IG*4$^2$(1).102.289 (Epid., iv B.C.), *IPE*1$^2$.184 (Olbia, iii A.D.). -ωτός, ή, όν, *covered with tiles*, applied to a *testudo* formed by Roman soldiers, Plb.28.11.2; ἡ κ. στέγη Str.11.3.1, 13.1.27.

**κερανίξαι**· κολυμβῆσαι, κυβιστῆσαι, Hsch.

**κεράνν-ῡμι**, also -ύω Alc.Com.15, Hyp.*Fr.*69; Ep. **κεραίω** and **κεράω** (qq.v.); subj. κεραννύω Pl.*Phlb.*61b: impf. ἐκεράννυν Luc.*VH* 1.7: fut. κεράσω [ᾰ] Them.*Or.*27 p.340 D.: aor. ἐκέρᾱσα Hp.*VM*3, (ἐν-) Pl.*Cra.*427c, poet. κέρᾱσα E.*Ba.*127 (lyr.), Ep. κέρασσα Od.5. 93, Ion. ἔκρησα Hp.*Int.*35:—Med., aor. ἐκερᾰσάμην Ti.Locr.95e, Ep. κεράσσατο Od.18.423:—Pass., fut. κραθήσομαι [ᾰ] Pl.*Ep.*326c, (συγ-) E.*Ion*406: aor. ἐκράθην [ᾱ] Th.6.5, E.*Ion*1016, Pl.*Phd.*86c; Ion. ἐκρήθην Hp.*VM*19; ἐκεράσθην Pl.*Phlb.*47c, *Ti.*85a, X.*An.*5.4. 29, Phylarch.10 J.: pf. κέκρᾱμαι Pi.*P.*10.41, etc.; Ion. κέκρημαι Hp. *VM*13, *Acut.*21; κεκέρασμαι Arist.*Fr.*549, D.H.*Comp.*24, *Anacreont.* 16.13, etc.: plpf. ἐκέκρᾱτο Sapph.51.1:—*mix, mingle* (diff. from μείγνυμι, v. κρᾶσις): 1. mostly of diluting wine with water, κερῶντάς τ' αἴθοπα οἶνον Od.24.364; κέρασσε δὲ νέκταρ ἐρυθρόν 5.93; κέρασον ἄκρατον Ar.*Ec.*1123, cf. Th.6.32: abs., τοῖς θεοῖς εὐχόμενοι κεραννύωμεν *let us mix a cup of wine*, Pl.*Phlb.*61b; ἂν μὴ κεράσῃ τις Antiph.85.2: c. dat. pers., *give to drink*, ἐν τῷ ποτηρίῳ ᾧ ἐκέρασε κεράσατε αὐτῇ διπλοῦν *Apoc.*18.6:—Hom. mostly in Med., ὅτε περ.. οἶνον.. ἐνὶ κρητῆρι κέρωνται *mix their* wine in the bowl, Il. 4.260, cf. Od.20.253; κρητῆρα κεράσσατο he *mixed* a bowl, 3.393, 18.423:—Pass., πῶς οὖν κέκραται [σκύφος]; E.*Cyc.*557; κύλιξ ἴσον ἴσῳ κεκραμένη a cup *mixed* half and half, Ar.*Pl.*1132; κεκρ. τρία

καὶ δύο Id.*Eq.*1187, cf. *AP*11.137 (Lucill.). 2. *temper, cool by mixing*, θυμῆρες κεράσασα *having mixed* (the water) *to an* agreeable *temperature*, Od.10.362. 3. generally, *mix, blend*, ἡδονὴν φθόνῳ Pl.*Phlb.*50a; τοῖς ὀνόμασι τὰ ῥήματα Id.*Sph.*262c; νοῦς μετ' αἰσθήσεων κραθείς Id.*Lg.*961d, cf. *Ti.* l. c.; πίστεως αἰσθήσει κεκραμένης Plot.4.7.15; ἀγωγὴν ἐξ ἀμφοῖν κ. Phld.*Acad.Ind.*p.77 M.; [οὐσία] οὐκ ἀπὸ τῶν ἄκρων κραθεῖσα Jul.*Or.*4.139a; of metals, ἀργυρίῳ πρὸς χαλκὸν κεκραμένῳ χρῆσθαι D.24.214: metaph., *temper, regulate*, of climates, ὧραι κάλλιστα κεκρημέναι most *temperate*, Hdt.3.106; ὧραι μετριώτατα κ. Pl.*Criti.*111e; ἔαρ κ. τῇ ὥρᾳ X.*Cyn.*5.5; [πλοῦτον] ἀρετᾷ κεκραμένον Pi.*P.*5.2; οὐ γῆρας κέκραται γενεᾷ no old age *is mingled with* the race, i. e. it knows no old age, ib.10.41, cf. *O.*10(11).104; ἐν ταῖς εὖ κεκρ. πολιτείαις Arist.*Pol.*1307$^{b}$30; of tempers of mind, ἤθει γεννικωτέρῳ κεκρᾶσθαι Pl.*Phdr.*279a; τοῖς ἤθεσιν..τούτοις ἡ φύσις κεράννυται Alex. 278b (iii p.744 K.); of Music, ἁρμονίας ῥυθμοῖς κραθείσας Pl.*Lg.*835b; τῆς εὖ κεκραμένης ἁρμονίας Arist.*Pol.*1290$^{a}$26; μετρίως κραθῆναι πρὸς ἄλληλα Pl.*Phd.* l. c. II. *compound*, ἐκ τῶν ἐπιτηδευμάτων τὸ ἀνδρείκελον Id.*R.*501b; οὐκ ἀπίθανον λόγον Id.*Phdr.*265b; θεόσυτος ἢ βρότειος ἢ κεκραμένη; A.*Pr.*116; φωνὴ μεταξὺ τῆς τε Χαλκιδέων καὶ Δωρίδος ἐκράθη Th.6.5. III. Gramm., in Pass., *coalesce by crasis*, τὸ ῥῆμα καὶ ὁ σύνδεσμος συναλοιφῇ κερασθέντα D.H.*Comp.*22. IV. *multiply into*, ὅταν ὁ τῆς δεκάδος λόγος τῷ τῆς ἑβδομάδος κερασθῇ *Theol.Ar.* 50. **-υτέον**, *one must mix*, Max.Tyr.5.4.

**κέραξ**, ακος, ὁ, = κέρας, in the senses θρίξ, τόξον, αἰδοῖον, Hsch.

⊛ **κερᾰοξόος**, ον, (ξέω) *polishing horn*; esp. *making it into bows*, etc., κ. τέκτων Il.4.110, *AP*6.113 (Simm.).

⊛ **κερᾰός**, ά, όν, (κέρας) *horned*, ἔλαφος Il.3.24; ἄρνες Od.4.85; τράγος Theoc.1.4; Ἄμμων *Epigr.Gr.*835 (Berytus). II. *made of horn*, τοῖχοι Call.*Ap.*63; βιός *AP*6.118 (Antip.). (Prob. fr. *κεραϝός, cf. Lat. *cervus.*)

**κερᾰοῦχος**, ον, (ἔχω) = κεροῦχος I, *AP*6.10 (Antip.).

**κεράρχης**, ου, ὁ, *commander of a* διφαλαγγαρχία, Ascl.*Tact.*2.10. 2. *commander of thirty-two elephants*, ib.9.1.

⊛ **κέρᾰς**, τό, Ep. gen. *κέρᾰος, Att. contr. κέρως; Ep. dat. κέρᾰϊ (elided) or κέραι or κέρᾳ Il.11.385, cf. Hdn.Gr.2.75, κέρᾳ also in Th. 2.90, 7.6: nom. pl. κέρᾱ (v. infr.), gen. κεράων, κερῶν, dat. κέρασι, Ep. κεράεσσι:—Att. Inscrr. have dual [κέρ]ατε *IG*1².301.109: pl. κέρατα ib.237.59; later Ep. κεράατα (⏑ – ⏑ ⏑) Nic.*Th.*291, κεράατος (⏑ – ⏑ ⏑) Arat.174, Q.S.6.225:—Hdt. has gen. κέρεος 6.111, dat. κέρεϊ 9.102: pl. κέρεα 2.38, κερέων ib.132; but Hp. has gen. sg. κέρως, pl. κέρατα, *Aër.*18. [In nom. and acc. κέρας, ᾰ always: in the obl. cases ᾰ in Ep., as κέρᾰσιν Od.3.384 (in contr. dat. κέρᾱͅ, nom. pl. κέρᾱ (cf. Batr.165), α is shortd. before a vowel, Il.11.385, Od.19.211); but ᾱ in Trag. and Com., κέρᾱτος Hermipp.43, κέρᾱτα E.*Ba.*921, κεράτων [ᾱ] prob. in S.*Tr.*519 (lyr.), κέρᾱσι A.*Fr.*185. In later Ep. the quantity varies.] (κέρας is prob. related to κάρα; cf. κεραός.) I. *the horn of an animal*, in Hom. mostly of oxen, Il.17.521, etc.; ταῦροι..εἰς κέρας θυμούμενοι E.*Ba.*743; ὀφθαλμοὶ δ' ὡς εἰ κέρα ἕστασαν his eyes stood fixed and stiff like *horns*, Od.19.211; as a symbol of strength, Lxx *Ps.*17(18).3, Diogenian.7.89, cf. Arist.*PA*662$^{a}$1; of elephants' *tusks*, Aret.*SD*2.13, Opp.*C.*2.494. 2. *antennae* of crustaceans, Arist.*HA*526$^{a}$31, 590$^{b}$27; of the silkworm's *grub*, ib.551$^{b}$10. II. *horn*, as a material, αἱ μὲν γὰρ [πύλαι] κεράεσσι τετεύχαται Od.19.563; *the horn* of animals' hoofs, Longus 2.28. III. *anything made of horn*, 1. *bow*, τόξον ἐνώμα..πειρώμενος..μὴ κέρα ἶπες ἔδοιεν Od. 21.395, cf. Theoc.25.206, Call.*Ep.*38, *AP*6.75 (Paul. Sil.); for Il.11. 385 v. infr. v. 1. 2. of musical instruments, *horn for blowing*, σημῆναι τῷ κέρατι X.*An.*2.2.4, cf. Arist.*Aud.*802$^{a}$17; also, *the Phrygian flute*, because it was tipped with horn (cf. Poll.4.74), αὐλεῖν τῷ κ. Luc.*DDeor.*12.1; καὶ κέρατι μὲν αὐλεῖν Τυρρηνοὶ νομίζουσι Poll.4.76, cf. Ath.4.184a. 3. *drinking-horn*, ἐκ τοῦ κέρατος αὖ μοι δὸς πιεῖν Hermipp.43, cf. X.*An.*7.2.23, *OGI*214.43 (Didyma, iii B. C.); ἐξ ἀργυρέων κ. πίνειν Pi.*Fr.*166, cf. *IG*1².280.77; ἀργυρηλάτοις κέρασι χρυσᾶ στόμια προσβεβλημένοις A.*Fr.*185; ἐκπιόντι χρύσεον κ. S.*Fr.* 483; for measuring liquids, Gal.13.435. 4. Ἀμαλθείας κ. *cornucopiae*, v. Ἀμάλθεια. IV. βοὸς κ. prob. a *horn guard* or *cover* attached to a fishing-line, Il.24.81, cf. Sch.; ἐς πόντον προΐησι βοὸς κέρας Od.12.253; ψάμμῳ κ. αἰὲν ἐρείδων *AP*6.230 (Maec.), cf. Aristarch.ap.Apollon.*Lex.* s. v. κέρᾳ ἀγλαέ, Arist.ap.Plu.2.977a (also expld. as a *fishing-line of ox-hair* (cf. infr. v. 1), ap.Plu.2.976f, cf. Poll.2.31; perh. an artificial *bait*). 2. *clyster-pipe*, Orib.8.32 7. 3. in pl., *horn points* with which the writing-reed was tipped, *AP*6.227 (Crin.). V. of objects shaped like horns, 1. a mode of dressing the hair, κέρᾳ ἀγλαέ Il.11.385 (unless the meaning be *bow*), cf. Aristarch. ad loc., Herodorus and Apion ap.Eust. ad loc.: hence κέρας is expld. as = θρίξ or κόμη, Apollon.*Lex.*, Hdn.Gr.ap.Eust. l. c., Poll.2.31, Hsch.; cf. IV. 1, and v. κεροπλάστης. 2. *arm* or *branch* of a river, Ὠκεανοῖο κ. Hes.*Th.*789; Νείλου Pi.*Fr.*201; τὸ Μενδήσιον κέρας Th.1.110; ἐν Ἰνδοῖς ἐν τῷ Κέρατι καλουμένῳ Arist.*Mir.*835$^{b}$5, cf. *Mu.*393$^{b}$5; τὸ κ. τὸ Βυζαντίων the 'Golden *Horn*', Str.7.6.2, cf. Plb.4.43.7. Sch.A.R.4.282; Ἑσπέρου Κ., name of a *bay*, Hanno *Peripl.*14, cf. Philostr.*VS*1.21.2. 3. *wing* of an army, Hdt.9.26, etc.; or fleet, Id.6.8, Th.2.90, etc.; κ. δεξιόν, λαιόν, A.*Pers.*399, E.*Supp.*704; τὸ εὐώνυμον κ. ἀναπτύσσειν X.*An.*1.10. 9. b. κατὰ κέρας προσβάλλειν, ἐπιπεσεῖν, to attack in *flank*, Th.3.78, X.*HG*6.5.16, etc.; κατὰ κ. προσιέναι, ἕπεσθαι, Id.*Cyr.*7.1.8 and 28; κατὰ κ. συμπεσών Plb.1.40.14; πρὸς κ. μάχεσθαι X.*Cyr.*7.1.22. c. ἐπὶ κέρας ἀνάγειν τὰς νέας to lead a fleet in *column*, Hdt.6.12, cf. 14; κατὰ μίαν ἐπὶ κέρως παραπλεῖν Th.2.90, cf. 6.32, X.*Cyr.*6.3.34, Eub.67.4; of armies, κατὰ κέρας, opp. ἐπὶ φάλαγγος, X.*Cyr.*1.6.43, cf. *An.*4.6.6, *HG*7.4.23; εἰς κ. Id.*Eq.Mag.*4.3; ἐκ κέρατος εἰς φάλαγγα καταστῆσαι Id.*Cyr.*8.5.15; οὐκ ἐλᾶτε πρὸς τὸ δεξιὸν κ.; Ar.*Eq.*243. 4. *corps of* 8192 *men*, = διφαλαγγαρχία, Ascl.*Tact.*2.6, Arr.*Tact.*10.7. b. = μεραρχία, Ascl.*Tact.*2.10. c. *contingent of thirty-two chariots*, ib. 8, Ael.*Tact.*22.2. 5. *sailyard*, = κεραία, *AP*5.203 (Mel.), *OGI*674.30 (Egypt, i A. D.), Luc.*Am.*6, *POxy.*2136.6 (iii A. D.). 6. *mountain-peak*, v.l. in *h.Hom.*1.8; *spur*, τὸ κ. τοῦ ὄρους X.*An.*5.6.7, cf. Lyc. 534: in pl., *extremities* of the earth, γῆς Philostr.*VA*2.18 (pl.). 7. in Anatomy, *extremities* of the uterus, Hp.*Superf.*1, Gal.7.266; of the diaphragm, Sor.1.57. b. ἁπαλὸν κ., = πόσθη, Archil.171, cf. Neophro (?) in *PLit.Lond.*77 *Fr.*2.19, E.*Fr.*278, *AP*12.95.6 (Mel.). 8. of the πήχεις of the lyre, χρυσόδετον κ. S.*Fr.*244 (lyr.) (rather than the *bridge*, because made of *horn*, Ael.Dion.*Fr.*133, Poll.4.62). VI. κέρατα ποιεῖν τινι to give him *horns*, cuckold him, prov. in Artem.2. 11; cf. κερασφόρος II. VII. = κερατίνης, Luc.*DMort.*1.2. VIII. = σταφυλῖνος ἄγριος, Dsc.3.52; = οἰνάνθη, dub. in Ps.-Dsc.3.120.

**κεράς** (A), άδος, ἡ, poet. fem. of κεραός, Eust.1625.45; but in Hsch., κερατ̈δες· τῶν προβάτων τὰ θήλεα, τὰ ἔνδον ὀδόντας ἔχοντα.

**κεράς** (B), Adv. *mixed*, glossed by κεραστικῶς, Call.*Fr.anon.*34.

⊛ **κερασβόλος**, ον, *struck by a horn*: σπέρμα κ. seed *that does not soften in boiling*, Thphr.*CP*4.12.13, cf. Plu.2.700c. II. metaph., *stubborn, inflexible* person, Pl.*Lg.*853d, cf. Plu. l. c.

**κερᾰσ-έα** and **-ία**, ἡ, = κερασός, *cherry-tree*, *Gp.*3.4.4, 10.41.2. **-ινον**, τό, *cherry-coloured dye*, *PHolm.*21.31. **-ιον**, τό, *fruit of the* κερασός, *cherry*, Diph.Siph.ap.Ath.2.51a, Dsc.1.113; also, *cherry-tree*, *Gp.*10.41.1.

**κερασκόμη**, ἡ, = κέρας VIII, Ps.-Dsc.3.52, 120 codd.

**κέρασμα**, ατος, τό, *mixture*, Zeno *Stoic.*1.36; μελῶν Iamb.*VP*15. 64 (pl.). 2. *drink poured out* (cf. κεράννυμι I. 1), *IGRom.*4.696 (Hieropolis); οἴνου ἀκράτου κ. Lxx *Ps.*74(75).8. 3. *mixed disease*, Gal.9.675.

**κερᾰσός** (on the accent v. Hdn.Gr.1.209), ὁ, *bird-cherry, Prunus avium*, Xenoph.39, Thphr.*HP*3.13.1, etc. (Assyrian *karšu.*)

⊛ **κεράστης**, ου, ὁ, *horned*, ἔλαφος S.*El.*568; κάνθαρος Id.*Ichn.*300; of a ram, ὦ κεράστα E.*Cyc.*52 (lyr.); Πάν Antip.*Oxy.*662.49, Corn. *ND*27; Σάτυροι Luc.*Bacch.*1:—fem. ⊛ **κεραστίς**, ίδος, of Io, A.*Pr.* 674. II. as Subst., *horned serpent* or *asp, Cerastes cornutus*, Nic. *Th.*258, Lxx *Pr.*23.32, D.S.3.50, Ael.*NA*1.57; οἱ κ. ὄφεις Call.Hist. 3. 2. *pest which destroys fig-trees*, Thphr.*HP*4.14.5, 5.4.5.

**κερασ-τής**, οῦ, ὁ, *one that mixes*, Ζεὺς πάντων κ. Orph.*Fr.*297. **-τικῶς**, Adv. *for mixing*, Suid. s. v. κεράς. ⊛ **-τός**, ή, όν, *mixed, mingled*, *APl.*4.83.

**κερασφορ-έω**, *have horns*. Philostr.*VA*2.13. ⊛ **-ος**, ον, *horned*, στόρθυγγες S.*Fr.*89; of Io, E.*Ph.*248 (lyr.), *Hyps.Fr.*3(1) iii 31 (lyr.); of Dionysos, Luc.*Bacch.*2; of rivers, Corn.*ND*22; τὸ κ. μέρος Pl. *Plt.*265b; τὸ κ. γένος *horned animals*, Gal.2.430, cf. Philostr.*VA* 2.13. II. *cuckold*, Lemm. to *AP*11.278 (Lucill.).

**κεράσχειλος**, ον, *with curved lips*, Hsch.

**κερᾱτ-άριον**, τό, Dim. of κέρας v. 5, Sch.E.*Hec.*1261 (s. v. l.), Eust. 1037.35. **-άρχης**, ου, ὁ, *commander of a body of thirty-two elephants*, Ael.*Tact.*23:—hence **-αρχία**, ἡ, ibid. **-αύλης**, ου, ὁ, = κεραύλης, Dosith.p.389 K., *Gloss.*

**κερατέα**, ἡ, = κερατωνία, *Gp.*11.1; dub. sens. in *POxy.*2146.9 (iii A. D.), *PGen.*75.8 (iii/iv A. D.).

**κερατεσσεῖς**· οἱ τοὺς ταύρους ἕλκοντες ἀπὸ τῶν κεράτων· καλοῦνται δὲ καὶ **κεραελκεῖς**, Hsch.

**κερᾱτήρ**, ῆρος, ὁ, etym. of κρατήρ, Ath.11.476a.

**κερᾰτηφόρος**, ον, = κερασφόρος I, Phaest.ap.Sch.Pi.*P.*4.28.

**κερατία**, ἡ, = κερατωνία, Str.17.2.2, Plin.*HN*26.52. II. **κεράτια**, τά, *fruit of the carob-tree*, Dsc.1.114, *Ev.Luc.*15.16, *PLond.*1. 131*.7 (i A. D.), Gal.6.615.

**κερᾱτ-ίας**, ου, ὁ, = κερασφόρος I, of Dionysos, D.S.4.4. II. kind of *comet*, Plin.*HN*2.90. ⊛ **-ίζω**, *butt with horns*: metaph., κ. τοῖς ποταμοῖς Lxx *Ez.*32.2, cf. Ph.1.57: c. acc., *gore*, ἐὰν κερατίσῃ ταῦρος ἄνδρα Lxx *Ex.*21.28. **-ίνης** [ῐ], ου, ὁ, *the fallacy called the Horns*: εἴ τι οὐκ ἀπέβαλες, τοῦτο ἔχεις· κέρατα δὲ οὐκ ἀπέβαλες· κέρατα ἄρα ἔχεις D.L.7.187; κερατίνας ἐρωτῶν *Com.Adesp.*294: acc. sg. **-ναν** Luc. *Symp.*23; cf. κερατίς. ⊛ **-ῐνος**, η, ον, *made of horn*, X.*An.*6.1.4, Pl. Com.50, etc.; κ. λύχνος Epicr.8; βωμὸς κ., = κερατών, Plu.2.983e, cf. Arist.*Fr.*489; σάλπιγξ Lxx *Ps.*97(98).6; also κ. alone, ib.*Jd.*3.27, *2Ki.* 2.28. ⊛ **-ιον**, τό, Dim. of κέρας, *small horn*, D.S.3.73, Arist.ap. Plu.2.977a. 2. of the *antennae* of the κάραβος, Arist.*HA*526$^{a}$7; of the hermit-crab, ib.529$^{a}$27. 3. in pl., *curved ends* of the womb (cf. κεραία II. 7), ib.510$^{b}$19. 4. musical instrument, perh. *fife* or *clarionet*, D.S.29.32, prob. for κεραμείου in Plb.26.1.4, cf. ib.1$^{a}$. 2. II. *carat*, $\frac{1}{1728}$ *of a pound*, Dsc.ap.Gal.19.775, Archig.ap.Aët. 6.37, Hero *Mens.*60.21, Just.*Nov.*32.1; = Lat. *siliqua*, *OGI*521.27 (Abydos, v/vi A. D.). III. = κερατωνία, Colum.*Arbor.*25. IV. v. κεράτια. **-ίς**, ίδος, ἡ, = κερατίνης, D.L.7.82 (s. v. l.). **-ισις**, εως, ἡ, *butting with horns*: metaph., of battering-rams, *impact*, Apollod. *Poliorc.*224.13 (pl.). **-ισμός**, ὁ, *loss on exchange of solidi for* κεράτια, *PMasp.*58 ii 11 (vi A. D.), Lyd.*Mag.*3.70 (pl.). **-ιστής**, οῦ, ὁ, *one that butts*, Lxx *Ex.*21.29, 36. **-ῖτις**, ιδος, ἡ, *horned*, μήκων κ. *horned poppy, Glaucium flavum*, Thphr.*HP*9.12.3, Dsc.4.65, Plin. *HN*20.205.

**κερᾱτο-βάτης** [ᾰ], ου, ὁ, gloss on κεροβάτας, Sch.Ar.*Ra.*230. **-γλύφος** [ῠ], ον, *working in horn*, Sch.D Il.4.110, *EM*505.11. **-ειδής**, ές, *like horn*, χιτών *external coat of the eye*, Cels.7.7.13, Poll.2.70, Aët.

7 1, etc. 2. applied to a part of the coat, opp. λευκός, Ruf.*Onom.* 27, cf. Gal.*UP*10.3 (distinguishing *cornea* from *sclera*). II. *horn-shaped*, λοβοί Dsc.2.158; γωνίαι J.*BJ*5.5.6; μορφή Sch.Arat. 779. III. *sounding like a horn*, ἦχοι D.H.*Comp.*14.

**κερᾰτοξόος**, ον, = κεραοξόος, Nonn.*D.*3.76 codd. (κεραο– Mein., Ludw.).

**κερᾰτο-ποιέω**, *make horn-shaped*, Sch.Arat.780. **-ποιός**, όν, gloss on κεραοξόος, Hsch. **-πους**, ὁ, ἡ, πουν, τό, gen. ποδος, *horn-footed, hoofed*, *Gloss.*

**κερᾰτουργός**, όν, = κεραοξόος, Sch.D Il.4.110, *EM*505.11.

**κερᾰτο-φάγος** [φᾰ], ον, *eating horn*, Hsch. s.v. ἶψ. **-φόρος**, ον, = κερασφόρος 1, Arist.*HA*499$^b$15, *PA*663$^b$35; θῆρες Opp.*C.*2.489. **-φῠέω**, *grow horns*, Sch.Ar.*Eq.*1341, *EM*505.6. **-φῠής**, ές, *growing horns, horned*, Ath.11.476a, *EM*541.18. **-φωνος**, ον, *sounding with the horn*, of the μάγαδις struck by the plectrum, Telest.4.

**κερᾰτ-όω**, *harden into horn*, Ael.*NA*12.18. **-ώδης**, ες, = κερατοειδής, *like antlers*, Thphr.*HP*5.1.6; τὸ κ., of the gizzard in fowls, Dsc.2.49. 2. *horned*, τὰ κ. τῶν ζῴων Arist.*HA*595$^a$13. II. v. κεραώδης. **-ών**, ῶνος, ὁ, *made of horns* (sc. βωμός), of an altar on Delos, *IG*2$^2$.1641.2 (iv B.C.), 11(2).161*A*101 (Delos, iii B.C.), *Inscr.Délos*442*A*188 (ii B.C.), Plu.*Thes.*21.

**κερατωνία**, ἡ, = κερωνία, κερατέα, *carob-tree, Ceratonia Siliqua*, Gal. 12.23, Aët.1.201, Hsch.

**κερᾰτῶπις**, ιδος, ἡ, *horned-looking*, μήνη Man.4.91.

**κεραύλ-ης**, ου, ὁ, *horn-blower*, Archil.172, Luc.*Trag.*33. **-ία**, ἡ, *horn-blowing*, Corn.*ND*6(pl.).

**κεραυν-εγχής**, ές, = ἐγχεικέραυνος, B.7.48. **-ειος**, ον, *wielding the thunder*, Ζεύς *AP*7.49 (Bianor). **-ία**, ἡ, = ἀείζωον μικρόν, Ps.-Dsc.4.89. **-ίας**, ου, ὁ, *thunder-stricken*, Hsch. **-ιον**, τό, *truffle, Tuber aestivum*, Thphr.*HP*1.6.5, Gal.19.731. II. *critical mark to indicate corrupt passages*, Isid.*Etym.*1.21.21, Sch.Il.i p.xliii Dind.; but πρὸς τὴν ἀγωγὴν τῆς φιλοσοφίας D.L.3.66. III. = κεραυνία λίθος, *PHolm.*5.40, Isid.*Etym.*16.13.5, etc. **-ιος**, α, ον, also ος, ον A.*Th.*430, E.*Ba.*594 (anap.):—*of a thunderbolt*, βολαί A. l.c.; φλόξ Id.*Pr.*1017; πέμφιξ S.*Fr.*538; πῦρ, λαμπάδες, E.*Tr.*80, *Ba.*244; θάνατος death *by the thunderbolt*, Call.*Aet.*3.1.64; λίθος *heliotrope*, *PHolm.*10.37, Porph.*VP*17, cf. Plin.*HN*37.132. 2. *thunder-smitten*, of Semele, S.*Ant.*1139 (lyr.), E.*Ba.*6; Καπανέως κ. δέμας Id. *Supp.*496; τὰ Κεραύνια the '*thunder-splitten peaks*', name of several mountain ridges, Str.6.3.5, etc. 3. κεραύνιος, ὁ, kind of *bandage*, Sor.*Fasc.*37. II. = κεραύνειος, [Ζεύς] Arist.*Mu.*401$^a$17, *Milet.*1(7). 278; applied to Philip, *AP*6.115 (Antip. ⟨Sid.⟩).

**κεραυνο-βλής**, ῆτος, ὁ, ἡ, = sq., Thphr.*HP*3.8.5, Tz.*H.*4.267. **-βλητος**, ον, *struck by lightning*, Ephor.17 J., Sch.S.*Ant.*1139, Hsch. s.v. λευκοστεφῆ, Suid. s.v. Σαλμωνεύς.

**κεραυνοβολ-έω**, *hurl the thunderbolt*, *AP*12.122 (Mel.), 140, Ps.-Luc.*Philopatr.*4, *Placit.*3.3.3. II. trans., *strike therewith*, οἰκίαν Eratosth.*Cat.*6. **-ία**, ἡ, *thunder-storm*, Str.13.4.11 (pl.), Plu.2. 624b (pl.). **-ιον**, τό, *thunderbolt*, Corn.*ND*19. **-ος**, ον, *hurling the thunder*, Ζεύς *IG*5(2).37 (Tegea); πῦρ τὸ κ. the *thunder-smiting* fire, *AP*12.63 (Mel.); κ. νεφέλαι Orph.*Fr.*256; of planetary influences, Vett.Val.14.17; title of the Roman *Legio XII Fulminata*, D.C.71.9. II. proparox. κεραυνόβολος, ον, Pass., *thunder-stricken*, of Semele, E.*Ba.*598 (lyr.), cf. D.S.1.13, etc.

**κεραυνο-βρόντης**, ου, ὁ, *thunderer*, Ζεῦ -βρόντᾶ Ar.*Pax*376. **-κλόνος**, ον, *causing the din of the thunderbolt*, *PMag.Par.*1.599. **-μάχης** [ᾰ], ου, Dor. **-χᾱς**, ὁ, *fighting with thunder*, *AP*12.110 (Mel.). **-πληκτος**, ον, = sq., Phld.*Ir.*p.94 W. **-πλήξ**, ῆγος, ὁ, ἡ, *thunder-smitten*, Alc.Com.2. **-πλους** (sic), epith. of Cerberus, perh. f.l. for **κεραύνοπλος**, *armed with the thunderbolt*, *PMag.Par.*1. 2262. **-ποιός**, όν, *causing thunderbolts*, Vett.Val.6.25.

**κεραυνός**, ὁ, *thunderbolt*, νῆα θοὴν ἔβαλε ψολόεντι κ. Od.23.330; βρόντησε καὶ ἔμβαλε νηῒ κ. 14.305; Διὸς πληγεῖσα κεραυνῷ 12.416; esp. as weapon of Zeus, Hes.*Th.*854, etc.; forged by the Cyclopes, ib.141; τὸν κ. τοῦ Διός Ar.*Av.*1538; καταιβάτης A.*Pr.*361; πυρωπός ib.668; ὁ πυρφόρος κ. Id.*Th.*445; κεραυνοῦ κρείσσονα φλόγα Id.*Pr.*922; κ. ἀργής Ar.*Av.*1747 (anap.); πτερόεις ib.576; κεραυνοῦ βέλος A.*Th.*453 (lyr.), S.*Tr.*1088; ὁ κ. λάμπων πυρί Ar.*Nu.*395; κ., πτεροφόρον Διὸς βέλος Id. *Av.*1714; κ. πίπτει, κατασκήπτει εἰς.., X.*HG*4.7.7, Plu.*Lyc.*31: pl., κεραυνοί *thunderbolts*, Hes.*Th.*690, Hdt.8.37, Epicur.*Ep.*2 p.46 U.; ποῦ ποτε κεραυνοὶ Διός; S.*El.*823 (lyr.), cf. Ar.*Pl.*125; τὰ τῶν κ. πτώματα Pl.*Ti.*80c; defined as ἔξαψις σφοδρὰ μετὰ πολλῆς βίας πίπτουσα ἐπὶ γῆς, i.e. *thunder and lightning*, Zeno *Stoic.*1.34. II. metaph., κεραυνὸν ἐν γλώττῃ φέρειν, of Pericles, *Com.Adesp.*10; τύπτειν κεραυνός *a thunderbolt* for striking, Antiph.195.4; Κεραυνός, as a name of great soldiers, Plu.*Arist.*6. III. title of Zeus, *IG* 5(2).288 (Mantinea, v B.C.), *Rev.Arch.*40.388 (Emesa). (Perh. cf. κεραΐζω.)

**κεραυνοσκοπ-εῖον**, τό, *machine for making thunder* on the stage, Poll.4.127,130. **-ία**, ἡ, *divination by thunder and lightning*, D.S. 5.40.

**κεραυνοῦχος**, ον, *wielding the thunder*, [Ζεύς] Ph.Byz.*Mir.*3.1.

**κεραυνο-φαής**, ές, *flashing like lightning*, πῦρ E.*Tr.*1103. **-φόρος**, ον, *wielding the thunderbolt*, Ἔρως Plu.*Alc.*16, cf. 2.335a; κ. στρατόπεδον *Legio XII Fulminata*, D.C.55.23: as Subst., title of a priest at Seleucia in Pieria, *OGI*245.47 (ii B.C.).

**κεραυν-όω**, *strike with thunderbolts*, Hdt.7.10.ε', Pl.*Smp.*190c, Phld.*Piet.*131:—Pass., κεραυνωθείς Hes.*Th.*859, Pi.*N.*10.8, cf. Pl.*R.* 408c, etc. II. metaph., = καταδικάζω, Artem.2.9 (Pass.). **-ωσις**, εως, ἡ, *striking with thunder*, Str.16.2.7, Plu.2.996c (pl.); τοῦ Φαέθοντος Scymn.398.

**κέραφος**· χλευασμός, κακολογία, Hsch.; cf. σκέραφος.

**κεράω** (A), Ep. form of κεράννυμι, used in imper. κέρα *Com.Adesp.* 1211; part. κερῶν Od.24.364: impf. κέρων A.R.1.1185:—Med., subj. κέρωνται Il.4.260: imper. κεράασθε (lengthd. from -ᾶσθε) Od. 3.332: impf. κερόωντο 8.470.

**κεράω** (B), (κέρας) *make horned*, κερόωσι σελήνην Arat.780. II. *take post on the wing* or *flank*, Plb.18.24.9.

**κερᾰώδης**, ες, *horned*, i.e. high-peaked, of a hill, prob. in Call.*Ap.* 91 (κερατώδεος codd.).

**Κεράων**, ωνος, ὁ, hero worshipped by cooks at Sparta, Polem.Hist. 40.

**κερᾰώψ**, ὁ, ἡ, gen. ῶπος, *horned-looking*, σελήνη Max.337.

**κερβαλά**· ἀσθενῆ, μεγάλα, Hsch.

**Κερβέριοι**, οἱ, Comic form of Κιμμέριοι, read by Crates in Od.11. 14 (Κερβερέων Aristarch. (?)), and apptly. by Ar.*Ra.*187: with a play upon Κέρβερος, cf. *EM*513.45.

**Κερβεροκίνδῡνος** Τάρταρος *full of Cerberus-dangers*, Hsch.

**Κέρβερος**, ὁ, *Cerberus*, the many-headed dog of Hades, Hes.*Th.* 311, etc. II. name of a bird, Ant.Lib.19.3.

**κερβολέω**, = κερτομέω, Hsch.; perh. to be read in B.1.34.

**κερδ-αίνω**, fut. -ᾰνῶ A.*Pr.*876, Lys.8.20, etc.; Ion. -ανέω Hdt.1. 35, 8.60.γ'; κερδήσω *AP*9.390 (Menecr.), *Ep.Jac.*4.13, κερδήσομαι Hdt.3.72: aor. 1 ἐκέρδᾶνα Pi.*I.*5(4).27, And.1.134 codd., etc.; Ion. -ηνα Hom.*Epigr.*14.6, Hdt.8.5, also ἐκέρδησα Id.4.152, Hld.4.13, etc.: pf. κεκέρδαγκα D.C.53.5, κεκέρδακα Aristid.1.366 J., Ach.Tat.5. 25, Phalar.*Ep.*81.2, etc., κεκέρδηκα D.56.30 (προσ–), J.*BJ*1.20.2:—Pass., aor. part. κερδανθείς Phld.*Oec.*p.67 J.: pf. κεκερδημένος J.*AJ* 18.6.5: (κέρδος):—*gain, derive profit* or *advantage*, κακὰ κ. *make unfair gains*, Hes.*Op.*352; μέγιστα ἐκ φορτίων Hdt.4.152; τί κερδανῶ; what *shall I gain*? Ar.*Nu.*259; κ. τινί *gain by* a thing, E.*HF*604; σμικρὰ κερδανῶ φυγῇ A.*Ag.*1301; κέρδος κ. S.*OT*889 (lyr.); κ. ἐξ τάλαντα And. l.c.; τὸν χρόνον κερδαίνει ὃν ἔζη οὐ προσῆκον αὐτῷ Lys.13.84; κ. λόγον *win* fame, Pi.*I.*5(4).27; χρηστὰ κ. ἔπη *receive* fair words, S.*Tr.*231: c. part., *gain by* doing.., εἰ δὲ κερδανῶ λέγων E.*Hel.*1051 (prob.); πολεμοῦντες οὐ κερδαίνομεν Ar.*Av.*1591, cf. Th.5.93; οὐδὲν ἐκμαθοῦσα κερδανεῖς A.*Pr.*876; Μεγάροισι κερδανέομεν περιεοῦσι we *shall gain* by Megara's preservation, Hdt.8.60.γ'; also κ. ὅτι.. Hp. *Art.*46:—Pass., τὰ κερδανθέντα Phld. l.c. 2. abs., *make profit, gain advantage*, Hdt.8.5, Ar.*Pl.*520; τοῦ κ. ἔχου S.*Fr.*28, cf. 354; ἐξ ἅπαντος, ἀπὸ παντός, Id.*Ant.*312, X.*Mem.*2.9.4; παρά τινων Lys.20.7; πρὸς σοῦ S.*Tr.*191; opp. τὸ τιμᾶσθαι, Th.2.44; *traffic, make merchandise*, S.*Ant.*1037. II. in bad sense, *reap* disadvantage from a thing, διπλᾶ δάκρυα κ. E.*Hec.*518; κερδᾶναι τὸν πολὺ χείρω βίον ἀντὶ θανάτου X.*Ap.*9. III. *save* or *spare oneself, avoid*, μεγάλα κακά Philem. 92.10; ὕβριν *Act.Ap.*27.21; τὸ μὴ μιανθῆναι τὰς χεῖρας J.*AJ*2.3.2; ἐνόχλησιν D.L.7.14, cf. Him.*Or.*2.26, *AP*10.59 (Pall.). **-αῖος**· τὸ ἐπικέρδη τοῖς παθοῦσι, καθόσον ἐκβέβρασται, Hsch. **-ᾰλέος**, α, ον, (κέρδος) of persons and their arts, *crafty, cunning*, κ. κ' εἴη καὶ ἐπίκλοπος Od.13.291; βουλή Il.10.44; μῦθος Od.6.148; νοήματα 8.548; of Ionian women, Aeschin.Socr.20. b. esp. of the fox, Archil.89.5: hence ἡ κ. *the wily one, the fox*, Ael.*NA*6.64, etc.; cf. κερδώ 1. 2. of things, *profitable*, Pi.*P.*2.78, X.*Mem.*3.4.11, etc.; κερδαλεώτερόν ἐστι ὁμολογέειν τῷ Πέρσῃ Hdt.9.7.α'; τὰς ἐμπορίας τὰς κ. Ar.*Av* 594, cf. Isoc.2.18; τὸ κ. A.*Eu.*1008 (anap.); κ. ἔς τι Th.2.53. II. Adv. -λέως *to one's advantage*, opp. δικαίως, Id.3.56. **-ᾰλεόφρων**, ον, gen. ονος, *greedy of gain*, Il.1.149, 4.339; *crafty*, Opp.*C.*2.29. **-αντέος**, α, ον, *to be used profitably*, κ. τὸ παρόν M.Ant.4.26. **-αντός**, ή, όν, *that ought to be gained*: τὰ κερδαντὰ κερδαίνειν to make *fair gains*, Periand.ap.D.L.1.97. **-άριον**, τό, Dim. of κέρδος, *Gloss.* **-εία**, ἡ, = πανουργία, also ἀλωπεκία, Hsch.

**Κερδείη**, ἡ, epith. of Πειθώ, Herod.7.74.

**κερδέμπορος**, ον, *presiding over gain in traffic*, Ἑρμῆς Orph.*H.*28.6.

**Κερδέων**, ωνος, ὁ, epith. of Hermes, Herod.7.74.

**κερδ-ητικός**, ή, όν, *greedy of gain*, *Gloss.* **-ία**, ἡ, *greed of gain*, Phot. **-ίζω**, *gain*, Sch.rec.Pi.*O.*1.84. **-ίων**, ον, gen. ονος, Comp. (with no Posit. in use), formed from κέρδος, *more profitable*; Hom. only neut., ἐμοὶ δέ κε κέρδιον εἴη Il.6.410, or καί κεν πολὺ κέρδιον ἦεν 3.41, cf. 7.28; ἦ μάλα τοι τόδε κ. ἔπλετο θυμῷ Od.20.304: later in masc., οὔτοι ἅπασα κερδίων φαίνοισα πρόσωπον ἀλάθεια Pi.*N.*5.16. II. κέρδιστος, η, ον, Sup., *most cunning* or *crafty*, Σίσυφος.., ὃ κέρδιστος γένετ' ἀνδρῶν Il.6.153. 2. of things, *most profitable*, A.*Pr.*387; πρὸς τὸ κέρδιστον τραπείς S.*Aj.*743.

**κερδογᾰμέω**, *marry for gain*, Diogenian.6.22.

**κέρδοπα**, = χέδροπα, Hsch.

**κέρδος**, εος, τό, *gain, profit*, Od.23.140, etc.; ἐνόησεν ὅππως κ. ἔῃ how *some advantage* can be gained, what is *best* to be done, Il.10. 225; οὔ τοι τόδε κ. ἐγὼν ἔσσεσθαι ὀΐω ἡμῖν Od.16.311, etc.; ποιέεσθαί τι ἐν κέρδεϊ, c. inf., Hdt.2.121.δ', 6.13; κ. νομίσαι τι Th.7.68; ὅτι.. Id.3.33; ἤν τι.. δάσωνται κ. ἡγεῖσθαι X.*Cyr.*4.2.43; ἐκ πονηροῦ πράγματος κ. λαβεῖν Men.697; μέγ' ἐστὶ κ., ἦν.. Id.*Mon.*359; πρὸς τὸ κ. βλέπειν ib.364; part., πᾶν κ. ἡγοῦ ζημιουμένη φυγῇ E.*Med.*454; κ. ἐστί μοι, c. inf., τί δῆτ' ἐμοὶ ζῆν κ.; A.*Pr.*747; τί κ. ἦν αὐτῷ διαβάλλειν ἐμέ; Lys.8.13, cf. Ar.*Ec.*607, 610: pl., *gains, profits*, περιβαλλόμενος ἑωυτῷ κέρδεα Hdt.3.71; τὰ δειλὰ (v.l. δεινὰ) κ. S.*Ant.*326; τὰ κ. μείζω φαίνεσθαι τῶν δεινῶν Th.4.59; τὰ πονηρὰ κ. Antiph.270:—κ. (metaph.) opp. ζημία (damage), Arist.*EN*1132$^a$12, (lit.) opp. ζη-

μια (damages), ib.14; ζημίαν λαβεῖν ἄμεινόν ἐστιν ἢ κ. κακόν S.*Fr.* 807. 2. *desire of gain*, κέρδει καὶ σοφία δέδεται Pi.*P.*3.54; ἄνδρας τὸ κ. πολλάκις διώλεσεν S.*Ant.*222; εἰς τὸ κ. λῆμ' ἔχων ἀνειμένον E.*Heracl.*3: pl., κερδῶν ἄθικτος A.*Eu.*704; ἐν τοῖς κέρδεσιν μόνον δέδορκε S.*OT*388; μὴ 'πὶ κέρδεσιν λέγων Id.*Ant.*1061, cf. E.*Hec.* 1207; of persons, ἡμέτερα κ. τῶν σοφῶν (= ἡμῶν τῶν σ.) *you of whom we wise men make gain*, Ar.*Nu.*1202. 3. iron. (cf. κερδαίνω II), ἀστεῖόν γε κ. ἔλαβεν ὁ κακοδαίμων ib.1064. II. in pl., *cunning arts, wiles*, ὅς δέ κε κ. εἰδῇ Il.23.322, cf. 709, al.; κέρδεσιν, οὔ τι τάχει γε παραφθάμενος ib.515; φρένας ἐσθλὰς κέρδεά θ' Od.2.118, cf. 88; ἐγὼ δ' ἐν πᾶσι θεοῖσι μήτι τε κλέομαι καὶ κέρδεσιν 13.299; ἐνὶ φρεσὶ κέρδε' ἐνώμας 18.216; κακὰ κ. βουλεύουσιν 'they mean *mischief*'. 23. 217. (Cf. OIr. *cerd* 'art', 'craft', Welsh *cerdd* 'craft' or 'music'.)

❀ **κερδοσύνη**, ἡ, *cunning, craft*: dat. κερδοσύνῃ as Adv., *cunningly*, Il.22.247, Od.4.251, 14.31: pl., ἐπὶ κερδοσύνας τετραμμένοι Cleanth. *Hymn.*1.28.

**κερδοφόρος**, ον, *bringing gain*, Artem.2.30.

**κερδύφιον**, τό, Dim. of κέρδος, *Gloss.*

**κερδώ**, όος, contr. οῦς, ἡ, *the wily one* or *thief*, i.e. *the fox* (cf. κερδαλέος I.1b), Pi.*P.*2.78(cj.), Ael.*NA*7.47; κ. δολία Ar.*Eq.*1068; ποικίλη κ. Babr.19.3. II. = γαλέη, *weasel*, Artem.3.28.

**κερδῴζισιν** (dat. pl.), τοῖς, perh. name of a board of magistrates, *BCH*47.50 (Pieria).

❀ **κερδῷος**, α, ον, *bringing gain*, epith. of Apollo, Lyc.208, *IG*9(2). 512.20 (Larissa), 1234 (Phalanna); of Hermes, Plu.2.472b, Luc.*Tim.* 41, etc. II. (κερδώ) *fox-like, wily*, ἀλώπηξ Babr.77.2.

**κέρεα**, τά, Ion. nom. pl. of κέρας.

**κερεαλκής**, ές, *stout in the horns*, ταῦρος A.R.4.468; βόες v.l. for κεραελκέες in Call.*Dian.*179.

❀ **Κερεάτας**, ὁ, epith. of Apollo in Arcadia, Paus.8.34.5: perh. from κέρας, cf. Κάρνειος.

**κέρεβρον**, τό, = Lat. *cerebrum*, Gal.*UP*8.4 (κέλ- codd.).

**κερεῖνος**, *horned*, Aq., Sm., Quint.*Ps.*49(50).9. **κερεκόψαι**· ἢ σχίσαι ξύλα, Hsch. (post κερουτιᾷ). ❀ **κερητίζει**· βασανίζει, Id.

❀ **κέρθιος**, ὁ, a little bird, perh. *tree-creeper, Certhia familiaris*, Arist. *HA*616$^b$28.

**κέρκα**· ἀκρίς, Hsch. **κέρκαξ**· ἱέραξ, Id. **κερκάς**, άδος, ἡ, = κρέξ, Id. **κέρκαφα**· ἐγγύη, Id.

**κερκέτης**, ου, ὁ, *weight used to steady a ship under sail*, Paus.Gr.*Fr.* 118, Hsch.

**κερκήδης**, *querquedula*, *Gloss.*; cf. sq.

**κέρκηρις**, εως, ὁ (?), an aquatic *bird*, *PCair.Zen.*186.10 (iii B.C.), *BGU*1252.30 (ii B.C.); *querquedula cerceris*, Varro *LL*5.79; cf. foreg.

**κερκῑδ-ιαῖον**, τό, *wedge-shaped block*, *IG*1$^2$.373.107, 122. **-ιον**, τό, Dim. of κερκίς, *POxy.*1740.1 (iii/iv A.D.), 1742.5 (iv A.D.), *Gloss.*

**κερκῑδοποιική** (sc. τέχνη), ἡ, *the art of the shuttle-maker*, Arist.*Pol.* 1256$^a$6.

**κερκίζω**, *separate the web with the* κερκίς, Pl.*Cra.*388b, *Sph.*226b; εἰ αἱ κερκίδες ἐκέρκιζον αὐταί Arist.*Pol.*1253$^b$37.

**κερκιθαλίς**· ἐρῳδιός, Hsch.

**κέρκιον**, τό, Dim. of κέρκος, Aq., Sm., Thd.*Le.*7.3.

**κέρκιος**, ὁ, = κιρκίας, Cato ap.Gell.2.22.28, v.l. in Arist.*Mu.*394$^b$31.

❀ **κερκίς**, ίδος, ἡ, *weaver's shuttle*, χαμαὶ δέ οἱ ἔκπεσε κ. Il.22.448; χρυσείῃ κερκίδ' ὕφαινεν Od.5.62, cf. S.*Ant.*976 (lyr.), Pl.*Cra.*388a; ἱστοῖς κερκίδα δινεύουσα E.*Tr.*199 (lyr.); κερκίσιν ἐφεστάναι Id.*Hec.* 363; φωνὴ κερκίδος S.*Fr.*595: κερκίδος ὕμνοις ib.890 (lyr.); κερκίδος ἀοιδοῦ E.*Fr.*523 (lyr.): metaph., μήδεα ἀδαμαντίναις ὑφαίνεται κερκίσιν αἶσα *Lyr.Adesp.*ap.Stob.1.5.11. II. *any taper rod, of wood, ivory*, etc.; as, 1. *peg, pin*, used to rivet the μεσάβοιον to the ζυγός, Poll.1.252: *hair-pin* or *comb*, A.R.3.46. 2. *measuring-rod*, *AP*11.267; *gnomon* of a dial (prob.), *CIG*2681 (Iasus). 3. *great bone of the leg, tibia*, A.R.4.1520, Plu.*Alex.*45; = κνήμη, Heroph. ap.Ruf.*Onom.*123, Poll.2.191. b. *radius of the arm*, ib.142, Gal. *UP*2.13, al., Orib.47.6.1. 4. *organ* of the electric ray, Opp.*H.* 2.63. 5. *rod* for stirring liquids, Gal.12.683. 6. iron *dowel*, *IG*2$^2$.1668.52. 7. καμπύλοχοι κ., *of ploughs*, Orph.*Fr.*33. III. *wedge-shaped division of the seats in the theatre*, περὶ τὴν ἐσχάτην.. κ. καθιζούσας θεωρεῖν Alex.41, cf. Phld.*Acad.Ind.*p.26 M., *LW*1586 (Aphrodisias). 2. *tympanum* or *half-tympanum*, *IG*4$^2$(1).102.89, 112 (Epid., iv B.C.). IV. *aspen, Populus tremula*, Arist.*HA*595$^a$2, Thphr.*HP*3.14.2. 2. *Judas tree, Cercis Siliquastrum*, ib.1.11. 2. 3. *white bryony, Bryonia cretica*, Gal.14.186. 4. *pine-cone*, Sch.E.*Hec.*1153, Hsch. V. kind of *bird*, Id.

**κέρκ-ῐσις**, εως, ἡ, *plying the* κερκίς, *weaving*, Arist.*Ph.*243$^b$7. **-ιστική** (sc. τέχνη), ἡ, *art of weaving*, Pl.*Plt.*282b. **-ιστρα**, τά, *cost of weaving*, *POxy.*736.77 (i B.C./i A.D.). **-ῖτις**, ιδος, ἡ, a kind of *olive* (cf. Lat. *radius*), prob. in Colum.5.8.3.

**κερκίων**, ὁ, *an Indian talking bird*, perh. *talking myna, Gracula religiosa*, Ael.*NA*16.3.

**κέρκνος**· ἱέραξ, ἢ ἀλεκτρυών, Hsch.

**κερκο-λύρα** [ῠ], ἡ, = κρέκουσα λύρα, Alcm.142. **-πίθηκος** [ῐ], ὁ, *long-tailed ape*, Str.15.1.29, Plin.*HN*8.72, etc.

❀ **κερκορῶνος**, ὁ, an *Indian bird*, perh. f.l. for κερκίων, Ael.*NA*15.14.

**κέρκος**, ἡ, *tail* of a beast (not a bird), e.g. swine, Ar.*Ach.*785; dog, κέρκῳ σαίνειν Id.*Eq.*1031; κ. λαγῶ a hare's *scut*, ib.909; horse, Pl.*Phdr.*254d, Plu.*Sert.*16; of all sorts of beasts, Arist.*PA*689$^b$2, al.; of fishes, Id.*HA*565$^b$29; ἡ κ. ποιεῖ καλῶς, of omens in sacrificing, Ar.*Pax* 1054, cf. Sch. ad loc., Eub.130. 2. *membrum virile*, Ar.*Th.*239; ἡ ἀνώνυμος κ. Herod.5.45; of an animal, κ. βοός, used as a tawse, Id.3.68. II. *handle*, Luc.*Lex.*7. III. *small animal that injures the vine*, Hsch. 2. = ἀλεκτρυών, Id. IV. *tongue* of flame, Sch.E.*Ph.*1257.

❀ **κερκούρ-ιον**, τό, Dim. of κέρκουρος, only as pr. n. of a ἑταίρα, *AP* 5.43 (Rufin.). **-ίτης** [ῑ], ου, ὁ, *sailor belonging to a* κέρκουρος, *PSI* 6.614.22 (iii B.C.). ❀**-ος** (proparox.) or **κερκοῦρος**, ὁ, *light vessel, boat*, esp. of the Cyprians, Hdt.7.97, cf. Din.*Fr.*12.2, Moschio ap. Ath.5.208e, D.S.24.1 (pl.); used for Nile transport, *PCair.Zen.*54.3 (iii B.C.), etc.:—written **κέρκυρος** (as if from Κέρκυρα) Sch.Ar.*Pax* 142; **κέρκυρα** (pl.) Suid. s. v. Ναξιουργὴς κάνθαρος. II. a *sea-fish*, Opp.*H.*1.141. (Cf. Lat. *cercurus, cercyrus* in both senses.)

**κερκουροσκάφη** [ᾰ], ἡ, = foreg. I, *PLille* 22.5 (iii B.C.).

**κερκοφόρος**, ον, *having a tail*, of fishes, Arist.*HA*489$^b$31.

**κέρκυ**· διπλῆ αὕτη καὶ δικέλαδος καὶ διθύσανος· ἐχρῆτο δὲ αὐτῇ μᾶλλον ὁ ἐν Κῷ πρύτανις, Hsch.

❀ **Κέρκῡρα**, ἡ, and **Κερκῡραῖοι**, οἱ, = Κόρκυρα, Κορκυραῖοι, in codd. of Hdt., Th., and later Attic Inscrr., *IG*2$^2$.96, etc.; early Attic Inscrr. and Corcyraean coins have Κορ-, *IG*1$^2$.295, *BMus.Cat.Coins Thessaly* p.117, *Corinth* p.112.

**κερκώδης**, v.l. for κερχνώδης, Erot. s. h. v.

**κερκώπη**, ἡ, long-tailed *cicada*, Ar.*Fr.*51, Epil.4, Alex.92.2, Speus. ap.Ath.4.133b; acc. κερκώπαν Ael.*NA*10.44.

**κερκωπία**, ἡ, *trickiness*, Semon.34.

**κερκωπίζω**, (κέρκωψ II) *play the ape*, Zen.4.50, Hsch.

**κέρκωσις**, εως, ἡ, *growth on the os uteri*, Paul.Aeg.6.70, Aët.16. 106. II. *appearance of a tail* to a comet, *Cat.Cod.Astr.*8(3).174.

❀ **Κέρκωψ**, ωπος, ὁ, (κέρκος) *man-monkey*, name of a race of mischievous dwarfs connected by legend with Heracles, Diotim.ap. Suid. s. v. Εὐρύβατος; ἕδραι Κερκώπων, near Thermopylae, Hdt.7.216; subject of poem ascribed to Hom., Harp., Suid. 2. metaph., *knave*, Aeschin.2.40, LxxPr.26.22, Gal.14.648; γόης τις ἢ Κ. λόγων *Com.Adesp.*1307; οἱ Κέρκωπες or Κερκώπων ἀγορά, at Athens, *Knaves-market*, D.L.9.114, Eust.1430.35. II. *long-tailed ape*, Manil.4.668.

❀ **κέρμα**, ατος, τό, (κείρω) *fragment*, κέρματα θηρείων μελέων dub. l. in Emp.101.1; τὰ κ. τοῦ ἡνωμένου ἡνωμένα Dam.*Pr.*107, cf. Suid.; but mostly, 2. *coin*, ἐγκάψας τὸ κ. εἰς τὴν γνάθον Alex.128.7; μικροῦ πρίασθαι κ. τὴν ἡδονήν Eub.67.7, cf. Amphis 5, Antiph.131; collectively, *cash*, Theopomp.Com.30, Arr.*Epict.*2.10.14, al., *Cat.Cod. Astr.*7.244; esp. of copper money, opp. silver (ἀργύριον), *PGen.*77. 5 (ii/iii A.D.): freq. in pl., μικρὰ κ. Ar.*Av.*1108, cf. *Pl.*379, Eub.84. 1; διδοὺς κέρματα Test.ap D.21.107, cf. Theopomp.Hist.89a, *UPZ*81 iv 20, 145 xi 71 (ii B.C.), Alciphr.1.2, *AP*5.44 (Cillactor).

❀ **κερμᾰτ-ίζω**, *cut into pieces, chop up*, Pl.*R.*525e, Achae.7 (Pass.), etc.; κατὰ σμικρὰ τὰ σώματα κ. Pl.*Ti.*62a; κ. τι εἰς πολλά Arist.*PA* 662$^a$13: metaph., κ. τὴν ἀρετήν Pl.*Men.*79a. II. *coin into money*, χαλκείην δαίμονα *AP*11.271. III. *change into smaller coin*, *PGnom.* 237 (ii A.D.), *PRyl.*224(a).5 (Pass., ii A.D.). ❀**-ιον**, τό, Dim. of κέρμα, Philippid.23, Plu.*Cim.*10, Arr.*Epict.*3.2.8, *AP*11.346 (Autom.), Phld. *Vit.*p.27 J. (pl.); κ. συνηγμένον Men.*Her.*7; *cash*, *PHib.*1.45.8 (iii B.C.), al. **-ισμός**, ὁ, metaph., *breaking up small*, Olymp. *in Phd.* p.86 N. ❀**-ιστής**, οῦ, ὁ, *money-changer*, *Ev.Jo.*2.14. **-όομαι**, = κερματίζομαι, Procl.*in Prm.*p.973 S.

**κέρμηλος**· ἀφ' οὗ χαλκὸς γίνεται, Hsch.

**κερμίον**, τό, = κερμάτιον, *Cat.Cod.Astr.*7.93 (s.v.l.).

**κέρνα**· ἀξίνη, Hsch. II. pl. κέρναι, αἱ, *transverse processes of the vertebrae*, Poll.2.180 (v.l. κέρνα). **κέρνα**, τά, v. foreg. II. 2. v. κέρνος.

❀ **κέρνας**, ὁ, *priest who carries the* κέρνος (q. v.), *AP*7.709 (Alex.).

**κερνάω**, v. κιρνάω sub fin.

❀ **κερνί[ον]**, τό, Dim. of sq., dub. in *IG*2$^2$.1544.64.

**κέρνος**, εος, τό, Ammon.ap.Ath.11.476f, Hsch. (pl.):—also **κέρνος**, ου, ὁ, Sch.Nic.*Al.*217: pl. **κέρνα**, τά, Poll.4.103:—*earthen dish with small pots affixed for miscellaneous offerings*, Ath. l. c., etc.; wrongly expld., = λίκνον, Sch.Pl.*Grg.*497c.

**κερνο-φορέω**, *carry the* κέρνος, Sch.Pl.*Grg.*497c. **-φόρος**, ὁ, ἡ, *priest* or *priestess who bears it*, Nic.*Al.*217; κ. κόρη Ps.-Plu.*Fluv.*13.3; κ. ὄρχημα, ὄρχησις, Poll.4.103, Ath.14.629d.

**κερο-βάτης** [ᾰ], ου, ὁ, (κέρας) *horn-footed, hoofed*, κεροβάτας Πάν Ar.*Ra.*230 (lyr.): acc. to some Gramm., *he that goes with horns*, i.e. *the horned god*; acc. to Sch., *he that walks the mountain-peaks* (cf. κέρας V.6). **-βόας**, ου, ὁ, *horn-sounding*, λωτοί *AP*6.94 (Phil.). **-δετος**, ον, *bound with* or *made of horn*, τόξα E.*Rh.*33 (lyr.). **-ειδής**, ές, *horn-shaped*, ἕρπυλλος Nic.*Th.*909.

❀ **κερόεις**, -εσσα (contr. -οῦσσα), -εν, *horned*, Anacr.51, Simon. 30, S.*Fr.*89, E.*Ph.*828 (lyr.), Doroth.ap.Heph.Astr.3.7, etc.; κερόεις ὄχος carriage *drawn by horned cattle*, Call.*Dian.*113. II. *of horn*, λωτός *AP*7.223 (Thyill.).

**κεροίαξ**, ᾱκος, ὁ, in pl., *ropes belonging to the yard-arm*, Luc.*Nav.* 4; sine expl., Suid.; glossed κάροια (v.l. κάρυα), i.e. *blocks*, and κρίκοι, Sch.Luc. l. c.

**κερο-πλάστης**, ου, ὁ, *arranging the hair in horns* or *queues* (cf. κέρας V.1), *hairdresser*, Archil.57, Poll.2.31, Hsch. **-τῡπέω**, *butt with horns*:—Pass., of ships in a storm, [νῆες] κεροτυπούμεναι.. χειμῶνι *buffeted* by the storm, A.*Ag.*655.

**κερουλίς** and **κερουλκίς**, v. κερουχίς.

**κερουλκός**, όν, (ἕλκω) *drawing* a plough *by the horns*, Hsch. II. *drawing a bow of horn*, [Τρῶες] S.*Fr.*859 (lyr.). 2. Pass., of the bow itself, because *tipped with horn*, τόξα κ. E.*Or.*268. III. κ. κάλως, = κεραιοῦχος, Hsch.

**κερουτ-ιάω**, prop. of horned animals, *toss the horns*: metaph., of persons, *toss the head, give oneself airs*, Ar.*Eq.*1344:—hence **-(ι)ασμός**, ὁ, *hauteur*, Phot.

**κερουχίς**, ίδος, pecul. fem. of sq., αἶγες Theoc.5.145 (**κερουλίδες**, αἱ οὖλα κέρατα ἔχουσαι, **κερουλκίδες**, αἱ ὑπὸ τῶν κεράτων ἑλκόμεναι vv.ll. ap.Sch.).

**κεροῦχος**, ον, (ἔχω) *horned*, αἶξ Babr.45.5. II. κ. (sc. κάλως), ὁ, *brace of the yard-arm*, δελφινοφόρος κ. Pherecr.12.

**κεροφόρος**, ον, = κερασφόρος I, *horned*, βόες E.*Ba.*691.

**κέρπαθος**, ὁ, a kind of *incense*, Uran.12.

**κέρσα**· Ἀσιανὸν νόμισμα, Hsch. **κερσαῖον**, τό, Egyptian coin, Id. s. v. κορσίπιον. **κέρσης**· γάμος (leg. γάλλος), Id.

**κέρσιμος**, ον, (κείρω) *that may be nibbled*: τὸ κ. angler's *float*, Sch. Il.24.81; cf. κέρας IV, γέντιμος, γέρσυμον.

⊛ **κερτομ-έω**, *taunt, sneer at*, c. acc. pers., μή μιν κερτομέωσιν Od.16.87, cf. 18.350, A.*Pr.*986, E.*Ba.*1293: abs., *sneer*, μή τις.. κερτομέοι ἐπέεσσι Od.7.17; κατθανοῦσι κ. ἐπ' ἀνδράσιν Archil.64: freq. in part., τί με ταῦτα κελεύετε κερτομέοντες; Od.8.153; σὲ δὲ κερτομέουσαν ὀΐω ταῦτ' ἀγορευέμεναι 13.326, etc.; πότερα δὴ κερτομῶν λέγεις τάδε; S.*Ph.*1235: c. acc. cogn., παραιβόλα κερτομέουσιν *h.Merc.*56: c. dupl. acc., οὐκ ἐῶ σε κ. ἡμᾶς τόδ' αὖθις E.*Hel.*619; οὔ τί τυ κερτομέω Theoc.1.62:—Pass., ἄβουλος ὡς κεκερτομημένη E.*Supp.*321.—Rare in Prose, Gal.14.656; κ. τινά Anon.ap.Suid. **-ησις**, εως, ἡ, *jeering, mockery*, S.*Ph.*1236. **-ία**, ἡ, *mockery*, in pl., κερτομίας ἠδ' αἴσυλα μυθήσασθαι Il.20.202,433; κερτομίας καὶ χεῖρας ἀφέξω Od.20.263. **-ικός**, ή, όν, *jeering*, Sch.Il.16.261. Adv. -κῶς ib.8.448. **-ιος** (-εος *EM*102.46), ον, *mocking, taunting*, κερτομίοις ἐπέεσσιν πειρηθῆναι Od.24.240; Δία Κρονίδην ἐρεθίζειν Il.5.419; simply κερτομίοισι Δία προσηύδα 1.539, cf. Od.9.474; κ. ὀργαῖς S.*Ant.*956 (lyr.); ἐν κ. γλώσσαις ib.962 (lyr.). (Perh. for (σ)κερ-στομος, cf. σκέραφος, κέραφος.) **-ιστής** (καρτ- cod.)· χλευαστής, Hsch.

**κέρτομος**, ον, = κερτόμιος, κέρτομα βάζειν Hes.*Op.*788; χοροὶ κ. Hdt. 5.83 (v.l. κερτομίοισι), cf. D.H.7.72, Ael.*NA*5.54. II. *mocking, delusive*, παῖς *h.Merc.*338; χαρά E.*Alc.*1125; χάριτες Id.*Fr.*492.2; ἁρμονία, of Echo, *AP*7.191 (Arch.).—Poet. word used once by Hdt., and in late Prose.

**κερτύλλιον**, τό, perh. *basket*, *PFlor.*176.9 (iii A.D.); cf. καρτάλλιον.

**κερύχρη**, a kind of *cake*, Hsch.

**κερχᾰλέος**, α, ον, *rough, hoarse*, βήξ Hp.*Epid.*7.16; κερχαλέον ὑποσυρίζειν v.l. for κερχναλέον ib.7:—written **κερχναλέος**, Gal.19.111.

**κέρχανα** or **κερχάνεα**, *bones*, or *stumps of teeth*, Hsch.

**κερχνασμός**, ὁ, *roughness, hoarseness*, Gal.19.111.

**κέρχνη**, ἡ, kind of *hawk*, prob. *kestrel, Falco tinnunculus*, Hsch.:—also **κερχνηΐς**, contr. **κερχνῄς**, ῇδος, ἡ, Ar.*Av.*304, 589; **κεγχρηΐς**, ΐδος, ἡ, Arist.*HA*509$^a$6, Ael.*NA*2.43; **κεγχρίς**, Arist.*HA*558$^b$28, 594$^a$2, *GA*750$^a$7.

**κερχνίον**, τό, Dim. of κέρχνος (B) III, *IG*2$^2$.1533.19,23.

⊛ **κέρχν-ος** (A), ὁ, = κέγχρος, Hsch. s. v. κατακερχνοῦται, cf. Anaxandr.41.27, Gal.18(1).574. **-ος** (B), ὁ, *rough excrescence*, τραχὺς χελώνης κ. S.*Fr.*279. 2. of the throat, *roughness, hoarseness*, Hp.*Epid.*7.27. b. of sound, *harsh croaking*, S.*Ichn.*128. II. *silver-dust*, Poll.7.99. III. = κέρνος, *IG*1$^2$.313.17,314.23 (Eleusis). **-ος** (C), ον, *rough, hoarse*: τὸ κ. Gal.19.111. **-όω**, aor. inf. κερχνῶσαι· καταστίξαι καὶ οἷον τραχῦναι, Hsch. s. v. κατακερχνοῦται. **-ω**, *make rough* or *hoarse*: Hp.*Int.*40:—Pass., *to be so*, Id.*Morb.*2.53. II. intr. in Act., *to be hoarse*, Id.*Int.*23, Diocl.*Fr.*147, Gal.7.173. **-ώδης**, ες, *rough*, v.l. for κεγχρώδης, Hp.*Epid.*6.6.5; ἀγγεῖα κ. *embossed* cups, Erot. II. *hoarse*, Hp.*Art.*41 (v.l. **κερχώδης** ap.Gal.18(1).574). 2. *causing hoarseness*, βρῶμα Hp.*Art.*50. ⊛**-ωμα**, ατος, τό, in pl., *roughnesses*, Hsch.; also, = τὰ κερχνωτά, Id. II. = κέγχρωμα, Id. (pl.). **-ωτός**, ή, όν, *roughened*, Id. s. v. κατακερχνοῦται: τὰ κ. *embossed plate*, Id.

**κερχώδης**, v. κερχνώδης II. **κερῳδός**, ὁ, *horn-blower*, *Gloss.*

**κερωνία**, ἡ, Ion. for κερατωνία, Thphr.*HP*4.2.4, cf. 1.11.2; *ceraunia*, Plin.*HN*13.59.

**κέρωνται**, v. κεράω (A).

**κερῶνυξ**, ὗχος, ὁ, ἡ, *with horn hoofs*, Πάν D.P.995.

**Κεσαρεών**, v. Καισαρεών.

**κέσκεον**, τό, *tow*, Herod.9a; **κέσκι⟨ον⟩**, Hsch.

**κέσκετο**, Ion. 3 sg. impf. of κεῖμαι, Od.21.41.

**κέστερ**· νεανίας (Argive), Hsch.

**κεστιανὰ** μῆλα, a kind of *apple*, Gal.10.469,911.

**κεστός**, ή, όν, (κεντέω) *stitched, embroidered*, κ. ἱμάς, of Aphrodite's *charmed girdle*, Il.14.214, Corn.*ND*24. 2. later, κεστός, ὁ, as Subst., κεστοῦ δεσπότις, of Aphrodite, Call.*Aet.Oxy.*2080.55; κεστοῦ φωνεῦσα μαγώτερα *AP*5.120 (Phld.), cf. 6.88 (Antiphanes Maced.), Luc.*DDeor.*20.10; ἅπαντα τὸν κ. ὑποζώσασθαι to put on all her *charms*, Alciphr.1.38; Κεστοί, title of work by Africanus.

**κέστρα**, ἡ, *hammer*, S.*Fr.*20. 2. *bolt hammered in* to pack τόνοι in a torsion-engine, Ph.*Bel.*61.14, Hero *Bel.*108.12. II. a *fish*, = σφύραινα, Ar.*Nu.*339, Stratt.28, Antiph.97, Speus.ap.Ath.7.323b.

**κέστρειον**, τό, perh. *storehouse for* κέστροι II, *arsenal*, *IG*11(2).165.38, 199*A*77 (Delos, iii B.C.).

⊛ **κεστρ-εύς**, έως, ὁ, *mullet*, = νῆστις, Hp.*Int.*30, Ar.*Fr.*156, Pl.Com.29, Arist.*HA*591$^a$22, Antig.*Mir.*93, Hices. and Dorio ap.Ath.7.307d, Alciphr.1.7; as nickname of a starveling (since its stomach was found empty), Euphro 2; κ. νηστεύει, prov. of those too honest to make gains, Ath.7.307c, cf. Lib.*Ep.*332.2. **-εύω**, *to be starving*, Hsch.

**κεστρῖνίσκος**, ὁ, Dim. of sq., Clearch.73.

**κεστρῖνος**, ὁ, = κεστρεύς, Anaxandr.34.8, Hyp.*Fr.*188. II. in pl., *pieces of the fish* κέστρα, *EM*506.45, Phot.

**κεστρίον**, τό, Dim. of κέστρος II, *IG*2$^2$.1487.94 (pl.).

**κέστρον**, τό, = βεττονική, Dsc.4.1; *cestros*, Plin.*HN*25.84. 2. = σαξίφραγος, *Stachys alopecuros*, Gal.6.339. II. (κεντέω) *serrated implement*, used in encaustic painting, Plin.*HN*35.149.

⊛ **κέστρος**, ὁ, *sharpness* or *roughness on the tongue*, Hsch. 2. *first sprout of seeds*, Id. II. *bolt discharged from engines*, invented in the war with Perseus, Plb.27.11.1 (s.v.l.), D.H.20.1.

**κεστρο-σφενδόνη**, ἡ, *engine which discharges* κέστροι II, Liv.42.65. **-φόρος**, ὁ, *one who carries* κέστροι II, *IG*3.1102 (pl.). **-φύλαξ** [ῠ], ακος, ὁ, *officer in charge of* κέστροι II, ib.1094, al.:—hence **-φῠλᾰκέω**, ib.735,736.

**κέστρ-ωσις**, εως, ἡ, *encaustic painting*, Hsch. **-ωτός**, ή, όν, *with the point hardened in the fire*, ξύλον Id. II. *executed by the encaustic process*, Plin.*HN*11.126.

**κετεύω**, word of doubtful meaning in *IG*5(1).268 (Sparta).

**κευθάνω**, poet. for κεύθω, impf. ἐκεύθανον Il.3.453.

**κευθῆνες**· οἱ καταχθόνιοι δαίμονες, Suid.

**κεύθ-ησις**, εως, ἡ, = ἀπόκρυψις, as etym. of κύησις, Sor.1.43. **-μα**, ατος, τό, = κευθμών, f.l. in Thgn.243 (leg. κεύθεσι). **-μός**, ὁ, = sq., Il.13.28 (pl.), Lyc.317, Call.*Jov.*34. **-μών**, ῶνος, ὁ, (κεύθω) *hiding place, hole*, μαιομένη κευθμῶνας ἀνὰ σπέος Od.13.367; ὥς τε σύες, πυκινοὺς κευθμῶνας ἔχοντες in the close-barred *sties*, 10.283; κευθμῶνες ὀρέων *hollows* of the mountains, Pi.*P.*9.34; κ. Κιθαιρῶνος Orac.ap. Hdt.7.141; Ἰδαῖον ἐς κευθμῶν' E.*Hel.*24; Μαλέας ἄκροι κ. Id.*Cyc.*293; ἕδρας τε καὶ κευθμῶνας ἐνδίκου χθονός A.*Eu.*805. 2. of the nether world, γαίης ἐν κευθμῶνι Hes.*Th.*158; Ταρτάρου μελαμβαθὴς κ. the deep black *vault* of T., A.*Pr.*222; νεκρῶν E.*Hec.*1; ἠλιβάτοις ὑπὸ κ. Id.*Hipp.*732 (lyr.).—Rare in Prose, as Str.11.2.10.

**κεῦθος**, εος, τό, = κευθμών, ὑπὸ κεύθεσι γαίης in *the depths* of the earth, Il.22.482, Od.24.204, Hes.*Th.*300, cf. Pi.*N.*10.56, A.*Eu.*1036 (lyr.): in sg., κ. [Ἀπίας χθονός] Id.*Supp.*778 (lyr.), cf. Epic. in *Arch. Pap.*7.7; κ. νεκύων S.*Ant.*818 (anap.); κ. οἴκων the *innermost* chambers, like μυχός, E.*Alc.*872 (lyr.); κεύθεα νηοῦ, = ἄδυτον, Musae.119; κ. πόντου Opp.*H.*4.607.

⊛ **κεύθω**, fut. κεύσω Od.3.187: aor. 1 ἔκευσα (ἐπ-) 15.263: Ep. aor. κύθε [ῠ] 3.16, Eratosth.4, redupl. subj. κεκύθω [ῠ] Od.6.303: pf. κέκευθα Il.22.118: plpf. ἐκεκεύθειν, κεκ-, Od.9.348, Hes.*Th.*505:—Pass., Il.23.244, etc.: pf. κέκευται Hsch., part. κεκυθ(η)μένη Antim.3. (Perh. cogn. with Lat. *custos*, OE. *hȳdan* 'hide'.):—poet. Verb, *cover, hide*, esp. of the grave, ὅπου κύθε γαῖα where earth *covered* him, Od.3.16 (also in Pass., εἰς ὅ κεν αὐτὸς ἐγὼν Ἄϊδι κεύθωμαι, i. e. till I am in the grave, Il.23.244); ἢν οὐδὲ κατθανόντα γαῖα κ. A.*Pr.*570 (lyr.), cf. E.*Hec.*325; ὁπότ' ἄν σε δόμοι κεκύθωσι, i. e. when thou hast entered the house, Od.6.303, cf. S.*OT*1229, E.*Hec.*880: in pf., *contain*, ὅσα πτόλις ἥδε κέκευθε Il.22.118; οἷόν τι ποτὸν.. νηῦς ἐκεκεύθει Od.9.348; Ἀρχεδίκην ἥδε κέκευθε κόνις Simon.111, cf. 95; εἴπερ τόδε κ. αὐτὸν τεῦχος, of a cinerary urn, S.*El.*1120, cf. A.*Ch.*687; ἃ κ. δέλτος ἐν πτυχαῖς E.*IA*112:—Med., *Epigr.Gr.*1081 (Ilium). 2. *conceal*, and in pf., *keep concealed* or *hidden*, δόλῳ δ' ὅ γε δάκρυα κεῦθεν Od.19.212; ὅς χ' ἕτερον μὲν κεύθῃ ἐνὶ φρεσίν ἄλλο δὲ εἴπῃ Il.9.313; μῆτιν ἐνὶ στήθεσσι κέκευθε Od.3.18, cf. 8.548, 24.474; οὐκέτι κεύθετε θυμῷ βρωτὺν οὐδὲ ποτῆτα no more can ye *disguise* your eating and drinking, 18.406; κ. φόνον Emp.100.5; κ. [τι] ἔνδον καρδίας A.*Ch.*102, cf. 739; σιγῇ κ. S.*Tr.*989 (anap.); κακόν τι κεύθεις καὶ στέγεις ὑπὸ σκότῳ E.*Ph.*1214; μῦθος ὃν κεύθω Id.*Supp.*295; τί κεύθων.. σοφόν; Id.*Heracl.*879; κ. μῆνιν *cherish* anger, like πέσσειν χόλον, ib.762 (lyr.); πάντα δόλον κεύθοισα v.l. in Theoc.1.50. 3. c. dupl. acc., οὐδέ σε κεύσω [ταῦτα] nor *will* I *keep* them *secret from* thee, Od.3.187, cf. Eratosth. l. c. II. in Trag. sts. intr., *to be concealed, lie hidden*, S.*OT*968, *Aj.*635 (lyr.): esp. in pf., A.*Th.*588, S.*Ant.*911, *El.*868 (lyr.).

**κεῦτλον**, τό, dub. sens. in *PTeb.*112 intr. (ii B.C.), 190 (i B.C.).

**κεφᾰλ-άδιον**, τό, Dim. of κεφάλαιον, *EM*240.2 (leg. -ᾴδιον). **-αία**, ἡ, *inveterate headache*, Antyll.ap.Orib.9.13.1, Aret.*SD*1.2, Gal.10.513; prob. in Thphr.*HP*9.11.2.

⊛ **κεφάλαι-ος** [ᾰ], α, ον, (κεφαλή) *of the head*: metaph., *principal, chief*, ῥῆμα κ. (with a play on κεφαλίτης λίθος) Ar.*Ra.*854; τὸ κ. μέρος *PMasp.*151.16 (vi A.D.): Sup. -ότατος v.l. in Pl.*Grg.*494e. II. mostly Subst. κεφάλαιον, τό, = κεφαλή, *head, parts about the head*, esp. of fish, θύννου κ. τοδί Callias Com.3: in pl., Amphis 35, Sotad. Com.1.5; also κ. ῥαφανῖδος Ar.*Nu.*981; of an infant, Leonid.ap. Aët.6.1. 2. *chief* or *main point*, κ. δὴ παιδείας λέγομεν τὴν ὀρθὴν τροφήν Pl.*Lg.*643c; esp. in speaking or writing, *sum, gist of the matter*, κεφάλαια λόγων Pi.*P.*4.116; κ. τοῦ παντὸς λόγου Men.*Georg.*75, cf. Cic.*Att.*5.18.1; τὰ κ. συγγράφων Εὐριπίδῃ drawing up the *heads* of the play, Antiph.113.5: freq. in Prose, Th.4.50, Pl.*Grg.*453a, etc.; κ. τῶν εἰρημένων Isoc.3.62, cf. 5.154; κ. τῆς οἰκονομίας Phld.*Rh.*1.68 S. (pl.); ἐν κεφαλαίῳ, or ὡς ἐν κ., εἰπεῖν to speak *summarily*, X.*Cyr.*6.3.18, Pl.*Smp.*186c, al.; ἐν κεφαλαίοις ὑπομνῆσαι, ἀποδεῖξειν, περιλαβεῖν τι, Th.6.87, Lys.13.33, Isoc.2.9; βραχυτάτῳ κ. μαθεῖν Th.1.36; τύπῳ καὶ ἐπὶ κεφαλαίου (v.l. -αίῳ), opp. ἀκριβέστερον, Arist.*EN*1107$^b$14; ἐπὶ κ. Plb.1.65.5, 3.5.9; ἐπὶ κεφαλαίων D.19.315, etc.; esp. in an argument, *summing up*, ἐν κεφαλαίοις Pl.*Ti.*26c; κεφαλαίῳ δέ.., Lat. *denique*, Decr.ap.D.18.164; τὸ δ' οὖν κ. ib.213; τὸ δὲ κ. τῶν λόγων, ἄνθρωπος εἶ Men.531.10; συναγαγεῖν

τὸ κ. *to sum* up, Arist.*Metaph.*1042ᵃ4. **3.** metaph., of persons, *the head* or *chief*, ὅ τι περ κ. τῶν κάτωθεν, of Pericles, Eup.93; τὸ κ. οὐδέπω λογίζομαι, τὸν δεσπότην Men.*Pk.*173; ὅ τι περ τὸ κ. Luc.*Harm.* 3, *Gall.*24, *Philops.*6; τὰ κ. τῶν μαθημάτων, of philosophers, Id.*Pisc.* 14; τὸ κ. τοῦ πολέμου App.*BC*5.50; οἱ τὸ τῆς στάσεως κ. ἦσαν ib.43; τὸν Θαλῆν τῶν σοφῶν τὸ κ. Jul.*Or.*3.125d: hence, of qualities, etc., σχεδόν τι τὸ κ. τῶν κακῶν (sc. avarice) Apollod.Gel.4; τὸ κ. τῆς εὐδαιμονίας ἡ διάθεσις Diog.Oen.57. **4.** Rhet., *head, topic* of argument, D.H.*Comp.*1, *Rh.*10.5, Str.1.2.31. **5.** of money, *capital*, opp. interest or income, Pl.*Lg.*742c, D.27.64, etc. **b.** *sum total*, *IG*1².91.23, al., Lys.19.40, D.27.10; πολλοῦ κ. for a large *sum*, *Act. Ap.*22.28, cf. Aristeas 24, Plu.*Fab.*4, etc.; κ. ἀργυρικά *PRyl.*133.15 (i A.D.); also σιτικὰ καὶ ἀργυρικὰ κ. *PSI*4.281.31 (ii A.D.). **6.** *crown, completion* of a thing, τὸ μὲν κ. τῶν ἀδικημάτων the *crowning act* of wrong, D.27.7; δύο ταῦτα ὥσπερεὶ κ. ἐφ' ἅπασι.. ἐπέθηκε Id.21. 18. **7.** *chapter, section*, *PGnom.Prooem.*, Ammon.*in Int.*1.17, al., Chor.in *Hermes* 17.223; distd. from τίτλος, Suid. s.h.v. **-όω,** *bring under heads, sum up*, Th.3.67, al.:—Med., Arist.*MM*1207ᵇ22; κ. τινὰ *characterize generally*, Pl.*R.*576b; τὰς δυνάμεις τινῶν Phld.*Vit.* p.17 J.:—Pass., *to be summed up*, Arist.*Metaph.*1013ᵇ30; κ. ἑκάστην τῶν ἀρετῶν περὶ ἴδιόν τι κεφάλαιον *Stoic.*3.73; κεφαλαιοῦσθαι ἐννακισχιλίων ἑξακοσίων [σταδίων] *to amount in all to*.., Str.2.1.39; εἰς δύο ἀρτηρίας ἡ πάντων ἀγγείων κ. σύνοδος *is combined in*.., Gal.4.657, cf. Porph.*Sent.*44; κεφαλαιούσθω διότι.. Phld.*Rh.*2.35 S. **II.** *smite on the head*, *Ev.Marc.*12.4. **-ώδης,** ες, *capital, principal*, *Stoic.*2.75, Luc.*DMort.*20.1: Comp., νόμοι Ph.2.183, cf. Luc.*Salt.*61, Hierocl. *in CA*27p.484M.: Sup., Hp.*Decent.*6, Luc.*Pseudol.*10; τὸ -ῶδες *the general character summed up in a definition*, Arr.*Epict.*2.12.9. **II.** *summary*, ἐξήγησις Plb.2.14.1; ὑπογραφή D.H.2.72. Adv. **-δῶς** Arist.*Rh.*1415ᵇ8, *Metaph.*988ᵃ18, Plb.1.13.1, D.H.*Comp.*8, etc.: Sup. -έστατα Epicur.*Ep.*1 p.31 U. **-ωμα,** ατος, τό, *sum total*, Hdt. 3.159. **II.** *collective expression*, τοὺς τὰς ἰδέας κεφαλαιώματα λέγοντας τοῦ ἐντρέχοντος κοινοῦ τοῖς πολλοῖς Procl.*in Prm.*p.564 S. **-ωσις,** εως, ἡ, *comprehension of several notions in a general term*, Sch.S.*OC* 916. **-ωτής,** οῦ, ὁ, = Lat. *capitularius, secretary and treasurer of a group of landowners or artisans, acting as recruiting officer, tax-collector*, etc., *PThead.*22.4 (iv A.D.), *PLips.*40 iii 17 (iv/v A.D.), 48.9 (pl., iv A.D.), al., *Cod.Theod.*11.24.6.7 (pl.); τοῦ ἡγεμονικοῦ πολυκώπου *PGrenf.*2.80 (pl., v A.D.); ταρσικαρίων *PLips.*89 (iv A.D.); πιττακίων *Sammelb.*4422.2; πλινθουργῶν ib.5175.21 (vi A.D.), al. **II.** in pl., = Lat. *optimates*, Olymp.Hist.p.452 D. **-ωτία,** ἡ, *function of* κεφαλαιωτής, *PLips.*52.14 (iv A.D.).

**κεφᾰλαλγ-έω,** *suffer from headache*, Hp.*Aph.*5.64, Sor.2.29, Dsc. 1.30, Arr.*Epict.*3.22.73, Gal.6.589, *BCH*48.517 (Palestine). **-ής,** ές, *suffering from headache*, Plu.2.147f, Ruf.ap.Orib.7.26.129, 143. **II.** Act., *causing headache*, X.*An.*2.3.15, Thphr.*HP*8.4.6, Diph.Siph.ap.Ath.2.54a, Ph.1.390, 2.99, Plu.2.133c, Gal.17(2).818, etc. (-αλγός is a common f.l.). **-ία,** ἡ, *headache*, in pl., Hp.*Aph.*3. 13, Arist.*Pr.*860ᵃ37, Str.16.2.41, *IG*4²(1).126.27 (Epid.). **-ικός,** ή, όν, *suffering from headache*, Hp.*Coac.*283; *inclined to headache*, Gal.6.438, 15.125. **II.** *causing headache*, Diocl.*Fr.*126, Gal.17(2). 754. **III.** τὰ κ. *symptoms of headache*, Hp.*Prorrh.*1.103.

**κεφᾰλᾰραία,** ἡ, = φάλαρον, Anon.*in Rh.*210.15.

**κεφᾰλ-αργία,** ἡ, later form for κεφαλαλγία, Luc.*Jud.Voc.*4:— hence **-αργέω,** *PMag.Par.*1.136; *give* one *a headache*, Hsch. s.v. ὠτοκοπεῖ.

**✱κεφᾰλή,** ἡ, *head* of man or beast, Hom. (v. infr.), Alc.15, etc.; once in A., *Th.*525 (lyr.), once in S., *Aj.*238 (anap.), also in E., *Fr.*308 (anap.), *Rh.*226 (lyr.), al.; ἄλλου οὐδενὸς ἐμψύχου κ. γεύσεται Αἰγυπτίων οὐδείς Hdt.2.39; κεφαλῇ.. μείζονες taller *in stature*, Il.3. 168; so μείων.. κεφαλήν ib.193 Aristarch.: freq. with Preps., **a.** κατὰ κεφαλῆς, Ep. κὰκ κεφαλῆς, *down over the head*, κόνιν.. χεύατο κὰκ κεφαλῆς Il.18.24, cf. Od.8.85, etc. **b.** κατὰ κεφαλήν, Ep. κὰκ κεφαλήν *on the head*, Ἐρύλαον.. βάλε πέτρῳ μέσσην κὰκ κεφαλήν Il.16. 412, cf. 20.387,475: in Prose, *from above*, X.*HG*7.2.8: c. gen., *above*, κ. κ. τινῶν γενέσθαι ib.7.2.11; τὸ κ. κ. ὕδωρ, of rain water, Thphr. *HP*4.10.7 (-ῆν codd.), *CP*6.18.10 (-ῆς): in Archit., *upright*, *IG*2². 463.42; also, *per head, each person* (cf. infr. 1. 2), Arist.*Pol.*1272ᵃ14, Lxx *Ex.*16.16; κατὰ κεφαλὴν τῶν κωμητῶν *PPetr.*2 p.17 (iii B.C.). **c.** ἐς πόδας ἐκ κεφαλῆς from *head* to foot, Il.23.169; τὰ πράγματα ἐκ τῶν ποδῶν ἐς τὴν κ. σοι πάντ' ἐρῶ Ar.*Pl.*650. **d.** ἐπὶ κεφαλήν *head foremost*, ἐπὶ κ. κατορύξαι to bury *head downwards*, Hdt.3.35; ἐπὶ κ. ὠθέεσθαι to be thrust *headlong*, Id.7.136, cf. Hyp.*Fr.*251; ἐπὶ κ. ὠθεῖν τινα ἐκ τοῦ θρόνου Pl.*R.*553b; ἐπὶ τὴν κ. εἰς κόρακας ὤσαν Men.*Sam.* 138; εὐθὺς ἐπὶ κ. εἰς τὸ δικαστήριον βαδίζειν D.42.12; οὐ βουλόμενος πολίτας ἄνδρας ἐπὶ κ. εἰσπράττειν τὸν μισθὸν *recklessly*, Hyp.*Lyc.*17; ἐπὶ ταῖς κεφαλαῖς περιφέρειν carry *on high*, in token of admiration, Pl. *R.*600d. **2.** as the noblest part, periphr. for the whole person, πολλὰς ἰφθίμους κ. Il.11.55, cf. Od.1.343, etc.; ἶσον ἐμῇ κ. no less than my*self*, Il.18.82; ἑᾷ κ. Pi.*O.*7.67; esp. in salutation, φίλη κ. Il.8.281, cf. 18.114; ἠθείη κ. 23.94; Ἄπολλον, ὦ δία κ. E.*Rh.*226 (lyr.): in Prose, Φαῖδρε, φίλη κ. Pl.*Phdr.*264a; τῆς θείας κ. Jul.*Or.* 7.212a: in bad sense, ὦ κακαὶ κεφαλαί Hdt.3.29; ὦ μιαρὰ κ. Ar.*Ach.* 285: periphr. in Prose, πεντακοσίας κεφαλὰς τῶν Ξέρξεω πολεμίων Hdt.9.99: in bad sense, ἡ μιαρὰ καὶ ἀναιδὴς αὕτη κ. D.21.117, cf. 18. 153; ἡ κ. τῶν αὐτοῦ *PRein.*57.8 (iv A.D.); μεγάλη κ. a great *personage*, Vett.Val.74.7; cf. supr. 1 b fin. **3.** *life*, ἐμῇ κ. περιδείδια Il.17.242; σύν τε μεγάλῳ ἀπέτεισαν, σὺν σφῇσιν κεφαλῇσι 4.162; παρθέμενοι κεφαλάς staking *their heads* on the cast, Od.2.237; τὴν κ. ἀποβαλέεις Hdt.8.65. **4.** in imprecations, ἐς κεφαλὴν τράποιτ' ἐμοί on my *head* be it! Ar.*Ach.*833; ἐς τὴν κ. ἅπαντα τὴν σὴν τρέψεται Id.*Nu.*40; ἃ σοὶ καὶ τοῖς σοῖς οἱ θεοὶ τρέψειαν εἰς κ. D.18.290; ἐς κ. σοί (sc. τράποιτο) Ar.*Pax* 1063, *Pl.*526; σοὶ εἰς κ. Pl.*Euthd.*283e; τὰ μὲν πρότερον.. ἐγὼ κεφαλῇ ἀναμάξας φέρω Hdt.1.155; οἷς ἂν.. τὴν αἰτίαν ἐπὶ τὴν κ. ἀναθεῖεν D.18.294; τὸ αἷμα ὑμῶν ἐπὶ τὴν κ. ὑμῶν *Act.Ap.* 18.6. **II.** of things, *extremity*, **a.** in Botany, κ. σκορόδου *head* (= *inflorescence*) of garlic, Ar.*Pl.*718, cf. Plb.12.6.4; κ. μήκωνος Thphr.*HP*9.8.2; ῥίζα κ. ἔχουσα πλείονας *tubers*, Dsc.3.120. **b.** in Anatomy, κεφαλαὶ τῆς κάτω γνάθου, prob. the condyloid and coronoid processes, Hp.*Art.*30; ἡ κ. τοῦ ὄρχεως, = ἐπιδιδυμίς, Arist.*HA*510ᵃ 14, cf. Gal.4.565; μηροῦ, κνήμης κ., Poll.2.186,188; of the *base* of the heart, Gal.*UP*6.16; but, *apex*, Hp.*Cord.*7; of the *sac* in poulps, Arist.*PA*654ᵃ23, 685ᵃ5; of muscles, *origin*, Gal.*UP*7.14. **c.** generally, *top, brim* of a vessel, Theoc.8.87; *coping* of a wall, X.*Cyr.*3. 3.68; *capital* of a column, *CIG*2782.31 (Aphrodisias), Lxx 3*Ki.*7.16, Poll.7.121. **d.** in pl., *source* of a river, Hdt.4.91 (but sg., *mouth*, οἶδα Γέλα ποταμοῦ κεφαλῇ ἐπικείμενον ἄστυ Call *Aet.Oxy.*2080.48): generally, *source, origin*, Ζεὺς κ. (v.l. ἀρχή), Ζεὺς μέσσα, Διὸς δ' ἐκ πάντα τελεῖται (τέτυκται codd.) Orph.*Fr.*21a; *starting-point*, κ. χρόνου *Placit.* 2.32.2 (κρόνου codd.), Lyd.*Mens.*3.4; κ. μηνός ib.12. **e.** *extremity* of a plot of land, *PPetr.*3 p.72 (iii B.C.), *PFlor.*50.83 (iii A.D.). **III.** Ὁμηρείη κ. *bust* of Homer, *IG*14.1183.10. **IV.** κ. περίθετος *wig, head-dress*, Ar.*Th.*258. **V.** metaph., κ. δείπνου *pièce de résistance*, Alex.172.15. **2.** *crown, completion*, κεφαλὴν ἐπιθεῖναι Pl.*Ti.*69b; ὥσπερ κ. ἀποδοῦναι τοῖς εἰρημένοις Id.*Phlb.*66d, cf. *Grg.*505d; ὥσπερ κεφαλὴν ἔχουσα ἐπιστήμη Arist.*EN*1141ᵃ19; *consummation*, σχεῖν κ. Pl.*Ti.*39d. **3.** *sum, total*, πάσας ἐργηγείας *Tab.Heracl.*1.36; of money, *IG*12(9).7 (Carystus, iv B.C.), *SIG*245 ii 36 (Delph., iv B.C.). **4.** *band* of men, Lxx *Jb.*1.17; *right-hand half* of a phalanx (opp. οὐρά), Arr.*Tact.*8.3, Ael.*Tact.*7.3. **5.** Astron., κ. τοῦ κόσμου, of Aries, Heph.Astr.1.1. (*ghebh-*, cf. κεβλή and Engl. *gable*.)

**κεφᾰλη-γερέτης,** ου, Dor. **-τᾶς,** ὁ, *head-collector*, Comic epith. of Pericles, formed after the Homeric νεφεληγερέτης, from the peaked shape of his skull, Cratin.240. **✱-γονος,** ον, *springing from the head*, κάλυκες Nic.*Fr.*74.25.

**κεφᾰλ-ηδόν,** Adv. *like a head*, f.l. in Opp.*C.*3.437. **II.** *individually*, νέμειν μερίδας κ. *Inscr.Prien.*362.25 (iv B.C.). **-ῆφιν,** Ep. gen. and dat. of κεφαλή, Il.11.350, 10.30, al.; **-φι** Od.20.94. **-ίδιον,** τό, Dim. of κεφαλή, Poll.2.42; as an article of food, *POxy.*1656.22 (pl., iv/v A.D.). **✱-ίζω,** *behead*, *BGU*341.9. **✱-ικός,** ή, όν, *of* or *for the head*, of remedies, etc., κ. ἔμπλαστροι Dsc.3.88, cf. Asclep.ap. Gal.13.543; δυνάμεις Dsc.3.48 (v.l. κεφαλαλγικαῖς), cf. *Arch.Pap.* 4.270 (iii A.D.); δέλτοι Gal.2.607; κεφαλική, ἡ, name of a herb, Griffith & Thompson *Demotic Magical Papyrus* verso iv 10. Adv. **-κῶς** *after the manner of a head*, *Corp.Herm.*10.11. **II.** *touching the head* or *life*, πράγματα *PMag.Leid.V.*5.13; *capital*, δίκη *POxy.*2104. 15 (iii A.D.); τιμωρία *Rev.Bibl.*35.285 (Jerusalem), *Cod.Just.*1.12.3.2 (Theodosius II), Just.*Nov.*85.3.1; κίνδυνος ib.123.31. Adv. **-κῶς,** κολασθήσεσθαι to be punished *capitally*, Hdn.2.13.9; τιμωρεῖσθαι Just. *Nov.*123.31, cf. *Cod.Just.*9.4.6.4. **III.** *belonging to an individual*, μερίς *PMasp.*151.89 (vi A.D.). **IV.** κ. σμίλη *sharp, strong* chisel, Gal.2.607. **-ίνη** [ῑ], ἡ, *root of the tongue*, supposed to be the seat of taste, hence also called γεῦσις, Poll.2.107. **-ῖνος,** ὁ, *a sea-fish*, = βλεψίας, Dorio ap.Ath.7.306f. **-ιον,** τό, Dim. of κεφαλή, ἵππου κ., as an ornament, *IG*2².1466.13, cf. Dsc.4.148, Sor.1.119, al., Plu. 2.641b; κ. γλυκύ, of a person, *Sammelb.*5807.12. **-ίς,** ίδος, ἡ, Dim. of κεφαλή, *little head*, σκορόδου Luc.*DMeretr.*14.3; *head* of a nail, Ath.11.488c; *extremity*, τῶν σκυταλίδων Antyll.ap.Orib.44.23. 74. **II.** *capital* of a column, Ph.2.147, Chor.p.118 B. (pl.), *PLond.* 3.755ᵛ6 (iv A.D.), *Gp.*14.6.6 (pl.): pl., = κρόσσαι, Eust.903.6. **III.** *toe-cap* of a shoe, Arist.*Rh.*1392ᵃ31, cf. Anon. ad loc.; of the *foot* of a table, Aristeas 68. **IV.** *rope attached to the bow* of a ship, Polyaen. 3.9.38 (pl.). **V.** κ. βιβλίου *roll*, Lxx *Ez.*2.9, *Ps.*38(39).8, al. **-ισμός,** ὁ, *multiplication table of single numbers from one to ten*, Arist. *Top.*163ᵇ 25 (pl.), cf. Suid. **-ίτης** [ῑ] λίθος *corner*-stone, Hsch. **-ῖτοπαραμήκης** λίθος *oblong corner*-stone, *POxy.*498.22 (ii A.D.).

**Κεφαλλήν,** ῆνος, ὁ, *Cephallenian*, pl. in Il.2.631, etc.: sg. in S.*Ph.* 791. **✱Κεφαλληνία,** ἡ, *Cephallenia*, Hdt.9.28.

**κεφᾰλο-βᾰρής,** ές, *with a head at the root*, of bulbous plants, Arist. *Long.*467ᵃ34, Thphr.*HP*1.6.8. **-βρωτος,** ον, *eaten away at the top*, [βιβλία] *Arch.Pap.*6.101 (ii A.D.). **-δεσμος,** ὁ, *head-band*, Sch.A.*Supp.*121:—Dim. **✱-δέσμιον,** τό, Sch.Il.14.184. **-ειδής,** ές, *shaped like a head*, ὀρίγανος Hp.*Int.*6; λοβός Dsc.2.110; παρεξοχή Apollod.*Poliorc.*220.20; κορμός Oenom.ap.Eus.*PE*5.36. **-θλαστος,** ον, *bruised in the head*: τὰ κ. *contusions of the head*, Thphr.*HP* 9.20.4. **-κλαστα,** τά, *injuries to the head*, Ruf.*Interrog.*58. **-κλάστης,** ου, ὁ, a surgical instrument, *Hermes* 38.284. **-κρούστης,** ου, ὁ, = κρανοκολάπτης, Sch.Nic.*Th.*763. **-ποιητικός,** ή, όν, *head-making*, δύναμις Phlp.*in GA*193.21. **-πους,** ποδος, ὁ, in pl., lamb's or goat's *trotters*, Cass.Fel.40 (s.v.l.). **-ρριζος,** ον, *with a bulbous root*, Thphr.*HP*1.14.2.

**κέφᾰλος,** ὁ, a species of *mullet*, Hp.*Int.*6, Arist.*HA*543ᵇ16, Archipp.12, Ephipp.12.2, Gal.6.708, Opp.*H.*1.111, Ael.*NA*1.3,12,13. 19; κεστρέα τὸν κ. Archestr.*Fr.*45.2.

**κεφᾰλο-τομέω,** *cut off the head*, less Att. than καρατομέω, Thphr. ap.*AB*104, cf. Phryn.320. **-τόμος,** ον, *cutting off the head*, Str. 11.14.14. **-τρύπᾰνον** [ῠ], τό, *trepan*, Gal.14.785.

**κεφᾰλ-ουργός,** ὁ, *foreman of works*, *LW*1666ᶜ (Lydia). **-ώδης,**

ες, = κεφαλοειδής, *like a head*, Thphr.*HP*8.8.5, 9.8.4. **-ωμα**, ατος, τό, *sum total*, *IG*5(1).1433.18 (Messene), *SIG*241*B*122 (Delph., iv B.C.). **-ών**, ῶνος, ὁ, *fan-palm*, *Chamaerops humilis*, Pall.*Agr*.5.4.5. II. = κεφαλωτόν, *BGU*1118.12 (i B.C.). III. = *capito*, *Gloss.* **-ωτός**, ή, όν, *with a head, headed*, Arist.*Cat*.7ᵃ16; of plants *with a head*, πράσον Dsc.2.149, cf. Epaenet.ap.Ath.9.371e, Mnesith.Cyz.ap.Orib.*inc*.15.18, *Gp*.12.1.8: Subst. -ωτόν (sc. πράσον), τό, *BGU*1120.16 (i B.C.); also, of a bolt, *with a flat head*, περόνη κ. Ph.*Bel*.76.3.

**κεχᾰλασμένως**, Adv., (χαλάω) *slackly*, Gal.14.793.

**κεχᾰρισμένως**, Adv., (χαρίζομαι) *acceptably*, Ar.*Ach*.248, Pl.*Phdr*.273e, D.S.17.47; κ. ἄρχειν Isoc.2.15, cf. X.*Eq.Mag*.1.1 (Sup.); ὄχλοις κ. λέγειν Plu.2.6b.

**κεχᾰρῑτωμένως**, Adv., (χαριτόω) gloss on ἐπιχαρίττως, Sch.Ar.*Ach*.867.

**κέχηνα**, v. χάσκω.

**Κεχην-αῖοι**, ων, οἱ, Comic word (from κέχηνα) for Ἀθηναῖοι, *Gapenians* for *Athenians*, Ar.*Eq*.1263. **-ότως**, Adv., (κέχηνα) *open-mouthed*, πιεῖν Moer.p.404 P. **-ώδης**, ες, *forming a hiatus*, τὸ κ. Sch.D.T.p.146 H.

**κεχιασμένως**, Adv., (χιάζω) *like a* X, *cross-wise*, *Theol.Ar*.19.

⊕**κεχρημένος**, *needy*, v. χράω C. VI.

**κεχῠμένως**, Adv., (χέω) *profusely*, πρὸς τὰς δόσεις κέχρηται τῷ βαλλαντίῳ Alciphr.3.65.

**κεχωρίδαται**, v. χωρίζω.

**κεχωρισμένως**, Adv., (χωρίζω) *separately*, Arist.*Pol*.1291ᵃ29, Aët.16.8.

**κέω**, v. κείω. **κεώδης**· καθαρός, and **κεώσατο**· καθήρατο, Hsch.; cf. κηώδης, κήϊα. **κεῶεν** ὄζει· εὐωδεῖ, Id. (Neut. of *κεώεις = κηώεις.) ⊕**κεωρεῖν**· πασχητιᾶν, Id.; **κεωρία**, ἡ, Theognost.*Can*.105.

**Κέως**, ἡ, *Ceos*, one of the Cyclades, *IG*12(5).532.7, Str.10.5.6, etc.:—hence **Κεῖος**, Ion. **Κήϊος**, ὁ, a *Ceian*, Hdt.5.102, etc.; οὐ Χῖος, ἀλλὰ Κεῖος not a (roguish) Chian, but an (honest) *Ceian*, proverb in Ar.*Ra*.970; ἀκόλαστόν τινα.., καὶ οὐδαμῶς Κεῖον Pl.*Prt*.341e, cf. *Lg*.638b; prov., ἐν Κέῳ τίς ἡμέρα; Crates Com.29.5. (Not to be confused with **Κέος** *IG*4²(1).122.117, or with **Κέος** Hdt.8.76 (cf. *Wiener Sitzb*.211(1).30).)

**κῇ**, Ion. for πῇ or ποῖ, Hdt.1.32, 8.67: but κῃ enclit. for πῃ or που, Id.5.22,40, 8.8, al.: also **κῆ**, Aeol. = ἐκεῖ, Sapph.51.

**κῆαι, κήαι**, v. καίω.

⊕**κῆβος**, ὁ, a long-tailed monkey, perh. the *nisnas monkey*, *Cercopithecus pyrrhonotus*, Arist.*HA*502ᵃ17, Gal.*UP*11.2; **κῆπος**, Agatharch.75, Str.16.4.16 (as v.l.), Ael.*NA*17.8.

**κηγχός**, Ion., = κῆ ἀγχός, A.D.*Adv*.184.9; cf. κῆχος.

**κηδάζω, κηδαλίζω**, = καθαίρω, Hsch. **κηδαίνω**, collat. form of κήδω, Id. **κήδαλον**· αἰδοῖον, κέρας, σκάλαθρον, Id.

**κηδ-εᾱκός** (κῆδος I. 2 b), ὁ, *undertaker*, *IGRom*.4.353ᵇ.23 (Pergam., ii A.D.). **-εία**, ἡ, *care for the dead, funeral*, A.R.2.836; κ. καὶ περιστολή D.H.3.21, *BGU*896.7 (ii A.D.), cf. Onos.36.1, etc.; *mourning*, ἐξανίστασθαι ἐκ τῆς κηδείας *SIG*1219.14 (Gambreum, iii B.C.). II. *connexion by marriage, alliance*, κηδείαν ξυνάψαι τινί E.*Supp*.134; συνάγειν ἀνθρώπους εἰς κ. X.*Mem*.2.6.36; κ. συνάπτεσθαι πρός τινα Plb.1.9.2; ἡ πρὸς αἵματος ἢ κατὰ..κηδείαν Arist.*Pol*.1262ᵃ11; κηδεῖαι ἐγένοντο κατὰ τὰς πόλεις ib.1280ᵇ36; ἐκ τῆς πρὸς Διονύσιον κ. ib.1307ᵃ39. **-ειος**, ον, *cared for, beloved*, τρεῖς τε κασιγνήτους, τούς μοι μία γείνατο μήτηρ, κηδείους Il.19.294. 2. Act., *careful of*, or *caring for*, c. gen., τροφαὶ κ. τέκνων E.*Ion*487 (lyr.). II. *of a funeral* or *tomb, sepulchral*, χοαί A.*Ch*.87, 538; κ. θρίξ *offered on a tomb*, ib.226; κ. οἰκτοισιν E.*IT*147 (lyr.).

⊕**κηδεμον-εύω**, *to be a guardian*, παίδων Just.*Nov*.94.2:—Pass., *to be a ward*, ib.18.9. **-εύς**, έως, ὁ, = κηδεμών, A.R.1.271, *APl*.4.41 (Agath.). ⊕**-ία**, ἡ, *care, solicitude*, Pl.*R*.463d, Phld.*Mort*.25, Ph.2.179, D.C.43.17, *POxy*.1070.21 (iii A.D.); ἡ κ. τῶν Ἀθηνῶν the *general charge* of her affairs, *IG*3.632, cf. *CIG*3187 (Smyrna); ἡ τοῦ αὐτοκράτορος περὶ πάντας κ. *BGU*372 I 12 (ii A.D.). **-ικός**, ή, όν, *provident, careful*, φίλος Plb.*Fr*.80; νουθέτησις Phld.*Lib*.p.13 O.; παρρησία Plu.2.55b; ἀνήρ Epict.*Gnom*.63; τὸ κ., = foreg., Plb.31.27.12, Cic.*Att*.2.17.3, Muson.*Fr*.14 p.73 H.: Comp., J.*BJ*1.28.2: Sup., Ph.2.288. Adv. -κῶς *OGI*56.15 (Canopus, iii B.C.), Muson.*Fr*.15ᴬ p.79 H., Luc.*Symp*.46, etc.; κ. ἔχειν πρός τινα Plb.4.32.4; κ. ὑποδεῖξαι, ἀποκρῖναι, J.*AJ*11.6.6, Sor.1.28.

⊕**κηδεμών**, όνος, ὁ, (κήδω) *one that has charge of* a person or thing, Hom. (only in Il.) always of *persons attending to the dead*, 23.163, 674. 2. generally, *one who cares for* others, *protector, guardian*, Thgn.645, S.*Ph*.195 (anap.), Ar.*V*.242, X.*Mem*.2.7.12: pl., Phld.*Mort*.23; of tutelary heroes, X.*Cyr*.3.3.21; κ. τῆς πόλεως Pl.*R*.412c; τᾶσδε φυγᾶς..κ. *protector*, A.*Supp*.76 (lyr.); τοῦ ζῆν ἡμῶν καὶ τοῦ φρονεῖν κ. Pl.*Lg*.808b; κ. οὐκ ἔφεδρον βίου Men.663; of a legal *guardian*, *POxy*.888.2 (iii/iv A.D.), etc.; τῶν δακτύλων Alex.148; of a female, Simon.116, S.*Ant*.549. II. = κηδεστής, E.*Med*.990 (lyr.); *patron*, opp. ξυγγενής, Ar.*V*.731.

**κήδεος**, ον, = κήδειος, only in Il.23.160 οἷσι κήδεός ἐστι νέκυς to whom *the charge of burying* him belongs (κηδεός acc. to Sch.Patm. D. in *BCH*1.142).

**κήδεσαι, κήδεσκον, κηδέσκετο**, v. κήδω.

⊕**κηδεστ-ής**, Dor. **κᾱδεστάς** *AP*7.712 (Erinna), οῦ, ὁ: (κῆδος, κηδεύω):—*connexion by marriage*, Pl.*Lg*.773b, X.*Mem*.1.1.8, Arist.*Pol*.1312ᵇ16, Cerc.17.25 (pl.), Ph.2.555 (pl.), etc.; esp. 1. *son-in-law*, Antipho 6.12, Isoc.10.43. 2. *father-in-law*, Ar.*Th*.74, 210, D.19.118, etc.; also, *step-father*, Id.36.31. 3. *brother-in-law*, E.*Hec*.834, And.1.50, Lys.13.1, Is.6.27, D.30.12, Timae.84. **-ία**, ἡ, *connexion by marriage*, X.*HG*2.4.21 (pl.). **-ικός**, ή, όν, *of affinity*, οἰκειότης Eust.942.36. ⊕**-ρια**, ἡ, *female attendant, keeper*, *PTeb*.378.4 (iii A.D.); *guardian*, *PThead*.18.2 (iii/iv A.D.). 2. *mother-in-law*, *Gloss.* **-ωρ**, ορος, ὁ, = κηδεμών I, Man.4.514.

**κήδ-ευμα**, ατος, τό, *connexion* or *alliance by marriage*, E.*Med*.76, Pl.*Lg*.773b. 2. poet. for κηδεστής, *one who is so connected*, S.*OT*85, E.*Or*.477. **-εύσιμος**, gloss on κήδεος, Hsch. **-ευσις**, εως, ἡ, = κηδεία I, Ael.*NA*10.48; = κηδεμονία, Plot.6.7.26. **-ευτής**, οῦ, ὁ, = κηδεμών I, Arist.*Pr*.922ᵇ26. **-εύω**, (κῆδος) *take charge of, tend*, S.*OT*1323 (lyr.), *OC*750; πόλιν Id.*Fr*.683.4, E.*IT*1212; νύμφην Id.*Med*.888; νόσημα Id.*Or*.883. 2. esp. *attend to* a corpse, *bury*, ἐν ξένῃσι χερσὶ κηδευθεὶς τάλας S.*El*.1141, cf. E.*Rh*.983; μ' ἔθαψε καὶ ἐκήδευσεν *IG*14.1860: also in Prose, Plb.5.10.4, etc.; ταφῇ κηδευθεῖσα ταῖς τῶν ἐναντίων χερσί Demad.9, cf. Plu.*Alex*.56; βασιλέων κηδευομένων Arist.*Fr*.519, cf. Wilcken *Chr*.499 (ii/iii A.D.); κεκηδευμένος νεκρὸς ἐν μέλιτι J.*AJ*14.7.4; εἰς ἣν [σορὸν] οὐδενὶ ἐξέσται ἕτερον πτῶμα κηδεῦσαι *CIG*3028.3 (Ephesus), cf. *POxy*.1067.6 (iii A.D.). 3. = κηδεμονεύω, in Pass., *Cod.Just*.3.10.1.1. II. *contract a marriage*, of the bridegroom, *ally oneself in marriage*, τὸ κηδεῦσαι καθ' ἑαυτὸν ἀριστεύει μακρῷ A.*Pr*.890 (lyr.): c. acc. cogn., κ. λέχος *marry*, S.*Tr*.1227: c. dat. pers., *ally oneself with*.., E.*Hipp*.634, *Fr*.395, D.59.81, Men.*Epit*.427, etc.; κ. ὅτῳ θέλουσιν Arist.*Pol*.1307ᵃ37; *become the son-in-law of*, Moer.p.368 P.:—in Pass., *to be married*, E.*Ph*.347 (lyr.). 2. c. acc. pers., *make one's kinsman by marriage*, Id.*Hec*.1202; also κ. τὴν θυγατέρα τινί *to marry* her to some one, J.*AJ*6.10.2: abs., οἱ κηδεύσαντες *those who formed the marriage*, E.*Med*.367. **-ιστος**, η, ον, Sup. formed from κῆδος, *most worthy of one's care, most cared for*, κήδιστοί τ' ἔμεναι καὶ φίλτατοι Il.9.642; κ. ἑτάρων ἦν κεδνότατός τε Od.10.225. II. κήδιστοι, οἱ, *those nearest allied by marriage*, 8.583. **-ομαι**, v. κήδω. **-ομένως**, Adv., κ. ἔχειν to be *provident*, Aristid.*Or*.53 p.619 D.

⊕**κῆδ-ος**, Dor. **κᾶδος**, εος, τό, (κήδω) *care about*, c. gen., τῶν ἄλλων οὐ κῆδος the others *do* not *matter*, Od.22.254. 2. *anxiety, grief*, Il.13.464, al. (v. infr. II): mostly in pl., *troubles*, Ἀργείοισι πολύστονα κήδε' ἐφῆκεν Il.1.445; Τρώεσσι δὲ κήδε' ἐφῆπται ἐκ Διός 2.69; ὅσ' ἐμῷ ἔνι κ. θυμῷ 18.53, cf. Od.4.108; ὁππόσα κήδε' ἀνέτλης 14.47. b. esp. for the dead, *funeral rites, mourning*, πατέρι δὲ γόον καὶ κήδεα λυγρὰ λεῖπ' Il.5.156, etc.; θάνατος καὶ κ. 4.270; κήδε' ἐμῶν ἑτάρων *mourning for* them, 22.272; κ. στονόεντα Archil.9, cf. A.*Ch*.469 (lyr.), Plu.*Sol*.12, etc.: sg., κᾶδος φθιμένου θήκασθαι Pi.*P*.4.112, cf. *N*.1.54; ἅμα κήδεϊ when there is a death in the family, Hdt.2.36; ἐς τὸ κ. ἰέναι to attend *the funeral*, Id.6.58, cf. *SIG*1218.18 (Iulis, v B.C.); ἐπὶ τὸ κ. ἀφικέσθαι Isoc.19.31; θυραῖον κ. ἐς τάφον φέρειν E.*Alc*.828; ὅταν οἰκεῖον..κ. γένηται Pl.*R*.605d; εἰς τὰ κήδη..οἱ συγγενεῖς ἀπαντῶσι attend at *funerals*, Arist.*EN*1165ᵃ20. 3. *object of care*, Ἰλίῳ κ. ὀρθώνυμον, of Helen, with a play on signf. II, A.*Ag*.699 (lyr.). II. *connexion by marriage*, Hdt.7.189; κ. ἐγγενές A.*Supp*.331; κ. Ἀδράστου λαβών, i.e. having married his daughter, E.*Ph*.77, cf. S.*OC*379; κατ' ἐπιγαμίαν τῷ ἀσκητῇ κ. συνάπτειν Ph.1.553; τὸ κ. ξυνάψασθαι τῆς θυγατρός contract the *marriage* for one's own daughter, Th.2.29; so some wrongly explain Il.13.464, cf. 15.245, 16.516 (v. supr. I. 2 a). **-οσύνη**, ἡ, *yearning*, in pl., A.R.1.277, 3.462, 4.1473. **-όσῠνος**, ον, *anxious*; = κήδειος I. 2, πούς E.*Or*.1017 (anap.). ⊕**-ω**, Hom. (v. infr.), etc.: impf. ἔκηδον Il.5.404, Ep. κήδεσκον Od.23.9: fut. κηδήσω Il.24.240:—**Med.** and **Pass.**, pres. in Hom., etc.; Dor. imper. κάδευ Call.*Lav.Pall*.140: Ep. impf. κηδέσκετο Od.22.358: fut. κεκᾰδήσομαι Il.8.353: aor. imper. κήδεσαι A.*Th*.139 (lyr.): pf. κέκηδα (in pres. sense) Tyrt.12.28. I. Act., *trouble, distress*, c. acc. pers., ὃς τόξοισιν ἔκηδε θεούς Il.5.404; μῆλα δὲ κήδει (sc. χειμών) 17.550; ὅττι ἑ κήδοι Od.9.402; ὅτι μ' ἤλθετε κηδήσοντες Il.24.240; Λύγδαμιν οὐ γὰρ ἐμὴ τῆμος ἔκηδε κάσις Call.*Aet*.3.1.23:—Act. only in Ep. and Eleg. II. Med. and Pass., *to be concerned, care for*..: c. gen., of persons or cities, κήδετο γὰρ Δαναῶν Il.1.56; τίη δὲ σὺ κήδεαι οὕτως ἀνδρῶν; 6.55; ὀλλυμένων Δαναῶν κεκαδησόμεθ' 8.353, cf. 11.665; ὅς τέ μευ κηδέσκετο παιδὸς ἐόντος Od.22.358, cf. Hdt.1.209, 9.45, S.*Aj*.203 (anap.), Th.6.14, Pl.*Chrm*.173a, Ph.1.359, etc.; Ἄργεος Call.*Lav.Pall*. l.c.; καὶ γαμέτου κήδεο καὶ τεκέων *mourn for*.., *Epigr.Gr*.243.25 (Pergam.): c. gen. rei, τῶν ἀλφίτων Ar.*Nu*.106; τῆς πολιτείας Arist.*Pol*.1320ᵃ6; τῶν ἔργων *POxy*.1682.13 (iv A.D.): folld. by a Verb, κ. μὴ ἀπόλωνται Hdt.7.220; κ. ἵνα μὴ δύῃ Pl.*Plt*.273d; κ. φόβῳ τοῦ πνιγῆναι Aët.8.63: abs. in part. κηδόμενος, η, ον, *caring for* a person, *anxious*, φιλέουσά τε κηδομένη τε Il.1.196; ἀνέρι κηδομένῳ *distressed*, 16.516; freq. in Hom. at end of verse, κηδόμενός περ, κηδομένη περ, Il.7.110, 1.586; εὐνοῶν τε καὶ κ. Ar.*Nu*.1410; Dor. καδόμενος Pi.*O*.6.47. b. *bury*, c. gen., Ael.*Fr*.106. 2. Inscrr., *take charge of*, τοῦ μνημείου τούτου ἡ γερουσία κ. *SIG*1244 (Cos, ii/iii A.D.), cf. 1228 (Ephesus, iii A.D.).

**κηδωλός**· ὁ φροντίζων καὶ κηδόμενος ὅλων, Suid.

**κῆεν**, Ep. 3 sg. aor. 1 Act. of καίω, Il.21.349.

⊕**κηθάριον**, τό, Dim. of κηθίς, *voting-urn, ballot-box*, Ar.*V*.674.

**κηθεῖν**· βοηθεῖν, and **κηθοί**· βοηθοί, Hsch.; cf. κέαθοι. **κήθευον**· συνεπορεύοντο, Id. **κῆθι**, v. ἐκεῖθι.

**κήθιν**, τό, prob. = κήθιον, *PLond*.2.402ᵛ.23 (ii B.C.).

⊕**κηθίς**, ίδος, ἡ, *dice-box*, prob. in Poll.7.203:—Dim. **κήθιον**, Hermipp.27, **κηθίδιον**, Poll.10.150.—Wrongly written **κητίον**, Alciphr.1.39, Ath.11.477d cod. A:—**χείτιον**, Ion. **κείθιον**, Eust.1259.36. (Ath. l. c. derives it from χέισεται, fut. of χανδάνω.)

**κῆθυ**, f. l. for κῆθι. **κηΐα**· καθάρματα, Hsch.; cf. κεΐα.

**κηκ-άζω** (κηκαδεῖ Hsch.), *abuse, revile*, Lyc.1386. **-άς**, άδος, ἡ, said to be Ion. word for κακός, *mischievous*, κ. ἀλώπηξ Nic.*Al.*185; *abusive*, κηκάδι σὺν γλώσσῃ Call.*Fr.*253. **-ασμός**, ὁ, *abuse, insult*, Lyc.545 (pl.), 692.

**κηκίβαλος**, ὁ, kind of *shell-fish*, Epich.42.2 (leg. κικ-, cf. **κικοβαυλιτίδες**).

**κηκίδιον**, τό, *ink-gall*, Philum.ap.Aët.16.117(107), Hdn.*Epim.*65, Eust.956.1: used as yellow dye, written **κικίδιον**, Ps.-Democr.ap. Zos.Alch.p.160B.

**κηκῖδοφόρος**, ον, *bearing gall-nuts*, Agathocl.ap.Eust.994.43.

**κηκίς** [ῐ], ῖδος, ἡ, *anything gushing* or *bubbling forth, ooze*, of fat or juices drawn forth by fire, κηκὶς πισσήρης φλογὸς A.*Ch.*268; κ. φόνου *bubbling* blood, ib.1012; μυδῶσα κ. *juices* drawn by fire from a sacrificial victim, S.*Ant.*1008; κ. πορφύρας *dye* of the murex, A.*Ag.* 960. **II.** *oak-gall*, Hp.*Nat.Mul.*32,al., Thphr.*HP*1.2.1, 3.8.6, Dsc.1.107; *the dye made therefrom*, D.27.10,43; used as *ink*, Eust. 955.64; esp. invisible ink, Ph.*Bel.*102.32.

**κηκίω**, Dor. **κᾱκίω** Hsch.:—*gush, bubble forth*, θάλασσα.. κήκιε πολλὴ ἂν στόμα τε ῥινάς τε much brine *gushed* up through his mouth, Od.5.455, cf. A.R.1.542; ἐκ βυθοῦ κηκῖον αἷμα S.*Ph.*784: c. acc. cogn., *bubble with, send forth*, κήκιε πόντος ἀϋτμήν A.R.4.929:—Med., *ooze*, αἱμάδα κηκιομέναν ἑλκέων S.*Ph.*697. [ῐ Ep.: ῑ S. ll. cc.]

**κήκραν**· ἐκεκράγ[ε]σαν, Hsch. **κηλαίνω**, = κηλέω, Id.

⊛ **κήλας**, ὁ, an Indian stork, *adjutant*, *Leptoptilus argala*, Ael.*NA* 16.4.

**κηλάς**, άδος, ἡ, prop. *mottled* (cf. κηλίς), of clouds denoting wind, not rain, Thphr.*Sign.*31, prob. in 51: hence κ. ἡμέρα a *windy* day, Hsch., dub. in Call.*Fr.*63 P. **II.** κηλὰς αἴξ, ἡ, a she-goat *with a mark* (σημεῖον τυλοειδές) *on her forehead*, Hsch.

**κηλ-άστρα**, ἡ, *milk-pail*, Hsch. **II.** *holly*, *Ilex Aquifolium*, Id.: —also **-αστρος**, ἡ, Thphr.*HP*3.4.5, 4.1.3:—more freq. **-αστρον**, τό, ib.1.9.3, 3.3.1, al.

**κήλεος**, ον, (καίω) *burning*, Hom. always in dat. in the phrase πυρὶ κηλέῳ (disyll.), Il.8.235, 18.346, Od.8.435, Hes.*Th.*865; always at end of line, exc. ἐνέπρησεν πυρὶ κ. νῆας ἐΐσας Il.8.217:—once in form **κήλειος**, σὺν πυρὶ κ.15.744:—also **κηλός**, *dry*, Hsch.; cf. καυαλέος.

**κηλ-έστης**, ου, ὁ, *beguiler*, Suid., Zonar. ⊛ **-έω**, *charm, bewitch, beguile*, esp. by music, κόρην ὕμνοισι E.*Alc.*359; ᾠδαῖς Pl.*Ly.*206b; κηλῶν τῇ φωνῇ ὥσπερ Ὀρφεύς Id.*Prt.*315a, cf. Luc.*Ind.*12; οὕτως ἐκήλει, of Pericles as an orator, Eup.94.6; ἐπᾴδων κ. *charm* by incantation, Pl.*Phdr.*267d; τῷ με κηλήσεις τρόπῳ; Achae.17.2; of bribery, Theopomp.Com.30:—Pass., κηλεῖται ἀοιδαῖς Archil.ap.Phld.*Mus.* p.20K., cf. Pi.*Dith.*2.22; ὑπὸ σοῦ ὥσπερ ὄφις κηληθῆναι Pl.*R.*358b; ὑπὸ δώρων κηλούμενος Id.*Lg.*885d; ὑφ' ἡδονῆς κηληθεὶς Id.*R.*413c; ἐφ' οἷς κατορθώσαντες εὐφρανθήσονται, τούτοις κεκήληνται Aeschin.1.191; παρὰ ταῖς Σειρῆσιν Arist.*EE*1230b35: rarely in good sense, παιδείᾳ τὸν νοῦν κηληθεὶς Pl.*Ep.*333c.

**κήλη**, Att. **κάλη** [prob. ᾱ], ἡ, *tumour*; esp. *rupture, hernia*, Hp.*Aër.* 7 (pl.), *AP*6.166 (Lucill.), 11.342. **2.** *hump* on a buffalo's back, Arist.*HA*606a16, in acc. pl. κάλας (v.l. χαίτας); in human beings, Eup.276.1, Gal.7.729, Artem.3.45; καλήτης καὶ κάλη Ἀττικοί.., κηλήτης καὶ κήλη Ἴωνες Phryn.*PS*p.81 B. (Cf. ONorse *haull*, OSlav. *kyla*, both = *hernia*.)

⊛ **Κηλ-ηδόνες**, αἱ, the *Charmers*, mythical songstresses, like the Sirens, but harmless, Pi.*Fr.*53, cf. Ath.7.290e. **-ηθμός**, ὁ, *rapture, enchantment*, κηληθμῷ δ' ἔσχοντο Od.11.334. **-ηθρον**, τό, = sq., Phryn.*PS* p.80B. **-ημα**, ατος, τό, *charm, spell*, in pl., Ibyc. 2, E.*Tr.*893: sg., Id.*Hyps.Fr.*26(32).

**κηλήνη**· μέλαινα, Hsch.

**κήλ-ησις**, εως, ἡ, *bewitching, charming*, ἔχεων, νόσων, Pl.*Euthd.* 290a: *enchantment* by eloquence, δικαστῶν κ. τε καὶ παραμυθία ibid.; by music and sweet sounds, Id.*R.*601b, *Stoic.*3.97. **-ήτειρα**, ἡ, *enchantress*, glossed by ἡσυχάστρια, Hsch. **-ητήριος**, ον, *charming, appeasing*, χοαί E.*Hec.*535; ᾄσματα Suid.; τὸ κ., = κήληθρον, S. *Tr.*575. **-ήτης**, ου, ὁ, (κήλη) *one who is ruptured*, Str.17.3.4, Gal. 10.988, D.C.73.2, *AP*11.342, Luc.*Epigr.*39:—Att. **καλήτης** Phryn. *PS*p.81 B. **-ητικός**, ή, όν, *charming*, τὸ κ. τῆς ἐπιστήμης Ath.14. 633a. **-ήτωρ**, ορος, ὁ, *charmer*, Orph.*Fr.*297a.6.

**κηλίβανα**, = σιδηρᾶ καλύμματα, as etym. of κλιβανάριοι, Lyd.*Mag.* 1.46.

**κηλῖδ-όω**, Dor. **κᾱλ-** Ecphant. (v. infr.):—*stain, soil*, τὰ ἱμάτια Arist. *Insomn.*460a12 (Pass.):—Pass., D.C.77.11: metaph., *defile, sully*, E.*HF*1318, Ecphant.ap.Stob.4.7.64:—Pass., Ph.1.156. **-ωτός**, ή, όν, *stained, soiled*, Suid., *Gloss.*

⊛ **κηλικτάς**, ᾶ, ὁ, Lacon., *charmer*, prob. in Plu.2.220f.

**κηλίς** [ῑ], ῖδος, ἡ, *stain, spot, defilement*, esp. of blood, A.*Eu.*787 (lyr.), S.*El.*446, E.*IT*1200, etc.: generally, οὐ ῥᾴδιον ἐκμάξαι τὴν.. κηλῖδα [ἐκ τοῦ κατόπτρου] Arist.*Insomn.*459b32; ἐν ἱματίῳ καθαρῷ καὶ αἱ μικραὶ κ. ἔνδηλοι Id.*GA*780b32; ἱμάτιον κηλίδων μεστὸν Thphr.*Char.* 19.7. **2.** metaph., *stain, blemish*, S.*OT*1384; κ. συμφορᾶς ib.833; κακῶν Id.*OC*1134; ἐστάθη τὴν ἀσπίδα ἔχων, ὃ δοκεῖ κ. εἶναι τοῖς Λακεδαιμονίοις X.*HG*3.1.9; *ignominious punishment*, θεία κ. προσπίπτει τῷ δράσαντι Antipho 3.3.8; τῆς κ. εἰς ὑμᾶς ἀναφερομένης ib.11; τιμωρίας καὶ κηλῖδας πάσας αὐτοῖς ἀνῆκεν Hdn.6.8.8. **3.** Medic., *naevus*, Lycus ap.Orib.9.44.3.

⊛ **κῆλον**, τό, *shaft* of an arrow, *arrow*, only pl., κῆλα θεοῖο *the shafts* of Apollo, as the cause of sudden death, Il.1.53,383; πιφαυσκόμενος τὰ ἃ κῆλα, of Zeus during a snowstorm, 12.280; στεροπὴν καὶ αἰθαλόεντα κεραυνόν, κῆλα Διός Hes.*Th.*708: metaph., [φόρμιγγος] κῆλα καὶ δαιμόνων θέλγει φρένας Pi.*P.*1.12; φρικώδεα κῆλα πιφαύσκων Orph. *A.*10:—also **κῆλεα** νηῶν, = κᾶλα, ships' *timbers*, Hes.*Fr.*206 (s. v.l.).

**κηλόν**· ξηρόν, Hsch.; cf. κήλεος, καυαλέος.

**κηλοτομ-ία**, ἡ, *operation for hernia*, Paul.Aeg.6.63. **-ικός**, ή, όν, *of herniotomy*, τέχνη Gal.*Thras.*24. **-ος**, ὁ, *herniotomist*, ibid. (v.l. -τομικόν).

**κηλόω** (A), aor. 1 inf. -ῶσαι, = ἀμβλῶσαι, ἐπὶ τῶν ἐμβρύων, *An. Par.*4.257:—Pass., *have an abnormal delivery*, Ptol.*Tetr.*149.

**κηλόω** (B), collat. form of κηλέω, expld. by εὔχεσθαι θεῷ, Hsch.

**κήλυγμα**, = κίνυγμα, Hsch.

⊛ **κήλων**, ωνος, ὁ, (κῆλον) *swipe, swing-beam*, for drawing water, *IG* 11(2).154*A* 8 (Delos, iii B.C.), *PLond.*1.131r.303 (i A.D.), Hsch. **II.** ὄνος κ. *he-ass*, Archil.97, cf. Eust.1597.28, Ph.2.307; *stallion*, Hsch., Suid., prob. in Plaut.*Poen.*1168: hence of Pan, Cratin.321.

⊛ **κηλών-ειον**, Ion. **-ήϊον**, τό, = foreg. 1, Hdt.1.193, 6.119, Ar.*Fr.*679, Arist.*Mech.*857a34, Aen.Tact.39.7, *PCair.Zen.*155 (iii B.C.), Gal.*UP* 7.7:—written **κηλώνιον**, Apollod.*Poliorc.*162.8, al. **-εύω**, *suspend on a fulcrum* or *pivot*, Hero *Spir.*1.20 (Pass.):—Pass., Ath.Mech.29. 14, 30.4.

**κηλωστά** or **κηλωτά**, ῶν, τά, *stews, brothels*, Lyc.1387.

**κήμιψ**· φλὲψ γεώδης (-ῶδες cod.) ἐν πέτραις (μέτρ- cod.), Hsch.

⊛ **κημός** (Dor. **κᾱμός**, cf. εὐκαμία), ὁ, *muzzle*, put on a led horse, to prevent it from biting, X.*Eq.*5.3, *AP*6.246 (Phld. or Marc. Arg.): pl., cj. in Ph.1.698: metaph., κημοὺς στόματος *muzzles* or *gags*, A. *Fr.*125. **2.** *nose-bag* for horses, Hsch. **3.** *cloth* used by bakers *to cover the nose and mouth*, Ath.12.548c. **4.** = φορβειά, Phot. **II.** *wicker vessel like an eel-basket*, for fishing, *weel*, S.*Fr.*504. **2.** *funnel-shaped top* of the voting-urn, Ar.*Eq.*1150 (lyr., et ibi Sch.), *V.*99, al. **III.** a *female ornament*, Hsch., Phot.

**κῆμος**, ἡ, = λεοντοπόδιον, Dsc.4.133, Orph.*A.*920.

**κημ-όω**, (κημός) *muzzle* a horse, X.*Eq.*5.3. **II.** Medic., = φιμόω, τὸν ὀφθαλμόν Sch.Ar.*Eq.*1147. **III.** *fit with the* κημός I.4, πολιῷ δ' ἐπὶ πολλάκι λωτῷ κημωθεὶς (cj. Herm. for κνημωθεὶς) κώμους εἶχε σὺν Ἐξαμύῃ Hermesian.7.38. **-ωσις**, εως, ἡ, *muzzling*, Hsch. (also **κίμωσις**).

**κήνεον**· καθαρόν, Hsch.

**κῆνος**, Aeol. and Dor. for κεῖνος, ἐκεῖνος, Sapph.2.1, *Epigr.Gr.*991. 13 (Balbilla), *SIG*1025.25 (Cos, iv/iii B.C.); **κήνοθεν**, *thence*, Alc. 86. **κηνούει**· ἐκεῖ, and **κηνῶ**· ἐκεῖθεν, Hsch.

**κηνσίτωρ**, ὁ, = Lat. *censitor*, *PAmh.*2.83.3 (iii/iv A.D.).

⊛ **κῆνσος**, ὁ, = Lat. *census*, *Ev.Matt.*22.19, *IGRom.*4.1213 (Thyatira), 3.41 (Nicaea), *PAmh.*2.83.2 (iii/iv A.D.). **II.** *poll-tax*, *Ev. Matt.*17.25.

**κήνυγμα**, written for κίνυγμα (q.v.), Hsch. **κηνύει**· καλεῖ, Id.

⊛ **κήξ**, κηκός, ἡ, a sea-bird, perh. the *tern* or *sea-swallow*, ἄντλῳ δ' ἐνδούπησε πεσοῦσ' ὡς εἰναλίη κήξ Od.15.479:—also in the forms **καύαξ**, = λάρος, Hsch., and **καυήξ** Hippon.2 (nisi leg. καύης, q.v.), Antim.*Eleg.*6, Euph.130, Call.*Fr.*167, Lyc.741, *AP*7.652 (Leon.); **κῆϋξ**, Babr.115.2, Dionys.*Av.*2.7.

**κήομεν** (or κείομεν), Ep. for κήωμεν, v. καίω.

**κηπάδιον**, τό, a kind of vine(?), *PFlor.*148.14 (iii A.D.).

⊛ **κηπ-αῖος**, α, ον, (κῆπος) *of* or *from a garden, cultivated*, κ. σίκυες Arist.*Pr.*926b7, cf. Dsc.2.146, Gal.6.627 (v. l.), etc.; κ. παράδεισοι *garden-like* parks, Clearch.6. **II.** κηπαία (sc. θύρα), ἡ, *garden-door, back-door*, Hermipp.47.9, cf. Poll.1.76; prov., ταῖς κ. θύραις 'by the back-stairs', D.L.7.25, cf. Gal.2.98. **2.** *a herb, Sedum Cepaea*, Dsc.3.151. **-εία**, ἡ, in pl., *gardens*, Pl.*Lg.*845d, D.S.5.43, J.*BJ*5.2. 2. **-ειος**, α, ον, v.l. for κηπαῖος, Nic.*Th.*88. **-ευμα**, ατος, τό, *garden*, κηπεύματα Χαρίτων Ar.*Av.*1100, cf. Apollod.Hist.ap.Ath.15.682d, Dicaearch.1.13. **-εύς**, Dor. **κᾱπ-**, έως, ὁ, *gardener*, Philyll.14, *AP*9. 329 (Leon.). **-εύσιμος**, ον, = κηπευτός, Alex.Trall.*Febr.*7, Sch.Nic. *Th.*66. **-ευτής**, οῦ, ὁ, = κηπεύς, *Gloss.* **-ευτός**, ή, όν, *cultivated, grown in a garden*, Dsc.3.45, *Gp.*12.30.7, Paul.Aeg.1.13. **-εύω**, *rear in a garden*, λάχανα, σῖτον, Luc.*VH*1.34, Herm. *in Phdr.*p.202 A.:—Pass., Dsc.3.43; τὰ κηπευόμενα *garden plants*, Arist.*PA*668a 18, Thphr.*HP*7.1.1, Gal.6.542; Ἠριδανὸς ὕδασι κ. κόρας, i.e. the Phaethontids, who became poplars, Eub.67.6: metaph., *tend, cherish*, βόστρυχον E.*Tr.*1175. **II.** *cultivate like a garden*, Thphr. *CP*4.6.7 (Pass.), Hld.9.4 (Pass.): metaph., *vivify, freshen*, Αἰδὼς κ. δρόσοις [τὸν λειμῶνα] E.*Hipp.*78; ὁπόσα ὁ ποταμὸς κ. Philostr.*VA*2. 26. **-ίδες** Νύμφαι, αἱ, *garden*-Nymphs, prob. in Aristaenet. 1.3. **-ίδιον**, τό, Dim. of κῆπος, Plu.2.1098b, D.L.3.20. **-ίον**, τό, Dim. of κῆπος, *SIG*46.15 (Halic., v B.C.), Plb.6.17.2, Gal.2.211, *PSI*1.77.18, etc.: metaph., *appendage*, κ. καὶ ἐγκαλλώπισμα πλούτου Th.2.62. **II.** = κῆπος II, Luc.*Lex.*5.

**κηπο-κόμας**, ου, ὁ, *one who has his hair cut in the fashion called* κῆπος, *Com.Adesp.*34D. ⊛ **-κόμος**, ὁ, *gardener*, *BCH*32.500 (Aphrodisias), Hsch. **-λᾰχᾰνία**, ἡ, *kitchen-garden*, *POxy.*1917. 55 (vi A.D.). **-λάχᾰνον**, τό, = foreg., *PLond.ined.*2489.13 (iv A.D.). **-λόγος**, ον, *teaching in a garden*, of Epicureans, *AP*6.307 (Phan.). **-παράδεισος**, ὁ, *garden and orchard in one*, *PSI*8.917.5 (i A.D.). **-ποιΐα**, ἡ, *making of a garden*, *Gp.*12.2.1.

⊛ **κῆπος**, Dor. **κᾶπος** (also *Inscr.Cypr.*135.20 H.), ὁ, *garden, orchard*, or *plantation*, Od.7.129, 24.247,338; πολυδένδρεος 4.737; of any rich, highly cultivated region, as Ἀφροδίτας κᾶπος, i.e. Cyrene, Pi. *P.*5.24; Διὸς κ., i.e. Libya, ib.9.53 (but Διὸς κῆποι, also of heaven, S. *Fr.*320 (lyr.); Φοίβου παλαιὸς κ., of the eastern sky, ib.956, cf. Pl.*Smp.* 203b; cf. Ὠκεανοῦ κ. Ar.*Nu.*271); κ. Εὐβοίας S.*Fr.*24; οἱ Μίδεω κῆποι,

in Macedonia, Hdt.8.138; of the country round Panormus, Call. Hist.2; the *enclosure* for the Olympic games, Pi.*O*.3.24; οἱ ἀπὸ τῶν κ. the scholars of Epicurus, because he taught in a *garden*, S.E.*M*. 9.64, cf. D.L.10.10; οἱ Ἀδώνιδος κ., v. Ἄδωνις; οἱ Ταντάλου κ., prov. of illusory pleasures, Philostr.*VS*1.20.1: metaph., Χαρίτων νέμομαι κᾶπον, i.e. poetic art, Pi.*O*.9.27; ἐκ Μουσῶν κ. τινῶν.. δρεπόμενοι τὰ μέλη Pl.*Ion* 534a; τοὺς ἐν τοῖς γράμμασι κ. σπείρειν Id.*Phdr.* 276d. **II.** *a fashion of cropping the hair*, Poll.2.29, Ael.Dion.*Fr.* 230. **III.** *pudenda muliebria*, D.L.2.116. **IV.** v.l. for κῆβος (q.v.).

⊛ **κηπο-τάφιον** [τᾰ], τό, *tomb in a garden*, *BGU*1120.7 (i B.C.):—also ⊛ **-τάφος**, ὁ, or **-τάφον**, τό, *Papers of Amer.Sch. at Athens* 3.621 (Ilias): cf. Lat. *cepotaphium*. **-τύραννος** [ῠ], ὁ, *tyrant of the garden*, epith. of the Epicurean philosopher Apollodorus, D.L.10.25.

**κηπουργ-ία**, ἡ, *gardening*, Poll.7.101. **-ικός**, ή, όν, *skilled in gardening*, ib.141.

**κηπουρ-έω**, *practise gardening*, Phleg.*Mir*.8, Poll.9.13. **-ϊκός**, ή, όν, *of* or *for a garden*, θρίδακες *BGU*1118.13 (i B.C.); θύραι (made of lettuce-stems) v.l. in Thphr.*HP*7.4.5. **-ικός**, ή, όν, *of* or *for gardening*, νόμοι, νόμιμον, Pl.*Min*.316e, 317b; κηπουρικαὶ θύραι *garden trellis*, Thphr.*HP*7.4.5; κ. κτένες, πλατυλίσγιον, Ph.*Bel*.100.10, Apollod.*Poliorc*.220.18; κ. λάχανον *Hippiatr*.7: κηπουρικά, τά, treatise on gardening by Caesennius, etc., Plin.*HN*1.19 *Ind.Auct.*, 19. 177. **II.** *skilled in gardening*, cj. in Poll.7.141. Adv. **-κῶς** ibid. **-ός**, ὁ, (οὖρος) *keeper of a garden*, ὄφις Euph.154. **II.** *gardener*, *IG*2².10 (v B.C.), Thphr.*HP*7.2.5, *PCair.Zen*.59.6 (iii B.C.), Plb.18.6.4, *Ev.Jo*.20.15, Philostr.*Her.Prooem*.2, *CIG*4082 (Pessinus); title of play by Antiph.:—also **κηπωρός**, Archipp.44, Pl.*Min*.316e, *PFay*.101ʳii 4 (i B.C.).

**κηπρίαρτος**, v. κοπριαίρετος.

⊛ **Κήρ**, ἡ, Aeol. **Κᾶρ** Alc. (v. infr.), gen. Κηρός, acc. Κῆρα; Dor. pl. **Κᾶρες** Hipparch.ap.Stob.4.34.8 (v.l. Κῆρες), but sg. κήρ Trag. in lyr. (v. infr.):—*the goddess of death* or *doom*, Κῆρ.. Θανάτοιο Od.11.171, etc.; Κῆρες.. Θανάτοιο Il.2.834, etc.; ἐν δ' Ἔρις ἐν δὲ Κυδοιμὸς ὁμίλεον ἐν δ' ὀλοὴ Κ. Il.18.535; ἐμὲ μὲν Κ. ἀμφέχανε στυγερή, ἥ περ λάχε γιγνόμενόν περ 23.79; διχθάδιαι Κῆρες, of Achilles, 9.411; Κῆρες μυρίαι 12.326; Κῆρες Ἀχαιῶν, Τρώων, 8.73,74; Κ. νηλεόποινοι Hes.*Th*.217; Κ. Ἐρινύες A.*Th*.1060 (anap.); Κ. ἀναπλάκητοι S.*OT*472 (lyr.), cf. *Tr.* 133 (lyr.), Pi.*Fr*.277, E.*El*.1252, *HF*870 (troch.); ἁρπαξάνδρα Κ., of the Sphinx, A.*Th*.777 (lyr.): prov., θύραζε Κῆρες (v.l. Κᾶρες), οὐκ ἔνι (v.l. ἔτ') Ἀνθεστήρια, of those who want the same always, Zen. 4.33, Suid. s.v. θύραζε. **II.** as Appellat., *doom, death*, esp. when *violent*, rarely without personal sense in Hom., τὸ δέ τοι κὴρ εἴδεται εἶναι that seems to thee to be *death*, Il.1.228; κῆρ' ἀλεείνων 3.32, al.; φόνον καὶ κ. φέροντες 2.352, al.: freq. later, ὑπὰ κᾶρι.. διννάεντ' Ἀχέροντ' ἐπέραισε Alc.*Supp*.7.7; μέλαιναν κῆρ' ἐπ' ὄμμασιν βαλών E.*Ph*.950. **2.** νοσῶν παλαιᾷ κηρί *plague, disease*, S.*Ph*.42, cf. 1166 (lyr.): in a general sense, βαρεῖα μὲν κ. τὸ μὴ πιθέσθαι grievous *ruin* it were not to obey, A.*Ag*.206 (lyr.); ἐλευθέρῳ ψευδεῖ καλεῖσθαι κ. πρόσεστιν οὐ καλή an unseemly *disgrace*, S.*Tr*.454. **3.** pl. sts. in Prose, *blemishes, defects*, [τοῖς καλοῖς] κ. ἐπιπεφύκασιν Pl.*Lg*.937d; [τόποι] ἰδίας ἔχουσι κῆρας Thphr.*CP*5.10.4; κ. σύμφυτοι D.H.2.3, cf. 8.61; ἁμαρτίαι καὶ κ. Plu.*Cim*.2; σῶμα ἀκήρατον τῶν ἐκτὸς κ. Ti.Locr. 95b, cf. Ph.1.368, al.: rarely sg., συνήθειαν ὥσπερ τινὰ κ. Plu.*Ant*.2, cf. Ph.1.440. (Perh. cogn. with κεραΐζω.)

⊛ **κῆρ**, τό, perh. contr. from κέαρ (sed v. infr.); Hom. always κῆρ, dat. κῆρι, Adv. κηρόθι (q.v.); Trag. always κέαρ (no other case):—*heart*, κῆρ γηθεῖ ἐνὶ στήθεσσι Il.14.139; κ. ἄχνυται ἐν θυμῷ 6.523, cf. 7.428; ἄλλα δέ οἱ κ. ὅρμαινε φρεσὶν ᾗσιν Od.18.344, cf. 7.82; τῷ κε.. αἶψα μεταστρέψειε νόον μετὰ σὸν καὶ ἐμὸν κ. Il.15.52; θαλέων ἐμπλησάμενος κ. 22.504, cf. 19.319; τοῦ δ' οὔ ποτε κυδάλιμον κ. ταρβεῖ, of a boar or lion, 12.45: dat. κῆρι as Adv., *with all the heart, heartily*, ὅν τε Ζεὺς κῆρι φιλήσῃ 9.117: mostly strengthd., περὶ κ. φιλεῖν (περί Adv., either *exceedingly* or *throughout*) 13.430; περὶ κ... τιμᾶν τινα Od.5.36, etc.; ἀπέχθωνται περὶ κ. Il.4.53; περὶ κ... ἐχολώθη 13.206; νεμεσσῶμαι π. κῆρι ib.119; for λάσιον κ. v. λάσιος; later κῆρ ἅσα βόρηται dub. in Sapph.*Supp*.25.18; ἐμὸν κέαρ οὐ γεύεται ὕμνων Pi.*I*.5(4).20, cf. *N*. 7.102, B.16.108, etc.; κέαρ ἀπαράμυθον A.*Pr*.187 (lyr.); ἠλγύνθην, ἠχθέσθην κέαρ, ib.247, 392, etc.; paratrag., τὸ κέαρ ηὐφράνθην Ar. *Ach*.5. (With nom. κῆρ cf. OPruss. *seyr*, Arm. *sirt*, 'heart', I.-E. *k̑ērd*- (cf. καρδία); κέαρ is perh. a later formation on the analogy of ἔαρ: ἦρ.)

**κῆρα**, ἡ, Lat. *cera, wax tablet*, *POxy*.2110.4 (iv A.D.).

**κηραίνω** (A), (κήρ) *harm, destroy*, A.*Supp*.999, Ph.1.653:—Pass., *to be injured, spoiled, perish*, *Placit*.2.4.12, Hierocl. *in CA*14 p.451 M. **II.** intr., *to be blemished* or *imperfect*, Ph.1.280, al.

**κηραίνω** (B), (κῆρ) *to be sick at heart, anxious*, E.*HF*518; τι *at* a thing, Id.*Hipp*.223 (anap.); ἐπί τινι Max.93; κ. περί τι Ph.2.205, al.

**κηρᾰμύντης**, ου, ὁ, (ἀμύνω) *averter of evil*, epith. of Heracles, Lyc. 663.

**κηράνθεμος**, ὁ, = κήρινθος, Dsc.2.82 (pl.), 5.9.

⊛ **κηραφίς**, ίδος, ἡ, a kind of *locust*, Nic.*Al*.394; = κάραβος, Hsch.

**κηρ-ᾰχάτης** [χᾱ], ου, ὁ, *wax-agate*, Plin.*HN*37.139. **-έλαιον**, τό, *wax-oil*, a kind of *salve*, Gal.6.445, 13.953. **-εμβροχή**, ἡ, *fomentation with melted wax*, Alex.Trall.12.

**κηρέσιος**, ον, (κήρ) *deadly, pernicious*, Hsch.

**κηρεσσῐφόρητος**, ον, *urged on by the* Κῆρες, ἐξελάαν... κύνας κηρεσσιφορήτους Il.8.527.

**κηρία**, ἡ, v. κειρία.

**κηριάζω**, *spawn*, of the purple-fish (πορφύρα), whose spawn is like a honeycomb (κηρίον), Arist.*HA*546$^{b}$25, *GA*761$^{b}$32.

**κηριάπτης**, *ceriforus, ceriolum*, *Gloss.*:—Dim. ⊛ **κηριαπτάριον**, τό, *PMasp*.340 *B*77 (vi A.D.).

**κηρ-ίδιον**, τό, Dim. of κηρίον, *honeycomb*, Aët.5.137 (pl.). **-ίζω**, *have a waxy appearance*, Zos.Alch.p.215 B. **-ίνη** [ῐ], ἡ, = κηρίων II, Hsch., Phot. **II.** (sc. ἔμπλαστρος) name of a *plaster*, Asclep.ap. Gal.13.936.

**κήρινθος**, ὁ, *bee-bread*, = ἐριθάκη, Arist.*HA*623$^{b}$23, Plin.*HN*11.17, Hsch. **II.** kind of *ulcer*, Id.

⊛ **κήρῐνος**, η, ον, (κηρός) *waxen*, Ar.*Ec*.1035, Archipp.3 D., Pl.*Tht.* 191c, 197d; κηρίνα ὀπώρα, i.e. *honey*, Alcm.75. **II.** metaph., *pliable as wax*, τοὺς θυμοὺς.. κηρίνους ποιεῖν Pl.*Lg*.633d; κηρίνας τὰς ὑπολήψεις ἔχειν Arr.*Epict*.3.16.10. **2.** *wax-coloured, pallid*, Suid. s.v. ἐκηριώθην. **3.** of women, '*made up' with cosmetics*, Philostr. *Ep*.22, cf. *VA*2.22.

**κηριο-ελκός**, ὁ, *one who makes wax lights*, *PRyl*.374.3 (i B.C./ i A.D.). **-κλέπτης**, ου, ὁ, *stealer of honeycombs*, title of Theocritus' nineteenth Idyll.

**κηριολάριον**, *cerilarium*, *Gloss.*

⊛ **κηρίολος**, ὁ, prob. *wax taper* or *wax figure*, *CIG*3028.5 (Ephesus).

⊛ **κηρίον**, τό, (κηρός) *honeycomb*, mostly in pl., *h.Merc*.559, Hes.*Th*. 597, Hdt.5.114, etc.; κ. καὶ λίβανον, as offerings, *Supp.Epigr*.3.774 (Crete, i B.C.): sg., Pl.*R*.552c, Theoc.19.2, *IG*5(2).514.14 (Lycosura, ii B.C.); τὸ κ. τοῦ μέλιτος Lxx 1*Ki*.14.27; used in Medicine, Hp. *Morb*.2.45, 3.17; παιδίον κηρίῳ βεβυσμένον having its mouth stopped with *a piece of honeycomb*, Ar.*Th*.506, cf. Sch. ad loc., Sor.1.86; κ. σφηκῶν Hdt.2.92: κηρία, τά, *honey*, Hippon.36, Aristo ap.Ath.2. 38f. **2.** metaph., of a book of poems, *AP*9.190: pl., title of Anthologies, Gell.*Praef*.6. **3.** metaph., of anything pleasant, τῆς ἐπιθυμίας τὸ κ. Lib.*Ep*.112.1. **II.** *a cutaneous disease*, = μελικηρίς, Dsc.2.135 (pl.), Gal.7.728, al.

**κηριόομαι**, Pass., *to be panic-stricken*, Hsch. (cf. eund. s.v. ἐκηριώθη), Suid., prob. in *Anacreont*.13.18.

**κηριοποιός**, όν, *making honeycombs*, Arist.*HA*623$^{b}$7.

**κηρίς**, ίδος, ἡ, = κιρρίς, Diph.Siph.ap.Ath.8.355d, Alex.Trall.7.1, 8.2, al.

**κηρῖτις** (sc. λίθος), ἡ, a precious stone *like wax*, Plin.*HN*37.153.

**κηρι-τρεφής**, ές, (τρέφω) *born to misery*, ἄνθρωποι Hes.*Op*.418, cf. Orac.ap.Sch.E.*Ph*.638. **-φάτοι**, οἱ, (θείνω) = ὅσοι νόσῳ τεθνήκασιν, Hsch.

**κηρι-ώδης**, ες, *arranged like a honeycomb*, Thphr.*HP*3.13.3. **-ωμα**, ατος, τό, *rheum in the eyes*, S.*Fr*.715. **-ων**, ωνος, ὁ, *wax light, waxen torch*, Plu.2.263f, Gal.17(2).267. **II.** *whip*, Hsch. and Phot. s.v. κηρίναι.

**κηρο-γονία**, ἡ, *formation of wax* or *combs*, Lxx 4*Ma*.14.19. **-γρᾰφέω**, *paint with wax*, *Inscr.Délos* 290.112 (iii B.C.), Callix.2 (Pass.). **-γρᾰφία**, ἡ, *painting with wax*, i.e. *encaustic painting*, πᾶς τόπος κηρογραφίᾳ κατεπεποίκιλτο Id.1. **-δέτης**, ου, Dor. **-δέτας**, ὁ, = sq., κάλαμος E.*IT*1125 (lyr.). **-δετος**, ον, (δέω A) *bound* or *joined with wax*, μέλι *APl*.4.305 (Antip.); σῦριγξ Euph.ap.Ath. 4.184a; κ. πνεῦμα the breath *of the wax-joined pipe*, Theoc.*Ep*.5. 4. **-δομέω**, *build with wax*, of bees, Ps.-Phoc.174. **-ειδής**, ές, *like wax, waxen*, σώματα Pl.*Ti*.61c, etc.: metaph., of the soul, Ph.1.64. **2.** *wax-coloured*, *PSI*4.444.3 (iii B.C.), Dsc.1.119.

**κηρόθεν**, Adv., (κῆρ) *from the heart*, *EM*511.20.

**κηρόθι**, Adv., (κῆρ) *with all the heart, heartily*, in Hom. always folld. by μᾶλλον, ἀπήχθετο κ. μ. Il.9.300; χολώσατο κ. μ. 21.136, cf. Od.5.284, etc.; φίλει δέ με κ. μ. 15.370; τίον δ' ἐ κ. μ. Hes.*Sc*.85.

⊛ **κηρό-κλυστος**, ον, *coated with wax*, *PSI*6.594.20 (iii B.C.). **-μάρμᾰρος**, ὁ, *cement* for making drainpipes watertight, Steph. *in Hp.* 2.384 D. **-μελι**, ιτος, τό, *honey in the comb*, Sch.rec.Theoc.7.83, prob. in Zos.Alch.p.113 B.

**κηρόν**· λεπτόν, νοσερόν, Hsch. **κηρόομαι**, Pass., (κήρ II) *to be destroyed, injured*, *EM*322.13.

**κηροπᾰγής**, ές, *fastened with wax*, θαλάμαι *AP*6.239 (Apollonid.), cf. Man.1.242.

**κηροπάζουσα**· βαστάζουσα, Hsch.

**κηρόπισσος**, ὁ, *wax-pitch*, an ointment, Hp.*Morb*.2.18, cf. *Gloss.*

**κηροπλαστ-έω**, *mould of* or *in wax*, Hp.*Art*.62; κ. Ἔρωτα Eub. 41; *mould as in wax*, ἐκηροπλάστεεν τὸν ἄνθρωπον ἡ φύσις Aret.*SD* 2.13. **2.** *make wax cells*, D.S.17.75, 19.2. ⊛ **-ης**, ου, ὁ, *modeller in wax*: *modeller*, Pl.*Ti*.74c, Ptol.*Tetr*.180. ⊛ **-ικός**, ή, όν, ἡ -κή (sc. τέχνη) Poll.7.165; ἡ ὕλη [ἐστὶν ἄμορφος] πρὸς -κήν Ocell.2.3. **-ος**, ον, (πλάσσω) *moulded of wax*, μελίσσης κ. ὄργανον S.*Fr*.398.5: metaph., of a girl, *AP*9.570 (Phld.). **2.** = κηρόδετος, δόναξ A. *Pr*.574 (lyr.).

⊛ **κηρο-ποιός**, όν, *making wax*, Sch.Ar.*V*.1075. **-πώλης**, ου, ὁ, *wax-chandler*, *Gloss.*

⊛ **κηρός**, ὁ, *bees-wax*, Od.12.48, Theoc.1.27, etc.; *honeycomb*, Id. 20.27; εὐπλαστότερον κηροῦ Pl.*R*.588d; used as a cosmetic, Philostr. *Ep*.22; in encaustic painting, *IG*4²(1).102.272 (Epid., iv B.C.), 14. 1320; for writing tablets, *POxy*.736.16 (i A.D.), etc.: hence λόγους εἰς γραμμάτιον καὶ κηρὸν ἐρχομένους Lib.*Ep*.886.1. **2.** *sealing-wax*, Luc.*Alex*.21. **3.** κ. Τυρρηνικός *white wax* used in medicine, Gal.13. 411, Dsc.1.70. **II.** pl. κηροί *wax tapers*, Hld.9.11. (Panhellenic η, *IG*4².l.c., Theoc. ll. cc., cf. κήρινος, κηρόδετος, κηροχυτέω; Lat. *cera*.)

**κηροσσαίων**· παλαιῶν, Hsch.

**κηροτᾰκίς**, ίδος, ἡ, *hot palette, hot plate*, used by painters for keep-

ing wax paints hot, and by alchemists, *PHolm.*6.33, Syn.Alch.p.60 B., Zos.Alch.p.158 B., etc.

**κηρο-τέχνης**, ου, ὁ, *modeller in wax*, Anacreont.10.9. ⊛ **-τρόφος** (A), ον, (κήρ) *death-breeding, deadly*, ὄφις Nic.*Th.*192. **-τροφος** (B), ον, (κηρός) *waxen*, δῶρα μελισσῶν *AP*6.236 (Phil.).

**κηρούει**· ἐκεῖ (Cret.), Hsch. (nisi leg. κηνούει).

**κηρουλκός**, όν, (κήρ, ἕλκω) *bringing destruction*, Lyc.407.

**κηρόφιν**, *from the heart*, Hsch.

**κηρο-φορέω**, *produce wax*, Suid. **-φόρον**, *cerostatarium*, *Gloss.* **-χίτων** [ῐ], ωνος, ὁ, ἡ, *clad in wax*, λαμπάς *AP*6.249 (Antip.). **-χρως**, ωτος, ὁ, ἡ, *wax-coloured*, κόμαι Chaerem.1.5 (fort. κιρρό-, q.v.). **-χῠτέω**, *mould as in wax*, Ar.*Th.*56 (anap.); κηροχυτεῖ τὰν ψυχάν Hippod.ap.Stob.4.1.94. **-χῠτος**, ον, *moulded of wax*, κ. μέλιγμα, of the melody of Pan, Castorio 2.5; dub. in Pl. *Epigr.*32.

**κηρόω**, *wax over*, [δέλτον] Herod.3.15, cf. Tryph.*Trop.*p.195 S. (Pass.), *PMag.Par.*1.3214:—Pass., Hp.*Art.*30; κεκηρῶσθαι τὰ ἔσωθεν [τῆς κλεψύδρας] Aen.Tact.22.25; *to be fastened with wax*, [σῦριγξ] κεκήρωτο Longus 2.35. II. Med., *form for oneself in wax*, ἄγγεα *AP*9.226 (Zon.).

**κήρτεα**· τὰ κέρδη, Hsch.

⊛ **κήρυγ-μα**, ατος, τό, (κηρύσσω) *that which is cried by a herald, proclamation*, S.*Ichn.*13, etc.; κ. ποιέεσθαι Hdt.3.52; ἐκ τοῦ κ. *by proclamation*, Id.6.78; πόλει κ. θεῖναι S.*Ant.*8; τῷ κ. ἐμμένειν Id.*OT* 350, cf. *Ant.*454; κ. ἀνειπεῖν Th.4.105; κηρύσσειν Aeschin.3.154; κ. γιγνόμενον D.18.83; *announcement* of victory in games, D.C.63.14; *mandate, summons*, S.*Ant.*162 (anap.); *reward offered by proclamation*, X.*HG*5.4.10, Aeschin.3.33. II. *preaching*, *Ev.Luc.* 11.32, al. **-μός**, ὁ, = κήρυξις, Sch.B Il.21.575.

**κηρύκ-αινα** [ῠ], ἡ, fem. of κῆρυξ, Ar.*Ec.*713. II. at Alexandria, a kind of *charwoman*, Suid. **-εία**, Ion. **-ηΐη**, ἡ, *office of herald* or *crier*, Hdt.7.134 (pl.), Pl.*Lg.*742b, *IG*2².145; ἐπὶ κηρυκείαν ἀποστέλλεσθαι on an *embassy*, Lex ap.Aeschin.1.21. 2. *crier's pay*, Is.*Fr.* 46. **-ειον**, Ion. **-ήϊον**, Dor. **κᾱρύκειον**, τό, *herald's wand*, Hdt.9.100, Th.1.53, *IG*12(8).51.24 (Imbros, ii B.C.), Ph.2.560; κ. συμπεπλεγμένα ἐκ τῶν θαλλῶν, = ἱκετηρίαι, Din.1.18: prov., τὸ κ. ἢ τὴν μάχαιραν 'peace or the sword', Phot.: as signet, *Tab.Heracl.* 1.4, 2.3; **-ιον**, Ar.*Fr.*518, Hsch. s.v. δράκοντα; also with ῠ, *AP* 11.124 (Nicarch.). 2. the constellation *Caduceus*, Hipparch.ap. Gem.3.13 (-ιον codd.), Vett.Val.7.6. II. *tax on auction sales*, *PSI*5.543.59 (iii B.C.), *PEleph.*14.12 (iii B.C.); *auctioneer's fee*, *SIG* 1011.23 (Chalcedon, iii/ii B.C.), Suid.; φέρειν ἠξίου κηρύκιον stooped to win a *tale-bearer's fee*, Jul.*Or.*2.96a. III. *the stone* whence the herald made his proclamations, Hsch., Suid. IV. *surgical machine*, Orib.49.4.64. **-ειος**, ον, *of a herald*, γράμμα S.*Fr.* 784; γραφή Anon.ap.Suid. II. **Κᾱρυκήϝιος**, ὁ, Boeot. title of Apollo, *Schwyzer* 440.10,11 (Tanagra, Thebes, vi B.C.). **-ευμα**, ατος, τό, *proclamation, message*, A.*Th.*651. **-ευσις**, εως, ἡ, = κηρυκεία, Suid. **-εύω**, *perform the office of a herald*, Pl.*Lg.*941a, Aeschin.1.19; κ. τινί *to be* his *herald*, Lycurg. in *Gött.Nachr.*1922.45, Philoch.36: c. gen., κ. τῆς βουλῆς *IG*3.1128 (ii A.D.). II. trans., *proclaim, notify*, τινί τι A.*Supp.*221, cf. E.*Tr.*787 (anap.). **-ηΐη**, **-ήϊον**, Ion. for κηρυκεία, -ειον. **-ίδαι**, v. κῆρυξ I. 1a. ⊛ **-ικός**, ή, όν, *of heralds*, φῦλον, ἔθνος, Pl.*Plt.*260d, 290b: ἡ -κή (sc. τέχνη) ib.260e. **-ῖνος**, η, ον, *of a herald*, ῥάβδος Suid. II. **-ίνη**, ἡ, = κηρύκαινα, Hsch., Phot.; but (sc. ἀρχή), *crier's office*, *CPR*232.29 (ii/iii A.D.). **-ιοειδής** (-κοειδ- cod.), ές, *like a herald's staff*, Hsch. s.v. Ἑρμῆς. **-ιον**, τό, v. κηρύκειον. II. *eye-salve*, Alex.Trall. 2. III. in pl., *sharp, pointed stones*, Paul.Aeg.6.88. **-ιοφόρος**, ον, *bearing a herald's staff*, *EM*812.26 (prob.), *Gloss.* **-τικός**, ή, όν, = κηρυκικός, Gal.1.227. **-τός**, ή, όν, *announced by public herald*, στέφανος Inscr. cit. ad *BMus.Inscr.*1032.10, *BCH*17.545. **-ώδης**, ες, *like* (that of) *the trumpet-shell* κῆρυξ (II), Arist.*HA*527ª28.

**κηρύλος** [ῠ], ὁ, fabulous sea-bird, sts. identified with ἀλκυών, or the male of that species (cf. Antig.ap.Hsch.), Alcm.26.2, Archil.141 (cf. 49 D.), Arist.*HA*593ᵇ12, Clearch.73, Ael.*NA*5.48: **κειρύλος**, Ar. *Av.*300 (cf. Sch. ad loc., Hsch.), applied to the barber Sporgilos (from κείρω).

**κήρῡνος**, ὁ, *a throw of the dice*, Eub.57.2; **κάρυννος**, Phot.

⊛ **κῆρυξ**, ῡκος, ὁ, Aeol. **κᾶρυξ** [ᾱ] Sapph.*Supp.*20a.2, Pi.*N.*8.1:—but **κήρῡκος**, ου, ὁ, *EM*775.26: (κηρύσσω):—*herald, pursuivant*: generally, *public messenger, envoy*, κ. λιγύφθογγοι Il.2.50, al.; κηρύκων, οἳ δημιοεργοὶ ἔασιν Od.19.135; κ. Διὶ φίλοι Il.8.517; κ., Διὸς ἄγγελοι ἠδὲ καὶ ἀνδρῶν 1.334; θεῶν κ., of Hermes, Hes.*Op.*80, cf. *Th.*939, A.*Ag.* 515, *Ch.*124: distd. from πρέσβεις, as being *messengers between nations at war*, Sch.Th.1.29, cf. A.*Supp.*727, Pl.*Lg.*941a, D.12.4: used interchangeably with ἀπόστολος, Hdt.1.21: as pr. n. of a family at Athens, Th.8.53, And.1.116, Paus.1.38.3, Poll.8.103; functioning as μάγειροι at festivals, Clidem.3,17; Κηρυκίδαι Phot. b. as fem., Pi.*N.*8.1, Nonn.*D.*4.11. 2. *crier*, who made proclamation and kept order in assemblies, etc., Ar.*Ach.*42 sq.; ὁ κ. ἀνεῖπεν And.1.36, etc.; ὁ τῶν μυστῶν κ., at Eleusis, X.*HG*2.4.20, cf. *SIG*845 (Eleusis, iii A.D.), Philostr.*VS*2.33.4. 3. *auctioneer*, ὑπὸ κήρυκος πωλεῖν Thphr.*Fr.*97: ἀπέδοτο πάντα τὰ ἔργα ὑπὸ κήρυκα *IPE*1².32*B*35 (Olbia, iii B.C.), cf. *PHib.*1.29.21 (iii B.C.); ἀποδίδοσθαι ὑπὸ κήρυκι Ammon. *Diff.*p.81 V. (v.l. ὑπὸ κήρυκα Ptol.Asc.p.399 H.). 4. generally, *messenger, herald*, θεοὶ κήρυκες ἀγγέλλουσι S.*OC*1511, cf. E.*El.*347; of the cock, Ar.*Ec.*30; of writing, Id.*Th.*780 (anap.); κ. καὶ τάφος εἰμὶ βροτοῦ *IG*14.1618; of Homer, ἡρώων κάρυκ' ἀρετᾶς ib.1188: metaph., κ. καὶ ἀπόστολος 1*Ep.Ti.*2.7, al. II. *trumpet-shell*, e.g. *Triton nodiferum*, and smaller species, Arist.*HA*528ª10, al., Hp.*Vict.*2.48, Diocl.*Fr.*133, Macho ap.Ath.8.349c, Gal.4.670, Alciphr.1.7, Alex. Trall.3.7. [ῡ exc. acc. pl. κήρῠκας Antim.19 (s.v.l.), cf. κηρῠκιον *AP* 11.124 (Nicarch.): but accented κῆρυξ, Hdn.Gr.1.44, etc.] (Cf. Skt. *kārú*s 'poet', *kīrtis* 'fame'.)

**κήρυξις**, εως, ἡ, *proclaiming*, as a subject of competition, D.C.63.8, 14.

⊛ **κηρύσσω**, Att. **-ττω**, Dor. **κᾱρύσσω**: impf. ἐκήρυσσον Il.2.444, Th. 1.27, -υττον And.1.112: fut. -ύξω Ar.*Ec.*684, Dor. καρυξῶ Id.*Ach.* 748: aor. ἐκήρυξα Hdt.1.194 (ἀπο-), etc., Aeol. part. καρύξαισα Pi.*I.*4(3).25: pf. κεκήρῦχα (ἐπι-) D.19.35:—Pass., fut. κηρυχθήσομαι X. *Cyr.*8.4.4, Aeschin.3.230, κηρύξομαι E.*Ph.*1631: aor. ἐκηρύχθην S. *OT*737, etc.: pf. κεκήρυγμαι E.*Fr.*1, Th.4.38:—*to be a herald, officiate as herald*, κηρύσσων γήρασκε Il.17.325. b. *to be an auctioneer*, D. 44.4. 2. *make proclamation as a herald*, λαὸν κηρύσσοντες ἀγειρόντων let them convene the people *by voice of herald*, Il.2.438, cf. 444, Od.2.8; κήρυσσε, κῆρυξ A.*Eu.*566, etc.: impers., ἐκήρυξε (sc. ὁ κῆρυξ) τοῖς Ἕλλησι συσκευάζεσθαι *proclamation was made*.., X.*An.*3.4. 36; κηρυξάτω Id.*Cyr.*4.5.42. II. c. acc. pers., *summon by herald*, κ. ἀγορήνδε..Ἀχαιούς Il.2.51, Od.2.7; πόλεμόνδε Il.2.443; κ. τινά *summon* one to a place, Ar.*Ach.*748:—Pass., τίς ἐκηρύχθη πρώτην φυλακήν; who *was summoned* to the first watch? E.*Rh.*538 (anap.). 2. *proclaim* as conqueror, Plu.2.185a; Φαβωρῖνον ἡ εὐγλωττία ἐν σοφισταῖς ἐκήρυττεν Philostr.*VS*1.8.1:—Pass., μήτε κηρυχθήσεσθαι μήτε ἆθλα λήψεσθαι X.*Cyr.*8.4.4; ὥστε τὴν πόλιν κηρυχθῆναι καὶ αὐτὸν στεφανωθῆναι Lys.19.63; *proclaim* as a criminal, D.25.56, cf. S.*El.*606; κηρύσσω τὸν Ἔρωτα *AP*5.176 (Mel.):—Pass., of a country, *to be proclaimed, extolled*, στεφάνοις ἀρετᾶς E.*Tr.*223 (lyr.). 3. *call upon, invoke*, θεούς Id.*Hec.*146 (anap.); κηρύξας δαίμονας κλύειν A.*Ch.*124a:—Pass., *to be called*, τοῦ κεκήρυξαι πατρός; E.*Fr.*1; κηρυσσομένοισι.. ἀπ' ἐσθλῶν δωμάτων Id.*Andr.*772 (lyr.). III. c. acc. rei, *proclaim, announce*, τινί τι A.*Ag.*1349, *Ch.*4, 1026; αὐδάν E.*Ion* 911 (lyr.); ἀγῶνας Ἀργείοισι S.*Aj.*1240; *proclaim* or *advertise* for sale, etc., Hdt.6.121 (Pass.), Plu.2.207a, etc.; κ. ἀποικίαν *proclaim* a colony, i.e. *invite* people to join as colonists, Th.1.27; κ. ὃς βούλοιτο.. *make proclamation* for some one who would.., Hdt.2.134:—Pass., of a crime, *to be proclaimed*, Antipho 2.3.2; τὰ κεκηρυγμένα Th.4.38. 2. *declare, tell*, τοῦτ' ἐκηρύχθη πόλει this *news was spread* in.., S.*OT*l.c.; τοῦτο κ. πόθι παῖς ναίει Id.*Tr.*97 (lyr.); ὃ εἰς τὸ οὖς ἀκούετε, κηρύξατε ἐπὶ τῶν δωμάτων *Ev.Matt.*10.27: abs., S.*El.* 1105. 3. *proclaim, command publicly*, τινί τι A.*Th.*1048, S.*Ant.* 32, 450, etc.; εὐφημίαν, σιγὴν κ., Id.*Fr.*893, E.*Hec.*530: c. dat. pers. et inf., κ. αὐτοῖς ἐμβαλεῖν κώπαισι Pi.*P.*4.200; ἐκήρυξαν, εἰ βούλονται, τὰ ὅπλα παραδοῦναι Th.4.37:—Pass., ᾔδησθα κηρυχθέντα μὴ πράσσειν τάδε; S.*Ant.*447. 4. of a cock, *crow*, *AP*5.2 (Antip.Thess.). IV. *preach, teach publicly*, *Ev.Matt.*3.1, al.

**κηρ-ώδης**, ες, *wax-like*, dub. l. for κηριώδης, Gal.10.476 (Comp.); = μαλθώδης, Id.19.120. ⊛ **-ωμα**, ατος, τό, = κηρωτή, *wax-salve, cerate*, Hp.*Acut.*(*Sp.*) 5, 33 (both pl.), Orib.*Fr.*63 (pl.). 2. *layer of mud* or *clay forming the floor of the wrestling-ring* in the times of the Empire, Lat. *ceroma*, *locus exercitii utilis..aequali et molli ceromate stratus*, Cael.Aur.*Salut.Praec.*35 (ed. V. Rose *Anecd.Gr.*2.199), cf. Plu.2.638c, Plin.*HN*35.168, Mart.4.19.5, al.; *a ceromate nos haphe excepit*, out of the *mud* into the dust, Sen.*Ep.*57.1: metaph. for *the wrestling-ring* or *wrestling*, ἐν παλαίστραις καὶ κηρώμασι Plu.2.79cf, cf. Plin.*HN*35.5. 3. *waxed tablet* or *board*, *IG*7.413.59 (S. C. de Orop.). **-ωματικός**, ὁ, *one who deals in* κηρώματα 1, *POxy.*43ᵛiii 21 (iii/iv A.D.); Lat. *ceromaticus*, *of* or *with a* κήρωμα 1, *defricationes*, Cass.Fel.55; but, *bespattered with* κήρωμα 2, Juv.3.68. ⊛ **-ωματιστής**, οῦ, ὁ, *one who anoints with* κήρωμα 1, Sch.Ar.*Eq.*490. ⊛ **-ών**, ῶνος, ὁ, (κηρός) *bee-hive*, Sch.Ar.*Ec.*737. ⊛ **-ωσις**, εως, ἡ, *material of bees-wax*, Arist.*HA*553ᵇ28. **-ωτάριον**, τό, *wax plaster*, Sor.1.50, Damocr.ap.Gal.13.225.

**κηρωτή**, ἡ, (κηρόω) = κήρωμα 1, *cerate* or *salve*, used medically, Hp.*Off.*12, *Art.*14, Ar.*Ach.*1176, Ph.*Bel.*96.18; κ. οἰνανθίνη, ῥοδίνη, Dsc.1.109, 2.110; κ. ὑγρά Gal.11.391; used as a cosmetic, Ar.*Fr.* 320.1.

**κηρωτο-ειδής**, ές, *like a cerate*, Gal.13.118, Aët.16.61; **-ώδης**, ες, Gal.12.813. **-μάλαγμα** [μᾰ], ατος, τό, *wax plaster*, Id.13.1006.

**κησσόν**· εὔοδμον, Hsch. (i.e. κηῶεν). **κήτα**, ἡ, = καλαμίνθη, Id. (cf. καιετάεις).

**κητ-εία**, ἡ, *fishing for large fish*, esp. *the tunny*, Ael.*NA*13.16. 2. *the place where it is carried on*, Str.5.4.4 (pl.), Ath.7.283c (pl.). ⊛ **-ειος**, ον, (κῆτος) *of sea monsters*, νῶτα Mosch.2.119; γέννες Nonn.*D.*30. 240; πέλωρα *Inscr.Perg.*324.28: generally, *monstrous*, Hsch. II. **Κήτειοι**, οἱ, an unknown race in Mysia, Od.11.521, cf. Str.13.1. 70. **-ημα**, ατος, τό, *salted tunny*, = ὠμοτάριχος, dub. in Diph.Siph. ap.Ath.3.121b. **-ήνη**· πλοῖον μέγα ὡς κῆτος, Hsch.

**κήτιον**, = γήτειον, used as an emetic, Cratin.266. II. v. κήθιον.

**κητό-δορπος** συμφορά, ἡ, *supplying food for sea-monsters*, Lyc. 954. **-θηρεῖον** (-θήριον codd.), τό, *magazine of implements for the fishery of large fish*, Ael.*NA*13.16. **-ομαι**, Pass., *grow to a sea-monster*, ib.14.23.

**κῆτος**, εος, τό, *any sea-monster* or *huge fish*, δελφῖνάς τε κύνας τε καὶ εἴ ποθι μεῖζον ἕλῃσι κῆτος Od.12.97, cf. 5.421, Il.20.147, Mosch.2. 116; of seals, Od.4.446, 452; of the monster to which Andromeda was exposed, E.*Fr.*121, cf. Ar.*Nu.*556, *Th.*1033; of the tunny, Archestr.*Fr.*34.3. 2. in Natural History, of the spouting *cetacea*,

Arist.*HA*566$^{b}$2, *PA*669$^{a}$8, 697$^{a}$16. II. name of a constellation, Arat.354, Eudox.ap.Hipparch.1.2.20.

**κητο-τρόφος,** ον, *nourishing sea-monsters*, Eust.294.16. **-φάγος** [ᾰ], ον, *eating sea-monsters*, prob. f.l. for σιτοφάγος, Paus.10.12.3. **-φόνος,** ον, *killing sea-monsters*, *AP*6.38 (Phil.), Opp.*H*.5.113.

**κητ-ώδης,** ες, of fish, *cetaceous*: τὰ κ. *animals of the whale kind*, Arist.*Resp*.476$^{b}$13, cf. *HA*591$^{b}$26; of *coarse* fishes (dogfish, etc.), Gal.6.728, Xenocr.ap.Orib.2.58.84, Alex.Trall.1.15. II. generally, *monstrous*, ἐλέφαντες καὶ ἄλλα ζῷα κ. D.S.2.54. ⊛ **-ώεις,** εσσα, εν, Homeric epith. of Lacedaemon, κοίλη Λακεδαίμων κητώεσσα Il.2.581, Od.4.1; perh. *full of hollows* or *ravines*, variously expld. ap. Str.8.5.7, Apollon.*Lex*., etc.; cf. καιετάεσσα. II. in later Ep., *cavernous*, of the wooden horse, Q.S.12.314. 2. = κήτειος, πώεα Nonn.*D*.43.251; φάλαγξ ib.1.274.

**κῆϋξ,** ϋκος [ῡ], v. κήξ.

**κήϋος,** α, ον, perh. *purificatory*, or *burnt* (καίω), θύεν τρικτεύαν κηύαν *IG*2$^{2}$.1126.34 (Amphict. Delph.); cf. κεῖα, κήϊα.

**Κηφεύς,** έως, ὁ, *Cepheus*, Hdt.7.61, etc.: name of a constellation, Eudox.ap.Hipparch.1.2.11.

⊛ **κηφήν,** ῆνος, ὁ, *drone*, Diph.126.7, Arist.*HA*553$^{b}$5, 624$^{b}$12; κηφήνεσσι εἴκελος ὀργήν, of a *lazy vagabond*, Hes.*Op*.304, cf. *Th*.595, Ar.*V*.1114; ὡς ἐν κηρίῳ κ. ἐγγίγνεται Pl.*R*.552c; of literary plagiarists, *AP*7.708 (Diosc.), Plu.2.42a: metaph., of worn-out, decrepit persons, ποῦ γαίας δουλεύσω γραῦς, ὡς κ.; E.*Tr*.192 (lyr.), cf. *Ba*.1365; cf. κόθουροι:—also **καφάν,** Hsch.

**Κηφῆνες,** οἱ, *Cephenes*, old name of the Persians, Hdt.7.61.

**κηφήν-ιον,** τό, Dim. of κηφήν, *drone's grub*, Arist.*HA*623$^{b}$34; *drone's cell*, ib.624$^{a}$2. **-ώδης,** ες, *like* (*that of*) *a drone*, ἐπιθυμία Pl.*R*.554b; of theories, *useless, otiose*, Cleom.2.1; of a person, κ. καὶ γέρων γενόμενος Phld.*Mort*.38.

**Κηφίσιος,** Dor. **Κᾱφ-,** ὁ (sc. μήν), name of month at Cos, *SIG* 953.27 (ii B.C.).

**Κηφῑσός,** Dor. **Κᾱφ-,** ὁ, *Cephisus*, name of various rivers, 1. in Phocis, running into Lake Copais, Il.2.522, Pi.*P*.4.46:—fem. λίμνη **Κηφισίς,** Il.5.709, *h.Ap*.280:—Dor. **Κᾱφ-,** of the nymph Copais, Pi.*P*.12.27:—Adj. **Κηφίσιος,** α, ον, Dor. **Κᾱφ-,** Id.*O*.14.1. 2. at Athens, S.*OC*687 (lyr.), etc. 3. in Argolis, etc., Str.9.3.16, etc.:—freq. written Κηφισσός in codd., but -σ- in derivs. in Att. Inscrr.

**κηχί** (also **κηχή, κῆχυ** Cyr.), = ῥύπος, Hsch.

**κῆχος** (also **κῆγχος** Hsch., **κηγχός** A.D.*Adv*.184.9), only in phrase ποῖ κ.; which some Gramm. expl. by ποῖ γῆς; *whither away?* some by ποῖ δή; *say whither?* as, ποῖ κ.; Answ. εὐθὺς Σικελίας Ar.*Fr*.656; ποῖ κ.; Answ. ἐγγὺς ἡμερῶν γε τεττάρων Pherecr.165.

**κη-ώδης,** ες, (κη- cogn. with κήϊα, καίω; -ώδης with ὄδωδα) *smelling as of incense, fragrant*, μιν κηώδεϊ δέξατο κόλπῳ Il.6.483; κηώδεα φύετο πάντα D.P.941; cf. κεώδης. **-ώεις,** εσσα, εν, = foreg., ἐν θαλάμῳ εὐώδεϊ κηώεντι Il.3.382; ἐς θάλαμον..κηώεντα 6.288, etc.; μύρον *AP*7.218.9 (Antip. Sid.); ἄνθεα Nonn.*D*.12.257: neut. κηῶεν Hsch.; cf. κεῶεν.

**κία·** ἡ μέθη, Cyr., Zonar.

**κιάθω,** lengthd. for κίω, only in compd. μετακιάθω (exc. ἐκίαθεν Hsch.); cf. κίατο. **κιανθείς·** ἑταίρα κιανγάλη (λίαν καλή Mein.), Hsch. **κιάντωρ·** κιναιδῶς, Id. **κίασθαι·** κεῖσθαι, and **κίατο·** ἐκινεῖτο, Id. **κίβαλος·** διάκονος, Id. **κίββα·** πήρα (Aetol.), Id.

**κιβδηλ-εία,** ἡ, *adulteration*, Pl.*Lg*.916d, 920c. **-ευμα,** ατος, τό, *an adulteration*, ib.917e. **-εύω,** *adulterate*, κ. τὸ νόμισμα Arist.*EN*1165$^{b}$12: metaph., τὸ ἀρετῆς νόμισμα Ph.1.241; [νομίσματα] οὐ κεκιβδηλευμένα Ar.*Ra*.721; of merchandise, Pl.*Lg*.917b. II. metaph., εὖ κ. τι *trick* it *out*, E.*Ba*.475; *counterfeit*, τἀληθῆ Max.Tyr.28.3; τὴν ἀληθῆ προφητείαν Ph.2.343, cf.1.156 (Pass.). **-ία,** Ion. **-ίη,** ἡ, *adulteration, dishonesty*, Ar.*Av*.158, D.C.52.35; *charlatanry*, κ. δημοειδής Hp.*Art*.78. ⊛ **-ιάω,** prop. *look like adulterated gold*: metaph., *look bilious, have the jaundice*, Arist.*Pr*.859$^{b}$1. ⊛ **-ος,** ον, *adulterated, base*, esp. of coin, χρυσοῦ κιβδήλοιο καὶ ἀργύρου Thgn.119, cf. E.*Med*.516; στατῆρες κ. *IG*2$^{2}$.1388.61; κ. λόγος τοῦ τόκου Pl.*R*.507a; τιμαί, opp. ἀληθεῖς, Id.*Lg*.728d; ἐν δὲ κιβδήλῳ τόδε this may prove *false*, E.*El*.550; τὸ σὰν κίβδαλον *spurious*, Pi.*Dith*.2.3; ἱμάτιον ἐκ δύο ὑφασμένον κ. Lxx *Le*.19.19. II. metaph., *fraudulent, dishonest*, opp. ἀληθής, of men, Thgn.117; κίβδηλον (cj. -λοι)..ἦθος ἔχοντες Id.965; τοῦτο θεὸς κιβδηλότατον ποίησε Id.123; κ. καὶ ἀπατεών, κ. καὶ ἀγαθοφανέες, Democr.63, 82; δίκαιον Arist.*Rh*.1375$^{b}$6; of oracles, etc., *deceitful*, Hdt.1.66,75, 5.91, Max.Tyr.28.3 (Sup.); of women, κ. ἀνθρώποις κακόν E.*Hipp*.616; κ. ἐπιτηδεύματα Pl.*Lg*.918a. (Poll.7.99 cites **κίβδος,** = *dross* or *alloy of gold*; Sch.Ar.*Av*.158 expl. κιβδηλία as *the dross of silver*; Hsch. also cites **κίβδης,** = κακοῦργος, ⟨κά⟩πηλος, χειροτέχνης, and Poll. **κίβδωνες** (v.l. κιβδῶνες Phot.), = μεταλλεῖς, *miners*.)

**κιβικία,** sine expl., Hsch.; cf. κιμβικία. **κιβίνδα·** κατὰ νώτου, Id.; cf. κυβησίνδα.

⊛ **κίβῐσις** [κῐ], ἡ, Cypr. for πήρα (Hsch.), *pouch, wallet*, such as Perseus wore, Hes.*Sc*.224, Pherecyd.11 J., Call.*Fr*.177 (**κίβησις** Suid., Orion 87; **κύβεσις** and **κυβησία** Hsch.; cf. κίββα).

**κιβλεῦραι·** στοχάσασθαι, Hsch. **κίβος,** v. κιβωτός.

⊛ **κῐβώριον,** τό, *seed-vessel of the* κολοκασία, a kind of *Nymphaea*, containing the κύαμος Αἰγύπτιος, Nic.*Fr*.81.3, D.S.1.34, *POxy*.105.18 (ii A.D.); κ. ἢ κιβώτιον Dsc.2.106; of the plant itself, Sor.1.57. II. *cup*, either from the material or the shape, Did.ap.Ath.11.477f, Hegesand.21; used liturgically, *PMag.Par*.1.1110.

**κῖβωτ-άριον,** Dim. of κιβωτός, *small box* or *chamber*, Hero *Aut*.28.4, cf. *CIG*2860ii 12 (Milet.). **-ίδιον,** τό, = foreg., *IG*11(2).147 *B*10 (Delos, iv B.C.). **-ιον,** τό, = foreg., Ar.*Pl*.711, Arist.*Metaph*.1042$^{b}$18, *IG*1$^{2}$.330.20, 2$^{2}$.1388.75, Plu.*Alex*.26, *CPR*22.8 (ii A.D.); *box* for drawing lots, Arist.*Ath*.63.2; *voting-urn*, *SIG*418 *A*7 (Delph., iii B.C.); *ark*, Luc.*Tim*.3.

**κῑβωτο-ειδής,** ές, *like a chest*, Hsch. s.v. θίβη. **-ποιός,** ὁ, *maker of chests*, Plu.2.580e.

⊛ **κῑβωτός,** ἡ, *box, chest, coffer*, Hecat.368 J., Simon.239, Eup.228.4, Ar.*Eq*.1000, *V*.1056 (anap.), Lys.12.10, Thphr.*Char*.18.4, *IG*2$^{2}$.1388.73; κ. δίθυρος, τετράθυρος, ib.1$^{2}$.330; ἱερά, δημοσία κ., *Inscr.Délos* 442 *A* 2,75 (ii B.C.); Noah's *ark*, Lxx *Ge*.6.14; the *ark* of Moses, ib.*Ex*.25.9(10), al.; πέπτωκεν εἰς κ. has been deposited in the *archives*, *UPZ* 126 (iii B.C.), etc.; opp. κίστη (q.v.). (Perh. a v.l. in Il.24.228, cf. Sch.ad loc. Suid. cites **κίβος** as the radic. form.)

**κίγκαλος,** v. κίγκλος.

**κίγκασος,** ὁ, name of a throw at dice, Hsch.; cf. κίκκασος.

**κιγκλ-ίζω,** *wag the tail*, as the bird κίγκλος does: metaph., *change constantly*, οὐ χρὴ κιγκλίζειν ἀγαθὸν βίον, ἀλλ' ἀτρεμίζειν Thgn.303. **-ίς,** ίδος, ἡ, mostly in pl. κιγκλίδες, *latticed gates* in the δικαστήριον or βουλευτήριον, by which the δικασταί or βουλευταί were admitted to pass through the δρύφακτοι or bar, Ar.*Eq*.641, *V*.124: metaph., ῥητορεία κιγκλίδων ἐπιδέουσα καὶ βήματος requiring *the practice of the bar* and the assembly, Plu.2.975c: sg., Lib.*Or*.12.38; ἐντὸς τῆς κ. διατρίβειν live *in court*, Luc.*Merc.Cond*.21; αἱ διαλεκτικαὶ κ. logical *quibbles*, behind which one ensconces oneself, Jul.*Caes*.330c. 2. *any latticed gates*, *IG*2$^{2}$.1668.65 (sg.), 3.162 (pl.). II. later, = δρύφακτοι, Plu.*Caes*.68: sg., Id.*Galb*.14. III. prob. = Lat. *fidiculae*, an instrument of torture, Id.*Luc*.20. **-ῐσις,** εως, ἡ, *quick, jerking movement*, Hp.*Art*.71. **-ισμός,** ὁ, = foreg., ib.14; = τάραχος, Men.478.

**κιγκλοβάτης** [ᾰ], ου, ὁ, *moving like the* κίγκλος, *jerking*, Ar.*Fr*.140.

⊛ **κίγκλος,** ὁ, prob. *dabchick*, *Podiceps ruficollis*, Ar.*Fr*.29, Autocr.1, Anaxandr.41.66, Arist.*HA*593$^{b}$5: prov., κίγκλου πτωχότερος 'poor as a church mouse', because it had no nest of its own, Men.221, cf. Ael.*NA*12.9:—Suid. has **κίγκαλος,** but κιγκάλους is unmetrical as a fish-name in Numen.ap.Ath.7.326a.

**κιγκράμας,** = κύχραμος, Hsch.

**κίγκρημι,** = κεράννυμι, Dor. 3 sg. κίγκρητι Orph.*Fr*.32(b) iv 2; cf. κίγκρα· κίρνα, Hsch.

**κιγχάνω** [ᾰ], v. κιχάνω [ᾱ]. **κίδαλον,** τό, *onion*, Hsch.

**κίδᾰρις,** εως, ἡ, *Persian head-dress*, prob. = τιάρα, κυρβασία, Ph.2.152,155, Poll.7.58, etc.:—also **κίταρις** in Ctes.*Fr*.29.47, Plu.*Art*.28, *Pomp*.42, etc.; Cypr. **κίτταρις** Hsch. 2. *turban of Jewish high priest*, Lxx *Ex*.28.4, al. II. *an Arcadian dance*, Ath.14.631d.

**κίδᾰφος,** η, ον, *wily*, Hsch.:—as Subst. **κίδαφος, κιδάφη** (cf. σκιδάφη), **κινδάφη, κινδάφιος,** = σκίνδαφος, Id., cf. Phot.; **κιδᾰφεύω,** = πανουργέω, Hsch.

**κίδναι,** αἱ, *roasted barley*, Hsch. (fort. κίδραι = τὰ χίδρα).

**κίδναμαι,** Pass. of κίδνημι (only found in the compd. ἐπικ-), poet. for σκεδάννυμαι, used only in pres. and impf., *to be spread abroad* or *over*, of the dawning day, ὑπεὶρ ἅλα κίδναται ἠώς Il.23.227, cf. 8.1; ὀδμὰ κατὰ χῶρον κ. Pi.*Fr*.129.6; κιδναμέναν μελιαδέα γᾶρυν prob. in Simon.41: once in Trag., ὕπνος ἐπ' ὄσσοις κ. E.*Hec*.916 (lyr., v.l. for σκίδ-); κολοιῶν κρωγμὸς..κιδνάμενος *AP*7.713 (Antip.).

**κιδνόν·** ἐνθάδε (Paph.), Hsch.

**κιείνησις,** εως, ἡ, coined as etym. of κίνησις, Pl.*Cra*.426d.

**κιέλλη,** ἡ, *radiance, hoar-frost*, or *mist*, Hsch. **κιθάναλλον,** v. κιττάναλον.

⊛ **κῐθάρ-α,** Ion. **-η** [θᾰ], ἡ, *lyre*, Hdt.1.24, Epich.79, E.*Ion*882 (anap.), etc.; cf. κίθαρις. II. = κίθαρος, *thorax*, *Hippiatr*.46: in pl., *ribs* of the horse, ib.38. **-ᾰοιδός,** ὁ, poet. uncontr. form of κιθαρῳδός: Sup. -ότατος Ar.*V*.1278, Eup.293:—late Boeot. **κιθαραϝυδός** *IG*7.3195.19 (Orchom.). **-ηφόρος,** ὁ, *Lycian coin stamped with a cithara*, *Ath.Mitt*.14.412 (Myra). ⊛ **-ίζω,** Att. fut. -ιῶ Antiph.141: (κίθαρις):—*play the cithara*, φόρμιγγι..ἱμερόεν κιθάριζε Il.18.570, Hes.*Sc*.202; λύρῃ δ' ἐρατὸν κιθαρίζων *h.Merc*.423; ἕρπει ἄντα τῶ σιδάρω τὸ καλῶς κιθαρίσδεν Alcm.35, cf. X.*Smp*.3.1, *Oec*.2.13; ᾄδειν καὶ κ. Phld.*Mus*.7 K.; κιθαρίζειν οὐκ ἐπίσταμαι I am not a 'high-brow', Ar.*V*.989, cf. 959; ἀρχαῖον εἶν' ἔφασκε τὸ κ. Id.*Nu*.1357: prov., ὄνος κιθαρίζειν πειρώμενος, like ὄνος πρὸς λύραν (v. λύρα), Luc.*Pseudol*.7; τὸ κιθαριζόμενον *music composed for the cithara*, Plu.2.1144d. **-ιον,** τό, Dim. of κίθαρος II, Ptol.Euerg.9 J. **-ις,** ιος, ἡ, acc. κίθαριν, = κιθάρα, Hom. (who never uses the latter form), Od.1.153, al., cf. Alc.*Supp*.17, Pi.*P*.5.65, Ar.*Th*.124 (lyr.). II. *playing on the cithara*, οὐκ ἄν τοι χραισμῇ κ. Il.3.54, cf. Od.8.248; κ. καὶ ἀοιδή Il.13.731. **-ῐσις,** εως, ἡ, *playing on the cithara*, Pl.*Prt*.325e; κ. ψιλή, i.e. without the voice, Id.*Lg*.669e, cf. *Pae.Delph*.15; αὔλησις καὶ κ. Phld.*Mus*.p.23 K. ⊛ **-ισμα** [ᾰ], ατος, τό, *that which is played on the cithara, a piece of music for it*, Pl.*Prt*.326b, Max.Tyr.7.6, Ach.Tat.2.1, D.C.63.26; κ. ἐκ Βακχῶν Εὐριπίδου *SIG*648 *B*8 (Delph., ii B.C.). ⊛ **-ισμός,** ὁ, = κιθάρισις, Call.*Del*.312. **-ιστέον,** *one must play the cithara*, Pl.*Sis*.389c. **-ιστήριος,** α, ον, *used to accompany the cithara*. αὐλός Ephor.3 J., Aristox.*Fr.Hist*.67. II. Subst. -τήριον, τό, *performance on the cithara*, *BGU*1125.26 (pl., i B.C.). ⊛ **-ιστής,** οῦ, ὁ, *player on the cithara*, *h.Hom*.25.3, Hes.*Th*.95, Ar.*Eq*.992 (lyr.), *Nu*.964, Arist.*Po*.1455$^{a}$3, *OGI*51.43, etc. II. κ. λίθος stone at Megara *which rang* on being struck, *APl*.4.279 tit. **-ιστικός,** ή, όν, *skilled in cithara-playing*, Pl.*Hp.Mi*.375b (in Comp. -ώτερος), *Ion* 540d, etc.: ἡ -κή (sc. τέχνη) *art of cithara-playing*, Id.*Grg*.501e, Arist.*Po*.1447$^{a}$15. Adv.

-κῶς Plu.2.404f. -ίστρια, ἡ, fem. of κιθαριστής, Arist.*Ath.*50.2, Theopomp.Hist.111a, Theophil.12.5, *AJA*18.1 (Sardis. iii/ii B.C.), *IG*12(8).178 (Samothrace); name of a play by Anaxandrides. -ιστρίς, ίδος, ἡ, = foreg., Nic.Dam.66.26 J. (pl.), Lemma to *AP*5.221 (Agath.). -ιστύς, ύος, ἡ, *the art of playing the cithara*, ἐκλέλαθον κιθαριστύν Il.2.600, cf. Phanocl.1.21. (Ion. word.) ※-ος, ὁ, = θώραξ II, *chest*, Hp.*Loc.Hom.*3, etc. II. kind of *flatfish*, sacred to Apollo, Epich.65, Pherecr.39, Call.Com.3, Arist.*HA*508$^{b}$17, *Fr.*319, Opp.*H.*1.98. (Derived from Κιθαιρών by Duris 80 J.)

**κῐθᾰρῳδ-έω**, *sing to the cithara*, Pl.*Grg.*502a. -ησις, εως, ἡ, *singing to the cithara*, D.C.63.8. -ία, ἡ, = foreg., Pl.*Lg.*700d (pl.), *Ion* 533b. -ικός, ή, όν, *of* or *for cithara-playing*, νόμοι Ar.*Ra.*1282; ᾠδή Pl.*Lg.*722d; ἡ ὑποδωριστὶ -ωτάτη τῶν ἁρμονιῶν Arist.*Pr.*922$^{b}$15: ἡ -κή (sc. τέχνη), = κιθαρῳδία, Pl.*Grg.*502a. Adv. -κῶς Phlp.*in de An.*153.29. ※-ός, ὁ, (κιθάρα, ἀοιδός) *one who plays and sings to the cithara*, Hdt.1.23, *IG*1$^{2}$.547, Pherecr.6.1, Phld.*Mus.*p.28 K., etc.: as fem., κ. γυνή Alciphr.3.33. II. *a fish*, found in the Red Sea, with body striped like the strings of a lyre, Ael.*NA*11.23.

**κίθρα**, ἡ, dub. sens., τῆς (τὰς) ἐκ κίθρας σταφυλῆς (-λάς) Herod. Med. in *Rh.Mus.*58.100,110.

**κῐθών**, Ion. for χιτών, Hdt.1.8, al., also *POxy.*2149.6 (ii/iii A.D.), etc.:—Dim. **κῐθώνιον** *IG*2$^{2}$.1464.13, *POxy.*2149.20, etc.; **κῐθωνίσκος** *IG*2$^{2}$.1523.18.

**κιθώνη**, Ion., = χιτώνη (q.v.), *Milet.*1(7).202.

**κικαῖος**· ἴσον ἐλλύχνιον τὸ τῶν καρπῶν λέπος, Hsch.

**κίκᾰμα** (**κικαμία** Hsch.), ων, τά, *kind of vegetable* resembling καυκαλίς, Nic.*Th.*841. **κικέα**, v. κίκι fin.

**κίκελος**· τροχός, Hsch. **κίκερος**· ὁ χερσαῖος κροκόδειλος, Id.

※**κίκι**, τό (on the accent v. Hdn.Gr.1.354, 2.766; κῖκι codd. Str. et Orib.), *castor-oil*, Hdt.2.94, Pl.*Ti.*60a, *PHib.*1.121.17, al. (iii B.C.), Ruf.ap.Orib.7.26.39, etc.; also, *the castor-oil tree, Ricinus communis*, Str.17.2.5, Dsc.4.161; gen. τοῦ κίκεως Gal.11.649, 12.26; κίκιος Hdn. Gr.2.767; also τῆς κικέας Aët.8.30, Paul.Aeg.7.20.

**κικίβαλος**, ὁ, kind of *shell-fish*, prob. in Epich.42; cf. κικοβαυλιτίδες.

**κικίδιον**, v. κηκίδιον. **κίκιμον**· τῆς κορώνης τὸ κόπριον, Hsch.

**κίκιννος** [κῐκ], ὁ, *ringlet*, Cratin.353, Ar.*V.*1069 (lyr.; cf. Poll.2.98), Theoc.11.10, 14.4, *AP*5.196 (Mel.), Gal.18(1).790.

**κίκῐνος**, η, ον, *made from the* κίκι-*tree*, ἔλαιον Dsc.1.32, Gal.11.870.

**κίκιον**, τό, = κρότωνος ῥίζα, Gal.19.115; = κίκι, cj. in Thphr.*HP* 1.10.1.

**κικιουργός**, ὁ, *castor-oil worker*, *PTeb.*5.173 (ii B.C.), etc.

※**κικιοφόρος**, ον, *bearing* κίκι, γῆ *PPetr.*3p.135 (cf. p.xvii) (iii B.C.).

**κίκιρρος**, ὁ, *cock*, Hsch.: **κίκκα**, ἡ, *hen*, Id.

**κικκᾰβαῦ**, onomatop., *cry in imitation of the screech-owl's note*, Ar. *Av.*261: **κικκάβη**, ἡ, *screech-owl*, Sch. ad loc.; cf. **κικκάμη**, *noctua*, *Gloss.*:—hence **κικκᾰβάζω** (-ίζω Phot.), *shriek like a screech-owl*, cj. Dobree for κακκ- in Ar.*Lys.*761.

**κίκκᾰβος**, ὁ, name of a small coin used in the nether world, Pherecr.(ip.167 K.) ap.Poll.9.83; also, = κίμβιξ, Phot. s. v. κίμβικας:—hence Dim. **κικκάβιν** (= -**βιον**)· ἐλάχιστον, οὐδέν, Hsch.

**κίκκασος**· ὀβολοῦ ὄνομα, Phot.; but ὁ ἐκ τῶν παραμηρίων ἱδρὼς ῥέων, καὶ βόλου ὄνομα, Hsch.; cf. κίγκασος. **κίκκη**· συνουσία, κτλ., Id. **κικκίδαι**· μινδῶνσ.., Id. **κικκιλόνδις**· παιδὸς ἀφόδευμα, Id. **κικκός**· ἀλεκτρυών, κλέπτης, διαχώρησις, Id.

**κικλήσκω**, poet. redupl. form of καλέω, used only in pres. and impf., *call, summon*, Il.11.606, 17.532, Od.22.397; κλήδην εἰς ἀγορὴν κ. Il.9.11:—Med., ἄμυδις κικλήσκετο πάντας ἀρίστους 10.300. 2. *invite*, 2.404. 3. *invoke, implore*, 9.569, A.*Supp.*212, 217, *Eu.*508 (lyr.), S.*OT*209 (lyr.), E.*Tr.*470, etc. II. *accost, address*, ψυχὴν Πατροκλῆος Il.23.221. III. *call by name*, τὴν.. ἄνδρες Βατίειαν κ. 2.813, cf. 14.291; τὸν ἐπίκλησιν κορυνήτην ἄνδρες κ. 7.139, cf. Pi.*P.* 4.119, *Fr.*87.4, A.*Ag.*712 (lyr.), E.*El.*118 (lyr.); οὔνομα Θεσμοφάνην με.. κίκλησκον *IG*3.1337:—Pass., νῆσός τις Συρίη κικλήσκεται *there is an island called* Συρίη, Od.15.403; ἀφ' οὗ δὴ Ῥήγιον κικλήσκεται A.*Fr.* 402; πατρὸς Στρυμόνος κικλήσκεται E.*Rh.*279, 652.—Also in late Ion. Prose, Aret.*SA*2.6, *SD*1.6 (Pass.), al.; cf. κλῄσκω.

**κικνία**· μικρὰ φθειρία, Hsch. **κίκνωψ**· θηρίον, Id. (cf. κνώψ, κινώπετον). **κικοβαυλιτίδες**· κογχυλίου τι γένος μέλαν, καὶ τὰ ἐκ στέατος σκωλήκια, Id.; cf. κικίβαλος. **κίκους**· ὁ νέος τέττιξ, Id. **κικριβιντίς**· ἀνδράχνη, Id.; cf. κιχληβῶτις.

※**κῐκῠμίς**, ίδος, ἡ, = κικκάβη, *screech-owl*, Lat. *cicuma*, Call.*Fr.*318: **κίκυμος** or **κίκυβος**, ὁ (also = λαμπτήρ), Hsch.

**κῐκῠμώ⟨σσ⟩ω**, *to be purblind like an owl*, Hsch., cf. Suid.

**Κίκυννα** [ῐ], ἡ, *Cicynna*, an Attic deme, Theognost.*Can.*101 (-υνα cod.): **Κῐκυννεύς**, έως, ὁ, *an inhabitant thereof*, *IG*2$^{2}$.1654.32, al., Ar. *Nu.*210: **Κῐκυννόθεν** *from Cicynna*, ib.134: **Κῐκυννοῖ** *at Cicynna*, Lys.17.5.

**κῖκυς**, ἡ, *strength, vigour*, poet. word, οὐ γάρ οἱ ἔτ' ἦν ἲς ἔμπεδος οὐδέ τι κ. Od.11.393, cf. *h.Ven.*237, Alc.137 (dub.); σοὶ δ' οὐκ ἔνεστι κ. οὐδ' αἱμόρρυτοι φλέβες A.*Fr.*230.

**κῑκύω**, = ἰσχύω, Hdn.Gr.2.533, *Et.Gud.*321.53, Suid.

***κίκω**, Dor. aor. 1 ἔκιξα, = ἤνεγκα, Simm.26.7; cf. κίξαντες· ἐλθόντες, and κίξατο· εὗρεν, ἔλαβεν, ἤνεγκεν, Hsch.; cf. ἀποκίκω.

**κιλάριος**· ὁ ἥλιος, Hsch. **κιλίας**· στρουθὸς ἄρσην, Id.

※**Κῐλῐκ-ῐαρχία**, ἡ, *presidency of the provincial council of Cilicia*, *OGI* 578.13 (pl., Tarsus, iii A.D.). -ίζω and Med. -ίζομαι, *play the Cilician*, i.e. *to be cruel and treacherous like the Cilicians*, Eust.741.21, Hsch. -ιον, τό, *coarse cloth*, strictly of Cilician goat's hair, Procop. *Pers.*2.26; used for sails, *PLond.*3.1164$^{h}$10 (iii A.D.); for mats hung to deaden the impact of missiles, Lat. *cilicium*, *Gloss.* -ισμός, ὁ, *Cilician behaviour*, i.e. *drunken butchery*, Theopomp.Hist.289a.

**Κίλιξ** [ῐ], ῐκος, ὁ, *a Cilician*, mostly in pl., Il.6.397, 415: as fem., Κίλιξ χώρα *Trag.Adesp.*162:—but regul. fem. **Κίλισσα** (q.v.):—Adj. ※**Κῐλίκιος**, α, ον, A.*Pr.*353; Κ. τράγοι *Com.Adesp.*806; -ιος as fem., Str.2.1.31, Dsc.1.4: ἡ **Κιλικία** (sc. γῆ), *Cilicia*, Hdt.2.34, etc.

**Κίλισσα** [ῐ], ης, ἡ, *Cilician woman*, A.*Ch.*732; as the name of a slave, Sch.Ar.*Pax* 362. 2. Adj., fem. of Κιλίκιος, νέες Hdt.8.14.

**κίλλαι**· ἀστράγαλοι, ἢ ὄνοι, Hsch.

※**κιλλακτήρ**, ῆρος, ὁ, *ass-driver*, Dor. word, Poll.7.56, 185.

**κιλλαμαρύζειν**· κατιλλώπτειν, Hsch.

**κιλλίβας** [λῐ], αντος, ὁ, mostly in pl. κιλλίβαντες, *three-legged stand* (Sch.Ar.*Ach.*1121, Hsch.), κιλλίβαντες ἀσπίδος a shield-*stand*, Ar. l.c.; *painter's easel*, Poll.7.129; *part of a chariot-frame*, Id.1.143; *bearers* of a platform, Moschio ap.Ath.5.208c, cf. *BGU*1127.11 (i B.C.): sg., *stand* or *pedestal* of σαμβύκη II, Bito 58.6 (pl., 62.3); cf. κελλίβας. (κίλλος, βαίνω; cf. *easel* = Germ. *Esel*, *clothes-horse*, etc.)

**Κιλλικύριοι** or **Καλλικύριοι**, οἱ, *class of serfs at Syracuse*, Arist. *Fr.*586, prob. in Hdt.7.155.

**κίλλιξ**, ικος, ὁ, *ox with crooked horns*, Hsch. II. = στάμνος, Id.

**κιλλοβόροι**, οἱ, = κιλλίβαντες (in a chariot), Poll.1.143.

**κίλλος**, ὁ, *ass*, *Sammelb.*5224.63 (written **κεῖλος** ib.29,40), Hsch.; Dor. acc. to Poll.7.56; cf. κίλλαι. 2. = τέττιξ πρωϊνός (Cypr.), Hsch.

**κιλλός**, ή, όν, *ass-coloured, grey*, θερίστριον Eub.103, cf. Hsch., Phot., Eust.1057.56:—also **κίλλιος**, α, ον, Poll.7.56.

**κίλλουρος**, ὁ, *wagtail*, Hsch.

**κιμαί**· χυμὸς πύρινος, and **κιμαός**· χυλὸς μορέας, Hsch.

**κιμβ-άζει**· στραγγεύεται, Hsch. -εία, ἡ, *stinginess*, Arist.*VV* 1251$^{b}$5, Hsch. (where for σκιφία read σκνιφία):—prob. f.l. for -ικεία or -ικία, cf. Phot. and Suid. s.v. κίμβικα, Arist. l.c. ap.Stob.3.1. 194. -εύει· ὀδοιπορεῖ, Hsch. -ιξ, ῑκος, ὁ, *niggard, skinflint*, Xenoph.21, Arist.*EN*1121$^{b}$22, *MM*1192$^{a}$9, *EE*1232$^{a}$14, Chamael.ap. Ath.14.656d, Plu.2.632c. II. metaph., of an author, *fond of petty details*, Ath.7.303e.

**κίμερος**· νοῦς (Phryg.), Hsch.

**κιμμερικόν** (sc. ἱμάτιον), τό, *woman's garment*, Ar.*Lys.*45, 52 (κιμβ- cod. R, Hsch.).

**Κιμμέριοι**, οἱ, *Cimmerians*, a mythical people dwelling beyond the Ocean in perpetual darkness, Od.11.14; later, a nomad people of the steppes, who invaded Asia Minor, Hdt.1.15, etc.:—also **Κίμμεροι**, Lyc.695:—Adj. **Κιμμερικός**, ή, όν, *Cimmerian*: Κ. ἰσθμός *the Crimea*, A.*Pr.*730; Κ. Βόσπορος Str.1.1.10, al.:—also **Κιμμέριος**, α, ον, Hdt.4.12; ἡ Κιμμερίη (sc. γῆ) ibid.: **Κιμμερίς**, ίδος, ἡ, Arist.*Fr.* 478, Apollod.2.1.3.

**κίμπτω**, = σκίμπτω, Hsch.

**Κίμωλος** [ῐ], ἡ, *Cimolus*, an island in the Cyclades:—Adj. **Κῑμώλιος**, α, ον, ἰσχάδες Amphis 40: **Κῑμωλία** (with or without γῆ), ἡ, *Cimolian earth*, a white clay, like *fuller's earth*, used in baths and barbers' shops, and in medicine, Ar.*Ra.*713 (lyr.), Str.10.5.1, Dsc.5.156.

**Κῑμώνιος**, α, ον, *of* or *belonging to Cimon*, ἐν τοῖς Κ. ἐρειπίοις among the ruins of his edifices, Cratin.151. **κίμωσις**, v. κήμωσις.

**κῑνάβευμα**, ατος, τό, *knavish trick*, in pl., Phot., Hsch.; ἀποκινναβευμάτων is f.l. in Ar.*Fr.*699 (where κἀνἀβευμάτων, = κανάβων, is prob. cj.).

**κῑνάβρ-α**, ἡ, *rank smell of a he-goat*, Luc.*Bis Acc.*10, Poll.2.77; also of men, Luc.*DMar.*1.5, al.; also, *goatish beard*, Id.*DMort.*10.9: metaph., = κιμβεία, Phot. -άω, *smell like a goat*, Ar.*Pl.*294. -εύεσθαι· σκευωρεῖσθαι, Phot. -εύματα· ἀποκαθάρματα ὄζοντα, Hsch.

**κῑνάδ-ιον** [ᾰ], τό, Dim. of sq., Harp. -ος, εος, τό, Sicil. word for *fox* (Sch.Theoc.5.25, cf. *EM*514.13), Call.Com.1 D.: hence, *cunning rogue*, τοὐπίτριπτον κίναδος S.*Aj.*103; ὦ συκοφάντα καὶ ἐπίτριπτον κ. And 1.99; πυκνότατον κ. Ar.*Av.*430, cf. *Nu.*448, D.18.162, 242, Theoc. l.c. (ὦ κίναδε, ὦ κιναδεῦ codd.): generally, *beast, monster*, Democr.259. -ρα· ἀλώπηξ, Hsch.

**κῑνάθ-ίας**· κρυπτός, Hsch. -ίζειν, *hoard as a miser*; also, = μινυρίζειν, κινεῖν, Id.:—hence -ισμα, ατος, τό, *rustling motion*, as of wings, A.*Pr.*124 (anap.): -ισμός, ὁ, Phot.; also κίναθος, = θησαυρισμός, Id.

**κῑναιδ-εία**, ἡ, *unnatural lust*, Aeschin.1.131, Demetr.*Eloc.*97. -εύομαι, *to be a* κίναιδος, Sch.Luc.*JTr.*8. -ία, ἡ, = κιναιδεία, Aeschin.2.99, Luc.*Demon.*50, D.C.45.26. -ίας, ου, ὁ, stone found in head of κίναιδος II, Plin.*HN*37.153. -ίζω, *practise unnatural vice*, Antioch.Astr. in *Cat.Cod.Astr.*7.113. -ιον, τό, = ἴυγξ, Hsch., Phot.; = σεισοπυγίς, Sch.Theoc.2.17. -ισμα, ατος, τό, *unnatural lewdness*, Eust.1784.54.

**κῑναιδο-γράφος** [ᾰ], ον, *writing of obscene things*, *AB*429, *An.Ox.* 2.318. -λογέω, *talk of obscene things*, Str.14.1.41. -λογία, ἡ, *obscene talk*, *An.Ox.*2.318. ※-λόγος, ον, *talking of obscene things*, D.L.4.40; *writing obscene books*, Ath.14.620f.

※**κίναιδ-ος** [ῑ], ὁ, *catamite*, Pl.*Grg.*494e, etc.: generally, *lewd fellow*, Herod.2.74, *PSI*5.483.1 (iii B.C.), Arcesil.ap.Plu.2.126a. 2. *public dancer*(?), *PTeb.*208 (i B.C.), perh. also *CIG*4926 (Philae). 3. pl., *obscene poems*, D.L.9.110. II. a *sea-fish*, Plin.*HN*32.146. III. = κιναίδιον, Gal.12.740, 800. -ώδης, ες, *after the fashion of catamites*, κουρά Sch.Ar.*Ach.*849. -ῶς, v. κιάντωρ.

**κῑνάκης** [ᾰ], ὁ, = ἀκινάκης, S.*Fr.*1061.

**κίνᾰμον**, **κινάμωμον**, v. κιννάμωμον.

**κῑνάρ-α** [ᾰρ], ἡ, *artichoke, Cynara Scolymus*, Ptol.Euerg.1 J., Colum. 10.235, *BGU*249.25 (i A.D.), Dsc.3.8, Ath.2.70a, Gal.6.636; cf. κυ-

*νάρα.* **-εών,** ῶνος, ὁ, *artichoke-bed*, *PFlor.*50.72 (iii A.D.). **-ηφάγος** [φᾰ], ον, *eating artichokes*, Juba ap.Ath.8.343f.

**κιναρύζεσθαι·** τὸ θρηνεῖν μετὰ τοῦ γογγύζειν, καὶ κινεῖσθαι, Hsch. **κίναρχος·** ἄψυχος, Id.

**κῑνᾰχύρα** [ῠ], ἡ, *sieve for bolting flour*, Ar.*Ec.*730.

**κίνδαλος,** ὁ, v. κύνδαλος. **κίνδαξ,** ακος, ὁ, ἡ, = σκίναξ, Hsch., Phot. ***κινδάπτω,** aor. ἐκίνδαψεν· ἔψηλεν, Hsch.; ἐκινδάψα(σ)κεν· ὑπέψηλεν, Id. **κινδαψός,** ὁ, v. σκινδαψός.

**κίνδος,** ὁ, a fragrant herb, Mnesim.4.63 (anap.).

**κίνδυν,** ῡνος, ὁ, v. κίνδυνος.

**κινδύν-ευμα** [ῡ], ατος, τό, *hazard, venture*, S.*OC*564, *Ant.*42, E.*IT*1001, Pl.*R.*451a, etc. **-ευτέον,** *one must venture*, ἐν ἀσπίσιν σοι πρῶτα κ. E.*Supp.*572, cf. *IT*1022, Plb.4.11.7: Adj. -τέος, α, ον, *Gloss.* **-ευτής,** οῦ, ὁ, *venturesome person*, Th.1.70, D.C.*Fr.*70.6. **-ευτικός,** ή, όν, *venturesome, adventurous*, Arist.*Rh.*1367$^b$4. ⊛**-εύω,** fut. -σω Hdt.8.60.α', etc.: pf. κεκινδύνευκα Lys.3.47, Plb.5.61.4:—Pass., mostly in pres.: fut. κινδυνευθήσομαι D.30.10, κεκινδυνεύσομαι Antipho 5.75: aor. and pf., v. infr. 3: (κίνδυνος):—*to be daring, run risk*, κ. πρὸς πολλούς, πρὸς τοὺς πολεμίους, Hdt.4.11, X.*Mem.*3.3.14; κ. εἰς τὴν Αἴγυπτον *venture* thither, Pherecr.11. b. abs., *make a venture, take a risk*, Hdt.3.69, Ar.*Eq.*1204; *to be in dire peril*, Th.3.28, 6.33, etc.; *to be in danger*, Arist.*EN*1124$^b$8, etc.; of a sick person, Hp.*Aph.*(*Sp.*)7.82, *Coac.*374; esp. *engage in war*, Isoc.1.43; τοῦ χωρίου κινδυνεύοντος the post *being in peril*, Th.4.8; ὁ κινδυνεύων τόπος the place *of danger*, Plb.3.115.6. 2. c. dat., κ. τῷ σώματι, τῇ ψυχῇ, Hdt.2.120, 7.209; κ. ἁπάσῃ τῇ Ἑλλάδι *run a risk with* all Greece, i.e. endanger it all, Id.8.60.α'; στρατιῇ Id.4.80; τίσιν οὖν ὑμεῖς κινδυνεύσαιτ' ἄν..; *in* what points..? D.9.18; κ. τοῖς ὅλοις πράγμασι, τῷ βίῳ, Plb.1.70.1, 5.61.4; τῷ ζῆν *PTeb.*44.21 (ii B.C.): freq. with Preps., κ. ἐν τοῖς σώμασι Lys.2.63; οὐκ ἐν τῷ Καρὶ ἀλλ' ἐν υἱέσι Pl.*La.*187b (Pass.); κ. περὶ [τῆς Πελοποννήσου] Hdt.8.74; περὶ τῆς ψυχῆς Antipho 2.4.5, Ar.*Pl.*524; περὶ τοῦ σώματος And.1.4; περὶ ἀνδραποδισμοῦ Isoc.8.37; περὶ τῆς μεγίστης ζημίας Lys.7.15; περὶ τῆς βασιλείας πρὸς Κῦρον D.15.24; περὶ αὐτῷ Antipho 5.6; περὶ τοῖς φιλτάτοις Pl.*Prt.*314a; but κ. περὶ δισχιλίους *go into battle* with a force of 2,000, Eun.*Hist.*p.244 D.; ὑπὲρ καλλίστων Lys.2.79. 3. c. acc. cogn., *venture, hazard*, τοὺς ἐσχάτους κινδύνους Antipho 5.82; κινδύνευμα Pl.*R.*451a; μάχην Aeschin.2.169; τὴν ψευδομαρτυρίαν *hazard* a prosecution for perjury, D.41.16 codd. (τῶν -ιῶν Blass):—Pass., *to be ventured* or *hazarded*, μεταβολὴ κινδυνεύεται *there is risk* of change, Th.2.43; ὁποτέρως ἔσται, ἐν ἀδήλῳ κινδυνεύεται *remains in hazardous* uncertainty, Id.1.78; τὰ μέγιστα κινδυνεύεται τῇ πόλει D.19.285; κεκινδυνευμένον *a venturous enterprise*, Pi.*N.*5.14; τὰ κινδυνευθέντα, = τὰ κινδυνεύματα, Lys.2.54; τῶν ἤδη σφίσι καλῶς κεκινδυνευμένων Arr.*An.*2.7.3; τὸ φιλοπόλεμον καὶ κεκ. D.S.2.21. 4. c. inf., *run the risk* of doing or being.., τὸν στρατὸν κινδυνεύσει ἀποβαλεῖν Hdt.8.65; κακόν τι λαβεῖν Id.6.9; ἀπολέσθαι Id.9.89; διαφθαρῆναι Th.3.74; ἀποθανεῖν Pl.*Ap.*28b, etc.; τοῦ συντριβῆναι Lxx *Jn.*1.4; then, b. to express *chance*, i.e. what *may possibly* or *probably happen*: c. pres., pf., or aor. inf., κινδυνεύουσι οἱ ἄνθρωποι οὗτοι γόητες εἶναι they *run a risk of being reputed* conjurers, Hdt.4.105; κινδυνεύσομεν βοηθεῖν we *shall probably have* to assist, Pl.*Tht.*164e, cf. 172c; κ. ἡ ἀληθὴς δόξα ἐπιστήμη εἶναι *seems likely* to be.., ib.187b; κινδυνεύσεις ἐπιδεῖξαι χρηστὸς εἶναι you *will have the chance of* showing your worth, X.*Mem.*2.3.17, cf. 3.13.3; κ. ἀναμφιλογώτατον ἀγαθὸν εἶναι ib.4.2.34, cf. Pl.*Ap.*40b; τὰ συσσίτια κινδυνεύει συναγαγεῖν he *probably* organized the σ., Id.*Lg.*625e; κινδυνεύω πεπονθέναι ὅπερ.. Id.*Grg.*485e: c. fut. inf., dub. in Th.4.117; κινδυνεύει impers., *it may be, possibly*, as an affirmat. answer, Pl.*Sph.*256e, *Phdr.*262c; out of courtesy, when no real doubt is implied, κινδυνεύεις ἀληθῆ λέγειν you *may very likely* be right, Id.*Smp.*205d. 5. Pass., *to be endangered* or *imperilled*, ἐν ἑνὶ ἀνδρὶ πολλῶν ἀρετὰς κ. Th.2.35; τὰ χρήματα κινδυνεύεται τῷ δανείσαντι D.34.28:—but Pass. in sense of Act. dub. in *GDI*3569.4 (Calymna). ⊛**-ος,** ὁ, heterocl. dat. κίνδῡνι (as if from κίνδυν) Alc.138, cf. Sapph.161:—*danger, hazard, venture*, whether abstract or concrete, πᾶσίν τοι κ. ἐπ' ἔργμασιν Thgn.585, cf. 637; ὁ μέγας κ. ἄναλκιν οὐ φῶτα λαμβάνει Pi.*O.*1.81; κ. γαλέης *danger of* or *from* her, Batr.9; κ. ἀϋτᾶς Pi.*N.*9.35; τὸν κ. τῆς μάχης Th.2.71; κίνδυνον ἀναρριπτέειν to run *a risk*, Hdt.7.50, etc.; ῥῖψαι E.*Rh.*154; κἀνὰ κίνδυνον βαλῶ A.*Th.*1033; κίνδυνον ἀναλαβέσθαι, ὑποδύεσθαι, Hdt.3.69, X.*Cyr.*1.5.12; αἵρεσθαι, ἄρασθαι, ἀρεῖσθαι, E.*Heracl.*504, Antipho 5.63, And.1.11; ξυνάρασθαι Th. l.c.; ἐγχειρίσασθαι Id.5.108, etc.; ὑπομεῖναι X.*Cyr.*1.2.1; μετὰ τοῦ δικαίου ποιούμενος τοὺς κ. Isoc.14.42; κινδύνῳ περιπίπτειν Th.8.27; ἐν κινδύνῳ αἰωρεῖσθαι, εἶναι, Id.7.77, Antipho 5.7; ἐπὶ κινδύνους χωρεῖν Th.2.39; πρὸς αὐθαιρέτους κ. ἰέναι Id.8.27; ἐς κ. ἐμβαίνειν X.*Cyr.*2.1.15; ἐς κ. καταστῆσαί τινα Th.5.99; κινδύνῳ βάλλειν τινά A.*Th.*1053; τὸν ἐπιόντα κίνδυνον Aeschin.3.148; τοὺς ἐπιφερομένους ἑαυτῷ κ. ib.163; τὸν κατειληφότα κ. τὴν πόλιν D.18.220; οὐ περὶ τῶν ἴσων ὁ κ. X.*HG*7.1.7; ἔνι κ. ἐν τῷ πράγματι Ar.*Pl.*348; κ. [ἐστι] c. inf., Pi.*N.*8.21, Lys.13.27, Pl.*Cra.*436b, etc.; πόλιν κ. ἔσχε πεσεῖν E.*Hec.*5; κ. ἀσφαλέστερος Antipho 2.2.9; κ. ἀνθρώπινοι.., θεῖοι And.1.139; ἐπὶ τῷ αὑτοῦ κ. at his own *risk*, Arist.*Pol.*1286$^a$14; ἰδίῳ ἡμῶν κ. *PLond.*2.356.4 (i A.D.); καθαρὸς ἀπὸ παντὸς κ. *PIand.*35.10 (ii/iii A.D.). 2. *trial, venture*, κ. ἀνεῖται σοφίας Ar.*Nu.*955. 3. *battle*, Plb.1.87.10, etc. **-ώδης,** ες, *dangerous*, Hp.*Prog.*14, *Art.*65 (Comp.); κ. καταφοραί Plb.8.20.3; τὸ κ., τὰ κ., J.*AJ*15.4.2, 14.8.2 (Sup.); κ. λόγοι Max.Tyr.24.5. Adv. -δῶς D.H.7.6, Gal.8.762.

**κίνερμοι·** οἱ μικροὶ ἰχθύες, Hsch.

⊛**κῑνέω,** aor. ἐκίνησα, Ep. κίνησα Il.23.730, etc.:—**Med. and Pass.,** fut. κινήσομαι (in pass. sense) Pl.*Tht.*182c, D.9.51, -ηθήσομαι Ar.*Ra.*796, Pl.*R.*545d, etc.: aor. Med. (Ep.) κινήσαντο Opp.*C.*2.582: aor. Pass. ἐκινήθην, Ep. 3 pl. ἐκίνηθεν Il.16.280: (cf. κίω):—*set in motion*, ἄγε κινήσας, of Hermes leading the souls, Od.24.5; simply, *move*, οὐδέ τι κινῆσαι μελέων ἦν 8.298; κ. θύρην 22.394; κ. κάρη Il.17.442, etc.; Ζέφυρος κ. λήϊον 2.147; κ. ὄμμα S.*Ph.*866; ναῦς ἐκίνησεν πόδα E.*Hec.*940 (lyr.), etc.; σκληρὰ ἡ γῆ ἔσται κινεῖν, i.e. plough, X.*Oec.*16.11; κ. δόρυ, of a warrior about to attack, E.*Andr.*607; κ. στρατιάν Id.*Rh.*18 (anap.); κ. ὅπλα Th.1.82; κ. σκάφην *rock* a cradle, Phylarch.36 J. b. in later Gr., *set in motion* a process of law, etc., *PKlein.Form.*405, etc. 2. *remove* a thing from its place, ἀνδριάντα Hdt.1.183; γῆς ὅρια Pl.*Lg.*842e; κ. τι τῶν ἀκινήτων *meddle with* things sacred, Hdt.6.134, cf. S.*Ant.*1061, Th.4.98; κ. τὰ χρήματα ἐς ἄλλο τι *apply* them to an alien purpose, Id.2.24; κ. τῶν χρημάτων Id.1.143, 6.70; κ. τὸ στρατόπεδον X.*An.*6.4.27, etc. (κινεῖν alone, Plb.2.54.2, cf. Lxx *Ge.*20.1, Plu.*Dio* 27); *change, innovate*, νόμαια Hdt.3.80; τοὺς πατρίους νόμους Arist.*Pol.*1268$^b$28; τῶν κειμένων νόμων Zaleuc.ap.Stob.4.2.19:—Pass., νόμιμα κινούμενα Pl.*Lg.*797b; ἰατρικὴ κινηθεῖσα παρὰ τὰ πάτρια Arist.*Pol.*1268$^b$35: so abs. in Act., *change treatment*, ib.1286$^a$13. 3. Gramm., *inflect*, τὰ ῥήματα ἐκίνει τὸ τέλος A.D.*Pron.*104.15:—more usu. in Pass., κατὰ τὸ τέλος κινεῖσθαι ib.104.10. 4. *alter* a manuscript reading, Str.7.3.4. II. *disturb*, of a wasps' nest, τοὺς δ' εἴ πέρ τις..κινήσῃ ἀέκων Il.16.264; *arouse*, κ. τινὰ ἐξ ὕπνου E.*Ba.*690; *urge on*, φόβος κ. τινά A.*Ch.*289; φυγάδα πρόδρομον κινήσασα *having driven* him in headlong flight, S.*Ant.*109 (lyr.); κ. ἐπιρρόθοις κακοῖσιν *attack, assail*, ib.413; μήτηρ κ. κραδίαν, κ. δὲ χόλον E.*Med.*99 (anap.); ἐάν με κινῇς καὶ ποιήσῃς τὴν χολὴν..ζέσαι Anaxipp.2; κ. τινά *incite* or *stir* one *up* to speak, Pl.*R.*329e, *Ly.*223a, X.*Mem.*4.2.2; κ. τὰ πολλὰ καὶ ἄτοπα *stir up*..questions, Pl.*Tht.*163a; *call in question* an assumption, τὰ μέγιστα κ. τῶν μαθηματικῶν Arist.*Cael.*271$^b$11, cf. Phld.*Sign.*27; κ. τὸ τὰ ἄκρα..ἀνταίρειν Str.2.1.12, cf. Plot.2.1.6; ὁ κινῶν [τὰ φαινόμενα] λόγος S.E.*M.*8.360:—Pass., S.*OC*1526; κινεῖται γὰρ εὐθύς μοι χολή my bile *is stirred*, Pherecr.69.5; κεκινῆσθαι πρός τι X.*Oec.*8.1. 2. *set going, cause, call forth*, φθέγματα S.*El.*18; πατρὸς στόμα Id.*OC*1276; μῦθον E.*El.*302; λόγον περί τινος Pl.*R.*450a; πάντα κ. λόγον Id.*Phlb.*15e; κ. ὀδύνην S.*Tr.*974 (anap.); κακά Id.*OT*636; πάθος Phld.*Mus.*p.4 K.; πόλεμον, πολέμους, Th.6.34, Pl.*R.*566e; Ἐμπεδοκλέα.. πρῶτον ῥητορικὴν κεκινηκέναι Arist.*Fr.*65. 3. Medic., κ. οὔρησιν, οὖρα, Dsc.2.109, 127; κοιλίαν ib.6. 4. sens. obsc., κ. γυναῖκα Eup.233.3 (nisi leg. ἐβίνουν), cf. Ar.*Ach.*1052 (v.l.), *Eq.*364, *Nu.*1103 (lyr., Pass.), al., *AP*11.7 (Nicander); κ. τὰ σκέλεα Herod.5.2. 5. phrases: κ. πᾶν χρῆμα *turn* every stone, *try* every way, Hdt.5.96; μὴ κ. εὖ κείμενον 'let sleeping dogs lie', Pl.*Phlb.*15c; μὴ κίνει Καμάριναν, ἀκίνητος γὰρ ἀμείνων Orac.ap.St.Byz.; κινεῦντα μηδὲ κάρφος 'not *stirring* a finger', Herod.3.67, cf. 1.55; μηδ' ὀδόντα κινῆσαι Id.3.49; κ. τὸν ἀπ' ἴρας πύματον λίθον 'play the last card', Alc.82 (s.v.l.). 6. in Law, πολιτικῶς κ. κατά τινος *employ* civil *action* against, *Cod.Just.*4.20.13.1.

B. Pass., *to be put in motion, go*, Il.1.47; ⟨κι⟩νηθεὶς ἐπήει dub. in Pi.*Fr.*101: generally, *to be moved, stir*, κινήθη ἀγορή, ἐκίνηθεν φάλαγγες, Il.2.144, 16.280; of an earthquake, Δῆλος ἐκινήθη Hdt.6.98, Th.2.8; θύελλα κινηθεῖσα S.*OC*1660; τί κεκίνηται; what *motion is* this? E.*Andr.*1226 (anap.); κινεῖσθαι, opp. ἑστάναι, *motion*, opp. rest, Pl.*Sph.*250b, etc.; ὥσπερ χορδαὶ ἐν λύρᾳ συμπαθῶς κινηθεῖσαι *vibrating* in unison, Plot.4.4.8. 2. of persons, *to be moved, stirred*, ὁ κεκινημένος *one who is agitated, excited*, Pl.*Phdr.*245b, cf. Vett.Val.45.25, al.; κ. παθητικῶς Phld.*Rh.*1.193 S. 3. of dancing, κ. τῷ σώματι Pl.*Lg.*656a. 4. *move forward*, of soldiers, S.*OC*1371, E.*Rh.*139, *Ph.*107; but κ. ἐκ τῆς τάξεως *leave* the ranks, X.*HG*2.1.22. 5. *to be disturbed* or *in rebellion*, D.C.39.54, 42.15, al. 6. κεκινημένος περί τι, Lat. *versatus in..*, Pl.*Lg.*908d.

**κῑν-ηθμός,** ὁ, *motion*, Pi.*P.*4.208. ⊛**-ηθρον,** τό, = κίνητρον, Poll.7.169. **-ημα,** ατος, τό, *movement*, οὔθ' ἡ γραμμὴ ἐκ στιγμῶν οὔθ' ἡ κίνησις ἐκ κινημάτων Arist.*Ph.*241$^a$4, cf. 232$^a$9, *Mu.*400$^a$8, etc.; of the *movements* of pantomimic actors, Luc.*Salt.*62. 2. *political movement*, Plb.5.29.3, al., Plu.*Fab.*20 (pl.). b. *uproar, excitement*, Lxx 1 *Ma.*13.44, Plu.*Aem.*18. 3. κινήματα τῆς σαρκός *impressions* of sense, Epicur.*Fr.*411; κ. λεῖον *Stoic.*2.25; κ. μελῳδητικὸν περὶ τὴν ψυχήν Thphr.*Fr.*89.1: abs., κινήματα *impressions, emotions*, Epicur.*Fr.*131: sg., Epict.*Fr.*14, S.E.*M.*11.83, etc. 4. Medic., *subluxation* of a bone, *partial dislocation*, Hp.*Fract.*47 (pl.). b. τὰ τῶν καιρῶν κ., of *periods* in disease, Gal.19.184. 5. Gramm., *inflexion*, Hdn.Gr.2.265, al. 6. pl., *moving things*, Max.Tyr.41.2.

⊛**κῑνησί-γαιος** [σῐ], ον, gloss on ἐννοσίγαιος, Hsch. **-πολος,** ον, *heaven-shaking*, *PMag.Par.*1.1372.

**κίνησις** [ῑ], εως, ἡ, *motion*, opp. rest (στάσις), Pl.*Sph.*250a; opp. ἠρεμία, Arist.*Ph.*202$^a$5, etc. 2. in Cyrenaic philos., λεία κ., = ἡδονή, τραχεῖα κ., = πόνος, D.L.2.86; also αἱ διὰ μορφῆς κατ' ὄψιν ἡδεῖαι κ. Epicur.*Fr.*67; αἱ κ. αἱ ἀνθρωπικαί human *emotions*, Arr.*Epict.*2.20.19. 3. *dance*, Ἄρεος κίνασις (sic) Tyrt.16, cf. Luc.*Salt.*63, *Ephes.*2 No.71; τραγικὴ ἔνρυθμος κ. *Inscr.Magn.*165. 4. *movement*, in a political sense, ἐν κ. εἶναι Th.3.75, cf. Plb.3.4.12; ἡ κ. ἡ Ἰουδαϊκή the Jewish *revolt*, *OGI*543.15 (Ancyra, ii A.D.); of the Peloponn. war, Th.1.1. 5. *change, revolution*, κινήσεις πολιτείας Arist.*Pol.*1268$^b$25. 6. *movement* of an army, Plb.10.23.1 (pl.); πολεμικαὶ κ. Ael.*Tact.*3.4, cf. Arr.*Tact.*20.1. b. *removal, change of abode*, Vett.Val.97.17 (pl.), al. 7. Gramm., *inflexion*, τοῦ ζῆμι κ. οὐχ εὕρηται *EM*410.38. 8. in Law, *punitive action*, βασιλικὴ κ. *Cod.Just.*1.3.43.10, cf. 10.27.2.7; also, *setting* a process *in motion*, *PLond.*5.1663.13 (vi A.D.).

**κῑνησῐ-φόρος**, ον, *causing motion*, Orph.*H*.10.21. **-φυλλος**, ον, *leaf-moving*, gloss on εἰνοσίφυλλος, Hsch., Apollon.*Lex*. **-χθων**, ον, gen. ονος, *earth-shaking*, Sch.S.*Ant*.154.

**κῑν-ητέος**, α, ον, *to be moved* or *excited*, Pl.*Amat*.134a; *to be altered*, Id.*Lg*.738d, Arist.*Pol*.1269$^a$25. II. κινητέον, *one must call into play*, τὴν ζωγραφίαν Pl.*R*.373a. 2. *one must excite*, ὀργὴν ἢ ἔλεον S.E.*M*.2.11. ⊛**-ητήρ**, ῆρος, ὁ, = κινητής, γαίης, γᾶς, *h.Hom*.22.2, Pi. *I*.4(3).19. **-ητήριος**, α, ον, = κινητικός, μύωψ A.*Supp*.307; ἀλγεινὰ θυμοῦ κ. ib.448; τὸ κ. *ladle*, = κίνητρον, Sch.Ar.*Eq*.980. **-ητής**, οῦ, ὁ, *one that sets going, author*, καινῶν ἐπῶν Ar.*Nu*.1397. 2. *seditious person, agitator*, Plb.28.17.12. ⊛**-ητικός**, ή, όν, *of* or *for putting in motion*, μόρια Arist.*Pol*.1290$^b$31; νεῦρα *motor* nerves, Gal.8.208; κ. βηχέων Hp.*Aph*.5.24; ἱδρώτων Dsc.5.112; οὔρων Xenocr.ap. Orib.2.58.50; ἐξ ἑαυτοῦ μόνον κ. *spontaneous*, Epicur.*Nat*.28.7: Sup. -ώτατος Arist.*Mete*.365$^b$30. Adv. -κῶς Procl.*in Alc*.p.52C. 2. metaph., *urging on, exciting*, λόγος κ. πρὸς ἀρετήν Aristo *Stoic*.1.88; τὸ -ώτατον τῶν ὄχλων Phld.*Rh*.1.198S., D.H.*Isoc*.13: abs., *stimulating*, X.*Oec*.10.12; τὸ μέλος κ. φύσει Phld.*Mus*.p.71K.; τὸ μήτε ὁρμῆς μήτε ἀφορμῆς -κὸν [ἀδιάφορον] *Stoic*.3.28, cf. 40, al. 3. *turbulent, seditious*, Plb.1.9.3, D.S.19.14, etc. II. (from Pass.) *movable, mobile*, Pl.*Ti*.58d, Arist.*HA*590$^a$33, *GA*775$^a$7 (Comp.), Plu.2.945f, 952e. **-ητός**, ή, όν, (fem. -ός Pl.*Ti*.37d) *moving* (intr.), l.c., cf. Plu.2.1012f; *liable to alteration*, Arist.*EN*1134$^b$29. 2. in Law, κ. οὐσία *movable* property, *Cod.Just*.1.11.10.1, cf. 1.2.15 *Intr*.; κ. καὶ ἀκίνητα *PLond*.3.1015.17 (vi A.D.). **-ητρον**, τό, *ladle* or *stick for stirring*, Eust.1675.57, Sch.Nic.*Th*.109, Sch.Od.11.128.

**κίννα**, ἡ, *way barley, wall-barley, Hordeum murinum*, Dsc.4.32.

⊛**κιννάβᾰρ-ι** [νᾰ], εως, τό, *cinnabar, bisulphuret of mercury*, whence *vermilion* is obtained, Arist.*Mete*.378$^a$26, Thphr.*Lap*.58, Dsc.5.94; thought by some to be *serpent's blood*, Dsc.l.c., Plin.*HN*33.116:—a masc. form **κιννάβαρις**, Anaxandr.14:—also **τεγγάβαρι** (q.v.). 2. = ἐρυθρόδανον, Ps.-Dsc.3.143 (-ρις). **-ίζω**, *have the colour of* κιννάβαρι, Dsc.5.76. **-ινος**, η, ον, *like cinnabar, vermilion*, Arist.*HA*501$^a$30, Ath.9.390b, Ael.*NA*4.21. **-ιον**, τό, name of an *eye-salve*, Gal.12.786.

**κίνναβος**, = κάναβος (for which it is prob. f.l.), Suid.

**κιννᾰμολόγος**, ὁ, = κιννάμωμον II, Plin.*HN*10.97.

**κιννᾰμον**, τό, later form for κιννάμωμον, Plin.*HN*12.86; *cinnamus*, *Gloss*.:—gen. **κῐνάμοιο**, Nic.*Th*.947.

**κιννᾰμωμ-ίζω**, *to be like* κιννάμωμον, Dsc.5.121. **-ινος**, η, ον, *prepared from* or *with* κιννάμωμον, Antiph.35, Dsc.1.61, Ath.10.439b. **-ίς**, ίδος, ἡ, an inferior kind of κιννάμωμον, Gal.12.26. **-ον**, τό, = Hebr. *ḳinnamon*, a superior kind of *cassia*, *Cinnamomum Cassia*, Hdt.3.111, Thphr.*HP*9.5.1, *PSI*6.628 (iii B.C.), *OGI* 214.59 (Didyma, iii B.C.), etc.: **κῐνάμωμον**, D.P.945 (pl.), also in codd. of D.S.1.91, v.l. in Hdt. l.c.; cf. κίνναμον. II. name of a fabulous Indian bird, said to make its nest of twigs of κιννάμωμον (cf. κινναμολόγος), Arist.*HA*616$^a$6, Antig.*Mir*.43, Ael.*NA*2.34.

⊛**κιννᾰμωμοφόρος**, ον, *bearing* κιννάμωμον, ἡ κ. (sc. γῆ) Str.1.4.2, al.

**κιννυρίδες**· τὰ μικρὰ ὀρνιθάρια, Hsch.

**κῑνούρης**, ὁ, *shaking the tail*, a sign of weakness in a horse, Hsch.

**κίνυγμα** [ῐ], ατος, τό, (κινύσσομαι) *anything moved about*, αἰθέριον κ. *a sport* for the winds of heaven, A.*Pr*.158 (anap.): misspelt κήνυγμα, Hsch., Phot.

**κίνῠμαι** [ῐ], = κινέομαι (only in pres. and impf.), *go, move*, Il.10.280, Od.10.556; ἐς πόλεμον.. κίνυντο φάλαγγες they *marched*.., Il.4.281, cf. 332, etc.; τοῦ καὶ κινυμένοιο *as it was stirred*.., 14.173, cf. A.R.1.1308; of dancing, *AP*5.128 (Autom.).

**κῐνύρα** [ῠ], ἡ, = Hebr. *kinnor*, a stringed instrument played with the hand, LXX 1*Ki*.16.23; with a plectron, J.*AJ*7.12.3.

**κῐνῠρίζω**, = sq., read by Zenod. in Il.9.612.

⊛**κῐνύρομαι** [ῡ], only pres. and impf. (unless the aor. κινύρατο be read in Mosch.3.43):—*utter a plaintive sound, lament*, Ar.*Eq*.11, A.R.1.292; οἰκτρὰ κινυρομένη Opp.*C*.3.217; πολλὰ κ. Q.S.6.81, al. 2. c. acc. pers., *bewail*, τινα Call.*Ap*.20. 3. once in Trag., c. acc. cogn., κινύρονται φόνον χαλινοί (L. Dind. μινύρονται ex Hsch.) the bridles *ring* murderously, A.*Th*.123 (lyr.).

**κῐνῠρός**, ά, όν, *wailing, plaintive*, Il.17.5; γόος A.R.4.605; πέτηλα Nonn.*D*.38.95; v. μινυρός.

**κῑνύσσομαι**, Pass., = κινέομαι, *waver, sway backwards and forwards*, A.*Ch*.196.

**κινύτιδος**· κινητικὸς χαραδριός, Hsch. **κῑνώ**, οῦς, ἡ, Dor. for κίνησις, Id., but found in Emp.123.2.

**κινώθαλον**, τό, expl. of κνώδαλον, Sch.Pl.*Ax*.365c.

**κῑνώπ-ετον**, τό, *venomous beast*, esp. *serpent*, Call.*Jov*.25, Nic.*Th*.27, 195:—also **-ηστής**, οῦ, ὁ, ib.141.

**κιξάλλ-ης**, ου, ὁ, *highway robber*, κ. καὶ λῃστής Democr.260; ὅστις κιξάλλας ὑποδέχοιτο *SIG*38.19 (Teos, v B.C.) (Hsch. **κιξάλης**· φώρ, κλέπτης, ἀλαζών: Phot. **κίξας**· τοὺς ἐν ὁδῷ λῃστάς: Jo.Gramm. in Hoffmann *Griech.Dial*. ii p.208 **κιττάλης**· κλέπτης). **-εύω**, *commit highway robbery*, *SIG* l.c.: **-ία**, ἡ, *highway robbery*, Hsch.

**κίξιος**· τέττιξ, Hsch.

**κιόκρᾱνον**, τό, *capital of a column*, *IG*1$^2$.372.29, 11(2).199*A*41 (Delos, iii B.C.), Pl.Com.72, X.*HG*4.4.5, Chor.p.84B.

**κῑον-ηδόν**, Adv., (κίων) *like a pillar*, γράφειν κ., i.e. in vertical lines from top to bottom, Sch.D.T.pp.183, 191 H. **-ικός**, ή, όν, *of a pillar*, φαντασία Eust.1390.18. **-ιον**, τό, Dim. of κίων, *small pillar*, Ph.*Bel*.76.15, Poll.7.73, *IG*3.162, *CIG*4608 (Palestine). II. *central column* in a snail's shell, Dsc.2.4. **-ίς**, ίδος, ἡ, Dim. of κίων, *uvula*, Id.1.107, Aret.*CA*1.8; esp. when inflamed, Gal.14.305. **-ίσκος**, ὁ, Dim. of κίων, Haussoullier *Milet* p.173, Ath.12.514c (pl.), J.*AJ*8.3.6 (pl.), Hero *Aut*.1.2, al.

**κῑονο-ειδής**, ές, *like a pillar*, Eust.1399.33. **-κρᾱνον**, τό, later form for κιόκρανον, Str.4.4.6 (as v.l.), D.S.5.47, etc. **-φορέω**, *bear the pillars* of heaven, of Atlas, Eust.1390.10. **-φορία**, ἡ, *bearing of pillars*, and **-φόρος**, ον, *pillar-bearing*, Id. ad D.P.66.

**κίουρος**, ὁ, *basket* for corn, or *measure*, Hsch. (Hebr. *kiyyôr* 'pot, basin'.)

**κιππαρός**, ὁ, dub. sens. in *BGU*470.3 (ii A.D., fort. κηπουρός).

**κίραφος**, ὁ, and Lacon. **κίρα**, ἡ, *fox*, Hsch. **κίρβα**, = πήρα, Id.; cf. κίββα. **κιρία**, v. κειρία. **κίρις**, v. κιρρίς.

**κιρκαία** (**κιρκέα** Gal.12.26), ἡ, *black swallow-wort, Vincetoxicum nigrum*, Dsc.3.119, Zopyr.ap.Orib.14.64.1: κιρκαία ῥίζα, used as a charm, Apollod.3.15.1. II. **κιρκαῖος** ἱέραξ, a kind of hawk, *PMag.Berol*.1.4. **κίρκας**, v. κιρκίας.

**κίρκασμα**· τοὺς βότρυας, Hsch.

**κίρκη**, ἡ, unknown *bird*, Ael.*NA*4.5.

**Κίρκη**, ἡ, *Circe*, Od.10.136, Hes.*Th*.957, etc.

**κιρκήλᾰτος**, ον (nisi leg. -ας), *chased by a hawk*, ἀηδών A.*Supp*.62 (lyr.).

**κιρκήσια** (sc. ἀγωνίσματα), τά, = Lat. *ludi Circenses*, Arr.*Epict*.4.10.21.

**κιρκίας**, ου, ὁ, = κίρκιος III, cj. for καικίας in Arist.*Mu*.394$^b$31 and for κίρκας in Id.*Vent*.973$^b$20.

**κιρκίον**, τό, Dim. of κίρκος III, *ring*, *BCH*29.544 (Delos, ii B.C.).

**κίρκιος**, ὁ, = θρασκίας, Agathem.2.7, *Gloss*.; cf. κέρκιος, κιρκίας.

**κίρκος**, ὁ, a kind of *hawk* or *falcon*, ἴρηξ κίρκος (where ἴρηξ is the generic term, κίρκος the specific), Od.13.87, cf. Il.22.139, A.*Pr*.857, Arist.*HA*620$^a$18, Opp.*C*.1.64; κίρκου λεπάργου A.*Fr*.304.5. (The species cannot be identified.) II. a kind of *wolf*, Opp.*C*.3.304. III. *circle*, mostly in form κρίκος (q.v.): hence, *ring*, *IG*11(2).161*B*49 (Delos, iii B.C.): poet. for Prose κρίκος acc. to Poll.1.94:—neut. pl. **κίρκα** ἢ καταδέσματα *PMag.Lond*.121.299. IV. later, = Lat. *circus*, Plb.30.22.2, Arr.*Epict*.3.16.14, Plu.*Aem*.32. V. unknown stone, Plin.*HN*37.153. VI. = κωπηλάτης, Hsch., Phot. VII. = ἡ τοῦ αἰγείρου βλάστησις, Hsch.

**κιρκόω**, *hoop round, secure with rings*, A.*Pr*.74.

**κιρνάω** and **-ημι**, collat., esp. poet., forms of κεράννυμι, only pres. and impf.:—*mix* wine with water, Hom. only in Od., μελίφρονα οἶνον ἐκίρνα (impf. of κιρνάω) 7.182, 10.356; κίρνη μελιηδέα οἶνον (impf. of κίρνημι) 14.78, 16.52; κιρνὰς αἴθοπα οἶνον (part.) 16.14; κιρνᾷ (v.l. κίρναται) κρητῆρα οἴνου Hdt.4.66; κρατῆρα μελέων κίρναμεν Pi.*I*.6(5).3; κόμπον κιρνάμεν *to mix the cup* of praise ib.5(4).25: inf. κιρνάναι Hp.*Mul*.2.113; part., κιρνάντες πόλιν Ar.*Fr*.683; Aeol. κίρναις (ἐγ-) Alc.34 codd. (fort. κέρναις); κιρνῶντες Hdn.8.4.9: impf., ἐκίρνη φάρμακον App.*Mith*.111:—Med., ἴσον ἴσῳ κίρνασθαι Ath.10.426b; κιρνᾶται Id.11.476a, A.D.*Pron*.74.7, κίρναται *Com.Adesp*.373; χθὼν δὲ πᾶσα καὶ θάλασσα κίρναται τεὰν χάριν *IG*4$^2$(1).130.23 (Epid.); part. κιρνάμενος Pi.*N*.3.78: impf. ἐκίρνατο (ἐν-) *Com.Adesp*.1203:—Pass., ποτὶ μῶμον ἔπαινος κίρναται Pi.*Fr*.181; κρητῆρες κιρνέαται *SIG*57.11 (Miletus, v B.C.); ἡ φύσις καὶ τὰ κιρνάμενα ταύτῃ Phld.*Ir*.p.59W. 2. *flavour by mixing*, κρήνη.. οὕτω δή τι ἐοῦσα πικρή, ἣ κιρνᾷ τὸν Ὕπανιν Hdt.4.52. 3. metaph., *temper*, μαλάττειν καὶ κιρνᾶν τὸ τῆς φύσεως αὔθαδες Plb.4.21.3. 4. τὸ χρύσιον κέρναν (Aeol.) ὑδαρέστερον *alloy* it, *IG*12(2).1.13 (Mytil., iv B.C.):—cf. ἀνα-, ἐγ-, ἐπι-, συγ-κίρνημι.

**κιρρά**, a *fish*, Hsch. **Κίρρα, Κιρραῖος**, v. Κρῖσα, Κρισαῖος.

**κιρράς**, άδος, ἡ, poet. fem. of κιρρός, Nic.*Th*.519.

**κιρρίς**, ίδος, ἡ, a *sea-fish*, = κηρίς, prob. a species of *wrasse*, Opp.*H*.1.129, 3.187. 2. species of ἱέραξ, *EM*515.15. 3. = λύχνος (Lacon.), ib.17. 4. = Ἄδωνις (Cypr.), ib.16. (Hsch. has κίρις in senses 2–4.)

⊛**κιρροειδής**, ές, *yellowish*, Apollod.*Fr.Hist*.214 J., Dsc.*Ther*.16, Philostr.*Im*.1.12.

**κιρροκοιλάδια**, τά, species of *fig*, Ath.3.78a.

⊛**κιρρός**, ά, όν, *orange-tawny*, between πυρρός and ξανθός, οἶνος Hp.*Acut*.52, cf. Arist.*Fr*.307, Mnesith.ap.Ath.1.32d, Nic.*Al*.44; τροχίσκος ὁ κ. Antyll.ap.Orib.10.24.10.

**κιρρόχρως**, ωτος, perh. to be read for κηρόχρως, Chaerem.1.5.

**κιρρώδης**, ες, *inclined to orange-tawny*, *Hippiatr*.104.

**κιρσο-ειδής**, ές, *varicose*, of veins, Hp.*Morb*.1.14; of the convolutions of the brain, Ruf.*Onom*.148; κ. παραστάτης, name for the πόρος σπερματικός, Gal.4.565. **-κήλη**, ἡ, *varicocele*, Cels.7.18, Gal.7.730.

**κιρσός**, ὁ, *enlargement of a vein, varicocele*, = ἰξία III, Hp.*Aph*.6.21 (pl.): of *varicose veins*, Apollon.*Mir*.42, Philostr.*Gym*.35, Gal.7.730: —also **κριξός**, Poll.4.196; **κρισσός**, *Hippiatr*.14, 77, Hsch.; cf. κισσός II.

**κιρσο-τομέω**, *remove varicocele*, Heliod.(?)ap.Orib.45.18.24:—also Pass., ib.45.18.5. **-τομία**, ἡ, *operation to remove varicocele*, ib.45.18.18, Paul.Aeg.6.82.

**κιρσουλκ-έω**, in Pass., *to be operated on for varicocele*, Heliod.(?) ap.Orib.45.18.31. **-ία**, ἡ, *this operation*, ib.45.18.30. ⊛**-ός**, ὁ, *instrument for this purpose*, ib.45.18.5, Gal.14.790.

**κιρσ-όω**, *cause to become varicose*, Gal.4.579:—usu. in Pass., *become varicose*, Id.18(1).499, Heliod.ap.Orib.45.19.1. **-ώδης**, ες, = κιρσοειδής, Hp.*Prorrh*.2.10, Gal.*UP*14.7 (Comp.), 10. **-ωσις**, εως, ἡ, *becoming varicose*, Heliod.(?)ap.Orib.45.18.29.

**κίρτος**, dub. sens., Simon.240.

**κίς**, ὁ, gen. κιός, acc. κῖν, *weevil*, κεῖνον [τὸν χρυσὸν] οὐ σὴς οὐδὲ κὶς δάπτει Pi.*Fr*.222: acc. pl. κίας Thphr.*CP*4.15.4. [κῖς Hdn.Gr.2.925

(oxyt., Choerob. *in Theod.*1.383): gen. κῑός Hdn.Gr.2.674: acc. κῖν Choerob. l. c.]

**κις**, Thess., = τις (q.v.).

**κῐσηρ-ίζω**, *rub with pumice-stone*, Nic.Dam.4 J., *Gloss.* **-ιον**, τό, Dim. of sq., *EM*515.28, *Gloss.* ⊛ **-ις** (**κίσηλις** *PHolm.*12.11, implied in Luc.*Jud.Voc.*4), εως (Luc. l. c., -ιδος Thphr. (v. infr.), cf. Choerob. *in Theod.*1.329 H.), ἡ, *pumice-stone*, Ar.*Fr.*320.4, Alex.124.9, Arist.*EN*1111ᵃ13, Thphr.*Lap.*22, etc. [ῐ in Comm. ll. cc., *AP*6.295 (Phan.): κίσσηρις is erroneous in Thphr. l. c., Asp. *in EN*65.4.]

⊛ **κῐσηροειδής**, ές, *like pumice-stone*, Diog.Apoll. in *Placit.*2.13.5, Thphr.*HP*3.7.5.

**κῐσηρ-όομαι**, Pass., *turn into pumice*, Thphr.*Lap.*20. **-ώδης**, ες, = κισηροειδής, Ephor.65(*e*) J., Dsc.5.74.

⊛ **κίσθος** (Dsc. (v. infr.), Hsch.) or **κισθός**, ὁ, *rock-rose*, Eup.14.5, Mnesim.4.63 (anap.), prob. l. for κισσός in Thphr.*HP*6.1.4, 6.2.1,2; κ. ἄρρην, = *Cistus villosus*, κ. θῆλυς, = *C. salvifolius*, Dsc.1.97: **κίστος**, Hp.*Liqu.*5, Gal.12.27:—Dsc. l. c. sq. distinguishes the species **κίσθαρος** or **κίσσαρος** from λῆδον, cf. Gal.12.28.

⊛ **κίσιρνις**, a *bird*, Hsch. **κίσπρα**· πικρὰ τὸ ἦθος, παλίγκοτος (Cos), Id.

**κίσσᾰ**, Att. **κίττᾰ**, ἡ, *jay, Garrulus glandarius*, Ar.*Av.*302, Antiph.302, etc.; σοῦ δ' ἐγὼ λαλιστέραν οὐπώποτ' εἶδον.., οὐ κίτταν Alex.92; prov., ἁ κίττα τὰν Σειρῆνα μιμουμένα Gal.8.632. 2. = ἰχθῦς ποιός, Hsch. II. '*longing*' *of pregnant women, craving for strange food*, Dsc.1.115, Sor.1.48, S.E.*M.*5.62: pl., Gal.8.343.

**κισσᾰβίζω**, Att. **κιττ-**, *scream like a jay*, Poll.5.90.

**κισσ-άμπελος**, ἡ, = ἐλξίνη, Dsc.4.39, cf. Gal.19.131: **κιττάμπελος**, Ps.-Dsc.4.39:—also **κισσ-άνθεμον**, τό, ibid., Gal.12.51; a kind of κυκλάμινος, Dsc.2.165.

**κίσσᾰρος**, ὁ, f. l. for κύσσαρος, Hp.ap.Erot.; = *hedera*, *Gloss.* II. = κίσθος, Dsc.1.97.

**κισσάω**, Att. **κιττ-**, (κίσσα II) *crave for strange food*, of pregnant women, Arist.*HA*584ᵃ19, Arr.*Epict.*4.8.35, Gal.6.422; κ. τῆς γηθυλλίδος Polem.Hist.36: metaph., κ. τῆς εἰρήνης Ar.*Pax*497 (lyr.): c. inf., *long* to do a thing, Id.*V.*349 (cf. Sch.); ἐκίττα ἡ πόλις ἐπὶ τῷ μειρακίῳ Longus 4.33. II. Act., *conceive*, Lxx *Ps.*50(51).7.

**κισσεοχαίτης**, ὁ, voc. -χαῖτα, *wreathed with ivy*, epith. of Apollo, *PMag.Berol.*2.98a.

**κισσ-εύς**, ὁ, *the ivy-crowned*, ὁ κ. Ἀπόλλων, ὁ βακχεύς, ὁ μάντις A.*Fr.*341. **-ήεις**, εσσα, εν, = κίσσινος, Nic.*Th.*510, Nonn.*D.*40.93. **-ηρεφής**, ές, (ἐρέφω) *ivy-clad*, Call.*Ep.* in *Berl.Sitzb.*1912.548, Philostr.*Dial.*2, prob. for κισσηφερής in Suid. **-ήρης**, ες, (ἀραρίσκω) = foreg., ὄχθαι S.*Ant.*1132 (lyr.).

**κισσηρίζω, κίσσηρις, κισσηροειδής, κισσηρόω**, incorrect forms for κισηρ-.

**κίσσ-ησις**, εως, ἡ, = κίσσα II, Gal.19.455. **-ητός**, ή, όν, *longed for*, Eust. ad D.P.946.

**κισσηφερής**, v. κισσηρεφής.

⊛ **κίσσῐνος**, η, ον, *of ivy*, E.*Ba.*177, 702; κ. ποτήρ Id.*Alc.*756; χρυσὸς κ. *ivy*-wreath of gold, Callix.2: **κίσσινον**, τό, name of a *plaster*, Orib.*Fr.*88.

**κισσίον**, τό, Dim. of κισσός, = ἀσκληπιάς, Ps.-Dsc.3.92.

**Κίσσιος**, α, ον, *of* or *from Cissia*, in southern Persia, γῆ Hdt.5.49, etc.; Κισσία ἰηλεμίστρια *hired* mourner, A.*Ch.*423 (lyr.).

**κισσό-βρῠος**, ον, *luxuriant with ivy*, Orph.*H.*30.4. **-δέτᾱς**, α, ὁ, Dor. for -δέτης, (δέω A) *bound* or *crowned with ivy*, of Bacchus, cj. in Pi.*Fr.*75.9 (κισσοδόταν, κισσοδαῆ codd.). **-δετος**, ον, = foreg., Nonn.*D.*14.262. **-ειδής**, ές, *like ivy*, Dsc.2.166, Gal.4.556: Subst. κ. (sc. γραμμή), ἡ, Math., the *cissoid curve*, Papp.54.21, Procl. *in Euc.*p.111 F. Adv. -δῶς Sch.Theoc.13.42. **-κόμης**, ου, ὁ, *ivy-crowned*, Διόνυσος *h.Hom.*26.1, cf. *IG*12(7).80 (Arcesine). **-κόρυμβος**, ὁ, *ivy-cluster*, *Hippiatr.*77. **-πλεκτος**, ον, *ivy-twined*, μέλεα κ., of dithyrambs, Antiph.209.7 corr. Mein.: codd. Ath. κισ⟨σ⟩όπληκτα, i. e. *ivy- (thyrsos-) stricken, frenzied*. **-ποίητος**, ον, *made of ivy*, δόρατα Luc.*Bacch.*1.

**κισσός**, Att. **κιττός**, ὁ, *ivy*, *Hedera Helix*, of three kinds, two *climbing* (μέλας and λευκός), and one *creeping* (also called ἕλιξ), Thphr.*HP*3.18.6, cf. Dsc.2.179, *h.Bacch.*40; ἀτενὴς S.*Ant.*826 (lyr.); κισσοῦ στέφανος *OGI*49.7 (Egypt, iii B.C.); sacred to Dionysus, κισσῷ.. στεφανωθεὶς Διόνυσον θεραπεύει E.*Ba.*81 (lyr.); κύκλῳ δὲ περί σε κ. εὐπέταλος ἕλικι θάλλει Ar.*Th.*999: hence οἰνωψ (or οἰνωπός) S.*OC*674 (lyr.). II. = κιρσός (Achaean), Hsch.

**κισσο-στέφᾰνος**, ον, *ivy-crowned*, of Dionysus, *AP*9.524.11. **-στεφής**, ές, = foreg., *Anacreont.*46.5: **κιττ-**, Alciphr.3.48. **-τόμος**, ον, (τέμνω) *ivy-cutting*: κισσοτόμοι (sc. ἡμέραι), αἱ, festival at Phlius, Paus.2.13.4. **-φάγος** [ᾰ], ον, Att. **κιττ-**, *ivy-eating*, Longus 3.5. **-φορέω**, Att. **κιττ-**, *to be decked with ivy*, like the Bacchanals, prob. in *IG*2.1285 (iv B.C.); of a tragic actor, *AP*7.707 (Diosc.); dub. l. in Plu.2.5b. **-φορία**, ἡ, *wearing of ivy-wreaths*, in pl., *IG*12(2).484.5 (Mytil.). ⊛ **-φόρος**, Att. **κιττ-**, ον, *ivy-wreathed*, of Dionysus, Pi.*O.*2.27, Ar.*Th.*988 (lyr.), *BCH*50.240 (Thasos, iii/ii B.C.); ὁ κ. παῖς Διός ib.529 (Marathon, ii A.D.): metaph., κ. διθύραμβοι Simon.148. 2. *luxuriant with ivy*, νάπη E.*Tr.*1066 (lyr.). ⊛ **-φυλλον**, τό, *ivy-leaf*, Διονύσου κ., as a brand, Lxx 3*Ma.*2.29. 2. *part of a torsion-engine shaped like an ivy-leaf*, Ph.*Bel.*70.33. II. = κυκλάμινος, Ps.-Dsc.2.164. ⊛ **-χαίτης**, ου, ὁ, *ivy-tressed*, i. e. *ivy-crowned*, only in voc., κισσοχαῖτ' (i. e. -χαῖτ[ᾰ]) ἄναξ Pratin.Lyr.1.17, Ecphantid.3 (ridiculed by Cratin.324). **-χᾰρής**, ές, *delighting in ivy*, Orph.*H.*52.12. **-χίτων** [ῐ], ωνος, ὁ, ἡ, *ivy-clad*, Id.*L.*261.

**κισσόω**, Att. **κιττ-**, *wreathe with ivy*, κρᾶτα κισσώσας ἐμόν E.*Ba.*205; κεκισσωμένος Alciphr.2.3.

**κισσύβιον** [ῠ], τό, *rustic drinking-cup* of wood, used by the Cyclops, Od.9.346; by Eumaeus, 14.78; κ. ἀμφῶες Theoc.1.27 (but expld. as μόνωτον ποτήριον, Philem.Gloss.ap.Ath.11.476f); ὀλίγῳ ἥδετο κ. Call.*Aet.*1.1.12.—So called, either as made of ivy-wood, Eumolp.ap.Ath.11.477a; or because adorned with ivy-wreaths, Poll.6.97: in late Prose, οἴνου κ. Prisc.p.316 D.

**κισσώδης**, ες, (κίσσα II) *longing like pregnant women*, Dsc.5.6.14.

**κισσ-ών**, ῶνος, ὁ, *ivy-grove*, Hdn.Gr.1.40, al. **-ωσις**, Att. **κιττ-**, εως, ἡ, *crowning with ivy*, Διονύσου *IG*2².1367.21 (pl.). **-ωτός**, ή, όν, *decked with ivy*, νεβρίς *AP*6.172.

**κιστᾱ-φορέω**, *bear the casket* in mystic processions, *BCH*37.97 (Macedonia, ii/iii A.D.). ⊛ **-φόρος**, ὁ, *one who bears it*, *CIG*2052 (Apollonia in Thrace); cf. κιστοφόρος I.

**κίστη**, ἡ, *basket, hamper*, Od.6.76, Ar.*Ach.*1098, al., Thphr.*HP*5.7.5, al., *PCair.Zen.*430.11, al. (iii B.C.), Euph.9, Call.*Hec.*1.2.13 (κείστη), etc.; *writing-case, desk*, Ar.*V.*529; *voting-urn*, *Notiz.Arch.*4.20 (Cyrene, Aug.); = ἀγγεῖον πλεκτόν, Hsch.; made of bark, Thphr. ll. cc.: hence distd. fr. κιβωτός, Ammon.*Diff.*p.81 V.

**Κίστῐβερ**, ὁ, = Lat. *quinquevir cis Tiberim*, *IG*14.1512.

**κιστίδιον**, τό, Dim. of κίστη, *basket*, Artem.1.2.

**κιστίς**, ίδος (εως Nic.Dam.52 J.), ἡ, Dim. of κίστη, Hp.*Mul.*1.104, dub. in Hld.4.11; κιστίδος used to balance ἀσπίδος, Ar.*Ach.*1138.

**κιστοειδής**, ές, *shaped like a chest*, Hsch. s. v. ὀγκίον.

**κίστος**, ὁ, v. κίσθος.

⊛ **κιστοφόρος**, ον, (κίστη) *carrying a basket* in mystic processions, prob. l. in D.18.260 (κιττοφόρος codd., κιστ- v.l. ap.Harp. s. h. v.); cf. κισταφόρος. II. Subst., *coin, with the basket of Dionysus as obverse*, Cic.*Att.*2.6.2, Liv.37.46.

**κίταρις**, εως, ἡ, = κίδαρις (q. v.).

**κιτρᾶτον**, τό, *spiced drink prepared from citron*, Alex.Trall.8.2.

**κιτρέα**, ἡ, *citron-tree*, *Citrus Medica*, *Gp.*10.7.8 (borrowed fr. Lat. *citrea*). **κίτρεος**, α, ον, = κίτρινος, *Stud.Pal.*20.245 (vi A.D.) (borrowed fr. Lat. *citreus*).

**κιτρῑνοειδής**, ές, *of a citron colour*, Sch.Theoc.5.95.

**κίτρῑνος**, η, ον, *of the citron-tree*, ξύλον D.C.61.10. II. *of a citron yellow*, *PMasp.*6 ii 82 (vi A.D.), Hdn.*Epim.*179. III. **κίτρινον**, τό, *a yellowish salve*, Paul.Aeg.7.18.

**κιτρῐοειδής**, ές, *citron-like*, Gal.14.392.

**κιτρῐον**, τό, = κιτρέα, *citron-tree*, *IG*4²(1).126.9 (Epid., ii A.D.), *POxy.*1764.19 (iii A.D.), *Gp.*10.8.1; θύρσοι ἐκ κιτρίων J.*AJ*13.13.5. II. = κίτρον, *citron*, Juba 24, Dsc.1.115.5, Ath.3.84d, Gal.12.77, *Gp.*10.7.8, Alex.Aphr.*Pr.*1.119 (borrowed fr. Lat. *citrium*, cf. Dsc. l. c.). [Parox. in Ath. l. c., v.l. in Dsc. l. c.]

**κιτρόμηλον**, τό, = sq., Dsc.3.104, *Gp.*10.76.7.

**κίτρον**, τό, *fruit of the* κιτρέα, *citron*, cited as Lat. word by Pamphil. ap.Ath.3.85c, cf. Gal.*Vict.Att.*10.

**κιτρό-φυλλον**, τό, *citron-leaf*, *Gp.*9.28.1. **-φυτον**, τό, *citron-tree*, ib.10.8.2. **-χρους**, ουν, *citron-coloured*, Tz.*H.*9.630.

**κίττα, κιττᾰβίζω, κιττάω, κίττησις**, Att. for κισσ-. **κιττάλης**, v. κιξάλλης. **κιττάναλον**· ἡ κρησέρα (κρήσσερα cod.), Hsch.; cf. gen. pl. κιθαναλλων dub. sens. in *PSI*5.485.2; χιταναλλων ib.19 (iii B.C.). **κίτταρις**, v. κίδαρις. **κίτταρος**, ὁ, *wearer of* κίδαρις (Cypr.), Hsch. **κιττός, κιττοφόρος, κίττωσις**, etc., Att. for κισσ-.

**κιττώ**, ἡ, kind of *cassia*, Hebr. *ḳiddah*, Dsc.1.13.

**κῐτών**, ῶνος, ὁ, Dor. (esp. Sicil.) for χιτών, Sophr.35; also *POxy.*1269.30 (ii A.D.), etc.:—Dim. **κιτώνιον**, τό, *PTeb.*406.14 (iii A.D.), etc.

**κίφος**, τό, Messen. for στέφανος, Paus.3.26.9. (For σκίφος, cf. σκιφατόμος.)

**κῐχάνω** [ᾰ], imper. κιχάνετε Il.23.407; inf. κιχάνειν Mosch.2.112: impf. ἐκίχᾰνον Il.3.383: aor. 3 sg. ἔκιχεν Od.3.169, κίχεν Il.24.160; 3 pl. κίχον 18.153; subj. 3 sg. κίχῃσι Od.12.122; part. κιχών 15.157: also non-thematic aor. ἐκίχην [ῐ], 2 sg. ἐκίχεις, like ἐτίθεις from τίθημι, 24.284; 1 pl. κίχημεν or ἐκ- 16.379; 3 dual κιχήτην Il.10.376; subj. κιχείω, κιχείομεν, 1.26, 21.128; opt. κιχείην 2.188; inf. κιχῆναι Od.16.357, κιχήμεναι Il.15.274; part. κιχείς 16.342:—after Hom. **κιγχάνω** [ᾰ] (cf. Eust.1525.16, Hsch., Phot.), first Sol.ap.Phot., A.*Ch.*622, S.*OC*1450 (both lyr.); misspelt κιχάνω E.*Hipp.*1444, *Hel.*597: fut. inf. κιχησέμεν A.R.4.1482: aor. ἔκιχον E.*Ba.*903 (lyr.), κίχον Pi.*P.*9.26, al.; subj. κίχω S.*Aj.*657, E.*Supp.*1069, *Alc.*22; inf. κιχεῖν B.1.67: aor. 1 ἐκίχησα Id.5.148, Opp.*H.*5.116, Musae.149:—Med. (in act. sense), κιχάνομαι Il.11.441, Od.9.266: fut. κιχήσομαι Il.10.370, S.*OC*1487: aor. 1 κιχήσατο Il.10.494, Od.6.51: aor. 2 part. κιχήμενος Il.5.187, 11.451:—poet. Verb (perh. used in the laws of Solon), *reach, hit*, or *light upon, meet with*, μή σε.. παρὰ νηυσὶ κιχείω Il.1.26, cf. Od.13.228; Ἄδμητον ἐν δόμοισιν ἆρα κ.; E.*Alc.*477; *reach, overtake*, ὃν κε.. ποσσὶ κιχείω Il.6.228; κιχήσεσθαι δέ σ' ὀΐω ib.341, cf. 21.605, Pi.*P.*2.50, B.5.148, etc.; τὰ φεύγοντα Id.1.67; ἵππους δ' Ἀτρεΐδαο κιχάνετε Il.23.407; σὲ δουρὶ κιχήσομαι *shall reach* thee, 10.370; εἰς ὅ κεν ἄστυ κιχείομεν till we *reach* it, 21.128; ἧός κε τέλος πολέμοιο κιχείω *arrive at* it, 3.291: sts. of things, βέλος ὠκὺ κιχήμενον the dart *that had just reached* him, 5.187; φθῆ σε τέλος θανάτοιο κιχήμενον 11.451. 2. rarely c. gen., like τυγχάνω, S.*OC*1487.

**κιχήλα**, ἡ, Dor. for κίχλη (q. v.).

**κιχήσιππον**, gloss on κελενδρύονα, Phot. **κίχησις**, εως, ἡ, (κιχάνω) *reaching, attaining*, Hsch. **κιχητός**· ὁ ἐμβάπτεται ὁ λιβανωτός (Cypr.), Id.

⊛ **κίχλη** [ῑ by nature], ἡ, *thrush* (a generic term, including various

species, Arist.*HA*617$^{a}$18), κ. τανυσίπτεροι Od.22.468, cf. Ar.*Av.*591, etc.:—Dor. **κιχήλα** Epich.157, Ar.*Nu.*339:—late Gr. **κίχλα** Alex. Trall.1.10, *Gp.*15.1.19. II. sea-fish, a species of *wrasse*, Epich. 60, Antim.ap.Ath.7.304e ('Antiphanes' codd.), Diocl.*Fr.*135, Arist. *HA*598$^{a}$11, Nic.*Fr.*59, Numen.ap.Ath.7.305c, Opp.*H.*1.126, 4.173: later **κίχλα,** Alex.Trall.1.15.

**κιχληβῶτις,** = ἀνδράχνη, Hsch.; cf. κικριβιντίς.

⊛ **κιχλ-ιδιάω,** Desider. of sq., *have a desire to titter*, *Com.Adesp.*1038. **-ίζω,** *titter, giggle*, Ar.*Nu.*983, Theoc.11.78, *AP*5.244 (Maced.); κιχλίζουσα καὶ μωκωμένη Alciphr.1.33, 3.27, cf. 74; *guffaw*, μέζον ἵππου κ. Herod.7.123: metaph., [ἡδονὴ] σεσαρυῖα καὶ κιχλίζουσα Ph.2.265:—Med., Ar.*Fr.*333.4. (Prop. *chirp like a thrush*, Gramm.ap. Valck.*Animadv. ad Ammon.*p.175 who writes **κιχλάζω**: wrongly expld. as *eat* κίχλαι, *live luxuriously*, Sch.Ar.*Nu.*979.) **-ισμός,** ὁ, *tittering, giggling*, Ar.*Nu.*1073 (pl., v.l. καχασμῶν), cf. *AB*271.

**κιχλοκόσσῦφος,** ὁ, = Lat. *turdus*, *Edict.Diocl.*4.27 (Aegira).

**κίχορα,** ων, τά, *chicory*, *Cichorium Intybus*, Nic.*Al.*429:—also **κιχόρη,** ἡ, Thphr.*HP*7.7.1: **κιχόριον,** τό, ib.1.10.7, al. (= ἀναγαλλίς, Dsc.2.178, s.v.l.); so called in Egypt, Plin.*HN*19.129: in pl., Ar.*Fr.* 293 (nisi leg. **κιχόρεια,** cf. Lat. *cĭchorēa*). [ῐ Nic.l.c., perh. metri gr.]

**κιχοριώδης,** ες, *of the genus of chicory*, φύλλον Thphr.*HP*9.16.4; τὰ κ. ib.7.11.3.

**κιχράω,** = sq., Lxx 1 *Ki.*1.28:—Med., *Gloss.*

**κίχρημι,** *lend*:—Med., κίχραμαι *borrow*, v. χράω:—Subst. **κίχρησις,** εως, ἡ, Tz.*H.*12.303.

**κίω,** κίεις A.*Ch.*680; imper. κίε Od.7.50, A.*Pers.*1068, *Supp.*852 (both lyr.); subj. κίῃς Od.1.311; opt. κίοι 9.42, A.*Supp.*504, κιοίτην, κίοιτε, Od.15.149, 3.347; part. κιών, κιοῦσα (for the accent cf. ἰών), 4.427, al.: impf. ἔκιον, Ep. 1 pl. κίομεν Il.21.456:—*go*, in Hom. almost always of persons, 2.565, 24.471, Od.4.427, etc.; of ships, Il.2.509:—Ep. Verb, Trag. only A.; as etym. of κίνησις, Pl.*Cra.*426c: in Hom. perh. always aor., unless impf. in Il.23.257. (Cf. κινέω, κίνυμαι, Lat. *cio*.)

⊛ **κίων** [ῑ], ονος, Hom. (not in Il.), mostly ἡ; ὁ Od.8.66, 473, 19.38, cf. Eumel.11, Ar.*V.*105, Hdt.4.184, etc.; ἡ Id.1.92, Pi.*P.*1.19, *IG*9(2).258.12 (Cierium, ii B.C.), al.:—*pillar*, freq. in Od. of roof-*pillars*, 19.38, al., cf. *h.Ap.*8; οἱ κ. οἱ ἐν τῷ Λυκείῳ Pl.*Euthd.*303b, cf. *SIG*969.10 (Piraeus, iv B.C.), al.; used as a flogging-post, S.*Aj.*108, Aeschin. 1.59: prov., ἔσθι' ἐλθὼν τοὺς Μεγακλέους κίονας eat the *pillars* of his hall, for, being a spendthrift, he had nothing else left to give, Ar.*Nu.* 815. 2. of natural objects, [Ἄτλας] ἔχει..κίονας αὐτὸς μακράς, αἳ γαῖάν τε καὶ οὐρανὸν ἀμφὶς ἔχουσι Od.1.53; [Ἄτλας] ἕστηκε κίον' (dual) οὐρανοῦ τε καὶ χθονὸς..ἐρείδων A.*Pr.*351; ὁ κ. τοῦ οὐρανοῦ (of Mount Atlas) Hdt.4.184; κίων οὐρανία, of Aetna, Pi.*P.*1.19; for *the Pillars* of Hercules, v. Ἡράκλειος I. II. *columnar gravestone*, *AP*7.163 (Leon.): distd. from στήλη, And.1.38; κ. τετράπλευρος an obelisk, *Epigr.Gr.*1061 (Constantinople); any *column* bearing an inscription, ἀγγράψαι ἐγ κίονα λιθίναν *IG*l.c. (cf. p.xii); ἔσται ἡ στήλη ἐπὶ τοῦ κείονος ib.2$^{2}$.1368.29 (ii A.D.). III. *uvula*, κ. ἀνεσπασμένος Hp. *Epid.*1.26.ε', cf. Arist.*HA*493$^{a}$3. IV. *division of the nostrils, cartilage of the nose*, Ruf.*Onom.*37, Poll.2.79, 80. V. kind of *meteor*, *Placit.*3.2.5. VI. kind of *wart*, Hp.*Nat.Mul.*65, *Mul.*2.212 (where κιών, oxyt.). (Cf. Arm. *siun* 'pillar'.)

**κλαγγ-άζω,** onomatop. word for the cry of cranes, Poll.5.89: hence, of the language of the Scythians, Porph.*Abst.*3.3. **-αίνω,** of hounds, *give tongue*, only pres., A.*Eu.*131. **-άνω,** of birds, *scream*, S.*Fr.*959.4; perh. of the lyre, *twang*, Id.*Ichn.*308. **-έω,** = κλαγγαίνω, of hounds, Theoc.*Ep.*6.5. **-ή,** ἡ, metapl. dat. κλαγγί Ibyc.56: (κλάζω):—*any sharp sound*, e.g. *twang* of the bow, Il.1.49; *scream* of birds, esp. cranes, to which are compared *confused cries of a throng*, 3.3, Od.11.605, cf. Il.2.100, 10.523; *grunting* of swine, Od. 14.412; later, *howling* of wolves and lions, *h.Hom.*14.4, cf. 27.8; *hissing* of serpents, Pi.*Dith.*2.18 (pl.), A.*Th.*381 (pl.); *baying* of dogs, X.*Cyn.*4.5, etc.; also, of musical instruments, Telest.4, Mnesim.4.57 (anap.); of song, S.*Tr.*208 (lyr.); κ. ἀηδόνειος (leg. -όνιος) Nicom. Trag.1; κ. δύσφατος, of Cassandra's prophecies, A.*Ag.*1152 (lyr.); of the *scream* of the Harpies, A.R.2.269. **-ηδόν,** Adv. *with a clang, noise, din*, Il.2.463:—also **-όν,** Babr.124.13, prob. in Id.135.3.

**κλάγ[γ]ος·** γάλα (Cret.), Hsch.; cf. γλάγος.

**κλαγγώδης,** ες, *shrill, strident*, of the voice after vomiting, Hp. *Coac.*550, *Prorrh.*1.17, cf. Gal.16.553, 18(2).301, *UP*7.7; wrongly expld. of ὄμματα εὐκίνητα by Demetr.Lac.ap.Erot.

**κλᾰγερός,** ά, όν, *screaming*, of cranes. *AP*6.109.8 (Antip.).

**κλαγκτός,** ή, όν, = foreg., φωναί Antiph.234.4.

**κλάδα, κλάδας,** metapl. acc. sg. and pl. of κλάδος (q.v.):—but κλᾶδα, κλᾶδας, Aeol. and Dor. acc. sg. and pl. of κλείς.

**κλᾰδᾰρόμ⟨μ⟩ᾰτοι·** εὔσειστοι τὰ ὄμματα, Hsch.

**κλᾰδᾰρόρυγχος,** ὁ, *clapper-bill*, = τροχίλος, Ael.*NA*12.15.

⊛ **κλᾰδᾰρός,** ά, όν, (dissim. fr.*κραδαρός, cf. κραδάω, κραδαίνω) *quivering, 'whippy' in the shaft*, δοράτια Plb.6.25.5; κάμακες *AP*9.322 (Leon., v.l. κλαμ-); *wavy*, ζωηφόρος κλαδαρὰ οἷον ἱμάς *Cat.Cod.Astr.*7.241.

**κλᾰδάσσομαι,** Pass., *rush violently, surge*, αἷμα κλαδασσόμενον διὰ γυίων Emp.100.22.

**κλᾰδάω,** *shake*, aor. inf. κλαδάσαι Hsch. (cf. κραδάω). II. (κλάδος) = κλαδεύω, f.l. for κλᾶν, Phryn.149, cf. Thom.Mag.p.193 R.

**κλᾰδ-εία,** ἡ, *pruning*, of the vine, *Gp.*3.14. **-εύματα,** τά, *leaves stripped off*, *Gloss.* **-ευσις,** εως, ἡ, = κλαδεία, Aq., Sm.*Ca.*2.12, *Gp.*4.5.2. **-ευτέον,** *one must prune*, ib.9.5.11. ⊛ **-ευτήριον,** τό, *pruning-knife*, Hsch. s.v. βράκετ⟨ρ⟩ον. II. pl. κλαδευτήρια, τά, *a festival at pruning-time*, Id. s.v. βίσβην. **-ευτής,** οῦ, ὁ, *pruner*, *Gloss.* **-εύω,** *prune* vines, Artem.1.51, *Gp.*3.14, Epigr. in *Rev. Phil.*19.178; condemned by Phryn.149. **-έω,** = foreg., Arr.*Ind.*11.10. **-εών,** ῶνος, ὁ, = κλάδος, Orph.*A.*925, prob. in *AP*9.78 (Leon.).

**κλᾰδη-φορέω,** *bear young branches*, Sch.E.*Ph.*791. **-φόρος,** ον, *bearing young branches*, Hdn.*Epim.*103.

**κλᾰδί,** metapl. dat. of κλάδος:—but **κλᾱδί,** Aeol., Dor. dat. of κλείς.

**κλάδινος,** *rameus*, *Gloss.*

⊛ **κλάδιον** [ᾰ], τό, Dim. of κλάδος, *twig* or *shoot*, ἀγρώστεως prob. in Philum.ap.Aët.5.124; κλαδίοις ἐλαιῶν αἰτοῦντες Lib.*Or.*16.46, cf. *BGU*1051.13 (i A.D.).

**κλᾰδίσκος,** ὁ, Dim. of κλάδος, Gal.12.35, *Anacreont.*18.4.

**κλαδοειδής,** *ramosus*, *Gloss.*

**κλάδος** [ᾰ], ου, ὁ, *branch, shoot* of a tree, Arist.*Juv.*468$^{b}$25, *GA*752$^{a}$20; *twig*, opp. ἀκρεμών, Thphr.*HP*1.1.9, 1.10.7: generally, *branch*, τῆς ἐλαίης τοὺς κλάδους Hdt.7.19: presented by suppliants, ἐλαίας θ' ὑψιγέννητον κλάδον A.*Eu.*43, cf. *Supp.*22 (anap.), S.*OT*3, 143; also of *laurel branches* used in temples, E.*Ion*80. 2. *plank*, *POxy.* 1738.4, al. (iii A.D.). 3. *branch* of a blood-vessel, Gal.15.141. 4. metaph., ἀπὸ νώτοιο δύο κλάδοι ἀΐσσονται two *arms*, Emp.29.1. 5. κ. ἐλέας, of a young girl, *Epigr.Gr.*368.7:—metapl. forms, dat. κλαδί *Scol.*9, prob. in *SIG*1025.33 (Cos, iv/iii B.C.); τῇ κ. Ael.*NA*4.38 codd. (cf. Eust.58.37); τῷ κ. Choerob. *in Theod.*1.138; acc. κλάδα *Lyr.Adesp.*122; cf. κλάδα[ν]· κλάδον, Hsch.; gen. pl. κλαδέων prob. in Philox.1.3; dat. pl. κλάδεσι Ar.*Av.*239 (lyr.), Ep. κλαδέεσσι Nic. *Fr.*74.19; acc. κλάδας ib.53.

**κλᾰδοτομ-έω,** *prune* vines, *PLond.*1821.382, *PHamb.*23.26 (v A.D.). **-ία,** ἡ, ibid.

**κλᾰδοῦχος,** v. κλειδοῦχος.

**κλᾰδώδης,** ες, *with many* κλάδοι, Sch.Nic.*Th.*544, Eust.1634.26.

**κλᾰδών,** όνος, ὁ, = κλάδος, Hsch. (pl.).

⊛ **κλάζω,** fut. κλάγξω A.*Pers.*948 (lyr.): aor. 1 ἔκλαγξα Il.1.46, A.*Ag.*201 (lyr.): aor. 2 ἔκλᾰγον *h.Pan.*14, B.16.127, Theoc.17.71, etc.: pf. κέκλαγγα X.*Cyn.*3.9, 6.23; subj. κεκλάγγω Ar.*V.*929; Dor. κέκλᾱγα Alcm.7; part. κεκληγώς, pl. κεκλήγοντες Il.17.756, -ῶτες v.l. ib. 16.430, κεκλαγώς Plu.*Tim.*26:—Pass., fut. κεκλάγξομαι Ar.*V.*930:—*make a sharp piercing sound*: 1. of birds, *scream*, οὐκ ἴδον.., ἀλλὰ κλάγξαντος (sc. ἐρῳδιοῦ) ἄκουσαν Il.10.276; of starlings and daws, οὖλον κεκλήγοντες 17.756, etc.; γεράνου φωνὴν ἐνιαύσια κεκληγυίης Hes.*Op.*449; of the eagle, Il.12.207, S.*Ant.*112 (lyr.), cf. *OT* 966, etc. 2. of dogs, *bark, bay*, οἱ μὲν κεκλήγοντες ἐπέδραμον Od. 14.30, cf. Ar.*V.*929, X.ll.cc., etc. 3. of things, as of arrows in the quiver, *clash, rattle*, ἔκλαγξαν δ' ἄρ' ὀϊστοί Il.1.46; of the wind, *whistle*, αἶψα γὰρ ἦλθε κεκληγὼς Ζέφυρος Od.12.408; of wheels, *creak*, A.*Th.*205 (lyr.): c. acc. cogn., κλάζουσι κώδωνες φόβον *ring forth* terror, ib.386; τί νέον ἔκλαγε σάλπιγξ..ἀοιδάν; B.17.3; of the sea, *roar*, ἔκλαγεν δὲ πόντος Id.16.127; of the musician, κιθάρᾳ κλάζεις παιᾶνας μέλπων E.*Ion*905 (lyr.); of Pan on his pipes, *h.Pan.*14; κλάζεις μέλισμα λύρας (of the τέττιξ) *AP*7.196 (Mel.). 4. of men, *shout, scream*, ὀξέα κεκληγώς Il.2.222, 17.88: c. acc. cogn., *shout aloud, ring forth*, κλάζοντες Ἄρη A.*Ag.*48 (anap.); γόον Id.*Pers.*948 (lyr.); Ζεὺς ἔκλαγξε βροντάν *pealed forth* thunder, Pi.*P.*4.23; also ἔκλαγξε κέαρ ὀλοαῖσι στοναχαῖς Id.*Pae.*8.20. 5. less freq. of *articulate* sound, ἄλλο μῆχαρ..μάντις ἔκλαγξεν *shrieked forth* another remedy, A.*Ag.*201 (lyr.); Ζῆνα..ἐπινίκια κλάζων *sounding loudly* the song of victory in honour of Z., ib.174 (lyr.).

**κλᾷθρον,** v. κλεῖθρον. **κλαιόν·** τὸ κανοῦν, Hsch. **κλᾱΐς,** gen. κλᾱῖδος and κλᾱΐδος, ἁ, Dor. for κληΐς, κλείς. **κλάϊστρον,** τό, Dor. for κλεῖστρον (q.v.).

**κλαίω,** old Att. **κλάω** (v. infr.) [ᾱ] never contracted; Aeol. **κλαΐω** *Lyr.Adesp.*65; Ep. 2 sg. opt. κλαίοισθα Il.24.619: Att. impf. ἔκλαον, Ep. κλαῖον Od.10.201, Ion. κλαίεσκον Il.8.364, Hdt.3.119, A.*Fr.*312: fut. κλαύσομαι, 2 sg. κλαύσῃ or κλαύσει, Il.18.340, Ar.*V.*1327 (lyr.), *Nu.*58, 933 (anap.), E.*Cyc.*554, etc., rarely κλαυσοῦμαι Ar.*Pax* 1081, 1277 (in mock heroic verses); Att. also κλαιήσω Hyp.*Dem.Fr.*10, κλᾱήσω D. 19.310, 21.99, later κλαύσω Theoc.23.34, D.H.4.70, *Ev.Jo.*16.20, Man. 3.143: aor. ἔκλαυσα, Ep. κλαῦσα Od.3.261:—Med., aor. ἐκλαυσάμην S.*Tr.*153, *AP*7.412 (Alc. Mess.):—Pass., fut. κλαυσθήσομαι Lxx *Ps.* 77(78).64, κεκλαύσομαι Ar.*Nu.*1436: aor. ἐκλαύσθην Lyc.831, J.*AJ*8. 11.1 (v.l. κλαυθείς), *IG*14.2128: pf. κέκλαυμαι A.*Ch.*687, S.*OT*1490, κέκλαυσμαι Lyc.273, Plu.2.115b. [κλάω [ᾱ] is recognized as Att. by A.D.*Adv.*187.26, and is found in codd. of Ar.*Av.*341, Pl.*Lg.*792a, *Phlb.*48a: ἔκλᾰε in later poetry, Theoc.14.32, dub. in Hermesian.7.33 (cf. κλέω A).] (κλᾰϝ-yω, cf. κλαυ-θμός, etc.) I. intr., *cry, wail, lament*, of any loud expression of pain or sorrow, κλαῖον δὲ λιγέως Od.10.201; πρὸς οὐρανόν Il.8.364; τῆς ἄρα κλαιούσης ὄπα σύνθετο Od.20.92; for the dead, Il.19.297, etc.; ἀμφὶ δὲ σὲ Τρῳαὶ καὶ Δαρδανίδες κλαύσονται 18.340; κλαίοντα καὶ ὀδυρόμενον Pl.*R.*388b, etc.; διὰ τί οἱ κλαίοντες ὀξὺ φθέγγονται; Arist.*Pr.*900$^{a}$20; δάκρυσι κ. D.C. 59.27; of infants, Sor.1.107, al.; of *crying* for joy, κλαῖον δὲ λιγέως, ἁδινώτερον ἤ τ' οἰωνοί κτλ. Od.16.216, cf. Eust.1799.57. 2. αὐτὸν κλαίοντα ἀφήσω I shall send him home *crying, howling*, i.e. *well beaten*, Il.2.263: freq. in Att., κλαύσεται *he shall howl*, i.e. *he shall suffer for it*, Ar.*V.*1327 (lyr.), *Pl.*174, al.; κλαύσομαι Id.*Nu.*58; κλαύσει μακρά you shall *howl* loudly, i.e. suffer severely, Id.*Pax* 255, cf. 1277; κλαύσῃ φιλῶν τὸν οἶνον E.*Cyc.*554; κλάοις ἄν, εἰ ψαύσειας A.*Supp.*925; κλαίων *to your sorrow* or *loss*, *at your peril*, S.*OT*401, 1152, *Ant.*754; κλάων ἄψῃ τῶνδε E.*Heracl.*270, cf. *Hipp.*1086; δεῦρ' ἔλθ' ἵνα κλάῃς Ar.*Nu.* 58; κλάειν ἔγωγέ σε λέγω (opp. χαίρειν σοι λέγω) Id.*Pl.*62, cf. Hdt.

4.127; κλάειν εἴπωμεν Eup.363; κλάειν κελεύων Λάμαχον Ar.*Ach.* 1131; κλάειν σε μακρὰ κελεύσας Id.*Eq.*433; σὲ δ' ἐὰν κλάειν μακρὰ τὴν κεφαλὴν *suffer* terribly in the head, Id.*Pl.*612 (anap.), cf. *V.*584. **II.** trans., *weep for, lament*, κλαῖεν ἔπειτ' Ὀδυσῆα, φίλον πόσιν Od.1.363, cf. Il.20.210; τι A.*Ag.*890, S.*El.*1117; τὰ αὑτοῦ πάθη Plu.*Alc.*33:— Pass., *to be mourned* or *lamented*, ἀνδρὸς εὖ κεκλαυμένου A.*Ch.*687: impers., μάτην ἐμοὶ κεκλαύσεται Ar.*Nu.*1436. **2.** *cry for*, of infants, μάμμας καὶ τιτθάς Arr.*Epict.*2.16.39. **III.** Med., *bewail oneself, weep aloud*, A.*Th.*920 (lyr.): pf. part. Pass. κεκλαυμένος *bathed in tears*, Id.*Ch.*457 (lyr.), 731, S.*OT*1490. **2.** trans., *bewail to oneself*, πάθη..πόλλ' ἔγωγ' ἐκλαυσάμην Id.*Tr.*153; κλαιόμενα τάδε βρέφη σφαγάς A.*Ag.*1096 (lyr.).

**κλαιωμῖλία**, poet. -ίη, ἡ, (ὁμιλία) *fellowship in tears*, *AP*9.573 (Ammian.).

**κλᾳκοφόρος**, ὁ, perh. *bearer of the key* (cf. κλᾴξ), name of hero worshipped at Epidaurus, $IG4^2(1)$.297; also, title of priest at Messene, ib.5(1).1447 (iii/ii B.C.).

✱**κλᾳκτός**, ά, όν, Dor. for κλειστός, *IG*5(1).1390.91 (Andania, i B.C.), *BCH*27.271 (Argos). **κλάλιον**, v. κλανίον.

**κλᾶμα** or **κλάμα**, ατος, τό, = κλάσμα, περονῶν *IG*4.1588.13,42 (Aegina, v B.C., pl.).

**κλᾰμᾰρός**, ά, όν, v.l. for κλαδαρός, *AP*9.322 (Leon.), cf. Hsch.

**κλαμβός**, ή, όν, *docked, cropped*, ὦτα *Hippiatr.*14, cf. 17.

✱**κλᾶμμα**, ατος, τό, Aeol. for κλῆμα, Alc.*Oxy.*1788 *Fr.*15 ii 19.

**κλαμμίς**· ἀναδενδράς, Hsch. **κλαμυστῆσαι**· βοῆσαι, καλέσαι, Id.

✱**κλανίον** (or **κλάνιον**), τό, *bracelet*, *POxy.*796 (i/ii A.D.), *PTeb.*417.37 (iii A.D.), Hsch., *Gloss.* (also **κλαρά** Hsch.):—written **κλάλιον**, *POxy.*114.11 (ii/iii A.D.), al.

**κλᾰνίσκιον**, = χλανίσκιον, *Jahresh.*16 *Beibl.*53 (Athens, iv B.C.).

**κλάννω**, = κλάω, *Gloss.*:—also **κλάνω**, *EM*1.50, al.

**κλᾴξ**, ᾳκός, ἡ, Dor. for κλείς, *key*, $IG4^2(1)$.102.110, al. (Epid., iv B.C.), 5(1).1390.92 (Andania, i B.C.), Theoc.15.33.

**κλᾳξῶ**, Dor. fut. of κλείω, *shut*, Theoc.6.32.

**κλαπάζειν**· χρονίζειν, Hsch.

**κλάπαι**, ῶν, αἱ, *wooden shoes, pattens*, D.C.77.4, cf. Suid. s. v. κωλοβάθρου. **2.** *the stocks*, Sch.Ar.*Pl.*276.

**κλάποι**, οἱ, = foreg. 2, Tz.*H.*13.300.

**κλαρά**, v. κλάνιον. **κλαραγεῖ** (-γείων cod.)· ἐλαφρῶς καθεύδει (Sicel), Hsch. **κλάρας**, = φοῖνιξ, Id. **κλάρες**· αἱ ἐπὶ ἐδάφου⟨ς⟩ ἐσχάραι, Id.

**κλάρια**, τά, v. κληρίον II.

**κλάριοι**· κλάδοι, Hsch.

**Κλάριος** [ᾱ], ὁ, Dor. for κλήριος (which is not found), *distributing by lot*, epith. of Zeus, A.*Supp.*360 (lyr.), Paus.8.53.9.

✱**Κλάριος** [ᾰ], ὁ, *of* Κλάρος, epith. of Apollo, *Rev.Phil.*22.260 (ii A.D.):—hence **Κλαριών**, ῶνος, ὁ, name of month at Notium, *Supp.Epigr.*4.566; at Ephesus, *Jahresh.*15 *Beibl.*207.

**κλᾶρος, κλᾱρόω, κλᾱρονομέω**, Dor. for κληρ-.

**κλᾱρῶται**, ῶν, οἱ, (κλᾶρος) in Crete, *serfs attached to the soil*, Ephor.29 J., Arist.*Fr.*586, Callistr.Hist.10.

**κλᾰσαυχενεύομαι**, (κλάω (A), αὐχήν) Pass., *walk with one's neck awry*, i.e. *with an affected air*, of the son of Alcibiades, Archipp.45.

**κλάσθεον**· κ(λ)εῖθρον, Hsch. (leg. κλᾴσθρον).

**κλᾰσῐβῶλαξ**, ἄκος, ὁ, ἡ, (κλάω A) *breaking clods*, *AP*6.41 (Agath.).

**κλάσ-ις** [ᾰ], εως, ἡ, (κλάω A) *breaking, fracture*, Pl.*Ti.*43e; ἡ κ. τῶν ἀμπέλων *breaking off the shoots and tendrils* of vines, Thphr.*CP*2.14.4 (pl.), cf. 3.7.5, al.; ἡ κ. τοῦ ἄρτου *Ev.Luc.*24.35. **2.** *bending* of the knee joint, Arist.*Pr.*$882^b33$; κ. ὄψεων *refraction*, Alex.Aphr. *in Mete.* 143.9; τὸ σαμεῖον περὶ ὃ ἁ κ. Archyt.ap.Simp. *in Ph.*785.25. **b.** κλάσιν λαβεῖν *to be deflected*, Plot.6.9.8; ὅταν κλάσιν ποιῇ καὶ γωνίαν, of a bandage, Erot. s. v. σκέπαρνος; of the labyrinth of the ear, Gal.*UP* 8.6. **II.** *modulation* of the voice, Ph.1.276, 2.266. **-μα**, ατος, τό, *fragment, morsel*, $IG2^2$.1425.347,368, Lxx 1*Ki.*30.12, D.S.17.13, *Ev.Marc.*6.43, Plu.*TG*19, *AP*6.304 (Phan.), 11.153 (Lucill.); μελάθρων κλάσματα *Inscr.Délos* 400.44 (ii B.C.). **II.** *lesion, rupture*, Vett.Val.110.31. **-μάτιον**, τό, Dim. of foreg., *IG*11(2).161*B*34, 162*B*27 (Delos, iii B.C.).

**κλάσσεται**· ἄρχεται (Syrac.), Hsch. post κασσαύριον.

**κλαστ-άζω**, *dress vines* (cf. κλάσις I.1): metaph., *trim, humble*, Ar.*Eq.*166. ✱**-ήριον**, τό, *knife for dressing vines*, Sch.Ar.*Eq.*166, Hsch. **-ης**, ου, ὁ, *vine-dresser*, Id.

**κλαστόθριξ**, perh. *curly-haired*, *PPetr.*3 p.15 (iii B.C.).

**κλαστός**, ή, όν, (κλάω A) *broken in pieces*, *AP*6.71 (Paul. Sil.). **II.** perh. = foreg., *PPetr.*1 p.54 (iii B.C.), *PCair.Zen.*374.6 (iii B.C.), *Arch.Pap.*1.65 (ii B.C.), etc.

**κλαυθμ-ηρός**, ά, όν, (κλαίω) *plaintive*, Sch.E.*Hec.*337. **-ονή**, ἡ, *weeping, wailing*, cited by Stob. fr. Pl.*Lg.*792a (κλαυμοναί codd.). **-ός**, ὁ, = foreg., Il.24.717, Od.4.212, 801, 17.8, A.*Ag.*1554 (pl., lyr.), Hdt. 1.111, 3.14, etc.; κλαυθμοὶ παίδων Arist.*Pol.*$1336^a35$, cf. Lxx *Ge.*45.2, al., *Ev.Matt.*8.12, Plu.*Rom.*19; κ. μετὰ δακρύων D.S.32.6. **-ῠρίζω**, *make to weep*, τὰ παιδία Plu.2.9a; τοὺς οἰκέτας prob. in Ath.8.364a:— Pass., *weep*, Pl.*Ax.*366d, Conon 48.4, D.S.4.20, etc. **II.** intr. in Act., Hp.*Progn.*24, Sor.1.88. **-ῠρίς**, ίδος, ἡ, in pl., = sq., Opp. *C.*4.248 (with many vv. ll.; κλαυθμυρμῶν cj. Lehrs). **-ῠρισμός**, ὁ, *crying like a child*, Is.*Fr.*163, Plu.*Lyc.*16, Steph. *in Hp.*1.228 D., f. l. in Opp.*C.*4.248 (pl.). **-ώδης**, ες, *broken as if by sobbing*, ἀναπνοαί Hp.*Aph.*6.54; φωναί Hierocl.p.58 A. **-ών**, ῶνος, ὁ, *place of weeping*, Lxx 2*Ki.*5.23, 24.

**κλαυκίθων**· λαμπρυνόμενος τὰς ὄψεις, Hsch. (i.e. γλαυκιόων).

**κλαῦμα**, ατος, τό, (κλαίω) always in pl., *weeping, wailing*, A.*Pers.* 705 (troch.), X.*Cyr.*2.2.14, etc.; κλαυμάτων πηγαί A.*Ag.*887; κλαυμάτων ἄξια And.4.39. **II.** *troubles, misfortunes*, Ar.*Pax* 249; κλαύμαθ' ὑπάρξει τινί, = κλαύσεται, S.*Ant.*932 (anap.).

**κλαυμονή**, v. κλαυθμονή.

✱**κλαυμῠρίζομαι**, = κλαυθμυρίζομαι, Men.*Epit.*432, Hierocl.p.29 A., Max.Tyr.9.3: cf. **κλαυμαριόμενον**· κλαίοντα (Tarent.), Hsch., and **κλαυμαρεῖται**· κλαίει, Id.

**κλαυσείω**, = sq., Apollon.*Lex.* s. v. ὀψείοντες.

**κλαυσιάω**, Desider. of κλαίω, *wish to weep*, τὸ θύριον φθεγγόμενον ἄλλως κ. the door *is like to weep*, i.e. *shall suffer* for creaking, Ar.*Pl.* 1099.

**κλαυσί-γελως** [ῐ], ὁ, acc. -γέλωτα Demetr.*Eloc.*28: dat. pl. -γέλωσι Plu.2.1097f:—*smiles mingled with tears*, πάντας κ. εἶχε X.*HG*7.2.9; nickname of Phryne, Ath.13.591c. **-μᾰχος**, ον, *Rue-the-fight*, parody on the name of *Lamachus* (*Ready-for-fight*), Ar.*Pax* 1293.

**κλαύσιμος**, η, ον, *plaintive*, *Gloss.*

**κλαῦσ-ις**, εως, ἡ, *weeping*, Andronic.Rhod.pp.570, 571 M. **-μα**, ατος, τό, = foreg., Porph.*Gaur.*12.4 (pl.). **-τήρ**, ῆρος, ὁ, *weeper*, Man. 4.192. ✱**-τικός**, ή, όν, *given to mourning*. Adv. -κῶς, ἔχειν Apollon. *Lex.* s. v. ὀψείοντες. **-τός**, ή, όν, (κλαίω) *to be bewailed, mournful*, S.*OC*1360:—also **κλαυτός**, A.*Th.*333 (lyr.), v. l. in S. l. c., cf. Hsch.

✱**κλάω** (A) [ᾰ], impf. ἔκλων (κατ-) Il.20.227, (ἀν-) Th.2.76: fut. κλάσω [ᾰ] J.*AJ*10.11.3, Luc.*DDeor.*11.1: aor. 1 ἔκλᾰσα, Ep. κλάσε Od.6.128, κατά-κλασσε Theoc.25.147:—Med., poet. aor. κλάσσατο *AP*7.124 (Diog. Laert.):—Pass., fut. κλασθήσομαι Arist.*Mete.*$373^a5$; aor. ἐκλάσθην Il.11.584: pf. κέκλασμαι Arist.*APo.*$76^b9$, etc.: aor. 2 part. κλάς (as if from κλῆμι) Anacr.153:—*break, break off*, ἐξ ὕλης πτόρθον κλάσε Od.6.128; ἐκλάσθη δὲ δόναξ Il.11.584; *break off* the luxuriant shoots of the vine, Thphr.*CP*1.15.1 (Pass.), Gal.6.134, Longus 3.29, etc.; κ. ἄρτον 1*Ep.Cor.*10.16, cf. 11.24 (Pass.). **2.** Geom., *deflect, inflect*, usu. of drawing a straight line 'broken back' at a line or surface, κλάσαι εὐθεῖαν τὴν ΑΓΒ ἐν λόγῳ τῷ δοθέντι Papp. 904.17; ἀπὸ δύο σημείων τῶν Β, Ε κλάσαι τὴν ΒΝΞΕ Id.122.3:—more freq. in Pass., Arist.*APo.* l. c.; ἡ κεκλασμένη (sc. γραμμή) Id.*Ph.*$228^b24$; αἱ κλώμεναι εὐθεῖαι Apollon.Perg.*Con.*2.52; ἐὰν ἀπὸ τῶν σημείων κλασθῶσιν ib.3.52; κεκλάσθω Euc.3.20, al.; of visual rays, Arist.*Mete.* $377^b22$, *Pr.*$912^b29$; of arteries, Gal.9.84: generally, καμπαῖς κεκλασμένας ὑποπορεύσεις Plu.2.968b; κεκλ. στολίδες ib.64a; τὰ κλώμενα τῶν ῥευμάτων their *broken* courses, ib.747d. **3.** metaph., *break, weaken, frustrate*, τὴν ἐλπίδα J.*BJ*3.7.13, cf. *Epigr.Gr.*348 (Cios): in pf. part. Pass., κεκλασμένη φωνή *weak, effeminate* voice, Hp.*Epid.*7.80, Arist.*Phgn.*$813^a35$ (also of the Siren's song, Vett.Val.108.28, cf. κ. ἀοιδή 242.10); τὰ κεκλ. τῶν ὀμμάτων *enfeebled* eyes, Arist.*Phgn.* $808^a9$; κεκλ. μέλη *varied by modulation*, Plu.2.1138c; ῥυθμὸς κεκλ. *broken* rhythm, Longin.41.1; τὸ κεκλ. καὶ παντοδαπόν (sc. τῆς λέξεως) Phld.*Rh.*1.198 S. **b.** of emotion, ἐκλάσθην πρὸς ἔλεον J.*Vit.*43.

**κλάω** (B) [ᾱ], Att. for κλαίω (q. v.).

**κλεαινός**, ή, όν, in Hsch. corrupt for κλεεννός.

**κλέβδην**, Dor. -δᾱν, Adv. *by stealth*, A.D.*Adv.*198.6, *EM*103.13.

**κλεεινός**, ή, όν, poet. (Ion.) form of κλεινός, Socr.ap.D.L.2.42.

**κλεεννός**, ά, όν, Lyr. (Aeol.) form of κλεινός, *famous*, Simon.120, Pi.*P.*4.280 (Sup.), 5.20, *Scol.*5.

**κλέζω**· καλῶ, φωνῶ, Hsch.

**κλεηδών**, όνος, ἡ, Ion. and Ep. for κληδών (q. v.). **κλέθος**· κληδόνα, Hsch. **κλεῖα**, poet. contr. from κλέεα, pl. of κλέος (q. v.).

**κλειδ-αγωγία**, ἡ, *procession of key-bearers*, *BCH*44.85 (Lagina). **-άρχης**, ου, ὁ, *keeper of the keys*, of St. Peter, Porph.*Chr.*23.

✱**κλειδᾶς**, ᾶ, ὁ, = κλειδοποιός, prob. in *BGU*429.14 (ii/iii A.D.).

**κλειδίον** (on the accent v. Hdn.Gr.1.356), τό, Dim. of κλείς, *little key*, κλειδία..Λακωνίκ' ἄττα, τρεῖς ἔχοντα γομφίους Ar.*Th.*421, cf. *Fr.* 16, $IG2^2$.1533.27 (iv B.C.); τὸ κ. τοῦ οἰκήματος Arist.*Mir.*$832^b23$: without dimin. sense, τὰ κ. τῶν οὐρανῶν Porph.*Chr.*26. **2.** *stopcock*, Hero *Spir.*1.24, *POxy.*2146.7 (iii A.D.). **II.** = κλείς III, of the tunny, Ath.7.315d; cf. κλιδία. **III.** a kind of *astringent pill*, Gal.13.87, 290, Paul.Aeg.3.40; or *astringent suppository*, κ. ὑπόθετον Alex.Trall.9.3. (κληδ- is not found.)

✱**κλειδοποιός**, ὁ, *locksmith*, *PTeb.ined.*, *PLips.*3 i 10 (iii A.D.), Sch. Paul.Al.*P.*2, *Cat.Cod.Astr.*5(3).88.

✱**κλειδουχ-έω**, Att. κληδ-, *to be a* κλειδοῦχος, κ. θεᾶς *to be* her *priestess*, E.*IT*1463: abs., -οῦντος Ἀρίστωνος *OGI*170 (Delos, ii/i B.C.). **II.** γλώσσης πικροῖς κέντροισι κληδουχούμενοι, perh. *kept in check*, E.*HF* 1288. **-ος**, Att. κληδ-, ον, (ἔχω) *holding the keys*: hence, *having charge* or *custody of* a place, Ἔρωτα τᾶς Ἀφροδίτας θαλάμων κληδοῦχον E.*Hipp.*540 (lyr.); Ἰώ, κ. Ἥρας her *priestess*, A.*Supp.*291, cf. Phoronis 4, E.*IT*131 (lyr.), $IG2^2$.974.23, 3.172.7; κ. Διός E.*Hyps.Fr.*3(1) iv 28; of Pallas, *tutelary goddess*, Ar.*Th.*1142 (lyr.); τῶν συνδέσμων ἑκάστου κ. Μοῖρα *protectress of*.., Plu.2.591b; of Aeacus, *IG*14.1746; κ. νεκύων πύλαι *AP*7.391 (Bass.); of Hecate, Orph.*Fr.*316. **II.** of the numbers 4 and 10, believed by the Pythag. to be *the keys of the order of nature*, *Theol.Ar.*22, 60: wrongly called κλαδοῦχοι (fr. κλάδος), through misunderstanding of Dor. κλᾳδ-, Lyd.*Mens.*1.15 (v. l. κλειδ-), *EM*253.50.

**κλειδοφορ-έω**, *bear keys*, = κλειδουχέω I, *BCH*44.72 (Lagina), etc.; **-ία**, ἡ, ib.11.13 (ibid.), *Supp.Epigr.*4.303 (Panamara). **-ος**, ἡ, *BCH* 5.186 (Lagina); κ. Ἑκάτης *Supp.Epigr.*4.301 (Panamara).

**κλειδο-φῠλάκιον** [ᾰ], τό, *safe for keeping keys*, prob. in *Supp.Epigr.* 4.270 (Panamara). **-φύλαξ** [ῠ], ἄκος, ὁ, ἡ, *one who keeps the keys*, Luc.*Am.*14.

**κλειδ-όω,** (κλείς) *lock up*, in Pass., ναὸς κεκλειδωμένος *SIG*996.19 (Smyrna), cf. *PMasp.*309.29 (vi A. D.), Sch.Ar.*Av.*1159, *Ec.* 361. **–ωμα,** ατος, τό, *fastening*, Suid. s. v. κλείθροις :—also ***–ωσις,** εως, ἡ, Sch.Ar.*Av.*1159.

**κλείζω,** fut. κλείξω, Dor. for κλῄζω.

**κλειθρ-ία** (sc. ὀπή), ἡ, *keyhole* or *chink* in a door, Luc.*Nec.*22 ; Ion. **κληϊθρίη** prob. in Pherecyd.Syr.ap.D.L.1.122 (vulg. κλειήθρης, which Menage corrects κληΐθρης or κλειθρίης, Dind. κληϊθρίης). **–ίον,** τό, Dim. of κλεῖθρον, Hero *Aut.*9.5, al. **–ιώδης,** ες, (κλειθρία) *full of chinks, Gloss.* ***–ον,** Ion. **κλήϊθρον,** Att. **κλῇθρον,** Dor. **κλᾷθρον** (v. infr.), τό, (κλείω A) *bar* for closing a door, in pl., κλήθρων λυθέντων A.*Th.*396 ; διοίγειν κλῇθρα S.*OT*1287, cf. 1294 ; κλῇθρα πύλης, δόμων, Id.*Ant.*1186, E.*HF*1029 (lyr.) ; κλῇθρα χαλάσθω Ar.*V.*1484 ; κλήθροισι τὰ προπύλαια πακτοῦν Id.*Lys.*264 ; διακόπτοντες ταῖς ἀξίναις τὰ κλεῖθρα X.*An.*7.1.17 ; σιδηρᾶ κ. Pl.*Ax.*37:b ; sg., ἀμφιδέαι.. ἀπὸ κλείθρου *IG*2[2].1627.319. 2. *boom* of a harbour, τοῦ λιμένος τὸ κ. Aen.Tact.11.3 : usu. in pl., τὰ στόματα τῶν λιμένων φράττειν τοῖς κ. Ph.*Bel.*94.42, cf. D.S.18.64 ; τὰ κ. τοῦ Πειραιέως Ath.12.535d. 3. ἐπὶ θάμνοις καὶ κλείθροις *fences, railings*, Gal.12.296. II. = κλειθρία, μεγάροιο διὰ κλήϊθρον ἔδυνεν *h.Merc.*146. 2. metaph., οἱ τὰ κ. ἔχοντες (sc. τῆς Πελοποννήσου), of the Corinthians, Str.8.6.20, cf. 9.4.15. 3. *entrance of the windpipe*, Hp.*Morb.*2.28. 4. as place-name, ἐν τοῖς Κλάθροις in the *Narrows*, *Mnemos.*42.332 (Argos).

**κλειθροποιός,** ὁ, *locksmith, Gloss.*

**κλείματα·** ὑποδήματα, Hsch. ; cf. κλῆμα III, κλίμα VI.

**κλεινία,** τά, *lock-gates* (?), *PKlein.Form.*1023 (iv/v A. D.).

**κλεινός,** ή, όν, Aeol. **κλεεννός** (q. v.), (κλέος) poet. Adj. *famous, renowned*, νῆσος Sol.19.3 ; freq. epith. of cities, Pi.*O.*3.2, 6.6, Epich.185 ; esp. of Athens, Pi.*Fr.*76, A.*Pers.*474, E.*Ph.*1758 (troch.) ; of persons, κ. οἰκιστήρ Pi.*P.*1.31 ; μνῆμα τόδε κλεινοῖο Μεγιστία Epigr.ap.Hdt.7.228 ; Διὸς κλεινὴ δάμαρ A.*Pr.*834 ; ὁ κ. Φιλοκτήτης S.*Ph.*575 ; ὁ πᾶσι κ. Οἰδίπους καλούμενος *all-renowned*, Id.*OT*8 ; also ironically, ὁ κ. νυμφίος Id.*El.*300 ; τόξοισι κλεινός A.*Pr.*872 ; of things, –ότερον γάμον Pi.*P.*9.112 ; τὰ κ. αἰνίγματα S.*OT*1525 (troch.) ; κ. ὄνομα Ar.*Av.*810 ; κ. τόξα S.*Ph.*654 : Sup., –ότατος στέφανος E.*IA*1529 (anap.) ; σοφία –οτάτη Ar.*Nu.*1024 : neut. pl. as Adv., στρατηλατήσας κλεινὰ E.*HF* 61 : rare in Prose, Pl.*Lg.*721c, *Sph.*243a ; καὶ τοῦτο κλεινὸν αὐτοῦ is *well-known* of him, Luc.*Per.*18. II. in Crete, = τὰ παιδικά, like Att. καλός, Ephor.149 J., Ath.11.782c.

**κλεῖξαι,** Dor. aor. 1 inf. Act. of κλείζω, κλῄζω (A) (q. v.).

**κλείπους·** κόσμος τις τοῦ καλουμένου γείσους, Hsch. **κλεῖρος·** κλειδίον, Id.

***κλείς,** ἡ, gen. κλειδός ; Att. acc. κλεῖν, v. infr. I. 3, III, later κλεῖδα *AP* 6.306 (Aristo), Plu.*Art.*9 : pl. κλεῖδες, κλεῖδας, contr. κλεῖς, v. infr. III, dat. κλεισίν Pl.*Ax.*371b :—Ion. **κληΐς** [ῑ], κληΐδος, κληΐδα, etc. (Hom. uses only the Ion. form) :—Dor. **κλᾱΐς,** κλαΐδος [ῐ] Simon.23, Pi.*P.*9.39 ; but acc. pl. κλαῖδας ib.8.4 ; acc. κλαΐδα or κλᾷδα Call.*Cer.*45 ; cf. κλᾴξ :—Aeol. **κλᾶϊς** (κλαῖς cod.)· μοχλός, Hsch. ; κλάϊς acc. κλάϊν *Et.Gud.*ap.Schaefer *Greg.Cor.*p.584 : pl. κλᾷδες (κλᾶδες cod.)· ζυγά, Hsch. :—old Att. **κλῄς,** κλῇδος, acc. κλῇδα E.*Med.*212 (anap.), 661 (lyr.) : κλείς and κλῄς in the same Att. Inscr., *IG*2[2].1414.44 and 47. (κλᾱϜίς, cf. Lat. *clavis, claudo.*) 1. *bar, bolt*, θύρας σταθμοῖσιν ἐπῆρσε (sc. Hera, from within) κληῗδι κρυπτῇ Il.14.168, cf. Od.21.241 ; κληῗδος ἱμάς ib.4.802, cf. 838 ; ἐπὶ δὲ κληῗδ' ἐτάνυσσεν ἱμάντι 1.442 ; = ἐπιβλής, Il.24.455. 2. *catch* or *hook*, passed through the door from the outside to catch the strap (ἱμάς) attached to the bar (ὀχεύς), ἐν δὲ κληῗδ' ἧκε, θυρέων δ' ἀνέκοπτεν ὀχῆας ἄντα τιτυσκομένη Od.21.47, cf. 50 ; οἴξασα κληῗδι θύρας Il.6.89 ; δοιοὶ δ' ἔντοσθεν ὀχῆες εἶχον ἐπημοιβοί, μία δὲ κληῒς ἐπαρήρει 12.456, cf. Parm.1.14. 3. later, *key*, τὴν κλεῖν ἐφέλκεται Lys.1.13 ; κλεῖν παρακλείδιον a false *key*, Pl.Com.77 : pl., κλῇδας οἶδα δώματος A.*Eu.*827, cf. E.*Ba.*448 ; Λακωνικὴ κ. Men.343 ; κυριεύοντα τῶν κ. *OGI*229.56 (Smyrna, iii B. C.) ; of a sacred *key* carried in processions, *SIG*900.14 (Panamara, iv A. D.), 996.24 (Smyrna, perh. i A. D.). 4. metaph., Ἁσυχία βουλᾶν τε καὶ πολέμων ἔχοισα κλαΐδας Pi.*P.*8.4, cf. 9.39 ; ἔστι κἀμοὶ κλῂς ἐπὶ γλώσσῃ, of silence, A.*Fr.*316, cf. S.*OC*1052 (lyr.) ; καθαρὰν ἀνοῖξαι κλῇδα φρενῶν E.*Med.*661 (lyr.) ; κλῇδας γάμου φυλάττει, of Hera, Ar.*Th.*976 (lyr.) ; of the *key* to a problem, Vett.Val.179.4. II. *hook* or *tongue* of a clasp, Od.18.294. 2. *stop-cock*, Hero *Spir.*1.25. III. *collar-bone*, prob. so called from its hook shape (v. supr. I. 2), Hom. (only in Il.), ὅθι κληῒς ἀποέργει αὐχένα τε στῆθός τε 8.325 ; κληῗδα παρ' ὦμον πλῆξ', ἀπὸ δ' αὐχένος ὦμον ἐέργαθεν ἠδ' ἀπὸ νώτου 5.146 ; ᾗ κληῗδες ἀπ' ὤμων αὐχέν' ἔχουσι 22.324, cf. Hp.*Aër.*7, *Art.*13 ; παῖσον ἡμᾶς ὑπὸ κλῇδος S.*Tr.*1035 ; τὴν κλεῖν συνετρίβην And.1.61 ; τὴν κλεῖν κατεαγώς D.18.67 : pl., Diog. Apoll.6, etc. ; τὰ πλάγια καὶ τὰς κλεῖδας Arist.*HA*513[b]35 ; αἱ κλεῖδες (v.l. κλεῖς) καὶ αἱ πλευραί, of the crocodile, ib.516[a]28 ; κλεῖδες ὀπταί roast *shoulder-bones* of the tunny (with play on I. 3, *visible* keys, opp. κρυπταὶ κλεῖδες of the Laconians), Aristopho 7.2, cf. Diph.Siph.ap. Ath.8.357a. IV. *rowing bench* in a ship, freq. in Od., always in pl. ; ἐπὶ κληῗσι καθίζειν 2.419, etc. ; κληῗδεσσιν ἐφήμενοι 12.215 ; once in Il., πεντήκοντ' ἔσαν ἄνδρες ἐπὶ κληῗσιν 16.170 ; δησάμενοι.. ἐπὶ κληῗσιν ἐρετμά Od.8.37. V. of promontories, straits, etc., Κληῗδες or Κληῗδες τῆς Κύπρου Hdt.5.108, cf. Str.14.6.3 ; πόντου κλῇδ', of the Bosporus, E.*Med.*212 (lyr.). VI. in pl., *sacred chaplets*, Id.*Tr.*256 (anap.) (Ephes., acc. to Hsch.). VII. in versification, *clausula, cadence*, Sch.Ar.*Pax* 1127.

**κλεισ-ία,** ἡ, *inn*, *IG*4[2](1).114.21, 30, 109 ii 151, al. (Epid.). II. v. sq. ***–ιάδες,** αἱ, *door opening into the* κλείσιον, *street-door* of a house, identified with the αὔλειος θύρα, Plu.*Publ.*20, Poll.4.125, 9.50 : written κλεισίαι in Ael.Dion.*Fr.*231 ; κλεισιάδες θύραι D.H.5.39 ; = δίθυροι πύλαι, Moer.p.227 P. ; but, *inner door*, opp. αὔλειος, ἐν οἰκίαις αὔλειοι πρόκεινται κλεισιάδων Ph.1.520 ; οἴκοι καταμένειν καὶ μηδὲ τὰς κ. ὑπερβαίνειν Id.2.82, cf. 4 ; οὐ μόνον τειχῶν ἐντὸς ἀλλὰ καὶ κλεισιάδων θαλαμευομένοις ἀποζῆν Id.ap.Eus.*PE*8.14 : metaph., μεγάλαι κ. ἀναπεπτέαται.. τῷ Πέρσῃ a wide *entrance*, Hdt.9.9, cf. Plu.*Alc.*10, Aristid. *Or.*38(7).21. II. *sluice-gates*, D.H.1.66. (Usu. written κλισ–, but κλεισ– Plu.*Publ.* l. c. codd.) **–ίον,** τό, *outhouse, shed*, τῆς οἰκίας τὸ κ. Antiph.21, cf. Lys.12.18, D.18.129 (here perh. = *brothel*), *IG*11(2). 158 *A* 56, 287 *A* 146 (Delos, iii B. C.), *BCH*35.243 (ibid., ii B. C.), *Ephes.* 2.75 (i B. C.) : pl., *sheds* for cattle, D.Chr.40.9. 2. *shrine, chapel*, Paus.4.1.7, *BCH*33.72 (Cappadocia). [First syll. long in Antiph. l. c. ; written κλεισίον *IG* l. c., *BCH*35 l. c., Hdn.Gr.1.356, 2.415, Ael. Dion. l. c. ; later κλισ– *Ephes.* l. c., *BCH*33 l. c., freq. in codd. ; prob. fr. κλίνω as 'lean-to', 'penthouse', rather than fr. κλείω as stated by Poll.9.50.]

**κλεῖσις,** εως, ἡ, (κλείω A) v. κλῇσις.

**κλεῖσμα,** ατος, τό, *barrier*, Tz.*H.*1.903.

**κλεισμός,** ὁ, *storing under lock and key*, οἴνου *POxy.*1578.7 (iii A. D.).

***κλεισούρα,** ἡ, *narrow pass, defile*, Procop.*Pers.*2.29, Suid. (also s. vv. ἐμβολήν, ὀχύρωμα).

**κλειστός,** Ion. **κληϊστός,** old Att. **κληστός,** ή, όν, *that can be shut* or *closed*, κληϊσταὶ σανίδες Od.2.344 ; χῶμα γαίας κ. E.*Fr.*617 ; βεβαίως κ. Th.2.17 ; κ. λιμήν Id.7.38 ; κ. ἀναβάσεις Aen.Tact.22.19, cf. Str.14.6.3, Scyl.29, al. ; κ. ὕδωρ Aristobul.35 J. ; θυρίδες κ. D.S.20.85, cf. Luc.*VH*1.24, Philostr.*Im.*1.13. 2. *closed*, διώρυγες Str.15.1. 50, al.

**κλεῖστρον,** τό, = κλεῖθρον, Luc.*Tox.*57, *PMag.Osl.*1.317 :—Dor. **κλᾴστρον** [ᾰ], γλεφάρων ἀδὺ κ. Pi.*P.*1.8 ; **κλᾷσθρον,** Hsch. (κλάσθεον cod.).

**κλειτοπόδιον,** part of a ship, Poll.1.85.

**κλειτορ-ιάζω,** *touch the* κλειτορίς, Ruf.*Onom* 111, Hsch., Suid. :—also **–ίζω,** v.l. in Poll.2.174. **–ίς,** ίδος, ἡ, *clitoris*, Ruf.*Onom.*111, etc. II. a gem, Ps.-Plu.*Fluv.*25.5.

***κλειτός,** ή, όν, (κλείω B) *renowned, famous*, ἐπίκουροι Il.3.451, 6.227, etc. ; βασιλῆες Od.6.54 ; γενεά Pi.*N.*6.61 ; of things, *splendid, excellent*, ἑκατόμβη Il.4.102, cf. Pi.*P.*10.33 ; Πανοπεύς, Ἰωλκός, Il.17.307, Pi.*P.*4.77.

**κλεῖτος** (A), εος, τό, poet. for κλέος, Alcm.96, cf. Hsch. s. v. κλειτή ; **κλῆτος,** Suid.

**κλεῖτος** (B), εος, τό, = sq., pl. κλείτεα A.R.1.599 cod. Laur. (v. l. κλίτεα) : elsewh. κλίτος (q. v.).

**κλειτύς,** ύος, ἡ, acc. pl. κλειτῦς Il.16.390 : (κλίνω) :—*slope, hillside*, Il. l. c., Od.5.470 ; Παρνησίαν ὑπὲρ κλειτύν S.*Ant.*1145 (lyr.), cf. Limen.2 ; Τιρυνθίαν πρὸς κ. S.*Tr.*271, etc. ; τὰ ἐγ Κλειτύϊ (place-name) *IG*12(5).1076.38 (Ceos, iv/iii B. C.). [ῡ in acc. κλειτύν Od. l. c., elsewh. ῠ S.*Tr.* l. c., etc. : freq. written κλι– in codd., but κλει– in *IG* and Limen. ll. cc., cf. Hdn.Gr.2.416.]

***κλείω** (A), fut. κλείσω X.*An.*4.3.20 (ἀπο–), Him.*Or.*22.7 ; rare fut. κατα-κλιῶ, v. κατακλείω : aor. ἔκλεισα X.*An.*7.1.36, Pl.*Ep.*348b : pf. κέκλεικα Thphr.*Char.*18.4, LXX 1 *Ki.*23.20, Luc.*Tox.*30 : plpf. ἐκεκλείκειν App.*Hann.*47 :—Med., aor. 1 ἐκλεισάμην (κατ–) X.*Cyr.* 7.2.5, (ἐγ–) Id.*HG*6.5.9 :—Pass., fut. κλεισθήσομαι (συγ–) ib.5.2.19 : aor. ἐκλείσθην D.23.110, etc. : pf. κέκλειμαι (later κέκλεισμαι f.l. in Ar.*V.*198) (v. infr.) :—Ion. **κληΐω** (ἀπο–) Hdt.4.7 : aor. ἐκλήϊσα Od. 24.166, (ἐξ–) Hdt.1.144, Ep. κλήϊσα Od.19.30 ; inf. κληῗσαι 21.382 :—Med., fut. κληϊσσομαι cj. in Nonn.*D.*2.310 :—Pass., aor. ἀπ-εκληΐσθην Hdt.1.165, 3.55, 58 : pf. κεκλήϊμαι 2.121.β', cf. 3.117, 7.129 (with vv.ll.) : plpf. ἀπ-εκεκλέατο 9.50 codd. :—old Att. **κλῄω** (also Trag., cf. *An.Ox.*1.226), fut. κλῄσω Th.4.8 : aor. ἔκλῃσα E.*Or.*1447 (lyr.), Th.2.4, Pl.*R.*560c : pf. κέκλῃκα (ἀπο–) Ar.*Av.*1262 :—Med., fut. κεκλήσομαι Id.*Lys.*1071 : aor. περι-κλῄσασθαι Th.7.52 :—Pass., aor. ἐκλῄσθην (κατ–, ξυν–) Id.1.117, 4.67, etc. : pf. κέκλῃμαι (v. infr.) :—Dor. fut. κλᾳξῶ Theoc.6.32 : aor. ἀπό-κλᾳξον, –κλᾴξας, Id.15.43, 77, ἔκλᾳξε Cerc.7.2, cf. κλάκαι (leg. κλᾷσαι)· κλεῖσαι, Hsch. :—Med., impf. κατ-εκλᾴζετο Theoc.18.5 :—Pass., aor. κατ-εκλᾴσθην Id.7.84, but part. συγκατα-κλαιχθείς *Chron.Lind.D.*62 : pf. 3 pl. κατα-κέκλᾳνται Epich.141.—Cf. κλῄζω (B). (κλείς) :—*shut, close, bar*, Hom. (only in Od.), κλήϊσεν δὲ θύρας *barred* the doors, 21.387 ; ἐκλήϊσεν ὀχῆας *shot* the bars, so as to close the door, 24.166 ; κλῄειν πύλας E. *HF*997, Pl.*R.* l. c., etc. ; κ. πηκτὰ δωμάτων Ar.*Ach.*479 ; κλεῖδες.., αἷς τὰς θύρας κλείουσιν Aristopho 7 ; Ἐτεοκλέους.. κλῄσας στόμα E. *Ph.*865 ; κανθώς Cerc. l. c. ; λάρυγγα Gal.6.65 :—Pass., βλέφαρα κέκλῃται S.*Fr.*711 ; ψυχῆς ἀνοῖξαι τὴν κεκλῃμένην πύλην Id.*Fr.*393 ; κεκλειμένης σου τῆς παρρησίας οὐ κιγκλίσιν.., ἀλλὰ.. ὀφλήμασι D.25.28. 2. *shut up, close, block up*, Βόσπορον κλῇσαι A.*Pers.*723 (troch.) ; κλῄσειν ταῖς ναυσὶν τοὺς ἔσπλους Th.4.8 :—Pass., Hdt.2.121.β' ; τὰ ἐμπόρια κεκλῇσθαι Lys.22.14 ; κεκλειμένων τῶν ἐμπορίων D.2.16. II. *shut in, enclose*, πόλιν.. πύργων μηχανῇ κεκλῃμένην A.*Supp.*956 ; cf. κλῄζω (B). III. *confine*, πλάστιγξ αὐχένα πώλων ἔκλῃε E.*Rh.*304 :—Pass., *to be confined*, χέρας βρόχοισι κεκλῃμένα Id.*Andr.*502 (lyr.) : metaph., ὅρκοις κεκλῄμεθα Id.*Hel.*977. 2. *deliver bound*, τινὰ εἰς τὰς τοῦ βασιλέως χεῖρας LXX 1 *Ki.*23.20.

**κλείω** (B), Ep. for κλέω (A), *celebrate* (q. v.).

**κλείω** (C), Ep. for κλέω (B), καλέω, *call* (q. v.).

**Κλειώ,** οῦς, ἡ, *Clio*, one of the Muses, Hes.*Th.*77, Pi.*N.*3.83 (Κλεοῦς metri gr. codd. recc.), etc. (κλέω (A), κλείω (B).)

**κλέμμα**, ατος, τό, (κλέπτω) *thing stolen*, E.*Hec.*618, Arist.*Pr.*952$^a$19; *money equivalent of thing stolen*, τὸ κ. ἐκτείσας διπλοῦν Pl.*Lg.*857b, cf. *Foed.Delph.Pell.*2*A* 14, *IG*5(1).1390.77 (Andania, i B.C.). **2.** *theft*, S.*Ichn.*67 (pl., lyr.), Ar.*Eq.*1203, Str.15.1.53. **II.** *stratagem* in war, Th.5.9; *fraud*, D.18.31, Aeschin.3.100; κ. ἐρωτικόν *clandestine* amour, Ael.*NA*1.2, cf. *AP*5.17 (Rufin.).

**κλεμμάδιος** [ᾰ], α, ον, *stolen*, Pl.*Lg.*955b, cf. Hsch., Phot.

**κλέμμιν**· δίφρον ἀνακλιτόν, Hsch. **κλεμμύειν**· κηρύσσειν, Id.

**κλεμμύς**, ύος, ἡ, = χελώνη, *tortoise*, Ant.Lib.32.2, Hsch.

**Κλεομενισταί**, οἱ, *partisans of Cleomenes*, Plb.2.53.2.

**κλεόνικον**, τό, = κλινοπόδιον, Dsc.3.95.

⊛ **κλέος**, τό, Dor. **κλέϝος** *GDI*1537 (Crissa, = Röhl *Imag.*$^3$ pp.87/8 No.1), only nom. and acc. sg. and pl.: Ep. pl. κλέᾰ (before a vowel) Hom. (v. infr. II. 1), κλεῖα (nisi leg. κλέεα) Hes.*Th.*100: (κλέω A):—*rumour, report*, τί δὴ κ. ἔστ' ἀνὰ ἄστυ; Od.16.461; κ. εὐρὺ φόνου 23.137; ὄσσαν.., ἥ τε μάλιστα φέρει κ. ἀνθρώποισι 1.283; σὸν κ. *news* of thee, 13.415: c. gen., μετὰ κ. ἵκετ' Ἀχαιῶν *the report* of their coming, Il.11.227, cf. 13.364; κείνου κατὰ κ. at *the news* of his coming, Pi.*P.*4.125; τῶν ἐμῶν κακῶν κ. S.*Ph.*251; *rumour*, opp. certainty, κ. οἶον ἀκούομεν οὐδέ τι ἴδμεν Il.2.486; γυναικογήρυτον κ. A.*Ag.*487 (lyr.). **II.** *good report, fame*, freq. in Hom., κ. ἐσθλόν Il.5.3; ἀνδρὸς τοῦ κ. εὐρὺ καθ' Ἑλλάδα Od.1.344: abs., τῷ μὲν κ., ἄμμι δὲ πένθος Il.4.197; τὸ δ' ἐμὸν κ. οὔ ποτ' ὀλεῖται 7.91, cf. 2.325; κ. εἶναί τινι to be *a glory* to him, 22.514; κ. οὐρανὸν ἵκει 8.192, Od.9.20; κ. οὐρανὸν εὐρὺν ἵκανε 8.74; κ. ἄφθιτον Sapph.*Supp.*20a.4, Ibyc.*Oxy.*1790.47, *GDI* l.c.; κ. ἀρέσθαι, εὑρέσθαι, Pi.*O.*9.101, *P.*3.111; γίνεσθε κατὰ κ. ὧδε μαχηταί in *renown*, *BCH*24.71 (Acraeph., iii B.C.); λαβεῖν S.*Ph.*1347; κ. αἰχμᾶς *glory in* or *for*.., Pi.*P.*1.66; τῆς μελλοῦς κ. A.*Ag.*1356; κ. σου μαντικόν ib.1098; μικροῦ δ' ἀγῶνος οὐ μέγ' ἔρχεται κ. S.*Fr.*938: less freq. in Prose, κ. ἀέναον Heraclit.29; μένοντι δὲ..κ. μέγα ἐλείπετο Hdt.7.220; κ. καταθέσθαι to lay up store of *glory*, Id.9.78; τιμὴν καὶ κ. ἔσχεν Ar.*Ra.*1035; πόρρω κ. ἥκει Id.*Ach.*646; κ. οὐρανόμηκες Id.*Nu.*459; κ. ἔχειν τὰ περὶ τὰς ναῦς Th.1.25; παρ' ἀνθρώποις ἀείμνηστον κ. ἔχει τινά X.*Cyn.*1.6; κ. ἀθάνατον καταθέσθαι Pl.*Smp.*208c; κ. τε καὶ ἔπαινος πρὸς ἀνθρώπων Id.*Lg.*663a; περὶ χώρας ἀκούειν κ. μέγα Lys.2.5; κ. ἕξειν ἔν τινι Ath.Mech.15.4; ποῖον κ., εἰ..; 1*Ep.Pet.*2.20: pl., ἄειδε δ' ἄρα κλέα ἀνδρῶν *the lays* of their achievements, Il.9.189, cf. 524, Od.8.73; κλέα φωτῶν μνήσομαι A.R.1.1. **2.** rarely in bad sense, δύσφαμον κ. ill *repute*, Pi.*N.*8.36; αἰσχρὸν κ. E.*Hel.*135, cf. Ar.*Fr.*796: both senses in Th.2.45 ἧς ἂν ἐπ' ἐλάχιστον ἀρετῆς πέρι ἢ ψόγου..κ. ᾖ of whom there is least *talk* either for praise or blame. (Cf. Skt. *śrávas* 'fame', Slav. *slovo* 'word', 'glory'; cogn. with κλέω (A), κλύω.)

**κλέπας**· νοτερόν, πηλῶδες· ἢ δασύ, ἢ ὑγρόν, Hsch.

**κλεπία**, ἡ, = κλοπή, Phot.

**κλέπιμος**, = κλόπιμος, *contraband*, ἔλαιον *PHib.*1.59.7 (iii B.C.), prob. in *PRev.Laws* 55.20 (iii B.C.).

⊛ **κλέπος**, εος, τό, = κλέμμα, Sol. ap.Poll.8.34.

**κλεπτ-άριον**, τό, Dim. of κλέπτης, = Lat. *furunculus*, Charis.p.552 K., *Gloss.* **-έλεγχος**, ον, *convicting a thief*, λίθος κ. a stone that had magic powers for this purpose, Aët.2.32. **-έον**, *one must conceal*, S.*Ph.*57. **-ήρ**, ῆρος, ὁ, = sq., Man.1.311, 4.304. **-ης**, ου, ὁ, *thief*, Il.3.11; τὸν πυρὸς κ. A.*Pr.*946; κλέπτα δύο Ar.*V.*928; opp. ἅρπαξ (a robber), Myrtil.4; λῃστὰς ἢ κλέπτας Pl.*R.*351c, cf. *Ev.Jo.*10.8; ὁ τοῦ κ. λόγος, a logical fallacy, Arist.*SE*180$^b$18. **2.** generally, *cheat, knave*, S.*Aj.*1135; κακῶν ἀλλοτρίων κ. D.45.59. **-ίδης**, ου, ὁ, Com. Patronym. of κλέπτης, *Son of a Thief*, Pherecr.219. **-ικός**, ή, όν, *thievish*: ἡ -κή (sc. τέχνη) *thievery*, Pl.*R.*334b, Luc.*DDeor.*7.2. Adv. -κῶς Eust.811.41. **-ις**, ιδος, ἡ, fem. of κλέπτης, *she-thief*, Alciphr.3.22. **-ίσκος**, ὁ, Dim. of κλέπτης, Eup.420. **-ίστατος**, η, ον, Att. Sup. formed from κλέπτης, *the most arrant thief*, Ar.*Pl.*27, Alciphr.3.20, Procop.*Arc.*21; κ. θεός S.E.*P.*3.215; κ. χεῖρες Adam.2.20: also Comp. -ίστερος, α, ον, Suid. s. v. Νεοκλείδου. **-οσύνη**, ἡ, *thievishness, knavery*, Od.19.396, Man.6.207: in Prose, κ. καὶ ἐπιορκία Phld.*Piet.*37.

**κλεπτο-τελωνέω**, *smuggle*, Men.Prot.p.22 D., Tz.*H.*13.527 (Pass.). **-τροφος**, ὁ, *thief of food*, Suid. s. v. δειπνολόχον.

**κλέπτρια**, ἡ, fem. of κλεπτήρ, Sotad.Com.2.

⊛ **κλέπτω**, Ion. impf. κλέπτεσκον Hdt.2.174: fut. κλέψω Ar.*Ec.*667, etc., κλέψομαι X.*Cyr.*7.4.13: aor. ἔκλεψα Il.5.268, etc.: pf. κέκλοφα Ar.*Pl.*369, 372, Pl.*Lg.*941d; later part. κεκλεβώς *IG*5(1).1390.75 (Andania, i B.C.):—Pass., aor. 1 ἐκλέφθην Hdt.5.84, E.*Or.*1580: aor. 2 ἐκλάπην [ᾰ] Pl.*R.*413b, X.*Eq.Mag.*4.17; later part. κλεπείς *BGU*454.19 (ii A.D.): pf. κέκλεμμαι S.*Ant.*681, Ar.*V.*57. (Cf. Lat. *clĕpere*, Goth. *hlifan* (κλέπτειν), *hliftus* (κλέπτης)):—*steal*, c. acc. or abs., Il.24.24, 71, 109; τῆς γενεῆς ἔκλεψε from that breed Anchises *stole*, i.e. foals of that breed, 5.268; κλέπτουσιν ἐφ' ἁρπαγῇ ἄλλοθεν ἄλλος Sol.4.13; κ. μοιχεύειν τε Xenoph.11.3; ἣν μηδὲν μήτε κλέπτῃ μήτε ἀδικῇ Democr.253; κ. τι παρ' ἀλλήλων Hdt.1.186; κ. ἐξ ἱερῶν Pl.*Lg.*857b; *carry off*, κλέψεν Μήδειαν Pi.*P.*4.250; πυρὸς σέλας κ., of Prometheus, A.*Pr.*8; κλέψαι τε χἀρπάσαι βίᾳ S.*Ph.*644; κ. τοὺς μηνύοντας *spirit away* the deponents, Antipho 5.38; ἐξ ἐπάλξεων πλεκταῖσιν ἐς γῆν σῶμα κ. *let* it *down secretly*, E.*Tr.*958, cf. 1010; κ. μορφάς, of painters, *steal* forms (by transferring them to canvas), Luc.*Epigr.*41. **2.** in part. Act., *thievish*, κλέπτον βλέπει he has a *thief's* look, Ar.*V.*900; κλέπτον τὸ χρῆμα τἀνδρός he's an arrant *thief*, ib.933. **II.** c. acc. pers., *cozen, cheat*, πάρφασις, ἥ τ' ἔκλεψε νόον Il.14.217; οὐκ ἔστι Διὸς κλέψαι νόον Hes.*Th.*613; μὴ κλέπτε νόῳ Il.1.132; κλέπτει νιν οὐ θεός, οὐ βροτός, ἔργοις οὔτε βουλαῖς Pi.*P.*3.29; σοφία κλέπτει παράγοισα μύθοις Id.*N.*7.23; οὔτοι φρέν' ἂν κλέψειεν A.*Ch.*854, cf. S.*Tr.*243, etc.; τὴν γνώμην Hp.*Epid.*5.27; κ. τὴν ἀκρόασιν Aeschin.3.99:—Pass., κλέπτεται ὁ ἀκροατής Arist.*Rh.*1408$^b$5; προβαίνειν κλεπτόμενος to go on *blindfold*, Hdt.7.49; κλέπτεταί οἱ ἡ αὐγή his vision *becomes deceptive*, Hp.*Morb.*2.12; κλαπέντες ἢ βιασθέντες τοῦτο πάσχουσιν Pl.*R.* l.c.: impers., κλέπτεται *the deception is passed off*, Arist.*Rh.*1404$^b$24. **III.** *conceal, keep secret*, θεοῖο γόνον Pi.*O.*6.36; θυμῷ δεῖμα Id.*P.*4.96; *disguise*, διαβολαῖς νέαις κλέψας τὰ πρόσθε σφάλματ' E.*Supp.*416; τοῖς ὀνόμασι κ. τὰ πράγματα Aeschin.3.142; τοὺς ἑαυτῶν κ. X.*Eq.Mag.*5.2; κ. ἑαυτὸν ὀφθαλμῶν τε καὶ ὤτων Philostr.*VS*1.7.2; κ. τοῦ διανοήματος τὴν ἄδειαν Demetr.*Eloc.*239:—Pass., κλέπτεται τὸ μετρικόν ib.182, cf. Them. *in Ph.*276.26, Paul.Aeg.6.103. **IV.** *do secretly* or *treacherously*, δόλοισι κ. σφαγάς *execute* slaughter *by secret* frauds, S.*El.*37; πόλλ' ἂν..λάθρᾳ σὺ κλέψειας κακά Id.*Aj.*1137; κ. μύθους *whisper malicious* rumours, ib.188 (lyr.); κλέπτων ἢ βιαζόμενος *by fraud* or open force, Pl.*Lg.*933e; ταῦτα κλέπτοντες ταῖς πράξεσιν, i.e. λάθρᾳ πράττοντες, ib.910b; κλεπτομένη λαλιά *secret, clandestine*, Luc.*Am.*15, etc. **2.** *seize* or *occupy secretly*, τὰ ὄρη X.*An.*5.6.9, cf. 4.6.11, 15; τὴν ἀρχήν D.H.4.10. **3.** *effect* or *bring about clandestinely*, γάμον κ. δώροις Theoc.22.151:—Pass., *to be 'smuggled in'*, Arist.*Rh.Al.*1440$^b$21. **4.** *get rid of imperceptibly*, τὸ δοκεῖν.. D.H.*Rh.*8.7; τῇ ποικιλίᾳ τὸν κόρον Id.*Comp.*19:—Pass., τοῦ πόσου κλεπτομένου Plot.4.7.5.

**κλέτας**, τό, prob. = κλειτύς, Lyc.703, Nonn.*D.*5.59, al., *AP*9.665 (Agath.).

**κλεύθομαι**, subj. κλεύθωμαι, fut. κλεύσομαι, expld. by Gramm. as for κελεύθ-, read by Aristarch. for κεύθομαι in Il.23.244, cf. Sch. ad loc., Hsch., *EM*517.45.

**κλευτόν**· τλευτόν, Hsch.

**κλέψ**, ὁ, *thief*, prob. coined from βοῦκλεψ, Phryn.*PS* p.17 B.

⊛ **κλεψίαμβος** [ῐ], ὁ, a kind of *musical instrument*, Phillis ap.Ath.14.636b, Aristox.ib.4.182f, Poll.4.59. **II.** in pl., = μέλη τινὰ παρὰ Ἀλκμᾶνι, Hsch.

⊛ **κλεψί-γᾰμος** [ῐ], ον, *seeking illicit love*, Nonn.*D.*8.60. ⊛ **-κοίτης**, ου, ὁ, = foreg., Ismenias ap.Ps.-Callisth.1.46.

⊛ **κλεψῐμαῖος**, α, ον, = κλοπιμαῖος, *stolen*, Lxx *To.*2.13, *PLond.*2.422.3 (iv A.D.). Adv. -αίως, = Lat. *furtim*, Dosith.p.412 K.

**κλεψί-νοος** [ῐ], ον, *beguiling the mind*, Nonn.*D.*8.47, etc. **-νυμφος**, ον, = κλεψίγαμος, Lyc.1116. ⊛ **-ποτέω**, *drink unfairly*, Anon. ap.Suid., Poll.6.20. **-ρρῦτος**, ον, *secretly flowing*, name of a stream at Athens, *which flowed some distance under ground*, Hsch. **-τόκος**, ον, *concealing offspring*, Opp.*C.*3.11, Nonn.*D.*28.317. **-φρων**, ον, gen. ονος, (φρήν) *dissembling*, Ἑρμῆς *h.Merc.*413. **II.** = κλεψίνοος, Man.1.93. **-χωλος**, ον, *disguising lameness*, Luc.*Ocyp.*33.

⊛ **κλεψ-ύδρα**, Ion. **-ύδρη**, ἡ, (ὕδωρ) *pipette*, = ὑδράρπαξ, a small vessel with one or more perforations below and an air-vent above, for transferring small quantities of liquid, Emp.100.9, Arist.*Ph.*213$^a$27, *Pr.*914$^b$9, al., Hero *Spir.*2.27 (described in 1.7), Simp. *in Cael.*524.19, *in Ph.*647.26. **II.** *water-clock*, a water-butt with a narrow orifice underneath, through which the water trickled slowly, for measuring periods of time, used to time speeches in the law-courts, Ar.*V.*93, 857, Arist.*Ath.*67.2, etc.; πρὸς κλεψύδρας ἀγωνίζεσθαι Id.*Po.*1451$^a$8; τὴν ὀπὴν βῦσον τῆς κλεψύδρης Herod.2.43; for measuring military watches, Aen.Tact.22.24; for astronomical measurements, Procl.*Hyp.*4.74 (in the form of a perforated bowl floating on water, Gal. *Anim.Pass.*2.5); rarely for other purposes, Eub.p.182 K., Epin.2; εἰς τὴν ἐκπλήρωσιν τῆς κ. Herophil.ap.Marcellin.*Puls.*265. **III.** name of an ebbing well, in the Acropolis at Athens, Ar.*Av.*1695 (lyr.); at Ithome, Pap. in *Abh.Berl.Akad.*1904(2).14 (ii B.C.), Paus.4.31.6. **-ύδριον**, τό, Dim. of foreg., Philostr.*VS*2.10.1, 2.13.1.

⊛ **κλέω** (A), Ep. **κλείω** (as Hom. always in Act., but in Pass. only κλέομαι; Trag. only κλέω, in lyr.), *tell of, make famous, celebrate*, ἔργ' ἀνδρῶν..τά τε κλείουσιν ἀοιδοί Od.1.338, cf. *h.Hom.*32.19; ἐγὼ δέ κέ σε κλείω Od.17.418, cf. Hes.*Op.*1, *Th.*105, Stesich.35, *Inscr.Cos* 218.7, prob. in Hermesian.7.33; ἔν τ' ἀλύροις κλέοντες ὕμνοις E.*Alc.*447; Θέτιν..κλέουσαι Id.*IA*1046; κλέωᾱ τὸν Ἀμύκλαις σιόν, Lacon. for κλέουσα τὸν Ἀμ. θεόν, Ar.*Lys.*1299:—Med., γῆρυν, ἂν σοφοὶ κλέονται E.*Fr.*369.7:—Pass., *to be famed*: c. dat., *for* a thing, φρένες..ᾗς τὸ πάρος περ ἔκλε' (for ἐκλέεο) Il.24.202; ἐγὼ δ' ἐν πᾶσι θεοῖσι μήτι τε κλέομαι καὶ κέρδεσιν Od.13.299; κλέεσθαι ἐν φορμίγγεσσι *to be celebrated* in lyric strains, Pi.*I.*5(4).27; ἔνθ'..ἀγοραὶ Πυλάτιδες κλέονται where *are held the famous* meetings, prob. in S.*Tr.*639 (lyr.). **II.** c. acc. et inf., *sing* how.., B.15.13. (κλεϝ-, cf. κλέος, κλύω, Lat. *clueo*: Skt. *śrutás* (= κλυτός) 'famous', *śṛṇóti* 'hear'.)

**κλέω** (B), Ep. **κλείω**, = καλέω, *call*, A.R.1.217, 2.687, Opp.*H.*5.536: impf. κλεῖον Orph.*L.*195:—Pass., ἔνθα περ ἀκταὶ κλείονται Παγασαί A.R.1.238 (cf. καλέω II. 3a); κλείονται γαλεοί Opp.*H.*1.379; also κλέεται Nic.*Fr.*71.5: 2 sg. impf. ἔκλεο Call.*Del.*40.

**κλεώνιον**, τό, = ἑλένιον, Dsc.1.28: **κλεωναία**, ἡ, prob. in Ps.-Dsc. ibid., Hsch.

**κλήδεα**· φραγμοί, Hsch.

**κλῇδες**, old Att. nom. pl. of κλείς.

**κλήδην**, Adv., (καλέω) *by name*, Il.9.11.

**κληδον-ίζω**, prob. *give a sign* or *omen*, Hsch.:—Med., *to be a diviner*, Lxx *De.*18.10, 4*Ki.*21.6:—Pass., *receive an omen*, *PMag.Oxy.*886.13 (iii A.D.). **-ιος**, α, ον, *giving an omen*, = πανομφαῖος, title of Zeus, Sch.Il.8.250, Eust.169.27. **-ισμα**, ατος, τό, *sign, omen*, Luc.

*Pseudol.*17. ⊛ **-ισμός,** ὁ, *observation of a sign* or *omen*, v.l. in Lxx *De.*18.14.

**κληδουχέω, κληδοῦχος,** old Att. for κλειδ- (q. v.).

**κληδών,** όνος, ἡ, Ep. **κλεηδών** and **κληηδών,** (κλέω A) *omen, presage contained in a chance utterance*, χαῖρεν δὲ κλεηδόνι δῖος Ὀδυσσεύς Od. 18.117, 20.120; ὁ μὲν τῇ κ. οὐδὲν χρεώμενος (supr. φήμη) Hdt.5.72; κληδόνας τε δυσκρίτους ἐγνώρισ' αὐτοῖς A.*Pr.*486, cf. S.*El.*1110, Call.*Ep.*1.14: in later Prose, κληδόνων ἀκούσονται Lxx *De.*18.14 (v.l. -ονισμῶν), cf. Polystr.p.5 W.; μαντικὴ ἀπὸ κληδόνων Paus.9.11.7, cf. *PMag.Oxy.*886.22 (iii A. D.); δέχομαι τὴν κ. Luc.*Laps.*8: personified, in pl., Paus. l. c.; Φήμη καὶ Κ., = Lat. *Aius Locutius*, Plu.*Cam.* 30. II. *tidings*, κληηδὼν πατρός *news* of my father, Od.4.317: abs., *report, rumour*, ἐξ ἀμαυρᾶς κ. A.*Ch.*853, cf. Hdt.9.101; κληδόνες παλίγκοτοι A.*Ag.*863; κ. ἐν ἁπάσῃ τῇ πόλει κατεῖχεν, ὅτι.. And.1. 130. 2. *fame, repute*, κ. ἀϋτεῖ A.*Ag.*927; *glory*, παῖδες γὰρ ἀνδρὶ κ. σωτήριοι Id.*Ch.*505; κληδὼν καλή good *report*, S.*OC*258; κ. αἰσχρά E.*Alc.*315. III. *invocation*. λιτὰς δὲ καὶ κληδόνας πατρῴους A. *Ag.*228 (lyr.); κληδόνος βοή Id.*Eu.*397. b. *shouting*, S.*Ichn.* 232. 2. *name, appellation*, κ. ἐπωνύμους A.*Eu.*418.

⊛ **κλῄζω** (A), Ar.*Th.*117 (lyr.), etc.; Ion. **κληΐζω** Hp.*Art.*42, Dor. **κλεΐζω** v.l. in Pi.*O.*1.110, cf. Eust.1497.50: impf. ἔκλειζον *Epigr.Gr.* 254 (Cyprus, iv/iii B.C.): fut. κληΐσω Fr.Lyr.ap.Aristid.*Or.*50(26).31, κλῄσω *h.Hom.*31.18, A.R.3.993, Dor. κλεΐξω Pi. l. c.: aor. ἔκλησα E.*IA* 1522, Ar.*Av.*905 (lyr., κλεῖσον cod. R), 950, 1745, Nic.*Fr.*86 (ἔκλησε codd. Ath.), ἔκλεισα *IG*14.2258 (Etruria):—Pass., κληΐζομαι A.R.4. 1153, Ti.Locr.100d, *Epigr.Gr.*946 (Tralles), κλῄζομαι S.*OT*733, X. *Cyr.*1.2.1, etc., κλεΐζομαι Man.6.571: pf. κεκλῄϊσμαι, ἐκλῄϊσμαι, A.R. 4.618, 990: plpf. ἐκλῄϊστο ib.267, 1202:—*make famous, celebrate in song*, *h.Hom.* l. c., Pi. l. c.; κλῄσωμεν Ἄρτεμιν E.*IA*1522 (lyr.); κλῆσον, ὦ χρυσόθρονε, τὰν τρομεράν Ar.*Av.*950 (mock lyr.), cf. 1745; παλαὶ δὴ τήνδ' ἐγὼ κλῄζω πόλιν ib.921:—Pass., τὰν Ἀργὼ τὰν διὰ σοῦ στόματος ἀεὶ -ομέναν E.*Hyps.Fr.*3(1) ii 20 (lyr.). 2. *mention, speak of*, in Pass., πότερα γὰρ αὐτοῦ ζῶντος ἢ τεθνηκότος φάτις.. ἐκλῄζετο; A. *Ag.*631; οἷα κλῄζεται as *are said*, E.*Hel.*721; ἀφανὴς (sc. ὤν) κλῄζεται ib.126; θανὼν κλῄζεται he *is reported* to be dead, ib.132; κλῄζομαι ὡς προδοῦσ' ib.927. 3. *applaud, praise*, Hp.*Art.*42. 4. *invoke*, *PMag.Par.*1.271, al. 5. *summon*, δίκῃ ἀνεμωλίῳ ἐκλῄϊσσαν.. σὸν θεράποντα Maiist.38. II. *call*, σὲ νῦν μὲν ἥδε γῆ σωτῆρα κλῄζει S. *OT*48:—Pass., Φωκὶς μὲν ἡ γῆ κλῄζεται ib.733; ἔνθα κλῄζεται οὑμὸς Κιθαιρών where *is* the hill *called* my Cithaeron, ib.1452, cf. E.*Hyps. Fr.*3(1) iv 26; παῖς κ. Μενοικέως Id.*Ph.*10; πατρὸς Ἀθηνίωνος κ. *IG* 9(1).880.3 (Corc.), cf. 12(3).1190.7 (Melos): less freq. in Prose, οἱ Περσεῖδαι ἀπὸ Περσέως κλῄζονται X.*Cyr.*1.2.1, cf. Pl.*Ax.*371*b*, App. *BC*1.1; etym. of Κλειώ, Corn.*ND*14. (κλε(ϝ)-ίζω (fr. κλέος) 'celebrate' and κλη-ΐζω (fr. καλέω) 'call' were confused by the Greeks.)

⊛ **κλῄζω** (B), late form for κλείω (A), κλῄω, *shut*, *Hymn.Is.*159:— Pass., *AP*9.62 (Even.).

**κληηδών,** όνος, ἡ, Ep. for κληδών, Od.4.317.

⊛ **κλήθρ-α,** Ion. **-ρη,** ἡ, *alder, Alnus glutinosa*, Od.5.64, 239, Thphr. *HP*1.4.3, 3.3.1. **-ινος,** η, ον, *of the alder*, ξύλα Ath.Mech.17.15 (κλεῖθρ- codd.).

**κλῆθρον,** τό, = κλήθρα, *Gloss.* **κλῇθρον,** Att. for κλεῖθρον (q. v.).

**κλῆθρος,** ὁ, = κλήθρα, Philostr. Jun.*Im.*6.

**κληΐζω,** Ion. for κλῄζω (B). **κληϊθρίη,** ἡ, Ion. for κλειθρία.

**κλῄϊθρον,** τό, Ion. for κλῇθρον, κλεῖθρον, *h.Merc.*146.

**κληΐσκω,** = κληΐζω II, *call*, Hp.*Cord.*8 (Pass.).

**κλῆμα,** ατος, τό, Aeol. **κλᾶμμα** (q. v.), *twig* or *branch*, esp. *vine-twig*, Ar.*Ec.*1031, Hp.*Epid.*4.50, 6.3.8, Thphr.*HP*2.5.5, *CP*3.14.6, al.; ἀμπέλου κ. Pl.*R.*353a: generally, *cutting, slip*, ὁ βλαστὸς τοῦ κ. X.*Oec.*19.8, cf. Arist.*HA*550$^{b}$8: metaph., ἀνατετμήκασί τινες τὰ κ. τὰ τοῦ δήμου D.ap.Aeschin.3.166; of the navel string, πεῖσμα καὶ κ. τῷ γεννωμένῳ καρπῷ Democr.148. 2. *vine-switch, cane*, carried by Roman centurions, Lat. *vitis*, Plu.*Galb.*26, etc. II. = πιτυοῦσσα, Dsc.4.165; = πολύγονον, Plin.*HN*27.113. III. = ὑπόδημα, Hsch.; cf. κλείματα.

**κληματ-ίζω,** *prune vines*, Al.*Le.*25.4. **-ικός,** ή, όν, *of* or *for a vine-twig*, *Gloss.* **-ινος,** η, ον, *of vine-twigs*, πῦρ Thgn.1360; κονία Dsc.*Alex.*22; τέφρα Id.5.117, *Ther.*19, Antyll.ap.Orib.10.12.2. **-ίς,** ίδος, ἡ, Dim. of κλῆμα, *vine-branch*, Lxx *De.*32.32, Ph.1.612 (generally, *branch*, ib.527), Plu.2.527d, Philum.*Ven.*2.2: usu. in pl., *brushwood, faggots*, Ar.*Th.*728, 739, Th.7.53, Arist.*HA*550$^{b}$9, *Inscr.Délos* 338 *Aa* 23, 24 (iii B.C.): collect. in sg., ib.38, 354.57 (iii B.C.), Lxx *Da.*3. 46. II. *periwinkle, Vinca herbacea*, Dsc.4.7. 2. *traveller's joy, Clematis Vitalba*, ib.180, Gal.12.31. 3. prob. *bearbind, Convolvulus arvensis*, Plin.*HN*24.139. **-ῖτις,** ιδος, ἡ, Adj. *with long climbing branches*, name of a kind of ἀριστολοχεία, Dsc.3.4. II. Subst., = foreg. II. 2, Ps.-Dsc.4.180.

**κληματό-δεσις,** εως, ἡ, *wicker hurdle* or *mat*, v.l. for κλιμακόδεσις in Ath.Mech.36.6. **-ειδής,** ές, = κληματίς II. 2, Dsc.4.[180] ap.Gal. 12.31 (but not in Dsc.). **-εις,** εσσα, εν, *of vine-twigs*, τέφρη Nic. *Al.*530. **-ομαι,** Pass., (κλῆμα) *put forth tendrils*, κεκλημάτωται χλωρὸν οἰνάνθης δέμας S.*Fr.*255, cf. Thphr.*CP*2.10.3.

**κληματώδης,** ες, *like vine-shoots*, Dsc.3.24, Gal.12.78.

**κλήνιος·** ἔνδοξος, Hsch. **κληπικοί·** ἰσχνοί, καὶ ἄσιτοι, Id.

⊛ **κληρ-ικός,** ή, όν, *concerning inheritances*, τὰ κ. Harp. s. v. παρακαταβολή. 2. Astrol., *of* or *according to the* κλῆρος (A) II. 4, Vett.Val. 122.13. Adv. -κῶς Id.123.22. 3. Medic., dub. sens. in *BKT*3 p.33 (v/vi A. D.). II. Subst. κληρικός, ὁ, *cleric*, Astramps.*Orac.* 66 p.6 H., *Cod.Just.*1.1.3.2 (pl.), etc. **-ίον,** τό, Dim. of κλῆρος (A) II. 2, *AP*6.98 (Zonas), *PLond.*2.370.1 (ii/iii A. D.). II. Dor. **κλάρια** [ᾱ], τά, *bonds, notes for debt*, Plu.*Agis* 13.

**κληρο-δοσία,** ἡ, *distribution of land*, Lxx *Ps.*77(78).55, D.S.5. 53. ⊛ **-δοτέω,** *distribute land*, c. dat., Lxx 2*Es.*9.12; *settle on the land*, αὐτούς ib.*Ps.*77(78).55:—Pass., -εῖτο ἡ χώρα Ph.2.291.

⊛ **κληρονομ-έω,** *inherit*, c. gen. rei, ὥσπερ τῆς οὐσίας, οὕτω καὶ τῆς φιλίας τῆς πατρικῆς κ. Isoc.1.2, cf. Is.4.7, Lycurg.127; ὅς γ' ἐκεκληρονομήκεις τῶν.. χρημάτων πλεῖν ἢ πέντε ταλάντων D.18.312; μὴ πλειόνων ἢ μιᾶς [κληρονομίας] τὸν αὐτὸν κ. Arist.*Pol.*1309$^{a}$25: c. acc. rei, Lycurg.88, Luc.*DMort.*11.3, *BGU*19 ii 1 (ii A. D.), etc.: abs., Phld. *Mort.*24. 2. *acquire, obtain*, τὴν ἐπ' ἀσεβείᾳ δόξαν Plb.15.22.3; φήμην Id.18.55.8; θρόνον βασιλείας Lxx 1*Ma.*2.57; τὴν γῆν *receive possession of* the promised land, Palestine, ib.*Le.*20.24, *De.*4.1 (also, *obtain* all that God has promised, ib.*Ps.*36(37).11, cf. *Ev.Matt.*5.5); *obtain* salvation, ζωὴν αἰώνιον *Ev.Matt.*19.29. II. *to be an inheritor* or *heir*, τινος *of* a person, Luc.*Hist.Conscr.*20: more freq. τινα, Posidon.36 J., Plu.*Sull.*2, *PGnom.*5, al. (ii A. D.), *AP*11.202, etc.; κ. τινὰ τῆς οὐσίας D.C.45.47: metaph., σῆτες καὶ σκώληκες -ομήσουσιν αὐτόν Lxx *Si.*19.3:—Pass., *to be succeeded in the inheritance*, of parents, Ph. 2.172, 291, Luc.*Tox.*22; ὑφ' ὧν τὴν ῥητορικὴν ἐκληρονομήθη Philostr. *VS*2.26.6. III. *leave an heir behind* one, υἱοὺς υἱῶν Lxx *Pr.*13. 22. **-ημα,** ατος, τό, *inheritance*, Luc.*Tyr.*6. **-ία,** ἡ, *inheritance*, Isoc.19.43, etc.; ἡ κ. κατὰ τὴν ἀγχιστείαν *inheritance* as heir-at-law, D.43.3; κ. μὴ κατὰ δόσιν, ἀλλὰ κατὰ γένος Arist.*Pol.*1309$^{a}$23: metaph., εἰλήφασι τὴν τοῦ ὀνόματος κ. αἱ σωματικαὶ ἡδοναί have taken *possession* of.., Id.*EN*1153$^{b}$33. 2. *property, possession*, ἀνέζευξεν ἕκαστος εἰς τὴν κ. αὐτοῦ Lxx *Ju.*16.21(25), cf. 1*Ma.*2.56, 6.24. **-ιαῖος,** α, ον, *concerning inheritance*, *Cod.Just.*3.10.1.2, Just.*Nov.*119.6; *inherited*, *PMasp.*151.40 (vi A. D.). **-ικός,** ή, όν, *connected with inheritance*, δίκαιον *PFlor.*61.20 (i A. D.), etc.; δίκαια Asp. *in EN*77.14; δικαστήρια *OGI*482 (i A. D.); *hereditary*, *Gloss.* ⊛ **-ος,** Dor. **κλᾱρονόμος,** ὁ, (νέμομαι) *heir*, freq. *the heir in possession*, Is.1.44, Pl.*Lg.*923c; of the *heir apparent*, *SIG*884.53 (iii A. D.): c. gen. pers., Pl.*Lg.*923e, *IG*2$^{2}$. 1623.117, Epicur.*Fr.*217, *SIG*953.65 (Cnidus, ii B.C.): c. gen. rei, Lys.32.23; κληρονόμους τῶν αὑτοῦ καταστήσας Isoc.19.9, etc.: metaph., κ. τῆς εὐνοίας, τῆς ἀτιμίας, Id.5.136, D.22.34; τῆς ὑπὲρ τῶν νόμων [δίκης] Id.21.20; κλαρονόμος μοίσας τᾶς Δωρίδος Mosch.3.96; κ. καταλιπεῖν τινα Arist.*Pol.*1270$^{a}$28; κ. γράφειν τινά *AP*11.171 (Lucill.).

**κληροπᾰλής,** ές, *distributed by shaking the lots*, μοῖραι *h.Merc.*129.

⊛ **κλῆρος** (A), Dor. **κλᾶρος** Pi. (v. infr.), *Leg.Gort.*5.27, etc., ου, ὁ:— *lot*, κλῆρον ἐσημήναντο ἕκαστος, ἐν δ' ἔβαλον κυνέῃ Il.7.175; κλήρους ἐν κυνέῃ χαλκήρεϊ πάλλον 3.316, cf. Od.10.206; ἐκ κλῆρος ὄρουσεν Il.3. 325; ἐκ δ' ἔθορε κλῆρος κυνέης 7.182; ἐν δὲ κλήρους ἐβάλοντο 23.352; ἐπὶ κλήρους ἐβάλοντο Od.14.209, cf. *SIG*1023.94 (Cos); κλήρῳ πεπαλάσθαι Od.9.331; κλήρῳ λάχον ἐνθάδ' ἕπεσθαι Il.24.400, cf. 23.862, A.*Pers.*187, Hdt.3.83, etc.; πάντας ἀνέφεδρος ἐπαγκρατίασε τοὺς κ., i.e. he never drew a bye, *SIG*1073.29 (ii A. D.); κλήρου κατὰ μοῖραν E.*Rh.*545 (lyr.); διὰ τὴν τοῦ κ. τύχην Pl.*R.*619d, etc.; κλάροισι θεοπροπέων divining *by lots*, Pi.*P.*4.190: hence, of oracles, E.*Hipp.*1057, *Ph.* 838; Ἑρμῆς γὰρ ὢν κλήρῳ ποιήσεις οἶδ' ὅτι Ar.*Pax* 365; κ. Ἑρμοῦ E. *Fr.*39. 2. *casting of lots, drawing of lots*, κ. τίθεσθαι Id.*IA*1198, cf. *Tr.*186 (lyr.); δοκεῖ δίκαιον εἶναι πᾶσι τῶν ἀρχῶν μετεῖναι ἐν τῷ κ. X. *Ath.*1.2, cf. Arist.*Pol.*1300$^{a}$19, *IG*5(1).1390.116 (Andania, i B.C.); = Lat. *sortitio provinciarum*, Plu.*Aem.*10. 3. λαβὼν πίστιν.. κλήρου dub. sens. in *OGI*494.19 (i or ii A. D.). II. *that which is assigned by lot, allotment* of land, Hdt.2.109, Th.3.50, Pl.*Lg.*740b, Arist.*Pol.* 1265$^{b}$15, al.; λαβεῖν τᾶς χώρας ἐξαίρετον τὸν πρῶτον κλᾶρον *SIG*141.6 (Corc. Nigr., iv B.C.); κ. ἱππικός *OGI*229.102 (Smyrna, iii B.C.); περὶ τοῦ λάχους τριάκοντα καὶ ἑπτὰ κλάρων *Schwyzer* 289.88 (Priene, ii B.C.), cf. 313.4, al. 2. generally, *piece of land, farm, estate*, οἶκος καὶ κ. Il.15.498; οἶκόν τε κ. τε Od.14.64, cf. Hes.*Op.*37, 341, Pi.*O.*13. 62; κατέφαγε τὸν κ. Hippon.35.4; οἱ κ. τῶν Συρίων their *lands*, Hdt. 1.76, cf. 9.94, Call.*Del.*281, etc.; Κύπρου Πάφου τ' ἔχουσα.. κλῆρον, of Aphrodite, A.*Fr.*463; κατὰ κ. Ἰαόνιον Id.*Pers.*899 (lyr.); κλῆροι χθονός E.*Heracl.*876; τῶν λαβόντων ἐν Ὀρχομενῷ κλᾶρον ἢ οἰκίαν *IG* 5(2).344.12 (iii B.C.), cf. *SIG*169.61 (Iasus, iv B.C.); Πισαίοις ἐνὶ κλήροισι Nic.*Fr.*74.5. b. pl., *title-deeds*, *PGrenf.*1.14.11 (ii B.C.). 3. *legacy, inheritance, heritable estate*, Is.11.9, Pl.*Lg.*923d, Arist.*Ath.*9.2, *SIG*1186 (iv B.C.), *IG*2$^{2}$.1368.127, 154. b. collect., *body of inheritors*, *Leg.Gort.* l. c. 4. Astrol., certain *degrees* in the zodiac connected with planets and important in a nativity, *Cat.Cod.Astr.*1.169, 170, Ptol.*Tetr.*111, Vett.Val.59.21, al., Paul.Al.*K.*2 (cf. Sch.); κ. τύχης Ptol.*Tetr.*129. 5. generally, *province, sphere*, ἕνα θεὸν πολλῶν ἅμα προεστάναι κλήρων Dam.*Pr.*369. III. of the Levites, Κύριος αὐτὸς κλῆρος αὐτοῦ Lxx *De.*18.2: hence, of the Christian *clergy*, ἐν κλήρῳ καταλεγόμενος *Cod.Just.*1.3.38.2, Just.*Nov.*6.1.7, Astramps.*Orac.*98.7.

**κλῆρος** (B), ου, ὁ, *a beetle destructive in bee-hives, Clerus apiarius*, Arist.*HA*605$^{b}$11, 626$^{b}$17.

**κληρουργία,** ἡ, *inheritance*, Sm.*Ru.*4.7.

**κληρουχ-αρχέω,** *to be governor of a* κληρουχία, *Ath.Mitt.*35.47 (iv B.C.). **-έω,** *obtain by allotment*, esp. of conquered lands divided among the conquerors, κ. τῶν Χαλκιδέων τὴν χώρην Hdt.6.100, cf. *SIG* 332.6 (iv/iii B.C.), 502.41 (Samothrace, iii B.C.), App.*BC*5.74 (and in Med., ib.27): generally, ἄλλοι κατ' ἄλλους τόπους κληρουχήσαντες θεῶν Pl.*Criti.*109c. 2. *inherit*, Sm.*Ps.*81(82).8. II. *divide, allot* lands, D.S. 5.9, D.H.9.37, D.C.48.6: metaph., κ. τὴν ἐν ἄστροις τύχην Callistr. *Stat.*10. III. *settle one as an allotment-holder*, in Pass., *PCair. Zen.*254 (iii B.C.), *PTeb.*5.36 (ii B.C.). **-ημα,** ατος, τό, *allotment of*

*land*, App.*BC*3.2 :—also **-ησις**, εως, ἡ, Nic. Dam.130.27 J. (pl.). **-ία**, ἡ, *apportionment of land in a foreign country among citizens*, ἡ Σάμου κ. Arist.*Rh*.1384$^{b}$32, cf. Plb.4.81.2, D.S.15.23; esp. to soldiers on the active list, *PPetr*.3 p.163 (iii B.C.), *PTeb*.30.26 (ii B.C.); = Lat. *colonia*, D.H.8.75, Plu.*Flam*.2. **b.** in Roman Egypt, a numbered *division* of the land, *PTeb*.343$^{r}$.9 (ii A.D.), *Sammelb*.4414.5 (ii A.D.). **2.** collect., = οἱ κληροῦχοι, *the body of citizens who receive such allotments*, ἀποικίαις καὶ κληρουχίαις *IG*1$^{2}$.140.9; κ. ἐκπέμπειν Isoc.4.107 (pl.); κ. ἔγραφεν Plu.*Per*.34 (pl.). **II.** *inheritance*, Lxx *Ne*.11.20, Ph.2.290 (pl.). **-ικός**, ή, όν, *of* or *for a* κληρουχία, γῆ κ. land *for allotment*, Ar.*Nu*.203 (in Egypt, *land held by* κληροῦχοι, *PSI*4.344.6 (iii B.C.), *PTeb*.5.194 (ii B.C.)); τὰ κ. (sc. χρήματα) D.14.16; νόμος κ., = Lat. *lex agraria*, Plu.*CG*5. **-ος**, ὁ, (κλῆρος, ἔχω) *one who held an allotment of land*, esp. *an allotment in a foreign country assigned him as a citizen*, Hdt.5.77, Th.3.50, Aeschin.1.53, *IG*1$^{2}$.60.10, 2$^{2}$.114.9; esp. in Ptolemaic Egypt, *holder of land by military tenure*, *PCair.Zen*.3.6, 326.37, al. (iii B.C.), *PSI*4.344.7 (iii B.C.), *PPetr*.2 p.4 (iii B.C.), etc.: metaph., μητέρα πολλῶν ἐτῶν κληροῦχον *having* old age *for her lot*, S.*Aj*.508; Ἑρμῆ.. Φιλιππίδου κληροῦχε Alex.89. **2.** *one who distributed allotments* to citizens, Harp., Phot.; ὁ κ. θεός Ph.2.121. **3.** *holder of an inheritance*, Id.2.290, al. **4.** in Roman Egypt, *land-owner*, *landlord*, *PFay*.82.19 (ii A.D.), *Sammelb*.7193$^{r}$ii 2 (ii A.D.), etc. **II.** Pass., κ. γῆ land *distributed in allotments*, D.H.8.75.

⊛ **κληρ-όω**, Dor. **κλᾱρόω**, inf. κλαρώεν *Foed.Delph.Pell*.1 *A*6, κλαρώειν *SIG*647.33 (Stiris, ii B.C.): (κλῆρος A):—*appoint by lot*, ἐξ ἁπάντων τὰς ἀρχάς Isoc.7.22; ἀθλητάς Arist.*Rh*.1393$^{b}$5; διαιρετὰς τῶν κτημάτων *SIG*364.9 (Ephesus, iii B.C.); τὰ δικαστήρια ib.647.33; ἄλλον [ἱερόν] *IG*5(1).1390.6 (Andania, i B.C.); also, of the lot, *fall on*, οὓς ἐκλήρωσεν πάλος E.*Ion*416:—Med., *cast lots* for office, of candidates, ἂν ἔλθῃ κληρωσόμενος τῶν ἐννέα ἀρχόντων Lys.6.4, cf. 24.13; κ. ἱερωσύνης D.57.62; κληρουμένων ἐπιμελῶς Arist.*Ath*.27.4; ὃς ἂν κληρούμενος λαγχάνῃ Pl.*Plt*.298e:—Pass., *to be appointed by lot*, Arist.*Ath*.43.2, Decr.ib.30.5, *SIG*525.11 (Crete, iii B.C.), *IG*5(1).1390.132 (Andania, i B.C.), etc.; [πρόεδροι] κεκληρωμένοι D.24.89; κεκληρῶσθαι ἄρχειν Luc.*Luct*.2. **2.** *cast lots*, Pl.*Lg*.759c, 856d; κληρώσω πάντας I *will make* all *draw lots*, Ar.*Ec*.682; κ. τὰς φυλάς Plb.6.20.2:—Med., A.*Th*.55, Ar.*Ec*.836, D.21.133; ὅτε ἐκληροῦσθε when *you were drawing lots*, Id.19.1. **3.** Med., *have allotted one*, *obtain by lot*, δεσπότας E.*Tr*.29; ἱερωσύνην Aeschin.1.188; ἀμπέλων δεκανίαν *IGRom*.4.1675 (Lydia): metaph., *obtain as one's sphere* or *province*, τὸ ταὐτὸν ὁ δημιουργὸς ἐκληρώσατο Dam.*Pr*.321; Astrol., ἥλιος κληρωσάμενος τὴν ὥραν Vett.Val.61.1; κεκληρῶσθαι *to be in possession of*, *to have*, Hp.*Ep*.20, Procl.*Inst*.110; τὴν καρδίαν κεκλήρωται ἐπὶ τῇ φάρυγγι Ael.*NA*5.31. **II.** *allot*, *assign*, ὔμμε δ' ἐκλάρωσε πότμος Ζηνί Pi.*O*.8.15; μοίρας, τὴν μὲν ἐπὶ μονῇ, τὴν δ' ἐπὶ ἐξόδῳ Hdt.1.94; ἓν ἑκάστῳ ἐκλήρωσαν Th.6.42:—Pass., ἐκληρώθην δούλη E.*Hec*.100 (anap.). **2.** ὀμφὰν κ. *deliver* an oracle *by lot*, Id.*Ion*908 (lyr.). ⊛ **-ωσις**, εως, ἡ, *choosing by lot*, βίου Pl.*Phdr*.249b; κληρώσεις δικαστηρίων Id.*Lg*.956e, cf. Isoc.7.23: metaph., πικρὰν κ. αἵρεσίν τέ μοι βίου καθίστης, of a *choice* of evils, E.*Andr*.384. ⊛ **-ωτήριον**, τό, = κληρωτρίς, Ar.*Ec*.681, *Fr*.146, Eub.74.5, Arist.*Ath*.63.2 (unless in signf. II), *Not.Arch*.4.20 (Aug.). **II.** *place where elections by lot* or *distributions of jurors were held*, Arist.*Ath*.64.3, al., Plu.2.793d, Poll.9.44. **III.** *list of citizens*, so called because jurors were selected from it by lot, ἀναγραφῆναι εἰς τὰ κ. *OGI*229.53 (Smyrna, iii B.C.). ⊛ **-ωτής**, οῦ, ὁ, *one who presided over elections by lot* or *distributions of jurors*, Poll.9.44; Dor. κλᾱρωτὰς δικαστᾶν Maiuri *Nuova Silloge* 18. **-ωτί** or **-ωτεί**, Adv. *by lot*, Lxx *Jo*.21.4, al. **-ωτικός**, ή, όν, *of* or *for casting lots*, τὸ -κόν (sc. ἀγγεῖον) Ath.10.450b. **-ωτός**, ή, όν, *appointed by lot*, δύναμις Pl.*Lg*.692a; βασιλεῖς Id.*Plt*.291a; τὰ κ., opp. τὰ αἱρετά, Id.*Lg*.759b, cf. Isoc.12.153, etc.; ἀρχὴ κ., opp. χειροτονητή, Lex ap.Aeschin.1.21, cf. *SIG*589.38 (Magn. Mae., ii B.C.); δημοκρατικὸν μὲν.. τὸ κληρωτὰς εἶναι τὰς ἀρχάς, τὸ δ' αἱρετὰς ὀλιγαρχικόν Arist.*Pol*.1294$^{b}$8, cf. 1266$^{a}$9, al. **-ωτρίς**, ίδος, ἡ, *urn for casting lots* or *votes*, Sch.Ar.*V*.672, 750.

**κλῄς**, ῃδός, ἡ, old Att. for κλείς.

⊛ **κλῆσις**, εως, ἡ, (καλέω) *calling*, *call*, Pl.*Smp*.172a, X.*Cyr*.3.2.14, etc. **2.** *calling into court*, *summons*, *prosecution*, Ar.*Nu*.875, 1189, etc.; τὰς κλήσεις καλεῖσθαι ὅσας ἔδει Antipho 6.38; ἀφιέναι τὰς κ. X.*HG*1.7.13. **3.** *invitation* to a feast, Id.*Smp*.1.7; εἰς τὸ πρυτανεῖον D.19.32; κλήσεις δείπνων Plu.*Per*.7, cf. Parmenisc.ap.Ath.4.156d. **4.** *invocation*, θεῶν Men.Rh.p.333 S. **5.** *calling to aid*, Plb.2.50.7. **6.** *calling* in a religious sense, 1*Ep.Cor*.7.20. **II.** *name*, *appellation*, Pl.*Plt*.262d, 287e, Dsc.1.42; τοὺς θεοὺς εἶναι κ. ἱεράς Cleanth.*Stoic*.1.123; Φιλησίη τὴν κ. *by name*, *IG*14.2067; *reputation*, Phld.*Rh*.2.46 S. **III.** Gramm., αἱ κ. τῶν ὀνομάτων the *nominatives*, opp. αἱ πτώσεις (the oblique cases), Arist.*APr*.48$^{b}$41; ἔχειν θηλείας ἢ ἄρρενος κλῆσιν the *nominative form* of.., Id.*SE*173$^{b}$40, cf. 182$^{a}$18. **IV.** = Lat. *classis*, D.H.4.18.

⊛ **κλῇσις**, εως, ἡ, (κλείω A) *closing*, τῶν λιμένων Th.2.94, cf. 7.70:—written **κλεῖσις**, Aen.Tact.20.1.

**κλῃστός**, v. κλειστός. **κλῄσω**, fut. of κλῄω (q.v.) and κλῄζω.

**κλητ-έος**, α, ον, (καλέω) *to be called*, *named*, Pl.*R*.341d, 428c. **II.** κλητέον, *one must call*, ib.470d, Lxx *Ep.Je*.63, Max.Tyr.40.5, Iamb.*Myst*.3.9. **-εύω**, *summon into court*, or *give evidence that a legal summons has been served*, Ar.*Nu*.1218; τινα D.18.150; τινι Ar.*V*.1413, cf. Is.*Fr*.108, D.32.30:—Med., *procure the issuing of the summons*, κ. τὴν δίκην Arist.*Pr*.951$^{a}$27:—Pass., = ἐκκλητεύεσθαι, Is. l.c. ⊛ **-ήρ**, ῆρος, ὁ, *summoner*, or *witness who gave evidence that the legal summons had been served*, *IG*1$^{2}$.63.39, 65.47, Ar.*Av*.147, 1422, *V*.1408, D.40.28, al., Eub.94.9, Pl.*Lg*.846c; with a pun, ὁμοιότατος κλητῆρος πωλίῳ (κλητῆρος for ὄνου 'brayer'), Ar.*V*.189. **II.** generally, = κῆρυξ, A.*Supp*.622: metaph., Ἐρινύος κ. Id.*Th*.574. **-ικός**, ή, όν, *of* or *for invitation*, Men.Rh.p.424 S.; σχῆμα Hermog.*Inv*.4.3. **2.** *invocatory*, ὕμνοι Men.Rh.p.333 S.; τύπος Id.p.334 S. **3.** Gramm., *vocative*, ἡ -κή (sc. πτῶσις) D.T.636.7, A.D.*Pron*.6.9, al.; σύνταξις Id.*Synt*.46.8; τὸ κ. "ὦ" Hdn.Gr.1.473. **-ός**, ή, όν, *invited*, Aeschin.2.162, etc.; *welcome*, Od.17.386. **2.** *called out*, *chosen*, Il.9.165. **3.** *invoked*, Anon.ap.Suid. **4.** *summoned to court*, *PAmh*.2.79.5 (ii A.D.). **II.** Subst. κλητή (sc. ἐκκλησία), ἡ, *convocation*, Lxx *Ex*.12.16, *Le*.23.2 (pl.). **-ροί**· κλήτορες, Hsch. **-ρόν**· καλούμενον, κλῆσιν, Id. **-ωρ**, = κλητήρ, *SIG*344.43 (Teos, iv B.C.), *PPetr*.3 p.48 (iii B.C.), *PHal*.1.223 (iii B.C.), Hdn.Gr.2.937, Hsch.; found in many codd. of Docum.ap.D.18.55, 21.87, 47.27, Plu.2.128f, etc. **2.** *one who invites*, *host*, Timae.88a. **3.** *one who invokes* the gods, Procl.*in Cra*.p.100 P., *in R*.2.246 K.

**κλῄω**, old Att. for κλείω (A). **κλῑβᾰν-άριος**, **-εύς**, **-ίτης**, **-οειδής**, **-ος**, v. κριβ-. **κλιδία**· τάριχος, Hsch. (cf. κλειδίον II).

⊛ **κλίμα** [ῐ, cf. Scymn.521], ατος, τό, (κλίνω) *inclination*, *slope* of ground, ἑκάτερον τὸ κ. τῶν ὀρῶν Plb.2.16.3; ἡ πόλις τῷ ὅλῳ κ. τέτραπται πρὸς τὰς ἄρκτους Id.7.6.1, etc.; *scarp*, Apollod.*Poliorc*.140.7. **II.** = ἔγκλιμα I.2, τοῦ κόσμου Hipparch.1.2.22, cf. Gem.16.12, Cleom.1.2. **2.** terrestrial *latitude*, *latitudes*, *region*, τὸ μεσημβρινὸν κ. D.H.1.9; τὸ ὑπάρκτιον κ. Plu.*Mar*.11; τὰ πρὸς μεσημβρίαν κ. the southern *regions*, Plb.5.44.6, cf. 10.1.3, Str.1.1.10, *AP*9.97 (Alph.), Ath.12.523e, Vett.Val.6.14, etc.; κ. οὐρανοῦ Hdn.2.11.4. **3.** *direction*, *cardinal point*, τὰ τέτταρα κ. (viz. N., S., E., W.) Str.10.2.12, *Gp*.1.11.1, cf. Isid.*Etym*.13.1.3; τὸ νότιον κ. τοῦ κόσμου Plu.2.365b; κατὰ τὸ βόρειον κ. Arist.*Mu*.392$^{a}$3. **4.** *seven latitudinal strips in the* οἰκουμένη *on which the longest day ranged by half-hour intervals from 13 to 16 hours*, Eratosth.ap.Scymn.113, Id.ap.Str.2.1.35, 2.5.34, Gem.5.58, 16.17, Posidon.ap.Procl.*in Ti*.3.125 D. (cf. eund.ap.Cleom.1.10), Id.ap.Str.6.2.1, Marin.ap.Ptol.*Geog*.1.15.8, 1.17.1, Id.*Alm*.2.12, al., *Cat.Cod.Astr*.8(4).37. **5.** *seven astrological zones corresponding to Nos. 3–6 of* κλίμα II.4, Nech.*Fr*.5, al., Vett.Val.22.33, al., Firmic.2.11.2. **III.** metaph., *inclination*, *propensity*, Arr.*Epict*.2.15.20. **IV.** *fall*, ἑπταετεῖ κλίματι *by death* at seven years of age, *IG*14.2431. **V.** Gramm., *inflected form*, A.D.*Adv*.173.25. **VI.** = ὑπόδημα, Hsch.; cf. κλείματα.

**κλῑμᾰκ-εών**, ῶνος, ὁ, *stairway*, *Gloss*. **-ηδόν**, Adv., (κλῖμαξ) *like a ladder* or *stairs*, A.D.*Adv*.197.19: wrongly written κλημακιδόν in Hsch. s.v. προκρόσσας. ⊛ **-ίας**, f.l. for καμακίας, Id. **-ίδιον**, τό, = κλιμάκιον, cj. in Amips.12 (pl.). **-ίζω**, *use the wrestler's trick called* κλῖμαξ (signf. III), Ar.*Fr*.4 D., Poll.3.155. **2.** metaph., *pervert*, *distort*, τοὺς νόμους Din.*Fr*.9.1 (**κλιμάζω** Harp., Phot.). **3.** *rear* (?), of a horse, Ar.*Fr*.63$^{b}$. **-ιον**, τό, Dim. of κλῖμαξ, Ar.*Pax* 69, Hp.*Art*.6, Demioprat.ap.Poll.10.171, Aristopho 4; κ. ξύλινον περίχρυσον ὄφεσιν ἀργυροῖς διεζωμένον *IG*11(2).161 *B*35 (Delos, iii B.C.), cf. *PLond*.3.1164(*h*)9 (iii A.D.). **2.** = κλιμακτήρ I, Heliod.ap.Orib.48.60.1. **3.** *bier*, Hsch. s.v. κλιματοφόρος. **4.** = κλιμακίς 4, Hp.*Art*.6 (as τινὲς ap.Apollon.Cit.1). ⊛ **-ίς**, ίδος, ἡ, Dim. of κλῖμαξ, *small ladder* or *stair*, Plb.5.97.5 (pl.); *ship's ladder*, *IG*2$^{2}$.1622.149, 203, al., *AB*272 (pl.). **2.** *woman who makes a step-ladder of herself*, by letting persons step on her back to mount a carriage, Plu.2.50d, Ath.6.256d. **3.** *wooden groove* for διώστρα in a torsion-engine, Ph.*Bel*.54.7, Hero *Bel*.100.7. **4.** *surgical machine* for reducing dislocations, Orib.47.4.15. **5.** wooden *frame* with openings for coffers in ceilings, *IG*1$^{2}$.372, 373, *Inscr.Délos* 504 *A*13 (iii B.C.). **-ισμός**, ὁ, = κλῖμαξ III, Hsch. (-ίσκοι cod.).

**κλῑμᾰκό-δεσις**, εως, ἡ, f.l. for κληματό-, Ath.Mech.36.6. **-ειδής**, ές, *like a stairway*, λαβύρινθος Steph.*in Rh*.286.12; *like a ladder*, Apollon.Cit.1 (s.v.l.). **-εις**, εσσα, εν, *with steps*, Nonn.*D*.18.56; v.l. for κλωμ-, Il.2.729. **-φόρος**, ον, *bearing a ladder*, Plb.10.12.1, D.S.18.33, App.*Mith*.26. **2.** *bearing on a bier*, Hsch. (κλιματ- cod.).

**κλῑμακ-τήρ**, ῆρος, ὁ, *rung of a ladder*, E.*Hel*.1570, Ar.*Fr*.277, Hp.*Art*.78, *IG*2$^{2}$.244.80, 11(2).203 *A*43 (Delos, iii B.C.). **II.** Astrol., *critical point in human life*, determined by multiples of 7, as 35, 49, 63, Varr.ap.Gell.3.10.9, Epist.Aug.ib.15.7.3, Vett.Val.143.9, Ptol.*Tetr*.141, Heph.Astr.1.1, etc.; κ. ἑβδοματικοί *Theol.Ar*.53: generally, *danger*, Anon.ap.Suid. s.v. ἐγκοπή. **-τηρίζω**, *mark a critical period*, Vett.Val.233.35. ⊛ **-τηρικός**, όν, *climacterical*, [ἐνιαυτός] Gell.15.7.2, cf. Plin.*Ep*.2.20.3; κ. λόγος Vett.Val.148.20; κ. ὑπάντησις Ptol.*Tetr*.140. **-ώδης**, ες, *like stairs*, κατάβασις Str.12.2.5. **-ωτός**, ή, όν, *made like a ladder* or *stairs*, *terraced*, πρόσβασις Plb.5.59.9. **II.** κ. σχῆμα, = κλῖμαξ IV, Hermog.*Id*.1.12.

⊛ **κλῖμαξ**, ᾰκος, ἡ, (κλίνω) *ladder* (because of its *leaning aslant*), *SIG*1169.92 (Epid.); *scaling-ladder*, Th.3.23, X.*HG*7.2.7, etc.; κλίμακος προσαμβάσεις A.*Th*.466, cf. E.*Ph*.489; κλιμάκων ὀρθοστάτας προσβαλών Id.*Supp*.497; προσθεῖναι Th. l.c.; *boarding-ladder*, *gangway*, E.*IT*1351, 1382, Theoc.22.30; κ. σκύτιναι, στύππιναι, Ph.*Bel*.102.13, 16. **2.** *staircase*, Od.1.330, 10.558, al., *IG*2$^{2}$.463.46; κ. ξύλιναι ib.1668.84; κ. ἑλικτή winding *stair*, Callix.1. **II.** *frame with cross-bars*, on which persons to be tortured were tied, Ar.*Ra*.618, *Com.Adesp*.422. **2.** *ladder used in reducing dislocations*, Hp.*Art*.42; κ. ἰσχυροὺς ἔχουσα κλιμακτῆρας ib.78. **III.** *wrestler's trick*, ἀμφίπλεκτοι κ. S.*Tr*.521 (lyr.), cf. Hsch. s.v. ἐκ κλίμακος. **IV.** in Rhet., *climax*, Demetr.*Eloc*.270, Quint.9.3.54, Longin.23.1 (pl.). **V.**

*part of a chariot*, narrowing like steps, Poll.1.253. **VI.** in pl., *handrails* on either side of a bridge, Arr.*An.*5.7.5.

**κλῐμᾰτάρχης**, ου, ὁ, *governor of a province*, Lyd.*Mag.*3.68, *Mens.* *Fr.*2. **II.** in pl., order of divine beings *ruling terrestrial regions*, Procl. *in Cra.*p.25 P., Olymp. *in Alc.*p.20 C.

**κλῐμᾰτίας** (sc. σεισμός), ὁ, = ἐπικλίντης, Heraclit.*All.*38, Amm. Marc.17.7; prob. l. for καυματίας, Posidon.ap.D.L.7.154.

**κλῐμᾰτικός**, ή, όν, *pertaining to* κλίμα II, διαφοραί Vett.Val.300.23.

**κλῑν-άριον**, τό, Dim. of κλίνη, Ar.*Fr.*239, *Act.Ap.*5.15, Arr.*Epict.* 3.5.13, *POxy.*1645.9 (iv A.D.); τὰ κ. τὰ ἐνδιδόντα elastic *bedsteads*, Thphr.*HP*5.6.4. ❋**-άρχης**, ου, ὁ, *one who sits in the first place*, Ph.2.537; **-αρχος**, ὁ, *president of an Isiac confraternity*, *Sammelb.*5099. **-ειος**, α, ον, *of* or *for beds*, ξύλα D.27.10. ❋**-η**, ἡ, (κλίνω) *that on which one lies, couch*, used at meals or for a bed, ἐν κλίνῃ κλῖναί τινας Hdt.9.16, cf. Ar.*Ach.*1090; κλίνην στρῶσαι to make up a *couch*, Hdt.6.139, X. *Cyr.*8.2.6, *IG*2².1315; ἐπὶ κλίνης φερόμενος And.1.61, cf. *SIG*1169.31 (Epid.); ἐκ κλίνης ἀνίστασθαι, after illness, And.1.64; κ. μιλησιουργὴς ἀμφικέφαλος *IG*1².330; κ. ἐπίχρυσοι καὶ ἐπάργυροι Hdt.1.50, 9.80; κ. ἐλεφαντόποδες Pl.Com.208. **2.** *bier*, Th.2.34, Pl.*Lg.*947b, *IG* 12(5).593.6 (Ceos, v B.C.). **3.** *grave-niche*, ib.14.788 (Naples), 871 (Cumae). **II.** ἱερὰ κ., = Lat. *lectisternium*, *POxy.*1144.6 (i/ii A.D.), cf. *PGnom.*202 (ii A.D.); κ. τοῦ κυρίου Σαράπιδος, of a ceremonial *banquet*, *POxy.*110.2 (ii A.D.). **2.** generally, *banquet*, *PSI*5.483.2 (pl., iii B.C.). **-ήρης**, ες, *ill in bed*, Ph.2.317, J.*BJ*2.21.6, Plu.*Pyrrh.*11, Ath.12.554d, Gal.1.297, *BGU*45.14 (iii A.D.); -ήρη τινὰ τηρεῖν keep her *in bed*, Sor.1.46. **-ίδιον**, τό, Dim. of κλίνη, Ar.*Lys.*916, D.H.7.68, J.*AJ*17.6.3, Plu.2.751b; κ. κρεμαστόν Antyll.ap.Orib. 6.23.6, Herod.Med.ap.eund.6.25.4. **2.** = Lat. *lectica*, Plu.*Cor.* 24. **-ικός**, ή, όν, *of* or *for a bed*: as Subst., κλινικός, ὁ, *physician who visits his patients in their beds*, Gal.12.829, *AP*11.113 (Nicarch.); title of work by Democrates, Gal.13.349; ἡ -κή (sc. τέχνη) *his art* or *method*, Plin.*HN*29.4. **II.** *bed-ridden*, γέρων Aus.*Ep.*8. 34. ❋**-ίον**, τό, = κλινίδιον, Thphr.*HP*4.2.5. **-ίς**, ίδος, ἡ, = κλινίδιον, Cratin.137, Ar.*Th.*261. **II.** = ἐπὶ τῆς ἁμάξης νυμφικὴ καθέδρα, Hsch., cf. Poll.10.33.

**κλῑνο-καθέδριον**, τό, *easy chair*, Phot. s. v. κλιντήρ, *AB*272. **-κοσμέω**, *arrange dining-couches*, Plb.12.24.3. **-κόσμοι**, οἱ, *officials who arranged* κλῖναι *for ceremonies*, *AEM*19.224 (Constanza). **-πάλη** [ᾰ], ἡ, *bed-wrestling*, sens. obsc., Suet.*Dom.*22. ❋**-πετής**, ές, *bed-ridden*, Hp.*Morb.*1.14, X.*HG*5.4.58, etc. **-πηγία**, ἡ, *making of beds*, Thphr.*HP*3.10.1, 5.7.6. **-πήγιον**, τό, *place where beds are made*, Poll.7.159. **-πηγός**, ὁ, = κλινοποιός, Theognost.*Can.*96, *CIG*2135 (κλεινο-, loc. incert.). **-πήξ**, -πῆγος, ὁ, = foreg., Theognost.*Can.*40. **-πόδιον**, τό, an aromatic herb, the leaves of which are *like the feet of a bed*, *Calamintha Clinopodium*, *horse-thyme*, Dsc. 3.95, Gal.12.30, Plin.*HN*24.137. **-ποιός**, ὁ, *maker of beds* or *bedsteads*, Pl.*R.*597a, D.27.9:—hence ἡ -ποιική (sc. τέχνη) *the art of making beds*, Poll.7.159. **-πους**, ποδος, ὁ, pl., *feet of a bed*, *Gp.* 13.9.9: sg., generally, κ. τοίχου Hsch. s. v. θριγκός, *EM*455.55; σφιγγῶν ib.425.28 (pl.). **-πώλιον**, τό, *shop where couches are sold*, Crates *Ep.*18 (pl.). **-στρόφιον**, τό, *engine of torture*, Agath. 4.1 (pl.). **-τροχος**, ἡ, *sycamore*, *Acer Pseudo-Platanus*, dub. l. in Thphr.*HP*3.11.1.

**κλῑνουργός**, ὁ, = κλινοποιός, Pl.*R.*597a.

**κλῑνοχᾰρής**, ές, *fond of bed*, Luc.*Trag.*131.

❋**κλιν-τήρ**, ῆρος, ὁ, (κλίνω) *couch*, Od.18.190, Theoc.2.86, 113, 24.43, Call.*Iamb.*1.112 (sic Pap., not κλωστῆρας), Tryph.441, Luc.*Symp.*8, 44; νεκροδόκος κ. *bier*, *AP*7.634 (Antiphil.), cf. *Epigr.Gr.*450.5 (Batanaea). ❋**-τηρίδιον**, τό, Dim. of foreg., Phot. **-τήριον**, τό, Dim. of κλιντήρ, Ar.*Fr.*266, Phylarch.44 J. **-τηρίσκος**, ὁ, = foreg., *Michel*832.48 (Samos, iv B.C.).

❋**κλίνω** [ῑ], fut. κλῐνῶ Lyc.557, (ἐγκατα-) Ar.*Pl.*621: aor. 1 ἔκλῑνα Il.5.37, etc.: pf. κέκλῐκα Plb.30.13.2:—Med., aor. ἐκλινάμην Od.17. 340, etc.:—**Pass.**, fut. κλῐθήσομαι (συγ-) E.*Alc.*1090, (κατα-) D.S.8 *Fr.*19: fut. 2 κατα-κλῐνήσομαι Ar.*Eq.*98, Pl.*Smp.*222e, also κεκλίσομαι dub. in A.D.*Pron.*22.7: aor. 1 ἐκλίθην [ῐ] Od.19.470, S.*Tr.*101 (lyr.), 1226, E.*Hipp.*211 (anap.), freq. in Prose; poet. also ἐκλίνθην, v. infr. II. 1,2,3: aor. 2 ἐκλίνην [ῐ] only in compds., κατακλῐνῆναι Ar.*V.*1208, 1211, X.*Cyr.*5.2.15, etc.; ξυγκατακλινείς Ar.*Ach.*981: pf. κέκλῐμαι (v. infr.); inf. κεκλίσθαι A.D.*Synt.*325.3, but κεκλίνθαι v.l. ib.47.1. (κλῐ-ν-yω, fr. root κλῐ: κλει-, cf. κλειτύς; Skt. *śrá-yati* 'cause to lean', 'support', Lat. *clinare*, *clivus*.) :—*cause to lean, make to slope* or *slant*, ἐπὴν κλίνῃσι τάλαντα Ζεύς when he *inclines* or *turns* the scale, Il.19.223; Τρῶας δ' ἔκλιναν Δαναοί *made* them *give way*, 5.37, cf. Od.9.59; ἐπεί ῥ' ἔκλινε μάχην Il.14.510; ἔκλινε γὰρ κέρας.. ἡμῶν E.*Supp.*704; also ἐκ πυθμένων ἔκλινε.. κλῇθρα S.*OT*1262:—Med., Περσῶν κλινάμενοι [δύναμιν] *IG*1².763. **2.** *make* one thing *slope* against another, i.e. *lean, rest it*, τι πρός τι Il.23.171, cf. 510; ἅρματα δ' ἔκλιναν πρὸς ἐνώπια 8.435: c. dat., ἔστησαν σάκε' ὤμοισι κλίναντες, i.e. *raising* their shields *so that the upper rim rested* on their shoulders, 11.593. **3.** *turn aside*, μηκέτι τοῦδε βήματος ἔξω πόδα κλίνῃς S.*OC*193 (lyr.); ὄσσε πάλιν κλίνασα *having turned* back her eyes, Il.3.427; τὰς ἐκ τῶν ἀριστερῶν [φλέβας] ἐπὶ τὰ δεξιὰ κ. *turn to*.., Pl.*Ti.*77e. **4.** *make* another *recline*, ἐν κλίνῃ κλῖναί τινας *make* them *lie down* at table, Hdt.9.16; κλινόν μ' ἐς εὐνήν E. *Or.*227; κλίνατ', οὐ σθένω ποσίν Id.*Alc.*267 (lyr.): metaph., ἡμέρα κλίνει τε κἀνάγει πάλιν ἅπαντα τἀνθρώπεια *puts to rest, lays low*, S. *Aj.*131. **5.** in Magic, *make subservient*, ψυχήν *PMag.Par.*1. 1718. **6.** Gramm., *inflect*, τὰ ῥήματα A.D.*Synt.*212.20:—Pass., Id.*Pron.*12.7. **II.** Pass., *lean*, ἂψ δ' ὁ πάϊς πρὸς κόλπον ἐϋζώνοιο τιθήνης ἐκλίνθη Il.6.467; ὁ δ' ἐκλίνθη, καὶ ἀλεύατο κῆρα μέλαιναν he *bent aside*, 7.254; of a brasen foot-pan, ἂψ δ' ἑτέρωσ' ἐκλίθη *it was tipped over*, Od.19.470; of battle, *turn*, ἐκλίνθη δὲ μάχη Hes.*Th.*711; of a body in equilibrium, οὐδαμόσε κλιθῆναι Pl.*Phd.*109a, cf. Archim. *Fluit.*1.8, al. **2.** *lean, stay oneself* upon or against a thing, c. dat., ἀσπίσι κεκλιμένοι Il.3.135; κίονι κεκλιμένη, Od.6.307, 17.97; ἠέρι δ' ἔγχος ἐκέκλιτο καὶ ταχέ' ἵππω Il.5.356 (s. v. l.); ἐν δορὶ κεκλιμένος Archil.2 (also in Med., κλινάμενος σταθμῷ Od.17.340); κεκλιμένοι καλῇσιν ἐπάλξεσιν Il.22.3; πρὸς τοῖχον ἐκλίνθησαν Archil.34; ξύλα ἐς ἄλληλα κεκλιμένα Hdt.4.73; ὅταν τύχωσι (sc. αἱ ἄτομοι) τῇ περιπλοκῇ κεκλιμέναι when they chance to be *propped* (i.e. *checked*) by the interlacing with others, Epicur.*Ep.*1 p.8 U. **3.** *lie down, fall*, ἐν νεκύεσσι κλινθήτην Il.10.350, etc.; παραὶ λεχέεσσι κλιθῆναι *lie* beside her on the bed, Od.18.213, cf. S.*Tr.*1226: in pf., *to be laid, lie*, ἔντεα.. παρ' αὐτοῖσι χθονὶ κέκλιτο Il.10.472; φύλλων κεκλιμένων of *fallen* leaves, Od.11.194 (φύλλα κεκλ. in Thphr.*HP*3.9.2, *slanting* leaves); Ληθαίῳ κεκλιμένη πεδίῳ Thgn.1216; 'Αλφεοῦ πόρῳ κλιθείς *laid* by Alpheus' stream, Pi.*O.*1.92; ἐπὶ γόνυ κέκλιται *has fallen* on her knee, i.e. is humbled, A.*Pers.*931 (lyr.); ὑπτία κλίνομαι S.*Ant.*1188; τὸ μὲν πρῶτον ἐρρήγνυντο τὸ τεῖχος, ἔπειτα δὲ καὶ ἐκλίνετο X.*HG*5.2.5; οὐ νούσῳ.. οὐδ' ὑπὸ δυσμενέων δούρατι κεκλίμεθα *AP*7.493 (Antip. Thess.), cf. 315 (Zenod. or Rhian.), 488 (Mnasalc.), Epic.*Oxy.*214ʳ.3. **4.** *recline* at meals, κλιθέντες ἐδαίνυντο Hdt.1.211, cf. E.*Cyc.*543, *SIG* 1023.48 (Cos, iii/ii B.C.); κλίθητι καὶ πίωμεν cj. in *Com.Adesp.*1203, cf. E.*Fr.*691. **5.** of Places, *lie sloping towards* the sea, etc., *lie near*, ἁλὶ κεκλιμένη Od.13.235; [νῆσοι] αἵ θ' ἁλὶ κεκλίαται (Ep. for κέκλινται) 4.608: hence, of persons, *lie on, live on* or *by*, ['Ορέσβιος] λίμνῃ κεκλιμένος Κηφισίδι Il.5.709; ῥηγμῖνι θαλάσσης κεκλίαται 16.68, cf. 15. 740; δισσαῖσιν ἀπείροις κλιθείς S.*Tr.*101 (lyr.); πλευρὰ πρὸς ἀνατολὰς κεκλιμένη, τὸ εἰς τὰς ἄρκτους κ., Plb.2.14.4, 1.42.5; ὄρος Κοῖον ὃ κέκλιται πρὸς Παρνασσόν *SIG*826 *E* iii 37 (Delph., ii B.C.). **6.** metaph., τῷδε μέλει κλιθείς *having devoted himself to*.., Pi.*N.*4.15 (also in Act., *incline* towards, τῶν πραγμάτων ἐπὶ 'Ρωμαίους κεκλικότων Plb. 30.13.2). **7.** *wander from the right course*, κεκλιμένη ναῦς Thgn. 856. **III.** Med., *decline, wane*, καὶ κλίνεται (sc. τὸ ἦμαρ) S.*Fr.*255. 6. **IV.** intr. in Act., κ. πρὸς τὸ ξανθὸν χρῶμα *incline* towards.., Arist.*Phgn.*812ᵇ3; κλίνοντος ὑπὸ ζόφον ἠελίοιο as the sun *was declining*, A.R.1.452; ἅμα τῷ κλῖναι τὸ τρίτον μέρος τῆς νυκτός as it *came to an end*, Plb.3.93.7; ἡ ἡμέρα ἤρξατο κλίνειν *Ev.Luc.*9.12; ἡ πόλις ἐπὶ τὸ χεῖρον ἔκλινεν X.*Mem.*3.5.13; τὸ κλῖνον ἀναλήμψεσθαι *PFay.*20.14 (iii/iv A.D.). **2.** of soldiers, κ. ἐπ' ἀσπίδα, ἐπὶ δόρυ, *turn* to left, to right, Plb.3.115.9, etc.; κ. πρὸς φυγήν Id.1.27.8; also, *wheel*, Ascl. *Tact.*10.4.

❋**κλισία**, Ion. -ίη, ἡ, (κλίνω) *place for lying down* or *reclining*: hence, **I.** *hut, shed, booth*, **1.** for use in peace, *cot, cabin*, once in Il., 18.589, cf. Od.14.194, al. **2.** for use in war, *hut*, κ. εὐπηκτος, εὔτυκτος, Il.9.663, 10.566; κ. ὑψηλή 24.448: freq. in pl., *camp*, 1.487, al.; πῦρ ἐν κλισίῃσι βαλόντες Od.8.501:—not common after Hom. (σκηνή being used), B.12.135, etc.: used by Trag. in lyr. and anap., A.*Fr.*131, S.*Aj.*190, 1407, E.*IA*189: later with various meanings, Βάκχου κλισίαι, of wine-*shops*, *IG*14.889 (Sinuessa); εὐσεβέων κλισίη, of the grave, *Epigr.Gr.*237.4 (Smyrna, ii/i B.C.), cf. *IG*12(5).1104 (Syros, ii A.D.); *chapel*, ἡ κ. ἡ ἱερά *BCH*51.220 (Thasos), cf. *Arch. Pap.*1.219, *IG*4²(1).123.131 (Epid.); cf. κλεισία. **II.** *anything for lying* or *sitting upon, couch* or *easy chair*, Od.4.123; κ. δινωτὴν ἐλέφαντι καὶ ἀργύρῳ 19.55; ἐπ' ἀλλοτρίαν κ. ἐρχόμενος *IG*2².1368.74. **2.** *couch for reclining on at table*, Pi.*P.*4.133 (pl.); ᾧ ξυνὴν εἶχον ἐγὼ κ. Call.*Aet.*1.1.8; *place on such couch*, κ. ἄτιμος Plu.*Ant.*59, 2.148f; κ. ἄδοξος Hegesand.18. **3.** *nuptial bed*, E.*Alc.*994, *IT*857. **III.** *company* of people *sitting at meals*, *Ev.Luc.*9.14; *banquet*, εὐωχίαι τε καὶ κ. Onos.35.5; *room for company*, Luc.*Am.*12. **IV.** *way of lying, decubitus*, Hp.*Epid.*7.25; τὸ σχῆμα τῆς κ. Plu.*Sert.*26.

❋**κλισιάδες**, v. κλεισιάδες.

**κλισιάζω**, *visit shrines*, Them.*Or.*13.178d (fort. κλεισιάζω, cf. κλεισίον 2).

**κλῐσί-ηθεν**, Adv. *out of* or *from the hut*, Il.1.391, etc. **-ηνδε**, Adv. *into* or *to the hut*, ib.185. **-ον**, τό, *outbuildings round a* κλισία or *herdsman's cot*, περὶ δὲ κλίσιον θέε πάντῃ Od.24.208 (glossed by προστῷον, Ameriasap.Ael.Dion.*Fr.*231); dub. sens. in *IG*11(2). 156*A* 38,49 (Delos, iii B.C.).

❋**κλισίον**, v. κλεισίον.

❋**κλίσις** [ῐ], εως, ἡ, (κλίνω) *bending, inclination*, τραχήλου Plu.*Pyrrh.* 8; *sinking* of the sun, D.P.1095; ἀκτίνων ἰδεῖαν κ. Id.585; *bend* of a river or tunnel, Agatharch.23, 25. **II.** *lying down*, ἄρθρων E.*Tr.* 114 (anap.); *place for lying on*, μαλακὴ κ. ὕπνον ἑλέσθαι Opp.*H.*1. 25. **2.** = κλισία IV, Hp.*Epid.*7.77: pl., Ruf.*Ren.Ves.*1. **III.** *turning*, of soldiers, ἐπὶ δόρυ ποιεῖσθαι τὴν κ. to the right, ἐφ' ἡνίαν (or ἐπ' ἀσπίδα Ael.*Tact.*32) to the left, Plb.3.115.10, 10.23.2, etc.; expld. as ἡ κατ' ἄνδρα κίνησις Ascl.*Tact.*10.2. **IV.** *region, clime*, D.P. 615. **V.** *inflexion* of nouns and verbs, D.T.632.8 (pl.), A.D.*Pron.* 12.14, al.; αἱ κατὰ πρόσωπον κ. Id.*Synt.*130.16. **b.** *augment*, *EM* 23.53.

**κλισμάκιον**, τό, Dim. of κλισμός, *IG*2².1541.28.

❋**κλισμία**, τά, = κλισία II. 3, Call.*Aet.*3.1.16.

**κλισμός**, ὁ (fem. only in Theoc.15.85), (κλίνω) *couch*, κλισμούς τε θρόνους τε Od.1.145; χρύσεοι κ. Il.8.436; κ. βασιλῆϊος Thgn.1191, cf. Hp.*Mul.*2.149, E.*Or.*1440 (lyr.); κ. δίφροιο Arat.251. **II.** *inclination, slope*, Arist.*Col.*792ᵃ22.

**κλίτα·** *στοαί, ἢ σέλλας* (ἐλαίας cod.) *εἰς τὸ κατακλίνεσθαι*, Hsch.

**κλῐτ-έον,** *one must inflect*, τοὺς μύθους εἰς τοὺς ἀριθμοὺς καὶ τὰς πλαγίας πτώσεις Theon *Prog.*3. **-ικός,** ή, όν, *inflexional*, τὸ κ. μέρος A.D.*Synt.*180.10; κ. ἔκτασις *temporal* augment, Choerob. *in Theod.* 2.81, *EM*295.14.

**κλῖτος** [ῐ], εος, τό, = κλειτύς, Lyc.600; *cliff*, Id.737 (pl.). 2. = κλίμα II, *clime*, κ. βόρειον *AP*7.699. 3. *side*, Lxx *Ex.*26.18, al.; τὸ κ. τὸ δεξιόν ib.*Ez.*47.1; τὸ κ. τοῦ νότου ib.3*Ki.*7.39.

**κλῖτος,** εος, τό, v. κλεῖτος (B). **κλῖτύς,** v. κλειτύς.

**κλοιόπους,** ποδος, ὁ, *clog for the foot*, in pl., = κλάποι, Tz.*H.*13.300.

⊕**κλοιός,** ὁ, also with heterocl. pl. κλοιά in Choerob. in *An.Ox.*2.234:—old Att. **κλῳός** Ar.*V.*897, E.*Cyc.*235:—*dog-collar*, Ar. l.c., Eup.159.16, Plu.*Sol.*24, *Fab.*20; τοὺς δάκνοντας κύνας κλοιῷ δήσαντες X.*HG*2.4.41; κ. σιδήρειος Babr.100(99).6; of a horse, κλοιῷ δειρὴν πεπεδημένος *AP*9.19 (Arch.). 2. wooden *collar* worn by prisoners, X.*HG*3.3.11, E. l.c., Luc.*Tox.*32, Jul.*Ep.*89b. 3. χρύσεος κ. *collar* of gold, as an ornament, E.*Cyc.*184, Lxx *Ge.*41.42.

**κλοῖστρον** or **κλῷστρον,** τό, prob. = κλεῖστρον, Hsch. **κλοιτοιμωγεῖς·** ἀκουσταὶ θρήνου, Id. (fort. κλύετ' οἰμωγῆς· ἀκούετε θρήνου). **κλοιώτης,** ου, ὁ, *wearing a collar*, hence, = δεσμώτης, Id.; **κλοιωτός,** ή, όν, Id.

⊕**κλόκιον,** τό, = ἀμίς, Steph. *in Hp.*1.163 D., prob. for κλοβίῳ (κλωβίῳ) ib.159 D.

**κλον-έω,** mostly in pres.: fut. -ήσω Ar.*Eq.*361:—**Pass.** also mostly in pres.: fut. κλονήσομαι Hp.*Genit.*2: aor. part. κλονηθέν Id.*Nat. Puer.*30: (κλόνος):—poet. Verb, used also in Ion. and late Prose, as Ph. (v. infr.), Aq.*Ge.*45.24, al.: Hom. (only in Il.) *drive tumultuously* or *in confusion*, πρὸ ἕθεν κλονέοντα φάλαγγας Il.5.96; ὥς τ' ἠὲ βοῶν ἀγέλην ἢ πῶϋ μέγ' οἰῶν θῆρε δύω κλονέωσι 15.324; of winds, νέφεα κλονέοντε πάροιθεν 23.213, cf. Hes.*Op.*553; κλονέων ἄνεμος φλόγα εἰλυφάζει Il.20.492; ὣς ἔφεπε κλονέων πεδίον 11.496, cf. 526; Ἕκτορα δ' ἀσπερχὲς κλονέων ἔφεπ' 22.188; χερὶ κλονέειν τινά, of a pugilist, Pi.*I.*8(7).70; εὖτ' ἐν πεδίῳ κλονέων μαίνοιτ' Ἀχιλλεύς B.12.118; dub. sens. in Sapph.*Supp.*19.3: generally, *harass, agitate*, καί νιν οὐ θάλπος θεοῦ.., οὐδὲ πνευμάτων οὐδὲν κλονεῖ S.*Tr.*146; τόνδε.. ἆται κ. Id.*OC*1244 (lyr.), cf. Ar.*Eq.*361; πάθη κ. τὴν ψυχήν Ph.1.589; in physical sense, βῆχες κ. τὸν θώρηκα Aret.*CA*1.10:—Pass., *to be agitated*, Hp. ll.cc., *Morb.*4.55. 2. abs., of the winds, *rage*, D.P.464. II. Pass., *rush wildly*, ἵππους ἐχέμεν, μηδὲ κλονέεσθαι ὁμίλῳ Il.4.302; *to be driven in confusion*, ὑπὸ Τυδεΐδῃ κλονέοντο φάλαγγες 5.93, cf. 11.148, 14.59, etc.; λαίλαπι κλονεύμενοι Semon.1.15; ψάμαθοι κύμασιν ῥιπαῖς τ' ἀνέμων κλονέονται Pi.*P.*9.48; τὸ συμπόσιον ἐκλονεῖτο τῷ γέλωτι Luc.*Asin.*47; κλονεῖσθαι τὴν γαστέρα Ael.*NA*2.44. 2. abs., *to be beaten by the waves*, ἀκτὰ κυματοπλὴξ κλονεῖται S.*OC*1241 (lyr.); παρὰ δ' ἰχθύες ἐκλονέοντο beside the fishes *tumbled*, Hes.*Sc.*317; of bees, *swarm*, βομβηδὸν κ. A.R.2.133: metaph., κ. ἡ οἰκουμένη Ph.1.298; *to be shaken in credit, refuted*, τὸ κεκλονημένον ῥῆμα Porph.*Chr.*35. **-ησις,** εως, ἡ, *agitation*, Hp.*Morb.*4.48,55, Aq.*Jb.*3.17, dub. in Q.S.8.41.

**κλόνις,** ιος, ἡ, *os sacrum*, Antim.65: **κλόνιον,** τό, = ἰσχίον, ῥάχις, ὀσφύς, Hsch.: **κλονιστήρ,** ὁ, = παραμήριος μάχαιρα, παρίσχιον, Id. (Cf. Skt. *śróṇis* 'haunch', Lat. *clūnis.*)

**κλονο-ειδῶς,** Adv. *tumultuously*, Sch.D Il.22.448. **-εις,** εσσα, εν, *tumultuous*, *EM*521.22. **-κάρδιος,** ον, *heart-stirring*, epith. of the thunderbolt, Orph.*H.*19.8 (cj. Steph. pro χρονοκάρδιος).

**κλόν-ος,** ὁ, Hom. (only in Il.), *confused motion, turmoil*, esp. *battle-rout*, κατὰ κλόνον Il.16.331,713; κ. ἐγχειάων *throng* of spears, 5.167, 20.319; ἐν δὲ κλόνον ἧκε κακόν [Ἀπόλλων] 16.729; κ. ἀνδρῶν *throng* of men, Hes.*Sc.*148; Trag. (not in S.) only in lyr., ἱππιοχάρμας κλόνους *throngs* of fighting horsemen, A.*Pers.*106; ἀσπίστορας κλόνους Id.*Ag.*404; σκέψαι κλόνον.. Γιγάντων E.*Ion* 206: in later Prose, *trembling, confusion*, Aq.*Ez.*12.8, Them.*Or.*6.73b; *agitation* of mind, ὁ ἄφρων σάλον καὶ κ. ὑπομένει Ph.1.230. II. *agitation* in physiological sense, of wind in the bowels, Ar.*Nu.*387; κλόνου πάταγος Aret.*SD*1.7; οἱονεί τινα σφυγμὸν καὶ κ. ἔχοντος τοῦ πνεύματος Plu.2.681a; of the pulse, Gal.9.76; of the body generally, ib.651: generally, *shaking, agitation*, Alex.Aphr. *in Top.*466.25. **-ώδης,** ες, *agitated*, Gal.8.554, al. Adv. -δῶς Id.9.79.

**κλοπ-αῖος,** α, ον, *stolen*, πυρὸς πηγή A.*Pr.*110, cf. S.*Ichn.*76, E.*Alc.*1035. 2. *furtive, fraudulent*, κλοπαίων τε καὶ βιαίων Pl.*Lg.*934c; ἀφανισμός D.H.2.71. **-εία** (v.l. κλωπεία), ἡ, *brigandage*, Str.15.3.18. **-εῖον,** τό, *stolen property*, Max.600. **-εύς,** έως, ὁ, *thief*, S.*Ph.*77. 2. generally, *secret doer, perpetrator*, Id.*Ant.*493. **-εύω,** *plunder*, τὴν Ἰταλίαν App.*Ill.*15. II. v. κλοτοπεύω. **-ή,** ἡ, (κλέπτω) *theft*, ἁρπαγῆς τε καὶ κλοπῆς δίκη A.*Ag.*534: pl., ib.402 (lyr.), E.*Hel.*1175; κλοπῆς δίκη Pl.*Prt.*322a; ἱερῶν κλοπῆς δυοῖν ταλάντοιν γεγραμμένος Antipho 2.1.6, cf. Ar.*Eq.*444, Pl.*Euthphr.*5d (pl.); κλοπῆς ὀφλεῖν And.1.74; ἐπὶ κλοπῇ χρημάτων ἀποκτείνειν Lys.30.25; κ. τῶν θησαυρῶν *PAmh.*2.79.63 (ii A.D.); σκεῦος.. ἐκφέρειν ἐκ τοῦ ἱεροῦ ἐπὶ κλοπήν *SIG*997.5 (Smyrna); κλοπῆς ἐν ταῖς εὐθύναις ἑάλωκεν D.24.112, cf. Arist.*Ath.*54.2, Plu.*Per.*32; opp. ἁρπαγή, Pl.*Lg.*941b. 2. of authors, *plagiarism*, Porph.ap.Eus.*PE*10.3. II. *secret act* or *transaction, fraud*, κλέπτουσα μύθοις κλοπάς E.*HF*100; πράγματος μεγάλου κ. Aeschin.2.57; κλοπῇ *by stealth* or *fraud*, S.*Ph.*1025, E.*Ion* 1254; ποδοῖν κλοπὰν ἀρέσθαι, i.e. to steal away, S.*Aj.*246 (lyr.). III. in warfare, *surprise*, X.*An.*4.6.14. **-ικός,** ή, όν, *thievish*, τὸ κ. Pl.*Cra.*408a. ⊕**-ῐμαῖος,** α, ον, *acquired by theft*, Luc.*Icar.*20; βόες Ant.Lib.23.4. Adv. -αίως *Gloss.* **-ιμος,** ον (η, ον Ps.-Phoc.135), *thievish*, χεῖρες Id.154, *APl.*4.193 (Phil.); *gotten by fraud*, παραθήκη Ps.-Phoc.135. Adv. -μως Man.5.298. **-ιος,** α, ον, (κλώψ) *thievish, artful*, μῦθοι Od.13.295; χείρ *AP*9.249 (Maec.); ὁδός *APl.*4.123. **-ός,** ὁ, *thief*, *h.Merc.*276, Opp.*C.*1.517.

**κλοποφορ-έω,** *steal from, rob*, τινα Lxx *Ge.*31.26. **-ημα,** ατος, τό, *a theft*, Hdn.*Epim.*72. **-ία,** ἡ, *theft*, Zonar.

**κλότι-ον,** τό, or -ος, ὁ, a kind of *vessel* or *basket*, μήκων ἐν κλοτίῳ *PSI*4.428.2, cf. 51 (iii B.C., nisi leg. κλουίον).

**κλοτοπ-εύω,** *deal subtly, spin out time by false pretences*, οὐ γὰρ χρὴ κλοτοπεύειν Il.19.149; κ. περὶ τὸ νησίδιον, perh. to be read for κλοπεύω, Hld.1.30:—hence **-ευτής·** ἐξαλλάκτης, ἀλαζών, Hsch.

**κλουβός,** ὁ, later form for κλωβός, Tz.*H.*5.602, *Gloss.*; *kiln*, *POxy.*1923.14 (v/vi A.D.):—Dim. ⊕**κλουβίον,** τό, *small cage*, *PTeb.*413.14 (ii/iii A.D.):—written **κλουίον,** *crate*, ᾠῶν *POxy.*936.5 (iii A.D.).

**κλοῦστρον,** τό, a kind of *cake*, Chrysipp.Tyan.ap.Ath.14.647d.

**κλύβατις** [ῠ], ἡ, = ἑλξίνη, Nic.*Th.*537, Dsc.4.85.

**κλύδα,** τήν, metapl. acc. of κλύδων, as if from *κλύς, Nic.*Al.*170.

**κλῠδ-άζομαι,** *fluctuate*, of the fluid in pleurisy, Hp.*Loc.Hom.*14; of cranes flying, Max.Tyr.12.3. **-αξις,** εως, ἡ, *splashing* in the stomach, Diocl.*Fr.*141. **-ασμός,** ὁ, *surging of waves*, Str.4.1.7; *fluctuation* in an abscess, Paul.Aeg.3.65. **-άττομαι,** = κλυδωνίζομαι, D.L.5.66. **-άω,** *to be plastic*, Arist.*Pr.*966b7. **-ιος,** α, ον, *surging*: κλύδιον· πέλαγος, Hsch.

**κλύδων** [ῠ], ωνος, ὁ, *wave, billow*, and collectively, *surf, rough water*, Od.12.421; πόντιος κ. A.*Pr.*431 (lyr.), S.*OC*1687 (lyr.); κ. πελάγιος, θαλάσσιος, E.*Hec.*701, *Med.*29; Θρῄκιος κ. S.*OT*197 (lyr.); κ. ἄγριος Tim.*Pers.*146: in Prose, prob. in Th.2.84 (Phot., Suid., κλυδωνίῳ codd.), cf. Thphr.*Char.*25.2; πνεῦμα καὶ κ. Arist.*HA*548b13; κ. καὶ χειμών Id.*PA*685a32: pl., Lyc.474, Plb.10.10.3. 2. Medic., *splashing* in the stomach and chest, Gal.1.348, al.; of sound heard in pleurisy, Id.8.285; ἢν κ. ὑγρῶν ἀναπνέῃ ἐς τὰς διαπνοὰς *flood* of humours, Aret.*SA*1.5; of internal water in dropsy, Id.*SD*2.1. II. metaph., κ. κακῶν *sea* of troubles, A.*Pers.*599; κ. ξυμφορᾶς S.*OT*1527 (troch.); κ. ἔφιππος *flood* of chariots, Id.*El.*733; πολέμιος κ. E.*Ion* 60; πολὺς κ. δορός Id.*Supp.*474; ἔριδος κ. Id.*Hec.*116 (anap.); πόλις ἐν κλύδωνι τῶν ἄλλων πόλεων διαγομένη Pl.*Lg.*758a; κ. καὶ μανία D.19.314; ἐν χειμῶνι πολλῷ καὶ κ. τῆς πόλεως Plu.*Cor.*32, cf. M.Ant.12.14; κ. ἀλογίας Hierocl. *in CA* 26 p.479 M.

**κλῠδων-ίζω,** Suid.:—elsewh. in Pass., *to be buffeted, swept by heavy seas*, τὸν κυβερνήτην -ίζεσθαι καὶ ἀστοχεῖν θαλασσομαχοῦντα Vett.Val.354.26; -ομένη ναῦς Phlp. *in APo.*381.7: usu. metaph., *to be disturbed, thrown into confusion*, οἱ ἄδικοι κλυδωνισθήσονται Lxx *Is.*57.20; δῆμος ταρασσόμενος καὶ -ιζόμενος J.*AJ*9.11.3; *to be tossed about*, παντὶ ἀνέμῳ τῆς διδασκαλίας *Ep.Eph.*4.14. **-ιον,** τό, Dim. of κλύδων, *little wave, ripple*, E.*Hec.*48, etc.: pl., Id.*Hel.*1209: metaph., of a city, κλυδωνίου πολλαῖσι πληγαῖς ἄντλον οὐκ ἐδέξατο A.*Th.*795: collectively, *surf*, dub. l. in Th.2.84 (cf. κλύδων): without Dim. sense, Arr.*Peripl.M.Eux.*3. II. metaph., κ. χολῆς A.*Ch.*183. **-ισμα,** ατος, τό, gloss on κλυδώνιον, Suid.: **-ισμός,** ὁ, Hdn.*Epim.*179: **-ῶ,** = κλυδωνίζω, Suid.

**κλύζω,** Ep. impf. κλύζεσκον Il.23.61: Ep. fut. κλύσσω *h.Ap.*75: aor. inf. κλύσαι Poll.4.21 (v.l. κλεῖσαι):—**Pass.,** aor. ἐκλύσθην: pf. κέκλυσμαι (v. infr.):—of the sea, *wash, dash over*, c. acc., ἔνθ' ἐμὲ μὲν μέγα κῦμα.. κλύσσει *h.Ap.* l.c.: abs., *surge up*, κύματος δίκην κλύζειν πρὸς αὐγάς (Auratus for κλύειν) A.*Ag.*1182:—more freq. in Pass., ἐκλύσθη δὲ θάλασσα ποτὶ κλισίας Il.14.392; ἐκλύσθη δὲ θάλασσα.. ὑπὸ πέτρης *was dashed high* by the falling rock, Od.9.484,541; λιμὴν.. κλυζομένῳ ἴκελος seeming *to rise in waves*, Hes.*Sc.*209; ὕδασι.. ἐκλύζετο Batr.76; of land, *to be washed by the sea*, Plb.34.11.2. II. *wash away, purge*, κλύζουσι φαρμάκῳ χολήν S.*Fr.*854; ἔκλυζεν ποταμῷ κλύματα Call.*Aet.*3.1.25: metaph., θάλασσα κλύζει πάντα τἀνθρώπων κακά E.*IT*1193. 2. *wash, rinse out*, ἔκπωμα X.*Cyr.*1.3.9; τοὺς μυκτῆρας οἴνῳ with wine, Arist.*HA*603b11; *drench* with a clyster, Hp.*Acut.*19, *Mul.*1.75, al., Nic.*Al.*140, *AP*11.118 (Nicarch. or Callicter), etc.; dub. l. in Hp.*Flat.*12 (Pass.). 3. εἰς ὦτα κ. *put water* into the ears *and so cleanse* them, E.*Hipp.*654. 4. *coat with wax*, Πανιώνιον στεγνώσαντι καὶ κλύσαντι *IG*11(2).154 *A*36 (Delos, iii B.C.); κηρῷ κλύσαντι ib.219 *A*40:—Pass., κισσύβιον κεκλυσμένον ἁδεῖ κηρῷ Theoc.1.27. (Cf. Lat. *cluĕre*, = *purgare*, *cloaca*, Goth. *hlutrs*, OHG. *hlûtar* (MHG. *lauter*) 'pure'.)

**κλῦθι,** v. κλύω.

**κλύμενον,** τό, *honeysuckle, Lonicera etrusca*, Thphr.*HP*9.8.5, 9.18.6, Dsc.4.14. 2. *Scorpiurus vermiculata*, ib.13, Plin.*HN*25.70. 3. *bearbind, Convolvulus arvensis*, Ps.-Dsc.4.13. 4. = κισσός, Hsch., quoting κισσοῦ τε κλυμένοιο Antim.68.

⊕**κλύμενος** [ῠ], η, ον, = κλυτός, *famous* or *infamous*, Antim.68 (v. foreg. 4); ἔρως Theoc.14.26:—mostly as pr. n., Κλύμενος, god of the nether world, *AP*7.9 (Damag.), 189 (Aristodic.), Paus.2.35.4.

⊕**κλυντήρ,** ῆρος, ὁ, prob. late spelling of κλιντήρ, *IGRom.*1.730 (pl., Philippopolis).

**κλύσις** [ῠ], εως, ἡ, *drenching* by clyster, Hp.*Acut.*11.

**κλύσ-μα,** ατος, τό, *liquid used for washing out*, esp. *clyster, drench*, Hdt.2.77,87, Ruf.ap.Orib.8.24 tit. 2. *surf*, πέτραι παραθηγόμεναι τῷ κ. Luc.*Nav.*8. II. *place washed by the waves, sea-beach*, Plu.*Caes.*52, Luc.*DMar.*6.3, etc. III. of a κίναιδος, Poll.6.126; of a ἑταίρα, Id.7.39. **-ματικόν,** τό, = sq., Ruf.ap.Orib.7.26.191. **-μάτιον,** τό, Dim. of κλύσμα, *clyster*, Hp.*Epid.*3.17.γ', Ruf.*Ren.Ves.*1, etc. **-μός,** ὁ, = κλύσμα I, D.S.1.82, Dsc.3.96, Ruf.ap.Orib.7.26.18, Mnesith.ap.eund.8.38.1. **-τέον,** *one must wash out*, Aët.

4.20. II. **-τέος**, *α, ον*, *to be washed out*, Lycus ap.Orib.8.28.7. **-τήρ**, *ῆρος, ὁ*, *clyster-pipe, syringe*, Hdt.2.87, Phld.*Lib*.p.30 O., Sor.2.59, Lycus ap.Orib.8.33.3, Gal.10.358, Artem.5.79. II. = κλύσμα I, Nic.*Al*.139; *τρόφιμοι κ.* nutritive *enemata*, Lycus ap.Orib.8.34 tit. **-τήριον**, *τό*, Dim. of foreg., Gal.7.443: **-τηρίδιον**, *τό*, Sor.1.125, Orib.*Fr*.143, Paul.Aeg.3.23.

**κλῦτε**, v. *κλύω*.

**κλῠτό-βουλος**, *ον*, *famous in counsel*, Ἑρμείας Opp.*H*.3.26. **-δενδρος**, *ον*, *famous for trees*, Πιερίη *AP*4.2.1 (Phil.). ⊛**-εργός**, *όν*, *making κλυτὰ ἔργα*: hence, = *κλυτοτέχνης*, epith. of Hephaestus, Od.8.345; Τύχη *AP*10.64 (Agath.). **-καρπος**, *ον*, *glorious with fruit*, *κ. στέφανοι* Pi.*N*.4.76. **-μαντις**, *εως, ὁ*, *famous for prophecy*, Πυθοῖ Pi.*Pae*.6.2. **-μητις**, *ι*, gen. *ιδος*, *famous for skill*, epith. of Hephaestus, *h.Hom*.20.1; of Apollo, *Pae.Erythr*.p.137 P.; of Asclepius, *IG*4²(1).471 (Epid.), 14.1015, Philostr.Jun.*Im*.13 (-*μήτης* codd.); of a judge, *APl*.4.43. **-μοχθος**, *ον*, *famous for toil*, Καλλιόπα ib.362. **-νοος**, *ον*, *famous for wisdom*, *AP*3.4 (Inscr. Cyzic.). [κλῠ- metri gr.] **-παις**, *ὁ, ἡ*, gen. *παιδος*, *famous for one's children*, ib.9.262 (Phil.). **-πωλος**, *ον*, *with noble steeds*, Il. always epith. of Hades, 5.654, 11.445, 16.625; later *κ. λόχος*, of the heroes in the wooden horse, Tryph.92.

⊛**κλῠτός**, *ή, όν* (but *κλυτὸς Ἱπποδάμεια, κλυτὸς Ἀμφιτρίτη*, Il.2.742, Od.5.422): (*κλέω* A):—*renowned, glorious*, in Ep., etc., freq. as epith. of gods and heroes, *κ. ἐννοσίγαιος* Il.9.362; *Ἀμφιγυήεις* Hes.*Op*.70; Ἑρμᾶς Pi.*P*.9.59; Ἀθάνα B.16.7; *Νηρέος κόραι* ib.101; *Ἀχιλλεύς* Il.20.320; *Ὀδυσεύς* Od.24.409; also *κλυτὰ φῦλ' ἀνθρώπων* Il.14.361; *κ. ἔθνεα νεκρῶν* Od.10.526; *ὄνομα κ.* a *glorious* name, 9.364 (expld. by Sch. as the name *by which one is called*); of cities, etc., Ἄργος Il.24.437; Ἰταλία S.*Ant*.1118; *πόλις* E.*IA*263. **2.** of things, *noble, splendid*. *ἄλσος* Od.6.321; *δώματα* Il.2.854, etc.; *λιμήν* Od.10.87, 15.472; *αἰθήρ* B.16.73; *ἀγγελίαν* Pi.*O*.14.21; *ἐπικωμίαν ὄπα* Id.*P*.10.6; of animals, *κ. μῆλα* Od.9.308; *κλυτοῖς αἰπολίοις* S.*Aj*.375; *κ. ὄρνις*, = *ἀλεκτρυών*, Hsch., cj. in Nic.*Fr*.68.2: freq. of the works of human skill, *κλυτὰ ἔργα* Od.20.72; *εἵματα* 6.58; *τεύχεα* Il.5.435; *δαίς, ἀοιδαί, φόρμιγξ*, Pi.*O*.8.52 codd., *N*.7.16, *I*.2.2; *ἔναρα* S.*Aj*.177; *χρήματα* Crates Theb.10.6.—Used by Trag. only in lyr.

**κλῠτο-τέρμων ὥρα**, *ἡ*, = *ὡροσκόπος*, Man.4.28. **-τέχνης**, *ου, ὁ*, *famous for his art*, epith. of Hephaestus, Il.1.571, 18.143, Od.8.286. **-τεχνικός**, *ή, όν*; *τὸ αὐτοῦ κ.* his *fame in art*, Eust.1148.57. ⊛**-τοξος**, *ον*, *famous for the bow, renowned archer*, epith. of Apollo, Il.4.101, 15.55, Od.21.267, B.1.37. **-φεγγής**, *ές*, *brightly-beaming*, Man.2.148. ⊛**-φημος**, *ον*, *illustrious by fame*, Orph.*A*.216.

**κλύω**, Hes.*Op*.726, etc.: impf. *ἔκλυον* with aor. sense, poet. *κλύον* Id.*Th*.474, B.16.67; 3 sg. *ἔκλεεν* Maiist.58: aor. imper. *κλῦθι* Il.1.37, etc.; pl. *κλῦτε* Pi.*O*.14.4; also with Ep. redupl. *κέκλῠθι* Il.10.284, A.R.4.783, *κέκλῠτε* Il.3.86, etc.; also sg. *κέκλῠκε* Epich.190. (Cf. *κλέω* A.) [ῠ, exc. in imper. *κλῦθι* and *κλῦτε*.]:—*hear*, Hom., etc.; *κλύειν, ἀκοῦσαι* Ar.*Ra*.1173: poet. word (Com. only in mock Trag., Ar. l.c., *Av*.407, 416, Pherecr.145.1):—Constr.: c. gen. pers. et acc. rei, *hear* a thing *from* a person, *κέκλυτέ μευ..μῦθον Ἀλεξάνδροιο* Il.3.86, cf. Od.2.25, S.*OT*235, etc.; *τι ἔκ τινος* Od.19.93; *τι πρός τινος* S.*OT*429: c. gen. pers. only, esp. with part. added, *οὐδ' ἔκλυον αὐδήσαντος* Il.10.47, cf. Od.4.505, S.*OC*1406, 1642: c. acc. rei only, *ἀγγελίην ἔκλυεν* Od.2.30; *κ. βάξιν* Emp.112.11; *κλύε εὐχὰν Ζεύς* B. l.c., cf. A.*Pr*.124 (anap.), 588 (lyr.), etc.: c. gen. rei, *θεὰ δέ μευ ἔκλυεν αὐδῆς* Od.10.311; *θεὰ δέ οἱ ἔκλυεν ἀρῆς* 4.767; *κέκλυτέ μευ μύθων* 12.271, etc.: c. gen. objecti, *hear of* a person or thing, S.*OC*307, *Ant*.1182: with part., *κ. νεκροὺς θανόντας* A.*Th*.837 (lyr.); *ὃν κλύεις..ὄντα δεσπότην* S.*Ph*.261, cf. 427: less freq. c. acc. et inf., *ποῦ κλύεις νιν..ἱδρῦσθαι;* Id.*Tr*.68: *κ. ὁθούνεκα hear* that.., Id.*El*.1307: pres. with pf. sense, *have heard* or *learnt, know*, *εἰ καὶ μὴ κλύεις τῶν ἀγγέλων* Id.*OT*305, cf. *Ph*.261, *Tr*.422, 425; *λόγῳ κ.* E.*Hipp*.1004: abs. in part., *κλύοντες οὐκ ἤκουον* A.*Pr*.448, cf. S.*Ant*.691, etc. **2.** *perceive* generally, *μάλιστα δέ τ' ἔκλυον αὐτοί* they themselves *know* [the blessing] most, Od.6.185; *κλῦθι ἰδὼν ἀΐων τε* Hes.*Op*.9. II. *give ear to, attend to*, *τοῦ κλύον ἠδ' ἐπίθοντο* Il.15.300, etc.: imper., *κέκλυτέ μευ, πάντες τε θεοὶ πᾶσαί τε θέαιναι* 8.5; esp. in prayers, *give ear* to me, *κλῦθί μευ, Ἀργυρότοξε* 1.37: c. dat., *give ear to*, *καί τ' ἔκλυες ᾧ κ' ἐθέλησθα* (of Hermes) 24.335; *κλῦθί μοι* v.l. 5.115 (v. *ἐγώ* II); *κλῦτέ μοι εὐχομένῳ* Sol.13.2 = Crates Theb.10.2, cf. Epic.*Oxy*.214ʳ.10 (iii A.D.), Thgn.13; *comply with, obey*, *θυγατρὶ φίλῃ μάλα μὲν κλύον ἠδ' ἐπίθοντο* Hes.*Th*.474: also c. gen., *κακῶν κ. φρενῶν* A.*Ag*.1064; *οἴακος* Id.*Supp*.718; *τῶν ἐν τέλει* S.*Aj*.1352, cf. *OC*740, etc. III. in Trag. like *ἀκούω* III, *to be called* or *spoken of*: with Adv., *εὖ* or *κακῶς κ.*, A.*Ag*.468 (lyr.), S.*Tr*.721; *πρός τινος* Id.*El*.524; *κλύειν δικαίως* (nisi leg. *δίκαιος*) *μᾶλλον ἢ πρᾶξαι θέλεις* A.*Eu*.430: with a Noun, *κ. ἄναλκις μᾶλλον ἢ μιαιφόνος* Id.*Pr*.868.

**κλωβίον**, *τό*, Dim. of sq., *small cage*, Eust. ad D.P.1134, Hdn.*Epim*.72.

**κλωβός**, *ὁ*, *bird-cage*, *AP*6.109 (Antip.), Babr.124.3, Aesop.341. (Cf. *κλουβός, κλουβίον*, and Hebr. *kĕlûbh*.)

⊛**κλωγμός** (also **κλωσμός**, v. infr.), *ὁ*, (*κλώζω*) *clucking* of hens, Plu.2.129a (*κλωσμοῖς* codd.). II. *clucking sound* by which we urge on a horse, X.*Eq*.9.10, Poll.1.209. **2.** *clucking sound* by which Greek audiences expressed disapprobation, *hooting*, Orac.ap.Luc.*J.Tr*.31, Eust.1504.29: **κλωσμός**, Ph.2.599 (v.l. *κλωγμός*), Harp. s.v. *ἐκλώζετε*.

**κλῶδις·** *κλέπτης*, Hsch.

**Κλώδωνες**, *ων, αἱ*, Maced. name of female Bacchanals, Plu.*Alex*.2, Polyaen.4.1, cf. *EM*521.48, Hsch.

**κλώζω**, of the sound made by jackdaws, as *κρώζω* of crows, Poll.5.89. II. *make a similar sound in token of disapprobation, hoot*, D.21.226, Alciphr.3.71, Phot.:—Pass., Aristid.*Or*.34(50).7, etc.; cf. *κλώσσω*.

**Κλῶθες**, *ων, αἱ*, *Spinners*, name of the *Goddesses of fate*, *πείσεται ἅσσα οἱ αἶσα κατὰ Κλῶθές τε βαρεῖαι γεινομένῳ νήσαντο λίνῳ* Od.7.197 (v.l. *Κατακλῶθες*: v.l. ap.Eust. *ἅσσα οἱ Αἶσα κατακλῶθησι βαρεῖα*, with next line omitted).

⊛**κλώθω**, aor. *ἔκλωσα* Nonn.*D*.2.678, (*ἐπ-*) Od.3.208:—*twist by spinning, spin*, *λίνον* Hdt.5.12, cf. *POxy*.1414.5 (iii A.D.); *μίτον* Luc.*Fug*.12; *κ. ἄτρακτον turn* it, Luc.*J.Conf*.19:—Pass., *βύσσος κεκλωσμένη* Lxx *Ex*.35.6. **2.** esp. of the goddesses of fate, *spin* a man his thread of life or of fate, *κ. τινὶ τὰ οἰκεῖα* Arist.*Mu*.401ᵇ22:—poet. in Med., *ἐκλώσασθε πανάφθιτον ἦμαρ ἀοιδῷ* *AP*7.14 (Antip. Sid.); *ἑπτὰ δέ μοι μοῖραι..ἐνιαυτοὺς ἐκλώσαντο* *IG*3.1337; *τίς μοιρῶν μίτον ὔμμιν ἐκλώσατο;* ib.5(1).1355 (Abia):—Pass., *τὰ κλωσθέντα one's destiny*, Pl.*Lg*.960c. II. intr. in Act., *χυλῷ ἐνὶ κλώθοντι* Nic.*Al*.93 (expld. by Sch. *ὡς νῆμα κλωθομένῳ*), cf. 528.

**Κλωθώ**, *οῦς, ἡ*, *Spinster*, one of the three Μοῖραι, who spins the thread of life (cf. Κλῶθες), Hes.*Th*.218, *Sc*.258, Pl.*R*.617c, Luc.*Hist.Conscr*.38: late nom. pl. *Κλωθῶες* *IG*14.1389 i 14.

**κλωκυδά**, Adv. *in a squatting position*, Hsch.

**κλωμᾰκόεις**, *εσσα, εν*, *stony, rocky*, Il.2.729.

**κλῶμαξ**, *ἄκος, ὁ*, *heap of stones, rocky place*, Lyc.653: **κρῶμαξ**, Hsch.

**κλών**, gen. *κλωνός, ὁ*, *twig, spray, slip*, S.*OC*483, *Ant*.713, E.*El*.324, *Ion*423, Pl.*Prt*.334b, Thphr.*CP*1.3.1, Lxx *Jb*.18.13, Dsc.4.170. **2.** *κ. βύσσου thread* or *fibre*, Paul.Aeg.6.13:—Dim. (in signf. I) **κλῶναξ**, *ὁ*, Hsch.; **κλωνάριον**, *τό*, *Gp*.12.19.9, *Gloss*.; **κλωνίδιον**, *τό*, ib.; **κλωνίον**, *τό*, Thphr.*HP*3.13.5, 3.18.5, *IG*2².1468.9, *AP*12.256.8 (Mel.); **κλωνίσκος**, *ὁ*, Dsc.5.68.

**κλων-ίζω**, = *κλαδεύω*, Suid. **-ίτης** [ῑ], *ου, ὁ*, *with branches*, *πρέμνος* Hdn.*Epim*.72. ⊛**-ος**, *ramus*, *Gloss*.

**κλῳομάστιξ**, *ῑγος, ὁ, ἡ*, *one who is flogged with a collar on*, Com.*Adesp*.1039.

**κλῳός**, *ὁ*, old Att. for *κλοιός*.

**κλωπ-άομαι**, poet. for *κλέπτω*, Hsch. **-εία**, *ἡ*, *theft*, Pl.*Lg*.823b (pl.), Isoc.12.211, 218, v.l. in Str.15.3.18, Plu.*Phil*.4. II. name of a *dance*, Juba 74:—*κλοπεία* is freq. as v.l. **-εύω**, *steal*, X.*An*.6.1.1, *Lac*.2.7, Luc.*Cat*.1, *Tox*.49. **-ηδίς**, = *κλοπιμαίως*, Theognost.*Can*.163. **-ήϊος**, *η, ον*, Ion. and poet. for *κλοπαῖος*, A.R.3.1197, Max.434. **-ίδαι**, *οἱ*, mock-Attic deme-name (cf. Κρωπίδαι), Ar.*Eq*.79. **-ικός**, *ή, όν*, *thievish*, *τὸ κ.* v.l. for *κλοπ-* in Pl.*Cra*.408a. **2.** *stealthy, clandestine*, *βήματα, ἕδραι*, E.*Rh*.205, 512. **-ιτεύω**, = *-εύω*, Suid.

**κλωποπάτωρ** [ᾰ], *ορος, ὁ, ἡ*, *son of a thief* (i.e. Hermes), Theoc.*Syrinx*15.

**κλῶσις**, *εως, ἡ*, *spinning*, Corn.*ND*13. **2.** = *κλῶσμα*, Lyc.716.

**κλώσκω**, = *κλώθω*, Hsch.

⊛**κλῶσ-μα**, *ατος, τό*, (*κλώθω*) *clue*, Nic.*Fr*.72.1, Paus.6.26.7. **2.** *thread*, Lxx *Nu*.15.38. **3.** metaph., *thread of fate*, *κλώσματα θεῖα τελῶν* *IG*12(7).123 (Amorgos). **-μός**, *ὁ*, v. **κλωγμός**.

**κλώσσω**, *cluck*, prob. in Suid. s.v. **φωλάς**; cf. *κλώζω*.

⊛**κλωσ-τήρ**, *ῆρος, ὁ*, *spindle*, Theoc.24.70, A.R.4.1062. II. *thread, yarn*, *λίνου κ.*, of a *net* (periphr. for **κλωστὸν λίνον** Sch.), A.*Ch*.507, cf. E.*Fr*.1001. **2.** *skein*, Ar.*Ra*.1349 (lyr.), *Lys*.567, Plu.2.558d. **3.** metaph., *thread of fate*, *μοιρῶν κλωστῆρι* *Epigr.Gr*.292.6 (Heraclea ad Latmum), cf. *Arch.Pap*.1.220 (*κλωστείρων* is a mason's error for *-τήρων*); *μοιρίδιοι κ.* *IG*3.1339. ⊛**-τήριον**, *τό*, *spun thread*, dub. in *Ostr*.1525 (ii B.C.). **-τής**, *οῦ*, Dor. **-τάς**, *ὁ*, *spinner*, *IG*5(1).209.22 (Sparta), *EM*495.27. II. *web*, *κλωστοῦ..λίνοισι* dub. l. in E.*Tr*.537 (lyr., leg. *κλωστοῦ λίνοιο*).

**κλωστόμαλλος**, *ον*, gloss on *στρεψίμαλλος*, Eust.1638.17.

⊛**κλωσ-τός**, *ή, όν*, *spun*, *λίνον* Aen.Tact.18.14, cf. *κλωστήρ* II; *κόκκινον* Lxx *Le*.14.6; *βύσσος* J.*AJ*3.7.1; *κρόκη* Plu.*Sol*.12. **2.** metaph., of fate, *μοῖραι κλωστὸν ἔθεντο μίτον* *IG*3.1344. **-τρον**, *τό*, = *vermiculus*, *Gloss*.

**κλώψ**, *κλωπός, ὁ*, (*κλέπτω*) *thief*, Hdt.1.41, al., E.*Hel*.553, X.*An*.4.6.17, Aen.Tact.23.7, etc.

**κμέλεθρον**, *τό*, *beam*, Pamphil.ap.*EM*521.34 (pl.).

**κμητός**, *ή, όν*, *wrought*, Hsch., *EM*521.31:—found only in compds. **κνᾰδάλλω**, = *κνάω*, *scratch*, Hsch. **κνάζει·** *βοηθεῖ*, Id. **κναίω**, = *κνάω*, prob. l. for *καινιεῖ*, Lxx *Si*.38.28:—elsewh. only in compds. **κνᾱκίας, κνᾱκός, κνάκων**, Dor. for *κνηκ-*. **κνᾶμις**, v. *κνημίς*. **κνάμπτω**, v. *κνάπτω*. **κνάξ·** *γάλα λευκόν*, Hsch.; cf. **κναξζβί** (cj. *κνάξ*) Thespis 4.

⊛**κνάπτω** (v. sub fin.), *card* or *comb* wool, *dress* or *full* cloth (either with teasel or comb), *ἱμάτια* Dsc.4.159; *παρ' ἐμοὶ πόκος οὐ κνάπτεται* Xenocr.ap.D.L.4.10. **2.** of torture, *ἐπ' ἀσπαλάθων κνάπτοντες* Pl.*R*.616a (cf. *κνάφος* II): generally, *mangle, tear*, *μάστιγι* Cratin.275:—Pass., *δίνᾳ κναπτόμενοι*, of bodies *mangled* against rocks, A.*Pers*.576 (lyr.); *ἐκνάπτετ' αἰέν*, of Hector's body, S.*Aj*.1031, cf. Philostr.*VA*6.40. **3.** *κ. γλῶσσαν*, = *συνέχειν ἐντὸς τῶν ὀδόντων*, Com.*Adesp*.1313 (= Trag.*Adesp*.224). (Acc. Sch.Ar.*Pl*.166, *κνάπτω, κναφεύς*, etc., were old Att., *γνάπτω, γναφεύς*, etc., later Att., confirmed by Inscrr.: forms in *γν-* are found in Ionic, Papyri, and later Gr., e.g. Dsc. l.c.; *κνάμπτ-* Pl. l.c. (as v.l.), Philostr. l.c.: cf.

Welsh *cnaif* 'fleece', Engl. *nap* (on cloth), Lett. *knābt* 'pick', 'peck'.)

**κνάπτωρ** or **γνάπτωρ**, ορος, ὁ, poet. for κναφεύς, Man.4.422.

**κναστήριον**· ἐνήλατο⟨ν⟩ (Lacon.), Hsch.

**κνάφαλλον**, τό, v. κνέφαλλον.

**κνᾰφᾰλώδης** or **γνᾰφ-**, ες, *like* κνέφαλλον, φύλλα Dsc.3.32, cf. Alex.Trall.1.15.

**κνᾰφ-εῖον**, Ion. **-ήϊον**, τό, *fuller's shop*, Hdt.4.14, Plu.*Cic.*1; **γνᾰφ-**, *IG*2².1638.28 (iv B.C.), codd. of Lys.3.15, 23.2, cf. *POxy.*1488.9 (ii A.D.), etc. * **-εύς**, έως, ὁ, *fuller, cloth-carder* or *dresser*, *IG*1².436 (vi B.C.), Hdt.4.14, Ar.*V.*1128, *Ec.*415: as fem., A.*Ch.*760; **γνᾰφ-**, Hp.*Epid.*1.21, Lys.3.16 codd., X.*Ages.*1.26, and usu. in later Gr., Herod.4.78, *PCair.Zen.*206.48 (iii B.C.), *IG*12(2).271 (Mytilene), *POxy.*736.37 (i A.D.), etc.; but κναφεύς *PLand.*43.13 (ii A.D.). II. γναφεύς, kind of *fish*, Dorio ap.Ath.7.297c. **-ευτικός**, later Att. **γνᾰφ-**, ή, όν, *belonging to a fuller*: ἡ κν. (sc. τέχνη) *fuller's art*, Pl.*Plt.*282a; ἡ γν. Id.*Sph.*227a. **-εύω** or **γνᾰφ-**, *clean cloth*, Ar.*Pl.*166. * **-ικός**, later **γνᾰφ-**, ή, όν, = κναφευτικός, Dsc.4.160, Suid. s.v. κνάφος; **γνᾰφική** (sc. ἐργασία), ἡ, *fuller's trade*, *PLond.*2.286 (i A.D.). **-ισσα**, ἡ, *female fuller*, *PLand.*43.8 (vi A.D.): in form **γνάφ-**, *PGoodsp.Cair.*30 xxix 24 (ii A.D.). * **-ος**, ὁ, *prickly teasel*, Alc.Com.35; used by fullers to card or clean cloth, Sch.Ar.*Pl.*166. 2. = ἱπποφαές, Gal.19.106. II. *carding-comb*, also used as an instrument of torture, ἐπὶ κνάφου ἕλκειν τινά Hdt.1.92 (κναφηΐου codd.), cf. Hp.*Mul.*2.114, Plu.2.858e (γναφ-), Hsch. **-ω**, = κνάπτω, v.l. in Dsc.4.159 (γν-).

**κνάψ** (gender and declens. unknown), = δαλός, Hdn.Gr.1.404.

* **κνάψις**, later **γνάψις**, εως, ἡ, *dressing* of cloth, Sch.Ar.*Pl.*166.

**κνάω**, κνᾷ Plu.2.61d, but in correct Att. κνῇ, inf. κνῆν (v. ἐπικνάω) corrupted to κνεῖν Moer.p.234 P., Hsch., Ion. κνᾶν Hdt.7.239: fut. κνήσω Hp.*Coac.*460 (prob. l.): aor. ἔκνησα Id.*Int.*23, Pl.*Smp.*185e (prob. l.), Arist.*Pr.*965ᵃ23, (κατ-) Ar.*V.*965; but κνᾶσαι· ὀλέσαι, λυπῆσαι, Hsch.; 3 sg. Ep. impf. ἐπι-κνῆ Il.11.639:—Med., inf. κνῆσθαι Pl.*Grg.*494c, later κνᾶσθαι Plu.2.89e, etc.: fut. κνήσομαι Herod.4.51: aor. ἐκνησάμην Luc.*Bis Acc.*1, Dor. ἐκνᾱσ- Theoc.7.110:—Pass., κνᾶται Gal.10.979: pf. κατα-κέκνησμαι Id.13.1022:—*scrape, grate*, ἐπὶ δ' αἴγειον κνῆ τυρόν Il. l. c., cf. Hp.*Int.* l. c.; τὸν κηρὸν κνᾶν *to scrape it off*, Hdt. l. c. (nisi leg. ἐκκν-), cf. Gal.13.1022:—Pass., prob. for κνισθεῖσα in Thphr.*HP*9.20.4. II. *scratch*, τῇ χειρὶ Hp.*Fract.*21; τὸν περὶ τὰς μασχάλας τόπον Arist. l. c.:—Med., *scratch oneself*, ἀφθόνως ἔχειν τοῦ κνῆσθαι Pl.*Grg.* l. c.; κνώμενος τὸ κρανίον Timocl.2.5 D.; τὸ βρέγμα κνήσῃ Herod. l. c.; [ἔλαφοι] κνώμενοι [τὰ κέρατα] πρὸς τὰ δένδρα Arist.*HA*611ᵇ16; δακτύλῳ κνᾶσθαι τὴν κεφαλήν Plu.*Pomp.*48: abs., Id.2.1091e, Jul.*Caes.*323b; τρίβειν τοὺς ὀφθαλμοὺς καὶ κνᾶσθαι Phld.*Rh.*2.143 S.; κνήσασθαι τὸ οὖς Luc. l. c.; κνησάμενον ἑνὶ τῶν ποδῶν τὴν πλευράν Gal.8.443. 2. Med., *itch*, Id.10.437,979. III. *tickle*, τὴν ῥῖνα prob. in Pl.*Smp.* l. c.:—Med., κνᾶσθαι τὰ ὦτα πτερῷ *tickle one's* ears, Luc.*Salt.*2, etc.: metaph., τοῦτο κνῇ καὶ γαργαλίζει καὶ ἀναπείθει Plu.2.61d:—Pass., οὐ παρέργως ἐκνώμην πρὸς αὐτά Luc.*Nec.*3.

**κνεφ-άζω**, (κνέφας) *cloud over, obscure*, A.*Ag.*131 (lyr.). **-αῖος**, α, ον, also ος, ον Ar.*Ra.*1350 (lyr.):—*dark*, Ταρτάρου βάθη A.*Pr.*1029, cf. E.*Alc.*593 (lyr.). 2. *in the dark*, κ. ἐλθών having come *in the dark*, i.e. *at nightfall*, Hippon.63; also, *early in the morning*, ἀνεφάνη κ. Ar.*V.*124, cf. *Ra.* l. c., *Lys.*327 (lyr.), etc.

* **κνέφαλλον**, τό, *wool torn off* in carding or fulling cloth, *flock*, used for stuffing cushions or pillows: hence, *cushion, pillow*, E.*Fr.*676, Cratin.99, Eup.228, Ar.*Fr.*19, etc. (prob. in *IG*1².330.22, cf. Demioprat.ap.Poll.10.39); κνάφαλλον, γνάφαλλον (cf. κνάπτω, γνάπτω) are freq. as vv.ll.; **γνάφαλλα**, *PCair.Zen.*298 (iii B.C.); Aeol. **γνόφαλλον** Alc.34.6.

* **κνέφᾰς**, τό, Att. gen. κνέφους Ar.*Ec.*290, *Com.Adesp.*35, later κνέφατος Plb.8.26.10; dat. κνέφα X.*HG*7.1.15, κνέφεϊ *AP*7.633 (Crin.), as if from **κνέφος**, cited by Hsch., Suid., Phot.: (cf. δνόφος):—*darkness*, Hom. (only in nom. and acc.), of the *evening dusk, twilight*, εἰς ὅ κε.. δύῃ τ' ἠέλιος καὶ ἐπὶ κ. ἱερὸν ἔλθῃ Il.11.194, 209: later, generally, *darkness*, δυσάλιον κ. A.*Eu.*396 (lyr.); νυκτός Id.*Pers.*357, cf. E.*Ba.*510, etc.; τὸ κατὰ γᾶς κ. Id.*Hipp.*836 (lyr.): metaph., τοῖον ἐπ' ἀνδρὶ μύσος πεπόταται A.*Eu.*378 (lyr.). 2. *morning twilight*, πρῴ πάνυ τοῦ κνέφους Ar.*Ec.*290; ἅμα κνέφᾳ at *dawn*, X. l. c., *Cyr.*4.2.15.

**κνέωρον**, τό, = sq., Dsc.4.172, Plin.*HN*13.114, Hsch. II. *pudenda muliebria*, Phot., Hsch.

**κνέωρος**, ὁ, *spurge-flax, Daphne Gnidium*, Thphr.*HP*6.1.4; κ. λευκός, *Daphne oleoides*, ib.6.2.2; κ. μέλας, *Thymelaea hirsuta*, ib.1.10.4, 6.2.2.

**κνῆ**, v. κνάω.

* **κνήδιον**, τό, in pl., prob. = κνίδια, *nettles* or *nettle-seeds*, *Stud.Pal.*22.75.7,16 (iii A.D.).

**κνηθ-ιάω**, Desider. of κνήθω, *desire to scratch, itch*, Hdn.Gr.2.949, *EM*116.25. **-μός**, ὁ, *itching*, Nic.*Al.*251, 422. **-ω**, later form of κνάω, *scratch*, ὡς λέγεται, κνήθειν οἶδεν ὄνος τὸν ὄνον *AP*12.238.8 (Strat.), cf. Moer.p.234 P.:—Med., κνήθεσθαι εἰς τὰς ἀκάνθας τὰ ἕλκη *to get* one's sores *scratched*, Arist.*HA*609ᵃ32. 2. Pass., *itch*, Paul.Aeg.6.60; κνηθόμενοι τὴν ἀκοήν 2*Ep.Ti.*4.3; *to be provoked*, Arist.*Pr.*957ᵇ15.

**κνηκ-άνθιον**, τό, = κνῆκος, Ps.-Democr.ap Zos.Alch.p.160 B. **-ίας**, ου, Dor. **κνᾱκίας**, ὁ, (κνηκός) name for the *wolf*, Babr.122.12. **-ινος**, η, ον, *of* or *from* κνῆκος, ἔλαιον *PRev.Laws*53.15, al. (iii B.C.), *PTeb.*122.11 (i B.C.), Dsc.1.36. **-ιον**, τό, = τρίφυλλον, Id.3.109 (v.l. κνίκιον). 2. = σάμψυχον, Ps.-Dsc.3.39. * **-ίς**, ῖδος, ἡ, *pale spot*, esp. in the heavens, Call.*Fr.anon.*36; κ. νεφώδεις Cleom.2.1 (pl.), cf. Plu.2.581f, Anon.*Intr.Arat.*p.126 M. II. *pale-coloured antelope*, Hsch. III. *fine skin*, Id. IV. = μελανία, Id. **-ίτης** [ῑ] λίθος, a kind of *gem*, Hermes Trism. in *Rev.Phil.*32.272.

**κνηκο-ειδής**, ές, *like* κνῆκος, Hsch. s.v. κνηκίς. **-πῡρος**, ον, *made of yellow wheat*, ἡδοναὶ τραγημάτων Sopat.17.

* **κνῆκος**, ἡ, Thphr.*HP*6.4.5, *PCair.Zen.*223.4 (iii B.C.), *PRev.Laws* (v. infr.), but ὁ Thphr.*HP*1.13.3, *CP*5.18.4, Dsc. (v. infr.), Gal.6.354, al.:—also **κνήκη**, ἡ, Sch.Theoc.3.5, 7.16 codd.:—*safflower, Carthamus tinctorius*, Hp.*Acut.*64, *Vict.*2.54, Diocl.*Fr.*140, Anaxandr.41.56, Arist.*HA*550ᵇ27, Thphr. *HP*6.1.3, *PRev.Laws*39.5, al. (iii B.C.), Dsc.4.188, Asclep.ap.Gal.*Nat.Fac.*1.13. II. κ. ἀγρία (ἄγριος Dsc.3.93), of two kinds, *Carthamus leucocaulos* and *blessed thistle, Cnicus benedictus*, Thphr.*HP*6.4.5; πώγωνι θάλλων ὡς τράγος κνήκῳ χλιδᾷς you are as wanton as a goat surfeited with *thistles*, S.*Ichn.*358 (nisi leg. κνηκῷ 'you swagger with your *yellow* (cf. sq.) beard': κνικωι Pap.). (Freq. written κνίκος or κνῖκος in codd., as Arist. l. c., Thphr.*CP*6.9.3, Gal. ll. cc., 11.612, etc., but always κνηκ- in Papyri, exc. S.*Ichn.* l. c.; prob. named from its colour, cf. sq.)

**κνηκός**, ή, όν, Dor. **κνᾱκός**, ά, όν, *pale yellow, tawny*, of the goat, Thespis 4, Theoc.7.16, *AP*6.32 (Agath.); so in oracular style, *Epigr.Gr.*1034.23; of the wolf, Babr.113.2; cf. **κνακός**· ψαρός, ἵππος, Hsch. (Perh. cogn. with Skt. *kāñcanam* 'gold', OPruss. *cucan* 'brown', OE. *hunig* 'honey'.)

**κνηκο-συμμῑγής**, ές, Dor. **κνᾱκ-**, *mixed with* κνῆκος, Philox.3.19. **-φόρος** (sc. γῆ), ἡ, *bearing safflower*, *Sammelb.*4369 ii 36, al. (iii B.C.).

**κνηκώδης**, ες, = κνηκοειδής, Thphr.*HP*1.11.3, 6.6.6.

**κνήκων**, Dor. **κνάκων** [ᾱ], ωνος, ὁ, (κνηκός) name for the *goat*, Theoc.3.5.

**κνῆμα**, v. κνῆσμα.

**κνημ-αῖος**, v. κνημιαῖος. **-αργος**, ον, *white-legged*, Theoc.25.127. * **-η**, Dor. **κνάμα** [νᾱ], ἡ, *part between knee and ankle, leg, shank*, Il.4.147, Od.8.135, Hdt.6.75, 125, 7.75, E.*Ph.*1394, etc.; of a horse, X.*Eq.*1.5, 12.10: prov., ἀπωτέρω ἢ γόνυ κνάμα 'blood is thicker than water', Theoc.16.18. 2. Anat., *tibia*, Gal.2.774, Ruf.*Onom.*123. 3. in plants, *stem between two joints*, Thphr.*HP*9.13.5; κνήμη (v.l. μνήμου) μελίνης dub. sens. in S.*Fr.*608. II. *spoke* of a wheel, Poll.1.144, Eust.598.4. (Cf. OIr. *cnāim* 'bone', OE. *hamm* 'ham'.) **-ία**, ἡ, = ἀντικνήμιον, Hsch. 2. *leg* of a chair, Id., Phot. 3. *spoke* of a wheel, Lys.*Fr.*95. II. in pl., = τὰ τῆς ἁμάξης περιθέματα, Hsch. 2. = φθοραί, Id.; cf. κνημόω. **-ιαῖος**, α, ον, *of the calf* or *leg*, Hp.*Oss.*16 (written **κνημαῖος** Gal.19.112). * **-ίδιον**, τό, dub. sens. in *IG*2².1641.52 (pl.); κ. χαλκᾶ ib.1648.18. **-ῑδοφόρος**, ον, *wearing greaves*, Hdt.7.92:—also **-ῑδωτός**, ή, όν, *Gloss.* * **-ίον**, τό, Dim. of κνήμη, *PLond.*3.1166.2 (i A.D.).

**κνημῑοπᾰχής**, ές, *thick as one's leg*, Ar.*Fr.*722.

* **κνημίς**, ῖδος, ἡ, Aeol. acc. **κνᾶμιν** Eust.265.18 (corrupted to κνῆμιν in Choerob. *in Theod.*1.327); Aeol. nom. pl. **κνάμῑδες** Alc.15.4: (κνήμη):—*greave, legging*, κνημῖδας μὲν πρῶτα περὶ κνήμῃσιν ἔθηκε ἀργυρέοισιν ἐπισφυρίοις ἀραρυίας Il.19.369; τεῦξε δέ οἱ κνημῖδας.. κασσιτέροιο 18.613; κ. ὀρειχάλκοιο φαεινοῦ Hes.*Sc.*122; βόειαι κ. ox-hide *leggings*, Od.24.229, cf. Plb.11.9.4; sg., Il.21.592, Luc.*Rh.Pr.*18. II. *spoke of a wheel*, D.S.18.27. III. = κνημός I, D.P.714.

**κνημοπᾰχής**, ές, = κνημιοπαχής, Thphr.*HP*9.4.3.

**κνημ-ός**, ὁ, *projecting limb, shoulder* of a mountain (above the foot, Eust.1498.42), Hom. (always in pl.), Ἴδης κνημοί Il.2.821, al., cf. Od.4.337: sg., *h.Ap.*283, Orph.*A.*465. 2. δημόσιος κ. public *grove*, prob. in *TAM*2(1).64 (Telmessus). II. Arg., = ὀρίγανος, Eust.265.40. **-όω**, aor. **-ῶσαι**, = περιχῶσαι, φράξαι, φθεῖραι, κλεῖσαι, ἐλθεῖν, Hsch.; **-οῦμαι**, = φθείρομαι, and **-ωθῆναι**, = φθαρῆναι, Id.; κνημωθείς is prob. f.l. for κημωθείς in Hermesian.7.38. **-ώδης**, ες, *well-legged*, gloss on κνήμαργος, Hsch.

**κνήνιον**, τό, dub. sens. in *Supp.Epigr.*1.413 (Gortyn, v B.C.). (Fort. leg. τῶν κτηνίων Cret. gen. pl. of κτῆνος).

**κνησ-είω**, = sq., Suid. **-ιάω**, Desider. of κνάω, *desire to scratch, itch*, Ar.*Ec.*919 (lyr.), Pl.*Grg.*494c,e, Jul.*Or.*7.206d.

**κνῆσις**, εως, ἡ, (κνάω) *scratching*, τρῖψις καὶ κ. Pl.*Phlb.*46d; κ. κροτάφων καὶ ὤτων Aret.*CA*1.1: pl., Pl.*Phlb.*51d: metaph., *tickling*, ἕνεκα ..κνήσεως ὤτων Plu.2.167b. II. (from Pass.) *itching, irritation*, κ. περὶ τὰ οὖλα Pl.*Phdr.*251c, cf. Gal.10.437.

**κνησίχρῡσος**, ον, *scraping gold*, ῥίνη *AP*6.92 (Phil.).

**κνῆσ-μα**, ατος, τό, in pl., *scrapings*, Hp.*Nat.Puer.*17 (κνήματα Gal.19.112): metaph., κ. λόγων Pl.*Hp.Ma.*304a. II. *sting, bite*, X.*Smp.*4.28 (v.l. κνῆμα); ψήκτρης κ., periphr. for a *comb*, *AP*6.233 (Maec.). * **-μονή**, ἡ, = sq., Archig.ap.Aët.3.167, Orib.*Fr.*116, *App.Anth.*3.158 (pl.), *Gp.*12.34. * **-μός**, ὁ, = κνῆσις, *itching*, Hp.*VM*16, Arist.*HA*578ᵇ3; ἡ ἀκαλήφη κ. ποιεῖ Diph.Siph.ap.Ath.3.90a; *scratching*, Plu.2.126b (pl.); in a pleasurable sense, *titillation*, Arist.*GA*723ᵇ34, *Pr.*878ᵇ7. 2. metaph., *irritation*, Plu.2.61a. **-μώδης**, ες, *affected with itching*, Hp.*Aph.*6.9, Aret.*SD*1.15, Gal.10.261. II. *accompanied with itching* or *irritation*, Arist.*Pr.*887ᵃ35, Gal.7.197. Adv. **-δῶς** Id.19.70. III. *causing irritation*, ἅλες Str.11.13.2. **-τέον**, *one must chafe*, τὰ σκέλη Paul.Aeg.3.9. * **-τήρ**, ῆρος, ὁ, *scraping-knife*, Nic.*Th.*85, *Al.*308. II. *slayer, destroyer*, Hsch. III. gloss on κνῆστρον, Erot. **-τιάω**, = κνησιάω, Plu.*Fr.inc.*149, Gal.7.197, Phlp. *in APr.*277.5: metaph., ἀκοαὶ κνηστιῶσαι Jul.*Ep.*111. **-τικός**, ή, όν, *irritating*, λόγοι Sch.E.*Hipp.*304. **-τις**, εως and ιος, ἡ, cheese-grater, Il.11.640, Nic.*Th.*696

(contr. dat. κνῆστι), *AP*6.305 (Leon.). 2. τυροῦ κ. cheese-*gratings*, Porph.*VP*34. II. = κνησμός, Opp.*H*.2.427. III. = ῥάχις, *spine*, Hsch., perh. to be read in Od.10.161 (v. ἄκνηστις). -τίς, ίδος, ἡ, *hollow hair-pin*, Plu.*Ant*.86. -τός, ή, όν, *scraped, rasped*, κ. ἄρτος Artem.Eph.ap.Ath.3.111d; but λάχανα κνηστά (v.l. κνιστά) *chopped up*, Ar.*Fr*.908 (= Antiph.79). ✱-τρίον, τό, *scraper*, ἰχθύων, σκυτῶν, *Edict.Diocl.* in *IG*5(1).1115*B* i 14,15 (Geronthr.):—in late form -τρίν, ἀργυροῦν *IG*3.238*a*; cf. *Gloss*. ✱-τρον, τό, *stinging plant, Daphne oleoides*, Hp.*Mul*.1.80, 2.169 (expld. = κνηστήρ by Erot.); = θυμελαία, Dsc.4.172.

**κνήφη**, ἡ, *itch*, Lxx*De*.28.27, Hsch. s.v. ξύσμα, Suid. s.v. Ἀφροδίτη:—hence **κνηφῶ**, *prurio*, *Gloss*. **κνηφός**, *semen candidum*, dub. in *Gloss*.

**κνιδᾶται** (κνηδ- cod.)· δάκνεται· ἴσως ἀπὸ τῆς πόας, Hsch.:—also **κνίδοντες** (fort. κνιδῶντες)· κνίδῃ μαστιγοῦντες, Id.

**κνίδη** [ῑ], (κνίζω) *nettle, Urtica*, Hp.*Vict*.2.54, Arist.*HA*522ᵃ8, Theoc.7.110, Nic.*Th*.880, *AP*12.124 (Artemo); = ἀκαλήφη, Dsc.4.93 (un-Attic, acc. to Moer.p.66P.). II. *sea-nettle, Actinia*, Arist.*HA*548ᵃ23.—Both senses combined, Archestr.*Fr*.9.7.

✱**Κνίδιος** [ῐ], α, ον, (Κνίδος) *of* or *from Cnidos*: οἱ Κνίδιοι *the Cnidians*, Hdt.1.174, al. II. κόκκος K., ὁ, *berry of the shrub* κνέωρον (*Daphne Gnidium*), used as a purgative, Eub.128, Thphr.*HP*9.20.2, Dsc.1.36, 4.172. III. Κνίδιον, τό, a measure of wine, *POxy*.150 (vi A.D.), etc. IV. v. κνήδιον.

**Κνιδιουργής**, ές, *of Cnidian manufacture*, Sch.Ar.*Pax*142.

**Κνιδόθεν**, Adv. *from Cnidos*, Luc.*Lex*.7.

**Κνιδόκοκκος**, ὁ, = κόκκος Κνίδιος, Alex.Trall.8.2.

**Κνίδος** [ῐ], ου, ἡ, *Cnidos*, *h.Ap*.43, etc.

**κνιδόσπερμον**, τό, *nettle-seed*, Gal.19.732:—also✱**κνιδόσπερμα**, ατος, τό, Alex.Trall.5.6.

**κνίδωσις** [ῑ], εως, ἡ, *itching*, such as is caused by a nettle, Hp.*Prorrh*.2.30 (pl.).

**κνίζα**, ἡ, = κνίδη, *Gloss*. II. cited by Eust. fr. Anacr.87: v. κνυζός.

✱**κνίζω**, fut. κνίσω [ῐ] Ar.*Ra*.1198: aor. ἔκνισα Pi.*P*.8.32, Herod.4.59, etc.; Dor. ἔκνιξα Pi.*I*.6(5).50:—**Pass.**, aor. ἐκνίσθην E.*Andr*.209, Theoc.4.59: *scratch, gash*, παῖδα..γυμνὸν ἣν κνίσω..οὐχ ἕλκος ἕξει; Herod. l. c.; κνίζων συκάμινα (to make them ripen) Lxx*Am*.7.14, cf. Ath.2.51b. 2. *pound, chop up*, or *grate*, dub. in Thphr.*HP*9.20.4 (fort. κνησθεῖσα). II. *tickle*, Arist.*HA*587ᵇ7 (Pass.), Phld.*Lib*.p.58O. (Pass.). 2. usu. metaph., of love, *chafe, tease*, τὸν Ἀρίστωνα ἔκνιζε τῆς γυναικὸς ταύτης ἔρως Hdt.6.62, cf. E.*Med*.568; κἠγὼ μὰν κνίζω τινά Theoc.5.122; of other feelings, as satiety, κόρος κνίζει Pi.*P*. l. c.; anxiety, Ξέρξην ἔκνιζε ἡ γνώμη Hdt.7.12; τὰ σμικρὰ οὐδέν μιν κνίζει (sc. τὸν θεόν) ib.10.ε'; ἔκνιζέ μ' αἰεὶ τοῦθ' S.*OT*786; τὸ βούλεσθαί μ' ἔκνιζε E.*IA*330 (troch.); *provoke, tease*, Ar.*V*.1286; οὐ κατ' ἔπος κνίσω τὸ ῥῆμ' ἕκαστον *will* not *attack* every word, Id.*Ra*. l. c.; *provoke to jealousy*, Alciphr.1.32; in good sense, ἀδεῖά νιν ἔκνιξε χάρις Pi.*I*.6(5).50:—Pass., E.*Med*.555, *Andr*. l. c.; ἐρωτίδα τᾶς ποκ' ἐκνίσθη Theoc.4.59, cf. Luc.*DMeretr*.10.4; κνιζόμενος ὑπ' ἔρωτος ἐπὶ τῇ παιδί App.*Pun*.10; ἐκνίσθης; *does that touch you?* Men.*Per*.16. b. *provoke*, ὀργὰν κνίζον αἰπεινοὶ λόγοι Pi.*N*.5.32, cf. *P*.11.23.

**κνίκιον**, τό, v. κνήκιον. **κνίκος**, v. κνῆκος. **κνιπά**· πτιλή, Hsch.

**κνιπεία**, ἡ, *miserliness*, Doroth. in *Cat.Cod.Astr*.6.81.

**κνιπεῖν**· σείειν, ξύειν μέλαθρα καὶ δοκούς, Hsch.

**κνίπειον** [ῐ] αἷμα, blood *of a* κνίψ, mystical name for substance used in Alchemy, Zos.Alch.p.188B.

**κνιπεύω**, *to be miserly*, Doroth. in *Cat.Cod.Astr*.6.81.

**κνιπίδος**· πέρασμα δορᾶς, Hsch.

✱**κνιπολόγος**, ὁ, (κνίψ, λέγω) *gatherer of wood-insects*, name of one of the woodpeckers, Arist.*HA*593ᵃ12.

**κνιπ-όομαι**, of the eyes, *to be inflamed*, Hsch. s.v. κεκνιπωμένοι; of fruits, *to be mildewed*, ibid. -ός, ή, όν, *niggardly, miserly*, *AP*11.172 (Lucill.). (Cf. Γνίφων (a standing name of old misers in the new Att. Comedy), σκνιπός.) -ότης, ητος, ἡ, *irritation* of the eyes, Hp.*Loc.Hom*.13; expld. as = ξηροφθαλμία, Erot.

**κνίς**, κνιδός, ἡ, = κνίδη, acc. sg. κνίδα [ῑ] Opp.*H*.2.429: pl. κνίδες Sm.*Is*.55.13, cf. Aq., Thd.ib.34.13.

**κνῖσα**, Ep. **κνίση** [ῑ], ης, ἡ, *steam and odour of fat* which exhales from roasting meat, *smell* or *savour of a burnt sacrifice* (ἡ λιπαροῦ θυμιάσεως, opp. λιγνύς, Arist.*Mete*.387ᵇ6, cf. 388ᵃ5); κνίση δ' οὐρανὸν ἷκεν ἑλισσομένη περὶ καπνῷ Il.1.317; κνίσην δ' ἐκ πεδίου ἄνεμοι φέρον οὐρανὸν εἴσω 8.549, cf. Ar.*Av*.193, 1517: generally, *odour of savoury meat*, Id.*Ach*.1045 (lyr.), Alex.261.4; αἱ ἐκ τῶν αἱμάτων καὶ σαρκῶν κ. Porph.*Abst*.2.42; of eructations, Xenocr.ap.Orib.2.58.152. II. *that which causes this smell, fat caul* (cf. κνῖσα· ἐπίπλους, *AB*1095), in which the flesh of the victim was wrapped and burnt, μηρούς τ' ἐξέταμον κατά τε κνίσῃ ἐκάλυψαν Il.1.460, cf. Od.18.45, 119, etc.; κνίσῃ τε κῶλα συγκαλυπτὰ A.*Pr*.496:—κνίσσα, κνίσση are incorrect forms, cf. Hdn.Gr.2.901, al.

**κνισ-ᾱλέος**, α, ον, *filled with the steam of fat*, Hsch. -άριον, τό, Dim. of κνῖσα II, Sch.Il.1.66. ✱-άω, (κνῖσα) *fill with the savour of burnt sacrifice*, κ. ἀγυιάς (never τὰς ἀγυιάς) *make* them *steam with sacrifice*, Ar.*Eq*.1320, *Av*.1233, Orac.ap.D.21.51; κ. βωμούς E.*Alc*.1156; intr., κ. βωμοῖσι *raise the steam of sacrifice* on.., Orac.ap.D.21.52; κ. παρὰ τοὺς βωμούς Luc.*JTr*.22. -ήεις, Dor. -άεις, εσσα, εν, (κνῖσα) *full of the steam of burnt sacrifice*, δῶμα Od.10.10; μήλων κνισάεσσα πομπά Pi.*O*.7.80: dat. contr. κνισᾶντι Id.*I*.4(3).66. -ρός, ά, όν, = foreg., Achae.7.

✱**κνίσ-μα**, ατος, τό, in pl., *scratches*, μή που κνίσματ' ὄνυξιν ἔχῃ; *AP*12.67; μή σε [κν]ισμάτων [γεύσω] dub. in Herod.9.4: metaph., *irritation*, Phld.*Lib*.p.16O.; of lovers' *quarrels*, *AP*7.219 (Pomp. Jun.). -μός, ὁ, *itching, tickling*, S.*Fr*.537; *irritation*, Ar.*Pl*.974; lovers' *quarrel*, Alciphr.1.29. II. tune for the flute, Trypho ap. Ath.14.618c.

**κνισο-διώκτης**, ου, ὁ, *Fat-hunter*, name of a mouse, v.l. Batr.232. -κόλαξ, ᾰκος, ὁ, *dinner-parasite*, Asius 1, cf. Phryn.*PS*p.81B. cod. (κνισοκόλαξ cj. Kaibel). -λοιχία, ἡ, *love of fat* or *roast meat*, Sophil.5. -λοιχός, όν, *licker of fat* or *savoury meat, gourmand*, Antiph.64, Amphis 10.

**κνῖσος**, εος, τό, = κνῖσα, *Com.Adesp*.608, Sch.Il.2.423.

**κνισός**, ή, όν, = κνισήεις, τὸ κ. Ath.3.115e. 2. = λίχνος, Comp. κνισότερος Id.12.549a.

**κνισοτηρητής**, οῦ, ὁ, = κνισοδιώκτης, *Com.Adesp*.1042.

**κνισόω**, = κνισάω, Matro *Conv*.82: metaph., τὰς ἑαυτῶν ψυχὰς κ. Ph.1.628. II. *turn into fatty smoke*, in Pass., δέλεαρ κεκνισωμένον *savoury* bait, Arist.*HA*534ᵇ5; ὑποθυμιατέον βδέλλαις -ουμέναις Antyll.ap.Orib.10.19.4; εἰ κνισοῦται τὰ σιτία κατὰ τὴν γαστέρα Gal.8.37, cf. 6.691, 706; ὁ ἰχθὺς κ. Alex.Aphr.*Pr*.2.17. 2. κ. τὸν ζωμόν *burn* the soup, Luc.*Sat*.23. III. Pass., *become greasy*, of oil after boiling, Heliod.ap.Orib.10.37.3; τὸ ἐκ τῆς ἑψήσεως κεκνισ(ω)μένον ἔλαιον prob. in Sor.1.69.

**κνίσσα**, **κνισσάω**, etc., v. κνῖσα, etc.

**κνιστός**, ή, όν, v. κνηστός.

**κνισ-ώδης**, ες, (κνῖσα) *steaming like roast meat, fatty*, Arist.*HA*534ᵃ23; opp. ἀπίμελος, Id.*PA*675ᵇ11; κνισῶδες ἐρυγγάνειν Gal.8.35, cf. Phlp.*in APo*.378.16; κ. ἀπεψία Alex.Trall.*Febr*.1; *greasy*, of oil, Gal.6.289. II. metaph., τὸ μνημονευόμενον ἀμαυρὸν καὶ κ. Plu.2.1088f. -ωτός, ή, όν, *steaming*, of a burnt sacrifice, A.*Ch*.485.

**κνίφος**, τό, = κνίδη, Hsch. (pl.).

**κνίφω**, **κνιφιάω**, cited without expl. by Hdn.Gr.2.949.

✱**κνίψ**, ὁ (ἡ v.l. in Arist., v. infr.), gen. κνῑπός, nom. pl. κνῖπες, = σκνίψ, small creatures which infest fig and oak trees and devour the fig-insect (ψήν), Ar.*Av*.590, Arist.*HA*534ᵇ19, Thphr.*HP*2.8.3, 4.14.10; small ants acc. to Arist.*Sens*.444ᵇ12. II. pl., = ὄμματα περιβεβρωμένα, Hsch.

✱**κνόος**, contr. **κνοῦς**, ὁ, = χνόη, Phot., cf. Hsch. II. *sound of footsteps*, A.*Fr*.237.

**κνῦ**· τὸ ἐλάχιστον, Hsch.

**κνύζᾰ** (A), ἡ, (κνύω) *itch*, Philox.Gramm.ap.*EM*523.2, Eust.1746.6, 23.

✱**κνύζᾰ** (B), ἡ, = κόνυζα, Theoc.4.25, 7.68 (pl.), *Hippiatr*.32 (sg.).

✱**κνύζᾰ** (C), ἡ, *corrupt, wrinkled*, cited from Anacr. by Hdn.Gr.2.901; cf. κνυζός.

**κνυζ-έομαι**, prop. of a dog, *whine, whimper*, κνυζεῖσθαι (v.l. -ᾶσθαι) S.*OC*1571 (lyr.), cf. Theoc.6.30; κυνηδὸν κνυζούμενον S.*Fr*.722, cf. Ar.*V*.977; of children, D.H.1.79; ἐν ὕπνῳ κνυζεῦνται (v.l. -ῶνται) φωνεῦντα φίλαν ποτὶ ματέρα τέκνα Theoc.2.109:—also Act. **κνυζῶ** Poll.5.64 (κνύζω Anon.ap.Suid.), κνυζεῖ Opp.*C*.1.507: **κνυζάομαι** (cf. supr.), Ael.*NA*1.8, 11.14: **κνύζομαι**, Gal.19.112, Hsch.; for Sophr.53 v. κνυζόω. -ηθμός, ὁ, prop. of dogs, *whining, whimpering*, opp. barking or snarling, κύνες τε ἴδον καὶ ῥ' οὐχ ὑλάοντο, κνυζηθμῷ δ' ἑτέρωσε διὰ σταθμοῖο φόβηθεν Od.16.163; of wild beasts, A.R.3.884; of young bears, Opp.*C*.3.169 (pl.); of children, Ath.9.376a. -ημα, ατος, τό, = foreg., of infants, ἄσημα κ. Hdt.2.2, Him.*Or*.23.4, cf. Max. Tyr.41.3. -ομαι, v. κνυζέομαι. ✱-ός, ή, όν, *cloudy, misty*, ἀήρ Hsch. II. of persons, *blear-eyed*, Id.; κνυζή τις ἤδη καὶ πέπειρα γίνομαι Anacr.87 (κνύζη, κνίζη codd.). -όω, (κνυζός) *make dim* or *dark*, κνυζώσω δέ τοι ὄσσε πάρος περικαλλέ' ἐόντε Od.13.401, cf. 433. (Perh. connected with κνύζα A.) II. Dor., = ξύω, *scratch*, *EM*522.54, prob. in Sophr.53 (Pass.).

**κνύζωψ**· λάχανον ὅμοιον σελίνῳ, Hsch. **κνυθόν**· σμικρόν, and **κνύθος**· ἄκανθα μικρά, Id.

**κνῦμα**, ατος, τό, (κνύω) *scratching*, κ. τῶν δακτύλων, of a person feeling for the door-handle in the dark, Ar.*Ec*.36, cf. Gal.19.112.

**κνύξ**, ἡ, Egypt. name for καπνός II, Ps.-Dsc.4.109.

**κνύος** [ῠ], τό, *itch*, Hes.*Fr*.29.1.

**κνυπόω**, = ῥιγκόω, Hsch.

**κνῦσα**, ἡ, *scab*: as term of abuse, Herod.7.95.

**κνύω**, *scratch*, πόθῳ μου 'κνῦεν ἐλθὼν τὴν θύραν Ar.*Th*.481, cf. Men.1021.

**κνωδᾰκ-ίζω**, (κνώδαξ) *hang* a body *on pins* or *pivots*, so that it turns as on an axis, ἐκνωδακισμένον ἀγγεῖον Hero *Spir*.2.4. ✱-ιον, τό, Dim. of κνώδαξ, *pivot*, ib.1.38. -οφύλαξ [ῠ], ακος, ὁ, *warder of the pivot* of the celestial sphere, *PMag.Par*.1.678 (pl.).

**κνωδάλ-ιον** [ᾰ], τό, Dim. of sq., prob. in Hsch. s.v. ζωυφίοις. -ον, τό, any *wild creature*, Od.17.317; κνώδαλ' ὅσ' ἤπειρος πολλὰ τρέφει ἠδὲ θάλασσα Hes.*Th*.582; but also, of an ox or ass, *h.Merc*.188; of beasts generally, κνωδάλων τε καὶ βροτῶν A.*Ch*.601 (lyr.); κ. πτεροῦντα καὶ πεδοστιβῆ, of birds and beasts, Id.*Supp*.1000; κ. βροτοφθόρων ib.264; of sea-monsters, κνώδαλ' ἐν βένθεσι πορφυρέας ἁλὸς Alcm.60.5, cf. A.*Ch*.587 (lyr.); ἔζευξα πρῶτος ἐν ζυγοῖσι κνώδαλα Id.*Pr*.462; ἀνημέρωσα κνωδάλων ὁδόν (sc. Theseus) S.*Fr*.905, cf. *Tr*.716; of boars, lions, E.*Supp*.146; asses, Pi.*P*.10.36; serpents, Id.*N*.1.50, Nic.*Th*.98, Pl.*Ax*.365c; κώνωπες νυκτὸς κ. δισπτέρυγα *AP*5.150 (Mel.); of persons, as a term of reproach, ὦ παντομισὴ κ. A.*Eu*.644: Com., *brutes, beasts*, τρία κ. ἀναιδῆ Cratin.233, cf. Ar.*Lys*.477; also ἁβρὰ Μουσᾶν κ.

dainty *prey* of the Muses, Cerc.7.9. **-ώδης**, ες, *monstrous*, Tz. *H*.5.521.

**κνώδαξ**, ἄκος, ὁ, (cf. κνώδων) *pin* or *pivot* on which a body or machine turns, καθάπερ ἐπὶ κνώδακος τῆς τοῦ δευτέρου σπονδύλου ἀποφύσεως ἡ κεφαλὴ ἐπιστρέφεται Gal.14.720, cf. 723; *axis* of a sphere, Orph.*Fr*.247.26: more freq. in pl., Hero*Spir*.1.43, S.E.*M*.10.93, Orib.49.22.21. II. pl., *sockets* in which the axes of a drum turn, Ph.*Bel*.75.45. III. = χρυσοχοϊκὸν ὄργανον, and in pl., = οἱ ἐν τοῖς φυσητῆρσιν ἀσκοί, Hsch.

**κνώδη**· χωρία, θηρία, Hsch.

**κνώδων**, οντος, ὁ, in pl. κνώδοντες, two *projecting teeth* on the blade of a hunting spear, X.*Cyn*.10.3,16, Philostr.*Im*.1.28; ξίφους διπλοῖ κ., i.e. a two-edged sword (cf. Sch.), S.*Ant*.1233: sg., φασγάνου κνώδοντι *IG*14.1374.11; κνώδων alone, = *sword*, S.*Aj*.1025, Lyc.466, 1109, 1434. (Cf. Lith. *kándu* 'bite'.)

**κνῶος**· ἡσυχία πάντων, Hsch. **κνωπεύς**, έως, ὁ (also **κνουπεύς**), *bear*, Id.

**κνωπόμορφος**, ον, (κνώψ) *shaped like a beast*, Lyc.675.

**κνώσσω**, *slumber*, Od.4.809, Simon.37.6, Pi.*O*.13.71, *P*.1.8, Theoc. 21.65, *AP*5.293.11 (Agath.), etc.: prov., Λάτμιον κνώσσεις 'you sleep like a top', Herod.8.10.

**κνώψ**, ὁ, gen. κνωπός, shortd. for κινώπετον, Nic.*Th*.499, 520, 751. II. = τυφλός, Zonar.

**κοακτήρ**, ῆρος, ὁ, attendant in the mysteries at Sparta, *IG*5(1). 210, 212; **κοιακτήρ**, ib.211. **κοάκτωρ**, = Lat. *coactor*, *Gloss*.

**κοαλδδεῖν**, Lydian for *king*, Hsch.

**κοάλεμος** [ᾱ], ὁ, *stupid fellow, booby*, Ar.*Eq*.198, Aeschin.Socr.16; addressed as a god or demon, Ar.*Eq*.221; nickname of the grandfather of Cimon, Plu.*Cim*.4. (From κοέω, ἠλεός acc. to Sch.Ar.*Eq*. 198, cf. Tim.*Lex*., etc.)

**κόαλοι**· βάρβαροι, Hsch. **κοάξ**, onomatop., to express the croaking of frogs, βρεκεκεκὲξ κοὰξ κοάξ Ar.*Ra*.209, al. **κόαρον**· ἐλάχιστον, Hsch. **κοάω**, v. κοέω. **κοβάθια**, v. κωβάθια. **κόβαθος**, sine expl., *PLond*.1821.362 (in a list of cups). **κόβακτρα**· κολακεύματα, πανουργήματα, Hsch.

**κοβᾰλ-εία**, ἡ, *impudent knavery*, Din.*Fr*.6.8. **-εύω**, *carry as a porter*, χόρτον *POxy*.146 (vi A.D.); θρύα εἰς οἶκον *PLond*.1. 131r.296 (i A.D.), cf. *EM*524.28, Suid. **-ίκευμα**, ατος, τό, *knavish trick*, Ar.*Eq*.332 (pl.). **-ισμός**, ὁ, *porterage, transport*, *PLond*.3.965.9 (iii A.D.). **-ος**, ὁ, *impudent rogue, arrant knave*, Ar.*Eq*.450, *Ra*.1015, *Pl*.279, D.C.53.3; of Midias, Phryn. Com.4: in pl., *mischievous goblins*, invoked by rogues, Ar.*Eq*.635; of the owl, κ. καὶ μιμητής Arist.*HA*597b23. II. Adj. κόβαλα, τά, *knavish tricks, rogueries*, Ar.*Eq*.417, *Ra*.104; ὕβριστον ἔργον καὶ κ. Pherecr.162. (For the orig. sense cf. κοβαλεύω.)

**κόβαρος**· ἄνθρωπος, Hsch. **κόβειρος**, ὁ, *jester*, Id.: Adj., in pl., κόβειρα· γελοῖα, Id. **κοβελίσκον**· τρύβλιον, Id. **κόγκαλος**· κονιορτός, Id. (leg. κονίσαλος). **κόγξ**, onomatop., sound made by the voting-pebble as it fell into the urn, Id. **κογχαλίζω**, of shells, *murmur*, Id.

**κογχ-άριον**, τό, Dim. of sq., Str.16.2.41 (pl.), Aret.*CA*2.5. **-η**, ἡ, *mussel* or (perh.) *cockle*, Emp.76.1, Sophr.25, X.*An*.5.3.8, Arar. 8.2, Posidipp.14.2; including several species, Arist.*HA*528a22, 547b13, 622b2; ἀνέχασκον ἐμφερέστατα ὀπτωμέναις κόγχαισιν Ar.*Fr*. 68; κόγχην διελεῖν to open a *mussel*, prov. of an easy task, Telecl. 19; κόγχης ἄξιον, i.e. worthless, Hsch., Suid. 2. *shell-full*, a small measure of capacity, Pherecr.143.3, Hp.*Nat.Mul*.32, *Morb*.3. 15, Thphr.*HP*9.6.2. II. *anything like a mussel-shell*, esp. *shell-like cavity* in the body, as, 1. *hollow of the ear*, Ruf.*Onom*.44, Poll.2. 86. 2. *knee-pan*, ib.188. III. *case round a seal* attached to documents, Ar.*V*.585. IV. *niche* for a statue, *CIG*4556 (Palestine); *apse*, *Epigr.Gr*.446.3 (Medjed). V. *fourth part of a sphere*, Hero*Stereom*.1.40. (Cf. Skt. *śaṅkhás* 'conch-shell'.) **-ίζω**, *dye purple*, *PGrenf*.2.87.22. **-ίον**, τό, Dim. of κόγχη, Antiph.71, Str. 16.4.17 (pl.). II. = κόγχη II. 1, Gal.14.701. **-ιστής**, οῦ, ὁ, *dyer*, *PGrenf*.2.87.9 (pl.). **-ιστική**, ἡ, *trade of purple-dyeing*, ib. 14. **-ίτης** [ῑ] λίθος, ὁ, *shelly marble*, found near Megara, Paus. 1.44.6.

**κογχο-γενής**, ές, *born from a shell*, of Aphrodite, *Cat.Cod.Astr*.1. 173. **-ειδής**, ές, *of the mussel kind*, Str.3.2.7. II. Subst. κ. (sc. γραμμή), ἡ, Geom., *conchoid curve*, Nicomedes ap.Procl.*in Euc*. p.272 F. Adv. **-δῶς** *in the form of a shell*, κοιλαίνεσθαι Chor.p.86 B. **-θήρας**, α, ὁ, *mussel-catcher*, Epich.42.8.

**κόγχος**, ὁ (ἡ Paus.1.44.6, cf. Plb.6.23.5), = κόγχη I, A.*Fr*.34, Epich. 42.9, Crates Theb.7; κόγχων (gen. pl.) Arist.*HA*528a24 (but κόγχαι ib.22). 2. = κόγχη I. 2, *shell-full*, κ. ἁλῶν Phryn.Com.49, cf. Dsc. 1.30. II. *anything like a mussel-shell*, 1. *upper part of the skull*, Lyc.1105. 2. *boss* of a shield, Plb. l. c. 3. *small iron crucible*, Dsc.5.95. 4. *socket of the eye*, Poll.2.71 (pl.). 5. *knee-pan*, ib.188. III. *soup of lentils boiled with the pods*, Timo 3.

**κογχυλαγόνες**· γυναῖκες, νύμφαι, Hsch.

**κογχῠλ-ευτής**, οῦ, ὁ, *murex-fisher*, Just.*Nov*.38.6. **-ευτική**, ἡ, *trade of murex-fishing*, ibid. **-η**, ἡ, = κόγχη, v.l. in Ph.1.536, cf. *AP*9.214 (Leo). **-ιαβάφος** [βᾰ], ὁ, *purple-dyer*, Maiuri *Nuova Silloge* 571 (Cos). **-ίας** (sc. λίθος), ὁ, = κογχίτης, Ar.*Fr*.193. **-ιάτης** [ᾱ], ου, ὁ, = κογχίτης, X.*An*.3.4.10, Philostr.*VA*2.20. **-ιᾱτός**, ή, όν, = -ιωτός, *PLeid.X*.95. **-ιον**, τό, Dim. of κογχύλη, *small kind of mussel* or *cockle*, Epich.42.1, Sophr.24, Arist.*HA*547b7, *PA* 661a22, al., *POxy*.1449.21 (iii A.D.). 2. any *mollusc* or *its shell*, Hdt.2.12, Hp.*Vict*.2.48, Diocl.*Fr*.133; used to cover seals, Sch.Ar. *V*.583; *fossil shell*, Plu.2.367b. II. = κόχλος, Crito ap.Gal.12.660, Dsc.2.8. **-ιος**, α, ον, *purple*, χρῶμα *PLeid.X*.95. **-ιώδης**, ες, *like a mollusc shell*, κ. λίθοι *fossil shells*, Xanth.3; βόθρος Str.1. 3.4. **-ιωτός**, ή, όν, (κογχύλιον II) *dyed with purple*, *Gloss*.; cf. κογχυλιατός.

**κογχ-ώδης**, ες, f.l. for κοχλιώδης, Ath.3.86b. **-ωτός**, ή, όν, *having a boss* (cf. κόγχος II. 2), ψυκτήρ *PCair.Zen*.327.103 (iii B.C.).

**κόδαλα**· ἰχθῦς, κεστρεύς, Hsch. **κοδαλεύομαι**, = ἐνδομυχῶ, *to be a stay-at-home*, '*loafer*', Id.

**κοδομ-εία**, ἡ, *barley-roasting*, Poll.1.246. **-εῖον**, τό, *vessel for roasting barley*, Id.6.64 (pl. written κοδομία, Hsch.). **-εύς**, έως, ὁ, *one who roasts barley*, Hsch., perh. to be read in *Ostr.Strassb*. 583 (iii B.C.):—fem. **-εύτρια**, Poll.1.246, Phot. **-εύω**, *roast barley*, Hsch. **-ή**, ἡ, = ἡ -εύουσα, Poll.6.64, cf. 10.109 (pl.); ὄνομα θεραπαίνης, Hsch., Phot. **-ηΐον**, τό, = κοδομεῖον, Suid.

**κοδράντης**, ου, ὁ, = Lat. *quadrans*, = ¼ *of an as*, *Ev.Matt*.5.26.

**Κόδρος**, ὁ, *Codrus*, legendary King of Athens: hence Κόδροι, οἱ, of *old-fashioned persons*, Hsch.

**κοδύμᾰλον** [ῠ], τό, *quince* or *medlar*, Alcm.90; = κυδώνιον, Hsch., who has **κοδώνεα**, τά, *winter figs*, or a kind of καρύαι Περσικαί.

**κοέω**, contr. **κοῶ**, *mark, perceive, hear*, ἄστρωτος εὕδω καὶ τὰ μὲν πρᾶτ' οὐ κοῶ Epich.35 (prob.); σὺ δ' οὐ κοεῖς Anacr.4.14; κοεῖν Hellad. in Phot.*Bibl*.p.531 B.; ἐκόησεν τοὔνεκεν.. Call.*Fr*.53, cf. Sch.Ar. *Eq*.198: etym. of Κοῖος, Corn.*ND*17: also (from **κοάω**) κοᾷ· ἀκούει, πεύθεται, and ἐκοᾶμες· ἠκούσαμεν, ἐπυθόμεθα, Hsch.; ἔκομεν (sic).. ἠσθόμεθα, Id. (κοϝ-, cf. Skt. *kavis* 'wise', Lat. *caveo*.)

**Κόης**, v. Κοίης. **κοθᾰρός**, **κόθαρσις**, v. καθαρός, κάθαρσις. **κοθεῖ**· αἰσθάνεται, νοεῖ, Hsch. **κόθημα**, τό, = αἰδοῖον, Id.

**κόθορνος**, ὁ, *buskin, high boot*, Hdt.1.155, 6.125, Ar.*Lys*.657, Lysipp.2, etc.; worn by tragic actors in heroic characters: hence, 2. emblem of Tragedy in the person of Dionysus, Ar.*Ra*.47, 557. 3. since the buskins might be worn on either foot, ὁ Κόθορνος, nickname for a *trimmer* or *timeserver*, such as Theramenes, X.*HG*2.3.31: prov., εὐμεταβολώτερος κοθόρνου Zen.3.93, etc.

**κοθοῦριν**· ἀλώπεκα, Hsch.; cf. κόλουρις. **κόθουρος**, ον, *dock-tailed*, i.e. *without a sting*, κηφῆνες Hes.*Op*.304. **κοθώ**, οῦς, ἡ, = βλάβη, Hsch.

**κοΐ**, onomatop., to express the *squeaking* of young pigs, Ar.*Ach*. 780, cf. Hdn.Gr.1.505.

**κοία**, ἡ, = σφαῖρα, Antim.69. II. = κλέψημα (sic), Hsch.

**κοιάζω**, = ἐνεχυράζω, Hsch.; cf. κωάζειν. **κοιακτήρ**, v. κοακτήρ. **κοίβινος**, = *covinnus*, *Gloss*. **κοιγά**· κοῖλα, Hsch. **κοίδιον**, τό, written for κῴδιον, *PCair.Zen*.20 (iii B.C.).

**κοΐζω**, *cry* κοΐ, *squeak like a young pig*, Ar.*Ach*.746.

**κοίῃ**, Ion. for ποίᾳ, dat. sg. fem. of ποῖος (q. v.).

**Κοιηΐς**, ΐδος, ἡ, = Κοιογενής, dub. l. in Call.*Del*.150: **Κοιαντίς**, Orph.*H*.35.2.

**Κοίης** or **Κόης**, ου, ὁ, priest in the mysteries of Samothrace, Hsch., who also has **κοιᾶται**· ἱερᾶται, **κοιώσατο**· ἀφιερώσατο, καθιερώσατο.

**κοΐκινος**, η, ον, (κοΐξ) *made of palm-leaves*, Str.17.2.5; cf. κοῦκι.

**κοικύλλω**, *look gaping about*, Ar.*Th*.852, dub. in Demetr.Lac. 1014 p.92 F.

**κοιλ-αγγίτας**, α, ὁ, *deep gorge*, *IG*5(2).444 (Megalopolis). **-αίνω**, aor. ἐκοίληνα Hdt.2.73; Att. ἐκοίλᾶνα Th.4.100:—Med., Ep. aor. κοιλήνατο Nonn.*D*.12.332:—Pass., aor. ἐκοιλάνθην Hp.*Epid*.7.52: pf. κεκοίλασμαι Id.*Medic*.11; -αμμαι *EM*233.51: (κοῖλος):—*hollow, scoop out*, τὸ ᾠόν Hdt. l. c.; πέτρην κοιλαίνει ῥανὶς ὕδατος ἐνδελεχείῃ Choeril.10; κ. δένδρα, of the woodpecker, Arist.*HA*614b14; κ. χῶμα, i.e. *dig* a grave, Theoc.23.43; κ. τὰς χεῖρας Ath.11.479a; κ. ὄμματα *APl*.4.142, cf. Opp.*H*.4.19:—Pass., *to be* or *become hollow*, ἔντοσθε, of ulcers, Hp.*Medic*. l. c.; ὀφθαλμοὶ κ. Id.*Acut*.30; κ. κατὰ τὸν κενεῶνα καὶ κατὰ τὰ ἄρθρα Id.*Art*.52; of poor timber, *go into holes*, Thphr.*HP*3.12.1. II. *make empty, make poor*, Lyc.772. 2. *allow to lapse*, of payments, *BGU*1156.18 (i B.C.), *PSI*4.287.16 (iv A.D.), etc. **-αῖος**, α, ον, = κοῖλος, Gal.18(2).568. **-ανσις**, εως, ἡ, *hollowing*, Alex.Aphr.*in SE*105.10, Paul.Aeg.6.90, Eust.159.35 (pl.). **-άς**, άδος, ἡ, Subst., *hollow*, δρυός Ps.-Phoc.173, cf. Thphr. *Fr*.169; in a wall, Lxx *Le*.14.37; in a rock, Str.12.3.11; *deep valley*, Pl.*Epigr*.5.6, Lxx *Ge*.14.8, al., *BGU*995 iii 4 (ii B.C.), *SIG*827 iii 11 (Delph., ii A.D.), Plb.5.44.7, D.S.3.15. II. Adj., fem. of κοῖλος, νεφέλαι Thphr.*Sign*.51 (nisi leg. κηλ-); εὐνή Tryph.194. **-ᾰσία**, ἡ, in pl., *indentations* in beams, Hero*Bel*.104.2. **-ασμα**, ατος, τό, *hollow*, Lxx *Is*.8.14; *groove*, Apollod.*Poliorc*.182.7, Ath.Mech.36.6; *interior* of a lamp, Hero*Spir*.2.22. **-έμβολον**, τό, *hollow wedge*, as an order of battle, Ael.*Tact*.37.7, Arr.*Tact*.29.6:—Adj. **-έμβολος**, ον, Ascl.*Tact*.11.5.

**Κοίλη**, ἡ, v. κοῖλος I. 2. **κοιλήπατα**, τά, *giblets of poultry*, *Gloss*.

**κοιλί-α**, Ion. **-η**, ἡ, (κοῖλος) *cavity of the body*, i.e. *thorax with abdomen*, Hp.*Art*.46 (including ἡ ἄνω κ., = *thorax*, ἡ κάτω, = *abdomen*, acc. to Gal.15.896); τὰ κατὰ κ. νουσήματα diseases of the *thoracic cavity*, Hp.*Aff*.6. 2. *belly, abdomen*, Hdt.2.87, *IG*4²(1). 122.32 (Epid.), etc.: specified as ἡ κάτω κ. Ar.*Ra*.485, Hp.*Ulc*.3, Pl.*Ti*.73a, 85e, Arist.*Somn*.456a3, *PA*650a13, etc.; opp. ἡ ἄνω κ., *stomach*, Pl.*Ti*.85e, Arist.*PA* l. c.; κ. alone freq. = *stomach*, Id.*HA* 489a2, etc.; of birds, Id.*PA*674b22; also, *paunch* or *rumen* of animals, Id.*HA*507b5: hence, of gluttons, δουλεύειν τῇ ἑαυτῶν κ. *Ep.Rom*.16. 18, cf. *Ep.Phil*.3.19. 3. *intestines*, κ. κείνη Hdt.2.40, cf. 86, 92, etc.; of animals, κ. ὑεία pig's *tripe*, Ar.*Eq*.356; κοιλίας ἥμισυ *SIG*1025.51

(Cos, iv/iii B.C.): pl., *tripe and puddings*, Ar.*Eq.*160, *Pl.*1169. b. phrases, κ. σκληρὰν ἔχειν to be costive, Theopomp.Com.62.2; κατὰ κοιλίαν νοσεῖν *Com.Adesp.*730; τὴν κ. λύειν to relax the *bowels*, Arist. *Pr.*863ᵇ29, 864ᵇ14; αἱ κ. λύονται, ἀναλύονται, ib.947ᵇ13, *GA*728ᵃ15; εὔλυτοί [εἰσι] Id.*Pr.*876ᵇ31; ἐὰν ἡ κ. στῇ Id.*HA*588ᵃ7; κ. καταρραγεῖσα Hp.*Coac.*126; [οἶνος] κοιλίας μαλακτικός, κοιλίας ἐφεκτικά, Mnesith. ap.Ath.1.33b, 2.59c; κ. ἐκλύειν, ὑπάγειν, μαλάσσειν, Dsc.2.72,163, 171; κ. ῥέουσαι D.S.5.41. 4. *excrement*, esp. in pl., κ. συνεστηκυῖαι *excrements* of firm consistency, Hp.*Aër.*10; opp. κ. ἐφυγραινόμεναι Id. *Epid.*1.10; κ. ὑγρή Id.*Prorrh.*1.38; στερεή, σκληρή, Id.*Acut.*(*Sp.*)56, *Epid.*4.23; οὔρησις καὶ κ. ἀχρόως ibid. II. any *cavity* in the body, *ventricle, chamber*, as in the *lungs, heart, liver, brain*, κ. αἱ τὸ πνεῦμα δεχόμεναι καὶ προπέμπουσαι Id.*Art.*41; ἡ δὲ καρδία ἔχει μὲν τρεῖς κ. Arist.*HA*496ᵃ4, cf. 513ᵃ27. 2. *socket* of a bone, Hp.*Art.*61. 3. supposed *cavities inside the muscles*, Erasistr.ap.Gal.4.375,707, Antyll. ap.Orib.8.6.30, 7.9.4; cf. νηδύς. 4. *womb*, Hp.*Mul.*1.38, al., *Ev. Jo.*3.4. III. any *hollow* or *cavity*, in the earth, Arist.*Mete.*349ᵇ4, 350ᵇ23, al.; in the clouds, ib.369ᵇ2, al. IV. perh. finger-*tip*, Aret. *SD*1.8 (pl.). **-ακός**, ή, όν, *of the bowels*, ἀρρώστημα Plu.*Ant.*49; διάθεσις Gal.8.388; τὰ κ. Dsc.1.42. II. of persons, *suffering in the bowels*, ib.73, Ruf.ap.Orib.8.24.30, Philagr.ib.5.20.2, Plu.2.101c, Gal.6.525. **-αλγέω**, *have pain in the bowels*, Id.14.467. **-αργία**, ἡ, by dissim. for κοιλιαλγία, *pain in the bowels*, *Rev.Ét.Gr.*41.74 (Damascus).

**κοιλίδιον**, τό, Dim. of κοιλία, Str.14.5.14, dub. in Hsch. s.v. κόλαβρον; written κυλίδιον, *Sammelb.*1941 (iv A.D.), *PLond.*3.1259.38 (iv A.D.).

**κοιλιο-δαίμων**, ονος, ὁ and ἡ, *one who makes a god of his belly*, of a parasite, Eup.172, cf. Ael.*Fr.*109, Ath.3.97c. **-δεσμος**, ὁ, *belly-band*, *Gloss.* ※**-λῦσία**, ἡ, (λύω) *looseness of the bowels*, περὶ κοιλιολυσίαν γίνεσθαι to take *laxative* medicine, Cic.*Att.*10.13.1, cf. Sor.1. 46, *AB*323. ※**-λῦτέω**, *suffer from looseness of the bowels*, Hsch. s.v. βδέλεσθαι. **-λῦτικός**, ή, όν, *laxative*, *Gp.*10.51 tit. **-πώλης**, ου, ὁ, *tripe-seller*, Ar.*Eq.*200. **-στροφία**, ἡ, *colic*, Sch.Nic.*Al.*597.

**κοιλίσκος**, ὁ, *scoop-shaped knife*, for surgical uses, Gal.10.445, Id. ap.Orib.46.21.17, Paul.Aeg.6.90 (κυκλίσκος is v.l. in Gal. l. c. and an unnecessary conjecture in Orib., Paul.Aeg. ll. cc.):—Adj. **κοιλισκωτός**, ἐκκοπεύς Paul.Aeg. l. c. (v.l. κυκλισκωτός).

**κοιλῖτική** (sc. νόσος), ἡ, disease *in the bowels*, *Cat.Cod.Astr.*2. 161.

**κοιλι-ώδης**, ες, *like a belly*, ὑποδοχαί Arist.*PA*678ᵇ30. **-ωσις**, v. κοίλωσις.

**κοιλο-γάστωρ**, ορος, ὁ, ἡ, (γαστήρ) *hollow-bellied, hungry*, A.*Th.* 1040: metaph., κ. κύκλος, of a *hollow* shield, ib.496. **-γένειος**, ον, *with a dimple in the chin*, *PPetr.*3p.26 (iii B.C.), *PGrenf.*1.10.13, 1.34.4 (ii B.C.). **-γώνιος**, ον, *having a re-entrant angle*, Zenodor. ap.Procl.*in Euc.*p.165 F. **-κρότᾰφος**, ον, *with hollow temples*, Aret.*SD*2.7. **-μισχος**, ον, *with hollow stalk*, Thphr.*HP*3.7. 5. **-πεδος**, ον, *lying in a hollow*, νάπος Pi.*P.*5.39. **-πίτυξ**· ὁπλίτης (fort. -πήληξ), τινὲς δὲ ὀϊστός, Hsch. **-ποιέομαι**, = κοιλαίνω II. 2, μηδένα μῆνα *BGU*1134.13 (i B.C.). **-ριζών**, = πάναξ, Theognost.*Can.*21.

※**κοῖλος**, η, ον, Aeol. and Ion. κόϊλος, prob. in Alc.15.5, Mimn.12.6; **κόϊλος**, α, ον, Anacr.9 (Comp. -ώτερα), cf. A.D.*Pron.*87.5, Hdn.Gr.2. 927:—*hollow*, Hom. mostly as epith. of ships, κ. νῆες Il.1.26, al. (later κ. ναῦς *hold* of the ship, Hdt.8.119, X.*HG*1.6.19, D.32.5; so ἡ κ. alone, Theoc.22.12, Callix.1; τὰ κ. App.*BC*5.107); κ. λόχος, κ. δόρυ, of the Trojan horse, Od.4.277, 8.507; κ. σπέος 12.93; κ. πέτρα A. *Eu.*23, S.*Ph.*1081 (lyr.); κ. κάπετος, of a grave, Il.24.797, S.*Aj.*1165 (anap.), cf. *Ant.*1205; κ. τάφρος E.*Alc.*898 (anap.); κ. νάρθηξ Hes. *Op.*52; ἄχερδος S.*OC*1596; κ. φλέψ *vena cava*, Hp.*Loc.Hom.*3, Gal. 2.786, 4.665; σφόνδυλος κ. Pl.*R.*616d; of vessels, ἀγγήϊα Hdt.4.2; κρατήρ S.*OC*1593; ζύγαστρον Id.*Tr.*692; κύλικος.. κοῖλον κύτος Pl. Com.189; κ. ἄργυρος καὶ χρυσός silver and gold *plate*, Theopomp. Hist.283a, cf. S.*Fr.*378, Arist.*Oec.*1350ᵇ23, etc.; κ. ἐκκοπεύς Gal.10. 445; νόμισμα κ. dub. sens. in Numen.ap.Eus.*PE*11.18; *sunk*, γράψαι εἰς σανίδα κοῖλα γράμματα *SIG*1011.15 (Chalcedon, iii/ii B.C.), cf. Longin.*Rh.*p.199 H. (but κ. γραμμή *curved* line, Hero*Bel.*75.15); ἀλέαν εἰς τὸ θύρωμα κοίλαν *curved* canopy, *Rev.Arch.*22.63 (Callatis, iii B.C.); κ. ὑποδήματα boots that reach to mid-leg, Ael.*NA*6.23 (κοῖλα ποσσὶν ὑποδέεσθε Ezek.*Exag.*181, cf. Poll.7.84); κ. δέμνια *empty* bed, S.*Tr.*901; κ. χείρ, of a beggar, *AP*12.212 (Strat.); κ. ἱστίον Poll.1.107; κοῖλος μήν *short* month, Gem.8.3, cf. κοιλοποιέομαι, κοῖλος II. 3: Comp., -ότερος ὁλμοῦ Epich.81. 2. of Places, *lying in a hollow* or *forming a hollow*, κ. Λακεδαίμων *the vale of* L., Od.4.1; κ. Θεσσαλίη Hdt.7.129; κ. Ἄργος S.*OC*378, 1387; Αὐλίδος κ. μυχοί E. *IA*1600; κ. τόποι Plb.3.18.10: as pr. n., Κ. Συρία the district between Lebanon and Anti Lebanon, Id.1.3.1, etc.; τὰ Κ. τῆς Εὐβοίης Hdt. 8.13; ἡ Κ. the *valley* of the Ilissus, name of Attic deme, Id.6.103, etc.: Comp., κοιλότερα τῆς κάτωθεν χώρας Arist.*Mete.*352ᵇ33. b. κ. λιμήν harbour *lying between high cliffs*, Od.10.92: κ. αἰγιαλὸς embayed beach, 22.385; ἐν τῷ κ. καὶ μυχῷ τοῦ λιμένος Th.7.52. c. κ. ὁδός *hollow* way, Il.23.419; κ. ἄγυια Pi.*O.*9.34. d. κ. ποταμός a river *nearly empty* of water, Th.7.84; τοῦ ποταμοῦ κοίλου ῥυέντος Socr.ap. Ath.9.388a; but κ. ποταμὸς *with deep bed*, Plb.21.37.4. e. τὰ κ. καὶ τὰ δασέα *ravines* grown with copsewood, Ar.*Nu.*325. 3. κ. ἅλς, θάλασσα, the sea *full of hollows*, i.e. *with a heavy swell* on, A.R. 2.595, Plb.1.60.6. 4. κ. νοσήματα *internal* complaints, Philostr. *VA*3.44. II. metaph., 1. of the voice, *hollow*, κόχλον ἑλὼν μυκήσατο κοῖλον Theoc.22.75 (though here κοῖλον may agree with κόχλον); φθέγγεσθαι κ. καὶ βαρύ Luc.*Ner.*6, Philostr.*VA*3.38; ὁ -ότατος τῶν φθόγγων Aristid.Quint.1.10. 2. Philos., *hollow, empty, void of content*, αἱ κ. ἐνέργειαι, opp. αἱ ἀμείνους, Herm.*in Phdr.*p.170 A.: more freq. in Comp., κοιλοτέρα θεωρία, ζωή, ib.pp.67,68 A.; τὰ -ότερα, opp. τὰ ὑπέρτερα, ib.p.143 A., cf. Dam.*Pr.*96; χωρῶν πρὸς τὸ κ. ib. 379. 3. ἡμέραν κ. ποιεῖσθαι *allow payments to lapse* for a day (cf. κοιλαίνω II. 2), *BGU*1136.5 (i B.C.); οὐδεμίαν δόσιν κ. ποιεῖσθαι ib. 1146.15 (i B.C.). III. *concave*, τὸ κ., opp. τὸ κυρτόν, Arist.*Ph.* 222ᵇ3, *EN*1102ᵃ31; κοῖλα καὶ ἐξέχοντα Philostr.*Im.*2.20; of military formations, Ascl.*Tact.*11.1. 2. *bending, yielding*, κλῆθρα S. *OT*1262; σταθμὰ θυρῶν Theoc.24.15. IV. Subst. κοῖλον, τό, *hollow, cavity*, Pl.*Phd.*109b, al.; esp. of *cavities* in the body, τὰ κ. γαστρός E.*Ph.*1411; τὰ κ. [τῆς καρδίας] the *ventricles*, Arist.*HA*496ᵃ 13; τὸ κ. τῶν νεφρῶν ib.497ᵃ11; τὸ τῶν χειρῶν κ. Apollod.ap.Ath. 11.479a; τὸ κ. τοῦ.. ποδὸς Hp.*Epid.*5.48: prov., τὸ κ. τοῦ ποδὸς δεῖξαι to show 'a clean pair of heels', Hsch.; τὰ κ. τῶν ὀφθαλμῶν, τοῦ προσώπου, Hp.*Mul.*2.119, *Nat.Mul.*9 codd. (sed leg. κύλα); τὰ κ. alone, *hollows of the side, flanks*, like κενεών, Arist.*HA*630ᵃ3. 2. κοῖλος· θυρεῶν, οὐκ ἔχων θύρας, Hsch.

**κοιλο-σταθμέω**, *provide with a coffered ceiling* or *panels*, οἶκον κέδροις Lxx 3*Ki.*6.9; ξύλοις ἔσωθεν ib.15. ※**-σταθμος**, ον, *with coffered ceilings, panelled*, οἶκοι ib.*Hg.*1.4; θυρίδας κοιλοστάθμους *PPetr.*3p.143 (iii B.C.):—Subst. **-σταθμος**, ὁ, *coffered ceiling*, τὸν κ. τοῦ ναοῦ.. ποιῆσαι *IG*11(2).287 *A*96 (Delos, iii B.C.):—also※**-σταθμον**, τό, ib.*B* 146. **-στομία**, ἡ, *hollowness of voice*, Quint.1.5.32. **-συρτος**· ὁ χωλός, Suid. **-σώματος**, ον, *hollow-bodied*, κύτος Antiph.52.2.

**κοιλότης**, ητος, ἡ, *hollowness*: *a hollow*, τῆς γῆς Arist.*Mete.*354ᵃ12, cf. *HA*529ᵃ21, Thphr.*Vent.*30; κ. ὀρέων Lxx *Wi.*17.19; κ. ἐν ῥινί, = σιμότης, Them.*in Ph.*42.3. II. *concavity*, Arist.*Metaph.*1025ᵇ33; *concave moulding* in architecture, Procop.*Ecphr.*p.157 B. (pl.). III. metaph., *shortage of cash*, Phld.*Oec.*p.71 J.

**κοιλοφθαλμ-ία**, ἡ, *sunkenness of eyes*, Phryn.Com.77. **-ιάω**, *have sunken eyes*, Cratin.288, Gal.6.444, Alex.Aphr.*Pr.*1.98, Orib. *Eup.*1.13. **-ος**, ον, *hollow-eyed*, X.*Eq.*1.9, Arist.*Phgn.*811ᵇ25, *PLond.*1.3 (ii B.C.), Poll.1.191, 2.62.

**κοιλο-φυής**, ές, *hollow by nature, hollow*, Opp.*H.*4.653. **-φυλλος**, ον, *hollow-leaved*, Thphr.*HP*1.10.8. **-φωνος**, ον, *hollow-voiced*, Hsch. s.v. ληκυθιστής. Adv. **-νως**, λαρυγγίζειν Phld.*Rh.*1.200 S. **-χείλης**, ες, *hollow-rimmed*, κύμβαλα *AP*6.94 (Phil.).

**κοιλ-όω**, *hollow out*, in Pass., κεκοιλωμένον ἔδαφος Dsc.3.48; τὰ κεκοιλωμένα τῆς πέτρας D.S.3.13. **-ώδης**, ες, *cavernous*, φάραγξ Babr.20.2; δίφροι Suid. s.v. χαμαίζηλοι. ※**-ωμα**, ατος, τό, *hollow, cavity*, Arist.*Spir.*483ᵇ23, *Mu.*395ᵇ34 (pl.), Anon.Lond. 23.20 (pl.), Thphr.*HP*3.8.3 (pl.), Babr.86.1, Ruf.*Onom.*145; [τοῦ νώτου] *PMag.Par.*1.1846; τὰ κ. τῶν νεφῶν Epicur.*Ep.*2p.44 U., cf. 1 p.9 U. 2. *basin* into which rivers discharge, Plb.4.39.2 (pl.), 8; *bed* of a torrent, Id.4.70.7: generally, of *hollow places, low-lying land*, Lxx *Ge.*23.2, Agatharch.32; κ. ἔμβροχον *BGU*571.12 (ii A.D.); *excavation*, *PPetr.*2p.43 (pl., iii B.C.). II. *ulcer* on the cornea, Gal.14.773, Aët.7.29. III. Astrol., = ταπείνωμα, Paul.Al.*A.*2, *Cat.Cod.Astr.*8(1).243 (pl.). IV. metaph., τὰ κ. τῆς εὐτυχίας *weak points* in.., Phld.*Vit.*p.12 J. **-ῶνυξ**, ὕχος, ὁ, ἡ, *hollow-hoofed*, ἵπποι Stesich.49. **-ῶπαν**· περίζωμα, Hsch. **-ώπης**, ες, *hollow-eyed*, κοιλώπεες αὐγαί *hollow* eyes, Nic.*Al.*442:—fem. **-ῶπις**, ιδος, in general sense, = sq., πέτρα *AP*6.219.5 (Antip.). **-ωπός**, όν, *hollow to look at*: *hollow*, ἀγμός E.*IT*263. **-ωσις**, εως, ἡ, *cavity*, Hp.*Carn.*15, Sor.1.82; *hollowing out*, of flutes, Nicom.*Harm.*4, 10 (pl., κοιλιώσ- codd.). **-ωτέα**, prob. = κολουτέα, Hsch.

※**κοιμ-άω**, fut. -ήσω, Dor. -άσω [ᾱ]: aor. ἐκοίμησα, Ep. κοίμησα Od. 12.372:—Med., fut. -ήσομαι *OGI*383.43 (Commagene, i B.C.), D.H. 4.64, Luc.*DDeor.*4.4, etc.: Ep. aor. κοιμήσατο, -αντο, Il.11.241, 1. 476:—Pass., fut. -ηθήσομαι S.*Fr.*574.6, Luc.*Asin.*40, Alciphr.1.37. 3. etc.: aor. ἐκοιμήθην Od.14.411, al., E.*Andr.*390, Pl.*R.*571e, etc.: pf. κεκοίμημαι Aeschrio 8.2, Luc.*Gall.*6:—*lull, put to sleep*, κοίμησον.. Ζηνὸς ὑπ' ὀφρύσιν ὄσσε φαεινώ Il.14.236; ἦ με.. κοιμήσατε νηλέϊ ὕπνῳ Od.12.372; βλέφαρα μὴ κοιμῶν ὕπνῳ A.*Th.*3; *put to bed*, τὸν δ' αὐτοῦ κοίμησε Od.3.397; of a hind, ἐν ξυλόχῳ.. νεβροὺς κοιμήσασα 4. 336. 2. metaph., *still, calm*, ἀνέμους, κύματα, Il.12.281, Od.12. 169; φλόγα A.*Ag.*597; κύματος μένος Id.*Eu.*832; εὔφημον.. κοίμησον στόμα Id.*Ag.*1247; also, *soothe, assuage*, κοίμησον δ' ὀδύνας Il.16. 524; ᾧ (sc. φύλλῳ) κοιμῶ τόδ' ἕλκος S.*Ph.*650. II. Med. and Pass., *fall asleep, go to bed*, Il.1.476, al., Hdt.1.9, etc.; of animals, *lie down*, κατὰ ἤθεα κοιμηθῆναι Od.14.411: c. acc. cogn., ποῖόν τινα ὕπνον ἐκοιμῶ; X.*Hier.*6.7; βαθὺν κοιμηθῆναι (sc. ὕπνον) Luc. *DMar.*2.3. 2. metaph., ὅπως ἂν κοιμηθῇ [τὸ ἐπιθυμητικόν] Pl. l. c. 3. of the sleep of death, κοιμήσατο χάλκεον ὕπνον Il.11. 241; ἱερὸν ὕπνον κ. Call.*Ep.*11.2: abs., *fall asleep, die*, S.*El.*509 (lyr.), Aeschrio l. c.; ἐκοιμήθη μετὰ τῶν πατέρων Lxx 3*Ki.*2.10, al., cf. *PFay.*22.28 (i A.D.), *Ev.Matt.*27.52, *Ev.Jo.*11.11, etc.; in epitaphs, *IG*14.1683, etc.; κ. τὸν αἰώνιον ὕπνον ib.929. 4. κοιμῶντο.. παρὰ μνηστῇς ἀλόχοισι Il.6.246, cf. 250: hence, of sexual intercourse, *lie with* another, Od.8.295, Pi.*I.*8(7).23; οὔ τινι κοιμηθεῖσα Hes.*Th.*213; παρά τινι Hdt.3.68; σὺν δεσπόταισι E. l. c.; μετά τινος Timocl.22.2; ἀπὸ γυναικὸς ἀνὴρ τὰν νύκτα κοιμαθείς *Berl.Sitzb.* 1927.157 (Cyrene). 5. *keep watch at night*, A.*Ag.*2, X.*Cyr.*1.2. 4.6, *POxy.*933.25 (ii A.D.), etc. 6. of things, *remain during the night*, οὐ μὴ κοιμηθήσεται ὁ μισθὸς παρά σοι ἕως πρωΐ Lxx *Le.*19.13; ἡ κιβωτὸς ἐκοιμήθη ἐκεῖ ib.*Jo.*6.10. 7. c. acc., *dream of*, μέταλλα

χρύσεια Luc.*Gall.*6. -ήθρα, ἡ, *sleeping-place*, Suid. s. v. *ἰαυθμοί*. -ημα, ατος, τό, *sleep*. in pl., S.*Ichn.*268; κ. αὐτογέννητα *intercourse* of the mother with her own child, Id.*Ant.*864 (lyr.): sg., Erot. s. v. κωματώδεες. ※-ησις, εως, ἡ, *lying down to sleep*, κοιμήσεις ἐπὶ θύραις Pl.*Smp.*183a; ἡ κ. τοῦ ὕπνου *Ev.Jo.*11.13. II. the *sleep of death*, Lxx *Si.*46.19, 48.13, *Tab.Defix.Aud.*242.30 (Carthage, iii A.D.). ※-ητήριον, τό, *sleeping-room*, *IG*7.235.43 (Oropus, iv B.C.), Dosiad.ap.Ath.4.143c (also -ητηρία, ἡ, *EM*550.56). II. *burial-place*, *IG*3.3545. -ητικῶς, Adv. *sleepily*, κ. ἔχειν *EM*485.18. -ίζω, post-Hom., = κοιμάω, *put to sleep*, κ. ὄμμα E.*Rh.*826 (lyr.); σὲ.. ἐκοίμισεν Ἀδρήστεια λείκνῳ ἐνὶ χρυσέῳ Call.*Jov.*47; *harbour for the night*, οἶκος ἐν ᾧ τοὺς ξένους κοιμίζουσιν Dosiad.ap.Ath.4.143c, cf. Lxx 3*Ki.*3.20; *still, calm*, ἄημα πνευμάτων ἐκοίμισε στένοντα πόντον, i.e. the winds *suffered* the sea *to rest*—by ceasing, S.*Aj.*674; θάλασσαν ἀγρίαν ἐκοίμισαν (sc. οἱ δαίμονες) *AP*9.290 (Phil.): metaph., κ. τὸν λύχνον *put* it *out*, Nicopho 7; μεγαλαγορίαν κ. *lay* pride *to sleep, quench, stifle* it, E.*Ph.*184 (lyr.); κ. θυμόν Pl.*Lg.*873a; τὰς λύπας X.*Smp.*2.24; πόθον *AP*12.19*(Mel.); ἐλπίδας οὐ θάλαμος κοίμισεν, ἀλλὰ τάφος ib.7.183 (Parmen.):—Pass., παῖς κοιμίζεται E.*Hec.*826; τὸ θηριῶδες κ. Pl.*R.*591b. 2. of the sleep of death, καλῶ δ'.. Ἑρμῆν χθόνιον εὖ με κοιμίσαι S.*Aj.*832; Τιτάνων γενεὰν.. Ζεὺς κοιμίζει φλογμῷ E.*Hec.*473 (lyr.), cf. *Hipp.*1386 (lyr.):—Med., κοίμισαί μ' ἐς Ἄιδου Id.*Tr.*594 (lyr.). 3. Gramm., *soften the accent* (from acute to grave), Sch. D.T.p.23 H., Sch.Il.7.334; cf. sq. II. -ισις, εως, ἡ, *putting to sleep*, *IG*12(5).329 (Paros, unless written for -ησις). II. *softening of the accent*, Sch.D.T.p.23 H.: -ισμός, ὁ, ibid. -ιστής, οῦ, Dor. -τᾱς, ὁ, *one who puts to bed*, metaph., λύχνος *AP*12.50 (Asclep.). -ιστικός, ή, όν, *of* or *for putting to sleep*, Sch.Il.3.382.

**κοιν-άν**, ᾶνος, ὁ, Dor. and Arc. for κοινῶν, Pi.*P.*3.28, *IG* (1).334.4 (Locr., v B.C.), 5(2).6.21 (Tegea, iv B.C.). ※-ανία, Dor. for κοινωνέω, Foed.Dor.ap.Th.5.79. -ανία, = κοινωνία, Aesar.ap. Stob.1.49.27; perh. to be read in Pi.*P.*1.97. -ανικός, = κοινωνικός, Archyt.ap.Stob.1.48.6. -άριον, τό, Dim. of κοινόν (v. κοινός A. VIII), in form *cynarium*, *CIL*13.10021.199. -άσομαι, -άσας, Dor. for κοινώσ-; v. κοινόω. ※-εῖον, τό, *common hall*, *Test.Epict.*4.30. 2. *association, club*, *IG*12(3).104.12 (Nisyros). 3. *brothel*, Hdn.Gr.1.372, *Bull.Soc.Arch.Alex.*6.282 (iii A.D.), Hsch. (κοινίον cod.); cf. ξυνεῖον. II. *common fund*, *IG*4.757*A*44 (Troezen): pl., ib.*B*2, al. ※-εών, ῶνος, ὁ, = κοινωνός, prob. in E.*HF*149, 340. -ῆ, v. κοινός B. II. -ισμός, ὁ, *mixture of dialects*, v.l. in Quint.8.3.59.

**κοινοβῐάρχης**, ου, ὁ, *head of a* κοινόβιον, *PMasp.*151.149 (vi A.D.).

**κοινό-βῐος**, ον, *living in community with others*, Ptol.*Tetr.*119, Iamb. *VP*5.29. II. as Subst. **κοινόβιον**, τό, *life in community*, dub. l. in Gell.1.9 fin. 2. *monastery*, Just.*Nov.*123.36, al., *PSI*8.953.9 (vi A.D.). -βιότης, *consortium*, *Gloss.*

**κοινοβουλ-ευτικός**, ή, όν, *deliberative*, Hippod.ap.Stob.4.1.94. -έω, *deliberate in common*, X.*Lac.*13.1:—Med., Hsch. -ης, ου, ὁ, = σύνεδρος, in pl., Id. -ία, ἡ, *common counsel*, Sch.Il.22.261 (pl.). -ιον, τό, *common council*, Plb.28.19.1, Str.8.7.3, *OGI*490.12 (Apamea, ii A.D.), 568.11 (Tlos, iii A.D.), etc.; *place of assembly*, App.*BC*1.51. ※-ος, ον, gloss on ξύμβουλος, Sch.Ar.*Th.*928. II. Subst. -βουλος, ὁ, *member of local senate*, *IGRom.*3.7 (Nicomedia).

**κοινο-βωμία**, ἡ, *community of altar*, of gods worshipped in common, ἀνάκτων τῶνδε κοινοβωμίαν σέβεσθε A.*Supp.*222. -γάμια [γᾰ], ων, τά, *promiscuous concubinage*, Clearch.49. -γενής, ές, *hybridizing*, opp. ἰδιογενής, φύσις Pl.*Plt.*265e. -γονία, ἡ, *mixing of breeds*, opp. ἰδιογονία, ib.d. -δήμιον, τό, *common assembly of the people*, Hsch. -δημος, ον, *common to the people, public*, πανήγυρις Ph.1.678. ※-δίκιον [δῐ], τό, *common court in which matters in dispute between different cities were settled*, *GDI*5040.58 (Hierapytna); τῶν Κρηταιέων *IG*12(3).254 (Anaphe); to be read for -δίκαιον, Plb. 22.15.4. 2. in Egypt, *court for disputes between Greeks and Egyptians*, *PMagd.*21.12, 23.9 (iii B.C., abbrev.). -δίκος, ον, *enjoying a common right*, Orac.ap.Phleg.1 J. -εργής, ές, *working in common*, μόρια Simp.*in Epict.*p.37 D. -θᾰνής, ές, *of common death*, κ. Μοιρῶν γήραϊ *IPE*2.91[1] (Panticap.). -θῡλᾰκέω, *have a common purse*, Ar.*Fr.*797. -καθέτας· συνθηκοφύλακας, Hsch. (Perh. for -καταθ-). -κρᾱτηρόσκῠφος, ὁ, *filling his cup from the common bowl*, Cerc.4.16. -λεκτέω, *use the language of common life*, κοινολεκτούμενα ἐπιρρήματα A.D.*Adv.*169.20, cf. *EM*184.11. -λεκτος, ον, *in the language of common life*: Adv. -τως Sch.Theoc.6.18. -λεκτρος, ὁ, ἡ, *bedfellow, consort*, A.*Ag.*1441: as Adj., δάμαρ Id.*Pr.*560 (lyr.). -λεξία, ἡ, *ordinary language*, Serv. ad Verg.*A.*8.31, Eust.956.1. -λεχής, ές, *paramour*, S.*El.*97 (anap.), cf. Eust. 653.34. -λογέομαι, fut. -ήσομαι Plb.21.39.2: aor. ἐκοινολογησάμην Hdt 6.23, Th.8.98, etc.: later aor. Pass. ἐκοινολογήθην Plb.2.5.4, al., *SIG*568.4 (Halasarna, iii B.C.): pf. κεκοινολόγημαι *OGI*315.37 (Pessinus, ii B.C.), D.C.49.41: plpf. ἐκεκοινολόγηντο Th.7.86: (λόγος):—*commune, take counsel with*, τινι Hdt.6.23, Th.8.98, etc.; πρός τινα Id.7.86, Plb.18.34.5, Jul.*Caes.*335c; κ. ἀλλήλοις περί τινος Arist. *Pol.*1268[b]7; πρός τινα ὑπέρ τινος Plb.10.42.4; κ. περί τινος *deliberate* on.., D.S.19.46; κ. πρὸς τὸ οὖς τινι Luc.*Deor.Conc.*1. II. Pass., γράμματα -λογούμενα κατὰ μίμησιν signs *used with common* (i.e. direct) *significance*, opp. ἀλληγορούμενα, Porph.*VP*12. -λογία, ἡ, *consultation*, Hp.*Praec.*8, *PFay.*12.15 (ii B.C.), Gal.8.151. 2. *discussion, conference*, Plb.2.8.7, al., Plu.*Ages.*25, al., Alex.Aphr.*in Metaph.*296.23; philosophical *dialogue*, Phld.*Rh.*1.109: pl., ib.243 S. 3. *communication by speech*, Iamb.*Myst.*7.4 (pl.). 4. in Magic, *use of* τὰ κοινά (cf. κοινός III. 4), *PMag.Par.*1.2080 (pl.). II. = ἡ κοινὴ διάλεκτος, Phot. -μετρέω, *measure corn-rent by agreement*, *POxy.*1689.35 (iii A.D.). -μήτωρ, ορος, ὁ, ἡ, *having a common mother*, Theognost.*Can.*21. -νοημοσύνη, ἡ, (νοέω) *regard for the feelings of others*, M.Ant.1.16. -πᾰθής, ές, *sympathetic, sociable*, ἔθη φιλάνθρωπα καὶ κ. D.H.1.41. -πλοος, ον, contr. -πλους, ουν, *sailing in common*. ναὸς κ. ὁμιλία, i.e. shipmates, S.*Aj.*872. -ποιέω, *make common property*, τὰ τῶν ἀγαθῶν ἔπαθλα Phld.*Rh.*1.217 S., cf. 2.256 S.; δόξαν Alex.Aphr.*in Metaph.*83.30:—Med., *regard as common*, *Inscr.Prien.*113.27 (i B.C.), al.:—Pass., *to be in common*, S.E. *P.*3.173. 2. *generalize*, λόγον Herm.*in Phdr.*p.128 A., Simp.*in Ph.*1275.6; κ. τὴν δόξαν αὐτῶν τοῖς περὶ Δημόκριτον *shows the common ground of* their view and that of D., Id.*in Cael.*617.22:—Med., Alex. Aphr.*in SE*17.13. II. *communicate*, τὰ μυστήρια Sch.Ar.*Av.*1073. -ποιός, όν, *creating community*, Dam.*Pr.*36. -πολῑτεία, ἡ, *citizenship of a* κοινόν or league, *SIG*622*B*12 (Vaxos, from Delphi, ii B.C.). -πορφῠροῦς, ᾶ, οῦν, *dyed with purple of inferior quality*, *CPR*21.17 (iii A.D.). -πους, ὁ, ἡ, πουν, τό, gen. ποδος, *of common foot*, κ. παρουσία, i.e. the arrival *of persons all together*, S.*El.*1104. -πρᾱγέω, *act in common with, have dealings with*, c. dat., Plb.4.23.8, 5.57.2, D.S.19.6: abs., κ. περί τινος Plb.30.4.16, cf. Ph. 2.201, Plu.*Galb.*6. 2. *share in*, c. gen., ἀδικημάτων Ph.2.72; ἀγαθῶν ib.444. ※-πρᾱγία, ἡ, *common enterprise, joint* or *concerted action*, Plb.5.95.2, D.S.11.1, 15.8, Plu.*Per.*17.

※**κοινός**, ή, όν, also ός, όν S.*Tr.*207 (lyr.):—*common* (opp. ἴδιος), not in Hom. (v. ξυνός); ἐκ κοινοῦ *shared in common*, Hes.*Op.*723; ἔσται γὰρ βίος ἐκ κ. Ar.*Ec.*610; of a *common* altar, Simon.140; τὸ τέμενος εἶναι κ. *SIG*1044.29 (Halic., iv/iii B.C.); κ. ἔρχεται κῦμ' Ἀΐδα Pi.*N.*7.30; τρεῖς.. κ. ὄμμ' ἐκτημέναι, of the Gorgons, A.*Pr.*795; κ. ὠφέλημα θνητοῖσιν φανείς, of Prometheus, ib.613; τὰς γυναῖκας εἶναι κοινάς Pl. *R.*457d: prov., κοινὸν τύχη A.*Fr.*389, cf. Men.*Mon.*356; κοινὰ τὰ τῶν φίλων E.*Or.*735 (troch.), Pl.*Phdr.*279c, Men.9, etc.; κ. Ἑρμῆς 'share the luck', Id.*Epit.*67, 100; κ. ἀρωγά *common* aid (i.e. for all), S.*Ph.*1145 (lyr.); ἐν δὲ κοινὸς ἀρσένων ἴτω κλαγγά and let the shouts of males rise *jointly*, Id.*Tr.*207 (lyr.); κ. πόλεμον πολεμεῖν X.*Hier.*2.8; τὸν ἀέρα τὸν κ. Men.531.8; κ. τὸν ᾅδην ἔσχον οἱ πάντες βροτοί Id. 538.8; κ. ἀγαθὸν τοῦτ' ἐστί, χρηστὸς εὐτυχῶν Id.791: c. dat., κ. τινί *common to* or *with* another, ὑμῖν φῶς.. καὶ τοῖσδ' ἅπασι κ. A.*Ag.*523; ὁ δαίμων κ. ἦν ἀμφοῖν ἅμα Id.*Th.*812; θάλατταν κ. ἐᾶν τοῖς ἡττημένοις And.3.19; οἰκία.. κοινοτάτη ἀεὶ τῷ δεομένῳ Id.1.147; [πολιτεία] τίς κοινοτάτη; Arist.*Pol.*1289[b]14, cf. 1265[b]29; κοινόν τι χαρᾷ καὶ λύπῃ δάκρυα X.*HG*7.1.32; τὸν ἥλιον τὸν κ. ἡμῖν Men.611: c. gen., πάντων αἰθὴρ κ. φάος εἱλίσσων A.*Pr.*1092 (anap.), cf. *Pers.*132 (lyr.), *Eu.*109, Pi.*N.*1.32; κ. τῶν Λακεδαιμονίων τε καὶ Ἀθηναίων *shared in by* both.., Pl.*Mx.*241c, etc.: with Preps., τὸ ἐπὶ πᾶσι κ., v. infr. V; κ. κατ' ἀμφοτέρων A.D.*Synt.*144.19; οὐ γίγνεταί μοί τι κ. πρός τινα *AP*11.141 (Lucill.), cf. Iamb.*Myst.*5.7; μέρος κ. πρός τινα *shared with*.., *CPR*22.11 (ii A.D.), etc.; κ. μεταξύ τινων *Stud.Pal.*1.7 ii 11 (v A.D.). II. in social and political relations, *public, general*, τὸ κ. ἀγαθόν the *common* weal, Th.5.90; κ. λόγῳ Id.5.37, Hdt.1.141; κ. στόλῳ ib.170; ἀδικήματα D.21.45; ὁ τῆς πόλεως κ. δῆμιος Pl.*Lg.*872b; κοινότατον *of public* or *general interest*, ib.724b, cf. Arist.*Rh.*1354[b]29; of constitutions, *popular, free*, κοινοτέραν εἶναι τὴν ἐκείνου μοναρχίαν τῆς αὐτῶν δημοκρατίας Isoc.10.36. 2. τὸ κ. the *state*, τὸ κ. Σπαρτιητέων Hdt.1.67: abs., of one's own state, Ar.*Ec.*208, etc.; τὸ κ. ὠφελεῖται Antipho 3.2.3, cf. X.*Cyr.*2.2.20; τὰς ὠφελείας ἅπασιν εἰς τὸ κ. ἀπεδίδου Isoc.10.36. b. esp. of *leagues* or *federations*, τὸ κ. τῶν Ἰώνων Hdt.5.109; τῶν συμμάχων Isoc.14.21; τῶν Βοιωτῶν *SIG*457.10 (Thespiae, iii B.C.), Plb.20.6.1 (pl.), etc.; ἄνευ τοῦ πάντων κοινοῦ (sc. τῶν Θεσσαλῶν) Th.4.78; also, of *private associations*, *Test.Epict.*1.22, *SIG*1113 (Lorymia), al.; of *guilds* or *corporations*, τὸ κ. τῶν τεκτόνων *POxy.*53.2 (iv A.D.); of *boards* of magistrates, τὸ κ. τῶν ἀρχόντων ib.54.12 (iii A.D.). c. *the government, public authorities*, Th.1.90, 2.12, etc.; τὰ κ. Hdt.3.156; ἀπαγγεῖλαι ἐπὶ τὰ κ. Th.5.37; ἀπὸ τοῦ κ. *by public authority*, Hdt.5.85, 8.135; σὺν τῷ κ. *by common consent*, Id.9.87. d. *the public treasury*, χρημάτων μεγάλων ἐν τῷ κ. γενομένων Id.7.144; ἐν τῷ κ. καὶ ἐν τοῖς ἱεροῖς Th.6.6, cf. 17; χρήματα δοῦναι ἐκ τοῦ κ. Hdt.9.87; ἔχειν ἐν κοινῷ (without the Art.), Th.1.80, cf. Sch. adloc. e. *common right* or *rights* of citizens, τὸ κ. τὸ τῶν πολιτῶν Arist.*Pol.*1283[b]41. 3. τὰ κ. *public affairs*: πρὸς τὰ κ. προσελθεῖν, προσιέναι, to enter *public life*, D. 18.257, Aeschin.1.165; but also, *the public money*, Ar.*Pl.*569, D.8.23 (in full, τὰ κ. χρήματα X.*HG*6.5.34, Arist.*Pol.*1271[b]11); τὰ κ. τῆς πόλεως, opp. τὰ ἁγνά, *BMus.Inscr.*4.481*.383; ἀπὸ κοινοῦ *at the public expense*, X.*An.*4.7.27, 5.1.12; ἐκ κοινοῦ φαγεῖν Euphro 8.4, cf. Antiph. 230; ἐκ κ. from *common funds*, at *joint expense*, *PGrenf.*1.21.19 (ii B.C.). III. *common, ordinary*, τὰ κ. εἰδέναι Pl.*Ax.*366b; διὰ τῶν κ. ποιεῖσθαι τὰς πίστεις Arist.*Rh.*1355[a]27; κοινοτάτη τῶν αἰσθήσεων [ἡ ἁφή] Id.*EN*1118[b]1; τὰ κ. *commonplaces*, Men.*Sam.*27, *Epit.*309; so κ. τόπος Hermog.*Prog.*6, Aphth.*Prog.*7; ἡ κ. ἔννοια or ἐπίνοια, Plb. 2.62.2, 6.5.2; κ. νοῦς, φρένες, *common* sense, Phld.*Rh.*1.37 S., 202 S.; κ. καὶ διήκουσαι κακίαι *general* and all-pervading vices, Id.*Sign.*28; κ. καὶ δημώδη ὀνόματα Longin.40.2; κ. καὶ ἐν μέσῳ κείμενα ὀνόματα D.H.*Lys.*3; ἡ κ. διάλεκτος *every-day* language (free from archaisms and far-fetched expressions), Id.*Isoc.*2; πεφευγὼς τὸ κ. Phld.*Acad. Ind.*p.53 M. 2. Gramm., *ordinary, 'regular'* Greek, opp. special dialects, διάλεκτοί εἰσι πέντε, Ἀτθὶς Δωρὶς Αἰολὶς Ἰὰς καὶ κ. Sch.D.T. p.14 H., cf. D.S.1.16, Theodos.*Can.*p.37 H., etc.; ἡ κ. alone, A.D. *Conj.*223.24; τὸ κ. ἔθος, ἡ κ. ἐκφορά, Id.*Adv.*155.10, *Pron.*4.27;

οἱ κ. the writers *who use this language*, Sch.D.T.p.469 H., *EM*405.23. b. *colloquial, vulgar Greek*, Moer.pp.201 (Comp., prob. for καιν–), 243 P., al. c. ἡ κ. διάλεκτος *demotic* Egyptian, Manetho ap. J.*Ap*.1.14. 3. *common, of inferior quality*, χρυσός *POxy*.905.5 (ii A.D.), 1273.6 (iii A.D.). 4. in magical formulae, of *words added at will* by the user, '*and so forth*', freq. in Pap., *PMag.Osl*.1.255, *PMag.Par*.1.273, al.; κοινὰ ὅσα θέλεις ib.2.53; ὁ κ. λόγος *PMag.Lond*.46.435; cf. κοινολογία. IV. of Persons, *connected by common origin* or *kindred*, esp. of brothers and sisters, κ. σπέρμα Pi.*O*.7.92, cf. S.*OT*261, *OC*535 (lyr.); κ. αἷμα Id.*Ant*.202, cf. 1; κ. πατήρ, μήτηρ, *PAmh*.2.152.9 (v/vi A.D.), *PFlor*.47.11 (iii A.D.); also κ. Χάριτες Pi.*O*.2.50. 2. *one who shares in* a thing, *partner*, ἐν θύμασιν κ. ποεῖσθαί τινα S.*OT* 240; κ. ἐν κοινοῖσι λυπεῖσθαι Id.*Aj*.267, cf. Ar.*V*.917; also κ. τῷ θεῷ *belonging in part* to the god (who claims tithe of his substance), *Berl.Sitzb*.1927.161 (Cyrene). 3. *lending a ready ear to all, impartial*, μὴ οὐ κ. ἀποβῆτε Th.3.53; *neutral*, ib.68; κοινοὺς τῷ τε διώκοντι καὶ τῷ φεύγοντι Lys.15.1; μέτριος καὶ κ. Arist.*Ath*.6.3; κοινοί, οἱ, *arbitrators*, *GDI*1832.10 (Delph.); κ. μεσίτης *PStrassb*.41.14 (iii A.D.); of a capital city, δεῖ..κοινὴν εἶναι τῶν τόπων ἁπάντων *easily accessible* on all sides, Arist.*Pol*.1327$^{a}$6. b. *courteous, affable*, X.*Cyn*.13.9; κ. ἅπασι γενέσθαι Isoc.5.80; τῇ πρὸς πάντας φιλανθρωπίᾳ κ. Democh.2 J.; ἔχειν τὰς κ. φρένας Phld.*Rh*.1.202 S. c. in bad sense, κοινή, ἡ, *prostitute*, Vett.Val.119.30, Porph.*Hist.Phil*.12 (pl.). d. of events, κοινότεραι τύχαι *more impartial*, i.e. *more equal*, chances, Th.5.102; ἔστιν ἐν τῷ κ. πᾶσι c. inf., And.2.6. V. in Logic, *general, universal*, τὸ κ. λαμβάνειν περί τινων, τὸ ἐπὶ πᾶσι κ., Pl.*Tht*.185b, c; τὰ κ. λεγόμενα ἀξιώματα Arist.*APo*.76$^{b}$14; αἱ κ. ἀρχαί ib.88$^{a}$36; κ. ἔννοιαι *axioms*, heading in Euc.; *general*, κ. ὅρος Arist.*Metaph*.987$^{b}$6; κοινὰ καὶ στοιχειώδη *general* principles, Phld.*Rh*.1.69 S.; κ. σημεῖον, opp. ἴδιον, Id.*Sign*.14; κ. κρίσις *objectively valid* judgement, Id.*Po*.5.22; ὄνομα κ. Str.10.2.10; *abstract*, ὁ κ. ἄνθρωπος καὶ λογισμῷ ληπτός Dam.*Pr*.341. VI. Gramm., 1. κ. συλλαβή *common* syllable, capable of being long or short, D.T.633.17, Heph.1.4. b. κ. ποιήματα, poems which are both κατὰ στίχον and συστηματικά, e.g. the Sapphic stanza, Id.pp.58,59 C.; also, poems *of ambiguous metrical form*, Id.p.60 C. 2. v. supr. III. 2. 3. of gender, κ. γένος D.T.634.19; of nouns, A.D.*Pron*.30.7, al., *EM*143.33, 305.19, etc. 4. ἀπὸ κοινοῦ λαμβάνειν, of two clauses taking a word *in common*, A.D.*Synt*.122.14, al.; κοινὸν or ἐκ κοινοῦ παραλαμβάνεσθαι, ib.20,28, al. VII. of forbidden meats, *common, profane*, φαγεῖν κ. καὶ ἀκάθαρτον *Act.Ap*.10.14, cf. *Ep.Rom*.14.14; κ. χερσὶ ἐσθίειν *Ev.Marc*.7.2. VIII. κοινόν, τό, name of an *eye-salve*, *CIL* 13.10021.3, al.

B. Adv. κοινῶς *in common, jointly*, E.*Ion*1462; τὰ κοινὰ κ. δεῖ φέρειν συμπτώματα Men.817: Comp., ἐν Κρήτῃ -οτέρως [ἔχει τὰ τῶν συσσιτίων] Arist.*Pol*.1272$^{a}$16. 2. *publicly*, κ. μᾶλλον ὠφέλησαν ἢ ἐκ τῶν ἰδίων ἔβλαψαν Th.2.42, etc. 3. *sociably, like other citizens*, οὐδὲ κ. οὐδὲ πολιτικῶς ἐβίωσαν Isoc.4.151; ἴσως καὶ κ. πρός τινα προσφέρεσθαι Arist.*Rh.Al*.1430$^{a}$1; κ. καὶ φιλικῶς Plu.*Ant*.33; μετρίως καὶ κ. ἀσπάζεσθαι Id.*Arat*.43. 4. *in general*, Diph.Siph.ap.Ath.3.81a; ἡ κ. σύνεσις, τὸ κ. "ἄνθρωπον", Phld.*Vit*.p.34 J., *Mort*.38; opp. ἰδίως, Demetr.Lac.*Herc*.1014.41, Plu.*Marc*.8, cf. Longin.15.1; κοινότερον εἰπεῖν Phld.*Rh*.1.256 S.; -οτέρως Orib.*Fr*.93. 5. *in the common dialect*, A.D.*Pron*.82.27, al.: Comp. -ότερον Id.*Synt*.159.5. 6. *in plain language*, opp. σοφιστικῶς, Plu.2.659f; *in the ordinary* or *wide sense*, opp. κυρίως, Them.*in APo*.5.5: Comp., M.Ant.2.10. II. fem. dat. **κοινῇ**; Dor. **κοινᾷ** *SIG*56.11 (Argos, v B.C.); Boeot. **κυνῆ** ib.635.31 (Acraeph., ii B.C.):—*in common, by common consent*, Hdt.1.148, 3.79, S.*OT*606, *OC*1339, E.*Hipp*.731, Th.1.3, etc.; κ. πᾶσι καὶ χωρίς Arist.*Pol*.1278$^{b}$23, cf. *Ath*.40.3; κ. μετά τινος, κ. σύν τινι, Pl.*Smp*.209c, *SIG*346.27 (iv B.C.), X.*Mem*.1.6.14, etc.; ἰδίᾳ τε καὶ κ. Alex.291: also neut. pl. κοινά S.*Ant*.546. 2. *publicly*, καὶ κ. καὶ ἰδίᾳ X.*HG*1.2.10, *Mem*.2.1.12, etc. 3. as Prep. c. dat., *together with*, E.*Ion*1228, *Hel*.829, *Fr*.823. III. with Preps., εἰς κοινόν *in common, in public*, ὑμῖν τῇδέ τ' ἐς κ. φράσω A.*Pr*.844; πᾶσιν ἐς κ. λέγω Id.*Eu*.408, cf. Ar.*Av*.457 (lyr.), Pl.*Lg*.796e; εἰς κ. γνώμην ἀποφαίνεσθαι D.19.156; εἰς τὸ κ. λέγειν, ἀγορεύειν, Pl.*Tht*.165a, X.*An*.5.6.27; εἰς τὸ κ. *for public use*, Pl.*Lg*.681c. 2. ἀπὸ κοινοῦ, ἐκ κοινοῦ, v. A.I.1, II.3, VI.4. 3. ἀφεῖσαν ἐν κοινῷ ζητεῖν, Lat. *rem in medio reliquerunt*, Arist.*Metaph*.987$^{b}$14; but οἱ ἐν κ. γιγνόμενοι λόγοι, = οἱ ἐξωτερικοὶ λόγοι, Id.*de An*.407$^{b}$29. 4. κατὰ κοινόν, opp. κατ' ἰδίαν, *jointly, in common*, Lex ap.D.21.94, Plb.4.3.5; prob. for κατὰ κοινοῦ Id.11.30.3.

⊛ **κοινο-τᾰφής**, ές, *in which all must be buried*, Λύσιλλαν κατέχει κ. θάλαμος *Ath.Mitt*.10.405 (iv B.C.). **-τάφιον** [ᾰ], τό, *public grave*, Ulp. ad D.18.208 (p.111 Dobson). **-τελής**, ές, *with the authority of the state*, δόγμα *IG*11(4).1150 (Delos, ii B.C.).

**κοινότης**, ητος, ἡ, *sharing in common, community*, τῶν γυναικῶν καὶ παίδων καὶ τῆς οὐσίας Arist.*Pol*.1274$^{b}$10; ἡ περὶ τὰ τέκνα κ. καὶ τὰς γυναῖκας ib.1266$^{a}$34; κ. φωνῆς *common* language, i.e. not peculiar or dialectal, Isoc.15.296, cf. D.H.*Th*.54, *Pomp*.2. 2. *common* or *universal quality*, Pl.*Tht*.208d, Plot.1.3.4; opp. ἰδιότης, Epicur.*Ep*.1 p.17 U.; κ. τοῦ ἵππου A.D.*Pron*.26.20: pl., *common features*, Phld.*Ir*.p.71 W., *Mort*.34, Plu.*Comp.Lyc.Num*.1; esp. in Medicine, term of the 'Methodic' school, Gal.1.80, al., cf. Plu.2.129d (pl.). 3. *generality, vagueness*, τῶν ὁμολογιῶν D.H.2.39, etc.; *ambiguity*, ὀνόματος Epicur.*Nat*.14.10, cf. Demetr.Lac.*Herc*.1014.48, Diog.Oen.27. II. in Politics, *absence of privileges* or *distinctions*, πολιτείας (sc. δημοκρατίας) ἣ μάλιστα κοινότητα δοκεῖ προῃρῆσθαι And.4.13. 2. *affability*, X.*HG*1.1.30; *accessibility*, λιμένων Aristid.*Or*.23(42).24, al. III. Gramm., *use of a common word* in two clauses, esp. in phrase ἐν κοινότητι παραλαμβάνεσθαι, A.D.*Synt*.122.27, al. 2. *common gender*, ib.55.2, al. IV. concrete, the *general body* of a βουλή, *POxy*.2110.29 (iv A.D.). 2. κ. τῶν ἀγρευτῶν, = κοινόν (cf. κοινός II. 2b), *Sammelb*.6704.4, al. (vi A.D.).

**κοινό-τοκος**, ον, *of* or *from common parents*, ἐλπίδες κ. hopes *in one born of the same parents*, i.e. *a brother*, S.*El*.858 (lyr.). **-τροφικός**, ή, όν, (τρέφω) *of* or *for group rearing*, ἐπιστήμη Pl.*Plt*.264d, 267d; ἡ -κή (sc. ἐπιστήμη) *group rearing*, ib.261e, 264b, etc. **-φᾰγία**, ἡ, *eating of what is common* or *profane*, J.*AJ*11.8.7. **-φῐλής**, ές, *with common affection*, κ. διανοίᾳ A.*Eu*.985 (lyr., κοινωφελεῖ codd.). **-φρων**, ον, gen. ονος, *like-minded with*, τινι E.*Ion*577, *IT*1008. **-φῠής**, ές, *of common origin*, πρόοδος Dam.*Pr*.52 bis.

**κοιν-όω**, fut. κοινώσω A.*Ch*.673: aor. ἐκοίνωσα Th.8.48, Pl.*Lg*.889d; Dor. ἐκοίνᾱσα Pi.*P*.4.115:—Med., fut. κοινώσομαι Id.*N*.3.12 codd. (leg. -άσομαι (Dor.)), E.*Med*.499: aor. ἐκοινωσάμην A.*Ag*.1347, Is.11.50, etc.:—Pass., aor. ἐκοινώθην E.*Andr*.38, Pl.*Ti*.59b: pf. κεκοίνωμαι (in med. sense) E.*Fr*.493:—*communicate, impart* information, κ. τινί τι A.*Ch*.717 (in 673 an acc. must be supplied), E.*Med*.685, Ar.*Nu*.197, Th.4.4, etc.; μῦθον ἔς τινας E.*IA*44 (anap.); κ. τινὶ περί τινος A.*Supp*.369; νυκτὶ κοινάσαντες ὁδόν *having imparted* their journey to night alone (i.e. travelling by night without consulting any one), Pi.*P*. l.c. 2. *make common, share*, κοινώσαντας τὴν δύναμιν κοινὰ καὶ τὰ ἀποβαίνοντα ἔχειν Th.1.39, cf. Pl.*Lg*. l.c.; v.l. for ἐκοινώνησε in Arist.*Pol*.1264$^{a}$1:—in Med., κοινάσομαι [ὕμνον] λύρᾳ Pi.*N*. l.c.: aor. Med. in act. sense, Hp.*Jusj*.; κ. τὴν οὐσίαν τῇ τοῦ παιδός *unite* one to the other, Is. l.c. 3. *make common, defile*, τὸν ἄνθρωπον *Ev.Matt*.15.11; γαστέρα μιαροφαγίᾳ Lxx 4*Ma*.7.6:—Med., *deem profane*, *Act.Ap*.10.15. II. Med., c. acc., *undertake together, make common cause in*, βουλεύματα A.*Ag*.1347; κοινούμεθα.. ἐγώ τε καὶ Λάχης τὸν λόγον Pl.*La*.196c; τὸ πρᾶγμα D.32.30; κοινουμένη τὰς ξυμφοράς σοι E.*Ion*608, cf. 858; κοινοῦσθαι τὸν στόλον Th.8.8; τὴν τύχην X.*Vect*.4.32. 2. *take counsel with, consult*, esp. an oracle or god, X.*An*.6.2.15, v.l. in *HG*7.1.27: generally, πρός τινας Pl.*Lg*.930c; περὶ πάντων ἑαυτοῖς Plb.7.16.3; τοῖς ἰατροῖς περί τινων Gal.*Consuet*.5; τοῖς φίλοις περὶ τὸ πρακτέον Hdn.7.8.1; ὧν ἄν τις κοινώσαιτο δόξαις *agree with*, Arist.*Metaph*.993$^{b}$12: abs., οὔτ' ἠθέλησας οὔτ' ἐγὼ 'κοινωσάμην S.*Ant*.539; simply, *communicate*, τὰ κατ' ἐμὲ τῇ βουλῇ Alciphr.3.72; μηδὲν τῇ γυναικὶ χρήσιμον Men.*Mon*.361. 3. c. gen., *to be partner* or *partaker*, τινος of a thing, E.*Ph*.1709, *Cyc*.634, Lys.12.93, etc.; τινί τινος with one in.., E.*Andr*.933. 4. *come to terms*, μοι Pl.*Smp*.218e. III. Pass., *have communication with*, λέχει E.*Andr*.38, cf. 217: metaph., ἀλλήλοις Pl.*Lg*.673d; ξανθῷ χρώματι -ωθέν, i.e. *tinged with* yellow, Id.*Ti*.59b. **-ωμα**, ατος, τό, *intercourse*, esp. *sexual*, Dionys.Minor 1, cf. Socr.*Ep*.35,36. 2. gloss on δαμώματα, Hsch. II. *mortised joint*, Ph.*Bel*.57.19. **-ωμάτιον**, τό, *band, tie*, ib.64.3. ⊛ **-ών**, ῶνος, ὁ, Dor., Arc. **κοινάν**, ᾶνος (q.v.), = κοινωνός, which is much more freq., X.*Cyr*.7.5.35, 8.1.16, 36, 40; of *partners* in a tax-farming syndicate, *PRev.Laws* 10.10, al. (iii B.C.).

⊛ **κοινων-έω**, fut. -ήσω Pl.*R*.540c: pf. κεκοινώνηκα Id.*Phdr*.246d, etc.:—Pass., fut. κοινωνήσομαι (v. infr.): pf. κεκοινώνημαι Id.*Lg*.801e:—*have* or *do in common with, share, take part in* a thing *with* another, c. gen. rei et dat. pers., τῆς πολιτείας κ. τινί ib.753a; κ. πόνων καὶ κινδύνων ἀλλήλοις ib.686a, cf. X.*HG*2.4.21; κ. αὐτοῖς ὧν ἔπραττον ib.6.3.1; σιτήσεώς τισι Din.1.101: also in act. sense, *give a share of*.., βρωτοῦ μηδενὸς μηδένα τούτῳ κ. D.25.61; τὰ περὶ τὰς κτήσεις τοῖς συσσιτίοις ὁ νομοθέτης ἐκοινώνησε (v.l. ἐκοίνωσε) Arist.*Pol*.1264$^{a}$1; πυρὸς ἢ ὕδατος κ. Luc.*Alex*.46; πάντων ἐκοινώνει μοι τῶν ἀπορρήτων Id.*Philops*.34. 2. κ. τινός *have a share of, take part in* a thing, χθονός A.*Supp*.325; μύθου Id.*Ch*.165; κακῶν Id.*Th*.1038; γάμων S.*Tr*.546; τάφου E.*Or*.1055; τύχης Id.*Med*.302; σίτου καὶ ποτοῦ X.*Mem*.2.6.22; τῆς πολιτείας Arist.*Pol*.1268$^{a}$18, etc.; τῶν αὐτῶν κ. πάντων *share* all things *in common*, ib.1257$^{a}$22; ἱερῶν *SIG*1106.7 (Cos, iv/iii B.C.); θυσίας *Inscr.Magn*.44.19 (Decr. Corc.); ἦθος παιδείας κεκοινωνηκός Aristeas 290; φύσεως κεκοινώνηκε σαρκίνης Phld.*Sign*.27; πάθους, of infection, Gal.12.312. b. of *partnership* in business, *BGU*969.13 (ii A.D.), etc. 3. κ. τινί *go shares with, have dealings with* a man, Ar.*V*.692, *Av*.653, Pl.*R*.343d, etc.; also of things, κοινωνεῖν μὲν ἡγοῦμαι καὶ τοῦτο τοῖς πεπολιτευμένοις I think that this also *is concerned with* my public measures, D.18.58; στολὴν φοινικίδα.. ἥκιστα..γυναικείᾳ κ. *has* least *in common with*.., X.*Lac*.11.3; οὐδὲν τραγῳδίᾳ κ. Arist.*Po*.1453$^{b}$10, cf. *SE*179$^{b}$16: Medic., *sympathize*, of bodily parts, Hp.*Mul*.1.38:—Pass., ἐγκώμια κεκοινωνημένα εὐχαῖς *united with*.., Pl.*Lg*.801e. 4. with Preps., φύσις ἡ θήλεια τῇ τοῦ ἄρρενος γένους κ. εἰς ἅπαντα Id.*R*.453a; κ. περί τινος Plb.31.18.6. 5. c. acc. cogn., κ. κοινωνίαν τινί Pl.*Lg*.881e; κ. ἴσα πάντα τοῖς ἀνδράσι Id.*R*.540c: rarely c. acc. rei, κ. φόνον τινί *commit* murder *in common with* him, E.*El*.1048. 6. abs., *share in an opinion, agree*, σκόπει.., πότερον κοινωνεῖς καὶ ξυνδοκεῖ σοι Pl.*Cri*.49d. 7. *communicate, join*, ἡ ἐρυθρὰ θάλασσα κ. πρὸς τὴν ἔξω.. Arist.*Mete*.354$^{a}$2. 8. *form a community*, Id.*Pol*.1280$^{a}$26, etc. II. of sexual intercourse, κ. γυναικί, ἀνδρί, Pl.*Lg*.784e, Luc.*DDeor*.1.2, 10.2, *PFlor*.36.6 (iv A.D.):—Pass., ὑπὸ μηδενός ποτε κοινωνήσεται εἰ μὴ ὑπὸ σοῦ μόνου *PMag.Osl*.1.293. **-ημα**, ατος, τό, *that which is communicated*: pl., *acts of communion, communications, dealings between man and man*, Pl.*R*.333a, *Lg*.738a, Arist.*Pol*.1280$^{b}$17; κ. πρός τινα J.*AJ*16.7.3; πρὸς ἀλλήλους Plu.2.158c; ψυχροῦ καὶ θερμοῦ κ. ib.951e:

in sg., *communication*, λόγων Phld.*Oec*.p.46 J.; *common enterprise*, Id.*Vit*.p.33 J.; *business partnership*, *Sammelb*.5658.8. 2. *point of junction*, Hp.*Epid*.2.4.2. 3. *connexion*, Nic.Dam.128 J. **-ησις**, εως, ἡ, *reciprocal recognition*, παίδων Pl.*Plt*.310b. 2. *partnership*, *BGU*1024 v 19 (iv A.D.). **-ητέον**, *one must share in*, τινός τινι Pl.*R*.403b; φιλίας Ph.2.401; ὀνειδῶν Plu.*Pomp*.44. **-ητικός**, ή, όν, v.l. for κοινωνικός, Plb.2.44.1; -κή (sc. ἐπιστήμη) *social science*, coupled with πολιτική, Plu.2.746a:—hyperdor. **-ᾱτικός**, *generous*, *liberal*, Diotog.ap.Stob.4.7.62. ❀**-ία**, ἡ, *communion*, *association*, *partnership*, κ. μαλθακά Pi.*P*.1.97; οὔτε φιλία ἰδιώταις οὔτε κ. πόλεσιν Th.3.10; ὅτῳ δὲ μὴ ἔνι κ., φιλία οὐκ ἂν εἴη Pl.*Grg*.507e; ἐν ταῖς κ. τε καὶ ὁμιλίαις Id.*Lg*.861e, cf. *Smp*.182c; ἡ περὶ..ἀνθρώπους πρὸς ἀλλήλους κ. ib.188c; ἐν διαλύσει τῆς κ. Id.*R*.343d; ἡ τῶν γυναικῶν κ. τοῖς ἀνδράσι, viz. co-education, ib.466c; ἀνθρωπίνη κ. human *society*, Id. *Plt*.276b; ἡ κ. ἡ πολιτική Arist.*Pol*.1252$^a$7; αὕτη ἡ κ., of marriage, ib.1334$^b$33; πόλις ἡ γενῶν καὶ κωμῶν κ. ib.1281$^a$1; *fellowship*, *Act.Ap*.2.42, al.; ἡ πρὸς τὸν Δία κ. Arr.*Epict*.2.19.27. b. *joint-ownership*, *PLond*.2.311.2 (ii A.D.), etc. 2. c. gen. objecti, λυγραὶ.. τῶν ὅπλων κ. E.*HF*1377; γάμων Pl.*Lg*.721a; γυναικῶν Id.*R*.461e; ἡ ἡδονῆς τε καὶ λύπης κ. συνδεῖ ib.462b; τῶν πόνων Id.*Ti*.87e; βοηθείας καὶ φιλίας D.9.28; βίου, of marriage, *BGU*1051.9 (Aug.); ἡ κ. τοῦ ἁγίου πνεύματος 2*Ep.Cor*.13.14 (later, of Holy *Communion*, Just. *Nov*.7.11); κ. τῶν ἱερῶν *Supp.Epigr*.4.247 (Panamara); τίς θαλάσσης βουκόλοις κ.; what have herdsmen *to do with* the sea? E.*IT*254; τίς δαὶ κατόπτρου καὶ ξίφους κ.; Ar.*Th*.140; λύπη μανίας κοινωνίαν ἔχει τινά Alex.296; opp. ἀκοινωνησία, Dam.*Pr*.423. II. *sexual intercourse*, E.*Ba*.1276; γυναικὸς λαμβάνειν κοινωνίαν Amphis 20.3. III. *charitable contribution*, *alms*, *Ep.Rom*.15.26, *Ep.Hebr*.13.16, *Jahresh*.4 *Beibl*.37. 2. *charitable disposition*, opp. πλεονεξία, *Corp.Herm*.13.9. IV. Pythag. name for 2, *Theol.Ar*.8. **-ικός**, ή, όν, *held in common*, τὰ κ. property *held by corporations*, D.14.16, cf. *BCH*20.16 (Delph., iv B.C., prob.); κ. ἐλαιών *BGU*1037.14 (i A.D.), cf. *PGiss*.30.7 (ii A.D.). b. *relating to partnerships*, [δίκαι] Arist. *Ath*.52.2. c. κοινωνικά, τά, *tax on corporations*, *PTeb*.5.59 (ii B.C.), 100.10 (ii B.C.). 2. *social*, ἰσότης κοινωνική [ἡ δικαιοσύνη] Pi.*Def*. 411e; κ. ἀρετή Arist.*Pol*.1283$^a$38; [φιλίαι] Id.*EN*1161$^b$14. 3. *sociable*, κ. καὶ φιλικὴ διάθεσις Plb.2.44.1, cf. Plu.2.43d; φύσει ἐσμὲν κ. Epicur. *Fr*.525, cf. Arr.*Epict*.3.13.5: Sup., τὸν ἄνθρωπον ἡ φύσις κατεσκεύασε -ώτατον Ph.*Fr*.71 H.; τὸ -κόν *sociability*, J.*BJ*2.8.3. b. of certain signs of the zodiac, *Cat.Cod.Astr*.1.166. 4. *giving a share of*, τῶν ὄντων Luc.*Tim*.56: abs., κ. ὁ Ἑρμῆς *ready to share luck with others*, prov. in Arist.*Rh*.1401$^a$20; *liberal*, 1*Ep.Ti*.6.18, Ptol.*Tetr*.69; opp. φθονερός, Gal.4.817. 5. c. dat., *in communion* with, τῇ ἐκκλησίᾳ Just. *Nov*.8 *Jusj*. II. Act., *receptive*, *sharing in*, φωτός Str.17.1.36. III. Adv. -κῶς, χρῆσθαι τοῖς εὐτυχήμασι to suffer others *to partake in* one's good fortune, Plb.18.48.7; κ. βιῶναι D.S.5.9; ζῆν κ. καὶ φιλικῶς Plu. 2.1108c, etc. 2. Medic., *by sympathy*, κ. σπᾶσθαι prob. in Aët.3.140. **-ῑμαῖος**, α, ον, = foreg. I. 1, πράγματα, τοῖχος, *PLond*.5.1728.8, *PMon*.16.19 (vi A.D.). **-οποιέω**, = κοινωνέω, *Gloss*. ❀**-ός**, ὁ, also ἡ, *companion*, *partner*, τινος of or in a thing, A.*Ag*.1037, 1352, *Supp*.344, Men.*Epit*.499; τῆς ἐπιβουλῆς Antipho 5.68; ἱερῶν Pl.*Lg*. 868e; τῆς ἀρχῆς Th.7.63, 8.46; ὁ τοῦ κακοῦ κ. *accomplice* in.., S.*Tr*. 730; ἀνοσίων αὐτοῖς ἔργων Pl.*Ep*.325a; κ. περὶ νόμων Pl.*Lg*.810c; τινι in a thing, E.*El*.637: c. dat. pers., κ. ἀλλήλοις τῶν τιμῶν with each other, X.*Mem*.2.6.24. 2. abs., *partner*, *fellow*, S.*Aj*.284, Pl. *R*.333b, *Phdr*.239c, etc.; ὁ σὸς κ., οὐχ ὁ ἐμός D.18.21; ἴσοι καὶ κ. Arist.*EN*1133$^b$3; κοινωνοὶ λιμένων, of a *societas publicanorum* which farmed harbour-dues, *BCH*10.267 (Syme); of *joint-owners*, *PAmh*. 2.100 (ii/iii A.D.). 3. *familiar spirit*, Lxx 4*Ki*.17.11. II. as Adj., = κοινός, ξίφος E.*IT*1173.

**κοίν-ωσις**, εως, ἡ, *mingling*, Plu.2.430e. II. *sharing*, Asp.*in EN*181.1. **-ωφελής**, ές, *of common utility*, Ph.2.424, al., Gal.14.296, *POxy*.1409.19 (iii A.D.), Just.*Nov*.7.2.1: Comp., Max.Tyr.41.1: Sup., Ph.1.389. **-ωφελία**, ἡ, *common utility*, Phld.*Rh*.1.174 S. (pl.), D.S.1.51: on the form (-εια Just.*Nov*.7.12 *Ep*.), cf. *EM*462.21.

❀**κοῖξ**, ῖκος, ὁ, *doum-palm*, *Hyphaene thebaica*, Thphr.*HP*1.10.5, etc. 2. *palm-leaf basket*, Pherecr.78, Antiph.63:—Dor. **κοῖς** Epich.113 (also *BGU*972.5).

**Κοιο-γενής**, ές, *born of Coios*, i.e. Latona, Pi.*Fr*.88.2:—fem. **Κοιογένεια** A.R.2.710; **Κοιηΐς** (q.v.).

❀**κοιόλης**, ὁ, = ἱερεύς, Hsch., Suid. **κοῖον**· ἐνέχυρον, Hsch. **κοῖος** (A), η, ον, Ion. for ποῖος, α, ον.

**κοῖος** (B), ὁ, Maced. for ἀριθμός, Ath.10.455e. II. Carian for πρόβατον, Sch.Il.14.255.

**κοιπποίβα**· πᾶν σπέρμα (Achaean), Hsch.

**κοιρᾰν-έω**, poet. Verb, *to be lord* or *master*, *rule*, *command*, in Hom., 1. of a military leader, ὣς ὅ γε κοιρανέων δίεπε στρατόν Il.2.207, cf. 4.250; μάχην ἀνὰ κοιρανέοντα 5.824; πόλεμον κάτα κοιρανέουσιν ib.332. 2. of a king in peace, Λυκίην κάτα κοιρανέουσιν 12.318; of the suitors (princes) in Ithaca, Od.1.247, al. II. later c. gen., *to be lord of*, Hes.*Th*.331, A.*Pers*.214: c. dat., θεοῖσι κ. Id.*Pr*.49; Ep. impf. κοιρανέεσκεν A.R.2.998: abs., τὸν νῦν κοιρανοῦντα A.*Pr*.958: c. acc., *lead*, *arrange*, χορούς Pi.*O*.14.9:—Pass., Call. *Del*.167. **-ηος**, Dor. for κοιράνειος, *belonging to a sovereign*, κάρτος Melinno ap.Stob.3.7.12. ❀**-ία**, Ep. -ίη, ἡ, *sovereignty*, D.P.464, *APl*.5.358. **-ίδης** [νῐ], ου, ὁ, *member of a ruling house*, S.*Ant*.940 (anap., pl.), *Sammelb*.5829 (pl.). **-ικός**, ή, όν, *royal*, λέοντες, ὀφθαλμοί, Opp.*C*.3.41,47, cf. Epic. in *BKT*5(1).p.119. ❀**-ος**, ὁ, poet. Noun (Boeot. for *king*, *AB*1095), *ruler*, *leader*, *commander*, 1. in war or peace, ἡγεμόνες Δαναῶν καὶ κ. Il. 2.487; κοίρανε λαῶν 7.234; οὐκ ἀγαθὸν πολυκοιρανίη· εἷς κ. ἔστω, εἷς βασιλεύς 2.204. 2. generally, *lord*, *master*, Od.18.106, Pi.*N*.3.62, A.*Ag*.549, S.*OC*1287, E.*Med*.71, al.—Rare in fem., Orph.*Fr*.38.

**κοῖς**, v. κοῖξ. **κοίσκαι**· δίκαιοι, Hsch. **κοισσοί**· κορμοί, Id.

**κοιτ-άζω**, (κοίτη) *put to bed*, Hsch.; esp. of cattle, *fold*, ποιμένων κοιταζόντων πρόβατα Lxx *Je*.40(33).12; *cause to rest*, ποῦ ποιμαίνεις, ποῦ -άζεις ἐν μεσημβρίᾳ; ib.*Ca*1.7. 2. Med., Dor. aor. ἐκοιταξάμην, *go to bed*, *sleep*, ἀνὰ βωμῷ θεᾶς κοιτάξατο νύκτα Pi.*O*.13.76, cf. Lxx *De*.6.7. b. *encamp*, *bivouac*, Aen.Tact.10.26 (Pass.), Plb.10.15.9, *POxy*.1465.9 (i B.C.); perh. to be read in Eup.341. II. intr., in Act., *have a lair*, of a lion, Aesop.114: *nest*, of birds, *BGU*1252.11 (ii B.C.). III. *parcel out* lands (cf. κοίτη v), ib.619.4 (ii A.D.). **-αῖος**, α, ον, (κοίτη) *abed*, κ. γίγνεσθαι ἐν τῇ χώρᾳ to *pass the night* in the country, Decr.ap.D.18.37; but τάξας ἡμέραν ἐν ᾗ δεήσει πάντας ἐν Ἀριμίνῳ γενέσθαι κ. *encamp*, Plb.3.61.10; κ. ἔρχεσθαι Id.*Fr*.177. II. Subst., τὸ κ., = κοίτη I. 2, *lair* of a wild beast, Plu.*TG*9. 2. τὰ κ. ἐπισπένδειν take a *last cup*, '*night-cap*', Hld.3.4. ❀**-άριον**, τό, Dim. of κοίτη, Sch.Od.14.51. **-άριος**, α, ον, *for beds*, σινδόνες *Edict.Diocl*. 28.16,31. **-ᾰσία**, ἡ, *cohabitation*, Lxx *Le*.20.15. ❀**-ασμός**, ὁ, *folding*, βοῶν *PMeyer* 12.24 (ii A.D.), etc. **-αστέον**, *one must put to bed*, κύνας Arr.*Cyn*.9 tit. **-ᾱτήριον**, τό, *dormitory*, *bed-chamber*, *Berl.Sitzb*.1927.164 (Cyrene). ❀**-η**, ἡ, (κεῖμαι) = κοῖτος I, once in Hom., Od.19.341 (v.l. οἴκῳ); *bedstead*, *IG*1$^2$.330.16, al., Wilcken *Chr*.244.3 (iii B.C.), etc.; esp. *marriage-bed*, A.*Supp*.804 (lyr.), S.*Tr*.17; οὐ γὰρ ἐκ μιᾶς κ. ἔβλαστον Id.*Fr*.546; τᾶς ἀπλήστου κ. ἔρος E.*Med*.152 (lyr.), etc.; ἀνάνδρου κοίτας λέκτρον ib.436 (lyr.); also πετρίνη κοίτη, of a cave, S.*Ph*.160 (anap.); τειρομέναν νοσερᾷ κ. on a sick-*bed*, E.*Hipp*.132 (lyr.); κοίταν δ' ἔχει νέρθεν, of one dead, S.*OC*1706 (lyr.); κ. σκληρά Pl.*Lg*.942d, Aret.*CA*1.1: pl., ἔννυχοι κ. Pi.*P*.11.25; νυμφίδιοι κ. E. *Alc*.249 (lyr.): metaph., of the sea, ἐν μεσημβριναῖς κοίταις..εὕδοι πεσών A.*Ag*.566; of the *bed* of a river, Procop.*Aed*.5.5, Phlp. *in Ph*. 586.21, Lyd.*Mens*.4.10. 2. *lair* of a wild beast, *nest* of a bird, etc., E.*Ion*155 (lyr.); χελιδόνων Aët.16.15; κ. ποιεῖσθαι, of the spider, Arist.*HA*623$^a$12; of the fish ἐξώκοιτος, Thphr.*Fr*.171.1. 3. *quarters*, τῶν φυλακιτῶν *BGU*1007.14 (iii B.C.), cf. *PTeb*.179 (ii B.C.); v. infr. VI. 4. *pen*, *fold* for cattle, *PLips*.118.15 (ii A.D.). II. *act of going to bed*, τῆς κοίτης ὥρη *bed*-time, Hdt.1.10, 5.20; τραπέζῃ καὶ κοίτῃ δέκεσθαι to entertain 'at *bed* and board', ibid.; τὴν σκηνὴν εἰς κ. διέλυον for *going to bed*, X.*Cyr*.2.3.1 (but κεῖσθαι κοίταν *to lie still* in death, A.*Ag*.1494 (lyr.)). III. *lodging*, *entertainment*, *PTeb*. 122.1 (i B.C.), al. IV. of *sexual connexion*, κ. διδόναι Lxx *Nu*.5.20, cf. *Le*.18.20; κ. σπέρματος ib.15.16; κ. ἔχειν ἐκ.. to become pregnant by a man, *Ep.Rom*.9.10; in bad sense, *lasciviousness*, ib. 13.13 (pl.). V. *parcel*, *lot* of land, *PAmh*.2.88.9 (ii A.D.), *PRyl*. 168.9 (ii A.D.). VI. *chest*, *case*, or *basket*, Pherecr.122, Eup.76, *IG* 2$^2$.120.37,40, Men.129.2, *PPetr*.2 p.10 (iii B.C., unless in signf. I. 3), Luc.*Ep.Sat*.21; αἱ μυστικαὶ κ. Plu.*Phoc*.28. **-ίδιον**, τό, Dim. of κοιτίς, Sch.Luc.*Gall*.21. **-ίς**, ίδος, ἡ, Dim. of κοίτη VI, *box*, *AP* 6.254.6 (Myrin.), Philostr.*VA*4.39; v.l. for κιστίς in Hld.4.11; gloss on φωριαμός, Sch.A.R.3.802; *basket*, Men.*Epit*.164; κ. πλεκτὰς ἐκ φοίνικος Arr.*An*.3.4.3; of Moses' *ark*, J.*AJ*2.9.5.

❀**κοῖτος**, ὁ, (κεῖμαι) *resting-place*, *bed*, κοίτοιο μεδώμεθα Od.3.334, cf. 2.358; οἱ δ' ἐπὶ κοῖτον ἐσσεύοντο 14.455; στυγερὸς δ' ὑπεδέξατο κ., of birds, 22.470; *stall*, *fold*, Arat.1116; ἀπάγειν ἐπὶ κοῖτον *pen*, Longus 1.8. II. *sleep*, ἐπὴν νὺξ ἔλθῃ, ἕλῃσί τε κ. ἅπαντας Od.19.515; κοίτοιο ὥρη *bed*-time, ib.510; ἐπ' ἠῶ κ. *lying abed* till dawn, Hes.*Op*. 574; τὸν ὑπασπίδιον κοῖτον ἰαύειν sleep under arms, E.*Rh*.740 (lyr.); κ. ποιέεσθαι go to *bed*, Hdt.7.17; ἐς κ. παρεῖναι Id.1.9.

❀**κοιτών**, ῶνος, ὁ, *bed-chamber*, Ar.*Fr*.6, *PTeb*.120.14 (i B.C.), D.S.11.69, etc.; ὁ ἐπὶ τοῦ κοιτῶνος *chamberlain*, *Act.Ap*.12.20, Arr.*Epict*.3.22.15; ἐπὶ κ. Σεβαστοῦ, = Lat. *cubicularius Augusti*, *CIG*2947 (Caria, ii A.D.), cf. *IG*14.2143, al.: rejected by the Atticists, who hold δωμάτιον to be correct, cf. Poll.1.79, Phryn.227. 2. *grave*, *IG*14. 464 (Catana). 3. *nursery*, ἐν κ. εἶναι to be an infant, minor, Just. *Nov*.155 *Praef*. II. *landing-place*, *Stad*.128.

**κοιτωνιάρχης**, ου, ὁ, *chamberlain*, Tz.*H*.6.486.

**κοιτων-ικός**, ή, όν, *for a bedroom*, κλίνη *Gloss*. II. Subst. κοιτωνική, ἡ, *bed-cover*, *Ostr*. in *Sammelb*.4292 (written -ονική). **-ιον**, τό, Dim. of κοιτών, *Stud.Pal*.20.67.32, Sch.Ar.*Lys*.160. **-ίσκος**, ὁ, = foreg., Artem.4.46, Procop.*Aed*.1.3. **-ίτης** [ῑ], ου, ὁ, *chamberlain*, Arr.*Epict*.1.30.7, Gal.14.624, *POxy*.471.84 (ii A.D.); κ. Καίσαρος *IG*14.1664.

**κοιτωνοφύλαξ** [ῠ], ακος, ὁ, *guardian of the bed-chamber*, Apion ap. Hsch. s.v. θαλαμηπόλος.

**κοιφί**, v. κῦφι. **κοιφόν**· κοῖλον, Hsch. (i.e. κυφόν).

**κοκάλια** (vv.ll. κοκκάλια, κωκάλια), ων, τά, small shell-fish like a periwinkle, Arist.*HA*528$^a$9.

❀**κόκκᾰλος**, ὁ, *kernel of the* στρόβιλος, Hp.*Acut*.(*Sp*.)30, 34; = κῶνος, Gal.15.848, cf. 12.55; coupled with ὀστρακίς, Ath.3.126a; = Κνίδιος κόκκος, Dsc.ap.Gal.19.113.

**κοκκάριον**, τό, Dim. of κόκκος III, *pill*, Ruf.ap.Orib.8.47.11 (pl.).

**κοκκηρός**, ά, όν, *made from* κόκκος II, πορφύρα *Edict.Diocl*.24.8.

❀**κοκκίζω**, *pick the kernel out of fruit*, κοκκιεῖς ῥόαν A.*Fr*.363, Ar.*Fr*. 610.

**κοκκῐνίζω**, *to be scarlet*, Sch.Opp.*H*.3.25, 5.271.

**κοκκῐνο-βᾰφής**, ές, = κοκκοβαφής, Callix.2:—also **-βᾰφος**, ον, Sch. rec.Pi.*O*.6.66. **-ειδής**, ές, *like the scarlet berry*, Sch.Theoc.7.58.

**κόκκ-ῐνος**, η, ον, *scarlet*, Herod.6.19, *Ep.Hebr*.9.19, *PHamb*.10.24

(ii A. D.), Plu.*Fab.*15; κ. γενόμενος *blushing*, *Com.Adesp.*19.3D. II. Subst. κόκκινα, τά, *scarlet clothes*, ἐν κ. περιπατεῖν, κ. φορεῖν, Arr.*Epict.*3.22.10, 4.11.34; -ων βαφαί *PHolm.*21.41: sg., Lxx *Ex.*25.4. -ίον, τό, Dim. of κόκκος I, Dsc.3.55 (interpol.); χαμαιμήλων Philotim.ap. Orib.5.33.7. 2. Dim. of κόκκος III, *pill*, Gal.12.496, Alex.Trall. 5.4. -ίς, ίδος, ἡ, = αἴγειρος, Hsch. II. in pl., *scarlet slippers*, Herod.7.61.

**κοκκο-άξ**· κορώνη, Hsch. **-βάρη**· γλαῦξ, Id. **-βαφής**, ές, *scarlet-dyed*, *scarlet*, Thphr.*HP*3.7.5, Ael.*NA*17.38, Philostr.*Im.*2.5. **-βαφία**, ἡ, *scarlet raiment*, Id.*VA*4.21. **-βόας**, v. κοκκυβόας. **-δαφνον**, τό, *laurel berry*, Paul.Aeg.3.28. **-θραύστης**, ου, ὁ, glossed ὄρνις ποιός, perh. *grosbeak*, Hsch. **-λάχανον**, *maccum*, *Gloss.* **-λέκτης**, ου, ὁ, *gatherer of grains* (cf. sq.), *PLond.*1821. 225. **-λογέω**, *sift grains* of weeds from wheat, *POxy.*1031.16 (iii A. D.); = Lat. *racemor*, Dosith.p.432K., *Gloss.* **-μαν**, τό, v. κουκούμιον.

**κοκκόνοι**· οἱ πυρῆνες τῶν ἐλαιῶν, Hsch.

**κοκκο-ποιόν**· κοκκοβαφές, Hsch. **-ριζον**, τό, name of a *drug*, *Hippiatr.*2.

**κόκκος**, ὁ, *grain*, *seed*, as of the pomegranate, *h.Cer.*372, 412, Hdt. 4.143, Hermipp.36, Hp.*Mul.*1.37, *PTeb.*273.47 (ii/iii A. D.); κ. Βαβυλώνιος Philostr.*Ep.*54; of the poppy, Euphro 11.11; of the pine, *IG* 14.966.12; of wheat, Philum.*Ven.*3.3; of weeds in corn, *PLond.*5. 1697.13 (vi A. D.): cf. Κνίδιος: metaph., νόου δέ μοι οὐκ ἔνι κ. *not a grain* of sense, Timo 66.3. 2. a measure, Dsc.2.166, Orib.*Fr.* 35. II. '*berry*' (*gall*) *of kermes oak*, used to dye scarlet, Thphr. *HP*3.7.3, Gal.12.32: hence, *scarlet* (the colour), Dromo 1.4, *PHolm.* 22.1. 2. κ. or κ. βαφική, ἡ, *kermes oak*, *Quercus coccifera*, Dsc.4. 48, Paus.10.36.1. III. *pill*, Alex.Trall.5.4. IV. in pl., *testicles*, *AP*12.222 (Strat.). 2. *pudenda muliebria*, Hsch.

**κοκκούμιον**, v. κουκούμιον. **κοκκοχλύζειν**· συλλαβίζειν, Hsch.

**κόκκυ**, *cuckoo!* the bird's cry, Ar.*Av.*505; as an exclam., *now! quick!* (ταχύ Suid.), κόκκυ, πεδίονδε ib.507; κόκκυ, μεθεῖτε *quick*—let go, Id.*Ra.*1384; οὐδὲ κ., = οὐδὲ βραχύ, *AB*105. (Onomatop.)

**κοκκύαι**, οἱ, v. κοκύαι.

**κοκκυβόας** ὄρνις, *cock*, '*chanticleer*', S.*Fr.*791 (κοκκο- codd. Eust.).

**κοκκυγ-έα**, ἡ, *wig-tree*, *Rhus Cotinus*, cj. in Thphr.*HP*3.16.6, cf. Plin.*HN*13.121:—but **κοκκυγία**· ἀνεμώνη (Croton.), Hsch. **-ινος**, η, ον, *purple-red*, and **-όω**, *dye red*, Id. s. v. κεκοκκυγωμένον.

**κοκκύζω**, Dor. -ύσδω Theoc.7.124: pf. κεκόκκῦκα Ar.*Ec.*31: (κόκκυ):—*cry cuckoo*, Hes.*Op.*486; also of the cock, *crow*, Cratin.311, Pl.Com.209, Diph.63, Hyp.*Fr.*262S.; Μοισᾶν ὄρνιχες ποτὶ Χῖον ἀοιδὸν ἀντία κοκκύζοντες Theoc.7.48, cf. Arist.*HA*631$^b$9, Poll.5.89. II. *cry like a cuckoo* or *cock*, *give a signal by such cry*, Ar.*Ra.*1380, *Ec.*31.

**κοκκῡ-μηλέα**, ἡ, *plum-tree*, *Prunus domestica*, Arar.20, Thphr. *HP*3.6.4, Dsc.1.121, Gal.12.32; κ. περὶ τὴν Θηβαΐδα *sebesten*, *Cordia Myxa*, Thphr.*HP*4.2.10. **-μηλον**, τό, *plum*, Archil.173, Hippon. 81, Alex.272.5, Thphr.*HP*1.10.10, Gal.6.613. **-μηλος**, ὁ, = -μηλέα, Com. (fort. Arar.20) ap.Poll.1.232. **-μηλών**, ῶνος, ὁ, *plum-orchard*, *Gloss.*

**κόκκυξ**, ῡγος, ὁ, *cuckoo*, Hes.*Op.*486, Epich.164, Ar.*Av.*504, Arist. *HA*563$^b$14, 618$^a$8; sacred to Hera, Paus.2.17.4; χειροτόνησάν με—κόκκυγές γε τρεῖς, i.e. three fellows who voted over and over again, Ar.*Ach.*598, cf. κόκκυγες· ἐπὶ ὑπονοηθέντων πλειόνων εἶναι καὶ ὀλίγων ὄντων, Hsch.; μῆλον κόκκυγος, = κοκκύμηλον, Nic.*Fr.*87. 2. *stammerer*, nickname of Battus, Sch.Pi.*P.*4.1. II. a sea-fish, *piper*, *Trigla cuculus*, said to make a sound like *cuckoo*, Hp.*Int.*21, Arist. *HA*535$^b$18, 598$^a$15, Numen.ap.Ath.7.309f, Speus.ap.eund.7.324f, Opp.*H.*1.97. III. = ὄλυνθος, a fig that ripens early, Nic.*Th.* 854. IV. Medic., *os coccygis*, Ruf.*Onom.*114, Gal.2.762; but τρητὸς κ., = the whole *os sacrum*, Poll.2.183. V. mark on a horse's shoulder, *Hippiatr.*14, 26, 115.

**κόκκυς**· λόφος, Hsch.

**κοκκ-υσμός**, ὁ, *crying cuckoo*: in men, *the sound of a very high voice*, Nicom.*Harm.*11.1, *Exc.*4 (pl.). **-υστής**, οῦ, ὁ, *crower*, *screamer*, Timo 43.1.

**κόκκων**, ωνος, ὁ, *pomegranate-seed*, Sol.40, Hp.*Mul.*1.37 (cf. Gal. 19.113), *Sammelb.*6779.51 (iii B. C.). II. *mistletoe-berry*, Hsch.:—Dim. **κοκκωνίδιον**, *Gloss.*

**κοκκωτόν**, *bacatum*, *granitum*, *Gloss.*

**κοκρύδων**· λῃστῶν, κλεπτῶν, Hsch. (but **κοκρύδες** = **κροκύδες**, Epich.181).

**κοκρύνδακοι**· κυλλοί, Hsch.

**κοκύαι**, οἱ, *ancestors*, *AP*9.312 (Zonas): fem., Call.*Fr.anon.*37 (v. l. κοκκ-).

**κόκχος**, ὁ, perh. = Lat. *coculum*, *PHamb.*10.36 (ii A. D.).

**κολαβρ-εύομαι**, = sq., Hsch. **-ίζω**, *dance a wild Thracian dance*, Id.: **-ισμός**, ὁ, name of such dance, Ath.14.629d (καλαβρ- codd.), Poll.4.100. II. Pass., *to be derided*, Lxx *Jb.*5.4. **-ος**, ὁ, *a song to which the* κολαβρισμός *was danced*, Ath.4.164e, Demetr. Sceps.ap.eund.15.697c. II. *young pig*, Hsch., Suid.

**κολάζω**, fut. κολάσω And.1.136, Lys.31.29, X.*Cyr.*7.5.8, Pl.*Lg.* 714d, etc.: aor. ἐκόλασα Ar.*V.*927, Th.3.40:—**Med.**, fut. κολάσομαι Theopomp.Com.27, X.*HG*1.7.19; twice contr. in Ar., 2 sg. κολᾷ *Eq.*456, part. κολώμενος *V.*244: aor. ἐκολασάμην Th.6.78, Pl.*Mx.* 240d:—**Pass.**, fut. -ασθήσομαι Th.2.87, etc.: aor. ἐκολάσθην Id.7. 68: pf. κεκόλασμαι Antipho 3.4.8, D.20.139:—*check*, *chastise*, τὰς ἐπιθυμίας Pl.*Grg.*491e; τὸ πλεονάζον Plu.2.663e, etc.; τὴν ἀμετρίαν Gal.6.29:—Pass., *to be corrected*, τὸ ἐν μέλιτι χολῶδες -άζεται Hp. *Acut.*59, cf. X.*Oec.*20.12: pf. part. Pass., *chastened*, εὐπειθὲς καὶ κεκολ. Arist.*EN*1119$^b$12; δίαιτα Luc.*Herm.*86; ῥήτωρ κεκ. Poll.6. 149; ἰσχὺς κ. ἐς ῥυθμούς Philostr.*VS*1.17.3; also of an athlete, ἀπέριττος τὰ μυώδη καὶ μὴ κεκ. Id.*Gym.*31. 2. *chastise*, *punish*, τινα E.*Ba.*1322, Ar.*Nu.*7, etc.; τὰ σέμν' ἔπη κόλαζ' ἐκείνους *use* your proud words *in reproving* them, S.*Aj.*1108: c. dat. modi, λόγοις κ. τινά ib.1160; θανάτῳ E.*Hel.*1172, Lys.28.3; πληγαῖς, τιμωρίαις, Pl. *Lg.*784d, Isoc.1.50; ἀτιμίαις Pl.*Plt.*309a:—Med., *get* a person *punished*, Ar.*V.*406, Pl.*Prt.*324c, v. l. X.*Cyr.*1.2.7:—Pass., *to be punished*, etc., Antipho 3.3.7, X.*Cyr.*5.2.1, etc.; of divine *retribution*, Plu.2.566e; *suffer injury*, Ael.*NA*3.24. 3. of a drastic method of checking the growth of the almond-tree, Thphr.*HP*2.7.6:—Pass., Id.*CP*1.18.9; cf. κόλασις I. 4. Pass. c. gen., *to be badly in need of*, *PFay.*120.5 (i/ii A. D.), cf. 115.19 (ii A. D.), *BGU*249.4 (ii A. D.).

**Κολαινίς**, ίδος, ἡ, obscure epith. of Artemis, Hellanic.163J., Ar. *Av.*874, Metag.1, *IG*3.216, Paus.1.31.5.

**κολᾰκ-εία**, ἡ, *flattery*, *fawning*, Democr.268, Pl.*R.*590b, *Grg.*463c, 465b, Thphr.*Char.*2, etc.; πολλὴν κολακείαν πεποίηται Aeschin.3.162, cf. Cic.*Att.*13.27.1; περὶ κολακείας, title of treatise by Phld. **-ευμα**, ατος, τό, *piece of flattery*, X.*Oec.*13.12 (pl.), Plu.*Demetr.*17. II. of a person, Sch.S.*Aj.*381. **-ευτέος**, α, ον, *to be flattered*, Luc.*Merc. Cond.*38, etc. II. -ευτέον, *one must flatter*, Ap.Ty.*Ep.*7, Sch.rec.A. *Th.*705. **-ευτής**, οῦ, ὁ, = κόλαξ, *Gloss.* **-ευτικός**, ή, όν, *sycophantic*, Luc.*Cal.*10; ἡ -κή (sc. τέχνη), = κολακεία, Pl.*Grg.*464c; κ. τέχναι Phld.*Lib.*p.42O.: Sup., Gal.10.4. Adv. -κῶς Str.17.1.43 (v.l. κολακικῶς), Poll.4.51, Charito 8.4. **-εύω**, *to be a flatterer*, Ar.*Eq.*48, Pl.*R.*538b, *Grg.*521b, Antiph.144.2, Diod.Com.2.34, Phld.*Ir.*p.66 W. 2. c. acc., *flatter*, And.4.16, X.*HG*5.1.17, Isoc.4.155, Ephipp.6, etc.; τὴν πόλιν Pl.*Alc.*1.120b: metaph., τὴν κατάποσιν κ. Muson.*Fr.*18$^A$p.97H.:—Pass., *to be flattered*, *be open to flattery*, Democr.115, D.8.34, etc. 3. metaph., *soften*, *render mild*, Alex. Trall.1.11, al. **-ικός**, ή, όν, = κολακευτικός, Arist.*EE*1222$^b$4: ἡ -κή (sc. τέχνη), = κολακεία, Pl.*Grg.*502d, *Sph.*222e: Comp. -ώτερος Luc.*Pr.Im.*22: Sup. -ώτατος, πρὸς τοὺς ὑπερέχοντας Plb.13.4.5. Adv. -κῶς Poll.4.51, Aristaenet.1.16, Chor. in *Rh.Mus.*49.521, v.l. in Str. 17.1.43. **-ίς**, ίδος, ἡ, fem. of κόλαξ; then, = κλιμακίς 2, Clearch. 25, Plu.2.50d.

**Κολᾰκοφωροκλείδης**, ου, ὁ, *flattering son of a thief*, parody on the name of Hierocleides, Hermipp.38, Phryn.Com.17.

**Κολᾰκώνῠμος**, ὁ, *parasite-named*, Com. distortion of the name Kleonymos, Ar.*V.*592.

**κόλαξ**, ᾰκος, ὁ, *flatterer*, *fawner*, Ar.*Pax* 756, Lys.28.4, Pl.*Phdr.* 240b, etc.; τύχης κόλακες Antipho Soph.65; πάντες οἱ κ. θητικοὶ καὶ οἱ ταπεινοὶ κ. Arist.*EN*1125$^a$1, cf. 1108$^a$29, Thphr.*Char.*2.1; *parasite*, Eup.159.1, Antisth.ap.D.L.6.4. 2. in later Gr., = Att. γόης, Moer. p.113P. II. lisping pronunciation of κόραξ, Ar.*V.*45.

**κολαπ-τήρ**, ῆρος, ὁ, *chisel*, *IG*11(2).199*A*86 (Delos, iii B. C.), 7.3073. 132 (Lebad.), Plu.2.350d, Luc.*Somn.*13. **-τός**, ή, όν, *engraved*, κ. γράμμα *an inscription*, *Sammelb.*5629 (Egypt, iii B. C.). **-τω**, of birds, *peck*, κολάψασα ἐξέλεψεν τὸν νεοσσόν, of a hen, Hp.*Nat.Puer.*30; κ. τὰ ἕλκη, τὰ ὄμματα, Arist.*HA*609$^a$35, $^b$6; τὸ ἧπαρ, of the eagle and Prometheus, Luc.*Sacr.*6 codd.; τινα, of a crane, *AP*11.369 (Jul. Antec.): metaph., of a man, ᾠὰ κ. Anaxil.18.4; of rain-drops breaking up the soil, Thphr.*Fr.*30.2; of horses, *strike* with the hoof, App. *Pun.*129; of Pegasos, *produce by striking* the ground with his hoof, κρήνην *AP*15.25.19 (Besant.). 2. *carve*, *engrave*, γράμμα εἰς αἴγειρον ib.9.341 (Glauc.); τὸ δόγμα κολαφθὲν εἰς στάλαν *IG*14.256 (Phintias), cf. 952 (Acragas), Πολέμων 1.30 (Demetrias), Luc.*Dips.*6, *PLeid.X.*36.

**κόλ-ᾰσις**, εως, ἡ, *checking the growth* of trees, esp. almond-trees, Thphr.*CP*3.18.2 (pl.). 2. *chastisement*, *correction*, Hp.*Praec.*5, Pl.*Ap.*26a, al., Th.1.41; opp. τιμωρία, Arist.*Rh.*1369$^b$13; of divine *retribution*, *Ev.Matt.*25.46, al.: pl., Pl.*Prt.*323e, al., Phld.*Ir.*p.52 W. **-ασμα**, ατος, τό, *chastisement*, Ar.*Fr.*385, X.*Cyr.*3.1.23, Critias 25.4D., *AP*5.217.7 (Agath.). **-ασμός**, ὁ, = κόλασις, Plu. *Alc.*13, al.

**κολασσία**· ἀνδριάντος σκιά, καὶ τὸ ἐς ὕψος ἀνάστημα, Hsch.

**κολ-άστειρα**, ἡ, fem. of κολαστήρ, *AP*7.425 (Antip. Sid.). **αστέος**, α, ον, *to be chastised*, *punished*, Pl.*Grg.*527b. II. κολαστέον, *one must prune*, *check*, τὰς ἐπιθυμίας ib.492d. **-αστήρ**, ῆρος, ὁ, = κολαστής, Arr.*Fr.*144J.: as Adj., στρατιῶται Eun.*VS*p.480B. **-αστήριος**, ον, = κολαστικός, δύναμις Ph.1.269, al. II. Subst. κολαστήριον, τό, *house of correction*, Luc.*Nec.*14, *VH*2.30. 2. *instrument of correction*, κολαστήρια θαλάσσης, of the whips of Xerxes, Plu.2.342f. 3. = κόλασμα, X.*Mem.*1.4.1. **-αστής**, οῦ, ὁ, *chastiser*, *punisher*, Ζεύς τοι κ. τῶν ὑπερκόπων ἄγαν φρονημάτων A.*Pers.*827, cf. S.*OT*1148, E. *Heracl.*388, Pl.*Lg.*863a, Epicur.*Sent.*34, Phld.*Mort.*17, etc.; κ. τῶν ἀδικούντων Lys.27.3, cf. Gorg.*Fr.*6; νόμοι κ. Critias 25.6D.; *tormentor*, in Hades, Plu.2.567d (pl.). **-αστικός**, ή, όν, *corrective*, *punitive*, -κή, ἡ, Pl.*Sph.*229a; δύναμις Ph.1.496; τὸ -κόν Plu.2.458b; τὸ κ. εἶδος Luc.*Phal.*1.8: c. gen., φάρμακα κ. τῆς κακίας Gal.14.760. 2. *given to punishing*, Jul.*Caes.*312d. **-άστρια**, ἡ, fem. of κολαστήρ, ῥάβδος Ezek.*Exag.*121.

**κολάττη**· κόλακα, Hsch. (perh. Boeot. for κολάσαι).

**κολᾰφ-ίζω**, *slap*, *buffet*, τινα *Ev.Matt.*26.67, *Sammelb.*6263.23:—Pass., 1*Ep.Cor.*4.11. **-ος**, ὁ, (κολάπτω) *buffet*, = κόνδυλος, Epich. 1 (as pr. n.), cf. Hsch., *Gloss.*; cf. Lat. *colaphus*.

**κόλαψ**, *stirps*, *Gloss.*

**κολέα**, ἡ, name of a *dance*, Hsch.:—also **κολία**, Id. **κολεάζω**,

sheathe: ⊛ –ασμός, ὁ, *sheathing*, Id. :—also –αρχος· κακόσχολον ὄνομα, Id. **κολεῖν**· ἐλθεῖν, Id.

**κολεκάνος** or **κολοκάνος**, ὁ, *lank, lean person*, dub. in Stratt.64.

**κολεόν**, Ep. and Lyr. usu. **κουλεόν**, τό, *sheath, scabbard*, ἕλκετο δ' ἐκ κολεοῖο μέγα ξίφος Il.1.194; κολεῷ μὲν ἄορ θέο Od.10.333; ἂψ δ' ἐς κουλεὸν ὦσε μέγα ξίφος Il.1.220; ξίφεος μέγα κουλεόν 3.272; ἀτὰρ περὶ κουλεὸν ἦεν ἀργύρεον 11.30, cf. Od.11.98, Pi.*N.*10.6; κολεῶν ἐρυστὰ..ξίφη S.*Aj.*730; φάσγανον κώπης λαβὼν ἐξεῖλκε κολεοῦ E.*Hec.*544; ἐν κολεῷ X.*Cyr.*1.2.9; μάχαιρα ἐλεφάντινον τὸ κολεὸν (sic) ἔχουσα *IG* 2².1382.16 (κολεόν ib.1388.47); κολεὰ δύο ib.11(2).203 *B* 39 (Delos, iii B.C.); κ., μέγα λώτινον ἔργον Theoc.24.45. 2. in insects, *sheath, wing-case*, Arist.*HA* 531ᵇ24.

**κολεόπτερος**, ον, *sheath-winged*, of beetles, Arist.*HA* 490ᵃ14, al.

⊛ **κολεός**, ὁ, = κολεόν, Hecat.22 J., Hsch., *Gloss.*; also, = λάρναξ, ὑδρία, Hsch. 2. v. κολιός. II. in form **κουλεός**, ὁ, *sheath of the heart, pericardium*, Hp.*Cord.*3.

**κολεοφόροι**, οἱ, *sheath-bearers*, name of a Comedy, *IG* 14.1097.

**κόλερος**, α, ον, (κόλος, ἔρος B) *short-wooled*, οἶες Arist.*HA* 596ᵇ 5. 2. κολερά· νόθα, νωθρά, Hsch. (Accent varies in codd.; κολέρον Theognost.*Can.*131.)

⊛ **κολετράω**, *trample on*, τινα Ar.*Nu.*552.

**κοληβάζω**, = ἐγκοληβάζω, Hsch. **κολία**, v. κολέα.

⊛ **κολίανδρον**, τό, = κορίανδρον, *Gp.*12.1.2, 16.4.5, Sch.Ar.*Eq.*679.

**κολίας**, ου, ὁ, *coly-mackerel, Scomber colias*, Epich.62, Ar.*Fr.*414, Arist.*HA* 598ᵃ24, Opp.*H.*1.184.

**κολίδιον**, τό, Dim. of foreg., Xenocr.ap.Orib.2.58.152.

⊛ **κολιός**, ὁ, *green woodpecker, Picus viridis*, Arist.*HA* 593ᵃ8, al. (vv. ll. κολεός, κελεός).

⊛ **κόλλᾰ**, ης, ἡ, *glue*, Hdt.2.86, Hp.*Art.*33, Arist.*Ph.*227ᵃ17, *IG* 2².1672.68. 2. *flour-paste*, Dsc.2.85.

**κολλᾰβίζω**, play a game, in which one holds his eyes, while the other strikes him, and bids him guess which hand he has been struck with, Poll.9.129.

**κόλλᾰβος**, ὁ, = κόλλοψ, Luc.*DDeor.*7.4, Iamb.*VP* 26.118 (pl.). II. kind of *cake* or *roll* (cf. κόλλυβος I. 3), Ar.*Ra.*507, *Pax* 1196, *Fr.*497, 506, Philyll.4.

⊛ **κολλάριον**, = Lat. *collarium*, *Gloss.*

⊛ **κολλ-άω**, (κόλλα) *glue, cement*, τι περὶ τὸν τράχηλον, τι πρός τι, Pl.*Ti.*75d, 82d; ἐπιστύλια ἐπὶ τοὺς κίονας *IG* 2².1668.46; *mend* a broken vessel, ib.11(2).161 *A* 111 (Delos, iii B.C.), *POxy.*1449.15 (iii A.D.). 2. *join* one metal or other substance to another, κ. χρυσὸν ἔν τε λευκὸν ἐλέφαντα, i. e. *make* [a crown] *inlaid with* gold and ivory, Pi.*N.*7.78:—Pass., κολλώμενα *glued together*, opp. γομφούμενα, Ar.*Eq.*463; ὁ κολλώμενος σίδηρος *welded* iron, Plu.2.619a; στραγγαλὶς χρυσᾶ κεκολλημένη *POxy.*1449.23 (iii A.D.). II. generally, *join fast together, unite*, ἄλφιτον ὕδατι Emp.34; χαλκὸν ἐπ' ἀνέρι κολλᾶν, of one applying a cupping-glass, Cleobulina 1, cf. Gal.*Thras.*23; *close up* wounds, Id.11.440:—Pass., κολλέεσθαι, of poison entering the system, Hp.*Ep.*19 (*Hermes* 53.66); κολλᾷ καὶ συνδεῖ πάντα ἤθη [ὁ πόθος] Pl.*Lg.*776a:—Pass., *cleave to*, κεκόλληται γένος πρὸς ἄτᾳ *is indissolubly bound* to.. (Blomf. for προσάψαι), A.*Ag.*1566 (lyr.); λόγος εἰς τὰ σπλάγχνα κολληθείς Philem.113.4; of persons, κ. τινί *Act.Ap.*5.13; of things, ὁ κονιορτὸς ὁ κολληθεὶς τινι *Ev.Luc.*10.11: sens. obsc., *AP* 11.73 (Nicarch.). III. *put together, build*, Pi.*O.*5.13:—Med., *fit together*, τροχάλεια Arat.530. –**εψός**, οῦ, ὁ, (κόλλα, ἕψω) *glue-boiler*, *IG* 2².1558.10, Poll.7.183.

**κολλήγ-ας**, α, ὁ, = Lat. *collega*, *IG* 14.1063 (nisi n. pr.): gen. pl., *Sammelb.*7252.25. –**ιον**, τό, = Lat. *collegium*, D.C.38.13, *IGRom.*1.1314 (Egypt), etc.

**κολλ-ήεις**, εσσα, εν, (κόλλα) *glued together, close-joined*, ξυστά Il.15.389, cf. 678; ἅρματα Hes.*Sc.*309. ⊛ –**ημα**, ατος, τό, (κολλάω) *that which is glued* or *fastened together*, Hp.*Art.*33, *IG* 11(2).287 *B* 152 (Delos, iii B.C.); βυβλιδίου κ. Antiph.162; esp. of the *sheets of papyrus gummed together* to form a roll, *PMag.Par.*1.2068, 2513, *BGU* 16.9 (ii A.D.), etc. II. hymenic *obstruction*, Aët.16.108 (98). –**ήσιμος**, η, ον, *glued together*, prob. in *Gloss.*; Subst. –**μον**, τό, *volume of* κολλήματα, *Stud.Pal.*1.28.8 (iii A.D.). ⊛ –**ησις**, εως, ἡ, (κολλάω) *gluing*, Hp.*Art.*39, Gal.18(1).456, Thphr.*HP* 5.7.4; *soldering*, κ. σιδήρου Hdt.1.25, Plu.2.156b; κ. χρυσίου Thphr.*Lap.*26; σωλήνων *POxy.*915 (vi A.D.). II. generally, *fixing tight, close fastening*, Hp.*Art.*33; of the cupping-glass, Arist.*Rh.*1405ᵇ3. b. *closing up* of wounds, Heliod.ap.Orib.45.6.2, Gal.11.440, 12.102. c. *binding material*, ἡ πρὸς ἄλληλα κ. ἰχώρ ἐστι καὶ ὑγρότης μυξώδης Arist.*Spir.*485ᵃ1. 2. Rhet., *union of a verse quotation with prose*, Hermog.*Meth.*30. 3. metaph., *close friendship*, Eun.*Hist.*p.267 D. 4. Astron., *apparent contact* of planet with fixed star, Ptol.*Alm.*8.4 (pl.); of two planets on the same meridian, Vett.Val.115.17. –**ητέον**, *one must fasten on, apply*, δρώπακα Philum.ap.Orib.45.29.18; σικύαν Herod.Med. in *Rh.Mus.*58.81. –**ητήρ**, ῆρος, ὁ, *soldering-iron*, *Gloss.* –**ητήριον**, τό, *glue*, Ph.*Bel.*77.50, *Gloss.* –**ητής**, οῦ, ὁ, *one who glues* or *fastens*, *PTeb.*316.70 (i A.D.), *Sammelb.*805 (iii A.D.), *Gloss.* –**ητικός**, ή, όν, *glutinous*, Arist.*Pr.*928ᵃ5 (Comp.), Plu.2.952b; δύναμις κ. τραυμάτων *closing up* wounds, Dsc.3.85; κ. φάρμακον Gal.11.439; κ. ἔργα *plumber's* work, *PLond.*3.1177.283 (ii A.D.): Dor. **κολλᾱτικόν**, τό, = κόλλα, *IG* 4²(1).102.69 (Epid.).

⊛ **κολλητίωνες**, οἱ, *military police-agents*, *POxy.*1100.19 (iii A.D.), Keil-Premerstein *Dritter Bericht* Nos.9, 28, 55.

**κολλ-ητός**, ή, όν, *glued together, closely joined*, θύραι, σανίδες, Od.23.194, 21.164; ἅρμα, δίφρος, ξυστόν, Il.4.366, 19.395, 15.678; ὄχοι E.*Hipp.*1225; ὕδασι καὶ γῆ κ. Pl.*Plt.*279e; ὑποκρητηρίδιον *with figures welded* on, Hdt.1.25, cf. Paus.10.16.1. –**ητρα**, τά, *cost of plumber's labour*, *POxy.*736.91 (i A.D.). –**ίζω**, late form for κολλάω, *Gp.*4.14.1.

**κολλίκιον** [λῑ], τό, Dim. of κόλλιξ, Greg.Cor.p.549 S.

**κολλίκιος** [λῑ], α, ον, *κόλλιξ-shaped*, ἄρτοι Ath.3.112f.

**κολλῑκοφάγος** [ᾰ], ον, *roll-eating*, epith. of Boeotians, Ar.*Ach.*872, prob. in Ephipp.1.

**κόλλιξ**, ῑκος, ὁ, *roll* or *loaf of coarse bread*, Hippon.35.6, Nicopho 15; κ. Θεσσαλικός Archestr.*Fr.*4.12. II. Medic., = τροχίσκος, rubbed up and taken in wine, Hp.*Int.*23, cf. Gal.19.103; = κολλύριον I. 1, Hp.*Epid.*2.6.29.

**κολλιστής**, = κολλητής, *Gloss.*

**κολλοβάλοισι**, dat. pl., dub. sens. in *Tab.Defix.* in *Rh.Mus.*55.85 (Crete, iii B.C.).

**κολλομελέω**, *patch verses together*, Com. word, Ar.*Th.*54.

**κολλοπ-εύω**, *to be a* κόλλοψ II. 2, Pl.Com.186.5. –**ίζω**, (κόλλοψ I. 1) *tighten with screws*, Hsch.

**κολλοποδιώκτης**, ου, ὁ, (κόλλοψ II. 2) Com. name for a gross debauchee, Sch.Ar.*Nu.*347, Eust.1915.16, Suid. s. v. ἀγρίους.

**κολλοπόω**, *glue together*, because glue was boiled out of κόλλοψ II. 1, Achae.22, *EM* 323.22.

**κολλοπώλης**, ου, ὁ, (κόλλα) *dealer in glue*, Poll.7.183.

⊛ **κολλόροβον**, τό, *shepherd's staff* or *crook*, *BGU* 759.13 (ii A.D., written κολλωρ–); applied to the so-called *club* of Orion and Bootes (which has this form), Hipparch.1.7.15, 2.6.1ᵇ, Ptol.*Alm.*7.5, 8.1. II. masc. and neut., dub. sens., apptly. a weight or a coin, *Sammelb.*6954. III. pl., v. l. for κιλλοβόροι in Poll.1.143. IV. κολόροβοι, gloss on σκοιά, Hsch.; κολόροβον, gloss on κορύνη, Id.

⊛ **κολλούρ-α**, ἡ, *roll* or *loaf* of bread (?), *PLond.ined.*2172; cf. κολλύρα. –**ιον**, τό, Dim. of foreg., *POxy.*1731.8 (iii A.D.). II. v. κολλύριον.

**κολλουρίς**, ίδος, ἡ, *marsh-mallow*, *Gloss.*

**κόλλουρος**, ὁ, an unknown *fish*, Marc.Sid.22.

⊛ **κόλλοψ**, οπος, ὁ, *peg* or *screw* by which the strings of the lyre were tightened, Od.21.407, cf. Pl.*R.*531b, Luc.*DMar.*1.4: metaph., τῆς ὀργῆς..τὸν κόλλοπ' ἀνεῖμεν Ar.*V.*574. 2. *bar* by which a windlass was turned, Arist.*Mech.*852ᵇ12. II. *thick skin on the upper part of the neck* of oxen, Ar.*Fr.*646; and of swine, ib.506.3. 2. metaph., = ἀνδρόγυνος, *cinaedus*, Eub.11, Diph.43.22, *AP* 12.42 (Diosc.), cf. Hsch.

**κολλῠβάτεια**, v. κουλυβάτεια.

**κολλῠβ-ιστήριον**, τό, *money-changer's office*, *PTeb.*485 (ii B.C.). ⊛ –**ιστής**, οῦ, ὁ, *small money-changer*, Lys.*Fr.*149 S., Men.1023, *PPetr.*3 p.173 (prob. l.), *Ev.Matt.*21.12, etc.: condemned by Phryn.404. –**ιστικός**, ή, όν, *of a money-changer*, τράπεζα *Ostr.Strassb.*9 (iii B.C.), *BGU* 1118.23 (i B.C.), etc. –**ος**, ὁ, *small coin*, κολλύβου *for a doit*, Ar.*Pax* 1200, Eup.233, Call.*Fr.*85: masc. acc. to Phryn.404, Hsch.:—but neut. **κόλλῠβον**, τό, Poll.9.72. 2. *small gold weight*, Thphr.*Lap.*46. 3. neut. pl. κόλλυβα, τά, *small cakes* (cf. κόλλαβος II), Sch.Ar.*Pl.*768; cf. κόλλυβα· τρωγάλια, Hsch. II. κ., ὁ, *rate of exchange*, *IG* 12(5).817 (pl., Tenos, ii B.C.), *SIG* 672.32 (Delph., ii B.C.); *agio*, Cic.*Verr.*2.3.78.181, *Att.*12.6.1, *PFay.*56.7 (ii A.D.), etc. (Cf. Hebr. *ḥālap* 'change', 'exchange'.)

**κολλύρ-α** [ῠ], ἡ, prob. = κόλλιξ I, Ar.*Pax* 123, *Fr.*413, Plaut.*Poen.*137, Lxx 2 *Ki.*13.6, *POxy.*397 (i A.D.), Ath.3.111a; cf. κολλούρα. 2. used of τὰ ἐκ τέφρας πεπλασμένα (cf. κόλλιξ II), Thphr.ap.Hsch. –**ίζω**, *bake* κολλῦραι, Lxx 2 *Ki.*13.6. –**ικός**, ή, όν, *made of* κολλῦραι, *jus collyricum*, Plaut.*Pers.*95. –**ιον** [ῠ], τό, Dim. of κολλύρα, *pessary*, Hp.*Mul.*1.51 (in form κολλούριον), Dsc.1.1; used as substitute for a probe, Cels.7.4.4; *pellet*, *PHolm.*1.16, *PLeid.X.*69. 2. *eye-salve*, *Apoc.*3.18, *IG* 14.966.16 (ii A.D.), *PFlor.*177.20 (iii A.D.); stamped with the physician's seal, *CIL* 13.10021.64, al.: freq. in pl., Arr.*Epict.*2.21.20, 3.21.21, etc.; *salve* in general, *POxy.*1088 (sg. and pl., i A.D.):—on κ. I. 1 and I. 2, Antyll.ap.Orib.10.23.1–19. 3. = κολλύρα I, Lxx 3 *Ki.*12.24. II. *fine clay on which a seal can be impressed*, Luc.*Alex.*21. (Freq. written κολλούριον, as Hp. l. c. (v. l.), *PHolm.*, *PLeid.X.*, *PFlor.* ll. cc.)

**κολλῡριοποιέομαι**, *to be made into collyrium*, Dsc.*Eup.*1.197 (-λουρ-).

**κολλῡρίς**, ίδος, ἡ, Dim. of κολλύρα, Lxx 2 *Ki.*6.19, v.l. 13.6.

**κολλῡρίων**, ωνος, ὁ, a bird of the *thrush* kind, perh. *fieldfare*, *Turdus pilaris*, Arist.*HA* 617ᵇ9.

**κολλῡρόω**, in pf. part. Pass., κεκολλυρωμένον· λευκῷ κεχρισμένον, Hsch. (–όμενον cod.). **κολλύχνιον**· καρύου λέπισμα, Id.

⊛ **κολλώδης**, ες, *glutinous, viscous*, Pl.*Cra.*427b, Arist.*HA* 568ᵇ11, 623ᵇ30 (Sup.), Thphr.*CP* 5.16.4, Heraclid.Tarent.ap.Ath.3.120c, Aret.*SD* 1.11; of rheum in the eye, *PMed.Strassb.*p.6, Philum.*Ven.*14.2.

**κολλώροβον**, v. κολλόροβον.

**κόλλωτες**, οἱ, a kind of *stone*, Thrasyll.ap.Ps.-Plu.*Fluv.*16.2.

**κολόβαξ**, = κολόβιον, *Gloss.*

**κολοβ-ανθής**, ές, *bearing stunted* (i.e. *papilionaceous*) *flowers*, such as peas, Thphr.*HP* 8.3.3:—also **κολοβοανθής**, ib.6.5.3. –**ίζω**, *mutilate*, in Pass., *IG* 12(3).323 (Thera, i B.C./i A.D.). ⊛ –**ιομαφόριον**, τό, *short* μαφόριον (q.v.), *Sammelb.*7033.36 (v A.D.). –**ιον**, τό, *sleeveless* (or *short-sleeved*) *tunic*, *POxy.*921.6, 16 (iii A.D.), *PTeb.*406.17 (iii A.D.), Serv. ad Virg.*A.*9.616. 2. of the senatorial *clavus*, Ps.-Acro ad Hor.*Sat.*1.5.36.

**κολοβο-διέξοδος**, ον, *having a curtailed passage*, of stars whose rising and setting is invisible owing to sunrise and sunset, Ptol.*Phas.* p.8 H., al. **-κέρᾱτος**, ον, *with stunted horns, short-horned*, Sch. Il.16.117. **-κερκος**, ον, *with a docked tail*, Lxx *Le.*22.23. **-μάχη** [ᾰ], ἡ, *the interrupted battle*, name for Il.8, Sch.B Il.8 init.; also **-μᾰχία**, ἡ, Sch.Leid.Il.13.745 in Valck.*Animadv. ad Ammon.*p.181; cf. κόλος 3. **-ρῖν**, ῖνος, ὁ, ἡ, *slit-nosed*, Lxx *Le.*21.18:—**-ρῖνος**, ον, *with broken nose*, Roussel *Cultes Égyptiens* 220 (Delos, ii B.C.).

**κολοβός**, όν (also -ός, ή, όν Artem.2.3, *IG*v. infr.), *docked, curtailed*, c. gen., κολοβὸς ἀγέλη κεράτων Pl.*Plt.*265d; κ. χειρῶν *APl.*4.186 (Xenocr.). 2. abs., *maimed, mutilated*, X.*Cyr.*1.4.11; οὐδὲν κ. προσφέρομεν πρὸς τοὺς θεούς, ἀλλὰ τέλεια καὶ ὅλα Arist.*Fr.*101; ζῷα κ. Id.*GA*746ᵃ30, cf. 721ᵇ17; ὄνος κ. *PCair.Zen.*215.10 (iii B.C.), *PGen.*23.5 (i A.D.), *BGU*806.4 (i A.D.); of trees, *stunted*, τὰν ἐλαίαν τὰν κολοβάν *IG*14.352 i 11 (Halaesa), cf. Dsc.1.76; ἄνθη Thphr.*HP*8.3.3; of persons, *undersized*, Procop.*Arc.*8: generally, *short*, ἐσθῆτες Artem. l.c.; χιτὼν Dam.*Isid.*138; ξίφος Lyd.*Mag.*1.12; of a period in Rhet., *curtailed, incomplete*, Arist.*Rh.*1409ᵃ18 (so in Comp. -ώτερόν πως ὑφᾶναι τὸν λόγον Chor. in *Philol.*54.123); ὄνομα *half-uttered*, Them.*Or.*1.4b; of a cup, *broken, chipped*, Arist.*Metaph.*1024ᵃ15, Theopomp.Hist. 243; of a wall, *dwarf*, τειχίον, τεῖχος, App.*Mith.*26, Procop.*Aed.*2.1; of a cone, *truncated*, Hero *Stereom.*2.42: metaph., ἀρετή Max.Tyr.37.1; κίνησις, in paralysis, Gal.7.588; κ. κῦμα, = κωφόν, Sch.Ar.*Eq.*689. Adv. -βῶς *elliptically*, opp. σαφῶς, ἐρωτᾶσθαι Arist.*SE*176ᵃ40. II. κολοβόν, τό, a measure, *PLond.*5.1694.22, al. (vi A.D.).

**κολοβόστᾰχυς**, υ, *with short spikes*, of flowers, Dsc.1.7.

**κολοβότης**, ητος, ἡ, *stuntedness*, Plu.2.800e (pl.). 2. κ. πνεύματος *shortness* of breath in speaking, Id.*Dem.*6.

**κολοβοτράχηλος** [ᾰ], ον, *stump-necked*, Adam.2.21.

**κολοβουρος**, ον, *stump-tailed*, Hsch. s.v. κόθουρος.

**κολοβ-όω**, *dock, curtail, mutilate*, Arist.*Fr.*101, Plb.1.80.13; τὰς χεῖρας καὶ τοὺς πόδας Lxx 2*Ki.*4.12:—Pass., *to be mutilated, imperfect*, Arar.3, Thphr.*HP*3.6.3; τῆς γυναικὸς τὴν ῥῖνα κολοβοῦσθαι D.S.1.78; τῇ φώκῃ κεκολοβωμένοι πόδες Arist.*HA*487ᵇ23, cf. *GA*771ᵃ2: c. gen., κεκολοβῶσθαι τῶν ἐκτὸς μορίων Id.*PA*695ᵇ2. II. of Time, *curtail, shorten*, τὰς ἡμέρας *Ev.Marc.*13.20, cf. *Ev.Matt.*24.22 (Pass.). **-ώδης**, ες, *stunted, stumpy*, δάκτυλοι Polem.*Phgn.*51 (v.l.). **-ωμα**, ατος, τό, *the part taken away in mutilation*, Arist. *Metaph.*1024ᵃ13, Gal.10.1002; = ἔλλειψις μορίου, Antyll.ap.Orib.45.25.1. **-ωσις**, εως, ἡ, *mutilation*, Arist.*IA*708ᵇ8. 2. *shortening*, [χορδῶν] Iamb.*in Nic.*p.121 P.

**κολοι-άρχης**, ου, ὁ, *chief of jackdaws, jackdaw-general*, Ar.*Av.*1212. **-άω**, *scream like a jackdaw*, Poll.5.89. **-διον**· παραξιφίδιον, Hsch. **-δορον**· ξύλον μάχας ποιούντων ἐπεισφερόμενον (ἐπεσφαιρωμένον Salmasius), Id. **-ή**· φωνή, Id.; cf. κολῳός.

**κολοιός**, ὁ, *jackdaw, Corvus monedula*, Il.16.583, 17.755, Ar.*V.*129, *Av.*50, al., Thphr.*Char.*21.6, *Sign.*39, Arat.963, al., Ael.*NA*4.30, Dionys.*Av.*3.18; κραγέται κολοιοί Pi.*N.*3.82:—Arist.*HA*617ᵇ16 distinguishes three species, κορακίας, λύκος, βωμολόχος (qq.v.): he also mentions a web-footed κολοιός, found in Lydia and Phrygia, which is prob. the *little cormorant, Phalacrocorax pygmaeus*; cf. Ath.9.395e (citing Ar.*Ach.*875):—Proverbs: κολοιὸς ποτὶ κολοιόν 'birds of a feather flock together', Arist.*EN*1155ᵃ34, etc.; κολοιὸς ἀλλοτρίοις πτεροῖς ἀγάλλεται 'borrowed plumes', Luc.*Apol.*4; κύκνον ἡγοῦ τὸν κ. 'your geese are swans', Lib.*Ep.*42.3; of impudent noisy talkers, πολλοὶ.. σφε κατακρώζουσι κολοιοί Ar.*Eq.*1020; of Agathocles, Timae.145. (Cf. κολῳός, κολῳάω.)

**κολοιτία**, ἡ, a *tree* which grew in the Lipari islands, *Cytisus aeolicus*, Thphr.*HP*1.11.2; called **κολουτέα**, ib.3.17.2 (for 3.14.4 v. κολυτέα); **κολοιτέα, κολωτέα** (-οτ- cod.), **κοιλώτεα**, Hsch. II. *sallow, Salix cinerea*, found about Mount Ida, Thphr.*HP*3.17.3.

**κολοίφρυξ**· Ταναγραῖος ἀλεκτρυών, Hsch.

**κολοιώδης**, ες, *daw-like*, i.e. *flocking together*, Plu.2.93e.

**κολοκάνος**, ὁ, v. κολεκάνος.

**κολοκάσιον** [ᾰ], τό, Nic.*Fr.*82, Diph.Siph.ap.Ath.3.73a, Dsc.2.106; or **κολοκασία**, ἡ, Plin.*HN*21.87, v.l. in Dsc. l.c.:—*the root of* κύαμος Αἰγύπτιος, *Nelumbium speciosum*, ll.cc., Verg.*E.*4.20, etc. 2. Κολοκασία, surname of Athena at Sicyon, Ath.3.72b.

**κολοκορδόκολα**, ων, τά, Com. word, perh. = *tripe*, *AP*10.103 (Phld.).

**κολόκῡμα**, ατος, τό, *large heavy wave* before it breaks, *swell* that is the forerunner of a storm: metaph., of the swelling threats of Cleon, Ar.*Eq.*692 (expld. as κόλον κῦμα, Sch. ad loc.; τυφλὸν κῦμα, Hsch.; κωφὸν κῦμα, Suid.).

**κολοκύνθ-η**, Arist.*HA*591ᵃ16, al. (v.l. -ττη), Sor.1.124, etc.; Att. **-κύντη**, ἡ (cf. Phryn.401), Thphr.1.13.3, 7.1.2, al., Mnesim.4.30 (v.l. -τα, -θα), also Hp.*Vict.*2.54; acc. -την Epicr.11.16, *PMag.Leid.V.*12.25, etc.:—later **κολόκυντᾰ** (acc. -ᾰν) *PCair.Zen.*300.3 (iii B.C.), Lxx *Jn.*4.7 cod. A, *Gp.*12.19.7, Artem.1.67 (v.l.), Luc.*VH*2.37 (v.l.), Hsch. s.v. κυκύϊζα; gen. -της *PCair.Zen.*292.132, 319 (iii B.C.); acc. pl. -τας *PSI*6.553.14 (iii B.C.), *BGU*1120.13 (i B.C.); **κολόκυνθᾰ** *PSakk.* in *Rev.Égypt.*3.123 (iii B.C., also -τα ib.120, 122), Lxx l.c., Arist.*Pr.*923ᵃ14 codd., Dsc.2.134, 4.176, Luc. l.c., Hdn.Gr.1.253, v.l. for -θη (nom. sg.) in Gal.6.794, but nom. -θη, acc. -θην ib.561, al. codd.; nom. pl. -θαι *Edict.Diocl.*6.26, 27:—*round gourd, Cucurbita maxima*, Alc.*Oxy.*1788 *Fr.*4.6 (Aeol. acc. pl. -ταις), Hp.*Morb.*2.67, 69 (in acc. -θην, v.l. -την), Hermipp.79, Ar.*Fr.*569.6, Metag.16 (-θης codd.), Diocl.*Frr.*125, 141, Diph.Siph. et Mnesith.ap.Ath.2.59b; κ. Ἰνδική Menodorus ib.59a, Ph.*Bel.*89.43; κ. ἀγρία *colocynth, Citrullus Colocynthis*, Dsc. l.c.: symbolic of health, from its juicy nature, ὑγιώτερον κολοκύντας Epich.154, Sophr.34; as a lily was of death, ἢ κολοκύντην ἢ κρίνον *living* or dead, Diph.98, cf. Men.934:—for λημᾶν κολοκύνταις, v. λημάω. **-ιάς**, άδος, ἡ, *made from gourds*, βρωτὺς *AP* 11.371 (Pall.). **-ινος**, η, ον, *made* or *obtained from gourds*, ἔλαιον *PRev.Laws* 39.6 (written κολυκυνθ-, cf. 59.21, also κολυκυντ- 40.10, κολοκυντ- 55.9, al., iii B.C.); πλοῖα Luc.*VH*2.37:—hence Com. name **κολοκυνθο-πειρᾶταί**, οἱ, *gourd-pirates*, ibid. II. ἀμπέλου κολοκυν[θίνης], a kind of vine, *PCair.Zen.*33.14 (iii B.C.). **-ίς**, ίδος, ἡ, = κολόκυνθα ἀγρία, Dsc.4.176, Gal.12.34, al. **-ος**, ὁ, = κολοκύνθη, *AP*9.532 tit., *PLond.*5.1881 (vi A.D.); κ. ἄγριος Ps.-Dsc.4.176:—written **κολύκιντος** *PTeb.*131 (ii/i B.C.). **-ών**, ῶνος, ὁ, *gourd-patch*, *PHamb.*99.8 (i A.D.).

**κολοκύντ-η**, v. κολοκύνθη:—Dim. **-ιον**, τό, Phryn.Com.61. **-ινος**, v. κολοκύνθινος. **-ος**, ὁ, = κολόκυνθος, *AP*9.532.

**κολοκώνας**· τὰς βαλβῖδάς τινες, Hsch.

**κόλον**, τό, = ἡ τροφή, as etym. of κόλαξ, βουκόλος, δύσκολος and κοιλία, Ath.6.262a, copied by Eust.1817.53, 62 (who adds ἄκολος); applied to some form of preserved food in *PSI*5.535.39, 46 (iii B.C.). II. *colon*, part of the large intestine, Ar.*Eq.*455, Arist.*PA*675ᵇ7, Nic. *Al.*23, Poll.2.209.

**κολόροβ-ον** and **-ος**, v. κολλόροβον IV.

**κόλος**, ον, *docked*, δόρυ Il.16.117; of oxen, *stump-horned* or *hornless*, τὸ γένος τῶν βοῶν τὸ κ. Hdt.4.29; ὦ κόλε, addressed to a he-goat, Theoc.8.51 (s.v.l.); of the κεράστης, Nic.*Th.*260. 2. a kind of goat *without horns*, prob. the animal described by Str.7.4.8, Hsch. 3. κόλος μάχη, name of Il.8, Sch.Il.8 init.; cf. κολοβομάχη.

**Κολοσσηνός**, ή, όν, *Colossian*, Str.12.8.16.

**κολοσσ-ιαῖος**, α, ον, *colossal*, D.S.11.72 (-ττ-), al.; κ. μεγέθη Ph. 1.2; κ. τὸ μέγεθος Luc.*Herm.*71; κ. ἄγαλμα, ἀνδριάς, Hdn.1.15.9, *BGU*362 vi 5 (iii A.D.). **-ικός**, ή, όν, = foreg., εἰκών *AJA*17.29 (Sardis, i B.C.), D.S.2.34 (in form **κολοττ-**); ἔργα Str.1.1.23, cf. Plu.2.780a: generally, *enormous, gigantic*, κεφαλὴν κ. ἔχων [ἄνθρωπος] Phld.*Sign.*2.

**κολοσσο-βάμων** [ᾱ], ον, gen. ονος, *with colossal stride*, Lyc.615. **-ποιός**, ὁ, *maker of colossal statues*, Hero *Deff.*135.13. **-πόνος**, ὁ, = foreg., Man.4.570.

**κολοσσ-ός**, ὁ (also ἡ, v. infr.), **κολοττ-** D.S.1.67:—*colossus, gigantic statue*, in Hdt. always of Egyptian works, 2.130, al.: of other *colossal statues*, Thphr.*Fr.*128, Sopat.1, Plb.18.16.2, Plin.*HN*34.45, Luc.*Hist.Conscr.*23, D.C.66.15; ὁ κ. ὁ ἡμαρτημένος Longin.36.3; dub. in *IG*1².577, 12(3).1015. 2. generally, *statue*, A.*Ag.*416 (lyr.), *Schwyzer* 89.17 (Argos, iii B.C.), Theoc.22.47; of small *images*, κολοσσὸς (acc. pl.), .. ἔρσενα καὶ θήλειαν ἢ καλίνος ἢ γαΐνος *Berl.Sitzb.*1927.167 (Cyrene): also fem., τὰς κ. ibid. **-ουργία**, ἡ, *making of a colossus*, Str.1.1.23.

**κολοσυρτός**, ὁ, poet. word, *noisy rabble*, ἀνδρῶν ἠδὲ κυνῶν Il.12.147, cf. 13.472; τὸν Ἀθηναίων Ar.*V.*666; παιδαρίων καὶ γραϊδίων Id. *Pl.*536: abs., *tumult, uproar*, Hes.*Th.*880:—hence **κολοσυρτέω**, = θορυβῶ, Hsch.

**κολούλια**, τά, *gasteropod molluscs*, Xenocr.ap.Orib.2.58.79; written *coluthia*, Plin.*HN*32.84, 147.

**κολουρ-αῖος**, η, ον, = κόλουρος, κ. πέτρη a *steep, abrupt* rock, Call. *Fr.*66. **-ία**, ἡ, = ἀποτομία, Hsch. **-ῖτις**· γῆ (Sicel), Id.

**κολουρό-κωνος**, ὁ, *truncated cone*, Hero *Metr.*3.22. **-πῡρᾰμίς**, ίδος, ἡ, *truncated pyramid*, Theo Sm.p.42 H.

**κόλουρ-ος**, ον, (κόλος, οὐρά) *dock-tailed, stump-tailed*, metaph., ὥσπερ ὑπὸ γήρως ἀπτῆνα καὶ κ. Plu.*Flam.*21:—fem. **κόλουρις**, of the fox in the fable, Timocr.3; cf. κοθοῦριν. 2. generally, *truncated*, πυραμίς Nicom.*Ar.*2.14. II. κόλουροι (sc. γραμμαί), αἱ, *colures*, two great circles passing through the equinoctial and solstitial points, intersecting at the poles, Hipparch.1.11.17 (sg.), Theo Sm. p.132 H., etc. (in full οἱ κ. κύκλοι Gem.2.21): sg., *Theol.Ar* 55. III. a kind of *fig*, Ath.3.75d. **-ωσις**, εως, ἡ, = κολόβωσις 1, Iamb.*Protr.* 21.κζ'.

**κόλ-ουσις**, εως, ἡ, *docking, cutting short*, ἡ τῶν ὑπερεχόντων σταχύων κ. Arist.*Pol.*1311ᵃ21, cf. Thphr.*CP*2.15.4, 5.17.5 (pl.); κ. δυνάμεως Plu.*Arist.*7. **-ουσμα**, ατος, τό, *that which is cut off, a piece*, Hsch. **-ουστός**, ή, όν, *docked, without horns*, Id. s.v. κόλον.

**κολουτέα**, ἡ, v. κολοιτία.

**κολούω**, Il.20.370, E.*Fr.*92, Pl.*Lg.*731a: fut. -ούσω Plu.*Alc.*34: aor. ἐκόλουσα Pl.*Prt.*343c, Arist.*Pol.*1274ᵃ8:—Pass., fut. -ουθήσομαι Gal.9.529: aor. ἐκολούθην Th.7.66, -ούσθην A.*Pers.*1035 (lyr.): pf. κεκόλουμαι *AP*7.234 (Phil.), Plu.*Ages.*31, etc., -ουσμαι D.C.*Fr.* 57.23: (κόλος):—*cut short, dock, curtail*, [ἀστάχυας] Hdt.5.92.ζ'; στάχυν σπάθῃ κ. φασγάνου E.*Fr.*373; *prune*, τὸν βότρυν Thphr.*CP* 2.15.5; [τὰ δένδρα] βελτίω κολουόμενά φασι γίγνεσθαι ib.2, cf. *IG*9(2).1109.81 (Coropa): c. gen., τὴν δ' ἐκόλουσεν οὐρῆς *docked* her of her tail, Opp.*H.*4.484. II. Hom. always metaph., τὸ μὲν τελέει, τὸ δὲ μεσσηγὺ κολούει part he brings to pass, part he *cuts off* half-accomplished, of the threats of Achilles, Il. l.c.; μηδὲ τὰ δῶρα.. κολούετε *curtail* them not, Od.11.340; ἐο δ' αὐτοῦ πάντα κολούει *cuts off* all his hopes, 8.211; κολούειν εἰς τὰ τῆς τέχνης ἔργα *hinders* performance in the art, Gal.5.733. 2. like κολάζω, which is more freq. in Prose, τὰ ὑπερέχοντα κ. *put down, abase* those who are exalted, Hdt.7.10.ε', cf. Arist.*Pol.*1284ᵃ37, 1313ᵃ40; δῆμον E.*Fr.*92; τοὺς ἄλλους κ. διαβολαῖς Pl.*Lg.* l.c., cf. *Ap.*39d; τὸ ῥῆμα *discredit* it, Id.*Prt.* l.c.; τὴν ἐν Ἀρείῳ πάγῳ βουλὴν Arist.*Pol.*1274ᵃ8; κ. καὶ θεραπεύειν, κ. καὶ ταπεινώσειν τινά, Phld.*Lib.*p.60 O., Plu.*Alc.* l.c.:—Pass., *to be balked*,

*thwarted*, σθένος ἐκολούσθη A.l.c.; νούσῳ κεκολουμένος *AP*l.c.; ἐπειδὰν ᾧ ἀξιοῦσι προὔχειν κολουθῶσι when *they are worsted* in a matter in which they claim superiority, Th.l.c.; ἀτιμαζόμενα καὶ κολουόμενα Pl.*R*.528c, cf. *Euthd*.305d, Plu.*Ages*. l.c.

❀**κολοφών**, ῶνος, ὁ, *summit, top, finishing*, κολοφῶνα ἐπιτιθέναι put *the finishing touch* to.., Pl.*Euthd*.301e, *Lg*.673d; τὸν κ. προσβιβάζειν Id.*Tht*.153c; κ. ἐπάγειν τῷ λόγῳ Ael.*NA*13.12; κολοφῶν ἐπὶ τῷ λόγῳ εἰρήσθω Pl.*Lg*.674c; κ. τοῦ λόγου *Com.Adesp*.433; later κ. τῆς ἀσεβείας *height* of impiety, Jul.*Gal*.333c; of persons, ὁ κ. τῆς ἀδικίας the *arch*-criminal, Lib.*Decl*.30.12; τῶν ἀτοπημάτων κ. Zos.4.15. (Expld. by Str.14.1.28 from the belief that the cavalry of Colophon was so excellent that it always decided the contest.) II. sort of *ball* for playing with, Plu.2.526e. III. = κολοιός, Hsch. 2. kind of *sea-fish*, Id.

**κολοφωνέω**, *put the crown on*, ἐπὶ πᾶσι τούτοις Steph. *in Hp*.1.248 D.

**Κολοφώνιος**, α, ον, *of* or *from Colophon* in Ionia, Hdt.1.147, etc.; K. σχῆμα, a figure of speech, such as using ἡ κεφαλὴ τῷ ἀνθρώπῳ for τοῦ –που, Lesb.Gramm.7: Subst., ἡ Κολοφωνία (sc. ῥητίνη), *Colophonian gum, resin*, Dsc.1.71, Gal.13.475, *Hippiatr*.20, al., *PGrenf*.1.52.7 (iii A. D.); also, = σκαμμωνία, Ps.-Dsc.4.170; Κολοφώνιον (sc. ὑπόδημα), τό, kind of *shoe*, Rhinth.4; also, a measure used in Egypt, *Ostr*.1166, 1265 (ii A. D.); but also, a kind of *vegetable*, *PTeb*.419.21 (iii A. D.).

**κολόχειρ**, ὁ, ἡ, *maimed in the hand*, Hsch.

**κολπ-αβρός**, όν, Ion. for κολφ-αβρός, *soft of bosom*, Eust.1745.60. –**άριον**, τό, Dim. of κόλπος III.6, Archig.ap.Aët.9.39. –**ίας**, ου, ὁ, *swelling in folds*, πέπλος A.*Pers*.1060. 2. name of a wind, *blowing from the gulf*, Ph.Bybl.ap.Eus.*PE*1.10, Ach.Tat.*Intr.Arat*.33. –**ίζω**, *form into a bosom* or *fold*, Suid. –**ίτης** [ῑ], ου, ὁ, *dwelling on a bay*, Philostr.*VA*3.35, 6.16.

**κολποειδής**, ές, *like a bay*, Ael.*NA*14.8. Adv. –δῶς Str.9.1.1.

**κόλπος**, ὁ, *bosom, lap*, παῖδ' ἐπὶ κόλπῳ ἔχουσα Il.6.400; ἂψ ὁ πάϊς πρὸς κόλπον ἐκλίνθη ib.467; ἡ δ' ἄρα μιν κηώδεϊ δέξατο κόλπῳ (cf. III. 1) ib.483; ἱμάντα τέῳ ἐγκάτθεο κ. put the girdle in thy *bosom*, 14.219; εἰς κόλπον πτύσαι Thphr.*Char*.16.15 (cf. πτύω); ἐν κόλπῳ εἶχες ὄφιν Thgn.602; ὁ κ. 'Αβραάμ *Ev.Luc*.16.22; freq. of pet birds or animals, τρέφειν ἐν κ. Herod.6.102; κυνίδιον ἐν κόλπῳ τιθηνούμενον *lapdog*, Plu.2.472c; κίσσαν ἐκ μέσων τῶν κόλπων ἁρπάσας Luc.*Jud.Voc*.8; so τὸ θυγάτριον ἐκ κόλπων τῶν ἐμῶν ἀναρπάσαντα Hld.4.14: metaph., εἰς τοὺς εὐανθεῖς κ. λειμώνων Ar.*Ra*.373 (lyr.); λειμώνων φύλλων τ' ἐν κόλποις ναίω Id.*Av*.1094 (lyr.); also τὰ ὑπὸ κόλπον, = τὰ ἀφροδίσια, Luc.*Alex*.39. 2. = αἰδοῖον γυναικεῖον, esp. *vagina*, Sor.1.16, al., Ruf.*Onom*.196, Poll.2.222: pl., Sor.1.70[b], S.E.*M*.5.62. b. κόλποι τῆς ὑστέρας supposed *sinuses* in the womb, Hp.*Nat.Puer*.31, Sor.1.9 (sg.), Gal.*UP*14.4. c. in poets more vaguely of the whole *sinus genitalis, womb*, in pl., E.*Hel*.1145 (lyr.), Call.*Jov*.15: sg., Id.*Del*.214; δεσποίνας ὑπὸ κόλπον ἔδυν Orph.*Fr*.32c.8; θεὸς διὰ κόλπου ib.31124: metaph., of the grave, σῶμα σὸν ἐν κόλποις.. γαῖα καλύπτει *IG*2.3839, cf. 3412, *Epigr.Gr*.214.7 (Rhenea); κ. ἡμερῶν, of the *womb* of time, Ezek.*Exag*.39. d. of other cavities, οἱ κ. τῆς κοιλίας, in the ἐχῖνος, Arist.*HA*530[b]27; of the *ventricles* of the heart, Poll.2.216. II. *fold of a garment*, esp. as it fell over the girdle, freq. in pl., δεύοντο δὲ δάκρυσι κ. Il.9.570, cf. A.*Pers*.539 (anap.), etc.: also in sg., κ. βαθὺν καταλιπόμενος τοῦ κιθῶνος Hdt.6.125; κόλπον ἀνιεμένη letting down the *bosom of her robe*, i.e. baring her breast, Il.22.80; ἐπὶ σφυρὰ κόλπον ἀνεῖσαι Theoc.15.134; κρύψε δὲ παρθενίαν ὠδῖνα κόλποις, i.e. she concealed her pregnancy *by the loose folds of her robe*, Pi.*O*.6.31; κατακρύψασ' ὑπὸ κόλπῳ Od.15.469; κόλπῳ φέρουσα.. πεπλώματος A.*Th*.1044; ὑπὸ κόλπου (v.l. –ῳ) χεῖρας ἔχειν 'keep one's hand in one's *pocket*', of a stingy person, Theoc.16.16; ὑπὸ κόλπου Luc.*Herm*.37, 81, *Hes*.2, *Merc.Cond*.27; ὑπὸ κόλπον Hsch. s. v. μασχαλοληπτεῖ, v.l. in Luc.*Ind*.12. III. any *bosom-like hollow*: 1. of the sea, first in a half-literal sense, of a sea-goddess, Θέτις δ' ὑπεδέξατο κόλπῳ received him *in her bosom*, Il.6.136, cf. supr. I. 1: generally, δῦτε θαλάσσης εὐρέα κ. 18.140, cf. Od.4.435; εἴσω ἁλὸς εὐρέα κ. Il.21.125: in pl., κατὰ δεινοὺς κ. ἁλός Od.5.52; also κόλποι αἰθέρος Pi.*O*.13.88; 'Ερέβους ἐν ἀπείροσι κ. Ar.*Av*.694. 2. *bay, gulf*, 'Ερμιόνην 'Ασίνην τε, βαθὺν κατὰ κ. ἐχούσας, i.e. βαθὺν κατεχούσας κόλπον, Il.2.560; Μηλιεὺς κ. A.*Pers*.486; κ. 'Ρέας, i.e. the Adriatic, Id.*Pr*.837; Τυρσηνικὸς κ. S.*Fr*.598, cf. Hdt.2.11, 7.58, 198, Th.2.90, etc. 3. *vale*, κ. 'Αργεῖος Pi.*P*.4.49; Νεμέας Id.*O*.9.87, cf. 14.23; 'Ελευσινίας Δηοῦς ἐν κόλποις S.*Ant*.1121 (lyr.); κ. Τροίας E.*Tr*.130 (lyr.); Πιερικὸς κ. Th.2.99, cf. X.*HG* 6.5.17. 4. of a fortified site, *salient*, Ph.*Bel*.86.8. 5. ὁ κ. τοῦ ἅρματος *bottom* of the chariot, Lxx 3*Ki*.22.35. 6. *fistulous ulcer* which spreads under the skin, Dsc.1.128, Heliod.ap.Orib.44.8.22, Gal.11.125. IV. in Tactics, *enveloping force*, Onos.21.5.

**κολποφακῆ**, Com. formation with play on βολβοφακῆ, Ath.13.584d.

❀**κολπ-όω**, *form into a swelling fold*; esp. *make* a sail *belly*, πνοιῇ.. λίνα κολπώσαντες *AP*9.363.10 (Mel.); ἄνεμος κ. τὴν ὀθόνην Luc.*VH* 1.9; χιτῶνας κολπώσαντες τῷ ἀνέμῳ, καθάπερ ἱστία ib.13:—Pass., *swell out*, of membranes, Hp.*Nat.Puer*.16; κολποῦται ὑμὴν φυσώμενος Arist.*HA*510[b]32; of Europa's garment, Mosch.2.129; κολποῦται Ζέφυρος εἰς ὀθόνας *AP*10.5 (Thyill.); of a bay, *curve*, Plb.34.11.5: Medic., *contain a sinus*, Heliod.ap.Orib.44.8.22: metaph. in pf. part. Pass., κεκολπωμένος *turgid*, of style, D.H.*Dem*.19. –**ώδης**, ες, *embosomed, embayed*, τὰν κολπώδη πτέρυγ' Εὐβοίας Αὖλιν E.*IA*120, etc.; *full of bays*, θάλασσα D.C.48.50. 2. *winding*, παράπλους Plb.4.44.7. II. metaph., of language, *turgid*, μηδὲν ἔχειν κ. D.H.*Dem*.18. –**ωμα**, ατος, τό, *bellying* or *bulging out*, of the centre in a line of battle, Plu.*Mar*.25. II. *garment with ample folds*, worn by kings in Tragedy, Poll.4.116, *An.Par*.1.19. –**ωσις**, εως, ἡ, *forming into a fold*, κ. πτερῶν *arching* of wings before the wind, Hdn.1.15.5. –**ωτός**, ή, όν, *formed into folds*, χιτῶνες Plu.2.173c; κολπωτὰν ὀθόναισι.. τρόπιν ἰθύνεσκον with *swelling* sails, *Hymn.Is*.153.

**κόλσασθαι**· ἱκετεῦσαι, Hsch.

**κολύβδαινα**, ἡ, kind of *crab*, Epich.57.

**κόλυβος**· ἔπαυλις, Hsch.; cf. καλύβη.

**κολύβριον**, τό, = μολόβριον (q.v.).

**κόλυθροι**, οἱ, *testicles*, Arist.*Pr*.913[b]20.

**κόλυθρον** or –**τρον**, τό, *ripe fig*, Philem.Gloss.ap.Ath.3.76f.

**κολυθροφιλάρπαξ**, ἄγος, ὁ, *one who loves to seize* κόλυθροι, prob. in Lyr. in *Philol*.80.334.

**κολύκιντος**, = κολόκυνθος (q.v.). **κολυκρίζοντες**· ἐκτελοῦντες, Hsch.

**κολύμβ-αινα**, ἡ, = κολύβδαινα, Archig.ap.Gal.13.174. ❀–**άς**, άδος, ἡ, less Att. form of κολυμβίς, κ. ἐλαία olive *swimming*, i.e. *pickled in brine*, Diph.Siph.ap.Ath.2.56b, *PSI*5.535.27 (iii B. C.), cf. Call.*Iamb*.1.273, Gal.6.609, al. II. as Subst., 1. = κολυμβίς, Ath.9.395e. 2. a shrub, = στοιβή, Gal.14.18. –**ατος**, ἡ, a plant, *Gp*.2.4.1. –**άω** (Dor. –**φάω** acc. to *EM*526.2), *dive, plunge headlong*, εἰς τὸν Τάρταρον Pherecr.108.21; εἰς τὰ φρέατα Pl.*Prt*.350a, cf. *La*.193c, Str.17.1.44, etc.; εἰς κολυμβήθραν μύρου Alex.300. 2. *swim*, τοὺς δυναμένους κολυμβᾶν *Act.Ap*.27.43, cf. *Hippiatr*.26. ❀–**ήθρα**, ἡ, *place for diving, swimming-bath*, Pl.*R*.453d, D.S.11.25; κ. μύρου Alex.300. II. *wine-vat, tun*, D.S.13.83. III. *reservoir, cistern*, Lxx 4*Ki*.18.17. IV. *baptismal font*, *POxy*.147 (vi A. D.). –**ησις**, εως, ἡ, pearl-*fishery*, *Peripl.M.Rubr*.35 (pl.), 58, Sch.Ptol.*Geog*.6.7.11. –**ητέον**, *one must swim*, Sch.Pl.*R*.453d. –**ητήρ**, ῆρος, ὁ, = sq., A.*Supp*.408. –**ητής**, οῦ, ὁ, *diver*, Th.4.26, Pl.*Prt*.350a, Arist.*PA*659[a]9, *Sammelb*.3747 (i B. C.), etc. II. *one who draws water from a well*, Hsch. (pl.). –**ητικός**, ή, όν, *of* or *for diving*: ἡ –κή (sc. τέχνη) the *art of diving*, Pl.*Sph*.220a. –**ίς**, ίδος, ἡ, *diver*, name of a bird, prob. *grebe*, *Podiceps minor*, Ar.*Av*.304, Arist.*HA*593[b]17, Alex.Mynd.ap.Ath.9.395d; cf. κολυμβάς II. 1: as Adj., κ. αἴθυιαι Arat.296. –**ιστής**, οῦ, ὁ, = –ητής, Sch.Opp.*H*.1.173. –**ιτεύω**, *plunge into a tank*, *PMasp*.9ii30 (vi A. D.). ❀–**ος**, ὁ, = κολυμβίς, Ar.*Ach*.876. II. = κολύμβησις, ἅμιλλα κολύμβου Paus.2.35.1, cf. Str.16.2.42, *AP*9.82 (Antip. Thess.), Plu.2.162f (pl.), Herod.Med.ap.Orib.10.39.3, Antyll.ib.6.27.4, X.*Eph*.3.2. 2. = κολυμβήθρα I, Hero *Mens*.19.

**κολύμφατος**· φλοιός, λεπίδιον, Hsch. **κολυμφάω**, v. κολυμβάω. **κολυρίζοντες**· ἐκκενοῦντες, Id. **κολυτέα**, ἡ, *bladder-senna, Colutea arborescens*, Thphr.*HP*3.14.4. **κόλυτρον**, τό, v. κόλυθρον. **κολύφανον**· φλοιός, λεπύριον, Hsch. (cf. κελύφανον). **κολυφρόν**· ἐλαφρόν, Id. **κόλφος**, = κόλπος, *Gloss*.

❀**κολχικόν**, τό, *meadow saffron, Colchicum speciosum*, Dsc.4.83.

**κόλχος**, ὁ, f.l. for κόχλος, *AP*9.551 (pl., Antiphil.), *APl*.4.37 (Leont.).

**Κόλχος**, ὁ, *Colchian*, Hdt.1.2, etc.:—Adj. **Κολχικός**, ή, όν, *Colchian*, Id.2.105:—poet. also **Κόλχος** στόλος A.R.4.485:—fem. **Κολχίς**, ίδος, Hdt.1.2 (but also Μηδεία τῇ Κόλχῳ Pl.*Euthd*.285c): as Subst. Κολχίς (sc. γῆ), *Colchis*, Hdt.1.104, etc.; (sc. γυνή) E.*Med*.132 (anap.).

❀**κολῳάω**, (κολῳός) *brawl, scold*, Il.2.212; Ion. κολῳέω Antim.37.

❀**κολῶμαι**, Att. fut. Med. of κολάζω (q.v.).

❀**κόλων**, ωνος, ὁ, = Lat. *colonus*, *Syria*5.347 (Dura).

**Κολωναί**, ἡ, = Κολωνός II, Call.*Fr*.428.

**κολωνεία**, ἡ, = Lat. *colonia*, *CIG*2811*b* (Aphrodisias), *POxy*.653 (ii A. D.), etc.; also **κολωνία** (q.v.).

❀**κολώνη**, ἡ, *hill, mound*, Il.2.811, 11.757, *Lyr.Adesp*.74; esp. *sepulchral mound, barrow*, S.*El*.894; later, *hill-top, peak*, D.P.150, al.; ὁπότ' ἀνθρώπων μεγάλας πλήσαιτο κ. Arat.120. (Cf. Lat. *collis, culmen*, Engl. *holm*.)

**Κολωνῆθεν**, Adv. *from the deme* Κολωνός (q.v.), D.21.64, *IG*2[2].650, etc.

**κολωνία**, ἡ, *grave* (Elean), Hsch. II. = Lat. *colonia*, *Act.Ap*.16.12, *Epigr.Gr*.908 (Batanaea); cf. κολωνεία.

**κολωνοειδής**, ές, *like a hill* or *barrow*, Sch.A.R.2.649.

**κολωνός**, ὁ, = κολώνη, *hill*, *h.Cer*.272, 298, Hes.*Fr*.122.1, Hdt.4.181, 7.225, etc.; κ. λίθων *heap* of stones, Id.4.92, X.*An*.4.7.25; *hill-top, peak*, A.R.1.1120. II. *Colonus*, deme of Attica, sacred to the hero Colonus (ἱππότης Κ. S.*OC*59); Οἰδίπους ἐπὶ Κολωνῷ, title of play by Sophocles:—hence **Κολωνεύς**, έως, ὁ, *one of the deme Colonos*, *IG*2.944.48. 2. K. ἀγοραῖος, mound in the Athenian ἀγορά, Κολωνόν.., οὐ τὸν ἀγοραῖον, ἀλλὰ τὸν τῶν ἱππέων Pherecr.134; labourers were hired there, *Com.Adesp*.35 D., hence called **Κολωνέται** or **Κολωνῖται**, Hyp.*Fr*.8.

❀**κολῳός**, ὁ, *brawling, wrangling*, κολῳὸν ἐλαύνετον Il.1.575, cf. A.R.1.1284.

**κόλωψ**· ἀμφιάτωρ, Hsch.

❀**κομάκτωρ**, ορος, ὁ, dub. sens., Rhinth.9, *Inscr.Magn*.217 (pl., i B. C.).

**κομανίαν**· πορνί, δαψιλῆν ἀνίαν, Hsch.

**κόμαρι**, εως, τό, red dye obtained from root of *Comarum palustre*, *PHolm*.14.2,5, al., Maria ap.Zos.Alch.p.155 B.:—also **κόμμαρι**, εως,

τό, PHolm.13.37, 16.5, al.; **κόμαρις** and **κώμαρις**, ἡ, Anon.Alch. pp.351,9 B.; **κόμαρον**, τό, ib.p.350 B., PHolm.25.15.

**κομᾰρίς**, ίδος, ἡ, a fish, Epich.47.

**κόμᾰρος**, ἡ, Ar.Av.620, Thphr.HP3.16.4, also ὁ, Amphis 38, Alciphr.3.12:—strawberry-tree, Arbutus Unedo, Ar. l. c., Thphr.HP1.5.2, Theoc.5.129, 9.11, Gal.12.34, Longus 2.16.

**κομᾰροφάγος**, ον, eating the fruit of the arbutus, Ar.Av.240.

**κομάς**· θεραπείας, καὶ τὰ συοφόρβια, Hsch.

**κοματροφέω**, = κόμην τρέφω, IG12(7).259.8 (Amorgos).

⊛ **κομάω**, Ion. -έω, (κόμη) let the hair grow long, Ἄβαντες ὄπιθεν κομόωντες Il.2.542; κάρη κομόωντες Ἀχαιοί 3.43, al.; κ. τὴν κεφαλήν Hdt.4.168; τὰ ὀπίσω κ. τῆς κεφαλῆς ib.180; τὰ ἐπὶ δεξιὰ τῶν κεφαλέων κ. ib.191; τὸ γένειον τῇ κεφαλῇ ὁμοίως κ. X.Smp.4.28; ξανθοτάτοις βοτρύχοισι κ. Pherecr.189; ἄρσεσιν οὐκ ἐπέοικε κ. Ps.-Phoc.212; Λακεδαιμόνιοι.. οὐ γὰρ κομῶντες πρὸ τούτου ἀπὸ τούτου κομᾶν Hdt.1.82, cf. Arist.Rh.1367$^a$29, Philostr.VA3.15; ἐλακωνομάνουν ἅπαντες.., ἐκόμων Ar.Av.1282; μὴ φθονεῖθ' ἡμῖν (sc. τοῖς ἱππεῦσι) κομῶσι Id.Eq.580; κομῶν καὶ αὐχμηρός Arist.Rh.1413$^a$9, cf. D.H.6.26; ἔνορκον ἂν ποιησαίμην μὴ πρότερον κομήσειν (in token of a vow) πρίν.. Pl.Phd.89c; ἀνὴρ μὲν ἐὰν κομᾷ, ἀτιμία αὐτῷ ἐστι· γυνὴ δὲ ἐὰν κομᾷ, δόξα αὐτῇ ἐστιν 1Ep.Cor.11.14-15. 2. plume oneself, give oneself airs, τοιοῦτος ἀνὴρ ὢν ποιητὴς οὐ κομῶ Ar.Nu.545, cf. Pl.170; οὗτος ἐπὶ τυραννίδι ἐκόμησε aimed at the monarchy, Hdt.5.71; ἐπὶ τῷ κομᾷς; on what do you plume yourself? Ar.V.1317; μηδὲν ταύτῃ γε κομήσῃς Id.Pl.572; κ. ἐπὶ κάλλει Plu.Caes.45, cf. Luc.Nigr.1; ἐπ' Ἠρίννῃ κ., of her lover, AP11.322 (Antiphan.): c. dat., Opp.C.3.192. II. of horses, χρυσέῃσιν ἐθείρῃσιν κομόωντε Il.8.42, 13.24. III. of the hair itself, to be long, Opp.C.3.28. IV. metaph., of trees, plants, etc., [οὖθαρ ἀρούρης] μέλλεν ἄφαρ ταναοῖσι κομήσειν ἀσταχύεσσιν soon were the fields to wave with long ears, h.Cer.454; μᾶζαι βώλοις κομῶσαι Cratin.165; ἁ δὲ καλὰ νάρκισσος ἐπ' ἀρκεύθοισι κομάσαι Theoc.1.133, cf. 4.57; αἴγειρος φύλλοισι κομόωσα A.R.3.928; ὄρος κεκομημένον ὕλῃ Call.Dian.41; ἡ γῆ φυτοῖς κομῶσα Arist.Mu.397$^a$24, cf. Ael.Fr.75; κομῶντα λήϊα Procop.Gaz.Ep.23. V. ἀστέρες κομόωντες, = κομῆται, Arat.1092.

**κόμβα**, = κορώνη (Polyrrhen.), Hsch. **κομβακεύομαι**, = κόμπους λέγω, Id. ⊛ **κόμβαλα**· παίγματά τινα, Id. **κόμβησαν**· ποιὸν ἦχον ἀπετέλεσαν, Id., Cyr. **κομβίζων**· φυσῶν, Hsch.

**κομβίον**, τό, = περόνη, buckle, Eust.794.13, Sch.E.Hec.1170.

**κομβο-θηλεία**, ἡ, buckle, Sch.E.Hec.1170; cf. κομποθήλυκα. -**λύτης** [ῠ], ου, ὁ, cut-purse, Hsch.

⊛ **κόμβ-ος**, ὁ, roll, band, girth, Anon.ap.Suid.; cf. κομποθηλαία. II. pl., = γομφίοι, Hsch. -**όω**, bind up, fasten, Gloss.:—Med., gird oneself, Hsch. ⊛ -**ωμα**, ατος, τό, robe, Id.: in pl., ornamental bands, Suid.

**κομέτιον**, τό, = Lat. comitium, IG14.951.

⊛ **κομέω** (A), Ep. impf. κομέεσκον Od.24.390:—Ep. Verb, take care of, tend, in Il. of horses, τούτω μὲν θεράποντε κομείτων 8.109, cf. 113, h.Ap.236; of dogs, Od.17.310, 319, Hes.Op.604; elsewh. in Od. always of men, γέροντα ἐνδυκέως κομέεσκεν 24.390, cf. 6.207, etc.; of children, σὺ δὲ τοὺς κομέειν ἀτιταλλέμεναί τε 11.250; κούρην.. κομέουσι τοκῆες IG3.1335, cf. Supp.Epigr.1.567 (Karanis, iii B.C.). (Prob. cogn. with κάμνω, q.v.)

**κομέω** (B), Ion. for κομάω.

**κόμ-η**, ἡ, hair of the head, Il.22.406, etc.: less freq. in pl., κὰδ δὲ κάρητος οὔλας ἧκε κόμας Od.6.231; κόμαι Χαρίτεσσιν ὁμοῖαι (i.e. κόμαις Χαρίτων) Il.17.51; κόμην κείρειν, κείρεσθαι (v. κείρω); κόμην τρέφειν to let the hair grow long, Hdt.1.82; κ. φορεῖν PGnom.188 (ii A.D.); κόμη δι' αὔρας ἀκτένιστος ἄσσεται S.OC1261; καθεῖσαν εἰς ὤμους κόμας E.Ba.695; κόμαι πρόσθετοι false hair, wig, X.Cyr.1.3.2, etc.; δοῦλος ὢν κόμην ἔχεις; Ar.Av.911; κόμης ἀναπλέως unkempt, Plu.Cic.30. 2. of the beard, Arr.Epict.4.8.4. 3. gill or branchia of the cuttle-fish, dub. in Arist.HA550$^b$18: pl., arms or suckers, Max.Tyr.4.5. II. metaph., foliage of trees, Od.23.195, Cratin.296, etc.; δόνακος App.BC4.28; of herbs, Dsc.4.164.7, Gal.6.268; of corn, λήϊου κ. Babr.88.3; λειμώνων κόμαι IG14.1389ii11; esp. = τραγοπώγων, Thphr.HP7.7.1, Dsc.2.143. III. luminous tail of a comet, Arist.Mete.343$^a$1, 346$^a$15. ⊛ -**ήεις**, εσσα, εν, leafy, Orph.Fr.258.

⊛ **κόμης**, ητος, ὁ, = Lat. comes, κ. πρώτου βαθμοῦ CIG4361 (Side), cf. IG14.1076, Zos.5.2, Cod.Just.1.4.20, etc.: gen. pl. κομίτων IG3.635:—Adj. **κομητικός**, ή, όν, PLond.1.113.6$^c$.24.

**Κομητᾰμῡνίας**, ου, ὁ, Com. adaptation of the name Amynias, Coxcomb-amynias (cf. κομάω 1), Ar.V.466.

**κομήτης**, ου, ὁ, (κομάω) wearing long hair, of the Persians, Orac. ap.Hdt.6.19; of dissolute men, Pherecr.14, Ar.Nu.348, 1101, etc.; ὁ ἐν Σάμῳ κ., prov. variously expld., Duris 62 J., etc.; also, simply, with hair on the head, opp. φαλακρός, Pl.R.454c, cf. Grg.524c; κ. τὰ σκέλη Luc.Bacch.2. 2. metaph., κ. ἰός a feathered arrow, S.Tr.567; κ. λειμών a grassy meadow, E.Hipp.210 (anap.); θύρσος κισσῷ κομήτης Id.Ba.1055. II. κομήτης, with or without ἀστήρ, ὁ, comet, Arist.Mete.343$^b$5, Epicur.Ep.2 p.52 U., etc. III. = τιθύμαλλος χαρακίας, Dsc.4.164.1.

**κομία**· εὐωχία, Hsch. **κομίατον**, τό, = Lat. commeatus, furlough, Id.

**κομῐδή**, ἡ, (κομίζω) attendance, care, Hom., etc.; in Il., of care bestowed on horses, 8.186, 23.411; in Od., of care bestowed on men, 8.453, 14.124; also, care bestowed on a garden, οὔ τι πρασιὴ τοι ἄνευ κομιδῆς κατὰ κῆπον 24.247, cf. 245: hence dat. κομιδῇ used as Adv. (q.v.). 2. provision, supplies, ἐπεὶ οὐ κ. κατὰ νῆα ἦεν ἐπηετανός 8.232. II. carriage, conveyance, esp. of supplies and provisions, τῶν ἐπιτηδείων τὴν περὶ τὴν Πελοπόννησον κ. Th.4.27; ὅθεν ῥᾴδιαι αἱ κ. ὧν προσέδει Id.6.21, cf. Isoc.11.14, etc.; λίθων IG4$^2$(1).103.75 (Epid.); gathering in of harvest, τοῦ καρποῦ, καρπῶν κ., X.Cyr.5.4.25, Arist.Pol.1335$^a$21; σίτου κ. Plb.5.95.5. b. Medic., removal, extraction, ὀδόντων Sor.2.62 (pl.); ἡ διὰ τομῆς κ. (sc. of stone in bladder) Gal.1.391. 2. (from Med.) carrying away for oneself, rescue, recovery, κατὰ Ἑλένης κομιδὴν Hdt.9.73; esp. recovery of a debt, D.38.9, Arist.EN1167$^b$31, Oec.1349$^a$7; μὴ ἔστω αὐτῷ κ. PHal.1.259 (iii B.C.). 3. (from Pass.) going or coming, ποιεύμενοι ταύτῃ τὴν κ. endeavouring to pass this way, Hdt.6.95; escape, safe return, κομιδῆς πέρι.. αὐτῷ μελήσειν ὥστε ἀσινέας ἀπικέσθαι ἐς τὴν Ἑλλάδα Id.8.19; οὔτε τις κ. τὸ ὀπίσω φανήσεται ib.108, cf. 4.134, al.; μένων δ' ὁ θεῖος ἀνὴρ πρίατο μὲν θανάτοιο κομιδὰν πατρός Pi.P.6.39, cf. A.R.3.1140, 4.1275.

**κομῐδῇ**, Adv. (dat. of foreg., orig. 'with care') exactly, just, ἐστὶ κ. μεσημβρία Ar.Fr.347; κ. δ' ὥσπερ ἦν D.1.22. 2. entirely, altogether, quite, with Verbs, κ. μεθύειν Pl.Smp.215d, cf. Antiph.74.12; κ. ἀπειρηκέναι Id.191.14; Πομπήϊον ἀπέστρεψε κ. τοῦ Κικέρωνος Plu.Cic.30: more freq. with Adjs., κ. ἕτερον Pl.Tht.159a; εἰς στενὸν κ.. καταστήσεται D.1.22; κ. μικρά Id.18.295; σαπροὺς κ. (sc. ἰχθῦς) Antiph.218.4; βαρὺς κ. Eub.41.7; κ. ἀναίσθητος Arist.EN1114$^a$10; κ. φαῦλος ib.1166$^b$5: with Substs., Θετταλὸν λέγεις κ. τὸν ἄνδρα quite a Thessalian, Antiph.276; μειρακύλλιον ὢν κ. D.21.78; νέος κ. ib.80: with an Adv., κύκλῳ κ. all round us, Pl.Chrm.155d: with a neg., κ. γὰρ οὐκ ἦν οὐδαμοῦ nowhere at all, Antiph.129.10; ὥστε μὴ κ. μοναρχίαν εἶναι none at all, Plu.Per.11; κ. ἀτέχνως without any art at all, Pl.Grg.501a. 3. freq. in answers, κομιδῇ μὲν οὖν just so, Ar.Pl.833, 834, 838, Pl.Tht.155a, Sph.221c, al.; κ. γε quite so, Id.R.442a, 453e, al.

⊛ **κομίζω**, fut. κομιῶ Od.15.546, Hdt.2.121.γ', Ar.Ec.800, etc.; κομίσω only late, as AP6.41 (Agath.): aor. ἐκόμισα, Ep. ἐκόμισσα Il.13.579, κόμισσα Od.18.322, κόμισα Il.13.196; Dor. ἐκόμιξα Pi.P.4.159: pf. κεκόμικα Hdt.9.115, etc.:—Med., fut. κομιοῦμαι Ar.V.690, Th.1.113, etc.; Ion. -ιεῦμαι, v. infr. II.4; late κομίσομαι Phalar.Ep.135: aor. ἐκομισάμην Hdt.6.118, etc.; Ep. ἐκομισσ- or κομισσ-, Od.14.316, Il.8.284:—Pass., fut. -ισθήσομαι Th.1.52, D.18.301: aor. ἐκομίσθην Hdt.1.31, Th.5.3, etc.: pf. κεκόμισμαι D.18.241: but more freq. in med. sense, v. infr. II.2: (κομέω):—take care of, provide for, τόν γε γηράσκοντα κομίζω Il.24.541; τόνδε τ' ἐγὼ κομιῶ Od.15.546; ἐμὲ κεῖνος ἐνδυκέως ἐκόμιζε 17.113, etc.; κόμισσε δὲ Πηνελόπεια, παῖδα δὲ ὣς ἀτίταλλε 18.322, cf. 20.68: rare in Trag., A.Ch.262, 344; receive, treat, φιλίως, οὐ πολεμίως κ. Th.3.65 codd.:—more freq. in Med., καί σε.. κομίσσατο ᾧ ἐνὶ οἴκῳ Il.8.284, cf. Od.14.316; Σίντιες.. ἄφαρ κομίσαντο πεσόντα Il.1.594; κομίζεσθαί τινα ἐς τὴν οἰκίαν And.1.127, cf. Is.1.15:—Pass., οὔ τι κομιζόμενός γε θάμιζεν not often was he attended to, Od.8.451. 2. of things, attend, give heed to, τὰ σ' αὐτῆς ἔργα κόμιζε Il.6.490, Od.21.350; κτήματα μὲν.. κομιζέμεν ἐν μεγάροισι 23.355; δῶμα κ., of the mistress of the house, 16.74, etc.; τὸν χρυσόν Hdt.1.153; ἔξω κ. πηλοῦ πόδα keep it out of the mud, A.Ch.697:—Med., ἔργα κ. Δημήτερος Hes.Op.393; Δημήτερος ἱερὸν ἀκτὴν μέτρῳ εὖ κομίσασθαι ἐν ἄγγεσιν store up.., ib.600. II. carry away so as to preserve, Ἀμφίμαχον.. κόμισαν μετὰ λαὸν Ἀχαιῶν they carried away his body, Il.13.196 (so in Med., κόμισαί με carry me safe away, 5.359, cf. E.IT774); of things, τὴν δὲ κόμισσε κῆρυξ the herald took up the mantle, that it might not be lost, Il.2.183; [τρυφάλειαν] κόμισαν.. ἑταῖροι 3.378, cf. 13.579; later, simply, save, rescue, ἄνδρ' ἐκ θανάτου Pi.P.3.56; ἄρουραν πατρίαν σφίσιν κόμισον Id.O.2.14; of the dead, νεκρὸν κ. carry out to burial, E.Andr.1264, cf. S.Aj.1397:—in Med., Is.8.21; also, simply, carry the body home, opp. θάπτω, A.Ch.683, cf. Hdt.4.71. 2. carry off as a prize or booty, χρυσὸν δ' Ἀχιλεὺς ἐκόμισσε Il.2.875; κόμισσα δὲ μώνυχας ἵππους 11.738; τέσσαρας ἐξ ἀέθλων νίκας ἐκόμιξαν four victories they won, Pi.N.2.19; ἔπαινος, ὃν κομίζετον τοῦδ' ἀνδρὸς S.OC1411:—in Med., Orac.ap.Hdt.1.67:—later freq., get for oneself, acquire, gain, δόξαν ἐσθλὴν v.l. in E.Hipp.432; τριώβολον Ar.V.690; τὴν ἀξίαν Pl.R.615c; τὰ ἆθλα αὐτῆς ib.621d; κ. τί τινος S.OT580; τι παρά τινος Th.1.43; τι ἀπὸ τινος X.Cyr.1.5.11; gather in, reap, καρπὸν Hdt.2.14: pf. Pass. in med. sense, ὑμεῖς τοὺς καρποὺς κεκόμισθε you have reaped the fruits, D.18.231; κεκόμισται χάριν Id.21.171; ὡμολόγει κεκομίσθαι τὴν προῖκα Id.27.14, cf. Is.5.22; simply, receive, ἐνηρόσιον SIG1044.31 (Halic., iv/iii B.C.); ἐπιστολὴν PCair.Zen.186 (iii B.C.); μισθὸν IG4$^2$(1).99.24 (Epid., ii B.C.); ἀπ' ἀλλήλων χρέας Phld.D.3 Fr.84. 3. receive a missile in one's body, ἀλλά τις Ἀργείων κόμισε χροΐ (sc. τὸν ἄκοντα) Il.14.456, cf. 463:—Med., ὥς δή μιν σῷ ἐν χροΐ πᾶν κομίσαιο (sc. τὸ ἔγχος) 22.286. 4. carry, convey, κόμισαν δέπας 23.699, cf. Od.13.68, Hdt.5.83, etc.; κομίζοις ἂν σεαυτὸν betake thyself, S.Ant.444:—Pass., to be conveyed, journey, travel, by land or sea, Hdt.5.43, etc.; εἴσω κομίζου get thee in, A.Ag.1035, cf. Pr.394; κ. παρά τινα betake oneself to him, Hdt.1.73: in this sense fut. and aor. Med. sts. occur, κομιεύμεθα ἐς Σῖριν Id.8.62; οἱ ἂν κομίσωνται.. ἐς Βαβυλῶνα Id.1.185; ἔξω κομίσασθ' οἴκων E.Tr.167 (lyr.). 5. bring to a place, bring in, introduce, κόμιζέ νύν μοι παῖδα S.Aj.530; import, Pl.R.370e, etc.; ξενικοῦ κομισθέντος νομίσματος Id.Lg.742c; κ. τὴν φιλοσοφίαν εἰς τοὺς Ἕλληνας Isoc.11.28; οἱ κομίσαντες τὴν δόξαν ταύτην Arist.EN1096$^a$17, cf. Metaph.990$^b$2:—in Med., [τὸν ἀνδριάντα] ἐπὶ Δήλιον Hdt.6.118; ποίμνας ἐς δόμους S.Aj.63, cf. Ar.V.833. 6. conduct, escort, τί μέλλεις κομίζειν δόμων τόνδ' ἔσω; S.OT678 (lyr.), cf. Ph.841 (hex.), Th.7.29, Pl.Phd.113d, etc.; κ. ἐξ ὀμμάτων γυναῖκα τήνδε take her from my sight, E.Alc.1064; κ. ναῦς Th.2.85; ἄρχοντα Id.8.61. 7. bring back from exile, Pi.P.4.106 (dub.);

τεὰν ψυχὰν κ. (from the world below), Id.*N*.8.44; πάλιν κ. Pl.*Phd.* 107e, etc. 8. *get back, recover*, Pi.*O.*13.59; τέκνων..κομίσαι δέμας E.*Supp.*273 (hex.), cf. 495:—Med., *get back for oneself*, τὸν παῖδα Id. *Ba.*1225, cf. *IT*1362; τὴν βασιλείαν Ar.*Av.*549; τοὺς ἄνδρας Th.1.113, cf. 4.117; τοὺς νεκροὺς ὑποσπόνδους κ. Id.6.103; τὰ πρέποντα Id.4.98; ἃ νῦν ἀπολαβεῖν οὐ δυνάμεθα διὰ πολέμου, ταῦτα διὰ πρεσβείας ῥᾳδίως κομιούμεθα Isoc.8.22; esp. of money, *recover* debts, etc., Lys.32.14, And.1.38, D.4.7, etc.; διπλάσια Lys.19.57; τόκους πολλαπλασίους Pl.*R.*556a, etc.; κ. τιμωρίαν παρά τινος Lys.12.70; κ. τὴν θυγατέρα *take back one's* daughter (on the death of her husband), Is.8.8. 9. metaph., *rescue from oblivion*, ἀοιδοὶ καὶ λόγοι τὰ καλὰ ἔργ' ἐκόμισαν Pi.*N.*6.30. 10. *bring, give*, θράσος..ἀνδράσι θνῄσκουσι κ. A.*Ag.* 804 (anap.):—Act. and Med. combined, χθὼν πάντα κομίζει καὶ πάλιν κομίζεται *gives* all things and *gets* them *back* again, Men.*Mon.*539, cf. 89, 668. 11. *cite* as an authority, Θεμιστοκλέα Phld.*Rh.*2. 205S. 12. Medic., *extract, remove*, Gal.2.632. III. Pass., *come* or *go back, return*, Hdt.4.76, al.; ἐκομίσθησαν ἐπ' οἴκου Th.2.33, cf. 73; κομισθεὶς οἴκαδε Pl.*R.*614b.

**κόμιον**, τό, Dim. of κόμη, Arr.*Epict.*2.24.24, 3.22.10. II. = προκόμιον, *Dialex.*2.13.

**κομίσκη**, Dor. -ā, ἡ, Dim. of κόμη, Alcm.1.101 Diehl.

**κομισ-τέος**, α, ον, *to be gathered in*, καρπὸς οὐ κ. A.*Th.*600. II. κομιστέον, *one must bring*, νέους εἰς δείματα κ. Pl.*R.*413d. 2. *one must carry*, Dsc.2.76.6. 3. *one must remove, draw off*, τὸ οὖρον διὰ τοῦ καθετῆρος Sor.2.59, cf. 87. **-τή**, ἡ, = κομιδή I, Hsch. **-τήρ**, ῆρος, ὁ, = sq. II, E.*Hec.*222, Plu.*Per.*12. **-τής**, οῦ, ὁ, *one who takes care of*, νεκρῶν E.*Supp.*25. II. *conductor*, Id.*Andr.*1268. **-τικός**, ή, όν, *fit for taking care of*; of foods, *strengthening*, Hp.*Aff.*54, 55. II. *fit for carrying*, κ. πλοῖα transports, Hyp.*Fr.*166. **-τός**, ή, όν, *brought*, J.*AJ*17.4.1. **-τρια**, ἡ, fem. of κομιστήρ, = τροφός, *AB* 267, Hsch.; as epith. of Nature, Orph.*H.*10.16. ⊛**-τρον**, τό (usu. in pl., sg. in *SIG* (v. infr.), Poll.7.133), *reward for saving*, ψυχῆς κ. A.*Ag.*965. 2. *reward for returning lost property*, *SIG*1184.4 (Cnidus). 3. *payment for maintenance* (?), *Leg.Gort.*3.37. II. *reward for bringing*, E.*HF*1387.

**κόμμα**, ατος, τό, (κόπτω) *stamp* or *impression of a coin*, χαλκίοις..κοπεῖσι τῷ κακίστῳ κόμματι Ar.*Ra.*726: prov., πονηροῦ κόμματος of bad *stamp*, Id.*Pl.*862, 957; χρυσίον κόμμασιν ἀποσμώμενον (sic leg. pro ἀποσπ-) cleansed *by blows of the die*, Luc.*Pisc.*14. 2. *coinage*, ἴδιοί τινες [θεοί], κ. καινόν Ar.*Ra.*890, cf. *Ec.*817; Σεύθα κόμμα, on Thracian coins, *BMus.Cat.Coins Thrace* p.201 (V B.C.); οἱ τὸ τοῦ νομίσματος κ. μεταχειριζόμενοι, = Lat. *triumviri monetales*, D.C.54. 26. 3. metaph., μαλθακωτέρου κόμματος, of the female body, Ph. 1.639. II. *that which is cut off, piece*, ἰχθύων *Gp.*18.14.2. 2. *refuse of corn* in threshing, *chaff*, Din.*Fr.*18.4 (pl.). 3. *short clause* in a sentence, Cic.*Orat.*62.211, Phld.*Rh.*1.165S., D.H.*Comp.*26, Quint.9.4.22, etc.; defined as τὸ κώλου ἔλαττον Demetr.*Eloc.*9; cf. κομμάτιον 3. III. *contusion*, Critoap.Gal.13.878.

**κομμ-ᾰτίας**, ου, ὁ, (κόμμα II.3) *one who speaks in short clauses*, Philostr.*VS*2.29. **-ᾰτικός**, ή, όν, *consisting of short clauses*, μικρὰ καὶ κ. ἐρωτήματα Luc.*Bis Acc.*28; εἶδος τοῦ λόγου Hermog.*Id.*1.9, cf. 1.1. Adv. -κῶς D.H.*Dem.*39; κ. καὶ γοργῶς Eust.200.33. II. κομματικόν (sc. μέλος), τό, = κομμός (A), Poll.4.53. **-άτιον**, τό, Dim. of κόμμα II.1: in pl., *small logs*, Alciphr.1.1. 2. *metrical phrase*, Eup.362. b. part of παράβασις in Comedy, Heph.*Poëm.*8.2. 3. *short clause*, ἔλαττον κώλου κ. D.H.*Comp.*26.

⊛**κόμμι**, τό, *gum*, Hdt.2.86, 96, Hp.*Art.*33, etc.; obtained from *Acacia arabica*, Thphr.*HP*9.1.3, Dsc.1.101.—Foreign word, Ath.2. 66f, prob. Egypt. *kemai*, commonly indecl., as in ll. cc., Gal.18(1). 808; also declined, gen. κόμμεως Hp.*Mul.*2.192, Gal.10.374; dat. κόμμει Str.12.7.3 (fem.), Dsc.1.66, Gal.12.718, κόμμιδι Crobyl.10, v.l. Hdt.2.86 (ap. *AB*104).

**κομμ-ίδιον**, τό, Dim. of foreg., *Hippiatr.*11, Sch.Nic.*Al.*109. **-ῐδώδης**, ες, *gummy*, Thphr.*CP*5.10.2. **-ίζω**, *to be like gum*, κ. τῇ ὄψει καὶ τῇ δυνάμει Dsc.1.64. **-ιώδης**, ες, = κομμιδώδης, Arist. *HA*628ᵇ27.

**κομμός** (A), ὁ, (κόπτω) *striking*; esp. *beating of the head and breast in lamentation*, ἔκοψα κομμὸν Ἄριον A.*Ch.*423 (lyr.), cf. Bion 1.97 (pl.); hence, 2. in the Att. Drama, *dirge, lament*, sung alternately by one or more of the chief characters and the chorus, κ. δὲ θρῆνος κοινὸς χοροῦ καὶ ἀπὸ σκηνῆς Arist.*Po.*1452ᵇ24.

**κομμός** (B), ὁ, (κομέω) *care bestowed on dress* or *adornment*, Suid.

**κομμός** (C), ὁ, in pl., *molar teeth*, Hsch.; cf. κόμπος III.

**κομμ-όω**, *beautify, embellish*, αὐτούς Arist.*SE*164ᵇ20, cf. Luc.*Bis Acc.*31 (prob.); λόγους Them.*Or.*27.336c, cf. *Or.*28.343b:—Med., Eup.421. **-ώ**, οῦς, ἡ, *priestess who adorned* the seated statue of Athena on the Acropolis of Athens, *AB*273. **-ῶ**· πλεκτάναι, Hsch. **-ωμα**, ατος, τό, *embellishment*, Luc.*Hist.Conscr.*8. **-ωσις**, εως, ἡ, *embellishment*, Ath.13.568a (pl.). II. (κόμμι) *stop-wax*, prob. in Arist.*HA*623ᵇ31, cf. Plin.*HN*11.16, Hsch. **-ωτής**, οῦ, ὁ, *dresser*, esp. *hairdresser*, in pl., Arr.*Epict.*2.23.14, Them.*Or.*20. 238a; *beautifier, embellisher*, τινος Luc.*Merc.Cond.*32: metaph., ὥσπερ γυναικὸς πολυτελοῦς τῆς τραγῳδίας κομμωταί Plu.2.348f: abs., Gal.*Thras.*35. **-ωτικός**, ή, όν, *of* or *for embellishment*, ἄσκησις Luc.*Am.*9; ποικιλία Them.*Or.*24.303c; τίνι διαφέρει τοῦ κ. τὸ κοσμητικὸν τῆς ἰατρικῆς μέρος Gal.12.434, cf. *UP*1.9: ἡ -κή (sc. τέχνη) *the art of embellishment*, Pl.*Grg.*463b, Phld.*Rh.*2.183S.: metaph., of style, κόσμος τις ἐπικείμενος ἔξωθεν κ. Hermog.*Id.*1.12, cf. 9, Them.*Or.*24.303c. Adv. -κῶς, ἔχειν Sch.Ar.*Pl.*1064. **-ώτρια**, ἡ, fem. of κομμωτής, *dresser, tirewoman*, Ar.*Ec.*737, Pl.*R.*373c, Jul. *Caes.*335b. **-ώτριον**, τό, *tiring-instrument*, Ar.*Fr.*320.8.

**Κομνοκάριος**, ὁ (sc. μήν), name of month at Dreros, *SIG*527.106 (iii B.C.).

**κομοτροφέω**, *let the hair grow*, Str.4.4.3, *Cat.Cod.Astr.*8(4).165.

**κομπάζω**, fut. -άσομαι B.7.42:— = κομπέω, *boast, brag*, A.*Th.*436, *Ag.*1671, etc.; κ. μέγα S.*Aj.*1122; μάτην E.*Hipp.*978; κ. ἐπί τινι *speak big* against.., A.*Th.*480 (but also, *boast* of.., Phld.*Rh.*1.24S.): c. acc., κ. λόγον *speak big* words, A.*Ag.*1400, etc.; κ. γέρας *boast* one's office, Id.*Eu.*209; οὐ πατρῴαν τὴν τέχνην ἐκόμπασας S.*El.*1500: c. inf., *boast that*.., A.*Ag.*1130, E.*Ba.*340; κ. ὡς.. X.*Oec.*10.3, Plu. *Crass.*18:—Pass., *to be made a boast of, be renowned*, οὕνεκ' ὄλβου E.*HF*64; φόβος..κομπάζεται fear *is loudly spoken*, A.*Th.*500; τίνος δὲ..παῖς πατρὸς κομπάζεται; of what father *is he said to be* the son? E.*Alc.*497.—Rare in early Prose, Lys.6.18, 48, X.*Smp.*4.19, *Oec.* l. c. II. = κομπέω I.2, *ring* a jar to test its soundness, *PLond. ined.*2327 (iii B.C.). III. ἐκομπάσθη· ἠπατήθη, εἰς ὄγκον διετέθη, Hsch., cf. Suid.

**κόμπαλος**· παλαιστροφύλαξ, Hsch.

**Κομπ-ᾱσεύς**, έως, ὁ, Com. word, *one of the* Κόμπος-*deme, Bragsman*, Ar.*Av.*1126. **-ᾱσία**, ἡ, *ringing* of wine-jars (cf. κομπάζω II), *POxy.*1631.16 (iii A.D.). **-ασμα**, ατος, τό, usu. in pl., *boasts*, A. *Pr.*363, *Th.*551, 794, Ar.*Ra.*940, Alex.ap.*POxy.*1801.51: sg., Μακεδονικὸν κ. Arr.*Ind.*5.10. **-ασμός**, ὁ, = foreg., Plu.*Sull.*16. **-αστής**, οῦ, ὁ, *braggart*, Ph.2.273 (pl.), Plu.*Crass.*16, Sch.Ar.*Ach.*595 in *POxy.* 856.56. II. *one who rings* wine-jars to test their soundness (cf. κομπάζω II), *PSI*8.953.3 (vi A.D.). **-αστικός**, ή, όν, *braggart*, Poll.9.146. Adv. -κῶς ib.147. **-έω**, (κόμπος) *ring, clash*, κόμπει χαλκὸς ἐπὶ στήθεσσι φαεινός Il.12.151. 2. c. acc., κ. χύτραν *ring* a pot to see if it be sound, D.L.6.30 (restored from Eust.896.61 for σκοποῦμεν), cf. 2.78. II. metaph., *boast, brag*, τί κομπέω παρὰ καιρόν; Pi.*P.*10.4; κ. ἄλλως Hdt.5.41; ὡς σὺ κομπεῖς E.*Or.*571: c. acc. cogn., κ. μῦθον *speak a boastful* speech, S.*Aj.*770; ὑψήλ' ἐκόμπεις ib. 1230. 2. c. acc., *boast of*, κ. γάμους A.*Pr.*947:—Pass., ὁπλῖται, ὅσοιπερ κομποῦνται *are boasted of*, Th.6.17, cf. Phld.*Rh.*2.33S. 3. c. acc. et inf., *boast that*.., E.*El.*815; κ. ὅπως.. *boast* how.., S.*OC* 1149.—Like κομπάζω, rare in Prose. **-ηγόρος**, ον, *speaking boastfully*, Hsch. s. v. ἀερολέσχης. **-ηρός**, ά, όν, *resounding*, λέξεις (in the Dithyramb) Anon.*in Rh.*177.3, cf. Sch.E.*Ph.*600. Adv. -ρῶς Anon.*in Rh.*161.29.

**κομποθηλαία** (-θυλ- cod.), ἡ, gloss on στρόφος, = ζώνη, Sch.rec. A.*Th.*871; cf. sq. **-θήλυκα**, τά, v.l. for πόρπακας (the ends of a seton) in *Hippiatr.*2; cf. foreg. and κόμβος, κομβίον, κομβοθηλεία.

**κομπο-λᾰκέω**, *talk big, be an empty braggart*, Ar.*Ra.*961:—also -λᾰκυθέω, Tz.*H.*9.414. **-λᾰκύθης** or ⊛**-λάκυθος**, ου, ὁ, *braggart*, Ar.*Ach.*589, 1182, perh. with a play on *Lamachus*. **-λογία**, ἡ, *boastful speaking*, Men.Prot.p.17D.

⊛**κόμπος** (A), ὁ, *din, clash*, esp. such as is caused by the collision of two hard bodies, as when a boar whets his tusks, ὑπαὶ δέ τε κ. ὀδόντων γίγνεται Il.11.417, 12.149; *stamping* of dancers' feet, πολὺς δ' ὑπὸ κ. ὀρώρει Od.8.380; *ringing* of metal, E.*Rh.*383 (anap., pl.). II. metaph., *boast, vaunt*, ὁ κ. οὐ κατ' ἄνθρωπον φρονεῖ A.*Th.*425, cf. 473, *Ag.*613; οὐ πεπλασμένος ὁ κ., ἀλλὰ καὶ λίαν εἰρημένος Id.*Pr.*1031; Ζεὺς γὰρ μεγάλης γλώσσης κόμπους ὑπερεχθαίρει S.*Ant.*127 (anap.); κ. πάρεστι, i.e. I am proud of the deed, Id.*Aj.*96: rare in Prose and Com., ὅρα μὴ μάτην κ. ὁ λόγος εἰρημένος ᾖ Hdt.7.103; οὐ λόγων..κ. τάδε, μᾶλλον ἢ ἔργων..ἀλήθεια Th.2.41; ἀλαζονεία καὶ κ. τοῦ ψηφίσματος Aeschin.3.237; κ. κενοὶ ψοφοῦσιν Alex.25.9; of rhetorical *bombast*, Epicur.*Sent.Vat.*45. 2. rarely in good sense, *praise*, Pi.*I.*1.43, 5(4).24. III. in pl., *molar teeth*, Hsch.

⊛**κομπός** (B), ὁ, = κομπαστής, E.*Ph.*600 (troch.); κ. λόγος *EM*527. 47.—On the accent, v. Hdn.Gr.1.187.

**κομποφακελορρήμων**, ον, gen. ονος, *pomp-bundle-worded*, derisive epith. of Aeschylus in Ar.*Ra.*839, because of his long compounds:—hence **κομποφακελλορρημοσύνη**, ἡ, Lyd.*Mag.*3.7.

**κομπ-όω**, = κομπέω, D.C.43.22 (Pass.). **-ώδης**, ες, *boastful, vainglorious*, κομπωδεστέρα προσποίησις Th.2.62; τὸ ἀνθρώπειον κ. Id. 5.68; τὸ κ. καὶ σοβαρόν Plu.*Sull.*16. Adv. -δῶς Sch.Th.8.81.

**Κομ-ύρια**, τά, festival of Zeus Panamaros, *BCH*11.384, *Supp. Epigr.*4.294, al. **-ύριον**, τό, sanctuary of Zeus, *BCH*11.380.

**κομψ-εία**, ἡ, (κομψός) *daintiness, refinement*, esp. of language, τὰς ..τοιαύτας κομψείας such-like *refinements*, Pl.*Phd.*101c, cf. Phld.*Rh.* 1.224S., Luc.*Prom.*8. II. κομψεία, Ἀττικῶς· πανουργία, Ἑλληνικῶς, Moer.p.237P. **-ευμα**, ατος, τό, *ingenious invention*, Arist. *Mete.*349ᵃ30; σεμνῶν ὀνομάτων Luc.*Am.*54 (pl.); *quibble*, Gal.6.228 (pl.). **-ευρῑπικῶς**, Adv. *with Euripides-quibbles* (shortd. from κομψευριπιδικῶς), Ar.*Eq.*18. **-εύω**, *refine upon*, κόμψευέ νυν τὴν δόξαν aye, *quibble on* the word δόξα (referring to the previous line), S.*Ant.*324:—mostly in Med., *to be smart, ingenious*, ἥδεσθαι κομψευόμενος to be fond *of clever inventions*, Hp.*Art.*70 (glossed πανουργευόμενος, Erot.); ὁ τοῦτο κομψευσάμενος he who *invented* this *subtlety*, Pl.*R.*489b; πρέπει..σοφιστῇ τὰ τοιαῦτα κομψεύεσθαι Id.*La.*197d; κ. ὡς... Id.*R.*436d: pf. Pass. in med. sense, αὐτὸ τοῦτο καὶ κεκόμψευται he *has advanced* this *dainty paradox*, Id.*Phdr.*227c; οἱ τὰ πολιτικὰ κεκομψευμένοι Ph.1.448. 2. Pass., of things, προσαγώγιον κεκομψευμένον *neatly made*, Pl.*Phlb.*56c; ὁ λόγος ὑπὸ τῶν τοιούτων κεκόμψευται σχημάτων D.H.*Isoc.*14.

**κομψο-λόγος**, ον, *fine speaking*, ἰατροί Aesop.168. **-πρεπής**, ές, *ingenious-seeming*, μοῦσα Ar.*Nu.*1030; τὸ κ. *Vit.Aeschyli.*

**κομψ-ός**, ή, όν, *nice, refined, gentlemanly*, ἐσμὲν ἅπαντα κομψοὶ ἄνδρες we are perfect *gentlemen*, Eup.159, cf. Ar.*V.*1317; κ. ἐν συνουσίᾳ Id.*Nu.*649; τὸ θῆλυ τοὺς πόδας ἔχει κομψοτέρους *more delicate, finer*, Arist.*Phgn.*809$^{b}$9. **2.** *smart, clever, ingenious*, of persons or their words and acts, ὁ πρῶτος εὑρὼν κ. ἦν τραγήματα Alex.185; κ. θεαταί Cratin.169, cf. 307; Θηραμένης ὁ κ. Ar.*Ra.*967; Σικελὸς κ. ἀνήρ Timocr.6, cf. Pl.*Grg.*493a; κ. περί τι *clever* about.., Id.*R.*495d(Sup.), *Cra.*405d; of a dog's instinct, κ. τὸ πάθος αὐτοῦ τῆς φύσεως Id.*R.*376a; μὰ γῆν.., μὴ 'γὼ νόημα κομψότερον ἤκουσά πω a *more ingenious* device.., Ar.*Av.*195; τὸ πρᾶγμα κ. [ἐστι] Id.*Th.*93, cf. 460(lyr., Comp.), Dionys.Com.3.1; esp. in a sneering sense, *over-ingenious*, κομψός γ' ὁ κῆρυξ καὶ παρεργάτης λόγων E.*Supp.*426; τρίβων γὰρ εἶ τὰ κομψά versed in *subtleties*, Id.*Rh.*625; μή μοι τὰ κομψὰ ποικίλοι γενοίατο, ἀλλ' ὧν πόλει δεῖ Id.*Fr.*16; τὸ κ. *refinement, subtlety*, Arist.*Pol.*1265$^{a}$12; τῶν ἰατρῶν ὅσοι κ. ἢ περίεργοι Id.*Resp.*480$^{b}$27; κ. σοφίσματα E.*Fr.*188.5; τοῦτ' ἔχει -ότατον this is the *subtlest* part of it, Pl.*Tht.*171a; κομψότερος.. ὁ λόγος ἢ κατ' ἐμέ *too subtle* for me, Id.*Cra.*429d:—but in Pl. and Arist., usu. *clever*, esp. *skilful in technique*, with at most a slight irony (κομψοὺς Πλάτων οὐ τοὺς πανούργους, ἀλλὰ τοὺς βελτίστους Moer.p.206 P.). **3.** more generally, *nice, good, pleasant*, πάντων δὲ κομψότατον τὸ τῆς πόας Pl.*Phdr.*230c; τὰ κ. ταῦτα χλανίσκια that *nice* suit of yours, Aeschin.1.131. **II.** Adv. -ψῶς *cleverly*, Ar.*Ach.*1016(lyr.), Pl.*Cra.*399a, etc.: Comp. -οτέρως Isoc.15.195; κ. ἔχειν to be *well*, 'nicely' in health, *PPar.*18.3(ii B.C.), cf. *PLond.ined.*2126(ii/iii A.D.), etc.; κομψότερον σχεῖν to get *better* in health, *Ev.Jo.*4.52, cf. Arr.*Epict.*3.10.13, *POxy.*935.5(iii A.D.): Sup. -ότατα *nicely*, Ar.*Lys.*89; λέγεσθαι κομψότατα *most cleverly*, Pl.*Tht.*202d.—Chiefly found in Att. Com. and Prose; Trag. only in E. (Orig. sense uncertain; = στρεβλός, Erot. (citing Euripides); = στρογγύλος, Hsch.) **-ότης**, ητος, ἡ, *elegance, prettiness, daintiness*, esp. of language, Isoc.12.1 (v.l. κοσμιότητος), Pl.*Ep.*358c(pl.); κ. ἱστορική, φυσική, Plu.2.353e.

**κονᾰβ-έω**, (κόναβος) Ep. Verb, *resound, clash, ring*, esp. of metallic bodies, ἀμφὶ δὲ πήληξ σμερδαλέον κονάβησε Il.15.648, cf. 21.593: late in pres., *AP*11.144(Cereal.); *re-echo*, ἀμφὶ δὲ νῆες σμερδαλέον κονάβησαν ἀϋσάντων ὑπ' Ἀχαιῶν Il.2.334, 16.277; ἀμφὶ δὲ δῶμα σμ. κον. Od.17.542; ἀμφὶ δὲ γαῖα σμ. κον. Hes.*Th.*840: late in Prose, of a river, Sch.Opp.*C.*2.145. **-ηδόν**, Adv. *with a noise, clash*, *AP*7.531(Antip. Thess.). ⊛ **-ίζω**, = κοναβέω, περὶ στήθεσσι δὲ χαλκὸς σμερδαλέον κονάβιζε Il.13.498, cf. 21.255; αὐτὰρ ὑπὸ χθὼν σμ. κον. ποδῶν 2.466, cf. Orph.*H.*38.9. **-ος**, ὁ, *ringing, clashing, din*, κόναβος.. ἀνδρῶν ὀλλυμένων νηῶν θ' ἅμα ἀγνυμενάων Od.10.122, v.l. for ὅτοβος ap.Sch.Hes.*Th.*709.—Ep. word, once in Trag., κ. χαλκοδέτων σακέων A.*Th.*160(lyr.), cf. Luc.*Hist.Conscr.*22.

**κονάριχον**· γλαφυρόν, Hsch. **κοναρός**, ά, όν, *well-fed, fat*, Id.; *vigorous, active*, Id. (also in Comp.).

**κονβενταρχέω**, τῶν Ῥωμαίων *to be president of a conventus civium Romanorum*, *IGRom.*4.818(Hierapolis).

**κόνδαξ**, ᾱκος, ὁ, gambling game played with an unpointed dart, *Cod.Just.*3.43.1.4: metaph., παίζων κόνδακα, of sexual intercourse, *AP*5.60(Rufin.).

**κόνδοι**· κεραῖαι, ἀστράγαλοι, Hsch.

⊛ **κονδο-κέρατος**, ον, *short-horned*, Al.*Le.*22.23. **-λύχνια, -λύχνιος**, = *statarium*, *Gloss.* **-μονόβολον**, τό, name of a gambling game, *Cod.Just.*3.43.1.4.

**κονδός**, v. κοντός (B).

⊛ **κόνδῠ**, υος, τό, *drinking-vessel*, Men.293, Hipparch.Com.1.6, *IG*11(2).287*B*133, al. (Delos, iii B.C.), *PPetr.*2p.108(iii B.C.), Pancrat. ap.Ath.11.478a; as a measure, LXX *Ge.*44.2, al.: pl., κόνδυα ἀργυρᾶ Alex.Magn.Epist.ap.Ath.11.784a.

**κονδῠλ-ίζω**, (κόνδυλος) *strike with the fist*, Hyp.*Fr.*98 (Act. and Pass.), Aristid.2.95J.: metaph., *maltreat, oppress*, ὀρφανούς LXX *Ma.*3.5; εἰς κεφαλὰς πτωχῶν ib.*Am.*2.7; also αὐτὴν εἰς ἀνάμνησιν κ. Lib.*Decl.*26.20:—Pass., ὑπὸ συνηθείας ἀεὶ κεκονδυλισμένος inured to *buffetings*, Longin.44.4, cf. D.L.2.21. **-ιον**, τό, Dim. of κόνδυ, *IG*11(2).147*B*10(Delos, iv B.C.), al.; κ. Σικυώνιον *BGU*1300.12(iii/ii B.C.). **II.** Dim. of κόνδυλος, f.l. in Axionic.6.3(pl.). **-ισμός**, ὁ, *striking with the fist, maltreatment*, Artem.2.15, LXX *Ze.*2.8. **-ιστής**, οῦ, ὁ, horse which injures its hoofs in the stable, *Hippiatr.*10(v.l.). **-οειδής**, ές, = κονδυλώδης, ἐξοχαί Ruf.*Oss.*15. **-όομαι**, Pass., *swell up*, κονδυλοῦνται αἱ στολίδες Aspasia ap.Aët.16.118, cf. Hsch. **-ος**, ὁ, *knuckle*, Arist.*HA*493$^{b}$28: pl., Hp.*Art.*2; κονδύλοις ἡρμοττόμην (v. ἁρμόζω I.4); κονδύλοις νουθετεῖν τινα Ar.*V.*254: so in sg., ib.1503; δοῦναι κόνδυλόν τινι Plu.2.439d; κονδύλους αὐτῷ δεῖδι (= δίδου) *POxy.*1185.12(ii/iii A.D.); κονδύλῳ καθικέσθαι τινός Plu.*Alc.*7, etc.; κονδύλοις [πατάξαι], opp. ἐπὶ κόρρης (a slap in the face), D.21.72: prov., κολλύραν καὶ κόνδυλον ὄψον ἐπ' αὐτῇ pudding and *knuckle*-sauce to it, i.e. a good thrashing, Ar.*Pax*123, ubi v. Sch.; λόγον ἔχειν τοῦ κ. προχειρότερον Plu.*Cat.Mi.*1; νὴ τοὺς κ. οὓς ἠνεσχόμην, Com. oath, Ar.*Eq.*411. **II.** generally, *knuckle of any joint*, as of the humerus, Gal.18(2).617; of the humerus and elbow, Poll.2.141; of the finger (middle joint), Ruf.*Onom.*84; ποδός Luc.*Ocyp.*28. **2.** *knot* in a string, Paul.Aeg.6.25. **III.** *any hard, bony knob*, of the teeth, Hp.*Epid.*4.19, 25. **-ώδης**, ες, *knobby*, Id.*Mochl.*1, Dsc.1.107, Gal.2.755. **-ωμα**, ατος, τό, *knob, callous lump*, Hp.*Haem.*4,5, Dsc.*Eup.*1.209, Gal.13.533. **-ωσις**, εως, ἡ, = foreg., Hp.*Haem.*4,5. ⊛ **-ωτός**, ή, όν, *knobby*, χρυσίς *IG*2$^{2}$.1400.36: neut. as Subst., ib.40, prob. in ib.1386.10.

**κονέω**, (κόνις) *raise dust*: hence, *hasten*, Hsch.; = ὑπηρετεῖν, *EM*268.29: elsewh. only in compd. ἐγκονέω.

**κονή**, ἡ, (καίνω) *murder*, Hsch.(pl.): hence, = κώνειον, Ps.-Dsc.4.78.

**κονητής**, οῦ, ὁ, *servant*, Hsch.

⊛ **κονί-α**, Ion. and Ep. -ίη, ἡ, (κόνις): **1.** *dust*, ποδῶν ὑπένερθε κ. ἵστατ' ἀειρομένη Il.2.150; ὑπὸ δέ σφισιν ὦρτο κ. 11.151: in pl., κὰδ δ' ἔπεσ' ἐν κονίῃσι Od.18.98; ἐν κονίῃσι πεσών Il.17.315, etc.; πρηνέες ἐν κονίῃσιν 2.418, cf. Hes.*Sc.*365; μιάνθησαν δὲ ἔθειραι αἵματι καὶ κονίῃσι Il.16.796: also Trag. in lyr., A.*Ag.*64, E.*Andr.*112, *Supp.*821. **2.** *sand*, Il.21.271. **3.** *ashes*, in pl., κατ' ἄρ' ἕζετ' ἐπ' ἐσχάρῃ ἐν κονίῃσι Od.7.153, cf. 160: sg., κ. δρυΐνη *Gp.*13.4.2. **II.** *pearl-ash, lye, soap-powder*, λούειν ἄνευ κονίας Ar.*Lys.*470 (with a play on ἀκονιτί), cf. *Ach.*18, *Ra.*711, Pl.*R.*430b: pl., Thphr.*HP*4.10.4 (nisi leg. κονιάσεις). **2.** *alkaline fluid* used for washing, Gal.12.35, al.; κ. στακτή Id.13.569. **b.** κ. ἀπὸ τῆς ἱερᾶς σποδοῦ καὶ τοῦ ἱεροῦ ὕδατος, as a medicine, *SIG*1171.12(Lebena). **III.** = τίτανος, Erot. s.h.v.; κ. ἄσβεστος *quicklime*, Heraclid.Tarent.ap.Gal.12.958; κ. μέλαινα *IG*2$^{2}$.1672.197. **2.** *plaster, stucco*, ib.4$^{2}$(1).103.278(Epid.), *POxy.*1450.4(iii A.D.), Eust.382.36. [Hom. uses ῐ in the quadrisyll. case κονίῃσι, ῑ in the trisyll.: Trag. and Com. ῐ in lyr. (dact. and anap.), A.*Ag.*64, E.*Andr.*112, Ar.*Ra.*711; ῑ in iamb., Id.*Ach.*18, *Lys.*470.] **-άζω**, in Pass., *to be sprinkled with ashes*, *Gp.*13.4.2; v.l. for κεκονιμένος, Sm.2*Ki.*1.2. **-ᾰλος**, ὁ, = κονίσαλος III, *IG*12(3).540(Thera). **-ᾱμα**, Ion. -ημα, ατος, τό, *stucco, plaster*, Hp.*Epid.*7.11, Arist.*GA*726$^{b}$27, *Col.*791$^{b}$27, 794$^{b}$32, Thphr.*CP*4.16.1, *PSI*5.545.19(iii B.C.), etc.: in pl., οἰκοδομαὶ πολυτελεῖς καὶ κονιάματα D.S.20.8; also, *whitewashing*, D.13.30. ⊛ **-ᾱσις**, εως, ἡ, *plastering with stucco, whitening*, *IG*11(4).1246(Delos, iii/ii B.C.), 7.2712.35(Acraeph.), 4$^{2}$(1).102.39, al.(Epid.), 2$^{2}$.1672.203, *Gp.*2.27.5, cj. in Thphr.*HP*4.10.4(pl.). **-ᾱτήρ**, ῆρος, ὁ, *plasterer*, *IG*4$^{2}$(1).102.251(Epid.). ⊛ **-άτης** [ᾱ], ου, ὁ, = foreg., *IG*11(2).146*A*74(Delos, iv B.C.), *Sammelb.*6823.20(i A.D.), *POxy.*1450.6(iii A.D.); gloss on ἐξαλίπτης, Gal.19.98, cf. Sch.Ar.*Av.*1150; title of play by Amphis. **-ᾱτικός**, ή, όν, in neut. pl., *stucco decorations*, *IGRom.*1.743(Trajana Augusta); κ. ἔργα *PPetr.*3p.290(iii B.C.), *POxy.*2145.2(ii A.D.). **-ᾱτός**, ή, όν, *plastered* or *daubed*, X.*An.*4.2.22, Thphr.*HP*8.11.1, *PPetr.*3p.290(iii B.C.). **-άω**, (κονία III) *plaster with lime* or *stucco*, D.3.29, 23.208, *IG*2$^{2}$.1672.107, 140, 179, *Inscr.Magn.*100$^{b}$.40, etc.:—Med., κ. τοὺς ἐγχελεῶνας *have* them *plastered*, Arist.*HA*592$^{a}$4:—Pass., Bito 55.9, Plu.*Comp.Arist.Cat.Ma.*4, *IG*7.2712.35(Acraeph.); τάφοι κεκονιαμένοι *Ev.Matt.*23.27. **2.** generally, *daub over*, as with pitch, ἀγγεῖα κεκονιαμένα D.S.19.94. **3.** metaph., κ. τὸ πρόσωπον *paint, disguise* it, Philostr.*Ep.*22:—Pass., κεκονιαμένοι LXX *Pr.*21.9 (κεκονιαμένους is f.l. for κεκονιμένους Them.*Or.*7.91d).

**κονιβᾰτία**, ἡ, (βαίνω) *dusty walk*, Hp.*Vict.*3.68 (prob. l. for σχοινοβατίῃσι).

⊛ **κονίζω**, v. κονίω. **II.** κονίζειν, name of a garment, dub. in Hsch. s.v. διακονίς. ⊛ **κόνικλος**, v. κύνικλος.

**κονίλη** [ῑ], ἡ, *marjoram, Origanum viride*, Diocl.*Fr.*150, Nic.*Th.*626, Dsc.3.29, Gal.12.91. **II.** *organy, Origanum heracleoticum*, Dsc.3.27.

⊛ **κόνιμα**, v. κόνισμα.

**κόνιον**, τό, = κονία, Suid.; dub. sens. in *POxy.*739.7(i A.D.). **II.** v. κώνειον. **κονιόπους** and **κονιορτόποδες**, v. κονίποδες.

**κονῐορτ-ός**, ὁ, (κόνις, ὄρνυμι) *dust raised* or *stirred up, cloud of dust*, Hdt.8.65; ὁ κ. δῆλος αὐτῶν ὡς ὁμοῦ προσκειμένων Ar.*Eq.*245, cf. Th.4.44; κ. τῆς ὕλης νεωστὶ κεκαυμένης, i.e. *a cloud* of wood-ashes, ib.34; κ. καὶ ζάλη Pl.*R.*496d: in pl., Diocl.*Fr.*147. **2.** generally, *dirt, sweepings*, σαρώματα.. σὺν τῷ κ. Wilcken *Chr.*198.16(iii B.C.). **II.** metaph., *dirty fellow*, χαίρει τις αὐχμῶν ἢ ῥυπῶν, κ. ἀναπέφηνεν Anaxandr.34.6, cf. Aristopho 10.8; Εὐκτήμων ὁ κ. D.21.103. ⊛ **-όω**, *cover with dust*, Thphr.*HP*2.7.5. **-ώδης**, ες, *dusty*, Arist.*HA*557$^{b}$3, *Cael.*313$^{a}$20, Thphr.*CP*4.16.1, Dsc.1.26, Gal.14.49.

⊛ **κόνῐος**, α, ον, (κόνις) *dusty*, χέρσος Pi.*N.*9.43. **II.** *causing dust*, epith. of Zeus, Paus.1.40.6.

**κονίποδες** [ῑ], οἱ, *dusty-foots*, name for the serfs at Epidaurus, Plu.2.291e; also κονιορτόποδες Hsch. s.v. κονίποδες. **II.** kind of *shoe covering a small part of the foot*, Ar.*Ec.*848, Poll.7.86: in *EM*529.2, and Suid., **κονιόπους**.

**κόνις**, ιος, Att. εως or εος E.*Cyc.*641, ἡ: dat. κόνι contr. fr. κόνιι, Il.24.18, Od.11.191, Att. κόνει:—*dust*, κόνιος δεδραγμένος Il.13.393; as an emblem of a countless multitude, εἴ μοι τόσα δοίη ὅσα ψάμαθός τε κ. τε 9.385; κ. δέ σφ' ἀμφιδεδήει Hes.*Sc.*62; κόνιν, ἄναυδον ἄγγελον στρατοῦ A.*Supp.*180; αἷμα κ. πίνει, ἀνασπᾷ, Id.*Th.*736(lyr.), *Eu.*647; κ. διψία S.*Ant.*247, 429; of the grave, κ. κατακρύπτει χάριν Pi.*O.*8.79, cf. S.*OC*406, *El.*435, etc.; κόνει φύρειν κάρα, in sign of mourning, E.*Hec.*496; ἡ ἐπίχρυσος κ. gold *dust*, Poll.7.97. **2.** *ashes*, ἐν κόνι ἄγχι πυρός Od. l.c.; κόνιν αἰθαλόεσσαν χεύατο κὰκ κεφαλῆς Il.18.23, cf. Theoc.24.93. **II.** the *dust* of the κονίστρα, Arist.*IA*709$^{a}$14, Luc.*Anach.*29, Ath.12.518d: metaph., of toil, πάντα ἡμῖν μία κ. dub. in Luc.*DMort.*1.3: in Plu.2.697a κόνιν (*lye*) is prob. an error for κονίαν. **III.** = κονία III, Jul.*Ep.*80. [κόνῐν Il.18.23; κόνῐ (shortd. fr. κόνι before a vowel) 24.18, Od. l.c.; κονῑς, κονῑν, A.*Pr.*1084(anap.), *Supp.*180, 783(lyr.): ῐ in gen., v. supr.] (Cf. Lat. *cinis.*)

**κονίς** (on the accent v. Hdn.Gr.1.94), ίδος, ἡ, mostly in pl., κονίδες *eggs of lice, fleas, and bugs, nits*, Arist.*HA*539$^{b}$11, 556$^{b}$24, Antyll.ap.

Orib.10.21.1; *κόνιδες* (sic), gloss on *δόρκαι*, Hsch. (Cf. OE. *hnitu* 'nit'.)

**κονῑσᾰλέος**, α, ον, *dusty*, Antim.52, Euph.23.

**κονίσᾰλος** [ῐ], in later Mss. sts. wrongly *κονίσσαλος*, ὁ, (*κόνις*) *cloud of dust*, ὣς ἄρα τῶν ὑπὸ ποσσὶ κ. ὄρνυτ' ἀελλής Il.3.13; λευκοὶ ὕπερθε γένοντο κονισάλῳ 5.503, cf. 22.401. II. the mixed *dust, oil and sweat* on wrestlers, Gal.12.283. III. a demon of the same class as Priapus, Ar.*Lys.*982 (ubi v. Sch.), Pl.Com.174.13, cf. Str.13.1.12, *SIG*1027.10 (Cos). 2. *lascivious dance*, Hsch.

**κόνῑσ-ις**, εως, ἡ, *exercise in the arena*, δρόμου..καὶ πάλης καὶ κονίσεως (v.l. *κινήσεως*) Arist.*Cael.*292$^a$26. II. f.l. for *κόμμωσις* (q.v.), Id.*HA*623$^b$31. ⊛ **-μα**, ατος, τό, = *κονίστρα*, *IG*5(1).938 (Cythera):—also **κόνῑμα**, *BCH*23.566 (Delph., iii B.C.). **-τήριον**, τό, = *κονίστρα*, Vitr.5.11.2, *IGRom.*4.293*a*i 19 (Pergam., ii B.C.). **-τικός**, ή, όν, *liking to roll in the dust*, of birds, opp. *λοῦσται*, Arist.*HA*633$^a$29. ⊛ **-τρα**, ἡ, *place covered with dust*: hence, *rolling place*, such as birds make in the dust, ib.613$^b$9. 2. *arena in a wrestling school*, Lyc.867, Plu.2.638c; δρόμοι καὶ κ. καὶ γυμνάσια Ael.*NA*11.10, cf. 6.15, Eust.382.32; also in a theatre, Suid. s.v. *σκηνή*.

⊛ **κονίω** [ῑ], fut. *κονίσω* [ῑ]: aor. *ἐκόνῑσα* Il. (v. infr.):—Med., Ph.2.173, fut. *κονιοῦμαι* v.l. in Ph. l.c. (as if from *κονίζω*, cf. Hsch. s.v. *κονίζεσθαι*): aor. *ἐκονῑσάμην* Ar.*Ec.*1177, Luc.*Anach.*31, etc.:—Pass., pf. *κεκόνῑμαι* Il.21.541, Hes.*Op.*481, Ar.*Ec.*291: plpf. *κεκόνῑτο* Il.22.405 (in Mss. sts. incorrectly *ἐκόνισσα, κεκόνισμαι, κεκόνιστο*, Il.21.407, Theoc.1.30, *AP*9.128):—*make dusty, cover with clouds of dust*, εὐρὺ κονίσουσιν πεδίον, of persons in hasty flight, Il.14.145. 2. *cover with dust*, ἐκόνισε δὲ χαίτας 21.407:—Pass., κεκονιμένοι φεῦγον *all dusty* fled they, ib.541; κεκόνιτο κάρη 22.405; κεκονιμένος *all dusty*, i.e. *in haste*, Ar.*Ec.*291, cf. 1177, Luc.*DDeor.*24.1, *Tim.*45, etc. 3. Pass., *to be sprinkled as with dust*, κισσὸς ἑλιχρύσῳ κεκονιμένος Theoc.1.30. 4. Med., *roll in the dust*, like birds, horses, etc., Arist.*HA*633$^b$4, 557$^a$12 (leg. *κονίωνται*), Polem.Hist.59; but, of wrestlers, *sprinkle themselves with dust*, Diocl.*Fr.*141, Gal.6.162, Luc.*Anach.* l.c.: hence, *prepare for combat*, Ph. l.c., Eust.1113.63; αὐτὸς ἐφ' ἑαυτοῦ κονισάμενος Max.Tyr.5.8. II. intr., κονίοντες πεδίοιο *galloping o'er the dusty* plain, in Il. always of horses, 13.820, 23.372, 449; of men racing, Od.8.122; of an advancing army, A.*Th.*60, cf. *Pers.*163 (troch.).

**κονιώδης**, ες, *ash-like*, Hp.*Coac.*571.

**κόννα**· *σποδός*, Hsch.

⊛ **κόννᾰρος**, ὁ, a prickly evergreen, *Zizyphus Spina-Christi*, Theopomp.Hist.129, Agathocl.6:—neut. **κόνναρον**, τό, *its fruit*, Hsch.

**Κοννᾶς** or **Κόννος**, ὁ, a famous harpist who taught Socrates, Pl.*Euthd.*272c, but died in want, Cratin.317, Ar.*Eq.*534: hence prov., Κόννου θρῖον *trifle*, Sch.Ar.*V.*673; altered to Κ. ψῆφος by Ar. l.c.

**κοννέω**, contr. **κοννῶ**, *know*, *κοννεῖς* A.*Supp.*130, 164 (both lyr.), cf. Hsch.

**κοννοειδῆ**· εἰς ὀξὺ λήγων, Hsch. (leg. *κωνο-*).

⊛ **κόννος**, ὁ, kind of *trinket*, Suid., citing Plb.10.18.6 (where *κόνος*). 2. *beard*, Luc.*Lex.*5. 3. = *σκόλλυς* (Lacon.), Hsch. s.v. *ἱέρωμα*; and **κοννοφόρος**, ον, = *σκολλυφόρος*, Id.

**κοννόφρων**, = *ἄφρων*, *Com.Adesp.*93.

⊛ **κοντάκιον**, τό, *essay*, κ. μου εἰς τὴν γεωμετρίαν Steph.*in Rh.*284.33, cf. 277.29.

**κοντάριον** (A), τό, = *κέντρον* 9, Heph.Astr.2.11 (pl.).

**κοντάριον** (B), τό, Dim. of *κοντός* (A), *spear*, Anon.*in Rh.*236.5, Sch.E.*Hec.*14; **κοντᾰρᾶτος**, ὁ, *one armed with a spear*, Anon.*in Rh.*103.21; **κοντᾰριοθήκη**, ἡ, *spear-case*, Sch.Opp.*H.*2.356.

**κονταφόρος**, ὁ, = *κοντοφόρος*, *Gloss.*

⊛ **κόντῑλος**, ὁ, Dim. of *κοντός* (A) (sens. obsc.), Eup.334.

**κοντο-βολέω**, *strike with a pole*, Str.10.1.12. ⊛ **-κῡνηγέσιον**, τό, *wild-beast hunt with pikes*, *IGRom.*4.1632.7 (Philadelphia). **-παίκτης**, ου, ὁ, (*παίζω*) *acrobat who balanced a pole on his head*, *SIG*847.4 (Delph., ii/iii A.D., written **-πέκτης**), *AB*652. **-πλεύριον**, τό, *short side*, interpol. in *Hippiatr.*115 (pl.). **-πορεία**, ἡ, *short road*, as pr. n., Ptol.Euerg.6 J., Plb.16.16.4.

⊛ **κοντός** (A), ὁ, *pole, punting-pole*, Od.9.487, Hdt.2.136, 4.195, E.*Alc.*254 (lyr.), Th.2.84, Epicr.10, Diocl.*Fr.*142, *IG*12(5).647.30 (Ceos). 2. *pike*, Luc.*Tox.*55. 3. *crutch*, Gal.*UP*3.5 (pl.). 4. *goad*, *PCair.Zen.*362$^r$.34 (iii B.C.).

**κοντός** (B), ή, όν, *short*, Adam.2.20, Palch. in *Cat.Cod.Astr.*1.95, interpol. in *Hippiatr.*115:—also written **κονδός**, Sor.1.16 (interpol.), Aët.16.111 (Comp.), prob. in *JRS*18.30 (Sup.). Adv. Comp. κονδότερον ἐπιβαίνειν, of a horse, take *shorter* steps, *Hippiatr.*30.

**κοντοφόρος**, ον, *carrying a pole* or *pike*, Plb.*Fr.*225, Luc.*Alex.*55.

**κόντ-ωσις**, εως, ἡ, *fishing with a pole*, Ael.*NA*12.43. **-ωτίτης** [ῑ], ου, ὁ, *puntsman*, *PCair.Zen.*492.2 (iii B.C.). **-ωτός**, ή, όν, *furnished with a pole*: κοντωτόν (sc. πλοῖον), τό, *punt*, *PHib.*1.39.4 (iii B.C.), D.S.19.12, App.*Prooem.*10.

⊛ **κόνυζα**, ης, ἡ, name of various species of *Inula*, *fleabane*, Hecat.154 J., Arist.*HA*534$^b$28, Thphr.*HP*6.2.6, Gal.12.35, etc.; poet. *κνύζα* Theoc.4.25, 7.68; κ. ἄρρην, = κ. μείζων, Dsc.3.121, *Inula viscosa*; κ. θήλεια Thphr. l.c.; = κ. μικρά, Dsc. l.c., *I. graveolens*, cf. Nic.*Th.*875; a third species, = *I. britannica*, Thphr. l.c., Dsc. l.c.

**κονυζ-ήεις**, εσσα, εν, *like Inula*, Nic.*Th.*615. **-ίτης** [ῑ] οἶνος, ὁ, wine *flavoured with* κόνυζα, Dsc.5.53, *Gp.*8.10.

**Κονώνειος**, α, ον, *of Conon*: κονωνεία (sc. κύλιξ), cup so named, *IG*11(2).287*B*133 (Delos, iii B.C.), cf. Ister 38.

**κόον**, v. *κῷον*.

**κοόρτις**, ιος, ἡ, the Roman *cohors*, Plb.11.23.1, 11.33.1, etc.

**κόος**, ὁ, *cavity* in the earth, Hsch. (pl.); from Lacon. *κόον*, = *μέγα*, *EM*396.29.

**Κοούτιος**, ὁ (sc. *μήν*), name of month at Chaleion, *GDI*1734, al.

**κοπάδιον**, τό, = *κόπαιον*, *Gloss.*

⊛ **κοπάζω**, aor. *ἐκόπασα* (v. infr.): pf. *κεκόπακα* Hsch.:—*grow weary*, τοῦ πολέμου Lxx *Jo.*14.15; τοῦ θυμοῦ ib.*Es.*2.1; of an abnormal pulsation, *abate*, Hp.*Epid.*7.2; esp. of natural phenomena, ἐκόπασε (sc. ὁ ἄνεμος) Hdt.7.191, cf. *Ev.Matt.*14.32; ὅταν ἡ λίμνη κοπάσῃ Arist.*Pr.*935$^a$18; ἐκόπασε τὸ πῦρ Lxx *Nu.*11.2; of heat, Longus 1.8.

**κόπαιον**, τό, (*κόπτω*) *piece*, Alciphr.3.7, Callistr.ap.Suid. s.v. *σελάχιον*.

**κοπᾰν-ίζω**, *bray, pound*, Lxx 3*Ki.*2.46e (Pass.), Alex.Trall.12 (Pass.). **-ισμός**, ὁ, *braying*, Hsch. s.v. *κόπος*. **-ιστήριον**, τό, *vessel for braying, mortar*, Id. s.v. *ἀλήθινον*, *Gloss.* ⊛ **-ον**, τό, *pestle*, Eust.1324.32. II. = *κοπίς*, A.*Ch.*860 (anap.). **-ος**, ὁ, = *σκέπανος*, Sch.Opp.*H.*1.106.

**κοπάριον**, τό, a sort of *probe*, Sever.ap.Aët.7.92, Paul.Aeg.3.81, 6.62.

**κοπάς**, άδος, ἡ, (*κόπτω*) *pruned, lopped*, Thphr.*HP*1.3.3: as Subst., *brushwood*, ξυλοκοπία τῆς κ. *PSI*4.323.3 (iii B.C.), *PCair.Zen.*118.5 (iii B.C.), al.: also in pl., κοπάδες, αἱ, *PSI*5.537.16 (iii B.C.).

**κόπασμα**, ατος, τό, *abatement*, of a flood, Tz.*H.*6.833 (pl.).

**κόπελλα**· *αἰδοῖα*, Hsch. **κόπερρα**, Aeol., = *κοπρία*, Hdn.Gr.2.605.

**κοπετόκτῡπος**, ον, *causing the noise of lamentation to be heard*, epith. of Hecate, *PMag.Par.*1.2867 (nisi leg. *καπετό-*).

**κοπετός**, ὁ, *noise*, Eup.347; esp. of lamentation, = *κομμός*, *Act.Ap.*8.2, Plu.*Fab.*17 (pl.), *AP*11.122 (Nicarch.).

**κοπεύς**, έως, ὁ, *one who brays* or *pounds*, employed in oil-factories, *PRev.Laws* 45.5 (iii B.C.), cf. Agatharch.26; *carpenter*, *PFlor.*175.14 (iii A.D.): generally, *one who cuts*, τινος A.D.*Synt.*301.28. II. *chisel*, D.S.1.35, Luc.*Somn.*13.

⊛ **κοπή**, ἡ, *cutting*, χόρτος εἰς κοπὴν καὶ ἐπινομήν *POxy.*499.15 (ii A.D.). 2. *cutting in pieces, slaughter*, Lxx *Jo.*10.20, *Ep.Hebr.*7.1. 3. κ. τριχός, tax levied on γερδιοραβδισταί, *PAmh.*2.119.4 (200 A.D.), cf. *PFay.*58.7 (ii A.D.). 4. *breaking up*, [νεφῶν] Arist.*Mu.*394$^a$34. 5. *pounding* in a mortar, Alex.Aphr.*Pr.*1.67. 6. *dressing* of stone, *CPHerm.*127 (iii A.D.). 7. *striking, minting*, νομίσματος *Inscr.Délos* 461 *Aa*76 (ii B.C.). 8. *divorce*, Aq.*De.*24.3 (1). II. = *κόπος* II, φλοίσβου μετὰ κοπήν S.*Fr.*479 codd. Eust. (sed leg. *κόπον*).

**κόπηθρον**, τό, a wild vegetable, Hsch.

**κοπ-ηρός**, ά, όν, = *κοπιαρός*, Hdn.*Epim.*179. **-ία**, ἡ, *rest from toil*, Hsch. (pl.); but, = Lat. *labor*, Serv.Dan. ad Virg.*G.*1.150. **-ιᾰρός**, ά, όν, *wearying*, in Comp. *-ώτερος*, Arist.*Pr.*880$^b$16, Thphr.*Lass.*7, 9. ⊛ **-ιάτης** [ᾱ], ου, ὁ, *grave-digger*, *Cod.Theod.*13.1.1, 16.2.15, Just.*Nov.*59.2, *Gloss.*:—also **κοπιᾶς**, ᾶτος, ὁ, in dat. pl. *κουπιᾶσιν* (sic) *BCH*24.306 (Philippi). ⊛ **-ιάω**, fut. *-άσω* [ᾱ]: aor. *ἐκοπίᾱσα* Men.*Phasm.*36: pf. *κεκοπίᾱκα* *Apoc.*2.3: (*κόπος*):—*to be tired, grow weary*, Ar.*Th.*795, *Fr.*318.8, Lxx *De.*25.18, al.; κ. τὰ σκέλη Alex.147, Men. l.c.; κ. ὑπὸ ἀγαθῶν *to be weary of* good things, Ar.*Av.*735; ἐκ τῆς ὁδοιπορίας *Ev.Jo.*4.6; τῇ διανοίᾳ Erasistr.ap.Gal.*Consuet.*1: c. part., κ. ὀρχούμενοι Ar.*Fr.*602; ζῶν *AP*12.46 (Asclep.); μὴ κοπιάτω φιλοσοφῶν Epicur.*Ep.*3 p.59 U., cf. Plu.2.185e: aor. part. κοπιάσας, *defunctus laboribus*, *IG*14.1811:—Med. in act. sense, Arist.*Pr.*881$^a$14. II. *work hard, toil*, *Ev.Matt.*6.28, etc.; μεθ' ἡδονῆς κ. Vett.Val.266.6; εἴς τι 1*Ep.Ti.*4.10, cf. *Ep.Rom.*16.6; ἔν τινι 1*Ep.Ti.*5.17; ἐπί τι Lxx *Jo.*24.13: c. inf., *strive, struggle*, μὴ κοπία ζητεῖν *Lyr.Alex.Adesp.*37.7. III. = *κοπάζω*, *come to rest*: *arrive at a state of saturation*, *PLeid.X.*30 (iii/iv A.D.).

⊛ **κοπίδερμος**, ὁ, = *μαστιγίας*, *Gloss.*

**κοπίζω** (A), (*κόπις* A) *talk idly, lie*, Hsch.

**κοπίζω** (B), *celebrate the κοπίς* (*κοπίς* (B) II), Ath.4.138f.

⊛ **κόπις** (A), ιδος, ὁ, *prater, liar, wrangler*, E.*Hec.*132 (anap.), Lyc.763, 1464; κοπίδων ἀρχηγός Heraclit.81, cf. Pythag.ap.Sch.E.*Hec.*134. (Prob. from *κόπτω*.)

⊛ **κοπίς** (B), ίδος, ἡ, (*κόπτω*) *chopper, cleaver*, Hermipp.46 (anap.), Ar.*Fr.*138, S.*Fr.*894, D.S.12.24, etc.; νερτέρων κ., prob. for *κόνις*, S.*Ant.*602 (lyr.); *broad curved knife*, used by the Thessalians, E.*El.*837; by Orientals, X.*Cyr.*2.1.9, 6.2.10: as Adj., κ. μάχαιρα E.*Cyc.*241: metaph., of Phocion, ἡ τῶν ἐμῶν λόγων κ. D.ap.Plu.*Phoc.*5. 2. (parox.) κέντροιο κ. *sting of a scorpion*, Nic.*Th.*780; cf. κόπιες· κέντρα ὀρνίθ⟨ε⟩ια, Hsch. II. among the Lacedaemonians, *feast given on certain festivals to strangers*, Cratin.164, Eup.138, Philyll.16.

**κοπίσκος**, ὁ, Dim. of *κοπίς*, = *λίβανος σμιλιωτός*, Dsc.1.68.

**κοπιώδης**, ες, = *κοπώδης*, Hp.*Epid.*1.26.ς', Arist.*Pr.*885$^b$2: Comp., ib.$^a$17; κ. πυρετοί Hp.*Prorrh.*1.142, Gal.7.626.

⊛ **κόπ-ος**, ὁ, (*κόπτω*) *striking, beating*, ὀξύχειρι σὺν κόπῳ (Pauw for *κτύπῳ*) A.*Ch.*23 (lyr.); στέρνων κόπους (Seidler for *κτύπους*) E.*Tr.*794 (anap.); = *κοπανισμός*, Hsch. II. *toil and trouble, suffering*, A.*Supp.*210 (pl.); ἀνδροδάϊκτος κόπος Id.*Fr.*132 ap.Ar.*Ra.*1265; *pain* of a disease, S.*Ph.*880; κόπους παρέχειν τινί to give *trouble*, *Ev.Matt.*26.10, al., *PTeb.*21.10 (ii B.C.), *BGU*844.10 (i A.D.); κόπον ἔχειν Phld.*Mus.*p.62 K.; πάντα κ. ἀναδεξάμενος *SIG*761*B*6 (Delph., i B.C.). 2. *fatigue*, Hp.*VM*21, Gal.6.190; κόπου ὕπο from *very weariness*, E.*Ba.*634; κόπῳ παρεῖμαι Id.*Ph.*852; κόπῳ δαμέντες, ἁλίσκεσθαι, Id.*Rh.*764, Th.7.40; τῷ κ. ξυνεῖναι Ar.*Pl.*321; τὰ γόνατα κ. ἕλοι μου Id.*Lys.*542: in pl., E.*Rh.*124; κόποι καὶ ὕπνοι Pl.*R.*537b, cf. X.*Eq.*4.2, 2*Ep.Cor.*6.5, etc.; περὶ κόπων title of work by Thphr. 3. *work, exertion*, καμάραν ἀφ' ἰδίων κόπων ἐποίησεν *IG*12(7).384 (Amor-

gos), cf. *BGU*884.10 (i A.D.); κόπῳ κόπον λύειν prov. in Orib.*Eup.* 1.2.8. ⊛-όω, *weary*, D.Chr.11.96; βαρυτέροις γυμνασίοις Id.18.6:—Pass., = κοπιάω, Batr.189, Antyll.ap.Orib.6.1.1, Plu.2.312f, Gal. 18(2).914; ὑπὸ τῆς ὁδοιπορίας J.*AJ*2.15.3.

**κόππα**, τό, = Hebr. ק (*Koph*), a letter (ϙ) standing between π and ρ in early Greek alphabets, *IG*14.2420, etc.; later displaced by κ, but surviving in Latin as Q and retained in Greek as a numeral = 90, e.g. *PSI*8.958.24 (iv A.D.): prov., οὐδὲ κόππα γιγνώσκων Parmeno 1.

**κοππ-ᾰτίας**, ὁ, *branded with the letter Koppa* as a mark, ἵππος κ. Ar. *Nu.*23 (with a play on κόπτω), 438, *Fr.*42. **-ᾰφόρος**, ον, = foreg., Luc.*Ind.*5.

**κοπρ-ᾰγωγέω**, *carry dung*, Dor. inf. κοπραγωγῆν Ar.*Lys.*1174. **-ᾰγωγός**, όν, *carrying dung*, γαστήρ Pl.Com.222; κ. ῥιπίς CratesCom. 13. **-ᾰνα**, τά, *excrements*, Hp.*Epid.*1.26.β', Aret.*SA*2.5. **-εαῖος**, ὁ, a quasi-pr. n., formed from κόπρος, *Dungy*, Ar.*Ec.*317. **-ειος**, α, ον, *full of dung, filthy*, ἀνὴρ κ. *stinkard*, Id.*Eq.*899, with play on signf. II. II. in Attica, of the deme Κόπρος, *IG*1².301.39:—later **Κόπριος**, misspelt Κύπριος, Is.3.2 codd., cf. Decr.ap.D.18. 73. **-εύω**, = κοπρίζω, Hsch.:—written **κοπρεόω**, *SIG*986.14 (Chios, v/iv B.C.). **-έω**, v. κοπρίζω. **-εών**, ῶνος, ὁ, = κοπρών, Tz. *H.*6.520. **-ηγέω**, *carry dung*, *PFay.*118.19 (ii A.D.). ⊛**-ηγία**, ἡ, *conveyance of dung*, ib.110.11 (i A.D.). ⊛**-ηγός**, όν, *conveying dung*, πλοῖον *PLond.*2.317.8 (ii A.D.): Subst. -ηγόν, τό, *dung-cart*, *PFay.* 119.33 (pl., 100 A.D.). **-ία**, ἡ, (cf. κόπερρα) *dunghill*, Semon.7.6 (pl.), Stratt.43, Arist.*Mir.*845$^a$5 (pl.), Lxx *Jb.*2.8, Asclep.ap.Gal.12.634, etc.; in Egypt, *rubbish-heap*, *PRyl.*2.162.17 (ii A.D.), etc.; ἀναιρεῖσθαι ἀπὸ κοπρίας, of foundlings, *PGnom.*238, cf. 115 (ii A.D.), *POxy.*3717 (i A.D.). II. *refuse*, ἐν σείσματι κοσκίνου διαμένει κ. Lxx *Si.* 27.4; *manure*, *Ev.Luc.*13.8 (v.l. κόπρια). **-ιαίρετος**, *sportellarius*, *Gloss.*:—also **-ίαρτος**, (αἴρω) *taken from the rubbish-heap*, i.e. *foundling*, prob. for κηπρ- in *PGnom.*210 (ii A.D.). **-ιακός**, ἡ, όν, *concerning manure*, *PGoodsp.Cair.*30 xxxiv 16 (ii A.D.). **-ίας**, ου, ὁ, (κόπρος) in pl., *buffoons*, a word first used under the Roman emperors, D.C.50.28, 73.6: Lat. *copreae*, Suet.*Tib.*61. (Perh. so called because ἐκ κοπρίας ἀναιρεθέντες, or because of their obscenity.) ⊛**-ίζω**, Ep. fut. -ίσσω, *dung, manure*, τέμενος μέγα κοπρίσσοντες Od.17.299 (v.l. for κοπρήσοντες), cf. Thphr.*CP*3.9.1, 4.12.2, *Sammelb.*5126.27 (iii A.D.); *act as manure*, of leguminous plants, Thphr.*HP*8.9.1. **-ιήμετος**, ον, *vomiting excrement*, Hp.*Epid.*2.1.9. **-ινος**, η, ον, *full of dung, filthy*, *Gloss.*; κόπρινοι σκώληκες worms *in excrement*, Hp.*Superf.* 28. **-ιον**, τό, = κόπρος, Id.*Acut.*56, Ruf.ap.Orib.8.24.8, *PFay.*110. 5 (i A.D.), etc.: pl., Heraclit.96, *OGI*483.81 (Pergam.), Sor.2.56, Plu.*Pomp.*48. 2. generally, *dirt, filth*, *BGU*1115.50 (i B.C.); esp. in Magic, *dirt* taken from spot where a corpse has lain, in pl., *PMag. Par.*1.1396, 1441. **-ισις**, εως, ἡ, *dunging, manuring*, Thphr.*HP* 8.6.3. **-ισμός**, ὁ, = foreg., Id.*CP*3.9.2, *POxy.*729.10 (ii A.D.), *Gp.* 2.39.6. **-ιώδης**, ες, = κοπρώδης, Hp.*Coac.*590, Thphr.*CP*2.6.3; *full of dung*, τόπος *PSI*6.696.10 (iii A.D.).

**κοπρο-βολεῖον**, τό, *dunghill*, Eust.1404.64. **-βόλος**, ον, *for spreading dung*, πτύον *EM*94.3. **-δοχεῖον**, τό, and **-δόχος**, ὁ, *cesspool*, *Gloss.* **-θέσιον**, τό, *place where dung is put*, *Gp.*2.22. 3. **-θήκη**, ἡ, = foreg., *Gloss.* **-λογέω**, *collect dung*, Ar.*Fr.* 662, *Sammelb.*6222.25 (iii A.D.). **-λόγος**, ὁ, *dung-gatherer*, Ar. *Pax*9; *scavenger*, Arist.*Ath.*50.2: hence, *dirty fellow*, Ar.*V.*1184.

**κόπρον**, τό, used for κόπρος, ἡ, acc. to Gal.12.290.

**κοπρο-ξύστης**, ου, ὁ, *one who clears out manure*, *UPZ*119.40 (ii B.C.). **-ποιέω**, *prepare manure*, *Ostr.Strassb.*748 (ii A.D.). **-ποιός**, όν, *producing excrement*, *EM*529.15, *Gloss.*

⊛**κόπρος**, ἡ, *excrement, ordure*, of men and cattle, Od.9.329, al., Hdt. 3.22, etc.: in pl., Euph.96.4; esp. as used in husbandry, *dung, manure*, Pl.*Prt.*334a, Thphr.*HP*2.7.4. 2. generally, *filth, dirt*, κυλινδόμενος κατὰ κόπρον Il.22.414, 24.640, cf. *BGU*1116.14 (i B.C.). II. *dunghill, byre*, Il.18.575, Od.10.411, Call.*Dian.*178; καθίσαι τινὰς ἐπὶ κόπρου Men.544.5. (In this sense oxyt. κοπρός acc. to Eust.1165. 15.) (Cf. Skt. *śákṛt*, gen. *śaknás* 'excrement'.)

**κοπροσύνη**, ἡ, *manuring*, *PSI*4.296.18 (vi A.D.).

**κοπροσύρα**· τὰ συρόμενα κόπρια, Hsch.

**κοπρο-φᾰγέω**, *eat dung*, Hsch., Suid. s.v. βοῦς Κύπριος. **-φάγος** [φᾰ], ον, *dung-eating*, Gal.12.249, Diogenian.3.49, Hsch. s.v. βοῦς Κύπριος. **-φορά**, ἡ, *load of dung*, *IG*12(7).62.20 (Amorgos, iv B.C., pl.). **-φορέω**, *cover with dung or dirt*, τινα Ar.*Eq.*295. **-φόρος**, ον, *carrying dung*, Poll.7.134; ὄνος Id.1.226; κόφινος κ. *dung-basket*, X.*Mem.*3.8.6.

**κοπρ-όω**, fut. -ώσω Sch.Ar.*Pl.*313:—*befoul with dung*, κοπρῶσαι τὸν τρίβωνα Arr.*Epict.*4.11.34:—Pass., κεκοπρῶσθαι, -ωμένος, ib.29. 18. **-ώδης**, ες, *like dung*, Hp.*Prorrh.*1.146, Arist.*PA*675$^b$30; *faecal*, Aret.*CA*1.2. 2. generally, *dirty, impure*, Pl.*Tht.*191c (Comp.), 194e. **-ών**, ῶνος, ὁ, *place for dung, privy*, Ar.*Th.*485, D.25.49, Eub.53.2, *IG*2.1058.11, etc.: prov., εἰς κοπρῶνα θυμιᾶν, of useless work, Phot. s.v. ὄνου πόκαι. **-ωσις**, εως, ἡ, *dunging, manuring*, Thphr.*HP*2.7.1.

**κοπ-τάριον**, τό, Dim. of κοπτή (κοπτός II. 2), *lozenge*, Dsc.4.188, Orib.8.47.16, Archig.ap.eund.8.46.10, Gal.13.58. 2. Dim. of κοπτή (κοπτός II. 1), *PGoodsp.Cair.*30 xlii 5 (ii A.D.). **-τέον**, *one must pound*, φάρμακον Asclep.ap.Gal.13.341, cf. 969, Dsc.2.76, *Gp.*3.7. 1. ⊛**-τή**, ἡ, = θαλάσσιον πράσον, Dionys.Utic.ap.Ath.14.648e. II. v. κοπτός II. 2. **-τήριον**, τό, *place where grain was beaten out*, *PCair.Zen.*464.9, al. (iii B.C.). ⊛**-τικός**, ἡ, όν, *murderous*, Tz.*H.* 12.872. Adv. -κῶς Hdn.*Epim.*134. **-τόν**, τό, = κοπτή (κοπτός II. 1), Hsch. (pl.). 2. name of various plasters, Orib.*Fr.*74, Alex. Trall.7.8.

**κοπτοπλᾰκοῦς**, οῦντος, ὁ, = κοπτή (κοπτός II. 1), Chrysipp.Tyan. ap.Ath.14.647f.

**κοπτοραν**, v. κοπτούρα.

⊛**κοπτός**, ή, όν, *chopped small* or *pounded*, ἰσχάς Cratin.371; τυρός Antiph.133.8. II. κοπτὴ σησαμίς, a cake of *pounded* sesame, Artem.1.72 codd.; κοπτή alone in this sense, Sopat.17, *AP*12.212 (Strat.), *POxy.*113.31 (ii A.D.), Alex.Trall.1.15. 2. **κοπτή**, ἡ, *lozenge, pastille*, Dsc.2.103, Archig.ap.Orib.8.46.8.

**κοπτούρα**, ἡ, *mortar* for flour-making, *PSI*7.787.5 (ii A.D.), *Stud. Pal.*20.131 (vi A.D.): acc. sg. written κοπτοραν Wilcken *Chr.*323.22 (ii A.D.).

**κοπτουργία**, ἡ, *making of* κοπταί, *POxy.*1454.6 (ii A.D.); nisi leg. κοπτουρία *pounding* of wheat into flour.

**κόπτρα**, τά, *wages for cutting*, ἀράκου *PLond.*3.1171 (i B.C.), cf. *PLips.*106.7 (i A.D.).

⊛**κόπτω**, Od.18.28, etc.: fut. κόψω Hippon.83, Men.*Pk.*64, etc.: aor. ἔκοψα, Ep. κόψα Il.13.203: pf. κέκοφα (ἐκ-) X.*HG*6.5.37, (περι-) Lys.14.42, (συγ-) Pl.*Tht.*169b; Ep. part. κεκοπώς Il.13.60 (v.l. -φώς, -πών), Od.18.335:—Med., fut. κόψομαι Lxx *Ez.*6.9: aor. ἐκοψάμην Hdt.4.166:—Pass., fut. κεκόψομαι (ἀπο-) Ar.*Nu.*1125, (ἐκ-) Id.*Ra.* 1223, (κατα-) X.*An.*1.5.16, κοπήσομαι Lxx *Je.*8.2, Gal.13.759: aor. ἐκόπην A.*Ag.*1278, Ar.*Ra.*723, Th.8.13: pf. κέκομμαι A.*Pers.*683:—*cut, strike*, 1. *smite*, σ' ἀμφὶ κάρη κεκοπὼς χερὶ στιβαρῇσι Od.18.335: c. dupl. acc., κόψε δὲ παπτήναντα παρήϊον *smote* him *on* the cheek, Il.23.690. 2. *smite* with weapons, κόπτοντες δούρεσσι μετάφρενον Od.8.528; τοῖσι Πέρσῃσι εἵποντο κόπτοντες Hdt.6.113: metaph. in Pass., with play on words, αἰεὶ κόπτῃ ῥήμασι καὶ κοπίσιν *AP*11.335. 3. *smite, slaughter* an animal with an axe or mallet, κόψας ἐξόπιθεν κεράων βοὸς Il.17.521, cf. Od.14.425, X.*An.*2.1.6; in Trag., A.*Ag.*1278, *Eu.*635, E.*El.*838. 4. *cut off, chop off*, κεφαλὴν ἀπὸ δειρῆς κόψεν Il.13.203; χεῖράς τ' ἠδὲ πόδας κόπτον Od.22.477; κ. [τὰ γέρρα] ταῖς μαχαίραις X.*An.*4.6.26; κ. δένδρα *cut down* or *fell* trees, Th.2.75, X. *HG*5.2.39, 43; κ. τὴν χώραν *lay it waste*, ib.3.2.26, 4.6.5:—in Pass., of ships, *to be shattered, disabled* by the enemy, Th.4.14, 8.13:—metaph., φρενῶν κεκομμένος A.*Ag.*479 (lyr.); τὸν ὕπνον ἁ φροντὶς κόπτοισα *preventing*, Theoc.21.28; [πνεῦμα] κοπτόμενον *being suddenly stopped, arrested*, Arist.*Mete.*367$^a$10. 5. *strike, beat* a horse, to make him go faster, κόψε δ' Ὀδυσσεὺς τόξῳ Il.10.513; also σκηπανίῳ Γαιήοχος ἀμφοτέρω (sc. Αἴαντε) κεκοπὼς πλῆσεν μένεος 13.60. 6. *hammer, forge*, κόπτε δὲ δεσμούς 18.379, Od.8.274: later, *stamp* metal, i.e. *coin* money, κ. νόμισμα *IG*12(5).480.11 (Siphnos, Athenian Law), Xenoph.4, Hdt.3.56:—Med., *coin oneself* money, *order to be coined*, κ. χρυσοῦ καὶ ἀργύρου νόμισμα Id.1.94, cf. 4.166:—Pass., of money, *to be stamped* or *coined*, [νομίσμασιν] μόνοις ὀρθῶς κοπεῖσι Ar.*Ra.*723, cf. 726. 7. *knock* or *rap at*, τὴν θύραν Id.*Nu.*132, *Pl.*1097, And. 1.41, X.*HG*5.4.7, Men.*Epit.*538, Phld.*Vit.*p.30 J., Plu.*Alc.*8, etc.; without θύραν, οὗτος, τί κόπτεις; Ar.*Ec.*976. 8. *pound, bray* in a mortar, κυπέρου κεκομμένου Hdt.4.71; ἀσταφίδα κεκ. Alex.127.4; ἔλαιον κεκ., i.e. *pure* oil, Lxx 3*Ki.*5.11. 9. *knock, dash about*, τὸ ὕδωρ ὅταν κοπῇ Pl.*Ti.*60b; κόνις..κοπτομένη..ὑφ' ἅρμασι Hes. *Sc.*63; θάλασσα κοπτομένη πνοιαῖς Theoc.22.16. 10. of birds, *peck*, Arist.*HA*609$^b$5; ὁ ἁλιάετος..τὰ λιμναῖα κ. *preys* on the lagoon life, ib.593$^b$24; σπειρὴν κ. *peck* at, Arat.449; of fish, *gnaw*, Arist.*HA* 620$^b$17; of a snake, *strike*, Il.12.204:—Pass., of wood or seeds, *to be worm-eaten*, Thphr.*HP*3.18.5, 8.11.2. b. *munch, masticate*, dub. in Chionid.6. 11. ὁ ἵππος κ. τὸν ἀναβάτην *jars* his rider *by his paces*, X.*Eq.*1.4:—Pass., ib.8.7, Hp.*Aër.*21. 12. κ. ὄνους *dress, prepare* mill-stones for use, Alex.13; *set, sharpen*, Herod.6.84:—Med., *AP* 11.253 (Lucill.). 13. metaph., *tire out, weary*, μήθ' ὑμῖν ἐνοχλῶ μήτ' ἐμαυτὸν κ. D.*Prooem.*29, cf. Alciphr.2.3; λέγων φαίνου τι δὴ καινόν.., ἢ μὴ κόπτε με Hegesipp.1.3, cf. Sosip.1.20; μὴ κόπτ' ἔμ', ἀλλὰ τὰ κρέα Alex.173.12; κ. τὴν ἀκρόασιν D.H.*Comp.*19; κ. τὰ ὦτα Poll.6.119; κ. ἐρωτήμασιν ἀκαίροις Plu.*Phoc.*7, cf. Moer.p.74 P.:—Pass., *to be worn out*, κοπτόμενοι ἀεὶ ταῖς στρατείαις D.2.16. II. Med. κόπτομαι, *beat* or *strike oneself, beat one's breast* or *head* through grief, κεφαλὴν δ' ὅ γε κόψατο χερσίν Il.22.33, cf. Hdt.2.121.δ' (also Act. τί κόπτεις τὴν κεφαλήν; Men.*Her.*4); κόπτεσθαι μέτωπα Hdt.6.58 (with μαχαίρῃσι added 2.61): abs., Pl.*Phd.*60b, *R.*619c: pf. Pass., [πόλις] κέκοπται A.*Pers.* 683:—Act. c. acc. cogn., ἔκοψα κομμὸν Ἄριον Id.*Ch.*423 (lyr.). 2. κόπτεσθαί τινα *mourn for* any one, κόπτεσθ' Ἄδωνιν Ar.*Lys.*396, cf. *Ev.Luc.*8.52; but also ἐπί τινα *Apoc.*1.7, 18.9 (v.l. αὐτῇ). (Cf. Lith. *kapóti*, Lett. *kapāt* 'chop small', 'beat', 'stamp', Lat. *capo* 'capon', perh. σκέπαρνον.)

**κοπώδης**, ες, *wearying, wearing*, πυρετοί v.l. in Hp.*Prorrh.*1.142; βάρη Arist.*Pr.*881$^a$19 (Comp.); βαρὺ καὶ κ. (sc. τὸ ὕδωρ) *causing pain*, Alex.198; κ. διάθεσις Gal.6.320: Comp. -ωδέστεραι συμφοραί Procop. *Arc.*13: c. gen., κ. ὑποχονδρίων *causing pain in..*, Hp.*Acut.*16. 2. metaph., *wearisome, boring*, D.H.*Dem.*58, Plu.2.47f; φράσις ib. 1011a. II. Pass., *wearied, worn out*, Hp.*Prorrh.*1.38, Gal.7.547. Adv. Comp. -ωδέστερον, ἔχειν Plu.2.130c.

**κόπωσις**, εως, ἡ, *weariness*, σαρκός Lxx *Ec.*12.12.

**Κόρα**, ἡ, v. κόρη (B).

**Κοραγεῖν**· τὸ ἀνάγειν τὴν Κόρην (sc. Persephone), Hsch.:—hence **Κοράγια**, τά, of a ritual procession at Mantinea, *IG*5(2).265.16 (i B.C.); **Κοράγιον**, τό, sanctuary where this rite took place, ib.266.41; **Κοραγοί**, οἱ, celebrants of the rite, ib.265.27.

**κοραῖος**, α, ον, *of a maiden*, ἠλακάτης δὲ κοραίης Epic.in *Arch.Pap.*7.8.

**κοράκ-ειον** [ᾰ], τό, = κορώνεως, Sch.Ar.*Pax*627. **-εύομαι**, gloss on κοράττω, Hsch. **-εύς**, έως, ὁ, kind of *fish*, prob. = κορακῖνος, Id. **-εως**, ω, ὁ, = κορώνεως, Hermipp.51. **-ησία**, ἡ, name of a herb, Pythag.ap.Plin.*HN*24.156. **-ήσιον**, τό, dub. sens. (prob. a kind of jar) in *PSI*5.535.48 (iii B.C.). II. name of place in Pamphylia, hence **-ησιωτικὸν** μέλι *PCair.Zen.*12.33 (iii B.C.). **-ιαί**, αἱ, perh. *the Rookeries*, name of a place in Delos, *IG*11(2).199*A*6 al. (iii B.C.). **-ίας**, ου, ὁ, *chough*, *Pyrrhocorax alpinus*, Arist.*HA* 617$^b$16, Hsch. 2. as Adj., *raven-black*, Id. **-ῑνίδιον**, τό, Dim. of κορακῖνος II, Pherecr.56, Anaxandr.27, *PSI*3.206.20 (iii A.D.). **-ῑνίς**, ίδος, ἡ, fem. form of κορακῖνος II, *Gp.*20.25.2. ⊛**-ῖνος**, η, ον, *like a raven, raven-black*, *AB*104, Vitr.8.3.14; κ. σφραγίς, remedy for sore throat, Gal.13.826. **-ῖνος**, ὁ, *young raven*, Ar.*Eq.*1053. 2. = κορακίας, Hsch. II. a fish, Epich.44, Ar.*Lys.* 560, Philyll.13.3, Alex.18, Numen.ap.Ath.7.308e, Arist.*HA*610$^b$5; found in the Nile, Str.17.2.4, J.*BJ*3.10.8, *PFay.*116.4 (ii A.D.); so called from its black colour, Opp.*H.*1.133; acc. to Ath.7.309a διὰ τὸ τὰς κόρας κινεῖν. **-ιον**, τό, Dim. of κόραξ II. 2, *Sammelb.*1.26 (iii A.D.), Eust.73.21. II. a plant, = ἱεράκιον, Arist.*Mir.*837$^a$20.

**κορᾰκίσκος**, ὁ, Dim. of κόραξ, *Gloss.*

**κορᾰκοειδής**, ές, *like a raven, of raven kind*, Arist.*HA*488$^b$5:—also **κορᾰκώδης**, ες, Id.*GA*756$^b$21, *PA*662$^b$7. 2. *like a crow's beak*, ἀπόφυσις τῆς ὠμοπλάτης Gal.*UP*13.12, cf. eund.2.275.

**κόρᾰκος**, ὁ, a plaster, Paul.Aeg.7.17. II. pl., Scythian for φίλιοι δαίμονες, Luc.*Tox.*7.

⊛**κορᾰκόω**, *close, fasten up* (cf. κόραξ II. 2), of a tomb, *Mon.Ant.*23. 202 (Termessus):—Pass., Judeich *Altertümer von Hierapolis* 209.

**κοραλλ-ίζω**, *resemble coral*, Dsc.1.13. **-ικός**, ή, όν, *like coral*, Ps.-Democr.Alch.p.56 B.; cf. κορωλλικός. ⊛**-ιον**, τό, *Peripl. M.Rubr.*28, al., Dsc.5.121, Alciphr.1.39, dub. sens. in Alex.Trall. 1.15; **κοράλιον** S.E.*P.*1.119; **κουράλιον** Thphr.*Lap.*38, D.P.1103, Luc.*Apol.*1 (s. v. l.); **κωράλλιον** or **-άλιον**, Att. acc. to Hdn.Gr.2. 537:—*coral*, esp. *red coral*, ll. cc.: sts. interpr. as Dim. of κόρη in Luc. and Alciphr.; cf. κωράλιον. ⊛**-ιοπλάστης**, ου, ὁ, *one who makes images of coral*, *CIG*3408 (Magn. Sip.).

⊛**κόραξ**, ᾰκος, ὁ, *raven*, *Corvus corax* (not in Hom.); πάντα τάδ' ἐν κοράκεσσι καὶ ἐν φθόρῳ 'food for *crows*', Thgn.833; κόρακες ὣς ἄκραντα γαρύετον Διὸς πρὸς ὄρνιχα θεῖον Pi.*O.*2.87; ἐπὶ σώματος δίκαν κόρακος.. σταθεῖσα A.*Ag.*1473 (lyr.); κόρακες ὥστε βωμῶν ἀλέγοντες οὐδέν Id.*Supp.*751 (lyr.); κόραξι καὶ λύκοις χαρίζεσθαι Luc.*Tim.*8; in imprecations, ἐς κόρακας 'go and be hanged', Ar.*V.*852, 982; βάλλ' ἐς κ. Id.*Nu.*133; ἀπόφερ' ἐς κ. Id.*Pax* 1221; οὐκ ἐς κ. ἐρρήσετε; ib.500; ἔρρ' ἐς κ. Pherecr.70; πλεῖτω ἐς κ. Ar.*Eq.*1314; οὐκ ἐς κ. ἀποφθερεῖ; Id.*Nu.* 789; ἐς κ. οἰχήσεται Id.*V.*51; ἐξελῶ σ' ἐς κ. ἐκ τῆς οἰκίας Id.*Nu.*123; ἐς κ. ἔρρειν ἐκ τῆς Ἀττικῆς Alex.94.5: as a prophet of bad weather, Arist.*Fr.*253, Thphr.*Sign.*16, Plu.2.129a, etc.; of fair weather, Arat.1003, *Gp.*1.2.6, etc.; λευκὸς κ., prov. of something unheard of, *AP*11.417, Luc.*Epigr.*43; but white ravens are mentioned by Arist. *HA*519$^a$6. 2. *cormorant*, *Phalacrocorax carbo*, ib.593$^b$18. 3. the constellation *Corvus*, Arat.449, Ptol.*Tetr.*27, etc. 4. title of a grade in the mysteries of Mithras, Porph.*Abst.*4.16. II. *anything hooked* or *pointed like a raven's beak*, cf. κορώνη II, 1. *engine for grappling ships*, Plb.1.22.3, App.*BC*5.106. b. *siege-engine*, Ph.*Bel.*100.18, D.S.17.44. 2. *hooked door-handle*, Posidipp.7, *AP*11.203, Alex.Aphr.*in SE*25.17; *hook* on a machine, Hero *Aut.* 15.3, Orib.49.4.16, Ath.Mech.36.10, Bito 50.9: generally, *hook*, *Sammelb.*1.24 (iii A.D.). 3. *instrument of torture*, Luc.*Nec.*11 (s. v. l.). 4. = κατακλείς, Hero *Bel.*79.11. 5. *point* of a surgical knife, σμιλαρίου Heliod.ap.Orib.44.10.5; κατιάδος Id.ap.Sch.Orib. 44.14.4. 6. *cock's bill*, Hsch. III. *tub-fish* (cf. κορακῖνος), Diph.Siph.ap.Ath.8.356a. IV. a plaster, Philum.ap.Aët.5.127, Orib.*Fr.*84. (Cf. κορώνη, Lat. *corvus, cornix*, etc.)

**κόραξε**· πόρθει, Hsch.

**Κοραξοί**, οἱ, *Coraxi*, a Colchian tribe, Hecat.210 J., Hellanic.70 J., Arist.*Mete.*351$^a$11: in sg., Phoen.1.14:—Adj. **Κοραξικός**, ή, όν, λῶπος Hippon.3.

⊛**κοραξός**, ή, όν, *raven-black*, Str.12.8.16, Ps.-Plu.*Fluv.*18.8. II. **κόραξος**, ὁ, a fish, Xenocr.ap.Orib.2.58.32.

⊛**κοράσ-ίδιον**, τό, = sq., Arr.*Epict.*1.18.22, al. ⊛**-ιον**, τό, in later Gr., Dim. of κόρη, *little girl, maiden*, Philippid.36, *AP*9.39 (Music.), *IG*7.3325 (Chaeronea), *GDI*1705, al. (Delph.), *PStrassb.*79.2 (i B.C.), Lxx *Ru.*2.8, *Ev.Matt.*9.24, etc. [ᾰ, *AP* l.c.] **-ίς**, ίδος, ἡ, *woman*, Steph.*in Hp.*1.75 D. **-ιώδης**, ες, *girlish*, *Com.Adesp.*146, Plu.2.528a.

**κοράσσει**· ὀρχεῖται, καὶ ἄκλητος ἐλήλυθε, Hsch.:—also **κοράττειν**· κορακεύεσθαι, Id.

**κόραυνα**, ἡ, barbarism for κόρη, Ar.*Av.*1678.

**κόραφος**, ὁ, name of a bird, Hsch.

**κορβᾶ**· ἡ τοῦ κόρματος καὶ Κορύβαντος (-αντίας cod.) αἰτία, Hsch.

**κορβᾶν** (indecl.), Hebr. *qorbān*, *gift* or *votive offering for the service of God*, *Ev.Marc.*7.11, J.*AJ*4.4.4:—hence **κορβανᾶς**, ὁ, *the treasury of the temple* at Jerusalem, *Ev.Matt.*27.6, J.*BJ*2.9.4 (v.l. κορβωνᾶς).

**κορδᾰκ-ίζω**, *dance the* κόρδαξ, Hyp.*Phil.*7, D.Chr.33.9, D.C.50.27, Jul.*Mis.*350b. **-ικός**, ή, όν, *like the* κόρδαξ: hence, of metrical sound, *tripping, running*, ῥυθμὸς κ., of trochaic metres, Arist.*Rh.* 1408$^b$36 (Comp.), cf. Cic.*Orat.*57.193. **-ισμα**, ατος, τό, *dancing of the* κόρδαξ, Hsch. s.v. κολλικόνομον. **-ισμός**, ὁ, = foreg., *licentious dancing*, D.2.18 (pl.), Nicopho 25, Chor. in *Hermes* 17.222 (pl.). **-ιστής**, οῦ, ὁ, *dancer of the* κόρδαξ, prob. in *IG*12(7).246 (Amorgos), cf. *PTeb.*231 (i B.C.).

⊛**κόρδαξ**, ᾰκος, ὁ, *cordax*, a dance of the old Comedy, κόρδακα ἑλκύσαι to dance *it*, Ar.*Nu.*540, cf. 555, Luc.*Salt.*22, 26; ὀρχεῖσθαι νήφων τὸν κ. Thphr.*Char.*6.3; regarded as indecent, l.c., cf. Ath.14.631d; also in cult of Artemis at Sipylus, Paus.6.22.1; at Elis, ibid.; οἱ περὶ τὸν Πύθιον Ἀπόλλωνα κ. *IG*12(7).246 (Amorgos).

**κορδίκιον**, τό, dub. sens., of an article of furniture, *POxy.*1449.53 (iii A.D.), *PLond.*2.429.11 (iv A.D.).

**κορδίνημα**, v. l. for σκορδίνημα (q. v.), Erot.

**κορδῠβαλλῶδες** πέδον, τό, Luc.*Trag.*223, said to be for κορδυλοβαλλῶδες (κορδύλη, βάλλω), a beaten floor.

**κορδύλειος** [ῠ], α, ον, *made from* κορδύλη III, ταρίχη prob. in Ath. 3.120f.

**κορδύλη** [ῡ, cf. Lat. *cordȳla*, Mart.3.2.4, al.: **κορδύλα** *EM*485.39], ἡ, *club, cudgel*, Hsch. 2. *bump, swelling*, Semon.35, *EM*310. 49. II. *wrapping for the head, head-dress*, in Cyprian, Sch.Ar. *Nu.*10, *EM*310.51. III. = σκορδύλη, Str.12.3.19; **κορύδῡλις** [ρῠ] in Numen.ap.Ath.7.304e.

⊛**κορδύλος**, ὁ, prob. *water-newt*, *Triton palustris*, Arist.*HA*589$^b$27, *PA*695$^b$25; **κουρύλος** [ρῡ] in Numen.ap.Ath.7.306c.

**κόρδυς**· πανοῦργος, Hsch.

**κορ-εία** (A), ἡ, (κορέω) *brushing*: *attendance*, prob. in Hsch. ⊛**-εία** (B), ἡ, (κορεύομαι) *maidenhood*, D.Chr.7.142, *AP*5.216 (Paul. Sil.), 293.19 (Agath.). ⊛**-ειος**, α, ον, (κόρη) *of a maiden*: τὸ κ., = κόρευμα, Sch.E.*Alc.*178. II. Κόρεια (sc. ἱερά), τά, *the festival of Kore* (Persephone), Plu.*Dio* 56, Hsch. 2. Κόρειον, τό, *her temple*, *IG*14.217 (Acrae), *Ath.Mitt.*49.5 (Attica, iii B.C.).

**Κορειτήα**, ἡ, prob. = *Κορῑτεία, perh. *performance as attendant of Kore* at Lycosura, ἐν.. τέκνων -ήαις *IG*5(2).516.11.

**κορέννῡμι**, Them.*Or.*16.213a; **κορεννύω**, *Gloss.*; **κορέω**, Nic.*Al.* 195; **κορέσκω**, ib.225, 360, 415: fut. κορέσω Hdt.1.212; Ep. κορέεις Il.13.831, κορέει 8.379, 17.241: aor. ἐκόρεσα 16.747, A.*Pr.*166 (lyr.); poet. ἐκόρεσσα Theoc.24.128, *AP*7.204 (Agath.):—**Med.**, κορέννυμαι Orph.*L.*732, opt. κορέοιτο Nic.*Al.*263: aor. ἐκορεσάμην, Ep. ἐκορεσσ–, κορεσσ–, Il.11.562, Od.20.59:—**Pass.**, fut. κεκορήσομαι Max.117: aor. ἐκορέσθην Od.10.499; Ep. 3 pl. -θεν Ar.*Pax* 1283 sq.: pf. κεκόρεσμαι X.*Mem.*3.11.3 (nowhere else in early Prose), Plu.*Dem.*23, *APl.*4.190 (Leon.); Ion. κεκόρημαι Il.18.287, Hes.*Op.*593, Sapph. 48, Ar.*Pax* 1285 (v. infr.): pf. part. Act. (with pass. sense) κεκορηώς, -ότος, Od.18.372, Nonn.*D.*5.34, Coluth.120: also fut. (in intr. sense) κορήσουσι Lxx *De.*31.20:—*satiate, fill* one *with* a thing, c. dat., κορέεις κύνας ἠδ' οἰωνοὺς δημῷ καὶ σάρκεσσι Il.13.831; μολπῇ θυμὸν κ. A.R. 3.897: c. gen. rei, κορέσαι στόμα ἐμᾶς σαρκός S.*Ph.*1156 (lyr.): c. acc. only, τίς ἂν κορέσειεν ἅπαντας; Thgn.229; πρὶν ἂν ἡ κορέσῃ κέαρ A. l. c.:—Med., *satisfy oneself*, c. gen., ἐκορέσσατο φορβῆς Il.11.562; οἴνοιο κορεσσάμενος καὶ ἐδωδῆς 19.167; ὄφρ'.. κρειῶν κορεσαίατο θυμόν *might satisfy their* desire with flesh, Od.14.28: metaph., φυλόπιδος κορέσασθαι Il.13.635: c. part., κορεσσάμεθα κλαίοντε 22.427; ἐκορέσσατο χεῖρας τάμνων δένδρεα 11.87:—Pass., *to be glutted, satiated*, δαιτὸς κεκορήμεθα θυμὸν ἐΐσης Od.8.98; κεκορήμεθ' ἀέθλων 23.350; κεκορημένος ἦτορ ἐδωδῆς Hes.*Op.*593; βορᾶς κορεσθεὶς E.*Hipp.*112; πολέμου ἐκόρεσθεν Ar.*Pax* 1283: c. part., κλαίων.. κορέσθην Od.4.541; οὔ πω κεκόρησθε ἐελμένοι; Il.18.287: rarely c. dat. rei, κριθαῖσι κορεσθεὶς Thgn.1269; πλούτῳ κεκορημένος Id.751; ὕβρι Hdt.3.80: abs., dub. in Sapph.48.—Cf. κορίσκομαι. (Cf. Lith. *šérti* 'feed'.)

**κορεστ-ικῶς**, Adv. *to satiety*, Sch.Arat.1049. **-ός**, ή, όν, *sated*; *to be sated*, *Gloss.*

**κόρ-ευμα**, ατος, τό, = κορεία (B), *maidenhood*, E.*Alc.*178 (pl.). **-εύομαι**, Pass., fut. κορευθήσομαι ib.313: (κόρη):—*pass one's maidenhood*, E. l. c. II. *to be deflowered*, Pherecyd.92(*b*) J.

**κορέω** (A), *sweep out*, δῶμα κορήσατε ποιπνύσασαι Od.20.149; τὴν αὐλὴν κόρει Eup.157; κ. τὸ παιδαγωγεῖον D.18.258. II. = ἐξυβρίζω, Hsch.: hence κεκορημένος, sens. obsc., Anacr.5.

**κορέω** (B), v. κορέννυμι. **κορζία**, v. καρδία.

⊛**κόρη**, ἡ, orig. κόρϝα (v. infr. B), with -η even in Att. Prose and Trag. dialogue; Dor. and Aeol. **κόρα**, Ar.*Lys.*1308 (lyr.), Alc.14, also Trag. in lyr. as A.*Supp.*145, S.*OT*508, E.*Tr.*561, and in the pr. n.: **κούρα** Pi.*O.*13.65, and twice in Trag. (in lyr.), v. infr. I. 3: Ion. **κούρη**, as always in Hom. (κόρη first in *h.Cer.*439): Dor. also **κώρα** Theoc.6.36, also Boeot., Corinn.*Supp.*1.48, 2.60 (but κόρα *IG*7.710–12, Ar.*Ach.*883, cf. κορικός, κόριλλα):—fem. of κόρος, κοῦρος. 1. *girl*, ἠΰτε κούρη νηπίη ἥ θ' ἅμα μητρὶ θέουσ' ἀνελέσθαι ἀνώγει Il.16.7; μήτε παῖδα μήτε κόραν *Schwyzer* 324.12 (Delph., iv B.C.); ἔτεκε κόραν *IG*4$^2$ (1).121.22 (Epid.); with reference to virginity, *maiden*, κόρην.. οὐκέτ', ἀλλ' ἐζευγμένην S.*Tr.*536; παῖς κ. Ar.*Lys.*595, D.21.79 codd.; παρθενικὴ κ. E.*Epigr.*2; ἀδελφὴ κ. Th.6.56; ἀνεδέξαντο τὰς κόρας πέμψειν ἐν Ἴλιον *Schwyzer* 366 *A* 2 (Tolophon, iii B.C.); of Nymphs, Pi.*P.*3. 78; ἐνάλιοι κ. sea-*nymphs*, Ar.*Th.*325 (lyr.): Com., πρέσβειρα πεντήκοντα Κωπᾴδων κορᾶν, of eels, Id.*Ach.*883; τευθὶς καὶ Φαληρικὴ κ., i.e. ἀφύη, Eub.75.4; of maiden-goddesses, however old, as the Eumenides, A.*Eu.*68, S.*OC*127 (lyr.); the Phorcids, A.*Pr.*794; the Sphinx, S.*OT*508 (lyr.); the Fates, Pl.*R.*617d. 2. of a bride, Od.18.279; young wife, Il.6.247, E.*Or.*1438 (lyr.), Hdn.3.10.8; or concubine, as Briseis, Il.1.98, 337, 2.689; καταχύσματα.. κατάχει τοῦ νυμφίου καὶ τῆς κ. the *bride*, Theopomp.Com.14; of a ἑταίρα, *AP*5.4 (Stat.Flacc.), 219 (Agath.). 3. with gen. of a pr. n. added, *daughter*, νύμφαι κοῦραι Διὸς Il.6.420, cf. Sapph.65, E.*Hel.*168 (lyr.), *Andr.*897, etc.; κ. Διός, of Athene, A.*Eu.*415; Δητῴα κόρη, of Artemis, Id.*Fr.*170, S.*El.*570; κ. Ἰναχεία, κ. Θεστιάς, A.*Pr.*589, E.*Hel.*133; Γῆς τε καὶ Σκότου κόραι, i.e. the Furies, S.*OC*40; in Thess. Prose, Αἰσχυλὶς

Σατύροι (gen.) κόρα *IG*9(2).1035 (Gyrton): without gen., *Berl.Sitzb.* 1927.7 (Locr., v B.C.): in voc., κούρα *my daughter*, A.*Th.*148, S.*OC* 180 (both lyr.); κόραι Ar.*Pax* 119. 4. metaph., of a *colony*, Κύμης κ. Hom.*Epigr.*1.2; of *newly launched* ships, Lyc.24. II. *puppet, doll*, as a child's plaything, Hyp.*Fr.*199 (v. infr. v), D.Chr.31.153; *small votive image*, Pl.*Phdr.*230b. III. *pupil* of the eye, because a little image appears therein (v. Pl.*Alc.*1.133a), κύκλοπα κούρην Emp.84.8, cf. S.*Fr.*710, E.*Hec.*972, al., Ar.*V.*7, Hp.*Prorrh.*2.20, Gal.*UP*10.4, Ruf.*Onom.*23; αἱ καλούμεναι κ. *IG*4²(1).122.67 (Epid., iv B.C.); Κ. κόσμου, title of Hermetic tract, Stob.1.49.44 tit. IV. *long sleeve* reaching over the hand, X.*HG*2.1.8. V. *the Attic drachma*, because it bore a head of Athena, misinterpr. of Hyp.l.c. ap. Poll.9.74. VI. = ὑπέρεικον, Hp.ap.Gal.19.113. VII. Archit., *female figures as supports, Caryatids*, τοὺς λίθους..τοὺς ἐπὶ τῶν κορῶν *IG*1². 372.86 (Erechtheum).

B. Κόρη, Dor. Κόρα (Cret. Κώρα *GDI*5047), Ion. Κούρη, Arc.(?) Κόρϝα *IG*5(2).554 (provenance unknown), ἡ:—*the Daughter* (of Demeter), *Persephone*, τῇ Μητρὶ καὶ τῇ Κόρῃ (v.l. Κούρῃ) Hdt.8.65; ναὶ τὰν Κόραν Ar.*V.*1438; Δημήτηρ καὶ Κ. Id.*Th.*298, X.*HG*6.3.6, *IG*2.1217, etc.; τῆς Κόρης ἁρπασθείσης Isoc.4.28: less freq. Κ. Δήμητρος E.*Alc.*358, cf. Ar.*Ra.*337; Κ. τὴν Διὸς καὶ Δήμητρος Isoc.10.20. II. Δηοῦς κ., in Com., = *flour*, Antiph.52.9; so μεμαγμένη Δήμητρος κ. Eub.75.10.

**κόρ-ηθρον**, τό, *besom, broom*, Luc.*Philops.*35, Artem.5.79. **-ημα**, ατος, τό, *sweepings, refuse*, Ar.*Fr.*474: in pl., Hermipp.47.10 (anap.). II. *besom, broom*, Ar.*Pax* 59, Eup.157, 228.4, Gal.12.93.

**κορθέλαι**· σύστροφοι (also συστροφαί), σωροί, Hsch.:—also ⊛**κορθίλη** and **κόρθις**, Id.:—but ⊛**κόρθιλος**, = βασιλίσκος, Id.

**κορθύνω** or **κορθύω**, (κόρθυς) *lift up, raise*, Ζεὺς κόρθυνεν ἑὸν μένος *raised high* his wrath, Hes.*Th.*853; εὖτέ με θυμὸς κορθύσῃ *Hymn.Is.* 150:—Pass., κῦμα κορθύεται *waxes high, rears its crest*, Il.9.7; ὕπερθε δὲ..ἁλὸς κορθύεται ὕδωρ A.R.2.322.

⊛**κόρθυς**, υος, ἡ, lengthd. form of κόρυς, *heap*, Anon.ap.Suid. s.v. κορθύεται, Hsch.; in Theoc.10.46, κόρθυος ἁ τομά the swathe *of mown corn*.

**κορθῶ**· βλάβη, Hsch. **κόρι**, abbreviated for κόριον, = κορίαννον, Bilabel Ὀψαρτ. p.10, al. **κοριάλαι**· τρίγλαι, Hsch.

⊛**κορίαννον** (**κορίανδρον** *Gloss.*, **κορίαμβλον** Hsch.) [ῐ], τό, *coriander, Coriandrum sativum*, the plant or seed, Alc.Com.17, Anaxandr.50, Thphr.*HP*7.1.2: freq. in pl., Anacr.123, Ar.*Eq.*676, 682, etc. II. *ring worn on the forefinger*, Poll.5.101, Hsch.

⊛**κορίαξος**, ὁ, a kind of *fish*, Alex.Trall.1.12, al.

**Κοριάσια**, τά, *festival of Kore*, *IG*7.47 (Megara).

⊛**κορίδιον**, τό, Dim. of κόρη, *GDI*1699, al. (Delph.), *IG*9(1).384 (Naupactus); censured by Poll.2.17, but allowed by Phryn.56. II. perh. for κόρι, = κορίαννον, Pap. in *Philol.*80.341.

⊛**κορίζομαι**, (κόρη, κόριον A) *fondle, caress*, Ar.*Nu.*68; cf. ὑποκορίζομαι, κουρίζω (A).

**κορίζω** (A), (κόρις) *to be infested with bugs*, *Gloss.*

**κορίζω** (B), (κόρος C) *sweep*: hence, *sift, clean*, *BGU*1120.40 (Pass., i B.C.).

**κορῐκός**, ή, όν, = παρθενικός, χιτών *Schwyzer* 462 *B* 29 (Tanagra, iii B.C.), cf. Poll.2.17. Adv. -κῶς *like a girl*, τρυφᾶν Ph.2.89; βαδίζειν Ael.*NA*2.38; αἰσχύνεσθαι Alciphr.3.2: Comp. -ώτερον Eust.1571.43. II. *belonging to Kore*, πεπλοποιία Dam.*Pr.*339.

**κόριλλα**, ἡ, Boeot. Dim. of κόρα, *IG*7.713, al. (Tanagra), 2901 (Coronea).

**κοριναῖος**, Maced. word, = νόθος, Marsyas Phil.24J.

**Κορινθι-άζομαι**, *practise fornication*, because Corinth was famous for its courtesans, Ar.*Fr.*354:—Act. in Hsch. **-αστής**, οῦ, ὁ, *whoremonger*, title of plays by Philetaerus, Ath.13.559a, and Poliochus, Id.7.313c.

⊛**Κορίνθιος**, α, ον, *Corinthian*, Hdt., etc.; Κ. κόρη *courtesan*, Pl.*R.* 404d; ἑταῖραι Κ. Ar.*Pl.*149; οἶνος Κ. Alex.290; Κ. κάδοι Diph.61.3. Adv. -ίως *in Corinthian fashion*, οἶκος Κ. ἐστεγασμένος *J.AJ*8.5.2:—fem. **Κορινθιάς**, άδος, ἡ, St.Byz.:—also **Κορινθιακός**, ή, όν, X.*HG*6. 2.9; Κ. γλυφαί Ph.1.666: **Κορινθικός**, *AP*6.40 (Maced.).

**Κορινθιουργής**, ές, (ἔργον) *of Corinthian workmanship* or *style*, κρατῆρες Callix.2; κιόκρανον Str.4.4.6, cf. *AJA*31.351.

**Κορινθοειδής**, ές, *of Corinthian style*, κέραμος Κ. προστεγαστήρ *SIG* 245 I 35 (Delph., iv B.C.).

⊛**Κόρινθος**, ὁ and ἡ, *Corinth*, the city and country, ἀφνειὸς Κ. Il.2. 570, Pi.*Fr.*122.2; ὀφρυόεντα Κ. Orac.ap.Hdt.5.92.β', cf. Plb.4.67.8, Str.8.6.20; but ἡ Κ. Hdt.3.50, Th.1.25, etc.; εὐδαίμων Κ. Hdt.3.52; famed for its luxury and extravagance, whence prov. οὐ παντὸς ἀνδρὸς εἰς Κ. ἐσθ' ὁ πλοῦς Ar.*Fr.*902a. II. son of Zeus, reputed founder of Corinth, Paus.2.1.1: prov., Διὸς Κόρινθος, used of persons who are always repeating the same old story, Pi.*N.*7.105, cf. Ar.*Ra.* 443, *Ec.*828, Pl.*Euthd.*292e. III. Adv. **Κορινθόθι**, *at Corinth*, Il. 13.664; **Κορινθόθεν**, *from C.*, *Michel* 1087 (Olympia, v B.C.).

**κοριοειδής**, ές, (κόρη) *like the pupil of the eye, dark-gleaming*, κορακῖνοι Epich.44. 2. (κόριον B) *like coriander*, Dsc.2.176.

⊛**κόριον** (A), τό, Dim. of κόρη, *little girl*, Lys.*Fr.*1.5 (ironically), Theoc.11.60; Megar. κώριον Ar.*Ach.*731.

**κόριον** (B), τό, shortd. for κορίαννον, Nic.*Al.*157, *Th.*874, *PCair. Zen.*292.16, al. (iii B.C.), *PTeb.*190 (i B.C.), Dsc.3.63, Gal.12.36: pl., Hp.*Mul.*1.66. II. κ. ἔνυδρον, = ἀδίαντον, Ps.-Dsc.4.134. III. κ. ἄγριον, = καπνός II, ib.4.109.

⊛**κόρις**, ιος, Att. εως, ὁ, *bug, Cimex lectularius*, οἱ κόρεις Ar.*Nu.*634 (with a play on Κορίνθιοι, cf. 710), *Ra.*115, al.: also fem., Sor.2.29, Phryn.277 (acc. to Suid. with gen. κόριδος, wh. is not found in Classical Gr., cf. [Gal.]14.538). II. kind of *fish*, = ἔσχαρος, Dorio ap. Ath.7.330a. III. a kind of *St. John's wort, Hypericum empetrifolium*, Dsc.3.157, Aët.16.17.

**κορίσκη**, ἡ, Dim. of κόρη, Pl.Com.69.12, Timocl.22:—hence **κορίσκιον**, Poll.2.17.

**κορίσκομαι**, = κορέννυμαι, *become saturated*, c. gen., ὑγρασίης Hp. *Gland.*6; κ. φλέγματος οἱ πνεύμονες ib.14: abs., *to be irked*, Id.*Art.*35.

**κορίσκος**, ὁ, Dim. of κόρος (B): as pr. n. Κορίσκος (pupil of Plato, D.L.3.46) is used to denote *any supposed person*, like J. S. Mill's 'Duke of Wellington', Arist.*APo.*85ᵃ24, *Ph.*219ᵇ21, al.

**κόριψ**· νεανίσκος, Hsch.; cf. κόρος (B). **κορκόδειλος, κορκόδριλλος, κορκοδρίλλιον**, v. κροκόδιλος. **κορκόδρυα**· ὑδρόρυα, Id. ⊛**κόρκορα**, a bird (Perg.), Id. **κόρκορος**, v. κόρχορος.

**κορκορῠγή**, ἡ, *rumbling noise, tumult*, in pl., A.*Th.*345 (lyr.), Ar. *Pax* 991 (anap.): in sg., Id.*Lys.*491.

⊛**κορκορυγμός**, ὁ, = foreg., of the bowels, Ps.-Luc.*Philopatr.*3.

**κορκότιλος**, v. κροκόδιλος. **κορκούτης**· αἰδοῖον ἀνδρῶν, Hsch. (post κορμός). **Κόρκῡρα, Κορκῡραῖος**, v. Κερκ—. **κορκυρεύεται**· ἀπον⟨ο⟩εῖται, Id.

**κόρμα**, ατος, τό, = κοῦρμι, Posidon.15J. II. v. κορβᾶ.

**κορμ-άζω**, *saw up into logs*, D.H.20.15 (Pass.). **-ηδόν**, Adv. *like logs*, Hld.9.18. ⊛**-ίον**, τό, Dim. of κορμός, *small log*, *IG*11(2). 233.13 (Delos, iii B.C.), *Stud.Pal.*10.259.11 (v A.D.). II. *trunk* or *body* of an undershirt, Anon.*in Rh.*106.3. 2. κορμίν, τό, *barrel* of a horse, interpol. in *Hippiatr.*115.

**κορμίω**, Cret., = κοσμέω, *GDI*5016, al.

⊛**κορμολογία**, ἡ, *collecting of* κορμοί (cf. κορμός (A) 2), *Sammelb.*5126. 25 (iii A.D.).

⊛**κορμός** (A), ὁ, (κείρω) *trunk* of a tree (with the boughs lopped off), Od.23.196, E.*Hec.*575, *HF*242; κ. ἐλάας Ar.*Lys.*255; κ. ἐλάϊνοι *PCair.Zen.*431 (iii B.C.); κορμοὶ ξύλων *logs* of timber, Hdt.7.36, *PCair.Zen.*154.2 (iii B.C.); κ. ναυτικοί, i.e. oars, E.*Hel.*1601. 2. ἀπὸ κορμοῦ εἰς κορμόν, in measurement of an irrigated vineyard, prob. from *block* to *block*, i.e. from *sluice* to *sluice*, *PFlor.*50.2, al. (iii A.D.); cf. κορμολογία.

**κόρμος** (B), Cret., = κόσμος, *GDI*5024, al.

⊛**κορνικουλάριος**, ὁ, = Lat. *cornicularius*, *CIG*4453 (Syria): written κορνουκλάριος *Sammelb.*6221 (ii A.D.).

**κόρνος**· κεντρομυρσίνη (Sicel), Hsch.

**κόρνοψ**, οπος, ὁ, a kind of *locust*, like πάρνοψ, Str.13.1.64 (but κορνώπιδες = κώνωπες, Hsch.):—hence **Κορνοπίων**, ωνος, ὁ, *Locust-scarer*, title of Heracles at Oeta, Str.l.c.

⊛**κόροιβος**, ὁ, *fool*, Hsch.; οὐχ οὕτω κ. ὁ Ἀλέξανδρος Ps.-Gem. in Iriarte *Cat.Cod.Matrit.* p.391. (Fr. pr. n. Κόροιβος, Euph.71, etc.)

**κοροῖτις**· ἀλώπηξ, Hsch. **κόροιφος**, v. κόρυφος III.

⊛**κοροκόσμιον**, τό, *girl's toy* or *ornament*, of masks placed at crossroads, *AB*102, cf. Sch.Theoc.2.110. II. *pupil of the eye*, *PLond.* 1821.27.

**κοροκότας** or **-κόττας**, v. κροκόττας.

**κορόνους**, coined as etym. of Κρόνος, Dam.*Pr.*267; cf. κορός (B).

**κορο-πλᾰθικός**, ή, όν, *belonging to the art of modelling*, τύπος Procl. *in Ti.*1.335D. **-πλάθος** [ᾰ], ὁ, *modeller of small figures, image-maker*, Pl.*Tht.*147b, Isoc.15.2, Luc.*Lex.*22; name of a play by Antiphanes:—in Hellenistic Gr. **-πλάστης**, ου, ὁ, *EM*530.11, Moer. p.234P.

**κόρος** (A), ὁ, *satiety, surfeit*, αἶψά τε φυλόπιδος πέλεται κ. ἀνθρώποισιν Il.19.221; αἰψηρὸς δὲ κ. κρυεροῖο γόοιο Od.4.103; πάντων μὲν κ. ἐστί, καὶ ὕπνου καὶ φιλότητος Il.13.636; ἀπὸ κ. ἀμβλύνει αἰανὴς ἐλπίδας Pi.*P.*1.82; κόρον ἔχει μέλι Id.*N.*7.52; κ. ἔχειν δακρύων, κακῶν, E.*Alc.* 185, *Ph.*1750 (lyr.); also κόρον ἡ τούτων συνουσία ἔχει Pl.*Phdr.*240c; ἐς κ. ἰέναι τινός Philox.2.38; ἄχρι κόρου D.19.187; ἐς κόρον Luc. *Merc.Cond.*26, Gal.15.500, *Vict.Att.*8; πρὸς ἡδονήν τε καὶ κ. *gormandizing*, Hp.*VM*14: in mystical sense, opp. χρησμοσύνη, Heraclit. 65. 2. *the consequence of satiety, insolence*, Pi.*O.*2.95, *I.*3.2; πρὸς κόρον *insolently*, A.*Ag.*382 (lyr.): freq. as cause or consequence of ὕβρις, τίκτει τοι κόρος ὕβριν, ὅταν κακῷ ὄλβος ἕπηται ἀνθρώπῳ Thgn. 153, cf. Sol.8; ὕβριν κόρου ματέρα Pi.*O.*13.10; κόρον, ὕβριος υἱόν Bacis ap.Hdt.8.77. (Cf. κορέννυμι.)

⊛**κόρος** (B), ὁ, Ion. **κοῦρος**, as always in Hom., Pi., and lyr. passages of Trag. (exc. E.*Alc.*904), sts. in late Gr., *Rev.Ét.Gr.*42. 247 (Varna); Dor. **κῶρος** Theoc.15.120:—*boy, lad* (even before birth, ὃν..γαστέρι μήτηρ κοῦρον ἐόντα φέροι Il.6.59, cf. Call.*Del.*212), κοῦρος πρῶτον ὑπηνήτης Il.24.347; πρωθῆβαι Od.8.262; τότε κοῦρος ἔα, νῦν αὖτέ με γῆρας ὀπάζει Il.4.321; σὺν κόροις τε καὶ κόραις A.*Fr.*43: in mock Trag., Οἰδίπου..παῖδε, διπτύχῳ κόρῳ Ar.*Fr.*558: rare in Prose, Pl.*Lg.*772a; *male infant*, ἔτεκε κόρον Conon 33.3, cf. *IG*4²(1).121.5 (Epid., iv B.C.); in Il. of warriors, 9.86, 12.196, al.; κοῦροι Βοιωτῶν, Ἀθηναίων, Ἀχαιῶν, 2.510, 551, 562; λεκτοὶ Ἀθηναίων κ. E.*Supp.*356; also, of *servants* waiting at sacrifices and feasts, Il.1.470, al.; at Sparta, κόροι, = ἱππεῖς, Archyt.ap.Stob.4.1.138. 2. with gen. of pr. n., *son*, Od.19.523, etc.; Θησέως κ. S.*Ph.*562, cf. *Tr.*644 (lyr.); τῶν ὀλωλότων κόροι E.*Supp.*107; Κεκροπιδῶν κόροι, periphr. like παῖδες, Eub.10.6. 3. *puppet, doll*, used in Magic, S.*Fr.*536. II. *shoot, sprout*, of a tree, κόρους πλεκτοὺς..μυρρίνης Lysipp.9, cf. Hp.ap.Gal. 19.113, *EM*276.28, Hsch.; cf. κόρυς (B). III. for Comp. v. κουρότερος. (Acc. to Eust.582.20, al., from κείρω, of *one who has cut his hair short on emerging from boyhood*: but κόρ(ϝ)ος (masc. of κόρη) perh. cogn. with Lat. *Ceres, Cerus, cresco*.)

⊛ **κόρος** (C), ὁ, *besom*, Hsch.

⊛ **κόρος** (D), ὁ, Hebr. *kor*, a dry measure containing, acc. to J.*AJ* 15.9.2,10 Att. medimni (about 120 gallons), Lxx *Nu.*11.32, al., *Ev. Luc.*16.7, cf. Eupolem.ap.Alex.Polyh.18.

**κορός** (A), Adj. *dark, black*, Sch.D Il.1.170: etym. of κόραξ, *EM* 529.30.

**κορός** (B), Adj. *pure*, Procl.*Theol.Plat.*5.3 (where θεοῦ κόρου καὶ νοῦ ὄντος), Id. ad Hes.*Op.*111, *EM*540.5, cf. Pl.*Cra.*396b (Κρόνος = κορὸς νοῦς).

**κόρρη**, Att. for κόρση.

**κόρσακις**, = τράγος, Cratin.338, ap.Hsch. (Κορσάτης Salmasius); obscurely expld. by Did. ἀπὸ τῆς κόρσης, Κόρσαι γὰρ τῆς Κιλικίας.

**κορσᾶς**, ὁ, pl. ᾶτες, *barber*, *BGU*, iv 15 (iii A.D.).

**κορσεῖα**, τά, (κόρση) *temples*, Nic.*Al.*135; **κόρσεα**, ib.414.

**κόρσεον**, τό, = κόρσιον (q.v.), in pl., *PTeb.*112.7 (ii B.C.), 189 (i B.C.):—written **κορσαῖον** D.S.1.10.

**κορσεύς**· κουρεύς, Hsch.

⊛ **κόρσ-η**, ἡ, Att. **κόρρη**, Dor. **κόρρα** Theoc.14.34, Aeol. **κόρσα** Alc. 34.5:—*temple, side of the forehead* (in this sense not in pl., for wh. κρόταφοι is used, but cf. Ruf.*Onom.*13, Poll.2.40), ξίφει ἤλασε κόρσην Il.5.584, cf. 13.576; τὸν ῥ' Ὀδυσεὺς.. βάλε κόρσην ἡ δ' ἑτέροιο διὰ κροτάφοιο πέρησεν αἰχμή 4.502, cf. Call.*Dian.*78. 2. in Att., πατάξαι ἐπὶ κόρρης smack on the *jaw*, Pherecr.155b (*CAF* iii p.716), D.21.147; ὅταν κονδύλοις, ὅταν ἐπὶ κόρρης [τύπτῃ], i.e. with the fist, or with the open hand, ib.72; ἐπὶ κόρρης τύπτειν Pl.*Grg.*486c, 508d, 527a; ῥαπίζειν ἐπὶ κ. Hyp.*Fr.*97 (ἐρραπίσθη τὴν γνάθον ibid.); πὺξ ἐπὶ κόρρας ἤλασα Theoc. l.c.; later κατὰ κόρρης πατάσσειν Luc.*DMort.*20.2, *Gall.*30, cf. *EM*529.39. 3. in pl., *hair*, λευκὰς δὲ κ. τῇδ' ἐπαντέλλειν νόσῳ A.*Ch.*282, cf. Poll.2.32 (perh. the white *down* in psoriasis): in sg., ναὶ μὰ τήνδε τὴν τεφρὴν κόρσην Herod.7.71 (unless in signf. 1.4). 4. *head*, κ. ἀναύχενες Emp.57.1, cf. Nic.*Th.*905, Opp.*C.*1.25; Att. for *the whole head and neck*, Ael.Dion.*Fr.*235; Ion. for *head*, Eratosth.ap.Did. in Miller *Mél.*400. II. *part of a temple gate*, Vitr. 4.6.3. III. in pl., = κρόσσαι, Hsch.; also, = κλίμακες, Id. (Perh. cogn. with κάρα.) -ήεις, εσσα, εν, = κορσοειδής, prob. in Orph. *L.*498. -ης, ου, ὁ, nickname of the first man *who shaved his beard* at Athens, Chrysipp.*Stoic.*3.198.

**κόρσιον**, τό, *tuber of the Nile water-lily, Nymphaea stellata*, Thphr. *HP*4.8.11, Str.17.2.4; cf. κόρσεον: **κορσίπιον**, Hsch. **κορσίς**· πυγή, Id.

**κορσοειδὴς** λίθος, ὁ, a stone of *greyish colour* (κόρση 1. 3), Plin.*HN* 37.153.

**κορσός**, ὁ, = κορμός, Hsch. (Cf. κοῦρος (B).)

**κορσ-όω**, (cf. κουρά, κείρω) = κείρειν, Hsch.; cf. ἀεικορσώσασθαι, ἀκόρσωτον, ἀποκορσόομαι. -ωτήρ, ῆρος, ὁ, *barber*, Call.*Fr.anon.* 128, Poll.2.32:—also -ωτεύς, έως, Charon 9. -ωτήριον, τό, *barber's shop*, ibid. -ωτός, ή, όν, = κροσσωτός (which is v.l.), Lyc. 291.

**κορταία** (sc. γῆ), ἡ, = χορτ-, *pasture-land*, *POxy.*2113.19 (iv A.D.).

**κόρταλος, κόρταφος**, v. κρόταλον, κρόταφος. **κορτερά**, v. κρατερός. **κορτέω**, v. κροτέω. **κόρτη**, ἡ, a Parthian garment, Hsch. **κόρτος**· ὁ ἐν τοῖς κυσὶ κροτός (prob. κροτών), Id.

**Κορῠβάντ-ειος**, α, ον, *Corybantian*, *AP*6.165 (Phal.). II. τὸ Κορυβαντεῖον (not -άντειον Hdn.Gr.1.375) *temple of the Corybantes*, Str.10.3.21. -ιασμός, ὁ, *Corybantic frenzy*, D.H.2.19 (pl.), Longin. 39.2. -ιάω, *celebrate the rites of the Corybantes, to be filled with Corybantic frenzy*, Pl.*Cri.*54d, *Smp.*215e, *Ion* 533e, 536c; κ. περί τι *to be infatuated* about a thing, Longin.5: in Ar.*V.*8, comically, of a drowsy person *nodding and suddenly starting up*, cf. Plin.*HN*11. 147. -ίζω, *purify by Corybantic rites*, Ar.*V.*119:—Pass., *to be subjected to such rites*, Iamb.*Myst.*3.9, Cels.ap.Orig.*Cels.*3.16. -ικός, ή, όν, *Corybantic*, σκιρτήματα Plu.2.758b, cf. Porph.*Abst.*2.21; οἱ τὰ Κ. τελούμενοι D.H.*Dem.*22. -ίς, ίδος, ἡ, pecul. fem of Κορύβας, Nonn.*D.*2.695. -ισμός, ὁ, *purification by Corybantic rites*, Hsch. -ώδης, ες, *Corybant-like, frantic*, Luc.*JTr.*30.

**Κορύβᾱς** [ῠ], αντος, ὁ, *Corybant, priest of Cybele in Phrygia*, Hsch.: pl., Str.10.3.7, D.S.5.49, Luc.*Salt.*8; also associated with Dionysus, in pl. Κορύβαντες, E.*Ba.*125 (lyr.), *Hipp.*143 (lyr.), Ar.*Lys.*558, Nonn.*D.*9.162, Str. l.c.: metaph., of *drunken persons*, Posidipp.26. 22.—Cf. Κύρβαντες. II. *enthusiasm*, ὁ τῆς ποιητικῆς κ. Luc.*Hist. Conscr.*45. III. fabulous gem, Ps.-Plu.*Fluv.*18.8.

**κορυγγεῖν**· κερατίζειν, Hsch. (leg. κορύπτ-). **κορύγης**, Dor., = κῆρυξ, Id.

**κορύδιον**, τό, Aetol. Dim. of κόρη, *JHS*13.346 (Naupactus).

**Κορύδιος**, ὁ (sc. μήν), name of month at Mitylene, *IG*12(2).81.

⊛ **κορῠδός**, ἡ, (κόρυς) *lark*, esp. *crested lark*, *Alauda cristata*, Ar.*Av.* 472, al. (on the accent v. Hdn.Gr.1.142):—also **κόρῠδος**, ὁ, Pl.Com. 266, Pl.*Euthd.*291b, Arist.*HA*559ᵃ2, 614ᵃ33: prov., κ. ἐν ἀμούσοις φθέγγεται, 'au royaume des aveugles les borgnes sont rois', Eust. 1072.40.—Other forms are: **κορυδών**, ῶνος, ὁ, Arist.*HA*609ᵃ7; **κορυδαλλή**, ἡ, Epich.45; **κορυδαλλίς**, ίδος, ἡ, πάσαισιν κορυδαλλίσιν χρὴ λόφον ἐγγενέσθαι Simon.68, cf. Theoc.7.23; **κορυδαλλός**, ὁ, Id. 10.50, Babr.72.20; **κορύδαλος**, Arist.*HA*617ᵇ20, 633ᵇ1.

**κορύδῠλις**, εως, ἡ, v. κορδύλη III.

**κόρυζ-α**, ης, ἡ, *mucous discharge from the nostrils, rheum*, Ruf. *Onom.*33, Gal.5.253; κορύζης τὴν ῥῖνα μεστός Luc.*DMort.*6.2; also, *running at the nose*, Gal.7.107; in this sense in pl., Hp.*Prog.*14, Gal. 10.513; *inflammatory nasal catarrh*, Hp.*VM*18, Gal.10.513, 18(2). 180. II. metaph., *drivelling, stupidity*, Luc.*DMort.*20.4, *Hist. Conscr.*31, *Alex.*20; κορύζης καὶ λέμφου ἔμπλεως Lib.*Decl.*33.29. -ᾶς, ᾶ, ὁ, *driveller, sniveller*, Men.1003. -άω, *have a catarrh, run at the nose*, Pl.*R.*343a (with a play on signf. II), Arist.*Pr.*861ᵃ18; ἀλεκτρυόνα γέροντα ἤδη καὶ -ῶντα Luc.*JTr.*15. II. metaph., *drivel*, ἐκορύζων αἱ πόλεις Plb.38.12.5, cf. Phld.*D.*1.11. -ιᾷ, *pipitat*, *Gloss.* -ώδης, ες, *suffering from catarrh*, ἀπὸ κεφαλῆς Hp.*Epid.* 6.3.2, cf. 2.3.11.

**κορῠθ-άϊξ** [ᾰ], ϊκος, (ἀΐσσω) *helmet-shaking*, i.e. *with waving plume*, κορυθάϊκι πτολεμιστῇ Il.22.132. -αιόλος (on the accent v. Hdn. Gr.1.228, Eust.352.28), ον, (αἰόλλω) *moving the helmet quickly*, i.e. *with glancing helm*, epith. of Hector, Il.2.816, etc.; once of Ares, 20. 38; κ. νείκη Ar.*Ra.*818.

**Κορυθαλία** or -θαλλία, ἡ, title of Artemis at Sparta, Polem.Hist. 86; also in Italy, Hsch. s.v. κυριττοί. II. = εἰρεσιώνη, Id.:—also **κορυθάλεια, κορυθάλη, κορυθαλίς**, *EM*303.32, 531.53, 276. 28. ⊛ **Κορυθαλλίστριαι**, αἱ, girls who dance in honour of Κορυθαλλία, Hsch. **κορύθιον** [ῠ], τό, Dim. of κόρυς, *Gloss.* ⊛ **κόρῠθος**, ὁ, (κόρυς) *crested* τροχίλος, Hsch.; but also, = περικεφαλαία, Id. II. **Κόρυθος**, title of Apollo, *Bull.Soc.Roy.Lettres de Lund* 1928–9 iv 40; **Κόριθος**, ib.39. **κορυλλίων**, a bird (perh. = κολλυρίων), Hsch.

**κορυμβ-άς**, άδος, ἡ, (κόρυς) *string running round a net*, Hsch. -η, ἡ, = κόρυμβος II, Asius *Fr.Ep.*13.5 K. -ήθρα, ἡ, = sq., Ps.-Dsc.2. 179. -ηλος, ὁ, sq., Nic.*Fr.*74.18. ⊛ -ίας, ου, ὁ, *white-berried ivy*, *Hedera Helix*, Thphr.*HP*3.18.6. ⊛ -ιον, τό, Dim. of κόρυμβος III, Dsc.3.94. II. = λυχνὶς στεφανωματική, Ps.-Dsc.3.100. ⊛ -ίτης [ῑ] κισσός, = κορυμβίας, Archig.ap.Aët.5.84.

**κορυμβο-ειδής**, ές, *clustered*, Dsc.2.24. -ομαι, Pass., *to be formed into a* κόρυμβος, κόμη χρυσῷ στρόφῳ κεκορυμβωμένη Nic.Dam. 62 J.

⊛ **κόρυμβος**, ὁ, pl. both κόρυμβοι and heterocl. κόρυμβα (v. infr.), (κόρυς, κορυφή) *uppermost point*, once in Hom., νηῶν.. ἄκρα κόρυμβα *high-pointed sterns* of ships, Il.9.241 (= ἄφλαστα, ἀκροστόλια, Hsch., but the meaning was disputed, Ar.*Fr.*222); νεὼς κόρυμβα A.*Pers.* 411, cf. E.*IA*258 (lyr.); ἀφλάστοιο κόρυμβα A.R.2.601; ἄφλαστα καὶ κ. Lyc.295. 2. the *top* of a hill, φεύγοντες ἐπὶ τοῦ ὄρεος τὸν κ. Hdt. 7.218, cf. D.H.9.23; ἐπ' ἄκρον κ. ὄχθου A.*Pers.*659 (lyr.). II. = κρωβύλος, κ. τῶν τριχῶν Heraclid.Pont.ap.Ath.12.512c; ἀσκητὸς εὐσπείροισι κορύμβοις *AP*6.219 (Antip.), cf. *Com.Adesp.*1331. III. *cluster of the ivy fruit*, κόρυμβα ἀμφὶ κρητὶ κίσσιν' ἔστεπτο prob. in Herod.8.33, cf. Corn.*ND*30, *AP*12.8 (Strat.), Plu.2.648f, Him.*Or.* 13.7: generally, *cluster of fruit or flowers*, Mosch.3.4, Nonn.*D.*12.224.

**κορυμβοφόρος**, ον, *cluster-bearing*, κισσός Longus 2.26. 2. *ivy-crowned*, Διόνυσος, γυναῖκες, Nonn.*D.*14.311, 24.102.

**κορυμβώδης**, ες, v.l. for κορυμβοειδής, Dsc.3.24.

**κόρυμνα**, *necklace*, Hsch.

**κορυν-άω**, (κορύνη II) *put forth knobby buds*, Thphr.*HP*4.12.2. -η, ἡ, *club*, freq. shod with iron for fighting, *mace*, σιδηρείῃ κορύνῃ ῥήγνυσκε φάλαγγας Il.7.141, cf. 143; ξύλων κορύνας ἔχοντες Hdt.1.59; κορύναις τύπτειν Arist.*Pol.*1311ᵇ28. 2. *shepherd's staff*, Theoc. 7.19. II. in plants, *knobby bud* or *shoot*, Thphr.*HP*3.5.1, al. III. = πόσθη, Nic.*Al.*409, *AP*5.128 (Autom.). [ῠ in Hom. and Theoc.7. 19, 9.23; ῡ in E.*Supp.*715, Theoc.25.63, Nic. l.c.] -ησις, εως, ἡ, *putting forth of knobby buds*, Thphr.*HP*3.5.1, Phan.Hist.25, Arr.*Fr.* 24 J. ⊛ -ήτης, ου, ὁ, *club-bearer, mace-bearer*, Il.7.9, 138, Paus.8. 11.4. -ηφόρος, ον, *club-bearing*, νύμφαι Epic. in *Arch.Pap.*7.7: as Subst., κ., οἱ, *club-bearers*, the body-guard of Peisistratos, Hdt.1. 59, Plu.*Sol.*30, D.L.1.66. II. *peasants* at Sicyon, Poll.3.83.

**κορυνθ-εύς**, έως, ὁ, *basket*, Hsch. II. *cock*, Id. -ος, ὁ, kind of *cake*, Id. II. epith. of Apollo, near Asine, Ἀρχ.Δελτ.2.17.

**κορῠνιόεις**, εσσα, εν, *knobby*, πέτηλα v.l. for κορωνιόωντα, Hes.*Sc.* 289.

**κορυνομάχος**, gloss on κορυνήτης, Hsch.

**κορυνώδης**, ες, *knobby*, Thphr.*HP*6.4.2.

**κόρυξ**· νεανίσκος, Hsch.

**κορύπτης**, ὁ, = κορυπτίλος, *EM*532.9, Hsch. s.v. κυρίττολος.

**κορυπτιάω**, = γαυριάω, in impf., Hsch.

**κορυπτίλος** [ῐ], ὁ, *one that butts with the head*, Theoc.5.147: **κυρίττολος**· κορύπτης, πλήκτης, Hsch.; **κορυπτόλης**· κερατιστής, Id.

**κορύπτω**, fut. -ψω Orac.ap.Luc.*JTr.*31:—*butt with the head*, Theoc. 3.5, perh. to be read in Lucil.1241 Marx; etym. of Κορύβαντες, Str. 10.3.21; *butt at*, τινα Tz. ad Lyc.558:—Med., v. κορύσσω ad fin.

**κόρυρ**· θριγκός, Hsch. (Dialect form of sq.)

**κόρῠς**, ῠθος, ἡ, acc. κόρυθα Il.11.351, al., E.*Ba.*1186 (lyr.), κόρυν Il. 13.131, Luc.*DDeor.*20.10, Philostr.*Her.*12.1; poet. dat. pl. κορύθεσσι S.*Ant.*116 (lyr.):—*helmet*, freq. in Hom. (esp. in Il.); αὐγὴ χαλκείη κορύθων ἄπο λαμπομενάων 13.341; κ. χαλκήρης, χαλκοπάρηος, 15.535, Od.24.523; τετράφαλος Il.22.315; ἱπποδάσεια 3.369. II. *scalp* of a lion, E. l.c.

**κορύσσω**, Ep. impf. κόρυσσε Il.21.306; poet. inf. -έμεν Pi.*P.*8. 75:—**Med.**, aor. ἐκορυσσάμην, part. κορυσσάμενος Il.19.397:—**Pass.**, pf. κεκόρυθμαι, part. κεκορυθμένος, freq. in Hom. (v. infr.): (κόρυς):—poet., chiefly Ep., Verb, prop. *furnish with a helmet*: hence, 1. generally, *fit out, equip, marshal*, πόλεμόν τε κορύσσων Il.2.273; κλόνον ἀνδρῶν Hes.*Sc.*148; μάχην ib.198; μάχας ἔργον Pi.*I.*8(7).58; φιλαιμάτους ἀλκάς E.*Rh.*933:—in Hom. mostly Pass. and Med., *equip, arm oneself*, τὼ δὲ κορυσσέσθην Il.4.274; ὄπιθεν δὲ κορυσσάμενος βῆ Ἀχιλλεύς 19.397; Αἴας δὲ κορύσσετο νώροπι χαλκῷ 7.206; κεκορυθμένος αἴθοπι χαλκῷ 5.562, etc.; of things, δοῦρε δύω κεκορυθμένα χαλκῷ *headed with* brass, 3.18, 11.43: abs., ἔγχος, βριθὺ μέγα στιβαρὸν κεκο-

ρυθμένον 16.802: c. acc., ὅπλων κεκορυθμένος ἔνδυτ' E.*IA*1073 (lyr.): metaph., ἔριδι κ. Id.*Andr.*279 (lyr.). 2. *furnish, provide*, βίον κορυσσέμεν ὀρθοβούλοισι μαχαναῖς Pi.*P.* l. c. II. *make crested*, κόρυσσε δὲ κῦμα ῥόοιο *reared* his *crested* wave, Il.21.306:—Pass., *rear its head*, of a wave, πόντῳ μέν τε πρῶτα κορύσσεται Il.4.424, cf. A.R.2.71; of Eris, ἥ τ' ὀλίγη μὲν πρῶτα κορύσσεται Il.4.442; χείμαρρε, τί δὴ τόσον ὧδε κορύσσῃ; *AP*9.277 (Antiphil.); of clouds, Theoc.25.94, etc.; also of birds, Thphr.*Sign.*16: metaph., Δῆμος..πρὸς πνεῦμα βραχὺ κ. *Com. Adesp.*1324; cf. κορθύνω. (κορύττεται 'butts' Agath.1.4 is prob. f.l. for κορύπτεται: aor. Med. κορύξασθαι, δίκην ἀλεκτρυόνος Ath.3.127a, dub. l. in Hp.*Ep.*17.)

**κορυστής**, οῦ, ὁ, *helmed man, armed warrior*, ἕλεν ἄνδρα κορυστήν Il.4.457, 8.256; δύω Αἴαντε κορυστά 13.201, 18.163.

**κορυστός**, ή, όν, (κορύσσω II) *raised up, heaped up*, esp. of full measure, opp. ψηκτός, *IG*2².1013.22, al.; cf. κορυτόν· ἐπίμεστον, Hsch.

**κορύτει**· τῇ κεφαλῇ, Hsch.

**κορῠφ-ᾱγενής**, ές, *head-born*, prop. epith. of Athena: in Pythag. philosophy, of an equilat. triangle, like Τριτογένεια II, Plu.2.381f. **-αία**, ἡ, *head-stall of a bridle*, X.*Eq.*3.2, 5.1, 6.7, Poll.1.147. II. *tuft on the crown of the head*, Luc.*Lex.*5, Eust.1528.18. **-αινα**, ἡ, a fish, = ἵππουρος, Dorio ap.Ath.7.304c, Hsch. ❋ **-αῖον**, τό, *upper rim of a hunting-net*, prop. neut. of sq., X.*Cyn.*10.2, Poll.5.31. II. in pl., *head-parts* of animals sacrificed, prob. in *SIG*1002.12 (Milet., v/iv B. C.). III. Archit., *central block* of tympanum, *IG*1².373.100, 115; *ridge-beam* of a roof, ib.2².1668.49, 52. ❋ **-αῖος**, ὁ, *head man, chief, leader*, αὐτὸς ἕκαστος βουλόμενος κ. εἶναι Hdt.3.82; τῶν ἀνδρῶν τοὺς κ. ib.159, cf. 6.23, 98, Pl.*Tht.*173c; οἱ κ. *party-leaders*, Plb.18.4.6, cf. Phld.*Sto.Herc.*339.11; in the Drama, *leader of the chorus*, ἡγεμὼν τῆς φυλῆς κ. D.21.60 codd., cf. Arist.*Pol.*1277ᵃ11, Posidon.15J., etc.; κ. ἑστηκώς standing *at the head of the row*, Ar.*Pl.*953. II. as Adj., *at the top*, ὁ κ. πῖλος the *apex* of the Roman *flamen*, Plu.*Marc.*5; τὰ κ. τῆς νίκης the *crowning fruits* of.., Hdn.8.3.5; κ. τέλος τῶν πραγμάτων Id.7.5.2; τοῦ λαμπροῦ -αῖον (sc. αἴτιον) Phld.*Po.*2.41. 2. epith. of Zeus, *CIG*4458.4 (Seleucia in Pieria); of the Roman *Jupiter Capitolinus*, Paus.2.4.5: Sup. κορυφαιότατος in later Gr., κ. ἀρχαί *CIG*3885 (Eumeneia), cf. Plu.2.1115b, Luc.*Sol.*5, *Hist.Conscr.*34. **-αιότης**, ητος, ἡ, *headship, supremacy*, *Corp.Herm.*18.16. **-άς**, άδος, ἡ, *edge of the navel*, Hp.ap.Gal.19.113. ❋ **-ή**, ἡ, (κόρυς) *head, top*: hence, 1. *crown, top of the head*, of a horse, Il.8.83, X.*Eq.*1.11; of a man or god, *h.Ap.*309, Pi.*O.*7.36, Hdt.4.187, *Sammelb.*6003.8 (iv A. D.): between βρέγμα and ἰνίον, Arist.*HA*491ᵃ34; τὸ ὀστέον τῆς κ. Hp.*VC*2. 2. *top, peak* of a mountain (so mostly Hom.), οὔρεος ἐν κορυφῇς Il.2.456; ὄρεος κορυφῇσι 3.10, cf. Alcm.60.1; κορυφαὶ γαίας B.5.24; κ. Οὐλύμποιο Il.1.499, cf. Ar.*Nu.*270; Αἴτνας μελάμφυλλοι κορυφαί Pi.*P.*1.27; τηλαυγέ' ἄγ κορυφάν Id.*Pae.*7.12; κ. πόληος Alc.*Supp.*17.6; ἀστρογείτονας κ. A.*Pr.*722, cf. Hdt.4.49, 181, 9.99. 3. generally, *summit, top*, κατὰ κορυφὴν ἐσβαλεῖν ἐς τὴν κάτω Μακεδονίαν *straight over the summit, ridge*, Th.2.99, cf. *IG*4²(1).71.11 (Epid., iv B. C.), *OGI*383.125 (Nemrud Dagh, i B. C.); κατὰ κ. [τῆς στήλης] ἔσφ[ιγ]γον (sc. ταύρους) Pl.*Criti.*119e; ἵσταται κατὰ κ. ὁ ἥλιος *in the zenith*, Plu.2.938a; τὸ κατὰ κ., with or without σημεῖον, *the zenith*, Gem.5.64, etc., cf. Plu.*Mar.*11, Procl.*Hyp.*4.59; ταῖς τῶν κατὰ κ. λίθων ἐμβολαῖς by the stones falling *vertically*, Plb.8.7.3. 4. *apex, vertex* of a triangle, Id.2.14.8; of the Delta, Pl.*Ti.*21e; *point* of an angle, τὸ ἐπὶ τὴν κ. μέρος Plb.1.26.16, etc.; *apex* of a cone, Arist.*Mete.*362ᵇ3; κατὰ κορυφὴν *vertically* opposite, of angles, Euc.1.15; of halves of double cone, Apollon. Perg.1 *Def.* 5. *extremity, tip*, κορυφαὶ [κλημάτων], τῶν συγκυπτων, Thphr.*CP*3.14.8, Ath.Mech.22.8; in Anatomy, *the os coccygis*, Poll.2.183: in pl., *finger-tips*, Ruf.*Onom.*85, cf. Poll.2.146: Medic., of an abscess, ἐς κορυφὴν ἀνισταμένης ἀποστάσιος coming to a *head*, Aret.*SA*1.7. II. metaph., λόγων κορυφαί *the sum* of all his words, Pi.*O.*7.69, cf. *Pae.*8.23; ἔρχομαι ἐπὶ τὴν κ. ὧν εἴρηκα Pl.*Cra.*415a; but λόγων κ. ὀρθάν true *sense* of legends, Pi.*P.*3.80; κορυφὰς ἑτέρας ἑτέρῃσι προσάπτων μύθων springing *from peak to peak*, i. e. treating a subject disconnectedly, Emp.24; κ. ὁ λόγος ἐπιθεὶς ἑαυτῷ having reached its *conclusion*, put *the finishing touch* to itself, Plu.2.975a; κ. τοῦ κακοῦ *height, full development* of.., Aret.*SD*1.6; τοῦ πάθεος κ. ἴσχοντος ib.1.16. 2. *height, excellence of..*, i. e. *the choicest, best*, κορυφαὶ πολίων Pi.*N.*1.15; κ. ἀρετᾶν ib.34, cf. *O.*1.13; κ. ἀέθλων, of the Olympic games, Id.*O.*2.13, cf. *N.*9.9; φιάλαν.. πάγχρυσον κ. κτεάνων Id.*O.*7.4; ὁ καιρὸς παντὸς ἔχει κορυφάν is the *best* of all, Id. *P.*9.79. 3. κορυφᾷ Διὸς εἰ κρανθῇ πρᾶγμα his *head*, i. e. his nod, A.*Supp.*92. 4. ἡ τῆς οἰκουμένης κ., of Rome, Lib.*Or.*59.19. **-ῆνδε**, Adv. *to the top*, Orph.*L.*112. **-ιον**, τό, = κολούλιον, Xenocr. ap.Orib.2.58.79 (pl.). **-ίς**, ίδος, ἡ, = κορυφή, *Gloss.* ❋ **-ιστήρ**, ῆρος, ὁ, = κορυφαῖον I, Poll.5.31. 2. = κορυφαία I, Hsch. s. v. κεκρυφάλους (-αστῆρας cod.). ❋ **-ιστής**, οῦ, ὁ, *fillet* or *diadem*, esp. as a woman's head-dress; also, = κεκρυφάλου τὸ μέσον ῥάμμα, Id. ❋ **-ος**, ὁ, = κορυφή I. 3, *IG*4²(1).71.17, al. (Epid.). II. pet name for a child (?), *PTeb.*414.7 (ii A. D.). III. Alexandrian word for ὁ ὡς κόρη οἰφώμενος, Sch.Theoc.4.62 (v. l. κόροιφος). **-όω**, *bring to a head*, ἰόνθους Archig.ap.Orib.*Syn.*8.58; τὴν περὶ τὰ πρέμνα γῆν *Gp.*5.26.9:—Pass., [κῦμα] κυρτὸν ἐὸν κορυφοῦται *rises with* arching *crest* (cf. κορύσσω II), Il.4.426; κορυφουμένων [ἑλκέων] ὅκως ἐν θαλάσσῃ κύματα Aret.*SD*2.9: metaph., τὸ ἔσχατον κορυφοῦται βασιλεῦσι kings *are on the highest pinnacle*, Pi.*O.*1.113; κορυφουμένου τοῦ πολέμου *coming to a crisis*, J.*BJ*6.2.9; πόθου κορυφούμενον σάλον Aristaenet.1.10. II. *roof over*, ὀπαῖον Plu.*Per.*13. III. Pass., *to be concluded*, κεκορυφωμένου τοῦ κεφαλαίου Phld.*Rh.*1.122S.; κορυφούμενος εἰς ἓν ἀριθμός *being summed up*, *AP*7.429 (Alc. Mityl.):—Med., *sum up*, τὴν οὐσίαν τοῦ θεοῦ Jul.*Or.*4.143b. **-ώδης**, ες, *peaked, pointed*, Hp.*Epid.*6.1.10. **-ωμα**, ατος, τό, *top, summit*, Ath.Mech.36.7. **-ών**, ῶνος, ὁ, = foreg., *Gloss.* **-ωσις**, εως, ἡ, *apex* of a pyramid, Nicom.*Ar.*2.14.

**κορφῶς**· ἐλαφρῶς, Hsch.

**κόρχορος**, ὁ, = ἀναγαλλὶς ἡ κυανῆ, *blue pimpernel, Anagallis caerulea*, Ps.-Dsc.2.178; παροιμιαζόμενος διὰ πικρότητα Thphr.*HP*7.7.2; **κόρκορος** in Ar.*V.*239, Nic.*Th.*626: prov., κ. ἐν λαχάνοισι, 'a tailor among kings', Sch.Ar. l. c., etc. II. *jute, Corchorus olitorius*, Plin. *HN*21.89.183. III. *fat*, Hsch.

**κορχυρέα**, ἡ, *subterranean channel, culvert*, *IG*9(1).692.8 (Corc., ii B. C.).

**κορωλλικός**, ή, όν, *made of coral*, εἰκόνες *BCH*12.85 (temple of Zeus Panamaros).

**κορωνεκάβη** [ᾰ], ἡ, *a Hecuba, as old as a crow*, *AP*11.67 (Myrin.).

**κορώνεως** (sc. συκῆ), ἡ, *a fig of raven-grey colour*, Ar.*Pax*628.

❋ **κορών-η**, ἡ, a sea-bird, possibly *shearwater, Puffinus Kuhlii* or *P. anglorum*, τανύγλωσσοί τε κορῶναι εἰνάλιαι Od.5.66, cf. 12.418, Arist.*HA*593ᵇ13, Thphr.*Sign.*16, Arat.950, Ael.*NA*15.23; λάροι καὶ αἴθυιαι καὶ κ. Arr.*Peripl.M.Eux.*32 (but confounded with λ. and αἴ. by Sch.Od.1.441, cf. Hsch.). 2. *crow* (including the *hooded crow, Corvus cornix*, and prob. also the *rook, C. corone*), μή τοι ἐφεζομένη κρώξῃ λακέρυζα κ. Hes.*Op.*747; συκῆ πετραίη πολλὰς βόσκουσα κ. Archil.19: distd. from κολοιός, Ar.*Av.*5 (cf. 7); ἐννέα τοι ζώει γενεὰς λακέρυζα κ. ἀνδρῶν γηράντων Hes.*Fr.*171; πέντ' ἀνδρῶν γενεὰς ζώει λακέρυζα κ. Ar.*Av.*609; πολιαὶ κ. ib.967; κορώνην δευτέραν ἀναπλήσας having lived out twice a full *crow's-age*, Babr.46.9; ὑπὲρ τὰς κορώνας βεβιωκώς Poll.2.16: prov., κορώνη σκορπίον [ἥρπασε] 'caught a Tartar', *AP*12.92 (Mel.), cf. Zen.4.57, Hsch., Suid.; invoked at weddings, Ael.*NA*3.9. 3. κ. Δαυλία, = ἀηδών, Ar.*Fr.*716. II. *anything hooked* or *curved*, like a crow's bill, 1. *door-handle*, θύρην δ' ἐπέρυσσε κορώνῃ ἀργυρέῃ Od.1.441; ἱμάντα.. ἀπέλυσε κορώνης 21.46; χρυσέη κ. 7.90, cf. Poll.7.107, al. 2. *tip of a bow*, on which the bow-string was hooked, πᾶν δ' εὖ λειήνας χρυσέην ἐπέθηκε κ. Il.4.111, cf. Od.21.138: generally, *end, tip*, Artem.5.65: metaph., v. infr. 7. 3. *curved stern of a ship*, Arat.345. 4. *tip of the plough-pole* (ἱστοβοεύς), upon which the yoke is hooked or tied, A.R.3.1318, Poll.1.252. 5. *coronoid process* of the ulna, Hp.*Art.*18, Gal.*UP*2.14, Id.18(2).617; of the jaw, Id.*UP*11.20, 18(1).426. 6. kind of *crown*, Hsch. 7. κ. παννυχική *crown*, i. e. *culmination*, of a festival, Posidipp.ap.Ath.10.414d; cf. μέχρι τῆς κ. Call.*Fr.*2.5P.: generally, χρυσῷ βίῳ (with play on βιῷ) χρυσῆν κορώνην ἐπιθεῖναι Luc.*Peregr.*33, v. supr. II. 2. ❋ **-ιάω**, of a horse, *arch the neck*, *AP*9.777 (Phil.); of a man, *to be ambitious*, Plb.27.15.6; κ. καὶ γαυριῶντα D.Chr.78.33. II. κορωνιόωντα πέτηλα *curving* leaves, Hes.*Sc.*289. **-ῑδεύς**, έως, ὁ, *young crow*, Cratin.179. **-ίζω**, *bring to completion* (cf. κορωνίς II. 2 b), ἐξ δεκάδας κεκορώνικε *IPE*2.298.9 (Panticapaeum). **-ίης**, Att. -ίας, ου, ὁ, (κορωνιάω) *arching the neck*, ἵππος ὡς κ. Semon.18 (κορωνίτης codd. *EM*). ❋ **-ιος**, ον, *with crumpled horns*, Hsch. II. Κορώνιος, ὁ (sc. μήν), name of month at Cnossus, *GDI*5015.28. ❋ **-ίς**, ίδος, ἡ, acc. -νίν Hes.*Fr.*123.3 (as pr. n.):—*crook-beaked*: hence, generally, *curved*, in Hom. always of ships, παρὰ νηυσὶ κορωνίσι Il.18.338, al.; twice in Od., ἐν νήεσσι κ. 19.182, cf. 193. 2. of kine, *with crumpled horns*, Theoc.25.151. II. as Subst., *anything curved* or *bent*: 1. *wreath, garland*, Stesich.29, Hsch. 2. *curved line* or *stroke, flourish with the pen* at the end of a book or chapter, scene of a play, etc., *AP*11.41 (Phld.), Heph.*Poëm.* p.73C., Isid.*Etym.*1.21.26, Sch.Ar.*Nu.*510, al.; ἐγὼ κ. εἰμι γραμμάτων φύλαξ *PLit.Lond.*11; ἐπιτιθέναι τὴν κ. τῷ συγγράμματι Plu.2.66e; ἀπὸ τῆς ἀρχῆς μέχρι τῆς κ. ib.334c, etc. b. metaph., *end, completion*, ἐπιθεῖναι κορωνίδα τινί Luc.*Hist.Conscr.*26, cf. Gal.1.643; ἡ κ. τοῦ βίου Plu.2.789a; ἡ κ. τῶν ἀγαθῶν Hld.10.39, etc. 3. *mark of crasis* ('), as in τοὔνομα, θοἰμάτιον, τοὐμόν, etc., *An.Ox.*1.372, Sch. D.T.p.147H., *EM*763.10 (found in parchments of *Lyr.Alex.Adesp.*31.20 (ii A. D.), Sapph.*Supp.*2.4 (vii A. D.), etc.). **-ισμα**, ατος, τό, *crow-song*, a begging-song sung by strollers, Hagnocles ap.Ath.8.360b. ❋ **-ισταί**, οἱ, *singers of the crow-song*, title of work by Hagnocles. v. foreg.

❋ **κορωνοβόλος**, ον, *shooting crows*: κορωνοβόλον, τό, *sling* or *bow for crow-shooting*, etc., *AP*7.546.

**κορωνόν**, τό, = κορώνη II. 5; τοῦ πήχεως Gal.*UP*2.15, al.; τὰ τῆς κεφαλῆς κ. *condyles*, Id.2.460. 2. κόρωνα, τά, *elbows*, Herod.Med. ap.Orib.10.18.7, Orib.*Fr.*97; κορωνά Luc.*Trag.*122.

**κορωνο-πόδιον**, τό, Dim. of κορωνόπους, Aët.1.224, *Gp.*20.9, *PMag.Osl.*1.283. **-ποδώδης**, ες, *like crow's feet*, Thphr.*HP*1.10.5. **-πους**, ποδος, ὁ, *hartshorn, Plantago Coronopus*, ib.7.8.3, *CP*2.5.4, Dsc.2.130, Gal.12.40.

❋ **κορωνός**, ή, όν, *curved, crooked*, of the coronoid process of the jawbone, Hp.*Art.*30; βοῦς κ. *with crumpled horns*, Archil.39. II. = γαῦρος, ὑψαυχενῶν, *EM*530.27; κορωνὰ βαίνειν, = κορωνιᾶν, Anacr.151.

**κοσάλανον**· τὸ βραχύ, καὶ τὸ δίκαιον, Hsch. **κοσάλεφοι**· κόλαφοι, Id. **κόσβατοι**, v. κοσυβάτας. **κόσκικοι**· οἱ κατοικίδιοι ὄρνιθες, Id.

**κοσκῐν-ευτήριον**, τό, *winnowing-place*, *PRyl.*215.34 (ii A. D.). ❋ **-ευτής**, οῦ, ὁ, *one who sifts, winnows*, *PSI*4.365.18 (iii B. C.), *PCair.Zen.*292.484 (iii B. C.), al. **-ευτικόν**, τό, *fee for sifting*, *PPetr.*3p.215 (iii B. C.); πυροῦ *PRyl.*71.10 (i B. C.), cf. *PTeb.*92.10 (ii B. C.), al. **-εύω**, *sift*, in Pass., Democr.164, *PHib.*1.98.19 (iii B. C.), etc.; κοσκίνῳ

–ευέσθω *Gp.*3.7.1. –ηδόν, Adv. *as in a sieve*, Luc.*Tim.*3, *Sat.* 24. –ίζω, = κοσκινεύω, Asclep.ap.Gal.13.326, Aq., Sm.*Am.*9.9, *Gp.*13.15.4. II. metaph., *thrash, beat*, Hierocl.*Facet.*209 (Pass.). –ιον, τό, Dim. of κόσκινον, Chrysipp.Tyan.ap.Ath.14.647f. –ισις, εως, ἡ, *sifting*, *PFlor.*388.9 (ii A.D.), Phlp. *in GA* 54.2 : interlinear gloss on ἀλευρόττησις, *Et.Gud.*

**κοσκῐνό-γῡρος**, ὁ, = τηλία, Sch.Ar.*Pl.*1038. –μαντις, εως (also ιδος, Choerob. *in Theod.*1.200, al.), ὁ and ἡ, *diviner by a sieve*, Philippid.37, Theoc.3.31, Artem.2.69.

* **κόσκῐνον**, τό (for the gender v. Ar.*Fr.*480, Poll.10.149), *sieve*, Semon.7.59, Ar.*Nu.*373, *Fr.*227, Democr.164, etc.; φορεῖν ὕδωρ τετρημένῳ κοσκίνῳ Pl.*Grg.*493b; ἐν Ἅιδου κοσκίνῳ ὕδωρ φέρειν, alluding to the punishment of the Danaids, Id.*R.*363d; κοσκίνοις μαντεύεσθαι Ael.*NA*8.5, cf. Luc.*Alex.*9; κ. ἀλωνικὸν ἀπὸ βύρσης, ἀπὸ δέρματος, κ. πλεκτόν, *Edict.Diocl.*15.56, al., cf. Poll.6.74, *Gp.*2.19.5, al. II. κ. Ἐρατοσθένους *table* for finding prime numbers, Nicom.*Ar.*1.13.

**κοσκῐνο-ποιός**, ὁ, *sieve-maker*, Philyll.14, Poll.7.160. –πώλης, ου, ὁ, *dealer in sieves*, Nicopho 19. –ράφος [ᾰ], ὁ, *one who sews (leather) sieves*, *PTeb.*540 (ii A.D.). –ρῖνος (–ριος cod.)· εἰς κοσκίνου κατασκευὴν ῥινός, Hsch.

**κοσκίνωμα**, ατος, τό, *grating*, Sm., Thd.*Ex.*35.16.

**κοσκυλμάτια**, ων, τά, *cuttings of leather*: Com., of *the scraps of flattery* offered by the tanner Cleon to his patron Δῆμος, Ar.*Eq.*49, cf. Sch.

**κοσμᾱγός**, ὁ, *guide of the universe*, name of an order of divine beings in the Chaldaean system, Dam.*Pr.*112.

**κοσμαῖα**, τά, *ornaments*, *CPR* 30 ii 1 (vi A.D., nisi leg. κοσμα⟨ρ⟩ίων).

**κοσμᾶν**· ἐρίζειν, ἀγνωμονεῖν, Hsch.

* **κοσμ-αρίδιον**, τό, Dim. of κόσμος II, *POxy.*903.29 (iv A.D.). * –άριον, τό, = foreg., Ath.11.474e, Hsch. s. v. καλαμίς, al. –άρχης, ου, ὁ, *governor of the universe*, Dam.*Pr.*132. * –έω, *order, arrange*, esp. *set* an army *in array, marshal* it, Il.14.379; κοσμῆσαι ἵππους τε καὶ ἀνέρας 2.554:—Pass., ἐπεὶ κόσμηθεν ἅμ' ἡγεμόνεσσιν ἕκαστοι 3.1; πένταχα κοσμηθέντες *marshalled* in five bodies, 12.87; of a population, διὰ τρίχα κοσμηθέντες 2.655; once in Od., of hunters, διὰ δὲ τρίχα κοσμηθέντες 9.157:—Med., κοσμησάμενος πολιήτας *having arranged his* men, Il.2.806; so after Homer, κ. στρατόν (v.l. for κοιμήσων) E.*Rh.*662; τάξεις κεκοσμημέναι X.*Cyr.*2.1.26, cf. Pl.*Phdr.*247a; ἐπὶ τάξις πλεῦνας ἐκεκοσμέατο Hdt.9.31. 2. generally, *arrange, prepare*, δόρπον ἐκόσμει Od.7.13; κ. ἀοιδήν *h.Bacch.*59; ἔργα Hes.*Op.*306; στέφανον E.*Hipp.*74; τράπεζαν X.*Cyr.*8.2.6; εἰς τάφον λέβητα S.*El.*1401:—Pass., δεῖπνον κεκόσμηται Pi.*N.*1.22; δεῖ οὕτω κοσμηθῆναι ὅκως.. Democr.266; τὸ κοσμηθὲν αἷμα, = τὸν οἰκεῖον κόσμον κτησάμενον, Gal.5.551. II. *order, rule*, τὴν πόλιν κ. καλῶς τε καὶ εὖ Hdt.1.59, cf. S.*Aj.*1103; Σπάρτην ἔλαχες, κείνην κόσμει E.*Fr.*723 (anap.); κ. ἐμαυτόν *restrain* myself, Id.*Hyps.Fr.*34(60).46; τὰ ἄλλα ἐκεκοσμέατό οἱ Hdt.1.100; τόν γε νοῦν κοσμοῦντα πάντα κοσμεῖν Pl.*Phd.*97c:—Pass., τὰ κοσμούμενα *orderly institutions*, S.*Ant.*677: pf. part., of persons, *orderly*, ταπεινὸς καὶ κεκοσμημένος Pl.*Lg.*716a; τεταγμένον τε καὶ κ. πρᾶγμα Id.*Grg.*504a. 2. in Crete, *hold office of* κόσμος III, οἱ κεκοσμηκότες Arist.*Pol.*1272a35, cf. Plb.22.15.1; Cret. κοσμίω *Leg.Gort.*1.51, etc.; also κορμίω (q. v.). III. *adorn, equip, dress*, esp. of women, *h.Hom.*6.11, Hes.*Op.*72; κοσμῆσαί τινα πανοπλίῃ Hdt.4.180; τριπόδεσσι κ. δόμον Pi.*I.*1.19; τινὰ πλούτῳ ὑπερβάλλοντι Hdn.3.10.6: c. dupl. acc., πρίν σε νυμφικὸν ἰστέφανον κοσμήσαμεν *JRS*17.51 (Phrygia, iv A.D.):—freq. in Med., κοσμέεσθαι τὰς κεφαλάς *to adorn their* heads, Hdt.7.209; κοσμεῖσθαι σῶμα ὅπλοις E.*Ph.*1359; ἐν φοινικίσι κοσμησάμενοι *having decked themselves*, Pl.Com.208:—Pass., χρυσῷ κοσμηθεῖσα *h.Ven.*65; παῖσα δ' Ἄρῃ κεκόσμηται στέγα Alc.15.1; ἵπποι κεκοσμημένοι ὡς κάλλιστα Hdt.7.40; κεκ. ἐσθῆτι ποικίλῃ καὶ χρυσοῖσι στεφάνοις Pl.*Ion* 535d, cf. S.*Ph.*1064, Th.6.41, etc. 2. metaph., *adorn, embellish*, λόγους E.*Med.*576; λόγους ῥήμασί τε καὶ ὀνόμασι κεκοσμημένους Pl.*Ap.*17c; τραγικὸν λῆρον Ar.*Ra.*1005; κ. ἔργον ἄριστον ib.1027; τὸ λογικὸν ἔχεις ἐξαίρετον, τοῦτο κόσμει Arr.*Epict.*3.1.26; λόγον εὐρυθμίαις Isoc.5.27; αὐτὸν λόγοις Pl.*La.*196b, cf. 197c; ἐπὶ τὸ μεῖζον κ. Th.1.21; τὸν..τὴν ἐκείνου ἀρετὴν κοσμήσοντα (in speaking) D.18.287:—Pass., ἦθος σεμνότητι –μημένον Phld.*Acad.Ind.* p.52 M. 3. *honour*, λουτροῖς σ' ἐκόσμησ' S.*El.*1139; κ. τάφον Id.*Ant.*396; νέκυν E.*Tr.*1147; κ. καὶ τιμᾶν X.*Cyr.*1.3.3; of persons, *adorn, be an honour to*, πατρίδα Thgn.947; νᾶσον εὐκλέα Pi.*N.*6.46; Σαλαμῖνα κ. πατρίδα E.*Fr.*530.3; [τὴν πόλιν] αἱ τῶνδε ἀρεταὶ ἐκόσμησαν Th.2.42. 4. *bury*, *JHS*25.172, al. (Isauria). IV. Pass., *to be assigned, ascribed to*, ἐς τὸν Αἰγύπτιον νομὸν αὗται [αἱ πόλεις] ἐκεκοσμέατο Hdt.3.91; ἐς Πέρσας κεκοσμέαται Id.6.41; esp. of philosophic schools, κατὰ τὴν Ἀκαδημίαν κοσμεῖσθαι S.E.*P.*1.231; οἱ κατὰ διαφόρους αἱρέσεις κοσμούμενοι Id.*M.*11.77. –ημα, ατος, τό, *ornament, decoration*, esp. in dress, X.*Cyr.*7.3.7, Luc.*Salt.*32, etc.: τὰ πολέμου κ. Pl.*Lg.*956b; of *adornments* buried with the dead, *BGU* 1024.iv 44 (iv A.D.): metaph., of the virtues, Luc.*Im.*11. * –ησις, εως, ἡ, *ordering, arrangement*, ταῖς τῆς ψυχῆς τάξεσι καὶ κοσμήσεσι Pl.*Grg.*504d, cf. *Criti.*117b (sg.): *adornment*, Arist.*Oec.*1344a19; pl., Plu.*Thes.*23: metaph., *dignity*, ἡ τῆς πόλεως καὶ τοῦ βουλευτηρίου κ. *BGU* 1024 viii 10 (iv A.D.). * –ητεία, ἡ, *office of* κοσμητής, *CPR*20.7 (iii A.D.). –ήτειρα, ἡ, fem. of –ητήρ, Orph.*H.*10.8. II. κ. τῆς Ἀρτέμιδος, title of *a female magistrate* at Ephesus, *SIG*1228 (Ephesus, iii A.D.), *CIG*2823. –ητέον, *one must adorn*, Porph.*Marc.*19. –ητεύω, *hold office of* κοσμητής (q. v.), *IG*2².1009.49, *PFlor.*57.75 (ii A.D.), *CPR*20.1 (iii A.D.), *IG*3.735, al., *BGU*362 i x 6 (iii A.D.):—also –ητέω *IG*3.736. –ητήρ, ῆρος, ὁ, = κοσμητής, Epigr.ap. Aeschin.3.185. II. at Itanos, title of eponymous magistrate, *SIG*463.15 (iii B.C.), *Supp.Epigr.*2.512.22. –ητήριον, τό, *dressing-room*, Paus.2.7.5. II. = κόσμητρον, Hsch. s. v. κάλλυντρα. * –ητής, οῦ, ὁ, *orderer, director*, πολέμου Epigr.ap.Aeschin.3.185; πόλεως κ. *legislator*, Pl.*Lg.*844a; title of Zeus, Paus.3.17.4. 2. at Athens and elsewhere, *magistrate in charge of the* ἔφηβοι, Arist.*Ath.*42.2, *IG* 2².665.10, 17 (iii B.C.), 1009.33 (ii B.C.), al., Pl.*Ax.*366e, Teles p.50 H., *POxy.*519.8 (ii A.D.), *PFay.*85 (iii A.D.), etc. II. *adorner*, X.*Cyr.*8.8.20. 2. *cleaner* or *polisher* of temple-statues, *IG*11(2).154*A* 20 (Delos, iii B.C.). –ητικός, ή, όν, *skilled in ordering* or *arranging*, τινος Arist.*Oec.*1344b26, Andronic.Rhod.p.575 M. Adv. –κῶς Hierocl.*Prov.*p.465 B. II. ἡ –κή (sc. τέχνη) *art of dress and ornament*, Pl.*Sph.*227a, *Plt.*282a: –κά, τά, title of work by Crito, Gal.12.446: –κόν, τό, *cosmetic*, *PTeb.*540 (ii A.D.); title of work by Cleopatra, Gal.12.432. –ητός, ή, όν, *well-ordered, trim*, πρασιαί Od.7.127. –ήτρια, ἡ, = κοσμήτειρα, Hsch. s. v. Σαραχηρώ. –ητρον, τό, *broom*, Sch.Ar.*Pax* 59, Suid. s. v. κάλλυντρα. –ήτωρ, ορος, ὁ, poet. for κοσμητής (in late Prose, Jul.*Gal.*49e), *one who marshals an army, commander, leader*, Ἀτρεΐδα.. δύω, κοσμήτορε λαῶν Il.1.16, 375; δοιὼ.. κοσμήτορε λαῶν 3.236; ἐν χερσὶν ἔθηκε δέπας κοσμήτορι λ. Od.18.152; *guide, director*, παιδός A.R.1.194. 2. *one who adorns*, ἡρώων κ. Ὅμηρον Epigr.ap. Arist.*Fr.*76. 3. = κοσμητής I. 2, *IG*3.740, al. –ιαῖος, α, ον, (κόσμος IV) *of the size of the universe*, Democr.ap.*Placit.*1.12.6. –ίδιον, τό, Dim. of κόσμος II, *adornment*, metaph., τῆς πόλεως *Mélanges Beyrouth* 7.395 (Cappadocia; written –ήδιον). * –ίζω, *clean*, Hsch. s. v. σαρῶ. * –ικός, ή, όν, (κόσμος IV) *of the world* or *universe*, σχήματα Procl. *in Euc.*p.65 F.; τὰ κ. πάντα v.l. in Arist.*Ph.*196a25, cf. Philol. (?) 23; ἡ κ. διάταξις Plu.2.119f; κ. ὀχλήσεις Luc.*Paras.*11; κλίσεις (v.l. κλήσεις) Suid. s. v. Ὀρφεύς: Astrol., κ. κέντρα (opp. γενεθλιαλογικά) Vett.Val.79.26. Adv. –κῶς Id.119.15, Ptol.*Tetr.*112. II. *of this world, earthly*, *Ep.Hebr.*9.1; *worldly*, ἐπιθυμίαι *Ep.Tit.*2.12. 2. *secular, lay*, opp. clerical, Just.*Nov.*123.1.2. * –ιον, τό, Dim. (in form) of κόσμος, D.S.25.15, Plu.2.141d, *BGU*1024 v 27 (iv A.D.); κ. ἡμέρας Secund.*Sent.*5; τὰ τῆς ἀρχῆς κ. the *insignia* of office, D.S.38/9.16; τὰ βασιλικὰ κ. Plu.*Demetr.*45; στρατηγικά Id.*Ant.*17. –ιος, α, ον, (–ος, ον, Gal.16.606, Sor.1.3), *well-ordered, regular, moderate*, δαπάνη Pl.*R.*560d; οἴκησις Id.*Criti.*112c; κόσμιόν ἐστι, c. inf., is *a regular practice*, Ar.*Pl.*565. 2. of persons, *orderly, well-behaved*, δίκαιοι καὶ σοφοὶ καὶ κ. ib.89; κ. καὶ σώφρων Lys.21.19; κ. καὶ εὔκολοι Pl.*R.*329d; κ. καὶ φρόνιμος ψυχή Id.*Phd.*108a; χρηστὸς εἶ καὶ κ. Nicopho 16; ἥτις ἐστὶ κοσμία γυνή Anaxandr.56, cf. Arist.*Pol.*1277b23; κ. ἐν διαίτῃ Pl.*R.*408b; πρὸς τοὺς θεοὺς Id.*Smp.*193a; οἱ κοσμιώτατοι φύσει Id.*R.*564e; of a patient, *quiet*, Hp.*Acut.*65: freq. in Oratt., of *honest, orderly* citizens, Lys.26.3, etc.; τοὺς πολίτας –ιωτέρους ποιεῖν Isoc.20.18; *modest*, ὁμιλία X.*Mem.*3.11.14 (Sup.); τὸ κ. *decency, order*, S.*El.*872, Pl.*Lg.*802e. Adv. κοσμίως *regularly, decently*, Ar.*Pl.*709, 978, al.; κ. ἔχειν Pl.*Phd.*68c; κ. ἥκομεν *as befits* us, Id.*Sph.*216a; κ. βιοῦν Lys.3.6: Comp. –ιώτερον, βεβιωκέναι Isoc.15.162: Sup. –ώτατα, τὰς συμφορὰς φέρειν Lys.3.4. II. Subst. κόσμιος, ὁ, (κόσμος IV) = κοσμοπολίτης, Plu.2.600f, Arr.*Epict.*1.9.1. –ιότης, ητος, ἡ, *propriety, decorum*, Ar.*Pl.*564, Pl.*Plt.*307b, Zeno *Stoic.*1.58, etc.; κ. καὶ σωφροσύνη Pl.*Grg.*508a; opp. ἀκολασία, Arist.*EN*1109a16: pl., τὰς αἰσχύνας καὶ κ. Phld.*Mus.*p.44 K.

* **κοσμο-γένεια**, ἡ, = sq., Jul.*Gal.*49a. –γονία, ἡ, *creation* or *origin of the world*, Cleom.1.1; applied to the poem of Parmenides, Plu.2.756f. –γρᾰφία, Ion. –ίη, ἡ, *description of the world*, title of work by Democritus, D.L.9.46. –γράφος [ᾰ], ον, *describing the world*, Jo.Gaz.2.3. –διοικητικός, ή, όν, *governing the world*, Stob.2.7.3f. –ειδής, ές, *like the celestial globe*, Horap.1.10. Adv. –δῶς ib.59. –κόμης, ου, ὁ, *dressing the hair*, κτείς *AP*6.247 (Phil.). * –κράτωρ [ᾰ], ορος, ὁ, *lord of the world*, epith. of οὐρανός, Orph.*H.*4.3; Ζεὺς Μίτρας Ἥλιος κ. *Not.Scav.*1912.323 (Rome). 2. of the Emperors, *IG*14.926, *Sammelb.*4275, cf. Ptol.*Tetr.*175, Heph.Astr.1.1. 3. Astrol., *ruler of the* κόσμος, i. e. *planet*, Id. in *Cat.Cod.Astr.*6.68, Vett.Val.171.6; οἱ ἑπτὰ κ. Dam.*Pr.*131; οἱ κ. τοῦ σκότους τούτου the *cosmic rulers* of this sinful world, *Ep.Eph.*6.12; οἱ κ. οἱ τὰ ὑπὸ σελήνην στοιχεῖα διοικοῦντες Iamb.*Myst.*2.3. –λογικός, ὁ, title of work by Ion, Sch.Ar.*Pax* 835. –πλαστέω, *frame the world*, Ph.1.437. –πλάστης, ου, ὁ, *framer of the world*, ib.329, 526. –πληθής, ές, *filling the world*, κατακλυσμός Lxx 4*Ma.*15.31. –πλόκος, ον, *holding together the world*, of Apollo, *AP*9.525.11. –ποιέω, *make the world*, Ph.1.5, Plu.2.719d, 877c (Pass.), *Stoic.*2.112 (ap.Alex.Aphr.*Mixt.*225.2), Iamb. *in Nic.*p.79 P. 2. *frame a system* or *theory of the world*, Arist.*Metaph.*1091a18, *Cael.*301a13; κ. ἕκαστον τῶν ἀστέρων *assert* them *to be worlds*, *Placit.*2.13.15. 3. *bestow order upon, organize*, τὴν ὕλην Dam.*Pr.*270. * –ποίησις, εως, ἡ, Archit., *ornamentation*, *POxy.*498.30 (ii A.D.). –ποιητής, οῦ, ὁ, *creator of the world*, Herm.ap.Stob.1.49.44. –ποιητικός, ή, όν, *creative*, δύναμις Ph.1.4. –ποιία, ἡ, *creation*, Arist.*Metaph.*985a19, *Stoic.*2.191, Str.15.1.59, Ph.1.1, Dam.*Pr.*270, etc. 2. title of a work by Empedocles, Arist.*Ph.*196a22; applied to the opening chapters of Genesis, Ph. l. c. II. = κόσμησις, *CPHerm.*p.79 W. –ποιός, όν, *creating the world*, *Placit.*1.25.3, Dam.*Pr.*309, al.; θεός *Theol.Ar.*43: Subst. –ποιός, ὁ, *creator*, Ph.1.2. –πολις, ὁ, a magistrate among the Locrians, Plb.12.16.6 (dat. –πόλιδι), and 9 (acc. –πολιν); at Thasos, *IG*12(8).386, 459; at Lyttus in Crete, *CIG*2583; at Cibyra, *IGRom.*4.908; at Miletus, title of the ἀρχιπρύτανις, *Milet.*1(7).230, 231. –πολίτης [ῑ], ου, ὁ, *citizen of the world*, Ph.1.1, al., D.L.6.63:—fem. –πολῖτις as

Adj., ψυχαί Ph.1.657. **-πρεπής**, ές, *suitable for the universe*, Euryph. ap.Stob.4.39.27.

**κόσμος**, ὁ, *order*, κατὰ κόσμον in *order*, *duly*, εὖ κατὰ κ. Il.10.472,al.; οὐ κατὰ κ. *shamefully*, Od.8.179; μὰψ ἀτὰρ οὐ κατὰ κ. Il.2.214: freq. in dat., κόσμῳ καθίζειν to sit *in order*, Od.13.77, cf. Hdt.8.67; οὐ κ... ἐλευσόμεθα Il.12.225; κ. θεῖναι τὰ πάντα Hdt.2.52, cf. 7.36, etc.; διάθες τάδε κ. Ar.*Av.*1331; κ. φέρειν bear *becomingly*, Pi.*P.*3.82; δέξασθαί τινα κ. A.*Ag.*521; σὺν κόσμῳ Hdt.8.86, Arist.*Mu.*398ᵇ23; ἐν κόσμῳ Hp.*Mul.*1.3, Pl.*Smp.*223b; κόσμῳ οὐδενὶ κοσμηθέντες *in* no sort of *order*, Hdt.9.59; φεύγειν, ἀπιέναι οὐδενὶ κ., Id.3.13, 8.60.γ', etc.; ἀτάκτως καὶ οὐδενὶ κ. Th.3.108, cf. A.*Pers.*400; οὐκέτι τὸν αὐτὸν κ. no longer *in* the same *order*, Hdt.9.66; οὐδένα κ. ib.65,69; ἦν δ' οὐδεὶς κ. τῶν ποιουμένων Th.3.77: generally, of things, *natural order*, γίνεται τῶν τεταρταίων ἡ κατάστασις ἐκ τούτου τοῦ κ. Hp.*Prog.*20. 2. *good order, good behaviour*, = κοσμιότης Phld.*Mus.* p.43K.; *discipline*, D.18.216; οὐ κ., ἀλλ' ἀκοσμία S.*Fr.*846. 3. *form, fashion*, ἵππου κόσμον ἄεισον δουρατέου Od.8.492; κ. ἐπέων ἀπατηλὸς Parm.8.52; ἐξηγεομένων..τὸν κ. αὐτοῦ the *fashion* of it, Hdt.3.22; κ. τόνδε..ὁ καταστησάμενος who established this *order* or *form*, Id.1.99. 4. of states, *order, government*, μεταστῆσαι τὸν κ. Th.4.76, cf. 8.48,67; μένειν ἐν τῷ ὀλιγαρχικῷ κ. 8.72, etc.; esp. of the Spartan *constitution*, Hdt.1.65, Clearch.3: pl., πόλεων κόσμοι Pl.*Prt.*322c. II. *ornament, decoration*, esp. of women, Il.14.187, Hes.*Op.*76, Hdt.5.92.η'; γυναικεῖος κ. Pl.*R.*373c, etc.; of a horse, Il.4.145; of men, Hdt.3.123, A.*Th.*397, etc.; γλαυκόχροα κόσμον ἐλαίας, of an olive-wreath, Pi.*O.*3.13, cf. 8.83, *P.*2.10, etc.; κ. κυνῶν X.*Cyn.*6.1; κ. καὶ ἔπιπλα Lys.12.19; κ. ἀργυροῦς a *service* of plate, Ath.6.231b; ἱερὸς κ. *OGI*90.40 (Rosetta, ii B.C.): pl., *ornaments*, A.*Ag.*1271; οἱ περὶ τὸ σῶμα κ. Isoc.2.32: metaph., of ornaments of speech, such as *epithets*, Id.9.9 (pl.), Arist.*Rh.*1408ᵃ14, *Po.*1457ᵇ2, 1458ᵃ33; ἀδυμελῆ κ. κελαδεῖν to sing sweet songs of *praise*, Pi.*O.*11(10).13 (s.v.l.). 2. metaph., *honour, credit*, Id.*N.*2.8, *I.*6(5).69; κόσμον φέρει τινί it does one *credit*, Hdt.8.60,142; γύναι, γυναιξὶ κόσμον ἡ σιγὴ φέρει S.*Aj.*293; κ. τοῦτ' ἐστὶν ἐμοί Ar.*Nu.*914; οἷς κόσμος [ἐστὶ] καλῶς τοῦτο δρᾶν Th.1.5; ἐν κόσμῳ καὶ τιμῇ εἶναί τινι D.60.36; of persons, σὺ ἔμοιγε μέγιστος κ. ἔσει X.*Cyr.*6.4.3; ἡ μεγαλοψυχία οἷον κ. τις τῶν ἀρετῶν Arist.*EN* 1124ᵃ1. III. *ruler, regulator*, title of chief magistrate in Crete, *SIG*712.57, etc.; collectively, *body of κόσμοι*, ib.524.1; τοῦ κ. τοῖς πλίασι ib.527.74: also freq. in pl., ib.528.1, al., Arist.*Pol.*1272ᵃ6, Str.10.4.18,22; cf. κόρμος. IV. Philos., *world-order, universe*, first in Pythag., acc. to *Placit.*2.1.1, D.L.8.48 (cf. [Philol.]21), or Parm., acc. to Thphr.ap.D.L.l.c.; κόσμον τόνδε οὔτε τις θεῶν οὔτε ἀνθρώπων ἐποίησεν, ἀλλ' ἦν ἀεὶ καὶ ἔστιν καὶ ἔσται πῦρ Heraclit.30; ὁ καλούμενος ὑπὸ τῶν σοφιστῶν κ. X.*Mem.*1.1.11: freq. in Pl., *Grg.*508a, *Ti.*27a, al.; ἡ τοῦ ὅλου σύστασίς ἐστι κ. καὶ οὐρανὸς Arist.*Cael.*280ᵃ21, cf. Epicur.*Ep.*2p.37 U., Chrysipp.*Stoic.*2.168, etc.; ὁ κ. ζῷον ἔμψυχον καὶ λογικόν Posidon.ap.D.L.7.139, cf. Pl.*Ti.*30b: sts. of the *firmament*, γῆς ἁπάσης τῆς ὑπὸ τῷ κόσμῳ κειμένης Isoc.4.179; ὁ περὶ τὴν γῆν ὅλος κ. Arist.*Mete.*339ᵃ20; μετελθεῖν εἰς τὸν ἀέναον κ., of death, *OGI*56.48 (Canopus, iii B.C.); but also, of *earth*, as opp. heaven, ὁ ἐπιχθόνιος κ. Herm.ap. Stob.1.49.44; or as opp. the underworld, ὁ ἄνω κ. Iamb.*VP*27.123; of any *region* of the universe, ὁ μετάρσιος κ. Herm.ap.Stob.1.49.44; of the sphere whose centre is the earth's centre and radius the straight line joining earth and sun, Archim.*Aren.*4; of the sphere containing the fixed stars, Pl.*Epin.*987b: in pl., *worlds*, coexistent or successive, Anaximand. et alii ap.*Placit.*2.1.3, cf. Epicur.l.c.; also, of stars, Νὺξ μεγάλων κ. κτεάτειρα A.*Ag.*356 (anap.), cf. Heraclid.et Pythagorei ap.*Placit.*2.13.15 (= Orph.*Fr.*22); οἱ ἑπτὰ κ. the Seven *planets*, *Corp.Herm.*11.7. 2. metaph., *microcosm*, ἄνθρωπος μικρὸς κ. Democr.34; ἄνθρωπος βραχὺς κ. Ph.2.155; of living beings in general, τὸ ζῷον οἷον μικρόν τινα κ. εἶναί φασιν ἄνδρες παλαιοί Gal.*UP*3.10. 3. in later Gr., = οἰκουμένη, *the known* or *inhabited world*, *OGI*458.40 (9 B.C.), *Ep.Rom.*1.8, etc.; ὁ τοῦ παντὸς κ. κύριος, of Nero, *SIG*814.31, cf. *IGRom.*4.982 (Samos); ἐὰν τὸν κ. ὅλον κερδήσῃ *Ev.Matt.*16.26. 4. *men in general*, φανέρωσον σεαυτὸν τῷ κ. *Ev.Jo.*7.4, cf. 12.19; esp. of the *world* as estranged from God by sin, ib.16.20, 17.9, al., 1*Ep.Cor.*1.21, etc. 5. οὗτος ὁ κ. this present *world*, i.e. *earth*, opp. heaven, *Ev.Jo.*13.1; regarded as the kingdom of evil, ὁ ἄρχων τοῦ κ. τούτου ib.12.31. V. Pythag. name for *six*, *Theol.Ar.*37; for *ten*, ib.59.

**κοσμο-σάνδᾰλον**, τό, Dor. = ὑάκινθος, *larkspur, Delphinium Ajacis*, Cratin.98, Pherecr.131.4, Paus.2.35.5. **-τρόφος**, ον, *feeding the world*, of Egypt, Man.1.2; Ῥώμη *IG*14.1108*c*19.

**κοσμουργ-έω**, *create the world*, Procl.*in Ti.*1.334D. **-ός**, ὁ, *creator of the world*, Iamb.*in Nic.*p.10P., Dam.*Pr.*270.

**κοσμο-φθόρος**, ον, *destroying the world*, *AP*11.270. **-φλεγής**, ές, *setting the world on fire*, δαλός Eleg.ap.Jo.Sic.in Rh.6.57 W. **-φόρος**, ὁ, *one who carries ornaments in procession*, *Jahresh.*18 *Beibl.*287 (Ephesus), *Cat.Cod.Astr.*8(4).136. II. Archit., *ornamental frieze*, *Rev.Phil.*44.251 (Didyma, ii B.C.).

**κοσμώ**, οῦς, ἡ, *priestess of Pallas*, Lycurg.*Fr.*48, Ister 16.

**κοσμωτός**, ή, όν, *made into a world*, Aristo Stoicus ap.Simp.*in Cat.*188.35.

**κόσος**, η, ον, Ion. for πόσος.

**κόσσᾰβος**, ὁ, Ion. and older Att. for κότταβος.

**κόσσαι**, αἱ, gloss on αὐλοί (*cannons* of a horse), Sch.Opp.*C.*1.189.

**κόσσος**, ὁ, *box on the ear, cuff*, Suid.:—hence **Κοσσοτράπεζος**, Com. name for a parasite, Alciphr.3.69, Hsch. s.v. παράσιτος.

**κοσσύμβη**, ἡ, v. κοσύμβη.

**κοσσῠφ-ίζω**, *sing like a blackbird*, Hero *Spir.*2.35. **-ος**, Att. **κόττῠφος**, ὁ (also **κόσσυκος**, *Gloss.*), *blackbird, Turdus merula*, ὁ μὲν ἕτερος μέλας, ..ὁ δ' ἕτερος ἔκλευκος Arist.*HA*617ᵃ11; ἑξῆς κ. ἦλθε μόνος γεύσασθαι ἕτοιμος Matro *Conv.*87, cf. Theoc.*Ep.*4.10, *AP*12.142 (Rhian.), 9.76 (Antip.), 343 (Arch.); v. κόψιχος. II. a sea-fish, Diocl.*Fr.*135, Gal.6.718; μελάγχρως Numen.ap.Ath.7.305c; ὁ θαλάττιος Ael.*NA*1.14sq. III. name of a peculiar breed of poultry at Tanagra, Paus.9.22.4.

**κοσταί** or **κόσται**, ῶν, αἱ, = ἀκοστή, *barley*, Hsch. II. κ., οἱ, kind of *fish*, Diph.Siph.ap.Ath.8.357a.

**κοστάριον**, τό, prob. = κόστος, Str.16.4.26 (pl.).

**κοστίας**· κοιλίας, κόμορος, Hsch.

**κόστος**, ὁ, root used as *spice*, *Saussurea Lappa*, Thphr.*HP*9.7.3, Dsc.1.16, D.S.2.49, *Peripl.M.Rubr.*39, al., *OGI*214.60 (Didyma, iii B.C.):—also **κόστον**, τό, Thphr.*Od.*32 (but κόστα, τά, dub. sens., of wooden parts of a cart, *Edict.Diocl.*15.19). II. = ἑλένιον, *Gp.*11.27.2.

**κοσυβάτας**, ὁ, *sacrificer*, *Supp.Epigr.*1.414.10 (Gortyn, v/iv B.C.); cf. κόσβατοι (sic, post κοστίας)· οἱ ἐπὶ θυσιῶν τεταγμένοι, Hsch.

**κοσύμβ-η**, ἡ, = Att. κρωβύλος, Poll.2.30 (v.l. κορσύμβην, κοσσάμην). 2. = ἐγκόμβωμα, *shepherd's coat*, D.Chr.72.1, *EM*311.5, cf. 349.45:—written **κοσσύμβη** or **κόσσυμβος**, Hsch. **-ος**, ὁ, *fringe*, v.l. for sq., Lxx *Ex.*28.35. II. *hair-net*, ib.*Is.*3.18. **-ωτός**, ή, όν, *tasselled, fringed*, τοὺς κ. τῶν χιτώνων ib.*Ex.* l.c.

**κοσώλυφος**· βόθυνος, ὄχθος, ἀνάστημα γῆς, ἢ σπέρμα, Hsch.

**κοταίνω**, = κοτέω, A.*Th.*485 (lyr.):—also **κοτάω**, *Et.Gud.* s.v. ἐνεκότουν.

**κότε, κοτέ**, Ion. for πότε, ποτέ.

**κοτεινός**, ή, όν, = κοτήεις, cj. for σκοτεινόν in Pi.*N.*7.61 Boeckh.

**κότερον, κότερα**, Ion. for πότερον, πότερα.

**κοτ-έω**, (κότος) Ep. and Lyr. Verb, used in the forms cited below, without distinction of voice, *bear one a grudge, be angry at* him, c. dat. pers., κοτεσσάμενος Τρώεσσιν Il.5.177, cf. 18.367; Τυδέος υἱι κοτέσσατο Φοῖβος 23.383; τῷ δ' ἄρ' Ἀχαιοὶ ἐκπάγλως κοτέοντο 2.223; τοῖσίν τε κοτέσσεται (Ep. for κοτέσηται) 5.747, 8.391, Od.1.101; λέοντε δύω ἀμφὶ κταμένης ἐλάφοιο ἀλλήλοις κοτέοντες Hes.*Sc.*403: prov., κεραμεὺς κεραμεῖ κοτέει καὶ τέκτονι τέκτων Id.*Op.*25: c. dat. rei, βασιλῆος ἀτασθαλίᾳ κοτέων Pi.*Supp.*13a31: c. gen. rei, ἀπάτης κοτέων *angry at* the trick, Il.4.168; κοτεσσαμένη τό γε θυμῷ, οὕνεκα.. 14.191: abs., οὐδ' ὄθομαι κοτέοντος 1.181, cf. 23.391; κεκοτηότι θυμῷ (Ep. pf. part.) with *angry* heart, 21.456, Od.9.501, 19.71: aor. κοτέσασα *h.Cer.*254; Διωνύσῳ κοτέσασα Euph.14. **-ήεις**, εσσα, εν, *wrathful, jealous*, θεός Il.5.191, cf. A.D.*Adv.*189.12.

**κοτίκας**, ὁ, = ἀλέκτωρ, Hsch. **κοτίλλιν**· ἀνδρὸς αἰδοῖον, Id.:—also **κότιλον**, Id. s.v. κόθημα.

**κοτῖνάς**, άδος, ἡ, *grafted upon a wild olive*, ἐλαία Poll.6.45. II. *fruit of the wild olive-tree*, Hp.*Morb.*3.16.

**κοτῖνηφόρος**, ον, *producing wild olive-trees*, Mosch.*Fr.*3.2. II. *winning a crown of wild olive*, Ζηνὸς κ. ἆθλον *Inscr.Magn.*181.

**κότῖνος**, ὁ (also ἡ Theoc.5.32), *wild olive-tree*, Ar.*Av.*621 (anap.), *Pl.*943; τοὺς νικῶντας στεφανώσας κοτίνου στεφάνῳ (sc. at Olympia) ib.586, cf. *AP*9.357, Thphr.*HP*4.13.2; τὰ ξύλα τὰ ἀπὸ τοῦ κ. *IG*11(2).287*A*22 (Delos, iii B.C.): distd. from ἀγριελαία by Sch.Pl.*Phdr.*236b (in neut. κότινον, τό), but identified by Dsc.1.105. (In Ar.*Pl.*592 the v.l. κοτίνῳ στεφάνῳ may point to κοτινῷ dat. of Adj. κοτινοῦς.)

**κοτῖνοτράγος** [ᾰ], ον, *eating wild olive-berries*, Ar.*Av.*240.

**κότιξις**· μέλους τι εἶδος, Hsch. **κοτίς**, v. κοττίς.

**κοτόεις**, εσσα, εν, = κοτήεις, A.D.*Adv.*189.12, *EM*34.57.

**κότορνος**, ὁ, v.l. in Hdt.6.125, as Ion. form for κόθορνος.

**κότος**, ὁ, *grudge, rancour, ill-will*, more inveterate than χόλος, Il.1.82 (cf. 81); τοῖσιν κ. αἰνὸν ἔθεσθε 8.449; τοῖσιν κότον αἰνὸν ἐνήσεις 16.449; κότον ἔνθετο θυμῷ Od.11.102; ὁπόταν τις ἀμείλιχον καρδίᾳ κότον ἐνελάσῃ Pi.*P.*8.9: freq. in A., δαιμόνων κότῳ, Λοξίου κ., *Ag.*635, 1211; βαρὺς..Ζηνὸς ἱκεσίου κ. *Supp.*347; τοῦ θανόντος ἡ Δίκη πράσσει κότον exacts *vengeance* for him, *Fr.*266.5; never in S., once in E.(?), *Rh.*828 (lyr.).—Poet. and late Prose, D.H.9.51.

**κοττᾰβ-εῖον** or **-ειον**, τό, *metal basin for the game of cottabos*, Dicaearch.Hist.34, *IG*11(2).161*C*60 (Delos, iii B.C.), Ath.15.667f. 2. *prize won at the game*, in pl., Pl.Com.46.7, Eub.16, Hegesand.32, Call.*Fr.*2P. **-ία** (fort. **-ίας**)· οὐλόθριξ, Hsch. **-ίζω**, fut. -ιῶ Antiph.55.4:—*play at the cottabos*, Ar.*Pax*343 (lyr.), Antiph.l.c. II. = ἐμέω, Poll.6.111, *EM*533.15. **-ικός**, ή, όν, *used in the cottabos*, ῥάβδος Hermipp.47.5. **-ινορ**, Lacon., = κοτταβεῖον, Hsch. **-ιον**, τό, = κοτταβεῖον 2, Arist.*Rh.*1373ᵃ23, *Com.Adesp.*587. **-ίς**, ίδος, pecul. fem. of κοτταβικός: as Subst., = κοτταβεῖον 1, Hegesand.32; κεραμεᾶ κ. Harmod.1. **-ισις**, εως, ἡ, *playing at the cottabos*, Plu.2.654c. **-ισμός**, ὁ, = foreg., prescribed as a cure for καχεξία, Philum. (?) ap.Orib.*Syn.*9.21.5, Paul.Aeg.3.47. **-ος**, ὁ, Ion. and older Att. **κόσσᾰβος** (A.*Fr.*179.4 (pl.), E.*Fr.*631 (pl.)), *the cottabos*, a Sicilian game (Anacr.53, Critias 2.1 D.), of throwing heel-taps into a metal basin, described by Ath.15.665d sqq., Sch.Ar.*Pax*342, 1243, Poll.6.109, Suid. s.v. κοτταβίζειν: κ. is found in various senses, 1. *the game itself*, Anacr.l.c., Critias l.c., Pl.Com.69.4, etc. 2. *the prize*, = κοτταβεῖον 2, Eup.86, cf. Ath.15.667d. 3. *the wine thrown*, = λάταξ, E.l.c., Antiph.55.5. 4. *the basin*, = κοτταβεῖον 1, Cratin.116, Eup.l.c., Antiph.55.12. (κότταβος ἀσπίδων is prob. f.l. for κόναβος Anon.*Rh.*3.210S.)

**κοττάνα**, ἡ, = παρθένος (Cret.), Hsch.

**κοττάναθρον** (fort. κοττόβαθρον), τό, *perch for fowls*, Hsch.

**κοττάνη**, ἡ, implement used in fishing, Ael.*NA*12.43.

**κόττᾰνον**, τό, *small* kind of *fig*, Ath.9.385a, prob. in Id.3.119b: Lat. *cottanum*, Plin.*HN*13.51.

**κοττάρια**· τὰ ἄκρα τῆς κέγχρου, Hsch. **κοττεῖν**· τύπτειν, δορατεῖν, Id. **κοττίδικα**· πλατάγη, κρόταλον, Id.

**κοττίζω**, (κόττος III) = κυβεύω, Sch.Luc.*Lex*.3.

**κόττικοι**· αἱ περικεφαλαῖαι, Hsch.

**κοττίς**, ίδος, ἡ, Dor. for κεφαλή, Poll.2.29, Phot. s. v. προκότταν:—in Hp. written **κοτίς**, *occiput*, *Morb*.2.20, cf. Erot.*Fr*.56, Gal.19.113.

**κοττ-ισμός**, = κυβεία, *Gloss*. ⊛ **-ιστής**, *aleator*, ib.

**κοττοβολεῖν**· τὸ παρατηρεῖν τινα ὄρνιν, Hsch.

⊛ **κόττος**, ὁ, = ἀλεκτρυών, prob. in Ezek.*Exag*.261, cf. Hsch.; also, *horse*, Id. II. a river-fish, Arist.*HA*534$^a$1. III. = κύβος, *Cod.Just*.1.4.25 (529 A.D.).

**κόττῠφος**, ὁ, Att. for κόσσυφος.

**κοτύλ-εα** [ῠ], ἁ, = sq. 3, *SIG*1026.25 (Cos, iv/iii B.C.): Coan form of κοτύλα, = κοτύλη. ⊛ **-η**, ἡ, *anything hollow* (πᾶν τὸ κοῖλον κοτύλην ἐκάλουν οἱ παλαιοί Apollod.ap.Ath.11.479a, cf. Sch.Il.22.494). 1. *small vessel, cup*, Il.22.494, Od.15.312, 17.12, Ar.*Fr*.350, cf. Ath.11.478d: prov., πολλὰ μεταξὺ πέλει κοτύλης καὶ χείλεος ἄκρου ib.e, Zen.5.71. b. metaph., = κοτύλων, D.H.19.5. 2. *cup* or *socket* of a joint, esp. of the hip-joint, κατ' ἰσχίον, ἔνθα τε μηρὸς ἰσχίῳ ἐνστρέφεται, κοτύλην δέ τέ μιν καλέουσι Il.5.306 sq., cf. Hp.*Loc.Hom*.6, Gal.18(2).519: also, *socket* of the arm, Hp.*Art*.7. 3. *liquid measure*, containing 6 κύαθοι or a ½ ξέστης, i.e. nearly *a ½ pint*, Hdt.6.57, Th.4.16, 7.87, Ar.*Pl*.436; κ. Ἀττική, Αἰγινητική, Hp.*Epid*.7.3, *Nat.Mul*.33. b. *dry measure*, ἀλφίτων.. τρεῖς χοίνικας κοτύλης δεούσας Ar.*Fr*.465; ἀλφίτων κ. μίαν Alex.221.17; prob. also a smaller measure, perh. = τρύβλιον, ὀξύβαφον, Hp.*Mul*.1.6. 4. *hollow of the hand*, Apollod. l. c., Poll.9.122, Eust.550.5; cf. ἐγκοτύλη. 5. = κοτυληδών I, Luc.*DMar*.4.3. 6. in pl., *cymbals*, χαλκόδετοι κ. A.*Fr*.57.6 (anap.). **-ηδονώδης**, ες, *of the nature of a* κοτυληδών, *warty*, ἐξοχή, ἔκφυσις, Gal.2.905. ⊛ **-ηδών**, όνος, ἡ, *any cup-shaped hollow* or *cavity*: 1. in pl., *suckers on the arms* (πλεκτάναι) *of the poulp* or *octopus*, Od.5.433, in Ep. dat. πρὸς κοτυληδονόφιν, cf. Arist.*HA*524$^a$2, *PA*685$^b$3, Thphr.*HP*9.13.6, Ath.11.479b; also on the feet of the κάραβος, Arist.*HA*527$^a$25: sg., Luc.*Musc.Enc*.3. 2. in pl., *cotyledons*, foetal and uterine vascular connexions (in animals), Hp.*Aph*.5.45, Arist.*GA*745$^b$33, al.: wrongly expld. as κοιλότητες.. ἐν αἷς τὴν ἀνατροφὴν τοῦ ἐμβρύου γίνεσθαι Diocl.*Fr*.27, cf. Gal.2.905. 3. = κοτύλη 2, *socket of the hip-joint*, Ar.*V*.1495, Arist.*HA*493$^a$24, *Milet*.6.22 (iii B.C.). 4. *hollow of a cup*, Nic.*Al*.626. 5. plant, prob. *navelwort*, *Cotyledon Umbilicus*, Hp.*Steril*.230, Nic.*Th*.681, Dsc.4.91, Gal.12.41; another species, *C. sterilis*, Dsc.4.92. **-ήρῠτος**, ον, (ἀρύω) *that can be drawn in cups*, i.e. *flowing copiously, streaming*, αἷμα Il.23.34. 2. ὄξος κ. *a measure of* vinegar, Nic.*Th*.539. **-ιαῖος**, α, ον, *holding a* κοτύλη, Antig.Car. ap.Ath.10.420a, D.L.2.139; λήκυθοι Hippoloch.ap.Ath.3.129b:—also written **-ιεῖος**, *PCair.Zen*.89.4 (iii B.C.). **-ίδιον**, τό, Dim. of κοτύλη, Eust.1541.52. **-ίζω**, *sell by the* κοτύλη: hence, *sell by retail*, opp. ἀθρόα πιπράσκειν, Arist.*Oec*.1347$^b$8, cf. *PAmh*.92.6 (ii A.D.), Phryn.*PS*p.79 B.; μηδὲ ἐξ ἀμφορέων μηδὲ ἐκ πιθάκνης μηδ' ἐξ ψευδοπίθου κοτυλιζέτω μηδείς *BCH*50.214 (Thasos, v B.C.): metaph., μηδὲν κ., ἀλλὰ καταπάττειν χύδην Pherecr.168; κίρναντες.. τὴν πόλιν ἡμῶν κοτυλίζετε τοῖσι πένησιν Ar.*Fr*.683. ⊛ **-ίς**, ίδος, ἡ, = κοτύλη 2, Hp.*Int*.18, cf. Gal.19.114. **-ίσκος**, ὁ, Dim. of κοτύλη, *little cup*, Ar.*Fr*.380, etc.:—also **ἰσκη**, ἡ, Pherecr.69; **-ίσκιον**, τό, Ar.*Ach*.459. II. a kind of *cake*, Heracleo ap.Ath.14.647b. III. *pit* used for sacrificing to Earth, Hsch. **-ισμός**, ὁ, *sale by retail* of oil, *Stud.Pal*.22.177.23 (ii A.D.). **-ιστής**, οῦ, ὁ, *one who plays the game* ἐγκοτύλη, Jul.*Mis*.360a. **-ιστί**, Adv., = κατὰ κοτύλην, *UPZ* 94.42 (ii B.C.), spelt **-ειστί**). **-οειδής**, ές, *cup-shaped*, χώρη Hp. *Art*.79. ⊛ **-ος**, ὁ, = κοτύλη, Hom.*Epigr*.14.3, Alc.139 (nisi potius Alc.Com.), Ar.*Fr*.71, Pl.Com.46.9, *IG*2$^2$.1541.14, cf. Ath.11.478b, 482b. **-ώδης**, ες, *like a* κοτύλη, ἀγγεῖον ib.480b. **-ων**, ωνος, ὁ, *nickname of a toper*, Plu.*Ant*.18.

**κότυμβον**, τό, = μακρὸν πλοῖον, *Peripl.M.Rubr*.44.

**κότυνα**· σκύβαλα, Hsch.

**κοῦ, κου**, Ion. for ποῦ, που. **κοῦα**· ἐνέχυρα, and **κουάσαι**· ἐνεχυριάσαι, Hsch.; cf. κοῖον, κῷα. **κούαγμα**· σκῆμα, Id. **κούαμα**· μέλαν (Lacon.), Id. (fort. κουάνια (= κυάνεα)· μέλανα).

**κουβαρίς**, ίδος, ἡ, = ὄνος III, Dsc.2.35 tit. ⊛ **κουβηζός**· στηβεύς, Hsch. **κουδριγάριον** ἄλειμμα, = Lat. *quadrigarium*, *charioteer's* ointment, *Hippiatr*.130. **κουκᾶ**· πάππων, ἡ κυκεῶνα, Hsch.

**κοῦκι**, τό, *doum palm*, *Hyphaena thebaica*, Lat. *cuci*, Plin.*HN*13.62; *fibre* thereof, *PBaden* 35.23 (i A.D.).

**κούκινος**, η, ον, *of the doum-palm*, φύλλα *Peripl.M.Rubr*.33. 2. *made of its fibre*, σόλια *POxy*.1742.7 (iv A.D.); κούκινα ὑποδεδεμένος *PMag.Par*.1.935; κ. πλέγματα prob. (for κόκκινα, v.l. κόκινα) in Str.17.2.5.

**κουκιοφόρος**, ον, *producing* κοῦκι, τὸ κ. δένδρον *doum-palm*, Thphr. *HP*4.2.7 (-όφορον codd.).

**κοῦκκος**, ὁ, = κόκκυξ I, Suid. s. h. v.

**κούκκουμα**, ἡ, = Lat. *cucuma*, *jar*, *POxy*.1160.23 (iii/iv A.D.):—hence Dim. **κουκκούμιον**, τό, Arr.*Epict*.3.22.71; **κουκούμιον** *POxy*.1290.3 (v A.D.):—also **κούκουμος** *Stud.Pal*.20.67.16 (ii/iii A.D.), *Gloss*.: pl. **κοκκόμανα** *PHamb*.10.36 (ii A.D.).

**κουκούφας**, ὁ, Egyptian name for ἔποψ, Horap.1.55: gen. κοκκούφατος *PMag.Berol*.2.18:—Dim. **κοκκοφάδιον** *PMag.Lond*.121.411.

**κουλεόν, κουλεός**, v. κολεόν, κολεός. **κουλιβός**· ἡ πίτυς, Hsch.

**κουλῠβάτεια** [βᾰ], ἡ, = κλύβατις, Nic.*Th*.589, 851.

**κουμᾶσι**· τὸ τῶν ὀρνίθων οἴκημα, Hsch. **κούνημα**· κόκων ἢ ὁ κύων, Id. ⊛ **κούνικλος**, v. κύνικλος. **κούνουπες** (-οῦνες cod.), = κώνωπες, Id. **κουπῖον**, τό, = καμάρα ἡ ἐπὶ τῶν ἁμαξῶν γινομένη, Id.

⊛ **κουρά**, Ion. **-ρή**, ἡ, (κείρω) *cropping* of the hair, τῶν τριχῶν τὴν κ. κείρεσθαι Hdt.3.8; κουρᾶς δεῖσθαι Arist.*PA*658$^b$20; ἐν χρῷ κ. Diocl. *Fr*.141: freq. as a sign of mourning, κ. πενθίμῳ E.*Alc*.512, *Or*.458; κουραῖσι καὶ θρήνοισι Id.*Hel*.1054; κουραῖς διατετιλμένης φόβην S.*Fr*.659.7. 2. generally, *cropping, lopping*, δρυοτομικὴ καὶ κ. σύμπασα Pl.*Plt*.288d; of animals that feed on grass, Arist.*PA*693$^a$17. 3. *shearing* of sheep, Porph.*Abst*.3.26, *PThead*.8.6 (iv A.D.). II. *that which is cut off*: 1. *lock of hair*, A.*Ch*.226. 2. *wool shorn, fleece*, *PCair.Zen*.433.26 (pl., iii B.C.); κουρᾷ κοσμοῦντα θρέμματα Porph.*Abst*.3.19: pl., κουρὰς προβάτων καὶ γάλα βοῶν ib.18. 3. *cut-off end*, σφηνός Ph.*Bel*.67.12; δοκῶν *Inscr.Délos* 442 *A* 157 (ii B.C.); ἡ κάτω κ., of a rod, Hero *Dioptr*.5: in pl., *slips* of wood, Ph. *Bel*.57.22.

⊛ **κουράλιον**, τό, poet. for κοράλλιον (q.v.).

**Κουράλιος**, ὁ (sc. μήν), name of month at Kophoi and Pyrasos, *IG* 9(2).102, 132.

**κουράς**, άδος, ἡ, = ὀροφή, Hsch. s. v. ἐγκουράδες. 2. *painting on a ceiling*, Id.

⊛ **κουράτωρ**, ορος, ὁ, = Lat. *curator*, *IGRom*.4.243 (Troad), etc.:—hence **κουρατορεύω**, *serve as curator*, *IG*14.1062 (iii A.D.): aor. part. κουρατορεύσας *IGRom*.4.1169 (Attalia), 1638 (Philadelphia); κεκουρατορευκώς ib.1640 (ibid.). ⊛ **κουρατορία**, ἡ, *office of curator*, *PGiss*.104.3 (iv A.D.), etc.

**Κουραφροδίτη**, ἡ, *virgin-Aphrodite*, Procl.*H*.5.1.

**κούρβα**, *scortum*, *Gloss*.

**κουρβών**, ῶνος, ὁ, *arm*, *PLond*.1821.288.

**κουρ-εακός**, ή, όν, *gossiping* (cf. sq.), κ. καὶ πάνδημος λαλιά Plb.3.20.5. ⊛ **-εῖον**, τό, (κουρά) *barber's shop*, the lounging-place where news and scandal were picked up, καί τοι λόγος γ' ἦν.. πολὺς ἐπὶ τοῖσι κουρείοισι τῶν καθημένων Ar.*Pl*.338, cf. *Av*.1441; πόλλ' ἔμαθον ἐν τοῖσι κ. ἐγὼ ἀτόπως καθίζων κοὐδὲ γιγνώσκειν δοκῶν Eup.180, cf. Lys.24.20, D.25.52, *AP*6.307 (Phan.), *Sammelb*.6762.2 (iii B.C.); εἰς κ. 'to my barber's bill', Lys.32.20 (v.l.); ἐν κουρείοις ἢ μυροπωλίοις Phld.*Ir*. p.47 W. II. κούρειον, proparox. (Hdn.Gr.1.372), *victim offered for boys and feasted on by the* φράτερες *at the feast* κουρεῶτις, S.*Fr*.126, Is.6.22 (κούριον codd.), *IG*2$^2$.1237.28, *Inscr.Prien*.362.13 (iv B.C.). ⊛ **-εος**, ὁ, epith. of Apollo, from foreg. II, *SIG*927 (Teos). ⊛ **-εύομαι**, (κουρά) *take the tonsure*, i.e. enter a monastery, of a nun, Just.*Nov*.134.10.1; *have the hair cut*, of four year-old children, Sch.Nic.*Al*.417. ⊛ **-εύς**, έως, ὁ, (κείρω) *barber, hair-cutter*, Pl.*R*.373c, Philyll.14, *PMagd*.15.1 (iii B.C.), Luc.*Ind*.29; ὁ κ. τὰς μαχαιρίδας λαβὼν ὑπὸ τῆς ὑπήνης κατακερεῖ—τὴν εἰσφορὰν (παρὰ προσδοκίαν for τὸ γένειον) Eup.278; as a purveyor of gossip, Plu.2.177a, 509a. 2. *shearer*, κουρεῖ τῷ κείραντι τὰς αἶγας *PCair.Zen*.176.54 (iii B.C.). II. a bird, said to chirp with a sound *as of clipping*, Hsch. **-εύσιμος**, η, ον, *for cutting hair*, σίδηρος Sch.E.*Or*.966. ⊛ **-ευτής**, οῦ, ὁ, *barber*, *Gloss*. **-ευτικός**, ή, όν, = κουρεύσιμος, Sch.E. l. c.; μαχαιρίδια Olymp.*Vit.Pl*.p.3 W. **-εύτρια**, ἡ, fem. of κουρεύς, κουρευτής, Plu.*Ant*.60. **-εύω**, only in Pass., v. κουρεύομαι. **-εών**, ῶνος, ὁ, name of month at Magnesia on Maeander, *SIG*807 (i A.D.):—also **Κουρηϊών**, *Inscr.Magn*.4.4, al. **-εῶτις** (sc. ἡμέρα, Hsch.; κ. ἑορτή Alciphr.3.46), ιδος, ἡ, the third day of the Ἀπατούρια, on which children were presented to the φράτερες, and boys competed in recitation, Pl.*Ti*.21b; ἡ κ. Ἀπατουρίων *IG*2$^2$.1237.28. (Perh. from κείρω, κουρά, because the child's hair is said to have been cut on that day, Hsch.)

**κούρη**, Ion. for κόρη. **κουρή**, Ion. for κουρά.

**κουρ-ήϊος**, η, ον, Ep. for κόρειος, *youthful*, ἄνθος *h.Cer*.108. **-ηϊών**, v. Κουρεών. ⊛ **-ητες**, ων, οἱ, (κόρος B, κοῦρος A) *young men*, esp. *young warriors*, κούρητες Παναχαιῶν, Ἀχαιῶν, Il.19.193, 248. II. as pr.n., Κουρῆτες (Hdn.Gr.1.63, al.), Dor. **Κωρῆτες**, *divinities* coupled with Nymphs and Satyrs, Κ. θεοὶ φιλοπαίγμονες ὀρχηστῆρες Hes.*Fr*.198; worshipped in Crete, Κωρῆτας καὶ Νύμφας καὶ Κύρβαντας *GDI*5039.14 (Hierapytna); Κωρῆσι τοῖς πρὸ καρταιπόδων ib.iv p.1036 (Gortyn); Κ. Διὸς τροφεῖς λέγονται Str.10.3.19, cf. 11, E.*Ba*.120 (lyr.), Orph.*H*.38.1, *Fr*.151, etc.: prov., Κουρήτων στόμα, of prophecy, Zen.4.61. (Sg. only late, ὁ Κορόνους δηλοῖ νοῦν καὶ τὸν Κουρῆτα τούτου Dam.*Pr*.267.) 2. *armed dancers* who celebrated orgiastic rites, Str.10.3.7: hence used to translate Lat. *Salii*, D.H.2.70; Κουρήτων Βάκχος ἐκλήθην ὁσιωθείς E.*Fr*.472.14 (lyr.). 3. at Ephesus, *religious college* of six members, συνέδριον Κουρήτων *Ephes*.2 No.83c, cf. *SIG*353.1 (iv B.C.), Str.14.1.20. III. pr. n. of a people who fought with the Aetolians, Il.9.529, al. **-ητικός**, ή, όν, *of* or *concerning the* Κουρῆτες, τὰ Κ. treatises on the Κ., Str.10.3.7: hence, in Neo-Platonic theology, *ministrant*, ὁ πρῶτος πατὴρ καὶ ὁ τρίτος οὐ παράγει κ. τάξιν Dam.*Pr*.278; κ. θεότης Procl.*in Ti*.3.310 D.; κ. τάξις Id.*Theol.Plat*.5.35; κ. τριάς ibid. (here derived fr. Κούρη = Κόρη). II. ὁ Κ. (sc. πούς) *the Cretic*, Sch.Ar.*Nu*.651; *the third paeon* (⏑ ⏑ — ⏑), Choerob. *in Heph*.p.218 C. **-ῆτις**, ιδος, fem. Adj., *of the* Κουρῆτες, i.e. of Pleuron, γῆ Epigr.ap.Str.10.3.2; χώρα Apollod.1.7.6. II. Pythag. name for *nine*, *Theol.Ar*.58. **-ητισμός**, ὁ, *armed dancing*, of the *rites of the Salii*, D.H.2.71.

**κοῦρι**, τό, liquid measure in Egypt, *Ostr*.1126, 1127 (vi/vii A.D.).

**κουρί-ας**, ου, ὁ, *one who wears his hair short*, ἐν χρῷ κ. Luc.*Fug*.27, *Vit.Auct*.20, D.L.6.31; cf. ἐγχρωκουρίας. **-άω**, of hair, *need clip-*

*ping*, πώγων εἰς ὑπερβολὴν κουριῶν Luc.*Gall.*10. II. of persons, ἐν χρῷ κ. *need* close *clipping*, Pherecr.30, Plu.*Alc.*23; ἄνθρωπος ἀεὶ -ιῶν Luc.*Lex.*10. 2. *wear rough, untrimmed hair*, Ael.*NA*7.48; κ. τὸ γένειον Alciphr.3.55, cf. Hp.*Ep.*17, Artem.1.19 (interpol.).

❋ **κουρ-ίδιος**, α, ον, (κοῦρος (A), κούρη, cf. sq. III) *wedded*, Ion. and poet. Adj., used sts. of the husband, κουρίδιον ποθέουσα πόσιν Il.5.414; κουριδίῳ τεύξασα πόσει φόνον Od.11.430; κουριδίοιο φίλοιο οὐκέτι μέμνηται 15.22: more freq. of the woman, *lawful, wedded wife*, κουριδίης ἀλόχου Il.1.114; ἀλλά μ' ἔφασκες Ἀχιλλῆος θείοιο κ. ἄλοχον θήσειν (Briseis to Patroclus) 19.298; κ. ἄκοιτις, ἀκοίτης, A.R.3.243, 4.1072; κ. γυναῖκες, opp. παλλακαί, Hdt.1.135, 5.18, cf. 6.138, Aristox.*Fr. Hist.*72: in poet. epitaphs, μνῆμ' ἀλόχῳ.. θήκατο κουριδίῃ *IG*3.1376.10, cf. 7.2539.9 (Thebes); ἀνὴρ κ. in prose epitaphs, *CIG*3827*l* (Cotiaeum), 4176 (Amasia), cf. Parth.27.2, Jul.*Or.*3.110c: as Subst., κ., ἡ, *wedded wife*, Q.S.5.445. 2. of things, νωΐτερον λέχος αὐτῶν κουρίδιον our own *lawful marriage* bed, Il.15.40, cf. Ar.*Pax*844; δῶμα κ. house *of my wedlock*, Od.19.580; κ. γάμοι Archil.18; κ. τέκνα *born in wedlock*, *CIG*3333 (Smyrna). 3. *nuptial, bridal*, κ. χιτῶνες *AP*9.602 (Even.); θάλαμοι A.R.3.1128. II. epith. of Apollo in Laconia, Hsch. **-ίζω** (A), (κοῦρος A) intr., *to be a youth*, σάκος.., ὃ κουρίζων φορέεσκε Od.22.185, cf. A.R.1.195; *to be a girl*, Id.3.666; παῖς ἔτι -ίζουσα Call.*Dian.*5, cf. Arat.32. 2. *cry like a babe*, Call.*Jov.*54. 3. of dolphins, κ. ἐὸν σθένος *attain* the strength of *youth*, Opp.*H.*1.664. II. trans., *bring up from boyhood* or *to manhood*, ἄνδρας Hes.*Th.*347. III. κουρίζεσθαι· ὑμεναιοῦσθαι, Hsch. **-ίζω** (B), (κείρω, κουρά) *clip, shear*, aor. 1 κούριξαν· ἀπέκειραν, Id.:—Pass., κυπάρισσος ἡ κουριζομένη which sprouts *when clipped*, Thphr.*HP*2.2.2. ❋**-ικός**, ή, όν, (κουρά) *for cutting the hair*, μάχαιραι Plu.*Dio*9: as Subst., κουρικός (sc. δίφρος), ὁ, *barber's* chair, *Sammelb.*4292; δίφρου τετραπόδου καὶ κουρικοῦ ξυλίνου *POxy.*646 (ii A. D.). II. (κοῦρος A) *like a youth*. Adv. -κῶς Apollon.*Lex.* s. v. κουρίξ. **-ιμος**, η, ον, also ος, ον Agatho 3, cf. II. 3: (κουρά):—*of, for cutting hair*, σίδαρος E.*Or.*966 (nisi cum κάρα jungendum). II. Pass., *shorn off*, χαίτη A.*Ch.*180; θρὶξ E.*El.*521, Agatho l. c. 2. *shorn*, κρᾶτα E.*Tr.*279 (lyr.); κ. σχῆμα ἀναλαμβάνειν *tonsure*, Plu.*Pel.*34. 3. as Subst., ἡ κούριμος *Tragic mask* for mourners, *with the hair cut close*, *AP*7.37 (Diosc.), cf. Poll.4.140. **-ίξ**, Adv., (κουρά) *by the hair*, ἔρυσάν τέ μιν εἴσω κουρὶξ Od.22.188; κ. ἑλκομένη A.R.4.18. **-ιος**, ον, (κοῦρος A) *youthful*, ἄνθος, in an interpol. verse after Il.13.433, cf. Orph.*A.*1339; ἥβη Orac. ap.Paus.9.14.3. **-ίς**, ίδος, ἡ, (κουρά) in pl., μάχαιραι κουρίδες *shears*, Cratin.37. II. = κομμώτρια, title of plays by Antiphanes, Alexis, and Amphis, cf. Men.1024, Plb.15.25.32, *POxy.*1489.9 (iii A. D.): κούρισσα, *EM*528.4. III. κουρίς or κωρίς, Dor. for καρίς, Epich.31, 89, Sophr.26.

**κούρκουμον**, τό, = κημός, Hsch. s. v. ἐν κημῷ.

**κοῦρμι**, τό, *kind of beer* made from barley, Dsc.2.88; cf. κόρμα.

**κουρο-βόρος**, ον, *devouring children*, A.*Ag.*1512 (lyr.). **-γονία**, ἡ, *begetting of boys*, κ. καὶ θηλυγονίη Hp.*Genit.*8. **-θάλεια** [θᾰ], ἡ, *nursing-mother*, epith. of δάφνη, διὰ τὸ κουροτρόφον τοῦ Ἀπόλλωνος Sch.Od.19.86.

**κοῦρος** (A), ὁ, Ep. and Ion. for κόρος (B) (q.v.).

❋ **κοῦρος** (B), ὁ, (κείρω, κορσός) *loppings, twigs stripped from a tree*, μηδὲ ξύλα μηδὲ κοῦρον μηδὲ φρύγανα μηδὲ φυλλόβολα *IG*2².1362.6.

**κουρο-σύνη** [ῠ], Dor. -σύνα, ἡ, (κοῦρος A) *youth, youthful prime*, χαίρων κουροσύνᾳ Theoc.24.58, cf. *AP*6.281 (Leon.), 309 (Id.), 9.259 (Bianor). **-σῦνος**, ον, *youthful*, θρίξ ib.6.156 (Theodorid.), with play on κούριμος, *shorn*; wrongly expld. as τὸ ὑπὲρ τῆς κουρᾶς θυόμενον, Suid. ❋ **-τερος**, α, ον, Comp. form of κοῦρος (A) (cf. βασιλεύς, λεύτερος), *young*, opp. *elder*, Il.4.316, Od.21.310, Hes.*Op.*[447]: as fem., A.R.1.684. **-τοκέω**, *bear boy-children*, Hp.*Genit.*7. **-τόκος**, ον, *bearing boy-children*, E.*Supp.*957 (lyr.). **-τρόπος**, v. κουροτρόφος. **-τροφέω**, *rear as a child*, κ. τὸν Δία Str.10.3.19; παῖδας Ph.2.463: metaph., θυγατέρας Id.1.441; ἡ φύσις κ. ἅπαντα Phleg.*Fr. Hist.*44. 2. *breed men*, γῆ κουροτροφοῦσα Philostr.*VA*8.7. ❋ **-τρόφος**, ον, *rearing children*, rare in lit. sense, γυνὴ νεοτόκος καὶ κ. Aret.*CA*2.3: usu. metaph., ἀγαθὴ κ. good *nursing-mother*, of Ithaca, Od.9.27, cf. Pi.*Fr.*109; κ. Ἑλλάς E.*Tr.*566 (lyr., s. v. l.); Ἀπόλλωνος κ., of Delos, Call.*Del.*2, 276: freq. as epith. of goddesses, as Hecate, Hes.*Th.*450; Ἄρτεμις D.S.5.73; Λοχία *Supp.Epigr.*3.400.9 (Delph., iii B. C.); of the Roman goddess Rumina, Plu.2.278d; esp. of Aphrodite, Hom.*Epigr.*12; called ἡ Κ. alone, *IG*1².840.9, Ar.*Th.*299, Pl. Com.174.7, Luc.*DMeretr.*5.1; αἱ πύλαι αἱ κατὰ Κουροτρόφον, at Delos, *IG*11(2).203*A*46 (iii B. C.):—in form **Κουροτρόπος**, ὁ (sc. μήν), name of Acarnanian month, ib.5(1).29.11 (Sparta).

❋ **κουρούλλιος** or **-ούλιος**, ον, = Lat. *curulis*, *IG*5(1).533.18 (Sparta), 4.588.13 (Argos), D.C.39.32, 54.2.

**κουρσεύω**, *seize, ravage*, τὴν Ἐπίδαυρον Anon.*in Rh.*204.34, cf. Babr.179 (paraphr.).

❋ **κούρσωρ**, ορος, ὁ, = Lat. *cursor*, *Edict.Diocl.* in *IG*2².1120:—hence Adj. **κουρσώριος**, *Edict.Diocl.*9.14.

**κουρύλος** [ῠ], ὁ, = κορδύλος, Numen.ap.Ath.7.306c.

**κουρώδης**, ες, *like a boy*, μολπή Aus.*Ep.*8.15.

**κουρῶν**· πρέπων, Hsch.

❋ **κουσσούλιον**, τό, *cloak*, *Sammelb.*7033.36 (v A. D.).

❋ **κουστούμην-α**, τά, *Crustumerian pears*, Aët.5.138. **-ᾶτον**, τό, *drink made from Crustumerian pears*, ibid.

❋ **κουστωδία**, ἡ, = Lat. *custodia*, *Ev.Matt.*27.65.

**κούστωρ**, ὁ, = Lat. *custos*, ἁρμόρω(ν) κ. *Sammelb.*6961, al. (Nubia).

**κουτάλη**, ἡ, Dor. for σκυτάλη, *EM*555.18 (cod. Par.); sed v. κώταλις.

**κούταρον**· τῶν ὀπισθίων (ὀσπητίων cod.) τοῦ βοὸς ἡ σὰρξ ὑπὲρ τὰ ἄρθρα, Hsch. **κουτίδες**· συκαλλίδες, Id.:—also **κουτίδια**, τά, *nets for catching* συκ., Id.

**κουφ-εία**, ἡ, perh. *potsherd* (cf. κοῦφος I. 6), *PTeb.*5.199 (pl., ii B. C.). **-ηγός**, ὁ, *one who conveys* κουφεῖαι, *PFlor.*335.4 (iii A. D.). ❋**-ίζω**, Att. fut. -ιῶ S.*Aj.*1287: pf. κεκούφικα *OGI*90.12 (Rosetta, ii B. C.): I. *to be light*, κουφίζουσαν ἄρουραν Hes.*Op.*463, cf. E.*Hel.*1555; of a sufferer, *to be relieved*, κουφίζειν δοκῶ S.*Ph.*735, cf. Hp.*Aph.*2.27. II. trans., *lighten, make light*, τὸ κενὸν ἐμπεριλαμβανόμενον κ. τὰ σώματα Arist.*Cael.*309ᵃ6:—Pass., Id.*PA*663ᵇ13: hence, 1. *lift up, raise*, S.*Ant.*43, *Tr.*1025 (lyr.); αἴρων κουφιῶ σ' ἐγώ Ar.*Av.*1762 (lyr.); ἀσπίδ' ἀμφὶ βραχίονι κουφίζων E.*Ph.*121 (lyr.); ἅλμα κουφιεῖν *make a light* leap, S.*Aj.* l. c.; κ. πήδημα E.*El.*861 (lyr.); δύστηνον αἰώρημα κουφίζω, = δύστηνος αἰωροῦμαι, Id.*Supp.*1047:—Pass., *to be lifted up, soar*, [τῷ πτερῷ] ᾧ ψυχὴ κουφίζεται Pl.*Phdr.*248c, cf. 249a; σώματα -όμενα ὑπὸ τοῦ κύματος Jul.*Or.*1.27c. 2. *lighten of* a load, ὄχλου πλήθους τε κ. χθόνα *lighten* earth *of* a multitude, E.*Hel.*40; κουφισθεὶς τοῦ βάρους Thphr.*HP*4.16.2: abs., *lighten* ships *of their cargo*, τῷ ταχυναυτοῦντι κουφίσαντες προσβάλλειν Th.6.34; κουφισθεισῶν τῶν νεῶν Plb.20.5.11, cf. 1.60.8. b. of persons, *relieve* from burdens, X.*Mem.*2.7.1, *Cyr.*6.3.24; τὸν δῆμον τῶν εἰσφορῶν D.S.13.64, cf. *IG*12(7).506.16 (Amorgos, iii B. C.); τόκων τοὺς χρεωφειλέτας Plu.*Caes.*37; *relieve* (contractors), Plb.6.17.5; τῆς ὑπερηφανίας Phld.*Vit.*p.16 J.; κ. τοὺς νοσοῦντας Plu.2.116c:—Pass., *to be relieved*, ὅταν σῶμα κουφισθῇ νόσου *from*.., E.*Or.*43; τοῦ πάθους Arist.*Pr.*873ᵇ22; λέξασα κουφισθήσομαι ψυχήν E.*Med.*473: fut. Med. κουφιεῖσθαι in pass. sense, Aristid.2.145 J.: metaph., τῇ τῶνδε εὐκλείᾳ κουφίζεσθε *feel your burdens lightened* by.., Th.2.44; κουφίζονται οἱ λυπούμενοι Arist.*EN*1171ᵃ29, cf. *Pol.*1342ᵃ14; ἐλπίδι κ. ματαίᾳ Ael.*NA*11.33. 3. c. acc. rei, *lighten, assuage*, ἀλγηδόνας E.*Fr.*573; συμφορὰς λόγῳ κ. D.60.35; κ. ἔρωτα Theoc.29.9; τὸ πάθος Plu.*Alex.*52; τὰ ὀφλήματα Id.2.807d: abs., *give* or *procure relief*, κ. οὐδέν, ἀλλά.. Hp.*Epid.*1.7, cf. Arist.*GA*725ᵇ9:—Pass., νομίζοντες κεκουφίσθαι τὸν πόλεμον αὐτοῖς Plb.1.17.2. b. *cancel* a debt, *POxy.*126.8 (vi A. D.), etc.:—Med., *PMasp.*95.10 (vi A. D.). 4. ἑαυτοὺς κ. *cheapen* themselves, dub. in Epicur.*Nat.*112 G. 5. *subtract*, ἀπὸ τῶν μοιρῶν Heph.Astr.2.1. **-ικὸν τρόπον**· κωμητικὴν ὄρχησιν, Hsch. **-ισις**, εως, ἡ, *lightening, alleviation, relief*, Th.7.75; κούφισιν φέρειν J.*AJ*17.6.2, D.C.42.28. **-ισμα**, ατος, τό, = foreg., E.*Ph.*848 (pl.), Plu.2.114c. **-ισμός**, ὁ, = κούφισις, ἀκληρημάτων D.S.25.17; συμφορᾶς J.*AJ*4.8.23; πάθους Plu.2.79c; πένθους κ. *Epigr.Gr.*406.8 (Iconium): abs., Carneisc.*Herc.*1027.15; *remission* of taxation, *Cod.Just.*10.16.13 *Intr.*: Medic., *alleviation*, Erasistr.ap. Gal.5.139; κ. ποιέεσθαι, of remittent fevers, Aret.*CA*1.1 (pl.). II. *elision*, Eust.150.24 (pl.), al. **-ιστήρ**, ῆρος, ὁ, *ring-pad* round a trepan-opening, Heliod.(?) ap.Orib.46.19.11. **-ιστικός**, ή, όν, *lightening*, Arist.*Cael.*310ᵃ32; κ. τῶν ἐπαχθῶν *relieving from*.., Hierocl.p.54 A.: Medic., *alleviating*, Antyll.ap.Orib.6.21.27 (Sup.).

**κουφο-λῐθος**, ὁ, *talc* or *talc-powder*, *PHolm.*2.21, al., *PLeid.X.*6, Alex.Aphr.*in Mete.*161.6, 15, Aët.2.68. **-λογέω**, *talk lightly*, App.*Hisp.*18, Them.*Or.*11.152b. **-λογία**, ἡ, *light talk*, Th.4.28, App.*Hisp.*38, Plu.2.855b. **-λόγος**, ον, *lightly talking*, Poll.6.119; κουφολόγον οἱ σοφισταὶ χρῆμα Philostr.*VA*7.16. **-νοος**, ον, contr. **-νους**, ουν, *light-minded, thoughtless*, εὐηθία A.*Pr.*385; ἔρωτες S.*Ant.*617 (lyr.); ὄρνιθες ib.342 (lyr.); τὸ κουφόνουν, = κουφόνοια, App.*Hisp.*9; of persons, Corn.*ND*25: freq. in Adam., 1.14, al.: heterocl. pl. κουφόνοες in Polem.*Phgn.*5. Adv. κουφόνως App.*BC*4.124. **-ξυλαία** or **-έα**, ἡ, = χαμαιάκτη, Orib.*Fr.*118. **-πους**, πουν, gen. ποδος, *light-footed*, Hsch. s. v. ψαυκρόποδα. **-πτερος**, ον, *light-winged*, αὖραι Orph.*H.*81.6.

❋ **κοῦφος**, η, ον, *light, nimble*, Hom. only in neut. pl. as Adv., κοῦφα ποσὶ προβιβάς stepping *lightly* on, Il.13.158, cf. Hes.*Sc.*323; κοῦφα βιβῶν Pi.*O.*14.16; κ. ποσὶν ἄγ' ἐς κύκλον Ar.*Th.*954 (lyr.); also κούφοις ποσί Pi.*O.*13.114; κουφοτάταις πτερύγων ἀκμαῖς Ar.*Ra.*1353; πήδημα κ. ἐκ νεὼς ἀφήλατο A.*Pers.*305; κ. ἐξᾶραι πόδα S.*Ant.*224; κ. ἅλμα E.*El.*439 (lyr.); κ. αἴρειν βῆμα Id.*Tr.*343; οὐ τοῖς κούφοις ὁ δρόμος Lxx*Ec.*9.11: metaph., κουφότεραι.. ἀπειράτων φρένες *too buoyant*, Pi.*O.*8.61. 2. metaph., *easy, light*, τελεῖν.. κούφαν κτίσιν to make achievement *easy*, ib.13.83; κ. εἰ δοίης τέλος A.*Th.*260; κ. νύξ an *easier* night, of a sick person, Jul.*Mis.*342a (Comp.); περίπατος Sor.1.46; τὸ ὅσιον ἅπαν κ. ἔργον *OGI*383.120 (Nemrud Dagh, i B. C.); of government, *light*, κουφοτέραν βασιλείαν *less oppressive*, Isoc.9.51; ἡ εὔκλεια κουφοτέρα φέρειν X.*Cyr.*8.2.22; of an antagonist, *easy-going*, κουφότατος ἦν κρατῆσας Id.*Ages.*11.12; δεσπότην ἀπράγμονα καὶ κ. ἐξαπατᾷ θεράπων Men.*Per.Fr.*1. 3. *unsubstantial, airy, vain*, τὸ νέον.. κούφας ἀφροσύνας φέρον S.*OC*1230 (lyr.); οὐδὲν ἄλλο πλὴν.. κούφην σκιάν Id.*Aj.*126; ἐλπίδος τι εἶχον κούφης Th.2.51; κ. καὶ πτηνοὶ λόγοι Pl.*Lg.*717c; κ. πρᾶγμα *a trifle*, ib.925a; κ. γράμματα a *small* letter, E.*IT*594; of persons, = κουφόνους, Hdn.5.7.1; τὸ κοῦφον τοῦ νοῦ *levity*, Paus.5.21.14, cf. Hdn.7.8.6. 4. *light* in point of weight, opp. βαρύς, Pl.*Phlb.*14d, *R.*438c (Comp.), etc.; κούφα σοι χθὼν ἐπάνωθε πέσοι may earth lie *lightly* on thee, E.*Alc.*462 (lyr.), cf. *Hel.*853; κούφη σοι κόνις ἥδε πέλοι *IG*14.1942.4; κούφη σεῖο γαῖ' ὀστέα κεύθοι ib.329 (Himera); κ. πνεύματα *light* airs, S.*Aj.*558; ὀστᾶ τε καὶ κ. κόνις Men.538.3; τὸ κουφότατον.. τῶν κακῶν.. πενία Id.*Kith.Fr.*2. b. Medic. in various uses, σικύαι κοῦφαι *dry* cuppings, Philum.ap.Orib.45.29.17, cf. Sor.2.11, etc.; also κούφου μένοντος τοῦ ἰοῦ *on the surface*, Philum.*Ven.*7.3; μὴν κ. the eighth month of pregnancy, Sor.1.56; of food, *easy to*

digest, light, Arist.EN1141b18, etc. c. of troops, light-armed, οἱ κ. τῶν στρατιωτῶν Hell.Oxy.6.4; ὡπλισμένοι κουφοτέροις ὅπλοις X.Mem.3.5.27; κούφη στρατιά Plu.Fab.11; τὰ κ. τῆς δυνάμεως Plb.10.25.2. d. of ships, lightly-laden, Th.6.37, 8.27. 5. light, slight, ἁμαρτήματα Pl.Lg.863c; κουφότερα γυμνάσια, opp. ἀναγκαῖα, Arist.Pol.1338b40; κ. ἐργασίαι ib.1321a25. 6. empty, κεράμια Gp.7.24.2, cf. PLond.5.1656.6 (iv A.D.), PFlor.314.8 (v A.D.): hence as Subst., κοῦφον (sc. κεράμιον), τό, jar, in pl., POxy.1631.16 (iii A.D.), PFay.133.6 (iv A.D.), PStrassb.1.10 (vi A.D.). 7. Act., relieving, assisting, χερὶ κούφᾳ Pi.P.9.11: prob. to be taken in this sense in Theoc.11.3. II. Adv. -φως lightly, nimbly, κ. ὀροῦσαι A.Eu.112; κ. ἐσκευασμένοι, of soldiers, Th.4.33; ὡπλισμένοι X.Mem.3.5.26, etc.; κ. ἔχειν to be relieved, Arist.Pr.873a16. 2. metaph., lightly, with light heart, κουφότερον μετεφώνεε Od.8.201; κ. νοῆσαι Sapph.Supp.5.14; κ. φέρειν, opp. δεινῶς φ., E.Med.449, 1018; ὡς κουφότατα φέρειν Hdt.1.35; διάγουσα κούφως doing well, of a patient, Hp.Epid.1.26.δ'. 3. lightly, with ease, A.Pr.701.

**κουφό-σκευος**, ον, light-armed, Hsch. **-τέλεια**, ἡ, remission of taxation, OGI669.29: pl., ib.26 (Egypt, i A.D.), POxy.1434.3 (ii A.D.).

**κουφότης**, ητος, ἡ, lightness, Hp.Aër.8, Pl.Ti.65e, Lg.625d, Arist.Cael.300b24, etc.; agility, Jul.Or.2.53c: pl., Pl.Lg.897a, Arist.PA648b7; κ. τροφῆς lightness, digestibility, Thphr.CP4.9.4. 2. metaph., triviality, levity, Phld.Vit.p.27J., D.H.7.17. 3. relief, μόχθων E.Fr.119. 4. lightness, of style, Phld.Rh.1.178S.

**κουφοφορέομαι**, Pass., rise by one's own lightness, S.E.M.9.71 (cj. for κουφοφορεῖσθαι).

**κοφῖν-ηδόν**, Adv., gloss on φορμηδόν, EM798.56. **-ιον**, τό, Dim. of κόφινος, PPetr.3p.152 (iii B.C.). **-όομαι**, Pass., have a basket put over one: in Boeotia a way of exposing insolvent debtors, Nic.Dam.103J. **-οποιός**, ὁ, basket-maker, Gloss. ⊛**-ος**, ὁ, basket, acc. to AB102 less Att. than ἄρριχος, found in Ar.Av.1310, Fr.349, Pl.Com.41, X.Mem.3.8.6, IG2².1672.65, Thphr.Char.4.11, PPetr.3p.312 (iii B.C.); in later times used specially by Jews, Juv.3.14, 6.542, cf. Ev.Matt.16.9. II. Boeotian measure, containing nine Attic choenices, i.e. about two gallons, κ. σίτου IG7.2712.65, cf. Stratt.13, Arist.HA629a13, Hsch. **-ώδης**, ες, like a basket, πλέγμα Sch.Ar.Ach.332.

**κόφος**, ὁ, prob. = κόφινος, basket-load, Arch.Pap.5.381 (i A.D.).

**κοχλάδιον**, τό, = κοχλίδιον, Sch.Opp.H.1.138.

**κοχλάζω**, = καχλάζω, Plu.2.590f (κολάζειν codd.), Gloss.: aor. subj. κοχλάσῃ, of boiling water, PHolm.3.1.

**κοχλᾶκ-ιστ(ής?)**, dub. sens. in Stud.Pal.20.211.13 (v/vi A.D.). **-ώδης**, ες, gravelly, Thphr.HP9.9.6.

**κόχλαξ**, ᾶκος, ὁ, = κάχληξ, LXX 1Ki.14.14, Dsc.2.70 (pl.), Apollod.Poliorc.139.12. 2. = λίθος μυλίτης, Gal.19.118.

**κόχλασμα**, ατος, τό, plashing of water, Hsch. s.vv. ἀπόβρασμα, πομφόλυξ.

⊛**κοχλι-άζων**, οντος, ὁ, in a machine, a kind of κοχλίας, Orib.49.20.6 (v.l. -άξων). **-άριον**, τό, spoon: as a measure, spoonful, Dsc.2.42, Philagr.ap.Orib.5.19.1, Gal.6.271, Gp.7.13.1: later Gr. for Att. λιστρίον, acc. to Phryn.293. ⊛**-ας**, ου, ὁ, (κόχλος) snail with a spiral shell, Batr.165, Achae.42, Philyll.21, etc.; ἀπιστότεροι εἶ τῶν κοχλιῶν, for they shrink into their shells on the least alarm, Anaxil.34, cf. Arist.HA523b11, 527b35; ὥσπερ κ. σεμνῶς ἐπηρκὼς τὰς ὀφρῦς Amphis 13.3; βολβός, κτείς (codd. τις), κοχλίας Theoc.14.17; κοχλιῶν ἀγγεῖα PSI6.553.11 (iii B.C.). II. anything twisted spirally, 1. automaton in form of snail, Democh.4J. 2. reel, spool, roller, Bito 47.4, Gp.8.29. 3. screw, Bito 58.10; esp. for raising water, screw of Archimedes, Moschioap.Ath.5.208f, Str.17.1.30, 52, D.S.1.34, 5.37, PLond.3.1177.73 (ii A.D.). 4. spiral stair, διὰ κοχλίου τὴν ἀνάβασιν ἔχει Str.17.1.10, Procop.Pers.1.24. 5. part of surgical machine, Orib.49.20.6.

**κοχλ-ίδιον**, τό, Dim. of κόχλος 2, BGU1118.15 (i B.C.), Epict.Ench.7, EM534.22. **-ιοειδής**, ές, spiral, Hsch. s.v. πολύδονος; κ. γραμμή conchoid, Simp. in Ph.60.14, in Cat.192.20. Adv. -δῶς by means of a screw, Ph.Byz.Mir.1.4. **-ιοκογχύλιον**, inferior kind of murex, Ps.-Democr.Alch.p.42 B.

**κοχλιός**, ὁ, = κοχλίας, Gloss.; screw of διόπτρα, Paul.Aeg.6.73, Aët.16.89.

**κοχλίς**, ίδος, ἡ, Dim. of κόχλος, in pl., Luc.Cat.16, Man.5.24. II. precious stone found in Arabia, Plin.HN37.194.

**κοχλι-ῶρυξ**, ῠχος, ὁ, = sq., Gloss. **-ώρῠχον**, τό, = κοχλιάριον, Poll.6.87, 10.89.

⊛**κοχλοειδής**, ές, = κοχλιοειδής, γραμμή conchoid, Papp.244, etc.

⊛**κόχλος**, ὁ, shell-fish with a spiral shell, used for dyeing purple, Lat. murex, Arist.HA528a1, AP5.227 (Paul. Sil.); used as a trumpet, E.IT303, Theoc.22.75, Mosch.2.124: also fem., Naumach.ap.Stob.4.31.76, Paus.3.21.6; Κασπίῃ ἐν κ., of a large sea-shell, A.R.3.859. 2. land snail, Arist.Mir.846b13. 3. kohl, Eust.728.47.

**κόχος**, ὁ, full stream, Sch.Theoc.2.107.

**κοχύ**· πολύ, πλῆρες, Hsch.

⊛**κοχῠδέω**, stream forth copiously, ποταμοὶ .. Ἀχιλλείοις μάζαις κοχυδοῦντες ἐπιβλὺξ gushing with cakes, Pherecr.130.4: Ion. impf. κοχύδεσκεν (v.l. κοχύεσκεν) Theoc.2.107.

**κοχύζω**, = foreg., cj. for κοκκύζει in Stratt.61 (Casaubon). (This and the foregoing words may be reduplicated forms from the root of χέω.)

**κοχώνη**, ἡ, perineum, Hp.Epid.5.7: in pl., Id.Mul.2.131, Eup.77, Ar.Fr.482, etc.; ἕαται ὅκως νεοσσοὶ τὰς κοχώνας θάλποντες Herod.7.48: dual. τὼ κοχώνᾱ Ar.Eq.424, 484. (Variously expld. by Gramm. ap.Erot.Fr.17; = γλουτοί, acc. to Poll.2.183.) (Cf. Skt. jaghánam 'buttock', 'pudendum'.)

⊛**κόψα**· ὑδρεία, Hsch. **κόψειον**, τό, = ἱππομάραθον, Sch.Nic.Th.596. **κόψενα**· παραστάτης, χαλκός, Hsch. **κοψία**· χύτρα, Id.

**κόψῐχος**, ὁ, = κόσσυφος 1, Ar.Av.305, 806, 1081, Aristopho 10.5, Anaxil.22.21. II. = κόσσυφος II, Orib.inc.13.25.

**Κόωνδε**, v. Κῶς.

**κρᾶ**, shortd. jestingly for κράνος (as δῶ for δῶμα), AP6.85 (Pall.).

**κρααίνω**, v. κραίνω.

**κρᾱ̆ρα**· κόσκινον ἢ ὄρυγμα, Hsch. (Elean for κρησέρα).

**κράατος, κράατι, κράατα**, v. κράς.

⊛**κραβάτιον**, τό, Dim. of κράββατος (κράβατος), Arr.Epict.3.22.74.

⊛**κραβάτριος**, ὁ, perh. = κοιτωνίτης, IPE2.297.

**κραββᾰτοποιός**, ὁ, couch-maker, Gloss.

⊛**κράββᾰτος**, ὁ, also **κράβᾰτος**, Sammelb.4292.9, v.l. in Ev.Marc.2.4, **κράβακτος**, v.l. in NT (cod. Alex.), PTeb.406.19 (iii A.D.) (whence Dim. **κραβάκτιον**, τό, PGrenf.2.111.32 (v/vi A.D.), and Adj. **κραβακτήριος**, α, ον, PMasp.6 ii 46 (vi A.D.)):—also **κράβακτον**, τό, l.c.97 (vi A.D.), **κράβαττος**, Arr.Epict.1.24.14, v.l. in NT (cod. W), Gloss., cf. grabattus, Virg.Mor.5:—couch, mattress, pallet, Rhinth.11, Crito Com.2; but condemned as un-Attic by Phryn.44; freq. in later Gr., ἐπὶ κλιναρίων καὶ κραββάτων Act.Ap.5.15, etc., cf. Arr.Epict. l.c., PLond.2.191.16 (ii A.D.).

**κράβη**, ἡ, = κράμβη, PPetr.3p.328 (iii B.C.).

**κράβος**, ὁ, = λάρος, Hsch.

**κράβυζος**, ὁ, kind of shell-fish, Epich.42.

**κραγγών**, όνος, ἡ, a kind of καρίς, prob. Squilla mantis, Arist.HA525b2: with v.l. **κράγγη**, ἡ, ib.21, 29. II. = κίσσα, Hsch.

**κρᾱγέτης**, ου, ὁ, (κράζω) screamer, chatterer, κολοιοί Pi.N.3.82.

**κράγιον**· σύστρεμμα (σύνστριμμα cod.) ἐν κεφαλῇ, Hsch.

**κρᾰγός**, οῦ, ὁ, bawling, Com. formation in the phrase κραγὸν κεκράξεται (cf. βάδον βαδίζεται) Ar.Eq.487, cf. Hsch.:—on the accent v. Hdn.Gr.2.20.

**κρᾰδαίνω**, (v. κραδάω) swing, ἀπάνευθε πόνοιο νόου φρενὶ πάντα κραδαίνει Xenoph.25; wave, brandish, ἔγχος E.HF1003; λόφους Ar.Ach.965; δόρυ Anacreont.27 A9; shake, χθόνα δ' ἐκ πυθμένων .. πνεῦμα κραδαίνοι A.Pr.1047 (anap.):—Pass., αἰχμὴ .. κραδαινομένη κατὰ γαίης quivering [after it fixes itself] in the ground, Il.13.504, cf. Plb.6.25.5, AP6.97 (Antiphil.); [ἀκόντιον] ὡς μάλιστα -όμενον χρὴ ἐξικέσθαι Arr.Tact.39.2, cf. 41.2; of a bell, to be set in vibration, Phlp. in de An.355.23, al.; σημεῖα -όμενα Procop.Pers.2.10. 2. agitate, τὸ σῶμα, of epilepsy, Praxag.(?) ap.Herod.Med. in Rh.Mus.58.76; of hiccough, Antyll.ap.Orib.8.6.24; κ. πόλιν, of an earthquake, D.H.16.6: metaph., agitate, τὴν Πελοπόννησον Plu.Alc.15; τὴν Ἀσίαν Id.Ant.37:—Pass., to be agitated, tremble, ἡ ὄψις (of fixed stars) .. κραδαίνεται Arist.Cael.290a22, Thphr.Vert.8: aor. ἐκραδάνθην Plu.Alex.74, etc.

**κράδᾰλος** [κρᾱ], ὁ, (κράδη I) fig-tree branch, Hsch.

**κρᾰδᾰλός**, ή, όν, quivering, Eust.1165.20.

**κρᾰδάμωμον**, τό, metri gr. for καρδάμωμον, Androm.ap.Gal.14.41.

**κράδ-ανσις** [κρᾰ], εως, ἡ, quaking, of the earth, Epicur.Ep.2p.48U. **-ασμός**, ὁ, vibration, cj. for foreg. in Epicur. l.c., cf. Nicom.Harm.4, 10; tremor, agitation, Simp. in Cael.453.6; τῶν δοράτων Marcellin.Puls.492. ⊛**-άω**, = κραδαίνω, only in part., κραδάων δολιχόσκιον ἔγχος Il.7.213, Od.19.438; ὀξὺ δόρυ κραδάων Il.13.583, 20.423. II. of trees, suffer from blight (κράδη II), Thphr.HP4.14.4. (Cf. Skt. kūrdati 'leap', Lat. cardo 'that which turns, pivot'.)

**κραδευταί**, v. κρατευταί.

**κρᾰδεύω**, = κραδάω I, Hsch.

⊛**κράδη** [ᾰ], ἡ, quivering spray at the end of a branch, esp. of fig-trees, ἐν κράδῃ ἀκροτάτῃ Hes.Op.681, cf. Thphr.CP5.1.3, Nic.Th.853; τέττιγες .. ἐπὶ τῶν κραδῶν ᾄδουσιν Ar.Av.40: generally, branch, esp. fig-branch, Hp.Superf.33, Thphr.HP2.1.2; κ. ἐριναῖ E.Fr.679; κ. τῶν συκῶν PSI5.449.6 (pl., iii B.C.); κράδῃσι βάλλεσθαι, of the φαρμακός, Hippon.4, cf. 8; κράδης ὀπὸς fig-juice, Hp.Ulc.12. 2. fig-tree, Ar.Pax627, v. Sch. II. diseased formation of small shoots in trees, Thphr.HP1.8.5. III. scenic contrivance for exhibiting actors in Comedy hovering in the air, like the μηχανή in tragedy, Poll.4.128.

**κρᾰδησίτης**· φαρμακός, ὁ ταῖς κράδαις βαλλόμενος, Hsch.; cf. κράδη I. 1, κραδίας II.

**κρᾰδηφορία**, ἡ, bearing of fig-tree branches at a festival, Plu.2.671e.

**κρᾰδία**, ἡ, Dor. for κραδίη, also in Trag.; v. καρδία.

**κρᾰδιαῖος**, α, ον, of or belonging to the heart: metaph., κόσμου κ. κύκλον Procl.H.1.6. II. made of fig-shoots, λίκνον Orph.Fr.199 (codd. Procl.); sed leg. τὸ⟨ν⟩ κ. Διόνυσον.

**κρᾰδίας**, Ion. -ίης, ου, ὁ, (κράδη) curdled with fig-juice, τυρός Hsch. II. κ. νόμος air played on the flute while the φαρμακοί were whipped with fig-branches, Id.; ascribed to Mimnermus by Hippon.96.

**κρᾰδίη**, ἡ, Ion. and Ep. for καρδία.

**κρᾰδοπώλης**, ου, ὁ, one who sells fig-branches, i.e. ἀγροῖκος, Eust.1409.64.

**κράδος** [ᾰ], ὁ, blight in fig-trees, etc., which blackens the boughs, Thphr.HP4.14.4. II. = κράδη I, v.l. for κλάδοις in Dsc.1.128.

**κρᾰδοφάγος** [φᾰ], ον, eating the young branches of the fig-tree, and as Subst., = ἀγροῖκος, Com.Adesp.1049 (κραδα- Hsch.).

⊛**κράζω**, not common in pres., Ar.Eq.287, Arist.HA609b24, Po.1458b31, Thphr.Sign.52, POxy.717 (i B.C.), etc.: fut. κεκράξομαι Eup.1, Ar.

*Eq.*285, 487, *Ra.*258, Men.*Sam.*204, later κράξω *AP*11.141 (Lucill.), *Ev.Luc.*19.40: aor. 1 ἔκραξα Thphr.*Sign.*53, Lxx *Jd.*1.14, *AP*11.211 (Lucill.); imper. κρᾶξον [ᾱ by nature] Hdn.Gr.2.14; ἐκέκραξα freq. in Lxx, *Nu.*11.2, al.: aor. 2 ἔκρᾰγον (ἀν-) Antipho 5.44, Ar.*Pl.*428, etc., ἐκέκραγον Lxx *Is.*6.4 (unless impf. of *κεκράγω): freq. in pf. with pres. sense, κέκρᾱγα (v. infr.) (late κέκρᾰγα *AP*5.86 (Rufin.)); imper. κέκραχθι Ar.*Ach.*335, *V.*198, Men.*Sam.*235; pl. κεκράγετε Ar.*V.*415: plpf. ἐκεκράγειν Id.*Eq.*674, X.*Cyr.*1.3.10:—post-Hom., *croak*, of the raven, S.*Fr.*208, Thphr. l.c.; of frogs, κεκραξόμεσθα Ar.*Ra.* l.c., cf. 265: generally, *scream, shriek, cry*, σὺ δ' αὖ κέκραγας A.*Pr.*743; παιδίον κεκραγός Men.*Sam.*11, 24; *bawl, shout*, κεκραγὼς καὶ βοῶν Ar.*Pl.*722, cf. D.18.132; κεκραγέναι πρός τινα *to call to*.., Ar.*Ra.*982; κραγὸν κεκράξεται Id.*Eq.*487 (cf. κραγός): c. acc. cogn., μέλος κέκραγα A.*Fr.*281.5; ποῖον (sc. περὶ ποίου) κέκραγας ἀνδρὸς ὧδ' ὑπέρφρονα; S.*Aj.*1236:—rare in early Prose, X. l.c., D. l.c., cf. *POxy.*717.1 (i B.C.), etc.; ἐκεκράγει ὅτι.. Plb.ap.Ath.6.274f; κεκράγασιν ὡς.. Phld.*Rh.*1.108 S.: c. acc. et inf., ib.2.98 S. 2. c. acc. rei, *call, clamour for*, ἐμβάδας Ar.*V.*103.

⊛ **κραίνω**, Od.19.567: fut. κρᾰνέω Emp.111.2; Att. contr. κρᾰνῶ A.*Ch.*1075, E.*Supp.*375 [κρᾶνῶ in compd. ἐπικρανεῖ A.*Ag.*1340 codd., nisi leg. -κράνῃ vel -κραίνει]: aor. ἔκρᾱνα ib.369; Ep. and Ion. ἔκρηνα, inf. κρῆναι, Od.5.170, Herod.7.69 (dub.):—Med., fut. inf. in pass. sense κρᾰνέεσθαι Il.9.626: aor. ἐπ-εκρήναντο Q.S.14.297:—**Pass.**, fut. κρανθήσομαι A.*Pr.*911: aor. ἐκράνθην Pi.*P.*4.175, E.*Hec.*219: κέκρανται 3 sg. pf. Pass., A.*Supp.*943, also 3 pl., E.*Hipp.*1255 (sed leg. συμφορά).—Hom. (v. infr.) mostly uses the Ep. pres. κραιαίνω, impf. ἐκραίαινεν, aor. imper. κρήηνον, κρηήνατε, inf. κρηῆναι: 3 sg. pf. Pass. ἐπι-κεκράανται Od.4.616: plpf. ἐπι-κεκράαντο ib.132: aor. ἐκράάνθην Theoc.25.196. (Orig κραίνω (ἐκράαινεν has Ms. authority in Il.5.508, ἐπεκράαινε in 2.419, ἐπεκρήαινε in 3.302; cf. κρᾱ́ανον· τέλεσον Hsch., ἐπικραᾶναι· τῇ κεφαλῇ ἐπινεῦσαι, τελέσαι Id.), contr. κραίνω, κρῆναι, etc. and by distraction κραιαίνω, κρηῆναι, etc.: κρᾱ́ινω from κρασ-ṇ-yω (κάρα, κρᾱ́ατα) = κεφαλαιόω 'achieve'.):—poet. Verb, *accomplish, fulfil*, τόδε μοι κρήηνον ἐέλδωρ Il.1.41, 504, cf. Od.17.242; οἱ μὲν φέρτεροί εἰσι νοῆσαί τε κρῆναί τε better than I both to conceive and *accomplish*, 5.170; κρῆνον νῦν καὶ ἐμοί.. ἔπος ὅττι κεν εἴπω 20.115; καί τε κραίνουσιν ἕκαστα, of the Thriae, *h.Merc.*559; ἐπεὶ μούνῳ σοι ἐγὼ κρανέω τάδε πάντα Emp. l.c.; μαντεύματα κ. *give true* oracles, E.*Ion* 464 (lyr.); δίκας θνατοῖσι κραίνων B.12.45; τοῦ δ' ἐκραίαινεν ἐφετμάς Il.5.508, cf. Pi.*O.*3.11; οἵ ῥ' ἔτυμα κραίνουσι those dreams *come true*, Od.19.567; freq. in A., esp. of Fate, as *Pr.*512, al., cf. S.*OC*914, *Tr.*127 (lyr.), etc.:—Pass., with fut. Med., *to be accomplished, brought to pass*, οὐ γάρ μοι δοκέει μύθοιο τελευτὴ τῇδέ γ' ὁδῷ κρανέεσθαι Il.9.626; πατρὸς δ' ἀρὰ.. τότ' ἤδη παντελῶς κρανθήσεται A.*Pr.*911, cf. 213; κέκρανται ψῆφος the vote *hath been cast*, Id.*Supp.*943; ψῆφος ἡ κρανθεῖσα E.*Hec.*219; λάχη τάδ' ἐφ' ἁμὶν ἐκράνθη A.*Eu.*347 (lyr.);—for the phrase ἐπὶ χείλεα κεκράαντο, v. ἐπικραίνω; of a person, ἐκράνθην I *was perfected* (Sch. ἐπετελέσθην), Pi.*Pae.*9.34. 2. *ordain*, A.*Ag.*369 (lyr.), E.*El.*1248, *Supp.*139. II. = τιμᾶν, Hsch.; so perh. in *h.Merc.*427 κραίνων ἀθανάτους τε θεοὺς καὶ γαῖαν ἐρεμνήν, ὡς ἐγένοντο (less prob. *finishing* [*the tale of*] the gods and earth, how they were made). III. abs., *exercise sway, reign*, ὧδε καὶ γὰρ κατὰ δῆμον.. ἀρχοὶ κραίνουσι Od.8.391: c. acc. cogn., κ. σκῆπτρα *sway* the staff of rule, S.*OC*449; θέμιστας Orph.*A.*1297. 2. after Hom., c. gen., *reign over, govern*, στρατοῦ, τῆς χώρας, τῆσδε γῆς, χθονός, S.*Aj.*1050, *OC*296, 862, 926: in later Ep. c. dat., Orph.*A.*475: c. acc., κ. Διὸς οἴκους *IG*14.433 (Tauromenium); ἐπὶ σπλῆνα κ., of a vein, *dominate*, Aret.*CA*2.2, cf. *CD*1.2. IV. intr., *come to an end, result* in a thing, ποῖ δῆτα κρανεῖ; A.*Ch.*1075 (anap.); of disease, *culminate, be at its worst*, Aret.*SD*2.8, *CA*1.1. 2. Medic., of bones, etc., *terminate*, ὅπῃ κραίνουσι Hp.*Art.*45, cf. Aret.*SD*1.7, 8; *extend*, ἀπὸ ἥπατος ἐς νεφρούς Id.*CA*2.6.

**κραιπᾰλ-άω**, *to be intoxicated*, Ar.*Pl.*298, Plb.15.33.2, Ph.1.260, Plu.*Dem.*7, Luc.*Bis Acc.*17, etc.; μειρακίων τινῶν -ώντων Epicur.*Fr.*114. 2. *have a sick headache after a debauch*, κραιπαλῶν ἔτι ἐκ τῆς προτεραίας Pl.*Smp.*176d; ἐχθὲς ὑπέπινες, εἶτα νυνὶ κραιπαλᾷς Alex. 286; εἰ τοῦ μεθύσκεσθαι πρότερον τὸ κραιπαλᾶν παρεγίγνεθ' ἡμῖν Id. 255.1; παρέξω Λέσβιον, Χῖον.., ὥστε μηδένα κραιπαλᾶν Philyll.24. 3. *carouse, revel*, D.C.77.17, Alciphr.1.34. **-η**, ἡ, *drinking-bout*, ἐκ κραιπάλης Ar.*Ach.*277, *V.*1255; τὰς κεφαλὰς ὑγιεῖς ἔχειν ἐκ κ. Alex. 9.8; κ. καὶ μέθη *Ev.Luc.*21.34; χθεσινὴ κ. Luc.*Laps.*1, cf. Procop. *Goth.*1.3. 2. *intoxication*, Men.*Kol.*47, Alciphr.1.37, Them.*Or.*2.36a. 3. *drunken headache*, Hp.*Aër.*3, Arist.*Pr.*873ᵃ37, etc.

⊛ **κραιπᾰλό-βοσκος** δίψα thirst *which draws on drunkenness*, Sopat. 25. **-κωμος**, ον, *rambling in drunken revelry*, Ar.*Ra.*217.

**κραιπᾰλώδης**, ες, *given to drunkenness*, Plu.2.647e. 2. Adv. -δῶς *in a drunken manner*, αὐτοσχεδιάζειν Phld.*Rh.*2.22 S.

⊛ **κραιπνός**, ή, όν, *swift, rushing*, Βορέης, θύελλαι, Od.5.385, 6.171; πομποῖσιν ἅμα κραιπνοῖσι φέρεσθαι Il.16.671, 681: in Hom. freq. ποσσὶ κραιπνοῖσι Il.23.749, etc.; κραιπνῷ ποδὶ A.*Pers.*95 (lyr.); πηδήμασιν κραιπνοῖσι S.*Ichn.*213; κ. βέλος Pi.*P.*4.90; κυλινδέσκοντο -ότεραι ἢ ἀνέμων στίχες, of the Symplegades, ib.209; σθένει κραιπνοί Id.*Fr.*133: metaph., *hasty, rash*, κραιπνότερος νόος, of a youth, Il.23.590. Adv. -νῶς, ἀνόρουσε 10.162; προσεβήσετο 14.292; διέπτατο 15.83; θέομεν Od.8.247: neut. pl. as Adv., κραιπνὰ ποσὶ προβιβάς 17.27; κ. διωκέμεν ἠδὲ φέβεσθαι Il.5.223, etc.

**κραιπνό-σῦτος**, ον, *swift-rushing*, A.*Pr.*281 (anap.). **-φόρος**, ον, *swift-bearing*, αὖραι ib.132 (lyr.).

**κραῖρα**, ἡ, (κέρας, κεραία) *top, head, extremity*, Hsch. (Att. acc. to Eust.710.49). 2. = ἀκροστόλιον, Hsch. **κραῖρος**, ὁ, = foreg., Id.

⊛ **κράκτης**, ὁ, later form for κεκράκτης, Adam.2.24, Tz.*H.*8.438.

**κρακτικός**, ή, όν, (κράζω) *noisy*, Luc.*Gall.*4, Sch.Ar.*V.*34, cj. in Tz. ad Hes.*Op.*744: Sup. -ώτατος Luc.*Symp.*12.

**κράκτρια**, ἡ, pecul. fem. of κράκτης, Hsch. s.v. λακέρυζα.

**κρᾶμα**, ατος, τό, (κεράννυμι) *mixture*, Ti.Locr.95e, Plu.2.1109e, etc.; κ. ψυχῆς καὶ σώματος Ph.1.372; esp. *mixed wine*, Lxx *Ca.*7.2, *OGI*383.148 (Nemrud Dagh, i B.C.), Plu.2.140f, Dsc.1.113 (misspelt κραμμα *PMag.Lond.*121.174); also of medicines, Hp.*Mul.*2.211, Archig.ap.Gal.13.265. 2. = χρέμμα, Aristipp.ap.D.L.2.67. 3. *alloy* of metals, Str.13.1.56. **κραμάσαι**, v. κρεμάννυμι.

**κρᾱμάτ-ινος**, η, ον, *made of an alloy*, σκεῦος *PLeid.X.*14 (κραμμ-Pap.). **-ιον**, τό, Dim. of κρᾶμα, *wine and water*, Dsc.*Eup.*1.197, Sor.1.63.

**κρᾱματοποιέω**, *mix*, τὸ ποτὸν τῷ οἴνῳ *Hippiatr.*34.

**κράμβαλα**· μνημεῖα, Hsch.

**κραμβᾰλέος**, α, ον, (κράμβος A) *dried, parched, roasted*, Ath.9.376c, 381c.

**κραμβᾰλίζω**, = καπυρίζω, κατασείω, Hsch.:—but **κραμβᾰλιαστύς**, ἡ, *loud laughter* (to be read for χαραμβαλιαστύς), Id. (post χρᾶν).

**κραμβασπάρᾰγος**, ὁ, = κραμβοσπάραγον, *Gloss.* **κραμβατέλος**· ξηρὸς καὶ καπυρός, Hsch.

**κραμβ-ειν**, v. κραμβίον. ⊛ **-η**, ἡ, *cabbage, Brassica cretica*, Batr. 163 (pl.), Hippon.37, Telecl.27 (pl.), *PHib.*1.121.30 (iii B.C.), etc.; of three kinds, Eudem.ap.Ath.9.369d, cf. Nic.*Fr.*85; = ῥάφανος (q.v.), Arist.*HA*551ᵃ16; κ. ἥμερος, ἀγρία, Dsc.2.120, 121. 2. κ. θαλασσία, *sea-cole, Convolvulus Soldanella*, ib.122, Gal.12.43. 3. μὰ τὴν κράμβην Anan.4, cf. Epich.25, or μὰ τὰς κράμβας Eup.74, Comic form of oath to avoid sacred names, Ath.9.370b. ⊛ **-ήεις**, εσσα, εν, *like a cabbage*, Nic.*Al.*330. **-ίδιον**, τό, Dim. of κράμβη, Antiph. 6. **-ίον**, τό, *decoction of cabbage*, Hp.*Mul.*1.63, 2.121, Gal.19.114: Sicel for κώνειον, Erot., Hsch.—written **κραμβειν**, *POxy.*1479.10 (i B.C.). **-ίς**, ίδος, ἡ, *cabbage-caterpillar*, Ael.*NA*9.39.

**κράμβος** (A), η, ον, = ξηρός, Hsch. II. of sound, (cf. καπυρός) *loud, ringing*, κ. γέλως Id.; κραμβότατον στόμα Ar.*Eq.*539.

**κράμβος** (B), ὁ, *blight in grapes, when they shrivel* before they are ripe, Thphr.*CP*5.10.1.

**κραμβο-σπάρᾰγον** [σπᾰ], τό, *sprouting broccoli*, *Gp.*12.1.2. **-φάγος** [φᾰ], ον, *Cabbage-eater*, name of a frog, v.l. in Batr.218.

**κράμβωτον**, = ἰκτῖνος, Hsch.

⊛ **κράνα**, v. κρήνη. II. = κεφαλή, Hsch.

**κρᾰνᾰήπεδος**, ον, *with hard rocky soil*, *h.Ap.*72.

**κρᾰνάϊνος**, = κρανέϊνος, *h.Merc.*460 codd. (ῑ metri gr.), Hp.*Fract.*30, X.*Eq.*12.12, Str.12.7.3, Dsc.*Eup.*1.120; ῥάβδοι *BGU*1253.4 (ii B.C.).

**κραναοίκορον**· μοῖρά τις τοῦ ἱερείου, Hsch.

⊛ **κρᾰνᾰός**, ή, όν, poet. word, *rocky, rugged*, in Hom. always of Ithaca (exc. in Il.3.445 where it is pr. n. of an island), Il.3.201, Od. 1.247, al.; of Delos, Pi.*I.*1.3; freq. of Athens, Id.*O.*7.82, etc.: hence as pr. n., Κραναὰ πόλις Athens, Ar.*Ach.*75; simply αἱ Κρανααί Id.*Av.*123; ἡ Κραναά, of the Acropolis, Id.*Lys.*481; Κραναοί *the people of Attica*, Hdt.8.44, Str.9.1.18; παῖδες Κραναοῦ (Cranaos being a mythic king of Athens) A.*Eu.*1011 (anap.). 2. generally, *hard*, χέλυς Opp.*H.*5.396; of a fishing-rod, ῥάβδος κ. ib.4.364. 3. *stinging*, κ. ἀκαλῆφαι Ar.*Fr.*560. **κρᾶνέα**, ἡ, v. κράνεια.

⊛ **κράν-ειᾰ** [ᾰ], ἡ, (κράνον) *cornelian cherry, Cornus mas*, κ. τανύφλοιος Il.16.767; ἀψάμενον βρόχον αἰπὺν ἀφ' ὑψηλοῖο κ. Demetr.Troez. 1; καρπὸς κρανείης, as food for swine, Od.10.242; ἰσχυρότατον ἡ κ. Thphr.*HP*5.6.4; τόξον κρανείας *of cherry-wood*, E.*Fr.*785; ῥάβδος κρανείας Ael.*NA*1.23, 12.43; κρανείας τάλαντον *of cornel-wood*, *IG*11(2).161 A 104 (Delos, iii B.C.); κράνεια alone, = *spear*, *AP*6.123 (Anyte):—also **κρανία**, Hp.*Mochl.*42 (gen. -ίης), Dsc.1.119, Gal.12.41, Arr.*An.*2.3.7; **κρανέα**, *Gp.*10.87.4. **-εῖνος**, η, ον, *made of the wood of* κράνεια, τόξα Hdt.7.92; παλτὸν X.*HG*3.4.14, cf. *Cyr.*7.1.2; ξυστά Arr. *An.*1.15.5, etc.—Freq. written **κρανάϊνος** (q.v.). ⊛ **-ειον**, τό, *fruit of* κράνεια, Amphis 38, Anaxandr.41.54 (prob.), Thphr.*HP*3.2.1: dat. pl. written κρανέοις ib.4.4.5:—later **κράνιον**, Gal.6.620, al. (pl.). **-εών**, ῶνος, ὁ, *grove of cornelian cherry-trees*, *Gloss.* **-ία**, ἡ, v. κράνεια.

**κρᾰνίδιον**, τό, Dim. of κράνος (A), *small helmet*, *IG*2².1421.123. 2. [κρᾱν-] Dim. of κρανίον, Paul.Aeg.6.74.

**κράνινος** [ᾰ], η, ον, = κρανέϊνος, τόξα Paus.1.21.5.

**κρανίξαι**· ἐπὶ κεφαλὴν ἀπορρίψαι, Hsch.; cf. κερανίξαι.

**κρᾱνιόλειος**, ον, *bald-crowned, bald-headed*, *Com.Adesp.*1050.

**κρᾱνίον**, τό, (κάρα) *upper part of the head, skull* (κεφαλῆς τὸ τριχωτὸν μέρος Arist.*HA*491ᵃ31, cf. Gal.2.739); of horses, ὅθι τε πρῶται τρίχες ἵππων κρανίῳ ἐμπεφύασι Il.8.84; of men, Pi.*I.*4(3).54, E.*Cyc.*683, Cratin.71, Pl.*Euthd.*299e, etc.: generally, *head*, Amphis 16. II. *headache*, *Hippiatr.*103 (v.l. κατακράνιον).

**κράνιον** [ᾰ], τό, = κράνειον (q.v.).

**κράννα**, Aeol. for κράνα, κρήνη (q.v.).

**κρᾱνο-κολάπτης**, ου, ὁ, *poisonous spider*, Philum.*Ven.*15.1, Sch. Nic.*Th.*764. **-κοπέω**, *cut heads off*, φυτά *PRyl.*152.17 (i A.D.).

**κράνον** [ᾰ], τό, = κράνεια, Thphr.*CP*3.1.4 and 10.2. 2. = κράνειον, Philagr.ap.Orib.5.20.5, v.l. in Gal.6.620. (Cf. Lat. *cornum*.)

**κρᾱνο-ποιέω**, *make helmets*: metaph., of one who *talks big and warlike*, Ar.*Ra.*1018:—hence **-ποιΐα**, ἡ, Poll.7.155. **-ποιός**, ὁ, *helmet-maker*, Ar.*Pax*1255, *SIG*1177 (= *Tab.Defix.*69), Poll.1.149, 7.155.

**κράνος** (A) [ᾰ], εος, τό, *helmet*, Hdt.1.171, 4.180, al., A.*Th.*385, E.*El.*470 (lyr.), Ar.*Ach.*584, 1103, X.*Cyr.*6.1.51, *IG*1².278.49, Plu.2.

789d, Jul.*Or.*2.53b. 2. metaph., τὸ δὲ τοῦδε κ. ὁ κοινὸς ἀὴρ Aret. *SD*2.6. II. *ship's ram*. Tim.*Pers.*21. (The ᾰ shows that it is akin to κρᾰναός (*hard*), rather than to κρᾱνίον.)

**κράνος** (B) [ᾰ], ου, ἡ, later form for κράνον, *Gp.*7.35.1. 2. *rod of cherry-wood*, *PTeb.*39.31 (ii B.C.); χιτῶνι καὶ κράνῳ καὶ πιλίῳ ib.230 (ii B.C.) (here perh. = κράνος A).

**κρᾰνουργός**, ὁ, *maker of helmets*; and **-ουργία**, ἡ, Poll.7.155.

**κράν-τειρα**, ἡ, fem. of sq. II, *APl.*4.220 (Antip.), Orph.*Fr.* 176. **-τήρ**, ῆρος, ὁ, (κραίνω) *one that accomplishes*: κραντῆρες, οἱ, *wisdom-teeth*, which come last and *complete the set*, Arist.*HA*501$^b$25 (κριτῆρες cited by *EM*742.37), Poll.2.93: generally, *teeth*, Nic.*Th.* 447 (sg.), Ruf.*Onom.*51: in sg., a boar's *tusk*, Lyc.833. II. *ruler*, κραντῆρα βοῶν ταῦρον Orph.*A.*313. **-τήριος**, α, ον, *accomplishing*, Hsch. **-της**, ου, ὁ, = κραντήρ, [πημάτων] κ. χρόνος Lyc.305. ⊛ **-τωρ**, ορος, ὁ, = κραντήρ, κ. ἐλευθερίας Epigr.ap.Paus.8.52.6. II. *ruler, sovereign*, E.*Andr.*508(lyr.), *AP*5.116 (Samos).

**κράος**· ἐν ᾧ τὴν γῆν σκάλλουσι, καὶ ἡ σκαλευομένη ἄμπελος, Hsch.

**κρᾰπᾰτᾰλίας**, ὁ, = ληρώδης, Pherecr.99.

**κρᾰπᾰτᾰλός** (**κραπαταλλός** Hdn.Gr.1.158), ὁ, a worthless kind of *fish*, hence = μωρός, Hsch.: Κραπαταλοί, title of play by Pherecrates, in which he says that the κραπαταλός is used for δραχμή in Hades, Poll.9.83.

**κράριον**, τό, perh. = κλάνιον, *PTeb.*550 (ii A.D.).

⊛ **κράς**, poet. form of κάρα, nom. only Simm.4; gen. κρᾱτός Il.5.7, al., Trag. (v. infr.); dat. κρᾱτί Od.9.490, S.*OC*313, Ar.*Ra.*329, κράτεσφι Il.10.156; acc. κρᾶτα Od.8.92, Trag. (v. infr.): pl., gen. κράτων Od. 22.309; dat. κρᾱσί Il.10.152; acc. κρᾶτας E.*Ph.*1149, *HF*526: gender rarely determinate, κρατὸς fem. E.*El.*140(lyr.), cf. Sch.E.*Hec.* 432, *Ph.*1159; κρᾶτα, τό, is nom. in S *Ph.*1457 (anap.), acc. ib.1001, *OT*263, cf. *Tr.*1016(lyr.); but acc. κρᾶτα, τόν, Ion Trag.61: pl. κρᾶτα, τά, Pi.*Fr.*8, perh. S.*OC*473:—Hom. also has gen. and dat. κράατος, κράατι, pl. nom. κράατα [all ‒ ◡ ◡], but no nom. κρᾶας is found:—*head*, ἐκ κράατος ἀθανάτοιο Il.14.177; σῷ δ' αὐτοῦ κράατι τείσεις Od. 22.218, etc.; ὑπὸ κρᾱτεσφι under his *head*, Il.10.156: metaph., *top, peak*, κρατὸς ἀπ' Οὐλύμποιο Il.20.5; ἐπὶ κρατὸς λιμένος at *the head* or *far end* of the bay, Od.9.140, 13.102. II. Adv. κρῆθεν, used by Hom. in the phrase κατὰ κρῆθεν *down from the head, from the top*, δένδρεα.. κατὰ κρῆθεν χέε καρπόν *from their tops*, Od.11.588, cf. *h.Cer.* 182, Hes.*Th.*574: hence, *from head to foot, entirely*, Τρῶας δὲ κατὰ κρῆθεν λάβε πένθος Il.16.548 (perh. for κατ' ἄκρηθεν = κατ' ἄκρης, v. ἄκρα); also ἀπὸ κρῆθεν Hes.*Sc.*7.

**κρᾶς**· κρέας, τινὲς δὲ κεφαλή (i.e. κράς), Hsch.

**κρασβόλος**, ον, shortd. from κερασβόλος (q.v.), Hsch.

**κρασ⟨ε⟩ίδιον**, τό, *paste*, Ruf.ap.Orib.8.47.20.

**κρασέρα**· ἀλευροτήσις (κράσσεα· ἀλευρωτίς cod.), Hsch.; cf. κρησέρα, κραῖρα.

**κρᾶσις** (Ion. **κρῆσις** Hp.*Vict.*1.32), εως, ἡ: (κεράννυμι):—*mixing, blending* of things which form a compound, as wine and water, opp. mechanical mixture (defined as an εἶδος μίξεως in which the constituents are liquids, Arist.*Top.*122$^b$26, cf. *Stoic.*2.153; περὶ κράσεως, title of work by Alex.Aphr.): first in A., τὴν δευτέραν γε κ. ἥρωσιν νέμω *Fr.*55, cf. Staphyl.9, Ath.10.426b (pl.); κράσεις ἠπίων ἀκεσμάτων *modes of compounding*.., A.*Pr.*482; ἡ τῶν ἐναντίων κ. Pl. *Lg.*889c; τὴν τῶν νεύρων φύσιν ἐξ ὀστοῦ καὶ σαρκὸς κράσεως.. συνεκεράσατο Id.*Ti.*74d; ἐκ κράσεως πρὸς ἄλληλα Id.*Tht.*152d; τὴν ἁρμονίαν κ. καὶ σύνθεσιν ἐναντίων εἶναι Arist. *de An.*407$^b$31; χρωμάτων ἀκριβὴς κ. Luc.*Zeux.*5, cf. Arist.*Col.*792$^a$4. 2. *temperature* of the air, κρᾶσιν ὑγρὰν οὐκ ἔχων [αἰθήρ] E.*Fr.*779.2; τὰς ὥρας κ. ἔχειν τοιαύτην ὥστε.. Pl.*Phd.*111b, cf. Poll.6.178; ἡ κ. τῶν ὡρέων *temperate climate*, Hp. *Aër.*12; ὅσα περὶ κράσεις *climates*, Arist.*Pr.*lib. xiv tit. 3. *temperament*, of the body or mind, κ. σώματος ib.871$^a$24, cf. 953$^a$30; διανοίας ib.909$^a$17; κ. μελαγχολική ib.954$^b$8: pl., αἱ τῶν σωμάτων κράσιες Ti.Locr.103a, cf. Plot.3.1.6: so in Medic., Hp.*Nat.Hom.*4, etc.; περὶ κράσεων, title of work by Galen. 4. metaph., *combination, union*, κ. καὶ ἁρμονία τούτων ἡ ψυχή Pl.*Phd.*86b, cf. 59a; μουσικῆς καὶ γυμναστικῆς κ. Id.*R.*441e, etc. 5. Gramm., *crasis*, i.e. the combination of the vowels of two syllables into one long vowel or diphthong, e.g. τοὔνομα for τὸ ὄνομα, ἁνήρ for ὁ ἀνήρ, τἄρα for τοι ἄρα, A.D.*Adv.*128.2, *EM*822.56, etc.; also, *synaeresis* of vowels, e.g. εὖ for ἐΰ, ib.392.54; but opp. ἔκθλιψις and συναίρεσις, *An.Ox.*1.371.

**κρασπεδίτης** [ῑ], ου, ὁ, *hindmost person in a chorus*, opp. κορυφαῖος, Plu.2.678e.

⊛ **κράσπεδ-ον**, τό, *edge, border, skirt*, esp. of cloth, Theoc.2.53; of the *fringe* or *tassel* worn by Jews, *Ev.Matt.*9.20: mostly in pl., ἄκροισι λαίφους κρασπέδοις (v. ἄκρος I. 2 b) E.*Med.*524; κράσπεδα στεμμάτων Ar. *V.*475, cf. Diph.43.30; χρυσᾶ κ. Chamael.ap.Ath.9.374a, Chrysipp. *Stoic.*3.36,37. 2. metaph., mostly in pl., *skirts* or *edge* of a country, S.*Fr.*602, E.*Fr.*381; of a mountain, X.*HG*4.6.8; πρὸς κρασπέδοισι στρατοπέδου on *the skirts* of the army, E.*Supp.*661; τοὺς πελταστὰς ἐπὶ τὰ κ. ἑκατέρωθεν καθίστασθαι X.*HG*3.2.16: also in sg., Τιμολέοντα ὥσπερ ἐκ κ. τινὸς λεπτοῦ τῆς πολίχνης τῇ Σικελίᾳ προσηρτημένον Plu. *Tim.*11; κ. αἰγιαλοῦ *AP*7.78 (Dionys. Cyzic.). 3. Medic., *affection of the uvula, fimbria*, Aret.*SA*1.8. **-όομαι**, Pass., *to be bordered* or *edged*, ὕφεσι κεκρασπεδῶσθαι E.*Ion* 1423.

⊛ **κρασταῖναι**· διάκονοι γυναῖκες, Hsch.

⊛ **κραστήριον**, τό, *rack, manger*, Poll.7.142, 10.166. II. in pl., *bed-posts*, Phryn.155.

**κραστίζομαι**, *consume green fodder*, Sophr.166, cf. *EM*535.23, *AB*273.

**κράστις** (**κρᾶστις** Harp.), εως, ἡ, = γράστις (q.v.), *green fodder*, esp. for horses (ἡ κ. τῶν ἵππων *PGrenf.*1.42.11 (ii B.C.)), Ar.*Fr.*798, Din.*Fr.*46.2, Arist.*HA*595$^b$26, Thphr.*HP*8.7.5, al., *PTeb.*61(*b*).318 (ii B.C.), Poll.7.142.

**κρᾶτα**, τό, *head*: v. κράς.

**κραταιά**, ἡ, = χελιδόνιον μέγα, Ps.-Dsc.2.180.

**κρᾰται-βάτης** [βᾰ], ου, Dor. **-τᾱς**, α, ὁ, *striding in might*, epith. of Zeus, *IG*4.669 (Nauplia). **-βῐος**, ον, *strong with violence*, Choerob. in *An.Ox.*2.318, Eust.1938.1. **-βολος**, ον, *hurled with violence*, E. *Ba.*1096. **-γονος**, ἡ, = κραταιόγονον, Thphr.*HP*9.18.5 (prob. l.):—also **-γονον**, τό, Ps.-Dsc.3.124, Hsch. **-γος**, ὁ, *thorn, Crataegus Heldreichii*, Thphr.*HP*3.15.6. **-γύᾰλος** [ῠ], ον, *with strong γύαλα, strongly arched*, θώρηκες Il.19.361. **-γών**, όνος, ὁ, = κράταιγος, Thphr.*HP*3.15.6. **-ίς**, ἡ, (κρατύς) of the stone of Sisyphus, ὅτε μέλλοι ἄκρον ὑπερβαλέειν, τότ' ἀποστρέψασκε κραταιίς when it was just about to surmount the top, then did *mighty weight* turn it back, dub. in Od.11.597 (taken as Adv., *violently*, by Aristarch.; as κράται' ἴς (where κράταια may be an old fem. of κρατύς like πλάταια (cf. Skt. *pr̥thivī*), pl. Πλαταιαί, fem. of πλατύς) by Ptol.Asc.ap.Hdn.*Gr.*2. 153). II. (proparox.) as pr. n., *the Mighty* one, name of the mother of Scylla, Od.12.124. **-λεως**, ων, gen. ω, (κραταιός, λᾶας) *of hard stones, rocky*, χθών A.*Ag.*666; πέδον E.*El.*534. **-όγονον**, τό, *willow-weed, Polygonum Persicaria*, Dsc.3.124, Gal.12.44; cf. κραταίγονον. **-ός**, ά, όν, poet. form of κρατερός, *strong, mighty*, μοῖρα κραταιή Il.16.334, etc.; of men, Od.15.242, 18.382, Pi.*N.*4.25, B.17. 18; of a lion, κραταιοῦ θηρὸς ὑφ' ὁρμῆς Il.11.119; ἔγχος Pi.*P.*6.34; κ. ἔπος word *of power*, ib.2.81; σθένος κ. A.*Pr.*428 (lyr.); κ. μετὰ χερσὶν S.*Ph.*1110 (lyr.); κραταιᾶς χειρὸς E.*HF*964; κραταιῷ.. βραχίονι *Trag. Adesp.*416; ἔχει χεῖρα κραταιάν Cratin.Jun.8.4 (hex.); χεῖρα κραταιοτέρην *AP*11.324 (Autom.); *fierce*, κ. καύματος ὥρα Poet.ap.Callistr. ap.Ath.3.125c: freq. in later Prose, κ. λίθος *hard* stone, Ph.*Bel.*80. 22, *Supp.Epigr.*2.829 (Damascus, iii A.D.); ἐν χειρὶ κ. with a *mighty* hand, Lxx *Ex.*13.3, al.; κ. ἀγών Plb.2.69.8; τόξα κ. Plu.*Crass.*24; ἐπὶ τὸ κ. Luc.*Anach.*28: Comp., Ph.1.14: Sup., Id.2.383; esp. in magical and mystical writings, ἐν φωτὶ κ. καὶ ἀφθάρτῳ *PMag.Lond.* 121.563; θεοὶ κ. ib.422; οἱ κ. the *Mighty Ones*, Iamb.*Myst.*8.4, Dam. *Pr.*351: Astrol., κ. ἡγεμόνες, divinities presiding over certain periods of the month, Porph.ap.Eus.*PE*3.4; ἀστέρες, ζῴδιον, *Cat.Cod.Astr.* 8(4).227; also ὁ κ. [μηνὸς Φαρμοῦθι] *POxy.*465 i 12 (ii A.D.): c. gen., *ruling over*, ὦ τῶν πάντων ζώντων τε καὶ τεθνηκότων κραταιοί *PMag. Leid.V.*7.8; ὁ μέγιστος κ. θεὸς Σοκνοπαῖος Wilcken *Chr.*122.1 (i A.D.). Adv. **-ῶς** Lxx *Jd.*8.1, Ph.1.276, Pap. in *Arch.f.Religionswiss.*18.259 (iii A.D.).

**κρᾰταιό-της**, ητος, ἡ, = κράτος, Lxx *Ps.*45(46).3. **-φρων**, ον, gen. ονος, *stern*, Τιτάν *PMag.Berol.*2.85. **-χειρ**, χειρος, ὁ, ἡ, *mighty of hand*, *Ath.Mitt.*24.257 (Thrace). **-χθων**, ονος, ὁ, ἡ, *wielding power over the earth*, *PMag.Lond.*121.353, *PMag.Par.*1.1355. ⊛ **-ω**, *strengthen*, τὰς χεῖράς τινος Lxx 1*Ki.*23.16, al.:—Pass., ib.30.6, al., *Ev.Luc.*1.80, 1*Ep.Cor.*16.13, etc.; κ. ὑπέρ τινα *to be too strong for* him, *prevail against* him, Lxx 2*Ki.*10.11, al. 2. Pass., *to be determined*, κ. τοῦ πορεύεσθαι ib.*Ru.*1.18. II. intr. in Act., *prevail*, ἐπί τινας ib.2*Ki.*11.23; ὑπέρ τινας ib.3*Ki.*21(20).23. III. Med., *control*, πάθη λόγῳ Ph.1.420.

**κρᾰταί-πεδος**, ον, *with hard ground* or *soil*, οὖδας Od.23.46. **-πῑλος**, ον, *with strong* πῖλος, A.*Fr.*430. **-πους**, ὁ, ἡ, -πουν, τό, gen. ποδος, *stout-footed*, ἡμίονοι Hom.*Epigr.*15.9; cf. καρταίπους. **-ρῑνος**, ον, *hard-shelled*, χελώνη Orac.ap.Hdt.1.47. **-ωμα**, ατος, τό, *strength*, Lxx *Ps.*42(43).2. **-ωνον**, τό, = κραταιόγονον, Ps.-Dsc.3. 124. **-ωσις**, εως, ἡ, = κραταίωμα, Lxx *Ps.*59(60).7.

**κρατάνιον**, τό, kind of *cup*, Polem.Hist.20.

**κρᾰτερ-αίχμης**, ου, Aeol., Dor. **-ᾱς**, *mighty with the spear* (in form καρτ-), Pi.*I.*6(5).38. **-αλγής**, ές, *cruel*, *IG*7.96 (Megara, iv A.D.). **-αύχην**, ενος, ὁ, ἡ, *strong-necked*, Pl.*Phdr.*253e: in form καρτ- (v.l. κρατ-), Hp.*Epid.*6.1.2. **-ῖτις** (sc. λίθος), ιδος, ἡ, hard yellowish stone, Plin.*HN*37.154. **-όδους**, οντος, ὁ, ἡ, *strong-toothed*, Hsch. (glossed by καρτερούμενοι).

**κρᾰτερός**, ά, όν, Ep. form of καρτερός, *strong, stout, mighty*, in Hom. mostly of bodily strength, κρατερός περ ἐὼν καὶ χερσὶ πεποιθώς Il.16.624, cf. 6.97, Pi.*I.*5(4).31, etc.; epith. of Ares, Il.2.515; of lions, Od.4.335; χεῖρες ib.288, Pi.*P.*11.18: with collat. notion of *stern, harsh*, of Hades, Il.13.415, cf. 21.566. 2. of things, conditions, etc., *mighty, fierce*, κ. ὑσμῖναι 2.345; ἀνάγκη 6.458; κρατερῆφι βίηφιν 21.501; σθένος B.17.40; πάλα Id.10.20; βέλος, τόξον, Il.5. 104, 8.279; βιός Od.24.170; δεσμός, δεσμοί, Il.5.386, Od.8.336; *hard*, χῶρος h.*Merc.*354; σίδηρος ὅπερ κρατερώτατός ἐστιν Hes.*Th.*864. 3. of passions, etc., *strong, vehement*, λύσσα Il.9.239; ἔρις 13.358; μένος 7.38; πένθος 11.249; ἄλγεα Od.15.232: of acts and words, κ. ἀμφίβασις Il.5.623; κ. μῦθος a *harsh, rough* speech, 1.25; μῦθον ἀπηνέα τε κ. τε 15.202. II. Adv. **-ρῶς** *strongly, stoutly*, μάχεσθαι 12.152; ἑστάμεναι 15.666; ἔχεσθαι 16.501, 17.559; νεμεσᾶν 13.16; κὰδ δ' ἔβαλε κ. dashed *roughly* to earth, Od.4.344; κ. ἀγόρευσεν, ἀπέειπεν, *sternly*, Il.8.29, 9.431; in Prose, Anon.ap.Stob.4.31.34.—Once in Trag., κ. γυιοπέδαι A.*Pr.*168 (anap.); elsewh. καρτερός. (κορτερά· κρατερά, ἰσχυρά, Hsch., is prob. Aeol.)

**κρᾰτερο-φόρος**· γενναῖος, Hsch. ⊛ **-φρων**, ον, gen. ονος, (φρήν) *stout-hearted, dauntless*, epith. of Heracles, Il.14.324; the Dioscuri, Od.11.299; Odysseus, 4.333; a wild beast, Il.10.184; ἀδάμαντος ἔχον κρατερόφρονα θυμόν Hes.*Op.*147, cf. Orph.*Fr.*164; Διὸς κρατερόφρονι κούρῃ, of Athena, *IG*1$^2$.503.

**κρᾰτέρ-ωμα**, ατος, τό, kind of *bronze*, Hsch. **-ῶνυξ**, ὕχος, ὁ, ἡ, (ὄνυξ) *strong-hoofed, solid-hoofed*, ἵπποι Il.5.329, 16.724, al.; ἡμίονοι 24.277, Od.6.253; *strong-clawed*, λύκοι κρατερώνυχες ἠδὲ λέοντες 10.218; *with strong nails*, χείρ Matro *Conv.*28.

**κράτεσφι** [ᾰ], Ep. dat. of κράς (q. v.).

**κρᾰτευ-ταί**, ῶν, οἱ, *stone* or *metal blocks on which a spit rests*, Il.9.214, cf. Sch., Paus.Gr.*Fr.*236; μολύβδινοι κ. Eup.171, cf. *IG*2².1425.388 (written **κραδευταί** ib.1425.415, 1541.20). 2. in Archit., *stones which support* a pavement, ib.7.3073.105, al. (Lebad.). 3. leaden *pigs* of specified weight, *IG*1².371.13. **-τήριον**, τό, = foreg. 1, Poll.6.89. ⊛ **-ω**, = κρατέω, pf. κεκράτευκα, *IG*14.1794.

⊛**κρᾰτ-έω**, Aeol. **κρετέω**, aor. inf. **κρέτησαι** Sapph.*Supp.*9.5:—Med., aor. ἐπι-κρατησάμενοι v. l. in Gal.*UP*6.13:—Pass., fut. κρατήσομαι Aristid.1.501 J. and, with v. l. κρατηθήσομαι, Th.4.9:—*to be strong, powerful*: hence, I. abs., *rule, hold sway*, Ἦλιδα.., ὅθι κρατέουσιν Ἐπειοί Od.13.275, 15.298; μέγα κρατέων ἤνασσε with mighty *sway*.., Il.16.172; ἅπας δὲ τραχύς, ὅστις ἂν νέον κρατῇ A.*Pr.*35; ὁ κρατῶν *the ruler*, Id.*Ag.*951, 1664, S.*Ant.*738, etc.; θώπτε τὸν κρατοῦντ' ἀεί A.*Pr.*937; οἱ κρατοῦντες Id.*Ch.*267, S.*OT*530, etc.; τὸ κρατοῦν E.*Andr.*133(lyr.), Pl.*Lg.*714c, Arist.*Pol.*1255ᵃ15; ἡ κρατοῦσα the *lady of the house*, A.*Ch.*734. 2. in Poets, c. dat., *rule among*, μέγα κρατέεις νεκύεσσιν Od.11.485; ἀνδράσι καὶ θεοῖσι 16.265; Φθίᾳ *rule in* Phthia, Pi.*N.*4.50; ἐν Ἰλιάδι χθονί E.*El.*4. 3. c. gen., *to be lord* or *master of, rule over*, πάντων Ἀργείων, πάντων, Il.1.79, 288, cf. Od.15.274; Ὀλύμπου A.*Pr.*149(lyr.); δωμάτων Id.*Ag.*1673; ὅπλων S.*Aj.*1337; κ. τοῦ βίου *to be master of*.., And.1.137; αὐτοῦ κ. S.*Aj.*1099, Antipho 5.26, cf. S.*OC*405; ἡδονῶν καὶ ἐπιθυμιῶν Pl.*Smp.*196c, etc.; τῶν πραγμάτων D.2.27; τοῦ μὴ πείθεσθαι τοῖς νόμοις κρατῆσαι *to be above* obedience.., X.*Lac.*4.6. II. *conquer, prevail, get the upper hand*, abs., A.*Ag.*324, etc.; πολλῷ ἐκράτησαν Hdt.5.77; εἰ τὰ τοῦ Μήδου κρατήσειε Th.3.62; ὁ μὴ πειθόμενος κρατεῖ Pl.*Phdr.*272b; ἔνθα τἀναιδὲς κρατεῖ Diph.111: c. dat. modi, κ. τῇ γνώμῃ *prevail* in opinion, Hdt.9.42; πάλᾳ, ἱπποδρομίᾳ, Pi.*O.*8.20, *I.*3.13; μάχῃ E.*HF*612; ταῖς ναυσί Ar.*Ach.*648; τῷ Φοινίκων ναυτικῷ Th.1.16; also θουρίῳ ἐν Ἄρει S.*Aj.*614 (lyr.); ἐν τοῖς πολέμοις Ar.*Pl.*184: c. acc. cogn., κ. στάδιον B.6.15, cf. 7; ὀκτὼ νίκας E.*Epigr.*1; τὸν ἀγῶνα D.21.18; τὴν μάχην v. l. for τῇ μάχῃ in D.S.18.30; τὴν πρεσβείαν Philostr.*VS*1.21.6; πάντα *in* all things, S.*OT*1522; οἱ κρατοῦντες *the conquerors*, X.*An.*3.2.26; τὰ κατὰ πόλεμον κρατούμενα τῶν κρατούντων εἶναί φασιν Arist.*Pol.*1255ᵃ7. b. *to be superior*, πλήθους ἕκατι ναυσὶν κρατῆσαι A.*Pers.*338: abs., *to be the best*, Critias 2.7 D. c. of reports, etc., *prevail, become current*, φάτις κρατεῖ A.*Supp.*293, S.*Aj.*978; λόγος κ. A.*Pers.*738; νόμιμα δὲ τὰ Χαλκιδικὰ ἐκράτησεν Th.6.5; κρατεῖ ἡ φήμη παρά τισι Plb.9.26.11. 2. c. inf., *prevail so that*, κ. τῷ πλήθει ὥστε μὴ αὐτίκα τὰς πύλας ἀνοίγεσθαι Th.4.104: impers., κατθανεῖν κρατεῖ *'tis better to*.., A.*Ag.*1364; κρατεῖ μ' ἂ γιγνώσκοντ' ἀπολέσθαι E.*Hipp.*248 (anap.). 3. c. gen., *conquer, prevail over*, τῶν ἐναντίων S.*Fr.*85, cf. *OC*646, A.*Th.*955(lyr.), etc.; κ. τινὸς τὸν ἀγῶνα Philostr.*Her.*2.5: metaph., τό τοι νομισθὲν τῆς ἀληθείας κρατεῖ S.*Fr.*86; κ. τῆς διαβολῆς *get the better of* it, Lys.19.53; ὁ λόγος τοῦ ἔργου ἐκράτει *surpassed, went beyond* it, Th.1.69; ἡ φύσις.. τῶν διδαγμάτων κρατεῖ *is better than*.., Men.*Mon.*213, cf. 169. b. of food, *digest, assimilate*, Hp.*VM*3, 14, Mnesith.ap.Ath.2.54b, Phylotim.ib.3.79c:—Pass., Hp.*Epid.*6.5.15; τῆς τροφῆς μὴ κρατηθείσης Plu.2.654b. 4. c. acc., *conquer, master*, Pi.*N.*10.25, A.*Pr.*215, *Th.*189, E.*Alc.*490, Ar.*Nu.*1346, *Av.*420, X.*An.*7.6.32, etc.; μάχῃ, τῷ πολέμῳ τινά, Th.6.2, Aeschin.2.30; τῷ λόγῳ τινά Ar.*V.*539; πάχει μάκει τε in.., Pi.*P.*4.245; *outdo*, τοὺς φίλους εὖ ποιῶν X.*Hier.*11.15; τῷ διαφθαρῆναι χρήμασιν ἢ μὴ κεκράτηκα Φίλιππον D.18.247; *surpass*, κρατεῖ δὲ ὁ τῆς ἡδονῆς [βίος] τὸν τῆς φρονήσεως Pl.*Phlb.*12a:—Pass., *to be overcome*, A.*Th.*750 (lyr.), etc.; ὕπνῳ Id.*Eu.*148 (lyr.); ὑπὸ τοῦ ὕπνου Hdt.2.121.δ'; ὑπὸ τῶν ἡδονῶν Pl.*Lg.*633e. III. *become master of, get possession of*, τῆς ἀρχῆς, τῶν νεκρῶν, Hdt.1.92, 4.111; πολλὰ φρονέοντα μηδενὸς κ. Id.9.16; σέθεν A.*Supp.*387; οὕτω ἡ βουλή σου ἐκράτει Lys.13.26; κ. τῆς γῆς Th.3.6; ναυσὶ τῆς θαλάσσης Pl.*Mx.*240a; κ. τῆς λέξεως *have* it *at command, remember* it, Ath.7.275b; *master* by the intellect, πάντων τῶν τῆς ἱστορίας μερῶν Plb.16.20.2:—Pass., *to be mastered*, δεῖ ἐν ταῖς τέχναις καὶ ἐπιστήμαις ταῦτα κρατεῖσθαι Arist.*Pol.*1331ᵇ38, cf. *Po.*1456ᵃ10 (prob. for κροτεῖσθαι). IV. *lay hold of*, τῆς χειρός Lxx *Ge.*19.16, *Ev.Matt.*9.25, *Ev.Marc.*9.27. 2. c. acc. rei, *seize, win and keep*, esp. by force, πᾶσαν αἶαν A.*Supp.*255; θρόνους S.*OC*1381; *seize, hold fast, arrest*, τινα Batr.63, Plb.8.18.8, *Ev.Matt.*14.3; τένοντα Batr.233; τὰς χεῖράς τινος *PLips.*40 iii 2 (iv/v A. D.); *secure, grasp*, τὴν ἀκατονόμαστον Τριάδα Zos.Alch.p.230 B. 3. *hold up, support*, τινα D.H.4.38; *maintain* a military post, X.*An.*5.6.7; *hold fast*, τὰς παραδόσεις 2*Ep.Thess.*2.15; *keep, retain*, *PTeb.*61(*b*).229 (ii B. C.):—Pass., οὐκ ἦν δυνατὸν κρατεῖσθαι αὐτὸν ὑπ' αὐτοῦ (sc. τοῦ θανάτου) *Act.Ap.*2.24; ἡ κτῆσις τοῖς τέκνοις κεκράτηται *has been reserved* for, *settled* upon, *POxy.*237 viii 36 (ii A. D.). 4. in Law, *possess a title to*, κ. καὶ κυριεύειν c. gen., *PTeb.*319.19 (iii A. D.), etc. b. *sequester, place under embargo*, *OGI*669.23 (Pass., Egypt, i A. D.), *BGU*742 iii 6 (Pass., ii A. D.). 5. *hold in the hand*, ὁ κρατῶν τοὺς ἑπτὰ ἀστέρας ἐν τῇ δεξιᾷ αὐτοῦ *Apoc.*2.1; πόαν Dsc.3.93; ἄρτον Plu.2.99d; σκῆπτρον Ath.7.289c, cf. Luc.*Am.*44, Ach.Tat.1.6, etc.; δακτύλιον *PMag.Lond.*46.451 (iv A. D.). 6. *endure, put up with*, τὸν ἀργυροπράτην *POxy.*1844 (vi A. D.). V. *control, command*, A.*Ag.*10, E.*Hec.*282:—Pass., αἰσχρὰ τῷ νόμῳ κρατούμενα *controlled* by.., Ar.*Av.*755; κρατεῖσθαι ὑπὸ τοῦ προβουλεύματος D.H.9.52; διαθέσει Porph.*Sent.*27. VI. *repair, make good*, τὸ βεδέκ (Hebr.) τοῦ οἴκου Lxx 4*Ki.*12.5. ⊛ **-ημα**, ατος, τό, *support*, of a bandage, Gal.18(2).538, Heracl.ap.Orib.48.15.3, Heliod.ib.27.3; *fulcrum*, Id.ib.49.19.2. 2. *grasp, grip* of the hand, Procl.*Par.Ptol.*36. 3. *handle*, Sch.Luc.*JTr.*31, *Icar.*10.

⊛**κρᾱτήρ**, Ion. and Ep. **κρητήρ**, ῆρος, ὁ, (κεράννυμι) *mixing vessel*, esp. *bowl, in which wine was mixed with water*, κ. ἀργύρεος, χρύσεος, Il.23.741, 219; [κ.] ἀργύρεος ἔστιν ἅπας, χρυσῷ δ' ἐπὶ χείλεα κεκράανται Od.4.615; οἶνον δ' ἐκ κρητῆρος ἀφυσσόμενοι δεπάεσσιν ἔκχεον Il.3.295, cf. 247; κρητῆρι δὲ οἶνον μίσγον ib.269; κρητῆρα κερασσάμενος Od.7.179, 13.50; οἶνον ἔμισγον ἐνὶ κρητῆρσι καὶ ὕδωρ 1.110, cf. Sapph.51, Alc.45, S.*OC*159(lyr.), Ar.*Ec.*841; κρατῆρα κεράσαι Orac.ap.D.21.53, cf. Th.6.32; κρητῆρα καὶ ὑποκρητήριον *SIG*2 (Sigeum, vi B. C.); πίνοντες κρητῆρας drinking *bowls of wine*, Il.8.232; κρητῆρα στήσασθαι ἐλεύθερον *to set up a bowl of wine* to be drunk in honour of the deliverance 6.528, cf. Od.2.431; κρητῆρα ἐπιστέψασθαι ποτοῖο, v. ἐπιστέφω; κρατῆρος μέρος μετασχεῖν A.*Ch.*291; σπονδὴ τρίτου κρατῆρος S.*Fr.*425. 2. metaph., κ. ἀοιδᾶν, of the messenger who bears an ode, Pi.*O.*6.91; κ. κακῶν, of a sycophant, Ar.*Ach.*937 (lyr.); τοσόνδε κρατῆρ' ἐν δόμοις κακῶν πλήσας.. ἐκπίνει A.*Ag.*1397; αἵματος κρατῆρα πολιτικοῦ στῆσαι, of civil war, D.H.7.44. 3. a constellation, the *Cup*, Ptol.*Tetr.*27. II. *any cup-shaped hollow, basin* in a rock, S.*OC*1593, cf. Pl.*Phd.*111d. 2. *mouth* of a volcano, *crater*, Arist.*Mu.*400ᵃ33 (pl.), Plb.34.11.12 (pl.), Luc.*Trag.*23.

**κρᾱτηρ-ία**, ἡ, foreg., *bowl* for compounding drugs, etc., Dsc.4.150, Zos.Alch.p.231 B. ⊛**-ίαρχος**, ου, ὁ, = συμποσίαρχος, dub. in Dumont-Homolle *Mélanges d'arch. et d'épigr.* p.457 (Thrace, κρατηριακος lapis). ⊛ **-ίζω**, Ion. **κρητηρ-** prob. in *SIG*57.24 (Milet., v B. C.):—in aor. Pass. κηκρατηρίχ⟨θ⟩ημες, *drink out of the* κρατήρ, i. e. *get drunk*, as we might say, *drink from the bottle* instead of the glass, Sophr.106 (prob. l., cf. ἐκρατηρίχθημεν· ἐμεθύσθημεν, Hsch.). II. Act., *mix a bowl of wine*, κρητηρίσα⟨ντες κρητῆρα⟩ς τέσσερας prob. in *SIG* l. c., cf. *AB*274; esp. for the orgies, D.18.259, Phot. **-ιον**, Ion. **κρητ-**, τό, Dim. of κρατήρ, Hp.*Nat.Mul.*34; as a measure, *POxy.*2049 (vi A. D.):—also **-ίδιον**, τό, in pl., *IG*7.3099 (Lebad.), J.*AJ*3.6.7. ⊛**-ίσκος**, ὁ, *IG*11(2).203*A* 35 (Delos, iii B. C.), Ath.11.479c; κ. τοῦ ὀφθαλμοῦ *sockets*, Hsch. (pl.).

⊛**κρᾱτηροφόρος**, ον, *bearing a bowl*, Ῥέα Sch.Nic.*Al.*217.

**Κράτης**, ὁ, mystical title, *PMag.Leid.V.*7.18.

**κρᾰτησι-βίας**, ὁ, = κραταίβιος, Pi.*Fr.*16. **-μάχος**, ον, *conquering in the fight*, Id.*P.*9.86. **-πους**, ποδος, ὁ, ἡ, *victorious in the foot-race*, ib.10.16.

**κρᾰτησιππος**, ον, *victorious in the race*, ἅρμα Pi.*N.*9.4.

**κράτησις** [ᾰ], εως, ἡ, *might, power, dominion*, Lxx *Wi.*6.3, Man. ap.J.*Ap.*1.26. 2. ἡ Καίσαρος κ. (sc. Αἰγύπτου), an era in Egypt (viz. the capture of Alexandria, 30 B. C.), *BGU*174 (i A. D.), *PFay.*89.2 (i A. D.), etc. 3. *accession* of an Emperor, *BGU* 62 iv 6, al. (iii A. D.). 4. *prevalence, predominance*, ἡ τῆς ἀπλανοῦς κ. Simp.*in Cael.*475.30, 476.5. II. *possession*, βίου κ. *BMus.Inscr.*918 (Halic.); κ. τοῦ ἐν ὕλῃ σκοτεινοῦ Plot.1.6.3. 2. in Law, *title to possession*, Mitteis *Chr.*31 iii 32 (ii B. C.); κ. καὶ κυρεία *BGU*1187.7, etc. 3. Medic., *retention*, κ. ἐπίμονος σπέρματος (i. e. conception) Sor.1.43; opp. ἔκκρισις, Gal.8.440. b. κ. τῶν ὑδάτων, i. e. drought, *Cat.Cod.Astr.*7.184. 4. *holding firm, steadying*, Gal.18(2).826, Olymp. *in Mete.*96.11.

**Κρᾰτήτειος**, ον, *of Crates*, γραφή Str.2.3.8.

**κρᾰτ-ητέον**, *one must keep to*, τῆς συμμετρίας Aët.9.35. ⊛ **-ητής**, οῦ, ὁ, *one who holds or possesses*, ἱερῶν Procl.*Par.Ptol.*228. **-ητικός**, ή, όν, *fit for winning*, νίκη κ. δύναμις Pl.*Def.*414a. 2. *ruling, controlling*, δύναμις κ. τῶν προνοουμένων Procl.*Inst.*121; κ. τῶν ὅλων Id. *in Ti.*1.69; αἱ κ. δυνάμεις, opp. αἱ ὑπουργικαί, Id. *in Prm.*p.736 S. 3. *promoting retention* (cf. κράτησις II. 3), συλλήψεως Aët.1.142. 4. Astrol., *predominant*, Vett.Val.333.5. **-ητός**, ή, όν, *capable of being grasped, mastered*, διανοίᾳ Porph.*Marc.*8. **-ήτωρ**, ορος, ὁ, = κρατητής, word coined by Alexarchus, Heraclid.Lemb.5. 2. Astrol., *ruling star*, Ptol.*Tetr.*198.

**κρατίζομαι**, f. l. for κραστίζομαι in Sophr.166.

**Κρᾰτίνειος** [ῑ], α, ον, *used by* the Comic poet *Cratinus*, ὄνομα D.H.*Rh.*11.10; μέτρον Heph.15.21.

**κρᾰτιστ-⟨ε⟩ία**, ἡ, the rank of *excellency*, *POxy.*1204.15 (iii/iv A. D.). **-εύω**, *to be mightiest, best, most excellent*, ὁ κρατιστεύων λόγος Pi.*Fr.*180; ὦ κρατιστεύων κατ' ὄμμα, of the Sun, S.*Tr.*102 (lyr.); ὁ κ. *the conqueror*, opp. ὁ ἡττηθείς, Arist.*HA*614ᵃ4; τὰ κ. J.*BJ*1.2.8. 2. *to be superior*, τῷ σώματι καὶ τῇ ψυχῇ X.*Mem.*1.4.14; ἔν τινι ib.2.6.26; τἆλλα Id.*Cyr.*1.5.1. 3. c. gen. pers., πάντων And.3.18; τῶν ἡλικιωτῶν κ. ἐν τοῖς ἀγῶσι *to be first of* them, Isoc.9.22. **-ής**, οῦ, ὁ, = κρατητής, ὦ βασιλέων κύριοι καὶ κρατισταί *PMag.Leid.V.*7.15. **-ίνδην**, Adv. *by choosing the best*, Poll.1.176. ⊛ **-ος**, η, ον, Ep. **κάρτ-** (as always in Hom.), isolated Superl. from κρατύς, *strongest, mightiest*, Il.1.266, etc.; θεῶν κ., i. e. Zeus, Pi.*O.*14.13; κ. Ἑλλήνων, i. e. Achilles, S.*Ph.*3: in Prose, εἰ τοὺς κ. ἐνικήσαμεν Th.7.67; Λημνίων τὸ κ. *the best* of their men, Id.5.8; τὸ δυνάμεως κ. *the strength* or *flower of*.., X.*Cyr.*6.1.28, etc.; of things, καρτίστην.. μάχην *fiercest* fight, Il.6.185; δεσμὸς κ. Ti.Locr.99a. 2. generally, *best, most excellent*, as Sup. of ἀγαθός, Pi.*I.*1.17, S.*Ant.*1050, etc.: colloquially, "ἄνδρα κ." εἰπών Thphr.*Char.*5.2; οἱ κράτιστοι *the aristocracy*, X.*HG*7.1.42, v. ἀγαθός I; τὰ κ. τῆς χώρας ib.3.4.20. b. as a title or mode of address, κράτιστε Θεόφιλε *Ev.Luc.*1.3; esp. = Lat. *egregius*, ὁ κ. ἡγεμών *PFay.*p.33 (i A. D.); ὁ κ. ἐπίτροπος *BGU*891 (ii A. D.); ἡ κ., of a woman of the *equester ordo*, *IG*14.

1346; also, = Lat. *clarissimus*, of Senators, ὁ κ. ἀνθύπατος ib.9(1).61; ὁ κ. συγκλητικός *IGRom*.3.581, etc.; ἡ κ. βουλή *POxy*.2108.6 (iii A.D.). c. with modal words added, κ. τὴν ψυχήν Th.2.40; πάντων πάντα κ. *best* of all in.., X.*An*.1.9.2; ἔν τινι Id.*Mem*.3.4.5; εἴς τι Pl. *Phlb*.67b; περί τι Id.*Plt*.257a; πρός τι X.*HG*3.4.16: c. inf., *best at* doing, Th.2.81, Pl.*Phdr*.267d, X.*Mem*.1.4.1, etc.: c. part., τῶν ἡλίκων κ. εἶναι ἀκοντίζων καὶ τοξεύων Id.*Cyr*.1.3.15. 3. neut. folld. by inf., φυγέειν κάρτιστον to flee were *best*, Od.12.120, cf. E.*El*. 379, Ar.*Eq*.80, etc.: in pl., κράτιστα.. ἐλεῖν E.*Med*.384: abs., ὅπερ κ. the *main point*, Th.1.143. 4. Adv. usages, ἀπὸ τοῦ κρατίστου *in all good faith*, Plb.8.17.4; κατὰ τὸ κ. D.H.2.22: neut. pl. κράτιστα as Adv., X.*HG*3.4.16, *Ages*.1.25.—The Comp. in use is κρείσσων (q.v.).

**κρᾱτο-βρώς**, βρῶτος, ὁ, ἡ, *devourer of heads* or *brains*, Lyc. 1066. **-γενής**, ές, *head-born*, θεός, of Athena, Porph.*Antr*. 32. **-δετον**· σφενδόνην δεδεμένην, τὰ γὰρ ἄκρα τῆς σφενδόνης κεφαλὰς ἐκάλουν, Hsch. s.v. κραστόδετον (incomplete s.v. κρατόδετον). **-πλᾰγής**, ές, *struck on the head*, cj. Lob. for -παγής in Man. 4.284 (-πάλης Koechly).

**κρᾰτορία**, ἡ, *power, might*, θεοῦ *Gloss*.

⊛ **κράτος** [ᾰ], Ion. and Ep. **κάρτος**, εος, τό, both in Hom.; Aeol. **κρέτος** Alc.25:—*strength, might*, in Hom. esp. of *bodily strength*, ἔπεφνε δόλῳ, οὔ τι κράτεΐ γε Il.7.142; ἔχει ἥβης ἄνθος, ὅ τε κ. ἐστὶ μέγιστον 13.484, etc.; τὸ γὰρ αὖτε σιδήρου γε κ. ἐστίν this (i.e. τὸ βάψαι) is what gives *strength* to iron, Od.9.393: generally, δικαία γλῶσσ' ἔχει κ. μέγα S.*Fr*.80; μηχανῆς ἔστω κ. A.*Supp*.207; κατὰ κράτος with *all one's might* or *strength*, πολιορκεῖσθαι Th.1.64; πολεμεῖν Pl. *Lg*.692d; ἐξελέγχεσθαι D.34.20, etc.: freq. in phrase αἱρεῖν κατὰ κ. take *by storm*, Th.8.100, Isoc.4.119, etc.; also ἀνὰ κράτος διώκειν X. *Cyr*.1.4.23; ἐλαύνειν Id.*An*.1.8.1, etc.; ἀπὸ κράτους D.S.17.34; πρὸς ἰσχύος κράτος, opp. λόγῳ, S.*Ph*.594. 2. personified, Κ. Βία τε A. *Pr*.12; Κ. καὶ Δίκη Id.*Ch*.244. II. *power*, τοῦ γὰρ κ. ἐστὶ μέγιστον, of Zeus, Il.2.118, etc.; τοῦ γὰρ κ. ἔστ' ἐνὶ οἴκῳ Od.1.359, cf. Il.12.214; Ζηνὸς κ. Pi.*O*.6.96, cf. A.*Pr*.527 (lyr.); ἐκπίπτειν κράτους, of Zeus, ib. 948; τὸ κ. τοῦ θεοῦ Lxx *Ps*.61(62).11, etc.: pl., ὑποχείριος κράτεσιν ἀρσένων A.*Supp*.393 (lyr.), cf. S.*Ant*.485; esp. of political power, *rule, sovereignty*, ὁ μαιόμενος τὸ μέγα κρέτος ὀντρέψει τάχα τὰν πόλιν Alc. l.c.; τὸ κ. περιθεῖναί τινι Hdt.1.129; ἐς τὸ πλῆθος φέρειν τὸ κ. Id.3.81; τὸ πᾶν κ. ἔχειν to be *all-powerful*, Id.7.3; ἀρχὴ καὶ κ. τυραννικόν S.*OC* 373; βασιλεὺς πρῶτος ἐν κράτει Ὀδρυσῶν ἐγένετο in *real power*, Th.2. 29; later τὸ κ. τῶν Ῥωμαίων *POxy*.41 i 2 (iii/iv A.D.): in pl., κράτη καὶ θρόνους S.*Ant*.173, cf. *OT*586, etc.; θρόνων κράτη sovereign *power*, Id.*Ant*.166. 2. c. gen., *power over*, τὸ Περσέων κ. ἔχοντα Hdt.3.69; τὸ κ. εἶχε τῆς στρατιῆς Id.9.42; πᾶν κ. ἔχων χθονὸς A.*Supp*.425 (lyr.); τῶν ἄλλων δαιμόνων E.*Tr*.949; δὸς κ. τῶν σῶν δόμων A.*Ch*.480; δωμάτων ἔχειν κ. Ar.*Th*.871; τὸ τῆς θαλάσσης κ. Th.1.143; μετὰ κράτους τῆς γῆς Id.8.24; ὧν ἂν ᾖ τὸ κ. τῆς γῆς whoever have *possession* of the land, Id.4.98; κ. ἔχειν ἑαυτοῦ Pl.*Plt*.273a: pl., ἀστραπᾶν κράτη νέμων S.*OT*201 (lyr.). 3. of persons, *a power, an authority*, Ἀχαιῶν δίθρονον κ. A.*Ag*.109 (lyr.), cf. 619, *Th*.127 (lyr.). III. *mastery, victory*, freq. in Hom., Il.1.509, 6.387, Od.21.280; κ. ἄρνυσθαι S.*Ph*. 838 (lyr.); νίκη καὶ κράτη A.*Supp*.951; ἀέθλων κ. *victory in*.., Pi.*I*. 8(7).4; νίκη καὶ κ. τῶν δρωμένων S.*El*.85; κ. ἀριστείας *the meed* of highest valour, Id.*Aj*.443; νίκη καὶ κ. πολεμίων Pl.*Lg*.962a; κ. πολέμου καὶ νίκη D.19.130. IV. Medic., in pl., *ligaments*, Hp.*Mul*. 2.167. 2. = ταρσός, *back of the hand*, Poll.2.144. V. Pythag. name for *ten*, *Theol.Ar*.59.—This word and its derivs. take two forms, κρατ- and καρτ-; the latter is mostly Ep., as κάρτος, κάρτιστος, καρτύνω, but in κρατερός and καρτερός the reverse holds, v. κρατερός fin.; κρατέω, κρατύς have no form καρτ-. (κρατ- and καρτ- from κ𝔯τ-, weak form of κρετ-, cf. κρέτος, κρέσσων.)

**κρᾰτός**, gen. sg. of κράς (q.v.).

**κρᾰτυν-τήριος**, α, ον, *strengthening, making firm*, Hp.*Mul*.1.78; κρατυντήρια, τά, title of work of Democritus *in support of his doctrines*, S.E.*M*.7.136, D.L.9.47, Suid.; κρατυντήρια· κατισχύοντα, Hsch. **-τικός**, ή, όν, = foreg., κ. φάρμακα, for loose teeth, Archig.ap.Gal.12.873, v.l. in Dsc.1.30, prob. l. in Antyll.ap.Orib. 6.34.3. **-τός**, ή, όν, *confirmed, upheld*, τὴν πάντα κρατυντὰ Orph. *Fr*.47.6. **-τωρ**, ορος, ὁ, *ruler, controller*, πυρός *PMag.Leid.W*.8. 21. **-ω**, Ep. καρτ-, (κράτος, κρατύς) *strengthen*, κ. τὰς Συρηκούσας Hdt.7.156; τὴν πόλιν Th.1.69; τείχη Id.3.18; κ. τινὰ δορυφόροισι Hdt.1.98; κ. ἑωυτὸν τῇ τυραννίδι ib.100:—also in Med. (so only in Hom.), ἐκαρτύναντο φάλαγγας they *strengthened their* ranks, Il.11. 215, 12.415; κρατυνάμενοι [τὴν Ἄντανδρον] Th.4.52, cf. 114; τὴν προβολήν Plu.*Aem*.20; πίστεις κ. *confirm* their pledges, Th.3.82; σπείραισιν ἐκαρτύναντο βοείαις χεῖρας Theoc.22.80; ἐκαρτ. μέλαθρον A.R.2.1087; οἵ μιν.. ἐκαρτ. κεραυνῷ Id.1.510; καρτ. τὴν αἰσυμνητείην Thrasyb.ap. D.L.1.100:—Pass., *wax strong*, ἔσχε τὴν βασιληίην καὶ ἐκρατύνθη Hdt.1.13; τείχεσιν ἐκεκράτυντο D.C.40.36, cf. D.H.3.72; ἐν χρόνῳ κρατυνθὲν ἔθος Lxx *Wi*.14.16. b. *confirm* an impression, S.E. *M*.8.364 (Pass.); an agreement, *PLond*.1.113⁵1 (vi A.D.). 2. *harden*, opp. ἁπαλύνω, τοὺς πόδας ἀνυποδησίᾳ X.*Lac*.2.3, cf. Gal.4. 748 (Pass.):—Pass., ὀστέα κρατύνεται *consolidate*, Hp.*Fract*.7. II. *rule, govern*, c. gen., S.*OT*14, E.*Ba*.660: c. acc., ἄκρα κρατύνων Emp. 100.19, cf. 73.2, A.*Pers*.900 codd. (lyr.); πτόλιν Id.*Supp*.699 (lyr.): c. acc. cogn., κράτος κ. Id.*Ag*.1471 (lyr.): abs., Id.*Pr*.150 (lyr.), 404 (lyr.); τὰ πρῶτα μὲν δόρει κρατύνων, πρῶτα δ' οἰωνῶν ὁδοῖς S. *OC*1314. 2. c. gen., *become master, get possession of*, τῶν ὅπλων Id.*Ph*.366, cf. 1059, 1161 (lyr.): c. acc., *possess*, λέκτρα Corinn. *Supp*.2.55; βασιληΐδα τιμὰν κ. *hold, exercise*, E.*Hipp*.1281 (lyr.), cf. A.*Supp*.372 (lyr.); τὴν πολιτικὴν ἀρετήν Him.*Or*.14.28. III. καρτύνειν βέλεα *ply, throw* them *stoutly*, Pi.*O*.13.95; κ. ἐνὶ χερσὶν ἐρετμά A.R.2.332. IV. c. acc. et inf., *insist* that.., D.L.7.83, cf. Procl.*Hyp*.3.54.

**κρᾰτύς** [ῠ], ὁ, *strong, mighty*, in Hom. always epith. of Hermes, κρατὺς Ἀργειφόντης Il.16.181, 24.345, Od.5.49. (For a doubtful fem. κράταια, v. κραταιίς.)

**κρᾰτυσμός**, ὁ, *strength, firmness*, Hp.*Epid*.6.8.11.

**κράτωρ** [ᾰ], ορος, ὁ, *ruler, potentate*, of God, *Gloss*.

⊛ **κραύγαζος**, ὁ, = κραύγασος, Ptol.*Tetr*.164.

**κραυγ-άζω**, = κράζω, of dogs, *bay*, *Lyr.Adesp*.135; of ravens, *croak*, Arr.*Epict*.3.1.37; of men, *cry aloud, shout*, D.54.7, Lxx 2*Es*.3.13, *Ev.Jo*.18.40, Polem.*Cyn*.40, Gal.8.287; κ. "μὴ θυμοῦ" Phld.*Ir*.p.70 W.; κραυγάζω κοὐκ ἐπακούει *Riv.Fil*.57.380 (Aptera). **-ανάομαι**, = foreg., παιδίον ἀσπαῖρόν τε καὶ κραυγανώμενον (v.l. -γόμενον) Hdt.1. 111, cf. Sch.Call.*Aet.Oxy*.2079.20. **-αρ**· ὁ ἰσχυρός, Hsch. **-ασίδης**, ου, ὁ, as if a Patron. of κραύγασος, *Croaker*, name of a frog in Batr. 243. **-ασμός**, ὁ, *screaming*, Diph.16; censured by Phryn. 317. ⊛ **-ᾰσος**, ὁ, *bawler, shouter*, *Gloss*. ⊛ **-αστής**, οῦ, ὁ, *crier, bawler*, gloss on βαβάκτης, *AB*223:—fem. **-άστρια**, Hsch. s.v. μηκάδες. **-αστικός**, ή, όν, *vociferous*, Procl.*Par.Ptol*.230, Sch.Il. 1.575; τὸ κ. Sch.Ar.*Pax*1078. Adv. -κῶς Sch.Ar.*Eq*.485. **-ή**, ἡ, *crying, screaming, shouting*, τίς ἥδε κ.; Telecl.35; κραυγὴν θεῖναι, στῆσαι, E.*Or*.1510, 1529; ποιεῖν X.*Cyr*.3.1.4; κραυγῇ χρῆσθαι Th.2. 4; κ. γίγνεται Lys.13.71; rarely of a *shout of joy*, *PPetr*.3p.334 (iii B.C.), *Ev.Luc*.1.42: in pl., Aeschin.1.34, Vett.Val.2.35; κραυγὴ Καλλιόπης, as an instance of bad taste, cited from Dionys.Eleg.(7) by Arist.*Rh*.1405ᵃ33. **-ίας** ἵππος, ὁ, a horse *that takes fright at a cry*, Hsch.

**κραυγός**, οῦ, ὁ, *woodpecker*, Hsch.:—also **κραυγόν** (leg. -γών), Id.

**κραῦρ-α**, ἡ, (κραῦρος) *fever*, a disease in swine and cattle, Suid., Phot., prob. in *GDI*5001 (Gortyn). **-άω**, *suffer from fever*, of cattle, Arist.*HA*604ᵃ17; of swine, ib.603ᵇ7. **-όομαι**, Pass., *become dry* or *parched*, Ph.2.174, D.C.66.21. **-ος** (A), ου, ὁ, = κραῦρα, Arist.*HA*604ᵃ14; also, *a disease of bees*, prob. in Hsch. (καυρούς cod.). **-ος** (B), α, ον, also ος, ον Arist.*PA*655ᵃ25:—*brittle, friable* (κραῦρον τὸ τελέως ξηρόν, ὥστε καὶ πεπηγέναι δι' ἔλλειψιν ὑγρότητος Id.*GC*330ᵃ6), Pl.*Ti*.60d (Comp.); of wood, Thphr.*HP*1.6. 2, al., Eust.1906.11; opp. μαλακός, γλίσχρος, Arist.*PA*1.c., *GA*734ᵇ 32; of meat, θερμότερον ἢ κραυρότερον ἢ μέσως ἔχον (apptly.) *dry and cold*, Eub.7. **-ότης**, ητος, ἡ, *brittleness*, opp. γλισχρότης, Thphr. *HP*1.5.4, Gal.6.799.

**κραῦσον**· τὸ πῦρ, Hsch. **κράφα**· ᾧ οἱ κηπουροὶ τοὺς βώλους ἀπάγουσιν, Id.

⊛ **κρε-άγρα**, ἡ, (κρέας, ἀγρέω) *flesh-hook*, to take meat out of the pot, Ar.*Eq*.772 (ubi v. Sch.), *V*.1155, Anaxipp.6.2, Lxx 1*Ki*.2.14, *PLond*. 2.191.10 (ii A.D.), etc.: generally, *hook to seize* or *drag by*, Ar.*Ec*. 1002. **-άγρευτος**, ον, *tearing off the flesh*, Lyc.759. **-άγριον**, τό, Dim. of κρεάγρα, *IG*2².1541.13. **-αγρίς**, ίδος, ἡ, = κρεάγρα, *AP*6.306 (Aristo).

**κρεάδιον**, τό, Dim. of κρέας, *morsel, slice of meat*, Ar.*Pl*.227, Cephisod.8, Hp.*Epid*.7.3, Porph.*Abst*.1.37: pl., Ar.*Fr*.591, Alex. 110.15, X.*Cyr*.1.4.13, Phld.*Ir*.p.41 W.; σφυρίδαν κρεδίων (sic) *BGU* 814.25 (iii A.D.): sg. written κρεάδινον Orib.*Eup*.4.72.1.

**κρεᾱ-δοσία**, ἡ, *distribution of meat*, *Inscr.Prien*.111.174 (i B.C.), *IG*7.2712.68 (Acraeph.). **-δοτέω**, *distribute meat*, *OGI*764.54 (Pergam., ii B.C.), *Inscr.Prien*.123.6 (i B.C.).

**κρεάνας**· ἐλπίδας, Hsch.

**κρεᾱ-νομέω**, pf. κεκρεανόμηκα Is.9.33:—*divide the flesh* of a victim among the guests, l.c., Luc.*Prom*.20; *distribute meat*, τῇ βουλῇ *IG*2².847.25: generally, *divide, cut piecemeal*, D.S.34.12:—Med., Sopat.20: with pl. subject, *divide among themselves*, Theoc.26. 24. **-νομία**, ἡ, *distribution of meat*, Theopomp.Hist.205 (pl.), *IG* 2².1245.5, Luc.*Prom*.5: pl., *IG*2².334.25, Porph.*Abst*.2.30. **-νόμος**, ὁ, (νέμω) *one who distributes the flesh of victims*, E.*Cyc*.245: as Adj., *mangling*, τέκνων Lyc.202, cf. 762.

⊛ **κρέας**, τό, Dor. **κρῆς** (q.v.), Ep. **κρεῖας** dub. cj. in Anan.5.3; Att. gen. κρέως S.*Fr*.728; Cret. κρίως *GDI*5128 (Vaxos): pl. κρέα *IG*1².84. 26, etc.; gen. κρεῶν Od.15.98, Hdt.1.73, *IG*1².10.7, Ar.*Ra*.191, etc.; Ep. κρειῶν Il.11.551, al., κρεάων [ᾰ] *h.Merc*.130; dat. κρέασι Il.12. 311, κρέεσσι Orac.ap.Hdt.1.47, κρεάεσσι Epic. in *Arch.Pap*.7.4. [κρέᾰ Hom., E.*Cyc*.126, Ar.*V*.363, al., κρέ' elided Od.3.65, 470, Ar.*Th*. 558, κρέᾱ Antiph.20 (s.v.l.).]:—*flesh, meat*, Od.8.477, etc.: ἄρνειον κ. piece of lamb, Pherecr.45, cf. Ar.*Pl*.1137; ἐρίφειον Antiph.222.6; τρία κρέα [ἢ] καὶ πλεῖω X.*Cyr*.2.2.2; τέτταρα.. κρέα μικρά Antiph. 172.3 (anap.): pl., mostly in collect. sense, *dressed meat*, Od.3.65, etc.; κ. ἑφθά Hdt.3.23; κ. ἀνάβραστα, ὠπτημένα, Ar.*Ra*.553, *Pl*.894; κ. ὀρνίθεια Id.*Nu*.339; βοῶν Id.*Pax*1280; βόεια Pl.*R*.338c; δαῖτα παιδείων κρεῶν A.*Ag*.1242, 1593; κ. Ἀθηναίοις μερίζειν, νέμειν τῷ δήμῳ, *IG*2².334.15, 24. 2. *carcass*: hence, *body, person*, τοὐδε τοῦ κρέως (i.e. ἐμοῦ) S. l.c. (satyric): in Com. addresses, like κάρα, ὦ δεξιώτατον κρέας Ar.*Eq*.421, cf. 457: prov., ὁ λαγὼς τὸν περὶ τῶν κρεῶν [δρόμον] τρέχει 'to save one's bacon', Zen.4.85, cf. Plu.2.1087b; so νεναυμάχηκε τὴν περὶ τῶν κρεῶν Ar.*Ra*.191, v. Sch. (κρεϝας, cf. Skt. *kravís* 'raw meat', Lat. *cruor*.)

**κρεγμός**, ὁ, (κρέκω) *sound of stringed instruments*, Epich.109 (pl.), A.R.4.909, cf. Poll.4.63.

**κρεηδόκος**, ον, = κρειοδόκος, *AP*6.101 (Phil.).

**κρεη-φᾰγέω**, v. κρεοφαγέω. **-φάγος** [ᾰ], = κρεοφάγος, Porph. *in Cat.*84.15.

**κρειοδόκος**, ον, *containing flesh*, *AP*6.306.8 (Aristo).

**κρεῖον**, τό, (κρέας) *meat-tray, dresser*, Il.9.206 :—Ion. **κρήϊον** Hsch. II. = κρέας, Euph.155.

**κρεῖος**, ὁ, v. κριός III, VII. **κρείουσα**, ἡ, v. κρείων.

**κρειοφάγος**, f.l. for κριο-, Nic.*Th.*50.

**κρεΐσκος**, ὁ, Dim. of κρέας, *morsel of meat*, Alex.189.

**κρεισσονεύω**, *to be better*, Hdn.*Epim.*69.

**κρεισσότεκνος**, ον, *dearer than children*, ὄμματα dub. in A.*Th.*784 (lyr.).

**κρεισσόω**, = κρεισσονεύω, *EM*299.22, Eust.64.15.

**κρείσσων**, ον, gen. ονος, as always in Ep. and old Att.; later Att. **κρείττων**; Ion. **κρέσσων** Hp.*Fract.*3, al., v.l. in Dionys.Trag. (v. infr. II); Dor. **κάρρων** (q.v.); Cret. **κάρτων** *Leg.Gort.*1.15 :—Comp. of κρατύς (v. κράτιστος), *stronger, mightier*, κ. βασιλεύς, ὅτε χώσεται ἀνδρὶ χέρηϊ Il.1.80; esp. in battle, κρείσσοσιν ἶφι μάχεσθαι 21.486; Διὸς κ. νόος ἤέ περ ἀνδρῶν 16.688; κεραυνοῦ κρέσσον..βέλος Pi.*I.*8(7).36, cf. Hdt.7.172, Hp. l.c., etc.; κρείσσων χεῖρας Antipho 4.4.7; τὸ τοῦ κ. συμφέρον Pl.*R.*338c, cf. Democr.267: hence, *having the upper hand, superior*, ὁππότερος δέ κε νικήσῃ κ. τε γένηται Il.3.71; κ. ἀρετῇ τε βίῃ τε 23.578: as Law-term, of witnesses, κάρτοναvs ἦμεν *prevail*, *Leg. Gort.* l.c. 2. freq. as Comp. of ἀγαθός, *better*, κρέσσονες one's *betters*, esp. in point of rank, Pi.*O.*10(11).39, *N.*10.72 (but also, *the stronger, more powerful*, E.*Or.*710, Th.1.8, etc.); ἐς τοὺς τοκέας καὶ ἐς τοὺς κρέσσονας τεθυμῶσθαι Hdt.3.52, cf. *SIG*685.134 (Magn. Mae., ii B.C.); οἱ κ. corps of guards at Thebes, Plu.2.598e; κρείσσονες θεοί, of the *greater* gods, as opp. to Oceanus, A.*Pr.*902 (lyr.); ὁ κ. Ζεύς Id. *Ag.*60 (anap.); οἱ κ. the *Higher Powers*, Id.*Fr.*10, Pl.*Sph.*216b, *Euthd.*291a, etc.; τὰ κρείσσω, = τὰ θεῖα, E.*Ion* 973; τὸ κ. the *Almighty, Providence*, *Corp.Herm.*18.11, Jul.*Ep.*204, Agath.1.16, Procop.Gaz. *Pan.*p.492; τὰ κρείσσονα one's *advantages*, τὰ ὑπάρχοντα ἡμῖν κρείσσω καταπροδοῦναι Th.4.10. 3. c. inf., οὔ τις ἐμεῖο κρείσσων..δόμεναι no one has *a better right* to.., Od.21.345; οὐκ ἄλλος κ. παραμυθεῖσθαι Pl. *Plt.*268b; κρεῖσσόν ἐστι c. inf., 'tis *better* to.., κ. γάρ ἐστιν εἰσάπαξ θανεῖν ἢ..πάσχειν κακῶς A.*Pr.*750, cf. 624, Hdt.3.52, etc.; τὸ μὴ εἶναι κ. ἢ τὸ ζῆν κακῶς S.*Fr.*488, cf. Apollod.Com.6; also κρείσσων εἰμί c. part., κ. γὰρ ἦσθα μηκέτ' ὢν ἢ ζῶν τυφλός thou wert *better* not alive, than living blind, S.*OT*1368, cf. *Aj.*635 (lyr.); κ. ἦν ὁ ἀγὼν μὴ γεγενημένος Aeschin.1.192, cf. D.H.6.9. II. c. gen. or ἤ, *too great for, surpassing, beyond*, ὕψος κ. ἐκπηδήματος A.*Ag.*1376; of evil deeds, κρείσσον' ἀγχόνης *too bad* for hanging, S.*OT*1374; κρεῖσσον δεργμάτων *too bad* to look on, E.*Hipp.*1217; θαυμάτων Id.*Ba.*667; λέγε τι σιγῆς κρεῖσσον (κρέσσον *PSI*9.1093) ἢ σιγὴν ἔχε Dionys.Trag. 6; κρείσσον' ἢ λέξαι λόγῳ τολμήματα E.*Supp.*844; κ. ἢ λόγοισιν (sc. εἰπεῖν) Id.*IT*837; ἀναρχία κ. πυρός Id.*Hec.*608; πρᾶγμα ἐλπίδος κ. γεγενημένον *worse* than one expected, Th.2.64; κ. λόγου τὸ κάλλος X.*Mem.*3.11.1; κ. τῆς ἡμετέρας δυνάμεως Id.*Cyr.*7.5.9. III. *having control over, master of*, esp. of desires and passions, τῶν ἡδονῶν Democr.214; τοῦ ἔρωτος X.*Cyr.*6.1.34; γαστρὸς καὶ κερδέων ib.4.2.45; αὑτῶν *over* themselves, Pl.*Phdr.*232a, al.; κ. χρημάτων *superior to* the influence of money, Th.2.60, Isoc.1.19; τῶν συμμάχων κ. X. *Ath.*2.1; also, *putting oneself above*, κ. τοῦ δικαίου Th.3.84; κρείσσους ὄντες..τῷ λογισμῷ ἐς τὸ ἀνέλπιστον τοῦ βεβαίου having reasoned themselves into an absolute belief of the hopelessness of certainty, ib.83; φαύλους καὶ κρείττους τῆς παιδείας, = οὓς παιδευθῆναι ἀδύνατον (just below), Arist.*Pol.*1316$^{a}$9. IV. *better, more excellent*, ἁρμονίη ἀφανὴς φανερῆς κ. Heraclit.54; κ. ἐπ' ἀρετήν Democr.181; ὁ κρείττων λόγος (opp. ὁ ἥσσων) Ar.*Nu.*113; κατὰ τὸ κ. in a *higher* sense, opp. κατὰ τὸ χεῖρον, Dam.*Pr.*7. V. Adv. κρεισσόνως Antipho 4.4.6, Iamb.*Myst.*7.4; also κρεῖσσον S.*OT*176 (lyr.), *OGI*90.31 (Rosetta, ii B.C.). (κρέσσων from κρέτ-yων, cf. κρέτος; κάρτων and κάρρων from κάρτ-yων, cf. κάρτος; κρείσσων (like μείζων) prob. took ει from ὀλείζων.)

**κρειττ-όομαι**, Pass., of the vine, *to be diseased, have excrescences*, Thphr.*HP*4.14.6, *CP*5.9.13 :—Subst. **-ωσις**, εως, ἡ, ibid.

⊛ **κρείων**, οντος, ὁ, *ruler, lord, master*, Ep. word, used in Il. mostly of kings and chiefs, esp. of Agamemnon, 1.130, al. (Com. in parody, of Diomedes, Cratin.68); of gods, ὕπατε κρειόντων, of Zeus, Il.8.31, etc.; of Poseidon, εὐρὺ κ. ἐνοσίχθων 11.751; as an honorary epithet, κ. Ἐτεωνεύς, of a squire of Menelaus, Od.4.22 :—so fem. **κρείουσα** (once in Hom.), κρείουσα γυναικῶν, of a concubine of Priam, Il.22.48; Ἀντιόπη κ. *queen* Antiope, Hes.*Fr.*110.6, cf. Call. *Del.*219; Dor. κρείοισα Theoc.17.132 :—after Hom. in the form **κρέων**, Pi.*P.*8.99, *N.*3.10, 7.45; of Zeus, A.*Supp.*574 (lyr.) :—fem. **κρέουσα**, B.3.1: hence pr. n. Κρέων, Κρέουσα. (A participial form (κρείειν γὰρ τὸ ἄρχειν ἔλεγον οἱ παλαιοί Artem.2.12): κρείων may be due to metrical lengthening or represent *κρήων.)

**κρειῶν**, Ep. gen. pl. of κρέας.

**κρεκάδια**, ων, τά, a kind of *tapestry*, Ar.*V.*1215.

**κρέκελος**· θρῆνος, Hsch.

**κρεκτός**, ή, όν, *struck so as to sound*, of stringed instruments: generally, *played, sung*, νόμος A.*Ch.*822 (lyr.), cf. S.*Fr.*463.

**κρέκω**, *weave*, ἱστόν Sapph.90; πέπλους E.*El.*542. 2. *strike* a stringed instrument with the plectron, μάγαδιν Diog.Ath.1.10; βάρβιτα D.H.7.72: generally, *play on* any instrument, αὐλόν Ar.*Av.*682 (lyr.): less freq. c. dat., κρέκειν δόνακι *APl.*4.231 (Anyte): c. acc. cogn., πηκτίδων ψαλμοῖς κ. ὕμνον Telest.5; λωτὸς ᾠδὰν κρέκει *Pae. Delph.*12; ἐν κιθάρᾳ νόμον ἔκρεκον *AP*9.584. 3. of any sharp noise, βοὴν πτεροῖς κ. Ar.*Av.*772 (lyr.), cf. *AP*7.192 (Mnasalc.); κίσσα κρέξασα ἁρμονίαν ib.191 (Arch.), cf. Hp.ap.Gal.19.114. (Cf. ONorse *hræll* (**hrahilaz*) 'weaver's sley', OE. *hrægel* 'dress', 'garment', perh. Lett. *krekls* 'shirt'.)

**κρεμ-άθρα**, ἡ, *rope hung from a hook*, Arist.*Rh.*1412$^{a}$14; οὑπὶ τῆς κ. ἀνήρ, of Socrates, Ar.*Nu.*218 (*basket* or *fowl-perch*, Sch.). ⊛ **-άννῡμι**, Pl.*Lg.*830b, etc.; **-ύω**, Arist.*HA*612$^{a}$10, Thphr.*CP*4.3.3; **κρεμάω**, Arist.*Mir.*831$^{a}$8, Ael.*NA*5.3, etc.; **κρεμνάω**, Demetr.*Eloc.*216, *Gp.*4.15.15; **κρεμάζω**, Lxx *Jb.*26.7 (v.l. κρεμνῶν): pres. part. **κρεμάντες** Ath.1.25d: fut. κρεμάσω [ᾰ] Alc.Com.8, Lxx *Ge.*40.19; Att. κρεμῶ, ᾷς, ᾷ, Ar.*Pl.*312 (lyr.); Ep. κρεμόω Il.7.83: aor. 1 ἐκρέμᾰσα Ar.*Th.*1028, Ep. and Lyr. κρέμασα Od.8.67, Pi.*P.*4.192; Dor. inf. κραμάσαι *IG*4$^{2}$(1).122.3 (Epid.); pf. κεκρέμᾰκα Corn.*ND*17 :—**Med.**, aor. inf. κρεμάσασθαι Hes.*Op.*629, subj. ἐκ-κρεμάσωμαι *AP*5.91 (Rufin.) :—**Pass.**, **κρέμαμαι**, Pi.*P.*5.34, Ar.*Av.*1387 (also κρεμᾶται *Anacreont.*16.17); inf. κρέμασθαι Hp.*VM*10, *Acut.*30, Antiph.74.4; subj. κρέμωμαι Hp.*Art.*70, Arist.*Rh.*1415$^{a}$13; opt. κρεμαίμην Ar.*Ach.*945, *V.*298, *Nu.*870: impf. ἐκρεμάμην, ω, ατο, Il.15.21, etc.: fut. κρεμήσομαι in pass. sense, Ar.*Ach.*279, *V.*808, *PCair.Zen.*202.9 (iii B.C.): aor. ἐκρεμάσθην Ar.*Th.*1053, etc.: pf. imper. κεκρεμάσθω Apollod. *Poliorc.*181.7, v.l. in Archim.*Quadr.*13: plpf. κατα-κεκρέμαστο D.S. 18.26. (Cf. κρημνός, Goth. *hramjan* 'crucify'): I. *hang up*, σειρὴν..ἐξ οὐρανόθεν κρεμάσαντες Il.8.19; τόξον ἐκ πίτυος A.*Fr.*251; ἀπὸ κάλω κ. σαυτόν Ar.*Ra.*122; καὶ κρεμόω προτὶ νηόν will bring them to the temple and *hang them up* there as an offering, Il. 7.83; κ. τινὰ τῶν ὄρχεων Ar.*Pl.*312; κ. [τὰς ὗς] τῶν ὀπισθίων σκελῶν *by* the hind legs, Arist.*HA*632$^{a}$23; κρεμάσας τὸ νόημα, in allusion to Socrates in his basket, Ar.*Nu.*229, cf. Alex.126.17; κρεμάσαι τὴν ἀσπίδα *hang up* one's shield, i.e. have done with war, Ar.*Ach.*58; τὴν πανοπλίαν Id.*Av.*436 :—so in Med., πηδάλιον κρεμάσασθαι *hang up one's* rudder, i.e. give up the sea, Hes.*Op.*629. 2. *hang*, τινα Arist.*Pol.*1311$^{b}$39, *Oec.*1352$^{a}$11; *crucify*, Plu.*Caes.*2, etc. II. Pass., *to be hung up, suspended*, ὅτε τ' ἐκρέμω (2 sg. impf.) ὑψόθεν when *thou wert hanging*, Il.15.18, cf. 21; μηδ' ὁ Ταντάλου λίθος τῆσδ' ὑπὲρ νήσου κρεμάσθω Archil.53; *to be hung up* as a votive offering, Pi.*P.*5.34, cf. Hdt.1.34, 66, etc.; τὰ σπλάγχνα οἱ δοκέει κρέμασθαι Hp.*VM*10; κάτω κρέμανται S.*Fr.*431; κρεμήσεται..ἐπὶ τοῦ παττάλου Ar.*V.*808; κ. ἐφ' ἵππων X.*An.*3.2.19; ἐκ ποδῶν κατωκάρα κ. Ar.*Ach.*945; αἱ μέλιτται κ. ἐξ ἀλλήλων Arist.*HA*627$^{b}$13: metaph., ἀμφὶ φρασὶν ἀμπλακίαι κρέμανται Pi.*O.*7.25; μῶμος κρέματαί τινι censure *hangs over* him, ib.6.74; δόλιος αἰὼν ἐπ' ἀνδράσι κ. Id.*I.*8(7).14; κρέμασθαι ἔκ τινος *to be wholly taken up with* a thing, Pl.*Lg.*831c; ὁ ἐκ τοῦ σώματος κρεμάμενος X.*Smp.*8.19. 2. *to be hanged*, of persons, E. *Hipp.*1252, Aristopho 9.10, *PCair.Zen.* l.c. 3. metaph., *to be in suspense*, ἵνα μὴ κρέμηται ἡ διάνοια Arist.*Rh.*1415$^{a}$13; κ. [ὁ λόγος] Gal. 18(2).754. 4. = ὀκλάζω, Arat.65 (ubi v. Sch.). **-άς**, άδος, ἡ, fem. Adj. *beetling*, πέτρα A.*Supp.*795 (lyr.). **-ᾰσία**, *suspendium*, *Gloss.* **-ᾰσις**, εως, ἡ, *hanging up*, Hp.*Art.*74, Orib.8.6.16. **-ασμα**, ατος, τό, = sq., Sch.rec.A.*Pr.*157. ⊛ **-ασμός**, ὁ, *suspension*, of a broken rib, unsupported by reason of the emptiness of the stomach, Hp.*Art.*49: generally, ib.76, Heliod.ap.Orib.49.9.15. **-αστάριον**, τό, *chandelier*, Anon.*in Rh.*211.2. **-αστέον**, *one must hang*, Sor. 1.51, *Gp.*16.1.11. **-αστήρ**, ῆρος, ὁ, *suspender*: οἱ κρεμαστῆρες *the muscles by which the testicles are suspended*, Gal.4.635, 18(2).998, Poll.2.173; = ὄρχεις, *PLips.*42.19 (iv A.D.), *Hippiatr.*30; but, *vasa deferentia*, Ruf.*Onom.*197, *Sat.Gon.*10, Paul.Aeg.6.61; a supposed *muscle suspending the ovaries*, Sor.1.12. 2. *stalk* by which a grape-cluster hangs, *Gp.*5.2.11, 5.17.5. II. = ταρσός I, Eust. 1625.14. **-αστός**, ή, όν, *hung, suspended*, γυνή S.*OT*1263; κ. αὐχένος *hung by* the neck, Id.*Ant.*1221: c. gen., *hung from* or *on* a thing, παραστάδος κρεμαστὰ τεύχη E.*Andr.*1122; κ. ἀρτάνη, i.e. a halter, S.*OT*1266; βρόχοι κ. E.*Hipp.*779; σκεύη κ. the *rigging* of ships, opp. ξύλινα σκ., X.*Oec.*8.12; τὰ κ. ἱστία Hermipp.63.12; κλινίδιον κ. *hammock*, Plu.*Per.*27; κ. ποτιστρέα *PTeb.*527 (ii A.D.); κ. σταφυλή, i.e. dried grapes, Alex.Trall.8.1; οἱ κ. κῆποι *hanging* gardens, Plu.2.342b; κ. παράδεισος Beros.ap.J.*AJ*10.11.1; κρεμαστά, τά, *fortresses*, Lxx *Jd.*6.2. **-άστρα**, ἡ, Hellen. for κρεμάθρα (Moer. p.242 P.), Eust.1625.17, v.l. in Arist.*Rh.*1412$^{a}$14. 2. *stalk by which a flower hangs*, Thphr.*HP*3.16.4. **-αστρον**, τό, *larder*, *Gloss.* **-άω**, v. κρεμάννυμι.

⊛ **κρέμβᾰλ-α**, τά, *castanets*, *Carm.Pop.*3. **-ῐάζω**, *mark time with castanets*, Hermipp.31 (-ίζουσι codd. Ath.), cf. Hsch. ⊛ **-ῐαστύς**, ύος, ἡ, *rattling with castanets*, to give the time in dancing, *h.Ap.*162 (v.l. -αστής, οῦ, ὁ).

**κρέμβολα**, τά, *bobbins, reels*, Hsch. **κρέμ⟨μ⟩υον**, τό, = κρόμμυον, Id. **κρεμόω**, Ep. fut. of κρεμάννυμι. **κρέμυς**, υος, ἡ, = χρέμυς, Arist.*Fr.*294. **κρεμών**, = ἀκρεμών, Eratosth.27. **κρέννω**, Thessal. for κρίνω (q.v.).

**κρέξ**, ἡ, gen. κρεκός, a long-legged bird, perh. *corn-crake, Rallus crex*, or *ruff, Machetes pugnax*, τούτους (sc. λίθους) ἐτύκιζον αἱ κρέκες τοῖς ῥύγχεσιν Ar.*Av.*1138, cf. Arist.*PA*695$^{a}$22, Ael.*NA*4.5; sacred to Athena, Porph.*Abst.*3.5; [ἡ ἶβις] μέγαθος ὅσον κ. Hdt.2.76; a name of ill omen to the newly-married, Euph.4: hence διαάρπαγος κρέξ, of Helen, Lyc.513. 2. metaph., *noisy braggart*, Eup. 423. II. *hair*, Hsch., Suid.: acc. κρέκαν Eust.1528.18.

**κρεο-**, representing stem of κρέας in Compds., freq. written κρεω- in codd.

**κρεο-βορέω**, *eat flesh*, D.S.24.1 (κρεω-). ⊛ **-βόρος**, ον, *fed on flesh*, A.*Supp.*287 (Abresch for κρεόβροτος). **-δαισία**, ἡ, *distribution*

*of meat*, Demetr.Sceps.ap.Ath.10.425c, Plu.2.643a. **-δαιτέω,** *distribute meat*, Zonar. **-δαίτης,** ου, ὁ, *distributor of meat, carver at a public meal*, Plu.*Lys.*23, *Ages.*8, Poll.6.34, 7.25: κρεω , Phld.*Vit.* p.26 J.:—fem. **κρεοδαῖτις** ἀρχή Poll.6.34. **-δείρα,** ἡ, (δείρω) *flaying-knife*, Id.7.25 (κρεωδ- codd.). **-δοσία,** ἡ, = κρεοδαισία, Zonar., v.l. in Plu.*Demetr.*11: **-δοτέω,** Zonar.: **-δότης,** ου, ὁ, = κρεοδαίτης, *CIG* 4485 (Palmyra), Suid. **-δόχος,** ον, = κρειοδόκος, Sch.Il.9.206, Hsch. s.v. κρήϊον, *EM*536.57 (κρεω-). **-θέτης,** ου, ὁ, *butcher*, *Gloss.* (κρεω- cod.). **-θηκάριος,** ὁ, *one who has charge of the larder*, title of priest, *Supp.Epigr.*4.357 (Panamara). **-θήκη,** ἡ, *larder*, Hsch. s.v. κρήϊνον. **-κάκκαβος,** *a mess of meat hashed with fat and blood*, Ath.9.384d. **-κοπέω,** *cut up like meat*: hence, *hack in pieces*, κ. δυστήνων μέλη A.*Pers.*463; μέλη ξένων E.*Cyc.*359 (lyr.). **-κόπος,** ὁ, *cutter up of flesh*, D.H.12.2.8 (pl.), *Gloss.* **-ποιός,** ὁ, *butcher*, ib. **-πωλέω,** *deal in butcher's meat*, Poll.6.33, 7.25. **-πώλης,** ου, ὁ, *seller of meat, butcher*, Macho ap.Ath.13.580c, cf. *AP*11.212 (Lucill.), Thphr.*Char.*9.4 (κρεω-). **-πωλικός,** ή, όν, *of* or *for a butcher*, τράπεζα Plu.2.643a:—fem. **-πωλις** ἀγορά *the meat* market, Hsch. s.v. κάπηλα. ⊛**-πώλιον,** τό, *butcher's shop*, D.S.12.24, Str.17.2.4, Plu.2.277e, Poll.7.25. **-σιτέω,** *live on meat*, Id.6.33. **-στάθμη,** ἡ, *butcher's steelyard*, Ar.*Fr.*799. **-τομέω,** = κρεοκοπέω, Tz.*H.*13.410.

⊛**κρεουργ-έω,** *cut up like a butcher*, J.*AJ*13.12.6: hence, *butcher, mangle*, Luc.*Syr.D.*55, D.L.9.108:—Pass., Ph.2.544, D.C.75.7. **-ηδόν,** Adv. *like a butcher, in pieces*, τοὺς ἄνδρας κ. διασπᾶν Hdt. 3.13 (Ion. κρεοργ-). **-ία,** ἡ, *cutting up, butchering*, Πέλοπος Luc. *Salt.*54. **-ικός,** ή, όν, *of* or *for a butcher* or *his trade*, *Gloss.* **-ός,** όν, *working*, i.e. *cutting up, meat*: κρεουργὸν ἦμαρ a day *of slaughter and feasting*, A.*Ag.*1592. **II.** Subst. κ., ὁ, *butcher* or *carver*, Poll. 7.25.

**κρεο-φᾰγέω,** Ion. **κρεηφ-,** *eat flesh*, Hp.*Salubr.*7, Plb.2.17.10 (v.l. κρεα-), Str.16.4.17, Ph.2.398 (vv.ll. κρεω-, κρεη-):—Pass., κάμηλοι κρεοφαγούμεναι D.S.2.54. **-φαγία,** Ion. **κρεηφᾰγίη,** ἡ, *eating of flesh*, Hp.*Acut.*37, D.S.3.31, Ph.2.235 (vv.ll. κρεω-, κρεη-), Porph. *Abst.*1.15, al.; κ. τῶν θηρίων Str.16.4.9; χρῆσθαι κρεοφαγίᾳ Plu.2. 132a (κρεω-). ⊛**-φάγος** [ᾰ], ον, *eating flesh, carnivorous*, Hdt.4.186, Arist.*PA*693ᵃ3, etc.; cf. κρεηφάγος.

**κρέσσων,** v. κρείσσων.

**κρετέω, κρέτος,** Aeol. for κρατέω, κράτος (qq.v.).

**κρεω-,** v. κρεο-.

**κρεώδης,** ες, *fleshy*, Arist.*HA*491ᵇ25, 583ᵇ10; ὀσμὴ κ. odour *of flesh*, Thphr.*Fr.*167; κ. τροφή *meat* diet, Gal.10.849; τὰ κ. Id.6.600.

**κρέων,** v. κρείων.

**κρεών,** ὁ, *larder*, *Gloss.* (dub.).

⊛**κρήγῠος,** ον, Dor. **κράγῠος** [ᾱ] Cerc.7.14, Lysis *Ep.*3:—*good, useful* or *agreeable*, once in Hom., οὐ πώ ποτέ μοι τὸ κ. εἶπας Il.1.106; ἄλλο μὲν οὐδὲν κ. *AP*7.284 (Asclep.); οὐδὲ γουνάτων πόνος κρήγυον *a good symptom*, Hp.*Coac.*31; τό τοι μέγα κρήγυον ἔσται Nic.*Th.*935; ποτὶ οὐδὲν κράγυον σχολάζοντες Lysis l.c. Adv. κρηγύως ἐπαιδεύθην Call.*Iamb.*1.196; νομίμως καὶ κ. *honourably*, Perict.ap.Stob.4.28. 19. **2.** by a misunderstanding of Hom., *true, real*, εἴπατέ μοι τὸ κ. Theoc.20.19, cf. Hp.*Ep.*17, *AP*7.648 (Leon.), Anon.ap.Stob.3. 28.21: as Adv., *in good earnest*, πορθεῖς με τὸ κ. *AP*5.57 (Arch.). **3.** of persons, *good, serviceable*, οὐκ ἐπίστανται, οὐδὲ κ. διδάσκαλοί εἰσι Pl.*Alc.*1.111e; εἰ δ' ἐσσὶ κ. τε καὶ παρὰ χρηστῶν Theoc.*Ep.*19; παρ' οἴνῳ κ. *AP*7.355 (Damag.); esp. of a woman, *honest*, Herod.4.46, 6.39.

**κρηδεμνόκομος,** ον, *wearing the* κρήδεμνον, Aus.*Ep.*8.13.

⊛**κρήδεμνον,** Dor. **κρᾱδ-,** τό, (κράς, δέω) *woman's head-dress* or *veil*, a kind of *mantilla*, κ. ὅ ῥά οἱ (sc. Ἀνδρομάχῃ) δῶκε χρυσέη Ἀφροδίτη Il.22.470; κρηδέμνῳ δ' ἐφύπερθε καλύψατο δῖα θεάων 14.184: pl., [Πηνελόπεια] ἄντα παρειάων σχομένη λιπαρὰ κ. Od.1.334; δμωαί τε καὶ αὐτή,.. ἀπὸ κ. βαλοῦσαι 6.100, cf. E.*Ph.*1490 (lyr.). **II.** metaph. in pl., *battlements* which *crown* a city's walls, Τροίης ἱερὰ κ. Il.16.100, cf. Od.13.388, *h.Cer.*151, B.*Fr.*16.7; πέτρινα κ. E.*Tr.*508: sg., Θήβης κρήδεμνον Hes.*Sc.*105. **2.** *cover, lid* of a wine-jar, Od.3.392.

⊛**κρήδεσμον·** κεφαλόδεσμον, Hsch. **κρηῆναι, κρήηνον,** v. κραίνω. **κρηθεῖν·** κατολογεῖν, Id. **κρῆθεν,** Adv., v. κράς II.

**κρῆθμον,** τό, *samphire, Crithmum maritimum*, Hp.*Nat.Mul.*2, al., Call.*Fr.*64, Lyc.238 (pl., accented κρηθμοῖσι), Nic.*Th.*909. (Neut. in Dsc.2.129, Ruf.*Ren.Ves.*1.18 (pl.); masc. **κρῆθμος,** ὁ, Eust.582. 16, *crethmus* Plin.*HN*26.158; **κρίθμος** (sic), Hdn.Gr.1.167.)

⊛**κρή-ϊνον,** τό, *larder*, Hsch. (s.v.l.). **-ϊον,** τό, Ion. for κρεῖον, kind of *bride-cake*, Philet.ap.Ath.14.645d: pl., = ζῴδια (i.e. cakes in shape of animals), Hsch. **II.** v. κρεῖον I.

**κρημν-άω,** = κρήμνημι, D.L.6.50, *PHolm.*8.11 (κριμ-). **-ηγορέω,** (κρημνός) *speak rugged words*, Tz. ad Hes.*Op.*p.10 G. ⊛**-ημι,** = κρεμάννυμι, *hang*, ἄγκυραν ποτὶ..ναὶ κρημνάντων Pi.*P.*4.25, cf. Arist.*Mir.* 831ᵃ8 (v.l.); κρήμνη (imper.) σεαυτὴν ἐκ.. ἀντηρίδος E.*Fr.*1111 (= Eup.455); *crucify*, τούσδε ἐκρήμνη (impf.) App.*Mith.*97:—Pass., κρήμναμαι *hang, be suspended*, E.*El.*1217 (lyr., κριμν-), App.*BC*1.71; *float in air*, ὑπερθ' ὀμμάτων κρημναμενᾶν νεφελᾶν A.*Th.*229 (lyr.). **-ίζω,** *hurl down headlong*, κατὰ τοῦ τείχους Lxx 2*Ma.*6.10: metaph., ἐπὶ ἀτάκτους ἡδονὰς ἑαυτοὺς κ. Plu.2.5b:—Pass., J.*BJ*2.3.3, *Cat.Cod. Astr.*8(4).156. **-ισις,** εως, ἡ, *hurling down headlong*, Sch.Th. 7.45. ⊛**-ισμός,** ὁ, = foreg., Ptol.*Tetr.*151, Doroth. in *Cat.Cod.Astr.* 5(3).84 (pl.).

**κρημνο-βᾰτέω,** *haunt precipices*, Ctes.ap.Lyd.*Mens.*4.14, Str.15. 1.56, Ph.2.444, S.E.*M.*11.126, Longus 3.28. ⊛**-βάτης** [ᾰ], ου, Dor. **-ᾱς,** ὁ, *climber of steeps*, Πάν *AP*9.142, cf. Polyaen.4.3.29. **2.** *rope-dancer*, Hsch. **-γρᾰφος,** ον, *written in rugged style, uncouth*, ῥήματα Tz. ad Hes.*Op.*p.9 G.

**κρημνο-κοπέω,** *boast, indulge in 'tall talk'*, Phot., Suid. **-ποιός,** όν, *speaking crags*, i.e. *using big, rugged words*, of Aeschylus, Ar.*Nu.* 1367.

⊛**κρημνός** (A), ὁ, heterocl. pl. **κρημνά,** τά, v.l. for κρημνούς in Eus. Mynd.63:—*overhanging bank*, in Hom. (only Il.) of the *bank* of a river, *edge* of a trench, 12.54, 21.175, 234, 244, cf. Pi.*O.*3.22; κ. θαλάσσας Id.*Fr.*201; κ. μαλακοί Arist.*HA*615ᵇ31; later, *beetling cliff, crag*, ἀπὸ τοῦ κ. ὠθέειν Hdt.4.103; ἀναθεῖναι ἐπὶ κρημνόν τιν' Ar.*Pl.*69; κατὰ τῶν κ. ἅλλεσθαι down from the *cliffs* of Epipolae, Th.7.45; κατὰ κ. ῥιφέντες Pl.*Lg.*944a; οἱ K., the *Screes*, on the Sea of Azof, Hdt.4.20, 110. **2.** in pl., *edges* of an ulcer, Hp.*Loc.Hom.*29. **3.** *labia pudendi*, ib.47, Poll.2.174, Ruf.*Onom.*112.

**κρημνός** (B), v. κριμνός.

**κρημνοφοβέομαι,** *to be afraid of precipices*, Hp.*Ep.*19 (*Hermes* 53. 70).

**κρημν-ώδης,** ες, *precipitous*, Th.7.84, Dsc.4.144, Onos.10.17, etc.; τὸ κ. τῆς ὄχθης Plu.*Tim.*31: Sup., Hdn.6.5.5. **-ώρεια,** ἡ, *steep mountain-ridge*, Hdn.*Epim.*232.

**κρημοφόρος,** ὁ, dub. sens., οἰνοχόαι καὶ κρημοφόροι *IG*2².1425.358.

**κρην-άγγη·** ἀρχὴ ἐπὶ τῆς ἐπιμελείας ὕδατος, Hsch. ⊛**-αῖος,** α, ον, (κρήνη) *of, from a spring* or *fountain*, Νύμφαι κρηναῖαι, = Κρηνιάδες, Od.17. 240; κ. ὕδωρ *spring* water, Hdt.4.181; ποτόν S.*Tr.*14, *Ph.*21; νασμοί E.*Hipp.*225 (anap.); γάνος, i.e. the water of Dirce, A.*Pers.*483; λιβάδες *AP*9.549 (Antiphil.); K. πύλαι the gate *of Dirce* (v. Sch.), E.*Ph.* 1123. ⊛**-η,** Dor. **κράνα** *IG*4²(1).121.6 (Epid.), etc.; Aeol. **κράννα** ib.12(2).103 (Mytil.): ἡ:—*well, spring, fountain*, μελάνυδρος, καλλιρέεθρος, Il.16.3, Od.10.107, cf. Pi.*P.*1.39, al., Pl.*Phd.*112c, etc.; opp. φρέαρ (q.v.), Hdt.4.120, Th.2.48; ἐμπλησαμένη τὴν ὑδρίαν.. ἀπὸ κρήνης Ar.*Lys.*328; κ. οἴνου E.*Ba.*707; ὀμνύω.. κράνας καὶ ποταμοὺς *SIG* 527.34 (Dreros, iii B.C.): poet. in pl., for *water*, S.*OC*686, *Ant.*844 (both lyr.); κρηνῶν ἐπιμελητής, title of official at Athens, *IG*2².338. 11, Arist.*Ath.*43.1, cf. Pl.*Lg.*758e, Arist.*Pol.*1321ᵇ26, *OGI*483.159 (Pergam.). **-ηθεν,** Adv. *from a well* or *spring*, *AP*15.25.18 (Besant.). **-ήϊος,** ον, = κρηναῖος, metaph., of the source of things, ἀρχή Orac.ap.Dam.*Pr.*344. **-ηνδε,** Adv. *to a well* or *spring*, Od. 20.154. **-ιάς,** άδος, ἡ, pecul. fem. of κρηναῖος, Νύμφαι Κρηνιάδες A.*Fr.*168 (hex.). **-ίδιον,** τό, Dim. of κρήνη, Arist.*Mir.*841ᵇ9, Antig. *Mir.*142, etc. **-ίον,** τό, = foreg., *Inscr.Délos* 290.75 (iii B.C.), Str.3. 4.17, *IGRom.*4.1657 (Almura). **-ίς,** ῖδος, ἡ, = κρήνη, E.*Hipp.*208 (anap.), Call.*Fr.anon.*98, Theoc.1.22 (Dor. κρᾶν-), D.H.1.32. **II.** pl. Κρηνῖδες, αἱ, ancient name for Philippi in Macedonia, Str.7 *Fr.*34, App.*BC*4.105; τὰ ἐγ Κρηνῖσιν, as local place-name, *IG*12(5).544 *B*2. 47 (Ceos). ⊛**-ῖτις,** ιδος, ἡ, *growing near a spring*, βοτάναι Hp.*Ep.* 16. **-ῶν·** καρηβαρῶν, Hsch. **-οῦχος,** ον, *ruling over springs*, of Poseidon, Corn.*ND*22.

**κρηνο-φῠλάκιον** [ᾰ], τό, *office of the* κρηνοφύλαξ, Poll.8.113. **-φύλαξ** [ῠ], ακος, ὁ, *warden of the springs*, *IG*11(2).159 *A*61, 161 *A*85 (Delos, iii B.C.); at Athens, *official in charge of the* κλεψύδρα, Poll.8. 113, Phot. **2.** bronze lion *which stood over the spring that supplied the* κλεψύδρα, Poll. l.c., Phot.

**κρηπῑδ-αῖον,** τό, *basement of a house*, Lys.*Fr.*185 S.:—also **-ειον,** *IG*14.915 (Ostia). ⊛**-ιαῖος,** α, ον, *belonging to a substructure* or *foundation*, [λίθοι] ib.1².313.90, cf. *Rev.Phil.*50.67 (Didyma, ii B.C.). ⊛**-ιον,** τό, Dim. of κρηπίς, *kerb*, ib.43.213, *Cinquantenaire de l'école des hautes études* p.89 (Didyma, ii B.C., pl.).

**κρηπῑδοποιός,** ὁ, *boot-maker*, Ath.13.568e.

**κρηπῑδ-ουργός,** οῦ, ὁ, = foreg., Din.*Fr.*89.20. **-όω,** (κρηπίς) *furnish with boots*:—Pass., *put on one's boots*, Anon.ap.Suid. **2.** *furnish with a quay*, D.C.60.11; *furnish with a foundation, found*, Id. 51.1:—Pass., *to be supported*, ἐπὶ θατέρου σκέλους Plu.2.233b. **-ωμα,** ατος, τό, *foundation*, *Inscr.Magn.*293, *JHS*15.127 (Termessus), D.S. 13.82, Aq.*Ez.*43.14.

⊛**κρηπίς,** ῖδος, ἡ, *man's high boot* (cf. *AB*273), *half-boot*, Hegem. *Parod.*4, X.*Eq.*12.10, Thphr.*Char.*2.7 (dub.): distd. from ὑποδήματα, Aristocl.Hist.8; κ. λευκαί, a mark of effeminacy, Timae.82. **b.** κρηπῖδες *soldiers' boots*, i.e. *soldiers* themselves, Theoc.15.6. **2.** *shoe-shaped cake*, Poll.6.77. **II.** generally, *groundwork, foundation, basement* of a building or altar, Hdt.1.93, S.*Tr.*993 (anap.), E.*Ion* 38 (pl.), *HF*985, X.*An.*3.4.7, *IG*1².372.67; κ. καὶ στυλοβάτας ib.4²(1).102.7 (Epid.); τύμβου 'πὶ κρηπῖδ' E.*Hel.*547: metaph., βάλλεσθαι κρηπῖδα σοφῶν ἐπέων Pi.*P.*4.138; κ. ἀοιδᾶν βαλέσθαι ib.7.3; ἐβάλοντο φαεννὰν κρηπῖδ' ἐλευθερίας Id.*Fr.*77; κ. γένους E.*HF*1261; ἡ ἐγκράτεια ἀρετῆς κ. X.*Mem.*1.5.4, cf. Onos.4.4; οὐδέπω κακῶν κ. ὕπεστιν we have not yet got to the *bottom* of misery, A.*Pers.*815; κ. θαλάσσης Opp.*H.*3.453, 5.48; κ. καὶ ἕδρα νόσου *foundation* and seat of disease, Max.Tyr.13.7. **2.** *walled edge* of a river or canal, *quay*, Hdt.1. 185, 2.170, Plb.5.37.8, *PTeb.*382.9 (i B.C.); *abutment* of a bridge, *Epigr.Gr.*1078.3 (Adana); *tiers* of seats in a theatre, *IG*11(2).203 *A* 95 (Delos, iii B.C.). **III.** *ox-tongue, Helminthia echioides*, Thphr. *HP*7.8.3, Plin.*HN*21.99. **IV.** a bandage, Sor.*Fasc.*59.

⊛**Κρής,** ὁ, gen. Κρητός, mostly in pl. Κρῆτες, ῶν, *Cretan*, Il.2.645, etc.: prov., ὁ Κρὴς τὸν πόντον (sc. ἀγνοεῖ), of those who feign ignorance, Alcm.115, cf. Str.10.4.17:—fem. **Κρῆσσα,** ης, Sapph.54: in pl., title of play by Aeschylus: as Adj., *Cretan*, Κρῆτα τρόπον Simon. 31; Κρὴς ταῦρος Apollod.2.5.7; μητρὸς.. Κρήσσης S.*Aj.*1295:—regul. Adj. **Κρήσιος,** α, ον, Id.*Tr.*119, E.*Hipp.*372 (both lyr.), Limen.39, etc.:—more freq. **Κρητικός,** ή, όν (q.v.).

**κρῆς**, Dor. for κρέας, Sophr.25, Ar.*Ach.*795, Theoc.1.6.

**κρησέρ-α**, ἡ, Ion. **κρησέρη**, Elean **κραάρα** (q. v.), *flour-sieve, bolting-sieve*, Hp.*Steril.*222 (but expld. as a *straining-cloth* by Erot.), Ar.*Ec.*991, Gal.*Nat.Fac.*2.3, Aret.*CA*1.4, Poll.6.74:—Dim. **-ιον**, τό, Id.10.114, Zonar. II. *fine net for fishing*, Phot. **-ίτης** [ῑ] ἄρτος, ὁ, bread *of sifted flour*, Diph.26.

**κρησίαι**· καλλίονες, Hsch. **Κρήσιος**, α, ον v. Κρής. **κρησίπαιδα** (fort. -πεδα)· ἐν Σαμιακῇ θυσίᾳ . . μέρη ἱερείων, Id. ⊛ **Κρῆσσα**, v. Κρής.

⊛ **κρηστήριον**, τό, perh. = κρεῖον 1, *IG*2².1543 (iv B. C.).

⊛ **κρησ-φύγετον** [ῠ], τό, (φεύγω) *place of refuge, retreat*, Hdt.5.124, al., D.H.4.15, Luc.*Eun.*10, al. (Etym. dub.; expld. by *EM*538.1 as *refuge from the Cretan*, i. e. Minos.) **-φύγιον** [ῠ], τό, = foreg., Steph.*in Rh.*253.2.

**Κρηταιεύς**, Att. **Κρηταεύς** *IG*2².687.25: ὁ:—*Cretan*, A.R.1.1129, Plb.6.46.3, *GDI*5160 (Mylasa), *AP*7.448 (Leon.):—fem. **-αιίς**, ίδος, ib.6.299 (Phan.):—also **Κρηταῖος**, α, ον, A.R.2.1233, *AP*14.129.

**κρητάριον**, τό, Dim. of Lat. *creta, piece of chalk*, *Gp.*2.42.2 (κριτ-), Aët.2.10, Charis.p.553 K., *Hippiatr.*49.

⊛ **Κρητάρχης**, ου, ὁ, *president of the κοινόν of Crete*, *CIG*2744 (Aphrodisias).

⊛ **Κρήτη**, ἡ *Crete*, Il.2.649, etc.: pl., Κρητάων εὐρειάων Od.14.199, 16.62: **Κρήτηθεν** or **-θε**, *from Crete*, Il.3.233, Q.S.5.350, Porph. *Abst.*2.21: **Κρήτηνδε** *to Crete*, Od.19.186.

**κρήτη**, ἡ, = Lat. *creta, chalk*, *PMag.Lond.*121.858:—hence prob. **κρητηρία**, ἡ, ib.169; cf. κρητάριον.

**κρητήρ**, ῆρος, ὁ, Ion. and Ep. for κρατήρ (q.v.). **κρητηρίζω**, v. κρατηρίζω.

**Κρητ-ίζω**, (Κρής) *speak like a Cretan*, D.Chr.[11.23]. II. *play the Cretan*, i. e. *lie*, πρὸς Κρῆτας or Κρῆτα κ. 'diamond cut diamond', Plb. 8.18.5, Plu.*Aem.*23, *Lys.*20. ⊛ **-ικός**, ή, όν, *Cretan*, A.*Ch.*616 lyr.), Ar.*Ra.*849, etc.; τὸ Κ. πέλαγος Th.4.53, etc. Adv. **-κῶς** *in Cretan fashion*, Ar.*Ec.*1165. II. **Κρητικόν** sc. ἱμάτιον), τό, *short garment*, used at sacred rites, Id.*Th.*730, Eup.311. 2. **Κρητικός** (sc. πούς), ὁ, a metrical foot [– ⏑ –], = ἀμφίμακρος, Heph.3.2, cf. A.D. *Pron.*50.16; so ἔγειρε . ., Μοῦσα, Κ. μέλος Cratin.222; τὸ Κ. (sc. μέτρον) Heph.13.1; Κ. ῥυθμός, ῥυθμοί, D.H.*Comp.*25, Str.10.4. 16. **-ισμός**, ὁ, *Cretan behaviour*, i. e. *lying*, Plu.*Aem.*26.

⊛ **Κρητογενής**, ὁ, *born in Crete*, epith. of Zeus, *GDI*5075.73 (Latos).

**κρῖ**, τό, Ep. for κριθή, *barley*, only as nom. and acc., κρῖ λευκὸν Il. 8.564, Od.4.41, al.

⊛ **κρῖβᾰν-άριος**, ὁ, in form **κλῖβ-**, *armoured cavalryman*, *Zeitschr. Deutsch.Pal.Vereins*44.93 (Jerusalem, iv/v A. D.), *Stud.Pal* 20.135.4 (vi A. D.), Lyd.*Mag.*1.46; cf. Lat. *clibanarius*, *Cod.Theod.*14.17.9, etc. II. *baker*, dub. in *CIL*4.677, *Stud.Pal.*20.131.4 (vi A. D.). **-εῖον**, τό, *bakery*, *BGU*1117.24 (i B. C., κλ-). **-εύς**, έως, ὁ, *baker*, *POxy.*1142.10 (iii A. D., κλ-), Man.1.80 (κλ-). **-η**, ἡ, or **-ης**, ὁ, *a cake*, Alcm.20 (-ωτος codd. Ath.), cf. Hsch. **-ίκιος**, ον, = κριβανίτης, Ath.3.113b (κλ-). **-ικός**, ή, όν, *belonging to a bakery*, σκεύη *BGU*1117.11 (i B. C., κλ-). **-ιον**, τό, *baking-oven*, *PLond.*5.1733.23 (vi A. D.). **-ιος**, ον, *for baking*, ἐργαστήριον *BGU*1117.8 (i B. C., κλ-), cf. *PTeb.*351.6 (ii A. D.). **-ίτης** [ῑ], ου, ὁ, *baked in a pan* (κρίβανος), of bread, Ar.*Fr.*125, Epich.52, Amips.5, Sophr.27 (also κλ- Id.28), Gal.6.489, etc.; ὁ κ. (sc. ἄρτος) *loaf so baked*, Ar.*Ach.*1123: hence, comically, βοῦς κ. ib.87.

**κρῖβᾰνοειδής**, ές, in form **κλῖβ-**, *shaped like a κρίβανος*, Dsc.1.72. 4; ἔσοπτρον Anthem.p.151 W.

**κρῖβᾰν-ον** [ῑ], τό, = sq., Pherecr.169. ⊛ **-ος**, ὁ, Att. for **κλίβανος** (which is called Dor. in *EM*538.19, cf. Epich.143, and is the usu. form in Pap., *PPetr.*3p.328 (iii B. C.), etc.), *covered earthen vessel*, wider at bottom than at top, wherein bread was baked by putting hot embers round it, Hdt.2.92 (in form κλιβ-), A.*Fr.*309, Ar.*Ach.*86, *V.*1153, al., Antiph.176.5; οὕτως εἰμὶ ὡς εἰς κρίβανον *POxy.* 1842.7 (vi A. D.); *potter's oven*, *PCair.Zen.*271.9 (iii B. C., κλ-). 2. *funnel-shaped vessel*, used for drawing water, Str.16.2.13 (κλ-). II. *underground channel* or *vaulted passage*, in irrigation works, *Sammelb.*7188.17 (ii B. C., κλ-). 2. *hollow, cavern in a rock*, Ael.*NA* 2.22. ⊛ **-ωτός**, ή, όν, *baked in a κρίβανος*, hence κριβανωτὸς (sc. ἄρτος), ὁ, Alcm.20 codd. Ath.), Ar.*Pl.*765; κ. ζῷα Eust.1286.19.

**κρίγδανον**· πέλτη, ἀσπίς, Hsch.

⊛ **κρῐγή**, ἡ, (κρίζω) *gnashing of teeth*, Sch.Ar.*Av.*1520:—also **κριγμός**, Zonar. II. *shrieking*, νεκρῶν Hippon.54. III. κριγή· ἡ γλαύξ, Hsch.

**κριδδέμεν**, Boeot. for κρίζειν (= γελᾶν), Stratt.47.7.

**κρίδιον** [ῐ], τό, contr. from κριΐδιον, Dim. of κριός, Hsch. **κρίες**· ἡ χελιδών, Id. **κρίζαος**· ψώρα, κρίζα, Id. **κριζόν**· ἐπίλεκτον, διάφορον, Id.

⊛ **κρίζω**, aor. 1 ἔκριξα Ael.*NA*5.50, Hsch.: aor. 2 and pf. (v. infr.):—*creak*, κρίκε ζυγόν Il.16.470. II. of persons, *screech*, ὥσπερ Ἰλλυριοὶ κεκριγότες Ar.*Av.*1521; χαμαιτύπη κρίζει τις Men.879; in Boeot., *laugh*, v. κριδδέμεν. (Onomatop.)

**κρῑηδόν**, Adv., (κριός) *like a ram*, Ar.*Lys.*309.

**κρίθα**· κρίθινον, καὶ ἵππου ἀρρώστημα, Hsch.

**κρῑθ-αία**, ἡ, (κριθή) *barley pottage*, Hom.*Epigr.*15.7. **-άλευρον** [ᾰ], τό, *barley-meal*, Aët.12.71. **-άμῖνος** [ᾰ], η, ον, = κρίθινος, ἄλευρα Polyaen.4.3.32. **-ανίας**, ου, ὁ, *like barley*: κ. πυρός a branching cereal, perh. *millet*, Thphr.*HP*8.2.3. **-άριον**, τό, Dim. of κριθή, *BGU*33.11 (pl., ii/iii A. D.), *PTeb.*420.21 (iii A. D.), Thom.Mag.p.202 R. **-άχῡρον** [ᾰ], τό, *mixture of barley and chaff*, *PFlor.*377.14 (vi A. D.). **-άω**, of a horse, *to be barley-fed, wax wanton*, κριθῶν πῶλος A.*Ag.*1641; κριθώσης ὄνου S.*Fr.*876. ⊛ **-ή**, ἡ, mostly in pl., *barley-corns, barley* (cf. κρῖ), the meal being ἄλφιτα: πυρῶν ἢ κριθῶν Il.11. 69, cf. Od.9.110, 19.112, Ar.*Eq.*1101; κριθῶν μέδιμμνον *IG*4²(1).40.7 (Epid.); "τὰς οὐλοχύτας φέρε δεῦρο"—"τοῦτο δ' ἐστὶ τί;"—"κριθαί" Strato Com.1.35; οἶνος ἐκ κριθέων πεποιημένος a kind of *beer*, Hdt.2. 77; ἐκ κριθῶν μέθυ A.*Supp.*953, cf. Arist.*Fr.*106; κριθαὶ πεφρυγμέναι, = κάχρυς, Th.6.22, cf. Moer.p.213 P.: pl., also of *species of barley*, Thphr. *HP*8.1.1: sg., *PGrenf.*2.29.9 (ii B. C.); κ. Ἰνδική *millet, Sorghum halepense*, Thphr.*HP*8.4.2. II. *pustule on the eyelid, stye*, Hp. *Epid.*2.2.5, Gal.12.742. III. *barley corn, the smallest weight*, Thphr.*Lap.*46. IV. in sg., = πόσθη, Ar.*Pax*965. (The connexion with Lat. *hordeum*, OHG. *gersta* is doubtful.)

**κριθθός**, όν, dub. sens., κἠπὶ τὸν κριθθὸν κοῖλον *GDI*5016.11 (Gortyn).

**κρῑθί-ᾱσις**, εως, ἡ, a disease of horses, *surfeit caused by over-feeding with barley*, X.*Eq.*4.2, *Hippiatr.*8, al. **-άω**, of a horse, *suffer from κριθίασις*, Arist.*HA*604b8. II. = κριθάω, *wax wanton*, Cleanth. *Stoic.*1.132, Cerc.17.36, Babr.62.2, cf. Poll.7.24.

**κρῑθ-ίδιον**, τό, Dim. of κριθή, *decoction of barley*, Hp.*Nat.Mul.*53 (s. v. l.). 2. in pl., *a little barley*, Posidon.36 J., Luc.*Asin.*3, 47. **-ίζω**, *feed with barley*, Aesop.178, Babr.76.2. **-ικός**, ή, όν, *consisting in barley*, φόρος *BGU*922.7 (iii A. D.). ⊛ **-ῖνος**, η, ον, *made of* or *from barley*, κόλλιξ, ἄρτος, Hippon.35, Luc.*Macr.*5; ἄχυρον, ἄλευρον, Thphr.*HP*8.4.1, *PEleph.*5.25 (iii B. C.), Plu.2.397a; τὸ κ. ποτόν Hp.*Acut.*64; κ. ὕδωρ ib.(*Sp.*)30; κ. οἶνος *beer*, Plb.34. 9.15; πόμα Plu.2.752b: metaph., κ. Δημοσθένης, 'gingerbread Demosthenes', nickname of Dinarchus, Hermog.*Id.*2.11. **-ίον**, τό, Dim. of κριθή, Luc.*Asin.*17, Longus 3.30.

**κρίθμος**, v. κρῆθμον.

**κρῑθό-γιτον**· ἀπόβριμα (fort. -κριμα) κριθῆς, Hsch. **-κανον**· σπέρμα μελανθίῳ ὅμοιον, Id. ⊛ **-λόγος**, ον, *gathering barley*: among the Opuntii, a *magistrate who kept the barley for sacrifices*, Plu.2.292c: —hence **-λογία**, ἡ, *Cod.Theod.*14.26.1. **-μαντεῖα**, τά, *divination by barley*, Oenom.ap.Eus.*PE*5.25. **-μαντις**, εως, ὁ, *one who divined by barley*, Suid. s. v. προφητεία. **-πομπία**, ἡ, *sending of barley*, Eratosth.ap.Hsch. s. v. Ῥοίκου κ. ⊛ **-πῡρον**, τό, *wheat mixed with barley*, *PPetr.*3p.206, al. (iii B. C.), *PSI*5.532.6 (iii B. C.), *PFay.*101 iii 4 (i B. C.): acc. pl. -πυρα *PCair.Zen.*498 (iii B. C.). ⊛ **-πώλης**, ου, ὁ, *dealer in barley*, *Hippiatr.*1. **-τράγος** [ᾰ], ον, (τραγεῖν) *barley-eating*, Ar.*Av.*231. **-φαγία**, ἡ, *barley-diet*, a punishment in the Roman army, Plb.6.38.4. **-φάγος** [ᾰ], ον, *living on barley*, ὄρνιθες D.C.*Fr.*43.33, cf. Sch.Ar.*Av.*232. ⊛ **-φόρος**, ον, *bearing barley*, Thphr.*HP*8.8.2, Str.8.6.16. **-φῠλάκία**, ἡ, *office of controller of export of barley*, Hsch.

**κρῑθ-ώδης**, ες, *like barley, made of it*, κριθώδεις πτισάναι, = ὅλη πτισάνη, opp. χυλός, Hp.*Acut.*40. **-ώλεθρος**, ον, *barley-wasting*, of horses that will not fatten, Phryn.*PS*p.79 B.

⊛ **κρίθων** (κρίθον cod.)· ἐπώνυμον ἀνδροκιδάλου, Hsch. **κρίκα**· κρίκον, Id. **κρικαδιᾶν**· τὸ ἐναλλάξαι τοὺς δακτύλους ὥσπερ κρίκους ([.]ρυβοὺς cod.), Id., cf. **κρικαδίαν** (acc. sg.), Sch.Il.23.34. **κρίκε**, v. κρίζω.

⊛ **κρῐκ-έλλιον**, τό, Dim. of sq., *hoop of a ring*, Alex.Trall.8.2. **-ελλος**, ὁ, = *circulus*, Gloss.

**κρῐκ-ηλᾰσία**, ἡ, (κρίκος, ἐλαύνω) *trundling of hoops*, Antyll.ap. Orib.6.26.1. ⊛ **-ιον**, τό, Dim. of κρίκος, *Inscr.Délos*380.100 (ii B. C.), *POxy.*1300.5 (v A. D.).

**κρῐκο-ειδής**, ές, *ring-shaped, annular*, Gal.14.715, *Placit.*1.3. 18. **-ομαι**, Pass., *to be secured by a ring*, κεκρίκωνται τὸ χεῖλος χαλκῷ κρίκῳ *they have a* brass *ring through* the lip, Str.17.2.3; *to be infibulated*, Heliod.ap.Orib.50.11.1. **-ποιέομαι**, *to be formed into a ring*, Heracl.ap.Orib.48.13.1.

⊛ **κρίκ-ος** [ῐ], ὁ, Homeric form of κίρκος, *ring*, on a horse's breast-band, to fasten it to the peg (ἕστωρ) at the end of the carriage-pole, Il.24.272. 2. *eyelet-hole* in sails, through which the reefing-ropes were drawn, Hdt.2.36, cf. Poll.1.94, *PLond.*3.1164(*h*)8 (iii A. D.). 3. *curtain-ring*, Thphr.*HP*4.2.7, J.*AJ*3.6.2. 4. *finger-ring*, Arist.*Pol.*1324b14; part of a finger-ring, *Inscr.Délos*461*Ba*6, al. (ii B. C.). 5. *nose-ring*, S.E.*P.*3.203. 6. *armlet*, Plu.*Dem.* 30. 7. *link in a chain*, Id.2.304b, Alex.Aphr.*Pr.*2.67, Iamb. *Comm.Math.*7; ἐκ κρίκου λεπτοῦ πεποιημένα ὑφάσματα *chain* armour, Jul.*Or.*37d. 8. *hoop*, Antyll.ap.Orib.6.26.2. 9. *ring* of a spanner, Hero*Bel.*101.13; of a ring-bolt, Apollod.*Poliorc.*166.15; of an armillary sphere, Procl.*Hyp.*6.2 (pl.). **-ωμα**, ατος, τό, *ring, circle*, Eust.726.16. **-ωσις**, εως, ἡ, *infibulation*, Heliod.ap.Orib. 50.11.1. **-ωτός**, ή, όν, *ringed, made of rings*, Caryst.7; θώραξ Eust.528.24; κ. σφαῖρα *armillary* sphere, Gem.16.10(pl.), Gell.3.10. 3, Ptol.*Geog.*7.6, *Alm.*1.6 (pl.); ἀστρολάβος Sch.Ptol.90.

⊛ **κρίμα**, ατος, τό, (κρίνω) *decision, judgement*, Chrysipp.*Stoic.*3.58, Plb.23.1.12, Lxx *Ps.*118(119).7, al., *Ep.Rom.*11.33, Arr.*Epict.*2.15. 8; περί τινος M.Ant.8.47; *verdict* on a literary work, Phld.*Po.*5. 23. 2. *decree, resolution*, δήμου D.H.4.12; ἱερομνημόνων *BCH*27. 107, cf. *IGRom.*3.58,66 (Prusias). 3. *legal decision*, *PPetr.*3p.56 (iii B. C.), *SIG*826*E* ii 29 (Delph., ii B. C.); *decision* of arbitrators, ib. 421.44 (Thermum, iii B. C.); esp. *sentence, condemnation*, Lxx *De.*21. 22, al., *Ev.Marc.*12.40, etc. II. *matter for judgement, question*, οὐκ εὔκριτον τὸ κρῖμα A.*Supp.*397. 2. *law-suit*, Lxx *Ex.*18.22, 1*Ep.Cor.*6.7. III. = κρίσις, *judging, judgement*, *Ev.Jo.*9.39, *Act. Ap.*24.25, etc. [ῐ in A. l. c. (nisi leg. **κρεῖμα**): ῑ in post-classical poetry; freq. written κρίμα in codd.]

**κριμν-ῆστις**· πλακοῦντος εἶδος, Hsch. **-ίτης** [ῑτ] ἄρτος, ὁ, bread *made of* κρίμνον, *coarse* bread, Archestr.*Fr.*4.13 (κριμματίαν codd.), Iatrocl.ap.Ath.14.646a. ※ **-ον,** τό, *coarse barley meal,* Hp.ap.Gal.19.115, Eup.11.5 D. (prob.), Arist.*HA*501b31 (pl.), *PRyl.*280v (ii A.D.); *grounds* in gruel, Call.*Fr.*205. 2. *coarse loaf, AP*6.302 (Leon.), Babr.108.9. 3. in pl., *crumbs,* Herod.6.6; κρίμνα χειρῶν, = ἀπομαγδαλιά, Lyc.607. ※ **-ος,** ἡ, a purple dye, *PHolm.*8.43 (κριμνον Pap.); κρημνός Ps.-Democr.Alch.p.42 B.; κριμνούς· λευκάς τινας βοτάνας, Hsch. **-ώδης,** ες, *like coarse meal,* of sediment in urine, Hp.*Aph.*7.31; κ. ἐλλέβορος S.E.*P.*1.130; κριμνώδη κατανείφειν snow *thick as meal,* Ar.*Nu.*965.

**κρῑνάνθεμον,** τό, *houseleek,* Hp.*Nat.Mul.*32. 2. = ἡμεροκαλλές, Ps.-Dsc.3.122.

**κρίνη**· κνίδη, Hsch.

**κρίνινος** [ῐ], η, ον, *made of lilies,* μύρον *PMag.Lond.*46.223 (iv A.D.); ἔλαιον Gal.11.872, *PMag.Lond.*121.631 (iii A.D.); κ., τό, *PMag.Leid.W.*9.13 (ii/iii A.D.).

**κρῐνο-ειδής,** ές, *like a lily,* Dsc.3.128. **εις,** εντος, ὁ, name of one of the Idaean Dactyls, Sch.Il.22.391. II. -εις, εσσα, εν, *like a lily,* κεραυνός dub. cj. in *Supp.Epigr.*4.386 (Panamara). **-μῠρον,** τό, = κρίνινον μύρον, Gal.19.71.

※ **κρίνον** [ῐ], τό, heterocl. pl. κρίνεα Hdt.2.92; dat. κρίνεσιν Cratin.98, Ar.*Nu.*911, etc.:—*white lily, Lilium candidum,* Thphr.*HP*6.6.8, Theoc.11.56, Nic.*Fr.*74.27, Dsc.3.102; κ. πορφυροῦν *Turk's cap lily, L. chalcedonicum,* Thphr.*HP*6.6.3, cf. Dsc. l. c.: prov., κρίνου γυμνότερος Jul.*Or.*6.181c: hence, of a needy man, Poll.6.197, etc.: symbolic of death, v. κολοκύντη. 2. *Egyptian bean, Nelumbium speciosum,* Hdt.2.92. II. kind of *choral dance,* Apolloph.2. III. kind of *loaf,* Ath.3.114f. IV. *architectural ornament, IG*11(2).161 *A* 72 (Delos, iii B.C.).

**κρῐνοστέφανος,** ον, *lily-crowned,* Aus.*Ep.*8.14 (κριννο- metri gr.).

※ **κρίνω** [ῑ], Ep. 3 sg. ind. κρίνησι (δια-) f.l. in Theoc.25.46: fut. κρῐνῶ, Ep., Ion. κρῐνέω (δια-) Il.2.387: aor. ἔκρῑνα Od.18.264, etc.: pf. κέκρῐκα Pl.*Lg.*734c, etc.:—Med., fut. κρῐνοῦμαι E.*Med.*609, but in pass. sense, Pl.*Grg.*521e: aor. ἐκρῑνάμην Il.9.521, etc.:—Pass., fut. κρῐθήσομαι A.*Eu.*677, Antipho 6.37, etc.: aor. ἐκρίθην [ῐ] Pi.*N.*7.7, etc.; 3 pl. κρίθεν Id.*P.*4.168, ἔκριθεν A.R.4.1462; Ep. opt. κρινθεῖτε (δια-) Il.3.102, part. κρινθείς 13.129, Od.8.48, inf. κρινθήμεναι A.R.2.148: pf. κέκρῐμαι Pi.*O.*2.30, And.4.35, etc.; inf. κεκρίσθαι (ἀπο-) Pl.*Men.*75c:—Aeol. κρίννω dub. in *IG*12(2).278 (Mytil.): aor. ἔκριννε ib.6.28 (Mytil., ἐπ-); inf. κρίνναι ib.526*b*15:—Thess. pres. inf. κρεννέμεν ib.9(2).517.14 (Larissa):—*separate, put asunder, distinguish,* ὅτε τε ξανθὴ Δημήτηρ κρίνῃ.. καρπόν τε καὶ ἄχνας Il.5.501, etc.; κρῖν' ἄνδρας κατὰ φῦλα 2.362, cf. 446; ἥλιος ἠῶ καὶ δύσιν ἔκρινεν Emp.154.1; κ. τὸ ἀληθές τε καὶ μή Pl.*Tht.*150b; τούς τε ἀγαθοὺς καὶ τοὺς κακοὺς X.*Mem.*3.1.9, etc.:—also Med., ἀντία δ' ἐκρίναντο δέμας καὶ σήματ' ἔθεντο χωρὶς ἀπ' ἀλλήλων Parm.8.55:—Pass., κρινόμενον πῦρ Emp.62.2. II. *pick out, choose,* ἐν δ' ἐρέτας ἔκρινεν ἐείκοσιν Il.1.309; ἐκ Λυκίης.. φῶτας ἀρίστους 6.188, cf. Od.4.666, 9.90, 195, 14.217, etc.; κ. τινὰ ἐκ πάντων Hdt.6.129; κρίνασα δ' ἀστῶν.. τὰ βέλτατα A.*Eu.*487; δίδωμί σοι κρίναντι χρῆσθαι S.*OC*641, etc.:—Med., κρίνασθαι ἀρίστους *to choose* the best, Il.9.521, cf. 19.193, Od.4.408, 530, etc.:—Pass., *to be chosen out, distinguished,* ἵνα τε κρίνονται ἄριστοι 24.507; esp. in partt., κεκριμένος *picked out, chosen,* Il.10.417, Od.13.182, al., Hdt.3.31; κρινθείς Il.13.129, Od.8.48; ἀρετᾷ κριθείς *distinguished for..,* Pi.*N.*7.7; κριθέντων ἐν τοῖς ἱερέοις *approved..,* *GDI*2049.15 (Delph.); ἀσπίδα.. κεκριμένην ὕδατι καὶ πολέμῳ *proved* by sea and land, *AP*9.42 (Leon.); ἐν ζῶσι κεκριμένα *numbered* among.., cj. in E.*Supp.*969 (lyr.); εἰς τοὺς ἐφήβους κριθείς Luc.*Am.*2. 2. *decide* disputes, κρίνων νείκεα πολλά Od.12.440; ἔκριναν μέγα νεῖκος.. πολέμοιο 18.264: c. acc. cogn., οἳ.. σκολιὰς κρίνωσι θέμιστας *judge* crooked judgements, Il.16.387; κ. δίκας Hdt.2.129; κρῖνε δ' εὐθεῖαν δίκην A.*Eu.*433, etc.; πρώτας δίκας κρίνοντες αἵματος ib.682; κρινεῖ δὲ δὴ τίς ταῦτα; Ar.*Ra.*805; κ. κρίσιν Pl.*R.*360e; ἄριστα κ. Th.6.39; κρίνουσι βοῇ καὶ οὐ ψήφῳ *they decide the question..,* Id.1.87; μίσει πλέον ἢ δίκῃ κ. Id.3.67; τὸ δίκαιον κ. Isoc.14.10; τῷ τοῦτο κρίνεις; by what *do you form* this *judgement?* Ar.*Pl.*48; κ. περί τινος Pi.*N.*5.40, Pl.*Ap.*35d, Arist.*Rh.*1391b9, etc.:—Pass., ἀγὼν κριθήσεται A.*Eu.*677; κἂν ἰσόψηφος κριθῇ (sc. ἡ δίκη) ib.741: impers., κριθησόμενον *a decision being about to be taken,* Arr.*An.*3.9.6. b. *decide* a contest, e.g. for a prize, ἀγῶνα κ. Ar.*Ra.*873; ἔργον ἐν κύβοις Ἄρης κρινεῖ A.*Th.*414: c. acc. pers., κ. τὰς θεὰς *decide* their *contest,* i.e. *judge* them, E.*IA*72:—Pass., Id.*Supp.*601 (lyr.); αἱ μάχαι κρίνονται ταῖς ψυχαῖς X.*Cyr.*3.3.19:—Med. and Pass., of persons, *have* a contest *decided, come to issue,* κρινώμεθ' Ἄρηϊ Il.2.385, cf. 18.209; ὁπότε μνηστῆρσι καὶ ἡμῖν.. μένος κρίνηται Ἄρηος Od.16.269; βίηφι κ. Hes.*Th.*882; *dispute, contend,* Ar.*Nu.*66; περὶ ἀρετῆς Hdt.3.120; οὐ κρινοῦμαι.. σοι τὰ πλεῖονα E.*Med.*609; δίκῃ περί τινος κρίνεσθαι Th.4.122; κρίνεσθαι μετά τινος v.l. in Lxx *Jd.*8.1, *Jb.*9.3; πολλαῖς μάχαις κριθείς Nic.Dam.20 J.; *compete* in games, c. acc. cogn., κριθέντα Πύθια *JRS*3.295 (Antioch. Pisid.): pf. part., *decided, clear, strong,* κεκριμένος οὖρος Il.14.19; πόνοι κεκρ. *decided, ended,* Pi.*N.*4.1. c. *win* a battle, τὴν μάχην Ἀννίβας ἔκρινε Plb.3.117.11. 3. *adjudge,* κράτος τινί S.*Aj.*443:—Pass., τοῖς οὔτε νόστος.. κρίθη Pi.*P.*8.84; τὰ κριθησόμενα *the sum adjudged to be paid, PLips.*38.13 (iv A.D.). b. abs., *judge, give judgement,* ἄκουσον.. καὶ κρῖνον Ar.*Fr.*473; ἀδίκως κ. Pherecr.96, cf. Men.*Mon.*287, 576. c. Medic., *bring to a crisis,* τὸ θερμὸν φίλιόν [ἐστι] καὶ κρῖνον Hp.*Aph.*5.22; κ. τὰ νοσήματα Gal.*Nat.Fac.*1.13, al.:—Pass., of a sick person, *come to a crisis,* ἐκρίθη εἰκοσταῖος Hp.*Epid.*1.15 (also impers. in Act., ἔκρινε τούτοισιν ἑνδεκαταίοισιν *the crisis came..,* ib.18); τοῦ πάθους κριθέντος D.S.19.24. 4. *judge of, estimate,* πρὸς ἐμαυτὸν κρίνων [αὐτόν] *judging of* him by myself, D.21.154; πρὸς ἀργύριον τὴν εὐδαιμονίαν κ. Isoc.4.76:—Pass., ἴσον παρ' ἐμοὶ κέκριται Hdt.7.16.α'; εὔνοια καιρῷ κρίνεται Men.691. 5. *expound, interpret* in a particular way, τὸ ἐνύπνιον ταύτῃ ἔκριναν Hdt.1.120, cf. 7.19, A.*Pr.*485, etc.:—in Med., ὁ γέρων ἐκρίνατ' ὀνείρους Il.5.150. 6. c. acc. et inf., *decide* or *judge that..,* Hdt.1.30, 214, Pl.*Tht.*170d, etc.; κρίνω σὲ νικᾶν A.*Ch.*903; so, with the inf. omitted, ἀνδρῶν πρῶτον κ. τινά S.*OT*34; Ἔρωτα δ' ὅστις μὴ θεὸν κρίνει μέγαν E.*Fr.*269; τὴν πόλιν ἀθλιωτάτην ἔκρινας Pl.*R.*578b; ἐκ τῶν λόγων μὴ κρῖνε.. σοφόν Philem.228:—Pass., Ἑλλήνων ἕνα κριθέντ' ἄριστον S.*Ph.*1345, cf. Th.2.40, etc. 7. *decide in favour of, prefer, choose,* κρίνω δ' ἄφθονον ὄλβον A.*Ag.*471, cf. *Supp.*396 (both lyr.); τὴν ἐλπίδα τῆς τύχης πάρος S.*Tr.*724; τινὰ πρό τινος Pl.*R.*399e, cf. *Phlb.*57e; τι πρός τι Id.*Phd.*110a (Pass.); εἴ σφε κρίνειεν Πάρις E.*Tr.*928, cf. Ar.*Av.*1103, *Ec.*1155; *choose between,* δύ' ἔσθ' ἃ κρῖναι τὸν γαμεῖν μέλλοντα δεῖ, ἤτοι προσηνῆ γ' ὄψιν ἢ χρηστὸν τρόπον Men.584. 8. c. inf. only, *determine* to do a thing, *UPZ*42.37 (ii B.C.), *Ep.Tit.*3.12, 1*Ep.Cor.*2.2, etc.; ζῆν μεθ' ὧν κρίνῃ τις ἂν (sc. ζῆν) with whom he *chooses* to live, Men.506; but τὸ βιάζεσθαι οὐκ ἔκρινε D.S.15.32. 9. *form a judgement of* a thing, μὴ κρῖν' ὁρῶν τὸ κάλλος Men.*Mon.*333. III. in Trag., *question,* αὐτὸν.. ἅπας λεὼς κρίνει παραστάς S.*Tr.*195; εἴ νιν πρὸς βίαν κρίνειν θέλοις ib.388; καὶ κρῖνε κἀξέλεγχ' Id.*Ant.*399; μὴ κρῖνε, μὴ 'ξέταζε Id.*Aj.*586; σέ τοι, σὲ κρίνω Id.*El.*1445. 2. *bring to trial, accuse,* D.2.29, 18.15, 19.233; κ. θανάτου *judge* (in matters) of life and death, X.*Cyr.*1.2.14; κ. τινὰ προδοσίας Lycurg.113; περὶ προδοσίας Isoc.15.129; κ. τινὰ κακώσεως ἐπαρχίας, Lat. *repetundarum,* Plu.*Caes.*4:—Pass., *to be brought to trial,* Th.6.29; θανάτου (δίκῃ add. cod. B) Id.3.57; Λεωκράτους τοῦ κρινομένου Lycurg.1; κρίνομαι πρὸς Σωφρόνην; Men.*Epit.*529; τρὶς κρίνεται παρ' ὑμῖν περὶ θανάτου D.4.47; ἐκρίνετο τὴν περὶ Ὠρωποῦ κρίσιν θανάτου Id.21.64: c. gen. criminis, κρίνεσθαι δώρων Lys.27.3: κ. ἐπ' ἀδικήματι Plu.2.241e: abs., ὁ κεκριμένος Aeschin.2.159. 3. *pass sentence upon, condemn,* D.19.232:—Pass., *to be judged, condemned,* κακούργου.. ἐστὶ κριθέντ' ἀποθανεῖν Id.4.47; μὴ κρίνετε, ἵνα μὴ κριθῆτε *Ev.Matt.*7.1; τὰ κεκριμένα *the judgement* of a court, *PRyl.*76.8 (ii A.D.). (κρῐ-ν-yω ἐ-κρῐ-ν-σα, cf. Lat. *cerno* (from *crĭ-n-), *crībrum* (from *crei-dhrom).)

**κρῐν-ωνιά,** ἡ, prop. *bed of lilies,* Suid.; but, = κρίνον, Thphr.*HP*2.2.1, 6.6.9. **-ωτός,** ή, όν, *adorned with lilies,* κεφαλίδες Aristeas 68.

**κριξός,** ὁ, Dor. for κιρσός (q. v.).

**κρῑο-βόλιον,** τό, *sacrifice of a ram, IG*14.1018 (iv A.D.). II. pl., *ephebic contest in which a ram was caught and sacrificed, OGI*764.27 (Pergam., ii B.C.). **-βόλος,** ον, *ram-slaying,* κ. τελετή, = foreg. 1, *IG*14.1018 (iv A.D.). **-γενής,** ὁ, name of a lozenge, Paul.Aeg.4.41, 7.12. **-δόχη,** ἡ, *frame of a battering-ram,* Ath.Mech.13.10, al. **-ειδής,** ές, *like a ram,* Suid. s. v. κριός. **-θεος,** ὁ, = ἀμμωνιακόν, Ps.-Dsc.3.84. **-κέρᾰτος,** ον, *with ram's horns,* θεός Ps.-Callisth.1.8. **-κέφαλος,** ον, *ram-headed,* Hermes Trism. in *Rev.Phil.*32.254. **-κοπέω,** *batter with a battering-ram,* Plb.1.42.9, App.*Mith.*36: abs., Ath.Mech.14.11, Apollod.*Poliorc.*143.7. **-μᾰχέω,** *manoeuvre with a battering-ram,* ib.185.14. **-μορφος,** ον, *ram-formed,* Sch.rec.A.R.1.256. **-μυξος,** ον, (μύξα) *like a drivelling ram, sheepish,* Cerc.15.

**κριον** (crion), = vervecina, *Gloss.* (Perh. contr. from *κρίειον (sc. κρέας).)

**κρῑο-πρόσωπος,** ον, *ram-faced,* ἄγαλμα Διός Hdt.2.42, 4.181; Ζεύς Luc.*Sacr.*14, etc. 2. *with a ram as figurehead,* ναῦς Nymphis 18. **-πρῳρος,** ον, = foreg. 2, πλοῖον, σκάφος, Sch.Pl.*Mx.*243a, Sch.A.R.2.168.

※ **κρῑός,** ὁ, *ram,* Od.9.447, 461, Hdt.2.42, etc.; κριοὶ ἄγριοι Id.4.192: prov., κριὸς τροφεῖα ἀπέτεισεν, of ingratitude, because a ram butts at those who have brought him up, Zen.4.63, Suid., Hsch.; κριοὺς ἐκγεννᾶν τέκνα Eup.99; κριοῦ διακονία, of thankless service, Suid., Hsch.; τὸν κριὸν ὡς ἐπέχθη the 'shearing of the *ram*', in allusion to the ode of Simonides in honour of Crius of Aegina, Ar.*Nu.*1356. 2. *battering-ram,* X.*Cyr.*7.4.1, *IG*2².468, Plb.1.48.9, Ath.Mech.14.1, J.*BJ*3.7.19, etc. 3. the constellation *Aries,* Eudox.ap.Hipparch.1.2.13, Euc.*Phaen.*p.6 M., Arat.238, J.*AJ*3.10.5, etc. II. a *sea-monster,* Ael.*NA*9.49, 15.2, Opp.*H.*1.372, 5.33, etc. III. kind of *mussel,* Hegesand.36 (κρεῖος cod. A Ath.). IV. *volute* on the Corinthian capital, *twisted like a ram's horn,* Hsch. V. kind of *ship,* Poll.1.83. VI. part of an irrigation-system, dub. sens. in *BGU*14iii9 (iii A.D.). VII. *a variety of* ἐρέβινθος, Thphr.*HP*8.5.1, *PCair.Zen.*192.8 (iii B.C.), Dsc.2.104, Gal.6.533: misspelt κρεῖος in Sophil.8: Lat. *cicer arietinum,* Petron.35, etc.; *est enim arietino capiti simile,* Plin.*HN*18.124. (Prob. cogn. with κέρας.)

**κρῑό-στᾰσις,** εως, ἡ, *station, position for a battering-ram,* Ph.*Bel.*92.19. ※ **-τάφος** [ᾰ], ον, ὁ, *one who buries sacred rams, PTeb.*72.411 (ii B.C.). ※ **-φάγος** [ᾰ], ον, *devouring rams,* epith. of a divinity, Hsch. **-φόρος,** ον, *carrying battering-rams,* χελῶναι Ph.*Bel.*99.44, Ath.Mech.8.14, Apollod.*Poliorc.*138.18, D.S.20.48, 91; μηχαναί App.*Pun.*98, Anon.ap.Suid. s. v. προσηρεικότος. II. *bearing a ram,* epith. of Hermes, Paus.9.22.1. **-ω,** pf. part. Pass. κεκριωμένον *made into a ram,* Hsch. s. v. Γαλλίμ (ante γαιηούχῳ).

**Κρῖσα,** ης, ἡ, *Crisa,* a city in Phocis, near Delphi, Il.2.520; **Κρίση,** *h.Ap.*282, etc.:—Adj. **Κρισαῖος,** α, ον, *Crisaean,* ib.446, Hdt.8.32:—also **Κίρρα,** Pi.*P.*3.74, al., *SIG*241.45, al. (Delph., iv B.C.), Paus.10.37.4 (but Κρῖσα distd. fr. Κίρρα by Leocrines ap.*EM*515.20, Str.9.3.3, Ptol.*Geog.*3.14.4); **Κύρρα,** *Marm.Par.*53, v.l. in Ptol. l.c.;

**Κίρσα**, Alc.*Oxy.*1789*Fr.*6.9 (dub.), *EM* l. c.; κόλπος **Κιρραῖος**, dub. in Hecat.105 J.: also **Κρῖσα**, Pi.*I.*2.18; **Κρῖσαῖος**, Id.*P.*5.37, al.

**κρισίαι**· τάξεις ἱππικαί, Hsch.

**κρίσῐμος** [ῐσ], ον, (κρίσις) *decisive, critical*, κ. ἡμέρα the *crisis* of a disease, Hp.*Aph.*7.85, al., Arist.*Ph.*230$^b$5; κ. γὰρ αὕτη γίγνεται (sc. the seventh day) Men.890; also κ. φάεα *AP*11.382.11 (Agath.); ἐν κρισίμοις Hp.*Epid.*1.7: Comp. -ώτερος Id.*Acut.*23. Adv. -μως Id. *Epid.* l. c.

**κρῐσιολογία**, ἡ, *litigation*, *Cat.Cod.Astr.*8(4).130 (pl.).

⊛**κρίσις** [ῐσ], εως, ἡ, (κρίνω) *separating, distinguishing*, τοῦ πλέω καὶ τοῦ μὴ πλέω Meliss.7; τῶν ὁμοιογενῶν, τῶν διαφερόντων, dub. l. in Arist.*EN*1165$^a$34. 2. *decision, judgement*, περὶ τούτων Parm.8. 15; τὴν Κροίσου κ. Hdt.3.34; ἐν θεῶν κρίσει A.*Ag.*1289; κατὰ δύναμιν καὶ κ. ἐμήν Hp.*Jusj.*1; κ. οὐκ ἀληθής no certain *means of judging*, S.*OT*501 (lyr.); πολίτης ὁρίζεται τῷ μετέχειν κρίσεως καὶ ἀρχῆς Arist. *Pol.*1275$^a$23; κρίσεως προσδεόμενα Epicur.*Nat.*32 G., cf. *Herc.*1420.3; αἱ τῶν πολλῶν κ. Phld.*Mus.*p.75 K.; Κρίσις, title of a play by Sophocles on the Judgement of Paris; κ. τινός *judgement on* or *respecting*, τῶν μνηστήρων Hdt.6.131; ἀέθλων Pi.*O.*3.21, *N.*10.23; μορφῆς E.*Hel.*26; ἡ τῶν ὅπλων κ., referring to the story of Ajax, Pl.*R.*620b, cf. Arist.*Po.*1459$^b$5; κρίσιν..τοῦ βίου πέρι ὧν λέγομεν Pl.*R.*360e; κ. ἀμφ' ἀέθλοις Pi.*O.*7.80; κ. διημαρτημένη *Stoic.*1.50; κ. συνετή Cleanth.ib.128; *power of judgement*, κρίσει πραγμάτων διαφέρεσθαι Plb.18.14.10; κατὰ κρίσιν with *judgement, advisedly*, Id.6.11.8. 3. *choice, election*, κ. ποιεῖσθαι τῶν ἀξίων Arist.*Pol.*1321$^a$30, cf. 1271$^a$10. 4. *interpretation* of dreams or portents, Lxx *Da.*2.36, D.S. 17.116, J.*AJ*2.5.7. II. *judgement* of a court, οὐδὲν ἂν τῆς ὑμετέρας κ. ἔδει Antipho 4.4.2; *trial, suit*, προκληθέντας ἐς κρίσιν περί τινος Th.1.34; καθιστάναι ἑαυτὸν ἐς κ. ib.131; κρίσιν ποιεῖν τινι Lys. 13.35; κρίσεως τυχεῖν to be put on one's *trial*, Pl.*Phdr.*249a; εἰς κ. ἄγειν Id.*Lg.*856c; ἡ κ. γίγνεταί τινι ibid.; κρίσιν ὑποσχεῖν ib.871d, D.21.125; τὰς κρίσεις ποιεῖσθαι περί τινος Isoc.4.40, cf. Th.1.77; τὰς κ. διαδικάζειν Pl.*Lg.*876b; κρίσιν λελογχότα Μειδίᾳ ἐξούλης Test.ap. D.21.82; αἱ κ. τῶν συμβολαίων Plu.2.447e. b. *result of a trial, condemnation*, X.*An.*1.6.5. c. ἡμέρα κρίσεως Day of *Judgement*, *Ev.Matt.*10.15. 2. *trial* of skill or strength, πρὸς τόξου κρίσιν in archery, S.*Tr.*266; δρόμου.., οὗ πρώτη κ. Id.*El.*684; κ. ποιεῖν ὁπότερος εἴη τὴν τέχνην σοφώτερος Ar.*Ra.*779; θεῶν ἔριν τε καὶ κ. Pl. *R.*379e. 3. *dispute*, περί τινος Hdt.5.5, 7.26. III. *event, issue*, κρίσιν σχεῖν to be *decided*, of a war, Th.1.23, Plb.31.29.5; κρίσεως τυχεῖν Id.1.59.11; ἐν τοῖς πεπολιτευμένοις τὴν κ. εἶναι νομίζω I suppose the *issue* depends upon my public measures, D.18.57. 2. *turning point* of a disease, *sudden change* for better or worse, Hp. *VM*19 (pl.), Gal.9.550, etc.; κ. ξύντομος ἐπὶ τὸ κάκιον Hp.*Judic.*34, cf. Gal.18(2).231. IV. middle of the spinal column, Poll.2.177.

**κρίσμιον**· φυλάκιον, Hsch.

**κρίσσιον**, τό, *thistle*, *Carduus pycnocephalus*, Dsc.4.118.

**κρισσοκάβων**, ωνος, ὁ, *suffering from varicocele*, of horses, *Hippiatr.* 14.

⊛**κρισσ-ός**, ὁ, = κιρσός, Andreas ap. Dsc.4.118, *Hippiatr.*77, Hsch. II. *knot* in oaks from which mistletoe springs, Id. **-ώδης**, ες, Att. for κιρσώδης, Gal.19.123, Hsch. s. v. βδαλοί (κροσσ- cod.).

**κρίτανος**· τέρμινθος, Hsch.

**κρῐτ-έος**, α, ον, *to be decided* or *judged*, Hp. *de Arte* 9. II. κριτέον *one must decide* or *judge*, Pl.*Grg.*523e, etc. **-ήρ**, ῆρος, ὁ, = κριτής, *IG*4.493 (Mycenae). II. *interpreter* of dreams, Nic.Dam.66.9 J. III. f.l. for κραντήρ (q. v.), Arist.ap.*EM*742. 37. ⊛**-ήριον**, τό, *means for judging* or *trying, standard*, freq. of the mental faculties and senses, ἔχων αὐτῶν τὸ κ. ἐν αὑτῷ Pl.*Tht.*178b, cf. *R.*582a, Plu.2.448b, etc.; τὸ αἰσθητήριον καὶ κ. τῶν..χυμῶν Arist. *Metaph.*1063$^a$3, cf. Epicur.*Ep.*1 p.5 U. (pl.), *Sent.*24, al.; περὶ κριτηρίου, title of works by Epicurus (D.L.10.27), Posidonius (Diocl.ap. D.L.7.54), and Ptolemy: generally, χρόνον εἶναι μέτρον καὶ κ. τάχους *measure, test*, Zeno *Stoic.*1.26, etc. 2. *court of judgement, tribunal*, Pl.*Lg.*767b; καθίζειν κ. Plb.9.33.12, cf. *PHib.*1.29(a) (iii B. C.), 1 *Ep. Cor.*6.2, *IG* 4.951.20, Paus.2.20.7, *POxy.*2134.6 (ii A. D.), etc. b. *decision* of a tribunal, *judgement*, *SIG*826 *K*9 (Delph., ii B. C.). **-ής**, οῦ, ὁ, voc. κριτή Hippon.118: (κρίνω):—*judge, umpire*, A.*Supp.*397, Hdt.3.160, etc.; ἐν πέντε κριτῶν γούνασι κεῖται Epich.229; κ. τῶν ἀληθῶν, opp. δοξαστής, Antipho 5.94; κριταὶ ἀπὸ τοῦ ἴσου, opp. ἀγωνισταί, Th.3.37; τῶν..λεγομένων μὴ κακοὺς κ. Id.1.120; κ. περί τινος Lys.16.21, Pl.*Phlb.*65a; at Athens, usu. of *the judges in the poetic contests*, Ar.*Ach.*1224, *Nu.*1115, *Av.*445, cf. And.4.21; rarely, = δικαστής, Demad.3: so metaph. in Aeschin.3.232; πάντα τὰ στοιχεῖα κριτὴν εἴληφε, i. e. each element has found favour with some philosopher, Arist.*de An.*405$^b$8, cf. *Pol.*1337$^a$42; of the *Judges* of Israel, Lxx *Jd.*2.16, al.; κ. δοθείς, = Lat. *judex datus*, *POxy.*1195.1 (ii A. D.); ἐπίλεκτος κ., = *judex selectus*, *OGI*567.10 (Attalia, ii A. D.). 2. κ. ἐνυπνίων *interpreter* of dreams, A.*Pers.*226. II. κριτάς· ὀδόντας, Hsch.; cf. κραντήρ.

**Κρῐτῐάζω**, *imitate the style of Critias*, Philostr.*VS*1.16.2; Κριτιάζουσα ἠχώ ib.2.1.14.

**κρῐτ-ῐκός**, ή, όν, *able to discern, critical*, δύναμις σύμφυτος κ. Arist. *APo.*99$^b$35; οὐκ ἔχει ῥῖνα κριτικὴν πρὸς τοὔψον Posidipp.1.4; αἰσθήσεις κ. Phld.*Mus.*p.8 K.; τὸ κ. *the power of discerning*, Arist.*de An.*432$^a$16; ἡ κριτική (sc. τέχνη) Pl.*Plt.*260c, etc.: c. gen., ἡ γεῦσις τῶν σχημάτων κριτικωτάτη Arist.*Sens.*442$^b$17, cf. Thphr.*Sens.*43, Ocell.2.7; of persons, [τὸν ὅλως πεπαιδευμένον] περὶ πάντων ὡς εἰπεῖν κ. τινὰ νομίζομεν εἶναι Arist.*PA*639$^a$9: esp. in language, *grammarian, scholar, literary critic*, Pl.*Ax.*366e, Phld.*Po.*5.24, Str.9.1.10, etc.; of Crates, Ath. 11.490e, who distd. κ. and γραμματικός, S.E.*M.*1.79; εἰ δύναταί τις εἶναι κ. καὶ γραμματικός, title of work by Galen (*Libr.Propr.*17); but τῶν ὕστερον γραμματικῶν κληθέντων πρότερον δὲ κ. D.Chr.53.1, cf. Apollod.ap.Clem.Al.*Strom.*1.16.79; οἱ κ. τῶν λόγων Philostr.*VS* 2.1.14; πρὸς τοὺς κ., title of work by Chrysippus, *Stoic.*2.9; ἡ κ., opp. ἡ γραμματική, Taurisc.ap S.E.*M.*1.248, cf. Sch.*DT*p.3 H. Adv. -κῶς, ἔχειν τινός Artem.4*Praef.*, cf. Erot.*Praef.*p.7 N., Men.Rh. p.391 S. 2. *of* or *for judging*, ἀρχὴ κ. the office *of judges*, opp. ἀρχὴ βουλευτική, Arist.*Pol.*1275$^b$19. II. = κρίσιμος, ἑβδομάς Ph.1.45 (Sup.), cf. Plu.2.124f, Gal.9.93, al. Adv. -κῶς Id.*UP*17.2, al. **-ός**, ή, όν, *separated, picked out, chosen*, Il.7.434, Od.8.258. 2. *choice, excellent*, Pi.*P.*4.50, S.*Tr.*27, 245, etc.; δάμαλις *SIG*1026.6 (Cos, iv/iii B. C.).

**κρῑ-ώδης**, ες, *ram-like*, Ph.1.113. **-ωμα**, ατος, τό, = κριός I.2, dub. in Apollod.*Poliorc.*139.1. II. = κριός V, Aq.*Ez.*40.14. ⊛**-ωπός**, όν, = κριοπρόσωπος I, Trag.ap.Phot.p.151 R.; = κριός VII, *POxy.*1801. 26.

**κρίως**, Cret. gen. sg. of κρέας (q. v.).

⊛**κροαίνω**, only pres. part., of a horse, *stamp, strike with the hoof*, θείῃ πεδίοιο κροαίνων Il.6.507 (where Sch.A rejects the expl. ἐπιθυμῶν, quoting Archil.176, cf. κρυαίνω); κροαίνοντες πεδίοισι (v. l. -ίοιο) Opp. *C.*1.279: abs., Philostr.*Im.*1.30: metaph., *luxuriate, wanton*, of a rhetorician, Id.*VS*1.25.7; also πλήκτρῳ λιγυρὸν μέλος κ. *striking*, *Anacreont.*58.6.

**κρόβαλος**· ὁ μαλλὸς τῶν παιδίων, καὶ αἱ τρίχες τῶν αἰδοίων, Hsch. **κροβάντιον**· πολίον, Id.

**κροιός**· νοσώδης, ἀσθενής, Hsch.; = κολοβός, Theognost.*Can.*21; ἐάν τις τῶν λίθων ἔχει τι κροιόν *IG*2$^2$.244.63 (iv B. C.); ἐγκολλᾶν τῶν λίθων τὰ κροιά, 'Αρχ.'Εφ.1923.39. (Cf. Lith. *kreĩvas* 'crooked'.)

**κρόκα**, heterocl. acc. sg. of κρόκη.

**κροκάλη** [ᾰ], ἡ, = κρόκη II, *AP*7.479 (Theodorid.): pl., *sea-shore, beach*, E.*IA*210 (lyr.), *AP*7.651 (Euph.), 6.186 (Diocl.); κροκάλην.. ἠϊόνα ib.7.294 (perh. f. l. for ἠϊόνος) (Tull. Laur.): in late Prose, Agath.2.2.

**κρόκαλον**· τὸ πανοῦργον παιδίον, Hsch.

⊛**κροκᾶτον**, τό, *yellow parchment*. *Edict.Diocl.Asin.*7.38.

**κρόκεος**, ον, (κρόκος) *saffron coloured*, Pi.*P.*4.232 (nisi leg. κροκόεν), E.*Hec.*468 (lyr.), *Ion*889 (lyr.).

**κρόκες**, αἱ, metapl. nom. pl. of sq.

⊛**κρόκη**, ἡ, heterocl. acc. κρόκα Hes.*Op.*538, nom. pl. κρόκες *AP*6. 335 (Antip.): nom. **κρόξ** only in Hsch.: (κρέκω):—*thread which is passed between the threads of the warp, woof*, Hes. l. c., Hdt.2.35, Pl. *Plt.*282d,e, *Cra.*388b; κ. καὶ στήμων *PLille*6.12 (iii B. C.); νῶσαι μαλθακωτάτην κ. Eup.319, cf. Men.892; κρόκας ἐμβάλλειν Arist.*HA* 623$^a$11. 2. generally, *thread*, Hp.*Morb.*2.18, Luc.*Nav.*26, etc. 3. = κροκύς, *flock* or *nap of woollen cloth*, ἐν 'Εκβατάνοισι γίγνεται κρόκης χόλιξ; Ar.*V.*1144: pl., μαλακαῖσι κρόκαις *with cloths of* soft *wool*, Pi.*N.* 10.44; κρόκαισι *with flocks of wool*, S.*OC*474; τρίβωνες ἐκβαλόντες.. κρόκας having lost *the nap*, worn out, E.*Fr.*282.12; τῆς κ. φορουμένης *the wool* being torn to pieces, Ar.*Lys.*896, cf. *Th.*738; κρόκη θαψίνη yellow *wool*, *IG*1$^2$.330.17. II. = κροκάλη, *pebble* on the sea-shore, Arist.*Mech.*852$^b$29; ἐν κρόκῃσι on *the pebbles of the shore*, Lyc.107, 193, etc.

**κροκ-ήϊος**, η, ον, *of saffron*, ἄνθος *h.Cer.*178. **-ηρός**, ά, όν, *made with saffron*, φάρμακον Gal.13.182, Paul.Aeg.6.8. ⊛**-ίας**, ου, ὁ, *saffron-coloured stone*, Plu.2.375e; dub. in S.*Ichn.*186 (lyr.). **-ίζω**, *to be like saffron*, Dsc.2.179; ὀσμὴ -ουσα Plu.*Them.*8. **-ῐνος**, η, ον, *of* or *made from saffron*, μύρα *AP*11.34 (Phld.), cf. Thphr.*Od.*27, Plb. 30.26.1, Apollon.ap.Gal.12.475, Aret.*CA*1.6; τὸ κ. Lxx *Pr.*7.17, Dsc.1.54. 2. *yellow*, Stratt.69, Thphr.*HP*1.13.1, 3.4.5, *POxy.* 1679.5 (iii A. D.), Democr.Eph.ap.Ath.12.525c:—the form κρόκιος in Artem.1.77 is corrupt.

**κρόκιον**, τό, Dim. of κρόκη, *woollen fillet*. Anticl.13.

**κροκίς**, ίδος, ἡ, *fly-trap*, *Silene Muscipula*, Apollod.ap.Plin.*HN*24. 167. II. = κροκύς I, *Gloss.*

**κροκισμός**, ὁ, *weaving, web*, Sch.S.*OC*475.

⊛**κρόκκαι**, αἱ, *pebbles*, Hsch. **κροκκάω**, *cluck*, of birds, *Gloss.*

**κροκό-βαπτος**, ον, *saffron-dyed*, A.*Pers.*660. ⊛**-βᾰφής**, ές, = foreg., Sch.Pi.*N.*1.58: metaph., ἐπὶ δὲ καρδίαν ἔδραμε κ. σταγών the *sallow, sickly* blood-drop such as might be supposed to run to the heart of dying men, A.*Ag.*1121 (lyr.). ⊛**-δῑλέα**, ἡ, *dung of the* κροκόδιλος χερσαῖος, used as an eye-salve, Plin.*HN*28.108. **-δίλεον** [ῑ], τό, *sea-holly*, *Eryngium maritimum*, Dsc.3.10, Gal.12.47. **-δῑλιάς**, άδος, ἡ, = foreg., ib.565; ἀρτεμισία κ. Alex.Trall.*Febr.*6. **-δίλῐνος** [δῑ], η, ον, = sq., [*ambiguitates*] Quint.1.10.5. **-δῑλίτης** [ῑτ] (sc. λόγος), ου, ὁ, a sophistic fallacy, Chrysipp.*Stoic.*2.93. **-δῑλοβοσκός**, ὁ, *feeder of sacred crocodiles*, *BGU*734 ii 7 (iii A. D., abbrev.). **-δῑλόβρωτος**, ον, = sq., Aët.13.6 tit. **-δῑλόδηκτος**, ον, *bitten by a crocodile*, Dsc.5.109. **-δῑλοειδής**, ές, *in the form of a crocodile*, *PMag. Leid.V.*3.15 (κορκ- Pap.). **-δῑλοπάρδᾰλις**, εως, ἡ, fabulous animal, *IG*14.1302 (Praeneste). ⊛**-δῑλος**, ὁ, prop. Ion. word for *lizard*, acc. to Hdt.2.69, etc.; κ. τριπήχεες χερσαῖοι, of the *desert monitor*, genus *Varanus*, Id.4.192; of other *lizards*, Arist.*Fr.*362, Lxx *Le.*11. 30, Ael.*NA*1.58; κ. μικρός, in a fountain at Chalcedon, Str.12.4.2; cf. **κροκύδιλος** Hippon.119 (-δειλ- Eust.; **κρεκύδειλος** *Et.Gen.* in *Indogerm.Forsch.*15.7). 2. *crocodile* found in the Nile, Hdt.2. 68 sq.; also in Indian rivers, Id.4.44, cf. Ael.*NA*12.41; ὁ κ. ὁ ποτάμιος Arist.*HA*492$^b$24, cf. 558$^a$18. (Correctly written **κροκόδιλος**

*PCair.Zen.*354.13, 443.4 (iii B.C.), *PTeb.*63.25 (ii B.C.), etc.; later -δειλος *PAmh.*2.45.8 (ii B.C.), etc., freq. in codd.; **κορκόδιλος** *PCair.Zen.*370.5 (iii B.C.); **κορκότιλος** *Stud.Pal.*20.75 ii 16 (iii/iv A.D.); **κορκόδριλλος** and Dim. **κορκοδρίλλιον**, *Gloss.* **-δῑλοτάφιον** [ᾰ], τό, *burial-place of sacred crocodiles*, *PGrenf.*2.14(*d*) (iii B.C.), *PTeb.*88.4 (ii B.C., κορκ-), *BGU* 303.9 (i B.C.). **-ειδής**, ές, *saffron-coloured*, Arist.*Col.*795ᵇ1, Sch.Pi.*N.*1.58; χολή Aret.*SD* 1.15. **-είμων**, ον, gen. ονος, *saffron-clad*, Sch.D II.8.1. ❋**-εις**, εσσα, εν, *saffron coloured*, prob.l. in Pi.*P.*4.232, cf. Sapph.*Supp.*22.7; δαῦκον Thphr.*HP*9.15.5; κισσός Theoc.*Ep.*3; στολίδος κ. τρυφᾷ E. *Ph.*1491 (lyr.); χιτών Phalaec.ap.Ath.10.440d. 2. κροκόεις (sc. χιτών), ὁ, = κροκωτός, *dress-robe of saffron*, ὃς ἐμὲ κροκόεντ' ἐνέδυσεν Ar.*Th.*1044. **-μαγμα**, ατος, τό, *residuum* after the *saffron-unguent has been expressed*, Dsc.1.27, Asclep.ap.Gal.13.210, *PMasp.*141 ii*a* 23 (vi A.D.). 2. *a compound drug*, Damocr.ap.Gal.14.133, Paul. Aeg.7.12. **-μέριον**, τό, = κημός, Ps.-Dsc.4.133. **-μηλον**, τό, *conserve of quince and saffron*, Alex.Trall.*Febr.*7. **-νητική** (sc. τέχνη), ἡ, (κρόκη I. 1) *the art of spinning the woof*, opp. στημονονητική, Pl.*Plt.*283a. **-πεπλος**, ον, *with yellow veil*, Ἠώς Il.8.1, 19.1, al.; Ἐνυώ Hes.*Th.*273; of a river-nymph, ib.358; of the Muses, Alcm.85A.

❋**κρόκος**, ὁ (ἡ, Str.14.5.5), *saffron*, *Crocus sativus*, Il.14.348, *h.Cer.* 6, Hippon.41, S.*OC*685 (lyr.), Cratin.98 (pl.), A.R.3.855, cf. Thphr. *HP*4.3.1, al., Dsc.1.26, etc. b. κ. λευκός, *C. cancellatus*, Thphr.*HP* 7.7.4. c. κ. ἀκανθώδης, = κνῆκος, ibid. 2. *saffron* (made from its stigmas), Ar.*Nu.*51, etc.; κρόκου βαφάς A.*Ag.*239 (lyr.); κ. Ἀραβικός *Edict.Diocl.* in Ἀθηνᾶ 18.6. 3. *saffron meadow*, Eust.1698. 30. 4. σὺν κρόκῳ ᾠὸν *yolk* of egg, Alex.Trall.1.1: pl., ᾠῶν τὰ κρόκα Paul.Aeg.3.78.

❋**κροκόττας**, α, ὁ, an Indian wild beast, supposed to be a hybrid between wolf and dog, perh. really the *hyena*, Ctes.*Fr.*87, Agatharch. 77, *Peripl.M.Rubr.*50, *IG*14.1302 (Praeneste): **κροκούττας** Str.16. 4.16: **κορικόττας** Ael.*NA*7.22, Porph.*Abst.*3.4, Plin.*HN*8.107: **κοροκότας** D.C.76.1.

❋**κροκόω**, *crown with yellow ivy* (cf. κροκόεις 1), *AP*13.29 (Nicaenet., Pass.). II. (κρόκη) *weave*, Dionys.ap.St.Byz. s.v. Δαρσανία. 2. *wrap in wool*, Phot.

**κροκῠδ-ίζω**, *pick loose flocks off a garment*, τὸ κάταγμα κροκυδίζουσαν Philyll.22, Gal.10.928; of persons in delirium, *twitch the blankets*, Aret.*CA*1.1. **-ισμός**, ὁ, *picking of flocks*, Gal.19.412:—hence **-ιον**, τό, Dim. of κροκύς, Id.10.867, Theognost.*Can.*125.

**κροκῠδολογέω**, = κροκυδίζω, Hp.*Epid.*7.25.

**κροκῠλεγμός**, ὁ, = κροκυδισμός, Hsch.

❋**κροκύς** [ῠ], ύδος, ἡ, (κρόκη I. 3) *flock* or *nap on woollen cloth*, Hdt.3. 8, Luc.*Fug.*28, etc.; *piece of wool*, Hp.*Prog.*4, Plu.*Sull.*35; κροκύδα ἀφαιρεῖν, typical of a flatterer, Thphr.*Char.*2.3: metaph., ἀνήσω κροκύδα μαστιγουμένη Ar.*Fr.*651. 2. κ. ἑδρική *suppository*, Herod. Med. in *Rh.Mus.*58.72, cf. Aët.3.161.

❋**κροκύφαντος** [ῠ], ον, (κρόκη, ὑφαίνω) *woven*: as Subst., gloss on κεκρύφαλος, Erot., Eust.1280.59: metaph., *network* of the human body, in contempt, M.Ant.2.2.

**κροκ-ώδης**, ες, *saffron-coloured*, Dsc.1.27, Aret.*SD*1.15; *containing saffron*, Id.*CA*2.2; κολλύριον Gal.12.715, cf. *CIL*13.10021.66. II. *like the* κρόκη or *thread of the woof*, Pl.*Plt.*309b. **-ωτίδιον**, τό, Dim. of κροκωτός 2, Ar.*Lys.*47, *Ec.*332. ❋**-ώτινος**, η, ον, = κροκωτός 1, Ezek. *Exag.*260, *CPR*27.9 (ii A.D.), *PHamb.*10.24 (ii A.D.). ❋**-ώτιον**, τό, = κροκωτίδιον, Poll.7.56. ❋**-ωτός**, ή, όν, *saffron-dyed*, *saffron-coloured*, Pi.*N.*1.38. 2. as Subst., κροκωτός (sc. χιτών), ὁ, *saffron-coloured robe*, worn by gay women, Ar.*Th.*138, *Ec.*879; as an offering in temples, *IG*1².386.22, 2².1514.60,62; worn by Dionysus (or at his festivals) over the χιτών, Cratin.38, Ar.*Ra.*46; by effeminate men, παρθένος δ' εἶναι δοκεῖ φορῶν κροκωτούς (prob. for κροσ-) Arar.4, cf. Callix.2, Duris 12 J., etc.: neut. pl. κροκωτά (sc. ἱμάτια) v.l. in Ar. *Lys.*44.

**κροκωτοφορ-έω**, *wear the* κροκωτός, Ar.*Lys.*44, 219. **-ος**, ον, *wearing the* κροκωτός, Plu.2.785e.

**κρολίαζε**· πλησίαζε θᾶττον, Hsch. (Lydian). **κρόμβος**· ὁ κόνδυλος, καὶ ὁ καπυρός, Id.: Sup. -ότατον· καπυρώτατον, κατακεκονδυλωμένον, Id.

**κρομβόω**, *roast*, χοιρίδια κ. ὅλα Diph.90.

❋**κρομμύδιον**, τό, *small onion*, *Gp.*12.1.2 (κρομύδιν codd.), Sch.Opp. *H.*3.173.

**κρομμυογήτειον**, τό, = γήτειον, *horn-onion*, Thphr.*HP*4.6.2.

❋**κρομμῠον**, τό, Ep. κρόμῠον, *onion*, *Allium Cepa*, κρομύοιο λοπόν Od.19.233; κρόμυον ποτῷ ὄψον Il.11.630, cf. Hdt.2.125, 4.17; freq. in Ar., *Lys.*798, etc.; κελεύω κρόμμυα ἐσθίειν, = κλαίειν κελεύω, Bias ap.D.L.1.83. 2. τὰ κ. *the onion-market*, Eup.304. II. κ. σχιστόν, *a variety of Allium Cepa, shallot*, Thphr.*HP*7.4.7. (Written κρόμμυον in *PCair.Zen.*269.4, 300.3, *PSI*4.332.13, *PPetr.*3 p.328 (all iii B.C.), freq. in codd. (confirmed by metre in Ar., etc.); κρόμυον Hom. ll. cc. (perh. metri gr.), *POxy.*1584.23 (ii A.D.), *Stud.Pal.* 22.75.8 (iii A.D.), etc.: prob. assim. fr. κρέμμυον, cf. place-name Κρεμμυών B.17.24, etc.)

**κρομμῠοξῠρεγμία**, ἡ, *a belch of onions and crudities*, Ar.*Pax*529.

**κρομμῠο-πώλης**, ου, ὁ, *dealer in onions*, *PPar.*5 xx 8 (ii B.C., in form κρομβυο-, cf. Wilcken *Ostr.* i p.691), Poll.7.198. **-πώλιον**, τό, *onion-shop*, Hsch. ❋**-φακον**, τό, *onions mixed with lentils*, *PLille* 34.11 (iii B.C.).

**κρόμπος** or **κρομπός**, ὁ, dub. sens., τὸν λόφον τὸν ἰν τῷ κρόμποι *Schwyzer* 664.12, cf. 16 (Orchom. Arc., iv B.C.).

**κρόμῠον**, v. κρόμμυον.

**Κρον-εῖον**, τό, *temple of Cronos*, *PGrenf.*1.11 i 16 (ii B.C.). **-ια**, ων, τά, v. Κρόνιος. **-ιάς**, άδος, ἡ, fem. of Κρόνιος: αἱ Κ. (sc. ἡμέραι), = *Saturnalia*, Plu.*Cic.*18. ❋**-ίδης** [ῐ], ου, ὁ, Patron., *son of Cronos*, i.e. *Zeus*, Il.1.498, al.; Ζεὺς Κ. 2.111, al. II. Lacon. **Κρονίδαρ**, *an aged man*, Hsch. **-ικός**, ή, όν, = sq.; Κ. ἀστήρ the planet *Saturn*, *AP*11.227 (Ammian.); ζῴδια Paul.Al.*O.*3; Κ. ἑορτή, = *Saturnalia*, Plu.*Pomp.*34, Porph.*Antr.*23; Κ. λόφος, = Κρόνιον, Pi.*O.*5.17; also Κ. ὄχθος ib.9.3. II. *old-fashioned, out of date*, Ar. *Pl.*581, Pl.*Ly.*205c (Comp.); πρᾶγμά τι γιγνόμενον ἀεί, Κρονικόν Alex. 62.2, cf. *Com.Adesp.*1052. 2. prov., Κ. λῆμαι, of the short-sighted, Diogenian.5.63, Hsch. **-ιος**, α, ον, (Κρόνος) *of Cronos* or *Saturn*, ὦ Κρόνιε παῖ A.*Pr.*577, Pi.*O.*2.12; Κ. ἅλς the Adriatic, A.R.4.327, 509; but Κ. πόντος the North Sea, Orph.*A.*1081. b. Astrol., Κρόνιον ὄμμα εἰς τὸν οἶκον ἐνέσκηψε, i.e. disaster, Hld.2.24. 2. Κρόνια (sc. ἱερά), τά, *festival of Cronos* at Athens on the twelfth of Hecatombaeon (hence called μὴν Κρόνιος, Plu.*Thes.*12); ὄντων Κρονίων D.24.26; Κ. ἐνστάντων Alciphr.3.57; later, = Lat. *Saturnalia*, D.H.4.14, Plu.2.272e, etc. 3. Κρόνιον (sc. ὄρος), τό, *the hill of Cronos*, near Olympia, Pi.*O.*1.111; = Lat. *templum Saturni*, D.C. 45.17. 4. Κρόνιον, τό, = δελφίνιον, Ps.-Dsc.3.73. II. = Κρονικός II, Κρονίων ὄζειν to smell *of the dark ages*, Ar.*Nu.*398, cf. Sch. ad loc. **-ιππος**, ὁ, *an old dotard*, Ar.*Nu.*1070. ❋**-ίων**, ωνος, ὁ, *son of Cronos*, i.e. *Zeus*, Il.1.397, al.; Ζεὺς Κρονίων ib.502, al.: gen. Κρονίονος only Il.14.247, Od.11.620. II. Κρονιών (sc. μήν), name of a month at Samos, etc., *SIG*976.2 (ii B.C.), al. [Hom. has ῑ in Κρονίων, Κρονίονος, in other cases ῐ: but Tyrt.2.1, Pi.*P.*4.23, etc., use ῐ in Κρονίων.]

**Κρονο-δαίμων**, ονος, ὁ, = Κρόνος II, *Com.Adesp.*1053. **-θήκη**, ἡ, *receptacle for old follies*, ib.1054. **-ληρος**, ὁ, *old twaddler*, Plu. 2.13b, *Com.Adesp.*1052.

❋**Κρόνος**, ὁ, *Cronos*, Hes.*Th.*137, *Op.*111, Il.8.479, 14.203, A.*Pr.* 203, *Eu.*641; οἷς δὴ βασιλεὺς Κ. ἦν 'in the golden age', Cratin.165; ὁ ἐπὶ Κρόνου βίος Arist.*Ath.*16.7.—Later interpreted as, = χρόνος, cf. Arist.*Mu.*401ᵃ15. 2. ὁ τοῦ Κ. (sc. ἀστήρ) the planet *Saturn*, Id. *Metaph.*1073ᵇ35, *Mu.*392ᵃ24, 399ᵃ11; so later Κρόνος, ὁ, *Placit.*2.32.1, Cleom.2.7; ἡ τοῦ Κ. ἡμέρα *Saturday*, D.C.37.16. II. nickname for *a dotard, old fool*, Ar.*Nu.*929, *V.*1480, Pl.*Euthd.*287b, Hyp.*Fr.* 252.

**κρόνος**, ὁ, = κόρνος, *Gloss.*

**Κρονότεκνος**, ὁ, *father of Cronos*, epith. of Uranos in Orph.*H.*4.8.

**κροντᾷ**· καταστήπεται, Hsch. **κρόξ**, v. κρόκη. **κρόπιον**, τό, *two-edged axe*, Id. (cf. κρώπιον).

**κροσός**, Rhod. for κρωσσός, *Chron.Lind.*B.9.

**κρόσσαι**, ῶν, αἱ, prob. = *stepped copings of parapets*, κρόσσας μὲν πύργων ἔρυον καὶ ἔρειπον ἐπάλξεις Il.12.258; κροσσάων ἐπέβαινον ib.444 (expld. by Aristarch. as *scaling ladders*). 2. *courses, steps* of the Pyramids, Hdt.2.125.

**κρόσσ-ιον** and **-οφθον** (-όφθοον cod.), τό, = κημός, Ps.-Dsc.4.133.

**κροσσ-ίον**, τό, Dim. of sq., Hdn.*Epim.*72. ❋**-οί**, οἱ, *tassels, fringe*, Poll.7.64, Hsch.; *lappets*, θώρακος Gal.18(1).818. **-όω**, assumed as etym. of sq., *EM*541.8, *Et.Gud.*349.33. **-ωτός**, ή, όν, also ός, όν Lyc.1102:—*tasselled, fringed*, l. c., Plu.*Luc.*28, Poll.4.120, *POxy.*1273.14 (iii A.D.): Subst. κροσσωτός (sc. χιτών), ὁ, Lxx *Ps.* 44(45).14; cf. κροκωτός 2. II. (κρόσσαι) *stepped*, σταυροῖσι -ωτὴ πτέρυξ, of a wall, Lyc.291 (v.l. κορσ-).

**κρόσταλλος**, = κρύσταλλος, Hsch. **κρόστινα**· φυλακτήρια, Id.

**κρόσφος**, ὁ, = γρόσφος, Eust.795.35.

**κροταίνω**, poet. collat. form of κροτέω, Opp.*C.*4.247.

❋**κροτάλ-ια** [ᾰλ], ων, τά, *ear-rings with pendants of pearl*, which *rattled* against each other, Petron.67, Plin.*HN*9.114. **-ίζω**, *use rattles* or *castanets*, τινὲς τῶν γυναικῶν, κρόταλα ἔχουσαι, κροταλίζουσι Hdt.2.60: hence ἵπποι κείν' ὄχεα κροτάλιζον *rattled* them *along*, Il.11.160. II. later, *clap, applaud*, Anaxil.2, D.Chr.31. 162, Alciphr.2.4:—Pass., Ath.4.159e, 11.503f. **-ισμός**, ὁ, *applause*, *Gloss.* **-ίστρια**, ἡ, *female castanet-player*, *Sammelb.*6945 (iii A.D.); Lat. *crotalistria*, of the stork, from the noise made by its mandibles, Publilius ap.Petron.55. **-ιστρίς**, ίδος, ἡ, = foreg., *POxy.* 475.17, 24 (ii A.D.). ❋**-ον**, τό, (κροτέω) in pl., *clapper*, used in the worship of Cybele, *h.Hom.*14.3, Pi.*Fr.*79, Hdt.2.60, Arist.*Mir.*839ᵃ1; of Dionysus, E.*Hel.*1308 (lyr.), cf. *Cyc.*205: generally, in dances, *AP* 5.174 (Mel.), 11.195 (Diosc.). II. sg., metaph., of persons, '*rattle*', Ar.*Nu.*260, 448 (anap.); οἶδ' ἄνδρα, κρόταλον δριμύ E.*Cyc.*104. III. a name for the *narcissus*, Eumach.ap.Ath.15.681e. IV. κόρταλος σημαίνει τὸν κρότον τῆς ψυχῆς *EM* post κορυθαίολος (cod. Voss.); κορτάλων is perh. required by the metre in E.*Hyps.Fr.*1 ii 9 (lyr.).

**κροτᾰφ-ίζω**, *strike on the temples*, *PLips.*40 iii 24 (iv/v A.D.). **-ιος**, α, ον, *on* or *of the temples*, Gal.14.720. **-ίς**, ίδος, ἡ, *pointed hammer*, resembling the κέστρα, *IG*2².1672.120, Poll.10.147. **-ιστής**, οῦ, ὁ, *one who strikes on the temples*, *Gloss.*, Hsch. s.v. κόβαλος. **-ίτης** [ῑ] μῦς, ὁ, *temporal* muscle, Hp.*Art.*30, Gal.*UP*16.6, Antyll.ap.Orib. 7.16.2, *Arch.Pap.*4.270 (iii A.D.):—fem. **-ίτιδες** πληγαί blows *on the temples*, Hp. l. c. **-ος**, ὁ, *side of the forehead*, Il.4.502, 20. 397, Ar.*Ra.*854: mostly in pl., *temples*, Il.13.188, al., Hdt.4.187, Hp.*Prog.*2, etc.; πρᾶτον ἴουλον ἀπὸ κροτάφων καταβάλλων Theoc.15. 85, cf. 11.9, *IG*5(1).1355 (Abia); τοὺς κ. πολιοῦνται πρῶτον Arist.*GA* 784ᵇ35. 2. generally, *side edge, profile*, Procl.*Hyp.*3.6; κύκλου ib.17; of a brick, *PMag.Par.*1.30; κατὰ κρόταφον *sideways, horizontally*, Hero *Bel.*98.2, Ph.*Bel.*64.25, cf. 60.7; ἐπὶ κρόταφον *on its side*,

ib.66.13. II. metaph., *slope* of a mountain, A.*Pr.*721; ὑπὸ κροτάφοις Ἑλικῶνος Philiadas ap.St.Byz. s.v. Θέσπεια. III. *back of a book*, Anon.ap.Suid. IV. *edge* or *narrow side* of a stele, *IG*4$^2$(1).109 iii 162, iv 129 (Epid.). (κόρταφος *EM*541.23, *Et.Gud.*, Zonar., prob. to be read in Pl.Com.84; **κότραφος** *PMag.Osl.*1.152, etc.)

⊛ **κροτ-έω**, poet. κορτέω Hsch., cf. ἀνακροτέω: (κρότος):—*make to rattle*, of horses, ὄχεα κροτέοντες *rattling* them *along*, Il.15.453, cf. *h.Ap.*234. II. *knock, strike*, λέβητας Hdt.6.58; θύρσῳ γῆν E.*Ba.*188; τοῖς ἀγκῶσι τὰς πλευράς D.54.9; τινα Plu.2.10d: sens. obsc., *IG*12(7).414 (Amorgos, cf. διακροτέω 1):—Pass., *to be beaten* by rain, Ael.*NA*16.17. 2. *clap* in sign of applause, κ. τὰς χεῖρας, τὼ χεῖρε, Hdt.2.60, X.*Cyr.*8.4.12; ταῖς χερσί Thphr.*Char.*19.10: abs., *applaud*, X.*Smp.*9.4, D.21.226, etc.; ἐν θεάτρῳ Thphr.*Char.*11.3: c. acc., κ. τινά D.L.7.173:—Pass., Arist.*Po.*1456$^a$10 (sed leg. κρατεῖσθαι), Pl.*Ax.*368d, etc.; τέλειος ῥήτωρ καὶ κεκροτημένος Phld.*Rh.*2.128 S.; παρὰ Ὁμήρῳ κεκρότηται τὰ σώφρονα συμπόσια *are commended*, Ath.5.182a (sed leg. (συγ)κεκρ.). b. also in sign of disapproval, Plu.2.533a. 3. κ. ὀδόντας *gnash* the teeth, Archil.*Supp.*2.9. 4. of a smith, *hammer, weld together*, Luc.*Lex.*9: metaph., in Pass., *to be wrought*, κεκρότηται χρυσέα κρηπίς Pi.*Fr.*194, cf. Lyc.888: hence ἐξ ἀπάτας κεκροτημένοι ἄνδρες *one mass of* trickery, Theoc.15.49; εὐθὺς τὸ πρῆγμα κροτείσθω 'strike while the iron is hot', *AP*10.20 (Adaeus). 5. *rattle, clash*, χαλκώματα Plu.2.944b: c. dat., κ. ὀστράκοις καὶ ψήφοις *make a rattling noise* with them, in order to collect a swarm of bees, Arist.*HA*627$^a$16; κ. κυμβάλοις Luc.*Alex.*9; satirically, ἡ τοῖς ὀστράκοις κροτοῦσα [Μοῦσ' Εὐριπίδου] Ar.*Ra.*1306, cf. Ael.*NA*2.11. 6. *strike the woof home with the weaver's sley*, σινδόνες λίαν κεκροτημέναι *close-woven*, Str.15.1.67. **-ημα**, ατος, τό, *work wrought with the hammer*: metaph., of Odysseus, '*piece of mischief*', S.*Fr.*913, E.*Rh.*499. **-ησίγομφος** [ῐ], ον, *with chattering teeth*, Cerc.6.4. **-ησις**, εως, ἡ, *clapping, striking*, χειρῶν, as a sign of grief, Pl.*Ax.*365a; [σιδήρου] Ph.*Bel.*71.44 (pl.); τοῦ πνεύματος D.H.*Comp.*14 (v.l. for κροῦσις). **-ησμός**, ὁ, = κρότος, [ἀσπὶς] πυκνοῦ κροτησμοῦ τυγχάνουσα A.*Th.*561. **-ητικός**, ή, όν, *plausible*, αἴτησις Dosith.p.427 K. **-ητός**, ή, όν, *stricken, sounding with blows*, κάρα A.*Ch.*428. 2. κ. ἅρματα *rattling, bumping* chariots, S.*El.*714; κροτητὰ πηκτίδων μέλη music *struck from* the harp, Id.*Fr.*241. II. τὰ κροτητά, 1. *cakes* of some kind, E.*Fr.*467.4. 2. *much-trodden places*, Thphr.*HP*6.6.10.

**κρότιον**, τό, = κατανάγκη, Ps.-Dsc.4.131.

**κροτοθόρῠβος**, ὁ, *loud applause*, Epicur.*Fr.*143, Plu.2.45f, 1117a, Eun.*Hist.*p.259 D.

**κρότος**, ὁ, *rattling noise*, made to collect a swarm of bees, Arist.*HA*627$^a$16; κ. ποδῶν *beat* of the feet in dancing, E.*Heracl.*783 (pl.), *Tr.*546 (both lyr.); κ. σικιννίδων Id.*Cyc.*37; ὁ τῶν δακτύλων κ. *snapping* of the fingers, Ael.*NA*17.5; ἐνόπλιος κ. *clash* of arms, Plu.*Mar.*22; ὁ κ. τῶν λόγων Luc.*Dem.Enc.*15 (but perh. 'welding'); ἡ εὔροια καὶ ὁ τῆς γλώσσης κ. Philostr.*VS*2.25.6; ῥυθμοῖο κ. *APl.*4.226 (Alc. Mess.). 2. κ. χειρῶν *clapping* of hands, *applause*, Ar.*Ra.*157: abs., X.*An.*6.1.13, etc.; θόρυβον καὶ κ... ἐποιήσατε D.21.14, cf. 19.195. b. in token of ridicule, γέλως καὶ κ. Pl.*La.*184a.

**κροτών**, ῶνος, ὁ, *tick, Ixodes ricinus*, Arist.*HA*552$^a$15, Agatharch.58, Dsc.1.77, Plu.2.55e: prov., ὑγιέστερος κροτῶνος Men.318 (but Str.6.1.12 has Κρότωνος). II. *castor-oil tree, Ricinus communis* (cf. κίκι), Hp.*Mul.*2.201, Thphr.*HP*1.10.1, 3.18.7, *PRev.Laws*39.3, al. (iii B.C.), etc. 2. in pl., *seeds* of the tree, *PCair.Zen.*499.10 (iii B.C.); in full, κ. κίκεως Gal.19.743. III. *part of the ear*, Poll.2.85. (Hdn.Gr.1.36 distinguishes κροτών from Κρότων the place-name.)

**κροτώνη**, ἡ, *excrescence on trees*, esp. *on the olive*, = γόγγρος II, Thphr.*HP*1.8.6. II. in pl., *fragments of bronchial cartilage*, Hp.*Morb.*2.53, cf. Gal.19.115.

**κροτωνο-ειδές**, τό, = κροτών II, Hp.*Nat.Mul.*32. **-φόρος**, ον, *bearing castor-oil plants*, [γῆ] *Sammelb.*6797.16, al. (iii B.C.), *PPetr.*2p.110 (= 3p.69) (iii B.C.).

**κρουερ(οῦ)**· τοῦ φοβεροῦ, Hsch.; cf. κρυερός.

**κροῦμα**, ατος, τό, (κρούω) *beat, stroke*, Ar.*Ec.*257 (sens. obsc.):—also **κροῦσμα** *AP*6.27 (Theaet.), Poet.*de herb.*121, Porph.*Abst.*1.43; κρούσμασι καὶ στρέμμασι *blows* and sprains, Paul.Aeg.3.78, cf. Poll.2.199. 2. *sound produced by striking stringed instruments* with the plectron, *note*, κρούεται τὰ κρούματα.., τὰ μὲν ἄνω, τὰ δὲ κάτω Hp.*Vict.*1.18, cf. Ar.*Th.*120 (lyr.), Pl.*R.*333b, *Min.*317d, etc.; τὸ πόημα οὐχ ὡς τερέτισμα καὶ κ. νοοῦμεν Phld.*Po.*2p.228 H.; also of wind instruments, κρούματα τὰ αὐλήματα καλοῦσιν Plu.2.638c, cf. Poll.4.83, 7.88; σαλπιστικὰ κ. Id.4.84; τοιαῦτα..νιγλαρεύων κ. Eup.110; αὐλεῖ..σαπρὰ κ. Theopomp.Com.50; ἡ τοῦ κρούματος ἁρμονία the *melody* (on the pan-pipes), Ach.Tat.8.6, cf. *APl.*1.8 (Alc. Mess.); so, *musical air, melody*, *BGU*1125.4 (i B.C.); ᾠδαὶ καὶ κ. Jul.*Or.*2.49d:—also **κροῦσμα**, *AP*5.291.8 (Agath.).

**κροῦμαι**· μύξαι, Hsch.

⊛ **κρουμ-ατικός**, ή, όν, *of* or *for playing on a stringed instrument*, σοφίη *AP*11.352.2 (Agath.): in a general sense, ἡ κ. μουσικὴ ἡ διὰ τῶν αὐλῶν Suid. s.v. Ὄλυμπος; διάλεκτος κ. style *in playing*, Plu.2.1138b; λέξεις κρουσματικαί sounds of *music*, i.e. *inarticulate* sounds without sense, Plb.3.36.3. **-άτιον**, τό, Dim. of κροῦμα, *musical phrase*, Ach.Tat.1.5, Sch.Ar.*Eq.*276, *Pl.*290. **-ατοποιός**, ὁ, *musician*, Macho ap.Ath.8.337c, Aristodem.8; *composer of instrumental music*, Phld.*Mus.*pp.95, 99 K.

**κροῦναι**· τὰ ἄφορα δένδρα, Hsch.; also, = κρῆναι τέλειαι, Id.

**κρουν-εῖον**, τό, kind of *drinking vessel*, Epig.6. **-ηδόν**, Adv. *like a spring, gushing*, Lxx 2*Ma.*14.45, Ph.2.96, Harp.Astr. in *Cat.Cod.Astr.*8(3).136. **-ίζω**, *discharge liquid in a slender stream*, of the ῥυτόν (q.v.), κ. λεπτῶς Doroth.ap.Ath.11.497e:—Med., *catch the liquid so running in one's mouth*, Epin.2.3. **-ίον**, τό, Dim. of κρουνός, Hdn.Gr.1.356, 360. **-ίσκος**, ὁ, = foreg., *cock, tap* of the clepsydra, Sch.Luc.*Pisc.*28. **-ισμα**, ατος, τό, *gush, stream*, *APl.*1.12. **-ισμάτιον**, τό, Dim. of foreg., *small nozzle* or *spout*, Hero *Spir.*1.8; *small pipe*, ib.29. **-ισμός**, ὁ, *gushing out of water*, Aq. 2*Ki.*5.8. II. Medic., *douche*, Aët.5.119, Paul.Aeg.2.52. **-ίτης** [ῑ], ου, ὁ, fem. **-ῖτις**, ιδος, *of springs*, Νύμφαι Orph.*H.*51.10. ⊛ **-ός**, ὁ, *spring, well head*, whence streams (πηγαί) issue, Il.22.147, 208; χείμαρροι ποταμοὶ..κρουνῶν ἐκ μεγάλων 4.454, cf. Pi.*O.*13.63, Men.530.22, *PLond.*3.1177.290 (ii A.D.), etc.; κρουνοὶ κρηναίου ποτοῦ S.*Tr.*14. 2. metaph., κ. αἵματος E.*Rh.*790, cf. *Hec.*568; κρουνοὶ Ἀφαίστοιο *streams* of lava from Etna, Pi.*P.*1.25; of *streaming* perspiration, Hp.*Aph.*7.82, Lib.*Ep.*316.3: metaph., *torrent of words*, θαρρῶν τὸν κ. ἀφίει Ar.*Ra.*1005. 3. *watercourse*, Str.5.3.8. 4. *spout, nozzle*, Hero *Spir.*2.25, al.

**κρουνοχυτρολήραιος**, ὁ, *pourer forth of washy twaddle*, with collat. notion of *water-drinker*, Com. word in Ar.*Eq.*89.

**κρούνωμα**, ατος, τό, = κρουνός 2, κ. βρότειον Emp.6.3.

**κρουπαλίας**· κλεῖδας, Hsch.

**κρούπεζαι**, αἱ, *high wooden shoes*, used in Boeotia for treading olives, and worn on the stage by flute-players to beat time, Paus.Gr.*Fr.*239, Poll.7.87 (sg.), Phot.:—also **κρούπαλα**, τά, S.*Fr.*44; **κρούπετα**, Hsch.

⊛ **κρουπέζιον**, τό, Dim. of foreg., Poll.10.153, Hsch.

**κρουπεζό-ομαι**, Pass., *have wooden shoes on*, Hsch. **-φόρος**, ον, *wearing wooden shoes*, of the Boeotians, Cratin.310.

**κρουσῐδημέω**, parody on κρουσιμετρέω, *cheat the people*, Ar.*Eq.*859.

**κρουσίης**· ἐλλιπής, Hsch.

**κρουσί-θῠρος** [ῐ], ον, *knocking at the door*: τὸ κ. (sc. μέλος) *serenade*, Trypho ap.Ath.14.618c. **-λύρης** [ῠ], ου, ὁ, *striking the lyre*, Orph.*H.*31.3. **-μετρέω**, *cheat in measuring* corn, *by striking off too much from the top of the measure*, Hsch., Poll.4.169. **-μέτρης**, ου, ὁ, *false measurer, cheat*, Sch.Ar.*Nu.*450.

**κροῦσις**, εως, ἡ, *striking, smiting, collision*, αἱ πρὸς ἀλλήλας κ., of atoms, Epicur.*Nat.Herc.*1431.16; ἡ πρὸς ἄλληλα κ. τῶν ὅπλων Plu.*Aem.*32; ποδὸς κρούσει χρώμενος *spurring* with the heel, of a rider, Id.*Alex.*6. 2. *tapping* or *ringing* of earthen vessels, to see whether they are sound: hence, generally, *scrutiny*, Suid. 3. metaph., of sophistical *attempts to deceive, chicanery*, Ar.*Nu.*318. 4. *playing on a stringed instrument*, Plu.*Per.*15, 2.1137b, etc.: generally, *instrumental music*, Plb.30.22.5; κρούσεις καὶ μέλη Phld.*Mus.*p.13 K.; παρὰ τὴν κροῦσιν λέγειν, of the recitative, ᾄδειν, of the air sung *to the accompaniment of instrumental music*, Plu.2.1141a; κ. ὑπὸ τὴν ᾠδὴν *heterophone accompaniment*, ib.b.

**κροῦσμα**, **κρουσματικός**, v. κρουμ-.

**κρουσ-μός**, ὁ, = κροῦσις 4, Procl.ap.Phot.*Bibl.*p.320 B. II. κ. ὀδόντων *gnashing* of teeth, Aus.*Ep.*8.8. **-τέον**, *one must knock at*, τηνδεδί (sc. θύραν) Ar.*Ec.*989. ⊛ **-της**, ου, ὁ, = Lat. *petulcus*, Dosith.p.397 K. ⊛ **-τικός**, ή, όν, *fit for striking, butting*, of a ram, Ph.1.113. II. *able to sound the right note*, ὄργανα Arist.*Pr.*918$^a$33; κ. θίξις χορδῶν, opp. ἠθική, Plu.2.802f. 2. metaph., of a rhetorician or sophist, *striking, impressive*, Ar.*Eq.*1379; τὸ κ. *striking eloquence*, Luc.*Dem.Enc.*32. **-τός**, ή, όν, *played by striking*, ὄργανα Nicom.*Harm.*2. II. κρουστὰ γράμματα· ἀπὸ τοῦ παρακρούεσθαι καὶ μὴ εὐθέως λέγειν, Phot.

**κρουτεῖται**· κοκκίζει, Hsch. **κρουφάδαν**, v. κρυφάδην.

⊛ **κρούω**, fut. -σω E.*El.*180: aor. ἔκρουσα X.*An.*4.5.18, Hyp.*Fr.*201: pf. κέκρουκα Diogenian.3.38, (ἐκ-) Pl.*Phdr.*228e, (προσ-) D.21.206:—Med., aor. ἐκρουσάμην Th.7.40:—Pass., aor. ἐκρούσθην Eratosth.*Cat.*32: pf. κέκρουμαι (ἀπο-) X.*HG*7.4.26, or -ουσμαι (ἀπο-) Ar.*Ach.*459:—*strike, smite*, ῥυτῆρι κ. γλουτόν S.*Fr.*501; κρούσας δὲ πλευρὰ [τῶν ἵππων] E.*Fr.*779.6; τὸν λυχνοῦχον Lys.*Fr.*83; τοῖς ποσὶ τὴν γῆν Arr.*An.*7.1.5; also εἰς τὴν χεῖρα τοῖς δακτύλοις κ. *with the* fingers, D.C.40.16: metaph., κνῖσα κ. ῥινὸς ὑπεροχάς *tickles*, Ephipp.3.3. 2. *strike* one *against* another, *strike together*, κ. χεῖρας *clap* the hands, E.*Supp.*720; τὰ ὅπλα κρουόμενα πρὸς ἄλληλα Th.3.22; τὰς ἀσπίδας πρὸς τὰ δόρατα X.*An.*l.c.: metaph., ἀλλήλων τοὺς λόγους τοῖς λόγοις ἐκρούομεν ἄν *would have knocked* their heads together, Pl.*Tht.*154e. 3. κ. πόδα (i.e. κ. τὴν γῆν τῷ ποδί), in dancing, E.*El.* l.c. (lyr.); ἴχνος ἐν γᾷ κ. Id.*IA*1043 (lyr.). 4. metaph. from *tapping* an earthen vessel, to try whether it rings sound (cf. κροῦσις 2): *examine, try, prove*, κρούετε ἀπολαμβάνοντες τὸ καλόν Pl.*Hp.Ma.*301b; κἂν διαπειρώμενος κρούσῃς [τὸν κόλακα] Plu.2.64d. 5. *strike* a stringed instrument with a plectron, Simon.183, Pl.*Ly.*209b: generally, *play* any instrument (v. κροῦμα, κρουματικός), αὐλεῖ..κρούων ἰαστί *Com.Adesp.*415; c. dat., κ. κρεμβάλοις, = κρεμβαλίζειν, Ath.14.636d. 6. κ. τὴν θύραν *knock at* the door *on the outside*, Ar.*Ec.*317, 990 (with play on signf. 8), X.*Smp.*1.11, Pl.*Prt.*310b, 314d, etc.; κόπτειν is better Att. acc. to Phryn.154; later κ. ἐπὶ τὴν θύραν Lxx *Jd.*19.22. 7. κ. σταθμὸν ἑτερόζυγον, = κρουσιμετρέω, Ps.-Phoc.15; ὡς μήτε κρούσῃς μήθ' ὑπὲρ χεῖλος βάλῃς S.*Fr.*796; κρούων γε μὴν αὐτὰς ἐωνούμην Eup.184. 8. sens. obsc., *AB*101, cf. Ar.*Ec.*990; κ. πέπλον E.*Cyc.*328. 9. Med., κρούεσθαι πρύμναν *back water*, Th.1.51, 54, 3.78; αἱ πρύμναν κρουόμεναι νῆες Arr.*An.*5.17.7 (also in Act., Plb.16.3.8); κ. ἐπὶ π. τὴν ναῦν App.*BC*5.119: hence κρούεσθαι τὸ πτερόν *fly backwards*,

Ael.*NA*3.13:—also in Act., Plot.2.9.18. 10. **κρούειν** ἀκράτῳ, v. πατάσσω II.2. (Cf. Lith. *krùšti* 'bruise', 'pound', Lett. *krausēt* 'thresh'.)

**κρυαίνω**, = ἱμείρω, Theognost.*Can.*21 (cf. Archil.176).

**κρῠβ-άζω**, = ἀποκρύπτω, Hsch.:—hence **-αστός**, = κρυπτός, prob. l. for κυρβαστός, *EM*547.46.

**κρύβακτος**, ὁ, dub. sens. in *Stud.Pal.*20.230.8 (iv A.D.).

**κρύβ-δᾰ**, Adv., (κρύπτω) *without the knowledge of*, c. gen., κ. Διός Il.18.168; Ὀρέστου κ. A.*Ch.*177. 2. abs., *secretly*, Pi.*P.*4.114. **-δην**, Dor. **-δᾱν**, Adv. *secretly*, Od.11.455, 16.153, Hp.*Mul.*1.54, Ar.*V.*1018, etc.; κ. ψηφίζεσθαι Lex ap.And.1.87, cf. Lys.12.91, Pl.*Lg.*766b, Arist.*Rh.Al.*1433ᵃ23, *IG*2².1237.82. 2. c. gen., = foreg. 1, κ. πατρός Pi.*P.*3.13. **-ες**· νεκροί, Hsch. **-ῆ**, Adv., = κρύβδην, v.l. in Lxx 2*Ki.*12.12, cf. 3*Ma.*4.12, *POxy.*83.14 (iv A.D.):—also **-ήν**, *Corp.Herm.*13.1 (s.v.l.). **-ηλος**, ον, *hidden*, Hsch.:—also **-ήτης**, ου, ὁ, *one hidden in the earth*, and **-ήσια**, τά, = νεκύσια, Id. **-ω**, late form of κρύπτω, Conon 50.2, Phlp.*in APr.*448.17, *PMag.Par.*1.385, *PMag.Leid.V.*10.10, *Gp.*2.24.2, Sch.E.*Hec.*739:—Pass., Lxx 4*Ki.*11.3, al. (also v.l. in Hp.*Mul.*2.154); mostly found in compds.

*κρῠερός, ά, όν, but ἀρῆς κρυεροῖο Hes.*Th.*657: (κρύος):—*icy, cold, chilling*. in Hom. only metaph., κρυεροῖο γόοιο Od.4.103, al.; κρυεροῖο φόβοιο Il.13.48; κρυεροῦ Ἀΐδαο Hes.*Op.*153; θανάτου τελευτή E.*Fr.*916.6 (anap.); πάθεα Ar.*Ach.*1191 (lyr.); θάλαμος, of the grave, *Epigr.Gr.*241.4 (Smyrna): in the lit. sense, *icy-cold*, κ. νέκυς Simon.114.5, cf. Ar.*Av.*951, 955, Hdn.1.6.1, etc.

**κρύμα**· εὕρημα, Hsch.

**κρῡμ-αίνω**, *make cold*, Hdn.*Epim.*75. *-**αλέος**, α, ον, *icy, chilly*, Heraclit.*All.*50, S.E.*M.*9.83. **-νός, -νώδης**, dub. forms for κρυμός, κρυμώδης (qq.v.).

**κρῡμοπᾰγής**, ές, *frost-congealing*, Βορέης Orph.*H.*80.2.

**κρῡμός**, ὁ, (κρύος) *icy cold, frost*, Hdt.4.8, 28, etc.; ἀνὰ κρυμόν in *frost*, Nic.*Th.*681: in pl., κατὰ τοὺς κρυμούς Str.11.2.8, cf. D.H.1.37, Onos.10.5, Polyaen.3.9.34, Ael.*NA*2.1. II. *chill, cold fit*, S.*Fr.*507, Hp.*Morb.*4.53, Call.*Aet.*3.1.19 (nisi leg. καυμός), Ruf.ap.Orib.45.30.21; κ. χολῆς E.*Fr.*682, cf. Dsc.3.53 (pl.). (κρυμνὸς ἢ κρυμός, Hsch.)

**κρῡμοχᾰρής**, ές, *delighting in frost*, f.l. in Orph.*H.*51.13 for δρυμο-.

**κρυμυεῖ**· ῥιγᾷ, πέφρικε, Hsch.

**κρῡμ-ώδης**, ες, *icy-cold, frozen*, Hp.*Vict.*2.65 (κρυμν- codd.), D.P.780, Men.Prot.p.47 D.; Ἄλπεις *AP*9.561 (Phil.): Comp., Ph.2.298, Metop.ap.Stob.3.1.116: Sup., Ael.*NA*3.13. **-ώσσω**, *to be stiff with cold*, Theognost.*Can.*21.

**κρῠ-όεις**, εσσα, εν, *chilling*, in metaph. sense, φόβου κρυόεντος Il.9.2; κρυόεσσα Ἰωκή 5.740; ἐν πολέμῳ κρυόεντι Hes.*Th.*936; συντυχία Pi.*I.*1.37: later in lit. sense, *icy-cold*, ἅλς, πάγος, A.R.1.918, *AP*6.221 (Leon.); Τάρταρος Orph.*Fr.*222; of Saturn, *Cat.Cod.Astr.*1.172; cf. ὀκρυόεις. **-όομαι**, Pass., *to be icy-cold*, κρυοῦται *it freezes*, *Gloss.* **-ος**, εος, τό, *icy cold, frost*, Hes.*Op.*494, Pl.*Ax.*368c, Jul.*Or.*6.181d; κ. ἰσχυρόν Arist.*Mete.*367ᵃ22: metaph., κακόν με καρδίαν τι περιπίτνει κρύος A.*Th.*834, cf. *Eu.*161 (both lyr.). II. κ., ὁ, = κρύσταλλος, Sch.Ar.*Nu.*766. (Cf. Lat. *crusta*.)

*κρυπ-τάδιος [ᾰ], α, ον (and ος, ον A.*Ch.*946 (lyr.)), *secret, clandestine*, κρυπταδίῃ φιλότητι Il.6.161; κρυπταδίου μάχας A.l.c.; κρυπτάδια φρονέοντα Il.1.542. Regul. Adv. **-ίως** Man.2.195, 6.182. **-τεία**, ἡ, (κρυπτεύω) *secret service* at Sparta, Pl.*Lg.*633b; employed against the Helots, Arist.*Fr.*538; ὁ ἐπὶ τῆς κ. τεταγμένος Plu.*Cleom.*28. II. *hiding-place*, Agath.5.19 (pl.). **-τέον**, *one must hide*, S.*Ant.*273, *AP*5.251 (Paul. Sil.). **-τεύω**, *hide oneself, lie concealed*, E.*Ba.*888 (lyr.), X.*Cyr.*4.5.5:—Pass., = ἐνεδρεύομαι (cf. Hsch.), E.*Hel.*541. *-**τή**, ἡ, *crypt, vault*, Callix.1. II. v. κρυπτός ad fin. *-**τήρ**, ῆρος, ὁ, = sq., τόποι Sch.Opp.*H.*3.235. **-τήριος**, α, ον, *convenient for concealing*, ἄντρον Orac.ap.Paus.8.42.6; κρυπτήριον, τό, *dungeon*, prob. l. in E.*Cret.*48. **-της**, ου, ὁ, *member of the Spartan* κρυπτεία, Id.*Fr.*1126 (s.v.l.). **-τικός**, ή, όν, *obscuring*, Alex.Aphr.*in Top.*528.12, 530.1. Adv. **-κῶς**, πυνθάνεσθαι Arist.*Top.*156ᵃ14; εἰπεῖν Alex.Aphr.*in SE*100.10. **-τίνδα**, Adv. *hide-and-seek*, Theognost.*Can.*15. **-τορχος**, ὁ, *with undescended testicles*, *PSI*3.252.25 (iii A.D.). *-**τός**, ή, όν, *hidden, secret*, κληῖδι κρυπτῇ Il.14.168, cf. Ar.*Th.*422; ἐπεποίητο οἱ κ. διῶρυξ Hdt.3.146; κ. τάφρος a trench *covered and concealed* by planks and earth, Id.4.201: freq. in Trag., κ. λόγος A.*Ch.*773; ἔπη S.*Ph.*1112 (lyr.); κρυπτᾷ ἐν ἥβᾳ, of young Orestes who was *concealed* in Phocis, Id.*El.*159 (lyr.); κ. πένθος E.*Hipp.*139 (lyr.), etc.; κρυπτῇ ψήφῳ Arist.*Rh.Al.*1424ᵇ1; τῆς πολιτείας τὸ κ. *the secret character* of the [Spartan] institutions, Th.5.68; ἡ κρυπτή (sc. ἀρχή) *secret service*, used by the Athenians in the subject-states, *AB*273; also, = κρυπτεία I, Heraclid.*Pol.*10; of persons, *in disguise*, Ar.*Th.*600, E.*El.*525: Medic., *deep-seated*, καρκίνος Hp.*Aph.*6.38, *Mul.*2.133, Gal.5.116; κ. πάθος *BGU*316.28 (iv A.D.). *-**τω**, Ep. Iterat. κρύπτασκε Il.8.272, -εσκε *h.Cer.*239: fut. κρύψω Od.4.350, etc.: aor. 1 ἔκρυψα, Ep. κρύψα 11.244: pf. κέκρῠφα (συγ-) D.H.*Comp.*18:—**Med.**, fut. κρύψομαι S.*Tr.*474, E.*Ba.*955: aor. ἐκρυψάμην S.*Aj.*246 (lyr.), etc.:—**Pass.**, fut. κρυφθήσομαι *Dialex.*2.4, κρυβήσομαι E.*Supp.*543, Lxx *Je.*39(32).27, κεκρύψομαι Hp.*Mul.*1.36: aor. ἐκρύφθην, Ep. κρ-, Il.13.405, E.*Ba.*955, ἐκρύβην [ῠ] *Ev.Jo.*8.59, Aesop.127, Apollod.3.2.2, (κατ-) Alciphr.3.47; part. κρῠφείς S.*Aj.*1145: pf. κέκρυμμαι Od.11.443, Pi.*O.*7.57, etc.; Ion. 3 pl. κεκρύφαται Hes.*Th.*730, Hp.*Mul.*2.163:—*hide, cover*, in Hom. with collat. notion of protection, κεφαλὰς.. κορύθεσσι κρύψαντες Il.14.373; ὁ δέ μιν σάκεϊ κρύπτασκε φαεινῷ 8.272, cf. 13.405 (Pass.); κ. με.. πόδα S.*OC* 114; later, simply, *hide*, κ. φάος ὀμμάτων Pi.*N.*10.40; *cover*, τινά τινι A.*Eu.*461, etc.; ὑφ' εἵματος κ. χεῖρα E.*Hec.*343:—Med., κάρα κρυψάμενος *having cloaked his* head, S.*Aj.*246 (lyr.); φύει τ' ἄδηλα καὶ φανέντα κρύπτεται *hides in its own bosom*, ib.647; παῖδά μ' ἐκρύψατο κρωσσός *IG*14.1909:—Pass., *hide oneself, lie hidden*, οὐρανῷ κρύπτεται E.*Hel.*606; δαλὸς κρύπτεται ἐς σποδιάν Id.*Cyc.*615 (lyr.); ὑφ' εἵματος κρυφείς S.*Aj.*1145: c. acc. cogn., κρύψει σὺ κρύψιν ἥν σε κρυφθῆναι χρεών E.*Ba.* l.c. 2. *cover in the earth, bury*, Hes.*Op.*138, S.*OC*621 (Pass.); χθονί ib.1546 (Pass.); τάφῳ Id.*Ant.*196; ἐν κατώρυχι ib.774; κατὰ χθονός ib.25; ὑπὸ γᾶν Pi.*P.*9.81; γῇ κ. Hdt.2.130 (Pass.), cf. S.*Ant.*946 (lyr., Pass.):—Pass., Τιτῆνες ὑπὸ ζόφῳ.. κεκρύφαται Hes.*Th.* l.c.; ἐν βένθεσιν νᾶσον κεκρύφθαι Pi.*O.* l.c. 3. Astron., *occult*, Theo Sm.p.193 H., al.:—Pass., of stars not seen in any part of the night, κεκρύφαται Hes.*Op.*386; of the heliacal *setting* of stars, Ptol.*Phas.*p.8 H. 4. *conceal, keep secret*, οὐδέν τοι ἐγὼ κρύψω ἔπος Od.4.350, cf. Ar.*Th.*74, etc.; κ. τι ἔνθα μή τις ὄψεται S.*Aj.*658, cf. *Tr.*903, *El.*436:—Med., πᾶν σοι φράσω τἀληθές, οὐδὲ κρύψομαι Id.*Tr.*474:—Pass., τὸ μὲν φάσθαι, τὸ δὲ καὶ κεκρυμμένον εἶναι Od.11.443; φάρμακα κεκρ. *secret*, E.*Andr.*32; κεκρ. νάπη *secret*, S.*OT*1398; κεκρ. παγίς Men.689; κεκρ. σκευωρία *secret* intrigue, Mitteis *Chr.*31 vi 14 (ii B.C.); κρυπτόμενα πράσσεται *in secret*, opp. ἐπὶ μαρτύρων, Antipho 2.3.8, cf. Th.6.72. b. *connive at*, S.*El.*825 (lyr.). 5. c. dupl. acc., *conceal* something from one, μή με κρύψῃς τοῦτο A.*Pr.*625, cf. S.*El.*957, E.*Hec.*570, Ar.*Pl.*26, Lys.32.7, etc.; so κ. τι πρός τινα S.*Ph.*588. 6. in Rhet., *argue so that the opponent is unwarily led to an adverse conclusion*, Arist.*Top.*156ᵃ7. 7. Medic., in Pass., *to be suppressed*, of the menses or lochia, Hp.*Mul.*1.36, 154, 2.163. II. intr., *lie hidden*, τὰ μὲν.. ὄμματα βλέποντα, τὰ δὲ κρύπτοντα E.*Ph.*1117 (s.v.l.); also κ. τινά *conceal oneself from*.., *h.Hom.*1.7.—(καλύπτω is simply *cover*; κεύθω *cover* so that no trace of it can be seen; κρύπτω *keep covered*, esp. for purposes of concealment.)

*κρυσταίνομαι, Pass., *to be congealed with cold, freeze*, Nic.*Al.*314.

**κρυσταλλ-ίζω**, *to be clear as crystal*, *Apoc.*21.11. *-**ῐνος**, η, ον, *icy*, χεῖρες Hp.*Epid.*7.25. II. *of crystal*, κύλιξ D.C.54.23; νίπτρα *AP*9.330 (Nicarch.). **-ιον**, τό, = ψύλλιον, Dsc.4.69 (Sicel). II. *rock-crystal*, in pl., *PHolm.*11.43, Anon.Alch.p.359 B.

*κρυσταλλο-ειδής, ές, *like ice*, πῆξις Epicur.*Ep.*2 p.45 U., cf. Lxx *Wi.*19.21; v.l. for -ώδης in Str.4.6.6. Adv. **-δῶς** *Placit.*2.11.2. II. *like crystal*, ἴασπις Dsc.5.142; κ. ὑγρόν the *crystalline lens*, Ruf.*Onom.*153, Gal.*UP*8.5, al.; κ. χιτών Poll.2.71: Astron., τὸ κ. the *crystalline sphere*, *Placit.*2.14.3. **-ομαι**, Pass., *to be frozen*, Ph.2.174, Anon.ap.Gell.17.8.7. **-πηκτος**, ον, *congealed to ice, frozen*, E.*Rh.*441:—also **-πήξ**, ῆγος, ὁ, ἡ, A.*Pers.*501.

*κρύσταλλος, ὁ, (κρύος, κρυσταίνομαι) *ice*, Il.22.152, Od.14.477, Hdt.4.28, S.*Fr.*149; κρύσταλλος ἐπεπήγει οὐ βέβαιος Th.3.23; ὁ παῖς τὸν κρύσταλλον prov., of persons who cannot keep a thing, but do not wish to let it go, Zen.5.58. 2. = νάρκη, *numbness, torpor*, Opp.*H.*3.155. II. *rock-crystal*, D.P.781, Str.15.1.67, Ael.*NA*15.8, etc.: also fem., *AP*9.753 (Claudian.): as Adj., οἱ κ. λίθοι D.S.2.52.

**κρυσταλλοφᾰνής**, ές, *of the look or transparency of crystal*: κρυσταλλοφανῆ, τά, *glass ware*, Str.16.2.25.

**κρυσταλλώδης**, ες, *icy, glacial*, Ptol.*Tetr.*94, D.C.49.31; of water, *clear*, *PHolm.*25.33.

**κρυτοπώλης**, v. γρυτοπώλης.

**κρύφ-ᾰ** [ῠ], Adv., (κρύπτω) = κρύβδα, *without the knowledge of*, c. gen., Th.1.101. 2. abs., *secretly*, Aen.Tact.2.4; *by ballot*, Th.4.88; *obscurely*, κ. καὶ δι' αἰνιγμάτων Plu.2.1125e. **-ᾷ**, Adv. Dor. for κρυφῇ, Pi.*O.*1.47, *Fr.*203. **-άδην**, Boeot. **κρουφάδαν**, = foreg., Corinn.*Supp.*2.59:—also **-άδις**, Hdn.Gr.1.512; **-άδεια**, ib.496. **-αῖος**, α, ον, also ος, ον Phld.*Piet.*101, Luc.*Ocyp.*166:—*hidden*, Pi.*I.*1.67, A.*Ch.*83 (lyr.), S.*Aj.*899, Pl.*Ti.*77c; ἐν κρυφαίοις Lxx *Je.*23.24, al. 2. *secret, clandestine*, δρασμός A.*Pers.*360; ἔκπλους ib.385; ἔπος S.*Fr.*935; ἀδικίαι Phld. l.c. Adv. **-ως** A.*Pers.*370, Aen.Tact.18.8.

**κρύφαλον**· σαβάκανον, Hsch. **κρυφανδόν** (-άνδων cod.), = κρυφηδόν, Id.

**κρύφασος**, ὁ, *a certain throw of the dice*, Poll.7.204.

**κρῠφ-ῆ**, Adv. *secretly, in secret*, S.*Ant.*85, 291, 1254, X.*Smp.*5.8, etc.:—Dor. **κρῠφᾷ** (q.v.); also ἐν κρυφῇ Lxx *Jd.*4.21, 9.31. **-ηδόν**, Adv., = foreg., opp. ἀμφαδόν, Od.14.330, cf. Q.S.14.60. **-ία**, ἡ, *concealment, hiding*, *PFlor.*284.8 (vi A.D.). **-ιαστής**, οῦ, ὁ, *interpreter of dreams*, Aq.*Ge.*41.8, al. **-ιμαίως**, Adv. *secretly*, Sch.Ar.*Pax*730. **-ιμος**, ον, = κρύφιος, Man.1.159, al., *PMag.Par.*1.1353, *PMag.Lond.*122.15, *Cat.Cod.Astr.*8(4).185: Comp., Dam.*Pr.*275.

**κρυφίνους**· ὑπούλους, Hsch. (cf. κρυψίνους).

**κρύφ-ιος** [ῠ], α, ον, also ος, ον E.*IT*1328, Th.7.25:—*hidden, concealed*, θυμός Pi.*P.*1.84; ὄφις S.*Ph.*1328. 2. *secret, clandestine*, ὀαρισμοί Hes.*Op.*789; λέχος S.*Tr.*360; εὐναί E.*El.*719 (lyr.); ἔρωτες Musae.1; ψᾶφοι Pi.*N.*8.26; κ. εἰσῆλθον E.*HF*598. Adv. **-ίως** Ps.-Luc.*Philopatr.*9. 3. *occult*, Procl.*Inst.*121, Dam.*Pr.*151; *latent*, ib.192, 201. Adv. **-ίως** ib.153. 4. voc. κρύφιε *such an one*, Lxx *Ru.*4.1. 5. κρύφιος, ὁ, fabulous gem, Ps.-Plu.*Fluv.*13.4. 6. κρύφιος, ὁ, title of a grade of initiates in the mysteries of Mithras, *CIL*6.751a, 753 (pl.). **-ιότης**, ητος, ἡ, *secrecy, obscurity*, Suid. s.v. ἀδηλία, Sch.Opp.*H.*2.258, Sch.E.*Ph.*1214. **-ιώδης**, ες, *mysterious*, Eust.1942.62 (Comp.).

**κρῠφο-γενής**, ές, *secretly born*, Hsch. s.v. κυθηγενέσι. **-νους**, ουν, = κρυψίνους, *EM*20.49; cf. κρυφίνους.

**κρῠφ-ός**, ό, = κρυφιότης, Emp.27.3 (dub.); κρυφὸν θέμεν to throw *a cloud* over.., Pi.*O*.2.97 (κρύφιον codd.). II. *lurking-place*, Lxx 1*Ma*.2.36, 1.53. (On the accent v. Hdn.Gr.1.225.) ※ **-ω**, late form of κρύπτω, only impf., Q.S.1.393, *AP*7.700 (Diod.), Nonn.*D*.7.45, al.

**κρυψί-γονος** [ῐ], ον, *secretly born*, Orph.*H*.50.3. ※ **-δομος**, ον, *dwelling in secret places*, ib.51.3 (Casaub. for κρυψίδρομος, *running secretly*). **-λογος**, ον, *keeping a matter secret*, Hdn.*Epim*. 38. **-μέτωπος**, ον, *hiding the forehead*, Luc.*Lex*.7. **-νοος**, ον, contr. **-νους**, ουν, *hiding one's thoughts, dissembling*, X.*Cyr*.1.6.27, Gal.8.362, D.C.67.1, Eun.*Hist*.p.254 D.; opp. παρρησιαζόμενος, X. *Ages*.11.5. Adv. **-νως** Poll.4.51. **-ποθος**, ον, *with concealed longing*, *EM*543.48.

**κρύψιππος**, ό, nickname of Chrysippus, D.L.7.182.

**κρυψιπυρίς**, *pigra*, *Gloss*.

**κρύψις**, εως, ἡ, (κρύπτω) *hiding, concealment*, κρυφθῆναι κρύψιν E. *Ba*.955, cf. Plb.10.46.3; opp. φάσις, of stars, *disappearance* below the horizon, Gem.13.2, al., Ti.Locr.97b (pl.); *occultation*, TheoSm. p.192 H. (pl.); *heliacal setting*, Metrod.*Herc*.831.10, Ptol.*Alm*.8.4, *Tetr*.4, TheoSm.p.137 H.; of new moon, Ptol.*Tetr*.22; *disappearance*, Plu.2.366d. 2. *suppression*, ἐπιμηνίων Gal.19.495. 3. *concealment* of stolen goods, Arist.*Rh*.1372ᵃ32. 4. *mystery, secret*, κρύψιν μεγάλην ἀνυμνοῦντες Dam.*Pr*.52 bis.

**κρυψί-φρων**, φρονος, ὁ, ἡ, = κρυψίνοος, Eust.1574.20. **-χολος**, ον, *dissembling one's anger*, Id.54.8.

**κρυψ-όρχης**, ου, ὁ, *with undescended testicles*, Sor.1.109. **-ορχις**, εως, ἡ, *undescended testicles*, Gal.19.448.

**κρῠώδης**, ες, *icy, chill*, Plu.2.653a, Poll.5.109.

**κρωβύλ-η** [ῠ], ἡ, *hair-net*, Serv. ad Virg.*Aen*.4.138, Hdn.Gr.1. 323. **-ος** (parox., v. Hdn.Gr.1.163), ὁ, *roll* or *knot of hair on the crown of the head*, worn at Athens, κρωβύλον ἀναδούμενοι Th.1.6, cf. Antiph.189, Sch.Ar.*Nu*.980. 2. nickname of the orator Hegesippus, Aeschin.3.118. 3. name of a πορνοβοσκός: prov., Κρωβύλου ζεῦγος 'a precious pair', Lib.*Ep*.91.2, Hsch., etc. II. *tuft of hair* on a helmet, X.*An*.5.4.13. **-ώδης**, ες, *like the* κρωβύλος, Luc.*Lex*.13.

**κρωγ-μα**, ατος, τό, = sq., Hdn.*Epim*.73. **-μός**, ό, *croaking, cawing of a crow* or *chough*, *AP*7.713 (Antip.), Jul.*Mis*.337c (pl.).

**κρώζω**, fut. κρώξω, prop. *croak*, of the κορώνη, Hes.*Op*.747, cf. Ar. *Av*.2, 24, Arat.953, Luc.*Asin*.12, Poll.5.89; also of other birds, as cranes, Ar.*Av*.710; of young halcyons, Luc.*VH*2.40; also, of men, *croak out*, τι Ar.*Lys*.506, *Pl*.369; of a wagon, *creak, groan*, Babr.52. 5. (Onomatop.)

**κρωκαλέον**· παιδίον πανοῦργον, Hsch.; cf. κρόκαλον.

**κρωμᾰκίσκος**, ὁ, *young pig*, Antiph.215 (dub.).

**κρῶμαξ**, ᾰκος, ό, *heap of stones*, = κλῶμαξ, Hsch.:—hence **κρωμᾰκόεις**, = κρημνώδης, Id.; **κρωμᾰκωτός**, ή, όν, Paphlagon. word, Eust. 330.40. [κρώμᾱξ, ᾱκος, acc. to Hdn.Gr.(?) in *Philol*.39.354.]

**κρώπιον**, τό, *scythe, bill-hook*, Pherecyd.154 J.:—in Hsch. κρώβιον (κρόβ- cod.).

**κρῶπος**, ὁ, = κρωσσός, Theognost.*Can*.21, Zonar.

**κρῶσσαι**, αἱ, v.l. for κρόσσαι, Hdt.2.125.

**κρωσσίον**, τό, Dim. of sq., *AP*9.272 (Bianor).

※ **κρωσσός**, ὁ, *water-pail, pitcher*, mostly in pl., A.*Fr*.96 (anap.), S. *OC*478, E.*Ion* 1173, *Cyc*.89: in sg., Theoc.13.46. 2. *cinerary urn*, πένθιμε κρωσσέ Erinn.5, cf. Mosch.4.34: also fem., με.. ὀλίγη ἐκρύψατο κ. *Epigr.Gr*.697a.

※ **κρωτάνεροι**· βάναυσοι πολῖται, καὶ ἐξελευθεριῶται, Hsch.

**κτά, καίνω, κτάμεν, -εναι, κτάμενος, κτάνε, κτάνθεν**, v. κτείνω.

**κτάντης**, ου, ὁ, (κτείνω) *murderer*, Dosiad.*Ara* 10.

**κτάομαι**, Ion. **κτέομαι**, only as v.l. in Hdt.8.112: fut. κτήσομαι Archil.6.4, Thgn.200, A.*Eu*.289, Th.6.30, Pl.*R*.417a, etc. (in pass. sense, Plot.2.9.15, s.v.l.); κεκτήσομαι A.*Th*.1022, E.*Ba*.514, Pl.*Grg*. 467a (ἐκτήσομαι in *La*.192e, and prob. in Emp.110.4): aor. ἐκτησάμην, Ep. κτ-, Od.14.4, Pi.*Pae*.2.59, etc.: pf. κέκτημαι Hes.*Op*.437, etc., ἔκτημαι Il.9.402, A.*Pr*.795, Hdt.2.44, and sts. in Pl. (κεκτήμεθα and ἐκτῆσθαι in following lines, *R*.505b, ἐκτῆσθαι τοῦ κεκτῆσθαι ἕνεκα *Tht*. 198d); Ion. 3 pl. ἐκτέαται Hdt.4.23; subj. κέκτωμαι Isoc.3.49, Pl. *Lg*.936b; opt. κεκτῄμην, ῇτο, ib.731c, 742e, κεκτῴμην E.*Heracl*.282 codd.: plpf. ἐκεκτήμην And.1.74, 4.41, Lys.2.17, etc.; poet. κεκτήμην E.*IA*404; Ion. 3 pl. ἐκτῆντο Hdt.2.108; Att. 1 pl. ἐκτήμεθα f.l. in And.3.37: for fut. and aor. Pass., v. infr. III. I. pres., impf., fut., and aor., 1. *procure for oneself, get, acquire*, κτήμασι τέρπεσθαι τὰ γέρων ἐκτήσατο Πηλεύς Il.9.400, etc.; [οἰκῆας] Od. l.c.; γῆν A.*Eu*. l.c., cf. *Pers*.770; of horses, *win* (as a prize), Pi.*N*.9.52; κτήσασθαι βίον ἀπό τινος *to get one's* living from a thing, Hdt.8.106; *win* favour, and the like, χάριν ἀπό τινος, ἔκ τινος, S.*Tr*.471, *Ph*.1370; παρά τινος X. *Smp*.4.43; τὴν εὔνοιαν τὴν παρὰ τῶν Ἑλλήνων Isoc.5.68; κ. φίλους, ἑταίρους, S.*Aj*.1360, E.*Or*.804 (troch.); κτήσασθαι παῖδας ἐξ ὁμοσπόρου Id. *IT*696, cf. S.*OT*1499, Hdt.8.105; παῖδας ἐς δόμους κτήσασθαι E.*Fr*.491, cf. *Supp*.225; πολλάκις δοκεῖ τὸ φυλάξαι τἀγαθὰ τοῦ κτήσασθαι χαλεπώτερον εἶναι D.1.23. b. of consequences, *bring upon oneself*, αὐτῷ θάνατον S.*Aj*.968; *incur*, θεᾶς ὀργὴν ib.777; κακά Id.*El*.1004; ξυμφορὰς E.*Or*.543; ἔχθραν πρός τινα Th.1.42; δυσσέβειαν κ. *get* a name for impiety, S.*Ant*.924; κακὸν λόγον πρὸς ἀστῶν E.*Heracl*.166, cf. *IT*676; ἐκ τῶν πόνων τὰς ἀρετὰς κ. Th.1.123. c. κ. τινὰς πολεμίους *make* them so, X.*An*.5.5.17; οὔ ποτ' εὔνουν τὴν ἐμὴν κτήσῃ φρένα S.*Ph*. 1281. 2. *procure* or *get* for another, ἐμοὶ δ' ἐκτήσατο κεῖνος Od.20. 265; μέγαν τέκνοις πλοῦτον ἐκτήσω A.*Pers*.755 (troch.), cf. X.*Oec*.15. 1. II. in pf. and plpf. with fut. κεκτήσομαι, *to have acquired*, i.e. *possess, hold* (opp. χρῆσθαι, Pl.*Euthd*.280d), οὐδ' ὅσα φασὶν Ἴλιον ἐκτῆσθαι Il.9.402, cf. X.*Cyr*.8.3.46, Pl.*Phdr*.260b; ὅπλα μὴ ἐκτῆσθαι Hdt.1.155, cf. S.*Ph*.778; στρατὸν πλεῖστον ἐκτημένοι Hdt.7.161; κοινὸν ὄμμ' ἐκτημέναι A.*Pr*.795; φωνὴν βάρβαρον κεκτ. Id.*Ag*.1051; κεκτ. τινὰ σύμμαχον E.*Ba*.1343; κ. κάλλος X.*Smp*.1.8; ἀρετὴν Pl.*Prt*.340e; τέχνην Lys.24.6; ποίησιν *to be master of* it, Pl.*Lg*.829c: dub. in aor., ἀγορὰς κτησάμενοι *having* market-places, Hdt.1.153 (leg. στησάμενοι): with impers. subject, πραγμάτων ἀγῶνας κεκτημένων *involving* effort, Epicur.*Sent*.21:—the diff. between pres. and pf. appears from X.*Mem*.1.6.3, ἃ [χρήματα] καὶ κτωμένους εὐφραίνει καὶ κεκτημένους.. ποιεῖ ζῆν: later, pres. in pf. sense, *Ev.Luc*.18.12. b. of evils, ἄγος κεκτήσεται θεῶν A.*Th*.1022; κακά E.*Hel*.272; φθόνον Pl.*Lg*.870c. c. *have in store*, opp. ἔχω, *have in hand*, ready for use, ἔχων τε καὶ κεκτημένος.. κακά S.*Ant*.1278; ἔχειν τε καὶ κεκτῆσθαι τὸ ψεῦδος Pl.*R*. 382b, cf. *Tht*.197b, 198d, *Cra*.393b; κ. ἱμάτιον *own*, opp. ἔχειν (*wear*), Id.*Tht*.197b. d. abs., *to be a property-owner*, τῶν ἐκτημένων ἐν τῇ χώρᾳ *SIG*633.73 (Milet., ii B.C.), cf. 888.15 (iii A.D.). 2. ὁ κεκτημένος *owner, master* (esp. of slaves), as Subst., Ar.*Pl*.4, etc.; οἱ κ. A.*Supp*.337; of a husband, E.*IA*715; ἡ κεκτημένη my *mistress*, S. *Fr*.762, Ar.*Ec*.1126, Men.*Pk*.61, al., cf. Phryn.Com.48. III. aor. 1 Pass. ἐκτήθην in pass. sense, *to be gotten*, ἃ ἐκτήθη Th.1.123, 2.36; *to be obtained as property*, δουλόσυνος πρὸς οἶκον κτηθεῖσα E.*Hec*.449 (lyr.), cf. D.H.10.27, etc.: fut. κτηθήσομαι Lxx *Je*.39(32).43. (Act. κτάω very late, *PLond*.1.77 (vi A.D.).)

**κτάτεσι**· κτήμασι, Hsch.

**κτεᾰν-ηχής**· πένης, Hsch. **-ισμός**, ὁ, *getting wealth*, Man.4. 41 (pl.). (Fort. κτεατ-.) ※ **-ον**, τό, (κτάομαι) = κτῆμα, Pi.*P*.1.2, Epic.ap.Sch.S.*OC*378 (Antim.(?)); κ. φιλίης, of a child, *Epigr.Gr*. 388 (Apamea). 2. usu. in pl. κτέανα, *possessions, property*, Hes. *Op*.315, Sol.4.12, Pi.*O*.3.42, *N*.9.32; δημοσίων κ. Xenoph.2.8; used in lyr. by A.*Th*.729, *Ag*.1573, E.*Ion*490; by S.(?) in hexam. ap. Sch.S.*OC*378 (cf. *Fr*.242); by Eub. in a mock heroic line, 139: in Prose, Hp.*Ep*.27; *property in cattle*, Theoc.25.109; cf. κτῆνος:— Hom. only in heterocl. dat. pl. κτεάτεσσι (cf. κτέαρ), Il.23.829, Od. 14.115, cf. Pi.*O*.5.24, E.*Fr*.791.3 (hex.): dat. pl. κτεάτοις Hdn.Gr. 2.936. (Cf. Avest. *šaēta*- 'property', 'wealth'.)

※ **κτέαρ**, τό, = foreg., formed as nom. to dat. pl. κτεάτεσσι in later Poetry, Maiist.32, *AP*9.52 (Carph.), 9.752 (Asclep. or Antip.Thess.), 11.27 (Maced.), Q.S.4.543.

**κτεάτ-ειρα** [ᾰτ], ἡ (as if fem. of *κτεᾰτήρ), *possessor*, Νὺξ μεγάλων κόσμων κ. A.*Ag*.356 (anap.). **-ίζω**, *gain, win*, δουρὶ δ' ἐμῷ κτεάτισσα Il.16.57; πολλὰ κτεατίσσας Od.2.102, 19.147, cf. Eumel.2, etc.: —Med., *get for oneself, acquire*, Ep. fut. κτεατίσσομαι Man.6.677, aor. κτεατίσσατο A.R.2.788: pf. Pass. in med. sense, ὅσ' Ἐκηβόλος ἐκτεάτισται *h.Merc*.522: plpf., ἃ ἐκτεάτιστο Μίδης Call.*Aet*.3.1.47; τὰ δὲ κτεατίζεται αὐτός Theoc.17.105.

※ **κτείνω**, Ep. subj. κτείνωμι Od.19.490; Aeol. **κτέννω** Hdn.Gr.2. 303 (and aor. 1 part. κτέννais Alc.33.5), but καίνω Id.140 acc. to Eust.1648.5 (leg. Ἀλκμᾶνι); Ep. Iterat. κτείνεσκε Il.24.393: fut. κτενῶ, Ep. κτενέω Od.16.404, -έεις Il.22.13, -έει ib.124, al. (κτενεῖ 15. 65, 68), part. κτανέοντα only 18.309 (but in compos. κατα-κτανέουσιν 6.409): aor. 1 ἔκτεινα 19.296, etc.: aor. 2 ἔκτᾰνον 2.701, etc.: pf. not found uncompounded: plpf. ἀπ-εκτονήκειν Plu.*Tim*.16:—Pass., fut. κτανθήσομαι Sch.T Il.14.481: Ep. 3 pl. aor. ἔκτᾰθεν Il.11.691, Od.4. 537, κτάθεν Q.S.1.812; ἐκτάνθην *AP*14.32, (ἀπ-) Lxx 1*Ma*.2.9, *Ev. Marc*.8.31, D.C.65.4: aor. 2 ἀπ-εκτάνην [ᾰ] Gal.14.284: pf. ἐκτάνθαι (ἀπ-) Plb.7.7.4:—Hom. also uses non-thematic forms, 3 sg., 1 and 3 pl. aor. ἔκτᾰ Od.11.410, al. (κατ- Il.15.432), ἔκτᾰμεν Od.12.375, ἔκτᾰν 19.276, Il.10.526 (ἔκτα also in S.*Tr*.38, E.*HF*423 (lyr., with ᾱ)); 1 pl. subj. κτέωμεν Od.22.216; inf. κτάμεν (κατα-) Il.9.458, κτάμεναι [ᾰ] 5.301, al.; part. κτάς (κατα-) 22.323, also in Trag., A.*Th*. 965 (lyr.), E.*IT*715: aor. Med. in pass. sense, 3 sg. ἀπ-έκτᾰτο Il.15. 437; inf. κτάσθαι ib.558 (prob. in pass. sense); part. κτάμενος 22.75, Hes.*Op*.541, Pi.*Fr*.203 codd., A.*Pers*.923 (lyr.), Cratin.95:—*kill, slay*, freq. in Poets, also in early Att., Lex Draconis in *IG*1².115.20; but in Prose and Com. ἀποκτείνω prevailed; usu. of men, less freq. of slaying an animal, as Il.15.587, Od.12.375, 19.543, Ar.*Av*.1063 (lyr.); Οὖτίς με κτείνει δόλῳ *seeks to kill* me, Od.9.408, cf. S.*OC*993; ὁ κτανών *the slayer, murderer*, A.*Eu*.422; οἱ κτανόντες Id.*Ch*.41 (lyr.), 144, etc. 2. *put to death*, Th.1.132, Arist.*HA*625ᵃ16, al.; esp. in legal language, εἰ.. ἐν δίκῃ ἔκτεινεν ὁ κτείνας Pl.*Euthphr*.4b, cf. *Prt*. 322d, *Lg*.871e, al., Lys.10.11. 3. of things, ὥστε καὶ κτείνειν so as *to be fatal*, of the plague, Th.2.51 (so in Pass., εὖτ' ἂν ὑπὸ τοῦ κακοῦ κτεινέωνται when the disease *is proceeding towards a fatal termination*, Aret.*SD*1.5); τὰ φύλλα [ἀποκύνου].. κτείνει κύνας Dsc.4. 80. 4. *put an end to*, θέρος [νοῦσον] κτείνει Aret.*SD*1.16. (Pass. in Hom. and Ion. Prose, Il.11.668, 14.60, Od.11.413, Hdt.4.43, etc.; but Trag. almost always used θνήσκω or καταθνήσκω as the Pass., Com. Poets and Prose writers ἀποθνήσκω.) (Cf. Skt. *kṣatás* 'wounded'.)

※ **κτείς**, κτενός, ὁ, *comb*, Pherecr.100; πύξινος κ. *AP*6.211 (Leon.), *Edict.Diocl*.13.3, cf. Luc.*Am*.44: hence, of toothed objects, 1. *comb in the loom*, by which the threads of the warp are kept separate, *AP*6.247 (Phil.); κναφικὸς κ. *comb* for carding wool, Tim.*Lex*. s.v. κνάφος. 2. *rake*, *AP*6.297.5 (Phan.), Ph.*Bel*.100.10 (pl.). 3. *horn* of the lyre, Hsch.: pl., of the constellation Lyre, Eratosth.*Cat*. 24. 4. *fingers*, χερῶν ἄκρους κτένας A.*Ag*.1594. 5. *ribs*, Opp. *C*.1.296, Hsch. 6. *virilia, pubes*, Hp.*Aph*.7.39, *Art*.51; *pudenda*

*muliebria*, Call.*Fr.*308, *AP*5.131 (Phld.), Ruf.*Onom.*109, Sor.2. 18. 7. in pl., *cutting-teeth, incisors*, Poll.2.91. 8. *bivalve shell-fish, scallop*, Philyll.13, Archipp.24, Anaxandr.41.62 (anap.), Alex. 170, prob. in Theoc.14.17, cf. Arist.*HA*525ᵃ22, al. b. dual κτένε, perh. = *scallopings* (ornaments on a garment), *IG*1².386.8; cf. κτενωτός. 9. *caruncula lachrymalis*, Arist.*HA*491ᵇ25 (cf. Gal.4.796). 10. *bandage*, Sor.*Fasc.*25. (For πκτεν-, cf. πέκω, Lat. *pecten*: the correct form (κτείς) of the nom. is found in *IG*2².1425.376; later κτήν, q.v.)

**κτεν-ίζω**, *comb*, τινα Anaxil.39, cf. *PSI*4.404.4 (Pass., iii B.C.); *curry* horses, ψήκτραισιν ἵππων τρίχας E.*Hipp.*1174: metaph., ὁ δὲ Πλάτων τοὺς ἑαυτοῦ διαλόγους κτενίζων καὶ βοστρυχίζων D.H.*Comp.* 25:—Med., κτενίζεσθαι τὰς κόμας *comb one's hair*, Hdt.7.208: so abs., Ar.*Fr.*603, Antiph.148.4:—Pass., ἐκτενισμένος *with one's hair combed*, Archil.165, cf. Semon.7.65; εἰ κτενισθείη *Hippiatr.*94. **-ιον**, τό, Dim. of κτείς 1, *POxy.*1142.7 (iii A.D.); of κτείς 8, Epich.42.3 (pl.). 2. in pl., = κτείς 3, Hsch. **-ιοποιός**, ὁ, *comb-maker*, *Gloss.* **-ισμός**, ὁ, *combing*, E.*El.*529 (pl.), Diocl.*Fr.* 141. **-ιστής**, οῦ, ὁ, *hairdresser*, Gal.13.1038, *PTeb.*322.23 (ii A.D.), *Gloss.* **-ιστικός**, ή, όν, *for hairdressing*, ζεῦγος κ. σιδηροῦν *POxy.*1035.12 (ii A.D.). **-ιστός**, ή, όν, *combed, carded*, λίνον Sm. *Is.*19.9.

**κτενο-ειδής**, ές, *like a comb*. Adv. -δῶς *Gloss.* **-ποιός**, ὁ, = κτενιοποιός, ib. **-πώλης**, ου, ὁ, *dealer in combs*, Poll.7.198.

**κτεν-ώδης**, ες, = κτενοειδής, Xanth.3; τὸ κ. Phan.Hist.29. **-ωτός**, ή, όν, perh. *scalloped*, χιτωνίσκος *IG*2².1514.30; κτενωτή· ὑφαντή, Hsch.; cf. πεντέκτενος, κτείς 8b.

**κτέομαι**, Ion. for κτάομαι.

**κτέρ-ας**, τό, = κτέανον, *possession*, Il.10.216, 24.235, cj. in Simon. 107.9, *Trag.Adesp.* in *Gött.Nachr.*1922.27. 2. *gift*, A.R.4. 1550. **-εα**, τά (no sg. in use), *funeral gifts*, burnt with the dead, Mosch.4.33, Hsch.: generally, *funeral honours*, ἐπὶ κτέρεα κτερεΐξαι Od.1.291, cf. 2.222, Il.24.38, etc.; ἔλαχον κτερέων Od.5.311; τῶν ὁσίων ἀντίασεν κτερέων *Epigr.Gr.*514 (Maced.). 2. later, *wrappers for the dead, shroud*, ἐνὶ κτερέεσσιν ἐλυσθεὶς A.R.1.254. **-εΐζω**, fut. -ΐξω Od.2.222: aor. κτερεΐξαι 1.291:—Ep. Verb., = κτερίζω: 1. c. acc. pers., *bury with due honours*, σὸν ἑταῖρον ἀέθλοισι κτερέϊζε Il. 23.646; κτερεΐζέμεν Ἕκτορα δῖον 24.657; τύμβῳ κτερέϊξε παῖδα *IG*12 (5).308 (Paros), etc. 2. c. acc. cogn., κτέρεα κ., v. κτέρεα. **-ες**· νεκροί, Hsch. **-ίζω**, fut. κτεριῶ Il.18.334: aor. ἐκτέρῐσα 24.38, Simon.109 (κτέρεα):—poet. Verb, = κτερεΐζω, οὔ σε πρὶν κτεριῶ Il. 18.334; τὸν δὲ κτεριοῦσιν Ἀχαιοί 22.336; ἔμ', εἴ κε θάνω, κτεριοῦσί γε δῖοι Ἀχαιοί 11.455; τάφῳ κ. τινά S.*Ant.*204; τούσδ' εἷς τάφος ἐκτέρισε Simon.l.c.: abs., E.*Hel.*1244; δημοσίᾳ κ. *IG*2.1678 (iv B.C.), cf. *Sammelb.*2119 (iii B.C.). 2. c. acc. cogn., τοί κέ μιν ὦκα ἐν πυρὶ κήαιεν καὶ ἐπὶ κτέρεα κτερίσαιεν Il.24.38, cf. Od.3.285. **-ίσματα**, τά, = κτέρεα, only pl., S.*OC*1410, *El.*434, 931, E.*Supp.*309, *Tr.*1249, *Hel.*1391. **-ιστής**, οῦ, ὁ, *undertaker*, Hsch. s.v. ταφῆες.

**κτέω, κτέωμεν**, v. κτείνω.

**κτηδών**, όνος, ἡ, *line of fissure* in the fibre of wood, Thphr.*HP*5.1.9 sq.; κτηδόνες ξύλου *grain* of wood, Hero *Bel.*96.12, cf. Suid. 2. Medic. in pl., *fibres of the heart*, Hp.*Cord.*10, cf. Erot. s.v. ἶνες. b. *layers* in the cornea of the eye, Ruf.*Anat.*10. c. κ. πιμελῆς *fibres* in a piece of fat, Sor.1.118. 3. *layers* of slate, Dsc.5.127. 4. *gills* of a mushroom, Id.3.1. 5. *shreds* of lint, Gal.8.415. (Cf. εὐκτέανος (B), εὐθυκτέανον, ἰθυκτέανον.)

**κτῆμα**, ατος, τό, (κτάομαι) *anything gotten, piece of property, possession*, sg. once in Hom., μή νύ τι.. δόμων ἐκ κτῆμα φέρηται Od.15. 19; later ταύτας [γυναῖκας] ἐξείλεθ' αὑτῷ κ. S.*Tr.*245; ἡδὺ κ. τῆς νίκης λαβεῖν Id.*Ph.*81, cf. *OT*549, *Ant.*702, E.*Or.*230, 703, etc.; κ. ἐς αἰεί Th.1.22; ὡς ἡδὺ καὶ μακάριον τὸ κ. Pl.*R.*496c, etc.; of a slave, παλαιὸν οἴκων κ. E.*Med* 49, cf. Pl.*Phd.*62d, X.*Oec.*1.6, *Vect.*4.42; κ. ἔμψυχον Arist.*Pol.*1253ᵇ32; of a calf, J.*AJ*6.14.3; κ. πάντων ἐστὶ τιμιώτατον ἀνὴρ φίλος Hdt.5.24. 2. freq. in pl., *possessions*, in Hom. of *heir-looms*, δόμοις ἐν κτήματα κεῖται Il.9.382, Od.4.127; also, of all kinds of *property*, freq. in Od., κ. δαρδάπτουσιν 14.92, cf. 18.144, al.; διέλαχον.. κτημάτων παμπησίαν A.*Th.*817, etc.; Ἔρως ὃς ἐν κτήμασι πίπτεις who fallest upon *wealth*, i.e. on *the wealthy*, S.*Ant.*782 codd. (lyr.): sts., χρήματα καὶ κ. *property* in money and *chattels*, Pl.*Lg.* 728e, cf. Isoc.1.28; = κτήνη, Pl.*Grg.*484c, *Phd.*62b; opp. ἀγρολ, *personal* (opp. real) *property*, Is.5.43; less freq. of *landed property*, κ. ἔχων ἐν Βοιωτίᾳ D.18.41 (sg. as v.l.), Hdn.2.6.3: later freq. in sg., *estate, farm, field*, etc., *Act.Ap.*5.1, *BGU*530.21 (i A.D.), etc.; ἀμπελικὸν κ. *vineyard*, *PRyl.*157.4 (ii A.D.). 3. in pl., *materials*, κ. πιλητά Gal.*UP*6.4, 7.22.

**κτηματ-ίδιον**, τό, Dim. of foreg., *small estate*, *PMasp.*21.19 (vi A.D.). **-ικός**, ή, όν, *possessed of wealth, opulent*, Plb.5.93.6, D.S. 18.10, Plu.*Sol.*14; οἱ κ., = Lat. *possessores*, App.*BC*1.12. II. *belonging to an estate* or *farm*, γεωργοί *POxy.*136.18 (vi A.D.); τὰ τῶν κ. ἔργα *PFlor.*161.6 (iii A.D.). **-ιον**, τό, Dim. of κτῆμα, Alciphr. 1.36, *PTeb.*616 (ii A.D.), *PFay.*133 (iv A.D.). **-ίτης** [ῑ], ου, ὁ, = κτηματικός 1, Lycurg.*Fr.*93, Socr.*Ep.*29.5.

**κτημᾰτοφύλαξ** [ῠ], ἄκος, ὁ, *estate bailiff, steward*, *Gloss.*

**κτηματ-ωνέω**, *purchase properties*, of commissioners for temples, *Supp.Epigr.*2.580.10 (Teos, ii B.C.); Ἀπόλλωνι καὶ Ἀρτέμιδι *LW*338 (Mylasa). **-ώνης**, ου, ὁ, *commissioner who purchases* temple-*properties*, *Supp.Epigr.*2.538 (Mylasa, ii B.C.), 565.11 (Olymos, i B.C.); γενομένης τῆς ὠνῆς τοῖς κ. εἰς τὸ τοῦ θεοῦ ὄνομα *LW*416 (Mylasa). **-ωνία**, ἡ, *purchase of properties*, *Supp.Epigr.*2.580.12 (Teos, ii B.C.).

**κτήν**, ὁ, later nominative form for κτείς (q.v.), ὁ κ. τοῦ ποδός, = ταρσός, Jo.Alex. περὶ τῶν διαφόρως τονουμένων p.16 Egenolff (Vratisl. 1880).

**κτην-αγωγία**, *evectio*, *Gloss.* **-αφαίρεσις**, εως, ἡ, *cattle-lifting*, *PMasp.*2 ii 25 (vi A.D.). **-ηδόν**, Adv., (κτῆνος) *like beasts*, Hdt.4. 180. **-ίατρος**, ὁ, *cattle-doctor*, *Gloss.* **-ίτης** [ῑ], ου, ὁ, *belonging to beasts*, ib.

**κτηνοβάτης** [ᾰ], ου, ὁ, (βαίνω A. II. 1) *one guilty of bestiality*, Sch.Ar. *Ra.*432, 965.

**κτῆνος**, εος, τό, (κτάομαι) mostly in pl. κτήνεα, contr. κτήνη, *flocks and herds*, *h.Hom.*30.10, Hdt.1.50, 2.41, Pl.*Criti.*109c, *PStrassb.*98. 9 (ii B.C.), *SIG*633.73 (Milet., ii B.C.); κ. τὰ δημιοπληθῆ A.*Ag.*129 (lyr.); of beasts in general, Heraclit.29; opp. ἄνθρωποι, Democr.57; of swine, Plb.12.4.14; ὑϊκὰ κ. *BGU*757.20 (i A.D.). 2. in sg., a single *beast*, as *an ox* or *sheep*, Hdt.1.132, Hp *Cord.*2, X *An.*5.2.3; *horse* or *mule for riding*, *Ev.Luc.*10.34, *Act.Ap.*23.24; of a domestic animal, opp. θηρίον, M.Ant.5.11. (Late dat. pl. κτῆσι *PFlor.*258.6, etc.)

**κτηνοστάσιον**, *jumentarium*, *Gloss.*

**κτηνοτροφ-εῖον**, τό, *cattle-stall*, *Gp.*15.8 tit. **-έω**, *keep cattle*, Str.12.2.9, Ph.2.89, *Hippiatr.*53. **-ία**, ἡ, *cattle-keeping*, Str.17. 2.3, D.H.3.36 (pl.), Ph.1.304, *BGU*969.12, al. (ii A.D.), Plu.*Publ.*11 (pl.). **-ος**, ον, *keeping cattle, pastoral*, βίος D.S.1.74; γῆ κ. a land *of pasture*, Lxx *Nu.*32.4: as Subst., *cattle-keeper*, Ph.1.304: pl., *PFay.*18(*b*) (i B.C.), Dsc.2.147, *BGU*969.11 (ii A.D.).

**κτην-ύδριον**, τό, Dim. of κτῆνος, *PStrassb.*92.12 (iii A.D.), *PFlor.* 120.6 (iii A.D.). **-ώδης**, ες, *like a beast*, Lxx *Ps* 72(73).22, Aesop. 324b; αἴσθησις Ph.1.151: Comp., Hsch. Adv. -δῶς, γράφειν Tz. ad Lyc.797.

**κτησ-είδιον**, τό, Dim. of κτῆσις, Arr.*Epict.*1.1.10; v.l. for συγκτησείδιον in Jul.*Ep.*4. **-ίβιος** [σῐ], ον, (κτάομαι) *possessing property*, Paul.Al.*L.*4. **-ιος**, α, ον, (κτῆσις) *belonging to property*, χρήματα κ. *property*, A.*Ag.*1009 (lyr.); κ. βοτόν a sheep *of one's own flock*, S.*Tr.* 690. II. *domestic*, Ζεὺς κ. *the protector of house and property*, A. *Supp.*445, Hp.*Insomn.*89, Orac.ap.D.21.53, Antipho 1.16: pl., τοὺς κ. Δίας Anticl.13; also Ἀθηνᾶ κ. Hp.l.c.; ὁ θεὸς ὁ κ. Plu.2.828a; κ. βωμός the altar *of* Ζεὺς κτήσιος, A.*Ag.*1038; θεοὶ κ., = Lat. *Penates*, D.H. 8.41. **-ιππος**, ον, *possessing horses*, pr. n. in Od., cf. Luc.*Fug.*26.

**κτῆσις**, εως, ἡ, (κτάομαι) *acquisition* (opp. ἀπόλαυσις, Arist.*Rh.* 1410ᵃ6), κ. τινὸς ποιεῖσθαι Th.1.8, 13; ἡ φιλοσοφία κ. ἐπιστήμης Pl. *Euthd.*288d; ῥᾳδίαν ἔχει (τὴν) κτῆσιν Alcid.*Soph.*5; κατ' ἔργου κτῆσιν according to *success in* the work, S.*Tr.*230. II. (from pf.) *possession*, λέχους, πλούτου, etc., ib.162, *El.*960, etc.; κ. ἔχειν τῶν μετάλλων ἐργασίας Th.4.105; ἡ τῶν χρημάτων κ. Pl.*R.*331b; διὰ τὴν τῶν υἱέων κ. on account of *your having* sons, Id.*Ap.*20b; ἱματίων Id.*Phd.*64d; φέροντας.. ἀγαθοῦ κτῆσιν οὐδενὸς D.18.308; κ. ἐκ δεσπότου καὶ δούλου [συνέστηκεν] Arist.*Pol.*1277ᵃ8; *holding*, opp. χρῆσις ('using'), Id. *EN*1098ᵇ32; *ownership*, opp. χρῆσις ('usufruct'), *POxy.*237 viii 35, al.; τὰς κτήσεις βεβαίας εἶμεν *IG*4²(1).76.25 (Epid., ii B.C.). 2. as collective, = κτήματα, *possessions, property*, διὰ κτῆσιν δατέοντο Il.5. 158; κ. ὄπασσεν Od.14.62; πατρῴα κ. S.*El.*1290; μετρίης κτήσιος ἐπιμέλεσθαι Democr.285; ἡ ἰδία κ. *POxy.*237 viii 32 (i A.D.): in pl., Hdt.4.114, etc.; ἀρετῆς βέβαιαι.. αἱ κ. μόναι S.*Fr.*194; esp. *lands, farms*, D.H.8.19, D.S.14.29, etc.: also in sg., *farm, estate*, *PFlor.* 155.6 (iii A.D.).

**κτη-τέος**, α, ον, *to be possessed*, Pl.*Lg.*742a. II. κτητέον, *one must get*, Id.*R.*373a. **-τικός**, ή, όν, *acquisitive, skilled in getting*, τῶν οὐκ ὄντων Isoc.12.242: abs., *industrious*, Str.16.4.26: ἡ -κὴ τέχνη the art *of acquiring property*, Pl.*Sph.*219c, cf. Arist.*Pol.*1253ᵇ23; τὸ κ. Phld.*Oec.*p.35 J. 2. *acquired by purchase*, δοῦλος, δούλη, *PRyl.* 111(*b*).6 (ii A.D.), *PLips.*4.11 (iii A.D.). II. Gramm., *possessive*, [ὄνομα] D.T.634.25; ἀντωνυμίαι A.D.*Pron.*16.15; τὰ κ. ib.14.21. Adv. -κῶς Id.*Synt.*160.13. **-τορικός**, ή, όν, *of an owner*, *PGiss.*124.7 (vi A.D.). **-τός**, ή, όν, (κτάομαι) *that may be gotten* or *acquired*, ληϊστοὶ μὲν.. βόες.., κτητοὶ δὲ τρίποδες Il.9.407, cf. E.*Hipp.*1295 (anap.), Pl.*Prt.*324a, al. 2. *worth getting, desirable*, Id.*Smp.*197d, *Hp.Mi.*374e. II. *acquired, gained*, Id.*Lg.*841e; κτητὴ *female slave*, opp. γαμετή, Hes.*Op.*406; κ. μέρος οἰκίας *PLond.*3.1164(*f*).11 (iii A.D.). **-τωρ**, ορος, ὁ, *possessor, owner*, D.S.34/5.2.31, *POxy.* 237 viii 31 (i A.D.), A.D.*Pron.*22.6, *AP*7.206 (Damoch.), Procop.*Arc.* 26: c. gen., οἰκιῶν κ. *Act.Ap.*4.34.

**κτίδεος** [ῐ], α, ον (from ἰκτίς: **κτίς** only in Hsch. s.v. κτιδέα), for ἰκτίδεος (which is not in use), *of a marten*, κτιδέη κυνέη *marten-skin* helmet, Il.10.335, 458.

**κτίζω**, Emp.23.6, etc.: fut. -ίσω A.*Ch.*1060: aor. ἔκτισα Od.11.263, etc.; poet. ἔκτισσα Pi.*P.*1.62, A.*Pers.*289 (lyr.), κτίσσα Il.20.216, κτίσα Pi.*P.*5.89: pf. ἔκτικα *Lyr.Alex.Adesp.*1.8, D.S.7.5, 15.13:—Med., poet. aor. ἐκτίσσατο Pi.*O.*10(11).25, *Fr.*1.4 (ἐκτήσ- codd.):—Pass., fut. κτισθήσομαι Str.*Chr.*5.38, D.H.1.56: aor. ἐκτίσθην Th.1. 12, etc.: pf. ἔκτισμαι Hdt.4.46, Hp.*Art.*45, E.*Fr.*360.9:—*people* a country, *build houses and cities in* it, κτίσσε δὲ Δαρδανίην Il.l.c.; κ. χώρην, νῆσον, Hdt.1.149, 3.49. 2. of a city, *found, build*, Θήβης ἕδος ἔκτισαν Od.l.c., cf. Hdt.1.167, 168, Th.6.4, *PCair.Zen.*169 (iii B.C.); ἀποικίαν A.*Pr.*815:—Pass., *to be founded*, Σμύρνην τὴν ἀπὸ Κολοφῶνος κτισθεῖσαν *founded by emigrants from* Colophon, Hdt.1.16, cf. 7.153, 8.62; μήτε ἄστεα μήτε τείχεα ἐκτισμένα no *fixed* cities or walls, Id. 4.46; -ομένη πόλις Phld.*Rh.*2.155 S. 3. κ. ἄλσος *plant* a grove, Pi.*P.*5.89; βωμὸν *set up* an altar, Id.*O.*7.42; ἑορτάν, ἀγῶνα, *found, establish* it, ib.6.69, 10(11).25 (Med.); τὸν Κύρνον.. κτίσαι, ἥρων ἐόντα *establish* his worship, Hdt.1.167; δαῖτάς τινι A.*Ch.*484 (Pass.); τάφον τινί S.*Ant.*1101; αἵρεσιν Phld.*Rh.*1.77 S.; σύνοδον *IG*2².1343.12

(i B.C.). 4. *produce, create, bring into being*, γόνῳ τινά A.*Supp*.172 (lyr.); *bring about*, τελευτήν ib.140 (lyr.), cf. *Ch*.441 (lyr.); ὁ τὴν φιλίην ἐκτικώς *Lyr.Alex.Adesp*. l. c.; of painters, δένδρεα.. καὶ ἀνέρας ἠδὲ γυναῖκας Emp. l. c.; ἵπποισι τὸν χαλινὸν κτίσας *having invented* it, S.*OC*715 (lyr.). 5. *make* so and so, ἐλεύθερον κ. τινά A.*Ch*.1060; ἔνθεον κτίσας φρένα Id.*Eu*.17, cf. 714; ποταπὰν εἴ σέ τις θεῶν κτίσαι E.*Supp*.620 (lyr.), cf. A.*Pers*.289 (lyr.). 6. *perpetrate* a deed, S.*Tr*. 898. (Cf. Skt. *kṣéti* 'reside', *kṣitis* (= κτίσις) 'habitation'.)

**κτῐλ-εύω**, *make tame, tame*, Pi.*Fr*.238 (Pass.). **-ίς**· τιθασός, πρᾶος, ἡγεμών, Hsch. ❀ **-ος**, ον, *tame, docile, obedient*. χρὴ δέ σε πατρὶ.. κτίλον ἔμμεναι Hes.*Fr*.222; ἦσαν δὲ κτίλα πάντα καὶ ἀνθρώποισι προσηνῆ Emp.130; μῆλα (sheep) Nic.*Th*.471; κύνες Parth.10.3; ἱερέα κτίλον Ἀφροδίτας Aphrodite's *cherished* priest, Pi.*P*.2.17; κτίλα ᾠέα, perh. their *cherished* eggs, Nic.*Th*.452. II. Subst. κτίλος, ὁ, *ram*, Il.3.196, 13.492, Opp.*C*.1.388, 4.211, Q.S.1.175. **-όω**, *tame, make tractable*, in Med., ἐκτιλώσαντο τὰς λοιπὰς τῶν Ἀμαζόνων *got* them *tamed*, Hdt.4.113:—Pass., pf. part. ἐκτιλωμένος Paus.Gr.*Fr*.241.

**κτίν**, = κτείς, *Gloss*.; cf. κτήν.

**κτίννυμι**, collat. form of κτείνω, App.*BC*1.71 (vv.ll. κτεινύντες, κτεννύντες). 4.35; **κτιννύω**, Polyaen.1.23,25, Plot.3.2.15:—Pass., κτιννύμενος App.*BC*1.2; κτιννύεσθαι J.*AJ*18.8.3:—more freq. in compd. ἀποκτίννυμι (cf. ἀποκτείνυμι), cf. Phryn.*PS*p.51 B.; κτεινύω and ἀποκτιννύναι are correct acc. to Choerob. in *An.Ox*.2.233.

**κτίς**, v. κτίδεος.

**κτίσ-ις** [ῐ], εως, ἡ, (κτίζω) *founding, settling*, Th.6.5; ἀποικιῶν Isoc. 12.190, cf. Plb.9.1.4 (pl.), etc. 2. loosely, = πρᾶξις, κούφα κ. an easy *achievement*, Pi.*O*.13.83. 3. *creation*, κ. κόσμου *Ep.Rom*. 1.20; ἀπ' ἀρχῆς κτίσεως *Ev.Marc*.10.6, 13.19, etc. II. *created thing, creature*, Lxx *Ju*.9.12, *Ev.Marc*.16.15, *Ep.Rom*.8.19, etc.: in pl., Lxx *To*.8.5. III. *authority created* or *ordained*, 1*Ep.Pet*.2. 13. ❀ **-μα**, ατος, τό, *colony, foundation*, Call.*Aet.Oxy*.2080.77; Παρίων Str.7.5.5, cf. D.H.1.59; Λακωνικὸν κ. Str.5.3.6; also, of a temple, J.*BJ*2.6.1: generally, *building*, *PSI*1.84.8 (pl., iv/v A.D.). 2. = κτίσις II, Lxx *Wi*.9.2 (pl.), 3*Ma*.5.11, *Ep.Jac*.1.18. II. = κτίσις I. 1, Eust.1382.50. **-μός**, ὁ, *foundation*, πόλεως *IGRom*.4.914 (Cibyra). **-τεῖον**, τό, *sanctuary of a founder*, *PLips*.97 xiii 7 (iv A.D., -ιον Pap.). **-τήρ**, ῆρος, ὁ, = sq., *AJA*23.364 (Corinth, iv B.C.). ❀ **-της**, ου, ὁ, *founder*, Arist.*Fr*.484, *OGI*111.9 (Egypt, ii B.C.), Luc.*Macr*.13; of Apollo as founder of Cyrene, *Berl.Sitzb*.1903. 85: pl., Call.*Aet.Oxy*.2080.64; ὁ τῆς στοᾶς κ., i.e. Zeno, Ath.8.345c, D.L.2.120: metaph., ἰατρικῆς κ. *IG*14.1759. 2. *builder*, *POxy*. 2144.8 (iii A.D.). II. *restorer*, τῆς πατρίδος Plu.*Cic*.22. III. *Creator*, ὁ κ. ἁπάντων Lxx *Si*.24.8, al. **-τός**, ή, όν, *wrought*, λάεσσιν *h.Ap*.299. 2. *built*: neut. κ., τό, *building*, *PFay*.117.23 (ii A.D.). **-τρια**, ας, ἡ, fem. of κτίστης I, *IGRom*.3.802 (Syllium). ❀ **-τύς**, ύος, ἡ, Ion. for κτίσις, Hdt.9.97. ❀ **-τωρ**, ορος, ὁ, = κτίστης, Αἴτνας Pi.*Fr*.105; Ἀσιάδος χθονὸς E.*Ion*74; ὁ τῆς στοᾶς κ., of Zeno, Ath.9.370c; ἀγαθῶν.. εὑρετὴν καὶ κτίστορα Diph.(?)138.

**κτίτερ**· κτίστης, Hsch.; cf. sq.

❀ **κτίτης** [ῐ], ὁ, = κτίστης, ἀγώνων *SIG*711 *L* 5 (pl., Delph., ii B.C.). II. generally, *inhabitant*, E.*Or*.1621.

❀ **κτοίν-α** or **κτοῖνα**, ἡ, (κτίζω) Rhod. name for *a local division*, like Att. δῆμος *township*, *IG*12(1).694, 1033, al.; cf. κτύναι· ἢ κτοῖναι· χωρήσεις προγονικῶν ἱερείων, ἢ δῆμος μεμερισμένος, Hsch. (also **πτοίνα** *BCH*10.261). ❀ **-άτης** [ᾱ], ου, ὁ, *member of a κτοίνα*, *IG*12(1).694. 14:—also **-έτης**, ib.157.9, 12(3).1270 *A* 13 (Syme).

**κτόνος**, ὁ, *murder*, Zonar.

**κτῠπ-έω**, Ep. Iterat. κτυπέεσκον Q.S.9.135: aor. 1 ἐκτύπησα E.*Ph*.1181, Arr.*Tact*.40.6; poet. κτύπησα S.*OC*1606, E.*Or*.1467 (lyr.): Ep. aor. 2 ἔκτυπον Il.8.75, al., S.*OC*1456 (lyr.), κτύπον Il.8.170:—Pass., v. infr.: (κτύπος):—*crash*, as trees falling, μεγάλα κτυπέουσαι πῖπτον Il.23.119; freq. of thunder, Ζεὺς ἔκτυπε 8.75, cf. 7.479, Od.21. 413, etc.; ἔκτυπεν αἰθήρ S.*OC*1456 (lyr.); of the sea, Pl.*R*.396b. 2. *ring, resound*, κτυπέει δέ θ' ὑπ' αὐτοῦ ὕλη (sc. χειμάρρου) Il.13.140; ἀμφὶ δ' ἐκτύπουν πέτραι *rang* with the cries of Heracles, S.*Tr*.787; Διὸς βρονταῖσιν εἰς ἔριν κ. E.*Cyc*.328; δρομήμασιν Id.*Med*.1180; τοῖν ποδοῖν κ. *stamp loudly* with.., Ar.*Ec*.545, cf. Gal.7.60; εἰ.. ἐμπεσὼν [δόρυ] τῷ θυρεῷ κτυπήσειε Arr. l. c.; σιδηρῷ ὑποδήματι Luc.*Salt*.83: c. acc. cogn., φόβον κτυπεῖν, like κλάζειν Ἄρη, E.*Rh*.308. II. causal, *make to ring* or *resound*, χθόνα Hes.*Sc*.61; τύμπανα Opp.*C*.4.247: c. dupl. acc., κτύπησε κρᾶτα.. πλαγάν (v.l. πλαγῇ) *made* it *ring* with a blow, E.*Or*. l. c.: metaph., κ. ἐν τοῖς συμβουλευτικοῖς τόποις τὰς ὀνομασίας Phld.*Rh*.1.208 S.:—Pass., *resound*, Ar.*Pl*.758, *Th*.995 (lyr.); κτυπηθῆναι τὰ ὦτα Philostr.*VA*6.26. **-ημα**, ατος, τό, = κτύπος, βροντῆς Critias 25.32 D.; κ. τυμπάνων D.C.51.17, cf. Jul.*Or*.7.220b; κ. χειρός E.*Andr*.1211 (lyr.). **-ητής**, οῦ, ὁ, *one who makes a noise*, Suid. s. v. πίτυλος. **-ία**, ἡ, = ὁ ἐπιθαλάμιος κτύπος, Hsch. **-ος**, ὁ, *crash, bang, din*, κ. θεῶν ἔριδι ξυνιόντων Il.20.66, cf. 12.338, A.*Th*.100, etc.; of thunder, S.*OC* 463 (lyr.), A.*Pr*.923; of the trampling of feet, περί τε κ. ἦλθε ποδοῖιν Od.16.6, cf. S.*Ph*.202; *rattling* of chariots or *sound* of horses' feet, Il.10.535, al., S.*El*.714, Ar.*Eq*.552 (lyr.); of a storm, A.*Ag*.1533 (lyr.); *noise* made by one knocking at the door, Id.*Ch*.653; ὀξύχειρ κ., of the *beating* of breasts by mourners, ib.23; στέρνων κ. E.*Supp*.87: in pl., κ. χερῶν Id.*Ph*.1351 (lyr.); of the *sound* of many voices, S.*OC*1500; of gates shutting, Aen.Tact.20.4; κτύπου ἀχὼ χάλυβος A.*Pr*.133 (lyr.); rarely of musical sound, σαλπίγγων κ. B.*Fr*.3.9.—Rare in Prose, Th.7.70, Pl.*Criti*.117e, X.*Cyr*.7.1.35, Aen Tact. l. c.

**'κτώ**, for βκτώ, as pronounced by fishmongers, Amphis 30.12.

❀ **κτῶ**, v. κτάομαι.

❀ **κῠάθ-ειον** ᾰ, τό, = κυάθιον, Dim. of κύαθος II, Nic.*Th*.591. **-ιαῖος**, α, ον, *contained in a κύαθος*, ὕδωρ *a ladleful of* water, Them. *in Ph*.135. 26, Simp. *in Ph*.174.30, Phlp. *in Mete*.24.22, Id. in *GA*92.22. ❀ **-ίζω**, *ladle out* wine, Antiph.115, Diph.107. II. κ. ταῖς ναυσὶν ἐκ θαλάττης *draw water* from the sea with the ships (*as one draws wine* from a bowl), of the engines of Archimedes lifting the Roman ships out of the water, Plb.8.6.6. **-ιον**, τό, Dim. of κύαθος, Pherecr.107, *PLond*.5.1657.11 (iv/v A.D.):—also ❀ **-ίς**, ίδος, ἡ, Sophr.3. **-ίσκος**, ὁ, κ. τῆς μηλωτρίδος *spoon-shaped end* of certain probes, Heliod.ap. Orib.46.11.26, cf. Gal.19.122, Archig.ap.eund.12.652, *Hermes*38. 282. 2. *spoon-shaped probe*, Diocl.*Fr*.191. ❀ **-ος**, ὁ, *ladle*, for drawing wine out of the κρατήρ, Anacr.63.5, Pl.Com.176, Archipp. 21, X.*Cyr*.1.3.9, *PEleph*.5.3 (iii B.C.), etc.; cold metal *ladles* were applied to bruises, Arist.*Pr*.890[b]7; κύαθον αἰτήσεις τάχα you'll need a *ladle* shortly (from being so soundly beaten), Ar.*Lys*.444; ὑπωπιασμέναι.. καὶ κυάθους προσκείμεναι with *ladles* applied, Id.*Pax* 542, cf. E.*Fr*.374, Apolloph.3. II. *Attic measure holding two* κόγχαι or *four* μύστρα, about $\frac{1}{12}$ *of a pint*. Gal.19.753, cf. 10.516. III. κύαθοι κλειδῶν ἀνεστηκότες filled-out *hollows* round the collar-bones, Philostr.*Gym*.48. **-ότης**, ητος, ἡ, coined by Plato, *cuphood*, D.L. 6.53. **-ώδης**, ες, *like a cup*, Eratosth.ap.Ath.11.482a; κλεῖδες Philostr.*Gym*.29.

**κῠαίνω**, = κυέω, Hsch.

**κῠᾰμ-ευτός**, ή, όν, *chosen by beans*, i.e. *by lot*, X.*Mem*.1.2.9, etc.; κ. ψηφοφορίαι voting *by beans*, Plu.2.12e. **-εύω**, *choose by lot*, δικαστάς *IG*1[2].41.19, 2[2].1172.13; ἔκ τινων Arist.*Ath*.8.1, 22.5:—Pass., *IG*1[2].10.8, Jusj.ap.D.24.150. ❀ **-ιαῖος**, α, ον, *of the size of a bean*, Dsc.2.133, Luc.*Herm*.40. **-ίας** (sc. λίθος), ου, ὁ, *precious stone like a bean*, Plin.*HN*37.188. **-ίδες**, *fabacia*, *Gloss*. **-ίζω**, *to be ripe for marriage* (cf. κύαμος III), Ar.*Fr*.582. ❀ **-ινος**, η, ον, *of beans*, ἔτνος Henioch.4.7, Gal.12.12; ἄλευρον Id.10.177. **-ιον**, τό, Dim. of κύαμος, Eust.948.30, *CIG*5109.30 (Nubia). **-ιστός**, ή, όν, f.l. for κυαμευτός, Plu.2.597a. **-ῖτις** (sc. ἀγορά), ιδος, ἡ, *bean-market*, ib.837c.

**κῠᾰμόβολος**, ον, *chosen by beans*, i.e. *by lot* (rather than **κυᾰμοβόλος** (parox.), *voting with the bean*), δικαστής S.*Fr*.288.

❀ **κύᾰμος** [ῠ], ὁ, *bean*, *Vicia Faba*, κ. μελανόχροες Il.13.589, cf. Emp. 141, *IG*2[2].1013.19, etc.; χλωροί Batr.125; κ. Ἑλληνικός Dsc.2.105; abominated by Pythagoreans, Arist.*Fr*.195, etc.; also, of the plant, Thphr.*CP*4.14.2. 2. *Egyptian bean*, *Nelumbium speciosum*, Id. *HP*4.8.7; usu. Αἰγύπτιος κ., Nic.*Fr*.81, D.S.1.10, Dsc.2.106, Gal.6. 532, 19.780. II. *lot* by which public officers were elected at Athens and elsewh. (because those who drew *white beans* were chosen), Plu.*Per*.27; ὁ τῷ κυάμῳ λαχὼν Ἀθηναίων πολεμαρχέειν Hdt. 6.109; ἐπίσκοπος.. τῷ κυάμῳ λαχών Ar.*Av*.1022; οἱ πεντακόσιοι ⟨οἱ⟩ λαχόντες τῷ κ. Lex ap.And.1.96; βουλὴ ἡ ἀπὸ τοῦ κ. Th.8.66, cf. Arist. *Ath*.24.3, 32.1; ἄρχοντας ἀπὸ κ. καθιστάναι X.*Mem*.1.2.9; κυάμοισι τὰς ἀρχὰς αἱρέεσθαι Luc.*Vit.Auct*.6; κύαμον ἐδέξατο *Schwyzer*701 *B* 30 (Erythrae, v B.C.); κυάμῳ πατρίῳ S.*Fr*.404. III. *swelling of the paps* at puberty, Ruf.*Onom*.92, Poll.2.163, cf. Eust.749.21. IV. *woodlouse*, Gal.12.367.

**κῠᾰμο-τρώξ**, ῶγος, ὁ, *bean-eater*, Ar.*Eq*.41 (with allusion to κύαμος II). **-φαγία**, ἡ, *eating of beans, bean-diet*, Luc.*VH*2.24.

**κῠᾰμ-ών**, ῶνος, ὁ, *field of* κύαμος I. 2, Thphr.*HP*4.8.8, Str.17.1.15, *BGU*1119.11 (i B.C.). ❀ **-ωνίτης** [ῑ], ου, ὁ, *bean-grower*, *POxy*.43ᵛ iii 2 (iii A.D.).

**κῠᾰν-αιγις** [ᾰν], ιδος, ἡ, *she of the dark Aegis*, i.e. Pallas, Pi.*O*.13. 70. **-άμπυξ**, ῠκος, ὁ, ἡ, *with dark* ἄμπυξ, Θήβα Id.*Fr*.29.3; Δᾶλος Theoc.17.67; μίτρη Nonn.*D*.6.114. **-ανθής**, ές, *of dark hue*, of the sea, B.12.124. **-αυγέτις**, ιδος, pecul. fem. of sq., Orph.*H*. 23.1. ❀ **-αυγής**, ές, *dark-gleaming*, ὀφρύες E.*Alc*.261 (lyr.); τὰς βολὰς τῶν ὀφθαλμῶν ἐστὶ κ. Alciphr.3.1; of the sea, κ. Ἀμφιτρίτη D.P. 169, etc.; πηγή *Supp.Epigr*.4.467.25 (Milet., iii A.D.): com. of dithyrambs, Ar.*Av*.1389. ❀ **-αῦλαξ**, ᾰκος, ὁ, ἡ, *dark furrowed*, Orac.ap. Hld.2.26.

**Κυάνεαι** (νῆσοι or πέτραι), αἱ, *Dark-rocks*, two small islands at the entrance of the Euxine, Hdt.4.85, D.19.273, Str.7.6.1, cf. Συμπληγάδες: Κυάνεα πελάγη, of the adjacent sea, is f.l. in S.*Ant*.966. [ῠ, metri gr., S. l. c.]

**κῠᾰν-έμβολος**, ον, = κυανόπρῳρος, πρῷραι E.*El*.436, Ar.*Ra*.1318; τριήρεις Id.*Eq*.554.—Only in lyr. ❀ **-εος**, α, ον, contr. **κυᾰνοῦς**, ῆ, οῦν Pl.*Ti*.68c, etc., prob. in A.*Pers*.81 (lyr.), Euph.51.7 (cf. κύανος II):—*made of κύανος* (q. v.), κάπετος Il.18.564; δράκοντες 11.26, cf. 39, Hes.*Sc*.167. II. *of the colour of κ., dark-blue, glossy*, of the swallow, Simon.74; of the halcyon, Arist.*HA*616[a]15; of the skin of the porpoise, ib.566[b]12; of the *deep* sea, E.*IT*7, cf. Arist.*Pr*. 932[a]31; πόντου κ. δίναι Xenarch.1.7; κ. χρῶμα Pl. l. c.; τὸ κ. ἐξ ἰσάτιδος καὶ πυρώδους Thphr.*Sens*.77. 2. generally, *dark, black*, of the mourning veil of Thetis, Il.24.94; of clouds, 5.345, 20.418, Od.12.75; of the brows of Zeus, Il.1.528; χαῖται 22.402; γενειάδες Od.16.176; ἄνδρες, of Africans, Hes.*Op*.527; γαῖα ψάμμῳ κυανέη (of the bottom of Charybdis) Od.12.243; κ. χθών, of Delos, Pi.*Fr*.87.4; κ. θάλαμος, of the chamber of Persephone, Sapph.119; φάλαγγες κ. *dark* masses of warriors, Il.4.282; κυάνεον Τρώων νέφος 16.66: metaph., Κῆρες κ. Hes.*Sc*.249; κ. δνόφος Simon.37.8; λόχμα Pi.*O*.6.40; Ἀίδης *IG*14.1389 ii 25. [ῠ, metri gr., in dactylic verse, Hom., etc.]

**Κυανεψιών** v. Κυανοψιών.

**κυᾰν-έω**, *to be dark in colour*, D.P.1111, Phryn.*PS*p.80 B. [ῡ, metri gr.] **-ίζω**, = foreg., Dsc.1.1, *Placit*.3.5.12; of varicose veins, Gal.13.460. **-ῖτις**, ιδος, ἡ, *bluish grey*, ὄψιες (in glaucoma) Hp. *Vid.Ac*.1.

**κυᾰνο-βενθής**, ές, *with dark-blue depths*, prop. of the sea; com. of a cup, Ar.*Fr*.165. **-βλέφᾰρος**, ον, *dark-eyed*, *AP*5.60 (Rufin.). **-ειδής**, ές, *dark-blue, deep-blue*, κ. ἀμφ' ὕδωρ (i.e. the sea) E.*Hel*.179 (lyr.), cf. Arist.*GA*779ᵇ33, *Col*.796ᵃ18. **-θριξ**, ὁ, ἡ, gen. τριχος, *dark-haired*, Orph.*A*.1194; χαίτη *AP*6.250 (Antiphil.). **-κρήδεμνος**, ον, *with dark-blue* κρήδεμνον, Q.S.4.381. **-πεζα**, ἡ, *with feet of* κύανος, τράπεζα Il.11.629. [ῡ, metri gr.] ⊛**-πεπλος**, ον, *dark-veiled*, of Demeter mourning for her daughter, *h.Cer*.319, 360, 374; of Leto, Hes.*Th*.406. [ῡ, metri gr.]. **-πλόκᾰμος**, ον, *dark-haired*, B.5.33, al., Q.S.5.345. **-πλοκος**, ον, = foreg., Pi.*Pae*.6.83. **-πρῴρειος**, ον, = sq., Od.3.299: **-πρῴειρα**, Simon.241. **-πρῳρος**, ον, *dark-prowed*, of ships, Il.15.693, 23.852, Od.9.482, 539: fem. κυανόπρῳρᾰ, B.16.1. **-πτερος**, ον, *with blue-black feathers*, like the raven, ὄρνις E.*Andr*.862 (lyr.): generally, *dark-winged*, τέττιξ Hes.*Sc*. 393. **-πτέρυξ**, ῠγος, ὁ, ἡ, = foreg., παῖς Ἀφροδίτας Cerc.5.2.

⊛**κύᾰνος** [ῠ], ὁ (later ἡ, v. infr. 1.3, 7), *dark-blue enamel*, esp. used to adorn armour, δέκα οἶμοι μέλανος κυάνοιο Il.11.24, cf. 35; πτύχες κυάνου Hes.*Sc*.143; also θριγκὸς κυάνοιο, of a cornice, Od.7. 87; so perh. in *IG*1².367.7, 4²(1).102.244 (Epid.). 2. *lapis lazuli*, κ. αὐτοφυής (opp. σκευαστός) Thphr.*Lap*.39, al., Dsc.5.91, etc. (perh. also in Pl.*Phd*.113c); κ. ἄρρην, θῆλυς, Thphr.*Lap*.31: also an imitation made in Egypt, ib.55. 3. *blue copper carbonate*, Hp.*Cord*.2, Gal.12.233 (ὁ and ἡ), Luc.*Lex*.22; βαπτὴ κ. *AP*6.229 (Crin.). 4. *blue cornflower*, Plin.*HN*21.68. 5. a bird, perh. *blue thrush*, *Turdus cyanus*, Arist.*HA*617ᵃ23, Ael.*NA*4.59. 6. *sea-water*, Hsch. 7. fem., *the colour blue*, Alex.Aphr. *in Mete*.162.4. II. as Adj., = κυάνεος, Nic.*Th*.438 (unless κυανός as in Phlp. *in GC*23.11, codd. Pl. l. c.): Comp. **-ώτερος** *Anacreont*.16.11: Sup. **-ώτατος** Philostr.*Im*.1.6. [ῠ in dactylic verses, metri gr., cf. κυάνεος, etc.]

**κυᾰνόστολος**, ον, *dark-robed*, στήθεα Bion 1.4.

**κυᾰνοῦς**, ῆ, οῦν, v. κυάνεος.

**κυᾰν-οφρυς** [ᾰ], υ, gen. υος, *dark-browed*, Theoc.3.18, 17.53.

**κυᾰνο-χαίτης**, ου, ὁ, *dark-haired*, in Hom. usu. of Poseidon, perh. in reference to the *dark blue* of the sea, Il.20.144, Od.9.536, cf. Hes. *Th*.278; Ἀρείων Thebais 4; of a horse, *dark-maned*, Il.20.224, Hes. *Sc*.120: voc. κυανοχαῖτα *h.Cer*.347:—also nom. **κυανοχαῖτα** Il.13. 563, 14.390; treated as indeclin. and joined with dat., κυανοχαῖτα Ποσειδάωνι Antim.27. [ῡ, metri gr.] **-χροος**, ον, *dark in hue*, ῥόθια E.*Hel*.1502 (lyr.); πέπλος Nech.ap.Vett.Val.241.18; ἑρπετά Opp.*H*.2.599. **-χρως**, ων, gen. ωτος, = foreg., πλόκαμος E.*Ph*. 308 (lyr.); θαλάττης ἔδαφος Alcid.ap.Arist.*Rh*.1406ᵃ5. **-χρωτος**, ον, = foreg., Orph.*H*.70.6, Man.1.327. [ῡ, metri gr., Orph. l. c.; ῠ, Man. l. c.]

⊛**Κυανοψιών**, ῶνος, ὁ, name of month in Ceos, *Ath.Mitt*.49.138 (iv B.C.); at Cyzicus, *GDI*5703:—also **Κυανεψιών** *IGRom*.4.157; cf. Πυανοψιών.

**κυᾰν-ώπης**, ες, *dark-eyed*, [ἵπποι] Opp.*C*.1.307:—fem. **-ῶπις**, ιδος, Ἀμφιτρίτη Od.12.60, cf. Hes.*Sc*.356; Νύμφαι Anacr.2.2; Μοῦσα *IG* 14.1942; νᾶες κυανώπιδες B.12.160, cf. A.*Pers*.559 (lyr.), *Supp*.743 (lyr.). **-ωπός**, όν, *dark of aspect*, σέλας *Trag.Adesp*.541.3, cf. Androm.ap.Gal.14.41; δύσις *AP*4.3ᵇ.36 (Agath.). **-ωσις**, εως, ἡ, (as if from *κυανόω) *dark-blue colour*, Plu.2.879d codd.

**κύαρ**, τό, *a hole*, as *the eye* of a needle, etc., Hp.*Morb*.2.33, cf. *Acut*.(*Sp*.)61; *orifice* of the ear, Poll.2.86.

**κυβάβδα**· αἷμα (Amathus), Hsch.

**κῠβάζω**, (κύβη) *set on the head, turn upside down*, Hsch.

**κυβαία** (sc. ναῦς), ἡ, kind of *boat*, *PCair.Zen*.2.3, al. (iii B.C.); Lat. *cybaea*, Cic.*Verr*.4.8.17, 5.17.44:—Dim. **κυβαίδιον** or **κυβᾴδιον**, τό, *PSI*6.594.3 (iii B.C.).

**κυβαΐζοντες**· λάσωνες, Hsch.

**κυβάλης**, ὁ, *cinaedus*, Eust.1431.46; cf. κυπάτης.

**κῠβᾰλικός**, ή, όν, *rascally*, ἀργυρίοισι -οῖσι cj. in Timocr.1.6; cf. κυβηλικός, κόβαλος.

**κύβας**, ου, ὁ, = σορός, Hsch. (συρός cod.). **κῠβάω**, (κύβος) gloss on πεττεύει, Id. 2. = κυβάζω, *EM*543.16. **κύββα**, ἡ, = κύμβη (A), Hsch. ⊛**κύβδᾰ**, Adv., (κύπτω) *with the head forwards, stooping forwards*, sens. obsc., κ. ἦν πονευμένη Archil.32, cf. Ar.*Eq*.365, *Th*.489, S.*Ichn*. 122.

**κυβέβις**, v. κύβηβος.

⊛ **κύβεθρον**, τό, = κυψέλη II, Hsch.; cf. κύβερτον.

**κῠβεία**, ἡ, *dice-playing*, Pl.*Phdr*.274d, X.*Mem*.1.3.2, Aen.Tact.5.2, Men.481.10 (pl.), etc.: metaph., ἐν τῇ κ. τῶν ἀνθρώπων by the *trickery* of men, *Ep.Eph*.4.14.

**κῠβείας**, ου, ὁ, a kind of πηλαμύς, Opp.*H*.1.183.

**κῠβεῖον**, τό, *gaming-house*, Aeschin.1.78.

**κύβειρος**, = ἀναιδής, Suid. ⊛ **κύβελα**, τά, *lairs* of wild beasts, Hsch.

**Κυβέλειον**, τό, = ἴον, Ps.-Dsc.4.121.

**κυβέλη**, ἡ, = κύαρ, *EM*543.1.

⊛**Κῠβέλη**, ἡ, *Cybele*, E.*Ba*.79 (lyr.), Ar.*Av*.877, etc.:—from **Κύβελον**, τό, or **Κύβελα**, τά, mountain in Phrygia, D.S.3.58, Str.12.5.3:—hence Adj. **Κῠβεληγενής**, St.Byz.:—also **Κῠβήβη**, Hippon.120 (dub.), Hdt.5.102, *Anacreont*.11.1; equated with Aphrodite by Charon Hist.(*FHG* iv p.627):—fem. Adj. **Κῠβηλίς**, ίδος, ἡ, *Cybelian*, Κυβηλίδος ὄργανα Ῥείης Nonn.*D*.10.387, 14.214, cf. Hippon.121, prob. in St.Byz. s. v. Κυβέλεια:—also **Κῠβεληΐς**, Nonn.*D*.14.10, al.

**κῠβεπίκῠβος**, ὁ, = κυβόκυβος, Theodoret.*Therap*.6.52.

⊛**κῠβερν-άω**, *steer*, νῆα κυβερνῆσαι Od.3.283, cf. Pi.*O*.12.3 (Pass.), Pl.*Plt*.298e, etc.: abs., *act as helmsman*, αὐτὸς ἑαυτῷ Ar.*Eq*.544. 2. *drive*, κ. ἅρματα Pl.*Thg*.123c; τὸν δρόμον τῶν ἵππων Hdn.7.9.6. 3. metaph., *guide, govern*, Pi.*P*.5.122, Antipho 1.13, Pl.*Euthd*.291d, etc.; τὴν δίκην ὀρθῇ γνώμῃ κυβερνᾶτε Herod.2.100. 4. *act as pilot*, i.e. perform certain rites, in the Ship of Isis, *IGRom*.1.817 (Callipolis). II. Med., = Act., κυβερνωμένης τῆς διανοίας Arist.*Pr*.964ᵇ 17; ὁ κυβερνώμενος μουσικῇ Marcellin.*Vit.Thuc*.49:—Pass., σῇ κυβερνῶμαι χερί S.*Aj*.35; μιᾷ γνώμῃ τῇ Κύρου ἐκυβερνᾶτο X.*Cyr*.8.8.1; ἡ ἰατρικὴ.. διὰ τοῦ θεοῦ τούτου κυβερνᾶται Pl.*Smp*.187a, cf. *R*.590d, Antiph.40.8, etc.; cf. κυμερῆναι. **-ήσια** (sc. ἱερά), ων, τά, *festival* at Athens in *memory of the steersman* of Theseus, Plu.*Thes*.17. **-ησις**, Dor. **-ᾱσις**, εως, ἡ, *steering, pilotage*, Pl.*R*.488b. 2. metaph., *government*, πολίων of cities, Pi.*P*.10.72 (pl.), cf. 1*Ep.Cor*.12.28 (pl.); θεοῦ by a god, Plu.2.162a. **-ήτειρα**, ἡ, fem. of κυβερνητήρ, τύχη *AP*10.65 (Pall.), cf. Nonn.*D*.1.89. **-ητέον**, *one must direct*, Pl. *Sis*.389d. **-ητήρ**, Dor. **-ᾱτήρ**, ῆρος, ὁ, = κυβερνήτης, Od.8.557, etc.: metaph., Pi.*P*.4.274: as Adj., κ. χαλινός Opp.*C*.1.96. **-ητήριος**, α, ον, = κυβερνητικός, Orac.ap.Plu.*Sol*.14. ⊛**-ήτης** (Aeol. κυμερνήτης, q. v.), ου, ὁ, *steersman, pilot*, Il.19.43, Od.9.78, A.*Supp*. 770, Hdt.2.164, Ar.*Th*.837, Th.7.70, Pl.*R*.341c, etc.; *skipper* of Nile-boat, ναύκληρος καὶ κ. *PHib*.1.39.6 (iii B.C.), cf. *PGiss*.11 (ii A.D.), etc. 2. metaph., *guide, governor*, E.*Supp*.880, Pl.*Phdr*.247c; as an official title, *PMasp*.89 iii 1 (vi A.D.). ⊛ **-ητικός**, ή, όν, *good at steering*, Pl.*R*.488d,e; νοῦς καὶ ἀρετὴ κ. Id.*Alc*.1.135a: Comp. **-ώτερος** Id.*R*.551c: Sup. **-ώτατος** X.*Mem*.3.3.9: ἡ **-κή** (sc. τέχνη) *pilot's art*, Pl.*Grg*.511d, cf. Iamb.*Myst*.3.26; τὸ **-κόν** Pl.*Plt*.299c; τὰ **-κά** Id.*Alc*.1.119d. Adv. **-κῶς** D.Chr.4.25. 2. metaph., ἡ τῶν ἀνθρώπων **-κή** Pl.*Clit*.408b, etc. **-ῆτις**, ιδος, fem. of κυβερνήτης, epith. of Isis, *POxy*.1380.69 (ii A.D.). **-ιον**, *gubernium, Gloss*. **-ισμός**, ὁ, = κυβέρνησις, Aq.*Na*.3.1. ⊛ **-ος**, *gubernita, Gloss*.

**κυβέρτιον**, τό, Dim. of sq., Suid. and Phot. s. v. κυψέλη. **κύβερτον**, gloss on κύψελον, Hsch. **κύβεσις**· ἡ (ἡ cod.) κίβισις· πήρα, Id.

**κῠβ-ευτήριον**, τό, *gambling-house*, Plu.2.621b, Poll.7.203, D.C. 65.2. **-ευτής**, οῦ, ὁ, *dicer, gambler*, S.*Fr*.947, Eup.11.8 D., X.*HG* 6.3.16, Men.965, Vett.Val.202.6; οἱ Κυβευταί, name of plays by Antiphanes, etc. **-ευτικός**, ή, όν, *of* or *for dice-playing*, ὄργανα Aeschin. 1.59; ἐργαλεῖα Poll.9.97. II. *skilled in dice-playing*, Pl.*R*. 374c. ⊛**-εύω**, *play at dice*, Cratin.195, Ar.*Ec*.672, Isoc.15.287, etc. 2. metaph., *run a risk* or *hazard*, περὶ διπλασίων X.*HG*6.3.16, cf. Plu.*Art*.17; περὶ τοῖς φιλτάτοις Pl.*Prt*.314a; κ. τῷ βίῳ Plb.*Fr*. 6. II. trans., *run the risk of, venture on*, κυβεύων τὸν πρὸς Ἀργείους Ἄρη E.*Rh*.446:—Pass., *to be staked*, *AP*7.427.13 (Antip. Sid.). 2. c. acc. pers., *cheat, defraud*, Arr.*Epict*.2.19.28, cf. 3.21.22. **-εών**, ῶνος, ὁ, = κυβευτήριον, Tz.*H*.10.558.

**κύβη**, ἡ, *head*, only as etym. of κυβιστάω, *EM*543.22; cf. κύμβη (B).

**Κῠβήβη**, ἡ, = Κυβέλη (q. v.). II. an Arcadian boot, Hsch.

**κύβηβος**, ον, (κύβη) *stooping with the head*, *EM*543.10. II. **Κύβηβος** [ῠ], ὁ, *minister of Cybele*, Semon.36; cf. κυβέβις· γάλλος, κτλ., Hsch.: generally, *one ecstatic* or *frantic*, Cratin.82:—hence **κῠβηβάω**, *to be frantic*, Phot., Hsch., cf. *EM*543.11 (-βειν codd.):—Hsch. also has the forms **Κυβήκη** (Hippon.120) and **Κύβηκος**.

**κῠβηλ-ίζω**, *strike with an axe*, Hsch. **-ικός**, ή, όν, *as with an axe*, κ. τρόπον *Com.Adesp*.869; cf. κυβαλικός. **-ις**, εως, ἡ, *axe, cleaver*, Philem.13, Anaxipp.6.6, Lyc.1170. II. = τυρόκνηστις, Cratin.315.

**Κῠβηλίς**, ίδος, ἡ, v. Κυβέλη.

**Κῠβηλιστής**, οῦ, ὁ, = ἀγερσικύβηλις, Cratin.62.

**κύβηνα**· σκήνωμα, Hsch. **κυβήνη**, ἡ, = γλαύξ, Id. **κύβηξ**, ηκος, ἡ, abusive term for *old woman*, *Com.Adesp*.57 D.

**κύβης**, ου, ὁ, = κυβευτής, Hsch. **κυβησίνδα** [παίζειν], play *at* ἐγκοτύλη, Poll.9.122, cf. Hsch., Phot. **κυβητίζω**· ἐπὶ κεφαλὴν ῥίψω, Hsch.

**κυβιάριον**, τό, *crate of salt fish*, *POxy*.1657.9 (iii B.C.).

**κῠβ-ίζω**, (κύβος) *make into a cube*, τὸ πλῆθος τῷ σχήματι Plu.2.979f; of numbers, *raise to the cube*, Hero *Metr*.3.22:—Pass., Procl.*Hyp*.4. 102, *Theol.Ar*.33; *to be multiplied*, Hippol.*Haer*.1.2.10. **-ικός**, ή, όν, *cubic*, σχῆμα, εἶδος, Pl.*Ti*.55c,d; σώματα Gal.9.523; πλοῖον κυβικὴ σανίς Secund.*Sent*.17. Adv. **-κῶς** *cubically*, Plu.2.404f: metaph., ἑστῶσα παγίως καὶ κ. Dam.*Pr*.266. 2. of numbers, *raised to the cube*, Arist.*Pr*.910ᵇ36.

**κύβιον** [ῠ], τό, *flesh of the* πηλαμύς *salted in* κύβοι, Hices.ap.Ath. 3.118b, Posidipp.16, cf. Gal.12.893: pl., *PCair.Zen*.66.11 (iii B.C.), *PSI*5.535.37 (iii B.C.).

**κῠβιοσάκτης**, ου, ὁ, *dealer in salt fish*, nickname of the son-in-law of the thirteenth Ptolemy, Str.17.1.11; of Vespasian, Suet.*Vesp*.19.

**κυβισίς**· κήλη, Hsch.

**κῠβισμός**, ὁ, prop. *cubing*: *making into a solid*, *Theol.Ar*.36.

**κῠβιστ-άω**, Ion. **-έω** Opp.*C*.4.263: (κύβη):— *tumble head foremost*, ἦ μάλ' ἐλαφρὸς ἀνήρ, ὡς ῥεῖα κυβιστᾷ Il.16.745, cf. 749; of fish, κατὰ καλὰ ῥέεθρα κυβίστων ἔνθα καὶ ἔνθα *tumbled* or *plunged about*, 21. 354, cf. Opp. l. c.; esp. of professional tumblers, Pl.*Smp*.190a; κ. εἰς ξίφη, εἰς μαχαίρας, X.*Smp*.2.11, *Mem*.1.3.9, Pl.*Euthd*.294e. **-ημα**, ατος, τό, *somersault*, Luc.*Anach*.18. **-ής**, οῦ, ὁ, = *κυβιστητής (*tumbler*), dub. in M.Bulard *La relig. domestique dans la colonie ital. de Délos* 482 (vase). **-ησις**, εως, ἡ, *somersault*, in pl., Plu.2.401c, Luc. *Anach*.16. **-ητεία**, ἡ, = foreg., Suid. **-ητήρ**, ῆρος, ὁ, *tumbler*, δοιὼ δὲ κυβιστητῆρε κατ' αὐτοὺς μολπῆς ἐξάρχοντες ἐδίνευον κατὰ μέσσους Il.

18.605, Od.4.18. 2. *diver*, Il.16.750. 3. *one who pitches headlong*, E.*Ph.*1151. II. later as Adj., *tumbling*, κυδοιμός Tryph. 192. **-ιάω**, *turn a somersault*, Gloss.

**κῠβῐτίζω**, (κύβιτον) *nudge* or *poke with the elbow*, Epich.213.

**κύβῐτον** [ῠ], τό, *elbow*, Lat. *cubitum*, Hp.*Loc.Hom.*6; Sicilian for Att. ὠλέκρανον, Ruf.*Onom.*79, cf. Poll.2.141: wrongly expld. as κυβοειδὲς ὀστάριον by Bacch.ap.Erot.

**κῠβο-ειδής**, ές, *like a cube, cubical*, Epicur.*Nat.*14.5, Str.16.1.5, Dsc.5.98, Gal.5.668, Heliod.ap.Orib.49.4.47; ὀστοῦν Gal.*UP*3.7, al. **-κῠβος**, ὁ, *cube multiplied by cube*, i.e. *sixth power*, Hippol. *Haer.*1.2.10. II. *sixth power of unknown quantity*, $x^6$, Dioph.1 *Def.*1, Sch.Iamb.*in Nic.*p.131 P.:—hence **κῠβοκῠβοστόν** (sc. μόριον), τό, *fraction corresponding to* κυβόκυβος, $1/x^6$, Dioph.1 *Def.*3.

**κύβος** [ῠ, v. sub fin.], ὁ, *cube*, Ti.Locr.98c; esp. *cubical die*, marked on all six sides, mostly in pl., *dice*, Hdt.1.94, etc.; κύβων βολαί S. *Fr.*429; ἐν πτώσει κύβων Pl.*R.*604c; περὶ κύβους τὰς διατριβὰς ποιούμενοι Lys.16.11: prov., ἀεὶ γὰρ εὖ πίπτουσιν οἱ Διὸς κ., i.e. God's work is no mere chance, S.*Fr.*895; ἔργον ἐν κύβοις Ἄρης κρινεῖ A.*Th.* 414; ἄλλα βλήματ' ἐν κύβοις βαλεῖν E.*Supp.*330; ψυχὴν προβάλλοντ' ἐν κύβοισι δαίμονος Id.*Rh.*183: later in sg., οἶδ' ὅτι ῥιπτῶ πάντα κύβον κεφαλῆς..ὕπερθεν ἐμῆς *AP*5.24 (Phld.); τὸν περὶ τῶν ὅλων ἀναρρίψων κύβον Plu.*Fab.*14, cf. Luc.*Pr.Im.*16; ἐφ' ἑνὸς ἀνδρὸς ἀναρρίπτειν τὸν κ. Id.*Harm.*3; ἀνερρίφθω κ., Lat. *jacta esto alea*, Men.65.4, Plu.*Caes.* 32; ἔσχατον κύβον ἀφιέναι try one's luck for the last time, Id.*Cor.* 3. 2. of the single *pips on the dice*, βέβληκ' Ἀχιλλεὺς δύο κύβω καὶ τέσσαρα he has thrown two *aces* and a four, E.*Fr.*888: prov., τρὶς ἕξ..ἢ τρεῖς κύβους βάλλειν 'all or nothing', Pl.*Lg.*968e, cf. Pherecr. 124. 3. in pl., *gaming-table*, Hermipp.27. II. *cubic number*, Pl. *R.*528b, Arist.*APo.*76ᵇ8. III. *anything of cubic shape*: *vertebra*, Rhian.57. 2. *block* of stone, *PCair.Zen.*276 (iii B.C.); of wood, *IG*2².463.57, 7.3073.187 (Lebad., ii B.C.). 3. *piece of salt fish*, Alex.187.4. 4. kind of *cubic cake*, Eup.424, Heraclid.ap.Ath.3. 114a. 5. *hollow above the hips* of cattle, Simaristus ib.9.399b. 6. *part of an irrigation-machine*, *BGU*1546 (iii B.C.), *PLond.*3.1177.216 (ii A.D.). [κῦβος only in late Poets, *AP*14.8; *coebus* Aus.*Idyll.*11.3.]

**κῠβοστόν** (sc. μόριον), τό, *fraction corresponding to* κύβος, i.e. $1/x^3$, Dioph.1 *Def.*3.

**κύβωλον**, τό, = κύβιτον, Poll.2.141.

**κυγχνίδα**, v. κυλιχνίς.

**κυδάγχας**· μάχας, λοιδορίας, and **κυδαγχόμενα**· λοιδορούμενα, Hsch.; cf. sq.

**κῡδάζω**, (κῦδος) *revile, abuse*, Ἄμυκε, μὴ κύδαζέ μοι τὸν πρεσβύτερον ἀδελφεόν Epich.6:—in Med., c. dat., τήνῳ κυδάζομαί τε κἀπ' ὧν ἠχθόμαν Id.35.6; οὔ τοι γυναιξὶ δεῖ κυδάζεσθαι· τί γάρ; A.*Fr.*94: c. acc., ὦ πέπον ἦ μάλα δή με κακῷ ἐκυδάσσαο μύθῳ A.R.1.1337:—Pass., *to be reviled*, S.*Aj.*722.

**κῡδ-αίνω**, fut. κυδᾰνῶ Lyc.721, etc.: Ep. aor. κύδηνα Il.23.793; Dor. ἐκύδανα Pi.*P.*1.31: (κῦδος):—*give* or *do honour to*, τινα Il.10.69, 13.348,350; ἠμὲν κυδῆναι θνητὸν βροτὸν ἠδὲ κακῶσαι Od.16.212; Ζεύς, ὅς μιν..τίμα καὶ κύδαινε Il.15.612; [Αἰνείαν] ἀκέοντό τε κύδαινόν τε they healed and *glorified* him, by restoring strength and beauty, 5.448; πάτρα κυδαίνων Τεγέαν Pi.*O.*10(11).66, cf. *P.*1.31; πατρίδα κ. Simon. 151; σφ' ἀρετὴ κυδαίνουσ' ἀνάγει..ἐξ Ἀΐδεω Id.99.4; πρὸ τοῦ κήπου κ. τὸν περίπατον Plu.2.635a. II. *delight* or *gladden by marks of honour*, κύδαινε δὲ θυμὸν ἄνακτος Od.14.438, cf. Il.23.793. III. seldom in bad sense, *flatter, fawn upon*, Hes.*Op.*38, cj. in Max.Tyr. 20.1. IV. Med., *pride oneself*, ἐπὶ πατράσι Onos.1.24.—Poet. and late Prose. **-άλῐμος** [ᾰ], ον, also η, ον *IG*5(1).599 (Sparta): (κῦδος):—*glorious, renowned*, in Hom. epith. of heroes, Il.17.378, Od.14.206, al.; of nations, Il.6.184,204; κ. κῆρ a *noble* heart, of Agamemnon and Achilles, 10.16, 18.33; the suitor Eurymachus, Od. 21.247; the lion, Il.12.45; ἱερεῖς..τιμαῖς -ους Man.2.226. **-άνω** [ᾰ], = κυδαίνω, only pres. and impf., *exalt*, τοὺς μὲν ὁμῶς μακάρεσσι θεοῖσι κυδάνει Il.14.73. II. *to be triumphant*, Ἀχαιοὶ μὲν μέγα κύδανον 20.42.

**κύδαρ**· τάφος, Hsch.

**κύδαρος**, ὁ, kind of *small ship*, Antiph.321:—also **κύδαρον**, τό, *POxy.*1197.10 (iii A.D.), *AB*274, *EM*543.39; Lat. *cydarum*, Gell.10. 25, *CIL*8.27790 (Althiburos).

**κῡδάττω**, = κυδάζω, Hsch. **κῡδέστερος**, irreg. Comp. of κυδρός.

**κῡδήεις**, εσσα, εν, *glorious*, δῶρα *AP*9.697, cf. Man.2.231: Dor. fem. **κυδάεσσα** [δᾱ], παρθένε *IG*4²(1).134.12 (Epid.).

**κῡδῐ-άνειρα** [ᾰν], ἡ, (κῦδος) fem. Adj. *bringing men glory* or *renown*, Homeric epith. of μάχη, Il.4.225, al.; once of the ἀγορή, 1.490; of Φύσις, Orph.*H.*10.5. II. Pass., *glorified by men, famous for men*, Σπάρτα *APl.*1.1 (Damag.). **-άω**, Ep. Verb, only pres. and impf., *bear oneself proudly, exult*, in Il. always in Ep. part. κυδιόων, 2.579, 21.519, cf. *h.Cer.*170; of a horse, Il.6.509: c. dat., *exult in*, κυδιόων λαοῖσι Hes.*Sc.*27; εὐφροσύνῃ..κυδιόωσι *h.Hom.*30.13: Iterat. κυδιάσκον A.R.4.978, Q.S.13.418.

**κύδ-ῐμος** [ῡ], ον, = κυδάλιμος, epith. of Hermes, *h.Merc.*46, al., Hes.*Th.*938; ἄεθλα Pi.*O.*14.24. **-ιστος**, η, ον, Sup. of κυδρός, *most honoured, noblest*, in Hom. freq. of Zeus and Agamemnon, Ζεῦ κύδιστε μέγιστε Il.2.412, al.; Ἀτρεΐδη κ. 1.122, al.; of Athena, 4. 515, Od.3.378; of Hera, *h.Ven.*42; of Leto, *h.Ap.*62; of Anchises, *h.Ven.*108; κύδιστ' Ἀχαιῶν A.*Fr.*238 (lyr.). 2. of things, *greatest*, κύδιστ' ἀχέων Id.*Supp.*13 (anap.): in Trag., Comp. **κῡδίων** [ῑ], ον, gen. ονος, τί μοι ζῆν δῆτα κύδιον; what *profits it* me to live? E.*Alc.*960 (s.v.l.), cf. *Andr.*639 (v.l. κύδιστον).

**κυδνός**, ή, όν, = κυδρός, Hes.*Th.*328 (v.l. κυδρή), *IG*14.2117; v.l. for κυδρός, Hes.*Op.*257.

**κῡδοιδοπάω**, *make a hubbub*, Ar.*Pax*1152, *Nu.*616.

**κῡδοιμ-έω**, *make an uproar, spread confusion*, τὼ δ' ἂν' ὅμιλον ἰόντε κυδοίμεον Il.11.324, cf. Q.S.13.480. II. trans., *drive in confusion*, ἡμέας εἶσι κυδοιμήσων ἐς Ὄλυμπον Il.15.136. (In later Prose, Phld. *Piet.*145.) **-ός**, ὁ, *din of battle, uproar, hubbub*, Τρώων δὲ κλαγγή τε καὶ ἄσπετος ὦρτο κυδοιμός Il.10.523, cf. 18.218; κυδοιμὸν ἐμβαλεῖν (mock-heroic) Ar.*Ach.*573; ὀρνίθων κυδοιμοί cock-*fights*, Theoc.22. 72:—Κυδοιμός personified, as companion of Ἐνυώ and Ἔρις, Il.5.593, 18.535, cf. Emp.128.1, Ar.*Pax*255.—Ep. word, used by Ar. and in later Prose, as Plb.5.48.5, Luc.*Bis Acc.*10, etc.

**κῦδος**, εος, τό, *glory, renown*, esp. in war, ὡς ἄν μοι τιμὴν..καὶ κ. ἄρηαι Il.16.84; ἐκ δὲ Διὸς τιμὴ καὶ κ. ὀπηδεῖ 17.251; Ἕκτορι κ. ὄπαζεν (sc. Ἀπόλλων) 16.730; ὁπποτέροισι πατὴρ Ζεὺς κ. ὀρέξῃ 5.33; κ. ἀρέσθαι to win *glory*, 12.407, etc.; κύδεϊ γαίων 1.405, 5.906; of a person, μέγα κ. Ἀχαιῶν *glory* of the Achaeans, of Odysseus, 9.673, Od.12. 184; of Nestor, Il.14.42, Od.3.79.—Ep. word, also in Alc.*Supp.*23. 13, Hdt.7.8.α', Democr.215, Pi.*P.*2.80, al., A.*Th.*317 (lyr.), *Pers.*455 (not in S. or E.); in a mock-heroic line, Ar.*Eq.*200; never in Att. Prose.

**κύδος**, ὁ, *reproach, abuse*, Sch.S.*Aj.*722, Sch.A.R.1.1337.

**κυδρόομαι**, Pass., = κυδιάω, Ael.*NA*4.29, 11.31, Polyaen.4.3.5.

**κῡδρός**, ά, όν, (κῦδος) = κυδάλιμος, in Hom. always in fem., as epith. of Hera and Leto, Διὸς κυδρὴ παράκοιτις Il.18.184, Od.11.580; of Pallas, *h.Hom.*28.1; Δίκη Hes.*Op.*257 (v.l. κυδνή); θεαί, of the Nymphs, A.*Fr.*168 (hex.); rarely of a mortal woman, Od.15.26: masc. first in *h.Merc.*461, Alcm.9; of a man, X.*Ap.*29; of a horse, κυδρῷ τῷ σχήματι φέρεται Id.*Eq.*10.16; κυδρότερον πίνειν to drink *more lustily*, Ion Eleg.2.10.—Poet. word, used once in Trag., and twice by X.—Besides regul. Comp. κυδρότερος Xenoph.2.6, B.1.54, we find κυδίων, -ιστος (v. κύδιστος), also κυδέστερος Plb.3.96.7: Sup. κυδίστατος Nic.*Th.*3; κυδότερος, -ότατος *EM*543.29.

**Κῠδων-ᾶτον**, τό, *drink made from quinces*, Aët.5.139; κ. τριπτόν *drug compounded of quinces*, Paul.Aeg.7.11. **-έα**, ἡ, *quince-tree*, *Pyrus Cydonia*, *PCair.Zen.*486.2 (iii B.C.), *Gp.*4.1.12:—also **Κῠδωνία**, ἡ, ib.10.24. **-ιάτης** [ᾱ], ου, ὁ, *inhabitant of Cydonia* in Crete, Plb.4.55.4, Str.10.4.12, etc. **-ιάω**, *swell like a quince*, μαζὸς κυδωνιᾷ *APl.*4.182 (Leon.); κυδωνιῶντες οἱ μαστοὶ τὴν ἀμπεχόνην ἐξωθοῦσι Aristaenet.1.1, cf. 3. **-ιος**, α, ον, (Κυδωνία) *Cydonian*, μᾶλα *quinces*, Stesich.29, cf. Alcm.143, Canthar.6, Phylarch.10J.; μηλίδες Ibyc. 1.1; κυδώνια, τά, Dsc.1.115. II. metaph., *swelling like a quince*, κ. τιτθία, of a young girl's breasts, Ar.*Ach.*1199. 2. κυδώνιον· μέγα καὶ ἀξιόλογον, ἢ ἀπατηλόν, δόλιον, λοίδορον (cf. κύδος), Hsch. **-ίτης** [ῑ] οἶνος, ὁ, *quince*-wine, Dsc.5.20.

**κῠδωνόμελι**, τό, *drink made from quinces and honey*, Dsc.5.21, Orib.5.25.16.

**κυέω**, older and more Att. form of κύω, Il.23.266, etc. (Aeol.(?) part. fem. κύεσσα Hsch.; Arc. κύενσα *IG*5(2).514.12 (Lycosura); Coan κυεῦσα *Schwyzer*251 *B*3, written κυεοσα ib.*A*61 (iv/iii B.C.)): impf. 3 sg. ἐκύει Il.19.117: fut. κυήσω Hp.*Mul.*1.17, *Steril.*214, κυήσομαι v.l. in *Mul.*1.76: aor. ἐκύησα Ar.*Th.*641, Pl.*Smp.*203c, etc.: pf. κεκύηκα Philem.107, D.C.45.1, S.E.*P.*2.106:—Med., v. infr.:—Pass., fut. -ηθήσομαι Gal.*UP*16.10: aor. ἐκυήθην Plu.2.567f: pf. κεκύηται Porph. *Abst.*1.54:—*bear in the womb, be pregnant with*, ἐκύει φίλον υἱόν Il.19. 117; of a mare, βρέφος ἡμίονον κυέουσα 23.266: metaph., of the soul, κυοῦσι γὰρ πάντες..καὶ κατὰ τὸ σῶμα καὶ κατὰ τὴν ψυχήν Pl.*Smp.*206c; ἐκύησε τὸν Ἔρωτα ib.203c; ἃ κυεῖ περὶ ἐπιστήμης [the thoughts] with which he *is in travail*.., Id.*Tht.*184b, cf. 210b; ἃ τῇ ψυχῇ προσήκει καὶ κυῆσαι καὶ κυεῖν (v.l. τεκεῖν) both *to have conceived* and *to bring forth*, Id.*Smp.*209a:—Pass., of the embryo or foetus, Id.*Lg.* 789a, *Epin.*973d, Arist.*GA*777ᵃ23; of fruits, *to be formed*, Thphr.*HP* 4.2.4:—Med., *bring forth*, Opp.*C.*3.22; ἡ κεκυημένη, Lat. *foeta*, *Et. Gud.* s.v. κοκίας: metaph., τὰς εὐτυχεῖς ὠδῖνας κυησαμένη Him.*Or.* 7.4. b. in Botany, *produce flowers*, Thphr.*HP*6.4.8. 2. abs., *to be big* or *pregnant, conceive*, ἐκύησε Hdt.5.41; στεριφὴ γάρ εἰμι κοὐκ ἐκύησα πώποτε Ar.*Th.*641, cf. *Lys.*745, Men.*Sam.*303, etc.; κυέουσαν ἐκ τοῦ προτέρου ἀνδρός Hdt.6.68, cf. And.1.125, Lys.13.42; γυνὴ κυεῖ δέκα μῆνας; Men.413; πεντ' ἔτη ἐκύησε *IG*4²(1).121.3 (Epid.). (Cf. κύω, Skt. *śváyati* 'swell', Lat. *inciens* 'pregnant'.)

**Κύζῐκος**, ἡ, *Cyzicus*, Hdt.4.14, etc., cf. Str.12.8.11:—Adj. **Κυζικηνικός**, ή, όν, βάμμα Ar.*Pax*1176:—more freq. **Κυζικηνός**, ή, όν, Κ. στατήρ a gold coin, Lys.32.6, D.34.23, etc.; without στ., Lys.12.11, X.*An.*6.2.4, D.21.173; Κ. ἔμπλαστρος, name of a plaster, Heras ap. Gal.13.814.

**κύ-ημα** [ῡ], ατος, τό, *that which is conceived, embryo, foetus*, Hp. *Epid.*7.6, al., Pl.*R.*461c, Arist.*GA*719ᵇ33, etc. II. in Botany, *that which is swollen as the result of growth*, e.g. base of flower-head, Thphr.*HP*6.4.3: of a cabbage-sprout, Dsc.2.120, Gal.6.642. **-ηρός**, ά, όν, *pregnant*, Hsch.; also, = ἁπαλόν, βλαστόν, Id. **-ησις**, εως, ἡ, *conception*, joined with γέννησις, Pl.*Plt.*274a, cf. *Mx.*238a, Arist.*PA* 689ᵃ18, *GA*721ᵃ20, al., Corn.*ND*24 (pl.); *pregnancy*, *PLond.*2.361. 6 (i A.D.): metaph., πρὸς ἀρετῆς κύησιν Plu.2.3a codd. (leg. κτῆσιν). II. = κύημα II, Thphr.*HP*6.4.8. **-ητήριος**, α, ον, *aiding conception*, πρόσθετον κ. Hp.*Nat.Mul.*109: as Subst. κυητήριον, τό, Id.*Mul.*1.75, al.

**κύθε, κεκύθωσι**, v. κεύθω.

**Κῠθέρεια**, ἡ, *Cythereia*, surname of Aphrodite, Od.8.288, 18.193, from the city Κύθηρα in Crete, or from the island Κύθηρα; Κυπρογενής

Κ. *h.Hom.*10.1; Κ.'Αφροδίτη Musae.38 (s.v.l.):—also **Κυθήρη**, *Anacreont.*14.11; **Κυθείρη** v.l. in Opp.*C.*1.39; **Κυθέρη**, *AP*6.209 (Antip. Thess.), Epigr.ap.Luc.*Symp.*41; **Κυθηριάς**, άδος, *AP*6.190 (Gaet.), 206 (Antip. Sid.); **Κυθερηϊάς**, Man.4.359.

**Κυθερηΐς**, ΐδος, ἡ, Adj. *of Cythereia*, Man.4.207.

**κυθηγενής**, ές, (κεύθω) *born in secret*, *Eleg.Alex.Adesp.*1.9, Hsch.

**Κύθηρα** [ῠ], τά, *Cythera*, mod. *Cerigo*, Od.9.81, etc.: **Κυθηρόθεν**, Adv. *from Cythera*, Il.15.438: poet. **Κυθέρηθεν** (for Κυθη-), Hermesian.7.69:—Adj. **Κυθήριος**, α, ον, Il.10.268, etc.; ἡ Κυθηρία (sc. γῆ) X.*HG*4.8.7.

**Κυθηροδίκης** [ῐ], ου, ὁ, *Spartan magistrate sent annually to govern the island of Cythera*, Th.4.53, *BSA*27.228 (Sparta, ii A.D.).

**κύθιον**, τό, name of an *eye-salve*, Cels.6.6.7.

**κυθνόν**, = σπέρμα, Hsch.; also, *drug which prevents conception* (leg. ἄκυθνον), Id.

**Κυθνώλης**, ες, (Κύθνος, ὄλλυμι) Κ. συμφορά, prov. of *utter ruin*, from the extirpation of the Cythnians by Amphitryon, Arist.*Fr.*523.

**κυθνώνυμος**, v. κυθώνυμος.

***κύθρα**, **κυθρίδιον**, **κύθρινος**, **κυθρίς**, **κυθρόκαυλος**, **κυθρόπους**, **κύθρος**, Ion. and later Greek for χύτρ- (q.v.).

**κυθώδης**, ες, *evil smelling*, Hsch.

**κυθώνῠμος**, ον, *of hidden name*, epith. of Oedipus, Antim.55: written κυθν- by Hsch.

**κυΐντατα**· οἰκτρότατα, Hsch.

**κυΐξ**, ὁ, name of a bulbous plant, Thphr.*HP*7.13.9.

***κυΐσκομαι**, Pass., of the female, *conceive*, *become pregnant*, Hdt.2.93, 4.30, Arist.*HA*543ᵇ19, etc.; κυϊσκομένη τε καὶ τίκτουσα Pl.*Tht.*149b; of plants, Thphr.*CP*3.2.8. II. Act. κυΐσκω in same sense, Hp.*Aph.*5.62, Philostr.*VA*1.22, *Gp.*14.1.3, Gal.4.513; but 2. causal, of the male, *impregnate*, Him.*Or.*1.7.

**κυΐτις** (sc. λίθος), ἡ, a gem, Plin.*HN*37.154.

**κυκαίνω**, prob. = κυκάω, Suid.

**κυκάν**, ᾶνος, ὁ, Dor. for κυκεών, *IG*4²(1).121.102 (Epid.).

***κῠκ-άω**, *stir*, of one curdling milk, Il.5.903; *mix*, τινι with a thing, τυρόν τε καὶ ἄλφιτα καὶ μέλι χλωρὸν οἴνῳ.. ἐκύκα Od.10.235, cf. Il.11.638; φάρμακα κ. Hp.*Ep.*17; ἅλμην κύκα τούτοισιν Ar.*V.*1515, cf. Dsc.5.79: metaph., αἴ μή τί τ' εἴπην γλῶσσ' ἐκύκα κακόν Sapph.28:—Med., *mix for oneself*, Ar.*Pax*1169 (lyr.). II. *stir up*, ἄνω τε καὶ κάτω τὸν βόρβορον Id.*Eq.*866; ἄνεμοι κ. τὸ πέλαγος Alciphr.1.10; of intrigue, ἕτερόν τι κ. Men.*Epit.*211: hence, *throw into confusion* or *disorder*, νιφάδι καὶ βροντήμασι.. κυκάτω πάντα A.*Pr.*994; κ. τὴν βουλήν Ar.*Eq.*363; τὴν Ἑλλάδα Id.*Pax*270; κ... πάντα καὶ ταραττέτω ib.320, cf. Pl.*Phd.*101e, Epicur.*Nat.*14.7, etc.: in Hom. only Pass., *to be confounded*, *panic-stricken*, τὼ δὲ κυκηθήτην Il.11.129; τρὶς δὲ κυκήθησαν Τρῶες 18.229; κυκήθησαν δέ οἱ ἵπποι 20.489; of a river, *to be churned up*, *seethe*, πάντα δ' ὄρινε ῥέεθρα κυκώμενος 21.235, cf. 324; of Charybdis, Od.12.238; κλύδων' ἔφιππον ἐν μέσῳ κυκώμενον S.*El.*733; of mental *disquiet*, θυμὲ κήδεσιν κυκώμενε Archil.66; ὑπ' ἀνδρὸς τοξότου κυκώμενος *hustled* by him, Ar.*Ach.*707. **-εών**, ῶνος, ὁ, acc. κυκεῶνα Hp.*Acut.*39, Pl.*R.*408b, etc., shortd. κυκεῶ Od.10.290, 316, *h.Cer.*210, Eup.11.4 D., 12.6 D., Ep. acc. κυκειῶ Il.11.624, 641; Dor. κυκάν (q.v.): (κυκάω):—*potion*, *posset*, containing barley-groats, grated cheese, and Pramnian wine, Il. l.c.; also honey and magical drugs, Od.10.316, cf. 234 sq.; other ingredients, *h.Cer.*210, cf. Hp. l.c., Thphr.*Char.*4.1, etc.; κ. βληχωνίας Ar.*Pax*712; ὁ κ. διίσταται ⟨μὴ⟩ κινούμενος Heraclit.125, cf. Chrysipp.*Stoic.*2.269, M.Ant.9.39. II. metaph., *mixture*, *medley*, Luc.*Vit.Auct.*14, *Icar.*17. **-ηθμός**, ὁ, *confusion*, *disturbance*, Max.Tyr.16.9, 17.10. **-ήθρα**· ταραχή, Hsch. **-ηθρον**, τό, *ladle for stirring*: metaph., *turbulent fellow*, *agitator*, Ar.*Pax*654; κ. μεγάλων πραγμάτων J.*AJ*17.5.8, cf. Cels.ap.Orig.*Cels.*5.63. **-ημα**· τάραχος, Hsch. **-ησις**, εως, ἡ, *stirring up*, *mixing*, Pl.*Ti.*68a, Epicur.*Nat.Herc.*1431.8. **-ησίτεφρος** [ῐ], ον, *mixed with ashes*, κονία Ar.*Ra.*710 (lyr.). **-ησμός**, ὁ, = κύκησις, S.*Ichn.*117. **-ητής**, οῦ, ὁ, *stirrer*, *agitator*, term applied to Heraclitus by Epicur.*Fr.*238, cf. Ptol.*Tetr.*166.

**κύκκαρος**· τὸ ἐλάχιστον, Hsch.

**κυκλ-άζω**, *go round about*, *surround*, Hsch. **-αίνω**, *make round*, Id.

**κυκλάμῑνος** [ᾰ], ἡ, Theoc.5.123, Dsc.2.164; also ὁ, Thphr.*HP*7.9.4, 9.9.3; **κυκλάμῑς**, ἡ, Orph.*A.*917:—*Cyclamen graecum*, etc., ll. cc.; also κ. ἑτέρα *honeysuckle*, *Lonicera Periclymenum*, Dsc.2.165.

***κυκλάνεμον**, τό, κ. γυναικείοις, ἅπερ ἀνεμόσουριν (dub. sens.) καλοῦσιν, Olymp.*in Mete.*200.20.

***κυκλάς**, άδος, ἡ, *encircling*, αἱ Κυκλάδες νῆσοι the *Cyclades*, islands in the Aegaean Sea, which *encircle* Delos, Hdt.5.31, Th.1.4, Isoc.4.136, 12.43, cf. Theoc.17.90, Str.10.5.1: without νῆσοι, Th.2.9; so Κυκλάδας νησαίας πόλεις the cities of those islands, E.*Ion*1583. 2. *recurrent*, of Time, Orph.*H.*53.7. II. Subst. κυκλάς (sc. ἐσθής), ἡ, *a woman's garment with a border all round it*, Prop.4(5).7.40. 2. *part of an irrigation-machine*, *PLond.*3.776.10 (vi A.D.).

**κυκλᾶτός**, ή, όν, *shod*, of horses, *PMasp.*279.18 (vi A.D.).

**Κυκλειών**, ῶνος, ὁ, name of month at Ceos, *Ath.Mitt.*49.138 (iv B.C.).

***κύκλ-ευμα**, ατος, τό, *water-wheel*, *PSI*1.77.18 (vi A.D.). ***-ευτήριον**, τό, = foreg., *PGiss.*56.8 (vi A.D.), etc. **-ευτής**, οῦ, ὁ, *tender of water-wheel*, *PLond.*1.131.32, al. (ii A.D.). ***-εύω**, *wind round*, περὶ τὸν περινεὸν κ. τὸ ὀθόνιον Hp.*Art.*14. 2. *traverse*, μιᾶς ἡμέρας κ. περίοδον Str.6.3.7, cf. J.*AJ*9.3.1, *Supp.Epigr.*2.530 (Puteoli); ἥλιος κ. τὴν γῆν Cleom.1.2. 3. *work a water-wheel*, *PLond.*1.131.495 (ii A.D.). b. *irrigate by means of a water-wheel*, *PGrenf.*1.58.7 (vi A.D.). II. *circumvent*, *surround*, App.*BC*4.71 (Pass.). ***-έω**, *wheel along*, in Hom. only once, κυκλήσομεν ἐνθάδε νεκροὺς βουσὶ καὶ ἡμιόνοισιν Il.7.332. 2. *move round* or *in a circle*, ὁδοῖς κυκλῶν ἐμαυτὸν εἰς ἀναστροφήν S.*Ant.*226; ἐπ' ἀνδρὶ δυσμενεῖ βάσιν κυκλοῦντα, metaph., from dogs *questing about* for the scent, Id.*Aj.*19; σὸν πόδ' ἐπὶ συννοίᾳ κυκλεῖς E.*Or.*632, cf. Ar.*Av.*1379; κ. πρόσωπον, ὄμμα, look *round*, look *about*, E.*Ph.*364, Ar.*Th.*958 (lyr.); = κυκλεύω I, Hp.*Fract.*4. 3. *bring round*, *repeat*, τὸν αὐτὸν λόγον Arist.*Cael.*300ᵃ33. II. Med. and Pass., *form a circle round*, *encompass*, *encircle*, μηνοειδὲς ποιήσαντες τῶν νεῶν ἐκυκλεῦντο ὡς περιλάβοιεν αὐτούς Hdt.8.16 (elsewh. κυκλόομαι); ἴδεσθέ μ' οἷον ἄρτι κῦμα.. κυκλεῖται *encompasses* me, S.*Aj.*353 (lyr.). 2. *go round and round*, *revolve*, τὴν αὐτὴν φορὰν κ. Pl.*R.*617a; χρόνου.. κατ' ἀριθμὸν κυκλουμένου Id.*Ti.*38a; οὑμὸς αἰεὶ πότμος ἐν πυκνῷ θεοῦ τροχῷ κυκλεῖται S.*Fr.*871; ὁ βίος ἀγαθοῖς τε καὶ κακοῖς κ. πάντα τὸν αἰῶνα D.S.18.59; δι' ἀλλήλων αὐτοῖς -εῖται τὸ κακόν, of the vicious circle in disease, Gal.10.360. 3. *assemble in knots*, X.*An.*6.4.20, *Cyr.*6.2.12. 4. metaph., of sayings, etc., *to be current*, *pass from mouth to mouth*, τὸ κυκλούμενον παρὰ πᾶσιν ἔπος Plu.2.118c. III. intr. in Act., *revolve*, *come round and round*, πολλαὶ κυκλοῦσι νύκτες ἡμέραι τ' ἴσαι (but read κυκλοῦνται as L had originally) S.*El.*1365; δελφῖνες.. πέριξ κυκλοῦντες Plu.2.160f. **-ηδόν**, Adv. *in a circle*, περιβλέψας τὸ πλῆθος Posidon.36 J. **-ησις**, εως, ἡ, *revolution*, Pl.*Ti.*39c, *Plt.*271d, Iamb.*Myst.*8.6. **-ιαῖος**, α, ον, *of* or *for wheels*, τροχοί *IG*1².349.13. **-ιακός**, ή, όν, only neut. pl., τὰ κ. *treatise on the circle*, by Philippus of Opus, Suid. s.v. φιλόσοφος. **-ιάς**, άδος, ἡ, *round*, τυροὶ κυκλιάδες *AP*6.299 (Phan.). **-ίζω**, *cause to revolve*, τὰ ἐναντία περὶ τὴν μένουσαν οὐσίαν Olymp. *in Phd.*p.145 N.:—Pass., *revolve*, ib.p.130 N., al.; *to be enclosed as in a circle*, ἡ οἰκουμένη -ίζεται ἐν τέτταρσι μέρεσιν Agatharch.64. II. intrans. in Act., *revolve*, Dam.*Pr.*23. ***-ικός**, ή, όν, *circular*, *moving in a circle*, σῶμα Arist.*Cael.*289ᵃ30, κίνησις *Placit.*2.7.5; περίοδος D.S.2.36: metaph., Procl.*Inst.*33. Adv. -κῶς, κινεῖσθαι Arist.*Cael.*272ᵇ24. 2. *of a circle*, λόγος Iamb. *in Nic.*p.61 P.; κ. ἀριθμός a number *which ends in the same digit when squared*, Nicom.*Ar.*2.17. 3. Astrol., *subordinate*, *ruling in rotation*, Vett.Val.175.17. b. -κὰ ἔτη *the minimum duration of life corresponding to a planet*, Balbill. in *Cat.Cod.Astr.*8(4).236, 237. 4. -κός (sc. πούς), ὁ, a form of anapaest in which the long syllable is shorter than a normal long, D.H.*Comp.*17. II. κυκλικοί, οἱ, the *poets of the Epic cycle* (cf. κύκλος), Sch.Il.3.242, al.; also ἡ κ. Θηβαΐς Ath.11.465e; but τὸ ποίημα τὸ κ. *commonplace*, *conventional* poem (cf. IV), Call.*Epigr.*30.1. III. f.l. for κύκλιος II, χορός Lys.21.2; τῶν κυκλικῶν (v.l. κυκλίων) αὐλητῶν Luc.*Salt.*2. IV. *in common use*, ἡ κ. (sc. ἔκδοσις) the *vulgate*, Sch.Od.16.195, 17.25: but Adv. -κῶς *conventionally*, οὐ κ. τὰ ἐπίθετα προσέρριπται ib.7.115.

**κυκλιοδῐδάσκᾰλος**, ὁ, *teacher of the cyclic chorus*, i.e. *dithyrambic poet* (v. κύκλιος II), Ar.*Av.*1403.

***κύκλ-ιος**, α, ον (ος, ον Eup.5 D.), (κύκλος) *round*, *circular*, ἀσπίς Archestr.*Fr.*13.3; ὕδωρ κύκλιον, of the Delian lake (cf. τροχοειδής), E.*IT*1104 (lyr.). II. κύκλιος χορός, ὁ, *circular* or *cyclic chorus*, prop. of any which were danced *in a ring round an altar*, chiefly used of *dithyrambic choruses*, opp. those which were arranged in a square (τετράγωνοι Timae.44), Ar.*Nu.*333, *Ra.*366, *Fr.*149.10, X.*Oec.*8.20, Aeschin.3.232, etc.; ἐν τῷ ἀγῶνι τῶν κ. χορῶν *Schwyzer*91.26 (Argos, iii B.C.); τῶν κ. (without χορῶν) Ἀρχ.Ἐφ.1913.7 (Nisyros, iii B.C.), cf. *Inscr.Cos*13.4; ἐν τοῖς κ. ἀγῶσιν *OGI*213.38 (Didyma, iv/iii B.C.); invented by Arion, Arist.*Fr.*677: hence κύκλιον ὠρχήσαντο Call.*Del.*313; εἱλισσόμεναι κύκλια E.*IA*1055 (lyr.). 2. κ. μέλη *dithyrambs*, Ar.*Av.*918; κύκλιος ἀναβολή Eup. l.c. 3. = κυκλικός II, *AP*11.130 (Poll.). 4. = χορίαμβος, Sch.Heph.p.303 C. III. name of month at Epidaurus, *IG*4²(1).115.23 (iv/iii B.C.), al. IV. κυκλίῳ, = κύκλῳ, c. gen. (cf. κύκλος I), *BGU*938.4 (iv A.D.). **-ίσκιον**, τό, Dim. of sq. I. 2, Dsc.2.83, Democr.ap.Gal.14.95. **-ίσκος**, ὁ, Dim. of κύκλος, *small circle* in a diagram, Ptol.*Hyp.*1.9, al.; as part of an instrument, Id.*Alm.*1.12. 2. *small round cake* of wax, Dsc.2.83; *lozenge*, = τροχίσκος, Hp.*Mul.*2.188, Gal.12.276, Lycus ap. Orib.8.25.23, Aët.15.37. II. *ring to pass the reins through*, Gal.2.323. 2. *circular opening* of a coop, Ph.*Bel.*78.1. 3. f.l. for κοιλίσκος (q.v.). III. *round spot*, Clytus 1. **-ισκωτός**, ή, όν, v.l. for κοιλισκωτός (q.v.). **-ισμός**, ὁ, *circular motion*, *circularity*, Simp. *in Ph.*1280.33, Olymp. *in Phd.*pp.141, 145 N., Hsch. s.v. ἀλάθεας ὥρας. **-ίστρια**, ἡ, *dancer in cyclic chorus*, *IG*2.4112.

**Κυκλο-βορέω**, *brawl like the torrent Cycloborus*, Ar.*Ach.*381. **-βόρος**, ὁ, torrent in Attica, κεκράκτης, Κυκλοβόρου φωνὴν ἔχων Id.*Eq.*137; φῆμην δ' ἔγωγε τὸν Κ. κατιέναι Id.*Fr.*636. **-γάλων**· γλίσχρων, σμικρολόγων, Hsch. (Fort. συλλογάδων.) **-γρᾰφέω**, *describe a circle*, S.E.*M.*3.26, 9.420, Simp. *in Cael.*209.22. II. *use periphrasis*, D.H.*Dem.*19. **-γρᾰφία**, ἡ, *description*, *tracing of a circle*, Simp. *in Cael.*210.5. **-γράφος** [γρᾰ], ον, *writing on a cycle* of subjects, of Dionysius Scytobrachion, Procl. ad Hes. p.6 G., Tz.*H.*12.184. **-δίωκτος** [ῐ], ον, *driven round in a circle*, *AP*9.301 (Secund.). **-ειδής**, ές, *circular*, Euc.*Opt.*36, Onos.21.6, Ath.7.328d; τὸ κ. Plu.2.1004c. Adv. -δῶς Gal.*Phil.Hist.*100, Porph. *in Cat.*133.4. **-εις**, εσσα, εν, poet. for κυκλικός, *circular*, ἀγορᾶς θρόνος S.*OT*161 (lyr.); ἴτυς *AP*7.232 (Antip.). **-έλικτος**, ον, *revolving in a circle*, Orph.*H.*8.11.

**κυκλόθεν**, Adv. *from all around*, κ. ὁδὸς περιέχει Lys.7.28, cf. Hp.

*Fract.*33, Thphr.*HP*4.6.10 (dub. l.), etc.: c. gen., Lxx 3*Ki.*18.32, al., *Apoc.*4.3: c. dat., Lxx 3*Ki.*6.5: spelt κύκλωθεν, *IPE*1².175 (Olbia), and sts. in codd., but this spelling is condemned by Theognost.*Can.* 156, and arose from a supposed connexion with κύκλῳ.

**κυκλόθι**, Adv. *around*, A.D.*Adv.*194.17.

**κυκλο-μόλυβδος**, ὁ, *round lead-pencil*, *AP*6.63 (Damoch.). **-ποιησάμενοι**, f.l. for κύκλον ποι- in X.*Cyr.*7.1.40. **-πορέω**, *go by a circuitous way*, Str.7.1.4. **-πορία**, ἡ, *going round, circuitous way*, Id.2.1.39, 11.13.4: pl., Id.16.4.23. **-πόρος**, ον, *moving in a circle*, βία Heraclit.*All.*12.

**κύκλος**, ὁ (Dor. ἁ, v. infr. II. 11), also with heterocl. pl. κύκλα Il., etc., v. infr. II. 1, 3, 9, III. 1:—*ring, circle*, ὁππότε μιν δόλιον περὶ κύκλον ἄγωσιν, of the *circle* which hunters draw round their game, Od.4.792; κ. δέκα χάλκεοι (concentric) *circles* of brass on a round shield, Il.11.33, cf. 20.280; but ἀσπίδος κύκλον λέγω the round shield itself, A.*Th.*489, cf. 496, 591. 2. Adverbial usages, κύκλῳ *in a circle* or *ring, round about*, κ. ἁπάντῃ Od.8.278; κ. πάντῃ X.*An.*3.1.2; πανταχῇ D.4.9; τὸ κ. πέδον Pi.*O.*10(11).46; κ. περιάγειν Hdt.4.180; λίμνη.. ἐργασμένη εὖ κ. Id.2.170; τρέχειν κ. Ar.*Th.*662; περιέπλεον αὐτοὺς κ. Th.2.84; οἱ κ. βασιλεῖς X.*Cyr.*7.2.23; ἡ κ. περιφορά, κίνησις, Pl.*Lg.*747a, Alex. Aphr.*in Top.*218.3: freq. with περί or words compounded therewith, *round* about, κ. πέριξ A.*Pers.*368, 418; περιστῆναι κ. Hdt.1.43; βωμὸν κ. περιστῆναι A.*Fr.*379; ἀμφιχανὼν κ. S.*Ant.*118 (lyr.); περιστεφῆ κ. Id.*El.*895; περισταδὸν κ. E.*Andr.*1137; κ. περιιέναι Pl.*Phd.*72b, etc.; τοῦ φλοιοῦ περιαιρεθέντος κ. Thphr.*HP*4.15.1; so κ. περὶ αὐτήν *round* about it, Hdt.1.185; περὶ τὰ δώματα κ. Id.2.62; also κύκλῳ c. acc., without περί, ἐπιστήσαντες κ. σῆμα Id.4.72; πάντα τὸν τόπον τοῦτον κ. D.4.4: c. gen., κ. τοῦ στρατοπέδου X.*Cyr.*4.5.5; τὰ κ. τῆς Ἀττικῆς D.18.96, cf. *PFay.*110.7 (i A.D.), etc.: metaph., *around* or *from all sides*, S.*Ant.*241, etc.; κεντουμένη κύκλῳ ἡ ψυχὴ *all over*, Pl.*Phdr.* 251d; τὰ κ. the *circumstances*, Arist.*Rh.*1367ᵇ29, *EN*1117ᵇ2; ἡ κ. ἀπόδειξις, of arguing *in a circle*, Id.*APo.*72ᵇ17, cf. *APr.*57ᵇ18: with Preps., ἐν κ. S.*Aj.*723, *Ph.*356, E.*Ba.*653, Ar.*V.*432, etc.; ἅπαντες ἐν κ. Id.*Eq.*170, *Pl.*679: c. gen., E.*HF*926, Th.3.74; κατὰ κύκλον Emp.17.13. II. *any circular body*: 1. *wheel*, Il.23.340; in which sense the heterocl. pl. κύκλα is mostly used, 5.722, 18.375; τοὺς λίθους ἀνατιθεῖσι ἐπὶ τὰ κύκλα on the *janker*, *IG*1².350.47. 2. *trencher*, *SIG*57.32 (Milet., v B.C.), *Abh.Berl.Akad.*1928(6).29 (Cos), Poll.6.84. 3. *place of assembly*, of the ἀγορά, ἱερὸς κ. Il.18.504; ὁ κ. τοῦ Ζηνὸς τὠγοραίου *Schwyzer*701 *B*6 (Erythrae, v B.C.); ἀγορᾶς κ. (cf. κυκλόεις) E.*Or.*919; of the *amphitheatre*, D.C.72.19. b. *crowd of people standing round, ring* or *circle of people*, κ. τυραννικός S.*Aj.*749; κύκλα χαλκέων ὅπλων, i.e. of armed men, dub. in Id.*Fr.*210.9, cf. X. *Cyr.*7.5.41: abs., E.*Andr.*1089, X.*An.*5.7.2 (both pl.), Diph.55.3. c. *place in the* ἀγορά *where domestic utensils were sold*, Alex.99. 4. *vault* of the sky, ὁ κ. τοῦ οὐρανοῦ Hdt.1.131, Lxx 1*Es.*4.34; πυραυγέα κ. αἰθέρος *h.Hom.*8.6, cf. E.*Ion* 1147; ὁ ἄνω κ. S.*Ph.*815; ἐς βάθος κύκλου Ar.*Av.*1715; νυκτὸς αἰανῆς κ. S.*Aj.*672; γαλαξίας κ. the milky way, *Placit.*2.7.1, al., Poll.4.159; also ὁ τοῦ γάλακτος κ. Arist. *Mete.*345ᵃ25; πολιοῖο γάλακτος κ. Arat.511. b. μέγιστος κ. great *circle*, Autol.*Sph.*2, al.; μ. κ. τῶν ἐν τῇ σφαίρᾳ Archim.*Sph.Cyl.*1.30, cf. Gem.5.70; κ. ἰσημερινός, θερινός, etc., Ph.1.27; χειμερινός Gem.5.7, Cleom.1.2; ἀρκτικός, ἀνταρκτικός, Gem.5.2, 9; ὁ κ. ὁ τῶν ζῳδίων Arist. *Mete.*343ᵃ24; ὁ ὁρίζων κ. the horizon, Id.*Cael.*297ᵇ34; παράλληλοι κ., of *parallels* of latitude, Autol.*Sph.*1: in pl., *the zones*, *Stoic.*2.196. 5. *orb, disk* of the sun and moon, ἡλίου κ. A.*Pr.*91, *Pers.*504, S.*Ant.*416; πανσέληνος κ. E.*Ion* 1155; μὴ οὐ πλήρεος ἐόντος τοῦ κύκλου (sc. τῆς σελήνης) Hdt 6.106: in pl., *the heavenly bodies*, *IG*14.2012 *A*9 (Sulp. Max.). 6. *circle* or *wall round* a city, esp. round Athens, ὁ Ἀθηνέων κ. Hdt.1.98, cf. Th.2.13, etc.; οὐχὶ τὸν κ. τοῦ Πειραιῶς, οὐδὲ τοῦ ἄστεως D.18.300. b. *circular fort*, Th.6.99, al. 7. *round shield*, v. sub init. 8. in pl., *eye-balls, eyes*, S.*OT*1270, *Ph.*1354; ὀμμάτων κ. Id.*Ant.*974 (lyr.): rarely in sg., *eye*, ὁ αἰὲν ὁρῶν κ. Διός Id.*OC*704 (lyr.). 9. οἱ κ. τοῦ προσώπου *cheeks*, Hp.*Morb.*2.50; κύκλα παρειῆς Nonn.*D.*33.190, 37.412; but κύκλος μαζοῦ, poet. for μαζός, is f.l. in Tryph.34. 10. κ. ἐλαίης an olive *wreath*, Orph.*A.*325 (pl.). 11. *cycle* or *collection of legends* or *poems*, κύκλον ἱστορημέναν ὑπὲρ Κρήτας *GDI*5187.9 (Crete); esp. of *the Epic cycle*, ὁ ἐπικὸς κ. Ath. 7.277e, Procl.ap.Phot.*Bibl.*p.319 B., cf. Arist.*Rh.*1417ᵃ15; of the corpus of legends compiled by Dionysius Scytobrachion, Ath.11. 481e, cf. Sch.Od.2.120; κ. ἐπιγραμμάτων Suid. s. v. Ἀγαθίας; cf. κυκλικός II. III. *circular motion, orbit* of the heavenly bodies, κύκλον ἰέναι Pl.*Ti.*38d; οὐρανὸς.. μιᾷ περιαγωγῇ καὶ κύκλῳ συναναχορεύει τούτοις Arist.*Mu.*391ᵇ18; *revolution* of the seasons, ἐνιαυτοῦ κ. E.*Or.* 1645, *Ph.*477; τὸν ἐνιαύσιον κ. the yearly *cycle*, ib.544; ἑπτὰ.. ἐτῶν κ. Id.*Hel.*112; μυρία κύκλα ζώειν, i.e. *years*, *AP*7.575 (Leont.): hence κ. τῶν ἀνθρωπηΐων ἐστὶ πρηγμάτων human affairs revolve in *cycles*, Hdt.1.207; φασὶ.. κύκλον εἶναι τὰ ἀνθρώπινα πράγματα Arist.*Ph.*223ᵇ 24, al.; κ. κακῶν D.C.44.29; κύκλου ἐξέπταν, i.e. from the *cycle* of rebirths, Orph.*Fr.*32c.6. b. ἐν τοῖς κ. εἶναι to be in *train*, of an affair, *PEleph.*14.24 (iii B.C.). 2. *circular dance* (cf. κύκλιος), χωρεῖτε νῦν ἱερὸν ἀνὰ κ. Ar.*Ra.*445, cf. Simon.148.9, E.*Alc.*449 (lyr.). 3. in Rhet., *a rounded period*, περιόδου κύκλος D.H.*Comp.*19, cf. 22, 23. b. period which begins and ends with the same word, Hermog.*Inv.*4.8. 4. in Metre, a kind of *anapaest*, v.l. for κυκλικός in D.H.*Comp.*17. IV. *sphere, globe*, Pl.*Lg.*898a. [ῡ by nature, S.*Ant.*416, *Aj.*672, etc., but freq. long by position in Hom. and Trag.]

**κυκλόσε**, Adv., (κύκλος) *in* or *into a circle*, περὶ δ' αὐτὸν ἀγηγέραθ' ὅσσοι ἄριστοι κ. Il.4.212; διαστάντες τανύουσι κ. stretch [the skin] *outwards on all sides*, 17.392, cf. Onos.17, A.D.*Adv.*193.8, Ael.*NA* 3.13, etc.

**κυκλο-σοβέω**, *whirl round*, πόδα cj. in Ar.*V.*1523 (lyr.). **-στρεφέομαι** (fort. -στροφ-), *proceed by cyclical recurrence*, Vett.Val.344. 2. **-τερής**, ές, (τείρω) *made round by turning* (τὴν γῆν ἐοῦσαν κυκλοτερέα ὡς ἀπὸ τόρνου Hdt.4.36): generally, *round, circular*, κυκλοτερὲς μέγα τόξον ἔτεινε stretched it *into a circle*, Il.4.124; ἄλσος πάντοσε κυκλοτερές Od.17.209; ὀφθαλμός, λιμήν, Hes.*Th.*145, *Sc.* 208; σφαῖρος Emp.27.4; φῶς Id.45; [ὄρος] κυκλοτερὲς πάντῃ Hdt.4. 184; πλοῖα κυκλοτερέα ἀσπίδος τρόπον Id.1.194; κ. κοιλίαι, of the sockets of bones, Hp.*Art.*61; αὐχήν Pl.*Smp.*190a; κώθων Henioch. 1; οἰκοδόμημα X.*HG*4.5.6; κ. ὁ ὄγκος τῆς γῆς Arist.*Cael.*294ᵃ8; γράφουσι κ. τὴν οἰκουμένην Id.*Mete.*362ᵇ13; πεδίον κ. τὸ σχῆμα Str.4.1.7. Adv. -ρῶς *Placit.*1.12.3, Ach.Tat.*Intr.Arat.*21, Dsc.3.90, Gal.*UP*16. 11. [ῠ always, by position.] **-τέρμων**, ον, gen. ονος, *moving in a cycle*, βίος *IG*5(2).472 (Megalopolis).

**κυκλοῦχος**, ὁ, perh. *linch-pin*, *IG*2².1549 (pl.).

**κυκλοφορ-έομαι**, Pass., *revolve*, Arist.*Mu.*391ᵇ22, f.l. in Heraclit. *All.*36. **-ητικός**, ή, όν, *moving in a circle, circular*, οὐσία Ph.1. 514; τρόπος Dam.*Pr.*23; σῶμα Thphr.*Fr.*35, Iamb.*Myst.*5.4. Adv. -κῶς S.E.*M.*10.58. **-ία**, ἡ, *circular motion*, opp. εὐθυφορία, Arist. *Ph.*227ᵇ18; τῶν φορῶν ἡ κ. πρώτη ib.265ᵃ13, cf. *de An.*407ᵃ6, Thphr. *Vert.*9; τῶν ψυχῶν Dam.*Pr.*102; τὰς ἑπτὰ καὶ τὴν ὀγδόην κ., of the heavenly *spheres*, Jul.*Or.*4.146c. **-ικός**, ή, όν, = κυκλοφορητικός, Ph.1.627, Plu.2.1004c, Gal.*UP*15.8 (v.l. -ητικήν), Them.*in APo.*17. 1. Adv. -κῶς *Placit.*1.7.32.

**κυκλ-όω**, fut. -ώσω E.*Cyc.*462: pf. κεκύκλωκα Plb.3.116.10:—Med., fut. -ώσομαι X.*Cyr.*6.3.20: aor. ἐκυκλωσάμην Hdt.9.18, Th.5. 72:—Pass., fut. κυκλωθήσομαι (v.l. -ώσομαι) D.H.3.24: pf. κεκύκλωμαι Th.4.32 (in med. sense (ἐγ-) Ar.*V.*395): aor. ἐκυκλώθην X. *Cyr.*6.3.20: (κύκλος):—*encircle, surround*, Ὠκεανὸς.. κυκλοῖ χθόνα E. *Or.*1379 (lyr.); πόλιν.. κυκλώσας Ἄρει φονίῳ Id.*IA*775 (lyr.); ὅταν κυκλώσωσι [τοὺς ἰχθῦς] Arist.*HA*533ᵇ27:—more freq. in Med., κυκλώσασθαί τινας Hdt.3.157, 9.18, Plb.1.17.13; κ. αὐτοὺς ἐς μέσον Hdt.8.10, cf. A.*Th.*121 (lyr.), Call.*Hec.*1.1.14, etc.: such forms as κυκλοῦνται, ἐκυκλοῦντο, etc., may belong to κυκλόω or to κυκλέω, Th.4.127, 7.81, etc.: abs., κυκλούμενοι *by an enveloping movement*, Hdt.8.76:—Pass., *to be surrounded*, A.*Th.*247, Th.7.81:—joined with Med., εἰ οἱ κυκλούμενοι κυκλωθεῖεν X. l. c. 2. *go round*, τὸ θυσιαστήριον Lxx *Ps.*25 (26).6:—Pass., κυκλωθεὶς τὸν Ἀδρίαν D.S.4.25. II. *move in a circle, whirl round*, Pi.*O.*10(11).72; οὕτω κυκλώσω δαλὸν ἐν φαεσφόρῳ Κύκλωπος ὄψει E.*Cyc.*462; κ. ἀεὶ τὸ σῶμα Hermipp.4; οἱ κυκλοῦντες [τὴν θάλασσαν] ἄνεμοι Plb.11.29.10; ἵετο κυκλώσας βαλιὰ πτερὰ θῆλυς ἀήτης Call. in *PSI*9.1092.53, cf. Archil.92b Diehl: metaph., πολλοὺς λογισμοὺς ἡ πονηρία κυκλοῖ *revolves, agitates*, Men.378:—Med., *hurl*, βέλη Him.*Or.*7.17:—Pass. (or Med.), *go in a circle*, X.*An.*6.4.20; *dance* or *whirl round*, Call.*Dian.*267, Arat.811: metaph., δίναις κυκλούμενον κέαρ A.*Ag.*997 (lyr.). III. *form into a circle*, κ. τόξα *AP*12.82 (Mel.), cf. Him.*Or.*17.5; incorrectly, κ. τόξοιο νευρήν Babr. 68.5:—Pass., *form a circle*, of a bow, E.*Ba.*1066; also [τάφρος] περὶ τὸ πεδίον κυκλωθεῖσα *being drawn in a circle*, Pl.*Criti.*118d. IV. abs., κυκλώσατε ἐπὶ τὸν βασιλέα κύκλῳ Lxx 4*Ki.*11.8; ἐκύκλωσα ἐγὼ καὶ ἡ καρδία μου τοῦ γνῶναι ib.*Ec.*7.26(25). V. = λακκίζειν, ἀμπέλους Philostr.*Her.*2.8. **-ώδης**, ες, = κυκλοειδής, *circular*, κ. παραλλαγή a distortion of several vertebrae *forming a curve*, opp. γωνιώδης, Hp.*Art.*48. 2. *round the outside*, opp. ἐν μέσῳ, Id.*Epid.* 7.84. **-ωθεν**, late form for κυκλόθεν (q.v.). **-ωμα**, ατος, τό, *that which is rounded into a circle*: 1. *wheel*, κ. Ἰξίονος E.*Ph.* [1185]. 2. βυρσότονον κ. *drum*, Id.*Ba.*124 (lyr.). 3. *coil* of a serpent, D.S.3.36. 4. of natural objects, αἰθέριον κ., of the sun, Secund.*Sent.*5; κόσμος ἀπλανὲς κ. ib.1.

**Κυκλώπ-ειος**, α, ον (in Eust.1634.35, al., ος, ον), (Κύκλωψ) *Cyclopean*, used of prehistoric architecture attributed to the Cyclopes, applied to Mycenae, E.*El.*1158 (lyr.); to ancient buildings near Nauplia, Str.8.6.2. 2. prov., κ. βίος *uncivilized* life, Id.11.4.3, Max.Tyr.21.7 (v.l. -ιος). **-ία** (better **-εία**), ἡ, *the tale of the Cyclops* in Od.9, Philostr.*VA*6.11, Ael.*VH*13.14. **-ικῶς**, Adv. *like the Cyclopes*, κ. ζῆν to live *an unsocial life*, Arist.*EN*1180ᵃ28.

**κυκλώπιον**, τό, (ὤψ) *white round the ball of the eye*, f.l. for κύκλῳ πῖον, Arist.*HA*533ᵃ9. II. Κυκλώπιον, τό, Dim. of Κύκλωψ, E.*Cyc.* 266.

**Κυκλώπιος**, α, ον, = Κυκλώπειος, πρόθυρα Pi.*Fr.*169.6; γᾶ, i.e. Mycenae, E.*Or.*965 (lyr.), cf. *IA*265 (lyr.), *HF*15; τροχός, of the 'circuit of the walls' of Mycenae, S.*Fr.*227; v. Κυκλώπειος 2:—pecul. fem. **Κυκλωπίς**, ίδος, ἑστία E.*IT*845 (lyr.).

**κύκλ-ωσις**, εως, ἡ, *surrounding, enveloping*, esp. in battle, X.*HG* 4.2.20, Plb.3.65.6, Plu.*Them.*12, Onos.21.1 (pl.); πρὶν καὶ τὴν πλέονα κ. σφῶν αὐτόσε προσμεῖξαι before the larger body *that was endeavouring to surround* them came up, Th.4.128. 2. *way round*, Plu.*Flam.*4. **-ωτός**, ή, όν, *rounded*, A.*Th.*540.

**Κύκλωψ**, ωπος (acc. -ωπα, v. infr.), ὁ, *Cyclops*, freq. in pl., one-eyed giant savages, Od.9.106, Hes.*Th.*139, Th.6.2, etc.: prop. *Round-eyed*, Κύκλωπες δ' ὄνομ' ἦσαν ἐπώνυμον, οὕνεκ' ἄρα σφέων κυκλοτερὴς ὀφθαλμὸς ἕεις ἐνέκειτο μετώπῳ Hes.*Th.*144: hence as Adj., κ. σελήνη the *round-eyed* moon, Parm.10.4; κύκλωπα κούρην, of the pupil of the eye, Emp.84.8: sg. in Od. always of *Polyphemus*, 1.69, al. 2. mythical builders of prehistoric walls at Tiryns, Mycenae, etc., Hellanic.88 J., Pherecyd.12, 35(*a*) J., B.10.77, Str.8.6.11; τὰ

Κυκλώπων βάθρα, i.e. Mycenae, E.*HF*944. **3.** Κύκλωπες, οἱ, a throw of the dice, Eub.57.6.

**κυκν-άριον**, τό, Dim. of κύκνος III, Aët.7.8, Gal.14.765. ❀ **-ειος**, α, ον, also ος, ον LXX 4*Ma*.15.21:—*of a swan*, πτίλον S.*Fr*.1127.3; στόμα *AP*7.12: τὸ κ. (sc. ᾆσμα or μέλος) ᾄδειν *a swan's dying song*, Chrysipp.*Stoic*.3.199, Ael.*NA*2.32; κ. πρὸς φιληκοΐαν φωναί LXX l. c.: prov., τὸ κ. ἐξηχεῖν, ἐξᾷσαι, to make a last appeal, Plb.30.4.7, 31.12.1, cf. D.S.31.5. **II.** Κύκνειος, α, ον, *of Cycnus*, μάχα Pi.*O*.10(11).15. **-ίας** ἀετός, ὁ, a kind of *white eagle*, Paus.8.17.3. **-ῖτις**, ιδος, pecul. fem. of Κύκνειος, βοή S.*Fr*.499.

**κυκνό-θρεπτος**, ον, *reared by swans*, Steph. *in Rh*.301.18, Sch.Lyc.237. **-κάνθαρος**, ὁ, a kind of ship *between* κύκνος II *and* κάνθαρος III, Nicostr.Com.10. **-μορφος**, ον, *swan-shaped*, or *white as a swan*, A.*Pr*.795. **-πτερος**, ον, *swan-plumed*, of Helen in reference to Leda and the swan, E.*Or*.1386 (lyr.).

**κύκνος**, ὁ, *swan*, *Cycnus olor*, κύκνων δουλιχοδείρων Il.2.460, cf. Hes.*Sc*.316, Pl.*R*.620a, Eratosth.*Cat*.25, etc.; sacred to Apollo, Ar.*Av*.870, Pl.*Phd*.85b, Call.*Ap*.5: Com., βάτραχοι κ. Ar.*Ra*.207; κύκνου δίκην τὸν ὕστατον μέλψασα θανάσιμον γόον A.*Ag*.1444: hence, metaph., *minstrel, bard*, *AP*7.19 (Leon.). **II.** kind of ship, prob. from its prow being curved like a *swan's* neck, Nicostr.Com.10. **III.** *eye-salve*, Gal.12.708,759, etc. [ῡ by position in Ep.; ῠ Pi.*O*.2.82, Theoc.16.49 in pr. n. Κύκνος.]

**κύκνοψις**, εως, ὁ, ἡ, *swan-like*, *AP*11.345.

**κυκύϊζα**· γλυκεῖα κολόκυντα, and **κύκυον**· τὸν σικυόν, Hsch.; cf. Lat. *cucumis*.

**κύλα**, ων, τά, *the parts under the eyes*, Hp.*Nat.Mul*.15; τὰ κ. τοῦ προσώπου ἐξερυθριᾷ ib.9, cf. *Mul*.1.37; τὰ κ. τῶν ὀφθαλμῶν ὑπόχλωρα Sor.1.44, cf. Hsch., Phot.:—also **κυλάδες**, αἱ, Eust.1951.18; **κυλίς**, Poll.2.66; cf. κύλλαβοι, κύλλια. **2.** sg., *groove above upper eyelid*, Ruf.*Onom*.21. (κῦλον Hdn.Gr.1.378; κοῖλα Suid., freq. as v.l., cf. Sch.Theoc.1.38; but κῠλ- in κυλοιδιάω.)

❀ **κυληβίς**· κολοβή, Hsch.

**κυλίδιον**, v. κοιλίδιον.

**κῠλῐκ-εῖον**, τό, *sideboard, stand for drinking-vessels*, Ar.*Fr*.104, Anaxandr.29, Eub.62, *PCair.Zen*.14.9 (iii B. C.). **II.** *carousal*, Cratin.Jun.9. **-ειος**, ον, *of a cup*, ζητήματα discussions *over wine*, Poll.6.108. **-ηγορέω**, *talk over one's cups*, Ath.11.461e, 480b, Poll.6.29. **-ηγόρος**, ον, *one who talks over his cups*, Eust.1632.18. **-ήρῠτος**, ον, (ἀρύω A) *drawn in cups*, i.e. *abundant*, αἷμα Call.*Fr.anon*.188. **-ιον**, τό, Dim. of κύλιξ, *small cup*, Thphr.*HP*5.9.8, Lyc.*Fr*.2.1, Philet.ap.Ath.11.498a, LXX *Es*.1.7, Aristeas 319 codd.:—also **-ίς**, ίδος, ἡ, dub. in Ath.11.480c. **-οφόρος**, ον, *carrying cups*, Hld.7.27. **-ώδης**, ες, *like a cup*, Sch.Theoc.2.2.

**κῠλινδ-αίνω**, = κυλίνδω, Max.Tyr.20.1 codd. (κυδαίνων cj. Reiske). **-έω**, v. κυλίνδω. **-ήθρα**, ἡ, = ἀλινδήθρα (q. v.). **-ησις**, εως, ἡ, *rolling, wallowing*, ἐν γυναίοις Plu.*Ant*.9. **II.** metaph., *constant practice, skill*, ἐν λόγοις Pl.*Sph*.268a.

**κῠλινδρ-ικός**, ή, όν, *cylindrical*, Archim.*Sph.Cyl*.1.11, Hero *Spir*.1.37, Theo Sm.p.195 H., al. Adv. **-κῶς** Plu.2.682d. **-ιον**, τό, Dim. of κύλινδρος, Archim.*Aren*.1.14, Ptol.*Alm*.5.1, Iamb.*Protr*.3, Procl.*Hyp*.6.7. **-ίσκος**, ου, ὁ, = foreg., *IG*11(2).161 *B*48, al. (Delos, iii B. C.). **-οειδής**, ές, *cylindrical*, Euc.*Phaen*.p.4 M., *Placit*.2.27.4, Cleom.2.2, Gal.8.895, Hero *Spir*.2.34. Adv. **-δῶς** Eust.1604.58. ❀ **-ος**, ὁ, *rolling stone, tumbler*, Chrysipp.*Stoic*.2.283, A.R.2.594, Veget.*Mil*.4.8, *Carm.Aur*.57; a child's *marble*, Gal.18(1).462. **2.** *roller, cylinder*, Democr.155, Ath.Mech.10.4, Plu.2.682d, *CIG*3546.9 (Pergam.); *pivot*, *IG*11(2).287 *A*115 (Delos, iii B. C.); περὶ σφαίρας καὶ κ., title of work by Archimedes. **3.** *roll of a book, volume*, D.L.10.26. **4.** name of a fabulous stone, Ps.-Plu.*Fluv*.19.4. **5.** fiery *envelope* of the axis of the κόσμος, Herm.ap.Stob.1.49.44. **-όω**, *roll, level with a roller*, Thphr.*HP*2.4.3 (Pass.). **-ώδης**, ες, = κυλινδροειδής, ib.8.5.3. **-ωτός**, ή, όν, *levelled with a roller*, ἅλως Nic.*Fr*.70.1.

❀ **κῠλίνδω**, Ep., Lyr., Trag., also Telecl.1.8, Ar.*Eq*.1249, *Nu*.375 (Pass.):—in Prose (always in Att.) more freq. **κυλινδέω** (for which καλινδέω is freq. v.l.), also Ar.*Av*.502 (Med.), v.l. in Semon.7.4:—later **κυλίω** (q. v.): fut. κυλινδήσω late, *IG*14.1389 ii 35 (ii A. D.): aor. ἐκύλῖσα Sosith.2.20, Theoc.23.52, *AP*7.490 (Anyt.), also (εἰσ-) Ar.*Th*.651, (ἐξ-) Pi.*Fr*.7:—Med., impf. Ar.*Av*. l. c.: fut. κυλίσομαι (προ-) App.*Ital*.5.4: aor. ἐκυλισάμην (ἐν-) Luc.*Hipp*.6:—Pass., fut. κυλισθήσομαι (ἐκ-) A.*Pr*.87: aor. ἐκυλίσθην, Ep. κυλ-, Il.17.99, S.*El*.50, *Fr*.363; later κυλινδηθείς Str.14.2.24: pf. κεκύλισμαι Luc.*Hist. Conscr*.63, Ath.11.480c: plpf. κεκύλιστο Nonn.*D*.5.47:—*roll*, ὀστέα ..εἰν ἁλὶ κῦμα κυλίνδει Od.1.162, cf. 14.315; Βορέης μέγα κῦμα κυλίνδων 5.296; οἶδμα.. κυλίνδει βυσσόθεν θῖνα S.*Ant*.590 (lyr.); κυλίνδετ' εἴσω τὸν δυσδαίμονα *trundle* him in, Ar.*Eq*. l. c.; ὁλοιτρόχους, λίθους κυλινδεῖν, X.*An*.4.2.3, 4.7.4; ἔνθα Νεῖλος.. γάνος κυλίνδει A.*Fr*.300.3: metaph., πῆμα θεὸς Δαναοῖσι κυλίνδει *rolls* calamity upon them, Il.17.688; στυγερὴν δὲ κυλινδήσει κακότητα *IG* l. c. **2.** *revolve* in mind, Pi.*N*.4.40. **3.** *roll away*, ἐλπίδας *AP* l. c. **II.** Med. and Pass., *to be rolled, roll*, freq. in Hom., τρόφι κῦμα κυλίνδεται Il.11.307, cf. Od.9.147, Alc.18; πέδονδε κυλίνδετο λᾶας ἀναιδής Od.11.598, cf. Il.13.142, 14.411; νῶϊν δὴ τόδε πῆμα κυλίνδεται 11.347, cf. Od.2.163, 8.81; *toss* like a ship at sea, κυλίνδοντ' ἐλπίδες Pi.*O*.12.6; *to be whirled round* on a wheel, of Ixion, Id.*P*.2.23; κυλινδόμενα φλόξ *whirling* flame, ib.1.24; [νεφέλαι] κυλινδόμεναι Ar.*Nu*. l. c.; μεταξύ που κυλινδεῖται τοῦ τε μὴ ὄντος καὶ τοῦ ὄντος *is tossed about* between.., Pl.*R*.479d. **2.** of persons, κυλίνδεσθαι κατὰ κόπρον *roll, wallow* in the dirt (in sign of grief), Il.22.414; κλαίων τε κυλινδόμενός τ' Od.4.541, cf. Ar.*Av*. l. c.; *wander to and fro*, ψυχὴ.. περὶ τάφους κυλινδουμένη Pl.*Phd*.81d; ἐν δικαστηρίοις Id.*Tht*.172c; πρὸ ποδῶν κ. Id.*R*.432d; in petitions, παρὰ πόδα τῶν ἰχνῶν τινος κ. *PMasp*.5.8 (vi A. D.), etc.: metaph., ἐν ἀμηχανίῃσι κυλίνδομαι Thgn.619; ἐν ἀμαθίᾳ κ. *wallow* in.., Pl.*Phd*.82e, *Plt*.309a; ἐν πότοις καὶ γυναιξίν Plu.2.184f; κατὰ τὰ βιβλία Gal.9.647. **b.** *to be rolled, whirled headlong*, ἐκ δίφρων κυλισθείς S.*El*.50; *roll over*, of the embryo, Arist.*HA*586[b]25. **c.** *to be rolled up*, κυλισθεὶς ὡς ὄνος like a wood-louse, S.*Fr*.363. **3.** of Time, κυλινδομέναις ἁμέραις Pi.*I*.3.18. **4.** of words, *to be tossed from mouth to mouth*, i.e. *be much talked of*, τοὔνομ' αὐτῆς ἐν ἀγορᾷ κυλίνδεται Ar.*V*.492; κ. πᾶς λόγος παρὰ τοῖς ἐπαΐουσιν Pl.*Phdr*.275e.

**κυλίνθιον**· προσωπεῖον ξύλινον, Hsch.

❀ **κύλιξ** [ῠ], ῐκος, ἡ, (ὁ, *IG*1[2].283.137) *cup*, esp. *wine-cup*, Phoc.11, Sapph.5, Alc.41, Pi.*Fr*.124.3, B.*Fr*.16.3, Hdt.4.70, etc.; κ. κεραμέα Pl.*Ly*.219e; κ. χελιδονεία, ἡδυλεία, *IG*11(2).154 *B*6,50 (Delos, iii B. C.); κυλίκων τέρψις S.*Aj*.1200 (lyr.); κ. φιλοτησία Ar.*Lys*.203, Alex.291; κ. ἴσον ἴσῳ κεκραμένη Ar.*Pl*.1132; πλήρεις κ. οἴνου.. ἠντλουν Pherecr.108.30; πίνειν τε πολλὰς κ. Eub.150.8; ἐπὶ τῇ κύλικι λέγειν, = κυλικηγορεῖν, Pl.*Smp*.214b; ἐπὶ τῆς κ. φλυαρεῖν D.L.2.82; ἡ παρὰ τὴν κ. θρασύτης Plu.*Ant*.24; περιελαύνειν τὰς κ. push round *the cup*, X.*Smp*.2.27; οἱ πρὸς ταῖς κ. *cup*-bearers, Hdn.3.5.5. **II.** Cypr., = κοτύλη, Glaucon ap.Ath.11.480f.

**κυλιούχιον**, v. κυνούχιον. **κυλίς**, v. κύλα.

**κύλῐσις**, εως, ἡ, *rolling*, esp. of athletes in the dust after anointing, Arist.*Ph*.201[a]18, *Metaph*.1065[b]19; opp. βάδισις, Id.*Ph*.227[b]18. **II.** *revolution* in an orbit, Id.*Cael*.290[a]10. **III.** *roll, parcel*, ἱματίων *PSI*4.428.37 (iii B. C.).

**κῠλ-ίσκη**, ἡ, Dim. of κύλιξ, D.H.2.23, Poll.6.95, 10.66:—hence Dim. **-ίσκιον**, τό, Id.6.98, 10.66, cf. Ar.*Ach*.459 codd. (κοτυλίσκιον Ath.11.479b.) **-ισμα**, ατος, τό, *roll*, Sm.*Ez*.10.13, *Hippiatr*.79, 117; κ. κανθάρου, ball of dung rolled by a beetle, *PMag.Berol*.1.223. **II.** = κυλίστρα, *Hippiatr*.8; v.l. for sq., 2*Ep.Pet*.2.22. **-ισμός**, ὁ, *rolling*, ibid., Thd.*Pr*.2.18; κ. τοῦ πνεύματος ἐν ταῖς ἀρτηρίαις Ruf.*Syn.Puls*.8.11: pl., *Hippiatr*.75. **-ιστήριον**, τό, = κυλίστρα, *Gloss*. **-ιστικός**, ή, όν, *practised in rolling*: Subst. κ., ὁ, *wrestler, who struggles on while rolling in the dust*, Sch.Pi.*I*.4.81. **-ιστός**, ή, όν, *fit for rolling, large*, gloss on ῥυτός, *EM*707.3. **II.** *twined in a circle*, epith. of a kind of garland, Alex.272.5, Antiph.51. **III.** Subst. **κυλιστός**, ὁ, *roll of papyrus, large letter*, or *packet* of letters, *PHib*.1.110.51, al. (iii B. C.); *parcel*, ἱματίων *Sammelb*.1.2 (iii A. D.). **-ίστρα**, ἡ, *place for horses to roll in*, Poll.1.183, *Hippiatr*.5, Sch.Ar.*Ra*.935; cf. καλίστρα.

❀ **κῠλίχν-η**, ἡ, *small cup*, Alc.41.2, Ar.*Fr*.498. **II.** *pot* for medical preparations, Hsch.:—Dim. **-ιον**, τό, Ar.*Eq*.906 (spelt **κυλύχνιον** *IG*11(2).287 *B*53, al. (Delos, iii B. C.)): **-ίς**, ίδος, ἡ, Achae.14, Antiph.208; also, = κυλίχνη II, Hsch. (corrupted to κυγχνίδα Hp.ap.Gal.19.115).

❀ **κῠλίω** [ῑ], later form of κυλίνδω: (προσ-) κύλιε Ar.*V*.202, (ἀνα-) κυλῖον Alex.116:—*roll along*, γαστέρας αἱμοβόρως ἐκύλιον, of serpents, Theoc.24.18; κυλίουσιν [ἀλλήλους] ἐν τῷ πηλῷ Luc.*Anach*.6; λόγοις τοὺς ῥήτορας κ. *rolling* them over, *Com.Adesp*.294 codd.: freq. in later Gr., LXX *Jo*.10.18, al.: metaph., ἐκ κισσηρεφέος κεφαλῆς εὔϋμνα κυλίων ῥήματα Call.*Epigr*. in *Berl.Sitzb*.1912.548:—Pass., *roll, whirl along*, Arist.*Cael*.290[a]25, al.; of bees, *grovel*, Id.*HA*625[b]5; πρὸς τοῖς ἑαυτοῦ γόνασι κυλιομένην D.H.8.39; κ. περὶ τὴν ἀγορὰν *to be always loitering* there, Arist.*Pol*.1319[a]29; *roll about*, in pantomime, Id.*Po*.1461[b]31. **2.** *roll up*, ἣν κυλίουσι κόπρον (sc. κάνθαροι) Id.*HA*552[a]17.

**κύλλα**· σκύλαξ (Elean), Hsch. **κύλλαβοι**· ὑπώπια, Id.; cf. κύλα.

**κυλλαίνω**, = κυλλόω, ὦτα κ. κάτω *let* them *hang* down, prob. in S.*Fr*.687. **II.** intr., *halt, limp*, metaph., κυλλαίνων ὁ νοῦς Ph.*Fr*.58 H.

**κύλλαιος**· βόστρυχος, Hsch. **κυλλάραβις**, = δίσκος; also a gymnasium at Argos, Id.

**κύλλᾰρος**, ὁ, *hermit-crab*, *Pagurus*, Arist.*HA*530[a]12 (v.l. σκύλλαρος).

**κυλλᾶστις**, ιος, Ion. and later Gr. (cf. *UPZ*46.15, 53.15 (ii B. C.)) **-ῆστις**, ιος, ὁ, *Egyptian bread made from* ὄλυρα, Hdt.2.77, Hecat.323(*b*) J., Phanod.5, Ar.*Fr*.257, prob. in *POxy*.1742.1 (iv A. D.).

**κυλλήβδην**· κολοβόντα, κτλ., Hsch.

**Κυλλήνη**, ἡ, *Cyllene, a mountain in Arcadia*, Il.2.603, etc.:—hence ❀**Κυλλήνιος**, epith. of Hermes, *h.Merc*.318, etc.; of Pan, *AP*6.96 (Eryc.), *BCH*27.295 (Crete).

**κύλλια**· ὑπώπια μελανά, Hsch. **κύλλοβος** (κόλλ- cod.)· ξηρὰ συκῆ, Id.

**κυλλο-ποδίων** [ῐ], ονος, ὁ, (πούς) *club-footed, halting*, epith. of Hephaistos, Il.18.371, 20.270: voc. κυλλοπόδῖον 21.331. **-πους**, ὁ, ἡ, πουν, τό, gen. ποδος, *club-footed*, Aristodem.8; θεοί Agatharch.7.

❀ **κυλλ-ός**, ή, όν, *club-footed and bandy-legged*, opp. βλαισός, Hp.*Art*.53, cf. 62; κ. πούς ib.53, Ar.*Av*.1379. **2.** generally, *deformed, contracted*, κ. οὖς Hp.*Art*.40; *crippled in the arm*, κ. ἠκόντιζεν ἀμείνονα *AP*11.84 (Lucill.), cf. *Ev.Matt*.15.30, Gal.*UP*1.17, al.; ἔμβαλε κυλλῇ (sc. χειρί) put into *a crooked hand*, i.e. *with* the fingers *crooked* like a beggar's, to catch an alms, Ar.*Eq*.1083, cf. Sch. ad loc. **2.** of things, *crooked*, κ. κυκλάς *PLond*.3.776.10 (vi A. D.). **II.** κυλλά, τά, *choliambi*, Herod.8.79. ❀ **-όω**, *crook, flex*, τὸ μέρος Gal.18(1).

637:—Pass., *become club-footed and bandy-legged*, Hp.*Art*.53: pf. part. κεκυλλωμένα ib.62. -ωμα, ατος, τό, *club-foot*, Gal.18(1).670. -ωσις, εως, Ion. ιος, ἡ, = foreg., Hp.*Art*.62, Gal.18(1).668.

**Κυλλύριοι**, οἱ, = Κιλλικύριοι (nisi hoc legend.), Hdt.7.155.

**κυλοιδιάω**, (κύλα, οἰδάω) *have a swelling below the eye, have a black eye*, κυλοιδιᾶν ἀνάγκη Ar.*Lys*.472; *have dark rings under the eyes*, κ. ὑπ' ἔρωτος Theoc.1.38: generally, *have a swollen face*, Antyll.ap. Orib.10.27.15, Nic.*Al*.478.

**κύλον**, τό, v. κύλα.

* **κῦμα**, ατος, τό, (κύω) *anything swollen* (as if *pregnant*): hence, I. *wave, billow*, of rivers as well as the sea, in sg. and pl.; κ. θαλάσσης Il.2.209, al.; κ. ῥόοιο 21.263; κ. διιπετέος ποταμοῖο ib.268, 326; κύματ' ἐπ' ἠϊόνος κλύζεσκον 23.61; κύματ' εὐρεῖ πόντῳ βάντ' ἐπιόντα τε S.*Tr*.114 (lyr.): less freq. in Prose, κύματος ἐπαναχώρησις Th.3.89: collectively, ὡς τὸ κ. ἔστρωτο when the *swell* abated, Hdt.7.193, cf. Arist.*Mete*.344$^b$35, al. 2. metaph., *flood* of men, κ. χερσαῖον στρατοῦ A.*Th*.64, cf. 114 (lyr.), 1083 (anap.). b. of *the waves of adversity*, etc., κ. ἄτης, κακῶν, Id.*Pr*.886 (anap.), *Th*.758 (lyr.), E.*Ion* 927; συμφορᾶς Id.*Hipp*.824; κελαινοῦ κ. μένος, of passion, A.*Eu*. 832; κ. κατακλυσμὸν φέρον νόσων Pl.*Lg*.740e. c. phrases: μάτην με κῦμ' ὅπως παρηγορῶν A.*Pr*.1001; πρὸς κῦμα λακτίζειν E.*IT*1396; ἐκ κυμάτων.. γαλήν' ὁρῶ Id.*Or*.279; ἐπ' ἠόνι κύματα μετρεῖν Theoc. 16.60; ἀριθμεῖν τὰ κύματα Luc.*Herm*.84. 3. Archit., *waved moulding, cyma*, Λέσβιον κ. A.*Fr*.78. II. from κύω (as κύημα from κυέω), *foetus, embryo*, νεόσπορον Id.*Eu*.659; γέμουσαν κύματος θεοσπόρου E.*Fr*.106; of the earth, κ. λαμβάνειν A.*Ch*.128; δισσὸν κῦμ' ἐλόχευσε τέκνων *AP*6.200 (Leon.). 2. *young sprout* of plants, Thphr.*HP*1.6.9; esp. of a cabbage, Gal.6.642.

* **κῦμ-αίνω**, fut. κυμανῶ Xuthus ap.Arist.*Ph*.216$^b$25: aor. ἐκύμηνα Arr.*An*.2.10.3: aor. 1 Pass. ἐκυμάνθην Plu.*Ant*.65: (κῦμα): —*rise in waves, swell*, ἐπὶ πόντον ἐβήσετο κυμαίνοντα over the *billowy* sea, Il.14. 229, cf. Od.4.425, 570, etc.; of a pot, *boil*, Call.*Fr.anon*.41; κ. ἄνω καὶ κάτω Pl.*Phd*.112b; κυμανεῖ τὸ ὅλον Xuthus l. c.; κ. τῇ πορείᾳ *undulate*, of caterpillars, Arist.*HA*551$^b$7; τὰ ἄποδα.. κυμαίνοντα προέρχεται Id.*IA*709$^a$24; of a line of soldiers, Plu.*Pomp*.69, cf. Arr.*An*. l. c. 2. metaph., of restless passion, *swell, seethe*, κυμαίνοντ' ἔπη A.*Th*.443; ἄνθος ἥβας κυμαίνει Pi.*P*.4.158; αἱ ψυχαὶ κ. μειζόνως, with passion, Pl.*Lg*.930a; κ. ἐκ τῆς ἐπιθυμίας Ael.*NA*7.15; ἐς τὴν ὁμιλίαν ib.15.9. 3. trans., *toss on the waves*, τὸ δέπας Pherecyd.18(a) J.; *agitate*, τὴν θάλατταν Luc.*DMar*.7.1; οἴστρῳ κ. θεούς *APl*.4.196 (Alc. Mess.):—Pass., *to be agitated*, τὸ πέλαγος κ. Hp.*Flat*.3, Plu. *Ant*. l. c., cf. Opp.*H*.4.676; πόθῳ Pi.*Fr*.123.3; *vibrate*, Nicom.*Harm*. 3. II. (κῦμα II) *to swell, to be pregnant*, κ. γαστέρα Opp.*C*.1.359; κύστιδα ib.4.443; μαζοὶ.. γάλα -ουσι Marc.Sid.91:—Med., Σεμέλης κυμαίνετο γαστήρ Nonn.*D*.8.7. -ανσις, εως, ἡ, *undulation*, Arist. *IA*709$^a$27.

**κύμαρος**, = κόμαρος, Hsch.

**κῦμάς**, άδος, ἡ, (κύω) *pregnant woman*, in pl., Hsch.

**κῦμᾰτ-ηδόν**, Adv. *like a wave*, Lyd.*Ost*.53. -ηρός, ά, όν, = sq., *Gloss*. -ίας, ου, Ion. -ίης, ὁ, *surging, billowy*, κ. ὁ ποταμὸς ἐγένετο Hdt.2.111; πόρος A.*Supp*.546 (lyr.); πορθμός Cerc.5.11. 2. Act., *causing waves, stormy*, ἄνεμος Hdt.8.118. -ίζομαι, Pass., *to be agitated by the waves*, Arist.*HA*622$^a$18; *toss about like waves*, ἐν τῇ κοιλίᾳ κ. τὰ σιτία Gal.19.717; of the pulse, Id.8.482, 9.180. (Act. only late, Sch.E.*Ph*.1105.) * -ιον, τό, Dim. of κῦμα I. 3, *IG*1$^2$.372. 166, al., 4$^2$(1).102.58 (Epid., iv B. C.), *SIG*245 *G*168 (Delph., iv B. C.), Lxx *Ex*.25.10(11), 23(24), Vitr.4.3.6; κ. πύξινον διπλοῦν Ph.*Bel*.62. 12; of the *volute* on the Ionic capital, Vitr.4.1.7. 2. *groove*, Hero *Aut*.3.1.

**κῦμᾰτο-āγής**, ές, (ἄγνυμι) *breaking like waves*, ἆται S.*OC*1243 (lyr.). -βόλος, ον, (βάλλω) *throwing up waves*, *Gloss*. -δρόμος, ον, *running over the waves*, Sch.Lyc.789; -δρομέω, ibid. -ειδής, ές, *like waves*: *stormy*, οἱ νότοι Arist.*Pr*.942$^a$6. Adv. -δῶς Democr.126. -εις, εσσα, εν, poet. for κυματίας, Arist.*Fr*.640.18, Opp.*H*.1.4. -λήγη, ἡ, *Wave-stiller*, a Nereid, Hes.*Th*.253. -πλήξ, ῆγος, ὁ, ἡ, *wave-beaten*, ἀκτά S.*OC*1241 (lyr.); σκόπελος *AP*10.7 (Arch.); *tossed by the waves*, of fish, Hp.*Vict*.2.48, Archestr.*Fr*.11, Mnesith.ap.Ath.8. 358b. -φθόρος, ον, *plundering by sea*, ἁλιαίετος E.*Fr*.636 (κυματότροφος *fed from the sea*, Ruhnk.). -φορτίδες· κόγχοι, Hsch.

**κῦμᾰτ-όω**, *cover with waves*, of the wind, τὸ πεδίον Plu.*Alex*.26:—Pass., of the land, *to be swept by the sea*, Hld.9.4, cf. 10.16 (metaph.). II. Pass., *rise in waves*, of the sea, ἡ θάλασσα κυματωθεῖσα Th.3.89; ὁ ποταμὸς ἐκυματοῦτο, ὥσπερ θάλασσα Luc.*VH*2.30: metaph., of the air when agitated by the voice, *Stoic*.2.140, 234. * -ωγή, ἡ, (ἄγνυμι) *place where the waves break, beach*, Hdt. 4.196, 9.100, Luc.*Herm*.84, etc.: in pl., Democr.164. -ώδης, ες, = κυματοειδής, *on which the waves break*, γῆ Arist.*Pr*.934$^b$10, 9 (Comp.); αἰγιαλός Plu.*Fab*.6; *billowy*, πέλαγος Scymn.190: metaph., of the pulse, σφυγμὸς κ. Gal.9.505. Adv. -δῶς Id.8.551. -ωσις, εως, ἡ, *flow* of the tide, Str.1.3.8; κλύδων καὶ κ. Ph.1.14: metaph., κυματώσεις καὶ στροφαί, of life, Id.*Fr*.63 H.

* **κυμβᾰλ-ίζω**, *play the cymbals*, Men.326, Lxx *Ne*.12.27, Arr.*Ind*. 7.8, Chor. in *Rev.Phil*.1.10. -ιον, τό, Dim. of κύμβαλον, Hero *Aut*.14.1, 2. II. = κοτυληδών 5, Dsc.4.91. -ισμός, ὁ, *playing on cymbals*, Alciphr.3.66. -ιστής, οῦ, ὁ, *player upon cymbals*, D.C.50.27. -ίστρια, ἡ, fem. of foreg., Lat. *cymbalistria*, Petron. 22. -ῖτις, ιδος, ἡ, = κυμβάλιον II, Gal.2.905.

**κυμβᾰλοκρούστης**, ου, ὁ, = κυμβαλιστής, *Gloss*.

* **κύμβᾰλον**, τό, (κύμβος) *cymbal*, X.*Eq*.1.3: mostly in pl., Pi.*Fr*.79 B., A.*Fr*.451 G, Men.245.3, *PHib*.1.54.13 (iii B. C.), Lxx 1*Ki*.18.6, Phld.*Mus*.p.49 K., D.S.2.38, Plu.2.144e, etc.

**κυμβατευταί**· ὀρνιθευταί, Hsch.; cf. κύμβη (B).

* **κύμβᾰχος**, ον, (κύμβη B) *head-foremost, tumbling*, ἔκπεσε δίφρου κύμβαχος ἐν κονίῃσιν Il.5.586; κ. ἐπ' ὤμους Hld.10.30, cf. Lyc.66, Eust.584.16. II. Subst., ὁ, *crown of a helmet*, κόρυθος.. ἱπποδασείης κ. ἀκρότατος Il.15.536.

**κυμβεῖον**, v. κυμβίον.

* **κύμβη** (A), ἡ, *hollow of a vessel*: *drinking-cup, bowl*, Nic.*Al*.164, 389, *Th*.948, Philem.Gloss.ap.Ath.11.483a; = ὀξύβαφον, Hsch. II. *boat*, S.*Fr*.127; Phoenician acc. to Plin.*HN*7.208. III. *knapsack, wallet*, Hsch. (Cf. κύμβος.)

* **κύμβη** (B), ἡ, = κύβη, *head*, *EM*545.27: hence, a kind of *bird*, perh. *tumbler*-pigeon (cf. κύμβαχος), πτεροβάμονες κύμβαι Emp.20.7.

**κυμβητιάω**, *hurl headlong*, *EM*545.27.

* **κυμβίον**, τό, Dim. of κύμβη (A) I, *small cup*, *IG*2$^2$.1522.32, 11(2). 145.48 (Delos, iv B. C.), Theopomp.Com.31, Philem.84, Alex.2.6, D.21.158, cf. Ath.11.481d; also, Dim. of κύμβη (A) II, Hsch., Suid.: **κυμβεῖον**, Pherecr.66, Paus.Gr.*Fr*.242.

* **κύμβος**, ὁ, = κύμβη (A), *cup*, Nic.*Th*.526: heterocl. dat. κύμβεϊ or κύμβεσι Id.*Al*.129. (Cf. Skt. *kumbhás* 'pot', Irish *cum* 'vase', etc.)

**κυμερνήτης**, ου, ὁ, Aeol. = κυβερνήτης, *EM*543.3:—also **κυμερῆναι**, Cypr. = κυβερνῆσαι, *Schwyzer* 685(1).

**κυμηχα**· κύαμον, Hsch. **κυμινᾶτον**, τό, *preparation of* κύμινον, *Gloss*. **κυμίνδαλα**· καταστροφή (Tarent.), Hsch.

* **κύμινδις** [ῠ], ὁ (or ἡ, v. Sch.Il.14.291), gen. -ιδος Pl.*Cra*.392a:—name of a bird, ἥν τ' ἐν ὄρεσσι χαλκίδα κικλήσκουσι θεοί, ἄνδρες δὲ κύμινδιν Il. l. c., cf. Ar.*Av*.1181, Arist.*HA*615$^b$6.

**κῦμῑν-εύω**, (κύμινον) *strew with cummin*, Orac.ap.Luc.*Alex*. 25. -ινος, η, ον, *of cummin*, Alex.Trall.1.3.

**κῦμῑνο-δόκον**, τό, *box for cummin, spice-box*, placed on the table like a salt-cellar, Nicoch.2:—also -δόκη, ἡ, Apollod.Gel.2; -δόχη, ἡ, Poll.10.93; -θήκη, ἡ, Demioprat.ibid. -κίμβιξ, ῑκος, ὁ, *skinflint* (cf. κυμινοπρίστης), *Com.Adesp*.1055.

* **κύμῑνον** [ῠ], τό, *cummin*, Hp.*Acut*.23, Antiph.142.2, Alex.127.6, Lxx *Is*.28.25, *PTeb*.112.13 (ii B. C.), etc.; κύμινον ἔπρισεν, prov. of a skinflint, Sophr.110, cf. Men.1025, Theoc.10.55; κ. ἥμερον, *Cuminum Cyminum*, Dsc.3.59, cf. Thphr.*HP*1.11.2, Nic.*Th*.601; κ. ἄγριον (ἀγρότερον ib.710), *wild cummin*, *Lagoecia cuminoides*, Dsc. 3.60; κ. ἄγριον ἕτερον, *Nigella arvensis*, ib.61; κ. αἰθιοπικόν Diocl. *Fr*.87. (Cf. Hebr. *Kammōn*.)

* **κῦμῑνο-πρίστης**, ου, ὁ, (πρίω) *cummin-splitter*, i. e. *skinflint*, Arist. *EN*1121$^b$27, Posidipp.26.12: as Adj., κ. ὁ τρόπος ἐστί σου Alex. 251. -πριστοκαρδᾰμογλύφος [γλῠ], ον, *cummin-splitting-cress-scraper*, strengthd. for foreg., Ar.*V*.1357. -πώλης, ου, ὁ, *cummin-seller*, *PMasp*.146.2, al. (vi A. D.). -τρῖβος, ον, *rubbed with cummin to flavour it*, κ. ἅλς Archestr.*Fr*.13.7.

**κῦμῑνώδης**, ες, *like cummin*, Thphr.*HP*8.7.3.

**κῦμο-δέγμων**, ον, gen. ονος, *receiving* or *meeting the waves*, ἀκτή E. *Hipp*.1173. -δόκη, ἡ, *Wave-receiver*, a Nereid, Il.18.39, Hes.*Th*. 252. -θᾰλής, ές, *abounding with waves*, of Poseidon, Orph.*H*. 17.5. -θόη, ἡ, (θοός) *Wave-swift*, a Nereid, Il.18.41, Hes.*Th*. 245. -κτῠπος, ον, *wave-sounding*, Αἰγαῖος E.*Hyps.Fr*.3(1)ii 28 (lyr.); μυχοί Simm.13. * -πλήξ, ῆγος, ὁ, ἡ, = κυματοπλήξ, Hdn.Gr. 1.46. -πόλεια, ἡ, *Wave-walker*, daughter of Poseidon, Hes.*Th*. 819. * -ρρόον· τὸν ὑπὸ τῶν κυμάτων ῥοῦν, Hsch. -ρρώξ, ῶγος, ὁ, ἡ, *breaking the waves*, Hdn.Gr.1.46. -τόκος, ον, *of child-birth*, ἐν γαστρὸς κυμοτόκοις ὀδύναις *IG*9(2).638 (Larissa). -τόμος, ον, *wave-cleaving*: ὁ κ. *cutwater* of a bridge, Suid., cf. *BCH*26.166 (Syria, vi A. D.; κοιμ- lapis).

**Κῦμώ**, οῦς, ἡ, *Wavy*, a Nereid, Hes.*Th*.255.

**κῠνᾱγέσιον, κυνᾱγέτας, κυνᾱγέτις, κυνᾱγία**, v. κυνηγ-.

* **Κυνᾱγίδας**, α, ὁ, title of Heracles, *BCH*47.292 n.2 (Macedonia, ii B. C.); also **Κουνᾱγίδας**, ib.291.

**κῠνᾱγός**, Dor. for κυνηγός, (ἄγω) *hound-leader*, i. e. *huntsman*, A. *Ag*.695 (lyr.), etc.; as Adj., τὴν κυναγὸν Ἄρτεμιν S.*El*.563; κυναγὲ παρσένε *huntress*-maid, Ar.*Lys*.1270 (lyr.); Ἔρως ὁ Κύπριδος κ. Tim. Com.2:—fem. **κυνηγίς**, ίδος, *huntress*, name of a comedy by Philetaerus; also (sc. ναῦς), *hunting-boat*, *Theb Ostr*.77 (i A. D.).—Trag. and Com. use κυναγός even in trim., cf. Phryn.399, and v. κυνηγία:—later **κυνηγός** Arist.*HA*579$^b$28, Callix.2, *PPetr*.3 p.115 (iii B. C.), *SIG*459.2 (Beroea, iii B. C.), D.S.2.25, Plu.*Luc*.8; = Lat. *bestiarius*, gladiator who fights with beasts, Just.*Nov*.115.3.10; κυνᾱγός in this sense, *Milet*.1(9).314.

**κῠν-άγχη**, ἡ, (κύων, ἄγχω) *dog-quinsy*, Arist.*HA*604$^a$5, Ant.Lib. 23.2; cf. ὑάγχη: hence, II. *sore throat*, Hp.*VM*19, *Prog*.23, *Aph*. 3.16 (all pl.), Porph.*Abst*.3.7: συνάγχη is a constant v.l., but Gal. distinguishes κυνάγχη as *an inflammation of the larynx*, συνάγχη *of the interior muscles of the throat*, παρασυνάγχη *of the exterior muscles*, 8.248, 17(2).706. III. *dog's collar*, *AP*6.34 (Rhian., v.l. κυνακτάν), 35 (Leon.). IV. *pillory*, Hsch. -άγχης, ου, ὁ, *dog-throttler*, title of Hermes, Hippon.1. * -αγχικός, ή, όν, *suffering from* κυνάγχη, Gal.17(1).596; πάθος κ., = κυνάγχη, D.S.36.13. -αγχον, τό, = ἀπόκυνον, Dsc.4.80. -αγχος, ὁ, = σύναγχος, Gal.15. 787. -ᾰγωγός, ὁ, (ἄγω) *leader of hounds, huntsman*, X.*Cyn*.9.2, Arr.*Cyn*.7.6, 25.6, Philostr.*Im*.1.28.

**κυνάδης**· ἀνελεύθερος, Hsch. (but Κυνάδης, title of Poseidon at Athens, Id.). **κυναίγινθος**, = αἴγινθος (i. e. αἴγιθος) μικρός, *Gloss*. **κυναίδης**· λίαν ἀναιδής, Hsch. **κυναιρίου**, v. κυνερίου.

**κῠνάκανθα** [ᾰκ], ἡ, *dog-thorn*, perh. = κυνόσβατος, Arist.*HA* 552$^{b}$3.

**κυνακίας·** ἱμάντες, οἱ ἐκ βύρσης τοῦ σφαγιασθέντος τετράχειρι Ἀπόλλωνι βοὸς ἔπαθλα διδόμενοι (–ομένου cod.), Hsch. **κυνακρίς**, *gillus* (fort. *gryllus*), *Gloss.*

**κῠν-ακτής**, οῦ, ὁ, (ἄγω) *dog-leash*, v. κυνάγχη III. **-ᾰλώπηξ**, εκος, ἡ, *mongrel between dog and fox*, nickname of a πορνοβοσκός, Ar.*Lys.*957; of Cleon, Id.*Eq.*1067, al.; of the Cynics, Luc.*Peregr.* 30.

**Κῠνᾰμολγοί**, οἱ, *dog-milkers*, name of Libyan tribe, D.S.3.31.

**κῠνάμυια** [νᾰ], ἡ, *dog-fly*, i. e. *shameless fly*, abusive epith. applied by Ares to Athena, and by Hera to Aphrodite, Il.21.394,421, cf. Ath.3.126a, 4.157a:—later **κυνόμυια**, Ezek.*Exag.*138, *AP*11.265 (Lucill.), Ael.*NA*4.51, Luc.*Gall.*31, etc.; ὦ γαστὴρ κυνόμυια *APl.* 1.9; of the plague of flies in Egypt, Lxx *Ex.*8.21(17), *Ps.*77(78).45.

**κῠνάνθρωπος**, ον, *of a dog-man*, νόσος κ. a malady *in which a man imagines himself to be a dog*, Gal.19.719, Antioch.Astr. in *Cat.Cod. Astr.*7.115.

⊛**κυνάπαιδες**, dub. sens. in Sophr.ap.Sch.Gen.Il.21.395.

**κῠνάρα** [ᾰρ], ἡ, = κινάρα, S.*Fr.*348, cf. Scyl. or Polemo ap.Ath.2.70c, Gal.6.636; ἄκανθα κυνάρα Hecat.291 J.:—also **κύνᾰρος** ἄκανθα S.*Fr.*718 (expl. as = κυνόσβατος by Did.ap.Ath. l. c.).

⊛**κῠν-άριον**, τό, Dim. of κύων, *little dog, puppy*, Pl.*Euthd.*298d, X.*Cyr.*8.4.20, Theopomp.Com.90, Alc.Com.33, *Ev.Matt.*15.26; *small waxen image of a dog* used in magic, *PMag.Par.*1.2945: less correct than κυνίδιον acc. to Phryn.157; but κυνάριον καὶ κυνίδιον δόκιμα Id. *PS* p.84 B. **-άς**, άδος, pecul. fem. of κύνεος, *of a dog*, ἡμέραι κ. *the dog*-days, Plu.2.380d. **II.** mostly as Subst., **1.** (sc. θρίξ), *dog's hair*, of a bad fleece, Theoc.15.19. **2.** = κυνάρα, Hsch. **3.** among the Spartans, = ἀπομαγδαλιά (q. v.), Polem.Hist.77, Poll.6.93. **4.** kind of *nail*, Sch.Od.7.91, Eust.1570.48. **-αστρος**, ὁ, late word for the *dog-star*, Sch.Opp.*H.*1.46, Sch.Lyc.397, Eust.514.27, Steph.*in Rh.*304.3. **-άω**, = κυνίζω, *play the Cynic*, Luc.*Demon.* 21.

**κυνδάλ-η** [ᾰ], ἡ, = sq., Hsch. **-ισμός**, ὁ, *game of knocking out one peg with another*, Poll.9.120:—hence **κυνδᾰλοπαίκτης**, ου, ὁ, *one who plays at it*, ibid., Hsch. (-στης cod.).

**κύνδᾰλος**, ὁ, *wooden peg*, Poll.10.188: pl. κύνδαλα Id.9.120.

**κυνδός·** ἄπαικτος, ἀπαράλλακτος, Hsch.

**κυνέα**, ἡ, = λινόζωστις ἀγρία ἄρρην, Ps.-Dsc.4.190.

**κυνεάγας·** κυδώδων, Hsch. **κυνεγκέφᾰλος**, ὁ, *spinal marrow*, Id.

**κῠνέη**, Aeol. **κυνία** Alc.15.2, Att. contr. **κυνῆ** *IG*1$^{2}$.279.62, etc.: ἡ:—prop. (sc. δορά) *dog's skin* (so only Anaxandr.65), used for making soldiers' caps: hence in Ep., generally, *helmet*, κ. ταυρείη, κτιδέη, Il.10.257,335; κ. χαλκήρης, χαλκοπάρῃος, 3.316, 12.183; κ. χρυσείη 5.743; once of a peasant's *cap*, αἰγείη κ. Od.24.231; later περὶ τῇσι κεφαλῇσι [εἶχον] ἐκ διφθερέων πεποιημένας κυνέας leathern caps, Hdt.7.77, cf. Ar.*Nu.*268, *V.*445; of the πέτασος, ἡλιοστερὴς κυνῆ Θεσσαλίς S.*OC*314; Ἀρκὰς κ., = Ἀρκαδικὸς πῖλος, Id.*Fr.*272, cf. Paus.Gr.*Fr.*72; but usu. *helmet*, λάμπραι κ. Alc. l. c.; κ. ἐπίχρυσος *IG*1$^{2}$. l. c.; τὴν κ. ἐοῦσαν χαλκέην Hdt.2.151; κ. Κορινθίη Id.4.180; Βοιωτία D.59.94, Thphr.*HP*3.9.6. **2.** Ἄϊδος κ. mythical *helmet* which rendered the wearer invisible, worn by Athena, Il.5.845; by Perseus, Pherecyd.11 J., cf. Hes.*Sc.*227, Ar.*Ach.*390, Pl.*R.*612b; Πλούτων κ. ἔχει τοῦ ἀφανοῦς πόλου σύμβολον Porph.ap.Eus.*PE*3.11.

⊛**κύνειος** [ῠ], α, ον, *of, belonging to a dog*, ἱμὰς Ar.*V.*231; κ. θάνατος a *dog's* death, ib.898; τὰ κ. *dog's flesh*, Id.*Eq.*1399, S.E.*P.*3.225; κυνεία, ἡ, = κ. κόπρος, Archig.ap.Gal.12.954, Aët.15.15.

⊛**κύνειρα** [ῠ], ἡ, (εἴρω A) *dog-leash*, *Com.Adesp.*1056.

**κυνελφεῖ·** κρύπτει, Hsch.

**κύνεος** [ῠ], α, ον, (κύων) = κύνειος, *AP*12.238 (Strat.), Orph.*Fr.* 224b.5. **II.** metaph., *shameless, unabashed*, Il.9.373, Hes.*Op.* 67; κέαρ A.R.3.641; μένος Timo 58.2. **III.** = Κυνικός, σοφισταί D.C.66.15.

**κυνέπασαν·** ἐξέδεισαν, κτλ., *Com.Adesp.*1057. **κυνερίου** (-αιρίου cod.) ἢ **κυνουρίου·** ἀργολύκου, Hsch.

**κῠνέω**, Ep. impf. κύνεον Od.21.224: fut. κῠνήσομαι E.*Cyc.*172; later κύσω [ῠ], poet. κύσσω Babr.129.17: aor. ἐκύνησα v.l. in Arist. *HA*560$^{b}$31; Poet. ἔκῠσα, Ep. κύσα, ἔκυσσα, κύσσα, v. infr.:—*kiss*, κάρη δ' ἔκυσ' Od.23.208; λάβε γούνατα καὶ κύσε χεῖρας Il.24.478; κύνεον.. κεφαλήν τε καὶ ὤμους Od.21.224: c. acc. pers. et partis, κύσσε δέ μιν κεφαλήν 16.15, cf. 19.417; Τηλέμαχον.. δῖος ὑφορβὸς πάντα κύσεν 16.21; κύσον με Ar.*Nu.*81, cf. *Av.*141, etc.; κ. τινὰ χειρός A.R. 1.313: pres. in E.*Alc.*183, *Med.*1141, Ar.*Ach.*1208, *Pax*1138(lyr.):—rare in Prose, Luc.*Alex.*55; κ. [ἀλλήλας], of pigeons, *bill*, Arist. l. c. **2.** = προσκυνέω, E.*Cyc.* l. c., *AP*6.283.

**κῠνηγ-εσία**, ἡ, later form for sq. II, D.L.6.31; = Lat. *venatio*, κ. ἐπετέλεσεν *CIG*2719 (Stratonicea):—Dor. **κυνᾱγ-** *AP*7.338, 6.183 (Zos.). ⊛**-έσιον**, τό, *hunting-establishment, pack of hounds*, Hdt.1.36, X.*Cyn.*10.4; also, *pack of wolves hunting together*, opp. λύκοι μονοπεῖραι, Arist.*HA*594$^{a}$31. **II.** *hunt, chase*, ἐπὶ τὸ κ. ἐξιέναι, πρὸς τὸ κ. προσιέναι, X.*Cyn.*6.11; ἀπιέναι ἐκ τοῦ κ. ib.26, cf. 7.11: in pl., E.*Hipp.* 224 (anap.), Isoc.7.45, X.*Cyn.*3.11, 6.4, Plu.*Alex.*40: metaph., κ. τὸ περὶ τὴν Ἀλκιβιάδου ὥραν Pl.*Prt.*309a; παρακαλεῖσθαί τινα ἐπὶ τὸ κ. Id. *La.*194b. **2.** = κυνήγιον 2, *CIG*2511 (Cos), 4157 (Sinope). **III.** *that which is taken in hunting, game*, X.*Cyn.*6.12. **-έσσω**, Att. -ττω, = sq., Phryn.*PS* p.84 B., Theognost.*Can.*143: hence aor. 1 subj. κυνηγέσω S.*Ichn.*44 (cf. Pass. inf. κυνηγεσ(ε)ῖσθαι *PGrenf.*2.71 ii 12 (iii A.D.)). **-ετέω**, Dor. **κυνᾱγ-**, *hunt*, Ar.*Eq.*1382, X. *Cyn.*5.34, etc.: c. acc., ὗς ἀγρίους κ. Aeschin.3.255, cf. Plb.31.14.3: metaph., *persecute, harass*, A.*Pr.*572 (lyr.); *hunt down*, τινας Plu. *Mar.*43: c. acc. cogn., κ. τέκνων διωγμόν E.*HF*898 (lyr.): abs., *quest about*, like a hound, S.*Aj.*5. ⊛**-έτης**, ου, ὁ, Dor. (never in Trag.) **κυνᾱγέτᾱς** Pi.*N.*6.14:—*huntsman*, Od.9.120, E.*HF*860 (troch.), *Hec.* 1174, Pl.*R.*432b, X.*Cyn.*6.11, al., *OGI*20 (iii B.C.); in pl. of certain δαίμονες, Pl.Com.174.16, *SIG*1040.9 (Piraeus, iv B.C.): metaph., of one who seeks fame, Pi. l. c.:—fem.⊛**-έτις**, Dor. **-ᾱγέτις**, ιδος, *huntress*, Ach.Tat.8.12; epith. of Artemis, Corn.*ND*34: as Adj., κ. αἰγανέα *AP*6.115 (Antip.). **-ετικός**, ή, όν, *of* or *for hunting, fond of the chase*, Pl.*Euthphr.*13a: ἡ -κή (sc. τέχνη) ibid., Phld.*Mus.*p.24 K.; οἱ κ. λόγοι Onos.*Praef.*1; ὁ κ. [λόγος], title of Xenophon's work on Hunting: τὰ -κά, of Oppian's poem. **-έτις**, ιδος, ἡ, fem. of κυνηγέτης (q. v.). **-έω**, Dor. **-ᾱγέω** Bion 1.60: pf. Pass. κεκυνηγῆσθαι Plb.31.29.4: (κυνηγός):—*hunt, chase*, later form of κυνηγετέω, ὅταν κυνηγήσῃ [ὁ ἀετός] Arist.*HA*619$^{a}$33, cf. Plu.*Pel.*8, etc.: metaph., *pursue, persecute*, τινα Pl.*Ep.*349c, etc. **-ητήρ**, ῆρος, ὁ, = κυνηγέτης, Man.4.337. **-ία**, ἡ, *hunt, chase*, Arist.*Rh.*1371$^{a}$5, Plb.8.25.4, D.S.3.36, etc.:—Trag. in Dor. form **κυνᾱγία** (cf. κυναγός) S.*Aj.*37 (cod. Med.), E.*Hipp.*109, and so prob. in Id *Ba.*339 (pl.). **-ικός**, ή, όν, *of* or *for hunting*, τόποι *PGrenf.*2.71 i 15 (iii A.D.). **-ιον**, τό, later form for κυνηγέσιον, *hunt, chase*, Ath.15.677e: in pl., Plb.10. 22.4, D.S.5.29 (v. l. -ίαις), etc. **2.** *beast-hunt* in the Amphitheatre, = Lat. *venatio*, *CIG*3847b8 (Nacolea), *OGI*533.7 (Ancyra). **3.** in pl., *game preserves*, D.S.2.8, Philostr.*VA*2.14. **4.** *prey*, κυνήγια λεόντων ὄναγροι Lxx *Si.*13.19. **-ίς, -ός**, v. κυναγός.

**κῠν-ηδόν**, Adv., (κύων) *like a dog*, S.*Fr.*722, Ar.*Eq.*1033, *Nu.*491, Luc.*Tim.*54. **-ηλᾰσία**, Ep. -ίη, ἡ, *hunting with dogs*, Call.*Dian.* 217. **-ηλᾰτέω**, *follow the hounds*, Euph.132, Nic.*Th.*20. **-ήποδες**, οἱ, (κύων VIII) *fetlocks* of a horse, X.*Eq.*1.15, Poll.5.65.

**κυνητίνδᾰ** (sc. παιδιά), ἡ, *game of kissing*, Crates Com.23 (lyr.).

**κυνθάνω**, = κεύθω, Hsch. **κύνθιον**, = κυλίνθιον, Id.

**Κύνθος**, ὁ, *Cynthus*, a mountain in Delos, birth-place of Apollo and Artemis, *h.Ap.*26:—Adj.⊛**Κύνθιος**, epith. of Apollo, Call.*Del.*10; Δήλιε, Κυνθίαν ἔχων.. πέτραν Ar.*Nu.*596 (lyr.):—also **Κυνθογενής**, ές, *AP*15.25.9 (Besant.).

**κῠνία**, ἡ, v. l. for κυνέα in Ps.-Dsc.4.190. **II.** v. κυνέη.

**κῠν-ίδιον**, τό, Dim. of κύων, *little dog, puppy*, Ar.*Ach.*542, Pl.*Euthd.* 298e, X.*Oec.*13.8, Phld.*Lib.*p.10O.: pl., Eup.207, Arist.*Rh.*1406$^{b}$ 28; cf. κυνάριον. **-ίζω**, fut. κυνιῶ *Stoic.*3.162, Apollod.ib.261:—*play the dog*: metaph., *live like a Cynic*, ll. cc., Arr.*Epict.*3.22.1, Luc. *Peregr.*43, Ath.13.588f, Jul.*Or.*6.182a.

⊛**κύνικλος**, ὁ, = Lat. *cuniculus, rabbit*, Plb.12.3.10 (κούνικλος ap. Ath.9.400f), prob. in Gal.6.666; in Ael.*NA*13.15 **κόνικλος**.

**κῠνικός**, ή, όν, (κύων) *dog-like*, X.*Cyr.*5.2.17 (v.l. for ὑϊκόν); τὸ κ. καὶ θηριῶδες τῶν ὀρέξεων Plu.2.133b; κ. σπασμός *unilateral facial paralysis*, Cels.4.3.1, Gal.18(2).930; κ. καύματα heat *of the dog-days*, Polyaen.2.30.3: metaph., ὁ ἄνθρωπος κ. *currish, churlish*, Lxx 1*Ki.*25.3. Adv. -κῶς, σπώμενοι Heliod.ap.Orib.48.38 tit.; *in dog-language*, opp. βοϊκῶς, etc., Porph.*Abst.*3.3. **II.** Κυνικός, ὁ, *Cynic*, as the followers of the philosopher Antisthenes were called, from the gymnasium (Κυνόσαργες) where he taught, D.L.6.13; or from their resemblance to dogs in several respects, Diog.Cyn.ap.eund.6. 60, Metrod.16, Polystr.p.20 W., Elias *in Cat.*111.2, etc.; Κράτητι τῷ κ. Men.117; κ. αἵρεσις, ἄσκησις, φιλοσοφία, Ph.1.352, J.*AJ*6.13.6, Jul.*Or.*6.187a; παρρησία κ. Plu.2.69c; τὸ κ. τῆς παρρησίας Id.*Brut.* 34. Adv. Comp. -ώτερον Id.2.601e.

**κυνίξεις·** ἀκροβολισμοί, Hsch.

**κῠν-ίσκη**, ἡ, *bitch-puppy*, Ar.*Ra.*1360. **-ίσκος**, ὁ, *puppy*, nickname of Zeuxidamus in Hdt.6.71. **2.** metaph., *little Cynic*, Luc. *Pisc.*45. **-ισμός**, ὁ, *Cynical philosophy* or *conduct*, Apollod.*Stoic.* 3.261, Luc.*Bis Acc.*33, Poll.5.65, Jul.*Or.*6.182c. **-ιστέον**, *one must practise Cynic philosophy*, ib.7.204a tit. **-ιστί**, Adv. *like a dog*, Posidon.5 J.

**κυνίσφειλον·** ἀπατητικόν, Hsch.

**κῠνο-βάμων** [ᾱ], ον, gen. ονος, = sq., Hsch. ⊛**-βάτης** [ᾰ], (κύων VIII) *with short, stiff fetlocks*, of a horse, *Hippiatr.*115; of an ass, ib. 14. **-βλώψ**, ῶπος, ὁ, ἡ, *with a dog's look*, Hsch. **-βορά**, ἡ, *dog's food*, Sch.Ar.*Pl.*293 (as etym. of κινάβρα), Tz.*H.*13.279. **-βοσκός**, ὁ, *feeder of sacred jackals*, Sammelb.5796 (i B.C.). **-βρωτος**, ον, *devoured by dogs*, Neanth.25 J., Phld.*Mort.*33, Antioch.Astr. in *Cat.Cod.Astr.*7.115. **-γᾰμία**, ἡ, *dog-wedding*, used by Crates the Cynic of his own marriage, Suid. s. v. Κράτης. **-γλωσσος**, ον, *dog-tongued*: hence **1.** κυνόγλωσσος, ὁ, kind of *fish*, Epich. 44. **2.** *hound's tongue, Cynoglossum Columnae*, Nic.*Fr.*71:—also **-γλωσσον**, τό, Ps.-Dsc.4.127, Zopyr.ap.Orib.14.62.1. **-δέσμη**, ἡ, (κύων VII, δεσμός) *fibula for the prepuce*, Phryn.*PS* p.85 B. (pl.), Phot.:—also **-δέσμιον**, τό, v.l. in Poll.2.171. **-δεσμος**, ὁ, *dog-leash*, Longus 2.14. **-δηκτικός**, ή, όν, *for dog-bite*, [ἔμπλαστρος] Theodor.ap.Philum.*Ven.*4.15. **-δηκτος**, ον, *caused by a dog's bite*, ἕλκη Arist.*HA*630$^{a}$8, cf. Heras ap.Gal.13.558, Dsc.1.123, 2.28; *bitten by a dog*, *Gp.*12.17.14.

**κῠνόδους**, οντος, ὁ, *canine tooth*, prop. of dogs, Arist.*PA*661$^{b}$9, *HA*501$^{b}$7; of lions, ib.579$^{b}$12; of men, Hp.*Aph.*3.25, Epich.21 (in form κυνόδων); of horses, X.*Eq* 6.8, Arist.*HA*576$^{b}$17; of a serpent's *fang*, Nic.*Th.*130, 231. **2.** in pl., *teeth* of a saw, Ael.*NA*10.20.

**κῠνοδρομ-έω**, *run* or *chase with dogs*, X.*Cyn.*6.17: metaph., ἐκυνοδρομοῦμεν ἀλλήλους ζητοῦντες Id.*Smp.*4.63. **-ία**, Ion. -ίη, ἡ, *hunting with dogs*, Hp.*Vict.*3.68 (pl., v.l. νυκτο-), Call.*Dian.*106.

**κῠνόδων**, *οντος, ὁ*, v. *κυνόδους*.

**κῠνοειδής**, *ές*, *like a dog*, Arist.*HA*502$^a$21 (Comp.), Gal.4.604:— Sicel name for *ψύλλιον*, Ps.-Dsc.4.69, cf. Plin.*HN*25.140.

**κῠν-όζολον**, *τό*, (*ὄζω*) = *χαμαιλέων μέλας*, so called from its smell, prob. in Dsc.3.9, cf. Ps.-Dsc.ibid. II. = *δρακοντία μικρά*, ib.2.167.

**κῠνο-θαρσής**, *ές*, *impudent as a dog*, Theoc.15.53: **-θρᾰσής**, A.*Supp.*758 (lyr.). **-θηρες**, *οἱ*, corrupt in Ps.-Dsc.4.77. **-κάρδᾰμον**, *τό*, = *κάρδαμον*, ib.2.155. **-καύματα**, *τά*, *the heat of the dog-days*, Aët.6.83, Alex.Trall.9.3:—hence **-καυματικαί** (sc. *ἡμέραι*), *dog-days*, *Gloss.* **-κεντρον**, *τό*, a plant, Hsch. **-κεφάλιον** [ᾰ], *τό*, = *ἀντίρρινον*, Sch.Orib.2.744, Ps.-Dsc.4.130; = *ψύλλιον*, ib.69, cf. *PMag. Lond.*46.198:—also **-κεφᾰλίδιον**, ib.121.602; but **-κεφάλαιον**, = *ἀνεμώνη*, Hsch. **-κεφᾰλιστί**, Adv. *after the manner of the κυνοκέφαλος*, *PMag.Lond.*46.27. **-κεφᾰλοειδὴς** *πίθηκος*, *ὁ*, = *κυνοκέφαλος* 2, Gal.2.534. **-κεφᾰλοκέρδων**, *ωνος*, *ὁ*, = sq. 2, *PMag.Leid. W.*4.28. ⊛ **-κέφᾰλος**, *ον*, *dog-headed*: *οἱ* Κ., *Dog-heads*, name of a people, Hdt.4.191, cf. Ctes.*Fr.*57.22, A.*Fr.*431. 2. *dog-faced baboon*, *Simia hamadryas*, Pl.*Tht.*161c, 166c, Arist.*HA*502$^a$19, etc.; sacred animal in Egypt, Luc.*Tox.*28, *JTr.*42. 3. *κυνοκέφαλον*, *τό*, = *ψύλλιον*, Dsc.4.69; = *ἀντίρρινον*, Xenocr.ap.Sch.Orib.2.744. [*κυνοκεφάλλῳ* at the close of an iambic tetrameter, Ar.*Eq.*416, where λλ is attested by Phryn.*PS* p.85 B., Phot.] **-κλόπος**, *ὁ*, *dog-stealer*, Ar.*Ra.*605. **-κοπέω**, *beat like a dog*, Id.*Eq.*289. **-κόριον**, *turbisci semen*, *Gloss.* **-κορον**, = *satyrion*, ib. **-κράμβη**, *ἡ*, = *κυνέα*, Ps.-Dsc.4.190. 2. = *ἀπόκυνον*, Dsc.4.80, *Gp.*13.4.7 and 7.1. **-κτόνος**, *ον*, *killing dogs*: κ., *τό*, = *ἀκόνιτον*, Dsc.4.76. **-λογέω**, *talk of the dog-star*, Ath.1.23a. **-λοφα**, *τά*, *processes of the spine*, Poll.2.180.

**κῠνολύγματε**, epith. of the Moon in *PMag.Par.*1.2549: perh. for **κυνολολύγματε**, *howling like a dog*.

**κῠνό-λῠκος**, *ὁ*, = *κροκόττας*, Ctes.*Fr.*87. **-λυσσος** or **-λυσσον**, *ὁ* or *τό*, *hydrophobia*, Andreas ap.Cael.Aur.*CP*3.98. **-μαζον**, *τό*, = *χαμαιλέων μέλας* prob. in Dsc.3.9, cf. Apul.*Herb.*110. **-μᾱλον**, *τό*, Dor. for *κυνόμηλον*, = *κοκκύμηλον*, Hsch. **-μαντεία**, *ἡ*, *divination by dogs*, *Gloss.* **-μᾰχέω**, *fight with dogs*, Poll.5.65; *ἐν φρέατι* κ., prov. *ἐπὶ τῶν δυσφεύκτων*, Hsch. **-μᾰχον**, *τό*, = *κυνόμαζον*, Orib.12 s.v. *χαμαιλέων μέλας*. **-μόριον**, *τό*, = *ὀροβάγχη*, Dsc.2.142. **-μορον**, *τό*, = *κυνόσβατος*, Gal.12.426; also, = *ἀπόκυνον*, Id.11.835. **-μορφος**, *ὁ*, = *κρόκος*, Ps.-Dsc.1.26. **-μυια**, *ἡ*, v. *κυνάμυια*. II. = *ψύλλιον*, Dsc.4.60.

**κύνοπλον**, *τό*, *corona* in the horse's foot, *Hippiatr.*95, 106.

**κῠνο-πόδιον**, *τό*, = *πολύγονος*, *Gloss.* **-πους**, *ποδος*, *ὁ*, = *κυνήπους*, *Hippiatr.*77, 115. **-πρᾰσον**, *τό*, *dog-leek*, a plant, ib.69. ⊛ **-πρηστις** (-*πρῖστις* cod.), *ιδος*, *ἡ*, (*πρήθω*) a venomous insect, *whose sting makes dogs swell up* and die, Hsch.; cf. *βούπρηστις*. **-πρόσωπος**, *ον*, *dog-faced*, Luc.*DMar.*7.2, *VH*1.16, S.E.*P.*3.219; of men, like *κυνοκέφαλος*, Ael.*NA*10.25.

**κῠνόπτικον**, *τό*, an eye-salve, Alex.Trall.2.

**κῠνο-ραιστής**, *οῦ*, *ὁ*, (*ῥαίω*) *dog-tick*, *Ricinus communis*, Od.17.300, Arist.*Rh.*1393$^b$26, *HA*557$^a$18. ⊛ **-ροδον**, *τό*, *dog-rose*, *Rosa canina*, Thphr.*HP*4.4.8. II. = *ἀντίρρινον*, Ps.-Dsc.4.130. **-ρράφιον** [ᾰ], *τό*, (*κύων* VII) a surgical instrument, *Hermes* 38.282.

**κῠνορτικός**, *ή*, *όν*, *urging on hounds*, *σύριγμα* S.*Ichn.*167.

**κῠνορχίας**, *ὁ*, a throw of the dice, Hsch.

**Κῠνόσαργες**, *εος*, *τό*, *Cynosarges*, a gymnasium outside the city of Athens, sacred to Heracles, for the use of those who were not of pure Athenian blood, Hdt.5.63, 6.116, And.1.61, D.23.213, Paus.1.19.3.

**κῠνόσ-βᾰτος**, *ἡ* (also *ὁ* Thphr. (v.infr.), Ath.2.70d), *white rose*, *Rosa sempervirens*, Arist.*Fr.*561, Theoc.5.92, Dsc.1.94, Plu.2.294e, etc.; *καρπὸς τοῦ* κ. Thphr.*HP*9.8.5:—also **-βᾰτον**, *τό*, ib.3.18.4. II. = *κάππαρις*, Dsc.2.173; = *βάτος*, Ps.-Dsc.4.37; = *σμῖλαξ τραχεῖα*, ib.142. **-ουρα**, *ἡ*, *dog's-tail*, a name for the constellation *Ursa Minor*, Arat.36, Aglaosth.ap.Eratosth.*Cat.*2. ⊛ **-ουρίς**, *ίδος*, *ἡ*, *a breed of Spartan hounds*, from the Laced. tribe so called, Call.*Dian.*94. II. = *κυνόσουρα*, Nonn.*D.*1.166; epith. of Ἄρκτος, Man.2.24.

**κῠνόσουρος**, *ον*, *ᾠά addled* eggs, Arist.*HA*560$^a$5; cf. *οὔριος* IV.

**κῠνο-σπάρακτος** [ᾰ], *ον*, *torn by dogs*, S.*Ant.*1198. **-σπάς**, *άδος*, *ὁ*, *ἡ*, = foreg., Nonn.*D.*46.341. **-σπαστος**, *ὁ*, = *ἀγλαοφῶτις*, Ael.*NA*14.24, 27.

**κῠνοσσόος**, *ον*, *cheering on hounds*, Nonn.*D.*1.233, etc.

**κῠνό-στομον**, *τό*, *distance between thumb and first finger*, = *λιχάς*, Hero *Geom.*4.4. **-σφᾰγής**, *ές*, *worshipped with sacrifices of dogs*, Lyc.77. **-σφη** (-*λφη* cod.)· *σίλφη*, Hsch. **-τρόφος**, *ον*, *keeping dogs*, Ctes.*Fr.*62.

⊛ **κῠνουλκός**, *ὁ*, (*ἕλκω*) *dog-leader*, Nic.Dam.56 J.

**κυνοῦπες**· *ἄρκτοι* (-*τος* cod.) (Maced.), Hsch. (Fort. *κυνουπεύς*, = *κνουπεύς*, *κνωπεύς*.)

**κύνουρα** [ῠ], *ων*, *τά*, *sea-cliffs*, Lyc.99.

**κυνοῦραι**· *ἀστράγαλοι*, Hsch.

⊛ **κῠνούχιον**, *τό*, Dim. of sq. III, corr. Casaub. for *κυλιούχιον* in Thphr.*Char.*18.4.

⊛ **κῠνοῦχος**, *ὁ*, (*ἔχω*) *dog-leash*, *AP*6.298 (Leon.), acc. to Suid., but more prob. in signf. III; *κλοιὸς* κ. *dog-collar*, ib.107 (Phil.). II. *calf-skin sack*, for carrying hunting-nets, etc., X.*Cyn.*2.9; also, for use as a *clothes-locker* in the gymnasium, Poll.10.64. III. *purse*, *money-bag*, *PCair.Zen.*22.22 (iii B.C.), *Inscr.Délos* 442 *A* 7, 461 *A a* 7 (ii B.C.), Ael.Dion.*Fr.*206, Hsch., Phot.

**κῠνοφᾰγέω**, *eat dog's flesh*, S.E.*P.*3.225, Porph.*Abst.*1.14.

**κυνοφάλιον**, *sabina*, *Gloss.*

**Κυνόφαλοι**, *οἱ*, name of a tribe at Corinth, *Com.Adesp.*1360.

**κῠνοφθαλμίζομαι**, *look impudent*, *Com.Adesp.*1058.

**κῠνο-φόντις** *ἑορτή*, *ἡ*, (*θείνω*) a festival, *in which dogs were killed*, Ath.3.99e. **-φρων**, *ον*, gen. *ονος*, *dog-minded*, *shameless of soul*, A.*Ch.*621 (lyr.). **-χάλκη**, *ἡ*, = *πολύγονον ἄρρεν*, Ps.-Dsc.4.4.

**κύντερος**, *α*, *ον*, Comp. Adj. formed from *κύων*, *more dog-like*, i.e. *more shameless* (cf. *κύων* II), Hom. only in neut., *ἐπεὶ οὐ σέο κύντερον ἄλλο* Il.8.483; *οὐ..κ. ἄλλο γυναικός* Od.11.427; *οὐ γάρ τι στυγερῇ ἐπὶ γαστέρι κ. ἄλλο* 7.216; *more horrible*, *κ. ἄλλο ποτ' ἔτλης* 20.18: later in masc., *κυνῶν κύντερος* Anon.ap.Suid. s.v. *Διονυσίων*. 2. Sup. **κύντατος**, *η*, *ον*, *μερμήριζε.., ὅ τι κύντατον ἔρδοι* Il.10.503; *κ. ἐνιαυτός* *h.Cer.*306; *κ. ἀνδρῶν* A.R.3.192; once in Trag., *τὰ κ. ἄλγη κακῶν* E.*Supp.*807 (lyr.); in later Prose, Phld.*Ir.*p.24 W. II. Comp. **κυντερώτερος** A.*Fr.*432, Pherecr.106: Sup. **κυντατώτατος** Eub.85, but **κυντότατος** Arist.*Fr.*77.

**κῠνῠλαγμός**, *ὁ*, *the howling of dogs*, Stesich.85.

**κυνύπισμα**· *τὸ ἀπὸ στεμφύλων ποτόν* (Cypr.), Hsch.

**κῠν-ώ**, *οῦς*, *ἡ*, *bitch*: hence, = *ἀναιδεστάτη*, Hsch.: as pr. n., Hdt.1.110; title of Hecate, *PMag.Par.*1.2279. **-ώδης**, *ες*, *dog-like*, *θηρίον* Arist.*GA*746$^a$35, cf. Heraclit.*Incred.*2; *αἰδοῖον* Arist.*HA*502$^b$24 (Comp.); *ὄρεξις ravenous*, Gal.7.131, cf. Alex.Trall.7.1. Adv. **-δῶς** Antyll.ap.Orib.6.23.5. II. metaph., *despicable*, Phld.*Rh.*2.175 S., *Piet.*95 (Sup.); *currish*, *ill-tempered*, Id.*Lib.*p.44 O. **-ώπης**, *ου*, *ὁ*, (*ὤψ*) *dog-eyed*, i.e. *shameless one*, Il.1.159:—fem. **-ῶπις**, *ιδος*, *ἡ*, *ἐμεῖο κυνώπιδος εἵνεκ'*, says Helen, Od.4.145, cf. Il.3.180; *κ. εἵνεκα κούρης*, of Aphrodite, Od.8.319; of Hera, Il.18.396; of the Erinyes, E.*Or.*260, *El.*1252; *παλλακὴ* κ. Cratin.241. **-ωτός**, *ὁ*, *dog's ear*, name of a throw of the dice, *An.Ox.*2.21; prob. in Eub.57 (but *κυνῶτες* Poll.7.205). **-ωψ**, *ωπος*, *ὁ*, *rib-grass*, *Plantago lanceolata*, Thphr.*HP*7.7.3.

**κῠόεις**, *εσσα*, *εν*, *pregnant*, *Abh.Berl.Akad.*1928(6).22 (Cos, iii B.C.).

⊛ **κύος** [ῠ], *εος*, *τό*, = *κύημα*, Ar.*Fr.*609, *IG*12(5).646 (Ceos).

**κῠο-τοκία**, *ἡ*, *production of young*, in birds, Alex.Aphr.*Pr.*2.68. **-τροφία**, *ἡ*, *nourishment of the foetus*, Hp.*Salubr.*6 (pl.).

**κύουρα**, *ἡ*, a plant, used to procure abortion, Agatho Sam.ap.Stob.4.36.12.

**κῠοφορ-έω**, *to be with young*, *be pregnant*, Hp.*Nat.Mul.*12 (v.l.), Lxx *Ec.*11.5; *ἔκ τινος* by.., Luc.*DDeor.*1.2; of the earth, Ph.1.9: metaph., ib.130: c. acc., *τινα with* or *of*.., ib.251, Hld.10.18: metaph., *ἡ διάνοια κ. πολλά* Ph.1.183:—Pass., D.S.1.7; *βρέφος κυοφορηθέν* Artem.4.67, cf. 84, Porph.*Marc.*32, Phlp.*in APo.*280.17. **-ησις**, *εως*, *ἡ*, *pregnancy*, Sor.2.53, *Theol.Ar.*50. **-ία**, *ἡ*, = foreg., Lxx 4*Ma.*15.6 (pl.), Sor.1.47, Hierocl.p.63 A. (pl.), v.l. in Artem.1.14. ⊛ **-ος**, *ον*, *pregnant*, *fertile*, *γῆ EM*546.8, cf. *PLond.*1821.161.

⊛ **κύπαιρ-ος** [ῠ], Dor. for *κύπειρος*, Alcm.16:—Dim. **-ίσκος**, Id.38.

**κύπαλον**· *μεμειρασμένον*, Hsch.

**κῠπᾰρισσ-ίας**, *ου*, *ὁ*, *Euphorbia aleppica*, Dsc.4.164, Ruf.ap.Orib.7.26.108. II. a kind of comet, prob. in Seneca *QN*1.15.4. **-ῐνος**, Att. **-ίττῐνος**, *η*, *ον*, *of cypress-wood*, *σταθμός* Od.17.340; *μέλαθρον* Pi.*P.*5.39; *λάρνακες* Th.2.34; *μνῆμαι* Pl.*Lg.*741c; *ξυλεία* Plb.10.27.10; also, *made* or *drawn from the cypress*, κ. *οἶνος* Dsc.5.36; *ῥητίνη* Gal.13.589. **-ιον**, Att. **-ίττιον**, *τό*, Dim. of *κυπάρισσος*, Alciphr.*Fr.*6.1 (pl.). **-ιος**, *ὁ*, title of Apollo in Cos, *Abh.Berl.Akad.*1928(6).32 (iv B.C.). (Cf. Κυφαρισσία.)

⊛ **κῠπᾰρισσόκομος**, *ον*, *with cypress foliage*, Sch.Il.13.132.

**κῠπᾰρισσ-όροφος**, *ον*, *ceiled with cypress-wood*, E.*Hyps.Fr.*32.10; *θάλαμοι* prob. (for -*τρόφοι*) in Mnesim.4.1 (anap.). ⊛ **-ος**, Att. **-ιττος**, *ἡ*, *cypress*, *Cupressus sempervirens*, *εὐώδης* Od.5.64, cf. Hdt.4.75, Hermipp.63.14, Phld.*Mort.*38, Dsc.1.74, Arr.*An.*7.19.4; *ἐλαφρά* Pi.*Fr.*154; *ῥαδινά* Theoc.11.45; *ἄρρην καὶ θήλεια* Thphr.*HP*1.8.2. II. *cypress-wood* as timber, *SIG*251 *H* ii 9 (Delph., iv B.C.), *IG*4$^2$(1).102.26 (Epid., iv B.C.), 2$^2$.1672.191. **-ών**, *ῶνος*, *ὁ*, *cypress grove*, Str.16.1.4.

⊛ **κύπασσις** [ῠ] (-*ασίς* Hsch.), *εως* (*ιδος* Alc.15.6), *ὁ* (*ἡ* v.l. in Hecat.284 J.), *short frock*, reaching to a man's mid-thigh, Alc. l.c. (in form *κυπάττιδες*), Ion Trag.59, Lys.*Fr.*58 S.; also worn by women, Ar.*Fr.*519, *AP*6.202 (Leon.), cf. 272 (Pers.), 358 (Diotim.); *κ. Περσικαί* Hecat. l.c.; *κ. χερμάδων* prob. for *κύπας τις χ.* in Lyc.333:—Dim. **κῠπασσίσκος**, *ὁ*, Hippon.18.

**κυπάται**· *κίναιδοι*, *μαλακοί*, Hsch.; cf. *κυβάλης*.

**κύπειρις** [ῠ], *ιδος*, *ἡ*, = sq. 2, Nic.*Al.*591:—also **κύπηρις**, *εως*, *ἡ*, *POxy.*374 (i A.D.).

**κύπειρον** [ῠ], *τό*, *galingale*, *Cyperus longus*, eaten by horses, Il.21.351, Od.4.603. 2. *C. rotundus*, Thphr.*HP*4.10.5; cf. sq. and *κύπερος*.

⊛ **κύπειρος** [ῠ], *ὁ*, = foreg., *h.Merc.*107, Ar.*Ra.*243 (lyr.), Pherecr.109, Thphr.*HP*1.8.1, and 10.5, Theoc.1.106.

**κῠπελλίς**, *ίδος*, *ἡ*, = *κύπελλον*, Eust.1776.31.

**κῠπελλομάχος** [ᾰ], *ον*, *at which they fight with cups*, *εἰλαπίνη AP*11.59 (Maced.).

**κύπελλον** [ῠ], *τό*, (*ἀπὸ τῆς κυφότητος* Ath.11.482e) *big-bellied drinking-vessel*, *beaker*, *goblet*, freq. in Hom., *χρύσεια κύπελλα* Il.3.248; *κύπελλα οἴνου* 4.345; *κύπελλα καὶ μεσομφάλους* Ion Trag.20 (lyr.); also of a *milk-vessel*, Q.S.6.345. II. at Syracuse, in pl., *fragments of bread left on table*, Philet.ap.Ath.11.483a.

⊛ **κῠπελλο-τόκος**, *ον*, *breeding cups*, *τράπεζα* Nonn.*D.*47.62. **-φόρος**,

ον, *carrying cups*, *App.Anth.*3.166 (Procl.). **-χάρων** [ᾰ], ωνος, ὁ, *delighting in cups*, Eust.1776.31.

**κύπερ-ίζω**, *resemble* κύπερος, Dsc.1.7. **-ον**, τό, *rope made of* κύπειρος, Hsch. (pl.). **-ος**, ὁ, Ion. for κύπειρος, *Cyperus rotundus*, Hp.*Nat.Mul.*58, Hdt.4.71 : also in later Gr., Dsc.1.4, Plu.2.383e, Gal.12.54, *PSI*6.718.4 (iv/v A.D.). II. κ. ἕτερος *turmeric*, *Curcuma longa*, Dsc.1.5.

**κύπη**, ἡ, a kind of *ship*, Hsch. 2. *hut*, Id. II. = τρώγλη, Id.

**κύπηρις**, v. κύπειρις :—hence **κῡπηρολογέω**, *gather* κύπειρις. *POxy.* 374 (i A.D.).

**κῡπόω**, (cf. κύπτω) *overthrow*, Lyc.1442.

**κυπριάζω**, = ἀνθέω (prob. f.l. for κυπρίζω), Suid.

**Κυπριακός**, ή, όν, *Cyprian*, D.S.14.110, etc.

**Κυπρίδιος**, α, ον, (Κύπρις) *of love*, ὄαροι *AP*10.68 (Agath.); κέλευθος ib.5.274 (Paul. Sil.); κῦμα ib.234 (Maced.).

**κυπρίζω**, *bloom*, Lxx *Ca.*2.13.

**κυπρῐνέλαιον**, τό, = κύπρινον, Alex.Trall.3.3.

**κύπρῐνος** (A), η, ον, *made of copper*, ἧλος *PMag.Lond.*121.466.

**κύπρῐνος** (B), η, ον, *made from the flower of* κύπρος, ἔλαιον *Edict. Diocl.Delph.*10 :—esp. as Subst. **κύπρῐνον** (sc. μύρον), τό, *oil* or *unguent made from the flower of the* κύπρος, Apollon.Heroph.ap.Ath.15. 688f, Dsc.1.55, Aret.*CA*1.2 ; also of a plaster, Androm.ap.Gal.13. 494.

**κυπρῖνος**, ὁ, *carp*, Arist.*HA*533ᵃ29, 538ᵃ15, *Fr.*321, Opp.*H.*1.101.

**κύπριον**, τό, = ἀρνόγλωσσον, Hsch.

⊛ **Κύπριος**, α, ον, *of Cyprus, Cyprian*, Pi.*P.*2.16, Hdt.3.19, etc.; λίθος Κ., a kind of σμάραγδος (found in Cyprus, Thphr.*Lap.*25), Achae.5, cf. Plin.*HN*37.66 ; Κ. ἄρτοι Eub.77 ; Κ. παραπέτασμα Ar.*Fr.*611 ; Κ. τάριχος Posidipp.17 ; βοῦς Κ., prov. of an *unclean feeder*, Diogenian.3.49, Suid., etc.; Κ. κάλαμος, = δόναξ, Dsc.1.85. 2. ⊛**Κυπρία**, ἡ, = Κύπρις, Pi.*O.*1.75. 3. **Κύπρια, τά**, an Epic poem introductory to the Il., Hdt.2.117, Arist.*Po.*1459ᵇ2.

**κύπριος**, α, ον, *of copper*, γραφεῖον *PMag.Par.*1.1847.

**Κύπρις**, ῐδος, ἡ, acc. Κύπριν and Κύπριδα, Il.5.330,458 :—*Cypris*, a name of *Aphrodite*, from the island of Cyprus, Il. ll.cc. (never in Od.), Sapph.5.1, Corinn.*Supp.*2.58 (Κούπρις), etc.; joined with Ἀφροδίτη, *h.Ven.*2 ; Κ. βασίλεια Emp.128.3. 2. metaph., of a beautiful girl, *a Venus*, Opp.*H.*4.235. II. as Appellat., *love, passion*, E.*Ba.*773 ; Κύπριν ὑφαρπάζειν Ar.*Ec.*722 ; λαθραία Κ. Eub. 67.8 ; ἐν πλησμονῇ τοι Κ. Men. *Mon.*159, cf. B.*Fr.*16.4, E.*Fr.* 951. III. = sq., Eust.1574.24, Sch.Od.7.125. [ῠ by nature ; in Ep. ῡ by position ; never in Com., exc. in parodies.]

**κυπρισμός**, ὁ, *bloom* of the olive or vine, Lxx *Ca.*7.12, Eust.1095. 23.

**Κυπρο-γενής**, ές, (γενέσθαι) *Cyprus-born*, Κ. Κυθέρεια *h.Hom.*10. 1 : standing alone, Hes.*Th.*199 (acc. -γενέα (prob.)), Sol.26, Pi.*O.* 10(11).105, etc. :—fem. **-γένεια**, ἡ, Κ. Ἀφροδίτη Ar.*Lys.*551 ; Κ. θεά Panyas.13.3 : abs., Pi.*P.*4.216, Plu.*Art.*28 :—Aeol. **Κυπρογένηα** Sapph.*Supp.*14.8, Alc.60, Theoc.30.31.

⊛**Κύπρος**, ἡ, *Cyprus*, Od.17.442, al. (never in Il., exc. in Adv. (v. infr.)). Adv. **Κυπρόθεν**, *from Cyprus*, *AP*9.487 (Pall.); **Κυπρόθε**, Call.*Sos.*9.7 ; **Κύπρονδε**, *to Cyprus*, Il.11.21.

**κύπρος**, ἡ, *henna*, *Lawsonia inermis*, Lxx *Ca.*1.14, *AP*4.1.42 (Mel.), Dsc.1.95, J.*BJ*4.8.3. 2. = κύπρινον μύρον, Thphr.*Od.*25, *PPetr.*2 p.114 (iii B.C.), etc. II. *a measure of corn*, Alc.141, *SIG*302 (Gambreum, iv B.C.), *Rev.Ét.Gr.*19.237 (Aphrod.). 2. = κεφάλαιον ἀριθμοῦ, Hsch.

**κυπτάζω**, Frequentat. of κύπτω, *keep stooping, go poking about, potter about* a thing, ἀμφ' ἄλητα Sophr.39 ; περί τινα Ar.*Lys.*17 ; τί κυπτάζεις ἔχων περὶ τὴν θύραν; Id.*Nu.*509 ; εἰώθασι μάλιστα περὶ τὰς σκηνὰς..κλέπται κ. Id.*Pax*731 ; περὶ τὸν τεθνεῶτα Pl.*R.*469d : abs., κυπτάζοντα ζῆν Id.*Amat.*137b. 2. abs., *cower*, D.C.49.30, 63. 28. II. = κύπτω 5, Phlp. *in Ph.*329.14.

⊛**κυπτόν**· ταπεινούμενον, Hsch.

⊛**κύπτω**, fut. κύψω Lxx *Ps.*9.31(10.10): aor. ἔκυψα (v. infr.): pf. κέκῡφα Hp.*Steril.*217 :—*bend forward, stoop*, πλευρά, τά οἱ κύψαντι παρ' ἀσπίδος ἐξεφαάνθη Il.4.468 ; ἔλαβεν..κύψας ἐκ πεδίοιο Il.17.621, cf. 21.69 ; ὁσσάκι γὰρ κύψει' ὁ γέρων πιέειν μενεαίνων κτλ. Od.11.585 ; κ. ἐς τὴν γῆν Hdt.3.14 ; κάτω κ. Ar.*V.*279 (lyr.), Thphr.*Char.*24.8 ; κεκυφότες εἰς γῆν καὶ εἰς τραπέζας Pl.*R.*586a ; χαμᾶζε Plu.*Ant.*45 : freq. in aor. part. with another Verb, ἔθει κύψας ran *with the head down*, i.e. *at full speed*, Ar.*Ra.*1091 (anap.); ὁμόσ' εἶμι κύψας Id.*Ec.*863 ; ἐς τὴν γῆν κύψασα κάτω βαδίζει Id.*Fr.*395 ; κύψας ἐσθίει eats *stooping*, i.e. *greedily*, Id.*Pax*33 ; sens. obsc., Hippon.22 Diehl. 2. *hang the head from shame*, οὗτος, τί κύπτεις; Ar.*Eq.*1354, *Th.*930 ; or sorrow, Amphis 30.6, Euphro 1.27 ; or thought, Epicr.11.21,23 (anap.). 3. *bow down under a burden*, D.18.323. 4. κύψαι, = ἀπάγξασθαι, Archil.35, cf. Phot. 5. of animals, *to be bowed forward*, opp. the erect figure of man, Arist.*PA*657ᵃ15 ; κέρεα κεκυφότα ἐς τὸ ἔμπροσθε horns *bent* forward, of certain African oxen, Hdt.4.183 ; ἐπὴν ὁ στόμαχος [τῆς ὑστέρης] ἐς τὸν ἀρχὸν κεκύφῃ Hp. l. c.

⊛ **κύρα**, v. κύριος B. 2. **κυρβάδωμεν**· κρύψωμεν, Hsch.

**κυρβαίη**, dub. sens., epith. of μάζα, Hom.*Epigr.*15.6 (κυρκαίη Suid. s. v. Ὅμηρος).

⊛ **Κύρβας**, αντος, ὁ, shortd. form of Κορύβας, Pherecyd.48 J.; dat. pl. Κυρβάντεσι S.*Fr.*862 ; gen. pl. Κυρβάντων Lyc.78, Call.*Jov.*46.

⊛ **κυρβᾰσία**, ἡ, *Persian bonnet* or *hat*, with a peaked crown, prob. much like the τιάρα (q. v.), Hdt.5.49, 7.64 ; ὥσπερ βασιλεὺς ὁ μέγας διαβάσκει ἐπὶ τῆς κεφαλῆς τὴν κ. τῶν ὀρνίθων μόνος ὀρθήν (sc. ὁ ἀλεκτρυών) Ar.*Av.*487 (cf. Sch.); a cover for a poultice for a woman's breast is compared to it in shape, Hp.*Mul.*2.186, cf. Aret.*CA*1. 10. II. = Lat. *apex* (of the *flamines*), D.H.2.70.

**κύρβεις**, εων, αἱ, Ar.*Av.*1354, Lys.30.20, etc.; οἱ, Cratin.274 (but ταῖς codd. of Plu.*Sol.*25), Arist.*Ath.*7.1, Euph.6 : κύρβιες *AP*4.4 (Agath.); acc. pl. κύρβιας A.R.4.280, *AP*4.3ᵇ.37 (Agath.) : sg., v. infr. III, acc. κύρβιν Nonn.*D.*12.55 ; dat. κύρβιδι ib.37 : (perh. akin to κόρυμβος) :—at Athens, *triangular tablets*, forming a three-sided pyramid, turning on a pivot, upon which the early laws were inscribed, Cratin. l. c., Ar. l. c., Pl.*Plt.*298e, Lys.30.17, Arist. l. c. ; described as being of wood, Plu. l. c.; of brass, Sch.Ar. l. c. ; of stone, Apollod.*Fr. Hist.*107(a) J. ; by some identified with ἄξονες, Eratosth.ap.Sch. A.R.4.280, Plu. l. c.; by others distd. from them, Ar.Byz.ap.*EM* 547.52, Sch.A.R. l. c., *AB*274, Hsch. II. later, of all *pillars* or *tablets with inscriptions*, Pl. l. c., Porph.*Abst.*2.21 ; of maps, A.R. l. c. ; of wall-pictures, Nonn.*D.*12.32 ; κ. γηραλέαι, of Homer's poems, *AP*15.36 (Cometas), cf. 4.4 (Agath.) : metaph., the *pillars* of Heracles, ib.4.3ᵇ.37 (Id.). III. in sg., metaph., of the Spartan scytale, Achae.19 ; of a *pettifogging lawyer*, as if *a walking statute-book*, Ar.*Nu.*448 (anap.); κ. ἑταιρικῶν κακῶν, of a ἑταίρα, Aristaenet. 1.17, cf. Zen.4.77.

**κύρβη**, ἡ, dub. sens., κ. ἀργυρᾶ ἐν σανιδίῳ προσηλωμένη *IG*11(2). 161 *B*76, 199 *B*10 (Delos, iii B.C.).

⊛ **κύρβος**, εος, τό, = κύρβις, Call.*Fr.*564.

**κῡρεία**, ἡ, contr. from κυριεία (q. v.).

**Κύρειος** [ῡ], α, ον, *of Cyrus* : οἱ Κ., his troops, X.*HG*3.2.7, al.

**κῠρέω**, A.*Pr.*332, S.*Tr.*386 : impf. ἐκύρουν [ῠ] Id.*El.*1331 : fut. κῠρήσω A.*Ch.*707, Hdt.1.112 : aor. ἐκύρησα Hes.*Op.*755, Archil.18, Hom.*Epigr.*6.6, Hdt.1.31, E.*Hec.*215 (lyr.): pf. κεκύρηκα Pl.*Alc.* 2.141b :—also **κύρω** [ῡ], Parm.8.49, A.R.2.363, *AP*9.710, etc.: impf. ἔκῡρον S.*OC*1159 ; Ep. κῦρον Il.23.821, *h.Cer.*189, *h.Ven.*174: fut. κύρσω Democr.243, S.*OC*225 (lyr.): aor. ἔκυρσα, part. κύρσας Il.3.23, Hes.*Sc.*426, *Op.*691, E.*Med.*1363 :—Med., κύρομαι [ῡ] in act. sense, Il.24.530 :—poet. Verb, of which the two forms are used as required by the metre, and some tenses occur in Ion. and (rarely) in other Prose : I. folld. by a case, *hit, light upon*, 1. c. dat., *meet with, fall in with*, ἄλλοτε μὲν..κακῷ..κύρεται ἄλλοτε δ' ἐσθλῷ Il.24.530 ; πήματι κύρσαι Hes.*Op.*691 ; λέων ὣς σώματι κύρσας Id.*Sc.* l. c. ; ἅρματι κύρσας *having struck against* it, Il.23. 428 ; μέγα δένδρεον αἰθέρι κῦρον *reaching to*.., Call.*Cer.*38, cf. A.R.2.363, 4.945, *AP*9.710 ; so ἐν πείρασι κ. Parm.8.49. b. of things, κυρεῖν τινι *befall* or *be granted to* him, S.*OC*1290, *Tr.* 291, E.*Hec.*215 (lyr.); also εἰς ὅ τι κύρει ἕκαστα 'which way the wind blows', Timo 48.5. 2. c. gen., *hit* the mark, ἔκυρσας ὥστε τοξότης..σκοποῦ A.*Ag.*628 ; *reach to* or *as far as*, μελάθρου κῦρε κάρη *h.Cer.*189 ; *meet with, find*, αἰδοίων βροτῶν κυρῆσαι Hom.*Epigr.*6.6 ; πικροῦ δ' ἔκυρσας..μνηστῆρος A.*Pr.*739 ; Ἰαόνων ναυβατᾶν κύρσαντες Id.*Pers.*1012 (lyr.); αἰθερίας νεφέλας κύρσαιμι *would I could reach*.., S.*OC*1082 (lyr.). b. *attain to, obtain*, γάμων Archil.18 ; τέκνων κ. Hdt.1.31 ; καθαρσίου ib.35 (v.l.); βασιλήτης ταφῆς ib.112 ; δίκης Id. 9.116 ; ἀτιμίης πρός τινων Id.7.158 ; κυρήσει νοστίμου σωτηρίας A. *Pers.*797 ; στυγερᾶς μοίρας τῆσδε κυρήσας ib.910 (anap.); κυροῦντα τῶν ἐπαξίων Id.*Pr.*70 ; βίου λῴονος κυρῆσαι S.*OT*1514 ; δυσπότμων γάμων κυρήσας Id.*Ant.*870 (lyr.); μητρὸς ὡς κακῆς ἐκύρσατε E.*Med.* 1363, cf. *Ion* 1105 (lyr.); ἀμοιβῆς ἔκ τινος κυρεῖν Id.*Med.*23, cf. *Supp.* 1170 ; ἀγαθῶν Pl.*Alc.*2.141b, Herod.3.57 ; λητῆς Id.2.45 ; τόσσων ἐκύρησεν ὅσ' οὐ πευσεῖσθε βέβαλοι Theoc.3.51. 3. less freq. c. acc., *reach, find*, τί νῦν..κυρῶ; A.*Ch.*214 ; βίον εὖ κυρήσας Id.*Th.*699 (lyr.); ἐπ' ἀκταῖς νιν κυρῶ E.*Hec.*698 ; τέρμονα κύρειν dub. cj. in Id.*Hipp.* 746 (lyr.), cf. Opp.*H.*1.34. b. *obtain*, κυρούντων τὰ πρόσφορα A.*Ch.* 714. II. abs., *happen, come to pass*, τί ποτ' αὐτίκα κύρσει; S.*OC*225 (lyr.); καλῶς, εὖ κυρεῖ *turns out* well, A.*Th.*23, S.*El.*799 ; of a person, Ἀτρείδην εἰδέναι κυροῦνθ' ὅπως *how he fares*, A.*Ag.*1371 ; also ἕτερα ἀφ' ἑτέρων κακὰ κυρεῖ *follow*, E.*Hec.*690 (lyr.); ἄλλα δ' ἐξ ἄλλων κ. Id.*IT* 865 (lyr.). 2. *to be right, hit the mark*, γνώμῃ κυρήσας by intelligence, S.*OT*398 : c. part., τόδ' ἂν λέγων κυρήσαις in saying, A.*Supp.* 589 (lyr.); ἐπεικάζων κυρῶ; S.*El.*663. b. *to be successful, prosper*, Democr.243. 3. as auxil. Verb, c. part., *turn out, prove to be* so and so, σεσωσμένος κυρεῖ A.*Pers.*503, cf. *Ag.*1201 ; ποῦ ποτ' ὢν κυρεῖς; S.*Ph.*805 ; θύων ἔκυρον Id.*OC*1159 ; ἐχθρὸς ὢν κυρεῖ E.*Alc.* 954 ; εἰ κυρεῖ τις πέλας..οἶκτον ἀΐων A.*Supp.*58 (lyr.): with part. omitted, acting merely as the copula, ἐκτὸς αἰτίας κυρεῖς Id.*Pr.*332, cf. *Pers.*598 ; ποῦ γῆς κυρεῖ; S.*Aj.*984 ; φονέα σε φημὶ..κυρεῖν Id.*OT* 362 ; ἐν κακῷ τῳ φαίνῃ κυρῶν Id.*Ph.*741 ; ἐν πύλαισι..κυρεῖ E.*Ph.* 1067 ; ἔνθα πημάτων κυρῶ Id.*Tr.*685. 4. κ. πρός.. *refer to*, οὔτ' εἶπον οὐδὲν πρός ⟨σε⟩ κῦρον *Trag.Adesp.*226 ; τὰ πρὸς διαβολὴν κυροῦντα Plb. 12.15.9.

**κυρηβ-άζω**, fut. -άσω Ar.*Eq.*272 :—prop. *butt with the horns*, like goats or rams, Sch.Ar. l. c. : metaph., τὸ σκέλος κυρηβάσει *he shall butt against* my leg, Ar. l. c. : aor. Med. κυρηβάσασθαι Cratin. 462. II. metaph. in Med., = λοιδοροῦμαι, Hsch. (κυριβ- cod.), Phot. **-ᾰσία** and **-ᾰσις**, εως, ἡ, *butting* with the horns, Sch.Ar. *Eq.*272, Suid. **-άτης** [ᾰ], ου, ὁ, *quarreller*, prob. in Hsch. (κυριβ- cod.). **-ῐα**, ων, τά, *husks, bran*, Cratin.295, Hp.*Nat.Mul.*58, Epicur.*Fr.*293, etc. II. *bran-shop*, Ar.*Eq.*254. **-ῐοπώλης**, ου, ὁ, *dealer in bran*, Id.*Fr.*696 (lyr.). **-ίων**, ωνος, ὁ, nickname of Epicrates, D.19.287, Ath.6.242d. **-ος**, ὁ, = κυρηβάτης, Hsch. (-ιβος cod.).

**κύρημα** [ῠ], ατος, τό, = κύρμα, *windfall*, Phot., Suid.

**⊛Κυρηναϊκός**, ή, όν, *Cyrenaic*: οἱ Κ. *the disciples* of Aristippus *of Cyrene*, D.L.2.85; Κυρηναϊκὴ φιλοσοφία, αἵρεσις, Str.17.3.22, D.L. 1.18.

**⊛Κυρήνη**, ἡ, *Cyrene*, Hdt.4.162, etc.:—Adj. **Κυρηναῖος**, α, ον, ib. 199, etc. [ῠ in Hes.*Fr.*128.2, Pi.*P.*4.2, al., Call.*Ap.*73, 94; ῡ Ar. *Th.*98, A.R.2.500.]

**κῡρί-α**, ἡ, *authority, power*, Arist.*Mir.*837ᵃ5, etc.; *possession, control*, οἴνου Plb.6.11ᴬ.4; ταμιείου Id.6.13.1; τοῦ ἐπαποστεῖλαι στρατηγόν Id.6.15.6; κυρίαν ἔχειν περί τινος Id.6.14.10.—The form **κυρεία** is freq. found in Pap. and Inscrr. from i B.C., as *BGU*1123.6 (i B.C.), *PAmh.*2.95i6 (ii A.D.), and codd., as Plb.6.11ᴬ.4, Lxx *Da.*11.5, Thd. *Da.*4.19, 6.26(7), Ph.2.52 (v.l.), Ath.10.440f (v.l.), *EM*427.9, and is required by metre in Man.4.606: contr. from **κυριεία** (q.v.). II. fem. of κύριος (q.v.). **-άζεις**· ἀποκακεῖς, Hsch. **⊛-ακός**, ή, όν, (κύριος) *of* or *for an owner* or *master*, *Stud.Pal.*22.177.18 (ii A.D.); but usu. *of the Roman Emperor*, ὁ κ. φίσκος *the fiscus*, *CIG*2827 (Aphrod.), *Supp.Epigr.*2.567 (Caria (?)); κ. ψῆφοι, λόγος, *OGI*669.13, 18 (Egypt, i A.D.); κ. χρῆμα *POxy.*474.41 (ii A.D.). II. esp. *belonging to the Lord* (*Christ*): Κ. δεῖπνον *the Lord's Supper*, 1*Ep.Cor.*11.20; ἡ Κ. ἡμέρα *the Lord's day*, *Apoc.*1.10; τὸ Κυριακόν (sc. δῶμα) *the Lord's house*, Edict.Maximini ap.Eus.*HE*9.10. III. Subst. κυριακός, ὁ, spirit invoked in magic, *PMag.Par.*1.916. **-εία**, ἡ, *proprietary rights*, Mitteis *Chr.*31 v 37 (ii B.C.), *IG*2².1006.28 (ii B.C.), *SIG*685.133 (pl., Magn. Mae., ii B.C.), *BGU*1187.7 (i B.C.):—written **κυριήα** *Mon. Anc.Gr.*17.22:—later contr. **κυρεία, κυρία** (q.v.). **-ευτικός**, ή, όν, *concerning rights of property*, χρηματισμοί *Sammelb.*5232.22 (i A.D.); δίκαιον *Stud.Pal.*20.117.4 (v A.D.). Adv. -κῶς *with full proprietary rights*, *PAmh.*2.99(*b*).5 (ii A.D.), *PStrassb.*29.8, al. (iii A.D.). **⊛-εύω**, *to be lord* or *master of*, πάντων X.*Mem.*2.6.22, cf. Arist.*EN*1160ᵇ35; τῆς Ἀσίας X.*Mem.*3.5.11; μυρίων γῆς πήχεων Men.1099, cf. *PEleph.* 14.14 (iii B.C.), etc.; τῶν γενημάτων *PTeb.*105.47 (ii B.C.); τῆς θαλάττης Agatharch.5; ὧν ἁ πόλις..κυριεύει *IG*5(2).510.4 (Arc., ii B.C.); κυριεύειν τὴν γυναῖκα τοῦ ἀνδρός D.S.1.27; σανίδων Phld.*Mort.*24; νεκρῶν καὶ ζώντων *Ep.Rom.*14.9; κρατεῖν καὶ κ. *PStrassb.*14.22 (iii A.D.); *gain possession of, seize*, ζωγρίᾳ τινῶν Plb.1.7.11, al., cf. Ph.*Bel.*80. 41: later c. acc., τὰ σώματα καὶ τὴν βοῦν κ. *PGrenf.*1.21.13 (ii B.C.); τοῦ κυριεύοντος τὴν ὅλην οἰκουμένην *PMag.Lond.*121.838: abs., *to be dominant*, Chrysipp.*Stoic.*2.244:—Pass., *to be dominated, possessed*, ὑπό τινος Arist.*Mir.*838ᵃ10. b. Astrol., of planets, κ. τοῦ σχήματος Ptol.*Tetr.*169, cf. Vett.Val.63.23:—Pass., οἱ -όμενοι τόποι Ptol. *Tetr.*112. 2. *to have legal power* to do, c. inf., Lex ap.Aeschin. 1.35. II. ὁ κυριεύων (sc. λόγος, wh. is expressed in Arr.*Epict.*2. 19.1), a logical puzzle, Plu.2.615a, Luc.*Vit.Auct.*22, etc., cf. *Stoic.* 2.93.

**κῡρίζω**, = κυρίσσω, *EM*548.2:—Pass., κυρίζεσθε· τρίβεσθε, Hsch.

**κύριθον**· τὴν σφαῖραν, Hsch. **κύριθρα**, τά, *wooden masks*, Id.; cf. κυριττοί.

**κυρίλλιον**, τό, *narrow-necked jug*, = βομβύλιος, Poll.10.68.

**κύριξις** [ῠ], εως, ἡ, *butting with the horns*, Ael.*NA*16.20.

**κῡριοκτόνος**, ον, *slaying a sovereign lord*, κ. πράξεις, of those who killed the son of Saul, J.*AJ*7.2.1.

**κῡριο-λεκτέω**, *use words in their proper* or *literal sense*, Alex.Aphr. *in SE*166.6; opp. τροπολεκτέω, in Pass., Eust.633.26, 836.58; κυριολεκτῶν, opp. καταχρηστικῶς, Phlp. *in de An.*490.19. **-λεξία**, ἡ, *use of literal*, opp. *figurative, expressions*, Herm. *in Phdr.*p.192 A., Eust. 624.41. **-λογέω**, = κυριολεκτέω, Magnus ap.Gal.8.640, Steph. *in Hp.*2.420 D. **-λογία**, ἡ, = κυριολεξία, Agatharch.21 (pl.), Phld. *Rh.*1.174 S., Longin.28.1, Magnus ap.Gal.8.641; *proper meaning* of a word, A.D.*Adv.*190.3; = ἀκριβολογία, Gal.18(2).526.

**⊛κύριος** [ῡ], α, ον, also ος, ον A.*Supp.*732, E.*Heracl.*143, Arist.*Pol.* 1306ᵇ20:—Thess. **κῦρρος** *IG*9(2).517.20 (Larissa, iii B.C.): (κῦρος) (not in Hom.): I. of persons, *having power* or *authority over*, c. gen., Ζεὺς ὁ πάντων κ. Pi.*I.*5(4).53, cf. *P.*2.58; ἐμῶν τε καὶ σῶν κ. πιστωμάτων A.*Ag.*878; πρὶν ἄν σε κ. στήσω τέκνων put thee *in possession of*.., S.*OC*1041; κύριοι πολιτείας Antipho 3.1.1; κ. καταλύσεως Th.4.20; εἰρήνης καὶ πολέμου X.*HG*2.2.18; -ώτατοι τοῦ ἱεροῦ Th.5.53 (but ὁ -ώτατος θεὸς τοῦ ἱεροῦ, of the god to whom a temple is dedicated, *OGI*90.39 (Rosetta, ii B.C.)); τῶν αὑτοῦ κ. Pl.*Lg.*929d, cf. Isoc. 19.34, etc.; θανάτου κ. τινός *with power of* life and death over, Pl. *Criti.*120d; κ. περί τινος Arist.*Pol.*1286ᵃ24. 2. κύριός εἰμι c. inf., I *have authority* to do, *am entitled* to do, A.*Ag.*104 (lyr.); οὗτος κ. ὁρκωμοτεῖν (prob. for -ῶν) E.*Supp.*1189; κ. ἀπολέσαι, σῶσαι δ' ἄκυροι And.4.9, cf. Th.5.63, 8.5; -ώτεροι δοῦναι *better able* to give, Id.4.18; οὐ..κ. οὔτε ἀνελέσθαι πόλεμον οὔτε καταλῦσαι X.*An.*5.7.27; δοῦλοι κ. μαστιγοῦν τοὺς ἐλευθέρους Ephor.29 J.; αἱ ἀρχαὶ κ. κρίνειν Arist. *Pol.*1287ᵇ16; also κ. τοῦ μὴ μεθυσθῆναι *having power* not to.., Id. *EN*1113ᵇ32: c. acc. et inf., κ. εἶναι ἢ τοίαν εἶναι [πόλιν] ἢ τοίαν Pl.*R.* 429b. 3. folld. by a dependent clause, κ. γενέσθαι, ὅντινα δεῖ καταστήσασθαι Is.6.4. 4. c. part., πριαμένους τι ἢ πωλοῦντας κυρίους εἶναι Th.5.34; κ. ἦν πράσσων ταῦτα Id.8.51, cf. Plb.6.37.8, 18.37.10; κύριοι ἐόντω συλέοντες Schwyzer 337.13 (Delph.). 5. abs., *having authority, supreme*, τί τῶνδε κυριωτέρους μένεις; A.*Supp.*965; -ώτερος σέθεν E.*Ba.*505; ὁ πατὴρ μέχρι τούτου κ. [ἐστί] Arist.*Rh.*1402ᵃ1; τὸ κ. the *sovereign power* in a state, Id.*Pol.*1281ᵃ11, cf. Pl.*R.*565a, etc.; τὰ κ. the *supreme authorities*, D.19.259, Arist.*Rh.*1365ᵇ27; τὰ τῆσδε τῆς γῆς κ. S.*OC*915; at Athens, κ. ἐκκλησία a *sovereign* or *principal* assembly, Ar.*Ach.*19, Arist.*Ath.*43.4, *IG*1².42.22, al., 2². 493.8, etc.; ἀγορὰ κ. ib.1298.7. II. of things, ὁ τῆς ὥρας τῆς καταρχῆς κ. [ἀστήρ] Serapio in *Cat.Cod.Astr.*1.99: but usu. abs., *authoritative, decisive*, δίκαι E.*Heracl.*l.c., And.1.88, Pl.*Cri.*50b; μῦθος -ώτερος *of more authority*, E.*IA*318 (troch.); -ωτάτη τῶν ἐπιστημῶν [ἡ πολιτική] Arist.*Pol.*1282ᵇ15; αἱ -ώτεραι ἀρχαί Id.*Cael.*285ᵃ26, cf. *Metaph.*997ᵃ12; [ἡ φρόνησις] τῆς σοφίας κυριωτέρα Id.*EN*1143ᵇ 34; -ωτέρα ἡ καθόλου [ἀπόδειξις] Id.*APo.*86ᵃ23; τάραχος ὁ -ώτατος Epicur.*Ep.*1 p.30 U.; of *sovereign* remedies, -ωτάτη τῶν καθάρσεων Pl.*Sph.*230d; -ωτάτη κένωσις Gal.1.299; *important, principal*, κ. δόξαι, of certain doctrines of Epicurus, Phld.*Ir.*p.86 W.; τὰ -ώτατα μέρη τῆς φύσεως Epicur.*Sent.*9; -ώτερα μέρη τοῦ σώματος Philostr.*Gym.*50; τὰ -ώτατα the *principal* organs, Gal.1.385 (but, the *most important matters*, Epicur.*Sent.*16); τὸ -ώτατον τῆς Ἐφέσου Philostr.*VS*1.22.4: Gramm., κ. τόνος *principal* accent, D.T.*Supp.* 674.32. 2. opp. ἄκυρος, *valid*, νόμος, δόγματα, D.24.1, Pl.*Lg.* 926d; κ. ποιεῖν [τὴν γνῶσιν], opp. ἄκυρον π., D.21.92, cf. 39.15; τὰς συνθήκας κυρίας ποιεῖν Lys.18.15; ἡ συγγραφὴ ἥδε κ. ἔστω *PEleph.* 1.14 (iv B.C.); ἔστω τὰ κριθέντα κ. Lex ap.D.21.94; so τὰς τῶν ἄλλων δόξας κ. ποιεῖν Pl.*Tht.*179b. 3. of times, etc., *ordained, appointed*, ἡ κυρίη ἡμέρη Hdt.5.50, cf. 93 (pl.); ἡ κ. τῶν ἡμερέων Id.1.48, 6.129; κ. ἐν ἡμέρᾳ A.*Supp.*732; τόδε κ. ἦμαρ E.*Alc.*105 (lyr.), etc.; κ. μήν, of a woman with child, i.e. the ninth month, Pi.*O.*6.32; ὅταν τὸ κ. μόλῃ φάος (prob.) the *appointed* time, A.*Ag.*766 (lyr.); κ. μένει τέλος Id.*Eu.*544 (lyr.); ἡ κ. [ἡμέρα] D.21.84, cf. Test.ib.93; but αἱ κ. [ἡμέραι], = κριτικαί, Hp.*Aff.*9. 4. *legitimate, lawful*, ὕπνος πόνος τε, κ. ξυνωμόται A.*Eu.*127, cf. 327; κύρι' ἔχοντες having *lawful power*, ib. 960 (lyr.). 5. ἡ κ. ἀρετή goodness *proper, real* goodness, Arist.*EN* 1144ᵇ4; [φλοιὸς] ὁ κ. Thphr.*HP*4.15.1; Rhet. and Gramm., κ. ὄνομα the *real* or *actual*, hence *current, ordinary*, name of a thing, opp. μεταφορά, γλῶττα, Arist.*Rh.*1404ᵇ6, 1410ᵇ12, *Po.*1457ᵇ3, cf. D.H. *Comp.*21, D.L.10.13, etc.; σπάνει κυρίου ὀνόματος for lack of a *current* term, D.H.*Comp.*24; -ώτατα ὀνόματα *most ordinary* terms, ib.3 (hence also κ. ὄνομα *proper, personal* name, Plb.6.46.10, A.D.*Pron.* 10.11, al., Hdn.7.5.8; ὄνομα alone in this sense, Diog.Bab.*Stoic.*3. 213); κ. [λέξεις] Phld.*Rh.*1.181 S.; κατὰ τὸν κ. τρόπον, opp. καταχρωμένη, ib.1.59 S. III. Adv. κυρίως, v. sub voc.

B. Subst. **κύριος**, ὁ, *lord, master*, τοῖσι κ. δωμάτων A.*Ch.*658, cf. 689, S.*Aj.*734, etc.; ὁ κ. alone, *head* of a family, *master* of a house (cf. Sch.Ar.*Eq.*965), Antipho 2.4.7, Ar.*Pl.*6, Arist.*Pol.*1269ᵇ10; τοὺς κ. τῶν οἰκιῶν *PTeb.*5.147 (ii B.C.); also, *guardian* of a woman, Is.6. 32, *PGrenf.*2.15 i 13 (ii B.C.), etc.: generally, *guardian, trustee*, Is. 2.10, D.43.15, 46.19, Men.*Epit.*89, etc. b. later κύριε, as a form of respectful address, *sir*, *Ev.Jo.*12.21, 20.15, *Act.Ap.*16.30 (pl.), *PFay.* 106.15 (ii A.D.), etc. 2. fem. κυρία, ἡ, *mistress, lady of the house*, Philem.223, Lxx *Is.*24.2, etc.; κ. τῆς οἰκίας Men.403: in voc., *madam*, D.C.48.44; applied to women from fourteen years upwards, Epict. *Ench.*40. (In later Gr. freq. written **κύρα**, *PGrenf.*1.61.4 (vi A.D.), etc.) b. epith. of Ἶσις, *OGI*180 (Egypt, i B.C.), etc. 3. of gods, esp. in the East, Σεκνεβτῦνις ὁ κ. θεός *PTeb.*284.6 (i B.C.); Κρόνος κ. *CIG*4521 (Abila, i A.D.); Ζεὺς κ. *Supp.Epigr.*2.830 (Damascus, iii A.D.); κ. Σάραπις *POxy.*110.2 (ii A.D.); ἡ κ. Ἄρτεμις *IG*14. 1124 (Tibur, ii A.D.); of deified rulers, τοῦ κ. βασιλέος θεοῦ *OGI*186.8 (Egypt, i B.C.); οἱ κ. θεοὶ μέγιστοι, of Ptolemy XIV and Cleopatra, *Berl.Sitzb.*1902.1096: hence, of rulers in general, βασιλεὺς Ἡρώδης κ. *OGI*415 (Judaea, i B.C.); of Roman Emperors, *BGU*1200.11 (Augustus), *POxy.*37 i 6 (Claudius), etc. 4. ὁ Κύριος, = Hebr. *Yahweh*, Lxx *Ge.*11.5, al.; of Christ, 1*Ep.Cor.*12.3, etc.

**⊛κῡρι-ότης**, ητος, ἡ, *dominion*, *Ep.Eph.*1.21: in pl., *Ep.Col.*1. 16. 2. later, concrete, *authority*, *PMasp.*151.199 (vi A.D.), etc. II. *proper, legitimate use of a term*, Dam.*Pr.*306; = Lat. *proprietas*, Dosith.p.376 K. **⊛-όω**, = κυρόω, dub. in Phld.*Piet.*107 (Pass.).

**κυρίσσω**, Att. -ττω, fut. -ίξω (v. infr.), *butt with the horns*, like rams, Arist.*GA*769ᵇ20, cf. Phot.; of bulls, ὁ ταῦρος δ' ἔοικεν κυρίξειν A.*Fr.*23, cf. Pl.*Grg.*516a; κ. ἀλλήλους σιδηροῖς κέρασι Id.*R.*586b; μόσχος κυρίττων Gal.4.602; ὁ κυρίττων (sc. λόγος), a logical puzzle, Chrysipp.*Stoic.*2.94: metaph., of floating corpses *knocking against* the shore, κ. ἰσχυρὰν χθόνα A.*Pers.*310.

**κυριττοί**, οἱ, *players who wear wooden masks*, in Italy, Hsch.; cf. κύριθρα.

**κῡριωνῠμ-έω**, *call by a proper name*, Eust.635.6 (Pass.). **-ία**, ἡ, *use of a proper name*, Id.652.40, etc. **-ικῶς**, Adv. *by a proper name*, οὐ κ. εἶπε τὸν Πᾶνα Pediasim. ad Theoc.*Syrinx*3.

**⊛κῡρίως**, Adv. of κύριος, *like a lord* or *master, with full authority*, τὰς πόλεις κ. παρείληφεν Isoc.4.137; κ. ζημιοῦν Arist.*Ath.*3.6, *SIG*1004. 11 (Oropus, iv B.C.). II. *surely, by fixed decree*, A.*Ch.*785 (lyr.). 2. *regularly, lawfully*, κ. ἔχειν to be *fixed, hold good*, Id.*Ag.*178 (lyr.), Is.7.26; κ. γίγνεσθαι Pl.*Lg.*925c; κ. αἰτεῖσθαι, *suo jure*, S.*Ph.*63; δόντος τοῦ πατρός D.36.32. III. *precisely, exactly*, διέψευσθαι τὸ ἀληθές Pl.*Prm.*136c. IV. *properly*, πρώτως καὶ κ. Arist.*EN*1157ᵃ 31; τὸ κ. [ἐν καὶ εἶναι] Id. *de An.*412ᵇ9; esp. of words, *in the proper sense*, opp. μεταφορᾷ or κατὰ μεταφοράν, κ. κατά τινος κατηγορεῖσθαι Id.*Top.*123ᵃ35, cf. 139ᵇ36; κ. λέγεσθαι Id.*Metaph.*1015ᵃ14, cf. Str. 3.5.5, Phld.*Po.*5.19, etc.; ἡ λέξις αὕτη τοῦτο σημαίνει κ. Plb.2.22.1; *properly speaking*, D.T.632.23: Comp. -ώτερον, λέγεσθαι Arist.*EN* 1098ᵃ6: Sup. -ώτατα, λέγεσθαι Id.*Cat.*14ᵃ27. V. *in a special* (i.e. exceptional) *sense*, Olymp. *in Mete.*306.29.

**κυρκαίη**, v. κυρβαίη.

**κυρκᾰν-άω**, *mix*: metaph., *plot*, κ. ὄλεθρόν τινι Ar.*Th.*429, cf. 852: in literal sense, Hp.*Mul.*1.57 (Pass.), cf. *EM*543.53. **-η**, ἡ, = ταραχή, ib.548.43, cf. Hdn.Gr.1.421.

**κύρμα**, ατος, τό, (κύρω) *that which one meets with* or *finds*: hence,

booty, prey, spoil, κ. γίγνομαι, c. dat., ἀνδράσι δυσμενέεσσιν ἕλωρ καὶ κύρμα γένησθε Il.5.488; κυσὶ κύρμα γενέσθαι 17.272; οἰωνοῖσιν ἕλωρ καὶ κ. γ. Od.3.271; θήρεσσιν 5.473; φώκῃσι καὶ ἰχθύσι 15.480. II. of a person, *one who gets booty, swindler*, Ar.*Av.*431.

**κύρνα·** κρανία, Hsch. **κύρνικα·** κώδια, Id.

**Κύρνος,** ἡ, *Cyrnus*, ancient name of Corsica, Hdt.1.165:—Adj. **Κύρνιοι,** οἱ, Id.7.165; Κυρνία γῆ, prov. of *a nest of robbers*, Diogenian. 5.75. II. Appellat. **κύρνος,** ὁ, *bastard* (Maced.), Phot., cf. Hsch.

**Κῦρος,** ὁ, *Cyrus*: 1. ὁ πρότερος, *the elder Cyrus*, Hdt.1.46, etc. 2. ὁ νεώτερος, the brother of Artaxerxes, X.*An.*1.1.1, etc.

**κῦρος,** εος, τό, *supreme power, authority*, κ. ἔχειν ἀμφί τινος A.*Supp.* 391; τῶν πρηγμάτων τὸ κ. ἔχειν Hdt.6.109; ἅπαν τὸ κ. ἔχειν Th.5.38, cf. Pl.*Grg.*450e, al.; κ. ἔχειν περί τινος Id.*Cra.*435c; τὸ κ. τῆς ἐνεργείας *principle* or *origin* of a function, Gal.10.459. 2. concrete, *one invested with authority*, Pl.*Lg.*700c. II. *confirmation, validity*, ἔχειν κ., = κεκυρῶσθαι, S.*OC*1779 (anap.), cf. *POxy.*2110.12 (iv A.D.), etc.; ἡ νῦν.. ὑπάρξει κ. ἡμέρα καλῶν S.*El.*919; κ. λαβεῖν, of a law, *to be ratified*, D.C.38.17, al.:—κῦρος and all derivs. are post-Hom. (Cf. Skt. *śūras* 'valiant', OIr. *caur* 'hero', Welsh *cawr* 'giant'.)

**※κυρόω,** fut. -ώσω Hdt.6.86.β': (κῦρος):—*confirm, ratify*, δόμοις.. τήνδ' ἐκύρωσας φάτιν A.*Pers.*227 (troch.); τῇδ' ἐκύρωσεν φάτις ib.521; ταῦτα Hdt. l. c.; τὸν γάμον Id.6.126; ἡ ἐκκλησία κυρώσασα ταῦτα διελύθη Th.8.69; Ζεῦ, ταῦτα κυρώσειας Ar.*Th.*369 (lyr.); μοῖραν Pl.*R.* 620e; τὴν γνώμην Plb.1.11.1; τὰς διαλύσεις Id.1.17.1:—Med., *accomplish one's end*, λόγῳ κυροῦται τὰ πάντα Pl.*Grg.*451c, cf. d:—Pass., *to be ratified, determined*, ἐκεκύρωτο ὁ γάμος Κλεισθένεϊ Hdt.6.130; οὐδὲ κυρωθῆναι ἔμενον τὸ πρῆγμα Id.8.56, cf. Th.4.125; τοὺς κυρωθέντας τῶν νόμων] And.1.85, cf. D.20.93; τὸ ψήφισμα τὸ κυρωθὲν περὶ τούτων *IG*7.303.45 (Orop.); κυρωθέντος τοῦ δόγματος Plb.1.11.3; of a contract, *to be sanctioned*, *PPetr.*2p.44 (iii B.C.); in auctions, *to be knocked down*, *BGU*992 i 9 (ii B.C.); ὁ κυρωθεὶς the highest bidder, to whom an object is knocked down, *PRev.Laws* 48.17 (iii B.C.): generally, ποῖ κεκύρωται τέλος; at what point *hath* the end *been fixed* or *determined?* A.*Supp.*603, cf. *Ch.*874, E.*Hipp.*746 (v. l.); πρὶν κεκυρῶσθαι σφαγάς before it *has been accomplished*, Id.*El.*1069: c. inf., ἐκεκύρωτο συμβάλλειν *it had been decided* to fight, Hdt.6.110; ἐκυρώθη ναυμαχέειν Id.8.56. 2. κ. δίκην *decide* it, A.*Eu.*581, 639. 3. c. acc. et inf., *decree* or *ordain* that.., τηρηθῆναι τὸν νόμον Arist.*Fr.* 593. 4. of arguments or doctrines, *confirm, establish*, Phld.*Po. Herc.*1676.3; κ. ὅτι.. Id.*Sign.*7.

**κύρρασι·** τοῖς κέρασιν ἐπιτυχεῖν (cf. **κυρσεῖν** similarly expld.) κρούσαντ.., Hsch.

**κυρσάνιος,** ὁ, Lacon. word, = νεανίας, contemptuously, *whippersnapper*, Ar.*Lys.*983, 1248; cf. σκυρθάλια.

**κύρσεος,** = πρωκτός, Gal.19.116.

**κυρσερίδες·** τὰ τῶν μελισσῶν ἀγγεῖα, κυψελίδες, Hsch. **κυρσίον·** μειράκιον, Id.; cf. κυρσάνιος. **κυρσός,** *gibberosus*, Gloss.

**κυρτ-αίνω,** *rise into a heap* or *hump*, ἡ γῆ ἐκύρτανε *PMag.Leid.W.* 4.42, al. II. *to be bent, stoop*, ὑπὸ τῆς βίας Suid. s.v. ὑβός. **-αύχην,** ὁ, ἡ, gen. ενος, *with bulging neck*, Quint.1.5.70. **-εία,** ἡ, *fishing with the κύρτη*, Ael.*NA*12.43. **-εύς,** έως, ὁ, *one that fishes with the κύρτη*, Herod.3.51, Opp.*H.*3.352:—also **-ευτής,** οῦ, ὁ, *AP*6.230 (Maec.). **-η,** ἡ, = κύρτος, *weel, lobster-pot*, Hdt.1.191, D.S.3.19; used as a *sieve* or *riddle*, σχοινίδι κ. Nic.*Al.*625. 2. *bird-cage*, Archil.177. **-ήν,** *gibbus*, Gloss. **-ία,** ἡ, (κύρτος) *wicker-work*: a *wicker shield*, D.S.5.33. **-ιάω,** (κυρτός) *to be hunchbacked*, νῶτά τε κυρτιόωντας Man.4.119. **-ίδιον,** τό, Dim. of κυρτίς, *strainer*, Dsc.1.52. **-ιον,** τό, part of a chariot, Poll.1.143. **※-ίς,** ίδος, ἡ, *weel, lobster-pot*, Opp.*H.*3.600; *strainer*, Nic.*Al.*493, Dsc.1.52, Gal. 13.55.

**κυρτο-βόλος,** ὁ, (κύρτος) *fisherman*, -βόλων συνεργασία, Μουσ. Σμυρν.1873/5.65 (Smyrna). **-ειδής,** ές, Astrol., of signs under which *hunchbacks* are born, Thrasyll. in *Cat.Cod.Astr.*8(3).100, Vett. Val.11.13. 2. of the moon, ἐξ ἀμφοτέρων -ειδής, = ἀμφίκυρτος, Paul. Al.*G.*4. 3. gloss on κυφός, *EM*545.35. **-νεφέλη** (fort. κυσθο-), epith. of a ἑταίρα, *Com.Adesp.*1059.

**※κύρτ-ος,** ὁ, = κύρτη I, Sapph.120, Pl.*Sph.*220c, *POxy.*520.20 (ii A.D.); τῷ τοῦ κ. πλέγματι Pl.*Ti.*79d; μήτε ἐγρηγορόσιν μήτε εὕδουσι κύρτοις ἀργὸν θήραν διαπονουμένοις *weels* that secure a lazy prey for men whether asleep or awake, Id.*Lg.*823e (hence prov. εὕδοντι κ. αἱρεῖ Diogenian.4.65), cf. Lib.*Ep.*86.1; κύρτῳ θηρεύουσι τοὺς ἰχθῦς Arist. *HA*603ª7. 2. *bird-cage*, λυγοτευχὴς *AP*9.562 (Crin.). **-ός,** ή, όν, *bulging, swelling*, κῦμα Il.4.426; κύματα κυρτὰ φαληριόωντα 13. 799, cf. Sosicr.2; θάλασσα κυρτὸν ἐπαφρίζῃ Mosch.*Fr.*1.5; τὼ δέ οἱ ὤμω κυρτώ *humped*, Il.2.218, cf. *AP*11.120; τὸ κ. τῶν ὤμων Jul. *Or.*6.201b: hence, *hunchbacked*, *PFay.*121.15 (i/ii A.D.); βραχίων κ. πέφυκεν ἐς τὸ ἔξω μέρος Hp.*Fract.*8; κ. τροχός E.*Ba.*1066; κυρτὴ κάμηλος Babr.40.2; καρίδες Ophel.1: Comp. κυρτότερος Phlp. *in Ph.* 696.26: Sup. κυρτότατον φύλλον Thphr.*HP*3.10.5. 2. *convex*, opp. κοῖλος, οὔσης [τῆς γῆς] κυρτῆς καὶ σφαιροειδοῦς Arist.*Mete.*365ª 31; περὶ τὰς ἐκλείψεις [ἡ σελήνη] ἀεὶ κυρτὴν ἔχει τὴν ὁρίζουσαν γραμμήν Id.*Cael.*297ᵇ28; κ. ἐπιφάνεια *convex* surface of a shield, Plb.6. 23.2; of blood-vessels, *bulging*, Sor.1.44. **-ότης,** ητος, ἡ, *humped shoulders, stoop*, ἡ Πλάτωνος κ. Plu.2.26b; *convex surface* of a bone, etc., Gal.*UP*2.7, 12.5 (pl.), al.; of the spherical moon, Plu. 2.922d; of the earth, Cleom.1.8; τῆς θαλάσσης Str.1.1.20, Theo Sm. p.123 H. 2. *convexity*, opp. κοιλότης, of a line, Arist.*Ph.*217ᵇ3, *Mete.*386ª1, cf. Hero *Spir.*1.23. **-όω,** *hump up, make convex*, κυρτῶν νῶτα, of a bull preparing to charge, E.*Hel.*1558; τὴν χεῖρα ὑπὲρ τοῦ μετώπου κεκυρτωκότες Ath.14.629f; καταιγίδες εἰς οὐρανὸν κυρτοῦσι τὰ κύματα Lib.*Or.*59.138; λαίφεα *AP*10.15 (Paul. Sil.); κ. ὀστοῦν *make* the skull *bulge*, Antyll.ap.Orib.46.27.6:—Pass., κῦμα περιστάθη, οὔρεϊ ἶσον, κυρτωθέν Od.11.244; κυρτοῦσθαι ῥάχιν Opp.*C.*3.273; of leeches, Opp.*H.*2.602: in Prose, οἱ φοίνικες ὑπὸ βάρους πιεζόμενοι ἄνω κυρτοῦνται ὥσπερ οἱ ὄνοι οἱ κανθήλιοι X.*Cyr.*7.5.11; *become hunchbacked*, Sor.1.112: aor. 1 Med. ἐκυρτώσαντο *bulged*, δειρήν Nonn. *D.*37.564. **-ώδης,** ες, = κυρτοειδής 1, ζῴδιον *Cat.Cod.Astr.*7. 205. **-ωμα,** ατος, τό, *bulge*, κ. τοῦ ὀστέου its natural *convexity*, Hp. *Fract.*8; μεταφρένου Luc.*Ind.*7; τὸ κατὰ τὴν ῥάχιν κ. D.S.2.54: in pl., of the earth's *convexity*, Cleom.1.2, 2.6. 2. *rotundity*, ἀσκοῦ Hp. *Art.*47; *swelling*, Id.*Prog.*11 (pl.); of sham pregnancy, Id.*Prorrh.*2. 26; *outside of bowl* of a cup, Ath.11.488d; *convex front* of half-moon formation, Plb.3.113.8, Onos.21.6. **-ών,** ῶνος, ὁ, *hunchback*, Crates Theb.9. **-ωσις,** εως, ἡ, *bulging*, of blood-vessels, Sor. 2.8. 2. *convexity* of the sea's surface, Theo Sm.p.122 H. 3. *being humpbacked*, Gal.18(1).494, Vett.Val.109.35; τοῦ σώματος Ptol.*Tetr.*151 (pl.). II. κύρτωσις· τὸ μέσον τῆς ῥάχεως, *EM*774. 12. **※-ωτός,** ή, όν, *hunchbacked*, Vett.Val.13.2.

**κύρω,** v. κυρέω.

**κύρ-ωσις** [ῡ], εως, ἡ, *ratification*, Th.6.103, *Sammelb.*4512 (ii B.C.), etc.; τῶν λεγομένων J.*AJ*4.8.44; πᾶσα.. ἡ κ. διὰ λόγων ἐστί Pl. *Grg.*450b. **-ωτήρ,** ῆρος, ὁ, *one who has the κῦρος, sovereign*, Hsch. **※-ωτής,** οῦ, ὁ, *one who ratifies or confirms*, *IG*2².1678*a A* 27.

**κύσαι** [ῠ], Ep. κύσσαι, aor. inf. of κυνέω:—but **κῦσαι** of κύω.

**κυσανίζει·** ὁμιλεῖ, Hsch. **κυσέρη·** πυθμήν, χάσμα, Id. **κυσήγη·** ῥοιά, Id.

**κυσθοκορώνη,** = νύμφη, *Com.Adesp.*1060.

**※κύσθος,** ὁ, *pudenda muliebria*, Eup.233, Ar.*Ach.*782, al. II. **κύσθος,** εος, τό, a marine substance used in dyeing, *PHolm.*22.42.

**κυσιάω,** = πασχητιάω, *Com.Adesp.*1061.

**κυσίβαλον,** etym. of σκύβαλον, Suid. s. v. σκυβαλίζεται.

**κυσο-βάκχαρις,** ιδος, ὁ, = ὁ τὸν κυσὸν μυρίζων, *Com.Adesp.*1062. **-δακνιᾷ·** ψωριᾷ, Hsch. **-δόχη,** ἡ, a sort of stocks, Alciphr.3. 72. **-κόλαξ,** v. κυνοκόλαξ. **-λάκων** [ᾰ], ωνος, ὁ, = παιδεραστής, from the Spartans being accused of the practice, Aristarch.ap. Hsch., *Com.Adesp.*1063. **-λαμπίς,** ίδος, ἡ, = πυγολαμπίς, Hsch. **-λέσχης,** ου, ὁ, *obscene talker*, *Com.Adesp.*1066. **-νίπτης,** ου, ὁ, = πόρνος, ib.1064.

**κυσός,** ὁ, = κύσθος I, Hsch. II. = πυγή, Id. III. = κύστις, Herod.2.44, *Lyr.Adesp.*25. [ῡ Heiod. l. c., prob. in Call.*Iamb.*1. 159; ῠ dub. in *Lyr.Adesp.* l. c.; κῦσος Theognost.*Can.*72.]

**※κυσο-χήνη,** ἡ, = κυσοδόχη, Hsch. II. = εὐρυπρωκτία, Id., Phot. **-χωλος,** = ἐγκυσίχωλος, *Com.Adesp.*6 D. (κυσινό- cod. Phot.).

**κύσσα, κύσσαι,** v. κυνέω.

**κύσσαρος,** ὁ, = κυσός II, ἀρχός II, Hp.*Nat.Puer.*17, Gal.19.176, Erot.

**※κύστεροι·** ἀγγεῖα τῶν μελισσῶν, καὶ τυρίσκοι (fort. ὑρίσκοι), Hsch.

**κύστη,** ἡ, = ἄρτος σπογγίτης, Hsch.; but, = *fiscella* (i.e. κίστη), Gloss.

**κύστιγξ,** ιγγος, ἡ, Dim. of κύστις, Hp.ap.Gal.19.116.

**κύστιον,** τό, (κύστη) *plant which bears its fruit in a bladder*, = ἀλικάκκαβον, Hsch.

**κύστις,** εως, ιος, also ιδος Aen.Tact.31.12 (cf. infr. II), ἡ: (κύω):—*bladder*, Il.5.67, 13.652, S.*Fr.*394, Hp.*Art.*41, Pl.*Ti.*91a, Ph.*Bel.* 102.40, etc.; ὥσπερ κύστιν φυσᾶν, of the wind swelling out the clouds, Ar.*Nu.*405; κ. ὑεία used as a *pouch*, Id.*Fr.*504; οἴνου κύστεις μεστάς Phanod.19. II. in pl. κύστιδες, *bags* under the eye, Arist.*Phgn.* 811ᵇ14: sg., Adam.1.22. III. *ulcer* on horse's back, *Hippiatr.*26.

**κυστεφῖλος,** ὁ, *end of catheter*, which carried the *folliculus*, Cael. Aur.*TP*2.23.

**κύταρον·** ζωμήρυσις, Hsch.

**κύτῐν-ος,** ὁ, *flower of the pomegranate*, Thphr.*HP*2.6.12, Dsc.1. 110, Gal.12.917, Cael.Aur.*TP*4.52; properly the *calyx*, Thphr.*CP* 1.14.4, cj. in *HP*1.13.5; also ὑοσκυάμου κ. Dsc.1.10. II. = ὑποκιστίς, ib.97. **-ώδης,** ες, *like a κύτινος*, Thphr.*HP*4.10.3.

**κυτίς,** ίδος, ἡ, *small chest, trunk*, Sch.Ar.*Pax*665 (leg. κοιτίς).

**※κυτισηνόμος,** ον, (νέμομαι) *eating κύτισος*, [χελύνη] Nic.*Al.*560.

**※κύτισος** [ῠ], ὁ (ἡ Theoc.5.128, 10.30), *tree-medick, Medicago arborea*, Hp.*Nat.Mul.*93, Cratin.98.8, Eup.14.3, Arist.*HA*522ᵇ28, Thphr. *HP*4.16.5, *CP*5.15.4, Theoc. ll. cc., Dsc.4.112. II. *bastard ebony, Laburnum vulgare*, Thphr.*HP*1.6.1, 5.3.1.

**κυτμίς,** ίδος, ἡ, a kind of soothing *ointment*, Luc.*Alex.*22 (pl.), 53.

**κυτογάστωρ,** ορος, ὁ ἡ, *with capacious belly*, prob. for κυάστορας in *AP*6.305 (Leon.).

**※κύτος** [ῠ], εος, τό, (κύω) *hollow*, κύκλου, of a shield, A.*Th.*495; ἀσπίδος E.*Fr.*185; θώρηκος Ar.*Pax*1224; περίπλευρον κ. E.*El.*473 (lyr.); λέβητος Id.*Cyc.*399; τρίποδος Id.*Supp.*1202; κύλικος Pl.Com.189; λοπάδος Xenarch.1.10; *hold* of a ship, Plb.16.3.4. 2. *vessel, jar*, A.*Ag.*322, 816, S.*El.*1142, etc.; πλεκτὸν κ. *basket*, E.*Ion*37; κοιλοσώματον κ. Antiph.52.2. 3. of any hollow container, τὸ τῆς κεφαλῆς κ. Pl.*Ti.*45a; τὸ ὄπισθεν κ. *occiput*, Arist.*PA*656ᵇ26; τοῦ θώρακος τὸ κ., i.e. the chest, Pl.*Ti.*69e; ποδῶν κ. Achae.4.4 (leg. πλευρῶν); τὸ ἄνω κ. Arist.*GA*742ᵇ14 (also of plants, = αἱ ῥίζαι, 741ᵇ35, al.); τὸ λοιπὸν ἅπαν κ., of the uterus, Gal.*UP*14.14, cf. Sor.1.9; of the fourth stomach of the ox, Phlp. *in APo.*417.14; τὸ τῆς ψυχῆς κ., i.e. the body, Pl.*Ti.*44a: hence, abs., *body*, ἀνδρείῳ κύτει S.*Tr.*12; *trunk*, διὰ παντὸς τοῦ κ. Pl.*Ti.*74a; τὸ ἀπ' αὐχένος μέχρι αἰδοίων κ. Arist.*HA*

491a29, cf. PA686b14; τὸ ὅλον κ. τοῦ σώματος D.S.1.35, cf. Archig. ap.Gal.13.262: metaph., of the πόλις, Pl.Lg.964e; τὸ σύμπαν τῆς πόλεως κ. τείχεσιν ἠσφάλισται Plb.5.59.8. 4. κ. ἀστέριον starry *vault* of heaven, Vett.Val.172.32.

**κύτρα**, Sicil. for χύτρα, Greg.Cor.p.341 S.

**κυττάρ-ιον** [ᾰ], τό, Dim. of κύτταρος, Arist.GA760b34, 770a29. **-ον**, τό, = sq., Ar.Th.516 (nisi leg. κύτταρος). ❀ **-ος**, ὁ, *cell of a honey-comb*, Id.V.1111, Arist.HA551b5, 554a18, 555a1. 2. pit in the receptacle of *Nelumbium speciosum*, Thphr.HP4.8.7. b. male flower of the pine, ib.3.3.8, 3.7.3. c. = ἐχῖνος III. 1, τῶν δρυῶν οἱ κ., Hsch. 3. metaph., τοὐρανοῦ τὸν κ. the *pinnacle of the dome* of heaven, Ar.Pax 199.

**κυττοί**, οἱ, *receptacles*, Hsch.

**κῡφάγωγ-έω**, *carry the neck arched* (v. sq.), Lib.Decl.31.15. **-ὸς** ἵππος, ὁ, a horse *that goes with the neck arched*, X.Eq.7.10.

**κύφαλα**, τά, etym. of κύμβαλα, EM545.33.

**κῡφάλέος**, α, ον, poet. for κυφός, AP6.297 (Phan.).

**Κῡφάρισσ-ία**, ἡ, = Κυπαρ-, epith. of Artemis Agrotera, IG5(1).977 (Lacon.). **-ινος**, = κυπ-, ib.4.1588.7 (Aegina, v B.C.). ❀ **-ίτας** [ῑ], α, ὁ, epith. of Pan, BCH27.295 (Crete).

**κύφελλα** [ῠ], τά, (cf. κύπελλον):—only in Alexandrian Poets, 1. *hollows of the ears*, Lyc.1402. 2. *clouds of mist*, Call.Fr.300; κ. ἰῶν *clouds* of arrows, Lyc.1426.

**κύφερον ἢ κυφήν**· κεφαλήν (Cret.), Hsch.

**κῦφι**, εος, and εως, τό, *an Egyptian compound incense*, Dsc.1.25, Plu.2.372d, 384b, Gal.13.199, Damocr.ap.eund.14.117:—freq. written **κοῖφι**, Ath.2.66f, Aristid.Or.47(23).26 (κοιφὶ), PMag.Lond.46.221, 121.538.

**κῡφο-γέρων**, οντος, ὁ, *old man bent with age*, Steph. in Hp.2.276 D. **-ειδής**, ές, *of the nature* or *quality of* κῦφι, Androm.ap.Gal.13.198, Archig.ap.Aët.16.88. **-νωτος**, ον, *crook-backed*, Antiph.217.18. **-ομαι**, Pass., *have curvature of the spine*, Hp.Art.41; κυφοῦται ῥάχις ibid., cf. Gal.7.782.

❀ **κῡφός**, ή, όν, (κύπτω, κέκῡφα) *bent forwards, stooping, hunchbacked*, ὃς δὴ γήραϊ κ. ἔην καὶ μυρία ᾔδη Od.2.16; κ. ἀνήρ, πρεσβύτης, Ar.Ach.703, Pl.266; σφόνδυλοι ἕλκονται ἐς τὸ κ., in *curvature* of the spine, Hp.Art.41; τρίγλαι κ. Epich.64; freq. of shrimps, from their form, Eub.111, Matro Conv.64, AP5.184 (Asclep.); τῶν καρίδων αἱ κυφαί *shrimps*, e.g. *Palaemon squilla*, Arist.HA525b1, cf. 549b12; of birds, Id.IA710b18; also ὑπὸ κ. ἄροτρον IG14.2012.14 (Sulp. Max.); cf. κύφων I. II. *curved, round*, of a cup, Ath.11.482e.

**κῦφος**, εος, τό, *hump, hunch*, Hdn.Gr.1.225, Aët.ap.Phot.Bibl. p.180 B.. II. = κύπελλον, EM549.8.

**κῡφ-ότης**, ητος, ἡ, *a being bent* or *humpbacked*, Hld.6.11. II. *rotundity*, Ath.11.482e. **-ω**, = κύπτω, κύφοντα ὀφθαλμοῖς *with downcast* eyes, Lxx Jb.22.29. **-ωμα**, ατος, τό, *hump on the back*, Hp.Art.41 (sg. and pl.); κυφώματα σπονδύλων Ruf.ap.Orib.45.30.43. ❀ **-ων**, ωνος, ὁ, (κυφός) *crooked piece of wood, bent yoke of the plough*, Thgn.1201: κύφωνες, οἱ, *two bars* in the frame of a chariot, Poll.1.143. II. *pillory*, ἐν τῷ κ. αὐχένα ἔχειν Cratin.115, cf. Ar.Pl.476, 606; δεθῆναι ἐν τῷ κ. Arist.Pol.1306b2; μαστιγούσθω ἐν τῷ κ. OGI483.177 (Pergam.). 2. *one who has had his neck in the pillory, knave*, Archil.178, Luc.Pseudol.17. III. part of a woman's dress, Posidipp.44. IV. Archit., *curved beam*, IG4²(1).102.224, al. (Epid., iv B.C.). V. part of a water-wheel, PLond.3.1177.213 (ii A.D.). **-ώνιον**, τό, a kind of *salve*, Alex.Trall.1.10. **-ωνισμός**, ὁ, *punishment by the κύφων*, Sch.Ar.Pl.476. **-ωσις**, εως, ἡ, *being humpbacked*, Hp.Art.41, 47 (pl.), Gal.18(1).74.

**κύχραμος**, ὁ, a bird that migrates with quails, perhaps *corn-crake, Rallus crex*, or *water-rail, Rallus aquaticus*, Arist.HA597b17 (vv.ll. κέχραμος, κίχραμος).

**κυψάλη**, ἡ, = sq., PSI4.358.8 (iii B.C.).

❀ **κυψέλη**, ἡ, *any hollow vessel*: *chest, box* (whence Cypselus was called), Hdt.5.92.ε', Plu.2.164a, Paus.5.17.5; ἑξμέδιμνος κ., of *a corn-chest*, Ar.Pax631; *bee-hive*, Plu.2.601c: metaph., κυψελαὶ φρονημάτων *boxes* full of thoughts, Com.Adesp.703. II. *hollow of the ear*, Poll.2.85, Hsch.: hence, 2. = κυψελίς II, *ear-wax*, κυψέλην.. ἔχεις.. ἐν τοῖς ὠσίν, prov. of stupid men, Com.Adesp.620, cf. Eup.213, Alex.Aphr.Pr.2.63.

**Κυψελίδαι**, οἱ, *descendants of Cypselus*, Thgn.894, Hdt.6.128, Pl.Phdr.236b.

**κυψέλ-ιον**, τό, Dim. of κυψέλη I, *bee-hive*, Arist.HA627b2. **-ίς**, ίδος, ἡ, = foreg., of swallows' or sand-martins' nests, ib.618a34. II. *wax in the ears*, Ruf.Onom.223, Aret.SD1.15, Luc.Lex.1, Lib.Decl.26.35:—also **-ίτης** ῥύπος, ὁ, EM549.24.

**κυψελόβυστος**, ον, (βύω) *stopped up with wax*, ὦτα Luc.Lex.1.

❀ **κύψελος**, ὁ, = ἄπους II, Arist.HA618a31. 2. κύψελον· κύβερτον μελισσῶν, Hsch. II. = κυψελίς II, Tz.H.8.199.

❀ **κύω**, post-Hom. form of κυέω (aor. 1 in Ep., v. infr. II): I. in pres. and impf., of females, *conceive*, Λάβδα κύει τέξει δὲ κτλ. Orac.ap.Hdt.5.92.β', cf. Ar.Fr.609, Pl.Lg.789e, etc.; κύω μῆνα ὄγδοον ἤδη Luc.DMeretr.2.1; κ. ἀπό τινος Id.Gall.19: metaph., κύει πόλις ἥδε Thgn.39. 2. rarely c. acc., *to be pregnant with*, οὐδὲ κύουσι πολλὰ κυήματα Arist.HA543b22; παιδίον Luc.DMeretr.2.4: metaph., ἡ ψυχή μου ἀεὶ τοῦτο κύουσα (al. κυοῦσα) διῆγεν X.Cyr.5.4.35:—Pass., *to be born in the womb*, τὰ κυόμενα παιδία Arist.Pr.860a21, Jul.Or.2.99c. II. in aor. Act. ἔκῡσα, causal, of the male, *impregnate*, metaph., ὄμβρος ἔκυσε γαῖαν A.Fr.44.4:—aor. Med. ἐκῡσάμην, of the female, *conceive*, οὓς τέκε κυσαμένη Hes.Th.125, cf. 405, h.Hom.1.4; Ζηνί by Zeus, Asius Fr.Ep.1.3 K.; ὅσσους.. Τυφάονι κύσατο Κητώ Euph.112.—The forms κυέω and κύω seem synonymous, but κυέω (κυῶ) is the better-attested form in Att. Prose (κύοντα only v.l. in Pl. Tht.151b, κύοντες is read in Arist.HA544a23 (v.l. κύονες, ποιοῦντες), κύοντα ib.585a3, κυόμενα (v.l. -ούμενα) Pr. l.c., κυόμενον (v.l. -ούμενον) GA730b4, but κυοῦντες HA610b3; ἐκύομεν Lxx Is.59.13).—The pres. κύω has ῡ in verse, but forms of κυέω can be restored by altering the accent.—The causal sense belongs only to the aor. ἔκῡσα.

❀ **κύων** [ῠ], ὁ and ἡ, both in Hom., the masc. more freq., gen. κυνός, dat. κυνί, acc. κύνα, voc. κύον Il.8.423, κύων Archipp.6: pl., nom. κύνες, gen. κυνῶν, dat. κυσί Il.17.272, al., Ep. κύνεσσι 1.4, acc. κύνας:—*dog, bitch*, Hom., etc.; of *shepherds' dogs*, Il.10.183, 12.303; *watch-dogs*, 22.66; but in Hom. more freq. of *hounds*, Il.8.338, al.; κυσὶ θηρευτῇσι 11.325; κύνε εἰδότε θήρης 10.360; later, when of *hounds*, mostly in fem., S.Aj.8, E.Hipp.18, etc.; κ. Λάκαινα Pi.Fr.106, S.l.c., X.Cyn.10.1, cf. Arist.HA608a27, al.; Μολοττικαὶ κ. Alexis Hist.ap.Ath.12.540d, etc.; but Ἰνδικοί Arist.GA746a34, cf. Hdt.1.192: prov., κυσὶν πεινῶσιν οὐχὶ βρώσιμα 'not fit for a dog', Com.Adesp.1205.4; χεῖρον ἐρεθίσαι γραῦν ἢ κύνα Men.802; κύνα δέρειν δεδαρμένην 'flog a dead horse', Pherecr.179; ἡ κ. κατακειμένη ἐν τῇ φάτνῃ 'dog in the manger', Luc.Ind.30, al.; χαλεπὸν χορίῳ κύνα γεῦσαι it's ill to let a dog 'taste blood', Theoc.10.11; νὴ or μὰ τὸν κύνα was a favourite oath of Socrates, Pl.Ap.22a (cf. Sch.), Grg.482b; used familiarly at Athens, Ar.V.83; οἷς ἦν μέγιστος ὅρκος.. κύων, ἔπειτα χήν· θεοὺς δ' ἐσίγων, of primitive men, Cratin.231. II. as a word of reproach, freq. in Hom. of women, to denote shamelessness or audacity; applied by Helen to herself, Il.6.344, 356; by Iris to Athena, 8.423; by Hera to Artemis, 21.481: of the maids in the house of Odysseus, Od.18.338, al.: later, in a coarse sense, Ar.V.1402; ἡ ῥαψῳδὸς κ., of the Sphinx, S.OT391, cf. A.Fr.236 (lyr.); of men, κακαὶ κ. Il.13.623; implying recklessness, 8.299, 527, Od.17.248, 22.35; also of offensive persons, compared to yapping dogs, Lxx Ps.21(22).17, Ep.Phil.3.2; κ. λαίθαργος, = λαθροδήκτης, metaph., of a person, S.Fr.885, cf. E. Fr.555: prov., μὴ δῶτε τὸ ἅγιον τοῖς κ. Ev.Matt.7.6. 2. metaph., of persons, *watch-dog, guardian*, τῶν σταθμῶν κ., of Agamemnon, A. Ag.896; δωμάτων κ., of Clytemnestra, ib.607, cf. Ar.Eq.1023. 3. of the Cynics, ἀρέσκει τούτοις κυνῶν μεταμφιέννυσθαι βίον Phld.Sto.Herc. 339.8: hence, *Cynic philosopher*, Arist.Rh.1411a24, AP7.65 (Antip.), 413 (Id.), Plu.2.717c, Ath.5.216b, Epigr.ap.D.L.6.19, 60, Baillet *Inscriptions des tombeaux des rois* 172. III. freq. in Mythology of the *servants, agents* or *watchers* of the gods, Διὸς πτηνὸς κύων, of the eagle, A.Pr.1022, cf. Ag.136 (lyr.), S.Fr.884; of the griffins, Ζηνὸς ἀκραγεῖς κ. A.Pr.803; of the Furies, μετάδρομοι.. πανουργημάτων ἄφυκτοι κ. S.El.1388 (lyr.), cf. A.Ch.924, E.Fr.383; Pan is the κύων of Cybele, Pi.Fr.96: Pythag., Περσεφόνης κύνες, of the planets, Arist. Fr.196: so Com., Ἡφαίστου κ., of sparks, Alex.149.16; of various mythical beings, as Cerberus, κ. Ἀΐδαο Il.8.368, cf. Od.11.623, X. An.6.2.2; Harpies, A.R.2.289; of Hecate, in Mithraic worship, Porph.Abst.4.16; of the Βάκχαι, Λύσσας κ. E.Ba.977 (lyr.); Λέρνας κ., of the hydra, Id.HF420 (lyr.); of a great fish, Τρίτωνος κ. Lyc. 34. IV. *dog-fish* or *shark*, Od.12.96, cf. Epich.68, Cratin.161, Arist.HA566a31; κ. ἄγριος, κ. γαλεός and κ. κεντρίτης or κεντρίνη, Opp.H.1.373, Ael.NA1.55; ξιφίας κ., of the *sword-fish*, Anaxipp. 2.3. V. = σείριος (q.v.), *dog-star*, i.e. *the hound of Orion*, Il.22. 29; in full, σειρίου κυνὸς δίκην S.Fr.803, cf. A.Ag.967; κυνὸς ψυχρὰν δύσιν S.Fr.432.11; πρὸ τοῦ κυνός Eup.147; μετὰ κυνὸς ἐπιτολήν, περὶ κ. ἐ., Arist.Mete.361b35, HA602a26; ἐπὶ κυνὶ ib.600a4, Syngr.ap.D. 35.13; ὑπὸ κύνα Arist.HA547a14, D.S.19.109; περὶ κύνα Thphr.CP 3.3.3; μετὰ κύνα Id.HP1.9.5; also of the whole constellation, Arat. 327, Gal.17(1).17. VI. *the ace, the worst throw* at dice, Poll.9.100, Eust.1289.63. VII. *frenum praeputii*, Antyll.ap.Orib.50.3.1: with pun on the prov. ap.Pherecr. l.c. (supr. 1), Ar.Lys.158: with pun on signf. v, AP5.104 (Marc. Arg.). VIII. *fetlock of a horse*, Hippiatr. 77. IX. *unilateral facial paralysis*, Gal.8.573. X. = ἀπομαγδαλία, Dsc.ap.Eust.1857.19. XI. ξυλίνη κ., = κυνόσβατος, Orac.ap.Did ap.Ath.2.70c. XII. *piece in the game of* πόλεις, Cratin.56.3 (dub.). (Cf. Skt. śvā, gen. śúnas, Lith. šuõ, gen. šuñs, Lat. canis, Goth. hunds (κύων), etc.)

**κω**, v. πω. **κῷα**, v. Κῷος III. 3. **κωαί**· ἀστράγαλοι, Hsch. (ante κώϊον, fort. κῷα). **κωάζω**, = ἀστραγαλίζω, Id. 2. = ἐνεχυράζω, Id. (also in form κοιάζω).

**Κῳακός**, ή, όν, *of Cos*: Κῳακαὶ προγνώσιες or αἱ Κῳακαί, title of work by Hippocrates of Cos.

❀ **κῶας**, τό, in Hom. nom. acc. sg. κῶας; pl. κώεα, dat. κώεσι; later contr. κῶς (q.v.):—*fleece*, στόρεσαν λέχος,.. κῶεά τε ῥῆγός τε Il.9.661, cf. Od.23.180; ἀδέψητον βοέην στόρεσ', αὐτὰρ ὕπερθε κώεα πόλλ' οἴων 20.3, cf. 142; χεῦεν ὑπὸ χλωρὰς ῥῶπας καὶ κῶας ὕπερθεν 16.47; φέρε δὴ δίφρον καὶ κῶας ἐπ' αὐτοῦ 19.97; ἵδρυσεν παρὰ δαιτὶ κώεσιν ἐν μαλακοῖσι 3.38, cf. 17.32; of the *Golden Fleece*, κ. αἰγλᾶεν χρυσέῳ θυσάνῳ Pi.P.4. 231; ἔπλεον ἐπὶ τὸ κ. ἐς Αἶαν Hdt.7.193; μέγα κ. Mimn.11.1; τὸ χρύσειον κ. Theoc.13.16.—Cf. κῴδιον.

❀ **κωβάθια**, τά, *arsenical sulphides of cobalt*, Ps.-Democr.Alch.p.51 B. (κοβ-), Zos.Alch.p.188 B. (κωβ-, v.l. κοβ-):—hence **κωβαθηκαύστης**, ου, ὁ, 'arsenic-burner', applied to Nilus, ib.190 B. (vv.ll. κωβατικ-, κωβαθιοκ ).

**κώβαλοι**, οἱ, *pomegranate flowers*, Hsch. **κῶβαξ**· ὁ μέγας τέττιξ, Id. **κωβάριον**, *globus*, Gloss. **κωβήλη**, ἡ, *needle*, Hsch. II. *sexual intercourse*, Id., Phot. **κωβηλίνη**, ἡ, (foreg. I) *needlewoman*, Hsch. **κωβιδάριον**, v. κωθάριον.

**κωβίδιον**, τό, Dim. of sq., Anaxandr.27.4, Sotad.Com.1.22, Arist. *Fr.*309. [–βῐ– Anaxandr. l.c. (anap., s.v.l.), but –βῑ– Sotad. l.c. (iamb.).]

**κωβιός**, ὁ, a fish of the *gudgeon* kind, Semon.15, Epich.66, Hp. *Int.*21, Pl.*Euthd.*298d, Antiph.26.19, Men.*Kol.Fr.*7. II. = τιθύμαλλος χαρακίας, Dsc.4.164; = τ. δενδροειδής, Plin.*HN*26.71.

**κωβῖτις**, ιδος, ἡ, *like the gudgeon*, ἀφύη Arist.*HA*569$^b$23, cf. Hices. ap Ath.7.285b.

**κωβιώδης**, ες, *like a* κωβιός, Plu.2.980f.

**κῳδάριον** [ᾰ], τό, Dim. of κῴδιον, Cratin.41, Ar.*Ra.*1203, Anaxandr. 34.11.

**κωδᾶς**, ᾶτος, ὁ, *dealer in sheepskins*, *POxy.*1519.4 (iii A.D.).

**κώδεα**, v. sq. II.

**κώδεια**, ἡ, *head*, ὁ δὲ φῆ, κώδειαν ἀνασχών Il.14.499; of plants, *head*, e.g. of garlic, *bulb*, Nic.*Al.*432; of the poppy, *capsule*, Gal. 12.73:—also **κωδία**, ἡ, dub. in Ar.*Fr.*117 (κώδυα Harp. Epit., κώδεια Suid.), f.l. for κώδεια in Poll.2.38, for κωδύα in Dsc.4.63 (pl.), Orib. 11 s.v. μικρὰ μήκων, for κώδυια in Arist.*Pr.*914$^b$7; **κώδειον** or –ιον, *Gloss.* (cf. **κώδυον**); **κωδίς**, Hsch.; cf. κωδύα, κώδων II. II. *cup shaped like a poppy-head*, in form **κώδεα**, *Inscr.Délos* 298*A* 169 (pl.), 300*B* 13 (iii B.C.).

**κῴδιο**, barbarism for sq., Ar.*Th.*1180.

***κῴδιον**, τό, Dim. of κῶας, *sheepskin*, *fleece*, Ar.*Eq.*400, *Ra.*1478, Pl. *Prt.*315d, Men.*Sam.*189, *IG*1$^2$.80.17, 11(2).287*A* 24 (Delos, iii B.C.), *PPetr.*2 p.108 (iii B.C.), etc.; of the *Golden Fleece*, Luc.*Gall.*1. II. Δῖον κ. ram's *fleece* used in purificatory ceremonies, Polem.Hist.87, 88.

**κῳδιοφόρος**, ον, *clad in sheepskin*, Str.17.2.3.

**κωδύα**, ἡ, *head*, i.e. *capsule*, of the poppy, Thphr.*HP*9.12.4, Damocr.ap.Gal.13.40, Dsc.4.63 (v.l. –ίαις), 64, Sor.1.120 (τῇ διακωδίων cod.), Ruf.*Ren.Ves.*1.15; imitated as an ornament of ἧλοι, *IG* 2$^2$.1457.14, 1544.38, al.; *head*, i.e. *fruit*, of the Nile water-lily, *Nymphaea stellata*, Thphr.*HP*4.8.10; of the Egyptian bean, *Nelumbium speciosum*, ib.7. [κωδύᾱ acc. to Hdn.Gr.1.302, and so in Damocr. l.c., but κώδυα in Ar.*Fr.*117 ap.Harp.Epit., Phot., cf. sq.]

**κώδυια**, ἡ, *head*: hence, *bulb*, *cup* of the κλεψύδρα, Arist.*Pr.*914$^b$ 27 (vv.ll. κωδύαν, κωδίαν: these forms, as well as κώδεια (q.v.), are prob. derived from κώδυια).

**κώδυον**, τό, *head*, i.e. *inflorescence*, of purse-tassels, *Muscari comosum*, Thphr.*HP*6.8.1. (From κωδύα as κάρυον from καρύα, etc.)

***κώδων**, ωνος, ὁ (Att. ἡ S.*Aj.*17, dub. in Ar.*Pax* 1078), *bell*, ὑπ' ἀσπίδος δὲ τῷ χαλκήλατοι κλάζουσι κ. φόνον A.*Th.*386, cf. 399, E.*Rh.*308; χαλκοστόμου κώδωνος ὡς Τυρσηνικῆς, i.e. a trumpet, S. l.c. (where Sch. expl. κώδων as τὸ πλατὺ τῆς σάλπιγγος, i.e. the *mouth* of the trumpet, cf. Ath.5.185a, Poll.2.203); carried on rounds of inspection to challenge sentries, τοῦ κώδωνος παρενεχθέντος Th.4.135; ἐφοδεύειν κώδωνι Plu.*Arat.*7, cf. Luc.*Merc.Cond.*24, Sch.Ar.*Av.*843. 2. *crier's bell*, hence ταῦθ' οὗτος μόνον οὐ κώδωνας ἐξαψάμενος διαπράττεται 'is his own trumpeter', D.25.90: metaph., ἡ κ. ἀκαλανθίς (ὅτι λάλον τὸ ζῷον Sch.) Ar.*Pax* 1078 (perh. κύων is the true reading, v. *App. Prov.*1.12); cf. κρόταλον. II. = κωδύα, τῆς μήκωνος Dieuch.ap. Orib.4.6.2.

**κωδων-ίζω**, *try*, *prove by ringing*, of money, Ar.*Ra.*723 (Pass.); ὅ τι ποιεῖ κ. ib.79: metaph., βούλομαι κωδωνίσας πέμψαι σε Anaxandr. 15.5:—wrongly expld. by Hsch. from the challenging of sentries (cf. κώδων I. 1). II. Pass., *to have one's name noised abroad*, *EM* 325.21. –ιον, τό, Dim. of κώδων, J.*AJ*3.7.4, Phlp. *in de An.*356. 20, prob. in *BGU*162.10 (ii/iii A.D.). cf. Hdn.*Epim.*71.

**κωδωνό-κροτος**, ον, *of* or *with jingling bells*, σάκος S.*Fr.*859 (lyr.); κ. κόμποι E.*Rh.*383 (anap.). –**φᾰλᾰρόπωλος**, ον, *with jingling harness*, coined by Ar.*Ra.*963, as a parody on Aeschylus. –**φορέω**, *carry the bell round*, *inspect sentinels*, Ar.*Av.*842, Nicopho 26, D.C.54. 4:—Pass., ἅπαντα κωδωνοφορεῖται Ar.*Av.*1160. 2. of a ship, *carry a bell*, Philostr.*VA*3.57. II. Pass., of a king, *to be attended by men with bells*, Str.15.1.58.

**κῶθα**· ποτήρια, Hsch.

**κωθάριον**, τό, Dim. of sq., cj. in Anaxandr.27.3 (κωβῖδαρίων codd.).

**κῶθος**, ὁ, Sicel name for κωβιός, Numen.ap.Ath.7.304e, 309c.

**κωθύλους**· ὄνους, Hsch.

***κώθων**, ωνος, ὁ, *Laconian drinking-vessel*, used by soldiers, Archil. 4, Ar.*Eq.*600, X.*Cyr.*1.2.8, Critias 34 D., *IG*2$^2$.47.6, etc.; κ. στρεψαύχην Theopomp.Com.54; πυριγενής Henioch.1; φαεινός Ar.*Pax* 1094 (parod.); of earthenware or metal, *IG*4$^2$(1).121.79, al. (Epid.), Ath.11.483b, c: κ. χαλκοῖ *IG*1$^2$.313.55, al., cf. 2$^2$.1425.393. II. *drinking bout*, *carousal*, εἰσῆλθεν ἐπὶ κώθωνα πρὸς τὸν βασιλέα Macho ap.Ath.13.583b, cf. Plu.*Ant.*4, etc.; *religious banquet*, *BCH*51.220 (Thasos). III. Sicel, = κῶθος, Nic.*Fr.*141, Apollod.ap.Ath.7. 309c. IV. the inner harbour at Carthage, Str.17.3.15, App.*Pun.* 127.

**κωθων-ία**, Ion. –ίη, ἡ, *deep potation* (not of wine), Aret.*SD*2. 13. –**ίζω**, *make drunken*, Hsch., Phot.:—Pass., *drink hard*, κ. ταῖς μεγάλαις (sc. κύλιξι) Arist.*Pr.*872$^b$28, cf. Lxx *Es.*3.15, Mnesith. ap.Ath.11.484a, Phylarch.1 J., Gal.*UP*4.13; κ. ἀφ' ἡμέρας, *de die potare*, Plb.23.5.9; κεκωθωνισμένος *inebriated*, Eub.126, cf. *PSI*5.172. 23 (ii B.C.). –**ιον**, τό, Dim. of κώθων, *AJA*31.350 (vase, v B.C.), *IG* 7.303.56 (Oropus), *PMag.Par.*1.2952, *Gp.*20.10. –**ισμός**, ὁ, *tippling*, Arist.*Pr.*863$^b$25, Mnesith.ap.Ath.11.484a (pl.). –**ιστήριον**, τό, *banqueting house*, D.S.5.19. *–**ιστής**, οῦ, ὁ, *toper*, Ath.10. 433b.

**κωθωνο-ειδής**, ές, *like a* κώθων, Suid. s.v. προχόῳ. –**πλύτης** [ῠ], ου, ὁ, *one who cleans the fish* κώθων, Sophr.45. –**ποιός**, ὁ, *κώθων-maker*, Dinarch.*Fr.*89.19. –**χειλος**, ον, *with the lip* or *rim of a* κώθων, κύλιξ Eub.56.3 (–χειρος codd.).

**Κώϊος**, α, ον, contr. Κῷος (q.v.).

**κώκαλον**· παλαιόν, καὶ εἶδος ἀλεκτρυόνος, Hsch.

**κώκ-ῡμα**, ατος, τό, *shriek*, *wail*, in pl., λιγέα κ. A.*Pers.*332; ὀξέα S. *Aj.*321; ὄρθια Id.*Ant.*1206. –**ῡτίς**, ίδος, ἡ, *born from Cocytus*, Νύμφη Opp.*H.*3.487. –**ῡτός**, ὁ, *shrieking*, *wailing*, κωκυτῷ τ' εἴχοντο καὶ οἰμωγῇ Il.22.409, cf. 447, Pi.*P.*4.113, A.*Ch.*150 (pl.); κωκυτὸν ἱέναι, ἠχεῖν, S.*Aj.*851, *Tr.*867; ἀνάγειν E.*Ph.*1350 (lyr.): also in late Prose, Luc.*Luct.*12, Ach.Tat.1.13. II. as pr. n. Κωκῡτός, ὁ, *Cocytus*, *River of Wailing* (cf. Ἀχέρων), Od.10.514, A.*Ag.*1160, E.*Alc.* 458 (lyr.), etc. –**ύω** [v. fin.], fut. –ύσω A.*Ag.*1313, –ύσομαι Ar.*Lys.* 1222: aor. ἐκώκῡσα S.*Ant.*28; Ep. κώκυσα Il.18.37:—Med., *AP*7.412 (Alc. Mess.):—*shriek*, *wail*, in Ep. and Trag. always of women, Il.18. 37, Od.2.361, etc.; κλαῖον καὶ ἐκώκυον 19.541: freq. with Adv., λίγ' ἐκώκυε Il.19.284, cf. Od.4.259, etc.; ὀξὺ δὲ κωκύσασα (opp. βαρὺ στενάχων, of the man) Il.18.71; κώκυσεν δὲ μάλα μέγα 22.407: also in late Prose, Plu.2.357c, etc.; even of men, Luc.*DMort.*21.1, Longus 2.21; and so Ar., as an execration, μακρὰ κωκύειν κελεύω σε *Ra.*34; οἰμώζοι γ' ἂν καὶ κωκύοι *Ec.*648. 2. c. acc., *lament* or *shriek over* one dead, also prop. of women, κώκυσ' ἐν λεχέεσσιν ἑὸν πόσιν Od.24. 295; ἐμὴν μοῖραν κ. A.*Ag.*1313, cf. S.*Ant.*28, al.: Com., of men, κωκύσεσθε τὰς τρίχας μακρά Ar.*Lys.*1222: also in late Prose, as Porph.*Abst.*4.9, etc. (Cf. Skt. *kāuti* 'cry' (intens. *kokūyate*), Lith. *kaũkti* 'shriek', etc.) [ῠ in Hom. before a vowel, ῡ before a conson. (v. supr.): later ῡ sts. before a vowel, κωκῡοι Ar.*Ec.* l.c., κωκῡουσα Bion 1.23, Q.S.3.779, κωκῡεσκε ib.460.]

**κωλαβοί**· λάσταυροι, Hsch.

**κωλακρετ-έω**, *to be a* κωλακρέτης, *IG*1$^2$.25.9: aor. 1 ἐκωλακρέτησαν *CIG*3660 (Cyzicus). *–**ης**, ου, ὁ, name of a financial official in early Athens and elsewhere (cf. foreg.), *IG*1$^2$.19.13, al., Arist.*Ath.* 7.3, Ar.*V.*695, *Av.*1541; κωλακρέτου γάλα, comically for the μισθὸς δικαστικός, Id.*V.*724. (Written κωλαγρ– in Cod. Rav. of Ar., Tim. *Lex.*; derivation from κωλᾶς ἀγρεῖν or ἀγείρειν perh. implied by Suid. s.v. κωλακρέτης.)

**κωλανιζόμενοι**· τάχει χρώμενοι, ἀνέμοις ἴσα, Hsch. **κωλαρίας**· τοὺς ἐκ τῆς ἀγέλης παῖδας, Id. (Fort. κωραλίας.)

**κωλάριον**, τό, Dim. of κῶλον, *fragment of a verse*, *hemistich*, Ael. Dion.*Fr.*168, Sch.Ar.*Pax* 179.

**κωλέα**, ἡ, = κωλῆ (q.v.); also expld. by ἀγκαλίς, δέσμη χόρτου, Hsch. **κώλειρ**, *prize given in a contest*, Id. ***κωλεός**, ὁ, = κωλῆ, Epich.82, 92, Hp.ap.Gal.19.116. **κωλετίναις** (–τήν– cod.)· ἀσκαλαβώταις, Hsch.

***κωλῆ**, ἡ, contr. from κωλέα, which occurs in Anaxipp.1.38, Lxx 1*Ki.*9.24: κωλία (v. κωλίαν) is a dialectal form: (κῶλον):—*thighbone with the flesh on it*, *ham*, esp. of a swine, Ar.*Pl.*1128, *Fr.*224, X. *Cyn.*50.30, Pl.Com.17 (pl.), Amips.7; ἐρίφου Xenoph.6.1; βοὸς κ. Luc.*Lex.*6; the portion of the priestess at a sacrifice, *IG*2$^2$.1361.5, *SIG*1015.10 (Halic.), etc. II. *membrum virile*, Ar.*Nu.*989, 1019.

**κωλήβη**· μήποτε ὁ λάσταυρος· κώληβοι γὰρ οἱ ταῖροι, Phot.

**κωλήν**, ῆνος, ἡ, = κωλῆ, *thigh*, *leg*, κωλῆνες νεβρῶν E.*Fr.*677, cf. Eup.47; κ. ὑείων κρεῶν *hams*, Hp.*Epid.*7.62: in pl., *bones of the leg*, Arist.*HA*516$^b$1:—Dim. **κωληνάριον**, τό, Sch.Ar.*Pl.*1129.

**κώληξ**, ηκος, ὁ, = sq., Sch.Ar.*Pl.*1129.

**κώληψ**, ηπος, ἡ, (κωλῆ) *hollow of the knee*, = ἰγνύα, Il.23.726, Nic. *Th.*424.

**κωλίαν**· ἰγνύαν κτλ., Hsch.

**Κωλιάς** (sc. ἄκρα), άδος, ἡ, *Colias*, a promontory of Attica, Hdt.8. 96; with a temple of Aphrodite, St.Byz.: hence, as epith. of the goddess, Ar.*Nu.*52, *Lys.*2; Κωλιάδες γυναῖκες Orac.ap.Hdt. l.c. 2. (sc. γῆ), *potter's clay* of high repute, *dug at Colias*, Plu.2.42d.

***κωλίζω**, in Pass., *to be arranged according to* κῶλα, τὰ κεκωλισμένα βιβλία Olymp.Hist.p.463 D.; esp. of poetical works, *to be arranged according to metrical* κῶλα, Ar.Cod.Ven.Subscr.

**κωλῐκ-εύομαι**, Pass., *suffer from colic*, Alex.Aphr.*Pr.*2.72, Alex. Trall.8.2. –**ός**, ή, όν, (κῶλον II. 6) *suffering in the colon*, *having colic*, prob. l. in Dsc.2.54, Gal.8.40; ἡ κ. διάθεσις *colic*, from its being seated in the colon and parts adjacent, Id.8.384; κ. φάρμακα remedies *for colic*, Id.13.266; κ. ἀντίδοτος Androm.ap.eund.13.276. Adv. –κῶς Gal.19.3.

**κωλοβαθρ-ιστής**, οῦ, ὁ, *one that goes on stilts*, Hsch. s.v. καδαλίων. –**ον**, τό, *stilt*, Artem.3.15 (v.l. καλ–).

***κωλο-ειδής**, ές, *in members*. Adv. –δῶς Sopat.in Rh.8.9 W. –**μετρία**, ἡ, (κῶλον II. 4) *measurement of metrical phrases*, Suid. s.v. Εὐγένιος.

***κῶλον**, τό, *limb*, *member* of a body, esp. *leg*, A.*Pr.*325, S.*OC*183 (lyr.), *Ph.*42, etc.; δρομάδι κ. E.*Hel.*1301 (lyr.); κ. ταχύπουν Id.*Ba.*168 (lyr.): mostly in pl., A.*Pr.*81, S.*OC*19; χεῖρες καὶ κῶλα E.*Ph.*1185: generally, of *arms* and *legs*, and of animals, *fore* and *hind legs*, τὰ ἐμπρόσθια κ. Pl.*Ti.*91e; τὰ ἔμπροσθεν καὶ τὰ ὄπισθεν κ. Arist.*HA*498$^a$ 3, cf. *PA*690$^a$20, etc.; δέρμα, τρίχας, ὄνυχάς τε ἐπ' ἄκροις τοῖς κώλοις ἔφυσαν Pl.*Ti.*76e. 2. = κωλῆ I, A.*Pr.*496. 3. of plants, *limb*, *arm*, σκολιῆς ἄγρια κ. βάτου *AP*7.315 (Zenod. or Rhian.): in pl., also, *internodes* of the νάρθηξ, Corn.*ND*30. II. generally, *member*, 1. of a building, *side* or *front*, of a square or triangular building, Hdt.2.126, 134, 4.62, 108, Pl.*Lg.*947e. b. *upright* of a ladder, Apollod.*Poliorc.* 182.5, al. 2. *limb* or *lap of the race-course*, διαύλου θάτερον κ. A.

*Ag.*344. 3. Rhet., *member* or *clause of a* περίοδος, Arist.*Rh.*1409ᵇ 13, Phld.*Rh.*1.165 S., D.H.*Comp.*22, Quint.9.4.22, Demetr.*Eloc.*1, Hermog.*Id.*1.3, 2.3; στίζομεν κατὰ κῶλον Castor in Rh.3.721 W.; διελὼν πρὸς κῶλον, of Origen in his Hexapla, Eus.*HE*6.16. 4. in verse, *metrical unit containing fewer than three* συζυγίαι *without catalexis*, Heph.*Poëm.*1; *element of a* στροφή, D.H.*Comp.*19, etc. 5. ῥινοῦ εὔστροφα κ., poet. for *a sling*, *AP*7.172 (Antip. Sid.). 6. incorrect form for κόλον (q. v.), Isid.*Etym.*4.7.38, etc.; cf. κωλικός.

**κωλο-πλάστης**, ου, ὁ, *manufacturer of artificial limbs* (as votive offerings), *PGiss.*20.20 (ii A. D.). **-τομέω**, prop. *cut off limbs*: generally, *cut* or *mow down*, Δημήτερα Epic.ap.Plu.2.377d.

**κώλ-ῡμα**, ατος, τό, *hindrance*, τί γὰρ ἐμπόδιον κ. ἔτι μοι; E.*Ion* 862 (anap.); κ. θεῶν ἢ ἡρώων Th.5.30; βασιλικὸν κ. *PFrankf.*1.100 (iii B.C.): pl., κωλύματα καὶ βλάβαι D.H.9.9: c. inf., *hindrance against*, ἅμαξα κ. οὖσα προσθεῖναι [τὰς πύλας] Th.4.67; κωλύματα μὴ αὐξηθῆναι [τὸ Ἑλληνικόν] Id.1.16: c. gen., κ. φορᾶς *impediment* to motion, Pl.*Cra.*418e; ἐνεργείας Ocell.4.12: c. dat., [τῷ αἵματι] Hp.*Flat.*8: κ. καὶ σῖνος πρὸς εὐκαρπίαν Thphr.*CP*2.7.5. II. *defence against* a thing, σβεστήρια κ. Th.7.53: c. gen., κ. δηλητηρίων Hdn.1.17.10. **-ῡμάτιον**, τό, Dim. of foreg., *catch* or *clutch* in a machine, Hero *Spir.*1.17, al. **-ύμη** [ῡ], ἡ, = κώλυμα, ἐπὶ κωλύμῃ for the purpose of *hindering*, Th.1.92; ταῖς κ. ταύταις ἱκανῶς.. εἰρχθῆναι by these *impediments*, Id.4.63; a poetical word in Th., cf. D.H.*Amm.*2.3.

**κωλυπηγορέω**, *talk grandly* or *at random*. πρὸς τὸ παρὸν δόξης ἕνεκεν τῆς οἰκείας f.l. in Sever.*Clyst.*p.43 D. (κυλικηγορoῦμεν cj. Dietz).

**κωλῡσ-ανέμας**, ου, ὁ, or **-άνεμος**, ὁ, *checking the winds*, epith. of Empedocles, Timae.94, Suid. s. v. Ἐμπεδοκλῆς; cf. ἀλεξάνεμος.

**κωλῡσί-δειπνος** [ῐ], ον, *interrupting the banquet*, applied to a species of κοχλίας, Apollod.ap.Ath.2.63d, cf. Plu.2.726a. **-δρόμης**, ου, ὁ, *one who obstructs the course*, Luc.*Trag.*198. **-εργέω**, *hinder, obstruct operations*, Plb.6.15.5, Ph.1.64,240, J.*AJ*15.11.7. **-εργός**, όν, *hindering from work*, τοῦ φιλοσοφεῖν Iamb.*Protr.*21.κβ'.

⊛**κώλῡ-σις**, εως, ἡ, *prevention*, ἕνεκα κωλύσεως Pl.*Sph.*220c; κωλύσεις τῶν συμπερασμάτων Arist.*Top.*161ᵃ15, cf. Phld.*Mort.*19; εἰς κώλυσιν μὴ ἐντελὲς τὸ κράτος εἶναι App.*BC*1.1: in Astrol. sense, Vett. Val.142.24 (pl.). **-τέον**, *one must hinder*, X.*Hier.*8.9, Gal.10.649, al. 2. **-τέος**, α, ον, *to be hindered* or *stopped*, Hp.*Art.*58, D.H.10.40. **-τήρ**, ῆρος, ὁ, = κωλυτής, τῶν ἀδικούντων Archyt.3; θεοὶ.. τῶν κακῶν κ. Porph.ap.Eus.*PE*4.9; ἀριθμὸς κ. τῶν περαιτέρω ἐπιμορίων Iamb.*in Nic.*p.52 P. ⊛**-τήριος**, α, ον, *preventive*, σημεῖα κ. τινός *of*.., D.H.11.62; θῦσαι τὰ κωλυτήρια (sc. ἱερά) Iamb.*VP*28.141, Apollon.*Mir.*4: as Subst. **κωλυτήριον**, τό, παρατριμμάτων Dsc.1.103. **-τής**, οῦ, ὁ, *hinderer*, τῆς διαβάσεως Th.3.23, cf. D.18.72; πηλὸν.. κωλυτὴν παρασχεῖν Pl.*Criti.*109a: abs., *OGI*5.7 (Scepsis, iv B.C.), Vett. Val.139.19. **-τικός**, ή, όν, *preventive*, τινος *of* a thing, X.*Mem.*4.5.7 (Comp.), Arist.*Rh.*1362ᵃ29, *EN*1096ᵇ12, Thphr.*Ign.*45, Epicur.*Ep.*2 p.52 U., Porph.*Abst.*2.47: abs., in Astrol., ἀστὴρ ἄπρακτος καὶ κ. Vett.Val.178.30. **-τός**, ή, όν, *to be hindered*, Arr.*Epict.*2.5.8, al.; ὑπό τινος ib.1.17.27.

**κωλύφιον**, τό, Dim. of κωλῆν, condemned by Phryn.60: Lat. *colyphium*, Plaut.*Pers.*92 (pl.), Juv.2.53 (pl.), etc.

⊛**κωλύω**, fut. -ύσω Ar.*Nu.*1448: aor. ἐκώλῡσα E.*Alc.*897 (anap.), Pl.*Mx.*244c: pf. κεκώλῡκα Din.1.101, Phld.*Rh.*2.63 S.:—Pass., fut. κωλυθήσομαι Lxx *Si.*20.2(1), Luc.*VH*2.25: also in med. form -ύσομαι Th.1.142: aor. ἐκωλύθην Id.2.64, etc.: pf. κεκώλῡμαι ib.37. [ῡ always before a conson.: common before a vowel, κωλῡόμεσθα E.*Ion* 391, κωλῡέτω Id.*Ph.*990, κώλῡεν Pi.*P.*4.33, κώλῡει Alc.55 (= Sapph.22 Lobel), Ar.*Eq.*(v. infr.), *Fr.*100, Anaxil.25, Men.*Epit.*10.]:—*hinder, prevent*:—Constr.: 1. c. acc. et inf., κ. ἐκρέειν τὸν Νεῖλον Hdt.2.20; κώλυεν [μιν] μεῖναι Pi. l. c.; τί δῆτα καὶ σὲ κωλύει ⟨λαβεῖν⟩ κέρδος; E.*Fr.*794, cf. *IT*507, etc.; ὅς σε κ. τὸ δρᾶν S.*Ph.*1241; φεύγειν οὐδεὶς κ. νόμος D.23.52: with neg. added (rare in Att. Prose), κ. τινὰ μὴ θανεῖν E.*Ph.*1268; μὴ προσεύχεσθαι X.*HG*3.2.22, etc.:—Pass., χρημάτων σπάνει Th.1.142; τοῦ ὕδατος πιεῖν *from* drinking the water, Pl.*R.*621b; κωλυόμεσθα μὴ μαθεῖν E.*Ion*391; μὴ οὐ πονηρὸν εἶναι D.H.2.3. b. rarely c. part. pro inf., κ. τινὰ πόλεμον εἰσάγοντα Id.7.25:—Pass., μὴ κωλύοντας περαιούμενοι Th.1.26. c. with relat. clause, κωλύειν εἴ τις ἐπαγγέλλεται, = τινὰ μὴ ἐπαγγέλλεσθαι, D.4.15; ἐκωλύσαμεν, ἵνα γένησθε.. J.*BJ*6.6.2. 2. c. gen. rei, κ. τινά τινος *hinder* one *from* a thing, X.*HG*3.2.21, *An.*1.6.2, etc.; κ. τινὰ ἀπό τινος Id.*Cyr.*1.3.11, 3.3.51:—Pass., τῆς ὁρμῆς ἐκωλύθησαν Plb.6.55.3. 3. c. acc. rei, *prevent*, E.*IA*1390 (troch.), X.*An.*4.2.24:—Pass., ἐν τούτῳ κεκωλῦσθαι ἐδόκει τὰ πράγματα Th.2.8, cf. 4.14; ταῦτα.. μὴ ἐν ὑμῖν κωλυθῇ Id.2.64; μηδὲ.. δαπάνῃ κεκωλύσθω *let there be no hindrance* by reason of expense, Id.1.129. b. *withhold*, τι ἀπό τινος Lxx *Ge.*23.6, *Ev.Luc.*6.29. 4. c. acc. pers., *hinder*, Th.1.35; τοὺς δρῶντας μοχθηρὰ Arist.*EN*1113ᵇ26. 5. abs., οὐδ' ὁ κωλύσων παρῆν S.*Ant.*261, cf. *El.*1197; εἶτ' οἱ κωλύουσιν Ar.*Pax*499; of the tribune's *intercessio*, Plu.*TG*10; τὸ κωλῦον *hindrance*, X.*An.*4.5.20, D.1.12: freq. an inf. may be supplied, εἶτα τίς σε κωλύει (sc. γεωργεῖν); Ar.*Fr.*100; αὐτοὶ ὠφελούμενοι τοὺς πολεμίους κωλύσετε [ὠφελεῖσθαι] Th.6.91, cf. 2.37 (Pass.). 6. freq. in 3 pers., οὐδὲν κωλύει *there is* nothing *to hinder*, c. acc. et inf., ὁμόφημον τὸν Ἀργεῖον εἶναι κ. οὐδέν Hdt.7.149; οὐδέν σε κωλύσει σεαυτὸν ἐμβαλεῖν ἐς τὸ βάραθρον Ar.*Nu.*1448, cf. Pl.*Phdr.*268e; ὃν διαμάττειν οὐ κ. Ar.*Av.*463; τί κ. ἡμᾶς διελθεῖν; Pl.*Tht.*143a, etc.; οὐδὲν κ., abs., as a form of assent, *be it so*, Ar.*Eq.*723, 972, Pl.*Euthd.*272d, etc.; τί γὰρ κ.; Id.*Euthphr.*9d, cf. *Plt.*292a, al.; τό γ' ἐμὸν οὐδὲν κ. Id.*Grg.*458d; μὴ τὸ σὸν κωλυέτω E.*Ph.*990; οὐ τἀμὰ κωλύσει Plu.2.151c, etc.; οὔτε ἐκεῖνο κωλύει ἐν ταῖς σπονδαῖς neither *is* that *any hindrance*, Th.1.144 (wrongly expld. as = κωλύεται by D.H.*Amm.*2.7); οὔτε μίαν δυοῖν τὴν αὐτὴν εἶναι κ. nor *is there any hindrance* to one of two being the same, Arist.*Ph.*202ᵇ9.

**κωλώτης**, ου, ὁ, = ἀσκαλαβώτης, Arist.*HA*609ᵇ19, Babr.204, Hsch.; epith. of Dionysus, Suid.

**κωλωτοειδής**, ές, *shaped like a lizard*, Hp.*Epid.*4.56.

⊛**κῶμα**, ατος, τό, (perh. cogn. with κεῖμαι, κοιμάω) *deep sleep*, αὐτῷ.. μαλακὸν περὶ κῶμα κάλυψα Il.14.359; ἥ με.. μαλακὸν περὶ κῶμ' ἐκάλυψεν Od.18.201; κακὸν δέ ἑ κῶμα καλύπτει Hes.*Th.*798; αἰθυσσομένων δὲ φύλλων κ. κατάρρει Sapph.4; ὕπνου κ. Theoc.*Ep.*3.6: metaph., of the effect of music, Pi.*P.*1.12.—Not in Trag. 2. Medic., *lethargic state, coma*, κῶμα συνεχές, οὐχ ὑπνῶδες Hp.*Epid.*3.6, cf. Gal.7.643, Sch.Nic.*Al.*458.

**κωμάδιος** [ᾰ], α, ον, *of a* κῶμος, Sch.D.T.p.542 H.

**κωμάζω**, fut. -άσω [ᾰ] Pi.*N.*9.1, -άσομαι Id.*P.*9.89, *AP*5.63 (Asclep.), Luc.*Luct.*13; Dor. -άξομαι Pi.*I.*4(3).72: aor. ἐκώμᾰσα E.*HF* 180; poet. κώμ- Pi.*N.*10.35; Dor. imper. -άξατε ib.2.24: pf. κεκώμᾰκα *AP*5.111 (Phld.): (κῶμος):—*revel, make merry*, νέοι κώμαζον ὑπ' αὐλοῦ Hes.*Sc.*281; κωμάζοντα μετ' αὐλητῆρος ἀείδειν Thgn.1065, cf. S.*Fr.*764, E.*Alc.*815, etc.; κ. μετὰ μέθης Pl.*Lg.*637a; κ. καὶ παιωνίζειν D.18.287; ὀρχούμενος καὶ κ. Theopomp.Hist.153; κ. μεθ' ἡμέραν Lys.14.25, Phld.*Acad.Ind.*p.47 M.; *go in festal procession*, Σικυωνόθεν εἰς Αἴτναν Pi.*N.*9.1; ὃς ἐν ταῖς πομπαῖς ἄνευ τοῦ προσώπου κ. D.19.287: metaph., νήσους κώμασον εἰς μακάρων Call.*Epigr.* in *Berl.Sitzb.*1912.548; esp. in Egypt, *take part in religious processions*, *PGnom.*200, 214 (ii A. D.): hence trans., *carry* images, etc., *in procession*, ναόν, ξόανον κ., ib.211, *BGU*362 vii 17 (iii A. D.):—Pass., χρὴ τὰς θεὰς κωμάζεσθαι *Sammelb.*421 (iii A. D.). II. esp. *celebrate a* κῶμος in honour of the victor at the games, κ. σὺν ἑταίροις Pi.*O.*9.4, etc.: c. acc. cogn., ἑορτὰν κ. Id.*N.*11.28; τὸν καλλίνικον μετὰ θεῶν ἐκώμασεν E.*HF* l. c. 2. c. dat. pers., *approach with a* κῶμος, *sing in* his *honour*, Pi.*I.*7(6).20 (in fut. Med., Id.*P.*9.89); ἡ Ἀφροδίτη κ. παρὰ τὸν Διόνυσον Plu.*Ant.*26. 3. c. acc. pers., *honour* or *celebrate* him *in* or *with the* κῶμος, Pi.*N.*10.35, *I.*4(3).72; κ. Δία Τιμοδήμῳ *celebrate* Zeus for Timodemos' sake, Id.*N.*2.24. III. *break in upon in the manner of revellers, serenade*, of lovers, Alc.56; ἐπὶ γαμετὰς γυναῖκας Is.3.14, cf. Luc.*DMar.*1.4; κ. ποτὶ τὰν Ἀμαρυλλίδα Theoc.3.1, cf. Ath.8.348c; παρά τινι Arr.*An.*7.24.4; εἴς τινα Alciphr.1.6; ἐπὶ τὰς ἑταιρίδων θύρας Ath.13.574e: generally, *burst in*, εἰς τόπον *APl.*4.102; of evil, ἄτη ἐς πόλιν ἐκώμασεν Tryph.314; θρῆνος εἰς ὑμέναιον *AP*7.186 (Phil.); of Alexander, καθ' ὅλης τῆς ὑφ' ἡλίῳ Him.*Ecl.*2.18: prov., ὗς ἐκώμασεν, 'a bull in a china-shop', Diogenian.8.60; εἰς μελίττας ἐκώμασας 'you have raised a hornet's nest about your ears', Paus.Gr.*Fr.*160, Zen.3.53, etc.

⊛**κωμαίνω**, *to be drowsy*, Hp.*Morb.*2.22; but κωμαίνεσθαι· κείρασθαι, Hsch. (post κωμική).

⊛**κωμαῖος**, α, ον, *of a village*, St.Byz. s. v. Κώμη; epith. of Apollo at Naucratis, Herm. Hist.2.

**κώμακον**, τό, an aromatic plant, perh. *spice-nutmeg*, Thphr.*HP*9.7.2 (but acc. to Plin.*HN*12.135, 13.18 a kind of *cinnamon*); also a fruit, Thphr. l. c.

**κώμαξ**, ακος, ὁ, *debauchee*, Eust.1749.28.

**κωμ-άριον**, τό, gloss on ἀγρίδιον, Hsch. ⊛**-αρχέω**, *to be* κωμάρχης, *GDI*3069 (Selymbria), Keil-Premerstein *Dritter Bericht* No.109 (Lydia, iii A. D.): c. acc., *administer as* κωμάρχης, τὴν κώμην *PAmh.*2.33.11 (ii B. C.). **-άρχης**, Dor. **-άρχας**, ου, ὁ, (κώμη) *head man of a village*, X.*An.*4.5.10,24, al. codd., *PRev.Laws* 40.3 (iii B. C.), D.H.4.14, *IG*12(1).128 (Rhodes), *CIG*3420 (Philadelphia), 3641 *b* 66 (Lampsacus), *OGI*527.10 (Hierapolis), etc. **-αρχία**, ἡ, *office of* κωμάρχης, *PTeb.*24.63 (ii B. C., pl.). ⊛**-αρχος**, ὁ, *leader of a* κῶμος, Πολέμων 1.45 (Attica, iv B. C., pl.). II. = κωμάρχης, *PCair.Zen.*379.15 (iii B. C.), *PTeb.*43.8 (ii B. C.), Poll.9.11:—hence Com. Patron. **-αρχίδης**, Ar.*Pax* 1142. ⊛**-ᾰσία**, ἡ, *procession of the images of the gods* in Egypt, αἱ τῶν θεῶν κ. *OGI*194.25 (i B. C.), cf. *PGnom.*199 (ii A. D.), Wilcken *Chr.*41 iv 14 (iii A. D.); αἱ τοῦ νέου ἔτους κ. *PStrassb.*90.18 (i B. C.). **-ασμός**, ὁ, *revelling*, prob. in J.*AJ*17.9.5 (pl.). ⊛**-αστήριον**, τό, *meeting-place of* κωμασταί 3 in Egypt, *Sammelb.*5051 (Taposiris). II. metaph. of heaven, as the *place of procession* of the Sun and Star-gods, *PMag.Par.*1.1608, *PMag.Leid.W.*17.27, etc. **-αστής**, οῦ, ὁ, *reveller*, Pl.*Smp.*212c, X.*HG*5.4.7, etc.; *member of a* κῶμος, Πολέμων 1.46 (Attica, iv B. C.); title of play by Epicharmus. 2. epith. of Dionysus, Ar.*Nu.*606 (lyr.). 3. in Egypt, *one who carries sacred images in procession*, κ. θεῶν *POxy.*519 (ii A. D.), cf. 1265.9 (iv A. D.). **-αστικός**, ή, όν, *of* or *fit for a* κῶμος, ᾠδή Ael.*NA*9.13; μέλη D.H.19.8, cf. Ph.1.372. Adv. **-κῶς** Ael.*VH*13.1. **-άστωρ**, ορος, ὁ, poet. for κωμαστής 1, Man.4.493.

⊛**κωμᾶται**· μαγεύει, Hsch.

**κωμᾰτ-ίζομαι**, Pass., *to be in a state of* κῶμα, Hp.*Epid.*7.11, Antyll. ap.Orib.10.19.7. ⊛**-ώδης**, ες, *lethargic*, Hp.*Epid.*1.26.β', 3.6.

**κωμέτας**, α, ὁ, Dor., = κωμήτης, *IG*4.497.11 (Mycenae, ii B. C.).

⊛**κώμη**, ἡ, *unwalled village*, opp. fortified city (said to be Dor. = Att. δῆμος, Arist.*Po.*1448ᵃ36, cf. κωμῳδία), Hes.*Sc.*18, Hdt.5.98; opp. πόλις, Pl.*Lg.*626c; κατοικῆσθαι κατὰ κώμας Hdt.1.96; πόλεσιν ἀτειχίστοις καὶ κατὰ κ. οἰκουμέναις formed of *scattered villages*, Th.1.5; πόλεως.. κατὰ κ. τῷ παλαιῷ τῆς Ἑλλάδος τρόπῳ οἰκισθείσης ib.10, cf. 3.94; διοικίζεσθαι κατὰ κώμας X.*HG*5.2.5; κατὰ κ. κεχωρισμένοι Arist.*Pol.*1261ᵃ28. II. *quarter, ward* of a city, διελόμενοι τὴν

μὲν πόλιν κατὰ κώμας, τὴν δὲ χώραν κατὰ δήμους Isoc.7.46, cf. Pl.*Lg.* 746d.

**κωμ-ηγέτης,** ου, ὁ, *leader of a* κῶμος, *OGI*97.10 (Egypt, ii B.C., κωμεγ- lapis). **-ηδόν,** Adv. *in villages,* ζῆν Str.3.2.15; οἰκεῖν D.S.5.6, D.H.1.9, etc. **-ήτης,** ου, ὁ, *villager, countryman,* Pl. *Lg.*762a, 763a, X.*An.*4.5.24, Call.*Hec.Fr.*23 M., *UPZ*120.3 (-ίτης, ii B.C.), D.H.4.14, etc. II. in a city, *one of the same quarter* or *district,* Ar.*Nu.*965, *OGI*488.3 (Philadelphia), *CIG*3695*b* (Aesepus): more generally, Φεραίας κωμῆται χθονός *dwellers in,* E.*Alc.*476; θυρέτρων τῶνδε κωμῆται θεοί *neighbours,* Ion Trag.37. ❋ **-ητικός,** ή, όν, *of a* κώμη, τὰ κ. *funds of the* κ., *PRyl.*221.29 (iii A.D.), *PTeb.*340 i 10 (iii A.D.); κ. κατάστασις Just.*Nov.*38.6; *delivered by a* κ., χόρτος *Sammelb.*4496.18 (vi A.D.). II. *rustic, peasant,* γύναιον Porph. *Chr.*64. **-ῆτις,** ιδος, fem. of κωμήτης, Ar.*Lys.*5, *Fr.*274. **-ήτωρ,** ορος, ὁ, = κωμήτης, St.Byz. s.v. κώμη.

**κωμῐκ-εύομαι,** *speak like a comic poet,* Ps.-Luc.*Philopatr.*22, *EM* 92.27. **-ός,** ή, όν, (κῶμος) *of* or *for comedy, comic,* later form for κωμῳδικός, κ. ὑποκριτής Aeschin.1.157; ποητάς *SIG*711 *L* 15 (Delph., ii B.C.); κ. χορός, ὄρχησις, Arist.*Pol.*1276$^b$5, Demetr.Lac.*Herc.*1012.21; προσωπεῖον Luc.*Bis Acc.*33; ἱλαρῷ καὶ κ. προσώπῳ Id.*Cal.*24, cf. Plu.*Ant.*29. II. Subst. κωμικός, ὁ, *comedian,* i.e. either *comic actor,* Alex.98.13; or *comic poet,* Plb.12.13.3, Phld.*Mus.*p.16 K. (pl.), Plu.2.62e, etc.; ὁ κ., κατ' ἐξοχήν, = Aristophanes, Luc.*Prom.Es* 2, etc. Adv. -κῶς Ph.1.473, D.L.5.88.

**κώμιον,** τό, Dim. of κώμη, Str.10.5.3, Plu.2.773b.

**κῶμο,** for κῶμος, barbarism in Ar.*Th.*1176.

**κωμογραμμᾰτ-εία,** ἡ, *office of* κωμογραμματεύς, *PTeb.*9.4 (ii B.C.), *Sammelb.*5672, 6025 (both ii A.D.). **-εύς,** έως, ὁ, *clerk of a* κώμη, *PPetr.*3 p.224 (iii B.C.), *PTeb.*19.9 (ii B.C.), *OGI*665.31 (Egypt, i A.D.), J.*AJ*16.7.3, etc.

**κωμο-δρομέω,** *run through villages,* Poll.9.11. **-κάτοικος,** ὁ, *settler in a* κώμη, *PRyl.*233.7 (ii A.D.), *PLips.*99 ii 18 (iv A.D.). ❋ **-μισθωτής,** οῦ, ὁ, *official of a* κώμη *who leases out land, PTeb.*183 (ii B.C.).

**κωμόομαι,** Pass., *fall into lethargic sleep,* κεκωμῶσθαι Hp.ap.Gal.19.111.

**κωμο-πλήξ,** ῆγος, ὁ, ἡ, *revel-smitten,* i.e. *inebriated,* Hdn.Gr.1.46. **-πολις,** εως, ἡ, *village-town,* i.e. a place not entitled to be called a πόλις, Str.12.2.6, al., *Ev.Marc.*1.38.

**κῶμος,** ὁ, *revel, carousal, merry-making,* εἰς δαῖτα θάλειαν καὶ χορὸν ἱμερόεντα καὶ ἐς φιλοκυδέα κ. *h.Merc.*481, cf. Thgn.829, 940; πίνειν καὶ κώμῳ χρᾶσθαι Hdt.1.21, cf. E.*Alc.*804, etc.; κῶμοι καὶ εὐφροσύναι B.10.12; δεῖπνα καὶ σὺν αὐλητρίσι κῶμοι Pl.*Tht.*173d; ἑορταὶ καὶ κ. Id.*R.*573d; ἐν κώμῳ εἶναι, of a city, X.*Cyr.*7.5.25; ἔρχεσθαί τισιν ἐπὶ κῶμον Id.*Smp.*2.1; ἐπὶ κῶμον βαδίζειν Ar.*Pl.*1040; esp. in honour of gods, τοῖς ἐν ἄστει Διονυσίοις ἡ πομπὴ.. καὶ ὁ κ. Lex ap.D.21.10, cf. *IG*2.971, etc.; κώμῳ θυραμάχοις τε πυγμαχίαισι Pratin.Lyr.1.8; χοροῖς ἢ κώμοις Ὑακίνθου E.*Hel.*1469 (lyr.). 2. concrete, *band of revellers,* κ. εὐίου θεοῦ Id.*Ba.*1167 (lyr.); esp. of the *procession* which celebrated a victor in games, Pi.*P.*5.22, etc.: generally, *rout, band,* κ. Ἐρινύων A.*Ag.*1189; of an army, κ. ἀναυλότατος E.*Ph.*791 (lyr.); κ. ἀσπιδηφόρος Id.*Supp.*390; *band* of hunters, Id.*Hipp.*55; of maidens, Id.*Tr.*1184; of doves, Id.*Ion* 1197. II. *the ode sung* at one of these festive processions, Pi.*P.*8.20, 70, *O.*4.10, B.8.103; μελιγαρύων τέκτονες κώμων Pi.*N.*3.5, cf. Ar.*Th.*104, 988 (both lyr.).

**κωμοφύλαξ** [ῠ], ᾰκος, ὁ, *warden of a* κῶμος, *BGU*742 i 1 (ii A.D.).

❋ **κωμύδριον,** τό, Dim. of κώμη, Porph.*Chr.*64. II. perh. Dim. of κῶμος, Steph.*in Rh.*285.19.

**κώμῡς,** ῡθος, ἡ, *bundle, truss* of hay, etc., Cratin.299, Theoc.4.18: in pl., of bamboos, Agath.5.21. II. *branch of laurel,* placed before the gates, Hsch. III. κώμυς, ὁ, *reed-bed,* in pl., Thphr.*HP*4.11.1.

**κωμῳδ-έω,** *treat after the manner of* κωμῳδοί: hence, *satirize, lampoon, ridicule,* κωμῳδεῖ τὴν πόλιν ἡμῶν Ar.*Ach.*631, cf. Pl.*R.*395e, 452d, Ael.*VH*13.43, etc.; κ. τοὺς τραγῳδούς Arist.*Po.*1458$^b$32; κ. τινὰ ἐπί τινι Ath.8.341e, cf. Sch.Ar.*V.*42: abs., Ar.*Pl.*557:—Pass., Id.*V.*1026, *Ra.*368, Plu.2.712a, etc.; μὴ κωμῳδεῖσθαι ὀνομαστί τινα Sch.Ar.*Av.*1297; τὸ κοινὸν καὶ κεκωμῳδημένον, of the parasites, Alex.116.2; κεκωμῳδημένα *made matter for comedy,* Pl.*Lg.*816d. 2. κωμῳδεῖν τὰ δίκαια, = κωμῳδοῦντα εἰπεῖν τὰ δ., Ar.*Ach.*655. 3. generally, *make fun of, ridicule,* Lys.24.18. II. *to be a* κωμῳδός 3, *write comedies,* c. acc. cogn., κ. κωμῳδίας Luc.*Pisc.*25; *write in a comedy* (introducing a quotation), Phld.*Vit.*p.38 J. **-ημα,** ατος, τό, *matter for comedy,* τὰ τοῦ γέλωτος κ. laughter such as comedy produces, Pl.*Lg.*816d. **-ητέον,** *one must ridicule,* Aristid.*Or.*29(40).25. **-ία,** ἡ, *comedy,* Ar.*Ach.*378, *Nu.*522, Pl.*R.*394c, etc.; κ. ἀρχαία Plu.*Luc.*39, 2.711f, M.Ant.11.6; μέση ibid., Ath.11.482c; νέα Plu.2.712b, M.Ant. l.c.: κ. παλαιαί, καιναί, Arist.*EN*1128$^a$22; κωμῳδιῶν ποιηταί *OGI*51.34 (Egypt, iii B.C.): generally, *play,* Plu.2.665e: metaph., βίου τραγῳδία καὶ κ. Pl.*Phlb.*50b. (From κῶμος: wrongly expld. by Dorian writers from κώμη, cf. Arist.*Po.*1448$^a$37.) **-ιακός,** ή, όν, = sq., Sch.Ar.*Ach.*380. **-ικός,** ή, όν, *of comedy, comic,* ἔπη Ar.*V.*1047; τερπνόν τι καὶ κ. Id.*Ec.*889; σκωραμὶς κ. ib.371; μορμολυκεῖον Id.*Fr.*31; ἐν μιμήσει κ. Pl.*R.*606c. Adv. -κῶς Ath.3.90b.

**κωμῳδιο-γράφος** [ᾰ], ὁ, *comic writer,* Plb.12.13.7, D.S.12.14. **-ποιός,** later form for κωμῳδοποιός, Clearch.3, Ath.1.5b, etc., cf. Moer.p.240 P.

**κωμῳδό-γελως,** ωτος, ὁ, = κωμῳδός, *AP*13.6 (Phal.). **-γράφος** [ᾰ], ὁ, = κωμῳδιογράφος, *AP*7.708 (Diosc.), Phld.*Mus.*p.88 K. **-δῐδασκᾰλία,** ἡ, *rehearsing a comedy, training the chorus:* generally, *the comic poet's part,* Ar.*Eq.*516. **-δῐδάσκᾰλος,** ὁ, *comic poet,* because he trained the actors and chorus, ib.507, *Pax* 737, Lys.*Fr.*53, Arist.*de An.*406$^b$17: κωμῳδιοδιδ. is f.l. in D.Chr.15.7, Aristid.2.129 J. **-λοιχέω,** *play the parasite,* περί τινα Ar.*V.*1318. **-ποιητής,** οῦ, ὁ, = κωμῳδοποιός, Id.*Pax* 734, Poll.4.111. **-ποιΐα,** ἡ, *writing of comedies,* Plu.2.348b. **-ποιός,** ὁ, *comic poet,* Pl.*Ap.*18d, *Phd.*70c, *R.*606c, al., Arist.*Po.*1449$^a$4, *IG*11(2).113.26 (Delos, iii B.C.), Phld.*Mus.*p.99 K., etc.

**κωμῳδός,** ὁ, late Boeot. **κωμαϝυδός** (i.e. κωμαοιδός) *IG*7.3195.23 (Orchom.):—prop. *singer in the* κῶμος or *comic chorus,* χορὸς κωμῳδῶν Arist.*Po.*1449$^b$1; κωμῳδοῖς χορηγεῖν Lys.21.4, Arist.*EN*1123$^a$23: hence, in pl., in the sense *performance of comedy,* κωμῳδῶν ὄντων ἐν Κολυττῷ Aeschin.1.157; ἀνειπεῖν Διονυσίων τοῖς κ. *at the performance,* *IG*2$^2$.1202.15; οὐδέ τοι ὑποκριταὶ κωμῳδοῖς τε καὶ τραγῳδοῖς οἱ αὐτοί Pl.*R.*395a, cf. *Phdr.*236c, *Lg.*935d; καινῇ κωμῳδῶν, v. καινός. 2. later, *comic actor,* Chares 4 J., *PCair.Zen.*417.11 (iii B.C.), Plu.*Cic.*5, *IG*4$^2$(1).99.25 (Epid., i/ii A.D.): generally, *actor,* M.Ant.12.36, Ath.14.620d. b. perh. *singer of comic lyrics,* *SIG*424.57 (Delph., iii B.C.); χορευταὶ κωμῳδοῦ ib.690.18 (ibid., ii B.C.). 3. later still, *comic poet,* ὁ κ., of Aristophanes, Phryn.*PS* p.79 B., cf. Sch.D.T. p.19 H.: this sense is doubtful in Pl.*Lg.* l.c.

**κωμῳδοτρᾰγῳδία,** ἡ, *serio-comedy,* title of plays by Alcaeus Comicus and Anaxandrides, Harp., Phot., Suid. s.v. ἀδηφάγος: metaph., of human life, Porph.*Marc.*2, Id.ap.Stob.3.21.28.

**κῶνα,** ἡ, = πίσσα, acc. κῶναν Dsc.1.72: gen. κώνης *Hippiatr.* 26. **κώνα·** βέμβιξ, Hsch.

**κωνάριον,** τό, Dim. of κῶνος, Hero *Spir.*1.41. 2. esp. *pineal gland in the brain,* from its shape, Gal.*UP*8.14, al.

**κωνάω,** (κῶνος II. 3) *spin a top:* generally, = περιδινέω, Ar.*Fr.*520, Hsch., Phot., *EM*551.24. II. (κῶνος I. 3) *cover with pitch,* *IG*11(2).203 *A* 33 (Delos, iii B.C.), *PCair.Zen.*366.23 (iii B.C.), Phot., Suid., *EM*551.22.

**κωνει-άζομαι,** Pass., *to be dosed with hemlock,* Str.10.5.6: Κωνειαζόμεναι, title of a play by Menander. **-ον,** τό, *hemlock, Conium maculatum,* Hp.*Steril.*224, Thphr.*HP*1.5.3, 9.8.3, Nic.*Al.*186, Dsc.4.78, etc. 2. = νάρθηξ, Call.*Iamb.*1.122, Hsch. II. *hemlock-juice,* poison by which criminals were put to death at Athens, Ar.*Ra.*124; κώνειον πεπωκώς Pl.*Ly.*219e; τὸ κώνειον ἔπιεν X.*HG*2.3.56, cf. And.3.10; κώνεια πιεῖν Ar.*Ra.*1051.

**κώνης,** pl. **-ητες·** θύρσοι, Hsch.

**κών-ησις,** εως, ἡ, (κωνάω II) *pitching:* hence, *daubing,* f.l. for κόμμωσις, Arist.*HA*623$^b$31. **-ητικός,** ή, όν, *for pitching:* neut. -κόν, τό, *BGU*1532 (iii B.C.). **-ίας** οἶνος, ὁ, *pitched* wine, Hp.ap.Gal.19.116. **-ικός,** ή, όν, (κῶνος) *cone-shaped, conical,* Epicur.*Nat.*14.5, Plu.2.410d; esp. in Math., κ. ἐπιφάνεια, γραμμαί, τομαί, Archim.*Sph.Cyl.*1.9, al., Papp.672.10, 662.15; κωνικά, τά, *Conic Sections,* title of work by Apollonius Pergaeus, cf. Archim.*Con.Sph.*3; κ. στοιχεῖα Id.*Quadr.*3; κ. ὅροι Papp.922.17; κ. προβλήματα Apollon.Perg.*Con.* 1 *Praef.* **-ίον** or **κώνιον,** τό, Dim. of κῶνος, *small cone,* κωνία μαστῶν *AP*5.12 (Phld.). II. *small pine-cone,* Posidon.3 J. **-ίς,** ίδος, ἡ, (κῶνος II) = ὑδρίσκη, Hsch. **-ῖτις,** ιδος, ἡ, (κῶνος I. 1) *extracted from pine-cones,* πίσσα Rhian.75.

**κωνο-ειδής,** ές, *conical,* σχῆμα Archim.*Con.Sph.Praef.*, al., Ph.*Bel.*86.51; of the creative fire, Cleanth.*Stoic.*1.111; of the *apex* of the Roman *flamen,* D.H.2.70; σκιά Cleom.2.2, etc.; σκίασμα D.C.60.26; τὸ κ. *conoid,* Archim.*Con.Sph.Praef.*, etc. Adv. -δῶς *Placit.*4.15.3, Cleom.2.2, Phlp.*in de An.*140.34. II. metaph., *concise, pointed,* ἑρμηνεία συνεστραμμένη καὶ οἷον εἰπεῖν κ. Corn.*Rh.*p.387 H. III. neut. -ειδές, τό, = κωνάριον II, Gal.2.723 (but κ. μόριον odontoid process of the second vertebra, 2.461). **-καρπος,** ὁ, *pine-cone, Gloss.* **-κόλουρος,** ὁ, = κολουρόκωνος, Hero *Metr.*3.22.

❋ **κῶνος,** ου, 1. masc., the fruit of the πεύκη, *pine-cone,* = στρόβιλος, Ps.-Hdt.*Vit.Hom.*20, Thphr.*HP*3.9.5, Theoc.5.49, Dsc.1.69, etc.; used in Orphic rites, Orph.*Fr.*31.29. 2. *edible seed* of the πίτυς, Mnesith.ap.Ath.2.57b; πιτύϊνοι κ. Alex.Mynd.ibid., cf. *IG*2$^2$.1013.19, *OGI*629.163 (Palmyra, ii A.D.). 3. fem., *pine tree,* Pl.*Epigr.*25 (prob.), Plu.2.64cc. II. from likeness of shape, 1. *cone,* Democr.155, Arist.*Mete.*362$^b$2, etc.; γραμμαὶ κατὰ κῶνον ἐκπίπτουσαι so as to form *a cone,* ib.375$^b$22, cf. 345$^b$6; ὀρθογωνίου, ὀξυγωνίου, ἀμβλυγωνίου κώνου τομά, names for *parabola, ellipse,* and *hyperbola,* Archim.*Con.Sph.Praef.* b. ὁ κ. τῆς γῆς *conical shadow* of the earth, Simp.*in de An.*133.5, cf. Phlp.*in de An.*348.27; τῆς νυκτὸς ὁ κ. εἰς ὀξὺ λήγει Dam.*Pr.*213. c. ὁ τῆς ὄψεως κ. *cone* of vision, Gal.7.95, cf. Phlp.*in de An.*333.27 (pl.). 2. *cone* or *peak* of a helmet, *AP*9.322 (Leon.). 3. = στρόβιλος, *spinning top,* Hsch. 4. *iron pole round which grain is piled in conical shape,* *PGrenf.*2.17.3 (ii B.C.), Gal.19.76. 5. στέφανος χρυσοῦς ἐπὶ κώνου δάφνης dub. sens. in *Inscr.Délos* 442 *B* 56 (ii B.C.). III. as place-name, πρὸς τῷ ἀνδροφόνῳ κώνῳ dub. sens. in *IG*3.61 *A* ii 15 (ii A.D.).

**κωνόσαρτον·** ξύει, Hsch.

**κωνο-τομέω,** *produce by means of conic sections,* τριάδας Eratosth.35.8. **-φόρος,** ον, *bearing cones,* Thphr.*HP*3.9.4; esp. κωνοφόρος (sc. πεύκη), ἡ, *stone-pine, Pinus pinea,* ib.2.2.6; also of the thyrsus, *AP*6.165.4 (Phal.).

**κωνωπ-εών,** ῶνος, ὁ, = sq. 2, *AP*9.764 tit. (Paul. Sil.). **-ιον,** τό, Dim. of κώνωψ, Gal.7.96, Phlp.*in de An.*291.33, *Gp.*2.5.12. 2. *couch with mosquito-curtains,* Lxx *Ju.*10.21, 13.9, Sor.1.85 (written κωνόπιον *Stud.Pal.*20.211.11 (v/vi A.D.)). (Lat. *cōnōpĭum,* later *cōnōpēum*). **-οειδής,** ές, *like a gnat,* θηρία Thphr.*HP*3.14.1, Dsc.1.84. **-οθήρας,** ου, ὁ, *gnat-catcher,* a bird, Hsch. **-οσφράντης,**

ου, ὁ, *Gnat-smeller*, name of a parasite, Alciphr.1.21. **-ώδης,** ες, = κωνωποειδής, Sch.Ar.*V*.351.

⊛ **κώνωψ,** ωπος, ὁ, *gnat. mosquito*, A.*Ag*.892, Hdt.2.95, Orac.ap.Ar. *Eq*.1038, Arist.*HA* $535^a3$, $552^b5$; μήτε ὡς λέων ἀναστρέφου μήτε ὡς κ. Metrod.*Fr*.60.

**κῶος,** ὁ, mostly in pl. κῶοι, *caves, dens*, Str.8.5.7, St.Byz. s.v. Κῶς. II. = κῶς (A) II, ibid.

⊛ **Κῷος,** α, ον, *of, from the island* Κῶς, *Coan*, *IG*1$^2$.195.7, al., Hdt.7.164, etc.; **Κώϊος** Call.*Fr*.254. II. as Subst. Κῷος (sc. βόλος), ὁ, *the highest throw with the* ἀστράγαλοι, opp. Χῖος, Hsch.; τὰ κῷα are *the inner*, τὰ χῖα *the outer, sides* of the *huckle*-bones (ἀστράγαλοι), Arist.*HA* $499^b28$ (κῶλα and ἰσχία codd.), cf. *Cael*. $292^a29$ (v.l.). III. **Κῷον** (sc. ἱμάτιον), τό, *a light semi-transparent garment, made at Cos*, Hsch. 2. a measure of wine, *Ostr.Fay*.44 (ii/iii A.D.), *BGU*531 ii 8: pl. written κόα, *Sammelb*.7199.2, al. (ii A.D.). 3. = ἐνέχυρον, Hsch. (also κώϊον); cf. κῷον, κοῖα.

**κώπαιον,** τό, (κώπη) *handle of an oar*, Hsch.

**Κωπαΐς,** αΐδος, contr. **Κωπᾴς,** ᾷδος, ἡ, *of* or *near Copae* (in Boeotia), ἡ Κ. λίμνη Lake *Copais*, Hdt.8.135, Str.9.2.27; ἡ Κ. alone, Ath.7.297d. 2. ἐγχέλεις Κωπαΐδες eels *from Lake C.*, Ar.*Ach*.880; Κωπᾷδ' ἔγχελυν ib.962: without Subst., Κωπᾴδων σπυρίδας Id.*Pax* 1005 (anap.); Κωπᾴδων ἁπαλῶν τεμάχη Stratt.44.

**κωπάω,** v. -έω. **κωπέτας·** σφονδύλους μεγάλους ἰχθύων, Hsch.

⊛ **κωπ-εύς,** έως, ὁ, (κώπη) always in pl. κωπέες, Att. κωπῆς, *pieces of wood fit for making oars, spars*, Hdt.5.23, Ar.*Ach*.552, *Lys*.422, And. 2.11, *IG*1$^2$.46.11, 2$^2$.1609.95, al. **-εύω,** *propel with oars*, βᾶριν *AP* 7.365 (Zon.). II. (κώπη 2) κεκώπευται στρατός it *has the sword drawn*, Anon.ap.Hsch. **-έω** or **-άω,** *furnish with oars*, in pf. Pass., κεκώπηται ἡ ναῦς Hsch.: pl. κεκώπηνται *IG*2$^2$.1604.73. II. *furnish with handles*, κοῦφα κεκωπημένα *BGU*1143.15 (i B.C.). III. = foreg. II, Hsch. s.v. κεκώπηται. ⊛ **-εών,** ῶνος, ὁ, = κωπεύς, Thphr. *HP*5.1.7: pl., ib.4.1.4.

**κώπ-η,** ἡ, *handle* (v. fin.); esp. 1. *handle of an oar*, Hsch.: hence, *the oar* itself (not in Il.), ἐμβαλέειν κώπῃς Od.9.489; κώπῃσιν ἁλὸς ῥηγμῖνα..τύπτετε 12.214, cf. Sapph.120, etc.; οἱ τὰς κ. ξύοντες Thphr. *HP*5.1.6, cf. κωποξύστης; κώπαν σχάσον, metaph., 'stay thy hand', Pi.*P*.10.51; νερτέρᾳ προσήμενος κώπῃ, = θαλαμίτης, metaph., of a man of low rank, A.*Ag*.1618; πομπίμοις κώπαις ἐρέσσων S.*Tr*.561; παραπέμπειν ἐφ' ἕνδεκα κώπαις, a prov. of dub. origin, meaning 'to escort with all the honours', Ar.*Eq*.546, cf. Eust.1540.44, Suid. s.v. ἐφ' ἕνδεκα; κώπαισι πλεῖν take to the *oars*, when the wind fails, Men. 241; κώπαις ποιεῖσθαι τὸν πλοῦν Arist.*IA* $710^a19$: poet., to express ships, κλεινᾷ σὺν κώπᾳ, of Agamemnon's fleet, E.*IT*140 (lyr.), cf. *Hel*.1272, 1452 (lyr.). 2. *handle of a sword, hilt*, ἐπ' ἀργυρέῃ κώπῃ σχέθε χεῖρα Il.1.219, cf. Od.8.403; ξίφεος δ' ἐπεμαίετο κώπην 11.531; χεῖρα κώπης ἐπιψαύουσαν S.*Ph*.1255; φάσγανον κώπης λαβών E.*Hec*. 543. 3. *handle of a key*, κώπη δ' ἐλέφαντος ἐπῆεν Od.21.7. 4. *haft of a torch*, E.*Cyc*.484 (anap.). 5. *handle* or *spoke* by which a mill is turned, *PSI*5.530.10 (iii B.C.), Agatharch.26, *PRyl*.167.11 (i A.D.), Luc.*Asin*.42. 6. *haft of a whip*, Hsch. s.v. Κερκυραία μάστιξ. 7. pl., *spars* or *bars* used in building-operations, *IG*1$^2$.313.135. (Cf. Lat. *cap-io*, Engl. *haft*, etc.) **-ήεις,** εσσα, εν, *hilted*, φάσγανα Il.15.713, al. **-ῆλα·** κοπεώδη, μακρά, Hsch. **-ηλᾰσία,** ἡ, *rowing*, Arist.*Mete*. $369^b11$, Str.9.2.17, *PSI*4.289.2 (iii A.D.), Sch.Ar.*Ra*.271. **-ηλᾰτέω,** *pull an oar, row*, opp. κυβερνῆσαι, Arist.*Rh.Al*. $1435^a28$, cf. Plb.1.21.1, etc. 2. metaph., *of any similar motion forwards and backwards*, as of a carpenter using an auger, τρύπανον κ. E.*Cyc*.461. **-ηλάτης** [ᾰ], ου, ὁ, (ἐλαύνω) *rower*, Plb.34.3.8, Lxx *Ez*.27.8, *PSI*4.289.18 (iii A.D.); κ. πολύπους *nautilus*, Clearch.47. **-ηλᾰτικός,** ή, όν, *of rowers*, ἐπίφθεγμα Hsch. s.v. ἄρρυ; πόνοι Sch.Opp.*H*.4.76. **-ήλᾰτος,** ον, *formed like an oar*, dub. in Hsch. (κωπῆλα cod.). **-ήρης,** ες, (ἀραρίσκω) *furnished with oars*, στόλος A.*Pers*.416; στρατός S.*Fr*.142. 16; σκάφος E.*Hel*.1381; πλοῖον Th.4.118; κωπῆρες (sc. πλοῖον), τό, Plu.*Ant*.65, etc. II. *holding the oar*, χείρ E.*Tr*.160 (lyr.). **-ητήρ,** ῆρος, ὁ, = τροπωτήρ, Hermipp.54, Agath.5.21, cf. Poll.1.92; v. ἐπικωπητήρ. **-ίον,** τό, Dim. of κώπη, Ar.*Ra*.269, Ael.*NA*13.19, *PRyl*. 110.14 (iii A.D.). 2. in pl., *false ribs*, Poll.2.181.

**κωπο-ξύστης,** ου, ὁ, (κώπη, ξύω) *oar-maker*, *SIG*1000.17 (Cos), *Gloss*. **-πώλης,** ου, ὁ, *oar-dealer*, dub. in *Jahresh*.23 *Beibl*.172 (fort. ῥωπο-).

**κωπώ,** οῦς, ἡ, *wreathed staff used in the* δαφνηφόρια in Boeotia, Procl.ap.Phot.*Bibl*.p.321 B.

**κώρα,** ἡ, Dor. for κούρη, Theoc.6.36, Call.*Lav.Pall*.27, 138, *Cer*. 9. II. = ὕβρις, Hsch.

⊛ **κωράλιον·** παιδάριον, κόριον, Hsch.; cf. κοράλλιον.

**κωρᾰλίσκος,** ὁ, Dim. of κῶρος (= κοῦρος A), Hdn.Gr.2.926, Phot.; title of play by Epilycus.

**κωραλλεύς,** έως, ὁ, *coral-fisher*, Hsch. **κωρία,** ἡ, Dor. for κουρεύτρια, Id. **κωριδάμνας·** ἀκρίς, Id. **κωρίθιον·** χόρτον, Id.

**κώριον,** τό, Dor. for κόριον (A) (q.v.).

**κωρίς,** ίδος, ἡ, = καρίς, Semon.15, Epich.89. II. = ψαλίς, Hsch.

**κωρισμός,** ὁ, Dor. for *κουρισμός, *education, upbringing*, κωρισμοῖς ἐδίδαξα μελίφροσι *Hymn.Is*.41.

**κῶρος,** ὁ, Dor. for κοῦρος (A), κόρος (B), Call.*Lav.Pall*.85, Theoc.1. 47, etc.

**Κωρῠκαῖος,** ὁ, v. Κώρυκος.

**κωρύκ-ιον** [ῠ], τό, Dim. of κώρυκος, Poll.10.172, Suid.: **-ίδιον,** Hsch.

**Κωρύκιος** [ῠ], α, ον, *Corycian*, ἄντρον, a cave on Mt. Parnassus, Hdt.8.36 (also Κωρύκιον, τό, Plu.2.394f: pl., Κ. ἄντρα Aristonous 1. 35); prov. for a 'snug retreat', Ceb.26; Νύμφαι Κ. S.*Ant*.1128 (lyr.); κορυφαὶ Κ. the peaks of Parnassus, E.*Ba*.559 (lyr.). II. v. Κώρυκος fin.

**Κωρῠκίς,** ίδος, ἡ, fem. of foreg., πέτρα A.*Eu*.22.

**κωρῠκίς,** ίδος, ἡ, Dim. of κώρυκος I. 1, Epich.113, Ar.*Fr*.415. II. *leaf-gall in elms*, Thphr.*HP*3.14.1.

**Κωρῠκιώτης,** ου, ὁ, *of Corycus*, epith. of Hermes, Orph.*H*.28.8.

**κωρῠκο-βολία,** ἡ, *exercise with punching-bag*, Aret.*CD*2.13 (pl.). **-μᾰχία,** Ion. -ίη, ἡ, = foreg., Hp.*Vict*.2.64, 3.78.

⊛ **κώρῠκος,** ὁ, *leathern sack* or *wallet for provisions*, Od.5.267, 9.213, Ar.*Lys*.1210 (lyr.), Pherecr.78, Antiph.160.3. 2. in the gymnasium, *leathern sack hung up for punching*, Sor.1.49, Antyll.ap.Orib. 6.33.1, Philostr.*Gym*.57, Luc.*Lex*.5; ζυγομαχῶν τῷ κωρύκῳ (with play on Κωρύκῳ) *Com.Adesp*.207; πρὸς κώρυκον γυμνάζεσθαι, prov. of *labour in vain*, Diogenian.7.54: metaph., of parasites, ἑαυτοὺς ἀντὶ κωρύκων λέπειν παρέχοντες ἀθληταῖσιν Timocl.29. 3. *leathern quiver*, Hsch. II. *scrotum*, *Hippiatr*.73. III. = κόγχη (Maced.), Hegesand.36.

**Κώρῠκος,** ὁ, *Corycus*, a promontory of Cilicia, *h.Ap*.39, etc.:— Adj. **Κωρυκαῖος,** α, ον: the inhabitants were infamous for *spying out* the destination and value of ships' cargoes and then piratically seizing them, Ephor.27 J., etc.: hence Κωρυκαῖος, prov. of *spies* and *eavesdroppers*, Str.14.1.32, Cic.*Att*.10.18.1, prob. in Call.*Iamb*.1. 143; Κ. ἠκροάσατο, 'a little bird told me', Men.150; μὴ κατακούσειεν δέ μου ὁ Κ., 'low be it spoken', Diox.2: — also **Κωρύκιον** σκάφος *piratical* craft, Alciphr.1.8.

**κωρῠκώδης,** ες, *like a sack*, Thphr.*HP*3.15.4.

**Κῶς,** ἡ, gen. Κῶ, *Cos*; Ep. **Κόως** *h.Ap*.42: acc. Κῶν Il.2.677; **Κόωνδε,** Adv. *to Cos*, 14.255, 15.28; cf. Κῷος, Κῳακός:—prov., ὃν οὐ θρέψει Κ., ἐκεῖνον οὐδὲ Αἴγυπτος Eust.983.33.

**κῶς** (A), τό, contr. for κῶας, Nicoch.12. II. at Corinth, *public prison*, St.Byz., cf. Hsch.; cf. κῶος. III. masc. pl. κῶες, οἱ, *prisoners*, at Corinth, St.Byz.

**κῶς** (B), Ion. for πῶς, Hdt. II. enclit. **κως,** Ion. for πως, Id.

**κώτᾰλις,** ἡ, *ladle, stirrer*, gloss on λάκτιν, *EM*555.18 (σκυτάλην codd.), Suid., Eust.1675.56.

**κώτᾰλος,** ὁ, name of *a musical air*, Hedyl.ap.Ath.4.176d.

**κωτ-άρχης,** ου, ὁ, priest of the Κάβειροι at Didyma, *CIG*2880, 2881: —also **-αρχος,** ib.2882:—fem. **-αρχις,** ιδος, ἡ, *Milet*.1(7) No.265.

**κωτῐλάς,** άδος, ἡ, poet. fem. of κωτίλος, *twitterer*, Boeot. name for the swallow, Stratt.47.6.

**κωτῐλ-ία,** ἡ, *prattle*, esp. *flattery*, *Gloss*. **-ίζω,** = sq., Call.*Iamb*. 1.277.

⊛ **κωτίλλω,** only pres., *prattle, chatter*, usu. with collat. notion of *coaxing, wheedling*, αἱμύλα κωτίλλουσα Hes.*Op*.374; μαλθακὰ κ. Thgn.852; ἡδέα κωτίλλοντα καθήμενον οἰνοποτάζειν Phoc.11; ἀνάνυτα κ. Theoc.15.87; ἑλικτὰ ἔπη Lyc.1466; κ. καὶ λιγαίνειν, of a speech in court, *to be lively, tripping*, D.H.*Dem*.44. II. trans., *cajole, beguile with fair words*, εὖ κώτιλλε τὸν ἐχθρόν Thgn.363; μή κώτιλλέ με *tease* me not *by prating*, S.*Ant*.756; τοιαῦτα κωτίλλουσα τὴν ἀχαΐνην Babr.95.87.

**κωτίλος** [ῐ], η, ον, *chattering, babbling*, Thgn.295, S.*Fr*.683.3; of women, Theoc.15.89; κωτίλε (-ιλλε codd.) 'chatterbox', gloss on τέττα, Hellad.ap.Phot.*Bibl*.p.531 B.; of the swallow, *twittering*, Anacr.154, Simon.243; generally, of animals, *vocal*, opp. σιγηλός, Arist.*HA* $488^a33$. II. metaph., *lively, expressive*, ῥήματα Theoc. 20.7; ὄμμα κ. *speaking* eye, *AP*5.130 (Phld.); *persuasive*, φίλτρα ib.7.221; κ. ἁρμονία, μουσική, *babbling*, i.e. *light*, music, D.H.*Dem*. 49, Plu.2.1136b; κῶλα πολὺ τὸ κ. ἔχοντα D.H.*Dem*.40; κωτίλας ἄνακτα μοίσας *IG*4$^2$(1).130.16 (Epid.).

**κώφαγρος,** *ruppo rusco* (?), *Gloss*.

**κωφ-άω,** (κωφός) *make dumb, silence*, πᾶσαν ἰωήν Opp.*C*.3.286:— Pass., *grow dumb* or *deaf, become stupid*, ὑπ' ἀπαιδευσίας κεκωφημένος Clearch.6. II. generally, *maim, injure*, Hsch. **-εία,** ἡ, *stupor, depression*, Phld.*D*.1.24. **-εύω,** *hold one's peace*, Lxx 2*Ki*.13.20, al. **-έω,** = κωφάω II, *mutilate*, prob. l. S.*Fr*.234. **-ησις,** εως, ἡ, *maiming, mutilation*, Hsch. **-ητέος,** α, ον, = βλαπτέος, Id. ⊛ **-ίας,** ου, ὁ, a burrowing snake, perh. = τύφλωψ, Ael.*NA*8. 13. ⊛ **-ός,** ή, όν, *blunt, dull, obtuse*, opp. ὀξύς, κ. βέλος Il.11.390, cf. E.*Fr*.495.27; κ. καλάμη *AP*12.25 (Stat. Flacc.). II. metaph., 1. of sound, *mute, noiseless*, κύματι κωφῷ Il.14.16; κωφὴν γὰρ δὴ γαῖαν ἀεικίζει is maltreating *dumb, senseless* earth, 24.54; τὰ μὲν ἄλλα ἔσκε κωφά the other parts sounded *dull*, opp. to the ringing of the hollow parts when struck, Hdt.4.200: neut. pl. as Adv., κωφὰ δὲ πόντος κεῖτο Orph.*A*.1103; ὁ κ. λιμήν, prob. the bay of Munychia, as opp. to the noisy Piraeus, X.*HG*2.4.31; κωφότερος ὁ ψόφος ἔσται, i.e. *muffled*, Aen.Tact.19; τῶν μεταλλικῶν κωφότατος [ὁ σίδηρος] *rings least*, Plu.2.721f; κωφοὶ ἄνεμοι D.S.3.51. 2. after Hom., of men or animals, *dumb*, Parm.6.7, etc.; καὶ κωφοῦ συνίημι καὶ οὐ φωνεῦντος ἀκούω Orac.ap.Hdt.1.47; οὐ..παρὰ κωφὸν ὁ τυφλὸς ἔοικε λαλῆσαι, i.e. is not so *dumb* but that he will answer the blind fool who assails him, Cratin.6; κωφότερος κίχλης Eub.29; κ. χάρις a *mute* gift (sc. an epitaph), *Epigr.Gr*.298 (Teos); so κωφοῖς δάκρυσι *IPE*2. 299 (Panticapaeum); κ. τάφοι prob. in *IG*12(8).441.26; κ. προσωπεῖον *mute* figure on the stage, Ph.2.520, cf. Plu.2.791e; κ. πρόσωπον Cic. *Att*.13.19.3; κ. καὶ ἄλογος, of a house, *with no echoes*, Luc.*Dom*. 1. b. *deaf*, *h.Merc*.92, Heraclit.34, A.*Th*.202, *Ch*.881; λήθην κωφήν, ἄναυδον S.*Fr*.670; ὅσοι γίνονται κ. ἐκ γενετῆς, πάντες καὶ ἐνεοὶ γίνονται

Arist.*HA*536ᵇ3 (hence of a ***deaf and dumb*** person, Hdt.1.34, *BGU* 1196.49 (i B.C.), cf. Hsch.); c. gen., κωφὴ ἀκοῆς αἴσθησις Antiph.196. 5, cj. in Pl.*Lg*.932a; κ. Ἑλλάδος φωνᾶς *deaf* of one's Greek ear, i.e. ignorant of Greek, *Dialex*.6.12; σπαράγματα κωφὰ τοῦ βεβαιοῦντος Plu.2.1108d. **c.** metaph., νοῦς ὁρῇ καὶ νοῦς ἀκούει· τἆλλα κωφὰ καὶ τυφλά Epich.249; κ. πέτρος Moschio Trag.7; μαψαῦραι Call.*Fr*.67; ἐρημία D.S.3.40: neut. pl. as Adv., κωφὰ χλιαίνεσθαι *feebly*, *AP*12.125 (Mel.). **3.** ὄμμα κ. *vacant, lack-lustre* eye, Arist.*Phgn*.807ᵇ23. **4.** of the senses in general, *dull*, Thphr.*Sens*.19 (Comp.). **5.** of the mind, *dull, obtuse*, ἐγὼ ὁ πάντα κ. S.*Aj*.911, cf. Pi.*P*.9.87; τὸ τῆς ψυχῆς ποιεῖν κ. Pl.*Ti*.88b: κωφοί, οἱ, 'the Dullards', title of satyr-play by Sophocles. **b.** of things, *senseless, unmeaning, obscure*, κ. καὶ παλαί' ἔπη S.*OT*290; κ. διήγησις Plb.3.36.4, cf. 5.21. 4; ὑπόνοια Phld.*Mus*.p.71 K.; σκῶμμα Plu.2.712a; but κ. εὐπραγίαι is prob. f.l. for κοῦφαι, D.C.38.27. Adv. -φῶς *obscurely*, Vett.Val.251. 25: Comp. -ότερον, ἐνοχλεῖν *less acutely*, Phld.*Vit*.p.21 J. **-ότης**, ητος, ἡ, *deafness*, Hp.*Epid*.3.17.ς', Pl.*Alc*.1.126b, Plu.2.167c; *dullness of hearing*, ib.38b: metaph., D.19.226, Phld.*Rh*.2.118 S. **-όω**, *numb, deaden*, ὀδύνας κωφοῖ Hp.*Liqu*.1, cf. Gal.19.116:—Pass., Hp. *Morb*.2.8: metaph. in Pass., κ. πρὸς μάθησιν Ph.1.548; κεκωφωμένος πρὸς τὰ τεχνικὰ θεωρήματα S.E.*M*.1.34. **2.** *deafen*, in Pass., ὁκόσοισιν ἂν τὰ ὦτα κωφωθῇ Hp.*Aph*.4.60, cf. Ph.1.224. **3.** *put to silence*, in Pass., *become dumb*, Lxx *Ps*.38(39).3. **II.** *maim, injure*, in Pass., Hp.*Loc.Hom*.2, cf. Erot. s.v. κωφωθῇ. **III.** Pass., of water, *lose its freshness*, Hp.*Vict*.1.35. **-ωμα**, ατος, τό, *deafness*, Id.*Epid*.5.52 (κύφ- codd.). **-ωσις**, εως, Ion. ιος, ἡ, = foreg., Id.*Aph*.4.28, *Coac*.186, al., Gal.9.758; *injury*, κ. ὀφθαλμῶν ἢ ἀκοῆς Hp.*Mul*.1.41. **2.** metaph., *dullness*, Pempel.ap.Stob.4. 25.52.

**κωχεύω**, f.l. for ὀκωχεύω, S.*Fr*.327.

**κώψ**, ὁ, = σκώψ, v.l. in Arist.*HA*617ᵇ31 ap.Ath.9.391c and Ael.*NA* 15.28, Alex.Mynd.ap.Ath. l.c.

# Λ

**Λ λ, λάμβδα**, or better **λάβδα** (v. sub voc.), τό, indecl., twelfth (later eleventh) letter of the Gr. alphabet: as numeral λʹ = 30, but ͵λ = 30,000.

**λᾱ-**, insep. Prefix with *intensive* force, as in λακαταπύγων, λακατάρατος; cf. also λαί-μαργος.

⊛**λάα**, = λεία (*booty*), Pi.*O*.10(11).44 (λαΐα codd. vett.), *IG*7.37 (Megara), cf. Hsch. s. v. λαιάν.

**λάαγες**· οἱ χλωροὶ βάτραχοι, Cyr.

**λααν**·. . καὶ θυλάκιον, ἐν ᾧ οἱ ἡνίοχοι τὰς μάστιγας ἀποτίθενται, Hsch., cf. Poll.7.116 (where the same thing is called σάργαλος).

**λάανα**· ἐπίστατον, Hsch.; i.e. λάάνα, = λάσανα.

**λααξός**, v. λαοξόος.

**λᾱάρχ-ημα**, ατος, τό, dub. sens., ἐν τῷ λααρχή(ματι) ἐ[κτεθήτω] *PTeb*.64(*a*).145 (ii B.C.). ⊛**-ης**, ου, ὁ, *commander of a* λααρχία, *Inscr.Mus.Alex*.31 (iii/ii B.C.). **-ία**, ἡ, *division of native μάχιμοι, settled in cleruchies*, *PTeb*.61(*a*).112, 62.258, al. (ii B.C.). **-ος**, ου, ὁ, = λαάρχης, *PStrassb*.91.2 (i B.C., in dat. -ῳ).

⊛**λᾶας**, ὁ (also ἡ, *AP*7.491 (Mnasalc.), Nic.*Th*.45), acc. λᾶαν (λᾶα Call.*Fr*.104), gen. and dat. λᾶος, λᾶϊ: dual λᾶε: pl. λᾶες *APl*. c., gen. λάων, dat. λάεσι, Ep. λάεσσι, all which forms occur in Hom., exc. λάεσι, which appears in *Epigr.Gr*.455.2 (Bostra), *IG*14.499 (Catana):—also masc. **λᾶος**, ὁ λᾶυ (sic) ὅδε *Inscr.Cypr*.93 H.; acc. λᾶον Puchstein *Epigr.Gr*.p.76 (Memphis), *Riv.Fil*.56.224 (Cyrene); gen. λάου S.*OC*196 (lyr.) codd. (cf. Hdn.Gr.1.109), *Leg.Gort*.10.36; acc. pl. λάους Hes.*Fr*.115, Simon.ap.Sch.Il.*Oxy*.1087.40; dat. λάϋς (= λάοις) Corinn. *Supp*.1.23 (fem.), cf. Serv. ad Virg. *G*.1.63:—poet. Noun (also in dialects, v. supr.), *stone*, esp. of stones thrown by warriors, ὅσον τ' ἐπὶ λᾶαν ἵησιν Il.3.12, cf. 7.268, al.; λ. ἀναιδής, of the stone of Sisyphus, Od.11.598; ὅς μιν λᾶαν θῆκε turned her into *stone*, 13.163, cf. Il. 2.319.

**λαβά**· σιαγών, Hsch. **λαβάβηρ**· λακανίσκη, Id. **λαβαντίς**, ίδος, ἡ, name of a vegetable, gloss on ἰφύα, Id.

**λᾰβάργῠρος**, ον, *taking money*, ὡρολογητής Timo 18.

**λαββάνω**, = λαμβάνω, *Foed.Delph.Pell*.1 *B* 14.

**λάβδα**, τό, indecl., *the letter* λ, Ar.*Ec*.920 (Sch.), Eup.359 (prob.), Pl.*Cra*.434c, Arist.*HA*514ᵇ18, Callias ap.Ath.10.453d, Phld.*Po*.2 *Fr*.42: the form **λάμβδα**, Ar.*Ec*. l. c. cod. R, v.l. in Arist. l. c., etc., is incorrect. (Hebr. *lāmedh*.)

⊛**λαβδᾰκισμός**, ὁ, (λάβδα) a defect in pronunciation, Quint.*Inst*.1.5.32 (pl.), Diom.453 K.

**λαβδοειδής**, ές, *formed like a* Λ, ὀστοῦν λ. the *os hyoïdes*, Gal.18(2).957, Orib.25.8.1; ῥαφή the suture in the skull between the occiput and sinciput, Gal.*UP*9.5, Ruf.*Onom*.133; διάγραμμα *Theol.Ar*.3. (**λαμβδ-** is freq. written in codd. and is v.l. in Gal.*UP* l. c., Orib. l. c., but **λαβδ-** Poll.2.37, 4.133.)

**λάβδωμα**, ατος, τό, *a figure like that of* Λ, Iamb. *in Nic*.p.14 P.

**λᾰβ-ή**, ἡ, (λαβεῖν) *handle, haft*, λάβαν τῶ ξίφεος Alc.33.2, cf. D.27.20, etc.; λαβαὶ ἀμφίστομοι, of a cup, S.*OC*473, cf. Ar.*Pax* 1258. **II.** as a pugilistic term, *grip, hold*, βελτίων οὐκ ἔστιν ἐν μάχαις λ. πώγωνος Alexander Magnus ap. Plu.2.180b, cf. Plu.*Thes*.5; ὥσπερ ἀθλητὴς λ. ζητεῖν Id.*Fab*.5: metaph., τὰς λ. τοῦ φαρμάκου Gal.11.426. **III.** metaph., *handle, occasion*, μὴ μεθῇς τὸν ἄνδρ', ἐπειδή σοι λ. δέδωκεν Ar.*Eq*.841; λ. γὰρ ἐνδέδωκας ib.847, cf. *Lys*.671, D. *Prooem*.2; ὡς ἅπαξ παρέδωκεν λ. Ar.*Nu*.551; ὥσπερ παλαιστὴς τὴν αὐτὴν λ. πάρεχε Pl.R.544b; ὁ λόγος ἡμῖν οἷον λ. ἀποδίδωσιν Id.*Lg*.682e; λ. παραδιδόναι εἰς ἔλεγχον Plu.*Cic*.20; εἰλημμένος ἦν προσήκει λ. ὑπὸ φιλοσοφίας Id.2.78b; εἰλήμμεθα λαβὴν ἄφυκτον Nicoch.3 D.: so in pl., τὰς ὁμοίας. . λ. λαβεῖν A.*Ch*.498; εἰς τὰς ὁμοίας λ. ἐληλυθας Pl.*Phdr*.236b; τὰ μαθήματα φαίη τις ἂν λαβὰς εἶναι φιλοσοφίας Xenocr.ap.Plu.2.452d, cf. D.L.4.10; ἐν λαβαῖς εἶναι or γενέσθαι to be at *grips*, of wrestlers, Plu.*Eum*.7, 2.979a; εἰς λαβὰς ἥκειν Id.*Luc*.3; of an orator, ἀφύκτους [δεῖ εἶναι] τὰς λ. D.H.*Dem*.18, cf. 20; λαβὰς ἀντιλογίας διδόναι *opportunities* for refutation, Id.*Rh*.8.15; also in friendly sense, φιλικαὶ λ. Plu.2.660b. **IV.** *attack* of fever, Hp.ap.Gal.19.116. **V.** *taking, accepting*, ἐν ἀργύρου λαβῇ A.*Supp*.935; *catching*, of a ball, Gal.*Parv.Pil*.3. **VI.** *turn*, of a bandage, Id.10.432. **VII.** Anat., in pl., *insertions, attachments* of muscles, Id.18(2).1006. **VIII.** *eye* of a needle, Aen.Tact.18.10. **-ήροις**· ποτιστηρίοις, Hsch. **-ίδιον**, τό, Dim. of λαβίς II, *pair of tweezers*, Dsc.1.68.7, Gal.12.687, *PHolm*.6.11. **II.** Dim. of λαβή I, ὑποδέρειν διὰ τοῦ λ. τοῦ σμιλαρίου Leonid.ap.Aët.6.1. **-ῐδόω**, *seize with pincers*, interpol. in Dsc.*Eup*.1.50. ⊛**-ιον**, τό, Dim. of λαβή I, *haft*, Str.12.2.10. **-ιρος**· βόθυνος, Hsch. ⊛**-ίς**, ίδος, ἡ, = λαβή, *handle*, Gal.2.704; *hilt*, Lxx *Jd*.3.22, *EM*594.9. **II.** Act., *holder*, i.e. **1.** *forceps*, Hp.*Steril*.244, *Hermes* 38.282 (cod. Laur.), Apollon. ap.Gal.12.659. **2.** *clamp, clasp*, Plb.6.23.11; λ. σιδηραῖ *Inscr. Délos* 442 *B* 168 (ii B.C.). **3.** *tongs* or *snuffers* to trim lamps, Lxx *Ex*.38.17(37.23), *Nu*.4.9, v.l. in J.*AJ*8.3.7. **4.** = πυράγρα, Cyr.

**λαβρᾰγορ-έω**, *talk boldly, brag*, Anon.*in Rh*.159.2, 161.34. **-ης**, ου, ὁ, *bold, rash talker, braggart*, Il.23.479.

**λαβράζω**, = λαβρεύομαι, Nic.*Al*.160, Tz.*H*.1.743, Hsch.; also, = λαβρόομαι, Lyc.260.

**λαβράκιον** [ρᾱ], τό, Dim. of λάβραξ, Antiph.222.2, Amphis 35.

⊛**λαβράκτης**, ου, ὁ, = λαβραγόρης, Pratin.Lyr.5.

**Λαβράνιος**, ὁ, epith. of Zeus in Cyprus, Myres *Cesnola Collection* p.550.

**λάβραξ**, ᾰκος, ὁ, (λάβρος) a ravenous sea-fish, *Labrax lupus*, the *bass*, Alc.107, Eup.150 (pl.), Diph.66.10, Arist.*HA*567ᵃ19, 591ᵃ11, Ptol.Euerg.1 J.; ὁ πάντων ἰχθύων σοφώτατος Ar.*Fr*.595; λάβρακες Μιλήσιοι, prov. of greedy persons, Apostol.10.38, cf. Ar.*Eq*.361.

**λαβρ-εία**· ἡ τοῦ λόγου ἔκληψις, Hsch.; = ἡ φλυαρία, Zonar. **-εύομαι**, (λάβρος) *talk rashly, brag*, τί πάρος λαβρεύεαι; Il.23.474; μύθοισι λαβρεύεαι ib.478. **2.** λαβρεύονται· ῥέουσι μεγάλα βουλεύονται, θορυβοῦσι σφόδρα, Hsch. **-ηγορέω**, *boast*, Tz. ad Hes.*Op*.477.

**λαβροβόρος**, ον, *ravenously devouring*, στόματα Pancrat.*Oxy*.1085.18.

**λαβρόνιον**, τό, = λαβρώνιον, Hsch.:—also **λαβρόϊον**, Id.

**λαβρό-ομαι**, *rush violently*, χεῦμα. . λαβρωθὲν σκότῳ *wild* and dark, Lyc.705. **-πόδης**, ου, ὁ, *rapid of foot, rushing*, χείμαρρε *AP*9.277 (Antiphil.). **-ποσία**, ἡ, *excessive drinking*, *Hippiatr*.8. **-ποτέω**, (πίνω) *drink hard*, *AP*5.109 (Marc. Arg.): c. acc., κύλικας ib.10.18 (Id.).

⊛**λάβρος**, ον (also α, ον Damocr.ap.Gal.13.917): **I.** in Hom. only of wind and water, *furious, boisterous*, Ζέφυρος λάβρος ἐπαιγίζων Il.2.148, cf. Od.15.293, Thphr.*Vent*.50; ὡς ὅτε κῦμα θοῇ ἐν νηῒ πέσῃσι λάβρον Il.15.625; ποταμὸς. . λ. ὕπαιθα ῥέων 21.271; ὅτε λαβρότατον χέει ὕδωρ Ζεύς 16.385; λ. ὄμβρος Hdt.8.12; καπνός, σέλας, Pi.*O*.8.36, *P*.3.40; πνεῦμα A.*Pers*.110 (lyr.); πῦρ E.*Or*.697; λάβρον αὐχέν', of the Hellespont personified, Tim.*Pers*.84; simply, *huge, mighty*, λίθος Pi.*N*.8.46; ὕδατα λαβρότερα, expld. by ἀθροώτερα, Arist.*Mete*.348ᵇ10: neut. as Adv., λάβρον ἐπαιγίζων. . Ἔρως *AP*5.285.2 (Paul. Sil.). **II.** after Hom., of men, *boisterous, turbulent*, esp. in talking, *hasty*, Thgn.634; λάβροι παγγλωσσίᾳ Pi.*O*.2.86; λ. στόμα Simon.177, S.*Aj*.1147; λ. ὄμμα E.*Hel*.379 (anap., s. v. l.). **2.** *fierce*, δράκοντος λαβρόταται γένυες Pi.*P*.4.244, cf. E.*HF*253; *violent, impetuous*, λ. πρὸς τὴν ἐπιθυμίαν τὴν τῆς τροφῆς Arist.*GA*717ᵃ23 (Comp.); λάβρῳ χρώμενοι τῷ ποτῷ D.S.5.26; λάβρος εἰς Βάκχον ὀλισθών *AP*11.25 (Apollonid.); λαγνεῖαι λαβρόταται Ti.Locr.103a; ἐπιθυμία Arist.*GA*717ᵃ28; Ἔρως *AP*5.267 (Paul. Sil.); λάβρῳ μαχαίρᾳ E.*Cyc*.403. **III.** Adv. λάβρως *violently, furiously*, [ἵπποι] ἄνακτα φέρουσι λάβρως Thgn.988 (cf. λαβροπόδης, -συτος); λ. ὕει Thphr.*HP*4.7.1; ἄνεμοι καταιγίζοντες λ. D.S.5.26; ἀθρόως καὶ λ. App.*Hisp*.18, cf. *Hann*.48; διδόναι [τὸ ὀξύμελι] κατ' ὀλίγον καὶ μὴ λ. Hp.*Acut*.58, cf. Ph.1.452. **2.** *eagerly, greedily*, λ. διαρταμᾶν (of the eagle) A.*Pr*.1022; τῇ βρώσει χρῆται λ. (of the lion) Arist.*HA*594ᵇ18, cf. Ph.1.71.—Poet. word, used also in Ion. and late Prose. [λᾱ- by position in Ep.: λᾰ- E.*Or*. l. c., *HF*861 (troch.), *AP*11.25 (Apollonid.).]

**λαβροσιάων**· χορτασμοῦ ἀκόσμου, Hsch. (χορτασμὸν cod.).

**λαβροστομ-έω**, (στόμα) *talk boldly, rashly*, A.*Pr*.329. **-ία**· ἡ διάχρηστος λαλιά, Hsch.

⊛**λαβρο-σύνη**, Dor. -νᾱ, ἡ, (λάβρος) *violence, greed*, *AP*6.305 (Leon.), Opp.*H*.5.366: also in pl., ib.2.130. **2.** *bold talking*, Tryph.423 (pl.). **-σῠτος**, ον, (σεύω) *rushing furiously*, A.*Pr*.600 (lyr.). **-της**, ητος, ἡ, = λαβροσύνη, Muson.*Fr*.18ᴮp.100 H., Ath.7.310f; λ. ἐν τῷ πίνειν Id.11.484c. **-φᾰγέω**, *eat greedily*, D.L.6.28.

**λάβρυς**, = πέλεκυς, Lydian word, Plu.2.302a.

**λαβρύσσει**· λαβρεύει, Hsch.; also, = δειλαίνει, Id.

**λαβρώνιος**, ὁ, *large wide cup*, Men.503, Diph.80.1:—also **λαβρωνία**, ἡ, Eust.1066.3; **λαβρώνιον**, τό, Men.24.4, Hsch. (λαβρό- cod.); cf. λαβρόνιον.

**λάβυζος**, ἡ, an unknown *spice-plant*, Dinon 18.

**λᾰβῠρινθοειδής**, ές, = -ώδης, Vett.Val.276.31.

⊛**λᾰβύρινθ-ος** [ῠ], ὁ, *labyrinth* or *maze*, a large building consisting of numerous halls connected by intricate and tortuous passages: in Egypt, Hdt.2.148, cf. Str.17.1.37; in Crete, Call.*Del*.311, D.S.1.61: pl., σπήλαια καὶ ἐν αὐτοῖς οἰκοδομητοὶ λαβύρινθοι Str.8.6.2; name of a building at Rome, *IG*14.1093; also at Miletus, *Milet*.7.56, *Supp. Epigr*.4.446 (iii/ii B.C., pl.). **2.** prov. of tortuous questions or arguments, ὥσπερ εἰς λ. ἐμπεσόντες, οἰόμενοι ἤδη ἐπὶ τέλει εἶναι περικάμψαντες πάλιν ὥσπερ ἐν ἀρχῇ. . ἀνεφάνημεν ὄντες Pl.*Euthd*.291b; λαβυρίνθων σκολιώτερα D.H.*Th*.40; λόγοι λαβυρίνθοις ὅμοιοι Luc.*Bis Acc*.21; λόγων λαβύρινθοι Id.*Icar*.29; of ant-hills, Gal.*UP*1.3; of the *rete mirabile Galeni*, Id.5.608; of Lycophron's poem, *AP*9.191; as name of a philosopher, Luc.*Symp*.6. **II.** *any wreathed* or *coiled up body*, εἰνάλιος λ. the twisted *sea-snail*, *AP*6.224 (Theodorid.); ἐκ σχοίνων λ. *bow-net* of rushes, Theoc.21.11. ⊛**-ώδης**, ες, *labyrinthine, contorted*, ἀστράγαλος Arist.*HA*499ᵇ25; οἴκημα Procop.*Arc*.4: metaph., δόξα Ph.1.192; ἐρωτήσεις Luc.*Fug*.10.

**λαγαγεῖ**· ἀφρίζει, Hsch. (betw. λαγαρόν and λαγάσσαι).

**λαγαίω**, *release*: inf. λαγαίεν *GDI*4982.4, 4989.6 (Crete): 3 sg. aor. subj. λαγάσει *Leg.Gort*.1.9, al.: aor. inf. λαγάσαι *GDI*4979.46, *Leg.Gort*.1.5; cf. λαγάσσαι.

⊛**λαγανίζω**, f.l. for γαληνίζω, Hp.*Morb.Sacr*.13.

⊛**λάγᾰνον** [λᾰ], τό, *a thin broad cake*, of meal and oil, like ἴτριον, Diocl.*Fr*.116; λ. ἄζυμα Lxx *Le*.2.4, cf. Matro *Parod.Fr*.4, Gal.6.492, *POxy*.1211.5 (ii A.D.), Ar.*Ec*.843 as cited by Ath.3.110a (πόπανα codd. Ar.); λ. τηγανιστόν J.*AJ*7.4.2 (cf. λ. ἀπὸ τηγάνου Lxx 2*Ki*.6.19); ἑλκύειν λ., cf. Lat. *tracta*, Chrysipp.Tyan.ap.Ath.14.647e:—

Dim. **λᾰγάνιον**, τό, Id.ap.Ath.14.648a, *UPZ*89.2 (ii B.C.), *PLond.*2.190.34 (iii A.D.).

**λᾰγᾰνοφᾰκῆ**, ἡ, *lentil pudding* or *cake*, Bilabel 'Οψαρτ.p.11.

**λᾰγᾰρίζομαι**, Pass., dub. sens., Ar.*V.*674 ἐκ κηθαρίου λαγαριζόμενον, expld. by Sch. τὰ λαγαρὰ ἐσθίοντα, ὅ ἐστιν εὔθραυστα καὶ εὐτελῆ τινα, i.e. *getting a poor living* out of the ballot-box. II. prob. *scrape*, Pherecr.121. III. *jog* or *nudge with the elbow*, = σκαλεύειν, Hsch. (v.l. λαγαρυζόμενον in Ar. l.c., λαγυριζόμενοι in Pherecr. l.c.). B. intr. in Act., of the pulse, Archig.ap.Gal.8.662.

**λαγαρίττεται**· μετριεύεται, Hsch.

**λᾰγᾰρο-ειδῶς**, Adv. *like a* στίχος λαγαρός (4), Eust.399.41. **-κυκλος**, ον, *somewhat convex*, of the lyre or cithara, Id.1464.64 (cf. λαγαρός 1). **-ομαι**, Pass., *to be* or *become slack*; ποταμὸς -ούμενος *in the act of thawing*, *AP*9.56 (Phil.).

**λᾰγᾰρός**, ά, όν, *hollow, sunken*, of an animal's flanks, X.*Cyn.*4.1; of the right ventricle, -ωτέρη Hp.*Cord.*4; λαγαρᾷ..τῇ γαστρί Philostr.*Im.*2.21; τὰς λ. (sc. γαστέρας) Ar.*Ec.*1167; λ. κύκλοι *sunken, flattish*, of the tortoise, Philostr.*Im.*1.10; λ. ποπάνευμα (cf. λαγαρίζομαι I) *AP*6.231 (Phil.): Comp., Hp. l.c.: Sup., κατὰ τὸ -ώτατον in the *least defensible* part, Plu.*Cam.*25. 2. *slack, loose*, αὐχὴν λ. τὰ κατὰ τὴν συγκαμπήν X.*Eq.*1.8; of camels, D.S.2.54. Adv. -ρῶς, ἱππασθείς Philostr.*Im.*2.2. b. metaph., τὴν πόλιν ἀντὶ λαγαρᾶς καὶ ὑποσόμφου μεστὴν ἐποίησεν ἀγλαΐας Them.*Or.*18.222d. Adv. Comp. -ώτερον, opp. σφοδρότερον, πλῆξαι τὴν χορδήν Theo Sm.p.72 H. 3. *thin, narrow*, δρυμῶνες (cj.) X.*Cyn.*6.5; of columns, *lanky*, D.H.16.3, Plu.*Publ.*15; of men, *emaciated*, Thphr.*HP*9.10.3. 4. in Metric, στίχος λ., opp. προκοίλιος, a '*thin-waisted*' verse, with a short syllable for a long one in the interior, like Il.23.493, cf. Ar.*Ec.*1167, Plu.2.397d, Ath.14.632e, Sch.Heph.p.289 C. 5. in Arist.*HA*622$^b$23 (Comp., s.v.l.), where it is an epith. of spiders, some expl. it to mean *lank, meagre*, some *agile, nimble*. 6. of plasters, *porous, absorbent*, Orib.*Fr.*74. (Cf. λαγαίω, Lat. *laxus*, ONorse *slak-r*, Engl. *slack*: perh. akin to λήγω.)

**λᾰγᾰρότης**, ητος, ἡ, *slackness*, Hld.9.15, Anon.ap.Suid. s.v. λαγαρόν. II. of a verse, v. foreg. 4, Eust.1464.63.

❀**λᾰγᾰρύζομαι**, v. λαγαρίζομαι.

**λᾰγᾰρ-ώδης**, ες, *sunken, flattish*, Sch.Ar.*Ach.*245. **-ωσις**, εως, ἡ, = λαγαρότης II, Eust.1103.18.

**λαγάσσαι**· ἀφεῖναι, Hsch. (cf. λαγαίω). **λαγβατόν**· ἀνατετραμμένον, οἱ δὲ λάγαν ἐμβάλλοντες, Id. **λάγγα**· ἡ τῇ τροφῇ διδομένη μερίς, Id.

**λαγγάζω**, *slacken* (= ἐνδίδωμι, *AB*106), Antiph.37, Phot.s.v. λογγάσω; λαγγάζει· ὀκνεῖ, οἱ δὲ λαγγεῖ, Hsch.; λαγγάσαι· περιφυγεῖν, Id.; cf. λαγγαρεῖ. **λαγγανώμενος**· περιστάμενος, στραγγευόμενος, Id. **λαγγαρεῖ**· ἀποδιδράσκει, Id. **λαγγεύει**· φεύγει, Id.

**λαγγών**· ὁ εὐθὺς λανθάνων τοῦ ἀγῶνος καὶ φόβου, *EM*554.15. II. *trader, merchant*, Cyr.

**λάγδην**, Adv. = λάξ, τὰ σώφρονα λ. πατεῖται S.*Fr.*683.3.

**λάγειος** [ᾰ], α, ον, = λαγῷος, λ. κρέα Hp.*Aff.*43, Orib.3.3.6; κρέας λάγειον Sor.1.51. (From Ion. λαγός = λαγώς.)

**λαγερός**· σμῖλαξ, Hsch. **Λάγεσις**· θεός (Sicel), Id.

❀**λᾱγέτᾱς**, α, ὁ, (λαός, ἀγέομαι) Dor. *leader of the people*, Pi.*O.*1.89, *P.*4.107, S.*Fr.*221.12, Hsch. (-έτης).

**λαγη(νάριος)**, ὁ, dub. sens. in *IGRom.*3.837 (Cilicia).

**λαγηνάρχος**· ὁ ἐξουσίαν ἔχων τοῦ οἴνου, Hsch. (λαγίν- cod., before λάγνα).

**λάγηνος, λαγήνιον**, v. λαγυν-.

**λᾰγῐδ-εύς**, έως, ὁ, (λαγώς) *leveret*, Plu.2.971d, Ael.*NA*7.47. II. *rabbit*, Str.3.2.6. **-ιον**, τό, Dim. of λαγώς, M.Ant.10.10, Poll.5.15.

**λάγῐνος** [ᾰ], η, ον, *of the hare*, γέννα A.*Ag.*119 (lyr.).

**λάγιον** [ᾰ] (not λαγίον, *EM*431.20), τό, Dim. of λαγώς, *leveret*, X.*Cyn.*5.13. II. [ᾰ or ᾱ?] a kind of *cup* or *vase*, *Inscr.Délos* 399 *B* 149, 461 *Bb* 40, al. (ii B.C.).

**λάγκατα**· πεπατημένα, Cyr. (i.e. λάγβ-). **λάγκει**· ἐῴκει, Hsch.

**λάγκη**, *lanx*, *Gloss.*

**λαγκία**, ἡ, Lat. *lancea*, D.S.5.30:—hence **λαγκιάριος**, ὁ, *lancearius*, *CIG*4004 (Iconium), Lyd.*Mag.*1.46.

**λαγκίολα** (Lat. *lanceola*), ἡ, = λογχῖτις, Ps.-Dsc.3.144.

**λάγκλα**, ἡ, = Lat. *lanx*, *dish*, *BGU*781 v 18 (i A.D.):—Dim. **λάγκλιον**, τό, ib.iv 1, *Gloss.*

**λαγκρύζεσθαι**· λοιδορεῖσθαι, Phot. **λάγματα**· ἱερὰ ἀπάργματα, Id. **λάγνα**· κάμπτρα, κιβωτός, Cyr.

❀**λαγν-εία**, Ion. -είη, ἡ, *the act of coition*, Hp.*Nat.Puer.*20, Arist.*HA*575$^a$21; *semen*, Hp.*Nat.Puer.*21, cf. Gal.19.117. II. *salaciousness*, X.*Mem.*1.6.8, *AP*10.45.8 (Pall.): pl., Ti.Locr.103a. **-ευμα**, ατος, τό, *coition*, Hp.*Nat.Puer.*31; *semen*, Id.*Int.*47. **-εύω**, *have sexual intercourse*, commonly of the man, Id.*Aër.*21, al.:—Pass., of the woman, Id.*Epid.*5.25, Procop.*Aed.*1.9; πρός τινος Id.*Arc.*17. II. *to be lecherous*, Plu.2.136d. ❀**-ης**, ου, ὁ, Att. for λάγνος acc. to Phryn.161, Phot. (but cf. Poll.6.188); voc. λάγνα Eub.55; acc. λάγνην *Com.Adesp.*388. **-ος**, η, ον, *lecherous, lustful*, prop. of the male (as μάχλος of the female), Critias 44 D., Ti.Locr.104e; of animals, Arist.*HA*575$^a$20; of the female, λάγνης γυναικός Anaxandr.60: irreg. Comp. λαγνίστερος Ph.2.307: irreg. Sup. λαγνίστατος Arist.*HA*575$^b$30; but -ότατος Choerob.*in Theod.*2.76 H., *Hippiatr.*33. Adv. Comp. -ίστερον Ph.2.207, al.

**λᾰγό-γηρως**, gloss on μύξος, Suid.; on μυγαλῆ, Sch.Luc.*Gall.*24 ap.Bast *Ep.Crit.*p.169. **-δαίτης**, ου, ὁ, (δαίω B) *hare-devourer*, A.*Ag.*123 (lyr.). **-θήρας**, ου, ὁ, *hare-hunter*, in voc. -θηρᾶ or -θῆρα *AP*9.337 (Leon.). II. a kind of *eagle*, Hsch. **-θηρέω**, *hunt hares*, Ar.*Lys.*789 (lyr.). **-κτονέω**, *kill hares*, *AP*10.11 (Satyr.). **-κύμῖνον** [ῡ], τό, *a kind of cummin*, = λαγώπους 2, v.l. in Ps.-Dsc.4.17. **-νάτη**, gloss on λαγώπυρος, Gal.19.117.

**λᾰγορεῖς**· ἐκκλησίαι, Hsch. (fort. λάγορσις). **λᾰγός**, οῦ, ὁ, v. λαγώς. **λᾰγοτροφεῖον**, v. λαγωτρ-.

**λᾰγόφθαλμος**, = λαγώφθαλμος, *PMed.Stras* b.p.6 K.

**λαγρόν ἢ λαγρός**· κραββάτιον, Hsch. **λαγρονίτης**· εἶδος πλακοῦντος, Id.

❀**λᾰγύν-ιον** [ῠ], τό, Dim. of λάγυνος, Diph.3.2, *BGU*1095.17 (i A.D.), Dsc.2.83 (v.l. -ήν-), Gal.10.835. **-ίς**, ίδος, ἡ, Dim. of λάγυνος, Plu.2.614f. **-ίων**, ωνος, ὁ, name for a parasite, *Hardbottle*, Ath.13.584f.

**λᾰγῡνοθήκη**, cj. for λαχανο- in Alex.Magn.ap.Ath.11.784b.

**λάγῡνος** [ᾰ], ὁ (fem. in Thessaly, Arist.*Fr.*499, cf. Rhian.75, Ath.11.499b), *flask, flagon*, Diph.29, 60.8, Nicostr.Com.11, *AP*6.248 (Marc. Arg.): also in later Prose, Plu.2.509d (fem.), *POxy.*1294.6 (fem., ii/iii A.D.). 2. a measure (perh. = Κνίδιον), *Ostr.*42, 150, *PFay.*104.3 (iii A.D.), Eratosth.ap.Ath.7.276b (fem.):—**λάγηνος** is freq. v.l., arising prob. from Lat. *lagena*, and admissible only in late writers, e.g. Gal.11.663. [ῡ only in late Poets, *AP*11.298.]

**λᾰγῡνοφόρια**, τά, *the flagon-bearing*, a feast at Alexandria, Eratosth.ap.Ath.7.276b. **λαγυρίζομαι**, v. λαγαρίζομαι.

❀**λαγχάνω**, fut. λήξομαι Pl.*R.*617e; Ion. λάξομαι (cf. λάξις) Hdt.7.144: aor. ἔλᾰχον Il.9.367, etc.; Ep. ἔλλαχον *h.Cer.*87, v.l. for ἔλλαβεν in Theoc.25.271; Ep. λάχον Il.4.49, al.; Aeol. opt. 1 sg. λαχόην Sapph.9 (λαχοίην A.D.*Synt.*247.25); for λέλᾰχον v. infr. IV: pf. εἴληχα A.*Th.*376, 423, etc.; plpf. εἰλήχει Pl.*Phd.*107d; poet. and Ion. λέλογχα Pi.*O.*1.53, B.9.39, Emp.20.3, E.*Tr.*282 (lyr.), Hdt.7.53, Test.ap.D.21.82, D.H.4.82, etc., but not in early Att. Prose; 3 pl. λελογχᾶσι(ν) Od.11.304, Emp.102, but λελάχᾱσι Id.115.5; part. λελαχώς Phld.*D.*1.17; Dor. 3 sg. λελόγχει Theoc.4.40: plpf. ἐλελόγχει Luc.*Am.*18:—**Pass.**, aor. ἐλήχθην Lys.17.8, Is.9.24, D.38.20: pf. εἴληγμαι E.*Tr.*296, D.30.34; 3 pl. λελάχαται Perict.ap.Stob.4.28.19: I. c. acc. rei, *obtain by lot*, of spoils, opp. ἐξαιρεῖσθαι, Od.14.232, cf. Il.9.367, etc.: generally, *obtain as one's portion*, τὸ γὰρ λάχομεν γέρας ἡμεῖς 4.49; λαχόντα τε ληΐδος αἶσαν 18.327; πρὸς δαιμόνων ὄλβον Pi.*N.*9.45; μέζονας μοίρας λ. Heraclit.25; μοῖραν ἴσην, ὡς αὐτοί περ ἐλάγχανον Od.20.282, cf. Hdt.7.144: with inf. added, ἔλαχον πολιὴν ἅλα ναιέμεν I *had* the sea *for my portion* to dwell in, Il.15.190, cf. Pi.*O.*6.34, A.*Eu.*931 (anap.); ἔλαχ' ἄναξ δούλην σ' ἔχειν E.*Tr.*278, cf. 282 (lyr.); of a deity as presiding over one's life, ἐμὲ μὲν Κὴρ..λάχε γεινόμενόν περ Il.23.79; τῷ σκληρῷ μάλα δαίμονος ὅς με λελόγχει Theoc.4.40; δαίμων ὁ τὴν ἡμετέραν μοῖραν εἰληχώς Lys.2.78; ὦ δαῖμον, ὅς με..εἴληχας Alciphr.3.49: also, esp. in pf., *to be the tutelary deity of* a place, *protect* it, [Πὰν] πάντα λόφον..λέλογχε *h.Hom.*19.6; θεοῖσι οἳ Περσίδα γῆν λελόγχασι Hdt.7.53; παῖ Ῥέας, ἃ πρυτανεῖα λέλογχας Pi.*N.*11.1; of Athena, ἣ τὴν ὑμετέραν πόλιν ἔλαχε Pl.*Ti.*23d, cf. E.*Or.*319 (lyr.), *Ph.*1576 (lyr.): metaph., ἀκέρδεια λέλογχεν θαμινὰ κακαγόρους Pi.*O.*1.53: freq. of persons *who have a post assigned to them by lot*, κλήρῳ νῦν πεπάλασθε διαμπερές, ὃς κε λάχῃσι Il.7.171, cf. 179, 23.354, 862: c. inf., κλήρῳ λάχον ἐνθάδ' ἕπεσθαι 24.400; so πάλῳ λαχεῖν A.*Th.*55, Hdt.4.94, cf. 3.128; ὡς ἐν πύλαις ἕκαστος εἴληχεν πάλον A.*Th.*376: abs., πρὸς Θύμβρης ἔλαχον Λύκιοι *had their post assigned* near Thymbra, Il.10.430; ἐπί, ἐν πύλαις λ., A.*Th.*423, 451, etc.; λαχών alone, Hdt.3.128, etc.; λ. τινὰ διδάσκαλον *have him assigned to one by lot*, Antipho 6.11. 2. at Athens, *obtain* an office *by lot*, ἀρχὰς λαχεῖν, opp. χειροτονηθῆναι (to be elected), D.57.25, cf. Ar.*Av.*1111; οὐδεμίαν [ἀρχὴν] λαχὼν οὐδὲ χειροτονηθεὶς Aeschin.1.106: more freq. c. inf., ὁ τῷ κυάμῳ λαχὼν πολεμαρχέειν *he who had the lot* to be polemarch, Hdt.6.109; ἔλαχον πρότεροι ἀποδιδόναι Th.5.21, cf. 35; λαχὼν..ἱερομνημονεῖν Ar.*Nu.*623; λαχόντος βουλεύειν *when I became* Member of Council *by lot*, D.21.111, cf. 59.3, Pl.*Grg.*473e: c. gen., λαχεῖν τῶν ἐξιόντων *to be chosen by lot* as one of.., D.21.133; also οἱ ταμίαι οἱ λαχόντες *IG*1$^2$.91.21; λαχεῖν βασιλεύς, ἐπιμελητής, ἱερεύς, etc., Lys.6.4, Din.2.10, D.57.47, etc.; ἐπίσκοπος τῷ κυάμῳ λαχών Ar.*Av.*1022; οἱ πεντακόσιοι ⟨οἱ⟩ λαχόντες τῷ κυάμῳ Lex ap.And.1.96: abs., κληρούντων τοὺς λαχόντας *those on whom the lot fell*, Th.3.50, cf. Pl.*Lg.*765c; τοὺς λαχόντας προέδρους *SIG*465.6 (Athens, iii B.C.); rare exc. in Athens, λαχὼν ἱερεύς ib.762.12 (Dionysopolis, i B.C.), etc. 3. as Att. law-term, λαγχάνειν δίκην *obtain leave to bring* a suit (esp. a private suit), prob. because the presiding magistrates decided the order of hearing by lot; λ. δίκην τινί *against* one, Pl.*Euthphr.*5b, *Lg.*938b, cf. Aeschin.2.99; ἔγκλημά τινι D.34.16; τὸν εἰληχότα τοῦ κλήρου τὴν δίκην the person *suing* for the inheritance, Is.8.3: without τὴν δίκην, εἴληχε μὲν αὐτῷ τῆς θυγατρὸς τῆς Εὐκτήμονος ὡς οὔσης ἐπικλήρου he *has claimed* Euctemon's daughter.., Id.6.46, cf. D.48.20; λ. τινὶ τοῦ συμβολαίου Lys.17.3; λ. φόνου ἐμαυτῷ D.21.120; also λ. τῷ υἱεῖ τῆς ἐπικλήρου *prosecute the claim* on his son's behalf, And.1.121, cf. 124; λ. δίκην τινὶ εἰς τοὺς Ἀμφικτύονας χιλίων ταλάντων ὑπέρ τινος D.59.98, cf. Isoc.16.2: abs., λ. πρὸς τὸν ἄρχοντα Is.11.33: metaph., τοῦ σώματος [τῇ ψυχῇ] δίκην λαχόντος Democr.159:—Pass., πρὸς οὓς αἱ δίκαι ἐλήχθησαν Lys.17.8; πρὸ τοῦ τὴν δίκην ληχθῆναι D.54.28: impers., τούτοις λαγχάνεται *proceedings are taken*, Id.23.76. II. c. gen. partit., *become possessed of* a thing, ὥς κεν Ἀχιλλεὺς δώρων ἐκ Πριάμοιο λάχῃ Il.24.76; ἔλαχον κτερέων Od.5.311, cf. Thgn.934, Pi.*I.*8(7).69, *Fr.*75.6, B.1.56, 9.39, *Lyr.Adesp.*53, Emp.102, 115.5, Democr.21; εὖ πραπίδων λαχόντα A.*Ag.*380 (lyr.); χρυσῆς..τιμῆς λαχεῖν S.*Ant.*699; οὔ τι μὴ λάχωσι τοῦδε συμμάχου Id.*OC*450; γέν-

νας ἀφθίτου λαχόντες Id.*Fr.*278; διπλοῦ βίου λαχόντες E.*Supp.*1086; πατρῴων οὐ λαχών not *having obtained* thy patrimony, Id.*Tr.*1192; τῆς εὐπρεπεστάτης τελευτῆς Th.2.44; δείπνου τε καὶ ὕπνου λαγχάνομεν X.*Hier.*6.9; also χθονὸς λαχεῖν τοσοῦτον ἐνθανεῖν μόνον S.*OC*790; γάμου μέρος λαχοῦσα Id.*Ant.*918; τύμβου κοινὸν εἰληχὼς μέρος Id.*El.* 1135; τῆς γῆς τὸ πρὸς Νότον εἴληχε Παλλάς Id.*Fr.*24.8. III. abs., *draw lots*, κατάστασις ἡ διὰ τοῦ λαγχάνειν γιγνομένη Isoc.7.23, cf. D.S. 4.63, etc.; περί τινος D.21 Arg.2 §§3,4, *Ev.Jo.*19.24. IV. causal only in Ep. redupl. aor. λέλᾰχον, *put in possession of* a thing, *grant* one *the rights of..*, ὄφρα πυρός με Τρῶες.. λελάχωσι θανόντα Il.7.80, cf. 15.350, 23.76: later this aor. is used intr. in *AP*7.341 (Procl.). V. intr., *fall to one's lot* or *share*, ἐς ἑκάστην [νῆα] ἐννέα λάγχανον αἶγες nine goats *were allotted* to each, Od.9.160; αἰὼν δυσαίων ἔλαχεν E. *Hel.*214 (lyr.); ὅσοις.. τὸ σωφρονεῖν εἴληχεν Id.*Hipp.*80; τὸ λαχὸν μέρος ἑκάστῳ τῷ θεῷ Pl.*Lg.*745e, cf. *Epin.*992d; τὴν πρὸς Νότον λαχεῖν φασι Δευκαλίωνι Str.9.5.23.

**λᾰγωβολ-εῖον**, τό, *place for catching hares*, Suid. ⊛**-ία**, ἡ, *hare-shooting*, Call.*Dian.*2 (pl.). **-ον** (parox.), τό, *staff* or *stick* for *flinging at hares*, also used as a *shepherd's staff* or *crook*, Theoc.4.49, 7.128, *Ep.*2, *AP*6.188 (Leon.), D.H.14.2, etc.:—also **λαγωοβόλον**, *AP*6. 296 (Leon.).

**λᾰγωδάριον**, τό, Dim. of λαγώς, Ph.1.256,318.

**λᾰγωδάτον** κοιμᾶσθαι *sleep with the eyes open*, Steph.*inHp.*1. 94 D. (s. v.l.).

**λᾰγωδίας**, ου, ὁ, a bird, = ὦτος, Alex.Mynd.ap.Ath.9.390f.

**λᾰγῴδιον**, τό, Dim. of λαγώς, *leveret*, Ar.*Ach.*520, *PFlor.*177.13 (iii A. D.).

**λᾰγώδων**, ον, gen. οντος, = ἐξώδων, *Hippiatr.*115.

**λᾰγώειος**, α, ον, *of* or *belonging to a hare*, Opp.*C.*1.491,519.

**λαγωΐνης**· ὄρνις ποιός, Hsch. **λᾰγωΐς**, ίδος, ἡ, kind of bird or fish, Hor.*Sat.*2.2.22.

⊛**λᾰγών**, όνος, ἡ, also ὁ, Hp.*Int.*25, Aret.*SD*2.11: (λαγαρός):—*the hollow on each side below the ribs*, *flank*, Hp. l. c., Ar.*V.*1193, Chaerem. 14.3, Arist.*HA*493$^a$18, al.: freq. in pl. λαγόνες, *flanks*, Batr.222, E. *IT*298, Ar.*Ra.*662, etc.; λαγόνων ὀστᾶ *iliac* bones, Gal.2.507, cf.772; prop. of men, but also of animals, E.*El.*826, X.*Cyn.*4.1, 5.10, Theoc. 25.246; θύννου λαγόνες Antiph.132.5 (anap.). 2. pl., in later Greek, *womb*, Naumach.ap.Stob.4.22.32, λύσις αἰνίγματος ap.Arg.E. *Ph.* II. metaph., any *hollow*, κοίλη λ. *hollow* of a cup, Eub.43; λαγόνεσσι φαρέτρης *AP*6.326 (Leon. Alex.); πρός τινι λ. τοῦ κρημνοῦ Plu.*Arat.*22; esp. of a mountain, *flank*, D.H.3.24, 9.23, Cleom.1.8, Call.*Fr.*185 (pl.); *bank* of a river, λαιᾷ ποταμοῦ.. λαγόνι *AP*6.287 (Antip.); *sides* of a grave, *IG*14.2001; χθονίαι ib.7.117 (Megara).

**λᾰγώνεια**· λαγοῦ κρέα, Hsch. **λᾰγωοβόλον**, τό, v. λαγωβόλον. **λᾰγωός**, οῦ, ὁ, Ep. for λαγώς (q. v.).

**λᾰγῷος**, α, ον, contr. for λαγώϊος, *of the hare*, κρέα Ar.*Ach.*1110; τρίχες Plu.2.138f; τὰ λ. (sc. κρέα) *hare's flesh*, Hp.*Vict.*2.46: and generally, *dainties*, *delicacies*, ζῆν ἐν πᾶσι λαγῴοις Ar.*V.*709, cf. *Ach.* 1006, *Pax* 1196, Telecl.32, Pl.Com.174.10, etc.

**λᾰγωοφόνος**, ον, poet. for λαγωφόνος, Opp.*C.*1.154.

**λᾰγώ-πους**, ποδος, ὁ, ἡ, *rough-footed like a hare*: hence, as Subst., 1. *ptarmigan*, Plin.*HN*10.133; cf. λαγώς II. 2. a downy plant, *hare's foot trefoil*, *Trifolium arvense*, Dsc.4.17, Gal.12. 56. (-πουν Dsc., Gal. ll. cc., but -πους Orib.15.1.11.) **-πῡρος**, ἡ, = foreg. 2, Hp.*Ulc.*15.

**λᾰγώς** or **λαγῶς**, ὁ, gen. λαγώ or λαγῶ (λαγῶς, λαγῶ, acc. to Hdn.Gr. 1.245, 2.629); acc. λαγών Ar.*V.*1203, *Frr.*212, 252, but λαγώ or λαγῶ X.*Cyn.*3.3 (this form is condemned by Luc.*Sol.*3, but cf. Ath.9.400a): pl., nom. λαγῴ Eup.143; acc. λαγώς Arist.*HA*619$^b$9:—Ion. **λαγός**, οῦ, Hdt.1.123, al., and so καθ' ἡμᾶς, Ath.9.400a; also in Dor., Epich. 60, and Trag. and Com., S.*Fr.*111, Amips.18, Alex.123, Philem.89. 5:—Ep. **λᾰγωός**, οῦ, also in X.*Cyn.*10.2 codd., Arist.*HA*606$^a$24, *EN* 1118$^a$18, Luc.*Symp.*38, etc., and cf. infr. III, V:—*hare*, ἢ κεμάδ' ἠὲ λαγωόν Il.10.361; πτῶκα λαγωόν 22.310; πρόκας ἠδὲ λαγωούς Od. 17.295; τοὶ δ' ὠκύποδας λαγὸς (Dor. for λαγούς) ἧρευν Hes.*Sc.*302; λαγὼ δίκην like *a hare*, A.*Eu.*26: prov., ἐστὶν λαγώς, of a coward, Posidipp.26.9; λαγὼ βίον ζῆν lead a *hare's* life, D.18.263; δειλότερος λαγὼ Φρυγός Prov.ap.Str.1.2.30; ὁ λ. οὗτος this *coward*, Philostr.*VA* 4.37; λαγὼς καθεύδων, of persons feigning sleep, Zen.4.84, cf. X. *Cyn.*5.11; λ. τὸν περὶ τῶν κρεῶν τρέχων, of persons seeking to escape imminent death, Zen.4.85. II. a bird *with rough feathered feet*, mentioned with the swallow, Artem.4.56, cf. Ant.Lib.21.5; cf. λαγωδίας, λαγώπους. III. a kind of *sea-slug*, *Lepus marinus*, Epich. l. c., Amips. l. c.; ὁ θαλάττιος λαγωός *sea-hare*, *Aplysia leporina*, Plu. 2.983f, Gal.11.688, al., cf. Nic.*Al.*465, Dsc.2.18. IV. a constellation, Arat.338, Eudox.ap.Hipparch.1.2.20. V. a kind of bandage, τῷ λαγωῷ ἐπιδέσμῳ Heliod.ap.Orib.46.18.2, cf. 48.27 tit., Sor. *Fasc.*7. (Prob. *slack-ear*, cf. λαγαρός, οὖς.)

**λᾰγω-σφᾰγία**, poet. -ίη, ἡ, *killing of hares*, *AP*6.167 (Agath.). **-τροφεῖον**, τό, Lat. *leporarium*, *Gloss.* (also λαγοτρ-, as Colum.8. 1). **-τροφέω**, *feed* or *keep hares*, Eust.1821.32.

**λᾰγώφθαλμος**, ον, lit. *hare-eyed*: hence, *unable to close the eye*, owing to shortening of the upper eyelid, Dem.Ophth.ap.Aët.7. 75, cf. Gal.14.681, Aët.7.2, Paul.Aeg.6.10; v. λαγόφθαλμος:—also **λαγωόφθαλμος**, Eust.812.2; τὸ λ. this condition of eyes, Gal.19.439.

**λᾰγω-φόνος**, ὁ, *hare-killer*, epith. of a species of eagle, Arist.*HA* 618$^b$28:—also **λαγωοφόνος** (q. v.). **-χειλος**, ον, *having a hare-lip*, Gal.14.681.

**λάδανον**, v. λήδανον.

**λάδας**· ἔλαφος νεβρίας, Hsch.

**λάδδουσθη**, Boeot., = λάζυσθαι, *IG*7.3054.6 (Lebad., iv B. C.).

**λαδοίατο**· λαμβάνοιτο, Hsch. (cf. λάζομαι). **λάδομαι**· γνώμην τίθεμαι, Id. **λᾶδος**, v. λῆδος.

**λαδρέω**, *flow strongly*, λαδρέοντι τοὶ μυκτῆρες Sophr.135.

**λαδωγενής**· ἡ Ἀφροδίτη, ὅτι ἐπὶ τῷ ἐν Ἀρκαδίᾳ ποταμῷ Λάδωνι ἐγεννήθη, Hsch.

**λαδωνίς**, ίδος, ἡ, = δάφνη, Gal.12.426.

**λαεδός**, ὁ, an unknown bird, Arist.*HA*610$^a$9 (vv. ll. λαιδός, λιβυός): prob. = λαιός (A).

**λαεντιάριος**· λιθοξόος, Hsch.

**λᾱεργής**, ές, *made of stone*, Nic.*Th.*708 (v. l. εὐεργής).

**λαέρκινον**, τό, name of the plant καρπήσιον at Side in Pamphylia, Gal.14.72.

**λᾱέρτης**, ου, ὁ, a kind of *ant*, Ael.*NA*10.42; a kind of *wasp*, ibid. II. as pr. n., *Laertes*, the father of Odysseus, Od.1.430, al.:—also **Λαέρτιος**, ου, S.*Ph.*87, 417, etc.; **Λάρτιος**, ib.402 (lyr.), 1286, *Aj.*1, etc.

**λαζίνης**· χαραδρίας, καλλαρίας ἰχθῦς, Hsch. (cf. μαζίνης).

**λάζομαι**, Ep., Ion., and Megar. for λαμβάνω, used by Hom. only in Ep. 3 sg. impf. λάζετο (ἐλάζετο only in Il.5.371), and 3 pl. opt. λαζοίατο (v. infr.); Dor. imper. λάσδεο Theoc.8.84, λάζευ Id.15.21, *Trag.Adesp.*381:—Act., λάζω Achaean acc. to *AB*1095:—*seize*, *grasp*, ἔγχος Il.8.389; πέτρον, μάστιγα, ἡνία, 16.734, 5.840, al.; λ. τινὰ ἀγκάς *take* one in her arms, ib.371; ὀδὰξ λαζοίατο γαῖαν *may they bite* the dust, 2.418: metaph., πάλιν δ' ὅ γε λάζετο μῦθον he *took* back, i. e. *retracted* his speech, 4.357, Od.13.254; also in Ion. Prose, πεφυκὸς νόσους λάζεσθαι disposed *to take* them, Hp.*Loc.Hom.*1; ὀδύνη λάζεται [τὸν ἐγκέφαλον] pain *seizes* or *attacks* it, Id.*Morb.*2.20. 2. *receive*, λαζόμενος τῶν θυομένων πάντων τὰ δέρματα.. *SIG*1010.4 (Chalcedon), cf. 1011.18 (ibid., iii/ii B. C.). II. Ep., Ion., also **λάζυμαι**, ἐπὶ βουσὶν ἐλάζυτο.. Ἑρμῆν *h.Merc.*316; λάζυται τὴν γονὴν *grasps* it, Hp.*Mul.*1.10, cf. Aret.*SD*2.13; φόβος [αὐτὸν] λάζυται Hp.*Morb.*2.72, cf. Aret.*SD*2.12: this form is alone used by Trag. and Com. (exc. in imper. ἀντιλάζου E.*Or.*452), λάζυσθε Id.*Med.*956, *Ba.*503; λάζυσθαι Id.*HF*943: c. gen., λάζυσθε κύλικος Ar.*Lys.*209 (also in compds. ἀντι-, ἐπι-, προ-, προσ-, qq. v.); Boeot. inf. λάδδουσθη (q. v.).

**λάζω**, = λακτίζω, λάξας τράπεζαν Lyc.137, cf. Sch.E.*Hec.*64; λάζειν· ἐξυβρίζειν, Hsch.

**λάη**· ὀφθαλμοί, Cyr.

**λᾱθάνεμος** [ᾰν], ον, Dor. for ληθ-, *escaping wind*, ὥρα Simon.12.3.

**λάθαργος** [λᾰ], ὁ, *bit of leather*, Nic.*Th.*423, cf. Hsch. II. = σκώληξ, Id. III. v. λαίθαργος.

**λαθασμός**, ὁ, = λήθη, Hsch.

**λᾱθέμεν**, Dor., = λήθειν, Pi.*O.*1.64.

**λαθήβας**· γέροντας, Hsch.

**λᾰθητικός**, ή, όν, *likely to escape detection*, Arist.*Rh.*1372$^a$21.

**λᾰθῐ-κηδής**, ές, (κῆδος) *banishing care*, εἴ ποτέ τοι λαθικηδέα μαζὸν ἐπέσχον Il.22.83; οἶνον λαθικάδεα (leg. -κάδεον) Alc.41.3; Διώνυσος *IGRom.*4.360.15 (Pergam.), cf. *Epic.Alex.Adesp.*8.10, *AP*9.524.12, Plu.2.657d; λ. τέχνης ἰδμοσύνη *APl.*4.273 (Crin.). **-νοστος**· ὁ βραδύνων ἐπανελθεῖν, Hsch. ⊛**-πήμων**, ον, gen. ονος, *banishing sorrow*, prob. cj. for λυσιπήμων (q. v.) in Orph.*H.*2.11. **-ποινος**, ον, *forgetful of vengeance*, Hsch.

**λᾱθίπονος** [ῐ], ον, (λήθη) *forgetful of sorrow*, S.*Aj.*711 (lyr.); βίοτος ὀδυνᾶν λ. a life *forgetting*, i. e. *free from*, *pain*, Id.*Tr.*1021 (hex.).

**λᾰθῐ-πορφῠρίς**, ίδος, ἡ, = πορφυρίς, *which feeds in the dark*, Ibyc.8 (λαθιπόρφυρας and ἀδοιπορφυρίδες codd. Ath.). **-φθογγος**, ον, *robbing of voice*, epith. of death, Hes.*Sc.*131. **-φροσύνη**, ἡ, *forgetfulness*, A.R.4.356 (pl.). ⊛**-φρων**, ον, gen. ονος, *forgetful*, *heedless*, *foolish*, Hsch.

**λάθος** [ᾰ], εος, τό, *escape from detection*, εἰ λάθος ἔσται μου τῷ δρασμῷ Astramps.*Orac.*89p.7 H.

**λᾶθος**, εος, τό, Dor. for λῆθος, = λήθη, Theoc.23.24.

**λᾱθοσύνα**, Dor., = λήθη, E.*IT*1279 (lyr., s. v. l.).

**λάθρα**· αἱ δίκαι (Elean), Hsch. **λάθρα, λάθρᾳ**, v. λάθρη.

**λαθρ-άδαν**, = λάθρᾳ, Corinn.*Supp.*1.13. **-αιόκοιτος**, ὁ, *adulterer*, *fornicator*, Vett.Val.75.16. **-αιοπρᾱγέω**, *deal secretly*, Phld. *Lib.*p.20 O. **-αῖος**, ον, also α, ον Eub.67.8, Lyc.1198:—*secret*, *clandestine*, ἄτη λ. A.*Ag.*1230; εἰσδέδεγμαι πημονήν.. λαθραῖον, of a person, S.*Tr.*377; λ. ὃς ἀσκεῖ κακά practises *secret* frauds, ib.384, cf. Arist.*EN*1131$^a$6; λ. ὠδίς one born in *secret* child-birth, E.*Ion*45; λ. θάνατον ἐπιβουλεύειν τινί And.4.15; λ. Κύπρις Eub. l. c.: Comp. λαθραιότερον, γένος Pl.*Lg.*781a. II. Adv. -αίως A.*Pr.*1077 (anap.), E.*El.*26, etc.: Sup., ὡς μάλιστα δύνανται λαθραιότατα Antipho 1. 28. 2. λ. τῆς μητρός *clam matre*, f. l. for λάθρᾳ in Alciphr.3.27. 3. *involuntarily*, οὖρα.. προϊόντα λ. Hp.*Coac.*136; *without obvious cause*, λ. τελευτῶσι Id.*Prorrh.*1.128. **-ακάζων**· χαλιναγωγῶν (Sicel), Hsch. **-επίβουλος**, ον, *secretly plotting*, Vett.Val.10.30.

**λάθρη** [ᾰ], Att. **λάθρᾳ**, Adv., (λανθάνω) *secretly*, *by stealth*, ὁ δέ οἱ παρελέξατο λάθρη Il.2.515; ἀνήρ, ὃς ἐμίσγετο λάθρη Od.15.430; λάθρη κτείναντες *treacherously*, 17.80; ἀλλά τε λάθρη γυῖα βαρύνεται *imperceptibly*, Il.19.165: in Trag. and Att., S.*Aj.*1137, *OT*386, Ar.*Ra.*746, Th.4.39, Pl.*R.*347b, etc. 2. c. gen., λάθρη τινός *unknown to* one, λάθρη Λαομέδοντος Il.5.269; λάθρη τῶν ἄλλων στρατηγῶν Hdt.8.112, cf. 9.90, S.*OT*787, *OC*354, Ar.*V.*347, X.*An.*1.3.8.—Freq. written λάθρα, λάθρη in codd. and Pap., but λάθραι (i. e. λάθρᾳ) in *UPZ*19. 28 (ii B. C.) and in some of the best codd., as the Laurentian of Sophocles, also in *POxy.*16 of Th. l. c. (i A. D.):—other forms are

λάθρᾳ, *h.Cer.*240, E.*Fr.*1132.28; **λαθρηδόν**, *AP*7.202 (Anyt.); **λαθρηδά**, Luc.*Cal.*21; **λαθρηδίς**, Hdn.Gr.1.512 (-δως (sic), Cyr.).

✱ **λαθρ-ίδιος** [ῐδ], α, ον, also ος, ον Vett.Val.16.6:— = λάθριος, Orph. *A.*888, Vett.Val. l.c., f.l. in Luc.*Bis Acc.*33. Adv. -ίως *AP*5.126 (Marc. Arg.), 261 (Paul. Sil.). **-ῐμαῖος**, ον, = λάθριος, Vett.Val.117. 26, Hsch. s. v. σκότιον. ✱ **-ιος**, ον, also α, ον Man.6.207:—later form of λαθραῖος, κλέμματα S.*Ichn.*66 (lyr.); ἐρετμοί Pl.Com.3; ἐπιθυμίαι Men.535.7; φιλάματα, εὐνά, Bion 2.6; of a person, ἐπ' οὔατα λάθριος εἶπεν Call.*Ap.*105; λ. γαμέτης *Epigr.Gr.*336.5 (Troas); of a place, λ. νάπος Theoc.20.39 codd. (Λάτμιον Wilamowitz): neut. pl. as Adv., *secretly*, Call.*Del.*241; λάθρια μὲν γελάοισα *treacherously* (v.l. for λάθρῃ), Theoc.1.96. II. Λαθρίη, ἡ, epith. of Aphrodite, *AP*6.300.1 (Leon.).

**λαθρό-βολος**, ον, *secretly set*, δόναξ *AP*9.824 (Eryc.). **-δάκνης**, ου, ὁ, *biting secretly*, λαθροδάκναι κόριες, of the Grammarians, ib.11.322 (Antiphan.):—also **-δήκτης**, ου, ὁ, Phryn.*PS*p.87 B. **-κοιτέω**, *live in secret marriage*, and **-κοιτία**, ἡ, Tz.*H.*1.441, 527 (pl.). **-νυμφος**, ον, *secretly married*, Lyc.320. **-πῖνος**, ον, *drinking secretly*, Rhetor. in *Cat.Cod.Astr.*7.216.1 cod. **-πόδης**, ου, ὁ, *stealthy-paced*, *AP* 9.409 (Antiphan.).

✱ **λαθροῦν**· βλάπτειν, Cyr.

**λαθροφᾰγ-έω**, *eat secretly*, Metag.15. **-ος**, ον, *eating secretly*, Hsch. s. v. ζοπαδασπίδας, ζοφοδερκίας.

**λαθῠρίς**, ίδος, ἡ, *caper spurge*, *Euphorbia Lathyris*, Dsc.4.166, Gal. 12.56, 14.208, al.

✱ **λάθῠρος**, ὁ, kind of *pulse*, *chickling*, *Lathyrus sativus*, Anaxandr. 41.43 (pl.), Alex.162.12 (both anap.), Thphr.*HP*8.3.1, Plu.2.286e: heterocl. pl. λάθυρα Babr.74.6.

**λαί**· ἐπὶ τῆς αἰσχρουργίας, Hsch. (αἰσχρολογίας Phot.).

**λαι-**, **λαισ-**, insep. prefix with intens. sense (cf. λα-) in λαίμαργος, λαίσκαπρος, λαίσπαις. **λαΐα**, v. λᾴα.

**λαιαί**, αἱ, *stones*, used as weights to keep the threads of the warp straight in the upright loom (cf. ἀγνύς), Arist.*GA*717ᵃ35, 787ᵇ26; or to move automata, in sg., Hero *Aut.*2.8, al.: nom. sg. λέα *EM* 558.57, λεία Hero l.c., *Spir.*2.27: nom. pl. λεῖαι Gal.4.564, al., Poll. 7.36: acc. pl. λεάς Hsch., λαιάς Arist. ll.cc.

✱ **λαίβα**· ἀσπίς, τρίβων, πέλτη, Hsch. ✱ **λαίγματα**· πέμματα, οἱ δὲ σπέρματα, ἱερὰ ἀπάργματα, Id., cf. Cyr., Phot. (λάγμ-); v. λαῖμα.

✱ **λαΐγξ**, ιγγος, ἡ, Dim. of λᾶας, *small stone, pebble*, λάϊγγες Od.5.433; λάϊγγας 6.95. II. generally, *stone*, A.R.1.402, al.

**λαίδης**· αἰχμαλωτός, Cyr. **λαίδιον**· ἀριστερόν, εὐώνυμον, Hsch. **λαῖδος** or **λᾷδος**, v. λῇδος.

**λαιδρός**, ά, όν, *bold, impudent*, Call.*Aet.*3.1.4, Nic.*Th.*689, *Al.*563, Max.438 (Comp.), Hsch.

**Λᾱΐειος**, α, ον, *of Laius*, Arg.metr. ad S.*OT.*

✱ **λαίθαργος**, ον, said to mean *biting secretly* (λαθεῖν, δάκνω), i. e. without barking, of a dog, σαίνεις δάκνουσα καὶ κύων λ. εἶ S.*Fr.*885, cf. Orac.ap. Ar.*Eq.*1068; also, = λαθραῖος, λαιθάργῳ ποδὶ *Trag.Adesp.* 227: **λάθαργος** in Phryn.*PS*p.87 B.: **λήθαργος**, Hsch.

**λαιθαρύζειν**· λαμυρῶσαι, διαπράξασθαι, Hsch.

✱ **λαικ-άζω**, fut. -άσομαι (v. infr.), *wench*, Ar.*Eq.*167, *Th.*57; λαικάσομ' ἄρα, i. e. I'll do anything rather, Cephisod.3; οὐχὶ λαικάσει; a vulgar form of execration, Strato Com.1.36. II. *deceive*, Suid., *EM*555.15. **-ᾰλέος**, α, ον, = sq., Luc.*Lex.*12. ✱ **-αστής**, οῦ, ὁ, *wencher*, Ar.*Ach.*79:—fem. ✱ **-άστρια**, *strumpet*, ib.529, 537, Pherecr. 149, Men.*Pk.*235:—also **-άς**, άδος, Aristaenet.2.16 (s.v.l.).

✱ **λᾱϊκ-ός**, ή, όν, (λαός) *of* or *from the people*: hence, *unofficial, civilian*, *PLille* 10.4 (iii B.C.), *PStrassb.*93.4 (ii B.C.). 2. *common* (opp. consecrated), of bread, Aq., Sm., Thd.1*Ki.*21.4(5); of a place, opp. *holy*, Sm., Thd.*Ez.*48.15. II. as Subst., *layman*, opp. κληρικός, *Cod.Just.*1.1.3.2, 1.3.38.2, Just.*Nov.*6.5. **-όω**, *make common, desecrate*, Aq.*De.*20.6.

**λαιλᾰπ-ετός**, v. λαῖλαψ. **-ίζω**, *agitate by storms*, Aq.*Is.*54. 11. **-ώδης**, ες, *stormy*, οὐρανός Hp.*Epid.*1.4; λ. ὕδωρ rain *which falls in a hurricane*, ib.6.4.17.

**λαίλας**· ὁ μὴ ἐκ γένους τύραννος, Cyr., Suid.; Lydian acc. to Hsch.

**λαιλᾰφέτης**, ου, ὁ, *sender of storms*, *PLeid.*W.8.21. (For λαιλαπαφέτης, cf. ἀνεμοφέτης.)

**λαιλάχει**· ψοφεῖ, Cyr.

✱ **λαῖλαψ**, ᾰπος, ἡ, *furious storm, hurricane*, βαῖνον ἐρεμνῇ λαίλαπι ἶσοι Il.12.375; κελαινῇ λ. ἶσος 11.747; ἄνεμος σὺν λαίλαπι πολλῇ 17. 57; Ζέφυρος βαθείῃ λ. τύπτων 11.306; Ζέφυρος μεγάλῃ σὺν λ. θύων Od. 12.408, cf. 426; ὅτε τε Ζεὺς λαίλαπα τείνῃ Il.16.365; ὦρσεν ἔπι ζαῆν ἄνεμον.. λ. θεσπεσίην Od.12.314, cf. 9.68; ὡς δ' ὑπὸ λαίλαπι.. βέβριθε χθών Il.16.384, cf. Semon.1.15; Νότου λαίλαπι Anacr.113; λαίλαπι χειμωνοτύπῳ A.*Supp.*33 (anap.), cf. Lxx *Jb.*21.18, Plb.30.11.6; acc. to Arist.*Mu.*395ᵃ7, a *whirlwind sweeping upwards*: metaph., ἔτλης λαίλαπα δυσμενέων *AP*7.147 (Arch.).—Not found in early Prose, but common later, cf. λ. ἀνέμου *Ev.Marc.*4.37, Plu.*Tim.*28; spelt λαῖλαμψ *Sammelb.*4324.15:—a form **λαιλαπετός**, ὁ, occurs in Sch. A Il.11.495, Hsch.

**λαῖμα**, ατος, τό, dub. in Ar.*Av.*1563 (λαῖτμα cod. Ven., λαῖγμα (cf. λαίγματα) Bentley).

**λαιμ-αγχία**, ἡ, *starvation diet*, f.l. for λιμαγχία in Cael.Aur.*TP*1. 171. **-άζουσιν**· ἐσθίουσιν ἀμέτρως, Hsch. **-αργέω**, = λαιμάσσω, Porph.*Abst.*1.53. **-αργία**, ἡ, *gluttony*, Pl.*R.*619b, *Lg.*888a, Epicur.*Fr.*471; ἡ περὶ τὴν τροφὴν λ. Arist.*PA*696ᵇ30. **-αργος**, ον, *greedy, gluttonous*, Id.*HA*591ᵇ1, Thphr.*CP*1.22.1, etc.; λ. πρὸς τὴν τροφήν Arist.*PA*675ᵃ20. Adv. -γως, ἐσθίειν Stob.4.56. 34. **-αργότης**, ητος, ἡ, *greediness*, Ph.1.686. **-άσσω**, Att. -ττω, (λαιμός B) *to be greedy* or *hungry*, Ar.*Ec.*1179 (lyr.), Herod.6.97; cf. λαιμώσσω. **-αστρον**, τό, *'greedy beast'*, term of abuse, Id.4.46, 7.18. ✱ **-άω**, = λαιμάσσω, Cyr., Hsch., Phot.; v. λαιμώσσω.

**λαιμητόμος**, ον, = λαιμοτόμος, *AP*6.101 (Phil.).

**λαιμίζω**, (λαιμός) *cut the throat, slaughter*, βοῦν Lyc.326.

**λαιμο-δάκής**, ές, (δάκνω) *throat-biting*, ἀκίδες *AP*6.5.2 (Phil.). **-πέδη**, Dor. -δᾱ, ἡ, *dog-collar*, ib.35 (Leon.). II. *springe* for catching birds, ib.109.8 (Antip.). **-ρρῠτος**, ον, (ῥέω) *gushing from the throat*, σφαγά E.*Hel.*355 (lyr.).

**λαιμός** (A), ὁ, *throat, gullet*, in Hom. always of men, βάλε δουρὶ λαιμὸν ὑπ' ἀνθερεῶνα Il.13.388; τὸν δ' Ὀδυσεὺς κατὰ λαιμὸν.. βάλεν ἰῷ Od.22.15; οὔ πως ἂν ἔμοιγε φίλον κατὰ λαιμὸν ἰείη οὐ πόσις οὐδὲ βρῶσις Il.19.209; λ. ἀπαμήσειε 18.34: metaph., *neck* of a bottle, *AP* 9.232 (Phil.): also in pl., E.*Ph.*1092; so of animals, Id.*Supp.*1201, Ar.*Av.*1560.—Rare in early Prose, as Hp.*Cord.*2, but commoner later, as Luc.*Nigr.*16, Gal.15.656, Porph.*Marc.*33, Jul.*Or.*6.193b.

**λαιμός** (B), ή, όν, = λαμυρός II, Heraclit.*Incred.*2 (cj.), Hsch.: neut. pl. as Adv., λαιμὰ βακχεύειν *impudently*, Men.106.

**λαιμό-τμητος**, ον, *with the throat severed*, κάρα E.*Ph.*455; λ. ἄχη *cut-throat* woes, Ar.*Th.*1054. **-τόμας**, α, ὁ, *throat-cutter*, prob. cj. for -τόμος, Περσεύς E.*El.*459 (lyr.). **-τομέω**, *cut the throat of*, μῆλα A.R.2.840; τινα Str.7.2.3, Plu.*Oth.*2: abs., A.R.4.1601:—Pass., *have one's head cut off*, S.E.*M.*1.264. **-τόμος**, ον, *throat-cutting*, χείρ E.*IT*444 (lyr.); σίδαρος Tim.*Pers.*142; σφαγίς *AP*6.306 (Aristo). II. proparox. **λαιμότομος**, ον, *with the throat cut*, E.*Hec.*208 (lyr.); *severed at the throat*, κεφαλά Id.*IA*776 (lyr.); Γοργοῦς λ. ἀπὸ σταλαγμῶν the blood dripping from the Gorgon's *severed head*, Id.*Ion*1054 (lyr.).

**λαιμωδῶ**· δραπετεύω, Suid. **λαιμώρη**· ἡ λαμυρίς, Id. II. = πρυτανεῖον, Cyr.

✱ **λαιμώσσω**, = λαιμάσσω, Hippon.76 (λαιμᾷ Bgk., metri causa), Nic. *Al.*352 (v.l. for λαιμάσσοντα).

**λαῖνα**, ἡ, = Lat. *laena*, Str.4.4.3, Juba 7.

✱ **λᾱΐνεος**, α, ον, = λάϊνος, Il.22.154, E.*Ph.*115 (lyr.), Theoc.23.58.

✱ **λαΐνθη**· λάρναξ λιθίνη, Cyr.

✱ **λάϊνος** [ᾰ], η, ον, (λᾶας) *of stone* or *marble*, οὐδός Il.9.404, Od.8.80; τεῖχος Il.12.178; λάϊνον ἕσσο χιτῶνα thou hadst put on a coat *of stone*, i. e. hadst been stoned to death, 3.57; of sculpture, Simon.110; λ. τάφος S.*OC*1596; μνῆμα λ. E.*El.*328; ἄπελθε λαΐνων σταθμῶν *Trag. Adesp.*44. 2. metaph., *stony-hearted*, λάϊνε παῖ Theoc.23.20. [ᾱ only *Epigr.Gr.*314 (Smyrna, iii A.D.).]

**λαϊνόχειρ**· σκληρόχειρ, Hsch.

**λᾱϊνῠφής**, ές, *woven of stone*, λ. ὅδε τύμβος *Mon.Ant.*23.85 (near Adalia).

✱ **λαῖον** (**λᾷον**), τό, Dor. for λήϊον, Sophr.95 (pl.). II. λαῖον, τό, *ploughshare*, A.R.3.1335.

**λαιόπους**, ποῦν, gen. ποδος, *left-footed*, Cyr.

✱ **λαιός** (A), ὁ, a kind of thrush, prob. the *blue thrush*, *Petrocichla cyanus*, Arist.*HA*617ᵃ15, Ant.Lib.19.3.

**λαιός** (B), ά, όν, *left*, λαιᾷ μὲν ἴτυν προβάλεσθε (sc. χειρί) Tyrt.15. 3; λαιᾶς χειρός *on the left* hand, A.*Pr.*714; πρὸς λαιᾷ χερί E.*HF*159; λαιοῖσι *on the left*, Parm.17; ἐπὶ λαιὰ κεκλιμένον Arat.160, cf. Heliod. ap.Stob.4.36.8; οἱ τὸ λ. ἔχοντες (sc. μέρος) D.S.13.99; ἐς λαιὰν ἐσιόντων χῆρα (Dor.) *IG*14.1721.3; τῇ λαιᾷ τοῦ δεξιοῦ λαβόμενος κέρως Philostr.Jun.*Im.*4. (Poet., but not in Hom., who uses ἀριστερός: also in later Prose, τὰ διδόμενα τῇ δεξιᾷ δέχεσθαι τῇ λαιᾷ χειρί Prov. ap.Plb.38.10.9, cf. Jul.*Or.*2.57d, etc.) (Orig. λαιϝός, cf. Lat. *laevus*, Slav. *lěvŭ*: in Hsch. we have λαίβα, i. e. λαίϝα, = ἀσπίς, because borne on the left arm; cf. λαῖφα, λαῖτα, λαφός.)

**λαιοστάτης**, = ἀριστεροστάτης, interpol. in Poll.4.106.

**λαιοτομέω**, (λᾷον) *reap corn*, Theoc.10.3.

**λαῖπος**· κίναιδος, λάσταυρος, Hsch. **λαιπτύηρον**· ἀναπεπλασμένον, ἰσχυρόν, Id. **λαΐς**, Dor. for ληΐς. **λαισαινοφόρος**· ὁπλοφόρος, Id. **λαισάς**· ἡ παχεῖα ἐξωμίς, Id. **λαίσασθαι**· κτήσασθαι, Id. (Dor. for ληΐσασθαι).

**λαισήϊον**, τό, *animal's skin with hair left on*, used as a shield, βοείας ἀσπίδας εὐκύκλους λαισήϊά τε πτερόεντα Il.5.453 = 12.426, cf. *Scol.*28. 2: used by the Cilicians, Hdt.7.91.

**λαίσιτος**· κίναιδος, πόρνη, Hsch.

**λαίσ-καπρος**, ον, *very lustful*, Hsch., Suid., *EM*558.39. **-παις**· βούπαις, Λευκάδιοι, Hsch.

**λαῖτα**· πέλτη, Hsch.

**λαῖτμα**, ατος, τό, poet. Noun, *depth* or *gulf* of the sea, μέγα λ. θαλάσσης Od.4.504, 5.174, 9.260; ἁλὸς ἐς μέγα λ. Il.19.267, cf. Od.8. 561; also alone, λ. μέγ' ἐκπερόωσιν 7.35, cf. 5.409, 7.276, Theoc.13. 24, A.R.1.1299.

**λάϊτος**, **λάϊτον**, **λάϊτρον**, v. λήϊτος, etc. **λαῖφα**· ἀσπίς, Hsch. **λαιφαί**· ἀναιδεῖς, θρασεῖς, κτλ., Id.

✱ **λαιφάσσω**, = λαφύσσω, Nic.*Th.*477. II. = ψηλαφάω, Cyr.

**λαίφη**, ἡ, rare collat. form of sq., Call.*Fr.*245.

✱ **λαῖφος**, εος, τό, poet. Noun, *shabby, tattered garment*, ἀμφὶ δὲ λαῖφος ἕσσω Od.13.399; τοιάδε λαίφε' ἔχοντα 20.206: generally, λ. λυγκός a lynx's *skin*, *h.Hom.*19.23; of *bedding*, *h.Merc.*152. II. *piece of cloth* or *canvas, sail*, Alc.18.7, *h.Ap.*406; καθήσειν λ. (metaph.) A.*Eu.*556 (lyr.), cf. E.*Med.*524, *Or.*341 (lyr.); στολμοὶ λαίφους A.*Supp.*715; στείλασα λ. ib.723: pl., S.*Tr.*561, E.*Hec.*112 (anap.), Aret.*SD*2.11, etc.: metaph., Ἄρης ἔθραυε λαίφη τῆσδε γῆς E.*Rh.*323.

✱ **λαιφύς**· δάπανος ἢ βορός, Hsch.

**λαιψηροδρόμος**, ον, *swift running*, E.*IA* 207 (lyr.).

**λαιψηρός**, ά, όν, *light, nimble, swift*, λαιψηρά τε γοῦνα Il.22.204, al.; of persons, *light-footed, swift*, 21.264; λ. βελέεσσιν ib.278; ἀνέμων λ. κέλευθα 14.17; λ. δρόμος, πόδες, Pi.*P*.9.121, *N*.10.63, B.*Scol.Oxy. Fr*.4.9; γνάθοι E.*Alc*.494; πόλεμοι Pi.*O*.12.4: neut. pl. as Adv., *swiftly*, E.*Ion* 717 (lyr.), Opp.*H*.1.237: regul. Adv. -ρῶς ib.5.660.

✻ **λαίω**, = λάω (B), Cyr.

**λᾰκάζω**, = λάσκω, *shout, howl*, A.*Th*.186, *Supp*.872 (lyr.).

**λᾰκάθη** [κᾰ], ἡ, f.l. for λακάρη (q.v.).

✻ **Λάκαινα** [λᾰ], ἡ, fem. of Λάκων, prop. *Laconian woman* (Phryn. 321), Λ. κόρη Thgn.1002, cf. E.*Hec*.441, etc.: abs., of Helen, Id. *Andr*.486 (lyr.); Λάκαιναι, αἱ, title of play by Sophocles: freq., esp. in Trag., Ion. Prose, and X., as fem. Adj., = Λακωνική, Λ. χώρη Hdt. 7.235; χθών, γαῖα, γᾶ, E.*Andr*.151, *Tr*.1110 (lyr.), *Hel*.1473 (lyr.); λίθος *Laconian* marble, Luc.*Hipp*.5; πόλις E.*Andr*.194, 209; κύων X.*Cyn*.10.4; σκύλαξ Pl.*Prm*.128c; ἡ Λ. (sc. κύλιξ) *Laconian* cup, Ar.*Fr*.216.

✻ **λᾰκάν-η** [κᾰ], ἡ, Hellenistic form of Att. λεκάνη, Suid. **-ίσκη**, ἡ, Dim. of foreg., Hsch. s. v. λαβάβηρ.

**λακάρα** or **λακάρη**, ἡ, a tree, prob. *bird-cherry, Prunus avium*, Thphr.*HP* 3.3.1, 3.6.1; vv.ll. λευκάρα, λακάθη: in Hsch. also **λακάρτη**.

**λάκας**· φάραγγας, Hsch.

**λᾰκαταπύγων** [ῡ], ον, gen. ονος, = καταπύγων with intens. prefix λα-, Ar.*Ach*.664.

**λᾰκατάρᾱτος** [ᾰρ], ον, = κατάρατος with intens. prefix λᾰ-, Phot. (λακκ- cod.).

**λάκαφθον**, τό, *an aromatic bark*, an ingredient of the Egypt. κῦφι, Paul.Aeg.7.22. (Perh. = νάρκαφθον.)

**λᾰκάω**, *burst asunder*, σίδηρος λακᾷ *PMag.Par*.1.3074:—Pass., ἕως λακηθῇ τὸ πέταλον *PLeid.V*.6.22.

**λάκε** [ᾰ], v. λάσκω.

**Λᾰκεδαιμ-ονιάζω**, = Λακωνίζω, Ar.*Fr*.95. ✻ **-ων**, ονος, ἡ, voc. -ον v.l. in Pi.*P*.10.1:—*Lacedaemon*, the capital of Laconia, Od.13.414, etc.; also, *Laconia* itself, Il.2.581, Hdt.1.67, etc.: also as Adj., Διὸς Λακεδαίμονος Id.6.56; Λ. γῆς E.*Hel*.474:—but regul. Adj. ✻**Λακεδαιμόνιος**, α, ον, of persons, Hdt.7.228, etc., Λακωνικός being commonly used of things; but Λακεδαιμόνιοι ἀστέρες Call.*Lav.Pall*.24.

**λακεδάμα**· ὕδωρ ἁλμυρὸν ἁλσὶ πεποιημένον, ὃ πίνουσιν οἱ τῶν Μακεδόνων ἀγροῖκοι, Hsch.

**λᾰκεδών**, όνος, ἡ, *bawling, wild talk*, Timo 65 (pl.).

**λᾰκεῖν**, aor. 2 inf. of λάσκω. **λακέμεναι**· φαγέσθαι, Hsch.

**λᾰκέρνιον**, τό, Dim. of Lat. *lacerna, cloak, Fouilles de Doura-Europos* 378.

**λᾰκερός**, ά, όν, (λάσκω) *talkative*: expld. by εἰκαῖος, Hsch.

✻ **λᾰκέρ-υζα**, ἡ, (λάσκω) *one that screams* or *cries*, λ. κορώνη *a cawing* crow, Hes.*Op*.747, Ar.*Av*.609, A.R.3.929 (pl.); λ. κύων *a yelping* dog, *Lyr.Adesp*.135 (masc. λακέρυζος restored by Toup in *AP*9.317 for λακόρυζος). **-ύζω**, *make a noise*, *EM*555.30:—Med., Hsch. (λακεράζεσθαι cod.), Phot., Suid. **-ωτάν**· συνεσταλμένον, Hsch.

**λᾰκέτᾱς**, ὁ, *the chirper*, i. e. the cicada, Ael.*NA*10.44.

**λᾰκέω**, Dor. for ληκέω (q. v.). **λάκη**· ῥάκη (Cret.), Hsch. **λακηδῆξαι**· διαρρῆξαι, Id. **λακηθμόν**· ὃν οἱ Ἀττικοὶ γλωσσόκομον καλοῦσιν, Id.

✻ **λάκημα** [ᾰ], ατος, τό, *fragment* broken off, *PLeid.V*.6.22; ὄρους *cleft*, Zos.Alch.p.186 B.; dub. sens. in *Sammelb*.4425 xi 24 (ii A. D.), *BGU*34 ii 3 (iii A. D.).

**λακίδαι**· βάλλει, Hsch. **λακιδαίμονος**· ψοφοῦντος, ἠχοῦντος, Id. **λακιδοφορῶν**· οὐχ ὑγιής, Id.

**λᾰκῐδόω**, (λακίς) = sq. 1, in Pass., of lacerating sensations, Dsc. *Alex.Prooem.*

**λᾰκ-ίζω**, *tear*, Lyc.1113, *AP*9.117 (Stat. Flacc.):—Pass., ib.4.3[b].14 (Agath.); λακισθεὶς ὑπὸ λύκων *MAMA* 1.286 (Phrygia). 2. *split*, καλάμους *POxy*.326 (i A. D., λακήσῃ Pap.). II. = θωπεύω (s. v.l.), Hsch. ✻ **-ίς**, ίδος, ἡ, *rent, rending*, Alc.18.8 (pl.); μὴ . . ἐν πέπλοις πέσῃ λ. A.*Pers*.125 (lyr.); ἐμπίτνω ξὺν λακίδι λίνοισι Id.*Supp*.131 (lyr.), cf. 903: freq. in pl., λακίδες ἐσθημάτων, ὑφασμάτων, Id.*Pers*. 835, *Ch*.28 (lyr.); λακίδες πέπλων *ragged* robes, *tatters*, Ar.*Ach*.423: in late Prose, of the *rent* or *gap* made in a ship by the enemy's beak, D.S.13.99, 14.72. **-ισμα**, ατος, τό, *that which is torn*: in pl., *tatters*, E.*Tr*.497. **-ιστός**, ή, όν, *torn, rent, split*, Antiph.181; μόρος λ. death *by rending*, *Trag.Adesp*.291.

**λακκ-αῖος**, α, ον, (λάκκος) *from the cistern*, ὕδωρ λ. Anaxil.3, Thphr. *Char*.20.9, *Stad*.12. **-άριος**, ὁ, *cistern-keeper*, *Gloss.* **-ίζω**, *dig a pit*, Suid. s. v. ἐλάκκισε.

**λακκό-πεδον**, τό, *scrotum*, Aristag.6, Ruf.*Onom*.106; λακόπεδον in Poll.2.172. **-πλουτος**, ὁ, *pit-wealth*, Com. nickname of Callias, who was said to have found a *buried* treasure, Plu.*Arist*.5: prov., of any rich man, Alciphr.1.9. **-ποιός**, όν, *making wells* or *cisterns*, *Gloss.* **-πρωκτία**, ἡ, *lewdness*, Eup.351.4. ✻ **-πρωκτος**, ον, *loose-breeched* (cf. εὐρύπρωκτος), Ar.*Nu*.1330, Call.Com.11 (cj. for λευκό-), Cephisod.3.

✻ **λάκκος**, ὁ, *pond* in which water-fowl were kept, Hdt.7.119. b. contemptuously, of the Sea of Galilee, Porph.*Chr*.55. 2. *cistern, tank*, Ar.*Ec*.154, Alex.174.9, Lxx *Ge*.37.20; τὸν λ. συντρίψας D. 29.3. 3. *pit, reservoir*, Hdt.4.195; *pit* for storing wine, oil, or grain, X.*An*.4.2.22, Machoap.Ath.13.580a; ὁ λ. τῶν λεόντων Thd. *Da*.6.7(8), al.: metaph., ἀνήγαγέ με ἐκ λάκκου ταλαιπωρίας Lxx *Ps*. 39(40).2; καταβαίνειν εἰς λ. ib.27(28).1, al.:—written **λάκος**, *PCair. Zen*.176.276 (iii B. C.). 4. Κούρτιος λ., = Lat. *lacus Curtius*, D.H. 2.42. 5. a kind of garment, λ. χρωμάτινος *Peripl.M.Rubr*.6.

**λακκοσκαπέρδας**, = λακκόπρωκτος, *Com.Adesp*.1362.

**λακκ-οσχέας**, ου, ὁ, *with hanging scrotum*, Luc.*Lex*.12, Poll.2.172, Ruf.*Onom*.107. (Single -κ- in Poll. l. c.) ✻ **-όω**, *hollow out*, *PLond*.2.191.10 (Pass., ii A. D.). **-ώδης**, ες, *full of pits*, *Gp*.3.3.11.

**λακοπεῖν**· πυνθάνεσθαι; **λακόπιον**· πυθίον; **λάκοποι**· ἀρχή τις, ἔνθα οἱ κλέπται κρίνονται, Hsch. **λάκος**· ἦχος, ψόφος, Id.

**λακπᾰτ-έω**, for λὰξ πατέω, *trample on*, Pherecr.136, prob. in Luc. *Lex*.10 (λὰξ πατ- codd.). **-ητος**, ον, *trampled on, trodden down*, S.*Ant*.1275 (λαξπάτητον Eust., v.l. λεωπάτητον).

**λακτίζω**, pf. λελάκτικα Ar.*Nu*.136:—*kick with the heel* or *foot*, λ. ποσὶ γαῖαν, of a defeated boxer, Od.18.99, cf. 22.88; φλὸξ αἰθέρα λακτίζουσα καπνῷ flames *lashing* heaven with smoke, Pi.*I*.4(3).66; κραδία δὲ φόβῳ φρένα λακτίζει my heart '*knocks at* my ribs' for fear, A.*Pr*.881 (anap.); [ἔρως] λ. κραδίην *AP*12.16 (Strat.); τὸν πεσόντα λακτίσαι *trample on* the fallen, A.*Ag*.885; λ. βωμὸν εἰς ἀφάνειαν *trample on* the altar so as utterly to destroy it, ib.383 (lyr.); τὴν θύραν λ. *kick at* the door, Ar. l. c.; λ. ἀλλήλους Pl.*R*.586b; of horses, λ. τὸ λυποῦν Arist.*PA*690[a]21; ἑαυτόν Pl.*Grg*.516a; ὑπὸ ἵππου λακτισθεὶς X.*An*. 3.2.18: metaph., λ. πολλὴν χάριν E.*Rh*.411; βοῦς ὁ λακτίσας ὑμᾶς, of a clumsy-footed person, Herod.7.118:—Med. in act. sense, *Mim. Oxy*.413.65. 2. abs., *kick, struggle*, Batr.90; of horses, X.*Eq. Mag*.1.4: freq. in prov. λ. ποτὶ κέντρον, πρὸς κέντρα, *kick* against the pricks, Pi.*P*.2.95, A.*Ag*.1624, E.*Ba*.795, *Act.Ap*.26.14, etc.; so πρὸς κῦμα λ. E.*IT* 1396.

✻ **λάκτιμα**· λάκτισμα, Hsch., cf. *PGen*.56.27 (iv A. D.).

**λάκτις**, ιος, ἡ, *pestle*, Call.*Fr*.178, Nic.*Th*.109.

**λάκτ-ισμα**, ατος, τό, *a kick*, given or received, S.*Ichn*.213, Lyc. 835, D.S.4.59, Ael.*Tact*.19.2; λ. δείπνου . . τιθεὶς *kicking away* the table, A.*Ag*.1601. **-ισμός**, ὁ, *kicking*, in pl., Hsch. s. v. σκαρθμοῖς. **-ίσσω**, Tarent. for λακτίζω, Heraclid.ap.Eust.1654.25, cf. 824.28, *An.Ox*.1.62. **-ιστής**, οῦ, ὁ, *one who kicks* or *tramples*, ἵπποι λ. *kicking* horses, X.*Mem*.3.3.4; of a man, Plu.2.10c; ληνοῦ λ. *treader* of the winepress, *AP*9.403 (Maec.). **-ιστικός**, ή, όν, *of kicking*: ἡ λ. (sc. τέχνη) *kicking* in wrestling, opp. πυκτική, Oenom. ap.Eus.*PE*5.34.

**λάκυθος**, Dor. for λήκυθος. **λάκυρος**· στεμφυλίας οἶνος, Hsch.

**λακχά**, ἡ, = ἄγχουσα, Ps.-Democr.Alch.p.42 B.

✻ **Λάκων** [ᾰ], ωνος, ὁ, *a Laconian* or *Lacedaemonian*, prop. of men, as Λάκαινα of women (Phryn.321), Pi.*P*.11.16, Hdt.7.161, Th.3.5, Ar. *Ach*.303, etc. (never in Trag.): also as Adj., *Laconian*, λόγος S.*Fr*. 176; πέπλοι *AP*6.292 (Hedyl.). II. Λάκων, ὁ, a throw of the dice, Eub.57.

✻ **Λᾰκων-ίζω**, *imitate Lacedaemonian manners, dress*, etc., Pl.*Prt*. 342b sq., X.*HG*4.8.18, D.54.34; Λ. τῇ διαίτῃ Plu.*Alc*.23; τῇ φωνῇ Id. 2.150b: hence, *speak laconically*, ib.513a, etc.; = *titubo*, *Gloss.* II. *act in the Lacedaemonian interest*, X.*HG*4.4.2, etc. III. = παιδεραστέω, Ar.*Fr*.338, Eup.351.1. ✻ **-ικός**, ή, όν, *Laconian*, ἄνδρες Ar.*Lys*. 628, etc.; κλειδίον, a kind of key, Id.*Th*.423, cf. Aristopho 7.4, Men. 343; Λακωνικὸν πνέων Ar.*Lys*.276; βραχυλογία τις Λ. Pl.*Prt*.343b; ἐλάττω ἔχειν γῆν τὸν ἀγρὸν ἐπιστολῆς Λακωνικῆς Prov. in Str.1.2.30, cf. Longin.38.5. Adv. -κῶς Diph.96; συντόμως καὶ Λ. D.S.13.52. II. as Subst., 1. ἡ Λακωνική (sc. γῆ) *Laconia*, Ar.*Pax* 245, etc. b. Λακωνικαί (sc. ἐμβάδες), αἱ, *Laconian shoes*, used by men, Id.*V*.1158, *Th*.142, *Ec*.74, 269, al. 2. τὸ -κόν *the state of Lacedaemon*, Hdt.7. 235; τῆς ὁμιλίας τὸ Λ. *Laconian* fashion, Plu.*Cleom*.32. 3. τὸ Λ. *Laconian steel*, St.Byz. s. v. Λακεδαίμων. 4. Λακωνικόν, τό, *female garment*, διαφανῆ Λ. Lxx *Is*.3.23. **-ιον**, τό, = Λακωνικός II. 4, *PGiss*. 21.5 (ii A. D.). **-ίς**, ίδος, ἡ, fem. of Λακωνικός, γαῖα *h.Ap*.410; θεραπαινίδες Max.Tyr.29.6. ✻ **-ισμός**, ὁ, *imitation of Lacedaemonian manners*, esp. of their short and pointed way of talking, Cic.*Fam*. 11.25.2. II. *acting in the Lacedaemonian interest*, X.*HG*4.4.15, 7.1.46. **-ιστής**, οῦ, ὁ, *one who imitates the Lacedaemonians*, Plu. *Phoc*.10. II. *one who takes part with them*, X.*HG*1.1.32. III. pl., *dancers in a square figure*, Timae.41.

**Λᾰκωνο-μᾰνέω**, *to be mad on Spartan ways*, Ar.*Av*.1281. **-σημος**, ον, *with stripes in Laconian fashion*, *POxy*.114.7 (ii/iii A. D.), *PTeb*. 406.14 (iii A. D.).

**λάλ**, name for the letter λάμβδα, *PLond*.3.909a 7 (ii A. D.).

**λάλαβις**· λαίλαψ, κτλ., Hsch.

**λαλάγγη**, ἡ, and **λαλάγγιον** or **λαλάγκιον**, τό, = λάγανον, Sch.Ar. *Pl*.138, Suid. s. v. κολλύρα.

✻ **λᾰλᾰγ-έω**, *babble*, Pi.*O*.2.97; μὴ λαλάγει τὰ τοιαῦτ' ib.9.40; of birds and grasshoppers, *chirrup, chirp*, Theoc.5.48, 7.139; humorously, of the swallow which announces spring, Cic.*Att*.9.18.3 (dub. l.), 10.2.1, alluding to *AP*10.1 (Leon.); of Echo, ib.6.54.9 (Paul. Sil.). ✻ **-ή**, ἡ, *prattle*, Opp.*H*.1.135. ✻ **-ημα**, ατος, τό, = foreg., *AP*6.220.15 (Diosc.). **-ητής**, οῦ, ὁ, *prattler*, Hsch.

✻ **λᾰλάζω**, = λαλαγέω, ὥστε κῦμα λ. Anacr.90; but λαλάξαι· τὴν γλῶσσαν ἐξελεῖν, Hsch.

**λάλαξ** [λᾰλ], ἄγος, ὁ, *babbler, croaker*: a name of the green frog (κέρβερος), and of a bird, Hsch.; cf. βάβαξ.

✻ **λαλαχεύομαι**, = λαχνόομαι, *POxy*.294.25 (i A. D.).

**λᾰλ-έω**, *talk, chat, prattle*, ἕπου καὶ μὴ λάλει Ar.*Ec*.1058, cf. *V*.1135; ἡ μὲν χελιδὼν τὸ θέρος . . λαλεῖ Philem.208; λαλεῖς . . ἀμελήσας ἀποκρίνασθαι Pl.*Euthd*.287d: c. dat., *talk to* one, λαλῶν ἐν ταῖς ὁδοῖς σεαυτῷ Ar.*Eq*.348; αὐτοῖς Philem.11; πρὸς αὐτοὺς Alex.9.10; λ. περί τινος Pherecr.2, Ar.*Lys*.627; ὑπέρ τινος Posidipp.26.3; opp. λέγω, λαλεῖν

ἄριστος, ἀδυνατώτατος λέγειν Eup.95; λαλῶν μὲν.., λέγων δέ.. D.21.118 (s.v.l.); λαλεῖν τι ἡμῖν ὅπως ἂν ἡμᾶς ὕπνος λάβῃ Thphr.*Char.*7.10: hence, b. generally, *talk, speak*, S.*Ph.*110 (v.l. for λακεῖν); καινὴν διάλεκτον λ. Antiph.171; Ἀττικιστὶ λ. Alex.195.4. c. metaph., ζωγραφία λαλοῦσα (of poetry), opp. ποίησις σιωπῶσα (of painting), Simon. ap.Plu.2.346f. 2. *talk of*, τινα Alciphr.*Fr.*5.2; ἀλλήλαις λαλέουσι τεὸν γάμον αἱ κυπάρισσοι Theoc.27.58; ἅμαξαν *Stoic.*2.92:—Pass., πρᾶγμα κατ' ἀγορὰν λαλούμενον Ar.*Th.*578. 3. in later writers, = λέγω, *speak*, λαλεῖ οὐθὲν τῶν ἄλλων ζῴων πλὴν ἀνθρώπου Arist.*Pr.*899a1: freq. in Lxx, *Ge.*12.4, al.; βασιλέως ἐναντίον Ezek.*Exag.*118; πρός τινα *Act. Ap.*3.22, cf. Luc.*Vit.Auct.*3, etc.; περὶ τῆς λέξεως Phld.*Po.*5.32, cf. *Rh.*1.189 S., al.; χειροῖν ἅπαντα λαλήσας, of a pantomime, *IG*14.2124: abs., εἴ τι μὴ λίθος, τοὔργον, ἐρεῖς, λαλήσει Herod.4.33, cf. 6.61; ἐλάλησεν ὁ κωφός *Ev.Matt.*9.33:—Pass., λαληθήσεταί σοι ὅ τι σε δεῖ ποιεῖν *it shall be told* thee.., *Act.Ap.*9.6. II. *chatter*, opp. articulate speech, as of locusts, *chirp*, Theoc.5.34; μεσημβρίας λαλεῖν τέττιξ (sc. εἰμί), a very grasshopper to *chirp* at midday, Aristopho 10.6; ἀνθρωπίνως λ. Strato Com.1.46. III. of musical sounds, αὐλῷ λαλέω Theoc.20.29; of trees, v. supr. I. 2; δι' [αὐλοῦ ἢ σάλπιγγος] λ. Arist. *Aud.*801a29; of Echo, D.C.74.14: also c. acc. cogn., μάγαδιν λαλεῖν *sound* the μάγαδις, Anaxandr.35. **–η**, ἡ, = λαλιά, *Com.Adesp.*12a D. (pl.), Luc.*Lex.*14. **–ηθρος**, ον, *talkative*, Lyc.1319, *AP*4.1.13 (Mel.), 12.136. **–ημα**, ατος, τό, *talk, prattle*, Eub.109, Mosch.1.8. II. *prater*, S.*Ant.*320; ποικίλων λαλημάτων E.*Andr.*[937]. 2. *a person talked about, by-word*, Lxx 3*Ki.*9.7, al. III. *style*, Nausiph. 2. ® **–ησις**, εως, ἡ, = λαλιά, Ar.*Fr.*803, *AB*438.4. **–ητέος**, α, ον, *to be talked of*, *AP*7.47. **–ητικός**, ή, όν, *given to babbling*, Ar. *Eq.*1381. **–ητός**, ή, όν, *endowed with speech*, Lxx *Jb.*38.14. II. *talked of*, *EM*588.54. **–ητρίς**, ίδος, ἡ, *talker, prattler*, *AP*5.236.7 (Agath.). ® **–ιά**, poet. –ιή, ἡ, *talk, chat*, λαλιὰν ἀσκῆσαι, ἐπιτηδεῦσαι, Ar.*Nu.*931 (anap.), *Ra.*1069; πέρας ποιεῖ λαλιᾶς Men.66.3, cf. Hermesian.7.78, *AP*7.440 (Leon.); *common talk, report*, Plb.3.20.5; τῆς εὐανδρίας τινός Lxx 2*Ma.*8.7; ἀχέων *APl.*4.134 (Mel.); λαλιάν τινα ποιεῖν Lxx *Si.*42.11; in good sense, *discussion*, ἡ περὶ βυβλίων λ. Plb. 31.23.4, cf. 36.12.3; *speech, conversation*, *Ev.Jo.*8.43; *matter, subject*, Lxx *Ec.*3.18. 2. *loquacity*, Aeschin.2.49, Thphr.*Char.*7, Arist. *Phgn.*806b18, Men.*Sam.*46. II. *a form of speech, dialect*, *Ev.Matt.* 26.73; ἡ λ. σου ὡραία Lxx *Ca.*4.3; *style*, Phld.*Rh.*2.27 S. **–ιός**, ά, όν, poet. for λάλος, *AP*5.148 (Mel.), 170 (Id.), 7.417 (Id.), *IG*14.1892 (i A.D.). (On the accent v. Hdn.Gr.1.123.) **–ιότης**, ητος, ἡ, *garrulity*, *Gloss.*

**λάλλαι**, αἱ, *pebbles*, from their *prattling* in the stream, restored for ἄλλαι in Theoc.22.39, from Hsch., *EM*555.47.

**λαλλοῦσα**, misspelling of λαλέουσα, *App.Anth.*2.681.9 (Egypt).

® **λᾰλο-βᾰρῠ-παρα-μελο-ρυθμο-βάτης** [βᾰ], ου, Dor. **–ᾱς**, ὁ, *heavy-going discordant talker*, Com. word in Pratin.Lyr.1.13 (s.v.l.).

**λᾰλόεις**, εσσα, εν, poet. for sq., *AP*9.122 (perh. Evenus).

® **λάλος** [ᾰ], ον, *talkative, babbling, loquacious*, E.*Supp.*462, Ar.*Pax* 653, Pl.*Grg.*515e, Theoc.5.75; λ. τρόπις, of Argo, Orph.*A.*709; λ. γῆρας *AP*7.417.10 (Mel.); of women, dub. in Arist.*Pol.*1277b23; of birds, Id.*HA*536a24 (Comp.): metaph., λάλοι πτέρυγες *AP*7.195 (Mel.); λ. κερκίς *AJA*17.162 (Cyrene); of the swallow, Arr.*An.*1. 25.8; ὕδωρ *Anacreont.*11.7; τὸ λ., = λαλιά, Philostr.*Im.*1.5; of style, ἡ ἰδέα τοῦ λόγου λ. μᾶλλον ἢ ἐναγώνιος Id.*VS*2.30: irreg. Comp. λαλίστερος Ar.*Ra.*91, Alex.92, Men.416, Arist.*HA* l.c.: Sup. λαλίστατος E.*Cyc.*315, Men.164.

**λαλύνει**· πάσσει, πατεῖ, Hsch. **λάμας**· μύξας, Id. (Cf. λήμη: λαμάς· μῦς cod.)

**Λᾱμᾰχίππιον**, τό, burlesque word, *little jockey-Lamachus*, Ar.*Ach.* 1206.

**λάμαχος**· ἄμαχος, ἀκαταγώνιστος, Hsch. **λάμβαι**· τὰ χάσματα, ἢ οἱ μόνοι τῶν ἀνθρώπων, καὶ ἰχθῦς, Id.; cf. **λάμβα**, *sapula*, *Gloss.*

® **λαμβάνω**, fut. λήψομαι (λήψω only late, v.l. in Lxx 1*Ma.*4.18); Ion. λάψομαι *GDI*5497.3, al. (Milet., iv/iii B.C.), 5597.11 (Ephesus, iii B.C.), corrupted to λάμψομαι in Mss. of Hdt.1.199; Dor. fut. 2 sg. λαψῇ Epich.34.2, Theoc.1.4,10, inf. λαμψεῖσθαι *PSI*9.1091.19; Hellenistic λήμψομαι *PPar.*14.47 (ii B.C.), *CIG*4224c (add.) (Telmessus), 4244 (Tlos), al.: aor. 2 ἔλᾰβον, Ep. ἔλλᾰβον Il.24.170, etc.; Ion. Iterat. λάβεσκον Hes.*Fr.*112, Hdt.4.78,130; imper. λαβέ Il.1.407, etc.; written λάβε in Med. Ms. of A.*Eu.*130, but λαβέ Att. acc. to Hdn. Gr.1.431: pf. εἴληφα S.*OT*643, Ar.*Ra.*591 (lyr.), etc. (dub. in Archil. 143); Ion., Dor., Arc. λελάβηκα Hdt.4.79, *IG*4$^{2}$(1).121.68 (Epid., iv B.C.), 5(2).6.14 (Tegea, iv B.C.), also Eup.426; inf. λελαβήκειν *IG* 4$^{2}$(1).121.59 (Epid.), *PSI*9.1091.7: plpf. εἰλήφειν Th.2.88, Ion. 3 sg. λελαβήκεε v.l. in Hdt.3.42 (κατα–); Dor. pf. subj. 3 sg. (παρ–) λελόνβῃ *GDI*5087b1 (Crete):—Med., aor. 2 ἐλαβόμην, Ep. ἐλλ–, Od. 5.325, etc.; Ep. redupl. λελαβέσθαι 4.388:—**Pass.**, fut. ληφθήσομαι S.*Ph.*68, Th.6.91, κατα-λελήψομαι Aristid.*Or.*54 p.677 D.: aor. ἐλήφθην Ar.*Eq.*101, etc.; Ion. ἐλάφθην *SIG*58.8 (Milet., v B.C.), (κατ–) *GDI*5532.7 (Zeleia), ἐλάμφθην Hdt.2.89, 6.92, 7.239 (–λάφθ– by erasure in cod. B); Hellenistic ἐλήμφθην *IG*14.1320, *Ev.Marc.* 16.19 (ἀν–); Dor. ἐλάφθην Archim.*Aren.*1.13: pf. εἴλημμαι D.24.49, Ar.*Pl.*455; but in Trag. usu. λέλημμαι, A.*Ag.*876, E.*Ion* 1113, *IA* 363 (troch.), *Cyc.*433, cf. Ar.*Ec.*1090 (δια–); so later προ-λέληπτε (sic) *Supp.Epigr.*2.769 (Dura); Ion. λέλαμμαι (ἀπο–) Hdt.9.51, (δια–) 3.117; inf. ἀνα-λελάφθαι Hp.*Off.*11 (acc. to many codd., Hsch. and Erot., –λελάμφθαι vulg.); Ion. 3 pl. λελήφαται *An.Ox.*1.268; Dor. pf. imper. λελάφθω Archim.*Con.Sph.*3, al.:—in the fut., aor. Pass., and pf. Pass. the α is short by nature in Ion., prob. long in Dor. and in Doricized Hellenistic forms such as λαμψοῦνται *Test.Epict.*5.14, λάμψεσθαι *IG*5(1).1390.67 (Andania, i B.C.); it is marked long in Aeol. λᾱ́μψεται Alc.*Supp.*5.9:—of these tenses Hom. uses only aor. Act., and aor. Med. twice (v. supr.); the Homeric pres. is λάζομαι.—The word has two main senses, one (more active) *take*; the other (more passive) *receive*: I. *take*, 1. *take hold of, grasp, seize*, μάστιγα καὶ ἡνία Od.6.81: freq. with χειρί or χερσί added, χειρὶ χεῖρα λαβόντες Il.21.286; χερμάδιον λάβε χειρί 5.302; χείρεσσι λαβὼν περιμήκεα κοντόν Od.9.487; ἐν χείρεσσι λάβ' ἡνία Il.8.116; ἐν χεροῖν λ. S.*OT*913; διὰ χερῶν λαβών Id.*Ant.*916; ἐς χέρας E.*Hec.*1242; ἐν ἀγκάλαις A.*Supp.*481, etc.; of an eagle, λ. ἄγραν ποσίν Pi.*N.*3.81: c. acc. of the thing seized, λ. γούνατα Il.24.465; but also c. acc. of whole, gen. of part seized, τὴν πτέρυγος λάβεν *caught* her *by* the wing, 2.316; τὸν δὲ πεσόντα ποδῶν ἔλαβε 4.463; γούνων λαβὼν κούρην Od. 6.142; λ. τινὰ τῆς ζώνης X.*An.*1.6.10, etc.: sts. c. gen. only, ἀγκὰς ἀλλήλων λαβέτην χερσί they *took hold of* one another with their arms, Il.23.711:—freq. in Med., v. infr. B. b. *take by violence, carry off as prize* or *booty*, Il.5.273, 8.191, Hdt.4.130, S.*Ph.*68 (Pass.), 1431, etc.; *capture* a city, Plb.1.24.11, 3.61.8; ἐκ πόλιος.. ἀλόχους καὶ κτήματα Od.9.41; of lions, λαβὼν κρατεροῖσιν ὀδοῦσιν Il.11.114; ἵνα δαῖτα λάβῃσιν 24.43; of an eagle, 17.678; of a dolphin, 21.24. c. λ. δίκην *take, exact* punishment, Lys.1.29,34, Isoc.4.181; ποινάς E.*Tr.* 360, etc. (rarely for δοῦναι δίκην, v. infr. II. 1e); λ. τιμωρίαν D.18. 280. 2. of passions, feelings, etc., *seize*, μένος ἔλλαβε θυμόν Il.23. 468; Ἀτρεΐωνα.. χόλος λάβεν 1.387; ὁππότε κέν μιν γυῖα λάβῃ κάματος 4.230; τὸν δὲ τρόμος ἔλλαβε γυῖα 24.170, al.; δὴν δέ μιν ἀμφασίη ἐπέων λάβε Od.4.704; τοὺς Ἀθηναίους θάρσος ἔλαβε Th.2.92; ἄχος X.*Cyr.* 5.5.6; δέος Pl.*Lg.*699c; ἐπειδὴ καιρὸς ἐλάμβανε when the occasion *came to* them, i.e. *occurred*, Th.2.34, D.C.44.19; of fevers and sudden illnesses, *attack*, Hp.*Morb.*1.19, Th.2.49, Ar.*Ec.*417, etc. (cf. λάζομαι, λῆψις): Pass., λαμβάνεσθαι νόσῳ, ὑπὸ [νόσου], S.*Tr.*446, Hdt.1. 138; ἔρωτι X.*Cyr.*6.1.31, etc. (reversely of the person, λ. θυμόν, etc., v. infr. II. 3). b. of a deity, *seize, possess*, τινα Hdt.4.79:—Pass., τῇ Ῥέᾳ λαμβάνονται Luc.*Nigr.*37. c. of darkness, etc., *occupy, possess*, εὖτ' ἂν κνέφας τέμενος αἰθέρος λάβῃ A.*Pers.*365. 3. *catch, overtake*, as an enemy, Il.5.159, 11.106,126, etc.; λ. τινὰ στείχοντα θύραζε Od.9.418; ζῶντες ἐλάμφθησαν Hdt.9.119; simply, *find, come upon*, S.*OT*1031, E.*Ion* 1339. 4. *catch, find out, detect*, Hdt.2.89 (Pass.); ποίῳ λαβών σε Ζεὺς ἐπ' αἰτιάματι; A.*Pr.*196; τὸν αὐτόχειρα τοῦ φόνου λ. S.*OT*266: freq. c. part., κἂν λάβῃς ἐψευσμένον ib.461; κλέπτοντα Κλέωνα λάβοιμι Ar.*V.*759; λ. τινὰ ψευδόμενον Pl.*R.*389d; τοῦτον ὑβρίζοντα λαβόντες D.21.97: with Adj., ὅπως μὴ λήψομαί σε προπετῆ Men.*Epit.*570:—Pass., δρῶσ' ἐλήφθης S.*Tr.*808; ἐπ' αὐτοφώρῳ δεινὰ δρῶντ' εἰλημμένω Ar.*Pl.*455; ληφθεῖσαν ἐπ' αὐτοφώρῳ μηχανωμένην τι Antipho 1.3; ἐλήφθη μοιχός Lys.13.66: in good sense, οὐκ ἂν λάβοις μου μᾶλλον οὐδέν' εὐσεβῆ S.*Ph.*1051. 5. λ. τινὰ πίστι καὶ ὁρκίοισι *bind* him by.., Hdt.3.74; ἀραῖον λαβεῖν τινα S.*OT*276 codd. 6. c. dupl. acc., *take as*, λαβὼν πρόβλημα σαυτοῦ παῖδα τόνδ' Id.*Ph.*1007; ξυμπαραστάτην λ. τινά ib.675; τοὺς Ἕλληνας λ. συναγωνιζομένους Isoc.5.86. 7. τὴν Ἴδην λαβὼν ἐς ἀριστερὴν χεῖρα *taking, keeping* Ida to your left (nisi leg. λαβών, ἐς..) Hdt.7.42; ἐν δεξιᾷ λ. τὴν Σικελίαν Th.7.1; λ. τὸ στρατόπεδον κατὰ νώτου *take* in rear, i.e. be behind, Hdt.1.75; cf. ἀπείργω II. 2, ἔχω (A) A. I. 7. 8. λ. Ἑλληνίδα ἐσθῆτα *assume* it, Id.4.78, cf. 2.37; λ. ζυγόν Pi.*P.*2. 93. b. *take* food or drugs, Diocl.*Frr.*121 (Pass.), 140, Sor.1. 125, Gal.15.469. 9. *apprehend by the senses*, ὄμμασιν θέαν S. *Ph.*537, cf. 656; πρόσφθεγμά τινος ib.234; ὁρᾶται, ἢ ἄλλῃ τινὶ αἰσθήσει λαμβάνεται Pl.*R.*524d. b. *apprehend with the mind, understand*, φρενὶ λ. τὸν λόγον Hdt.9.10; νόῳ Id.3.41; τῇ διανοίᾳ Pl. *Prm.*143a; λ. ἐν ταῖς γνώμαις βεβαίως X.*Cyr.*3.3.51; ἐν νῷ Plb.2. 35.6: abs., λ. τὴν ἀλήθειαν Antipho 1.6; μνήμην παρὰ τῆς φήμης λ. Lys.2.3, cf. Pl.*Phdr.*246d, etc. c. with Adv. added, *take*, i.e. *understand* in a certain manner, ταύτῃ ταῦτα ἐλάμβανον Hdt.7.142; λάβετε [τοὺς λόγους] μὴ πολεμίως Th.4.17; τὸ πρᾶγμα μειζόνως ἐλάμβανον *took* it more seriously, Id.6.27, cf. 61; ὀρθῶς λ. τὸν φιλοκερδῆ Pl.*Hipparch.*227c; λ. τι οὕτω, ὧδε, Arist.*SE*174b27, *Rh.Al.* 1423a4; ὀργῇ καὶ φόβῳ τὸ γεγονὸς λ. Plu.*Alc.*18: with παρά c. acc., λαμβάνω σε παρὰ βουκόλον.. *PMag.Par.*1.2434:—Pass., τρίτου καθεστῶσαι ἐπὶ πρώτου λαμβάνονται *are used for* the first person, A.D.*Pron.*78.22; with ἐς, εἰ ἐς κόρην λαμβάνοιτο *be taken* for a girl, Philostr.*Im.*2.32: less freq. c. dupl. acc., ὡς μεθυστικὰς λ. [τὰς ἁρμονίας] Arist.*Pol.*1342b25, cf. S.E.*P.*1.179; τῆς νίκης ἆθλον τὴν ὑπεροχὴν τῆς πολιτείας λ. Arist.*Pol.*1296a31; τοῦτο λ. γιγνόμενον Id.*Mete.* 346a7; also λ. περί τινος τί ἐστι Id.*EN*1142a32, cf. 1140a24, al.: also c. inf., λ. τι εἶναί τι Id.*Mete.*389a29, al.: with a relat. clause, οὕτω δεῖ λαμβάνειν, ἀλλ' οὐχ ὅτι.. Id.*Metaph.*1053a27, cf. Str.2.5.1; εἰλήφθω ὁ ἄδικος ποσαχῶς λέγεται Arist.*EN*1129a31: in bad sense, πρὸς δέους λ. τι Plu.*Flam.*7; πρὸς ἀτιμίας Id.*Cic.*13; λ. δι' οἴκτου E. *Supp.*194; but also ἐν χάριτι καὶ δωρεᾷ λ. *receive* as a favour, Plb.1. 31.6. d. in Logic, *assume, take for granted*, ἅπαν ζῷον λαμβάνει ἢ θνητὸν ἢ ἀθάνατον Arist.*APr.*46b6; λ. τὰς περὶ ἕκαστον ἀρχάς ib.53a2, etc.:—Pass., τὰ ἐξ ἀρχῆς ληφθέντα ib.26b30; αἱ εἰλημμέναι προτάσεις ib.33a15, cf. Phld.*Rh.*2.46 S., *Sign.*35, *Oec.*p.5 J., S.E.*P.*2.89. e. *take*, i.e. *determine, estimate*, τὴν ξυμμέτρησιν τῶν κλιμάκων Th.3.20; ἐντεῦθεν τὸ μέγεθος τῶν ἁμαρτημάτων Lycurg.66; τὴν τιμωρίαν ποθεινοτέραν λ. Th.2.42. 10. *take in hand, undertake* (cf. ληπτέον), λ. τι ἐπὶ τὸ σωφρονέστερον, opp. συνταχύνειν, Hdt.3.71; μηδένα πόνον λαβόντες without *taking* any trouble, Id.7.24; παλαισμάτων λ. φροντίδα Pi.*N.*10.22. 11. *take in, hold*, τὸ στρατόπεδον πεζοὺς λ. περὶ τετρα-

κισχιλίους Plb.3.107.10. 12. part. λαβών freq. seems pleonastic, but adds dramatic effect, λαβὼν κύσε χεῖρα *took and* kissed, Od.24.398, cf. Il.21.36: so in Trag. and Com., τί μ' οὐ λαβὼν ἔκτεινας; S.OT1391, cf. 641; τῇ νῦν τόδε πῖθι λαβών Cratin.141, etc. b. ingressive of ἔχων (ἔχω (A) A.I.6), ἑτάρους τε λ. καὶ νῆα..ἦλθον Od.15.269, cf. S.Tr.259. II. *receive*, 1. *have given one, get, receive*, prop. of things (AB106), ἄποινα Il.6.427; τὰ πρῶτα 23.275; ἀντίποινα S.El.592, v. infr. e; παρὰ βασιλέος δῶρα Hdt.8.10, cf. Ar.Eq.439; πρός τινος S.El.12, etc.; ἀπὸ τῶν συκοφαντῶν X.Mem.2.9.4; *gain, win*, κλέος Od.1.298, S.Ph.1347, etc.; ἀρετάν Pi.O.8.6; κόσμον Id.N.3.31 codd. (v.l. ἔλαχες Sch.); ἀλκήν S.OT218, etc.; πρὸς τὸ μνηστεύεσθαι λ. ἡλικίαν *attain*.., Isoc.10.39; λ. νόστον E.IT1016, etc.; λ. τὴν ἀρχὴν τῆς θαλάττης Isoc.5.61; μοναρχίαν S.Ant.1163; τέρψιν Id.Tr.820; χάριν Id.OT1004; κέρδος Ar.Ach.906: also in bad sense, λ. ὀνείδη S.OT1494; συμφοράν E.Med.43; θάνατον Id.Hel.201 (lyr.); γέλωτα μωρίαν τε *incur*.., Id.Ion600; αἰτίαν ἀπό τινος Th.2.18, etc.:—for λ. θυμόν, etc., v. supr. I.2 et infr. 3. b. *receive hospitably*, Od.7.255, cf. S.OC284 (ἔλαβες τὸν ἱκέτην ἐχέγγυον) which approaches this sense; καλῶς λ. τινά *treat* well, BGU843.10 (i/ii A.D.). c. *receive in marriage*, Hdt.1.199, 9.108, E.Fr.953.27, X.HG4.1.14, Isoc.10.39, PEleph.1.2 (iv B.C.), Men.Pk.436; τοῖς λαμβάνουσιν ἐξ αὐτῶν, i.e. those who married their daughters, SIG1044.14 (Halic., iv/iii B.C.); also of the father taking a daughter-in-law, τῷ υἱῷ λ. τινά Men.Pk.447. d. λ. ὄνομα, ἐπωνυμίαν, *receive* a name, Pl.Plt.305d, Smp.173d. e. λ. δίκην *receive*, i.e. *suffer*, punishment, Hdt.1.115; τὴν ἀξίην λ. *get* one's deserts, Id.7.39; δίκην γὰρ ἀξίαν ἐλάμβανεν E.Ba.1312; λ. ζημίας D.11.11. f. λ. ὅρκον *receive* an oath, Arist.Rh.$1377^{a}8$; λ. πιστά X.An.3.2.5, al.; λ. λόγον *demand* an account, τινος for a thing, παρά τινος from a person, Id.Cyr.1.4.3, D.8.47. g. λ. ἐν γαστρί *conceive*, Hp.Prorrh.2.24; κῦμα λ., of the earth, A.Ch.128. h. *receive as produce, profit*, etc., οἶνον ἐκ τοῦ χωρίου Ar.Nu.1123; [χρήματα] ἐκ τῆς ἀρχῆς Pl.R.347b; λ. ἑκατὸν τῆς δραχμῆς, ὀβολοῦ, *purchase* for.., Ar.Pax1263, Ra.1235, cf. Nu.1395; πόθεν ἄν τις τοῦτο τὸ χρῖμα λάβοι; X.Smp.2.4. i. λ. πεῖράν τινος, v. πεῖρα. 2. *admit of*, ὁ μέγας κίνδυνος ἄναλκιν οὐ φῶτα λαμβάνει Pi.O.1.81. b. *admit, initiate*, τοὺς ἐς τὰ τῆς τέχνης εἰλημμένους Hp.Decent.17. 3. of persons conceiving feelings and the like, λ. θυμόν *take* heart, Od.10.461: freq. in periphrasis, λ. φόβον, = φοβεῖσθαι, S.OC729; αἰδῶ λ., = αἰδεῖσθαι, Id.Aj.345; λ. ὀργήν, = ὀργίζεσθαι, E.Supp.1050: so generally λ. ἀρχήν, = ἄρχεσθαι, Id.IA1124; λ. ὕψος, ἐπίδοσιν, αὔξησιν, = ὑψοῦσθαι, ἐπιδιδόναι, αὐξάνεσθαι, Th.1.91, Isoc.4.10, Arist.GA$732^{b}5$, etc.; λ. κακόν τι Ar.Nu.1310; λ. νόσον *take* a disease, Pl.R.610d; λ. μορφήν, τέλος, etc., Arist.GA$762^{a}13$, $744^{a}21$, etc.; αἱ οἰκίαι ἐπάλξεις λαμβάνουσαι *receiving* battlements, *having* battlements *added*, Th.4.69, cf. 115. 4. c. inf., *receive permission to*.., SIG996.6 (Smyrna, i A.D.).

B. Med., *take hold of, lay hold on*, c. gen., [σχεδίης] Od.5.325; τῆς κεφαλῆς, τῶν γουνάτων, Hdt.4.64, 9.76; χειρός E.Med.899, etc.; τοῦ βωμοῦ And.1.126, etc.: c. dupl. gen., μου λαβόμενος τῆς χειρός Pl.Chrm.153b. 2. *seize and keep hold of, obtain possession of*, ἀρχῆς S.OC373; καιροῦ λαβόμενος *seizing* the opportunity, Is.2.28; λ. ἀληθείας Pl.Plt.309d: rarely c. acc., τόν..λελαβέσθαι Od.4.388. 3. *lay hands upon*, χαλεπῶς λαμβάνεσθαί τινος *lay* rough *hands on* him, *deal* hardly *with* him, Hdt.2.121.δ'. 4. of place, λ. τῶν ὀρῶν *take to* the mountains, Th.3.24, cf. 106; Δήλου λαβόμεναι (sc. αἱ νῆες) *reaching* Delos, Id.8.80. 5. *find fault with, censure*, τινος Pl.Lg.637c, Philostr.VA4.22. 6. λαβέσθαι ἑαυτοῦ *check* oneself, Hld.2.24.

**λάμβδα, λαμβδοειδής,** v. λάβδα, λαβδοειδής.

**Λάμιᾰ** [ᾰ], ἡ, *a fabulous monster said to feed on man's flesh*, a bugbear to frighten children with, Ar.V.1177, Duris17J., etc. II. λάμια, ἡ, *a fierce shark*, Arist.HA$540^{b}18$, Gal.6.727, Plin.HN9.78; cf. λάμνα, λάμβαι.

**λάμια** [ᾰ], τά, = χάσματα, Choerob. in An.Ox.2.239 (where Λοίμια), EM555.50; cf. λάμβαι, λάμος.

**λᾶμμα,** ατος, τό, = *vitta*, Gloss. (pl.).

**λάμνα** or **-η,** ἡ, = Λάμια II, Opp.H.1.370, 5.36.

⊛**λᾶμνα,** = Lat. *lāmina*, PMag.Par.1.2153, PLond.1.124.26.

**Λᾶμνος, Λαμνόθεν, Λαμνιάς,** Dor. for Λημν-.

**λαμόπτης·** ὁ ἐπὶ τηλίας, Hsch. (Prob. = *blear-eyed*, cf. λήμη: perh. λ.· ὀπτιλίας; cf. ὀπτιλίασις.)

**λάμος,** = *ingluvies*, Sch.Hor.Ep.1.13.10.

**λαμπᾰδαρχ-έω,** *act as* λαμπαδάρχης, IG12(5).173 ii 13 (Paros), BCH36.392 (Delos), CIG3498 (Thyatira), SIG667.62 (Athens, ii B.C.); of a woman, Ephes.3.151 No.68. **-ης,** ου, ὁ, *holder of the office of* λαμπαδαρχία, JHS7.150 (Samos), CIG (add.) 3886 (Eumenia):—also **-αρχος,** IG12(5).176 ii (Paros), 11(2).203A65 (Delos, iii B.C.), AJA19.446 (Opunt. Locr., iii B.C.). **-ία,** ἡ, *superintendence of the* λαμπαδηδρομία, Arist.Pol.$1309^{a}19$ (pl.), Rh.Al.$1437^{b}1$, SIG1003.26 (pl., Priene, ii B.C.). **-ισσα,** ἡ, fem. of λαμπαδάρχης, Ephes.3.151 No.68.

**λαμπᾰδ-εία,** ἡ, *torchlight procession*, Inscr.Prien.195.13 (iii/ii B.C.). **-εῖον,** τό, *torch-holder*, IG$2^{2}$.1541.15, 1543 (Eleusis, iv B.C.). **-εύω,** *make into a* λαμπάς, D.S.20.7. II. Pass., *to be lighted by torches*, Sch.S.OC1048. 2. *to be handed on like a torch* (in the race), Ph.1.478. III. Med., = λαμπαδίζω, Ael.Fr.286.

**λαμπᾰδη-δρομία,** ἡ, *torch-race*, Sch.Ar.Ra.131 (pl.); cf. λαμπάς (A) II. **-φορέω,** *carry the torch, run in the torch-race*, Aristid.Or.47(23).22, cf. EM244.40. **-φορία,** Ion. **-ίη,** ἡ, = λαμπαδηδρομία, Hdt.8.98. ⊛**-φόρος,** ὁ, *torch-bearer*, A.Ag.312, Ar.Fr.442, IG$2^{2}$.1250, $2.965^{b}28$: **-οι,** title of play by Philetaerus; but also, *candelabra*, JRS18.162 (Jerash, iii A.D.).

⊛**λαμπᾰδ-ίας,** ου, ὁ, *kind of comet resembling a torch*, Chrysipp.Stoic.2.201, Plin.HN2.90, Lyd.Mens.4.116. 2. the star *Aldebaran*, Ptol.Tetr.23; called **λαμπαύρας** in Procl.Par.Ptol.33. **-ίειος,** α, ον, *belonging to a torch*, ὕσπληξ IG11(2).203B96 (Delos, iii B.C.). **-ίζω,** *run the torch-race*, Sch.Ar.Ra.131; *take part in a torch-bearing procession*, τοὺς λαμπαδίξοντας (Dor. fut.) SIG671A11 (Delph., ii B.C.). **-ικός,** ή, όν, *of torches*, δρόμος λ. the *torch*-race, Sch.Lyc.732. **-ιον,** τό, Dim. of λαμπάς, *small torch*, λαμπάδια ἔχοντες διαδώσουσιν ἀλλήλοις, of the torch-race, Pl.R.328a, cf. λαμπάς (A) II.2; λαβὼν στέφανον..καὶ λ. Plu.Pyrrh.13, etc. 2. *bowl* of a lamp, Lxx Ex.38.16(37.19), Za.4.2. II. *lint* for wounds, Ar.Ach.1177, D.C.68.8. 2. *top-knot*, coiffure of Theban women, Dicaearch.1.19. 3. kind of comic mask, Poll.4.151, 154, Hld.10.39. **-ιος,** α, ον, *torch-bearing*, epith. of the moon-goddess, PMag.Par.1.2557. 2. *of a torch*, πῦρ Hld.1.18 codd. **-ιστής,** οῦ, ὁ, *runner in torch-race*, τὸ κοινὸν τῶν λ. SIG1068.2 (Patmos, iii/ii B.C.), cf. 671A10 (Delph., ii B.C.); subject of painting by Pyrrho, D.L.9.62. II. λ. ἀγών, = λαμπαδηφορία, Sch.Ar.Ra.131. **-ίτης** [ῑ], ου, ὁ, = foreg., Abh.Berl.Akad.1928(3).20 (Pergam., iii B.C., pl.).

**λαμπᾰδο-δρομέω,** *run in the torch-race*, Sch.Ar.V.1198. **-δρομία,** ἡ, = λαμπαδηδρομία, AB228 (read -μιῶν for -μίων). **-δρομικός,** ή, όν, *of* or *for the torch-race*, λ. ἀγών, = λαμπαδηφορία, Sch.Pi.O.13.56. **-εις,** εσσα, εν, *torch-bearing*, Orph.H.40.11. **-ποιός,** ὁ, *torch-maker*, Gloss.

**λαμπᾰδουχ-έω,** *hold* or *carry a torch*, Ephes.2.20 (ii A.D.), Sch.Ar.Ra.1119. **-ία,** ἡ, *torch-carrying*, Lyc.1179 (pl.). **-ος,** ον, *torch-carrying, bright-beaming*, ἁμέρα E.IA1506 (lyr.); λ. δρόμος, λ. ἀγών, = λαμπαδηφορία, Lyc.734, Sch.Ar.Ra.131.

**λαμπᾰδοφόρος,** ὁ, *torch-bearer*, τοῦ βασιλέως BGU1233.6 (ii B.C.).

**λαμπάζω,** poet. for λάμπω, Man.4.318.

**λαμπάκτῑς,** ἡ, (ἀκτίς) *shining*, of Venus, Doroth. in Cat.Cod.Astr.2.82.

⊛**λαμπάς** (A), άδος, ἡ, *torch*, A.Th.433, Th.3.24, etc.; πευκίνη λ. S.Tr.1198; *beacon-light*, A.Ag.8, 28, etc.; λαμπάδας ἅψασθαι light *torches*, Ar.Th.655; λαμπάδας τινάσσων, in Bacchic ceremonies, Id.Ra.340 (lyr.); used in festal processions, φαίνετε τούτῳ (sc. τῷ Αἰσχύλῳ) λαμπάδας ἱεράς ib.1525 (anap.), cf. Th.102 (lyr.). 2. *faggot*, Plb.3.93.4; any *light, lamp*, λαμπάδες ἀργυραῖ Lxx Ju.10.22; *wax-light*, Plu.2.263f; λ. κηροχίτων AP6.249 (Antip.); later of *oil-lamps*, Ev.Matt.25.3. 3. metaph., of the sun, Parm.10.3, S.Ant.879 (lyr.), etc.; ἡ 'πιοῦσα λ. the coming *light*, i.e. the next day, E.Med.352; of lightning, δαμασθεὶς λαμπάσιν κεραυνίοις Id.Supp.1011, cf. Ba.244, 594 (lyr.); of the Cyclops' eye, Cratin.459. 4. *meteor*, Arist.Mu.$395^{b}11$, D.S.16.66, D.C.37.25. II. *torch-race*, = λαμπαδηδρομία, Hdt.6.105, X.Vect.4.52; λαμπάδα δραμεῖν, τρέχειν, run *the race*, Ar.V.1203, Thphr.Char.27.4; τὰς λ. δραμεῖν IG$2^{2}$.1030.9; ἐν ταῖς λ. διηγωνίσθαι ib.1039.20; λαμπάδα φέρειν Ar.Ra.1087 (anap.); ἀφιεμένην τὴν λ. θεῶ see the start, ib.131; τὰς λ. συντελεῖν IG$2^{2}$.1011.9; λ. ἔσται..ἀφ' ἵππων τῇ θεῷ Pl.R.328a; λαμπάδι νικᾶν win in it, And.4.42, cf. IG$2^{2}$.957, al.; λαμπάδα ν. win it, ib.3.106, al.; οἱ νικήσαντες τὴν λ. ib.122, cf. Milet.1(7).203a14 (ii B.C.). 2. metaph., of life, λαμπάδα γὰρ ζωᾶς με δραμεῖν..ἤθελε δαίμων Epigr.Gr.231 (Chios); καθάπερ λαμπάδα τὸν βίον παραδιδόντας ἄλλοις ἐξ ἄλλων Pl.Lg.776b. III. = λυχνὶς ἀγρία, Ps.-Dsc.3.101.

**λαμπάς** (B), άδος, poet. Adj., *torch-lit*, λ. ἀκταί, of Eleusis, S.OC1049 (lyr.); ἑορταὶ λ. Lys.Fr.105 S.

**λαμπαύρας,** ὁ, v. λαμπαδίας. **λάμπεσκε,** Ion. Iterat. of λάμπω.

**λαμπετ-άω,** = λάμπω, *shine*, only in Ep. part. λαμπετόων *shining*, ὄσσε δέ οἱ πυρὶ λαμπετόωντι ἐΐκτην Il.1.104 = Od.4.662, cf. Hes.Sc.390; ἄστρα λαμπετόωντα Id.Th.110; τείρεα λ. A.R.3.1362. **-ης,** ου, ὁ, *the lustrous one*, coined to expl. λαμπετόωντι, Sch.Il.1.104:—fem. **λαμπέτις,** ιδος, Luc.Trag.103: also pr. n. **Λαμπετίη,** a daughter of Helios, Od.12.132; as epith. of Selene, Orph.H.9.9.

**λάμπη,** ἡ, = λαμπάς, *torch*, A.Eu.1042 (lyr., cod. Med. e manu prima), E.Supp.993 (lyr., s. v.l.); so Herm., after Sch., took ἀνήλιος λάμπα in A.Eu.387 (lyr.), *light* not of the sun, i.e. nether gloom, but v. λάπη 3. II. = λάπη (q.v.).

⊛**λαμπηδών,** όνος, ἡ, *lustre*, of the eyes, D.S.3.37 (pl.), S.E.P.1.45; χαλκοῦ Plu.Aem.18; of lightning, Epicur.Ep.2 p.45 U.: metaph., Plot.5.3.8. 2. *brilliance*, Lib.Or.59.103; of ebony, Jul.Caes.307d.

**λαμπήν-η,** ἡ, *covered chariot*, S.Fr.441, Men.29, Posidipp.10, Lxx 1 Ki.26.5; at Tegea, = ἀπήνη, Polem.Hist.ap.Sch.Pi.O.5 Arg.: Astrol., ἐν ἰδίαις λ., of planets when in certain favourable aspects, Ptol.Tetr.51. **-ικός,** ή, όν, *like a* λαμπήνη, ἅμαξαι Lxx Nu.7.3.

**λαμπηρός,** ά, όν, (λάμπη II) *covered with scum, slimy*, Hp.ap.Gal.19.117.

**λαμπ-ής,** epith. of the sun, Doroth. in Cat.Cod.Astr.2.82 cod. **-ίας·** ὁ ἥλιος, Hsch.

**Λάμπος,** ὁ, one of the horses of Eos, *Bright*, Od.23.246; cf. Φαέθων.

**λάμπουρις,** ιδος, ἡ, (οὐρά) *fox*, A.Fr.433, Lyc.344, 1393 (on the accent v. EM474.4). II. v.l. for λαμπυρίς in Suid. s.v. πυριλαμπίς.

**λάμπουρος,** ον, *bright-tailed*, epith. of foxes, Epic.Alex.Adesp.2.13; as a dog's name, *Firetail*, Theoc.8.65. (Prob. from λαμπρός, οὐρά, with dissimilation.)

**λαμπρ-αυγής,** ές, *lustrous*, Man.4.415:—irreg. fem. **λαμπραυ-**

**γέτις,** Id.1.301, 4.201. **-ειμονέω,** *wear white* or *splendid garments*, Charito 3.1. **-είμων,** *ονος, ὁ, ἡ, clad in splendid robes*, Hp.*Ep.* 15. **-ίζομαι,** Pass., *to be made bright*, Pempel.ap.Stob.4.25.52.

**λαμπρό-βῐος,** *ον, living splendidly*, Paul.Al.*M*.3. **-ειδής,** *ές, bright-looking*, v.l. for λαμπρός in Gal.*UP*8.6. **-είμων,** *ονος, ὁ, ἡ*, = λαμπρείμων, Suid., Phot. **-ζωνος,** *ον, with bright zone*, Hsch. s.v. ἀβρομίτρας. **-μοιρία,** *ἡ*, in pl., = λαμπραὶ μοῖραι (cf. λαμπρός IV), *Cat.Cod.Astr.*8(1).243, 8(4).207. **-πους,** *ὁ, ἡ, πουν, τό*, gen. *ποδος, bright-footed*, Sch.D Il.1.538.

⊛ **λαμπρός,** *ά, όν*, fem. *-ή* in Ep. (Il.17.269, Hom.*Epigr.*3.3), but *-ά* in Hes.*Th.*19, 371:—*bright, radiant*, of the sun and stars, λ. φάος ἠελίοιο Il.1.605; ἀστήρ 4.77; *-ότατος*, of Sirius, 22.30 (and of the same, λαμπρὸν παμφαίνησι 5.6); λαμπρὰ σελήνη Hes. ll.cc., cf. Th.7.44; πρὶν ἡμέραν λ. γενέσθαι D.H.3.27; of the eyes, S.*OT*1483, E.*Hec.*1045, etc., v. infr. II. 3; of metallic bodies, λ. φάλοι, κόρυθες, Il.13.132, 17.269: neut. as Adv., θώρηκες λαμπρὸν γανόωντες 13.265. **2.** of white cloths and the like, *bright*, λαμπρὸς δ' ἦν ἠέλιος ὥς [ὁ χιτών] Od.19.234; δέρμα..-ότατον λευκότητι Hdt.4.64; λ. ἐσθής, = Lat. *toga candida*, Plb.10.5.1. **3.** of water, *clear, limpid*, A.*Eu.*695, Hp.*Aër.*5, X.*HG*5.3.19; of air, λ. ἠήρ Hp.*Aër.*15; αἰθήρ E.*Med.*829 (Sup., lyr.). **4.** of sound or voice, *clear, distinct*, Pl.*Phlb.*51d, D.19.199; λαμπρὰ κηρύσσειν E.*Heracl.*864; φωνὴ -οτέρα Arist.*HA*545$^{a}$12; opp. φ. ἀσαφής, Id.*Aud.*801$^{b}$22; λαμπρὸν ἀνολολύξαι Plu.2.768d; cf. λάμπω I. 2. **5.** metaph., of *vigorous* action, λ. ἄνεμος a *keen* wind, Hdt.2.96, cf. A.*Ag.*1180; λ. ἤδη καὶ μέγας καθιείς swooping down like a *fresh* and mighty breeze, Ar.*Eq.*430, cf. 760; λαμπρὸς φανήσεται he will come *furiously* forth, E.*Heracl.*280; λ. μάχη a *keenly contested* battle, Plb.10.12.5; -ότερος κίνδυνος Id.1.45.9. Adv. -ρῶς, ἐπικείμενοι *vigorously*, Th.7.71; *utterly*, λ. ἡττῆσθαι, λ. περιεστοιχίσθαι, Hld.4.4, 9.1. **6.** metaph. also, *clear, manifest*, μαρτύρια A.*Eu.*797; ταῦτ' ἐπειδὴ λαμπρὰ συμβαίνει S.*Tr.*1174; ἴχνη X.*Cyn.*5.5; γεγενημένης τῆς νίκης λ. ἤδη Th.7.55; λ. φυγή *decisive*, Arr.*An.*2.11.3. Adv. -ρῶς, κοὐδὲν αἰνικτηρίως A.*Pr.*833; λελυμένων λ. τῶν σπονδῶν Th.2.7; λ. νικᾶν Arr.*An.*2.10.4; λαμπρῶς ἐλέγετο it was said *without concealment*, Th.8.67. **II.** of persons, *well-known, illustrious* by deeds, station, etc., λ. ἐν τῇσι Ἀθήνῃσι Hdt.6.125; ἐν τοῖσι πολέμοισι ἐὼν -ότατος Id.7.154; λ. ἐν [τοῖς κινδύνοις] D.19.269; -οτάτους γενομένους τῶν καθ' ἑαυτούς Th.1.138; ἐξ ἀδόξων γενέσθαι λ. Isoc.5.89; λ. ἐς γένος E.*El.*37; ἐν λόγοις Id.*Supp.*[902]; as honorary title, -ότατος, = Lat. *clarissimus*, *IG*14.911, 7.91, etc.; of cities, councils, etc., ἡ λαμπρὰ τῶν Μιλησίων μητρόπολις *SIG*906*A*4 (iv A.D.), cf. 867.4 (Sup., Ephesus, ii A.D.); of actions, etc., ἔργον οὐδὲν ἀπ' αὐτῶν λ. γίνεται Hdt.3.72; τὸν βίον λ. ποιεῖσθαι S.*OC*1144; τὸ λ. φῶς ἀποσβεννὺς γένους *Trag.Adesp.*9. **2.** *magnificent, munificent*, λ. ἐν ταῖς λειτουργίαις Isoc.3.56, cf. D.21.153 (Sup.); ὁ λ. καὶ πλούσιος οὗτος ib.174. Adv. -ρῶς, χορηγεῖν Antipho 2.2.12, Arist.*EN*1122$^{b}$22. **3.** *bright, joyous*, λ. ὥσπερ ὄμματι, of the bearer of good news, S.*OT*81, cf. X.*HG*4.5.10; λαμπρὸν ἐξέπεμψα *with bright hopes*, S.*El.*1130; λ. ταῖς ἐλπίσιν Jul.*Or.*2.64b; also ὄμματι δέρκομαι λαμπρόν, of one *clear in conscience*, Pi.*N.*7.66. **III.** of outward appearance, *splendid, brilliant*, νυμφίον..λ. ὄντα Ar.*Pax*859; of a horse, *IG*2$^{2}$.956.87, X.*Eq.*11.1; in dress, Id.*Cyr.*2.4.5 (Sup.); of youthful bloom, ὥρᾳ ἡλικίας λ. Th.6.54; of *healthy* look, Hp.*Aër.*24; of property, dress, etc., εἴ τί γ' ἔστι λ. καὶ καλόν Ar.*Pl.*144, cf. E.*Fr.*316.5; κατασκευή X.*Smp.*1.4 (Comp.); λ. κάλλος *beaming* beauty, Pl.*Phdr.*250b, etc.: more generally λ. τι ποιεῖν X.*Cyr.*5.4.15; τὸ λ. *splendour*, Pi.*N.*8.34; λ. γενέσθαι βουλόμεσθα τοὺς γάμους Euang.1.3. Adv. -ῶς, opp. λιτῶς, Phld.*Mort.*30: Sup. -ότατα X.*Cyr.*2.4.1; later -οτάτως *JHS*44.26 (Ancyra, ii A.D.). **2.** of language, *brilliant*, τῶν διθυράμβων τὰ λ. Ar.*Av.*1388; λ. λέξις *ornamental* diction, Arist.*Po.*1460$^{b}$4; λόγος Hermog.*Id.*1.9. **IV.** Astrol., of degrees in a zodiacal sign, ἑκάστου ζῳδίου λαμπρὰς μοίρας ἐξέθεντο Heph.Astr.1.1, al. **V.** for Adv. -ρῶς, v. supr. I. 5 and 6, II. 2, III. 1.

**λαμπρότης,** *ητος, ἡ, brilliancy, splendour*, λ. καὶ τάξις τοῦ στρατεύματος X.*An.*1.2.18; of a horse, Id.*Eq.*11.9; of arms, Plb.11.9.1, Arr.*An.*1.14.4. **2.** *clearness, distinctness*, Plu.*Phil.*11. **II.** metaph., *brilliancy, splendour*, Hdt.2.101; ἡ παραυτίκα λ. Th.2.64, cf. 7.69; ἀπὸ οἵας λαμπρότητος..ἐς οἵαν..τελευτὴν ἀφῖκτο Id.7.75, cf. 6.31: pl., *distinctions*, τιμαὶ καὶ λ. Id.4.62; ἔν τινος λαμπρότητι in *distinction* for a thing, Id.6.16; λ. τῶν πράξεων D.S.16.66, cf. Arr.*An.*2.7.7. **2.** *munificence*, D.21.158. **3.** *brilliancy* of style, Plu.2.25b; λαμπρότητες τοῦ λόγου, Lat. *lumina orationis*, Philostr.*VS*1.23.2. **4.** λ. ψυχῆς *magnanimity*, Plb.32.8.1, D.S.4.40. **5.** as a title, ἡ σὴ λ. your *Serenity, Serene Highness*, *PGrenf.*1.59 (v/vi A.D.).

**λαμπρό-τοξος,** *ον, with radiant bow*, Sch.D Il.1.37, Eust.32.45. **-φᾰής,** *ές, bright-beaming*, Orph.*H.*78.2, Man.4.53, *Cat.Cod.Astr.*1.173. **-φᾰνής,** *ές, appearing brilliant*, Paul.Al.*N.*2, Lyd.*Mag.*2.16. **-φεγγής,** *ές, brightly shining*, *PMag.Par.*1.386.

**λαμπρόφθαλμος,** *ον, bright-eyed*, Hsch. s.v. γλαυκῶπις.

**λαμπρό-φωνος,** *ον, clear-voiced*, Hp.*Aër.*5, Plu.2.840a: Sup. -ότατος D.18.313:—hence **-φωνεύομαι,** Hdn.*Philet.*p.436 P., Hsch. s.v. βαλανεύειν; and **-φωνία,** Ion. *-ίη, ἡ, clearness and loudness of voice*, Hdt.6.60. **-ψῡχος,** *ον, high-minded*, Arar.15, Ptol.*Tetr.*162. Adv. -χως, *munificently*, ἐπιμελητεύειν *Klio*17.187 (i A.D.).

**λαμπρ-υντής,** *οῦ, ὁ, bearing oneself proudly*, ἵππος Antisth.ap.D.L.6.7. **-υντικός,** *ή, όν, making bright and clean*, προσώπου Dsc.2.135, cf. Critoap.Gal.12.446. **-ύνω,** mostly in pres. and impf. (v. infr.), *make bright* or *brilliant*, τὸν ἵππον X.*Eq.*10.1, cf. *App.Anth.*3.158; μὴ χρώμασιν (ὄμμασιν codd. Stob.) τὸ σῶμα λ. *deck with bright colours*, Antiph.264; λαμπρύνει τὴν φωνήν (of garlic) *makes* the voice *clear*, Dsc.*Eup.*1.87:—Med., ἐλαμπρύνοντο τὰς ἀσπίδας *polished their* shields, X.*HG*7.5.20:—Pass., of a shield, *to be polished* or *bright*, Id.*Lac.*11.3; also εὕδουσα φρὴν ὄμμασιν λαμπρύνεται *is lightened* with eyes, A.*Eu.*104; λελάμπρυνται κόρας S.*Fr.*710; also, *to become manifest* or *notorious*, ἐν ἡμῖν ὁ ψόγος -ύνεται E.*El.*1039. **II.** Med., *make oneself splendid, pride oneself on* a thing, ὄχοις καὶ στολῇ -ύνεται ib.966; γένει Onos.1.22; *distinguish oneself in* or *by*.., ὅσα..χορηγίαις ἢ ἄλλῳ τῳ -ύνομαι Th.6.16; μειρακίων -υνομένων ἐν ἅρμασιν Ar.*Eq.*556; λ. ἐν οἷς οὐ δεῖ Arist.*EN*1122$^{a}$33, etc.; περὶ τὰς εὐωχίας Str.14.1.20; πολλὰ καὶ μεγάλα λαμπρυνάμενος πρὸς τὸ θεῖον Plu.*Nic.*26; τὰ ἄλλα ἐλαμπρύνατο Id.*Alex.*70; ἐπί τινι Philostr.*VA*2.43; πολλὰ περὶ τῶν Μηδικῶν ἔργων Plu.2.870d. **-υσμα,** *ατος, τό, ornament*, Phryn.*PS*pp.82, 124 B., Hsch. s.v. γλαινοί, *EM*232.40.

**λαμπ-τήρ,** *ῆρος, ὁ*, (λάμπω) *stand* or *grate* for pine and other wood used *for lighting rooms*, Od.18.307 sq., 343, 19.63; ὦ χαῖρε, λ. νυκτός *thou that lightest up* the night, of a beacon-fire, A.*Ag.*22; ἕσπεροι λαμπτῆρες the evening *watch-fires*, S.*Aj.*286; ἡλίου λαμπτῆρες E.*Rh.*60. **b.** epith. of Dionysus, Paus.7.27.3. **2.** *lantern*, E.*IA*34 (anap.), Hp.*Int.*26, X.*Smp.*5.2, Aen.Tact.22.21, *PCornell*1.85; λ. ἀντιπεφραγμένος, of a horn-*lantern*, Philist.15, cf. Emp.84.3; λ. μὴ ἔχοντι τὸ κύκλῳ δέρμα Arist.*HA*531$^{a}$5. **-τήρια** (sc. ἱερά), *τά, feast of Dionysus* λαμπτήρ, Paus.7.27.3. **-τηροκλέπτης,** *ου, ὁ, lamp-stealer*: metaph., of Perseus, who stole the eye of the Graeae, Lyc.846. **-τηρουχία,** *ἡ, holding of torches*: pl., λαμπτηρουχίαι *the beacon-watches*, A.*Ag.*890. ⊛ **-τηροφόρος,** *ον, carrying lights*, παῖδες Socr.Rhod.1 J.

**λαμπῠρ-ίζω,** *shine like a glow worm*, Thphr.*Lap.*58, 59, Dsc.5.84; *shine steadily*, opp. σπινθηροβολέω, of Venus, *PMag.Par.*1.2940: c. acc., *illuminate*, τὴν ὅλην οἰκουμένην *PMag.Berol.*2.103, cf. *PLeid.V.*3.15:—Med., abs., *shine*, *PMag.Lond.*121.603. **-ίς,** *ίδος, ἡ, glow-worm*, = λάμπουρις II, Arist.*PA*642$^{b}$34.

⊛ **λάμπω,** Il.13.474, etc.; Ion. Iterat. λάμπεσκεν Emp.84.6, Theoc. (v. infr.): fut. -ψω S.*El.*66, *AP*6.249 (Antip.): aor. ἔλαμψα Hdt.6.82 (v.l.), S.*OT*473 (lyr.), Ar.*V.*62, Pl.*Ep.*335d: pf. λέλαμπα (in pres. sense) E.*Andr.*1025, *Tr.*1295 (both lyr.):—**Med.,** *h.Hom.*31.13, etc.: impf. ἐλαμπόμην, Ep. λαμπ-, Il.6.319, E.*Med.*1194: fut. λάμψομαι (ἐλλ-) Hdt.1.80:—**Pass.,** fut. λαμφθήσομαι (ἐλλ-) Plot.2.9.3: aor. ἐλάμφθην J.*BJ*4.10.1 (περι-): from these late forms of Pass. must be distd. the similar Ion. forms of λαμβάνω:—*give light, shine*, of the gleam of arms, τῆλε δὲ χαλκὸς λάμφ' ὥς τε στεροπή Il.10.154, cf. 11.66; λάμπε δὲ χαλκῷ, of Hector, 12.463; φῶς λάμπεσκεν Emp. l.c.; ἀπ' ὀφθαλμῶν δὲ κακὸν πῦρ..λάμπεσκε Theoc.24.19; of the eyes, ὀφθαλμὼ δ' ἄρα οἱ πυρὶ λάμπετον Il.13.474; of the sun, Sol.13.23, etc.; of fire, S.*Ant.*1007; ἄλσος λάμπεν ὑπὸ δεινοῖο θεοῦ Hes.*Sc.*71:—Med., κόρυθος -ομένης Il.16.71; λάμπετο δουρὸς αἰχμή 6.319; δαΐδων ὕπο -ομενάων 18.492, Od. (only in this phrase) 19.48, 23.290; χαλκὸς ἐλάμπετο Il.22.134; of a person, -όμενος πυρί 15.623; τεύχεσι λ. 20.46, Hes.*Sc.*60; ὄσσε -έσθην Il.15.608; πεδίον..λάμπετο χαλκῷ 20.156, etc. **2.** of sound, *ring loud and clear*, παιὰν δὲ λάμπει S.*OT*186 (lyr.), cf. 473 (lyr.); cf. λαμπρός I. 4. **3.** metaph., *shine forth, be famous* or *conspicuous*, λάμπει κλέος Pi.*O.*1.23; ἀρετά Id.*I.*1.22, E.*Andr.*776 (lyr.); δίκα δὲ λάμπει μὲν ἐν δυσκάπνοις δώμασιν A.*Ag.*773 (lyr.); τέκνων οἷς ἂν λάμπωσιν νεάνιδες ἧβαι E.*Ion*476 (lyr.); κάλλος Pl.*Phdr.*250d. **b.** Astrol., of a planet, *occupy a favourable position*, Ptol.*Tetr.*51. **4.** of persons, φαιδρὸς λάμποντι μετώπῳ with *beaming* face, Ar.*Eq.*550 (anap.); *shine, gain glory*, οὐδ' εἰ Κλέων γ' ἔλαμψε Id.*V.* l.c.; ἐν ἄλλοις βουσὶν ἰὼν λάμπεσκεν Theoc.25.141. **II.** trans., *cause to shine, illumine*, δόλιον ἀκταῖς ἀστέρα λάμψας E.*Hel.*1131 (lyr.), cf. *Ion*83 (anap.), *Ph.*226, *AP* l.c., *Trag.Adesp.*33, etc.—Found chiefly in poetry and Com., though the pres. and impf. occur in X.*An.*3.1.11 (Med.), *Mem.*4.7.7, Pl.*Phdr.*250d, Arist.*de An.*419$^{a}$4, and late Prose, and the aor. in Hdt.6.82 (v.l.), Arist.*Mu.*395$^{a}$15, Plu.*Tim.*3, etc.

**λαμπώδης,** v. λάπη.

⊛ **λᾰμῡρ-ία,** *ἡ*, (λαμυρός III) *wantonness*, of women, Plu.*Sull.*35, *Luc.*6; of a man, Id.*Ant.*24; *pertness*, Id.2.66c, 1124b. **-ίς,** *ίδος, ἡ*, = λωγάνιον, Sch.Luc.*Lex.*3. **-ός,** *ά, όν, full of abysses*, θάλασσα *EM*555.57: hence, **II.** *gluttonous, greedy*, γάστρις καὶ λ. Epicr.5.8 = Antiph.89.5; γαστρὶ χαριζόμενος τῆς οὐ λαμυρώτερον οὐδὲν Timo 7; ὀδόντες Theoc.25.234; κάρηνον Nic.*Th.*293. **III.** metaph., *wanton, impudent*, -ώτερον λέγειν X.*Smp.*8.24; Ἀλκιβιάδου ἡ ἄγαν λ. πολιτεία Plu.*Comp.Alc.Cor.*1; λάμυρόν τι προσβλέπειν τινί Id.*Mar.*38; λ. ἱστορίη *AP*7.450 (Diosc.); of women, *coquettish*, ib.5.161 (Asclep.); of Eros, λαμυροῖς ὄμμασι πικρὰ γελᾷ ib.179 (Mel.); λαμυρὰς Πόθων ἀέλλας Cerc.5.10: later in good sense, *piquant, arch*, like ἐπίχαρις, Phryn.259; *charming*, Plu.*Caes.*49, Eun.*VS*p.467 B. **IV.** *bright*, τὰ λευκὰ τῶν ὀφθαλμῶν -ώτατα (in pneumonia) Aret.*SA*2.1.

**λαμφθῆναι,** Ion. aor. inf. Pass. of λαμβάνω; cf. also λάμπω.

**λαμψάνη,** *ἡ*, = λαψάνη (q.v.).

**λάμψις,** *εως, ἡ, shining*, ἀστέρων, ἀστραπῶν, ἡλίου, Ph.1.72, 2.187, *Gp.*2.5.12: metaph., of the law, Lxx *Ba.*4.2.

**λάμψομαι,** fut. Med. of λάμπω, and also Ion. fut. of λαμβάνω. **λᾶν·** δρᾶν, ἢ λίθον, Hsch. **λανηθάς·** δευτερίας οἶνος, Id.

⊛ **λανθᾰνόντως,** Adv. pres. part. of λανθάνω, *secretly*, Gal.12.292, Hdn.7.9.11, 8.7.3, D.C.66.5.

⊛ **λανθάνω,** Pi.*Fr.*75.13, etc.:—also **λήθω** (which is the form of the Act. generally used in compds., δια-λανθάνω being the sole exception), Il.23.323, S.*OT*1325 (lyr.), X.*Smp.*4.48; Dor. **λάθω** [ᾱ] S.*El.*

222 (lyr.); inf. λαθέμεν Pi.O.1.64: impf. ἐλάνθανον Il.13.721, etc.; ἔληθον Od.19.151, S.El.1359: Ep. λῆθον Il.15.461; Ion. λήθεσκεν 24.13: fut. λήσω Od.11.102, Ar.Ec.98, etc.; Aeol. inf. λάσην Alc.Supp.22.8; Dor. λασῶ Theoc.14.9, al., so (in late writers) λήσομαι, v. infr. c. II: aor. 1 ἔλησα Nic.Al.280 (but Hom. has ἐπ-έλησα, Alc. ἐξ-έλᾰσα, in causal sense): aor. 2 ἔλᾰθον Il.17.676, etc. (for λέλᾰθον, v. infr. B): pf. λέληθα Semon.7.9, Sol.13.27; Aeol. part. λελάθων Alc.Supp.26.8: plpf. ἐλελήθειν, Att. -ήθη, Th.8.33, Ar.Eq.822, Nu.380, Luc.Pr.Im. 15; Ion. 3 sg. ἐλελήθεε Hdt.6.79. B. causal ληθάνω, aor. 2 λέλᾰθον, v. infr. B. C. Med. and Pass., λανθάνομαι Arist.Po.1455ᵃ25 (s. v. l.), λήθομαι Il.11.790, A.Ag.39; Dor. λάθομαι [ᾱ] Pi.O.8.72: Ep. impf. λανθανόμην Od.12.227: fut. λήσομαι 1.308; Dor. λασεῦμαι Theoc.4.39, also λελήσομαι E.Alc.198: aor. 1 ἐλησάμην or λησάμην only in late Ep., Maiist.47, Mosch.3.62 (Dor. λāσ-), Q.S.3.99, etc.; also ἐλήσθην, Dor. inf. λασθῆμεν Theoc.2.46, cf. διαλανθάνω: aor. 2 ἐλᾰθόμην, Ep. λαθ-, Il.13.835, E.Hipp.289: rare in Prose exc. in compds., Plu.Caes.38; also Ep. redupl. λελάθοντο, etc., v. infr. C: pf. λέλησμαι S.El.342, Pl.Phdr.252a; Ep. λέλασμαι, part. λελασμένος, etc.; cf. ἐπιλήθω.

A. in most of the act. tenses, *escape notice* (freq. joined with a neg.):—Constr.: 1. c. acc. pers. only, *escape* his *notice*, λάθε δ' Ἕκτορα Il.22.277; οὐδέ σε λήσει 23.326; οὐ λῆθε Διὸς πυκινὸν νόον 15.461, cf. Od.11.102, al.; [τοῦτον] οὐκ ἔστι λαθεῖν ὄμματα φωτός A.Ag. 796 (anap.); οὐ λάθει μ' ὀργά S.El.222 (lyr.), cf. Ph.207 (lyr.); τουτί μ' ἐλελήθειν Ar.Nu.380; εἰ λανθάνει σε perhaps you *don't know*, Men. Sam.78: impers., λεληθέναι οὐ θαυμάζω τὸ πλῆθος περὶ τούτου it *escaped the notice of* the people, X.Hier.2.5; σὲ δὲ λέληθεν περὶ τοῦτο ὡς.. Pl. Lg.903c. 2. most freq. with a part. added, in which case we usually translate the part. by a Verb, and express λανθάνω by an Adv., *unawares, without being observed*; either, a. c. acc. pers., ἄλλον τινὰ λήθω μαρνάμενος I *am unseen by* others while fighting, i. e. I fight *unseen* by them, Il.13.273; πάντας ἐλάνθανε δάκρυα λείβων Od.8.93, cf. 12.17,220, 19.88, al., Pi.O.1.64, 6.36, Hdt.8.25: freq. in Trag. and Att., μὴ λάθῃ με προσπεσών lest he come on *unseen* by me, S.Ph.46, cf. 156 (lyr.); ὅπως μὴ λήσουσιν αὐτοὺς αἱ νῆες.. ἀφορμηθεῖσαι should put to sea *without their observing* them, Th.8.10; or, b. without an acc., φονέα ἐλάνθανε βόσκων he maintained the murderer *unawares*, Hdt.1.44; λέληθας ἐχθρὸς ὤν S.OT415; δουλεύων λέληθας Ar.V. 517; συνέβη δὲ ὑπερημέρῳ γενομένῳ λαθεῖν D.21.89: the reflex. Pron. may be supplied and is sts. added, λέληθεν αὑτὸν τοῖς ξυνοῦσιν ὢν βαρύς S.Fr.103; ἕως σαυτὸν λάθοις διαρραγείς Ar.Pax32, cf. Nu.242, X.An.6.3.22: sts., however, a different object must be supplied from the context, βάλλοντες ἐλάνθανον (not ἑαυτούς, but Τρῶας) Il. 13.721; ἐλάνθανε [πάντας] ἔχων Hdt.8.5; μὴ διαφθαρεὶς λάθῃ [τινὰ ὁ βίος] S.Ph.506; μὴ λάθῃ [ἡμᾶς] φύγδα βὰς A.Eu.256 (lyr.), cf. Th. 4.133, etc.—In a few examples this constr. is reversed, and λαθών is put in the part., as in our idiom, ἀπὸ τείχεος ἅλτο λαθών (for ἔλαθεν ἁλόμενος) Il.12.390; ἡ.. λήθουσά μ' ἐξέπινες S.Ant.532. 3. rarely c. acc. et inf., μή σε λαθέτω ὑπερτιθέμεν *let* it not *escape* thee to.., i. e. *forget* not to.., Pi.P.5.23; ἔλαθεν αὐτὸν σύνθημα δοῦναι Plu.Arist. 17; σφᾶς λέληθε Θεόδωρον εἶναι *it has been unnoticed* that it was.., Paus.9.41.1. 4. folld. by a relat. clause, οὐδέ με λήθεις, ὅττι θεῶν τίς σ' ἦγε thou *escapest* me not, it is *not unknown* to me, that some god led thee, Il.24.563; οὐδὲ ἑ λήθει, ὅππως.. 23.323; ἐδόκεες θεοὺς λήσειν οἷα ἐμηχανῶ thou thought'st to *escape* the gods' *notice* in.., Hdt.8.106; οὔκουν με.. οἷα πράττεις λανθάνει Ar.Eq.465; οὐ λανθάνεις με, ὅτι.. X.Mem.3.5.24, cf. Smp.3.6,13; ὁ γείτων λ. τινὰ οὐ μόνον ὅτι πράττει, ἀλλ' εἰ.. Pl.Tht.174b. 5. abs., *escape notice* or *detection*, S.Tr.455, Th.1.37,69, al.; λάθε βιώσας Epicur.Fr.551; λανθάνει τὸ οὖρον προσπῖπτον Hp.Coac.464.

B. causal, *make one forget* a thing, c. gen. rei, in compds. ἐκληθάνω, ἐπι-λήθω; the simple Verb only in Ep. redupl. aor. 2, ὄφρα.. λελάθῃ ὀδυνάων that.. he *may cause* him *to forget* his pains, Il.15.60; πόλιν λελάθοιτε συντυχιᾶν Lyr.Adesp.140.9: but II. in late Ep., λέλαθον, = ἔλαθον, *escaped notice of*, ἐὸν νόον, τοκῆας, A.R.2.226, 3.779, cf. Orph.A.876.

C. Med. and Pass., *let* a thing *escape one, forget*, 1. *forget* simply, in pres. (abs.), σὺ δὲ λήθεαι Il.11.790: c. gen., Κίρκης μὲν ἐφημοσύνης.. λανθανόμην Od.12.227, cf. Pi.O.8.72; οὔ ποτε λήσομαι αὐτῶν Od.1.308; ἄλγος, οὔ ποτ' οὐ λελήσεται E.Alc.198: mostly in aor. 2, ἀλκῆς λαθέσθαι A.Supp.731; νόστου τε λαθέσθαι Od.9.97; πῶς ἂν.. Ὀδυσῆος.. λαθοίμην; 1.65: also in redupl. aor., οὐδὲ σέθεν.. θεοὶ μάκαρες λελάθοντο Il.4.127; μή τίς μοι ἀπειλάων λελαθέσθω 16.200; οὐ δυνάμην Ἄτης λελαθέσθ' 19.136 (but in Hes.Th.471 like the Act., ὅπως λελάθοιτο τεκοῦσα that she might bear *unknown*): so in pf., τῶν δὲ λέλασται Il.5.834; ἐμεῖο λελασμένος 23.69; κείνου λελῆσθαι S. El.342, etc.; ἑταίρων πάντων λέλησται Pl.Phdr.252a: with a relat. clause, λελασμένος ὅσσ' ἐπεπόνθει Od.13.92: fut. Med. in pass. sense, once in S., οὐδέ ποτε λησόμενον οἷον ἔφυ κακόν never *will be forgotten*, El.1249 (lyr.); cf. ἐπιλανθάνω. 2. *forget purposely, pass over*, ἢ λάθετ' ἢ οὐκ ἐνόησεν either he *chose to forget it*.., Il.9.537; μαθοῦσιν αὐδῶ, κοὐ μαθοῦσι λήθομαι A.Ag.39. II. in later writers fut. Med. is used like Act., *escape notice*, ἡμᾶς Arist.APr.66ᵃ31, cf. A.R.3.737, Luc.Sacr.14: abs., Alciphr.3.52.

**λανίζει**· λαγγάνει, βρέχει, Hsch. **λανὸν κῆρ**· σοφωτάτη ψυχή, Id. **λανόν**· λίθον, Id. **λᾶνός**, Dor. for ληνός.

**Λάνοτρος**, ὁ, name of a month at Tauromenium, IG14.427 ii 1, al.

❀ **λάξ**, Adv. *with the foot*, λ. ἐν στήθεσι βὰς ἐξέσπασε μείλινον ἔγχος Il. 6.65, cf. 16.503; λ. προσβάς 5.620, 16.863; λ. ποδὶ κινήσας 10.158, Od.15.45; λ. ἔνθορεν 17.233; λ. δ' ἐφ' ὁρκίοις ἔβη Archil.Supp.2.13; so later βοῦς μοι ἐπὶ γλώσσης κρατερῷ ποδὶ λ. ἐπιβαίνων Thgn.815; λ. ἐπίβα δήμῳ Id.847; λ. πατεῖσθαι (cf. λάγδην) to be *trodden under foot*, A.Eu.110, Ch.644 (lyr.); ἀθέῳ ποδὶ λ. ἀτίσαι Id.Eu.542 (lyr.); λ. ἐπορούσας πλῆξε A.R.2.106; παίει τε λ. πύξ Philem.1.6 D.: also in late Prose, Luc.Asin.31, al.:—for the form cf. γνύξ, πύξ, ὀδάξ.

**λαξ-εία**, ἡ, *quarrying*, POxy.498.6 (ii A. D.). **-ευμα**, ατος, τό, *hewn work in stone*, Anon.Prog. in Rh.1.640 W. **-ευσις**, εως, ἡ, *cutting of stone*, Sch.Theoc.6.18. ❀ **-ευτήριον**, τό, *stone-cutter's tool*, Lxx Ps.73(74).7. **-ευτής**, οῦ, ὁ, *stone-hewer*, Man.1.77. **-ευτικός**, ή, όν, *of* or *for a stone-cutter* or *his art*, διαβήτης Eust.341.28; ἡ λ. τέχνη Anon Prog. in Rh.1.640 W., Phot. **-ευτός**, ή, όν, *hewn out of the rock*, Lxx De.4.49, Ev.Luc.23.53. **-εύω**, *hew in stone*, Lxx Ex. 34.1, al.; also, *hew* wood, ib.Is.9.10(9):—Pass., ἐκ λίθων λελαξευμένων ib.Ju.1.2, cf. J.AJ12.7.6. **-ικός**, ή, όν, = λαξευτικός, POxy.498. 34 (ii A. D.). II. λαξικά, τά, *tax on stone-cutting*, PFay.44.6 (i B. C.). **-ιμος**, η, ον, *hewn*, PLond.3.856.30 (i A. D.).

❀ **λάξις** (not λᾶξις), ιος, ἡ, (λαχεῖν) Ion. for λῆξις (A), *that which is assigned by lot, an allotment of land*, Hdt.4.21; μοίρης λ. SIG57.35 (Miletus, v B. C.); so prob. καί σφε τεὴν ἐκρίναο λάξιν Call.Jov.80.

**λάξομαι**, Ion. for λήξομαι, fut. of λαγχάνω.

**λαξόος**, ὁ, contr. from λαοξόος, prob. in Timo 25.1: in pass. sense, λάξοος *hewn from stone*, S.Fr.212 (lyr.).

**λαξός**, v. λαοξόος. **λαξπάτητος**, v. λακπάτητος.

**λᾱο-βότειρα**, ἡ, *feeder of the people*, γαῖα Orph.L.714. **-βότος**, ον, (βόσκω) = λαοτρόφος, Hsch.

**λᾱογρᾰφ-έω**, *enrol in the class subject to poll-tax*, only in Pass., POxy.711.3 (i B. C.), etc. **-ία**, ἡ, *enrolment, census*, Lxx 3Ma.2. 28: *assessment for poll-tax*, κατ' ἄνδρα PTeb.103.1 (i B. C.), al.; later, *poll-tax*, BGU1613 B ii 7 (i A. D.), etc. ❀ **-ος**, ὁ, *officer in charge of enrolments*, Sammelb.4299.1 (iii A. D.).

**λᾱο-δάμᾱς** [δᾰ], αντος, ὁ, *subduer of peoples*, Ἄρης A.Th.343 (lyr.). II. in Hom. only as pr. n., Il.15.516; voc. -δάμᾱ Od.8.141, 153. **-δῐκος**, ον, *tried by the people*, σοφίη Socr.ap.D.L.2.42. **-δογμᾰτικός**, ή, όν, *suited to public opinion, popular*, ἀποφάσεις prob. l. in Plb.34.5.14, cf. 34.1.6, 34.12.2. Adv. -κῶς f. l. ibid. ❀ **-δόκος**, ον, *receiving the people*, dub. in IG7.53.12 (Megara) = Simon.107.10 (δαμοδόκων Bgk.); in Hom. as pr. n. **Λαόδοκος** (proparox.).

**Λαοίτας**, title of Zeus at Elis, Paus.5.14.4, 5.24.1.

**λᾱο-κᾰτάρᾱτος** [ᾰρ], ον, *accursed by the people*, Sm.Pr.11.26. **-κρᾰτέομαι**, Pass., *live under mob-rule*: and **-κρᾰτία**, ἡ, *mob-rule*, Men.Rh. p.359 S. **-κρίτης** [ῑ], ου, ὁ, *judge in native court* in Egypt, Mitteis Chr.8.12 (iii B. C.), 31 vii 3 (ii B. C.), PTeb.5.216 (ii B. C.). **-μέδων**, οντος, ὁ, *ruler of the people*, in Hom. as pr. n.

**λᾶον**, v. λάϊον.

❀ **λᾱοξόος**, ὁ, (λᾶας, ξέω) *sculptor*, Ptol.Tetr.179, IG3.1308:—also **λαξόος** (q. v.); **λααξός**, *stone-cutter*, PCair.Zen.172 (iii B. C.); **λαξός**, ib.176 (iii B. C.), PTeb.121.13 (i B. C.), etc.:—Adj. **λᾱοξοϊκός**, ή, όν, σκεῦος Hsch. s. v. ὄρυξ, cf. Vett.Val.11.14.

**λᾱοξουργέω**, incorrect form for λαξεύω, Sch.Od.14.223.

**λᾱοπᾰθής**, ές, *suffered by the people*, A.Pers.945 (lyr.).

**λαόπαις**· βούπαις, Hsch. **λαοπίζειν**, coined as etym. of λαπίζειν (q. v.), τοὺς λαοὺς εἰς ὄπιν ἄγειν.. διὰ τῆς ἀλαζονείας, Id.

**λᾱο-πλάνος** [πλᾰ], ὁ, *misleader of the people*, J.AJ8.8.5 (pl.). **-πόρος**, ον, *serving as a passage for the people, man-conveying*, λ. μαχαναί a bridge, A.Pers.113 (lyr.).

**λαοργός**· ἀνόσιος (Sicel), Hsch. (cf. λεωργός).

❀ **λᾱός**, ὁ, Ion. **ληός** Hippon.88, Hdt.5.42 (v.l. λαόν, which is in all Mss. in 4.148), cj. in Mimn.14.9; Att. **λεώς**, which is also used in Hdt.1.22, 8.136, while the form λαός is sts. used in Trag., and once or twice even in Com. (v. infr. I. 3): also in Inscrr. and Pap. (v. infr.) and in late Prose, as Foed.Byz.ap.Plb.4.52.7 (pl.), Str.14.4.3 (pl.), Plu.2.1096b, etc. (both forms in pr. nn., Λεωβώτης Hdt.7.204, Λαβώτας X.HG1.2.18, etc.). 1. in Il., λαός (λαοί) usu. means *men*, i. e. soldiers, both of the whole army and smaller divisions, κριτὸς ἔγρετο λ. Ἀχαιῶν 7.434; λαὸν ἀγείρειν 16.129; πολὺν ὤλεσα λαόν 2.115: pl., ἅμα τῷ γε.. ἄριστοι λ. ἕποντ' ib.578; στίχες ἀσπιστάων λ. 4.91; periphr., στρατὸς λαῶν ib.76; λαῶν ἔθνος 13.495; mostly including both *foot and horse*, as 2.809; but sts. λαός denotes *foot*, as opp. horse, 7.342; also, *a land army*, opp. a fleet, 4.76, 9.424, 10.14; also, *the common men*, opp. their leaders, 2.365, 13.108; but 2. in Od., λαοί, more rarely λαός, almost always means *men* or *people*; as *subjects* of a prince, e. g. 3.214, 305, al. (λαοί is sts. so used in Il., e. g. 17.226, 24.611; λαοὶ ἀγροιῶται country-*folk*, 11. 676; *work-people*, 17.390); of *sailors*, Od.14.248; so after Hom., ναυτικὸς λεώς seafaring *folk*, A.Pers.383; πᾶς ὁ χειρῶναξ λεώς S.Fr.844; ὁ γεωργικὸς λεώς Ar.Pax920 (lyr.): in sg., *slave*, τὸν Εὐρυσθέως λεών, of Heracles, Hecat.23 J.; and so perh. λεὼς αὔτοικος GDI5533e (Zeleia): more generally, μέροπες λαοί, i. e. *mankind*, A.Supp.90 (lyr.); λ. ἐγχώριοι the natives, ib.517, cf. Od.6.194; esp. in Egypt, of the fellahīn, PRev.Laws 42.11–16 (iii B. C.), PSI4.380.5 (iii B. C.), etc.; *civil population*, opp. priests and soldiers, OGI90.12 (Rosetta, ii B. C.), cf. 225.8 (Milet., iii B. C.), al. 3. *people assembled*, as in the theatre, ὁ πολὺς λαῶν ὄχλος Ar.Ra.676, cf. 219 (both lyr.); esp. in the Ecclesia, αἱ στίχες τῶν λαῶν Id.Eq.163: hence the phrase ἀκούετε λεῴ hear *O people!*—the usual way of beginning proclamations at Athens, like our *Oyez!* Sus.1.1, Ar.Pax 551, Av.448; τιμῶσιν οἱ πάντες λεῴ ib. 1275; δεῦρ' ἴτε, πάντες λεῴ Arist.Fr.384; Ἀττικὸς λεώς A.Eu.681; ὁ πολὺς λεώς *the multitude*, Pl.R.458d, etc. 4. in Lxx, *of the*

*people*, as opp. priests and Levites, 1*Es.*5.46; in *NT*, of *Jews*, opp. Gentiles, *Ev.Matt.*2.6, *Ev.Luc.*2.10, al., cf. *SIG*1247 (Jewish tombstones); of *Christians*, opp. heathen, *Act.Ap.*15.14, al. II. *a people*, i.e. all who are called by one name, first in Pi., Δωριεῖ λαῷ *O.*8.30; Λυδῶν δὲ λαὸς καὶ Φρυγῶν A.*Pers.*770; ξύμπας Ἀχαιῶν λαός S.*Ph.*1243, cf. *OT*144, etc.; ἱππόται λαοί, i.e. the Thessalians, Pi. *P.*4.153, cf. 9.54, *N.*1.17. (The resemblance between λαός *people* and λᾶος *stone* (cf. λᾶας) is implied in Il.24.611 λαοὺς δὲ λίθους ποίησε Κρονίων (in the story of Niobe); and so Pi. explains the word from the legend of Deucalion, *O.*9.46, cf. Epich.122, Apollod.1.7.2; but cf. Philoch.12.) (From λᾱϝ-, as shown by the pr. names ΛαϝοπτόλεμοςGDI3151, ϝιόλαϝος ib.3132 (Corinth): hence prob. λήϊτον.)

**λᾶος**, irreg. gen. of λᾶας. II. **λᾶος**, ὁ, *stone*, v. λᾶας.

**λᾱο-σεβής**, ές, *worshipped by the people*, ἥρως Pi.*P.*5.95. **-σσόος**, ον, (σεύω) *rousing* or *stirring the nations*, epith. of the war-deities Ares, Eris, Il.17.398, 20.48; of Athena, 13.128, Od.22.210; of Apollo, Il.20.79: also of men, as Amphiaraus, Od.15.244; of Electryon, Amphitryon, Hes.*Sc.*3,37; λαοσσόοι ἀγῶνες assemblies *to which the people flock*, Pi.*P.*12.24.

**λᾱο-τέκτων**, ονος, ὁ, *stone-worker*, *AP*7.380 (Crin.). **-τίνακτος** [ῐ], ον, *stirred by a stone*, ὕδωρ ib.9.272 (Bianor). **-τομέω**, *hew stone*, *Sammelb.*4279 (i A.D.). **-τόμος**, ον, *stone-cutting*, ὄργανα Men.Prot.ap.Suid. s.v. σπαλίων. II. = λατόμος, Man.6.416, *Epigr.Gr.*1021 (Antinoe), *AJA*7.47 (Corinth), *POxy.*134.16 (vi A.D.); λ. πέτρης Man.4.325.

**λᾱοτρόφος**, ον, *nourishing* or *tending the people*, πόλις Pi.*O.*5.4; τιμὰ λ. an office *useful to the people*, ib.6.60.

⊛ **λᾱοτύπος** [ῠ], ον, *cutting stones*, σμῖλαι *AP*7.429.3 (Alc.). II. as Subst., *stone-cutter, statuary*, *APl.*4.59 (Agath.).

**λᾱο-φθόρος**, ον, *ruining the people, destructive*, c. gen., στάσις Ἑλλήνων λ. Thgn.781. **-φόνος**, ον, *slaying the people*, δόρυ B.12.120; Διομήδης Theoc.17.53; ξίφος *IG*14.1294. ⊛ **-φόρος** and **λεωφόρος**, ον, *bearing people*, λαοφόρον καθ' ὁδόν on *a highway, thoroughfare*, Il.15.682; λαοφόρου ἐπέβησαν..κελεύθου Theoc.25.155; ὑπὲρ τῶν μάλιστα λεωφόρων (v.l. λαοφ-) πυλέων over the gates of greatest *thoroughfare*, Hdt.1.187. 2. Subst., λ. (sc. ὁδός), ἡ, *highway*, τὰς λεωφόρους μὴ βαδίζειν Pythag.ap.Porph.*VP*42, Ael.*VH*4.17, cf. Iamb.*Protr.*21.δ', D.L.8.17; λεωφόρους πρὸς ἐκτροπάς E.*Rh.*881 (λαοφ- codd.; λεωφόρου *from the highway*, cj. Vater); τῶν ἐκ τῆς χώρας λ. εἰς τὴν πόλιν..τεταμένων Pl.*Lg.*763c, cf. Ph.1.16, Paus.9.2.2, Jul.*Or.*6.184d, 7.225c, and v. λεώβατος. II. λεωφόρος, ἡ, = πόρνη, Anacr.157. [λεω- as monosyll. in E. l.c.]

**λάπαγμα** [λᾰ], ατος, τό, and **λᾰπαγμός**, ὁ, *evacuation*, Hsch.

**λᾰπαδνός**, όν, metri gr. for ἀλαπαδνός, restored by Musgrave in A.*Eu.*562.

**λᾰπάζειν**· ἐκκενοῦν, ἀφ' οὗ καὶ τὸ ὄρυγμα, Hsch. (cf. λαπάσσω).

**λᾰπᾰθοειδής**, ές, *like a dock* or *sorrel leaf*, φύλλα f.l. in Ps.-Dsc.2.166.

⊛ **λάπᾰθον** [λᾰ], τό, *monk's rhubarb, Rumex Patientia*, Epich.161, Thphr.*HP*7.1.2, al.; λ. ἄγριον *dock, Rumex conglomeratus*, ib.7.6.1, Dsc.2.114:—also **λάπαθος**, ὁ or ἡ, Thphr.*HP*1.6.6, al., *EM*57.17 (fem. in Steph. *in Rh.*311.32); and **λαπάθη**, ἡ, *EM*551.15. II. *pitfall for wild beasts*, Phot., Suid.:—also **λάπαθος**, ὁ, Democr.122 (pl.).

**λᾰπακτικός**, ή, όν, (λαπάσσω) *laxative*, Xenocr.ap.Orib.2.58.9, Gal.6.457, 11.711.

**λάπαξις** [λᾰ], εως, Ion. ιος, ἡ, *evacuation* of the bowels, Arist.*Ph.*197$^{b}$24, *Pr.*935$^{b}$30, Gal.19.199; [ὑστέρης] Aret.*CA*2.10.

**λᾰπάρᾱ** [πᾰ], Ep. and Ion. **-ρη**, ἡ, (λαπαρός) *the soft part of the body* between the ribs and hip, *flank*, Il.6.64, 16.318, al. (not in Od.), Epich.90, Hdt.2.86, etc.: pl., *flanks*, Id.6.75, Diocl.*Fr.*193, Hp.*Flat.*9, etc.; sg. also, *side* of the chest, Id.*Loc.Hom.*14, Erot.:—λαπάρα and κενεών are distd. by Hp.*Morb.*2.55, *Int.*17, Gal.18(2).762,764. II. *sausage* or *haggis*, *AP*9.486 (Pall.).

**λᾰπᾰρ-ός**, ά, όν, *slack, loose*, τὸ λ. τῆς πλευρῆς, = λαπάρα, Hp.*Art.*50; of the bowels, Id.*Prog.*11; λαπαρὸς εἰλεός Id.*Epid.*2.6.26, Orib.8.28.5; λ. γίνεσθαι have the bowels *opened*, Arist.*Pr.*935$^{b}$28; ἵππος λ. ὢν ἀλγεῖ Id.*HA*604$^{b}$16 (nisi leg. λαπάρας ἀνέλκει); of a dislocated joint, ὄπισθεν λαπαρόν, ἔμπροσθεν ἐξέχον Hp.*Mochl.*24; *hollow*, of a cushion, μέσον κατὰ μῆκος ποιήσαντα λαπαρόν Id.*Fract.*16; πλευρέων ὀδύναι λαπαραί, perh. *slight*, Id.*Epid.*6.3.18 (so perh. λ. εἰλεός above). Adv. -ρῶς, ὑποχονδρίου ἔντασις λαπαρῶς, i.e. without swelling, ib.3.1.β' (opp. μετ' ὄγκου acc. to Gal. ad loc.). II. *lewd, lecherous*, Hsch. **-ότης**, ητος, ἡ, *looseness*, of the bowels, Hp.*Epid.*4.45.

**λᾰπάσσω**, Att. **-ττω**, *empty*, διάρροιαι..τὴν γαστέρα λαπάσσουσαι Hp.*Prog.*8; οὐκ ἐλάπαξεν οὐδέν *had* no *evacuations*, Id.*Epid.*4.31; τὰ παρ' οὖς λαπάσσει *causes* the tumours by the ear *to discharge*, Id.*Coac.*201, *Prorrh.*1.167:—Pass., esp. in aor. ἐλαπάχθην, of the bowels, *to be emptied*, Id.*VM*11, *Acut.*(*Sp.*)42, Arist.*Pr.*935$^{b}$30: abs., ἐλαπάσσετο *internal relief took place*, Hp.*Epid.*6.2.19: pf. inf. λελαπάχθαι Ath.8.363a. 2. *soften*, ὅκως..τὰ σκληρυνόμενα λαπαχθῇ Hp.*Ulc.*10. II. *sack* a town (cf. ἀλαπάζω), λαπάξειν ἄστυ Καδμείων βίᾳ A.*Th.*47, 531, dub. in Id.*Ag.*130.

**λάπη** [ᾰ], ἡ, *scum* which forms on the surface of wine, vinegar, or other liquids left to stand, Erot.: **λάμπη** in Dsc.5.76, Plu.2.1073a, Gal.16.704, Orib.*Syn.*9.13.2:—hence **λαμπῶδες**, of urine, *with a scum on it*, Hp.*Coac.*182, *Prorrh.*1.92; but Erot. read **λαπῶδες**, and **λαππώδης** (ἀπὸ τοῦ **λάππειν**) occurs in Gal. l.c. 2. *phlegm*, Hp.*Morb.*2.15, *Int.*12; μεστοὶ λάπης Diph.17.15; cf. λέμφος. 3. metaph., ἀνηλίῳ λάπᾳ (Wieseler for λάμπᾳ) in sunless *filth* or *damp*, of the nether world, A.*Eu.*387 (lyr.).

**λᾰπ-ίζω**, = συρίζω, S.*Fr.*1062; *swagger, rodomontade*. Cic.*Att.*9.13.4, *AB*277, Phot.; cf. λαοπίζειν. **-ικτής**, = λαπιστής, Id. **-ισμα**, ατος, τό, *swaggering, boasting*, Cic.*Att.*9.13.4. **-ίσσω**, Att. **-ττω**, = λαπίζω, Phot. (-ήττειν cod.). **-ιστής**, οῦ, ὁ, *swaggerer*, Lxx *Si.*20.7:—fem. **-ίστρια**, Phot.

**λάπος**· θής, δοῦλος, Hsch. **λάππειν, λαππώδης**, v. λάπη. **λάπτας**· τοὺς ῥοφοῦντας, Id. II. λαπτής, f.l. for λάπης, Id.

**λαπτικός**, ή, όν, *fit for emptying* (v. λάπτω sub fin.), Eust.1413.3.

**λαπτυήρ**· σφοδρῶς πτύων, Hsch.

**λάπτω**, fut. -ψω Il.16.161, (ἀπο-) Ar.*Nu.*811: aor. ἔλαψα *Epic.Alex.Adesp.*1.10, Lxx *Jd.*7.5, (ἐξ-) Ar.*Ach.*1229: pf. λέλᾰφα Id.*Fr.*598:—Med., fut. λάψομαι (ἐκ-) Id.*Pax*885: aor. ἐλαψάμην Pherecr.95:—*lap with the tongue*, of wolves, λάψοντες γλώσσῃσιν..μέλαν ὕδωρ Il. l.c., cf. Lxx l.c., Plu.2.971a; πίνει τὰ καρχαρόδοντα λάπτοντα Arist.*HA*595$^{a}$7; τῇ γλώττῃ λ. Ael.*NA*6.53; cf. κάπτω. 2. *drink greedily*, αἷμα λέλαφας Ar.*Fr.* l.c., cf. *Epic.Alex.Adesp.* l.c.; οἶνον Ath.10.443e:—also in Med., λεπαστὴν λαψαμένοις *gulp down*, Pherecr. l.c.—In Ath.8.363a λαπάττειν shd. be restored for **λάπτειν**, unless it was an error of the writer, as in Eust.1413.3.

**λαπώδης**, v. λάπη.

**λάρβᾰσον**, τό, = στίβι, Dsc.5.84.

**λαρδηγός**, ὁ, *purveyor of salted meat*, *OGI*521.25 (Abydos, v/vi A.D.).

⊛ **λάρδος**, ὁ, *salted meat*, Lyd.*Mens.*4.92, Hero *Stereom.*2.54, *PLond.ined.*2147 (iv A.D.).

**λαρίεθος**· φλόϊνον στεγάστριον, Hsch.

**λάριμνον**, τό, Arabic name for *frankincense*, Str.16.4.19:—written **λάριμναν** by Agatharch.101.

**λᾱρῑνός**, ή, όν, *fatted, fat*, ταῦρος Xenoph.6.2; βοῦς Ar.*Pax*925; σύες Eratosth.20: metaph., λ. ἔπος Ar.*Av.*465:—hence **λᾱρῑνεύομαι**, *grow fat*, Sophr.104.

**λάρῑνος** [ᾱ], ὁ, a kind of *sea-fish*, Opp.*H.*3.399 (v.l. λάριμος), Hsch.:—hence **λᾱρῖναῖον** κύρτον· οἱ ἁλιεῖς τὸν ἐκ λε⟨υ⟩κέας, ἢ μέγαν, Id.:—**λᾱρῑνευτής**, οῦ, ὁ, = ἁλιεύς, Id.

**λάριξ**, ικος, ἡ, *larch, Larix europaea*, Plin.*HN*16.43. II. *Venice turpentine, terebinthina veneta*, Dsc.1.71, Gal.13.410, al.; = *coagulum*, *Gloss.* [*lărīces*, Lucan.9.920, of the trees.]

**λᾰρίς**, ίδος, ἡ, = λάρος, *AP*7.652 (Leon.), 654 (Id.).

⊛ **Λάρῑσα** [ᾱρ], ἡ (not Λάρισσα, v. Arc.77.14, *IG*9(2).60.5, 525.5, al., but Λαρισσέοις ib.9(2).603), *Larissa*, a name of many old Greek cities, Il.2.841, etc.; Pelasgic acc. to Str.9.5.19, 13.3.2: an Ion. form Λήρισαι (in Aeolis) occurs in Hdt.1.149; orig. it denoted a *citadel*, such as *the Larissa* of Argos, St.Byz., Sch.A.R.1.40. II. Adj. **Λᾱρῑσαῖος**, α, ον, *Larissaean, of* or *from Larissa*, Th.2.22, X.*HG*3.1.7, etc.; Ion. **Ληρισ-** Hdt.9.1 and 58:—also **Λαρίσιος** and **Λαρισηνός** as epith. of Zeus, Str.9.5.19, 13.3.2. 2. **Λᾱρῑσαῖοι** ἑψητῆρες *Larissaean* pots for boiling, *AP*6.305 (Leon.); **λᾱρῑσοποιοί** for λαρισαιοποιοί, either *makers of Larissaean pots*, or *makers of Larissaean citizens*, of the δημιουργοί (magistrates), Gorg.ap.Arist.*Pol.*1275$^{b}$30.

**λαρκ-ᾰγωγός**, ὁ, *coal-basket carrier*, ὄνος E.*Fr.*283 (troch.). **-ίδιον**, τό, Dim. of λάρκος, Ar.*Ach.*340:—also **-ίον**, Poll.10.111. **-ος**, ὁ, *charcoal-basket*, Ar.*Ach.*333, Alex.208, Lys.*Fr.*139 S. (Dissim. fr. νάρκος, cf. ναρκίον.)

**λαρκοφορέω**, *carry a* λάρκος, D.C.52.25.

**λαρνάκιον**, τό, Dim. of λάρναξ, Sm.1*Ki.*6.8, *Sammelb.*5939.3 (Cyrenaica).

**λαρνᾰκό-γυιος**, ον, epith. of Pan, apptly. from a pun on χηλή, *hoof*, and χηλός, = λάρναξ, Theoc.*Syrinx* 16. **-φθόρος**, ον, *killing in a box* or *chest*, Lyc.235.

⊛ **λάρναξ**, ᾰκος, ἡ, (rarely ὁ, v. infr. 3) *coffer, box, chest*, e.g. for household stores, Il.18.413, Hdt.3.123; λ. δαιδαλέα B.5.141, cf. Simon. (v. infr.). 2. *cinerary urn* or *coffin*, [ὀστέα] χρυσείην ἐς λάρνακα θῆκαν Il.24.795; λάρνακας κυπαρισσίνας ἄγουσιν ἅμαξαι..· ἔνεστι δὲ τὰ ὀστᾶ κτλ. Th.2.34, cf. *CIG*4003, 4007 (Iconium), 4441 (Adana), al.; the *ark* of Deucalion, Plu.2.968f, Luc.*Syr.D.*12, Apollod.1.7.2; of the Ark, *AP*1.62 (Christian); esp. an *ark* in which children were exposed, Simon.37.1, A.R.1.622, D.S.5.62, etc. 3. *drinking trough*, ὁ λ. οὗτος *IG*12(1).961 (Chalce). (Dissim. fr. νάρναξ, q.v.)

**λᾰροειδής**, ές, (λάρος) *like a sea-mew*, Tz. ad Lyc.76.

⊛ **λάρος** [ᾰ], ὁ, a ravenous sea-bird, perh. *sea-mew, gull*, Od.5.51, Arist.*HA*542$^{b}$17, 593$^{b}$3: hence, metaph., of greedy demagogues, as Cleon, λ. κεχηνὼς ἐπὶ πέτρας δημηγορῶν Ar.*Eq.*956; Κλέωνα τὸν λ. δώρων ἑλόντες Id.*Nu.*591, cf. *Av.*567, Matro *Conv.*9, Timocl.4.9; also of fools, Luc.*Tim.*12, Sch.Ar.*Pl.*913.

⊛ **λᾱρός**, όν, poet. Adj. *pleasant to the taste, dainty, sweet*, in Hom. always of taste, λαρὸν παρὰ δεῖπνον ἔθηκας Il.19.316; λαρὸν τετυκοίμεθα δόρπον Od.12.283, 14.408; λαρόν τέ οἱ αἷμ' ἀνθρώπου *sweet* to it [the fly] is the blood of man, Il.17.572; μέθυ λαρόν A.R.1.456: Ep. Sup. λαρώτατος, οἶνος Od.2.350: Comp. λαρότερον as Adv., Simon.183.10. 2. *pleasant to the smell*, ἀϋτμή Mosch.2.92; ἄνθεα λαρὰ φύοις *IG*14.1362; λαρὸν ὄδωδεν D.P.936. 3. *pleasant to the eye, lovely*, *AP*9.525.12; ἄνθεμα λ. ib.15.11 = *IG*12(1).783 (Lindos). 4. *pleasant to the ear, sweet to hear*, ἔπος A.R.3.933, *AP*7.602 (Agath.); λαρὰ φθέγξατο Βακχυλίδης ib.9.571; λ. χείλεα *uttering sweet sounds*, *APl.*4.226 (Alc.). [As ˘ ˘ can always be substituted for λᾱ- in Hom. and the Sup. is -ώτατος, λᾱρός is prob. contr. fr. λᾰᾰρός or λᾰερός (this perh. fr. λαϝ-, cf. ἀπο-λαύω).]

**Λάρτιος**, ὁ, Trag. for Λαέρτης (q.v.).

**λάρτιος**, α, ον, name of a hard Rhodian stone, πέτρα *SIG*581.98 (Hierapytna, iii/ii B.C.); λίθος *IG*12(1).2.7, cf. 677.7, 1033.22; στάλα (i.e. made of such stone) *Supp.Epigr.*3.674.9 (Rhodes, ii B.C.).

**λᾰρυγγ-ιάω**, = sq. I, βραγχὰ λαρυγγιόων *AP*11.382.2 (Agath.). **-ίζω**, *shout lustily*, D.18.291, Phld.*Rh.*1.200S., Luc.*Am.*36; of the raven, *croak*, Anon.ap.Suid.: c. acc. cogn., *bawl out*, τάδε Ath.9.383f. II. trans., *outdo in shouting*, λαρυγγιῶ τοὺς ῥήτορας Ar.*Eq.*358; acc. to others, *will cut* their *throats*, v. Sch. **-ικός**, ή, όν, *gluttonous*, Pherecr.32. **-ιον**, τό, Dim. of λάρυγξ, Gal.14.474. **-ισμός**, ὁ, *croaking*, Plu.2.129a (pl.). **-ός**· ματαιολόγος, Hsch.

**λᾰρυγγο-τομέω**, *cut open the windpipe*, Gal.14.734, Paul.Aeg.6.33: **-τομία**, ἡ, ibid. **-φωνος**, ον, *sounding from the throat*, Sopat.16.

**λάρυγξ** [ᾰ], υγγος, ὁ, *larynx* or *upper part of the windpipe*, Arist. *HA*493ᵃ6; used in sounding the vowels, ib.535ᵃ32: but in Poets confused with φάρυγξ (gullet) (cf. Arist.*HA*535ᵃ29), E.*Cyc.*158; χωρεῖν κατὰ τοῦ λ. Pherecr.108.7, cf. Crobyl.8; of gluttons, ἀνόσιοι λάρυγγες Eub.139; ἐκ τοῦ λ. ἐκκρεμάσας τινά Ar.*Eq.*1363; τὸν λάρυγγ' ἂν ἐκτέμοιμί σου Id.*Ra.*575: metaph., λ. γλυκύς *speech*, Lxx *Si.*6.4. II. = τραχεῖα ἀρτηρία, Meno *Iatr.*8.30.

**λαρυδοί**· στῦλοι οἱ ἐν τῷ ἀρότρῳ, Hsch. **λαρύζει**· βοᾷ, ἀπὸ τοῦ λάρυγγος, Id.

**λᾰρύνω**, *coo* like a dove, Anon.*devoc. animal.* in *Stud.Ital.*1.95, 3.496.

**λαρωντιδῶν**· ἐν τοῖς ἀθροίσμασιν ἔλεγον, ὡς ἐπῳδῶν, Hsch. **λᾶς**, = λᾶας, Id.; v. λαστρυγυλίας. ❀**λάσα**· τράπεζα πληρεστάτη, Id. II. **Λάσα**, = Λάρισα, Id.: Adj. ❀**Λασαῖος** *IG*9(2).517.19. **λάσαγγες**· οἱ περὶ τὰς Λίμνας χλωροὶ βάτραχοι, Hsch.

❀**λάσᾰνα** [λᾰ], τά, (cf. λάανα) always in pl., *trivet* or *stand for a pot*, Ar.*Pax* 893 (ubi v. Sch.), Diocl.Com.8. II. *night-stool*, Hp.*Fist.*9, Cratin.49 (cj. Mein. for λαχάνοις), Pherecr.88, Eup.224, Ar.*Fr.*462: also in sg., like Lat. *lasanum*, Hp.*Superf.*8, *AP*11.74.8 (Nicarch.):—hence **λᾰσᾰνοφόρος**, ὁ, *slave who had charge of the night-stool*, Plu.2.182c, 360d:—also **λᾰσᾰνίτης** [ῑ] δίφρος *BGU*1116.25 (i B.C.).

**λάσαρον** (= ὀπὸς δριμύς, Hsch.) or **λάσαρ**, τό, = ὀπὸς σιλφίου, *asafoetida*, *Hippiatr.*3, Aët.1.306, 15.5, Alex.Trall.12: Dim. **λασάριον**, τό, Aët.8.61, *Gloss.*

**λασάσθω**· χλευαζέτω, Hsch.

❀**λάσειος**, ον, prob. = λάσιος, δελματικὴ λ. *Edict.Diocl.*19.30.

**λᾰσεῦμαι**, Dor. fut. Med. of λανθάνω. ❀**λασθαίνειν**· κακολογεῖν, Hsch.

**λάσθη**, ἡ, *mockery, insult*, = Att. χλεύη, ἐπὶ γέλωτί τε καὶ λάσθῃ Hdt.6.67, cf. *AP*7.345.

**λασθῆμεν**, Dor. aor. inf. Pass. of λανθάνω. **λάσθον**· αἰσχρόν, Hsch. **λάσθω**· χλευαζέτω, and **λάσθων**· κακολογῶν, Id.

**λᾰσῐαύχην**, ενος, ὁ, ἡ, (λάσιος) *with rough, shaggy neck*, of the centaur, *h.Merc.*224, cf. λασιαύχενα χαίταν Ar.*Ra.*822 (lyr.); of the bear, *h.Hom.*7.46; of the horse, S.*Ant.*350 (lyr.); λ. βύρσα Theoc.25.272: also with a neut., λασιαύχενος ἄντρου v.l. Id.*Ep.*5.5.

**λασιδεύς**· θρασύς, ἄπληστος, Hsch. **λασῖνος**· ἄφρων, ἐπιλήσμων, Id.

**λᾰσῐό-θριξ**, τρῐχος, ὁ, ἡ, *shaggy*, Opp.*H.*4.369, Nonn.*D.*38.350, Orph.*Fr.*169. **-κνημος**, ον, *hairy-legged*, Opp.*C.*2.186. **-κωφος**, ον, *deaf from hair growing in the ears*, cited from Pl.(*Phdr.*253e) by Synes.67d, Phot., Suid., from a false reading, found in cod. B.

**λᾰσιόμᾱλον**· μῆλον τὸ ἔχον χνοῦν, Hsch.:—hence **λᾰσίμηλον**, τό, *peach*, shd. perh. be read in Antig.Car.ap.Ath.3.82b (ἡ δ' ἀριμήλων codd.).

**λάσιον** [ᾰ], τό, *a rough cloth*, Sapph.89 (pl.); λάσιον ἐπιβεβλημένος Theopomp.Com.36, cf. Artem.Gramm.ap.Erot.; perh. to be read for σίαλον in Hp.*Acut.*(*Sp.*)37.

**λᾰσιόπους**, πουν, gen. ποδος, *shaggy-footed*, Aesop.238.

❀**λάσῐος** [ᾰ], α, ον, later also ος, ον Luc.*Prom.*12, etc. (cf. λάσειος):—*shaggy, woolly*, of sheep, Il.24.125, Od.9.433; λ. θῆρες, of sheep and goats, opp. deer (στικτοὶ θ.), S.*Ph.*184 (lyr.); μέλισσαι Theoc.22.42; τὰ -ώτατα, of horses, X.*Eq.*2.4; in men, λ. κῆρ was in the heroic age a mark of strength, Il.2.851, 16.554, cf. Pl.*Tht.*194e; ἐν.. στήθεσσιν λασίοισι, of Achilles, Il.1.189; τὸ στῆθος ἐπαινεῖν χρὴ τετράγωνόν τε ἐὸν καὶ λ. Hp.*Prorrh.*2.7; whereas afterwards a hairy breast was looked upon as a sign of dissoluteness or coarseness, Ar.*Nu.*349; or of intrigue and cunning, Ἀγαθοκλεῖος λάσιαι φρένες ἤλασαν ἔξω πατρίδος Alex.Aetol.5; also λ. κεφαλή Pl.*Ti.*76c; περὶ ὦτα λ. Id.*Phdr.*253e; λ. τὰ σκέλη Luc.*DDeor.*4.1; λ. ὀφρύς Theoc.11.31; μηρῶν τρίχες *AP*11.326 (Autom.): τὸ λ. *hairiness*, Luc.*DMar.*1.1. Adv. τῶν ὀφρύων -ίως ἔχειν Philostr.*VS*2.1.7. II. generally, *bushy, overgrown*, αἴης λάσιον μένος Emp.27.2; χωρίον X.*HG*4.2.19, cf. Pl.*Cra.*420e; δρυμός Theoc.25.134; δρῦς Id.26.3; ἐκ τῶν λ. τὰ θηρία ἐξελᾶν X.*Cyr.*1.4.16; διὰ τῶν λ. ἐπιγενόμενοι Id.*An.*6.4.26: c. dat., *overgrown with..*, γῆ ὕλαις λάσιος Luc.*Prom.* l.c.

**λᾰσῐό-στερνος**, ον, *hairy-breasted*, παρδάλιες *AP*7.578 (Agath.). **-της**, ητος, ἡ, *shagginess*, Eust.1638.39. **-τρῐχος**, ον, = λασιόθριξ, Opp.*C.*1.474.

**λασιουργίας**· ἱστουργίας, δημιουργίας, Hsch. (i.e. ταλασ-).

**λᾰσιόφρυς**, υ, gen. υος, *with bushy eyebrows*, Hsch. s.v. μελάνοφρυς. **λᾰσῐοχαίτης**, ου, ὁ, *with shaggy hair*, Hdn.*Epim.*166.

**Λασίσματα**· ὡς σοφιστοῦ τοῦ Λάσου καὶ πολυπλόκου, Hsch. **λασιτός**· κίναιδος, ἡ **λεσιτός**· πόρνη, Id. (cf. λαίσιτος). **λασιχνεύουσα**· πλανωμένη (Sicel), Id.

**λᾰσῐ-ών**, ῶνος, ὁ, (λάσιος II) *thicket*, Nic.*Th.*28,489. **-ῶτις**, ιδος, fem. Adj., = λασία, λασιώτιδος ὕλης *Epic.Alex.Adesp.*9 vi 20.

**λασκάζει**· φλυαρεῖ, θωπεύει, Hsch.

**λάσκω**, impf. ἔλασκον E.*El.*1214 (lyr.): fut. λᾰκήσομαι Ar.*Pax* 381, 384: aor. 1 ἐλάκησα [ᾰ] ib.382 (δια-λακήσας Id.*Nu.*410 is prob. from διαλακέω, Dor. for -ληκέω): aor. 2 ἔλᾰκον, Ep. λάκον Il.14.25, al.: aor. 1 ἔληξα Herod.8.65: pf. λέληκα Il.22.141, Arist.*HA*618ᵇ31, λέλᾱκα A.*Pr.*407 (lyr.), Ar.*Ach.*410 (paratrag.); part. fem. λελᾰκυῖα Od.12.85:—Med., v. infr. II:—*ring, rattle, crash*: I. of things, *ring* when struck, λάκε χαλκὸς νυσσομένων ξίφεσίν τε καὶ ἔγχεσι Il.14.25; λάκε δ' ἀσπίς 20.277; also λάκε δ' ὀστέα the bones *cracked, broke with a crash*, 13.616; λάκε δ' ἀμφὶ πυρὶ ὕλη *crackled*, Hes.*Th.*694; ἔλακον ἀξόνων βριθομένων χνόαι *creaked* under the weight, A.*Th.*153 (lyr.):—this sense occurs only in aor. 2 Act. II. of animals, *scream*, of the falcon, ὀξὺ λεληκώς Il.22.141; of the nightingale in the falcon's talons, τί λέληκας; Hes.*Op.*207; also, of dogs, *howl, bay*, Σκύλλη.. δεινὸν λελακυῖα Od. l.c.; rare in Prose, οὐ μινυρίζει οὐδὲ λέληκεν, of the black eagle, Arist. l.c.:—this sense occurs only in pf., exc. in Ep. aor. Med., κύνες λελάκοντο *h.Merc.*145. III. of human beings, *shout, scream, cry aloud*, λέληκεν ἣν καὶ μηδέν' ἀνθρώπων ὁρᾷ Semon.7.15; φόβος μυχόθεν ἔλακε A.*Ch.*35 (lyr.), cf. S.*Ant.*1094, etc.; τί λέλακας; Ar.*Ach.* l.c.; μή νυν λακήσῃς Id.*Pax* 382: hence of Oracles, *utter*, A.*Ag.*1426 (lyr.), S.*Tr.*824 (lyr.), Ar.*Pl.*39; also, *sing*, πρὸς αὐλόν E.*Alc.*346. 2. c. acc. cogn., *shriek forth, utter aloud*, ὀλολυγμόν A.*Ag.*596; στονόεν λέλακε χάρα Id.*Pr.* l.c.; λ. βοάν E.*El.* l.c., cf. *Ion* 776 (anap.); ἀγγελίας Id.*IT*461 (anap.); πῆμα A.*Ag.*865; ῥῆμα γενναῖον Ar.*Ra.*97: c. dupl. acc., τοιαῦτα λάσκεις τούς.. φίλους; E.*Andr.*671:—in this sense only in Trag. and (rarely) Com.

**λασκωρεῖ**· διαφεύγει, Hsch. **λασταγεῖ**· ψοφεῖ, Id. **λάσται**· πόρναι, Id. **λαστάρνη**· μάστιξ, Id.

**λασταυροκάκκαβον**, τό, *an aphrodisiac dish*, Chrysipp.ap.Ath.1.9c.

❀**λάσταυρος**, ὁ, epith. of a κίναιδος, Theopomp.Hist.217(a), cf. *AP*12.41 (Mel.); as general term of abuse, Phryn.173: **λαστρίς** is cited as a Dim. in *EM*159.30.

**λαστήριον**, v. λῃστήριον. **λαστρυγυλίας**· λίθος τετριμμένος, Hsch. (Fort. λᾶς (= λᾶας) τρυμαλίας.)

**λᾰσῶ**, Dor. fut. of λανθάνω.

**λᾰτᾰγ-εῖον**, τό, *the vessel into which the* λάταξ *falls*, Suid. **-έω**, *throw the* λάταγες, λ. κοττάβους Luc.*Lex.*3. **-η**, ἡ, = λάταξ I, Dicaearch.Hist.34 (Sicilian); but Thess. or Rhod. acc. to Clitarch.ap.Ath.15.666c.

**λάταξ** [ᾰ], ἄγος, ἡ, usu. in pl. λάταγες, in the game of κότταβος, *the drops of wine in the bottom of the cup which were thrown into a basin with a splash*, λάταγες ποτέονται κυλίχναν ἀπὸ Τηΐαν Alc.43; ἀπ' ἀγκύλης.. ἵησι λάταγας Cratin.273, cf. Hermipp.47.7 (anap.), Critias 2.2 D., Call.*Fr.*102: so collectively in sg., ξανθὴ Ἀφροδισία λ. S.*Fr.*277 (lyr.). II. *a water-quadruped*, perh. beaver, Arist.*HA*487ᵃ22, 594ᵇ32.

**λατάσσω**, = λαταγέω, τὶν τάνδε λατάσσω (Dor.) Kretschmer *Griech. Vaseninschr.*p.87.

**Λᾰτιάριος**, ὁ, = Lat. *Latiaris*, epith. of Jupiter, D.H.4.49: **Λατιάρια**, τά, *the Latin festival*, in honour of *Jupiter Latiaris*, D.C.47.40.

**Λᾰτίνη** [ῑ], ἡ, *Latium*, Plb.3.22.13, Str.5.3.10.

**Λᾰτῑνοήθης**, ες, *following Latin customs*, Eust.1658.62.

❀**Λᾰτῖνος**, η, ον, *Latin*, Thphr.*HP*5.8.1; ἑορταὶ Λ., = Lat. *feriae Latinae*, D.H.4.49; ἡ Λ. φωνή, ἡ Λ. διάλεκτος, Str.6.1.6.

**Λάτιον** [ᾰ], τό, = Lat. *jus Latii*, Str.4.1.12, 4.2.2.

**λατμενεία**· δουλεία, Hsch. (cf. ἀτμενία).

**Λάτμιος**, α, ον, *Latmian*, Λάτμιον κνώσσεις (sc. ὕπνον), i.e. like Endymion on Latmos, Herod.8.10; cj. for λάθριον in Theoc.20.39.

**Λᾱτογενής**, ές, Dor. for Λητογενής.

❀**λᾱτομ-εῖον**, τό, *stone-quarry*, Str.12.2.8:—written **λᾱτόμιον** *SIG* 1182.12 (Ephes., iii B.C.), Str.5.3.10, 9.1.13, *CIG*2032, 2043; **λᾱτόμιν** *AEM*8.224 and 225. **-εύω**, = sq., *PSI*4.423.27 (iii B.C.). **-έω**, *quarry*, γῆν Posidon.57 J.; πέτραν *IG*4²(1).122.25 (Epid.), cf. D.S.5.39; λίθους *PCair.Zen.*499.38 (iii B.C.), Antig.*Mir.*161: abs., *PCair.Zen.*296.34 (iii B.C.), Agatharch.25, J.*AJ*8.2.9:—Pass., λελατόμηται *PPetr.*2p.12 (iii B.C.); τὰ -ούμενα θραύματα D.S.3.12. II. λ. λάκκον *hew it out*, Lxx *Ex.*21.33, cf. *De.*6.11 (Pass.). **-ημα**, ατος, τό, *stone hewn from a quarry*, D.S.3.13. **-ητός**, ή, όν, *hewn out of a rock*, κλῖμαξ Str.14.5.5, al. 2. of stones, *hewn*, Lxx 4*Ki.*12.12(13). **-ία**, ἡ, *quarrying of stone*, *PHib.*71.7 (iii B.C.), *IG*4²(1).102.17 (Epid.); τῷ στρώματι ib.40: mostly in pl., = *quarries*, Man.ap.J.*Ap.*1.26, Str.8.5.7, *AP*11.253 (Lucill.); of *the quarries* at Syracuse used as a prison, Plu.2.334c; also in sg., *PCair.Zen.*176.215 (iii B.C.). ❀**-ικός**, ή, όν, *for quarrying stones*, σίδηρος D.S.3.12. **-ιον**, v. λατομεῖον. ❀**-ίς**, ίδος, ἡ, *stone chisel*, χαλκαῖ λ. Agatharch.29. **-ος** (parox.), ὁ, (λᾶας, τέμνω) *quarry-man, stonecutter*, *IG*4.823.50 (Troezen), *PCair.Zen.*499.2, al. (iii B.C.), Lxx 3*Ki.*5.15(29), J.*AJ*11.4.1, *CIG* add.)4528b (Lebanon).

**λάτος**, ὁ, *the great Nile perch*, *Perca* (*Lates*) *niloticus*, Archestr.*Fr.*51, Str.17.1.40, 47, 2.4.

**λατραβιάζειν**· ἐσπουδασμένως καὶ ἀσήμως λαλεῖν, Hsch.; cf. **λατράζειν**· βαρβαρίζειν, Id. **λατραβός**, = λαμυρός, and **λατραβία** (λατραπία cod.), = λαμυρία μετὰ ἐρυθριάσεως, Id.:—also **λατραβῶν**· ἀλαζονευόμενος, and **ἐλατράβιζον**· τὸ βωμολοχεύειν καὶ πανουργεῖν

**λατραβίζειν** ἔλεγον, Id. **λατράζειν,** v. λατραβιάζειν. **λατραίω,** v. λατρεύω. **λάτραψ·** ὑετός, Id.

**λατρ-εία,** ἡ, *the state of a hired labourer, service,* A.*Pr.*966; ἐπίπονον ἔχειν λ. S.*Tr.*830 (lyr.): pl., οἵας λατρείας ἀνθ' ὅσου ζήλου τρέφει Id. *Aj.*503, cf. E.*Ph.*225 (lyr.), etc.: metaph., *the business* or *duties* of life, Plu.2.107c. 2. λ. τοῦ θεοῦ, θεῶν, *service to* the gods, divine *worship,* Pl.*Ap.*23c, *Phdr.*244e (pl.): abs., Lxx *Ex.*12.25, al., *Ep. Rom.*9.4, etc. **-ειος,** v. λάτριος. **-είω,** *render as offering,* Δί *SIG*9 (Pass., Olympia, vi B.C.):—also **-αίω,** prob. in *Inscr.Olymp.* 1.7. (Both Elean for λατρεύω, from -ηϝ-yω.) **-ευμα,** ατος, τό, in pl., *service for hire,* πόνων λατρεύματα painful *service,* S.*Tr.*357. 2. *service paid to the gods, worship,* E.*IT*1275 (lyr.). II. = λάτρις, *slave,* Id.*Tr.*1106 (lyr.). **-εύς,** έως, ὁ, *hired servant,* Lyc.393. **-ευσις,** εως, ἡ, *servitude, Gloss.* **-ευτικός,** ή, όν, *servile,* Ptol.*Tetr.* 160, Vett.Val.335.34, al. **-ευτός,** ή, όν, = foreg., ἔργον Lxx *Ex.* 12.16. **-εύω,** Elean **λατρείω** (q.v.), *work for hire* or *pay,* Sol. 13.48: *to be in servitude, serve,* X.*Cyr.*3.1.36; παρά τινι Apollod.2. 6.3. 2. λ. τινί *to be subject* or *enslaved to,* S.*Tr.*35, etc.: c. acc. pers., *serve,* E.*IT*1115 (lyr.), f.l. in Id.*El.*131: metaph., λ. πέτρᾳ, of Prometheus, A.*Pr.*968; μόχθοις λατρεύων τοῖς ὑπερτάτοις βροτῶν S.*OC*105; λ. νόμοις *obey,* X.*Ages.*7.2; λ. καιρῷ, = Lat. *temporibus inservire,* Ps.-Phoc.121; τῷ κάλλει λ. *to be devoted to..,* Isoc.10. 57; λ. ἡδονῇ Luc.*Nigr.*15. 3. *serve* the gods *with prayers and sacrifices,* λ. Φοίβῳ E.*Ion* 152 (lyr.): c. acc. cogn., πόνον λ. τινί *render due* service, ib.129 (lyr.); πόνον.. τόνδ' ἐλάτρευσα θεᾷ *IG*2.1378. **-ιος,** α, ον, *of a servant* or *service,* μισθός Pi.*O.*10.28; λατρίαν Ἰαολκὸν παρέδωκεν gave Iolcos *into slavery,* Id.*N.*4.54 (ubi codd. λατρείαν contra metrum); λ. ἔργα Man.1.275. **-ις,** ιος, ὁ and ἡ, *hired servant,* and in fem. *handmaid,* Thgn.302, 486, S.*Tr.*70, E.*Supp.*639, *Supp.Epigr.* 1.405 *B* 1 (Samos, iii A.D.); Ἑρμῆν.. δαιμόνων λάτριν E.*Ion* 4; ἡμιγύναικα θεῆς λάτριν ὅς.. [Simon.]179.9; of *slaves,* E.*IA*868 (troch.): fem., Id.*Hec.*609; ἡ θεῶν λ. *handmaid* of the gods, Id.*HF*823; τὴν Ἀπόλλωνος λ., of Cassandra, Id.*Tr.*450 (troch.), cf. Phld.*Piet.*91: metaph., μίτου πολυδινέα λ., of the spindle, *AP*6.39 (Arch.); Φοίβου λ., of the raven, ib.9.272 (Bianor). ⊛ **-ον,** τό, *pay, hire* (λ.· ὁ μισθός, Suid., *EM*557.35), λάτρων ἄτερθεν without *charge* or *payment,* A. *Supp.*1011. **-ώδης,** ες, *servile,* Vett.Val.5.26, Heph.Astr.1.1.

**λάττα·** μυῖα (Polyrrhen.), Hsch. **λα(τ)ταία·** παραξιφίς, καὶ ἡ περὶ ζώνην μάχαιρα, Id.

**λᾰτύπ-έω,** *build of stone,* Lyc.523. ⊛ **-η,** ἡ, *the chips of stone in hewing, IG*2².244.82 (iv B.C.), *Rev.Phil.*50.67 (ii B.C.), Str.17.1.34. II. *gypsum, lime,* Plu.2.954a, Poll.9.104 (cf. Sch.Pl.*Tht.*146a), Paul.Aeg. 4.14, Sch.Ar.*Nu.*260. **-ικός,** ή, όν, *of* or *for hewing,* σμίλη Hsch. s.v. εὐσμίλωτα (-ηλ- cod.); ἡ λ. τέχνη Porph.*Hist.Phil.*11. **-ος** (parox.), ὁ, *stone-cutter, mason,* Hp.*Fract.*31, S.*Fr.*530, Gal.*Thras.* 43, *CIG*(add.)3827*v*, al. (Cotiaeum); cf. λαοτύπος.

**λᾰτύσσω,** *clap, strike,* in Med., πέρδικες.. λατυσσόμενοι πτερύγεσσι Opp.*C.*2.430:—Pass., Id.*H.*1.628.

**Λατώ,** Dor. for Λητώ.

**λαυκᾰνίη,** ἡ, *throat,* φαίνετο δ' ᾗ κληῗδες ἀπ' ὤμων αὐχέν' ἔχουσι, λαυκανίην Il.22.325 (cf. 24.642: λευκανίη is v.l. ibid. (cf. Ruf.*Onom.* 48, 68) and prevails in later Ep., as Orph.*L.*554 (pl.); λευκανίηθεν Opp.*H.*1.755; -ηνδε A.R.2.192).

**λαυκελαρχέω,** *hold a priestly office, IG*14.716, al. (Naples).

⊛ **λαύκη·** φοβερά, Hsch. (Cf. λυκεῖον.) **λαύξει·** κρατεῖ, δαίνυται, εὐφραίνει, Id. **λαυξία·** δαρήσ.. (Cret.), Id. **λαῦξις,** = λῆξις (A), Id.

⊛ **λαύρα,** Ep. and Ion. **-ρη,** ἡ, *alley, lane, passage,* Od.22.128, 137, Pi. *P.*8.86, Hdt.1.180, Hermesian.7.65, Herod.1.13, *POxy.*1449.6 (iii A.D.), etc.; ἡ τῶν Σαμίων λ. an *alley* or *bazaar* at Samos, where women sold delicacies of all kinds, Clearch.22; εὐδαιμόνων λ., at Alexandria, Ath.12.541a; *avenue,* Theoc.*Ep.*4.1; *path,* Plu.*Crass.*4. 2. = ἄμφοδον II, *POxy.*242 (i A.D.). II. *sewer, privy,* Hippon. in *PSI*9. 1089.10: pl., Ar.*Pax* 99, 158 (both anap.), J.*AJ*15.9.6.

**Λαύρειον,** τό, promontory in the south of Attica, famous for its silver-mines, Hdt.7.144, Th.2.55, *EM*533.34, etc.; **Λαύρεον,** *IG*2². 1582.67, al.; later **Λαύριον,** Paus.1.1.1:—Adj. **Λαυρ-εωτικός** or **-ειωτικός,** ή, όν, *of Mt. Laurium,* Ar.*Av.*1106, Plu.*Nic.*4.

**λαῦρος,** freq. f.l. for λάβρος.

**λαυροστάται** [ᾰ], οἱ, (λαύρα, στῆναι) *the choreutae who stood in the middle,* generally the bad ones, Cratin.422.

**λαῦσαι·** περιπτεῦσαι τοῖς δεσπόταις, Hsch. **λαυστήρ·** μοχθηρός, ὅμοιον δὲ τῇ δυνάμει τὸ ὄνομα, ἢ οἴκου λαύρα, Id. **λαύστρανον·** τινὲς λύκον, τινὲς φρέατος ἅρπαγα, Id. **λαυφθάζει·** σπεύδει, Id. **λαυφθάσσει·** λάβρως ἐσθίει, Id. **λαυχάνη·** γλῶσσα, Id. **λάφατον,** = λάπαθον, *Gloss.* **λαφθία·** ἡ ἀσπίς, ὅπλον, Hsch. **λάφνη·** δάφνη (Pergaean), Id. **λαφνίσκος,** = *britia* (dub. sens.), *Gloss.* (περὶ θρεμμάτων). **λαφός·** ὁ ἀριστερᾷ χειρὶ χρώμενος, Hsch.

⊛ **Λαφρία,** ἡ, epith. of Artemis, Paus.4.31.7, etc., cf. Str.10.2.21, Ant.Lib.40.2; of Athena, Lyc.356, etc.:—so ⊛**Λάφριος,** of Hermes, Id.835.

**Λάφρια,** τά, festival at Delphi, *GDI*2561 *D* 8; at Hyampolis, *IG* 9(1).90:—also **Λαφρίεια,** τά, *Supp.Epigr.*2.258.35 (Delph., iii B.C.).

**Λαφρ-ιάδαι·** φρατρία ἐν Δελφοῖς, Hsch. ⊛ **-ιαῖος,** ὁ, month in Aetolia, *GDI*1908. ⊛ **-ιος,** ὁ, month in Phocis, ib.1719, al.; at Gytheion, *IG*5(1).1145.28, etc.

**λάφ-υγμα** [λᾰ], ατος, τό, (λαφύσσω) *greedy attack,* λαφύγματα νούσων *IG*14.1363.13 (Rome). **-υγμός,** ὁ, *gluttony,* Ar.*Nu.*52, Eup.148; personified, *AP*6.305 (Leon.). **-ύειν·** τὸ εἰς αὐτὸν ἀσχημονεῖν, Hsch. ⊛ **-ύκτης,** ου, ὁ, *gourmand,* Arist.*EE*1232ᵃ 16. **-υξις,** εως, ἡ, = λαφυγμός, Ath.8.362f.

**λάφῡρα** [λᾰ], τά, Arg. **φάλυρα** *SIG*56.9 (v B.C.):—*spoils* taken in war, A.*Th.*278, 479, E.*HF*417 (lyr.), S.*Aj.*93; ἀρετᾶς λ. Id.*Tr.*646 (lyr.), cf. X.*HG*5.1.24, Aen.Tact.16.8, *Marm.Par.*53, Lxx *Ju.*15.7:—also in sg. **λάφυρον,** Hellanic.143 J., Plb.2.62.12, *IG*12(7).386.23 (Amorgos), Plu.2.330d, Ach.Tat.4.13, al.; τὸ λ. ἐπικηρύττειν κατά τινων give public authority for plundering a people, Plb.4.26.7; cf. ῥύσιον, σύλη.

**λᾰφῡρᾰγωγ-έω,** *carry off as booty,* Str.6.3.1, J.*AJ*13.14.3, Plu. *Galb.*5 (in fut. Med.), etc.: metaph., πόλεμος οὐ λ. ἀρετήν Id.2.5f:—Pass., Sch.E.*Med.*256. II. *plunder,* πόλιν Apollod.2.7.7: abs., Ph.1.152. **-ητικός,** ή, όν, gloss on ἀγελείη, Sch Lips.Il.4.128 Bekker. **-ία,** ἡ, *carrying off booty,* Heph.Astr.3.7, Sch.E.*Or.* 1434, Procl.*in Alc.*p.214C. **-ός,** όν, *carrying off booty,* Sch.D Il. 4.128, Sch.ib.10.460, prob. l. for φυγαγ- in Polyaen.8.16.6.

**λᾰφῡρ-εύω,** *plunder,* Lxx *Ju.*15.11; **-έω,** Aq.*Is.*59.15.

**λᾰφῡροπωλ-εῖον,** v. λαφυροπώλιον. **-έω,** *sell booty,* abs., X.*An.* 6.6.38: c. acc., λείαν Plb.5.24.10, etc.; λ. αἰχμαλώτους *sell* them *as booty,* D.S.17.14. **-ης,** ου, ὁ, *seller of booty, one who has bought up booty to retail,* X.*An.*7.7.56, Dionys.Com.3.16 (s.v.l.). II. in pl., at Sparta, *officers* attached to the king's staff, *who took charge of the booty,* X.*Lac.*13.11, *HG*4.1.26. **-ιον,** τό, *sale of booty, IG*5(2).6.11 (Tegea, iv B.C.). 2. *place where booty is sold,* Str.14.3.2, D.H.9. 56:—written **-εῖον** in Plb.4.6.3.

**λᾰφύσσω,** Att. **-ττω,** fut. λαφύξω Ael.*Fr.*156: aor. ἐλάφυξα Orph. *L.*120, etc.:—**Med.** (v. infr.), aor. inf. λαφύξασθαι Lyc.321:—*swallow greedily, gulp down,* of the lion, αἷμα καὶ ἔγκατα πάντα λαφύσσει Il.11. 176; of dogs, Luc.*Asin.*27; of wild beasts, eagles, etc., Q.S.10.316, etc.; also, of bears, *tear open,* ὄνυξι τὴν γαστέρα Ael.*NA*4.45: metaph., of fire, *consume, AP*5.238 (Paul. Sil.); of disease, Aret.*CA*2.3:—Med., of men, *eat gluttonously, gorge,* λαφύσσεται λαφυγμόν Eup. 148, cf. Lyc. l.c.—Poet. Verb used in late Prose, as Ph.1.550 (abs.).

**λᾰφύστιος,** α, ον, (λαφύσσω) *gluttonous, APl.*1.15*, Lyc.215. II. Pass., *devoured,* Id.791. III. title of Zeus among the Minyae, Hdt.7.197; of Dionysus in Boeotia, *EM*557.51; of devotees of Dionysus, γυναῖκες Lyc.1237.

**λάφωνοι·** λίαν ἄφωνοι, Hsch.

**λᾰχαίνω,** (from λαχάν-yω, cf. λάχανον) *dig,* μεγάλην ἐλάχαινε.. τάφρον Mosch.4.96, cf. Opp.*H.*3.121; κρῆναι ἃς ἐλάχηνεν A.R.3.222; λαχαινέμεν ἔργα σιδήρου *dig* iron mines, Call.*Fr.*305; σκαπανῇ λ. αἶαν Orph.*Fr.*280 (prob.).

⊛ **λᾰχᾰν-άριον,** τό, = *holerarium, Gloss.* ⊛ **-ᾶς,** ᾶ, ὁ, *greengrocer,* Hdn.Gr.2.657. **-εία,** ἡ, *culture of pot-herbs,* κῆπος -είας a garden *of herbs,* Lxx *De.*11.10, cf. *PCair.Zen.*269.22 (iii B.C.), *PPetr.*3p.236 (iii B.C.), *PTeb.*60.39 (ii B.C.), al., Sch.Od.7.127 (pl.), Ptol.*Tetr.* 81. II. = λαχανισμός, J.*BJ*4.9.8. **-ευμα,** ατος, τό, = foreg. I, Procl.*Par.Ptol.*118 (pl.). **-εύς,** έως, ὁ, = λαχανοπώλης, Id.*Proll.ad Hes.*p.5 G. ⊛ **-ευτής,** οῦ, ὁ, = foreg., *POxy.*43ᵛ iii 12 (iii A.D.), 1139.2 (iv A.D.). ⊛ **-εύω,** *plant vegetables, PSI*4.403.13 (iii B.C.):—Pass., *to be planted with vegetables* or *produce them,* Str.5.4.3, App.*Pun.*117, *PStrassb.*122.5 (ii A.D.); τὰ -όμενα *vegetables,* Sor.1.87. 2. Pass., *to be used as pot-herbs,* λαχανεύεται ἑφθόν Dsc.2.119. II. Med., *gather herbs,* Luc.*Lex.*2. **-ηλόγος,** ον, *gathering vegetables, AP* 9.318 (Leon.). **-ηρός,** ά, όν, *of vegetable kind,* τὸ λ. Thphr.*HP*7. 1.1: pl., τὰ λ. *vegetables, pot-herbs,* ib.1.11.3, 6.1.2, *CP*6.9.3. **-ηφόρος,** ον, *bearing,* i.e. *sowing, vegetables,* Man.4.258. ⊛ **-ιά,** ἡ, *garden-bed, PCair.Zen.*329.16 (pl., iii B.C.), Hsch. s.v. πρασιαί. **-ίδιον,** τό, Dim. of λάχανον, Id. s.v. κιχόρια. **-ίζω,** *to be at grass,* of horses, *Hippiatr.*130:—Med., *gather vegetables, EM*558.14. II. Lat. *lachanizare,* = *betizare,* i.e. *languere,* Suet.*Aug.*87. III. Pass., *become green,* Gal.17(1).343. ⊛ **-ικός,** ή, όν, = λαχανηρός, *Inscr. Magn.*116.42 (ii A.D.). II. λαχανικόν (sc. τέλος), τό, *tax on market-gardeners,* dub. in *Ostr.*787 (i A.D.), *Sammelb.*2085. **-ιον,** τό, Dim. of λάχανον, D.L.2.139, Sch.Ar.*Oxy.*856 i (*b*)37, *PHamb.*23. 26 (vi A.D.). **-ιος,** α, ον, = λαχανηρός, γῆ λ. *garden*-ground, Jul. *Caes.*329d; τὸ τέλος τῆς λαχανίας (sc. γῆς; fort. -ιᾶς) tax on *market-gardens, Ostr.*787 (i A.D.). **-ισμός,** ὁ, *cutting* or *gathering of vegetables,* ἐπὶ -ισμὸν ἐξελθεῖν Th.3.111, cf. *PTeb.*117.73 (i B.C.). II. *being at grass,* of horses, *Hippiatr.*129.

**λᾰχᾰνο-ειδής,** ές, *of the colour of vegetables,* Tz.ap.Sch.Nic.*Al.* 570. **-θήκη,** ἡ, *dish* or *pot for vegetables,* Alex.Magn ap Ath.11. 784b (s.v.l.). **-κοπικός,** ή, όν, *for pounding vegetables,* λίθοι *POxy.*1913.65 (vi A.D.).

⊛ **λάχᾰνον** [λᾰ], τό, mostly in pl., *garden-herbs,* opp. wild plants, *vegetables,* Cratin.313, Epicr.11.15, al., Pl.*R.*372c, Thphr.*HP*1.3.1, etc.; but also λ. ἄγρια Ar.*Th.*456, *Pl.*298: sg. is rarer, οὐδὲ λ. οὐδὲν.. δρῶ not *a single herb,* Cratin.191; ὥστε μηδὲ λ. γενέσθαι ἐν τῷ κήπῳ D.50.61; ἐν τῷ λ. τούτῳ, i.e. the lettuce, Eub.14, cf. 54, Epicr.11. 25. 2. in pl. also, *the vegetable-market,* Ar.*Lys.*557, Alex.46.8, Diph.32.22.

**λᾰχᾰνο-πράτης** [πρᾱ], ου, ὁ, *greengrocer, PAmh.*2.148.2 (v A.D.), *PLond.*1.113.6(*a*)7 (vi A.D.). **-προβάλλω,** *expose vegetables for sale, PMasp.*164.7 (vi A.D.). **-πτερος,** ὁ, *vegetable-winged,* Luc. *VH*1.13.

**λᾰχᾰνοπωλ-εῖον,** τό, *greengrocer's shop, POxy.*1461.22 (iii A.D.), nisi leg. **-ιον.** **-ης,** ου, ὁ, *greengrocer,* Critias 70 D., Arr.*Epict.*3. 3.3, al., *PFay.*23.13 (ii A.D.), *BGU*337.22 (ii/iii A.D.):—fem. **-ήτρια,** ἡ, Ar.*Th.*387. **-ικός,** ή, όν, *belonging to a greengrocer,* ἐργαστήριον

*POxy*.1461.6 (iii A.D.). **-ιον**, τό, *vegetable-market*, Sch.Ar.*Lys.* 556, Suid. ⊛**-ις**, ιδος, ἡ, = -ήτρια, Ar.*V*.497, Alexand.Com.7.

**λαχανό-σπερμον**, τό, *vegetable seed*, *PFay*.89 (i A.D.), *BGU*454.13 (ii A.D.), etc. **-φᾰγία**, Ion. -ίη, ἡ, *vegetable diet*, Hp.*Int*.34, *Epid.* 7.82. **-φόρος**, = -ηφόρος, Sch.Od.7.127.

**λᾰχᾰν-ώδης**, ες, = λαχανηρός, Thphr.*HP*1.3.4, 7.1.1, Muson.*Fr.* 18$^{A}$ p.95 H., Dsc.2.126, Gal.6.644; λαχανώδη *the vegetable kind*, Arist.*Pr*.20tit. **-ωνῠμία**, ἡ, *naming after* λάχανα, Tz.*H*.4.558.

**λάχε, λαχεῖν**, v. λαγχάνω.

**λάχεια** [λᾰ], ἡ, obscure word read (prob.) by Aristarch. in two passages of Od., νῆσος ἔπειτα λάχεια..τετάνυσται 9.116; ἔνθ' ἀκτή τε λάχεια καὶ ἄλσεα Περσεφονείης 10.509; expld. by εὔσκαφος καὶ εὔγειος, παρὰ τὸ λαχαίνεσθαι, ὅ ἐστι σκάπτεσθαι πυκνῶς, Hsch., cf. Apollon.*Lex.*, Eust.1619.30, 1667.13, Sch.; cf. λάχανον, λαχύφλοιος: Zenod. read ἐλάχεια, cf. *h.Ap.*197.

⊛**λᾰχειδής**, ές, epith. of the toad in Nic.*Al*.568 (perh. from same root as foreg.; but prob. corrupt).

**Λάχεσις** [ᾰ], εως, Ion. ιος, ἡ, (λαχεῖν) *Lachesis*, one of the three Fates, *Disposer of lots*, Hes.*Th*.218, *Sc*.258, Pi.*O*.7.64, etc.; as the goddess of *distribution*, Plu.2.644a, cf. Arist.*Mu*.401$^{b}$20. **II.** as Appellat., *lot*, *destiny*, Bacis ap.Hdt.9.43: pl., Μοιρῶν Λαχέσεων *IG* 5(1).602.8 (Sparta, iii A.D.).

⊛**λάχ-η** [ᾰ], ἡ, = λῆξις, ἀποκλήρωσις, Hsch.; τάφων πατρῴων λάχαι (λαχαί codd.) *a share* in their fathers' tombs, A.*Th*.914 (lyr.). **-ησις**, εως, ἡ, = λάχεσις II, Sch.Lyc.1141. **-ισμός**, ὁ, *casting of lots*, *Gloss.*

**λαχμητήριον**, τό, (λαχεῖν) = λάχος, λαχμός (A), Eust.674.24.

**λαχμός** (A), ὁ, = λάχος, Sch.Theoc.8.30, Eust.1521.48.

**λαχμός** (B), ὁ, = λακτισμός, Antim.54.

**λαχμός** (C), ὁ, v.l. for λάχνος (A) in Od.9.445, cf. Eust.1638.39, Hsch.

**λαχν-αῖος**, α, ον, = λαχνήεις, *AP*9.439 (Crin.). ⊛**-η**, ἡ, *soft woolly hair*, *down*, as of the first beard, πρίν σφωϊν..πυκάσαι γένυς εὐανθέϊ λάχνῃ Od.11.320; ὅτε λάχναι νιν μέλαν γένειον ἔρεφον Pi.*O*.1.68; of the *thin hair* on Thersites' head, ψεδνὴ δ' ἐπενήνοθε λ. Il.2.219; of the *soft nap* or *pile* on cloth, οὔλη δ' ἐπενήνοθε λ. 10.134; of the *scanty hairs* on the elephant, Luc.*Philops*.24; of the *hair* or *fur* of wild beasts, λάχνῃ δέρμα κατάσκιον Hes.*Op*.513; of the bear's or polecat's *fur*, Opp.*C*.3.140, Nic.*Th*.690; of sheep's *wool*, S.*Tr*.690, Opp.*C*.2.379; of ox's *hair*, A.R.1.325: in pl., of the hedgehog's *quills*, Plu.2.98d, Opp.*H*.2.369. **II.** metaph., *leafage*, Nic.*Al*.410, Opp.*H*.4.167,380 (pl.). **-ήεις**, Dor. **-άεις**, εσσα, εν, contr. **-ῆς** Hdn.Gr.2.618:—*woolly*, *hairy*, *shaggy*, Φῆρες Il.2.743; στήθεα 18.415; στέρνα Pi.*P*.1.19; συὸς δέρμα Il.9.548; λ. ὄροφος *downy*, *soft* thatch, 24.451.

**λαχνό-γυιος**, ον, *with shaggy limbs*, θῆρες E.*Hel*.378 (lyr.). **-ομαι**, Pass., *grow hairy* or *downy*, of a youth's chin, Sol.27.6, *AP*12.178 (Strat.).

**λάχνος** (A), ὁ, = λάχνη, *wool*, Od.9.445; v.l. λαχμός (C).

**λάχνος** (B), ὁ, *glutton*, *Gloss.*; cf. λάγνος, λίχνος.

**λαχν-ώδης**, ες, = λαχνήεις, λαχνῶδες οὖδας χλόης the ground *downy with* grass, E.*Cyc*.541; gloss on v.l. ἔγχνοα in Nic.*Th*.762. **-ωσις**, εως, ἡ, *covering with hair*, Hp.*Hebd*.5.21 R.

⊛**λάχος** [ᾰ], εος, τό, (λᾰχεῖν) *allotted portion*: **I.** *lot*, *destiny*, Thgn.592, S.*Ant*.1303 (so Bothe for λέχος). **2.** *appointed office*, A.*Ch*.361 (lyr.), *Eu*.334 (lyr.): pl., ib.310 (anap.), 347, 386 (both lyr.). **II.** *portion obtained by lot*, *share*, Pi.*O*.7.58, *N*.10.85, A.*Eu*.400, X.*An*.5.3.9; ἐν τῷ τρίτῳ λ., = τὸ τρίτον or τρίτως, A.*Eu*.5; νυκτὸς τρίτατον λ. Mosch.2.2, cf. A.R.1.1082; ἤματος Id.3.1340.—Poet. word, used by X., and found in dialects, τῶν χρημάτων τὸ λ. *IG*5(2).262.20 (Mantinea, v B.C.), cf. *Schwyzer*289.88 (Rhodian, ii B.C.).

**λᾰχύφλοιος**, ον, κάρυον Nic.*Al*.269, expld. by Sch. ἐλάχιστον φλοιὸν ἔχοντος, as if it were ἐλαχύφλοιος, cf. λάχεια (vv.ll. δασύ-, ταχύ-, τασύ-φλοιος).

**λάψ**, Adv. (Tarent.), sine expl., Hdn.Gr.1.404, al. **λάψα**· γογγυλίς (Pergaean), Hsch.

**λαψάνη** (so *PPetr*.3p.152 (iii B.C.)) or **λαμψάνη**, ἡ, the herb *charlock*, *Brassica arvensis*, Dsc.2.116, Gal.7.285.

**λαψάρων**· τῇ χειρὶ ποτίζων, ἢ ἁπτόμενος, Hsch.

**λάψις**, εως, ἡ, (λάπτω) *lapping*, opp. σπάσις and κάψις, Arist.*HA* 595$^{a}$10.

**λάψομαι**, Ion. fut. of λαμβάνω (q.v.).

**λάω** (A) [ᾰ], = βλέπω, οὐδέ κεν αὐτὸν αἰετὸς ὀξὺ λάων ἐσκέψατο *h.Merc.* 360; γηθήσειε λάων is probably v.l. for γ. ἰδών in Il.13.344 (*POxy.* 769); cf. λάετε· σκοπεῖτε, βλέπετε, Hsch., Cyr.

**λάω** (B) [ᾰ], *seize*, *hold*, κύων ἔχε ποικίλον ἐλλόν, ἀσπαίροντα λάων *gripping* it as it struggled, Od.19.229; ὁ μὲν λάε νεβρὸν ἀπάγχων *gripped* the fawn as he was throttling it, ib.230.—Also expld. by ἀπολαυστικῶς ἔχων (Aristarch.) or ἀπολαυστικῶς ἐσθίων (Sch., Hsch. s.v. λάων, who refers it alternatively to λάω (A), but also has λάε· ἐψόφησεν, οἱ δὲ ἐφθέγγετο; cf. λαήμεναι· φθέγγεσθαι, Cyr.).

***λάω** (C), v. λῶ.

**λᾱώδης**, ες, (λαός) *popular*, Ph.1.80, Plu.*Crass*.3.

**λέα**, ἡ, v. λαιαί.

**λεάδα**· ἡ ἐξοχὴ τῶν πετρῶν, Hsch.; cf. λεδδά.

**λεάζω**, *to be smooth*, opp. τρίχας ἔχειν, Arist.*PA*658$^{a}$21.

**λέαινα**, ἡ, fem. of λέων, *lioness*, Hdt.3.108: metaph., δίπους λ., of Clytaemnestra, A.*Ag*.1258; λεαίνας μαζὸν ἐθήλαζεν, as a symbol of ferocity, Theoc.3.15, cf. 23.19. **II.** λ. ἐπὶ τυροκνήστιδος, = σχῆμά τι συνουσίας, Ar.*Lys*.231. **III.** pl., *women dedicated to Mithras*, Porph.*Abst*.4.16 (cf. λέων VI); title of Hecate, ibid. **IV.** name of several salves, Orib.*Fr*.75, Aët.7.86, Paul.Aeg.7.17.

⊛**λεαίνω**, also **λειαίνω**, Sol.4.35, Nic.*Th*.95, *Gp*.4.12.13: fut. λεᾰνῶ Arist.*PA*674$^{b}$21; Ep. λειᾰνέω Il.15.261: aor. 1 ἐλέηνα Hdt.1.200, Nic.*Fr*.70.15, -ᾱνα Arist.*GA*788$^{b}$31, ἐλείανα *IG*1$^{2}$.372*E*11,373.174; Ep. ἐλείηνα, λείηνα, Il.4.111, Od.8.260:—**Med.**, Muson.*Fr*.18$^{B}$ p.101 H.: Ep. aor. λειηνάμην Nic.*Th*.646:—**Pass.**, Pl.*Plt*.270e: aor. ἐλεάνθην Dsc.3.158, S.E.*P*.1.130; Ion. subj. λειανθέωσι Hp.*Mul*.2.168; part. λειανθείς *Gp*.11.13.2, Philotim.ap.Orib.4.10.1: pf. inf. λελειάνθαι Thphr.*Fr*.30.2, Ph.2.510; part. λελεασμένος Democr.ap.Gal.13.989, Dsc.5.75, Dieuch.ap.Orib.4.6.2, Porph.*Abst*.4.7, λελειασμένος Ph.1.302:—*smooth*, *polish*, of a worker in horn or stone, πᾶν δ' εὖ λειήνας Il.4.111, cf. *IG* ll. cc.; ἵπποισι κέλευθον πᾶσαν λειανέω I will *smooth* the way, Il.15.261; λείηναν δὲ χορόν Od.8.260, λ. τὰ τραχυνθέντα Pl.*Ti*.66c; λ. τὰ κηρία, of bees, Arist.*HA*625$^{b}$19:—Pass., λεαινόμενοι τὰ σώματα Theopomp.Hist.195. **2.** *triturate*, *pound in a mortar*, Hdt. l.c.; *grind down* (of the teeth), X.*Mem*.1.4.6, Arist.*Ph*.198$^{b}$26, *HA*501$^{b}$31, Nic.*Th*.95, Ph.1.63:—Med., *grind small*, Nic.*Th*.646:—Pass., Philotim.ap.Orib. l.c. **b.** generally, *crush*, *extirpate*, τὰ φυόμενα Hdt.4.122. **3.** *smooth away*, τὰς τῶν σκυτῶν ῥυτίδας Pl.*Smp*.191a, cf. *Plt*. l.c. (Pass.): metaph., *smooth* or *soften down*, τὸν Μαρδονίου λόγον Hdt.8.142; τὸ ἐπίχολον λ. τῷ ὕπνῳ Philostr.*Im*.2.11: *polish* style, D.H.*Comp*.16: metaph., also, λ. τὴν κατάποσιν *tickle* the palate, Muson. l.c.; τὴν ἀκοήν D.H.*Comp*.12: abs., [ὁ χυλὸς] λεαίνει *lubricates*, *soothes*, Thphr.*CP*6.2.1. **II.** intr., *to be smooth*, Arist.*Pr*.936$^{a}$15.

**λέαν-σις** or **λείανσις**, εως, ἡ, *grinding down*, Antyll.ap.Orib.10.23.17; τροφῆς Anon.Lond.*Fr*.2.1, cf. Gal.14.714. **-τειρα**, ἡ, fem. of λεαντήρ, κίσηρις *AP*6.295 (Phan.). **-τέον**, *one must grind down*, Dsc.5.88. **-τήρ**, ῆρος, ὁ, *grinder*, i.e. *pestle*, Antyll.ap.Orib.10.23.14. **-τήριον**, τό, *polisher*, *PLeid.X*.56. **-τικός**, ή, όν, *good for lubricating* or *soothing*, of sweet wine, Arist.*Pr*.872$^{b}$34; χυμὸς λ. Thphr.*CP*6.1.3; *laxative*, cj. in Aristox.*Fr.Hist*.ap.Gell.4.11: c. gen., λ. ἀρτηρίας Diph.Siph.ap.Ath.2.57c. Adv. **-κῶς** Eust.118.9.

**λεβηρίς**, ίδος, ἡ, *skin* or *slough* of serpents, Hp.*Mul*.1.78, 2.191, J.*AJ*3.7.2; of beans, *shell*, Hsch.: prov., κενότερος λεβηρίδος Stratt.10D.; so τυφλότερος λ. Ar.*Fr*.35; λεπτότερον τὸ δέρμα λεβηρίδος Alciphr.3.19. **II.** *rabbit* (cf. λέπορις) Str.3.2.6; Massiliote word acc. to Polemarch.ap.Erot. **III.** a bird of ill-omen, Phot.

⊛**λέβης**, ητος, ὁ, *kettle*, *cauldron*, Il.21.362, Pi.*O*.1.26; τρίπους λ. A.*Fr*.1; used for gifts and prizes, Il.23.259, al.; *brazier*, Th.4.100. **b.** *coin stamped with a cauldron*, *GDI*4979, al. (Crete). **II.** in Od., mostly the *basin* in which the purifying water (χέρνιψ) was handed to the guests before meals, made of silver, 1.137, al.; but in 19.386, a *pan* for washing the feet; δολοφόνος λ., of the *bath* in which Agamemnon was slain, A.*Ag*.1129 (lyr.). **III.** basin used as a *cymbal* or *drum*, Hdt.6.58; of the *gong* at Dodona, Call.*Del*.286. **IV.** *cinerary urn*, A.*Ag*.444 (lyr.), *Ch*.686, S.*El*.1401. **V.** generally, *casket*, Id.*Tr*.556: *pan* for colours, Luc.*Bis Acc*.8. **VI.** *vase* of cauldron shape on the roof of the temple of Zeus at Olympia, Paus.5.10.4. **VII.** *air-vessel* used like a diving-bell, Arist.*Pr*.960$^{b}$32.

**λεβητ-άριον**, τό, Dim. of foreg., Poll.10.66,95, etc. **-ίζω**, *put into* or *boil in a cauldron*, σάρκας Lyc.199. **-ιον**, τό, Dim. of λέβης, *IG*2$^{2}$.1541.16 (iv B.C.), 11(2).161*C*88 (Delos, iii B.C.), Anaxipp.6.5, Men.1027, cf. Poll.6.92, 10.76; *small brazier*, Antyll.ap.Orib.8.12.3.

**λεβητο-ειδής**, ές, *like a kettle* or *basin*, ἀγγεῖον Eust.1298.36, etc. **-χάρων** [ᾰ], ωνος, ὁ, *pot-friend*, Cerc.11.

**λεβητώδης**, ες, = λεβητοειδής, Ath.11.468e.

**λεβίας**, ου, ὁ, a kind of *fish*, Ar.*Fr*.414 (λέβιοι codd. Ath.), Ephipp.12.4, Diph.17.9, etc.

**λεβίνθιοι**· ἐρέβινθοι, Hsch.

**Λεβύα** [ῠ], ἡ, = Λιβύη, *Berl.Sitzb*.1927.156 (Cyrene):—hence **Λεβῠᾱφῐγενής**, ές, *sprung from Libya*, Ibyc.57.

⊛**λεγεών**, ῶνος, ἡ, = Lat. *legio*, *Ev.Matt*.26.53, *Ev.Marc*.5.9, Plu.*Rom*.13,20, *IGRom*.3.670, al.:—freq. written **λεγιών**, ib.214.3, al.:—hence **λεγιονάριος**, ὁ, ib.913.3, al.

**λεγιώνη**, ἡ, = λεγεών, *SIG*830 (Delphi, ii A.D.).

**λέγμα**· τὸ εἰπεῖν, Hsch.

**λέγνη**, ἡ, = sq., Sch.Call.*Dian*.12, Hsch.

**λέγνον**, τό, *coloured edging* or *border* of a garment parallel to the ὤα or selvage, Poll.7.62, Hsch. **2.** τὰ λέγνα τῆς ὑστέρης *border* of the womb, Hp.*Mul*.2.144.

**λέγνος**· ἄνανδρος, σῖτος ὁ μὴ ἁδρός, Hsch.

**λεγν-όω**, in aor. inf. λεγνῶσαι· ποικῖλαι, Hsch. **-ώδης**, ες, = sq., Id., Phot. **-ωτός**, ή, όν, *with a coloured border*, χιτών Call.*Dian*.12; λ. ῥάβδοι Nic.*Th*.726.

**λέγξ**· ποιὸν ἦχον ἀπετέλεσεν, Hsch.

**λέγος**, η, ον, *lewd*, λέγαι γυναῖκες Archil.179.

***λέγω** (A), *lay*, pres. erroneously inferred from λέξομαι, ἔλεκτο, etc.; v. λέχομαι.

⊛**λέγω** (B), *pick up*, etc.: tenses for signf. I and II, fut. λέξω Od.24.224: aor. ἔλεξα A.*Pers*.292:—**Med.**, fut. in pass. sense λέξομαι E.*Alc*.322: aor. ἐλεξάμην Il.21.27 (trans.); Ep. ἐλέγμην Od.9.335; λέκτο 4.451:—**Pass.**, aor. ἐλέχθην Il.3.188: also post-Hom. in these senses, but only in compos., esp. with ἀπο-, ἐκ-, κατα-, συν-; post-Hom. pf. εἴλοχα (κατ-, συν-), Pass. εἴλεγμαι, in these senses rarely λέλεγμαι (v. the compds.); also fut. λεγήσομαι (συλ-): aor. 2 ἐλέγην (κατ-, συν-):—*gather*, *pick up*, ὀστέα..λέγωμεν Il.23.239, cf. Od.24.

72, Pi.*P.*8.53; αἱμασιάς τε λέγων *picking out stones for building* walls, Od.18.359 (ubi v. Sch., cf. λογάς 2), cf. 24.224:—Med., *gather for oneself*, ἐπὶ δὲ ξύλα πολλὰ λέγεσθε Il.8.507; ὀστέα λευκὰ λέγοντο 24.793; φάρμακα λέξασθαι A.R.3.807. 2. Med., *choose for oneself, pick out*, λέξαιτο.. ἄνδρας ἀρίστους Od.24.108; κούρους Il.21.27:—Pass., *to be chosen*, εἰ.. λεγοίμεθα πάντες ἄριστοι 13.276. II. *count, tell*, ἐν δ' ἡμέας λέγε κήτεσιν he *counted* us among the seals, Od.4.452; and in aor. Med., Il.2.125; ἐγὼ πέμπτος μετὰ τοῖσιν ἐλέγμην I *reckoned myself*.., Od.9.335; λέκτο δ' ἀριθμόν he *told him over* the number, 4.451:—Pass., μετὰ τοῖσιν ἐλέχθην I *was counted* among these, Il.3.188. b. so, but not freq., after Hom., λ. ποντιᾶν ψάφων ἀριθμόν Pi.*O.*13.46, cf. A.*Ag.*570; καθ' ἓν ἕκαστον λ. Isoc.2.45; also καὶ σὲ δ' ἐν τούτοις λέγω *count* you among.., A.*Pr.*973; λ. τινὰ οὐδαμοῦ *count* him as naught, S.*Ant.*183; κέρδος λ., εἰ.. *count* it gain, that.., ib.462:—Med., λέξατο πάντας [ναύτας] Pi.*P.*4.189:—Pass., λέγεσθαι ἐν τοῖς ἱππικωτάτοις X.*Oec.*11.20; ἐνὶ πρώτησι λέγεσθαι Call.*Del.*16: fut. Med. in pass. sense, ἐν τοῖς οὐκέτ' οὖσι λέξομαι E. l.c. 2. *recount, tell over*, οὔ τι διαπρήξαιμι λέγων ἐμὰ κήδεα Od.14.197; σὺ δέ μοι λέγε θέσκελα ἔργα 11.374; τὰ ἕκαστα λέγων 12.165; ὅσα τ' αὐτὸς.. ἐμόγησε, πάντ' ἔλεγ' 23.308: so in Trag., λ. τύχας, πάθη, μόχθους, etc., A.*Pr.*633, *Pers.*292, *Ag.*555, etc.; also Ἀγαμέμνονι.. λέγ' ὀνείδεα *repeated* reproaches against him, Il.2.222; so perh. ψεύδεα πολλὰ λ. Hes.*Th.*27 (but v. infr. III):—Med., τί σε χρὴ ταῦτα λέγεσθαι; why need'st thou *tell the tale* thereof? Il.13.275; and so, μηκέτι ταῦτα λεγώμεθα νηπύτιοι ὥς ib.292, cf. Od.3.240, 13.296; μηκέτι νῦν δήθ' αὖθι λεγώμεθα Il.2.435. III. *say, speak*, first in Hes.*Th.*27 (v. supr. II. 2): fut. λέξω Emp.38.1, A.*Ag.*859, Hdt.4.14, Th.2.48, Antipho 6.33, etc.: aor. ἔλεξα Anacr.45, Pl.*Sph.*217e, Antipho 1.15 (rare in Pl. and the Orators, common in some dialects, as Boeotian, *IG*7.504.2 (Tanagra), Thessalian, ib.9(2).461.21, Ionic, v.l. in Hp.*Aër.*12): pf. λέλεχα Gal.16.249, λέλεγα and λέλογας Hsch. (εἴρηκα in correct writers):—Pass., fut. λεχθήσομαι Th.5.86, Pl.*Ti.*67c, etc.: also fut. Med. in pass. sense, S.*OC*1186, E.*Hec.*906 (lyr.), etc.; and λελέξομαι Th.3.53 (v.l. λέξεται), Pl.*R.*457b: aor. ἐλέχθην (never ἐλέγην in this sense) S.*OT*1442, Th.6.32, etc.: pf. λέλεγμαι Pi.*N.*8.20, Hdt.2.21, S.*Ph.*389, etc. (εἴλεγμαι in this sense only in compd. δι-): rare in compds. (only ἀντιλέγω, ἐπιλέγω, καταλέγω, προλέγω), the pres. in most compds. being supplied by ἀγορεύω, the fut. by ἐρῶ, the aor. by εἶπον, the pf. by εἴρηκα: 1. *say, speak*, never in Hom., first in Hes. l.c., freq. from Hdt. and Trag. downwds.; of all kinds of *oral* communications, ἐκέλευε λέγειν εἴ τι θέλοι Hdt.8.58; so λέγοις ἄν *speak, say on*, Pl.*Plt.*268e, etc.; λ. μῦθον A.*Pers.*698 (troch.); ψευδῆ λ. Id.*Ag.*625; ἀληθῆ λ. Pl.*Phlb.*12b (so in Pass., λόγος λέλεκται πᾶς S.*Ph.*389); of oracles, *say, declare*, Hdt.8.136; ὥσπερ τοὔνομα λέγει *indicates*, Pl.*Prt.*312c: with Preps., λ. ἀμφί τινος A.*Th.*1017, E.*Hec.*580; περί τινος Xenoph.34.2, Democr.165, S.*Aj.*151 (anap.), Th.2.48; ὑπέρ τινος in his defence, S.*El.*555, X.*HG*1.7.16; κατά τινος against him, Thgn.1240a, X.*HG*1.5.2; λ. ἐπί τισι εὐχὰς ἀγαθάς *express* good wishes for them, A.*Supp.*625 (anap.); λ. τά τινος take his part, D.8.64; λ. πρός τι in reference or in answer to.., S.*Ant.*753, etc.; εἴς τι X.*Mem.*1.5.1. 2. c. acc. et inf., *say* that.., Pi.*P.*2.59, etc.: with neg. οὐ, Pl.*R.*348c, etc., but μή ib.346e, X.*Smp.*4.5 (Pass.), and usu. in later Gr., LXX *Ge.*38.22; λ. μὴ εἶναι ἀνάστασιν *Ev.Matt.*22.23: freq. also folld. by ὡς, ὅτι (generally so in the Act. voice) when the subject of the relative clause may become the object of the principal Verb, γυναῖκα λέγουσιν, ὡς κάθηται.. X.*Cyr.*7.3.5, etc.: rarely c. part., λ. Οἰδίπουν ὀλωλότα *speak of* him as dead, S.*OC*1580; λέγουσιν ἡμᾶς ὡς ὀλωλότας A.*Ag.*672; λέξασ' ἀδελφῷ σ' ἐνθάδ' ὄντα E.*Hel.*888:—Pass., λέξεται ἔχων Id.*IT*1047, cf. A.*Ag.*170 (cj.). 3. λέγειν τινά τι *say* something *of* another, esp. κακὰ λ. τινά *speak* ill *of* him, *revile* him, Hdt.8.61; ἀγαθὰ λ. τινάς Ar.*Ec.*435; τὰ ἔσχατα, τὰ ἀπόρρητα λ. ἀλλήλους, X.*Mem.*2.2.9, D.18.123; also εὖ or κακῶς λ. τινά, A.*Ag.*445 (lyr.), S.*El.*524, cf. 1028; εὖ λ. τὸν εὖ λέγοντα X.*Mem.*2.3.8. 4. *call by name*, ἃς τρέμομεν λ. S.*OC*128 (lyr.): c. dupl. acc., *call* so and so, λέγοιμ' ἂν ἄνδρα τόνδε τῶν σταθμῶν κύνα A.*Ag.*896, cf. S.*OC*939 codd., Hdt.1.32, etc. 5. λ. τινὰ ποιεῖν τι *tell, command* one to do, A.*Ch.*553, S.*Ph.*101, X.*Cyr.*4.1.22, etc.: so with τινι, S.*OC*840, D.19.150 (no obj. expressed in A.*Ag.*925, S.*OC*856); λέγε τὸν ἐρωτῶντα ἵνα.. εἴπῃ σοι.. Astramps.*Orac.*p.1 H.; ὡς ὁ νόμος λέγει D.22.20; ὁ λέγων μὴ μοιχεύειν *Ep.Rom.*2.22. 6. λ. τι *say something*, i.e. *speak to the point* or *purpose*, βούλῃ λέγειν τι, καὶ λέγων μηδὲν κλύειν; S.*Ant.*757; λέγω τι; *am I right?* the answer being λέγεις, Id.*OT*1475; κινδυνεύεις τι λέγειν Pl.*Cra.*404a; ἴσως ἄν τι λέγοις X.*Mem.*2.1.12, cf. *Cyr.*1.4.20; opp. οὐδὲν λέγει *has no meaning*, *no authority*, οὐδὲν λ. τὸ σωφρόνως τραφῆναι Ar.*Eq.*334, cf. *V.*75; οὐδὲν λέγεις *nonsense!* Id.*Th.*625; but οὐδὲν λέγειν, also, *say what is not, lie*, Id.*Av.*66, Pl.*Ap.*30b; also εὖ γε λέγεις, εὖ λέγεις, εὖ ἂν λέγοις, *good news!, that is well!*, ib.24e, *Grg.*447b, *Prt.*310b; καλῶς, ὀρθῶς λ., *you are right*, X.*Mem.*3.3.4, 3.6.8; κοὔπω λέγω *and what is more*, Herod.7.44; τί λέγεις; τὸν ἔποπα παῖ καλεῖς; Ar.*Av.*57, cf. *Ec.*298 (lyr.). 7. pleon., ἔφη λέγων Hdt.3.156, 5.36; ἔλεγε φάς Id.1.122; ἔφασκε λέγων Ar.*Av.*472; ἦ δ' ὃς λέγων Id.*V.*795; ὡς ἔφη λέγων S.*Aj.*757; καὶ λέγων εἶπεν οὕτω πως D.8.74, etc. 8. at the beginning of letters or documents, Ἄμασις Πολυκράτεϊ ὧδε λέγει.., Μαρδόνιος τάδε λέγει.., etc., Hdt.3.40, 8.140.α', etc.; τὰ γράμματα ἔλεγε τάδε Id.1.124, etc.; γράμμασι λέγον τάδε, of an inscription, Th.6.54: in Roman edicts, Μᾶρκος Μέττιος Ῥοῦφος.. λέγει *POxy.*237 viii 28 (i A.D.). 9. *wish to say, mean*, οὔτοι γυναῖκας ἀλλὰ Γοργόνας λέγω A.*Eu.*48; τί τοῦτο λέγει, πρὸ Πυλοιο; what *does* πρὸ Πυλοιο *mean?* Ar.*Eq.*1059, cf. 1021, 1375, *Ec.*989, Pl.*Phd.*60e: freq. in Platonic dialogue, πῶς λέγεις; how *do you mean?* in what *sense do you say this?* *Ap.*24e, al.; ἢ πῶς λέγομεν; or what *do we mean to say? Grg.*480b; πῶς δὴ οὖν αὐτὸ λέγεις; *Phdr.*265c; ποῖόν τί ποτε ἄρα λέγοντές φασι.. what they can possibly *mean* by saying.., *Tht.*181c, al.: c. dupl. acc., τοιοῦτόν τι σὲ λέγειν τὸ κρεῖττον *Grg.*489d, al.: freq. (esp. in Trag.) to explain more fully, εἴσω κομίζου καὶ σύ, Κασάνδραν λέγω you, *I mean* Cassandra, A.*Ag.*1035; ὁ μάντις, υἱὸν Οἰκλέους λ. Id.*Th.*609, cf. 658 (v.l.), *Pr.*946; ποταμός, Ἀχελῷον λέγω S.*Tr.*9, cf. 1220, *Ph.*1261, E.*Ph.*987; ἐμὲ λέγων *meaning* me, Isoc.12.215; τὸ δ' ὑμεῖς ὅταν λέγω, τὴν πόλιν λ. D.18.88: sts., however, the word after λέγω is put in appos. with the word to be expld., Ἀντικλείας.., τῆς σῆς λέγω τοι μητρός A.*Fr.*175, cf. *Th.*658 cod. M; περὶ τῶνδε.., λέγω δὲ Φωκέων D.19.152; παρ' ὧν.., τούτων τῶν τὴν Ἀσίαν οἰκούντων λέγω Id.8.24, cf. Pl.*Smp.*202b: abs., μηδενὸς ὄντος ἐν [τῇ χώρᾳ] λέγω D.1.27. b. περὶ ἃς (sc. ἀπολαύσεις) λέγομεν τὸν σώφρονα in regard to which we *use the term* 'temperate', Arist.*EN*1148$^a$5, cf. Pl.*Grg.*494b. 10. ὡς λέγουσι as *they say*, S.*Ant.*23, etc.; ὡς λ. μοι Id.*OC*1161:—Pass., λέγεται *it is said*, c. acc. et inf., X.*Mem.*1.2.30, al.; but also πατρὸς λέγεται γενέσθαι.. Id.*Cyr.*1.2.1; θανεῖν ἐλέχθη he *was said* to have been killed, S.*OT*292; so λεγόμενον ἐρέω Pi.*P.*5.108: τὸ λεγόμενον abs., *as the saying goes*, Th.7.68, cf. Pl.*Grg.*447a, *Smp.*217e, etc.; τὸ λ. δὴ τοῦτο Id.*Grg.*514e: ὁ λεγόμενος γραῶν ὕθλος the *so-called*.., Id.*Tht.*176b; οἱ λ. αὐτόνομοι εἶναι X.*HG*6.3.8; οἱ λ. ὅτι.. *of whom it is said* that.., Id.*Cyr.*8.6.16. 11. of orators, *speak* (emphatically), λέγειν δεινός S.*OT*545, X.*Cyr.*1.5.9, etc.; λέγειν ἠσκηκότες S.*Fr.*963, cf. Eup.95 (v. λαλέω); λ. τε καὶ πράσσειν δυνατώτατος Th.1.139; οἱ ἐν τῷ πλήθει λέγειν δυνάμενοι Isoc.3.8, cf. D.19.286; *plead* one's cause in a court of law, Id.23.78; δίκας λέγειν ὑπέρ τινος *speak* as an advocate for.., Din.1.111. 12. *boast of, tell of*, τὴν ἑαυτοῦ ῥώμην X.*Cyr.*1.3.10; in Poets, *sing of*, θέλω λ. Ἀτρείδας *Anacreont.*23.1. 13. *recite* what is written, λαβὲ τὸ βιβλίον καὶ λέγε Pl.*Tht.*143c; and freq. in Oratt., as λέγε τὸν νόμον D.21.8 and 10, etc.; of lectures, ἀκούσατέ μου σχόλια λέγοντος Arr.*Epict.*3.21.6, cf. 15.8 (the sense of Lat. *lego, read*, occurs only in the compds. ἀναλέγομαι, ἐπιλέγομαι). 14. *say* or *send word* by another, X.*An.*1.9.25, 7.4.5. 15. *maintain* as a thesis, οἱ τὰς ἰδέας λέγοντες Arist.*Ph.*193$^b$36, *Metaph.*1036$^b$14. 16. *nominate*, Lat. *dicere* [*dictatorem*], D.C.*Fr.*36.26 (Pass.). (Cf. Lat. *lĕgo, legio, legulus* ('olive-gatherer').)

**λεγωνῆσαι**, = παῖσαι, Ar.*Fr.*804.

**λεδδά·** ἡ ἐξοχὴ τῶν πτερνῶν, Hsch.; cf. λεάδα. **λεδρεῖται·** φροντίζει, θέλει, βούλεται, Id. **λεή·** ὁμοίως, Id.

**ληλ-ᾱσία**, Ep. -ίη, ἡ, *plundering, robbery*, X.*Hier.*1.36, Ps.-Phoc. 46 (pl.), A.R.2.303, Plu.*Eum.*9 (pl.). **-ατέω**, (λεία, ἐλαύνω) *drive away booty*, esp. *cattle*, S.*Aj.*343, E.*Rh.*293, X.*HG*4.4.15, al., Aen.Tact.16.8. 2. c. acc. loci, *plunder, despoil*, τὸ πεδίον, τὴν πόλιν, τὴν χώραν, Hdt.2.152, 5.101, Hdn.3.9.3, cf. *Hell.Oxy.*16.5, Plu.*Cam.*17; *ravage*, κώμην *PMasp.*2 iii 3 (vi A.D.):—Pass., *to be plundered*, τὰ ἐκ τῆς χώρας ληλατηθέντα Aen.Tact.16.11: metaph., τῇ γαστρὶ ληλατεῖσθαι *to be a slave to*.., Plu.2.133a. **-ατησις** [ᾰ], εως, ἡ, = ληλασία, Aen.Tact.16.5.

**λεία** (A), ἡ, (λεῖος) *tool for smoothing stone*, S.*Fr.*531. II. v. λααί.

⊛ **λεία** (B), Ion. **ληΐη**, Dor. **λᾱΐα** (Pi.*O.*10(11).44), ἡ, *booty, plunder*, freq. in Hdt. (v. infr.), etc. (Hom. and Hes. always use ληΐς); esp. of cattle, opp. ἄνθρωποι, Pi. l.c., Th.2.94 (v. infr. 4); λείας ἀπαρχὴν βοῦς S.*Tr.*761, cf. *Aj.*54, 145 (anap.): pl., ἐφθαρμένας εὑρίσκομεν λείας ἁπάσας ib.26; rarely of persons, ἀγόμεθα λεία E.*Tr.*614; *prey* of hunters, Id.*Rh.*326 generally, *booty*, Th.8.3, X.*HG*1.2.4, 1.3.2; τοὺς λοιποὺς ληΐην θέσθαι give them up *as plunder*, Hdt.4.202; λείαν ποιεῖσθαι τὴν χώραν, = ληλατεῖν τὴν χώραν, Th.8.41; λείαν ἄγειν X.*Cyr.*5.3.1; ἐπὶ λείαν ἐκπορεύσονται Id.*An.*5.1.8, etc.; κατὰ ληΐην ἐκπλῶσαι Hdt.2.152: pl., διεσκεδασμένοι κατὰ τὰς ἰδίας λείας X.*HG*1.2.5: prov., Μυσῶν λεία, of anything that may be plundered with impunity, Stratt.35, D.18.72, Arist.*Rh.*1372$^b$33. 2. *plunder* (as an act), ζῶσι ἀπὸ ληΐης καὶ πολέμου Hdt.4.103. 3. *stolen property*, τὴν λ. ἀποδοῦναι *PCair.Zen.*145.16 (iii B.C.), cf. *PSI*4.438.10–13 (iii B.C.). 4. *flocks and herds, cattle*, ἀπογραφὴ λείας *PHib.*1.33.2 (iii B.C.), cf. *PPetr.*3 p.279 (iii B.C.), *BGU*1012 (ii B.C.), D.S.19.21,97; ἀτέλεια τῆς λ. *OGI*748.9 (Cyzic., iii B.C.). (Lit. *the people's property*, cf. Lat. *populari* 'plunder'.)

**λειαίνω, λείανσις**, v. λεαίνω, λέανσις.

**λείαξ**, ακος, ὁ, (λεῖος) *beardless boy*, *EM*562.19; **λίαξ** in Hsch.

⊛ **λειαύστηρος**, ον, *with the harshness softened*, Poll.6.15.

**λείβ-δην**, Adv., (λείβω) *in drops*, *EM*781.26. ⊛**-ηθρον**, τό, *wet country* or *place*, Eup.428, e Phot. (ubi λίβηθρα et sic Kock), cf. Ael.Dion.*Fr.* 244. 2. *channel*, Phot., *Lex.Rhet.*ap.Eust.1235.58. II. Λείβηθρον, τό, mountain district of Thrace inhabited by Orpheus, Str.9.2.25, etc.; τὸ Λιβήθριον Paus.9.34.4: the inhabitants were proverbially dull, whence the phrases ᾄδειν ἀμουσότερα Λειβηθρίων Aristaenet.1.27; Λειβηθρίων ἀνοητότεροι Thugen. 4: the **Λειβηθρίδες** or Λειβηθρίδες (-ιάδες, -ιαι) Νύμφαι were freq. confounded with the Muses, Str.9.2.25, 10.3.17, Paus. l.c., Orph.*Fr.*342. **-ω**, Il.1.463, etc.: aor. inf. λεῖψαι, part. λείψας, 7.481, 24.285:—**Med.**, aor. ἐλειψάμην E.*Alc.*1015:—**Pass.**, Hes.*Sc.*390, E. (v. infr.):—*pour, pour forth*, used like σπένδω in a religious sense, οἶνον λείβειν *make a libation of* wine, Il.1.463, Od.3.460; μέθυ 12.362; also λείβειν (without οἶνον) Il.24.285; ἐξ ἀσαμίνθου κύλικος λ. Cratin.234; esp. with a dat. of the gods to whom the libation is made, λεῖψαι Κρονίωνι Il.7.481; θεοῖς Od.2.432; in full, Διὶ λ. αἴθοπα οἶνον Il.6.266, cf. 10.

579: rare in Trag., σπονδὰς θύειν τε λ. τ' A.*Supp.*981; σπονδὰς θεοῖς λ. E.*Ion*1033:—Med., σπονδάς Id.*Alc.* l.c. II. like εἴβω (q.v.), *let flow, shed*, δάκρυα λ. Il.13.88,658, Od.5.84, 16.214; δάκρυ λ. A. *Th.*51; ἐκ δ' ὀμμάτων λείβουσι δυσφιλῆ λίβα (δία cod. M) Id.*Eu.*54; δι' ὄμματος ἀστακτὶ λ. δάκρυον S.*OC*1251; τήκειν καὶ λ. (abs.) melt and *liquefy* one's spirit, Pl.*R.*411b:—Pass., of the tears, *to be shed, pour forth*, E.*Ph.*1522 (lyr.), X.*Cyr.*6.4.3; but also, of persons, λείβομαι δάκρυσιν κόρας *have my* eyes *running with* tears, E.*Andr.*532 (lyr.). 2. of other liquids, κόμαι λείβουσιν ἔλαια *drip with* oil, Call.*Ap.*38:—Pass., ἀφρὸς περὶ στόμα λείβεται Hes. l.c., cf. Pl.*Ti.* 82d; ὅπλα λύθρῳ λ., τύμβος λ. μέλιτι, *AP*6.163 (Mel.), 7.36 (Eryc.): metaph., of sound (cf. χέω), θρῆνον..λειβόμενον..σὺν καμάτῳ Pi.*P.* 12.10. III. in Pass., also, *melt* or *pine away*, Ar.*Eq.*327 (lyr.), Plu.2.681b.—σπένδω was nearly equiv. in sense, and was used in Att. Com. and Prose (exc. Pl. and X. ll. cc.).

**λειεντερ-ία**, ἡ, (λεῖος, ἔντερον) *passing one's food undigested*, Hp. *Aër.*10 (pl.), *Aph.*3.22 (pl.), Gal.7.327, al. **-ικός**, ή, όν, = sq., Hp. *Epid.*3.8, Ruf.ap.Orib.5.3.4, 8.24.30, Gal.8.389. ® **-ιώδης**, ες, *affected with* λειεντερία, κοιλίαι Hp.*Aph.*4.12.

**λεΐζομαι**, Ion. and poet. for ληΐζομαι (q.v.).

**λεικνάριον, λεικνίζω, λεῖκνον**, ff.ll. for λικν-. **λείκρικα**· σειραί, σχοινία, πλέγματα, Hsch. (Cf. λέκρικα.)

**λείκτης**, ου, ὁ, (λείχω) = Lat. *cunnilingus*, Sch.Ar.*Pax*883, Teucer in *Cat.Cod.Astr.*8(4).196.

**λειμᾰκ-ίδες**, αἱ, λ. νύμφαι *meadow*-nymphs, Orph.*A.*646 Ruhnk. (λιμνακίδων codd., λιμναίων Hermann). **-ώδης**, ες, *like meadows, grassy*, Hp.*Aër.*18, 24: Comp. λειμακέστεροι, f.l. for -κωδέστεροι, ib.13.

® **λεῖμαξ**, ᾰκος, ἡ (not ὁ, Hdn.Gr.1.524), = λειμών, *meadow*, E.*Ph.* 1571, *Ba.*867 (both lyr.), *Lyr.Alex.Adesp.*22, *AP*9.788.10. 2. *garden*, Pherecr.109. II. = Lat. *limax, snail*, Hsch.

**λεῖμμα**, ατος, τό, (λείπω) *remnant, residue*, Phld.*Herc.*1251.6 (pl.), Plu.*Nic.*17; τοῦ παιδὸς τὰ λείμματα *what was left* of him, his *remains*, Hdt.1.119; so, of persons, Lxx4*Ki.*19.4, *Ep.Rom.*11.5. 2. in Music, *interval* of $\frac{256}{243}$ *left* over when two τόνοι of $\frac{9}{8}$ are measured off from the διὰ τεσσάρων ($\frac{4}{3}$), Ptol.*Harm.*1.10, Gaud.*Harm.*13, 15, Adrast.ap.Theon.Sm.p.68 H., al., Procl. in *Ti.*2.168, 179 D.; misunderstood as the number 13 (256 − 243) by Plu.2.1017f, cf. Anon.ap. Theon.Sm.p.69 H. b. in Rhythmic, the shortest pause, λ. ἐν ρυθμῷ χρόνος κενὸς ἐλάχιστος Aristid.Quint.1.18. 3. in Medicine, *intermission* in fever, Steph. in *Gal.*1.268 D. (sg. and pl.). 4. *deficiency*, μὴ γενέσθαι μήτε δανεισμὸν μήτε λ. περὶ ταύτας τᾶς εἰσφορᾶς *IG*5(1). 1432.9 (Messene, i B.C./i A.D.).

**λειμματιαῖος**, α, ον, in Music, *of the* λεῖμμα 2, λόγος Theo Sm. p.69 H.

**λειμόδωρον**, τό, a wild plant, prob. *strangleweed, Orobanche cruenta*, Thphr.*CP*5.15.5.

® **λειμών**, ῶνος, ὁ, *any moist, grassy place, meadow*, Il.2.467, etc.; ἀμφὶ δὲ λειμῶνες μαλακοὶ ἴου ἠδὲ σελίνου θήλεον Od.5.72; μαλακὸς λ. Hes.*Th.*279; βαθύς A.*Pr.*653; λ. βούχιλος, βουθερής, Id.*Supp.*540 (lyr.), S.*Tr.*188: metaph., λειμῶνα Μουσῶν δρέπων Ar.*Ra.*1300; ἐς λειμῶνα ποταμίων ποτῶν into the smooth river-water, S.*Fr.*659; χυτῆς λειμὼν θαλάσσης, of a sponge, *AP*6.66.7 (Paul. Sil.); πλούτου καὶ νεότητος λειμῶνας ἀφθόνους Pl.*Sph.*222a, cf. *Phdr.*248c. 2. *flowers*, Ὧραι λειμῶνας βρύουσι Him.*Or.*1.19. II. *pudenda muliebria*, E.*Cyc.*171. III. later, freq. metaph. for *any bright, flowery surface*, as *a blooming face, a peacock's tail*, Ach.Tat.1.19, 1.16; *an embroidered robe*, λ. ὁ περὶ τὰς ἐσθῆτας Philostr.*Im.*2.1; also λ. λέξεων, title of work by Pamphilus, Suid.*Praef.*, cf. Plin.*HN Praef.*24, Gell. *Praef.*6:—and as Dim. **λειμωνάριον**, τό, Phot.*Bibl.*p.161 B.

**λειμων-ήρης**, ες, *belonging to a meadow*, βοτάνη Suid. ® **-ιάς**, άδος, poet. fem. of λειμώνιος, νύμφη λ. *meadow-nymph*, S.*Ph.*1454 (anap.), A.R.2.655; cf. λειμακίδες. ® **-ιάτης** λίθος, ὁ, a stone *of grass-green colour*, Plin.*HN*37.172. **-ιον**, τό, *Statice limonium, sea-lavender* or *snakeweed*, Dsc.4.16, Plin.*HN*20.72; as an ornament, λ. χρυσοῦν *Inscr.Délos*442 B11 (ii B.C.). ® **-ιος**, α, ον, (λειμών) *of a meadow*, κἀπὸ γῆς λ. δρόσοι A.*Ag.*560; ἄνθεα Id.*Fr.*374; φύλλα Theoc.18.39; ἀράχναι Arist.*HA*555b7; ἀνεμώνη ἡ λ. *Anemone pavonina, scarlet anemone*, Thphr.*HP*6.8.1 (= ἀ. ἀγρία, q.v.); also λειμωνία, ἡ, a thorny plant, prob. = σκόλυμος, *golden thistle, Scolymus hispanicus*, ib.6.4.3. (λειμωνίᾳ is corrupt in S.*Aj.*601 (lyr.).) **-ίς**, ίδος, poet. fem. of λειμώνιος, D.P.756. **-οειδής**, ές, *like meadows, grassy and flowery*, Ceb.17. **-όθεν**, Adv. *from a meadow*, Il.24. 451:—also **-θε**, Theoc.7.80.

**λειν[ ]**· ἔρια (Cypr.), Hsch. **λειξοῦρα**· τὸ δῶρον, ἐκ τοῦ λείχω, Id.; *gluttony*, Suid. s.v. λεῖξαι (wh. = Lat. *lixae*).

**λείξουρος**, ον, *gluttonous*, Zonar.

**λειό-βᾰτος**, ὁ, a fish, *skate* or *ray*, Pl.Com.137, Arist.*HA*566a32; another name for the ῥίνη acc. to Ath.7.312b: but distd. from the ῥίνη by Archestr.*Fr.*46. II. = ὁ ὁμαλὸς τόπος, Suid. Cf. λεώβατος. **-γένειος**, ον, *smooth-chinned, beardless*, Hdt.5.20. **-γλωσσος**, ον, *smooth-tongued, flattering*, Sm., Thd.*Pr.*6.24. **-θᾰλασσία**, ἡ, a kind of radish, Thphr.*HP*7.4.2 codd.: but **λειοθασία** is to be restored from Ath.2.56f, cf. Plin.*HN*19.76 (-thasium). **-κάρηνος** [ᾰ], ον, *smooth-headed, bald-headed*, Poll.2.26. **-καυλος**, ον, *smooth-stalked*, Thphr.*HP*7.8.2. **-κόνιτος**· ἡ τελείως κῦμα κόνις διαλελυμένη, λείως γὰρ τελείως, Hsch.; cf. λεωκόνιτος. **-κῡμονέω**, *to be upon a smooth sea*, interpol. in Suid. **-κύμων** [ῡ], ον, gen. ονος, *having low waves*, θάλαττα λ. Luc.*VH*2.4, *Scyth.*11. **-μερος**· ταχυδιάνοιος, Hsch. (post λεῖον, fort. λειόπορος). **-μῑτος**, ον, *smoothing the warp*, κάμακες *AP*6.247 (Phil.).

**λειοντῆ**, ἡ, poet. for λεοντῆ, *lion's skin*, *APl.*4.185.

**λειοντοπάλης** [ᾰ], ου, Dor. **-ᾱς**, α, ὁ, *wrestler with a lion*, *AP*9.237 (Eryc.).

**λειοποι-έω**, *make smooth, file down* a bone, Heliod.ap.Orib.46.11. 29. II. *pound fine*, Orib.9.40.2, *Gp.*20.26. **-ησις**, εως, ἡ, *filing down* of a bone, Heliod.ap.Orib.46.12.3.

**λειόπους**, ὁ, ἡ, πουν, τό, gen. ποδος, *flat-footed*, Gal.18(1).613.

® **λεῖος**, α, ον, *smooth* to the touch, [αἴγειρος] Il.4.484; λ. ὥσπερ ἔγχελυς Ar.*Fr.*218, cf. Eup.338; χῆμαι, χηραμβίς, *PCair.Zen.*82.12 (iii B.C.), Hsch.s.v. χήμη; τὰ τραχέα καὶ τὰ λ. X.*Mem.*3.10.1; freq. in Pl., *Cra.*414b, al., Arist.*Cat.*10a17, etc.; also, of cloths, *smooth, plain, not embroidered*, ὑφαντά τε καὶ λ. Th.2.97; λ. ὕφασμα Pl.*Plt.*310e; λεῖα ἐκπεποιημένα worked *smooth*, of marble, *IG*1².372.134; also λεία ἐργασία ib.372.165; *unsculptured*, Ἀθήνης ἕδος Call.*Fr.*105.4; of plate, *unembossed*, φιάλαι *IG*11(2).161 B27 (Delos, iii B.C.), *Inscr. Délos*442 B78 (ii B.C.). 2. in Hom., chiefly of *level* places or countries, λεῖος δ' ἱππόδρομος ἀμφὶς Il.23.330; ἐν λείῳ πεδίῳ ib.359; λ. ὁδὸς Od.10.103, Hes.*Op.*288 (ap. X., Pl., etc., ὀλίγη codd.); λ. ἄροσις Od.9.134; λεῖα δ' ἐποίησεν made a *smooth place*, Il.12.30; πεδίον λ. Hdt.2.29; χωρίον λειότατον Id.7.9.β'; ἡ -οτάτη τῶν ὁδῶν Id. 9.69; λ. θάλασσα a *smooth* sea, Id.2.117; λ. χώρα καὶ ἄξυλος X.*Ath.* 2.12; λ. βάσεις *flat* feet, Gal.6.856. b. c. gen., χῶρος..λεῖος πετράων *smooth* (i.e. *free*) *from* rocks, Od.5.443, 7.282. 3. *smooth-skinned, without hair*, of animals, Arist.*HA*582b35, Lxx *Ge.*27.11; -ότατον τῶν ζῴων ἐστὶν ἄνθρωπος Arist.*HA*583a6; esp. of youths, *smooth-chinned, beardless* (cf. λείαξ), Theoc.5.90, cf. *AP*12.13 (Strat.); also, of fish, *smooth*, ἱππίδια Epich.44; opp. λεπιδωτοί, Arist.*HA*505a 26; [γαλεός] the *smooth* shark, *Mustelus laevis*, ib.565b2, Opp.*H.*1. 380; τὸ λ. Hp.*Epid.*3.14, 6.3.16; λείη ὑπόστασις a *smooth* or *uniform* sediment, Id.*Coac.*462; [γάλα] λ. καὶ ὁμαλὸν καὶ συνεχὲς ἑαυτῷ Sor. 1.91. 4. metaph., *smooth, soft*, πνεῦμα Ar.*Ra.*1003; of the sound of the voice, Pl.*Plt.*307a, *Ti.*67b, *Phlb.*51d; διάλεκτος Phld.*Po.Herc.* 994.36; of the taste, Ti.Locr.100e sq.; also λ. μῦθοι A.*Pr.*647; [τὸ] ἥμερόν τε καὶ λ. [τοῦ ἤθους] Pl.*Cra.*406a; λ. πάθημα, opp. τραχύ, Id. *Ti.*63e; λ. κινήματα τῆς σαρκός Epicur.*Fr.*411; λ. κίνησις, Cyrenaic phrase for ἡδονή, D.L.2.86, cf. Luc.*Par.*10, Alex.Aphr. *in Top.*94.32; λ. ἡσυχίη *AP*7.278 (Arch. Byz.); ὡς -οτέρου ἐλέους ὑπάρχοντος (sed leg. τελειοτέρου) Plb.20.9.11; τὸ λ., = λειότης, τῆς ἑρμηνείας D.H. *Lys.*24; τὸ λ. καὶ ὁμαλὲς τῆς συνθέσεως Demetr.*Eloc.*48. Adv. λείως *smoothly, gently*, Pl.*Tht.*144b, Plu.2.384a; καί με κωτίλλοντα λ. τραχὺν ἐκφανεῖν νόον Sol.ap.Arist.*Ath.*12.3. II. *rubbed* or *ground down*, Dsc.1.3, al., *PHolm.*19.39; cf. λειόω II: λεῖον, τό, *fine sand*, *Inscr.Délos*500 A9 (iii B.C.). (Prob. λειϝος, cf. Lat. *lēvis*.)

**λει-όστρᾰκον**, τό, *smooth-shelled*, a kind of oyster, Arist.*HA*528a 21, *Fr.*304, Xenocr.ap.Orib.2.58.128. **-ότης**, ητος, ἡ, *smoothness*, opp. τραχύτης, σπλάγχνων A.*Pr.*493; χαλινοῦ X.*Eq.*10.6 sq.; κατόπτρων Pl.*Ti.*46c; of the skin, Id.*Grg.*465b: in pl., Id.*Ti.*65c, Arist.*PA*648b6. 2. of the voice or pronunciation, [φωνῆς] Id.*GA* 786b10, Demetr.*Eloc.*299; λ. ὀνομάτων D.H.*Vett.Cens.*2.2; τῇ λ. δουλεύειν, of Isocrates, Phld.*Rh.*1.199 S. = D.H.*Isoc.*13.

**λειο-τρῑβέω**, = λειόω II.1, Gal.12.423, Heras ap.eund.13.39, etc.:—Pass., Dsc.1.7. (Written λεοτρ-, *PMag.Leid.W.*1.25, and prob. in *SIG*1172.7 (Lebena).) **-τρῐχέω**, = sq., Arist.*HA*595b26. **-τρῐχιάω**, *have smooth hair*, Sophr.26.

**λειουρία**, ἡ, *diabetes*, Ruf.*Ren.Ves.*6.3 (restd. fr. Aët.11.1).

**λείουρος**· αἴλουρος, Hsch. **λείουσι**, poet. for λέουσι, dat. pl. of λέων. **λειούσματα ἢ λεγούσματα**· εἶδος καταφράκτου, Γαλάται, Id.

**λειό-φλοιος**, ον, *smooth-barked*, Thphr.*HP*1.5.2, *CP*5.7.2 (Comp.). **-φυλλος**, ον, *smooth-leaved*, Id.*HP*7.4.4; κράμβη Eudem.ap.Ath.9. 369e. **-χρως**, ωτος, ὁ, ἡ, *smooth-skinned*, Arist.ap.Ath.7.312f (ὁμόχρους codd. Arist.*HA*543a25). **-ω**, *make smooth*, Aq.*Pr.*28.23:—Pass., *to be polished, smoothed*, Arist.*Col.*793a16, Heliod.ap.Orib.46. 12.2. II. *pound fine, triturate*, Gal.*UP*11.8, *PSI*6.718.4 (iv/v A.D.):—Pass., Ruf.ap.Orib.8.47.4, Marc.Sid.83. 2. *emulsify, levigate*, κόμμι Crito ap.Gal.13.36, cf. Ps.-Democr.Alch.p.55 B.

**λειπανδρία** and other compds. freq. written in medieval Mss. with λειπ- (λειπο-, λειφ-) will be found, with few exceptions, under λῐπ- (λῐπο-, λῐφ-): metrical evidence, where available, favours λῐπ-, which is also certain in λιποτελέω: but λειπ- is certain in λειπογνώμων, and for many other words no trustworthy evidence of the spelling exists; cf. Choerob. in *An.Ox.*2.239.

® **λειπογνώμων**, ον, gen. ονος, *lacking* γνώμονες II.6, οἷς *IG*2².1357 (iv B.C.), cf. Ister 53, Poll.1.182, Luc.*Lex.*6, *EM*4.4, Hsch. (Freq. misspelt λιπογνώμων in codd.)

**λειπτέον**, *one must leave, abandon*, E.*HF*1385, Pl.*Cri.*51b, etc.

**λειπῠρ-ία, -ίας, -ικός, -ώδης**, v. λιπ-.

® **λείπω**, impf. ἔλειπον Il.19.288, etc.: fut. λείψω 18.11: aor. 1 ἔλειψα, part. λείψας Ar.*Fr.*965 (= Antiph.32), elsewh. only late, Plb.12.15. 12 (παρ-), Str.6.3.10 (παρ-), Ps.-Phoc.77 (ἀπ-), etc.; uncompounded, Ptol.*Alm.*10.4, Luc.*Par.*42, Ps.-Callisth.1.44 (cod. C); also in later Poets, Man.1.153, Opp.*C.*2.33, and in Inscrr., *Epigr.Gr.*522.16 (Thessalonica), 314.27 (Smyrna), etc.: but correct writers normally use aor. 2 ἔλῐπον Il.2.35, A.*Pers.*984 (lyr.), etc.: pf. λέλοιπα Od.14. 134: plpf. ἐλελοίπειν (Att. -η) X.*Cyr.*2.1.21:—**Med.**, in prop. sense chiefly in compds.: aor. 2 ἐλιπόμην Hdt.1.186, 2.40, E.*HF*169, etc. (in pass. sense, Il.11.693, al.):—**Pass.**, fut. Med. in pass. sense λείψομαι Hes.*Op.*200, Hdt.7.8.α', 48; also λειφθήσομαι S.*Ph.*1071, λελεί-

ψομαι Il.24.742, Th.5.105, etc.: aor. ἐλείφθην, λείφθην Pi.*O*.2.43; Ep. 3 pl. ἔλειφθεν *h.Merc.*195: pf. λέλειμμαι Il.13.256, Democr.228, Pl.*Ti.*61a, etc.: plpf. ἐλελείμμην Il.2.700; Ep. λέλειπτο 10.256: Ep. aor. also ἔλειπτο A.R.1.45, etc.: 1. *leave, quit*, Ἑλλάδα, δώματα, etc., Il.9.447, Od.21.116, etc.: with a neg., [σκόπελον] οὔ ποτε κύματα λείπει Il.2.396; νιν.. χιὼν οὐδαμὰ λ. S.*Ant.*830(lyr.); χερσὶν ὕπο Τρώων λείψειν φάος ἠελίοιο, i.e. die, be killed, Il.18.11; λ. τὸν βίον ὑπό τινος Pl.*Lg.*872e; λ. βίον, βίοτον, etc., S.*El.*1444, E.*Hel.*226(lyr.), etc.; αὐτόχειρι σφαγῇ λ. βίον Id.*Or.*948. b. conversely, τὸν δ' ἔλιπε ψυχή Il.5.696, Od.14.426; τὸν.. λίπε θυμός Il.4.470; ἔπειτά με καὶ λίποι αἰών 5.685, cf. Od.7.224; λίπε δ' ὀστέα θυμός Il.16.743; ψυχὴ δὲ λέλοιπεν (sc. ὀστέα) Od.14.134; νῦν δ' ἤδη πάντα λέλοιπεν (sc. ἐμέ) ib.213; in these two last passages some take it intr., *is gone*, v. infr. II. 2. *leave behind, leave at home*, παιδὶ τὸν ἐν μεγάροισιν ἔλειπες Od.13.403, cf. Il.5.480; esp. of dying men, *leave* (as a legacy), Ἀτρεὺς δὲ θνήσκων ἔλιπεν πολύαρνι Θυέστῃ [τὸ σκῆπτρον] 2.106; πατέρι γόον καὶ κήδεα λυγρά 5.157, cf. S.*Aj.*973; παῖδα ὀρφανὸν λ. ib.653; λ. ἄρρενας, θυγατέρας, Pl.*Lg.*923e, 924e; λ. εὔκλειαν ἐν δόμοισι A.*Ch.*348 (lyr.):—also in Med., *leave behind one* (as a memorial to posterity), μνημόσυνον λιπέσθαι Hdt.1.186, 6.109, al.; λιπέσθαι τιμωρούς E.*HF*169; διαδόχους ἐμαυτῷ Plu.*Aem.*36, etc. b. *leave standing, leave remaining, spare*, οἰκίαν οὐδεμίαν X.*An.*7.4.1; μηδένα Id.*HG*2.3.41, Pl.*R.*567b, etc. 3. *leave, forsake*, Il.17.13, etc.; λ. τινὰ χαμαί Pi.*O*.6.45; εὕδοντα S.*Ph.*273; τὴν αὑτοῦ φύσιν λ. ib.903; λ. τὴν τάξιν Pl.*Ap.*29a, etc.; λ. ἐράνους *fail in paying*.., D.27.25, cf. 25.22; λ. δασμόν, φοράν, X.*Cyr.*3.1.1,34; λ. μαρτυρίαν, ὅρκον, *fail in*.., D.49.19, 59.60, λ. δίκην *allow* it *to go by default*, *SIG*134*b*24(Milet., iv B.C.); λοιβὰς.. οὐ λίπε *neglected* them not, *IG*3.1337.8. b. conversely, λίπον ἰοὶ ἄνακτα they *failed* him, Od.22.119. 4. Math., *lose* or *drop* something, i.e. have something subtracted from it, τὸ ΚΡ λιπὸν τὸ ΒΟ the area ΚΡ *minus* the area ΒΟ, Apollon.Perg.3.12, cf. Ptol.*Alm.*10.4, al., Dioph.2.21. II. intr., *to be gone, depart*, *Epigr.Gr.*149.2 (Rhenea); v. supr. I. 1 b. 2. *to be wanting* or *missing*, οὔ τί πω ἔλιπεν ἐκ τοῦδ' οἴκου.. αἰκία S.*El.*514(lyr.); οὔποτ' ἔρις λείψει κατὰ πόλεις E.*Hel.*1157(lyr.); τὸ κακοτυχὲς οὐ λέλοιπεν ἐκ τέκνων Id.*HF*133(lyr.); λείπουσιν αἱ ἐκ τῆς κεφαλῆς [τρίχες] Arist.*HA*518$^a$24; ἔτι ἕν σοι λείπει *Ev.Luc.*18.22; τί λείπει τῶν ἐπιτηδείων αὐταῖς; Plb.10.18.8; τί γάρ σοι λείπει; Arr.*Epict.*2.22.5, cf. Diog.Oen.64; [εἰς τὴν προκειμένην πραγματείαν] τὸ ὑφ' οὗ γίνεται.. μὴ ῥηθὲν οὐ λείπει *is* not *needed*, Marcellin.*Puls.*69: c. inf., λείπει μὲν οὐδ' ἃ πρόσθεν ᾔδεμεν τὸ μὴ οὐ βαρύστον' εἶναι *nihil absunt quin*.., S.*OT*1232: so c. gen., βραχὺ λείπει τοῦ μὴ συνάπτειν Plb.2.14.6, etc.; πρότασις τῆς προειρημένης λείπουσα ὑποθέσει a proposition *containing less* in the hypothesis than that aforesaid, Papp.648.1: freq. with numerals, κεφάλαιον γίγνεται μικροῦ λείποντος πέντε καὶ δέκα τάλαντα Lys.19.43; οὐ πολὺ λεῖπον τῶν ἐνενήκοντα ἐτῶν Plb.12.16.13; τριήρεις πέντε λείπουσαι τῶν ἑκατὸν εἴκοσι D.S.13.14: generally, παντὸς μὲν οὖν λείπει Pl.*Lg.*728a; ὁ λιπών ib.759e; τὸ λεῖπον *what is lacking*, Plb.4.38.9, etc.; esp. Gramm., *to be incomplete*, of a phrase, λειπούσης τῆς φράσεως A.D.*Adv.*159.28, al.; *to be wanting, omitted*, λείποντος τοῦ καί Id.*Conj.*225.24: also c. dat., λείπει ἡ "κεῖνος" φωνὴ τῷ ε̄ Id.*Adv.*147.17. b. of the moon, *to be invisible* (cf. λειψιφαής), Plot.2.3.5. c. λείποντα εἴδη, in Algebra, = λείψεις, *negative* terms, Dioph.1 *Def.*10.

B. Pass., *to be left, left behind*, ἄλοχος Φυλάκῃ ἐλέλειπτο Il.2.700; οἱ δ' οἶοι λείπονται Od.22.250, etc.; also ὀπίσσω, μετόπισθε, κατόπισθε λ., Il.3.160, 22.334, Od.21.116; παῖδες.. μετόπισθε λελειμμένοι *left behind* in Troy, Il.24.687; μόνα.. νὼ λελειμμένα S.*Ant.*58, etc.; τὸ λειπόμενον βίου (v.l. βιοτᾶς) Ariphron 1 (= *IG*3.171). b. Math., *to be subtracted*: τὸ ἀπὸ τῆς ΔΦ λειφθὲν ὑπὸ τοῦ ἀπὸ τῆς ΔΑ ποιεῖ.., the square on ΔΦ *subtracted* from the square on ΔΑ gives.., Ptol.*Alm.*10.7. 2. *remain, remain over and above*, τριτάτη δ' ἔτι μοῖρα λέλειπται Il.10.253; ἐμοὶ δὲ λελείψεται ἄλγεα λυγρά 24.742; ὀλίγων σφι ἡμερέων λείπεται σιτία Hdt.9.45; ὃ πᾶσι λ. βροτοῖς.. ἐλπίς E.*Tr.*681; αὐτόνομοι ἐλείφθημεν Th.3.11; ἕως ἄν τι λείπηται Id.8.81: impers., λείπεται *it remains*, Pl.*Tht.*157e: c. acc. et inf., πεπληρῶσθαί με Id.*Phdr.*235c. 3. *remain alive*, πολλοὶ δὲ λίποντο Od.4.495, cf. A.*Pers.*480, X.*An.*3.1.2. II. c. gen., 1. *to be left without, to be forsaken of*, κτεάνων λειφθεὶς καὶ φίλων Pi.*I*.2.11; σοῦ λελειμμένη S.*Ant.*548; but στρατὸν λελειμμένον δορός *which has been left* by the spear, i.e. not slain, A.*Ag.*517. 2. *to be left behind in a race*, Il.23.407,409, Od.8.125; λελειμμένος οἰῶν *lingering behind* the sheep, 9.448; λείπετ'.. Μενελάου δουρὸς ἐρωήν he *was left* a spear's throw *behind* Menelaus, Il.23.529; ἐς δίσκουρα λέλειπτο he *had been left behind* as much as a quoit's throw, ib.523; κίρκοι πελειῶν οὐ μακρὰν λελειμμένοι A.*Pr.*857, cf. E.*Hipp.*1244; τοῦ κήρυκος μὴ λείπεσθαι not *to lag behind* the herald, Th.1.131; but ἀπό τινος *to be left behind by* one, Il.9.437,445; λ. βασιλέος or ἀπὸ βασιλέος *by* the king, Hdt.8.113, 9.66; λείπεσθαι τοῦ καιροῦ *to be behind* time, X.*Cyr.*6.3.29; τῆς ναυμαχίης Id.7.168; τῆς ἐξόδου Id.9.19; but. λείπου μηδὲ σύ, παρθέν', ἀπ' οἴκων *fail* not [to come] from the house, i.e. follow us, dub. in S.*Tr.*1275(anap.): abs., *to be left behind, be absent*, Hdt.7.229, 8.44. 3. *come short of, be inferior to*, τινος, like ἐλαττοῦσθαι, ἡττᾶσθαι, ὑστερεῖσθαί τινος, because the Verb has a comp. sense, Id.7.48, etc.; οὐκ ἔσθ' ὁποίας λείπεται τόδ' ἡδονῆς *falls short of*.., E.*Fr.*138.3; λείπεσθαί τινος ἔς τι or ἔν τινι, Hdt.1.99, 7.8.α' (v. infr. 4); περί τι Plb.6.52.8; πρός τι S.*Tr.*266; καμήλους ταχυτῆτι οὐ λειπομένας ἵππων Hdt.7.86; ξύνεσιν οὐδενὸς λ. Th.6.72; πλήθει λ. X.*HG*7.4.24; πλήθει ἡμῶν λειφθέντες Id.*An.*7.7.31; οὐδ' ἔτι θηρὸς ἐλείπετο δερκομένοισιν, i.e. resembled.., Epic. in *Arch.Pap.*7 p.4: also c. gen. rei, λειφθῆναι μάχης E.*Heracl.*732; οὐδὲν σοῦ ξίφους λελείψομαι Id.*Or.*1041: Math., τὸ ἐγγραφὲν τοῦ περιγραφέντος ἐλάσσονι λείπεται the inscribed figure *falls short of* the circumscribed by less than.., Archim.*Con.Sph.*21: also c. dat. rei, λειφθῆναι μάχῃ A.*Pers.*344: c. part., οὐδὲν ἐμοῦ λείπει γιγνώσκων X.*Oec.*18.5; λέλειψαι τῶν ἐμῶν βουλευμάτων *you come short of, understand not* my plans, E.*Or.*1085; λέλειμμαι τῶν ἐν Ἕλλησιν νόμων Id.*Hel.*1246: abs., *to be defeated*, Plb.1.62.6; ὑπό τινος *AP*11.224 (Antip.); λείπεσθαι ἐν [τῇ ἀγορανομίᾳ], Lat. *repulsam ferre*, Plu.*Mar.*5, etc.: abs., in part., ἄνδρας λελειμμένους *inferior* men, A.*Fr.*37; also, λειπόμενοι *the poor*, *IG*14.1839.7. 4. *to be wanting* or *lacking in* a thing, *fail of* or *in*, c. gen., ὀδυρμάτων ἐλείπετ' οὐδέν S.*Tr.*937; γνώμας λειπομένα σοφᾶς Id.*El.*474(lyr.); λελειμμένη τέκνων E.*Ion*680; λελ. λόγου *failing to heed* my word, S.*Aj.*543; μῆνας ἓξ.. λειπόμενος (sc. τῶν εἴκοσι ἐτῶν) *Epigr.Gr.*519 (Thessalonica); also, λ. ἐν τῷ μὴ δύνασθαι μηδ' ὁρᾶν S.*OC*495; v. supr. 3. 5. *to be in need of*, τῆς σῆς βοηθείας A.D.*Synt.*289.28. (I.-E. *leiqʷ-*, cf. Lat. *li-n-quo*, Skt. *ric-*, pres. 3 sg. *ri-ṇa-k-ti* 'leaves', etc.)

**λειπώδῖν**, ῖνος, ἡ, *past bearing children*, Suid.

**λείρ-ῐνος**, η, ον, *made of lilies*, χρῖσμα Dsc.3.102; ἔλαιον Gal.19.119. II. *like a lily*, ἄνθος prob. in Thphr.*HP*3.18.11. ⊛ **-ιόεις**, εσσα, εν, prop. *like a lily*, but in Hom. only metaph., χρόα λειριόεντα *lily* skin, Il.13.830; of the cicadae, ὄπα λειριόεσσαν their *delicate* voice, 3.152; of the Muses' voice, Hes.*Th.*41; Ἑσπερίδες Q.S.2.418. 2. *of the lily*, κάρη Nic.*Al.*406. ⊛ **-ιον**, τό, *Madonna lily, Lilium candidum*, prob. in Thphr.*HP*9.16.6; = κρίνον, Dsc.3.102, cf. *h.Cer.*427, Hp.*Mul.*2.179, A.R.1.879. II. *polyanthus narcissus, Narcissus Tazetta*, Thphr.*HP*6.8.1, 7.13.4, Dsc.4.158. III. *autumn narcissus, Narcissus serotinus*, Thphr.*HP*6.6.9; *narcissus* in general, ib.1.13.2. **-ιοπολφᾰνεμώνη**, ἡ, *omelet made with lilies*, etc., Pherecr.130.8. **-ιος**, ον, = λειριόεις, ἄνθεμον Pi.*N*.7.79. II. of the voice, A.R.4.903, Orph.*A*.252. III. of the eyes of youth, ὄμματα B.16.95. **-ιώδης**, ες, *like a lily*, εὐωδία Thphr.*HP*3.13.6. **-ός**, ά, όν, = λειριόεις, of the voice, τέττιξ γλυκεροῖς χείλεσι λειρὰ χέων *IG*14.1934*f*6.

**λειρώς**· ὁ ἰσχνὸς καὶ ὠχρός. καὶ **ληρίας** λέγουσι κύνας, τὰς κατισχνωμένας καὶ ἀποβαλούσας τρίχας. ἢ τὸν μικρὸν λαγών, Hsch. **λεϊστός**, ή, όν, v. ληϊστός.

⊛ **λείστριον**, τό, = λίστριον, *tool for smoothing stone*, *IG*7.3073.119, al. (Lebadea).

**λείτειραι**· ἱέρειαι, Hsch. (Cf. λήτειρα). **λειτῖνος**· πέμματος εἶδος, Id. **λειτνεία**, dub. sens. in *POxy.*1740.12 (iii/iv A.D.). **λειτόν**· βλάσφημον, Hsch.

⊛ **λειτορεύω** (λείτωρ), = ἱερεύω, *IG*9(2).397.1, 1228.3, al. (Thess.), *Arch.Pap.*9.215 (Egypt?).

⊛ **λειτουργ-έω**, earlier Att. **λητουργέω** *IG*2$^2$.1147.6 (iv B.C.), etc. (λειτ- 2$^2$.665.11 (282 B.C.)): pf. λελειτούργηκα Lys.18.7, Is.6.60, Isoc.15.145: I. at Athens, *serve public offices at one's own cost*, And.1.132, al., D.27.64: c. acc. cogn., λ. τὰ προσταττόμενα Is.6.61; δύο λειτουργίας D.50.9, cf. Lys.3.47; λ. ὑπέρ τινος *serve* these *offices* for another, Is.3.80, 6.64; τὰ λελειτουργημένα *public services performed*, D.21.169. II. generally, *perform public duties, serve the state*, τῇ πόλει X.*Mem.*2.7.6; ἐκ τῆς ἰδίας οὐσίας ὑμῖν λ. Isoc.8.13; τὸ ταῖς οὐσίαις λειτουργοῦν, ὃ καλοῦμεν εὐπόρους Arist.*Pol.*1291$^a$34; τοῖς σώμασιν καὶ τοῖς χρήμασιν λ. Id.*Ath.*29.5; λ. τοῖς σώμασιν D.21.165; τὸ περὶ τὰς ἀρχὰς λ. Arist.*Pol.*1291$^a$35; λ. τῇ πόλει ταύτην τὴν λειτουργίαν ib.37, cf. Plb.6.33.6; λ. πρὸς τεκνοποιΐαν Arist.*Pol.*1335$^b$28; ἄρχειν καὶ λ. *POxy.*1119.16 (iii A.D.). III. generally, *serve* a master, c. dat., οἱ ἐνὶ λειτουργοῦντες τὰ τοιαῦτα δοῦλοι [εἰσι] Arist.*Pol.*1278$^a$12, cf. *PSI*4.361.15 (iii B.C.), Nic.Dam.4 J.; λ. τρισὶν ἀνδράσιν, of a prostitute, *AP*5.48 (Gallus). 2. *perform religious service, minister*, ἐπὶ τῶν ἱερῶν D.H.2.22; τῷ Κυρίῳ *Act.Ap.*13.2, etc. (Written λιτ- in *Rev.Ét.Anc.*32.5 (Athens, i B.C.), etc.. cf. λειτούργιον, λειτουργός.) **-ημα**, ατος, τό, *performance of a public service*, D.H.6.40, Plu.*Ages.*36, *POxy.*1412.14 (iii A.D.), Jul.*Or.*1.21d. 2. *performance of religious ritual*, Lxx *Nu.*4.32. **-ησία**, ἡ, = foreg. 1, prob. l. in Philostr.*VS*2.26.1; *tenure of municipal office*, *POxy.*1413.17 (iii A.D.). **-ήσιμος**, ον, *for service*, σκεύη Lxx 1 *Ch.*28.13. **-ία**, ἡ, earlier Att. λητ- *IG*2$^2$.1140.14 (386 B.C.):—at Athens, and elsewhere (e.g. Siphnos, Isoc.19.36; Mitylene, Antipho 5.77), *public service* performed by private citizens at their own expense, And.4.42, Lys.21.19, etc.; λ. ἐγκύκλιοι ordinary, i.e. annual, *liturgies*, D.20.21; λειτουργίαι μετοίκων, opp. πολιτικαί, ib.18. II. *any public service* or *work*, *PHib.*1.78.4 (iii B.C.), etc.; ὁ ἐπὶ τῶν λειτουργιῶν τεταγμένος, in an army, *the officer who superintended the workmen, carpenters*, etc., Plb.3.93.4; οἱ ἐπί τινα λ. ἀπεσταλμένοι Id.10.16.5: generally. military *duty*, *UPZ*15.25 pl., ii B.C.). 2. generally, *any service* or *function*, ἡ πρώτη φανερὰ τοῖς ζῴοις λ. διὰ τοῦ στόματος οὖσα Arist.*PA*650$^a$9, cf. 674$^b$9,20, *IA* 711$^b$30; φιλικὴν ταύτην λ. Luc.*Salt.*6. 3. *service, ministration, help*, 2 *Ep.Cor.*9.12, *Ep.Phil.*2.30. III. *public service* of the gods, αἱ πρὸς τοὺς θεοὺς λ. Arist.*Pol.*1330$^a$13; αἱ τῶν θεῶν θεραπεῖαι καὶ λ. D.S.1.21, cf. *UPZ*17.17 (ii B.C.), *PTeb.*302.30 (i A.D.), etc.; *the service* or *ministry* of priests, Lxx *Nu.*8.25, *Ev.Luc.*1.23. **-ικός**, ή, όν, *of* or *for* λειτουργία, Lxx *Ex.*31.10, al.; ἡμέραι (in temples) *PTeb.*88.6 (ii B.C.); *ministering*, πνεύματα *Ep.Hebr.*1.14: Subst. -κόν (sc. τέλος), τό, prob. a tax paid in lieu of labour performed, *PPetr.*2 p.129 (iii B.C.), *PTeb.*5.49 (ii B.C.), al.:—in form **λειτουργιακός** *Cat.Cod.Astr.*7.209.19. **-ιον**, τό, *subsidiary action springing out of a trial*, Plin.*Ep.*2.11,12 (λιτ- codd., cf. λειτουργέω ad fin.). ⊛ **-ός**, ὁ, (λήϊτος, ἔργον) *one who performed a* λειτουργία (q.v.), *POxy.*82.3 (iii A.D.), etc.; λ. τῶν

ἐν παισὶ λειτουργιῶν *CIG*2881.13, cf. 2882, 2886(Branchidae). II. *public servant*, ἡ στάσις τῶν λ. [τοῦ Σαλωμῶνος] Lxx 3*Ki.*10.5; of *workmen, carpenters*, etc., οἰκοδόμοι καὶ λ. *PPetr.*3 p.139 (iii B.C.), cf. Plb.3.93.5; at Magnesia, an official of the γερουσία, *Inscr.Magn.*116.17; = Lat. *lictor*, Plu.*Rom.*26: metaph., λ. τῆς χρείας μου *ministering* to my need, *Ep.Phil.*2.25. 2. *private servant*, Lxx 2*Ki.*13.18. III. in religious sense, *minister*, [θεοῦ] ib.*Ps.*102(103).21, *Ep.Rom.*13.6, al.; τῶν θεῶν D.H.2.22, cf. 73; τῶν ἁγίων λ. *Ep.Hebr.*8.2; θεοῖς λιτουργοί (sic) *Rev.Ét.Anc.*32.5 (Athens, i B.C.); *attendant* at sacrifices, *acolyte*, *IG*3.1005, al. IV. Astrol., λειτουργοί, οἱ, astral gods *subordinate* to the δεκανοί, Iamb.*Myst.*9.2, Firm.2.4.4, Mart.Cap.2.200.

* **λείτωρ**, ορος, ὁ, *priest*, ἀρωγὸς λ. *Ath.Mitt.*12.283 (Athens); **λείτορες**· ἱέρειαι (fort. ἱερεῖς), Hsch.; cf. λείτειραι, λειτορεύω, δμολείτωρ, ληπῆρες, λήτωρ.

**λειφαιμέω, λείφαιμος**, v. λιφ–; cf. λειπανδρία. **λείφητρα**· λείψανα, Hsch.

* **λειχήν**, ῆνος, ὁ, *tree-moss, lichen*, implied in Thphr. (cf. λειχηνιάω). 2. a kind of *liver-wort*, that grows on damp rocks, Dsc.4.53; but ἵππειος λ., = ἱππολειχήν, Nic.*Th.*945. 3. a *lichen-like eruption* on the skin of animals, esp. on the chin, *mentagra*, A.*Ch.*281 (pl.), Hp.*Aph.*3.20 (pl.), Thphr.*Sud.*14 (pl.), Lxx *Le.*21.20, Gal.14.75, Aët.8.16; also, of the ground, *blight, canker*, A.*Eu.*785 (lyr.). 4. in horses, the normal *callosity on foreleg, chestnut*, Dsc.2.43 (pl.), Cael.Aur.*TP*1.138 (pl.).—In codd. freq. written λιχήν.

**λειχήν-η**, ἡ, = μυρτάκανθον, Dsc.4.144. **-ιάω**, *have the* λειχήν I, of olives, Thphr.*CP*5.9.10. **-ικός**, ή, όν, *for eruptions*, τροχίσκος Gal.12.832: **-κή** (sc. ἔμπλαστρος) ib.835; **-κόν** (sc. φάρμακον) Orib.*Fr.*78, Aët.8.16, etc. **-ώδης**, ες, *like the* λειχήν, Hp.*Epid.*4.20, Gal.6.750, al.

**λειχήνωρ**, ορος, ὁ, *Lick-man*, name of a mouse, Batr.202:—so also **λειχομύλη** [ῠ], ἡ, *Lick-meal*, name of a mouse, ib.29; **λειχοπίναξ** [ῐ], ακος, ὁ, *Lick-platter*, ib.100, 230.

* **λείχω**, fut. λείξω Lxx *Mi.*7.17: aor. ἔλειξα A. (v. infr.), Ar. (v. infr.):—Pass., aor. part. ἐκ-λειχθέν Dsc.3.36:—*lick up*, Hdt.4.23, A.*Eu.*106, *Ag.*828; λ. δημιόπρατα Ar.*Eq.*103; simply, *lick*, ἅλα Arist. *HA*580ᵇ31; βοῦς ὁπλὴν λ. Thphr.*Sign.*15. (Cf. Skt. *lih-* 'lick', etc.)

**λειψανδρία**, ἡ, (λεῖψις) = λιπανδρία, Hsch., v.l. in J.*BJ*3.3.2, for λειπανδρία or λιπανδρία:—hence in later Gr., Adj. **λείψανδρος**, Sch. E.*Or.*249; Verb **λειψανδρέω**, Tz.*H.*1.779.

**λειψᾰνηλόγος**, ον, *gathering remnants*, *AP*6.92 (Phil.).

* **λείψᾰνον**, τό, (λείπω) *piece left, remnant*, Ἀργοῦς E.*Med.*1387: metaph., of a man, λ. φίλων, Φρυγῶν, Id.*El.*554, *Tr.*716; τὸ νῦν αὐτῆς [τῆς γῆς] λ. Pl.*Criti.*110e, cf. 111a; δάκρυα.. στοργᾶς λείψανον *AP*7.476 (Mel.); μειδιάματος λ. *traces* of a smile, Chor.in *Rev.Phil.*1.230. 2. freq. in pl., *remains* of the dead, λείψαν' ἐκβάλλειν κυσίν E.*Fr.*469; λείψανα θανόντος S.*El.*1113; τὰ λ. τοῦ σώματος Pl.*Phd.*86c; βωμὸς λ. φωτὸς ἔχει *CIG*(add.)4079*b* (Ancyra), al.; but λ. τῶν ἀγαθῶν ἀνδρῶν *their deeds, good name*, etc., E.*Andr.*774 (lyr.); *remnants* of youth, Ar.*V.*1066 (lyr.); λ. τῶν Ἰλιακῶν παθημάτων *sequels* to.., Longin.9.12.

**λειψεδᾰφία**, ἡ, (ἔδαφος) *loss of soil* (by washing away), *POxy.*1911.98, 1912.129 (vi A.D.).

**λεῖψις**, εως, ἡ, *omission*, τοῦ ἄρθρου A.D.*Synt.*78.9. 2. *failure, lack*, ἀγαθῶν *Cat.Cod.Astr.*8(1).182. II. Math., *negative term* in an algebraic expression, opp. ὕπαρξις, λ. ἐπὶ λεῖψιν πολλαπλασιασθεῖσα ποιεῖ ὕπαρξιν *a minus* multiplied by *a minus* gives a plus, Dioph.1 *Def.*9: dat. λείψει c. gen., *minus*, Id.2.21.

**λειψῐ-φᾰής**, ές, *waning*, σελήνη Max.455, cf. Heph.Astr.2.34. **-φωτέω**, *wane*, *Cat.Cod.Astr.*8(2).108.18. **-φωτος**, ον, *waning*, Paul.Al.*M.*4, *Cat.Cod.Astr.*8(2).107.13, al.:—also **-φως**, Vett.Val.191.6, Eust.811.63; but ἥρωες.. λιψόφωτες (sic) *who have quitted the light of day*, *PMag.Par.*1.1409.

**λειψό-θριξ**, τρῐχος, ὁ, ἡ, τό, *having lost their hair*, μέρη Ael.*NA*14.4. **-σέληνον**, τό, *the moon's first* or *last quarter*, when it is hidden, Paraphr.Poet. *de herb.*7.

**λειψυδρία**, ἡ, *want of water*, Thphr.*CP*5.12.1, Plb.34.9.6, Str.16.1.10, D.S.1.52, *Sammelb.*4416.14 (ii A.D.). **Λειψύδριον**, τό, *a waterless district* near Mt. Parnes in Attica, *Scol.*14, Hdt.5.62, Ar.*Lys.*665.

**λείω**, v. λῶ.

**λειώ-δης**, ες, = λεῖος, *smooth, even*, Suid. **-κόρης**· ὁ τελείως ἐκκεκαυμένους τοὺς ὀφθαλμοὺς ἔχων, Hsch. (λειοκ- cod.).

**λειώλης**, ες, = πανώλης, *IG*12(1).737 (Camirus, vi B.C.); cf. **λεώλης**· τελείως ἐξώλης, Hsch.

**λείωμα**, ατος, τό, (λειόω) *pigment-powder*, τὰ ἄκρατα λ., τὰ ὑδαρέστερα λ., Thphr.*Lap.*55.

**λείων**, v. λέων. **λείως**, Adv. of λεῖος (q.v.). II. v. λέως.

**λεί-ωσις**, εως, ἡ, (λειόω) *trituration*, σιτίων Gal.*UP*11.8, cf. 9, Erasistr.ap.eund.19.372; f.l. in Plu.2.129d. 2. *levigation* of a powder, Zos.Alch.p.177 B., al. **-ωτέον**, *one must make smooth*, δρεπάνῳ τομήν *Gp.*9.5.6.

**λέκαιος**· ὁ ἀποτεταλμένος, Hsch. (post λεκανίσκη). **λεκαλέος**, f.l. for λαικαλέος in Luc.*Lex.*12.

**λεκάν-η** [ᾰ], ἡ, (λέκος) *dish, pot, pan*, Ar.*Nu.*907, *V.*600, al., *PGrenf.*1.14 (ii B.C.), etc.; *basin*, *IG*4²(1).122.57 (Epid., iv B.C.); *hod*, Ar.*Av.*840, 1143, *IG*2².1672.184; cf. λακάνη:—Dim. **-ίδιον**, τό, Poll.10.84, Eust.1402.16: **-ιον**, τό, Ar.*Ach.*1110, Polyzel.4, Orib.*Fr.*88, v.l. in X.*Cyr.*1.3.4: **-ίς**, ίδος, ἡ, Ar.*Fr.*805, Plu.2.828a, Luc.*Am.*39: **-ίσκη**, ἡ, Ar.*Fr.*805, Telecl.1.11. (Perh. fr. Bab. *lahannu.*)

**λεκᾰνό-μαντις**, εως, ὁ, *dish-diviner*, Str.16.2.39, Ptol.*Tetr.*181, Artem.2.69:—hence **-μαντεία**, ἡ, *PMag.Par.*1.221, Ps.-Callisth.1.1. **-πωλις**, ιδος, ἡ, *for the sale of dishes*, στωία *IG*12(2).14.12 (Mytil., dub.).

**λέκᾰνος**, ὁ, or **-ον**, τό, *wine-bowl*, λεκάνου ψυκτήρ *IG*2².1425.348; fort. **λεκανοψυκτήρ**.

**λεκᾰνοσκοπία**, Ep. **-ίη**, ἡ, *the inspecting of a dish*, in order to divine, Man.4.213.

**λεκάριον**, τό, Dim. of λέκος, *little dish*, X.*Cyr.*1.3.4 (v.l. **-άνια**, pl.), Herm.Hist.2, Gal.18(1).240, Poll.10.86.

**λεκίθ-ιον** [ῐθ], τό, *bean-meal*, *PHolm.*19.41. **-ίτης** [ῑτ] ἄρτος, ὁ, bread *made of pulse*, Seleuc.ap.Ath.3.114b, cf. *Carm.Pop.*41.11.

**λεκῐθο-ειδής**, ές, = λεκιθώδης, Hp.*Morb.*2.47. **-πώλης**, ου, ὁ, Suid.:—fem. **-πωλις**, ιδος, *peasepudding-seller*, Ar.*Pl.*427, Luc.*Lex.*3.

**λέκῐθος** (A), ὁ, *gruel* of pulse or cereals, πτισάνης Hp.*Mul.*1.109; φακῶν ib. 52, cf. 2.192, Ar.*Lys.*562, Pherecr.22, Alex.258, etc.; defined in Gal.6.782. II. = φακῶν τὸ ἔνδον τοῦ λέπους, Id.19.117.

**λέκῐθος** (B), ἡ, *yolk of an egg*, Hp.*Mul.*2.205, freq. in Arist., as *HA*562ᵃ29, al.; σμῆχε ἀπὸ λ. Nic.Dam.4 J.

**λεκῐθώδης**, ες, (λέκιθος B) *yolk-coloured*, Hp.*Epid.*4.14, Thphr.*HP*4.8.11, Aret.*SD*1.15, etc.

**λεκίς, λεκίσκιον, λεκίσκος**, v. λέκος.

* **λέκκη**· χλαῖνα, Hsch. (cf. δεκτή, λόκκη):—also **λακτή** (post λεκτοί).

* **λέκος**, εος, τό, *dish, pot, pan*, Demioprat.ap.Poll.10.87, Hippon.58, Phoen.2.2:—Dim. forms **λεκ-ίς**, ίδος, ἡ, Epich.126, Iamb.*VP* 26.119 (pl.); = παροψίς, Hsch.; **-ίσκος**, ὁ, Hp.ap.Poll. l.c.:—hence **-ίσκιον**, τό, a small measure or weight, Hp.*Acut.*(*Sp.*)63, 69; cf. λεκάνη.

**λέκρανα**, τά, = ἀγκῶνες, Hsch., Phot.; cf. ὀλέκρανον. **λέκρικα**· σειραί, σχοινία, Hsch.; cf. λείκρικα. **λεκροί**, = λικροί (q.v.).

**λεκ-τέος**, α, ον, (λέγω B) *to be said* or *spoken*, Pl.*R.*378b. II. λεκτέον, *one must say* or *speak*, περί τινος X.*Lac.*2.12; [λόγους] Pl.*R.*392a; ὅτι.. Arist.*EN*1145ᵃ15. **-της**, ου, ὁ, *speaker, Gloss.*

**λεκτίκιον**, τό, Dim. of Lat. *lectīca, litter*, Alex.Trall.10.

**λεκτικός**, ή, όν, *good at speaking, able to speak*, X.*Mem.*4.3.1, *Cyr.*5.5.46 (Sup.); ἡ **-κή** (sc. τέχνη) *the art of speaking*, Pl.*Plt.*304d. II. *suited for speaking*, οἱ λ. τῶν λόγων speeches *in common colloquial style*, opp. ποιητικῶς συγκείμενοι, D.61.2; μάλιστα λ. τῶν μέτρων τὸ ἰαμβεῖόν ἐστι Arist.*Po.*1449ᵃ24, cf. *Rh.*1408ᵇ33. Adv. **-κῶς** *in prose*, D.H.*Comp.*25. 2. *related to expression, stylistic*, ὁ λ. τόπος the province *of expression*, ib.1,4; opp. πραγματικός, *of style*, opp. matter, ἀρεταί Id.*Pomp.*1; μέρος Id.*Th.*34. III. Adv. **-κῶς** *with the force of a word*, of the termination -θεν, A.D.*Adv.*195.16; *verbally, Stoic.*3.214.

* **λεκτίς**, ίδος, ἡ, *litter*, Sm.*Is.*66.20.

**λέκτο**, v. λέγω (B), λέχομαι.

* **λεκτός**, ή, όν, (λέγω B) *gathered, chosen, picked out*, of stones, λ. ἐκ γαίης λάους Hes.*Fr.*115.3; στόλος A.*Pers.*795; ἠθέων λεκτοί S.*OT* 19, etc. II. *capable of being spoken, to be spoken*, ἔστ' ἐκείνῳ πάντα λεκτά Id.*Ph.*633; κακὸν οὐ τλητὸν οὐδὲ λεκτόν E.*Hipp.*875; οὔτε λ. οὔτε πιστόν Ar.*Av.*423 (lyr.): λεκτόν, τό, *an expression* (opp. mere φωνή), A.D.*Adv.*136.32; *a word* (with a meaning), Id.*Pron.*59.1, al.; τὰ λ. *predications*, Cleanth.*Stoic.*1.109; but later, *expressions, phrases* (including statements, questions, commands, wishes, etc.), *Stoic.*2.58, 61, al.; coupled with προτάσεις and ἀξιώματα, Plot.5.5.1.

**λεκτρίτῃ** θρόνῳ· ἀνάκλισιν ἔχοντι, Hsch.

**λέκτρον**, τό, (λέχομαι) *couch, bed*, Hom. (esp. in Od.); λέκτρονδε *to bed*, Od.8.292: also in pl., Il.22.503, Od.20.58, etc.; Arc. for κλίνη acc. to *AB*1095. II. later, mostly in pl., *marriage-bed*, Pi.*N.*8.6 (sg.); παρθένοις γαμηλίων λ. ἀπείροις A.*Fr.*242; λέκτρων εὐναί Id.*Pers.*543 (anap.); λέκτρων κοῖται E.*Alc.*925 (anap.); κοίτας λέκτρον Id.*Med.*436 (lyr.); but τὸ δυσπάρευνον λ. S.*Tr.*791: hence γῆμαι λέκτρα τινός wed one, E.*Med.*594; λέκτρα προδοῦναι, αἰσχῦναι, etc., Id.*Or.*939, *Hipp.*944, etc.; ἀλλότρια, νόθα, δοῦλα λέκτρα, of illicit connexions, Id.*HF*345, *Andr.*928, *Ion*819; cf. λέχος. 2. *the fruit of marriage, a child*, Agathyll.ap.D.H.1.49 (pl.).

**λεκτροχᾰρής**, ές, *enjoying the marriage-bed*, Orph.*H.*55.9.

**λεκχώ**, v. λεχώ.

**λελᾰβέσθαι**, v. λαμβάνω. **λελάθη, λελάθοντο, λελαθέσθαι**, v. λανθάνω. **λέλᾱκα, λελάκοντο, λελᾰκυῖα**, v. λάσκω. **λέλαμμαι**, v. λαμβάνω, λέπω. **λέλασμαι**, v. λανθάνω. **λελάχητε, λελάχωσι**, v. λαγχάνω. **λελέγια**· κόχλακες, ἢ κοχλώδεις τόποι, Hsch. **λελεπρίς**· ἰχθῦς ποιός, ἡ καλουμένη φυκίς, Id.

**λεληθότως**, Adv. pf. part. of λανθάνω, *imperceptibly*, Pl.*Ax.*365c, Cic.*Att.*6.5.3, *Fam.*9.2.3, D.H.*Comp.*22, *Anacreont.*15.16, Luc.*Am.*13; *secretly*, Lxx 2*Ma.*6.11, 8.1.

**λέληκα**, v. λάσκω. **λέλησμαι**, v. λανθάνω. II. **λέλησμαι**, v. ληΐζομαι.

**λελίημαι**, old Ep. pf., *strive eagerly*, Il., but only in part. λελῑημένος, λ. ὄφρα τάχιστα ὤσαιτ' Ἀργείους 5.690, cf. 4.465: as Adj., *eager*, βὰν δ' ἰθὺς Δαναῶν λελιημένοι 12.106, cf. 16.552: in later Ep. c. gen., *eager for* a thing, λελιημένοι ἠπείροιο A.R.1.1164: also 3 sg. plpf. with inf., αὐδῆσαι λελίητο Id.3.1158, cf. 646, 4.1009: 2 sg. pf., λελίησαι ἀκούειν Theoc.25.196, cf. Orph.*Fr.*280.4: 3 pl. plpf. λελίηντο prob. cj. in Id.*L.*118. II. in phys. sense, αἰθὴρ ἐκτὸς ἔσω λελιημένος *rushing*, Emp.100.18.

**λελικκός**, ὁ, a kind of *fish*, Hsch. **λελιμμένος**, v. λίπτομαι. **λελιχμότες**, v. λιχμάω.

**λελογισμένως**, Adv., (λογίζομαι) *according to calculation*, λ. ὅκως..

Hdt.3.104; λ. πράσσοιμι μᾶλλον ἢ σθένει E.*IA*1021; ὀρθῶς καὶ λ. Plu. *Galb.*5.

**λελοχυῖα**, v. λέχομαι.

**λελῠμένως**, Adv., (λύω) *mildly, chronically*, of fever, Hp.*Coac.*470, cf. Gal.16.672; *openly, freely*, τι περί τινος δηλῶσαι Chio *Ep.*7.3.

❊ **λεμβαρχ-έω**, *command a* λέμβος, perh. metaph. in religious sense, *IGRom.*1.817 (Callipolis). **-οι**· λιπόδερμοι. (καὶ οἱ ἐφολκίοις πλέοντες), Hsch. (cf. λέπανος).

**λεμβ-ευτικός** λόγος, title of work by Heraclides 'Lembos', D.L.5.94. **-ος**, ὁ, a ship's *cock-boat*, D.32.6: metaph., of a *parasite*, ὄπισθεν ἀκολουθεῖ κόλαξ τῳ; λέμβος ἐπικέκληται Anaxandr.34.7. II. *fishing-boat*, Theoc.21.12. 2. *fast-sailing galley, felucca*, used either to precede a fleet, Plb.1.53.9; or as a light transport, Id.2.3.1, cf. 5.109.3, *SIG*569.19 (Halasarna, iii B.C.), *PPetr.*2 p.64 (iii B.C.). **-ώδης**, ες, *like a* λέμβος II. 2, πλοῖον Arist.*IA*710ᵃ31.

**λεμεῖσα**, v. λέμυσος.

❊ **λέμμα**, ατος, τό, (λέπω) *that which is peeled off, rind, husk*, Hp.*Mul.*2.117, Ar.*Av.*674, Alex.266.3; τῆς.. σαρκοειδοῦς φύσεως λ. Pl.*Ti.*76a. 2. ἰχθύων λέμματα *scales*, Poll.6.51. 3. metaph., *a mere husk*, of one who has been swindled, Anaxil.33.5.

**λέμνα**, ἡ, a water-plant, *star-grass, Callitriche verna*, Thphr.*HP* 4.10.1.

**λέμυσος** or **λεμύσης**, ου, ὁ, Egyptian name of a kind of priest, *Sammelb.*1007 (i A.D.); cf. **λεμεῖσα**, *PTeb.*122.1 (i B.C.).

**λέμφ-ος**, ὁ (Hsch., pl.) or τό (Tz.*H.*6.331), = κόρυζα, μύξα, Lib. *Decl.*33.29, cf. Moer.p.251 P., Hsch. 2. λ., οἱ, *putrescent carcasses*, Phot., Eust.1761.18. II. Adj. *snotty, drivelling*, Men.493, *Epit.*344. **-ώδης**, ες, *drivelling*, Sch.Luc.*Lex.*18.

**λεντίκιον**, τό, = sq., prob. in *POxy.*1741.10 (iv A.D.).

❊ **λέντιον**, τό, = Lat. *linteum, cloth, napkin, towel*, *Peripl.M.Rubr.*6 (pl.), *Vit.Aesop.Oxy.*2083.48, *Ev.Jo.*13.4, *Inscr.Magn.*116.34, *BSA* 27.228 (Sparta, ii A.D.):—hence ❊**λεντι-άριος**, ὁ, prob. *attendant at the bath*, *IG*3.1160.72, 14.2323: **-ὑφαντής**, οῦ, ὁ, *towel-weaver*, *Supp. Epigr.*4.541 (Ephesus).

**λέξεο**, Ep. imper. aor. Med. of λέχομαι (q.v.).

❊ **λεξ-ίδιον** [ῐδ], τό, Dim. of λέξις, Arr.*Epict.*2.1.30, Gal.13.575, etc.:—in Mss. freq. λεξείδιον, which is called Attic by Choerob. in *EM*560.11, cf. Did.ib.230.10; but cf. ὀφίδιον. **-ίδριον**, τό, = foreg., Sch. D.T.p.227 H. (v.l. -ύδριον).

❊ **λεξῐθηρέω**, *hunt after words*, Plu.ap.Gell.2.9.

**λεξῐκογράφος** [ᾰ], ὁ, *lexicographer*, *EM*221.33.

**λεξικός**, ή, όν, *of* or *for words*, λεξικόν (sc. βιβλίον), = λέξεις (v. λέξις II.3), *AB*1094, Phot. tit.

**λέξις**, εως, ἡ, (λέγω B) *speech*, opp. ᾠδή, Pl.*Lg.*816d; λ. ἢ πρᾶξις *speech* or action, Id.*R.*396c; ὁ τρόπος τῆς λ. ib.400d; τὰ λέξει δηλούμενα orders given *by word of mouth*, Arr.*Tact.*27.2. 2. *diction, style*, ἡ ἐνθάδε λ. the *style* used here (in courts of justice), Pl.*Ap.*17d; Μούσης λ. poetical *diction*, Id.*Lg.*795e, cf. Arist.*Rh.*1410ᵇ28, *Po.*1450ᵇ13, etc.; περὶ Λέξεως, title of work by Ephorus, Theon *Prog.*2. II. *a single word* or *phrase*, Arist.*Rh.*1406ᵇ1, Epicur.*Nat.*28 p.4 V., al. (pl.), D.T.633.31, Plb.2.22.1, etc.; even a meaningless *word*, such as βλίτυρι, Diog.*Stoic.*3.213; ταῖς λ. κέχρηται ταῖς αὐταῖς Plb.6.46.10; αὐταῖς λέξεσι or κατὰ λέξιν *word for word*, D.H.*Pomp.*2, Plu.2.869d, Ath.11.493d, D.L.2.113; later ἐπὶ λέξεως *PLond.*5.1713.14 (vi A.D.), *Vit.Arist.*p.438 Rose, etc.; collectively, κρατῶ καὶ τῆς λ. *the very words*, Ath.7.275b, cf. Epicur.*Nat.*28 p.15 V., Gal.12.403. 2. κατὰ λέξιν *as the phrase goes*, *AP*11.140 (Lucill.); παρὰ λέξιν *incorrectly*, Cic.*Att.*16.4.1. 3. Gramm., *a word peculiar in form* or *signification*: hence λέξεις is the older term for *a glossary*, Ῥοδιακαὶ λέξεις *a glossary of* Rhodian *phrases*, Ath.11.485e; cf. γλῶσσα II. 2. 4. *text* of an author, opp. exegesis, Asp.*in EN*122.27, Arr.*Epict.*3.21.7, Dam.*Pr.*165, 169.

**Λεξῐφάνης** [ᾰ], ου, ὁ, *Phrase-monger*, title of dialogue by Lucian.

**λέξο**, Ep. aor. imper. Med. of λέχομαι.

❊ **λεοντ-άγχης**, ου, ὁ, *lion-strangling*, voc. λεοντάγχ' ὦνα (i.e. ὦ ἄνα) prob. in Call.*Epigr.*36. ❊**-άριον**, τό, Dim. of λέων, *CIG*4558 (Palestine), *BGU*781 iii 8 (i A.D.), Gal.12.773. II. as fem. pr. n., Epicur.ap.D.L.10.5. **-έη** (fem. of λεόντεος), contr. -ῆ (sc. δορά), ἡ, *lion's skin*, Hdt.7.69, Ar.*Ra.*46, al., Pl.*Cra.*411a, Anaxandr.65: poet. **λειοντῆ**, *APl.*4.185:—also **λεοντεία**, Anon.ap.Suid. **-εία**, ἡ, *ferocity*, f.l. in Ps.-Polem.*Phgn.*1.17 (p.326 F.). ❊**-ειος**, α, ον, also late ος, ον, v. infr. 3, *of a lion*, τῆς λ. (δορᾶς) A.*Fr.*109; δέρμα Theoc.24.136; στέαρ Gal.13.631, al. 2. *lion-like*, δύναμις Epich.[301]; βία *AP*9.221 (Marc. Arg.). 3. ἡ λεόντειος πόα, = ὀροβάγχη, *Gp.*2.42.3. **-εος**, α, ον, = foreg. I, γάλα dub. in Alcm.34.5. **-ηδόν**, Adv. *like a lion*, Lxx 2 *Ma.*11.11. **-ιανός**, ή, όν, Astrol., *born under the sign Leo*, *Cat.Cod.Astr.*7.112. **-ίασις**, εως, ἡ, *the early stage of* ἐλεφαντίασις, Ruf.ap.Orib.45.27.2, Gal.14.757. **-ιάω**, *suffer from foreg.*, Id. l. c.; *to be like a lion*, Tz.*H.*4.937. **-ῐδεύς**, έως, ὁ, *lion-cub*, Ar.Byz.ap.Ael.*NA*7.47. **-ική**, ἡ, a plant, = κακκαλία, Dsc.4.122 (v.l. λεαντική). II. a dye, *PLeid.X.*98. **-ικός**, ή, όν, *of a lion*, τὰ λ., in Mithraic mysteries, Porph.*Abst.*4.16, *Antr.*15. **-ιον**, τό, Dim. of λέων, Theognost.*Can.*123. II. = λεοντίασις, Aret.*SD* 2.13. ❊**-ίς**, ίδος, ἡ, *lion-shaped ornament* on a building, Keil-Premerstein *Dritter Bericht* No.117.

**λεοντο-βάμων** [ᾰ], ον, gen. ονος, (βῆμα) *resting on a lion* or *lion's feet*, σκάφη A.*Fr.*225. **-βᾰσις**, εως, ἡ, *base in form of a lion*, *IG*2².1425.349, 381, 1544.64 (pl.), Roussel *Cultes Égyptiens* p.220, *Michel*832.45 (Samos). ❊**-βότος**, ον, *feeding* or *keeping lions*, Nonn.*D.*1.21. II. proparox. **λεοντόβοτος**, *fed on by lions*, χώρα Str.16.1.24. **-δάμᾱς** [δᾰ], acc. -δάμαν, ὁ, *lion-taming*, κύων Pi.*Fr.*74ᵃ Schroeder (= Luc. *Pr.Im.*19). ❊**-δέρης**, ου, ὁ, (δέρος) *like a lion's skin, tawny*, Orph. *L.*619. **-δίφρος**, ον, *in a chariot drawn by lions*, Ῥέη *AP*6.94 (Phil.). **-ειδής**, ές, *lion-like*, Ael.*NA*12.7, *Gp.*19.2.1. **-κέφᾰλος**, ον, *lion-headed*, παραιετίδες, of gargoyles, *IG*2².1627.303, prob. in 1666 *B* 19, 29, cf. Luc.*Herm.*44:—also **-κεφᾰλή**, ἡ, *lion-headed gargoyle*, *SIG* 241.107, 117 (Delph., iv B.C.), in Dor. form -ά), *IG*4².(1).102.294, 303 (Epid.). **-κόμος**, ον, *tending* or *rearing* lions, Opp.*C.*3.53, Philostr. *Her.*10.5. **-κρᾶνον**, τό, = Ἀμαζονικὸν ὅπλον, *Com.Adesp.*1365. **-κρουνον**, τό, *lion's-head spout*, *IG*7.3099 (Lebad.). **-μάχος** [ᾰ], ον, *fighting with a lion*, Epic.*Oxy.*412.40, Hdn.Gr.1.232:—also **-μάχᾱς**, Theoc.*Ep.*22.2. **-μῐγής**, ές, (μείγνυμι) *half-lion, half something else*, Poll.5.38. **-μορφος**, ον, *lion-shaped*, Horap.1.21, *Sammelb.*5620.14, *Cat.Cod.Astr.*8(4).252. **-μύρμηξ**, ηκος, ὁ, *half-lion, half-ant*, Hdn.Gr.1.46. **-πέτᾰλον**, τό, a plant, *Leontice Leontopetalum*, Dsc.3.96, Gal.12.57. **-πόδιον**, τό, = foreg., Dsc.3.96; = ζῳόνυχον, Ps.-Dsc.4.133. **-πους**, ὁ, ἡ, πουν, τό, gen. ποδος, *lion-footed*, E.*Fr.*540; of vessels, *IG*11(2).161 *B*10, *C*55, al. (Delos, iii B.C.). ❊**-πρόσωπος**, ον, *lion-faced*, Sch.E.*Ph.*411, *POxy.*465.162 (ii A.D.), *PMag. Par.*1.2113. **-τροφία**, ἡ, *rearing* or *breeding of lions*, Ael.*NA*6.8.

**λεοντοῦχος**, ον, (ἔχω) *holding a lion*, epith. of Asclepios at Ascalon, Marin.*Procl.*19.

**λεοντο-φόνος**, ον, *lion-killing*, νῖκαι *AP*6.74 (Agath.); λ., ἡ, *lion-slayer*, *BMus.Inscr.*1061 (Cyrene, ii A.D.). II. λεοντοφόνον, τό, a Syrian insect *that poisons lions*, Arist.*Mir.*845ᵃ28, cf. Ael.*NA*4.18. **-φόρος**, ον, *bearing the figure of a lion*, Luc.*Herm.*44. **-φυής**, ές, *of lion nature*, ἄγρα E.*Ba.*1196 (lyr.); κυλίκιον.. ὦτα ἔχον -φυᾶ Roussel *Cultes Égyptiens* p.235 (Delos, ii B.C.). ❊**-χασμα**, ατος, τό, = λεοντόκρουνον, *CIL*10.1554 (Puteoli). **-χλαινος**, ον, *clad in a lion's skin*, *APl.*4.94 (Arch.). **-χορτος**, ον, *eaten by a lion*, βούβαλις A.*Fr.*330 (-ταν cod. Eust.). **-χρους**, ουν, *lion-coloured*, Heph.Astr.1.1. **-ψῡχος**, ον, (ψυχή) *lion-hearted*, Sch.D Il.5.639.

**λεοντώδης**, ες, *lion-like*, ἤθη Arist.*Pol.*1338ᵇ19; παῖς λ. τὴν φύσιν Plu.*Alex.*2; τὸ λ. the *leonine element*, Pl.*R.*590a, Plot.1.1.7; *lion-heartedness*, Plu.*Fab.*1. Adv. -δῶς Posidon.15 J.

**Λεοντών**, ῶνος, ὁ, a month at Alexandria, Ptol.*Alm.*9.7.

**λεόπαρδος**, ὁ, *leopard*, Gal.5.134, *Edict.Diocl.*8.39, Theognost. *Can.*98.

**λεοτριβέω**, = λειοτριβέω (q.v.).

**λεουργός**, όν, = λεωργός, blamed as φορτικόν by Poll.3.134, quoting X.(*Mem.*1.3.9, where λεωργότατον is now read).

**λεπᾰδεύομαι**, (λεπάς) *fish for limpets*, Hsch., Phot.

**λεπαδν-ιστήρ**, ῆρος, ὁ, *end of the* λέπαδνον, Poll.1.147. **-ον**, τό, *broad leather strap* fastening the yoke (ζυγόν) to the neck, and joined to the girth (μασχαλιστήρ), mostly in pl., Il.5.730, 19.393, A. *Pers.*191, Ar.*Eq.*768, *PFay.*348 (ii/iii A.D.): sg., *AP*4.3ᵇ1 (Agath.): so metaph., ἀνάγκας ἔδυ λέπαδνον A.*Ag.*218 (lyr.):—later **λέπαμνον** acc. to Apollon.*Lex.* s. v. λέπαδνα. II. λέπαδνα σιδηρᾶ iron *baskets*, *PLond.*1821.112.

**λεπάζω**, = πέσσω, in pf. Pass., Stratt.77, Hsch.

**λεπαῖος**, α, ον, (λέπας) *of a scaur* or *cliff*, ὀφρύη E.*Heracl.*394; *rocky, rugged*, χθών, νάπαι, Id.*Hipp.*1248, *IT*324.

**λέπανος** ἢ **λέπανθος**· λιπόδερμος (Tarent.), Hsch.

❊ **λέπαργος**, ον, (λέπος) *with white coat* or *feathers*, κίρκος A.*Fr.*304.5; of a sheep or goat, Theoc.4.45. II. as Subst., λ., ὁ, of an ass, Nic.*Th.*349.

**λέπας**, τό, *bare rock, scaur*, Simon.114.1, A.*Ag.*283, 298, E.*Ph.*24, al.; Ἀκραῖον λ. Th.7.78. (Only nom. and acc. sg.)

**λεπάς**, άδος, ἡ, *limpet*, Alc.51 (s. v. l.), Epich.42.2, 114, Hermipp. 31, Arist.*HA*528ᵇ1, al.; ὥσπερ λεπὰς προσεχόμενος τῷ κίονι Ar.*V.*105, cf. *Pl.*1096.

**λέπασμα**, ατος, τό, *coat, skin, membrane*, gloss on χιτών, Sch.Nic. *Th.*184.

**λεπαστή** (so Hdn.Gr.1.345) or **λεπάστη**, ἡ, (λεπάς) *limpet-shaped drinking-cup*, Ar.*Pax*916, Pherecr.95, Cratin.423 (pl.):—also **λεπαστίς**, ίδος, ἡ, *AJA*31.349 (vase), Hsch.

**λέπαστρον**· σκεῦός τι ἁλιευτικόν, Hsch.

**λεπέω** or **λεπόω**, impf. ἐλέπουν· οἷον ἐλέπιζον τύπτων καὶ μαστιγῶν, Hsch.

❊ **λεπίδ-ιον**, τό, (λεπίς) *small plate, capsule*, used to close a tube, Hero *Spir.*1.3. II. a Syrian plant, *pepperwort, Lepidium latifolium*, used in cases of scurvy, Dsc.2.174, Gal.12.58, 13.350:—in Ath.3.119b, 9.385a. λέπιδι or -δυν, τό. ❊**-ίσκη**, ἡ, Dim. of λεπίς, *IG*12(8).51.19 (Imbros, ii B.C.).

**λεπῐδο-ειδής**, ές, *like scales*, of bones, Gal.2.713; λ. προσκολλήματα, of sutures, Id.*UP*9.18. **-ομαι**, Pass., *to be covered with scales*, τὰ λελεπιδωμένα, = τὰ λεπιδωτά, S.E.*P.*1.50. II. τὰ ὀστέα λεπιδοῦται the bones *scale off*, Hp.*Fract.*33.

❊ **λεπῐδωτός**, ή, όν, *scaly*, δέρμα, of the crocodile, Hdt.2.68; ἰχθύες Arist.*HA*505ᵃ24, al.; σῶμα Paul.Aeg.6.78. 2. θώρηξ λ. a cuirass *covered with scales*, Hdt.9.22, cf. D.C.78.37. II. as Subst. λ., ὁ, a fish of the Nile *with large scales*, Hdt.2.72; = κυπρῖνος, Dorio ap. Ath.7.309b. (Prob. *Cyprinus bynni.*) 2. a kind of *gem*, Orph.*L.*287.

**λεπ-ίζω**, (λέπος) *peel off the husk, skin* or *bark*, mostly in Pass., Antiph.217.10 (codd. Ath.), Thphr.*HP*9.2.7, Arist.*Mir.*830ᵃ15 (s. v. l.), Ph.*Bel.*88.45, Dsc.1.36; of the tongue, Aët.8.40:—Act. in Lxx *Ge.*30.37, al. II. (λεπίς) *strip* an object of its covering *of metal*

*plates*, Plb.22.4.7, 10.27.11 (Pass.). **-ιον**, τό, Dim. of λέπος, *thin rind, scurf*, Hp.*Coac.*458; λ. τοῦ ἄρτου Sor.1.80. ⊛ **-ίς**, ίδος, ἡ, (λέπω) *epithelial debris*, Hp.*Aph.*4.81; *layer* of the skull, *PMed.* in *Arch.Pap.*4.270; ᾠοῦ λ. egg-*shell*, Sch.Ar.*Pax* 198; *cup* of a filbert, *AP*6.22 (Zonas), 102 (Phil.); *coat* of an onion, Sch.Luc.*Hist.Conscr.* 26. **2.** collectively, *scales* of fish, λεπίδος σιδηρέης ὄψιν ἰχθυοειδέος Hdt.7.61; ὃ ἐν ὄρνιθι πτερόν, τοῦτο ἐν ἰχθύϊ ἐστὶ λ. Arist.*HA*486$^b$21; opp. φολίς, ib.490$^b$23, 517$^b$5; also of serpents, v.l. in Nic.*Th.*154, cf. Emp.82. **3.** of other things, λ. χαλκοῦ *flakes* that fly from copper in hammering, Dsc.5.78,79: abs., λεπίς Hp.*Mul.*1.63. **4.** *plate* of metal, Ph.*Bel.*69.50, Hero *Aut.*12.2, D.S.20.91, Plu.*Phoc.*18; collectively, λ. σιδηρᾶ *BGU*544.8 (ii A.D.); of gold and silver, Plb.10.27.10; λ. ἀργυρᾶ *PMag.Par.*1.258. **5.** λ. πρίονος *blade* of a saw, Heliod.ap.Orib.47.14.5. **6.** λεπίδες (sc. χιόνος) snow-*flakes*, cj. in Thphr.*HP*4.14.13, *CP*5.12.11. **-ισμα**, ατος, τό, *peel*, Lxx *Ge.*30.37, Dsc.1.23, Gal.19.106. ⊛ **-ιστής**, οῦ, ὁ, = ψευστής, Hsch., *EM* 436.11. **-ιστός**, ή, όν, *peeled*, Al.*Le.*23.14, Eust.1246.28.

**λέπορις**, ὁ, Sicel and Aeol. for *hare*, Lat. *lepus*, acc. to Varro *RR* 3.12, *LL*5.20; cf. λεβηρίς II.

**λέπος**, εος, τό, (λέπω) *rind, husk, scale*, Alex.266.7, Dsc.1.40; κυάμου Luc.*Icar.*19; σταφίδος Nic.*Th.*943; ἰχθύων λέπη Poll.6.51,94.

**λέπρ-α**, Ion. **-ρη**, ἡ, (λεπίς) *leprosy, which makes the skin scaly*, Hdt. 1.138, Hp.*Aph.*3.20 (pl.), *Prorrh.*2.43 (pl.), *Epid.*5.9 (sg.), *Morb.*1.3 (sg.), Arist.*Pr.*887$^a$34, Thphr.*Char.*19.2, *Sud.*14, Lxx *Le.*13.2. **-αίνομαι**, = λεπρύνομαι (q.v.), Nic.*Th.*156. **-άς**, άδος, ἡ, poet. fem. of λεπρός, *rough*, λεπρὰς πέτρα Theoc.1.40, cf. Opp.*H.*1.129. **-άω**, *have* or *catch leprosy*, Lxx *Nu.*12.10; *become scaly* or *rough*, λ. τὴν κύστιν Hp.*Epid.*5.17 (cf. *Aph.*4.77); τὴν ῥάκιν λελέπρηκε Herod. 3.50; λεπρᾶν κεράμιον ὀξηρόν the vinegar-jar *is mouldy*, Ar.*Fr.* 723. **-ιάω**, = foreg., of the nails, Dsc.1.74, Orib.*Syn.*7.18.8; κορώνη λεπριᾷ Porph.*Abst.*3.7; λ. τὰς ὄψεις Sch.Ar.*Av.*149. **-ικός**, ή, όν, *good for leprosy*, Dsc.2.62, 3.88, *POxy.*1088.14 (i A.D.). **-όομαι**, *become leprous*, Lxx 4*Ki.*5.1,27, *PHolm.*3.16. **-ός**, ά, όν, *scaly, scabby, rough*, of places, cj. Coraës in Hp.*Aër.*13,24, etc.; so βουνὸς λ. *Schwyzer* 289.169 (Priene, ii B.C.); ἀκταὶ λ. Lyc.642; Λ. ἀκτή as pr. n., Hippon.47. **II.** *leprous*, Thphr.*CP*2.6.4, Lxx *Le.*13.44: as Subst., *leper*, *Ev.Marc.*1.40, etc.; λ. ὄνυχες, prob. *psoriasis unguium*, Hp.*Liqu.*4, Dsc.2.114; τὸ λ., = λέπρα, ἡ, Lxx 4*Ki.*5.11; ἱμάντας ἐκ λεπρῶν (sc. δερμάτων, for the toughest leather, acc. to Sch., was supposed to be made of *mangy* skins) Ar.*Ach.*724 (but Sch. prefers ἐκ Λεπρῶν, pr. n. of a *Tannery* outside the walls); λ. βαυβῶν Herod. 6.36. **-ύνομαι**, *to be rough and scaly*, of snakes, Nic.*Th.*156 (as v.l.), 262. **-ώδης**, ες, *rough*, of the τρίγλη, named from its habitat (*rough* rocks), Ael.*NA*2.41; φλοιός Dsc.1.68. **II.** *of leprous character*, of a disease, Id.*Eup.*1.47,120, Ruf.ap.Orib.8.24.35; of a man, *suffering from a leprous disease*, Gal.12.315. **-ωσις**, εως, ἡ, *leprosy*, Tz.*H.*10.147.

**λεπτάγιον**, τό, dub. sens. in *PHib.*1.47.13 (iii B.C.).

**λεπτ-ᾱκῑνός**, ή, όν, poet. for sq., *AP*11.102 (Ammian. or Nicarch.). **-ᾰλέος**, α, ον, (λεπτός) *fine, delicate*, φωνή Il.18.571; ὑπήεισαν..λεπταλέον σύριγγες Call.*Dian.*243; also λ. φᾶρος, ἑανόν, A.R.2.31, 4.169; πόδες (of Hephaestus) Nonn.*D.*9.230; ἠήρ, λύγοι, etc., *AP*10.75 (Pall.), 7.204 (Agath.), etc.: metaph., μοῦσα Call.*Aet.Oxy.*2079.24; *feeble*, λεπταλέοι θυμοῖσι Man.1.165. **-άριον**, τό, a surgical instrument, *Hermes* 38.282. **-επίλεπτος**, ον, *thin-upon-thin*, i.e. *as thin as thin can be*, in Comp., *AP*11.110 (Nicarch.); cf. παππεπίπαππος, φαυλεπίφαυλος. **-ερέβινθος**, *cicer*, *Gloss.* **-ηκής**, ές, (ἀκή A) *fine-pointed, delicate*, Hsch., Phot. **-ίζω**, v. λεπτύνω I. **-ίον**, τό, *jar* (cf. λεπτός III.3), *POxy.*1153.4 (i A.D.), *Sammelb.* 4425 v 7, al. (ii A.D.), *BGU*14 iv 18 (iii A.D.). **-ίτιδες** [ῐτ] κριθαί, a kind of *fine barley*, *Gp.*3.3.12.

**λεπτό-βλαστος**, ον, *with feeble shoots*, Thphr.*CP*3.7.11. **-βυρσος**, ον, *thin-skinned*, Sch.Ar.*Eq.*316. **-γαστρος**, ον, *with a small belly*, Hp.*Epid.*4.30. **-γειος**, ον, Thphr.*CP*3.6.8, *HP*6.5.2, etc.:—also **λεπτόγεως**, ων, Th.1.2: (γῆ):—*of a thin* or *poor soil*: pl. λεπτόγεα, τά, *barren lands*, Hsch., Phot., Suid. **-γνώμων**, ον, gen. ονος, *subtle in mind*, Luc.*JTr.*27. **-γραμμος**, ον, *written small* or *neat*, Id.*Symp.*17. **-γρᾰφος**, ον, = foreg., Id.*Vit.Auct.*23. **-δερμία**, ἡ, *thinness of skin*, Thphr.*CP*3.5.3. **-δερμος**, ον, *with thin* or *fine skin*, Hp.*Morb.*2.74: Sup. -ότατος Arist.*PA*657$^b$2, *GA*781$^b$21. **-δομος**, ον, (δέμω) *slightly framed, slight*, πείσματα A.*Pers.*112 (lyr.). **-θριξ**, τρῐχος, ὁ, ἡ, *with fine hair*, ἔθειρα, of the eagle, B.5.28; λεπτότριχες Arist.*Pr.*966$^b$33; also λεπτότριχοι Id.*HA*518$^b$6: neut. pl. λεπτότριχα (which may come from either form), Id.*GA*783$^a$2: Comp. -τριχώτερος Id.*HA*538$^b$8. **-θριος**, ον, (θρῖον) *with thin, fine leaves*, κόνυζα Nic.*Th.*875. [Prop. ῑ, but ῐ l.c., metri gr.; cf. θρῖον.] **-ϊνος** [ῐ], ον, (ἴς A) *with fine fibres*, Thphr.*HP*3.9.3. **-κάλᾰμος** [κᾰ], ον, *with fine stalks*, ib.[8.9.2]. **-καρπος**, ον, *with small, delicate fruit*, Dsc.3.24. **-κάρῠον** [ᾰ], τό, *nut with a thin shell*, = Ποντικόν, Id.1.125, cf. *Gp.*10.3.3, Gal.6.609, 12.15:—hence **-ῠΐνος**, = *colurnus*, *Gloss.* **-καρφος**, ον, *with thin, light stem*, Dsc.3.23. **-κεραμεῖον**, τό, (λεπτός III.3) *jar-factory*, *PFlor.*50.104 (iii A.D.). **-κερᾰμεύς**, έως, ὁ, *potter, jar-maker*, ib.71.343 (iv A.D.), 73.5 (vi A.D.), *Sammelb.* 2137.4 (vi/vii A.D.). **-κνημος**, ον, *spindle-shanked*, Adam.2.2 (Comp.). ⊛ **-κοπέω**, *chop fine* or *small*, Dsc.1.12, 5.75 (both Pass.), Aq., Thd., Sm.*Is.*28.28. **-κτήτωρ**, ορος, ὁ, *small land-holder*, *PMasp.*212 (vi A.D.), *PLond.*5.1674.95 (vi A.D.). **-λάχᾰνον** [λᾰ], τό, *small vegetables*, *POxy.*1656.8 (iv/v A.D.). **-λῐθος**, ον, *covered with pebbles*, *Lyr.Alex.Adesp.*20.10.

**λεπτολογ-έω**, *speak subtly, chop logic, quibble*, Ar.*Nu.*320; περί τινος S.E.*M.*1.65; λ. τι *discuss in quibbling fashion*, Luc.*Bis Acc.*34, D.C.55.28:—also in Med., Luc.*Prom.Es*6; τι πρός τινα Id.*JConf.* 10. **-ία**, ἡ, *subtle argument, quibbling*, Hermipp.22, *Stoic.*1.89, Philostr.*VA*1.17. **II.** = κνιπότης, Phryn.*PS* p.85 B. **2.** *chicanery*, *PMasp.*151.201 (vi A.D.). **-ος**, ον, *speaking subtly, quibbling*, φρένες Ar.*Ra.*876 (hex.), cf. Philostr.*VS*1.21.1: in good sense, ἀλλ' ὅ γε λεπτολόγος σκῆπτρον Ἄρατος ἔχει Ptol.ap.Ach.Tat.*Intr. Arat.*p.79 M.

**λεπτομέρ-εια**, ἡ, *a consisting of small particles*, Ti.Locr.98e, *Placit.* 1.7.34, al.; of the soul, Epicur.*Ep.*1 p.20 U. **-ής**, ές, (μέρος) *composed of small particles*, as water and fire, opp. παχυμερής, Ti. Locr.100e; of the soul, Epicur.*Ep.*1 p.19 U.: Comp. -έστερος Arist. *Cael.*303$^b$19: Sup. -έστατος Id.*de An.*405$^a$6, al. **II.** *treated in detail* or *minutely*, Ptol.*Geog.*1.22.1 (Comp.), Tz.*H.*10.159. Adv. -ρῶς Phot.*Bibl.*p.4 B., Hsch. **2.** of persons, *refined* or *meticulous*, λ. καὶ δεδιδαγμένος *Cat.Cod.Astr.*8(2).124.

**λεπτομεριμν-ία**, ἡ, *attention to trifles*, Corn.*ND*18. **-ος**, ον, (μέριμνα) *meticulous*, *Cat.Cod.Astr.*8(2).124, cf. *Gloss.*

**λεπτο-μήλη**, ἡ, *slender probe*, *Hermes* 38.282. **-μητις**· ἡ δασεῖα ψυχή, Hsch. **-μῑτος**, ον, *of fine threads*, φάρος E.*Andr.*831 (lyr.); νεφέλη *AP*6.11 (Satyr.). **-νευρος**, ον, *with thin sinews*, Adam.2.2 (Comp.). ⊛ **-πηνος**, ον, (πηνίον) *of fine fabric*, ὕφος Eub.67.5 = 84. 4; v.l. **λεπτόνητος**, ον, (νέω) *fine-spun*, in the latter place (cod. A Ath.).

**λεπτοποι-έω**, *make fine* or *small*, Crito ap.Gal.13.878, Orib.50.11. 8. **-ησις**, εως, ἡ, *making fine*, Gal.10.742. **-ητέον**, *one must make fine* or *small*, Dsc.5.88.

**λεπτό-πους**, ὁ, ἡ, gen. ποδος, *with small, delicate feet*, Sch.Ar.*Av.* 1292. **-πρυμνος**, ον, *with slender stern*, ναῦς B.16.119. **-πῡγος**, ον, *with a thin* πυγή, Sch.Ar.*Eq.*1365. **-ραμφος**, ον, *having a slender bill*, στρουθίον Paul.Aeg.3.45. **-ρριζος**, ον, *with thin, delicate root*, Thphr.*HP*8.2.3, *Gp.*2.12.2, Sch.Theoc.5.123. **-ρρῠτος**, ον, *thinly-flowing*, ὕδωρ Hp.*Ep.*17.

⊛ **λεπτός**, ή, όν, (λέπω) rare in lit. sense, *peeled, husked*, ῥίμφα τε λέπτ' ἐγένοντο, of barley being *threshed out*, Il.20.497. **2.** *fine, small*, κονίη 23.506; κόνις S.*Ant.*256; τέφρα Ar.*Nu.*177; λεπτοῖς ἁλσί Alex.187.5: freq. in Hp., διατρήσεις λ. *Loc.Hom.*10, al.; of soil, *light*, Thphr.*HP*1.8.1. **3.** *thin, fine, delicate*, freq. in Hom., mostly of garments and the like, ὀθόναι Il.18.595; πέπλοι, φᾶρος, Od.7.97, 10.544; ἀράχνια 8.280; μήρινθος Il.23.854; -ότατος χαλκός 20.275; ἔβενος, ἐλέφας, σίδηρος *BCH*35.286 (Delos, ii B.C.); ῥινὸς βοός Il.20.276 (Sup.); δέρμα Arist.*HA*517$^b$27 (Sup.); τρίχες Id.*GA*783$^a$4 (Comp.); σάρξ E.*Med.*1189; χαλκὸς καὶ δόνακες Pi.*P.*12.25, cf. E.*Med.*949, Th. 2.49, etc.; λεπτὰ τὰ πρῴραθεν ἔχειν, of ships, to have the bows *thin and weak*, Id.7.36. **4.** of the human figure, mostly in bad sense, *thin, lean*, Alc.39; opp. παχύς, Hp.*Art.*8 (Comp.); ἐγὼ δὲ λεπτὴ κἀσθενὴς Ar. *Ec.*539; σοφιστῶν λεπτῶν, ἀσίτων Antiph.122.4; λ. καὶ αὐχμῶν Thphr. *Char.*26.5, cf. Ceb.10; λ. χείρ Hes.*Op.*497; στῆθος Ar.*Nu.*1018 (anap.); τράχηλος X.*Cyn.*5.30; λεπτὸς ⟨ἐκ⟩ τοῖν σκελοῖν Luc.*Nav.*2; λ. ὑπὸ μεριμνῶν Pl.*Amat.*134b; of animals, X.*Cyr.*1.4.11; also, *slender, taper* (opp. παχύς), δάκτυλος Pl.*R.*523d; ἀπολήγειν εἰς λεπτόν, of the fingers of a statue, Luc.*Im.*6. **5.** of space, *strait, narrow*, εἰσίθμη Od.6.264; ἀταρπός Alcm.81; ἐπὶ λεπτὸν τετάχθαι in *a thin line*, X. *Cyr.*5.4.46, cf. Plb.3.115.6; οὔτε εὐρεῖαν οὔτε λεπτὴν..ὁδόν Plu.2. 964c (ap.Porph.*Abst.*1.6). **6.** generally, *small, weak, impotent*, λεπτὴ μῆτις Il.10.226, 23.590; ἐλπίς Ar.*Eq.*1244, cf. ὀχέω II.3; ἀσφάλεια D.*Ep.*2.20; λ. ἴχνη *faint* traces, X.*Cyn.*5.5; λ. οὖας, of a child's ear, *tiny*, Simon.37.14; τὰ λ. τῶν προβάτων *small* cattle, i.e. *sheep and goats*, Hdt.8.137; λ. πλοῖα *small* craft, Id.7.36; ἄκραι λ. *small* headlands, Id.8.107; λ. κλιμάκια Ar.*Pax* 69; τὸ -ότατον τοῦ χαλκοῦ νομίσματος Plu.*Cic.*29; λ. χαλκός *OGI*485.12 (Magn. Mae.): without χαλκός, *Inscr.Perg.*374 D 7; ἀργύριον Ῥόδιον λ. *CIG*2693e 5 (Mylasa), cf. *TAM*2(1).15 (Telmessus); v. infr. III.2. Adv. -τῶς, ζῆν *poorly, meanly*, Men.*Mon.*682: neut. pl. as Adv., λεπτὰ λεύσσω κόραις E.*Or.*224. **7.** *light, slight*, λεπταῖς ὑπαὶ κώνωπος..ῥιπαῖσι A. *Ag.*892; λ. πνοαί *light* breezes, E.*IA*813; λεπταῖς ἐπὶ ῥοπῇσιν on *slight* turns of fortune, S.*Fr.*555. **8.** of size or quantity, λ. πυρίδια *small*, Ar.*Lys.*1206; λ. κύλικες Pherecr.143.5 (but f.l.): neut. pl. as Adv., λ. τῖλαι 'pluck into small pieces', Theoc.3.21. **9.** of liquids, *thin*, γάλα Hp.*Vict.*2.46; λεπτὰ ἀνεμέειν Id.*Coac.*310; λ. οἶνος *light* wine, Luc.*Merc.Cond.*18; also of food, λ. δίαιται Hp.*Aph.*1.4; λ. ὀψάρια *OGI*484.16 (Pergam.). Adv. -τῶς, διαιτᾶσθαι, διαιτᾶν, Gal. 19.191, Paul.Aeg.3.43. **10.** = λεπτομερής, *consisting of fine parts*, ὅσῳ -ότερον ἀὴρ ὕδατος Arist.*Ph.*215$^b$4, cf. *Cael.*303$^b$26, al. **II.** metaph., *subtle, refined*, νοῦς E.*Med.*529; -ότεροι μῦθοι ib.1082 (anap.); -ότατοι λῆροι Ar.*Nu.*359; πυκνῇ..λεπτὰ μηχανᾷ φρενί Id. *Ach.*445; λ. λογιστά Id.*Av.*318; λ. καὶ ἀκριβής Antipho 3.4.2; ἐς τὰς τέχνας παχέες, οὐ λεπτοί Hp.*Aër.*24; λόγοι λ...τρέφουσ' ἐκείνους Alex.220.8; cf. λεπτολόγος. Adv. -τῶς, μεριμνᾶν *Lyr.Adesp.*135; λ. καὶ πυκνῶς ἐξετάζειν Amphis 33.5: Comp. -οτέρως Anaxandr.36: also κατὰ λεπτόν *in detail*, *PPetr.*2 p.118 (iii B.C.), Cic.*Att.*2.18.2, Phryn. *PS* p.83 B., Phot. s.v. νιφετός; cf. κατάλεπτον, καταλεπτολογέω: τὰ κατὰ λεπτόν, title of poems by Aratus, Ach.Tat.*Intr.Arat.*p.79 M., Str.10.5.3; also of minor poems of Virgil; τῶν κατὰ λεπτὸν πόρων ἀραιώσεις, perh. *small* pores, Gal.15.201. **2.** rarely of the voice, *fine, delicate*, Arist.*HA*545$^a$7, Lyc.687; ἁρμονία E.*Fr.*773.23 (lyr.): neut. as Adv., λεπτὸν ἀμφιτιττυβίζειν Ar.*Av.*235 (lyr.); of sound, λ. ὑποτρύζουσα *AP*11.352.5 (Agath.); cf. λεπταλέος. **3.** of

smell, Pl.*Ti.*66e (Comp.). 4. of persons, *οἱ λ. the poor,* Plb.24.7.3; λεπτὴν πλέκειν, prov. of poor people, Hsch.; λεπτὰ ξαίνεις Suid. III. Subst. λεπτόν (sc. ἔντερον), τό, the *small intestine,* Hp.*Coac.*311,449. 2. (sc. νόμισμα) *a very small coin,* Ev.*Luc.*21.2, Phot. s. v. ὀβολός; cf. supr. I. 6. 3. (sc. κεράμιον) *jar, POxy.*920.4 (ii/iii A. D.), *PStrassb.*40.48 (vi A. D.); cf. λεπτίον, λεπτοκεραμεύς. 4. Astron. (sc. ἑξηκοστόν), division of a degree, πρῶτα λεπτά, = *minutes,* δεύτερα λ., = *seconds,* Gem.18.11,18; λεπτά alone, = *minutes, PLond.*1.98ʳ.47 (i/ii A. D.), *POxy.*1476 (iii A. D.).

**λεπτό-σαρκος**, ον, *with fine pulp,* κάρυον *Gp.*10.64.3, cf. Sch.Theoc. 5.94. **-σίνιον**, τό, a kind of fruit (?), *PPetr.*3 p.154 (iii B. C.). **-σκελής**, ές, *thin-shanked,* Arist.*PA*684ᵃ10: Comp. -έστερος Id.*HA*505ᵇ16. **-σπάθητος** [ᾰ], ον, *fine-woven,* χλανίδια *Trag.Adesp.* 7. **-σπάθιον** [ᾰ], τό, *thin spatula,* Cass.Fel.36. **-σπερμος**, ον, *with small seeds,* Dsc.4.93. **-στομος**, ον, *with small mouth,* Arist.*Fr.*304. **-σύνη**, ἡ, = λεπτότης, *AP*11.110 (Nicarch.). **-σύνθετος**, ον, *of fine texture,* καλύμματα Antiph.52.10. **-σχῐδής**, ές, *with narrow slit,* of sandals, Cephisod.4, cf. Dsc.3.24, Poll.7.85. Adv. -δῶς Dsc.4.186. **-σωμος**, ον, *with thin* or *taper body,* Eust. 1288.40. **-τᾰρίχιον** [ῐχ], τό, *small pickled fish, PLond.ined.*2184 (iii A. D.).

⊛ **λεπτότης**, ητος, ἡ, (λεπτός) *thinness,* opp. παχύτης, Hp.*VC*2. 2. *fineness, delicacy,* opp. πάχος, Pl.*R.*523e, al.; of soil, Arr.*Tact.*34.1; of the air, *tenuity,* Pl.*Ti.*58b, Arist.*Cael.*303ᵇ24, cf. *Ph.*215ᵇ28: in pl., opp. πάχη, Id.*HA*507ᵇ26; of the εἴδωλα, Epicur.*Ep.*1 p.10 U. 3. *thinness, meagreness,* of body, Pl.*Lg.*646b. II. metaph., *subtlety,* τῶν φρενῶν Ar.*Nu.*153, cf. Luc.*Bis Acc.*2.

**λεπτο-τομέω**, *cut small, mince,* Str.15.2.14. **-τράχηλος** [ᾰ], ον, *thin-* or *fine-necked,* Arist.*Phgn.*809ᵇ6 (Comp.), Alex.Mynd.ap. Ath.9.392c. **-τρητος**, ον, (τιτράω) *with small holes,* Dsc.5.120, Gal.13.638. **-τρῐχος**, ον, v. λεπτόθριξ.

**λεπτουργ-έω**, *do fine work,* of carvers and turners, Plu.*Aem.*37, 2.997d:—Pass., of a drug, *to be finely powdered,* Gal.11.404. 2. metaph., = λεπτολογέω, E.*Hipp.*923, Pl.*Plt.*262b; *recount in detail,* ib.294d; ὅσα ἔδρασεν ἡμᾶς ἀγαθὰ καθ' ἕκαστον λ. Jul.*Or.*3.123c. **-ής**, ές, *finely worked,* ἔσθος *h.Hom.*31.14: *cut up small,* ῥίζαι Nic.*Fr.*70.10. **-ία**, ἡ, *fine workmanship,* Bito 54.3, J.*AJ*3.6.4; esp. in wood, *cabinet-making, PMasp.*159.13 (vi A. D.): metaph., *working out in detail,* Them.*Or.*34 p.448 Dind.; ὀνομάτων Gal.18(1).460; *subtlety,* Procl.*in Prm.*p.518 S. **-ικά**, τά, *articles of fine workmanship, SIG* 880.66 (Pizus, iii A. D.). **-ός**, όν, *producing fine work,* esp. in wood, D.S.17.115 (as Subst.), *Edict.Diocl.*7.3; τέκτων λ. *PMasp.*158.6 (vi A. D.).

**λεπτο-ϋφής** [ῠ], ές, (ὑφαίνω) *finely woven,* Luc.*Am.*41, Alciphr.3.41. **-φαής**, ές, *feebly shining,* Nonn.*D.*5.170. **-φλοιος**, ον, *with thin bark,* Thphr.*HP*1.5.2, etc. **-φυής**, ές, = λεπτός, οὐρή Nonn. *D.*26.315; τύπος.. ἐλεφάντων ib.18.86. **-φυλλος**, ον, *with thin leaves,* Thphr.*HP*9.11.4, Sor.2.16, Anon.Vat.16, Alex.Aphr.*in Top.* 118.30: Comp., Thphr.*HP*3.9.5, 6.2.6. **-φωνος**, ον, *with small, weak voice,* Sapph.*Oxy.*1231 *Fr.*22.2, Arist.*HA*538ᵇ13 (Comp.). **-χειλής**, ές, *thin-lipped,* ib.528ᵃ29; v.l. λεπτόχειλος, ον. **-χρως**, ωτος, ὁ, ἡ, *with delicate skin,* dub. cj. in E.*Fr.*906. **-χῦλος**, ον, *with thin* or *little juice,* Thphr.*CP*6.16.5 (Comp.). **-ψάμᾰθος** [ψᾰ], ον, *with fine sand,* προστόμια A.*Supp.*3 (anap.), as Pauw for λεπτομαθῶν. **-ψηφος**, ον, *with small spots,* of red porphyry with white granules, Plin.*HN*36.57.

**Λέπτυνις**, ἡ, name for Persephone, Lyc.49.

⊛ **λέπτυν-σις**, εως, Ion. ιος, ἡ, *attenuation,* Hp.*Prorrh.*2.25; αἱ τοῦ ὑγροῦ λ. *evaporation,* Hero *Spir.*1 *Praef.* **-τέον**, *one must reduce,* τὸ πάχος Aët.16.61. **-τικός**, ή, όν, *of* or *for making thin, attenuating,* Dsc.5.88, Gal.6.572, Diph.Siph.ap.Ath.8.369d (also Comp., ib.e): c. gen., χυλὸς λ. αἵματος Id.ap.Ath.8.356d; τὸ φῶς λ. τοῦ ἀέρος *Stoic.* 2.143. **-ω**, fut. -υνῶ Lxx *Ps.*17(18).42: aor. 1 ἐλέπτυνα Hp.*Epid.* 6.1.5:—Pass., aor. ἐλεπτύνθην Id.*Aph.*5.46: pf. λελέπτυσμαι Id. *Morb.*1.19, Arist.*HA*511ᵇ22; inf. λελεπτύνθαι Ath.12.552e: (λεπτός):—*make thin* or *meagre,* αἱ ταλαιπωρίαι λ. [τὰ πρόβατα] Arist.*HA* 596ᵃ29, cf. *Pr.*882ᵃ27; λ. τὸ σχῆμα [τῶν ταγμάτων] Plb.3.113.8 (cf. λεπτυσμός); φωνὴν βαρεῖαν.. λεπτύνων Babr.103.5:—Pass., *to be reduced, grow lean* or *slender,* Hp.*Aph.*2.7, Arist.*HA*518ᵇ29, al.; τοὺς ὤμους λεπτύνεσθαι X.*Smp.*2.17; λελεπτυσμένος (-ισμένος cod.) κατὰ τὴν οὐράν, of a serpent, Philum.*Ven.*18.1; of things, *to be rarefied,* Damox.2.28, cf. Ph.1.642, S.E.*M.*10.25. 2. *comminute* or *liquefy* food in digestion, Plu.2.689d; -ύνουσα δίαιτα diet *productive of thin humours,* Gal.*Vict.Att.*3:—Pass., *become fluid,* opp. παχύνεσθαι, of foods, Hp.*VM*19; also -όμενα εἰς πνεῦμα διακρίνεται Arist.*Pr.*966ᵇ14. 3. *thresh, winnow,* λ. Δηοῦς καρπόν *AP*9.21.

**λεπτυξίς**· ἀπὸ τοῦ λέπους, καὶ τῆς χωρίσεως, Hsch.

**λεπτυσμός**, ὁ, *thinning,* Hp.*Epid.*6.3.16; τριχῶν Dsc.5.112; esp. of the line of battle, Ael.*Tact.*38.3.

**λέπτω**, v. λέπω II. 2.

**λεπῡρ-ίζομαι**, *to be contained in a husk,* Sch.Nic.*Th.*802. **-ιον**, τό, *small husk, thin peel,* etc., Hp.*Nat.Puer.*22, Arist.*HA*546ᵇ20, Theoc.5.95; *egg-shell,* Hp.*Nat.Puer.*13. **-ιόω**, *strip off the husk* (λεπυριῶσαι· ἐξαχυριῶσαι), Hsch. **-ιώδης**, ες, *like husks, consisting of coats* or *layers,* like the onion, Arist.*HA*546ᵇ30, Thphr.*HP* 4.6.2, 7.9.4, al.; cf. λεπυρώδης. ⊛ **-ον**, τό, (λέπος) *rind, shell, husk,* Batr.131, Lxx *Ca.*4.3, Dsc.*Eup.*1.89, Porph.*Gaur.*17.7.

**λεπῡρός**, ά, όν, *in a husk, peel, rind,* γενέθλη Nic.*Th.*136; ἀθέρων στάχυς ib.803.

**λεπῡρώδης**, ες, = λεπυριώδης, Thphr.*HP*1.6.7.

**λεπύχᾰνον** [ῠ], τό, = λέπυρον, *coat* of an onion, etc., Theopomp. Com.33, Plu.2.684a, Archig.ap.Gal.12.256,445; *rind,* ῥοᾶς Dsc.*Eup.* 1.74.

⊛ **λέπω**, fut. λέψω (ἀπο-) prob. in E.*Cyc.*237; Ep. inf. ἀπο-λεψέμεν Il.21.455: aor. ἔλεψα 1.236, Nic.*Fr.*82:—Med., Alex.49:—Pass., fut. λᾰπήσομαι (ἐκ-) Hp.(*Nat.Puer.*29) ap.Erot.: aor. 2 λᾰπῆναι Hsch., (ἐκ-) Ar.*Fr.*164: pf. λέλεμμαι (ἀπο-) Epich.158, but λέλαμμαι *IG*2².463.68:—*strip off the rind* or *husks, peel, bark,* περὶ γάρ ῥά ἑ χαλκὸς ἔλεψε φύλλα τε καὶ φλοιόν Il.1.236; κρόμμυον λ. Eup.255; κυάμου κολοκάσιον Nic. l. c.:—Pass., κάλαμος λελαμμένος *IG* l. c. II. metaph., in Com. Poets, *give a hiding to,* i. e. *thrash,* Pl.Com.12, Timocl.29, Apollod. Car. 5.10 (Pass.); Ἀφροδίτην *PBerol.* 13426 (Gercke-Norden *Einleitung*³ 1(9) p.42). 2. *eat,* Antiph.135; Phot. cites λέπτει (sic) = κατεσθίει from Eup.(*Fr.*427). III. Med., = δέφομαι: hence, *indulge in indecent gestures,* Alex.49, Mnesim.4.18 (anap.).

**λεπώδης**, ες, *bare, windswept,* etym. of ἐλεσπίς, *EM*328.24.

**Λέρνα**, ἡ, *Lerna,* a marsh in Argolis, the mythol. abode of the Hydra, Plu.*Cleom.*15, Paus.2.4.5; also Λέρνη, Cratin.347, Str.8.6.8, etc.: gen. Λέρνης A.*Pr.*652, etc.: prov., Λέρνη κακῶν an abyss of ills, Hsch.; so Λ. θεατῶν, of the theatre, Cratin. l. c.:—Adj. **Λερναῖος**, α, ον, Hes.*Th.*314, etc.; also ος, ον E.*Ion* 191 (lyr.):—Λερναία χολή, of malignant anger, *Trag.Adesp.*229.

**λέρος**, ὁ, a fish, Xenocr.ap.Orib.2.58.14.

**Λεσβ-άρχης**, ου, ὁ, *president of the council of Lesbos, IGRom.*3.87 (Amastris). **-ιάζω**, *do like the Lesbian women,* Lat. *fellare,* Ar.*Ra.* 1308, Luc.*Pseudol.*28. **-ίζω**, = foreg., in Att. fut. -ιεῖν, Ar.*V.*1346 codd. (leg. -ιᾶν). **-ίς**, ίδος, ἡ, *Lesbian woman,* Il.9.271, cf. Pherecr. 149:—also ⊛ **-ιάς**, άδος, Hermesian.7.52, *AP*9.26 (Antip.Thess.). **-ος**, ἡ, *Lesbos,* Il.24.544, Od.4.342, etc.; the seventh in magnitude of islands known to the Greeks, Alex.268.6:—hence Adv. **-όθεν**, *from Lesbos,* Il.9.664; **-όθι**, *at Lesbos, EM*25.15:—Adj. **Λέσβιος**, α, ον, Sapph.92, Hdt.1.23, etc.: prov., μετὰ Λέσβιον ᾠδόν, of those who are judged second best, Cratin.243; Λέσβιον κῦμα or κυμάτιον, v. κῦμα I. 3, A.*Fr.*78, Vitr.4.6.2; so τὸ Λέσβιον (without κ.) *PCair.Zen.* 445.11 (iii B. C.); Λεσβία οἰκοδομία Arist.*EN*1137ᵇ30; Λ. πώματος οὐκ ἔστιν ἄλλος οἶνος ἡδίων πιεῖν Alex.274, cf. Philyll.24; ἡδίων ὁ Λ. (sc. οἶνος), with a play on words, indicating a preference for Theophrastus (of Lesbos) over Eudemus (of Rhodes), Arist.ap.Gell.13.5. II. Λέσβιον, τό, 1. part of a ship, ἡ δευτέρα τρόπις acc. to Poll.1.85. 2. *drinking-cup,* Hedyl.ap.Ath.11.486b.

**λέσπιν**· μεγάλην. ὑδρηλήν. Δίδυμος τὴν καταδυομένην εἰς πέλαγος πέτραν. οἱ δὲ τὴν νοτεράν. ἄλλοι δὲ σπίδα βαθεῖαν. οἱ δὲ λόχμην, Hsch.

**λεσχ-άζω**, (λέσχη) *prate, chatter,* κακὰ λ. Thgn.613. **-αίνω**, = foreg., -ουσά τε καὶ ἀκούουσα καλά Perict.ap.Stob.4.28.19, cf. Call. *Fr.*98b. ⊛ **-αῖος**· ἐξηγητής, ὁμιλητής, Hsch.

**Λεσχανάσιος**, ὁ (sc. μήν), a month at Tegea, *IG*5(2).3.

**Λεσχανόριος**, v. Λεσχηνόριος.

**λεσχάραι**· οἷον αἱ σχολαί, κτλ. (cf. sq.), *EM*561.17.

⊛ **λέσχ-η**, ἡ, (prob. from *λέχ-σκη, cf. λέχος) orig. *couch*: hence, *funeral bier* or *tomb, IG*12(1).709 (Camirus); then, 2. *lounging place,* resort of idlers or beggars, οὐδ' ἐθέλεις εὕδειν χαλκήϊον ἐς δόμον ἐλθὼν ἠέ που ἐς λέσχην Od.18.329; πὰρ δ' ἴθι χάλκειον θῶκον καὶ ἐπαλέα λέσχην Hes.*Op.*493, cf. 501; κατίζων ἐν ταῖς λ. τῶν γερόντων Ps.-Hdt.*Vit.Hom.*12. 3. later, *public building* or *hall,* used as a *lounge* or *meeting-place,* esp. at Sparta and in other Doric cities, Cratin.164 (pl.), cf. Paus.3.14.2, Plu.*Lyc.*16, 24 (pl.); also in Attica, *IG*1².888, 2.1055.23, Procl. ad Hes.*Op.*491; at Delphi, *hall* adorned with paintings by Polygnotus, Luc.*Im.*7, Paus.10.25.1; at Cnidus, *council-chamber,* Plu.2.412d, cf. 298d; of the *council* of the Olympian gods, Ζεὺς ἃς λέσχας ἀπηξιώσατο (sc. τὰς Ἐρινῦς) A.*Eu.*366 (lyr.); also σύγκλητον τήνδε γερόντων λ. this specially summoned *council,* S.*Ant.*161 (anap.). II. *talk* or *gossip,* such as went on in the λέσχαι (cf. λεσχηνεύω, etc.), μακραὶ λ. E.*Hipp.*384, cf. *IA*1001 (pl.), Epicr.11.32 (pl., anap.), Lxx *Pr.*23.29 (pl.), *AP*13.6 (Phal.); in bad sense, *malicious gossip, scandal,* Vett.Val. in *Cat.Cod.Astr.*8(1).165 (pl.); also in good sense, *conversation, discussion,* γενομένης λ., ὃς γένοιτο.. ἄριστος Hdt.9.71; ἐκ λόγων ἄλλων ἀπικέσθαι ἐς λ. περὶ τοῦ Νείλου Id.2.32; λόγον εἴ τιν' οἴσεις πρὸς ἐμὰν λ. if thou hast aught to *discuss* with me, S.*OC*167 (lyr.); αἶσαν λέσχης οἶνος ἔχειν ἐθέλει Call. *Aet.*1.1.16; ἥλιον ἐν λέσχῃ κατεδύσαμεν Id.*Epigr.*2.3; λύω λέσχας, 'cut the cackle', prov. for breaking off *discussion* and setting to work in earnest, Pl.Com.223. **-ημα**, ατος, τό, *gossip,* v.l. in Hp.*Ep.*17 (pl.). **-ηνεύομαι**, Med., *chat,* πολλὰ τοῖσιν ἰδιώτῃσιν Hp.*Decent.* 7. **-ήν**, ῆνος, ὁ, *chatterer,* Timo 46.

**λεσχην-εῖ**· ὁμιλεῖ, μυθολογεῖ, Hsch. **-εία**, ἡ, *gossip,* Pl.*Ax.* 369d. ⊛ **-ευτής**, οῦ, ὁ, *gossip, chatterer,* Ath.14.649c. **-εύω**, *chat* or *converse with,* τοῖς πρέσβεσι App.*BC*2.91:—Med., Heraclit.5, Democr.85, Hp.*Decent.*7 (v.l.), *Prorrh.*2.4, *Morb.*1.19, Nic.Dam.3 J.:—Hdt. has the compds. περιλεσχήνευτος, προλεσχηνεύομαι. **-ίτης** [ῑ], ου, ὁ, = λεσχηνευτής, Suid. ⊛ **-όριος**, ὁ, epith. of Apollo, as *guardian of the meetings in the* λέσχαι, Cleanth.*Stoic.*1.123, Plu.2. 385c, Corn.*ND*32:—Dor. **Λεσχᾱνόριος**, ὁ (sc. μήν), a month in Thessaly, *IG*9(2).509, al.; in Crete, -ορία [νεμονηΐα] *Supp.Epigr.*1. 410 (iv B. C.). ⊛ **-ώτης**, ου, ὁ, *scholar, pupil,* Thales ap.D.L.1.43, Anaximen.ib.2.4. (On the accent v. Hdn.Gr.1.74.)

**λεσχηρεῖ**· κόπτει, ὁμιλεῖ, Hsch. (cf. λεσχηνεῖ).

**λεσχολογία**, ἡ, *superfluity of words, PMag.Par.*1.2085.

(i A.D.), *PLond.*2.303.16 (ii A.D.):—also **-χρως,** *BGU*228.4 (ii/iii A.D.).

**λευκομφάλιος** [ᾰ], ον, *with white navel* or *centre*, of fig-trees, Thphr. *CP*5.1.8.

**λευκόν,** τό, *white*, as a colour, τὸ λ. οἶδεν knows *white* from black, Ar.*Eq.*1279; opp. μέλαν, Pl.*Prt.*331d. **2.** *a white dress*, λευκὸν ἀμπέχει are dressed *in white*, Ar.*Ach.*1024; ἠμφιεσμένη λευκά Id.*Th.* 840. **3.** *white of egg*, Hp.*Nat.Mul.*32, Arist.*GA*753ᵃ35, Dsc.2. 50. **4.** τὰ λ. the *whites of the eyes*, Hp.*Prog.*2, Alex.222.9, cf. Arist.*HA*492ᵃ1. **5.** τὰ λ. the *menstrua alba* of young girls, Id.*GA*738ᵃ26, *HA*581ᵇ2; more generally, Hp.*Prorrh.*1.80, *Epid.* 4.22. **6.** of a *white formation* in testaceans, Arist.*HA*529ᵃ3.

**λευκό-νοτος,** ὁ, *the south wind which cleared the weather* (for the usual νότος brought rain), Arist.*Mete.*362ᵃ14: distd. from λιβόνοτος, Gal.16.410, 17(1).655. **-οινάριον,** τό, inscription of amphorae at Pompeii, *CIL*4*Suppl.*6564, al. (written λευκουν-). **-όπωρος,** ον, (ὀπώρα) *with white fruit*, *AP*9.563 (Leon.). **-πάρειος** [ᾰ], ον, *fair-cheeked*, ib.5.159 (Mel.). **-πάρῠφος,** ον, *with white-edged robe*, Alexander Magnus ap.Plu.2.180e. **-πέλιος,** ον, *pale-grey*, Erot. s.v. τὸ χρῶμα ἀφυῶδες. **-πεπλος,** ον, *white-robed*, Corinn.20: metaph., ἡμέρη λ., Lat. *dies albo notandus*, Hippon.32. **-πέτηλος,** ον, *white-leaved*, Poet. *de herb.*8. **-πετρον,** τό, *bare rock*, Plb.3.53.5, 10.30.5. **-πηχυς,** υ, *white-armed*, only in acc. pl. -πήχεις, E.*Ph.* 1351 (lyr.), and dat. pl. -πήχεσι, Id.*Ba.*1206. **-πλευρος,** ον, *with white sides*, Sch.Theoc.4.45. **-πληθής,** ές, *full of persons in white*, ἐκκλησία Ar.*Ec.*387. **-ποδήρης,** ες, *clad in white down to the feet*, in acc. -ήρην, Zos.Alch.p.117 B. **-ποίκῐλος,** ον, *motley-white*, Sch.Theoc.4.45. **II.** as Subst., λ., ἡ, name of *a gem*, Plin.*HN*37. 171. **-ποιός,** όν, *that makes white*, Sch.S.*Aj.*624. **-πους,** ὁ, ἡ, πουν, τό, gen. ποδος, *white-footed*, *bare-footed*, Βάκχαι E.*Cyc.*72 (lyr.), cf. Ar.*Lys.*665, *Anacreont.*8.5. **-πρωκτος,** ον, *with white* πρωκτός, a play on the words εὐρύπρωκτος and λευκός II. 1 c, conveying a notion of cowardice, Call.Com.11 (s. v. l.). **-πτερος,** ον, *white-winged*, of a ship, E.*Hipp.*752 (lyr.): generally, *white*, νιφάς A.*Pr.*993; Ἁμέρα E. *Tr.*848 (lyr.). **-πτέρυξ,** ῠγος, ὁ, ἡ, = foreg., prob. l. in Ion Eleg. 10. **-πῡγος,** ον, = λευκόπρωκτος, Alex.321. ⊛**-πῡρος,** ὁ, *fine wheat*, in pl., Ph.1.614.669. **-πυρρος,** ον, *pale-red*, τριχώματα Arist.*Col.*797ᵇ13; prob. to be read for λευκόπυρον μάλαγμα, Gal.13. 984. **-πωλος,** ον, *with white horses*, ἡμέρα A.*Pers.*386, S.*Aj.*673; τέθριππον Plu.*Cam.*7; epith. of the Dioscuri (cf. λεύκιππος), Pi.*P.*1. 66; at Thebes also of Amphion and Zethus, E.*HF*29; θεοί Id.*Ph.* 606. **-ρόδιος,** ον, *rose-pink*, *Sammelb.*7033.37 (v A.D.). **-ροδον,** τό, *the white rose*, *Gloss.* **-ρυγχος,** ον, *white-nosed*, of a horse, *Hippiatr.*104.

**λεῦκος,** ὁ, name of *a fish* (cf. λευκίσκος), Theoc.*Beren.*4, cf. Arist. *HA*567ᵃ20.

**Λεῦκος,** ὁ, divinity at Miletus, *Schwyzer*725 (vi B.C.).

⊛**λευκός,** ή, όν, *light, bright, clear* (opp. μέλας in all senses), αἴγλη Od. 6.45; λευκὸν (v.l. λαμπρόν)..ἠέλιος ὥς Il.14.185; λ. φάος S.*Aj.*708 (lyr.), cf. infr. II. 3; αἰθήρ E.*Andr.*1228 (anap.); of metallic surfaces, λέβης Il.23.268; λ. γαλήνη a *glassy* calm, Od.10.94; of water, *clear, limpid*, Il.23.282, Od.5.70, A.*Supp.*23 (anap.); λ. νᾶμα E.*HF*573; -ότατος ποταμῶν Call.*Jov.*19. **2.** metaph., *clear, distinct*, of the voice, Arist.*Top.*106ᵃ25, S.E.*M.*6.41: in literary sense, *clear*, λ. στίχος *AP*11. 347 (Phil.): prov., λευκὸς Ἑρμῆς, when a rogue was detected, Macar. 5.53. Adv. -κῶς, πάντα φαίνειν, of Hermes, Corn.*ND*16: Comp. -ότερον, διαλεχθῆναι Hld.7.20. **II.** of colour, *white*, freq. in Hom., varying from the pure *white* of snow ([ἵπποι] -ότεροι χιόνος Il.10.437) to the *grey* of dust (λευκοὶ ἐγένοντο κονισάλῳ 5.503); γάλα λ. 4.434; κρῖ 5.196; ἄλφιτα 18.560; ἡνία λεύκ' ἐλέφαντι 5.583; ὀδόντες 10. 263; ὀστέα 16.347; ἱστία 1.480; φᾶρος 18.353, etc.; λ. ἅρμα, = λεύκιππον, E.*Ph.*172; of the white horses used by tyrants, λ. ζεῦγος D. 21.158, cf. λεύκιππος; λ. λίθος marble, *OGI*219.36 (Sigeum, iii B.C.), etc., cf. λευκόλιθος; λευκῷ ⟨'ν⟩ λίθῳ λ. στάθμη a *white* line on a *white* stone, prov. of explanations which do not explain, S.*Fr.*330; ἡ λ. ῥίζα *white* root (= ἡ τοῦ δρακοντίου, acc. to Gal.19.118), Hp.*Morb.*2. 48, *Nat.Mul.*32; freq. of *white* or *grey* hair, λ. κάρη Tyrt.10.23; θρίξ S.*Ant.*1092; λ. γῆρας Id.*Aj.*625 (lyr.); λευκὰ γήρᾳ σώματα E.*HF* 909, etc. **b.** of the human skin, *white, fair*, sts. as a sign of youth and beauty, χρώς, πήχεε, Il.11.573, Od.23.240; λ. παρειά, παρηΐς, S.*Ant.*1239, E.*Med.*923; σάρξ, δέρη, ib.1189 (v.l.), *IA*875 (troch.); freq. with the notion of *bare*, κῶλον, πούς, Id.*Ba.*665, 863 (lyr.), *Ion* 221 (lyr.); cf. λευκόπους. **c.** of persons, *white-skinned*, Pl.*R.*474e: hence, *weakly, womanish*, Ar.*Th.*191, *Ec.*428, X.*HG*3.4.19; λευκῶν ἀνδρῶν οὐδὲν ὄφελος Macar.5.55; cf. λευκόπρωκτος, λευκόχρως. **d.** λευκαὶ φρένες in Pi.*P.*4.109 is expld. by Hsch. μαινόμεναι, *frantic, passionate* (cf. λευκῶν πραπίδων· κακῶν φρενῶν, Id.). **2.** λ. χρυσός, *pale* gold, i.e. gold *alloyed with silver* (prob. the same as ἤλεκτρον), opp. ἄπεφθος χρυσός, Hdt.1.50. **3.** metaph., *bright, fortunate, happy*, λευκὸν ἦμαρ νυκτὸς ἐκ μελαγχίμου A.*Pers.*301, cf. *Ag.*668; a *joyful* day or *holiday*, Call.*Aet.*1.1.2; λ. ἡμέρα a *happy* day, S.*Fr.*6, cf. Sch.Call.*Iamb.* in *PSI*9.1094.39; variously expld. in Phylarch. 83 J., Plu.*Per.*27; ἡ λ. ψῆφος the vote of acquittal, Luc.*Harm.*3, cf. Hsch. **III.** λεύκη, ἡ, λευκόν, τό, as Subst., v. sub vocc. (Cogn. with Lat. *lux*, etc.)

**λευκό-σαρκος,** ον, *with white flesh*, Xenocr.ap. Orib.2.58.44, Epaenet.ap.Ath.7.312b. **-σπᾰνος,** ον, *pale-grey*, of a coloured garment, *PHamb.*10.20 (ii A.D.). **-στερνος,** ον, *white-chested*, ὄνος *BGU*982.9 (ii A.D.). **-στεφής,** ές, *white-wreathed*, of pliant boughs, A.*Supp.*191, 334. **II.** λευκοστεφῆ· τὰ κεραυνόβλητα, Hsch. **-στικτος,** ον, (στίζω) *grizzled*, θρίξ E.*IA*222 (lyr.). **-στολος,** ον, *white-robed*, Orph.*Fr.*33. **-σφῠρος,** ον, *white-ankled*, Ἥβα Theoc.17.32. **-σώμᾰτος,** ον, *of white substance*, ἄρτοι Antiph.176.3.

⊛ **λευκότης,** ητος, ἡ, *whiteness*, Hp.*Aër.*20, Pl.*Tht.*156d, al.

**λευκο-τράχηλος** [ᾰ], ον, *white-necked*, Anatolius in *Cat.Cod.Astr.* 8(3).188. **-τρῐχα, -τρίχων,** v. λευκόθριξ. **-τρῐχέω,** *have white hair*, Str.6.1.13. **-τροφος,** ον, *white-growing*, μύρτα Ar.*Av.* 1100 (lyr.).

**λευκουργ-έω,** *provide with marble facing*, τὰς πυλίδας *CIG*2749 (Aphrodisias). ⊛ **-ός,** ὁ, (ἔργον) *worker in marble* or *white stone*, *BCH*32.500 (Aphrodisias), *Milet.*7.60 (Didyma), *Princeton Exp.Inscr.* Sect. B No.1170, *Wiener Denkschr.*44(6) p.31 No.70 (Cilicia, iii A.D.).

**λεύκουρος,** ον, *white-tailed*, Hsch. s.v. μάλουρος.

**λευκο-ῠφής** [ῠ], ές, *of a white web*, φᾶρος Eust.1530.56. **-φᾰής,** ές, *white-gleaming*, ψάμαθος E.*IA*1054 (lyr.); αὐγά prob. in Id.*Hyps.* *Fr.*3(1) ii 4 (lyr.); αὐχήν Nonn.*D.*15.232; cf. sq. **-φαιος,** ον, *whitish grey, ash-coloured*, πρόβατον *PHib.*1.32.13 (iii B.C.); χιτών *PCair.Zen.*433.9 (iii B.C.), cf. Ath.3.78a, Poll.7.129; καρπός prob. in Posidon.3 J.

**λευκ-όφθαλμος,** ἡ, *white-eye*, name of a gem, Plin.*HN*37. 171.

**λευκοφλεγμᾰτ-έω,** *have dropsy*, Hp.*Coac.*472. **-ία,** ἡ, *the beginning of dropsy* (also called λευκὸν φλέγμα), dub. in Cels.3. 21. **-ίας,** ου, ὁ, *one of a leuco-phlegmatous temperament*, Hp.*Epid.* 3.14. **2.** ὁ λ. ὕδερος *oedematous* dropsy, *anasarca*, Gal.10.82, al. **-ος,** ον, *suffering from white phlegm*, Hp.*Epid.*4.30. **-ώδης,** ες, *affected with dropsy*, ib.10.

**λευκό-φλοιος,** ον, *with white husk*, cj. in Posidon.3 J.; cf. λευκόφαιος. **-φόντης,** gloss on Ἀργειφόντης, Hsch. **-φορέω,** *wear white garments*, of ἔφηβοι, *IG*3.1132 (ii A.D.). **-φορῐνόχροος,** ον, *white-skin-coloured*, Philox.2.31. **-φόρος,** ον, *white-robed*, δαίμων *APl.*2.20 (Ammian.); *shining white*, Zos.Alch.p.118 B. **2.** *bearing white grapes*, ἄμπελοι *Gp.*5.2.2.

**Λευκοφρῠ-ηνά,** τά, festival of Artemis Leucophryene, *SIG*561.26 (Magn. Mae., iii B.C.), al. **-ηνή,** ἡ, epith. of Artemis at Magn. Mae., ib.558.12 (ibid.), al.

**λεύκοφρυς,** υ, gen. υος, *white-browed*, ἀγορή Orac.ap.Hdt.3.57. **II.** **λευκόφρυς,** v. λυκόφρυς.

**λευκο-φυής,** v.l. for λευκοφαής, Nonn.*D.*15.232. ⊛**-φυλλος,** ον, *white-leaved*, Dsc.4.103; ῥάβδος λ., name of a plant growing in the Phasis, Arist.*Mir.*846ᵃ29, Ps.-Plu.*Fluv.*5.2. **II.** λευκόφυλλον, τό, = ξηρόμυρον, Aët.16.128(118). **-χίτωνος** [ῐ], ον, *white-coated*, ἥπατα Batr.37. **-χλωρος,** ον, *pale-green*, Aret. *SD*1.8, 15. **-χριστος,** ον, *whitewashed*, ἐπάλξεις Ulp. ad D.3. 29. **-χροια,** ἡ, *whiteness, white colour*, *Placit.*3.1.1. **-χροος,** ον, contr. -χρους, ουν, *of pale complexion*, Arist.*GA*728ᵃ2, Aret.*SD* 1.13, etc.: generally, *white*, heterocl. acc. λευκόχροα κόμαν E.*Ph.* 322 (lyr.); pl. λευκόχροας Ptol.*Geog.*7.2.17:—also **-χροιος,** ον, Hp. *Epid.*2.1.10, Phlp. *in GA*53.3. **-χρῡσος,** ἡ, a gem *of pale gold colour*, Plin.*HN*37.128, 171: as Adj., Lyd.*Mag.*3.70. **-χρώματος,** ον, = λευκόχρως, Phint.ap.Stob.4.23.61ᵃ. ⊛ **-χρωμος,** ον, = foreg., κάμηλος *PGrenf.*2.74.7 (iv A.D.). ⊛**-χρως,** ωτος, ὁ, ἡ, *white-skinned, colourless*, Eub.35, Alex.98.18, Theoc.*Ep.*2.1, Arist.*Phgn.*808ᵇ 4. **-ψᾰρος,** ον, *whitish grey*, ὄνοι *Hippiatr.*14.

**λευκ-όω,** *whiten over*, [πυξίον] Aen.Tact.31.14; βωμόν *IG*2².1672. 140:—Med., λευκοῦσθαι τὰ ὅπλα *whiten their* shields, X.*HG*2.4.25, cf. 7.5.20; λ. πόδα *bare* the foot, *AP*9.403 (Maec.). **II.** mostly in Pass., *to be made* or *become white*, λευκωθεὶς κάρα μύρτοις Pi.*I.*4(3). 69; τοῖχος λελευκωμένος *whitened* or *plastered*, Pl.*Lg.*785a; γραμματεῖον λελευκωμένον, = λεύκωμα I, D.46.11; ὁ ἄνθρωπος οὐ λευκός ἐστιν ἀλλὰ λελεύκωται Arist.*Ph.*185ᵇ29; of a leper, Ph.1.346; λελευκωμένος πίναξ, of the list of proscribed, D.C.*Fr.*109.12. ⊛**-ώλενος,** ον, *white-armed*, epith. of Hera, Il.1.55, 195, etc.; of Persephone, etc., Hes.*Th.*913, Pi.*P.*3.98, etc.; of female slaves, Od.6.239, 18. 198, 19.60; λ. λίνον, perh. with a play on λευκόλινον, of a useless woman, Diogenian.6.22. **-ωμα,** ατος, τό, *tablet covered with gypsum*, used as a public *notice-board*, ἐς λ. γράψαι, ἀναγράφειν, Lys.9.6, Lex ap.D.24.23, *IG*12(5).647.40 (Ceos), *PHib.*1.29.9 (iii B.C.), etc.: hence ἐν λευκώμασιν γραφῆναι to be posted in a list of defaulters, 'to be sold up', *App.Prov.*2.63; of the *proscription-list*, D.C.47.3; of the *album* of senators, Id.55.3: hence οἱ τοῦ λ. senators, Procop.*Arc.*29. **II.** *whiteness*, Arist.*Phgn.*813ᵃ28. **2.** *a white spot in the eye*, caused by a thickening of the cornea, *PGrenf.*1.33.14 (ii B.C.), Dsc.3.84, Gal. 14.775, *Sammelb.*4414.6 (ii A.D.), Aët.7.39 tit. **-ωμᾰτίζομαι,** *to be affected with* λεύκωμα II. 2, Sch.A.*Pr.*499. **-ωμᾰτικός,** ή, όν, *good for* λεύκωμα II. 2, κολλούρια Paul.Aeg.3.22. **-ωματώδης,** ες, *of the nature of* λεύκωμα II. 2, πάθος Erot. s.v. ἀργεμον. **-ωπιάς·** λευκὸς ὀφθῆναι, Hsch. ⊛**-ωσις,** εως, ἡ, = λεύκωμα II. 2, interpol. in *Hippiatr.*11. **II.** *whitening*, Olymp.Alch.p.91 B.; of pearls, etc., *PHolm.*2.36, al. ⊛**-ωτής,** οῦ, ὁ, *whitewasher*, or **-ωτός,** ή, όν, *white-washed*, in dat. -ωτῇ, *IG*1².374.46.

**λευραι·** εὑρίσκω, Hsch.

⊛ **λευρός,** ά, όν (also ός, όν A.*Pr.*371), poet. Adj. *smooth, level, even*, λευρῷ ἐνὶ χώρῳ Od.7.123, Orac.ap.Hdt.1.67; Σικελίας λευροὺς γύας A. l. c.; λ. οἶμος αἰθέρος ib.396; ἐν ψαμάθῳ λευρᾷ E.*Hec.*700 (lyr.); πέδον, πέτρα, Id.*Ph.*836, *Ba.*982 (lyr.); ὁδοί Call. *Aet.Oxy.*2080. 67. **II.** *smooth, polished*, ξίφος Pi.*N.*7.27; δέρμα..λευρὸν ἔθηκε

**λεσχώδης**, ες, *given to scandal*, Vett.Val. in *Cat.Cod.Astr.*8(1). 169.

⊛ **λεσῶνις**, *PAmh.*2.35.11 (ii B.C.); gen. -ώνιος ib.41.15 (ii B.C.); dat. -ώνει ib.40.1 (ii B.C.); later gen -ώνου *Sammelb.*6154.31 (i B.C.), dat. -ώνῃ *BGU*37v (i A.D.): ὁ:—*chief administrator of a temple* in Egypt, ll. cc.:—hence **λεσωνεία**, ἡ, *his office*, *PAmh.*2.35.30 (ii B.C.), Wilcken *Chr.*92 i 13 (ii/iii A.D.):—written **λεσονία**, *BGU*719.10 (i/ii A.D.). (Egypt. *mr šn* = ἀρχιερεῖς.)

**λετμὸς** ἀναδρήσσει· τὸ σῶμα (Ἀ)μερίας φησί, Hsch. **λετωνῆσαι**· ἀφειδῶς παῖσαι κατὰ τῶν ἰσχίων, Id.

**λευγαία**, Maced., = ἴλη, as pr. n. of a regiment, Arr.*An.*2.9.3.

**λευγᾰλέος**, α, ον, (v. λυγρός): 1. of persons, *in sad* or *sorry plight*, *wretched*, πτωχῷ λ. ἐναλίγκιον Od.16.273; λ. ἐσόμεσθα 2.61. Adv. -έως, χωρεῖν to go *in ill plight*, Il.13.723. II. of conditions, etc., *sore*, *baneful*, νῦν δέ με λ. θανάτῳ εἵμαρτο ἁλῶναι, i. e. by drowning, 21.281, cf. Od.15.359; κήδεσιν..λευγαλέοισι ib.399; ἄλγεσι λ. 20.203; πολέμοιο μεθήσετε λ. Il.13.97; ἐν δαῒ λ. 14.387; φρεσὶ λ. πιθήσας 9.119; λ. ἐπέεσσιν 20.109; ἤθεα λ. Hes.*Op.*525; ποινή ib.754; κόρος Thgn.1174; ἀνίαι A.R.1.295; κέντρον Nic.*Th.* 836. 2. rarely of material objects, λ. χιτών *sorry* tunic, Philet. 17. 3. λευγαλέα· διάβροχος, Phot., cf. *EM*561.28 (prob. an error due to misunderstanding of S.*Fr.*785).

**λεύγη**, ἡ, a measure of milk, Hsch.

**Λευΐτης** [ῑ], ου, ὁ, *Levite*, *Ev.Luc.*10.32, Plu.2.671f:—fem. **Λευΐτις**, φυλή v.l. in J.*AJ*3.11.1; **Λευϊτικός**, ή, όν, *Ep.Hebr.*7.11; τὸ -κόν, title of book of *VT*.

⊛ **Λευκᾰθ-έα**, ἡ, goddess worshipped in Thessaly (= Λευκοθέα), *IG* 9(2).422 (Pherae), Ἀρχ.Ἐφ.1910.380 (Larissa). II. neut. pl. **Λευκάθεα**, τά, festival at Teos, *CIG*3066.25:—hence -**εών**, ῶνος (sc. μήν), ὁ, month at Chios, *GDI*5661.25 (iv B.C.); at Teos, *Supp.Epigr.* 2.579.21 (iv B.C.); at Magnesia on Maeander, *Inscr.Magn.*89.6:—also -**ιών**, at Lampsacus, *CIG*3641 *b* 17; -**εος**, at Astypalaea, *SIG* 780 (i B.C.).

**λευκᾰθ-έω**, = λευκαθίζω, perh. to be read in Hes.*Sc.*146 (ὀδόντων.. λευκὰ θεόντων codd.). -**εών**, v. Λευκαθέα. -**ίζω**, *to be white*, Hdt.8.27 (codd. opt.), *PLeid.X.*84, *Gloss.*; of spots on the body, Lxx *Le.*13.38; [τρίχες] λευκαθίζουσαι Babr.22.9; αἶγες χιόνι λ. Id. 45.3, cf. Ael.*NA*17.8,9; λ. οἱ λόφοι, of snow-clad hills, Alciphr.3. 30; οἰκία λ. γύψῳ Epict.*Gnom.*43; of fluids in the eye, *to be colourless*, Cass.*Pr.*27; of eyes, S.E.*P.*1.44:—Pass., λελευκαθισμένη *clad in white*, Lxx *Ca.*8.5. (λευκανθ- is read in Babr., but is against the metre. also in Ael., Alciphr., Epict., Cass., and S.E., and is v.l. in Hdt. l. c., Lxx *Ca.* l. c.; cf. λευκαθέω, ὑπολευκαθίζω.)

**λευκαία**, ἡ, a synonym (perh. a variety) of σπάρτος, used for cordage or tackle, Moschio ap.Ath.5.206f:—written **λευκέα** in *BGU*544. 5 (ii A.D.), Artem.3.59 (who dists. it from κάνναβις), Hsch. II. = λεύκη II. 1, λευκαίας στέφανος *IG*12(1).155 iii 79, iv 118:—hence **Λευκαῖος** Ζεύς, Zeus *of the white poplar*, Paus.5.5.5.

**λευκαίνω**, late aor. 1 inf. λευκᾶναι (v. infr.): pf. Pass. λελεύκασμαι Diph.Siph.ap.Ath.2.54b, Orib.*Fr.*102:—*make white*, λεύκαινον ὕδωρ ξεστῇς ἐλάτῃσιν Od.12.172; ἅλα ῥοθίοισι λ. E.*Cyc.*17; ἐς γένυν ἕρπει λευκαίνων ὁ χρόνος Theoc.14.70; *plaster with whitening*, λευκᾶναι τὰ λευκώματα *Ephes.*3 p.148:—Pass., *to be* or *become white*, Arist.*GA* 730a6, Sopat.8, A.R.1.545, Diph.Siph. l. c.: *to be clarified*, of oil, Orib. l. c. 2. *cause to appear white*, of the effect of dawn on lamplight, E.*IA*157 (anap.). II. Pass., *have a sensation of whiteness*, S.E.*M.*7.191, al. III. intr., *grow white*, E.*Hyps.Fr.*34(60) i 13, Arist.*Pr.*890a9, Lxx *Le.*13.19; ἀφροῖο with foam, Nic.*Al.*170.

**λευκ-άκανθα** [ᾰκ], ἡ, *white thistle*, *Tyrimnus leucographus*, Thphr. *HP*6.4.3, Plin.*HN*21.94 (v. infr.). 2. *tuberous thistle*, *Cnicus tuberosus*, Dsc.3.10, Gal.12.58, Plin.*HN*22.40:—in form -**άκανθος**, ἡ, ib.21.94, v.l. in Gal.6.623. -**άλφῐτος**, ον, *rich in pearl-barley*, Sopat.3. -**άμπυξ**, ῠκος, ὁ, ἡ, τό, *with white headband*, πῦρ Opp. *H.*4.238. -**άνθεμον**, τό, *white-flower*, like χρυσάνθεμον, name of several plants of the genus *Anthemis*, Dsc.3.137, Plin.*HN*21.163:—also -**ανθεμίς**, ίδος, ἡ, ib.22.53. -**ανθής**, ές, *white-blossoming*, Nic.*Th.*530: generally, *blanched*, *white*, καπνός Pi.*N.*9.23 (dub.); λ. κάρα S.*OT*742, cf. *AP*12.165 (Mel.). -**ανθίζω**, v. λευκαθίζω. -**ᾰνίη**, -**ᾰνίηθεν**, etc., v. λαυκανίη. -**ανίων** (?), dub. sens. in *PSI*8.944.5 (iv A.D.). ⊛ -**ανσις**, εως, ἡ, *a growing white*, Arist.*Ph.*224b15, Alex.Aphr.*in Top.*304.1; *clarification* of oil, Gal. 11.484. -**αντέον**, *one must bleach*, κηρόν Dsc.2.83. ⊛ -**αντής**, οῦ, ὁ, *one who makes* or *paints white*, *Gloss.* -**αντικός**, ή, όν, *of* or *for whitening*, δύναμις Sch.Pl.*Tht.*156d. Adv. -κῶς, διατεθῆναι *have a sensation of whiteness*, S.E.*M.*7.192. -**άντυξ**, ῠγος, ἡ, *bright-orbed*, of the moon, Doroth.ap.Heph.Astr.3.20. -**άργιλλος** or -**άργῑλος**, ον, *of* or *with white clay*, Str.9.5.19: as Subst., *leucargilion*, *white clay*, Plin.*HN*17.42. ⊛ -**άς**, άδος, fem. of λευκός: Λ. πέτρη as pr. n. of mythical and real promontories, Od.24.11, Anacr.19, cf. E. *Cyc.*166; Λ. alone, Th.1.30, etc. II. λ. ὀρεινή *mountain deadnettle*, *Lamium maculatum*, Dsc.3.99; λ. ἥμερος *dead-nettle*, *L. moschatum*, ibid. 2. epith. of ἤρυγγος, *white*, Nic.*Th.*849. ⊛ -**ασία**, ἡ, = λεύκωσις II, of artificial pearls, *PHolm.*3.6. -**ασμός**, ὁ, gloss on 'Laban', Ph.1.306. ⊛ -**ασπις**, ῐδος, ὁ, ἡ, *white-shielded*, of a Trojan, Il. 22.294; of the Carians, X.*HG*3.2.15; of a Maced. corps, Plu.*Cleom.* 23; in Trag. esp. of the Argives, A.*Th.*89 (lyr.), S.*Ant.*106 (lyr.), E.*Ph.*1099; κόραι λ. *Lyr.Adesp.*68. -**αυγής**, ές, *white-gleaming*, of a fish, Antiph.217.20. -**ᾰχάτης** [χᾱ], ου, ὁ, *white agate*, Plin.*HN*37. 139. -**έα**, v. λευκαία. -**ελεφάντινα**· λευκὰ ὡς ἐλεφάντινα, Hsch. (λεύκ' ἐλέφαντι Valck. from Il.5.583). -**ερῑνεός**, Att. -**ερίνεως**, ἡ, *white fig-tree*, Ath.3.76c: also as Adj., of the fruit, λ. ἰσχάδες Hermipp.68. -**έρυθρος**, ον, *whitish red*, χροιαί Arist.*Phgn.*806b4; of persons, Ptol.*Tetr.*143. -**ερῳδιός**, ὁ, *white heron* or *spoonbill*, *Platalia leucorodius*, Arist.*HA*593b2. -**η**, ἡ, a cutaneous disease, so called from its colour: a kind of *leprosy* or *elephantiasis*, λέπρην ἢ λεύκην ἔχειν Hdt.1.138; λειχῆνες καὶ λέπραι καὶ λεῦκαι Hp.*Prorrh.*2. 43; λ. ἀλφούς τε Pl.*Ti.*85a; [ἐξάνθημα] ὃ καλεῖται λ. Arist.*HA*518a 13, cf. *Pr.*891a26. II. *white poplar*, *Populus alba*, Thphr.*HP*1. 10.1, al.; used for chaplets, Ar.*Nu.*1007, Eup.14.4, D.18.260, Theoc. 2.121; later λεύκη λευκή *Hippiatr.*22. 2. a place at Athens where the taxes were let out to farmers of the revenue. prob. so called from a *poplar* in the place, And.1.133. III. = ἀνδρόσακες, Ps.-Dsc.3. 133. IV. in pl., *white spots* on the nails, Alex.Aphr.*Pr.*1.146. V. in pl., kind of κόγχοι, = ἀνδροφυκτίδες, Epich.42.11. VI. name of various plasters, Gal.13.414, al. VII. *white clay* or *chalk*, *Gloss.* -**ηναί**, αἱ, *chestnuts from* Λευκαί (or Λεῦκαι) on Mt. Ida, Gal.6. 778. -**ηπᾰτίας** or **λευχηπᾰτίας**, ου, ὁ, *white-livered*, i. e. *cowardly*, *Com.Adesp.*1072. -**ήπειρος**, ον, *with white soil*, [πέτραι] *Gp.*2.6. 39. -**ήρετμος**, ον, *with white oars*, Ἄρης E.*IA*283 (lyr.). -**ήρης**, ες, *white*, *blanched*, θρίξ A.*Pers.*1056, dub. in *PFay.*2 iii 32 (Lyr., ii A.D.).

**Λευκιανή**, ἡ, epith. of Artemis, *BCH*12.269 (Panamara).

**λεύκῐνος**, η, ον, (λεύκη II) *of white poplar*, στέφανοι Arist.*Oec.*1353b 27; μύρον Gal.13.631. 2. of soldiers, *decorated with chaplets of white poplar*, *OGI*266.14 (Pergam., iii B.C.). II. (λευκαία 1) *of hemp*, σχοινία Hsch. s. v. μεσχάλην.

**Λευκιππίδες**, αἱ, *daughters of Leucippus*, nymphs worshipped at Sparta, κόραι Λ. E.*Hel.*1466 (lyr.), cf. Paus.3.13.7.

**λεύκ-ιππος**, ον, *riding* or *driving white horses*, Ibyc.16, Stesich.86, Pi.*P.*4.117, S.*El.*706; of Persephone, Pi.*O.*6.95; λ. Ἀώς B.*Scol.Fr.* 24. 2. λ. ἀγυιαί *full of white horses*, Pi.*P.*9.83. -**ίσκος**, ὁ, a fish, *white mullet*, Hices.ap.Ath.7.306e, Gal.6.713. -**ίτης** [ῑ], ου, Dor. -ᾱς, ὁ, = λευκός II, of a ram, Theoc.5.147.

**λευκο-βᾰφής**, ές, gloss on λευκανθές, Sch.rec.S.*OT*742. -**βρᾰχίων** [ῐ], ον, gen. ονος, *with white arms* or *shoulders*, Suid. s. v. λευκώλενος, Sch.D Il.1.55. -**γειος**, ον, Thphr.*CP*2.4.4, Hsch. s. v. ἄργιλος; ⊛-**γεως**, ων, Str.9.5.18, Eust.332.21 (v. l. **λευκόγαιος**):—*of* or *with white earth*, ll. cc. -**γρᾰφέω**, *paint in white* on a coloured ground, Arist.*Po.*1450b2. -**γρᾰφία**, ἡ, *painting in white*, Phlp. *in Mete.*74.22. -**γρᾰφίς**, ίδος, ἡ, a kind of *clay for painting white*, Plin.*HN*27.103; = μόροχθος λίθος, Dsc.5.134, Aët.2.16. -**γρυψ**, *ossifragus*, *Gloss.* -**δέρμᾰτος**, ον, gloss on sq., Hsch. -**δίφθερος**, ον, *with a white skin*, Id. -**είμων**, = λευχείμων, τᾷ ἐσθᾶτι Melissa *Ep.* 11.1. -**έρυθρος**, ον, = λευκέρυθρος, Procl.*Par.Ptol.*203. -**ζωτος**· τῆς γῆς ἡ μὲν καλεῖται λ., ἡ δὲ μελάνζωτος, Hsch.

⊛ **Λευκοθέα**, Ep. -έη, ἡ, *the white goddess* (cf. Λευκαθέα), name of the sea-goddess Ino, Od.5.334, Pi.*P.*11.2. II. λ., ἡ, *the faculty of seeing white*, Aristo *Stoic.*1.86.

**Λευκόθιον**, τό, name of a building in Delos, *IG*11(2).154 *A* 24, al. (iii B.C.).

**λευκο-θρακία** (sc. ἄμπελος), ἡ, *a white* Bithynian *vine*, *Gp.*5.17. 4. -**θριξ**, τρῐχος, ὁ, ἡ, *white-haired*, *white*, λευκότριχα κριόν Ar. *Av.*971; λευκοτρίχων πλοκάμων E.*Ba.*112 (lyr.); -τριχες ἵπποι Call. *Cer.*121; τῶν λευκοτρίχων Arist.*GA*786a24; λ. πρόβατα Str.16.4. 26. -**θώραξ**, ᾱκος, ὁ, ἡ, *with white cuirass*, X.*An.*1.8.9.

**λευκ-ο(ί)κιον**, τό, *white house*, *PLond.*2.405.12 (iv A.D.).

**λευκό-ϊνος** [ῐ], η, ον, *made of* λευκόϊον, Thphr.*Od.*27, cf. Philonid. ap.Ath.15.675e (-ὅϊνον codd.); ὁ λ. (sc. στέφανος) *AP*11.34 (Phld.):—written **λευκόϊος**, Apollon.*Mir.*45 (s. v. l.). II. *of the colour of* λευκόϊον, δεῖγμα *POxy.*113.5 (ii A.D.). -**ῐον** [ῐ], τό, for λευκὸν ἴον, lit. *white-violet*: I. *gilliflower*, *Matthiola incana*, Theoc.7.64, Dsc.3. 123, etc. II. *snowdrop*, *Galanthus nivalis*, flowering very early, Thphr.*HP*6.8.1; joined with the narcissus and lily in *AP*5.143 (Mel.), 146 (Id.). III. λ. τὸ μέλαν, = ἴον τὸ μέλαν, Hp.*Nat.Mul.* 32. -**καρπος**, ον, *yielding white fruit*, Thphr.*HP*3.18.6. -**καυλος**, ον, *white-stalked*, ib.7.4.6: Comp., ib.5. -**κέρᾰτες**, v. λευκόκρας. -**κερκος**, gloss on μάλουρις, Hsch. -**κέφᾰλος**, ον, gloss on λευκόκρας, Id. -**κηρος**, ον, *made of white wax*, Id. s. v. Δατύς. -**κνημος**, ον, *white-legged*, Anatolius in *Cat.Cod.Astr.*8(3). 188.13. -**κομος**, ον, *white-haired*, Poll.4.139. -**κράμβη**, ἡ, *white cabbage*, *Gp.*12.1.4. -**κρας**· λευκοκέφαλος, Hsch.: pl. -κρατες (-κέρατες cod.)· ἢ διὰ τὸ τοὺς ἐν Εὐβοίᾳ βοῦς λευκοὺς εἶναι, ἢ ἴσως ἀντὶ τοῦ λαμπρούς, Id. -**κύμων** [ῠ], ον, gen. ονος, *white with waves* or *surf*, ᾐόνες E.*Or.*992 (lyr.). -**λῐθος**, ον, *made of white marble*, ἔργα *Supp. Epigr.*4.270 (Panamara); τὰ ἐν τῷ θεάτρῳ λ. *OGI*510 (= *Ephes.*2 No.39, ii A.D.); στήλη, στάλα λ., *IPE*1².40.42 (Olbia), al.; κρηπίς Str.5.3.8; στοαί Id.12.5.3: as Subst., -λίθου στάλα *IPE*1².357 (Chersonesus). ⊛ -**λῑνον**, τό, *white flax* for ropes and rigging, used esp. by the Phoenicians, Hdt.7.25,34,36, Ael.*NA*5.3. -**λόφας**, ᾱ, ὁ, = sq. 1, E.*Ph.*119 (lyr.). -**λοφος**, ον, *white-crested*, Anacr.82, Ar.*Ra.*1016, Philet.4. II. τοῦτ' ἀνὰ λευκόλοφον, prob. on this *white hill*, *AP* 7.636 (Crin.). -**μαινίς**, ίδος, ἡ, *the white sprat* (μαινίς), Polioch. 1. -**μαλλος**, ον, *with white wool*, Eust.403.44. -**μέλᾱς**, αινα, αν, *grey*, Hdn.*Epim.*163, Tz. ad Lyc.334. ⊛ -**μέτωπος**, ον, *with a white forehead*, *Hippiatr.*104, Hsch. s. v. φαλαρός. II. as Subst., name of a bird, *PPetr.*3 p.152 (iii B.C.), *PGrenf.*2.14b3 (iii B.C.), etc.; λ. ἄγριος *PMag.Par.*1.2395, 3148, cf. 2.209 (prob.). -**μήλινος**, ον, *pale-yellow*, ἔμπλαστρος Gal.13.460. -**μῠόχρους**, ουν, *white and mouse-coloured*, *BGU*1258.22 (ii B.C.); esp. of asses, ib.1066.6

βοός *AP*6.116 (Samus). **III.** λευρᾶς σωφροσύνης· τελείας, καὶ ταπεινῆς, κοίλης, ὁμαλῆς, μὴ τραχείας, Hsch.

**λεύσιμος**, ον, (λεύω) *stoning*, χεὶρ λ. E.*Or.*863; λ. καταφθοραί death *by stoning*, Id.*Ion* 1237 (lyr.); θανάτου λεύσιμον ἄταν ib.1240 (lyr.); θανεῖν λ. πετρώματι Id.*Or.*50; λ. δοῦναι δίκην ib.614, cf. *Heracl.*60; λ. ἀραί curses *that will end in stoning*, A.*Ag.*1616; *stoned*, θῦμα ib.1118 (lyr.).

**λευσμός**, ὁ, *stoning*, A.*Eu.*189, E.*Fr.*878.

⊛ **λεύσσω**, by good authors used only in pres. and impf. (in codd. sts. with single σ, as also in *IG* (v. infr.), *CIG*3284 (Smyrna), Hsch.); Ep. impf. λεῦσσον Od.8.200; Ion. λεύσσεσκον Emp.129.5: fut. λεύσω dub. in *AP*15.7, Man.6.93: aor. opt. λεύσσειε ib.487, λεύσσειεν ib. 620.—Poet. Verb, also used in Arc., *IG*5(2).16 (Tegea, iii B.C.), cf. Κλειτορίων..λεύσει· ὁρᾷ *AB*1096:—*look* or *gaze upon*, *see*, c. acc., Il. 1.120, al., Pi.*P.*4.145: c. part., πυρπολέοντας ἐλεύσσομεν Od.10.30; of the gods, ὁ εἰσαιὲν ὁρῶν κύκλος λεύσσει νιν Διός S.*OC*705 (lyr.); λεύσσετε..οἷα πάσχω Id.*Ant.*940 (anap.); used by Com. in mock Trag. phrases, Ar.*Th.*1052, *Ra.*992 (both lyr.). **2.** abs., *look*, *gaze*, λεύσσων ἐπὶ οἴνοπα πόντον Il.5.771; Κυκλώπων ἐς γαῖαν ἐλεύσσομεν Od.9.166; ἐς αὐτόν 8.171, cf. S.*OT*1254; στατὸν εἰς ὕδωρ Id. *Ph.*716 (lyr.); ἐς χέρας E.*Ph.*596 (troch.); πρόσσω καὶ ὀπίσσω λ. Il. 3.110; ὁ μὴ λεύσσων, like ὁ μὴ βλέπων, he that *lives* no more, S.*Tr.*828 (lyr.); so c. acc., εἰ λεύσσει φάος E.*Ph.*1084, cf. *Tr.*269 (lyr.). **3.** c. acc. cogn., λ. φονίου δέργμα δράκοντος A.*Pers.*81 (lyr.); λεπτά, δεινὸν λ. κόραις, E.*Or.*224, 389; φόνον λεῦσσόν τε προσώπῳ and *looked* murder, Theoc.25.137.

**λευστήρ**, ῆρος, ὁ, (λεύω) *one who stones*, E.*Tr.*1039; τὸν Κασσανδρέων λευστῆρα their *oppressor*, Ael.*NA*5.15; so perh. in Hdt.5.67, where the oracle tells Cleisthenes Ἄδρηστον μὲν εἶναι Σικυωνίων βασιλέα, ἐκεῖνον δὲ λευστῆρα (or perh. *a mere stone-thrower*, i.e. ψιλός: Suid., quoting Ael.*Fr.*115, makes it Pass., = ὁ καταλευσθῆναι ἄξιος). **II.** as Adj., λ. μόρος death *by stoning*, A.*Th.*199; λευστῆρα πρῶτον..ῥίψας πέτρον Lyc.1187, cf. Hsch.

**λευστός**, ή, όν, neut. pl. -ά· ὁρατά, λιθοβόλητα, Hsch.

**λευτον**, dub. sens. in *IG*5(2).3, εἰ δ' ἂν λευτον μὲ ἰνφορβίε (Tegea, iv B.C.).

**λευχ-ειμονέω**, *to be clad in white*, Pl.*R.*617c, *CIG*2715.8 (Stratonicea), Str.11.11.8, Ph.1.156. **-είμων**, ονος, ὁ, ἡ, (εἷμα) *clad in white*, Phint.ap.Stob.4.23.61ᵃ; λεώς Ph.2.188, cf. Orph.*H.*51. 11, Aristid.*Or.*48(24).31. **-ηπᾰτίας**, ου, ὁ, = λευκηπατίας, Suid.

⊛ **λεύω**, fut. λεύσω (κατα-) Ar.*Ach.*285: aor. ἔλευσα (κατ-) Hdt.9.5, Th.1.106:—Pass., fut. λευσθήσομαι J.*Ap.*2.27: aor. ἐλεύσθην S.*OC* (v. infr.), Hp.*Ep.*27: (λᾶας):—*stone*, Th.5.60; πέτροις λ. μνῆμα E.*El.* 328; τὸ λευσθῆναι πέτροις S.*OC*435, cf. E.*IA*1350.

**λεχαῖος**, α, ον, (λέχος I) *of* or *for a couch*, φυλλάς A.R.1.1182, cf. Theognost.*Can.*9. **II.** (λέχος 4) *in the nest*, τέκνων ὑπερδέδοικε λεχαίων for her *nestlings*, A.*Th.*292 (Lachm., for λεχέων).

⊛ **λεχεποίη**, ἡ, (λέχος, ποία) *grown with grass fit to make a bed*, i.e. *grassy*, *meadowy*, epith. of various towns, Il.2.697, *h.Ap.*224, *h.Merc.* 88:—masc. ⊛ **λεχεποίης**, ου, of the river Asopus, from its grassy banks, Il.4.383, Orac.ap.Hdt.9.43.—Hom. has both forms in acc. sg. only; the dat. occurs ap.Hdt. l.c.

**λεχέρνα**· ὑπὸ Ἀργείων ἡ θυσία ἐπιτελουμένη τῇ Ἥρᾳ, Hsch.

⊛ **λεχήρης**, ες, *bed-ridden*, E.*Ph.*1541 (lyr.).

**λεχήρια**· ἐνήλατα, Hsch. **λεχμάδ...**· ἤλεκτρον, Id. **λέχνη**· τρόπος, Id.

⊛ **λέχομαι**, *lie down*, pres. only in Hsch. λέχεται (λεύχεται cod.)· κοιμᾶται, cf. Theognost.*Can.*139: pf. part. λελοχυῖα (= λεχὼ γενομένη) Hsch.; other tenses in Ep.: fut. λέξομαι: aor. ἐλεξάμην; also 3 sg. aor. ἔλεκτο, λέκτο; imper. λέξο, λέξεο (v. infr.):—*lie down*, esp. to sleep, λέξεται ὕπνῳ *will lie* asleep, Il.4.131, cf. Od.7.319; λέξομαι εἰς εὐνήν 17.102: aor., πὰρ δ' Ἑλένη ἐλέξατο 4.305; τῷ ἔνι λεξάσθην Il. 14.350; λεξάσθων παρὰ τάφρον *let them bivouac*, 9.67, cf. 8.519; ἔλεκτο Od.19.50, Hes.*Sc.*46; λέκτο Od.4.453, al.; imper. λέξο Il.24.650, Od.10.320; λέξεο Il.9.617, Od.19.598. **II.** causal in Act., *lay asleep*, *lull to sleep*, λέξον με Il.24.635; ἔλεξα Διὸς νόον 14.252. (Goth. *ligan*, Engl. *lie*, etc.)

**λέχος**, εος, τό, poet. Noun, *couch*, *bed*, Il.1.609, al.: in Hom. freq. in pl., *bedstead*, Il.3.448, al. **2.** *bier*, usu. in pl., 24.589, 702, *IG Rom.*4.507*a* 25 (Pergam.), etc. **3.** *marriage-bed*: and generally, *marriage*, ἐμὸν λ. ἀντιόωσαν Il.1.31; δυὸν λ. εἰσαναβαίνοι 8.291; λ. δ' ἤσχυνε καὶ εὐνὴν Ἡφαίστοιο ἄνακτος Od.8.269, cf. 3.403; ἑτέρῳ λέχεϊ, i.e. in adultery, Pi.*P.*11.24; ἰὼ λ. καὶ στίβοι φιλάνορες A.*Ag.*411 (lyr.); τὸ σὸν λ. ξυνῆλθον S.*Aj.*491; λ. Ἡρακλεῖ..ξυστᾶσα Id.*Tr.*27; κρύφιον ὡς ἔχοι λέχος ib.360; λέχους γὰρ..ἁγνὸν δέμας (sc. ἐστί) E. *Hipp.*1003: freq. in pl., ἐκ λεχέων Pi.*P.*9.37; λεχέων Διὸς εὐνάτειρα A.*Pr.*895 (lyr.); τὰ νυμφικὰ λ. S.*OT*1243: ἱέμενοι λεχέων Id.*Tr.*514 (lyr.); γῆμαι μείζω λέχη make a great *marriage*, E.*El.*936; λ. τἀλλότρια ib.1089; μικρὰ μεγάλων ἀμείνω..λέχη ib.1099: hence for the concrete, λ. νεώτερον younger *spouse*, Sapph.75; σὰ λέχεα thy *spouse*, E.*El.*481 (lyr.); ὤλεσας κεδνὸν λ. Id.*Hipp.*835: used by Com. in poet. or mock Trag. passages, λ. γαμήλιον Ar.*Av.*1758; κουρίδιον λ. Id.*Pax*844; παιδὶ συμμεῖξαι λ. Id.*Th.*891. **4.** a bird's *nest*, A. *Ag.*50 (anap.), S.*Ant.*425.

**λέχοσδε**, Adv. *to bed*, Il.3.447, Od.23.294.

**λέχριος**, α, ον, also ος, ον Call.*Del.*236: (v. λικριφίς):—*slanting*, *crosswise*, with a Verb, λ. ὀκλάσας S.*OC*195 (lyr.); λ. ἐκπεσεῖν, χωρεῖν, E.*Hec.*1026 (lyr.), *Med.*1168; τιθέναι τὰς κεφαλὰς ἐπὶ γῆν λεχρίας X.*Cyn.*4.3: metaph., πάντα γὰρ λ. τἀν χεροῖν all the business in hand is *cross*, S.*Ant.*1345 (lyr.).

**λέχρις**, Adv. *crosswise*, λ. τέμνων ἄπο μήδεα πατρός Antim.35, cf. A.R.1.1235, 3.238, 1.160.

⊛ **λεχώ**, όος, contr. οῦς, Cyrenaic gen. λεχός *Berl.Sitzb.*1927.166, dat. λεχοῖ ib.158, *IG*5(1).713, al. (Sparta), λεκχοῖ *Schwyzer*323*D*13 (Delph., v/iv B.C.): ἡ: (λέχος):—*woman in childbed* or *one who has just given birth*, E.*El.*652, 654, 1108, A *Ec.*530, Sor.1.77, etc.; of an animal, Opp.*C.*3.208: pl. λεχοί Orph.*H.*2.10; acc. pl. λεχούς Sch. A.R.2.1010 (cod. Par.).

**λεχῶεν**· ὑλῶδες, βοτανῶδες, Hsch.

**λεχ-ωϊάς**, άδος, ἡ, fem. of sq., νύμφη λ., = λεχώ, Nonn.*D.*48. 848. **-ώϊος**, ον, (λεχώ) *of* or *belonging to childbed*, A.R.2.1014; λ. δῶρα presents *made at the birth*, *AP*7.166 (Diosc. or Nicarch.). **II.** neut. as Subst., Ῥείης..λεχώϊον *the place where* Rhea *bare her child*, Call.*Jov.*14. **-ωΐς**, ΐδος, ἡ, = λεχώ, A.R.4.136, Call.*Dian.*127, *Del.*56, *AP*6.348 (Diod.). **-ώς**, = λεχώ, dub. l. in Lxx *Ep.Je.* 28.

**λεώβατος**· ὁδός, καὶ ἰχθῦς σελαχώδης, Hsch.; cf. λειόβατος.

**λεώδης** (A), ες, (λεώς) = λαώδης, *popular*, *common*, *Gloss.*

**λεώδης** (B), = λιθόλευστος, Theognost.*Can.*9: **λιώδης**, Hsch.; fort. λεώλης. **λεωκόνητος, λεωκόνιτος**, v. λέως.

**Λεωκόρειον**, τό, *the temple of the daughters of Leos*, Th.1.20, 6.57.

**λεωκόρητος, λεώλεθρος, λεώλης**, v. λέως.

**λεωλογέω**, *number the people*, Phoen.1.8.

**λέῳμι, λέων**, v. λῶ.

⊛ **λέων**, οντος, ὁ, Ep. dat. pl. λείουσι Il.5.782, etc., λεόντεσσι *IG*12(2). 285 (Mytil., prob.):—*lion*, ὠμοφάγοι λ. Il. l.c.; αἴθων 18.161; χαροποί Od.11.611; ὀρεσίτροφος 6.130, cf. Hdt.7.126; cf. λίς: metaph., of Artemis, σὲ λέοντα γυναιξὶ Ζεὺς θῆκεν Zeus made thee a *lion* toward women (because she was supposed to cause their sudden death), Il. 21.483; used of savage persons, A.*Ch.*938 (lyr.); but also, of brave men, Id.*Ag.*1259, E.*Or.*1401 (lyr.), 1555; of a baby, Ar.*Th.*514 (but by way of contrast, of a coward, λέοντ' ἄναλκιν, of Aegisthus, A.*Ag.* 1224); οἴκοι μὲν λέοντες, ἐν μάχῃ δ' ἀλώπεκες Ar.*Pax*1189 (lyr.); ἀντὶ λέοντος πίθηκον γίγνεσθαι Pl.*R.*590b; ξυρεῖν ἐπιχειρεῖν λέοντα, of a dangerous undertaking, 'to bell the cat', ib.341c. **2.** *Leo*, the sign in the Zodiac, Eudox.ap.Hipparch.1.2.8, Euc.*Phaen.*p.12 M., Arat.148, *IG*14.1307. **3.** = λεοντῆ, *lion's skin*, Luc.*Hist.Conscr.*10. **4.** as an ornament, *BGU*387 ii 5 (ii A.D.). **II.** a kind of *crab*, Diph.Siph. ap.Ath.3.106c, Ael.*NA*14.9. **III.** a kind of *serpent*, Nic.*Th.*463, f.l. in Artem.2.13. **IV.** = λεοντίασις, Aret.*SD*2.13. **V.** a kind of *dance*, Ath.14.629f, Poll.4.104. **VI.** title of grade of initiates in the mysteries of Mithras, Porph.*Abst.*4.16. **VII.** a *sea-monster*, Ael.*NA*9.49, Opp.*H.*1.367, Nonn.*D.*1.273. **VIII.** = ὀροβάγχη, Dsc.2.142, *Gp.*2.42 tit.

**λεωπάτητος**, v. λέως.

**λεωπετρία**, ἡ, = λεία πέτρα, D.S.3.16 (= Agatharch.34), Lxx *Ez.* 24.8, al.; **λεωπέτρα** is f.l. in Hsch.; cf. λιοπέτριον.

**λεωργός**, όν, (Adv. λέως, ἔργον) *one who will do anything* (cf. ῥᾳδιοῦργος, πανοῦργος), *villainous*, A.*Pr.*5; of actions, λεωργὰ κἀθέμιστα (fort. καὶ θεμιστά) Archil.88.3: Sup. -ότατος X.*Mem.*1.3.9, Ael.*NA* 16.5; cf. λεουργός, λιτουργός.

**λεώς**, ώ, ὁ, Att. and Ion. for λαός (q.v.).

**λέως** or **λείως**, Ion. Adv. *entirely*, *wholly*, *at all*, λείως γὰρ οὐδὲν ἐφρόνεον Archil.112, cf. Hp.ap.Erot. et Gal.19.118:—elsewh. only found in the compds. **λεωργός** (q.v.); **λεω-κόνητος, -κόνιτος**, or **-κόρητος**, *utterly destroyed*, Theognost.*Can.*9, Hsch., Phot.: **λεώλεθρος, λεώλης**, ες, *utterly destroyed*, Hsch. (also **λειώλης**, q.v., cf. λιωλεθρία Hsch.): **λεωπάτητος** [ᾰ], ον, v.l. for λακπάτητος, S.*Ant.* 1275.—The Gramm. expl. it as shortd. for τελέως, A.D.*Pron.*58.12, Erot. l.c. (ubi λίως codd.), Gal. l.c. (ubi male λεῶς), *EM*560.31.

**λεωσφέτερος**, ον, only in Hdt.9.33, λεωσφέτερον ἐποιήσαντο Τεισαμενόν made him *one of their own people*, *their fellow-citizen*.

**λεωφόρος**, ον, v. λαοφόρος. **λῆ, λῆς**, etc., v. λῶ. ⊛ **ληβόλε**· λιθοβόλε, ἄξιε λιθασθῆναι, Hsch. **ληβολία**· δημοσία κοπρία, Id.

⊛ **λήγω**, Ep. aor. ἔλληξα A.R.2.84:—*stay*, *abate*, Ἰδομενεὺς δ' οὐ λῆγε μένος μέγα Il.13.424, cf. 21.305; λ. γόον *AP*7.549 (Leon. Alex., s.v.l.): c. gen., οὐδέ κεν ὧς ἔτι χεῖρας ἐμὰς λήξαιμι φόνοιο *would stay* my hands *from* slaughter, Od.22.63. **II.** more freq. intr., *leave off*, *cease*, of speaking, etc., οὐ λήξω, πρὶν.. Il.19.423; οὐδέ τ' ἔληγε θεὸς μέγας 21.248; ἐν σοὶ μὲν λήξω, σέο δ' ἄρξομαι 9.97, cf. Hes. *Op.*368; λ. [ἡ ἀτραπὸς] κατὰ Ἀλπηνὸν πόλιν *comes to an end* at.., Hdt.7.216, cf. Th.7.6; ἡ ἡμέρη ἔληγε Hdt.9.52, cf. X.*An.*7.6.6; of heat, wind, rain, etc., λ. μένος ἠελίοιο Hes.*Op.*414; λήξαντος οὔρου Pi.*P.*4.292; ψακὰς λ., νότος λ., A.*Ag.*1534 (lyr.), S.*Aj.*258 (anap.); ἅμα τῷ τοῦ σώματος ἄνθει λήγοντι Pl.*Smp.*183e. **2.** c. gen., *stop*, *cease from* a thing, ἔριδος, χόλοιο, φόνοιο, ἀπατάων, πόνου, χοροῖο, Il.1. 319, 224, 6.107, Od.13.294, Il.10.164, 3.394; ἀοιδῆς Hes.*Th.*48 (dub. l.); κλαυμάτων A.*Pers.*705 (troch.); θρήνων, γόων, S.*El.*104 (anap.), 353; ὀδύνης Pl.*Phdr.*255d; λ. τοῦ βίου, i.e. to *die*, X.*Ap.*8; φύλλα πτόρθοιο λ. Hes.*Op.*421; also λ. ἀπ' ἔργων A.R.4.928: c. dat., λ. τῇ αὐθαδίᾳ *PTeb.*16.9 (ii B.C.). **3.** c. part., ὁπότε λήξειεν ἀείδων Il. 9.191, cf. Od.8.87; οὐ πρὶν λήξω..ἐναρίζων Il.21.224; εὖτ' ἂν φλέγων..ἥλιος χθόνα λήξῃ A.*Pers.*365, cf. 831; τὸ σκέλος ῥίψαντες λήγομεν Ar.*Pax*332; λήγει κινούμενον Pl.*Phdr.*245c, etc. **4.** with Preps., λ. ἔς τι Hdt.4.39, Plot.3.2.2; ἐπὶ τῶν ὀνειδῶν App.*Hisp.*75 (73). **5.** Gramm., *terminate*, of a word, εἰς ē λ. A.D.*Pron.*11.9, cf. D.T.639.20; also λήγεσθαι c. dat., μακρᾷ, βραχείᾳ, *An.Ox.*2.

313. 6. *follow logically*, Them.*in Ph.*115.5; τὸ λῆγον, opp. τὸ ἡγούμενον, the *consequent*, opp. antecedent, Chrysipp.*Stoic.*2.70, S.E.*P.*2.111,112. 7. of months, = φθίνω, *IG*12(3).325.20 (Thera); also περὶ λήγοντα τὸν ἐνιαυτόν D.24.98; τοῦ χειμῶνος -οντος Th.5.81; so perh. εἰς τὸ λῆγον is to be read for εἰς τὸ λῆγος in *Gp.*12.1.4.

**Λήδα**, ας, ἡ, *Leda*, A.*Ag.*914, etc.:—the forms **Λήδη**, ης, only Ep., as Od.11.298.

**λήδᾰνον** or **λάδᾰνον** [λᾱ], τό, (λῆδον) = κίσθος, *gum-ladanum*, τὸ λήδανον, τὸ καλέουσι Ἀράβιοι λάδανον Hdt.3.112, cf. 107, Hp.*Mul.*2.189, Plu.2.397a, Ruf.ap.Gal.12.425, Heraclid.ib.436, Gal.12.28, al., Wilcken *Chr.*273 i 15 (ii/iii A.D.). (λη- Hdt. ll. cc., Hp. l. c. (cod. opt.), Plu. l. c., also (in verse) Ruf. l. c.; λα- Heraclid., Gal., Wilcken *Chr.* ll. cc., v. l. in Hp. l. c.).

**ληδάριον** [ᾰ], τό, Dim. of λῆδος, Ar.*Av.*715, 915 (v. l. ληδάριον).

⊛ **ληδεῖν**· κοπιᾶν, κεκμηκέναι, and **ληδήσας**· κεκμηκώς, κοπιάσας, Hsch.

**λήδιον** or **ληδίον**, τό, Dim. of λῆδος, *IG*2$^2$.1514.45, 1516.23, 1517.149, 151 (iv B.C.):—also **λῄδιον** or **ληδίον**, τό, Men.1028, Clearch.25, Macho ap.Ath.13.582d sq., Hsch.; cj. Toup for λήϊον, Suid.; cf. λῆδος, ληϊδιώδεις.

**λῆδον**, τό, *shrub* from which the gum λήδανον exudes, *Cistus cyprius*, Dsc.1.97, Plin.*HN*26.47.

⊛ **λῆδος**, Dor. **λᾶδος**, εος, τό, *a cheap common dress*, esp. *a light summer dress*, Alcm.97 (so Did.; **λᾶιδος** Hsch.): more freq. in Dim. forms, λήδιον or ληδίον, τό, and ληδάριον (qq. v.).

**λῄζομαι**, v. ληΐζομαι.

⊛ **λήθαιος** or **ληθαῖος**, α, ον, (λήθη) *of* or *causing forgetfulness*, πτερόν, of Sleep, Call.*Del.*234; σκότος Lyc.1127, etc. 2. of persons, *oblivious*, opp. ἔμφρων, S.E.*M.*7.129. II. *of* or *from Lethe*, ἄκατος *AP*9.279 (Bass.); v. λήθη II. III. λ. λίθος, = μελιτίτης λ., Ps.-Dsc.476 ed. Sarac.

**ληθάνεμος**, v. λαθάνεμος. **ληθάνω**, v. ἐκληθάνω, λανθάνω B.

⊛ **ληθαργ-έω**, *forget*, *PMag.Lond.*122.91:—Pass., *CIG*2804 (Aphrodisias), Sch.Pi.*N.*6.30. **-ία**, ἡ, *drowsiness*, *Com.Adesp.*344 (pl.). **-ικός**, ή, όν, *affected by lethargic fever*, Hp.*Coac.*136, Praxag. ap.Gal.17(1).889, Ruf.ap.Orib.7.26.129, 8.24.30, *AP*9.141. **-ος**, ον, (λήθη) *forgetful*, c. gen., ib.5.151 (Mel.), 12.80 (Id.): abs., Men.1029, Phld.*Rh.*1.6 S.:—later word for ἐπιλήσμων, acc. to Phryn.390. 2. *lethargic*, ἀλήθαργος (sic) εἰς ὕπνον ἐφερόμην *POxy.*1381.100 (ii A.D.). II. as Subst., ὁ and ἡ, *lethargy*, Hp.*Morb.*2.65, al., Lyc.241, Ant.Lib.23.2, Gal.10.931, Paul.Aeg.3.9: in pl., Arist.*Somn.*457$^a$3, Chrysipp.*Stoic.*3.57; coupled with μελαγχολία, ibid. b. *lethargic fever*, Hp.*Aph.*3.30. Cf. λαίθαργος. **-ώδης**, ες, = ληθαργικός, Dsc.*Ther.*15, Gal.7.466. Adv. -δῶς Dsc.4.64.

**ληθεδ-ᾰνός**, ή, όν, *causing forgetfulness*, φάρμακον Luc.*Salt.*79, *Philops.*39. **-ών**, όνος, ἡ, poet. for λήθη, *AP*7.17 (Tull. Laur.), *APl.*4.244 (Agath.).

**λήθ-η**, Dor. **λάθα**, ἡ, *forgetting*, *forgetfulness*, personified in Hes.*Th.*227; μηδέ σε λήθη αἱρείτω Il.2.33; [Περσεφόνη] βροτοῖς παρέχει λήθην, βλάπτουσα νόοιο Thgn.705; κακοῦ λ. S.*Ph.*878, cf. E.*Ba.*282, *Or.*213; λήθην ποιεύμενος τά μιν ἐόργεε *forgetting*.., Hdt.1.127; λ. ποιεῖν τινος S.*Fr.*259; Λήθην..κωφήν, ἄναυδον Id.*Fr.*670; χρόνος πάντα..ἐς λ. ἄγει Id.*Fr.*954; τῶν ἰδίων λ. λαβών Timocl.6.5, cf. Phld.*Rh.*1.254 S.; τῶν αὑτοῦ κακῶν ἐπάγεσθαι λ. Men.467; παρέχειν Pl.*Phdr.*275a; ἐμποιεῖν Id.*Phlb.*63e; λήθην ἐμποιῆσαι τῶν πεπραγμένων Isoc.1.8; εἰς λήθην ἐμβαλεῖν τινα Aeschin.3.205; λήθη λαμβάνει, ἔχει τινά, Th.2.49, D.18.283; λήθη τινὸς ἐγγίγνεταί τινι X.*Mem.*1.2.21; εἰς λ. ἀφιγμένα *forgotten*, Phld.*Ir.*p.19 W. II. after Hom., of *a place of oblivion* in the lower world, Λήθης δόμοι Simon.184.6; τὸ Λήθης πεδίον Ar.*Ra.*186; τὸ τῆς Λ. π. Pl.*R.*621a, D.H.8.52; Λ. ὕδωρ Luc.*DMort.*13.6, Paus.9.39.8, Aesop.168; also, ὁ τῆς Λήθης ποταμός, of the river Λιμαίας in Lusitania, Str.3.3.4, 5, cf. App.*Hisp.*73 (71). (Λήθη as pr. n. of a river is not found.) **-ηκέα**· εἰς λήθην ἄγοντα φάρμακα, Hsch. **-ήμων**, ον, only dat. pl. ληθήμοσι (ληθημόνοισι cod.)· ληθάργοις, Id. **-ιος**, ον, *causing forgetfulness*, πόμα Zonar. II. = λαθραῖος, Hsch.

**ληθομέριμνος**, ον, *banishing cares*, νύξ Orph.*H.*3.6 codd. (λυσιμ- Abel).

**λῆθον**· βαλιόν, Hsch.

**λῆθος**, Dor. **λᾶθος**, εος, τό, = λήθη, Theoc.23.24.

**ληθότης**, ητος, ἡ, = λήθη, Suid., Zonar.

**λήθω**, **λήθομαι**, collat. forms of λανθάνω, λανθάνομαι (q. v.).

**Ληθώ**, = Λητώ, Pl.*Cra.*406a.

**ληθώδης**, ες, (λήθη) *lethargic*, ὕπνος Hsch. s. v. κῶμα.

**ληϊάνειρα** [ῐᾰν]· ἡ ποιοῦσα τοὺς ἄνδρας γυναικῶν ἐρᾶν, Hsch.

**ληϊ-άς**, άδος, ἡ, poet. fem. of ληΐδιος, *taken prisoner*, *captive*, γυναῖκες Il.20.193; Ep. dat. ληϊάδεσσι A.R.1.612. ⊛ **-βοτήρ**, ῆρος, ὁ, (λήϊον A) *crop-consuming*, *crop-destroying*, Suid., etc.: fem., σῦς ληϊβότειρα Od.18.29.

⊛ **ληΐδιος**, α, ον, (ληΐς) *taken as booty*, *captive*, *AP*6.20 (Jul. Aegypt.), *APl.*4.203 (Id.), Tryph.679.

**ληϊδιώδεις**· τριβωνιώδεις (-ίδες cod.), Hsch.; cf. λήδιον.

**ληΐζομαι**, Ep. and Ion., Hes.*Op.*702, Hdt.4.112; **λῄζομαι**, X.*HG*5.1.1, *AP*9.410 (Tull. Sab.), etc.; also **λεΐζομαι**, ib.6.169; Att. impf. ἐλῃζόμην Th.1.24, etc.: Ep. fut. ληΐσσομαι Od.23.357: aor. ἐληϊσάμην Hdt.3.47, And.1.101; Ep. ληΐσσατο Il.18.28; Att. ἐλῄσατο E.*Tr.*866: pf. in pass. sense λέλῃσμαι, v. infr. II:—*seize*, *carry off as booty*, either men or things, δμῳαὶ ἃς Ἀχιλεὺς ληΐσσατο Il. l. c., cf. Od.1.398, 23.357, Hdt.3.47, 4.110, al.; ἐκ δόμων δάμαρτα.. ἐλῄσατο E. l. c.; ἐκ τῆς Ἀττικῆς X.*HG*5.1.1, etc.: generally, *win*, *acquire*, ὄλβον ἀπὸ γλώσσης ληΐσσεται Hes.*Op.*322; οὐ γάρ τι γυναικὸς ἀνὴρ ληΐζετ' ἄμεινον τῆς ἀγαθῆς ib.702, cf. Semon.6. 2. *plunder*, *despoil*, esp. by raids or forays, ἀλλήλους Th.1.5, cf. 3.85, 5.115, And.1.101, etc.; τὴν Κολχίδα X.*An.*4.8.23; τὴν θάλατταν D.S.11.88, Jul.*Or.*7.210a: metaph., λ. τὴν τῶν ζῴων φύσιν Pl.*Epin.*976a. 3. abs., *plunder*, *SIG*38 *B* 20 (Teos, v B.C.), Hdt.4.112, Lys.20.24 (prob.), etc. II. Act. ληΐζω occurs in several Mss. of Th.3.85, and all Mss. of Id.4.41:—so in Pass., *to be carried off*, ἐκ γῆς βαρβάρου λελῃσμένη E.*Med.*256; γυναικὸς..οὐ βίᾳ λελῃσμένης Id.*Tr.*373; ληϊσθεῖσα A.R.4.400; οὔ τί που λελῄσμεθ' ἐξ ἄντρων λέχος; I *have* not surely *had* my wife *carried off*.., E.*Hel.*475; ληϊζόμενος *robbed*, Luc.*Gall.*14.

**ληΐη**, ἡ, Ion. for λεία (q. v.). **λήϊμνος**· εὔβοτος, Hsch.

**ληΐνη**, ἡ, = Lat. *laena*, *cloak*, *PGiss.*76.5 (ii A.D.).

**ληϊνόμος** [ῐ], ον, *dwelling in the country*, *APl.*4.94 (Arch.).

**λήϊον** (A), Dor. **λᾷον** (q. v.), τό, *standing crop*, ὡς δ' ὅτε κινήσῃ Ζέφυρος βαθὺ λ. Il.2.147, al., cf. Hes.*Sc.*288, Hdt.1.19, Pherecr.20 (pl.); τοῦ σίτου τὸ λ. Arist.*HA*612$^a$32; λ. σίτου βαθύ Arr.*An.*1.4.1; λήϊά τε σταχύων *IG*14.1389 ii 10. 2. in later Poets, also, *corn-field*, Theoc.10.42 (in Dor. form); ληΐου κόμῃ Babr.88.3. 3. = λεία, *booty*, *SIG*3g (Susa, from Didyma, v B.C.).

**λήϊον** (B), τό, v. λήδιον.

**λη-ΐς**, Dor. **λᾱΐς**, ΐδος, ἡ, Ep. form of λεία, *booty*, *spoil*, mostly of cattle, ληΐδα δ' ἐκ πεδίου συνελάσσαμεν.., πεντήκοντα βοῶν ἀγέλας, κτλ. Il.11.677, cf. X.*Lac.*13.11; then of all kinds of *booty*, Il.9.138, 18.327, Od.10.41; πλαζόμενοι κατὰ ληΐδα 3.106: in A.*Th.*331 (lyr.), concrete for αἰχμάλωτοι, cf. A.R.1.695; cf. ληϊάς. 2. without any notion of plunder, *cattle*, *stock* (cf. λεία), ληΐδ' ἀέξειν, βουκολίας τ' ἀγέλας τε καὶ αἰπόλια πλατέ' αἰγῶν Hes.*Th.*444, cf. Theoc.25.97. **-ϊσθιῶν**· τρεπόμενος, Hsch. **-ϊσμαδία**· αἰχμάλωτος, λεληϊσμένη, Id. **-ϊστήρ**, ῆρος, ὁ, v. λῃστήρ. ⊛ **-ϊστής**, οῦ, ὁ, = Att. λῃστής, *h.Bacch.*7, Hdt.6.17, *SIG*38 *B* 20 (Teos, v B.C.), Democr.260, A.R.1.750. **-ϊστός**, ή, όν, *to be carried off as booty*, *to be won by force*, Il.9.406: also in form **λεϊστός**, ib.408, *Inscr.Prien.*268 c 5. **-ϊστύς**, ύος, ἡ, *plundering*, ζῆν ἀπὸ..ληϊστύος Hdt.5.6. **-ΐστωρ**, ορος, ὁ, = ληϊστήρ, Od.15.427, Nic.*Th.*347: in Prose **λῄστωρ**, *Sammelb.*4309.14 (iii B.C.) II. as Adj., ληΐστορι χαλκῷ *AP*9.649 (Maced.). **-ϊτιαί**· ἡγεμονίαι, στρατιαί, Hsch. **-ῖτις**, ιδος, ἡ, *she who makes* or *dispenses booty*, epith. of Athena, Il.10.460, Paus.5.14.6. II. Pass., = ληϊάς, A.R.1.818, Lyc.105.

**ληϊτοάρχαι**· οἱ καθηγούμενοι τῶν θυσιῶν καὶ ἑστιάσεων, καὶ ἀρχαὶ καὶ ἱερεῖς, Hsch. (Cf. λήταρχος.)

⊛ **λήϊτον**, τό, (λαός, λεώς) *town-hall*, *council-chamber*, as the Achaeans of Achaea Phthiotis called it, Hdt.7.197; = δημόσιον acc. to Plu.*Rom.*26, Id.2.280a:—Hsch. has **λάϊτον**· τὸ ἀρχεῖον, **λαΐτων**· τῶν δημοσίων τόπων; cf. λαιετόν, λαῖστρον, Suid., Zonar.:—Hsch. also quotes **ληΐτη**, **λητή**, = ἱέρεια, a *public priestess*.

**ληϊτουργέω**, **-ουργός**, early forms of λητ-, λειτ- (q. v.).

⊛ **ληκάω**, (ληκώ) = λαικάζω, aor. inf. ληκῆσαι Pherecr.177:—Pass., of the woman, Ar.*Th.*493; ληκούμεσθ' (sic) Pherecr. l. c. II. ληκᾶν· τὸ πρὸς ᾠδὴν ὀρχεῖσθαι, Hsch.

**ληκέω**, Dor. and later Gr. **λᾱκέω**, *crack*, *crackle*, Theoc.2.24; *burst asunder*, ἐλάκησε μέσος *Act.Ap.*1.18; λακῆσαι τὰς ψύλλας ποιήσεις *Gp.*13.15.5:—in Call.*Iamb.*1.183 P. the context is broken.

**λήκημα**, ατος, τό, (ληκάω) *wenching*, in pl., Epicur.*Fr.*414; or perh. from ληκέω (cf. sq.), *bawling*, = ἀνακραύγασμα.

**ληκητής**, οῦ, ὁ, (ληκέω) *bawler*, ἀγοραίων λ. ἐπέων Timo 42.

**ληκίνδα** παίζειν, *beat time*, *tattoo*, Luc.*Lex.*8, A.D.*Adv.*152.11.

**ληκτέον**, (λαγχάνω) *one must lay claim to*, ὅλου τοῦ κλήρου Is.7.23.

**ληκ-τήριος**, α, ον, (λήγω) *extreme*, νῆσον εἰς ληκτηρίαν to *the farthest bounds of* the island, Lyc.966, cf. 1391 (s. v. l.). **-τικός**, ή, όν, *causing to cease*, ὀδύνης v. l. in Hp.*Liqu.*6; *terminal*, [συλλαβαί] A.D.*Synt.*7.10; ζῴδιον *Cat.Cod.Astr.*7.194.18 (Rhetor. ex Teucro). **-τός**· καταληπτός, Hsch.

**ληκυθ-ιάδες**· ἐνώτια ποιά, Hsch. ⊛ **-ίζω**, *declaim in a hollow voice*, *as though speaking into a* λήκυθος, τραγῳδὸς Μοῦσα -ίζουσα Call.*Fr.*10.13 P., Phryn.*PS* p.86 B., Poll.4.114, 7.182: c. acc., θέσεις λ. *declaim* commonplaces, Str.13.1.54. **-ιον**, τό, Dim. of λήκυθος, *small oil-flask*, Ar.*Ra.*1200–1246, D.24.114, *PTeb.*221 (ii B.C.), Anon.ap. Suid., etc. II. name for the Trochaic hephthemimer, originating with the form ληκύ|θιον ἀπ|ώλεσ|εν in Ar. l. c., Heph.6.2. **-ισμός**, ὁ, *hollow*, *affected speaking*, Plu.2.1086e, Anon.ap.Suid. **-ιστής**, οῦ, ὁ, *one who declaims in a hollow voice*, S.*Fr.*1063.

**ληκῠθο-ποιός**, ὁ, *maker of oil-flasks*, Str.15.1.67. **-πώλης**, ου, ὁ, *seller of oil-flasks*, Poll.7.182.

⊛ **λήκῠθος** (Dor. **λάκυθος** [ᾱ] *IG*4$^2$(1).123.130 (Epid., iv B.C.)), ἡ, *oil-flask*, δῶκεν δὲ χρυσέῃ ἐν ληκύθῳ ὑγρὸν ἔλαιον Od.6.79, cf. 215, Hp.*Morb.*4.51, Ph.*Bel.*102.41, etc.; *casket for unguents*, *cosmetics*, etc., S.*Fr.*130; αἱ δὲ λήκυθοι μύρου γέμουσι Ar.*Pl.*810, cf. *Fr.*207; buried or burnt with the dead, Id.*Ec.*538, 996, 1032, cf. *IG*14.865, *CIG*8346*k*. 2. in pl., *rhetorical bombast*, Cic.*Att.*1.14.3, Plin.*Ep.*1.2.4. II. *projecting cartilage on the gullet*, *Adam's apple*, = βρόχθος, Clearch.72.

**ληκῠθοφόρος**, ον, *carrying an oil-flask*, Poll.3.154.

**ληκῠτία**, ἡ, = λήκυθος, *BGU*1160.11 (pl.).

**ληκώ**, οῦς, ἡ, *membrum virile* (whence ληκάω), Hsch., Phot.

⊛ **λῆμα**, ατος, τό, (λῶ) *will*, *desire*, *purpose*, Epich.182 (prob. l.): concrete, λ. Κορωνίδος *wilful* Coronis, Pi.*P.*3.25; μητρῷον λ. thy *proud* mother, S.*El.*1427; λήματος κάκη weakness *of will*, cowardice,

A.*Th.*616; ἥκιστα τοὐμὸν λ. ἔφυ τυραννικόν E.*Med.*348; ἐς τὸ κέρδος λ. ἔχων ἀνειμένον Id.*Heracl.*3, cf. 199, *Alc.*981 (lyr.), *Ba.*1000 (lyr.). II. *temper of mind, spirit*, either, 1. in good sense, *courage, resolution*, εὔτολμον ψυχῆς λ. Simon.140; γενναῖον λ. Pi.*P.* 8.45, cf. *N.*1.57; αἴθων λ. fiery *in courage*, A.*Th.*448; δύο λήμασιν ἴσους Ἀτρείδας Id.*Ag.*122 (lyr.); τοξουλκῷ λήματι πιστοί relying on their archer *spirit*, Id.*Pers.*55 (anap.); ἀρείφατον λ. Id.*Fr.*147; πέτρας τὸ λ. κἀδάμαντος E.*Cyc.*596; λ. οὐκ ἄτολμον Ar.*Nu.*457 (lyr.); καθ' Ἡρακλέα.. τὸ λ. ἔχων Id.*Ra.*463; or, 2. in bad sense, *insolence, arrogance, audacity*, ὅσον λ. ἔχων ἀφίκου S.*OC*877 (lyr.); ὦ λῆμ' ἀναιδές ib.960; δῆλον.. τἀνθρώπου 'στι τὸ λῆμα Ar.*Nu.*1350 (lyr.).—Poet. word, also used in Ion. Prose, in signf. *spirit, courage*, ἔργα χειρῶν τε καὶ λήματος Hdt.5.72; λήματος πλέος ib.111, cf. 7.99, 9.62: and in late Prose, as D.S.2.58 (pl.), J.*BJ*3.10.4, Luc.*Dem.Enc.*50, etc.; defined by Andronic.*Pass.*p.575 M.

**λημᾰλέος**, α, ον, (λήμη) *bleared*, of the eyes, Luc.*Lex.*4.

**λημᾰτ-ίας**, ου, ὁ, *high-spirited*, λ. κάνδρεῖος εἶ Ar.*Ra.*494; cf. sq. **-ιάω**, *to be high-spirited*, v.l. in Ar. l.c. **-ιον**, τό, Dim. of λῆμα, = φρόνημα, Hsch. (pl.). **-όομαι**, in pf. Pass. λελημάτωμαι· λῆμα ἔχω εἰς τὸ ἔργον, Id.

⊛**λημ-άω**, only pres., (λήμη) *to be bleared*, of the eyes, Hp.*Prorrh.* 2.18; *to be blear-eyed* or *purblind*, λημᾶν κολοκύνταις *to have one's eyes running* pumpkins, Ar.*Nu.*327, cf. Hsch.; λ. καὶ ἀμβλυώττειν Luc.*Tim.*2, etc.: metaph., Κρονικαῖς λήμαις λ. τὰς φρένας Ar.*Pl.* 581. **-η**, ἡ, *a humour that gathers in the corner of the eye, rheum*, Hp. *VM*19, *Prog.*2: in pl., *sore eyes*, Ar.*Lys.*301 (v. Sch.): metaph., ἡ τοῦ Πειραιέως λ. the *eye-sore* of Piraeus, of Aegina, Periclesap.Arist. *Rh.*1411ᵃ15, Plu.*Per.*8; Κρονικαὶ λῆμαι old prejudices *that dim the mind's eye*, Ar.*Pl.*581; ὄψεως λ. ἡ δεισιδαιμονία Plu.2.1101c. (Cf. λάμας.) **-ηρός**, ἡ, όν, *misty*, λημηρῇ νεφέλῃ εἰλυμένος ὄσσε Heliod. ap.Stob.4.36.8. **-ίον**, τό, Dim. of λήμη, Hp.*Coac.*214, *Epid.*1.5.

**λῆμμα**, ατος, τό, (λαμβάνω) *anything received*, opp. δόμα, Antig.ap. Plu.2.182e; λ. καὶ ἀνάλωμα *receipt* and expense, Lys.32.20, Pl.*Lg.* 920c, Anaxandr.26; ἀνενεγκεῖν (ἐν- Pap.) ἐν λήμματι place to *credit*, *PEleph.*15.4 (iii B.C.), cf. *BGU*346.2 (i B.C.), etc.: generally, *gain, profit*, D.5.12, etc.; λ. τι κέρδους Id.45.14; esp. of *unjust gain*, Din. 1.45; παντὸς ἥττων λήμματος unable to resist any temptation *of gain*, D.19.339; ὥσπερ ἂν τρυτάνη ἐπὶ τὸ λ. ῥέπειν Id.18.298; λ. λαβεῖν Id.21.28, 27.39: freq. in pl., S.*Ant.*313, D.8.25, etc.; τὰ λ. τοῦ ἀργυρίου Id.49.57; λημμάτων μετέχειν Id.58.40; τἀπὸ Θρᾴκης λ. ἕλκουσι δεῦρο Antiph.196. II. in Logic, *statement taken* as true, *assumption*; esp. *premiss* in a syllogism, ἐπὶ λ. τῷ τοιούτῳ A.D.*Synt.*242. 13; τὰ οἰκεῖα τῇ ἐπιστήμῃ λ. Arist.*Top.*101ᵃ14; λήμματα τιθέναι ib. 156ᵃ21, cf. Gell.9.16, Phld.*Rh.*1.9S.; prop. *the major premiss* (the minor being πρόσληψις), Crinis*Stoic.*3.269; later, ἀποδεικτικὰ λήμματα παρασχεῖν offer scientific *proofs*, Gal.14.627. III. *matter, substance*, or *argument* of a sentence, etc., opp. form or style (λέξις), D.H.*Dem.*20, Longin.15.10, etc.: hence, *title* or *argument* of an epigram, Lat. *lemma*, Mart.14.2; *theme* or *thesis*, Plin.*Ep.*4.27.3, Mart.10.59; *nutricis lemmata*, 'baby songs', Aus.*Ep.*12.90. IV. in Lxx, *burden* laid on one, *commission received*, esp. of *prophecy*, *Na.* 1.1, *Je.*23.33, al.; even, λῆμμα ἰδεῖν *Hb.*1.1, cf. *La.*2.14.

⊛**λημμᾰτ-ίζω**, *place to credit*, *PFlor.*361.7 (iii A.D.), etc. II. *assume, posit*, τὰ λελημματισμένα *premisses*, A.D.*Synt.*101.27. ⊛**-ικός**, ή, όν, *quick at seizing opportunity*, Hp.*Decent.*3. **-ιον**, τό, Dim. of λῆμμα, Ptol.*Alm.*1.10, Olymp.*in Mete.*261.27, Dam.*Pr.*233, 396, al., Zonar. **-ιστής**, οῦ, ὁ, *receiver* of taxes, *PKlein.Form.*51 (vi A.D.).

**Λημνιακός**, Dor. Λᾱμν-, v. Λῆμνος.

**Λημνιασταί**, οἱ, *worshippers of the Lemnian deities*, *IG*12(1).43 (Rhodes, i B.C.). ⊛**Λήμνιος**, v. Λῆμνος.

**λημνίσκος**, ὁ, *woollen fillet* or *ribbon*, by which chaplets were fastened, *IG*2².1297.11 (iii B.C.), al., Plb.18.46.12, Posidon.9 J., Plu. *Sull.*27, *AP*12.123; of *ribbons* attached to bird's feet, Callix.2; *surgical bandage*, Mnesith.ap.Orib.*inc.*15.16; *pledget*, Heliod.ap.Orib. 50.49.1, Gal.19.97, etc.

**Λῆμνος**, ἡ, Dor. **Λᾶμνος**, *Lemnos*, Il.1.593, al., Od.8.283; sacred to Hephaestus, Sch.A.R.1.851, etc.: **Λαμνόθεν**, Adv. *from Lemnos*, Pi. *P.*1.52: —Adj. **Λήμνιος**, α, ον, *Lemnian*, πῦρ S.*Ph.*800, Ar.*Lys.*299; Λ. ἔργα, prov. from the wickedness of certain Lemnian women, Hdt. 6.138, cf. A.*Ch.*631 (lyr.); Λ. ἄμπελοι Ar.*Pax* 1162:—also **Λημνιακός**, Dor. Λαμν- Call.*Fr.*1.44 P.:—also fem. **Λημνιάς** (Λαμνιάς), άδος, Pi.*O.*4.22; **Λημνίς**, ίδος, μίλτος Nic.*Th.*865.

**λημ-ότης**, ητος, ἡ, (λήμη) *soreness of eyes*, Sch.Ar.*Nu.*326. **-ύδριον**, τό, Dim. of λήμη, Gal.17(1).868.

**λημψαπόδοσις**, εως, ἡ, *receipts and payments*, *PLond.*1.77.50 (vi A.D.).

**λῆμψις**, = λῆψις (q.v.): **λήμψομαι**, = λήψομαι, v. λαμβάνω.

**λημ-ώδης**, ες, (λήμη) *full of rheum*, Alex.Trall.2. **-ωσις**, εως, ἡ, *secretion of rheum in the eyes*, *PMed.* in *Sitzb.Heidelb.Akad.*1913 (13).33, 41.

**λῆν**, inf. of λῶ; but λήν· λίαν, Hsch.

**Ληνᾰγέτας**, α, ὁ, (Λῆναι) *leader of Bacchanals*, θοᾶν Ληναγέτα Βακχᾶν *BMus.Inscr.*902 (Halic., iii B.C.).

**Λῆναι** (Ληναί Hsch.), αἱ, (ληνός I) *Bacchanals*, Heraclit.14, Str.10. 3.10, D.P.702, 1155, Theoc.26 tit. (Arc. acc. to Hsch.)

**Ληνᾰ-ΐζω**, *celebrate Bacchanal rites*, Heraclit.15. ⊛**-ϊκός**, ή, όν, *of* or *belonging to the* Λήναια, ἀγῶνες Posidipp.ap.Ath.7.414e; διδασκαλίαι Plu.2.839d; θέατρον Λ. Poll.4.121.

**ληναῖος**, α, ον, (ληνός I) *belonging to the wine-press*; esp. 1. epith. of Dionysus, as *god of the wine-press*, D.S.3.63. 2. Λήναια (sc. ἱερά), τά, *the Lenaea*, an Athenian (also Rhodian, *IG*12(1).125) festival held in the month Ληναιών (i.e. Gamelion) in honour of Dionysus, at which there were dramatic contests, esp. of the Com. Poets, Ar.*Ach.*1155 (lyr.). 3. Λήναιον, τό, *the Lenaeum*, the place at Athens where the Lenaea were held, οὐπὶ Ληναίῳ ἀγών the *Lenaean* dramatic contest, opp. τὰ κατ' ἄστυ, ib.504, cf. Pl.*Prt.*327d, Lex ap. D.21.10; Διονύσια τὰ ἐπὶ Ληναίῳ *SIG*1029.9 (iv B.C.).

**Ληνᾱ-ΐτης** [ῑ], ου, ὁ, = Ληναϊκός, θόρυβος Ar.*Eq.*547 (anap.). ⊛**-αιών**, ῶνος, ὁ, name of a month in many Greek calendars, Hes.*Op.*504, *SIG*1014.94 (Erythrae), etc. **-εύς**, έως, ὁ, epith. of Dionysus, ib.1024.24 (Myconos).

**λην-εύω**, = βακχεύω, Hsch. **-εών**, ῶνος, ὁ, *the place of the* ληνός I, *Gp.*6.1.3. **-ίδιον**, τό, Dim. of ληνός, *PTeb.*414.37 (ii A.D., prob.), *POxy.*2150.4 (iii A.D.). ⊛**-ίς**, ίδος, ἡ, *a Bacchante*, Eust.629.30, Suid. II. = ληνός 2 or 3, *PTeb.*414.31 (ii A.D.); = ληνός 4, *EM*478. 28 (λινίδα codd.).

⊛**ληνο-βάτης** [ᾰ], ου, ὁ, *one who treads the wine-vat*, Him.*Or.*6.2, 21. 6, *Sammelb.*5810.12 (iv A.D.), *Gloss.* **-πᾰτέω**, *tread the wine-press*, Hsch. s.v. τραπεῖν. **-πῖθος**, ὁ, *vat*, *PMasp.*97.2 (vi A.D.). **-ποιός**, ὁ, = ληνοβάτης, *Gloss.*

⊛**ληνός**, Dor. **λᾱνός** Theoc.7.25, *IG*14.150.5 (Syracuse): ἡ:—*anything shaped like a tub* or *trough*, Hp.*Mochl.*38; esp. 1. *wine-vat* in which the grapes are pressed, *PCair.Zen.*300.15 (iii B.C.), Theoc.7.25, 25.28, D.S.3.63. 2. *trough*, for watering cattle, *watering-place* for them, *h.Merc.*104, Lxx *Ge.*30.38, 41. 3. = κάρδοπος, *kneading-trough*, Men.116. 4. *socket into which the mast fitted*, = ἱστοπέδη, Asclep.Myrl.ap.Ath.11.474f, Poll.1.91. 5. *coffin*, Pherecr.5, *CIG*1979, al. (Thessalonica), *IG* l.c. 6. part of the brain, *the meeting-point of the sinuses of the dura mater*, still called *torcular Herophili*, Herophil.ap.Gal.2.712, cf. *UP*9.6. 7. *hollow of a chariot*, Hsch. (pl.). 8. in pl., *the lower parts of the nose*, Poll.2.80.

⊛**λῆνος**, εος, τό, *wool*: hence, *fillet*, A.*Eu.*44, Epic. in *Arch.Pap.*7 p.4 (pl.): in pl., *fleece*, A.R.4.173, 177.

**ληνών**, ῶνος, ὁ, = ληνεών, *PLond.*2.401.13 (ii B.C.).

**ληξιαρχ-ικός**, ή, όν, *belonging to the* ληξίαρχος: τὸ λ. γραμματεῖον the register of each Athenian deme, *IG*1².79.6, Is.7.27, D.44.35, Lycurg.76, etc. **-ος**, ὁ, the officer at Athens who kept order in the ἐκκλησία, Poll.8.104.

**ληξῐπύρετος** [ῠ], ον, (λῆξις B) *allaying fever*, Asclep.ap.Gal.14. 136:—also **ληξοπύρετος**, Gal.13.68, 1013.

⊛**λῆξις** (A), εως, ἡ, Ion. **λάξις** (q.v.), (λαγχάνω) *determination* or *appointment by lot*, ἀρχῆς Pl.*Lg.*765d. 2. *portion assigned by lot, allotment*, ib.740a, 747e, *Criti.*109c, 113b; cf. λάξις. b. *section* of a body, determined by lot, Arist.*Ath.*30.3, 31.3. c. pl., *fortunes*, αἱ διάφοροι τῆς ἀνθρωπείας ψυχῆς λήξεις Simp.*in de An.*4.6. 3. without the notion of lot or chance, *assigned sphere*, θεῶν καὶ τῶν εἰς θείαν λῆξιν πορευθέντων Jul.*Or.*6.187c; ἡ ἑτέρα λ. the other *world*, Hld.2.24; ἡ ἑῴα λ. the eastern *part of the empire*, Procop. Gaz.*Pan.*497.3; ἡ τῆς Ἀθηνᾶς λ. the *sphere* of Athena, Lib.*Or.*12. 36, *Decl.*1.175, *Ep.*1065.3; *province*, τὰς λ. [τῶν θεῶν] Herm. *in Phdr.* p.74 A.; *dwelling-place*, εἰ.. αἱ λ. τῶν ψυχῶν.. ὑποσέληνοί εἰσιν ib. p.104 A. II. as law-term, λ. δίκης or λ. alone, *written complaint lodged with the Archon, as the first step in private actions*, nearly, = ἔγκλημα, Pl.*R.*425d, Is.11.10, Aeschin.1.63, cf. λαγχάνω I.3; very rarely of *public actions*, as in D.39.17. 2. λ. τοῦ κλήρου, *an application to the Archon* (required of all except direct descendants) *to be put in legal possession of an inheritance*, τοῦ κλήρου λαχεῖν τὴν λ. ἠξίωσεν Is.3.2, cf. Arist.*Ath.*43.4.

⊛**λῆξις** (B), εως, ἡ, (λήγω) *cessation*, μόχθων, ἀνέμων, A.*Eu.*505 (lyr.), A.R.1.1086; of the flow of a river, Ph.1.175; τῆς ἐνεργείας λῆξιν λαμβανούσης Gal.*Phil.Hist.*17, cf. M.Ant.9.21. 2. *death, decease*, *PMasp.*19.6 (vi A.D.), etc. II. Gramm., *termination*, A.D. *Synt.*104.28; λ. ἡ εἰς σ̄ Id.*Adv.*195.27. III. *end, extremity*, τοῦ κόλου Sor.1.7.

**ληξῐ-φάρμᾰκον**, τό, = ληξιπύρετον, Asclep.ap.Gal.14.136. **-φωτος**, ον, *waning*, Heph.Astr.2.34; **-φωτέω**, *wane*, Anubion ap.eund. 2.5.

**λῃός**, ὁ, Ion. form of λαός (q.v.).

**ληπ-τέος**, α, ον, (λαμβάνω) *to be taken* or *accepted*, Pl.*Prt.*356b. II. neut. ληπτέον, *one must take hold*, Ar.*Eq.*603; ἔργον λ. *one must undertake*, X.*Mem.*1.7.2; *one must assume* in arguing, etc., Pl.*Phlb.* 61a; *one must take* or *choose*, ἐκ τούτων ἐπιστάτας λ. X.*Cyr.*8.1.10; λ. δὲ.. τίνας ὅρους λέγουσι Arist.*Pol.*1280ᵃ7. 2. *one must take, receive*, δμήρους δοτέον καὶ λ. X.*HG*3.2.18; *one must submit to*, πληγὰς ὑπὸ τῶν ἀμεινόνων Id.*Lac.*9.5. **-της**, ου, ὁ, *one who accepts*, Zonar. **-τικός**, ή, όν, *disposed to accept*, Arist.*EN*1120ᵇ15. II. *assimilative*, opp. ἐκκριτικός, Id.*Ph.*243ᵇ14. ⊛**-τός**, ή, όν, (λαμβάνω) *to be apprehended*, λόγῳ καὶ διανοίᾳ Pl.*R.*529d; τῷ λογισμῷ Max.Tyr.7.5; πρὸς αἴσθησιν Chryserm.ap.Gal.8.741. b. later, *to be apprehended by the senses*, opp. νοητός, *AP*11.354.6 (Agath.). 2. in Stoic philos., *acceptable*, not to be refused if offered, *Stoic.*3.32, 34. II. = ἐπίληπτος, Arist.*Pr.*896ᵇ6.

**ληρ-αίνω**, = ληρέω, Ph.1.77, Hsch.; f.l. for ληναΐζω in Heraclit. 15. **-εία**, ἡ, = λήρησις, Phld.*Mus.*p.92 K. **-έω**, (λῆρος A) *to be foolish* or *silly, speak* or *act foolishly*, S.*Tr.*435, Ar.*Eq.*536, al., Pl.*Tht.* 152b, etc.; ξυνθιασῶτης τοῦ ληρεῖν Ar.*Pl.*508; περί τινος Isoc.12.11, 33; λῆρον ληρεῖς Ar.*Pl.*517; ληρεῖς ἔχων (v. ἔχω B.IV.2) Id.*Ra.*512, cf. Pl.*Grg.*497b: c. acc., μὴ ληρήσῃς τὸν ἐκτιναγμόν σου *PFay.*114.

21 (i A.D.). 2. of a sick person, *to be delirious*, Hp.*Epid.*1.26.γ'. **-ημα**, ατος, τό, *silly talk, nonsense*, Pl.*Grg.*486c (pl.), Phld.*Mus.*p.72 K. (pl.), Gal.8.651 (pl.). **-ησις**, εως, ἡ, *silly talk, trifling*, Plu.2.504b, D.L.7.118; λ. τοῦ γήραος *dotage* of the old, Aret.*SD*1.6.

**ληρίας**, v. λειρώς.

**Ληρόκριτος**, name given by Epicurus to Democritus, D.L.10.8.

**ληροπετώδη**· ληρώδη, Hsch.

**λῆρος** (A), ὁ, *trash, trumpery*, of what is showy but useless, λήροις ἀναδῶν τοὺς νικῶντας Ar.*Pl.*589; τραγικὸς λ. Id.*Ra.*1005; λῆρόν τε τἄλλ' ἡγεῖτο τοῦ γνῶναι πέρι φύσεις ποιητῶν *no good* as connoisseurs of poets, ib.809; λ. πάντα πρὸς τὸ χρυσίον Antiph.232.1, cf. X.*An.*7.7.41; λ. εἶναι δοκεῖ τὸ νόμισμα, φύσει δ' οὐθέν *mere trash*, Arist.*Pol.*1257$^b$10; a mere *trifle*, Pl.*Phd.*72c, Men.*Epit.*60; λ. ἐστι τἄλλα πρὸς Κινησίαν there's *naught* to compare with Cinesias, Ar.*Lys.*860; οἱ ποιηταὶ λ. εἰσιν *useless, futile*, Xenarch.7.1; ποιητῶν λ. Cratin.306; ἐμὲ μὲν λ. ἡγεῖσθαι Pl.*Chrm.*176a, cf. *Tht.*176d, Luc.*DMeretr.*10.3; λεπτοτάτων λ. ἱερεῦ Ar.*Nu.*359; λῆροι καὶ παιδιαί, of flute-playing at banquets, Pl.*Prt.*347d; λῆροι καὶ φλυαρίαι *futile* nonsense, Id.*Hp.Ma.*304b; ὀδοὺς καὶ κρήνας καὶ λήρους D.3.29; παροψίδες καὶ λῆρος side-dishes and suchlike *trumpery*, Alex.261.5; παρεὶς λ. πολὺν ἀστακὸν ὠνοῦ Archestr.*Fr.*24, cf. 35.7; as an exclamation, λῆρος *nonsense! humbug!* Ar.*Pl.*23, cf. Eub.41.8. 2. *delirium*, Hp.*Epid.*1.26.γ' (as v.l. for παράληρος). II. as Adj., *silly*, ποιητής Luc.*Gall.*6, cf. *Rh.Pr.*17. Adv. -ρως Tz.*H.*13.337. (Perh. derived fr. sq.)

**λῆρος** (B) (Boeot. **λεῖρος** *IG*7.2421), ὁ, *gold ornament* on women's tunics, *AP*6.292 (Hedyl.), cf. Luc.*Lex.*9, Poll.5.101, Hsch. (Oxyt. in *AP* l.c., Hsch.)

**ληρωδ-έω**, *talk frivolously*, Phot.*Bibl.*p.4 B. **-ημα**, ατος, τό, = ληρωδία, Suid. s. v. Λεόντιος (pl.). **-ης**, ες, *frivolous, silly*, Pl.*Tht.*174d, Arist.*Rh.*1414$^b$15, *BGU*1011 ii 15 (ii B.C.), Phld.*Ir.*p.16 W., cj. in Lucil.187 Marx. **-ία**, ἡ, *frivolous talk*, Hdn.*Epim.*77.

**λησθέων**· στρεφόμενος, Hsch.; cf. ληϊσθιῶν.

**λησίμβροτος**, ον, (λήθω, βροτός) *taking men unawares, cheat, thief*, *h.Merc.*339.

**λῆσις** (A), εως, ἡ, (λήθω) = λῆστις, Hsch. s. v. ληθεδών (λύσις cod.); f. l. for λῆστις in Critias 6.12 D.

**λῆσις** (B), εως, ἡ, (λῶ) = βούλησις, αἵρεσις, Hsch.

**λησμαδία**· λελησμένη, Hsch.; cf. ληϊσμ-.

**λησμονηθέντες**, = *illimati, Gloss.* (dub.).

**λησμοσύνη**, ἡ, = λήθη, *forgetfulness*, κακῶν Hes.*Th.*55; τῶν νῦν θέσθαι λησμοσύναν S.*Ant.*151 (lyr.).

**λήσμων**, ον, gen. ονος, (λήθω) *unmindful*, Them.*Or.*22.268c.

**Λῆσος**· ὁ ἐν τῷ ῥάχει τοῦ σκορπίου λαμπρὸς ἀστήρ, Hsch.

**ληστάρχ-ης**, ου, ὁ, *chief of robbers*, Plu.*Crass.*22. **-ία**, ἡ, *chieftainship of robbers*, Lyd.*Mag.*3.72. **-ος**, ὁ, = ληστάρχης, D.S.33.1, App.*Hisp.*68, Polyaen.4.9.3, Wilcken *Chr.*20 iv 8 (ii A.D.).

**ληστ-εία**, ἡ, *robbery, piracy*, Th.1.5, Pl.*Lg.*823e, etc.; ἀπὸ ληστείας βίον ἔχειν, ζῆν, X.*An.*7.7.9, Arist.*Pol.*1256$^a$36: in pl., πόλιν.. κατὰ γῆν λῃστείαις πορθουμένην Th.8.40. **-εύω**, fut. -εύσω App.*Pun.*116:—Pass. (v. infr.), aor. ἐλῃστεύθην D.S.2.55:—*practise robbery* or *piracy*, Th.7.18, D.4.23; ἐν τῇ γῇ καὶ ἐν τῇ θαλάσσῃ D.C.36.3. 2. c. acc., *spoil, plunder*, Th.4.45, App.*Pun.*5, etc.:—Pass., Th.4.2, 5.14, D.S. l. c.; λῃστεύεται ἡ ὁδὸς *is infested by robbers*, Arr.*Epict.*4.1.91. **-ήρ**, ῆρος, ὁ, in Hom. **ληϊστήρ**, = λῃστής (q.v.), *robber*, esp. *pirate*, Od.3.73, etc.; λ. πολύπλαγκτοι 17.425, cf. 16.426, *AP*7.737, Man.3.258:—fem. **λῄστειρα**, ναῦς Ael.*NA*8.19. **-ήριον**, Dor. **λᾳστήριον**, τό, *band of robbers*, X.*HG*5.4.42, Aeschin.1.191, *PPetr.*3 p.59 (iii B.C.): in pl., *piratical vessels*, Clidem.5, *IGRom.*4.219 (Ilion). 2. *retreat* or *nest of robbers*, *SIG*581.52 (Crete, iii/ii B.C.), Str.14.1.32. II. *robbery*, Luc.*Cont.*11 (pl.). III. λᾳστήριοι (Dor.), οἱ, *pirates*, metaph., Axiop.6. **-ής**, οῦ, ὁ, Ion. **ληϊστής**, Dor. **λᾳστής**, (λῆϊς, ληΐζομαι) *robber, pirate*, E.*Alc.*766, X.*Cyr.*2.4.23, etc.; opp. κλέπτης, Pl.*R.*351c; esp. by sea, *buccaneer*, later πειρατής, And.1.138, etc.; λῃστοῦ βίον ζῆν Pl.*Grg.*507e; ληϊστὴς κατεστήκεε Καρχηδονίων he began a course of *piracies* upon them, Hdt.6.17, cf. Th.1.5, 8, 6.4; οἱ λ. αὐτοὺς ποριστὰς καλοῦσιν Arist.*Rh.*1405$^a$25; of irregular troops, *IG*12(2).526 (Eresos). II. metaph., λ. ἐναργὴς τῆς ἐμῆς τυραννίδος S.*OT*535; Κύπριδος Lyc.1143; λῃστὰ λογισμοῦ, of love, *APl.*4.198 (Maec.). **-ικός**, ή, όν, *piratical*, πλοῖον D.23.148; λῃστικῷ τρόπῳ *PTeb.*53.11 (ii B.C.). 2. ἡ -κή, = λῃστεία, Pl.*Sph.*222c. 3. τὸ -κόν, *piracy*, Th.1.4, 13; *piratical vessels*, Id.2.69. 4. Adv. -κῶς *in the manner of pirates*: Comp. -κώτερον, πλοῖα λ. παρεσκευασμένα Id.1.10, cf. 6.104. Cf. λῃστρικός.

**λῆστις**, εως, ἡ, = λήθη, E.*Cyc.*172, Critias 6.12 D.; λῆστιν ἴσχειν, = ἐπιλανθάνεσθαι, *forget*, S.*OC*584.

**λῃστο-διώκτης**, ου, ὁ, = *latrunculator, Gloss.* **-κτόνος**, ον, *slaying robbers*, *AP*11.280 (Pall.). **-πιαστής**, οῦ, ὁ, in pl., *thief-catchers*, a branch of the local police in Egypt, Wilcken *Chr.*472.2 (iii A.D.), *PFlor.*2.181 (iii A.D.). **-σαλπιγκτής**, οῦ, ὁ, *robber-trumpeter*, of the Tyrrhenians, inventors of the trumpet, Com. word in Men.1030; in Hsch. **ληϊστοσάλπιγξ**.

**λῃστ-ρικός**, ή, όν, = λῃστικός, for which it is a freq. v.l., of ships, τριακόντορος λ. (cf. λῃστρίς) Th.4.9, cf. App.*Pun.*25, etc.; λ. σκάφη D.S.3.43: metaph., of ἑταῖραι, τὰ λ. τῆς Ἀφροδίτης *AP*5.43 (Rufin.), 160 (Hedyl. or Asclep.); λ. τρόπῳ *BGU*1061.14 (i B.C.). 2. of persons, Str.7.2.2; also λ. δύναμις Plu.*Sert.*18; βίος λ. Arist.*Pol.*1256$^b$1; ἔθνη ib.1338$^b$23; τὸ λ. ἦθος Str.12.8.9; ὁ λ. πόλεμος App.*Mith.*96. Adv. -κῶς Str.2.5.26. **-ρίς**, ίδος, ἡ, fem. of foreg., νῆες λ. *pirate* vessels, D.52.5, cf. D.S.16.5, Plu.*Nic.*29, etc.; λ. γυνή Id.*Thes.*9, cf. Herod.6.10. **-ρών**, = *latrina, Gloss.* (dub.). **-ωρ**, v. λῄτωρ.

**λήσω, λήσομαι**, v. λανθάνω.

**λῄτ-αρχος**, ὁ, *public priest*, Lyc.991. (Cf. λήϊτον.) **-ειρα**, ἡ, *public priestess*, Call.*Fr.*123, Hsch.; cf. λείτειραι. **-η**, ἡ, v. λήϊτον. **-ῆρες**· ἱεροὶ στεφανηφόροι (Athamanian), Id.

**λῆτο**· ἐπελάθετο, Hsch. (Cf. **λήϊτο**· ἐπέθετο, Id).

**Λητογενής**, Dor. **Λᾱτ-**, ές, *born of Leto*, epith. of Apollo and Artemis, E.*Ion* 465 (lyr.), *AP*9.525.12:—fem. **Λᾱτογένεια**, A.*Th.*148 (lyr.).

**Λητοΐδης** [ῐ], ου, Aeol., Dor. **Λᾱτοΐδας**, α, ὁ, *son of Leto*, i.e. Apollo, *h.Merc.*253, Hes.*Sc.*479, Alc.*Supp.*30.3:—Pi.*P.*1.12 has Λᾱτοΐδας (trisyll.).

**λητ-ουργέω, -ουργία, -ουργός**, v. λειτ-.

**Λητώ**, Dor. **Λᾱτώ**, όος, contr. οῦς, ἡ, *Leto*, mother of Apollo and Artemis, Il.21.497, Hes.*Th.*406, cf. 918, al.; on the accent of the acc. sg., v. Hdn.Gr.2.33; voc. Λητοῖ Il.21.498, *h.Ap.*14, 62. (Dor. uncontr. acc. Λητόα Tyrannio ap.Sch.Gen.Il.21.497):—Adj. **Λητῷος**, α, ον, *of* or *born from Leto*, κόρη A.*Fr.*170, S.*El.*570; Dor. **Λᾱτῴα** *AP*6.280:—fem. also **Λητωϊάς**, άδος, Call.*Dian.*83, Opp.*C.*1.109, etc.; and **Λητωΐς**, Dor. **Λᾱτ-**, ΐδος, *AP*6.272 (Pers.), A.R.2.938. II. Λητῷον, τό, *temple of L.*, Arist.*EE*1214$^a$2, Str.14.3.6. III. Λητῷα, τά, festival in honour of L., *IG*11(2).161 *A*93 (Delos, iii B.C.).

**λήτωρ**, ορος, ὁ, *priest*, prob. in *IG*5(2).405 (Lusi); cf. λείτωρ, λειτορεύω, λητῆρες.

**ληχμός**, ὁ, = λῆξις (B), Antim.53.

**λῆψις**, εως, ἡ (later **λῆμψις** *POxy.*1088.45 (i A.D.), etc.), *taking hold, seizing, catching*, ῥύγχος.. πρὸς τὰς λ. τῶν ζῳδαρίων Arist.*PA*662$^b$9; αἱ καμπαὶ τῶν δακτύλων καλῶς ἔχουσι πρὸς τὰς λ. καὶ πιέσεις ib.687$^b$10; ἀπορώτερος ἡ λ. the *seizure* of them will be more difficult, Th.5.110; ἡ λ. τῆς πόλεως the *seizure* of it, Id.4.114, cf. 7.25. 2. *accepting, receiving*, ἥδιστον ὅτῳ πάρεστι λ. ὧν ἐρᾷ καθ' ἡμέραν S.*Fr.*356; ἡ τοῦ μισθοῦ λ. Pl.*R.*346d; opp. ἀπόδοσις, ib.332b; opp. ἀποβολαί (loss), Arist.*Rh.*1362$^a$35 (pl.): in pl., *receipts*, Pl.*R.*343d, *Alc.*1.123a, Arist.*EN*1122$^a$13, al. b. *taking* of medicine, προλούσας πρὸ τῆς λ. *POxy.* l.c. II. *attack* of fever or sickness, *seizure*, ἀπὸ τῆς πρώτης λ. Hp.*Epid.*1.6, cf. *Morb.*1.18, Arist.*Pr.*866$^a$26. III. in Logic, *assumption* (cf. λῆμμα II), Id.*APr.*24$^a$23, 24$^b$11. 2. τῇ ἡμετέρᾳ λ. from our *point of view*, Ascl.*Tact.*7.8. IV. *choice of matter*, in a poem, etc., Longin.10.3; cf. λῆμμα III. V. *choice of pitch*, in Music, Ocell.4.8, Aristid.Quint.1.11 bis. VI. Geom., τὴν τοῦ κέντρου τοῦ ἐκκέντρου λ. the *determination* of the centre of the eccentric circle, Procl.*Hyp.*5.56.

**ληψ-ολῐγό-μισθος** τέχνη, the art of *taking low pay*, cj. Hemsterh. in Ephipp.14.4 (ληψιγομ- codd.): Meineke **ληψι-λογό-μισθος** *receiving pay for words*.

**λῑ**, Adv., = λίαν, Epich.223; cf. λιπόνηρος.

**λῐάζομαι**, aor. ἐλιάσθην, Ep. 3 pl. λίασθεν Il.23.879: 3 sg. plpf. λελίαστο Mosch.4.118 (for Act. v. sub fin.):—*bend, incline*; and so, I. mostly of persons, *go aside, recoil, shrink*, ἐκ ποταμοῖο λιασθείς Od.5.462; ἀπὸ πυρκαϊῆς ἑτέρωσε λ. Il.23.231; νόσφι λ. 1.349, 11.80; ὕπαιθα λιάσθη he *shrank* beneath his attack, 15.520, cf. 21.255; δεῦρο λιάσθης hither *hast* thou *retired*, 22.12; παρὰ κληῖδα λιάσθη ἐς πνοιὰς ἀνέμων, of a vision, *disappeared* by the key-hole, Od.4.838: metaph., *stray from the straight path*, Emp.2.8; in A.R. of *parting, separating* from others, 1.94, 3.827, 1164:—once in Trag., πρὸς σ' ἐλιάσθην *hastened* to thee, E.*Hec.*98 (anap.). 2. *sink, fall*, πρηνὴς ἐλιάσθη Il.15.543; λιαζόμενον ποτὶ γαίῃ 20.420, cf. 418; ἐν γῇ Mosch. l.c. II. of things, ἀμφὶ δ' ἄρα σφι λιάζετο κῦμα *retired, drew back*, Il.24.96; πτερὰ πυκνὰ λίασθεν (for ἐλιάσθησαν) the dying bird's thick wings *dropped*, 23.879; where Aristarch. read λίασσεν it *dropped* its wings, though the Act. is not used exc. impf. λίαζον they *loosened* (the cables), Lyc.21.

**λιάζω** (A), v. foreg. sub fin.

**λιάζω** (B), (λίαν) *to be over-enthusiastic*, [παρὰ τὸ] λίαν λιάζειν A.D.*Pron.*34.27; λιάζειν· λίαν ἐσπουδακέναι, Phot.

**λιαίνω**, = χλιαίνω, Hsch. s.v. ἐλιάνθη; cogn. with λιαρός.

**λίαν** [v. fin.], Ion. and Ep. **λίην**, Adv. *very, exceedingly*, in Hom. with an Adv., λ. ἑκάς Od.14.496; λ. ἀεικελίως 8.231: with an Adj., λ. μέγα εἶπες 3.227, 16.243; νήπιος λ. τόσον 4.371, cf. 13.238; λ. λυπρός 13.243; λ. ἐνθύμιος ib.421: alone with a Verb, *very much, overmuch*, κεχολώατο λ. 14.282; λ. ἄχθομαι ἕλκος Il.5.361; οὔ τι λ. ποθὴ ἔσσεται not *exceedingly*, 14.368; μή τι λ. προκαλίζεο Od.18.20, cf. Il.6.486; also, in Hom., καὶ λίην, which always begins the sentence or verse, *surely, aye surely*, καὶ λ. κεῖνός γε ἐοικότι κεῖται ὀλέθρῳ Od.1.46, cf. 3.203, Il.1.553, al. II. after Hom.. ἀσχάλα μὴ λίην Archil.66.7, cf. Sol.6; λίην δὲ δειλιάζεις Anacr.ap.Ptol.Ascal.p.409 H.; λ. πιστεύειν to believe *implicitly*, Hdt.4.96; μὴ κάμνε λ. Pi.*P.*1.90; μὴ λ. στένε S.*El.*1172, cf. E.*Med.*158 (lyr.); ἀσπάζου αὐτὴν λ. *POxy.*936.13 (iii A.D.); καὶ λ. σαφῶς Ar.*Eq.*1231; λ. ἀσελγῶς Lys.24.15; λ. πόρρω Pl.*Prt.*310c; ἐντὸς λ. τῶν τειχῶν Th.7.5: with other words of like sense, πολὺ λ. Isoc.9.48; λ. πάνυ Antiph.184.2 (dub.), cf. Eust.972.46; κόμπος λ. εἰρημένος, opp. πεπλασμένος (compare our *very* and *verily*), A.*Pr.*1031:—in Trag. and Com. freq. betw. Art. and Noun, ἡ λ. φιλότης βροτῶν his *too great* love.., A.*Pr.*123 (anap.); τὸ λ. ποτόν Cratin.187; ἡ λ. τρυφή Men.587; τὰ λ. μειράκια Theopomp.

Com.29; αἱ πρὸς τυράννους λίαν ὁμιλίαι D.6.21; τὸ λ. excess, violence, E.Andr.866, Pl.Cra.415c. [Hom. has ῐ nine times, ῑ thirty-two times; the latter is found both in arsi and in thesi. In later Ep. and Trag. both quantities are found: ᾰ always.]

**λιαντήρ**, ῆρος, ὁ, = λεαντήρ, Gloss.

**λίαξ**, ὁ, v. λειάξ.

⊛ **λῐᾰρός**, ά, όν, warm, lukewarm, αἷμα, ὕδωρ, Il.11.477,830, Od.24.45, etc.; οὖρος λ. a warm, soft wind, 5.268; ὕπνος λ. gentle, balmy, Il.14.164, cf. A.R.3.300, etc.

**λίβα, λιβός**, acc. and gen. of λίψ (q.v.).

**λῐβ-άδιον** [ᾰ], τό, (λιβάς) small spring, πότιμα λ. Plu.2.913c; small stream, λ. ὀλεθρίου ὕδατος Str.8.8.4. II. in the common dialect, a wet place, Eust.1358.54, Thom.Mag.p.223 R.; = χωρίον βοτανῶδες, Hsch. III. = κενταύρειον τὸ μικρόν, Plin.HN25.68. **-άζω**, = λείβω, let fall in drops, Hsch., Phot.: Med., run out in drops, trickle, AP9.258 (Antiphan. Megalop.). II. γῆ λιβάζουσα land full of pools of water, Poll.1.238.

**λῐβᾰν-ᾶς**, ὁ, = λιβανοπώλης, PLond.3.604.281 (i A.D.), Sammelb. 410.1 (i/ii A.D.). **-ίδιον**, τό, Dim. of λίβανος, Men.260 (ἴδιον cod.; corr. Bentl.). **-ίζω**, smell like frankincense, Dsc.1.71, Gal.13.475. **-ινος**, η, ον, made of frankincense, Gloss. II. frankincense-coloured, POxy.114.5 (ii A.D.).

**Λῐβᾰνῖτις**, ιδος, ἡ, title of Aphrodite, Luc.Ind.3 codd.

**λῐβᾰνο-ειδής**, ές, = λιβανώδης, Dsc.3.83. **-θήκη**, ἡ, incense-box, POxy.978 (iii A.D.), Gloss. **-κᾰΐα**, ἡ, burning of incense, ib. **-μάννα**, ἡ, = μάννα λιβανωτοῦ, Orph.H.20 tit. **-μαντις**, εως, ὁ, also ἡ, one that divines from the smoke of frankincense, Eust. 1346.39. **-ομαι**, Pass., to be mixed with frankincense, οἶνος λελιβανωμένος Lxx 3Ma.5.45; λιβανῶ occurs in Hdn.Gr.1.451. **-πώλης**, Dor. **-ᾱς**, ου, ὁ, = λιβανωτοπώλης, in gen. pl. -πωλᾶν, SIG1000.15 (Cos, i B.C.).

⊛ **λίβᾰνος** [ῐ], ὁ, frankincense-tree, Boswellia Carterii, Hdt.4.75, Thphr.HP9.4.2, Dsc.1.68, etc.; ἱερόδακρυς λ. Melanipp.1.5. II. = λιβανωτός, frankincense, in which sense it is fem. in Pi.Fr.122.3, E.Ba.144 (lyr.); but masc. in PCair.Zen.69.13 (iii B.C.), AP6.231 (Phil.), 9.93 (Antip. Thess.), Edict.Diocl.('Αθηνᾶ 18.6, Tegea); indeterminate in Sapph.Supp.20c.2, S.Fr.1064, Anaxandr.41.37, SIG 247ii 19 (Delph., iv B.C.).

**λῐβᾰνο-φόρος**, ον, bearing frankincense, χώρα, δένδρα, Heraclid. Cum.4, Peripl.M.Rubr.29, Dsc.1.68 (nisi leg. λιβανωτοφ-); contributing frankincense, βάρβαροι (written **λιβανω-**) OGI199.20 (ii A.D.). ⊛ **-χροος**, ον, contr. **-χρους**, ουν, frankincense-coloured, Str. 15.1.37.

**λῐβᾰν-ώδης**, ες, frankincense-like, πόα Philostr.Im.1.29. **-ωτίδιον**, τό, Dim. of λιβανωτίς (B), small censer, Roussel Cultes Égyptiens p.217 (Delos, ii B.C.). **-ωτίζω**, fumigate with frankincense, Str.16.4.26. II. to be like frankincense, Dsc.3.84. **-ωτικός**, ή, όν, consisting in frankincense, φορτία Raccolta Lumbroso 119 (iii B.C.), OGI 132.11 (ii B.C.). II. of or for the manufacture of frankincense, [ἐργασία] PSI6.628.5 (iii B.C.). **-ώτῖνος**, η, ον, prepared with frankincense, μύρον Apollon.Herophil.ap.Ath.15.689b. **-ωτίς** (A), ίδος, ἡ, rosemary frankincense, λ. κάρπιμος Lecokia cretica, Thphr.HP9.11.10, Dsc.3.74.1, Gal.12.60; λ. καχρυφόρος Nic.Th.850. 2. λ. [κάρπιμος] ἑτέρα Ferulago galbanifera, Dsc.3.74.2. 3. λ. ἄκαρπος Rosmarinum sterile, ibid.; also, Lactuca graeca, Thphr.HP9.11.11, Dsc.3.74.4. 4. rosemary, Rosmarinus officinalis, Id.3.75, Gal.12.61. 5. = κόνυζα λεπτόφυλλος, Ps.-Dsc.3.121. ⊛ **-ωτίς** (B), ίδος, ἡ, = λιβανωτρίς, IG2².840.7, 11(2).110,111, al. (Delos, iii B.C.), Roussel Cultes Égyptiens p.217 (ibid., ii B.C.), Polyaen.4.8.2.

**λῐβᾰνωτο-πωλέω**, deal in frankincense, Ar.Fr.807. **-πώλης**, ου, ὁ, dealer in frankincense, Critias 70 D., Cratin.Jun.1.4.

⊛ **λῐβᾰνωτός**, ὁ, also ἡ Men.Sam.Fr.1:—frankincense, the gum of the tree λίβανος, used to burn at sacrifices, Xenoph.1.7, Hdt.1.183, 2.40.86, Ar.Nu.426, V.96, Ra.871, Thphr.HP4.4.14, etc.; λ. ὑπὲρ αὐτῶν ἐπιτιθέναι Antipho 1.18: called, when in small pieces, χόνδρος λιβανωτοῦ Luc.Sat.16; when pounded, μάννα λιβανωτοῦ Gp.6.6.1; cf. λιβανομάννα: the best kind was λ. ἄρρην Dsc.1.68, Alciphr. 2.4. 2. = λίβανος 1, Thphr.HP9.1.6. II. the frankincense-market, Eup.304, Chamael.ap.Ath.9.374b. III. = λιβανωτρίς, Apoc.8.3,5.

**λῐβᾰνωτοφόρος**, ον, bearing frankincense, Hdt.2.8, 3.107; ἡ λ. (sc. χώρα) Str.16.4.25, Peripl.M.Rubr.31.

⊛ **λῐβᾰνωτρίς**, ίδος, ἡ, censer, Carnead.ap.Plu.2.477b, Keil-Premerstein Zweiter Bericht No.20 (Thyatira), Ramsay Studies in the Eastern Rom. Provinces p.319 (Pisidia). Hsch.

**λῐβάς**, άδος, ἡ, (λείβω) anything that drips or trickles, esp. spring, fount, stream, S.Ph.1215 (lyr.), E.Andr.116,534 (lyr.); λ. νυμφαία Antiph.52.13; standing water, Babr.24.6: in pl., streams, λιβάσιν ὑδρηλαῖς.. πηγῆς A.Pers.613; δακρύων λιβάδες streams of tears, E.IT 1106 (lyr.); γάλακτος A.R.4.1735; also ἀραιὰ ἡ Αἴγυπτος καὶ ῥᾳδία λιβάδας διαδοῦναι Ephor.65 J.: in pl., also of pools of water that collect after rain, ὑπόνομοι λ. Str.8.6.21, cf. Gal.6.627, Gp.2.6.14; of marshes, Thphr.HP2.4.4; cf. λιβάζω. II. vessel that drips when under the influence of heat, a rudimentary thermometer, Hero Spir.2.8.

**λιβδύειν**· ἀφορίζειν, Hsch.

⊛ **λίβελλος**, ὁ, = Lat. libellus, petition, PGiss.40.2 (iii A.D.), etc. **λιβλάριος**, ὁ, = Lat. librarius, scribe, secretary, BGU423$^v$.3 (ii A.D.), PFlor.71.605 (iv A.D.), etc.

**λίβερνος**, ὁ, = Λιβυρνίς (ναῦς), BGU455.9 (i A.D.), etc.

**λῑβερτῖνος**, ὁ, = Lat. libertinus, freedman, IG14.1781, Act.Ap.6.9:—also ⊛ **λίβερτος**, = Lat. libertus, Plb.30.18.4.

**λίβηθρον**, v. λείβηθρον.

**λῑβηρός**, ά, όν, = ὑγρός, Hp.ap.Gal.19.118, EM564.50.

**λῐβιανόν**, τό, an eye-salve, Gal.12.762, Alex.Trall.2.

**λῐβικός**, ή, όν, (λίψ) western, PLand.52.23 (i A.D.), PFlor.50.3, al. (iii A.D.), etc.

**λῐβόνοτος**, ὁ, a wind between south-west and south, Arist.Mu.394$^b$34, Agatharch.2.7, Peripl.M.Rubr.57; cf. λιβοφοῖνιξ.

**λιβός**, gen. of λίψ.

**λίβος** [ῐ], εος, τό, (λείβω) = λιβάς, in pl., tears, A.Ch.448 (lyr.); v. λίπος. 2. = ἐπίσταγμά τι τῶν ὀμμάτων, Gal.19.118. II. = Lat. libum, Chrysipp.Tyan.ap.Ath.15.647d, cf. Ath.3.126a.

**λῐβοφοῖνιξ**, ικος, ὁ, = λιβόνοτος, Arist.Mu.394$^b$34.

**λιβρός**, ά, όν, = σκοτεινὸς καὶ μέλας, Hp.ap.Erot. (prob. referring to Aër.15 where διερῷ and θολερῷ codd. Hp., as epith. of ἠήρ); νὺξ expld. as either dark or (cf. λιβάς) dewy night, EM564.49; λιβρὸν σέλας Trag.Adesp.232; ὀλὸς λ. either black or dripping blood, AP 15.25.1 (Besant.); cf. λιμβρός.

⊛ **Λῐβῠ-άρχης**, ου, ὁ, governor of region on the west bank of the Nile, PRev.Laws 37.5 (iii B.C., pl.); governor of Libya, Plb.15.25.12. **-αφιγενής**, ές, v. Λεβυαφιγενής.

**Λιβύη** [ῠ], ἡ, Libya, Od.4.85, 14.295, Hdt.1.46, etc.; also for Africa generally, Id.4.42, al.; the west bank of the Nile, PTaur.8.9 (ii B.C.), PLond.1.3.8 (ii B.C.): prov., ἀεὶ Λιβύη φέρει τι καινόν or κακόν, Arist.HA606$^b$20, Zen.2.51:—Adv. **Λῐβύηθεν**, from Libya, D.P. 46,222:—also **Λῐβύηθε**, Dor. **-ᾱθε**, Nic.Al.368, Theoc.1.24:—Adj. **Λῐβῠκός**, ή, όν, Hdt.2.8, etc.; Λ. ὄρνεον, i.e. a strange, foreign bird, Ar.Av.65; Λ. λόγοι a kind of fables resembling those of Aesop, Arist.Rh.1393$^a$30; also, western, Ptol.Tetr.119; = δυτικός, Procl. Par.Ptol.29.

**λίβυον**, τό, wild lotus, f.l. in Ps.-Dsc.4.111 (Λιβυκόν cj. Wellmann).

**λιβυός**, ὁ, unknown bird, Arist.HA609$^a$20.

**Λῐβυρνοί**, οἱ, the Liburnians, a people on the Adriatic coast below Istria, Λιβυρνὴ πόλις Str.7.5.4, etc.:—Adj. **Λῐβυρνικός**, ή, όν, Liburnian, A.Fr.364: -κόν (sc. πλοῖον), τό, a light, swift vessel, felucca, such as was used by the Λιβυρνοί, Plu.Cat.Mi.54:—also **Λῐβυρνός**, ὁ, BGU709.23 (ii A.D.), prob. in Supp.Epigr.3.565.11 (Tyras, iii A.D.):—fem. **Λῐβυρνίς** (sc. ναῦς), ίδος, ἡ, Plu.Ant.67, etc.; -ίδες νῆσοι Str.7.5.5:—hence **Λῐβυρνάριος**, ὁ, Stud.Pal.20.123.33 (v A.D.).

**Λίβῠς** [ῐ], υος, ὁ, a Libyan, Hdt.4.181, al., S.El.702, etc.: and as Adj., = Λιβυκός, αὐλός E.Alc.346; Λ. καυλός, = σίλφιον, Antiph.217.13:—fem. **Λίβυσσα** [ῐ], Pi.P.9.105, S.Fr.11, Hdt.4.189, Call.Ap.86, Riv.Fil.57.379 (Crete):—also **Λῐβυστικός**, ή, όν, A.Eu.292, Fr.139, etc.; fem. also **Λῐβυστίς**, ίδος, ἡ, A.R.4.1753; cf. Λιβύη. II. harmless kind of serpent, Nic.Th.490. III. = λουτροφόρος 2, Hsch.

**Λῐβυστικόν**, τό, a herb, Gal.6.267, 12.62:—also **Λῐβυστιάς**, άδος, ἡ, Androm.ap.Gal.14.40:—hence **Λῐβυστικᾶτον**, τό, a drink made from it, Alex.Trall.8.2. [Identical with Λιγυστικόν, q.v.]

**Λῐβῠ-φοῖνιξ**, ικος, ὁ, Liby-Phoenician, i.e. Carthaginian, Plb.3.33.15, etc. **-φοίτης**, ου, ὁ, visiting Libya, Juba ap.Hsch.

**λίβω**, = λείβω, Hsch.

**λίγ-ᾰ** [ῐ], Adv. of λῐγύς (cf. τάχα, ὦκα, etc.), in loud, clear tone, ἀμφ' αὐτῷ χυμένη λίγ' ἐκώκυε Il.19.284, cf. Od.8.527; λίγ' ἄειδεν in clear, sweet tone, 10.254, cf. Alcm.59, Thgn.939; ζεφύρου λ. κινυμένοιο A.R. 4.837. **-αίνω**, (λιγύς) poet. Verb, cry out with a loud, clear voice, of heralds, Il.11.685; of mourners, A.Th.874 (lyr.); of shepherds, Mosch.3.81; also φόρμιγγι, σύριγγι λ., produce clear sounds on.., play on.., A.R.1.740, AP9.363.7 (Mel.): c. acc. cogn., μέλος λ. Bion 2.1, cf. Mosch.3.120; [οὐκ] ᾤετο δεῖν τὸν ἐν δικαστηρίοις λόγον κωτίλλειν καὶ λιγαίνειν D.H.Dem.44:—Med., Arat.1007:—Pass., of a person, to be made λιγύς, Ὁμήρῳ ὑπὸ Καλλιόπης λιγαινομένῳ Max.Tyr.3.8. II. trans., sing of, AP9.197 (Marin.). 2. charm, ὦτα φθεγξαμένη λ. Ph.2.267, cf. Hsch. λιγαίνει· τέρπει.

⊛ **λιγάνταρ**· εἶδος τέττιγος (Lacon.), Hsch. **λιγγούριον**, v. λυγκούριον.

**λίγδα**, v. λίγδος III. **λιγδαρεοχύται**· οἱ ἐν ταῖς λίγδαις τὰς ⟨σ⟩άρκας χέοντες, τουτέστι χοάναις, Hsch. **λιγδεύει**· ἀπηθεῖ, Id.

**λίγδην**, Adv., (v. λίζω) grazing, βάλε χεῖρ' ἐπὶ καρπῷ λίγδην Od.22.278; v. ἐπιλίγδην.

**λίγδος**, ὁ, = θυεία, mortar, Nic.Th.589,618, cf. S.Fr.35, and ἴγδις. II. clay mould, Poll.10.189, Ael.Dion.Fr.249. III. lye, used as soap, Eust.1229.27: so in Hsch., **λίγδα**· ἡ ἀκόνη, καὶ ἡ κονία.

**λίγειος** [ῐ], α, ον, later form of λιγύς, cj. Coraës for λίγιον, λόγιον (q.v.), Hld.6.5; λιγήϊα συρίζουσι (Schneid. for λιγέα) Opp.C.4.411. Adv. -είως Suid.

**λιγιπενές**· ἀσθενές, ἀγεννές, Hsch. (cf. ὀλιγηπελής). **λίγνον**, = bandum ('banner'), Gloss. (σίγνον Scaliger). ⊛ **λιγνύζων**, ὁ, v. λιθίζω.

**λιγνῠόεις**, εσσα, εν, smoky, sooty, καπνός A.R.2.133, 3.1291.

⊛ **λιγνύς**, ύος, ἡ (parox. in Call.Fr.1.57 P.), thick smoke mixed with flame, murky fire (such as is made by burning resinous substances, Arist.Mete.387$^b$6, al.), ἱέντα.. διὰ στόμα λιγνὺν μέλαιναν A.Th.494; στέροψ λ., of the fires seen by night on the two peaks of Parnassus, S.Ant.1127 (lyr.); λ. σῶμα καταιθαλοῖ Ar.Av.1241; λ. καὶ καπνός Id.

*Lys.*319; λιγνὺς πρόσεδρος S.*Tr.*794, expld. by Sch. of the *smoke* of the altar hanging round Heracles: pl., αἱ φλόγες καὶ αἱ λ. Plb.34.11.18, cf. Str.6.2.11. 2. *soot*, λ. ἐστι καπνώδης αἰθάλη Erot. s. v. γλῶσσα λιγνυώδης; used medicinally, Dsc.2.72, Gal.12.61. [ῠ Tryph. 322; but ῡ Call. l. c., and prob. in S.*Ant.* l. c.]

**λιγνῠώδης**, ες, *smoky, sooty, dark-coloured*, πνεῦμα Hp.*Coac.*255; γλῶσσα Id.*Epid.*3.17.ιβ'; opp. καπνώδης, Gal.9.470; ἀναθυμιάσεις, πνεύματα, Agath.2.15, 5.8.

**λίγξ** πλάγιος, = καμπτὴρ πλάγιος, Hsch.

⊕**λίγξε**, only aor. 1, λίγξε βιός the bow *twanged*, Il.4.125.

⊕**λῐγουρά**, Boeot. fem. of λιγυρός, Corinn.21:—also ⊕**λῐγουροκώτιλος**, α, ον, *clear and plaintive*, ἐνοπαί Ead.20.4.

**λιγρόν**· πικρόν, λιγυρόν, ἡδύ, γλυκύ, Hsch.

**λῐγῠάοιδος** [ᾰ], ον, *clear-singing*, Arc.86.

⊕**Λῐγῠαστάδης**, ου, ὁ, (λιγύς) name borne by Mimnermus, Sol.20.3, cf. Suid. s. v. Μίμνερμος.

**λῐγῠ-ηχής**, ές, poet. -ᾱχής, *clear-sounding*, κιθάρη *AP*9.308 (Bianor); Μοῦσαι *Ath.Mitt.*27.339; dub. in B.*Scol.Oxy.Fr.*4. **-θροος**, ον, = foreg., D.P.574, Coluth.276, etc. **-κλαγγής**, ές, *shrill*, νευρά B.5.73; *clear-voiced*, χοροί Id.13.14. **-κορτος**, ον, = sq., Alcm. 85 B. **-κροτος**, ον, *loud-rattling*, gloss on λιγυρώτατον, Suid.; cf. foreg. **-μακρόφωνος**, ον, epith. of heralds, Tim.*Pers.*232. **-μολπος**, ον, *clear-singing*, νύμφαι *h.Hom.*19.19. **-μῦθος**, ον, *clear-speaking*, *AP*7.343. **-πνοιος**, ον, *shrill-blowing, whistling*, ἄνεμοι *h.Ap.*28. **-πνοος**, ον, contr. **-πνους**, ουν, = foreg., Coluth.309, *IG*14.1934*f*7. **-πτέρῠγος**, ον, *chirping with the wings*, of the cicada, *AP*7.195 (Mel.).

**λῐγῠρίζω**, *sing loud* or *clear*, ᾠδήν Luc.*Lex.*2, cf. Hsch.

⊕**λιγύριον**, τό, a precious stone (Dim. of λίγυρος), Lxx *Ex.*28.19, J.*BJ*5.5.7.

**λῐγῠρόπνοος**, ον, = λιγύπνοος, Poll.4.72.

⊕**λῐγῠρός**, ά, όν, Boeot. fem. **λιγουρά** (q. v.), *clear, shrill*, ὦρτο δὲ κῦμα πνοιῇ ὕπο λιγυρῇ Il.23.215, cf. 5.526, 13.590; of a whip, 11.532, S.*Aj.* 242 (anap.); ἀκόνα (v. ἀκόνη); λιγυρὰ ἄχεα griefs *which vent themselves in shrill wailings*, E.*Med.*205 (lyr.); also (like λιγύς), of a *clear, sweet* sound, as of the Sirens, λιγυρῇ θέλγουσιν ἀοιδῇ Od.12.44; λιγυρὴν ἔντυνον ἀοιδήν ib.183; of a bird, Il.14.290; of locusts, Hes.*Op.*583; λ. σύριγγες Id.*Sc.*278: metaph., of poets, Id.*Op.*659; ἀοιδά Theoc. 15.135, etc.: neut. pl. as Adv., λιγυρὰ ἀείδειν Thgn.939: regul. Adv. -ρῶς Theoc.8.71.—Poet. word, used occasionally in Prose, λιγυρὸν ὑπηχεῖ echoes *shrilly*, Pl.*Phdr.*230c; φωνὴ λ., opp. λαμπρά, Arist. *HA*616b31, cf. *Aud.*804a29 (Comp.): also in later Prose, Plu.2.974a, Luc.*Salt.*72, *Phal.*1.11, etc. 2. metaph., συμβιῶναι.. ἥδιστος καὶ -ώτατος Isoc.*Ep.*4.4. II. *pliant, flexible*, of dogs' tails, X.*Cyn.* 4.1.

**λίγυρος**, ὁ, = λιγύριον, J.*AJ*3.7.5.

**λῐγῠρότης**, ητος, ἡ, *clearness, sweetness*, of Homer, prob. in Phld. *Herc.*1677.21.

**λῐγύς**, λίγεια (not λιγεῖα, Hdn.Gr.1.249), λιγύ; of sound, *clear, shrill*, λιγέων ἀνέμων λαιψηρὰ κέλευθα Il.14.17; ὦρτο δ' ἐπὶ λ. οὖρος Od. 3.176, cf. 4.357: more freq. of a *clear, sweet* sound, *clear-toned*, φόρμιγγι λιγείῃ, φόρμιγγα λίγειαν, Il.9.186, Od.8.67, etc.; of articulate sounds, *clear-voiced*, Μοῦσα λίγεια 24.62, Alcm.1; λ. Σειρήν Id.7; λ. ἀγορητής in Il. as epith. of Nestor, 1.248, 4.293; also of Thersites, 2.246; ἐπέων οἶμος λ. Pi.*O.*9.72. Adv. λιγέως, ἀγορεύειν Il.3.214: freq. also, λ. κλαίειν wail *shrilly*, 19.5, Od.11.391; ἰάχειν Hes.*Sc.* 233: neut. as Adv., λ. πνείοντες ἀῆται Od.4.567; λ. μέλπεσθαι Hes. *Sc.*206; λιγύ or λίγεα κλάζειν Mosch.4.24, A.R.4.1299. II. after Hes., mostly of sad sounds, as always in A., λ. κωκύματα *Pers.*332; κἀνακωκύσας λιγύ ib.468; λ. πάθεα *Supp.*113 (lyr.); of the nightingale, *Ag.* 1146 (lyr.), S.*OC*671 (lyr.); also of music, λίγεια λωτοῦ χάρις E.*Heracl.*892 (lyr.); αὐλοῦ λ. ἦχον, v. l. for γλυκὺν in Mosch. 2.98.—Poet. word (Μοῦσαι λίγειαι Pl.*Phdr.*237a).

**Λίγυς** [ῐ], υος, ὁ, ἡ, *Ligurian*, A.*Fr.*199.1, Hdt.5.9, Th.6.2, etc.: as Adj., Λ. στρατός A.*Fr.*199.9 (on the accent, v. Hdn.Gr.1.236.7):— Adj. **Λῐγυστικός**, ή, όν, *Ligurian*, S.*Fr.*598, Str.2.4.3; ἡ Λιγυστική *Liguria*, Arist.*Mete.*351a16, cf. 368b32:—also **Λῐγυστῖνος**, η, ον, σάγοι, χιτῶνες Str.4.6.2. II. τὸ λ. *bastard lovage, Laserpitium Siler*, Dsc.3.51.

**λῐγυ-σφάρᾰγος** [φᾰ], ον, *shrill-sounding*, φόρμιγγες Pi.*Parth.*2 *Fr.* 1.34. **-φθογγος**, ον, *clear-voiced*, in Hom. always epith. of heralds, Il.2.50, al., Od.2.6, etc.; αὐλίσκοι Thgn.241; ἀηδών Ar.*Av.*1380; ὄρνιθες B.5.23; μέλισσα (of a poet) Id.9.10; αὐδή Opp.*H.*5.620. **-φωνέω**, *sound clear* or *loud*, Sch.Theoc.8.30. **-φωνος**, ον, *clear-voiced, loud-voiced*, ἅρπη Il.19.350, cf. *h.Merc.*478; also of *sweet* sounds, Ἑσπερίδες Hes.*Th.*275, 518; ἀηδών Theoc.12.7; ἀοιδή Orph. *A.*5.

**λιδρίον**· τρύβλιον, Hsch. **λίζει**· παίζει, and **λίζουσι**· παίζουσιν, Id. **λιζόν**· ἔλαττον, Id. (i. e. ὀλιζον). **λίζω**, *graze*, Eust.1926. 37, as giving the Root of λίγδην, ἐπιλίγδην. **λιζῶνες**· ἐλάττονες, Hsch. (Cf. ὀλείζων, ὀλίγος.) **λίημος**· ψάμαθος, Id. (fort. ἄμμος). **λίην**, Ion. and Ep. for λίαν. **λίηνος**· λιθοπυργία, Id. **λίηφος**· δεινός, Id. **λῖθ'**, v. λῖτα.

**λῐθάγωγ-ία**, ἡ, *conveyance of stone*, *IG*1².347.37, *SIG*241*B*87 (Delph., iv B. C.). **-ός**, όν, *for conveying stones*, ναῦς *IG*1².336.8; μηχανή Poll.10.148. II. Subst. λ., ὁ, *stone-haulier*, *SIG*241*A*47, 244I38 (pl., Delph., iv B. C.).

⊕**λῐθ-άζω**, (λίθος) *fling stones*, Arist.*Pr.*881b1, Plb.10.29.5; ἐπὶ σκοπόν Str.15.1.43. 2. *throw like stones*, χρυσὸν εἴς τινα App.*Reg.* 4. II. *stone*, τινα Anaxandr.16, Lxx 2*Ki.*16.6, *Ev.Jo.*10.31:— Pass., dub. sens. in *IGRom.*4.494.13 (Pergam.). ⊕**-ᾰκός**, ὁ, = λίθαξ, Stesich.*Oxy.*1087.48; on the accent, v. Hdn.Gr.1.150. **-αβολεύς**, έως, ὁ, *surgical instrument for extracting stone*, Aët.16.110 (100). **-αξ**, ᾰκος, ὁ, ἡ, *stony*, λίθακι ποτὶ πέτρῃ Od.5.415. II. as fem. Subst., = λίθος, Arat.1112, Orph.*A.*613; κωφὴ λ., of a *gravestone*, *AP*7.392 (Heraclid. Sinop.); of a *precious stone*, Man.6.343; λ. τρητὴν σπόγγῳ εἰδομένην, of the pumice-*stone*, *AP*6.66 (Paul. Sil.). 2. in pl., *stony land*, Epic. in *Arch.Pap.*7.10, v. l. in Nic. *Th.*150; cf. ἕρμαξ.

**λῐθαργύρ-εος** [ῠ], α, ον, = sq., Stesich.30. **-ῖνος**, η, ον, *of* or *like* λιθάργυρος, Arist.*SE*164b23. **-ος**, ἡ, *litharge, lead monoxide*, Nic.*Al.*594, Gal.13.397, al.: sts. called λ. ἀργυρῖτις, to dist. it from λ. χρυσῖτις (flake *litharge*), Dsc.5.87. II. as Adj., = foreg., Achae.19.

**λῐθαργῠροφᾰνής**, ές, *like litharge*, Dsc.5.85.

**λῐθᾰρ-ίδιον**, τό, = sq., Alex.Trall.3.3. ⊕**-ιον**, τό, Dim. of λίθος, *stone*, Thphr.*HP*3.7.5, Phld.*Po.Herc.*1675.5, Dsc.1.68, 5.40, *PKlein. Form.*303 (vi A. D.). 2. a *gem*, *IG*11(2).287*B*46 (Delos, iii B. C.), *Annuario*6/7.405 (Perge), *PHolm.*5.4, al. (Condemned by Phryn. 158.)

⊕**λῐθ-άς**, άδος, ἡ, = λίθος, *stone*, σεῦεν κύνας.. πυκνῇσιν λιθάδεσσιν Od.14.36; θάλαμον δέμον.. πυκνῇσιν λ. 23.193; collectively, *shower of stones*, A.*Th.*158 (lyr.); *heap of stones*, λιθάδας τε καὶ ἕρμακας ἐνναίοντες, of snakes, Nic.*Th.*150 (v. l. λίθακας). **-άσβεστος**, ὁ, = *lapis calcinus*, Gloss. **-ασμός**, ὁ, *stoning*, Sch.A.*Th.*676. **-αστής**, οῦ, ὁ, *one who stones*, A.D.*Adv.*135.25. **-αστικός**, ή, όν, *by stoning*, μόρος Sch.A.*Th.*199. **-άω**, v. λιθιάω. **-εία**, ἡ, later written **λιθία**, a sort of *fine stone* or *marble*, Plb.4.52.7, Str.9.5.16, J.*AJ*8.2.9: collectively, *IG*11(2).287*A*89 (Delos, iii B. C.), *Sammelb.*5801.3 (i B. C., written -έα, and so in *Gloss.*). II. collectively, *precious stones, jewellery*, *OGI*132.8 (ii B. C.), Str.15.1.67, 16.4.22, D.S.1.46, *Peripl.M.Rubr.*56. **-ειος**, α, ον, = λίθινος, βολή Sch.A.*Pr.*561, 677; also -ος, ον Suid. **-έμπορος**, ὁ, *stone-merchant*, *IG*14.2247 (Picenum), *Supp.Epigr.*4.106 (Rome, ii A. D.). **-εος**, α, ον, = λίθινος, *of stone*, Il.23.202, Od.13.107. **-ηγός** (sc. ναῦς), ἡ, *stone-carrying vessel*, *PCair.Zen.*176.6, *PPetr.*2p.43, 3p.137 (all iii B. C.), *IG*11(2).203*B*97 (Delos, iii B. C.): pl., *Rev.Phil.*50.70 (Didyma, ii B. C.). **-ηλογής**, ές, (λέγω (B) I) *built of stones*, *AP*6.253 (Crin.).

**λῐθῐ-ᾰκός**, v. λιθικός. **-ᾱσις**, εως, Ion. ιος, ἡ, *the disease of the stone*, Hp.*Aph.*3.26 (pl.), Gal.10.917. II. *a callosity within the eyelid*, Id.14.771, Aët.7.82. **-άω**, only pres., *suffer from the stone*, Hp.*Aph.*4.79, al., Pl.*Lg.*916a, *IG*4²(1).121.68 (Epid., iv B. C.), Arist.*Pr.*895a37, Ruf.*Ren.Ves.*3, al., Philostr.*VS*1.25.11; (νοσήματα) -ιῶντα Hp.*Hum.*12:—also **λῐθάω**, which is restored in Pl. l. c., cf. Phot. s. v. λιθῶντας; also λιθόωσα· πολύλιθος, Hsch.

**λῐθ-ίδιον**, τό, Dim. of λίθος, *pebble, gem*, Pl.*Phd.*110d, Arist.*Pr.* 934b22, Plu.2.979b, Luc.*Hist.Conscr.*4. 2. *gravel* in the urine, Hp. *Coac.*578 (pl.); *stone* in the bladder, Paul.Aeg.6.60 (sg.). ⊕**-ίζω**, *look like a stone*: λιθίζων, name of a kind of *carbuncle*, v. l. in Callistr. ap.Plin.*HN*37.94 (sed leg. λιγνύζων). **-ικός**, ή, όν, *of* or *for stones*; ἔργα *Arch.Pap.*3.128 (ii B. C.); but usu. λιθικά (sc. βιβλία), τά, *a treatise upon precious stones*, title of Orphic poem, ap.Tz. (περὶ λίθων codd.); also βιβλία λιθιακά Eust. ad D.P.*Prooem.*; but Λιθικά, of D.P.'s work, Sch.Od.10.323. 2. *of* or *for stone* in the bladder, Paul.Aeg.6.60. **-ῐνος**, η, ον, also ος, ον *AP*9.719, D.L.2.33:— *made of stone*, Hippon.10, Ibyc.22, Hdt.3.88, Th.3.68, Herod.7. 109, *PHib.*1.27.26 (iii B. C.), etc.; λ. θάνατος, i. e. caused by seeing the Gorgon's head, Pi.*P.*10.48; so λ. εὐθὺς γίγνομαι Antiph.166.4; but, ἕστηκε λίθινος, of a statue, Hdt.2.141 (cf. ἵστημι A. I, B. III. 2); τὰ λ. *marble statues*, X.*Lac.*3.5; Ἑρμῆς λ. Eub.96; for Hdt.2.69, v. λίθος II. 1, ὕαλος II: metaph., καρδία Lxx *Ez.*11.19. Adv. -νως *like stone*, λ. βλέπειν πρός τινα, with allusion to the Gorgon, X.*Smp.* 4.24. **-ινότης**, ητος, ἡ, *stony quality*, dub. in Phld.*Herc.*862. 6. **-ιον**, τό, Dim. of λίθος, Paus.2.25.8. ⊕**-ιος**, Thess. for λίθινος, *IG*9(2).517.21 (Larissa). **-ίς**, ίδος, ἡ, = λιθίασις, Hp.*Morb.*4.55.

**λῐθό-βᾰσις**, εως, ἡ, *stone base* of a tripod, *BCH*29.541 (Delos). **-βλής**, ῆτος, ὁ, ἡ, *stoned*, θνήσκει λ. Tz.*H.*3.246. **-βλητος**, ον, *stone-throwing, pelting*, εὐστοχίη *AP*9.3. II. *set with stones*, κεκρύφαλα ib.5.269 (Paul. Sil.).

**λῐθοβολ-έω**, *pelt with stones, stone*, Lxx *Le.*20.2, al., D.S.17.41, *Ev. Matt.*21.35, Plu.2.1011e:—Pass., Lxx *Ex.*8.26(22). **-ήσιμος**, ον, = λιθοβόλος, Sch.E.*Or.*50:—also **-βόλητος**, Hsch. s. v. λευσίμου δίκης. **-ησις**, v. sq. **-ία**, ἡ, *throwing of stones*, Hp. *Fract.*2 (pl., v. l. for **λιθοβόλησις**), D.S.3.49. II. *stoning*, Sch. A.*Eu.*189. III. neut. pl. λιθοβόλια, τά, festival at Troezen, Paus. 2.32.2. **-ισμός**, ὁ, = λιθοβολία, Sch.A.*Th.*546. **-ίτης**, gloss on λιθολεύστης, Hsch. **-ος**, ον, (parox.) *throwing stones, pelting with stones*: -βόλοι, οἱ, *stone-throwers*, distd. from σφενδονῆται, Th.6. 69, cf. J.*BJ*3.7.18; γυμνῆτες λ. καὶ ἀκοντισταί Pl.*Criti.*119b: sg., as winner of a contest, *SIG*1061.6, 19 (Samos, ii B. C.). 2. -βόλος, ὁ, *engine for hurling stones*, Plb.8.5.2, Moschio ap.Ath.5.208c, Ath. Mech.18.6; distd. from καταπέλτης, D.S.20.48; also -βόλον, τό, Lxx 1*Ma.*6.51, J.*BJ*5.6.3; in full, λ. μηχαναί ib.4.9.12. II. proparox. λιθόβολος, ον, Pass., *struck with stones, stoned*, E.*Ph.*1063 (lyr.).

**λῐθό-γληνος**, ον, *stony-eyed*, Nonn.*D.*48.456. II. = λιθοδερκής, ib.47.592. **-γλύπτης**, ου, ὁ, *sculptor in stone*, Gloss. **-γλυφία**, ἡ, *a cutting in stone*, Man.4.130 (dat. pl.); λιθογλυφέεσσι cj. Rigler. **-γλύφος** [ῠ], ὁ, *sculptor*, Luc.*Somn.*18, Gal.1.7; *engraver*,

Dsc.5.147 (v.l. -γράφος); title of play by Philemon, Did. *in D.*9.62. **-γλώχῑν,** ὁ, ἡ, gen. ῖνος, *set with sharp stones,* ἀγυιαί Nonn.*D.*40.354, cf.6.138. **-γνωμικός,** ή, όν, *skilful in stones*: λ. (sc. βιβλίον), τό, *a work on stones,* by Philostr., Suid. s. v. Φιλόστρατος. ❋**-γνώμων,** ον, gen. ονος, = foreg., Jul.*Or.*2.91b. **-γόνος,** ον, = λιθοποιός II, Dsc.*Eup.*2.118. **-γράφος,** v. λιθογλύφος. **-δαίδᾰλος,** ον, *cunningly fashioned in stone, App.Anth.*2.534 (Halic.). **-δενδρον,** τό, *branching coral,* Dsc.5.121. **-δερκής,** ές, *petrifying with a glance,* Γοργώ *APl.*4.147 (Antiphil.). **-δερμος,** ον, *with stony hide,* Arist.*Rh.* post 1377ᵃ7 (interpol.). **-δικτέω,** (fort. -δικέω) *throw stones at,* Suid. ❋**-δμητος,** ον, *stone-built, AP*9.570 (Phld.). **-δόμητος,** ον, = foreg., J.*AJ*15.11.5. **-δόμος,** ὁ, *mason,* τέκτονες καὶ λιθοδόμοι joiners and *masons,* X.*Cyr.*3.2.11 codd. (sed leg. λιθοτόμοι). **-ειδής,** ές, *like stone,* Hp.*Morb.*4.55, Pl.*Ti.*74a, Gal.2.745, etc. **-εργής,** ές, sq. I, Μέδουσα Opp.*C.*3.222. **-εργός,** όν, *turning to stone,* Γοργώ *AP*6.126 (Diosc.). II. Subst., *stonemason,* Man.1.77. **-θεσία,** ἡ, *placing of stones,* Alex.Polyh.14. **-θήρας,** ου, ὁ, *stone-collector,* Tz.*H.*11.518.

**λῐθ-οικοδόμητος,** ον, *built of stone,* οἰκία Alex.Aphr. *in Top.*261.29.

**λῐθο-καλλής,** ές, *of beautiful stone,* μορφή *App.Anth.*2.534 (Halic.). **-κάρδιος,** ον, *stony hearted,* Sch.E.*Or.*121. **-κέφᾰλος,** ον, *with a stone in its head,* χρέμυς Arist.*Fr.*294. **-κολλα,** ἡ, *cement,* Dsc.5.145. ❋**-κόλλητος,** ον, *set with precious stones,* χιτών Callix.2; ποτήρια Thphr.*Char.*23.3, Parmenio ap. Ath.11.782a; κρατῆρες Theopomp.Hist.283(a); φιάλαι Agatharch.102; περιτραχήλιον Plu.*Alex.*32, cf. Men.372: metaph., χάλυβος λ. στόμιον a bit of steel *set with stones* (to make it sharper), S.*Tr.*1261 (lyr.). II. τὸ λ. *inlaid work, mosaic,* prob. in Str.16.4.19, cf. Thphr.*Lap.*35 (pl.). ❋**-κολλος,** ον, = foreg., *CIG*2852.47 (Branchidae). **-κομικόν,** τό, dub. sens. in *IG*1².336.9. **-κοπέω,** *pelt with stones, UPZ*16.18 (Pass., ii B. C.). **-κοπία,** ἡ, = ἡ ἐκ λίθων βολή, Suid. **-κοπικός,** ή, όν, *of* or *for stone-cutting,* σκεῦος Eust.1533.10. ❋**-κόπος,** ὁ, *stone-cutter,* Antipho Soph.92, D.47.65, *IG*3.307, prob. in 3455. **-κρήδεμνος,** ον, *with crown of stone,* of a cliff, Coluth.103. **-κτονία,** ἡ, *death by stoning, AP*9.157. **-λάβος** [ᾰ], ὁ, *instrument for extracting the stone,* Gal.14.787. **-λευστέω,** *pelt with stones,* Sch.Ar.*Ach.*233. **-λεύστης·** λιθοβολίτης, Hsch. **-λευστος,** ον, *stoned,* ὑπὸ τῶν ὄχλων D.S.3.47; λ. ποιῆσαί τινα Plu.2.313b, Sch.Call.*Iamb.* in *PSI*9.1094.25; λ. Ἄρης death *by stoning,* S.*Aj.*254 (lyr.). 2. *deserving to be stoned,* Call.*Epigr.*42.5, Alex.Aet.3.12.

❋**λῐθολογ-έω,** *build with unworked stones, IG*2².463.39, Poll.7.118; ὀπτάνιον *IG*2².1672.189. II. Pass., *to be demolished,* Aq.*Mi.*3.12. **-ημα,** ατος, τό, *foundation of unworked stone,* X.*Cyr.*6.3.25, *IG*2².463.45 (pl.), 1672.47. **-ία,** ἡ, *laying of a foundation of unworked stones,* ib.97. 2. *heap of stones,* Aq.*Ps.*78(79).1. **-ος,** ὁ, (λέγω (B) I) *one who picks out stones for building*: hence, *one who builds with stones picked out* to fit their places, not squared (cf. λογάς 2), *BSA*3.112 (Athens): so generally, *mason,* Pl.*Lg.*858b; λιθολόγοι καὶ τέκτονες *masons* and joiners, Th.6.44, cf. 7.43, X.*HG*4.4.18.

**λῐθοξό-ᾰνος,** ον, *adorned with statues,* Nonn.*D.*4.273. **-εῖον,** τό, *workshop of a* λιθοξόος, *Gloss.* **-ῐκός,** ή, όν, *of* or *for stone-cutting, Klio* 10.232, Eust.341.28. ❋**-ος,** ὁ, (ξέω) *stone-* or *marble-mason,* Luc.*Somn.*9, Max.Tyr.38.7, 39.5, f.l. in Timo 25. 2. *sculptor,* Plu.2.74d, *IG*3.1372, *AP*5.14 (Rufin.).

**λῐθο-ξύστης,** ου, ὁ, = foreg., *Cat.Cod.Astr.*7.117. ❋**-ποιέω,** *turn to stone,* v.l. in Luc.*DMar.*14.3. **-ποιός,** όν, *turning to stone,* Μέδουσα Id.*Im.*1. II. *producing stone* in the bladder, Alex.Aphr. *Pr.*1.109. ❋**-πρίστης,** ου, ὁ, *sawing stone* or *marble,* πρίων *IG*1².313.129, Poll.10.148. **-πυργία,** gloss on λίηνος, Hsch. **-ρρῖνος,** ον, *with stony skin,* χελώνη Emp.76.2.

❋**λίθος** [ῐ], ου, ὁ (v. infr. II), *stone,* Hom., etc.; esp. of the *stones* thrown by warriors, τρηχὺς λ., λ. ὀκριόεις, Il.5.308, 8.327; also, *stone-quoit,* Od.8.190: ἐλέσθαι.. ἐκ γαίας λίθον A.*Fr.*199.4; of *building-stones,* λίθοι βασιλικοί *PSI*4.423.28, *PCair.Zen.*499.20 (both iii B. C.): prov., ἐν παντὶ γάρ τοι σκορπίος φρουρεῖ λίθῳ S.*Fr.*37; λίθον ἕψειν 'to lose one's labour', Ar.*V.*280; also of stupid persons, 'blockheads', λίθοι Id.*Nu.*1202, cf. Thgn.568, Pl.*Hp.Ma.*292d, Gal.9.656; λ. τις, οὐ δούλη Herod.6.4; προσηγορεύθη διὰ τὸ μὴ φρονεῖν λ., of Niobe, Philem.101; ὥσπερ λίθον ζῆν Pl.*Grg.*494a sq.; λίθῳ λαλεῖς prov. of ἀναίσθητοι, Macar.5.61. 2. *stone* as a substance, opp. wood, flesh, etc., ἐπεὶ οὔ σφι λ. χρὼς οὐδὲ σίδηρος Il.4.510; λαοὺς δὲ λίθους ποίησε turned into *stone, petrified,* 24.611, cf. Pl.*Smp.*198c; so [νῆα] θεῖναι λ. Od.13.156; as an emblem of hard-heartedness, σοὶ δ' αἰεὶ κραδίη στερεωτέρη ἐστὶ λίθοιο 23.103, cf. Theoc.3.18. II. λίθος, ἡ, twice in Hom., Il.12.287, Od.19.494, just like masc., also in Theoc.7.26, Bion *Fr.*1.2: later mostly of *some special stone,* as the magnet is called Μαγνῆτις λ. by E.*Fr.*567 (but ἡ λίθος simply in Democr.11ᵏ, Arist.*Ph.*267ᵃ2, cf. v.l. *de An.*405ᵃ20); also Λυδία λ. by S.*Fr.*800 (but in B.*Fr.*10 J. Λυδία λ. = *touchstone*); Ἡρακλεία λ. by Pl.*Ion* 533d, Epicur.*Fr.*293; so of a *touchstone,* Pl.*Grg.*486d; ἡ διαφανὴς λ. *a piece of crystal* used for a burning-glass, Ar.*Nu.*767, cf. Luc.*Alex.*21; χυτὴ λ. was perh. a kind of *glass,* and so an older name for ὕαλος, Epin.1.8 (the same thing as the ἀρτήματα λίθινα χυτά in Hdt.2.69: cf. τὴν ὕαλον.. ὅσα τε λίθων χυτὰ εἴδη καλεῖται Pl.*Ti.*61c); λ. = *precious stone* is fem. in Hp.*Nat.Mul.*99, *IG*2².1421.92, 1460.21, but masc. in Hdt.2.44, etc.; in the sense of *marble* mostly masc., λευκὸς λ. Id.4.87 (simply λίθος 1.164), S.*Fr.*330 (λευκοὶ λ. is opp. πέτρινοι λ. *Supp.Epigr.*4.446.8 (Didyma)); Πάριος λ. Pi.*N.*4.81, Hdt.3.57; Ταινάριος λ. Str.8.5.7; λ. Θάσιος, Αἰγύπτιος, etc., Paus.1.18.6, etc.; κογχίτης Id.1.44.6; κογχυλιάτης X.*An.*3.4.10; but Παρία λ. Theoc.6.38, Luc.*Am.*13; cf. λυχνίας, -ίτης; πώρινος λ. *tufa,* Hdt.5.62. 2. collectively, πέφυκε λίθος.. ἄφθονος, ἐξ οὗ.. X.*Vect.*1.4. III. *grave-stone* (fem.), Call.*Epigr.*8.1. IV. at Athens, λίθος, ὁ, was a name for various *blocks of stone used for rostra* or *platforms,* as, 1. the βῆμα (q. v.) of the Pnyx, Ar.*Ach.*683, *Pax* 680, *Ec.*87. 2. another in the ἀγορά used by the κήρυκες, Plu.*Sol.*8; prob. the same as ὁ πρατὴρ λ., on which the auctioneer stood when selling slaves, etc., Poll.3.78, cf. 126. 3. an *altar* in the ἀγορά, at which the Thesmothetae, arbitrators, and witnesses took their oaths, Philoch.65, D.54.26 (restored from Harp. s. v. λίθος), Arist.*Ath.*7.1, 55.5, Plu.*Sol.*25; cf. λιθωμότης. 4. two *stones* on which litigants stood in the Areopagus, Paus.1.28.5. V. *piece on a draughtboard,* Alc.82, Theoc.6.18, cf. γραμμή III. 1: hence prov., πάντα λίθον κινεῖν Zen.5.63 (who explains it differently). VI. Medic., *stone in the bladder, calculus,* Arist.*HA* 519ᵇ19, Hp.*Morb.*4.55, al. VII. Δία λίθον ὀμνύναι, = Lat. *Jovem lapidem jurare,* Plb.3.25.6. VIII. λίθοι χαλάζης *hail-stones,* Lxx *Jo.*10.11. IX. λ. ὁ οὐ λ. the philosophers' *stone,* Zos. Alch.p.122 B.

**λῐθο-σπᾰδής** ἁρμός, a chasm in the vault *made by tearing out stones,* S.*Ant.*1216. **-σπερμον,** τό, *gromwell, Lithospermum officinale,* Dsc.3.141, Ps.-Gal.19.694. **-στεγής,** ές, *covered with stones,* Sch. Lyc.350. ❋**-στρωτος,** ον, *paved with stones,* S.*Ant.*1204; δρόμος *POxy.*2138.15 (iii A. D.), *PFlor.*50.97 (iii A. D.). 2. esp. of *tesselated work,* λ. ἔδαφος Str.17.1.28, Poll.7.121; λ., τό, *mosaic* or *tessellated pavement, IG*4² 1).110.19 (Epid., iv/iii B. C.). Lxx *Ca.*3.10, *Ev.Jo.*19.13, *CIG*2643 (Cyprus, -στρατ-), Roussel *Délos : Colonie Athénienne* p.422, Arr.*Epict.*4.7.37 (v. l.), etc.

**λῐθοτομ-εῖον,** τό, *quarry, IG*2².47.30. II. = λιθοτομία II, *Gloss.* **-έω,** *quarry,* Ph.1.235, Philostr.*VA*3.48:—Pass., *to be cut out of stone,* Luc.*JTr.*10. II. *cut for the stone,* Gal.1.168:—Pass., Dsc.5.15, Paul.Aeg.6.60. **-ία,** Ion. -ίη, ἡ, *stone-quarry, IG*2².1666 *B* 72: mostly in pl., *quarries,* Hdt.2.8, Th.7.86, 87, D.53.17; *marble quarries,* Thphr.*Lap.*6, Paus.1.32.1 (sg. in 1.18.9, 1.19.6), etc.; cf. λατομία. II. *cutting for the stone, lithotomy,* Gal.18(1).29, Paul. Aeg.6.60. **-ικός,** ή, όν *of* or *for stone-cutting*: ἡ -κή (sc. τέχνη), Porph.*Hist.Phil.*11, cf. *BCH*35.12 (Delos); *skill in lithotomy,* Gal. *Thras.*24. **-ιον,** τό, = λιθοτόμον II. b, *Hermes* 38.282. **-ος** (parox.), ον, *for cutting stones,* ὄργανα Agath.1.10: Subst. λ., ὁ, prob. for λιθοδόμος in X.*Cyr.*3.2.11; *quarryman, IG*1².347.36, 2².1680.4; *mason,* Gal.*Thras.*43, *PAmh.*2.76.9 (ii/iii A. D.). II. Subst., λ., ὁ, *surgeon who cuts for the stone,* Gal.1.125, *Thras.*24; but, *who cuts the stone* (internally), Ammonius ὁ λ. Cels.7.26.3. b. λ., τό, *knife for cutting for the stone,* Paul.Aeg.6.60.

**λῐθο-τράχηλος** [ᾰ], ον, *stony-,* i.e. *stiff-necked,* Jul.*Gal.*213b. **-τρῐβικός,** ή, όν, *of* or *for stone-polishing*: ἡ -κή (sc. τέχνη), *the art of so polishing,* Lys.*Fr.*69.

**λῐθουλκ-έω,** *draw* or *quarry stones,* Suid.: metaph., *drag slowly along,* Hsch. **-ία,** ἡ, *haulage of stone, IG*1².347.38, al. ❋**-ός,** όν, (ἕλκω) *quarrying stones,* Poll.7.118. II. as Subst. λ., ὁ, *instrument for extracting the stone,* Heliod.ap.Orib.45.6.2, Aët.16.111 (101), Paul.Aeg.6.60.

**λῐθουργ-εῖον,** τό, *quarry,* Is.5.44, Str.5.2.5, *IG*2².1123*b*. **-έω,** *work in stone, hew,* λίθον Lxx *Ex.*35.33: abs., Porph.*Hist.Phil.*11; *carve* a gem, *PMag.Berol.*1.68. II. *turn into stone, petrify,* γυῖα *AP*3.11 (Cyzic.), cf. Philostr.*Im.*1.11. **-ής,** ές, *worked in stone,* εἰκόνισμα S.*Fr.*574; βότρυς Aristeas 70. **-ία,** ἡ, *sculpture in marble, IG*1².347.39, D.S.4.76; *working at* or *in stone,* Thom. Mag.p.221 R.: in pl., *stone-quarries,* Brut.*Ep.*37. **-ικός,** ή, όν, *of* or *for a* λιθουργός, τέχνη Lxx *Ex.*28.11: -κά, τά, ib.31.5: ἡ -κή (sc. τέχνη), Lys.*Fr.*69: -κόν, τό, *sum spent on masonry, IG*1².374.317, al. ❋**-ός,** ὁ, *stone-mason,* Ar.*Av.*1134, Th.4.69, 5.82, etc.; *sculptor in marble,* opp. ἀνδριαντοποιός (in bronze), Arist.*EN*1141ᵃ10, cf. *Supp. Epigr.*3.464 (Thess., iv B. C.). 2. σιδήρια λιθουργά *a stone-mason's tools,* Th.4.4.

**λῐθουρία,** ἡ, *passing gravel with the urine,* Sch.Pi.*P.*1.87.

**λῐθοφορ-έω,** *carry stones,* Th.6.98. ❋**-ος,** ον, *carrying stones,* ὁλκάδες D.S.13.78; κεραῖαι Moschio ap. Ath.5.208d; ἱερεύς *IG*3.296. 2. as Subst. λ., ὁ, = λιθοβόλος I. 2, Plb.4.56.3.

**λῐθο-φρύγιον** [ῠ], τό, = λίθος φρύγιος (v. Dsc.5.123), Olymp.Alch. p.93 B., Paul.Aeg.3.59. **-ψήκτης,** ου, ὁ, (ψήχω) *stone-polisher, Cat.Cod.Astr.*8(4).216 (-ψύκτ- cod.). **-ψωκτος,** ον, (ψώχω) *rubbing* or *polishing stones,* Man.4.326.

**λῐθ-όω,** only in Pass. λιθόομαι, *to be petrified,* Arist.*PA*641ᵃ21, *GA*783ᵃ28, Plu.2.577f, Luc.*Asin.*4: impers., λιθοῦται *petrifaction takes place,* Arist.*Pr.*937ᵃ17. 2. λελιθωμένον, prob. = λιθόστρωτον, Poll.7.121. **-ώδης,** ες, *like stone, stony,* γῆ Hdt.4.23; ὁδός X.*Eq.*4.4; τόποι τραχεῖς καὶ λ. Arist.*HA*590ᵇ23; πεδίον (as pr. n.) Str.4.1.7: Comp., of plants, Arist.*GA*783ᵃ31: metaph., λ. [κέαρ] Pl.*Tht.*194e; Νιόβης αὐτῆς -ωδέστερος Lyd.*Mag.*3.61. Adv. -δῶς, ὅσα (sc. ὕδατα) προσπήγνυται τοῖς χαλκείοις λ. Ruf.*Fr.*66.16. **-ωδία,** ἡ, *stone-like hardness,* Eust.24.7. **-ωμότης,** ου, ὁ, *one that took an oath at the altar* (λίθος IV. 3), *Com.Adesp.*667. **-ώπης,** ες, (ὤψ) *gleaming with jewels,* ὀφθαλμοί, of the Wooden Horse, Tryph.68. 2. fem. **λιθῶπις,** ιδος, *turning one to stone by a look,* Nonn.*D.*30.265. **-ωσις,** εως, ἡ, *a turning into stone, petrifying,* Plu.2.953e. II. *work in stone,* λ. ποικίλη Aristeas 74.

**λικερτίζειν·** σκιρτᾶν, Hsch. **λίκηνον·** ἀγγεῖον ὀστράκινον,

Id. **λίκιγξ·** ἡ ἐλαχίστη βοὴ τῶν ὀρνέων, Sch.Ar.*Ach.*1034. **λικμάζειν·** περιλείχειν, Hsch.

**λικμ-αῖος,** α, ον, *presiding over winnowing*, of Demeter, *AP*6.98 (Zon.). ⊛**-άς,** άδος, ἡ, *winnowing fan*, = θρῖναξ, Hsch. (λιχμάς cod.). ⊛**-άω,** fut. -ήσω X.*Oec.*18.8: aor. ἐλίκμησα B.*Fr.*34:—*part the grain from the chaff, winnow*, ἀνδρῶν λικμώντων Il.5.500; σῖτον λ. X.*Oec.*18.6; καρπὸν ἀπ' ἀσταχύων B. l.c.: metaph., *scatter like chaff*, Lxx *Ez.*29.12; *make away with*, ib.*Is.*30.22; *crush, destroy*, ἐλίκμησάν μου τὸ λάχανον *BGU*146.8 (iii A.D.); ἐφ' ὃν δ' ἂν πέσῃ (sc. ὁ λίθος) λικμήσει αὐτόν *Ev.Luc.*20.18. **-ητήρ,** ῆρος, ὁ, *winnower* of corn, Il.13.590. **-ητήριον,** τό, *winnowing-fan, shovel*, Sm.*Je.*15.7, Thd.*Is.*30.14, Hsch. **-ητηρίς,** ίδος, ἡ, = foreg., Poll.1.245. **-ητής,** οῦ, ὁ, = λικμητήρ, *PFay.*101.4 (i B.C.), Poll.1.222, Aq., Sm.*Je.*51(28).2, Serv.Dan. ad Verg.*G.*1.166. **-ητικός,** ή, όν, *of* or *for winnowing*, πτύον Eust.135.43. **-ητός,** ὁ, *winnowing*, *AP*6.225 (Nicaen.). **2.** = ἀπώλεια, λικμητὸν ἀνθρώποις ἀπειλεῖ Lyd.*Ost.*20. **-ητρίς,** ίδος, ἡ, = λικμός, *PFay.*120.4 (i/ii A.D.), *Gloss.* **-ήτωρ,** ορος, ὁ, = λικμητήρ, metaph., λ. ἀσεβῶν Lxx *Pr.*20.20(26). **-ίζει·** ἀλοᾷ, Hsch. **-ός,** οῦ, ὁ, = λίκνον, Lxx *Am.*9.9, *Sammelb.*5220.2 (i A.D.), Serv.Dan. ad Verg.*G.*1.166, Hsch.

**λικν-άριον,** τό, Dim. of λίκνον, *Gloss.* **-ίζω,** = λικμάω, *PFay.*102.30 (ii A.D.), *Gloss.* **-ίτης** [ῑ], ου, ὁ, god *of the* λίκνον, epith. of Dionysus, Orph.*H.*46.1, 52.3, Plu.2.365a:—fem. **-ῖτις,** τροφή S.*Ichn.*269.

**λικνοειδής,** ές, = ῥυπαρός, Suid., Zonar.

**λίκνον,** τό (also λεῖκνον acc. to Hdn.Gr.2.543, and λικμός (q.v.)), *winnowing-fan*, i.e. a broad basket, in which the corn was placed after threshing, and then thrown against the wind so as to winnow the grain from the chaff, Arist.*Mete.*368$^{b}$29; sacred to Dionysus, and carried on the head at his festivals, *AP*6.165 (Phal.); also to Athena, S.*Fr.*844; cf. λικνίτης, λικνοφόρος. **II.** *cradle*, *h.Merc.*21.150, al., Call.*Jov.*48, Arat.268, Gal.6.37, etc.

**λικνο-στεφεῖ·** λίκνον στεφανούμενος θρησκεύει, Hsch. **-φορέω,** *carry the sacred* λίκνον, Polem.Hist.88. **-φόρος,** ον, *carrying the sacred* λίκνον *in procession*, D.18.260, Call.*Cer.*127.

**λικνόω** or **λικνέω,** = λικμάω, in part. dat. pl. λιγνοῦσιν (sic), dub. in *Ostr.Strassb.*748 (ii A.D.).

**λικριφίς,** Adv. *cross-wise, sideways*, λ. ἀΐξας Il.14.463, Od.19.451.

**λικροί·** οἱ ὄζοι τῶν ἐλαφείων κεράτων, Hsch. (also **λεκροί** Id.). **λίκτης,** ου, ὁ, (λείχω) *one that licks*, *Gloss.* (better **λείκτης**).

**λιλαίομαι,** only pres. and impf., *long* or *desire earnestly*, freq. in Hom., mostly c. inf., *long to be* or *do* so and so, τί με..λιλαίεαι ἠπεροπεύειν; Il.3.399; λ. πολεμίζειν 16.89; εὐνηθῆναι 14.331: metaph., of a lance, λιλαιομένη χροὸς ἆσαι *longing* to taste flesh, 21.168, cf. 11.574, 15.317; λιλαιομένη πόσιν εἶναι *longing for him* to be her husband, Od.1.15, 9.30, 32, 23.334: c. gen., *long for*, πολέμοιο, δδοῖο, βιότοιο, δόρποιο, Il.3.133, Od.1.315, 12.328, 13.31; also φόωσδε λιλαίεο *struggle* to the light of day, 11.223: so in later Ep., c. inf., A.R.3.394, al.: c. acc., Nonn.*D.*28.144: abs., ib.42.132.—Cf. λελίημαι.

**λιλεῖ·** φθονεῖ, ἐπιθυμεῖ, Hsch. **λιλουργετά·** ἐν τῷ σώματι ἐξανθήματα, Id. **λίλυ·** τὸ ὕδωρ (Libyan word), Id.

**λιμαγχ-έω,** in Pass., *to be weakened* or *reduced by hunger* or *low diet*, Hp.*Art.*8, *Prorrh.*2.4, *POxy.*37 i 14 (i A.D.), Gal.10.584. **-ία,** ἡ, *weakening by low diet*, Ruf.*Ren.Ves.*1.6. **-ικός,** ή, όν, *famished*, Hp.*Epid.*2.1.8. **-ονέω,** = λιμαγχέω, Id.*Art.*81, Antisth.ap.Stob.3.8.26, Lxx *De.*8.3, Gal.15.573. **-ονία,** ἡ, = λιμαγχία, Id.15.478. **-ονικός,** ή, όν, *of* or *for reducing by hunger*, Id.1.605.

**λιμαίνω** (λιμός), aor. 1 ἐλίμηνα, *suffer from famine*, of armies, Hdt.6.28, 7.25; of a country, Nic.Dam.45 J.

**λιμᾰλέος,** α, ον, *starved*, Hsch.

**λιμβ-εία,** ἡ, = λιχνεία, Hdn.*Epim.*77; **λιμβία,** Hsch. s.v. λιχνία. **-εύω,** = λιχνεύω, Hdn. l.c. **-ος** (or **λιμβός**), ον, = λίχνος, Hsch., Anon. *in EN*182.9, etc.

**λιμβός,** ὁ, = Lat. *limbus*, a dinner-dress, Lyd.*Mag.*2.4.

**λιμβρός,** ά, όν, = λιβρός II, *EM*564.52, Suid.

⊛**λιμεναρχ-έω,** *to be a harbour-master*, *IG*7.1826 (Creusis). **-ης,** ου, ὁ, *harbour-master*, *PGiss.*10.4 (ii A.D.), *Cod.Just.*7.16.38, *Gloss.*

**λιμεν-ήοχος,** ον, (ἔχω) *closing in the harbour*, ἄκρη A.R.2.965. **-ίζω,** *form a harbour*, Polyaen.4.7.7. ⊛**-ιον,** τό, Dim. of λιμήν, Str.5.2.6 (pl.), Marcian.*Epit.*8. ⊛**-ιος,** α, ον, *of the harbour*, epith. of Aphrodite, Paus.2.34.11; of Zeus, Ach.Tat.*Intr.Arat.*p.84 M.; cf. sq. ⊛**-ίτης** [ῑ], ου, ὁ, voc. λιμενῖτα, *god of the harbour*, of Priapus, *AP*10.1 (Leon.), cf. 10.17 (Antiphil.):—fem. **-ῖτις,** ιδος, of Artemis, ib.6.105 (Apollonid.). **2.** λ. φυλακτῆρες *custom-house* officers, Dam.*Isid.*186. **-ιτικός,** ή, όν, *of a harbour*, χρήματα *harbour-dues*, *Cod.Just.*10.30.4 (-ητικός codd.).

**λιμενο-ειδής,** ές, *like a harbour*, κόλπος Str.5.1.9. **-ποιΐα,** ἡ, *construction of harbours*, Tz.*H.*2.8 (pl.). **-ποιϊκά,** τά, *things belonging thereto*, Ph.*Bel.*49.3.

**λιμεν-ορμίτης** [μῑ], ου, ὁ, (λιμήν, ὅρμος) *god of harbours and mooring-places*, epith. of Priapus, *AP*10.5 (Thyill.).

**λιμενοσκόπος,** ον, *watching the harbour*, epith. of Zeus and Phoebus, Call.*Fr.*114, *AP*10.25 (Antip.): as fem., Call.*Dian.*259.

**λιμενουργία,** ἡ, *harbour-making*, Tz.*H.*11.621.

**λιμενοφύλαξ** [ῠ], ἄκος, ὁ, *harbour-watcher*, Aen.Tact.29.12: title of magistrate at Carystus, *IG*12(9).8 (ii B.C.), 9 (i B.C.); τὸν λι[μενοφυλακοῦντα Ἀ]θηναίων may perh. be restored, ib.2$^{2}$.133.23 (iv B.C.).

⊛**λιμήν,** ένος, ὁ, *harbour*, Il.1.432 (here distd. fr. ὅρμος, mooring-place), al., Pl.*Ti.*25a, etc.; Κανθάρου λ. a dockyard in the Piraeus, with a pun on κάνθαρος just above, Ar.*Pax*145 (ubi v. Sch.): freq. in pl., λιμένες νηῶν ὀχοί Od.5.404; λιμένες δ' ἔνι ναύλοχοι αὐτῇ 4.846; λιμένες τε πάνορμοι 13.195, cf. S.*Ph.*936, etc.: c. gen. objecti, λιμένες θαλάσσης *havens of refuge from* the sea, Od.5.418, cf. Hes.*Sc.*207. **II.** metaph., *haven, retreat, refuge*, Thgn.460; ἑταιρείας λ. *a haven of* friendship, S.*Aj.*683; οὗτος..λ. πέφανται τῶν ἐμῶν βουλευμάτων E.*Med.*769: c. gen. objecti, λ. κακῶν *from* ills, A.*Supp.*471; ὦ ναυτίλοισι χείματος λ. φανείς E.*Andr.*891; ὕπνον..τῶν καμάτων λ. Critias 6.20 D.; λ. τῆς πλάνης ἥδε ἡ γῆ μόνη λείπεται D.H.1.58. **2.** *gathering-place, receptacle*, πλούτου λ. A.*Pers.*250; μέγας E.*Or.*1077; παντὸς οἰωνοῦ λ. S.*Ant.*1000; Ἅιδου λ. *harbour* of death, ib.1284 (lyr.); ξείνων αἰδοῖοι λιμένες Emp.112.3; βοῆς τῆς σῆς ποῖος οὐκ ἔσται λ.; what place shall not *harbour* (i.e. receive) thy cry? S.*OT*420. **III.** = ἀγορά in Thessaly and Paphos, *IG*9(2).517.42 (Larissa), Gal.*Thras.*32, D.Chr.11.23 (interpol.). **IV.** *the source of birth, womb*, Emp.98.3, S.*OT*1208 (lyr.).

⊛**λιμηρός,** ά, όν, (λιμός) *hungry, causing hunger*, ἔρως Theoc.10.57; ἐργασίη *AP*6.47 (Antip. Sid.), cf. 285 (Nicarch.), 7.546, Alciphr.1.9, etc.

⊛**λιμηρός,** ά, όν, (λιμήν) *furnished with a good harbour*, special epith. of Epidaurus in Laconia, Th.4.56, 7.26; εὐλίμενον δὲ οὖσαν, βραχέως..λιμηρὰν εἰρῆσθαι, ὡς ἂν λιμενηράν Apollod.ap.Str.8.6.1.

**λίμινθες·** ἕλμινθες, Hsch.

⊛**λιμν-ᾱγενής,** ές, *born at* Λίμναι (v. λίμνη II), *BMus.Inscr.*1009 (Cyzic., ii B.C.), Hsch. ⊛**-άζω,** of the sea or rivers, *form stagnant pools*, Arist.*Mete.*352$^{b}$35, 356$^{a}$7; ὅσοι ποταμοὶ -άζουσιν εἰς ἕλη rivers which *stagnate* into marshes, Id.*Pr.*938$^{a}$3: impers., -άζει *stagnant pools are left* in them, Id.*Mete.*351$^{b}$8, 352$^{a}$5. **2.** of the blood, *to be stagnant*, Id.*HA*513$^{b}$4, Gal.*UP*14.10. **II.** c. acc., *form into a lake*, ὁ ποταμὸς λ. τὰς ἀρούρας Ph.2.98, cf. Str.8.8.4, D.Chr.11.76:—Pass., of land, *to be flooded*, J.*AJ*1.3.5, *PStrassb.*10.11 (iii A.D.). **III.** intr. in Act., of a country, *become a marsh*, ἐν τοῖς -άζουσι τόποις Arist.*Mete.*340$^{b}$37, cf. D.S.4.18, Str.8.5.1, etc. **-αῖον,** τό, v.l. for λιμνήσιον, Dsc.3.7. ⊛**-αῖος,** α, ον, (λίμνη) *of* or *from the marsh*, ὄρνιθας χερσαίους καὶ λ. both land-fowl and *water*-fowl, Hdt.7.119, cf. Ar.*Av.*272; of the crocodile, ἐὸν..τετράπουν, χερσαῖον καὶ λ. ἐστι Hdt.2.68; λ. κρηνῶν τέκνα, of frogs, Ar.*Ra.*211; of the beaver, Nic.*Al.*307; of an eel, Diph.Siph.ap.Ath.8.355d (vulg. λιμνία); λ. φυτόν *water*-plant, Plu.2.399f. **2.** of water, *stagnant*, Hp.*Aër.*7. **3.** *of* or *for marshes*, λ. πλοῖον, σκάφος, *PLond.*2.317.9 (ii A.D.), Hld.1.31; λ. ἄνεμοι Hsch. **II.** (Λίμναι) *of* or *from Limnae*, epith. of Dionysus, from his temple there, Call.*Fr.*37 P.: but Λιμναῖον, τό, *a temple of Artemis at Limnae*, on the borders of Laconia and Messenia, Str.8.4.9, cf. Paus.3.2.6: hence she was called **Λιμνᾶτις** v. λιμνήτης; also **Λιμναία,** epith. of Artemis at Sicyon and elsewhere, Id.2.7.6, etc. **-άς,** άδος, ἡ, poet. fem. of λιμναῖος, Theoc.5.17, Babr.115.1, Paus.3.7.4. **-ᾰσία,** ἡ, *marshy ground*, Arist.*Pr.*938$^{a}$7. **-ασμός,** ὁ, *irrigation, flooding*, *PFlor.*21.3 (iii A.D.), *POxy.*2121.41 (iii A.D.). **-αστεία,** ἡ, *irrigation works*, *BGU*91.5 (ii A.D.). **-αστής,** οῦ, ὁ, *supervisor of irrigation-works*, *PTeb.*209 (i B.C.), Wilcken *Chr.*392.4 (ii A.D.). **-εία,** ἡ, and **-ευσις,** εως, ἡ, = λιμνασία, Zonar. **-η,** ἡ, *pool of standing water* left by the sea or a river, Il.21.317: hence, *marshy lake, mere*, distd. from ἕλος, Pl.*Criti.*114e, *Lg.*824c; Βοιβηῒς λ. Il.2.711; Γυγαίη ib.865; Κηφισίς 5.709; λ. Γοργῶπις A.*Ag.*302; Μαιῶτις Id.*Pr.*419 (lyr.), cf. 729, *Pers.*871 (lyr.), Hdt.4.86; ἡ Βόλβη λ. Th.4.103; λ. τροχοειδής, at Delos, Hdt.2.170, cf. A.*Eu.*9. **b.** also, *artificial pool* or *basin*, Hdt.1.185, 191, al., *SIG*799 ii 3 (Cyzic., i A.D.). **2.** in Hom. and other Poets, *the sea*, Il.24.79, Od.3.1; βένθεσι λίμνης Il.13.21, 32: so in Trag. in lyr., λίμνᾳ πορφυροειδεῖ A.*Supp.*529; ἐπ' οἶδμα λίμνας S.*Fr.*476, E.*Hec.*446; Πόσειδον, ὃς γλαυκᾶς μέδεις..λίμνας S.*Fr.*371; Μηλίδα πὰρ λ. by the Malian *bay*, Id.*Tr.*636. **II.** Λίμναι, αἱ, (used without the article), *a quarter of Athens* (once prob. *marshy*), near the Acropolis, in which stood the Lenaeum, Ar.*Ra.*216, Th.2.15, Is.8.35, etc., cf. λιμναῖος II. **2.** *a quarter* or *suburb of Sparta*, Str.8.5.1. **3.** *a place in Messenia*, Id.8.4.9. **-ηθεν,** Adv. *from the lake* or *sea*, A.R.4.1579. **-ησία,** ἡ, = ἀδάρκη, Gal.7.600. **-ήσιον,** τό, = κενταύρειον τὸ μικρόν, Dsc.3.7; = κενταύρειον τὸ μέγα, Ps.-Dsc.3.6. **II.** = ἀδάρκη, Damocr.ap.Gal.13.1051.

**Λιμνήσιος,** ὁ, *Laker*, name of a frog, v.l. in Batr.223.

**λίμν-ησις,** εως, ἡ, = ἀδάρκη, v.l. in Gal.6.434. **-ήστινον** (sc. ἄκοπον), τό, *drug prepared from* λιμνήσιον II, Herod.Med. in *Rh.Mus.*58.92 (s.v.l.). **-ήστιον,** τό, = foreg., ib.104 (λημνίστιον ib.101). **-ηστις,** εως, ἡ, = κενταύρειον τὸ μέγα, Ps.-Dsc.3.6, cf. Aret.*CA*1.2, al.; = ἀδάρκη, Gal.6.434:—also **-ηστρίς,** ίδος, ἡ, = ἀδάρκη, Androm.ap.Gal.13.1036: gen. sg. **λημνίτιδος** (sic) Herod.Med. in *Rh.Mus.*58.101. **-ηστρον,** τό, = ἀδάρκη, Gal.12.424. ⊛**-ήτης,** ου, ὁ, fem. **-ῆτις,** Dor. **-ᾶτις,** ιδος, *living in marshes*, βδέλλα Theoc.2.56. **II.** epith. of Artemis at Limnae (v. λιμναῖος II), *IG*5(1).1431.38 (i A.D.), Paus.3.23.10, 4.4.2, al., Artem.2.35, Sch.Th.*Oxy.*853 x 14: voc. λιμνᾶτι *AP*6.280.

**λιμνι-άρχης,** ου, or **-αρχος,** ὁ, *superintendent of lakes*, *POxy.*117.20 (ii/iii A.D.). ⊛**-ον,** τό, Dim. of λίμνη, Arist.*Mir.*840$^{b}$33, dub. in Phld.*Mort.*32. **-ος,** α, ον, v. λιμναῖος I.1.

**λιμν-ιτικά,** τά, *taxes incident upon* γῆ λιμνιτική (prob. land *on the margin of the lakes*, which occurs in *PGen.ined.*), *PRyl.*213.32, al. (ii A.D.). **-ῖτις,** ιδος, ἡ, epith. of the moon, *Hymn.Mag.*5.46.

**λιμνό-βῐος,** ον, *living in a lake*, opp. χερσόβιος, Ael.*NA*6.10, Philum.*Ven.*36.1. **-ειδής,** ές, = λιμνώδης. Adv. -δῶς Eust. ad D.P.48. **-θάλασσα** [θᾰ], Att. **-ττα,** ἡ, *lagoon*, Xanth.3, Arist.

*HA*598$^{a}$20, *GA*761$^{b}$7. Gal.6.711; later, of the Dead Sea, Aët.1 *Praef.* **-μάχης** [ἄ], ου, ὁ, *candidate for the prize at the Lenaea*, v. λίμνη II. 1, Hsch. **-ομαι,** Pass., *become a marsh*, Thphr.*HP*5.4.6, *CP*5.12.3, Str.5.3.13.

**λίμνος,** ἡ, perh. = λίμνη, *POxy.*103.18 (iv A.D.).

**λιμνόστρεον,** τό, *edible oyster, which was kept in ponds by the sea* (λίμναι), Arist.*HA*528$^{a}$23, 547$^{b}$11, *GA*763$^{a}$30.

**λιμνοσώμᾰτος,** ον, *marsh-bodied*, ἐγχέλεις Eub.37 (s.v.l.).

**λιμνουργός,** ὁ, *one who works in* λίμναι, *fisherman*, Plu.*Mar.*37.

**λιμνο-φῠής,** ές, *marsh-born*, δόναξ *AP*6.23. **-χᾰρις,** ιτος, ὁ, *Grace of the marsh*, or **-χᾰρής,** *Love-marsh*, name of a frog, Batr.12, 212.

**λιμνώδης,** ες, *marshy*, ὕδωρ Hp.*Aër.*10, cf. Arist.*Mete.*353$^{b}$24; ὁ Πόντος ἐστὶ λ. διὰ τὸ πολλοὺς ποταμοὺς εἰς αὐτὸν ῥεῖν Id.*Pr.*932$^{a}$28. 2. of *marshy ground*, τὸ λ. τοῦ Στρυμόνος Th.5.7.

**λῑμοδοξ-έω,** *crave after fame*, Ph.2.273, 534. **-ία,** ἡ, *craving for fame*, Id.1.290.

**Λῑμοδωριεῖς,** οἱ, name given to colonists driven by famine from Peloponnesus, Hsch.

**λῑμο-θνής,** ῆτος, ὁ, ἡ, *dying of hunger*, A.*Ag.*1274. **-κίμβιξ,** ῑκος, ὁ, ἡ, *one who starves himself from avarice*, *Com.Adesp.*1073. **-κόλαξ,** ᾰκος, ὁ, *hungry flatterer*, ib.1074. **-κτονέω,** *treat by hunger*, *diet severely. starve*, Hp.*Acut.*(*Sp.*)56, Pl.*R.*589a, Lxx *Pr.*10.3:—Pass., *to be severely dieted*, Hp.*Mul.*1.12; *to be starved to death*, Str.11.11.3, Procop.*Arc.*25. **-κτονία,** Ion. **-ίη,** ἡ, *treatment by abstinence from food*, Hp. *Acut.*(*Sp.*)24, *Vict.*3.71, Gal.11.182: pl., Pl.*Prt.*354a. **-ξηρος,** ον, *wasted with hunger*, Hierocl.*Facet.*219–226. Adv. -ρως *Gloss.* **-ποιός,** όν, *causing hunger*, Erot. s.v. λεβηρίδος; Ζεύς Oenom.ap.Eus.*PE*6.7.

⊛ **λῑμός,** οῦ, ὁ (Dor. ἡ, acc. to Phryn.164, used by the Megarian in Ar.*Ach.*743, cf. Herod.2.17, Bion *Fr.*14.4; Λ. ἔχων γυναικὸς μορφήν Callisth.ap.Ath.10.452b; also *h.Cer.*311, Call.*Fr.anon.*43, Plb.1.84.9, *AP*9.89 (Phil.), *Ev.Luc.*15.14, *Act.Ap.*11.28):—*hunger, famine*, δίψα τε καὶ λ. Il.19.166; λιμῷ θανέειν Od.12.342; λιμὸν ὁμοῦ καὶ λοιμόν Hes.*Op.*243, cf. Th.2.54; λ. αἰανής Pi.*I.*1.49; λιμῷ συνεστεῶτας Hdt.7.170; σκότῳ λ. ξύνοικος A.*Ag.*1642; δείπνου προφήτην λιμόν Antiph.217.23; ἅπανθ' ὁ λ. γλυκέα πλὴν αὑτοῦ ποιεῖ Id.293; ὁ δὲ λ. ἐστιν ἀθανασίας φάρμακον Id.86.6: prov., ἀπολεῖτε λιμῷ Μηλίῳ, referring to the siege of Melos, Ar.*Av.*186: metaph., ἤδη γὰρ εἶδον..λιμόν τ' ἐν ἀνδρὸς πλουσίου φρονήματι, γνώμην δὲ μεγάλην ἐν πένητι σώματι E.*El.*371. II. *a hungry wretch*, Men.*Kol.*78, Posidipp.26.12, Eust.1828.6.

**λῑμο-φορεύς,** έως, ὁ, (φέρω) *causing hunger*, *AP*11.371 (Pall.). **-ψωρος,** ὁ, (ψώρα) *scurvy*, arising from hunger or bad food, Plb.3.87.2:—later **-ψώρα,** ἡ, *Hippiatr.*69.

⊛ **λιμπάνω,** collat. form of λείπω, Hp.*Morb.*4.55, Arat.128, Hdn.Gr.2.10: elsewh. only in compds. ἀπο-, κατα-, ὑπο-λιμπάνω; not in Hom. exc. as v.l. in Il.11.604 (*PTeb.*266).

**λιμφεύειν·** ἀπατᾶν, Hsch. **λιμφός·** συκοφάντης, ἢ μηνυτὴς παρανόμων, Id.

**λῑμ-ώδης,** ες, *famished, hungry*, λιμῶδές τι ἔχει τινά Hp.*Prog.*2; λιμῶδες ἐρυγγάνειν Alciphr.1.25; λ. τι ἀναφθέγγεσθαι Plu.2.751a, cf. Sm.*Jb.*30.7, Ath.6.270f; λ. τράπεζα *scanty*, Plu.2.703f; λεπτὸς καὶ λ. ὕπνος ib.325c. **-ωξις,** εως, ἡ, *starvation*, *Cat.Cod.Astr.*7.230, *PLond.*5.1676.27 (vi A.D.). ⊛ **-ώσσω,** Att. **-ττω,** *to be famished, hungry*, Str.15.2.5, J.*AJ*2.1.1, Babr.45.8, *AP*6.307.8 (Phan.), Luc.*Luct.*9, Alciphr.1.21: aor. ἐλίμωξα Apostol.10.53.

**λῐν-αγερτουμένη** (fort. -αγρε-)· ἐνημμένη λινά, κακοείμων, λινεργοῦσα, Hsch. **-αγρέτης,** ου, ὁ, *caught in the net*, Lyc.237. **-αῖος,** α, ον, *pertaining to flax*, φόρος *flax-*tax, *PBaden* 19.32 (ii A.D.). 2. *made of flax* or *linen*, Hp.*Steril.*221, *Morb.*2.34. (Perh. always a misspelling of λίνεος: λίναια ⟨·ἔρια⟩, Hsch. is a misspelling of λήνεα.)

**λίναμαι·** τρέπομαι, Hsch.

**λῐν-άριον,** τό, Dim. of λίνον, *thread*, Roussel *Cultes Égyptiens* p.213 (Delos, ii B.C.), Dsc.2.171, *PMag.Par.*1.1083. 2. *net*, D.Chr.7.71, Eust.574.32. **-άρμενον,** τό, *sail*, *POxy.*2136.6 (iii A.D.), *PLond.*3.1164*h*7 (iii A.D.). **-αυτιά,** sine expl., Hsch. **-άω,** only found in compds. δια-, ἐκ-, ἐπι-λινάω.

**λίνδεσθαι·** ἁμιλλᾶσθαι, Hsch.

**λίνδος,** ὁ, an aromatic plant, Mnesim.4.63, cf. Eust.315.18.

⊛ **Λίνδος,** ἡ, the town of *Lindos*, Il.2.656, etc.:—Adv. **Λινδόθεν** *from Lindos*, Call.*Aet.Oxy.*2080.49:—hence **Λινδιᾰκος,** ὁ (sc. λόγος), *Chron.Lind.B*65; **Λίνδιος,** α, ον, *Lindian*, *SIG*129.38, al.; Ἀθάνα Λινδία ib.725.11; **Λινδιασταί,** οἱ, religious guild at Lindos, *IG*12(1).161; **Λινδοπολίτας,** α, ὁ, *citizen of Lindos*, *SIG*725.12.

**λίν-ειος** [ῐ], α, ον, = λίνεος, Suid. **-έμπορος,** ὁ, *flax-merchant*, *POxy.* 414.7 (iii A.D.). ⊛ **-εος,** α, ον, contr. **-οῦς,** ῆ, οῦν, (λίνον) *of flax, linen*, κιθών, θώρηξ, Hdt.1.195, 3.47, etc.; ἱμάτιον Pl.*Cra.*389b; σφαῖρα Arist.*HA*616$^{a}$6; στολή *BGU*1036.14 (ii A.D.); νεφέλαι (i.e. nets) Call.*Aet.*3.1.37; ὅπλα λ. cables *of flax*, Hdt.7.36: also λινᾶ, τά, A.*Fr.*206, Ar.*Fr.*19: Subst. λινέη, ἡ, *tape-measure* used in building, *IG*7.3073.128 (Lebadea), cf. Bito 63.7, 9 (v.l. λιναία); cf. λιναῖος. **-εργέω,** gloss on λιναγερτουμένη, Hsch. **-εργής,** ές, *wrought of flax*, Lyc.716, D.P.1116. ⊛ **-εύς,** έως, ὁ, = κεστρεύς, Call.Com.3, Phot., Hsch. **-εύω,** *catch with nets*, λ. γυργαθοῖς *Peripl.M.Rubr.*15. **-έψιον,** τό, *tax on*, or *payment for, linen-boiling*, *Ostr.Bodl.* i 140, 141 (ii B.C.). ⊛ **-εψός,** ὁ, *linen-boiler, linen-cleaner*, *PCair.Zen.*304.6, *PSI*4.349.5, 6.566.7 (all iii B.C.). **-ικός,** ή, όν, *pertaining to flax*: -κή, ἡ, *tax on flax*, *PTeb.*347.12 (ii A.D.). **-ινος,** η, ον, = λίνεος, *Schwyzer* 462 *B*39, al. (Tanagra, iii B.C.).

**λινίς,** v. ληνίς II.

**λῐνο-γενής,** ές, *born* (i.e. made) *of flax*, ἐπενδύται S.*Fr.*439. **-δεσμος,** ον, = sq., σχεδία A.*Pers.*68 (lyr.). **-δετος,** ον, (δέω) *bound with flaxen cords*, χαλινοί E.*IT*1043; πέδη (of the Hellespont) Tim.*Pers.*85; λ. ὥσπερ μηλολόνθην τοῦ ποδός *tied* by the foot, Ar.*Nu.*764. **-δρῦς,** υος, ἡ, = χαμαίδρυς, χαμαίρωψ, Dsc.3.98. **-εργής,** ές, = λινεργής, Opp.*H.*3.444 (v.l. -ερκής). **-ερκής,** ές, *surrounding with nets* or *snares*, Nonn.*D.*26.55; cf. foreg. **-ζευκτος** δεσμός *flaxen bond*, Opp.*H.*4.79. **-ζωστις** (in codd. sts. wrongly **-ζῶστις**), εως (Gal.14.760, 19.128) and ιδος (Id.12.63, 19.96), Ion. ιος (Hp.*Epid.*7.92), ἡ, *mercury, Mercurialis annua*, Hp.*Mul.*2.135, *Epid.* l.c., Dsc.4.189: dat. λινοζώστῳ v.l. in Aret.*CA*1.2. 2. λ. ἀγρία ἄρρην *dog's mercury, Mercurialis perennis*, Ps.-Dsc.4.190. **-ζωστος,** ον, *bound with flaxen cords*, πλευραί, of ships, Tim.*Pers.*16. II. v. foreg. 1. **-θήρας,** ου, ὁ, *one who uses nets* or *snares*, *AP*7.172 tit. **-θώραξ,** ᾱκος, Ep. and Ion. **θώρηξ,** ηκος, ὁ, ἡ, *wearing a linen cuirass*, Il.2.529, 830; Ἀργεῖοι *AP*14.73; [Λυσιτανοί] Str.3.3.6.

**λῑνο-κᾰλάμη** [λᾰ], ἡ, = ἀμοργίς, *fine flax*, *PCair.Zen.*470 (iii B.C.), Cleopatra ap.Gal.12.433, Sch.Ar.*Lys.*736; collectively, *flax-straw*, used as thatch, Lxx *Jo.*2.6, cf. Eust. ad D.P.525, *POxy.*103.9 (iv A.D.), etc. **-κᾰλᾰμίς,** ίδος, ἡ, = λίνον (i.e. λινόσπερμον), Ps.-Dsc.2.103. **-κάλᾰμον** [κᾰ], τό, = λινοκαλάμη, *PMasp.*116.3 (pl., vi A.D.). **-κάρυκες·** οἱ τὰ λινὰ πωλοῦντες, Hsch. **-κλως,** v. λινουλκός. **-κλωστος,** ον, *spinning flax*, ἠλακάτη *AP*7.12. ⊛ **-κρῑθή,** ἡ, *flax mixed with barley*, *PLille* 1.38*f* (iii B.C.). **-κροκος,** ον, *flax-woven*, φᾶρος E.*Hec.*1081.

⊛ **λίνον** [ῐ], τό, *anything made of flax* (v. fin.) 1. *cord, fishing-line*, Il.16.408; *thread* spun from a distaff, E.*Or.*1431 (lyr.), Archipp.38, etc.: pl., E.*Tr.*537 (lyr.); *thread* for stringing jewels, ὅρμον χρυσείοισι λίνοισιν ἐερμένον *h.Ap.*103; ἄλλα παντοδαπὰ χρυσᾶ ἀνηρμένα ἐπὶ λίνου *IG*11(2).208.22 (Delos, iii B.C.); *thread* used as a *ligature*, Gal.2.669. 2. metaph., *thread of destiny* spun by the Fates, Il.20.128, Od.7.198, etc.: pl., τά γε μὰν λ. πάντα λελοίπει ἐκ Μοιρᾶν Theoc.1.139, cf. Call.*Lav.Pall.*104; ὑπὲρ τὸ λ., = ὑπὲρ μόρον, Luc.*JConf.*2. 3. prov., with or without neg., λίνον λίνῳ συνάπτειν, i.e. join like with like, deal with matters of like kind, Pl.*Euthd.*298c, Stratt.38, Arist.*Ph.*207$^{a}$17. 4. *fishing-net*, ἀψῖσι λίνου ἁλόντε Il.5.487, cf. κλωστήρ II; also, *hunting-net*, Theoc.8.58, 27.17; for catching birds, D.S.1.60, *AP*9.396 (Paul. Sil.), 343 (Arch.); λ. δορκάδεια *hunting-nets* for gazelles, *PCair.Zen.*524 (iii B.C.). 5. *linen, linen-cloth*, Il.9.661, Od.13.73, 118: pl., *linen cloths, linen garments*, A.*Supp.*121, 132 (both lyr.): sg., *linen garment*, *Apoc.*15.6; *sail-cloth*, Ar.*Ra.*364, A.R.1.565, etc. 6. *flax* for spinning, λίνου μεστὸν ἄτρακτον Ar.*Ra.*1347, cf. *PRev.Laws* 39.7 (iii B.C.), etc.; λ. Καρπάσιον *asbestos*, Paus.1.26.7. II. *the plant flax, Linum usitatissimum*, λίνον ἐργάζεσθαι Hdt.2.105, etc.; λίνου σπέρμα *linseed*, Th.4.26: pl., ἡ ἐκ τῶν λ. δημιουργία Pl.*Plt.*280c. 2. = θυμελαία, Dsc.4.172. 3. = χρυσόγονον, ib.56. 4. λ. πύρινον, an unknown plant, Thphr.*HP*9.18.6. 5. λ. ἀπὸ τῶν δενδρέων *cotton, Gossypium herbaceum*, Nearch.ap.Arr.*Ind.*1.16.1. III. v. Λίνος II. (Lith. *linaĩ* pl. 'flax', with ĭ as in Gr., but Lat. *līnum*, OE. *lín*, etc. with ī: ῑ also in the doubtful words λινόσαρκος, λινοπτάομαι, ἀμφίλινος.)

⊛ **λῑνό-πεπλος,** ον, *with linen robe*, *AP*6.231 (Phil.). **-πλεκτος,** ον, *twisted* or *plaited of flax*, Nonn.*D.*26.56 codd. **-πληκτος,** ον, *shy of the net*, of animals that have been caught and escaped, Plu.2.642a:—also **-πλήξ,** ῆγος, ὁ, ἡ, Hsch.: Sup. λινοπληγέστατος, ἰχθῦς Numen.ap.Ath.7.321b. **-πλόκος,** ὁ, *linen-weaver*, *Ostr.Strassb.*277.3 (ii A.D.). **-πλύνας·** τριβεύς, Hsch. ⊛ **-πλῠτής,** οῦ, ὁ, *flax-washer, flax-soaker*, prob. in Aët.8.16 (λινοπλήτων gen. pl., codd.). **-ποιός,** όν, *making linen*, Sch.Ar.*Th.*942. **-πόρος,** ον, *sail-wafting*, αὖραι E.*IT*410 (lyr.).

**λινοπτ-άζει·** ἐπιλινεύει, περιβλέπει, Hsch. **-άομαι,** (λινόπτης) *watch nets to see whether anything is caught*, Ar.*Pax* 1178 (λῑν-; dub. l.).

**λῐνό-πτερος,** ον, *sail-winged*, λ. ναυτίλων ὀχήματα A.*Pr.*468. **-πτέρυξ,** ῠγος, ὁ, ἡ, = foreg., Opp.*C.*1.121, 4.61.

**λῑν-όπτης,** ου, ὁ, (ὄψομαι) *one who watches nets to see whether anything is caught*, Arist.ap.Sch.Ar.*Pax* 1178, Poll.5.17, Hsch.

⊛ **λῐνο-πῡρος,** ὁ, *flax mixed with wheat*, *PLille* 31.13 (iii B.C.). **-πώλης,** ου, ὁ, *flax-merchant*, *Ostr.*45, al. (i/ii A.D.). **-ρρᾰφής,** ές, (ῥάπτω) *sewn of flax*, τυλεῖα S.*Fr.*468; λ. δόμος dub. sens. in A.*Supp.*134 (lyr.). II. *making nets*, ἁλιῆες Nonn.*D.*23.131.

⊛ **Λίνος** [ῐ], ὁ, *Linos*, a mythical minstrel, Hes.*Fr.*192, Theoc.24.105, Apollod.1.3.2. II. as Appellat., *the song* or *lay of Linos*, whether composed by him or upon him; λίνον δ' ὑπὸ καλὸν ἄειδε λεπταλέῃ φωνῇ sang *the lay of Linos* in accompaniment, Il.18.570, cf. Pi.*Fr.*139.5, Hdt.2.79, E.*HF*348 (lyr.), Ar.Byz.ap.Ath.14.619c, and v. οἰτόλινος. (In Il. l.c. Zenod. read λίνος and interpreted it of the string of the instrument, which was orig. made of flax acc. to Sch.)

**λίνος,** ὁ, = λίνον, τό, λίνος· τὸ δίκτυον, Suid.; λῖνος· τὸ λινάριον, *Et.Gud.*371; λῖνος also in *Gp.*2.40.3. II. **λίνοι,** οἱ, *the Bands*, a constellation, Gem.3.7.

**λῑνόσαρκος,** ον, *with soft, tender body* (as Eust. expld. it), τροφαλίς Antiph.49 (s.v.l.).

**λῐνό-σπαρτον,** τό, *Spanish broom, Spartium junceum*, Thphr.*HP*1.5.2. **-σπέρμινος,** η, ον, *of linseed*, ἔλαιον Aët.1.101. **-σπερμον,** τό, *linseed*, Dsc.2.103, Gal.6.549, Artem.1.68, Alex.Aphr.*Pr.*1.67, *POxy.*103.13 (iv A.D.):—also **λινόσπερμα,** ατος, τό, Cleopatra

ap.Gal.12.433, *Hippiatr.*54, Alex.Trall.12, v.l. in Gal.6.549. **-στᾰσία**, ἡ, *laying of nets*: *the nets laid*, *AP*6.179 (Arch.), 9.76 (pl., Antip.). **-στᾰτέω**, (ἵστημι) *lay nets*, Opp.*C*.4.64, Longus 2.13:—Pass., *to be surrounded and caught with nets*, Ath.5.219d. **-στολία**, ἡ, *wearing of linen, linen clothing*, Plu.2.352c (pl.), Man.4.344, Vett.Val.4.27. **-στολος**, ον, *clad in linen*, B.18.43, *Hymn.Is.* 1. **-στροφος**, ον, *twisted of flax*, θῶμιγξ Opp.*H*.3.76. II. -στροφον, τό, = *marrubium*, Plin.*HN*20.241, *Gloss.* **-τειχής**, ές, *with linen walls*, Dionys.ap.St.Byz. s. v. Γαζός. **-τόμοι**· οἱ τὰ λίνα διατέμνοντες καὶ ὑγιῆ δεικνύντες, i.e. conjurers, Hsch.

**λῐνούγιον**, τό, perh. = sq., *Sammelb.*7033.40, al. (v A. D.).

***λῐν-ούδιον** [ῠ], τό, *linen shirt*, *POxy.*114.8 (ii A. D.), 1066.10 (iii A. D.), etc. **-ουλκός**, όν, (ἕλκω) *of spun flax*, χλαῖνα Ion Trag. 40 (**λινόκλως** cj. Lobeck).

**λῐνουργ-εῖον**, τό, *linen factory*, prob. l. in Str.4.2.2 (pl.): sg., Id. 16.1.7. **-έω**, *make into linen*, τὴν καλάμην Sch.Pi.*P*.4.376. **-ία**, ἡ, *linen manufacture*, Str.11.2.17. **-ός**, όν, *working flax, spinning* or *weaving*, γυνή Alex.35. II. as Subst. λ., ὁ, *linen-weaver*, *PMagd.* 36.2 (iii B.C.), Str.3.4.9, *PRyl.*397.2 (iii A. D.), *Cat.Cod.Astr.*8(4).137; συντεχνία λ. *IGRom.*3.896 (Anazarba). 2. a kind of *goose*, Dionys.*Av.*3.23. 3. a kind of *stone*, Ps.-Plu.*Fluv.*22.3. 4. λινουργοί, οἱ, name given to the proletariate, D.Chr.34.21.

**λινοῦς**, ἡ, οῦν, contr. for λίνεος.

**λῐνοῠφ-ής** [ῠ], ές, *weaving linen*, *EM*558.49:—also ***λῐνόῠφος**, ον, *AB*302, *PGiss.*49 ii 27 (iii A. D.), *Cat.Cod.Astr.*8(4).216, etc.; cf. λίνυφος. **-ικός**, ή, όν, *pertaining to linen-weaving*, πῆχυς *POxy.* 669.33 (iv A. D.): -κός, ὁ, *linen-weaver*, *BGU*637.17 (iii A. D.): -κόν, τό, *tax on linen-weaving*, *POxy.*1438.12 (ii A. D., λινουψικόν Pap.). **-ιον**, *lintio*, *Gloss.* (fort. **λινουφίων**).

**λῐνοῦχος**, ον, *having* or *using nets*, *Gloss.*

***λῐνο-φακός**, ὁ, *flax mixed with lentils*, *PLille* 1.31.14 (iii B.C.). **-φάντης**, ου, misspelling for *λινοϋφ-, *linen-weaver*, *UPZ*85.14 (ii B.C.). **-φθόρος**, ον, *linen-spoiling*, ὑφασμάτων λακίδες A.*Ch.*27 (lyr.). **-φόρος**, ον, *flax-bearing*, of land, *PLond.ined.*2361[r] (iii B.C.). **-χίτων** [ῐ], ωνος, ὁ, ἡ, *with linen tunic*, Hsch., prob. l. in Him.*Or.*11.1. **-χλαινος**, ον, *with linen mantle*, D.P.1096, Nonn. *D.*26.58. **-χορτος**, ὁ, or **-χορτον**, τό, *joint crop of flax and grass*, *PBaden* 15.20 (i B.C.).

**λῐνῠφαντ-εῖον**, τό, *workshop for weaving flax*, *PMagd.*36.2 (iii B.C.), *PTeb.*5.238 (ii B.C.). **-ικός**, ή, όν, *of* or *for linen-weaving*, ἐργαλεῖα ib.242 (ii B.C.).

***λῐνῠφ-άριος**, ὁ, = λίνυφος, *Cod.Just.*11.8.13. **-εῖον**, τό, = λινυφαντεῖον, ἐπ' ἀμφόδου Λινυφείων *BGU*324.7 (ii A. D.). **-ος**, = λινόϋφος, *PTeb.*5.239 (ii B.C.), *POxy.*1281.4 (i B.C.), etc.; ἡ συντεχνία τῶν λ. guild of *linen-weavers*, *Papers of Amer.School* 1.97 (Tralles); ἡ ἱερὰ τέχνη λινύφων *JRS*18.171 (Jerash).

**λῐνῳδία**, ἡ, *the lament for Linos* (v. Λίνος II), Sch.B Il.18.570 (pl.).

**λῐνωνία**, ἡ, *purchase of flax*, *PPetr.*3 p.187, al. (iii B.C.).

**λίξ**· πλάγιος, καὶ λίθος πλατύς, Hsch.; also, = πνευμονία, νόσος, Id. **λιολεθρίᾳ**· παντελεῖ ὀλέθρῳ, Id. **λιοπέτριον**· λίθος λεῖος, Id.

**λίπα** [ῐ], used by Hom. as Adv. usu. in the phrase ἀλείψασθαι λίπ' ἐλαίῳ anoint oneself *richly* with oil, Il.10.577, 14.171, al.; χρῖσαι, χρίσασθαι λίπ' ἐλαίῳ, Od.3.466, 6.96, 10.364, Hes.*Op.*522: once without ἐλαίῳ, λοέσσατο καὶ λίπ' ἄλειψεν Od.6.227; so later, τῷ ῥοδίνῳ ἀλείφεσθαι λίπα Hp.*Mul.*2.150; ἐλαίῳ χρίων λίπα ib.147: also without a dat., χρίεσθαι λίπα ib.1.35; λίπα ἀλείψασθαι, ἀλείψεσθαι, Th.1.6, 4.68, cf. Thphr.*HP*9.8.5, etc. II. in Hp. sts. as Subst., neut. nom. or acc., χρῖσμα λίπα ἔστω *Mul.*2.133; μηδ' ἄλλο τι πῖον μηδὲ λίπα ἔχον ib.145; so λίπα ἀσκεῖν D.C.53.27. (Cf. λίπος.)

**λῐπάδελφος** [ᾰ], ον, *brotherless*, *Epigr.Gr.*241.9 (Smyrna).

**λῐπάζω**, = sq., Nic.*Th.*90, 112.

***λῐπαίνω**, aor. ἐλίπηνα Opp.*H*.4.357, ἐλίπᾱνα Axionic.4.10:—Med., aor. ἐλιπήνατο Euph.9.9; part. λιπηνάμενος *APl.*4.273 (Crin.):—Pass., aor. ἐκ-λιπανθῆναι Plu.*Mar.*21: pf. λελίπασμαι Democr.ap. Gal.13.225:—*oil, anoint*, τὴν κεφαλὴν ἐλαίῳ Hp.*Mul.*1.35; χρῶτα μύροις Anaxil.18.1; χαρᾶς ὕπο σῶμα λ. ἱδρῶτι Aspasia ap.Ath.5.219c; πάσμασι σῶμα λ. Axionic. l.c., cf. *PMag.Osl.*1.212; *of oiling* the τόνοι in a machine to preserve them, Ph.*Bel.*61.37:—Med., *anoint oneself*, *AP*l.c. 2. of rivers, *make fat, enrich*, χώραν ὕδασιν E.*Ba.* 575 (lyr.), cf. *Hec.*454 (lyr.); of Sciron swallowed by a sea-tortoise, χέλυος.. ἐλιπήνατο λαιμόν Euph. l.c. (s. v.l.). II. intr., of the eyes, *glisten* with tears, Epicur.*Fr.*120.

**λῐπανδρ-έω**, *to be in want of men*, Ephor.216 J. **-ία**, ἡ, *want of men*, Str.13.1.32, J.*BJ*3.3.2.

**λῐπανθρωπία**, ἡ, = foreg., Eust.23.39.

**λῐπαν-σις** [λῐ], εως, ἡ, *anointing*, Antyll.ap.Orib.10.29.1. **-τέον**, *one must anoint*, Herod.Med. in *Rh.Mus.*58.104. **-τικός**, ή, όν, *of* or *for anointing*, ἔλαιον Sch.Od.6.227.

**Λῐπάρα** [πᾰ], ἡ, *Lipara*, the largest of the Aeolian islands, Th.3.88, etc.:—Adj. **Λῐπᾰραῖος**, α, ον, *of Lipara*, αἱ Λ. νῆσοι *the group of these islands*, Plb.1.25.4, etc.; ἡ Λιπαραίων πόλις Arist.*Mete.*367[a]6; λίθος Λιπαραῖος a stone like *volcanic glass* or *obsidian*, Thphr.*Lap.*14, Orph. *L.*692.

***λῐπᾰρ-άμπυξ**, ῠκος, ὁ, ἡ, *with bright fillet* or *headband*, Μναμοσύνα Pi.*N.*7.15; parodied by Ar.*Ach.*671 (lyr.), as epith. of fish-sauce. **-αυγής**, ές, *bright-beaming*, πορθμίδες Philox.3.1.

**λῐπᾰρ-έω**, *persist, persevere, hold out*, of obstinate resistance, λιπαρήσομεν οὕτω, ὅκως ἂν ἔχωμεν Hdt.8.144: in part., τους Λυδοὺς τέως μὲν διάγειν λιπαρέοντας continued *to hold out*, under pressure of famine, Id.1.94: reversely, with part. added, λιπαρέετε μένοντες *persist* in holding your ground, Id.9.45; ἐλιπάρεε ἱστορέων *persisted* in inquiring, Id.3.51: c. dat., λ. τῇ πόσει *keep on* drinking, Id.5.19; λ. τῇ ἑταίρᾳ D.L.6.66. II. of persistent entreaty, 1. abs., *to be importunate*, λιπαρεόντων δὲ αὐτῶν Hdt.1.86, cf. 2.42, 9.111, A.*Pr.*520, Pl.*Cra.*413c, Men.*Epit.*54, Herod.6.28, 93; γενοῦ γλίσχρος προσαιτῶν λιπαρῶν τε Ar.*Ach.*452, cf. D.21.206. 2. c. acc. et inf., *beseech* one to do a thing, A.*Pr.*1004; also τοῦ με χρείας ὧδε λιπαρεῖς τυχεῖν; to obtain what request *dost thou so importune me?* S.*OT*1435; λιπαροῦντι μὲν τυχεῖν *importunate* to obtain, Id.*OC*776; ξυγγενέσθαι.. μ' ἐλιπάρει.. μάζαις *importuned* me to become acquainted with cakes, Telecl.38 (cj. Porson), cf. X.*Oec.*2.16; also λ. τινὰ ὅπως.. *PAmh.* 2.79.47 (ii A. D.); ἐξαιτήσεσθαι καὶ λιπαρήσειν παρ' ὑμῶν αὐτόν *entreat earnestly for* him at your hands, D.21.208; but also λ. βωμοὺς *importune*.., Plb.32.15.7:—Pass., *to be earnestly entreated*, ὑπό τινων X. *HG*3.5.12. **-ής**, ές, *persisting* or *persevering* in a thing, *earnest, indefatigable*, περί τινος Pl.*Cra.*413a; περί τι, πρός τι, Id.*Hp.Mi.*369d, 372b: also c. gen., παιδείας Luc.*Am.*6. 2. of things, λ. χειρουργία Ar.*Lys.*672; προθυμία Luc.*Abd.*4; λ. πυρετός an *obstinate* fever, Id.*Hist.Conscr.*1. II. *earnest in begging* or *praying, importunate*, c. part., λ. ἦσαν δεόμενοι Plu.*TG*6; ἀκοῦσαί τι βουλόμενοι λ. ἦσαν Id.2. 665e; λ. χείρ a hand *instant in prayer*, S.*El.*1378: c. gen., *fawning upon*, τῶν ἐν ἐξουσίᾳ Plu.2.776b; τὸ λ. *importunity*, Luc.*Herm.*24; πρὸς τὸ λ., = λιπαρῶς, S.*OC*1119. III. Adv. **-ρῶς** *earnestly, importunately*, Pl.*Lg.*931c; λ. ἔχων ἀκούειν longing *earnestly* to hear, Id.*Prt.*315e; λ. ἔχω γίγνεσθαί τι I am *importunate in desiring* that.., ib.335b. **-ησις**, εως, ἡ, *supplication*, D.H.1.81 (pl.). **-ητέον**, *one must be importunate*, X.*Ap.*23. **-ία**, Ion. **-ίη**, ἡ, *persistence, perseverance*, λιπαρίῃ τε καὶ ἀρετῇ ἀντέχομεν Hdt.9.21, cf. 70; *importunity*, Ael.*Fr.*61.

**λῐπᾰρ-ία**, ἡ, (λιπαρός) *fatness*, Dsc.1.40. **-ιάζω**, gloss on λιπαίνομαι, *An.Ox.*2.470. **-ίσχιος**, ον, dub. sens. in Lyr. in *Philol.*80.338.

**λῐπᾰρό-γειος**, ον, *with rich soil*, Sch.D Il.18.541. **-ζωνος**, ον, *bright-girdled*, θύγατρες B.8.49; Ἀέλιος E.*Ph.*175 (lyr.). ***-θρονος**, ον, *bright-throned*, A.*Eu.*806, *Lyr.Adesp.*140.6, Aristonous 2. 16. **-κρήδεμνος**, ον, *with bright headband*, Il.18.382, *h.Cer.*25, 459, etc.

**λῐπᾰρ-όμμᾰτος**, ον, *lustrous-eyed*, Licymn.4, Arist.*Phgn.*808[a]34.

**λῐπᾰρο-πλόκᾰμος**, ον, *with glossy locks*, Il.19.126, Pi.*Fr.*88. 1. **-ποιέω**, gloss on καταλιπαίνειν, Hsch.

***λῐπᾰρ-ός**, ά, όν, (λίπα) prop. *oily, shiny with oil*, once in Hom., *anointed*, λιπαροὶ κεφαλὰς καὶ καλὰ πρόσωπα Od.15.332; λ. χωρεῖν ἐκ βαλανείου Ar.*Pl.*616; θεᾶσθαι λιπαρὸν παρὰ τῷ Διονύσῳ Id.*Eq.*536, cf. *Nu.*1002; σοὶ δὲ μελήσει.. λιπαρῷ (Bentl. for -ρῶς) χωρεῖν ἐπὶ δεῖπνον Id.*Ec.*652; of oil or oily objects, *shiny*, Simon.148.4, X.*Mem.* 2.1.31, Pl.*Ti.*60a, 84a, Arist.*HA*520[a]27. 2. *fatty, greasy*, ἄρτος Ar.*Fr.*109; τὰ λ. *unctuous dishes*, ib.506.1; τὸ λ. *fatty substance*, Arist.*PA*651[a]24; λιπαραί (sc. ἔμπλαστροι), αἱ, *oily* plasters, Dsc.1.112, Gal.12.468: sts. opp. τὸ πῖον (which implies resinous substance), Arist.*Mete.*387[b]6, cf. *Col.*791[b]23: of vegetables *boiled in grease*, Hp. *Mul.*1.66. Adv. -ρῶς, ἕψειν boil *in grease*, Hp.*Mul.* l. c.; so λ. ἠρτυμένον Gal.9.677; ἀνατρίβειν massage *with a greasy* or *oily lubricant*, Hp.*Art.*9. II. of the healthy look of the human body or skin, *shining, sleek*, in Hom. in phrase λιπαροὶ πόδες *bright, smooth* feet, without a wrinkle on the skin, mostly of men's feet, in the line ποσσὶ δ' ὑπὸ λιπαροῖσιν ἐδήσατο καλὰ πέδιλα Il.2.44, al.: of Hera, 14.186; of Themis, Hes.*Th.*901; -ώτεροι ἐγένοντο Hdt.3.23; λ. στῆθος Ar.*Nu.* 1012; θηρία X.*Cyr.*1.4.11; χείλεα Luc.*Am.*13; *radiant*, θυγάτηρ Χρόνου B.7.1; ἄκοιτις Id.5.169. III. of condition or state of life, *rich, comfortable, easy*, γῆρας Od.11.136, 19.368, Pi.*N.*7.99; λ. εὐφροσύνη *AP*11.63 (Maced.). Adv. -ρῶς, γηρασκέμεν Od.4.210; πλήσαντα λ. κύκλον ἐτῶν ἑκατόν *Epigr.Gr.*451. IV. of things, *bright, brilliant*, λιπαρὴ καλύπτρη Il.22.406; λ. κρήδεμνα Od.1.334, etc.; χοροί Hes.*Th.*63; of city walls, Od.13.388; λ. δόμος B.15.29; νίκα Id.10.38; στέφανοι Id.1.47; λιπαρὰς τελέουσι θέμιστας *splendid* or *rich* tribute, Il.9.156, 298; also, of the *oily smoothness* of a calm sea, λ. γαλάνα Theoc.22.19, cf. Call.*Epigr.*6.5; also σέλας Theoc.23.8; and of smells, λ. ὀσμή *rich, savoury*, Arist.*de An.*421[a]30, cf. *Sens.*443[b] 10. V. of soil, *fat, rich, fruitful*, as epith. of places, Χίος, ἣ νήσων λιπαρωτάτη εἰν ἁλὶ κεῖται *h.Ap.*38; λ. πόλις Thgn.947; λ. Ὀρχομενός, Θῆβαι, Νάξος, Μαραθών, Pi.*O.*14.2, *P.*2.3, 4.88, *O.*13.110; λιπαραὶ Ἀθῆναι, favourite epith. with the Athenians, prob. with allusion to the Attic olive, first in Pi.*I.*2.20, *Fr.*76, cf. Ar.*Ach.*639, 640 (where he plays on the double sense of *brilliant* and *greasy*), *Nu.*300, *Fr.*110; λ. τὸ χρῆμα τῆς πόλεως, of Nephelococcygia, Id.*Av.*826; λ. χεύματα, of rivers, A.*Supp.*1028 (lyr.); λ. ὅρμος Call.*Del.*155; ἄντρον Orph.*H.* 59.4 (Hermann), etc. VI. Adv. λῐπαρῶς, v. supr. I, III. **-ότης**, ητος, ἡ, *fattiness*, ὑπάρχει ἐν γάλακτι λ. Arist.*HA*522[a]21, cf. *PA*652[a] 29: in pl., *fatty substances*, Hp.*Prog.*12. II. *brilliancy*, ὀμμάτων Plu.2.670f.

**λῐπᾰρό-τροφος**, ον, *richly fed*, μῆλα Pi.*Oxy.*1792 *Fr.*1.6. * **-χροος**, ον, *with shining body, sleek of skin*, Σελαναία λιπαρόχροε Theoc.2.165:—also **-χρως**, ωτος, ὁ, ἡ, acc. -χρων, ib.102.

**λῐπᾰρώψ**, ῶπος, ὁ, ἡ, *bright-looking*, τράπεζα Philox.2.1.

**λίπας** [ῐ], τό, = λίπος, used by Aret. in nom. λίπας, *CD*2.3, *SD*2.9; gen. λίπαος *CA*1.1; dat. λίπαϊ ibid.

**λίπ-ασμα** [ῐ], ατος, τό, *a greasy form of ulceration*, Hp.*Alim.*16, Heliod.ap.Orib.46.22.14, Gal.15.316. 2. *a fattening substance*, Plu.2.771b, Lxx *Ne.*8.10 (pl.). 3. *salve*, Man.4.345. 4.

λίπασμα ὀφθαλμῶν *a glistening*, i.e. a tear, Epicur.ap.Cleom.2.1 (p.89 U.). **-ασμός**, ὁ, *anointing*, Dsc.*Alex*.14, Paul.Aeg.2.48.

**λῐπ-αυγής**, ές, *deserted by light, dark, sunless*, *IG*12(5).891.5 (Tenos), Orph.*H*.18.2; *blind*, *AP*9.13 (Pl. Jun.). **-αυρέω**, (αὔρα) *to be calm*, λιπαυρεῖ (impers.) Hsch.

**λῐπ-άω**, (λίπας, λίπος) *to be sleek, radiant*, Ep. pres. λιπόω, v.l. for ῥυπόω, Od.19.72; part. λιπόων Call.*Fr*.141, *AP*6.324 (Leon.), Nic. *Al*.487, Q.S.10.274: regul. forms, ind. 3 pl. pres. λιπῶσιν Ph.1.542, part. λιπῶν Phryn.Com.38, Call.*Fr*.121, Plu.2.206f. II. trans., *anoint*, γυῖα Nic.*Th*.81. **-έλαιον**, τό, gloss on *pinguis olivi*, Serv. ad Verg.*E*.5.68.

**λῐπεργάτης** [ᾰ], ου, ὁ, *unemployed labourer* (s.v.l.), v. λιπερνήτης.

❀ **λῐπερν-έω**, *to be poor*, Suid. (who also has λιφερνῶν sine gloss.); **λῐφερνέω**, *to be meagre*, στάχυς J.*AJ*2.5.5:—but Hsch. has λιφερνοῦντες· ἐν συνδένδρῳ τόπῳ προσφιλῶς διάγοντες. ❀ **-ής**, ῆτος, *poor, forlorn, outcast*, ὦ λιπερνῆτες πολῖται Archil.50 (borrowed by Cratin. 198); context doubtful in *BCH*11.161 (Lagina); = *pupillus*, ὀρφανός, *Gloss*.:—also **-ήτης**, ου, ὁ, *AP*9.649 (Maced.), *EM*566.50, restored by Schäfer in Longus 2.22 for λιπεργάτης:—fem. **-ῆτις**, ιδος, Call. *Fr*.66e, Epic.*Oxy*.1794.17.

**λῐπεσάνωρ** [ᾱ], ορος, ἡ, *forsaker of her husband*, of Helen, Stesich. 26.5.

**λῐπήμεροι**· οἱ ἐν τῷ προσήκοντι χρόνῳ μὴ γεννώμενοι, Hsch. **Λιπ[ι]ῦϊα**, ἡ, *land that lacks rain*, coined as etym. of Λιβύη by Varro ap.Serv. ad Verg.*A*.1.22.

**λῐπό-βῐοι**· νεκροί, Hsch. **-βοτᾰνέω**, *lose* or *be without herbage*, Plu.2.182e. **-γάλακτος** [γᾰ], ον, = λιπόθηλος, Eust.1752.01; = *lacticularius, lacticulosus*, *Gloss*. **-γᾰμος**, ον, *having abandoned her marriage ties*, ἡ λ. *the adulteress*, of Helen, E.*Or*.1305 (lyr.); cf. λιπεσάνωρ. **-γληνος**, ον, *without eyeballs, sightless*, Nonn.*D*. 37.517. **-γλωσσος**, ον, *tongueless*, ib.26.281. **-γνώμων**, v. λειπογνώμων. **-γράμμᾰτος**, ον, *wanting a letter*, Suid. s.v. Νέστωρ, Eust.1379.55. **-γυιος**, ον, *wanting a limb, maimed, lame*, *AP*9.13 (Pl. Jun.). **-δεής**, ές, *with few wants*, Pythag. *Ep*.2. **-δερμέω**, *to be without skin*, *Hippiatr*.26. **-δερμος**, ον, *without a skin*, of ulcers. ibid.; *without a foreskin*, Sor.1.103; *circumcised*, Dsc.2.82, Crito ap.Gal.12.449, Gal.19.445, Paul.Aeg.6. 53. **-δρᾰνέω**, *fail in strength*, Gal.10.842. **-δρᾰνής**, ές, *lacking strength* (cf. ἀδρανής), Aret.*SD*2.6. **-ζύγων**· μοναζόντων, Hsch. **-θηλος**, ον, (θηλή) *deprived of the breast*, of late-born pigs (μετάχοιρα), which the sows will not suckle, *Gp*.19.6.8. **-θριξ**, τριχος, ὁ, ἡ, *hairless*, Ael.*NA*17.4, Nonn.*D*.11.510. **-θροος**, ον, *wanting voice, mute*, of Echo, ib.4.327.

**λῐποθῡμ-έω**, *fall into a swoon, faint*, Hp.*Art*.68, *Mul*.2.134, Plu. *Them*.10, Gal.1.139. **-ημα**, ατος, τό, = sq., Tz.*H*.12.391. **-ία**, ἡ, *swoon*, Hp.*Aph*.1.23, *Art*.68, Plu.*Pomp*.49, etc. **-ικός**, ή, όν, *subject to fainting fits*, Hp.*Liqu*.2, Antyll.ap.Orib.7.7.7. **-ιώδης**, ες, *swoon-like*, Archig.ap.Orib.8.1.26, Aët.9.40.

**λῐπό-κεντρος**, ον, *leaving a sting*, μέλισσαι *Lyr.Alex.Adesp*.7. 15. **-κοπρος**, **-κοπτος**, v. λιπόκωπος. **-κρεως**, ων, gen. ω, *losing flesh*, i.e. *wasted, thin*, Suid.: acc. pl. λ(ε)ιποκρέους in Tz.*H*. 11.60; neut. pl. -κρεα Phlp.*in GA* 200.22. **-κωπος**, ον, *without handle*, φασγανίδες cj. Toup in *AP*6.307 (Phan.) for λιποκόπτους or λιποκόπρους. **-μαρτῠρίου δίκη**, action *against a witness for non-appearance*, Poll.8.36, cf. D.49.19, Lys.*Fr*.321 S. **-μήτωρ**, ορος, ὁ, ἡ, *having left one's mother*, *AP*9.240 (Phil.). **-μορία**· δένδρον τὰ ἐκ τοῦ θωρακίου κατεαγός, ἐκ δὲ τῆς ῥίζης φέρον βλαστούς, Hsch. ❀ **-ναυς**, ὁ, ἡ, *deserting the fleet*, A.*Ag*.212 (lyr.) (or, *deserted by the allied fleet*); v. λιπόνεως. ❀ **-ναύτης**, ου, ὁ, *leaving the sailors*, Theoc.13.73, Anon.ap.Suid. **-ναυτίου γραφή**, indictment *against one who deserts his ship* or *duty at sea*, Poll.8.42. **-νεως**, ων, = λιπόναυς, D.50.65, Luc.*Cat*.3, Max.Tyr.9.7.

**λῐ-πόνηρος**· λίαν πονηρός, Hsch.: cf. λῖ.

**λῐπό-ξῠλος**, ον, *lacking wood*: metaph., *defective, feeble*, πίστις Emp.71.1, cf. 21.2. **-παις**, παιδος, ὁ, ἡ, *childless*, found in neut. pl., λέχη λιπόπαιδα Man.4.584. **-πατρις**, ιδος, ὁ, ἡ, *leaving one's country*, Nonn.*D*.1.131. II. *causing to forget one's country*, λ. ἐδωδή, i.e. the lotus, *AP*15.12 (Leo Phil.). **-πάτωρ** [ᾰ], ορος, ὁ, ἡ, *deserter of one's father*, E.*Or*.1305. **-πνόη**, ἡ, *death*, Tim.*Pers*. 106. ❀ **-πνοος**, ον, contr. **-πνους**, ουν, *breathless, dead*, *AP*12.132 (Mel.), *APl*.4.110.5 (Id.), 133.5 (Philostr.). II. *without wind, deadly still*, Ἅιδης Orph.*H*.18.9. **-πτόλεμος**, ον, *leaving the war*, Nonn.*D*.35.389. **-πτολις**, ιος, ὁ, ἡ, *leaving the city*, ib.9.78; **λιπόπολις**, Hsch. s.v. λιπερνής, Phot. s.v. λιπερνῆτις. **-πωγωνία**, ἡ, *want of beard*, Crates Com.22. **-ρρῑνος**, ον, *without skin*, of Marsyas, Nonn.*D*.1.44. 2. epith. of the salamander, perh. (from λίπος) *with greasy skin*, Nic.*Al*.537.

**λίπορτος**· βακτηρία, Hsch.

**λίπος** [ῐ], εος, τό, prop. *animal fat, lard, tallow*, Arist.*Long*.467ᵃ3, cf. *Pr*.935ᵇ20: pl., χηνὸς λίπη *AP*9.377.8 (Pall.); βεβρῶτες αἵματος λ. gorged with *fat* and blood, S.*Ant*.1022; but λ. αἵματος *a fleck* of blood, A.*Ag*.1428 (lyr., λίβος Casaub.); of vegetable oil, λ. ἐλαίας S.*Fr*.398, cf. Thphr.*HP*3.18.3, 8.7.3, Call.*Ap*.39. (Cf. λίπα, λιπαρός, λιπάω, λιπαίνω, Skt. *lip-* 'anoint', Lith. *lìpti* 'stick'.)

**λῐποσαρκ-έω**, *lose flesh*, opp. ἁδρύνομαι, Thphr.*HP*8.11.4 (dub. cj.), *Hippiatr*.26. **-ής**, ές, = λιπόσαρκος, *AP*11.374 (Maced.), Man.1.55, cj. for λειπόσαρκες in Opp.*C*.2.106. **-ία**, ἡ, *want of flesh*, Sch.Hes.*Sc*.268. **-ος**, ον, *lean, thin*, Hp.*Ep*.17, v.l. in Opp.*C*.2.106 (cf. sq.); σκῆνος λ., of the skeleton, *IG*14.2131 [ῑ]; of wounds, *leaving a hollow*, *Hippiatr*.77.

**λῐπό-σαρξ**, σαρκος, ὁ, ἡ, = foreg., prob. in Opp.*C*.2.106. **-σθενής**, ές, *powerless*, Nonn.*D*.14.101. **-σῑτέω**, *to be in want of corn* or *bread*, Suid. **-σκῐος**, ον, *casting no shadow*, δένδρεα Nonn.*D*. 2.93. 2. *unshadowed*, αὐχήν ib.10.186. **-στέφᾰνος**, ον, *falling from the wreath*, φύλλα *AP*6.71 (Paul. Sil.).

**λῐποστρᾰτ-έω**, *desert, refuse to serve in arms*, Sch.Ar.*Eq*.226. **-ία**, ἡ, *desertion from the army, refusal to serve*, Hdt.5.27, Th.6.76, D.H. 11.22:—also **-ιον**, τό, Th.1.99, Ph.2.132. **-ιώτης**, ου, ὁ, *deserter*, dub. l. in App.*Pun*.115.

❀ **λῐπο-τακτέω**, *desert one's post*, Lxx 4*Ma*.9.23, Ascl.*Tact*.3.6, Plu.2. 241a; λ. τῆς τοῦ θεοῦ τάξεως Ph.1.268. **-τάκτης**, ου, ὁ, *deserter*, D.H.8.79, Ph.1.144, J.*BJ*5.3.4, Max.Tyr.9.7: metaph., λ. Μουσῶν Jul.*Ep*.183. **-τακτος**, ὁ, = foreg., *Gloss*. **-ταξία**, ἡ, *desertion*, D.21.166 codd. (-ιον Cobet): metaph., διάλυσις τῶν ἐν τῷ ζῴῳ πάντων καὶ λ. συμβαίνει (after death) Anatolius ap.*Theol.Ar*.35. **-τάξιον**, τό, *desertion*, λ. διαπεπραγμένοι Ph.2.132:—elsewh. in gen. **-ταξίου γραφή**, indictment *for desertion*, Pl.*Lg*.943d, D.21.103; ἔνοχος λιποταξίου Lys.14.5; τὰ δ' ἐγχέλεια γράψομαι λιποταξίου, Com. phrase, Antiph.129.9, cf. Pl.Com.7, Ar.*Fr*.808, v. Poll.8.42.

**λῐπό-τεκνος**, ον, *childless*, οἶκος Pi.*Parth*.1.16. **-τελέω**, *to be in arrears with taxes*, *IG*9(1).334.14 (Oeanthea, v B.C.).

**λῐπότης**, ητος, ἡ, *fatness*, *Cat.Cod.Astr*.7.225.4.

**λῐπο-τονέω**, *become relaxed*, Nicom.*Harm*.4 (λειπ-, interpol.). **-τρῐχέω**, *grow bald*, Gal.14.530. **-τρῐχής**, ές, = λιπόθριξ, *AP*9.52 (Carph.); **-τρῐχος**, ον, Nonn.*D*.26.159.

**λῐπουργ-ός**, όν, *badly healed*, Heras ap.Gal.13.815:—hence **-ία**, ἡ, Asclep.ib.525, Heras ib.546.

**λίπουρος** [ῐ], ον, *without tail*, Call.*Fr*.28.2 P.

**λῐπο-φεγγής**, ές, = λιπαυγής, Man.1.65, Musae.238. **-φθογγος**, ον, = λιπόθροος, Nonn.*D*.26.288.

**λῐποψῡχ-έω**, *swoon*, S.*Fr*.496, Th.4.12, X.*HG*5.4.58, Xenarch.7. 12, Arist.*Somn.Vig*.456ᵇ15, D.S.12.62, Plu.2.347b, Arr.*An*.6.11. 2. **-ία**, ἡ, *swooning*, v.l. in Hdt.1.86, Hp.*Aph*.7.8, Arist.*Somn. Vig*.455ᵇ5, Plu.2.695a, Arr.*An*.6.10.2. **-ώδης**, ες, *like* λιποψυχία, *faint*, Hp.*Acut*.42.

**λιπόω, λιπόων**, v. λιπάω.

**λίπτομαι**, pf. λέλιμμαι, *to be eager*, οὔτε μεῖον οὔτ' ἴσον λελιμμένοι A. *Th*.355 (lyr.): c. gen., *to be eager for, long for*, μάχης λελιμμένος ib. 380:—later in Act. **λίπτω**, A.R.4.813, Lyc.131, Nic.*Th*.126. (Cf. λίψ· ἐπιθυμία, Hsch., ἔλιπεν, = ἐπιθυμητικῶς ἤσθιεν, Id., λιψουρία, and perh. Lith. *liẽpti* 'command'.)

❀ **λῐπῠρ-ία**, Ion. **-ίη**, ἡ, for λιπο-πυρία, *a malignant intermittent fever*, Hp.*Judic*.11:—also **λιπύριον**, τό, Id.*Morb*.2.51:—hence **-ίας**, ου, ὁ, *one who suffers from* λιπυρία, Gal.17(2).728, cf. 18(2).121, Ps.-Gal.19. 399:—Adj. **λειπῠρικός** (leg. **λῐπῠρικός**), ή, όν, *like* λιπυρία, Hp.*Coac*. 117; **λῐπῠριώδης**, ες, *of the nature of* λιπυρία, πυρετός Id.*Ep*.21.

**λῐπώδης**, ες, (λίπος) *fatty, oily*, Thphr.*HP*3.12.1 (Comp.).

**λῑραίνω**, (λιρός) *to be bold* or *shameless*, = ἀναιδεύομαι, Hsch.

**λίρινος, λιριόεις, λίριον**, less correct forms of λειρ-.

**λῑρός**, ά, όν (not λῖρος, Hdn.Gr.1.191), *bold, shameless, lewd*, Call. *Fr*.229, Alex.Aet.3.30.

**λῑρόφθαλμος**, ον, *lewd-eyed*, Suid.

**λίς**, ὁ, Ep. for λέων, *lion*, mostly in nom., ἐφάνη λὶς ἠυγένειος Il. 15.275, cf. 11.239, 18.318, Hes.*Sc*.172: acc., ἐπί τε λῖν ἤγαγε δαίμων Il.11.480, cf. Theoc.13.6: nom. pl. λῖες [ῐ] Euph.35, but λῖες Antim. 89: dat. pl. λίεσσι [ῐ] ibid. [λίς but λῖν, Aristarch.ap.Hdn.Gr.2.73, cf. 77.]

**λίς**, ἡ, Ep. = λισσή, *smooth*, λὶς πέτρη Od.12.64,79. II. v. λῖτα.

**λίσαι**, v. λίσσομαι.

**λισγάριον**, τό, *spade, mattock*, Sch.Theoc.4.10, Suid. s.v. σκαφεῖδιον. (Mod.Gr. λισγάρι, a kind of *rake* or *harrow*.)

**λίση**, v. λίσσομαι. **λίσκος**· δίσκος, Hsch. **λίσπη**, ἡ, v. λίσπος.

**λισπόπῡγος**, ον, *smooth-buttocked*, epith. of κίναιδοι, Phryn.*PS* p.86 B., Poll.2.184; cf. Suid. s.v. λίσποι:—also **λισπόπυξ**, Eust. 1288.46: acc. pl. λισπόπυγας Sch.Ar.*Eq*.1365.

❀ **λίσπος**, η, ον, *smooth, polished*, λίσπη γλῶσσα Ar.*Ra*.826 codd.; cf. λίσφος. 2. = λισπόπυγος, Poll.2.184; from λίσπος, = θηρίδιον λεπτὸν σφόδρα, acc. to Callistr.ap.Sch.Ar.*Ra*.848. II. Subst. **λίσπαι**, αἱ, *dice cut in two* by friends (ξένοι), each of whom kept half as a tally, Pl.*Smp*.193a:—so **λίσποι**, οἱ, Suid.

**λισσάνιος** [ᾰ], ον, Lacon. for ἀγαθός (Hsch., Phot.), ὦ λισσάνιε *my good friend*, Ar.*Lys*.1171 (λυσσάνιε cod. R).

**λισσάς**, άδος, Boeot. **λιττάς** Corinn.*Supp*.1.30, fem. of λισσός, λισσὰς αἰγίλιψ πέτρα A.*Supp*.794 (lyr.), cf. E.*Andr*.533 (lyr.), *HF* 1148, Theoc.22.37, Lyr.ap.Plu.2.90d: Subst. λισσάς (sc. πέτρα), *bare, smooth cliff*, Plu.*Mar*.23, *Crass*.9, Opp.*H*.2.320; of *a tombstone*, *Epigr.Gr*.256.

**λίσσομαι**, Hom., Lyr., Trag.; Ep. Iterat. λισσέσκετο Il.9.451: aor. 1 ἐλισάμην, Ep. ἐλλ. Od.11.35; imper. λίσαι Il.1.394; subj. 2 sg. λίση Od.10.526: aor. 2 inf. λιτέσθαι Il.16.47; opt. λιτοίμην Od.14. 406. (For pres. **λίτομαι**, v. sub voce):—*beg, pray*, either abs. or c. acc. pers., λισσομένη προσέειπε Δία Il.1.502; εὐχωλῇσι λιτῇσί τε ἔθνεα νεκρῶν ἐλλισάμην Od.11.35, etc.; the thing by which one prays is found with ὑπέρ, λ. ὑπὲρ τοκέων, ὑπὲρ ψυχῆς καὶ γούνων, Il.15.660, 22.338; λ. τινὰ ὑπὲρ πατρὸς καὶ μητέρος 24.467: or simply in gen.,

λ. Ζηνὸς ἠδὲ Θέμιστος Od.2.68; λ. τινὰ γούνων Il.9.451, Od.22.337 (for which in Il.6.45 we have λαβὼν ἐλλίσσετο γούνων, cf. Od.6. 142; τῇ ἑτέρῃ μὲν ἑλὼν ἐλλίσσετο γούνων Il.21.71; ἥπτετο χείρεσι γούνων ἱέμενος λίσσεσθ' 20.469); also in Trag., πρὸ..τέκνων σε λ. E. *Tr.*1045 (v. infr.): an inf. is freq. added, as οὐδέ σ' ἔγωγε λίσσομαι εἵνεκ' ἐμεῖο μένειν I do not *pray* thee to remain, Il.1.174, cf. 283, B.10. 69, Pi.*P.*4.207; πρός νυν θεῶν σε λ. ἐμοὶ πιθέσθαι S.*El.*428; καὶ μὴ προδοῦναι λ. *prays* her not to abandon him, E.*Alc.*202: more rarely with an acc. and inf. added, λίσσονται Δία..ἌΤην ἅμ' ἕπεσθαι they *pray* Zeus *that* Ate may follow, Il.9.511, cf. Od.8.30: sts. folld. by ὅπως, λίσσεσθαί μιν, ὅπως νημερτέα εἴπῃ *entreat* him to say the truth, 3.19; or by ἵνα, ib.327: in Trag. parenth., μὴ πρόλειπε, λ., πάτερ A. *Supp.*748; μή, λίσσομαί σ', αὔδα τάδε S.*Aj.*368, cf. *OT*650 (lyr.), Ar. *Pax*382. 2. c. acc. rei, *beg* or *pray for*, οἵ αὐτῷ θάνατον καὶ κῆρα λιτέσθαι Il.16.47: c. dupl. acc. pers. et rei, ταῦτα μὲν οὐχ ὑμέας ἔτι λίσσομαι this *I beg* of you no more, Od.2.210, cf. 4.347. 3. in Hom. freq. c. dat. modi, ἐπέεσσι Il.21.98, al.; εὐχῇσι Od.10.526; εὐχωλῇσι λιτῇσί τε ἐλλισάμην 11.35.—Rare in Prose, as Hdt.1.24, Lxx *Jb.*17.2, Luc.*Syr.D.*18; in Pl.*R.*366a there is a ref. to Il.9.501. [The λ- freq. makes position in Ep., Il.1.394, al.; written λλ after the augm., v. supr.]

**λισσ-ός**, ή, όν, *smooth*, Hom. (only in Od.), λισσὴ αἰπεῖά τε εἰς ἅλα πέτρη a *smooth* rock running sheer into the sea, 3.293; λισσὴ δ' ἀναδέδρομε πέτρη 5.412, cf. 10.4; λ. νῆσος A.R.2.382; λ. δειράδες *AP*15. 25.11 (Besant.). 2. *poor* (= δεόμενος, Hsch.): hence, *insolvent*, *SIG*527.115 (Dreros, iii B.C.). **-όω**, *render insolvent*, [λισ]σωθέντων dub. in ib.524.43 (Crete, iii B.C.); cf. foreg. 2. **-ωμα**, ατος, τό, *smoothness*, λ. τριχῶν the *crown* or *spot on the head from which the hair sets in different ways*, Arist.*HA*491ᵇ6. **-ωσις**, εως, ἡ, *setting of the hair from the crown of the head*, ib.491ᵇ8.

**λίσσωμεν**· ἐάσωμεν, Hsch.

**λιστός**, ή, όν, (λίσσομαι) *to be moved by prayer*, Il.9.497 (as quoted in Pl.*R.*364d): elsewh. only in compds. ἄλλιστος, τρίλλιστος.

**λιστρ-αίνω**, *dig round*, Suid. **-εύω**, = foreg., φυτόν Od.24. 227. **-ῆρες**· οἱ λιστρεύοντες, καὶ οἱ πρὸς ταῖς ὑποκαιομέναις χύτραις ἱστάμενοι σπινθῆρες, Hsch. **-ιον**, τό, Dim. of sq., = κοχλιάριον, Ar.*Fr.*809 (restd. fr. Phryn.*PS*p.88 B.), Hsch.; cf. λείστριον. **-ον**, τό, *tool for levelling* or *smoothing*, *spade*, *shovel*, Od.22.455, Lyc. 1348, Mosch.4.101:—later also **-ος**, ὁ, Sch.Nic.*Th.*29, *EM*587. 43. **-όω**, = λιστρεύω, Eust.1229.26. **-ωτός**, ή, όν, *levelled*, ἅλω δρόμος Nic.*Th.*29.

**λίσφ-ος**, η, ον, Att. for ἄπυγος, Moer.p.245 P.; said to be Att. for λίσπος (q.v.), Tz.ad Hes.*Op.*156. II. as Subst. λίσφοι, οἱ, = ἴσχια, *EM*567.20. **-ώσασθαι**· ἐλαττώσασθαι, Hsch.

**λίσχροι**, οἱ, = τὰ στροφικὰ τῶν σπερμάτων, i.e. *plants which were ploughed into the ground*, to serve for manure, as lupines in Italy, Hsch. II. λίσχρος· φειδωλός, Suid. Adv. -ρῶς Hsch.

⊛ **λῖτα, λιτί**, case forms of a noun of which no nom. sg. is found (unless σινδὼν λίς is right in *Michel*832.19 (Samos, iv B.C.)), *linen cloth*, ἑανῷ λιτὶ κάλυψαν they covered [the corpse] with a fine *linen cloth*, Il.18.352, 23.254; λῖτα may be acc. sg. or acc. pl., αὐτὴν δ' ἐς θρόνον εἷσεν ἄγων, ὑπὸ λῖτα πετάσσας, καλὸν δαιδάλεον Od.1.130; ἔβαλλε θρόνοις ἔνι ῥήγεα καλά, πορφύρεα καθύπερθ', ὑπένερθε δὲ λῖθ' ὑπέβαλλεν 10.353: understood as pl. by Ath.2.48c; used for covering a chariot, Il.8.441: in *AP*6.332 (Hadr.) λῖτα [ῐ] πολυδαίδαλα is prob. f.l. (Perh. akin to λίνον.)

**λῐτ-άζομαι**, = λίσσομαι, *IG*14.2525, *Arch.Anz.*19.8 (Milet.), Opp. *C.*2.373, Orph.*Fr.*333 (perh. Act.), *Inscr.Perg.* 324 (hymn to Zeus). **-αίνω** (fr. λιταν-yω, cf. λιτανός), = λιτανεύω, E.*El.*1215 (lyr.). **-αῖος**, *hearing prayer*, epith. of Zeus, *BCH*2.509 (coin of Nicaea); also in form λιδαῖος ib.24.389 (inscr. of Bithynia).

**λῐτᾰν-εία**, ἡ, *entreaty*, Lxx 2*Ma.*3.20, 10.16, *PTeb.*284.9 (i B.C.), Corn.*ND*12: pl., D.H.4.67; -εῖαι πρὸς τοὺς θεούς Jul.*Ep.*114, cf. Iamb.*Myst.*1.15. ⊛ **-ευτικός**, ή, όν, *of* or *for praying*, Sch.A.*Supp.* 809. **-ευτός**, ή, όν, *begged*, *entreated*, Hsch. s. v. ἀμφιλίτην. **-εύω**, in Hom. with λλ in augm. tenses, ἐλλιτάνευε, ἐλλιτάνευσα: (λιτανός):—*pray*, *entreat*, πάντας δ' ἐλλιτάνευε (v.l. δὲ λ.) Il.15.422:— Constr. same as λίσσομαι, either abs., Od.7.145: or c. acc. pers., Il. l. c., 9.581, etc.; that by which one prays in gen., γούνων ἐλλιτάνευσα Od.10.481; for which in Il.24.357 we have ἀλλ' ἄγε, γούνων ἁψάμενοι λιτανεύσομεν (Ep. for -ωμεν); also c. inf., 23.196: c. acc. pers. et inf., Hes.*Th.*469, Pi.*N.*8.8, etc.: c. Adj. neut., πολλὰ λ. τινά ib.5.32: rare in Att. Poets, Men.49 (dub. l.), and in Prose, X.*HG*2.4.26, Pl. *R.*388b, Lxx *Ps.*44(45).12; λ. τὸ θεῖον Str.15.1.60; τοὺς θεοὺς εὐχαῖς D.H.4.76. **-ός**, ή, όν, (λιτή) *praying*, *suppliant*, μέλη A.*Supp.* 809 (lyr.): as Subst. λιτανά, τά, = λιταί, ἀμφὶ λιτάν' ἕξομεν engage in *prayer*, Id.*Th.*102 (Seidler for ἀμφίλιταν or ἀμφὶ λιτάν).

**λῐταργ-ίζω**, Att. fut. -ιῶ, *slip away*, Ar.*Pax*562; cf. ἀπολιτ-. **-ισμός**, οῦ, ὁ, = σκιρτήματα, in pl., Sch.Ar.*Nu.*1255. **-ος**, ον, *running quick*, *An.Ox.*2.236, *EM*567.38, prob. in Semon.7.12 (λιτοργόν codd. Stob.).

⊛ **λῐτή**, ἡ, (λίτομαι) *prayer*, *entreaty*, mostly in pl., λιτῇσι ἐλλισάμην Od.11.34; καταβαίνειν ἐς λιτάς Hdt.1.116; λιταῖς ἀποτρέπει [αὐτὸν] μὴ πορεύεσθαι ib.105; λιταῖς πεῖσαί τινα Pi.*O.*2.80, cf. 8.8; μαλθάσσειν κέαρ λιταῖς A.*Pr.*1008; ηὔχετο λιταῖσι Id.*Pers.*499; λιτᾶν ἀκούειν Id. *Ag.*396 (lyr.); λιτὰς κλύειν Id.*Th.*172 (lyr.), cf. E.*Or.*1233, etc.; λιταῖς σεβίζειν S.*OC*1557 (lyr.); ἐπεύχεσθαι λιτάς ib.484; λ. δέχεσθαι Id.*Ant.* 1019; ἐν λιταῖς στέλλειν *with prayers*, Id.*Ph.*60; λιταὶ θεῶν *prayers to* the gods, E.*Supp.*262; but λιταὶ ἐμαυτοῦ ξυμμάχων τε *prayers for* myself, S.*OC*1309: also c. gen. of that by which one prays, γενείου τοῦδ'..ἐκτείναι λιτάς E.*Or.*290. (Poet., Ion. and late Prose, *BGU* 74.15 (ii A.D.).) II. Λιταί, αἱ, personified, *Prayers of sorrow and repentance*, Il.9.502 sq., *AP*11.361 (Autom.).

**λιτῆρα θαλλόν** (= *Trag.Adesp.*234)· τὸν ἱκέσιον, Hsch.

**λῐτί**, v. λῖτα.

**λῑτό-βῐος**, ον, (λιτός) *living plainly* or *sparingly*, Str.15.1.34. **-βόρος**· εὐτελῶς τραφείς, Hsch. **-δίαιτος** [δῐ], ον, *of a plain way of life*, D.H.2.49.

**λίτομαι** [ῐ], = λίσσομαι, *h.Hom.*16.5, Ar.*Th.*313, 1040 (both lyr.), *AP*5.150 (Mel.), 164 (Id.), Orph.*H.*41.9, Opp.*C.*2.367, *IG*14.902 (Capri).

⊛ **λῑτός**, ή, όν, *simple*, *inexpensive*, *frugal*, λιταὶ τράπεζαι Ps.-Phoc.81; οἱ λ. χυλοί Epicur.*Ep.*3 p.63 U.; λ. βίος Men.633, Crates Theb.10; τροφὴ λιτοτάτη Ath.5.191f; λιτὴ δίαιτα Plu.2.668f, cf. 125d, etc.; τὸ λ. τῆς διαίτης, κατὰ τὴν δίαιταν, Epicur.*Fr.*478, M.Ant.1.3; παρέξοδος (q.v.) -οτέρη Hp.*Decent.*8; λ. χλαμύδιον Men.442; τὰ ἱμάτια λ. καὶ σώφρονα Jul.*Caes.*317c; μίτρη λιτὴ στυππείου *Michel*832.17 (Samos, iv B.C.); ὑποκεφάλαια δύο ἡμιτυβίου λιτά ib.l.23; [ἀσπίδας] χαλκᾶς λιτὰς δύο, opp. περίχρυσος μία, *IG*2².1491.31 (iv B.C.); ἅλα λιτὸν ἐπέσθων *frugal* salt, Call.*Epigr.*48; λ. ὀξίς Nicostr.Com.9 (cj. for λοιπή); λ. ὕδωρ πίνων D.L.8.13; λ. χρίματα *simple* or *plain* unguents, Call. *Lav.Pall.*25; λ. ταφή Phld.*Mort.*30; λ. ζωμός *thin* (chicken-)broth, Gal.12.295; of medicines, ἡ διὰ κωδυῶν λιτή (sc. δύναμις) Critoap. Gal.13.38; ἡ διὰ μόρων λιτή Archig.ap.eund.12.973; λ. ἔμπλαστροι Androm.ap.eund.13.495, cf. 486; χάρτης λιτός, as a cargo, perh. *cheap* or *coarse* papyrus, *Cat.Cod.Astr.*1.104.28. 2. of persons, *poor*, λ. γενόμενος τοῖς ἔχουσι μὴ φθόνει dub. in Dionys.Com.10 (= Dionys.Trag.8); *frugal*, αὐτάρκεις καὶ λ. Plb.6.48.7; κατὰ τὴν ἐσθῆτα καὶ σίτησιν ἀφελὴς καὶ λ. Id.11.10.3; λ. περὶ δίαιταν Plu.2.709b. Adv. -τῶς *frugally*, Sotad.Com.1.6, *AP*7.156 (Isid.); λ. βιοῦν D.L. 6.105; λ. καὶ σωφρόνως ζῆν Ephor.149 J.; λαμπρῶς ἢ λ. ἐξενεχθέντας Phld. l. c. II. metaph., of style, *plain*, *simple*, *unadorned*, Arist. *Rh.*1416ᵇ25, D.H.*Th.*23, al. III. *paltry*, *petty*, *small*, τάφος *AP* 7.73 (Gemin.), cf. 7.18 (Antip. Thess.); of persons, opp. μέγας, Call. *Ap.*10; πολισμάτια Plb.32.8.3. Adv. -τῶς *slightly*, ἡψημένα Artem. 1.70; λ. ἑφθά Diocl.*Fr.*141; dub. sens. in Alc.*Oxy.*1788 *Fr.*2.11. [ῑ, but ῐ late, λῐτὰ δεῖπνα Nonn.*D.*17.59.]

⊛ **λῐτός** (A), ή, όν, epith. of γαῖα, dub. sens. in Alex.Aet.1, Orph. *A.*92; λιτὴ χθών· ἀπὸ τοῦ προσκυνεῖσθαι καὶ λιτανεύεσθαι, Hsch.

⊛ **λῐτός** (B), ή, όν, *suppliant*, *supplicatory*, θυσίαι Pi.*O.*6.78; ἐπαοιδαί Id.*P.*4.217.

⊛ **λῑτότης**, ητος, ἡ, (λῑτός) *plainness*, *simplicity*, κόσμου Democr.274; τῶν στεφάνων Thphr.*Fr.*142; τὴν λ. διώκουσι D.S.2.59; λ. διαίτης Cic.*Fam.*7.26.2; cj. for λεπτότης in Epicur.*Sent.Vat.*63. II. Gramm., a figure of speech, *assertion by means of understatement* (cf. μείωσις) or *negation*, Serv.ad Verg.*G.*2.125, Donat.ad Ter.*Hec.*775.

**λιτουργ-έω**, = κακὰ λέγω, Did.ap.Ammon.*Diff.*p.88 V. **-όν**· κακοῦργον, Hsch. (Cf. λίταργος.)

⊛ **λῑτρ-α**, ἡ, *a silver coin* of Sicily, Epich.9, Sophr.72, Diph.71, Posidipp.8.—On its value v. Arist.*Fr.*476, 510. II. as a weight, 12 ounces, *a pound*, [Simon.]141, Plb.21.43.19, D.S.14.116, Dsc.1.43, Plu.*TG*2, J.*AJ*14.7.1: metaph., λίτραν ἐτῶν ζήσας having lived *a pound* of years, i.e. 72 (in late times a pound of gold was coined into 72 pieces), *AP*10.97 (Pall.). III. measure of capacity, = 1 Italic κοτύλη, Gal.6.287. [ῑ as in Lat. *libra*; written λείτρα in *CIG*2040.7 (Bosp.).] (Both λῖτρα and Lat. *libra* prob. from early Italic **līþrā*.) **-αῖος**, α, ον, *weighing* or *worth a* λίτρα, χείλη *AP*11.204 (Pall.), cf. Gal.13.415. II. λ. κέρας a drinking-cup *holding* 1 λίτρα, ib.435. **-ασμός**, = *libratio*, *Gloss.* **-ιαῖος**, α, ον, = λιτραῖος 1, D.H.9.27. **-ίζω**, *weigh* or *deliver by weight*, *POxy.*1543.1 (iii A.D.). **-ίς**· πυξὶς σαματοδόχος, Hsch. (perh. πυξὶς σμηματοδόχος 'soap-box', λιτρίς being from λίτρον 1). ⊛ **-ισμός**, ὁ, *delivery by weight*, *PFlor.*31.21 (iv A.D.).

**λιτροδόκη**, ἡ, *box for holding* λίτραι, Phot. s.v. λίτρα.

**λιτρόμηλον**, τό, *an apple weighing a* λίτρα, Tz.*H.*9.347.

⊛ **λίτρον** [ῑ by nature], τό, older form for νίτρον, Hp.*Epid.*2.6.9 and 29, Hdt.2.86,87, Ar.*Fr.*320.1, Pl.*Ti.*60d, 65d (pl.), Thphr.*HP*3.7.6, Alex.1, dub. l. in Pl.Com.69.3. II. = λίτρα III, *PFay.*331 (ii A.D.).

**λιτροπώλης**, ου, ὁ, *seller of* λίτρον, *IG*2².1673.22 (iv B.C.).

**λιτροσκόπος**, ὁ, (λίτρα 1) *one who examines money*, *money-changer*, S.*Fr.*1065.

**λιτρώδης**, ες, = νιτρώδης, Pl.*Ti.*65e, Thphr.*Fr.*159, Gal.6.559: Comp. -εστέρα Ath.2.43b.

**λιττάς**, v. λισσάς.

**Λῐτυέρσης**, ου, Dor. **-έρσας**, ὁ, *Lityerses*, a bastard son of Midas, who used to challenge wayfarers to a reaping match, and bound the heads of the conquered in his sheaves, Ath.10.415b, Suid. 2. *a reaper's song named after him*, Men.264, Theoc.10.41, Ath.14.619a.

**λίτυον**, τό, = Lat. *lituus*, Plu.*Rom.*22.

**λῐφαιμ-έω**, *lack blood*, Arist.*Pr.*877ᵃ30, Gal.12.693; *bleed to death*, J.*AJ*8.15.5, App.*Gall.*10, Hsch. **-ία**, ἡ, *bloodlessness*, Ph.2. 512. **-ος**, ον, *lacking blood*, Emp.100.1; *pallid*, Hp.*Mul.*2.119, 125.

**λιχάζει**· ἐπιθυμεῖ, Hsch. II. in aor. inf. λιχάξαι· ῥῖψαι, βάλαι (Cret.), Id.

**λῐχᾰνοειδὴς τόπος**, ὁ, *locus of the* λίχανος II, Aristox.*Harm.* p.26 M.; ὁ λ. φθόγγος *the highest note of a* πυκνόν, Bacch.*Harm.*43, cf. Aristid.Quint.1.6.

**λῐχᾰνός**, όν, (λείχω) *licking*: ὁ λ., with or without δάκτυλος, *forefinger*, from its use in licking up, Hp.*Art.*37, al., Luc.*Tim.*54, Ath. 1.15d, *PLips.*12.9 (iii A. D.), etc. II. as Subst. **λῐχᾰνος** (sc. χορδή), ἡ, *the string struck with the forefinger*, and *its note*, Aristox. *Harm.*p.116 M., Arist.*Pr.*919ᵃ17, D.S.3.59, Plu.2.1029a, etc. III. Adj., λ. σωλήν *a tube of the alembic*, Zos.Alch.pp.225,236 B.

**λῐχάς**, άδος, ἡ, *the space between the forefinger* (λιχανός) *and thumb*, the lesser span, Hero *Geom.*4, Poll.2.158. II. = ἀπότομος, Hsch. III. λιχάδες· ὄστρεα πάντα, οἱ δὲ λίθοι καὶ ψῆφοι καὶ κογχύλια, Id.

**λιχήν**, ῆνος, ὁ, v. λειχήν.

**λιχμ-άζω**, = λιχμάω, Hes.*Sc.*235; γλώσσῃ λ. Nic.*Th.*229. II. trans., *lick*, Opp.*H.*2.250, Nonn.*D.*44.111; Ion. impf., λιχμάζεσκε δέρην Mosch.2.94. **-αίνω**, = λιχμάω, Opp.*C.*3.174. **-άς**· θρῖναξ, καὶ ἀπαλὴ πόα καὶ χαμαιπετής, ἣν τὰ ἑρπετὰ ἐπιλείχουσι, Hsch. **-άω**, fut. Med. -ήσομαι (ἀνα-) J.*AJ*8.15.4: aor. ἐλιχμησάμην ap.D.L.8.91:—*play with the tongue*, of snakes, in Ep. part., αἰνὸν λιχμώωντες Q.S.5.40: in irreg. pf. part., γλώσσῃσι λελιχμότες Hes.*Th.*826:—Med., ἑκατὸν.. κεφαλαὶ κολάκων.. ἐλιχμῶντο περὶ τὴν κεφαλήν *played like serpents* round.., Ar.*V.*1033, *Pax* 756 (ἐλιχνῶντο v.l. in Sch., Hsch.), cf. Theoc.24.20, Euph.51.6. 2. trans., *lick*, ὄφεσι.. λιχμῶσιν γένυν E.*Ba.*698:—Med., D.L. l.c., App.*Hisp.*96, *Mith.*38. II. Med., also, *lick up*, λιχμώμενος ἔρσην Nic.*Al.*569; used by Hom. only in the compd. ἀπολιχμάομαι. **-ήμων**, ον, gen. ονος, *licking*, of mice, Nic.*Al.*37. **-ήρης**, ες, *playing with the tongue*, of snakes, Id.*Th.*206.

**λιχνάομαι**, v. λιχμάω I. 1.

**λιχν-εία**, ἡ, *gluttony, luxuriousness in eating*, X.*Lac.*5.4, Luc.*Tim.* 55: pl., X.*Oec.*1.22, Pl.*R.*519b; περὶ τὰ φαῦλα Ath.5.220c. 2. in pl. also, *dainties*, Plu.2.225f: so in sg. in collective sense, Nic. Dam.56 J. **-ευμα**, ατος, τό, *a dainty, delicacy*, Sophr.24. **-εύω**, *gormandize*, περὶ τὰς πέτρας Luc.*Pisc.*48, cf. Arr.*Epict.*2.4.8, Plu.2. 713c. II. *desire greedily, covet*, τὰ δημόσια D.H.8.73; δόξαν Plu. *Comp.Dem.Cic.*2:—Med., *desire eagerly* to do, c. inf., Id.2.347a; *to be greedy*, λ. εἰς ὅρασιν Lib.*Descr.*30.3: c. gen., σαρκὸς ἀνθρωπείου λ. Sch.Il.*Oxy.*221 ix 35:—Pass., *to be lusted after*, Nic.Dam.1 J. codd. (dub.).

**λιχνο-βόρος**, ον, *eating tit-bits*, μῦς *AP*9.86 (Antiphil.). **-γραυς**, ᾱος, ἡ, *greedy old woman*, Timo 38.1.

**⊛λίχνος**, η, ον, also ος, ον E.*Hipp.*913, *gluttonous*, X.*Mem.*1.2.2, Pl.*R.*354b, Plb.3.57.7, Gal.6.716; τὰ περὶ τὴν τροφὴν λίχνοι Clitarch. 1 J.: c. gen., τῶν ἐν διαίτῃ ποικιλμάτων Epicur.*Sent.Vat.*69: metaph., λ. τὴν ψυχήν Pl.*R.*579b: Comp. -ότερος Sophr.62: Sup. -ότατος Arist.*HA*594ᵃ6. 2. metaph., *curious, inquisitive*, E. l.c.; ὄμματα λ. Call.*Fr.*107, *AP*12.106 (Mel.); *lewd*, Crates Theb.4: c. gen., *curious after*, τοῦ κεκρυμμένου E.*Fr.*1063.8; c. inf., λ. εἰμὶ καὶ τὸ πεύθεσθαι Call.*Fr.*98d. II. of things, *luxurious, appetizing*, ὄψα, ἐδέσματα, Gal.*Anim.Pass.*6.

**λιχνο-τένθης**, ου, ὁ, *greedy glutton*, Poll.6.122. **-της**, ητος, ἡ, = λιχνεία, Sch.Ar.*Av.*1690. **-φιλάργῠρος**, ον, *both epicure and miser*, Philyll.17 (s.v.l.).

**λιχνώδης**, ες, = λίχνος, Ael.*Fr.*325 (Sup.).

**λίψ** (A), ὁ, gen. λιβός, *the SW. wind*, Hdt.2.25, Arist.*Mete.*364ᵇ 2 (pl.), *Mu.*394ᵇ27, Theoc.9.11: pl., Plb.10.10.3. 2. *the South*, freq. in Lxx, *Ge.*13.14, al. 3. *the West*, opp. ἀπηλιώτης, *PTeb.* 14.19 (ii B. C.), Vett.Val.8.5, Paul.Al.*A.*2, Herm.ap.Stob.1.21.9, 1. 49.45; rarely in Lxx, 2*Ch.*32.30, 33.14, Thd.*Da.*8.5; λιβὸς or λίβα εἰς ἀπηλιώτην from *West* to East, *BGU*1037.15 (i A. D.), *CPR*28.21 (ii A. D.). 4. Astron., πρωινὸς λ., μεσημβρινὸς λ., ὀψινὸς λ., *position* of a star *on the W. horizon* at sunrise, midday, or sunset, Ptol.*Alm.* 8.4.

***λίψ** (B), ἡ, (λείβω) only gen. and acc. (λιβάς or λίβος being the nom. in use), *stream*, ἐξ ὀμμάτων λείβουσι.. λίβα (Burges for δία) A.*Eu.*54; ἀφθονέστερον λίβα f.l. in A.*Fr.*72; μέλιτος λίβα A.R.4. 1454. 2. = λοιβή, *libation*, φιλοσπόνδου λιβός A.*Ch.*292; εὐκταίαν λίβα Id.*Fr.*55.

**⊛λίψ** (C)· ἐπιθυμία (cf. λίπτομαι), πέτρα ἀφ' ἧς ὕδωρ στάζει, Hsch.

**λιψουρία**, ἡ, (λίπτομαι, οὖρον) *desire to make water*, A.*Ch.*756.

**λιώδης**· λιθόλευστος, Hsch. (Perh. λιώλης, cf. λεώλης.) **λιωργός**· κακοῦργος, Id. **λόβαι**· χεῖρες, Id.

**λόβ-ιον**, τό, Dim. of sq. I. 1, Gal.14.701; of sq. I. 2, Hsch. II. *fruit of the* σμῖλαξ, Dsc.2.146. **⊛-ός**, ὁ, *lobe of the ear*, εὔτρητοι (for wearing ear-rings) λ. Il.14.182, cf. *h.Hom.*6.8, Hp.*Prog.*2, Arist. *HA*492ᵃ16; ἄκροι λ. Lyc.1401. 2. *lobe of the liver*, to which special attention was paid in divination, A.*Pr.*495, E.*El.*827, Pl.*Ti.*71c, Euphro 7: generally, *liver*, A.*Eu.*159 (lyr.). 3. *lobe* of the lung, Gal.*UP*6.4, al.; of the whole *lung*, Hp.*Loc.Hom.*14. II. *capsule* or *pod* of leguminous plants (cf. ἔλλοβος), Thphr.*HP*1.11.2, etc.; esp. of φασίολοι or δόλιχοι, because they were eaten pod and all, Gal.6.557, Jul.*Or.*5.175c. 2. in rose leaves, *the white part*, elsewh. ὄνυξ, Gal.12.748.

**λογ-άδην** [ᾰ], Adv., (λογάς) *picked*, of troops, Plu.*Oth.*6. 2. mostly of stones for building, εἰργάζοντο λ. φέροντες λίθους καὶ ξυνετίθεσαν ὡς ἕκαστόν τι ξυμβαίνοι bringing the stones *as they picked them out*, Th.4.4, cf. 31, 6.66, D.H.*Comp.*22. **-αῖος**, α, ον, *chosen, picked*, Str.1.3.18 (paraphrasing Ibyc.22). **-αοιδικός**, ή, όν, *logaoedic*, of verses in which dactylic and trochaic rhythms are combined, so that they stand *between* λόγος *and* ἀοιδή, *between prose and poetry*, D.L.4.65, Heph.7, Aristid.Quint.1.23, *POxy.*220 xii 2.

**⊛λογᾰρ-ιάζω**, *calculate*, Eust. ad D.P.907, Sch.Ar.*Pl.*381:—hence **-ιασμός**, ὁ, *calculation*, Sch.Luc.*Cat.*4. **-ίδιον**, τό, = sq., *POxy.* 599 (i/ii A. D.). **-ιον**, τό, Dim. of λόγος, Ar.*Fr.*810 (pl.); λ. δύστηνα wretched *petty speeches*, D.19.255; τὰ ἐκ στοᾶς λ. Theognet.1.2; λογάρια δειπνεῖν dine off *mere words*, Ath.6.270d. II. *account*, *PTeb.*20.8 (ii B. C.), etc.

**⊛λογάς** (A), άδος, ὁ, ἡ, (λέγω) *picked, chosen*, mostly in pl. of *picked men*, λ. νεηνίαι Hdt.1.36,43, E.*Hec.*544, etc.; τριηκόσιοι Σπαρτιητέων λ. Hdt.8.124; λ. Περσέων τοὺς ἀρίστους χιλίους Id.9.63; Ἀργείων οἱ χίλιοι λ. Th.5.67; στρατηγῶν λογάδες E.*Andr.*324; of cattle, *PStrassb.*24.32 (ii A. D.); φωναὶ λογάδες *chosen* phrases, Phot.*Bibl.* p.491 B.: with collect. Nouns, στρατιὴ λ. ἡμιθέων *AP*15.51 (Arch.). 2. λ. λίθοι *unhewn stones, taken just as they were picked*, Paus.7.22.5; cf. λογάδην, λέγω B. I, λιθολόγος.

**⊛λογάς** (B), usu. in pl., **λογάδες**, αἱ, *whites of the eyes*, Sophr.49, Call.*Fr.*132, Nic.*Th.*292 (sg., Poll.2.70): generally, *eyes*, *AP*5.269 (Paul. Sil.).

**λογάω**, *to be fond of talking*, Luc.*Lex.*15. II. λογάω or λογέω, fut. 3 sg. λογήσει, perh. *will take account*, Tyrt.*Fr.*1.42 Diehl.

**⊛λογγ-άζω**, = λαγγάζω, A.*Fr.*112, Ar.*Fr.*811, cf. Phryn.*PS* p.87 B. **-άσια** [ᾰ], τά, *stones with holes in them*, through which mooring-cables were passed, Hsch., Phot. s. v. λογγάζειν:—sg. **λογγᾰσία**, Hsch.:—also **λογγῶνες**, οἱ, Syracusan acc. to *EM*569.42, cf. Suid.

**λογ-εία**, ἡ, *collection* of taxes or voluntary contributions, *PHib.*1. 51.2 (iii B. C.), *PTeb.*58.55 (ii B. C.), *POxy.*239.8 (i A. D.); *collection* for charity, 1*Ep.Cor.*16.1, Hsch.; for religious purposes, *GDI*4156 (Lindos), *PSI*2.262.3 (i A. D.); *perquisite*, *PPar.*5 xxvii 6 (ii B. C.). **⊛-εῖον**, τό, (λογεύς I) prop. *speaking-place*: in the theatre, *stage*, *IG*11(2).161 *D*126 (Delos, iii B. C.), Vitr.5.7.2, Plu.*Thes.*16, etc.: generally, *platform*, *Arch.Pap.*2.564 (pl.), unless λογείων = λογίων. 2. = στόμα, Poll.2.98. **-έμπορος**, ὁ, *phrase-monger*, Artem.2.70: a pecul. accent λογεμπόρος is mentioned by Eust.463.40, 1447.47. **-ευμα**, ατος, τό, *taxes collected*, *PRev.Laws* 56.15, al. (pl., iii B. C.). **-εύς**, έως, ὁ, *speaker*, Critias 54 D., Plu.2.813a. II. *prose-writer*, Sch. D.T.pp.114, 119 H. **⊛-ευτήριον**, τό, *office of the* λογευτής, *PRev. Laws* 11.13 (iii B. C.). **-ευτής**, οῦ, ὁ, *tax collector*, ib.9.2, al. (iii B. C.), *Ostr.*318, *PTeb.*90 (i B. C.), etc. **-ευτικόν**, τό, *cost of collection*, ib.105.24, cf. 5 (pl., ii B. C.). **-εύω**, *collect* contributions, taxes, etc., *PRev.Laws* 39.14 (iii B. C.), *PTeb.*5.139, al. (ii B. C.), Plb. 31.31.1, *GDI*4156 (Lindos), *IG*12(5).186.4 (Paros, ii B. C.), 12(7).237. 24 (Amorgos, i B. C.), *OGI*665.37 (i A. D.), 629.156 (ii A. D.). **-ία**, late spelling of λογεία (q. v.). **-ίατρος**, ὁ, *a physician only in words*, Gal.*Libr.Propr.*1, Id.15.159, al.:—hence **-ιατρεία**, ἡ, Ph.1.526 (v.l. λογοιατρεία). **-ίδιον**, τό, Dim. of λόγος, Isoc.13.20, Pl.*Erx.* 401e. 2. *little fable* or *story*, Ar.*V.*64. **-ίζομαι**, Att. fut. -ιοῦμαι Id.*Ra.*1263, Th.5.87, etc.: aor. ἐλογισάμην E.*Or.*555, Th.6. 31, etc.: pf. λελόγισμαι Lys.32.24,27, D.28.12:—Pass., v. infr. III: (λόγος):—prop. of numerical calculation, *count, reckon*, οὐκ ἐπισταμένους λογίζεσθαι Hdt.2.16; εὗρον λογιζόμενος Id.7.28, cf. 194, etc.; in full, λ. ψήφοισι Id.2.36; λόγισαι φαύλως, μὴ ψήφοις ἀλλ' ἀπὸ χειρός *calculate* roughly, not by rule, but off-hand, Ar.*V.*656: c. acc. rei, λ. τοὺς τόκους *calculate* the interest, Id.*Nu.*20; τρεῖς μνᾶς ἀναλώσας λογίσασθαι δώδεκα spend 3 minae and *set down* 12, Id.*Pl.*381. 2. c. acc. et inf., *reckon* or *calculate that*.., λ. μύρια εἶναι [τὰ ἔτεα] Hdt. 2.145; τὰς βλάβας, ἃς ἐλογίζεθ' αὑτῷ γεγενῆσθαι D.21.176: without acc., Θηριππίδῃ μισθὸν ἀποδεδωκέναι λ. Id.27.20. 3. λ. τινί τι *set down to* one's account, οὗτος.. τὸ ἥμισυ τούτοις.. λελόγισται Lys.32. 24, cf. 27; τἀνηλωμέν'.. οὐκ ἐλογιζόμην I *did* not *charge* them.., D. 18.113: metaph., τὰ παραπτώματα λ. τινί 2*Ep.Cor.*5.19. b. *audit the accounts of* a person, c. dat., τοῖς ὑπευθύνοις Arist.*Ath.*54.2; ταῖς ἀρχαῖς ib.48.3. II. without reference to numbers, *take into account, calculate, consider*, ταῦτα Hdt.9.53, cf. S.*Aj.*816, etc.; λ. τὰ ξυμφέροντα Th.1.76; λ. τι πρός τινας with them, D.5.24; also λ. περί τινος *calculate, form calculations* about.., Hdt.2.22, X.*Mem.*4.3. 11. 2. c. acc. et inf., *reckon, consider that*.., τὸν ἕτερον [παῖδα] οὐκ εἶναί μοι λ. Hdt.1.38; τὸν Πᾶνα τῶν ὀκτὼ θεῶν λ. εἶναι Id.2.46; λ. ὅτι.. or ὡς.., X.*HG*2.4.28, 6.4.6; ἐλογιζόμην πρὸς ἐμαυτὸν.., ὅτι.. And.1.52, Pl.*Ap.*21d: c. acc. et part., Σμέρδιν μηκέτι ὑμῖν ἐόντα λογίζεσθε Hdt.3.65: also with inf. omitted, *reckon* or *account* so and so, τὸν καθ' ἡμέραν βίον λογίζου σόν [εἶναι], τὰ δ' ἄλλα τῆς τύχης E.*Alc.* 789; πολὺν [εἶναι] τὸν κάτω χρόνον ib.692; λογίζεταί τ' ἐκεῖνα πάνθ' ἁμαρτίας Ar.*V.*745; μίαν ἄμφω τούτω τὼ ἡμέρα λ. *count* both days as one, X.*Cyr.*1.2.11. 3. c. inf. also, *count* or *reckon upon* doing, *calculate* or *expect* that.., ἐπισιτιεῖσθαι ἐλογίζοντο Hdt.7.176; ἐλογίζετο κατύπερθέ οἱ τὰ πρήγματα ἔσεσθαι Id.8.136; λογιζόμενοι ἥξειν ἅμα ἡλίῳ δύνοντι X.*An.*2.2.13; λελογισμένοι.. εἰσὶν.. διαζῆν E.*IA*922, cf. *Or.* 555 (dub. l.); τί λογίζομ'.. προσδοκῶν χάριν παρὰ γυναικὸς κομιεῖσθαι; Men.564. 4. *count upon*, εἴ τις δύο ἢ καί τι πλείους ἡμέρας λ., μάταιός ἐστιν S.*Tr.*944. 5. *conclude by reasoning, infer that*.., c. acc. et inf., Pl.*Grg.*524b, X.*Ages.*7.3; λ. ὅτι.. Id.*HG*6.1.5, cf. Pl.*Phd.*62e, al. 6. abs., τοὺς ἐπισταμένους λογίζεσθαι Archyt.3; ὁ σπουδαῖος λελόγισται ἤδη *has finished reasoning*, Plot.3.8.6, cf. 4. 4.12. III. Pass., mostly aor. ἐλογίσθην and (less freq.) pf. λελόγισμαι, also in pres., part. λογιζόμενον Hdt.3.95, freq. in later Gr., *PPetr.*3 p.340 (iii B. C.), *Ep.Rom.*4.5, etc.; χρήματα εἰς ἀργύριον λογισθέντα *counted* or *calculated* in silver, X.*Cyr.*3.1.33; ὁπλῖται ἐλογίσθησαν οὐκ ἐλάττους δισμυρίων Id.*HG*6.1.19; οὗτος λογισμὸς λογισθεὶς Pl.*Ti.*34b; οὐδ' ἐξ ἑνὸς λόγου λελογισμένου Id.*Phdr.*246c; τὸ λελογισμένον, = λογισμός, E.*IA*386, Luc.*Nigr.Prooem.*

**λογῐκ-εύομαι**, *to be merely arguing*, πρὸς ἐπίδειξιν Dam.*Pr*.320, cf. 162. **-ός**, ή, όν, (λόγος) *of* or *for speaking* or *speech*, μέρη λ. the organs *of speech*, Plu.*Cor*.38: λογική, ή, *speech*, opp. μουσική, D.H. *Comp*.11; λ. φαντασία *expressed in speech*, *Stoic*.2.61. 2. *of* or *in eloquence*, ἀγῶνες Philostr.*VS*1.22.1; ἀκροάσεις λ. καὶ ὀργανικαί *Supp. Epigr*.2.184.6 (Tanagra, ii B.C.). 3. *suited for prose*, ὁ ἡρῷος σεμνὸς καὶ οὐ λ. Demetr.*Eloc*.42; τὸ λ., opp. τὸ μεγαλοπρεπές, ib.41; of persons, *writing in prose*, D.L.5.85; ἐγκώμιον λ. *in prose*, *IG*9(2).531.43 (Thess.). II. *possessed of reason, intellectual*, μέρος Ti.Locr.99e, al.; τὸ λ. ζῷον Chrysipp.*Stoic*.3.95; ἀρεταὶ λ., = διανοητικαί, opp. ἠθικαί, Arist.*EN*1108b9. 2. *dialectical, argumentative*, οἱ λ. διάλογοι of Plato, such as the Theaetetus and Cratylus, D.L.3.58; in Arist. usu. like διαλεκτικός, λ. συλλογισμός *APo*.93a15, cf. *Top*.162b27; διὰ λογικωτέρων καὶ ἀκριβεστέρων λόγων *more abstract*, *Metaph*.1080a10; λ. δυσχέρειαι ib.1005b22; λ. ἀπόδειξις *GA*747b28; but also, *logical*, λ. συλλογισμοί, opp. ῥητορικοί, *Rh*.1355a13. Adv. **-κῶς** *dialectically*, *Metaph*.1029b13, *APo*.84a7, 88a19; φυσικῶς καὶ λ. *GC*316a11: Comp. **-ώτερον** *Cael*.275b12. b. Subst., ἡ λογική (sc. τέχνη) *logic*, Cic.*Fin*.1.7.22; also τὰ λογικά Id.*Tusc*.4.14.33; περὶ λογικῶν title of work, Democr.10b; τὸ λ., opp. τὸ φυσικόν, τὸ ἠθικόν, Zeno *Stoic*. 1.15, etc. 3. of the 'dogmatic' school of physicians, ἡ λ. αἵρεσις Gal.*Sect.Intr*.1. **-ότης**, ητος, ή, *rationality*, Id.19.481, Alex. Aphr. *in Metaph*.205.33, Eust.1953.44.

**λόγ-ιμος**, η, ον Hdt.2.98, also ος, ον Id.6.106: (λέγω B):—*worth mention, notable, famous*, πόλις ll. cc.; πόλισμα, ἔθνος, ἀνήρ, Id.1.143, 171, 9.64; λ. ἐς τὰ πρῶτα Id.9.16; **-ώτατος** ib.37; as epith. of temples in Egypt, ἱερὸν λ. *PTeb*.302.4 (i A.D.), etc. (ἐλλόγιμος is more freq.). **-ιον**, τό, *oracle*, esp. one preserved from antiquity, Hdt. 4.178, 203, 8.60.γ', Plu.*Thes*.26, *Lys*.22: more freq. in pl., *oracles*, Hdt.1.64, 8.62, 141, E.*Heracl*.405, Ar.*Eq*.120, al., Plu.*Fab*.4, *Marc*.3: distd. fr. χρησμοί, Th.2.8 (the former being *prose*, the latter *verse*, acc. to Sch., but this distn. does not hold), cf. Plu.*Pel*.20, *Nic*.13, 2.412c. 2. τὰ λ. Κυρίου the *sayings* of the Lord, Lxx *Ps*.11(12).6, cf. *Act.Ap*.7.38, *Ep.Rom*.3.2, 1*Ep.Pet*.4.11. II. τὸ λ. τῶν κρίσεων *the oracular breastplate* worn by the Jewish High-Priest, Lxx *Ex*.28. 26(30), cf. Ph.2.154; τὰ λόγια Aristeas 158. **-ιος**, α, ον, (λόγος) *of* or *belonging to* λόγοι: I. *versed in tales* or *stories* (cf. λόγος v), λόγιοι καὶ ἀοιδοί Pi.*P*.1.94, cf. *N*.6.45: hence of chroniclers (opp. poets), Περσέων οἱ λόγιοι Hdt.1.1; Αἰγυπτίων **-ώτατοι** Id.2.3, cf. 4.46; so later, οἱ -ώτατοι τῶν ἀρχαίων συγγραφέων Plb.6.45.1, cf. 38.6.1, D.S. 2.4, D.H.5.17, etc. 2. generally, *learned, erudite*, Democr.30, etc.; λ. περὶ τὴν ὅλην φύσιν Arist.*Pol*.1267b28; ὁ λ. Ἀκεστῖνος, of a *learned* physician, Hld.4.7; οἱ -ώτατοι Τυρρηνῶν, of the Tuscan haruspices, Plu.*Sull*.7; Χαλδαίων οἱ λ. Arr.*An*.7.16.5, cf. J.*AJ*17.6.2, etc.; λογιώτατος as title, *OGI*408.5 (Theb. Aeg.), *POxy*.902.1 (v A.D.), etc.; ὁ τῆς λ. μνήμης σχολαστικός *PMasp*.118.30 (vi A.D.). II. *skilled in words, eloquent*, τὸ μεγαλοπρεπὲς ὅπερ νῦν καὶ λόγιον ὀνομάζουσιν Demetr.*Eloc*.38, etc.; Arist. is said to have made Thphr. [τὸν] -ώτατον (of his disciples), Str.13.2.4; λ. ἐξ ἀφώνου γενόμενος Plu.*Pomp*.51; epith. of Hermes, as the god of eloquence, Luc.*Apol*.2, *Gall*.2 (Sup.), Jul.*Or*.4.132a; οἱ λ. θεοί Id.*Ep*.80; this sense is condemned by Phryn.176. Adv. **-ίως** *eloquently*, Plu.2.405a; ὡς ἐνῆν -ώτατα *as nearly in words as possible*, of the elephant, ib.968d. III. *oracular*, Ἀπόλλωνος δῶμα λόγιον *Berl.Sitzb*.1911.632 (Cyprus). **-ιότης**, ητος, ή, *eloquence*, Ph.2.93, Plu.2.205a; ascribed to Sophocles by Id. 2.348d. II. as title, from λόγιος I. 2, ἡ σὴ λ. *POxy*.902.13 (v A.D.), etc. **-ίς**, ίδος, ή, fem. derivative of λόγος, λογίδες σεμναί Anon.ap.*An.Ox*.1.225. **-ισις**, εως, ή, = λογισμός, Phryn.*PS* p.65 B. **-ισμα**, ατος, τό, *reckoning, account*, Antiph.243; ἐπὶ λόγισμα ἀργυρίου *JHS*9.248 = *BCH*50.491 (Cyprus). ⊛ **-ισμός**, ὁ, *counting, calculation*, τῶν ἡμερῶν Th.4.122; τυγχάνειν τοῦ ἀληθοῦς λ. Id.3.20; ἐκ τοιοῦδε λ. ἔξεστί τῳ σκοπεῖν Id.5.68; ἐν λ. ἁμαρτάνειν Pl.*R*.340d; ἀριθμὸς καὶ λ. Id.*Phdr*.274c; ἐπὶ λογισμὸν ἐλθόντες Id. *Euthphr*.7b; καθέζεσθαι ἐπὶ τοὺς λ. Aeschin.3.59: in pl., *numbers, arithmetic*, λογισμοὺς μανθάνειν X.*Mem*.4.7.8; λογισμούς τε καὶ ἀστρονομίαν καὶ γεωμετρίαν.. διδάσκειν Pl.*Prt*.318e, cf. *R*.510c, al. 2. *account, reckoning*, Lys.32.19, D.18.113, etc.; λ. λαμβάνειν hold an *audit*, Arist.*Pol*.1322b9. II. without reference to number, *calculation, reasoning*, τοῦ ξυμφέροντος λογισμῷ Th.2.40; καθιστάναι τινὰς ἐς λ. Id.6.34; λογισμῷ ἐλάχιστα χρώμενοι Id.2.11; ἐνδέχεταί τι λογισμὸν Id.4.92; λ. αὐτοκράτορι (v. αὐτοκράτωρ I. 4) ib.108; οὐ λογισμῷ δόντες τοὺς κινδύνους Lys.2.23; λογισμὸν περί τινος ἔχειν Pl. *Lg*.805a; ὅσον ἦν ἀνθρωπίνῳ λ. δυνατόν D.18.300, cf. 193; τοῖς λ. τοῖς ἰδίοις πταίων ἀεί Men.380; μετὰ λογισμοῦ πάντα πράττουσίν τινος Id. 617, cf. Philem.90.10, etc.; personified, opp. Θυμός, Cleanth.*Stoic*. 1.129. 2. *reason, argument*, X.*HG*3.4.27, Pl.*Ti*.34a. III. *reasoning power*, [Epich.]257.1, Democr.187, X.*Mem*.4.3.11, Epicur. *Sent*.16, al.: freq. in Arist., τὸ τῶν ἀνθρώπων γένος [ζῇ] καὶ τέχνῃ καὶ λογισμοῖς *Metaph*.980b28, cf. *de An*.415a8, al.—Only in Prose and Com.

**λογιστ-εία**, ή, *office of* λογιστής, *Bull.Inst.Français d'Arch.Orient*. 22.193 (Egypt. iii/ii B.C.), *Inscr.Délos* 396 *A* 19 (ii B.C.), *IG*12(1).83 (Rhodes, ii A.D.), *OGI*509.9 (Aphrodisias), *PKlein.Form*.1010 (iv/v A.D.), *Cod.Just*.10.56.1, etc. **-έον**, *one must reckon*, Vett.Val.264.9; λ. ἀπό.. *one must deduct* from.., τὴν τροφὴν.. ἀπὸ τῶν ἑβδομήκοντα μνῶν.. λογιστέον D.27.36. 2. *one must impute*, τινί τι Hld.1.15. II. *one must take into account*, τι Pl.*Ti*.62a. 2. *one must reason*, Men. 531.9. **-εύω**, *administer as* λογιστής, τοὺς Σμυρναίους Philostr.*VS* 1.19.2, cf. *Jahresh*.23 *Beibl*.54 (Mopsuestia), *IGRom*.3.6, *OGI*722.10 (iv A.D.), etc.: c. gen., *to be curator of*, τῆς κολωνίας, τῆς.. πόλεως, *IG* 5(1).524 (Laconia), *OGI*500.12 (Aphrodisias). II. metaph., ἡ φύσις λογιστεύει τὰ μόρια Sever.*Clyst*.p.6 D., cf. Suid. ⊛ **-ήριον**, τό, *the place* at Athens *where the* λογισταί *met*, Decr.ap.And.1.78 (pl.), Lys.20.10; later of any *office*, λ. τῶν νομαρχικῶν *Klio* 12.365 (Alexandria, ii B.C.), cf. *PPetr*.2 p.26 (iii B.C.), *PTeb*.24.38 (ii B.C.); στρατιωτικὸν λ. war-*office*, Str.16.2.10. 2. λογιστήρια, τά, = λογισταί, Arist.*Fr*.446; ἀνενεγκάτω ὁ ταμίας.. τῷ πρώτῳ λογιστηρίῳ at the first *meeting of the* λογισταί, *SIG*1219.36 (Gambreum, iii B.C.). II. *reckoning-board, abacus*, D.S.30.15; called τράπεζα λογιστηρία by Poll.10.158. **-ής**, οῦ, ὁ, *calculator, teacher of arithmetic*, Pl.*Plt*.260a, *R*.340d. 2. *calculator, reasoner*, λεπτῷ λογιστᾷ Ar.*Av*.318; δίκαιος λ. τῶν.. ὑπηργμένων D.1.10. II. *auditor*, esp. at Athens, in pl., a board which audited the accounts of magistrates going out of office, Aeschin.3.15, D.18.117, 229; also called εὔθυνοι acc. to Arist.*Pol*.1322b11, but distd. from them, Id.*Ath*.48.3, *IG*1².91, 2².956; also at Delos, ib.11(2).203 *A* 63 (iii B.C.); in Egypt, λ. Ὀξυρυγχίτου (sc. νομοῦ) *POxy*.84.2, etc.; λ. κώμης *PKlein.Form*.617 (v A.D.): metaph., λογισταὶ τῶν.. χορῶν, of the audience, Eup.223. 2. = Lat. *curator rei publicae*, an *Imperial commissioner and inspector of accounts*, *IGRom*.3.39 (Bithynia), etc. **-ικός**, ή, όν, *skilled* or *practised in calculating*, Pl.*Tht*.145a, X.*Mem*.1.1.7; οἱ φύσει λ. Pl.*R*.526b; of a mathematician, *AP*11. 267: Subst. ἡ **-κή** (with or without τέχνη), *practical arithmetic, the art of arithmetic*, opp. ἀριθμητική (the science of number), Pl.*Grg*. 450d, 451b, *R*.525a, al.; so τὸ **-κόν** Id.*Chrm*.174b; ἡ λ., opp. γεωμετρία, Archyt.4. II. *endued with reason, rational*, ζῷα Arist. *de An*. 434a7; [τὸ] λ. [μόριον τῆς ψυχῆς] ib.432a25; λ. ὄρεξις, opp. ἄλογος, Id.*Rh*.1369a2; τὸ λ. (sc. τῆς ψυχῆς) the *reasoning faculty*, Pl.*R*.439d, cf. Arist.*Top*.128b38; = τὸ βουλευτικόν, Id.*EN*1139a12. 2. *using one's reason, reasonable*, X.*HG*5.2.28, Men.*Epit*.541. III. **-κόν**, τό, *expenses of the* λογιστεία, *Inscr.Délos* 395.13, 399 *A* 96 (ii B.C.).

**λογιστονόμος**, ον, *regulating accounts*, Man.4.160.

**λογκούριον** (λογούριον cod.)· ὕαλος, Hsch. (cf. λυγκούριον, λογούριον).

**λογογρᾰφ-εύς**, έως, ὁ, = λογογράφος II, D.H.*Din*.11 codd. (-γράφῳ Sauppe). **-έω**, *to be a* λογογράφος II, *write speeches*, τισι for people, Plu.*Comp.Dem.Cic*.3; ἐπί τινα Id.*Dem*.6. II. *make into a story*, [μυθάρια] Jul.*Or*.7.208c. III. *keep accounts*, ψευδῶς λ., Ἑλληνικά 1.18 (Gytheum, i A.D.). **-ημα**, ατος, τό, *prose work*, Anon. in Rh. 3.571 W. **-ία**, ή, *writing of speeches*: and generally, *of prose*, Pl. *Phdr*.257e, 258b; ἱστορία καὶ ἡ ἄλλη λ. Hermog.*Id*.2.12; esp. *speech-writing* for money, Demad.8. 2. *office of official recorder* in a law-court, *PAmh*.2.82.7 (iii/iv A.D.). **-ικός**, ή, όν, *of* or *for writing speeches* or *prose*, ἀνάγκη λ. inevitable rules *for composition*, Pl. *Phdr*.264b; ἡ **-κή** (sc. τέχνη) Id.ap.Poll.2.121; ἡ λ. ἰδέα Ammon. *in Int*.4.30. **-ος**, ὁ, *prose-writer*, opp. poet (v. λόγος v), Arist.*Rh*. 1388b22, D.H.*Comp*.16.1: applied to the early Greek historians from Cadmus of Miletus to Hdt. by Th.1.21; cf. λογοποιός I: generally, *historian*, Plb.7.7.1; coupled with συγγραφεύς, D.H.1.73. II. *professional speech-writer*, Alex.124.19, Aeschin.1.94; as a term of reproach, διὰ πάσης τῆς λοιδορίας ἐκάλει λογογράφον Pl.*Phdr*.257c, cf. Din.1.111, D.19.246, Aeschin.3.173, Hyp.*Ath*.3: but without such implication, Χαιρήμων ἀκριβὴς ὥσπερ λ. Arist.*Rh*.1413b13. III. *accountant*, *POxy*.2115 (iv A.D.), etc. IV. *recorder* in a court, *PAmh*.2.82.3 (iii/iv A.D.).

**λογο-δαιδᾰλία**, Ion. **-ίη**, ή, *skill in adorning a speech*, Aus.*Ep*. 10.26. **-δαίδᾰλος**, ον, *skilled in tricking out a speech*, Pl.*Phdr*. 266e. **-δεής**, ές, *wanting in reason* or *reasonableness*, prob. l. in Arist.*Spir*.481b27. **-δειπνον**, τό, *feast of words, learned banquet*, Ath.1.b. **-διάρροια**, ή, *flux of words*, ib.22e, 4.159e. **-δῐδάσκᾰλος**, ὁ, *teacher of eloquence*, Poll.2.125. **-είδεια**, ή, *prosaic diction*, D.H.*Comp*.26. **-ειδής**, ές, *prose-like, prosaic*, στίχος Sch.Heph.p.292 C., cf. Hermog.*Id*.1.3 (Comp.), Eust.718.25, etc.; τὸ λ. *prose*, D.L.7.60; but also, *command of language*, Philostr. *VA*1.19. II. *resembling reason*, θηρία λογοειδῆ, λογοειδεῖς ἐνέργειαι Dam.*Pr*.18. III. *reasonable, rational*, Procl.*Inst*.111, *in Alc*. p.68C. ⊛ **-θεσία**, ή, *keeping of accounts*, *POxy*.136.33 (pl., vi A.D.); *audit*, *BGU*77.10 (ii A.D.), etc. II. *description, account*, Bito 44. 9. ⊛ **-θέσιος**, ὁ, *accountant*, Palchos in *Cat.Cod.Astr*.1.94.26: **-θέσια**, τά, *account-books*, ib.1.95.17. **-θετέω**, *call to account*, Epimyth. ad Aesop.406:—Pass., Mitteis *Chr*.372 ii 3. II. *keep accounts*, Antioch.Astr. in *Cat.Cod.Astr*.7.110.29. **-θέτης**, ου, ὁ, *auditor*, *BGU*77.10 (ii A.D.), al., *Cod.Just*.10.30.4, Procop.*Arc*.8, al. **-θεώρητος**, ον, *to be apprehended by the intellect alone*, of the pores, Cael. Aur.*TP*3.2.19, *CP*2.16, cf. Cic.ap.Macr.*Sat*.2.3.6. **-θήρας**, ου, ὁ, *word-catcher*, Ph.1.526, al. **-ῑατρεία**, ή, *healing only in words*, v. λογίατρος. **-κλοπία**, ή, *stealing of another's words* or thoughts, *plagiarism*, attributed to Empedocles by Timae.81. **-λεσχέω**, *prate*, Eust.437.24. **-λέσχης**, ου, ὁ, *prater*, *AP*11.140 (Lucill.). **-μάγειρος** [ᾰ], ὁ, *one who cooks up words*, Suid. s. v. Ἀντιφῶν. **-μᾰνέω**, *to have a passion for study*, Chio *Ep*.15.3. **-μᾰχέω**, *fight about words*, 2*Ep.Ti*.2.14. **-μᾰχία**, ή, *war about words, disputation*, 1*Ep.Ti*.6.4 (pl.), Porph.ap.Eus.*PE*14.10; title of Menippean satire by Varro, Nonius p.268 L., Porphyr. ad Hor.*Sat*.2.4. **-μῖμος**, ὁ, *writer* or *actor of spoken mimes*, Hegesand.13. **-μύθιον** [ῡ], τό, *fabulous legend*, Poll.2.123. **-πλάθος** [ᾰ], ὁ, *fable-maker*, e. g. Aesop, Phryn.*PS* p.86 B.

⊛ **λογοποι-έω**, *write, compose*, Pl.*R*.378d, *Lg*.636d; *write speeches*, Id.*Euthd*.289d. 2. *fabricate tales*, esp. of newsmongers, Th.6.38,

And.1.54, Lys.16.11, D.4.49, Thphr.*Char.*8.1; τὰς [συμφορὰς] αὐτοὶ λογοποιοῦσιν Lys.22.14; λ. κατὰ τῆς πόλεως Plb.28.2.4:—Pass., D.C. 37.35. **II.** Med., *settle accounts*, πρός τινας *PRyl.*136.4 (i A.D.), etc.:—Pass., *Ostr.*1179. **III.** Med., *make proposals*, ἰδίᾳ πρός τινα Luc.*DMeretr.*10.4. **-ημα**, ατος, τό, *idle tale, piece of gossip*, Antiph.166.2. **-ία**, ἡ, *tale-telling, newsmongering*, Thphr.*Char.* 8.1. **II.** *tale, piece of gossip*, Nic.Dam.130.20 J. (pl.), Charito 3.2 (pl.). **2.** *prayer*, Sm.*Ps.*101(102).1. **III.** *rendering of accounts*, *PLond.*5.1660.20 (vi A.D.). **-ικός**, ή, όν, *of* or *like a* λογοποιός: ἡ -κὴ τέχνη, = λογογραφική, Pl.*Euthd.*289c. **-ός**, ὁ, *prose-writer*; esp. *historian, chronicler*, Id.*R.*392a, Isoc.5.109, 11.37; applied by Hdt. to Hecataeus, 2.143, 5.36,125; to Hdt. himself by Arr.*An.*3.30.8. **2.** *writer of fables*, Αἴσωπος ὁ λ. Hdt.2.134, cf. Plu.*Sol.*28. **II.** at Athens, = λογογράφος II, *professional speech-maker*, Pl.*Euthd.*289d. **2.** with collat. sense of *tale-teller, newsmonger*, D.24.15, Thphr.*Char.*8.1, Plu.*Nic.*30.

**λογο-πρᾱγέω**, *write copiously*, Eust.1759.5. ***-πράκτωρ**, ορος, ὁ, dub. sens. in *PBaden* 26.40 (iii A.D.). **-πώλης**, ου, ὁ, *dealer in words*, Ph.1.526, Philostr.*VS*1.23.1.

***λόγος**, ὁ, verbal noun of λέγω (B), with senses corresponding to λέγω (B) II and III (on the various senses of the word v. Theo Sm. pp.72,73 H., *An.Ox.*4.327): common in all periods in Prose and Verse, exc. Epic, in which it is found in signf. derived from λέγω (B) III, cf. infr. VI. 1 a: **I.** *computation, reckoning* (cf. λέγω (B) II). **1.** *account* of money handled, σανίδες εἰς ἃς τὸν λ. ἀναγράφομεν *IG*1$^{2}$. 374.191; ἐδίδοσαν τὸν λ. ib.232.2; λ. δώσεις τῶν μετεχείρισας χρημάτων Hdt.3.142, cf. 143; οὔτε χρήματα διαχειρίσας τῆς πόλεως δίδωμι λ. αὐτῶν οὔτε ἀρχὴν ἄρξας οὐδεμίαν εὐθύνας ὑπέχω νῦν αὐτῆς Lys.24.26; λ. ἀπενεγκεῖν Arist.*Ath.*54.1; ἐν ταῖς εὐθύναις τοῦ τοιούτου λ. ὑπεχέτω Pl.*Lg.*774b; τὸν τῶν χρημάτων λ. παρὰ τούτων λαμβάνειν D.8.47; ἀδικήματα εἰς ἀργυρίου λ. ἀνήκοντα Din.1.60; συνᾶραι λόγον μετά τινος settle *accounts* with, *Ev.Matt.*18.23, etc.; δεύτεροι λ. a second *audit*, *Cod.Just.*1.4.26.1; ὁ τραπεζιτικὸς λ. banking *account*, Theo Sm.p.73 H.: metaph., οὐκ ἂν πριαίμην οὐδενὸς λ. βροτόν S.*Aj.*477. **b.** *public accounts*, i.e. branch of *treasury*, ἴδιος λ., in Egypt, *OGI*188.2, 189.3, 669.38; also as title of *treasurer*, ib.408.4, Str.17.1.12; ὁ ἐπὶ τῶν λ. *IPE*2.29 *A* (Panticapaeum); δημόσιος λ., = Lat. *fiscus*, *OGI*669.21 (Egypt, i A.D.), etc. (but later, = *aerarium*, *Cod.Just.*1.5.15); also Καίσαρος λ. *OGI*669. 30; κυριακὸς λ. ib.18. **2.** generally, *account, reckoning*, μὴ φῦναι τὸν ἅπαντα νικᾷ λ. excels the whole *account*, i.e. is best of *all*, S.*OC* 1225 (lyr.); δόντας λ. τῶν ἐποίησαν *accounting* for, i.e. paying the penalty for their doings, Hdt.8.100; λ. αἰτεῖν Pl.*Plt.*285e; λ. δοῦναι καὶ δέξασθαι Id.*Prt.*336c, al.; λαμβάνειν λ. καὶ ἐλέγχειν Id.*Men.*75d; παρασχεῖν τῶν εἰρημένων λ. Id.*R.*344d; λ. ἀπαιτεῖν D.30.15, cf. Arist. *EN*1104$^{a}$3; λ. ὑπέχειν, δοῦναι, D.19.95; λ. ἐγγράψαι Id.24.199, al.; λ. ἀποφέρειν τῇ πόλει Aeschin.3.22, cf. *Ev.Luc.*16.2, *Ep.Hebr.*13.17; τὸ παράδοξον τῶν συμβεβηκότων ὑπὸ λόγον ἄγειν Plb.15.34.2; λ. ἡ ἐπιστήμη, πολλὰ δὲ ὁ λ. the *account* is manifold, Plot.6.9.4; ἔχων λόγον τοῦ διὰ τί an *account* of the cause, Arist.*APo.*74$^{b}$27; ἐς λ. τινός on *account* of, ἐς χρημάτων λ. Th.3.46, cf. Plb.5.89.6, Lxx 2 *Ma.*1.14, *JRS* 18.152 (Jerash); λόγῳ c. gen., by *way* of, *Cod.Just.*3.2.5, al.; κατὰ λόγον τοῦ μεγέθους if we take into *account* his size, Arist.*HA*517$^{b}$27; πρὸς ὃν ἡμῖν ὁ λ. *Ep.Hebr.*4.13, cf. D.Chr.31.123. **3.** *measure, tale* (cf. infr. II. 1), θάλασσα..μετρέεται ἐς τὸν αὐτὸν λ. ὁκοῖος πρόσθεν Heraclit.31; ψυχῆς ἐστι λ. ἑαυτὸν αὔξων Id.115; ἐς τούτου (sc. γήραος) λ. οὐ πολλοί τινες ἀπικνέονται to the *point* of old age, Hdt.3.99, cf. 7.9.β′; ὁ ξύμπας λ. the full *tale*, Th.7.56, cf. *Ep.Phil.*4.15; κοινῷ λ. νομίσαντα common *measure*, Pl.*Lg.*746e; *sum, total* of expenditure, *IG*4$^{2}$(1).103.151 (Epid., iv B.C.); ὁ τῆς οὐσίας λ., = Lat. *patrimonii modus*, *Cod.Just.*1.5.12.20. **4.** *esteem, consideration, value* put on a person or thing (cf. infr. VI. 2 d), οὗ πλείων λ. ἢ τῶν ἄλλων who is of more *worth* than all the rest, Heraclit.39; βροτῶν λ. οὐκ ἔσχεν οὐδέν' A.*Pr.*233; οὐ σμικροῦ λ. S.*OC*1163: freq. in Hdt., Μαρδονίου λ. οὐδεὶς γίνεται 8.102; τῶν ἦν ἐλάχιστος ἀπολλυμένων λ. 4. 135, cf. E.*Fr.*94; περὶ ἐμοῦ οὐδεὶς λ. Ar.*Ra.*87; λόγου οὐδενὸς γίνεσθαι πρός τινος to be of no *account, repute* with.., Hdt.1.120, cf. 4.138; λόγου ποιήσασθαί τινα make one of *account*, Id.1.33; ἐλαχίστου, πλείστου λ. εἶναι, to be highly, lowly *esteemed*, Id.1.143, 3.146; but also λόγον τινὸς ποιεῖσθαι, like Lat. *rationem habere alicujus*, make *account* of, set a *value* on, Democr.187, etc.: usu. in neg. statements, οὐδένα λ. ποιήσασθαί τινος Hdt.1.4, cf. 13, Plb.21.14.9, etc.; λ. ἔχειν Hdt.1. 62,115; λ. ἴσχειν περί τινος Pl.*Ti.*87c; λ. ἔχειν περὶ τοὺς ποιητάς Lycurg.107; λ. ἔχειν τινός D.18.199, Arist.*EN*1102$^{b}$32, Plu.*Phil.*18 (but also, have the *reputation* of.., v. infr. VI. 2 e); ἐν οὐδενὶ λ. ποιήσασθαί τι Hdt.3.50; ἐν οὐδενὶ λ. ἀπώλοντο without *regard*, Id.9.70; ἐν σμικρῷ λ. εἶναι Pl.*R.*550a; ὑμεῖς οὔτ' ἐν λ. οὔτ' ἐν ἀριθμῷ Orac.ap. Sch.Theoc.14.48; ἐν ἀνδρῶν λ. [εἶναι] to be *reckoned, count* as a man, Hdt.3.120; ἐν ἰδιώτεω λόγῳ καὶ ἀτίμου *reckoned* as.., Eus.Mynd.*Fr.* 59; σεμνὸς εἰς ἀρετῆς λ. καὶ δόξης D.19.142. **II.** *relation, correspondence, proportion*, **1.** generally, ὑπερτερίης λ. *relation* (of gold to lead), Thgn.418 = 1164; πρὸς λόγον τοῦ σήματος A.*Th.*519; κατὰ λόγον προβαίνοντες τιμῶσι in inverse *ratio*, Hdt.1.134, cf. 7.36; κατὰ λ. τῆς ἀποφορῆς Id.2.109; τἄλλα κατὰ λ. in *like fashion*, Hp.*VM*16, *Prog.*17: c. gen., κατὰ λ. τῶν πρόσθεν ib.24; κατὰ λ. τῶν ἡμερῶν Ar. *Nu.*619; κατὰ λ. τῆς δυνάμεως X.*Cyr.*8.6.11; ἐλάττω ἢ κατὰ λ. Arist. *HA*508$^{a}$2, cf. *PA*671$^{a}$18; ἐκ ταύτης ἐγένετο ἐκείνη κατὰ λ. Id.*Pol.* 1257$^{a}$31; cf. εὔλογος: sts. with ὁ αὐτός added, κατὰ τὸν αὐτὸν λ. τῷ τείχεϊ *in fashion* like to.., Hdt.1.186; περὶ τῶν νόσων ὁ αὐτὸς λ. *analogously*, Pl.*Tht.*158d, cf. *Prm.*136b, al.; εἰς τὸν αὐτὸν λ. *similarly*, Id.*R.*353d; κατὰ τὸν αὐτὸν λ. in the same *ratio*, *IG*1$^{2}$.76.8; by parity of *reasoning*, Pl.*Cra.*393c, *R.*610a, al.; ἀνὰ λόγον τινός, τινί, Id.*Ti.*29c, *Alc.*2.145d; τοῦτον ἔχει τὸν λ. πρὸς..ὃν ἡ παιδεία πρὸς τὴν ἀρετήν is *related* to..as.., Procl.*in Euc.*p.20 F., al. **2.** Math., *ratio, proportion* (ὁ κατ' ἀνάλογον λ., λ. τῆς ἀναλογίας, Theo Sm.p.73 H.), Pythag.2; ἰσότης λόγων Arist.*EN*1131$^{a}$31; λ. ἐστὶ δύο μεγεθῶν ἡ κατὰ πηλικότητα ποιὰ σχέσις Euc.5 *Def.*3; τῶν ἁρμονιῶν τοὺς λ. Arist.*Metaph.*985$^{b}$32, cf. 1092$^{b}$14; λόγοι ἀριθμῶν numerical *ratios*, Aristox.*Harm.*p.32 M.; τοὺς φθόγγους ἀναγκαῖον ἐν ἀριθμοῦ λ. λέγεσθαι πρὸς ἀλλήλους to be expressed in numerical *ratios*, Euc.*Sect.Can. Proëm.*: in Metre, *ratio* between arsis and thesis, by which the rhythm is defined, Aristox.*Harm.*p.34 M.; ἐὰν ᾖ ἰσχυροτέρα τοῦ αἰσθητηρίου ἡ κίνησις, λύεται ὁ λ. Arist.*de An.*424$^{a}$31; ἀνὰ λόγον *analogically*, Archyt.2; ἀνὰ λ. μερισθεῖσα [ἡ ψυχή] *proportionally*, Pl. *Ti.*37a; so κατὰ λ. Men.319.6; πρὸς λόγον in *proportion*, Plb.6.30.3, 9.15.3 (but πρὸς λόγον ἐπὶ στενὸν συνάγεται narrows *uniformly*, Sor. 1.9, cf. Diocl.*Fr.*171); ἐπὶ λόγον *IG*5(1).1428 (Messene). **3.** Gramm., *analogy, rule*, τῷ λ. τῶν μετοχικῶν, τῆς συγκοπῆς, by the *rule* of the participles, of syncope, Choerob.*in Theod.*1.75 Gaisf., 1. 377 H.; εἰπέ μοι τὸν λ. τοῦ Αἴας Αἴαντος, τουτέστι τὸν κανόνα *An.Ox.* 4.328. **III.** *explanation*, **1.** *plea, pretext, ground*, ἐκ τίνος λ.; A.*Ch.*515; ἐξ οὐδενὸς λ. S.*Ph.*731; ἀπὸ παντὸς λ. Id.*OC*762; χὠ λ. καλὸς προσῆν Id.*Ph.*352; σὺν ἀφανεῖ λ. Id.*OT*657 (lyr., v.l. λόγων); ἐν ἀφανεῖ λ. Antipho 5.59; ἐπὶ τοιούτῳ λ. Hdt.6.124; κατὰ τίνα λ.; on what *ground?* Pl.*R.*366b; οὐδὲ πρὸς ἕνα λ. to no *purpose*, Id.*Prt.* 343d; ἐπὶ τίνι λ.; for what *reason?* X.*HG*2.2.19; τὸν λ. τοῦτον this *ground* of complaint, Aeschin.3.228; τίνι δικαίῳ λ.; what just *cause* is there? Pl.*Grg.*512c; τίνι λ.; on what *account? Act.Ap.*10.29; κατὰ λόγον ἂν ἠνεσχόμην ὑμῶν *reason* would that.., ib.18.14; λ. ἔχειν, with personal subject, εἶχον ἄν τινα λ. I (i.e. my conduct) would have admitted of an *explanation*, Pl.*Ap.*31b; τὸν ὀρθὸν λ. the true *explanation*, ib.34b. **b.** *plea, case*, in Law or argument (cf. VIII. 1), τὸν ἥττω λ. κρείττω ποιεῖν to make the weaker *case* prevail, ib.18b, al., Arist.*Rh.*1402$^{a}$24, cf. Ar.*Nu.*1042 (pl.); personified, ib.886, al.; ἀμύνεις τῷ τῆς ἡδονῆς λ. Pl.*Phlb.*38a; ἀνοίσεις τοὺς λ. αὐτῶν πρὸς τὸν θεόν Lxx *Ex.*18.19; ἔχειν λ. πρός τινα to have a *case, ground of action* against.., *Act.Ap.*19.38. **2.** *statement of a theory, argument*, οὐκ ἐμεῦ ἀλλὰ τοῦ λ. ἀκούσαντας prob. in Heraclit.50; λόγον ἠδὲ νόημα ἀμφὶς ἀληθείης *discourse* and reflection on reality, Parm.8.50; δηλοῖ οὗτος ὁ λ. ὅτι.. Democr.7; οὐκ ἔχει λόγον it is not *arguable*, i.e. *reasonable*, S.*El.*466, Pl.*Phd.*62d, etc.; ἔχει λ. D.44.32; οὐδεὶς αὐτὰ καταβαλεῖ λ. E.*Ba.*202; δίκασον..τὸν λ. ἀκούσας Pl.*Lg.*696b; personified, φησὶ οὗτος ὁ λ. ib.714d, cf. *Sph.*238b, *Phlb.*50a; ὡς ὁ λ. (sc. λέγει) Arist.*EN*1115$^{b}$12; ὡς ὁ λ. ὁ ὀρθὸς λέγει ib.1138$^{b}$20, cf. 29; ὁ λ. θέλει προσβιβάζειν Phld.*Rh.*1.41, cf. 1.19 S.; οὐ γὰρ ἂν ἀκούσειε λόγου ἀποτρέποντος Arist.*EN*1179$^{b}$27; λ. καθαίρων Aristo *Stoic.*1.88; λόγου τυγχάνειν to be *explained*, Phld.*Mus.*p.77 K.; ὁ τὸν λ. μου ἀκούων my *teaching*, *Ev.Jo.*5.24; ὁ προφητικὸς λ., collect., of *VT* prophecy, 2 *Ep. Pet.*1.19: pl., ὁκόσων λόγους ἤκουσα Heraclit.108; οὐκ ἐπίθετο τοῖς ἐμοῖς λ. Ar.*Nu.*73; of *arguments* leading to a conclusion (ὁ λ.), Pl. *Cri.*46b; τὰ Ἀναξαγόρου βιβλία γέμει τούτων τῶν λ. Id.*Ap.*26d; λ. ἀπὸ τῶν ἀρχῶν, ἐπὶ τὰς ἀρχάς, Arist.*EN*1095$^{a}$31; συλλογισμός ἐστι λ. ἐν ᾧ τεθέντων τινῶν κτλ. Id.*APr.*24$^{b}$18; λ. ἀντίτυπός τε καὶ ἄπορος, of a self-contradictory *theory*, Plot.6.8.7. **b.** ὁ περὶ θεῶν λ., title of a *discourse* by Protagoras, D.L.9.54; ὁ Ἀχιλλεὺς λ., name of an *argument*, ib.23; ὁ αὐξόμενος λ. Plu.2.559b; καταβάλλοντες (sc. λόγοι), title of work by Protagoras, S.E.*M.*7.60; λ. σοφιστικοί Arist.*SE* 165$^{a}$34, al.; οἱ μαθηματικοὶ λ. Id.*Rh.*1417$^{a}$19, etc.; οἱ ἐξωτερικοὶ λ., current outside the Lyceum, Id.*Ph.*217$^{b}$31, al.; Δισσοὶ λ., title of a philosophical treatise (= *Dialex.*); Λ. καὶ Λογίνα, name of play of Epicharmus, *quibble, argument*, personified, Ath.8.338d. **c.** in Logic, *proposition*, whether as premiss or conclusion, πρότασίς ἐστι λ. καταφατικὸς ἢ ἀποφατικός τινος κατά τινος Arist.*APr.*24$^{a}$ 16. **d.** *rule, principle, law*, as embodying the result of λογισμός, Pi.*O.*2.22, *P.*1.35, *N.*4.31; πείθεσθαι τῷ λ. ὃς ἄν μοι λογιζομένῳ βέλτιστος φαίνηται Pl.*Cri.*46b, cf. c; ἡδονὰς τοῖς ὀρθοῖς λ. ἑπομένας obeying right *principles*, Id.*Lg.*696c; προαιρέσεως [ἀρχὴ] ὄρεξις καὶ λ. ὁ ἕνεκά τινος *principle* directed to an end, Arist.*EN*1139$^{a}$32; of the final cause, ἀρχὴ ὁ λ. ἔν τε τοῖς κατὰ τέχνην καὶ ἐν τοῖς φύσει συνεστηκόσιν Id.*PA*639$^{b}$15; ἀποδιδόασι τοὺς λ. καὶ τὰς αἰτίας οὗ ποιοῦσι ἑκάστου ib.18; [τέχνη] ἕξις μετὰ λ. ἀληθοῦς ποιητική Id.*EN*1140$^{a}$10; ὀρθὸς λ. true *principle*, right *rule*, ib.1144$^{b}$27, 1147$^{b}$3, al.; κατὰ λόγον by *rule*, consistently, ὁ κατὰ λ. ζῶν Pl.*Lg.*689d, cf. *Ti.*89d; τὸ κατὰ λ. ζῆν, opp. κατὰ πάθος, Arist.*EN*1169$^{a}$5; κατὰ λ. προχωρεῖν according to *plan*, Plb.1.20.3. **3.** *law, rule* of conduct, ᾧ μάλιστα διηνεκῶς ὁμιλοῦσι λόγῳ Heraclit.72; πολλοὶ λόγον μὴ μαθόντες ζῶσι κατὰ λόγον Democr.53; δεῖ ὑπάρχειν τὸν λ. τὸν καθόλου τοῖς ἄρχουσιν universal *principle*, Arist.*Pol.*1286$^{a}$17; ὁ νόμος..λ. ὢν ἀπό τινος φρονήσεως καὶ νοῦ Id.*EN*1180$^{a}$21; ὁ νόμος..ἔμψυχος ὢν ἑαυτῷ λ. *conscience*, Plu. 2.780c; τὸν λ. πρόχειρον ἔχειν *precept*, Phld.*Piet.*30, cf. 102; ὁ προστακτικὸς τῶν ποιητέων ἢ μὴ λ. κοινός M.Ant.4.4. **4.** *thesis, hypothesis*, provisional *ground*, ὡς ἂν εἰ λέγοι λόγον maintain a *thesis*, Pl. *Prt.*344b; ὑποθέμενος ἑκάστοτε λ. provisionally assuming a *proposition*, Id.*Phd.*100a; τὸν τῆς ὁμοιότητος λ. *hypothesis* of equivalence, Arist.*Cael.*296$^{a}$20. **5.** *reason, ground*, πάντων γινομένων κατὰ τὸν λ. τόνδε Heraclit.1; οὕτω βαθὺν λ. ἔχει Id.45; ἐκ λόγου, opp. μάτην, Leucipp.2; μέγιστον σημεῖον οὗτος ὁ λ. Meliss.8; [ἐμπειρία] οὐκ ἔχει λ. οὐδένα ὧν προσφέρει has no *grounds* for.., Pl.*Grg.*465a; μετὰ λόγου

τε καὶ ἐπιστήμης θείας Id.*Sph.*265c; ἡ μετὰ λόγου ἀληθὴς δόξα (= ἐπιστήμη) Id.*Tht.*201c; λόγον ζητοῦσιν ὧν οὐκ ἔστι λ. *proof*, Arist. *Metaph.*1011$^a$12; οἱ ἁπάντων ζητοῦντες λ. ἀναιροῦσι λ. Thphr.*Metaph.* 26. **6.** *formula* (wider than *definition*, but freq. equivalent thereto), *term* expressing *reason*, λ. τῆς πολιτείας Pl.*R.*497c; ψυχῆς οὐσία τε καὶ λ. essential *definition*, Id.*Phdr.*245e; ὁ τοῦ δικαίου λ. Id.*R.*343a; τὸν λ. τῆς οὐσίας ib.534b, cf. *Phd.*78d; τὰς πολλὰς ἐπιστήμας ἑνὶ λ. προσειπεῖν Id.*Tht.*148d; ὁ τῆς οἰκοδομήσεως λ. ἔχει τὸν τῆς οἰκίας Arist. *PA*646$^b$3; τεθείη ἂν ἴδιον ὄνομα καθ' ἕκαστον τῶν λ. Id.*Metaph.*1006$^b$5, cf. 1035$^b$4; πᾶς ὁρισμὸς λ. τίς ἐστι Id.*Top.*102$^a$5; ἐπὶ τῶν σχημάτων λ. κοινός generic *definition*, Id.*de An.*414$^b$23; ἀκριβέστατος λ. specific *definition*, Id.*Pol.*1276$^b$24; πηγῆς λ. ἔχον Ph.2.477; τὸ ᾠὸν οὔτε ἀρχῆς ἔχει λ. fulfils the *function* of.., Plu.2.637d; λ. τῆς μίξεως *formula*, i.e. *ratio* (cf. supr. II) of combination, Arist.*PA*642$^a$22, cf. *Metaph.*993$^a$17. **7.** *reason*, *law* exhibited in the world-process, κατὰ λόγον *by law*, κόσμῳ πάντα καὶ κατὰ λ. ἔχοντα Pl.*R.*500c; κατ τὸν ⟨αὐτὸν αὖ⟩ λ. by the same *law*, Epich.170.18; ψυχῆς τὸ πᾶν τόδε διοικούσης κατὰ λ. Plot.2.3.13; esp. in Stoic Philos., the divine *order*, τὸν τοῦ παντὸς λ. ὃν ἔνιοι εἱμαρμένην καλοῦσιν Zeno *Stoic.*1.24; τὸ ποιοῦν τὸν ἐν [τῇ ὕλῃ] λ. τὸν θεόν ibid., cf. 42; ὁ τοῦ κόσμου λ. Chrysipp. *Stoic.*2.264; λόγος, = φύσει νόμος, *Stoic.*2.169; κατὰ τὸν κοινὸν θεοῖς καὶ ἀνθρώποις λ. M.Ant.7.53; ὁ ὀρθὸς λ. διὰ πάντων ἐρχόμενος Chrysipp.*Stoic.*3.4: so in Plot., τὴν φύσιν εἶναι λόγον, ὃς ποιεῖ λ. ἄλλον γέννημα αὐτοῦ 3.8.2. **b.** σπερματικὸς λ. generative *principle* in organisms, ὁ θεὸς σπ. λ. τοῦ κόσμου Zeno *Stoic.*1.28: usu. in pl., *Stoic.* 2.205, 314, al.; γίνεται τὰ ἐν τῷ παντὶ οὐ κατὰ σπερματικούς, ἀλλὰ κατὰ λ. περιληπτικούς Plot.3.1.7, cf. 4.4.39: so without σπερματικός, ὥσπερ τινὲς λ. τῶν μερῶν Cleanth.*Stoic.*1.111; οἱ λ. τῶν ὅλων Ph.1.9. **c.** in Neo-Platonic Philos., of regulative and formative *forces*, derived from the intelligible and operative in the sensible universe, ὄντων μειζόνων λ. καὶ θεωρούντων αὐτοὺς ἐγὼ γεγέννημαι Plot.3.8.4; οἱ ἐν σπέρματι λ. πλάττουσι..τὰ ζῷα οἷον μικρούς τινας κόσμους Id.4.3.10, cf. 3.2.16, 3.5.7; opp. ὅρος, Id.6.7.4; ἀφανεῖς λ. τῆς φύσεως Procl.*in R.*1.18 K.; τεχνικοὶ λ. ib.142 K., al. **IV.** inward *debate* of the soul (cf. λ. ὃν αὐτὴ πρὸς αὑτὴν ἡ ψυχὴ διεξέρχεται Pl.*Tht.*189e (διάλογος in *Sph.*263e); ὁ ἐν τῇ ψυχῇ, ὁ ἔσω λ. (opp. ὁ ἔξω λ.), Arist.*APo.*76$^b$25, 27; ὁ ἐνδιάθετος, opp. ὁ προφορικὸς λ., *Stoic.*2.43, Ph.2.154), **1.** *thinking*, *reasoning*, τοῦ λ. ἐόντος ξυνοῦ, opp. ἰδία φρόνησις, Heraclit. 2; κρῖναι δὲ λόγῳ..ἔλεγχον test by *reflection*, Parm.1.36; *reflection*, *deliberation* (cf. VI. 3), ἐδίδου λόγον ἑωυτῷ περὶ τῆς ὄψιος Hdt.1.209, cf. 34, S.*OT*583, D.45.7; μὴ εἰδέναι..μήτε λόγῳ μήτε ἔργῳ neither by *reasoning* nor by experience, Anaxag.7; ἃ δὴ λόγῳ μὲν καὶ διανοίᾳ ληπτά, ὄψει δ' οὔ Pl.*R.*529d, cf. *Prm.*135e; ὁ λ. ἢ ἡ αἴσθησις Arist.*EN* 1149$^a$35, al.; αὐτῷ μόνον τῷ λ. πιστεύειν (opp. αἰσθήσεις), of Parmenides and his school, Aristocl.ap.Eus.*PE*14.17: hence λόγῳ or τῷ λ. in *idea*, in *thought*, τῷ λ. τέμνειν Pl.*R.*525e; τῷ λ. δύο ἐστίν, ἀχώριστα πεφυκότα two in *idea*, though indistinguishable in fact, Arist. *EN*1102$^a$30, cf. *GC*320$^b$14, al.; λόγῳ θεωρητά *mentally* conceived, opp. sensibly perceived, *Placit.*1.3.5, cf. Demetr.Lac.*Herc.*1055.20; τοὺς λ. θεωρητοὺς χρόνους Epicur.*Ep.*1 p.19 U.; διὰ λόγου θ. χ. ib.p.10 U.; λόγῳ καταληπτός Phld.*Po.*5.20, etc.; ὁ λ. οὕτω αἱρέει *analogy* proves, Hdt.2.33; ὁ λ. or λ. αἱρέει *reasoning* convinces, Id.3.45, 6. 124, cf. Pl.*Cri.*48c (but, our *argument* shows, *Lg.*663d): also c. acc. pers., χρᾶται ὅ τι μιν λ. αἱρέει as the *whim* took him, Hdt.1.132; ἢν μὴ ἡμέας λ. αἱρῇ unless we *see fit*, Id.4.127, cf. Pl.*R.*607b; later ὁ αἱρῶν λ. ordaining *reason*, Zeno *Stoic.*1.50, M.Ant.2.5, cf. 4.24, Arr.*Epict.* 2.2.20, etc.: coupled or contrasted with other functions, καθ' ὕπνον ἐπειδὴ λόγου καὶ φρονήσεως οὐ μετεῖχε since *reason* and understanding are in abeyance, Pl.*Ti.*71d; μετὰ λόγου τε καὶ ἐπιστήμης, opp. αἰτία αὐτομάτη, of Nature's processes of production, Id.*Sph.*265c; τὸ μὲν δὴ νοήσει μετὰ λόγου περιληπτόν embraced by thought with *reflection*, opp. μετ' αἰσθήσεως ἀλόγου, Id.*Ti.*28a; τὸ μὲν ἀεὶ μετ' ἀληθοῦς λ., opp. τὸ δὲ ἄλογον, ib.51e, cf. 70d, al.; λ. ἔχων ἑπόμενον τῷ νοεῖν Id.*Phlb.* 62a; ἐπιστήμη ἐνοῦσα καὶ ὀρθὸς λ. scientific knowledge and right *process of thought*, Id.*Phd.*73a; πᾶς λ. καὶ πᾶσα ἐπιστήμη τῶν καθόλου Arist.*Metaph.*1059$^b$26; τὸ λόγον ἔχον Id.*EN*1102$^b$15, 1138$^b$9, al.: in sg. and pl., contrasted by Pl. and Arist. as *theory*, *abstract reasoning* with outward experience, sts. with depreciatory emphasis on the former, εἰς τοὺς λ. καταφυγόντα Pl.*Phd.*99e; τὸν ἐν λόγοις σκοπούμενον τὰ ὄντα, opp. τὸν ἐν ἔργοις (realities), ib.100a; τῇ αἰσθήσει μᾶλλον τῶν λ. πιστευτέον Arist.*GA*760$^b$31; γνωριμώτερα κατὰ τὸν λ., opp. κατὰ τὴν αἴσθησιν, Id.*Ph.*189$^a$4; ἐκ τῶν λ. δῆλον, opp. ἐκ τῆς ἐπαγωγῆς, Id.*Mete.*378$^b$20; ἡ τῶν λ. πίστις, opp. ἐκ τῶν ἔργων φανερόν, Id.*Pol.*1326$^a$29; ἡ πίστις οὐ μόνον ἐπὶ τῆς αἰσθήσεως ἀλλὰ καὶ ἐπὶ τοῦ λ. Id.*Ph.*262$^a$19; μαρτυρεῖ τὰ γιγνόμενα τοῖς λ. Id.*Pol.*1334$^a$6; ὁ μὲν λ. τοῦ καθόλου, ἡ δὲ αἴσθησις τοῦ κατὰ μέρος *explanation*, opp. perception, Id.*Ph.*189$^a$7; ἔσονται τοῖς λ. αἱ πράξεις ἀκόλουθοι *theory*, opp. practice, Epicur.*Sent.*25; in Logic, of *discursive reasoning*, opp. intuition, Arist.*EN*1142$^a$26, 1143$^b$1; *reasoning* in general, ib.1149$^a$ 26; πᾶς λ. καὶ πᾶσα ἀπόδειξις all *reasoning* and demonstration, Id. *Metaph.*1063$^b$10; λ. καὶ φρόνησιν Phld.*Mus.*p.105 K.; ὁ λ. ἢ λογισμός ibid.; τὸ ἰδεῖν οὐκέτι λ., ἀλλὰ μεῖζον λόγου καὶ πρὸ λόγου, of mystical vision, opp. *reasoning*, Plot.6.9.10.—Phrases, κατὰ λ. τὸν εἰκότα by probable *reasoning*, Pl.*Ti.*30b; οὔκουν τόν γ' εἰκότα λ. ἂν ἔχοι Id. *Lg.*647d; παρὰ λόγον, opp. κατὰ λ., Arist.*Rh.Al.*1429$^a$29, cf. *EN* 1167$^b$19; cf. παράλογος (but παρὰ λ. *unexpectedly*, E.*Ba.*940). **2.** *reason* as a faculty, ὁ λ. ἀνθρώπους κυβερνᾷ [Epich.]256; [θυμοειδὲς] τοῦ λ. κατήκοον Pl.*Ti.*70a; [θυμὸς] ὑπὸ τοῦ λ. ἀνακληθείς Id.*R.*440d; σύμμαχον τῷ λ. τὸν θυμόν ib.b; πειθαρχεῖ τῷ λ. τὸ τοῦ ἐγκρατοῦς Arist. *EN*1102$^b$26; ἄλλο τι παρὰ τὸν λ. πεφυκός, ὃ μάχεται τῷ λ. ib.17; ἐναντίωσις λόγου πρὸς ἐπιθυμίας Plot.4.7.13(8); οὐ θυμός, οὐκ ἐπιθυμία, οὐδὲ λ. οὐδέ τις νόησις Id.6.9.11: freq. in Stoic. Philos. of human *Reason*, opp. φαντασία, Zeno *Stoic.*1.39; opp. φύσις, *Stoic.*2.206; οὐ σοφία οὐδὲ λ. ἐστὶν ἐν [τοῖς ζῴοις] ibid.; τοῖς ἀλόγοις ζῴοις ὡς λ. ἔχων λ. μὴ ἔχουσι χρῶ M.Ant.6.23; ὁ λ. κοινὸν πρὸς τοὺς θεούς Arr.*Epict.* 1.3.3; οἷον [εἰκὼν] λ. ὁ ἐν προφορᾷ λόγου τοῦ ἐν ψυχῇ, οὕτω καὶ αὐτὴ λ. νοῦ Plot.5.1.3; τὸ τὸν λ. σχεῖν τὴν οἰκείαν ἀρετήν (sc. εὐδαιμονίαν) Procl.*in Ti.*3.334 D.; also of the *reason* which pervades the universe, θεῖος λ. [Epich.]257; τὸν θεῖον λ. καθ' Ἡράκλειτον δι' ἀναπνοῆς σπάσαντες νοεροὶ γινόμεθα S.E.*M.*7.129 (cf. infr. x). **b.** *creative reason*, ἀδύνατον ἦν λόγον μὴ οὐκ ἐπὶ πάντα ἐλθεῖν Plot.3.2.14; ἀρχὴ οὖν λ. καὶ πάντα λ. καὶ τὰ γινόμενα κατ' αὐτόν Id.3.2.15; οἱ λ. πάντες ψυχαί Id.3.2.18. **V.** *continuous statement*, *narrative* (whether fact or fiction), *oration*, etc. (cf. λέγω (B) II. 2), **1.** *fable*, Hdt.1.141; Αἰσώπου λόγοι Pl.*Phd.*60d, cf. Arist.*Rh.*1393$^b$8; ὁ τοῦ κυνὸς λ. X.*Mem.* 2.7.13. **2.** *legend*, ἱρὸς λ. Hdt.2.62, cf. 47, Pi.*P.*3.80 (pl.); συνθέντες λ. E.*Ba.*297; λ. θεῖος Pl.*Phd.*85d; ἱεροὶ λ., of Orphic *rhapsodies*, Suid. s.v. Ὀρφεύς. **3.** *tale*, *story*, ἄλλον ἔπειμι λ. Xenoph. 7.1, cf. Th.1.97, etc.; συνθέτους λ. A.*Pr.*686; σπουδὴν λόγου urgent *tidings*, E.*Ba.*663; ἄλλος λ. 'another *story*', Pl.*Ap.*34e; ὁμολογούμενος ὁ λ. ἐστίν the *story* is consistent, Isoc.3.27: pl., *histories*, ἐν τοῖσι Ἀσσυρίοισι λ. Hdt.1.184, cf. 106, 2.99; so in sg., *a historical work*, Id.2.123, 6.19, 7.152: also in sg., one *section* of such a work (like later βίβλος), Id.2.38, 6.39, cf. VI. 3d; so in pl., ἐν τοῖσι Λιβυκοῖσι λ. Id.2.161, cf. 1.75, 5.22, 7.93, 213; ἐν τῷ πρώτῳ τῶν λ. Id.5.36; ὁ πρῶτος λ., of St. Luke's gospel, *Act.Ap.*1.1: in Pl., opp. μῦθος, as *history* to legend, *Ti.*26e; ποιεῖν μύθους ἀλλ' οὐ λόγους *Phd.*61b, cf. *Grg.*523a (but μῦθον λέγειν, opp. λόγῳ (*argument*) διεξελθεῖν *Prt.* 320c, cf. 324d); περὶ λόγων καὶ μύθων Arist.*Pol.*1336$^a$30; ὁ λ...μῦθός ἐστι Ael.*NA*4.34. **4.** *speech*, delivered in court, assembly, etc., χρήσομαι τῇ τοῦ λ. τάξει ταύτῃ Aeschin.3.57, cf. Arist.*Rh.*1358$^a$38; δικανικοὶ λ. Id.*EN*1181$^a$4; τρία γένη τῶν λ. τῶν ῥητορικῶν, συμβουλευτικόν, δικανικόν, ἐπιδεικτικόν Id.*Rh.*1358$^b$7; τῷ γράψαντι τὸν λ. Thphr. *Char.*17.8, cf. λογογράφος II; ἐπιτάφιος λ. funeral *oration*, Pl.*Mx.*236b; esp. of the *body of a speech*, opp. ἐπίλογος, Arist.*Rh.*1420$^b$3; opp. προοίμιον, ib.1415$^a$12; *body of a law*, opp. proem, Pl.*Lg.*723b; *spoken*, opp. written *word*, τὸν τοῦ εἰδότος λ. ζῶντα καὶ ἔμψυχον οὗ ὁ γεγραμμένος εἴδωλόν τι Id.*Phdr.*276a; ὁ ἐκ τοῦ βιβλίου ῥηθεὶς [λ.] *speech* read from a roll, ib.243c; published *speech*, D.C.40.54; rarely of the *speeches* in Tragedy (ῥήσεις), Arist.*Po.*1450$^b$6, 9. **VI.** *verbal expression* or *utterance* (cf. λέγω (B) III), rarely a single *word*, v. infr. b, never in Gramm. signf. of vocable (ἔπος, λέξις, ὄνομα, ῥῆμα), usu. of a *phrase*, cf. IX. 3 (the only sense found in Ep.). **a.** pl., without Art., *talk*, τὸν ἔτερπε λόγοις Il.15.393; αἱμύλιοι λ. Od.1.56, *h.Merc.* 317, Hes.*Th.*890, *Op.*78, 789, Thgn.704, A.R.3.1141; ψευδεῖς Λ., personified, Hes.*Th.*229; ἀφροδίσιοι λ. Semon.7.91; ἀγανοῖσι λ. Pi.*P.* 4.101; ὄψον δὲ λ. φθονεροῖσιν *tales*, Id.*N.*8.21; σμικροὶ λ. brief *words*, S.*Aj.*1268 (s.v.l.), *El.*415; δόκησις ἀγνὼς λόγων bred of *talk*, Id.*OT* 681 (lyr.): also in sg., λέγ' εἴ σοι τῷ λ. τις ἡδονή speak if thou delightest in *talking*, Id.*El.*891. **b.** sg., *expression*, *phrase*, πρὶν εἰπεῖν ἐσθλὸν ἢ κακὸν λ. Id.*Ant.*1245, cf. E.*Hipp.*514; μυρίας ὡς εἰπεῖν λόγῳ Hdt.2.37; μακρὸς λ. *rigmarole*, Simon.189, Arist.*Metaph.*1091$^a$8; λ. ἠρέμα λεχθεὶς διέθηκε τὸ πόρρω a whispered *message*, Plot.4.9.3; ἑνὶ λόγῳ to sum up, in brief *phrase*, Pl.*Phdr.*241e, *Phd.*65d; *concisely*, Arist. *EN*1103$^b$21 (but also, = ἁπλῶς, περὶ πάντων ἑνὶ λ. Id.*GC*325$^a$1): pl., λ. θελκτήριοι magic *words*, E.*Hipp.*478; rarely of single words, λ. εὐσύνθετος οἷον τὸ "χρονοτριβεῖν" Arist.*Rh.*1406$^a$36; οὐκ ἀπεκρίθη αὐτῇ λ. answered her not a *word*, *Ev.Matt.*15.23. **c.** coupled or contrasted with words expressed or understood signifying act, fact, truth, etc., mostly in a depreciatory sense, λ. ἔργου σκιή Democr. 145; ὥσπερ μικρὸν παῖδα λόγοις μ' ἀπατᾷς Thgn.254; λόγῳ, opp. ἔργῳ, Democr.82, etc.; νηπίοισι οὐ λ. ἀλλὰ ξυμφορὴ διδάσκαλος Id.76; ἔργῳ κοὐ λόγῳ τεκμαίρομαι A.*Pr.*338, cf. S.*El.*59, *OC*782; λόγῳ μὲν λέγουσι..ἔργῳ δὲ οὐκ ἀποδεικνῦσι Hdt.4.8; οὐ λόγων, φασίν, ἡ ἀγορὴ δεῖται, χαλκῶν δέ Herod.7.49; οὔτε λ. οὔτε ἔργῳ Lys.9.14; λόγοις, opp. ψήφῳ, Aeschin.2.33; opp. νόῳ, Hdt.2.100; οὐ λόγῳ μαθών E.*Heracl.*5; ἐκ λόγων, κούφου πράγματος Pl.*Lg.*935a; λόγοισι εἰς τὸ πιθανὸν περιπεπεμμένα ib.886e, cf. Luc.*Anach.*19; ἵνα μὴ λ. οἴησθε εἶναι, ἀλλ' εἰδῆτε τὴν ἀλήθειαν Lycurg.23, cf. D.30.34; opp. πρᾶγμα, Arist.*Top.*146$^a$4; opp. βία, Id.*EN*1179$^b$29, cf. 1180$^a$5; opp. ὄντα, Pl.*Phd.*100a; opp. γνῶσις, 2*Ep.Cor.*11.6; λόγῳ in *pretence*, Hdt.1.205, Pl.*R.*361b, 376d, *Ti.*27a, al.; λόγου ἕνεκα merely as a matter of *words*, ἄλλως ἕνεκα λ. ἐλέγετο Id.*Cri.*46d; λόγου χάριν, opp. ὡς ἀληθῶς, Arist.*Pol.*1280$^b$8; but also, *let us say*, *for instance*, Id.*EN*1144$^a$33, Plb.10.46.4, Phld. *Sign.*29, M.Ant.4.32; λόγου ἕνεκα *let us suppose*, Pl.*Tht.*191c; ἕως λόγου, μέχρι λ., = Lat. *verbo tenus*, Plb.10.24.7, Epict.*Ench.*16: sts. without depreciatory force, the antithesis or parallelism being verbal (cf. 'word and deed'), λόγῳ τε καὶ σθένει S.*OC*68; ἔν τε ἔργῳ καὶ λ. Pl.*R.*382e, cf. D.S.13.101, *Ev.Luc.*24.19, *Act.Ap.*7.22, Paus.2.16.2; ὅσα μὲν λόγῳ εἶπον, opp. τὰ ἔργα τῶν πραχθέντων, Th. 1.22. **2.** *common talk*, *report*, *tradition*, ὡς λ. ἐν θνητοῖσιν ἔην Batr. 8; λ. ἐκ πατέρων Alc.71; οὐκ ἔστ' ἔτυμος λ. οὗτος Stesich.32; διξὸς λέγεται λ. Hdt.3.32; λ. ὑπ' Αἰγυπτίων λεγόμενος Id.2.47; νέον [λ.] *tidings*, S.*Ant.*1289 (lyr.); τὰ μὲν αὐτοὶ ὡρῶμεν, τὰ δὲ λόγοισι ἐπυνθανόμεθα by *hearsay*, Hdt.2.148: also in pl., ἐν γράμμασιν λόγοι κείμενοι *traditions*, Pl.*Lg.*886b. **b.** *rumour*, ἐπὶ παντὶ λ. ἐπτοῆσθαι Heraclit. 87; αὐδάεις λ. voice of *rumour*, B.14.44; περὶ θεῶν διῆλθεν ὁ λ. ὅτι.. Th.6.46; λ. παρεῖχεν ὡς.. Plb.3.89.3; ἐξῆλθεν ὁ λ. οὗτος εἴς τινας

ὅτι.. *Ev.Jo.*21.23, cf. *Act.Ap.*11.22; *fiction*, *Ev.Matt.*28.15. **c.** *mention, notice, description*, οὐκ ὕει λόγου ἄξιον οὐδέν worth *mentioning*, Hdt.4.28, cf. Plb.1.24.8, etc.; ἔργα λόγου μέζω beyond *expression*, Hdt.2.35; κρεῖσσον λόγου τὸ εἶδος τῆς νόσου beyond *description*, Th. 2.50; μείζω ἔργα ἢ ὡς τῷ λ. τις ἂν εἴποι D.6.11. **d.** the *talk* one occasions, *repute*, mostly in good sense, *good report, praise, honour* (cf. supr. I. 4), πολλὰ φέρειν εἴωθε λ... παίσματα Thgn.1221; λ. ἐσλὸν ἀκοῦσαι Pi.*I.*5(4).13; πλέονα..λ. Ὀδυσσέος ἢ πάθαν Id.*N.*7.21; ἵνα λ. σε ἔχῃ πρὸς ἀνθρώπων ἀγαθός Hdt.7.5, cf. 9.78; Τροίαν..ἧς ἁπανταχοῦ λ. whose *fame*, *story* fills the world, E.*IT*517; οὐκ ἂν ἦν λ. σέθεν Id.*Med.*541: less freq. in bad sense, *evil report*, λ. κακόθρους, κακός, S.*Aj.*138 (anap.), E.*Heracl.*165: pl., λόγους ψιθύρους πλάσσων *slanders*, S.*Aj.*148 (anap.). **e.** λ. ἐστί, ἔχει, κατέχει, the *story* goes, c. acc. et inf., ἔστ. τις λ. τὰν Ἀρετὰν ναίειν Simon.58.1, cf. S.*El.*417; λ. μὲν ἔστ' ἀρχαῖος ὡς.. Id.*Tr.*1; λ. alone, E.*Heracl.*35; ὡς λ. A.*Supp.*230, Pl.*Phlb.*65c, etc.; λ. ἐστί Hdt.7.129, 9.26, al.; λ. αἰὲν ἔχει S.*OC*1573 (lyr.); ὅσον ὁ λ. κατέχει *tradition* prevails, Th.1.10: also with a personal subject in the reverse construction, Κλεισθένης λ. ἔχει τὴν Πυθίην ἀναπεῖσαι has the *credit* of.., Hdt.5.66, cf. Pl.*Epin.*987b, 988b; λ. ἔχοντα σοφίας *Ep.Col.*2.23, v. supr. I. 4. **3.** *discussion, debate, deliberation*, πολλὸς ἦν ἐν τοῖσι λ. Hdt.8.59; συνελέχθησαν οἱ Μῆδοι ἐς τὠυτὸ καὶ ἐδίδοσαν σφίσι λόγον, λέγοντες περὶ τῶν κατηκόντων Id.1.97; οἱ Πελασγοὶ ἑωυτοῖσι λόγους ἐδίδοσαν Id.6.138; πολέμῳ μᾶλλον ἢ λόγοις τὰ ἐγκλήματα διαλύεσθαι Th.1.140; οἱ περὶ τῆς εἰρήνης λ. Aeschin.2.74; τοῖς ἔξωθεν λ. πεπλήρωκε τὸν λ. [Plato] has filled his dialogue with extraneous *discussions*, Arist.*Pol.*1264$^{b}$39; τὸ μῆκος τῶν λ. D.Chr.7.131; μεταβαίνων ὁ λ. εἰς ταὐτὸν ἀφῖκται our *debate*, Arist.*EN*1097$^{a}$24; ὁ παρὼν λ. ib.1104$^{a}$11; θεῶν ὧν νῦν ὁ λ. ἐστί *discussion*, Pl.*Ap.*26b, cf. *Tht.*184a, M.Ant.8.32; τῷ λ. διελθεῖν, διϊέναι, Pl.*Prt.*329c, *Grg.*506a, etc.; τὸν λ. διεξελθεῖν conduct the *debate*, Id.*Lg.*893a; ξυνελθεῖν ἐς λόγον *confer*, Ar.*Eq.*1300: freq. in pl., ἐς λόγους συνελθόντες *parley*, Hdt.1.82; ἐς λ. ἐλθεῖν τινι have *speech* with, ib.86; ἐς λ. ἀπικέσθαι τινί Id.2.32; διὰ λόγων ἰέναι E.*Tr.*916; ἐμαυτῇ διὰ λ. ἀφικόμην Id.*Med.*872; ἐς λ. ἄγειν τινά X.*HG*4.1.2; κοινωνεῖν λόγων καὶ διανοίας Arist.*EN*1170$^{b}$12. **b.** *right of discussion* or *speech*, ἢ 'πὶ τῷ πλήθει λ.; S.*OC*66; λ. αἰτήσασθαι ask *leave to speak*, Th.3.53; λ. διδόναι X.*HG*5.2.20; οὐ προυτέθη σφίσιν λ. κατὰ τὸν νόμον ib.1.7.5; λόγου τυχεῖν D.18.13, cf. Arist.*EN*1095$^{b}$21, Plb.18.52.1; οἱ λόγου τοὺς δούλους ἀποστεροῦντες Arist.*Pol.*1260$^{b}$5; δοῦλος πέφυκας, οὐ μέτεστί σοι λόγου *Trag.Adesp.*304; διδόντας λ. καὶ δεχομένους ἐν τῷ μέρει Luc.*Pisc.*8: hence, *time allowed for a speech*, ἐν τῷ ἐμῷ λ. And.1.26, al.; ἐν τῷ ἑαυτοῦ λ. Pl.*Ap.*34a; οὐκ ἐλάττω λ. ἀνήλωκε D.18.9. **c.** *dialogue*, as a form of philosophical *debate*, ἵνα μὴ μαχώμεθα ἐν τοῖς λ. ἐγώ τε καὶ σύ Pl.*Cra.*430d; πρὸς ἀλλήλους τοὺς λ. ποιεῖσθαι Id.*Prt.*348a: hence, *dialogue* as a form of literature, οἱ Σωκρατικοὶ λ. Arist.*Po.*1447$^{b}$11, *Rh.*1417$^{a}$20; cf. διάλογος. **d.** *section, division* of a dialogue or treatise (cf. v. 3), ὁ πρῶτος λ. Pl.*Prm.*127d; ὁ πρόσθεν, ὁ παρελθὼν λ., Id.*Phlb.*18e, 19b; ἐν τοῖς πρώτοις λ. Arist.*PA*682$^{a}$3; ἐν τοῖς περὶ κινήσεως λ. in the *discussion* of motion (i.e. *Ph.*bk.8), Id.*GC*318$^{a}$4; ἐν τῷ περὶ ἐπαίνου λ. Phld.*Rh.*1.219; *branch, department, division* of a system of philosophy, τὴν φρόνησιν ἐκ τριῶν συνεστηκέναι λ., τῶν φυσικῶν καὶ τῶν ἠθικῶν καὶ τῶν λογικῶν Chrysipp.*Stoic.*2.258. **e.** in pl., *literature, letters*, Pl.*Ax.*365b, *Epin.*975d, D.H.*Comp.*1, 21 (but, also in pl., *treatises*, Plu.2.16c); οἱ ἐπὶ λόγοις εὐδοκιμώτατοι Hdn.6.1.4; Λόγοι, personified, *AP*9.171 (Pall.). **VII.** *a particular utterance, saying*: **1.** *divine utterance, oracle*, Pi.*P.*4.59; λ. μαντικοί Pl.*Phdr.*275b; οὐ γὰρ ἐμὸν ἐρῶ τὸν λ. Pl.*Ap.*20e; ὁ λ. τοῦ θεοῦ *Apoc.*1.2, 9. **2.** *proverb, maxim, saying*, Pi.*N.*9.6, A.*Th.*218; ὧδ' ἔχει λ. ib.225; τόνδ' ἐκαίνισεν λ. ὡς.. Critias 21, cf. Pl.*R.*330a, *Ev.Jo.*4.37; ὁ παλαιὸς λ. Pl.*Phdr.*240c, cf. *Smp.*195b, *Grg.*499c, *Lg.*757a, 1*Ep.Ti.*1.15, Plu.2.1082e, Luc.*Alex.*9, etc.; τὸ τοῦ λόγου δὴ τοῦτο Herod.2.45, cf. D.Chr.66.24, Luc.*JTr.*3, Alciphr.3.56, etc.: pl., Arist.*EN*1147$^{a}$21. **3.** *assertion*, opp. oath, S.*OC*651; ψιλῷ λ. bare *word*, opp. μαρτυρία, D.27.54. **4.** *express resolution*, κοινῷ λ. by common *consent*, Hdt.1.141, al.; ἐπὶ λ. τοιῷδε, ἐπ' ᾧ τε.. on the following *terms*, Id.7.158, cf. 9.26; ἐνδέξασθαι τὸν λ. Id.1.60, cf. 9.5; λ. ἔχοντες πλεονέκτην a greedy *proposal*, Id.7.158: freq. in pl., *terms, conditions*, Id.9.33, etc. **5.** *word of command, behest*, A.*Pr.*17, 40 (both pl.), *Pers.*363; ἀνθρώπους πιθανωτέρους ποιεῖν λόγῳ X.*Oec.*13.9; ἐξέβαλε τὰ πνεύματα λόγῳ *Ev.Matt.*8.16; οἱ δέκα λ. the ten *Commandments*, Lxx *Ex.*34.28, Ph.1.496. **VIII.** *thing spoken of, subject-matter* (cf. III. 1b and 2), λ. τοῦτον ἐάσομεν Thgn.1055; προπεπυσμένος πάντα λ. the whole *matter*, Hdt.1.21, cf. 111; τὸν ἐόντα λ. the truth of the *matter*, ib.95, 116; μετασχεῖν τοῦ λ. to be in the *secret*, ib.127; μηδενὶ ἄλλῳ τὸν λ. τοῦτον εἴπῃς Id.8.65; τίς ἦν λ.; S.*OT*684 (= πρᾶγμα, 699); περί τινος λ. διελεγόμεθα *subject, question*, Pl.*Prt.*314c; [τὸ προοίμιον] δεῖγμα τοῦ λ. *case*, Arist.*Rh.*1415$^{a}$12, cf. III. 1b; τέλος δὲ παντὸς τοῦ λ. ψηφίζονται the end of the *matter* was that.., Aeschin.3.124; οὐκ ἔστεξε τὸν λ. Plb.8.12.5; οὐκ ἔστι σοι μερὶς οὐδὲ κλῆρος ἐν τῷ λ. τούτῳ *Act.Ap.*8.21; ἱκανὸς αὐτῷ ὁ λ. Pl.*Grg.*512c; οὐχ ὑπολείπει [Γοργίαν] ὁ λ. *matter for talk*, Arist.*Rh.*1418$^{a}$35; μηδένα λ. ὑπολιπεῖν Isoc.4.146; πρὸς λόγον to the *point*, apposite, οὐδὲν πρὸς λ. Pl.*Phlb.*42e, cf. *Prt.*344a; ἐὰν πρὸς λ. τι ᾖ Id.*Phlb.*33c; also πρὸς λόγου Id.*Grg.*459c (s.v.l.). **2.** *plot* of a narrative or dramatic poem, = μῦθος, Arist.*Po.*1455$^{b}$17, al. **b.** in Art, *subject* of a painting, ζωγραφίας λόγοι Philostr.*VA*6.10; λ. τῆς γραφῆς Id.*Im.*1.25. **3.** *thing talked of, event*, μετὰ τοὺς λ. τούτους Lxx 1*Ma.*7.33, cf. *Act.Ap.*15.6. **IX.** *expression, utterance, speech* regarded formally, τὸ ἀπὸ [ψυχῆς] ῥεῦμα διὰ τοῦ στόματος ἰὸν μετὰ φθόγγου λ., opp. διάνοια, Pl.*Sph.*263e; *intelligent utterance*, opp. φωνή, Arist.*Pol.*1253$^{a}$14; λ. ἐστὶ φωνὴ σημαντικὴ κατὰ συνθήκην Id.*Int.*16$^{b}$26, cf. Diog.Bab.*Stoic.*3.213; ὅθεν (from the heart) ὁ λ. ἀναπέμπεται *Stoic.*2.228, cf. 244; Protagoras was nicknamed λόγος, Hsch.ap.Sch.Pl.*R.*600c, Suid.; λόγου πειθοῖ Democr.181: in pl., *eloquence*, Isoc.3.3, 9.11; τὴν ἐν λόγοις εὐρυθμίαν Epicur.*Sent.Pal.*5 p.69 v. d. M.; λ. ἀκριβής precise *language*, Ar.*Nu.*130 (pl.), cf. Arist.*Rh.*1418$^{b}$1; τοῦ μὴ ᾀδομένου λ. Pl.*R.*398d; ἡδυσμένος λ., of rhythmical *language* set to music, Arist.*Po.*1449$^{b}$25; ἐν παντὶ λ. in all *manner of utterance*, 1*Ep.Cor.*1.5; ἐν λόγοις in *orations*, Arist.*Po.*1459$^{a}$13; λ. γελοῖοι, ἀσχήμονες, ludicrous, improper *speech*, Id.*SE*182$^{b}$15, *Pol.*1336$^{b}$14. **2.** of various modes of expression, esp. artistic and literary, ἔν τε ᾠδαῖς καὶ μύθοις καὶ λόγοις Pl.*Lg.*664a; ἐν λόγῳ καὶ ἐν ᾠδαῖς X.*Cyr.*1.4.25, cf. Pl.*Lg.*835b; *prose*, opp. ποίησις, Id.*R.*390a; opp. ψιλομετρία, Arist.*Po.*1448$^{a}$11; opp. ἔμμετρα, ib.1450$^{b}$15 (pl.); τῷ λ. τοῦτο τῶν μέτρων (sc. τὸ ἰαμβεῖον) ὁμοιότατον εἶναι Id.*Rh.*1404$^{a}$31; in full, ψιλοὶ λ. *prose*, ib.$^{b}$33 (but ψιλοὶ λ., = *arguments* without diagrams, Pl.*Tht.*165a); λ. πεζοί, opp. ποιητική, D.H.*Comp.*6; opp. ποιήματα, ib.15; κοινὰ καὶ ποιημάτων καὶ λόγων Phld.*Po.*5.7; πεζὸς λ. ib.27, al. **b.** of the constituents of lyric or dramatic poetry, *words*, τὸ μέλος ἐκ τριῶν..λόγου τε καὶ ἁρμονίας καὶ ῥυθμοῦ Pl.*R.*398d; opp. πρᾶξις, Arist.*Po.*1454$^{a}$18; dramatic *dialogue*, opp. τὰ τοῦ χοροῦ, ib.1449$^{a}$17. **3.** Gramm., *phrase, complex term*, opp. ὄνομα, Id.*SE*165$^{a}$13; λ. ὀνοματώδης noun-*phrase*, Id.*APo.*93$^{b}$30, cf. *Rh.*1407$^{b}$27; *expression*, D.H.*Th.*2, Demetr.*Eloc.*92. **b.** *sentence, complete statement*, "ἄνθρωπος μανθάνει" λόγον εἶναί φῃς..ἐλάχιστόν τε καὶ πρῶτον Pl.*Sph.*262c; λ. αὐτοτελής A.D.*Synt.*3.6, D.T.634.1; ῥηθῆναι λόγῳ to be expressed in a *sentence*, Pl.*Tht.*202b; λ. ἔχειν to be capable of being so expressed, ib.201e, cf. Arist.*Rh.*1404$^{b}$26. **c.** *language*, τὰ τοῦ λ. μέρη parts of *speech*, Chrysipp.*Stoic.*2.31, S.E.*M.*9.350, etc.; τὰ μόρια τοῦ λ. D.H.*Comp.*6; μέρος λ. D.T.633.26, A.D.*Pron.*4.6, al. (but ἓν μέρος ⟨τοῦ cod.⟩ λόγου one *word*, Id.*Synt.*340.10, cf. 334.22); περὶ τῶν στοιχείων τοῦ λ., title of work by Chrysippus. **X.** the *Word* or *Wisdom* of God, personified as his agent in creation and world-government, ὁ παντοδύναμός σου λ. Lxx *Wi.*18.15; ὁ ἐκ νοὸς φωτεινὸς λ. υἱὸς θεοῦ *Corp.Herm.*1.6, cf. Plu.2.376c; λ. θεοῦ δι' οὗ κατεσκευάσθη [ὁ κόσμος] Ph.1.162; τῆς τοῦ θεοῦ σοφίας· ἡ δέ ἐστιν ὁ θεοῦ λ. ib.56; λ. θεῖος..εἰκὼν θεοῦ ib.561, cf. 501; τὸν τομέα τῶν συμπάντων [θεοῦ] λ. ib.492; τὸν ἄγγελον ὅς ἐστι λ. ib.122: in *NT* identified with the person of Christ, ἐν ἀρχῇ ἦν ὁ λ. *Ev.Jo.*1.1, cf. 14, 1*Ep.Jo.*2.7, *Apoc.*19.13; ὁ λ. τῆς ζωῆς 1*Ep.Jo.*1.1.

**λογο-συλλεκτάδης** [ᾰ], ου, ὁ, *phrase-collector, plagiarist*, Eust.1309.2. **-τροπος**, ὁ, a shortd. form of syllogism, Crinis *Stoic.*3.269.

**λογούριον**· ὕελος (Lacon.), Hsch. (post λόγιος); cf. λογκούριον.

**λογοφίλης** [ῐ], ου, ὁ, *fond of words*, Ph.1.58:—also **-φῐλος**, ον, *fond of argument*, opp. φιλόλογος, Zeno *Stoic.*1.67.

**λογόω**, *introduce* λόγος *into*, τὸν κόσμον Procl. *in Ti.*2.244 D., cf. *in R.*2.350 K., al.:—Pass., Plot.3.8.2, 6.8.17; λελόγωται, τοῦτο δέ ἐστι μεμόρφωται Id.3.2.16. **2.** Math., *rationalize*, Iamb. *in Nic.*p.91 P., al. (Pass.).

**λογύδριον**, τό, = λογίδιον, Zos.Alch.p.190 B., Olymp.Alch.p.79 B., Lyd.*Mag.*3.73, Tz.*H.*12.247.

**λογχ-άζω**, gloss on δοράζω, Hsch. **-αῖος**, α, ον, (λόγχη A) *of* or *with a spear*, Suid. **-άριον**, τό, Dim. of λόγχη (A), Posidon.2 J., Luc.*Hist.Conscr.*25; as an ornament, *POsl.*46.12 (iii A.D.). **-εύω**, *pierce with a spear*, *AP*9.300 (in tit.). **-η** (A), ἡ, *spear-head*, Hdt.7.69; λ. δορός S.*Tr.*856, E.*Tr.*1318 (both lyr.): also in pl. of a single spear, *the point with its barbs*, τὸ ξυστὸν τῇσι λόγχῃσι ἐὸν ὁμοίως χρύσεον the shaft alike with *the spear-head*, Hdt.1.52, etc.; λόγχαι δ' ἐκαυλίζοντο καὶ ξυστὴ κάμαξ Ar.*Fr.*404, cf. X.*Cyn.*10.3 (where the shaft is ῥάβδος); οἱ κνώδοντες τῆς λόγχης the barbs *of the spear-head*, ib.16. **2.** *lance-shaped birth-mark*, *Trag.Adesp.*84. **II.** *lance, spear, javelin*, Batr.129; χαλκέας λόγχας ἀκμᾷ Pi.*N.*10.60, cf. S.*Tr.*512 (lyr.), etc.: metaph., ὀμμάτων ἄπο λόγχας ἵησιν Id.*Fr.*157; λόγχας ἐσθίων, prov. of a bragging coward, a 'fire-eater', Timocl.12.5. **III.** *troop of spearmen*, ξὺν ἑπτὰ λόγχαις S.*OC*1312, cf. *Ant.*119 (lyr.); μυρίαν ἄγων λόγχην E.*Ph.*442; λόγχης ἀριθμῷ πλείονος κρατούμεναι Id.*Fr.*286.12; χωρεῖτε, λόγχη Id.*Cret.*45. **-η** (B), ἡ, Ion. for λάχος, *lot* (cf. λέλογχα), Ion Hist.15, *SIG*1013.12 (Chios, iv B.C.), Hsch.; also λόγχαι· ἀπολαύσεις, Id. **-ήρης**, ες, *armed with a spear*, λ. ἀσπισταί *with spear* and shield, E.*IA*1067 (lyr.). **-ηφόρος**, ον, = λογχοφόρος, Sch.rec.A.*Pers.*147. **-ίδιον**, τό, Dim. of λόγχη (A), Hsch. s.v. ζιφύνια. **-ῐμος**, ον, *of a spear*, κλόνοι λ. the clash *of spears*, A.*Ag.*404 (lyr.). **-ίον**, τό, *small spear-head*, *IG*2$^{2}$.1541.17: pl., of ornaments composing a necklace, ib.11(2).161 *B*23, al. (Delos, iii B.C.); *small spears*, *Sammelb.*7247.25, al. (iii/iv A.D.). **-ίς**, ίδος, ἡ, = λόγχη (A), Lycophronid.2. **-ίτης** [ῑ], ου, ὁ, *spearman*, Hdn.*Epim.*78. **II.** λογχῖτις, ιδος, ἡ, plant *with spear-shaped seeds*, *Serapias Lingua*, Dsc.3.144, Gal.12.63. **2.** *Holly-fern*, *Aspidium lonchitis*, Dsc.3.145, Gal. l.c. **3.** shrub yielding τὸ Ἰνδικὸν λύκιον, Dsc.1.100.

**λογχο-δρέπᾰνον**, τό, *spear with sickle-shaped head, partisan*, Suid. s.v. Γοργόνες, Sch.Lyc.836. **-ειδής**, ές, *like a spear, lanceolate*, Dsc.4.144. **-ομαι**, Pass., (λόγχη A) *to be furnished with a point* or *head*, λελογχωμένον δόρυ Arist.*EN*1111$^{a}$13; ἀκόντιον -ωμένον σιδήρῳ Str.3.5.1; *to be ornamented with* λόγχαι, στολὴ χρυσῷ λελογχωμένη Lyd.*Mag.*2.4. **-ποιΐα**, ἡ, *manufactory of spears*, *An.Ox.*4.255 (prob. cj. for λοχιποιΐαν or λογοποιΐαν). **-ποιός**, ὁ, *spear-maker*, E.*Ba.*1208. **-φόρος**, ον, *spear-bearing*, Id.*Hec.*1089: as Subst.

λ., ὁ, *spearman, pikeman*, Ar.*Pax*1294, X.*Cyr.*2.1.5, Plb.3.84.14, *POxy.*1241 ii 16 (ii A.D.); χιλίαρχοι λ. *Sammelb.*6154.6 (i B.C.), *Bull.Soc.Arch.Alex.*7.64.

**λογχωτός**, ή, όν, *furnished with a point, lance-headed*, βέλος E.*Ba.* 761; ἔγχεα B.*Fr.*3.8, cf. *AP*6.172; *lanceolate*, Paul.Aeg.6.88. 2. *composed of*, or *ornamented with, spear-heads*, ὅρμος *IG*11(2).161 *B* 23, al.; φιάλη ib.l.75 (Delos, iii B.C.); λογχωτοὶ χιτῶνες Lyd.*Mag.* 1.17, cf. 2.4. II. λογχωτόν, τό, = χαλκανθές, interpol. in Dsc.5.98, cf. Plin.*HN*34.124.

**λογώδης**, ες, = λογοειδής I, μέλος Aristox.*Harm.*p.18 M. II. *verbal*, of an argument, Thphr.*Metaph.*16.

**λόε, λοέσσας, λοεσσάμενος, λοέσσομαι**, v. λούω. **λοετρόν, λοετροχόος**, v. λουτρ-. **λοέω**, v. λούω. **λοιάδες**· αἱ κόραι τῶν ὀφθαλμῶν, Theognost.*Can.*22; cf. λογάς (B). **λοίαξ**· ὁ ξηρὸς χόρτος, Hsch.

**λοιβ-αῖος**, α, ον, *of* or *belonging to a* λοιβή, Megaclid.ap.Ath.12. 512f. **-άομαι**, = σπένδω, Hsch. **-άσιον**, τό, = sq., Epich. 79 (pl.), cf. Ath.11.486a. **-εῖον**, τό, *cup for pouring libations*, Plu. *Aem.*33, *Marc.*2. ⊛**-ή**, ἡ, (λείβω) *pouring*, only in religious sense, *drink-offering*, λοιβῇ τε κνίσῃ τε with *drink-offering* and burnt-offering, Il.9.500, cf. 4.49, 24.70; σοὶ δ' αὖ λ. φέρον says Odysseus to the Cyclops, Od.9.349: later, like σπονδαί, χοαί (which are more freq.), in pl., Pi.*N.*11.6, S.*El.*52; λοιβαὶ Διός, offered to him, A.*Fr.*55.—Rare in Prose, λ. οἴνου Pl.*Lg.*906d, referring to Il.9.500. 2. of *water* generally, λ. Στυγός A.R.2.291. **-ίς**, ίδος, ἡ, = λοιβεῖον, Antim. ap.Ath.11.486a, *IG*2².1541.12 (Eleusis, iv B.C.).

**λοιγ-ήεις**, εσσα, εν, = sq., Nic.*Al.*207:—also **-ής**, ές, ib.256, *Th.* 921. **-ιος**, ον, (λοιγός) *pestilent, deadly*, λ. ἔργα Il.1.518,573; οἴω λοίγι' ἔσεσθαι I think there shall be *sorrow*, 21.533, 23.310; λ. πῆμα A.R.1.469: neut. pl. λοίγια, of poisons, Androm.ap.Gal.14. 37. **-ίστρια**· ὀλοθρεύτρια, Hsch.

**λοιγολαμπής**, ές, *balefully gleaming*, cj. for λογο- in Doroth.ap. *Cat.Cod.Astr.*1.173.7.

**λοιγός** (A), ὁ, *ruin, havoc*, of death by plague, ἡμῖν ἀπὸ λ. ἀμῦναι Il. 1.67; by war, 5.603, etc.; of *destruction* of ships, νεῶν ἀπὸ λ. ἀμύνων 16.80; λ. Ἐνυαλίου Pi.*N.*9.37; βοᾷ λοιγὸν Ἐρινὺς (Schütz λοιγὸς Ἐρινὺν) A.*Ch.*402 (lyr.); ἀνδροκμὴς λ. Id.*Supp.*679 (lyr.).—Poet. (not in Od.); mock-heroic in Cratin.171. (Cf. Lith. *pa-liegti* 'become feeble, sickly'.)

**λοιγός** (B), όν, = λοίγιος, Nic.*Th.*6,733; λ. Ἄρης *AP*7.368 (Eryc.).

**λοιγωντίαν**· φρατρίαν, Hsch.

⊛**λοιδορ-έω**, fut. -ήσω D.40.48: aor. ἐλοιδόρησα E.*Med.*873, etc.: pf. λελοιδόρηκα Pl.*Phdr.*241e:—Med. and **Pass.** (v. infr.), fut. -ήσομαι Ar.*Eq.*1400, etc.: aor. ἐλοιδορησάμην Is.6.59; Att. more freq. ἐλοιδορήθην D.9.54, 54.5 (v. infr.): (λοίδορος):—*abuse, revile*, τινα Hdt.3.145; θεούς Pi.*O.*9.37, cf. Ar.*Nu.*1140, X.*An.*3.4.49, *BGU* 1007.6 (iii B.C.), etc.: abs., E. l. c., etc.; sts. simply, *rebuke*, X.*Cyr.* 1.4.9; οἶνον εἰς ἐπίνοιαν λ. Ar.*Eq.*90, cf. Plu.2.175b (Pass.): with neut. Adj., ἐμαυτὸν πόλλ' ἐλοιδόρησα E.*Hel.*1171; οὐδὲν οὐδένα λ. Pl. *Tht.*174c; λ. ἔνια Arist.*EN*1128$^{a}$31: with a predicate added, [τὴν Τύχην] λ. τυφλὴν *reproach* fortune as blind, Plu.2.98a:—Med., *rail at one another*, Antipho 2.1.4, Ar.*Ra.*857, D.54.18:—Pass., λοιδοροῦντας ἢ λοιδορουμένους *reviling* or *reviled*, Isoc.2.47, cf. Phld.*Lib.*p.29 O.; λελοιδορημένος ὑπὸ.. *rebuked*.., X.*HG*5.4.29; οὐκ ἐν δίκῃ λοιδορηθεὶς Pl.*Phdr.*275e, cf. *Grg.*457d. II. Med. with aor. Pass. in act. sense, c. dat. pers., *rail at*, τινι Ar.*Eq.*1400, *Pl.*456, *Ec.*248, Pl.*R.* 395d, etc.; also λ. ἐπί τινι X.*Ages.*7.3; τινος Ach.Tat.1.6; εἴς τινα Luc.*Anach.*22; πρός τινα Lxx *Ex.*17.2: c. acc. cogn., πάντα τὰ αἰσχρὰ λοιδορέονται, ὅτι.. they *use* all kind of foul *reproaches*, saying that .., Hdt.4.184; λοιδορίαν ἣν ἐλοιδορήθη Κρατίνῳ περὶ τούτων D.21. 132.—Act. never has dat. exc. in later Gr., Lxx *Ex.*17.2, 2*Ma.*12.14, Epict.*Ench.*34, Ant.Lib.22.5; in And.1.67 (ἠναντιώθην καὶ ἀντεῖπον —καὶ ἐλοιδόρησα—ἐκείνῳ ὧν ἦν ἄξιος) the dat. (if correct) depends on the other verbs; as does the acc. in οὓς ὕβριζες καὶ ἐλοιδορου Hyp. *Dem.Fr.*(*a*).—Only the Act. is found in Trag. **-ημα**, ατος, τό, *railing, abuse*, Arist.*EN*1128$^{a}$30; τὸν πτωχὸν λ. ποιεῖσθαι Plu.2. 607a. **-ημάτιον**, τό, Dim. of foreg., Ar.*Fr.*90. **-ησις**, εως, ἡ, = λοιδορία, Pl.*Lg.*967c (pl.): personified as place-name, Lxx *Ex.* 17.7. **-ησμός**, ὁ, = λοιδορία, Ar.*Ra.*758. **-ητέον**, *one must rail at*, τινι Max.Tyr.3.3. **-ητικός**, ή, όν, *abusive*, Arist.*EE*1221$^{b}$ 14, Phld.*Ir.*p.72 W., Iamb.*VP*30.171, Sch.Heph.p.300 C. **-ία**, ἡ, *railing, abuse, reproach*, Antipho 2.1.4, Ar.*Fr.*346, Th.2.84, Pl. *Euthd.*288b, Phld.*Lib.*p.29 O., etc.; εἰς γέλωτα καὶ λ. ἐμβαλόντες D.10.75: pl., Lys.21.8, Pl.*Tht.*174c. **-ιστής**, οῦ, ὁ, = sq., Hsch. s. v. κόβειρος. **-ος**, ον, *railing, abusive*, ἔρις E.*Cyc.*534; πομπεῖαι Men.*Per.Fr.*4; ῥήματα *IG*14.1857; φωναί Phld.*Ir.*p.74 W. Adv. -ρως Str.14.2.28. 2. as Subst. λ., ὁ, *railer*, 1*Ep.Cor.*5.11, Plu.2.177d; τὸ λ., = λοιδορία, Arist.*Phgn.*808$^{b}$37, Plu.2.810d; λοίδορα *AP*5.175 (Mel.).

**λοῖθον**· λιμός, Hsch. **λοῖκορ**· κέγχρος, Id.

**λοιμ-εύομαι**, (λοιμός) *to be pestilent*, Lxx *Pr.*19.19. **-η**, ἡ, = λοιμός, *pestilence*, Hsch. (In Hp.*Praec.*13 λοιμίης is f.l. for λοίμης or λύμης.) **-ικός**, ή, όν, *pestilential*, Hp.*Ep.*1, Plb.1.19.1, Ph.2.102, Longin.44.9, etc.; λ. περίστασις, διάθεσις, *SIG*731.7 (Tomi, i B.C.), *IG*12(1).1032.7 (Carpathus); λ. διήγησις *about pestilence*, Gal.17(2). 168. Adv. -κῶς S.E.*M.*9.79. 2. *destructive*, λ. τοξεύματα Lyc. 1205. **-ιος**, ον, = foreg., epith. of Apollo at Lindos, Macr.*Sat.*1. 17.15.

**λοιμοποιός**, όν, *causing a pestilence*, Vett.Val.6.29.

**λοιμός**, ὁ, *plague*, once in Hom. (Il.1.61), cf. Hes.*Op.*243, Hdt. 7.171; λοιμοῦ σκηπτός A.*Pers.*715 (troch.); of the plague at Athens, Th.2.47,54, Pl.*Smp.*201d: pl., ib.188b, al.; coupled with λιμός, Hes. and Hdt. ll. cc., Th.2.54, Orac.ap.Aeschin.3.135. 2. of persons, *plague, pest*, D.25.80. II. as Adj., *pestilent*, Lxx 1*Ki.*1.16; ἀνὴρ λ. καὶ πονηρός ib.30.22, cf. *Act.Ap.*24.5; λ. οἶνος Sm.*Pr.*20.1.

**λοιμότης**, ητος, ἡ, *pestilent condition*, Lxx *Es.*8.13(16.7).

**λοιμοφόρος**, ον, *bringing plague, pestilential*, *Gloss.*

⊛**λοιμ-ώδης**, ες, *pestilential*, λ. νόσος *plague*, Hp.*Acut.*5, Th.1.23, Ph.1.408, al.; ἔτος λ. Arist.*Pr.*862$^{a}$5. **-ώσσω**, Att. -ττω, fut. -ξω, *to have the plague*, Gal.10.362, Luc.*Hist.Conscr.*15, *Scyth.*2, Max.Tyr.41.4, Sch.Ar.*Pl.*627; also ἐν λοιμώττοντι χωρίῳ a *plague-spot*, Procl. *in Alc.*p.256 C.

**λοιπ-ἄδάριον**, τό, Dim. of λοιπάς, Suid. **-ἄδάριος**, ὁ, *one who is in arrear with taxes*, *POxy.*136.33 (vi A.D.). **-άδιος** [ᾰ], α, ον, prob. = λοιπός, Sch.D.T.p.542 H. **-άζω**, *leave*, *Gloss.*:—Pass., *to be left over, remain*, *POxy.*1194.3 (iii A.D.), Sch.Ar.*Pl.*227, etc.; *to be in need*, Anon. *in EN*448.23 (v.l. λειπ-). **-άς**, άδος, ἡ, *remainder*, *PTeb.*112.50 (ii B.C., λοπ- Pap.), *PAmh.*2.152.3 (v/vi A.D.), etc. **-ασμός**, ὁ, *want*, cj. for ἐλειπασμός in Ps.-Luc.*Philopatr.*20. **-ημα**, ατος, τό, = λοιπάς, *PTeb.*281.24 (ii B.C.).

⊛**λοιπογρἄφ-έω**, *allow to remain in arrear, carry over* a debt, *PPetr.*3 p.154 (iii B.C.), *PTeb.*112.34, al. (ii B.C.), *CIG*2335.23 (Delos, i B.C.), *BGU*362 iii 21, al. (iii A.D.), Nech.ap.Vett.Val.279.12. ⊛**-ή**, ἡ, = sq., *Stud.Pal.*20.85 (iv A.D.). **-ία**, ἡ, *outstanding debt, arrears*, *BGU*567.2, al., Petersen-Luschan *Reisen in Lykien* p.54 No.96, *Gloss.* II. *carrying over* of debt or arrears, *PStrassb.*77.5 (iii A.D.).

⊛**λοιπός**, ή, όν, (λείπω) *remaining over*, not in Hom., freq. from Pi. and Hdt. downwards; λ. βίοτος Pi.*O.*1.97; λ. εὐχαί ib.4.15; λ. γένος ib.2.15; also λοιποί *descendants*, Id.*I.*4(3).39: in Prose the Art. is commonly added, and ὁ λ. either agrees with the Noun or takes a dependent genitive, αἱ λ. τῶν νεῶν Th.7.72; τὴν λοιπὴν (sc. ὁδὸν) πορευσόμεθα X.*An.*3.4.46; τὸ λ. τῆς ἡμέρας ib.16, etc. 2. λοιπόν [ἐστι] c. inf., *it remains* to show, etc., ἀποδεικνύναι, διελέσθαι, etc., Id. *Smp.*4.1, Pl.*R.*466d, etc.: also c. Art., τὸ λ. ἤδη ἡμῖν ἐστι σκέψασθαι, πότερον *what remains* for us is to.., ib.444e; διανομὴ τοίνυν τὸ λ. σοι ib.535a: without inf., ὃ δὲ λ. *quod superest*, A.*Ag.*1571 (lyr.); ὅ τι λ. πόνων Id.*Pr.*684; τὸ εὐπρεπείας πέρι.. λοιπόν Pl.*Phdr.*274b. 3. freq. of Time, ὁ λ. χρόνος *the future*, Pi.*N.*7.67; πρὸς τὸν λοιπὸν τοῦ χρόνου D.15.16; τὸν λ. χρόνον *for the future*, S.*Ph.*84; τοῦ λ. χρόνου Id.*El.*817; εἰς τὸν λ. χρόνον Pl.*Ep.*358b; ἐκ τοῦ λ. χρόνου D.59.46: so without Subst. in neut., τὸ λ. *henceforward, hereafter*, Pi.*P.*5.118, A.*Eu.*1031, S.*OT*795, etc.; τὸ λ. εἰς ἅπαντα.. χρόνον A.*Eu.*763; τὰ λ. Id.*Th.*66, S.*El.*1226, Th.8.21; ἐς τὸ λ. A.*Pers.*526, *Eu.*708, cf. *Inscr. Prien.*64 (ii B.C.); also τοῦ λ. Hdt.1.189, Ar.*Pax*1084; ἐκ τοῦ λ. X. *HG*3.4.9; ἐκ τῶν λ. Pl.*Lg.*709e, *Ep.*316d; καθεύδετε τὸ λ. sleep *now*.., *Ev.Matt.*26.45, *Ev.Marc.*14.41; ἑσπέρα δὲ ἦν λ. καὶ.. it was *now* evening, Jul.*Or.*1.24c. 4. τὸ λ. and τὰ λ. *the rest*, A.*Pr.*476, 697, 699, etc.; καὶ τὰ λ., = '*etc.*', Aristeas 190, Plu.2.1084c, etc.; also λοιπόν without the Art., as Adv., *for the rest, further*, and so freq., = ἤδη, *already*, λ. δή Pl.*Prt.*321c; αἰσχρὸν δὴ τὸ λ. γίγνεται Id.*Grg.* 458d. 5. λοιπόν, Adv. *then, well then*, Plb.1.15.11, al., Dsc.2.83, Arr.*Epict.*1.24.1; οὐδεμία λ. ἀμφισβήτησίς ἐστιν *BGU*969.19 (ii A.D.). b. *finally*, λ., ἀδελφοί, χαίρετε 2*Ep.Cor.*13.11.

**λοισθ-ήϊος**, ον, *of* or *for the last*, λοισθήϊον ἔκφερ' ἄεθλον the prize *for the last* in the race, Il.23.785: pl., λοισθήϊ' ἔθηκε *last prize*, ib. 751. **-ημα**, ατος, τό, = τέλος, πέρας, Hsch. **-ιος**, α, ον S.*Ant.* 895, etc.; also ος, ον A.*Ch.*500:—= sq., Pi.*P.*4.266, A.*Ag.*120 (lyr.), S.*Ant.*1220, etc.; τὰ λ. τοῦ βίου Id.*OC*583: neut. λοίσθιον as Adv., *last*, Id.*Aj.*468, *Ant.*1304; λ. ἄλλων A.R.2.559; τὸ λ. E.*HF*23; τὰ λ. Theoc.5.13. **-ος** (A), ον, *left behind, last*, Il.23.536, Lyc.163, Euph.51.13, etc.; ὁ θάνατος λοῖσθος ἰατρὸς κακῶν S.*Fr.*698: Sup. -ότατος *last of all*, Hes.*Th.*921; -οτάτας χάριτας *the last* honours (to the dead), *IG*14.1721.

**λοῖσθος** (B), ὁ, *beam*, λοῖσθοι ἐξ ὧστε μοχλοῖς χρῆσθαι *IG*2².1673.17 (iv B.C.); *boom, gaff*, or *spar*, E.*Hel.*1597.

**λοισθωνας**· τοὺς ἀκρατεῖς περὶ τὰ ἀφροδίσια, Hsch.: cf. **λοισθώνη**· ἡ θρασεῖα, Suid. **λοιτεύειν**· θάπτειν, and **λοίτη**· τάφος, Hsch.

**λόκαλος**, ὁ, an unknown bird, Arist.*HA*509$^{a}$21.

**λόκκη** (cf. Hdn.Gr.1.314), ἡ, archaic word in *AP*11.20 (Antip. Thess.); acc. to Hsch., = χλαμύς (λόκμη cod.); cf. λέκκη.

**λοκός**· λοκρός, φαλακρός, Hsch.

**Λοκρ-ιστί**, Adv. *in Locrian manner*: ἡ Λ. ἁρμονία Ath.14.625e. **-οί**, οἱ, *the Locrians*, of whom there were three tribes, *the Opuntian*, opposite Euboea, Il.2.527, Th.1.108, Str.9.3.1, 9.3.17; *the Epicnemidian*, on Mt. Cnemis on the Maliac Gulf, Id. ll. cc.; and *the Ozolian*, on the Corinthian Gulf, Th.1.5,103, etc.: *the Epizephyrian* or *Zephyrian* were a colony of the last on Mt. Zephyrium in lower Italy, Pi.*O.*10(11).13, Th.4.24 sq., 7.1, etc.: prov. Λοκρῶν σύνθημα, of deceit, Eust.275.43, Hsch., Suid.:—Adj. **Λοκρός**, ά, όν, *Locrian*, Lyc. 1429:—also **Λοκρικός**, ή, όν, Poll.4.65, etc.:—fem. **Λοκρίς**, ίδος, Pi. *P.*2.19; ἡ Λ. (sc. γῆ) Ar.*Av.*152, etc.

**λολλα**, ἡ, a plant, *PLond.*1.122.12 (iv A.D.).

**λολλώ**, ἡ, child's word for anything 'divinely nice', Hermipp.89.

**λόμβαι**· αἱ τῇ Ἀρτέμιδι θυσιῶν ἄρχουσαι, ἀπὸ τῆς κατὰ τὴν παιδιὰν σκευῆς. οἱ γὰρ φάλητες οὕτω καλοῦνται, Hsch. **λομβούς**· τοὺς ἀπεσκολυμμένους, Id. **λομβρός**, όν, in Comp. λομβρότερον, name of an indecent dance, Poll.4.105. **λόνδις**· βωμολόχος, εἴρων, Hsch.

**λόξ-ευμα**, ατος, τό, *obliquity*, in pl., Man.1.307, 4.479. **-εύω**,

= λοξόω, τὸν ὀφθαλμόν Lib.*Descr.*30.18; λελοξευμένα *obscure* or *symbolical language*, Syn.Alch.p.63 B.

**Λοξ-ίας**, ου, Ion. -ίης, εω, ὁ, epith. of Apollo, B.12.148, Hdt.1.91, A.*Eu.*19, al., S.*OT*410, Ar.*Eq.*1047, *Pl.*8, etc.; expld. because the Sun traverses the ecliptic (cf. II), Cleanth.*Stoic.*1.123; or from Apollo's 'crooked', i.e. ambiguous, oracles (cf. λοξός 3), Corn.*ND* 32, etc. II. (λοξός) *the zodiac* or *ecliptic*, from its *obliquity* to the equator, Anon.*Intr.Arat.*p.96 M. **-ικός**, ή, όν, *oblique*, λ. κύκλος *the ecliptic*, *Cat.Cod.Astr.*7.194 (Rhetorius).

⊛ **λοξο-βάμοισι** (leg. -βάμοσι, from -βάμων)· πλαγίως περιπατοῦσιν, Hsch. **-βάτης** [ᾰ], ου, ὁ, = foreg., Batr.295. **-βλεπτέω**, *look askance at*, Thom.Mag.p.93 R. **-ειδής**, ές, *oblique*, of the lower ribs, Ruf.*Oss.*25. ⊛ **-κέλευθος**, ον, *oblique*, δρόμος Nonn.*D.*5.233. **-κίνητος** [ῑ], ον, *moving athwart*, λ. κύκλος *the ecliptic*, Sch. Hes.*Op.*381 (p.208 G.) **-περιπάτητος** [ᾰ], ον, *walking sideways*, gloss on Batr.295. **-πορέω**, *go slantwise* or *sideways*, *Placit.*2.23.6. **-πορος**, ον, *moving aslant*, of the Moon, *Hymn.Is.*30.

**λοξ-ός**, ή, όν, *slanting*, *crosswise*, Hp.*Off.*11; λοξή (sc. γραμμή), ἡ, a *cross*-line, E.*Fr.*382.9; λοξὰ βαίνειν, of a crab, Babr.109.1; λ. ὄφις Call.*Epigr.*26; ὁ λ. κύκλος *the ecliptic*, Arist.*Metaph.*1071ᵃ16, Cleanth. *Stoic.*1.112, Arat.527, Gem.5.51, Cleom.1.4, Ptol.*Alm.*1.8 (without κύκλος Plot.5.8.7); of the milky way, Gem.5.68; τῶν ἀστέρων λ. γίνεται φορά Arist.*Mete.*342ᵃ27; λ. δρόμος Diog.Oen.8; λ. πορείας σχῆμα Plu.*Phoc.*2; λ. φάλαγξ, a phalanx of which one wing is in advance of the other, Ascl.*Tact.*10.1, Onos.21.8, Ael.*Tact.*30.3; λ. ζῴδια, i.e. λοξῶς ἀνατέλλοντα, Heph.Astr.3.1; οἱ λ. μῦες the *oblique* abdominal muscles, Gal.2.518, al.; λ. τῇ θέσει πρός τι *at an acute angle* to it, Thphr.*Sens.*73, cf. Arist.*Mu.*393ᵇ15. Adv. -ξῶς, τὰ λοξὰ [ἐπιδεῖν] Hp. l. c. 2. of suspicious looks, λοξὸν ὄμμασιν βλέπειν τινά look *askance* at one, Anacr.75.1; λοξὸν ὀφθαλμοῖς ὁρᾶν Sol.34; ὄμμασι λοξὰ βλέποισα Theoc.20.13; λοξῷ ὄμματι ἰδεῖν A.R.4.475; οὔπω Ζεὺς αὐχένα λοξὸν ἔχει Zeus has not yet turned his neck *aside*, i.e. withdrawn his favour, Tyrt.11.2; but αὐχένα λοξὸν ἔχει, of a slave, as type of dishonesty, Thgn.536: hence metaph., *mistrustful*, *suspicious*, in Adv. Comp. -ότερον, ἔχειν πρός τινα Plb.4.86.8. 3. of language, *indirect*, *ambiguous*, esp. of oracles, Lyc.14, 1467, Luc. *Alex.*10; λοξὰ ἀποκρίνασθαι Id.*DDeor.*16.1; ἐν τοῖς χρησμοῖς λ., of Apollo, Id.*JTr.*28. (Cf. λέχριος.) ⊛ **-ότης**, ητος, ἡ, *obliquity*, Str.2.1.37, *Placit.*5.9.2, Gem.2.24. 2. *ambiguity*, of oracles, Plu.2.409c.

**λοξοτρόχις**, ιδος, ἡ, *oblique-running*, of Lycophron's Cassandra, *AP*9.191; cf. λοξός 3.

⊛ **λοξ-όφθαλμος**, ον, *oblique-eyed*, Procl.*Par.Ptol.*204.

**λοξοχρήσμων**, ον, gen. ονος, *uttering ambiguous oracles*, Sch.Lyc. 1466.

**λοξ-όω**, *make slanting*, *cast sideways*, τὰς λογάδας Sophr.49:—Pass., *to be* or *become so*, Hp.*Mul.*1.33, Eudox.ap.Arist.*Metaph.*1073ᵇ20, 29, Str.6.2.1. **-ωσις**, εως, ἡ, *obliquity*, κατὰ λόξωσιν οὐρανοῦ Epicur.*Ep.*2 p.40 U.; of the ecliptic, Ocell.2.23, Str.6.2.1, Ptol.*Tetr.*98, *Placit.*2.12.2. 2. *ambiguity*, Tz. ad Hes.*Op.*412.

**λοπᾰδ-άγχης**, ου, ὁ, = sq., Eub.139. **-αρπᾰγίδης**, ου, ὁ, *dish-snatcher*, Epigr.ap.Hegesand.1. **-εύω**, *dress as a dish*, Philum.ap. Orib.45.29.25, *AB*105 (Pass.). ⊛ **-ιον**, τό, Dim. of λοπάς 2, Ar.*Pl.*812, Eub.9, 38, Alex.186.7, *PCair.Zen.*82 (iii B.C.), etc. II. *oyster*, *Gp.*20.18. **-ίσκος**, ὁ, = foreg. 1, Sch.Ar.*V.*962.

**λοπᾰδο-τεμᾰχο-σελᾰχο-γᾰλεο-κρᾱνιο-λειψᾱνο-δρῐμ-ὑποτριμμᾰτο-σιλφιο-κᾰρᾱβο-μελῐτο-κᾰτᾰκεχῡμενο-κιχλ-επῐκοσσῡφο-φαττο-περιστερ-ᾰλεκτρῡον-οπτο-κεφαλλιο-κιγκλο-πελειο-λᾰγῳο-σιραιο-βᾰφη-τρᾰγᾰνο-πτερύγων**, Com. word in Ar.*Ec.*1169 (as emended by Meineke), name of a dish compounded of all kinds of dainties, fish, flesh, fowl, and sauces.

**λοπᾰδο-φυσητής**, οῦ, ὁ, *dish-piper*, nickname of Dorion, a gluttonous flute-player, Mnesim.10:—perh. with a play on λωτός.

⊛ **λοπάς**, άδος, ἡ, *flat dish* or *plate*, in which food was served, Ar.*Eq.*1034, *V.*511, Men.*Sam.*150, Dsc.2.142, etc. b. *dish* in sense of food-preparation, Gal.6.653, al. 2. *frying-pan*, Eub.109, Arched. 2.4; distd. from τήγανον by Eub. l. c., Pl.Com.173.12. II. in Com. also, = σορός (ἡ), Theopomp.Com.92. III. *a disease of the olive*, Thphr.*HP*4.14.3; *rotting at the root*, of fig-trees, ib.5. IV. *shell-fish*, Luc.*Asin.*47; ὄστρεα καὶ λοπάδας Gal.4.670; v.l. for λεπάς, Thphr.*HP*4.6.7.

⊛ **λοπ-άω**, (λοπός) *let the bark peel off*, of trees which lose their bark on the return of the sap in spring, Thphr.*HP*3.5.1, 5.1.1, etc. II. of fig-trees, *rot at the root*, Id.*CP*5.9.9. **-ητός**, ὁ, *the time of bark peeling off*, Id.*HP*5.1.1. ⊛ **-ίδιον**, τό, Dim. of λοπίς III, λοπίδια παντοδαπὰ ἀπ' ἀνδριάντων *BCH*29.542 (Delos). ⊛ **-ίζω**, *peel off the bark* (with v.l. λεπίζω, which Phot. condemns), in Pass., Thphr.*HP*3.13.1, 4; cf. λοπίξαι· λαμπρῦναι ἢ λεπιδῶσαι, Hsch.:—the word occurs in broken context, *POxy.*218 *Fr.*(b)3. ⊛ **-ιμος**, ον, *easily stripped*, of nuts which have a skin and not a shell, Nic.*Fr.*76, Sor.ap.Gal.12.420, cf. Gal.6.621, Hsch. ⊛ **-ίς**, ίδος, ἡ, = λεπίς 2, Ar.*V.*790, Nic. *Al.*467, *Th.*154. II. λ. σιδηρᾶ iron *pin* to keep a βάλανος in place, Aen.Tact.20.3. III. *fragment* of ἀκρόβασις, *BCH*29.541 (Delos). IV. = λοπάς 1.1a, *Schwyzer*89.20 (Argos, iii B.C.). **-ισμα**, ατος, τό, = sq., Eust.1863.51, Phot. **-ός** or **λόπος**, ὁ, (λέπω) *peel*, κρομύοιο λ. Od.19.233. II. of a hide, λ. δέρματος *the outer part of a split piece of leather*, opp. αὐτὸ τὸ δέρμα, Hp.*Art.*33, cf. 38. 2. *peeling of the skin* after illness, Id.*Epid.*2.1.7.

**λορδ-αίνω**, = λορδόω, Hp.*Art.*46. **-ός**, ή, όν, *bent backward*, so as to be convex in front, opp. κυφός, Id.*Fract.*16, *Art.*48, Arist.*IA*707ᵇ18. ⊛ **-όω**, as neut., *bend oneself supinely*, so as to throw the head back, Hp.*Art.*46, Mnesim.4.55 (anap.):—Pass., Hp.*Art.*48, Procop. *Arc.*9: sens. obsc., Ar.*Ec.*10, *Fr.*140. **-ωμα**, ατος, τό, *a bending supinely*, Hp.*Mochl.*38 (pl.), *Art.*48. ⊛ **-ων**, ωνος, ὁ, *the demon of impure* λόρδωσις (cf. λορδόω sub fin.), cf. Κύβδασος (from κύβδα), Pl. Com.174.17. **-ωσις**, εως, ἡ, *a curvature* of the spine *which is convex in front*, Hp.*Art.*48, Gal.18(1).493, Sch.Theoc.5.43. **-ωτός**, = λορδός, dub. cj. in Erot. s. v. λορδότατον.

**λουδοτρόφος**, *lanista*, *Gloss.*

**λουέω**, impf. ἐλούεον, v. λούω. **λοῦκα**, *gruel made of wheat-meal* (Cauconian), Hsch.

**λούκουντλος**, ὁ, a kind of *cake*, Chrysipp.Tyan.ap.Ath.14.647d. (Lat. *lucunculus.*)

**λουλάκιον**, τό, a plant, Lyd.*Mens.*1.21.

**λοῦμα**, ατος, τό, (λούω) *stream*, *Epigr.Gr.*903.2 (Sardes). II. λούματα· τὰ τῶν πτισσομένων κριθῶν ἄχυρα (Cypr.), Hsch. (ἀούματα cod.); cf. ἀπολούω.

**λοῦμαι**, Att. for λούομαι.

**λουμενάριον**, τό (Lat. *luminarium*), *window*, *PGot.*7 (iv A.D.).

**λουνόν**· λαμπρόν, Hsch.

**λούπης**, ὁ, = ἰκτῖνος, Hierocl.*Facet.*257, Hdn.*Epim.*46.

**λούππις**, *milvus*, *Gloss.*

⊛ **λοῦσις**, εως, ἡ, *washing*, *bathing*, *PFlor.*384.23 (V A.D.), *Gloss.*; *cleaning*, τῶν βαλανείων *SIG*901.17 (Delph., iv A.D.).

**λοῦσον**· κόλουρον, κολοβόν, τεθραυσμένον, Hsch.; Cypr., acc. to Eust.1246.38.

**λοῦσσον**, τό, *pith of the fir-tree*, Thphr.*HP*3.9.7.

**λουσ-τέον**, *one must take a bath*, Archig.ap.Gal.13.168. **-της**, ου, ὁ, *one fond of bathing*, of certain birds, opp. κονιστικοί, Arist.*HA* 633ᵃ29; ἀωρὶ λ. M.Ant.1.16.

**λουταρίζημα**· ὅ τινες, ὄλισθον, Hsch. **λουτέον**, *one must wash*, τὰ βρέφη Sor.1.78.

⊛ **λου-τήρ**, ῆρος, ὁ, *washing* or *bathing-tub*, *Supp.Epigr.*4.263.10 (pl., Stratonicea, i A.D.), *CIG*2820 *A* 10 (Aphrodisias), *IGRom.*4.454 (pl., Pergam., i A.D.), Callix.2, Moschio ap.Ath.5.207f, Lxx *Ex.*30.18, al. **-τηρίδιον**, τό, Dim. of foreg., Hero *Spir.*1.37, *BGU*781 ii 12 (i A.D.), Dsc.1.43. **-τήριον**, τό, Dor. **λωτήριον** *Tab.Heracl.*1.184, = λουτήρ, Antiph.208, *IG*2².1425.371 (iv B.C.), *PLond.*2.193.21 (ii A.D.); λουτήρια μέγιστα A.*Fr.*366. II. a kind of *cup*, Epig.6. **-τηρίσκος**, ὁ, Dim. of λουτήρ, *Gloss.* **-τιάω**, Desiderat. of λούω, *wish to bathe*, Luc.*Lex.*2. **-τρικός**, ή, όν, *of* or *for bathing*, Hsch. s. v. ξυστρολήκυθον. **-τριον**, τό, *water that has been used in washing*, Ar.*Eq.*1401, *Fr.*306, Luc.*Lex.*4. II. = λουτήρ, λ. χαλκοῦν μέγα *CPR*p.125 (iii A.D.). ⊛ **-τρίς**, ίδος, ἡ, *woman employed to wash Athena's temple*, Hsch., Phot. II. ᾠὰ λ. *bathing drawers*, Theopomp.Com.37.

**λουτροδάϊκτος** [ᾰ], ον, *slain in the bath*, A.*Ch.*1071 (anap.).

⊛ **λουτρόν**, τό, in Hom. always **λοετρόν**, but contr. form in *h.Cer.*50, Hes.*Op.*753; Dor. **λωτρόν**, Hsch.: (λούω):—*bath*, *bathing-place*, Hom., always in pl., θερμὰ λοετρά hot *bath*, Il.22.444, al.; later θερμὰ λουτρά A.*Ch.*670, S.*Tr.*634 (lyr.), Crates Com.15, etc.; θερμὰ Νυμφᾶν λουτρά Pi.*O.*12.19; also called Ἡράκλεια λουτρά Ar.*Nu.*1051; λοετρὰ Ὠκεανοῖο Il.18.489, Od.5.275; σίτοισι καὶ λουτροῖσι in matters of eating and *washing*, Hdt.6.52; λουτρῷ χρωμένους Plu.2.1109b: sg. first in Hes. l. c.; τραπέσθαι πρὸς τὸ λ. Pl.*Phd.*115a, cf. X.*Oec.*9.7: in pl., *bathing-establishment*, τὰ δημόσια λ. *POxy.*1252 *B* 22 (iii A.D.), etc. 2. *water for bathing* or *washing*, ὑδάτων ἐνεγκεῖν λουτρά S.*OC*1599; ἐν λουτροῖς while *bathing*, X.*Cyr.*7.5.59; λοῦσαί τινα λουτρόν give one a *bath*, wash one with water, S.*Ant.*1201, Ar.*Lys.*469; λουτρὸν παρέχειν ib.377; λοῦσθαι λουτρόν *bathe*, A.*Fr.*366 (note); λουτρόν ἐστιν, οὐ πότος Alex.9; νυμφικὰ λουτρά *the conveying of water to the bride* (cf. λουτροφόρος), Poll.3.43; in *NT*, of baptism, *Ep.Eph.*5.26; λ. παλιγγενεσίας *Ep.Tit.*3.5. II. in Poets, = σπονδαί, *libations to the dead*, S.*El.*84, 434, E.*Ph.*1667, cf. Hsch. s. v. χθόνια λ.

**λουτρό-ομαι**, *bathe*, θερμοῖς Αἰδεψοῦ *IG*12(9).1240.11 (Aedepsus). **-ποιός**, ὁ, *bath-attendant*, title of play by Anaxilas. ⊛ **-φορέω**, *carry water for bathing*, Harp. ⊛ **-φόρος**, ον, *bringing water*: παῖς, παρθένος λ. at Athens the boy or girl who, as next of kin to the bridegroom, *fetched him water from the fountain Callirrhoe* on his wedding day, Harp. s. v., Paus.2.10.4, Poll.3.43: hence λ. χλιδή *marriage-ceremony*, E.*Ph.*348 (lyr.). 2. as Subst., λουτροφόρος, ἡ, *black urn* placed on the tomb of an unmarried person, D.44.18, 30, Poll.8.66; cf. λίβυς. **-χοέω**, *pour into the bath*, ὕδωρ *AP*9.627 (Marian.). ⊛ **-χόος**, ον, in Hom. always **λοετρ-**, Dor. **λωτρ-** Call.*Lav.Pall.*1, 15: *—pouring water into the bath*: Subst., *the slave who did this*, Od.20.297, X. *Cyr.*8.8.20: λ. τρίπους a three-legged cauldron, *in which water was warmed for bathing*, Il.18.346, Od.8.435.

⊛ **λουτρών**, ῶνος, ὁ, *bathing-room*, *bath-house*, X.*Ath.*2.10, Lyc.1103, *PSI*5.547.24 (iii B.C.), Ptol.Euerg.3 J. (pl.), Plu.2.734b, Procop. *Aed.*5.3; of a baptismal font, Id.*Arc.*17.

⊛ **λουτρωνικός**, ή, όν, *of the public baths*, *Cod.Just.*1.4.26 *Intr.*

⊛ **λούω**, contr. from **λοέω**, from which come impf. λόεον Od.4.252: aor. inf. λοέσσαι 19.320; part. λοέσσας Il.23.282: fut. Med. λοέσσομαι Od.6.221: 3 sg. aor. λοέσσατο ib.227; λοεσσάμενος Il.10.577, *Schwyzer*633 (Eresus, ii/i B.C.): also Ep. impf. ἐλούεον *h.Cer.*289.—Later forms, λούει Hdt.6.52; inf. λούειν Hp.*Morb.*2.20, Pl.*Phd.*115a: fut. λούσω Call.*Del.*95; Dor. λουσῶ Theoc.5.146: aor. ἔλουσα Anacr.47, S.*Ant.*901, Ar.*Lys.*19 (Ep. λοῦσα Il.16.679, etc.):—Med. λούονται Hdt.4.75; inf. λούεσθαι Il.6.508, Hp.*Epid.*5.70; part. λουόμενοι Hdt.3.23: fut. λούσομαι Ar.*Nu.*837, Pl.*Phd.*116a: aor. ἐλουσάμην ibid.; Ep.

λούσαντο Il.10.576; Dor. part. λωσάμενος *Berl.Sitzb.*1927.157 (Cyrene):—**Pass.**, aor. ἐλούθην Hp.*Mul.*1.11, later ἐλούσθην Lyc.446: pf. λέλουμαι, 3 sg. λέλουται Ar.*Pax*868; part. λελουμένος Il.5.6, later λέλουσμαι Lxx *Ca.*5.12 (cod. Vat.).—Another old form of the pres. was **λόω**, whence 3 sg. λόει *Scol.*25, 2 sg. Med. κατα-λόει Ar.*Nu.*838 (prob.): 3 sg. impf. λόε Od.10.361, 3 pl. λόον *h.Ap.*120; 3 sg. subj. Med. λόηται *IG*12(5).569.5 (Ceos, iii B.C.); inf. λόεσθαι Hes.*Op.*749:—to λόω also belong the foll. contr. forms, 3 sg. impf. ἀπ-έλου Ar.*V.*118, ἐλοῦμεν Id.*Pl.*657; pres. Pass. λοῦται Semon.7.63, X.*Cyr.*1.3.11, A.*Fr.*366 (note); λοῦνται, ἐλοῦτο, Hdt.1.198, 3.125, ἐλούμην Men.363; 3 pl. ἐλοῦντο X.*Cyr.*4.5.4, etc. (Dor. λῶντο, λώοντο, Call.*Lav.Pall.*72, 73); inf. λοῦσθαι Od.6.216, Hdt.3.124, Ar.*Nu.*1044, Pl.*Lg.*942b; part. λούμενος Ar.*Av.*1623, *Pl.*658, X.*Mem.*3.13.3: the forms ἐλούομεν, λούομαι, ἐλουόμην, etc., are rejected by Phryn.165, but are freq. found in codd., Lys.1.9, etc.: the imper. form λοῦ (glossed by λοῦσαι, Hsch.), if correct, is contr. for λόε: (Cf. Lat. *lăvo* [fr. *lovo]):—*wash*, prop. *wash the body* (νίζω being used of the hands and feet, πλύνω of clothes), τὸν δ' Ἥβη λοῦσεν Il.5.905; δμῳαὶ λοῦσαν καὶ χρῖσαν ἐλαίῳ Od.4.49, cf. 6.210; λοῦσ' ἐν ποταμῷ *bathed* me, i. e. *let* me *bathe*, 7.296; τίς ἄν σφε λούσειεν; A.*Th.*739 (lyr.); λούσαντες τὸν νεκρόν Hdt.2.86, cf. E.*Tr.*1152, S.*Ant.*901; λ. τινὰ ἀπὸ τῶν πληγῶν *Act.Ap.*16.33; also λό' ἐκ τρίποδος μεγάλοιο *washed* me [with water] from a great cauldron, Od.10.361; ὀϊστοὺς λοῦσεν φοινίσσᾳ.. Ἄρης ψακάδι Simon.106: c. acc. cogn., λουτρὸν λοῦσαί τινα, v. λουτρόν I. 2. **b.** rarely of things, λ. τὰ δύο μέρη τοῦ βαλανείου *PFlor.*384.30 (V A.D.). **2.** metaph., *purify*, τινὰ ἐκ τῶν ἁμαρτιῶν v.l. in *Apoc.*1.5. **II.** Med. and Pass., *bathe*, λοῦσθαι ποταμοῖο ῥοῇσι Od.6.216: also c. gen., λελουμένος Ὠκεανοῖο (of a star just risen) *fresh from* Ocean's *bath*, Il.5.6; λοέσθαι ποταμοῖο *bathe* in the river, 6.508; so ἀπὸ [κρήνης] λουόμενοι Hdt.3.23: c. acc. cogn., τὸ λουτρὸν ἡ Ῥέα λοῦται Arr.*Tact.*33.4: abs., λούσαντο Od.4.48, cf. Hdt.5.20, etc.; λελουμένος *fresh-bathed, after bathing*, Id.1.126, Ar.*Lys.*1064 (lyr.); ἐν βαλανείῳ λελουμένος Pl.*R.*495e; λούεσθαι ἐν πηλῷ Arist.*HA*595a31; εἰς λουτρῶνας Ptol.Euerg.3 J. (dub.): metaph., τόξα.. αἵματι λουσάμενα Simon.143, cf. Call.*Del.*95; λελουμένος τῷ φόνῳ Luc.*DMeretr.*13.3. **2.** in strict pass. sense, λοῦσθαι ὑπὸ τοῦ Διός, i. e. *to be washed* by the rain from heaven, Hdt.3.124, 125. **3.** in strict med. sense, c. acc., λοέσσασθαι χρόα *wash one's* body, Hes.*Op.*522, *Th.*5; λούονται (v. l. λοῦνται) ὕδατι τὸ σῶμα Hdt.4.75.

⊛**λόφα**· μίσχος, τὸ περίττισμα, καὶ τὸ τῆς γῆς ἔπαρμα, Hsch.

**λοφάδεια**· .. αὐχήν, οἷον κατὰ τοῦ αὐχένος, ἢ χωρίον ὃ καλοῦσι Λίβυσσα, Hsch.: gloss on κατὰ λοφάδεια which is v.l. for καταλοφάδεια (q.v.) in Od.10.169.

**λοφᾰδίας** and **λοφίας**, ου, ὁ, *first dorsal vertebra and skin over it*, Poll.2.178.

**λοφ-άω**, *have a crest* (λόφος), of larks, Babr.88.4. **2.** *suffer from having too much crest*, Ar.*Pax* 1211 (Com. word formed like βραγχάω, λιθάω, etc.); but λοφᾷ· λόφου ἐπιθυμεῖ, Hsch. **-εῖον**, τό, *crest-case*, Ar.*Ach.*1109; *any case*, Id.*Nu.*751. **-η**, ἡ, = λόφος, *crest*, D.S.17.90. **-ηφόρος**, ον, *crested*, of a lark, Babr.88.8. **-ιά**, Ion. **-ιή**, ἡ, (λόφος) *mane* or *bristly ridge* on the back of animals, *mane* of horses, *bristly back* of boars and hyenas (cf. Arist.*PA*658a30, *HA* 498b30, 579b16), φρίξας εὖ λοφιήν, of a wild boar, Od.19.446; ὀρθὰς ἐν λοφιῇ φρίσσει τρίχας ἀμφί τε δειρήν Hes.*Sc.*391; ἀντὶ λόφου ἡ λοφιὴ κατέχρα *the mane* served for a plume, Hdt.7.70, cf. 2.71. **2.** *back-fin* of dolphins and similar fishes, D.S.3.41, *AP*9.222 (Antiphil.), Philostr.*Im.*1.19. **II.** = λόφος II, *ridge*, Lxx *Jo.*15.2, al., *AP*9.249 (Maec.). **-ίας**, ου, Ion. **-ίης**, ὁ, *having a back-fin*, φάγρος Numen. ap.Ath.7.322f. **II.** v. λοφαδίας. ⊛**-ίδιον** [φῐ], τό, Dim. of λόφος II, Ael.*NA*16.15. **-ίζω**, *raise the* λόφος, Zonar. **-ίτης**, ου, ὁ, *dweller on the hills*, epith. of Pan, formed like πολιήτης, *AP*6.79 (Agath.). **-ιον**, τό, Dim. of λόφος III. 1, *small crest*, Sch. Ar.*Ach.*1108: also, = κάλλαιον, Sch.D.T.p.196 H. **II.** = λοφεῖον, Hsch. **-ιος**· ἀκρώμιον, ἢ ἀκρώνιον, Id. (Cf. λοφορρῶγα.) **-ίς**· περικεφαλαίας θήκη, Id.

**λοφνία**, v. λοφνίς. **λοφνίδια**· λαμπάδια, Hsch.

**λοφνίς**, ίδος, ἡ, *torch made of vine bark*, in pl., *AP*11.20 (Antip. Thess.), Lyc.48:—also **λοφνία**, Clitarch.Gloss.ap.Ath.15.701a, cf. Ath.15.699d.

**λοφό-εις**, εσσα, εν, *crested*, Tryph.68. **II.** *hilly*, Nonn.*D.*2.37. **-ομαι**, Pass., *to be raised up, grow into a ridge* or *hill*, Eust. ad D.P.638 (of Mt. Taurus). **-ποιός**, ὁ, *crest-maker*, Ar.*Pax* 545. **-πωλέω**, *sell crests*, Id.*Fr.*812. ⊛**-ρρῶγα**· τὸν ἀπερρωγότα τοὺς ὤμους, Hsch.

⊛**λόφος**, ὁ, *back of the neck*; of a horse, *withers*, Il.23.508; ὑποζυγίων Dsc.4.185; of a man, *nape of the neck*, Il.10.573: metaph., ὑπὸ ζυγῷ λόφον ἔχειν have *the neck* under the yoke, i.e. obey patiently, S.*Ant.*292; cf. εὔλοφος II. **II.** *crest of a hill, ridge*, Od.11.596, 16.471, Hdt.2.124; so always in Pi., as *O.*8.17, *N.*5.46, and in Th.4.124, Pl.*Lg.*682b. **III.** *crest* of a helmet, κυνέην.. ἵππουριν, δεινὸν δὲ λόφος καθύπερθεν ἔνευεν Il.16.138, cf. 6.469, 15.537; λευκοὶ ἵππιοι λ. Alc.15.2; χρύσεος λ. Il.18.612, cf. 19.383; τρεῖς κατασκίους λ. σείει A.*Th.*384, cf. Ar.*Ach.*575, 586; λόφων ἐπένευον ἔθειραι Theoc.22.186; of Carian origin acc. to Hdt.1.171; λ. τε σείων Κάρικον Alc.22; λ. ὑακινθοβαφής, on a Persian helmet, X.*Cyr.*6.4.2; λ. τρίχινοι *PSI*5.533.7 (iii B.C.); Ar. jeers at the λόφοι of Lamachus, *Ach.*575, 586, 965 sq., 1074.—Rare in any of these senses in Att. Prose. **2.** after Hom., *crest* or *tuft* on the head of birds, whether of feathers, as the lark's crest, Simon.68, cf. Arist.*HA*617b20; or of flesh, as the cock's *comb*, Ar.*Eq.*496, *Av.*1366, Arist.*HA*486b13, Phld.*Rh.*2.188 S.: metaph., ῥήματα.. ὀφρῦς ἔχοντα καὶ λόφους Ar.*Ra.*925. **3.** of men, *tuft of hair* upon the crown, λόφους κείρεσθαι shave so as to leave tufts, Hdt.4.175; Χῖος λ. a *tonsure* in the middle of the head, Eust.1462.38. **4.** of large fishes, = λοφιά, Plu.2.978a.

⊛**λόφ-ουρος** (**λοφοῦρος** Arist.*HA*501a6 Bekker), ον, in neut. pl., *pack-animals*, as horse, ass, mule, Arist.*HA*491a1, *GA*755b18, *IG* 12(1).677.23 (Rhodes, iv/iii B.C.); also called ὑποζύγια, Arist.*Pr.* 895b12 (cf. 15); τὰ ζυγὰ τῶν λ. Thphr.*HP*5.7.6; opp. τὰ μηρυκάζοντα, ib.3.10.2, cf. 2.7.4, Arist.*Pr.* l. c. **-ώδης**, ες, *like a ridge*, ὄγκος Id.*Mete.*367a4; *on a ridge*, πόλις Procop.*Aed.*5.6. **-ωσις**, εως, ἡ, *being crested*, ἡ λ. ἡ τῶν ὀρνέων their *crests*, Ar.*Av.*291. **-ωσός**· ἐπισήμων, Hsch. (fort. **-ωτός**· ἐπισήμων).

**λοχ-αγενεῖς**· ἡγεμόνες, στρατηγοί, ταξιάρχαι, ἄρχοντες τῆς ἐνέδρας, οἱ συνάγοντες τοὺς στρατιώτας, Hsch. (Perh. λοχαγερεῖς, from ἀγείρω.) ⊛**-ᾱγέτας**, α, ὁ, Dor. for λοχηγέτης (which is not found), = λοχαγός, A.*Th.*42, E.*Ph.*[974], *Supp.*502. **-ᾱγέω**, Dor. (borrowed by Att.) for λοχηγέω, *lead a* λόχος or *company* (commonly of 100 men), X.*An* 6.1.30, *Mem.*3.1.5, Is.9.14: c. gen., λόχου λοχηγέων Hdt.9.53, cf. 21. **II.** *consist of* λοχαγοί, -γοῦν ζυγόν Ascl.*Tact.*10.13, 11.1. **-ᾱγία**, ἡ, Dor. for λοχηγία (also used in Att., v. λοχαγός) *rank* or *office of* λοχαγός, X.*An.*1.4.15, 3.1.30, Arist.*Pol.*1322b 4 (pl.). ⊛**-ᾱγός**, ὁ (λόχος, ἄγω), Dor. for λοχηγός, *leader of an armed band*, S.*Ant.*141 (anap.), Theophil.3. **II.** esp. *commander of a company* (100 men), *captain*, X.*An.*3.1.32, Ascl.*Tact.*2.2, *PPetr.* 3p.8 (iii B.C.), etc.; cf. ταξίαρχος. **2.** in the Spartan army, *commander of a* λόχος, Th.5.66, X.*Lac.*11.4, etc.; in the Persian army, *captain* of 24 men, Id.*Cyr.*6.3.21, etc.; = Lat. *centurio*, Plu.*Cam.*37; also, = *curio*, D.H.2.7.—The word, like κυναγός, was always used in the Dor. form by Attic authors. **-άδην** [ᾰ], Adv. *from ambush, treacherously*, Nic.*Th.*125. **-άζομαι**, = λοχάω, Emp.84.8, *AP*9.251 (Even.):—Act. in Hsch. ⊛**-αῖος**, α, ον, = λόχιος, λοχαίας ἐξ ἕδρας prob. l. in E.*Alc.*846, cf. Artem.5.73 (as v.l. for λοχείους [δίφρους]); λ. ἔρως *clandestine* love, *AP*15.9 (Cyrus). **II.** *bearing down*, like heavy ears of corn, λ. σῖτος Phot., cf. Hsch.; and so prob. in Thphr.*CP*3.21.5, 23.5: hence metaph., *richly-blooming*, Arat.1057. **-άω**, Ep. aor. subj. Med. -ήσομαι Od.4.670:—*lie in wait for, waylay*, Τηλέμαχον λοχόωντες 16.369, cf. 4.847; ἢ μέν μιν λοχόωσι 13.425; τὸν δὲ.. οἴκαδ' ἰόντα λοχῶσιν 14.181; αὐτὸν ἰόντα λοχήσομαι 4.670; ἐλόχησαν τὰς γυναῖκας Hdt.6.138; σε.. λοχῶσιν.. Ἐρινύες S.*Ant.*1075. **2.** abs., *lie in wait, ambush*, ὅθι σφίσιν εἶκε λοχῆσαι Il.18.520; λοχᾷ ἐπὶ δένδρεον ἀναβάς Hdt.4.22; πρὸς δόμοις λοχᾷς ἐμοῖς E.*El.*225; πρὸς τοῖσι βωμοῖς Pherecr.141: but mostly in aor. part. with another Verb, ὄφρα.. σὺν παῖδα κατακτείνειε λοχήσας Od.22.53; λοχήσαντες τὴν νέα εἷλον Hdt.6.87, cf. 37; λοχήσας.. πολλοὺς διέφθειρεν Th.1.65, cf. 3.94:—Med., λοχησάμενος Od.4.388, 463; ἐγγὺς ὁδοῖο λοχησάμενος 13.268; later also λοχώμενος, λελοχημένος, *in ambush*, A.R.1.991, 3.7. **3.** c. acc. loci, *occupy with an ambuscade*, ἐλόχησαν τὴν ἐν Πηδάσῳ ὁδὸν Hdt.5.121. **4.** metaph., οἷον λοχῶντες τὴν πρὸς Ῥωμαίους φιλίαν *laying a trap* of friendship for them, Plb.3.40.6.—Rare in good Att. (v. Th. ll. cc.), but freq. in late Prose, as Plb. l. c., D.H.2.55, al., Plu.*Ant.*46:—Pass., Epicur.*Nat.*15.22, J.*BJ*3.6.2:—Med. only in Ep.

**λοχ-εία**, ἡ, *child-birth, childbed*, E.*IT*382, Call.*Del.*251; τὴν λ. εἴληχε she presides over *child-birth*, Pl.*Tht.*149b: in pl., Id.*Plt.*268b; of flowers, ἐπ' εὐκάρποισι λοχείαις *AP*10.16 (Theaet.); f.l. in E.*IT*206 (lyr.) for λόχιαι. **II.** = λόχευμα I, *APl.*4.132 (Theodorid.). **III.** = ἀρτεμισία, Ps.-Dsc.3.113. ⊛**-εῖος**, α, ον, and ος, ον, = λόχιος (q.v.), λοχείους ἡμέρας days *of thanks for safe delivery*, Plu.2.377c; θυέτωσαν.. αἱ τὰ λ. ἐκπορευόμεναι καὶ ζωννύμεναι *Milet.*1(7).204b9; λοχεῖα (sc. χωρία) λιποῦσα having left *the place where she bore the child*, E.*IT*1241 (lyr.); cf. λοχαῖος: Subst. λοχεῖα, τά, = λοχεία I, Hp.*Mul.*1.29, Ruf.ap.Orib.5.3.16. **2.** Λοχεία, ἡ, title of Artemis, = Λοχία, *IG*9(2).141, 142 (Theb. Phthiot.), Orph.*H.*36.3, etc. **-εός**, ὁ, = λόχος, *ambush*, only in Hes.*Th.*178. **-ευμα**, ατος, τό, *that which is born, child*, E.*Ion* 921 (anap.), *Ph.*816 (lyr.), *BCH*26.187 (Syria). **II.** in pl., = λοχεία, *child-birth*, E.*El.*1124: metaph., κάλυκος ἐν λοχεύμασιν in *the bursting* of the bud, A.*Ag.*1392. ⊛**-εύτρια**, ἡ, *woman in childbed*, metaph. as Adj., ἡ τοῦ ψεύδους λ. ποίησις Anon.ap. Suid. s. v. Ἀδάμ. **II.** *midwife*, Sch.D Il.16.187. ⊛**-εύω**, (λόχος II) *bring forth, bear*, παῖδα *h.Merc.*230, cf. Orph.*A.*184, etc.; γαστὴρ ἥ σ' ἐλόχευσε *AP*9.126; of the father, *beget*, Orph.*A.*136, cf. 13; of both parents, ib.159; metaph., *produce*, φλογὸς ἄσθμα Coluth.179:—Med., -ομένην σε.. ἔαρ ὕμνων *AP*7.12. **2.** of the midwife, *bring to the birth, deliver*, τινα E.*Ion* 948, 1596, cf. *El.*1129:—hence in Pass., *to be brought to bed, be in labour*, ἔνθ' ἐλοχεύθην Id.*Tr.*602 (lyr.); λοχευθεῖσ' ἀστραπηφόρῳ πυρί, of Semele, Id.*Ba.*3, cf. Plu.*Pel.*16: c. gen., λοχευθείσης αὐτοῦ τῆς μητρός Id.*Cic.*2. **3.** of a man, *practise couvade*, D.S.5.14. **II.** Med., in sense of Act., of the mother, E.*Ion* 921 (anap.), Arist.*HA*616a34, Call.*Del.*326; also of the birthplace, *APl.*4.295. **III.** Pass., of the child, *to be born*, S.*OC*1322; Τιτᾶνι λοχευθεῖσαν by the obstetric art of the Titan, E.*Ion* 455 (lyr.). **2.** metaph., generally, *lie embedded*, ἐν τεύχλοισι λ. Ar.*Pax* 1014 (anap.). ⊛**-ή**, ἡ, = λόχμη, *Supp.Epigr.*2.544 (Mylasa).

**λοχηγέω, λοχηγός**, ὁ, Ion. for λοχαγ-.

**λόχ-ησις**, εως, ἡ, *waylaying, entrapping*, Suid. **-ητής**, v. λοχίτης II. **-ητικός**, ή, όν, *lying in wait, treacherous*, Adam.2.2.

**λόχια**, τά, and **Λοχία**, ἡ, v. λόχιος.

**λοχιᾷ**· κρυφαία, γεννᾷ, αὔξει, καὶ ἄρτος τῇ Ἀρτέμιδι γενόμενος, καὶ ἁδροὺς ἀστάχυας ἔχουσα, Hsch. **λοχιάδες**· αἱ ὗλαι, Id.

⊛ **λοχίδιον** (-ιν Pap.), τό, dub. sens. in *POxy.*1290.8 (v A.D.).

⊛ **λοχίζω**, = λοχάω, *lie in wait for*:—Pass., λοχισθέντες διεφθάρησαν they were cut to pieces by *falling into an ambuscade*, Th.5.115, cf. D.C.41.51. 2. *place in ambush*, λοχίζει ἐς ὁδὸν κοίλην ὁπλίτας Th. 3.107; λ. ἐν τόπῳ D.H.2.55; c. dat. loci, Id.3.64 (nisi leg. (ἐν) χωρίοις); λοχίσαντος is prob. l. in Plu.*Oth.*7. 3. *beset with an ambuscade*, λελοχισμένον χωρίον D.H.1.79. II. *distribute men in companies* (λόχοι), and so, *put them in order of battle*, Hdt.1.103, Aen. Tact.1.5, Plu.*Sull.*27:—Pass., *to be so distributed*, Agatharch.*Fr. Hist.*17 J., D.H.2.14, etc. III. λοχίζει· ἐπιβουλεύεται, Hsch.

**λοχικός**, ή, όν, = sq., λ. κάθαρσις dub. in Steph.*in Hp.*1.201 D. (λοχ- codd.).

⊛ **λόχιος**, α, ον, *of* or *belonging to child-birth*, λ. νοσήματα *childbed*, E. *El.*656; ὠδίνων λοχίαις ἀνάγκαισι Id.*Ba.*89 (lyr.), cf. *Ion* 452 (lyr.); λόχιαι.. Μοῖραι prob. in Id.*IT*206 (lyr.); λοχίης ἐκ νηδύος A.R.4.706. 2. λοχίη, = Lat. *foeta* or *puerpera*, Opp.*C.*3.292. b. λόχιαι, αἱ, = λοχεῖαι, Euph.9.11. II. Λοχία, ἡ, epith. of Artemis, E.*IT*1097, *Supp.*958 (both lyr.), cf. *SIG*1219.33 (Gambreum, iii B.C.):—also Λοχεία, q.v. III. λόχια, τά, *discharge after child-birth*, Hp.*Nat. Puer.*18, Arist.*HA*573ᵃ9 (ἡ λοχίη κάθαρσις Hp.*Mul.*1.29, al.). 2. *child-birth*, *AP*7.375 (Antiphil.), 9.311 (Phil.).

⊛ **λοχ-ισμός**, ὁ, *placing in ambush*, Plu.*Phil.*13 (pl.). **-ίτης** [ῑ], ου, ὁ, *one of the same* λόχος or *company*, *fellow-soldier*, *comrade*, A.*Ag.* 1650, X.*Cyr.*2.2.7, etc.; ξὺν λοχίταις εἴτε καὶ μονοστιβῆ; with *attendants* or alone? A.*Ch.*768; πολλοὺς ἔχων ἄνδρας λοχίτας S.*OT*751:—fem. **λοχῖτις** ἐκκλησία, = Lat. *comitia centuriata*, D.H.4.20, App.*BC* 3.30, etc. II. *one who lies in wait*, Hsch., Suid. (leg. λοχητής).

**λοχμ-άζω**, *to be downy*, ἄρτι παρειὰ(ν) λοχμάζων Pisand.ap.Sch.Tl. 4.147. **-αῖος**, α, ον, *of the coppice*, Μοῦσα λ., of the nightingale, Ar. *Av.*737 (lyr.). **-η**, ἡ, (λέχομαι) *thicket*, *copse*, esp. as the *lair* of wild beasts, ἐν λόχμῃ πυκινῇ κατέκειτο μέγας σῦς Od.19.439; λόχμας ὕπο κυανέας Pi.*O.*6.40, cf. *P.*4.244; ἐχῖνος ὥς τις ἐν λόχμῃ κεῖσαι πεσών S.*Ichn.*121: in pl., λόχμαισι δοκεύσαις lying in wait *in the coppice*, Pi. *O.*10(11).30; μασχάλαι λόχμης δασύτεραι Ar.*Ec.*61, cf. *Lys.*800: prov., μία λ. δύο ἐριθάκους οὐ τρέφει Sch.Ar.*V.*922: also in Prose, Arist.*HA*615ᵃ17, Ael.*NA*13.14, Creophyl.ap.Ath.8.361d; λόχμη τῶν θηρίων Jul.*Mis.*338c. **-ιος**, ον, = λοχμαῖος, τράγος *AP* 6.32 (Agath.); τὰ λόχμια, = λόχμη, Ps.-Luc.*Philopatr.*10 (δόχμια codd.). **-ίς**, gloss on λοχμαία, Sch.Ar.*Av.*738. **-ώδης**, ες, *overgrown with bushes*, *bushy*, ὁδὸς Th.3.107: Sup., D.C.40.2. II. *growing in clumps* or *beds*, [δόναξ] Thphr.*HP*4.11.11 (Sup.); τὰ λ., a class of water plants, as reeds, rushes, sedges, etc., ib.4.8.1.

**λόχονδε**, Adv., v. λόχος I. 2.

**λοχός**, ἡ, Hellenistic form for λεχώ, Dsc.3.4 (in dat. pl. λοχοῖς), Moer.p.247 P. (λόχος codd.); cf. λοχώ.

**λόχος**, ὁ, (λέχομαι): I. *ambush*, i.e. 1. *place for lying in wait*, εἰ γὰρ νῦν παρὰ νηυσὶ λεγοίμεθα πάντες ἄριστοι ἐς λ. Il.13.277; ἐκ λ. ἀμπήδησε 11.379; κοῖλος λ., of the wooden horse, Od.4.277, 8.515; ξεστὸς λ. E. *Tr.*534 (lyr.); ὠδῖνων λ. Lyc.342; ξύλινος λ., of the enemy's ships, Orac. ap.Hdt.3.57. 2. *ambuscade*, ἑζέσθαι λόχον ἀνδρῶν take up one's post in *ambush*, Il.13.285; λόχον εἶσαι place *an ambush*, 4.392, Od.4.531; εἷσε δέ μιν κρύψασα λόχῳ Hes.*Th.*174; λόχον ἀρτύνειν Od.14.469; λόχονδ' ἰέναι Il.1.227; ὁππότε κρίνοιμι λόχονδε ἄνδρας ἀριστῆας Od.14. 217; φυτευέ οἱ θάνατον ἐκ λόχου Pi.*N.*4.60; δεινοῖς κρυπτομένα λόχοις Ἐρινὺς S.*El.*490 (lyr.); τὸν εὔαγρον τελειῶσαι λ. Id.*OC*1089 (lyr.). b. c. gen. objecti, λόχος θείοιο γέροντος *the way to ambush* him, Od.4. 395. 3. *the men that form the ambush*, μὴ λ. εἰσέλθῃσι πόλιν Il.8. 522, cf. E.*Andr.*1114, etc. b. *any armed band*, *body of troops* (of foot, rarely of horse, Arr.*Alan.*20), Od.20.49; also in Trag., A.*Th.*56, 460, S.*OC*1371, etc.: metaph., παρθένων ἱκέσιος λ. A.*Th.*111 (lyr.); θαυμαστὸς λ. γυναικῶν, of the Furies, Id.*Eu.*46, cf. 1026; ἐλάφων κεραὸς λ. *AP*9.244 (Apollonid.); ἐμῶν προγόνων λ. *OGI*383.48 (Nemrud Dagh, i B.C.). c. in historical writers, mostly, *a company*, reckoned at 24 men in X.*Cyr.*6.3.21, but at 100 in Id.*An.*3.4.21, 4.8.15; in the Spartan army, *the fourth* or *fifth part of a* μόρα (q.v.), Hdt.9.53, 57, cf. Th.5.68, Arist.*Fr.*541, etc.; ὁ Πιτανάτης λ. Th.1.20; ὁ ἱερὸς λ. the sacred *company* at Thebes, Din.1.73, Plu.*Pel.*18; also at Carthage, D.S.16.80, 20.10; later λ., = 16 men, Ascl.*Tact.*2.7, Ael.*Tact.*4.3, Arr.*Tact.*5.5; but of light-armed, 8 men, Ascl. l. c., Arr.*Tact.*14. 2. d. *any body of people united* for civil purposes, X.*Hier.*9.5, Arist. *Pol.*1309ᵃ12; αἱ ἐν λόχοις συντέλειαι (where λόχοι seems to represent συμμορίαι) Catal.ap.D.18.106. e. = Lat. *centuria*, D.H.4.16, App. *BC*1.59, etc. f. = Lat. *curia*, D.H.2.7. II. *child-birth*, A.*Ag.* 137 (lyr.): pl., Id.*Supp.*677 (lyr.). III. dub. sens. in *SIG*1002.8 (Milet., v/iv B.C.).

**λοχώ**, ἡ, = λεχώ, *Sammelb.*6652.3 (where λοχοῦς is used as nom. sg.); so perh. λοχῷ is to be read rather than λόχῳ ib.6227: nom. sg. λοχώς is v.l. in Lxx *Ep.Je.*28; cf. λοχός.

**λύα**, v. λύη. **λυάζει**· φλυαρεῖ, μωρολογεῖ, στασιάζει, Hsch.

⊛ **Λυαῖος**, α, ὁ, ἡ, (λύω) *loosener* or *deliverer*, epith. of the Great Mother, κακῶν λυαία Tim.*Pers.*132; of Dionysus (cf. Lat. *Lyaeus*), *Anacreont.*11.9, al., *IG*5(2).287 (Mantinea, i/ii A.D.).

**λυάω**, (λύη) = στασιάζω, ἀλλήλοις δ' ἐλύησαν Call.*Aet.Oxy.*2080. 76, cf. Choerob.*in Theod.*2.162 H.:—Med., λυᾶται Hsch.

**λυβάζειν**· λοιδορεῖν, Hsch.

**λύβερνος**, ὁ, = λιβυρνός, *war-galley*, *BGU*709.2 (ii A.D.).

**λύγαια**· τὰ περὶ ταῖς χερσὶ ψέλλια, Hsch.

**λυγαῖος**, α, ον, (λύγη) *shadowy*, *murky*, *gloomy*, νέφος S.*Fr.*525, E. *Heracl.*855; νυκτὸς ὄμμα λυγαίας Id.*IT*110, cf. A.R.2.1120; ἐσθὴς Lyc.973; εἱρκτή Id.351; θάλαμος *IG*12(8).92.10 (Imbros, ii/i B.C.). Adv. -αίως Eust.1756.28, Hsch. (-γαῶς cod.).

**λύγαος**, f.l. for λύγδος, Hsch.

**λυγγανόμενον**· λύζοντα ἐν τῷ κλαίειν, Hsch.; cf. λυγκαίνω.

**λύγγιος**, α, ον, *of a lynx*, δέρμα *Edict.Diocl.* in *IG*5(1).1115 *A* ii 65 (Geronthrae).

⊛ **λυγγούριον**, τό (derived by the ancients from λύγξ, οὖρον, and supposed to be the coagulated urine of the lynx, Dsc.2.81, Plu.2.962f, S.E.*P.*1.119), a kind of *amber* (glossed by ἤλεκτρον, Hsch., cf. Str. 4.6.2), Thphr.*Lap.*28, *IG*11(2).161 *B*49 (Delos, iii B.C.), al., 2².1534. 100, Str.4.5.3 (pl.):—also written **λυγκούριον**, **λιγκούριον**, and **λιγγούριον** in codd.; **λογγούριον** Aët.2.35.

⊛ **λυγγώδης**, ες, *attended with hiccup*, πυρετοί Hp.*Fract.*11, cf. *Acut.* (*Sp.*)30.

**λύγδη**, = λεύκη, *white poplar*, Hsch.

**λύγδην**, Adv., (λύζω) *with sobs*, κλάειν S.*OC*1621, cf. *AP*15.28.

**λυγδ-ίνεος** [ῐ], α, ον, = sq. 2, δειρή *AP*5.47 (Rufin.). ⊛ **-ῐνος**, η, ον, *of white marble*, βωμός *Africa Italiana* 1.325 (Cyrene, i B.C.), cf. *AP*6.209 (Antip. Thess.), Babr.30.1; λυγδίνη λίθος Philostr.*Im. Prooem.* 2. *marble-white*, λ. κώνια μαστῶν *AP*5.12 (Phld.); τράχηλος *Anacreont.*15.27. **-ος**, ἡ, *white marble*, *Peripl.M.Rubr.*24; λύγδου λειότερον *AP*5.27 (Rufin.); οἷά τε λύγδου γλυπτήν ib.193 (Posidipp. or Asclep.); ἡ Παρία λ. D.S.2.52, cf. Mart.6.13, 42.

**λῠγέα**, ἡ, = λύγος, Eust.834.37.

**λύγειος**, = λυγαῖος, Tz.*H.*5.725.

**λύγη** [ῠ], ἡ, *twilight*, App.*Ill.*25, cf. Suid., Eust.689.18.

**λῠγίζομαι**, Pass., (λύγη) *to be hidden*, λυγίσασθαι· κρυβῆναι, Theognost.*Can.* 2.

**λῠγ-ίζω**, Dor. fut. inf. λυγιξεῖν Theoc.1.97: (λύγος):—*bend* or *twist as one does a withe*, πλευρὰν λυγίσαντος ὑπὸ ῥώμης, of a dancer, Ar.*V.*1487; νεῦρα λελυγισμένα *twisted*, Hp.*Mochl.*4; τὰ λυγισθέντα τῶν ἄρθρων *twisted* joints, Gal.*Protr.*11; λυγίζειν ἀλλήλους, of wrestlers, Luc.*Anach.*1, cf. Philostr.*Im.*2.32: metaph., λ. μέλος Ael.*NA*2.11; cf. λύγισμα, λυγισμός. 2. *throw*, *master*, Ἔρωτα Theoc. l. c.:—Pass., *to be thrown* or *mastered*, Id.1.98; οὐδ' ἐλυγίχθη τὰν ψυχάν Id. 23.54. II. Pass., *bend* or *twist oneself like a withe*, *bend aside*, so as to avoid a blow, λυγίζεται καὶ συστρέφει τὸν αὐχένα Eup.339, cf. Pl. *R.*405c; στρέφου λυγίζου τε μύθοις S.*Ichn.*362 (lyr.); ἐλυγίσθησαν κατὰ τροχῶν Phalar.*Ep.*147.3; also of dancers, Luc.*Salt.*77, etc.; ὑπ' ὀρχησμῶν λελυγισμένον ἴχνος *AP*6.33 (Maec.): metaph., in pf. part. λελυγισμένος, *effeminate*, Anon.ap.Suid. s. v. ἁβρός; ἐπέων κόσμος λελ. *AP*11.20 (Antip. Thess.). 2. *turn*, *play*, as a joint in the socket, ἄρθρον ᾗ λυγίζεται S.*Tr.*779. **-ῐνος**, η, ον, *of agnus castus*, στέφανος λ. Heph.ap.Ath.15.673e; cf. λύγος. **-ιον**, τό, *switch*, Sch.D.T. p.195 H. **-ιος**, α, ον, = διωλύγιος, λ. τι ἀνακωκύσασα v.l. in Hld. 6.5. **-ισμα**, ατος, τό, *sprain*, Dsc.5.117; λυγίσμασι· συγκάμμασι, Hsch. **-ισμός**, ὁ, *a bending*, *twisting*, like the willow, hence of wrestlers, Luc.*Anach.*24, cj. in Philostr.*Im.*2.6 (λογ- codd.); of dancers, -ισμοὺς ὀρχεῖσθαι Id.*VA*4.21; γονάτων -ισμοί *PMich.* in *Class. Phil.*22.10: metaph., of *the windings and twistings* of a sophist, Ar. *Ra.*775 (pl.). **-ιστικός**, ή, όν, *readily twisting*, *supple*, of dancers, Poll.4.97.

**λυγκαίνω**, *sob*, Suid. s. v. ἀναλύζουσα. **λυγκαστήσει**· αὔξει παραπλησίως, ἢ λυγκάσαι, ῥεῦσαι, Hsch. (fort. ..ἢ λύγκας ἀγρεῦσαι).

⊛ **λύγκειος**, α, ον, (Λυγκεύς) *of Lynceus*, βλέμμα *App.Anth.*3.79 (Posidipp.).

**λυγκεύς**, έως, ὁ, an eye-salve, Gal.12.778, Paul.Aeg.7.16.

**λυγκίον**, τό, Dim. of λύγξ (A), Callix.2.

**λυγκούριον**, v. λυγγούριον.

**λυγμ-ός**, ὁ, (λύζω) = λύγξ (B), Hp.*Aph.*5.3, Arist.*Pr.*961ᵇ9, 963ᵃ 38 (pl.), Nic.*Th.*434 (pl.), J.*BJ*6.2.2. II. = ὀλολυγμός, Suid.; = θρῆνος, Hsch. **-ώδης**, ες, = λυγγώδης, Hp.*Art.*86.

⊛ **λύγξ** (A), ὁ, ἡ, gen. λυγκός (λύγγα in E.*Fr.*863 is perh. f.l. for λύγκα, but cf. λύγγιος):—*lynx*, *Felis lynx*, *h.Hom.*19.24; βαλιαὶ λύγκες E.*Alc.*579 (lyr.), cf. Arist.*HA*500ᵇ15, Thphr.*Fr.*175, etc. II. *caracal*, *Felis caracal*, Ael.*NA*14.6, Opp.*C.*3.85, etc. (cf. λυγγούριον). (OHG. *luhs*, Germ. *luchs*, Lith. *lūšis*.)

**λύγξ** (B), ἡ, gen. λυγγός, (λύζω) *hiccup*, Hp.*Aph.*5.58, al., Pl.*Smp.* 185d; λ. κενή an ineffectual *retching*, Th.2.49, cf. Aret.*CA*2.4: masc. in pl., τοῖς λυγξί Gal.1.356, but fem. in Id.15.846. II. λύγγα θηρατηρίαν dub. l. in S.*Fr.*474.1.

**λῠγό-δεσμος**, η, ον, *bound with willow-twigs*, epith. of Artemis, Paus.3.16.11. **-ειδής**, ές, *like agnus castus*, Dsc.4.144. **-πλόκος**, ον, *viminarius*, *Gloss.*

**λύγος** [ῠ], ἡ, also ὁ, Longus 3.27 codd.:— = ἄγνος, *agnus castus*, *Vitex Agnus-castus*, *withy*: in pl., *its twigs* or *withes*, τοὺς [the rams] συνέεργον ἐϋστρεφέεσσι λύγοισι Od.9.427, cf. 10.166, E.*Cyc.*225, etc.; in δίδη μόσχοισι λύγοισι Il.11.105, λύγοισι is the specific word added to the generic μόσχοισι (cf. σῦς κάπρος, ἴρηξ κίρκος, etc.): in late Prose, Arr.*Fr.*153 J.; used for wreaths, στεφανοῦται λύγῳ Anacr.41; cf. λύγινος. II. λυγῶς (sic cod., fort. λυγός) *screw-press* used by carpenters, Hsch. (but perh. λυγῶ⟨δε⟩ς).

**λῠγοτευχής**, ές, *made of withes*, κύρτος *AP*9.562 (Crin.).

**λῠγόω**, *tie fast*, ἱμάντι κατ' αὐχένος ἅμμα *AP*9.150 (Antip.); ἀλυκτοπέδῃσι λυγωθείς *APl.*1.15. II. *bend*, *overpower*, Δανάας ἐλύγωσεν ὅδε φρένα *AP*5.216 (Paul. Sil.).

**λυγροπαθής**, ές, *suffering mournfully*, βίοτος *IG*12(8).38.15 (Lemnos).

**λυγρός**, ά, όν, *baneful*, *mournful*, ὄλεθρος, γῆρας, Il.10.174, Od.24.

250, etc.; ἄλγεα Il.13.346; ἀνδροκτασίης ὕπο λυγρῆς 23.86; λ. δέος Archil.74.4; ὀνίαν..λύγραν (gen. pl.) Sapph.*Supp.*1.10; νεῖκος Pi.*N.*8.25; μάχαι B.10.68; πένθος A.*Ch.*17; ὀργά ib.835 (lyr.); πόνοι, νόσος, S.*OT*184 (lyr.), *Ph.*1424, etc.; λυγρά *bane, misery*, Il.24.531, Od.14.226; *ruin*, 3.303; ἔξοχα λυγρὰ ἰδυῖα *versed above all in banes*, 11.432, cf. Hes.*Th.*313; λυγρὰ νοεῦντες Id.*Op.*261. 2. with an act. force, σήματα λ. Il.6.168; φάρμακα λυγρά, opp. ἐσθλά, *baneful* drugs, Od.4.230, 10.236; γαστὴρ λυγρή the stomach *that cause of bane*, 17.473. 3. λ. εἵματα *sorry* garments, 16.457. II. of persons, *baneful, mischievous*, 9.454: more freq., *sorry*, i.e. *weak, cowardly*, Il.13.119,237, Od.18.107, A.*Fr.*361, S.*Ant.*823 (Sup., lyr.). III. Adv. -ρῶς *sorely*, λυγρῶς πεπληγυῖα Il.5.763. [ῠ by nature, Pi.*N.*8.25, Mosch.4.73, etc.]

**λῠγώδης**, ες, (λύγος) *like a willow*, ῥάβδοι Dsc.4.80; φυτά Eust.834.32.

**Λῡδία**, Ion. -ίη, ἡ, *Lydia*, Hdt.1.79, etc.:—hence **Λῡδιακά**, τά, *a history of Lydia*, by Xanthus, Ath.12.515e: **Λῡδικὴ ἀρχή** *Lydian empire*, Hdt.1.72.

**Λῡδίζω**, *speak Lydian*, Hippon.in *PSI*9.1089.1. II. *play the Lydian*, of Magnes, in reference to his play called Λυδοί, Ar.*Eq.*523; Λυδίζειν τὴν στολήν Philostr.*VA*5.32:—in Phot. and Suid. also **Λυδιάζω**.

**Λύδιος** [ῡ], α, ον, *of Lydia, Lydian*, αὐλοί Pi.*O.*5.19; σύκινα *PCair.Zen.*33.12 (iii B.C.); also ος, ον Luc.*VH*1.8, *Harm.*1: prov., παρὰ τὸ Λύδιον ἅρμα θέειν *to be left far behind*, Diogenian.6.28, Greg.Cypr.2.99, cf. Pi.*Fr.*206: Λυδία λίθος, ἡ, a siliceous stone used to assay gold, and first discovered in Lydia, elsewhere βάσανος, Λυδία γὰρ λίθος μανύει χρυσόν B.*Fr.*10; also Λ. πέτρη Theoc.12.36; and ἡ Λ. Anon. in *An.Ox.*3.216; Λ. λίθος, of the magnet, S.*Fr.*800: Λύδιον, τό, a kind of vase, Λ. μέζω *AJA*31.349.

**Λῡδιστί** [ῐ], Adv. *after the Lydian fashion*, Cratin.256; in Music, *in the Lydian mode*, Pl.*La.*188d; ἡ Λ. ἁρμονία Id.*R.*398e, cf. Arist.*Pol.*1342b32, Plu.2.1134b.

**λῡδίων**, ωνος, ὁ, Lat. *ludio, ludius*, D.H.2.71; cf. Λυδός III.

**Λῡδοπᾰθής**, ές, *voluptuous as a Lydian*, Anacr.155.

**Λῡδός**, ὁ, *a Lydian*, Alc.*Supp.*22.1, Sapph.*Supp.*5.19, Pi.*O.*1.24, Hdt.1.10, etc.: also as Adj. for Λύδιος, Λύδαισιν ἐμπρέπεται γυναίκεσσιν Sapph.*Supp.*25.6; Λυδὴ κερκίς, Λ. πηκτίς, S.*Fr.*45, 412. II. = λυδίων, App.*Pun.*66. III. f.l. for αὐλός, D.H.1.33.

⊛ **λύζω**, aor. ἔλυγξα Gal.15.846:—*to have the hiccup*, Hp.*Morb.*3.10. II. *sob violently*, from fear or cold, οἱ φοβούμενοι καὶ οἱ ῥιγοῦντες λύζουσιν Arist.*Pr.*962b33; λ. καὶ δακρύει Ar.*Ach.*690; γοερὸν λύζων *AP*7.218.12 (Antip. Sid.). (Cf. Ir. *slucim*, Welsh *llyncu*, MHG. *slucken* 'swallow'.)

**λύη** [ῠ], ἡ, (λύω) *dissolution, separation*: hence, *faction, sedition*, = στάσις, Hdn.Gr.1.306; Aeol., Dor. **λύα**, Alc.*Supp.*23.10, 5.11 (pl.), Pi.*N.*9.14.

**λυθάζω**, gloss on λύζω, Hsch. **λύθιος**· ἠθμός (Heraclea), Id.

⊛ **λύθρ-ον**, τό, or **-ος**, ὁ, *defilement from blood, gore*, Hom., only in dat., λύθρῳ..παλάσσετο χεῖρας Il.11.169, 20.503; αἵματι καὶ λύθρῳ πεπαλαγμένος 6.268, Od.22.402: masc. λύθρος *AP*9.323 (Antip.), Ph. ap.Gal.13.268, Poll.1.46, M.Ant.3.3, Jul.*Or.*2.71a: the neut. λύθρον only in *APl.*4.112: in Medic., of *the impure blood* in a woman's womb, Plu.2.496b, 997a: pl., ἐκ μητρῴων λύθρων Hp.*Ep.*17; of *blood* in general, M.Ant.2.2; of the *venom* of the hydra, Euph.50.2. [ῠ by nature, *APl.* l.c., *Epigr.Gr.*314 (Smyrna).] **-όω**, misspelling of λυτρόω, *redeem* a pledge, *CPR*12.17 (i A.D., Pass.). **-ώδης**, ες, *defiled with gore*, Lxx *Wi.*11.6, *AP*9.258 (Antiphan. Megalop.).

**λῠκάβας** [κᾰ], αντος, ὁ, *year*, τοῦδ' αὐτοῦ λυκάβαντος ἐλεύσεται ἐνθάδ' Ὀδυσσεύς within this very *year*, Od.14.161, 19.306 (but '*this very month*' acc. to D.Chr.7.84; perh. *day*, if Od.14.161–2 are spurious); εἶαρ..ὅλῳ λ. παρείη Bion *Fr.*15.15; αὖθι μένων λυκάβαντα *for a year*, A.R.1.198; but acc. λυκάβαν *IG*12(2).129 (Mytilene, late):—the word is freq. in metr. epitaphs, ib.4.622 (Argos), *Epigr.Gr.*231 (Chios), 228 (Ephesus): hence II. **λῠκᾰβαντίδες** ὧραι, αἱ, the hours *that make up the year*, *AP*5.12 (Phld.). (Arc. word, = ἐνιαυτός, acc. to *AB*1095.)

**λῠκάγχη**, ἡ, (λύκος) = κυνάγχη, Cael.Aur.*CP*3.1.

**Λύκαια**, τά, v. Λυκαῖος III.

**λύκαινα** [ῠ], ἡ, fem. of λύκος, *she-wolf*, Arist.*HA*580a18, Babr.16.8, Plu.*Rom.*2; of Artemis in Mithraism, Porph.*Abst.*4.16:—Dim. **λυκαίνιον**, τό, of a woman, Poll.4.150.

**λῠκαινόμορφος**, ον, *she-wolf-shaped*, Lyc.481.

**Λῠκαιονίκης** [νῑ], ου, ὁ, *victor at the* Λύκαια, *IG*5(2).549.

**Λῠκαῖος**, α, ον, *Lycaean, Arcadian*, epith. of Zeus, Pi.*O.*9.96, Hdt.4.203, etc.; τὸ τοῦ Λ. Διὸς ἱερὸν κατὰ τὸ Λ. ὄρος Str.8.8.2. II. **Λύκαιον**, τό, *his temple*, Plu.2.300a; Λ. σήκωμα E.*El.*1274. 2. *Mons Lycaeus* in Arcadia, Pi.*Fr.*100, Theoc.1.123. III. **Λύκαια** (sc. ἱερά), τά, *festival of Lycaean Zeus*, τὰ Λ. θῦσαι X.*An.*1.2.10, cf. *IG*2².993, *SIG*82 (iv B.C.), etc.; also, = Lat. *Lupercalia* (from λύκος, Lat. *lupus*), D.H.1.80, Plu.*Ant.*12.

**λῠκαιχλίας**· ὁ λυκόβροτος, Hsch. (fort. λυκόβρωτος, cf. αἶκλον).

**Λῠκαμβὶς** ἀρχή, phrase used of the Polemarch by Cratin.130.

**λῠκάνθρωπ-ος**, ὁ and ἡ, *were-wolf* or *man-wolf*, Marc.Sid. (cf. Suid. s.h.v.) ap.Gal.19.719, Aët.6.11, Paul.Aeg.3.16:—hence **-ία**, ἡ, a kind of madness, *in which the patient had the ravenous appetite and other qualities of a wolf*, Gal. l.c., Orib.*Syn.*8.9.

**Λῠκᾱονία**, ἡ, district in the S. of Asia Minor, X.*An.*1.2.19, etc.:—the people were **Λυκάονες**, οἱ, ib.3.2.23, Arist.*Fr.*151. Adv. **-ιστί**, *in Lycaonian*, *Act.Ap.*14.11.

**λῠκαυγής**, ές, (*λύκη) *of* or *at the grey-twilight*, Heraclit.*All.*7; τὸ λ. *early dawn*, Luc.*VH*2.12, Agath.4.20, etc.

**λύκαψος** [ῠ], ὁ, *viper's herb, Echium italicum*, Nic.*Th.*840; **λυκαψός** in Dsc.4.26 (with vv. ll.), Paul.Aeg.7.3:—also **λυκοψίς**, ίδος, ἡ, Gal.11.811.

**λῠκ-άων**, ονος, ὁ, = λυκάνθρωπος, Paul.Aeg.3.16. **-έη** (sc. δορά), ἡ, *wolf's-skin*, Il.10.459, Hsch.:—contr. **λυκῆ** App.*Hisp.*48, Poll.5.16. **-εία**, ἡ, *helmet of wolf-skin*, Plb.6.22.3. **-εῖον**· φοβερόν, Hsch.

⊛ **Λύκειον** [ῠ], τό, *the Lyceum*, a gymnasium at Athens, named after the neighbouring temple of Apollo Λύκειος, Ar.*Pax*356, X.*HG*1.1.33: a resort of Socrates, Pl.*Euthphr.*2a, *Euthd.*271a; here Aristotle used to discourse, whence his disciples were called Λύκειοι Περιπατητικοί, Elias *in Cat.*112.31. II. λύκειον, v. λύκιον I. 2.

**λύκειος** [ῠ], ον, S.*El.*7, E.*Rh.*208 (but λυκεία (q.v.) as Subst. in Plb.):—*of* or *belonging to a wolf*, δορά E. l.c., etc. II. Λύκειος (written **Λύκηος** *Milet.*1(7) No.282 (i B.C.)), epith. of Apollo, either as λυκοκτόνος (q.v.), or as *the Lycian god* (v. Λυκηγενής, Λύκιος), or (fr. *λύκη) as *the god of light*: Λύκει' Ἄπολλον A.*Ag.*1257; εὐμενὴς δ' ὁ Λ. ἔστω Id.*Supp.*686 (lyr.); in Id.*Th.*145 (lyr.) there is a play upon the doubtful meanings, Λύκει' ἄναξ, λύκειος γενοῦ στρατῷ δαΐῳ, *Lycean* lord, be *a very wolf* to the enemy; so τοῦ λυκοκτόνου θεοῦ ἀγορὰ Λύκειος (this ἀγορά being *an open place* in Argos near the temple of Apollo Λύκειος) S. l.c.; cf. Λύκειον. III. epith. of Pan, *IG*5(2).93 (Tegea). IV. Λύκειος, ὁ (sc. μήν), a month at Epidaurus Limera, ib.(1).932; Λύκεος, at Lamia (Thess.), ib.9(2).75.18, etc.

**λῠκῆ**, ἡ, contr. for λυκέη.

***λύκη** [ῠ], ἡ, *morning twilight*, only in Macr.*Sat.*1.17.37, as etym. of λυκόφως, ἀμφιλύκη; cf. λυκαυγής, λυκοειδής II, ἀμφιλύκη.

**Λῠκηγενής**, ές, epith. of Apollo, commonly expld. *Lycian-born*, i.e. at Patara, Il.4.101,119, cf. Heraclit.*All.*7, and v. λύκειος.

**λῠκ-ηδόν**, Adv., (λύκος) *wolf-like*, A.*Fr.*39. **-ηθμός**, ὁ, *a wolf's howl*, formed like μυκηθμός, Anon.ap.Suid.

**λυκηλάτους**· τὰς ἐγχελεῖς, Hsch.

**Λῠκία**, Ep. -ίη, ἡ, *Lycia*, Il.2.877, etc.: **Λυκίηθεν**, *from Lycia*, 5.105; **Λυκίηνδε**, *to Lycia*, 6.168,171.

**Λῠκι-άρχης**, ου, ὁ, *president of the* κοινόν *of Lycians*, Str.14.3.3, *OGI*495.14 (Cibyra), 568 (Tlos, iii A.D.):—hence **-αρχέω**, ib.556 (ibid.), etc.; and **-αρχία**, ἡ, *TAM*2(1).190.5 (Sidyma), etc. **-άρχισσα**, ἡ, fem. of Λυκιάρχης, ib.189a2 (ibid.).

⊛ **λῠκῐδεύς**, έως, ὁ, *wolf's cub*, Sol.ap.Plu.*Sol.*23, Theoc.5.38.

**Λῠκιοεργής**, contr. **-ουργής**, ές, *of Lycian workmanship*, προβόλους Λυκιοεργέας (λυκοεργέας and λυκεργέας codd.) Hdt.7.76 (quoted by Ath.11.486d); Λυκιουργεῖς φιάλαι D.49.31, cf. Poll.6.97: called βατιάκαι **Λυκιουργοί** in Epist.Alex.ap.Ath.11.784b (-ουργεῖς corr. Schw.).

⊛ **λύκιον**, τό, *dyer's buckthorn, Rhamnus petiolaris*, found in Cappadocia and Lycia, Dsc.1.100, Plin.*HN*12.30, 24.125, Gal.12.63. 2. λ. ἰνδικόν, = λογχῖτις, Dsc. l.c., Gal.12.216; also λύκειον Apollon.ap.Gal.12.616. II. *a decoction from* λ. I. 1, used medicinally, ib.63, *IG*14.2406.2,4.

**λύκιος**· κολοιοῦ εἶδος, Hsch.; cf. λύκος II.

⊛ **Λύκιος** [ῠ], α, ον, *Lycian*: **Λύκιοι**, οἱ, *the Lycians*, Il.2.876, etc.:—also **Λῠκιακός**, ή, όν, Luc.*Nav.*8; **Λυκιακά**, τά, *history of Lycia*, Ath.8.333d. II. epith. of Apollo (cf. Λύκειος), Pi.*P.*1.39, E.*Fr.*700, D.S.5.56, Paus.2.19.3: expld. ἀπὸ τοῦ λευκαίνεσθαι πάντα φωτίζοντος ἡλίου Antip.*Stoic.*3.249.

**Λῠκιουργής**, ές, contr. for Λυκιοεργής (q.v.).

**λυκίσκος**· ἡ μὴ ἔχουσα ἀξονίσκον τροχαλία, τρῆμα δὲ μόνον, ἢ ἄνοδος δόματος, Hsch. **λῠκοβᾰτίας** δρυμός· ἐν ᾧ οἱ λύκοι διατρίβουσι, Id. (post λυκαιχλίας).

**λῠκό-βρωτος**, ον, *eaten by wolves*, πρόβατα Arist.*HA*596b7, Plu.2.642b, Orib.*Eup.*4.88.11; perh. to be read in Hsch. s.v. λυκαιχλίας; cf. λυκόω. **-δίωκτος** [ῐ], ον, *wolf-chased*, δάμαλις A.*Supp.*351 (lyr., restored by Herm. for λευκοδίκτος). **-ειδής**, ές, *wolf-like*, Eust.856.51. II. = λυκαυγής, Poet.ap.Hsch. **-εργής**, ές, f.l. for Λυκιο- in Hdt.7.76. **-έρια**· ἐκ λυκείου δέρματος πεποινημένα, Hsch. (fort. -εργέα). **-θαρσής**, ές, *not fearing wolves*, *AP*7.703 (Myrin.); -θράσής in Hsch. **-καρίς**· θερμὸν ἀπ' ἀλφίτου πιεῖν, Id. **-κτονέω**, *slay wolves*, Sch.Ar.*Av.*368. **-κτόνος**, ον, *wolf-slaying*, epith. of Apollo, S.*El.*6, Plu.2.966a, Porph.*Abst.*1.22, and v. Λύκειος; λ. φαρέτρη *AP*13.22 (Phaedim.). II. **λυκοκτόνον**, τό, *wolf's-bane, aconitum*, Gal.11.820. **-λυγξ**, λυγκος, ὁ, *wolf-lynx*, Pap. in *Sitzb.Heidelb.Akad.*1923(2).14,23. **-μορφος**, ον, *wolf-shaped*, Tz. ad Lyc.481. **-πάνθηρος**, ὁ, *wolf-panther*, synon. of θώς in Hdn.*Epim.*60, cf. Eust.856.51. **-πέρσιον**, τό, an Egyptian plant, with a strong-smelling, yellowish juice, *Hyoscyamus muticus*, Gal.11.682.

**λῠκόποδες**, οἱ, f.l. for **λευκόποδες**, either *barefoot*, or *wearing white shoes*, in Ar.*Lys.*665 (lyr.); expld. by Arist.*Fr.*394 (ap.Sch. ad loc.) as οἱ τῶν τυράννων δορυφόροι (either from wearing wolf-skin footgear or from the device of a wolf on their shields).

**λῠκορραίστης**, ου, ὁ, *wolf-worrier*, κύνες *AP*7.44 (Ion), cf. 6.106 (Zon.).

⊛ **λύκος** [ῠ], ὁ, *wolf*, Il.16.156, 352; πολιός *grisly*, 10.334; κρατερώνυχες Od.10.218; ὀρέστεροι ib.212; ὠμοφάγοι Il.16.156; κοιλογάστορες A.*Th.*1041; the small Egyptian wolves mentioned by Hdt.2.67 were perh. *jackals*: various kinds distd. by Opp.*C.*3.293 sqq.: prov. λύκον ἰδεῖν *to see a wolf*, i.e. *to be struck dumb*, as was vulgarly believed of any one at whom a wolf got the first look (Pl.*R.*336d), Theoc.14.22; λύκου πτερά, of things that are not, 'pigeon's milk', Suid.; ὡς λ. χανών, of vain expectation, Eub.15.11, cf. Ar.*Fr.*337,

Euphro 1.31; λ. κεχηνώς Ar.*Lys.*629; πρίν κεν λ. οἶν ὑμεναιοῖ, of an impossibility, Id.*Pax* 1076, 1112, cf. Il.22.263; ὡς λύκοι ἄρν' ἀγαπῶσιν, of treacherous or unnatural love, Poet.ap.Pl.*Phdr.*241d; λύκου βίον ζῆν, i.e. live by rapine, Prov.ap.Plb.16.24.4; ἐκ λύκου στόματος, of getting a thing *praeter spem*, Zen.3.48; τῶν ὤτων ἔχειν τὸν λύκον 'catch a Tartar', Apollod.Car.18, cf. Plb.30.20.8; λ. ἀετὸν φεύγει, of the inescapable, Diogenian.6.19; λ. περὶ φρέαρ χορεύει, of those engaged in vain pursuits, ib.21. **II.** a kind of *daw*, Arist.*HA* 617$^{b}$17; cf. λύκιος. **III.** *a fish*, = καλλιώνυμος, Hices.ap.Ath.7.282d, *Gp.*18.14.1. **IV.** a kind of *spider*, Arist.*HA* 623$^{a}$2, Nic.*Th.*734, Plin.*HN*30.52. **V.** *anything shaped like a hook*: **1.** *a jagged bit* for hard-mouthed horses, Lat. *lupus*, Plu.2.641f; cf. λυκοσπάς. **2.** *hook* or *knocker* on a door, Hsch. **3.** *flesh-hook*, Poll.10.98. **VI.** nickname of παιδερασταί, *AP*12.250 (Strat.), cf. Pl.*Phdr.*241d. **VII.** *the flower of the iris*, Philin.ap.Ath.15.682a. **VIII.** a kind of *noose*, Gal.*UP*7.14, Heraclas ap.Orib.48.7, *Hippiatr.*74. **IX.** *a pastille used in dysentery*, Aët.9.49 (Latin version). **X.** = ὀροβάγχη, v.l. in marg. of Dsc.2.142. **XI.** an engine of war for defending gates, Procop.*Goth.*1.21. (Cf. Skt. *vṛ́kas*, Lith. *vilkas*, Slav. *vlĭkŭ*, Goth. *wulfs*.)

**λῠκό-σκορδον**, τό, = ἀμπελόπρασον, Ps.-Dsc.2.150. **-σκῠτάλιον** [ᾰ], τό, = σησαμοειδὲς τὸ μέγα, ib.4.149. **-σπάς**, άδος, ὁ, ἡ, *torn by wolves*, epith. of bees, Nic.*Th.*742 (because generated from corpses of oxen torn by wolves, Sch. ad loc.). **II.** of horses, Ἀτράκιον δήπειτα λυκοσπάδα πῶλον ἐλαύνει Call.*Fr.*474, where it may mean *drawn by the bit* (λύκος v. 1), cf. Plu.2.641f, or ἀποσπασθεῖσαν ἀπὸ λύκου as expld. by Choerob. *in Theod.*1.287, cf. Plu. l.c. (where horses bitten by wolves are said to become speedier); but οἱ λ. were *a breed of horses in lower Italy*, = ἵπποι αἱ Ἐνετίδες, Phot., cf. Hsch., Ael.*NA*16.24. ⊛**-σπαστος**, ον, = foreg. 1, Hsch. s.v. λελυκωμένα. **-στομος**, ὁ, *wolf-mouth*, a kind of *anchovy*, = ἔγγραυλις, Ael.*NA*8.18, *Gp.*20.46.1.

**Λῠκούργεια**, ἡ, the *trilogy* of Aeschylus *on the story of Lycurgus* king of Thrace, Ar.*Th.*135 (Λυκουργία codd.).

**λυκόφανον**· τὸν ἐχινόποδα (Messen.), Hsch.; cf. λυκόφων.

**λῠκ-όφθαλμος**, ἡ, *wolf-eye*, a precious stone, Plin.*HN*37.187.

**λῠκο-φῐλία**, ἡ, *wolf's* (i.e. *false*) *friendship*, Pl.*Ep.*318e, M.Ant.11.15. **-φίλιος** [φῐ], ον, *like wolf's friendship*, διαλλαγαί Men.833. Adv. -ίως Ael.Dion.*Fr.*251. **-φόρος**, ον, *branded with the mark of a wolf*, name of a swift breed of Venetian horses (cf. λυκοσπάς II), Str.5.1.9.

**λῠκόφρυς**, υος, ἡ, name for the plant ἀρτεμισία, cj. for λυσίκοπον in Poet. *de herb.*28; but **λευκόφρυς**, Ps.-Dsc.3.113.

**λῠκόφρων**, ονος, ὁ, ἡ, *wolf-minded*, = δεινόφρων, Hsch.; ἄνδρες λυκόφρονες quoted as poet. by Plu.2.988d:—in Hom. only as pr. n.

**λυκόφων**, ωνος, ὁ, a plant, Plu.*Lyc.*16, Id.2.237b:—in both places λυκοφάνους (= ἐχινόποδας, v. λυκόφανον) should prob. be read (λυκόφονας, λυκοφάνας codd.).

**λῠκόφως**, ωτος, τό, *twilight*, both of morning and evening, *gloaming* (cf. ἀμφιλύκη νύξ), Ael.*NA*10.26, Sch.Il.7.433, Hsch. s.v. λυκοειδέος, Eust.689.21, Sch.Ar.*Ra.*1385. (Variously expld. ll. cc.)

**λῠκόχροος**, ον, contr. **-χρους**, ουν, *wolf-coloured*, βαφή Eust.689.20.

**λῠκοψία**, ἡ, (ὄψις) = λυκόφως, Lyc.1432.

**λύκοψις**, and **λύκοψος**, vv.ll. for λυκαψός in Dsc.4.26.

**λῠκόω**, (λύκος) *tear like a wolf*:—Pass., *to be torn by wolves*, πρόβατα λελυκωμένα X.*Cyr.*8.3.41.

**λυκτά**· οὐκ ἀνεκτά, Hsch.

**λῠκ-ώ**, οῦς, ἡ, = λύκαινα, epith. of the Moon, *PMag.Par.*1.2276. **-ώδης**, ες, *wolf-like*, τῷ χρώματι Arist.*HA* 579$^{b}$15.

⊛**λῦμα** (A), ατος, τό, mostly in pl. (sg. in *Berl.Sitzb.*1927.159 (Cyrene)), *water used in washing*, or *dirt removed by washing*, *offscourings*, οἱ δ' ἀπελυμαίνοντο καὶ εἰς ἅλα λύματα βάλλον Il.1.314; ἀμβροσίῃ μὲν πρῶτον ἀπὸ χροὸς.. λύματα πάντα κάθηρεν 14.171; ἔκλυζεν ποταμῷ λύματα Call.*Aet.*3.1.25; of catarrhal discharges, *purgations*, Hp.*Gland.*12; λύμαθ' ἁγνίσας ἐμά, of the blood on his hands, S.*Aj.*655; τόκοιο λύματα, = τὰ λόχια, Call.*Jov.*17: generally, *offscourings*, *refuse*, γῆς Id.*Ap.*109; δόμων ἐκ λύματ' ἔνεικαν A.R.4.710; of ordure, Call.*Fr.*216; ἔκβολα λ. δαιτός Id.*Cer.*116; ἐκκλύζειν τὰ λ. τῆς πόλεως εἰς τὸν Τίβεριν Str.5.3.8, cf. Plu.2.518b. **II.** *moral filth*, *defilement*, in sg., λῦμα τῷ γήρᾳ τρέφῃ; S.*OC*805. **III.** = λύμη, *ruin*, A.*Pr.*692 (pl., lyr.): in sg., of a person, σύ τ', ὦ λῦμ' Ἀχαιῶν, i.e. Hector, E.*Tr.*591 (lyr.).

**λῦμα** (B), ατος, τό, (λύω) = ἐνέχυρον, Suid. (pl.).

**λῦμαίνομαι** (A), (λῦμα A) *cleanse from dirt*, of fullers, Hp.*Vict.*1.14; v. ἀπολυμαίνομαι.

⊛**λῦμ-αίνομαι** (B), fut. λῡμᾰνοῦμαι Isoc.11.49, D.24.1, etc.: aor. ἐλῡμηνάμην Hp.*VM*20 (v.l. -αίνετο), Hdt.8.28, E.*Andr.*719, Isoc.20.12, etc.: also with pass. forms, part. λυμανθέν A.*Ch.*290: pf. λελύμασμαι (3 sg. λελύμανται D.9.36, 21.173); part. -ασμένος X.*HG*7.5.18, D.45.27; inf. λελυμάνθαι Id.20.142, *PPetr.*3p.57 (iii B.C.): cf. διαλυμαίνομαι: some of these forms are also used in pass. sense, v. infr. II: (λύμη):—*outrage*, *maltreat*, esp. of personal injuries, scourging, binding, etc. (cf. D.23.33), but also in moral sense:—Constr.: **1.** c. acc., *outrage*, *maltreat*, ὅτι τὸν ξεῖνον.. δήσας λυμαίνοιτο Hdt.5.33; τὴν ἵππον ἐλυμήναντο ἀνηκέστως Id.8.28; ὀργῇ χάριν δούς, ἥ σ' ἀεὶ λυμαίνεται S.*OC*855; λ. λέχη *dishonour*.., E.*Ba.*354: c. acc. cogn. added, τοιαῦτα.. Σοφοκλέης λυμαίνεται.. ἐμὲ τὸν Τηρέα Ar.*Av.*100; λύμης ἥν μ' ἐλυμήνω πάρος E.*Hel.*1099; also in Att. Prose, λ. νόμους Lys.30.26, cf. D.18.312; τὰς ῥήσεις ἃς ἐλυμαίνου the speeches you *used to murder* (as an actor), ib.267; later simply, *harm*, *injure*, βλασφημεῖν καὶ -εσθαι τὸν σοφόν Phld.*Lib.*p.10 O., cf. *Ir.*p.33 W.; of things, *spoil*, *ruin*, νοῦσος λ. τὸ σῶμα Hp.*Morb.Sacr.*11, cf. *VM*6; τὰ -όμενα γαστέρας καὶ κεφαλὰς καὶ ψυχάς X.*Mem.*1.3.6; ὀψοποιία λ. τὰ ὄψα ib.3.14.5; λ. τὴν οἰκίαν Is.6.18; τοὺς χυλούς Thphr.*CP*6.17.5; τὰ παρόντα Epicur.*Sent.Vat.*35; θλίβει καὶ λ. τὸ μακάριον Arist.*EN* 1100$^{b}$28; λ. τοῦ ἀραχνίου *spoil part of* it, Id.*HA* 623$^{a}$20. **2.** c. dat., *inflict indignities* or *outrages upon*, νεκρῷ Hdt.1.214, 9.79; μειρακίοις Ar.*Nu.*928 (anap.); ἡ ὕβρις τοῖς ὅλοις πράγμασι λ. Isoc.20.9; ἡ κακία λ. τοῖς ὅλοις D.18.303; λ. τῇ καταστάσει X.*HG*2.3.26; τῇ ἑαυτοῦ δόξῃ ib.7.5.18; πονηροὶ.. αὐτοῖς -αίνονται Epicur.*Sent.Vat.*53; τοῖς.. προῃρημένοις *POxy.*1409.21 (iii A.D.).—The constr. with dat. is considered strictly Att., Sch.Ar.*Nu.*925; but X. almost always uses the acc., which is freq. also in the Oratt.; Pl. does not use the word at all. **3.** abs., *cause ruin*, ὅσα μετ' ἐλπίδων λυμαίνεται Th.5.103; πᾶν τὸ λυμαινόμενόν ἐστιν ἔνδοθεν Men.540.3; *cause damage*, *IG*5(2).6.16 (Tegea, iv B.C.); also, *inflict punishment*, ib.5(1).1390.26 (Andania, i B.C.). **4.** c. dat. modi, λυμαίνεσθαι [τινα] λύμῃσι ἀνηκέστοισι *treat* with the worst *ill-treatment*, Hdt.6.12; γλῶτταν ἡδοναῖς λ. *defile* it, Ar.*Eq.*1284. **5.** c. neut. Adj., τἆλλα πάντα λυμαίνεσθαι *inflict* all possible *indignities*, Hdt.3.16; αὐτῷ τάδ' ἄλλα Βάκχιος λ. E.*Ba.*632 (troch.), cf. Ar.*Av.*100 (supr. I. 1). **II.** Act. λυμαίνω, only late, Lib.*Decl.*13.6; but λυμαίνομαι is sts. Pass., δεδεμένος καὶ -όμενος Antipho 5.63; ὑπὸ τοιούτων ἀνδρῶν λυμαίνεσθε Lys.28.14; πλάστιγγι λυμανθὲν δέμας A.*Ch.*290; λελυμάνθαι D.20.142; λελυμασμένος Paus.7.5.4, 10.15.4; ἐλελύμαντο D.C.39.11; cf. διαλυμαίνομαι II. **-αντήρ**, ῆρος, ὁ, *spoiler*, *destroyer*, φιλίας X.*Hier.*3.3. **-αντήριος**, α, ον, *injurious*, *destructive*, δεσμά A.*Pr.*991: c. gen., *destroying*, *ruining*, γυναικὸς τῆσδε Id.*Ag.*1438; τῶνδε οἴκων Id.*Ch.*764. **-αντής**, οῦ, ὁ, = foreg., γάμος λ. βίου S.*Tr.*793: also **-αντικός**, ή, όν, Muson.*Fr.*8 p.34 H., Epict.*Gnom.*9: c. gen., δόγματα λ. οἴκων Arr.*Epict.*3.7.20; φυομένων (καρπῶν) Ph.2.429. ⊛**-άντωρ**, ορος, ὁ, = λυμαντήρ, Timo 65.

**λῦμαξ**, pl. **λύμακες**· πέτραι, Hsch. (cf. καταλυμακόομαι).

**λῦμαρ**, τό, poet. for λῦμα, λύμη, Max.238.

**λύμασις**, f.l. in A.*Supp.*877.

**λυμάχη**· ἡ εἰς διαφθορὰν λύπη, Hsch.

**λῡμ-εών**, ῶνος, ὁ, (λύμη) *destroyer*, *corrupter*, λ. ἐμός S.*Aj.*573; γυναικῶν E.*Hipp.*1068; σωτῆρες ἀλλὰ μὴ λυμεῶνες τῶν Ἑλλήνων] Isoc.8.141, cf. 4.80; λυμεῶνι σώματος θαλάσσᾳ Tim.*Pers.*81; ὁδουροὶ λ., of robbers, E.*Fr.*260, cf. J.*BJ*4.3.9; φόβος τῶν ἡδέων λ. X.*Hier.*6.6; κοινὸς λ. τῆς πόλεως *SIG*799.23 (Cyzic., i A.D.); τῆς τέχνης, of bad physicians, Gal.9.916; σκύλακας.. λ. τῶν ποιμνίων Jul.*Or.*2.87a; ὄφιν λ. ἀνθρωπίνης γενέσεως Id.*Gal.*93d. **-εωνεύομαι**, *play* or *act the* λυμεών, Plb.5.5.8. **-η**, ἡ, *outrage*, *maltreatment*, esp. by maiming, ἐπὶ λύμῃ for the sake of *insult*, Hdt.2.121.δ'; δόμων ἐπὶ λύμῃ A.*Th.*880 (lyr.); ὑπ' ἄφρονι λύμᾳ Id.*Eu.*377 (lyr.); ἄνδρα οὕτω αἰσχρῶς λύμῃ διακείμενον Hdt.2.162; ὧν διαφθειρομένων οὐκ ἂν γίγνοιτο μεγάλη λ. τῇ πόλει Pl.*Lg.*919c; λ. καρπῶν καὶ προβάτων X.*Oec.*5.6; χωρὶς τῆς ἄλλης λύμης besides the *mischief* done, Hp.*Fract.*3: freq. in pl., *outrages*, *indignities*, λυμαίνεσθαι λύμῃσι Hdt.6.12; χερσὶ καὶ λύμαισι καὶ πᾶσιν κακοῖς S.*El.*1196, cf. 1195; φθείρειν λύμαις ἐχθίσταις Ar.*Av.*1068; ταῖσδ' ἀδαμαντοδέτοισι λύμαις A.*Pr.*148 (lyr.), cf. 427 (lyr.); ἐπὶ ταῖς ἐρεθιζούσαις τὸν νουθετούμενον λύμαις Phld.*Lib.*p.8 O. **II.** *corruption*, καθάπερ σιδήρῳ μὲν ἰός, ξύλοις δὲ θρῖπες.. συμφυεῖς εἰσι λῦμαι Plb.6.10.3. **III.** *damage* in financial sense, πρὸς λύμην τῶν βασιλικῶν φόρων *PMasp.*2 iii 18 (vi A.D.), cf. 4.16 (vi A.D.); *injury* from disease, Ruf.*Fr.*64.

**λύμην**, v. λύω. ⊛**λυμνός**· γυμνός, Hsch. **λύμπρωσχος**· τὸ λυχνίον, Id. **λύξ**· λύτρον, Id. **λυπάη**, corrupt word in Luc.*Pseudol.*16. **λύπεια**· λιπαρά, Hsch.

**λῡπ-έω**, (λύπη) *grieve*, *vex*, whether in body or mind, τινα Hes.*Op.*401, Sapph.*Supp.*2.4, etc.; opp. εὐφραίνειν, E.*Alc.*239 (anap.); [ὁ θώραξ] λυπεῖ *distresses* by its weight, X.*Mem.*3.10.15: c. neut. Adj., λυπεῖν μηδὲν αὐτόν E.*Cyc.*338, cf. Hdt.8.144, X.*Cyr.*3.3.50; ταὐτὰ ταῦτα λυποῦντες, ἅπερ ἐγὼ ὑμᾶς ἐλύπουν Pl.*Ap.*41e: c. part., ἐλύπει αὐτὸν ἡ χώρα πορθουμένη X.*An.*7.7.12; οὐ σκοπεῖς ὅ τι μὴ λυπήσεις τοὺς ἄλλους ποιῶν D.21.135: folld. by interrog., καί μ' ἦμαρ.. λυπεῖ, τί πράσσει S.*OT*74, cf. *El.*59; οὐδὲν ἐλύπησεν [αὐτό], ὥστε μή.. *does* no *harm*.., Pl.*Cra.*393e; οὐδένα λυπήσας or -ασα, as formula in epitaphs, *IG*14.1857, 2.1868. **2.** abs., *cause pain* or *grief*, ἄγαν γε λυπεῖς S.*Aj.*589, *Ant.*573, cf. *OT*1231; τὸ λυποῦν Antiph.107, Men.410. **3.** in histor. writers, of cavalry and light troops, *harass*, *annoy* an army by constant attacks, Hdt.9.40, cf. 61, Th.6.66, X.*HG*6.3.14, *An.*2.3.23, etc.; λῃσταὶ.. τὴν Λακωνικὴν ἧσσον ἐλύπουν Th.4.53, cf. Ar.*Av.*1427. **II.** Pass. with fut. Med. (E.*Med.*474, etc.), *to be grieved*, *distressed*, λυπεῖσθαι φρένα Thgn.593 codd.; τῷ μήτε χαίρειν μήτε λυπεῖσθαι βροτούς A.*Fr.*266, cf. S.*Aj.*555, etc.; μήτε λυπέο μήτε.. *be* not *distressed*, Hdt.8.100; ὑπὸ θεραπαίνης ἐπίτηδες λ. Lys.1.11: c. acc. cogn., τὰς ἐσχάτας λ. λύπας Pl.*Grg.*494a, cf. *Phd.*85a; also διπλῇ τινι λύπῃ λ. Id.*Phlb.*36a: also c. acc. rei, *grieve about* a thing, S.*Aj.*1086; πρὸς τὰς ξυμφοράς Th.2.64; διά τι Pl.*Phlb.*52b; ἐπί τινι X.*Mem.*3.9.8: c. part., λυπῇ.. ἐστερημένη E.*Med.*286; ταῦτ' ἐλυπεῖθ' ὁρῶν D.18.217: abs., *feel pain*, E.*Ion*632, etc.; τὸ -ούμενον τῆς ψυχῆς Pl.*Lg.*689b; τὸ -εῖσθαι Id.*Prt.*354d. **-η**, ἡ, *pain of body*, opp. ἡδονή, Id.*Phlb.*31c, etc.; also, *sad plight* or *condition*, Hdt.7.152. **2.** *pain of mind*, *grief*, ib.16.α'; δῆγμα δὲ λύπης οὐδὲν ἐφ' ἧπαρ προσικνεῖται A.*Ag.*791 (anap.); τί γὰρ καλὸν ζῆν βίοτον, ὃς λύπας φέρει; Id.*Fr.*177, cf. S.*OC*1217 (lyr.), etc.; ἐρωτικὴ λ. Th.6.59; λύπας προσβάλλειν Antipho 2.

2.2; λ. φέρειν τινί And.2.8; opp. χαρά, X.*HG*7.1.32. **-ημα**, ατος, τό, *pain*, Antipho Soph.49 (pl.), D.C.55.17, f.l. in S.*Tr*.554. **-ηρός**, ά, όν, I. of things, *painful, distressing*, Hdt.5.106, S.*El*.553; τί σοι τοῦτ' ἐστὶ λ. κλύειν; Id.*OC*1176; τὰν δόμοισι λ. E.*Ion*623, etc.; ἀζημίους μέν, λ. δὲ ἀχθηδόνας *causing pain*, Th.2.37; τὰ λ. X.*Hier*. 1.8, cf. Men.555.3; βίος -ότερος Pl.*Lg*.733b; τὸ λ. Id.*R*.585a; opp. τὸ ἡδύ, Antipho Soph.49. II. of persons, 1. *causing sorrow*, λυπηρὸς ἡμῖν τούσδ' ἂν ἐκλίποι δόμους E.*Hipp*.796. 2. *causing pain, troublesome*, λ. κλύειν S.*El*.557; λ. οὐκ ἦν οὐδ' ἐπίφθονος πόλει E.*Supp*.893, cf. Ar.*Ach*.456, Th.1.76, etc.; of those who are *objects of jealousy and envy*, Id.6.16, cf. 2.64. III. of persons, *sad*, = ἄθυμος, Hsch., cf. Lxx *Pr*.17.22. IV. Adv. -ρῶς *painfully, so as to cause pain*, S.*Ph*.912; λ. δ' ἔχει, εἰ.. it is *painful* that.., Id.*El*.767, cf. E.*Ba*.1263. 2. *with pain, so as to feel* or *show pain*, λ. φέρειν τι Isoc.9.54, cf. Arist.*EN*1110$^{b}$12. **-ησίλογος** [ῐ], ον, *giving pain by talking*, Cratin.343. **-ητέον**, *one must feel pain*, X.*Ap*. 27. **-ητικός**, ή, όν, *feeling pain*, ἐπί τινι Arist.*MM*1192$^{b}$22. II. τὸ λ. the *capacity for feeling pain*, Plu.2.657a.

**λῡποτόκος**, ον, *pain-producing*, ἐκτὸς ἐὼν δακρύων καὶ λυποτόκων ὀδυνάων *BCH*4.406 (Halic.).

**λυπρό-βῐος**, ον, *leading a wretched life*, Str.7.5.12. **-γεως**, ων, *with poor soil*, Ph.2.294, App.*Hisp*.59 (-γειον codd., -γαιον Suid.).

**λυπρ-ός**, ά, όν, (λυπέω, cf. λυπηρός) *distressful, wretched, poor*, esp. of land, γαῖα Od.13.243, cf. Hdt.9.122, Arist.*HA*556$^{a}$4; of plants, Thphr.*CP*2.4.5; λ. τροφαί ib.6; of base coin, dub. l. in Id.*Char*.4.11; μισθάριον D.L.10.4. II. = λυπηρός, 1. of persons, *causing pain, offensive*, ἐμοί γε λυπρός A.*Eu*.174 (lyr.); λ. φανῇ E.*Med*.301. 2. of states and conditions, *painful, distressing*, A.*Pers*.1034 (lyr.), E.*Alc*. 370, etc.; τὸ τούτων λ. Id.*Supp*.38; f.l. in A.*Ch*.835 (lyr.). III. Adv. -ρῶς, ἔφερεν *aegre ferebat*, E.*Supp*.898; λ. πράττειν Plu.*Dio* 58; also λυπρὰ πράττειν Id.*Cim*.1. **-ότης**, ητος, ἡ, *wretchedness, poverty*, of land, Str.2.5.32, al.

**λυπρόχωρος**, ον, = λυπρόγεως, Str.9.4.11.

**λυπτά**· ἑταίρα, πόρνη, Hsch.

⊛ **λύρα** [ῠ], ἡ, *lyre*, a stringed instrument with a sounding-board formed of the shell of a tortoise (not in Il. or Od.), *h.Merc* 423, Margites 1, Pi.*O*.10(11).93, *N*.10.21, etc.; κέλαδος ἑπτατόνου λύρας E.*IT* 1129 (lyr.); τὸν ἄνευ λύρας θρῆνον (since the dirge was accompanied by the flute) A.*Ag*.990 (lyr.); λ. καὶ κιθάρα (q.v.) Pl.*R*.399d, cf. Aristid.Quint.2.16: prov. ὄνος λύρας (sc. ἀκούων), v. ὄνος; ἀνὴρ δὲ φεύγων οὐ μένει λύρας κτύπον Ar.*Fr*.11 D. II. *lyric poetry* and *music*, Pl.*Lg*.809c,e. III. the constellation *Lyra*, Anacr.99, Arat. 269; Μουσῶν λ., of the Pleiades, Pythag.ap.Arist.*Fr*.196. IV. a sea-fish, perh. *Trigla lyra*, Arist.*HA*535$^{b}$17.

**Λυραῖος**, ὁ, epith. of Hermes as ἔφορος μουσικῆς, Procl. *in Alc*. p.195 C.

⊛ **λῠρ-ᾱοιδός** (or rather λυράοιδος Hdn.Gr.1.229), ὁ, ἡ, *one who sings to the lyre*, *AP*7.612 (Agath.), *APl*.4.279:—contr. **λῠρῳδός**, *AP*6.118 (Antip.), Plu.*Sull*.33: Adj. -ῳδὸς ἁρμονία Callistr.*Stat*.7. **-ίζω**, *play the lyre*, Chrysipp.*Stoic*.3.140, *Anacreont*.42.12, Teucer in *Cat. Cod.Astr*.7.202. II. trans., *play on the lyre*, ποιήματα Phalar.*Ep*. 67.1. **-ικός**, ή, όν, *of* or *for the lyre, lyric*, μοῦσα *Anacreont*.2 B 2; τέχνη Plu.2.13b; τὰ κωμικὰ καὶ τραγικὰ καὶ λ. Phld.*Po*.2.35. II. as Subst. λ., ὁ, *lyrist*, *AP*11.78 (Lucill.), Plu.*Num*.4; or, *lyric poet*, Cic.*Orat*.55.183, Plu.2.1142b. **-ιον**, τό, Dim. of λύρα, Ar.*Ra*. 1304, *IG*2$^{2}$.1388.80:—also **-ίς**, ίδος, ἡ, Hdn.Gr.1.86. **-ισμός**, ὁ, *playing on the lyre*, Sch.Ar.*Pl*.242. ⊛ **-ιστής**, οῦ, ὁ, *player on the lyre*, Plin.*Ep*.9.17.3, Artem.4.72; un-Att. acc. to Hellad.ap.Phot. *Bibl*.p.529 B.:—fem. **-ίστρια**, ἡ, Sch.Juv.11.162.

**λυρίτης**· ζῷόν τι ταῖς δρυσὶν ἐντίκτον, Hsch. (fort. δρυΐτης).

**λῠρο-γηθής**, ές, *delighting in the lyre*, *AP*9.525.12, *An.Par*.4. 350. **-δμητος**, ον, *lyre-built*, epith. of Thebes, Nonn.*D*.25.415, al. **-εις**, εσσα, εν, *like the lyre*, σκινδαψός Theopomp.Coloph.ap.Ath. 4.183b. II. *fitted for the lyre, lyric*, *AP*7.30 (Antip. Sid., prob. for λυρόθεν). **-εργός**, όν, *playing on the lyre*, Orph.*A*.7. **-θελγής**, ές, *charmed by the lyre*, *AP*9.250 (Honest.). **-κτῠπία**, ἡ, *a striking of the lyre*, ib.6.54.10 (Paul. Sil.), *APl*.4.277 (Id.). ⊛ **-κτῠπος**, ον, *striking the lyre*, *IG*14.2134.6, *Epigr.Gr*.1023.2 (Nubia). 2. *twanging like a lyre*, of a bow-string, Lyc.918.

**λύρον**, τό, = ἄλισμα, Dsc.3.152.

**λῠροποι-ητικός**, ή, όν, *skilled at making lyres*, Poll.7.153; also -κή, ἡ, and Adv. -κῶς ibid. **-ία**, ἡ, *manufacture of lyres*, ibid. **-ικός**, ή, όν, = λυροποιητικός: ἡ -κή (sc. τέχνη) *the art* or *craft of lyre-making*, Pl.*Euthd*.289c. **-ός**, ὁ, *lyre-maker*, And.1.146, Pl.*Euthd*. 289b,d, *Cra*.390b, Anacr.30 (codd. Heph., μυρο- Bgk. from Poll.7. 177).

**λῠροφοῖνιξ**, ικος, ὁ, kind of *lyre*, Juba 73:—Dim. **-φοινίκιον**, τό, Poll.4.59.

**λυρτός**, ὁ, Epirote word for σκύφος, Seleuc.ap.Ath.11.500b.

**λῠρ-ῳδέω**, *play the lyre*, Tz.*H*.10.410. **-ῳδης**, ες, = λυρόεις, μέλη Epigr.ap.Eus.*PE*11.6. **-ῳδία**, ἡ, *song to be sung to the lyre*, Poll.4.58, Aristid.*Or*.37(2).21, Callistr.*Stat*.7. **-ῳδός**, v. λυραοιδός. **-ωνία**, ἡ, (ὠνέομαι) *buying of lyres*, Ar.*Fr*.240.

⊛ **Λῡσάνδρια** (better -εια as Hsch., Phot.), τά, *festival in honour of Lysander*, Plu.*Lys*.18.

**λῡσ-ᾱνίας**, ου, ὁ, (λύω, ἀνία) *ending sorrow*, λ. κακῶν Ar.*Nu*.1162 (lyr.), cf. Hsch.; dub. cj. in Theopomp.Com.30.4. **-έρως**, ωτος, ὁ, *deliverer from love*, Sch.Verg.*Aen*.4.520. **-ήνωρ**, ορος, ὁ, ἡ, *relaxing men*, οἶνος Tryph.449.

**λῡσί-γᾰμος** [ῐ], ον, *dissolving marriage*, ἀγγελίαι *AP*5.301.14 (Agath.). **-γυῖα**, ἡ, *relaxation of the limbs*, Hp.*Loc.Hom*.14.

**λῡσ-ίδρως**, ωτος, ὁ, ἡ, *freeing from perspiration*, Choerob. *in Theod*. 1.252.

**λῡσῐ-έθειρα**, ἡ, *with loose, dishevelled hair*, Nonn.*D*.19.331. ⊛ **-ζωνος**, ον, of a soldier, *unequipped, ungirded, unarmed*, Polyaen.8.24. 3. II. *loosing the zone*, i.e. ceasing to be a maid, Hsch., Suid.: hence as epith. of Eileithyia and Artemis, who *assisted women in travail*, Theoc.17.60, Corn.*ND*34, Orph.*H*.2.7, 36.5, etc. **-θριξ**, τρῐχος, ὁ, ἡ, *with loose hair*, *Gp*.12.8.5. **-κᾰκος**, ον, *ending evil*, ὕπνος Thgn.476. **-κομος**, ον, = λυσίθριξ, Philostr.*Ep*.16, Nonn.*D*.19. 331. **-κοπος**, ον, *freeing from fatigue*, Poet. *de herb*.28 cod. **-λαΐδες**, = θέρμοι (Lacon.), Polem.Hist.91. **-μάχειος** [ᾰ], α, ον, *of Lysimachus*, χρυσοῦς *IG*11(2).287 *B* 46 (Delos, iii B.C.), written -εος. II. Subst. **-μάχειος**, ὁ, *loosestrife*, *Lysimachia vulgaris*, Dsc.4.3, Gal. 12.64; also λυσιμάχειον, τό, Paul.Aeg.7.3. (Freq. written -ιον in codd.) **-μᾰχος**, -ον, *ending strife*, freq. as pr. n.; used with a play on the meaning, *AP*5.70 (Rufin. or Pall.), 11.210 (Lucill.):—fem. **λῡσῐμάχη**, Ar.*Pax*992 (anap.), *Lys*.554 (pl.). 2. **-μαχος**, ἡ, a gem, Plin.*HN*37.172. **-μβροτος**, ον, prob. = λυσήνωρ, Pi.*Pae.Oxy*. 1791.18. **-μελής**, ές, *limb-relaxing*, epith. of sleep, Od.20.57, 23. 343, Mosch.2.4, etc.; of love, Hes.*Th*.911, Archil.85, Sapph.40, etc.; of thirst, Thgn.838; of death, E.*Supp*.47 (lyr.); of wine, sickness, etc., *AP*11.414 (Hedyl.); of the Furies, Orph.*H*.70.9. ⊛ **-μέριμνος**, ον, *driving care away*, of Dionysus, *AP*9.524.12; of Hermes, Orph. *H*.28.6; of Artemis, ib.36.5; of Sleep, ib.85.5, etc.

**λύσιμος** [ῠ], ον, *able to loose* or *relieve*, μέλη A.*Supp*.811 (lyr.). II. Pass., *that can be redeemed, redeemable*, ἐνέχυρα Pl.*Lg*.820e. 2. *that can be solved, refutable*, συλλογισμός Arist.*APr*.70$^{a}$31. 3. τὰ λ. τῶν νόμων the legal texts read by fourth-year students (λύται), *AP* 5.291 tit. (Agath.). 4. *that can be melted*, κηρός Jul.*Ep*.193.

**λύσιος** [ῠ], α, ον, (λύσις) *releasing, delivering*, λύσιοι θεοί the gods *who deliver from curse* or *sin*, Pl.*R*.366a; esp. Λύσιος, as epith. of Dionysus, Plu.2.613c, Corn.*ND*30, Orph.*H*.50.2, cf. Paus.9.16.6; λύσιοι τελεταί, of Dionysus Λύσιος, Phot. s. h. v.; also Λύσειος, Orph. *H*.42.4; voc. Λυσεῦ, ib.52.2 (Κισσεῦ Lobeck).

**λῡσῐ-παίγμων**, ον, gen. ονος, *letting loose*, i.e. *giving, play* or *sport*, *Anacreont*.48.9. (As all other Adjs. (exc. sq.) compd. with λυσι- have ῡ, Herm. suggested λυροπαίγμων.) **-πήμων**, ον, gen. ονος, *ending sorrow* or *pain*, Orph.*H*.2.11, 59.20 codd. (λαθιπήμων Herm., cf. foreg.).

**λυσιπνεῖ**· φοβεῖται, Hsch.

**λῡσί-ποθος** [ῐ], ον, *delivering from love*, ἀγγελίαι *AP*5.268 (Agath.). ⊛ **-πόλεμος**, ὁ, name of a *war-engine* invented by Dorion, Pap. in *Abh. Berl.Akad*.1904(2).9 (ii B.C.). **-πόνιον**, τό, *a medicinal unguent*, Gal.12.771, Alex.Trall.1.16: also **-πονον**, τό, *an eye-salve*, *CIL*13. 10021.174, cf. 52,63. ⊛ **-πονος**, ον, *releasing from toil, labour-lightening*, θεράποντες Pi.*P*.4.41; λ. τελευτά death *that frees from care*, Id.*Fr*.131.1.

**λύσις** [ῠ], εως, Ion. ιος, ἡ, (λύω) *loosing, releasing, ransoming*, νεκροῖο Il.24.655; σώματος Lys.4.13; ἡ λ. τῆς αἰσθήσεως ἐγρήγορσις Arist.*Somn.Vig*.454$^{b}$27: c. gen. objecti, θανάτου λ. *deliverance from* death, Od.9.421, Thgn.1010; λ. ἔριδος Hes.*Th*.637; χρεέων Id.*Op*. 404; πενίης Thgn.180; λύσιν αἰτησόμενοι τῶν παρεόντων κακῶν Hdt. 6.139; πενθέων Pi.*N*.10.76; μόχθων τῶν ἐφεστώτων S.*Tr*.1171; τῶν δειμάτων Th.2.102; τῶν δεσμῶν Pl.*R*.515c; ἀπὸ τῶν δεσμῶν ib.532b; ἐκ χαλεπῶν Thgn.1385; βλασφημίας D.*Ep*.3.39; μάχης *PLips*.40 ii 16 (iv/v A.D.). 2. abs., οὐ γὰρ λ. ἄλλη στρατῷ πρὸς οἶκον no other *means of letting* the host *loose from port* for home, S.*El*.573. 3. *deliverance from guilt* by expiatory rites, ὅπως λ. τιν' ἡμὶν εὐαγῆ πόρῃς may'st grant us *a deliverance* such as may purify us, Id.*OT*921; οὐδ' ἔχει λύσιν [τὰ πήματα] admit not of *atonement*, Id.*Ant*.598 (lyr.); λύσεις τε καὶ καθαρμοὶ ἀδικημάτων Pl.*R*.364e; τῇ [τῆς φιλοσοφίας] λύσει καὶ καθαρμῷ *by* her *offer to release them*, Id.*Phd*.82d; αἱ νομιζόμεναι λ., in cases of homicide, Arist.*Pol*.1262$^{a}$32; λ. ἁμαρτημάτων *blotting out* of sins, Ph.2.151. 4. *redemption* of mortgage or pledge, [χωρίον] πεπραμένον ἐπὶ λύσει *IG*2.1103, al., cf. 12(7).55.14 (Amorgos), 12(8).18 (Lemnos). b. *release, discharge* from a financial obligation, λύσιν ποιήσασθαι τῆς συγχωρήσεως *BGU*1115.46 (i B.C.), etc. 5. for ὠμὴ λύσις, v. ὠμήλυσις. II. *loosing, parting*, λ. καὶ χωρισμὸς ψυχῆς ἀπὸ σώματος Pl.*Phd*.67d; simply, ἡ τοῦ σώματος λ. Id.*Ax*.371a; *dissolution*, πολιτείας Id.*Lg*.945c; νόμων ἢ πολιτείας Arist.*Pol*.1268$^{b}$30; βίου λύσιν ἔσχε *IG*14.140 (Syracuse); λ. κομήτου Phlp. *in Mete*.86.25; τῶν σφραγίδων αἱ λ. *breaking* them, Luc.*Alex*. 20. 2. *emptying, evacuation*, πείνη μέν που λ. καὶ λύπη; Pl.*Phlb*.31e; ἡ λ. τῶν κοιλιῶν, κοιλίας, Arist.*Pr*.947$^{b}$29, Dsc.1.64 (v.l.); *emission* of *semen*, Alex.Aphr.*Pr*.1.125 (pl.). 3. λ. πυρετοῦ *remission* of fever, Gal.11.28; λ., opp. κρίσις, Id.9.732; *cure*, Anon.Lond.3.20; τὰ πάθη defined as συστολαὶ καὶ λύσεις (v.l. χύσεις) τῆς ψυχῆς, opp. κρίσεις, Zeno *Stoic*.3.113 = 1.51. 4. as a technical term, a. *solution* of a difficulty, ἡ λ. τῆς ἀπορίας its *solution*, Arist.*EN*1146$^{b}$7, al.; ἔχει τινὰ λ. πρὸς ταύτην τὴν ἀπορίαν, ὅτι.. Id. *de An*.422$^{b}$28; οὐ συμβαίνει ἡ λ. Id.*EN*1153$^{b}$5; ὅταν τὸ θάμβος.. μὴ δύνηται τὴν λ. λαμβάνειν Epicur.*Ep*.1 p.29 U.; εὑρεῖν λ. τοῦ προβλήματος Plb.30.19.5; λ. εὑρέσθαι Phld.*Rh*.1.267 S.; also, *interpretation*, σημείων τεράτων τε λύσεις Orph.*A*.37. b. *refutation* of an argument, Arist.*SE*179$^{a}$27, *Rh*. 1402$^{b}$23, al. c. *unravelling* of the plot of a tragedy, opp. δέσις, Id.*Po*.1454$^{a}$37 (pl.), 1455$^{b}$24. d. *softening* of a strong expression, Longin.38.5. e. *resolution of one vowel into two*, as in ἥλιος, ἠέλιος,

like διαίρεσις, Demetr.*Eloc.*70. **f.** *looseness* of structure in writing, esp. asyndeton, ib.192, al. **g.** in metric, *resolution* of – into ⏑⏑, Heph.6. **5.** *divorce*, 1*Ep.Cor.*7.27; λ. γάμου Just.*Nov.*140 *Prooem.*, cf. 117tit. **III.** = δόρπου λ., *place* for banqueting (cf. κατάλυσις II), Pi.*O.*10(11).47.

**λῡσισωμᾰτέω**, *to be relaxed in body*, Hp.*Epid.*5.82.

**λῡσιτέλ-εια**, ἡ, *advantage, profit*, Thphr.ap.D.L.5.54, D.S.1.36, Lxx 2*Ma.*2.27, J.*AJ*16.9.1; λ. περὶ τὸν χρόνον *economy* in respect of time, i.e. by postponement of payments until they fell due, Plb.31.27.11; διὰ λυσιτέλειαν for the sake of *economy*, Dsc.5.8.—Rejected by the Atticists, Poll.5.136, Moer.p.248 P., Phot. **-έω**, prop. *indemnify for expenses incurred*, or *pay what is due*, and then '*pay*', i.e. *profit, avail* (cf. λύω v.2), c.dat., **I.** with subject expressed, οὔ φημ' ἂν λυσιτελεῖν σφῷν [τοῦτο] Ar.*Pl.*509; λυσιτελεῖ ἡμῖν ἡ δικαιοσύνη Pl.*Prt.*327b; δοῦλος τοιοῦτος οἷος μηδενὶ δεσπότῃ λυσιτελεῖν X.*Mem.*2.1.15. **2.** mostly impers., λυσιτελεῖ μοι *it profits* me, *is better* for me, c. part., οἷς οὐδ' ἅπαξ ἐλυσιτέλησε πειθομένοις Lys.25.27; πολλοῖς δὴ ἐλυσιτέλησεν ἀδικήσασι Pl.*Alc.*1.113d: c. inf., λ. προϊέναι Id.*Tht.* 181b; τεθνάναι νομίσασα λυσιτελεῖν ἢ ζῆν thinking it *better* to be dead than alive, And.1.125, cf. Pl.*R.*407a, X.*Cyr.*2.4.12 (v.l.), *PHamb.*27.17 (iii B.C.), etc.: c. dat. pers., *it profits* one to do so and so, οὐ γάρ οἱ λυσιτελέειν . . δικάζειν Hdt.1.97; ὅτι μοι λυσιτελοῖ ὥσπερ ἔχω ἔχειν Pl.*Ap.*22e, cf. X.*Hier.*7.13: sts. c.acc. pers., *it is good* that.., λυσιτελεῖ τὸν μέλλοντα κακῶς ἰητρεύεσθαι ἀμφότερα καταγῆναι τὰ σκέλεα Hp.*Fract.*19, cf. Pl.*R.*406d: abs., ἐλυσιτέλει γάρ Axionic.6.6. **3.** in bad sense, *conspire*, as gloss on ἐς τὸ κακὸν ἀλλήλοισι συντιμωρεῖ (Hp.*Acut.*17), Gal.15.494 (v.l. συντελεῖ). **II.** neut. part. as Subst., τὸ λυσιτελοῦν *profit, gain, advantage*, Th.6.85, Pl.*R.*336d, D.2.28; a wrong etym. is given in Pl.*Cra.*417c. **-ής, ές**, (λύω v.2, τέλος) prop. *paying for expenses incurred*: hence, *useful, profitable, advantageous*, τὸ πρᾶγμά μοι λ. Axionic.6.8; οὐδέποτ' . . -έστερον ἀδικία δικαιοσύνης Pl.*R.*354a, cf. 364a; ἐμπορεύματα -έστερα X.*Hier.*9.11; -εστάτην ζωὴν ζῆν Pl.*R.*344e; λυσιτελῆ *advantages*, Plb.4.38.8; τὸ -έστατον πρὸς ἀργύριον *what was most profitable* in point of money, D.20.13; τὰ λ. καὶ ἀλυσιτελῆ πρός τι Phld.*Mus.*p.93 K.; κτήσεις -έστεραι Id.*Oec.*p.68 J. **2.** *cheap*, X.*Vect.*4.30, D.H.7.37. **II.** rarely of persons, *profitable, advantageous*, Pl.*Phdr.*239c. **III.** Adv. -λῶς D.S.14.102: Sup. -έστατα Hdn.3.5.1. **2.** *cheaply*, τοῦ δέοντος πρίασθαι -έστερον Ael.*NA*10.50. **-ούντως**, Adv. *usefully, profitably*, X.*Oec.*20.21, Pl.*Alc.*2.146b; ἑαυτοῖς D.C.56.40.

**λῡσῐ-τόκος**, ον, *loosing the pains of child-birth*, θέαινα Nonn.*D.*41.166. **II.** Pass. **λῡσίτοκος**, *set free by birth*, θάλαμοι λ., i.e. eggs that have been laid, Opp.*C.*3.128. **-φάρμᾰκον**, τό, *remedy against spells*, *PMag.Osl.*1.178. **-φλεβής**, ές, *opening the veins*, *AP*6.94 (Phil.). **-φρων**, ονος, ὁ, ἡ, *releasing from care*, *Anacreont.*47.2. **-χίτων** [χῐ], ωνος, ὁ, ἡ, *with loose tunic*, Nonn.*D.*5.407.

⊛ **λῡσῐῳδός**, ὁ, *one who played women's characters in male attire*, Aristox.*Fr.Hist.*57, Posidon.4 J., Phld.*Ind.Sto.*7, Plu.*Sull.*36: so called from Λῦσις, who wrote songs for such actors, Str.14.1.41: distd. from μαγῳδός, ibid., but identified with μ. by Aristocl.Hist. 7: fem. ἡ λυσιῳδός Ath.Naucr.(*FGrH* 166)1 J. **II.** as Adj., λ. αὐλοί flutes *that accompanied such songs*, Ephor.3 J. (nisi leg. λυσιῳδ(ικ)ῶν).

**λυσκάζει**· περιφεύγει, Hsch.

⊛ **λύσσ-ᾰ**, Att. **λύττᾰ**, ἡ, *rage, fury*, in Hom. always of *martial rage*, κρατερὴ δέ ἑ λ. δέδυκεν Il.9.239; λ. ἔχων ὀλοήν ib.305; λ. δέ οἱ κῆρ αἰὲν ἔχε κρατερή 21.542. **2.** after Hom., *raging madness, frenzy*, such as was caused by the gods, as that of Io, λύσσης πνεύματι μάργῳ A.*Pr.*883 (anap.); of Orestes, Id.*Ch.*287, E.*Or.*254, etc.; of the Proetides, B.10.102; of Bacchic frenzy, ἐλαφρᾷ λ. E.*Ba.*851; θοαὶ Λύσσας κύνες, of the Furies, ib.977 (lyr.); λύσσῃ παράκοπος Ar.*Th.*680: strengthd., λ. μανιάς S.*Fr.*941.4; λύττα ἐρωτική Pl.*Lg.*839a; λ. alone, *of raging love*, Theoc.3.47; simply, *rage*, Phld.*Ir.*p.77 W.; *fanaticism*, περὶ τὰς αἱρέσεις Gal.8.148 (pl.). **3.** personified, Λύσσα *the goddess of madness*, E.*HF*823. **II.** *rabies*, in dogs, X.*An.*5.7.26, Arist.*HA*604ᵃ5, Gal.1.296; in horses, Porph.*Abst.*3.7. **2.** *the worm* under the tongue *of dogs*, removed from the belief that it produces rabies, Plin.*HN*29.100. **-αίνω**, *rave*, τινι against one, S.*Ant.*633. **-ᾰλέος**, α, ον, *raging mad*, κύνες A.R.4.1393; also λ. μανίη Man.4.539. **-άς**, άδος, ἡ, *raging mad*, Tim.*Fr.*3, *APl.*4.289; λ. μοῖρα E.*HF*1024 (lyr.). **-άω**, Att. λυττάω, Ep. part. λυσσώων Man.1.244, *AP*5.265 (Paul. Sil.):—*to be raging* in battle, Hdt.9.71; cf. λύσσα init. **2.** *rave, be mad*, S.*OT*1258, *Ant.*492, Pl.*R.*329c, Epicur.*Sent.Vat.*11, Man., *AP* ll. cc., etc.; λ. πρὸς μεῖξιν Ps.-Phoc.214; ἔρωτες λυττῶντες Pl.*R.*586c: c. inf., *desire madly* to do, Hld.2.20. **II.** of dogs, *suffer from rabies*, Ar.*Lys.*298, Arist.*HA*604ᵃ6; of wolves, Theoc.4.11; of horses, Arist.*HA* 604ᵇ13. **III.** causal, *make mad*, κἂν λελυσσήκῃ τινά (sc. τὰ δήγματα) Damocr.ap.Gal.13.821. (Hsch. has λύσσεται· μαίνεται.) **-ηδόν**, Adv. *furiously, madly*, Opp.*H.*2.573. **-ήεις**· μανιώδης, Hsch. **-ημα**, ατος, τό, *fit of madness*: in pl., *ravings*, εἴ μ' ἐκφοβοῖεν μανιάσιν λυσσήμασιν E.*Or.*270. **-ήρης**, ες, = λυσσαλέος, Orph.*H.*69.6, Man.6.560. **-ητήρ**, ῆρος, ὁ, *one that is raging* or *raving mad*, κύων Il.8.299; ἰὸς κυνὸς *AP*5.265 (Paul. Sil.). **-ητής**, οῦ, ὁ, = foreg., *App.Anth.*5.47; Dor. -ᾱτάς *AP*7.473 (Aristodic.). **-ητικός**, ή, όν, *driving mad*, πρὸς τἀφροδίσια Ael.*NA*12.10.

**λυσσό-δηκτος**, ον, *bitten by a mad dog*, Dsc.1.100 (interpol.), *Gp.*12.17.14, Herasap.Gal.13.431, M.Ant.6.57, Damocr.ap.Aët.15.14. **-δίωκτος** [ῐ], ον, *pursued by madness*, Orac.ap.X.Eph.1.6. **-μᾰνέω**, *rage, rave*, Man.4.216. **-μᾰνής**, ές, *raving mad*, *AP*11.232 (Call. Arg.); πλόκαμοι ib.6.219 (Antip.). **-μᾰνία**, ἡ, *paroxysm of madness*, Jul.*Ep.*114.

**λυσσ-όω**, *enrage, madden*:—Pass., *to be* or *grow furious*, Ps.-Phoc.122. **-ώδης**, ες, *like one raging, frantic*, of martial rage, Il.13.53. **2.** *of madness*, λ. νόσος S.*Aj.*452; of Dionysus, E.*Ba.*981 (lyr.); τὸ λ. τῶν ἡδονῶν Plu.*Fr.*18.12. **-ῶπις**, ιδος, ἡ, *with frantic glance*, Orph.*A.*979.

**λύται** [ῠ], οἱ, *law-students who were in their fourth year of study*, Just.*Const.omnem* 5; cf. προλύται.

**Λῡταῖος**, title of Poseidon in Thessaly, B.17.21, cf. St.Byz. s.v. Λυταί: **Λυταίη**, name for Thessaly, Hsch.

**λυταρίς**· μήκωνος εἶδος, Hsch. **λυταῶς**· σκοτεινῶς, Id.

**λύτ-ειρα** [ῠ], fem. of λυτήρ, Orph.*H.*10.17, 32.13. **-έον**, *one must refute*, Pl.*Grg.*480e; *one must open*, φλέβας Herod.Med. in *Rh.Mus.*58.89. **2.** Adj. λυτέος *that must be repealed*, νόμος D.24.78. ⊛ **-ήρ**, ῆρος, ὁ, (λύω) *one who looses, deliverer*, πόνων E.*El.*136 (lyr.); πόρον . . γάμου λυτῆρα (as Pauw for καὶ λυτήρια) A.*Supp.*807 (lyr.). **II.** *arbitrator, decider*, νεικέων Id.*Th.*940 (lyr.). **-ηριάς**, άδος, ἡ, = λύτειρα, Orph.*H.*14.8, 36.7. ⊛ **-ήριος**, ον, *loosing, delivering*, δαίμονες A.*Th.*175 (lyr.); λ. ἄκη, μηχανή, Id.*Supp.*268, *Eu.*646; πλοῦτον δωμάτων λυτήριον Id.*Ch.*820 (lyr.); λ. σημεῖον a symptom *of healing*, Hp.*Prog.*24: c. gen., ὅπως γένοιτο τῶνδ' ἐμοὶ λ. my *deliverer* from.., A.*Eu.*298; λυτηρίους εὐχὰς δειμάτων S.*El.*635; τόδ' ἂν κακῶν μόνον γένοιτο . . λ. ib.1490, cf. 447; τὸ μεθύειν πημονῆς λ. Id.*Fr.*758; also λ. ἐκ θανάτου E.*Alc.*224 (lyr.); λυτήριον λώφημα is prob. in S.*Tr.*554 (λ. λύπημα codd.). **II.** Subst. λυτήριον, τό, = λύτρον, τὸ λ. δαπανᾶν the *atonement* or *reward* for all costs, Pi.*P.*5.106; φόνοιο *expiatory offering*, A.R.4.704. **-ικός**, ή, όν, *able to loose, laxative*, τῆς κοιλίας Mnesith.ap.Ath.3.92c, cf. 91b; λ. φάρμακα Arist.*Pr.*949ᵃ5. **2.** λ. φάρμακον *antidote* to a poison, Thphr.*HP* 9.16.5. **3.** φάρμακον φλεγμονῆς λ. *dispersive* of inflammation, Gal.11.751, cf. 10.637. **II.** *able to refute, confutative*, of arguments, Arist.*Rh.*1403ᵃ25. **-ός**, ή, όν, *that may be untied*, Pl.*Ti.*41b, al. **II.** *that may be dissolved, soluble*, ὑφ' ὕδατος ib.60d, cf. Arist.*Mete.*383ᵇ13. Adv. -τῶς *solubly*, Id.*PA*649ᵃ32. **III.** of arguments and problems, *refutable, soluble*, Id.*Rh.*1357ᵇ13.

⊛ **λύτρ-ον**, τό, (λύω) *price of release*: **1.** *ransom*, mostly in pl. (later sg., D.S.20.84, Plu.2.295c, etc.), τῶν λ. τὴν δεκάτην the tithe *of the ransom-money*, Hdt.5.77; "Εκτορος λύτρα, title of Il.24 and of play by Aeschylus; λύτρα λαβεῖν τινος receive *as ransom* for.., Th.6.5; τῆς θυγατρὸς λύτρα φέρων Pl.*R.*393d; λύτρα ἀποδιδόναι, καταθεῖναι, pay *ransom*, D.53.11,13; εἰσενεγκεῖν εἰς λύτρα contribute towards *it*, ib.7; ἀφιέναι ἄνευ λύτρων release without *ransom*, X.*HG*7.2.16, cf. Aeschin.2.100, D.19.169, etc.; δώσουσιν ἕκαστος λύτρα τῆς ψυχῆς αὐτοῦ Κυρίῳ a *ransom* of his soul, Lxx *Ex.*30.12; sg. in *NT*, λ. ἀντὶ πολλῶν *Ev.Matt.*20.28, *Ev.Marc.*10.45; λ. ὑπὲρ γαμέτου *IG*14.607f (Carales); pl., *sum paid for manumission* of a slave, *POxy.*48.6 (i A.D.), etc. **b.** *sum paid for redemption of a pledge*, in pl., *PBad.*3.4 (ii B.C.). **2.** *atonement*, τί γὰρ λ. πεσόντος αἵματος; (so Canter for λυγρόν) A.*Ch.*48; of blood-money, Lxx *Ex.*21.30, al. **3.** generally, *recompense*, λύτρον καμάτων for toil, Pi.*I.*8(7).1; συμφορᾶς Id.*O.*7.77. **II.** a plant, = λυσιμάχειος, Ps.-Dsc.4.3. **-όω**, *release on receipt of a ransom, hold to ransom*, τινὰ χρημάτων ὅσων δοκεῖ *for* such a sum as is agreed on, Pl.*Tht.*165e; *redeem* a pledge, λ. τὰ ἱμάτια *POxy.*530.14 (ii A.D.), etc.:—Med., *release by payment of ransom, redeem*, παρὰ τῶν Αἰτωλῶν *IG*12(5).36 (Naxos, iii B.C.), cf. Lxx *Ex.*13.15, al.; τὴν χώραν χρημάτων οὐκ ὀλίγων Plb.18.16.1; ἡμᾶς ἀπὸ πάσης ἀνομίας *Ep.Tit.*2.14:—Pass., *to be ransomed*, ἐκ τῶν ἰδίων λελυτρῶσθαι D.19.170, cf. Arist.*EN*1164ᵇ34; αἵματι 1*Ep.Pet.*1.18. **II.** Pass., *to be released* from an obligation, *PEleph.*19.8 (iii B.C.). **III.** mistranslation of Hebr. 'rp 'break the neck', Lxx *Ex.*13.13. **-ών**, ῶνος, ὁ, = ἀπόπατος 2, ib.4*Ki.*10.27, *AB*433. **-ώσιμος**, η, ον, *redeemable*, Suid. s.v. λύματα, Phot. s.v. λύσιμα. **-ωσις**, εως, ἡ, *ransoming*, αἰχμαλώτων Plu.*Arat.*11, cf. Lxx *Le.*25.29, *Ev.Luc.*1.68, *Ep.Hebr.*9.12; *redemption* of a pledge, *PTeb.*120.41 (i A.D.). **2.** *release, discharge* from an obligation, *POxy.*1130.20 (v A.D.). **II.** λ. ὕδατος, = *spring* of water, Lxx *Jd.*1.15. **-ωτέον**, *one must ransom*, Arist.*EN*1165ᵃ1. **-ωτής**, οῦ, ὁ, *ransomer, redeemer*, Lxx *Ps.*18(19).15, *Act.Ap.*7.35. **-ωτός**, ή, όν, *redeemable*, Lxx *Le.*25.31.

**λύττα, λυττάω, λυττητικός**, etc., v. λυσσ-.

**λυττεῖ**· πολλὰ λαλεῖ, Hsch. **λύττος**, Cret. word for ὑψηλός, St.Byz. s.v. Λύκτος; λυττοί (sic)· οἱ ὑψηλοὶ τόποι, Hsch.

**λύτωρ**, ορος, ὁ, = λυτήρ, f.l. for ῥύτωρ in *AP*9.351 (Leon. Alex.). [ῡ is incorrect.]

**λυχν-αῖος**, α, ον, *of a lamp*, φῶς Procl.*Sacr.*p.149 B. **II. λυχναῖος** καὶ **λυχνεύς**· ὁ διαυγὴς λίθος, Hsch. ⊛ **-απτέομαι**, *light lamps*, Roehl *Sched.Epigr.*27 (= *CIG*3062). **-άπτης**, ου, ὁ, gloss on δᾳδοῦχος, Hsch.: pl. misspelt λυχνάπτοι, *POxy.*1453.4,8 (i B.C.). **-άπτιον**, τό, *meeting-place of the* λυχνάπται, *Sammelb.*1934 (Memphis). ⊛ **-άπτρια**, ἡ, fem. of λυχνάπτης, *IG*3.162. **-άριον**, τό, Dim. of λυχνία, *PLond.*5.1657.3 (iv/v A.D.). ⊛ **-αψία**, ἡ, acc. to Ath.15.701b less common form for λυχνοκαυτία, Cephisod.11, cf. *PAmh.*2.70.10 (ii A.D.), *IGRom.*4.1176 (Aegae), etc. **-έα** and **-εία**, ἡ, forms of λυχνία, *PHamb.*10.34 (ii A.D.), *PTeb.*406.12 (iii A.D.). **-εῖον**, τό, *lampstand*, Pherecr.85, *IG*2².1425.368, 4.1588.3 (Aegina), 11(2).161 *C*77, al. (Delos, iii B.C.); *stand* for ballot-balls, Arist.*Ath.*68.4; cf. λυχνίον:—Dim. **-είδιον** (-ίδιον [ῐ] codd.) Ar.*Frr.*14, 281, Crates Com. 3, Hermipp.62. **-έλαιον**, τό, *lamp-oil*, Alex.Trall.1.1. ⊛ **-εύς**,

ἕως, ὁ, = λυχνίτης, Callix.1, cf. Ath.15.699d, Hsch. s.v. λυχναῖος. -εών, ῶνος, ὁ, *place to keep lamps in*, Luc.*VH*1.29. -ία, ἡ, *lampstand*, *SIG*1106.118 (Cos, iv/iii B.C.), *IG*11(2).161*C*66,68 (Delos, iii B.C.), LXX *Ex.*25.30(31), al., *PGrenf.*1.14.6 (ii B.C.), *Ev.Matt.*5.15, Plu.*Dio*9, Luc.*Asin.*40, etc.: condemned by Phryn. 289. -ιαῖος, α, ον, *belonging to a lamp*, φῶς S.E.*P.*1.119, cf. Gal. 17(2).413, Olymp.*in Mete.*18.12, al. -ίας λίθος, ὁ, = λυχνίτης, Pl. Com.146. -ίδιον, τό, v. λυχνεῖον. ⊛ -ίον or -ιον, τό, = λυχνεῖον, Antiph.55.2, Theoc.21.36, Luc.*Symp.*46, *IG*5(2).514.16 (Lycosura, ii B.C.). 2. *lamp*, *PTeb.*406.12 (iii A.D.). ⊛ -ίς, ίδος, ἡ, *rose campion*, *Lychnis coronaria*, used for garlands, Thphr.*HP*6.8.3, *AP* 4.1.23 (Mel.), Dsc.3.100. 2. λ. ἀγρία *corn cockle*, *Agrostemma Githago*, ib.101, cf. Nic.*Th.*899 (ubi v. Sch.). b. = ἀντίρρινον, Dsc. 4.130, Plin.*HN*25.129. II. a precious stone *that emits light*, prob. *ruby*, Luc.*Syr.D.*32, cf. Dercyl.11 :—also **λύχνις**, ὁ, D.P. 329, Orph.*L.*271. -ίσκος, ὁ, Dim. of λύχνος II, Luc.*VH*2. 30. ⊛ -ίτης [ῑ], ου, ὁ, *a precious stone of a red colour*, Pl.*Erx.*400d, Str.17.3.11, Plin.*HN*37.104 (v.l.), Eust.ad D.P.327. II. λ. λίθος a name for Parian marble, which was quarried by lamplight, Varro ap.Plin.*HN*36.14. ⊛ -ῖτις, ιδος, ἡ, *candlewick*, *Verbascum mallophorum*, the leaves of which served as lampwicks, Plin.*HN*25.121, *BGU*485.10 (ii A.D.); = φλομίς, Dsc.4.103.

**λυχνό-βιος**, ον, *living by lamplight*, Senec.*Ep.*122. -ειδής, ές, *lamplike*, φῶς Iamb.*Protr.*21.κδ'. ⊛ -καΐα, Ion. -ΐη, ἡ, *lighting of lamps, illumination*, Cratin.227 (but cf. Cratin.9 D.), D.C.79.16; a *Feast of Lanterns* at Sais, Hdt.2.62, J.*Ap.*2.9 (pl.). -καυστέω, = sq., Cratin.9 D. -καυτέω, *light lamps*, τῆς πόλεως -ούσης D.C.63. 20: a pecul. form λυχνοκῶσα, = λυχνοκαυτοῦσα, in Telecl.60. ⊛ -καυτία, ἡ, = λυχνοκαΐα, λυχναψία, Ath.15.701a. -μαντεία, ἡ, *divination by means of a lamp*, *PMag.Lond.*121.540,556 (-τία Pap.), *PMag.Par.* 1.952 (-τία).

⊛ **λύχνον**, τό, = λύχνος, Hippon.22 Diehl, *BGU*338.1, al. (ii/iii A.D.).

**λυχνο-ποιέω**, *make lamps and lanterns*, And.*Fr.*5(6): -ποιΐα, ἡ, f.l. for -καΐαν, Them.*Or.*4.49a: -ποιός, ὁ, *maker of lamps* or *lanterns*, Ar.*Pax*690, Philetaer.4, *Cat.Cod.Astr.*8(4).215. -πολις, εως, ἡ, *city of lamps*, Luc.*VH*1.29. -πωλέω, *deal in lamps* or *lanterns*, Sch.Luc.*Tim.*30. -πώλης, ου, ὁ, *dealer in lamps* or *lanterns*, Ar. *Eq.*739.

⊛ **λύχνος**, ὁ, pl. λύχνοι Batr.180, Ar.*Eq.*1315, Antiph.70,152, *PPetr.*2p.72 (iii B.C.): freq. also λύχνα, Hdt.2.62,133, E.*Cyc.*514 (lyr.), Call.*Hec.*1.4.11, etc., prob. in Alc.41.1. (Fr. λυκ-sno-, cf. *λύκη) :—*portable light, lamp*, χρύσεον λ. Od.19.34; λύχνα καίειν, ἀνάπτειν, *light lamps*, Hdt. ll. cc.; ἅπτε, παῖ, λ. Ar.*Nu.*18; λύχνους ἅπτειν *to have an illumination*, Arr.*Epict.*2.17.37; λύχνους ἀποσβέσαι Ar.*Pl.*668; λ. ἀπεσβήκει had been put out, Pl.*Smp.*218b; περὶ λύχνων ἁφάς about *lamp-lighting time*, i.e. towards nightfall, Hdt.7.215, D.S.19.31; πάννυχος λ. παρακαίεται *lamps* are kept burning all night, Hdt.2.130; καύσεις λύχνων *Sammelb.*1161.14 (i B.C.); ἔλαιον ἡμῖν οὐκ ἔνεστ' ἐν τῷ λύχνῳ Ar.*Nu.*56; cf. κεράτινος. 2. in pl., οἱ λύχνοι or τὰ λύχνα *the lamp-market*, οὐκ τῶν λ. ib.1065. II. a fish, Str. 17.2.4, Hsch.; cf. Lat. *lucerna*, Plin.*HN*9.82.

⊛ **λυχνοῦχος**, ὁ, (ἔχω) *lampstand*, καὶ τὸν λ. ἔκφερ' ἐνθεὶς τὸν λύχνον Pherecr.40; διαστίλβονθ' ὁρῶμεν ὥσπερ ἐν καινῷ λ. Ar.*Fr.*8; ἐξελὼν ἐκ τοῦ λυχνούχου τὸν λύχνον Alex.102, cf. Lys *Fr.*83.

**λυχνο-φορέω**, *carry a lamp*, λυχνοφορίοντες (Lacon.) Ar.*Lys.*1003. -φόρος, ον, *carrying a lamp*, Posidon.36 J., Plu.*Pomp.*52, J.*Ap.*2.9.

**λυχν-ώδης**, ες, *like a lamp*, opp. πυρώδης, Heph.Astr.1.23. -ωμα, ατος, τό, = ὀθόνιον, Sch.Ar.*Ach.*1175; cf. λαμπάδιον II. 1.

⊛ **λύω**, poet. imper. λῦθι Pi.*Fr.*85: fut. λύσω [ῠ] Il.1.29, etc.: aor. ἔλῦσα 18.244, etc.: pf. λέλῠκα Th.7.18, Ar.*V.*992 (ἀπο-), etc.:—Pass., pf. λέλυμαι Il.8.103, etc.: plpf. ἐλελύμην [ῠ] Od.22.186, etc.: aor. ἐλύθην, Ep. λύθην [ῠ] 8.360, E.*Hel.*860, Th.2.103, etc.: fut. λῠθήσομαι Pl.*Ti.*41b, Isoc.12.116, etc., also λελύσομαι [ῡ] D.14.2, X. *Cyr.*6.2.37 (ἀπο-): Ep. aor. Pass. λύμην [ῠ] Il.21.80; λύτο [ῠ] ib.114, but λῦτο 24.1 (at beginning of line, v.l. λύτο); λύντο 7.16: also 3 sg. opt. plpf. λελῦτο Od.18.238:—**Med.**, fut. λύσομαι Il.1.13, etc.: aor. ἐλυσάμην 14.214: pf. Pass. λέλυμαι in med. sense, D.36.45, Arist.*Rh.* 1400$^a$22 (cf. δια-, κατα-λύω): fut. λύσομαι in pass. sense, (δια-) Th.2. 12, (ἐπι-) Lys.25.33 codd. (καταλύσεσθαι edd.), (κατα-) X.*Cyr.*1.6. 9.—Homer uses all tenses exc. pf. Act., pres. and fut. Pass. [In pres. and impf. ῡ always in Att., ῠ mostly in Ep., though Hom. has ῡ twice, ἔλῡεν Il.23.513, λῡει Od.7.74; also in compds., ἀλλύεσκεν 2.105, ἀλλύουσαν ib.109: in fut. and aor. 1 ῡ always: in other tenses ῠ always, exc. in the forms λελῦτο, λῦτο (v. supr.).] (Cf. Lat. *luo* (pay), *re-luo*, *solvo* (for *se-luo*), *solūtus*, etc.) :—*loosen*: I. of things, *unbind, unfasten*, esp. clothes and armour, λῦσε δέ οἱ ζωστῆρα, θώρηκα, Il.4. 215, 16.804; λ. παρθενίην ζώνην *loose* the maiden-girdle, of the husband after marriage, Od.11.245; of the wife, λύοι χαλινὸν ὑφ' ἥρωϊ παρθενίας Pi.*I.*8(7).48; ἔνθα παρθένει' ἔλυσ' ἐγὼ κορεύματα E.*Alc.*177; so ἔλυσας.. ἅγνευμα σόν Id.*Tr.*501; freq. of the tackling of ships, λ. πρυμνήσια, ἱστία, λαῖφος, etc., Od.2.418, 15.496,552, *h.Ap.*406, etc. (never in Il.); λ. πρύμνας, νεῶν πόδα, E.*Hec.*539,1020, etc.: abs., λύειν, of ships, *set sail*, λῦε, κυβερνήτα *APl.*1.6*.9 (Panteleus); ἀσκὸν λ. *untie* a skin (used as a bag), Od.10.47: freq. in Trag., λ. στολάς, πέπλον, S.*OC*1597, *Tr.*924; λ. ἡνίαν *slacken* the rein, Id.*El.*743; κλῄθρων λυθέντων when the gates have been *opened*, A.*Th.*396; λ. γράμματα, δέλτον, *open* a letter, E.*IA*38 (anap.), 307; λ. πέδας, δεσμά, A.*Eu.* 645 (Pass.), E.*HF*1123; ἀρβύλας A.*Ag.*945; ἀρτάνας.. δέρης ἔλυσαν *loosed* it from my neck, ib.876, cf. E.*Hipp.*781:—Med., ἀπὸ στήθεσφιν ἐλύσατο κεστὸν ἱμάντα *undid her* belt, Il.14.214; but λύοντο τεύχεα they *undid* the armour *for themselves*, i.e. stripped it off (others), 17.318; later λυσαμένα πλοκαμῖδας *unbinding her* hair, Bion 1.20, etc. b. in various phrases, στόμα λ. *open* the mouth, E.*Hipp.*1060, Isoc.12.96; γλῶσσαν λ. εἰς αἰσχροὺς μύθους Critias 6.9 D.; λ. βλεφάρων ἕδραν wake up, E.*Rh.*8 (anap.); λ. ὀφρύν *unfold* the brow, Id. *Hipp.*290; λ. ἄχος ἀπ' ὀμμάτων S.*Aj.*706 (lyr.), etc. 2. of living beings, a. of horses, etc., *unyoke, unharness*, opp. ζεύγνυμι, Od.4. 35; ἐξ ὀχέων, ὑπὲξ ὀχέων, Il.5.369, 8.504; ὑφ' ἅρμασιν 18.244; ὑπὸ ζυγοῦ Od.4.39; ὑπὸ ζυγόφιν Il.24.576; ὑπ' ἀπήνης Od.7.6 (also in Med., μὴ.. ὑπ' ὄχεσφι λυώμεθα μώνυχας ἵππους *unyoke* our horses, Il. 23.7; βόε λῦσαι Hes.*Op.*608); λύε μώνυχας ἵππους *loosed* them, Il.10. 498; λ. κύνα *let* him *loose*, X.*Cyn.*6.13, etc. b. of men, *release, deliver*, esp. from bonds or prison, and so, generally, from difficulty or danger, Il.15.22, Od.8.345, 12.53, D.24.206, etc.; ὁ λύσων *he that shall deliver*, A.*Pr.*771,785: c. gen. rei, τὸν.. θεοὶ κακότητος ἔλυσαν Od.5.397, cf. Pi.*P.*3.50, etc.; λ. τινὰ δεσμῶν A.*Pr.*1006; ὄκνου S. *Tr.*181; τὼ.. ἐκ δεσμοῖο λύθεν Od.8.360, cf. Pi.*O.*4.23, A.*Pr.*873, E.*Hipp.*1244, Pl.*R.*360c; also λ. δόμους ἁβρότατος *rob* the house of.., Pi.*P.*11.34; λ. τινὰ τῆς ἀρχῆς *depose* him from.., D.S.13. 92:—Med., prop. *get one loosed* or *set free*, λύσασθαί τινα δυσφροσυνάων Hes.*Th.*528; ὅσπερ Ἰὼ πημονᾶς ἐλύσατο A.*Supp.*1065 (lyr.):—Pass., λυθῆναι τὰς πέδας D.S.17.116; λέλυται γὰρ λαὸς ἐλεύθερα βάζειν, ὡς ἐλύθη ζυγὸν ἀλκᾶς *has been let loose* to speak, since the yoke *was loosed*, A.*Pers.*592 (lyr.). c. of prisoners, *release on receipt of ransom, admit to ransom, release*, Il.1.29, 24.137,555, etc.; λ. τινά τινι 1.20, 24.561, Od.10.298; Σαρπηδόνος ἔντεα καλὰ λύσειαν *would give* them *up*, Il.17.163; in full, λ. τινὰ ἀποίνων 11.106; χρημάτων μεγάλων Hdt.2.135 (Pass.); ἀνὴρ ἀντ' ἀνδρὸς λυθεὶς Th.5.3:—Med., *release by payment of ransom, get* a person *released, redeem*, Il.1.13, 24. 118, al., Od.10.284,385, Pl.*Mx.*243c, D.19.229; λύσασθαί τινας ἐκ πολεμίων Lys.12.20; ἵππον X.*An.*7.8.6; ὅσους αὐτὸς ἐλυσάμην τῶν αἰχμαλώτων D.19.169; λ. τινὶ τὸ χωρίον Id.50.28; ἑαυτοὺς λ. *pay their own ransom*, Id.19.169; *buy* from a pimp, Ar.*V.*1353. d. λελύσθαι τῶν νόμων, = Lat. *legibus solvi*, D.C.53.18. 3. *give up*, [θρόνον] λῦσον ἄμμιν Pi.*P.*4.155. II. *resolve a whole into its parts, dissolve, break up*, λ. ἀγορήν *dissolve* the assembly, Il.1.305; ἀγορὰς ἠμὲν λύει ἠδὲ καθίζει Od.2.69, etc.:—Pass., λῦτο δ' ἀγών Il.24.1; μὴ λυθείη ἡ στρατιά X.*Cyr.*6.1.2; πρὶν ⟨ἂν⟩.. ἡ ἀγορὰ (*market*) λυθῇ Id. *Oec.*12.1; λυθείσης τῆς συνουσίας Plb.5.15.3. 2. of concrete objects, σπάρτα λέλυνται, i.e. *have rotted*, Il.2.135; ῥαφαὶ δ' ἐλέλυντο ἱμάντων Od.22.186; λ. τὴν σχεδίην *break* it *up*, Hdt.4.97; [τὴν γέφυραν] X. *An.*2.4.17; τὴν ἀπόφραξιν ib.4.2.25. 3. esp. of physical strength, *loosen*, i.e. *weaken, relax*, λῦσε δὲ γυῖα *made* his limbs *slack* or *loose*, i.e. killed him, Il.4.469, al.; ὅς τοι γούνατ' ἔλυσα 22.335; πολλῶν τε καὶ ἐσθλῶν γούνατ' ἔλυσεν 5.176, etc.; ἀλλά οἱ αὖθι λῦσε μένος 16.332; πέλεκυς λῦσεν.. βοὸς μένος Od.3.450, cf. Il.17.29; but οἵ μοι καμάτῳ.. γούνατ' ἔλυσαν *made* my knees *weak* with toil, Od.20.118:—Pass., λύντο δὲ γυῖα, etc., as the effect of death, sleep, weariness, fear, Il. 7.16, etc.; καμάτῳ φίλα γυῖα λέλυντο 13.85, cf. Od.8.233; αὐτοῦ λύτο γούνατα καὶ φίλον ἦτορ Il.21.114,425; λύθη ψυχή τε μένος τε 5.296, etc.; λύθεν δέ οἱ ἅψεα πάντα Od.4.794, 18.189; λέλυνται γυίων ῥώμη A.*Pers.*913 (anap.); λύεται δέ μου μέλη E.*Hec.*438; λέλυμαι μελέων σύνδεσμα Id.*Hipp.*199 (anap.). b. λύει βλέφαρα *closes* her eyes *in sleep*, S.*Ant.*1302. c. metaph., λ. τὴν ἐν ταῖς ψυχαῖς πρὸς μάχην παρασκευήν X.*HG*7.5.22. 4. *undo, bring to naught, destroy*, πολίων κάρηνα Il.9.25; Τροίης κρήδεμνα 16.100, Od.13.388, cf. B.*Fr.*16.7; generally, *put an end to*, νείκεα Il.14.205; μελεδήματα 23.62; ἔριν E.*Ph.*81, *AP*9.316.12 (Leon.); πόλεμον Th.5.31; ἐπιμομφάν Pi.*O.*10(11).9; μέμψιν Democr.271; φόβον A.*Th.*270; φόβον καὶ τὴν ὑποψίαν Polystr.p.7 W., cf. Epicur.*Sent.*12; μοχθήματα S.*OC*1616; ἀνάγκας E.*Supp.*39; βίον, i.e. die, Id.*IT*692; αἰῶν' ἔλυσε, i.e. died, B.1.43; λ. τὸ τέλος βίου S.*OC*1720 (lyr.); μάχας Ar. *Pax*991 (anap.); νοσήματα Diocl.*Fr.*35 (Pass.), cf. Gal.6.476; κόπους Dsc.*Eup.*1.220; *forgive*, ἁμαρτήματα LXX *Jb.*42.9. b. in Prose, λ. νόμους *repeal* or *annul* laws, Hdt.3.82, D.3.10, Arist.*Pol.*1269$^a$15; οὐθὲν τῶν περὶ τὴν πολιτείαν ib.1298$^b$31; λ. ψήφῳ τὸ παράνομον Aeschin. 3.197 (Pass.), etc.; ἐπεὶ ἐκεῖνοι λέλυσαν τὰς σπονδὰς λελύσθαι μοι δοκεῖ ἡ ἐκείνων ὕβρις καὶ ἡ ἡμετέρα ὑποψία X.*An.*3.1.21; *rescind* a vote, ψῆφον λύει ὁ νόμος D.24.2; *revoke* a will, διαθήκην Is.6.33, etc. (but in Pass., *to be opened*, of a will, *POxy.*715.19 (ii A.D.), etc.); *unbind* a spell, Iamb.*Myst.*3.27:—Pass., λέλυται πάντα all *ties are broken*, all *is in confusion*, D.25.25. c. as a technical term, *solve* a difficulty, a problem, a question, λύεται ἡ ἀπορία Pl.*Prt.*324e, al.; λ. ζήτημα Gal.6.436. d. *refute* an argument, Pl.*Grg.*509a, Arist.*Rh.*1402$^b$ 24, al.; cf. λύσις II. 4b, λυτικός II. e. *unravel* the plot of a tragedy, opp. πλέκειν, Id.*Po.*1456$^a$10. f. λ. τὴν φάσιν, of the Moon, *pass out of*, Vett.Val.134.1, cf. 2. 5. *break* a legal agreement or obligation, τὸν νόμον Hdt.6.106; τὰς σπονδὰς Th.1.23,78, cf. 4.23, al.; τὰ συγκείμενα Lys.6.41; σίς κε τὰς ϝρήτας τάσδε λύσῃ whoso *breaks* this agreement, *Inscr.Cypr.*135.29 H. 6. in physical sense, *dissolve*, λύθεν, opp. πάγεν, Emp.15.4; τὸ θερμὸν λύει, opp. πήγνυσι, Arist.*Mete.*384$^b$11, cf. 382$^b$33 (Pass.); ἀμμωνιακὸν ὄξει λύσας Gal.11. 106; *melt*, παγείσας χιόνας Hdn.8.4.2; τι πυρὶ λ. *Hippiatr.*52. 7. of medicines, λ. τὴν κοιλίαν Arist.*Pr.*863$^b$29, cf. Hp.*Acut.*(*Sp.*)38, Diocl.*Fr.*140; so of the effects of terror, Arist.*Pr.*877$^a$32 (Pass.). 8. *resolve* into ◡◡, in Pass., Heph.8,10, Aristid.Quint.1.28. III. *solve, fulfil, accomplish*, τὰ τοῦ θεοῦ μαντεῖα S.*OT*407; ὅρκον Plb.6. 58.4. IV. *atone for, make up for*, τὰς πρότερον ἁμαρτίας Ar.*Ra.*

691; λύσων ὅσ' ἐξήμαρτον S.*Ph.*1224; λ. φόνον φόνῳ Id.*OT*101, E.*Or.*511; αἱ πρόσοδοι λύουσι τἀναλώματα Diph.32.5:—Med., τῶν πάλαι πεπραγμένων λύσασθ' αἷμα..δίκαις A.*Ch.*804 (lyr.). V. μισθὸν λύειν *pay* wages *in full*, *quit oneself of* them, used only in cases of obligation, X.*Ages.*2.31. 2. τέλη λύειν, = λυσιτελεῖν, *pay*, *profit*, *avail*, ἔνθα μὴ τέλη λύει φρονοῦντι where *it boots* not to be wise, S.*OT* 316: but more freq. λύει without τέλη, construed like λυσιτελεῖ, abs., λύει δ' ἄλγος E.*Med.*1362, cf. *PSI*4.400.16: c. dat. pers., φημὶ τοιούτους γάμους λύειν βροτοῖσιν E.*Alc.*628, cf. *Hipp.*441: c. inf., πῶς οὖν λύει..ἐπιβάλλειν; Id.*Med.*1112 (anap.); ἐμοί τε λύει τοῖσι μέλλουσιν τέκνοις τὰ ζῶντ' ὀνῆσαι *it is good for* me to benefit my living children by means of those to come, ib.566; λύει ἀπελθεῖν *UPZ*77 i 12 (ii B.C.): c. acc. et inf., λύει γὰρ ἡμᾶς οὐδέν, οὐδ' ἐπωφελεῖ,..θανεῖν *it is* not *expedient that* we should die (οὐδ' ἐπωφελεῖ being parenthetic), S.*El.* 1005; οὐ γάρ με λύει..κακορροθεῖσθαι E.*Sthen.Prol.*35; cf. λυσιτελέω.

⊛ **λῶ**, Dor. Verb, = θέλω: 1 sg. indic., λῶ τι μυσίξαι νέον Ar.*Lys.*981; 2 sg., αἰ λῇς, = εἰ θέλεις, Epich.170.7, 172.4, Ar.*Ach.*766, cf. 776; ὅ τι τὺ λῇς Epich.171.10; ὅ τι λῇς Ar.*Lys.*95; καὶ τὺ λῇς Crates Com.41 (cj.); ἥντινα λῇς Call.*Dian.*19; λῇς..τῆδε καθίξας..συρίσδεν; Theoc. 1.12; 3 sg., λῇ..λαβεῖν; Epich.170.8: 1 pl., ἁμές γε λῶμες αἴ τις..λῇ τοῦτ' ἀποδόμεν Ar.*Lys.*1162; 3 pl., ἐπιλέγω τοῖς θεοῖς, ὅτι λῶντι Epich. 35.12, cf. Theoc.4.14: subj., καἴ κά τις..λῇ τήνῳ λέγειν Epich.35.5, cf. *GDI*4982.2, *Leg.Gort.*3.18, al.; αἴ κα λῇς Theoc.5.21; κἂν λῆτε Ar. *Lys.*1105; λείωντι *Leg.Gort.*2.35, al.; but αἴ κα λῶντι *Inscr.Olymp.* 22 (Selinus): opt. 1 sg. λέῳμι Hsch.; 3 sg. λείοι *Leg Gort.*8.13, al., *GDI*5011.6, λέοι ib.5072*b*6, λῴη Epich.[285]; 3 pl. λείοιεν *GDI*4984.12; Elean 3 dual λεοίταν (or ληοίταν) *Inscr.Olymp.*16.3: inf., αἰ μὲν λῆν Foed.Lacon.ap.Th.5.77 (Ahrens, for ἐμενλῆν etc.): part. λέων *Abh.Berl.Akad.*1925(5).21 (Cyrene), λείοντος *Leg.Gort.*8.22, λείοντα *BCH*27.221 (Lato), etc.; ἐξέστω καὶ ἄλλῳ τῷ λῶντι *IG*9(1).694.118 (Corc.); συνδειπνέων τῷ λῶντι.., καὶ τῷ γα μηδὲ λῶντι Epich.35.1,2 (Ahrens for γαμηλιῶντι; μὴ λείοντι Brause); λῶσα Hsch.:—Med., 3 pl. pres. subj. λῶνται *IG*12(7).67.11 (Amorgos, Dor. dial.); 3 sg. λάηται· βούληται, Hsch.:—*wish*, *desire*, ll. cc. (Cf. λῆ-μα, λῆσις (B), perh. also λελίημαι: the dialects seem to point to λείω (fr. λεί-yω) as the original form, but the forms with λω- cannot have resulted from contr. of λειο-: a stem λαο- is doubtful, λάηται (βούληται) Hsch. being perh. corrupt.)

**λωβ-άζω**, = sq., f.l. for λωβᾶσθαι, Hp.*Ep.*17. **-άομαι**, Ion. **-έομαι** Id.*Art.*35 (as v.l.), **-εῦμαι** Herod.3.69; Dor. impf. ἐλωβῆτο Sophr.21: fut. -ήσομαι Pl.*Cri.*47d: aor. ἐλωβησάμην Hdt.3.154, cf. Theoc.5.109, etc.: for pf. and aor. Pass., v. infr.: (λώβη):—*outrage*, *maltreat*, c. acc. pers., also with cogn. acc. added, λώβην λωβᾶσθαί τινα *do* one *despite*, Il.13.623; esp. *maim*, *mutilate*, τινα Hdt. l. c.; ἑωυτὸν λωβᾶται λώβην ἀνήκεστον ibid.; ἀρτάναισι λωβᾶται βίον *brings* her life *to a shameful end* by the halter, S.*Ant.*54; ἀνδρῶν εὔνιδας λ. *dishonouring* them, E.*Or.*929; λ. τοὺς νέους *harm* their pupils, Pl.*Prt.*318d; of the effect of drudging work, τὰ σώματα λωβῶνται Arist.*Pol.*1258$^b$37; also λ. πόλιν Lys.26.9; [ἄστεα] κατ' ἄκρας Theoc. 16.89; *pillage*, πόλιν Plb.4.54.2; *damage* statues, etc., *IG*3.1417: less freq. c. dat., Ar.*Eq.*1408, Pl.*Cri.*47e, D.H.13.4, Orac.ap.Jul.*Ep.*88: abs., *act outrageously*, Il.1.232, 2.242. II. Act. λωβάω only Ps.-Phoc.38, and κατ-ελώβησαν in Plb.15.33.9: but pf. is used as Pass., λελωβημένος *mutilated*, Hdt.3.155, Pl.*Grg.*511a, *R.*611b, etc.; esp. of leprous persons, Man.ap.J.*Ap.*1.28: also aor. Pass., μεγάλας λώβας λωβηθείς Pl.*Grg.*473c: and Ion. pres. 3 pl. λωβέονται in Hp.*Art.* l. c. (v. l.); cf. ἀπο-, ἐκ-λωβάομαι. **-εία**, ἡ, *leprosy*, Zonar. **-εύω**, *mock*, *make a mock of*, τινα Od.23.15,26. **-η**, ἡ, *outrage*, *dishonour*, αἶσχος λώβη τε 18.225; λώβην λωβᾶσθαι (v. λωβάομαι); τείσετε λ. ye shall pay for the *outrage*, Il.11.142; ἀπὸ πᾶσαν ἐμοὶ δόμεναι..λ. 9.387; but λ. τείσασθαι exact retribution for *an outrage*, i.e. avenge it, 19.208, Od.20.169, S.*Aj.*181 (lyr.); ἐπὶ λώβᾳ for *ruin* or *destruction*, Id.*Ant.*792 (lyr.), cf. E.*Hec.*647 (lyr.); ὡς ἐπὶ λώβᾳ Id.*HF*882 (lyr.); λ. καὶ διαφθορά Pl.*Men.*91c, etc.; esp. *mutilation*, *maiming*, Hdt.3.154: pl., S.*Aj.*1392; λώβας λωβηθείς Pl.*Grg.*473c. 2. of persons, *a disgrace*, λώβην τ' ἔμεναι καὶ ὑπόψιον Il.3.42, cf. E.*El.*165 (lyr.), Herod.7.95; ποιητῶν λῶβαι, of the Grammarians, *AP*11.322 (Antiphan.); οὐ γὰρ Ἀρκάδεσσι λώβα no *insult* to the Arcadians, Alc. 38. II. *a form of leprosy*, Gal.14.757. **-ήεις**, εσσα, εν, *outrageous*, A.R.3.801, Tryph.261. **-ήμων**, ον, gen. ονος, = foreg., in acc. sg., λωβήμονα κῆρα Nic.*Al.*536 (v. l. λωβήτορα). ⊛ **-ησις**, εως, ἡ, = λώβη, Ptol.*Tetr.*151. **-ήτειρα**, fem. of sq., *AP*9.251 (Even.). **-ητήρ**, ῆρος, ὁ and ἡ, *foul slanderer*, Il.2.275, 11.385: generally, *destroyer*, of the Erinyes, S.*Ant.*1074; ἀοιδᾶν Tim.*Pers.*231. II. *worthless wretch*, Il.24.239, A.R.3.372, Tryph.21. **-ητής**, οῦ, ὁ, = foreg., λ. τέχνης *one who disgraces* his trade, Ar.*Ra.*93. **-ητός**, ή, όν, *despitefully treated*, *outraged*, λωβητὸν ἔθηκε (= ἐλωβήσατο) Il.24.531, cf. Hes.*Sc.*366; κείνης δρῶν λωβητὸν εἶδος S.*Tr.*1069; λωβητὸν αὐτὸν ἐκβαλεῖν Id.*Aj.*1388; μόχθῳ λωβᾶτός Id.*Ph.*1102 (lyr.). II. Act., *insulting*, *abusive*, αἰσχρὰ καὶ λ. ἔπη ib.607; λωβητὸν ἐμπόλημα *baneful*, Id.*Tr.*538, cf. Tryph.21 (v.l.). **-ήτωρ**, ορος, ὁ, = λωβητήρ, Opp.*H.*4.684, *AP*6.168 (Paul. Sil.), etc.: as fem., λωβήτορα κῆρα v.l. for λωβήμονα in Nic.*Al.*536. **-ός**, ή, όν, = λωβητός, coinage in *EM*570.37.

**λωγάλιοι**· ἀστράγαλοι ἢ πόρνοι, Hsch.; cf. sq. and v. λωγάς. **λωγάνιον**, τό, *dewlap of oxen*, Ambraciote and Epirote word, Luc.*Lex.* 3, cf. Dionys.Utic.ap.Sch. l. c.—In Suid. **λογάνιον** sine expl., in Hsch. **λωγάλιον**. **λωγάς**· πόρνη, Id.; cf. λωγάλιοι. **λώγασος**· ταυρεία μάστιξ, Id. **λωγάω**, = λέγω, Theognost.*Can.*149; ἐλώγη· ἔλεγεν, Hsch. (ἐλωγῆ· ἔλεγον cod.), Dor. contr. from ἐλώγαε. ⊛ **λώγη**· καλάμη, καὶ συναγωγὴ σίτου, Id.

**λῶδιξ**, ῑκος, ἡ, *blanket* or *counterpane*, Lat. *lodix*, *Peripl.M.Rubr.* 24, *BGU*1564.8 (ii A.D.):—Dim. **λωδίκιν** prob. in ib.93.24 (ii/iii A.D.); **λωδίκιον**, *Stud.Pal.*20.67.26 (ii/iii A.D.), etc.; cf. λωτίκιον.

**λώεσσαν**· τὴν ἅμαξαν, Hsch. (also **λώλεσσαν**). **λωϊσμόν**· χῶμα ἢ κλωσμένον, Id. **λωΐτερος**, v. λωΐων. **λωϊτήνη**· συμφερωτέρα, Id.

⊛ **λωΐων**, (λῶ), ὁ, ἡ, λώϊον, τό, gen. ονος; Att. **λῴων**, **λῷον**, A.*Pers.* 526; acc. sg. and neut. pl. λῴω S.*Ph.*1079, Pl.*Phlb.*11b; acc. pl. λῴους S.*Tr.*736: also an ο-stem λώϊος (Hdn.Gr.1.122, Thgn.800) from which come neut. pl. λώϊα Thgn.853, Theoc.26.32, and λῷα prob. in Thgn.96: gen. pl. τῶν λῴων *IG*12(9).1179.36 (Chalcis, ii A.D.):—*more desirable*, *more agreeable*, *better*, Hom. only in neut., πολὺ λώϊόν ἐστι, τόδε λ. ἐστι, Il.1.229, Od.2.169, al.; τῷ σε χρὴ δόμεναι καὶ λώϊον ἠέ περ ἄλλοι σίτου 17.417: as Adv., γνωσόμεθ' ἀλλήλων καὶ λώϊον 23. 109; μετρεῖσθαι Hes.*Op.*350; but οὐκ..ἄλλη τῆσδε λωΐων γυνή Semon. 7.30: also Comp. λωΐτερος, α, ον, also used by Hom. only in neut., λωΐτερον καὶ ἄμεινον Od.1.376, 2.141: masc. in A.R.3.850, etc.: fem. in Call.*Aet.*4.1.7, *AP*5.111.6 (Phld.).—In Trag. λῴων was used generally as Comp. of ἀγαθός, A.*Pers.*526, etc.; φρόνησιν λαβεῖν λῴω S. *Ph.*1079; λῷον φρονεῖ Id.*OT*1038; λῴους φρένας ἀμείψασθαι Id.*Tr.* 736; βίου λῴονος κυρῆσαι Id.*OT*1513; εἰς τὸ λῷον σὸν μεθέστηκεν κέαρ E.*Med.*911: sts. also in Prose, ἄμεινον καὶ λῷον Pl.*Lg.*828a; ἀμείνω καὶ λῴω Id.*Phlb.*11b; λ. καὶ ἄμεινον X.*An.*6.2.15, *SIG*398.41 (Cos, iii B.C.), 1044.4 (Halic., iv/iii B.C.), cf. *Berl.Sitzb.*1927.165 (Cyrene), etc. II. Sup. **λῷστος**, η, ον, Thgn.255; λῷστον δὲ τὸ ζῆν ἄνοσον S.*Fr.*356; τὰ λῷστα βουλεύων A.*Pr.*206, etc.; παραινέσαι τὰ λ. ib. 310; τὰ λ. λέγειν Id.*Ag.*1053, cf. Cratin.4 D.; ὦ λῷστε Πῶλε *my good friend*, like ὦ βέλτιστε, Pl.*Grg.*467b, cf. X.*Smp.*4.1, etc.

**λώκιον**, τό, a piece of furniture, *Stud.Pal.*20.46.25 (ii/iii A.D.), 67.40 (ii/iii A.D.).

**λώλεσσαν**, v. λώεσσαν. **λῶλον**· βρῶμα ἐκ γιγάρτων καὶ σύκων γενόμενον, παιδίοις πεφωσμένον, Hsch. **λωλώ**· ὅταν σῦκα μετὰ γιγάρτων φωσθῇ, Id.

⊛ **λῶμα**, ατος, τό, *hem*, *fringe*, *border*, of a robe, Lxx *Ex.*28.29(33), al.:—Dim. **λωμάτιον**, τό, *AP*11.210 (Lucill.).

**λῶντι**, v. λῶ.

⊛ **Λῷος** (cf. Hdn.Gr.1.112, Theognost.*Can.*57), ὁ, a Macedonian month, [Ep.Phil.]ap.D.18.157, Call.*Epigr.*46, *PCair.Zen.*88.12 (iii B.C.), Plu.*Alex.*3, J.*AJ*4.4.7, Gal.17(1).21, *Supp.Epigr.*2.480 (Scythia, iv A.D.), Jul.*Mis.*361d.

**λωπεύει**· ψεύδεται, Hsch.

⊛ **λώπ-η**, ἡ, (λέπω) *covering*, *robe*, *mantle*, δίπτυχον ἀμφ' ὤμοισιν ἔχουσ' εὐεργέα λώπην Od.13.224, cf. Theoc.25.254, A.R.2.32:—also **λῶπος**, εος, τό, Alc.*Supp.*18.2 (dub.), Hippon.3, Anacr.80, Herod. 8.36, Theoc.14.66, Ps.-Luc.*Philopatr.*22.—Only poetic in class. writers, though prose writers have the derivs. λώπιον, λωποδύτης. **-ία**, ἡ, = δέρμα, *EM*571.1 s.v. λῶπος. **-ίζω**, *uncover*, *strip*, Hsch., Suid.: found only in compds. ἀπολωπίζω, περιλωπίζω, etc.; S.*Tr.*925, ἐκ δ' ἐλώπισεν πλευράν, belongs to ἐκλωπίζω.—Cf. λοπίζω. **-ιον**, Dim. of λώπη, Arist.*Metaph.*1006$^b$26, *Top.*103$^a$10, *IG*4$^2$(1).122.127 (Epid.), *AP*6.245 (Diod.); ἐς τὰ λ.· ἡ τῶν ἱματίων ἀγορά (Tarent.), Hsch. **-ιστός**, όν, *with a patched cloak*, *Com. Adesp.*78.

⊛ **λωπο-δυσία**, ἡ, (λῶπος, δύω) prop. *slipping into* another's *clothes*: hence, *highway-robbery*, J.*BJ*4.3.4 (pl.), *Gloss.* **-δυσίου δίκη**, prosecution for λωποδυσία, Hermog.*Id.*2.6. **-δυτέω**, *steal clothes*, esp. from bathers or travellers, Pl.*R.*575b, X.*Mem.*1.2.62, Arist. *Pol.*1267$^a$4; λ. ἐσθῆτα Luc.*Bis Acc.*34; λ. τινὰ ἐσθῆτα Philostr.*VA* 8.7. II. generally, *rob*, *plunder*, Ar.*Ec.*565, *Pl.*165, Diph.32.14, Lxx 1 *Es.*4.24: c. acc. pers., Ar.*Ra.*1075, D.9.22; of plagiarists, λ. Ὅμηρον *AP*11.130 (Poll.). **-δύτης** [ῠ], ου, ὁ, *clothes-stealer*, esp. one who steals of bathers, or strips travellers, S.*Epigr.*4. II. generally, *thief*, *robber*, *footpad*, *IG*1$^2$.44.5, Antipho 5.9, Cratin.206, Ar.*Av.*497, *Ra.*772, Lys.10.10, Phld.*Rh.*2.144 S., etc.; λωποδυτῶν θάνατον αἱρεῖσθαι D.4.47; λ. ἀλλοτρίων ἐπέων *plagiarist*, *AP*11.130 (Poll.), cf. Arr.*Epict.*2.19.28.

**λῶπος**, τό, = λώπη (q. v.).

⊛ **λωρίκιον** [ῑκ], τό, Dim. of Lat. *lorica*, *corslet*, *Sammelb.*7249.18 (iii/iv A.D.). **λωρίον**, *gallica*, *Gloss.*

**λωροκάπιστρον** [ᾰ], τό, *halter*, gloss on ῥυτήρ, Sch.rec.S.*Aj.*235.

**λωρόν**· πικρόν, Hsch. (Cf. Lat. *lorum* 'sour wine'.)

⊛ **λῶρος**, ὁ, = Lat. *lorum*, *thong*, Sch.Ar.*Ach.*724, Moer.p.195 P., Pall. *in Hp.Fract.*12.278 C., Steph. *in Hp.*1.211 D. II. = χρυσήλατος ἐπωμίς, Lyd.*Mag.*2.2. III. *arch*, οἱ λῶροι καλούμενοι τοῦ νεώ Procop.*Aed.*1.1.

**λωρο-τομέω**, *cut into thongs*, Sch.Ar.*Eq.*764 (Pass.). ⊛ **-τόμος**, ον, *cutting thongs*, Hsch. s.v. σκυτοτόμος, Sch.Pl.*Grg.*517e, Rhetor. in *Cat.Cod.Astr.*8(4).216.

**λωρυμνόν**· βαθύτατα, κατώτατα, Hsch. **λῷστος**, v. λωΐων.

**λωστύς**, ύος, ἡ, dub. sens. in Ἀρχ.Ἐφ.1923.39 (Oropus, iv B.C.).

**λῶταξ**, ᾰκος, ὁ, = αὐλητής, Zonar., Eust.344.37.

**λωτάριον**, τό, *flower of lotus*, Steph. *in Gal.*1.335 D., Paul.Aeg.3. 59, 7.12 (pl.).

⊛ **λωτέω**, *play the flute*, Zonar. II. *bloom*, πεδία λωτεῦντα Il.12. 283 (v.l. for λωτοῦντα); cf. λωτόεις. III. λωτεῦσι δέ, πάχνη, ἀνθεῖ ποιοῦσιν αἰσχρότητες, Hsch.

**λωτήριον**, v. λουτ-.

**λωτίζομαι**, *cull the best*, A.*Supp.*963; Ἄρης γὰρ οὐδὲν τῶν κακῶν λ.

S.*Fr.*724 (prob. cj.):—Act. in Hsch., λωτίζειν· ἀπανθίζεσθαι, ἀπολλύειν.—Cf. ἀπολωτίζω.

**λωτίκιον**, τό, = λωδίκιον, Dim. of λῶδιξ, *Sammelb.*7033.38 (v A. D.).

**λώτ-ῐνον**, τό, = λωτός III, *PBaden* 15.18 (i B. C.), *PFay.*111.11, al. (i A. D.). ⊛ **-ῐνος**, η, ον, (λωτός III. 1) *lotus*, ξύλον Thphr.*HP*4.2.9, 5.5.6; χόρτος *PSI*4.432.3 (iii B. C.); καρπός Dsc.2.76. II. *made of lotus-wood*, ὑποθυμίδες Anacr.39; κολεόν, μέγα λ. ἔργον Theoc.24.45; λ. αὐλοί (cf. λωτός III. 1 a, b) Ath.4.182d: hence λ. ἀηδόνες, of flutes, E.*Fr.*931. 2. *covered with lotus*, ὄχθοι Ἀχέροντος Sapph. p.44 Lobel. 3. *made of the flowers of Nymphaea Nelumbo* (cf. λωτός II), στέφανος Ath.15.677d.

⊛ **λῶτις**, ἁ, dub. sens. (perh. = λοῦσις), *IG*2².1126.26 (Amphict. Delph., iv B. C.); dat. λώτι prob. in *SIG*243*D*25 (Delph., iv B. C.).

**λώτισμα**, ατος, τό, *a flower*: metaph., like ἄνθος and ἄωτος, *the fairest, choicest, best*, γῆς Ἑλλάδος λωτίσματα E.*Hel.*1593, cf. A.*Fr.*99.17ᵃ.

**λωτο-βοσκός**, όν, *lotus-eating*, φῦλον *Trag.Adesp.*236. **-ειδής**, ές, *lotus-like* (signf. III. 1), Thphr.*HP*4.2.12. **-εις**, εσσα, εν, *overgrown with lotus*, πεδία λωτοῦντα (v. l. -εῦντα) *lotus*-plains, Il.12.283; or. *blooming* (λωτέω II). **-μήτρα**, ἡ, *fruit-pulp* of λωτός II, Plin.*HN*22.56, *PMag.Par.*1.754.

⊛ **λωτός**, ὁ (λῶτα· ἄνθη, Hsch. is perh. for ἄωτα), name applied to various plants and trees (Thphr.*HP*7.15.3, Plin.*HN*14.101, cf. Hsch.) providing fodder or fruit: I. fodder plants, 1. *clover, trefoil, Trifolium fragiferum*, Od.4.603, Thphr.*HP*7.8.3, 7.13.5, Dsc.4.111. 2. *fellbloom, Lotus corniculatus*, Il.14.348, Plin.*HN*22.55. 3. = τῆλις, *fenugreek, Trigonella Foenum-graecum*, Dsc.2.102; λ. ἄγριος *wild fenugreek, T. gladiata*, Id.4.111, Gal.12.65. 4. *melilot, T. graeca*, Thphr.*HP*9.7.3. b. *Italian melilot, Melilotus messanensis*, Dsc.4.110, Gal. l. c. 5. = κύτισος, *Medicago arborea*, Ps.-Dsc.4.112. II. *Nile water-lily, Egyptian lotus, Nymphaea Lotus*, Hdt.2.92, Thphr.*HP*4.8.9, *PHib.*1.152 (iii B. C.), Dsc.4.113, Plin.*HN*13.107; the blue species (*Nymphaea stellata*), Thphr.*HP*4.8.11; also, *Nymphaea Nelumbo*, Ath.3.73a. III. of trees found in Libya, 1. *nettle-tree, Celtis australis*, Thphr.*HP*1.5.3, 4.3.1, Dsc.1.117, etc.; used for making flutes, Thphr.*HP*4.3.4: hence b. in E. (lyr.) and later poets, *flute*, λ... Μουσᾶν θεράπων *El.*716, cf. *Pae.Delph.*12, *AP*7.182 (pl., Mel.); Λίβυς λ. E.*Tr.*544, *Hel.*170, *IA* 1036, prob. in Limen.13. c. *pipe* inserted in the νάβλα, Sopat. 10. d. *tube* or *stalk* of vaginal speculum, Aët.16.89, Paul.Aeg.6.73. 2. tree growing among the Lotophagi, *Zizyphus Lotus*, λωτοῖο.. μελιηδέα καρπόν Od.9.94, cf. Hdt.2.96, 4.177, Thphr.*HP*4.3.1–4, Plb.12.2.2.

**λωτο-τρόφος**, ον, (λωτός I) *producing lotus*, λειμαξ E.*Ph.*1571 (anap.). **-φάγοι** [ᾰ], οἱ, (λωτός III. 2) *Lotus-eaters*, a mythical people on the coast of North Africa, Od.9.84, Hdt.4.177, cf. X.*An.*3.2.25, Scyl.22, Plb.1.39.2:—their country was perh. called **Λωτοφαγία**, ἡ, Thphr.*HP*4.3.2 (dub. l.): hence Adj. fem. **Λωτοφαγῖτις** Σύρτις Str.17.3.17. **-φόρος**, ον, *lotus-bearing*, λειμών Pherecr.109.

**λωτρόν, λωτροχόος**, Dor. for λουτρ–. **λωφάξαλος**· ἐμπηδήσας, Hsch. **λῶφαρ**· λώφημα, Id.

**λωφ-άω**, *rest, give over*, ὅδε μὲν τάχα λωφήσει Il.21.292; εἰ λωφήσω τρεῖς ὥρας dub. in Phld.*Herc.*1251.18. 2. c. gen. (cf. καταλωφάω), *take rest* or *abate from, recover from*, χόλου, πόθου, A.*Pr.*378, 654; πόνου S.*Aj.*61; τῆς ὀδύνης Pl.*Phdr.*251c; φιλοτιμίας λελωφηκυῖαν Id.*R.*620c; so λ. ἀπὸ νόσου καὶ πολέμου Th.6.12. 3. c. part., *cease* to do, πρήσων A.R.4.819, cf. *AP*5.187 (Leon.). 4. *abate*, of pain, Hp.*Int.*49; of a disease, Th.2.49, Pl.*Lg.*854c; of misfortunes, Th.7.77; of wind, Arist.*Mete.*367ᵃ7; of the sea, Id.*Pr.*934ᵇ15; ὅταν λωφήσωσιν οἱ λίθοι X.*An.*4.7.6. II. trans., *lighten, relieve*, ὁ λωφήσων γὰρ οὐ πέφυκέ πω A.*Pr.*27: c. gen., ἀχέων λωφήσετε θυμόν *relieve* your mind *from* pains, Emp.145.2. **-έω**, Ion. (Ep.) for foreg., A.R.2.648, 4.1627, Nonn.*D.*1.172. **-ήϊος**, α, ον, *relieving*; λ. ἱερά *expiatory* offerings, A.R.2.485. **-ημα**, gloss on λῶφαρ, *relief*, Hsch., cj. in S.*Tr.*554. **-ησις**, εως, ἡ, *abatement, cessation*, τοῦ πολέμου ἀπὸ τῆς Πελοποννήσου Th.4.81; τῶν ὀδυνῶν Aët.11.5.

**λώψ**· χλαμύς, Hsch. **λῴων**, neut. λῷοι, Att. contr. for λωΐων, λώϊον.

# M

**M μ, μῦ**, τό, Ion. μῶ Democr.19: indecl., thirteenth (later twelfth) letter of the Gr. alphabet: as numeral μʹ = 40, but ͵μ = 40,000.—In Inscrr. M stands for μύριοι or μυριάς: hence [M] for πεντακισμύριοι or πέντε μυριάδες, 50,000.

**μ'**, by elision for με; also for μοι, Ep. and Lyr., Il.6.165, al., Sapph.2.13, but rarely if ever in Trag., dub. in E.*Med.*721, *IA*814, S.*Aj.*190 (lyr.).

⊛ **μά** (A) [ᾰ], Particle used in asseverations and oaths, c. acc. of the deity or thing appealed to; in itself neither affirmative nor negative, but made so by prefixing ναί or οὐ, or, in Att., by the context: thus, I. ναὶ μὰ.., in affirmation, ναὶ μὰ τόδε σκῆπτρον yea *by* this staff, Il.1.234, cf. *h.Merc.*460; ναὶ μὰ γὰρ ὅρκον Pi.*N.*11.24; ναὶ μὰ Δία, ναὶ μὰ τὸν Δία, etc., Ar.*Ach.*88, Pl.*R.*407b, etc.; also μὰ ναί *Inscr.Cypr.*109 H. II. οὐ μὰ.., in negation, οὐ μὰ γὰρ Ἀπόλλωνα, οὐ μὰ Ζῆνα, nay, *by*.., Il.1.86, 23.43; οὐ μὰ τὴν δέσποιναν Ἄρτεμιν S.*El.*626; οὔ τοι μὰ τοὺς δώδεκα θεούς Ar.*Eq.*235; οὐ μὰ τὸν Δία, οὔκουν οὕτω γε.. Pl.*Tht.*142e. III. after Hom. μά is freq. used alone, 1. chiefly in negation when the negative follows, μὰ Δί' οὐκ εἶδον ἐμαυτοῦ ἀμείνω ὑλοτόμον *IG*1².1084; μὰ τὴν πατρῴαν ἑστίαν, ἀλλ' οὐχ ὕβρει λέγω τάδ' S.*El.*881; μὰ τοὺς παρ' Ἅιδῃ νερτέρους ἀλάστορας, οὔτοι ποτ' ἔσται τοῦτο E.*Med.*1059; μὰ τὸν Ἀπόλλω, οὔκ Ar.*Th.*269, cf. A.*Ag.*1432, E.*Cyc.*262, Pl.*Prt.*312e; μὰ τὴν γῆν, μή σύγε δῷς Anaxil.9; μὰ δαίμονας, οὐκ ἀπὸ ῥυσμοῦ εἰκάζω Call.*Epigr.*44; μὰ τὸν Δία δὲ οὐδὲ νομίζω.. *IG*2².1099.30 (ii A. D.); μὰ σέ, Καῖσαρ, οὐδεὶς σε νικᾷ D.C.61.20: with preceding neg., οὐδ' ὄναρ, μὰ τὰς Μοίρας Herod.1.11: in answers, when the negation is expressed in the question, οὐκ ἀφ μ' ἐάσεις; Answ. μὰ Δί', ἐπεὶ κἀγὼ πόνηρός εἰμι Ar.*Eq.*336, cf. 338 where οὐκ ἐάσω is to be supplied after μὰ Δί' from the question, cf. *Ra.*951, *Pl.*400): when ἀλλά follows, δύο δραχμὰς μισθὸν τελεῖς; Answ. μὰ Δί', ἀλλ' ἔλαττον Id.*Ra.*174 (where οὐ τελῶ is understood, cf. ib.753, 779, 1053, X.*Mem.*2.13.3): in μὰ γῆν, μὰ κρήνας, μὰ ποταμούς, μὰ νάματα Antiph.296 = Timocl.38, the context is missing. b. in reply to an imper., ἀπόδος αὐτό; Answ. μὰ τὸν Ἀπόλλω Ar.*Th.*748. 2. in later Gr. in affirmation, δακρύω μὰ σέ, δαῖμον *Annales du Service* 27.32 (Egypt); μὰ τὴν Ἄρτεμιν Ἀκοντίῳ γαμοῦμαι Aristaenet.1.10, cf. Ach.Tat.8.5. IV. in colloquial discourse, esp. Att. (cf. Greg.Cor.p.150 S., Ph.2.271), the name of the deity sworn by was often suppressed, to avoid a downright oath, μὰ τόν Ar.*Ra.*1374 (lyr.), Pl.*Grg.*466e; μὰ τήν Men.369; ναὶ μὰ τόν Call.*Fr.*66d, Ael.*NA*3.19; ναὶ μὰ τάς (sc. Χάριτας) Suid. s. v. ναὶ μὰ τό (codd. dett.); οὐ μὰ τὸν—οὐκ ὀμόσω *AP*12.201 (Strat.), cf. 7.112 (D.L.). V. μά is sts. omitted after ναί (q. v.); also after οὐ, οὐ τὸν πάντων θεῶν θεὸν πρόμον Ἅλιον S.*OT*660 (lyr.); οὐ τὸν Ὄλυμπον ib.1088 (lyr.); οὐ τόνδ' Ὄλυμπον Id.*Ant.*758, cf. *El.*1063 (lyr.).

**μά** (B), Thess. for δέ, *IG*9(2).258.11 (Cierium, ii B. C.), 461*A*9 (Crannon, ii B. C.); also found at beginning of sentence in *POxy.*1216.10 (ii/iii A. D.).

**μά** (C) [ᾱ], Elean for μή, *Schwyzer*413.5.

**μᾶ**, shorter Aeol. and Dor. form for μάτηρ, in the phrase μᾶ γᾶ, = μῆτερ γῆ, A.*Supp.*890, 899 (both lyr.): as an exclam. used by women (perh. = Demeter), Herod.1.85, 4.20; μᾶ, πόθεν ὤνθρωπος; Theoc.15.89.

**μαατρόν**· μωρόν (Lacon.), Hsch.

⊛ **μᾰγᾰδ-ίζω**, *play the* μάγαδις, Theophil.7. II. of a choir, *sing a succession of notes in octaves*, μ. ἐν τῇ διὰ πασῶν συμφωνίᾳ Arist.*Pr.*921ᵃ12, cf. 918ᵇ40. **-ιον**, τό, Dim. of μαγάς, *BGU*1125.21 (i B. C.), Ptol.*Harm.*1.8, 3.1, v.l. in Luc.*DDeor.*7.4. ⊛ **-ις**, ῐ, gen. μαγάδιδος Ath.14.634c; nom. pl. μαγάδιδες S.*Fr.*238 (anap.) codd. Ath., Phillis ap.Ath.14.636b; also, dat. μαγάδι prob. in X.*An.*7.3.32, Anaxandr.35; acc. μάγαδιν Alcm.91, Anacr.18, cf. Poll.4.61 (-ῖν Diog.Ath.1.10, ῐν dub. in Anacr. l. c.); nom. pl. μαγάδεις Hsch.:—*magadis*, an instrument with twenty strings arranged in octaves, Lydian acc. to Ath.14.634f, but ascribed to the Thracians by Canthar.9, and derived from Thrac. pr. n. Μάγδις by Duris 28 J.; played with the finger, Aristox *Fr.Hist.*66; = πηκτίς, ibid., Menaechm.4 J. II. *a Lydian flute* or *flageolet*, producing a high and a low note together, Ion Trag.23 (cf. Aristarch.ap.Ath.14.634d), Anaxandr. l. c., cf. Did.ap.Ath.14.634e, Hsch. [μᾰ, but μᾱ- S.*Fr.*238 (anap.), nisi leg. μᾰγάδιδες.]

**μᾰγάζω**, f.l. for μαγαδίζω in Hsch. s. v. μαγάδεις.

**Μᾰγᾰρικός**, ὁ, = Μεγαρικός, acc. to the tradesmen's pronunciation, esp. of pottery, St.Byz. s. v. Μέγαρα, cf. *POxy.*1851 (vi A. D.), prob. (for Μακ–) in *PLond.*5.1904 (vi A. D.).

**μαγαρ-ίς**, ίδος, ἡ, = μικρὰ σπάθη, Hsch. **-ίσκος**, ὁ, = πινακίσκος, Id.; cf. μαργαρίσκος.

⊛ **μάγαρον**, v. μέγαρον IV.

**μᾰγάς**, άδος, ἡ, *bridge of the cithara*, Ptol.*Harm.*1.8, 2.16, Philostr.*VS*1.7.1, 1.21.3, Hsch.

**μαγγάνα**, ἡ, Italic name for *wine-cask*, Suid.

⊛ **μαγγᾰν-άριος**, ὁ, *conjurer*, Rhetor. in *Cat.Cod.Astr.*8(4).213, *POxy.*1050.19 (ii/iii A. D.). II. *mechanical engineer*, Papp.1024.14, al. **-εία**, ἡ, *trickery*, esp. of magical arts, Pl.*Lg.*908d; μαγγανεῖαι καὶ ἐπῳδαί ib.933a; περίαπτα καὶ μ. Ph.2.267, Gal.11.792; τῆς Κίρκης ἡ μ. Them.*Or.*26.330b, cf. Jul.*Gal.*340a; μ. μαγειρικαί, of meretricious cookery, Ath.1.9c. **-ευμα**, ατος, τό, *trickery*, in pl., Pl.*Grg.*484a, *Lg.*933c; φάρμακα καὶ μ. *quack remedies*, Max.Tyr.23.3; of women, *meretricious arts*, Plu.*Ant.*25. **-ευτήριον**, τό, *haunt of impostors*, Them.*Or.*5.70b. **-ευτής**, οῦ, ὁ, *impostor, quack*, Suid., Phot. **-ευτικός**, ή, όν, *fit for trickery*, etc.; ἡ -κή (sc. τέχνη), *magical art*, Poll.7.209. **-εύτρια**, ἡ, fem. of μαγγανευτής, Hsch. s. v. βαμβακεύτρια. **-εύω**, (μάγγανον) *use charms* or *philtres*, of Circe, Ar.*Pl.*310: metaph., *play tricks*, D.25.80, Jul.*Gal.*340a; μ. πρὸς τὰς θεὰς *use superstitious means* to propitiate the goddesses, Plb.15.29.9; μ. ἐπί τινα Luc.*DDeor.*2.1, *BisAcc.*21: c. acc. cogn., μ. ἀπάτην *contrive means for* cheating, Ach.Tat.2.38. II. c. acc., *trick out, dress artificially*, of cooks, τὰ σιτία καὶ τὰ ὄψα μ. καὶ φαρμάττειν Plu.2.126a. ⊛ **-ον**, τό, *means for charming* or *bewitching* others, *philtre*, Heraclit.*All.*28, Hsch. II. μ. πολεμικόν, = Lat. *ballista, tormentum*, Gloss. III. *block of a pulley*, Hero *Bel.*84.12, *PLond.*3.1164*h*8 (iii A. D.). IV. = βάλανος II. 4, Sch.Ar.*V.*155, *Av.*1159, *Ec.*361. V. = γάγγαμον, *hunting-net*, Hsch.

**μαγδᾰλιά**, ἡ, later form of ἀπομαγδαλιά, Gal.19.119, cf. Damocr. ap.eund.13.823, Cass.Fel.66, Sch.Ar.*Eq.*412: **μαγδαλέα**, *Hippiatr.*62.

**μάγδωλος**, ὁ, *watch-tower*, *BGU*1550 (Ptol.), *PTheb.Bank* i 116 (ii B.C.), Meyer *Ostr.*40 (i A.D.), *PFay.*38.5 (iii/iv A.D.), Hsch.: also **μαγδώλ**, gen. τοῦ μαγδῶλος *PHamb.*62.8 (ii A.D.). (Hebr. *migdol*; place-name in Lxx *Nu.*33.7, cf. **Μαγδωλός**, a town in Egypt, Hecat. 317 J.; also **Μαγδῶλα** Μίρη *PAmh.*2.87 (ii A.D.), etc.)

**μαγδωλο-φῠλάκία**, ἡ, *manning of the watch-tower*, dub. in *PLond.* 3.1235.12 (ii A.D.), *PRyl.*101.5,8 (ii A.D.). **-φύλαξ** [ῠ], ἄκος, ὁ, *guard of the watch-tower*, *PFay.*108.13 (ii A.D.), *PTeb.*353.9 (ii A.D.), *PLond.*3.844.5 (ii A.D.).

**μᾰγεία**, ἡ, *theology of the Magians*, μ. ἡ Ζωροάστρου Pl.*Alc.*1. 122a. II. *magic*, Thphr.*HP*9.15.7 (pl.), *Act.Ap.*8.11 (pl.), *PMag. Berol.*1.127, etc.; τὴν γοητικὴν μ. οὐδ' ἔγνωσαν [οἱ μάγοι] Arist. *Fr.*36.

**μᾰγεῖον**, τό, (μάσσω) = ἐκμαγεῖον, Longin.32.5.

**μᾰγείρ-αινα**, ἡ, fem. of μάγειρος, οὐδεὶς..μαγείραιναν εἶδε πώποτε Pherecr.64. **-εία**, ἡ, = μαγείρευμα, Cato ap.Fronton.p.223 N. (pl.), Hdn.*Epim.*19. **-εῖον**, τό, *butcher's shop, cook-shop*, Arist.*HA*629$^a$33, *Mir.*833$^a$3, Babr.79.1. 2. *place where food is cooked, kitchen*, *IG*2$^2$.1301 (iii B.C.), *PCair.Zen.*6.55 (iii B.C.), *PSI*6.669.6 (iii B.C.), Lxx *Ez.*46.23, *Explor.Arch. de Délos* 11.262, Dsc.*Eup.*1.34, Gal.6. 721. 3. pl., *butchers' or cooks' quarter* of Athens, Antiph.203, Thphr. *Char.*6.9. (Written **μαγειρεῖον** *IG*, *PCair.Zen.* ll. cc., **μαγιρῖον** *PSI* l. c., **μαγιρέον** *Explor.Arch.de Délos* l. c.) **-ευμα**, ατος, τό, *that which is cooked, food*, Hsch. s. v. ὄψα (pl.), Eust.1402.16. **-ευτικός**, ή, όν, = μαγειρικός, *Proll.Hermog.* in Rh.6.52 W. **-εύω**, *to be a cook, cook meat*, Thphr.*Char.*6.5, Plu.2.704a, Porph.*Abst.*3.18: c. acc., μ. τὰ ἱερεῖα Ath.4.173d, cf. Chor. in *Rev.Phil.*1.232:—Pass., τὰ μαγειρευόμενα ὄσπρια Sch.Ar.*Pl.*1207. 2. *to be a butcher*, Babr.122.16. 3. metaph., *butcher, massacre*, Lxx *La.*2.21. ⊛**-ικός**, ή, όν, *fit for a cook* or *cookery*, ῥήματα Ar.*Eq.*216; νόμοι Pl.*Min.*316e; πῦρ Arist. *Spir.*485$^a$35; κοπίς Plu.*Lyc.*2; τάβλια *PFay.*104.4 (iii A.D.); σκεύη, τράπεζα, Ath.4.169b,173a; ἡ μαγειρικὴ τέχνη *cookery*, Pl.*R.*332c, Athenio 1.1; ἡ μ. ἐμπειρία Pl.*Grg.*500b; ἡ -κή alone, Id.*Plt.*289a, Dionys.Com.2.30, etc. Adv. -κῶς, ἐσκευασμένη τροφή, opp. ὠμή, S.E.*P.*1.56. 2. of persons, *skilled in cookery*, Pl.*Tht.*178d. Adv. -κῶς *in a cook-like way, like a true 'artist'*, Ar.*Ach.*1015, *Eq.*376, *Pax* 1017. 3. μαγειρικόν, τό, = μαγειρεῖον, *IG*14.352 i 71 (but, *expenses of dressing meat*, 2$^2$.334.28). 4. μαγειρική, ἡ, either the *meat-trade*, or *tax on butchers*, *PZen.* in *Arch.Pap.*8.79 (iii B.C.), *PUniv.Giss.*2.5 (ii B.C.). **-ίσκιον**, τό, Dim. of μάγειρος, of a silver cup in the form of a genre figure, Plin.*HN*33.157. **-ίσκος**, ὁ, Dim. of μάγειρος, Ath.7.292e. **-ισσα**, ἡ, fem. of sq., Lxx 1 *Ki.*8.13. **-ος**, ὁ, Dor. **μάγῑρος** *IG*4$^2$(1).144 (Epid., v B.C.), *SIG*241.16 (Delph., iv B.C.), *IG*9(1).976.7 (Corc., iv/iii B.C.); but Att. **μάγειρος** ib.2$^2$.10 *B*2 (v/iv B.C.), and so in Pap. of iii B.C., *PCair.Zen.*6.48, al., *PRev. Laws* 50.14, both forms freq. in later Inscrr., Pap., and codd.; Aeol. διὰ τοῦ ῑ **μάγοιρος** (s. v. l.) Philox.ap.*Et.Gud.* in Greg.Cor.p.606 S.:—*slaughterer, butcher* (*meat-salesman*), and *cook* (these functions being freq. combined in one person), Pl.*Euthd.*301d, *Lg.*849d, Babr.51.8, al., Ath.14.659c sq., Plu.2.175d, D.Chr.4.44, Max.Tyr.25.2: hence, Ἅιδου μ., of Polyphemus, E.*Cyc.*397; *public cook*, παρὰ τῶν μαγείρων, opp. π. τῶν ἰδιωτῶν, Ph.*Bel.*86.38, cf. Alex.257, Men.272, *Sam.* 68; *butcher, meat salesman*, Alex.98.23, Macho ap.Ath.6.243f, Aesop. 301; λόγος μαγείρου *butcher's bill*, *POxy.*108$^v$ (ii/iii A.D.), cf. *PRyl.* 228 intr. (i A.D.); μ. ὁ κατ' οἶκον, οἱ ἐν ἀγορᾷ μ., Artem.3.56, cf. Arr.*Epict.*3.19.5, 3.26.21, *PFlor.*166 (iii A.D.); περὶ μαγείρου τοῦ ἀποδράντος *PSI*4.329 (iii B.C.); officiating at sacrifices, Athenio 1.40; μ. τὸ γ' *IG*5(1).97.26 (i A.D.); acting as waiter, Matro *Conv.*11, 46, al.; not in Hom., but mentioned in Batr.40, Hdt.4.71, 6.60, S.*Fr.* [1122], Ar.*Ra.*517, al., freq. in Com.; opp. ὀψοποιός, Dionys.Com. 2.9; but = ὀψοποιός, Alex.149.14; ὅσον μαγείρου διαφέρει μάγειρος οὐκ οἶσθ' Nicom.Com.1.6; μάγειρος *cook for fish and meat*, opp. οἰνοχόος and σιτοποιός (baker), Ph.1.390 (pl.). **-ώδης**, ες, *butcherly*, φονικὴ καὶ μ. ψυχή Eun.*VS* p.480 B.

**μαγέτας** αὐλός, ὁ, *bewitching*, Hsch.

**μάγευμα** [ᾰ], ατος, τό, *piece of magic art*: in pl., *charms, spells*, E. *Supp.*1110, v. l. in Hp.*Morb.Sacr.*18; φάρμακα καὶ μ. ἀκολάστων γυναικῶν Plu.2.752c (pl.).

**μᾰγεύς**, έως, ὁ, (μάσσω) *one who kneads*, Poll.6.64, Hsch. (pl. μαγῆες). II. *one who wipes*, μαγῆα σπόγγον *AP*6.306 (Aristo).

⊛**μᾰγ-ευτής**, οῦ, ὁ, = μάγος, D.C.52.36. **-ευτικός**, ή, όν, *magical*: ἡ -κή (sc. τέχνη), *magic*, Pl.*Plt.*280e. 2. of persons, *addicted to magic*, Ptol.*Tetr.*70. ⊛ **-εύω**, *to be a Magus* or *skilled in Magian lore*, Plu.*Art.*3,6, Philostr.*VA*1.2. II. *use magic arts*, E.*IT*1338; καταγαγεῖν τὸν Δία μαγεύσαντας Plu.*Num.*15. III. trans., *bewitch*, e. g. by philtres, Ach.Tat.5.22:—Pass., Clearch.25, Luc.*Asin.* 54; πέπλον μεμαγευμένον φαρμάκοις Apollod.1.9.28. 2. *call forth by magic arts*, ἔμψυχα *AP*12.57 (Mel.), cf. Luc.*Asin.*11. ⊛ **-ιανός**, ή, όν, *inscribed with charms*, ψέλιον *BGU*1065.8 (pl., i A.D.), *POxy.* 259.12 (i A.D.).

**μᾰγίδιον**, τό, Dim. of μαγίς II, *Peripl.M.Rubr.*30, Sch.Ar.*Nu.* 1250.

**μᾰγῐκός**, ή, όν, *Magian*, λόγοι Plu.*Them.*29: Μαγικός, ὁ (sc. λόγος), title of work by Antisthenes, Suid. s. v. Ἀντισθένης, or Aristotle, D.L.1.1. II. *magical*, βίβλοι Ps.-Phoc.149; μ. τέχνη *magic*, Lxx *Wi.*17.7; ἡ μ. Ph.2.316. 2. of persons, *skilled in magic*, Ptol. *Tetr.*72.

**μάγιν**· ἀσπίδα, Hsch. **μαγιρέον, -ιρος**, v. μαγειρεῖον, -ειρος.

**μᾰγ-ίς**, ίδος, ἡ, (μάσσω) *any kneaded mass, cake*, Lxx *Jd.*7.13; *lump* of fat, Dsc.2.76; esp. *cake* offered to Hecate and Trophonius, S. *Fr.*734, Ar.*Fr.*813; Cypr. acc. to Ath.14.663b; described as a small *cheese-pudding*, Hp.*Mul.*2.133, cf. *Steril.*235. II. *kneading-trough* or *dresser*, Cratin.21, *BGU*40.8 (ii/iii A.D.), cf. Poll.10.81; *small table*, Epich.118, Cerc.12; also, *round pan* or *plate* for placing on the τρίπους, Poll.6.83. III. μαγίδες· αἷς ἀπομάττουσι καὶ καθαίρουσι, Hsch.

**μαγκίππιον**, *pistrina*, *Gloss.*

**μάγκορον**, τό, = σάκχαρ, Sch.Orib.2.745 D.

**μάγλα**, ἡ, kind of *spice*, *Peripl.M.Rubr.*12.

⊛**μάγ-μα**, ατος, τό, *thick unguent*, Plin.*HN*13.19, *PTeb.*273.17 (ii/iii A.D.); esp. μ. ἡδύχρουν, an ingredient in the Theriaca Andromachi, Androm.ap.Gal.14.39; also, of a plaster, Id.ap.eund.13.925; cf. ἡδύχρους. **-μός**, ὁ, *wiping, cleansing*, Hsch., cf. S.*Fr.*467 (dub.).

**Μάγνης**, ητος, ὁ, *Magnesian*, i.e. a dweller in Magnesia in Thessaly, Il.2.756, S.*El.*705, etc.; or in Magnesia in Lydia, Hdt.3.90, etc.: —fem. ⊛**Μάγνησσα** Theoc.22.79:—hence ⊛**Μαγνησίη**, ἡ, *Magnesia* in Asia, Hdt.3.122, al.; in Thessaly, Id.7.176, al.:—Adj. **Μαγνητικός**, ή, όν, *Magnesian*, A.*Pers.*492: fem. **Μαγνῆτις**, ιδος, ἵπποι Pi.*P.*2.45, cf. S.*Fr.*1066. 2. Μάγνης (sc. οἶνος), ὁ, Hermipp.82. b. a throw of the dice, Hsch. II. Μαγνῆτις λίθος, ἡ, *the magnet*, E.*Fr.*567, cf. Pl.*Ion* 533d, Eub.77, etc.: without λίθος, Sch.Pl.*R.*600a; also ἡ Μαγνησίη λίθος Hp.*Int.*21, cf. Ach.Tat.1.17; ἡ Μάγνησσα Orph. *L.*307; ὁ Μάγνης λίθος Porph.*Abst.*4.20; ὁ Μ. alone, Alex.Aphr. *Pr.*2.59; Μ. ὁ πνέων *PMag.Par.*1.2631; also ὁ Μαγνήτης λίθος Dsc. 5.130, Phlp. *in Ph.*403.23; ἡ Μαγνῆτις πέτρα Dsc.5.126. 2. Μαγνῆτις λίθος, also, *a mineral* resembling silver, prob. a kind of *talc*, Thphr.*Lap.*41. III. **μαγνησία**, ἡ, name of several ores and metallic amalgams, Zos.Alch.p.188 B., Maria ap.eund.p.192 B.

**Μαγνήτινος**, η, ον, made of Μαγνῆτις λίθος, καρδία *PMag.Par.*1. 3142.

⊛**Μάγος** [ᾰ], ου, ὁ, *Magian*, one of a Median tribe, Hdt.1.101, Str. 15.3.1: hence, as belonging to this tribe, 2. *one of the priests and wise men in Persia* who interpreted dreams, Hdt.7.37, al., Arist.*Fr.* 36, Phoen.1.5, *Ev.Matt.*2.1. 3. *enchanter, wizard*, esp. in bad sense, *impostor, charlatan*, Heraclit.14, S.*OT*387, E.*Or.*1498 (lyr.), Pl.*R.*572e, *Act.Ap.*13.6, Vett.Val.74.17: also fem., Luc.*Asin.*4, *AP* 5.15 (Marc. Arg.). II. μάγος, ον, as Adj., *magical*, μάγῳ τέχνῃ πράττειν τι Philostr.*VA*1.2; κεστοῦ φωνεῦσα μαγώτερα *AP*5.120 (Phld.). (OPers. *maguš* 'Magian'.)

**μᾰγοφόνια**, τά, *slaughter of the Magians*, a Persian festival, Hdt. 3.79:—also **-φονία**, ἡ, ἑορτὴ τῆς μ. Ctes.*Fr.*29.15.

**μαγύδαρις**, ἡ, *inflorescence of the σίλφιον*, Thphr.*HP*6.3.4; also its *seed* (or *root*), Dsc.3.80; also its *sap*, Hsch. II. another plant, distinct from σίλφιον, *Prangos ferulacea*, Thphr.*HP*1.6.12, 6.3.7, Dsc. l.c., *Gp.*2.35.9 (μαγοδ- codd.). [*măgūdăris* Plaut.*Rud.*633.]

**μᾰγῳδία**, ἡ, *rude pantomime*, Aristox.*Fr.Hist.*58:—also **μαγῳδή**, Hsch.: hence **-ῳδός**, ὁ, *performer in such pieces*, Str.14.1.41, Ath. 14.621c.

⊛**μᾰδᾰγένειος**, ον, Dor. for μαδηγένειος, Anon.ap.Phot.

**μᾰδαῖος**, α, ον, poet. for μαδαρός, ἕλκη Poet. *de herb.*83.

**μᾰδάλλει**· τίλλει, ἐσθίει, Hsch. (μαγδ- cod.): in pres. part., Id.

**μάδαρα**, τά, kind of *boat*, *Peripl.M.Rubr.*36 (μαδαράτε cod.).

**μαδαρεῖς**· τὰ πλατύλογχα τῶν κρεάτων (Celt.), Hsch. (πλατύτερα λόγχα codd.), cf. Str.4.4.3 (prob.) and Lat. *mataris*.

**μᾰδᾰριάω**, *suffer from falling hair*, Cleopatra ap.Gal.12.405.

**μᾰδᾰροκέφᾰλος**, ον, *bald-headed*, Tz.*H.*7.851.

⊛**μᾰδᾰρ-ός**, ά, όν, (μαδάω) *wet*, ἕλκεα μ. *running* sores, Hp.*Hum.* 14; *watery, pulpy*, Id.*Epid.*7.83, Arist.*HA*531$^b$14. 2. *bald*, κεφαλή Luc.*Epigr.*37. **-ότης**, ητος, ἡ, *baldness*, Hp.*Hum.*1, cf. Gal.16. 88; *falling off of the eyelashes*, Id.14.767. ⊛ **-όω**, *make bald*, v.l. in Lxx *Ne.*13.25. **-ωσις**, εως, ἡ, *falling off of the hair, baldness*, Gal.18(1).55, Vett.Val.109.31 (pl.); esp. from the eyelids, Gal.14. 413, Aët.7.80, Paul.Aeg.3.22.

**μᾰδ-άσκομαι**, = sq. 1, of an ulcer, Steph. *in Hp.*2.488 D. ⊛ **-άω**, *to be moist* or *sodden*, of a disease in fig-trees, Thphr.*HP*4.14.5. 2. of hair, *fall off*, Ael.*NA*15.18; of persons, *to be bald*, Ar.*Pl.*266, Longus 3.32, cf. Gal.16.88; μ. τὰς τρίχας Sotion p.186 W.; ἐάν τινι μαδήσῃ ἡ κεφαλή Lxx *Le.*13.40: abs., ἐὰν μαδήσῃ if *there is baldness*, Hp.*Mul.*2.189.

**μᾶδδα**, ἡ, Megar. for μᾶζα, Ar.*Ach.*732, 835.

**μάδεγμα**· δέλεαρ, πρόβλημα, οἱ δὲ **μάδευμα**, Hsch.

**μαδηγένειος**, v. μαδιγένειος.

⊛**μάδησις** [ᾰ], εως, ἡ, (μαδάω) *loss of hair, becoming bald*, τῆς κεφαλῆς Hp.*Epid.*3.4.

⊛**μᾰδῐγένειος**, ον, (μαδαρός, γένειον) *smooth-chinned*, Arist.*HA*518$^b$ 20 (prob. **μαδηγένειοι**, cf. μαδαγένειος and Poll.2.88).

**μᾰδ-ίζω**, f.l. for μαδάω, Hp.*Mul.*2.189. II. *pluck* or *singe bare*, *Hippiatr.*2 (Pass.). **-ῐσις**, εως, ἡ, = μάδησις (s. v. l.), μ. τριχῶν Hp. *Epid.*2.1.7. II. (μαδάω 1) ῥιζῶν Thphr.*CP*5.9.9.

**μάδισος**, ὁ, = δίκελλα, Hsch.:—also **μαδιβός**, Id.

**μᾰδιστήριον**, τό, *instrument for removing hair*, gloss on εὔστρα, Sch.Ar.*Eq.*1233. II. *place where depilation is carried on*, Michel 1199 (Arconnesos).

**μαδόνη**, ἡ, prob. f.l. for sq., Zopyr.ap.Orib.14.62.1.

**μάδος**, ὁ, = ἄμπελος λευκή, Dsc.4.182, *Eup.*1.171, Heraclid.Tar.ap. Gal.14.186, prob. cj. in Plin.*HN*23.21. (Connected with μαδάω, as the plant was also called ψίλωθρον.) II. = μαδωνάϊς, ib.25.75.

**μαδός**, ή, όν, (μαδάω) = μαδαρός 2, Hsch.

**μάδρυα**, τά, for μαλόδρυα, = κοκκύμηλα, Seleuc.ap.Ath.2.50a.

**μαδρυνθήσομαι**· κολασθήσομαι, ἐπιτριβήσομαι, Hsch.

**μαδών**, ῶνος, ὁ, transcription of Hebr. *'îš mādhôn* 'man of contention', Lxx 2*Ki*.21.20.

® **μαδωναΐς**, ἡ, Boeot. name of *νυμφαία*, Thphr.*HP*9.13.1.

**μαεῖται**· μωρολογεῖ, Hsch.; cf. *μαατρόν*.

® **μᾶζα**, ἡ, (μάσσω, on the accent v. Hdn.Gr.2.937; later **μάζα** Moer.p.258 P.) *barley-cake*, Archil.2, Hdt.1.200, Democr.246, etc.; ἀμολγαίη Hes.*Op*.590; κυρβαίη (v.l. κυρκ-) Hom.*Epigr*.15.6; φυστή Ar.*V*.610: distd. from ἄρτος (wheaten bread), Hp.*VM*8, cf. *Acut.* 37, *Aff*.52, Ar.*Ec*.606, Antiph.226.1, X.*Cyr*.1.2.11, Ath.3.114e; μ. καὶ ὕδωρ Epicur.*Ep*.3 p.64 U.; δουλίας μ. τυχεῖν to eat *the bread* of slavery, A.*Ag*.1041: prov., ἀγαθὴ καὶ μᾶζα μετ' ἄρτον, of second best things, Zen.1.12; μᾶζαν μεμαχώς having baked *a cake*, with a play on μάχην μεμαχημένος, Ar.*Eq*.55. II. generally, *lump, mass, ball*, Lxx *Bel*27, Suid.s.v. παλάθαι; χρυσοῦ J.*AJ*5.1.10, cf. Dsc.5.79: esp. in Alchemy, *amalgam*, ἀνέκλειπτος μ. *PHolm*.2.17, *PLeid.X*.7.

**μαζαγόας**, ὁ, *one who complains about bread*, Hsch.

**μαζαγρέτας**, α, ὁ, (ἀγείρω) *one who begs for barley-loaves*, Dor. word in Aristias 3.

**μαζάκις**· δόρυ Παρθικόν, Hsch. **μαζάρυγξ**· τὰ ἐπὶ τῷ πότῳ ἐπιόντα, Id.

**μαζάω**, *knead a barley-cake*, *BGU*1026 xxii 20 (iv A.D.), cf. Hsch. (μαζόντα cod.). II. like κριθάω, *wax wanton*, Suid.

**μαζέας**, ου, ὁ, = ἧπατος, Xenocr.ap.Orib.2.58.27.

**μαζεινὸς βοῦς**· ὁ ἐξ ἀλφίτων, Hsch. **Μαζεύς**, = Ζεύς (Phryg.), Id.

**μαζήρεοι**, οἱ, *bastards*, 1*Enoch* 10.9. (Hebr. *mamzēr*.)

**μαζηρὸς πίναξ**, trencher *for barley-cakes*, Poll.10.84.

**μαζίνης**, ὁ, f.l. for *μάξεινος*, Thphr.*Fr*.171.2.

**μαζ-ίον**, τό, Dim. of μᾶζα, Phryn.Com.61, Ath.14.646c, *Gp*.20.33; of the size and shape of a suppository, Hp.*Mul*.1.78, cf. Dsc.*Eup.* 1.204. **-ίσκη**, ἡ, = foreg., *barley-scone*, Ar.*Eq*.1105, 1166.

**μαζο-βόλιον**, τό, = μαζονόμος, Apollon.*Lex.* s.v. οὐλοχύτας. ® **-νομεῖον**, τό, = sq., Ar.*Fr*.417, Pl.Com.162:—also **-νόμιον**, Callix. 2. ® **-νόμον**, τό, *trencher for serving barley-cakes on*, Harmod.1, *IG* 7.3498.8,50 (Orop.), *OGI*214.50 (Didyma, iii B.C.), prob. in *IG*2$^{2}$.1478.14:—also **-νόμος**, ὁ, *POxy*.1449.58,60 (iii A.D.). **-πέπτης**, ου, ὁ, *barley-bread baker*, Hsch. **-ποιέω**, *make barley-bread*, Eust. 1766.42, Sch.Od.14.429. **-ποιός**, όν, *making barley-bread*, *Gloss.*

**μαζός**, v. μαστός. II. = μάξεινος, Epich.69.

**Μαζουσία ἀκτή**, name of a promontory in the Thracian Chersonese, Lyc.534 (= *breast-shaped* acc. to Tz. ad loc.), cf. Str.7 *Fr*.52.

**μαζο-φᾰγέω**, *eat barley-bread*, Hp.*Acut*.37. **-φάγος** [φᾰ], ον, (φαγεῖν) *eating barley-bread*, Id.*Morb*.2.48, Porph.*Abst*.1.47, Jul.*Or.* 6.198d. **-φορίς**, ίδος, ἡ, (φέρω) = μαζονόμος, Hsch.

**μαζύγιον**, τό, and **μαζύς**, ἡ, = μᾶζα II, *amalgam*, Zos.Alch.p.216 B.

**μαζῶνες**, οἱ, those who celebrated a festival of Dionysus at Phigalea, Harmod.1, cf. *IG*5(2).178 (Tegea).

**μαθαλίς**, ίδος, ἡ, kind of *cup* or *measure*, Blaes.2, Hsch.

**μαθᾶμαι**· ζητῶ, Hsch.

**μαθετάς**, ᾶ, ὁ, Dor. for μαθητής, *SIG*721.7 (Cnossus, found at Delos, ii B.C.).

**μάθ-η** [ᾰ], ἡ, = μάθησις, Emp.17.14, Hsch. **-ημα**, ατος, τό, (μαθεῖν) *that which is learnt, lesson*, τὰ παθήματα μαθήματα Hdt.1.207; μ. μαθεῖν S.*Ph*.918; μ. τινός or περί τι, Pl.*Smp*.211c, *R*.525d; προσπορεύεται πρὸς τὰ λοιπὰ μ. *PCair.Zen*.60.7 (iii B.C.); ἀφεῖσθαι τοὺς παῖδας ἀπὸ τῶν μ. *SIG*577.77 (Milet., iii/ii B.C.), cf. 578.28 (Teos, ii B.C.), al. 2. *learning, knowledge*, Ar.*Nu*.1231, *Av*.380, Th.2.39, *PSI*1.94.9 (ii A.D.), etc.; οἱ καθιστάμενοι ἐπὶ τῶν μ. *educational* authorities, *SIG*578.66 (Teos, ii B.C.); τὸ μ. τὸ περὶ τὰς τάξεις the *science* of tactics, Pl.*La*.182b: freq. in pl., Isoc.12.27, etc.; μαθημάτων φρόντιζε μᾶλλον χρημάτων· τὰ γὰρ μαθήματ' εὐπορεῖ τὰ χρήματα Philem. 232. 3. esp. *the mathematical sciences*, Archyt.1,3 tit.; τρία μ., i.e. arithmetic, geometry, and astronomy, acc. to Pl.*Lg*.817e, cf. Phld. *Ind.Sto*.66; later τὰ τέσσαρα μ. (ἁρμονική being added) *Theol.Ar*.17; Arist. distd. pure from mixed μ., τὰ φυσικώτερα τῶν μ., οἷον ὀπτικὴ καὶ ἁρμονικὴ καὶ ἀστρονομία *Ph*.194$^{a}$8; ἡ ἐν τοῖς μ. ἁρμονική *Metaph*.997$^{b}$21; τὰ μ. περὶ τὰ εἴδη ἐστίν *APo*.79$^{a}$7; οἱ ἀπὸ τῶν μ. *mathematicians*, Cleom.1.8. 4. *astrology*, *AP*7.687 (Pall.). 5. *creed*, *Cod.Just*.1.1.7.11, al. **-ημᾰτικεύομαι**, *employ mathematical reasoning*, μ. πέρα τοῦ δέοντος Dam.*Pr*.396, cf. Doxop. in Rh.2.132 W. **-ημᾰτικός**, ή, όν, = μαθητικός, *fond of learning*, Pl.*Ti*.88c. II. *scientific*, τὸ μ. εἶδος Id.*Sph*.219c; esp. *mathematical*, μαθηματικός, ὁ, *mathematician*, Arist.*Ph*.193$^{b}$31, *EN*1142$^{a}$17, Phld.*Acad.Ind*.p.16 M., Ceb.34: ἡ -κή (sc. ἐπιστήμη) *mathematics*, Archyt.1 tit., Arist.*Metaph*.1026$^{a}$14; αἱ -καί ib.26; φιλοσοφία μ. ib.19; τὰ μ. *mathematics*, Id.*EN*1151$^{a}$17; also, *mathematical entities*, Id.*Metaph*.1076$^{a}$17; γραμμὴ μ. a *mathematical* line, opp. γ. φυσική, Id.*Ph*.194$^{a}$11; κύκλοι μ. Id.*Metaph.* 1036$^{a}$4; ἁρμονικὴ ἥ τε μ. καὶ ἡ κατὰ τὴν ἀκοήν Id.*APo*.79$^{a}$1: Comp. -κωτέρα ὕλη *too mathematical*, Id.*Metaph*.992$^{b}$2. Adv. -κῶς ib.995$^{a}$6, Str.2.5.1, etc. 2. *astronomical*, οἱ μ. κανόνες Plu.2.974f; ἡ -κή *astronomy*, S.E.*M*.5.104. b. *astrological*, ἡ μ. τέχνη Sallust.9, cf. Gal. 19.529; ὁ μ. *astrologer*, M.Ant.4.48, S.E.*M*.5.2, Porph.ap.Eus.*PE* 6.1, etc. 3. among the Pythagoreans, οἱ μ. (opp. οἱ ἀκουσματικοί) *advanced students*, Porph.*VP*37, Iamb.*VP*18.81. **-ημᾰτοπωλικός**, ή, όν, *making a trade of science*: μ. γένος *the Sophists*, and ἡ -κή *their trade*, Pl.*Sph*.224e,b. **-ημοσύνη**, ἡ, *learning*, *IGRom*.4.607 (Phryg.). **-ησις**, εως, ἡ, (μαθεῖν) *the act of learning, getting of knowledge*, πεῖρά τοι μαθήσιος ἀρχά Alcm.63; μ. οὐ καλὴν ἐκμανθάνεις S. *Tr*.450; ὧν μάθησιν ἄρνυμαι of which things I gain *information*, ib. 711; μ. ἔχειν τινός E.*Supp*.915; ὁ χρόνος μ. δίδωσι ib.419; τὴν μ. ποιεῖσθαι περί τινος Th.1.68; ἡ περὶ τὸ ἓν μ. Pl.*R*.525a; μ. τέχνης *BGU*1021.8 (iii A.D.): in pl., νωθροὶ ἀπαντῶσι πρὸς τὰς μ. Pl.*Tht*.144b, cf. *R*.407b; μνῆμαί τε ἰσχυραὶ καὶ μ. ὀξεῖαι *faculties of learning*, Id. *Lg*.908c; ὁπλομαχίας μ. Ephor.54 J. 2. *desire of learning*, ἀλλά σοι μ. οὐ πάρα S.*El*.1032. 3. *education, instruction*, Hp.*Jusj.*, Pl.*Ap.* 26a; τοῦ φόβου τὴν μ. κρείττονα παρέξεσθαι X.*Cyr*.3.3.53; τὴν αὐλητικὴν ἤγαγον πρὸς τὰς μ. Arist.*Pol*.1341$^{a}$32.

**μᾰθητ-εία**, poet. -είη, ἡ, *instruction from a teacher*, Timo 54, D. Chr.4.41. **-έος**, α, ον, *to be learnt*, Pl.*Lg*.822c. II. μαθητέον, *one must learn*, Hdt.7.16.γ', Ar.*V*.1262, Pl.*Lg*.818d; τέχνας παρά τινος X. *Mem*.2.1.28. **-εύω**, *to be pupil*, τινι to one, Plu.2.832c. II. trans., *make a disciple of, instruct*, πάντα τὰ ἔθνη *Ev.Matt*.28.19, cf. *Act.Ap*.14.21:—Pass., *Ev.Matt*.13.52. ® **-ής**, οῦ, ὁ, *learner, pupil*, τῆς Ἑλλάδος Hdt.4.77, Mosch.3.95, etc.; of dancing, *SIG*1094.6 (Eleusis, iv B.C.): freq. in Att. of the *pupils* of philosophers and rhetoricians, οὐ θέμις πλὴν τοῖς μ. λέγειν Ar.*Nu*.140; οἱ Πρωταγόρου μ. Pl.*Prt.* 315a, al.; ἐμοὺς μαθητάς Id.*Ap*.33a: c. gen. rei, τούτου τοῦ μαθήματος μ. a *student* of it, Id.*R*.618c; μ. ἰατρικῆς a *student* of medicine, ib.599c; μ. περί τινος Id.*La*.186e; *apprentice*, *POxy*.725.15 (ii A.D.). **-ιάω**, Desiderat., *wish to become a disciple, wish to learn*, Ar.*Nu*.183, Ps.-Luc.*Philopatr*.14, *AP*15.38 (Cometas). **-ικεύομαι**, *make a display of learning*, Dam.*Pr*.192. **-ικός**, ή, όν, *disposed to learn*, τινος Pl. *R*.475e. 2. *easily taught, docile*, of animals having memory, -ώτερα Arist.*Metaph*.980$^{b}$21, cf. *HA*608$^{a}$27. Adv. Comp. -ώτερον Dam.*Pr.* 195 (nisi leg. μαθηματικ-). **-ός**, ή, όν, *learnt, that may be learnt*, ἀνθρώποις *by* men, X.*Cyr*.1.6.23; ἡ ἀσκητὸν ἢ μ. [ἡ ἀρετή] Pl.*Men.* 70a, cf. Arist.*EN*1099$^{b}$9; μ. τε καὶ διδακτά Pl.*Prt*.319c. **-ρια**, ἡ, = sq., D.S.2.52, *Act.Ap*.9.36, D.L.4.2. **-ρίς**, ίδος, ἡ, fem. of μαθητής, Ph.1.273.

**μάθος** [ᾰ], τό, poet. and Ion. for μάθησις, Alc.104, Ar.*Fr*.814; opp. πάθος, as μαθήματα to παθήματα, A.*Ag*.177 (lyr.). II. *custom*, πλέων τοῦ μάθεος Hp.*Mul*.1.6,61.

**μάθυιαι**· γνάθοι, Hsch. **μαί**· μέγα (Indian), Id.

® **μαῖα**, ἡ, *good mother*, form of address to old women, Hom. (only in Od.), always in voc., usu. addressed to Eurycleia, the nurse of Odysseus, Od.19.482, al.; but also to Eurynome the ταμίη, 17.499: hence not only of nurses, cf. *h.Cer*.147, Ar.*Ec*.915 (lyr.). 2. later, *foster-mother*, E.*Hipp*.243 (anap.), Antiph.159.6; also, a true *mother*, μαῖα δὴ κάτω βέβακεν E.*Alc*.393 (lyr.): metaph., of the earth, ἰὼ γαῖα μαῖα A.*Ch*.44 (lyr.), cf. S.*Fr*.959. 3. *midwife*, Pl.*Tht.* 149a, Isyll.54, Sor.2.3, al., etc. b. *lady doctor*, Gal.14.641. 4. in Dor., *grandmother*, Iamb.*VP*11.56, *IG*12(3).1120 (Melos). II. *large kind of crab*, Arist.*HA*525$^{b}$4, al. III. a plant, = λεπίδιον, Orib.*Fr*.102. (Prob. from same Root as μήτηρ.)

**Μαῖα**, ἡ, *Maia*, mother of Hermes, *h.Merc*.3, Alc.5, etc.; Ion. Μαίη, Hes.*Th*.938:—also **Μαιάς**, άδος, ἡ, Od.14.435, *h.Merc*.57, E. *Or*.997 (lyr.), etc. (Derived fr. μαῖα, = τροφός, by Porph.*Abst*.4.16.)

® **Μαίανδρος**, ὁ, *Maeander*, a river of Caria, Il.2.869, Hes.*Th*.339; noted for its windings, Hdt.2.29:—Adj. **Μαιάνδριος**, α, ον, πέδιον D.P.837, etc. II. metaph., *winding*, μαιάνδρους πολλοὺς ἑλίττει, of water, Philostr.*Im*.1.9; *winding pattern*, Aristeas 66, Str.12.8.15, J.*AJ*12.2.10.

**μαιανδρώδης**, ες, *winding*, Ph.*Bel*.86.5.

**μαι-άς**, άδος, ἡ, fem. of μαιευτικός, τέχνη Nonn.*D*.3.403. II. cf. Μαῖα. **-εία**, ἡ, *business of a midwife*, Pl.*Tht*.150d, 210c, cf. Procl. *in Alc.Praef.* **-ευμα**, ατος, τό, *product of a midwife's art, delivery*, σὸν μὲν παιδίον, ἐμὸν δὲ μαίευμα Pl.*Tht*.160e, cf. Iamb.*Myst*.8.3 (cj.). **-εύομαι**, (μαῖα I. 3) *serve as a midwife, act as one*, D.S.19. 34; ἡ Ἄρτεμις μ. Luc.*DDeor*.26.2. 2. *cause delivery to take place*, ἱκανὴ ἔκπληξις μαιεύσασθαι πρὸ τῆς ὥρας Philostr.*VA*1.5. 3. c. acc., *bring to the birth*, Marin.*Procl*.6; ὄρνιθας μ. *hatch* chickens, Anon.ap. Suid.; αἰετὸν κάνθαρος μαιεύσομαι, prov. of taking vengeance on a powerful enemy, Ar.*Lys*.695 (cf. Sch.). 4. *deliver* a woman, esp. metaph. in Pl. of the Socratic method, *Tht*.149b. II. Act., Poll. 4.208, Sch.Opp.*H*.4.506:—Pass., τὰ ὑπ' ἐμοῦ μαιευθέντα *brought into the world* by me, Pl.*Tht*.150e, cf. Philostr.*VA*5.13. **-ευσις**, εως, ἡ, *delivery of a woman in child-birth*, Pl.*Tht*.150b. **-ευτικός**, ή, όν, *skilled in midwifery*, ib.151c; ἡ μαιευτικὴ τέχνη or ἡ -κή alone, art *of delivery*, Id.*Plt*.268b; esp. metaph. of the Socratic method of eliciting from others what was in their minds without their knowing it, Id.*Tht*.161e, D.L.3.49 sq.; οἱ μ. διάλογοι of Plato, such as *Alc.* 1, *La.*, *Ly.*, Thrasyll.ib.59. Adv. -κῶς Poll.4.208. **-εύτρια**, ἡ, *midwife*, S.*Fr*.99, Gal.*Nat.Fac*.3.3. **-ήϊος**, ον, = μαιευτικός, Nonn. *D*.9.167.

**Μαιῆτις**, Ion. for Μαιῶτις.

**μαιήτωρ**, ορος, ὁ, (μαίομαι) *seeker*, σοφίης μαιήτορες Orac.ap.Porph. *Plot*.22.

**μαιθαῦ**· οἴμοι, Hsch. **μαίθη**· καρδία πρὸς τοῖς ἱεροῖς, Id. **μαίμα**· τῶν ὀρνίθων ἡ κοιλία, Id. **μαιμάζω**, = μαιμάω, Ph.1.391, cj. in Suid.

**μαίμακος**, ον, *violent*, *Trag.Adesp*.593 (dub.).

® **Μαιμακτήρ**, ῆρος, ὁ, prop. = Μαιμάκτης: as name of month at Phocaea, *Inscr.Prien*.64 (ii B.C.).

® **Μαιμακτηριών**, ῶνος, ὁ, the fifth Attic month (cf. Μαιμάκτης), *IG* 1$^{2}$.63.6, D.49.62, Arist.*HA*578$^{b}$13, 597$^{a}$24, D.S.3.48, cf. Harp. s.v.

® **Μαιμάκτης**, ου, ὁ, (μαιμάσσω) epith. of Zeus at Athens, *boisterous, stormy*, Harp., cf. Plu.2.458b.

**μαῖμαξ**, ᾶκος, ὁ, ἡ, = ταραχώδης, Hsch.

**μαιμάσσω**, = μαιμάω, *AP*9.272 (Bianor); ἐμαίμασσεν ἐκ κοιλίας μητρός Lxx *Jb*.38.8; dub. l., ib.*Je*.4.19.

**μαιμάχης**· ὑβριστής, Zonar.

**μαιμάω** (redupl., cf. *μάω), Ep. 3 pl. μαιμώωσι, part. μαιμώων, -ώωσα, Hom. (v. infr.); Aeol. part. μαιμάεντι· ἐνεργῶς κινουμένῳ, Hsch.: Ep. aor. μαίμησα Il.5.670:—Poet. Verb (Hom. only in Il.), *to be very eager, quiver with eagerness*, μαίμησε δέ οἱ φίλον ἦτορ Il. l. c.; μαιμώωσι πόδες καὶ χεῖρες 13.75; περὶ δούρατι χεῖρες ἄαπτοι μαιμῶσιν ib.78; μαιμώων ἔφετ' ἔγχεϊ 15.742: metaph., of a spear, αἰχμὴ δὲ διέσσυτο μαιμώωσα 5.661, cf. 15.542; δεινὸν μαιμώοντα Orac.ap.Hdt. 8.77: c. inf., λὶς μαιμώων χροὸς ἆσαι Theoc.25.253, cf. Lyc.529, etc.: not common in Trag., μαιμᾷ ὄφις the snake *rages*, A.*Supp*.895 (lyr.): c. gen., χεῖρα μαιμῶσαν φόνου *eager for* murder, S.*Aj*.50 (unless φ. goes with ἐπέσχε); μαιμώωσαι ἐδητύος A.R.2.269: in late Prose, μαιμῶσα ἐπιθυμία Ph.1.305, cf. 1.391 (ap.*POxy*.1173):—Pass., ἐς σίδηρον θύρσοι μαιμώοντο, prob. *rushed into, were suddenly changed into*, iron, D.P.1156.

**μαιμώσσω**, late form for μαιμάω, Nic.*Th*.470.

**Μαίνᾰλον**, τό, *Mount Maenalus* in Arcadia, sacred to Pan, Theoc. 1.124:—Adj. **Μαινάλιος**, α, ον, δειραί Pi.*O*.9.59; ἡ Μαιναλία (sc. χώρα) Th.5.64.

**μαίνανδρος**, ον, *mad after men*, γυνή Hdn.*Epim*.83.

⊕ **μαινάς**, άδος, ἡ, (μαίνομαι) *raving, frantic*, λύσσα v. l. in S.*Fr*.941.4; βάκχη E.*Ba*.915. 2. as Subst., *mad woman*, esp. *Bacchante, Maenad*, μαινάδι ἴση Il.22.460, cf. *h.Cer*.386, A.*Fr*.382, S.*OT*212 (lyr.), etc.; of the Furies, A.*Eu*.500 (lyr.); of Cassandra, E.*Tr*. 173 (lyr.). 3. = πόρνη, Poll.7.203 cod. A, Hdn.*Epim*.83. II. Act., *causing madness*, esp. of love, μαινὰς ὄρνις Pi.*P*.4.216.

**μαίν-η**, ἡ, *Maena vulgaris*, a small sprat-like fish, which was salted, *AP*9.412 (Phld.); cf. μαινομένη. **-ίδιον**, τό, Dim. of foreg., Ar. *Fr*.247, Pherecr.56, Arist.*HA*569ᵃ18. **-ίς**, ἡ, gen. ίδος Ar.*Ra*. 985, but ἶδος Opp.*H*.1.108:—Dim. of μαίνη, freq. in Com., Ar. l. c., Philyll.27, etc., cf. Arist.*HA*607ᵇ10, Speus.ap.Ath.7.313a, Numen. ap.Ath.7.328d, Dsc.*Eup*.1.78, Ael.*NA*12.28, Alciphr.1.6.

⊕ **μαινόλης**, ου, ὁ, *raving, frenzied*, μαινόλᾳ θύμῳ Sapph.1.18; a name of Dionysus, Ph.1.351, Corn.*ND*30:—fem. **μαινόλις**, not found in gen., B.*Scol.Fr*.11; διάνοιαν μαινόλιν A.*Supp*.109 (lyr.); ἀσέβεια μ. prob. cj. in E.*Or*.823 (lyr.). II. Act., *maddening*, of wine, Plu.2. 462b. (From μαίνομαι, as φαινόλης from φαίνομαι.)

⊕ **μαινόλιος**, α, ον, = foreg., of Dionysus, *AP*9.524.13.

⊕ **μαίνομαι**, fut. μᾰνοῦμαι Hdt.1.109, μᾰνήσομαι *AP*11.216 (Lucill.), D.L.7.118 (neither found in Att.): pf. with pres. sense μέμηνα A.*Pr*. 977, S.*El*.879, Ar.Byz.ap.Ath.13.586f; Dor. μέμᾱνα dub. in Alcm. 68; also in pass. form μεμάνημαι [ᾰ] Theoc.10.31: aor. Pass. ἐμάνην, part. μᾰνείς, inf. μᾰνῆναι, Hdt.3.30, E.*Ba*.1295: also aor. Med. ἐμηνάμην *CPHerm*.7.18 (iii A. D.); poet. 2 sg. ἐμήναο prob. in Bion 1.61, 3 sg. μήνατο Theoc.20.34; part. μηνάμενος *AP*9.35 (Antiphil.):—on the act. forms, v. infr. II.—Hom. uses only pres. and impf.:—*rage, be furious*, in Il. freq. of martial rage, μαίνεσθαι ἐάσομεν οὖλον Ἄρηα 5. 717, cf. 6.101, Od.9.350, etc.; χεῖρες ἄαπτοι μαίνονται Il.16.245; μαίνεται ἐγχείη ἀπὸ λοιγὸν ἀμῦναι ib.75; δόρυ μαίνεται ἐν παλάμῃσιν 8.111; *rage with anger*, πατὴρ.. φρεσὶ μαίνεται οὐκ ἀγαθῇσι ib.360; ἐνὶ φρεσὶ μ. ἦτορ ib.413; φρεσὶ μαινομένῃσιν 24.114; μαινομένᾳ κραδίᾳ A.*Th*. 781, E.*Med*.432 (both lyr.); μανείσᾳ πραπίδι Id.*Ba*.999 (lyr.); ὁ μανείς *the madman*, S.*Aj*.726; μ. καὶ παραπαίω Pl.*Smp*.173e, etc.; αἱ τῶν μεμηνότων αἰσθήσεις Aristocl.ap.Eus.*PE*14.20; *to be mad* with wine, Od. 18.406, 21.298; μεμηνότες ὑπὸ τοῦ ποτοῦ Luc.*DDeor*.18.2; of Bacchic frenzy, μαινόμενος Διώνυσος Il.6.132; [Θυιάδες] μαινόμεναι S.*Ant*. 1152 (lyr.); Διονύσῳ μαίνεσθαι Paus.2.7.5; ἐπὶ τῷ Δ. Alex.223; ὑπὸ τοῦ θεοῦ μ. *to be inspired by.., driven mad by..*, Hdt.4.79, cf. μάντις; τὸ μαίνεσθαι *madness*, S.*OC*1537; πλεῖν ἢ μαίνομαι *I am beside myself* with joy, Ar.*Ra*.103, 751; of madness in animals, Plu.2.641c, al.; later simply, = ὀργίζομαι, μαινόμενος ὅτι.. *PCair.Zen*.41.11 (iii B. C.): freq. with words of manner, ὁ δὲ μαίνεται οὐκέτ' ἀνεκτῶς Il.8.355; τάδε μαίνεται 5.185: c. acc. cogn., μεμηνότ' οὐ σμικρὰν νόσον A.*Pr*. l. c.; μ. μανίας Ar.*Th*.793; μ. μανίαν ἐρρωμένην Luc.*Ind*.22: c. dat., μ. γόοισι φρήν A.*Th*.967 (lyr.); τόλμῃ X.*Cyr*.1.4.24; πόνοις *at* or *because of..*, A.*Supp*.562 (lyr.); τοῖς εὑρήμασιν E.*Cyc*.465; ἐπί τινι (sc. φιλοτιμίᾳ) Id.*Ph*.535 (but ἐπί τινι, of love, Theoc.10.31); ἀμφί τινι Semon.7.33; εἰς τὴν ποιητικήν D.S.14.109; κατά τινος Luc.*Abd*. 1; ὑφ' ἡδονῆς S.*El*.1153. 2. of things, *rage, riot*, esp. of fire, ὡς ὅτ'.. ὀλοὸν πῦρ οὔρεσι μαίνηται Il.15.606, cf. Tryph.230; μαινόμενος οἶνος a *hot, strong* wine, Pl.*Lg*.773d; of feelings, ἐλπὶς μαινομένη Orac.ap.Hdt.8.77; ἔρις A.*Th*.935 (lyr.); ἄχεα S.*Aj*.957 (lyr.); μαινομένᾳ ξὺν ὁρμᾷ Id.*Ant*.135 (lyr.); σὺν μ. δόξᾳ E.*Ba*.887 (lyr.). 3. ἄμπελος μαινομένη, of a vine that is never done bearing fruit, Arist. *Mir*.846ᵃ38, Thphr.*CP*1.18.4. 4. μαινόμενα ἕλκη *malignant* ulcers, Asclep.ap.Aët.15.14. II. aor. 1 Act. ἔμηνα, in causal sense, *madden*, E.*Ion* 520 (troch., prob. in *IA*580 (lyr.)), Ar.*Th*.561; *enrage*, X.*HG*3.4.8: pres. μαίνω first in Orph.*H*.71.6. (Cf. μέμονα.)

**μαινομένη**, ἡ, = μαίνη, Sch.Luc.*Gall*.22:—Dim. **μαινομένιον**, τό, Alex.Trall.*Febr*.7.

**μαίομαι**, Aeol. **μαίομαι** and **μάομαι** [ᾰ] (v. infr.): fut. μάσσομαι Il.9.394 (Aristarch., recte): aor. 1, v. ἐπιμαίομαι:—*seek after, seek for*, γυναῖκα Il. l. c.; κευθμῶνας ἀνὰ σπέος *searching for* hiding-places in the cave, Od.13.367, cf. 14.356, Hes.*Op*.532, *h.Cer*.44, Pi.*O*.1.46, *Trag. Adesp*.509 (lyr.); *pursue*, ὁ μαιόμενος τὸ μέγα κρέτος Alc.25.1; δυνατὰ μαιόμενος Pi.*P*.11.51, cf. *N*.3.5; μ. ὄλεθρόν τινι *seek* one's destruction, Nic.*Th*.197: c. gen., A.R.4.1275: c. inf., *seek* to do, Pi.*O*.8.5, A. *Ch*.786 (lyr., dub.), S.*Aj*.287; *desire*, ἐγὼ δέ σ' ἐμαιόμαν (σε μὰ ὤμαν cod.) Sapph.*Supp*.18.1; καὶ ποθήω καὶ μάομαι Ead.23; Κρητῶν μαιομένων ὃς ἀναίνετο αὐταρχεῖν Pi.*Pae*.4.36.—Never used in Prose; for it appears in Pl.*Cra*.421a merely for an etym. purpose. (Prob. μᾰ(σ)-yo-, cf. μασ-τήρ, μασ-τρός, μασ-τεύω; but μᾱ- is found in μᾱτεύω, μᾱ-τήρ; perh. cogn. with μῶμαι.)

**μαῖον**, τό, = λαγώπους 2, Gal.1.649, Alex.Trall.9.1.

**μαιόομαι**, = μαιεύομαι, 1. of a midwife, *deliver* a woman, Call. *Jov*.35, Luc.*DDeor*.16.2, cf. Plu.2.999c; ὑμέας ἀφροσύνη μαιώσατο, τόλμα δ' ἔτικτε *AP*9.80 (Leon.); ἐμαιώσαντο νέον τόκον Εἰλείθυιαι *IG* 14.967: of Hephaestus at the birth of Athena, Corn.*ND*19: abs., *practise midwifery*, Sor.1.80: in pass. sense, ὑφ' ἧς μαιωθεῖσα Apollod. 1.4.1. 2. of the mother, *to be delivered of*, ἣν.. οὐ μαιώσατο μήτηρ Coluth.181, cf. Nonn.*D*.4.437, etc. II. of a nurse, *suckle*, μαζῷ τινα ib.8.186. III. Act. only late, of dawn *bringing forth* day, Jo.Gaz.1.58.

**Μάϊος** (with or without μήν), ὁ, = Lat. *Maius, May*, D.H.1.38, Plu. *Num*.19, etc.: as Adj., Καλάνδαι Μάϊαι the Calends *of May*, Id.*Rom*. 12.

**μαϊούλιον**, τό, prob. f. l. for μαρούλιον, Hsch. s. v. θριδακίναι (pl.).

**Μαῖρα**, ἡ, (μαρμαίρω) name of the dog-star, *the Sparkler*, Call.*Aet*. 3.1.35, *AP*9.555 (Crin.), Nonn.*D*.5.221; of Hecuba when changed into *a dog*, Lyc.334: in Hom. as pr. n., Il.18.48.

⊕ **μαιριάω**, Tarent. for κακῶς ἔχω, acc. to Hsch. s. v. Μαῖρα.

**μαίσων**, ωνος, ὁ, *native cook*, at Athens, Ath.14.659a; derived from μασᾶσθαι by Chrysipp.ibid., but acc. to Ar.Byz.ibid. it means *comic mask of a cook, sailor*, etc., named after an actor so called:—hence **μαισωνικὰ** σκώμματα, ib.b.

**μαιτῠρέω**, = μαρτυρέω, *Supp.Epigr*.4.31 (Camarina, ii B. C.).

**μαῖτυς**, Cret. and Epid. for μάρτυς (q. v.).

**μαίωσις**, εως, ἡ, (μαιόομαι) = μαίευσις, Plu.*Alex*.3, Sor.1.68 (pl.).

**μαιωστᾷ**· ἐρευνᾷ τῇ φύσει, Hsch.

**Μαιῶται**, Ion. **Μαιῆται**, οἱ, *Maeotians*, a Scythian tribe to the north of the Black Sea, Hdt.4.123, X.*Mem*.2.1.10. II. as Adj. **Μαιώτης**, ου, *Maeotian*, ποταμὸς Μ. the Tanais, Hdt.4.45:—fem. **Μαιῶτις** λίμνη *the Palus Maeotis, Sea of Azof*, A.*Pr*.418 (lyr.), etc.; ἡ λίμνη ἡ Μαιῆτις (Ion.) Hdt.1.104, etc.: **μαιώτης**, ου, ὁ, *a fish caught there, and in the Nile*, Archipp.26, Ael.*NA*10.19. 2. **Μαιωτικός**, ή, όν, αὐλὼν Μ., i.e. *the Cimmerian Bosporus*, A.*Pr*.731.

**μαιωτικός**, ή, όν, = μαιευτικός, τέχνη Plu.2.1000e; δίφρος Antyll. ap.Orib.10.19.2, Sor.1.35; μαιωτικός (sc. λόγος), ὁ, treatise on midwifery by Herophilus, Id.2.3.

**Μαιωτιστί**, Adv. *in Scythian fashion*, Theoc.13.56.

**μαίωτρα**, τά, *midwife's wages*, Luc.*DDeor*.8.

⊕ **μάκαρ** [v. infr.], ἄρος, ὁ, also **μάκαρς** Alcm.10, 11; μάκαρ as fem., E.*Hel*.375, *Ba*.565, Ar.*Av*.1722, Eub.104 (all lyr.), Orac.ap.D.S.8 *Fr*. 29, *AP*12.52 (Mel.), but usu. fem. μάκαιρα *h.Ap*.14, Alcm.37, Sapph. 1.13, Pi.*P*.5.11, E.*Alc*.1003 (lyr.), etc.; Boeot. μάκηρα Corinn.*Supp*. 1.15: with neut. Nouns in oblique cases, μακάρων ἐξ ἐτέων *AP*9.424 (Duris); μακάρων τεκέων Nonn.*D*.21.263. [μᾰκᾱρ Archil.*Supp*.3.5, Sol.14, Diph.126.6 (mock-Epic), elsewh. μᾰκᾰρ Il.3.182, etc.]:—*blessed, happy*, prop. epith. of the gods, as opp. mortal men, πρός τε θεῶν μ. πρός τε θνητῶν ἀνθρώπων Il.1.339: abs., μάκαρες *the blessed ones*, μακάρων μέγαν ὅρκον ὀμόσσαι Od.10.299, cf. Hes.*Op*.136, Sol.13. 3, Pi.*O*.1.52, A.*Supp*.1019 (lyr.); μ. χθόνιοι Id.*Ch*.476 (lyr.); οὐράνιοι μ. E.*HF*758 (lyr.); μ. ὀλίζονες lesser *gods*, Call.*Jov*.72.—In this sense always in pl., exc. in addressing single gods, as *h.Hom*.8.16, Sapph. l. c., Corinn. l. c., S.*Ph*.400 (lyr.), etc.: freq. in Inscrr., μ. Παιάν *IG*14.1015; μάκαιρα, of Persephone, ib.12(5).229 (Paros). II. of men, *blest, fortunate*, ὦ μάκαρ Ἀτρεΐδη Il.3.182, cf. 24.377, Thgn.1013, Pi.*P*.4.59, etc.; μάκαιρα Θήβα, ἑστία, etc., Id.*I*.7(6).1, *P*.5.11, etc.; esp. *wealthy*, ἀνδρὸς μάκαρος κατ' ἄρουραν Il.11.68, cf. Od.1.217. III. esp. μάκαρες, οἱ, *the blessed dead*, μ. θνητοῖς καλέονται Hes.*Op*.141; μακάρων νῆσοι the Islands *of the Blest*, ib.171; of an oasis in the African desert, Hdt.3.26: sg., μ. νᾶσος Pi.*O*.2.71; ἀπιὼν εἰς μακάρων δή τινας εὐδαιμονίας Pl.*Phd*.115d, cf. *Grg*.523b, *R*.519c, al.—This sense does not occur in Hom., and is the only usage found in Prose, μακάριος being the common form. IV. Sup. μακάρτατος Od.6.158, 11.483, S.*Fr*.410; μακάρων μακάρτατε, of Zeus, A.*Supp*.524 (lyr.).

⊕ **μακάρι**, *would that..*, Hsch. s. v. αἴθε, Suid. s. v. ὄφελες.

**μᾰκᾰρ-ία**, ἡ, *happiness, bliss*, Phld.*Herc*.1232 p.70 V.; κενὴ μ. Luc. *Herm*.71, *Nav*.12: hence, as a Com. euphem. for ἐς κόρακας, ἄπαγ' ἐς μακαρίαν Ar.*Eq*.1151; βάλλ' ἐς μ. Pl.*Hp.Ma*.293a; ἐς μ. τὸ λουτρόν Antiph.245. II. *foolishness, nonsense*, κεναὶ μ. Simp. *in Cael*.140. 31. III. = βρῶμα ἐκ ζωμοῦ καὶ ἀλφίτων, Hsch. **-ίζω**, Att. fut. -ιῶ Ar.*V*.429:—*bless, deem* or *pronounce happy, congratulate*, τινα Od.15.538, Pi.*N*.11.11, Hdt.7.45, S.*OT*1196 (lyr.), Antipho 2.4.4, E.*Ba*.911 (lyr.), etc.; τινά τινος for a thing, Ar.*V*.429, Lys.2.81, Phld.*Rh*.1.194 S.; τινὰ ἐπί τινι Id.*D*.1.15; also μ. τὴν ῥώμην τινός, = μ. τινὰ τῆς ῥώμης, Hdt.1.31; ironically, μακαρίσαντες ὑμῶν τὸ ἀπειρόκακον *blessing* your *happy* ignorance, Th.5.105: with neut. Pron., τουτί.. σε μόνον (cj.).. μακαρίζω Ar.*V*.588:—Pass., Th.2.51, D.L.6.45: c. dat. modi, σωφροσύνῃ καὶ ὁσιότητι μακαρισθεὶς X.*Cyn*.1.11. **-ίνη**, = ἀνδράχνη, Hsch. **-ιος**, α, ον, also ος, ον Pl.*Lg*.803c: collat. form. of μάκαρ, mostly used in Prose, but also in Poets, as Pi., and freq. in E., 1. mostly of men, *blessed, happy*, Pi.*P*.5.46, E.*Or*. 86, etc.; σοφοί τε καὶ μ. ἄνδρες Pl.*R*.335e; μ. τε καὶ εὐδαίμων ib.354a: distd. from εὐδαίμων by Arist.*EN*1101ᵃ7, 19: freq. in phrases such as μ. ὅστις.. νοῦν ἔχει Men.114, cf. *Mon*.357, 614, Phld.*Ir*.p.3 W.:

Sup., Id.*Piet.*104: in addresses, ὦ μακάριε *my good sir, my dear sir*, Pl.*Prt.*309c, *R.*432d, Men.*Pk.*219: c. gen., ὦ μ. τῆς τύχης *O happy you* for.., Ar.*Eq.*186, cf. *V.*1512, Pl.*Euthd.*303c; ἰὼ χελῶναι μακάριαι τοῦ δέρματος Ar.*V.*1292; ὦ μ. σύ τά τε ἄλλα καὶ αὐτὸ τοῦτο ὅτι.. X.*Cyr.*8.3.39. **2.** *prosperous*, οἱ μ., opp. οἱ ἐνδεεῖς, Arist.*EN*1157$^b$21, al.; κινδυνεύω σοι δοκεῖν μ. τις εἶναι Pl.*Men.*71a; τοὺς μ. καλουμένους ὁρῶ πονοῦντας ἡμῖν ἐμφερῆ Men.*Kith.Fr.*1.6; μακαριωτάτην.. πόλιν Καπύην Plb.3.91.6; ἐπιγονή *SIG*695.48 (Magn. Mae., ii B.C.). **3.** of the dead, like μακαρίτης, Pl.*Lg.*947e, cf. Ar.*Fr.*488.9; μακαρίας μνήμης *BCH*25.89 (Bithynia), *Sammelb.*4753.2, etc. **II.** of states, qualities, etc., μ. λέχος E.*Or.*1208; -ωτέρα πόλις Id.*Tr.*365; -ώταται τύχαι ib.328 (lyr.); βίος Cratin.238, cf. Pl.*R.*561d; τοῖς θεοῖς ἅπας ὁ βίος μ. Arist.*EN*1178$^b$26; μ. διάθεσις Phld.*Mort.*18; μ. ἐστιν ἡ τραγῳδία ποίημα Antiph.191.1; τὸ μακάριον *bliss*, Arist.*EN*1099$^b$2. **III.** Adv. -ίως E.*Hel.*909, Ar.*Pl.*629, Arist.*Pol.*1324$^a$24, etc.: Sup. -ώτατα Pl.*Lg.*733e. **-ιότης**, ητος, ἡ, *happiness, bliss*, ib.661b, Arist.*EN*1178$^b$22, Epicur.*Ep.*1 p.28 U., etc.; as a title of bishops, *Cod.Just.*1.3.42 *Intr.*, Just.*Nov.*3. **-ισμός**, ὁ, *pronouncing happy, blessing*, Pl.*R.*591d, Arist.*Rh.*1367$^b$33, Andronic. *Pass.*p.570 M., Plu.2.471c; *giving praise* or *thanks*, Epicur.*Sent. Vat.*52, Phld.*D.*3 *Fr.*86a. **-ιστέον**, *one must deem happy*, Plb.23.12.5. **-ιστής**, οῦ, ὁ, gloss on Ἀσήρ, J.*AJ*1.19.8. ⊛**-ιστός**, ή, όν, *deemed* or *to be deemed happy*, ἐς Ἀΐδα κατέβα πᾶσιν μ. ἰδέσθαι *IG*1$^2$.1085; πρὸς πάντων ἀνθρώπων Hdt.7.18; ἡ ὑπὸ τῶν πολλῶν μ. αἵρεσις Pl.*Phdr.*256c; πᾶσι Χαλδαίοις X.*Cyr.*7.2.6: abs., *enviable*, Ar.*V.*550, Epicur.*Sent.Vat.*17; μ. γάμος Ar.*Av.*1725; ὦ μακαριστὲ Κομᾶτα Theoc.7.83, cf. Call.*Epigr.* in *Berl.Sitzb.*1912.548 (fort. proparox., quasi-Sup. of μάκαρ): Comp. -ότερος Isoc.8.143: Sup. -ότατος *Lyr. Adesp.*139.6, X.*Mem.*2.1.33, Isoc.9.70, *Sammelb.*5765.4 (iii/iv A.D.), Man.1.209; αἱ -όταται φύσεις Phld.*Herc.*1232 p.70 V. Adv. -τῶς, διάγειν J.*AJ*2.6.1. **-ίτης** [ῑ], ου, Dor. **-τᾱς**, ὁ, like μάκαρ III, *one blessed*, i.e. *dead*, esp. of one *lately dead*, A.*Pers.*633 (lyr.), Ar.*Fr.*488.10, Men.1032, *PCair.Zen.*447.1 (iii B.C.): freq. in late writers, Plu.2.120b, Ath.3.113e; ὁ μ. σου πατήρ your *late* father, Luc. *DMeretr.*6.1, etc.:—fem. ⊛**-ῖτις**, ιδος, Theoc.2.70, Herod.6.55; ἡ μ. μου γυνή Luc.*Philops.*27. **II.** as Adj., μ. βίος, with a play on I, Ar.*Pl.*555. **-ος**, α, ον, = μακάριος, *Epigr.Gr.*454 (Trachonitis), 656, dub. in *IG*14.2258 (Lorium). **-τός**, ή, όν, = μακαριστός, *AP* 7.740.5 (Leon.).

⊛**μᾰκεδνός**, ή, όν, = μηκεδανός, *tall, taper*, αἴγειρος Od.7.106; ἐλάται Nic.*Th.*472; νάπαι Lyc.1273: as pr. n. of the Dorians, Δωρικόν τε καὶ Μ. ἔθνος Hdt.8.43, cf. 1.56; Μ. σκῦλα Hsch. (who glosses it by οὐράνια καὶ μεγάλα).

**Μᾰκεδον-ίζω**, *to be on the Macedonian side*, Plb.20.5.5, Plu.*Alex.* 30, etc.: *speak Macedonian*, Id.*Ant.*27, Ath.3.122a:—hence Adv. **-ιστί**, *in Macedonian*, Plu.*Eum.*14.

⊛ **Μᾰκεδών**, όνος, ὁ, ἡ, *Macedonian*, Hdt.6.44 (pl.), etc.:—also **Μακηδών** (q.v.):—fem. **Μακεδόνισσα**, Stratt.32. **II.** Adj. **Μακεδονικός**, ή, όν, Hdt.7.131, etc.: **-κόν** (sc. φάρμακον), τό, Gal.10.883. Adv. **-κῶς** Arr.*An.*7.12.2, Plu.*Cleom.*23; ἡ **Μακεδονία**, Ion. **-ίη**, *Macedon*, Hdt.5.17:—also ἡ **Μακεδονὶς** γῆ Id.7.127; **Μακεδονῖτις**, Ael.*NA* 15.20; but γῆ Μακεδών *AP*7.45 (Th.).

⊛ **μᾰκέλας**, ὁ, kind of priest in Lydia, Alex.Aet.9.2 codd.

**μᾰκέλη**, ἡ, = sq., Hes.*Op.*470, Theoc.16.32, A.R.4.1533.

**μάκελλα** [μᾰ], ης, ἡ, *mattock, pick*, used for digging and breaking up, Il.21.259, Luc.*Hes.*7: metaph., Τροίαν κατασκάψαντα Διὸς μακέλλῃ A.*Ag.*526; μ. Ζηνὸς ἐξαναστραφῇ S.*Fr.*727, cf. Ar.*Av.*1240.

**μακελλ-εῖον**, τό, = *laniatorium*, *Gloss.* **-ίτης**, = *corpodicina* (sic), ib.

⊛**μάκελλον**, τό, *enclosure*, *IG*4$^2$(1).102.107, al. (Epid., iv B.C.):—also **μάκελλος**, ὁ, Sch.Ar.*Eq.*137; **μάκελος**, ὁ, and pl. **μακελα, μάκελλα**, Hsch. **II. μάκελλος**, ὁ, = Lat. *macellum, market*, *IG*5(2).268.45 (Mantinea, i B.C.), 5(1).149 (Sparta), 1*Ep.Cor.*10.25, D.C.61.18, *PLond.ined.*2487.43 (iv A.D.):—hence ⊛**μακελλάριος**, ὁ, = Lat. *macellarius*, Aesop.134; = *laniator, lanio*, *Gloss.*: neut. **-άριον**, τό, *POxy.*1000 (vi A.D.).

⊛ **μακελλωτός**, ή, όν, *latticed*, θύραι *Inscr.Délos* 442 *B* 238 (ii B.C.).

**μᾱκεσίκρᾱνος**, ον, (μᾶκος) *tall-crested*, of the hoopoe, Hsch.

**Μάκέτης**, ου, ὁ, = Μακεδών, Gell.9.3, etc.:—fem. **Μάκέτις**, ιδος, Str.10.4.10, *AP*7.49 (Bianor); or **Μάκέτη**, ib.51 (Adaeus).

**Μᾱκηδών**, όνος, ὁ, poet. for Μακεδών, Hes.*Fr.*5.2 (pr. n. of eponymous hero), Call.*Del.*167; **Μακηδονίη**, ἡ, Hermesian.7.65, Epigr. ap.Paus.1.13.3.

⊛**μάκιρ** (μάκειρ *Peripl.M.Rubr.*8), *muttee-pal*, the fragrant resin of *Ailanthus malabarica*, Dsc.1.82, Plin.*HN*12.32, Gal.12.66.

**μᾱκιστήρ**, ῆρος, ὁ, *long and tedious*, μῦθος A.*Pers.*698 (troch.); μακιστῆρα καρδίας λόγον is corrupt in Id.*Supp.*466 (Sch. δηκτικόν, leg. μαστικτῆρα).

**μάκιστι**· λοιμός, Hsch. **μάκιστος**, Dor. for μήκιστος.

**μακκοάω**, fut. -άσω [ᾱ], *to be stupid*, μακκοᾷ καθήμενος Ar.*Eq.*396: pf. part. μεμακκοακώς (v.l. -ηκώς) *sitting mooning*, ib.62, cf. *Com.Adesp.* 1210, Luc.*Lex.*19.—Derived from Μακκώ, *a stupid woman*, by Suid.

**μάκκορ**· ἐργαλεῖον γεωργικὸν ὡς δίκελλα, Hsch.; cf. μάκελλα. **μακκούρᾳ**· χειρὶ σιδηρᾷ ᾗ χρῶνται πρὸς τοὺς ἵππους, Id. **μᾶκος**, τό, Dor. for μῆκος. **μακούνιον**· δίκτυον κιχλῶν, ὅπερ τινὲς νεφέλην, Id.

**μάκρα**, ἡ, later form of μάκτρα (q.v.), *bath-tub*, Eup.[Junior]136 (v.l.), *PCair.Zen.*14(*b*).10 (iii B.C.), Plb.30.29.3, *IG*5(1).1390.107 (Andania, i B.C.), Ariston ap.Phld.*Vit.*p.29 J., Dsc.3.139 (codd.opt.), Damocr.ap.Gal.13.352, Crito ap.eund.12.589, Artem.5.58, etc.; esp. *sarcophagus*, *Jahresh.*18 *Beibl.*46 (Elaeussa), *Wiener Denkschr.*44(6). 64,65 (Cilicia), *BCH*20.351 (Cyprus), *Arch.Pap.*2.561 No.97 (Egypt, i A.D.), *Princeton Exp.Inscr.*1152 (Syria, ii A.D.). [μᾰ- in verse, Damocr. l. c., prob. in Eup. l. c.]

⊛**μακραίων**, ωνος, ὁ, ἡ, *lasting long*, βίος A.*Fr.*350 (dub.), S.*OT*518; μακραίωνι.. σχολᾷ Id.*Aj.*193 (lyr.). **2.** of persons, *long-lived, aged*, Id.*OC*152 (lyr.); Μοῖραι μ. Id.*Ant.*987 (lyr.); τίς τῶν μ.; who *of the immortals?* Id.*OT*1099 (lyr.); μ. λαός Tim.*Pers.*219; of the stars, Corn.*ND*17.

**μακρακές**· τὸ εὔκυκλον, Hsch.

**μακράν**, Ion. **μακρήν**, acc. fem. of μακρός used as Adv., *far*, μ. ἀνωτέρω θακῶν A.*Pr.*314; μ. λελειμμένος left *far* behind, ib.857; οὐδέπω μακρὰν πτέσθαι σθένοντες S.*OT*16; ἀπελθεῖν Ar.*Ra.*438 (lyr.); ἰέναι X.*An.*3.4.17; ἔστ' οὐ μ. ἄπωθεν Ar.*Av.*1184; τοὔργον οὐ μ. λέγεις the business you speak of is not *far* to seek, S.*Ph.*26: c. gen., *far from*, βαρβάρου χθονός E.*IT*629; κἂν ᾖ τοῦ γένους μ. Pl.Com.192; τῶν πολεμίων Plb.3.50.8; οὐ μ. ἀπό τινος Id.3.45.2: in Comp., ἀποσκίδνασθαι μακροτέραν *to a greater distance*, Th.6.98; πορεύεσθαι μ. X. *An.*2.2.11: Sup., ὅτι μακροτάτην *as far as possible*, c. gen. loci, ib.7.8.20. **2.** μακρὰν λέγειν speak *at length*, A.*Th.*713, S.*El.*1259; μ. τείνειν A.*Ag.*1296, S.*Aj.*1040; ἐκτείνειν A.*Ag.*916. **II.** of Time, *long*, μ. ζῆν, ἀναμένειν, S.*El.*323, 1389 (lyr.); οὐ μ. *shortly*, E.*Or.*850, etc.; so οὐκ ἐς μακρήν Hdt.5.108, cf. A.*Supp.*925, Ar.*V.*454, etc.; εὐθύς, οὐκ εἰς μακράν D.18.36 (but, not *at length*, Phld.*Piet.*25).

**μακρ-απόδοτος**, ον, = μακροαπόδοτος, Jo.Sic. in Rh.6.195 W. **-αυχένοπλος**, ον, *furnished with long shafts*, πόδες ναός, i.e. oars, Tim. *Pers.*100. **-αύχην**, ὁ, ἡ, gen. ενος, *long-necked, long*, κλῖμαξ E. *Ph.*1173: neut. pl., τὰ μακραύχενα Hp.*Epid.*2.1.8, Arist.*HA*595$^a$11. **-έτειος**, ον, (ἔτος) *aged*, Suid. **-ηγορέω**, *speak at great length, be long-winded*, A.*Th.*1057, Hp.*Nat.Puer.*12, E.*Hipp.*704, Th.1.68, 2.36, Herod.2.60:—Pass., Porph.*Chr.*23. **-ηγορία**, Dor. **μακρᾱγ-**, ἡ, *long-windedness, tediousness*, Pi.*P.*8.30, Poll.2.121. **-ήγορος**, ον, *speaking at great length*, Ph.2.268, Tz.*H.*10.4. **-ημερία**, Ion. **-ίη**, ἡ, *the season of long days* (in summer), Hdt. 4.86.

**μακρο-απόδοτος**, ον, *with the apodosis far off*, λέξις Phlp. *in de An.* 582.32; σύνταξις Eust.1491.49; λόγος Sch.D.T.p.114 H. **-βάμων** [βᾱ], ον, gen. ονος, *taking long strides*, Arist.*Phgn.*813$^a$3. **-βῐος**, ον, (βίος) *long-lived*, Hp.*Aër.*4, Arist.*Rh.*1361$^b$33, Apollod.2.1.5; of plants, Thphr.*HP*4.13.1 (hence μακρόβιον, τό, = ἀείζωον τὸ μικρόν prob. cj. in Ps.-Dsc.4.89): Comp. -ώτερος Str.15.1.34, Arr.*Ind* 9.4: Sup. -ώτατος Hdt.3.114, Str.15.1.43; Αἰθίοπες οἱ μ., of a half-mythical, perh. Abyssinian, people, Hdt.3.23, Orph.*A.*1107; αἱ Μ., nymphs at Rhodes, Hsch. **II.** (βιός) *with a long bow*, gloss on ἄβιος, *EM*3.23. **-βιότης**, ητος, ἡ, *longevity*, Arist.*Rh.*1361$^b$32, Gal.14.297, Alex.Aphr. *in Top.*258.4; of plants, Thphr.*HP*4.13.2. **-βίοτος** [ῐ], ον, = μακρόβιος, *long*, αἰών A.*Pers.*262 (lyr.). **-βίωσις** [ῐ], εως, ἡ, = μακροβιότης, Lxx *Ba.*3.14. **-βολέω**, *throw far*, Ph.*Bel.*50.2, al. **-βολία**, ἡ, *a throwing far, a long shot*, Str.3.5.1 (pl.). **-βόλος**, ον, *far-throwing*, σφενδόνη Id.8.3.33 (Comp.), Eust.311.20 (Comp.). **-γένειος**, ον, *with a long chin*, Poll.4.145. **-γενυς**, υ, gen. υος, *with long jaw-bones*, Adam.2.23. **-γηραία**, ἡ, *extreme old age*, *PMasp.*314 iii 27 (vi A.D.). **-γηράω**, *attain extreme old age*, ib.89.19 (vi A.D.). **-γηρως**, ων, gen. ω, *long-lived*, *AP*11.159 (Lucill.), Dsc.2.16, *Cat.Cod.Astr.*8(4).159. Adv. -γήρως Artem.5.74. **-γόγγῦλος**, ον, *cylindrical*, σωλῆνες Epich.42.7, Sophr.24. **-δάκτῠλος**, ον, *long-toed*, Arist.*PA* 690$^b$7, 694$^b$16. **-δρόμος**, ον, *running long* or *far*, X.*Cyn.*5.21 (Sup.). **-ειδής**, ές, *tall*, *BGU*364.6 (vi A.D.). **-ηλος**, ον, *with long nails*, Theognost.*Can.*84. ⊛ **-ημέρευσις**, εως, ἡ, *length of days*, Lxx *Si.*1.12. **-ήμερος**, ον, *long-lived*, ib.*De.*4.40, Anatol. in *Cat. Cod. Astr.* 8(3).188, Eust.129.1: Comp., Philostr.*VS* 2.1.7. **-θεν**, Adv. *from afar*, Chrysipp.*Stoic.*3.199, Lxx *Jo.* 9.15, *PTeb.*230 (ii B.C.), Str.3.3.4, etc.; ἀπὸ μ. *Ev.Marc.*5.6; of Time, *from long since*, Plb.1.65.7. **-θι**, Adv. *at a distance*, Tz.*H.*8.137. **-θριξ**, τρῐχος, ὁ, ἡ, *long-haired*, *Gp.*18.9.6. **-θῡμέω**, *to be long-suffering*, ἐπί τινι towards one, Lxx *Si.*18.11, al., *Ev.Matt.*18.26; πρός τινα 1*Ep.Thess.*5.14. **2.** *to be slow* to help, *Ev.Luc.*18.7. **3.** *persevere*, Plu.2.593f. **4.** c. acc., *bear patiently*, Lxx *Ba.*4.25: imper. μακροθύμει *bear up!* Astramps.*Orac.* 90.7. **-θῡμία**, Ion. **-ίη**, ἡ, *long-suffering, patience*, Men.549, Str. 5.4.10, *Ep.Col.*1.11, J.*BJ*6.1.5, Aret.*SD*1.1. **2.** *forbearance*, Lxx *Pr.*25.15, Aristeas 188, *Ep.Eph.*4.2. **-θῡμος**, ον, *long-suffering, patient*, Lxx *Ex.*34.6, al.; ὄνος *AP*11.317 (Pall.). Adv. -μως, ἀκοῦσαί τινος *Act.Ap.*26.3. **-θώραξ**, ᾱκος, ὁ, ἡ, *long-chested*, Philostr.*Gym.* 36. **-ῐαμβεῖον**, τό, *long iambic line*, Jo.Sic. in Rh.6.103 W. **-καμπῠλαύχην**, ενος, ὁ, ἡ, *with long bending neck*, ἐρῳδιοί Epich.46. **-καταληκτέω**, *end with a long syllable*, Choerob. in *Theod.*2.355 H., Eust.26.36:—Med., Hdn.Gr. in *An.Ox.*3.229:—hence **-κατάληκτος**, ον, Did.ap.St.Byz. s. v. Πνύξ, A.D.*Pron.*11.10, al.; **-καταληξία**, ἡ, Choerob. l. c. **-καυλος**, ον, *long-stalked*, Dsc. 2.175 (Comp.). ⊛ **-κέντης**, ου, ὁ, gloss on γαιός (γαιῶς cod.), Hsch. **-κεντρος**, ον, *with long sting*, Arist.*HA*532$^a$17. **2.** of figs, *with long pedicle*, Jul.*Ep.*180. **-κερκος**, ον, *long-tailed*, Stratt.66.4, Arist.*HA*596$^b$5. **-κέφᾰλος**, ον, *long-headed*, Hp. *Epid.*2.1.8; of a Scythian tribe, Hes.*Fr.*62, Hp.*Aër.*14: Sup., Str.11.11.8. **-κοίλιος**, ον, *with large intestines*, Heph.Astr.2.2. **-κομέω**, *have long hair*, Str.11.11.8. **-κρᾶνοι**, οἱ, = μακροκέφαλοι, Apollod.ap.Tz.*H.*7.763. **-κωλία**, ἡ, *use of long*

clauses, Jo.Sic. in Rh.6.305 W. **-κωλος**, ον, *long-limbed*, *Gp.* 19.2.1; applied to a sling, Str.3.5.1. 2. of authors, *using sentences with long clauses*, Arist.*Rh.*1409b30. **-κωπος**, ον, *long-oared*, gloss on δολιχήρετμος, *EM*282.15. **-λοβος**, ον, *with long pods*, Thphr.*HP*8.5.2. **-λογέω**, *speak at length*, *use many words*, Pl.*Grg.*465b, *Tht.*163d, Isoc.3.63, Arist.*Rh.Al.*1440b 36, etc.; περί τινος Hp.*Art.*43; τὰ ῥηθέντα τί ἄν τις -λογοίη X.*HG*4.1.13. **-λογία**, ἡ, *length of speech*, opp. βραχυλογία, Pl.*Grg.*449c, *Prt.*335bsq., Arist.*Rh.*1418b25, Gal.10.425. **-λόγος**, ον, *speaking at length*, θεός *Com.Adesp.*14.1 D., cf. Axiop.1.11: Comp., Pl. *Sph.*268b; -ώτερος τοῦ συμμέτρου Philostr.*VS*1.10. Adv. -γως Gal. 17(1).744. **-μαλλος**, ον, *with shaggy* or *long wool*, cj. in Str.4.4.3 (ἀκρο- codd.). **-μισθος**, ον, *highly paid*, prob. in Procop.*Goth.*4. 25. **-νοσέω**, *have a lingering sickness*, Arr.*Epict.*3.16.12. **-νοσία**, ἡ, *lingering sickness*, Artem.1.31, Paul.Al.*S.*3. **-ξῦλος**, ον, *with long wood*, Eust.1107.62. **-πέπερι**, τό, *long pepper*, *Piper longum*, Gal.11.881. **-πεπλος**, ον, *long-robed*, Eust.682.2. **-περιοδεύτως**, Adv. *verbosely*, A.D.*Pron.*3.7. **-περίοδος**, ον, *making long periods*, Sch.Il.13.172. **-πλεκτος**, ον, gloss on τανύπλεκτος, Sch.Opp.*H.* 1.33. **-πνοια**, ἡ, *deep breathing*, Antyll.ap.Orib.6.36.4, Gal.7. 836. **-πνοος**, ον, contr. **-πνους**, ουν, *deep-breathed*, or (acc. to others) as Subst. μ., ὁ, *deep breathing*, Hp.*Epid.*2.3.7, 6.2.4: metaph., ἕλκεις μ. ζόαν..a *wearisome* life, E.*Ph.*1535 (lyr.). **-ποιέω**, *spin out* conclusions *at length*, Arist.*Metaph.*1090b30. **-πολος**, ον, *long*, πίτυλοι E.*Hyps.Fr.*3(1)iii 11 (lyr.). **-πόνηρος**, ον, *bearing malice for a long time*, Phot. **-πονία**, ἡ, *long labour*, v.l. in Aesop. 353 Chambry. **-πόρευτος**, ον, *far-journeying*, μ. βίος *PLit.Lond.*98 ii 12 (Dioscorus). **-πορέω**, *go, travel far*, Str.8.3.29. **-πορία**, ἡ, *long detour*, Id.14.1.9. ⊛**-πορος**, ον, *travelling far*, in Comp. -ώτερος, Procl.*in Prm.*p.472 S.; *completing an orbit in longer time*, Id. *Hyp.*1.24. **-πρόσωπος**, ον, *long-faced*, *PGrenf.*2.15 i 12, al. (ii B.C.), *PLond.*3.879 (ii B.C.), *Peripl.M.Rubr.*62, Anatol. in *Cat.Cod.Astr.*8 (3).188, etc. **-πτερος**, ον, *long-winged*, Arist.*PA*644a20. **-πτόλεμος**, ὁ, = Τηλέμαχος, Theoc.*Syrinx* 1. **-πτύστης**, ου, ὁ, *spitting far from one*, prov. of a 'big bug', Sch.Luc.*Nav.*15, *Apol.*7. **-πῦλος**, gloss on Τηλέπυλος, Sch.Od.10.82. ⊛**-πώγων**, ωνος, ὁ, ἡ, *long-bearded*, name of a tribe, Str.11.2.1. **-ρριζία**, ἡ, *length of root*, Thphr.*HP*1.7.1. **-ρριζος**, ον, *with long root*, ib.7.11.3: Comp. and Sup., ib.1.7.2. **-ρρυγχος**, ον, *long-beaked*, Ath.7.294f (Comp.); *prognathous*, Gal.2.222 (Comp.).

⊛**μακρός**, ά, όν [ᾰ by nature], *long*, whether of Space or Time, I. of Space, 1. in length, *long*, δόρυ Il.7.140; νέες, νῆες μ. *ships of war*, Hdt.7.21, Th.1.41, etc. (collect. in sg., A.*Pers.*380); πλοῖα μ. Hdt. 5.30, Th.1.14; ἐπὶ τὰ -ότερα measured by *the longer sides*, i.e. *lengthwise*, Hdt.1.50; τὰ μ. τείχη the *long* walls of Athens, Th.8.71, etc.; ἐν τῷ μακρῷ σκέλει τῷ ποτ τῷ Ποτειδανίῳ *SIG*247 iii 11 (Delph., iv B.C.); ἡ μακρά (sc. γραμμή), line traced by δικασταί to indicate the heavier penalty, Ar.*V.*106; ὁ μ. δρόμος the *long-distance* torch-race, *SIG* 1068.9 (Patmos, iii/ii B.C.), al., *OGI*339.83 (Sestos, ii B.C.). 2. in height, *tall, high*, μ. Ὄλυμπος, οὔρεα, δένδρεα, κίων, Il.15.193, 13. 18, 9.541, Od.1.127, etc.; of a man, μακρότερον καὶ πάσσονα θῆκεν ἰδέσθαι 8.20, cf. 18.195; μ. πύκτης *PLond.*3.1158.6 (iii A.D.). b. reversely, *deep*, φρείατα Il.21.197; φάραγξ Herod.8.17. 3. in distance, *long, far, remote*, κέλευθος Il.15.358; οἶμος Hes.*Op.*290; ναυτιλίαι Hdt.1.1; στόλος S.*Ph.*490; μ. ἐπιβοήθειαι *long* marches to aid, X.*Cyr.*5.4.47; *remote*, ἀποικία A.*Pr.*814; τὰ μακρότατα the *remotest parts*, Hdt.2.32: freq. in neut. sg. and pl. as Adv., μακρὰ βιβάς, βιβάσθων, with *long* strides, Il.7.213, 13.809; μακρὰ ῥίψαις, δισκήσαις, Pi.*P.*1.45, *I.*2.35; -ότερον σφενδονᾶν X.*An.*3.4.16; μακρὸν ἀῦσαι, βοᾶν, to shout *so as to be heard afar*, i.e. *loudly*, Il.3.81, 2.224; μακρὰ μεμυκώς 18.580; μακρὸν ἠχεῖν Pl.*Prt.*329a; κλάειν σε μακρὰ κελεύσας Ar.*Eq.*433 (v. κλαίω and infr. v); later by analogy, μακρὰ χαίρειν φράσας τῷ ναυπηγῷ Luc.*Nav.*2, cf. *Apol.*3, al., D.C.46. 3; cf. μακράν. 4. generally, *large in size* or *degree, great*, ἤπειρος A.*Eu.*75; ὄλβος Pi.*P.*2.26; πλοῦτος S.*Aj.*130; τιμήματα Arist.*Pol.* 1278a23, cf. 1297b4 (Sup.); οὐσία ib.1290b16, 1321a11; μακροτέρα ἀρετά Pi.*I.*4(3).13; ἐλπίσαντες μακρότερα μὲν τῆς δυνάμεως, ἐλάσσω δὲ τῆς βουλήσεως Th.3.39; μ. τραπεζῖται, perh. *big* bankers, *Cat.Cod. Astr.*7.222. 5. dat. μακρῷ, to strengthen Comp. and Sup., *by far*, μ. πρῶτος Hdt.1.34; ἄριστος μ. Id.9.71; ἀσθενεστέρα μ. A.*Pr.*514, cf. Pl.*Phlb.*66e; μ. μάλιστα Hdt.1.171, cf. A.*Eu.*30, etc.; κάκιστα δὴ μ. S.*Ant.*895: also with Verbs implying comparison, ἀριστεύει μ. A.*Pr.*890 (lyr.), cf. D.H.1.2. II. of Time, *long* (Hom. only in Od.), ἤματα, νύξ, 10.470, 11.373; αἰών v.l. in Pi.*N.*3.75; μ. χρόνος Hdt.1.32, etc.; οὐ μ. χρόνου for no *long* time, S.*Ant.*1078, etc.; διὰ μ. χρόνου A.*Pers.*741 (troch.); ἐν χρόνῳ μ. S.*OC*88, etc.; δι' αἰῶνος μ. A.*Supp.*582 (lyr.); τὸν μ. βίον Id.*Pr.*449; τοῦ μ. βίου S.*Aj.*473; μηνὶ -ότερος *by* a month, Hdt.1.32; μακρῷ (cf. I. 5) πρότερον Gal.8.958; μ. ἐέλδωρ a *long-cherished* wish, Od.23.54; μ. γόοι, ὀδύρματα, S.*El.*375, E.*Hec.*297. 2. *long, tedious*, Pi.*N.*4.33, etc.; λόγοι S.*El.*1335, Th. 3.60, etc.; μακρὰν ἔοικε λέξειν (sc. ῥῆσιν) Ar.*Th.*382; οὐδὲ εἷς Ὅμηρον εἴρηκεν μακρόν Philem.97.7; μακρόν [ἐστι] c. inf., Lat. *longum est*, Pi.*I.*6(5).56; μ. ἂν εἴη γράφειν X.*Ages.*7.1. Adv. -ρῶς, λέγεσθαι Antiph.268: Comp. -ότερον, ποιεῖς you are taking *too long*, *PCair.Zen.* 48.4 (iii B.C.), cf. Philippid.21. 3. Gramm., *long* in quantity, φωνήεντα Arist.*Po.*1458a11, D.H.*Comp.*15; μακρά (sc. συλλαβή), ἡ, A.D.*Pron.*92.12; ἡ φύσει μ. Id.*Adv.*179.16: Comp., φωνήεντι μακροτέρῳ Arist.*Po.*1458a1; also μακρά (sc. προσῳδία), ἡ, *mark of long quantity*, S.E.*M.*1.113, D.T.*Supp.*674.7; ᾱ μακρόν A.D.*Pron.*112. 6. III. neut. with Preps. in adverb. sense, διὰ μακροῦ (sc. χρόνου) after *a long time, long delayed*, E.*Hec.*320, *Ph.*1069; οὐ διὰ μακροῦ not *long after*, Th.6.15, 91, Pl.*Alc.*2.151b (also of place, οὐ διὰ μ. τῆς Ῥώμης D.H.9.56); διὰ μακρῶν E.*Fr.*420.1; διὰ μακρᾶς Phalar.*Ep.* 69.1; but διὰ μακρῶν *at great length*, Pl.*Grg.*449b, etc.; διὰ μακροτέρων Isoc.4.106; μικρῷ διὰ μ. at somewhat *greater length*, Arist. *Pol.*1279b11. 2. ὄλβος οὐκ ἐς μακρὸν ἔρχεται for no *long time*, Pi. *P.*3.105; ἐς τὰ μακρότατα to the *utmost*, Th.6.31; v. μακράν II. 3. ἐπὶ μακρόν *far, a long way*, πορεύεσθαι X.*Cyr.*5.4.47; of Time, Call. *Del.*255; ὅσον ἐπὶ μακρότατον οἷοί τε ἐγενόμεθα ἐξικέσθαι ἀκοῇ Hdt. 4.16, cf. 2.34 (ἐπί omitted 1.171 codd.); τοσόνδε ἐπὶ μ. ἐπυθόμην Id. 2.29; ἐπὶ μακρότερον *yet more*, Th.4.41. IV. regul. Comp. and Sup., v. supr.: irreg. Comp. μάσσων, Sup. μήκιστος, v. sub vocc. V. Adv. -ρῶς *at great length*, opp. συντόμως, Arist.*Rh.* 1416b4; *slowly*, Plb.3.51.2; μ. ἔχειν τοῖν σκέλοιν have *long* legs, Philostr.*Gym.*31; of pronunciation, D.H.*Comp.*15; μ. ἐκφέρειν συλλαβήν Str.13.1.68: but the Adv. is usu. expressed by neut. μακρόν or μακρά, cf. supr. I. 3; μακρὰ κλάειν to howl *loudly*, Ar.*Th.*211; οἰμώξει μ. Id.*Av.*1207, *Pl.*111; ὀτοτύζεσθαι μ. Id.*Lys.*520; τί μακρὰ δεῖ λέγειν; Antiph.33.5; also by μακράν (v. sub voc.); or by neut. with a Prep., v. supr. III: for Comp. and Sup. of the Adv., v. μακροτέρως, μακροτάτω: neut. pl. -ότερα as Adv., Pl.*Phdr.*250c, al.— Fem. μακρά not to be confused with μάκρα (q.v.). (Cf. Avest. *mas-* 'long', Lat. *măcer*.)

**μάκρος**, εος, τό, = μῆκος, *length*, Ar.*Av.*1131, cf. Sch.Il.23.419.

**μακρό-σημος**, ον, *with long border* (cf. πλατύσημος), *Sammelb.*1988 (iii/iv A.D.). **-σίδηρος** [ῑ], ον, gloss on δολίχαυλος, Eust.1620. 36. **-σκελής**, ές, *long-legged*, A.*Fr.*62, Arist.*PA*692b5, *HA*623a 26 (Comp.), Str.2.1.9. **-σκῖος**, ον, *with long shadow*, Ach.Tat. *Intr.Arat.*31. **-σπαρτον**, τό, *machine drawn by long ropes*, cj. for *macron sparton* (acc.), Cael.Aur.*TP*5.134. **-σύλλᾰβος**, ον, *consisting of long syllables*, Phld.*Po.Herc.*994.31, D.H.*Dem.* 38. **-σύνθετον**, τό, *use of long compounds*, Phld.*Po.Herc.*1676. 9. **-σφυκτος**, ον, *having a long* (i.e. spatially extended) *pulse*, Gal. 9.100.

**μακρο-τάτω**, Adv. Sup. of μακρός, *farthest off*, Crates *Ep.*11, Longus 3.17. **-τενής**, ές, = μακρότονος: metaph., τὸ μ. τῶν συμπερασμάτων Dam.*Pr.*263. **-τένων**, οντος, ὁ, ἡ, *far-stretching, long*, ἅλος *AP*6.96 (Eryc.). **-τέρως**, Adv. Comp. of μακρός, *for a longer time*, Hp.*Prorrh.*1.117; *to a greater degree*, Pl.*Sph.*258c; *at greater length*, Arist.*Rh.*1410b18: **-τέρω**, *farther off*, Id.*Pr.*901a22. ⊛**-της**, ητος, ἡ, *length*, τῶν ἡμερῶν Lxx *De.*30.20, al.; χρόνου Phld.*Lib.*p.28 O.: Gramm. of syllables, A.D.*Adv.*187.15, Plu.2.947e (pl.). **-τομέω**, *prune so as to leave the shoots long*, Thphr.*CP*3.14.2. **-τομος**, ον, *pruned so that the shoots are left long*, of vines, opp. βραχύτομος, ib.3.2.3. **-τονέω**, *lengthen the* τόνος in a torsion-engine, μ. τὸ μῆκος τῶν τόνων Ph.*Bel.*68.15. II. *persevere*, Lxx 2*Ma.*8.26 (v.l. for ἐμακροθύμησαν). **-τονία**, ἡ, *physical endurance*, Antyll.ap.Orib. 6.35.1. **-τονος**, ον, *far-stretching, long drawn out*, σχοῖνοι *AP*9. 299 (Phil.). Adv. -νως S.E.*M.*1.121. II. opp. βραχύτονος (q.v.), *with a long* τόνος, Ph.*Bel.*53.32 (Comp.). **-τράχηλος** [τρᾰ], ον, *long-necked*, *AP*5.134, Str.17.3.19 (Comp.), D.S.2.50, Gal.2.429 (Comp.). **-ϋπνία**, ἡ, *long sleep*, Eust.1951.19. **-φάρυγξ** [ᾰ], υγγος, ὁ, ἡ, *long-necked*, of a bottle, *AP*9.229 (Marc. Arg.). **-φλυᾱρήτης**, ου, ὁ, *tedious prater*, ib.11.134 (Lucill.). **-φυέω**, *grow long*, *PAmh.*2.150.25 (vi A.D.). **-φυής**, ές, *with elongated bodies*, Arist.*PA*696a6 (Comp.); of crops, *tall, well-grown*, *PFlor.*17.10 (iv A.D.). **-φυλλος**, ον, *long-leaved*, Dsc.3.26 (Comp.), Sch.D Od. 13.102. **-φωνέω**, *shout, sing aloud*, Hp.*Carn.*18. **-φωνος**, ον, *shouting aloud*, Hsch. s.v. τανύγλωσσοι. **-χειρ**, χειρος, ὁ, ἡ, *long-armed*, name of Artaxerxes I, Str.15.3.21, Plu.*Art.*1; of athletes, Philostr.*Gym.*31, 34. **-χηλος**, ον, *with long hoofs*, v.l. in Str.17. 3.19. **-χρονέω**, *last a long time*, Sm.*Jb.*12.12. **-χρονίζω**, = foreg., Lxx *De.*17.20, 32.27, *PFlor.*296.10 (vi A.D.). **-χρόνιος**, ον, *lasting a long time, lingering*, Hp.*Epid.*3.7; πυρετός Gal.17(2). 739 (Sup.); τὸ μ. *long duration*, Agatharch.83. 2. *dwelling a long time*, Lxx *Ex.*20.12, al. 3. *long-lived*, *Ep.Eph.*6.3; βοῦς Porph. *VP*24 (Sup.). **-χρονιότης**, ητος, ἡ, = *longinquitas* (sic), *Gloss.* **-ψῡχέω**, *have patience*, *PSI*4.299.11 (iii A.D.). ⊛**-ψῡχία**, ἡ, f.l. for μικροψυχία in Cic.*Att.*9.11.4. **-ψῡχος**, ον, *patient*: hence, *dilatory*, *PMag.Par.*1.2902.

**μάκρ-υμμα**, ατος, τό, *a thing put far away*, as abominable, Lxx 2*Es.*9.1, 11 (with v.l. μάκρυνσις). **-ύνω**, fut. μακρῠνῶ Lxx *Ec.*8. 13: fut. Pass. μακρυνθήσομαι ib.*Is.*49.19: pf. Pass. μεμάκρυμμαι ib. *Ps.*55(56) tit.:—*prolong*, ἡμέρας ib.*Ec.* l.c.; ἀνομίαν ib.*Ps.*128(129). 3. 2. *lengthen* a syllable, Sch.Il.16.390 (Pass.). II. *remove to a distance, put away*, τὴν βοήθειαν Lxx *Ps.*21(22).20, cf. 39(40).12; τοὺς ἀνθρώπους ib.*Is.*6.12:—Pass., *to be far off*, τόπου *from* a place, Hero *Spir.Praef.* 2. intr. in Act., *travel far*, c. gen., Lxx *Jd.*18. 22, cf. *Ps.*54(55).7. **-υσμός**, ὁ, *long interval*, Aq.*Ps.*55(56).1, 119 (120).5. **-ων**, ωνος, ὁ, *longhead*: Μάκρωνες, οἱ, a people of Pontus, Hdt.2.104, etc. **-ωσις**, εως, ἡ, *lengthening, prolonging*; esp. *dwelling on* a thing, Plb.15.36.2 (nisi leg. ἀκρόασις). **-ώτης**, ου, ὁ, (οὖς) *long-eared*, Tz.*H.*1.125.

**μακτήρ**, ῆρος, ὁ, expld. by Hsch. in three senses: I. = μάκτρα. II. = διφθέρα. III. = μακτρισμός.

⊛**μακτήριον**, τό, = μάκτρα, Plu.2.159d: pl. μακτήρια, prob. = *food*, Call.*Fr.*7.32 P., cf. Sch. II. μ.· ἱλαστήριον, κάλυμμα, ἱερὸν κρύφιον, Hsch.

**μάκ-της**, ου, ὁ, (μάσσω) *one who kneads*, Hsch. II. pl., = *gulatores*, Gloss. **-τός**, ή, όν, *kneaded* (but not boiled or baked), of poultices, Antyll.ap.Orib.9.24.3,4, cf. *Gloss.*; of barley, Sor.1.86. **-τρα**, ἡ, *kneading-trough*, Ar.*Ra.*1159, *Pl.*545, Hermipp.57, X.*Oec.*9.7. II. *bathing-tub*, only in form **μάκρα** (q.v.). III. *mortar* for pounding drugs, Nic.*Th.*708.

**μακτρ-ισμός**, ὁ, = ἀπόκινος, Ath.14.629c. **-ίστρια**, ἡ, *one who dances the* μακτρισμός, ib.d (μαρκτυπίας cod.).

⊛ **μάκτρον**, τό, *wiper, towel*, Alex.Trall.*Febr.*1.

**μᾱκών**, v. μηκάομαι. **μάκων** [ᾰ], **μᾱκώνειον, μᾱκωνίς**, v. μηκ–.

⊛ **μάλα** [μᾰλᾰ; but Hom. sts. uses the ult. long before λ, Il.3.214, 4.379; before μ, 10.172], Adv. *very, exceedingly*, prefixed or subjoined to Adjectives, Verbs, and Adverbs: 1. strengthening the word with which it stands, a. with Adjs., in Hom. most freq., μάλα πολλά *very* many, Od.1.1; μ. πᾶσα, μ. πάντα, *every one*, all *together*, Il.13.741, Od.2.306, etc.; μάλ' ἀσκηθής *all* unhurt, 5.26; ἀβληχρὸς μ. τοῖος *quite* gentle, 11.135; σαρδάνιον μ. τοῖον a *quite* sardonic smile, 20.302; μάλα μυρίοι 15.556, 16.121, etc.; ἐμέο πρότερος μ. *actually* before me, Il.10.124; later, μ. φιλόσοφοι, πλάτανος μάλ' ἀμφιλαφής, etc., Pl.*Prm.*126b, *Phdr.*230b, etc.: strengthd., μ. δὴ πρεσβύτης *very* old, X.*Cyr.*8.7.1; μ. γέ τινες ὀλίγοι Pl.*R.*531e. b. with Advs., πάγχυ μ., μ. πάγχυ, *quite* utterly, Il.12.165, 14.143; πάνυ μ. Pl.*Phd.*80c; εὖ μ. *right* well, Od.22.190, Pl.*Phd.*92d, etc.; μάλα..εὖ Od.23.175, cf. Pl.*Tht.*156a; μάλ' αὐτίκα (v. αὐτίκα); μάλ' αἰεί for ever and aye, Il.13.557, 23.717; ἄχρι μ. κνέφαος until *quite* dark, Od.18.370; μάλ' ὧδε *just* in this way, 6.258; μ. διαμπερές *right* through, Il.20.362; μ. μόλις (v. μόλις); to express repeated action, μάλ' αὖθις A.*Ag.*1345, *Ch.*654; μάλ' αὖ S.*El.*1410, etc.; μ. alone, ἔα, ἔα μ. A.*Ch.*870; οἲ μ. καὶ τόδ' ἀλγῶ Id.*Pers.*1045 (lyr.); εἶα μ. Ar.*Pax* 460sq. (so ἄλλος πύργος.., καὶ ἕτερος μ. ἐπὶ τούτῳ Hdt.1.181, cf. 7.186): freq. after καί, αὗται σ' ὁδηγήσουσι καὶ μάλ' ἀσμένως A.*Pr.*728, cf. *Ch.*879: with neg., μάλ' οὐ, μάλ' οὔ πως, Il.2.241, Od.5.103; οὐ μ. Hdt.1.93, 2.37, S.*Ph.*676 (lyr.). c. with Verbs, μήτ' ἄρ με μάλ' αἴνεε Il.10.249; μ. τ' ἔκλυον αὐτοῦ 1.218; ἡ δὲ μάλ' ἡνιόχευεν drove *carefully*, Od.6.319; μ... προπέμπει *in earnest*, A.*Th.*915 (lyr.), cf. *Eu.*368 (lyr.); καὶ μ. δοκοῦντας φρονίμους εἶναι X.*Cyr.*6.1.36; μ. πολιορκούμενοι Id.*HG*7.1.25. 2. strengthening an assertion, νῦν σε μ. χρὴ αἰχμητὴν ἔμεναι, i.e. now *or never*, Il.16.492; τῷ κε μάλ' ἤ κεν μεῖνε.. then *doubtless* he would have stayed, Od.4.733; σοὶ δὲ μάλ' ἕψομ' ἐγώ yes *indeed*.., Il.10.108; ἀλλὰ μάλ' ὤφελλες why *plainly*.., Od.4.472: freq. with another word, as ἦ μ. δή.. now *in very* truth, Il.5.422, etc.; ἦ δή που μ. 21.583; freq. ἦ μ. (without δή) 3.204, etc. 3. in Hom. sts. after εἰ, as εἰ μ. μιν χόλος ἵκοι if wrath come on him *ever so much*, Il.17.399, cf. Od.5.485, al.; καὶ εἰ μ. τις πολεμίζοι Il.9.318; also μ. περ c. part., μ. περ μεμαώς though desiring *never so much*, 13.317, cf. 14.58, 17.710, al.; καὶ μ. περ 1.217, cf. 17.571; καὶ εὐρέα περ μάλ' ἐόντα Od.18.385. 4. in Att. freq. in answers, *yes, certainly*, μ. γε Pl.*R.*555d, 564e, etc.; μ. τοι X.*Mem.*1.2.46; καὶ μ. Pl.*Phdr.*258c; καὶ μ. γε Id.*Tht.*148c, etc.; καὶ μ. δὴ ib.177a; καὶ μ. ἐπαύσατο *certainly* it stopped, Id.*Smp.*189a, etc. II. Comp. **μᾶλλον** [ᾱ by nature, Hdn.Gr.2.932], Ion. **μάλιον** [ᾰ] only in Tyrt.12.6, cf. Choerob.in *An.Ox.*2.240; late Dor. **μαλλότερον** Pempel.ap.Stob.4.25.52:—*more, rather*, Il.5.231, Od.1.351, al.: mostly folld. by ἤ, but in Prose also by a gen., μ. τοῦ ξυμφέροντος *more than* is expedient, Antipho 5.1; μ. τοῦ δέοντος Pl.*Grg.*487b, X.*Mem.*4.3.8 (sts. expressed by μᾶλλον alone, Pl.*Phd.*63d); οὐπώποτ' ἔργου μ. εἰλόμην λόγους E.*Fr.*394; παντὸς μ. most assuredly, Pl.*Lg.*715d (v. infr. 8); in Id.*Ap.*36d, οὐκ ἔσθ' ὅτι μ. πρέπει οὕτως, ὡς.., ὡς is prob. = ἤ (v. ὡς): denoting a constant increase, *more and more*, sts. doubled, μ. μ. E.*IT*1406, Ar.*Ra.*1001 (lyr.), Alex.29: in positive sense, *exceedingly*, κηρόθι μ. Il.9.300, Od.15.370, al.:—Usage: 1. freq. strengthened by other words, πολὺ μ. Il.9.700, etc.; ἔτι μ. 14.97, al.; μ. ἔτ' ἢ τὸ πάροιθεν Od.1.322; καὶ μ. Il.8.470; καὶ μ. ἔτι Od.18.22; ἔτι καὶ μ. Pi.*P.*10.57; ἔτι καὶ πολὺ μ. Il.23.386, 429, Hes.*Th.*428; ἐπὶ μ. Hdt.3.104; ἔτι ἐπὶ μ. Id.1.94; πολλῷ μ. Pl.*Phd.*80e, 1*Ep.Cor.*12.22: also modified, μᾶλλόν τι somewhat *more*, μ. τι περιημέκτεε Hdt.1.114, cf. 50, etc.; μ. ἤδη προσδεχομένου Th.8.71. 2. sts. with a second Comp., ῥηΐτεροι μ. Il.24.243, cf. Hdt.1.32, A.*Th.*673, *Supp.*279, S.*Ant.*1210, E.*El.*222, Pl.*Phd.*79e, Is.4.14 (s.v.l.), Arist.*Top.*116b24. 3. μᾶλλον δέ *much more*.., or *rather*.., to correct a statement already made, ὁ δεσπότης πέπραγεν εὐτυχέστατα, μ. δ' ὁ Πλοῦτος αὐτός Ar.*Pl.*634; πολλοί, μ. δὲ πάντες D.18.65, cf. Pl.*Smp.*173e; so ἢ μ. Corn.*ND*20, Simp.*in Ph.*25.16; οὐχὶ μ. ἤ.. not so, *but rather* so.., Th.2.87. 4. μ. δὲ καὶ ἡσυχαίτερα *more* or less *violent*, Id.3.82. 5. οὐδὲν μ. none *the more*, ib.79; οὐδέν τι μ. Pl.*Phd.*87d; μηδέν τι μ. ἤ.. S.*Aj.*280. 6. μ. ἤ.. folld. by οὐ in comparisons, where preference implies rejection or denial, πόλιν ὅλην διαφθεῖραι μᾶλλον ἢ οὐ τοὺς αἰτίους Th.3.36: preceded by another neg., Hdt.4.118, 5.94, 7.16.γ', etc.: by an interrog. which conveys a neg. force, τί δεῖ..μᾶλλον, ἢ οὐ..; X.*HG*6.3.15. 7. τὸ μ. καὶ ἧττον, a form of argument, *a fortiori*, Arist.*Rh.*1397b12. 8. παντὸς μ., v. πᾶς III. 4. III. Sup. **μάλιστα** *most of all, above all*, Hom., etc.; πᾶσι, μάλιστα δ' ἐμοί Od.21.353; μ. μὲν.., ἔπειτα or ἔπειτα δέ.., *first and above all*.., next.., S.*OT*647, cf. *Ph.*1285; μ. μὲν.., δεύτερον δὲ.. Is.2.20; μ. μὲν.., εἰ δὲ μή.. Hdt.8.22, Th.1.40, Pl.*R.*590d, D.20.25, etc.; τοῦτο δ' ἐστὶ μ. μὲν θάνατος, εἰ δὲ μή, πάντα τὰ ὄντα ἀφελέσθαι Id.21.152; μάλιστα μὲν.., μᾶλλον μέντοι.. Pl.*Smp.*180b; μάλιστα.., εἰ μὴ δ'.. S.*Ph.*617; δοκέων μιν μ. ταύτης ἂν πείθεσθαι *certainly*, Hdt.3.53; τί μ.; what *precisely?* Pl.*Grg.*448d, cf. *Men.*80b, *Smp.*218c: c. gen. partit., μ. πάντων Hdt.2.37, Pl.*Prt.*327a, cf. Th.4.86; τὸ μ. πάντων the *supreme* reality, Plot.5.5.11; τὸ μ. εἶναι the *highest degree* of being, Id.6.2.7. 1. strengthd., ὡς μ. *certainly*, A.*Supp.*294, Pl.*R.*460a, etc.; ὅσον μ. A.*Pr.*524; ὅσα ἐδύνατο μ. Hdt.1.185; ὡς δύναμαι μ. Pl.*R.*367b; ὡς οἷόν τε μ. Id.*Grg.*510b; εἰς ὅσον ἀνθρώπῳ δυνατὸν μ. Id.*Phdr.*277a; ὅτι μ. δύνασαι Id.*Sph.*239b; μακρῷ μ. Hdt.1.171; πολλῷ μ. Paus.1.42.3; παντὸς μ. D.H.3.35, etc. 2. with the Art., ἐς τὰ μ. *in the highest degree*, Hdt.1.20, 2.76, Th.6.104, 8.6, D.21.212: without ἐς, φίλοι τὰ μ. Hdt.2.147, cf. Th.1.92, D.21.62; τά γε μ. Pl.*Lg.*794d; εἰ τὰ μ. ἦσαν ἀληθεῖς if they were *ever so* true, D.18.95; εἰ τὰ μ. μή τινές, ἀλλὰ πάντες.. if (*to put an extreme case*) not some, but all.., Id.20.2; εἰ..δοκοίη τὰ μ. Id.18.21; ἀνὴρ δόκιμος ὁμοῖα τῷ μ. as famous as he that is *most* [famous], Hdt.7.118, cf. 3.8; τοῖς μάλισθ' ὁμοίως D.*Ep.*2.24. b. ἐν τοῖς μ. *especially, as much as any*, Th.8.90, Pl.*Smp.*173b, etc.: with a Sup., ἐν τοῖς μ. ὠμότατος Ael.*VH*14.40; φιλτάτη καὶ ἀναγκαιοτάτη ἐν τοῖς μ. Procop.*Arc.*4. 3. added to a Sup. (v. μάλα II. 2, πλεῖστον), ἔχθιστος μ., μ. φίλτατος, Il.2.220, 24.334; μ. κη ἐμφερέστατα Hdt.2.76; μ. φίλτατος E.*Hipp.*1421: to a Comp. (?), μ. δὴ ὀκνηρότεροι ἐγένοντο Th.4.55. 4. μάλιστα for μᾶλλον, μ. τῆς κόρης E.*IA*[1594]; μ. ἢ ἐμοί A.R.3.91. 5. with numerals, *in round numbers, about*, Th.3.29, 92, X.*HG*5.2.31, etc.; πεντήκοντα μάλιστα is 49 in Th.1.118; ἑκατοστὸς μ. 99th, Id.8.68; ἐς μέσον μάλιστά κῃ *about* the middle, Hdt.1.191, cf. 76; ἥμισυ μ. Th.1.93; μ. σφᾶς μεσοῦν δειπνοῦντας that they were *about* the middle of supper, Pl.*Smp.*175c; κου μ. Hdt.7.22; μ. πως Plb.2.41.13. 6. in answers, *most certainly*, Ar.*Pl.*827, etc.; μ. γε S.*OT*994, Ar.*Nu.*253; μ. πάντων Id.*Av.*1531; πάντων μ. Pl.*Grg.*453d; v. supr. I. 4. (Orig. perh. *fiercely*, cf. μαλερός.)

**μᾰλᾰβάθρ-ῐνος**, ον, *prepared with* μαλάβαθρον, μύρον Crito ap.Gal.12.448, cf. Dsc.1.63; ἔλαιον Sor.2.38. ⊛**-ον**, τό, *leaf of Cinnamomum Tamala* or *albiflorum*, *Peripl.M.Rubr.*56, 65, Dsc.1.12, Gal.12.66, Plin.*HN*12.129. [*mālŏbăthrum* Hor.*Od.*2.7.8.] (From Skt. *tamāla-pattra-* 'leaf of *tamāla-* (name of various trees)'.)

⊛**μάλαγμ-α** [μᾰ], ατος, τό, (μαλάσσω) *emollient*, Thphr.*Od.*59, Gal.13.946, *PCair.Goodsp.*30 x 6 (ii A.D.), etc. II. *soft materials, padding*, used in sieges to blunt the force of engines and weapons, Ph.*Bel.*91.7, 95.47; μ. τῆς ἀντιτυπίας Plu.2.618f, cf. Pl.*Ti.*70d, ap. Longin.32.5; μαλάγματος χάριν for *padding*, Ruf.ap.Orib.49.28.10; μ. ἕνεκα, of a shirt worn under armour, Sch.Il.21.31. **-ᾰτίζω**, *soften*, Zos.Alch.p.164B. **-ᾰτώδης**, ες, *like an emollient plaster*, Gal.12.409, Alex.Trall.12.

**μᾰλᾰκαίπους**, ὁ, ἡ, πουν, τό, gen. ποδος, poet. for μαλακόπους, *treading softly*, Ὧραι Theoc.15.103 (s.v.l.).

**μᾰλᾰκ-αύγητος**, ον, (αὐγή) *with languid eye*, ὕπνος Arist.*Fr.*675 (lyr.). **-εια**, τά, = μαλάκια, Opp.*H.*1.638. **-ευνέω**, (εὐνή) *lie on a soft bed*, Hp.*Insomn.*90, prob. in *Vict.*2.66. **-ευτικός**, ή, όν, *softening*, Sch.D Il.1.582 (nisi leg. μαλακτικός). **-ία**, Ion. **-ίη**, ἡ, (μαλακός) *softness*, Hp.*Aër.*20: hence, of persons, *moral weakness*, opp. καρτερία, Arist.*EN*1150a31, cf. Hdt.6.11, Th.1.122, Lys.10.11, X.*Smp.*8.8, D.11.22, etc.; τῇ σαυτοῦ ζυγομάχει μ. Men.201.5. 2. = κιναιδεία, Ph.2.306, Plu.*CG*4, D.C.58.4. 3. *weakliness, sickness*, Lxx *Ge.*42.4, *Ev.Matt.*4.23, Ps.-Hdt.*Vit.Hom.*36, *POxy.*1151.27 (v A.D.); μ. σώματος, opp. ψυχῆς, Phld.*Mus.*p.30K. II. *calmness of the sea, malacia ac tranquillitas*, Caes.*BG*3.15.3. ⊛**-ια**, τά, *cephalopod mollusca*, i.e. *water-animals of soft substance, without external shells*, Arist.*HA*523b2, *PA*654a10, al., Diocl.*Fr.*132. II. v. μαλάχιον. **-ιάω**, *become soft*, τῶν βοῶν, ἂν εἰς τὰς χηλὰς μαλακιῶσι, προσαλείφειν τὰ ἄκρα τῶν κεράτων Plu.2.559f codd. (fort. μαλκίωσι); v. μαλκίω. **-ίζομαι**, fut. μαλακισθήσομαι D.C.38.18: aor. ἐμαλακίσθην Th.2.42, al., Pl.*Sph.*267a, D.24.175: less freq. in med. form ἐμαλακισάμην, X.*Ap.*33, *Cyr.*4.2.21:—*to be softened* or *made effeminate, show weakness* or *cowardice*, οὔτε πλούτου τις..ἀπόλαυσιν προτιμήσας ἐμαλακίσθη, οὔτε πενίας ἐλπίδι Th. l. c.; of soldiers, μὴ ὄντος χωρίου.. ὅποι ἂν μαλακισθέντες σωθείητε Id.7.77; κἂν αὐτὸς μαλακίζηται X.*Cyr.*2.3.3; μ. πρὸς τὸν θάνατον *meet* death *like a weakling*, Id.*Ap.* l.c. 2. *to be softened, appeased*, Th.6.29; πρὸς τὸ παρὸν Id.3.40. 3. *to be weakly*, Arist.*HA*605a25, Thphr.*Char.*1.4, *PSI*4.420.16 (iii B.C.), *SIG*$^2$850.24 (Delph., ii B.C.): acc. to Phot. applied to men in Att., opp. ἀσθενεῖν, of women, but this is not so; cf. Alciphr.2.1.

**μαλακίννης**· παρθένος, Hsch.; cf. μαλκενίς.

**μᾰλάκ-ιον** [ᾰκ], τό, v. μαλάχιον. II. v. μαλάκια. **-ιστέον**, *one must display weakness*, Ph.2.162, Ach.Tat.6.17, v.l. (for μαλθ-) in Pl.*Alc.*1.124d. ⊛**-ίων**, ωνος, ὁ, Dim. of μαλακός, as a term of endearment, *darling*, Ar.*Ec.*1058.

**μᾰλᾰκό-γειος**, ον, (γῆ) *with soft soil*, χώρα Str.1.3.7. **-γνᾰθος**, ον, of a horse, *soft-mouthed*, Poll.1.219. **-γνώμων**, ον, gen. ονος, *mild of mood*, A.*Pr.*190 (anap.); gloss on εὔκολος, Sch.Ar.*Ra.*82. **-δερμος**, ον, *soft-skinned*, Arist.*HA*489b15, al. **-ειδής**, ές, *soft-sounding*, στίχος Sch.Heph.p.292C. **-θριξ**, τρῐχος, ὁ, ἡ, *soft-haired*, Arist.*GA*783a13. **-κισσος**, ὁ, = μῖλαξ λεία, *Gp.*2.6.31. **-κόλαξ**, ακος, ὁ, *voluptuous parasite*, Clearch.26. **-κρᾱνεύς**, έως, ὁ, *shrike, Lanius sp.*, Mod. Gr. κεφαλᾶς, Arist.*HA*617a32. **-λᾰλος**, ον, *speaking effeminately*, *Cat.Cod.Astr.*1.116. **-ποιέω**, *make soft, soothe*, D.Chr.32.57. **-ποιός**, όν, *making soft*, Sch. Theoc.5.51, Eust.155.33. **-πους**, ὁ, ἡ, πουν, τό, gen. ποδος, *tender-footed*, *Hippiatr.*95, 104. **-πτῠχής**, ές, dub. sens., ἄρτοι Philox.2.36. **-πύρηνος** [ῡ], ον, (πυρήν) *with soft kernel*, Thphr.*CP*2.11.7.

⊛**μᾰλᾰκός**, ή, όν, *soft*: I. of things subject to touch, εὐνή Il.9.

618; κώεα Od.3.38; τάπης μαλακοῦ ἐρίοιο 4.124; χιτών Il.2.42, *PSI* 4.364.5 (iii B.C.); πέπλοι Il.24.796; νειὸς μ. *fresh-ploughed* fallow, 18.541; λειμῶνες μ. *soft grassy* meadows, Od.5.72, cf. Il.14.349; πόας ἄνθος Sapph.54; τάπητες..-ώτεροι ὕπνω Theoc.15.125; of the skin or flesh, μ. παρειαί S.*Ant.*783 (lyr.); χρώς E.*Med.*1403 (anap.); σώματα X.*Mem.*3.10.1; πρόβατα μ. *soft-fleeced*, D.47.52; τόποι πεδινοὶ καὶ μ., opp. hard. rugged ground, Arist.*HA*607ᵃ10; οἱ κρημνοὶ οἱ μ. ib.615ᵇ31; μ. πέτρα *SIG*970.8 (iii B.C.), *PPetr.*2 p.6 (iii B.C.); μ. τέφρα a *slow* fire, Ph.*Bel.*89.36; so μ. πῦρ Androm.ap.Gal.13.26; μ. ἀνθρακιά Dsc.2.76; ὕδωρ μ., of *marsh* water, A.*Fr.*192.8 (anap.), Pl.*Ti.*59d (cf. μαλθακός); of soil, X.*Oec.*19.8, Pl.*Criti.*111b. Adv., μαλακῶς ἐνεύδειν, εὐδέμεναι, to sleep *softly*, i.e. *on soft bedding*, Od. 3.350, 24.255; μαλακώτατα καθεύδειν X.*Mem.*2.1.24; καθίζου μ. sit *softly*, i.e. *on a cushion*, Ar.*Eq.*785; ὑποστορεῖτε μ. τῷ κυνί Eub.90, cf. 108; but ὡς μ. ἐσθίεις what *dainty* food you have! Thphr.*Char.*2. 10. 2. μαλακά (sc. σκεύη), τά, *household utensils*, Men.*Per.Fr.*3, Diph.19. II. of things not subject to touch, *gentle*, θάνατος Od. 18.202; ὕπνος Il.10.2; κῶμα 14.359; μ. ἔπεα *soft, fair* words, 1. 582, 6.337; λόγοι Od.1.56; ἐπαοιδαί Pi.*P.*3.51; παρηγορίαι A.*Ag.*95 (anap.); αὖραι X.*Oec.*20.18; μ. βλέμμα *tender, youthful* looks, Ar. *Pl.*1022; μαλακὰ φρονέων ἐσλοῖς Pi.*N.*4.95; μ. οἶνος *mild*, Arist.*Pr.* 873ᵇ34; μ. [φωνή] *soft*, Id.*Aud.*803ᵃ8 (Comp.); of scent, *faint, delicate*, Thphr.*HP*6.7.4; of climate, *mild*, ib.6.8.1. Adv. μαλακῶς, αὐλεῖν Arist.*Aud.*803ᵃ20; ἐὰν τὰ σκληρὰ μ. λέγηται Id.*Rh.*1408ᵇ 9. 2. *light, mild*, -ώτεραι ζημίαι Th.3.45. III. of persons or modes of life, *soft, mild, gentle*, μαλακώτερος ἀμφαφάασθαι *easier* to handle, of a fallen hero, Il.22.373; ἐκ τῶν μ. χώρων μ. ἄνδρας γίνεσθαι Hdt.9.122; -ώτερον ἐκ σκληροτέρου τὸ τῆς ψυχῆς ἦθος Pl.*Lg.*666b; ἀρνίου -ώτερος Philippid.29; -ώτερον τὸ ἦθος τὸ τῶν θηλειῶν Arist.*HA* 608ᵃ25; ἀρρένων καὶ μ. ἠθῶν καὶ πράξεων Phld.*Mus.*p.92 K. 2. in bad sense, *soft*, μ. ἐν τῇ ξυναγωγῇ τοῦ πολέμου Th.2.18; μ. ἦν περὶ τοῦ μισθοῦ Id.8.29; πρὸς τὸ πονεῖν X.*Mem.*1.2.2. Adv. -κῶς, ξυμμαχεῖν Th.6.78; -ωτέρως ἀνθήπτετο attacked him *somewhat feebly*, Id.8.50; μ. φιλεῖν X.*Mem.*3.11.10. b. *faint-hearted, cowardly*, Th.6.13, X. *HG*4.5.16 (Comp.), etc. c. *morally weak, lacking in self-control*, Hdt.7.153 (Comp.); ἀντίκειται τῷ μ. ὁ καρτερικός Arist.*EN*1150ᵃ33: c. inf., μαλακὸς καρτερεῖν πρὸς ἡδονάς τε καὶ λύπας Pl.*R.*556c; τὸ τρυφῶν καὶ μ. Ar.*V.*1455 (lyr.); μ. οὐδὲν ἐνδιδόναι not to give in *from weakness* or *want of spirit*, Hdt.3.51,105, Ar.*Pl.*488; τὰ μ. *indulgences*, Epich.288, cf. X.*Cyr.*7.2.28. d. = παθητικός, *PHib.*1.54.11 (iii B.C.), 1*Ep.Cor.*6.9, Vett.Val.113.22, D.L.7.173. e. of music, *soft, effeminate*, μ. ἁρμονίαι Pl.*R.*398e, 411a, cf. Arist.*Pol.*1290ᵃ28; *tuned to a low pitch*, opp. σύντονος, χρῶμα μ. Cleonid.*Harm.*7, etc. f. of style, *feeble*, τὸ -ώτερον καὶ ταπεινότερον Phld.*Rh.*1.197 S. g. of reasoning, *weak, loose*, λόγος Isoc.12.4 (Comp.), cf. 5.149 (Comp.); λόγος λίαν μ. Arist.*Metaph.*1090ᵇ8. Adv. -κῶς, συλλογίζεσθαι to reason *loosely*, Id.*Rh.*1396ᵇ1 (Comp.); ἀποδεικνύειν -ώτερον Id.*Metaph.*1025ᵇ 13. 3. *weakly, sickly*, -κῶς ἔχειν to be *ill*, Hermipp.58, Ps.-Hdt. *Vit.Hom.*34, Luc.*DDeor.*9.1; -κῶς διάκειται *PCair.Zen.*263.3 (iii B.C.). IV. Adv. -κῶς, v. supr. I, II, III.

**μᾰλᾰκόσαρκος**, ον, *with soft flesh*, ζῷα Arist.*HA*486ᵇ9; οἱ μ. Id. *de An.*421ᵃ26, cf. Diocl.*Fr.*135 (Comp.).

**μᾰλᾰκόστρᾰκος**, ον, *soft-shelled, crustaceous*, Arist.*HA*490ᵇ11, al., Speus.ap.Ath.3.105b.

✻**μᾰλᾰκόσωμος**, ον, *effeminate*, Antioch.Astr. in *Cat.Cod.Astr.*7.113.

**μᾰλᾰκότης**, ητος, ἡ, *softness*, opp. σκληρότης, Pl.*R.*523e, *Tht.*186b, Arist.*Mete.*382ᵃ9, al.; ἡ μ. ὕπνος Herod.6.71; μ. ἱματίων D.L.5.67: in pl., Pl.*Cra.*432b. 2. of climate, *mildness*, Thphr.*HP*3.5. 4. II. *weakness, effeminacy*, Plu.*Oth.*9.

**μᾰλᾰκο-τρεφής**, ές, *softly-nurtured*, χάριτες *PLit.Lond.*99.6 (Dioscorus). -**τρῐχος**, ον, *with soft hair*, Gal.4.605, al.

**μᾰλᾰκόφθαλμος**, ον, *soft-eyed*, f.l. in Theodect.6.1.

**μᾰλᾰκό-φλοιος**, ον, *with soft bark*, Philox.3.20, Thphr.*CP*1.6. 4. ✻-**φρων**, ονος, ὁ, ἡ, *gentle-hearted*, Orph.*H.*59.15, 69.13. ✻-**φωνος**, ον, *with a soft voice*, D.H.*Dem.*40. -**χειρ**, χειρος, ὁ, ἡ, *soft-handed*, φαρμάκων μαλακόχειρα νόμον, of a physician's art, Pi.*N.*3.55. -**ψῡχέω**, *to be cowardly*, Lxx 4*Ma.*6.17. -**ψῡχος**, ον, *faint-hearted*, *Cat. Cod.Astr.*1.145. -**ω**, = μαλάσσω, Hsch. s. v. μαλθώσω.

**μᾰλακ-τέον**, *one must relax*, τὴν κοιλίαν Herod.Med.ap.Aët.5. 129. ✻-**τήρ**, ῆρος, ὁ, *one that melts and moulds*, χρυσοῦ μ. καὶ ἐλέφαντος Plu.*Per.*12. -**τικός**, ή, όν, *emollient*, χρίσματα Hp.*Vict.*2. 66; δύναμις Plu.2.659c; μ. οἶκος, of the outer chamber in a bath, Alex.Trall.*Febr.*5. -**τός**, ή, όν, *that can be softened*, as iron, Arist. *Mete.*385ᵃ13, al. -**υνσις**, εως, ἡ, = μάλαξις, Alex.Aphr.*Pr.*1.90 (prob.). -**ύνω**, *soften*, v.l. for μαλακευνέω in Hp.*Vict.*2.66; αἱ πυρώσεις τὸν σίδηρον -ουσιν Ph.*Bel.*71.43; Κύριος ἐμαλάκυνε τὴν καρδίαν μου Lxx *Jb.*23.16; *weaken*, χεῖρας καὶ πόδας Muson.*Fr.*19 p.107 H.:—Pass., *become soft, flag*, X.*Cyr.*3.2.5; ταῖς ψυχαῖς D.S.17. 10. -**ώδης**, ες, *softish*, λίθος St.Byz. s. v. Μονόγισσα.

**μάλαξις** [μᾰ], εως, ἡ, *softening*, Thphr.*HP*5.3.3; διὰ πυρός Plu.2. 430a; σιδήρου ib.c; μ. τῆς τροφῆς *digestion*, ib.700b.

**μάλασσος**· τράχηλος, Hsch.

**μᾰλάσσω**, Att. -ττω, fut. -ξω E.*Or.*1201: (μαλακός):—*make soft*, I. of dressing leather, *make it supple*, Luc.*Anach.*24; μ. δέρμα Hp.*Aph.* 5.22, of the human skin:—hence, with reference to Cleon's trade of tanner, μ. τινά *give* one *a hiding*, Ar.*Eq.*388: metaph., ἐν παγκρατίου στόλῳ μαλαχθείς *worsted* in it, Pi.*N.*3.16; χηλῇ μαλαχθείς *crushed* by the hoof, of a toad, Babr.28.6. 2. *soften* metal or other materials *for working*, ὥσπερ σίδηρον μ. Pl.*R.*411b:—Pass., Arist. *Mete.*383ᵃ31. 3. *calm*, μαλάξοντες βιατὰν πόντον, of the Dioscuri, *Lyr.Adesp.*133. II. metaph., *soften, appease*, σπλάγχνον, ὀργάς, E. *Or.*1201, *Alc.*771; χρόνος μαλάξει σε *will relieve* thee, ib.381, cf. 1085; [θωπεῖαι] τοὺς θυμοὺς μαλάττουσαι ποιοῦσιν κηρίνους interpol. in Pl.*Lg.* 633d; μ. τὸ τῆς φύσεως σκληρόν Plb.4.21.3; μ. τὰ ἤθη Plu.2.156d:—Pass., *to be softened, relent*, πρὸς θεῶν, μαλάσσου S.*Aj.*594; τί κακόν ποτ' ἔσθ' ὅτῳ μαλάττομαι; Ar.*V.*973; τῶν ψυχῶν -ομένων (by music) Phld.*Mus.*p.33 K.; μ. νόσου *to be relieved from* disease, S.*Ph.*1334; of fever, *remit*, Hp.*Epid.*3.17.ς', cf. *Coac.*380; τὰ πολλὰ τῶν δεινῶν ἡμέρας μαλάσσεται S.*Fr.*65.

**μαλατῆρες**· ναῦται, Hsch. **μαλατθᾷ**· αἱμωδιᾷ, Id. **μαλαφῶν**· ζητῶν, Id.

✻**μᾰλάχη** [λᾰ], ἡ, *mallow, Malva silvestris*, Hes.*Op.*41, Batr.161, Pherecr.131.1 (pl.), Thphr.*HP*7.7.2, 7.8.1, Mosch.3.99, etc.; σιτεῖσθαι ἀντὶ μὲν ἄρτων μαλάχης πτόρθους Ar.*Pl.*544:—also **μολόχη**, Epich.153, Antiph.158, Dsc.2.118 (cod. F). 2. μ. ἀγρία, = ἀλθαία 1, Thphr.*HP*9.15.5, Ps.-Dsc.3.146. 3. μ. κηπευτή *tree-mallow, Lavatera arborea*, Dsc.2.118, cf. Gal.6.628; μ. ἀποδενδρουμένη Thphr. *HP*1.3.2; ἄνθρακες -ης Xenocr.ap.Orib.2.58.48. (Perh. fr. μαλάσσω, because of its *laxative* properties, cf. Dsc. l. c., Plin.*HN*20. 221; the relation to Lat. *malva*, Engl. *mallow* is uncertain.)

✻**μαλάχιον**, τό, a woman's ornament worn round the neck, Ar. *Fr.*320.10 (ap.Phot.; **μαλάκιον** Hsch., Poll.5.98 (pl.); **μολόχιον** Clem.Al.*Paed.*2.124.2).

**μαλάχιος**, ὁ, a fish, Hsch.

**μάλβαξ**, ἄκος, ὁ, = μαλάχη, Luc.*Alex* 25.

**μάλδακον**, τό, = βδέλλιον, Dsc.1.67, Plin.*HN*12.35.

✻**μᾰλερός**, ά, όν, *fierce, raging*, in Hom. always epith. of fire, Il.9. 242, 20.316, 21.375, cf. Hes.*Sc.*18; πυρὸς μαλερὰ γνάθος A.*Ch.*325 (lyr.): metaph., *fiery, glowing*, ἀοιδαί Pi.*O.*9.22. 2. *fierce, violent, terrible*, πόθος A.*Pers.*62 (anap.); λέοντες Id.*Ag.*141 (lyr.); Ἄρης ὁ μ. S.*OT*190 (lyr.); πόνοι Arist.*Fr.*675.5 (lyr.): neut. pl. as Adv., *furiously*, E.*Tr.*1300 (lyr.). II. μαλεραὶ φρένες, = ἀσθενεῖς, *subdued, prostrate*, Call.*Fr.anon.*198.

✻**μάλευρον** [ᾰ], τό, = ἄλευρον, Alc.70, Achae.51, Theoc.15.116, v.l. in Hom.*Epigr.*14.3 (pl.), Hellad.ap.Phot.*Bibl.*p.531 B.

**μαλέω**, (μάλα) = αὐξάνω, *EM*76.41.

✻**μάλη** [ᾰ], ἡ, *arm-pit*, almost confined to the phrase ὑπὸ μάλης *under the arm* (cf. Ruf.*Onom.*76), esp. as the place for carrying concealed weapons, ξιφίδια ὑπὸ μ. ἔχοντας X.*HG*2.3.23; λαβὼν ὑπὸ μ. ἐγχειρίδιον Pl.*Grg.*469d, cf. Ptol.Euerg.3 J.; δόρυ δῆθ' ὑπὸ μ. ἥκεις ἔχων; Ar. *Lys.*985: Com., λαγύνιον ἔχων ὑπὸ μ. Diph.3.3; also, of fighting-quails, ὑπὸ μ. λαβεῖν Pl.*Lg.*789c; κρύπτειν ὑπὸ μ. Luc.*Ind.*23 (but ὑπὸ μάλην ἔχειν *Gall.*14); ὑπὸ τὴν μ. πατάξας Plb.*Fr.*202; παρὰ τὴν μ. ἢ ὑπὸ ζώνην, of a horse, *Hippiatr.*26. 2. *underhand, secretly*, οὐδ' ὑπὸ μ. ἡ πρόκλησις γέγονεν, ἀλλ' ἐν τῇ ἀγορᾷ μέσῃ D.29.12, cf. D.C.46.23.

✻**μάληκος**, ὁ, name of a bird, Hdn.Gr.1.151. (As pr. n. in Inscrr.)

**μαλητέον**· ζητητέον, Hsch.; cf. μαλαφῶν, μαλιεῖς.

**μάλθα** (Ar.*Fr.*157) or **μάλθη** (Cratin.204), ἡ, *mixture of wax and pitch* (cf. Fest.p.119 L.) for caulking ships, μάλθῃ τὴν τρόπιν παραχρίσας Hippon.50; for laying over writing-tablets, τὴν μάλθαν ἐκ τῶν γραμματείων ἤσθιον Ar. l. c.; ἐν μάλθῃ γεγραμμένη μαρτυρία D.46. 11; μάλθης ἄναγνα σώματ' ἐκμεμαγμένα fashioned of *wax* (and melting with terror), S.*Ichn.*140. II. a great *fish*, Ael.*NA*9.49, Opp. *H.*1.371; = πρῆστις, Suid. III. also expld. by μαλακία καὶ τρυφ[ερ]ή, and ῥύπος ξηρός, Hsch.

**μαλθ-άζω**, = μαλθάσσω, *soften*, τὸ δέρμα Aret.*SA*2.8. -**αίνω**, = foreg., τὸ ἀπότομον τᾶς βλάβας Diotog.ap.Stob.4.7.62.

**μαλθᾰκ-ευνία**, ἡ, (εὐνή) *soft bed*, *Com.Adesp.*56 (pl.). -**ία**, ἡ, = μαλακία, Pl.*R.*590b. -**ίζομαι**, Pass., *to be softened*, of persons, A.*Pr.*79, 952, E.*Med.*291; of the sun's heat, Gal.17(1).388. II. *relax, give in*, Pl.*R.*458b, al.; *to be a coward*, Id.*Smp.*179d; *to be remiss*, Id.*Ep.*317c. -**ινος**, η, ον, poet. for μαλθακός, χάρις *AP*9.567 (Antip.). -**ιστέον**, *one must be remiss*, Pl.*Alc.*1.124d: in pl. -**ιστέα**, Ar.*Nu.*727. ✻-**ός**, ή, όν, Aeol. μόλθακος Alc.*Oxy.*1789.1 ii 3:—*soft*, I. of things subject to touch, ἄνθεα *h.Hom.*30.15; δρόσος, γυῖα, Pi.*P.*5.99, *N.*4.4; γνόφαλλον Alc.34; τύλα Sapph.50; σιαγόνας μαλθακὰς τίθησι, of a boxer, S.*Fr.*112; μέχρις οὗ (ευ Pap.)..τὸ βρέγμα τῷ σκίπωνι μαλθακὸν θῶμαι Herod.8.8; of ground, *stoneless*, χῶρός ἐστι μ. A.*Fr.*199.5; τὰ μ. γαίας E.*Hipp.*1226; χρώς Id.*Med.*1075; μ. τινά, opp. στερεόν, Pl.*Phdr.*239c; μ. ὕδατα, of *marsh* water, Hp.*Aër.*1; μ. πῦρ a *slow* fire, Id.*Ulc.*12; μ. νηδύες *relaxed*, Id.*Aër.*7: Comp. -ωτέρα σικυοῦ Theopomp.Com.72: Sup., Eup.319. Adv. -κῶς, κατακεῖσθαι to recline *on soft cushions*, Ar.*Ach.*70; φιλήσατόν με μ. ib. 1200. II. mostly metaph., *faint-hearted, cowardly*, αἰχμητής Il. 17.588; ὄκνος Alc.*Oxy.* l. c.; μηδὲ μ. γένῃ A.*Eu.*74; τὸ μ. βίου E. *Supp.*883; μ. τι ἐνδιδόναι show signs of *relenting*, Id.*Hel.*508; also, *weak, feeble*, Ar.*V.*714. b. = κίναιδος, Cael.Aur.*TP*4.131. 2. in good sense, *gentle, mild*, ὕπνος Hes.*Fr.*121.4; μαλθακὰ κωτίλλων Thgn.852; οἶνος ὡς -ώτατος *mild, weak*, Hp.*Morb.*2.44; μ. φωνά, ἀοιδά, κοινωνία, φθέγμα, Pi.*P.*4.137, *N.*9.49, *P.*1.98, 8.31; μ. ὀμμάτων βέλος A.*Ag.*742 (lyr.); μ. λόγοι S.*Ph.*629; γῆρυς Ar.*Av.*233 (lyr.); ἐς τὸ μ. προσάγεσθαι to bring to *a mild temper*, E.*Or.*714; ὀργὴ γέροντος μ. *mellow* temper, S.*Fr.*894; μεταστρέφεσθαι πρὸς τὸ -ώτερον Ar.*Ra.* 539 (lyr.); of pain, -ωτέρας ποιεῖν [τὰς ὠδῖνας] Pl.*Tht.*149d. Adv. *gently, mildly*, τὸν κρατοῦντα -κῶς A.*Ag.*951; σκληρὰ μ. λέγειν S.*OC* 774: neut. as Adv., μαλθακόν σφ' ἐπόψεται A.*Ag.*1642: Comp. -ωτέρως, παραμυθούμενοι Pl.*Sph.*230a.—Mainly poet., esp. Lyr. and Trag. (μαλακός being the Prose word), but also in Hp. and

Pl. -ότης, ητος, ἡ, = μαλακότης, κοιλίης Hp.*Aër*.21; of broken-up soil, Arr.*Tact*.34.1.

**μαλθᾰκόφωνος**, ον, *soft-voiced*, ἀοιδά Pi.*I*.2.8.

**μαλθακ-τήριον**, τό, = μάλαγμα, Hp.*Superf*.27,29, Aret.*CA*1.8, *CD* 1.3. **-τικός**, ή, όν, = μαλακτικός, πνεύμονος Hp.*Acut*.53, Aret.*CD* 1.3. **-ύνω**, = μαλακύνω, τὰς φωνάς Sch.D.T.p.173 H. **-ώδης**, ες, *emollient*, Hp.*Ulc*.2,21, Gal.ap.Orib.51.36.25: sed v. μαλθώδης.

**μάλθαξις**, εως, ἡ, = μάλαξις, *by fomentations*, etc., Hp.*Acut*.22, Aret.*CD*1.14: in pathological sense, ἐντέρων Archig.ap.Aët.9.28, Aret.*SA*2.6.

**μαλθάσσω**, = μαλάσσω, *soften, soothe*, μ. κέαρ A.*Pr*.381; τινὰ λόγοις E.*HF*298; τί γάρ σε μαλθάσσοιμ' ἄν..; why *should I soothe* thee *with fair words?* S.*Ant*.1194: μ. κοιλίην *relax* the bowels, Hp.*Acut*.16, *Art*.40:—Pass., οὐδὲ μαλθάσσει λιταῖς A.*Pr*.1008; μαλθαχθεῖσ' ὕπνῳ *unnerved* by sleep, Id.*Eu*.134.

**μάλθη**, ἡ, v. μάλθα. **μαλθόω**, = μαλακόω, Hsch.

**μαλθώδης**, ες, (μάλθα) = μαλακτικὸς ἢ κηρώδης, Hp.ap.Gal.19.120: hence conjectured by Daremberg for μαλθακώδης in Hp.*Ulc*.2,21, Gal.ap.Orib.51.36.25.

**μάλθων**, ωνος, ὁ, *weakling*, opp. ἐργάτης, Socr.ap.Stob.4.15.16; = ὁ τὰ ἴδια λάθρᾳ καταφαγών, Lat. *nebulo, Gloss.*

**μάλιαν**· εὔφημον, ἥσυχον, πραεῖαν, Hsch.; cf. μαλιωτέρα.

**μαλι-ᾱσις**, εως, ἡ, = sq., *Gloss.* **-ασμός**, ὁ, *glanders*, Suid. **-άω**, *suffer from glanders, Hippiatr*.2. **-εῖς**· ζητεῖς, Hsch. **-ή**, ἡ, = μαλιασμός, Id.

**μαλιναθάλλη**, ἡ, an Egyptian plant, prob. *earth-almond, Cyperus esculentus*, Thphr.*HP*4.8.12: Salmas. ἀνθάλλιον, from *anthalium* in Plin *HN*21.88. **μάλινος** [ᾰ], v. μήλινος.

**μάλιον** [ᾰ], τό, Dim. of *μαλός (= μαλλός), *long hair, pigtail, AP*11.157 (Ammian.), Herm.Trism. in *Rev.Phil*.32.256 (prob.), 264. II. v. μάλα II.

**μαλίρ**· γῆ Κιμωλία, Hsch. **μᾶλις**, = μηλίς (B), *Hippiatr*.2. **Μᾱλίς**, ίδος, ἡ, Dor. for Μηλίς. **μάλιστα**, Adv. Sup. of μάλα, v. μάλα III. ⊛**μαλιωτέρα**· προσφιλεστέρα, Hsch.; cf. μάλιαν. **μαλκάω**, = ναρκάω, Sch.Nic.*Th*.382. **μαλκενίς**· παρθένος (Cret.), Hsch.; cf. μαλακίννης.

**μάλκη**, ἡ, *numbness from cold*, esp. in hands and feet, Nic.*Al*.540, *Th*.724, 382 (pl.), prob. in Plu.2.914a. 2. *chilblain*, Sch.Nic.*Th*.382 (pl.). II. μάλκην· τὸ ἐπικόπανον (Parian), Hsch.

**μαλκιάω**, = μαλκίω, in Ep. part. dat. μαλκιόωντι Arat.294 (v.l. μαλκίοντι ap.Stob.), read by Crates in Hes.*Op*.530 (μυλιόωντες codd.).

⊛**μάλκιος**, ον, (μάλκη) *freezing, benumbing*, πιὼν (sc. Mithridates) φάρμακον ἀσθενές τε καὶ μάλκιον Anon.ap.Suid.: Sup., τόδε μοι μαλκίστατον ἦμαρ Call.*Fr.anon*.45:—Hsch. has μαλκιώτατον· μαλακώτατον, and μαλκόν· μαλακόν; the latter is cj. in Poet.ap.Sch.Nic.*Th*.382.

**μαλκίω** [ῑ], *become numb with cold*, ἔλα, δίωκε, μή τι μαλκίων ποδί A.*Fr*.332; μέλλομεν καὶ μαλκίομεν D.9.35 (restored from Harp. and Phot. for μαλακιζόμεθα); αἱ κύνες μαλκίουσαι τὰς ῥῖνας οὐ δύνανται αἰσθάνεσθαι X.*Cyn*.5.2 (μαλακῶσαι codd., μαλακιούσας Poll.5.64, εἰ.. μαλακιοῦσι ib.49); πνεύματος ἀργαλέοιο πόνοιό τε μαλκίοντες (μαλκείοντα cod. A) Poet.ap.Sch.Nic.*Th*.382; οἶσθα δὲ ὡς ἐν κρύει σφοδρῷ γίνεται τὰ καύματα·.. ἰδίω θ' ἅμα καὶ μαλκίω (μαλακιῶ codd.) τὸ σῶμα Luc.*Lex*.2; of a bee in cold weather, μαλκίει (μαλακιεῖ codd.) τὰ μέλη Ael.*NA*5.12, cf. 1.32 (μαλακίει codd.); ἀμβλύνεσθαι τὸ κέντρον καὶ μαλκίειν (μαλκιεῖν codd.) ib.9.4; μαλκίουσαν (μαλκιοῦσαν codd.) ἐκ τῶν κρυμῶν τοῦ ζῴου τὴν ὄψιν ib.16; κεῖσθαί που ἐν κλινιδίῳ τρέμοντα καὶ μαλκίοντα (μαλακιῶντα, μαλκιῶντα codd.) Them.*Or*.4.50c; μαλκίειν (μαλακιῆν cod.)· τὸ ὑπὸ κρύους ναρκᾶν, Phryn.*PS*p.89 B., cf. Hsch. s.vv. μαλκίειν, μαλκίετον, *EM**574.21; v. μαλακιάω.

**μαλκόν**, v. μάλκιος.

**μἀλλά**, crasis for μὴ ἀλλά, v. μὴ ἀλλά.

**μαλλαθόντες**· ἐσθίοντες, Hsch.

**μαλλόδετος**, η, ον, *bound with wool*, μαλλοδέτας κύστεις S.*Fr*.394.

**μαλλοειδής**, ές, *woolly, PMasp*.6ii82 (vi A.D.).

**μᾶλλον**, Adv. Comp. of μάλα, v. μάλα II.

⊛**μαλλός**, ὁ, *flock of wool*, Hes.*Op*.234, *Schwyzer*725.5 (Milet., vi B.C.), A.*Eu*.45, S.*OC*475; μ. ἐρίου, εἰρίων, Aen.Tact.18.19, Herod.8.13. 2. *tress*, Hsch.; of men's hair, πλοκάμων μαλλοί E.*Ba*.113 (lyr.).

**μάλλυκες**· τρίχες, Hsch.

**μάλλ-ωσις**, εως, ἡ, *a being clothed with wool*, Sch.Pi.*P*.4.407. **-ωτάριον**, τό, *sheepskin, PSI*5.481.8 (v/vi A.D.). ⊛**-ωτός**, ή, όν, *fleecy*, μ. χλαμύδες cloaks *lined with wool*, Pl.Com.13; δοραί Str.11.2.19; χιτῶνες D.H.7.72, cf. *IG*2².1120 (iv A.D.), *Sammelb*.7033.44 (v A.D.):—written **μαλλουτός** in *PMasp*.6ii65 (vi A.D.).

**μαλόβαθρον**, v. μαλάβαθρον. ⊛**μᾱλοκόμος**, Dor. for μηλ-, *Hymn.Is*.164. ⊛**μᾶλον**, τό, Dor. for μῆλον.

⊛**μᾱλοπάραυος** [πᾰ], ον, Aeol. for μηλοπάρειος, Theoc.26.1; **μαλλοπάραυος**· λευκοπάρειος, Hsch.:—but acc. sg. **μαλοπαρουάν** and **μαλοπαραυάν**, of a mare, *white and chestnut* (cf. παρώας), *PPetr*.2 p.115 (= 3pp.xviii, 159) (iii B.C.).

⊛**μᾱλός** (A), ή, όν, epith. of a goat, *white*, Theoc.*Ep*.1.5, cf. Hsch.

**μᾱλός** (B), ή, όν, = ἀμαλός, only in ἄρνα μαλήν, a wrong division of ἄρν' ἀμαλήν, Il.22.310. **μαλοσσόα** ὁδός· ἣ τὰ πρόβατα βαδίζει, Hsch. (μαλόσα cod.); cf. ἱπποσόα, μηλοσόη. ⊛**μάλουρος**, ον, and fem. ⊛**μάλουρις**, *white-tailed*, Id. **μᾱλοφόρος**, **μᾱλοφύλαξ**, Dor. for μηλοφ-. **μαλόχιον**· σπαθητόν, Id.

**μαλόω**, (μάλη) *carry off under the arm, Mim.Oxy*.413.43.

⊛**μάματα**· ποιήματα, βρώματα, Hsch.; cf. μάμματα. **μαματίδες**· ἀναδενδράδες (Dolopian), Id. **μαμάτραι**· οἱ στρατηγοί, παρὰ Ἰνδοῖς, Id. **μἀμελεῖν**, Att. crasis for μὴ ἀμελεῖν.

**Μάμερσα**, ἡ, old epith. of Athena, Lyc.1417.

**Μάμερτος**, ὁ, = Osc. *Mamers*, = *Mavors, Mars*, Lyc.938, 1410:—hence **Μαμερτῖνοι**, οἱ, *Campanian mercenaries*, Plb.1.8.1, etc.

**μαμιρά**, ἡ, a medicinal root, Aët.12.64 (-ηρά), Alex.Trall.2, Paul.Aeg.7.3.

⊛**Μαμμάκῡθος** [ᾱκ], ὁ, Com. word for a *blockhead*, Ar.*Ra*.990 (pl.); title of play by Plato Com. or Aristagoras.

**μαμμᾶν** αἰτεῖν, *cry for food*, of children, Ar.*Nu*.1383. (Expld. by Sch.Pl.*Alc*.1.118e and Phot. as Arg. = *eat*, cf. Call.Com.29; but more prob. from μάμμη II, *cry for the breast*.)

**μάμματα**, τά, = βρώματα, Sch.Pl.*Alc*.1.118e; cf. μάματα.

⊛**μάμμ-η**, ἡ, child's word for *mother*, ὦ μάμμη Pherecr.70, cf. Men.*Sam*.28; Σισύφου ὦ μ. *AP*11.67 (Myrin.), cf. Epicur.*Fr*.176. II. *mother's breast*, Arr.*Epict*.2.16.43. III. later, *grandmother, POxy*.1644.12 (i B.C.), Ph.2.301, Plu.*Agis*4, Lxx4*Ma*.16.9, *SIG* 844*B*5 (Chaeronea, iii A.D.), etc. ⊛**-ία**, ἡ, *mother*, Ar.*Lys*.878, 890. **-ίδιον**, τό, Dim. of μαμμία, Plu.2.858c, Hld.7.10:—also **-ίον**, τό, Phryn.110. **-ικός**, ή, όν, *of a grandmother, PGrenf*.2.55.18,24 (ii A.D.), *BGU*410.18 (ii A.D.). II. = μητρικός, Hsch.

**μαμμό-θρεπτος**, ον, (μάμμη III) *brought up by one's grandmother*, Sch.Ar.*Ra*.1021, Aug.*in Psalm*.30; condemned by Phryn.267, cf. Poll.3.20. ⊛**-πάτωρ** [ᾰ], ορος, ὁ, *maternal grandfather, Inscr.Cypr*.159 H.

**μάμμος**· οἰκέτης, Hsch.

**μαμμωνῠμικῶς**, Adv. *after a grandmother's name, EM*796.57 (but -κόν, τό, in Sch.BIl.1.43).

**μαμμῷος**, α, ον, = μαμμικός I, *BGU*613.33 (ii A.D.).

**μαμωνᾶς**, ᾶ, *wealth, Ev.Luc*.16.9, al. (Aramaic word.)

**μάν**, Dor. and old Ep. for μήν.

**μανάκιν**, τό, = μανιάκιον, *necklace, POxy*.114.8 (ii/iii A.D.).

**μανάκις**, Adv. (μανός) *seldom*, Hsch.; μ. τῆς ἡμέρας Pl.Com.200.

**μανάσιος**, ὁ, corn-measure at Elis, *Schwyzer*419.5 (v/iv B.C.); cf. μνασίς, μνασίον.

**μαναύεται**· παρέλκεται (παν- cod.), Hsch.

⊛**μανδάκης**, ου, ὁ, *band to tie trusses*, e.g. of hay, etc., *truss*, τήλεως μανδάκαι *Sammelb*.1959 (Oxyrhynchus, iii A.D.), cf. *PFlor*.198.6 (iii A.D.), *Hippiatr*.26:—Adv. **-ηδόν**, *in the form of a band*, ib.52:—Dim. ⊛**-ιον**, τό, *bundle, truss, PRyl*.236.11 (iii A.D.).

⊛**μάνδᾰλ-ος**, ὁ, = βάλανος II.4, ZenoMed.ap.Erot. s.v. ἄμβην, Artem.2.10:—hence **-όω**, Hsch. s.v. τυλαρῶσαι; **-ωτός**, ή, όν, *with the bolt shot*,—τόν· εἶδος φιλήματος, perh. kiss *with the tongue protruded*, Phot., cf. Telecl.13: hence, *lascivious*, μέλος.. κατεγλωττισμένον καὶ μ. Ar.*Th*.132.

⊛**μανδ-ήλη**, ἡ, = Lat. *mantele, towel, Sammelb*.7033.42 (v A.D.):—Dim. **-ήλιν**, = -ήλιον, *Gloss.*

**μανδοτά**· σημεῖα, Hsch.

⊛**μάνδρα**, ἡ, *enclosed space*, 1. for cattle, *fold, byre*, Call.*Cer*.106, Theoc.4.61, Plu.2.648a; for horses, μάνδραις ἐν ἱππείαισιν S.*Fr*.659. 3: in reference to the bezel in which the stone of a ring, with a design of oxen, is set, Pl.*Epigr*.21, *AP*9.746 (Polemo), cf. Hld.5.14. 2. dub. sens. in *POxy*.984 (i A.D.). 3. *square* on a draught-board, Mart.7.72.8 (pl.).

**μανδρᾰγόρ-ας**, ου or α, ὁ, *mandrake* (μ. ἄρρην = *Mandragora officinalis*, μ. θῆλυς, = *M. autumnalis*, Dsc.4.75), Thphr.*HP*9.8.8, *CP*6.4.5, etc.; μανδραγόρου ῥίζα Hp.*Loc.Hom*.39; ὁ μ. τοὺς ἀνθρώπους κοιμίζει X.*Smp*.2.24; μανδραγόρᾳ ἢ μέθῃ συμποδίσαι Pl.*R*.488c; μανδραγόραν πεπωκόσιν ἐοίκαμεν D.10.6; ἐκ μανδραγόρου, ὑπὸ μανδραγόρα καθεύδειν, Luc.*Dem.Enc*.36, *Tim*.2. 2. *belladonna, Atropa Belladonna*, Thphr.*HP*6.2.9. II. epith. of Zeus, Hsch. **-ιζομένη**, ἡ, *the mandrake-drugged*, title of play by Alexis:—Act. in Suid. **-ικός**, ή, όν, *made of mandrake*, Alex.Trall.1.10. **-ίτης** [ῑ], ου, ὁ, *flavoured with mandrake*, οἶνος Dsc.5.71:—fem. **-ῖτις**, ιδος, ἡ, epith. of Aphrodite, Hsch.

**μάνδρευμα**, ατος, τό, = μάνδρα I, D.H.1.79.

**μανδύα** [ῠ], ἡ (**μανδύη** Poll.7.60, D.C.57.13, al.), **μανδύας**, ου, ὁ (Lxx *Jd*.3.16, al., Suid.), or **μανδύης** (Lyd.*Mag*.2.13), *woollen cloak*, Persian word acc. to Ael.Dion.*Fr*.252, Hsch.; but Λιβυρνικῆς μίμημα μανδύης χιτών A.*Fr*.364, cf. Artem.2.3, St.Byz. s.v. Λιβυρνοί.

**μανδῠοειδής**, ές, *like a* μανδύα, Eust.198.42, 794.21.

**Μανερῶς**, ῶτος, ὁ, *Maneros*, only son of the first king of Egypt; also a national dirge named after him, identified by Hdt.2.79 with the Greek Λίνος, cf. Eub.46, Nymphis 9, Plu.2.357e, Paus.9.29.7.

**μάνη** or **μάνα**, ἡ, = μανία, Ar.*Fr*.816; sed leg. μάμμη or μάμμα, = μαμμία.

⊛**μάνης** [ᾰ], ὁ, a kind of *cup*, acc. sg. μάνην, *IG*11(2).219*B*65,66, 226*B*9 (Delos, iii B.C.), Nico 1: nom. pl. μάνητες *PHib*.1.121.50 (iii B.C.): but acc. pl. μάνας *IG*11(2).110.22 (Delos, iii B.C.). II. *small bronze figure* used in the game of κότταβος (q.v.), Hermipp.47, Antiph.55.11, Nicoch.10. III. freq. in Com., as the name of a *Phrygian slave*, cf. Str.7.3.12: generally, *slave*, Sch.Ar.*Av*.523; applied to uncultured or dull people, Ar.*Ra*.965, al. IV. a throw of the dice, Eub.59.

**μανθάνω**, Pi.*P*.3.80, etc.: fut. μαθήσομαι Thgn.35, Parm.1.31, A.*Pr*.926, S.*Aj*.667, *OC*1527, Pl.*Phlb*.53e, etc.; Dor. μαθεῦμαι dub. in Theoc.11.60; late μαθήσω Gal.13.450, *Sect.Intr*.9 (cod. L): aor. ἔμαθον Pi.*N*.7.18, etc.; Ep. ἔμμαθον Od.17.226. μάθον (v. infr.): pf. μεμάθηκα Anacr.74, Xenoph.10, Emp.17.9, Ar.*Nu*.1148, Pl.*Euthphr*.9c, etc.:

plpf. ἐμεμαθήκη ib.14c; 3 sg. ἐμεμαθήκει Id.*Men.*86a; 3 pl. μεμαθήκεσαν Hp.*VM*10:—**Pass.**, used by good writers only in pres., as Pl. *Ti.*87b, *Men.*88b.—Hom. uses only the Ep. aor. forms μάθον, ἔμμαθες, ἔμμαθε:—*learn*, esp. *by study* (but also, *by practice*, Simon.147, Arist.*EN*1103$^a$32, *Metaph.*1049$^b$31, 980$^b$24; *by experience*, A.*Ag.*251 (lyr.), Arist.*APo.*81$^a$40), thrice in Hom., ἔργα κακά Od.17.226, 18.362: c. inf., μάθον ἔμμεναι ἐσθλός Il.6.444: freq. later, οὐδὲ μαθόντες γινώσκουσιν Heraclit.17; ἀεὶ γὰρ ἡβᾷ τοῖς γέρουσιν εὖ μαθεῖν A.*Ag.*584; ταλάντου τοῦτ' ἔμαθεν *for* a talent, Ar.*Nu.*876; οἱ μανθάνοντες *learners, pupils*, X.*Mem.*1.2.17; μ. τὰ Ὁμήρου ἔπη *learn by heart*, Id.*Smp.*3.5; μ. βέμβικα Ar.*Av.*1461; μ. τί τινος *learn* from.., Pi.*P.*3.80, A.*Pr.*701, S.*OT*575, etc.: with Preps., ἐσθλῶν ἄπ' ἐσθλὰ μαθήσεαι Thgn.l.c.; μ. καθ' Ὅμηρον Xenoph.l.c.; τι ἔκ τινος S.*El.*352; ἐκ ποίων ὀνομάτων μεμαθηκὼς ἦν τὰ πράγματα Pl.*Cra.*438a; παρά τινος A.*Ag.*859, S.*Ant.*1012, etc.; παρά τινος ὅτι.. Isoc.8.67; πρός τινος S.*OC*12; πρὶν μάθοιμ' εἰ.. Id.*Ph.*961: c. inf., *learn to*.., or *how to*.., Il.l.c., Pi.*P.*4.284, A.*Pr.*1068 (anap.), S.*Aj.*667; μ. σεαυτὸν αἰσχύνεσθαι Democr.244. II. *acquire a habit of*, and in past tenses, *to be accustomed to*.., c. inf., Emp.17.9, Hp.*VM*10; τοὺς μεμαθηκότας ἀριστᾶν Id.*Acut.*28; τὸ μεμαθηκός *that which is usual*, πρότερον ἢ ὕστερον τοῦ μ. Id.*Mul.*2.128; ἀργαὶ μανθάνουσι *acquire a habit of* idleness, 1*Ep.Ti.*5.13. III. *perceive, remark, notice*, τὸ πλῆθος Hdt.7.208; ἀλλήλους μ. ὁπόσοι εἴησαν X.*HG*2.1.1. 2. freq. c. part., μ. τὴν νέα ἐμβαλοῦσαν Hdt.8.88; ἔμαθον ταῦτα πρησσόμενα Id.1.160; ἵνα μάθῃ σοφιστὴς ὢν A.*Pr.*62; μὴ μάθῃ μ' ἥκοντα S.*Ph.*13, cf. E.*Ba.*1113; μάνθανε ὢν *know that* you are, S.*El.*1342; διαβεβλημένος οὐ μανθάνεις Hdt.3.1; εἰ μὴ μανθάνετε κακὰ σπεύδοντες Th.6.39. 3. with ὅτι, Pl.*R.*394b; with ὡς, Th.1.34, etc. IV. *understand* (cf. Pl.*Euthd.*277e), ὡς μάθω σαφέστερον A.*Ch.*767; ὄψ' ἐμάθεθ' ἡμᾶς E.*Ba.*1345; τὰ λεγόμενα Lys.10.15, etc.: c. dat. pers., εἴ μοι μανθάνεις if you *take* me, Pl.*R.*394c: freq. in Dialogue, μανθάνεις; *d'ye see?* Answ., πάνυ μανθάνω *perfectly!* Ar.*Ra.*195, cf. Pl.*Men.*84d, *Tht.*174b; εἶεν, μανθάνω Id.*R.*372e, cf. *Phd.*117b, etc. V. τί μαθών..; freq. in questions, lit. *under what persuasion, with what idea?* hence ironically for *why on earth?* τί δὴ μ. φαίνεις ἄνευ θρυαλλίδος; Ar.*Ach.*826, cf. *Nu.*402, 1506, *Lys.*599, *Pl.*908; τί τοῦτο μ. προσέγραψεν; D.20.127 (sts. with v.l. τί παθών; what possessed you to..? cf. πάσχω); imitated in later Greek, Ael.*Fr.*67; also indirectly, *because* (with a sense of disapprobation), ὅ τι μαθόντες τοὺς ξένους μὲν λέγετε ποιητὰς σοφοὺς Eup.357; ὅ τι μαθὼν..οὐχ ἡσυχίαν ἦγον Pl.*Ap.*36b; σοὶ εἰς κεφαλήν, ὅ τι μαθών μου καὶ τῶν ἄλλων καταψεύδῃ τοιοῦτο πρᾶγμα Id.*Euthd.*283e, cf. 299a: even with neut. subject, ὅμως δ' ἂν κακὰ ἦν, ὅ τι μαθόντα χαίρειν ποιεῖ Id.*Prt.*353d.

**μᾰνία** (A), Ion. **-ίη**, ἡ, (μαίνομαι) *madness*, Hdt.6.112, Hp.*Aph.*7.5, S.*Ant.*958 (lyr.), etc.; πολλὴν καταγνῶναι μ. τινῶν Isoc.4.133; μέχρι μανίας ἡ σφοδρὰ ἡδονὴ κατέχουσα Pl.*Phlb.*45e; μανίη νοῦσος Hdt.6.75: freq. in pl., Lex Solonis ap.D.46.14, Thgn.1231, A.*Pr.*879, 1057 (both anap.), etc. II. *enthusiasm, inspired frenzy*, μ. Διονύσου πάρα E.*Ba.*305; ἀπὸ Μουσῶν κατοκωχή τε καὶ μ. Pl.*Phdr.*245a; θεία μ., opp. σωφροσύνη ἀνθρωπίνη, ib.256b, cf. *Prt.*323b, X.*Mem.*1.1.16; τῆς φιλοσόφου μ. τε καὶ βακχείας Pl.*Smp.*218b. III. *passion*, ἐρωτικὴ μ. Id.*Phdr.*265b; μανίην μανεὶς ἀρίστην *Anacreont.*59.2: freq. in pl., Pi.*O.*9.39, *N.*11.48, E.*HF*835; ἐγγὺς μανιῶν ἐλαύνει Id.*Heracl.*904 (lyr.); μανίη τινός *mad desire for*.., Hermesian.7.85.

**μανία** (B), ἡ, = μανότης, *An.Ox.*2.393.

⊛ **μᾰνι-άκης**, ου, ὁ, *necklace, torc*, worn of gold by Persians and Gauls, Plb.2.29.8, 2.31.5, Lxx 1*Es.*3.6, Plu.*Cim.*9, Jul.*ad Ath.*284d, Lyd.*Mag.*1.46 (pl.):—also **-άκη**, ἡ, *PMon.*7.74 (vi A.D.):—Dim. **-άκιον**, τό, Sch.Theoc.11.41. **-ακός**, ή, όν, = μαινόμενος, *Gloss.* **-αξ**, = μανιάκης, ib.

**μᾰν-ιάς**, άδος, *frantic, mad*, μανιάσιν νόσοις S.*Aj.*59; λύσσας μανιάδος E.*Or.*327 (lyr.), cf. S.*Fr.*941.4: with neut. Subst. in dat. pl., μανιάσιν λυσσήμασι E.*Or.*270. **-ιάω**, *to be mad, rave*, J.*BJ*1.7.5.

**μανίκια**, τά, *cuffs*, Anon.*in Rh.*106.1. (Dim. of Lat. *manica*.)

**μᾰνῐκός**, ή, όν, (μανία) *of* or *for madness, mad*, μ. πράγματα Ar.*V.*1496; [νόσημα] Hp.*Aph.*3.20; βλέπει μανικόν τι she has a *madwoman's* eye, Ar.*Pl.*424; -ωτέρα ἡδονή Pl.*R.*403a; ἡ -κή *madness*, Id.*Phdr.*244c; μανικόν *symptom of madness*, Hp.*Prog.*3; οὐ μανικόν ἐστ' ἐν οἰκίᾳ τρέφειν ταῶς; Anaxandr.28, cf. Epicur.*Ep.*2 p.53 U.; νοσῶν τι μ. Timocl.6.12. Adv. -κῶς, περιφέρεσθαι X.*Cyn.*3.5; πυρέττειν Plu.*Alex.*75. 2. generally, *mad, extravagant*, Isoc.1.15, Pl.*Prt.*343c, etc.; σωφρόνημα λίαν μ. dub. l. in X.*Ages.*5.4; μ. ἱππωνίαι Id.*Eq.Mag.*1.12. Adv. -κῶς, διακεῖσθαι Pl.*Phdr.*249d; ἔχειν Id.*Sph.*216d; ἀλόγως καὶ μ. Isoc.5.65, cf. Phld.*Ir.*p.82 W. II. *disposed to madness*, Pl.*Smp.*173d (dub.); *unbalanced*, Id.*Sph.*242a. 2. *frenzied, enthusiastic, inspired*, εὐφυοῦς ἡ ποιητική ἐστιν ἢ μανικοῦ Arist.*Po.*1455$^a$33; ἐξίσταται τὰ εὐφυᾶ γένη εἰς -ώτερα ἤθη Id.*Rh.*1390$^b$29; νοσήματα μ. καὶ ἐνθουσιαστικά Id.*Pr.*954$^a$36. III. Act., *causing madness*, στρύχνος (-ον) Thphr.*HP*9.11.5, Dsc.4.73, Gal.11.767; μανικόν, τό, = δορύκνιον, Plin.*HN*21.179, cf. Dsc.*Alex.*6; φάρμακα Plu.*Arat.*54.

**μᾰνιόκηπος**, ον, (κῆπος III) of women, *madly lustful*, Anacr.158, *Com.Adesp.*1366.

**μᾰνίον**, τό, Dim. of μάνης I, *IG*11(2).287*B*138, al. (Delos, iii B.C.), *POxy.*1757.23 (ii A.D.).

**μᾰνιοποι-έω**, *madden, infuriate*, Phld.*Ir.*p.71 W. **-ός**, όν, *maddening*, Polyaen.8.43, Sch.Il.6.132.

**μᾰνι-ουργέω**, *drive mad*, c. acc., Polyaen.8.43. **-ώδης**, ες, *like madness*, νοσεύματα Hp.*Aër.*7, cf. *Coac.*475. 2. *like a madman, crazy*, ὑπόσχεσις Th.4.39; καὶ τὸ μ. μαντικὴν πολλὴν ἔχει E.*Ba.*299; μ. πάντα τἀνθρώπων ὅλως Alex.219.9; κύνας μ. καὶ δυσπειθεστάτας X.*Mem.*4.1.3: Comp. -έστερον ἢ κατά.. J.*AJ*2.12.2. Adv. -δῶς Gal.5.415, Paul.Aeg.3.6, Sch.Theoc.1.83. II. *causing madness*, Dsc.1.68, 4.68; ἱμάσθλη Πανός Nonn.*D.*10.4.

⊛ **μάννᾰ**, ἡ, μάννα λιβάνου frankincense *powder* or *granules*, Dsc.1.68.6; but μ. λιβανωτοῦ *gum* of λίβανος, Aen.Tact.35; μ. alone, of the powder, Hp.*Art.*36, *Epid.*2.2.18, Antyll.ap.Orib.7.21.8, Gal.12.722; = λιβάνου τὸ λεπτόν, *AB*108. II. **μάννα**, τό, = Hebr. *mān*, *manna*, Lxx *Ex.*16.35 (v.l. μάν), *Nu.*11.6, al., cf. J.*AJ*3.1.6.

⊛ **μαννάριον**, τό, perh. f.l. for μαμμάριον, as term of endearment, Luc.*DMeretr.*6.1, 7.4.

**μάννινον**, τό, = μάννα I, Asclep.ap.Gal.13.648.

**μάννος**, also **μόννος**, ὁ, *necklace*, Dor. word, Poll.5.99; **μάννος**, glossed μανιάκιον, Sch.Theoc.11.41.

**μαννοφόρος**, ον, *wearing a collar*, v.l. for ἀμνο- in Theoc.11.41.

**μαννώδης**, ες, *like μάννα* I: τὸ μ. *a μάννα-like drug*, Hp.*Epid.*7.47.

⊛ **μᾰνός** [v. fin.], ή, όν, of consistency, *loose* or *open in texture, rare*, opp. πυκνός, Emp.75.1, Hp.*VM*22, etc.; μ. ὀστοῦν, σάρκες, Pl.*Ti.*75c, 79c; τὰ μ. καὶ κοῦφα, opp. πυκνὰ καὶ βαρέα, ib.53a; of the tongue, σὰρξ μ. καὶ σομφή Arist.*HA*492$^b$33; of the female breasts, ib.493$^a$14; of the lungs, μ. καὶ πολύτρητος ὁ πνεύμων Aret.*SD*1.10. II. *rare, sparse, infrequent*, of hare-tracks, X.*Cyn.*5.4 (Sup.); of pleasures and pains, Pl.*Lg.*734c (Comp.); of hair, Arist.*HA*498$^b$25; of plants, *growing far apart*, Thphr.*HP*1.8.2; but of trees or plants, *spreading*, ib.3.11.5, al. 2. *happening rarely* or *at intervals*, in Adv. -νῶς, τοσούτῳ μανότερον so much *the less often*, X.*Cyr.*7.5.6; τῇ ἀναπνοῇ χρῆται μανότερον Arist.*Resp.*475$^b$25, cf. Thphr.*Sign.*32.—Att. for ἀραιός, acc. to Phryn.*PS* p.89 B. [ᾰ Telecl.61, cf. Hdn.*Gr.*2.13, and v. μανόστημος: ᾱ Emp.l.c. (prob. only Ion. in spite of Phryn.l.c.): Comp. μανότερος Pl.l.c., Arist.*Ph.*217$^a$6, *GA*782$^a$34 (later μανώτερος Gal.18(1).83): Sup. μανότατος X.l.c.] (Perh. for μᾰνϝός, cf. μάνυ, OIr. *menb* 'small'.)

**μανο-σπορέω**, *sow thinly*, Thphr.*HP*8.6.2. ⊛ **-σπορος**, ον, *thinly sown*, Id.*CP*3.21.5.

**μᾰνό-στημος**, ον, (στήμων) *open in warp and weft, gossamer*, πέπλοι A.*Fr.*297.

**μανότης**, ητος, ἡ, opp. πυκνότης, *looseness of texture, porousness*, σπληνός, ὀστῶν, Pl.*Ti.*72c, 86d; σαρκός Arist.*EN*1129$^a$22, cf. Thphr.*HP*1.5.4, al. II. *rarity, separateness*, Pl.*Lg.*812d; τῶν φυτευομένων Thphr.*CP*3.7.1.

⊛ **μανό-φυλλος**, ον, *with loosely-packed leaves*, Thphr.*HP*7.6.3. **-χροος**, ον, *with loose, flabby skin*, Id.*Sud.*19.

**μανόω**, (μανός) *make porous, loose*, ἡ κόπρος μανοῖ τὴν γῆν Thphr.*CP*3.6.1; τὸ σῶμα μανοῦν, of diaphoretic treatment, Orib.*Syn.*6.8.4:—Pass., Thphr.*HP*9.14.3, *Sens.*30; *to be rarefied*, of the soul, Dam.*Pr.*400.

⊛ **μαντ-εία**, Ep. **-είη**, Ion. **-ηίη**, ἡ, (μαντεύομαι) *prophetic power, power of divination*, h.*Merc.*533, 547, etc.; μαντείᾳ χρῆσθαι καθ' ὕπνον Pl.*Ti.*71d; *mode of divination*, Hdt.2.57; αἴνιγμα μαντείας ἔδει S.*OT*394; μαντείας δεῖται ὅ τι ποτὲ λέγεις Pl.*Smp.*206b; ἔτι ταῦτα μαντείας προσδεῖται; Aeschin.1.76: pl., *divinations*, h.*Merc.*472, S.*El.*499 (lyr.), Hdt.2.83, etc. 2. *conjecture*, ἡ περὶ τὸν θεὸν μ. Arist.*Cael.*284$^b$3; μαντείᾳ μᾶλλον ἢ κρίσει τἀληθὲς ἀναζητῶν Luc.*Herm.*49. II. *oracle, prophecy*, Pl.*Ap.*29a: pl., Tyrt.4.2, S.*OT*149, Lys.6.33; ὡς ἡ ἐμὴ μ. as I *divine*, Pl.*Phlb.*66b. 2. *oracular*, i.e. *obscure, expression*, Id.*Cra.*384a. **-εῖον**, Ion. and Ep. **-ήϊον**, τό, *oracle*, i.e., I. *oracular response*, mostly in pl., μαντήϊα Τειρεσίαο Od.12.272, cf. Hes.*Fr.*134.9, Hdt.2.174, Pl.*Ap.*33c: sg., Hdt.2.111, 9.33, Phld.*Mus.*p.87 K. II. *seat of an oracle*, Heraclit.93, A.*Eu.*4, Hdt.1.46, Th.2.17, Isoc.6.17; τὸ Πυθικὸν μ. S.*El.*33: in pl. of a single shrine, A.*Pr.*831, E.*Ion*66. III. *method, process of divination*, *PMag.Lond.*46.1. IV. in pl., *rewards of divination*, Lxx *Nu.*22.7. **-εῖος**, α, ον, also ος, ον E.*Ion*130 (lyr.); Ion. **-ήϊος**, η, ον:—poet. for μαντικός, *oracular, prophetic*, βωμός, μυχός, Pi.*O.*6.5, *P.*5.69, etc.; στέφη A.*Ag.*1265; ἕδρα E.l.c.; τρίπους *Pae.Delph.*18; ἐπ' Ἰσμηνοῦ τε μαντείᾳ σποδῷ, of the altar's embers, S.*OT*21; μ. ἄναξ, i.e. Apollo, E.*Tr.*454, cf. *Or.*1666, Ar.*Av.*722. **-ευμα**, ατος, τό, *oracle*, Pi.*P.*4.73, S.*OT*992, E.*Med.*685, etc.: pl., Pi.*P.*8.60, *Pae.*7.1, Pl.*Ep.*311d, *Supp.Epigr.*3.400 (Delph.), etc. **-εύομαι**, fut. -εύσομαι Od.17.154, Pi.*O.*6.38, A.*Ag.*1367, Hdt.1.46, etc.: aor. ἐμαντευσάμην Pl.*Ap.*21a, Aeschin.3.107; poet. μαντευσάμην Pi.*O.*7.31: pf. μεμάντευμαι Id.*P.*4.163:—Pass., v. infr. IV: (μάντις):—*divine, prophesy*, τί μοι θάνατον μαντεύεαι; Il.19.420; τί νύ μοι μαντεύεαι αἰπὺν ὄλεθρον; 16.859; ἐτεὸν μ. 2.300: abs., οὐ γὰρ ἀπείρητος μαντεύομαι Od.2.170, cf. 9.510, Il.1.107; τινι *to* one, Od.2.178, etc.: c. dat. modi, *draw divinations from* or *by means of*.., ῥάβδοισι Hdt.4.67: c. acc. cogn., μαντεῖα μ. A.*Eu.*716 (s.v.l.). 2. generally, *presage, forebode, surmise*, of presentiment, opp. knowledge, Pl.*Cra.*411b, *R.*349a, al.; μαντευσόμεσθα τἀνδρὸς ὡς ὀλωλότος A.*Ag.*l.c.; ἔστι γὰρ ὃ μαντεύονταί τι πάντες φύσει κοινὸν δίκαιον Arist.*Rh.*1373$^b$7; μ. τὸ συμβησόμενον ἐκ τῶν εἰκότων Id.*GA*765$^a$27. 3. of animals, *get scent of*, κύων ἄρτον μ. Theoc.21.45. II. *consult an oracle, seek divinations*, Pi.*O.*7.31, Hdt.1.46, 4.172, etc.; ἐν Δελφοῖσι Id.6.76; ἐπὶ Κασταλίᾳ Pi.*P.*l.c.; περί τινος Id.*O.*6.38, Hdt.8.36; ὑπέρ τινος E.*Ion*431; ὁ γὰρ θεὸς μαντευομένῳ μοὐχρησεν ἐν Δελφοῖς ποτε Ar.*V.*159, cf. *Av.*593; ταῦτα καὶ μ. this is *the question I ask the oracle*, E.*Ion*346; ἐτόλμησε τοῦτο μαντεύσασθαι Pl.*Ap.*21a; μαντείαν μ. παρὰ τῷ θεῷ Aeschin.l.c. III. later, of the god, *give an oracle*, ταῦθ' ὁρῶ τὸν Δία ὑμῖν μαντευόμενον D.18.253, cf. Luc.*Alex.*19, *Sol.*9. IV. in later Greek, Act. **μαντεύω**,

Plu.*Alex.*75, Arr.*Ind.*11.5, X.Eph.5.4, Him.*Or.*10.5, 14.34, 23.23: but aor. Pass., ἐμαντεύθη *an oracle was given*, Hdt.5.114: pf. part., τὰ μεμαντευμένα *the words of the oracles*, ib.45; τὰ ὑπὸ τοῦ θεοῦ μαντευσθέντα (sic) *IG*4²(1).122.81 (Epid., iv B.C.), cf. Hld.7.1. **-ευτέον**, *one must divine*, E.*Ion* 373, Pl.*Phlb.*64a. **-ευτής**, οῦ, ὁ, = μάντις, Hld.9.1. ⊛ **-ευτικός**, ή, όν, *of* or *for divination*: ἡ -κή (sc. τέχνη), = μαντεία, f.l. in E.*Ba.*299 as cited by Plu.2.432e. **-ευτός**, ή, όν, *foretold by an oracle*, γόνος E.*Ion* 1209; *prescribed by an oracle*, ἐθύετο τῷ Διί, ὥσπερ αὐτῷ μαντευτὸς ἦν X.*An.*6.1.22; μ. ἱερά Arist.*Ath.*54.6; λουτρά Philostr.*Her.*2.18; μ. λόγοι, group of orations by Aristides, *Or.*37(2) tit., Men.Rh.p.344 S. **-εύτρια**, ἡ, gloss on φοιβάστρια, Sch.Lyc.1468. **-ηΐη, -ήϊον, -ήϊος**, Ion. for μαντεία, etc.

⊛ **μαντῐ-άρχης**, ου, ὁ, in Cyprus, *president of a college of* μάντεις, *LW*2795: also ⊛ **-αρχος**, ὁ, Myres *Cesnola Collection* 1909.

⊛ **μαντικός**, ή, όν, *prophetic, oracular*, κλέος A.*Ag.*1098; μ. μυχοί, θρόνοι, Id.*Eu.*180, 616; τέχνη Id.*Fr.*350.6; μ. φῆμαι *oracular sayings*, S.*OT*723; τὸ μ. γένος, = μάντεις, Id.*Ant.*1055; τὸ μ. σπέρμα E.*IA*520; μ. ἐπίπνοια *prophetic* inspiration, Pl.*Phdr.*265b; λόγοι μ. ib.275b; μ. ζῷα Porph.*Abst.*2.48. 2. τέχνη μ. faculty *of divination, prophecy*, S.*OT*709, Arist.*Pol.*1274ᵃ28, etc.; more freq. ἡ μαντική alone, Hdt.2.49, 4.68; ἡ.. μ. ἡ τοῦ δαιμονίου, of Socrates, Pl.*Ap.*40a: in Poets without Art., A.*Pr.*484, S.*OT*311; also in Pl., μαντικὴν Ἀπόλλων ἀνηῦρεν *Smp.*197a; μ. ἔνθεος *Phdr.*244b, cf. Th.5.103. II. of persons, *like a prophet, oracular*, μ. γὰρ εἶ Pl.*Alc.*1.115a, cf. *Phd.*85b; Comp., Luc.*Hes.*7. Adv. -κῶς Ar.*Pax* 1026, Pl.*Smp.*198a, etc.

**μαντίλη** [ῐ], ἡ, f.l., perh. for Μαντίας, Pl.Com.185.

⊛ **μαντίον**, *paludamentum*, *Gloss.*

**μαντῐ-πολέω**, *prophesy*, A.*Ag.*979 (lyr.). **-πόλος**, ον, *frenzied, inspired*, Βάκχη E.*Hec.*121 (anap.); Ἀπόλλων Orac.ap.Luc.*JTr.*31: pl., as Subst., *diviners*, Man.6.306.

⊛ **μάντῐς**, ὁ, gen. εως, Ion. ιος; voc. μάντῐ: pl., gen. μάντεων (written μαντειον *IG*1².503); dat. μάντεσι Thgn.545: also fem., acc. sg. μάντιδα δάφνην *App.Anth.*6.122; nom. pl. μάντιδες Suid. s.v. Σίβυλλα:—*diviner, seer, prophet*, ἀλλ' ἄγε δή τινα μ. ἐρείομεν ἢ ἱερῆα ἢ καὶ ὀνειροπόλον Il.1.62, cf. Od.17.384; μάντι κακῶν *prophet* of ill, Il.1.106; with the Greek armies, Simon.94, *IG*1².929.129: distd. from χρησμολόγος, Th.8.1; μ. ἀνήρ Pi.*I.*6(5).51; of Apollo, A.*Ag.*1202, *Ch.*559, *Eu.*169 (lyr.); ὁ μάντις μάντιν ἐκπράξας ἐμέ, of Apollo and Cassandra, Id.*Ag.*1275; of the Pythian priestess, Id.*Eu.*29; of Amphiaraus, Id.*Th.*382, etc.: c. dat. pers., ὁ Θρῃξὶ μ. E.*Hec.*1267 (of Dionysus), cf. *Or.*363: c. acc. neut. Pron., μάντις.. οὐ καλὸς τάδε Id.*Heracl.*65: as fem., A.*Ag.* l.c., S.*El.*472 (lyr.), E.*Med.*239; μ. κόρα Pi.*P.*11.33. 2. metaph., *presager, foreboder*, μ. εἰμ' ἐσθλῶν ἀγώνων S.*OC*1080 (lyr.), cf. *Ant.*1160, A.*Th.*402; οὐδεὶς μ. τῶν μελλόντων S.*Aj.*1419 (anap.); γνώμη δ' ἀρίστη μ. E.*Hel.*757. 3. Adj., τοῦδε μάντεως χοροῦ of this *prophetic* band, dub. in S.*Fr.*113. II. a kind of *grasshopper*, the *praying mantis, Mantis religiosa*, Theoc.10.18, Dsc.*Eup.*1.149. III. *green garden-frog, Rana arborea*, so called as *predicting* the weather, Hsch. IV. a kind of *cabbage*, Nic.*Fr.*85.7. V. applied to comets, Herm.ap.Stob.1.21.9. (Deriv. from μαίνομαι by Pl.*Ti.*72a,b.)

**μαντῐχώρας**, ου, ὁ, v. μαρτιχόρας.

**μάντοι**, Dor. for μέντοι, *IG*4²(1).121.38 (Epid., iv B.C.).

⊛ **μαντο-σύνη**, ἡ, *the art of divination*, Il.1.72, Pi.*O.*6.66, Luc.*Astr.*1: pl., Il.2.832, 11.330, Emp.112.10, Man.6.317. **-σῠνος**, η, ον, *oracular*, τρίπους Corinn.*Supp.*2.64; κέλευμα E.*Andr.*1032 (lyr.); θεοῦ ἀνάγκαι Id.*IA*761 (lyr.).

⊛ **μαντῷος**, α, ον, = μαντεῖος, *AP*9.201 (Leo), 5.295 (Agath.).

**μάνυ·** πικρόν (fort. leg. μικρόν), Ἀθαμᾶνες, Hsch. **μάνυζα**, ἡ, = μώλυζα, Id.

**μᾶν-ύω, -ῡτής, -ῡτικός, -ῡσις**, Dor. for μην-.

**μᾰν-ώδης**, ες, *of loose texture*, Arist.*PA*695ᵇ26. **-ωσις**, εως, ἡ, *making loose* or *porous, rarefaction*, opp. πύκνωσις, Id.*Ph.*212ᵇ3, al., cf. Thphr.*CP*4.14.2, etc.; opp. πυκνότης, *Placit.*1.3.6. **-ωτικός**, ή, όν, *relaxing*, of south winds, Ptol.*Tetr.*29; *loosening*, ἀλείμματα Gal.10.760.

**μάξεινος**, ὁ, = γαλλερίας, Dorio ap.Ath.7.315f, prob. for μαζίνης in Thphr.*Fr.*171.2; cf. μαζός II.

**μάομαι**, v. μαίομαι. **μᾰπέειν**, Ep. aor. 2 inf. of μάρπτω (q.v.).

**μαππ-άριος**, ὁ, = *vexillarius*, *Gloss.* ⊛ **-ίον**, τό, Dim. of Lat. *mappa, napkin*, *POxy.*1051.17 (iii A.D.), *Gloss.*

**Μάρ** [ᾰ], Μᾱρός, ὁ, pl. Μᾶρες, a tribe near Colchis, Hes.(?)ap.Sch.Il.*Oxy.*221 iii 3, Hecat.205 J., Hdt.3.94, 7.79, *UPZ*149.4 (iii B.C.).

⊛ **μάραγδος** [μᾰ], ὁ, = σμάραγδος, *IG*11(2).161*B*44, 199*B*59 (Delos, iii B.C.).

**μάραγνα** [μᾰ], ἡ, = σμάραγνα, *lash, scourge*, διπλῆ μ. A.*Ch.*375 (lyr.), cf. E.*Rh.*817, Pl.Com.63, Poll.10.56.

**μάραγοι·** οἱ ἀπόκρημνοι τόποι, Hsch.

**μᾰρᾰθ-ίς**, ίδος, ἡ, = ἱππομάραθον, Ps.-Dsc.3.71. **-ίτης** [ῑ], ου, ὁ, *flavoured with fennel*, οἶνος Dsc.5.65, *Gp.*8.9. **-οειδής**, ές, *like fennel*, v.l. for μαράθῳ ὅμοια in Dsc.3.139. Adv. -οειδῶς, v.l. for μαράθῳ ὅμοια in Id.2.139. ⊛ **-ον** (proparox.), τό, *fennel, Foeniculum vulgare*, D.18.260, Anaxandr.41.58, Thphr.*HP*1.12.2, al.: pl., Epich.156, 159:—also **-ος**, ὁ, Python 1.13, but ἡ, Lyd.*Mag.*1.42; of doubtful gender, Hermipp.81, Lycus ap.Orib.8.32.4.

**μάρᾰθρον** [μᾰ], τό, less Att. form of μάραθον, Alex.127.5, *PTeb.*116.43 (ii B.C.), *UPZ*89.9 (ii B.C.), Dsc.3.70 codd., Gal.12.67, Hld.6.14.

**Μᾰρᾰθών**, ῶνος, ὁ, also ἡ, Pi.*O.*13.110: (μάραθον):—*Marathon*, so called from its being *overgrown with fennel* (Str.3.4.9), Od.7.80, Hdt.1.62, etc.: **Μαραθῶνι** *at M.*, Ar.*Eq.*781, etc.; ⊛ **Μαραθῶνάδε** *to M.*, And.1.107; **Μαραθωνόθεν** *from M.*, Aristid.2.218 J.:—Adj. **Μᾰρᾰθώνιος**, α, ον; Μ., τά, *festival in celebration of the victory of Marathon*, D.H.5.17.

**Μᾰρᾰθωνο-μάχης** [μᾰχ], ου, ὁ, *one who fought at Marathon*: prov. of *a veteran*, Ar.*Ach.*181, *Nu.*986:—also **-μάχος**, ὁ, *APl.*4.233.8 (Theaet.), D.L.1.56, and v.l. Ar.*Nu.* l.c.

⊛ **μᾰραίνω**, fut. μᾰρᾰνῶ Orph.*Fr.*262, *Epigr.Gr.*854 (Delos): aor. 1 ἐμάρᾱνα *h.Merc.*140, S.*OT*1328, etc.:—**Med.**, aor. ἐμαρηνάμην (v. infr.):—**Pass.**, fut. μᾰρανθήσομαι *Ep.Jac.*1.11, Gal.7.691: aor. ἐμᾰράνθην Il.9.212, Lyc.1231, etc.: pf. μεμάρασμαι Dsc.1.99, Luc.*Anach.*25, μεμάραμαι (leg. -αμμ-) v.l. in Dsc. l.c., Plu.*Pomp.*31: 3 sg. plpf. μεμάραντο Q.S.9.371:—*quench* fire, ἀνθρακιήν *h.Merc.* l.c.:—Pass., *die away, go slowly out*, of fire, φλὸξ ἐμαράνθη Il. l.c.; πυρκαϊὴ ἐμαραίνετο 23.228, cf. *AP*5.4 (Stat. Flacc.): distd. from σβέννυσθαι as that which goes out of itself, Arist.*Cael.*305ᵃ11; of rays of light, Arat.862. II. later, in various senses, ὄψεις μ. *quench* the orbs of sight, S. l.c.; esp. *waste, wither*, [νόσος] μαραίνει με A.*Pr.*597 (lyr.); γῆρας ἀμὲ μαραίνον ταριχεύει Sophr.54; κάλλος ἢ χρόνος ἀνάλωσεν ἢ νόσος ἐμάρανε Isoc.1.6; μάραινε [αὐτὸν] διωγμασι A.*Eu.*139; πίνος πλευρὰν μ. S.*OC*1260; πάνθ' ὁ μέγας χρόνος μ. Id.*Aj.*714 (lyr.), Philem.240; ἀδικία φθείρει [τὴν ψυχὴν] καὶ μ. Pl.*R.*609d:—Med., νέους ἐμαρήνατο δαίμων *IG*5(1).1355 (Abia):—Pass., *waste away*, καμάτοισι (v.l. ὑπὸ νούσοις) Emp.[156.3]; νόσῳ E.*Alc.*203; τὸ σῶμα οὐκ ἐμαραίνετο Th.2.49, cf. Pl.*Plt.*270e; but also of a tumour, *disappear*, Hp.*Epid.*7.84; αἷμα.. μαραίνεται χερός blood *dies away from* my hand, A.*Eu.*280; of a river, *dry up*, Hdt.2.24; μ. ἡ κίνησις Arist.*Pr.*901ᵃ26; of a musical sound, *die away*, ib.921ᵇ15; τὸ νοεῖν μ. Id.*de An.*408ᵇ24; of winds and waves, *abate*, Plu.*Pyrrh.*15, *Mar.*37; of wine, *lose its strength*, Id.2.692d; κῦδος μαρανθέν Lyc.1231, cf. 1127; μ. ἀκμή, δύναμις, Plu.*Fab.*2, *Caes.*3; τῶν ἐπιθυμιῶν καὶ ὀργῶν μεμαρασμένων Porph.*Abst.*3.26. (Perh. cf. Lat. *morbus*; signf. II may be the earlier in origin.)

**μαραίπους·** μεμαρασμένος τοὺς πόδας, Hsch.

**μαρὰν ἀθά**, Syriac phrase, = ὁ Κύριος ἥκει, 1*Ep.Cor.*16.22.

**μάραν-σις** [μᾰ], εως, ἡ, *causing to die away*, μ. πυρός, opp. σβέσις, Arist.*Juv.*469ᵇ22, cf. *Resp.*474ᵇ20; of the sun's action on wind, Id.*Mete.*361ᵇ21. II. *dying* or *fading away*, ib.372ᵇ19 (pl.); μαράνσει τὸν βίον ἐκλείπειν Id.*Pr.*871ᵇ17; διὰ μαράνσεως καὶ λήθης Porph.*Abst.*1.32. **-τικός**, ή, όν, *wasting away*, πόθος Sch.rec.A.*Pers.*59. II. *withered*, γέρων Phryn.*PS* p.57 B.

**Μαράξας**, ὁ, name of the month Ἀπελλαῖος, Hsch.

**μάραον**, τό, or **μάραος**, ὁ, = πίτταξις, Eust.1657.20.

**μᾰρασμ-ός**, ὁ, = μάρανσις, Gal.7.666; *withering*, τῆς ἀνθήσεως Dsc.2.166, cf. 3.86. **-ώδης**, ες, *wasting*, πυρετοί Antyll.ap.Orib.8.17.1, cf. Gal.7.315.

⊛ **μαράσσαι·** κύνες, ὄρνιθες, Hsch.

**μᾰράσσω**, read by Erot. for σμαραγέω in Hp.*Mul.*2.154.

**μᾰραυγ-έω**, *contract the pupil when exposed to light*, of cats' eyes, Plu.2.376f, cf. 599f. **-ία**, ἡ, *dazzling of the eyes*, Archyt.ap.Stob.3.1.196. II. **μαραύγεια** or **-αυγεία**, ἡ, a fish, Xenocr.ap.Orib.2.58.7.

**μαργαίνω**, (μάργος) only in pres., *rage furiously*, μαργαίνειν ἀνέηκεν ἐπ' ἀθανάτοισι θεοῖσι Il.5.882; σύες ἐπὶ φορυτῷ μαργαίνουσιν *are madly greedy* after.., Democr.147: abs., μαργαίνοντι χαριζόμενος βασιλῆϊ Coluth.198.

**μαργᾰρ-ίδης**, ου, ὁ, Ion. for μαργαρίτης, Praxag.ap.Phot.*Bibl.*p.22 B. **-ίς**, ίδος, ἡ, a kind of *palm-tree*, Plin.*HN*13.42. II. v. μαργαρίτης I. **-ίσκον·** πινακίσκον, Hsch.; cf. μαγαρίσκος. **-ῑτάριον**, τό, *small pearl*, *PHolm.*2.37 (pl.). ⊛ **-ίτης** [ῑ], ου, ὁ, *pearl*, Thphr.*Lap.*36, Ael.*NA*10.13: **-ῖτις** λίθος, ἡ, Androsth.ap.Ath.3.93b; **-ῖτις** alone, Isid.Char.20: **-ὶς** λίθος, ἡ, Philostr.*VA*3.53; **-ίς** alone, Hld.2.30. II. **-ίτης** χερσαῖος, an unidentified precious stone, Ael.*NA*15.8.

**μαργᾰρογονία**, ἡ, *the production of pearls*, Tz.*H.*11.460.

**μάργᾰρ-ον**, τό, = μαργαρίτης, *Anacreont.*22.14, *PHolm.*10.17, 29. **-ος**, ὁ and ἡ, *pearl-oyster*, Ael.*NA*15.8; but, = μαργαρίτης, Tz.*H.*11 passim.

**μαργάς**, ἡ, = δεσμός, Hsch. s.v. μαργαίνω.

⊛ **μαργ-άω**, (μάργος) only in part. μαργῶν *raging*, esp. in battle, A.*Th.*380; οἱ μαργῶντες S.*Fr.*842; φόνου μαργῶντος E.*HF*1005; μαργῶσαν χέρα Id.*Hec.*1128; [ἵπποι] μαργῶσαι φρένας Id.*Hipp.*1230, cf. Call.*Fr.*98a; μαργῶσα γνάθος *ravenous* jaw, A.*Fr.*258: c. inf., μ. ἱέναι δόρυ *madly eager* to.., E.*Ph.*1247. **-ήεις**, εσσα, εν, = μάργος, Hsch.

**μάργηλις**, εως or ιδος, ἡ, *pearl*, Philostr.*Im.*1.6.

**μάργης** or **μαργῆς** (contr. from μαργήεις), = μάργος, Suid.

**Μαργῑτ-εία**, ἡ, = Μαργιτομανία, Phld.*Rh.*1.139 S.; cf. sq. **-ης**, ου, ὁ, (μάργος) *Margites*, i.e. *madman*, hero of a mock-heroic poem of the same name, ascribed to Homer, Arist.*Po.*1448ᵇ30, etc.

**Μαργῑτομᾰνής**, *mad as Margites*, Phld.*Vit.*p.35 J.:—hence **-μᾰνία**, ἡ, Id.*Rh.*1.207 S.

**μαργ-όομαι**, Pass., = μαργάω, Pi.*N.*9.19, A.*Supp.*758 (lyr.). ⊛ **-ος**, η, ον, also ος, ον (A.*Eu.*67, Pl.*Lg.*792e):—poet. Adj. (used once by Pl.), *mad*, μάργε *madman!* Od.16.421; μαῖα φίλη, μάργην σε θεοὶ θέσαν 23.11, cf. Pi.*O.*2.96, etc.; θυμὸς μ. Thgn.1301; λύσσης πνεύματι μάργῳ A.*Pr.*884 (anap.); τάσδε τὰς μάργους, of the Furies, Id.*Eu.* l.c.; μάργοι ἡδοναί Pl. l.c.; of horses, *rampant, furious*, μάργων ἐπιβήτορες ἵππων Hom.*Epigr.*4.4, cf. A.*Th.*475; of wine, οἶνος δέ οἱ ἔπλετο μάργος Hes.*Fr.*121. 2. of appetite, *greedy, gluttonous*, μετὰ δ' ἔπρεπε γαστέρι μάργῃ Od.18.2; τὸ μ. σῆς γνάθου E.*Cyc.*310: metaph., οἴδματι μάργῳ Emp.100.7; μάργοις φλὸξ ἐδαίνυτο γνάθοις Phryn.Trag.5.4. 3. *lewd, lustful*, Thgn.581, A.*Supp.*741, E.*El.*1027, etc. **-οσύνη**, ἡ,

*gluttony*, Anacr.87, Luc.*Epigr.*2.10. II. *lust, wantonness*, Thgn. 1271 (pl.), A.R.3.797, al. -ότης, ητος, ἡ, (μάργος) *raging passion, madness*, S.*Fr.*846. 2. *gluttony*, Pl.*Ti.*72e. 3. *wantonness*, E.*Andr.*949.

⊛**μάρδος**, ὁ, kind of *flute*, Hdn.Gr.1.142.

**Μάρεια** [ᾰρ], Ion. gen. and dat. Μαρέης, Μαρέῃ, ἡ, *Marea* in Lower Egypt, Hdt.2.18,30, Th.1.104. II. a lake near it, Str.17.1.7; more commonly called ἡ **Μᾰρεῶτις** (λίμνη), ibid.:—also ὁ **Μᾰρεώτης** (οἶνος) Id.17.1.14: **Μαρεωτικὸς** (οἶνος) *PFay.*134.6 (iv A.D.), cf. *PRyl.* 227.26 (iii A.D.).

⊛**μάρη** [ᾰ], ἡ, = χείρ, *hand*, Pi.*Fr.*310. (Hence εὐμαρής, εὐμάρεια.)

**μαρήγει**· λαμβάνει, Hsch. **μαρηγηλλᾷ**· ἀμφιπονεῖ, στραγγεύεται, Id.

**Μᾰρῑαν-δῡνία**, ἡ, district in Bithynia, Eup.279:—Adj.⊛**-δῡνοί**, οἱ, Hdt.1.28, etc.: hence Μ. θρηνητήρ, of one who utters *wild, barbaric* laments, A.*Pers.*938 (lyr.); Μ. κάλαμοι *Com.Adesp.*415. **-δῡνίζω**, = εἰρωνεύω, Hsch.

⊛**μᾰριεύς**, έως, ὁ, *a stone that takes fire when water is poured on it*, Arist.*Mir.*833ᵃ27, Hsch. (μαριζεύς cod.).

⊛**μᾰρῑκᾶς**, ὁ, a foreign word for κίναιδος, Hsch.; under this name Eupolis attacked Hyperbolus, Ar.*Nu.*553.

**μᾰρῑλ-ευτής**, οῦ, ὁ, *charcoal-burner*, and -εύω, *burn charcoal*, Poll. 7.110. -η, ἡ, *embers of charcoal, coal-dust* (= ἡ ἐξ ἀνθράκων τέφρα Sch.Ar.*Ach.*349; = ἀμαυρὸν πῦρ, ὁ χνοῦς καὶ τὸ λεπτότατον τῶν ἀνθράκων, Suid.), Hippon.59, Cratin.257, *Com.Adesp.*443; μ. ἀνθράκων Hippon.71, cf. Ar.*Ach.*350: distd. from ἄνθρακες (charcoal) and σποδιή (ashes) by Hp.*Mul.*2.133; *hot embers*, Ruf.ap.Orib.4.2.20; λεπτῆς μ. Arist.*Pr.*967ᵇ5; χαλκεὺς γέμων κάπνου καὶ μαρίλης Jul.*Or.*7.233b: hence, ὦ Μᾰρῑλάδη *O son of Coaldust!* comic name of an Acharnian collier, Ar.*Ach.*609. -ιον, τό, pl. written μαρύλλια, = foreg., λαβὼν μ. ποίησον τέφραν *PLeid.X.*56.

**μᾰρῑλο-καύτης**, ου, ὁ, *charcoal-burner*, S.*Fr.*1067 (prob. = *Ichn.*34, pl.). -πότης, ου, ὁ, *coal-dust-gulper*, of a blacksmith, *APl.*1.15*.

⊛**μαρίν**· τὴν σύν (Cret.), Hsch.

**μᾰρῖνος**, ὁ, kind of *sea-fish*, dub. in Arist.*HA*570ᵃ32; v.l. for μύρινος, ib.602ᵃ1.

⊛**μάρις**, εως, ὁ, a liquid measure, containing six κοτύλαι, Arist.*HA* 596ᵃ6, Poll.10.184; or ten χόες, Polyaen.4.3.32.

**μαρίσκος**, ὁ, *bog-rush, Cladium Mariscus*, Plin.*HN*21.112.

⊛**μαρίω**, Dor. μαιριάω, *to be feverish*, Hsch. **μαρκάς**· μακάριος, εὔμοιρος, Id. (fort. μάκαρς).

**μαρμαίρω**, only pres. and impf.; impf. μαρμαίρεσκον Q.S.1.150: (redupl. from μαρ-, cf. μάρ-μαρος, ἀ-μαρ-ύσσω):—*flash, sparkle, gleam*, of any *darting, quivering* light, Hom. (only in Il.); ἔντεα μαρμαίροντα Il.12.195, cf. 16.664, al.; τεύχεα μ. 18.617; Τρῶες.. χαλκῷ μαρμαίροντες 13.801; σὺν ἔντεσι μαρμαίροντας 16.279; δώματα.. χρύσεα μαρμαίροντα 13.22; ὄμματα μαρμαίροντα the *sparkling* eyes of Aphrodite, 3.397; αὐγὴ μαρμαίρουσα κεραυνοῦ Hes.*Th.*699; μαρμαίρει δὲ δόμος χάλκῳ Alc.15.1; χρυσῷ ἐλέφαντί τε μ. οἶκοι B.*Fr.*16.9; νύκτα .. ἄστροισι μαρμαίρουσαν A.*Th.*401; χρυσῷ χαίταν μαρμαίρων, of Apollo, E.*Ion* 888 (lyr.); ἀστὴρ μαρμαίρων D.P.329; μαρμαίρουσι παρῆΐδες *AP*5.281 (Agath.), cf. Alciphr.3.67: also in late Prose, Phld. *Po.*2.40, Plu.*Caes.*6, Luc.*DMeretr.*13.3, Alciphr. l.c.

**μάρμαρ**· στερεόν, Hsch. **μαρμάραι**· αἱ τῷ ἐρυθροδάνῳ βεβαμμέναι, Id.

⊛**μαρμᾰρ-άριος**, ὁ, *marble-mason*, *IG*4.375 (Corinth), 14.1093. -ειος, α, ον, = sq., Hsch. ⊛ -εος, α, ον, *flashing, gleaming*, esp. of metals, αἰγίς, ἄντυξ, Il.17.594, 18.480; πύλαι Hes.*Th.*811; ἅλα μαρμαρέην the *twinkling* sea, Il.14.273; αὐγαὶ μ. Ar.*Nu.*287 (lyr.); ἄστρα Orph.*Fr.*168.13. II. *of marble*, λίθος *IG*7.2544 (Thebes); στήλη ib.14.1603; δόμος *AP*6.123 (Anyt.), cf. *PRyl.* 227.16 (iii A.D.). -εργᾰτέω, *work in marble*, Tz.*H.*9.127. ⊛ -ίζω, = μαρμαίρω, ἀκτῖνας προσώπου -ιζούσας Pi.*Fr.*123.2; ἡ -ίζουσα πέτρα, of quartz rock containing gold, D.S.3.12. ⊛ -ικός, ή, όν, either *prepared from marble* or *obtained from Marmarica* (*Barca*), ἄσβεστος *PHolm.*25.19. -ῐνος, η, ον, *of marble*, ἄγαλμα Theoc.*Ep.*10.2; τάφος *AP*7.649 (Anyt.); τροχοί D.S.17.45; εἰκών, ἄγαλμα, *GDI*3502 (Cnidus), *SIG*996.14 (Smyrna); λίθος J.*AJ*7.10.3. ⊛ -ῖτις, ιδος, ἡ, *like marble*, πέτρα Ph.Byz.*Mir.*2.3. II. = ἀγλαοφῶτις, Plin.*HN*24.160.

**μαρμᾰρο-γλύπτης**, ου, ὁ, = *marmorum sculptor*, *Gloss.* -γλῠφία, ἡ, *sculpture in marble*, Str.10.5.7. ⊛ -εις, εσσα, εν, = μαρμάρεος, Ὀλύμπου μ. αἴγλαν S.*Ant.*610 (lyr.). -κονία, ἡ, *stucco made from marble*, Sch.Hes.*Sc.*142.

**μάρμᾰρον**, τό, *marble*, Call.*Ap.*24, *SIG*909.5 (v A.D.). II. *sore on the feet of asses*, *Hippiatr.*53.

**μαρμᾰρο-ποιός**, όν, *working in marble*, *Gloss.* -πτερος, ον, *with gleaming wings*, κόλποι Ἀμφιτρίτας Tim.*Pers.*39 (prob.).

**μάρμᾰρος**, ὁ, *a crystalline rock*, which sparkles (μαρμαίρει) in the light, μάρμαρος ὀκριόεις Il.12.380, Od.9.499, cf. E.*Ph.*663 (lyr.), Ar. *Ach.*1172 (lyr.): as Adj., πέτρος μ. ὀκριόεις Il.16.735, cf. E.*Ph.*1401, etc. II. later, *marble*, μάρμαρον ἢ λίθον λευκήν Hp.*Mul.*2.185, cf. Thphr.*Lap.*9: also fem., μαρμάρου.. τῆς Πεντελικῆς μέταλλα Str. 9.1.23; μ. λίθος Id.14.1.35: hence, 2. *work in marble*, i.e. *tombstone*, τυκτὴ μ. Theoc.22.211. 3. *chips made by cutting marble* (masc.), Plu.2.660c, 954a, Dsc.5.79.

**μαρμᾰρουργός**, ὁ, *marble-mason*, Tz.*H.*9.131.

**μαρμᾰροφεγγής**, ές, *gleaming white*, στόματος παῖδες, of the teeth, Tim.*Pers.*103.

**μαρμᾰρόω**, *coat with marble stucco*, [κίονας] Jul.*Ep.*80:—Pass., *PMag.Berol.*1.109. 2. *line with marble*, κολυμβήθρα.. μεμαρμαρώσθω Hero *Stereom.*2.5. II. Pass., *to be turned to stone*, Lyc.826.

**μαρμᾰρῠγ-ή**, ἡ, *flashing, sparkling, gleaming*, λάμπει δ' ὑπὸ μαρμαρυγαῖς ὁ χρυσός B.3.17, cf. Pl.*Criti.*116c, Plu.*Caes.*69; ἡ τοῦ οὐρανοῦ μ. Dam.*Pr.*213; αἱ ἀπολάμπουσαι ἀπὸ τῶν ὀμμάτων μ. Damian.*Opt.*2, cf. Adam.1.16. 2. '*seeing sparks*', Hp.*Prog.*24 (pl.), Pl.*R.*518a. 3. of any quick motion, μαρμαρυγαὶ ποδῶν *the quick twinkling* of the dancers' feet, Od.8.265, cf. *h.Ap.*203. -μα, ατος, τό, = foreg. 2, Cael.Aur.*TP*1.62 (pl.). -ώδης, ες, '*seeing sparks*', ὄμματα Hp. *Acut.*42; μαρμαρυγῶδές τι πρὸ τῶν ὀφθαλμῶν Id.*Prorrh.*2.35.

**μαρμαρυκᾷ**· ἀπὸ τοῦ μαρμαίρειν, Hsch.

**μαρμᾰρ-ύσσω**, *flash, sparkle*, Them.*Or.*20.235b; of the eyes, Adam.1.16, al.; of stars, *twinkle*, Jul.*Gal.*356e. -ώδης, ες, *like marble*, *Et.Gud.*499.21. -ῶπις, ιδος, ἡ, *turning to stone by a glance*, Lyc.843; as riddling synonym for Ἀθηναία, Trypho *Trop.*p.195 S. -ωπός, όν, *with sparkling eyes*, Λύσσα E.*HF*884 (lyr.). ⊛ -ωσις, εως, ἡ, *production of* μάρμαρον II, *Hippiatr.*100. -ωσσός, ή, όν, *afflicted with* μάρμαρον II, ib.53.

**μάρνᾰμαι**, μάρνασαι Pi.*N.*10.86, μάρναται Il.4.513, μάρνανται E. *Med.*249; imper. μάρναο Il.15.475; subj. μαρνώμεσθα Hes.*Sc.*110; opt. μαρναίμεθα Od.11.513; inf. μάρνασθαι Il.5.33, E.*Tr.*731; part. μαρνάμενος Il.3.307, Tyrt.12.33, E.*Ph.*1574 (lyr.): impf. ἐμαρνάμην *Anacreont.*12.11; -αο, -ατο, Od.22.228, Il.12.40 (Ep. μάρνατο 11.498); 3 dual ἐμαρνάσθην 7.301; pl. ἐμαρνάμεσθα E.*Ph.*1142, *IT*1376; poet. μαρνάμεθα Od.3.108, B.5.125, μάρναντο Il.13.169: only pres. and impf.:—*fight, do battle*, τινι *with, against* another, Il.15.475, etc.; ἐπί τινι 9.317; πρός τινα E.*Tr.*731; σύν τινι *together with* another, *on his side*, Od.3.85; ἀμφί τινα *about* a fallen hero, Il.16.775; περί τινος *for* or *about* a person, ib.497; ἐναντίοι ἀλλήλοισι νίκης καὶ κράτεος πέρι μ. Hes.*Th.*647; γῆς πέρι καὶ παίδων Tyrt. l.c.; περὶ δορᾶς Κουρῆσι B. l.c.; μήλων ἕνεκ' Hes.*Op.*163: c. dat. instrum., ἔγχεϊ, χαλκῷ μ., Il.16.195, 497; φασγάνῳ, δορί, Pi.*P.*9.21, E.*Med.* l.c. 2. of boxers, Od.18.31. 3. *quarrel, wrangle*, Il.1.257. 4. *contend, strive*, Pi.*P.*2.65; ἀμφ' ἀρεταῖσι, ἐσλοῖσι πέρι, Id.*O.*5.15, *N.*5.47; κασιγνήτου πέρι ib.10.86; μ. φυᾷ *strive* with all one's natural powers, ib.1.25.—Ep. and Lyr. Verb, used also by E.; cf. βάρναμαι. (Cf. Skt. *mṛṇā́ti* 'crush'.)

**Μάρνας**, ὁ, name of Zeus at Gaza, St.Byz. s.v. Γάζα, *LW*2412*g* (Haurân), Marin.*Vit.Procl.*19; **Μαρνεῖον**, τό, his temple, Marc.Diac. *Vit.Porph.*64.

**μᾶρον**, τό, a kind of *sage, Teucrium Marum*, Mnesim.4.61 (anap.), Thphr.*Od.*33, Dsc.3.42.

**μαρούλιον**, τό, = θριδακίνη, *lettuce*, *Gp.*12.1.2, Alex.Trall.2, *Verm.* p.593 P.; cf. μαιούλιον.

**μάρπτις**, ὁ, *seizer, ravisher*, A.*Supp.*826 (lyr.); μάρπτυς (sic)· ὑβριστής, Hsch.

**μάρπτω**, impf. ἔμαρπτον Il.21.489; Ep. μάρπτον Emp.90.1: fut. μάρψω Il.15.137, E.*Ion* 158 (lyr.): aor. 1 ἔμαρψα Il.22.201, etc.: Ep. forms, 3 sg. subj. μάρπτῃσι Il.8.405: aor. 2 opt. μεμάποιεν Hes. *Sc.*252; inf. μᾰπέειν ib.231, 304: 3 sg. pf. μέμαρπεν ib.245; part. μεμαρπώς Id.*Op.*204, A.R.1.756:—Pass., μαρπτομένη Call.*Dian.* 195:—poet. (chiefly Ep.) Verb, *take hold of*, τινα Il.14.346, etc.: c. gen. partis, *catch by*.., αὐχένων χερσὶν ὄφιας Pi.*N.*1.45; μάρψας ποδὸς νιν S.*Tr.*779: c. dat. instrum., χεῖρας ἔμαρπτε σκαιῇ Il.21. 489; φάρμακα χερσίν Emp.23.3; χερσὶν ἡνίας E.*Hipp.*1188; γαμφηλῇσι δράκοντα Orac.ap.Ar.*Eq.*197; χερὶ ἀνθέματος *AP*6.199 (Antiphil.).—Special usages: in a hostile sense, *lay hold of, seize*, αὐτίχ' ἕνα μάρψας ἑτάρων Od.10.116; of sleep, τὸν ὕπνος ἔμαρπτε Il.23.62; γῆράς τε μέμαρπεν Hes.*Sc.*245, cf. καταμάρπτω; *overtake, catch* a fugitive, μή με μεταΐξας μάρψῃ ταχέεσσι πόδεσσι Il.21.564, cf. 22.201, Archil.59; but χθόνα μάρπτε ποδοῖιν *took hold of* ground with her feet, Il.14.228; ἕλκεα.., ἅ κεν μάρπτῃσι κεραυνός which the thunderbolt shall *inflict* (*by laying hold*), 8.405, 419; μ. σθένος *gain* strength, of a fallow field, Pi.*N.*6.11; εἴ σε μάρψει ψῆφος if the votes *shall condemn*, A.*Eu.*597; ἄσκοποι πλάκες ἔμαρψαν the unseen land *engulfed* him, S.*OC*1681 (lyr.); τόξοις μ. τινά E.*Ion* 158 (lyr.); τὰ ὄλβια τῦφος ἔμαρψεν Crates Theb.8; of death, μάρψεν Ἀΐδης *Trag.Adesp.* 208; esp. in epitaphs, μάρψασα μοῖρα *IG*4.620 (Argos), 7.115 (Megara), cf. 12(7).115 (Amorgos). (From μ̥πτω, cf. βράπτω.)

**μάρρον**, τό, *iron spade*, Hsch. (Semitic or Sumerian word, cf. Assyr. *marru* 'hoe', 'pick'.)

⊛**μάρσιππος**, ὁ, *bag, pouch*, X.*An.*4.3.11, *PPetr.*3 p.257 (iii B.C.), *PSI*4.427.1, al. (iii B.C.), *PCair.Zen.*69.14 (iii B.C.), LXX *Ge.*42.27, al., f.l. in D.S.20.41; *poultice*, Sor.2.10, 59; μ. λινοῦς, = κρησέρα, Gal.19.115:—Dim. μαρσίππιον, τό, Hp.*Acut.*21, Apollod.Car.13, *PCair.Zen.*10.27, al. (iii B.C.), *PPetr.*3 p.145 (iii B.C.), LXX *Pr.*1.14. [-ιπος, -ίππιον, Pap. ll. cc. and usu. in LXX; -ιπος, -ίπιον freq. v.l. in later codd., cf. *Gloss.*; -είπειον *UPZ*77 ii 13 (ii B.C., illiterate); -υπος, -ύπιον, *Gloss.*; -υπεῖον v.l. in LXX *Si.*18.33; -υππος, -ύππιον, Hsch. s. vv. ἀρυβαλίδα, ἀρύβαλλοι.]

**Μάρτιος**, ὁ (sc. μήν), Lat. *Martius, the month of March*, Plu.*Num.* 19, D.C.71.33.

**μαρτιχόρας**, ὁ, *man-eater*, i.e. *tiger*, described with fabulous attributes by Ctes.ap.Arist.*HA*501ᵃ26 (v.l. μαρτιοχώρας, μαντιχώρας), cf. Ctes.*Fr.*57.7, Id.ap.Paus.9.21.4 (μαρτιόρα codd.), et ap.Ael. *NA*4.21. (Cf. OPers. *martiya-* 'man', Avest. *khwar-* 'eat', Mod. Pers. *mard-khwār* 'man-eater'.)

**μάρτῠρ**, ῠρος, ὁ and ἡ, Aeol. for Att. μάρτυς, Hdn.Gr.1.47, al.; also Dor., *SIG*953.22 (Calymna, ii B.C.); cf. μάρτυρος, ἐπιμάρτυρος.

**μαρτῠρ-έω**, fut. -ήσω Pi.*O*.6.21:—Pass., fut. μαρτυρηθήσομαι Is.8.13, D.19.40; μαρτυρήσομαι in pass. sense, X. (v. infr. 9), D.57.37: aor. ἐμαρτυρήθην: pf. μεμαρτύρημαι Antipho6.16, used in act. sense, Lxx *Ge*.43.3:—*bear witness, give evidence*:—Constr.: 1. abs., Simon.4.7, Pi.*I*.5(4).48; μαρτυροῦντι πιστεύειν Antipho 2.2.7; ἐξέστω καὶ τοῖς δούλοις μαρτυρεῖν *PLille* 29.20 (iii B.C.), cf. *SIG*953.19 (Calymna, ii B.C.), etc. 2. c. dat. pers., *bear witness to* or *in favour of* another, *confirm* what he says, A.*Eu*.594, Hdt.8.94, etc.; μαρτυρέει μοι τῇ γνώμῃ, ὅτι.. *bears witness to* my opinion, that.., Id.2.18, cf. 4.29; μαρτυρεῖς σαυτῷ E.*Ion* 532; esp. *bear favourable witness to, give a good report of* a person, *IG*2².657 (iii B.C.), etc.; πάντες ἐμαρτύρουν αὐτῷ *Ev.Luc*.4.22. b. c. dat rei, μ. τῇ διαθήκῃ *POxy*.494.33 (ii A.D.), etc. 3. c. acc. rei, *testify to* a thing, Alc.102, Pi.*O*.13.108, S.*Ant*.515, Pl.*Phdr*.244d; μ. τινί τι Pi.*O*.6.21, A.*Supp*.797 (lyr.). 4. μ. περί τινος Pl.*Ap*.21a; ὑπέρ τινος D.29.54. 5. c. inf., *testify that* a thing is, Heraclit.34, S.*OC*1265, etc.; τίς σοι μαρτυρήσει ταῦτ' ἐμοῦ κλύειν; *that* he heard..? Id.*Tr*.422, cf. E.*Hipp*.977; ὁ κληθεὶς μαρτυρείτω ἀληθῆ μαρτυρεῖν *PHal*.1.225 (iii B.C.): rarely c. part., μαρτυρεῖτέ [μοι].. ῥινηλατούσῃ A.*Ag*.1184; μ. τισὶ παραγινομέναις D.H.8.46. 6. μ. τινὶ ὡς.. A.*Ag*.494, cf. Pl.*Grg*.523c; σώματα.. ὡς ἔστιν, αὐτὴ ἡ αἴσθησις.. μ. Epicur.*Ep*.1 p.6 U.; μ. ὅτι.. X.*Vect*.4.25. 7. μ. τινὶ τῆς συμμαχίας *testify to, acknowledge the value of* his alliance, J.*AJ*13.5.3. 8. c. acc. cogn., μαρτυρίαν μ. Is.11.25, Pl.*Erx*.399b; μ. ἀκοήν *give* hearsay *evidence*, D.57.4; μ. ψεῦδος, ψευδῆ, *bear* false *witness*, Amips.13, Diph.32.16; τὰ ψευδῆ Lys.19.4; τἀληθῆ Aeschin.1.46:—Pass., μαρτυρίαι μαρτυρηθεῖσαι D.47.1; μεμαρτύρηταί τι περί τινος Antipho6.16, cf. Lys.13.66. 9. impers. in Pass., παρ' ἄλλου ποιητοῦ μαρτυρεῖται *testimony is borne* by.., Pl.*Prt*.344d; οἶδα.. μαρτυρήσεσθαί μοι ὅτι.. X.*Mem*.4.8.10, cf. *Ap*.26; μεμαρτύρηται ὑμῖν *testimony has been given* before you, Lys.19.55, Is.9.5. 10. Pass., μαρτυρεῖταί μοι σοφία *is ascribed* to me, D.H.2.26; μαρτυροῦμαι ἐμπειρίαν I *have* it *ascribed to me*, Plu.2.58a, cf. Luc.*Sacr*.10; καλοκἀγαθίαν μαρτυρούμενος J.*AJ*15.10.5; μαρτυροῦμαι ἐπί τινι I *bear a character* for.., Ath.1.25f; ἄνδρας μαρτυρουμένους men *whose character is approved by testimony*, *Act.Ap*.6.3; τεχνίτας.. μαρτυρηθέντας ὑπό τινος *SIG*799.28 (Cyzicus, i A.D.); δι' ὅλης οἰκουμένης μαρτυρούμενον θεόν *Sammelb*.1070 (Abydos). II. Astrol., *to be in aspect with*, c. dat., Ptol.*Tetr*.123; μ. τὴν μοῖραν *Cat.Cod.Astr*.7.226:—Pass., Nech.ap.Vett.Val.279.23. **-ημα**, ατος, τό, *testimony*, E.*Supp*.1204. **-ησις**, εως, ἡ, *corroborative evidence*, ἡ ἀπὸ τῶν φαινομένων μ. Sor.1.41. **-ητέον**, *one must testify*, Dsc.*Praef*.2. ⊛**-ητικός**, ή, όν, *complimentary*, ψηφίσματα μ. καὶ τιμητικά *Jahresh*.13.201 (Alabanda, ii A.D.). ⊛**-ία**, ἡ, *testimony*, Διονύσου μαρτυρίῃσι Od.11.325, cf. Hes.*Op*.282 (pl.): freq. both sg. and pl., μ. τινός his *evidence*, Antipho2.2.7; μ. παρέχεσθαι Pl.*Smp*.179b; εἰς μ. κληθῆναι Id.*Lg*.937a; μαρτυριῶν ἀπέχεσθαι to refuse to give *evidence*, Ar.*Eq*.1316; ἐμβάλλεσθαι μ. ψευδῆ D.54.31; γράφειν μ. τινί *serve* him *with a subpoena*, Aeschin.1.45; μ. ἔχειν παρά τινων ἔκ τινων Arist.*Pol*.1338ª36: in non-legal sense, *commendation*, πάσης μ. ἐπιτήδειον (in sense of ἄξιον) *SIG*1073.17 (Olympia, ii A.D.): in pl., *demonstrations of favour*, *POxy*.41.18 (iii/iv A.D.). II. Astrol., *aspect*, Vett.Val.5.5, Gal.19.532, Man.1.124, Procl.*Par.Ptol*.255.

⊛**μαρτύριον** [ῠ], τό, *testimony, proof*, πρῶτον καὶ μέγιστον μ. Hdt.2.22, cf. Pi.*I*.4(3).10, etc.: freq. in pl., μαρτύρια θέσθαι Hdt.8.55, cf. A.*Ag*.1095 (lyr.), *Eu*.485, 797; μετ' ἀειμνήστου μ. Th.1.33; μαρτύριον δέ.., folld. by γάρ, *here is a proof, namely*.., ib.8, etc.; μέγα τόδε μ., ..γάρ Hdt.8.120. II. τὰ μ. *the tables of the Decalogue*, Lxx *Le*.16.13, al. III. *shrine of a martyr*, Aët.15.15(*a*)Z., *POxy*.941.4 (vi A.D.), etc.

**μαρτῠρογράφιον** [γρᾰ], τό, *written deposition*, Anon. *in Rh*.159.8.

⊛**μαρτύρομαι** [ῠ], fut. μαρτῠροῦμαι (δια-) Lxx *Ps*.80(81).9 (cod. Alex.): aor. ἐμαρτῠράμην Pl.*Phlb*.47d, App.*BC*2.47:—*call to witness, invoke*, c. acc. pers., Antipho1.29, S.*OC*813, etc.; esp. of the gods, Ἄρτεμιν, γαῖαν καὶ θεούς, E.*Hipp*.1451, *Ph*.626; δαίμονας, ὡς.. Id.*Med*.619: c. acc. et inf., ὑμᾶς δ' ἀκούειν ταῦτ' ἐγὼ μαρτύρομαι A.*Eu*.643, etc.: c. part., μαρτύρομαι τυπτόμενος I *call you to witness that*.., Ar.*Av*.1031, cf. E.*HF*858 (troch.). 2. c. acc. rei, *call* one *to witness* a thing, Hdt.1.44, Ar.*Ra*.528, *Pl*.932. 3. *protest, asseverate*, μ. ὅτι.. Id.*Nu*.1222, Th.6.80; ταῦτα Pl. l. c.: abs., μαρτύρομαι I *protest*, Ar.*Ach*.926, Lys.3.15. 4. c. acc. pers. et gen. rei, οἱ δὲ τῆς τῶν θεῶν.. παραγωγῆς τὸν Ὅμηρον μ. ὅτι.. *cite* Homer *as a witness* of.., Pl.*R*.364d; ἐμαυτὸν μ. τῆς φιλοτιμίας App. l. c.; μ. τινὶ ὅτι.. *Ep.Gal*.5.3; τοὺς ἀποστάντας μ. τῆς ἐπιορκίας *remind* them of.., App.*BC*5.129.

**μαρτῠροποι-έω**, *produce evidence*, *PLips*.40iii 14 (iv/v A.D.), *Gloss*.:—also in Med., *call to witness*, Corn.*ND*16. II. mostly in Med., *testify, certify on oath*, *IG*9(1).61.8 (Daulis, ii A.D.), Mitteis *Chr*.242.3 (ii A.D.), *Sammelb*.5217.20 (ii A.D.), etc. **-ημα**, ατος, τό, *statement on oath, affidavit*, *POxy*.1114.23 (iii A.D.), *BGU*1093.22 (iii A.D.), *Gloss*. **-ησις**, εως, ἡ, *affirmation on oath*, *Sammelb*.5217.18 (ii A.D.). II. = *contestatio*, *Gloss*. ⊛**-ία**, ἡ, Astrol., = μαρτυρία II, Ptol.*Tetr*.183 (pl.). II. = *testificatio*, *Gloss*.

**μάρτῠρος**, ὁ, Ep. form for μάρτυς, ἐστὲ μάρτυροι Il.2.302, etc.; also in Central Greece, *IG*9(1).226 (Drymaea), 364 (Naupactus), *GDI*1684, al. (Delph.), etc.: sg. once in Od., οἷσιν ἄρα Ζεὺς μάρτυρος 16.423, cf. *PGen*.54.6 (iv A.D.). (Zenod. rejected this form, but it is defended in Sch.Il.*Oxy*.1087.22.)

⊛**μάρτῠς**, ὁ, ἡ, Cret., Epid. **μαῖτυς** *Leg.Gort*.1.13, al., *IG*4²(1).42, Cret. also **μαίτυρς** *GDI*4998 v 11; gen. μάρτῠρος, acc. -ῠρα Hes.*Op*.371, etc., formed from **μάρτυρ** (q. v.), exc. acc. μάρτῡν Simon.84.4, Men.1034, Plu.2.49a; dat. pl. μάρτῡσι (but μάρτυρσι prob. in Hippon.51):—*witness* (not in Hom.), Hes. l. c., *h.Merc*.372, Thgn.1226, etc.; ἄμμιν μάρτυς ἔστω Ζεύς Pi.*P*.4.167, cf. A.*Eu*.664; ἁμέραι δ' ἐπίλοιποι μ. σοφώτατοι Pi.*O*.1.34; τούτων μάρτυρας καλῶ θεούς S.*Tr*.1248, cf. E.*Ph*.491; μάρτυρα θέσθαι τινά Id.*Supp*.261; μ. θεοὺς ποιεῖσθαι Th.4.87, etc.; μάρτυρι χρῆσθαί τινι Arist.*Rh*.1375ᵇ30; μάρτυρας παρέχεσθαι produce *witnesses*, Pl.*Grg*.471e, cf. D.27.51, etc.; μάρτυρες παρίστανται X.*Cyr*.1.6.16; μάρτυρα παράγεσθαι, μάρτυρας ἐπάγεσθαι, Pl.*Lg*.836c, *R*.364c; δικάζει ταῦτα μαρτύρων ὕπο A.*Supp*.934; μαρτύρων ἐναντίον Antipho1.28, Ar.*Ec*.448; ἐν μάρτυσι Pl.*Smp*.175e; τί δεῖται μάρτυρος; Id.*R*.340a. II. *martyr*, *Apoc*.2.13, etc. III. Astrol., *in aspect*, μάρτυρες ἀλλήλων Man.4.451. (Cf. μάρτυρ, μάρτυρος.)

**μᾱρυκ-άομαι, -ισμός**, Dor. for μηρυκ-. **μᾱρύομαι**, Dor. for μηρύομαι.

⊛**Μάρων** [ᾰ], ωνος, ὁ, name of Thracian priest who gave wine to Odysseus, Od.9.197: hence, of a strong wine, Cratin.135, E.*Cyc*.412; perh. also a throw of the dice, cf. Herod.3.25. II. **μάρων**, ονος, ὁ, ἡ, = λευκόψαρος, ὄνοι *Hippiatr*.14.

**μαρώνη**, *centauria*, *Gloss*.

⊛**μᾰσάομαι**, aor. 1 ἐμασησάμην Hp.*Epid*.7.11, Hsch. s. v. ἐμάσταζεν:—*chew*, ἀμυγδάλας μασᾶσθαι Eup.253; κρέας Ar.*Pl*.321; σηπίας Id.*Ec*.554; τι Hp. l. c.; πάπυρον Thphr.*HP*4.8.4; τὰ δέρματα τῶν θυρεῶν J.*BJ*6.3.3: abs., Ar.*Eq*.717, *V*.780, Thphr.*Char*.20.5: μασώμενον, τό, of a toothache remedy, Cass.Fel.32.—Not in Trag., or Att. Prose. II. *shoot out the lip*, as a mark of contempt, Philostr.*VA*7.21.

**μάσασθαι**, v. ἐπιμαίομαι. **μάσδα, μασδός**, Dor. for μᾶζα, μαζός.

**μάσδασνος**, ὁ, = Avest. *mazdayasna*, *worshipper of Mazda*, title of kings of the Sassanid dynasty, *OGI*432.1 (Naksh-i-Rustam).

⊛**μάσ-ημα** [μᾰ], ατος, τό, *something to chew, quid*, Antiph.244, Thphr.*HP*4.8.4. **-ησις**, εως, ἡ, *chewing*, Id.*CP*6.9.3, Ruf.*Anat*.19, Gal.6.626. **-ητά**, τά, *food which has to be chewed*, Sor.1.115. **-ητήρ**, ῆρος, ὁ, *chewer*, μῦς μ. a muscle *of the lower jaw*, used in *chewing*, Hp.*Art*.30, Gal.*UP*16.6, Simp. *in Cael*.664.4.

**μάσθλ-ημα**, ατος, τό, *leather*, Ctes.*Fr*.57.23 (pl.). ⊛**-ης**, ητος, ὁ, = ἱμάσθλη, *leather*, Hp.*Morb*.2.59; Aeol. **μάσλης**, perh. *leather shoe*, Sapph.19; *thong* of a whip, φοίνιον μάσθλητα δίγονον S.*Fr*.129: **μάσθλη** is dub., cf. ib.571, Hsch. II. metaph., *supple, slippery knave*, Ar.*Eq*.269, *Nu*.449 (anap.), Aristid.*Or*.34(50).61. **-ήτινος**, η, ον, *like leather* or *red as leather*, καρὶς μασθλητίνη Cratin.283, Eup.107.

**μασθ-ός**, ὁ, v. μαστός. **-ωτόν**, τό, or **-ωτός**, ὁ, = μαστάριον II, Zos.Alch.pp.199, 251 B.

**μᾰσῐ-**, intens. Prefix (like ἐρι-); cf. μαί.

**μασί-γδουπος**, ον, = ἐρίγδουπος, Hsch. **μασιτρίς**, gloss on νάρφη, Id.

⊛**μασκαύλης**, ου, ὁ, *laver*, Keil-Premerstein *Dritter Bericht* No.42 (Jewish, iii A.D.). (Cf. Talmudic *maskel, maskol* 'basin'.)

**μάσκη**· δίκελλα, Hsch.

**μάσμα**, ατος, τό, (μαίομαι) *search*, Cratin.424; = ζήτημα, Pl.*Cra*.421b.

**μασουάφιον**, τό, = sq., Aët.13.118, Paul.Aeg.7.23.

**μασουχᾶς**, ᾶ, ὁ, a compound remedy, Alex.Trall.7.1, Paul.Aeg.3.37, 7.23.

**μάσπετον**, τό, *the leaf of* σίλφιον, Antiph.88.4 (cj.), Thphr.*HP*6.3.1. 2. *the stalk of* σίλφιον, Dsc.3.80. 3. = *semen ferulae*, *Gloss*.

**μᾶσσαι**, said to be Aeol. for δῆσαι, Timae.39. II. **μάσσαι**· ζητῆσαι, καθαρίσαι, φυράσαι, Hsch. (μᾶσσαι cod.).

**Μασσαλία**, ἡ, *Marseilles*, Th.1.13, Arist.*Pol*.1321ª30, etc.:—hence **Μασσᾰλιῶται** or **-ῆται**, οἱ, D.32.8, D.S.14.93, etc.:—Adj. **-ωτικός**, ή, όν, Hp.*Mul*.1.78:—also **Μασσᾰλιήτης** οἶνος Ath.1.27c.

**μασσάομαι, -σσημα, -σσησις, -σσητήρ**, incorrectly written for μασάομαι, etc. **μάσσεται**, v. μαίομαι.

**μασσότερον**· πορρώτερον, Hsch.; ὡς ἔνι μ. Diusap.Stob.4.21.16 (nisi leg. -ότατον); cf. μάσσων.

⊛**μάσσω**, S.*Fr*.563; Att. **μάττω** Eup.340: fut. μάξω Ar.*Lys*.601 (anap.) (ἀνα- Od.19.92): aor. ἔμαξα Pherecr.183.2, Pl.*R*.372b, Arist.*Rh*.1416ᵇ31, Nic.*Th*.952: pf. μέμαχα Ar.*Eq*.55:—**Med.**, fut. μάξομαι (ἐμ-) Call.*Dian*.124: aor. ἐμαξάμην Hdt.1.200; poet. μαξάμην *AP*5.295 (Agath.):—**Pass.**, aor. 1 ἐμάχθην Aret.*CD*2.12: aor. 2 ἐμάγην [ᾰ] (v. ἐκμ-): pf. μέμαγμαι Ar.*Eq*.57, Th.4.16: freq. in compds. with ἀπό, ἐκ: —*knead, press into a mould*, esp. of barley-cakes which were subsequently moistened and eaten without baking (cf. μακτός), S. l. c., Ar.*Pax*14; μᾶζαν μεμαχότος Id.*Eq*.55 (also in Med., Hdt. l. c., Ar.*Nu*.788); ἐκ μὲν τῶν κριθῶν ἄλφιτα.., ἐκ δὲ τῶν πυρῶν ἄλευρα, τὰ μὲν πέψαντες, τὰ δὲ (viz. ἄλφιτα) μάξαντες Pl. l. c.: metaph., μάττειν ἐπινοίας Ar.*Eq*.539:—Med., εὐλόγου(ς) αἰτίας ματτόμενον Pall. *in Hp.Fract*.12.286C.:—Pass., μᾶζα μεμαγμένη Archil.2; μᾶζαν ὑπ' ἐμοῦ μεμ. Ar.*Eq*.57, cf. 1167; σῖτος μεμαγμένος dough *ready kneaded* (or *pressed into cakes*), Th. l. c., cf. Ar.*Pax*28; ὅστις ἀλφιτοσιτεῖ, ὕδατι μεμαγμένην (μεμιγ- codd.) ἀεὶ τὴν μᾶζαν ἐσθίει prob. cj. in X.*Cyr*.6.2.28, cf. Agathocl.6. II. *wipe*, ῥοδόπηχυς Ἠὼς μαξαμέ[νη χεῖρας ?] *Inscr.Prien*.287; cf. εἰσμάσσομαι. III. *take the impression of, cling close to*, Med. c. acc., *AP* l. c.

⊛**μάσσων**, ὁ and ἡ, neut. μάσσον (v. Hdn.Gr.2.942), gen. μάσσονος, poet. Comp. of μακρός (from μᾰκ-γων), *longer*, ἔτι μ. Od.8.203; μάσσον' ἢ ὡς ἰδέμεν *greater* than one else could see, Pi.*O*.13.113; μάσσον' ἀριθμοῦ *too many* for counting, Id.*N*.2.23; τὰ μάσσω μὲν τί δεῖ

λέγειν; A.*Ag*.598, cf. *Pers*.440; ὁ μ. βίοτος ib.708 (troch.); [ἔλαφοι] μάσσονες ἢ ταῦροι Call.*Dian*.102: c. acc. cogn., μῆκος μάσσων Nic.*Th*. 224: in Prose, μ. ὁδός X.*Cyr*.2.4.27; μάσσω δρόμον (prob.) Id.*Lac*. 12.5. Adv., μάσσον ὡς ἐμοὶ γλυκύ (nisi leg. μάσσον' ὤν) A.*Pr*.629.

**μάστα**· ἡγεμών, ἢ μεγάλως, Hsch.

**μαστάζω**, = μασάομαι, *chew, eat*, Nic.*Th*.918.

**μασταλίδες**· χάρακες, κάμακες, Hsch.

⊛ **μάσταξ**, ἄκος, ἡ (Lyc.687), (μασάομαι) *that with which one chews, mouth, jaws*, ἐπὶ μάστακα χερσὶ πίεζε he stopped his *mouth* with his hands, Od.4.287; με.. ἑλὼν ἐπὶ μάστακα χερσίν seizing me by the *mouth*, 23.76, cf. Alcm.144; ἀμαυρᾶς μάστακος προσφθέγμασι Lyc. l. c.; μάστακι ποππύζων *AP*5.284.6 (Agath.), cf. 293.16 (Id.). 2. v. μύσταξ. II. = μάσημα, *mouthful, morsel*, ὡς δ' ὄρνις ἀπτῆσι νεοσσοῖσι προφέρησι μάστακ', ἐπεί κε λάβῃσι Il.9.324, cf. Eust.753.62; μάστακα δοῖσα τέκνοισιν Theoc.14.39; of the olive, Call.*Iamb*.1. 271; others expl. in Il. l. c. as dat. μάστακι *in its beak*, Apollon.*Lex*. s. v. μάσταξ, Plu.2.494d. III. *locust*, S.*Fr*.716, Nic.*Th*.802, Clitarch.Gloss.ap.*EM*216.9. (Cf. μέστακα.)

**μαστάριον**, τό, Dim. of μαστός I. 2, Alciphr.1.31 (pl.). II. Dim. of μαστός II. 3, prob. in *IG*11(4).1307.23, 1308.2 (v. *Supp.Epigr*. 3.665) (Delos). III. *cover* of an alembic, Syn.Alch.p.60 B.

**μαστᾰρύζω**, *mumble*, like one with his mouth full, of an old man, Ar.*Ach*.689; cf. μασταρίζειν· μαστιχᾶσθαι, καὶ τρέμειν, κτλ., Hsch.:— also **μαστηρύζειν**· τὸ κακῶς μασᾶσθαι (Cyren.), Phot.

**μαστ-εία**, ἡ, *inquiry*, μ. τεχνική Olymp.*in Alc*.p.192 C. **-ειρα**, ἡ, fem. of μαστήρ, metaph., μῆνις μ. *demanding vengeance*, A.*Supp*. 163 (lyr.); glossed μαστιγωτική in Sch. l. c., whence μαστίκτειρα has been conjectured in A. l. c. **-είω**, = μαστεύω, *GDI*1570 (Dodona, dub.). **-ευσις**, εως, ἡ, *search*, *IG*4²(1).123.133 (Epid., iv B.C.); *investigation*, τινων Archim.*Spir.Praef*.; *search for*.., c. gen., γῆς ἀμείνονος D.H.1.56. **-ευτέον**, *one must inquire*, Max.Tyr.34. 4. **-ευτής**, οῦ, ὁ, = μαστήρ, X.*Oec*.8.13. **-εύω**, Ep. impf. **-εύεσκον** A.R.4.1394; poet. inf. μαστευέμεν Pi.*P*.3.59: poet. aor. μάστευσα ib.4.35:—*seek, search after*, c. acc. pers. vel rei, τὴν μαστεύων Hes.*Fr*.79.4; μαστεύων σε κιγχάνω μόλις E.*Hel*.597; ἄλλον ἄλλη μ. [Epich.]298, cf. *IG*4²(1).122.24 (Epid.); [χώραν] X.*An*.5.6. 25; τὰ φεύγοντα διώκειν καὶ μ. ib.7.3.11; *crave, need*, τὰ ἐοικότα πὰρ δαιμόνων μ. Pi.*P*.3.59; προφήτας δ' οὔτινας μαστεύομεν A.*Ag*.1099. 2. c. inf., *seek, strive* to do, Pi.*P*.4.35, *N*.8.43, X.*An*.3.1.43, *Cyr*.2.2.22; τὸν.. παῖδα μ. μαθεῖν, εἰ μηκέτ' εἴη E.*Ph*.36:—Med., Aesar.ap.Stob. 1.49.27, Philostr.Jun.*Im*.17:—Pass., ἀδονὰ σφοδρότερον -ομένα Metop.ap.Stob.3.1.115.—Poet. word (Hom. uses only ματεύω), also used by X., and in late Prose, Nic.Dam.4 J., etc. **-ήρ**, ῆρος, ὁ, (μαίομαι) *seeker, searcher*, τινος S.*OC*456, *Tr*.733, E.*Ba*.986 (lyr.): also in late Prose, Parth.1.1, Alciphr.1.11; μ. ἀναγκαίας ζωῆς Porph. *Abst*.2.5: as fem., Carc.5.5 (s. v. l.); cf. μάστειρα. II. μαστῆρες, οἱ, *officers appointed to ascertain and get possession of* the assets of public debtors and exiles at Athens, Hyp.*Fr*.133; at Amorgos, *IG* 12(7).62.54. **-ήριος**, α, ον, *good at search*, Ἑρμῆς A.*Supp*.920.

**μαστιάω**, = μαστίζω, only in Ep. part. μαστιόων, Hes.*Sc*.431.

**μαστῑγ-έω**, f.l. for μαστιγόω (q. v.). **-ία**, = *flagrum*, *Gloss*. (dub.). II. a kind of plant used in magic, *PMag.Par*.1. 3009. **-ίας**, ου, ὁ, (μάστιξ) *one that wants whipping, a rogue*, S.*Fr*.329 (pl.), Ar.*Eq*.1228, *Ra*.501, Pl.*Grg*.524c, Men.*Pk*.134, Plu. 2.829b, etc. **-ιάω**, Com. Desiderat. of μαστίζω, *long for*, i. e. *deserve, a whipping*, Eup.429. **-ιον**, ου, τό, Dim. of μάστιξ, *whip*, M.Ant.10.38.

**μαστῑγο-νομέομαι**, Pass., *to be governed by the scourge* (i. e. as slaves), D.S.8*Fr*.24. **-νόμος**, ον, = μαστιγοφόρος, Plu.2. 553a. **-φορέω**, *bear the scourge*, D.S.8*Fr*.24, *Mon.Ant*.23.68 (Perga). ⊛ **-φόρος**, ον, *scourge-bearing*, ὑπηρέται Arist.*Ath*.35.1; epith. of Ajax, Arg.S.*Aj*. II. Subst., *policeman*, esp. at the Games, Th.4.47, Luc.*Herm*.40: generally, of attendants on officials, μ. οἰκονόμου *PTeb*.121.58 (i B.C.), cf. 179 (ii B.C.); ἄνδρας μ. *PCair. Zen*.80.4 (iii B.C.).

**μαστῑγ-όω**, opt. μαστιγοίην (v. l. -οῖμι) Aeschin.2.157: fut. -ώσω X.*Cyr*.1.4.13: aor. -ωσα Hdt.7.54:—Pass., fut. μαστιγωθήσομαι Lxx *Ps*.72(73).5, μαστιγώσομαι Pl.*R*.361e, *IG*2².1362.9: aor. part. -ωθείς Phld.*Rh*.2.180 S.:—*whip, flog*, Hdt.1.114 (μαστιγέων codd.), 3.16, 7.54; μυρίκῃ ἢ μαλάχῃ Luc.*Ind*.3:—Pass., Lys.1.18, etc.; πληγὰς μαστιγούσθω *let him be whipped*, Pl.*Lg*.914b, cf. 845a; ψυχῆς ἠσκημένης καὶ μεμαστιγωμένης Max.Tyr.25.5. **-ώσῐμος**, ον, *that deserves whipping*, Luc.*Herod*.8. **-ωσις**, εως, ἡ, *whipping, flogging*, Charicles ap.Ath.8.350c (pl.). **-ωτέος**, α, ον, ἐστὶ μ. he *must be whipped*, Ar. *Ra*.633. **-ωτικός**, ή, όν, gloss on μάστειρα (q. v.), Sch.A.*Supp*.163.

⊛ **μαστ-ίζω**, Nonn.*D*.2.645, Dor. -ίσδω Theoc.7.108: Ep. aor. μάστιξα Il.5.768:—Pass., aor. ἐμαστίχθην v. l. in Hdt.1.114; part. μαστιχθείς *AP*9.348 (Leon. Alex.): (μάστιξ):—*whip, flog*, μάστιξεν δ' ἵππους Il. l. c., etc.; τυ.. ὑπὸ.. ὦμους μαστίσδοιεν (v. supr.) Theoc. l. c.: c. inf., μάστιξεν δ' ἐλάαν *whipped* them on or forward, Il.5.366, Od.6.82, etc.: metaph., ἵνα.. σε πολλοὶ μαστίζωσι λόγοις *Epigr.Gr*. 303.5 (Smyrna). 2. *stimulate* the bowels, Steph. *in Hp*.2.311 D.:— Pass., ib.312 D.—Ep. word, used twice in Com., Eup.72, Alex.133.5, also in Lxx *Nu*.22.25, *Wi*.5.11 (Pass.); and in late Prose, Plu.*Alex*. 42, Luc.*Pr.Im*.24, etc.; the Att. form being μαστιγόω. **-ίκτειρα**, ἡ, v. μάστειρα. **-ίκτωρ**, ορος, ὁ, *scourger*, A.*Eu*.159 (lyr.).

**μαστίον**, τό, *cup* in the form of a breast, *IG*7.3498.15, al. (Oropus).

⊛ **μάστ-ιξ**, ῖγος, ἡ, *whip, scourge*, mostly for driving horses, Il.5.748, etc.; μ. λιγυρῇ 11.532; ἵππου μ. horse-*whip*, Hdt.4.3; λιγυρὰ μ. διπλῆ S.*Aj*.242 (anap.); later, *scourge*, ὑπὸ μαστίγων διαβαίνειν to cross under *the lash*, of soldiers flogged on, Hdt.7.56, cf. 103; τοξεύειν ὑπὸ μ. X.*An*.3.4.25; τῇ μ. κνάπτειν Cratin.275; μάστιγ' ἔχων *whip* in hand, Ar.*Th*.933, Phryn.Com.36. II. metaph., *scourge, plague*, μάστιξ Διός Il.12.37, 13.812; μάστιγι θείᾳ.. ἐλαύνομαι A.*Pr*.682; πληγεὶς θεοῦ μάστιγι Id.*Th*.608; διπλῇ μ., τὴν Ἄρης φιλεῖ, i. e. fire and sword, Id.*Ag*.642; μ. [Θεοῦ], of sickness, *Ev.Marc*.5.34, cf. 3.10 (pl.); but μάστιξ Πειθοῦς the *lash* of eloquence, Pi.*P*.4.219:—Ion. μάστις (q. v.): μάστιγξ is not found. **-ῐς**, ιος, ἡ, Ion. for foreg., dat. μάστῑ Il.23.500; acc. μάστιν Od.15.182, *AP*6.234 (Eryc.):—also **μαστίδες**· ἀκίδες ἢ ἀγκύλαι, Hsch. **-ιστής**, οῦ, ὁ, *scourger*, v. l. for ὑπασπιστής, Lxx 4*Ma*.9.11.

**μαστῑχᾶτον**, τό, *mastich-wine*, Alex.Trall.8.2.

**μαστῑχάω**, *gnash the teeth*, Ep. dat. part. μαστιχόωντι Hes.*Sc*. 389:—Med., gloss on μασταρίζειν, Hsch.

**μαστῑχ-έλαιον**, τό, *mastich-oil*, Dsc.1.42 (in lemmate). ⊛ **-η**, ἡ, *mastich*, μ. τρώγειν *Com.Adesp*.338; obtained from σχῖνος, *mastich, Pistacia Lentiscus*, or from ἰξίνη, *pine-thistle, Atractylis gummifera*, Thphr.*HP*9.1.2, cf. Dsc.1.70; the latter distd. as ἡ ἀκανθική Thphr.*HP*6.4.9; used as a cosmetic, Luc.*Ind*.23, *Alex*. 21. **-ηρά** (sc. ἔμπλαστρος), ἡ, a plaster, Aët.15.15(a) Z. **-ῖνος**, η, ον, *prepared with mastich*, ἔλαιον Dsc.1.42, Gal.11.870, Philagr.ap. Orib.5.19.10.

**μαστίω** [ῐ], poet. form of μαστίζω in pres. and impf., *whip, scourge*, μάστιε νῦν Il.17.622, cf. Hes.*Sc*.466, Pancrat.*Oxy*.1085.15, Nonn.*D*. 1.179, al.:—Med., οὐρῇ δὲ πλευράς τε καὶ ἰσχία ἀμφοτέρωθεν μαστίεται Il.20.171.

**μαστό-δεσμος**, ὁ, = sq., Gal.18(1).774. **-δετον**, τό, *breast-band*, *AP*6.201 (pl., Marc. Arg.). **-ειδής**, ές, *like a breast*, Arist.*HA* 529ᵃ18; πλακοῦς Sosib.ap.Ath.3.115a; λόφος μ. a *small round* hill, Plb.5.70.6; πέτρα D.S.17.75; ἀποφύσεις *mastoid* processes, Gal.*UP* 11.20; ἐκφύσεις (in the womb) Diocl.*Fr*.27.

**μαστός**, ὁ, Ep., Ion. **μαζός**, Hom., Hdt. (exc. in 3.133, 5.18, where codd. give μαστός; twice in codd. of Trag., A.*Ch*.531, E.*Ba*.701); Dor. **μασδός** Theoc.3.16,48; later **μασθός** Lxx *Is*.32.12 (cod. A), al., Asclep.ap.Gal.13.934, *Apoc*.1.13 (v. l.), *IG*3.238*b*, *PMag.Lond*.121. 208, etc., also in codd. of A.*Ch*.545:—usage contradicts the statement of Gramm. that μαζός is *the man's breast*, μαστός *the woman's*:— *breast*, δεξιτερὸν κατὰ μαζόν Il.5.393; of men's breasts, βάλε δουρὶ στέρνον ὑπὲρ μαζοῖο 4.528; βάλε στῆθος παρὰ μαζόν 8.121, cf. Od.22.82, X.*An*.1.4.17, 4.3.6. 2. more freq. of *a woman's breast*, μαζὸν ἀνέσχε, of Hecuba pleading with Hector, Il.22.80; εἴ ποτέ τοι λαθικηδέα μαζὸν ἐπέσχον ib.83; γυναῖκά τε θήσατο μαζόν sucked her *breast*, 24.58; παῖς δέ οἱ ἦν ἐπὶ μαζῷ Od.11.448; σὺ δέ μ' ἔτρεφες.. τῷ σῷ ἐπὶ μαζῷ 19.483; so φαίνουσαι τοὺς μαζούς Hdt.2.85; τοὺς μ. ἀποταμοῦσα Id.4.202; ἐπὶ τοῦ μαστοῦ ἔφυ φῦμα Id.3.133; προὔκειτο μαστῶν περονὶς S.*Tr*.925; προσέσχε μαζόν, of the mother, A.*Ch*.531; μαστὸν ἀμφέχασκε, of the child, ib.545, cf. 897; μαστῶν ἀποσπάς S.*El*.776; πῶλον ἀφέλξων σῶν ἀπὸ μαστῶν E.*Hec*.142 (anap.), etc. b. rarely of animals, *udder*, Id.*Cyc*.55 (lyr.), 207, Call.*Jov*.48. c. generally, of the *breasts* of all mammalia, Arist.*HA*521ᵇ21, *PA*688ᵃ18 sq., *GA* 752ᵇ23. II. metaph., *any round, breast-shaped object*: 1. *round hill, knoll*, Pi.*P*.4.8, X.*An*.4.2.6, Call.*Del*.48. 2. *round piece of wool* fastened to the edge of nets, X.*Cyn*.2.6, cf. Poll.5. 29. 3. at Paphos, *breast-shaped cup*, Apollod.Cyren.ap.Ath.11. 487b, cf. *IG*7.3498 (Oropus), 11(4).1307.21 (Delos).

**μαστρ-εία**, ἡ, Elean μαστράα *Schwyzer* 409.6 (v B.C.):— = εὔθυνα, *IG*5(1).1433.15,16 (pl., Messen., i A.D.); μαστρίαι· αἱ τῶν ἀρχόντων εὔθυναι, Hsch. ⊛ **-ικός**, ή, όν, *concerning* μαστροί, νόμος *SIG*671 *A* 5 (Delph., ii B.C.).

**μαστροπ-εία**, ἡ, *pandering*, X.*Smp*.3.10, Plu.2.632e. ⊛ **-εύω**, = προαγωγεύω, τινα X.*Smp*.4.57; μ. τινὰ πρὸς τὴν πόλιν *seduce* one into public life, ib.8.42, cf. Luc.*Tim*.16: metaph., αἰσθήσεις μ. ἡδονῇ Ph.1.40. **-ικός**, ή, όν, *ready to pander*: Adv. Sup. μαστροπικώτατα Sch.S.*Aj*.520. **-ίς**, ίδος, ἡ, fem. of sq., Lib.*Decl*.40.46 (pl.). ⊛ **-ός**, ὁ and ἡ, *pimp* or *procuress*, Ar.*Th*.558, Diph.43.22 (both fem.), Luc.*Symp*.32 (masc.): metaph., X.*Smp*.4.57 (masc.), Luc.*Am*.16 (fem.). II. as Adj., μάστροπα ἔργα τελοῦντες, = μαστροπικοί, Man.4.306. **-ώδης**, ες, *like a pander*, λόγοι Sch.E. *Hec*.826.

⊛ **μαστρός**, ὁ, = μαστήρ II, title of financial officials, at Pellene, Arist. *Fr*.567; at Rhodes, *IG*12(1).677.35 (iii B.C.), al., cf. Hsch.; at Delphi, *SIG*671 *A* 3 (ii B.C.). (Cf. μαίομαι.)

**μαστρ-οφός**, ὁ, = μαστροπός, Hsch. **-υλλεῖον, -ύλλιον**, f.ll. for ματρυλεῖον (q. v.). **-υς**, υος, ἡ, = μαστροπός, Phot. s. v. ματρυλεῖον.

⊛ **μαστύς**, ύος, ἡ, Ion. for μάστευσις, Call.*Fr*.277.

**μαστώδης**, ες, = μαστοειδής, *Gloss*.

⊛ **μᾰσύντης**, ου, ὁ, = μασητήρ: nickname of a *parasite*, Hsch.

**μασχαλέον**· κάνεον, πίναξ, Hsch.; cf. μασχάλιον.

**μασχάλ-η** [χᾰ], ἡ, *arm-pit*, ὑπὸ μασχάλῃ *h.Merc*.242, etc.; in pl., Ar.*Ach*.852, *Ec*.60; μασχάλην αἴρειν, = κωθωνίζεσθαι, Cratin.298; οἰνωμένος μ. ἆραι Ael.*Ep*.15; of animals, λύκοι νεβρὸν φέρουσιν ἀμφὶ μασχάλαις A.*Fr*.39; μ. τῶν ἐμπροσθίων σκελῶν, of elephants, Arist. *PA*688ᵇ5. II. in trees and plants, *hollow at base of a shoot, axil*, Thphr.*CP*1.6.4; hence, *branch*, Id.*HP*3.15.1. 2. *young palm-twigs* for making baskets or ropes, Hsch. 3. *part of the olive-leaf*, Id.; *of the leaf of* ἀνδρόσαιμον, Dsc.3.156. III. *bay*, Str.6.2.3. 2. *corner*, ἁ βυβλίνα μ. *Tab.Heracl*.1.92. IV.

in a ship, *the part of the* πρῷρα *to which the* ἀρτέμων *is fastened*, Hsch. V. part of a dirigible χελώνη, Ath.Mech.34.5. -ήττει· ὑπὸ κόλπον καὶ ὑπὸ μάλην φέρει, Hsch. -ιαία πλίνθος, *corner-stone*, $IG1^2$.372.13,98; φλέψ *basilic* vein, Paul.Aeg.6.40, Steph. *in Gal.*1.304 D. ⊛-ίζω, *put under the arm-pits*: hence, *mutilate* a corpse, since murderers believed that by cutting off the extremities (nose, ears, etc.), stringing them together, and passing the string round the neck and under the arm-pits of the victim they would avert vengeance, A.*Ch.*439 (lyr., Pass.), S.*El.*445 (Pass.), cf. Ar.Byz.ap. Phot., Suid. s.v. μασχαλίσματα, *EM*118.29,*574.202, etc. -ιον, also -ινον, τό, *basket of palm-leaves*, Hsch., Sch.Orib.2.743 D.; cf. μασχαλέον. -ίς, ίδος, ἡ, = μασχάλη II, Thphr.*HP*3.7.5, Ctes.*Fr.*57. 28 (pl.). II. = μασχαλιστήρ I, Hsch. ⊛-ίσματα, τά, *extremities cut off from a corpse*, S.*Fr.*623. 2. *flesh of the shoulders*, laid on the haunches at sacrifices, Hsch., Suid. -ισμός, ὁ, *mutilation*, S.*Fr.*623. -ιστήρ, ῆρος, ὁ, *girth passing round the horse behind his shoulders* and fastened to the yoke by the λέπαδνον, Poll. 1.147, Hsch. II. generally, *girth, band*, A.*Pr.*71, Hdt.1.215; μ. ἔνλιθος *CPR*22.5 (ii A.D.). III. *second dorsal vertebra*, Poll.2. 178. -όν· τὸν χιτῶνα, Hsch.

**μᾰτᾴζω**, = ματάω, *speak* or *work folly*, S.*OT*891 (lyr.); σπλάγχνα δ' οὔ τι ματᾴζει my heart *is* not *deceived*, A.*Ag.*995 (lyr.).—On the form cf. Hdn.Gr.2.929, *EM*737.21:—**ματαΐζω**, J.*BJ*6.2.10, Suid. (ματᾴζω is prob. contr. fr. *ματαιΐζω.)

**μᾰταιάζω**, = foreg., Epicur.*Ep.*1 p.22 U. (v.l. -αΐζ-), Ph.1.222, al., Luc.*Luct.*16, Palaeph.10, S.E.*M.*9.282 (v.l. ματάζ-, i.e. ματᾴζ-).

**μᾰταιο-βαστάκτης**, *nugigerulus*, *Gloss.* -κομπος, ον, *idly boasting*, Sch.Ar.*Ach.*589. -κοπία, Ion. -ίη, ἡ, = ματαιοπονία, prob. in Hp.*Praec.*12. -λογέω, *talk idly*, Str.2.1.19, Aesop.417, Hsch. s.v. ἐμματάζων, Suid. s.v. θαλαττοκοπεῖς. -λογία, ἡ, *idle talk*, Diogenian.Epicur.2.16, 1*Ep.Ti.*1.6, Plu.2.6f, Vett.Val.150.24 (pl.), al., Porph.*Abst.*4.16. -λόγος, ον, *talking at random*, Telest.1. 9, *Ep.Tit.*1.10, Vett.Val.301.11. -λοιχός, v. ματιολοιχός. -μοχθέω, = ματαιοπονέω, Herm. *in Phdr.*p.66 A. -ποιός, όν, *acting foolishly*, Ath.5.179f. -πονέω, *labour in vain*, Democr.52, Plb.9.2.2, 24. 15.11, Aret.*SD*1.12. -πόνημα, ατος, τό, *work done in vain*, Iamb. *VP*5.24. -πονία, ἡ, *labour in vain*, Str.17.1.28, Plu.2.119e, Luc.*DMort.*10.8. -πόνος, ον, *labouring in vain*, τεχνίτης Ph.2. 500; ματαιοπόνον ἀποκαλεῖν τὴν φύσιν Gal.*UP*5.5, cf. Apollon.Cit. 3. -πρᾱγέω, -πρᾱγία, ἡ, = ματαιοπονέω, -πονία, Eust.543. 4. -πώγων, ωνος, ὁ, *having a beard in vain*, Sch.Theoc.14.28.

⊛**μάταιος** [μᾰ], α, ον A.*Pr.*331, *Th.*442, *Ag.*422 (lyr.), etc.; also ος, ον ib.1151, *Ch.*82, *Eu.*337 (all lyr.), S.*OC*780, E.*IT*628, Pl.*Sph.* 231b, D.1.18: (μάτη):— I. *vain, empty, idle*: 1. of words, acts, etc., μάταια νομίζομεν Thgn.141, cf. 487,492, etc.; μ. λόγοι *idle* tales or words, Hdt.7.10.η′; μ. ἔπεα ib.11; δόξαι φέρουσαι χάριν μ. A. *Ag.*422 (lyr.); μ. ὑλάγματα, ποιφύγματα, ib.1672, *Th.*281; μ. εὐχή E. l.c.; μάταια βάζειν τινά Id.*Hipp.*119; μ. τι δρᾶσαί τινα Id.*Cyc.*662 (lyr.); μ. ἂν εἴη πόνος Pl.*Ti.*40d; μ. ἡδονή S. l.c.; δοξοσοφία Pl.*Sph.* l.c.; ὄρεξις Arist.*EN*1094$^a$21; τὰ μ. ἀναλώματα *useless* expenses, *POxy.*58.20 (iii A.D.); but also, μ. ἔπος a word *of offence*, Hdt.3. 120. 2. of persons, *empty, foolish*, ματαιότεροι νόον Thgn.1025, cf. Hdt.2.173, S.*Tr.*863,888 (lyr.), Ar.*V.*338, Amips.9 (Sup.); φῦλον ματαιότατον Pi.*P.*3.21; *worthless*, S.*Ant.*1339 (lyr.). II. *rash, irreverent, profane*, freq. in A., μ. γλῶσσα *Pr.* l.c., *Ag.*1662 (troch.); φρονήματα *Th.*438; αὐτουργίαι μ., of matricide and the like, *Eu.* l.c.; χαρὰ μ. *mad* merriment, *Th.*442; μ. ἀνοσίων τε κνωδάλων *Supp.*762; τὸ μὴ μ. *seriousness, gravity*, ib.198; ψαύειν ματαίαις χερσί S.*Tr.* 565. III. Adv. -ως *idly, without ground*, ib.940, Emp.39.2, E.*Fr.*908.4; ὀχλεῖν τοῖς ἀνθρώποις Aen.Tact.6.1; μ. ἐρεῖν *to no purpose*, Pl.*Ep.*331d; ταλαιπωρῆσαι Polystr.p.31 W. -οσύνη, ἡ, = ματαιότης, Polem.*Phgn.*13, al.

**μᾰταιό-τεκνος**, ον, *having illegitimate children*, gloss on ἀλιτόκαρπος, Hsch., *EM*65.15. -τεχνία, ἡ, *useless art*, Quint.2.20.3, Gal. *Protr.*9; [*pictura*] apud veteres μ. dicta est, Serv.Dan.ad Verg.*A.*1. 464.

**μᾰταιότης**, ητος, ἡ, *vanity, purposelessness*, ματαιότης ματαιοτήτων Lxx *Ec.*1.2, cf. Ph.1.426; τῇ μ. ἡ κτίσις ὑπετάγη *Ep.Rom.*8.20; *folly*, ἀνθρώπων Phld.*Rh.*2.26 S.

**μᾰταιουργός**, όν, = ματαιοποιός, Ph.2.98.

**μᾰταιό-φημος**, ον, = ματαιολόγος, Phot. s.v. λῆρος. -φρονέω, gloss on ματᾴζω, Sch.S.*OT*891. -φροσύνη, = κενοφροσύνη, Phot. -φρων, ὁ, ἡ, gen. φρονος, *weak-minded*, Lxx 3*Ma.*6.11, Adam.2.24. -φωνία, ἡ, *idle talk*, Phot. and Suid. s.v. κενοφωνία. -φωνος, ον, *talking idly*, Hsch. s.v. μαψίφωνος.

**μᾰταιόω**, *bring to naught*, Sch.S.*Tr.*258, *Gloss.* 2. ματαιοῦσιν ἑαυτοῖς ὅρασιν *invent* a vision of their own, Lxx *Je.*23.16. II. more freq. in Pass., *to be brought to naught*, οὐ ματαιωθήσεται τὰ ῥήματα ib.*Ju.*6.4. 2. *become foolish, act foolishly*, ἐματαιώθην σφόδρα ib.1*Ch.*21.8, cf. *Ep.Rom.*1.21; μεματαίωταί σοι thou *hast done foolishly*, Lxx 1*Ki.*13.13.

⊛**μᾰταϊσμός** or **μᾰτασμός**, ὁ, = *crepitus ventris*, Pl.Com.61 (pl.), Seleuc.ap.Ath.2.76f (pl.).

**μάταν**, Adv., Dor. for μάτην. II. **μάταν**· ἡ λύγξ, ἔνιοι δὲ **ματακὸς** ἢ **ματακόν**, Hsch. **μάταξα**, ἡ, v. μέταξα. **μάταρος**· στέφανος μεμαρασμένος, Id. (fort. μαδαρός).

**μᾰτάω**, (μάτην):—poet. Verb, *to be idle, dally*, ἀπέκοψε παρήορον οὐδὲ μάτησε Il.16.474, cf. 23.510; μὴ τὼ μὲν (sc. ἵππω) δείσαντε ματήσετον 5.233; οὐ ματᾷ τοὔργον the work *lags* not, goes on apace, A.*Pr.*57; ματᾶν ὁδῷ *to loiter* by the way, Id.*Th.*37; ἰδώμεθ', εἴ τι τοῦδε φροιμίου ματᾷ *is in vain, is fruitless*, Id.*Eu.*142; of persons, *fail of* a thing, τινος Opp.*H.*3.102.

**μᾰτευ-τής**, οῦ, ὁ, = μαστευτής, κακεμπορίης Man.4.268. -ω, fut. -σω Il.14.110: aor. ἐμάτευσα Pi.*O.*5.24:—= μαστεύω, abs., *seek, search*, ἐγγὺς ἀνήρ, οὐ δηθὰ ματεύσομεν Il. l.c.; οἴκοθεν μάτευε Pi.*N.*3.31, cf. S.*OC*211 (lyr.). 2. c. acc., *seek for, search after*, ματεύει ὧν ἀνευρήσει φόνον A.*Ag.*1094, cf. *Ch.*219, S.*Ph.*1210 (lyr.), *Ichn.*13, etc.; θάνατον εὑρέμεν μ. ἐλάφῳ Simon.30 (cj.). 3. c. inf., *seek, strive to* do, μὴ ματεύσῃ θεὸς γενέσθαι Pi.*O.*5.24, cf. S.*OT*1052. 4. c. acc. loci, *search, explore*, ματεύει ἄλλος ἀλλοίαν κέλευθον B.9.35; πάντα Ar.*Th.*663; τὰ χωρία Theoc.21.65.

**μάτη** [ᾰ], ἡ, *folly, fault*, μάτας εἰπών speaking *folly*, Stesich.47, cf. A.*Ch.*918 (pl.); μάταισι πολυθρόοις with clamorous *lewdness*, Id.*Supp.* 820 (lyr.) (but expld. by Sch. as 'quest'); οὔ τί τοι μέτρον μάτας S.*Fr.*798. II. cf. μάτην ad fin.

***μάτημι** (A), Aeol., = ματεύω, in 2 sg. pres. μάτης, ἐξ ἑτέρω ἕτερον μ. Theoc.29.15:—Pass., Ion. ματεῖσθαι, = ζητεῖσθαι, Hp.ap.Erot. (Hsch. has ματεῖ· ζητεῖ.)

⊛***μάτημι** (B), Aeol., = πατέω, Alc.*Supp.*31.3: pres. part. fem. μάτεισαι Sapph.54.

**μάτην**, Dor. **μάταν** [μᾰ], Adv. *in vain*, *h.Cer.*308, Pi.*O.*1.83, etc.; μὴ πόνει μ. A.*Pr.*44; βλέποντες ἔβλεπον μ. ib.447; μ. ἐρεῖν ib.1007; with a Noun, τὸ μ. ἄχθος the *fruitless* burden, Id.*Ag.*165 (lyr.); Διὸς μ. ἄκοιτις his bedfellow *to no good end*, S.*Tr.*1149: as predicate, μ. ὁ μόχθος A.*Ch.*521. 2. *at random, without reason*, οὔ σε μ. τιμῶσι Thgn.523; ὅρα μὴ μ. κόμπος ὁ λόγος ᾖ Hdt.7.103, cf. E.*Supp.* 127; οὐ γὰρ δίκαιον . . τοὺς κακοὺς μ. χρηστοὺς νομίζειν S.*OT*609; ἵνα μὴ μ. θαρρήσῃς Pl.*Tht.*189d; ὁ νοσῶν μ., i.e. he that is mad, S.*Aj.*635 (lyr.), cf. Ar.*Pax*95 (anap.). 3. *idly, falsely*, λέγοντες εἴτ' ἀληθές, εἴτ' ἄρ' οὖν μ. S.*Ph.*345; λόγῳ μάτην θνήσκοντες Id.*El.*63, cf. 1298; μ. βέβακεν, of a dream, A.*Ag.*423 (lyr.).—Originally acc. of μάτη, and we find εἰς μάτην in Luc.*Trag.*28,241, Aristid.*Or.*33(51).3; ἐπὶ μ. *POxy.*530.8 (ii A.D.).

**μᾰτήρ**, ῆρος, ὁ, = μαστήρ, Hsch. **μάτηρ** [ᾱ], ἡ, Dor. for μήτηρ. **μᾰτηρεύω**, (ματήρ) = ματεύω, Id., Phot.

**μᾰτία**, Ion. -ίη, ἡ, (μάτη) *vain attempt, bootless enterprise*, ἡμετέρῃ ματίῃ Od.10.79. 2. *folly, error*, A.R.1.805, 4.367.

⊛**μᾰτίζω**, = ματεύω, in aor. inf. ματίσαι, Hsch. (leg. ματῆσαι).

**μᾰτιολοιχός**, ὁ (on the accent v. Hdn.Gr.1.231), Ar.*Nu.*451, expld. as = κρουσιμέτρης, from **μάτιον**, τό, *trifle, scrap*, by Sch. ad loc.: **ματαιολοιχός**· ὁ περὶ τὰ μικρὰ πανοῦργος καὶ λίχνος, Hsch.:—Bentley cj. **ματτυολοιχός** (in both places), v. ματτύη.

**μάτιον**, τό, Egyptian measure of capacity, *Arch.Pap.*5.178 No.32, *Ostr.*296 (ii A.D.), al., *PTeb.*314.18 (ii A.D.), *PLond.*5.1906 (vi A.D.), prob. in *PAmh.*2.130.5 (i A.D.); hence **ματιαῖον** μέτρον *Sammelb.* 4683.6.

**μάτος** [ᾰ], τό, or ὁ, *search*, Hp.ap.Gal.19.120.

**ματραδελφεός, ματρο-δόκος, -ξενος, ματρόθεν, ματρυιά**, Dor. etc. for μητρ-.

**μᾰτρῠλεῖον**, τό, *brothel*, Din.*Fr.*43.5, Men.*Epit.*429, Plu.2.752c; written **ματρύλλιον** or **μαστρύλλιον** ib.1094a, Poll.6.188.

**μάτρυλλος**, ὁ, fem. **μάτρυλλα**, ἡ, *pimp*, Phryn.*PS*p.84 B., Eust. 380.5.

**μάτρως, μᾱτρωσμός**, Dor. for μητρ-.

**ματταβεῖ**· περιβλέπει, ἀδημονεῖ; also **ματταβόμενος**· μέλλων καὶ ἀποκνῶν, **ματτάβης**· ἀπορῶν, and **μάτταβος**, ον, = μωρός, Hsch.

**ματτῠάζω**, *eat* or *dress a* ματτύη, Alex.49.

**ματτύη** [ῠ] (not -ύα), ἡ, Nicostr.Com.8, Sophil.4.5, Macho 1; but **ματτύης**, ου, ὁ, Artem.ap.Ath.14.663d; gender doubtful in Philem. 9,12, Alex.205:—*a rich, highly-flavoured dish*, made of hashed meat, poultry, and herbs, and served cold as a dessert, of Macedonian or Thessalian origin, cf. Poll.6.70 (ματύλλη codd.).—Especially freq. in the New Comedy acc. to Ath.14.662f: but **ματτυολοιχός** is prob. cj. for ματιολοιχός (q.v.).

**ματτῠοκόπης**, ου, ὁ, a nickname, = ματτυολοιχός, Amm.Marc.15. 5.4.

**μαῦδι**· λαοτομίον, Hsch. **μαυδός**, dub. sens. in Hdn.Gr.1. 142. **μαυκυρόν**· τὸ χλιαρόν, Hsch.

**μαῦλ-ις** (A), ιδος, or ιος, ἡ, *bawd, procuress*, Hsch.: hence, -ίζω, = μαστροπεύω, Id. s.v. μαστροπός, Sch.Ar.*Nu.*976: -ιστής, οῦ, ὁ, = μαστροπός, *Cat.Cod.Astr.*8(4).212, Phot. and Suid. s.h.v.: fem. -ίστρια, *EM*695.31, Sch.Ar.*Nu.*976, Suid. s.v. πυγοστόλος: -ιστήριον, τό, *bawd's hire*, Hippon.126; but also, *brothel*, *PLond.*5.1877.7 (vi A.D.).

⊛**μαῦλις** (B), ἡ, *knife*, acc. μαῦλιν Call.*Aet.*3.1.9; dat. μαύλιδι Nic. *Th.*706; nom. pl. μαύλιες *AP*15.25 (Besant.):—also **μαυλία**, ἡ, in acc. pl. -ίας, Sch.Th.1.6, Suid.

⊛**μαυρός**, όν, = ἀμαυρός, Hdn.Gr.1.193 (μαῦρος codd.); **μαῦρος** Hsch.; cited (without transl.) as properisp. by Gal.18(2).518.

⊛**μαυρόω**, = ἀμαυρόω, *darken, blind*: hence, *make powerless*, dub. in A.*Eu.*358 (lyr.), cj. in Pi.*I.*4(3).48. 2. metaph., *make dim* or *obscure*, ῥεῖα δέ μιν μαυροῦσι θεοί Hes.*Op.*325:—Pass., *become dim* or *obscure*, Thgn.192, A.*Ag.*296.

⊛**Μαύσσωλλος**, *SIG*167.2, al. (Mylasa, iv B.C.), or **Μαύσσωλος**, ib. 169.3 (Iasos, iv B.C.), or **Μαύσωλος** (as freq. in codd.), ὁ, *Mausolus*, a Carian noble, Hdt.5.118; another, called satrap or king, X.*Ages.* 2.26, D.15.3, *SIG* ll.cc., etc.:—Adj. **Μαυσσώλλειος** or -εος, τετράδραχμα *IG*11(2).161 *B*21, al. (Delos, iii B.C.): **Μαυσωλεῖον**, τό, *tomb*

*of M.* at Halicarnassus, Plin.*HN*36.30:—hence, as appellat., *mausoleum*, Str.5.3.8, Paus.8.16.4 (pl.).

⊛ **μᾰφόριον**, τό, = sq., *BGU*948.19 (iv/v A.D.), *Sammelb.*7033.39 (v A.D.).

⊛ **μαφόρτ-ης**, ου, ὁ, *veil, head-dress* of women and priests (cf. *Gloss.*), *BGU*845.15 (ii A.D.), etc.; also, = *peplus, ricinus*, *Gloss.*; Dim. ⊛ **-ιον**, τό, *POxy.*1295.19 (ii/iii A.D.), *PMeyer*23.6 (iv A.D.), etc.

**μάχαιρ-α** [μᾰ], ας (later -ης, dat. -ῃ, *PTeb.*16.14 (ii B.C.), *Ev.Luc.*21.24, etc.), ἡ, *large knife* or *dirk*, Il.11.844, 18.597, 19.252; μ. ἣ οἱ πὰρ ξίφεος μέγα κουλεὸν αἰὲν ἄωρτο 3.271; *carving-knife*, Pi.*O.*1.49, Hdt.2.61, Ar.*Eq.*489, Pl.*R.*353a, etc.; κοπίδες μ. E.*Cyc.*242; *sacrificial knife*, Ar.*Pax* 948, Pl.Com.91, *Michel* 832.52 (Samos, iv B.C.):—ἡ Δελφικὴ μ. a knife adapted to various purposes, Arist.*Pol.*1252$^{b}$2, cf. Hsch. s.v. Δελφικὴ μ.; prov., of greedy persons, because Delphian sacrificers claimed a share for the knife, *App.Prov.*1.94. 2. as a weapon, *short sword, dagger*, Pi.*N.*4.59, Hdt.6.75, 7.225, Lys.13.87, etc.; an assassin's weapon, Antipho 5.69; used by jugglers, Pl.*Euthd.*294e (pl.), etc.; later, *sabre*, opp. the straight sword (ξίφος), X.*Eq.*12.11, cf. *HG*3.3.7, *Cyr.*1.2.13, *Ev.Matt.*26.52, etc.; οἱ ἐπὶ τῆς μ., of a bodyguard, Arr.*Epict.*1.30.7; but, ἐπὶ μ. τασσόμενοι possessing power of life and death (*jus gladii*), *Cat.Cod.Astr.*8(4).173; μ. ἱππική cavalry *sabre*, *IG*11(2).161*B*99 (Delos, iii B.C.). 3. μ. κουρίδες, *shears* or *scissors*, Cratin.37; κεκαρμένος μοιχὸν μιᾷ μ., i.e. with one *blade*, Ar.*Ach.*849, cf. Poll.2.32 (where διπλῇ is f.l.), Hsch. s.v. μιᾷ μαχαίρᾳ; μ. κουρικαί Plu.*Dio* 9. 4. metaph., διὰ μαχαιρῶν καὶ πυρός Zen.3.19, cf. Posidipp.1.10; μ. τοῦ πνεύματος *Ep.Eph.*6.17, cf. Lxx *Is.*49.2. II. name of a precious stone, Arist.*Mir.*847$^{a}$5, Ps.-Plu.*Fluv.*10.5. III. part of the liver, Ruf.*Onom.*180. ⊛ **-ᾶς**, ᾶ, ὁ, *cutler*, *POxy.*1676.6 (iii A.D.). ⊛ **-ίδιον** [ῐ], τό, Dim. of μάχαιρα, Ph.2.530 (pl.), Luc.*Pisc.*45. **-ιον**, τό, = foreg., X.*An.*4.7.16, Men.765, *PEleph.*5.13 (iii B.C.), Str.12.2.10; *surgeon's* or *barber's knife*, Hp.*Medic.*6,7, Arist.*GA*789$^{b}$13, *Metaph.*1061$^{a}$4, *Com.Adesp.*327, Plu.*Brut.*13, Ruf.*Ren.Ves.*12.12. **-ίς**, ίδος, ἡ, butcher's *cleaver*, Ar.*Eq.*412; *knife*, μικρὰ μ. Plu.*Art.*19, cf. Luc.*Ind.*29; *dagger*, Str.16.4.17; pl., *shears, scissors*, ὁ κουρεὺς τὰς μ. λαβών Eup.278, cf. Poll.10.140.

**μᾰχαιρίων**, ωνος, ὁ, = ξιφίον, Dsc.4.20; v.l. μαχαιρώνιον.

**μᾰχαιριωτός**, ή, όν, = μαχαιρωτός, καυτήρ v.l. in Paul.Aeg.6.62.

**μᾰχαιρο-δέτης**, ου, ὁ, *sword-belt*, Hsch. **-θήκη**, ἡ, *case for knives*, *Michel* 832.52 (Samos, iv B.C.). **-κ[οπέω]**, *cut with a* μάχαιρα, dub. in *UPZ*119.40 (ii B.C.). **-μᾰχέω**, *fight with a* μάχαιρα, Plb.10.20.3:—Subst. **-μᾰχία**, gloss on ξιφιστύς, Hsch. **-ποιεῖον**, τό, *cutler's factory*, D.27.31. **-ποιός**, ὁ, *maker of cutlery*, Ar.*Av.*442, D.27.9, Plu.*Dem.*4, Luc.*Rh.Pr.*10. **-πώλης**, ου, ὁ, *cutler*, Poll.7.156. **-πώλιον** or **-εῖον**, τό, *cutler's shop*, Plu.*Dem.*15, Poll. l.c.

**μᾰχαιρ-ουργός**, όν, = μαχαιροποιός, Tz.*H.*6.132.

**μᾰχαιρο-φορά**, ἡ, *sword-bearing, wearing of arms*, Wilcken *Chr.*13.9 (i A.D.). **-φορέω**, *wear a sabre*, J.*AJ*18.2.4, *BJ*3.5.5. **-φόρος**, ον, *wearing a sabre*, of Egyptians, Hdt.9.32; μ. ἔθνος, of Persians, A.*Pers.*56 (anap.); of Thracians, Th.2.96, 7.27:—as Subst., *swordsman*, Plb.38.7.2, Plu.*Sull.*8, etc.; freq. of military *police* in Egypt, *PAmh.*2.38 (ii B.C.), *PTeb.*35.13 (ii B.C.), *OGI*737.6 (ii B.C.), *Sammelb.*46, *Ostr.Bodl.* iii 64, etc. **-φυλλον**, τό, = *gladiolus*, prob. in *Gloss.*

**μᾰχαιρ-ώνιον**, v. μαχαιρίων. **-ωτός**, ή, όν, *sabre-shaped*, πρίων Gal.18(2).331, cf. Paul.Aeg.6.62.

**μαχαίτας**, v. μαχητής.

**Μᾱχᾰν-εῖος**, ὁ (sc. μήν), month at Chalcedon, *SIG*1011.7 (iii/ii B.C.). **-εύς**, ῆος, ὁ, title of Zeus at Cos, ib.1026.10 (iv/iii B.C.); at Tanagra, *IG*7.548; at Argos, *SIG*56.29 (v B.C.), Paus.2.22.2. 2. (sc. μήν), month at Corcyra, *IG*9(1).694. **-ίς**, ίδος, ἡ, title of Athena at Cos, *SIG*1026.21 (iv/iii B.C.). **-ῖτις**, ιδος, ἡ, title of Aphrodite and Athena at Megalopolis, Paus.8.31.6, 8.36.5.

**μᾰχ-ᾱτάρ, -ᾱτάς**, v. μαχητής. **-άω**, (μάχη) *wish to fight*, Hsch. **-ετέον**, *one must fight*, Arist.*Rh.*1403$^{a}$9 (v.l. μαχητέον), Plu.2.181c. ⊛ **-η**, ἡ, (μάχομαι) *battle, combat*, freq. in Hom., usu. of armies, μ. καὶ φύλοπις Il.13.789; ἐπὶ ἶσα μ. τέτατο πτόλεμός τε 12.436; μ. ἐνοπή τε 12.35; μάχαι τ' ἀνδροκτασίαι τε 7.237; sts. of *single combat*, ib.158, 232, 263; μ. καὶ δηϊοτής ib.290; ναῶν ἐν μάχαις Pi.*N.*9.34; μάχαις καὶ ναυμαχίαις Lys.30.26; μάχῃ δορός A.*Ag.*439 (lyr.), etc.: with Verbs, μάχην μάχεσθαι fight *a battle*, Il.15.414, etc.; θήσονται μ. 24.402; μάχας εἰσήλυθον 2.798; ἀρτύνθη μ. 11.216; μ. ἤγειραν 17.261; μ. ὀρνύμεν, ὤτρυνον, 9.353, 12.277; συμφερόμεσθα μάχῃ 11.736; πειρᾶτο μάχας Pi.*N.*1.43; ἀντιάζειν τινὶ μάχαν ib.67; σὺν γυναιξὶ τὰς μ. ποιούμενος S.*El.*302, cf. X.*Cyr.*3.3.29; μάχην συνάψαι ἐμβολαῖς A.*Pers.*336; μ. συμβάλλειν τινί engage *battle* with.., E.*Ba.*837; διὰ μάχης τινὶ ἀπικέσθαι, ἔρχεσθαι, ἥκειν, Hdt.1.169, 6.9, A.*Supp.*475; διὰ μάχης ἐκβαλεῖν τινα Arist.*Pol.*1303$^{a}$35 (so ἐξέπεσον διὰ μάχης ib.34); εἰς μάχην πρός τινα ἐλθεῖν, μολεῖν, E.*Ba.*636 (troch.), *Ph.*694; ἐς μάχην ἐπεξιέναι τινί Th.2.23; μάχης γενομένης Pl.*Lg.*869c; μάχῃ κρατῆσαι conquer *in battle*, E.*HF*612, D.18.193 (with v.l. μάχην); νενικήκαμεν τὴν μεγάλην μ. X.*Cyr.*7.5.53; Μιλτιάδης ὁ τὴν ἐν Μαραθῶνι μ. τοὺς βαρβάρους νικήσας Aeschin.3.181; μάχη τινός *battle with* an enemy, Αἴαντος δ' ἀλέεινε μ. Il.11.542, cf. Hes.*Sc.*361; μ. ὑπέρ τινος Pi.*N.*7.42; περί τι Pl.*Lg.*919b: pl., *strifes*, ἔρις τε..πόλεμοί τε μάχαι τε Il.1.177; μάχας ἐν λόγοις ποιεῖσθαι Pl.*Ti.*88a, etc.: generally, *contention, strife*, Id.*Ep.*352c, etc.; μάχης ἐάν τις ἄρξηται *SIG*1109.72 (ii A.D.); μ. νομικαί *Ep.Tit.*3.9. 2. = ἀγών, *contest*, as for a prize in the games, Pi.*O.*8.58 (but ἄεθλα, opp. μάχαι πολέμου, Id.*O.*2.44). 3. *struggle*, μηχανή τε πολλὴ καὶ μ. ἦν περί τινος X.*Cyr.*7.5.38. II. *mode of fighting, way of battle*, ἡ μ. σφέων ἦν ἀπ' ἵππων Hdt.1.79; ἐπίστασθαι τὴν μ. τινῶν Id.7.9.α', cf. 7.85, X.*Cyr.*2.1.7. III. *field of battle*, interpol. in Id.*An.*2.2.6, 5.5.4. IV. in Logic, *contradiction, inconsistency*, Epict.*Ench.*52.1, S.E.*M.*7.392. **-ήμων**, ον, gen. ονος, *warlike*, Il.12.247; βῶλος, of the soil of Colchis, *AP*4.3$^{b}$.22 (Agath.). **-ηνδε**, *to battle*, Theoc.25.136. **-ητέον**, *one must fight*, Mnesim.7, Plu.*Pomp.*32. ⊛ **-ητής**, οῦ, ὁ, Aeol. **μαχαίτας** Alc.33; Dor. **μαχᾱτάς** Pi.*N.*2.13, etc.; Lacon. **μαχᾱτάρ** (-άταρ cod.) Hsch.: (μάχη):—*fighter, warrior*, μικρὸς μὲν ἔην δέμας ἀλλὰ μ. Il.5.801; θείειν ταχὺς ἠδὲ μ. Od.3.112; Τρῶάς φασι μ. ἔμμεναι ἄνδρας 18.261; φὼς μ. Pi.*N.* l.c.: as Adj., μαχατὰν θυμὸν αἰσχυνθῆμεν his *warrior* heart, ib.9.26: in later Prose, Lxx *Jo.*6.3, al. **-ητικός**, ή, όν, *fit for fighting*, ὀδόντες μ. Arist.*PA*662$^{b}$34; *warlike*, μ. παιδιαί Id.*Rh.*1371$^{a}$1; of persons, *pugnacious*, ib.1381$^{a}$32, etc.; μ. περὶ κέρδους ib.1372$^{b}$31: ἡ -κή (sc. τέχνη), *skill in fighting*, Pl.*Sph.*225a; τὸ -κόν ibid.; μ. ἵπποι *restive* horses, Id.*R.*467e. Adv. -κῶς *pugnaciously*, Id.*Tht.*168b; *in a hostile manner*, μ. διακείμενα Simp.*in Cael.*197.9. **-ητός**, ή, όν, *to be fought with*, κακὸν ἄγριον οὐδὲ μ. Od.12.119.

⊛ **μάχῐμ-ος** [ᾰ], η, ον, also ος, ον Hdt.7.185: (μάχη):—*fit for battle, warlike*, ἐπειδὴ μ. εἶ since you're *a fighting man*, Ar.*Av.*1368; αἱ μάχιμοι μυριάδες Hdt. l.c.; τὸ μ. the *effective force*, Th.6.23, X.*Cyr.*5.4.46; τὸ τῆς πόλεως μ. Pl.*Lg.*830c (but ἀνέωνται ἐς τὸ μ. = ἐς πόλεμον Hdt.2.165); μ. γένη Pl.*Mx.*240a; τὸ μ. γένος Id.*Ti.*24a, cf. Arist.*Pol.*1268$^{a}$36; τὸ μ. (sc. ἔθνος) Pl.*Criti.*110c; esp. in Egypt, οἱ μ. τῶν Αἰγυπτίων the *warrior caste*, Hdt.2.141, cf. 164; so later, of *native troops*, freq. in Pap., *PTeb.*61(*a*).109 (ii B.C.), etc.: Comp. -ώτερος Plb.2.22.6: Sup. -ώτατος Hdt.3.102, Ar.*Ach.*153, Th.1.110; τὰ μ. τῶν ἔργων Philostr.*Her.*2.19. Adv. -μως Arr.*Epict.*2.9.5. 2. = sq., *Gloss.* II. *disputable*, S.E.*M.*8.45. **-ώδης**, ες, *quarrelsome*, *AP*12.200 (Strat.).

**μαχλ-άς**, άδος, poet. fem. of μάχλος (also late Prose, Ph.1.40, al., Artem.4.11), Man.4.357, *AP*5.104 (Marc. Arg.), 301.2 (Agath.); of things, *wanton, luxuriant*, ἐλπίς ib.9.443 (Paul. Sil.). **-εύομαι**, *to be lewd*, in pf. part. Pass., μεμαχλευμένον ἦτορ Man.4.315. **-ης**, ου, ὁ, = μάχλος, Hsch.:—fem. **μαχλίς**, Id. **-ικός**, ή, όν, *like a* μάχλος, Man.4.184. **-οίονας**· τοὺς αὐτομόλους Αἰθίοπας, Hsch. **-οίων**· κρομμύων, Id. ⊛ **-ος**, ον, *lewd, lustful*, of women (λάγνος (q.v.) being used of men), μαχλόταται δὲ γυναῖκες Hes.*Op.*586, cf. Ephor.96 J.; μ. ἐς ἄνδρας Aeschrio 8.6, cf. Ach.Tat.8.1; of a man, Luc.*Alex.*11; of Ἡδονή personified, Ph.2.267. 2. metaph., *wanton, luxuriant*, ἄμπελος A.*Fr.*325. b. *wanton, insolent*, Ἄρης Id.*Supp.*636 (lyr.). **-οσύνη**, ἡ, *lewdness, lust*, of Paris, Il.24.30 (rejected by Aristarch. as a word peculiar to women, but used of Paris as effeminate), cf. Hes.*Fr.*28, Hdt.4.154, Adam.1.10, *AP*5.301.10 (Agath.). **-ότης**, ητος, ἡ, = μαχλοσύνη, *EM*594.24, Sch.Lyc.771.

**μάχομαι** [ᾰ], Ion. pres. opt. μαχέοιτο Il.1.272, μαχέοιντο ib.344 (v.l. μαχέονται); part. μαχεόμενος v.l. in Hdt.7.104 (elsewh. μαχόμενος, 9.75, al.); Ep. μαχειόμενος Od.17.471, μαχεούμενος 11.403, 24.113: Ep. impf. μαχέσκετο Il.7.140: fut. μαχήσομαι 23.621, Hdt.7.209; μαχέσομαι, δια-μαχεσόμεθα (as v.l.) Id.9.48; also in late Prose, J.*AJ*11.8.3, Plu.2.215f; μαχοῦμαι S.*OC*837, Ar.*Pl.*1076, etc., μαχεῖται even in Il.20.26, but μαχέονται 2.366; Ep. μαχέσσομαι v.l. for μαχήσομαι 1.298: aor. ἐμαχεσάμην Hdt.1.18, etc.; opt. μαχέσαιο Il.6.329; inf. μαχέσασθαι 17.178, also μαχέσσασθαι 15.633; opt. μαχεσσαίμεσθα Theoc.22.74; part. μαχεσσαμένω Il.1.304; later μαχήσασθαι Paus.1.27.1, (ἀνα-) D.S.19.93: pf. μεμάχημαι Th.7.43, Lys.7.41, Isoc.6.54: late aor. ἐμαχέσθην Plu.2.970f, Paus.5.4.9: fut. μαχεσθήσομαι only Sch.rec.A.*Th.*672:—*fight*, Hom., etc.; ὑσμῖνι μ. Il.2.863; πολεμίζειν ἠδὲ μ. ib.452, etc.; μάχην μ. X.*Ages.*5.5: in Hom. mostly of armies and persons fighting as parts of armies, but sts. of single combat, Il.3.91, 433, 7.51, 111, 279, Od.18.31, 39; between men and beasts, Il.15.633, Od.20.15; between beasts, Il.16.824:—Constr.: c. dat. pers., *fight with*, i.e. *against*, one, ἀνδράσιν ἶφι μ. Il.1.151, cf. S.*Ph.*1253, etc.; μ. ἀντία, ἐναντίον τινός, Il.20.88, 97; ἐπί τινι 5.124, etc.; πρός τινα 17.471, but πρὸς δαίμονα *against* heaven's will, ib.98 (in Att. Prose, mostly c. dat. or πρός, μ. τοῖς πολεμίοις D.4.47; πρὸς ἀλλήλους Isoc.4.116); μ. σὺν σοί,..θεά, *with thy help*, Od.13.390; μετὰ πρώτοισι μ. among the foremost, Il.5.575; μετὰ Βοιωτῶν μ. with them, in their ranks, 13.700; πρός τινας μετ' ἀλλήλων Isoc.10.53, cf. Pl.*Smp.*179a; κατὰ σφέας γὰρ μαχέονται *will fight* by themselves, Il.2.366 (but κατ' ἕνα μ. *fight* in single combat, Hdt.7.104); μ. πρό τινος before him: hence, metaph., for him, in his defence, Il.4.156, 8.56, X.*HG*5.4.33, etc.; ὑπὲρ τοῦ νόμου Heraclit.44; πάτρας ὕπερ E.*Ph.*1002; Ἕλλησιν ὑπὲρ Ἑλλήνων Pl.*Mx.*239b; περὶ δαιτί Od.2.245; but later usu. περί τινος, A.*Supp.*740, Cratin.163, Hdt.1.95; ἀμφί τινι Il.3.70, 91; ἀμφὶ νέκυι 16.565; εἵνεκά τινος 2.377: c. dat. instrum., τόξοισι, πελέκεσσι μ., 7.140, 15.711 (χερσὶ μαχέσσασθαι, of boxers, Od.18.39); μ. ἀπ' ἵππου *fight* from horseback, Hdt.9.63; τὸ μήπω μεμαχημένον *the force that had* not yet *come into action*, Th.7.43. 2. c. acc., *fight against*, only f.l. in Philostr.*Im.*2.23. II. generally, *quarrel, wrangle*, ἔριδι μ. Il.1.8; μ. ἐπέεσσιν ib.304, etc.; τινι 5.875, 13.118; τῷ παιδὶ μ. *make a scene* with.., Thphr.*Char.*23.8; *dispute, argue*, περί τι μ. Pl.*R.*342d, etc. III. *contend for the mastery* in games, etc., πὺξ μ. Il.23.621; *measure oneself with* or *against*, τινι 1.272; παγκράτιον μ. Ar.*V.*1190, 1195; μ. Ὀλυμπιάδα Philostr.*Gym.*21. IV. after Hom., *struggle against* a

force, ἀνάγκᾳ δ' οὐδὲ θεοὶ μ. Simon.5.21; ὄμβρῳ Alc.*Supp.*26.4; πρὸς ἡνίας μ. A.*Pr.*1010; πρὸς ἐπιθυμίας ἢ ἡδονάς Pl.*La.*191e; μ. τῷ λιμῷ, τῷ δίψει, X.*Cyr.*3.1.5. V. c. inf., *struggle, make an effort* to do, Arist.*HA* $552^{a}23$. VI. of arguments, propositions, etc., *to be in contradiction* or *inconsistent*, τρία ὁμολογήματα μ. αὐτὰ αὑτοῖς Pl.*Tht.* 155b, cf. Plb.16.28.4; μαχόμενα Phld.*Mus.*p.95 K., S.E.*P.*1.198, al.

**μᾰχομένως**, Adv. *self-contradictorily*, Str.2.1.40, S.E.*M.*1.281, Iamb.*Myst.*1.18.

**μάψ** (A), a bird, Hdn.Gr.1.404. [ᾱ by nature.]

**μάψ** (B), Adv. *in vain, without result*, μ. οὕτω..πολεμίζειν Il.2.120; *without aim or object*, 20.298. II. *vainly, falsely*, μ. ὀμόσαιμι 15.40; μ. αὔτως εὐχετάασθαι 20.348; *thoughtlessly, recklessly*, σῖτον ἔδοντας μ. αὔτως Od.16.111; μ. ἀτὰρ οὐ κατὰ κόσμον Il.2.214, 5.759; *in haste*, Od.3.138.—Ep. word, in compds. Poet., mostly Ep.

**μαψ-αῦραι**, ῶν, αἱ, (αὔρα) *random breezes, gusts of wind*, Hes.*Th.* 872, cf. Call.*Fr.*67 (al. divisim μὰψ αὖραι ἐπιπνείουσι θάλασσαν). II. as Adj., μαψαῦραι στόβοι *idle* boastings, Lyc.395. **-ίδιος**, ον (also η, ον, v. infr.), (μάψ B) *vain, false*, τὸ δ' ἐμὸν ὄνομα..μαψίδιον ἔχει φάτιν E.*Hel.*251 (lyr.); γλῶσσα μ. Theoc.25.188; *useless, worthless*, μαψιδίη κόνις *AP*7.602 (Agath.). II. in Hom. only Adv. μαψιδίως, = μάψ, *thoughtlessly, at random*, Il.5.374, al.; *without reason*, κεχολῶσθαι Od.7.310; *rashly, recklessly*, 2.58, 14.365; μ. ἀλάλησθε, of pirates, 3.72.

**μαψῐ-λόγος**, ον, *idly talking*, μ. οἰωνοί birds *whose cries convey no sure omen*, *h.Merc.*546. **-τόκος**, ον, *bringing forth in vain*, λαγόνες *AP*14.125 (Metrod.). **-φωνος**, ον, = μαψιλόγος, Hsch.

**μαψ-ῠλάκᾱς** [ᾰκ], α, ὁ, (ὑλάω, ὑλακτῶ) *idly barking*, i.e. *repeating* a thing *again and again*, Pi.*N.*7.105: μαψυλάκαν γλῶσσαν (fem.) prob. for μαψυλάκταν in Sapph.27.

**μάψωτος**· μάταιος, Hsch.

***μάω**, v. μαίομαι, μέμονα, μῶμαι.

**μεγα-βρεμέτης**, ου, ὁ, = μεγαλοβρεμέτης, ποταμός Orph.*A.*749. **-βυξος**, ὁ, a Persian pr. n. (Hdt.3.70, al.) and later title of generals and priests, *Bagabukhša*, lit. 'set free by God', Hdt.3.153, al., *SIG* 282.2 (Priene, iv B.C.), X.*An.*5.3.6, Str.14.1.23, App.*BC*5.9, Hsch., etc.:—hence **-βύξειοι** λόγοι, *boastings*, Id. (Usu. -βυζ- in codd., as Str., App., and Hsch. ll. cc., but -βυξ- in *SIG* l. c., v. l. in Hdt.3.153, 160, al., *-bux-* Quint.5.12.21 codd., *-byx-* Plin.*HN*35.93 codd. opt.) **-δάκτῠλος**, ὁ, *big toe*, Orib.ap.Aët.11.35. **-δωρος**, ον, = μεγαλόδωρος, ἄρουρα Opp.*C.*3.29. **-θαμβής**, ές, *greatly astounded*, ib.2.488. **-θαρσής**, ές, *very bold*, Hes.*Sc.*385, Man. 2.372.

**μέγᾰθος**, τό, Ion. for μέγεθος, Hdt.

**μεγάθῡμος** [ᾰ], ον, *great-hearted*, Ἀχιλλεύς Il.20.498, cf. Hes.*Th.* 734, etc.; Ἀχαιοί Il.1.123, al.; Ἀθήνη Od.8.520, 13.121, cf. Orac. ap.Phleg.*Fr.*36.3 J.; ταῦρος Il.16.488.

⊛ **μεγαίνητος**, ον, *illustrious*, B.1.44, 3.64.

**μεγαίρω**, aor. ἐμέγηρα, (from μέγας, cf. γεραίρω from γεραρός (γέρας)) prop. *regard as too great*: hence, I. *grudge* one a thing *as too great* for him, μέγηρε γάρ οἱ τό γ' Ἀπόλλων Il.23.865; ἐγὼ δέ τοι οὔ τι μεγαίρω Orac.ap.Hdt.1.66. 2. c. inf. pro acc. rei, μηδὲ μεγήρῃς ἡμῖν εὐχομένοισι τελευτῆσαι τάδε ἔργα *grudge* us not the accomplishment.., Od.3.55, cf. *h.Merc.*465: c. acc. et inf., μνηστῆρας..οὔ τι μεγαίρω ἔρδειν ἔργα βίαια I *complain* not that.., Od.2.235; ὃν οὐδέ κεν αὐτὸς ἀείδειν Φοῖβος..μεγαίροι Theoc.7.101: c. inf. only, ἀμφὶ δὲ νεκροῖσιν κατακαιέμεν οὔ τι μεγαίρω I *object* not to [your] burning them, Il.7.408: with inf. understood, τάων οὔ τοι ἐγὼ πρόσθ' ἵσταμαι, οὐδὲ μεγαίρω (sc. διαπέρσαι) 4.54, cf. Call.*Del.*163. 3. c. dat. pers. only, *feel a grudge towards*, Δαναοῖσι μεγήρας Il.15.473. 4. abs., ἢ πὺξ ἠὲ πάλῃ ἢ καὶ ποσίν, οὔ τι μεγαίρω I *care* not which, Od.8.206. 5. c. gen. rei, ἀμενήνωσεν δέ οἱ αἰχμὴν..Ποσειδάων, βιότοιο μεγήρας Poseidon baffled his spear *grudging* him the life [of Antilochus], Il.13.563; οὐ μ. τοῦδέ σοι δωρήματος A.*Pr.*626; μοι..ἐμέγηρε τόκοιο A.R.1.289. 6. Pass., *to be envied*, *AP*9.645.10 (Maced.). II. = βασκαίνειν, *bewitch*, ὄμμασι..ἐμέγηρεν ὀπωπάς A.R.4.1670. (Said to be a Salaminian word, Sch.Il.13.563: in late Prose, as etym. of Μέγαιρα, Corn.*ND* 10.)

⊛ **μεγᾰ-κήτης**, ες, (cf. κητώεις) *yawning, with mighty hollows*, μεγακήτεα πόντον Od.3.158; *with mighty maw*, δελφίς Il.21.22; *capacious*, νηῦς 8.222, 11.5, 600. (Also expld. as derived from κῆτος, μ. πόντος *teeming with monsters*, μ. νηῦς *with a monster as figurehead.*) ⊛ **-κλεής**, ές, *very famous*, acc. (as if from μεγακλής) μεγακλέᾰ Opp.*C.*2.4. II. parox. Μεγακλέης as pr. n. **-κῡδής**, ές, *much renowned*, *IG*3.1335, 12(5).677 (Syros), Man.2.150.

**μεγᾰλ-άδῐκος**, ον, *unjust in great matters*, opp. μικραδικητής, Arist.*Rh.* $1391^{a}29$. **-αλκής**, ές, = μεγαλοσθενής, Hsch.

⊛ **μεγᾰλάμπρως**, Adv. *splendidly, munificently*, προσφέρεσθαι πρὸς τὸν δῆμον *Michel* 731.4 (Ilium, ii B.C.).

⊛ **μεγᾰλ-άμφοδος**, ον, *with spacious ways*, Hsch. s. v. εὐρυόδεια. **-ανδροι**· μεγάλοι ἄνδρες, ἢ μεγάλοι κατὰ τὴν ἀνδρείαν, ἢ πολυανδροῦντες, Id. **-ᾱνορία**, **-άνωρ**, Dor. for μεγαλην-. ⊛ **-άρτια** (sc. ἱερά), τά, (ἄρτος) *feast of great loaves*, kept by the Delians in honour of Demeter, Semus 13. **-άρτιος**, ὁ (sc. μήν), month at Halos, *IG* 9(2).109. **-αρτος**, ον, epith. of Demeter in Boeotia, Polem.Hist. 39. **-αυχέω**, *boast, brag*, A.*Ag.*1528 (anap.), Lxx *Ez.*16.50, Ph. 1.284, *AP*5.272 (Agath.); ἐπί τινι Plb.12.13.10; ἐν ταῖς εὐπραγίαις Id.8.21.11; διά τι D.S.15.16:—also in Med., Pl.*Alc.*1.104c, *R.*395d; ἐπί τινι App.*BC*1.13. II. c. acc., *boast of*, μονομάχιον Id.*Gall.* 10. **-αύχημα**, ατος, τό, *matter for boasting*, τὸ μ. καὶ ἀξίωμα Ph. 2.434, cf. Sm.*Ez.*32.12. **-αύχην**, ενος, ὁ, ἡ, *with large neck*, Olymp.Hist.p.459 D., Apollon.*Lex.* s. v. ἐριαύχενας, Hsch. s. v. ἐρισφάραγος. ⊛ **-αυχής**, ές, = μεγάλαυχος, Orph.*H.*63.3, *IG*14.433 (Tauromenium), Man.3.34, Vett.Val.272.8. **-αυχητέον**, *one must boast*, Ph.1.217. **-αύχητος**, ον, *much vaunted*, Epigr.ap.Paus.1.13.3. ⊛ **-αυχία**, ἡ, *boasting, arrogance*, Pl.*Tht.*174d (pl.), *Ly.*206a, Lxx 4*Ma.*2.15. 2. *exultation*, Longin.7.2. **-αυχος**, ον, *boastful, vainglorious*, Pi.*P.*8.15, A.*Pers.*533 (anap.), Pl.*Ly.*206a (Comp.), Ph.1.121; τὸ μ., = foreg. 1, X.*Ages.*8.1. Adv. Sup. *-ότατα*, εἰπεῖν Max.Tyr.7.7.

**μεγᾰλεῖ-ος**, α, ον, (μέγας) *magnificent, splendid*, ῥήματα X.*Mem.* 2.1.34 (Comp.); κτῆμα ib.4.5.2; μ. τι διαπεπραγμένος Men.*Per.Fr.* 1, cf. Phld.*Rh.*2.6 S.; πίστιν -οτάταν prob. in Paean ap.Plu.*Flam.*16 (*Coll.Alex.*p.173 P.); τὸ μ. τῶν πράξεων, τῆς ἀθανασίας, Plb.8.1.1, *SIG*798.4 (i A.D.), cf. Vett.Val.70.1; τὰ μ. *mighty works*, Lxx *De.*11.2, al., *Act.Ap.*2.11. Adv. *-ως greatly*, ὠφελῶν τὴν πόλιν X.*Ages.*11.16, Plb.3.87.5; *magnificently*, μ. εἴρηκας Pl.*Hp.Ma.*291e; ὀψωνεῖν Antiph.192; θεοὺς μ. τιμᾶν X.*Oec.*11.9: Comp. *-ότερον* Pl.*Tht.* 168c; *-οτέρως*, γαμεῖν X.*HG*4.1.9. 2. of persons, *stately, haughty*, Id.*Mem.*4.1.4. 3. τὸ μ. τινός, as a title, *Highness*, *POxy.*1204.10 (iii A.D.), etc. 4. of style, *elevated*, Demetr.*Eloc.*14, al. Adv. Sup. *-ότατα*, ἑρμηνεῦσαι Philostr.*VS*1.21.1. **-ότης**, ητος, ἡ, *majesty, magnificence*, Lxx *Je.*40(33).9, *Ev.Luc.*9.43, Ath.4.130f, Dam.*Pr.*94; ἡ τῶν πυραμίδων μ. *OGI*666.26 (Egypt, i A.D.); of a person, *greatness*, *Supp.Epigr.*3.583.6 (Olbia, ii/iii A.D.). II. as a title, *Majesty*, ἡ σὴ μ. J.*AJ*8.4.3, cf. *CPHerm.*52.23 (iii A.D.); ἐν ταῖς μ. γενήσεται Vett.Val.70.4; also, = Lat. *majestas*, ἡ μ. τοῦ Ῥωμαίων δήμου *PGiss.*40 i 11 (iii A.D.). **-ωτός**, ή, όν, *amplified*, of compound words, prob. in Arist.*Po.* $1457^{a}35$.

**μεγᾰλ-έμπορος**, ὁ, *wholesale merchant*, Sch.Ar.*Av.*823. **-επίβολος**, ον, *attempting great objects*, Plb.15.37.1, D.S.1.19: μεγαλεπήβολος is v.l., cf. Suid. **-επίβουλος**, ον, *harbouring great designs*, Corn. *ND*22. **-ηγορέω**, *talk big, boast*, X.*An.*6.3.18: with neut. Adj., ἕκαστα ἐμεγαληγόρουν Id.*Cyr.*4.4.2, cf. 7.1.17; also τοιοῦτόν τινα λόγον μ. Polem.*Cyn.*45. II. trans., *extol highly*, Hdn.3.9.12. **-ηγορία**, ἡ, *big talking*, E.*Heracl.*356 (pl., lyr.), X.*Ap.*1, Man.2.468 (pl.). II. *elevation, sublimity* of diction, D.H.*Th.*27, Demetr.*Eloc.*29. **-ήγορος**, ον, *talking big, vaunting*, A.*Th.*565 (lyr.), X.*Cyr.*7.1.17. Adv. *-ρως* App.*Hisp.*19, *Mith.*70. 2. *lofty, magniloquent*, Longin.8.4. **-ηνορία**, Dor. **-ᾱνορία**, ἡ, *manliness, self-confidence*, Pi.*N.*11.44 (pl.). 2. *haughtiness*, E.*Ph.*184 (lyr., sed -ηγορ- Sch.). **-ήνωρ**, Dor. **-άνωρ**, ορος, ὁ, ἡ, (ἀνήρ) *high-souled*, epith. of Ἡσυχία, Pi.*Fr.* 109. 2. *haughty*, Id.*P.*1.52. **-ήτωρ**, ορος, ὁ, ἡ, (ἦτορ) *great-hearted*, Πάτροκλος Il.16.257; Κύκλωψ Od.10.200, cf. D.P.658, etc.: in Hom. always with pr. ns., exc. in phrase μεγαλήτορα θυμόν Il.9.629, Od.9.500, al.; μεγαλήτορες ὀργαί Pi.*I.*5(4).34. **-ήφᾰτος**, ον, *in lofty strain*, ὕμνος prob. for μελαν- in Orph.*A.*421 (μέλανα σκότον Abel). **-ίζομαι**, Pass., *to be exalted, bear oneself proudly*, μηδὲ μεγαλίζεο θυμῷ Il.10.69; *οὔτ' ἄρ τι μεγαλίζομαι οὔτ' ἀθερίζω* Od.23.174.—Ep. word.

**μεγᾰλικώτατος**, η, ον, late Sup. of μέγας, μ. δίφθογγος Sch.D.T. p.199 H.

**Μεγάλλειον** μύρον, a perfumed unguent named after the inventor Megallos (cf. Ar.*Fr.*536, Stratt.33), Pherecr.140, Anaxandr.46, Eub.90.6, Amphis 27, cf. Dsc.1.58:—wrongly written **μεγαλεῖον** in Thphr.*Od.*29, al.

**μεγᾰλό-βῐος**, ον, *illustrious in life*, Paul.Al.*N.*2. **-βλᾰβής**, ές, *greatly injuring*, Apollon.*Lex.* s. v. ἄτη. **-βόας**, α, ὁ, *loud-shouting*, κήρυκες Agath.4.1. **-βόος**, ον, gloss on ἠερίβοια, Eust.562.40. **-βοτος**, ον, gloss on ἱππόβοτος, Apollon.*Lex.* s. h. v. **-βουλος**, ον, *high-counselling*, Pap. in *Sitzb.Heidelb.Akad.* 1923(2).14, Sch.rec.A.*Pr.*18. **-βρεμέτης**, ου, ὁ, *loud-thundering*, Ζεύς Q.S.2.508. **-βρομος**, ον, *loud-roaring*, ὕδωρ Orph.*A.* 463. **-βρῡχος**, ον, *loud-bellowing*, λέων Q.S.5.188. **-βωλος**, ον, *with large clods*, Sch.D Il.1.155. **-γάστωρ**, ορος, ὁ, ἡ, *big-bellied*, Sch.A.*Th.*1035.

**μεγᾰλογκία**, Ion. **-ίη**, ἡ, *hugeness*, Democr.3.

**μεγᾰλο-γνωμονέω**, *entertain noble sentiments*, D.C.63.25. **-γνωμοσύνη**, ἡ, *loftiness of sentiment*, X.*Ages.*8.3. **-γνώμων**, ον, gen. ονος, *of lofty sentiments, high-minded*, Id.*Oec.*21.8: τὸ μ., = foreg., Philostr.*Ep.*73, cf. X.*Ages.*9.6. **-γρᾰφέω**, *write with* ω μέγα, opp. μικρογραφέω, Sch.A.*Pers.*297, Hdn.*Epim.*193, 200, Jo.Sic.in Rh.6.89 W., etc. **-γρᾰφία**, ἡ, *painting on a large scale*, Vitr.7.4.4. **-δάπᾰνος** [δᾰ], ον, *munificent*, διάθεσις *IGRom.*4.1302.27 (Aeolis). **-δενδρος**, ον, *full of large trees*, Str.3.2.3, 3.4.2. **-δηλος**, ον, *quite evident, manifest*, Sch.B Il.11.155. **-δοξία**, ἡ, *high opinion of oneself*, in pl., Suid. s. v. ψολοκομπία. **-δοξος**, ον, *very glorious*, Εὐνομία Pi.*O.*9.16; κύριος *OGI*90.1 (Rosetta, ii B.C.); Ῥώμη Plu. *Thes.*1, cf. Herm.ap.Stob.1.49.44. Adv. *-ξως* Lxx 3*Ma.*6.39. **-δουλος**, ὁ, *great slave*, opp. μικρόδουλος, Arr.*Epict.*4.1.55.

**μεγᾰλόδους**, οντος, ὁ, ἡ, *with large teeth*, gloss on ἀργιόδους, *EM* 137.6.

**μεγᾰλο-δῠνᾰμία**, ἡ, *great power*, Hsch. s. v. ἐρισθενέος. **-δύνᾰμος** [ῠ], ον, *very powerful*, Herm. *in Phdr.*p.176 A., *PMag.Lond.*121.881, *PMag.Leid.V.*11.24. **-δωρέομαι**, *make large presents*, J.*AJ*12.4.9. **-δωρία**, ἡ, *munificence*, Luc.*Sat.*4, *DMort.*6.4, *Anach.*9, Hld.9.24, *CPHerm.*121.13 (iii A.D.): pl., Hdn.2.3.9. **-δωρος**, ον, *munificent*, τύχη Democr.176, cf. Max.Tyr.17.2; μεγαλοδωρότατε δαιμόνων Ar.*Pax* 393 (lyr.), cf. Plb.10.5.6, *CPHerm.* $119^{v}$ iii 2 (iii A.D.):

τὸ μ.,= foreg., Plu.*Ant.*4,43. Adv. -ρως Poll.3.119, Jul.*Or.*6.194d. **-ειδῶς**, Adv. *on a large scale*, οἱ τὰ σώματα διηρθρωμένοι μ. Philostr.*Gym.*36. **-είμων**, ονος, ὁ, ἡ, *clad in a large robe*, Eust.1430.25. **-εργέω**, contr. **-ουργέω**, *do great things*, Ph.2.142:—Pass., Id.1.428, al. **-έργημα**, ατος, τό, *great achievement*, Id.2.107,174 (pl.). **-εργής**, contr. **-ουργής**, ές, *performing great deeds*, *Gloss.* Adv. -γῶς ib. **-εργία**, ἡ, *great achievement*, Plb.30.25.1 (s.v.l.); contr. **-ουργία**, Str.3.5.6, Ph.2.143, J.*AJ*2.7.1; *magnificence*, ib.8.3.2, al., Luc.*Cal.*17. **-εργικός**, ή, όν, contr. **-ουργικός**, = -εργής, Procl. *in Alc.*p.137C. **-εργός**, contr. **-ουργός**, όν, = μεγαλοεργής: τὸ μ., = μεγαλοεργία, Plu.*Caes.*58, Luc.*Alex.*4, Procl.*in Prm.*p.663S., al. **-ζηλος**, ον, *very zealous*, gloss on ἀγάζηλος, *EM*5.29. **-ζωνος**, ον, gloss on λιπαρόζωνος, Sch.E.*Ph.*175. **-ημέρευσις**, εως, ἡ, v.l. for μακροημέρευσις, Lxx *Si.*30.22. ® **-ηχος**, ον, *loud-sounding*, gloss on ἐρικλάγκτας, Sch.Pi.*P.*12.38; on ἐριβρεμέτης and ἐρίβρομος, Hsch. **-θριξ**, τρῐχος, ὁ, ἡ, *with strong* or *thick hair*, *Gloss.* ® **-θῡμος**, ον, = μεγάθυμος, Pl.*R.*375c, Thd.*Pr.*19.19. **-θῠτον**, τό, *great sacrifice*, Sch.Lyc.329 (ed. Bachm.).

**μεγάλοιτος** [ᾰ], ον, *very wretched*, Theoc.2.72.

**μεγᾰλο-καμπής**, ές, *with a large curve*, Orib.45.6.6. **-καρπος**, ον, *with large fruit*, Thphr.*HP*4.4.5. **-καυλος**, ον, *with large stalk*, ib.7.6.3. **-κερως**, ων, gen. ω, *with large horns*, Eust.634.56, Sch. Opp.*H.*2.290. **-κευθής**, ές, *concealing much*: *capacious*, θάλαμοι Pi.*P.*2.33. **-κέφᾰλος**, ον, *with large head*, Arist.*Somn.Vig.*457a23, *Pr.*955b7, Gal.19.454. **-κίνδῡνος**, ον, *braving great dangers*, *adventurous*, opp. μικροκίνδυνος, Arist.*EN*1124b8. **-κλεής**, ές, *glorious*, B.7.49, *Lyr.Adesp.Oxy.*860(*a*).10. **-κμής**, ῆτος, ὁ, ἡ, gloss on ἀνδροκμῆσι (i.e. *ἀδροκμῆσι), Sch.A.*Eu.*248. **-κοίλιος**, ον, *with large ventricles*, Arist.*PA*667a29; *with large intestinal canal*, Mnesith. ap.Orib.21.7.6,7 (Sup.):—written **-κοιλος** (= προγάστωρ) in Gal.6.467. **-κολπος**, ον, *full-bosomed*, Νύξ B.*Fr.*23 (leg. μελανό-). **-κορος**, ον, (κόρη III) *with large pupils*, Aët.7.54. **-κόρῠφος**, ον, *with lofty summits*, γῆ Lyc.Orator ap.Arist.*Rh.*1405b36. **-κοτος**, ον, gloss on ζάκοτος, Sch.Pi.*Pae.*9.18, *EM*407.16. Adv. -τως, gloss on ζαφελῶς, Hsch. **-κρακτος**, ον, *loud-screaming*, gloss on ἐρικλάγκτας, Sch.Pi.*P.*12.38. **-κρᾰτής**, ές, *far-ruling*, Ῥώμη *AP*9.657 (Marian.). **-κράτωρ** [κρᾰ], ορος, ὁ, = foreg., Lxx 3*Ma.*6.2. **-κτῠπος**, ον, gloss on ἐρίγδουπος, Hsch. **-κύμων** [ῡ], ον, gen. ονος, *making great waves*, Arist.*Pr.*942a14. **-κωλος**, ον, *large-limbed*, of a locust, Dsc.2.52. **-λᾰλος**, ον, *talking big* or *much*, *Gloss.* **-μαζος**, ον, (μᾶζα) = μεγάλαρτος (q.v.), epith. of Demeter in Boeotia, Polem. Hist.39. **-μᾰνής**, ές, *very frantic*, Sch.S.*Aj.*143. **-μασθος**, ον, *with large breasts*, *Gp.*19.2.4. ®**-μέρεια**, ἡ, *largeness of parts*, opp. μικρομέρεια, Arist.*Metaph.*989a6, Thphr.*Ign.*45. II. generally, *largeness of scale*, *great size*, μ. καὶ δύναμις Plb.1.26.9; τόπου *IG*9(2).1109.77 (Coropa). III. *lavishness*, *munificence*, *OGI* 168.58 (Syene, ii B.C.), *Sammelb.*4321.4 (ii B.C.). **-μερής**, ές, *consisting of large particles*, Pl.*Ti.*62a (Comp.), Arist.*Cael.*303b27. Adv. -ρῶς, κατάγνυται (of bone) Gal.14.792. II. *magnificent*, *sumptuous*, Plb.28.20.1; παρασκευὴ καὶ πότος Id.30.14.1; δεῖπνα *IG*7.2712.61 (Acraeph.), cf. Lxx 3*Ma.*5.8, etc. Adv. -ρῶς, χρῆσθαί τινι *OGI*339.68 (Sestos, ii B.C.), cf. Plb.16.25.3, 31.28.6, Lxx 3*Ma.*6.33, Phld.*Piet.*p.93G., Ant.Lib.18.1, etc.: Comp. -έστερον Plb.24.5.5. **-μέτωπος**, ον, gloss on εὐρυμέτωπος, *EM*396.50. **-μήτηρ**· ἡ τῆς μητρὸς μήτηρ, Hsch. **-μητις**, τι, *of high design*, *ambitious*, A.*Ag.*1426 (lyr.). **-μῑκρος**, ον, *great and small at once*: τὸ μ. Ph.2.61. **-μισθος**, ον, *receiving high pay*, Luc.*Apol.*15, *Herm.*57, Ath.13.569a. **-μοιρία**, ἡ, *magnificence*, Aristeas 21 (dub.). **-μῡκητής**, οῦ, ὁ, *loud bellower*, gloss on μεγάμυκος, Hsch. **-νοια**, ἡ, *magnanimity*, Pl.*Lg.*935b, J.*BJ*1.21.12, Plu.2.401d, Luc.*Apol.*9, Ael.*NA*15.22. II. *elevation of thought*, Luc.*Pisc.*22, Simp.*in Ph.*1147.5. III. as honorific title, ἡ ὑμετέρα μ. *PFlor.*303.7 (vi A.D.). **-νοος**, ον, contr. **-νους**, ουν, *great-minded*, *magnanimous*, Adam.1.11, al.; τὸ φύσει μ. J.*BJ*1.21.5, cf. 5.5.8, Luc.*Im.*18: metapl. pl. -νοες Polem.*Phgn.*29. II. *elevated in diction*, ὕμνοι Men.Rh. p.336S. (Comp. -ούστερος). **-πάθεια** [πᾰ], ἡ, *patience*, *fortitude*, Plu. 2.551c (s.v.l.). ®**-πάρηος** [πᾰ], ον, *with great cheeks*, Apollon.*Lex.* s.v. ἱππόβοτος. **-πενθής**, ές, gloss on νηπενθές, *EM*604.34. **-πετρος**, ον, *on the mighty rock*, Ἀκρόπολις Ar.*Lys.*482 (lyr.). **-πλούσιος**, ον, = sq., Sch.E.*Hec.*493. **-πλουτος**, ον, *exceeding rich*, Eub.37, D.S. 15.58. **-πνοος**, ον, contr. **-πνους**, ουν, *breathing strongly*, Apollon. *Lex.* s.v. ζαής. **-ποιέω**, *do great things*, Lxx *Si.*50.22. II. trans., *magnify*, τὰ ἴδια Hierocl.ap.Stob.4.27.20. **-πόλεμος**, ον, *great in war*, J.*AJ*12.11.2. **-πολις**, epith. of great cities, αἱ μεγαλοπόλιες Ἀθᾶναι Pi.*P.*7.1; μεγαλοπόλιες ὦ Συράκοσαι ib.2.1; ἁ μ. Τροία E.*Tr.*1291 (lyr.); Ἀθθίς *Pae.Delph.*8; ἡ λαμπροτάτη μ. Ἀλεξάνδρεια *PLips.*45.13 (iv A.D.); also of the κόσμος, Ph.1.4, al. ®**-πολίτης** [ῑ], ου, ὁ, *citizen of a large city*, ib.34, Poll.9.25. **-πόνηρος**, ον, *wicked in great things*, Arist.*Pol.*1295b9. **-πορνος**, ὁ, gloss on ἱππόπορνος, Phot. **-πους**, ὁ, ἡ, πουν, τό, gen. ποδος, *with large feet*, Arist.*HA*617a26. **-πρᾱγία**, ἡ, *great fortune*, App.*BC*5.52. **-πραγμοσύνη**, ἡ, *disposition to do great things*, *magnificence*, Plu.*Alc.*6, etc. **-πράγμων**, ον, gen. ονος, *disposed to do great deeds*, *forming great designs*, X.*HG*5.2.36, Plu.*Ages.*32. **-πρέπεια**, Ion. -είη, ἡ, *magnificence*, as a quality of persons, Hdt.1.139, 3.125, Pl.*R.*486a, Isoc.9.2, Arist.*EN*1107b17, etc. III. of style, *elevation*, D.H.*Comp.*16, *Th.*23, Demetr.*Eloc.*37. III. as a title, ἡ σὴ μ. Just.*Nov.*41 *Praef.*; ἡ αὐτοῦ μ. *POxy.*1163.4 (v A.D.). ® **-πρεπής**, ές, *befitting a great man*, *magnificent*, δεῖπνον μ. Hdt.5.18; δωρεὴν μεγαλοπρεπεστάτην Id.6.122; κάλλιστον ἔργον καὶ μεγαλοπρεπέστατον Ar.*Av.*1125; ταφή Pl.*Mx.*234c; προαίρεσις Hyp. *Epit.*40; πράξεις ib.1 (Comp.); δόξα 2*Ep.Pet.*1.17, etc. 2. of persons, Pl.*R.*487a, al., Arist.*EN*1107b17; τὸ μ. X.*Mem.*3.10.5; of a horse, Id.*Eq.*10.1 (Comp.): Sup., as honorific title, *PGrenf.*2.81 (*a*).14 (v A.D.), etc. 3. of style, μ. λόγοι Pl.*Smp.*210d; λέξις Arist. *Rh.Al.*1441b12; μεθιστάναι ἐπὶ τὸ -έστερον ib.1423b12. II. Adv. -πέως, Att. -πῶς, Hdt.6.128, X.*An.*1.4.17, etc.: Comp. -έστερον Id. *Vect.*6.1, Pl.*Ly.*215e: Sup. -έστατα Hdt.7.57. **-πτέρῠγος**, ον, *with great wings*, Lxx *Ez.*17.3,7. **-πτωχος**, ὁ, *magnificently poor*, Διογένης τοὺς μεγάλα καὶ ἀθρόα λαμβάνοντας μεγαλοπτώχους ἐκάλει Stob.3.10.62. **-πῠλος**, ον, gloss on εὐρυπυλής (-εύς cod.), Hsch. **-ρῑνος**, ον. (ῥίς) *with large nose*, Suid. s.v. χαροποὶ βόες. **-ρρέκτης**, ου, ὁ, *one who does great things*, Adam.2.39. **-ρρημονέω**, *to be a boaster*, Lxx *Ju.*6.17, Str.13.1.40. **-ρρημονία**, ἡ, *big talking*, Sch.S.*Ant.*1350 (pl.). **-ρρημοσύνη**, ἡ, = foreg., Lxx 1*Ki.*2.3, Philostr.*Her.*2.19, Anon.ap.Suid. s.v. σεμνομυθοῦσιν. **-ρρήμων**, ον, gen. ονος, *talking big*, Lxx *Ps.*11(12).4, Men.Prot.p.11 D.; in good sense, *magniloquent*, Philostr.*VA*6.11. Adv. -όνως Poll.9.147. **-ρριζος**, ον, *with large roots*, Dsc.2.156, dub. l. in Thphr *CP*2.3.8 (ἐλαιηρότεραι cj. Wimmer). **-ρρώξ**, ρρῶγος, ὁ, ἡ, *with large berries*, βότρυς Str. 15.2.14.

**μεγᾰλος**, v. μέγας.

**μεγᾰλό-σαρκος**, ον, *great of flesh*, Lxx *Ez.*16.26. **-σθενής**, ές, *of great strength*, Hom.*Epigr.*6, Pi.*P.*6.21, Corinn.2, Lxx 3*Ma.*5.13; epith. of Horus, Herm.ap.Stob.1.49.44; of Heracles, *IG*5(1).1119 (Geronthrae). **-σκῖος**, ον, gloss on δάσκιος, *EM*248.51. **-σμάρᾰγος** [σμᾰ], ον, *loud-resounding*, Luc.*JTr.*1. **-σοφιστής**, οῦ, ὁ, = μέγας σοφιστής, Ath.3.113d. **-σπλαγχνος**, ον, *with enlarged abdomen*, Hp.*Acut.*53; *with large viscera*, Mnesith.ap.Orib.21.7.6 (Sup.). 2. *causing the viscera to swell*, οἶνος μ. σπληνὸς καὶ ἥπατος Hp.*Acut.*50. II. *high-spirited*, ψυχή E.*Med.*109 (anap.). **-στάφῠλος** [στᾰ], ον, gloss on ἐριστάφυλος, Sch.D Od.9.358. **-στᾰχυς**, υ, *with large spikes*, νάρδος Dsc.1.7, cf. Thphr.*HP*8.4.3. **-στένακτος**, ον, gloss on ἀγάστονος, *EM*8.54. **-στερνος**, ον, *broad-chested*, Philostr.*Gym.*39. **-στηθος**, ον, = foreg., Mnesith.ap.Orib.21.7.6 (Sup.). **-στομος**, ον, *with large mouth*, Arist.*PA*662a25. **-στονος**, ον, *most piteous*, πήματα A.*Pr.*413 (lyr.). **-σφυκτος**, ον, *with a large pulse*, Gal.2.387,412, 8.710. **-σχήμων**, ον, gen. ονος, *magnificent*, A.*Pr.*408 (lyr.):—also **-σχημος**, ον, *bulky*, of particles, Thphr. *CP*6.1.6. ® **-σώμᾰτος**, ον, *large-bodied*, Eust.962.23, Sch.Opp.*H.*1.360. **-σωμος**, ον, = foreg., Sch.Ar.*Ra.*55, etc. **-τεχνος**, ὁ, *engineer*, Arist.*Mu.*398b14 (s.v.l.); τὸ μ., = ὕψος, *the sublime*, D.H. *Isoc.*3.

® **μεγᾰλότης**, ητος, ἡ, = μέγεθος, Chrysipp.*Stoic.*3.60.

**μεγᾰλό-τῑμος**, ον, *greatly honoured*, *PMag.Leid.W.*14.22, Pap.in *Sitzb.Heidelb.Akad.*1923(2).18; gloss on ἐρίτιμος, Hsch., *EM*374.55. Adv. -μως D.L.8.88. **-τολμος**, ον, *greatly adventurous*, J.*AJ*5.1.29, App.*Syr.*10 (Comp.), Luc.*Alex.*8. **-τοξος**, ον, *with large bow*, gloss on ἄβιοι, *EM*3.23. ® **-τράχηλος** [τρᾰ], ον, *large-necked*, gloss on ἐριαύχην, ib.142.12.

**μεγᾰλουργέω**, **-γής**, **-γία**, **-γικός**, **-γός**, v. μεγαλοεργ-.

**μεγᾰλ-ουχία**· μεγαλαυχία, ὑψηλοφροσύνη, Hsch. **-οῦχος**, ον, *lordly*, *overweening*, βία B.16.23 (nisi leg. -αυχον).

**μεγᾰλο-φᾰνής**, ές, = μεγαλοπρεπής 2, ὄνος Arist.(?) in *PLit.Lond.*112 (Sup.), cf. Paul.Al.*N.*2, Hsch., Phot. **-φαρής**, ές, gloss on βυσσοφαρής, Hsch. **-φεγγής**, ές, gloss on ζαφλεγέες, Id.

®**μεγᾰλ-όφθαλμος**, ον, *large-eyed*, Arist.*Phgn.*811b20, *PPetr.*3p.31 (iii B.C.), Plu.2.299b, Ptol.*Tetr.*143, Olymp.Hist.p.459 D.

**μεγᾰλό-φῐλος**, ον, *having great friends*, Paul.Al.*N.*2, *Cat.Cod. Astr.*8(4).136. **-φλεβος**, ον, *large-veined*, Arist.*PA*667a30. **-φρονέω**, *to be high-minded*, μ. ἐφ' ἑαυτῷ *to be confident* in oneself, X.*HG*6.2.39; πρὸς τὰς ἀνάγκας Lxx 4*Ma.*6.24; *to be generous*, D.C.43.21, al.:—Med., *display high spirit*, περὶ τῆς ἡγεμονίας J.*AJ*19.3.1. II. in bad sense, *to be arrogant*, Plu.*Dio*40, al.:—in Med., Pl.*R.*528c; ἐπί τινι D.C.43.14; τινι Philostr.*VA*8.5; πρός τινα.. ὡς.. ib.1.39. **-φροσύνη**, ἡ, *greatness of mind*, Pl.*Smp.*194b, Isoc.9.27, *IG*7.2713.10 (Oratio Neronis), Philostr.*VS*2.1.3; ὑπὸ μεγαλοφροσύνης *magnanimously*, Hdt.7.136. 2. in bad sense, *pride*, *arrogance*, ib.24; μ. γένους *pride* of family, Antipho 4.3.2: pl., *proud thoughts*, *AP*5.298 (Agath.). II. *elevation of thought*, Longin.7.3, Demetr. *Eloc.*298; ὕψος -φροσύνης ἀπήχημα Longin.9.2. **-φρων**, ονος, ὁ, ἡ, (φρήν) *high-minded*, *generous*, Protag.9; Ἡσυχία Ar.*Lys.*1289 codd. (lyr.), cf. Isoc.2.25: Comp., Id.12.60,242, Luc.*Am.*52; μ. εἰς δαπάνην Gal.13.954; τὸ μ. X.*Ages.*11.11. Adv. -όνως J.*AJ*6.6.5, *OGI*566.12 (Oenoanda): Sup. -έστατα, εἰπεῖν Philostr.*VS*2.1.3. 2. in bad sense, *arrogant*: in Adv. -όνως Pl.*Euthd.*293a, X.*HG*4.5.6. **-φυής**, ές, (φυή) *of noble nature*, ἄνδρα -έστερον ἢ κατ' ἄνθρωπον Plb.12.23.5, cf. Dam.*Pr.*54 (Comp.); οἱ μ. τῶν ἀνθρώπων S.E.*P.*1.12, cf. Arr. *Epict.*3.23.15; μ. ἤθη καὶ πάθη D.H.*Vett.Cens.*2.11; ἡ μ. αὐθεντία σου, as a title, Just.*Nov.*126.3 *Ep.* Adv. -φυῶς Arr.*Epict.*2.17.19. 2. *endowed with genius*, Phld.*Rh.*1.28S., D.L.1.38; τὸ μ. *lofty genius*, Longin.9.1; τὸ -έστατον Id.34.4. 3. *large*, ἀμφίβια (in the Nile), Str.15.1.22. II. Adv. -φυῶς in bad sense, *with exaggeration*, Cleom.2.1. **-φῠΐα**, ἡ, *nobleness of nature*, Iamb.*VP*23.103 (pl.), Phlp.*in de An.*529.14, Hsch. II. *genius*, *talent*, Longin.13.2, 36.4, Apollod.*Poliorc.*138.16. **-φυλλος**, ον, *large-leaved*, Thphr. *CP*2.10.2: Comp., Id.*HP*7.4.4. **-φωνέω**, part. -φωνῶν f.l. in Phot. s.v. ἱεροφωνῶν (leg. -φώνων). **-φωνία**, ἡ, *loudness of voice*,

Arist.*GA*787$^{a}$3, D.S.16.92. 2. *grandiloquence*, Luc.*Hist.Conscr.* 8, *JTr.*6, Philostr.*VS*1.21.5, Men.Rh.p.369S. **–φωνος,** *ον*, *loud-voiced*, Hp.*Epid.*6.4.19 (Sup.), Arist.*GA*787$^{a}$12, *Pr.*899$^{a}$9: Comp. *–ότερος* Luc.*Bis Acc.*11: Sup. *–ότατος* D.S.11.34. Adv. *–νως* Poll. 2.113, Suid. s.v. *τορόν.* 2. *loud-talker, bawler*, D.19.238. 3. *grandiloquent*, Philostr.*VS*2.10.1; *ποιητής* Id.*Ep.*16; *ὁ –ότατος*, of Pindar, Ath.13.564d; of Homer, Luc.*Musc.Enc.*5. **–χαρτος,** *ον*, *greatly rejoiced over*, gloss on *μεγήριτος*, Hsch. **–χάσμων,** *ον*, gen. *ονος*, *wide-gaping*, *χάνναι* Epich.67. **–ψόφητος,** *ον*, gloss on *ἀγάστονος*, *EM*8.54. **–ψοφος,** *ον*, *loud-sounding*, Hsch. s.v. *ἐρίγδουπος*, Sch.Ar.*Nu.*284. **–ψῡχέω,** *to be generous*, Hsch. s.v. *δαψιλέστατος.* **–ψῡχία,** Ion. *–ίη*, *ἡ*, *greatness of soul, high-mindedness, lordliness*, Democr.46, Isoc.9.59, Arist.*EN*1107$^{b}$22, 1123$^{a}$34, Plb.10.40.6, etc.; *μ. τῶν ἔργων* D.23.205, cf. D.S.1.58; *generosity*, *πρός τινας* *IG*2$^{2}$.1326.25: pl., Plb.1.64.5. 2. in bad sense, *arrogance*, D.18.68, v.l. in Luc.*Tim.*28. 3. *Quixotism*, Pl.*Alc.*2. 150c. **–ψῡχος,** *ον*, *high-souled, generous*, Isoc.9.3, Arist.*EN* 1123$^{b}$2; *εὐεργετικὸς καὶ μ.* Plb.22.21.3; *τὸ μ.*, = *μεγαλοψυχία*, Id.1. 20.11, 31.28.9, Plu.*Per.*36: Comp. *–ότερος*, *φαίνεσθαι* D.19.235, cf. Hyp.*Eux.*33. Adv. *–χως*, *ἔχειν πρός τινας* D.19.140; *χρήσασθαι τοῖς πράγμασι* Plb.1.8.4, cf. *OGI*194.11 (Egypt, i B.C.); *ἐνεγκεῖν συμφοράν* Plu.*CG*19. 2. *romantic, Quixotic*, Pl.*Alc.*2.140c.

⊛**μεγᾰλύνω,** fut. *μεγαλῠνῶ* Lxx *Ge.*12.2, al.: aor. *ἐμεγάλυνα* ib.*Ec.*2.4, al.:—Pass., fut. *–υνθήσομαι* ib.*Za.*12.11, al.: aor. *–ύνθην* ib.*Ma.*1.5, al.: pf. part. *μεμεγαλυμμένος* Aq.*Ps.*143(144).12: (*μέγας*):—*make great* or *powerful, exalt*, *τοὺς πολεμίους* Th.5.98:—Pass., *μεγαλύνεσθαι ἐκ τῶν συμβαινόντων* *gain great glory* by.., X.*HG*7.1.24, cf. *Ep.Phil.*1.20, *POxy.*1592.3 (iii/iv A.D.). II. *make great by word, extol, magnify*, *τὸ ὄνομά τινος* E.*Ba.*320; *μ. τὴν ἑαυτοῦ δύναμιν παρά τινι* Th.8.81; *ἑαυτόν* X.*Ap.*32; *μ. τὴν Λακεδαίμονα πρὸς Ἀθηναίους* Plu.*Cim.*16; *τοῦ θεοῦ τὴν δύναμιν* D.S.1.20: freq. in Lxx, ll.cc.:—Med., *boast oneself*, *περί τινος* Sapph.35; *γέννᾳ* in point of birth, A.*Pr.*892 (lyr.); *οὐδὲ μεγαλύνεται ἐπὶ τῷ ἔργῳ* X.*Hier.*2.17, cf. *Oec.*21.4; *ταῦτ' ἀκούων ἐμεγαλύνετο* Id.*Mem.*3.6.3. 2. *magnify, exaggerate*, Th.6.28, Phld. *Rh.*1.173S., *Ir.*p.45W., D.C.*Fr.*57.81, al.

**μεγᾰλ-ώδῠνος,** *ον*, gloss on *ἐριώδυνος*, Hsch. **–ωμα,** *ατος, τό*, *might*, *ῥάβδος μεγαλώματος* Lxx *Je.*31(48).17. ⊛**–ώνῠμος,** *ον*, *with a great name, giving glory*, *νίκα* S.*Ant.*148 (lyr.); *Ζεῦ* Ar.*Th.*315 (lyr.), cf. *Nu.*569 (lyr.); *κύριος* Lxx *Je.*39(32).19. II. Math. in Comp., *having a higher denominator*, Iamb.*in Nic.*p.50P., al. Adv. *–ωτέρως* ib.p.85P. **–ωπός,** *όν*, *large-eyed*, Opp.*C.*2.177.

**μεγάλως,** Adv. of *μέγας.*

⊛**μεγᾰλ-ωστί** [ῐ], Adv. of *μέγας*, *far and wide, over a vast space*, *κεῖτο μέγας μ.* Il.16.776, cf. 18.26; *κεῖσο μέγας μ.* Od.24.40, cf. Sapph. *Supp.*20a.18. II. v.l. for *μεγάλως*, Hdt.2.161, Arr.*An.*4.12.1, al. 2. = *μεγαλοπρεπῶς*, Hdt.5.67, 6.70, Plb.28.13.5, Luc.*Zeux.*8.—Ep., Ion., and late Prose. **–ωσύνη,** *ἡ*, *greatness, majesty*, Lxx 2*Ki.*7.21, al., Aristeas 192. **–ωφελής,** *ές*, (*ὄφελος*) *very serviceable*, Phld.*Mus.*p.104K., Corn.*ND*16, Plu.2.553c, Cleom.1.1 (Sup.), Sor. 2.14.

**μεγάμῡκος** [ᾰ], *ον*, *loud-braying*, *ὄνος* Hsch.

⊛**μεγάνωρ** [ᾱ], *ορος, ὁ, ἡ*, = *μεγαλήνωρ*, *πλοῦτος* Pi.*O.*1.2.

**Μέγᾰρα,** *τά*, *Megara*, Hdt.5.76, etc.; **Μέγαράδε** *to Megara*, Ar. *Ach.*524.

**Μεγᾰρ-εύς,** *έως, ὁ*, *citizen of Megara*, Thgn.23, etc.: pl. *Μεγαρέες, –εῖς, –ῆς*, Hdt.1.59, etc.: prov., *Μεγαρέων δάκρυα* 'crocodile's tears' (because of the quantity of onions grown near Megara), Zen.5.8. **–ίζω,** *side with the Megarians* or *speak their dialect*, *κλάων Μεγαριεῖς* Ar.*Ach.*822, cf. Sch. ad loc. 2. *follow the Megarian* philosopher Stilpo, D.L.2.113. **–ικός,** *ή, όν*, *Megarian*, Ar.*Ach.*522, etc.; *Μεγαρικοὶ κέραμοι*, and in the language of trade *Μεγαρικά*, *Megarian pottery*, Sch.Ar.*Nu.*1205; cf. *Μαγαρικός*: *Μεγαρικοί, οἱ*, *philosophers of the Megarian school*, Arist.*Metaph.*1046$^{b}$29, D.L.2.106; *οἱ Μ. διαλεκτικοί* Phld.*Rh.*1.279S.; *Μ. ἐρωτήματα* Chrysipp.*Stoic.*2.90: fem. **Μεγαρίς** (sc. *γῆ*), *Megarian territory*, Th. 2.31, etc. **–ιστί** [ῐ], Adv. *in the Megarian dialect*, Hdn.Gr.1. 506. **–όθεν,** Adv. *from Megara*, Sus.1, Ar.*V.*57. **–οῖ,** Adv. *at Megara*, Id.*Ach.*758, *IG*1$^{2}$.929.3.

⊛**μέγᾰρον,** *τό*, gen. pl. *μεγαρέων* Sophr.6: I. *large room, hall*; esp. 1. *the chief room* in the Homeric palace, *μ. πλεῖον δαιτυμόνων* Od.17.604, al. 2. *women's apartment*, 18.198: pl., 17.569, 19. 30. 3. *bedchamber*, 11.374. II. in pl., *house, palace*, freq. in Hom., *ἐνὶ* (*ἐν*) *μεγάροισι* Il.1.396, 418, al.: opp. *ἐπ' ἀγροῦ*, Od.22.47: later in sg., Pi.*O.*6.2, *P.*4.134. III. *sanctuary, shrine*, freq. in Hdt. (who uses the word in this sense only), 1.47, 65, 2.143, 6.134. 2. *tomb*, *Epigr.Gr.*453.2 (Batanaea). IV. *μέγαρα, τά*, *pits* sacred to Demeter and Persephone, into which young pigs were let down in the Thesmophoria, Paus.9.8.1, Porph.*Antr.*6, Sch.Luc.*DMeretr.*1:—also written **μάγαρον,** Men.1031. (For sense IV cf. Hebr. *mĕʿārāh* 'cave'.)

**μέγᾰρόνδε,** Adv. *to the hall, to the women's room*, Od.16.413, al.

**μέγαρ-σις,** *εως, ἡ*, (*μεγαίρω*) *jealousy, envy*, Hsch. **–τός,** *ή, όν*, *envious*, Id.

⊛**μέγᾰς,** *μεγάλη* [ᾰ], *μέγᾰ*, gen. *μεγάλου, ης, ου*, dat. *μεγάλῳ, ῃ, ῳ*, acc. *μέγᾰν, μεγάλην, μέγᾰ*; dual *μεγάλω, α, ω*; pl. *μεγάλοι, μεγάλαι, μεγάλα*, etc.: the stem *μεγάλο–* is never used in sg. nom. and acc. masc. and neut., and only once in voc. masc., *ὦ μεγάλε Ζεῦ* A.*Th.* 822 (anap.). I. *big*, of bodily size: freq. of stature, *εἶδος.. μ. ἦν ὁράασθαι* Od.18.4; *κεῖτο μ. μεγαλωστί* Il.16.776; *ἠΰς τε μ. τε* Od.9. 508; *φῶτα μέγαν καὶ καλόν* ib.513; *καλή τε μεγάλη τε* 15.418; *κάρτα μεγάλη καὶ εὐειδής* Hdt.3.1; *φύσιν τίν' εἶχε φράζε;* Answ. *μέγας* S.*OT*742. b. *full-grown*, of age as shown by stature, *νῦν δ' ὅτε δὴ μ. εἰμί* Od.2.314; *μήτε μέγαν μήτ' οὖν νεαρῶν τινα* A.*Ag.*358 (anap.); later, *elder* of two persons of the same name, Wilcken *Chr.*305 (iii B.C.); *Σκιπίων ὁ μ.* Plb.18.35.9. c. of animals, *μ. ἵπποι, βοῦς, σῦς*, Il.2.839, 18.559, Od.19.439; *αἰετός* Pi.*I.*6(5).50. 2. generally, *vast, high*, *οὐρανός, ὄρος, πύργος*, Il.1.497, 16.297, 6.386; *wide*, *πέλαγος, λαῖτμα θαλάσσης*, Od.3.179, 5.174; *long*, *ἠϊών, αἰγιαλός*, Il.12. 31, 2.210: sts. opp. *ὀλίγος*, *κῦμα οὔτε μέγ' οὔτ' ὀ.* Od.10.94; but usu. opp. *μικρός* or *σμικρός*, *πρὸς ἑαυτὸ ἕκαστον καὶ μ. καὶ σμικρόν* Anaxag. 3; *τὸ ἄπειρον ἐκ μεγάλου καὶ μικροῦ* Arist.*Metaph.*987$^{b}$26, etc. II. of quality or degree, *great, mighty*, freq. epith. of gods, *ὁ μ. Ζεύς* A. *Supp.*1052 (lyr.), etc.; *μεγάλα θεά*, of Demeter and Persephone, S. *OC*683 (lyr.); *θεοὶ μεγάλοι*, of the Cabiri, *IG*12(8).71 (Imbros), etc.; *Μήτηρ μ.*, of Cybele, *SIG*1014.83 (Erythrae, iii B.C.), 1138.3 (Delos, ii B.C.); *Μήτηρ θεῶν μ.* *OGI*540.6 (Pessinus), etc.; *Ἴσιδος μ. μητρὸς θεῶν* *PStrassb.*81.14 (ii B.C.); *μ. ἡ Ἄρτεμις Ἐφεσίων* *Act.Ap.*19.28; *τίς θεὸς μ. ὡς ὁ θεὸς ἡμῶν;* Lxx *Ps.*76(77).13; *ὁ μ. θεός* *Ep.Tit.*2.13; of men, *μ. ἠδὲ κραταιός* Od.18.382; *ὀλίγος καὶ μ.* Callin.1.17, etc.; *μέγας ηὐξήθη* rose *to greatness*, D.2.5; *ἤρθη μ.* ib.8; *βασιλεὺς ὁ μ.*, i.e. the King of Persia, Hdt.1.188, etc. (*θεῶν β. ὁ μ.*, of Zeus, Pi.*O.* 7.34); *βασιλεὺς μ.* A.*Pers.*24 (anap.); as a title of special monarchs, *Ἀρδιαῖος ὁ μ.* Pl.*R.*615c; *ὁ μ. Ἀλέξανδρος* Ath.1.3d; *ὁ μ. ἐπικληθεὶς Ἀντίοχος* Plb.4.2.7, etc.; *μ. φίλος* E.*Med.*549; *πλούτῳ τε κἀνδρείᾳ μ.* Id.*Tr.*674; *ἐπὶ μέγα ἦλθεν ἰσχύος* Th.2.97. 2. *strong*, of the elements, etc., *ἄνεμος, λαῖλαψ, Ζέφυρος*, Od.19.200, 12.408, 14.458; of properties, passions, qualities, feelings, etc., of men, *θάρσος, πένθος, ποθή*, etc., 9.381, Il.1.254, 11.471, etc.; *ἀρετή* Od.24.193, Pi. *O.*8.5; *θυμός* Il.9.496, E.*Or.*702; *κλέος* Il.6.446; *ἄχος* 9.9; *πυρετός* *Ev.Luc.*4.38 (incorrect acc. to Gal.7.275); *ἡ μ. νοῦσος* *epilepsy*, Hp. *Epid.*6.6.5, cf. Gal.17(2).341. 3. of sounds, *great, loud*, *ἀλαλητός, ἰαχή, πάταγος, ὀρυμαγδός*, Il.12.138, 15.384, 21.9, 256; *θόρυβοι, κωκυτός*, S.*Aj.*142 (anap.), E.*Med.*1176; *οὐκ ἔστι ὅκως τι νεῖκος ἔσται ἢ μέγα ἢ σμικρόν* Hdt.3.62; *μὴ φώνει μέγα* S.*Ph.*574. 4. generally, *great, mighty*, *ὅρκος* Il.19.113; *ὄλβος, τιμά*, Pi.*O.*1.56, *P.*4. 148; *μ. λόγος, μῦθος*, a *great* story, rumour, A.*Pr.*732, S.*Aj.*226 (lyr.); *ἐρώτημα* a *big*, i.e. *difficult*, question, Pl.*Euthd.*275d, *Hp.Ma.* 287b; *weighty, important*, *τόδε μεῖζον* Od.16.291; *μέγα ποιέεσθαί τι* to esteem *of great importance*, Hdt.3.42, cf. 9.111; *μέγα γενέσθαι εἴς τι* X.*HG*7.5.6; *μ. ὑπάρχειν πρός τι* Id.*Mem.*2.3.4; *μέγα διαφέρειν εἴς τι* Pl.*Lg.*780c; *οὐκ ἂν εἴη παρὰ μέγα τὸ δικολογεῖν* not of *great importance*, Phld.*Rh.*2.85S.; *τὸ δὲ μέγιστον* and what is *most important*, Th.4.70, cf. 1.142; *οἱ μέγιστοι καιροί* the *most pressing* emergencies, D.20.44; *μ. ὠνησάμενοι χρημάτων* for *large* sums, Plb. 4.50.3, etc. 5. with a bad sense, *over-great*, *μέγα εἰπεῖν* to speak *big*, and so provoke divine wrath, Od.22.288; *λίην μέγα εἶπες* 3. 227, 16.243; *μέγα ἔργον* 3.261, Pi.*N.*10.64; *ἔργων μ.* A.*Ag.*1546 (anap.); *ὠμὸν τὸ βούλευμα καὶ μ.* Th.3.36; *ἔπος μ., μ. λόγοι*, S.*Aj.* 423 (lyr.), *Ant.*1350 (anap.); *μ. γλῶσσα* ib.127 (anap.); *μηδὲν μέγ' εἴπῃς* Id.*Aj.*386; *μὴ μέγα λέγε* Pl.*Phd.*95b; *μὴ μεγάλα λίαν λέγε* Ar.*Ra.*835; *μέγα φρονεῖν* S.*OT*1078, E.*Hipp.*6; *μεγάλα φρονεῖν* Ar.*Ach.*988; *μεγάλα, μεῖζον ἢ δικαίως πνεῖν*, E.*Andr.*189, A.*Ag.*376 (lyr.); *μέγα τι παθεῖν* X.*An.*5.8.17; *μὴ μέγα λέγων μεῖζον πάθῃς* E. *HF*1244. 6. of style, *impressive*, Demetr.*Eloc.*278; *μεῖζον* *more striking*, ib.103. 7. of days, *long*, Gal.12.714.

B. Adv. *μεγάλως* [ᾰ] *greatly, mightily*, Od.16.432, Hes.*Th.* 429, Hdt.1.16, 30, al., X.*Cyr.*8.2.10, Parth.28.1, etc.; strengthd., *μάλα μ.* Il.17.723; *δμαθέντες μ.* A.*Pers.*907 (lyr.); with Adjs., Hdt. 1.4, 7.190. II. more freq. neut. sg. *μέγα* as Adv., *very much, exceedingly*, *μ. χαῖρε* *all* hail!, v.l. for *μάλα* in Od.24.402; esp. with Verbs expressing strong feeling, *μ. κεν κεχαροίατο* Il.1.256; *μ. κήδεται* 2.27, etc.: with Verbs expressing power, might, *μ. πάντων.. κρατέει* 1.78; *ὃς μ. πάντων.. ἤνασσε* 10.32; *πατρὸς μ. δυναμένοιο* Od.1.276, cf. Hom.*Epigr.*15.1, A.*Eu.*950 (anap.), E.*Hel.*1358 (lyr.), Ar.*Ra.*141, Pl.*R.*366a; *μ. δύνασθαι παρά τινι* Th.2.29; *πλουτέειν μ.* Hdt.1.32; or those expressing sound, *loudly*, *μ. ἰάχειν, ἀῦσαι, βοῆσαι, εὔξασθαι, ἀμβῶσαι*, Il.2.333, 14.147, 17.334, Od.17.239, Hdt.1.8 (also pl., *μεγάλ' εὔχετο* Il.1.450; *μ. αὐδήσαντος, μ. ἤπυεν*, Od.4.505, 9.399): strengthd., *μάλα μ.* Il.15.321; *μ. δ' ἔβραχε φήγινος ἄξων* 5.838, etc.: so in Trag. with all kinds of Verbs, *μ. στένειν, σθένειν, χλίειν*, A.*Ag.*711 (lyr.), 938, *Ch.*137: also in pl., *μεγάλα.. δυστυχεῖς* Id.*Eu.*791 (lyr.). 2. of Space, *far*, *μέγα προθορών* Il.14.363; *ἄνευθε μέγα* *far* away, 22.88; *οὐκ ἂν μέγα τι τῆς ἀληθείας παρεξέλθοις* Pl.*Phlb.*66b. 3. with Adjs., as *μέγ' ἔξοχος, μέγα νήπιος*, Il.2.480, 16.46; *μ. νήπιε* Orac.ap.Hdt.1.85; *μ. πλούσιος* Id.1.32, 7.190; *ὦ μέγ' εὔδαιμον κόρη* A.*Pr.*647: with Comp. and Sup., *by far*, *μέγ' ἀμείνονες, ἄριστος, φέρτατος*, Il.4.405, 2.82, 16.21.

C. degrees of Comparison (regul. *μεγαλώτερος, –ώτατος* late, *EM*780.1, 2): 1. Comp. *μείζων, ον*, gen. *ονος*, Ep., Att. (also Delph., *SIG*246*H*$^{2}$60 (iv B.C.)); Ion., Arc., Dor., Aeol. *μέζων, ον*, Heraclit. 25, Hp.*Acut.*44, Hdt.1.26, *IG*7.235.16 (Oropus), 5(2).3.18 (Tegea), Epich.62 (also early Att., *IG*1$^{2}$.22.65, but [*με*]*ίζων* ib.6.93, by analogy of *ὀλείζων* ib.76, 95); dat. pl. *μεζόνεσσι* Diotog.ap.Stob.4.7.62: written *μέσδων* in Sapph.*Supp.*7.6, Plu.*Lyc.*19: cf. **μέττον·** *μεῖζον*, Hsch. (dub.); later *μειζότερος* 3*Ep.Jo.*4 (used as title, *elder*, *POxy.* 943.3 (vi A.D.), etc.); *μειζονώτερος* A.*Fr.*434:—*greater, longer, taller*, Il.3.168, 9.202, etc.; freq. also, *too great*, *γέρας* Pl.*Sph.*231a; *Μηνόφιλος μείζων* M. *the elder*, *Ostr.Bodl.*v C2 (ii A.D.); as title, *μείζων*

κώμης *headman* of a village, *POxy*.1626.5 (iv A. D.), etc.: generally, *the higher authority*, *PLond*.2.214.22 (iii A. D.), *POxy*.1204.17 (pl., iii A. D.); οὔτε μεῖζον οὔτε ἔλαττον, a strong form of denial, *nothing whatever*, D.H.*Comp*.4; οὐδαμὰ προὔφηνεν οὔτε μείζον' οὔτ' ἐλάττονα S.*Tr*.324. Adv. μειζόνως E.*Hec*.1121, Th.1.130, X.*Cyn*.13.3, Isoc.9.21, etc.; Ion. μεζόνως Hdt.3.128, Herod.4.80, etc.: neut. as Adv., μεῖζον σθένειν S.*Ph*.456, E.*Supp*.216; μ. ἰσχύειν D.*Ep*.3.28; ἐπὶ μ. ἔρχεται S.*Ph*.259. 2. Sup. μέγιστος, η, ον, Il.2.412, etc.: neut. as Adv., μέγιστον ἴσχυσε S.*Aj*.502; δυνάμενος μ., c. gen., Hdt.7.5, 9.9: with another Sup., μέγιστον ἐχθίστη E.*Med*.1323: in pl., χαῖρ' ὡς μέγιστα S.*Ph*.462; θάλλει μ. Id.*OC*700 (lyr.); τὰ μέγιστ' ἐτιμάθης Id.*OT*1203 (lyr.); ἐς μέγιστον ib.521; ἐς τὰ μ. Hdt.8.111:—late Sup. μεγιστότατος *PLond*.1.130.49 (i/ii A. D.). (Cf. Skt. *majmán*- 'greatness', Lat. *magnus*, Goth. *mikils* 'great'.)

✻**μεγα-σθενής**, ές, = μεγαλοσθενής, Γαιάοχος, Λοξίας, Pi.*O*.1.25, A.*Eu*.61; Τιτυός A.R.1.181; also μ. χρυσός Pi.*I*.5(4).2; χρησμός A.*Ch*.269, cf. Trag.ap.*PGrenf*.2.1(*b*). **-συρνος**, kind of grape grown at Cnidus, Hsch. **-σχιδής**, ές, *with a great cleft*, Id. **-τιμος**, ον, = μεγαλότιμος, Ael.*VH*8.7. **-τολμος**, ον, = μεγαλότολμος, Man.3.49.

✻**μεγ-αυχής**, ές, = μεγάλαυχος, παγκράτιον Pi.*N*.11.21; δαίμων A.*Pers*.642 (lyr.). II. *boasting*, c. dat., σκάπτροισι *AP*7.427.7 (Antip. Sid.). ✻**-αύχητος**, ον, *glorious*, *Ath.Mitt*.27.339 (Acarnania, ii B. C.).

**μεγεθικός**, ή, όν, *quantitative*, διάστασις, συνέχεια, Simp.*in de An*.42.16,30; μέτρον Id.*in Ph*.636.28.

**μεγεθόομαι**, Pass., = μεγαλύνομαι, Xenocr.ap.Orib.2.58.28, Hsch. s. v. κύματι; τὸ μεμεγεθωμένον that which *possesses magnitude*, S.E.*M*.10.240.

**μεγεθο-ποιέω**, *increase*, μῆκος, πᾶσαν διάστασιν, S.E.*M*.7.108; τὴν ὀδύνην Aët.7.7. II. *invest with sublimity*, τὰ λεγόμενα Longin.40.1. **-ποίησις**, εως, ἡ, *enlargement*, Gal.19.448, Aët.16.115. **-ποιός**, όν, *productive of sublimity*, ῥυθμοί Longin.39.4.

✻**μέγεθος**, Ion. (not Hp.) **μέγᾰθος** Hdt. (v. infr.), also Philox.2.19, εος, τό: (μέγας):—*greatness*, *magnitude*, opp. πλῆθος, Anaxag.1, etc.; πλῆθος μὲν.. ἐὰν ἀριθμητὸν ᾖ, μ. δὲ ἐὰν μετρητὸν ᾖ Arist.*Metaph*.1020ᵃ9. I. in Hom. always *stature*, of men and women, εἶδος ἀκιδνοτέρη μέγεθός τ' εἰσάντα ἰδέσθαι Od.5.217, cf. 6.152; ἐς μ. καὶ κάλλος ὁρώμενος 18.219, cf. Pl.*Chrm*.154c; θηλειῶν ἀρετὴ σώματος κάλλος καὶ μ. Arist.*Rh*.1361ᵃ7: then, generally, *size*, μύρμηκες μεγάθεα ἔχοντες κυνῶν ἐλάσσονα Hdt.3.102; μ. λαβεῖν X.*Cyr*.1.4.3; ἡ ἐπίδοσις εἰς τὸ μ. Arist.*HA*560ᵃ20; of sound, *loudness*, βοῆς μ. Th.4.126: acc. as Adv., λίθου λάμποντος μέγαθος, = μεγάλως, Hdt.2.44; but usu., *in size*, τεῖχος κατὰ τὸν Ἀθηνέων κύκλον.. τὸ μ. Id.1.98; [δένδρεον] μέγαθος κατὰ συκέην μάλιστά κῃ Id.4.23; ὅσην δεῖ τὸ μ. τὴν πόλιν ποιεῖσθαι Pl.*R*.423b: also in pl., ποταμοὶ οὐ κατὰ τὸν Νεῖλον ἐόντες μεγάθεα Hdt.2.10, cf. 1.202; σμικροὶ τὰ μεγάθεα Id.3.107; κυαμιαῖοι τὰ μ. Luc.*Herm*.40; μεγέθη ἔργων καὶ διαθέσεων Epicur.*Nat*.43 G. 2. freq. in dat., μεγέθει.. ἐκπρεπεστάτη *in stature*, A.*Pers*.184; ἀνθρώπους μεγέθει μεγίστους καὶ ἥκιστα διαφόρους ἐς.. τὰ μεγέθεα Hp.*Aër*.12; πλήθεϊ μέγιστον καὶ μεγάθεϊ ὑψηλότατον, of a mountain, Hdt.1.203; κρητῆρες μεγάθεϊ μεγάλοι ib.51; μεγάθεϊ μέγιστος Id.7.117; μ. περιμήκεας Id.2.108; σμικρός ib.74; ἐλάττω τῷ μ. Arist.*HA*560ᵇ5. II. of quality and degree, *greatness*, *magnitude*, πόνων E.*Hel*.593; τῆς παρανομίας Th.6.15; τῆς ζημίας Lys.1.3; τῆς κολάσεως Pl.*Lg*.934b; *importance*, μ. ἐχούσας πράξεις D.H.*Isoc*.6. 2. *might*, *power*, E.*Ba*.273; δαίμονος μεγέθει πάντα ἐπέχοντος X.*Smp*.8.1. 3. *greatness*, *magnanimity*, Plu.*Alex*.14; περί τι Id.*Ant*.24. 4. Rhet., *loftiness*, *sublimity*, μ. περιτιθέναι τοῖς πράγμασιν D.H.*Comp*.17, cf. Demetr.*Eloc*.5, Hermog.*Id*.1.5, etc.; λόγων μ. Longin.4.1, al.: in pl., *sublime objects*, Id.9.1, al. III. Math., *magnitude*, Gorg.3; μ. ἔχειν Pl.*Ti*.57d, cf. Iamb.*Comm.Math*.3, etc.; *extension*, Plot.2.4.11: in pl., *magnitudes*, Pl.*Prt*.356c; τὰ μ. τὰ γεγραμμένα *IG*7.3073.102 (Lebad.). 2. Astron., *magnitude*, of stars, Cleom.1.11, Ptol.*Alm*.7 passim. IV. Gramm., *metrical length*, τὸ μέγιστον μ. τρίχρονον A.D.*Synt*.133.26, cf. *EM*419.50. 2. τὰ ἐν τῷ μέτρῳ μ. the recognized *lengths* of lines in a metre, Heph.12.3. V. τὸ μ. τινός, as title, his *Highness*, *POxy*.2107.8 (iii A. D.); τὸ σὸν μ. *Cod.Just*.8.10.12.1a.

**μεγεθ-ουργία**, ἡ, *doing* or *attempting great deeds*, Pl.*Ax*.370b. **-όω**, in Pass., v. -όομαι. ✻**-ύνω**, *increase in bulk*, *magnitude* or *number*, *enlarge*, Heliod.ap.Orib.46.8.13, Iamb.*Protr*.21.ιζ':—Pass., Cleom.1.9, Sor.1.15, 2.37, Iamb.*in Nic*.p.11 P.: aor. Med. in pass. sense, οὐδ' ἐμεγεθύνατο μὲν ἐμειώθη δέ Numen.ap.Eus.*PE*11.10. 2. Pass., *acquire magnitude*, *become quantified*, Plot.3.6.17, 6.4.1; τὰ μεμεγεθυσμένα *the world of magnitudes*, Id.2.4.10, cf. Porph.*Sent*.33; μετὰ τὸ μεγεθυνθῆναι τὴν ὕλην Phlp.*in de An*.543.34. II. *invest with sublimity*, τὰ δαιμόνια Longin.9.5:—Pass., *to be lofty* or *sublime*, of style, Id.13.1. III. Gramm., of a vowel, *lengthen*, οἱ τὸ ο μεγεθύνοντες Sch.E.*Ph*.629:—Pass., Tryphoap.A.D.*Pron*.65.23, cf. A.D.*Adv*.193.23.

**μεγήρῐτος**, ον, (ἐρίζω) *much contended for*, μ. τέκνα θεάων Hes.*Th*.240 (with v.l. **μεγήρᾰτα**, (ἐρατός) *passing lovely*, which is prob. l. in Pancrat.*Oxy*.1085.9).

**μεγιστάν**, ᾶνος, ὁ, *great man*, *grandee*, Lxx*Si*.4.7, 10.24: but usu. in pl., Men.1035, Lxx*Da*.5.23, *Ev.Marc*.6.21, Man.4.41, Artem.1.2, Vett.Val.61.16, Alex.Aphr.*in Top*.466.12, etc.

**μεγιστεύω**, *to be* or *become very great*, ἡ πόλις -εύσει App.*Syr*.58.

**μεγιστο-άνασσα** [ᾰν], ἡ, *greatest of queens*, of Hera, B.18.21. **-πάτωρ** [ᾰ], ορος, *greatest of fathers*, of Zeus, Id.5.199. **-πολις**, ι, *making cities greatest* or *most blest*, Ἁσυχία, μ. Δίκας θύγατερ Pi.*P*.8.2. **-σωμος**, ον, *of largest frame*, Tz.*H*.8.272. **-τῑμος**, ον, *most honoured*, Δίκα A.*Supp*.709 (lyr.).

**Μεγιστώ**, οῦς, ἡ, *Greatness*, personified, Emp.123.2.

**μεγύτης**, sine expl., Theognost.*Can*.44.

**μέδεα**, v. μέζεα.

**μεδέων**, οντος, ὁ, (μέδω) participial Subst., *guardian*, *ruler*, Hom. (only in Il.), always of Zeus, as connected with special places, Ἴδηθεν μεδέων *ruling* from Ida, Il.3.276, etc.; Δωδώνης μ. 16.234; also Κυλλήνης μ., of Hermes, *h.Merc*.2; Πάν, Ἀρκαδίας μ. Pi.*Fr*.95; Ἀπόλλων Τελμεσσοῦ μ. *SIG*1044.8 (Halic., iv/iii B. C.); τῷ μεδεῦντι Νείλεω δήμου (i. e. Apollo) Call.*Fr*.95; δελφίνων μ., of Poseidon, Ar.*Eq*.560 (lyr.); σοὶ τῷ πάντων μ. E.*Fr*.912.1 (anap.): c. dat. loci, Pi.*O*.7.88; μ. καὶ χθονὶ καὶ πελάγει *AP*6.30 (Maced.): generally, *ruler*, ἡμετέρῳ μεδέοντι Call.*Jov*.86. 2. fem. μεδέουσα, *guardian goddess*, of Aphrodite, Σαλαμῖνος μεδέουσα *h.Hom*.10.4; of Mnemosyne, Ἐλευθῆρος μεδέουσα Hes.*Th*.54; of Pallas, τῆς ἱερωτάτης μεδέουσα χώρας (Attica) Ar.*Eq*.585 (lyr.), cf. 763; νεὼς Ἀθηναίας τῆς Ἀθηνῶν μεδεούσης prob. in *IG*12(1).977.10 (Carpathos, iv B. C.), cf. *Supp.Epigr*.1.375, 376 (Samos), 3.3.5 (Athens), Plu.*Them*.10: generally, [Ἑλένη] μ. θαλάσσης E.*Or*.1690 (anap.); τόξων μ. Ἄρτεμιν Id.*Hipp*.167 (lyr.).—Aeol. participial form μέδεις (as if from μέδημι), Alc.5 (wrongly expld. as 2 sg. ind. by Apion ap.A.D.*Synt*.92.7); other forms in late poets, μεδέουσι Q.S.5.525; μεδέεις *Epigr.Gr*.975; μεδέοιεν *IG*14.1363.10.

**μεδιμν-αῖος**, α, ον, *holding a μέδιμνος*, Hsch.:—also **-ιαῖος**, α, ον, *GDI*4990 (Gortyn). ✻**-ος**, ὁ, Hdt.7.187, etc.; ἡ, only v.l. in Id.1.192:—a corn-measure, Hes.*Fr*.160.3; μ. Ἀττικός, Σικελικός, Hdt.1.192, Plb.2.15.1; σιτηρός *IG*2².1013.27; [σῖτον] κατὰ μέδιμνον συνωνούμενοι Lys.22.12; μεδίμνῳ ἀπομετρήσασθαι ἀργύριον X.*HG*3.2.27; ὁ γὰρ νόμος.. κωλύει παιδὶ μὴ ἐξεῖναι συμβάλλειν μηδὲ γυναικὶ πέρα μεδίμνου κριθῶν to make a contract for value exceeding *a medimnus*, Is.10.10: hence, οὐ κύριος ὑπὲρ μέδιμνόν ἐστ' ἀνὴρ οὐδεὶς ἔτι, i. e. he is no better than a woman, Ar.*Ec*.1025, cf. Sch. ad loc.; τῶν ἁλῶν μ., v. ἅλς (A). II. in Magna Graecia, = κρουνός 4, *pipe of a fountain*, D.S.12.10.

**μέδος**, ὁ, *mead*, Goth. word in Prisc.p.300 D. (Goth. **midus* not directly attested, cogn. with μέθυ.)

**μέδω**, *protect*, *rule over*, used by Hom. only in participial Subst. **μέδων**, οντος, ὁ, *lord*, *ruler*, freq. in pl., Ἀργείων, Φαιήκων ἡγήτορες ἠδὲ μέδοντες, Il.2.79, Od.7.136: once in sg., of Phorcys, ἁλὸς.. μέδων *lord* of the sea, 1.72: fem. Μέδουσα, as pr. n. of the Gorgon, Hes.*Th*.276, etc.: later as Verb, c. gen. loci, ὃς Αἰγαίου μέδεις πρωνός, of Poseidon, S.*Fr*.371 (lyr., s. v. l., πρῶνας codd.), cf. Ar.*Ra*.665; of Dionysus, ὃς.. μέδεις.. παγκοίνοις Ἐλευσινίας Δηοῦς ἐν κόλποις S.*Ant*.1119 (lyr.); τιμῆς ἄλλης ἄλλο μέδει Emp.17.28. II. **μέδομαι**, fut. μεδήσομαι Il.9.650, elsewh. pres. and impf.:—*provide for*, *be mindful of*, c. gen., πολέμοιο μεδέσθω 2.384; εἰ μέν κε.. νόστου τε μέδηαι Od.11.110; ὥς κ'.. δείπνοιο μέδηται 19.321; ὁππότε κεν.. κοίτου τε μέδηται 2.358, cf. 3.334; μεδώμεθα θούριδος ἀλκῆς, like ἀλκῆς μνήσασθαι, Il.4.418, 5.718; ἀλλ' ἄγε δὴ.. μεδώμεθα.. σίτου 24.618; ὄφρα.. νόστοιο μεδοίατο 9.622; δόρποιο μέδεσθαι 18.245; δόρποιο μέδοντο ὕπνου τε γλυκεροῦ ταρπήμεναι 24.2: later c. inf., πλεῦσαι μέδονται Orph.*A*.90. 2. *plan*, *contrive*, *devise*, τινί τι, always in bad sense, κακὰ δὲ Τρώεσσι μεδέσθην Il.4.21, 8.458. (Cf. Lat. *modus*, Osc. *med-dix* 'magistrate'.)

**μέζεα**, ων, τά, = μήδεα (cf. μῆδος B), Hes.*Op*.512, Lyc.762: sg. in Hsch.; **μέδεα**, Archil.138.

**μέζων**, **μεζόνως**, v. μέγας.

✻**μεθαιρέω**, only in Ep. aor. 2 (iterat.) μεθέλεσκον (v. infr.):—*catch in turn*, of a game at ball, [σφαῖραν] ἕτερος ῥίπτασκε ποτὶ νέφεα σκιόεντα ἰδνωθεὶς ὀπίσω· ὁ δ' ἀπὸ χθονὸς ὑψόσ' ἀερθεὶς ῥηϊδίως μεθέλεσκε, πάρος ποσὶν οὖδας ἱκέσθαι Od.8.376.

✻**μεθάλλομαι**, used by Hom. only in Ep. aor. part. μετάλμενος:—*leap*, *rush upon*, of warriors, οὔτασε.. μετάλμενος ὀξέϊ δουρί Il.5.336; οὔτασε δουρὶ μ. 14.443; Τρώεσσι μ. ἐν φόβον ὦρσε 13.362; of a lion, ἥρπαξε μ. 12.305, cf. Hld.10.30. 2. *rush after*, in a race, οὐκ ἔσθ' ὅς κέ σ' ἕλῃσι μ. Il.23.345. II. *leap from* one ship *to another* in a sea-fight, ἐς ἀλλήλους App.*BC*5.120; *spring from side to side*, *hither and thither*, τᾷ καὶ τᾷ τὸν Ἔρωτα μετάλμενον Bion *Fr*.10.6, cf. Hld.6.14, Them.*Or*.22.269c.

**μεθάμερα** [ᾱ], Dor. Adv. *by day*, *IG*4²(1).121.114 (Epid.).

**μεθᾱμέριος**, Dor. for μεθημέριος.

**μεθάπτομαι**, Pass., *have fastened to one*, θύρσος ἱστία μεθῆπται Philostr.*Im*.1.19.

**μεθαρμ-ογή**, ἡ, *transposition*, *re-tuning*, ἐν ταῖς τῶν τόνων (modes) μ. Ptol.*Harm*.2.11, cf. 3.1. **-όζω**, later Att. **-όττω**, *dispose differently*, *correct*, εἰ μή τι καιροῦ τυγχάνω, μεθάρμοσον (sc. με) S.*El*.31, cf. Luc.*Nigr*.12; *transpose*, δύο ὀνόματα Them.*Or*.2.33c: abs., *make a change*, D.H.7.66:—more freq. in Med., μεθάρμοσαι τρόπους νέους *adopt* new habits, A.*Pr*.311; μεθηρμοσάμεσθα βελτίω βίον τοῦ πρόσθεν E.*Alc*.1157; μ. τὸν ἀπράγμονα βίον D.H.11.22; ἐπὶ τὴν συνήθη δίαιταν μ. τὰς τραπέζας *restore* them to.., Plu.2.642f; μ. τι ἔς τι *AP*7.712 (Erinna), Ph.2.219 codd.; πρός τι *AP*9.584.12: c. gen., *from* a certain condition, Μοῦσα τῆς συνήθους μεθαρμοσαμένη σπουδῆς Luc.*Am*.4, etc.; *adapt oneself*, μεθηρμόσατο εἰς τὸ λέγειν S.E.*M*.9.53; πόλις ἡ πρὸς τὰ πράγματα μεθαρμοττομένη D.H.10.51: in Music,

*change the mode*, Iamb.*VP*25.113:—Pass., τὰ στοιχεῖα μεθαρμοζόμενα *having their order changed*, Lxx *Wi*.19.18. **-οσις**, εως, ἡ, *change*, δεσποτῶν Plb.18.45.6.

**μεθεδράζω**, *transplant*, of population, in Pass., *IPE*1$^{2}$.35 (i B.C.); οἱ μεθηδρασμένοι ὑπὸ.. Μιθραδάτου ib.6.

**μεθεκ-τέον**, (μετέχω) *one must share*. τινος Th.8.65; παιδιᾶς Pl. *R*.424e; νόμων Antiph.44.2: pl. μεθεκτέα Agath.2.14. **-τικός**, ή, όν, *participating in*, τῶν εἰδῶν Arist.*GC*335$^{b}$12; τὸ μ. *the participant*, Id.*Ph*.209$^{b}$35. **-τός**, ή, όν, *able to be shared in*, of the Platonic ideas, Id.*Metaph*.990$^{b}$28, al.; ὁ μ. θεός Dam.*Pr*.25bis. II. Act., *participant*, Procl.*Inst*.189.

**μεθέλεσκε**, v. μεθαιρέω.

⊛ **μεθελίτης**, dub. sens. in *PKlein.Form*.21 (vi A.D.):—also **μεθλίτης**, ib.674; hence **μεθλιτάριος**, *Sammelb*.4858.8 (vi A.D.).

**μεθελκ-υστέον**, *one must draw along*, [τὰς σικύας] λοξῶς Aët.11.5. **-ω**, *draw to the side*, ἡνίας *APl*.5.384,386; *divert*, τινὰ ἀπό τινος Ph.2.224:—Pass., ὑπό τινος Id.1.387; of cupping instruments, -έσθωσαν βιαίως ἄνω τε καὶ κάτω Orib.*Fr*.74.

**μεθέμεν**, v. μεθίημι. **μεθέν**, Dor. for ἐμέθεν, v. ἐγώ.

**μέθεξις**, εως, ἡ, (μετέχω) *participation*, οὐσίας μετὰ χρόνου *participation* of being in time, Pl.*Prm*.151e; χρόνου in time, ib.141d; αἱ μ. τῶν ἀρχῶν Arist.*Pol*.1278$^{a}$23. II. in Platonic philosophy, *participation* in the ideas, ἡ μ. τοῖς ἄλλοις..τῶν εἰδῶν Pl.*Prm*.132d, cf. Arist.*Metaph*.987$^{b}$10; ταὐτοῦ *in* the same, Pl.*Sph*.256b. III. in Logic, κατὰ μέθεξιν as *being contained* or *comprehended*, as genus or difference in species, Arist.*Top*.132$^{b}$35.

**μεθέορτος**, ον, (ἑορτή) *after the feast*, μεθέορτοι ἡμέραι, ἡ μ. (sc. ἡμέρα), *the morrow of it*, Antipho Soph.95, Plu.2.1095a; τὰ μ. *AB* 279.

⊛ **μεθέπω**, Ep. impf. μέθεπον; Aeol. 1 pl. πεδήπομεν Sapph.*Supp*.23.8: fut. μεθέψω Hsch.: poet. aor. part. μετασπών, Med. μετασπόμενος:—*pursue, follow after*, ποσὶ κραιπνοῖσι μετασπών Il.17.190, Od.14.33; ψεῦδος, of Ixion *pursuing* the phantom, Pi.*P*.2.37, cf. A.R.4.1339, Epic.ap.Ath.9.399a, Euph.9.12:—Med., ἀπιόντα μετασπόμενος βάλε δουρί Il.13.567: and c. dat., οὔ σοι μὴ μεθέψομαι S.*El*.1052. 2. c. acc., *go in search of*, ἡνίοχον μέθεπε θρασύν *drove in search of* a charioteer, Il.8.126; [ἔλαφον] μ. Pi.*O*.3.31. 3. *visit*, νέον μεθέπεις; *dost thou come* but now *to visit us?* Od.1.175. II. *cherish*, τινα Sapph. l.c. 2. *ply* a business, γεηπονίην Ps.-Phoc.161; αἶσαν Pi.*N*.6.13; νώτῳ μεθέπων ἄχθος *wielding*, i.e. *carrying*, a burden on his back, ib.57; μοῦσαν μ. *IG*3.399.3. III. causal, c. dupl. acc., Τυδεΐδην μέθεπε κρατερώνυχας ἵππους he *turned* the horses *in pursuit of* Tydeides, Il.5.329.—Only poet., mostly Ep. and Lyr.

**μεθερμην-ευτικός**, ή, όν, *fit for interpreting*, Sch.Pi.*O*.5.54, Sch.E.*Hec*.490. Adv. -κῶς Sch.Opp.*H*.1.688. **-εύω**, *translate*, Lxx *Si.Prol*., Str.17.1.29:—freq. in Pass., Plb.6.26.6, Aristeas 38, *PTeb*.164 i 2 (ii B.C.), D.S.1.11, D.H.4.76, *Ev.Matt*.1.23, etc.

**μεθ-ερπύζω**, = sq., Orph.*L*.427. **-έρπω**, *creep after, overtake*, Opp.*H*.1.543.

**μέθ-εσις**, εως, ἡ, (μεθίημι) *relaxation*, ψυχῆς Ph.1.354. **-ετέον**, *one must let go*, τοῦτον (v.l. τούτων) Pl.*Ti*.55d; *one must set scot-free*, τοὺς ἀνδροφονήσαντας Ph.2.298.

**μεθέτερος**, ον, *additional*, *POxy*.237 vii 42 (ii A.D.).

**μεθετικός**, ή, όν, *letting go, relaxing*, only in Adv. -κῶς Sch.D Il.6.523 (μεθητ- codd.).

**μέθη**, ἡ, (for μεθύω: μέθη, cf. πληθύω: πλήθᾱ) *strong drink*, καλῶς ἔχειν μέθης to be pretty well *drunk*, Hdt.5.20; ὑπερπλησθεὶς μέθης S.*OT*779; μέθῃ βρεχθείς E.*El*.326; ἡ ἀπειρία τῆς μ. Antipho 4.3.2; ἐσφαλμένος ὑπὸ μέθης Pl.*R*.396d; μανδραγόρᾳ ἢ μέθῃ συμποδίσαι τινά ib.488c; μ. εὐώδης παλαιός fragrant old *wine*, Hp.*Epid*.7.82. II. *drunkenness*, μ. αἰώνιος Pl.*R*.363d; πίνειν εἰς μέθην Id.*Lg*.775b; μέθῃ χρῆσθαι ib.674a; διὰ μέθης ποιήσασθαι..τὴν συνουσίαν Id.*Smp*.176e; κωμάζειν μετὰ μέθης Id.*Lg*.637b; τρεῖς εἶχεν προφάσεις, μέθην, ἔρωτα, ἄγνοιαν D.21.38: pl., *carousals*, Democr.159, Pl.*Lg*.682e; ἐν μέθαις Id.*Phdr*.256c, cf. Lxx *Ju*.13.15, *Ep.Rom*.13.13, etc. 2. metaph., ὑπὸ μέθης τοῦ φόβου ναυτιᾷ Pl.*Lg*.639b, cf. Metrod.*Herc*.831.18; μ. νηφαλίῳ κατασχεθεὶς ὥσπερ οἱ κορυβαντιῶντες Ph.1.16, cf. 2.320. III. Μέθη personified, in Art, Paus.2.27.3.

**μεθήκω**, fut. -ήξω D.C.64.7:—*come in quest of*, τινα E.*Tr*.1270, cf. Ar.*Eq*.937; ἔμελλε τὸν Ὄθωνα ἡ Δίκη μεθήξειν D.C. l.c.

**μέθημαι**, Pass., *sit among*, c. dat. pl., μνηστῆρσι Od.1.118.

**μεθημερῐνός**, ή, όν, (ἡμέρα) *by day*, φῶς Pl.*Ti*.45c; φυλακαί X.*Lac*.12.2; μ. γάμοι prostitution *in open daylight*, D.18.129, cf. Ph.1.155; τὸ μεθημερινόν (sc. μέρος) Pl.*Sph*.220d. 2. of fevers, *remittent quotidian*, Gal.17(1).221.

**μεθημέριος**, Dor. **-ᾱμέριος**, ον, = foreg., ἔφοδοι E.*Ion* 1050 (lyr.).

⊛ **μεθημοσύνη**, ἡ, *remissness, carelessness*, Il.13.121: pl., ib.108.

**μεθήμων**, ον, gen. ονος, (μεθίημι) *remiss, careless*, Il.2.241, Od.6.25, *Anacreont*.56.17.

**μεθίδρ-ῡσις**, εως, ἡ, *migration*, τινῶν εἰς.. Str.8.6.10; *removal*, Plu.2.927a. ⊛ **-ύω**, *place differently, transpose*, ἐπὶ τἀναντία τὸν βίον Pl.*Lg*.904e:—Med., *migrate*, Arist.*Ath*.19.2, D.H.6.52:—Pass., *keep moving*, ἄλλοθεν ἀλλαχόσε Plu.*Ages*.11.

**μεθιζάνω**, *change the position of*, τὰς σικύας Aret.*CA*2.4.

⊛ **μεθίημι**, μεθιεῖς (v.l. μεθίης), μεθιεῖ, Il.6.523, 10.121, Od.4.372; Ion. μετίει Hdt.2.70; 3 pl. μεθιᾶσι Pl.*Ti*.81d; Ion. μετιεῖσι Hdt.1.133; imper. μεθίει Pl.*La*.187b; Ep. subj. 3 sg. μεθίῃσι Il.13.234; inf. μεθιέναι, Ep. -ιέμεναι, -ιέμεν, ib.114, 4.351: impf. 3 sg. μεθίει 15.716, 16.762, 21.72, 3 pl. μέθιεν Od.21.377; Ep. μεθίεσκεν A.R.4.799: fut. μεθήσω Od.15.212; Ep. inf. μεθησέμεναι, -έμεν, 16.377, Il.20.361: aor. 1 μεθῆκα, Ep. μεθέηκα 23.434 (also ἐμέθηκα Phot.); part. μεθήσας Coluth.127: other moods from aor. 2, imper. μέθες S.*El*.448, Ar.*Ec*.958 (lyr.), etc.; subj. μεθῶ, Ep. μεθείω Il.3.414; opt. μεθείην S.*Ph*.1302; inf. μεθεῖναι, Ep. μεθέμεν Il.1.283; part. μεθείς A.*Pers*.699 (troch.), etc.:—**Med.**, first in Hdt., not in Att. Prose, fut. μεθήσομαι E.*Hipp*.326, Ar.*V*.416 (μετήσομαι in pass. sense, Hdt.5.35): aor. 2 μεθεῖτο S.*Tr*.197, μέθεσθε Id.*OC*1437; subj. dual and pl. μεθῆσθον, μεθῆσθε, Ar.*Ra*.1380, *V*.434; inf. μεθέσθαι S.*El*.1277:—**Pass.**, Ion. impf. ἐμετίετο Hdt.1.12: pf. 3 sg. μεθεῖται A.*Th*.79 (lyr.); pl. μεθεῖνται Pl.*Phlb*.62d; Ion. part. μεμετιμένος Hdt.6.1, etc.: Ion. aor. 1 μετείθη Id.1.114. [Generally ῐ in Hom. and Ep., ῑ in Att.: but ῑ in μεθιέμεν Il.14.364, μεθίετε 4.234, al., μεθιέμεναι 13.114: in μεθίει, 15.716, 16.762, 21.72, ῑ may be long by augment, but ῐ in μεθίεν Od.21.377.] I. trans., *set loose, let go* what is bound, stretched, or held back: hence 1. c. acc. pers., *release* a prisoner, Il.10.449, Hdt.1.24, etc.; μ. χεροῖν S.*OC*838; *let* a visitor *depart*, Od.15.212, cf. Pl.*La*.187b; *dismiss* a wife, Hdt.9.111: c. inf., *set one free* to do as he will, ἐμὲ μέθες ἰέναι ἐπὶ τὴν θήρην Id.1.37, cf. 40; also ἐλεύθερον μ. τινά E.*Hec*.551:—Pass., *to be let go, dismissed*, Hdt.1.12, 114, al.; but μεθεῖται στρατός *is let loose* (as if from a leash), A.*Th*.79 (lyr.). b. *give up, abandon*, μή χωσαμένη σε μεθείω Il.3.414; εἰ τοῦτον Τρώεσσι μεθήσομεν.. ἄστυ πότι.. ἐρύσαι 17.418. c. metaph., εἴ με μεθῄη ῥῖγος granting the cold *will quit hold of* me, Od.5.471. 2. c. acc. rei, *let go, let fall, throw*, τι ἐς ποταμόν ib.460, Hdt.2.70; μ. δεξιάν (v.l. δεξιᾶς) E.*Hipp*.333; μ. με χεῖρα S.*Ph*.1301; ταῦτα μὲν μέθες (sc. τὰ λουτρά) *lay down*, Id.*El*.448, cf. 1205; μ. ψυχήν *give up* the ghost, E.*Med*.1218; of liquids, *let flow, let drop*, πολλὰ τῶν δακρύων Hdt.9.16; ἰὸν ἀντιπενθῆ μεθεῖσα καρδίας A.*Eu*.783 (lyr.): c. acc. et inf., μ. τὰς συμπάσας [ἐπιστήμας] ῥεῖν εἰς.. Pl.*Phlb*.62d; of words, *utter*, γλῶσσαν Περσίδα μ. Hdt.6.29; λόγους, βρόμον μ., E.*Hipp*.499, 1202; μ. βλαστόν *let* it *shoot forth*, Hdt.6.37; of weapons, *let fly, discharge*, μετὰ δ' ἰὸν ἕηκε Il.1.48; μ. βέλος S.*Ph*.1300, cf. X.*Cyr*.4.3.9; ἐκ χερὸς λίθον, ἀπὸ γλώσσης λόγον, Men.1092; of plants, *put forth*, καρπούς Porph.*Abst*.2.13; μ. ξίφος ἐς γυναῖκα *plunge* it into her, E.*Or*.1133; but μ. οἱ τὰς αἰχμάς *laid* them *aside* as he ordered, Hdt.3.128, cf. 4.3, 9.62: elliptically, μεθῆκε (sc. τὰς ἡνίας) E.*Fr*.779.7; ναῒ μεθεῖναι *give* the ship *her way*, S.*Aj*.250 (lyr.). b. *relieve*, κῆρ ἄχεος Il.17.539. c. c. dat. pers. et acc., *give up to, surrender*, Ἕκτορι νίκην 14.364; στέμματ' ἀνέμοις E.*Ba*.350. d. *resign, throw aside*, χόλον Il.15.138, Od.1.77; Ἀχιλλῆϊ μεθέμεν χ. as a favour to Achilles, Il.1.283 (cf. II.3); μ. καρδίας χόλον from one's heart, E.*Med*.590; *give up* a scheme, Hdt.1.133; τὰ παρεόντα ἀγαθά ib.33; τὴν ἀρχήν Id.3.143; τὴν τυραννίδα Id.5.37; αἰδῶ A.*Pers*.699 (troch.); τὸ κόσμιον S.*El*.872; τἀφανῆ the search for the unknowable, Id.*OT*131; τεμένη..μέθες E.*Supp*.1212:—Pass., ἡ πρότερον γνώμη ἀποδεχθεῖσα μετείσθω Hdt.4.98. e. *forgive* one a fault, Ἀθηναίοισι τὰς ἁμαρτάδας Id.8.140.α'; *remit*, φόρον τῇσι πόλισι Id.6.59; τόνδε κίνδυνον μεθείς *excusing* you this peril, E.*Ph*.1229. f. *let in, introduce*, τὸ δεῖγμα εἰς τὰς ἄλλας πόλεις Pl.*Lg*.951d; τὸ μὲν τῶν ἐγκυρτίων εἰς τὸ στόμα μεθῆκεν Id.*Ti*.78c. II. intr., *relax* one's energies: 1. abs., *to be slack, remiss, dally*, Od.4.372, etc.; esp. in battle, Il.13.229, 20.361, etc. 2. c. inf., *omit* or *neglect* to do, ὅς τις μεθίῃσι μάχεσθαι 13.234, cf. 23.434; οἱ ἵπποι μετιέντες τὰς νομὰς νέμεσθαι Hdt.1.78; μ. τὰ δέοντα πράττειν X.*Mem*.2.1.33. b. *permit*, μεθεῖσά μοι λέγειν *having left it* for me to speak, *having allowed* me, S.*El*.628:—Pass., δύο πηγαὶ μεθεῖνται ῥεῖν Pl.*Lg*.636d. 3. c. gen. rei, *relax, cease from*, μεθιέντα.. στυγεροῦ πολέμοιο Il.6.330; ἀλκῆς 4.234; βίης Od.21.126; μεθιεὶς πολέμου (prob. for πόλεμον) Tyrt.12.44; μ. τῆς χρησμοσύνης Hdt.9.33; μέθιεν.. χόλοιο Τηλεμάχῳ [the suitors] *ceased from* wrath in deference to Telemachus, Od.21.377. b. c. gen. pers., *abandon, neglect*, Il.11.841. 4. c. part., κλαύσας καὶ ὀδυράμενος μεθέηκε after weeping and lamenting he *leaves off*, 24.48. III. Med., *free oneself from, let go one's hold of*, c. gen., παιδὸς οὐ μεθήσομαι E.*Hec*.400, cf. Ar.*Pl*.42, 75, etc.; σῶν γονάτων E.*Hipp*.326; τοῦ θρόνου Ar.*Ra*.830, etc.; σπουδασμάτων Metrod.*Herc*.831.15: in this sense the acc. is rarely used and perh. corrupt, ἐκεῖνο (fort. ἐκείνου) E.*Ph*.519; τόνδε (fort. τοῦδε) Ar.*V*.416; in S.*El*.1277 (lyr.) the constr. is μή μ' ἀποστερήσῃς τῶν σῶν προσώπων ἁδονάν, [ὥστε] μεθέσθαι [αὐτῆς], and in E.*Med*.736 ἄγουσιν οὐ μεθεῖ' ἂν ἐκ γαίας ἐμέ, the acc. is governed by ἄγουσιν.

**μεθιππεύω**, *ride away*, εἰς Λίγυας App.*Pun*.44.

**μεθίπταμαι**, *fly away to another* place, App.*Hisp*.73(71), *BC*4.83.

⊛ **μεθιστάνω**, later form of sq., *Milet*.3.148.54 (ii B.C.), D.S.2.57, A.D.*Adv*.191.13 (Pass.): **μεθιστάω**, D.S.18.58.

⊛ **μεθίστημι**: A. causal, in pres. and impf., fut. and aor. 1, *place in another way, change*, τοι ταῦτα μεταστήσω I *will change* thee this present, i.e. *give another instead*, Od.4.612; μ. τὰ νόμιμα πάντα Hdt.1.65; ὄνομα, τύχην, E.*Ba*.296, *Heracl*.935; τὸ μέγα εἰς οὐδὲν χρόνος μ. Id.*Fr*.304 (lyr.); μ. νόμους X.*HG*5.4.64; ταύτην τὴν πολιτείαν Pl.*R*.562c; ἐκ τοῦ παρόντος κόσμου τὴν πόλιν μεταστήσας Th.8.48; ἐς ὀλιγαρχίαν μ. [τὴν πολιτείαν] X.*HG*2.3.24; ἐξ ὀλιγαρχίας ἐς τὸ δημοκρατεῖσθαι μ. τοὺς Βυζαντίους ib.4.8.27; τὰ ἐκεῖ πάντα πρὸς Λακεδαιμονίους ib.2.2.5; also ἐκ τῆς καθεστηκυίας ἄλλην μ. [πολιτείαν] *introduce a new* polity, Arist.*Pol*.1301$^{b}$8; μ. βασιλείαν ἀντὶ τυραννίδος Pl.*Ep*.319d. 2. c. gen. partit., οὐ μεθίστησι τοῦ χρώματος he *changes* [nothing] *of* his colour, Ar.*Eq*.398 (lyr.). II. of persons, *set free*, τινὰ νόσου S.*Ph*.463; κακῶν, πόνων,

E.*Hel.*1442, *IT*991, cf. 775; ὕπνου Id.*Or.*133. 2. *remove by killing*, αὐτόν J.*AJ*18.6.2: so in Med., τὸν ἄνθρωπον ib.18.9.5. 3. *remove from one place to another*, Th.4.57; ὠστράκιζον καὶ μεθίστασαν ἐκ τῆς πόλεως Arist.*Pol.*1284ᵃ21; ἐς ἄλλην χθόνα μ. πόδα E.*Ba.*49:— aor. 1 Med. μεταστήσασθαι *remove from oneself* or *from one's presence*, Hdt.1.89, 8.101, And.1.12, Th.1.79; *banish*, Aeschin.3.129; μ. φρουρὰς ἐκ πόλεων Plb.18.44.4.

B. Pass., with aor. 1 μετεστάθην [ᾰ] E.*El.*1202 (lyr.), D.26.6, also aor. 2, pf., and plpf. Act.: I. of persons, *stand among* or *in the midst of*, c. dat., ἑτάροισι μεθίστατο Il.5.514. 2. *change one's position*, τυράννοις ἐκποδὼν μεθίστασο *make way* for them, E.*Ph.*40; *depart*, παλαιὸν εἰς ἴχνος A.*Supp.*538 (lyr.); ἐκ τῆς τάξιος Hdt.9.58; ἐκ τυραννικοῦ κύκλου S.*Aj.*750; ἔξω τῆς οἰκουμένης Aeschin.3.165; ἐκ φωτὸς εἰς σκότος μ. Pl.*R.*518a: c. gen., δεῦρ' Ἰωλκίας χθονὸς E.*Med.*551; θρόνων Id.*Ph.*75; μ. φυγῇ Id.*Med.*1295: abs., μετάσταθ', ἀπόβαθι S.*OC*162 (lyr.), cf. D.23.69; ὅταν μεταστῇ [ὄλβος] S.*Fr.*646.6. 3. c. gen. rei, *change, cease from*, κότου A.*Eu.*900; ξηρῶν τρόπων Ar.*V.*1451 (lyr.), cf. *Pl.*365; λύπης, κακῶν, E.*Alc.*1122, *Hel.*856; μ. βίου die, Id.*Alc.*21 (also μ. alone, J.*AJ*17.4.2, Plu.2.1104c; ἑκὼν μ. commit suicide, Vett.Val.94.9); μ. φρενῶν *change* from *one's* former mind, *change one's* mind, E.*Ba.*944. 4. *go over to* another party, *revolt*, Th.1.35, etc.; ἀπό τινος Id.8.76; παρά or πρός τινα, Id.1.107, 130. 5. *to be banished*, ὑπό τινων D.26.6. II. of things, *change, alter*, either *for the better*, τῆς τύχης εὖ μετεστεώσης Hdt.1.118; ἐς τὸ λῷον.. μεθέστηκεν κέαρ E.*Med.*911; or *for the worse*, ἐξ ἧς [πολιτείας] ἡ ὀλιγαρχία μετέστη from which oligarchy *arose by a change*, Pl.*R.*553e, cf. X.*HG*2.3.24, Arist.*Pol.*1301ᵃ22, Plb.6.9.10; εἴ τι μὴ δαίμων.. μεθέστηκε στρατῷ *hath changed* for them, A.*Pers.*158 (troch.); νέος μεθέστηκ' ἐκ γέροντος E.*Heracl.*796. 2. Medic., of pains, *change position*, εἰς τὴν ἄνω χώραν Gal.16.652.

**μέθλην**· τὸν ἄρνα, Hsch. **μεθλίτης, -άριος**, v. μεθελίτης.

***μεθοδ-εία** or **-ία**, ἡ, *craft, wiliness*, *Ep.Eph.*4.14: pl., μ. τοῦ διαβόλου ib.6.11. II. *method of collecting taxes* or *debts* (in form μεθοδία), *POxy.*1134.9 (v A. D.), 136.18 (vi A. D.). **-ευμα**, ατος, τό, *that which is regularly practised*, Phld.*Ir.*p.49 W. **-ευτέον**, *one must conduct*, διὰ παραδείγματος τὸ σκέμμα Sch.Pl.*Lg.*627a; τὴν ἐμβολὴν ὃν τρόπον ὑπογέγραπται Apollon.Cit.1. ***-ευτής**, οῦ, ὁ, *one who goes to work by rule*, Ptol.*Tetr.*165. 2. *master of method*, c. gen., μύθων πλάσεως Eust.2.5. **-ευτικός**, ή, όν, *regular*, Agatharch. 73. ***-εύω**, aor. with double augm. ἐμεθώδευσα D.L.8.83: pf. Pass. μεμεθώδευμαι Eust.1325.32: (μέθοδος):—*treat* or *practise by rule* or *method*, τέχνην Phld.*Rh.*1.31 S., Ph.ap.Eus.*PE*8.14, cf. D.H. *Th.*19, D.S.1.15; τὴν ἀλήθειαν ἐκ τῆς ἐμπειρίας μ. ib.81; τέχνας D.H. 2.28:—Pass., Ph.1.212. 2. *deal with*, i.e. *remove, avert* an impending misfortune, *PMag.Leid.W.*16.13. 3. c. acc. pers., *defraud*, '*get round*', Just.*Nov.*115.5.1:—Pass., ib.124.3; γυνὴ -εύεται ἐπαίνοις Charito 7.6:—abs. in Act., *employ craft*, Lxx 2*Ki.*19.27:—in Med., Plb.38.12.10, Arg.D.47. 4. Medic., *treat*, '*doctor*', in Pass., Orib.*Fr.*74, Paul.Aeg.6.26: metaph., πᾶς λίβανος δολοῦται τῇ.. ῥητίνῃ -ευομένῃ (v.l. -ευόμενος) Dsc.1.68. 5. *collect, exact* a tax or debt, *Cod.Just.*10.19.9.1, 1.3.38.2. **-ηγέω**, aor. μεθωδήγησα, *lead another way*, *AP*9.351 (Leon.Alex.). **-ικός**, ή, όν, *going to work by rule, methodical, systematic*, ἐπιστῆμαι Plb.10.47.12; τὸ μ. τῆς τέχνης Phld.*Rh.*1.23 S.: Comp., Id.*Sign.*28. Adv. -κῶς Plb.5.98.10; ἰατρὸς ἄνθρωπον ἀποκτείνει μ. Phld.*Rh.*1.19 S.: Comp. -ώτερον S.E.*M.*8. 141. II. τὰ μ., a lost work of Arist., prob. on Logic, *Rh.*1356ᵇ19, cf. D.H.*Amm.*1.8; αἱ μ. συντάξεις ib.6. III. οἱ μ. '*methodic*' physicians, opp. rationalists and empirics, Gal.*Sect.Intr.*6; μ. αἵρεσις Id. *Libr.Propr.*1; μ. ἰατρός Id.10.140, *Epigr.Gr.*306 (Smyrna). IV. in Surgery, μ. τρόποι *first-aid* treatment, Heliod.ap.Orib.49.1.1, 3. V. *crafty*, Vett.Val.4.14; τὰ μ. ib.16. ***-ιον**, τό, = ἐφόδιον, *OGI*229. 31 (Smyrna, iii B. C.), D.L.7.198, Hsch., dub. l. in *PCair.Zen.*44.25 (iii B. C.). II. = μέθοδος II. 2, Anon.ap.Suid., cf. Petron.36. **-ίτης**, ου, ὁ, = τεχνίτης (nisi leg. -ευτής), Hsch. ***-ος**, ἡ, (μετά, ὁδός) *following after, pursuit*, νύμφης μέθοδον ποιεῖσθαι Anon.ap.Suid. s. v. ζεῦγος ἡμιονικόν (*EM*409.35):—hence, II. *pursuit of knowledge, investigation*, Pl.*Sph.*218d, 235c, al.; μ. ποιεῖσθαι to pursue one's inquiry, ib.243d; ἐν τῇ πρώτῃ μ. Arist.*Pol.*1289ᵃ26: hence, *treatise*, Dam.*Pr.*451. 2. *mode of prosecuting such inquiry, method, system*, Pl.*Phdr.*270c, Arist.*EN*1129ᵃ6, *Pol.*1252ᵃ18, etc.; ἡ διαλεκτικὴ μ. Pl.*R.*533c, Arist.*Rh.*1358ᵃ4; joined with τέχνη, Id.*EN* 1094ᵃ1, cf. Phld.*Rh.*1.32 S.; μ. ἔχειν to have a *plan* or *system*, Arist.*Top.*101ᵃ29; ἡ περὶ τὸν πίνακα μ. Plu.*Rom.*12. 3. ἡ τοῦ πάντα κινεῖσθαι μ. the *doctrine* of motion, Pl.*Tht.*183c. 4. '*methodic*' *medicine*, ἰητὴρ μεθόδου.. προστάτα *Epigr.Gr.*306 (Smyrna), cf. Julian. ap.Gal.18(1).256. 5. Rhet., *means*, τῆς εὑρέσεως, τοῦ κατορθοῦν, τοῦ ἀνεπαχθῶς ἑαυτὸν ἐπαινεῖν, Hermog.*Meth.*2, 22, 25. b. *means of recognizing*, τῶν στάσεων Id.*Stat.*1, 2. c. *mode of treating* the subject-matter, Id.*Id.*1.1. III. *trick, ruse*, Plu.2.176a: pl., Vett.Val.242.11; μ. ἐρωτικαί Aristaenet.1.17; *stratagem*, Lxx 2*Ma.* 13.18.

**μεθολκή**, ἡ, *diversion, distraction*, Ph.1.459 (pl.), 559, Plu.2.517c.

**μεθομήρεος**, ὁ, μ. ἐρίφων prob. *companion of kids*, i.e. Pan, Pi. *Fr.*47.

**μεθομῑλέω**, *hold converse with*, c. dat., Il.1.269.

**μεθομοίωσις**, εως, ἡ, *transformation*, Eust.1742.16.

**μεθόπιον**, τό, = μετόπη, *SIG*246 ii 67 (Delph., iv B. C.), Hsch.; μ[..]όπια *IG*2².1666 A 39 (iv B. C.).

**μεθόπωρον**, τό, = μετόπωρον, Phld.*Piet.* in *Stud.Pal.*6.130, Hsch., and codd. of Hp.*Aër.*6, etc.:—hence **μεθοπωρινός**, = μετοπ-, Eudox. *Ars* 2.28, al.; μ. πυλαία *BCH*38.26 (Delph., ii B. C.); ἰσημερία μ. *Gloss.*

**μεθορίζω**· *determino*, *Gloss.*: μεθορίζει· μετέχει, Hsch.

***μεθόριος**, α, ον (also ος, ον Ph. (v. infr.)), (ὅρος) *lying between as a boundary*, γῆ μεθορία τῆς Ἀργείας καὶ Λακωνικῆς the *border* country *between*.., Th.2.27, 4.56: neut. pl., *borders, marches*, ἐν -ίοις τῆς Ἀττικῆς καὶ Βοιωτίας Th.2.18, cf. X.*Cyr.*1.4.16, etc.; τὰ μ. Τύρου καὶ Σιδῶνος v.l. in *Ev.Marc.*7.24; μεθόρια φιλοσόφου τε καὶ πολιτικοῦ Prodic.6: sg., τὸ μεθόριον Lxx *Jo.*19.27 cod. A: metaph., Pl.*Lg.* 878b; ὁ ὕπνος δοκεῖ εἶναι τοῦ ζῆν καὶ τοῦ μὴ ζῆν μ. Arist.*GA*778ᵇ30, cf. *HA*588ᵇ5, Hierocl. in *CA*20 p.462 M.; ἐν μεθορίῳ [εἶναι] Arist.*Pr.*943ᵇ26, Gal.6.255; ἡ Ἀράβων καὶ Ἀσσυρίων μεθορία (sc. χώρα) Plu.*Crass.* 22; ἡ μεθόριος Ph.2.514; ἔστι ἐν λιτότητι μεθόριος there is a *limit* to frugality, cj. in Epicur.*Sent.Vat.*63.

**μεθορκόω**, *bind by a new oath*, τὴν στρατιὰν ἐς ἑαυτόν App.*BC*4. 62. 2. μεθόρκ[ωσόν μ]οι ὅρκον *swear with* me an oath, Pap. in *Sitzb. Heidelb.Akad.*1923(2).14.

**μεθορμάομαι**, Pass., *rush in pursuit of, make a dash at*, μεθορμηθείς Il.20.192, Od.5.325.

**μεθορμίζω**, *remove from one anchorage to another*, intr. (sc. νέας), μ. εἰς Σηστόν X.*HG*2.1.25; μ. σκάφος Iamb.*VP*3.17: metaph., τοῦ νῦν σκυθρωποῦ.. μεθορμιεῖ σε E.*Alc.*798; ἐξ ἕδρας μεθώρμισα [πλόκαμον] Id.*Ba.*931:—Med., μεθορμίσασθαι μόχθων πάρα *to seek a refuge* from.., Id.*Med.*442 (lyr.), cf. 258; *sail from one place to another, put out from*, μετορμίζεσθαι ἐκ (or ἀπό).. ἐς.. Hdt.2.115, 7.183, cf. Th.6. 88: metaph., πρὸς εὐσέβειαν cj. in Ph.2.219.

**μέθῠ**, τό, *wine*, Hom., only in nom. and acc., πολλὸν.. μέθυ πίνετο Il.9.469; σῖτον καὶ μέθυ ἡδύ Od.4.746; ἐκ κριθῶν μ. A.*Supp.*953, etc.: gen. μέθυος first in Pl.*Epigr.*22, Nic.*Th.*582, Marc.Sid.50; dat. μέθυϊ *An.Ox.*3.255. (Cf. Skt. *mádhu* 'sweet, sweet drink, honey', OE. *medu* 'mead', Slav. *medŭ* 'honey', etc.)

**μεθῠδότης**, ου, ὁ, = μεθυδώτης, Jul.*Mis.*359c, *EM*575.46.

**μεθ-υδριάς**, άδος, ἡ, (ὕδωρ) νύμφη, = ὑδριάς, *water-nymph*, *APl.*4. 226 (pl., Alc.). **-υδρίδες**, αἱ, kind of small birds, Hsch. (-υθρ- cod.). **-ύδριον**, τό, properly *Between-waters*, name of a place in the heart of Arcadia, whence the waters ran different ways, some north, some south, Th.5.58.

**μεθῠδώτης**, ου, ὁ, *giver of wine*, of Dionysus, *AP*9.524.13, Orph.*H.* 47.1.

***μεθ-υμναῖος**, ὁ, (μέθυ) the *wine-god*, epith. of Dionysus, Plu.2. 648e, Orph.*Fr.*280, Epic. in *Arch.Pap.*7.4. **-ύμνιον**· τὸ μετὰ τὸν ὕμνον, ἢ ἡ μετὰ μέθης ᾠδή, Phot.

**μεθυπάρχω**, *exist after*, Phlp. in *GA*85.24; opp. προϋπάρχω, Simp. in *Cael.*368.6.

**μεθυπερβᾰτῶς**, Adv. *by changing the order of words*, Ammon. in *APr.*16.33.

**μεθῠ-πῖδαξ**, ἄκος, ὁ, ἡ, *gushing with wine*, βότρυς *AP*6.22 (Zon.). **-πλήξ**, ῆγος, ὁ, ἡ, *wine-stricken*, i.e. *drunken*, Call.*Fr.* 223, *APl.*4.306 (Leon.).

**μεθυπο-δέομαι**, Med., *put on another person's shoes*, Ar.*Ec.* 544. **-στρέψιμος**, ον, gloss on παλινόστιμος, Sch.Opp.*H.*1. 616. **-στρωσις**, εως, ἡ, *changing one's bedding*, Hp.*Fract.*16 (pl.), cf. Gal.10.431. **-χώρησις**, εως, ἡ, *expulsion*, τῆς τροφῆς Philum.(?) ap.Aët.9.23.

**μεθύσης** [ῠ], ου, ὁ, = μεθυστής, Ath.15.685f, Luc.*Sol.*5.

**μεθύσιον**· εἶδος ἀμπέλου, Hsch.

**μέθῠσις**, εως, ἡ, *drunkenness*, Thgn.838.

***μεθύσκω**, fut. -ύσω [ῠ] Lxx *De.*32.42: aor. 1 ἐμέθυσα ib.2*Ki.*11.13, Ep. -υσσα Nonn.*D.*3.11, *AP*5.260 (Agath.); inf. μεθύσαι Alex. (v. infr.):—Pass., fut. μεθυσθήσομαι Lxx *Ho.*14.8, Luc.*Luct.*13, D.L. 7.118: aor. ἐμεθύσθην Heraclit.117, E.*Cyc.*167, etc.; Aeol. inf. μεθύσθην Alc.35: pf. μεμέθυσμαι Hedyl.ap.Ath.4.176d:—Causal of μεθύω, *make drunk, intoxicate*, Διόνυσος οἶδε τὸ μεθύσαι μόνον Alex. 214; μ. ἑαυτὴν οἴνῳ Luc.*Syr.D.*22: metaph., πάνθ' ὅσα δι' ἡδονῆς μεθύσκοντα παράφρονας ποιεῖ Pl.*Lg.*649d; τὴν αἴσθησιν Thphr.*Od.* 46; Ἀθηνᾶ μεθύσασα ὕπνῳ τοὺς βαρβάρους Vett.Val.347.26. 2. *give to drink*, θηλὴ μεθύσκει με μητρυφῇ Babr.89.9; *moisten*, βωμοὺς ἐν γάλακτι, τέφρην, *AP*6.99 (Phil.), 11.8. II. Pass., = μεθύω, *drink freely, get drunk*, Alc. l. c., Hdt.1.133, etc.; ὀδμῇ, οἴνῳ, ib.202; πίνων οὐ μεθύσκεται X.*Cyr.*1.3.11: in aor. ἐμεθύσθην, *to be drunk*, ἀνὴρ ὁκόταν μεθυσθῇ Heraclit. l. c.; ἅπαξ μεθυσθεὶς E.*Cyc.*167, cf. Ar.*V.*1252; ἀνθρώπους οἵους μεθυσθέντας D.2.19: c. gen., νέκταρος *with* nectar, Pl.*Smp.*203b: metaph., ὅταν πόλις [ἐλευθερίας] μεθυσθῇ Id.*R.*562d: c. dat., ταῖς ἐξουσίαις *with* power, D.H.4.74:—in Hp. *Steril.*218 μεθυσκέτω is corrupt for μεθυσκέσθω. 2. *to be filled* with food, μ. σίτῳ Lxx *Ho.*14.8; cf. μεθύει· πεπλήρωται, Hsch.

**μέθυσμα**, ατος, τό, *an intoxicating drink*, Lxx 1*Ki.*1.15, *Je.*13.13, Ph.1.324, al.: metaph., ib.296.

**μεθῠσοκότταβος**, ον, *drunk with cottabus-playing*, Ar.*Ach.*525.

**μέθῠσος**, *drunk with wine*, prop. only fem., μέθυσος Ἀμαζών Hecat. 34 J.; μεθύση γραῦς Ar.*Nu.*555, cf. *V.*1402, Phryn.129, Poll.6.25. 2. later also, of men, μεθύσους τοὺς ἐμπόρους ποιεῖ Men.67.1, cf. *Com. Adesp.*384, Lxx *Pr.*23.21, 1*Ep.Cor.*5.11, Plu.*Brut.*5, Luc.*Tim.*55, S.E.*P.*3.195; *drunken, intemperate*, Ceb.34, Jul.*Caes.*330c.

**μεθῠσοχάρυβδις** [ᾰ], εως, ἡ, *wine-charybdis*, nickname for a drunken woman, *Com.Adesp.*1077.

**μεθυστάς**, άδος, fem., *drunken*: metaph., μεθυστάδες γάμων *Trag. Adesp.*238.

***μεθύστερος**, α, ον, *living after*, καλόν τ' ἀκοῦσαι καὶ λέγειν μεθυστέ-

*pois for posterity*, A.*Th.*581; μεθυστέρῳ ἐν χρόνῳ in *after* time, Cratin. 119. II. neut. as Adv., of time, *afterwards*, ἔπειτα μ. *h.Cer.*205; *so long after, so late*, A.*Ch.*516; οὐ μ. *in a moment*, Id.*Ag.*425 (lyr.); *too late*, S.*Tr.*710; τὸ μ. *hereafter*, Id.*Ph.*1133 (lyr.), Porph.*Abst.*4.2.

**μεθ-υστής**, οῦ, ὁ, *drunkard*, Arr.*Epict.*4.2.7, *AP*5.295 (Agath.). **-υστικός**, ή, όν, *intoxicating*, ἁρμονία Arist.*Pol.*1342ᵇ25. II. of men, *given to wine, drunken*, Pl.*R.*573c. **-ύστρια**, ἡ, fem. of μεθυστής, Theopomp.Com.93.

**μεθυ-σφᾰλέω**, *to be reeling-drunk*, Opp.*C.*4.204. **-σφᾰλής**, ές, *reeling-drunk*, ἴχνος *APl.*4.99, Nonn.*D.*18.151; λάγυνε μεθυσφαλές *AP*6.248 (Marc. Arg.); of a person, Nonn.*D.*19.59. ⊛**-τρόφος**, ον, *producing wine*, ἡμερίς Simon.183.1. **-χάρμων**, ον, gen. ονος, *rejoicing in wine*, Man.4.300.

**μεθύω** [ῠ], (μέθυ), only pres. and impf.: fut. and aor. Act. belong to μεθύσκω (μεθύσας is f.l. in Nonn.*D.*28.211; μεθύσαντας is f.l. for -τες in Plu.2.239a), aor. being supplied by Pass. of μεθύσκω:—*to be drunken with wine*, νευστάζων κεφαλῇ, μεθύοντι ἐοικώς Od.18. 240; μεθύων, opp. νήφων, Thgn.478,627, cf. Alc.*Supp.*4.12, Pi.*Fr.* 128, Ar.*Pl.*1048, *PHal.*1.193 (iii B.C.), etc.; μ. ὑπὸ τοῦ οἴνου X. *Smp.*2.26; τὸ μεθύειν *drunkenness*, Antiph.187.2, Alex.43; τὸ μ. πημονῆς λυτήριον S.*Fr.*758. II. metaph., 1. of things, *to be drenched, steeped* in any liquid, c. dat., e. g. βοείην.. μεθύουσαν ἀλοιφῇ Il.17.390; μεθύων ἐλαίῳ λύχνος Babr.114.1; [χείμαρρος] ὄμβροισι μ. *AP*9.277 (Antiphil.). 2. of persons, *to be intoxicated* with passion, pride, etc., ὑπὸ τῆς Ἀφροδίτης X.*Smp.*8.21; ὑπὸ τρυφῆς Pl.*Criti.* 121a; ἔρωτι Anacr.19; τῷ μεγέθει τῶν πεπραγμένων D.4.49; περὶ τὰς ἡδονάς Philostr.*VS*1.22.1; οὐ μ. τὴν φρόνησιν Alex.301; μ. τὸ φίλημα *AP*5.304. b. *to be stupefied, stunned*, πληγαῖς μεθύων Theoc.22.98; ἐξ ὀδυνάων Opp.*H.*5.228, cf. Nonn. l. c.

**μειᾰγωγ-έω**, (μεῖον) *bring the sacrificial lamb to the scale*, hence metaph., μ. τὴν τραγῳδίαν *weigh* it *as you would a lamb*, Ar.*Ra.*798:— hence **-εῖον**, τό, and **-ία**, ἡ, Suid.: **-ός**, ὁ, ὥσπερ μ. ἑστιῶν (τὴν πόλιν) Eup.116.

**μεῖγμα**, v. μίγμα.

⊛**μείγνυμι** or **μίγνυμι**, μ(ε)ίγνυσι Pl.*Lg.*691e; imper. μ(ε)ίγνυ Id. *Phlb.*63e:—also **μ(ε)ιγνύω**, Damox.2.60, Arist.*HA*627ᵃ23, Thphr. *Lap.*53, etc.: impf. ἐμ(ε)ίγνυν, pl. ἐμ(ε)ίγνυσαν (συν-) X.*Cyr.*8.1.46; poet. μ(ε)ίγνυον Pi.*N.*4.21: fut. μ(ε)ίξω Od.22.221 (μετα-), S.*OC* 1047 (lyr.), Pl.*Phlb.*64b: aor. ἔμ(ε)ιξα Archil.86, Pi.*I.*7(6).25, etc.; inf. μ(ε)ῖξαι Il.15.510: pf. μέμῐχα (συμ-) Plb.16.10.1, 38.13.5: plpf. ἐμεμίχειν [ῐ] (συν-) D.C.47.45:—**Med.** and **Pass.**, μ(ε)ίγνυμαι Pl. *Phd.*113c: impf. ἐμ(ε)ίγνυντο (ἐπ-) Th.2.1: fut. μ(ε)ίξομαι Od.6.136, 24.314, μεμ(ε)ίξομαι Hes.*Op.*179, μ(ε)ιχθήσομαι Aeschin.1.166 (ἀνα-), Palaeph.13; also μῐγήσομαι Il.10.365: aor. 1 ἐμίχθη ib.457, ἐμ(ε)ίχθην A.*Supp.*295, Hdt.2.181, Ph.*Bel.*70.5, etc.; inf. μιχθήμεναι Il. 11.438; but in Hom. and Att. more commonly aor. 2 ἐμίγην [ῐ]; Ep. μίγην Il.21.143; inf. μιγήμεναι 15.409, μιγῆν Parm.12.5; both forms in Trag., μ(ε)ιχθῆναι A. l. c., al. (v. infr.), μιγῆναι Id.*Pr.*738: Ep. aor. Pass. ἔμικτο Od.1.433, μίκτο Il.11.354, 16.813, A.R.3.1223; part. μίγμενος in trans. sense, Nic.*Al.*574: aor. Med. ἐμ(ε)ιξάμην Thphr. *CP*3.22.3: pf. μέμιγμαι Il.10.424, etc.; 3 pl. ἀνα-μεμ(ε)ίχαται Hdt.1. 146: plpf. ἐμέμικτο Il.4.438.—For the pres. and impf. Hom. and Hdt. always use μίσγω, which occurs once in Trag., S.*Fr.*271 (anap.), never in Com., sts. in Att. Prose, Th.6.104 (προσ-), Thphr.*Sens.*43; part. μίσγων Pl.*Ti.*41d; also impf. ἔμισγον Th.3.22 (προσ-), Pl.*Ti.* l.c.; also in later Prose, Plb.9.8.9 (προσ-), 18.32.2, 31.17.5 (συμ-), *PTeb.*12.7,18, 26.3 (συμ-, ii B.C.), etc.: Ep. impf. ἐμισγέσκοντο Od. 20.7. (In codd. usu. μι- in all tenses and derivs.; in Inscrr. and Pap. freq. μει-, e. g. μειγνύς Phld.*Mus.*p.13 K., μειγνύμενος Limen.14 (128/7 B.C.), ὀν-εμείχνυτο Sapph.*Supp.*20c.2 (= pp.21, 78 Lobel, ὀν-εμίγνυτο ib.20b.4): fut. inf. συν-μείσχι[ν] *IG*1².920 (vi B.C.): aor. συν-έμειξα *PPetr.*2 p.64 (iii B.C.); inf. συμ-μεῖξαι *PEleph.*29.11 (iii B.C.): pf. Pass. μέμειγμαι Phld.*Vit.*p.34 J.: aor. Pass. ἐμείχθην A.*Fr.*99.5 (Pap. of ii B.C.), E.*Antiop.*iv B45 (Pap. of iii B.C.), Phld.*Po.*2.12; similarly μεῖξις Id.*Mus.*p.65 K.; σύμ-μεικτος freq. in Att. Inscrr., *IG* 2².1388.63 (iv B.C.), al.; μεικτός *PCair.Zen.*292.25, al. (iii B.C.): μι- is found in συνανα-μιγνύμενα Phld.*D.*3.9, μιγνύωσι Id.*Ir.*p.41 K.: aor. inf. συμ-μῖξαι *SIG*568.6 (Halasarna, late iii B.C.): pf. part. Pass. μεμιγμένος Wilcken *Chr.*198.12 (iii B.C.): aor. part. Pass. μιχθεὶς *Pae. Erythr.*5 (iv B.C. and ii A.D., v.l. μει- ii A.D.); similarly σύμ-μικτος *AJA*31.350 (vase, v B.C.); the oldest forms were prob. μίσγω μείξω ἔμειξα μέμιγμαι ἐμίχθην (μίκτο) μεῖγμα μῖξις μικτός (cf. the forms of τεύχω, φεύγω, etc.); the μει- forms already in v B.C. had encroached, and after 150 B.C. were freq. written μι- (i. e. μῑ-)):—*mix*, strictly of liquids, οἶνον ἐνὶ κρητῆρσι καὶ ὕδωρ Od.1.110, etc.; also of a solid and liquid, θρόμβῳ δ' ἔμ(ε)ιξεν αἵματος φίλον γάλα A.*Ch.*546; of two solids, ἄλεσσι μεμιγμένον εἶδαρ Od.11.123; also μ. ἐκ γῆς καὶ πυρὸς Pl.*Prt.* 320d; μ(ε)ιγνὺς [ταῦτα] μετὰ τῆς οὐσίας Id.*Ti.*35b:—Med. for Act., *AP*7.44 (Ion), Nic.*Th.*603:—Pass., v. infr. B. II. generally, *join, bring together*, in various ways: 1. in hostile sense, μ(ε)ῖξαι χεῖράς τε μένος τε *join* battle hand to hand, Il.15.510; μ(ε)ίξαντες.. Ἄρευα Alc.31; Κόλχοισι βίαν μ. Pi.*P.*4.213; χερσὶν ἐναντία χεῖρας ἔμ(ε)ιξεν A.R.2.78; Ἄρη μ(ε)ίξουσιν S.*OC*1047 (lyr.):—Pass., μ(ε)ιγνυμένου πολέμου Callin.1.11. b. in good sense, ἀλώπηξ καιετὸς ξυνωνίην ἔμ(ε)ιξαν Archil.86. 2. *bring into connexion with, make acquainted with*, ἄνδρας.. μισγέμεναι κακότητι καὶ ἄλγεσι Od.20.203; Καδμεῖοί νιν.. ἄνθεσι μ(ε)ίγνυον *covered* him *with* flowers, Pi.*N.*4.21; reversely, ᾧ πότμον.. Ἄρης ἔμ(ε)ιξεν *upon* whom A. *brought* death, Id.*I.*7(6).25.

B. **Pass.**, with fut. Med. μείξομαι (v. sub init.):—*to be mixed up with, mingled among*, προμάχοισιν ἐμίχθη Il.5.134, etc.; ἐνὶ προμάχοισι μιγέντα Od.18.379; [σῆμα] οὔ τι μεμιγμένον ἐστὶν ὁμίλῳ 8.196; ἔόλπει μ(ε)ίξεσθαι ξενίῃ hoped to *hold intercourse* in guest-friendship, 24.314; Τρώεσσιν ἐν ἀγρομένοισιν ἔμιχθεν Il.3.209, cf. 10.180; ἐν ταῖς κακαῖσιν ἀγαθαὶ μεμ(ε)ιγμέναι E.*Ion* 399; *hold intercourse with, live with*, Od.7.247, etc.; ἐμίσγετο δαίμονι δαίμων Emp.59.1; αἷς οὐ μ(ε)ίγνυνται θεῶν τις A.*Eu.*69: abs., *hold intercourse*, θάμ' ἐνθάδ' ἐόντες ἐμισγόμεθ' Od.4.178. b. *to be mixed* or *compounded*, μεμ(ε)ιγμένον μέλι σὺν γάλακτι Pi.*N.*3.77; Κύπριδος ἐλπὶς.. μειγνυμένα Διονυσίοισι δώροις B.*Scol.Oxy.*1361 *Fr.*1.9; σύλλογος νέων καὶ πρεσβυτέρων μεμ(ε)ιγμένος Pl.*Lg.*951d, cf. E.*Fr.*997; μεμ(ε)ιγμένην πολιτείαν ἐκ κακοῦ τε καὶ ἀγαθοῦ Pl.*R.*548c; ἔκ τε ταὐτοῦ καὶ θατέρου καὶ τῆς οὐσίας μ. Id.*Ti.* 35b. 2. *to be brought into contact with*, κάρη κονίῃσιν ἐμίχθη his head *was rolled* in the dust, Il.10.457, Od.22.329; ὄτ' ἐν κονίῃσι μιγείης Il.3.55; οὐδ' ἔτ' ἔασε [ἔγχος].. μιχθήμεναι ἔγκασι φωτός she let not the spear *reach* them, 11.438; κλισίῃσι μιγήμεναι 15.409; ἐς Ἀχαιοὺς μίσγετο *went to join* them, 18.216; ἔσω μίσγεσθαι *to come among us* in the house, Od.18.49; μίσγεσθαι ὑπὲρ ποταμοῖο *to join* the rest across the river, Il.23.73: freq. in Pi. in various senses, c. dat. (with or without ἐν), *come to*, ἔν τ' Ὠκεανοῦ πελάγεσσι μίγεν *P.*4.251; Λακεδαιμονίων μιχθέντες ἀνδρῶν ἤθεσιν ib.257; ἐν αἱμακουρίαις μέμικται *is present at* that feast, *O.*1.91; φύλλοις ἐλαιᾶν μιχθέντα, στεφάνοις ἔμιχθεν (3 pl.), *come to*, i. e. *win*, the crown of victory, *N.*1.18, 2.22; μ. εὐλογίαις *I.*3.3; μ. ἐν τιμαῖς ib.2.29; μ. θάμβει *to be affected by* amazement, *N.*1.56; also βροτοὶ ξὺν κακοῖς μεμ(ε)ιγμένοι S.*El.*1485. 3. in hostile sense, *mix in fight*, Il.4.456, cf. Od.5.317; ἐν δαΐ, ἐν παλάμῃσι μ., Il.13.286, 21.469. 4. in Hom. and Hes. most freq. of the sexes, *have intercourse with*, both of the man and the woman, sts. abs., Il.9. 275, etc.: more freq. μιγῆναί τινι, of the man, 21.143, etc.; of the woman, Od.1.73; ἄρσενι θῆλυ μιγῆν Parm.12.5, cf. Pi.*P.*3.14, al.; but in Trag. only of the man, as μητρὶ μ(ε)ιχθῆναι, μιγῆναι, S.*OT*791, 995; but in Com. μ(ε)ιγνυμένας τοῖσιν ἀδελφοῖς Ar.*Ra.*1081 (anap.): in Prose pres. μίσγεσθαι in this sense, of the man, Hdt.2.64, etc.; of the woman, Id.1.5,190, Od.22.445; in full, φιλότητί τινι μιγῆναι, of the man, Il.6.165; of the woman, ib.161, Hes.*Th.*927, 970, etc.; ἐμισγέσθην φ., of the two, Il.14.295; ἐν φιλότητι μίσγεσθαι (with or without τινι), of the man, 2.232, 24.131; of the woman, *h.Hom.*33. 5; Διὸς φιλότητι μιγῆναι, Διὸς ἐν φ. μ., of the woman, Hes.*Th.*920, *h.Merc.*4; σῇ φ. μ., of the man, *h.Ven.*150; εὐνῇ μ., of the man, Od. 1.433; φιλότητι καὶ εὐνῇ, of the man, Il.3.445, cf. Od.15.420; of the woman, 5.126; but ἐν ἀγκοίνῃσι Διός 11.268: c. acc. cogn., φιλότης.., ἣν ἐμίγης Il.15.33.—The aor. 1 is not used in this sense by Hom., but occurs in the Hymns, *h.Ven.*46, al.; the aor. 1 is more freq. in Hes. and Pi. (Cf. Lat. *misceo*, Skt. *mekṣáyati* 'stir', *miśrás* 'mixed'.)

**μειδ-άμων** [ᾱ], ονος, ὁ, ἡ, *smiling*, *Hymn.Is.*147. **-άω**, *smile*, Ep. Verb, only 3 sg. aor. μείδησε Il.1.595, 5.426, Od.4.609, Hes.*Sc.* 115, etc.; part. μειδήσας, -σασα Il.1.596, etc.; inf. μειδῆσαι *h.Cer.* 204; μείδησε σαρδάνιον (v. Σαρδάνιος) Od.20.301; opp. γελᾶν, *laugh aloud*, μειδῆσαι γελάσαι τε *h.Cer.* l. c.; κάρχαρόν τι μειδήσας *grinning* so as to show his teeth, Babr.94.6:—pres. is supplied by **μειδιάω**, used by Hom. only in Ep. part. μειδιόων Il.7.212, 23.786; -ιόωσα 21. 491: later 3 sg. μειδιάει *h.Hom.*10.3, μειδιᾷ Theoc.30.5; part. μειδιάων *h.Hom.*7.14, μειδιῶσα Ar.*Th.*513; inf. μειδιᾶν Pl.*Prm.*130a: impf. ἐμειδία Luc.*DMeretr.*3.2; Ep. μειδιάασκε *PLit.Lond.*41, Q.S. 9.117: aor. 1 ἐμειδίασα Plu.2.172b, Luc.*DDeor.*20.11; inf. μειδιᾶσαι Apollod.1.5.3; part. μειδιάσας Pl.*Phd.*86d; Aeol. fem. -ιάσαισα Sapph.1.14. (Cf. Skt. *smáyati*, Lett. *smaidīt* 'smile', etc.) **-ημα**, ατος, τό, *smile*, Hes.*Th.*205 (pl.).

**μειδί-ᾱμα**, ατος, τό, *smile, smiling*, Luc.*BisAcc.*28: pl., Plu.*Sull.* 35, Corn.*ND*24:—also **-ᾱσις**, εως, ἡ, Poll.6.199, Porph.*Abst.*4.6: -ασμα, ατος, τό, Hsch.: **-ασμός**, ὁ, Poll. l. c., Sch.Ar.*Pl.*165. **-αστικός**, ή, όν, *conducive to smiling*: μ., τό, *hilarity*, ib.27. **-άω**, v. μειδάω.

**μεῖδος**· γέλως, Hsch.

**μειζον-άκις**, Adv. of μείζων, *multiplied by a larger number*, opp. ἐλαττονάκις, Nicom.*Ar.*2.17, cf. Iamb. *in Nic.*p.95 P. **-ία**, ἡ, *office of a* μείζων (cf. μέγας c. 1), *POxy.*1147.9 (vi A.D.). **-ότης**, ητος, ἡ, *greater magnitude*, Iamb.*VP*26.115, *in Nic.*p.33 P. **-ως, μειζότερος, μείζων**, v. μέγας.

**μείης**, ὁ, coined as etym. of μείς (= μήν), Pl.*Cra.*409c.

**μεῖλαξ**, ακος, ὁ, = λειμών, παράδεισος, Suid.

**μείλια**, τά, (μειλίσσω) *soothing things*, esp. of gifts, ἐγὼ δ' ἐπὶ μ. δώσω, of a bridal dowry, Il.9.147, cf. 289, Luc.*Epigr.*2; so of playthings, etc., A.R.3.146: sg., ib.135. II. *propitiations*, δαίμοσιν.. νόστῳ ἔπι μ. θέσθαι Id.4.1549; of *offerings* to the dead, *BCH*36.230 (Rhodes, iii B.C.): rarely in sg., μείλιον ἀπλοΐης *charm against* storms, Call.*Dian.*230; *offering* to a god, *AP*6.75 (Paul. Sil.). 2. *satisfaction, penalty*, μ. τείσειν A.R.3.594.

**μείλιγμα**, ατος, τό, (μειλίσσω) *that which soothes*, μειλίγματα θυμοῦ *scraps with which* the master *appeases* the hunger of his dogs, Od.10. 217; μειλίγματα προσφέρειν E.*Fr.*1053: sg., Nic.*Fr.*75: metaph., γλώσσης ἐμῆς μ. καὶ θελκτήριον A.*Eu.*886; μ. νούσου Nic.*Th.*896; λύπης Ph.2.28 (pl.); τῆς ὀργῆς Plu.*Pomp.*47; πλούτου μειλίγματα Epic.*Oxy.*1015.19. 2. pl., *propitiatory offerings* to the dead, A. *Ch.*15, *Eu.*107, Parth.12.1, Ant.Lib.25.5. 3. *darling, fondling*, Χρυσηΐδος μ., of Agamemnon, A.*Ag.*1439. II. *soothing song*, λιγεῶν μειλίγματα Μουσέων Theoc.22.221. 2. pl., μ. θρασειῶν μεταφορῶν *phrases which soften* bold metaphors, Longin.32.3.

**μειλικ-τήριος**, ον, *able to soothe*, εὐχαί Suid. s. v. Ποντίφιξ: Subst. μειλικτήρια (sc. ἱερά), τά, *propitiations*, νεκροῖσι A.*Pers*.610; cf. μείλιγμα I. 2. **-τικός**, ή, όν, = foreg. Adv. -κῶς Sch.Ar.*Pl*.233. **-τός**, ή, όν, only in *Lyr.Alex.Adesp*.35.8 (Mesom.(?)) μύθους μειλικτοὺς ἀνδρῶν ἔργοις, perh. *mingled* (cf. ἀμείλικτον· ἄμικτον, Hsch.). **-τρα**, τά, = μειλίγματα, A.R.4.712.

**μειλῐνεος**, α, ον, = μείλινος, Opp.*C*.4.383.

⊛ **Μειλῑνόη**, ἡ, euphem. name of Hecate, Orph.*H*.71 (Μηλ- codd.).

**μείλῑνος**, η, ον, Ep. for μέλινος (q. v.).

**μείλιξις**, εως, ἡ, *propitiation*, Anon.ap.Suid. s. v. μειλίγμασιν.

**μείλιον**, τό, v. μείλια. II. = μίλιον, freq. in Inscrr., as *BCH*37.149 (Thrace), *SIG*888.26 (ibid., iii A. D.).

⊛ **μειλίσσω**, fut. -ξω A.R.4.416: Ep. aor. Med. μειλίξατο Id.1.650: —*make mild, soothe, treat kindly*, τινα Theoc.16.28; esp. *appease, propitiate*: rarely c. gen., πυρὸς μειλισσέμεν (like πυρὸς χαρίζεσθαι) *to appease* [the dead] *by* fire, i. e. funeral rites, Il.7.410; of rivers, λιπαροῖς χεύμασι γαίας.. μειλίσσοντες οὖδας *gladdening* the soil with rich streams, A.*Supp*.1029 (lyr.); ὀργὰς μ. E.*Hel*.1339 (lyr.); μ. τινὰ λοιβαῖς, χύτλοις, Lyc.542, A.R.4.708. 2. *implore*, ἐγὼ κεῖνόν γε τεὰς ἐς χεῖρας ἱκέσθαι μειλίξω ib.416. II. Pass., μειλίσσομαι *to be soothed, grow calm*, *h.Cer*.290; *to be subdued*, πυρὸς μειλίσσετ' ἀϋτμή A.R.3.531. III. Med., *use soothing words*, μηδέ τί μ' αἰδόμενος μειλίσσεο μηδ' ἐλεαίρων *extenuate* not aught from respect or pity, Od.3.96. 2. *propitiate*, Κύπριν ἀοιδῇσιν θυέεσσί τε A.R.1.860; συκοφάντας ἀπομαγδαλιᾷ Philostr.*VA*7.23; *soften, subdue*, ἔθνη.. καθάπερ ζῷα τιθασεύων καὶ μ. Plu.2.330b. 3. *implore*, A.R.3.985, 4.1012.

**μειλίχ-η** [ῐ], ἡ, *boxing-glove which left the fingers bare*, Paus.8.40.3. **-ία**, Ep. -ίη, ἡ, *gentleness, softness*, μειλιχίῃ πολέμοιο *lukewarmness* in battle, Il.15.741; *kindness*, Hes.*Th*.206, A.R.2.1279, etc. 2. = ἱκετεία, Hsch. **-εῖον**, τό, *temple of* Ζεὺς Μειλίχιος, *IG*14.352 i 16 (Halaesa). ⊛ **-ιος**, α, ον, also ος, ον Plu.2.370d, cf. Hsch.:—*gentle, soothing*, Hom. mostly of speech, μειλιχίοις ἐπέεσσι Il.12.267, al.; μ. μῦθος Od.6.148, cf. B.10.90: without Subst., προσαυδᾶν μειλιχίοισι *with gentle words*, Il.4.256, 6.214; οἱ δέ τ' ἐς αὐτὸν τερπόμενοι λεύσσουσιν—ὁ δ' ἀσφαλέως ἀγορεύει—αἰδοῖ μειλιχίῃ Od.8.172; θεὸν ὣς ἱλάσκονται αἰδοῖ μειλιχίῃ Hes.*Th*.92. Adv. -ίως A.R.2.467, etc.: neut. as Adv., μειλίχιον μυκήσατο Mosch.2.97. II. later of persons, *mild, gracious*, Ζεὺς Μ. the protector *of those who invoked him with propitiatory offerings*, at Athens, *IG*1².866 (written **Μιλίχιος**), Th.1.126, X.*An*.7.8.4; at Orchomenus in Boeotia, *IG*7.3169 (written **Μιλίχιος** *BCH*50.422 (Thespiae)); in Argolis, Paus.2.20.1, etc.; of other divinities, as Dionysus, Plu.2.994a, etc.; Κύπρις *AP*5.225 (Paul. Sil.): Cret., Theraean **Μηλίχιος** *GDI*5046 (Hierapytna), al., *IG*12(3).406, 1316; early Ion. **Μειλίχιος** written **Μελ-** ib.12(5).727 (Andros); Arc. written **Μελίχιος** ib.5(2).90 (Tegea, perh. iv B. C.). III. μειλίχια (sc. ἱερά) *propitiatory offerings*, Plu.2.417c; so perh. μ. ποτά S.*OC*159 (lyr., but expld. by Sch. as referring to *honey* mixed in the drink-offerings).

**μείλιχμα**, ατος, τό, = μείλιγμα I. 2, in pl., *Schwyzer*725.2 (Milet., vi B. C., written μελ-).

**μειλῐχό-βουλος**, ον, *mild-counselling*, Procl.*H*.7.40. **-γηρυς**, υ, *soft-voiced*, γλῶσσα Tyrt.12.8. **-δωρος**, ον, *giving pleasing gifts*, [οἶνος] Hermipp.82.2; Ὑγίεια Hymn.ap.Stob.1.1.31a. **-θῡμος**, ον, *gentle-hearted*, *BCH*23.302 (Termessus). **-μειδος**, ον, Aeol. **μελλιχό-**, *soft-smiling*, Alc.55:—also **-μειδής** (-μετίδης cod.), Hsch.

⊛ **μειλίχος**, ον, Aeol. **μέλλιχος** Hdn.Gr.2.302, cj. in Sapph.100:—*gentle, kind*: I. in Il. always of persons, πᾶσιν γὰρ ἐπίστατο μ. εἶναι 17.671; μ. αἰεί 19.300, al.; epith. of Λητώ, Ὕπνος, Hes.*Th*.406, 763: c. gen., Ἄρτεμις μ. ὠδίνων *soother of*.., *AP*6.242 (Crin.): Sup. μειλιχώτατος *IG*7.115.1 (Megara): in late Prose, Jul.*Or*.2.86a, al. II. of things, once in Od., οὐ μ. ἔστιν ἀκοῦσαι οὔτ' ἔπος οὔτε τι ἔργον 15.374; μ. δῶρα *h.Hom*.10.2; ἔπεα Hes.*Th*.84; οἶνος Xenoph.1.6; αἰών, ὀργά, Pi.*P*.8.97, 9.43; τὸ μ. *gentleness*, Thgn.365; τὰ μείλιχα *joys*, Pi.*O*.1.30; μείλιχα μυθεῖσθαι Opp.*C*.3.219. Adv. -χως, μυθεύμενος Semon.7.18: neut. as Adv., μείλιχον ἀντιάαν A.R.1.971.

**μειλῐχόφωνος**, v. μελλιχόφωνος.

**μειλῐχώδης**, ες, *gentle*, τὸ μ. Cerc.18.10.

**μεῖξις, μειξοβάρβαρος, μείξοφρυς**, v. μίξις, etc.

**μεῖον** (A), ονος, τό, neut. of μείων (q. v.).

**μεῖον** (B), ου, τό, *lamb* or *sheep offered at the Athenian Apaturia* by a father who was enrolling his son among his φράτερες, τοῦ μείου *IG* 2².1237.5; τὰ μεῖα ib.60; παρέστησε μεῖον Is.*Fr*.124: expld. by Sch. Ar.*Ra*.810 (cf. Eratosth. and Apollod.ap.Harp.) as neut. of μείων, *too light!* from the cry of the φράτερες when the lamb was weighed; cf. μειαγωγέω.

**μεῖον** (C), ου, τό, = μῆον, v.l. in Dsc.1.3, Androm.ap.Gal.14.43.

⊛ **μειονεκτ-έω**, (ἔχω) *have too little, to be poor*, σὺν τῷ γενναίῳ μ., opp. σὺν τῷ ἀδίκῳ πλέον ἔχειν, X.*Ages*.4.5; *come short*, μ. εἰ μή.. Id.*Cyr*.8.6.23, cf. *Mem*.3.14.6; μ. ἔν τινι *fall short* in a thing, Id.*Hier*.1.11, 27: c. gen. rei, *to be short of* a thing, σίτων καὶ ποτῶν ib.2.1; μ. τῶν εὐφροσυνῶν ἔν τινι ib.1.29; τῶν δικαίων D.H.6.71: c. gen. pers. et dat. rei, τῇ εὐφροσύνῃ μ. τῶν ἰδιωτῶν X.*Hier*.1.18; opp. πλεονεκτέω, Hierax ap.Stob.3.9.54. **-ικός**, ή, όν, *disposed to take too little*, opp. πλεονεκτικός, ibid.

**μειονεξία**, ἡ, *taking less than one's due*, opp. πλεονεξία, X.*Cyr*.2.1.25, Hierax ap.Stob.3.9.54, Simp. *in Cael*.171.20.

**μειόνως, μειότερος**, v. μείων.

**μειοπῡρεξία**, ἡ, *remission of fever*, Aët.5.77, Steph. *in Gal*.1.268 D.

⊛ **μειότης**, ητος, ἡ, *minimizing*, A.D.*Conj*.250.9, 253.16. II. *minority*, Vett.Val.337.25.

**μειουρία, -ίζω, -ος**, v. μυουρία, -ίζω, -ος.

**μειόφρων**, ονος, ὁ, ἡ, (φρήν) *thoughtless*, Hsch.

⊛ **μειόω**, (μείων) *lessen, diminish*, opp. αὔξω, Phld.*Oec*.p.21 J. (Pass.); μ. τὸ χωρίον Plb.9.20.3; μ. τὸν ὁπλισμὸν τοῖς θώραξιν *diminish* the armour *by* the breast-pieces, D.H.4.16; μειούμενον φόρον *PFay*.26.15 (ii A. D.); *moderate*, τὴν ἄγαν κάθαρσιν X.*Eq*.5.9. 2. *lessen in honour, degrade*, τοὺς φίλους Id.*HG*3.4.9; τὴν ἐξ Ἀρείου πάγου βουλήν D.S.11.77. 3. *lessen by word, disparage*, τὰ τῶν πολεμίων X.*Cyr*.6.3.17, cf. *Hier*.2.17; αὔξειν καὶ μειοῦν Arist.*Rh*.1403ᵃ17. 4. *shorten* a syllable, D.H.*Comp*.11: generally, λέξεων κατὰ ποσότητα μεμειωμένων Hdn.Gr.2.909. II. Pass., *become smaller, decrease*, in size, etc., σπλὴν ἐμειοῦτο Hp.*Epid*.1.26.γ', cf. Pl.*Cra*.409c; σελήνη μειουμένη Arist.*Mu*.399ᵃ7, cf. Ph.2.153, al. 2. *become worse* or *weaker*, μ. τὴν διάνοιαν X.*Mem*.4.8.1: c. gen., *fall short of*, τῶν.. μεγάλα θυόντων ib.1.3.3; τῆς τοῦ σώματος ἰσχύος Id.*Cyr*.7.5.65.

**μειρᾰκεύομαι**, v. l. for μειρακιεύομαι, Alciphr.2.2.

**μειρᾰκῐ-εία**, ἡ, *boyish mischief*, prob. in Epicur.*Sent.Palat*.5 p.69 v. d. M. **-εξᾰπάτης** [πᾰ], ου, ὁ, *boy-cheater*, Epigr.ap.Hegesand.1. **-εύομαι**, lit. *play the boy*: hence, *to be bashful, coquettish*, Plu.*Ant*.10, Luc.*DMort*.27.9, etc. II. *attain puberty*, ἐς ἡλικίαν μ. Arr.*An*.4.13.1. **-ον**, τό, in form Dim. of μεῖραξ, *lad, stripling*, Antipho 3.3.11, Ar.*Nu*.917 (anap.), Pl.*R*.497e, *Prt*.315d, Men.*Georg*.46; ἔφηβος, μ., ἀνήρ, γέρων Id.18 D.; ἄχρι γενείου λαχνώσιος, ἐς τὰ τρὶς ἑπτά Hp.ap.Ph.1.26; παῖς, μ., νεανίσκος Arr.*Epict*.3.9.8; *under twenty-one*, Plu.*Brut*.27; *about twenty*, Luc.*DMort*.9.4; ἐκ μειρακίων μέχρι γήρως Isoc.15.93, cf. Aeschin.1.39; εἰς ἄνδρας ἐκ μειρακίων τελευτᾶν Pl.*Tht*.173b; ἐκ μειρακίου Is.5.40. 2. of adults, in a contemptuous sense, Plb.2.68.2, Plu.*Phil*.6. **-όομαι**, = μειρακιεύομαι II, X.*Lac*.3.1, Ph.1.531, Ael.*VH*12.1.

**μειρᾰκ-ίσκη**, ἡ, Dim. of μεῖραξ, *little girl*, Ar.*Ra*.411 (lyr.), and (in iron. sense) *Pl*.963. **-ίσκος**, ὁ, Dim. of μεῖραξ, *lad, stripling*, Alex.36.2, 178.7, Men.*Georg*.4, Satyr.*Vit.Eur.Fr*.39 xii 26, Jul.*Or*.7.223c; ἦν δὴ παῖς μᾶλλον δὲ μ. Pl.*Phdr*.237b.

⊛ **μειρᾰκιώδ-ης**, ες, *becoming a youth, youthful*, παιδεία Pl.*R*.498b: τὸ μ., of style, *foppish, affected*, D.H.*Isoc*.12, cf. *Pomp*.2, Longin.3.4. II. *characteristic of youth*, δόξα Pl.*R*.466b; ὑπερβολαί Arist.*Rh*.1413ᵃ29; βίος τῶν ἀσώτων Ph.1.678. Adv. -δῶς Plb.11.14.7, Phld.*Mus*.p.109 K.: Comp. -έστερον Din.*Fr*.66. **-ία**, ἡ, *boyishness*, Theognost.*Can*.26.

**μειρᾰκύλλιον**, τό, Dim. of μειράκιον, *stripling*, Ar.*Ra*.89, Anaxandr.33.12, Men.*Fab.inc*.2.33, Luc.*Par*.43; μ. ὢν κομιδῇ D.21.78:—also **-υλλίδιον**, v.l. in Lib.*Ref*.1.11.

**μεῖραξ**, ᾰκος, ἡ, *young girl, lass* (cf. Phryn.187), Cratin.301, Ar.*Th*.410, *Ec*.611, *Pl*.1071, 1079, Xenarch.4.3, Men.*Pk*.14: used as fem. of men, *qui muliebria patiuntur*, Cratin.55, Luc.*Sol*.5: in later writers masc., *boy, lad*, Herod.Med. in *Rh.Mus*.58.109, Aret.*SD*1.13, Hld.4.19. (Cf. Skt. *maryakás* 'manikin', *máryas* 'young man'.)

⊛ **μείρομαι** (A), Hes.*Op*.578 (ἀπο-), imper. μείρεο Il.9.616; elsewh. in Hom. and Hes. only 3 sg. ἔμμορε (which is prob. aor. (v. infr. II) and was so understood by later Ep. Poets, who have 2 sg. ἔμμορες A.R.3.4; 3 pl. ἔμμορον cited by *EM*335.24, ἐξ-έμμορον Nic.*Th*.791: but pf. 3 pl. ἐμμόραντι· τετεύχασι Hsch.); we also have (as if from μορέω) fut. μορήσω *EM*335.23: pf. μεμόρηκα Nic.*Al*.213; for pass. forms v. infr. III:—*receive as one's portion*, with collat. notion of its being *one's due*: c. acc., καὶ ἥμισυ μείρεο τιμῆς *take* half the honour *as thy due*, Il. l. c.; later, *divide*, ἀροτήσιον ὥρην τριπλόα μείρονται Arat.1054. II. in form ἔμμορε (ἔμμορες, etc.), *obtain one's share of*, c. gen., οὐ ποθ' ὁμοίης ἔμμορε τιμῆς Il.1.278; πάντα δέδασται, ἕκαστος δ' ἔμμορε τιμῆς 15.189, cf. Od.11.338; θεῶν ἐξ ἔμμορε τιμῆς 5.335; ἔμμορέ τοι τιμῆς ὅς τ' ἔμμορε γείτονος ἐσθλοῦ Hes.*Op*.347; ἐν δὲ διχοστασίῃ καὶ ὁ πάγκακος ἔμμορε τιμῆς Call.*Fr.anon*.373: later c. acc., A.R.3.208, Nic.*Al*.488. 2. c. part., like τυγχάνω, *happen* to be, νόημα.. μεμόρηκε.. ἐσφαλμένον ib.213. III. pf. Pass. εἵμαρται, inf. εἱμάρθαι B.13.1, App.*BC*2.4: impers., *it is allotted, decreed by fate*, εὖ εἱμάρθαι παρὰ δαίμονος B. l. c.: usu. c. acc. et inf., Pl.*R*.566a, *Phdr*.255b: freq. in plpf. εἵμαρτο *it was decreed*, νῦν δέ με λευγαλέῳ θανάτῳ εἵμαρτο ἁλῶναι Il.21.281; ἐκ γὰρ τῆς εἵμαρτο.. τέκνα γενέσθαι Hes.*Th*.894; εἰ.. οὕτως εἵμαρτο πρᾶξαι D.18.195, etc.: freq. also in part., θεῶν εἱμαρμένα δῶρα Thgn.1033; τὰ δ' ἄλλα.. σὺν θεοῖς εἱμαρμένα A.*Ag*.913; τοιαῦτα.. πρὸς θεῶν εἱμ. S.*Tr*.169; χρόνος εἱμαρμένος Pl.*Prt*.320d, cf. *Phd*.113a; εἴπερ εἱμαρμένον εἴη Id.*Mx*.243e; ἡ εἱμαρμένη (sc. μοῖρα) *destiny*, Id.*Phd*.115a, *Grg*.512e, D.18.205, etc.: later forms μέμορται Phot., Suid.: inf. μέμορθαι Aeol. acc. to Sch.Il.10.67, *EM*312.46: part. μεμορμένος, θάνατος, οἶκος, A.R.3.1130, *Epigr.Gr*.414.7 (Egypt); ἠρίον Alex.Aet.3.33; πότμος Lyc.430; κῆρες *AP*7.700 (Diod.); τὸ μ. Plu.*Mar*.39, Agath.1.1 (v.l. μεμαρμένον): Aeol. **ἐμμόρμενον** Alc.*Supp*.14.7: Dor. **ἐμβρᾱμένα** (q.v.); **βεβρᾱμένων**· εἱμαρμένων, Hsch.; μεμόρηται Man.6.13; μεμορημένος *AP*7.466 (Leon.); but μεμορημένον in Nic.*Al*.229 is from μορέω (q.v.); Dor. 3 sg. μεμόρακται (as if from μοράζω) *it receives a portion of*, τινος Ti.Locr.95a. IV. μείρομαι as Pass., *to be divided from*, τινος Arat.657.

**μείρομαι** (B), = ἱμείρομαι, c. gen., Nic.*Th*.402, *Inscr.Perg*.203.

⊛ **μείς**, μηνός, ὁ, nom. sg. **μείς** Il.19.117, Hes.*Op*.557, *h.Merc*.11, Anacr.6.1, Pi.*N*.5.44, Hdt.2.82, Hp.*Septim*.3 (v. l.), Pl.*Cra*.409c, *Ti*.39c, Arist.*GA*777ᵇ23, Thphr.*Sign*.27, Call.*Hec*.1.1.12, *SIG*1009.

27 (Chalcedon, iii/ii B.C.), 1047.46 (Amorgos, ii/i B.C.), *IG*9(1).682 (Corc., iv B.C.), Chrysipp.*Stoic.* 2. 199, Eudox. *Ars Prooem.*, 13.1, Ezek.*Exag.*153, Str.13.1.64, *Sammelb.*1191; Dor. μής *SIG*243*D*45 (Delph., iv B.C.), *IG*4²(1).102.10(Epid., iv B.C.), 42.6 (iii B.C.), *Tab. Heracl.*1.1; Elean **μεύς** *Schwyzer*418.15: nom. sg. μήν Hes.*Fr.*240 codd., *IG*1².377.14,al. (v B.C.), 387.32 (v B.C.), Th.5.54, X.*HG*4.5.1, 7.4.28, Lxx 1*Ki.*20.24,al., *SIG*672.85(Delph., ii B.C.); both μείς and μήν in Thphr.*Sign.*27: oblique cases formed from stem **μην-**, Aeol. **μηνν-** *IG*12(2).6.39,al. (Mytil.), Thess. **μειvv-** ib.9(2).258.5 (Cierium); dat. pl. μησί Hdt.4.43, 8.51 (v.l. μήνεσι(ν)), Pl.*Lg.*771b, μησίν *SIG*45.18 (Halic., v B.C.):—*month*, Il. l.c., etc.; τοῦ μὲν φθίνοντος μηνός, τοῦ δ' ἱσταμένοιο Od.14.162, cf. Hes.*Op.*780,*Th.*59; ἱσταμένου τοῦ μ. εἰνάτῃ Hdt.6.106, cf. Th.4.52, etc.; μηνὸς τετάρτῃ φθίνοντος on the fourth day *from* the end of *the month*, Foed.ap.eund.5.19; Μαιμακτηριῶνος δεκάτῃ ἀπιόντος, i.e. on the 21st, Decr.ap.D.18.37; μηνῶν φθινὰς ἁμέρα the last of the *month*, E.*Heracl.*779(lyr.); τελευτῶντος τοῦ μηνός at the end of *the lunar month* (when there was no moonlight), Th.2.4; ἐκείνου τοῦ μηνὸς *in the course of*.., X.*Mem.*4.8.2; κατὰ μῆνα *monthly*, Ar.*Nu.*1287, etc.; μισθὸν διδόναι κατὰ μ. D.50.10; κατὰ μῆνα ἕκαστον, κατὰ μῆνας, Pl.*Lg.*830d, 762b; ἑκάστου μηνός ib.760d; τοῦ μηνὸς ἑκάστου Ar.*Ach.*859(lyr.); τοῦ μηνός alone, *by the month*, Id.*Nu.*612, etc.; συνόδους ποιεῖσθαι δύο τοῦ μ. Pl.*Lg.*771d; τόκον δραχμὴν τοῦ μ. τῆς μνᾶς interest a drachma per mina *per month*, Aeschin. 3.104; μ. πλήρης, κοῖλος, civil *month* of 30 or 29 days respectively, Gem.8.3; μ. ἐμβόλιμος intercalary *month*, Hdt.1.32, *IG*12(7).237.56 (Arcesine), Eudox.*Ars*13.13. **2.** *crescent moon*, Thphr. l.c. (μείς); *the part of the month corresponding to a phase of the moon*, ibid. (μείς and μήν); *the visible part of the moon*, Chrysipp. l.c. (μείς). **3.** *ornament in form of crescent moon*, *IG*1².387.32 (v B.C., μήν). **b.** = μηνίσκος 1, prob. in Ar.*Av.*1115, cf. Cleom.2.5. **II.** as pr. n., the god *Lunus*, masc. of Μήνη, Luc.*JTr.*8. (I.-E. stem *mēns-* 'moon', 'month', cf. Lat. *mensis*, gen. pl. *mensum*, etc.)

**μεῖστος**, η, ον, Sup. of μείων, *least*, Hsch., *EM*676.14, Eust.134.45, Sch.Ar.*Pl.*627: neut. as Adv., μεῖστον *at least*, *Berl.Sitzb.*1927.8 (Locr., v B.C.). (From μέγ-ιστος.)

⊛**μεῖχμα**, ατος, τό, Aeol. for μεῖγμα, dub. in Alc.*Supp.*13.7.

**μεί-ωμα**, ατος, τό, (μειόω) *curtailment*: hence, *fine*, X.*An.*5.8.1. ⊛**-ων**, so in Dor., *Leg.Gort.*9.48,al., *Schwyzer*323*B*9 (Delph., iv B.C.), *Tab.Heracl.*1.114,al., Archyt.1, prob. in Epich.62 (μηονος cod., and so in Diotog.ap.Stob.4.7.62, etc.), and Arc., *IG*5(2).3.15, 18 (Tegea): neut. pl. μείονα Hes.*Op.*690, but μείω Ti.Locr.102b: masc. pl. μείους Xenoph.3.4, etc.: dat. pl. μειόνοις *IG*9(1).333 (Locr.):—irreg. Comp. of ὀλίγος or μικρός, *lesser*, *less*, Pi.*O.*1.35,al., A.*Ch.*519, B.1.63, etc.; τὸ μ. κρεισσόνων κρατύνει; A.*Supp.*596(lyr.), cf. Hp. *VM*8 (v.l., cf. Erot.), *Vict.*1.5,al. (not in other works of Hp.), freq. in X., *Cyr.*5.4.48,al., not in good Att. Prose or Com., nor in Hdt.; *younger*, S.*OC*374: neut. μεῖον as Adv., *less*, μ. ἰσχύσειν Διός A.*Pr.*510, cf. *Ch.*707: regul. Adv., μειόνως ἔχειν to be *of less value*, S.*OC* 104, cf. J.*AJ*19.2.2:—also **μειότερος**, α, ον, A.R.2.368, Arat.43, *AP*14.41, Man.2.147, *IG*14.2064. (μεί-γων, cf. μινύθω, Lat. *minuo*, *minus*.) **-ώνυμος**, ον, *with a smaller denominator*, of fractions, Iamb. *in Nic.*p.48 P. (Comp.). ⊛**-ωσις**, εως, ἡ, (μειόω) *diminution*, opp. αὔξησις, αἱ τῶν ὀστέων μ. Hp.*Mochl.*24, cf. Arist.*Cat.*15ᵃ14, *GC* 320ᵇ31, Thphr.*CP*4.4.11, Phld.*Oec.*p.68 J.(pl.), Alex.Aphr.*in Top.* 111.4: voc. μείωσι Orph.*H.*13.7; of the moon, *waning*, Cleom.2.5, *Placit.*3.17.3, Arr.*Epict.*1.14.4, Gal.9.905; *loss* of property, etc., Vett. Val.44.14(pl.), al. **-ωτέον**, *one must lessen*, Herod.Med.ap.Orib. 5.27.17. **-ωτής**, οῦ, ὁ, *causing diminution*, ἀστὴρ μ. τῶν προκτηθέντων Paul.Al.*N.*4. **-ωτικός**, ή, όν, *lowering* in description, *diminishing*, ὕψους Longin.42.1; ὑπαρχόντων Vett.Val.10.20; ποταμῶν Heph.Astr.1.20: Medic., πλήθους (plethora) Gal.1.146; *waning*, τὸ τῆς σελήνης μ. σχῆμα Vett.Val.41.6. **2.** *depreciatory*, Phld.*Rh.* 1.217 S. Adv. -κῶς S.E.*M.*3.42, D.L.7.53. **-ωτός**, ή, όν, *capable of diminution*, Herm.ap.Stob.1.10.15.

**μελάγ-γαιος**, ον, Hdt.2.12,4.198; **-γειος**, ον, Dicaearch.1.12, Thphr.*HP*8.7.2, *BGU*1529(Ptol.), Antyll.ap.Orib.9.11.6; **-γεως**, ων, gen. ω, Thphr.*CP*2.4.12:—*with black soil*, Hdt., Thphr. ll.cc.; πόλις μ. τῇ χρόᾳ Dicaearch. l.c. **-γραφής**, ές, *marked with black*, διφθέραι prob. for μελεγγρ- in E.*Fr.*627. **-καρπος**, v. μελάγκουρος. **-κερως**, ων, *black-horned*, of Agamemnon, A.*Ag.*1127 (lyr., the epith. being suggested by the preceding words, ἄπεχε τῆς βοὸς τὸν ταῦρον): but cod. Med. is corrected to μελαγκέρῳ (= μέλανι) agreeing with μηχανήματι. **-κευθής**, ές, *shrouded in gloom*, εἴδωλον B. *Fr.*25; *carrying darkness* (i.e. dark rain) *in its bosom*, νέφος Id.3.55 (prob. l.). **-κολπος**, ον, *black-bosomed*, Nonn.*D.*34.83. **-κόμης**, ου, ὁ, *black-haired*, Poll.2.24. **-κορυφίζω**, *pipe like the* μελαγκόρυφος, Hero *Spir.*2.32. **-κόρυφος**, ὁ, either *blackcap warbler*, *Motacilla atricapilla*, or *a kind of titmouse*, Ar.*Av.*887, Arist.*HA*592ᵇ 22, 616ᵇ4; αἱ συκαλίδες καὶ οἱ μ... μεταβάλλουσιν εἰς ἀλλήλους ib.632ᵇ 31, cf. Plin.*HN*10.86, *Gp.*15.1.23. **-κουρος**, ον, *black-haired*, Ἀσάφεια Emp.122.4 (v.l. -καρπος). **-κραιρα**, ἡ, *black-haired*, of the Sibyl, Lyc.1464, Arist.*Mir.*838ᵃ9. **-κράνινος** [ᾰ], ον, *plaited of rushes*, Philet.17.2; σφενδόναι Str.3.5.1 (-κραϊν- codd. in both places). **-κρᾶνίς**, ίδος, ἡ, *black bog-rush*, *Schoenus nigricans*, Thphr.*HP*4.12.1 (μελαγκράνισμα, μελαγκρανισμόν codd.), Plin.*HN* 21.113. (Fort. proparox.) ⊛**-κρηπῖς**, ῖδος, ὁ, ἡ, *with black shoes*, Eust.174.9, 1437.53. **-κροκος**, ον, (κρόκη) *with black woof*: *with black sails*, [ναῦς] A.*Th.*857 (lyr.). **-κωπος**, ον, *with black handle*, Sch.E.*Or.*821. **-χαίτης**, ου, Dor. **-τᾱς**, α, ὁ, *black-haired*, of Centaurs, Hes.*Sc.*186, S.*Tr.*837 (lyr.); of Hades, E.*Alc.*439 (lyr.). ⊛**-χῖμος**, ον, poet. for μέλας, *black*, *dark*, γυῖα, στρατός, A. *Supp.*719, 745 (lyr.); φάρη Id.*Ch.*11; πέπλοι, οἷς, E.*Ph.*372, *El.*513; νύξ A.*Pers.*301; τὰ μ. *dark spots in snow*, X.*Cyn.*8.1, cf. Poll.5.66.—For the form cf. δύσ-χιμος. **-χίτων** [ῐ], ωνος, ὁ, ἡ, *with black raiment*: hence, metaph., *darksome*, *gloomy*, φρήν A.*Pers.*115 (lyr.). **-χλαινος**, ον, *black-cloaked*, Mosch.3.27 (glossed by διαυγής, Hsch.). **II.** οἱ M., as pr. n. of a Scythian tribe, Hdt.4.20, etc. **-χλωρος**, ον, *dark olive-coloured*, *sallow*, v.l. in Hp.*Epid.*6.2.19, prob. in Arist. *Phgn.*812ᵃ19, cf. Gal.13.460, Vett.Val.111.9, Aret.*SD*2.1; χροιή ib. 1.5; χολή ib.15. **-χολάω**, *to be atrabilious*, *melancholy-mad*, Ar. *Av.*14, *Pl.*12, 366, 903, Pl.*Phdr.*268e, D.48.56, Alex.211, Men.*Sam.* 218, Gal.1.500, etc. **-χολία**, Ion. -ίη, ἡ, *atrabiliousness*, *melancholy*, freq. in pl., Hp.*Aër.*10, Ti.Locr.103a, Phld.*Ir.*p.28 W., Man.2. 366: sg., Aret.*SD*1.5. **-χολικός**, ή, όν, *of atrabilious* or *melancholic temperament*, τὰ μ. Hp.*Aph.*3.20; οἱ μ. ib.4.9; opp. πικρόχολος, Id.*Acut.*61. Adv. -κῶς Id.*Prorrh.*1.14, *Coac.*92, etc. **II.** *atrabilious*, *impulsive*, Pl.*R.*573c, Arist.*EN*1152ᵃ19. **-χολος**, ον, *dipped in black bile*, ἰοί S.*Tr.*573. **-χολώδης**, ες, *like black bile*, Aret.*SD*1.15. **-χροος**, ον, contr. **-χρους**, ουν, heterocl. nom. pl. μελάγχροες Hdt.2.104:—*black-skinned*, *swarthy*, of sunburnt persons, Hp.*Epid.*6.2.19, *PPetr.*3 pp.1, 19 (iii B.C.), Plu.*Arat.*20, etc.; μ. κόσσυφος Numen.ap.Ath.7.315b:—also **μελαγχροιής**, ές, of a hero's complexion, Od.16.175; **μέλαγχρος**, ον, as pr. n., Alc.21; **μελάγχρως**, ωτος, ὁ, ἡ, E.*Or.*321 (lyr.), *Hec.*1106 (lyr., v.l. μελανό-), Pl.*Phdr.*253e, *PPetr.*3 p.19,al. (iii B.C.), etc.:—Com. **μελαγχρής**, ές, Cratin.425, Eup.430, Antiph.135, Men.974, Anon.Iamb. in Gerhard *Phoinix* p.7, also *PCair.Zen.*76.9 (iii B.C.); μ. μᾶζα Polioch.2.2.

**μελάθρα**, ἡ, = sq. 1, *IG*11(2).146*A*64 (Delos, iv B.C.). **II.** = sq. II. 1, Hermesian.7.21 cod.

**μέλαθρον**, τό, Ep. gen. sg. μελαθρόφιν Od.8.279:—*roof-tree*, *ridge-pole*, μελαθρόφιν ἐξεκέχυντο l.c., cf. 11.278, *h.Ven.*173, *IG*11(2).161*A* 105 (Delos, iii B.C.), 199*A*113 (ibid., pl.); ἐπὶ προὔχοντι μελάθρῳ Od. 19.544: generally, *beam*, Lxx 3*Ki.*7.9(20); τὰ μ. τῶν θυρίδων *PRyl.* 233.5 (ii A.D.). **2.** *roof*, Il.2.414, Od.18.150. **II.** *house*, κυπαρίσσινον μ. Pi.*P.*5.40; οὐράνιον μ., of heaven, E.*Hec.*1101 (lyr.): mostly in pl., Alc.*Supp.*19.2, etc.; μ. ἐν βασιλείοις in the king's *halls*, A.*Ch.*343 (anap.), etc.; ἐς δόμων μ. Id.*Ag.*957; of a cave used as a dwelling, S.*Ph.*147, E.*Cyc.*491 (both anap.). **2.** *lair* of an animal, Opp.*C.*2.307. **3.** *cage*, ib.4.107,423. (Acc. to *EM*576.16 from μελαίνω, cf. καπνοδόκη; it is doubtful whether κμέλεθρον is cogn.)

**μελαθρόω**, *connect* or *fasten by beams*, Lxx 3*Ki.*7.42(5) (Pass.).

**μέλαινα**, ἡ, v. μέλας.

⊛**μελαινάς**, άδος, ἡ, *a blackish fish*, Cratin.161.

**μελαινίς**, ίδος, ἡ, *the black*, a name of Aphrodite at Corinth, Ath. 13.588c. **II.** a bivalve *sea-shell*, used as a drinking-cup, Sophr. 101, Herod.1.79; = πελωρίς, Xenocr.ap.Orib.2.58.97. **III.** μελαῖνις (sic) αἲξ καὶ βοῦς *from Melaenae*, Diosc.Gloss.ap.Gal.19.120.

**μελαινονεφής** (sic), ές, = μελανονεφής, *accompanied by black clouds*, of sunset and sunrise, *Cat.Cod.Astr.*8(1).138.

**μελαινόρῖνες**, f.l. for κελαινόρινες in S.*Fr.*29.

⊛**μελαίνω** (Act. not in Hom. or Hes.), aor. 1 inf. μελᾶναι Arist. *Mete.*371ᵃ23:—Pass., pf. μεμέλαμμαι Antyll.ap.Orib.10.36.1: aor. ἐμελάνθην S.*Aj.*919; Ep. 3 pl. μελάνθησαν Hes.*Sc.*300: (μέλας):—*blacken*, *make black*, Arist. l.c., *Pr.*966ᵇ22, Nic.*Al.*472: metaph., μ. φράσιν *use an obscure* expression, Ath.10.451c; μ. τὸ σαφές D.H. *Pomp.*2:—Pass., μελαίνετο δὲ χρόα καλόν she *had her* fair skin *stained black* (i.e. with blood), Il.5.354; μελανθὲν αἷμα S. l.c., cf. Gal.18(1). 33; of earth just turned up, ἡ δὲ μελαίνετ' ὄπισθεν Il.18.548; of ripening grapes, Hes. l.c.; of a newly-bearded chin, ib.167; αἱ λευκαὶ τρίχες ἐμελαίνοντο Pl.*Plt.*270e; of hair, *to be dyed black*, Ar.*Ec.*736; μεμελαμμένοι ὀδόντες Antyll. l.c. **2.** Medic., *cause* μελασμός (q.v.), Hp.*Aph.*5.20:—Pass., *turn black*, as a symptom of mortification, Id. *Art.*69, *Fract.*11. **3.** metaph., *blacken*, *misrepresent*, Simp. *in Cael.*290.24. **4.** Pass., *receive an impression of blackness*, S.E.*M.* 7.293. **II.** intr., = Pass., *grow black*, Pl.*Ti.*83a, Thphr.*Ign.*50, *AP*5.123 (Phld.), Plu.2.517c.

**μελαμ-βᾰθής**, ές, *darkly deep*, Ταρτάρου κευθμών A.*Pr.*221; ἀκταὶ Ἀχέροντος S.*Fr.*523 (v.l. -βαφεῖς); σηκὸς δράκοντος E.*Ph.*1010 (v.l. -βαφής); εἴδωλον v.l. in B.*Fr.*25; cf. μελαγκευθής. **-βᾰφής**, ές, *dark-dyed*, Poll.7.129; cf. foreg. **-βιος**, ον, *of dark and dreary life*, Hsch. **-βοος**, ον, *having black oxen*, Eust.562.39. **-βόρειος**, ον, (βορέας) *of the black north*: πνεῦμα μ. *the black north wind* in Southern Gaul and Palestine, Str.4.1.7, J.*BJ*3.9.3. **-βροτος** γῆ land *of negroes*, E.*Fr.*228.3; γείτονες μ. *negroes*, ib.771.4. **-βωλος**, ον, *with black soil*, Αἴγυπτος *AP*6.231 (Phil.), cf. Opp.*C.*3.508. **-πᾱγής**, ές, Dor. for -πηγής, *black-clotted*, αἷμα A.*Th.*737 (lyr.): generally, *black*, *discoloured*, [χαλκὸς] μ. πέλει Id.*Ag.*392 (lyr.). **-πεπλος**, ον, *black-robed*, epith. of Death, and Night, E.*Alc.*843, *Ion*1150, Alex. 89; *dark*, *black*, στολή E.*Alc.*427, cf. 819. **-πέραμον**· σκοτεινήν, Hsch. ⊛**-πέτᾰλος**, ον, *dark-leaved*, κλών *AP*4.1.14 (Mel.), 9.307 (Phil.). **-πετᾰλοχίτων** [ῐ], ωνος, *with a garment embroidered with black leaves*, γόνατα Tim.*Pers.*134. **-πετρος**, ον, *with black rocks*, Philet. 24. **-πόδεια**, τά, *festival of Melampus* at Aegosthena, *IG*7.223.22 (ii B.C.):⊛**-εῖον**, τό, *sanctuary of Melampus* at Aegosthena, ib.207, 208. **-πόδιον**, τό, = ἐλλέβορος μέλας, Thphr.*HP*9.10.4. **-πόρφῠρος**, ον, *dark purple*, Poll.4.119. **-πους**, ὁ, ἡ, πουν, τό, gen. ποδος, *black-footed*, ancient epith. of the Egyptians, Apollod.2.1.4, Eust.37.23: in Hom. only as pr. n., *Blackfoot*. **-πράσιον**, τό, = βαλλωτή, Dsc.3.

103. -πρῳρος, ον, *with black prow*, ναῦς *Hymn.Is.*146. ⊛-πῡγος, ον, *black-bottomed*, considered a mark of manhood, Eub.61; a name of Heracles, μ. τοῖς ἐχθροῖς *a very Heracles* to them, Ar.*Lys.*802 (lyr.), cf. Hdt.7.216: prov., μή τευ μ. τύχῃς take care not to 'catch a Tartar', Archil.110. II. of a kind of eagle, v. πύγαργος. -πῡρον, τό, *ball-mustard, Neslia paniculata*, Thphr.*HP*8.4.6, Gal.6.552 (also -πῡρος, ὁ, Thphr.*HP*8.8.3). II. = μύαγρον, Dsc.4.116. -φαής, ές, *whose light is blackness*, μελαμφαὲς οἴχεται δι' Ἔρεβος E.*Hel.*518 (lyr.); γαίας ἐς μ. μυχούς Carc.5.3. ⊛-φᾱρής, ές, (φᾶρος) *with dark shroud*, σκότος B.3.13. ⊛-φυλλος, ον, *dark-leaved*, δάφνα Anacr. 78 (= 92 Diehl, perh. pr. n.); δάφναι Theoc.*Ep.*1.3; κισσός D.P.573; of places, *dark with leaves*, Αἴτνας κορυφαί Pi.*P.*1.27; γῆ S.*OC* 482; ὄρη Ar.*Th.*997 (lyr.). II. as Subst. μελάμφυλλον, τό, = ἄκανθος, Dsc.3.17, Gal.11.818. -φωνος, ον, *with indistinct voice*, Id.5.384. -ψηφῖς, ῖδος, ὁ, ἡ, *with black pebbles*, of streams, Call. *Dian.*101, *Del.*76. -ψίθιος [ῐθ] (sc. οἶνος), ὁ, *wine made from black* ψίθιος, Dsc.5.6, Orib.*Fr.*64. -ψωρος, ον, *with black spots*, ἵπποι *PWis.*16 in *Aegyptus*9.244 (ii A.D.).

⊛μέλᾰν, ᾰνος, τό, (neut. of μέλας) *ink*, Pl.*Phdr.*276c; τὸ μ. τρίβων D.18.258, cf. Herod.5.66, etc.; μ. γραφικόν Dsc.1.69; used of a drawing material capable of erasure, Procl.*Hyp.*3.72. 2. μ. Ἰνδικόν *indigo*, *Peripl.M.Rubr.*39. II. *iris* of the eye, Arist.*HA*491ᵇ 21. b. *cornea*, Gal.14.772. 2. = αἰδοῖον, τὸ μ. τῷ μ. συναρμόσαι *PMag.Par.*1.403.

μελᾰν-άγριος ἄμπελος, *vitis nigra agrestis*, *Gloss.*: -άγριος, *malva agrestis*, ib. -άετος, ὁ, *black eagle*, Arist.*HA*618ᵇ28. ⊛-ᾱθὴρ σῖτος, ὁ, *dark kind of summer-wheat*, *Gp.*3.3.11 (-αἴθηρ Hsch.). -αιγίς, ίδος, ὁ and ἡ, *with dark aegis*, epith. of Erinys, A.*Th.*699 (lyr.); of Dionysus at Athens, Paus.2.35.1, Sch.Ar.*Ach.*146.—On the accent v. Hdn.Gr.1.85. II. [οἶνος] μ. *dark red* wine, Plu.2.692f. -αίων (μελανεών Bgk.), ωνος, ὁ, *the part of a ship covered with pitch*, Ar.*Fr.* 817. -αυγής, ές, *dark-gleaming*, νασμός E.*Hec.*153 (anap.), cf. Orph.*A.*513. -δανέως· ἀμπέλου εἶδος, Hsch. -δειρος, ὁ, a small bird, Id. -δετος, ον, *bound* or *mounted with black*, φάσγανα καλὰ μελάνδετα Il.15.713; μ. ξίφος *with iron scabbard*, E.*Ph.*1091; σάκος μ. *iron-rimmed* shield, A.*Th.*43; but μελάνδετον φόνῳ ξίφος E.*Or.*821 (lyr.). ⊛-δίνης [ῑ], ου, ὁ, *dark-eddying*, Γάγγης D.P. 577. -δόκος, ον, *holding ink*, κίστη, ἄγγος μ., *AP*6.65 (Paul. Sil.), 68 (Jul. Aeg.). -δόχιον, τό, *inkstand*, *Gloss.* -δρυον, τό, *heart of oak*, Thphr.*HP*1.6.2. II. v. μελάνδρυς. -δρυος, ον, *dark as the oak, dark-leaved*, πίτυς A.*Fr.*251, cf. Sch.Od.14.12. -δρῦς, ῠος, ὁ, *a large kind of tunny*, Pamphil.ap.Ath.3.121b:—hence μελάνδρυα (sc. τεμάχη), τά, *cheap cuts of tunny*, Xenocr.ap.Orib.2.58.146 (said to resemble black oak-roots, cf. Plin.*HN*9.48); and μελανδρύαι (sc. τόμοι), οἱ, Ath. l. c., 7.315e. -ειδέω, *look black*, Gal.19. 156. -ειμονέω, *to be clad in black*, Arist.*Mir.*840ᵇ7, Scymn.401, *IPE*1².34.24 (Olbia, i B.C.), Str.11.11.8, J.*BJ*4.4.3, Plu.2.838f, Lib. *Or.*30.8. -ειμοσύνη, ἡ, *wearing of black robes*, *Cat.Cod.Astr.*2. 161. -είμων, ον, gen. ονος, *black-clad*, μ. ἔφοδοι the assaults *of the black-robed ones* (the Furies), A.*Eu.*375 (lyr.); μ. ἑορτή a public lamentation, D.H.2.19, cf. Plb.2.16.13, J.*AJ*16.8.6; cf. μελανοείμων.

μελανέω, v. μελάνω.

⊛μελᾰν-ζοφος, ον, *blackly dark*, *EM*370.19. -ζωνος, ον, *with black girdle*, Nonn.*D.*31.116. -ζωτος, v. λευκόζωτος.

μελᾰνη-φόρος, ον, = μελανοφόρος, Orph.*H.*42.9; epith. of priests of Isis, at Delos, *SIG*977ᵃ2 (ii B.C.); at Eretria, Ἀρχ.Δελτ.1.148:—hence -φορέω, Tz.*H.*7.999.

μελαν-θέᾱ, ἡ, = μελάνων ὅρασις, opp. λευκοθέα, Aristo *Stoic.*1.86.

μελανθέλαιον, τό, *oil of* μελάνθιον, Dsc.1.37 (marg.).

μελ-άνθεμον, τό, v. l. for μηλάνθεμον, Dsc.3.137. -άνθεον, v. μελάνθιον. -ανθής, ές, (ἄνθος = *colour*) *black, swarthy*, γένος A.*Supp.* 154 (lyr.); μ. ῥοίζῳ σπερχόμενος πόντος *Hymn.Is.*150. -άνθινος, η, ον, *made from* μελάνθιον, Dsc.1.37, Gal.11.870. -άνθιον, τό, *a herb whose seeds were used as spice, black cummin, Nigella sativa*, Hp. *Mul.*1.74, *Steril.*230, Lxx *Is.*28.27, Dsc.3.79, *POxy.*1088.16 (i A.D.), *PMag.Par.*1.919, *Gp.*13.4.2, al.: gen. μελανθείου *PStrassb.*102.8 (iii B.C.); μελανθείου (with v. l. μελανθείης) Nic.*Th.*43; μελανθείου *PCair. Zen.*292.325, cf. 20 (iii B.C.): dat. μελανθείῳ *PTeb.*69.25 (ii B.C.).

μελάνθριξ, τρῐχος, ὁ, ἡ, = μελανόθριξ, Arist.*Phgn.*808ᵃ19.

⊛μελᾰν-ία, ἡ, (μέλας) *blackness*, opp. λευκότης, Arist.*Ph.*264ᵇ8, *Metaph.*1020ᵇ10, Str.12.8.18, etc.; μ. τῆς μορφῆς, of negroes, Agatharch.16; μ. οὐλῶν Dsc.1.34; μ. ἐκ τόκου Crito ap.Gal.12.447: in pl., Hierocl.p.35 A. II. *black cloud*, X.*An.*1.8.8 in pl., *black spots*, Plb.1.81.7. 2. *black pigment*, Thphr.*HP*5.3.1. -ια, τά, *festival of Dionysus* Μέλας, dub. in *SIG*1025.58 (Cos, iv/iii B.C.). -ίζω, *to be black* or *blackish*, Hices.ap.Ath.7.320d, Dsc.1.105, *Gp.*9.17.1:— Pass., Heliod.ap.Orib.50.7.2. ⊛-ιον, τό, Dim. of μέλαν, *ink*, *PMag. Par.*1.2013 (pl.), *PMag.Berol.*1.243a. -ιππος, ον, *with black horses*, νύξ A.*Fr.*69.5 (lyr.).

μελανίχροος, ον, *dark in colour*, οἶνος Hp.*Mul.*1.42 (s. v. l.).

μελᾰνό-βροχος, ον, gloss on ἐβαδίαστον, Hsch. -γειος, ον, = μελάγγειος, Sch.Nic.*Th.*566. -γραμμος, ον, *with black stripes*, Arist.*Fr.*298. -δέρμᾰτος, ον, *black-skinned*, Id.*HA*517ᵃ14. -δοχεῖον, τό, *inkstand*, Aq.*Ez.*9.2:—also -δόχον, Poll.10.60; and -δόκον, *PLond.*2.402ᵛ25 (ii B.C.). -ειδής, ές, *black-looking*, Arist.*Col.*795ᵃ33. -είμων, ον, gen. ονος, = μελανείμων, Hp.*Insomn.* 92 (v. l. μελανείμ-), Vett.Val.2.5. -εις, εσσα, εν, *darkish*, ὦτα Aret. *SD*2.13 (s. v. l.). -ζυξ, ῠγος, ὁ, ἡ, lit. *black benched*, i. e. manned with swarthy (Egyptian) rowers, μ. ἄτα A.*Supp.*530 (lyr.). -θριξ, τρῐχος, ὁ, ἡ, *black-haired*, Hp.*Epid.*1.19, Arist.*GA*786ᵃ25. -κάρδιος, ον, *black-hearted*, Στυγὸς πέτρα Ar.*Ra.*470. -κισεργός, dub. sens. in *Tab.Defix.Aud.*255 (Carthage, i A.D.). -κολπος, ον, *dark-bosomed*, Νύξ prob. for μεγαλόκολπος in B.*Fr.*23. -κόμης, v. l. for μελαγκόμης in Poll.2.24. -κωλος, ον, *black-limbed*, Zonar. -μαλλος, ον, *black fleeced*, Eust.403.42.

μελᾰν-όμμᾰτος, ον, *black-eyed*, Pl.*Phdr.*253d, Arist.*GA*779ᵇ14.

μελᾰνο-νεκῠείμων, ον, gen. ονος, *clad in black shroud*, Com. word in Ar.*Ra.*1336 (lyr.). -νεφής, ές, *with black clouds*, gloss on κελαινεφής, Sch.D Il.2.412. -ομαι, Pass., *to be* or *become black*, pf. Pass. μεμελάνωμαι Lxx *Jb.*30.30, Aët.16.75. -πλόκᾰμος, ον, *black-haired*, Sch.Pi.*O.*6.46. -ποιός, όν, *blackening*, Hsch. s. v. μελαινάων. -πους, ποδος, ὁ, ἡ, *black-footed*, gloss on κυανόπεζα, Sch.D Il. 11.628. -πτερος, ον, *black-winged*, φάσμα E.*Hec.*705 (lyr.); Νύξ Ar. *Av.*695; ἀλεκτορίδες *Gp.*14.7.9. -πτέρυξ, ῠγος, ὁ, ἡ, = foreg., ὄνειρος E.*Hec.*71 (anap.); *with black fins*, κορακῖνοι Ar.*Fr.*537. -πωλος, ον, *having black horses*, Sch.E.*Ph.*606. -ρράβδωτος, ον, *with black stripes*, Xenocr.ap.Orib.2.58.107. -ρριζον, τό, *black hellebore*, Ps.-Dsc.4.162.

μελᾰνός, ή, όν, = μέλας, *Gp.*7.15.6, *Stad.*57: neut. μελανόν, τό, *black pigment*, *Sammelb.*2251 (iv A.D.).

μελᾰνοσπᾰλάκισσα [ᾰκ], ἡ, fem. Adj. *dark mole-coloured*, ἵππος *PPetr.*3 p.159 (iii B.C.).

μελᾰν-όσσος, ον, *black-eyed*, v. l. (ap.Sch.) in Il.21.252; cf. μελάνοστος.

μελᾰνό-στερφος, ον, *black-skinned*, A.*Fr.*370 (μελαστ- cod. L, fort. μελανστ-). -στικτος, ον, *black-spotted*, Arist.*Fr.*299. -στολος, ον, *black-robed*, Plu.2.372e; epith. of Isis, *Epigr.Gr.*1023.3 (Egypt).

μελᾰν-οστος, ον, for μελᾰν-όστεος, *black-boned*, αἰετοῦ.. μελανόστου θηρητῆρος read for μέλανος τοῦ in Il.21.252 by Aristotle (cf. Sch. BT, Eust.1235.42); cf. μελάνοσσος.

μελᾰνο-συρμαῖος, ον, epith. of Egyptians in Ar.*Th.*857, with a double meaning, *with black trains to their robes* (σύρματα), and *fond of purges* (συρμαῖαι). -σώμᾰτος, ον, gloss on μελανόχρως, Sch.E. *Hec.*1105.

μελᾰνότης, ητος, ἡ, *blackness*, opp. λευκότης, Arist.*Ph.*244ᵇ17.

μελᾰν-ουργός, *atramentarius*, *Gloss.* -ουρίς, ίδος, pecul. fem. of sq., *AP*6.304 (Phan.). -ουρος, ὁ, (οὐρά) a sea-fish, *black-tail, Oblata melanura*, Epich.56, Cratin.221, Antiph.194.4, Arist.*HA*591ᵃ15, Speus.ap.Ath.7.313e, Numen.ib.d; μὴ γεύεσθαι μελανούρων Pythag. ap.Plu.2.12d. II. a kind of snake, perh. = διψάς, Ael.*NA*6.51.

μελᾰνόφαιος, ον, *dark grey*, opp. λευκόφ-, of figs, Ath.3.78a.

μελᾰν-όφθαλμος, ον, *black-eyed*, Hp.*Epid.*1.19, Arist.*GA*779ᵃ35, Philostr.*Gym.*25, *Gp.*17.2.1.

μελᾰνό-φλεψ, εβος, ὁ, ἡ, *black-veined*, Aret.*SD*2.1. -φορέω, *wear black*, Plu.2.557d. -φόρος, ον, *wearing black*, Sch.E.*Ph.*324.

μελᾰν-οφρυς, υ, gen. υος, *black-* or *beetle-browed*, Hdn.Gr.1.237, Hsch.

μελᾰνό-φυλλος, ον, = μελάμφυλλος, ἴων πτερά Chaerem.14. 13. -χλωρος, ον, = μελάγχλωρος, Procl.*Par.Ptol.*204. -χροος, ον, = μελάγχροος, Od.19.246: heterocl. nom. pl. κύαμοι μελανόχροες Il.13.589: gen. sg. -χροος Nic.*Th.*941: acc. sg. -χροα Orph.*L.*363: contr. -χρους *PLond.*2.333.23 (ii A.D.):—also μελανοχροιής, Suid.; -χρως, ωτος, ὁ, ἡ, = μελάγχρως, E.*Hec.*1106 (lyr., as v. l.), Arist. *Phgn.*808ᵃ17, Theoc.3.35; μελανόχρων Thphr.*Sens.*78.

μέλανσις, εως, ἡ, *a becoming black*, opp. λεύκανσις Arist.*Ph.*227ᵇ8, 230ᵃ23. 2. *dyeing black*, τριχῶν Alex.Trall.1.3.

μελᾰν-σπερμον, τό, = μελάνθιον, Dsc.*Eup.*2.97. -στερνος, ον, *black-breasted*, Jo.Gaz.2.126. -τειχής, ές, *black-walled*, δόμος Φερσεφόνας Pi.*O.*14.20. -τηρία, ἡ, *black pigment*, also used internally as a drug, Lat. *creta sutoria, shoemakers' black*, *IG*2².1672. 14,16,69, Arist.*Col.*794ᵃ20, Heraclid.Tar.ap.Cael.Aur.*CP*3.44, Dsc. 5.101, Gal.13.741, Luc.*Cat.*15, Scrib.Larg.208. -τήριον, τό, *spot, stain*, Sch.E.*Hec.*912. -τραγής, ές, *black when eaten*, σῦκον *AP* 6.299 (Phan.). -υδρος, ον, *with black water*, κρήνη μελάνυδρος, of water *which looks black* from its depth, Il.9.14, Od.20.158, Thgn. 959. -ω, intr., *grow black*, only in Il.7.64 Ζεφύροιο ἐχεύατο πόντον ἔπι φρίξ.., μελάνει δέ τε πόντος ὑπ' αὐτῆς (sc. τῆς φρικός), cf. Arist.*Pr.* 934ᵃ15; but Aristarch. read πόντον in the second clause and took μελάνει trans., = μελαίνει (sc. Ζέφυρος), *makes* the sea *black*:—later writers use μελανέω, intr. (which implies the reading μελανεῖ δέ τε πόντος), Thphr.*Ign.*50, A.R.4.1574, Arat.836; τὸ καλὸν μελανεῦντα Call.*Epigr.*53; μικκὴ καὶ μελανεῦσα *AP*5.120 (Phld.). -ώδης, ες, gloss on ἰοειδής, *EM*473.12. -ῶπις, ιδος, ἡ, fem. Adj. *black-looking*, σηπεδών Marc.Sid.64.

μελάρ-ρῑνος, ον, (ῥινόν) *black-skinned*, Nonn.*D.*14.395, al.

⊛μέλᾱς (μέλᾰς Rhian.58, where μέγας is corrupt for μέλας), μέλαινα, μέλᾰν; gen. μέλᾰνος, μελαίνης, μέλᾰνος, etc.; Ep. dat. μείλανι (metri gr.) Il.24.79: Aeol. nom. μέλαις, from *μέλανς, Choerob.*in Theod.* 1.123, Greg.Cor.p.599 S., hence restored in Sapph.57:—*black, dark*: in Hom. generally, *dark* in colour, οἶνος Od.5.265; μέλαν αἷμα, κῦμα, Il.4.149, 23.693; γαῖα μέλαινα 2.699, cf. Sapph.*Supp.*5. 2; ὕδωρ μέλαν Αἰσήποιο Il.2.825, cf. Od.4.359; νηῦς μ., from its being *pitched over*, Il.1.300, al.; of men, *dark, swarthy*, μέλανας δὲ ἀνδρικοὺς ἰδεῖν Pl.*R.*474e; ἰσχυρός τις ἦν, μ. D.21.71; τὰ μ. *black marks* about the ears of dogs, X.*Cyn.*5.23. II. *dark, murky*, ἕσπερος Od.1. 423; εὐφρόνα Pi.*N.*7.3. III. metaph., *black, dark*, θάνατος Il.2. 834, etc.; κήρ ib.859, etc.; ὀδύναι 4.117, etc. (the origin of the metaphor is seen in the phrases θανάτου μ. νέφος, ἄχεος νεφέλη μ., 16.

350, 18.22); μ. τύχα, ἀρά, A.*Supp.*89 (lyr.), *Th.*832 (lyr.); Ἐρινύς ib.993 (lyr.), cf. *Eu.*52; ἄτα Id.*Ag.*769 (lyr.); Ἄρης ib.1511 (lyr.); Ἅιδης S.*OT* 29; Ἅιδου μ. ἀνάγκα E.*Hipp.*1388 (lyr.), etc.; ἡμέραι μέλαιναι, = Lat. *dies atri*, Plu.*Luc.*27. 2. of the voice, *indistinct*, Arist.*Top.*106ᵃ25, Philostr.*VA*4.44; βραχὺ καὶ μ. φώνημα, of Nero, D.C.61.20. 3. *dark, obscure, enigmatical*, ἱστορίη *AP*11.347 (Phil.). 4. of character, *dark, malignant*, μ. φρήν, καρδία, Sol.42.4, Pi.*Fr.*123.4; μ. ἄνθρωποι Plu.2.12d; μ. ἦθος M. Ant.4.28. IV. Comp. μελάντερος, α, ον, *blacker, very black*, τοῦ δ' οὔ τι μελάντερον ἔπλετο ἔσθος Il.24.94: prov. of thick darkness, [νέφος] μελάντερον ἠΰτε πίσσα (v. ἠΰτε) 4.277: Sup. μελάντατος Hp. *VC*14, Ar.*Fr.*580, etc.:—Comp. also μελανώτερος Str.16.4.12: Sup. μελαινότατος *AP*11.68 (Lucill.), *Epigr.Gr.*320.4 (Thyatira). V. **μέλαινα** (sc. νοῦσος), ἡ, Medic., of diseases causing black secretions (such as *melaena*), Hp.*Morb.*2.73. VI. μέλαν, τό, v. sub voc. (Cf. Skt. *málam* 'dirt', *malinás* 'dirty', Lett. *melns* 'black'.)

**⊛μέλ-ασμα**, ατος, τό, *a black* or *livid spot*, Hp.*Fract.*11 (pl.), *Art.*86 (pl.), *Liq.*4 (sg.). II. *black hair-dye*, Apollod.Com.21, Poll.2.35, Crito ap.Gal.12.447. III. μ. γραμμοτόκον the solid *ink* in a pencil, *AP*6.63 (Damoch.). IV. in pl., *spots* in the moon, Cleom. 2.1. ⊛**-ασμός**, ὁ, *blackening* of flesh from mortification, Hp.*Aph.* 5.17 (pl.). 2. *dyeing black*, μελασμοὶ τριχῶν Dsc.1.112, Gal.12. 446. II. *black spot*, Plu.2.921f (pl.), Simp.*in Ph.*1294.20; on snakes, Plu.2.564d.

**μέλδω**, *soften by boiling*, γέντα βοὸς μέλδοντες Call.*Fr.*309; πυθομένοις μέλδουσιν ἅμ' ἰχθύσιν οὐλοὸν ἅλμην Man.6.464:—Hom. only in Med. (or Pass.), ὡς δὲ λέβης ζεῖ ἔνδον.., κνίσην μελδόμενος ἁπαλοτρεφέος σιάλοιο Il.21.363 (vv.ll. κνίσῃ and μελδομένου):—Pass., σάρκες μελδόμεναι Nic.*Th.*108. (Cf. Skt. *mṛdús*, Lat. *mollis* 'soft', OE. *meltan* 'melt', ONorse *maltr* 'rotten', Gr. βλαδύς.)

**μέλε** (A), Ep. 3 sg. impf. from μέλω, Od.5.6.

⊛**μέλε** (B), Att. voc., used as a familiar address to both sexes, ὦ μ. *my friend!* Ar.*Eq.*671, *Nu.*33, 1192, *V.*1400, *Pax* 137, *Ec.*120, 133; νὴ Δία, ὦ μ. Pl.*Tht.*178e; τί κόπτεις, ὦ μ.; Men.457: sarcastically, διαρραγείης, ὦ μ. Ar.*Av.*1257. (Gramm. expl. it by ὦ ἐπι-μελ-είας ἄξιε καὶ οἷον με-μελ-ημένε, Sch.Pl. l. c. (who says it was originally used by women only), or connect it with μέλεος, Sch.Ar.*Eq.*668: but it is perh. voc. of *μέλος 'good', cf. Lat. *melior*.)

**μελε-άγριον** or **-αγρον**, τό, a plant, Anon.ap.Suid. **-αγρίς**, ίδος, ἡ, *guinea-fowl, Numida ptilorhyncha*, etc., named after the hero Meleager, Arist.*HA*559ᵃ25, Clytus1, Scyl.112, Agatharch. 81. **-αγρος**· ἡ κατοικίδιος ὄρνις, Hsch.

**μελεάζω**, (μέλος) *execute a recitative*, Nicom.*Harm.*2.

**μελεαί** (-αιαί cod.)· ἀστράγαλοι, ἢ νωθροί, Hsch.

**μελεγγρἄφής**, ές, f.l. for μελαγγραφής (q. v.).

⊛**μελεδ-αίνω**, (μέλω) *care for, be cumbered about*, c. gen., πενίης Thgn.1129: c. acc., Archil.8, *SIG*2 (Sigeum, vi B. C.), Theoc.10.52: c. inf., γῆμαι κακὴν οὐ μελεδαίνει ἐσθλὸς ἀνήρ a well-born man *does* not *mind* marrying a woman of mean birth, Thgn.185. II. *care for, attend upon*, μ. τοὺς νοσέοντας Hdt.8.115; τὰς ὑστέρας Hp.*Mul.*1.17; τὴν ἄνθρωπον Aret.*CA*2.10. **-αντός**, ή, όν, *object of care*, Μαραθῶν ..μ. ἀνδράσιν *BCH*50.529 (Attica, ii A. D.). **-ή**, f.l. for μελέτη, Hp. *Mul.*1.67. **-ηθμός**, ὁ, *practice, exercise*, Orac. in *App.Anth.*6. 140. **-ημα**, ατος, τό, (μελεδαίνω) *care, anxiety*, Hom. always in pl., μελεδήματα πατρός *anxieties about* his father, Od.15.8; of sleep, λύων μ. θυμοῦ Il.23.62; μελεδήματα θεῶν *the care* of the gods [for men], E.*Hipp.*1103 (lyr.). II. *object of care*, Χαρίτων Ibyc.5; ἐμοὶ μ. ἰσχάς Alex.162.15 (anap.); Μοισᾶν *Epigr.Gr.*238 (Smyrna). **-ήμων**, ον, gen. ονος, *careful*, c. gen., ἔργων Emp.112.2; μ. κερκίδα πέπλων *AP* 6.39 (Arch.); δόμων φυλακὰν μ. ib.7.425 (Antip. Sid.). **-ών**, ῶνος, ἡ, = μελεδώνη II, Aret.*SD*1.6, Dioscorus in *PLit.Lond.*98 ii 20. II. in pl., = μελεδώνη I (q. v.), cj. in Hsch.; τῇσι μελεδώνεσι *sufferings* of a patient, Aret.*SD*2.4 (-δόσεσι codd., -δόσι Hude). **-ωνεύς**, έως, ὁ, poet. for μελεδωνός, Theoc.24.106. **-ώνη**, ἡ, *care, sorrow*, in pl., Od.19.517, Sapph.17, Theoc.21.5, Cerc.7.5; ἄγρυπνοι μελεδῶναι Phanocl.1.5: rare in Prose, Gal.18(1).363: in *h.Ap.*532, *h.Merc.* 447, Hes.*Op.*66, Thgn.883, the vulg. readings μελεδώνων, μελεδῶνας (as if from μελεδών) shd. prob. be corrected μελεδωνῶν, -ώνας; cf. μεληδών. II. in sg., = μελέτη, δέεται πολλῆς μ. Hp.*Mul.*1. 36. **-ωνός**, ὁ and ἡ, *attendant, guardian*, τῶν οἰκίων μ. *house-steward*, Hdt.3.61; ὁ μ. τῶν θηρίων *the keeper* of the crocodiles, Id.2. 65; μ. τῆς τροφῆς *one who provides* their food, ibid., cf. 7.31; μ. τῶν χρημάτων ib.38; μελεδωνοὶ τῶν ἱερῶν D.H.1.67; τοῦ τείχους Ael.*NA* 3.26; μ. λῃστῶν *agents* of pirates, Philostr.*VA*3.24; title of public officials in Samos, *SIG*976.63 (ii B. C.): metaph., of a learned man, πάσης πολύβυβλον ἀφ' ἱστορίης μ. *Ath.Mitt.*11.428 (Notium).

**μέλει**, impers., v. μέλω A. II.

**μελεΐνος**, η, ον, *ashen*, *IG*2².1672.307, Thphr.*HP*5.7.8; cf. μελίϊνος, μέλινος.

**μελεϊστί**, Adv. *limb from limb*, ταμών Il.24.409; διὰ μ. ταμών Od. 9.291, cf. 18.339; μ. κεδαιόμενος A.R.2.626; μ. ξαίνειν Philostr.*Her.* 19.18; cf. μελιστί.

**μελεο-πᾰθής**, ές, *having suffered wretchedly*, A.*Th.*961 (lyr.). **-πονος**, ον, *having done wretchedly*, ib.960 (lyr.).

**μέλεος**, α, ον, also ος, ον E.*Or.*207 (lyr.):—*idle, useless*, οὐδέ τί σε χρὴ ἑστάμεναι μέλεον σὺν τεύχεσιν Il.10.480; μελέη δέ μοι ἔσσεται ὁρμή Od.5.416; οὐ μ. εἰρήσεται αἶνος Il.23.795; μ. δέ οἱ εὖχος ἔδωκας a vaunt *unearned*, 21.473: neut. μέλεον as Adv., *in vain*, μέλεον δ' ἠκόντισαν ἄμφω 16.336. II. after Hom., *unhappy, miserable*, ὦ μέλεοι, τί κάθησθε; Orac.ap.Hdt.7.140, etc.; μέλεος γάμων *unhappy* in marriage, A.*Th.*779 (lyr.); ὤμοι ἐγὼ σοῦ μ. S.*Tr.*972 (lyr.), cf. E.*IT*868 (lyr.), Men.*Epit.*470. 2. of acts, conditions, etc., ἔργα A.*Ch.*1007 (anap.); θάνατοι, πάθα, Id.*Th.*879 (anap.), S.*Ant.*977 (lyr.); ὀνόματα Antiph.209.8. [μέλεοι is disyll. in A.*Th.*878 (lyr.), 945 (lyr.).]

**μελεόφρων**, ὁ, ἡ, gen. ονος, *miserable-minded*, E.*IT*854 (lyr.).

**μελερόν**· μαραντικόν, καυστικόν, Hsch.; cf. μαλερός.

**μελεσίπτερος**, ον, (μέλος B) *singing with its wings*, epith. of the cicada, *AP*7.194 (Mnasalc.).

⊛**μελετ-αίνω**, *take thought for, attend to*, c. gen., *Mnemos.*57.208 (Argos, vi B. C.). **-άω**, fut. -ήσω Th.1.80, etc., -ήσομαι Luc.*Sol.* 6, Philostr.*VS*1.24.2:—post-Hom. Verb, *take thought* or *care for*, c. gen., βίου, ἔργου, Hes.*Op.*316, 443: c. acc. rei, δόξαν ἀρετῆς Th. 6.11; of a physician, *treat* a case, Hp.*Int.*27, etc.:—Pass., of the patient, ib.26, etc. 2. *attend to, study*, οὐ δύναμαι ἀκοῦσαι, τοῦτο μελετῶν (sc. τὸ ἀκοῦσαι) Hdt.3.115; πλήθους δόξας μεμελετηκώς Pl. *Phdr.*260c. II. *pursue, exercise*, [μαντείην] *h.Merc.*557; μ. τοῦτο (sc. ἡμεροδρόμην εἶναι) Hdt.6.105: freq. in Att., μ. σοφίαν Ar.*Pl.* 511; τέχνας, ῥητορικήν, Pl.*Grg.*511b,c, 448d; *practise*, ἤθη, γαστριμαργίας, ὕβρεις, Id.*Phd.*81e; ὄρχησιν Id.*Lg.*813e; [νόμους] E.*Ba.*892 (lyr.); ἀστοῖς ἴσα χρὴ μελετᾶν S.*OC*171 (anap.); τὴν τῶν πολεμικῶν ἄσκησιν Arist.*Pol.*1333ᵇ39: generally, μ. ἄδικα Lxx *Jb.*27.4; ταῦτα μελέτα 1*Ep.Ti.*4.15; esp. *practise* speaking, *con over* a speech *in one's mind*, λογάρια δύστηνα μελετήσας D.19.255; ἀπολογίαν Id.46.1; also, *deliver, declaim* (cf. II. 5 b), λόγους D.C.40.54:—Pass., τὸ ναυτικὸν οὐκ ἐνδέχεται ἐκ παρέργου μελετᾶσθαι naval warfare cannot *be practised* 'en amateur', Th.1.142; εὐταξία μετὰ κινδύνων μελετωμένη discipline *put in practice* on the battle-field, Id.6.72, cf. Pl.*R.*455c. 2. c. inf., μετρίως ἀλγεῖν μελετᾷ σοφία *practises* moderation in grief, E. *Fr.*46; λαλεῖν μεμελετήκασί που Ar.*Ec.*119; also μ. τοξεύειν καὶ ἀκοντίζειν X.*Cyr.*1.2.12, cf. Antipho 3.2.3; μ. ποιεῖν καὶ λέγειν Lys.10.9; μ. ἀποθνῄσκειν, τεθνάναι, *practise* dying, death, Pl.*Phd.*67e, 81a, cf. Epicur.*Fr.*470. 3. less freq. c. part., μ. κυβερνῶντες X.*Ath.*1.20; with ὡς and part., Id.*Cyr.*5.5.47. 4. with Prep., μ. ἔν τινι Lxx *Jo.* 1.8, al. 5. abs., *study, train oneself*, Ar.*Ec.*164, Th.1.80, X.*HG* 3.4.16; ἦν τὸ ἱππικὸν μεμελετηκός ib.6.4.10: c. dat. modi, τόξῳ μ. καὶ ἀκοντίῳ Id.*Cyr.*2.1.21; ἐν τῷ μὴ μελετῶντι by want of *practice*, Th.1.142. b. esp. *practise oratory, declaim*, Pl.*Phdr.*228b; ἐπὶ τῶν καιρῶν μ. *extemporize a speech*, D.61.43; Ἑλληνιστὶ μ. Plu.*Cic.*4, cf. 2.131a, Luc.*Sol.*6, Philostr.*VS*1.24.2, *AP*11.145; of actors, Arist. *Pr.*904ᵇ3. 6. Medic., of disease, *threaten*, μ. τὴν τοῦ καρκινώματος γένεσιν Leonid.ap.Aët.16.43: abs., ἢν κρύβδην μελετήσῃ.. ἡ νοῦσος Aret.*SD*2.12:—Pass., ἀπειλᾷ καὶ μελετᾶται μανία Steph.*in Hp.*1.99 D., cf. Aët.16.63. 7. c. acc. pers., *exercise, train* persons, ἐμελέτησεν [αὐτοὺς] ὡς εἶεν.. X.*Cyr.*8.1.42: c. inf., οὓς ἀναβαίνειν ἐπὶ τοὺς ἵππους μελετᾷ Φείδων Mnesim.4.7:—Pass., μελετώμενοι ὑπ' αὐτῶν τὴν πτῆσιν, of eaglets, Philostr.*VA*1.7. III. Gramm., *to be accustomed*, c. inf., μεμελέτηκε τὸ τ εἰς θ τρέπεσθαι *An.Ox.*1.66; τὰ μὴ μελετήσαντα πάσχειν συναίρεσιν Theognost.*Can.*145.25. b. Medic., *acquire a habit*, μελετησάντων ἐκπίπτειν βραχιόνων Gal.14.782:—Pass., *become chronic*, μελετηθὲν τὸ πάθος Aët.16.67. **-η**, ἡ, *care, attention*, Hes.*Op.*412, Epich.[284]: pl., Emp.110.2: c. gen. objecti, μ. πλεόνων *care for* many things, Hes.*Op.*380; μελέτην τινὸς ἔχειν, = μελετᾶν, ἐπιμελεῖσθαι, ib.457; ἔργων ἐκ πολλοῦ μ. long-continued *attention* to action, Th.5.69: c. gen. subjecti, *care taken* by one, θεῶν μελέτη S.*Ph.*196 (anap.); of a trainer, B.12.191: abs., μελέτη κατατρύχεσθαι E.*Med.*1099 (anap.): pl., Emp.131.2. 2. Medic., *treatment*, Hp.*Fract.*31, 35 (pl.), *Art.*50. II. *practice, exercise*, ὀξεῖα μ. Pi.*O.*6.37; ἔχων μ. Id.*N.*6.54; ἡ δι' ὀλίγου μ. their short *practice*, Th.2.85; πόνων μ. *painful exercises*, of the Spartan discipline, ib.39; μάθησις καὶ μ. Pl.*Tht.*153b; μ. θανάτου Id.*Phd.*81a; ἡ ἐγκύκλιος τῶν προπαιδευμάτων μ. Ph.1.157. b. in a military sense, *exercise, drill*, μετὰ κινδύνων τὰς μελέτας ποιεῖσθαι to go through one's *exercises* in actual war, Th.1.18; ταῖς τῶν πολεμικῶν μ. Id.2.39; μ. ἐν ὅπλοις ποιεῖσθαι *IG*2².1028.19, al. c. freq. of orators, *rehearsal, declamation*, ταύτης τῆς μελέτης καὶ τῆς ἐπιμελείας D.18.309, al.; of actors, νήστεις ὄντες τὰς μ. ποιούμενοι making their *rehearsals*, Arist.*Pr.*901ᵇ 3. d. *matter* for discussion, μ. σοφισταῖς προσβαλεῖν Pi.*I.*5(4).28; *branch* or *object of study*, Pl.*Grg.*500d, al.; ὁ νόμος σου μ. μού ἐστιν Lxx *Ps.*118(119).77. 2. later, *theme, lecture*, Str.1.2.2, Plu.2.41d, Luc.*Rh.Pr.*17; *declamation*, μελέτῃσί τ' ἄριστον *IG*3.625; τὰς μ. μισθοῦ ποιεῖσθαι Philostr.*VS*1.21.5. 3. *pursuit*, μία οὐχ ἅπαντας θρέψει μ. Pi.*O.*9.107, cf. Pl.*Phd.*82a. III. *practice, usage*, ἃς οἱ πατέρες ἡμῖν παρέδοσαν μ. Th.1.85. 2. *habit*, Hp.*Mul.*1.17; ἢν ἐς μελέτην ἥκῃ τοῦ κακοῦ ὤνθρωπος Aret.*CA*1.5; ἐν μ. γίγνεσθαι ψόφων *become accustomed to* noises, Stob.*App.*p.22 G. IV. *threatening symptom* or *condition*, of disease, μελέτη καὶ προοίμιον ἐπιληψίας Posidon.ap.Aët. 6.12; ὀδύνη.. μ. λύσεως Aët.5.100, cf. Steph.*in Hp.*1.191 D. **-ημα**, ατος, τό, *practice, exercise*, Pl.*Phd.*67d, X.*Cyr.*8.1.43 (pl.), Critias 6.1; αἰσχρῶν ἔργων μ. E.*Fr.*910 (anap., nisi leg. μελέδημα); τὰ πρὸς πόλεμον μ. *practice for*.., X.*Eq.*11.13. 2. μελετήματα φωνῆς grammatical *examples*, A.D.*Synt.*277.26. **-ηρός**, ά, όν, *practising diligently*, X.*An.*1.9.5 (Sup.), Longin.*Rh.*p.203 H. (Sup.); συνουσίαι μ. *debating* societies, Philostr.*VS*1.23.2. **-ησις**, εως, ἡ, = μελέτη, *AB* 438. **-ητέος**, α, ον, *to be treated*, νοσήματα Hp.*Acut.*6. II. μελετητέον *one must study*, Pl.*Grg.*527b, Porph.*Abst.*1.31: c. inf., Iamb. *Protr.*5. **-ητήριον**, τό, *place for practice*, Plu.*Dem.*8. II. *instrument for practising*, Anaxandr.15.2. ⊛**-ητικός**, ή, όν, *mourning, cooing*, περιστεραί Lxx *Ez.*7.16; αὐλός, = *vasca*, *Gloss.* II.

ὕλη μ. a collection *of meditations*, D.L.3.47. **-ητός**, ή, όν, *to be gained by practice*, Pl.*Clit.*407b, Luc.*Im.*16. **-ωρ**, ορος, ὁ, (μέλω) *one who cares for, an avenger*, ἀμφί τινα S.*El.*846 (lyr.).

**μέλη**, ἡ, a sort of cup, Anaxipp.8.

**μεληδόν**, Adv., (μέλος) = μελεϊστί, κρέα μ. ὠπτημένα Posidon.22 J., cf. Al.*Ex.*29.17. II. *in order*, Zos.Alch.p.193 B.

**μελ-ηδών**, όνος, ἡ, = μελεδώνη I, Simon.39.1 (pl.), A.R.3.812 (pl.), *Anacreont.*14.6, *AP*5.292.3 (Paul. Sil.). **-ημα**, ατος, τό, (μέλω) *object of care, beloved object, darling*, of persons, μ. τῶμον Sapph. 126, cf. Ar.*Ec.*972 (lyr.), Men.*Pk.*214; νέαισιν παρθένοισι μ. Pi.*P.*10.59; Χαρίτων μ. Id.*Fr.*95; Κύπριδος ib.217; ὦ φίλτατον μ. δώμασιν A.*Ch.*235; ὦ γραῦ, τῷ θανάτῳ μ. Ar.*Ec.*905 (lyr.). II. *charge, duty*, A.*Ag.*1551 (anap.); μέλον πάλαι μ. μοι S.*Ph.*150 (lyr.). 2. *care, anxiety*, A.*Eu.*444, Theoc.14.2, etc. **-ησίμβροτος**, ον, *an object of care* or *love to men*, ῥίζα Pi.*P.*4.15. **-ησμός**, ὁ, *care, diligence*, *EM* 444.54. **-ητέον**, *one must take thought*, τοῦ λανθάνειν Pl.*R.*365e.

**Μελητίδης**, ου, ὁ, prov. at Athens for *a blockhead* (in form a patronymic from Μέλητος), Ar.*Ra.*991 (lyr., prob.), Luc.*Am.*53, etc.—In codd. usu. written Μελιτίδης: hence derived by Sch.Ar. l.c. and Eust.1735.51 from μέλι, though second syll. is long.

⊛**μέλῐ**, τό, gen. ῐτος, etc.; dat. μέλι Philox.3.17; gen. pl. μελίτων Emp.128.7 (nisi leg. μελιτῶν, cf. μελιτόν):—*honey*, Od.20.69, etc.; μ. χλωρόν Il.11.631, Od.10.234, Xenoph.38.1; ξανθόν Simon.47; παμφαές A.*Pers.*612; τὸ μέλι τἀττικόν Ar.*Pax* 252, cf. Men.708; various kinds, Thphr.*Fr.*190; said to be made from the palm (φοῖνιξ), Hdt.1.193, cf. 4.194; μ. θανάτου σύμβολον Porph.*Antr.*18. 2. in comparisons, of anything sweet, esp. of eloquence, μέλιτος γλυκίων ῥέεν αὐδή Il.1.249, cf. Pi.*O.*10(11).98; Σοφοκλέους τοῦ μέλιτι κεχριμένου Ar.*Fr.*581; ὕπνος γλυκίων μέλιτος Mosch.2.3; ἡ τῶν ἀνδρῶν [χολή] ἐστι πρὸς ἐκείνην μέλι Alex.146.6: prov. μήτε μοι μ. μήτε μέλισσα, of those who refuse to take 'the rough with the smooth', Sapph.113. II. *sweet gum* collected from certain trees, *manna*, Arist.*Mir.*831$^{b}$23; τὸ ὗον μ. Polyaen.4.3.32; μ. ἄγριον, μαινόμενον, D.S.19.94, Str.12.3.18. (Cf. Goth. *miliþ*, Lat. *mel.*)

⊛**μελία**, Ep. -ίη, ἡ, *manna ash, Fraxinus Ornus*, Il.13.178, 16.767, Musae.*Fr.*5 D., S.*Fr.*759, Thphr.*HP*3.11.3, etc.; τρίτον ἄλλο γένος . . ἐκ μελιᾶν Hes.*Op.*145. II. *ashen spear*, Il.19.390, 22.225, etc.

**μελιᾱδής**, ές, Dor. and Aeol. for μελιηδής.

**Μελίαι**, αἱ, a race of nymphs said to have sprung from the spot of earth on which fell the blood of Uranus, Hes.*Th.*187, Call.*Jov.*47, etc. (The name implies *ash-nymphs*.)

⊛**μελίαμβοι**, οἱ, *lyric iambics*, as written by Cercidas, D.L.6.76, prob. in St.Byz. s.v. Μεγάλη πόλις and Stob.4.16.7.

**μελίβδεσθαι**· μέλλειν, Hsch. (Fort. μέμβλεσθαι· μέλειν.)

⊛**μελῐ-βόας**, ὁ, *sweet-singing*, κύκνος E.*Fr.*773.34 (lyr.). **-βρομος**, ον, *sweet-toned*, βοὰ αὐλοῖο *AP*7.696 (Arch.). **-γᾱθής**, ές, Dor. for *-γηθής, *honey-sweet*, ὕδωρ Pi.*Fr.*198. **-γδουπος**, ον, *sweet-sounding*, ἀοιδαί Id.*N.*11.18. **-γενέτωρ**, τορος, ὁ, *producer of honey*, epith. of Ζεὺς Ἥλιος Μίθρας Σάραπις, *PMag.Lond.*46.6. **-γηρυς**, Dor. **-γᾱρυς**, υος, ὁ, ἡ, *sweet-voiced, melodious*, ὄψ Od.12.187; ἀοιδή *h.Ap.*519; παρθενικαί Alcm.26.1; ὕμνοι, κῶμοι, Pi.*O.*11(10).4, *N.*3.4; παιᾶνος ὀμφά Id.*Pae.*5.47; ἀηδών, of a woman, *IG*14.1942.—Poet. word, used by Pl.*Phdr.*269a. **-γληνος**, ον, *soft-eyed*, Hsch. **-γλωσσος**, ον, *honey-tongued*, πειθοῦς ἐπαοιδαί A.*Pr.*173 (anap.); ἀοιδαί B.*Fr.*3.2; ἀηδών, of a poet, Id.3.97; ἔπη Ar.*Av.*908 (lyr.); Πιερίδες *Epigr.Gr.*228*a* 2 (Ephesus).

**μέλιγμα**, ατος, τό, v.l. for μέλισμα, Mosch.3.55, 92.

**μελιειδής**, ές, f.l. for μελιηδής, Hp.*Aff.*55.

⊛**μελί-εφθον**, τό, *honey-jar*, *Peripl.M.Rubr.*6, 8:—Dim. **-έφθιον** (μελέφθ- Pap.), τό, *PLond.*2.964.4 (iii A.D.).

**μελίζω** (A), fut. -ιῶ Lxx *Le.*1.6: aor. ἐμέλισα D.H.7.72: pf. Pass. μεμέλισμαι Opp.*C.*3.159: (μέλος A):—*dismember, cut in pieces*, Pherecyd.32 J., D.H. l.c., Apollod.1.9.12. 2. Pass., *have the limbs fully formed*, Opp. l.c.

⊛**μελίζω** (B), Dor. **μελίσδω**, Dor. fut. Med. μελίξομαι Mosch.3.51: otherwise only pres. and impf.: (μέλος B):—*modulate, sing*, μελίσδειν σύριγγι Theoc.20.28:—mostly in Med., Pi.*Parth.*2 *Fr.*2.66, Pl.Com. 69.13, Theoc.1.2, 7.89, *APl.*4.307.5 (Leon.):—Pass., Phld.*Po.Herc.* 994 *Fr.*20. 2. *to be like music*, [λέξις] μελίζουσα μέν, οὐ μὴν μέλος D.H.*Dem.*50. II. trans., *celebrate in song*, τινὰ ἀοιδαῖς Pi.*N.*11.18; μ. πάθη A.*Ag.*1176 (lyr.). 2. *make musical*, τὴν ποιητικὴν S.E.*M.*6.16.—Never in Att. Prose.

**μελίζωρος**, ον, *of pure honey, sweet as honey*, ποτόν Phaedim.ap. Ath.11.498e, Nic.*Al.*351; ῥίζα μ. πάσασθαι Id.*Th.*663; τὸ μ., = μελίκρατον, Id.*Al.*205.

**μελιη-γενής**, ές, *ash-born*, A.R.4.1641.

**μελῐ-ηδής**, Dor. -ᾱδής, ές, Aeol. -άδης, (ἡδύς) *honey-sweet*, οἴνου . . μελιηδέος Il.4.346; οἶνός σε τρώει μελιηδὴς Od.21.293; λωτοῖο μελιηδέα καρπόν 9.94; τὼ μελιάδεος (sc. οἴνου) Alc.45, cf. Id.p.31 Lobel, Pi.*Fr.*166.1. 2. metaph., μελιηδέα θυμὸν ἀπηύρα Il.10.495; νόστον δίζηαι μελιηδέα Od.11.100; ἐμὲ μελιηδὴς ὕπνος ἀνῆκε 19.551; γᾶρυς Simon.41. **-θρεπτος**, ον, *honey-fed*, *AP*9.122 (Evenus?). ⊛**-θροος**, ον, contr. **-θρους**, ουν, *sweet-voiced*, κύκνος ib.5.124 (Bass.).

**μελίϊνος**, η, ον, = μελέϊνος, *IG*$2^{2}$.1672.155, al., Sch.D Il.5.655.

**μελίκακι**· σκεύασμά τι βρωτὸν μετὰ τυροῦ, Hsch.

**μελί-κηρᾱ** [ῐ], ἡ, *spawn of the murex*, as being like *a honeycomb*, Arist.*HA*546$^{b}$19. 2. gloss on κοπρίων (v.l. for κηρίων), Gal.19. 113. II. = μελικηρίς II, Pherecr.25. ⊛**-κήριον**, τό, (κηρός) *honeycomb*, Sm.*Ex.*16.31. **-κηρίς**, ίδος, ἡ, Medic., a kind of *cyst* or *wen*, from its resembling *a honeycomb*, Hp.*Prorrh.*2.42, Antyll.ap.Orib.45. 3 tit., cf. Sch.ad loc. II. *honey-cake*, Philox.2.17 (as f.l.). III. *honeycomb*, *POxy.*936.10 (iii A.D.), Sch.Ar.*Th.*523. IV. *kind of vine*, Eust.1656.63. **-κηρον**, τό, = foreg. III, Theoc.20.27 (dub.), Poll.1.254, Hsch. II. = foreg. IV, Ps.-Plu.*Fluv.*19.2. **-κηρος**, ὁ, *beeswax*, *PMed.Lond.*155 ii 1, 15. **-κηρώδης**, ες, *due to* μελικηρίς I, ἕλκος Aët.4.23. **-κομπος**, ον, *sweet-sounding*, ἀοιδαί Pi.*I.*2.32.

**μελῐκός**, ή, όν, (μέλος B) *lyric*, ποίησις Plu.2.348b: μελικός, ὁ, *lyric poet*, of Pindar, ib.1120c; τὸ μ. σχῆμα D.H.*Comp.*11. Adv. **-κῶς** *lyrically*, Sch.Ar.*Av.*209.

**μελικράς**, κρᾶτος, or **μελίκρᾱς**, ᾱτος, = sq., οἶνος Orib.*inc.*13.34; on the accent v. Hdn.Gr.ap.Choerob.*in Theod.*1.377.

**μελίκρᾱτον**, Ion. **-κρητον**, τό, (κεράννυμι) *drink of honey and milk* offered as a libation to the powers of the nether world, χοὴν χεῖσθαι πᾶσιν νεκύεσσι, πρῶτα μελικρήτῳ, μετέπειτα δὲ ἡδέϊ οἴνῳ Od.10.519, cf. *SIG*1025.34 (Cos); μελίκρατα γάλακτος E.*Or.*115; also, *a mixture of honey and water*, Hp.*Aph.*5.41, Arist.*Metaph.*1092$^{b}$29, *Com.Adesp.* 128, Antyll.ap.Orib.5.29.7, Gal.ap.Orib.5.14.1, cf. Sch.S.*OC*481, Thphr.*HP*9.11.2; μ. θερμόν *POxy.*1088.61.

**μελίκταινα**, ἡ, poet. for μελίτταινα, Nic.*Th.*555, Hsch.

⊛**μελικτής**, οῦ, ὁ, Dor. **-κτάς**, (μελίζω B) *singer, player*; esp. *flute-player*, Theoc.4.30, Mosch.3.7; cf. μελιστής.

**μελῐ-λώτῐνος**, η, ον, *made of melilot*, στέφανοι Alex.114, cf. Plu.2. 356f: neut. as Adv., μ. λαλεῖν to talk *sweetly as melilot*, Pherecr. 131.2. **-λωτον**, τό, *Peripl.M.Rubr.*49, and **-λωτος**, ὁ, Sapph. *Supp.*25.14, Thphr.*HP*7.15.3:—*melilot, Trigonella graeca*, a kind of clover, so called from the quantity of honey it contained, μ. ἀνθεμώδης Sapph. l.c., cf. Cratin.98, Arist.*HA*627$^{a}$8, Thphr. l.c. 2. *king's clover, Trigonella corniculata*, Dsc.3.40. II. a tree, acc. to Str.17.3.11. [ῐ: but ῑ Nic.*Th.*897.] **-μηλον**, τό, *Pyrus praecox, summer-apple, jenneting*, Dsc.1.115. 2. *apple grafted on quince*, *Gp.*10.20.1. II. *drink made from* I. 1, Antyll.ap.Orib.5.29.8, Herod.Med. in *Rh.Mus.*58.98.

**μελίνεως**· εἶδος ἀμπέλου, Hsch.

⊛**μελίνη** [ῐ], ἡ, = ἔλυμος, *Italian millet, Setaria italica*, Hdt.3.117; κνήμη μελίνης S.*Fr.*608: in pl., *millet-fields*, X.*An.*2.4.13, D.8. 45. II. name of an animal, δέρμα μελίνης ἄνεργον *Edict.Diocl. Geronthr.*8.29 (v.l. μελεινον *Aeg.*); perh. *badger*, cf. Lat. *mēles, mellina*. III. = τοῦ πολύποδός τι μέρος, Hsch.

**μέλινον**, τό, = μελισσόφυλλον, dub. in Varro *RR*3.16.

**μέλινος** (A), ὁ, = μελίνη I, cited by Harp. from X.*An.*1.2.22, 1.5.10 (μελίνην codd.), cf. Thphr.*HP*8.1.4, Diocl.*Fr.*113.

**μέλῐνος** (B), Ep. **μείλινος** (also in late Prose, μειλίνη ὕλη Orib.49. 3.1), η, ον, (μελία) *ashen*, μείλινον ἔγχος Il.5.655; δόρυ μείλινον ib.666, al.; ἷζε δ' ἐπὶ μελίνου οὐδοῦ Od.17.339.

**Μελῐνοφάγοι** [ᾰ], οἱ, *Millet-eaters*, a Thracian tribe, X.*An.*7.5.12.

**μελι-οῦχος**, ὁ, epith. of doubtful meaning applied in magical writings to various divinities, M. τύραννε, of Apollo, *PMag.Lond.*47.33; Ζεῦ Ἥλιε Μίθρα Σάραπι ἀνίκητε, M., Μελικέρτα, Μελιγενέτωρ ib.46. 5, cf. *PMag.Par.*2.45, *Tab.Defix.Aud.*22.32, 38.12. **-παις** σίμβλος, ὁ, the hive *with its honey-children*, *AP*12.249 (pl., Strat.). **-πηκτον**, Dor. **-πακτον**, τό, *honey-cake*, Antiph.78, 140, Philox.3.16. **-πνοος**, ον, contr. **-πνους**, ουν, *honey-breathing*, λίβανος *AP*6.231 (Phil.): metaph., μ. σῦριγξ Theoc.1.128; αὐδά Limen.13; Μοῦσα Tryph. 429. **-πτέρωτος**, ον, *honey winged*, μέλεα Μουσᾶν *Lyr.Adesp.* 81. **-πτορθος**, ον, *with sweet boughs*, of liquorice, Androm.ap. Gal.14.39. **-ρρᾰθάμιγξ**, ιγγος, ὁ, ἡ, *honey-dropping*, Nonn.*D.*12. 168, 21.160. **-ρροθος**, ον, *sweet-sounding*, Pi.*Fr.*246. **-ρροος**, ον, contr. **-ρους**, ουν, *flowing with honey*, *Gloss.* **-ρρῠτος**, ον, = foreg., κρῆναι Pl.*Ion* 534b.

**μέλις**, ὁ, barbarism for μέλι, Ar.*Th.*1192.

**μελίσδω**, Dor. for μελίζω (B).

**μελῐσῑδωνοφρῡνῐχήρᾱτα** μέλη, *honey-sweet Sidonian* lays *of Phrynichus*, Ar.*V.*220.

⊛**μελίσκιον**, τό, Dim. of μέλος B, Alcm.65 (-ίσκον codd. A.D.), Antiph.207.3.

**μέλισμα**, ατος, τό, (μελίζω B) *song*, Theoc.14.31, 20.28; cf. μέλιγμα. 2. *air, melody*, μ. λύρας *AP*7.196 (Mel.); *lyric poetry*, ib. 4.1.35 (Id.).

**μελισμάτιον**, τό, Dim. of foreg., v.l. in *AP*11.168 (Antiphan.).

**μελισμός**, ὁ, (μελίζω A) *dismembering, dividing*, opp. πλοκή, v.l. in D.H.*Lys.*11. II. (μελίζω B) *song*, Str.15.1.42.

**μελίσπονδα** (sc. ἱερά), τά, *drink-offerings of honey*, μ. θύειν Plu.2. 464c, 672b, cf. Porph.*Abst.*2.20.

⊛**μέλισσᾰ**, Att. -ττα, ης, ἡ, (perh. by haplology for μελι-λιχ-ya 'honey-licker', cf. Skt. *madhu-lih-* (corresp. with Gr. *μεθυ-λιχ-) 'bee') *bee*, Od.13.106, etc.; of *wild bees*, that live in rocks, Il.2.87, cf. 12.167; of *honey-bees*, that live in hives, Hes.*Th.*594; σμῆνος μελισσᾶν A.*Pers.*128 (lyr.), cf. Hdt.4.194, 5.10:—Phrases: ὥσπερ μέλιττα τὸ κέντρον ἐγκαταλιπών Pl.*Phd.*91c; ὄνος ἐν μελίτταις 'a hornets' nest', Crates Com.36; cf. μέλι I. 2 fin. II. the term μέλισσα was applied 1. to *poets*, from their culling the beauties of nature, ἔνθεν ὡσπερεὶ μ. Φρύνιχος . . μελέων ἀπεβόσκετο καρπὸν Ar.*Av.*748; μ. Μούσης Id.*Ec.*974 (lyr.); μ. Ἤρινναν Μουσῶν ἄνθεα δρεπτομέναν *AP*7. 13 (Leon. or Mel.); esp. of Sophocles, Sch.Ar.*V.*460. 2. to the *priestesses* of Delphi, Pi.*P.*4.60; of Demeter and Artemis, Sch.Pi. l.c., Porph.*Antr.*18; of Cybele, Did.ap.Lact.*Inst.*1.22. 3. in Neo-Platonic Philos., *any pure, chaste being*, of souls coming to birth, Porph.*Antr.*19; of the Moon, ib.18. III. = μέλι, *honey*, ὕδατος,

μελίσσης, μηδὲ προσφέρειν μέθυ S.*OC*481: metaph., γλώσσης μελίσσῃ καταρρυηκέναι Id.*Fr.*155; of poetry, *AP*9.505.6; ἑσμὸς μελίσσης appears to be corrupt in Epin.1.7. **IV.** = ὀβολός, Hsch.

**μελισσ-αῖος**, α, ον, *of bees*, αὐλαμός Nic.*Th.*611. **II.** **-αῖον**, τό, *apiarium*, *Gloss.* ⊛ **-ειος**, α, ον, = foreg., κηρίον μ. *honeycomb*, *Ev.Luc.*24.42 (v.l. μελίσσιον); μελίσσειον or μελίσσιον alone, Hsch. s.vv. νύμφη, σής, Suid., Sch.Nic.*Al.*547; also μελίσσιον· σμῆνος, Hsch. **II.** μελίσσειον, τό, *beehive*, *PCair.Zen.*467 (iii B.C.). **-εύς**, έως, ὁ, *bee-keeper*, Arist.*HA*626ᵃ10, *PMasp.*147.1 (vi A.D.). **-ήεις**, εσσα, εν, *rich in bees*, as a place-name, Nic.*Th.*11, Coluth.23. **-ία**, ἡ, = μελισσών, *Gp.*15.6.1. **-ιος**, v. μελίσσειος.

⊛ **μελισσο-βότᾰνον**, τό, *balm*, *Melissa officinalis*, Sch.Theoc.4.25. **-βοτος**, ον, *fed on by bees*, *AP*9.523, D.P.327. **-κόμος**, ον, *keeping bees*, A.R.2.131, Opp.*C.*4.275. **-κράς** (parox. cod.)· ἡ γλυκεῖα δέλτος, ἢ μέλιτι κεκραμένη, Hsch. **-νόμος**, ον, (νέμω) *keeping bees*: Μελισσονόμοι, αἱ, *priestesses* of Artemis (cf. μέλισσα II. 2), A.*Fr.*87. **-ομαι**, = μελιτόομαι (v. μελιτόω II), S.*Fr.*306 (μελιττ– codd.). **-πόλος**, Att. **μελιττ-**, ον, *keeping bees*, Arist.*Mir.*835ᵃ23. **-πόνος**, ον, = μελισσοκόμος, *AP*6.239 (Apollonid.). **-ρῦτος**, ον, *flowing from bees*, μ. νασμοί Orph.*A.*574. **-σόος**, ον, *guardian of bees*, of Pan, *AP*9.226 (Zon.). **-τευκτος**, ον, *made by bees*, κηρία Pi.*Fr.*152. **-τοκος**, ον, *produced by bees*: metaph., *honied*, ὕμνοι *AP*7.12. **-τρόφιον**, Att. **μελιττ-**, τό, = μελισσών, prob. for *melitrophia* (pl.) in Varro *RR*3.16. **-τρόφος**, Att. **μελιττ-**, ον, *feeding bees*, Σαλαμίς E.*Tr.*799 (lyr.); χώρα J.*BJ*4.8.3.

**μελισσουργ-εῖον**, τό, *beehive*, Aesop.289. **-έω**, Att. **μελιττ-**, *to be a bee-master*, Arist.*HA*624ᵃ21 (prob.), Poll.1.254. **-ία**, Att. **μελιττ-**, ἡ, *bee-keeping*, Arist.*Pol.*1258ᵇ18, D.S.5.65 (pl.), Sch.Nic.*Al.*448. **-ικός**, ή, όν, *of* or *for a bee-master*, Poll.7.147: τὰ -κά, *a poem on bee-keeping*, by Nicander, Ath.2.68c. **-ός**, Att. **μελιττ-**, ὁ, = μελισσεύς, Pl.*R.*564c, *Lg.*842d, Arist.*HA*554ᵃ2, Thphr.*HP*6.2.3, *PCair.Zen.*368.5, al. (iii B.C.), *PTeb.*5.140 (ii B.C.).

**μελισσο-φάγος** [φᾰ], ον, *eating bees*, Eust.179.6. **-φάτνη**, ἡ, *beehive*, Hsch. s.v. κυψελίδες. **-φονος**, *apiastra*, i.e. μέροψ, *Gloss.* ⊛ **-φυλλον**, τό, = μελισσοβότανον, Thphr.*HP*6.1.4, Dsc.3.104. ⊛ **-φῦτον**, τό, = foreg., Nic.*Th.*677.

**μελίσσω**, = μειλίσσω, *An.Ox.*2.218, Hsch.

**μελισσών**, Att. **-ττών**, ῶνος, ὁ, *bee-house, apiary*, Lxx 1*Ki.*14.25, Varro *RR*3.16, Gell.2.20.9.

**μελι-στᾰγής**, ές, *dropping honey*, κηρίον Babr.*Prooem.*18. **2.** *sweet as dropped honey*, λοιβαί A.R.2.1272; στόματα *AP*5.294 (Leont.); σταφυλαί Dioscorus in *PLit.Lond.*100 *D* 5. **-στακτος**, ον, = foreg. 2, Μοῦσαι *AP*4.1.33 (Mel.).

**μελιστής**, οῦ, ὁ, = μελικτής, *Anacreont.*59.8.

**μελιστί**, Adv., = μελεϊστί, J.*AJ*15.8.4, Hsch.

**Μελῐταῖος**, α, ον, *of* or *from Melita* (Malta), κυνίδιον **M.** *Maltese* lap-dog, Arist.*HA*612ᵇ10, cf. Thphr.*Char.*21.9, Str.6.2.11, etc.

⊛ **μελίτεια** [ῐ], ἡ, = μελισσοβότανον, Theoc.4.25, 5.130.

**μελίτειον** [ῐ], τό, (μέλι) *mead*, Plu.2.672b, *Cor.*3; cf. μελίτιον.

⊛ **μελῐτερπής**, ές, *honey-sweet*, μολπή Simon.184.9.

**μελιτέτροπα**· τὴν χλαμύδα οὕτω καλοῦσιν, Hsch. **μελιτήμερον**· ἡδύ, γλυκύ, Id.

**μελῐτηρός**, ά, όν, *of* or *for honey*, ἄγγος Ar.*Fr.*511; ἀγγεῖον Nic.*Fr.*138, Gal.11.377. **2.** *like honey*, χυλός Thphr.*HP*3.7.4. **3.** ἡ -ηρά, a plaster, Orib.*Fr.*99, Paul.Aeg.4.40.

**Μελῐτίδης**, f.l. for Μελητίδης (q.v.).

⊛ **μελίτ-ῐνος** [λῐ], η, ον, *made of honey*, τὸν πρὸς χάριν λόγον ἔφη μελιτίνην ἀγχόνην εἶναι Diog.ap.D.L.6.51; στεφάνια *POxy.*936.11 (iii A.D.). **-ιον**, τό, = μελίτειον, Porph.*Abst.*1.21 codd.; written -ῑν *IG*14.1890. **2.** μελίτια, = Lat. *mella*, *Gloss.* **-ισμός**, ὁ, Medic., *treatment with honey*, Mnesith.ap.Orib.*inc.*19.8 (pl.). **-ίτης** [ῑ], οἶνος, ὁ, *wine prepared with honey*, Dsc.5.7. **II.** μ. λίθος *honey-stone*, ib.133, Gal.12.195, Plin.*HN*36.140 (v.l.).

**μελῐτο-ειδής**, ές, *like honey*, οἶνος Hp.*Morb.*2.22. Adv. -δῶς Sor.1.91. **-εις**, εσσα, εν, *honied*, i.e. *sweet, delicious*, εὐδία Pi.*O.*1.98. **II.** *sweetened with honey*, μελιτόεσσα (sc. μᾶζα), ἡ, *honey-cake*, esp. used as a sacred offering, Hdt.8.41: Att. contr. **μελιτοῦττα**, like οἰνοῦττα, etc., Ar.*Nu.*507, *Lys.*601 (anap.), etc.; παγκαρπία μ. Thphr.*HP*9.8.7: with masc. Noun, μελιτοῦτται ναστοί Ar.*Av.*567 (s.v.l.); in Hsch. **μελιτοῦς** (sc. πλακοῦς), ὁ.

**μελιτόν**· κηρίον, ἢ τὸ ἑφθὸν γλεῦκος, Hsch.; v. μέλι.

**μελῐτο-ποιέω**, *produce honey*, Eust. ad D.P.936. **-ποιός**, όν, *producing honey*, ζῷον Sch.Nic.*Al.*547. **-πωλέω**, *sell honey*, Poll.7.198. **-πώλης**, ου, ὁ, *dealer in honey*, Ar.*Eq.*853, Antiph.125.5:—fem. **-πωλις**, ιδος, Poll.7.198. **-ρρῦτος**, ον, *flowing with honey*, νέκταρ *Lyr.Alex.Adesp.*7.18.

**μελῐτουργ-έω**, *make honey*, Arist.*HA*624ᵃ21 (leg. μελιττ-). **-ία**, ἡ, **-ός**, όν, dub. ll. for μελιττουργία, -γός.

**μελιτοῦς, μελῐτοῦττα**, v. μελιτόεις II.

**μελῐτό-φυλλον**, τό, = μελισσόφυλλον, Sch.Nic.*Al.*149. **-χροος**, ον, contr. **-χρους**, ουν, = μελίχροος, Sch.Nic.*Th.*797; δελματίκιον *Sammelb.*7033.38 (v A.D.). **-ω**, in Pass., *to be sweetened with honey*, μήκων μεμελιτωμένη Th.4.26. **II.** *to be filled with honey*, Plu.2.628d.

**μέλιττα**, ἡ, Att. for μέλισσα.

**μελίττ-αινα**, ἡ, = μελισσοβότανον, Dsc.3.104:—also **-αιον**, τό, Ps.-Dsc.ibid. Cf. μελίκταινα.

**μελίττιον**, τό, Dim. of μέλιττα, Ar.*V.*367 (lyr.). **II.** *cell of a bee's comb*: in pl., *honeycomb*, Arist.*HA*624ᵃ5; cf. μελίσσειος I.

**μελιττο-πτηχέω**, *frighten bees* by striking metal pans, so as to collect the swarm, dub. in Phot., Suid. **-πόλος**, ον, v. μελισσ-. **-τρόφιον, -τρόφος**, Att. for μελισσοτρ-.

**μελιττ-ουργός, -ουργέω, -ουργία**, Att. for μελισσ-. **-ώδης**, ες, *like a bee*, τὰ μ. τῶν ζῴων Arist.*PA*683ᵃ30. **-ών**, ῶνος, ὁ, Att. for μελισσών.

**μελῐτ-ώδης**, ες, *like honey*, χυμός Thphr.*CP*6.9.2, Plu.2.628c; τὰ γλυκέα καὶ τὰ μ. Luc.*Vit.Auct.*19; also, of Persephone, Theoc.15.94, Porph.*Antr.*18. **-ωμα**, ατος, τό, *honey-cake*, Batr.39, Philet.ap.Ath.14.646d, Archig.ap.Orib.8.1.7. **-ωσις**, εως, ἡ, *sweetening with honey*, *Gloss.*

**μελί-φθογγος**, ον, *honey-voiced*, Μοῖσαι, ἀοιδαί, Pi.*O.*6.21, *I.*2.7. **-φόρος**, ὁ, *carrying* or *containing honey*, of a jar, *Ostr.Strassb.*652 (ii/iii A.D.). ⊛ **-φρων**, ον, gen. ονος, (φρήν) *sweet to the mind, delicious*, ὕπνος Il.2.34, B.*Fr.*3.10; οἶνος Il.6.264, Od.7.182, etc.; μ. θυμός Hes.*Sc.*428; νόστος Simon.119; σκόλιον Pi.*Fr.*122.11; μ. αἰτίαν ῥοαῖσι Μοισᾶν ἐνέβαλε Id.*N.*7.11; μ. δεσμὸν ἐρώτων Coluth.95. **II.** Act., *whose care is honey*, Ἀρισταῖος A.R.4.1132. **-φυλλον**, τό, = μελισσόφυλλον, Nic.*Th.*554, Ps.-Dsc.3.104. **-φυρτος**, ον, *mixed with honey*, ἤθεος ἁρμονίη *AP*5.269 (Paul. Sil.). ⊛ **-χλωρος**, ον, *honey-yellow, olive-complexioned*, Pl.*R.*474e, Arist.*Phgn.*812ᵃ19, Theoc.10.27, Nic.*Th.*797; μ. ἦν ὁ Πάτροκλος Philostr.*Her.*19.9.

**μελίχματα**, τά, v. μείλιχμα.

**μελιχοίρινα**, τά, kind of *honey-cake* (cf. χοιρίνη), Roehl *Inscr.Gr.Antiq.*10 (Rhodes).

⊛ **μελίχροος**, ον, contr. **-χρους**, ουν, = μελίχλωρος, *AP*12.165 (Mel.), 244 (Strat.). **2.** = μελίχρως, *PPetr.*3p.4, al. (iii B.C.), *PCair.Zen.*76.9 (iii B.C.): in gen. μελιχρόου *PStrassb.*87.14 (ii B.C.). **II.** *honied*, οἶνος Hp.*Aff.*43 (sed leg. μελιχρόν).

**μελιχρός**, ά, όν, *honey-sweetened*, οἶνος Alc.34 (proparox.) Hp.*Morb.*2.12, Telecl.24 (lyr.). **2.** *honey-sweet*, ὀρομαλίδες Theoc.5.95; σῦκα *AP*6.191 (Corn. Long.). **3.** metaph., ὑποσχεσίαι A.R.4.359; μελιχρότατος περὶ τὰς ἐννοίας Philostr.*VS*1.22.1; epith. of Sophocles, *AP*7.22 (Simm.); τὸ μελιχρότατον τῶν ἐπέων Call.*Epigr.*29; τὸ μ. ἐν ταῖς ἀκοαῖς D.H.*Comp.*1, cf. *Dem.*48; λωτοὶ κλάζοντες ἴσον φόρμιγγι μελιχρόν *APl.*1.8 (Alc.): Comp. Adv. μελιχρότερον Hedyl.ap.Ath.11.473a. (Formed from μέλι, as πενιχρός from πενία.)

**μελιχρότης**, ητος, ἡ, *sweetness as of honey*, Sch.Theoc.7.82.

**μελίχρῡσος**, ον, *gold-honey-coloured*, ἔθειραι Opp.*C.*1.315; λίθοι Plin.*HN*37.128.

**μελιχρώδης**, ες, = μελίχλωρος, *AP*12.5 (Strat.).

**μελίχρως**, ωτος, ὁ, ἡ, *honey-coloured*, i.e. *with olive complexion*, freq. in Pap., as *PPetr.*3p.8, al. (iii B.C.), *Sammelb.*7169.17 (ii B.C.), cf. *AP*12.170 (Diosc.): also acc. pl. μελίχροας *honey-coloured*, κηρούς Q.S.3.224; of complexion, Ptol.*Tetr.*144: dat. sg. μελίχροϊ, νέκταρι Tryph.113.

**μέλκα**, ἡ, *cooling food made from sour milk*, = ὀξύγαλα, Gal.10.468; prob. for μέλκα, τά, in Alex.Trall.7.3: **μέλκη**, *Gp.*18.21.1.

**μέλκιον**· κρήνη, νύμφαι, παίγνιον, Hsch.

**μελλάκιον**, τό, Dim. of sq., *Sammelb.*2104 (Alexandria).

⊛ **μέλλαξ**, ακος, ὁ, = μεῖραξ, *youth, lad*, *PMag.Par.*1.343; *page*, *CIG* 4682 (Alexandria): pl. written μέλακες in Hsch.; cf. μίλαξ. (Prob. from μέλλω, like μελλείρην, μελλέφηβος.)

⊛ **μελλάρχων**, οντος, ὁ, *ἄρχων-designate*, Müller-Bees *Inschriften der jüdischen Katakombe* Nos.106, 136.

**μελλέβιος**· ἡμιθανής, καὶ μὴ συνιείς, ἢ ὁ ἐκδιδαγμένος, Hsch.

⊛ **μελλ-είρην** (-ίρην Hsch.), ενος, ὁ, at Sparta, *youth about to become an εἴρην* (q.v.), Plu.*Lyc.*17. **-ειρονία** (written **-νεία**), ἡ, *age of a μελλείρην*, *IG*5(1).296 (Sparta).

**μελλέ-ποσις**· ὁ μέλλων ἀνὴρ γίνεσθαι, Hsch. **-πταρμος**, ον, *just going to sneeze*, Arist.*Pr.*958ᵃ15.

⊛ **μελλέφηβος**, ον, *near puberty*, Censorin.*Nat.*14.8, Hsch. s.v. μελλίρην, Eust.763.21.

**μέλλ-ημα**, ατος, τό, *delay*, in pl., E.*IA*818, Aeschin.3.72, Plu.*Nic.*21. **-ησις**, εως, ἡ, *being about to do, threatening to do*, Th.1.69, 4.126, al.; opp. ὁρμή, Arist.*Rh.*1393ᵃ4. **II.** *unfulfilled thought* or *intention, delay*, Th.5.116, Pl.*Lg.*723d; διὰ βραχείας μελλήσεως *at short notice*, Th.5.66; μελλήσει οὐδεμιᾷ Procop.*Pers.*1.25. **2.** c. gen. rei, *putting off*, διὰ τὴν ἐκείνων μέλλησιν τῶν ἐς ἡμᾶς δεινῶν Th.3.12. **-ησμα**, ατος, τό, = sq., *PMasp.*131.2 (vi A.D.). ⊛ **-ησμός**, ὁ, *procrastination, indecision* of character, Epicur.*Sent.Vat.*14, D.H.7.17, Gal.1.576, Paus.4.21.4. **II.** *approach, threatening*, of disease, Aret.*SD*1.11. **-ητέον**, *one must delay*, E.*Ph.*1279, Ar.*Ec.*876, Pl.*Criti.*108e. **-ητής**, οῦ, ὁ, *one who delays* or *procrastinates*, Th.1.70, Arist.*EN*1124ᵇ24, Procop.*Goth.*3.1. **-ητιάω**, Desiderat. from μέλλω, *wish to delay*, Hsch. ⊛ **-ητικός**, ή, όν, *inclined to delay*, Arist.*Phgn.*813ᵃ5, Poll.9.138, Vett.Val.18.6. **-ιέρη**, ἡ, *probationary priestess, novice*, Plu.2.795e.

**μελλίχ-ιος**, Aeol. for μειλίχιος, dub. cj. in Sapph.100. **-όμειδος**, ον, *gently smiling*, Alc.55. **-ος**, v. μείλιχος. **-όφωνος**, ον, *soft-voiced*, Sapph.*Oxy.*1787*Fr.*6.6 (= Sapph.129, where μειλιχο- codd.).

⊛ **μελλό-γαμβρος**, ὁ, *about to be a brother-in-law*, Hsch. **-γᾰμος**, ον, *betrothed*, S.*Ant.*628 (codd. plurimi, anap.), Theoc.22.140, Euph.7. ⊛ **-γυμνᾰσίαρχος**, ὁ, γυμνασίαρχος-*designate*, *PLond.*2.1166.3 (i A.D.). **-δειπνικός**, ή, όν, *played* or *sung at the beginning of dinner*, μέλος Ar.*Ec.*1153. **-θάνᾰτος** [θᾰ], ον, *at the point of death*, Sch.Ar.*Pl.*277. **-κούρια**, τά, *coming-of-age celebration*, *POxy.*1484 (ii/iii A.D.). **-νῑκιάω**, *delay victory*, with a play on the name of Νικίας, the Athenian *Cunctator*, Ar.*Av.*640. ⊛ **-νυμφος**, ον, *about to be*

*betrothed* or *wedded*, esp. of females, S.*Ant*.633, D.C.58.7, *Epigr.Gr.* 364.3 (Cotiaeum); rarely of the male, Phryn.Com.78 (prob. for -νύμφιος), Lyc.174: in S.*Tr*.207 (lyr.), ἀνολολυξάτω (-ύξετε codd.) δόμοις.. ὁ μελλόνυμφος, we shd. read either δόμος.. ὁ μ. the *maidens* of the household or δόμοις.. ἁ (sc. κλαγγά) the shout *of the maidens*. **-παις**, ὁ, ἡ, gen. παιδος, *child in the tenth year*, Hsch. **-ποσις**, ὁ, ἡ, *about to become a husband* or *wife*, S.*Fr*.1068; cf. μελλέποσις. **-πρόεδρος**, ὁ, πρόεδρος-*designate*, *PGiss*.54.6 (iv/v A.D.). **-πρύτᾰνις** [ῠ], εως, ὁ, πρύτανις-*designate*, *POxy*.1414.24 (iii A.D.), 2110.13 (iv A.D.).

**μελλῠμέναιος**, ον, = μελλόνυμφος, *IPE*2.86 (Panticapaeum).

**μέλλω**, impf. ἔμελλον and ἤμελλον (v. infr.), Ep. μέλλον Il.17.278, Od.1.232, 9.378, B.12.164; Ep., Ion. μέλλεσκον Theoc.25.240, Mosch.2.109: fut. μελλήσω D.6.15, *Ev.Matt*.24.6: aor. ἐμέλλησα Th.3.55, X.*HG*5.4.65, etc., and ἠμ- (v. infr.):—**Pass.** and **Med.**, v. infr. v.—Only pres. and impf. in Hom., Hes., Lyr., and Trag.: aor. only in Prose (exc. Thgn., v. infr.): the impf. ἤμελλον with long augm. is established by the metre in Hes.*Th*.898, Thgn.906, Ar.*Ec.* 597, *Ra*.1038 (both anap.), A.R.1.1309 (cf. Sch. ad loc.), Call.*Del.* 58: aor. I ἠμέλλησα Thgn.259; ἤμελλον is not found in earlier Att. Inscrr., but occurs in Pap., as *PPetr*.2 p.146 (iii B.C.), Phld.*Rh*.1.145 S. (but ἔμελλον Hyp.*Ath*.7, Arist.*Ath*.25.3). I. *to be destined* or *likely to*, indicating an estimated certainty or strong probability in the present, past, or future (cf. Aristonic.ap.Sch.Il.10.326, 11.817, 16.46, al.): a. c. pres. inf. (or its equivalent), of a probability in the present, ὅθι που μέλλουσιν ἄριστοι βουλὰς βουλεύειν where *belike* the best are holding counsel, Il.10.326; ᾧ μέλλεις εὔχεσθαι to whom thou *doubtless* prayest, 11.364; μέλλεις δὲ σὺ ἴδμεναι *doubtless* thou knowest, Od.4.200; τὰ δὲ μέλλετ' ἀκουέμεν *belike* you have heard it, Il.14.125, cf. Od.4.94; οὕτω που Διὶ μέλλει ὑπερμενεϊ φίλον εἶναι Il.2.116; ὄλβον δὲ θεοὶ μέλλουσιν ὀπάζειν *methinks* it is the gods who give wealth, Od.18.19; εἰ δ' οὕτω τοῦτ' ἐστίν, ἐμοὶ μέλλει φίλον εἶναι *you may be sure* it is my good pleasure, Il.1.564. b. c. aor. inf., of a probability in the past, μέλλω που ἀπεχθέσθαι Διὶ πατρὶ I *must have* become hateful to father Zeus, 21.83; κελευσέμεναι δέ σ' ἔμελλε δαίμων a god *must surely have* bidden thee, Od.4.274; πολλάκι που μέλλεις ἀρήμεναι you *must* often *have* prayed, 22.322; μέλλω ἀθανάτους ἀλιτέσθαι I *must have* sinned against the immortals, 4.377; ἄλλοτε δή ποτε μᾶλλον ἐρωῆσαι πολέμοιο μέλλω at any other time rather than this I *may have* drawn back.., Il.13.777; μέλλει μέν πού τις καὶ φίλτερον ἄλλον ὀλέσσαι before now, *no doubt*, a man *has* lost.., 24.46, cf. 18.362; τοῦ δ' ἤδη μέλλουσι κύνες ταχέες τ' οἰωνοὶ ῥινὸν ἀπ' ὀστεόφιν ἐρύσαι Od.14.133; of a destiny in the past, ἔμελλεν οἷ αὐτῷ θάνατον.. λιτέσθαι he *was fated to have* been praying for his own death, Il.16.46; ἐπεὶ οὐκ ἄρ' ἔμελλον ἑταίρῳ κτεινομένῳ ἐπαμῦναι since I *was* (i.e. *am*) not *destined to have* succoured my comrade when they were slaying him, 18.98: c. pres. inf., οὐκ ἄρ' ἔμελλες ἀνάλκιδος ἀνδρὸς ἑταίρους ἔδμεναι he *was to turn out* no helpless man whose comrades you ate, Od.9.475. c. c. fut. inf., of a destiny or probability in the future, ἅ ῥ' οὐ τελέεσθαι ἔμελλον which *were* not *to be* accomplished, Il.2.36; τάχα δ' ἀνστήσεσθαι ἔμελλεν ib.694; ἐπεὶ οὐκ ἄρ' ἔμελλον ἔγωγε νοστήσας οἰκόνδε.. εὐφρανέειν ἄλοχον 5.686, Il.12.113, 22.356, Od.13.293, 384; μέλλον ἔτι ξυνέσεσθαι ὀϊζυῖ πολλῇ 7.270; περὶ τρίποδος γὰρ ἔμελλον θεύσεσθαι they *were to have* run.., Il.11.700, cf. E.*HF*463; χρόνῳ ἔμελλέ σ' Ἕκτωρ.. ἀποφθίσειν S.*Aj*.1027; ἔμελλον ἄρα παύσειν ποθ' ὑμᾶς τοῦ κοάξ Ar.*Ra*.268; φεύγεις; ἔμελλόν σ' ἄρα κινήσειν ἐγώ Id.*Nu*.1301, cf. *V*.460, *Pl*.103, *Ach*.347: c. pres. inf., καὶ γὰρ ἐγώ ποτ' ἔμελλον ἐν ἀνδράσιν ὄλβιος εἶναι I *had a chance* of being, *might have* been.., Od.18.138; μέλλεν ποτὲ οἶκος ὅδ' ἀφνειὸς καὶ ἀμύμων ἔμμεναι, ὄφρ' ἔτι κεῖνος ἀνὴρ ἐπιδήμιος ἦεν 1.232: c. aor. inf. (cf. infr. II), οὐδεὶς ἂν οὐδὲ μελλήσειε γενέσθαι ἀγαθός Arist.*EN*1105ᵇ11: with inf. understood, [τὰ μὲν] πάσχουσι, τὰ δὲ μέλλουσι [πάσχειν] A.*Pers*.814; ἀλλ' οὐχ ὁμὸς τοῦτο πέπονθεν βίος οὐ μὰ Δί' οὐδέ γε μέλλει no, not *likely!* Ar.*Pl*.551; οὐδὲν.. οὔτε ἐπάθετε οὔτε ἐμελλήσατε Th.3.55; οὔτ' ἐμὲ ἀπέφηνεν ἡ βουλὴ οὔτ' ἐμέλλησεν Din.1.49. d. in εἰ clauses, εἰ μέλλει πόλις εἶναι if it *is to* be a city, Pl.*Prt*.324e: c. fut. inf., εἰ μέλλομεν.. ἀνοίσειν if we *were to* refer.., Id.*Phd*.75b: c. aor. inf., εἰ μέλλομεν.. δηλῶσαι Id.*Lg*.713a, cf. *Smp*.184d, *Plt.* 268d, al.: so in part., τὴν μέλλουσαν οἰκήσεσθαι πόλιν καλῶς Arist. *Pol*.1261ᵃ3, etc. e. in final clauses, ξυνεπιμελέσθαι ᾗ μέλλει ἄριστα ἕξειν, = ᾗ ἄριστα ἕξει, Th.8.39; εἴχομεν ἂν.. ἐπιστάτην λαβεῖν.. ὃς ἔμελλεν.. ποιήσειν Pl.*Ap*.20b, cf. App.*Syr*.46, etc. f. in questions, the inf. being understood, τί οὐ μέλλω (μέλλεις, etc.); why *shouldn't* I? why *is it* not *likely* that I should?, i.e. *yes, of course*, τὸν υἱὸν ἑόρακας αὐτοῦ; Answ. τί δ' οὐ μέλλω (sc. ἑορακέναι); *of course* I have, X. *HG*4.1.6; τί δ' οὐ μέλλει, εἴπερ γε δρᾷ αὐτό; Pl.*R*.605c; πῶς γὰρ οὐ μέλλει; Id.*Phd*.78b, etc.; ἀλλὰ τί μέλλει; what (else) *would you expect?* i.e. *yes, of course*, Id.*R*.349d, *Hp.Mi*.373d. II. *to be about to*, in purely temporal sense, c. fut. inf., Ἕκτορα δῖον ἔτετμεν ἀδελφεόν, εὖτ' ἄρ' ἔμελλε στρέψεσθ' ἐκ χώρης Il.6.515; ὁ μέν μιν ἔμελλε γενείου.. ἀψάμενος λίσσεσθαι (perh. pres. inf.), ὁ δ' αὐχένα μέσσον ἔλασσε 10.454; ἄλεισον ἀναιρήσεσθαι ἔμελλε Od.22.9, cf. Il.23.544, 2.39, 6.52, 393; δειπνήσειν μέλλομεν, ἢ τί; Ar.*Av*.464, cf. *Eq*.931 (lyr.), Th.2.8, etc.: c. pres. inf., τί μέλλεις δρᾶν; Ar.*V*.1379, *Th*.215, cf. *Ec.* 760, *Ach*.493, *Av*.498, al.; μέλλω μαίνεσθαι *Lyr.Alex.Adesp*.1.23: more rarely c. aor. inf., παθεῖν A.*Pr*.625; κτανεῖν S.*OT*967 (nisi leg. κτενεῖν); ἀναλαβεῖν, λιπεῖν, θανεῖν, E.*Or*.292, *Heracl*.709, *Med*.393; ἀπολέσαι, λαβεῖν, Ar.*Av*.366, *Ach*.1159 (lyr.); προσθεῖναι Th.3.92; οὐδὲ ἐμέλλησαν οὐδὲ διενοήθησαν ἐνθέσθαι D.35.19: Phryn.316 wrongly condemns this constr.—The inf. is sts. omitted, τὸ μέλλειν ἀγαθά (sc. πράσσειν or πράξειν) the *expectation* of good things, E.*Or*.1182, cf. *IA*1118. III. *to be always going to do* without ever doing: hence, *delay, put off*, freq. in Trag. (also in Med. μέλλομαι, v. infr. IV fin.): in this signf. usu. folld. by pres. inf., S.*OT*678 (lyr.), *OC*1627, etc.; τοὺς ξυμμάχους.. οὐ μελλήσομεν τιμωρεῖν· οἱ δ' οὐκέτι μέλλουσι κακῶς πάσχειν we *shall* not *delay* to succour our allies, for their sufferings *are* not *being delayed*, Th.1.86: freq. with μὴ οὐ, A.*Pr*.627, S.*Aj*.540: with μή, τί μέλλομεν.. μὴ πράσσειν κακά; E.*Med*.1242: rarely folld. by aor. inf., Id.*Ph*.299 (lyr.), *Rh*.673: inf. is freq. omitted, τί μέλλεις; why *delayest thou?* A.*Pr*.36, cf. *Pers*.407, *Ag*.908, 1353, S.*Fr*.917, Th.8.78, etc.; μακρὰ μ. S.*OC*219 (lyr.); Ἄρης στυγεῖ μέλλοντας E. *Heracl*.723; ἴωμεν καὶ μὴ μέλλωμεν ἔτι Pl.*Lg*.712b; μέλλον τι.. ἔπος a *hesitating* word, which one hesitates to speak, E.*Ion* 1002; μέλλων σφυγμός a *hesitating* pulse, Gal.8.653. IV. part. μέλλων is used quasi-adjectivally, ὁ μ. χρόνος the *future* time, Pi.*O*.10(11).7, A.*Pr.* 839, Arist.*Top*.111ᵇ28: Gramm., ὁ μέλλων *the future tense*, D.T.638.23, A.D.*Synt*.69.28, etc.; ἡ μ. αὐτοῦ δύναμις his *future* power, Pl.*R.* 494c; μ. φυλάξασθαι χρέος Pi.*O*.7.40; τὸν μ. βλαστόν (καρπόν codd.) Thphr.*HP*4.15.1: esp. in neut., τὸ μέλλον, τὰ μέλλοντα *things to come, the future*, Pi.*O*.2.56, A.*Pr*.102, Th.1.138, 4.71, Pl.*Tht*.178e, etc.; opp. to what is simply future (τὸ ἐσόμενον), Arist.*Div Somn*.463ᵇ29, cf. *GC*337ᵇ4; εἰς τὸ μέλλον (sc. ἔτος) *Ev.Luc*.13.9, cf. *PLond*.3.1231.4 (ii A.D.), Plu.*Caes*.14:—also in Med., τὰ ἰσχυρότατα ἐλπιζόμενα μέλλεται your strongest pleas are hopes *in futurity*, Th.5.111:—but V. Pass. μέλλομαι, ὡς μὴ μέλλοιτο τὰ δέοντα that the necessary steps *might* not *be delayed*, X.*An*.3.1.47; ἐν ὅσῳ ταῦτα μέλλεται while these *delays are going on*, D.4.37: fut. μελλήσομαι dub. l. in Procop. *Goth*.2.30: pf. part. μεμελλημένος, = μέλλων, σφυγμός Gal.9.308.

**μελλώ**, οῦς, ἡ, poet. for μέλλησις, A.*Ag*.1356.

**μελο-γρᾰφία**, poet. -ίη, ἡ, (μέλος B) *song-writing*, *App.Anth*.3.186. II. *skill in musical notation*, *CIG*3088 (Teos), *SIG*960 (Magn. Mae., ii B.C.). **-γράφος** [ᾰ], ὁ, *writer of songs*, *AP*11.133 (Lucill.), Vett.Val.75.7. **-θεσία**, ἡ, (μέλος A) *assignment of parts of the body to the tutelage of signs* or *planets*, Antioch.Astr. in *Cat. Cod.Astr*.8(3).106.4, Porph. *in Ptol*.201. 2. of the Universe, *position of its parts* at the beginning of things, Paul.Al.*T*.2. II. = φυή, Sch.Opp.*H*.1.147, 214. **-κοπέω**, *mutilate*, Ptol.*Tetr*.201 (Pass.), Vett.Val.6.21 (Pass.). **-κόπησις**, εως, ἡ, *mutilation*, Procl.*Par.Ptol*.280. **-κοπία**, ἡ, = foreg., Sm.*Na*.3.1, Vett.Val.16.12 (pl.). **-κόπος**, ον, (μέλος A, κόπτω) = Lat. *articulator*, *Gloss.*

**μέλομαι**, v. μέλω A. III, B. II.

⊛ **μελοποι-έω**, *make lyric poems*, Ar.*Ra*.1328 (lyr.), *Th*.42 (anap.). 2. *compose music*, *IG*3.78 (ii A.D.). II. *set to music*, ἐλεγεῖα μεμελοποιημένα Plu.2.1134a; ψιλὴν λαβὼν τὴν λέξιν μ. Longin.28.2. 2. *express in song*, τὸν ἔρωτα Palaeph.48. 3. *write melodiously*, πᾶσαν τὴν ποίησιν Ath.14.632d.—A pf. part. Pass. with double redupl. μεμελοπεποιημένος, Id.10.453d. **-ητής**, οῦ, ὁ, = μελοποιός, *AP*11.143 (Lucill.). **-ΐα**, ἡ, *making of lyric poems* or *music for them*: generally, *music*, Arist.*Po*.1450ᵇ16, *Pol*.1341ᵇ24, Aristox.*Harm*.p.38 M., Phld.*Mus*.p.31 K., Ocell.4.8, Cleonid.*Harm*.14, Aristid.Quint.1.12. II *musical composition*, as opposed to *its practice*, Pl. *Smp*.187d, cf. *R*.404d. **-ός**, ὁ, *maker of songs, lyric poet*, Ar. *Ra*.1250, Pl.*Prt*.326a, etc.; ὁ Θηβαῖος μ., of Pindar, Ath.1.3c; ἡ Λεσβία μ., of Sappho, Luc.*Im*.18. II. as Adj., generally, *tuneful*, μέριμνα E.*Rh*.550 (lyr.).

⊛ **μέλος**, εος, τό, *limb*, in early writers always in pl., Il.7.131, Pi.*N.* 1.47, etc. (κατὰ μέλος is corrupt for κατὰ μέρος in *h.Merc*.419); μελέων ἔντοσθε within my *bodily frame*, A.*Pers*.991 (lyr.), cf. *Eu*.265 (lyr.); κατὰ μέλη (-εα) *limb by limb*, like μελεϊστί, Pi.*O*.1.49, Hdt.1.119; τὰ τοῦ σώματος μέλη καὶ μέρη Pl.*Lg*.795e; μέλη ποιεῖν *dismember*, Lxx 2 *Ma*.1.16: later in sg., *AP*9.141, Gal.*UP*12.3, al.; ἡ κατὰ μέλος τομή Str.2.1.30. 2. metaph., ἐσμὲν.. ἀλλήλων μέλη *Ep.Rom*.12.5, cf. 1 *Ep.Cor*.6.15. 3. *features, form*, οὐκέτ' ἐγὼ.. γονέων μ. ὄψομαι *BMus.Inscr*.1077 (Sudan).

B. esp. *musical member, phrase*: hence, *song, strain*, first in *h.Hom*.19.16 (pl.), of the nightingale (the Hom. word being μολπή), cf. Thgn.761, etc.; μέλη βοῶν ἄναυλα S.*Fr*.699; esp. of *lyric poetry*, τὰ Ἀρχιλόχου μ. Pi.*O*.9.1; ἐν μέλει ποιέειν to write in *lyric strain*, Hdt.5.95, cf. 2.135; ἐν μέλει ἤ τινι ἄλλῳ μέτρῳ Pl.*R*.607d, cf. D.H. *Comp*.11; Ἀδμήτου μ. Cratin.236; μέλη, τά, *lyric poetry, choral songs*, opp. Epic or Dramatic verse, Pl.*R*.379a, 607a, al.; [μ.] ἐκ τριῶν συγκείμενον, λόγου τε καὶ ἁρμονίας καὶ ῥυθμοῦ ib.398d. b. *lyric portion* of the Comic παράβασις, Heph.*Poëm*.8.2. 2. *music to which a song is set, tune*, Arist.*Po*.1450ᵃ14; opp. ῥυθμός, μέτρον, Pl.*Grg.* 502c; opp. ῥυθμός, ῥῆμα, Id.*Lg*.656c; Κρητικόν, Καρικόν, Ἰωνικὸν μ., Cratin.222, Pl.Com.69.12, 14: metaph., ἐν μέλει *properly, correctly*, ἐν μ. φθέγγεσθαι Pl.*Sph*.227d; παρὰ μέλος *incorrectly, inopportunely*, πὰρ μ. ἔρχομαι Pi.*N*.7.69; παρὰ μ. φθέγξασθαι Pl.*Phlb*.28b, *Lg*.696d; παρὰ μέλος λαμπρύνεσθαι Arist.*EN*1123ᵃ22, cf. *EE*1233ᵃ39. 3. *melody* of an instrument, φόρμιγξ δ' αὖ φθέγγοιθ' ἱερὸν μ. ἠδὲ καὶ αὐλός Thgn.761; αὐλῶν πάμφωνον μ. Pi.*P*.12.19; πηκτίδων μέλη S.*Fr*.241: generally, *tone*, μ. βοῆς E.*El*.756. [In *h.Merc*.502 θεὸς δ' ὑπὸ καλὸν ἄεισεν must be read for θεὸς δ' ὑπὸ μέλος ἄεισεν, and Ἕλλησιν δ' ᾄδων μέλεα καὶ ἐλέγους is corrupt in Epigr.ap.Paus.10.7.6.]

**μελοτῠπέω**, *strike up a strain, chant*, τι A.*Ag*.1153 (lyr.).

**μελουργ-έω**, *make music*, Sch.rec.Theoc.11.1, al. **-ός**, όν, = μελοποιός, Man.4.185.

**μελουρίς**, = μολουρίς, *EM*474.2.

**μέλοψ**, ὁ, in form *melops*, = *dulcis sonus, bonus cantor*, *Gloss.* (dub.).

**μέλπηθρα**, τά, (μέλπω) *means of playing, plaything*: Hom. (only in Il.) always in pl., of an unburied corpse, *sport, plaything*, κυνῶν μέλπηθρα γένοιτο *a sport* of dogs, 13.233; κυσὶν μέλπηθρα γενέσθαι 17.255.

**μελπήτωρ**, ορος, ὁ, (μέλπω) *singer*, Man.4.183.

**Μελπομένη**, ἡ, *Melpomene*, a Muse, prop. *the Songstress*, Hes.*Th.* 77: later esp. as the Muse of Tragedy, perh. from its connexion with Dionysus, cf. sq. II.1, Helbig *Wandgemälde Campaniens* No. 871.

⊛**μέλπω**, Il.1.474, Lasus 1, etc.: Ep. impf. μέλπον Hes.*Fr.*265: fut. μέλψω E.*Alc.*446, Ar.*Th.*989 (both lyr.), *APl.*1.8 (Alc.): aor. ἔμελψα A.*Ag.*245 (lyr.), 1445, Ar.*Th.*974 (lyr.):—**Med.** (v. infr. II):—poet. Verb, *celebrate with song and dance*, μέλποντες ἑκάεργον Il. l. c.; Φοῖβον Hes. l. c., cf. Pi.*Fr.*75.11; μ. τινὰ κατὰ χέλυν E. l. c.; τινὰ κώμοις Ar. *Th* 989 (lyr.); μ. ᾠδαῖς Σπάρτην Anaxandr.41.19 (anap.); μ. τὸν πόσιν E.*Tr.*339 (lyr.). 2. intr., *sing*, A.*Ag.*245, E.*IT* 429 (both lyr.): c. acc. cogn., μ. θανάσιμον γόον A.*Ag.*1445; ἰαχάν, βοάν, E.*Med.*150, *Tr.*547 (both lyr.); μ. τᾶς κιθάρας ἐνοπάν *let* it *sound*, Id.*Ion* 881 (lyr.): c. dat. instrum., μ. αὐλῷ *play* on.., *AP*6.195 (Arch.); μ. πτεροῖς, of the swan, *Anacreont.*58.9. II. Med. **μέλπομαι**, Hom. (v. infr.), E. *Ph.*787 (lyr.): aor. part. μελψάμενος *AP*7.19 (Leon.): fut. μέλψομαι in pass. sense, ib.9.521:—*sing* to the lyre or harp, μετὰ δέ σφιν ἐμέλπετο θεῖος ἀοιδός, φορμίζων Od.4.17, cf. 13.27; μέλπεο καὶ κιθάριζε *h.Merc.* 476; Μελπόμενος, epith. of Dionysus at Athens, Paus.1.2.5; *dance and sing*, as a chorus, μετὰ μελπομένῃσιν ἐν χορῷ Il.16.182, cf. *h.Hom.* 19.21; μέλπεσθαι Ἄρηϊ *to dance a war-dance* in honour of Ares, by a bold metaph. for *to fight on foot* (ἐνὶ σταδίῃ), Il.7.241: c. acc. cogn., στοναχὰς μέλποντο *let* them *sound*, E.*Andr.*1039 (lyr.), cf. *Ph.* l. c. (lyr.). 2. c. acc., *sing of, celebrate*, νόμους καὶ ἤθεα Hes.*Th.*66, cf. Pi.*P.*3.78; μ. χοροῖσι E.*Tr.*554 (lyr.).

**μελπῳδός**, όν, *singing songs*, restored in Hsch. for μελπόδιοι.

**μελύδριον**, τό, Dim. of μέλος A, *poor limb*, M.Ant.7.68 (pl.). II. Dim. of μέλος B, *ditty*, Ar.*Ec.*883, Theoc.7.51, Bion *Fr.*5.1.

⊛**μέλω**, Med. **μέλομαι**, used in both voices, either in neut. sense, *to be an object of care* or *thought*, or in act. sense, *care for, take an interest in.*

A. pres. μέλω: impf. ἔμελον, Ep. μέλον Od.5.6: fut. μελήσω, Ep. inf. μελησέμεν Il.10.51: aor. ἐμέλησα: pf. μεμέληκα; also Ep. and Lyr. μέμηλα, Dor. part. μεμᾱλώς dub. in Pi.*O.*1.89 (for Ep. forms of Med. v. infr. III. 2): almost always 3 sg. and pl., exc. in pres. (v. infr.):—*to be an object of care* or *thought*, sts. with a personal subject (not in Att. Prose): I. πᾶσι δόλοισιν ἀνθρώποισι μέλω by all manner of wiles *am I in* men's *thoughts*, i. e. *am well known* to them, Od.9.20; Ἀργὼ πᾶσι μέλουσα 12.70; μελήσεις ἄφθιτον ἀνθρώποις αἰὲν ἔχων ὄνομα Thgn.245; Εὐθυμίᾳ μέλων εἴην Pi.*Fr.*155; μέλει σφισὶ Καλλιόπα Id.*O.*10(11).14; ἵνα θανοῦσα νερτέροισιν μέλω E.*Andr.* 850 (lyr.); Ἔρως..οὐρανίδαισι μέλων Id.*Tr.*842; μέλων πολλοῖσι *AP* 5.121 (Diod.); ἡ μέλουσα ἀγέλη Them.*Or.*1.10a: pf. part., ἀρεταῖσι μεμαλότας *dear* to virtue, Pi.*O.*1.89 (dub.); μέλε γάρ οἱ [Ὀδυσσεύς] Od. 5.6; τὸν ξεῖνον δὲ ἐῶμεν..Τηλεμάχῳ μελέμεν 18.420: but more freq. of things, μή τοι ταῦτα..μελόντων *let* not these things *weigh on thy soul*, Il.18.463, Od.13.362; μηδέ τί οἱ θάνατος μελέτω φρεσί Il.24. 152; σοὶ χρὴ τάδε πάντα μέλειν 'tis good these things *should be a care* to thee, 5.490; πόλεμος δ' ἄνδρεσσι μελήσει 6.492; μελήσουσιν δ' ἐμοὶ ἵπποι 5.228; ᾧ τόσσα μέμηλε 2.25; οἷς ὕβρις μέμηλε κακή Hes.*Op.* 238; τοῖσιν..ἐνὶ φρεσὶν ἄλλα μεμήλει Od.1.151, cf. Il.2.614; ὅσα φημὶ μελησέμεν Ἀργείοισι 10.51; ἔλεγε..κομιδῆς πέρι τὴν ὥρην αὐτῷ μελήσειν Hdt.8.19; μέλει γὰρ ἀνδρὶ..τἄξωθεν A.*Th.*200; σοὶ χρὴ μέλειν ἐπιστολάς Id.*Pr.*3; οὗτος..δμωσὶν ἂν μέλοι πόνος E.*Supp.*939; ἃ τοῖσιν ἀστοῖς ἔμελεν Ar.*Ec.*459; τοῖσδε μελήσει γάμος E.*El.*1342 (anap.); τοῦτο ἴσασιν ἐμοὶ μεμεληκός X.*Ap.*20. 2. impers. c. inf., οὐκ ἔμελέν μοι ταῦτα μεταλλῆσαι Od.16.465; so in A.*Ag.*1250, Th.1.141, etc.; also, μοι ἐμέλησεν ὥστε εἰδέναι X.*Cyr.*6.3.19: united with the personal construction, οὗτος μητρὶ κηδεύειν μέλει E.*Rh.*983. 3. less freq. with a Conj., οὐ μέλειν οἱ ὅτι ἀποθνήσκει Hdt.9.72; σοὶ μελέτω ὅκως.. Id.1.9, cf. X.*An.*1.8.13, etc.; ὡς δὲ καλῶς ἕξει.., ἐμοὶ μελήσει Id.*Cyr.*3.2.13; ἐμοὶ τοῦτο μέλει, μή.. S.*Ph.*1121 (lyr.); οὐ τοσοῦτόν μοι μέλει εἰ.. Lys.21.12. 4. 3 sg. is freq. used impers. with the object in gen., and pers. in dat., ᾧ μέλει μάχας to whom *there is care* for the battle, who *careth* for it, A.*Ch.*946 (lyr.), cf. *Ag.*974; ἐμοὶ δ' ἔλασσον Ζηνὸς ἢ μηδὲν μέλει Id.*Pr.*938; θεοῖσιν εἰ δίκης μέλει S.*Ph.* 1036; Ζηνὶ τῶν σῶν μέλει πόνων E.*Heracl.*717; πάνυ μοι τυγχάνει μεμεληκὸς τοῦ ᾄσματος Pl.*Prt.*339b; also μέλει μοι περί τινος A.*Ch.*780, Ar.*Lys.*502, Pl.*Alc.*2.150d; μεμέληκέ μοι περὶ αὐτῶν Id.*Cra.*428b: less freq. with ὑπέρ, εἴπερ ὑπὲρ τοῦ κοινῇ βελτίστου δεῖ μέλειν ὑμῖν D. 21.37. 5. abs., μηδέ σοι μελησάτω A.*Pr.*334; οἶμαι θεοῖς τοῖς κάτω μέλειν, οἷ (nisi leg. οἷς) ἠδίκηνται Antipho 1.31. 6. freq. with a neg., οὐδέν μοι μέλει I *care* not, Ar.*Ra.*655; μή νυν μελέτω σοι μηδέν Id.*Pl.* 208; τῷ δ' οὐδὲν μ. Alex.178.2; so τί δέ σοι μέλει; Diph.73.10. II. μέλον ἐστι periphr. for μέλει, as τοῖσδ' ἔσται μ. S.*OC* 653, cf. 1433. 2. neut. part. used abs., οὐδὲν ἄρ' ἐμοῦ μέλον for *they took* no *thought* of me, Ar.*V.*1288; δῆλον ὅτι οἶσθα, μέλον γέ σοι *since you care about it*, Pl.*Ap.*24d; οὐδὲν αὐτῷ μ. τοῦ τοιούτου Id.*Phdr.*235a; μ. αὐτοῖς ἰσχυρῶς ὅπῃ τὸ μέλλον ἀποβήσοιτο X.*Cyr.*5.2.24; οὔτε σκοπούμεναι οὔτε μ. αὐταῖς ἄλλο ἢ χαρίζεσθαι Pl.*Grg.*501b. III. Med. is used by Poets and in Hp. like Act., μελόμεθα, -ησόμεθα, Hp.*Ep.*27; *to be an object of care*, Ἄρτεμιν ᾇ μελόμεσθα E.*Hipp.*60: mostly in 3 sg., ἐμοὶ δέ κε ταῦτα μελήσεται Il.1.523; μή τί τοι ἡγεμόνος γε ποθὴ μελέσθω *let* it not *weigh on* thy *mind*, Od.10.505; τἀντεῦθεν..αὐτῷ μελέσθω Λοξίᾳ A.*Eu.*61; τἀνθάδ' ἂν μέλοιτ' ἐμοί S.*El.*1436; γάμους..σοὶ χρὴ μέλεσθαι E.*Ph.*759, etc.; ἰαχὰν μελομέναν νεκροῖς ib.1302: rarely impers., σοὶ..μελέσθω φρουρῆσαι S.*El.*74; μέλεταί τινί τινος Theoc. 1.53, Orac.ap.Luc.*Alex.*24. 2. Ep. pf. and plpf. Pass. **μέμβλεται, μέμβλετο** (fr. μέ-μλ-εται, μέ-μλ-ετο), with pres. and impf. sense, ἦ νύ τοι οὐκέτι πάγχυ μετὰ φρεσὶ μέμβλετ' Ἀχιλλεύς (for μέλει); Il.19.343; μέμβλετο γάρ οἱ τεῖχος (for ἔμελε) 21.516; φόνος δέ οἱ οὐκ ἐνὶ θυμῷ μέμβλετο Od.22.12; ᾗσιν ἀοιδὴ μέμβλεται ἐν στήθεσσιν Hes. *Th.*61: hence later Ep. formed a pres. μέμβλομαι, 2 pl. μέμβλεσθε A.R.2.217; 3 pl. μέμβλονται, in act. sense (cf. B. II infr.), μ. πόνοισι Opp.*H.*4.77: the regul. pf. and plpf. (with pres. and impf. sense) also occur in later Poets, μεμέληται Opp.*C.*1.436; Φοίβῳ μεμελήμεθα *AP*10.17 (Antiphil.); μεμέληνται Call.*Fr.anon.*119, Opp.*C.*1. 349: 2 and 3 plpf. μεμέλησο, -το, *AP*5.219 (Agath.), Theoc.17.46; part. μεμελημένος, α, ον, *cared for*. πολλοῖς μεμελημέναι ἡρωΐναι Id.26. 36, cf. *AP*7.199 (Tymn.): aor. part. Pass. μεληθέν ib.5.200; cf. βέβλεσθαι.

B. with an object, *care for, take an interest in* a thing, c. gen., Hom. only in pf. part., μέγα πλούτοιο μεμηλὼς *busied with, attending to*.., Il.5.708; μέγα πτολέμοιο μεμηλώς 13.297: later in pres., οὐκ ἔφα τις θεοὺς βροτῶν ἀξιοῦσθαι μέλειν A.*Ag.*370 (lyr.); μέλειν μὲν ἡμῶν S.*Aj.*689; δεινόν σε..τικτούσης μέλειν Id.*El.*342: later c. dat., *care for*, μέλω κύρτοις *AP*10.10 (Arch. Jun.); θεοῖς μέλοντες Plu.*Sull.*7: abs., *to be anxious*, μέλει..κέαρ A.*Th.*288, cf. *Pers.*1049 (both lyr.); μελούσῃ καρδίᾳ E.*Rh.*770. 2. rarely c. acc., πεντήκοντα βοῶν ἀντάξια ταῦτα μέμηλας *thou hast invented*, *h.Merc.*437 (fort. μέμηδας). 3. c. inf., θεοὶ τῶν ἀδίκων μέλουσι (μέλλουσι codd. opt.) καὶ τῶν ὁσίων ἐπᾴειν E.*HF* 773 (s. v. l.). II. Med. μέλομαι, *care for, take care of*, c. gen., A.*Th.*177 (lyr.), S.*OT* 1466, E.*Hipp.*109, *Heracl.*354 (lyr.), A.R.1.967; τὰ λοιπά μου μέλου (where τὰ λ. is adverbial) S.*OC* 1138; μεμελημένοι ἀέθλων Opp.*H.*4.101: c. dat., ἐτητυμίῃ μεμελημένος Call. *Aet.*3.1.76; ἱππασίῃ μεμελημένον ἦτορ Q.S.4.500: c. acc., μέλομαι ῥόδον (prob. l. for μέλπομαι) *Anacreont.*53.2: with Preps., μέλεσθαι ἀμφί τι or τινος, A.R.2.376, 4.491; ἀμφ' αἰγῶν μεμελημένοι *AP*6.221 (Leon.); ἐμέλοντο περὶ σφίσιν A.R.3.1172: c. inf., μέλομαι..ἀείδειν Anacr.65; μελέσθω λαὸς ἐκπονεῖν δίκῃ A.*Supp.*367, cf. E.*Heracl.*96 (lyr.): aor. in same sense, c. gen., τάφου μεληθεὶς S.*Aj.*1184.

**μελῳδ-έω**, *chant, sing*, Ar.*Av.*226, 1381, *Th.*99:—Pass., *to be chanted*, τὰ ῥηθέντα ἢ μελῳδηθέντα Pl.*Lg.*655d, cf. Chamael.ap.Ath. 14.620c; *to be set to music*, Cleanth.ap.Phld.*Mus.*p.98 K.; τὰ μελῳδούμενα διαστήματα *used in music*, Plu.2.1019a. **-ημα**, ατος, τό, *melodic interval*, ib.1145a.

**μελώδης**, ες, *consisting of members* or *limbs*, *Gloss.*

**μελῳδ-ητικός**, ή, όν, *caused by melody*, κίνημα Thphr.*Fr.*89.1. **-ητός**, ή, όν, *to be sung, used in singing*, Plu.2.389f, etc. ⊛ **-ία**, ἡ, *singing, chanting*, E.*Rh.*923, etc. II. *chant, choral song*, μελῳδίας ποιητής Pl.*Lg.*935e, cf. 812d; *lullaby*, ib.790e: generally, *music*, Phld.*Mus.*p.12 K. ⊛ **-ικός**, ή, όν, *by means of melody*, πειθώ Aristid.Quint.2.10. **-ός**, όν, *musical, melodious*, κύκνος, ὄρνις, E.*IT* 1104 (lyr.), *Hel.*1109 (lyr.); ἀχήματα Id.*IA* 1045 (lyr.). II. Subst. μελῳδός, ὁ, = μελοποιός, Pl.*Lg.*723d, *AJP* 48.18 (Rome).

***μέμαα**, v. μέμονα.

**μεμᾰθημένως**, *by learning*, Ph.*Fr.*70 H.

**μεμαίκυλον**, v. μιμαίκυλον. **μεμαῖνα**· ἀληλλιμένα, Hsch. **μεμακυῖα**, v. μηκάομαι. **μεμαλισμένους**· μεμαλαγμένους, ἢ παραφρονοῦντας, μαινομένους, Id. **μεμάποιεν, μέμαρπον**, v. μάρπτω. **μεμβλάσαι**· συνδῆσαι, Id. **μέμβλεται, μέμβλετο**, v. μέλω. **μέμβλωκα**, v. βλώσκω. **μεμβλώντων**· τυχόντων, Id.

**μεμβράδιον**, τό, Dim. of μεμβράς, Alex.Trall.*Febr.*7 (where ἐμβράδια, v. l. **μεμβρίδια**).

**μεμβρᾰδοπώλης**, ου, ὁ, *dealer in anchovies*, Nicopho 19 (anap.).

**μεμβράνα**, ἡ, = Lat. *membrāna, parchment*, 2*Ep.Ti.*4.13, Charax 14, *POxy.*2156.9 (iv/v A. D.):—also **μέμβρανον**, τό, Lyd.*Mens.*1.28: hence Adj. **μεμβράϊνος**, *PMasp.*144.6 (vi A. D.), and Subst. **μεμβραϊνάριος**, prob. in *Stud.Pal.*20.194 (vi A. D.).

**μέμβραξ**, ακος, ὁ, a kind of *cicada*, Ael.*NA*10.44.

**μεμβράς**, άδος, ἡ, a small kind of *sprat* or *anchovy*, Ar.*V.*493, Eup. 28, Arist.*Fr.*302, *POxy.*788 (i B.C.), Ael.*NA*1.58, etc.; cf. βεμβράς.

**μεμβρ-ᾰφύα** [ῠ], ἡ, a kind of *anchovy*, Aristonym.2. **-ίδιον**, v. μεμβράδιον.

**μεμελᾰνωμένως**, Adv. *obscurely*, Phlp.*in GA*196.12.

**μεμελετηκότως**, Adv. *by practice*, Poll.1.157, dub. l. in X.*Eq.Mag.* 7.14.

**μεμελετημένως**, Adv. *in a practised manner*, Plu.*Pomp.*68.

**μεμελημένως**, Adv., (μέλω) *carefully*, ἔχειν Pl.*Prt.*344b.

**μεμελλημένως**, Adv. *hesitatingly*, J.*BJ*6.1.3.

**μεμερισμένως**, Adv., (μερίζω) *dividedly*, Dam.*Pr.*28; *in parts*, Aët. 12.2, Phlp.*in Ph.*517.11, al. 2. *at intervals*, Philum.ap.Orib.*Syn.* 9.21.1, cf. 9.13.1.

**μεμετιμένος**, Ion. for μεθειμένος, pf. part. Pass. of μεθίημι (q. v.).

**μεμετρημένως**, Adv. *according to a stated measure*, Luc.*Salt.* 67. II. = μετρίως, *IG*12(7).393.1, 407.12 (Amorgos), Gal.7.12, Orib.*Syn.*6.22, Sch.E.*Hipp.*253.

**μεμηκώς**, v. μηκάομαι.

**μέμηλε, μεμήλει, μεμηλώς**, v. μέλω A. I. 1, B. I.

**μεμηνῑμένως**, Adv., (μηνίω) *angrily*, Pl.*Ep.*319b.

**μεμηνότως**, Adv., (μαίνομαι) *madly*, J.*AJ*16.7.3.

**μεμηχᾰνημένως**, Adv., (μηχανάομαι) *by stratagem*, E.*Ion* 809.

**μεμῐασμένως**, Adv., (μιαίνω) *disgustingly*, Sch.Tricl.S.*Ant.*1080.

**μεμιγμένως**, Adv., (μείγνυμι) *mixedly*, opp. ἁπλῶς, Arist.*Sens.*442ᵃ 2; opp. χωρὶς ἕκαστον, Id.*HA*616ᵃ16.

**μεμῑσημένως**, Adv., gloss on δυσκόλως, Sch.Isoc.3.1.

⊛ **μέμνεο, μεμνέῳτο, μέμνημαι, μεμνῄμην**, v. μιμνῄσκω.

**μεμνονίδες**, αἱ, = Μέμνονες (cf. Μέμνων II), Paus.10.31.6.

**Μέμνων**, ονος, ὁ, (μένω) *the Steadfast* or *Resolute* (but cf. θρασυμέμνων), as pr. n., *Memnon*, Od.11.522, Hes.*Th.*984. 2. his statue at Thebes which was said to sound musically when struck by the light of the rising sun, Str.17.1.46, *Epigr.Gr.*988 (Balbilla), Luc. *Tox.*27:—hence **Μεμνόνειος** or **-όνιος**, α, ον, *of Memnon*, Str.17.1.42; **Μεμνόνειον**, τό, *the temple of M.*, in Egypt, Id.17.1.46; or at Susa, Id.15.3.2; τὰ βασιλήϊα τὰ Μεμνόνια Hdt.5.53; Μεμνόνιον ἄστυ, i.e. Susa, ib.54. II. a black bird, named after Memnon, Ael.*NA* 5.1, Q.S.2.647, Dionys.*Av.*1.8, cf. μεμνονίδες. III. μέμνων, a name for the ass at Athens, from its *patient* nature, Hsch.:—hence **μεμνόνεια** (sc. κρέα), τά, *ass's flesh*, Id.; also, *the market where it was sold*, Poll.9.48.

**μεμοιρᾱμένως**, Adv., (μοιράω) *by lot* or *fate*, Sch.A.R.1.973.

**μεμολυσμένως**, Adv. *in a 'simmering' fashion*, Gal.9.897 (leg. μεμωλ-).

**μέμονα**, redupl. pf. (with pres. sense) of root μεν-, weak form μᾰ- (fr. *mn̥-*), cogn. with μένος (cf. Il.5.135, 136), μαίνομαι: 1 sg. μέμονα Il.5.482; 2 sg. μέμονας 9.247, al.; 3 sg. μέμονε, μέμονεν, 12.304, 18.176, al.; 2 dual μέμᾰτον 8.413; 1 pl. μέμᾰμεν 9.641; 2 pl. μέμᾰτε 7.160; 3 pl. μεμάᾱσι 10.208, 236, al.; 3 sg. imper. μεμάτω [ᾰ] 20.355; inf. μεμονέναι Hdt.6.84; μεμάμεν Hsch.: plpf. 3 sg. μεμόνει prob. cj. in Theoc.25.64 (μέμοινε, μέμαεν codd.); 3 pl. μέμᾰσαν Il.13.337: mostly in pf. part. μεμᾱώς 5.301, al. (μεμᾰώς nom. sg. masc. only Il. 16.754); which in Ep. and Lyr. retains ω in oblique cases, μεμᾱῶτος, μεμᾱῶτες, exc. where we have μεμᾱότες, μεμάότε [ᾱ metri gr.], Il.2.818, 13.197; fem. μεμᾰυῖα 4.440, al. (μεμαότας is dub. l. in Pi.*O.*1.89):—*to be furiously* or *very eager*, c. pres. inf., λάβε φαίδιμος Ἕκτωρ ἑλκέμεναι μεμαώς Il.18.156; μάλιστα δὲ φαίδιμος Ἕκτωρ ἑλκέμεναι μέμονεν ib.176; μέμονέν τε μάχεσθαι Od.20.15; μέμασαν δὲ μάχεσθαι Il.13.135; ἀλεξέμεναι μεμαῶτε 1.590; ἐρεσσέμεναι μεμαῶτες 9.361; θεοὶ μεμαῶτα νέεσθαι ἔσχον Od.4.351; τοῦ.. μεμάασιν ἀκουέμεν ὁππότ' ἀείδῃ 17.520; μέμαμεν δέ τοι ἔξοχον ἄλλων κήδιστοί τ' ἔμεναι καὶ φίλτατοι we *would fain* be, Il.9.641: c. aor. inf., ἀποκτάμεναι μεμάασιν 20.165; μεμαὼς πόλιν ἐξαλαπάξαι 4.40; διαπραθέειν μεμαῶτες 9.532; γούνων ἅψασθαι μεμαώς 21.65; ἐξελθεῖν μεμαῶτα 22.413; Λυκίους ὀτρύνω καὶ μέμον' αὐτὸς ἀνδρὶ μαχήσασθαι 5.482; ἀμφελίξασθαι μεμαῶτες Pi.*N.*1.43: inf. omitted, ἐπεὶ μεμάασί γε πολλοί (sc. ἑταροί σοι γενέσθαι) Il.10.236: abs., *rage*, ἵνα τε δόρατα μέμονε δάϊα E.*IA*1495 (lyr.); γαστέρα.. μεμαυῖαν *ravenous*, Od.17.286; βῆ μεμαώς he strode on *eagerly*, Il.10.339; ἕλκ' ἐπὶ οἷ μεμαὼς ὥς τε λίς 11.239; ἆλτ' ἐπί οἱ μεμαώς 21.174, cf. 22.326; ἐν πέτρᾳ μεμαώς, of a fisher, *expectant*, Theoc.21.42: with Adv. of direction, πῇ μέματον; whither *so fast?* Il.8.413; πῇ μεμαυῖα κατ' Οὐλύμπου τόδ' ἱκάνεις; 14.298; πρόσσω μεμαυῖαι *pressing* forward, 11.615; ἀντικρὺ μεμαώς 13.137; ἰθὺς μεμαῶτι 22.284: so c. dat. instrum., μεμαότες ἐγχείῃσι 2.818. 2. *to be minded, purpose, intend*: c. pres. inf., οὔ ῥά τ' ἀπείρητος μέμονε σταθμοῖο δίεσθαι *has no mind* to be chased, Il.12.304; ἀλλ' ἄνα, εἰ μέμονάς γε καὶ ὀψέ περ υἷας Ἀχαιῶν τειρομένους ἐρύεσθαι (perh. fut. inf.) 9.247; ποσσῆμαρ μέμονας κτερεϊζέμεν Ἕκτορα δῖον; 24.657; ἣ καταλείψουσιν ..ἧε μένειν μεμάασι 22.384, cf. 10.208, 409, Od.5.375: c. aor. inf., πῇ τ' ἄρ μέμονας καταδῦναι ὅμιλον; Il.13.307; εἰ.. μέματον καταδῦναι ὅμιλον 10.433: c. fut. inf., sts. with sense of *hoping, expecting, presuming*, πῶς δὲ σὺ νῦν μέμονας, κύον ἀδεές, ἀντί' ἐμεῖο στήσεσθαι; 21.481; ἀλλ' ἄγε, πῶς μέμονας πόλεμον καταπαυσέμεν ἀνδρῶν; 7.36, cf. 2.543, 12.197, 200, 218; οὕτω δὴ μέμονας Τρώων πόλιν εὐρυάγυιαν καλλείψειν (ἐκπέρσειν Zenod.); 14.88, cf. 15.105; μέμονέν τε μάλιστα μητέρ' ἐμὴν γαμέειν καὶ Ὀδυσσῆος γέρας ἕξειν Od.15.521; σίτῳ ἐπιχειρήσειν μεμαῶτες 24.395: c. acc. cogn., μέμονεν δ' ὅ γε ἶσα θεοῖσι *deems himself* a match for.., Il.21.315; τί μέμονας; what *wishest* thou? A.*Th.*686 (lyr.): c. gen., μεμαυῖ' ἔριδος καὶ ἀϋτῆς Il.5.732; μεμαότε θούριδος ἀλκῆς *mindful* of.., 13.197 (cf. μεδώμεθα θούριδος ἀλκῆς 5.718); ἤ τινα καὶ Δαναῶν, ἀλκῆς μάλα περ μεμαῶτα, σχήσω ἀμυνέμεναι 17.181 (unless ἀλκῆς goes only with σχήσω), cf. 9.655, 20.256, Od.22.172: abs., διχθὰ δέ μοι κραδίη μέμονε φρήν Il.16.435; δίδυμα μέμονε φρήν E.*IT*655 (lyr.).

**μεμονωμένως**, Adv., (μονόω) *singly*, v.l. in Corn.*ND*14.

**μεμόρηται, μεμορημένος, μεμορμένος**, v. μείρομαι.

⊛ **μεμόριον**, τό, (Lat. *memoria*) *memorial chapel* or *shrine*, *BCH*17.290, Ramsay *Cities and Bishoprics* 2.736 (iii/iv A.D.).

**μεμορυχμένα**· μυσαρά, κτλ., Hsch. (v. μορύσσω). **μεμόσει**· μολύνει, Id.

**μεμουνωμένος**, Ion. pf. part. Pass. of μονόω.

**μεμπ-τέος**, α, ον, *to be blamed*, Gorg.*Hel.*19, A.D.*Pron.*49.13. II. **-τέον**, *one must blame, reject*, Str.1.2.1, Sor.1.21, Plot.3.2.7. ⊛ **-τός**, ή, όν, *blameworthy*, E.*Hel.*462, Phld.*Oec.*p.70 J.: Comp. μεμπτότερος Th.2.61: mostly with a neg., Pi.*Fr.*220, S.*OC*1036, Th.3.57, etc.; οὐ μ. not *contemptible*, Id.6.13, Pl.*Tht.*187c; in a question, Hdt.7.48. Adv., οὐδὲ τῶν ξένων μεμπτῶς μαχεσαμένων Plu.*Cleom.*28. II. Act., *throwing blame upon*, τινι S.*Tr.*446, where μεμπτός is fem.

**μεμυδότος**· βρέοντος, Hsch. **μέμῡκα**, pf. both of μυκάομαι and μύω. **μεμύκωται**· πεπύκνωται, Id. **μεμύλληκε**· διέστραπται, συνέστραπται, Id.

**μέμφειρα**, ἡ, = μέμψις, Telecl.62.

**μεμφητός**, ή, όν, = μεμπτός I, *PAmh.*2.63.5 (iii A.D.).

**μεμφίδες**· αἱ τῶν πτηνῶν ψυχαί, Hsch.

**Μεμφίτιον**, τό, *jar* of wine *from Memphis*, *PFlor.*213.6 (iii A.D.).

⊛ **μέμφομαι**, Thgn.797, etc.: impf. ἐμέμφετο Batr.70: fut. μέμψομαι Hes.*Op.*186, etc.: aor. ἐμέμφθην Hdt.1.77, 3.13, Pi.*N.*11.30 (κατα-), E.*Hipp.*1402, al., Th.4.85 (in pass. sense, Ph.1.301, A.D.*Synt.*67.22): but in Att. and Trag. commonly ἐμεμψάμην, as A.*Pr.*1073 (anap.), And.4.3, Th.1.143, also in Mimn.14.5, Hdt.2.24: pres. in pass. sense, D.L.6.47, Asp.*in EN*133.14: fut. μεμφθήσομαι Ps.-Men. in Meineke *Fragm.Com.Gr.* iv p.337:—*blame, censure*, first in Hes. (though ἐπιμέμφομαι occurs in Hom.): 1. c. acc. pers., μέμψονται δ' ἄρα τοὺς Hes.*Op.*186, cf. Thgn.797, Pi.*N.*7.64, S.*El.*384, etc.; μ. τύχην A.*Pr.*1073 (anap.); μ. τὸν θέντα τὸν νόμον And.4.3; κατὰ τὸ μαντήϊον οὐκ ὀρθῶς ὁ Κροῖσος μέμφεται (sc. τὸν Λοξίαν) Hdt.1.91; μ. τινὰ πρὸς τοὺς φίλους X.*Oec.*11.23; μ. τινὰ εἴς τι Id.*An.*2.6.30. b. c. acc. rei, οἶνε, τὰ μέν σ' αἰνῶ, τὰ δὲ μέμφομαι Thgn.873; μ. τὴν γνώμην, τὰ δῶρα, Hdt.1.207, 3.13; μ. τὴν φιλοσοφίαν Pl.*Euthd.*305b; ἄλλο οὐδὲν μ. X.*An.*7.6.39; μεμφθεὶς κατὰ τὸ πλῆθος τὸ ἑωυτοῦ στράτευμα Hdt.1.77; ταῦτα.. προτ' ἐμὸν θυμὸν ἐμεμψάμαν Theoc.30.24. 2. c. dat. pers. et acc. rei, *impute as blameworthy, cast in one's teeth*, Sapph.*Supp.*14.7 (prob.), Hdt.3.4, 4.180, Ar.*Nu.*525, *Av.*137, Th.1.143, etc.: also c. acc. cogn., τῷ Λοξίᾳ μέμψιν μ. Ar.*Pl.*10, etc.; μ. τινὶ ὅτι.. Hdt.9.6, cf. 6.92; οὕνεκα.. E.*Hel.*31; εἰ.. Th.4.85: c. dat. pers. et gen. rei, οὔποτ' ἀνδρὶ τῷδε κηρυκευμάτων μέμψει A.*Th.*652: c. gen. pers. et acc. rei, ὃ μάλιστα μέμφονται ἡμῶν which is the chief *complaint they make* against us, Th.1.84. 3. c. dat. pers. only, *to be dissatisfied with, find fault with*, A.*Th.*560, *Pr.*63, S.*Tr.*470, E.*Or.*285, *IA*899 (troch.), X.*Mem.*3.5.20, *Ep.Hebr.*8.8: with part. added, μ. ἡμῖν λογισαμένοις Luc.*Charid.*20; ὡς κακῶς βουλευομένοις Pl.*Phdr.*234b, cf. *Cri.*50d. 4. c. gen. rei only, *complain of*, οὐ μάχης.. μέμψει A.*Fr.*199.3; εἴ τι μέμφῃ τῆς ἐμῆς ἀπουσίας E.*Hec.*962; τιμῆς ἐμέμφθη of her [neglected] honour (cf. εὐχωλῆς ἐπιμέμφεται Il.1.93), E.*Hipp.*1402; μ. τῶν γεγενημένων Th.8.109. 5. c. inf. with μή, μ. μὴ πολλάκις βουλεύεσθαι *object* that one ought not.., Id.3.42. 6. abs., *find fault, complain*, A.*Supp.*137 (lyr.); ὅτι Arist.*EN*1162ᵇ18. in Law, οἱ μεμφόμενοι the *plaintiffs*, *GDI*4998 (Gortyn).

**μεμφωλή**, ἡ, = μέμψις, Hsch., Suid.

**μεμψῐ-βολέω**, *cast reproaches*, Phot., Suid. **-μοιρέω**, *grumble, complain of*, τινι Plb.18.8.3, D.S.17.77; τισὶν ἐπί τινι Plb.18.48.7; περί τινος D.S.17.79; ὅτι.. Luc.*Sacr.*1. II. *blame, bear a grudge against*, [τινὶ] οὐδέν Decr.ap.D.18.74, cf. Plu.*CG*8. **-μοιρητέον**, *one must complain*, τισὶν ὅτι Plb.4.60.9. **-μοιρία**, ἡ, *faultfinding*, Hp.*Ep.*20, Arist.*VV*1251ᵇ25, Thphr.*Char.*17.1, Epicurus in *PHerc.*176 p.46 V. **-μοιρος**, ον, *faultfinding, criticizing, querulous*, Isoc.12.8, Thphr.*Char.*17.2, Phld.*Lib.*p.42 O., *Ep.Jud.*16, Luc.*Tim.*13, etc.; τὸ μ. Plu.2.50b: Comp., γυνὴ ἀνδρὸς -ότερον Arist.*HA*608ᵇ 10.

⊛ **μέμψις**, εως, ἡ, *blame, censure*, μέμψιν δικαίαν μέμφομαι Ar.*Pl.*10; μ. ἐπιφέρειν τινί Id.*Ra.*1253 (lyr.); μ. λαβεῖν Men.576 (s.v.l.); ἔχειν μ. to incur *blame*, E.*Heracl.*974; φίλων μ. *censure* of them, S.*Fr.*472: pl., *censures*, Pl.*Lg.*684d; *complaints*, Arist.*EN*1162ᵇ5. 2. *ground of complaint*, μ. οὔτιν' ἀνθρώποις ἔχων A.*Pr.*445, cf. S.*Ph.*1309.

**μέν**, Particle, used partly to express certainty on the part of the speaker or writer; partly, and more commonly, to point out that the word or clause with which it stands is correlative to another word or clause that is to follow, the latter word or clause being introduced by δέ.

A. I. μέν used absolutely to express certainty, not followed by correlative δέ, *indeed, of a truth*, synonymous with μήν, as appears from the Ep. and Ion. form ἦ μέν in protestations and oaths (where Att. used ἦ μήν), καί μοι ὄμοσσον, ἦ μ. μοι πρόφρων ἔπεσιν καὶ χερσὶν ἀρήξειν Il.1.77, cf. 14.275; ἦ μέν τοι τάδε πάντα τελείεται Od.14.160, cf. Il.24.416; τοῦτον ἐξορκοῖ, ἦ μέν οἱ διηκονήσειν Hdt.4.154, cf. 5.93, etc.: with neg., οὐ μὲν γάρ τι κακὸν βασιλευέμεν Od.1.392, etc.; ὤμοσα, μὴ μὲν.. ἀναφῆναι 4.254, cf. Hdt.2.118, 179; ἔξαρνος ἦν, μὴ μὲν ἀποκτεῖναι Id.3.67, cf. 99: without neg., ἀνδρὸς μὲν τόδε σῆμα πάλαι κατατεθνηῶτος Il.7.89: also in Trag., ἀκτὴ μὲν ἥδε τῆς περιρρύτου χθονὸς S.*Ph.*1, cf. 159 (anap.), *OC*44, E.*Med.*676, 1129, etc.; καὶ μέν Il.1.269, 9.632, etc.; οὐδὲ μὲν οὐδὲ.. 2.703, 12.212; γε μέν, cf. γε I. 5. 2. an answering clause with δέ is sts. implied, τὴν μὲν ἐγὼ σπουδῇ δάμνημ' ἐπέεσσι her can I hardly subdue, [*but* all others easily], Il.5.893; ὡς μὲν λέγουσι as *indeed* they say, [*but* as I believe not], E.*Or.*8; καὶ πρῶτον μὲν ἦν αὐτῷ πόλεμος (with no ἔπειτα δέ to follow), X.*An.*1.9.14; so νῦν μέν σ' ἀφήσω I will let you go *this time*, Herod.5.81: to give force to assertions made by a person respecting himself, wherein opposition to other persons is implied, ὡς μὲν ἐμῷ θυμῷ δοκεῖ Od.13.154; δοκεῖν μέν μοι ἥξει τήμερον [τὸ πλοῖον] Pl.*Cri.*43d: hence with the pers. Pron., ἐγὼ μέν νυν θεοῖσι ἔχω χάριν Hdt.1.71; ἐγὼ μὲν οὐδέν (sc. θέλω) S.*Ant.*498; ἐμοῦ μὲν οὐχ ἑκόντος Id.*Aj.*455; ἐγὼ μὲν οὐκ οἶδα X.*Cyr.*1.4.12, cf. 4.2.45, etc.: with the demonstr. Pron., τούτου μὲν τοῦ ἀνθρώπου ἐγὼ σοφώτερός εἰμι Pl.*Ap.*21d: generally, to emphasize the preceding word, πολλὴ μὲν ἡ μεταβολή μοι γέγονεν great *indeed* has been the change, Is.1.1, cf. Simon.5.1, etc. 3. μέν is used alone in questions, when the answer is assumed, *I take it*, θέμις μὲν ἡμᾶς χρησμὸν εἰδέναι θεοῦ; E.*Med.*676, cf. *Ion* 520 (troch.), *Hipp.*316, S.*Ant.*634, Ar.*Av.*1214; Ἕλλην μέν ἐστι καὶ Ἑλληνίζει; Pl.*Men.*82b. II. μέν folld. by δέ in the correlative clause or clauses, *on the one hand, on the other hand*; commonly in Classical Gr., less freq. in later Gr. (rare in *NT*): 1. μέν.., δέ.. (or when the correlative clause is neg., μέν.., οὐδέ.., Il.1.318, 536), to mark oppo-

sition, Hom., etc.—The opposed clauses commonly stand together, but are freq. separated by clauses, parenthetic or explanatory; e.g. μέν in Il.2.494 is answered by δέ in 511,527 sq.; in X.*An*.1.9.2, πρῶτον μέν is answered by ἐπεὶ δέ in §6; in Id.*Mem*.1.1.2, πρῶτον μέν is answered by θαυμαστὸν δέ in 1.2.1. 2. to connect a series of clauses containing different matter, though with no opposition, Il.1.18 sq., 306 sq. (five δέ-clauses), 433 sq. (eight δέ-clauses), cf. X.*An*.1.3.14, 7.10 sq.: freq. when the members of a group or class are distinctly specified, παῖδες δύο, πρεσβύτερος μὲν Ἀρταξέρξης, νεώτερος δὲ Κῦρος ib.1.1.1; τάφρος.., τὸ μὲν εὖρος ὀργυιαὶ πέντε, τὸ δὲ βάθος ὀργυιαὶ τρεῖς ib.1.7.14; πρῶτος μέν.., δεύτερος δέ.., τρίτος δέ.. ib.5.6.9; τότε μέν.., τότε δέ.., at *one* time.., at *another*.., ib.6.1.9, etc.: esp. with the Art. used as a Pron., ὁ μέν.., ὁ δέ..; τὸ μέν.., τὸ δέ.., etc. 3. the principal word is freq. repeated, οἱ περὶ μὲν βουλὴν Δαναῶν, περὶ δ' ἐστὲ μάχεσθαι Il.1.258, cf. 288, Od.15.70; ἔνι μὲν φιλότης, ἐν δ' ἵμερος, ἐν δ' ὀαριστύς Il.14.216; Ξέρξης μὲν ἄγαγεν.., Ξέρξης δ' ἀπώλεσεν A.*Pers*.550, cf. 560, 694, 700 (all lyr.); χαλεπαίνει μὲν πρῳρεύς, χαλεπαίνει δὲ κυβερνήτης X.*An*.5.8.20. 4. one of the correlative clauses is sts. independent, while the other takes the part. or some other dependent form, ἐβλασφήμει κατ' ἐμοῦ.., μάρτυρα μὲν.. οὐδένα παρασχόμενος.., παρεκελεύετο δέ.. D.57.11; οἱ ἀμφὶ βασιλέα, πεζοὶ μὲν οὐκέτι, τῶν δὲ ἱππέων ὁ λόφος ἐνεπλήσθη X.*An*.1.10.12, cf. 2.1.7, 5.6.29; ὧν ἐπιμεμφομένα σ' ἁδεῖα μὲν ἀντία δ' οἴσω S.*Tr*.123, cf. *OC* 522 (both lyr.); χωρὶς μὲν τοῦ ἐστερῆσθαι.., ἔτι δὲ καὶ.. δόξω ἀμελῆσαι Pl.*Cri*.44b. 5. μέν and δέ freq. oppose two clauses, whereof one is subordinate to the other in meaning or emphasis, ἀλλ' ἐκεῖνο θαυμάζω, εἰ Λακεδαιμονίοις μέν ποτε.. ἀντῆρατε,.. νυνὶ δὲ ὀκνεῖτ' ἐξιέναι (for εἰ.. ἀντάραντες νυνὶ ὀκνεῖτε) D.2.24, cf. E.*IT*116, Lys.34.11, X.*Mem*.2.7.11, etc.: so in an anacoluthon, τρία μὲν ὄντα.. ναυτικά.., τούτων δ' εἰ περιόψεσθε τὰ δύο, κτλ., Th.1.36. 6. μέν is not always answered by δέ, but freq. by other equiv. Particles, as ἀλλά, Il.1.22 sq., 2.703 sq., Pi.*O*.9.1, A.*Pers*.176, X.*An*.1.7.17:—by μέντοι, Hdt.1.36, S.*Ph*.350, D.21.189, etc.:—by ἀτάρ, Il.6.84,124, A.*Pr*.342, S.*OT*1051 sq., Pl.*Tht*.172c, etc. (so μέν.., αὐτὰρ in Ep., Il.1.50, Od.19.513, etc.):—by αὖ, Il.11.108, Od.4.210:—by αὖθις, S.*Ant*.165:—by αὖτε, Il.1.234, Od.22.5:—by temporal Particles, πρῶτα μέν.., εἶτα.. S.*El*.261; πρῶτον μέν.., μετὰ τοῦτο.. X.*An*.6.1.5–7; μάλιστα μὲν δή.., ἔπειτα μέντοι.. S.*Ph*.350, cf. *OT*647:—rarely by μήν with neg., οὐδὲν μὴν κωλύει Pl.*Phdr*.268e; οὐ μὴν αὐταί γε Id.*Phlb*.12d. b. when the opposition is emphatic, δέ is sts. strengthd., as ὅμως δέ.. S.*OT*785, *Ph*.473, 1074, etc. (so ἀλλ' ὅμως *El*.450); δ' αὖ.. Il.4.415, X.*An*.1.10.5; δ' ἔμπης.. Il.1.561–2. c. μέν is sts. answered by a copul. Particle, κάρτιστοι μὲν ἔσαν καὶ καρτίστοις ἐμάχοντο ib.267, cf. 459, Od.22.475, S.*Aj*.1, *Tr*.689, E.*Med*.125 (anap.), etc.: rarely in Prose, τρία μὲν ἔτη ἀντεῖχον.., καὶ οὐ πρότερον ἐνέδοσαν Th.2.65 (dub.).

B. μέν before other Particles: I. where each Particle retains its force, 1. μὲν ἄρα, in Hom. μέν ῥα, Il.2.1, 6.312, Od.1.127, Pl.*Phdr*.258d, *R*.467d, etc. 2. μὲν γάρ S.*OT*62, Th.1.142, etc.:—in Hom. there is freq. no second clause, Od.1.173,392, cf. S.*OT*1062, etc.; μὲν γὰρ δή Il.11.825; μὲν γάρ τε 17.727. 3. μέν γε, when a general statement is explained in detail, Κορινθίοις μέν γε ἔνσπονδοί ἐστε Th.1.40, cf. 70, 6.86, Hdt.6.46, Antipho 5.14, Lys.13.27, Is.4.8, Ar.*Nu*.1382, *V*.564, E.*Fr*.909.4. 4. μὲν δή Il.1.514, Hdt.1.32, etc.: freq. used to express positive certainty, ἀλλ' οἶσθα μὲν δή S.*Tr*.627, cf. *OT*294; τὰ μὲν δὴ τόξ' ἔχεις Id.*Ph*.1308; esp. as a conclusion, τοῦτο μὲν δή.. ὁμολογεῖται Pl.*Grg*.470b, cf. X.*Cyr*.1.1.6, etc.: in closing a statement, τοιαῦτα μὲν δὴ ταῦτα A.*Pr*.500, etc.: used in answers to convey full assent, ἦ μὲν δή (cf. supr. A) Il.9.348, Od.4.33; καὶ μὲν δή.. γε Pl.*R*.409b; οὐ μὲν δή, to deny positively, Il.8.238, X.*Cyr*.1.6.9, Pl.*Tht*.148e, etc.; οὐ μὲν δή.. γε X.*An*.2.2.3, 3.2.14; ἀλλ' οὔ τι μὲν δή.. Pl.*Tht*.187a. 5. μὲν οὖν, v. infr. II. 2. II. where the Particles combine so as to form a new sense, 1. μέν γε *at all events, at any rate* (not in Trag.), τοῦτο μέν γ' ἤδη σαφές Ar.*Ach*.154, cf. *Nu*.1172, *Lys*.1165, *Ra*.80, Th.3.39; μέν γέ που Pl.*R*.559b, *Tht*.147a. 2. μὲν οὖν is freq. used with a corresponding δέ, so that each Particle retains its force, Od.4.780, Pi.*O*.1.111, S.*OT*244, 843, *Ph*.359, D.2.5, etc.: but freq. also abs., *so then*, S.*Ant*.65; ταῦτα μὲν οὖν παραλείψω D.2.3; esp. in replies, sts. in strong affirmation, παντάπασι μὲν οὖν Pl.*Tht*.158d; κομιδῇ μὲν οὖν ib.159e; πάνυ μὲν οὖν ib.159b; ἀνάγκη μὲν οὖν ib.189e; also to substitute a new statement so as to correct a preceding statement, *nay rather*, κακοδαίμων; Answ. βαρυδαίμων μὲν οὖν! Ar.*Ec*.1102; μου πρὸς τὴν κεφαλὴν ἀποψῶ wipe your nose on my head: Answ. ἐμοῦ μὲν οὖν.. *nay* on mine, Id.*Eq*.911, cf. A.*Pers*.1032 (lyr.), *Ag*.1090 (lyr.), 1396, S.*Aj*.1363, *El*.1503, *OT*705, Ar.*Ra*.241, Pl.*Cri*.44b, *Grg*.466a, 470b, *Prt*.309d, etc.; also μὲν οὖν δή S.*Tr*.153; καὶ δὴ μὲν οὖν Id.*OC*31; cf. οὐμενοῦν: in *NT* μενοῦν and μενοῦνγε, to begin a sentence, *yea rather*, *Ev.Luc*.11.28, *Ep.Rom*.9.20, etc., cf. Phryn.322, Hsch.—In Ion., μέν νυν is used for μὲν οὖν, Hdt.1.18, 4.145, etc. 3. by μέν τε, if δέ τε follows, the two clauses are more closely combined than by τε.., τε.., Il.5.139, al.; μέν τε is freq. answered by δέ alone, 16.28, al.; by ἀλλά, αὐτάρ, 17.727, Od.1.215, al.; perh. by ἠδέ, Il.4.341:—Hom. also uses μέν τε abs., when τε loses its force, as after ἦ, τίς, etc., Il.2.145, al. 4. μέν τοι in Hom. always occurs in speeches, where τοι can be regarded as the dat. of the Pron.: later, μέντοι is written as a single word, and is used: a. with a conj. force, *yet*, *nevertheless*, A.*Pr*.320, 1054 (anap.), S.*Tr*.413, etc.; and sts. stands for δέ, answering to μέν, v. supr. A.II.6a. b. as an Adv., in strong protestations, οὐ μέντοι μὰ Δία.. D.4.49; in eager or positive assent, *of course*, φαμέν τι εἶναι..; Answ. φαμὲν μέντοι νὴ Δία Pl.*Phd*.65d, al.: with a neg. to give emphasis to a question, οὐ σὺ μέντοι..; *why*, are you not..? Id.*Prt*.309a, cf. *Phdr*.229b, *R*.339b, etc.: sts. to express impatience, ὄμνυμι γάρ σοι—τίνα μέντοι, τίνα θεῶν; Id.*Phdr*.236d; τί μ. πρῶτον ἦν, τί πρῶτον ἦν; *nay* what *was* the first? Ar.*Nu*.787; οὗτος, σὲ λέγω μ. Id.*Ra*.171; σὺ μέντοι.. Luc.*Alex*.44: with imper., to enforce the command, τουτὶ μ. σὺ φυλάττου *only* take heed.., Ar.*Pax*1100, cf. *Av*.661, X.*An*.1.4.8: in answers, γελοῖον μέντἂν εἴη *nay* it would be absurd, Pl.*Tht*.158e; summing up a long temporal clause, And.1.130. c. μέντοι γε X.*Cyr*.5.5.24, etc.; οὐ μ. γε Diog.Apoll.5: in later Gr. μέντοιγε stands first in the sentence. μ. οὐ θέλω *PLond*.3.897.13 (i A.D.); also γε μέντοι A.*Ag*.938, S.*OT*778, 1292, E.*Hec*.600; ὅμως γε μ. Ar.*Ra*.61. d. καί μ. καί is used to add a point to be noted, Heraclit.28, Pl.*R*.331d; also καί.. μ., νῦν σοι καιρός ἐστιν ἐπιδείξασθαι τὴν παιδείαν, καὶ φυλάξασθαι μέντοι.. and *of course* to take care.., X.*An*.4.6.15 (v.l.), cf. 1.8.20, Pl.*Prt*.339c, *Tht*.143a. e. ἀλλὰ μέντοι *well, if it comes to that*, X.*An*.4.6.16; *well, of course*, Pl.*R*.331e, etc.; cf. μέντον.

C. for μέν after other Particles, see each Particle.

D. Position of μέν. Like δέ, it usu. stands as the second word in a sentence. But when a sentence begins with words common to its subordinate clauses, μέν stands second in the first of these clauses, as ἥδε γὰρ γυνὴ δούλη μέν, εἴρηκεν δ' ἐλεύθερον λόγον S.*Tr*.63; οἱ Ἀθηναῖοι ἐτάξαντο μέν.., ἡσύχαζον δέ.. Th.4.73, cf. 113, etc. It also attaches itself to words which mark opposition, as πρῶτον μέν, τότε μέν, ἐγὼ μέν, even when these do not stand first: sts. however it precedes them, ὡς μὲν ἐγὼ οἶμαι Pl.*Phdr*.228b; ὡς μέν τινες ἔφασαν X.*Cyr*.5.2.28. It generally stands between the Art. and Noun, or the Prep. and its Case: but if special stress is laid on the Noun, this is sts. neglected, as οἱ Τεγεᾶται μὲν ἐπηυλίσαντο, Μαντινῆς δὲ ἀπεχώρησαν Th.4.134; ἀνὰ τὸ σκοτεινὸν μέν.. Id.3.22; also τῇ σῇ μὲν εὐδαιμονίῃ, τῇ ἐμεωυτοῦ δὲ κακοδαιμονίῃ Hdt.1.87. II. μέν is freq. repeated: 1. when, besides the opposition of two main clauses, a subordinate opposition is introduced into the first, ὁ μὲν ἀνὴρ τοιαῦτα μὲν πεποίηκε τοιαῦτα δὲ λέγει, ὑμῶν δέ.. X.*An*.1.6.9, cf. 5.8.24, Th.8.104, D.18.214, 23.208. 2. in apodosi with the demonstr. Pron. or Adv., τὸν μὲν καλέουσι θέρος, τοῦτον μὲν προσκυνέουσι, τὸν δὲ χειμῶνα.. Hdt.2.121; ὅσοι μὲν δὴ νομοῦ τοῦ Θηβαίου εἰσί, οὗτοι μέν [νυν].. αἶγας θύουσι· ὅσοι δὲ.. νομοῦ τοῦ Μενδησίου εἰσί, οὗτοι δὲ.. ὄϊς θύουσι ib.42, cf. 3.108, al.; ὅτε μέν με οἱ ἄρχοντες ἔταττον.., τότε μὲν ἔμενον.., τοῦ δὲ θεοῦ τάττοντος,.. ἐνταῦθα δέ.. Pl.*Ap*.28e, cf. *Grg*.512a. 3. μέν used absolutely is freq. folld. by a correlative μέν, εἰ μὲν οὖν ἡμεῖς μὲν.. ποιοῦμεν Id.*R*.421a. III. μέν is sts. omitted (esp. in Poetry) where it is implied in the following δέ, φεύγων, ὁ δ' ὄπισθε διώκων Il.22.157; ἐλευθεροῦτε πατρίδ', ἐλευθεροῦτε δὲ παῖδας A.*Pers*.403; σφραγῖδε.. χρυσοῦν ἔχουσα τὸν δακτύλιον, ἡ δ' ἑτέρα ἀργυροῦν *IG*2².1388.45, cf. Ar.*Nu*.396, Pl.*Sph*.221e, Arist.*Po*.1447ᵇ14, etc.

**μεν-αίχμης**, ου, Dor. **-αίχμᾱς**, α, ὁ, *staunch soldier*, Anacr.70 (dub.): as Adj., χειρὶ μεναίχμᾳ *AP*6.84 (Paul. Sil.). **-ανδρος**, ον, *awaiting a man*, παρθένος Dionys.Trag.12.

**μενάσσει**· μολύνει, Hsch. **μενδῖται**, οἱ, v. μίνδις.

**μενεαίνω**, (μένος) *desire earnestly* or *eagerly*, c. pres. inf., μηδὲ θεοῖς μενεαινέμεν ἶφι μάχεσθαι Il.5.606, cf. Od.13.30, etc.: more freq. c. aor. inf., μενεαίνει Ἰλίου ἐξαλαπάξαι πτολίεθρον Il.4.32, etc.: rarely c. fut. inf., ἐρύσσεσθαι (v.l. -ασθαι) μενεαίνων 21.176, Od.21.125 (s.v.l.): when abs., an inf. may be supplied, σὺ δ' ἀσπερχὲς μενεαίνεις [διῶξαι] Il.22.10; μάλα περ μενεαίνων [καταφθῖσαι] Od.5.341, etc.: also c. gen., μ. μάχης *long for* battle, Hes.*Sc*.361: c. acc. rei, ὄλεθρον μ. τινί *purpose* death against another, Q.S.12.380. II. *to be angry, rage*, Il.19.68, 24.22,54; ἔριδι μενεήναμεν 19.58; μ. τινί *rage* against one, 15.104, Od.1.20, etc.; κτεινόμενος μενέαινε *wrestled with* death, Il.16.491 (Sch. expld. it by ἐλειποθύμει).—Ep., and Ps.-E.*Fr*.1132.51 (lyr.).

**μενεγχής**, ές, = μεναίχμης, A.*Eleg*.3.

⊕ **μενε-δήϊος**, ον, *standing one's ground against the enemy, staunch*, κραδίη Il.12.247, 13.228:—Dor. **-δάϊος** *AP*7.208 (Anyt.). ⊕ **-δουπος**, ον, *steadfast in the battle-din*, Orph.*A*.539. **-κράτης** [ᾰ], ες, *abiding in strength*, στῦλος Dionys.Trag.12. **-κτῦπος**, ον, *steadfast in the battle-din*, B.16.1, cf. Hsch.

⊕ **Μενέλᾱος**, ὁ, pr. n., *Abiding-men*, Hom., etc.:—Att. **Μενέλεως**, gen. εω, Trag. use either form, as the metre requires:—Dor. dat. Μενέλᾳ Pi.*N*.7.28; acc. Μενέλαν E.*Rh*.257 (lyr.); gen. Μενέλα Id.*Tr*.1100 (lyr.).

**μενε-μάχος** [ᾰ], ον, *staunch in fight*, App.*Hisp*.51. **-μηλάδες**, αἱ, *ewes*, v.l. for ἐπιμηλάδες, Call.*Ap*.51 (ap.Sch.). **-πτόλεμος**, ον, *staunch in battle, steadfast*, Il.19.48, etc.; ἥρως B.16.73; Περαιβοί, Κουρῆτες, Il.2.749, B.5.126.

**μενε-τέον**, (μένω) *one must remain*, Pl.*R*.328b, X.*HG*3.2.9, etc. **-τικός**, ή, όν, *long-suffering*, M.Ant.1.16. ⊕**-τός**, ή, όν, *inclined to wait, patient*, μενετοὶ θεοί Ar.*Av*.1620; of circumstances, οἱ καιροὶ οὐ μ. opportunities *will* not wait, Th.1.142. **-φύλοπις** [ῠ], ιος, ὁ, ἡ, *staunch in battle*, *AP*6.84 (Paul. Sil.), prob. cj. in Doroth. in *Cat.Cod.Astr*.8(4).223. **-χάρμης**, ου, ὁ, (χάρμη) = foreg. (not in Od.), Il.11.122,303, al.; Αἰτωλοί 9.529:—also ⊕**-χαρμος**, ον, 14.376.

**μέν-ημα**, ατος, τό, *room, cell*, *PKlein.Form*.785 (v/vi A.D.), *Sammelb*.5175.5 (vi A.D.). **-ητέον**, *one must wait for*, Gal.16.64.

**μενθήρη**, ἡ, = φροντίς, prob. in Panyas.12 (post v. 15), cf. Hsch., *EM*580.6 (pl.; μενθῆρες f.l. in Suid.).

**μενθηρίζω**, = μερμηρίζω, in fut. -ιῶ, Hsch., Phot.; cf. ἀμενθήριστος.

**μέννης·** *μένε κύριε*, Hsch.

® **μενοεικής,** *ές*, (*εἰκός, ἔοικα*) *suited to the desires, satisfying, agreeable, to one's taste*, mostly of meat and drink, *δαίς, δεῖπνον*, Il.9.90, Od.20.391; *ἐδωδή* 6.76; *σῖτον καὶ ὕδωρ καὶ οἶνον..ἐνθήσω μενοεικέ', ἅ κέν τοι λιμὸν ἐρύκοι* 5.166; *πάρα γὰρ μενοεικέα πολλὰ δαίνυσθαι* Il.9.227, cf. Od.16.429; *τῶν ἐξαιρεύμην μενοεικέα* 14.232; *τάφος μ.* a *plentiful* funeral feast, Il.23.29; *μενοεικέα ὕλην great store of* wood, ib.139; [*δῶρα,*] *χάρις*, 19.144, 23.650; *καί σφιν μενοεικέα ληΐδα δῶκα* Od.13.273, cf. Plu.*Phoc.*2.

**μενοιν-άω,** Ep. **-ώω** Il.13.79; 3 sg. *μενοινάᾳ* 19.164: Ep. impf. *μενοίνεον* 12.59; 3 sg. *ἐμενοίνα* Hes.*Sc.*368, *μενοίνα* Od.11.532, Theoc.25.62: aor. *μενοίνησεν* Od.2.36; subj. *μενοινήσωσι* Il.10.101; opt. *μενοινήσειε* 15.82 (but subj. *μενοινήησι* Aristarch.), Od.2.248: (*μένος*):—= *μενεαίνω*, *desire eagerly*, *φρεσὶν ᾗσι μ.* Od.2.34; *μετὰ φρεσὶ σῇσι* Il.14.264; *θυμῷ, ἐνὶ θυμῷ*, 19.164, Od.2.248: mostly c. acc. rei, ib.285, al.; *ἔργα πολλὰ μ.* Pi.*N.*11.45; *νόῳ ὅγε πολλὰ μενοίνα* Theoc. l.c.: also c. pres. inf., *μ. πολεμίζειν* Il.19.164, cf. Od.22.217: c. aor. inf., 2.248, 21.157, Pi.*P.*1.43; also *μενοίνεον εἰ τελέουσι were eager to see* whether.., Il.12.59: rarely abs., *ὧδε μενοινῶν* so *eager* [for battle], 15.293; *μ. τινί τι design* or *purpose* something against one, *κακὰ δὲ Τρώεσσι μενοίνα* Od.11.532: c. dat. rei alone, *strive for* a thing, *μ. χρήμασι* Thgn.461.—Ep. and Lyr., twice in Trag., in pres., *τί ποτε μενοινᾷ;* S.*Aj.*341; *νιν σφάξαι μενοινᾷς* E.*Cyc.*448; once in Ar., pres., *ἐξελεῖν ἡμῶν μενοινῶν..τἀνθρήνια* *V.*1080. **-ή,** *ἡ*, *eager desire*, Call.*Jov.*90, A.R.1.894, *AP*11.350 (Agath.). **-ής** (fort. *ᾗς*, contr. fr. *-ήεις*)· *πρόθυμος, φροντιστής*, Hsch.

® **μένος,** *εος, τό*, *might, force*, *μή μ' ἀπογυιώσῃς μένεος, ἀλκῆς τε λάθωμαι* Il.6.265; *μ. χειρῶν* 5.506 (more freq. *μ. καὶ χεῖρες* 6.502, al.); *μ. καὶ γυῖα* 6.27. 2. of animals, *strength, fierceness*, *παρδάλιος, λέοντος*, 17.20; of horses, *spirit*, ib.456, 476, etc.; *ἵππος κατασθμαίνων μένει* A.*Th.*393; *ὑπὸ χαρᾶς καὶ μένους*, of dogs, X.*Cyn.*6.15. 3. of things, *force, might*, [*ἔγχεος*] Il.13.444; *ἠελίοιο* Od.10.160; *πυρός* Il.6.182, Ar.*Ach.*665; *ποταμῶν* Il.12.18, cf. A.*Pr.*720; *ἄστρων θερμὸν μ.* Parm.11.3; *ἀνέμων* Emp.111.3; *χειμῶνος* E.*Heracl.*428; *χαλινῶν ἀναύδῳ μένει* A.*Ag.*238 (lyr.); *ἄτης* Id.*Ch.*1076 (anap.); *τὸ ἀπὸ τοῦ οἴνου μ.* Hp.*Acut.*63, cf. *VM*9. 4. *life*, *ἀπὸ γὰρ μ. εἵλετο χαλκός* Il.3.294; *λύθη ψυχή τε μ. τε* 5.296; *φυσῶσι μέλαν μ.* the black *life-blood*, S.*Aj.*1412 (anap.), cf. A.*Ag.*1067. II. of the soul, *spirit, passion*, *μ. ἀνδρῶν* the *battle-rage* of men, Il.2.387; *μ. Ἄρηος* 18.264: less freq. in pl., mostly in phrase *μένεα πνείοντες* 2.536, al.; *μένος καὶ θυμός* 5.470, al., *h.Cer.*361; *μ. καὶ θάρσος* Il.5.2, Od.1.321; *μ. ἔλλαβε θυμόν* Il.23.468; *μένεος δ' ἐμπλήσατο θυμόν* 22.312; *μένεος δὲ μέγα φρένες ἀμφὶ μέλαιναι πίμπλαντο* 1.103: also in Att., *ὀργῆς καὶ μένους ἐμπλήμενος* Ar.*V.*424; *ὅτε ζέσειεν τὸ τοῦ θυμοῦ μ.* Pl.*Ti.*70b; *μένους τὴν ψυχὴν πληρουμένην* Alcid.ap.Arist.*Rh.*1406$^a$2 (but *νοῦς..πληρωθεὶς μένους* filled with *spiritual exaltation*, Plot.5.5.8); *θυμὸς ὁ κρατέων τῷ μένεος* Theag.ap.Stob.3.1.117; *προθυμία καὶ μ., μ. καὶ θάρρος*, X.*Cyr.*3.3.61, *HG*7.1.31; *παντὶ μένει σπεύδων* Hes.*Sc.*364. 2. *intent, purpose*, [*Τρώων*] *μ. αἰὲν ἀτάσθαλον* their *bent* is aye to folly, Il.13.634: in pl., *intents*, *ἐμῶν μενέων ἀπερωεύς* 8.361: hence, *temper, disposition*, in compds., like *εὐμενής, δυσμενής*. III. in periphr., like *βίη*, etc., *ἱερὸν μένος Ἀντινόοιο*, for *Antinous* himself, Od.18.34; *μένος Ἀτρεΐδαο* Il.11.268; *μένε' ἀνδρῶν* 4.447, Od.4.363; *καταφθιμένου μ. ἀνδρός* Emp.111.9; *αἴης λάσιον μ.* Id.27.2; *αἰθέριον μ.*, = *αἰθήρ*, Id.115.9. (Cf. Skt. *mánas* 'spirit', 'passion', Gr. *μέμονα, μαίνομαι.*)

**μεντάγρα,** *ἡ*, a skin disease, a form of *lichen*, Plin.*HN*26.2, Gal.12.839, al., Aët.8.16.

**μεντιόπον·** *χλανίδα*, Hsch.

**μέντοινε,** = *μέντοι* (v. *μέν* B. II. 4), *Inscr.Magn.*17.44.

**μέντον,** = *μέντοι*, *PHib.*1.40.7 (iii B.C.), *PCair.Zen.*359.7 (iii B.C.), *IG*9(2).517.38 (Larissa, iii B.C.), ib.338.13 (Cyretiae, ii B.C.), Chrysipp.ap.Phot. s.v. *μέντοι*, v.l. in Il.8.448: Arg. and Cret. acc. to Heraclid.ap.Eust.722.58.

**Μεντορουργής,** *ές*, *wrought by Mentor*, Luc.*Lex.*7.

® **μένω,** Ep. inf. *μενέμεν* Il.5.486; Arc. pres. part. *μίνονσαι* *Schwyzer* 657.49 (Tegea, iv B.C.); Ep., Ion. impf. *μένεσκον* Il.19.42, Hdt.4.42: Ep., Ion. fut. *μενέω* Il.19.308, Hdt.4.119; Att. *μενῶ* Ar.*Ach.*564, etc.: aor. *ἔμεινα* Il.15.656, etc.: pf. *μεμένηκα* D.18.321; cf. **μίμνω**:—*stay, wait*: I. *stand fast*, in battle, *οὐδ' ἴφθιμοι Λύκιοι μένον, ἀλλὰ φόβηθεν* Il.16.659; *μενέω καὶ τλήσομαι* 11.317; *φεύγειν μηδὲ μένειν* Orac. ap.Hdt.1.55, cf. X.*Cyr.*3.3.45, S.*OT*295; *ἐμπέδως μ.* A.*Ag.*854; *ἀραρότως* Id.*Supp.*945; *μ. κατὰ χώραν*, of soldiers, Th.4.26. 2. *stay at home, stay where one is*, Il.16.838; *ἔντοσθε μένοντες* Hes.*Th.*598; *μ. αὐτοῦ* Hdt.8.62; *οἴκοι* A.*Fr.*317; *εἴσω δόμων* Id.*Th.*232; *κατ' οἶκον* E.*IA*656; *ἐν δόμοις* Pi.*N.*3.43, S.*Aj.*80; *ἔνδον* Amphis 1.3. b. *lodge, stay*, *παρὰ ματρί* Pi.*P.*4.186; *πρὸς τοὺς γονέας* Hp.*Ep.*13; *ἐκεῖ* Plb.30.4.10 codd. (fort. *οἴκοι*), cf. Alciphr.3.5. c. *μ. ἀπὸ ἧς ἀλόχοιο stay away, be absent* from.., Il.2.292; *ἀπὸ πτολέμοιο* 18.64: and so abs., *to be a shirker*, *ἴση μοῖρα μένοντι καὶ εἰ μάλα τις πολεμίζοι* 9.318. d. *οἱ μένοντες*, opp. *οἱ φεύγοντες* (exiles), *IG*1$^2$.10.27. 3. *stay, tarry*, *ἐς ἠέλιον καταδύντα* Od.17.570; *μενέουσι, εἰς ὅ κέ περ Τροίην διαπέρσομεν* Il.9.45; *loiter, be idle*, 11.666, A.*Pers.*796; *οἱ μένοντες* X.*An.*4.4.19, etc. 4. of things, *to be lasting, remain, stand*, *στήλη μένει ἔμπεδον* Il.17.434; *ἀσφαλὲς αἰὲν..μένει οὐρανός* Pi.*N.*6.4; *τάδ' αἰανῶς μένοι* A.*Eu.*672; *αἰῶνα δ' ἐς τρίτον μένει* Id.*Th.*744 (lyr.); opp. *φέρεσθαι*, Pl.*Phdr.*261d; *εἰ μηδὲν μένει* if nothing *is fixed*, Id.*Cra.*440a; *τὴν μεμενηκυῖαν κρίσιν* Phld.*Sto.*339.15; *οἱ μένοντες* (sc. *ἀστέρες*) *having no proper motion*, opp. *οἱ πλάνητες*, Arist.*Cael.*290$^a$21; *μένων κύκλος* Autol.12, al., Ptol.*Hyp.*1.3; *μένουσιν ἀριστοκρατίαι are stable, permanent*, Arist.*Pol.*1308$^a$3. b. *μ. παρά τινι remain* in one's possession, *CPR*18.37 (ii A.D.), etc. 5. of condition, *remain as one was*, of a maiden, Il.19.263; *τῶν βεβαίως μοι φίλων μενόντων* Ps.-Philipp.ap.D.12.11; *τὸ νόμισμα βούλεται μένειν* Arist.*EN*1133$^b$14: generally, *stand, hold good*, *ἢν μείνωσιν ὅρκοι* E.*Andr.*1000; *μένειν τὸ ὅρκιον κατὰ χώρην* Hdt.4.201; *εἰ τὰ πρότερον μένει ἡμῖν ὁμολογήματα* Pl.*Grg.*480b; *μ. τὰ βουλήματα καὶ οὐ μεταρρεῖ* Arist.*EN*1167$^b$7; of circumstances, *οὐ μενεῖν κατὰ χώραν τὰ πράγματα* Th.4.76; *οὐδαμὰ ἐν τὠυτῷ μ.*, of prosperity, Hdt.1.5; *μένειν ἐμπέδοις φρονήμασι* S.*Ant.*169; *μ. ἐπὶ τούτων* [*ἃ κατέστραπται*] *remain contented* with.., D.4.9; *μ. ἐπὶ τούτοις* Isoc.8.7; *ἐπὶ τούτῳ τῷ βίῳ μ. be content with..*, Pl.*R.*466c, cf. 496b; *μ. ἐλεύθερον* Men.145; of wine, *keep good*, Plb.12.2.8. 6. *abide* by an opinion, conviction, etc., *ἐπὶ τῷ ἀληθεῖ* Pl.*Prt.*356e; *μενέτωσαν ἐν τοῖς διαγνωσθεῖσι* Lex ap.D.21.94; *ὁ μένων* the party which *observes* an engagement, *PTeb.*391.24 (i A.D.). 7. impers. c. inf., *it remains* for one to do, *μένει..ἐκτίνειν θέμιν* A.*Supp.*435 (lyr.); *τοῖς πᾶσιν ἀνθρώποισι κατθανεῖν μένει* E.*Fr.*733. II. trans., of persons, *await, expect* (cf. *μίμνω*), *ἡμέρας μεῖναι φάος* Id.*Rh.*66; *τοὺς Ἰλλυριούς* Th.4.124, cf. 8.78; esp. *await* an attack without blenching, *Δαναοὶ Τρῶας μένον ἔμπεδον, οὐδὲ φέβοντο* Il.5.527, cf. A.*Th.*436; of a rock, *bide* the storm, Il.15.620; *ἀπορίαν γὰρ οὐ μενῶ* E.*Ph.*740: reversely of things, *τὸ μόρσιμον γὰρ τόν τ' ἐλεύθερον μένει awaits* him, A.*Ch.*103; *ἐπίξηνον μένει* (sc. *με*) Id.*Ag.*1277; *ἀγὼν γὰρ ἄνδρας οὐ μένει λελειμμένους* Id.*Fr.*37; *δεσμά με καὶ θλίψεις μένουσιν* *Act.Ap.*20.23. 2. c. acc. et inf., *wait for*, *ἦ μένετε Τρῶας σχεδὸν ἐλθέμεν; wait* ye *for* the Trojans to come nigh? Il.4.247; *οὐ μενῶ πόσιν μολεῖν* E.*Andr.*255; *μένον δ' ἐπὶ ἕσπερον ἐλθεῖν* they *waited for* evening's coming on, Od.1.422, etc.; *οὐκ ἔμειν' ἐλθεῖν τράπεζαν νυμφίαν* Pi.*P.*3.16; *τί μένεις..ἰέναι;* why *wait* to go? Thgn.351; *μένω δ' ἀκοῦσαι* I *wait*, i.e. *long*, to hear, A.*Eu.*677, cf. *Ag.*459 (lyr.). (Cf. OPers. *man-* 'wait', Lat. *maneo.*)

**μέρα·** *ὄμματα*, Hsch. **μέρα,** *ἡ*, = *μέρος*, *PGrenf.*1.58.12 (vi A.D.).

**μεράρχ-ης,** *ου, ὁ*, (*μέρος*) *distributing official* of a deme, *IG*2$^2$.1203 (pl.). 2. *commander of a division of* 2,048 *men*, Ascl.*Tact.*2.10, Arr.*Tact.*10.5; also, *commander of* 32 *elephants*, Ael.*Tact.*23. **-ία,** *ἡ*, *command of a μεράρχης*, Ascl. l.c., Arr. l.c.

**μέργιζε·** *ἀθρόως ἔσθιε*, Hsch. ® **μέρδει·** *κωλύει, βλάπτει*, and aor. part. Pass., *μερθεῖσα· στερηθεῖσα, ἀμερθεῖσα*, Id.

® **μέρεια,** *ἡ*, = *μερίς*, *Tab.Heracl.*1.18, 85: glossed by *φυλῆς μέρος ἐκ δέκα τρι⟨ακ⟩άδων συνεστός*, Hsch.

**Μερῐδ-άρπαξ,** *ἄκος, ὁ*, *Bit-stealer*, name of a mouse in Batr.260.

**μερῐδάρχ-ης,** *ου, ὁ*, *governor of a district* or *province*, *PTeb.*66.60 (ii B.C.), Lxx 1 *Ma.*10.65, J.*AJ*12.5.5. **-ία,** *ἡ*, *his office*, Lxx 1 *Es.*1.5, J.*AJ*15.7.3. **-ικά,** *τά*, a tax, perh. for his maintenance, *Sammelb.*7166.8 (iii A.D.), *PStrassb.*58.8 (iii A.D.).

**μερίδιον,** *τό*, *small part*, Arr.*Epict.*2.22.23, *Sammelb.*4630.16 (ii A.D.).

**μεριζομένως,** Adv., gloss on *μελεϊστί*, Sch.Opp.*C.*4.281.

® **μερίζω,** Dor. **-ίσδω,** Bion 2.31: Att. fut. *-ιῶ* Pl.*Prm.*131c: aor. *ἐμέρισα* Nicom.Com.1.27; Dor. part. *μερίξας* Ti.Locr.99d: pf. *μεμέρικα* D.H.*Pomp.*4:—Med., fut. *-ίσομαι* Sopat. in Rh.8.306 W., *-ιοῦμαι* Lxx *Pr.*14.18: aor. *ἐμερισάμην* Is.9.24, etc.: pf. *μεμέρισμαι* D.47.34 (v.l. *νενέμημαι*):—Pass., fut. *μεριοῦμαι* Arist.*PA*664$^a$27, *μερισθήσομαι* Plot.4.3.8, 6.4.4: aor. *ἐμερίσθην* Pl.*Ti.*56d, etc.: pf. *μεμέρισμαι* Id.*Prm.*144b, D.15.5, etc.: (*μερίς*):—*divide, distribute*, Pl.*Prm.*131c; *μ. τὸ ἄπειρον* Arist.*Ph.*204$^a$34; *μ.* [*ἀρχήν*] *τινα εἰς πλείους* Id.*Pol.*1321$^b$37; *καθ' ἕκαστον εἶδος πολιτείας μ. make a division*, ib.1304$^b$19: abs., *split up the amount*, ib.1268$^b$15: Arith., *μ. τι παρά τι, εἴς τι, divide* by.., Dioph.4.33, 34, al.: abs., Gal.5.223. 2. *assign a part, allot*, *ἐφ' ἕκαστον μ. τὸ φιλεῖν* Arist.*MM*1213$^b$5; *μ. τοὺς τόκους πρὸς τὸν πλοῦν allot* the interest according to the voyage, i.e. *pay only a part* of it, if a part only of the voyage has been performed, D.56.49; *allot, assign* spheres of duty, *τινι* *PHamb.*24.6 (Pass.); *apportion, allocate* funds, *IG*2$^2$.29.18, al., *SIG*577.22 (Milet., iii/ii B.C.) (Pass., *IG*2$^2$.1672.116, al.); *τὸ μὲν εἰς δαπάνην, τὸ δ' εἰς θησαυρισμόν* Phld.*Oec.*p.71 J., cf. *Sto.*339.15, Metrod.*Herc.*831.13; *bestow*, *POxy.*713.29 (i A.D.), etc.; *κατὰ τόπους μ. τὰς ἀναγραφάς divide, arrange* them, D.H.*Th.*9; *μ. τινὰ τοῖς ποιηταῖς*, i.e. make one a theme for several tragedies, Him.*Ecl.*4.18:—Pass., *to be delivered over*, *εἰς ὕβριν καὶ δουλείαν* Chor.p.216 B. 3. *sever, cut off*, *πελέκει χεῖρα* Him.*Or.*2.21. 4. *apply by turns*, *τὰς χεῖρας τῷ τε τείχει καὶ τῇ λύρᾳ* ib.21.12. II. Med., *μερίζεσθαί τι divide among themselves*, *χρήματα* Din.1.10, cf. Theoc.21.31; *τι μετά τινος* D.34.18; *πρός τινα τὴν ἀρχήν* Hdn.3.10.6; *take possession of*, *τι* D.34.35; *ἠρόμην αὐτὸν πότερα μεμερισμένος εἴη πρὸς τὸν ἀδελφόν* whether he *had gone shares* with his brother, Id.47.34. 2. c. gen. rei, *get a portion of*, Is.9.24. b. *take part in*, *τοῦ ἀδικήματος* Arist.*EN*1137$^a$2. III. Pass., *to be divided*, *κατὰ μέρος* X.*An.*5.1.9 (s.v.l.); *ἐπὶ πολλά* Hp.*Insomn.*86; *τὸ μερίζεσθαι τὰς οὐσίας εἰς ὁποσονοῦν πλῆθος* Arist.*Pol.*1265$^b$3; *μ. πρὸς ἑκάστην διοίκησιν* (sc. *αἱ πρόσοδοι*) *are distributed*, ib.1321$^b$32; *ἐς πᾶσαν πεῖραν μ.* make attempts in every direction, App.*BC*4.78, cf. Luc.*DDeor.*24.1; *μερίζεταί τι ἀπό τινος* Id.*Nav.*8. 2. *to be dispersed*, *ὕδωρ ὑπὸ πυρὸς μερισθέν* Pl.*Ti.*56d; *to be split up*, *ἄνθρωπος πληγῇ τινι μεριζόμενος* Democr.32: metaph., *have divided interests, disperse one's energy*, Chor.p.11 B.; also, *to be split into parties* or *factions*, Plb.8.21.9, App.*BC*1.1, Hdn.3.10.4; *μεμέρισται ὁ Χριστός;* 1 *Ep.Cor.*1.13. 3. *to be reckoned as part*, *ἐν τῇ ἀρχῇ τινος μ.* D.15.5.

**μερῐκ-εύω,** *make* or *represent as divisible*, Eust.48.31, Steph. *in Rh.*

267.23. **-ός,** ή, όν, *partial*, ἔκλειψις Cleom.2.6,al.; *minutely subdivided*, ἐν τοῖς μερικωτέροις [κλίμασι] Id.1.11. II. *particular, individual, special*, Aristipp.ap.D.L.2.87, Demetr.Lac.*Herc*.1055.16, Hero *Deff*.136.11 (Comp.), Porph.*Sent*.22, Jul.*Gal*.148c, etc.; μ. ψυχή, νοῦς, Procl.*Inst*.109, cf. Dam.*Pr*.397; μ. καὶ θνητὸν ζῷον Hierocl.*in CA* 24p.474M. Adv. -κῶς Gal.16.411, Porph.*Sent*.22, etc.; opp. καθολικῶς, A.D.*Adv*.123.1: Comp. -ώτερον ib.138.9.

**μέριμν-α,** ἡ, *care, thought, solicitude*, ὅν τε θαμιναὶ ἐπιστρωφῶσι μέριμναι *h.Merc*.44, cf. Pi.*O*.2.54, etc.; μ. τινός *care for*.., A.*Eu*.132, S.*OT*1460; ἀμφί τι A.*Th*.843 (lyr.); ἐλθεῖν ἐς τόδε μερίμνης E.*Ion* 244, cf. 404: pl., *cares*, Hes.*Op*.178, Emp.11.1, Sapph.*Supp*.13.8, Thgn. 343, etc.; γνώμαις δὲ λεπταῖς..ξύνειμι καὶ μερίμναις Ar.*Nu*.1404; λύπας, μερίμνας, ἁρπαγάς Diph.88.—Rare in early Prose, Hp.*Insomn*. 89, Pl.*Amat*.134b(pl.); later ἡ τοῦ βίου μ. *UPZ*20.29(ii B.C.); μ. καὶ φροντίς Aristeas 271; μ. τοῦ αἰῶνος *Ev.Matt*.13.22, cf. Vett.Val.131.3, etc. 2. concrete, *object of care* or *thought*, μεγάλην σε πατὴρ ἐφύτευσε μ. θνητοῖς ἀνθρώποισι *h.Merc*.160. 3. *pursuit, ambition*, esp. in pl., Pi.*O*.1.108, *N*.3.69; κουφόταται μ. B.1.69: sg., Pi.*P*.8.92. 4. Κηΐα μ. the Cean poet's *fancy*, B.18.11. 5. *anxious mind*, A.*Ag*. 460(lyr.). (Cf. Skt. *smárati* 'remember', Lat. *memor*.) ⊛ **-άω,** *care for, be anxious about, meditate upon*, ἔργον μεριμνῶν ποῖον..; S.*OT* 1124; esp. of philosophers, τὰ ⟨μὲν ἀ⟩φανῆ μ. Ar.*Fr*.672; οἱ λεπτῶς μεριμνῶντες *Lyr.Adesp*.135, cf. X.*Mem*.4.7.6; μ. περὶ τῆς τῶν πάντων φύσεως ib.1.1.14; πολλὰ μ. *to be cumbered with* many *cares*, Id.*Cyr*.8. 7.12; τοῖς μεριμνῶσίν τε καὶ λυπουμένοις Apollod.Com.3; μηθὲν τὴν ἀλήθειαν μεριμνᾶν Phld.*Rh*.1.135 S., cf. 2.143 S.; μεριμνήσω ὑπὲρ τῆς ἁμαρτίας μου Lxx *Ps*.37(38).18; μ. εἰς τὴν αὔριον *Ev.Matt*.6.34: c. inf., *to be careful* to do, ὁ μεριμνήσας τὰ δίκαια λέγειν D.21.192: with relat. clause, πολλὰ μ. ὅπως μὴ λάθῃς X.*Mem*.3.5.23; μεριμνῶ πῶς κλαύσω *AP*9.148; μὴ μεριμνᾶτε τῇ ψυχῇ τί φάγητε *Ev.Matt*.6.25:—Pass., *to be treated with anxious care*, *AP*10.52 (Pall.); τράπεζαι πολυτελῶς μεμεριμνημέναι Ath.14.641c; ἔννοια, ἀμφισβήτησις μ., Just.*Nov*.22. 26*Intr*., 44.1.3. **-ημα,** Dor. **-ᾱμα,** ατος, τό, *anxiety*, in pl., Pi. *Fr*.277, 278, S.*Ph*.186 (lyr.). ⊛ **-ητής,** οῦ, ὁ, *one who is anxious about*, λόγων E.*Med*.1226, cf. Porph.*Gaur*.12.7. **-ητικός,** ή, όν, *anxious*, Sch.S.*Tr*.109; *caused by anxiety*, ὄνειροι Artem.4.2.

**μεριμνο-ποιέω,** *cause care*, *Gloss*. **-ποιός,** όν, *causing care*, *Cat.Cod.Astr*.8(1).168. **-τόκος,** ον, *mother of cares*, βίοτος *AP*11. 382.20 (Agath.). **-φροντιστής,** οῦ, ὁ, '*minute philosopher*', Ar. *Nu*.101.

**μερινων,** gen. pl., dub. sens. in *BGU*1519 (Ptolemaic).

⊛ **μερ-ίς,** ίδος, ἡ, (μέρος) *part, portion*, Pl.*Sph*.266a, etc.; κρεῶν Pherecr.45 (lyr.), D.43.82, cf. Thphr.*Char*.30.4, Lxx *Ge*.43.34, Plu. *Ages*.17, Hippoloch.ap.Ath.4.130d; μ. δίκρεως *SIG*1013.4 (Chios, iv B.C.); γυναιξὶν μερίδας ποησάντωσαν ἴσας ib.1044.42 (Halic., iv/iii B.C.): metaph., Vett.Val.345.16; τὴν μ. τὴν ἐξ Ἀρείου πάγου *portion of sacrificial meat* allotted to a member of the court, Din.1.56; τὴν τοῦ Προμηθέως μ. Luc.*Merc.Cond*.26; μ. τῆς οὐσίας Men.235.5, cf. *PLond*.3. 880 (ii B.C.); *share* in a mine, D.42.3: generally, ἐκ τῶν λόγων μ. ἑκατέρῳ ἴση ἐστί (with vv.ll.), Antipho 5.51; ἐν προσθήκῃ μ. οὐ μικρά D.2. 14. 2. *contribution, quota*, μερίδ' εἰς σωτηρίαν ὑπάρχειν *contribute* to.., Id.21.70; μεγάλη..μ. καὶ πλεονεξία ib.184; τὰ δεῖπνα πρὸς μερίδα γίγνεται Plu.2.644c; ἀποστείλαντος μερίδα τοῦ φίλου Thphr.*Char*.17. 2. 3. *plot* of ground, Lxx 4*Ki*.9.21, al., *CIL*11.1147 pp.iii 2, vi 86, al. (Veleia); μ. γῆς *PStrassb*.84.3 (ii B.C.). b. *region, district*, *PPetr*. 3 pp.28,78 (iii B.C.), *PTeb*.32.18 (ii B.C.), *OGI*177.12 (Egypt, ii/i B.C.), *Act.Ap*.16.12, etc. c. Astrol., ἡ κάτω μ. S.E.*M*.5.15. d. metaph., *province*, Jul. *ad Them*.266b. II. *division, class*, πολιτῶν E.*Supp*. 238, cf. Jul. *ad Them*.253c; esp. in political sense, *party, faction*, Pl. *Lg*.692b, D.18.64; ἡ Σύλλα μ. Plu.2.203b. III. = μέρος IV. 3, εἰς ἀρετῆς μερίδα τὸ ψεύσασθαι τιθέμενος Id.*Mar*.29; χρυσὸν ἐν οὐδενὸς μερίδι ποιήσασθαι Paus.10.28.4. IV. of persons, κακὰ μ. you bad *lot!* *AP*7.433 (Tymn.), cf. 355.3 (Damag.). ⊛ **-ισμα,** ατος, τό, *part*, Orph.*H*.11.16, prob. in *PStrassb*.107.6 (iii B.C.). **-ισμός,** ὁ, *dividing, division*, Pl.*Lg*.903b, Thphr.*CP*1.12.6, etc.; ὁ τῶν θεῶν ἔσχατος μ. ἄχρι τῆς ὕλης προῆλθεν Dam.*Pr*.134; esp. *apportionment, allocation* of funds, Arist.*Ath*.48.2; *distribution* of money, *SIG*364.81 (Ephesus, iii B.C.); of victims, ib.1017.16 (Sinope, iii B.C.); οὐκ ἔνεστιν οὐδὲ εἷς παρ' ἐμοὶ μ., 'going shares', Men.*Epit*.244. 2. *partition*, τῆς Ἀκαρνανίας Plb.9.34.7. 3. *share of taxation, assessment*, *PTeb*. 58.38 (ii B.C.), 29.15 (ii B.C.), *Ostr.Bodl*. ii 18,41 (ii A.D.). 4. *role, part assigned*, in a religious ceremony, *IG*2$^{2}$.1368.65 (ii A.D.). 5. kind of gymnastic, Gal.*Thras*.47. II. Rhet., *division of subjects, arrangement*, in writing, D.H.*Is*.3 (pl.). b. *the art of dividing* a whole *into its parts*, Hermog.*Id*.2.1. 2. in Logic, *assignment* of the elements of a contradiction, Arist.*Metaph*.1027$^{b}$20. b. *definition*, D.L.7.62. 3. in Gramm., *classification* of parts of speech, A.D. *Synt*.23.8 (hence, concretely, *class*, ib.48.9, 109.4); *distribution* of the functions of inflexions, opp. σύγχυσις, ib.95.17. b. *analysis* of a sentence *into its component parts, parsing*, ib.140.11, Sch.D.T.p.214 H.; cf. ἐπιμερισμός. 4. in Metric, ὁ μ. ὁ τῶν μέτρων *division into feet, scansion*, S.E.*M*.1.159; also ὁ κατὰ γραμματικὴν μ. *division* of a line *into words*, ib.161. 5. Math., *quotient*, Dioph.4.22. **-ιστέον,** *one must divide*, τὸ καθόλου εἰς γένη Aristox.*Harm*.p.4 M.; *one must distribute*, Eust.83.12. II. Adj. μεριστέος, α, ον, *to be divided*, Just.*Nov*.156.1. ⊛ **-ιστής,** οῦ, ὁ, *divider, distributor*, *Ev.Luc*.12. 14, Poll.4.176, *PMag.Leid.W*.14.42; μ. χρόνων ζωῆς, of the lord of the horoscope, Vett.Val.62.4:—fem. **-ίστρια,** Sch.rec.A.*Th*. 711. **-ιστικός,** ή, όν, *fit for dividing*, gloss on μερόεν, Hsch. **-ιστός,** ή, όν, *divided*, Pl.*Prm*.144d; τὸ κατὰ τὰ σώματα μ. Id.*Ti*.35a; μ. ψυχαί, φύσεις, *separate, individual*, Jul.*Or*.4.151c; δημιουργία ib. 144a, *Or*.5.179b, cf. Plot.1.1.8; ὁ μ. λόγος reason *with its inevitable distinctions*, Dam.*Pr*.41. II. *divisible*, Pl.*Prm*.131c; μ. ψυχὴ ἢ ἀμερής Arist. *de An*.402$^{b}$1; ἅπαν [συνεχὲς] εἰς ἄπειρα μ. Id.*Ph*.239$^{a}$22, cf. Timo 76; ὅσα μ. τοῖς κοινωνοῦσι τῆς πολιτείας *divisible among* them, Arist.*EN*1130$^{b}$32; τὸ μ. Iamb.*Comm.Math*.1. Adv. -τῶς Id. *Myst*.1.18, Porph.*Sent*.33, Procl.*Inst*.195.

⊛ **μερῑτ-εία,** ἡ, *division* of property, *PFay*.97.16 (i A.D.). II. = μεριδαρχία, Hsch., Phot. (ubi μεριτία). **-εύομαι,** Med., *divide among themselves*, Lxx *Jb*.40.25. **-ης,** ου, ὁ, (μερίς) *partaker, sharer*, τῆς ὠφελείας D.32.25, cf. Plb.4.29.6, Them.*Or*.5.71b, al.; τινί τινος *with* one *in* a thing, Plb.13.8.2: in pl., *joint-owners*, *IG*2.1058. 8. **-ικός,** ή, όν, *of a* μερίτης, Lyd.*Mag*.3.70, Just.*Nov*.123.16*Intr*.

**μερμαίρω,** = μερμηρίζω, Suid.; **μερμέρω,** Hsch., Phot.; οἱ ἅπαντα μερμαιρόμενοι, = μεμφόμενοι, Gal.17(2).189 (s. v. l.).

**μερμέριος,** α, ον, = sq., κακόν Luc.*Lex*.11 (nisi leg. Τερμέριον), cf. Them.*Or*.21.261b.

⊛ **μέρμερος,** ον, *baneful*, Hom. (only in Il.) always in neut. pl., μέρμερα μητίσασθαι to devise *mischief*, 10.48; μ. ῥέζων 11.502; μ. μήσατο ἔργα 10.289, cf. 524; in Hom. always of *warlike deeds*, πολέμοιο μ. ἔργα 8.453; but μ. ῥέζων, of Zeus, Orph.*Fr*.21a; μ. ἔργα γυναικῶν the *ills* that women work, Hes.*Th*.603; μ. κακόν E.*Rh*. 509; βλάβη Lyc.949; ἀδρανίη Nic.*Th*.248. II. of persons, *captious, fastidious*, Pl.*Hp.Ma*.290e; ἔθνος Λατίνων D.P.350; μ. χρῆμα *crafty* creature, of a fox, Plu.2.988a; of a hound, Opp.*C*.1.490.—Ep. word, used in E. and Pl. ll. cc.

**μέρμηρ-ᾰ,** ἡ, poet. form of μέριμνα (not in Hom.), *care, trouble*, ἄμπαυμα μερμηράων rest *from troubles*, Hes.*Th*.55, cf. Thgn.1325; ἔρρετε μέρμηραι θυμαλγέες *IG*14.1942. 2. *morning-nap*, Sch.Ar. *V*.5, Hsch. ⊛ **-ίζω,** fut. -ίξω Od.16.261: Ep. aor. μερμήριξα (v. infr.): I. intr., *to be anxious* or *thoughtful, to be in doubt*: folld. by ὡς, etc., μερμήριζε κατὰ φρένα, ὡς Ἀχιλῆα τιμήσῃ *was debating* how he should.., Il.2.3; μερμήριξε.., ὅππως ἐξαπάφοιτο Διὸς νόον 14.159; μερμήριζεν, ὅπως ἀπολοίατο πᾶσαι νῆες Od.9.554: more freq. διάνδιχα μερμήριξεν, ἤ.., ἦε.. *debated anxiously* whether .., or.., Il.1.189; μερμήριξε δ' ἔπειτα κατὰ φρένα καὶ κατὰ θυμόν, ἤ.., ἤ.. 5.671; δίχα δὲ φρεσὶ μερμήριζεν, ἤ.., ἤ.. Od.22.333; δίχα θυμὸς ἐνὶ φρεσὶ μερμηρίζει, ἤ.., ἤ.. 16.73: c. aor. inf., διάνδιχα μ., ἵππους τε στρέψαι καὶ ἐναντίβιον μαχέσασθαι *debated anxiously* with himself, whether to turn back and fight (or not..), Il.8.167, cf. Od.10.438: with inf. in first clause and ἤ in second, μερμήριξε..κύσσαι καὶ περιφῦναι.., ἦ πρῶτ' ἐξερέοιτο 24.235 sq.: c. acc. rei, ἤ τι περὶ Τρώων..μερμηρίζεις; Il.20.17. II. trans., *devise, contrive*, πολλὰ φρεσὶ μερμηρίζων Od.1.427; ἀεικέα μ. 4.533, al.; δόλον..ἐνὶ φρεσὶ μ. 2.93; φόνον ἡμῖν μερμηρίζει ib.325; εἰ δύνασαί τιν' ἀμύντορα μερμηρίξαι 16.256.—Ep. Verb, censured in Prose by Luc.*Hist.Conscr*. 22, *Bis Acc*.2. ⊛ **-ικοί,** οἱ, = πειρᾶται, Hsch.

⊛ **μερμίλλων,** ωνος, ὁ, = Lat. *mirmillo* (*murmillo*), a light-armed gladiator, *CIG*3392 (Smyrna); **μορμίλλων,** pl. -ονες, *IG*12(8).547 (Thasos); **μουρμίλλων,** *CIG*2889 (Milet.); **μυρμύλλων,** *IGRom*.1. 773 (Hadrianopolis).

⊛ **μέρμῑς,** ῑθος, ἡ, *cord, string, rope*, Od.10.23, D.S.3.21 (v.l. μέρμινθα): dat. pl. μερμίθαις from **μέρμῑθα,** Agatharch.47; **μέρμῑθος,** ὁ, Hsch., Zonar. (Cf. μήρινθος.)

⊛ **μέρμνος,** ὁ, a sort of *hawk*, Call.*Aet.Oxy*.2080.68, Ael.*NA*12.4:—spelt **μέρμνης** in Hsch., *An.Ox*.1.64.

**μερόεν·** μεριστικόν, Hsch.

**μεροπήϊος,** ον, (μέροψ) *human*, ἔργα, γενεή, Man.4.215,474, cf. Opp. *C*.2.364:—fem. **-ηΐς,** ΐδος, ib.1.23.

**μεροποιός,** όν, *creating parts*, κίνησις πολλοποιὸς καὶ μ. Dam.*Pr*.221.

**μεροποσπόρος,** ον, *begetting men*, ὥρη Man.4.577.

⊛ **μέρος,** εος, τό, (μείρομαι) first in *h.Cer*.399 (v. infr. IV), *h.Merc*.53 (v. infr. II. 2):—*share, portion*, Pi.*O*.8.77, Hdt.1.145, *Berl.Sitzb*. 1927.167 (Cyrene), etc.; μέρος ἔχοντα Μουσᾶν B.3.71; ἔχει δόμων μ. E.*Ph*.483; κτεάνων μ. A.*Ag*.1574 (anap.); συμβαλέσθαι τὸ μ. D.41. 11; τὰ μ. τινῶν κομίζεσθαι ibid.; λαβεῖν τῆς μεθόδου τὸ μ. Arist. *Pol*.1295$^{a}$3; of work put out to contract, *allotment*, *IG*2$^{2}$.463.7, 26. 2. *heritage, lot, destiny*, μεθέξειν τάφου μ. A.*Ag*.507; ἔχετον κοινοῦ θανάτου μ. S.*Ant*.147 (anap.); τοῦτο γὰρ..σπάνιον μ. is a rare *portion*, E.*Alc*.474 (lyr.); ἀπὸ μέρους προτιμᾶσθαι from *considerations of rank* or *family*, Th.2.37. II. *one's turn*, ἐπεί τε αὐτῆς μ. ἐγίνετο τῆς ἀπίξιος Hdt.3.69; μ. ἑκατέρῳ νέμειν Id.2.173; ὅταν ἥκῃ μ. ἔργων *the turn* or *time* for.., A.*Ch*.827 (lyr.), cf. Pl.*R*.540b; ἀγγέλου μ. *his turn of duty* as messenger, A.*Ag*.291. 2. with Preps., ἀνὰ μέρος *in turn, successively*, E.*Ph*.478, Arist.*Pol*.1287$^{a}$17; κατὰ μέρος *h.Merc*.53, Th.4.26, etc.; κατὰ μ. λέγειν *severally*, Pl.*Tht*.157b; κατὰ μέρη ἄκουε ib.182b; τὰ κατὰ μέρος the *particulars*, Phld.*Sign*. 23, *D*.1.22; τὸ κατὰ μ. ἄστρον ib.3.9; ἐν μέρεϊ *in turn*, Hdt.1.26, al.; κλῦθί νυν ἐν μ., ἀντάκουσον ἐν μ., A.*Ch*.332 (lyr.), *Eu*.198; *by turns, in succession*, Id.*Ag*.332, 1192, Th.8.93; ἐν μ. καὶ ἐφεξῆς Pl. *Lg*.819b; ἐν τῷ μέρει *in one's turn*, Hdt.5.70, E.*Or*.452, Ar.*Ra*.32, 497, Pl.*Grg*.462a; ἐν τῷ μ. καὶ παρὰ τὸ μ. *in* and *out of turn*, X.*An*. 7.6.36; παρὰ μέρος *in turn, by turns*, ἄρχειν Plu.*Fab*.10, cf. Ant. Lib.30.1, Nicom.*Ar*.1.8.10, Iamb. *in Nic*.p.33 P.; [ἡ ψυχὴ] παρὰ μ. ἐν τῇ γενέσει γίνεται καὶ ἐν τοῖς θεοῖς ἐστιν Procl.*Inst*.206 (but also, *partially*, Alciphr.3.66). III. *the part one takes in* a thing, μέτεστι χὐμῖν τῶν πεπραγμένων μ. E.*IT*1299; ὑμέτερον μ. [ἐστί] c. inf., Pl.*La*.180a. 2. freq. in periphrases, τοὐμὸν μέρος, τὸ σὸν μ., *my*

or *thy part*, i.e. simply *I* or *me*, *thou* or *thee*, ὅσον τὸ σὸν μ. S.*OT*1509, cf. *Ant.*1062, Pl.*Cri.*45d: abs. as Adv., τοὐμὸν μ. *as to me*, οὐ καμῇ τοὐμὸν μ. S.*Tr.*1215, cf. E.*Heracl.*678; τὸ σὸν μέρος *as to thee*, S.*OC*1366; τοὐκείνου μ. E.*Hec.*989: rarely, κατὰ τὸ σὸν μ. Pl.*Ep.* 328e. IV. *part*, opp. the whole, ὡρέων τρίτατον μ. *h.Cer.*399, etc.; τρίτον κασιγνητᾶν μ., i.e. one of three sisters, Pi.*P.*12.11; μέρει τινὶ τῶν βαρβάρων Th.1.1; τὰ δύο μ. two-thirds, ib.104, Aeschin. 3.143, D.59.101; τρία μέρη.., τὸ δὲ τέταρτον Nic.Dam.130.17 J.; οὐδὲν ἂν μέρος οὖσαι φανεῖεν τῶν.. no *fraction* of.., i.e. infinitesimal compared with.., Isoc.5.43, cf. 12.54; ὅσα ἄλλα μ. ἐντὸς τοῦ Ἴστρου *parts of the country*, *regions*, Th.2.96, cf. 4.98; ξυγκαταδουλοῦν..τὸ τῆς θαλάσσης μ., i.e. the sea *as their part* of the business, Id.8.46: hence, *branch*, *business*, *matter*, Men.*Epit.*17, *Pk.*107, Plb.1.4.2, 1.20.8, al., *PRyl.*127 (i A.D.); τὰ τοῦ σώματος μέλη καὶ μ. Pl.*Lg.*795e; *division* of an army, X.*An.*6.4.23, etc.; *class* or *party*, Th.2.37, D.18.292; of the *factions* in the circus, πρασίνων μ. *POxy.*145.2 (vi A.D.); *party* in a contract or lawsuit, *BGU*168.24 (ii A.D.), *PRein.*44.34 (ii A.D.); *caste*, Str.15.1.39:—special uses, in Geom., *direction*, ἐπὶ θάτερον μ. interpol. in Archim.*Aequil.*1.13, cf. Euc.1.27, al.: Arith., *submultiple*, Id.7 *Def.*3, 4; τὰ μ. the *denominators* of fractions, Hero *Stereom.*2.14: Gramm., μ. τῆς λέξεως *part* of speech, Arist.*Po.*1456$^{b}$20, D.H.*Comp.* 2: more freq. μ. λόγου D.T.634.4, A.D.*Pron.*4.6, al.; μ. λόγου, also, = *word*, S.E.*M.*1.159, Heph.1.4 (v. λόγος IX. 3c); *section* of a document, Mitteis *Chr.*28.30 (iii B.C.), etc. 2. abs. as Adv., μέρος τι *in part*, Th.4.30, etc.; μέρος μέν τι.., μέρος δέ τι.. X.*Eq.*1.12; τὸ πλεῖστον μ. for the most *part*, D.S.22.10. b. with Preps., κατά τι μέρος Pl.*Lg.*757e; κατὰ τὸ πολὺ μ. Id.*Ti.*86d; ἐκ μέρους in *part*, γινώσκομεν 1*Ep.Cor.*13.9 (but ἐκ μ. τινός by the *side* of, Lxx 1*Ki.* 6.8; ἐκ μ. τῶν ὁρίων ib.*Nu.*20.16; ἐκ τοῦ ἑνὸς μέρους ib.8.2); ἐκ τοῦ πλείστου μ. for the most *part*, Hdn.8.2.4; ἀπὸ μέρους in *part*, Antip.*Stoic.*3.249, *BGU*1201.15 (i A.D.), 2*Ep.Cor.*2.5; ἐπὶ μέρους Luc.*Bis Acc.*2; τὰς ἐπὶ μέρους γράφειν πράξεις *special* histories, Plb. 7.7.6; αἱ ἐπὶ μ. συντάξεις Id.3.32.10; πρὸς μέρος *in proportion*, Th. 6.22, D.36.32. 3. ἐν μέρει τινὸς τιθέναι, etc., to put *in the class of*.., consider *as* so and so, εἰ ἐν ἀρετῆς τιθεῖς μέρει τὴν ἀδικίαν Pl.*R.*348e; οὐ τίθημ' ἐν ἀδικήματος μ. D.23.148; also ἐν τεκμηρίου μ. ποιεῖσθαι τἀδίκημα Id.44.50; ἐν οὐδενὸς εἶναι μ. to be *as* no one, Id.2.18; μήτ' ἐν ἀνθρώπου μ. μήτ' ἐν θεοῦ ζῆν Alex.240.2; ἐν προσθήκης μ. *as* an appendage, D.11.8; ἐν ὑπηρέτου καὶ προσθήκης μ. γίγνεσθαι Id.3.31; ἐν χάριτος μ. Id.21.165; τοῦτ' ἐν εὐεργεσίας ἀριθμήσει μ. ib.166; ἐν ἰδιώτου μ. διαγαγεῖν Isoc.9.24; ὡς ἐν παιδιᾶς μ. Pl.*R.*424d; also εἰς εὐεργεσίας μέρος καταθέσθαι D.23.17. 4. in local sense, *district*, *POxy.*2113.25 (iv A.D.). 5. in Neo-Platonism, *by way of species* or *element*, ἐν μέρει καὶ ὡς στοιχεῖον Dam.*Pr.*193; οὕτω ὁ μέγας Ἰάμβλιχος ἐνόησεν τὸ ἓν ὂν ἐν μέρει ἑκάτερον ib.176; πάντα μὲν ἅμα, ἐν μέρει δὲ ἕκαστον Plot.3.6.18.

⊛ **μέροψ**, *οπος*, ὁ, poet. word, used only in pl. as epith. of men, derived by Gramm. from μείρομαι, ὄψ, *dividing the voice*, i.e. *articulate* (cf. Hsch., Sch.Il.1.250), μ. ἄνθρωποι Il.l.c., Hes.*Op.*109, etc.; μ. βροτοί Il.2.285; μερόπεσσι λαοῖς A.*Supp.*90 (lyr.): hence as Subst., = ἄνθρωποι, Musae.*Fr.*13 D., A.*Ch.*1018 (anap.), E.*IT*1263 (lyr.), A.R.4.536, Call.*Fr.*418, *AP*7.563 (Paul. Sil.); a usage satirized by Strato Com., 1.6 sq. II. in sg. and pl., *bee-eater*, *Merops apiaster*, Arist.*HA*615$^{b}$25, Plu.2.976d; cf. εἴροψ.

**μέρτρυξ**, = γεράνιον, Ps.-Dsc.3.116.

**μερύτης**· ἀναιδής, Hsch. **μερῶν**· ἐλάσσων, Id. **μέρωον**· πωλίον, Id.

**μές**, Dor. for μέν, Greg.Cor.p.364 S. (perh. meaning the verbal endings -μες, -μεν).

⊛ **μέσᾰβον**, τό, (μέσος, βοῦς) *leathern strap*, by which the middle of the yoke was fastened to the pole, Hes.*Op.*469: Ep. pl. μέσσαβα Call.*Fr.*513 (expld. by Sch.Hes. as αἱ τοῦ ζυγοῦ γλυφαί): also masc. μέσαβοι Tz. ad Hes. l.c.:—v.l. **μεσάβοιον**, Poll.1.252.

⊛ **μεσᾰβόω**, poet. **μεσσ-**, *yoke*, *put to*, Lyc.817.

⊛ **μεσ-άγκῠλον**, τό, *javelin with a thong* (ἀγκύλη) for throwing it by, E.*Ph.*1141, *Andr.*1133, Men.562.2, Plb.22.3.9. **-άγριος** or **-άγροικος**, *ον*, *half-savage*, Str.13.1.25.

**μεσάδιος** [ᾰ], *α*, *ον*, *central*, Aeol. form acc. to Sch.D.T.p.542 H.

⊛ **μεσάζω**, = μεσόω, ὁ μεσάζων τόπος (v.l. νησίζων) D.S.1.32; πότερον ἄρχοιτο τὸ πάθος ἢ μεσάζοι Hp.*Ep.*18; νυκτὸς μεσαζούσης Lxx *Wi.* 18.14; μεσαζούσης ἡμέρας Hdn.7.5.2; of food, *to be half-cooked*, Bilabel Ὀψαρτ.p.11. II. Pass., *to be inserted in the middle*, *intervene*, αἱ μεσαζόμεναι λέξεις A.D.*Synt.*270.5, cf. *Conj.*255.20; of terms in an arithmetical series, *Theol.Ar.*39. 2. *occupy a central position*, τὴν γῆν ὁ μῦθος λέγει μεσάζεσθαι Eust.1389.38.

**μεσαῖος**, *α*, *ον*, = μέσος, Antiph.181: neut. as Subst., *middle*, Id. 72.

**μεσαιπόλιος**, *ον*, *half-grey*, *grizzled*, i.e. *middle-aged*, Il.13.361, App.*Hann.*6, Aesop.56, Tryph.168, Zos.1.51, *AP*5.233 (Paul. Sil.).

**μεσαίτατος**, **-τερος**, v. μέσος VI.

**μεσαίχμιον**, τό, (αἰχμή) = μεταίχμιον, Hsch.; possibly to be read in J.*BJ*5.1.4, D.C.*Fr.*5.5:—also Adj. **μεσαίχμιος**, γῆ Hsch.

⊛ **μέσακλον**, τό, *weaver's beam*, Lxx 1*Ki.*17.7:—but **μέσακμον**, Hsch., **μέσατμον**, Suid.

**μεσακόθεν**, Adv. (dissim. from *μεσαχόθεν), *in the midst*, *between*, *Schwyzer*664.7 (Orchom. Arc., iv B.C.).

**μέσακτος**, *ον*, (ἀκτή) *half-way between two shores*, *in mid-sea*, A. *Pers.*889 (lyr.): **μεσάκτιος**, *ον*, Sch. ad loc. II. (ἄγνυμι) *broken mid-way*, πλευρά A.*Fr.*210.

**μεσ-αμβρίη**, **-αμβρινός**, **-αμέριος**, v. μεσημ-. **μεσανύκτιον**, v. μεσο-.

**μεσ-άραιον** (sc. δέρμα), τό, = μεσεντέριον, Gal.2.561, Ruf.*Anat.* 50: pl., Steph. *in Hp.*1.134 D.:—hence Adj. **-αραϊκαὶ** φλέβες ib. 139 D.

**μεσάτιον**, τό, = μέσαβον, Poll.1.148, cf. 142.

**μέσᾰτος**, v. μέσσατος. II. Subst. μ., ὁ, *arbitrator*, *PKlein. Form.*402 (vi A.D.).

**μεσ-αύλη**, ἡ, = μέσαυλος I, prob. in Möller *Pap.Berl.Mus.*3.13 (vi A.D.). ⊛ **-αύλιον**, τό, (αὐλός) *piece of flute-music*, played in the intervals of the choral song, *Vit.Aesop.Oxy.*2083.27, Eust.862.19:—hence **-αυλικὰ** κρούματα Aristid.Quint.1.11. **-αύλιος**, *ον*, v.l. for μέσαυλος in Ph.2.327, cf. Phot., Suid. **-αυλον**, τό, v. sq. ⊛ **-αυλος**, *ον*, Ep. **μέσσ-**, Att. **μέτ-**: (αὐλή): I. in Hom. μέσσαυλος, ὁ, or μέσσαυλον, τό (gender unknown), prob. *the inner court*, *inside the* αὐλή, where cattle were put at night, Il.11.548, 17.112, 657, 24.29; used of the cave of the Cyclops, Od.10.435. II. Att. Prose and Com. μέταυλος (sc. θύρα), ἡ, *the door between the* αὐλή *and the inner part of the house*, Ar.*Fr.*371; in full, μέταυλος θύρα Lys.1.17; also θύραι μέσαυλοι E.*Alc.*549; *mesauloe*, Vitr.6.7.5. **-αύχην**, *ενος*, ὁ, *bound in the middle of the neck*, μεσαύχενας νέκυας, comically for wineskins (ἀσκοί), Ar.*Fr.*725 (v.l. δεσαύχενας Hsch., Phot., βυσαύχενας Poll.2.135 cod. A).

**μέσδων**, *ον*, Aeol. and Dor. for μέζων, μείζων (v. μέγας C).

**μεσεγγῠ-άω**, Act. only in aor. inf. μεσεγγυῆσαι Poll.8.28:—*deposit a pledge in the hands of a third party*, in Pass., τρία τάλαντα μεσεγγυηθέντα *being so deposited*, Lys.29.6:—Med., μεσεγγυήσασθαι ἀργύριον *have one's* money *deposited in the hands of a third party*, D. 30.3, cf. Antipho 6.50. ⊛ **-η**, ἡ, *security by means of a third party*, *Gloss.* **-ημα**, *ατος*, τό, *money* or *pledge deposited with a third party*, X.ap.Poll.8.28, Aeschin.3.125, Hyp.*Fr.*254, App.*BC*2.19, *BGU*592 ii 9 (ii A.D.). **-όομαι**, Med., = μεσεγγυάομαι, Isoc.13. 5:—Pass., τὸ μεσεγγυωθέν Pl.*Lg.*914d (v.l. -ηθέν). ⊛ **-ος**, ὁ, *third party*, *with whom a security is deposited*, Mitteis *Chr.*88.13 (ii A.D.), Hsch. II. **μεσέγγυον**, τό, *deposit*, *IG*7.3172.69 (Orchom. Boeot.). **-ωμα**, *ατος*, τό, = μεσεγγύημα, v.l. in Isoc.12.13.

**μεσειδιόω**, v. μεσιδιόω.

**μεσεμβολ-έω**, *intercalate* mean terms in a series, Nicom.*Ar.*1. 19:—Pass., Iamb. *in Nic.*p.85 P., *Theol.Ar.*39. II. Astrol., *intercept* the influence of a planet, Vett.Val.102.10, *Cat.Cod.Astr.*1.107 (Pass.), Porph. *in Ptol.*188; τὸν ἥλιον -ῆσαι τοῖς ἑπτὰ κοσμοκράτορσι Dam.*Pr.*341:—Pass., ὁ ἥλιος πανταχοῦ μεμεσεμβόληται ibid. III. θάλασσα μεσεμβολεῖ τοὺς Αἰθίοπας *comes in the middle of* the E., Str. *Chr.*1.32. **-ημα**, *ατος*, τό, *interval* between zodiacal signs, Heph.Astr.1.1. II. *parenthesis*, Sch.Opp.*H.*1.409, Sch.E.*Hec.* 705. **-ησις**, *εως*, ἡ, Astrol., *intervention* of a planetary influence, *interception*, Antioch.Astr. in *Cat.Cod.Astr.*8(3).107, Porph. *in Ptol.* 188. **-ία**, ἡ, = foreg., *Cat.Cod.Astr.*1.107 (pl.). **-ος**, *ον*, *intercepted*, Vett.Val.102.15.

**μεσ-εντέριον** (sc. δέρμα), τό, *membrane to which the intestines are attached*, Arist.*HA*495$^{b}$32, *PA*678$^{a}$14, etc.:—also **-έντερον**, τό, ib. $^{a}$15 (s.v.l.), Ruf.*Anat.*50. ⊛ **-έρκειος**, *ον*, (ἕρκος) *in the middle of the house*: Ζεὺς μ., = ἑρκεῖος, Hsch. (-έρκιος), Sch.Il.16.231. **-ευθύς**, ύ, gen. *εος*, *between the even ones*: Pythag. name for the number 6, as *half-way between* 2 *and* 10, the first and last of the even (εὐθεῖς) numbers in the denary scale, Clem.Al.*Strom.*6.139.2.

**μεσεύς**, *έως*, ὁ, = καικίας, Steph. *in Hp.*2.351 D.; cf. μέσης.

**μεσεύω**, *keep the middle* or *mean between* two, c. gen., Pl.*Lg.*756e; Πλάτων μεσεύων Πυθαγόρου καὶ Σωκράτους, τοῦ μὲν δημοτικώτερος τοῦ δὲ σεμνότερος ὤφθη Numen.ap.Eus.*PE*14.5. 2. abs., *stand midway*, μ. κατὰ τοὺς τόπους Arist.*Pol.*1327$^{b}$29. b. *to be neutral*, X. *HG*7.1.43, D.C.41.46.

⊛ **μέση** (sc. χορδή), ἡ, the *mese*, i.e. the top note of the lower tetrachord in the octave, originally the *middle string* of the seven-stringed (or of an earlier three-stringed) lyre, Pl.*R.*443d (cf. Sch.), Arist.*Metaph.*1018$^{b}$29, *Pr.*919$^{b}$20, Euc.*Sect.Can.*10; variously defined, Ptol.*Harm.*2.5, Cleonid.*Harm.*11, Bacch.*Harm.*65:—Dor. **μέσσα** Philol.6. II. Geom., *mean proportional*, v. μέσος III. 5. III. in punctuation (sc. στιγμή), dot placed midway between top and bottom of line, functioning as a *comma*, Satyr.6, D.T.630. 6, Sch.D.T.p.177 H.

⊛ **μεσηγύ**, Ep. **μεσσηγύ**, before a vowel or metri gr. **μεσσηγύς**—all in Hom.; **μεσηγύς** only in Orph.*Fr.*94: Adv., I. of Space, 1. abs., *in the middle*, *between*, οὐδέ τι πολλὴ χώρη μεσσηγύς Il.23.521, cf. 11.573; μηδέ τι μεσσηγύς γε..πάθῃσι *in mid-voyage*, Od.7.195. 2. more freq. c. gen., *between*, ὤμων μ. Il.8.259; στηθέων Theoc.25. 237; Κουρήτων τε μ. καὶ Αἰτωλῶν Il.9.549; μ. γαίης τε καὶ οὐρανοῦ 5.769; μ. Ἰθάκης τε Σάμοιό τε Od.4.845; μ. κόρυθός τε καὶ ἀσπίδος Hes.*Sc.*417; μ. θέρεός τε καὶ ὑετίου κρυστάλλου Eratosth.16.16. II. of Time, *meanwhile*, Aret.*CA*1.10; μεσηγὺ τούτου τοῦ χρόνου Hp. *Fract.*8. III. as Subst., τὸ μεσηγύ *the part between*, *h.Ap.*108, Thgn.553; τὸ μ. τῶν ὠμοπλατέων Hp.*Art.*16; ἤματος τὸ μεσηγύ *noon*, Theoc.25.216. IV. of quality, Orph.l.c. [ῠ exc. Od.4.845 μεσσηγὺς Ἰθάκης τε...]

**μεσ-ήεις**, *εσσα*, *εν*, *middling* (between ἔξοχος and χερειότερος), Il. 12.269. **-ῆλιξ**, *ικος*, ὁ, ἡ, *middle-aged*, Artem.1.31, Poll.2.12, *Gp.*1.12.16, Hsch.

⊛ **μεσημβρ-ία** (μέσος, ἡμέρα), Ion. **μεσαμβρίη** Hdt. (v. infr.), Arr. *Ind.*3.8, al.: ἡ:—*midday*, Ζεὺς ἐκ μεσημβρίης ἔθηκε νύκτα Archil.74.

3; ἐν μεσημβρίας θάλπει A.*Supp.*746; ἀποκλιναμένης τῆς μεσαμβρίης Hdt.3.104; μεσαμβρίης at *noon*, ibid.; ἔτρωγ'.. σῦκα τῆς μεσημβρίας Ar.*Fr.*463, cf. Eub.106, Pherecr.80, Ar.*V.*500; τῇ μεσαμβρίῃ Hdt. l.c.; ἐν μεσημβρίᾳ Th.6.100; νύκτα ἐν μ. ἐπαγόμενοι Pl.*Lg.*897d; ἅμα μεσημβρίᾳ X.*HG*5.3.1; ἐκ μεσημβρίας just after *noon*, Pl.*Ax.* 372; σμικρόν τι μετὰ μεσημβρίαν Ar.*Av.*1499; ἤδη ἦν μ. Pl.*Smp.* 220c; μ. ἵσταται 'tis high *noon*, Id.*Phdr.*242a. II. *the South*, Μολοσσῶν πρὸς μεσημβρίης Hecat.108J.; [ποταμὸς] ῥέων ἀπὸ μεσαμβρίης Hdt.1.6; κεῖται πόλις πρὸς μεσαμβρίην ib.142; τὰ πρὸς μ. Id.7. 113, cf. *IG*7.3073.95 (Lebad., ii B.C.). [μεσημβρῑη *APl.*4.369.] **-ιάζω**, *pass the noon*: μεσημβριάζοντα εὕδειν to sleep *at noon*, Pl.*Phdr.* 259a. 2. of the sun or stars, *culminate*, Poll.4.157,158; μεσημβριάζοντος τοῦ θεοῦ Porph.*Antr.*27. **-ιάς**, άδος, pecul. fem. of μεσημβρινός, Nonn.*D.*48.590. **-ιάω**, poet. for μεσημβριάζω I, part. -ιάων *AP*9.764 (Paul. Sil.). 2. = μεσημβριάζω 2, Ep. part. μεσημβριόων A.R.2.739, *Hymn.Mag.*2(2).20. ❋**-ίζω**, = μεσημβριάζω I, Str.15.1. 21, J.*AJ*7.2.1. **-ινός**, ή, όν, for μεσημερινός, Dor. **μεσαμβρινός**, ά, όν, *belonging to noon, noontide*, εὖτε πόντος ἐν μεσημβριναῖς κοίταις .. εὕδοι πεσών A.*Ag.*565; μεσημβρινοῖσι θάλπεσι in the *noonday* heats, Id.*Th.*431, cf. 381, Ar.*Av.*1096; κἂν ἔγρῃ μεσημβρινός Id.*V.*774, cf. *Ach.*40; μ. δαιμόνιον LXX *Ps.*90(91).6; ὁ μ. ᾠδός, of the cicada, *AP* 9.584.11; τὸ μεσαμβρινόν *at noon*, Theoc.1.15, 10.48, Luc.*Anach.*25: without the Art., Nic.*Th.*401; ὁ μ. κύκλος *the meridian*, Euc.*Phaen.* p.6 M., Gem.2.25: without κύκλος, Arist.*Mete.*362ᵇ11, 375ᵇ29, Hipparch.3.1.1, al., Str.2.1.10, Cleom.1.8, etc., cf. Theo Sm.p.131 H. II. *southern*, κέλευθος A.*Pr.*722; τὰ μεσημβρινά Th.6.2, Str. 2.1.12, etc.: Comp. -ώτερος Gem.14.10, Anon.*Geog.Comp.*18: Sup. -ώτατος Str.2.5.33, etc. [ῐ, but ῑ metri gr., on the analogy of ὀπωρινός, Call.*Lav.Pall.*72,73, Opp.*C.*2.17.] **-ιος**, α, ον, = foreg. II, [ῠδ.τα] Ruf.ap.Orib.5.3.17: **-ιον**, τό, = *meridies, Gloss.* **-ιστός**, ὁ, = ὡροσκόπος, dub. in Ps.-Ptol.*Centil.*49.

❋ **μεσ-ημέριος**, ον, = μεσημβρινός: τὸ μεσαμέριον *at midday*, Theoc.7. 21:—also -ήμερον, τό, *Gloss.* **-ήπειρος**, ον, *inland*, D.P.211, 1068.

**μεσηρ-εύω**, *to be neutral*, Philist.61. ❋**-ης**, poet. μεσσ-, ες, *in the middle, midmost*, γαίας ἕδρα E.*Ion*910 (lyr.); Σείριος ἔτι μ. is still *in mid-heaven*, Id.*IA*8 (anap.); μ. παντὸς Ὀλύμπου Eratosth.16.1.

**μέσης**, ου, ὁ, *a wind between* ἀπαρκτίας *and* καικίας, Arist.*Mete.*363ᵇ 30, 364ᵇ21; cf. μεσεύς.

**μεσήτιος**, ον, = μέσος, Hsch.

**μεσιάνη**, ἡ, name of a plaster, Gal.13.877.

**μεσίδι-ον**, τό, *object deposited* with a neutral party, *PSI*6.551. 10 (iii B.C.), *PMagd.*30.3 (iii B.C.), dub. in *PCair.Zen.*44.26 (iii B.C.). **-ος**, α, ον, = μέσος, [δικαστής] μ., = μεσίτης, Arist.*EN* 1132ᵃ23; ἄρχων μ. Id.*Pol.*1306ᵃ28. **-όω**, *deposit with* a neutral party or trustee, χειρόγραφόν τινι *PRein.*7.22 (ii B.C.):—Pass., ib. 32, *SIG*633.87 (Milet., ii B.C., written μεσειδ-): condemned by Phryn.98.

❋**μεσῑτ-εία**, ἡ, *mediation*, J.*AJ*20.3.2, Jul.*Mis.*354d; *arbitration*, *BGU*1676.5 (ii A.D.), 98.23 (iii A.D.), etc.; μ. κρίσεων Vett.Val.2.27 (pl.). 2. *pledging, mortgaging*, *BGU*445.9 (iii A.D.), etc. 3. *negotiation*, Babr.93.8. II. *lying between*, Nicom.*Ar.*1.7. ❋**-εύω**, *act as arbiter* or *mediator*, J.*AJ*16.4.3, *BGU*709.18 (ii A.D.), Babr.39. 2, etc.; τισι *BGU*906.7 (i A.D.), etc.; μ. ὅρκῳ *Ep.Hebr.*6.17; *act as go-between*, τῇ Πασιφάῃ πρὸς τὸν ἔρωτα τοῦ ταύρου Eust.1166.25. 2. trans., *mediate, negotiate*, τὴν διάλυσιν μ. Plb.11.34.3; τὰς συνθήκας *OGI*437.76 (Pergam., i B.C.), D.H.9.59, D.S.19.71; τὰς διαλλαγάς Nic.Dam.130.29J. 3. *pledge, mortgage* property, *CPR*1.19 (i A.D.), etc. 4. = μεσιδιόω, χειρόγραφον παρά τινι Möller *Pap.Berl. Mus.*2.11 (Pass., i A.D.), Suid. 5. *add as a third constituent*, χάλκανθον Zos.Alch.p.113B. II. intr., τὰ χρήματα μ. *lies on deposit with a stakeholder*, Plb.*Fr.*183. 2. *lie between*, μονάδος καὶ δεκάδος *Theol.Ar.*44. ❋**-ης**, ου, ὁ, *mediator, umpire, arbitrator*, *PLille* 28.11 (iii B.C.), Plb.28.17.8 (pl.), *Ep.Gal.*3.19, etc.; τῶν ὁμολογιῶν D.S.4. 54; θεοῦ καὶ ἀνθρώπων 1 *Ep.Ti.*2.5; *stakeholder*, *PStrassb.*1.41.14 (iii A.D.). 2. fem. μεσῖτις, ιδος, φιλίας μεσῖτιν τράπεζαν παραθέμενοι Luc.*Am.*27; φιλίας μ. ἡδονή ib.54. II. *in a middle position*, of a limb, Gal.18(2).861.

❋ **μέσκος**, ὁ, = κῴδιον, Nic.*Fr.*119.

**μέσμα**· μέστωμα, Hsch.

**μεσοβᾰσῐλ-εία**, ἡ, = Lat. *interregnum*, Plu.*Num.*2, D.C.39.31. **-ειος**, ον, *belonging to an interrex*, ἀρχή D.H.2.57. **-εύς**, έως, ὁ, = Lat. *interrex*, ib.58, Plu.*Num.*7, D.C.39.27.

**μεσό-βῐος**, ον, *of moderate means*, Serapio in *Cat.Cod.Astr.*8(4). 229, Vett.Val.233.17. **-βρᾰχυς**, υ, *having a short syllable in the middle*, name of the foot – – ᴗ – –, Diom.p.481 K. ❋**-γαιος**, ον, also α, ον, *inland, in the heart of a country*, μ. οἰκέειν Hdt.1.145; τὴν μ. τῆς ὁδοῦ the *inland* road, Id.7.124, 9.89; πόλεις Plb.2.5.2; ὁ μ., opp. οἱ παράκτιοι, *IG*5(2).268.25 (Mantinea, i B.C.): Comp. μεσογαιότερος (v.l. -ειό-) Str.13.1.51: Att. also **μεσόγεως**, ων, Pl.*Lg.*909c; Ep. **μεσσόγεως** Call.*Dian.*37. II. as Subst. μεσόγαια, ἡ, *inland parts, interior*, Hdt.1.175, 2.7,9, etc.; **μεσόγεια**, ἡ, Th.1.100,120, 6.88, D.18.301:—also **μεσόγαια**, τά, App.*BC*4.53. 2. μεσόγεια, ἡ, *continent*, Call.*Del.*168. III. Μεσόγειοι, οἱ, *inhabitants of the interior* of Attica, *IG*2².1245. **-γάστωρ**, ορος, ὁ, either, *one who is amidships*; or, *girt about the waist*, Epic.ap.Hsch. **-γεωτικός**, ή, όν, *inland, Gloss.* **-γονάτιον** [ᾰ], τό, (γόνυ) *space between two knots* or *joints*, Thphr.*HP*4.11.6. **-γρᾰφος**, ον, *written in the middle*: τὸ μ. *a mean proportional* found by the μεσόλαβος, Eratosth. 35.11 (pl.); μεσόγραφοι γραμμαί Plu.*Marc.*14. **-δάκτῠλον**, τό, *space between two fingers* or *toes*, Dsc.4.186 (condemned by Phryn. 172). **-δάκτυλος**, ὁ, *middle phalanx* of a finger, *Cat.Cod.Astr.* 7.238. **-δερκής**, ές, *looking towards the middle*: μ. ἀτραπός, = μεσουράνημα, Man.4.583.

**μεσόδμη**, ἡ, (δέμω, cf. *EM*581.5) Att. **μεσόμνη** *IG*2².1668.48,53:—*tie-beam*, τοῖχοι μεγάρων καλαί τε μεσόδμαι Od.19.37, cf. 20.354 (expld. by Aristarch. as = μεσόστυλα, by others as τὰ μεταξὺ τῶν δοκῶν διαστήματα, cf. Hsch.); κρεμάσαι χρὴ τὸν ἄνθρωπον τῶν ποδῶν πρὸς μεσόδμην Hp.*Art.*70; expld. as τὸ μέγα ξύλον ἀπὸ τοῦ ἑτέρου τοίχου πρὸς τὸν ἕτερον διῆκον Gal. ad Hp. l. c. (18(1).738), cf. *IG* ll. cc., *SIG* 248 *N*8 (Delph., iv B.C.), Q.S.13.451. 2. *box amidships*, in which the mast was stepped, ἱστὸν.. κοίλης ἔντοσθε μεσόδμης στῆσαν ἀείραντες Od.2.424. 3. *shelf* built between the floor of the gallery and the roof, pl., *IG*2².1668.74,85: sg., ib.78. II. μεσόδμα, Lacon. μεσσοδόμα, = γυνή, Hsch.

**μεσό-δοκον**, τό, and **-δοκος**, ὁ, = Lat. *zona, trabes, Gloss.* **-δόμιον**, τό, v. μεσολάνιον. **-δομος**, ἡ, = κατῆλιψ, Sch.Ar.*Ra.*571.

**μεσο-ειδής**, ές, (cf. μέση I) *in the region of the* μέση, i.e. *in the middle region of the voice*, μελοποιΐα Aristid.Quint.1.12. **-ζευγμα**, ατος, τό, *a word which belongs equally to what precedes and to what follows*, Diom.p.444 K.; also **-ζευξις**, εως, ἡ, Sacerd.p.456 K. **-ζύγιος** [ῠ] ἐρέτης, ὁ, = ζευγίτης, *EM*441.24.

**μεσόθεν**, ***μεσόθι**, v. μεσσ-.

**μεσόθριξ**, τρῐχος, ὁ, ἡ, *having middling hair*, Ptol.*Tetr.*143.

**μέσοι**, locative form from μέσος, *in the midst, between*, γαίας καὶ νιφόεντος ὠράνω μ. Alc.17.

**μεσό-κενος** σφυγμός, of the pulse, dub. sens. in Archig.ap.Gal.8. 944. **-κλαστος**, ον, (κλάω) *broken off in the middle* ( = λαγαρός), of hexam. verses with a trochee for a spondee in the interior, Ps.-Plu.*Metr.*3, Sch.Heph.pp.349, 350 C., interpol. in Sch.D.T.p.53 H. **-κνήμιον**, τό, *middle of the leg*, Str.15.3.19. **-κοιλος**, ον, *hollow, low-lying*, πόλις Plb.10.10.7, cf. Agathem.5.20. 2. *hollow in the middle*, of a stalk, Dsc.1.11; of the heart, Ruf.*Anat.*32; *grooved*, ξύλον Sor.1.83. 3. τὰ μ., = μεσόδμη I. 2, Luc.*Am.* 6. **-κοπος**, ον, (κόπτω) *of middle size* or *age*, Cratin.426, Xenarch.4.9. **-κουράδες**, αἱ, *trees broken by the force of the wind*, Hsch. **-κουρος**, ον, *shaven in the middle*, Poll.4.139. **-κρᾱνον**, τό, *crown of the head*, Orph.*Fr.*330. **-κρῐνής**, ές, *parting in the middle*: μ. (sc. κίων), ὁ, *pillar left as a support in working mines*, in pl., Plu.2.843d, Poll.3.87. **-κύνιον** [ῠ], τό, (κύων VIII) *pastern* of a horse, etc., *Hippiatr.*2. **-κωλον**, τό, *middle of a limb*, Sor.*Fasc.* 55. II. in pl., *part of the* μεσεντέριον *next to the* κῶλον, Hp.*Oss.* 1, *Epid.*6.4.6: sg., Gal.17(2).134.

**μεσολᾰβ-έω**, *seize, nip*, κιρσόν Antyll.ap.Orib.45.18.20, cf. eund. ib.7.14.4, Sor.*Fasc.*46 (Pass.); *interrupt*, νῆσος μ. τὸν πόρον *Peripl. M.Rubr.*25: freq. metaph., μ. τὰς τῶν διωκόντων ὁρμάς *intercept*, D.S.12.70, cf. 16.1, Alciphr.2.1; τὴν τῶν φλεβῶν ἔκρυσιν Timagoras ap.Stob.4.36.19; *interrupt*, τινα Plb.18.52.3: abs., μεσολαβήσας ἤρετο Id.16.34.5, etc.; τὴν ἀνάγκην.. οὐκ ἔστιν ἐποχῇ μεσολαβεῖν Metrod. *Herc.*831.6, cf. 12; of *intervening* causes, Alex.Aphr.*Febr.*27, al.; also, *perceive an interval*, Gal.9.69:—Pass., *to be intercepted*, of letters, Chryserm.ap.Stob.3.39.31; of planetary influences, Ἀφροδίτη μεσολαβουμένη Max.*Epit.*p.100 L.; μεσολαβηθῆναι ὑπὸ τῆς πεπρωμένης, i.e. die prematurely, Plb.*Fr.*184; μ. νόσῳ D.S.12.29; μεσολαβηθεὶς τὸν βίον *having one's* life *cut short in the midst*, Id.1.3, cf. *BCH*11.219 (Phrygia), Vett.Val.246.9; ἐὰν μεσολαβηθῇ [ἡ περιστερά] Sch.Od. 12.69. II. [λίθους?] κατὰ λόγον μεσολαβείτω perh. he *shall calculate* (cf. μεσόλαβος) the size of the stones in proportion, *BCH* 20.324 (Lebad.). **-ής**, ές, *held by the middle*, κέντρον A.*Eu.*157 (lyr.). **-ησις**, εως, ἡ, *grasping by the middle*, Eust.664.14. **-ος**, ὁ, or **-ον**, τό, *mesolabe*, a mathematical instrument used by Eratosthenes for finding mean proportional lines, Papp.54.31, Vitr.9 *Prooem.*14.

**μεσο-λάνιον** (fort. μεσόδμιον)· μεσοδόμιον, Hsch. **-λευκος**, ον, *middling white*, χιτὼν πορφυροῦς μ. a tunic of purple *shot with white*, X.*Cyr.*8.3.13, cf. Luc.*Alex.*11; μ. χιτών alone, *JHS*41.195 (Delos, ii B.C.), D.C.36.52; opp. πορφύρεος, Ephipp.ap.Ath.12. 537e; χλαμὺς μ. D.C.78.3. II. Subst., a precious stone, Plin. *HN*37.174. 2. = λευκὰς ὀρεινή, ib.27.102. **-μάζιον**, τό, *space between the breasts*, Heliod.ap.Orib.48.51.1. **-μακρος**, ον, *with a long syllable in the middle*, name of the foot ᴗ ᴗ – ᴗ ᴗ, Diom.p.481 K. **-μέλας**, name of a precious stone, Plin.*HN*37. 174. **-μηνία**, ἡ, *mid-month*, = Lat. *Idus*, Lyd.*Mens.*3.10. **-μήνιον**, τό, = foreg., *Gloss.* **-μήρια**, τά, *space between the hips* or *thighs*, Poll.2.188, Ptol.*Alm.*8.1, Gal.19.558, Aët.4.24: sg. in *Gloss.*

**μεσόμνη**, v. μεσόδμη.

**μεσομφᾰλ-ία**· ἡ μέσος τῶν Δελφῶν πόλις, Hsch. **-ιον**, τό, = ὀμφαλός, Poll.2.169; of a shield, Id.1.133. **-ος**, ον, *in mid-navel, central*, used esp. of Apollo's shrine at Delphi, μ. χρηστήρια, ἑστία, ἵδρυμα, μυχοί, μυχός, A.*Th.*747 (lyr.), *Ag.*1056, *Ch.*1036, E.*Or.*331 (lyr.), Aristonous 2.3; τὰ μ. γᾶς μαντεῖα S.*OT*480 (lyr.); λύχνου τὸ μ. the central boss, Batr.129; μ. ἄστρον Ὀλύμπου, of Aries, Nonn.*D.* 1.181. II. *with a navel* or *boss in the middle*, κύκλος, of the letter Θ, Agatho 4; of a φιάλη, Ion Trag.20 (lyr.), Theopomp.Com.3, Poll. 6.98; of a cake, Id.2.169.

**μέσον**, τό, v. μέσος III and V.

**μεσό-νεοι**, ων, οἱ, *rowers amidships*, who had the longest oars, Arist.*Mech.*850ᵇ10, *IG*12(1).43 (Rhodes, i B.C.):—hence κώπη **-νεως** (prob. for μέσον νεώς), Arist.*PA*687ᵇ18. **-νεφής**, ές, *with clouds*

*in the midst*, *Cat.Cod.Astr.*8(1).138. **-νύκτιος**, ον, *of* or *at midnight*, ἔκλειψις Arist.*Mete.*367$^b$26; ὥρα D.S.19.31, cf. *Anacreont.*31.1: with a Verb, μεσονύκτιον δέξασθαί τινα Pi.*I.*7(6).5; μ. ὠλλύμαν E.*Hec.*914 (lyr.): neut. as Adv., Theoc.13.69: as Subst. **-νύκτιον**, τό, Hp.*Morb.*2.48, Lxx*Jd.*16.3, Plu.*Caes.*43, Luc.*Merc.Cond.*26, Vett.Val.339.6; κατὰ τὸ μ. Str.2.5.42, *Act.Ap.*16.25; μεσονυκτίου *at midnight*, *Ev.Marc.*13.35; μεσονύκτου seems to be f.l. in Arist.ap.Sotion. p.185 W.—Poet. word acc. to Phryn.36:—the spelling **μεσᾱνύκτιον** is v.l. in *Ev.Marc.* l.c., cf. *POxy.*1768.6 (iii A.D.).

**μεσόνυξ**, ῠχος, Pythag. name for *one of the planets*, Stesich.87.

**μεσο-πᾱγής**, ές, Ep. **μεσσο-**, (παγῆναι) *fixed up to the middle*, μεσσοπαγὲς δ' ἄρ' ἔθηκε κατ' ὄχθης μείλινον ἔγχος drove it in *up to the middle*, Il.21.172:—Aristarch. preferred the v.l. **μεσσοπαλές**, *quivering up to the middle* (cf. Hsch.); but it is doubtful whether -παλές could mean *quivering*, and μεσσοπαγής is found in late Poets, as Nonn.*D.*1.233. **-πέρδην**, Adv., prob. Com. distortion of **-φέρδην**, term applied to a form of wrestling, *Com.Adesp.*1078. **-περσικός**, ή, όν, *half Persian*: -περσικαί or -κά a kind of *shoe*, Poll.7.94, Hsch. **-πλᾰτος**, ον, *broad in the middle*, Agathem.1.2. **-πλεύριος**, ον, *between the ribs*: μ. μύες *intercostal* muscles, Gal.2.498; μεσοπλεύριον, τό, *part between the ribs*, Ruf.ap.Orib.8.24.65: more freq. in pl., Id.*Onom.*93, Gal.8.77, Poll.2.167 (v.l. μεσόπλευρα). **-πλουτος**, ον, *moderately rich*, dub. in Alciphr.3.34 (leg. νεόπλ-); **μεσσόπλουτος**, Hsch. **-πολις**, ή, f.l. for μητρόπολις, Plu.2.301d. **-πόντιος**, ὁ, *amid the sea*, epith. of Poseidon at Eresos, Call.*Fr.*16. **-πορέω**, *to be half-way*, Men.1036, Thphr.*Char.*25.2, D.S.18.34, App.*BC*2.88: metaph., of a meal, Lxx*Si.*34(31).21; also μεσοπορούσης τῆς κατὰ τὴν ὀπώραν ἀκμῆς Dsc.1.109. **-πορία**, ή, *half-journey*, Ps.-Callisth.3.13. **-πορικόν**, τό, *half-way station*, Isid.Char.1. **-πόρος**, Ep. **μεσσ-**, ον, *going* or *passing in the middle*, Opp.*H.*5.46; μ. δι' αἰθέρος through *mid*-air, E.*Ion* 1152. **-πόρφῠρος**, ον, *mixed* or *shot with purple*, οὐχ ὅλως λευκὸν ἀλλὰ μ. Plu.*Arat.*53; χλαμύς D.C.78.3; τὰ μ. (sc. ἱμάτια) Lxx*Is.*3.20. **-ποτάμιος** [ᾰ], α, ον, *between rivers*, αἱ μ. (sc. χῶραι) Str.15.1.18; ἥδε ἡ μ. ib.30: esp. as pr. n. **Μεσοποτᾰμία** (sc. χώρα), ή, *Mesopotamia*, Plb.5.44.6, Str.11.12.2, etc.:—hence **Μεσοποτᾰμίτης** [ῐ], ου, ὁ, Luc.*Hist.Conscr.*24. II. *in the middle of the river*, ἐν μ. νήσῳ Plu.*Oth.*4. **-πτερύγια** [ῠ], τά, *the middle wing-feathers*, Ael.*NA*7.17. **-πτωτα** ὀνόματα words *inflected in the middle*, e.g. *quisque* or τίσποτε, Dosith.p.405 K. **-πύγιον** [ῠ], τό, *part between the buttocks*, Sor.1.102, Sch.Ar.*Pl.*122. **-πύλη** [ῠ], poet. **μεσσ-**, ή, *middle gate*, *AP*5.202 (Asclep.):—also **-πῦλον**, τό, Aen.Tact.39.3. **-πύργιον**, τό, *wall between two towers*, *curtain*, Ph.*Bel.*83.12 (pl.), Plb.9.41.1, D.S.17.24.

***μεσόριον**, ***μέσορος**, v. μεσούριον, μέσσορος.

**μεσόρομβος**, ὁ, kind of *bandage*, Hsch.

**μεσορρᾰγής**, ές, *rent in twain*, Opp.*H.*2.31.

**μέσος**, η, ον, also Arc. (v. ἰμέσος, μεσακόθεν); Ep. **μέσσος** (also Aeol., Sapph.1.12, *IG*11(4).1064*b*32, and Lyr., Pi.*P.*4.224, and sts. in Trag., E.*HF*403 (lyr.), S.*OC*1247 (lyr.), *Tr.*635 (lyr.), *Ant.*1223, 1236, *Fr.*255.5), Boeot., Cret. **μέττος**, *IG*7.2420.20 (iii B.C.), *GDI* 5000ii*b*2 (v B.C.):—*middle*, *in the middle*, I. of Space, esp. with Nouns, of the *middle* point or part, μ. σάκος Il.7.258; ἱστίον 1.481; οὐρανός *zenith*, Od.4.400; μ. ἀπήνης from *mid* chariot, S.*OT*812; ἐν αἰθέρι μ. in *mid*-air, Id.*Ant.*416; μ. μετώπῳ in the *middle* of the forehead, *PRyl.*128.30 (i A.D.): in Prose freq. preceding the Art., κατὰ μέσον τὸν σταθμόν X.*An.*1.7.14; ἐν μ. τῇ χώρᾳ ib.2.1.11; ἐκ μ. τῆς νήσου, κατὰ μ. τὴν νῆσον, Pl.*Criti.*113d, 119d; ἐπὶ μέσου τοῦ τμάματος at the *middle point* of the segment, Archim.*Aequil.*1.6; ἁ ἐπὶ μέσαν τὰν βάσιν ἀγομένα (sc. εὐθεῖα) ib.12: sts. following the Noun, ἐν τῇ ἀγορᾷ μέσῃ D.29.12: less freq. *midmost*, *central*, of three or more objects, μ. ὁδός Thgn.220, 331; ὁ μ. [δάκτυλος] Pl.*R.*523c; τὸ μ. στῖφος the *central* division of the army, X.*An.*1.8.13; μέσον, τό, *centre*, ἡ ἐπὶ τὸ μ. φορά Iamb.*Protr.*21. b. with a Verb, ἔχεται μ. *by the middle*, *by the waist*, prov. from the wrestling-ring, Ar.*Eq.*387 (lyr.), cf. *Ach.*571 (lyr.), *Nu.*1047, *Ra.*469; μέσην λαβόντα Id.*Ach.*274, cf. Hdt.9.107, D.53.17; ὁ πέπλος ἐρράγη μ. Philippid.25.5. c. c. gen., *midway between*, ἐντὸς καὶ πλήθους τὸ ὀλίγον μ. Pl.*Plt.*303a (also μ. ἐπ' ἀμφότερα, ibid.):—S. has μέσος ἀπὸ [τοῦ κρατῆρος] τοῦ τε πέτρου *OC* 1595. 2. of Time, Hom. only in phrase μέσον ἦμαρ *midday*, Il.21.111, Od.7.288, Pi.*P.*9.113; μέσαι νύκτες Sapph.52, Hdt.4.181, X.*An.*7.8.12, etc.; θέρευς ἔτι μέσσου ἐόντος Hes.*Op.*502; χειμῶνος μέσου Ar.*Fr.*569.1; μ. ἡμέρα Hdn.8.5.9; μ. ἡλικία *middle* age, Pl.*Ep.*316c: so μέσοι τὴν ἡλικίαν E.*Ep.*5; μέσος ἀκμῆς v.l. in Theoc.25.164. 3. metaph., *impartial*, Th.4.83, *PLond.*1.113(1).27 (vi A.D.). b. *intermediate*, freq. c. gen., μ. τις γέγονα χρηματιστὴς τοῦ τε πάππου καὶ τοῦ πατρός Pl.*R.*330b; ψιλὸν μὲν τὸ π̄, δασὺ δὲ τὸ φ̄, μέσον δὲ ἀμφοῖν τὸ β̄ D.H.*Comp.*14 (v. infr. d); ἡ τρίτη καὶ μ. τῶν εἰρημένων δυεῖν ἁρμονιῶν ib.24; ὁ μ. χαρακτήρ ib.21; *indeterminate*, Luc.*Par.*28; τὰ μ. *things indifferent* (neither good nor bad), *Stoic.*3.135, al.; of words such as τύχη, *EM*626.38; ζῴδια (neither lucky nor unlucky) Vett.Val.93.9; μ. δίαιτα Diocl.*Fr.*141, cf. Sor.1.46. c. Gramm., of Verbs, *middle*, Eust.1846.30, etc.; μ. διάθεσις, σχήματα, A.D.*Synt.*226.10, 210.18; μ. ἐνεστώς present *middle*, ib.278.25. d. Gramm., of consonants, Lat. *mediae*, i.e. β̄γ̄δ̄, D.T.631.23: but also of *semi-vowels*, Pl.*Phlb.*18c: of accent, ὀξύτητι καὶ βαρύτητι καὶ τῷ μέσῳ, i.e. the *circumflex*, Arist.*Po.*1456$^b$33. II. *middling*, *moderate*, 1. of size, μέσοι ὀφθαλμοί, ὦτα, γλῶττα, Id.*HA*492$^a$8, 33, $^b$31; μ. μεγέθει ib.496$^a$21, *PPetr.*1 p.37 (iii B.C.); μ. alone, *of middle height*, *PGrenf.*2.23(*a*) ii 3 (ii B.C.), *POxy.*73.13 (i A.D.), etc. 2. of class or quality, πάντων μέσ' ἄριστα Thgn.335; παντὶ μέσῳ τὸ κράτος θεὸς ὤπασεν A.*Eu.*529 (lyr.); μ. ἐν πόλει Phoc.12; μ. ἀνήρ a man *of middle rank*, Hdt.1.107; μ. πολίτης Th.6.54; τὰ μ. τῶν πολιτῶν Id.3.82 (so τῶν ἀνὰ πόλιν τὰ μ. Pi.*P.*11.52); οἱ μ., between οἱ εὔποροι and οἱ ἄποροι, Arist.*Pol.*1289$^b$31, 1295$^b$3; οἱ μ. πολῖται ib.1296$^a$19; τὸ μ. ib.1295$^b$37; μ. [πολιτεία] ib.1296$^a$7; ὁ μ. βίος Luc.*Luct.*9; *mediocre*, Pl.*Prt.*346d; τῶν ἑταιρῶν αἱ μ. Theopomp.Com.21. Adv. μέσως, ἱκανόν *fairly* adequate, Phld.*Rh.*2.4 S. III. μέσον, τό, *midst*, *intervening space*, mostly with Preps., a. ἐν μέσῳ, = ἐν μεταιχμίῳ, Il.3.69, 90; ἐν τῷ μ. *in the midst*, *Ev.Matt.*14.6; ἡ 'ν μέσῳ [μοῖρα] σῴζει πόλεις the *middle* class, E.*Supp.*244: without ἐν, ἔμβαλε μέσσῳ Il.4.444; ἔνθορε μέσσῳ 21.233; μέσσῳ ἀμφοτέρων 3.416, 7.277; τῶνδέ τ' ἐν μ. πεσεῖν E.*Ph.*583; ἐν μ. λόγους ἔχειν Id.*Hel.*630; μῆκος ἐν μ. χρόνου A.*Supp.*735; χρόνος οὐν μ. E.*Ph.*589 (troch.); τὰ ἐν μ. what *went between*, S.*OC*583; οἱ ἐν μ. λόγοι the *intervening* words, Id.*El.*1364, E.*Med.*819; κλίνης ἐν μ. Id.*Hec.*1150; ἐν μ. ἡμῶν καὶ βασιλέως *between* us and him, X.*An.*2.2.3; σοφίας καὶ ἀμαθίας ἐν μ. Pl.*Smp.*203e; ἐν μ. νυκτῶν at *mid*night, X.*Cyr.*5.3.52; ἆθλα κείμεν' ἐν μέσῳ *offered for competition* (cf. infr. b), D.4.5, cf. Thgn.994, X.*An.*3.1.21; ἡ τιμὴ ἐν τῷ μέσῳ ἔστω *deposited* with the court, Herod.2.90: without ἐν, καὶ μέσῳ πάντες καὶ χωρὶς ἕκαστος both *collectively* and severally, *IG*12(5).872.27, 31, 38, al. (Tenos): in pl., κεῖτο δ' ἄρ' ἐν μέσσοισι Il.18.507; ἐν μέσοισ' Xenoph.1.7; ἐν μέσῳ εἶναι τοῦ συμμεῖξαι to stand *in the way of*.., X.*Cyr.*5.2.26; ἡ γὰρ θάλαττα ἐν τῷ μ. is an *obstacle*, Id.*Ath.*2.2; οὐδεὶς ἐν μέσσῳ γείτων πέλεν Theoc.21.17; οὐδὲν ἂν ἦν ἐν μ. πολεμεῖν ἡμᾶς D.23.183; cf. ἰμέσος. b. ἐς μέσον, ἐς μ. ἀμφοτέρων, freq. in Hom. for ἐς μεταίχμιον, Il.4.79, 6.120; ἀνδρὶ δὲ νικηθέντι γυναῖκ' ἐς μέσσον ἔθηκε *deposited* her *as a prize* (cf. supr. a), 23.704; ἐς μ. δεικνύναι τινί τι Pi.*Fr.*42.3; ἐς μ. ἴεσθαι, ἐλθεῖν, παρελθεῖν, S.*Tr.*514 (lyr.), Theoc.22.183, Plu.*Agis*9; ἐς μέσον ἀμφοτέροισι.. δικάσσατε Il.23.574; ἐς τὸ μ. φέρειν bring forward *publicly*, Hdt.4.97, D.18.139; ἐς τὸ μ. λέγεσθαι Hdt.6.129; ἐς μ. Πέρσῃσι καταθεῖναι τὰ πρήγματα to give up the power *in common to all*, Id.3.80; ἐς μ. τὴν ἀρχὴν τιθεὶς ἰσονομίην ὑμῖν προαγορεύω ib.142. c. ἐκ τοῦ μέσου *away*, ἐκ μ. ἀνελεῖν D.10.36, 18.294; [χειρόγραφον] ἦρκεν ἐκ τοῦ μ. *Ep.Col.*2.14, cf. Arr.*Epict.*3.3.15; also ἐκ μ. *a half*, ἔτη ὀκτὼ καὶ ἔνατον ἐκ μ. Th.4.133; also ἐκ μ. κατῆστο remained *in the middle*, i.e. neutral (cf. ἐκ I.6 fin.), Hdt.3.83, cf. 4.118, 8.22, 73. d. διὰ μέσου *between*, τὸ διὰ μ. ἔθνος Id.1.104; διὰ μ. ποιεῖσθαι X.*Cyr.*6.3.3; διὰ μ. γενέσθαι *intervene*, of an event, Th.4.20: c. gen., διὰ μέσου τῆς πόλεως ῥεῖ ποταμός X.*An.*1.2.23; διὰ μ. ῥεῖ τούτων ποταμός ib.1.4.4, etc.; τὸ τούτων διὰ μ. Pl.*Lg.*805e; also οἱ διὰ μέσου the *middle* party, the *moderates*, Th.8.75, X.*HG*5.4.25; τὸ διὰ μ. the *middle* class, Arist.*Pol.*1296$^a$8; of Time, ὁ διὰ μ. χρόνος Hdt.9.112; ἡ διὰ μ. ξύμβασις an *interim* agreement, Th.5.26; διὰ μέσου, as a figure of speech, *use of parenthesis*, Hdn.*Fig.*p.95 S. e. ἀν (ὀν) τὸ μ. *in the midst*, Alc.18.3, Xenoph.1.11, Thgn.839; ἀνὰ μέσον *midway between*, Arist.*HA*496$^a$22, Antiph.13, Theoc.22.21, etc.; ἀνὰ μ. τοῦ ναοῦ καὶ τοῦ βωμοῦ *GDI*2010 (Delph.), cf. *PTeb.*13.9 (ii B.C.), al.; θρὶξ ἀνὰ μέσσον Theoc.14.9; ἀνὰ μέσσα Nic.*Th.*167; also ἀνὰ μέσον φέρε, = μετρίως, Men.531.18. f. κατὰ μέσσον, = ἐν μέσῳ, Il.5.8, 16.285, etc.: c. gen., κὰδ δὲ μέσον τάφρου καὶ τείχεος ἷζον *between*, 9.87. 2. μέσον, τό, *difference*, τὸ μ. πρὸς τὰς μεγίστας καὶ ἐλαχίστας *the average* between.., Th.1.10; πολλὸν τὸ μ., πολὺ τὸ μ., *the difference* is great, Hdt.1.126, E.*Alc.*914 (anap.); τὸ μ. οὐδὲν τῆς ἔχθρης ἐστί there is no *middle course* for our enmity, Hdt.7.11. 3. *middle state*, *mean*, τὸ μ. καὶ τὸ εὖ Arist.*EN*1109$^b$26; ποιήματα μέσα, opp. ὀγκώδη, *in the* (correct) *mean*, Phld.*Po.*5.5. Adv. -ως, ἀναστρέφεσθαι Id.*Rh.*1.155 S. 4. in Logic, τὸ μ. *the middle term* of a syllogism, opp. τὰ ἄκρα, Arist.*APr.*66$^a$30; also ὁ μ. (sc. ὅρος) ib.25$^b$33. 5. Math., *middle* terms in a proportion, Euc.6.16; μέση, or μέση (μέσος) ἀνάλογον a *mean proportional* (straight line or number), ib.13, 17, 8.11, 12, al.; μέσης εὕρεσις Arist.*de An.*413$^a$19, *Metaph.*996$^b$21; μέση *medial*, a specific kind of irrational (straight line), Euc.10.21, al.; μέσον ὀρθογώνιον (χωρίον) *medial* rectangle (area), ib.24, al. 6. Astron., ὁ διὰ μέσων τῶν ζῳδίων κύκλος the *ecliptic*, Hipparch.1.9.3, 4, Gem.2.21, Ptol.*Alm.*2.7: without κύκλος, Eudox.ap.Arist.*Metaph.*1073$^b$20, Hipparch.1.9.12; simply, ὁ διὰ μέσων D.L.7.146; but, ὁ μέσος [κύκλος] the *equator* of a rotating sphere, Arist.*Metaph.*1073$^b$30. 7. μέσα, τά, = μέζεα, Blaes.p.191 K. b. = κοιλία I.3, Herod.Med.ap.Orib.5.27.3, Gal.14.732: sg., Heph.Astr.1.1 (v.l. τὰ μέσα *Cat.Cod.Astr.*8(2).45). 8. Μέσον, τό, one of the law-courts at Athens, Phot., Sch.Ar.*V.*120. 9. οὐ τοῖς μέσοις τῆς βίας χρωμένη no *ordinary* force, Hierocl.p.15 A. IV. μέση, ή, as Subst., v. μέση. V. Adv. μέσον, Ep. μέσσον, *in the middle*, Il.12.167, Od.14.300: c. gen., *between*, οὐρανοῦ μ. χθονός (τε) E.*Or.*983 (lyr.), cf. Arr.*Epict.*2.22.10; *in the midst of*, μ. τῆς θαλάσσης Lxx*Ex.*14.27; μ. γενεᾶς σκολιᾶς *Ep.Phil.*2.15: also in pl., μέσα αἰετὸς οὐρανοῦ ποτᾶται E.*Rh.*530 (lyr.), cf. Nic.*Fr.*74.26. 2. regul. Adv. μέσως, πόλεώς τ' οὐ μ. εὐδαίμονος E.*Andr.*873, cf. *Hec.*1113, Isoc.9.23; καὶ μ. even *in a moderate degree*, even *a little*, Th.2.60; μ. ἔχειν πρός or περί τι to be *in the mean*.., Arist.*EN*1105$^b$28, 1119$^a$11; θερμότερον ἢ κραυρότερον ἢ μ. ἔχον Eub.7.1, cf. Sosip.1.53; μ. βεβιωκέναι *in a middle way*, i.e. neither well nor ill, Pl.*Phd.*113d; μ. μεθύων Men.226; μ. διατιθέναι *in an intermediate way*, D.H.*Comp.*14. b. Gramm., *in the middle voice*, A.D.*Synt.*276.21. VI. irreg. Comp. μεσαίτερος Pl.*Prm.*165b: Sup. μεσαίτατος Hdt.4.17, Arist.*Mu.*392$^b$33, Gem.9.3, etc.; poet. μεσσότατος A.R.4.649, Man.6.373. (Cf. Skt. *mádhyas* 'middle', Lat. *medius*, etc.)

**μεσο-σέληνον**, τό, *new moon, Gloss.* **-στάτης** [ᾰ], ου, ὁ, *inner beam* or *standard* in the plinth of a torsion-engine, Ph.*Bel.*55.12, Hero *Bel.*104.9, Apollod.*Poliorc.*165.10, al. **-στενος**, ον, *narrow in the middle*, ib.148.6. ⊕ **-στροφωνίαι** ἡμέραι, name of a festival at Lesbos, Hsch. **-στύλιον** [ῡ], τό, *space between columns*, *IG*5(2).123 (Tegea, pl.), Agatharch.102 (pl.):—also ⊕ **-στῦλον**, τό, Sch.Od.19.37, Hsch. s. v. μεσόδμαι, *Cod.Just.*1.4.26.8. **-συλλᾰβέω**, *use* one remedy *alternately* with another, Sever.ap.Aët.7.45. II. Pass., *to be intercepted*, Alex.Aphr.*Pr.*2.14. **-συλλᾰβία**, ἡ, *parenthesis*, Sch.E.*Med.*1085. ⊕ **-σφαιρος**, ον, *of middle globular size*, *Peripl. M.Rubr.*65. **-σχῐδής**, ές, *divided in the middle*, Thphr.*HP*3.11.1; δονακῆες *AP*6.64 (Paul. Sil.). ⊕ **-τᾰγής**, ές, *placed in the middle*, [ἀριθμοί] Iamb. *in Nic.*p.84 P. **-τακτος**, ὁ, dub. sens. in *CPR*154.13 (iii A. D.). **-τείχιος**, ον, *between the walls and outworks*, θέατρον App. *Hann.*37; τὸ μ. *the space between the wall and siege-works*, ib.29. **-της**, ητος, ἡ, (μέσος) *central position*, χώρας τε καὶ ἄστεος μεσότητας Pl.*Lg.*746a, f.l. in Arist.*Mir.*846ᵃ18 (cf. *Mu.*399ᵇ34); also of Time, τὸ νῦν ἐστι μ. τις Id.*Ph.*251ᵇ20; Αἰών.. ἀρχὴν μ. τέλος οὐκ ἔχων *SIG*1125.10 (i B. C./i A. D.). II. Math., *mean*, Pl.*Ti.*32a, 43d (pl.), etc.; μ. ἀριθμητική, ἁρμονική, Arist.*Fr.*47; γεωμετρουμένη Plu.2.1138d. 2. generally, *mean, state between two extremes* (ἔλλειψις and ὑπερβολή), μ. ἐστὶν ἡ ἀρετή Arist.*EN*1106ᵇ27, cf. 36; μ. ἡ ἀρετὴ καὶ βίων καὶ ἔργων καὶ τεχνῶν D.H.*Comp.*24; ἡ μ. ἐν πᾶσιν ἀσφαλεστέρα *Trag. Adesp.*547.6; αἱ μ. ἄρισται *AP*10.102 (Bass.). 3. *medium*, communicating between two opposites, ἡ αἴσθησις οἷον μ. τις τῆς ἐν τοῖς αἰσθητοῖς ἐναντιώσεως Arist.*de An.*424ᵃ4, cf. 431ᵃ11; *standard*, ὡς μ. χρώμενοι τῇ ἁφῇ Id.*Mete.*382ᵃ19. 4. τῆς λέξεως μ. *a style between* poetry and prose, D.H.*Vett.Cens.*2.11, cf. 5.2. 5. Gramm., *middle voice*, D.T.638.9, A.D.*Synt.*211.19. **-τοιχον**, τό, = sq., *Ep.Eph.*2.14, Hsch. s. v. κατῆλιψ. **-τοιχος**, ὁ, *party-wall*, *Milet.*7.56 (Didyma), *BCH*33.452 (Argos): metaph., τὸν τῆς ἡδονῆς καὶ ἀρετῆς μ. διορύττειν Eratosth.Cyren.ap.Ath.7.281d. II. as Adj., *having a party-wall*, οἰκίαι *PAmh.*2.98.9 (ii/iii A. D.). **-τομέω**, *cut in twain*, X.*Oec.*18.2; *halve, bisect*, Pl.*Plt.*265a. **-τομος**, poet. **μεσσο-**, ον, *cut through the middle, split*, κάλαμοι *AP*6.63 (Damoch.). **-τρῐβάκόν**, τό, *half-worn-out garment*, prob. in *POxy.*1645.10 (iv A.D.). **-τρίβας** [ῐ], α, ὁ, prob. from μέσα (μέσος III. 7), title of play by Blaesus, Ath.3.111c. **-τρῐβής**, ές, *half-worn-out*, Hsch. s. v. θύστινον. **-τῠχος**, ον, poet. **μεσσό-**, *of moderate fortune*, ἀνήρ Antioch.Astr. in *Cat.Cod. Astr.*1.109.

⊕ **μεσουρᾰν-έω**, *to be in mid-heaven*; of heavenly bodies, *culminate, be in the meridian*, Arist.*Mete.*373ᵇ13, Hipparch.1.7.11, etc.; μεσσουρανέουσα σελήνη Man.5.189. II. μ. ὑπὸ γῆν *to be at the nadir*, Gem.2.19. **-ημα**, ατος, τό, *culmination*, Str.3.5.8, Cleom.2.1, Ptol. *Alm.*8.4, Theo Sm.p.159 H., etc. 2. *mid-heaven, zenith*, *Apoc.*8.13, al. 3. μ. κόσμου title of Aries as having been on the meridian at the Creation, Vett.Val.5.26. 4. name of the tenth τόπος, Paul. Al.*N.*1. ⊕ **-ησις**, εως, ἡ, *culmination*, Str.2.1.18 (pl.), Gem.2.21, al., Ptol.*Alm.*8.4 (pl.), Plot.3.1.5 (pl.). **-ιος**, ον, *in mid-heaven, in the meridian*, Arist.*Mete.*378ᵃ8; -ιον, τό, = μεσουράνημα 1, Heph.Astr.2.11,18. **-ισμα**, ατος, τό, = μεσουράνημα 1 and 2, Theo Sm.p.133 H., Zos.Alch.p.118 B., Phlp.*in Ph.*455.10.

**μεσούριον**, τό, Ion. for *μεσόριον, *boundary*, D.P.17.

**μέσουροι** (sc. κάλοι), οἱ, *sail-ropes, halyards*, Sch.A.R.1.566.

**μεσο-φάλακρος** [φᾰ], ον, *bald on the crown*, Ptol.*Tetr.*143. **-φᾰνής**, Ep. **μεσσ-**, ές, *appearing in the middle*, Nonn.*D.*1.252. 2. *half-appearing*, of the half-moon, ib.38.247. **-φάραγγιον**, τό, *ravine between hills, Gloss.* **-φέρδην**, v. μεσοπέρδην.

⊕ **μεσ-όφθαλμος**, ον, *with middle-sized eyes*, Procl.*Par.Ptol.*202.

**μεσό-φθεγμα**, ατος, τό, = ἐφύμνιον, Sch.A.*Eu.*341. **-φλέβιον**, τό, *space between two veins, Gloss.*

**μεσ-όφρῠον**, τό, *space between the eyebrows*, *BGU*1258.15 (ii B. C.), *Placit.*4.5.2, 5.24.4, Ruf.*Onom.*17, Aret.*SD*2.13, Gal.2.744, Opp.*C.*1.179.

**μεσό-χθων**, ονος, ὁ, ἡ, *midland, in the interior*, D.H.1.49. **-χλοος**, ον, *greenish*, ἄρουρα Nic.*Th.*753. ⊕ **-χορος**, ον, *standing in mid-chorus*, of the coryphaeus, *Delph.*3(1) No.219. II. *leader of a claque*, Plin.*Ep.*2.14. **-χρόνιος**, ον, *having an average duration of life*, Vett.Val.314.31, Anon. in *Cat.Cod.Astr.*2.169, Astramps.*Orac.*11.9. **-χροος**, ον, *of mixed complexion*, Ptol.*Tetr.*145. **-χωρος**, ον, *midland, Gloss.*; τὸ μ. the *middle space*, Apollod.*Poliorc.*192.6.

⊕ **μεσόω**, (μέσος) *to be in* or *at the middle*, τόδ' ἴσθι, μηδέπω μεσοῦν κακόν A.*Pers.*435; ἐν ἀρχῇ πῆμα κοὐδέπω μεσοῖ E.*Med.*60; ἐπειδὴ τὸ δρᾶμα ἤδη μεσοίη Ar.*Ra.*924; esp. of Time, μεσοῦσα ἡμέρη *mid*day, Hdt.3.104; θέρους μεσοῦντος in *mid*summer, Th.5.57; ἐν [ἐνιαυτῷ] μεσοῦντι X.*HG*2.2.24; πρὸς ἥλιον μεσοῦντα towards *mid*day, Thphr.*CP*2.4.8; μεσούντων τῶν ζῳδίων Hipparch.2.3.19. 2. c. gen., *to be in the middle of*, τῆς ἀναβάσιος Hdt.1.181; τὰ δὲ καὶ μεσοῦν τούτων Pl.*R.*618b; μεσοῦντα τῆς ἀρχῆς *in the middle of* his time of office, Sch. Aeschin.3.12: and c. part., μεσοῦν δειπνοῦντας Pl.*Smp.*175c.

**μεσπίλ-η** [ῐ], ἡ, *medlar-tree*, *Mespilus germanica*, distd. as σατάνειος, Thphr.*HP*3.12.5. II. μ. ἡ ἀνθηδὼν *oriental thorn*, *Crataegus orientalis*, ibid. 2. μ. ἡ ἀνθηδονοειδὴς *hawthorn*, *Crataegus Oxyacantha*, ibid. ⊕ **-ον** (proparox.), τό, *medlar*, Archil.180, Hp.*Vict.*2.55, Amphis 38, Agatharch.96, Gal.12.71, al. b. μ. σητάνιον, = μεσπίλη 1, Dsc.1.118. 2. *azarole*, *Crataegus Azarolus*, ibid. [ῐ Archil. and Amphis ll. cc.; ῑ in Eub.74.4.] **-ώδης**, ες, *like a medlar*, καρπός Thphr.*HP*3.15.6.

**μέσπλη**, Scythian word for the *moon*, Hsch.

**μεσπόδι**, Thess., = μέσφα, *IG*9(2).517.13 (Larissa, iii B. C.).

⊕ **μέσσαβον**, = μέσαβον, Hsch. **μεσσαῖον**· τὸ ὑπὸ τοὺς τραχήλους ὑποτιθέμενον, Id.

⊕ **μέσσᾰτος**, η, ον, irreg. Sup. of μέσσος, *midmost*, ἐν μεσσάτῳ for ἐν μέσῳ, Il.8.223; Att. **μέσατος**, υἱός Ar.*V.*1502, cf. Men.267, Theoc.21.19, *IG*14.2012*A* 33 (Sulp. Max.), Opp.*C.*1.112, D.P.204:—in later Ep. **μεσσάτιος**, Call.*Dian.*78, D.P.296, Opp.*C.*4.442. (For the form, cf. νέος νέατος, τρίτος τρίτατος.)

**μέσσαυλος, μέσσαυλον, μεσσηγύ, -γύς**, v. μεσ-.

**μεσσηγῠ-δορπο-χέστης**, = ὁ μεσηγὺ δόρπου χέζων, Hippon.127.

**μεσσήρης**, v. μεσήρης. **μεσσίδιος**· μέσος, ἴσος, Hsch.

**μεσσο-γενής**, ές, *middle-aged*, Hsch. **-γεως**, v. μεσόγαιος. **-θεν**, poet. for μεσόθεν, Adv. *from the middle*, μ. ἰσοπαλές Parm.8.44, cf. A.R.1.1168: c. gen., μ. ὕλης *AP*9.661 (Jul. Aeg.); **μεσόθεν**, Ti.Locr.95e. **-θῐ**, Adv., for *μεσόθι, *in the middle*, Hes.*Op.*369, etc.: c. gen., νηός A.R.2.172; ζώνης Opp.*C.*1.92.

**μεσ⟨σ⟩οικέται**· μέτοικοι, ἢ οἱ τὰς λαγόνας οἰκοῦντες, Hsch. **μέσ⟨σ⟩οπα**· ἱμάντα τὸν περὶ τὸν ζυγὸν καὶ τὸ ἄροτρον δεδεμένον, Id.; cf. μέσαβον. **μεσσο-παγής, -παλής**, v. μεσοπ-. **-πλουτον** προσόψημα· τὸ σκώληκα ποιῆσαν, Id. **-ρης**· ὁ μέσος ὠκεανοῦ καὶ οὐρανοῦ τόπος, Id.

**μέσσορος**, ὁ, for *μέσορος, *boundary-stone*, *Tab.Heracl.*1.63, al.

**μέσσος**, η, ον, Ep. and Aeol. for μέσος (q. v.).

**μεσ⟨σ⟩οτύλαρον**· αἰδοῖον, Hsch. **μεσ⟨σ⟩όψηρον**· ἡμίξηρον, Id. **μεσσωτήρ**· ὁ μεσιτεύων κατὰ τὸν ἀγῶνα, Id.

⊕ **μέστα**, Dor., = μέσφα, μέστα κα ἡ κρίσις ἐπιτελεσθῇ *SIG*712.39 (Crete, ii B. C.), cf. *Berl.Sitzb.*1927.160,164 (Cyrene); cf. μέστε, μέττα.

**μέστακα**· τὴν μεμασημένην τροφήν, Hsch.; cf. μάσταξ.

**μέστε**, Arc., = μέσφα, μέστ' ἂν ἀέλιος ὀν[τέλλοι] *IG*5(2).4.12 (Tegea); [μέ]στε ζατὸν ἔοι ἄμοινα ib.22.

**μεστ-ός**, ή, όν, *full*, ἄγγεα Hom.*Epigr.*15.5; ἐποίησεν τὴν πόλιν μεστήν Ar.*Eq.*814; ἔγχεον μεστήν *a full cup*, Diph.20, cf. Alex.58; μὴ μεστὰς ἀεὶ ἕλκωμεν Antiph.207.1; of persons, οἶνον πίνεις μ. ὢν Alex.164, cf. Anaxandr.15. II. c. gen., *full of*, ἀργυρίου.. ἀρτάβη μεστή Hdt.1.192; τὸ στόμα.. μεστὸν βδελλέων Id.2.68; μ. ὕδατος Ar.*Nu.*383; ἀλφίτων, οἴνου, ἐλαίου, Id.*Pl.*806 sq.; ὄνος.. οἴνου μ. *laden with*.., Id.*V.*617; ἱμάτιον κηλίδων μ. Thphr.*Char.*19.7. 2. metaph., πάντα μ. ἐλπίδων ἀγαθῶν εἶναι X.*HG*3.4.18; μεστοὶ σπουδῆς, ἀταξίας, Id.*Smp.*1.13, *Mem.*3.5.6; πολλῆς ἀνοίας μ. Isoc.5.45; σοφία μ. ἐλέους καὶ καρπῶν ἀγαθῶν *Ep.Jac.*3.17; φόβου καὶ ἐρώτων μ. Pl.*R.*579b; ἀπάτης μ. Id.*Phd.*83a, etc.; ἐλευθερίας Id.*R.*563d; μ. θεάτρου *full of* theatric pride, i. e. spoilt by applause, Id.*Smp.*194b; ὑπερηφανίας καὶ ὑπεροψίας μ. v. l. in D.21.195. b. *sated with*, c. gen., E.*IT*804; μ. εἰρήνης σαπρᾶς Ar.*Pax*554; τινος (of a person) Plu.2.541d: c. part., μ. ἤ θυμούμενος, i. e. had had my *fill* of anger, S.*OC*768; μ. ἐγένετο ἀγανακτῶν D.48.28; μεστοὶ τοῦ συνεχῶς λέγοντος Id.12.308; also μ. τὸν θυμόν Plu.*Alex.*13. **-ότης**, ητος, ἡ, *fullness, Gloss.* **-όω**, *fill full of*, c. gen. rei, ὀργῆς μ. τινά S.*Ant.*280:—Pass., *to be filled* or *full of*, κτύπου Id.*El.*713, cf. *Ant.*420; of persons, παρρησίας μεστοῦσθαι καὶ ἐλευθερίας Pl.*Lg.*649b; ὕβρεώς τε καὶ ἀδικίας ib.713c: abs., Procop.*Arc.*13; and in medic. sense, ἀγγεῖα μεμεστωμένα Gal.1.394, cf. 8.932. **-ωμα**, ατος, τό, *fullness*, Orac.ap.Eus.*PE*4.9 (pl.). **-ωσις**, εως, ἡ, *filling full, saturation*, φαίνεται ἄπειρον πᾶν κατὰ τὴν ἑαυτοῦ μ. ὂν Dam.*Pr.*200; *plenitude*, τῆς οἰκείας τελειότητος Herm. *in Phdr.*p.145 A. II. in Lit. Crit., *overcrowding with detail*, Syrian. *in Hermog.*1.36 R.

**μεσύμνιον**, τό, an exclamation *in the middle of a strophe*, Heph. *Poëm.*7.1.

⊕ **μέσφᾰ**, Adv., poet. for μέχρι, *until*, c. gen., μέσφ' ἠοῦς Il.8.508; *as far as*, μ. αὐτῶν γονάτων Arat.725: c. acc., μ. τό γ' ἐχθές Theoc.2.144; μ. τὰ πρυτανήϊα Call.*Cer.*129: with Preps., μέσφ' ἐς Id.*Del.*47; μέσφα ποτί prob. in *AP*12.97 (Antip.); μ. παρά Arat.599. 2. before ὅτε, μέσφ' ὅτε *even till*.., c. aor. ind., Call.*Dian.*195, *Hec.*1.1.4: without ὅτε, as a Conj., *until*, c. ind., Id.*Cer.*93, A.R.2.1227, *AP*7.614.10 (Agath.): c. subj., D.P.586; μέσφα κε Opp.*H.*1.754; *while*, μέσφ' οὐ ὁ δαίμων οὔρια φυσιάει Cerc.4.49. 3. *meantime*, Call.*Lav.Pall.*55.

**μέσφι**, = foreg., *as far as, up to*, c. gen., Aret.*SD*1.7,10,13, 2.5,13: as Conj., μ. διαχωρέει Id.*CA*2.4; μέσφι ἂν c. subj., Id.*CD*2.13.

**μεσῳδ-ικός**, ή, όν, *belonging to* or *like a* μεσῳδός, Heph.*Poëm.*4.4, cf. Sch. ad loc. **-ός**, ἡ, *portion of a choral ode, coming between* the strophe and antistrophe, without anything to correspond with it, Heph.*Poëm.*7.2.

**μέσωρος**, ον, *between the ages, adolescent*, Hsch.; also of things, *suited to boys and men*, Id.; ὅπλα Poll.7.158.

⊕ **μετά** [ᾰ, but ᾱ in S.*Ph.*184 (s. v. l., lyr.)], poet. **μεταί**, dub., only in μεταιβολία; Aeol., Dor., Arc. **πεδά** (q. v.): Prep. with gen., dat., and acc. (Cf. Goth. *miþ*, OHG. *miti, mit* 'with'.)

**A.** WITH GEN. (in which use μ. gradually superseded σύν, q. v.), I. *in the midst of, among, between*, with pl. Nouns, μετ' ἄλλων λέξο ἑταίρων Od.10.320; μ. δμώων πῖνε καὶ ἦσθε 16.140; τῶν μέτα παλλόμενος Il.24.400; πολλῶν μ. δούλων A.*Ag.*1037; μ. ζώντων εἶναι S.*Ph.*1312; ὅτων οἰκεῖς μέτα Id.*OT*414; μ. τῶν θεῶν διάγουσα Pl.*Phd.*81a (but κεῖσθαι μ. τινός *with* one, S.*Ant.*73): sts. the pl. is implied, μετ' οὐδενὸς ἀνδρῶν ναίειν, i. e. *among* no men, Id.*Ph.*1103 (lyr.), etc. II. *in common, along with, by aid of* (implying a closer union than σύν), μ. Βοιωτῶν ἐμάχοντο Il.13.700, cf. 21.458; συνδιε-

πολέμησαν τὸν πόλεμον μ. Ἀθηναίων *IG*1².108.7; μ. ξυμμάχων ξυγκινδυνεύσειν Th.8.24, cf. 6.79, etc.; μ. τῆς βουλῆς *in co-operation with* the council, *IG*1².91.10: in this sense freq. (not in Il., Od., Pi., rare in early Gr.) with sg., μετ' Ἀθηναίης *with*, i.e. *by aid of*, Athena, *h.Hom.* 20.2; μ. εἷο Hes.*Th.*392; μ. τινὸς πάσχειν, δρᾶν τι, A.*Pr.*1067 (anap.), S.*Ant.*70; μ. τινὸς εἶναι to be *on* one's *side*, Th.3.56; μ. τοῦ ἠδικημένου ἔσεσθαι X.*Cyr.*2.4.7; μ. τοῦ νόμου καὶ τοῦ δικαίου Pl.*Ap.*32b: generally, *with, together with*, with Subst. in sg. first in Hdt. (in whom it is rare exc. in the phrase οἱ μ. τινός, v. infr.), as κοιμᾶσθαι μ. τινός 3.68, Timocl.22.2; εὕδειν μ. τινός Hdt.3.84; οἱ μ. τινός his *companions*, Id.1.86, al., Pl.*Prt.*315b: freq. with Prons., μετ' αὐτοῦ S. *Ant.*73; μετ' ἐμοῦ Ar.*Ach.*661 (anap.), etc.: less freq. of things, στέγη πυρὸς μ. S.*Ph.*298; μ. κιθάρας E.*IA*1037 (lyr.); μ. τυροῦ Ar.*Eq.*771, etc.; τὴν δίαιταν μεθ' ὅπλων ἐποιήσαντο Th.1.6, cf. E.*Or.*573; ὄχλος μ. μαχαιρῶν καὶ ξύλων *Ev.Matt.*26.47: indicating community of action and serving to join two subjects, Κλεομένης μετὰ Ἀθηναίων C. *and* the Athenians, Th.1.126: with pl. Verb, Δημοσθένης μ. τῶν ξυστρατήγων σπένδονται Id.3.109, etc.; of things, *in conjunction with*, ἰσχύν τε καὶ κάλλος μετὰ ὑγιείας Pl.*R.*591b; γῆρας μ. πενίας ib.330a. III. later, *in one's dealings with*, ὅσα ἐποίησεν ὁ θεὸς μετ' αὐτῶν *Act.Ap.* 14.27; ὁ ποιήσας τὸ ἔλεος μετ' αὐτοῦ *Ev.Luc.*10.36; τί ἡμῖν συνέβη μ. τῶν ἀρχόντων *PAmh.*2.135.15 (ii A.D.): even of hostile action, σὺ ποιεῖς μετ' ἐμοῦ πονηρίαν Lxx *Jd.*11.27, cf. 15.3; πολεμῆσαι μ. τινός *Apoc.*12.7, cf. Apollod.*Poliorc.*190.4 codd. (but μ. may be a gloss), Wilcken *Chr.*23.10 (v A.D.), *OGI*201.3 (Nubia, vi A.D.): to denote the union of persons with qualities or circumstances, and so to denote manner, τὸ ἄπραγμον.. μὴ μ. τοῦ δραστηρίου τεταγμένον Th.2.63, etc.; ἱκετεῦσαι μ. δακρύων Pl.*Ap.*34c; οἴκτου μέτα S.*OC*1636; μετ' ἀσφαλείας μὲν δοξάζομεν, μετὰ δέους δὲ.. ἐλλείπομεν Th.1.120, cf. *IG*2². 791.12; μ. ῥυθμοῦ βαίνοντες Th.5.70; ὅσα μετ' ἐλπίδων λυμαίνεται ib.103, etc.; ψυχὴν ὁσίως βεβιωκυῖαν καὶ μετ' ἀληθείας Pl.*Grg.*526c, cf. *Phdr.*249a, 253d; also, *by means of*, μετ' ἀρετῆς πρωτεύειν X.*Mem.* 3.5.8; γράφε μ. μέλανος *PMag.Lond.*121.226. 2. serving to join two predicates, γενόμενος μ. τοῦ δυνατοῦ καὶ ξυνετός, i.e. δυνατός τε καὶ ξυνετός, Th.2.15; ὅταν πλησιάζῃ μ. τοῦ ἅπτεσθαι Pl.*Phdr.* 255b. IV. rarely of Time, μ. τοῦ γυμνάζεσθαι ἠλείψαντο, for ἅμα, Th.1.6; μετ' ἀνοκωχῆς *during..*, Id.5.25.

B. WITH DAT., only poet., mostly Ep.: I. *between, among* others, but without the close union which belongs to the genitive, and so nearly = ἐν, which is sts. exchanged with it, μ. πρώτοισι.. ἐν πυμάτοισι Il.11.64: 1. of persons, *among, in company with*, μετ' ἀθανάτοισι Il.1.525; μετ' ἀνθρώποις B.5.30; μ. κόραισι Νηρῇος Pi.*O.*2.29; μ. τριτάτοισιν ἄνασσεν *in* the third generation (not μ. τριτάτων *belonging to* it), Il.1.252; of haranguing an assembly, μετ' Ἀργείοις ἀγορεύεις 10.250, etc.; *between*, of two parties, φιλότητα μετ' ἀμφοτέροισι βάλωμεν 4.16. 2. of things, μ. νηυσίν, ἄστρασι, κύμασιν, 13.668, 22.28, Od.3.91; δεινὸν δ' ἐστὶ θανεῖν μ. κύμασιν Hes. *Op.*687; χαῖται δ' ἐρρώοντο μ. πνοιῇς ἀνέμοιο Il.23.367; αἰετῷ.. ἐπέτοντο μ. π. ἀ. Od.2.148. 3. of separate parts of persons, *between*, μ. χερσὶν ἔχειν to hold *between*, i.e. *in*, the hands, Il.11.4, 184, S. *Ph.*1110 (lyr.), etc.; τὸν μ. χ. ἐρύσατο Il.5.344; ὅς κεν.. πέσῃ μ. ποσσὶ γυναικός, of a child being born, 'to fall *between* her feet', 19. 110; so μ. γένυσσιν, γαμφηλῇσιν, 11.416, 13.200; μ. φρεσί 4.245, etc. II. to complete a number, *besides, over and above*, αὐτὰρ ἐγὼ πέμπτος μ. τοῖσιν ἐλέγμην I reckoned myself to be *with* them a fifth, Od.9.335, cf. Il.3.188; Οὖτιν.. πύματον ἔδομαι μ. οἷς ἑτάροισι last *to complete the number*, i.e. *after*, Od.9.369, cf. A.*Pers.*613, Theoc.1.39, 17.84. III. c. dat. sg., only of collect. Nouns (or the equivalent of such, μεθ' αἵματι καὶ κονίῃσιν Il.15.118), μ. στροφάλιγγι κονίης 21. 503; στρατῷ 22.49; μ. πρώτῃ ἀγορῇ 19.50, etc.; μετ' ἀνδρῶν.. ἀριθμῷ Od.11.449; μετ' ἄλλῳ λαῷ A.*Ch.*365 (lyr.).

C. WITH ACCUS., I. of motion, *into the middle of, coming into* or *among*, esp. where a number of *persons* is implied, ἵκοντο μ. Τρῶας καὶ Ἀχαιούς Il.3.264; μ. φῦλα θεῶν 15.54, cf. Od.3.366, al.; μ. μῶλον Ἄρηος Il.16.245; μ. λαὸν Ἀχαιῶν 5.573, al.; μ. στρατόν, μεθ' ὅμιλον, μεθ' ὁμήγυριν, 5.589, 14.21, 20.142: so of birds, ὥς τ' αἰγυπιὸς μ. χῆνας (though this may be referred to signf. 2), 17.460; of *things*, εἴ τινα φεύγοντα σαώσειαν μ. νῆας 12.123; με μ... ἔριδας καὶ νείκεα βάλλει plunges me *into* them, 2.376; of place, μ. τ' ἤθεα καὶ νομὸν ἵππων 6.511; δράγματα μετ' ὄγμον πῖπτον *into the midst of* the furrow, 18.552. 2. *in pursuit* or *quest of*, of persons, sts. in friendly sense, βῆ δ' ἰέναι μ. Νέστορα went *to seek* Nestor, Il.10.73, cf. 15.221: sts. in hostile sense, βῆναι μ. τινά to go *after*, pursue him, 5.152, 6.21, al.; also of things, πλεῖν μ. χαλκόν to sail *in quest of* it, Od.1.184; ἵκηαι μ. πατρὸς ἀκουήν *in search of* news of thy father, 2.308, cf. 13.415; οἴχονται μ. δεῖπνον Il.19.346; πόλεμον μέτα θωρήσσοντο they armed *for* the battle, 20.329; ὡπλίζοντο μεθ' ὕλην prepared *to seek after* wood, 7.418, cf. 420; μ. δούρατος ᾤχετ' ἐρωήν 11.357; μ. γὰρ δόρυ ἦει οἰσόμενος 13.247. II. of sequence or succession, 1. of Place, *after, behind*, λαοὶ ἕπονθ', ὡς εἴ τε μ. κτίλον ἕσπετο μῆλα like sheep *after* the bell-wether, Il.13.492, cf. Od.6.260, 21.190, *h.Ven.*69; ἔσχατοι μ. Κύνητας οἰκέουσι Hdt.4.49; μ. τὴν θάλασσαν *beyond, on the far side of* the sea, Theo Sm.p.122 H. 2. of Time, *after, next to*, μ. δαῖτας Od.22.352; μεθ' Ἕκτορα πότμος ἑτοῖμος *after* Hector thy death is at the door, Il.18.96; μ. Πάτροκλόν γε θανόντα 24.575, cf. Hdt. 1.34; μετ' εὐχάν A.*Ag.*231 (lyr.), etc.; μ. ταῦτα *thereupon, thereafter*, *h.Merc.*126, etc.; τὸ μ. ταῦτα Pl.*Phlb.*34c; τὸ μ. τοῦτο Id.*Criti.* 120a; μετ' ὀλίγον ὕστερον shortly *after*, Id.*Lg.*646c; μ. μικρὸν Luc. *Demon.*8; μ. ἡμέρας τρεῖς μ. τὴν ἄφεδρον Dsc.2.19; μ. ἔτη δύο J.*BJ* 1.13.1; μ. τρίτον ἔτος Thphr.*HP*4.2.8; μ. χρυσόθρονον ἠῶ *after* daybreak, *h.Merc.*326: but μετ' ἡμέρην *by* day, opp. νυκτός, Hdt.2.150, cf. Pl.*Phdr.*251e, etc.; μεθ' ἡμέραν, opp. νύκτωρ, E.*Ba.*485; μ. νύκτας Pi.*N.*6.6; μ. τὸν ἑξέτη καὶ τὴν ἑξέτιν *after* the boy or girl has attained the age of six years, Pl.*Lg.*794c. 3. in order of Worth, Rank, etc., *next after*, following Sup., κάλλιστος ἀνὴρ.. τῶν ἄλλων Δαναῶν μετ' ἀμύμονα Πηλεΐωνα Il.2.674, cf. 7.228, 12.104, Od.2.350, Hdt.4. 53, X.*Cyr.*7.2.11, etc.; κοῦροι οἵ.. ἀριστεύουσι μεθ' ἡμέας Od.4.652, cf. Isoc.9.18: where Sup. is implied, ὃς πᾶσι μετέπρεπε.. μ. Πηλεΐωνος ἑταῖρον Il.16.195, cf. 17.280, 351; μ. μάκαρας *next to* the gods, A.*Th.* 1080 (anap.); also μάχεσθαι μ. πολλοὺς τῶν Ἑλλήνων to be *inferior* in fighting *to* many.., Philostr.*Her.*6. III. *after, according to*, μ. σὸν καὶ ἐμὸν κῆρ *as* you and I *wish*, Il.15.52; μετ' ἀνέρος ἴχνι' ἐρευνῶν 18.321; μετ' ἴχνια βαῖνε Od.2.406. IV. generally, *among, between*, as with dat. (B. I), μ. πάντας ὁμήλικας ἄριστος best *among* all, Il.9.54, cf. Od.16.419; μ. πληθύν Il.2.143; μ. τοὺς τετελευτηκότας *including* those who have died, *PLond.*2.260.87 (i A.D.); μ. χεῖρας ἔχειν Hdt.7.16.β', Th.1.138, *POxy.*901.9 (iv A.D.), cf. X.*Ages.*2. 14, etc.

D. μετά with all cases can be put after its Subst., and is then by anastrophe μέτα, Il.13.301, but not when the ult. is elided, 17. 258, Od.15.147.

E. abs. as ADV., *among them, with them*, Il.2.446, 477, etc.; *with him*, οὐκ οἶον, μ. καὶ Γανυμήδεα A.R.3.115. II. *and then, next afterwards*, opp. πρόσθε, Il.23.133. III. *thereafter*, 15.67, Hdt.1. 88, 128, 150, A.*Ag.*759 (lyr.), etc.; μ. γάρ τε καὶ ἄλγεσι τέρπεται ἀνήρ one feels pleasure even in troubles, *when past*, Od.15.400; μ. δέ, for ἔπειτα δέ, Hdt.1.19, Luc.*DMort.*9.2, etc.

F. μέτα, = μέτεστι, Od.21.93, Parm.9.4, Hdt.1.88, 171, S.*Ant.* 48, etc.

G. IN COMPOS.: I. *of community* or *participation*, as in μεταδίδωμι, μετέχω, usu. c. gen. rei. 2. of action *in common with* another, as in μεταδαίνυμαι, μεταμέλπομαι, etc., c. dat. pers. II. *in the midst of*, of space or time, as in μεταδήμιος, μεταδόρπιος I; *between*, as in μεταίχμιον, μεταπύργιον. III. of *succession* of time, as in μεταδόρπιος 2, μετακλαίω, μεταυτίκα. IV. of *pursuit*, as in μεταδιώκω, μετέρχομαι. V. of *letting go*, as in μεθίημι, μεθήμων. VI. *after, behind*, as in μετάφρενον, opp. πρόσθε. VII. *reversely*, as in μετατρέπω, μεταστρέφω. VIII. most freq. of *change* of place, condition, plan, etc., as in μεταβαίνω, μεταβάλλω, μεταβουλεύω, μεταγιγνώσκω, etc.

**μεταβαίνω**, fut. -βήσομαι *h.Ven.*293: aor. μετέβην, imper. μετάβηθι Od.8.492, μετάβα Alex.14: pf. -βέβηκα:—Med., aor. 3 sg. μετεβήσετο or -σατο A.R.4.1176:—*pass over* from one place to another, μετὰ δ' ἄστρα βεβήκει (for μετεβεβήκει) the stars *had passed over* the meridian, Od.12.312, 14.483 (but τοῦ ἄστρου μεταβαίνοντος μίαν ἡμέραν διὰ τεσσάρων ἐτῶν *OGI*56.42 (Canopus, iii B.C.)); μ. ἐς τὴν Ἀσίην Hdt.7.73, cf. 1.57; μ. ἐξ οἰκίας εἰς οἰκίαν *Ev.Luc.*10.7: abs., *change one's abode*, *PTeb.*316.20 (i A.D.): metaph., ᾗ τὸ δίκαιον μεταβαίνει according as right *passes over* (from one side to the other), A. *Ch.*308 (anap.). 2. in writing or speaking, *pass from one subject to another*, μετάβηθι *change thy theme*, Od.8.492; μεταβάντες *changing their course, turning round*, Hdt.8.4; μεταβήσομαι ἄλλον ἐς ὕμνον *h.Ven.* l.c.; ἐπανέλθωμεν ὅθεν δεῦρο μετέβημεν Pl.*Cra.*438a; ἀπὸ τοῦ ψέγειν πρὸς τὸ ἐπαινεῖν Id.*Phdr.*265c; ἀπ' ἐμψύχων ἐπ' ἄψυχα μ. Phld. *Rh.*1.172 S.; μεταβαίνων ὁ λόγος *advancing step by step*, Arist.*EN* 1097ᵃ24. 3. *pass from one state to another, change*, [αἱ πολιτεῖαι] οὐκ εὐθὺς μ. Id.*Pol.*1292ᵇ18, etc.: freq. with Preps., μ. ἐκ μείζονος εἰς ἔλαττον Pl.*Prm.*165a; of changes of fortune in a drama, μ. εἰς εὐτυχίαν Arist.*Po.*1455ᵇ27; μ. ἐκ τῆς τιμαρχίας εἰς τὴν ὀλιγαρχίαν Pl.*R.*550d; μεταβαίνει τυραννὶς ἐκ δημοκρατίας *comes on after..*, ib.569c; μεταβεβήκαμεν ἐκ τοῦ θανάτου εἰς τὴν ζωήν 1*Ep.Jo.*3.14; ἀπὸ τοῦ παιδὸς εἰς τὸν ἄνδρα Luc.*Am.*24; μ. εἰς ἀλεκτρυόνα Id.*Gall.*4. 4. in the Epicurean logic, *make a transition*: hence, *infer*, esp. from analogy or resemblance, λόγος ὁ μεταβαίνων ἀπό τινος ἐπί τι Phld.*D.*3.12, cf. *Sign.* 5, al. 5. c. acc., *pass to another* place or state, ἄνω μεταβὰς βίοτον E.*Hipp.*1292 (anap.); μ. τόπον ἐκ τόπου S.E.*M.*10.52. b. *go after, follow* a pursuit *eagerly*, Opp.*H.*4.418. II. causal in aor. I μεταβῆσαι, *carry over* or *away*, τινὰ ποτὶ δῶμα Διὸς -βᾶσαι Pi.*O.*1.42; *change*, ἄστρων ὁδοὺς E.*El.*728 (lyr.).

⊛**μεταβάλλω**, fut. -βαλῶ Ar.*Av.*1568: aor. μετέβαλον:—*throw into a different position, turn quickly* or *suddenly*, Hom. only once, in tmesi, μετὰ νῶτα βαλών Il.8.94; χαλεπῶς μ. δέμας E.*Hipp.*204 (anap.), cf. Gal.15.556; μ. θοἰμάτιον ἐπιδέξια Ar. l.c.; μ. γῆν *turn*, i.e. *plough*, the earth, X.*Oec.*16.14; μετέβαλε Κύριος ἄνεμον ἐκ θαλάσσης Lxx *Ex.* 10.19; μ. ποταμόν *change the course of* a river, Jul.*Or.*3.126d. II. *turn about, change, alter*, τὸ οὔνομα Hdt.1.57; τὴν πολιτείαν Arist.*Pol.* 1292ᵇ21; [οἱ Βρίγες] τὸ οὔνομα μετέβαλον [ἐς Φρύγας] Hdt.7.73; τὰς φυλὰς μετέβαλε [ὁ Κλεισθένης] ἐς ἄλλα οὐνόματα Id.5.68; μ. μορφήν τινος εἰς ἀνδρὸς φύσιν E.*Ba.*54; [τινὰ] ἐπὶ κακόν Ar.*Th.*723; ἐπὶ τὸ βέλτιον Pl.*R.*381b; μ. δίαιταν *change* one's way of life, Th.2.16; μ. ὕδατα *drink different* water, Hdt.8.117; ὀργὰς μ. E.*Med.*121 (anap.); μ. τοὺς τρόπους Ar.*Pl.*36, Eup.357.7; μ. τὸ ἔθος Th.1.123; μ. εὔνοιαν *lose* it, ib. 77; μ. χώραν ἐκ χώρας Pl.*Tht.*181c: freq. with Adjs., etc., implying change, μ. ἄλλους τρόπους *change and adopt* other ways, E.*IA*343 (troch.); μ. ἄλλας γραφάς ib.363 (troch.); εἶδος καινὸν μουσικῆς μ. Pl. *R.*424c; πόλις ἄλλοτ' ἄλλον -βάλλουσα τύραννον Plu.*Tim.*1; μ. ἀντὶ τοῦ "ὁμο-" "ἀ-" Pl.*Cra.*405d; ἐμαυτὸν ἄνω κάτω μετέβαλλον Id. *Phd.*96b; ἄνω καὶ κάτω τὰς δόξας μ. Id.*R.*508d: c. acc. cogn., πολλὰς

μεταβολὰς..μ. ὑδάτων καὶ σίτων ib.404a. **b.** *translate*, νόμον εἰς τὴν Ἑλλάδα φωνήν J.*AJProoem.*3, cf. 12.2.13 (Pass.). **c.** *stir* with a spoon, Dsc.3.22 (Pass.). **III.** intr., *undergo a change*, μ. ἐς εὐνομίην Hdt.1.65, cf. Antipho 2.4.9; μ. εἰς ὀλιγαρχικὸν ἐκ τοῦ τιμοκρατικοῦ Pl.*R.*553a, etc.; μ. ἐπὶ τοὐναντίον Id.*Plt.*270d; ὅταν εἰς ἑτέραν -βάλῃ πολιτείαν ἡ πόλις Arist.*Pol.*1276b14, cf. 1301a20: impers., μεταβάλλει διὰ πλειόνων ζῴων *changes run* through a series of creatures, Thphr.*HP*2.4.4: c. gen. rei, *come in exchange for* or *instead of*, καιναὶ καινῶν μεταβάλλουσαι..συντυχίαι E.*Tr.*1118. **b.** *vary*, μεταβάλλειν τὰς ἐπιστήμας τοῖς τόποις Phld.*Rh.*2.115 S. **2.** *change one's course*, μεταβαλὼν πρὸς Ἀθηναίους *turning* to the Athenians, Hdt.8.109: aor. part. μεταβαλών abs., *instead, in turn*, μεταβαλόντας ἀντὶ Κρητῶν γενέσθαι Ἰήπυγας Id.7.170, cf. E.*Ion* 1614, Pl.*Smp.*204e, *Grg.*480e: also pres. part. μεταβάλλων Id.*Tht.*166d.

**B.** Med., *turn round, shift* a load, μεταβαλλόμενος τἀνάφορον Ar.*Ra.*8; προβαλλομένους τὰ ὅπλα ἢ μεταβαλλομένους X.*An.*6.5.16. **2.** *cause to be removed*, σῖτον *PHib.*1.45.6 (iii B.C.), etc. **b.** *order to be paid, remit*, *POxy.*1153.8 (i A.D.), 1419.5 (iii A.D.). **II.** *change what is one's own*, μ. τὰ ἱμάτια *change one's* clothes, X.*Mem.*1.6.6; μ. τοὺς τρόπους Ar.*V.*1461 (lyr.); μετεβάλλετ' ὀπωπάν *changed her* appearance, Erinn. in *PSI*9.1090.53+13 (p.xii). **2.** *exchange*, τίς μεταβάλοιτ' ἂν ὧδε σιγὰν λόγων; silence *for* words, S.*El.*1261; [τὴν ἄσαρκον τροφὴν] ὑγείας καὶ ῥώμης μεταβαλέσθαι *have given up* asceticism *in exchange for* health and strength, Porph.*Abst.*1.2; *barter, traffic in*, οἴνου μεταβαλλόμενος καὶ σίτου πρᾶσιν Pl.*Lg.*849d; μ. τὰ ἀλλότρια ἔργα Id.*Sph.*223d; μ. ἐν τῇ ἀγορᾷ X.*Mem.*3.7.6, cf. D.S.5.13. **III.** *turn oneself, turn about*, ἄνω καὶ κάτω Pl.*Grg.*481e, Din.1.17; esp. **2.** *change one's purpose* or *mind*, Hdt.5.75, *SIG* 22.20 (v B.C.), *Act.Ap.*28.6, etc.; *change sides*, Th.1.71, 8.90, X.*HG* 2.3.31; πρός τινα Axionic.6.10. **3.** *turn* or *wheel round*, μ. ἐπ' ἀσπίδα X.*Cyr.*7.5.6; τὸ δόρυ εἰς τοὔπισθεν μ. Id.*Eq.*8.10: abs., *turn about*, μεταβαλλόμενος τοῖς ἔξω περιεστηκόσι λοιδορήσεται Aeschin.3.207.

**μεταβάπτω**, *change by dipping*, Luc.*Am.*40: metaph., αὐτοὺς μ. ἡ φιλοσοφία Id.*Bis Acc.*8:—Pass., *change one's complexion*, Id.*Anach.*33.

**μεταβᾰσᾰνίζω**, *test* a theory *afterwards*, Gal.18(2).862.

**μετά-βᾰσις**, εως, ἡ, *moving over, shifting*, e.g. of the body in walking, from one leg to the other, Hp.*Mochl.*20; *change of position*, Epicur.*Ep.*1 p.16 U.: pl., ib.p.17 U. **2.** *passing over*, ἐς τὸ ἕτερον πλοῖον v.l. in Antipho 5.22; *migration, change of residence*, εἰς Κόρινθον ἐξ Ἀθηνῶν Plu.2.78d; μ. ποιεῖσθαι ἐπί.. *BGU*137.6 (ii A.D.). **II.** *change*, τῶν πολιτειῶν γένεσις καὶ μ. Pl.*Lg.*676c; δοκεῖ ἡ μ. ἐντεῦθεν γίγνεσθαι Id.*R.*547c; τῶν νομίμων Arist.*Pol.*1303a22 (pl.); ἡ μ. ἐκ [τῶν φυτῶν] εἰς τὰ ζῷα συνεχής ἐστιν Id.*HA*588b11; μ. ἀπὸ ποιότητος εἰς ποιότητα Sor.2.15; αἱ τῆς τραγῳδίας μ. Arist.*Po.*1449a37; but ἡ μ. the *reversal of fortune* in a drama, ib.1455b28. **III.** *transition* from one subject to another, Luc.*Hist.Conscr.*55; as a figure in Rhet., Quint.9.3.25. **2.** *inference* or *procedure by analogy*, Phld.*Rh.*1.105 S., *Sign.*19, S.E.*M.*8.194; ἡ κατὰ τὸ ὅμοιον μ. Phld.*Sign.*38, al.; also in Medicine, ἡ τοῦ ὁμοίου μ. Gal.1.118. **-βᾰτέον**, *one must pass over*, ἐπί τι Ph.1.22. **2.** *one must argue by analogy*, ἀπ' ἐκείνου ἐπὶ τοῦτο S.E.*M.*8.202. **3.** *one must have recourse to* a fresh treatment, Herod.Med. in *Rh.Mus.*58.89, Paul.Aeg.3.32. **-βάτης** [ᾰ], ου, ὁ, = Lat. *desultor, trick-rider*, Hsch. s.v. ζευγηλάτης. **-βᾰτικός**, ή, όν, *able to pass from one place to another*, τὸ μ. ἀφ' ἑτέρου εἰς ἕτερον *Placit.*4.8.6; μ. κίνησις motion *involving change of place*, ib.4.6.1, Ph.1.397, S.E.*M.*9.195; μ. ὄργανα organs *of motion*, Gal.4.546. Adv. -κῶς, κινεῖν *Placit.*3.13.3, cf. Ph.1.176, Alex.Aphr.*in Top.*43.32. **2.** *discursive*, φαντασία μ. καὶ συνθετική S.E.*M.*8.276, cf. Procl.*in Prm.* p.628 S., *in Ti.*1.244 D. Adv. -κῶς Id. *in Prm.*l.c., *in Ti.*1.246 D.; *by the process of analogical* or *discursive reasoning*, εἰ καὶ τὸ νοητὸν μ. ἀπὸ τοῦ αἰσθητοῦ νοοῦμεν S.E.*M.*3.25; νοῦν..ἅμα πάντα γιγνώσκοντα καὶ οὐ μ. Dam.*Pr.*100; opp. ἀμεταβάτως, Procl.*Inst.*211. **II.** *exchanging, bartering*: τὸ -κόν *the petty dealers*, dub. in Hippodam.ap. Stob.4.1.94 (leg. -βλᾰτικόν). **III.** Gramm., *not reflexive*, of pronouns, A.D.*Pron.*24.15. Adv. -κῶς ib.44.14. **-βᾰτός**, ή, όν, *allowing of passage* from part to part, i.e. *divisible, extended*, Epicur.*Ep.*1 p.17 U.

**μεταβῐάζομαι**, *do violence to*, τὴν φύσιν Aret.*CD*1.4.

**μεταβῐβ-άζω**, Att. fut. -βιβῶ, causal of μεταβαίνω, *carry over, transfer*, τοὺς ἐπιβάτας ἐς κοίλην ναῦν X.*HG*1.6.19; τὴν γλῶσσαν τῶν ταρσῶν, i.e. from ankle to ankle, Procop.*Arc.*4; τινὰ ἐπὶ θάτερα Pl.*Lg.*795c; εἰς ἀγαθὰ Ar.*Pax*947 (lyr.); τὸ ἀπὸ τῶν κοινῶν ἔθος ἐπὶ τὰ ἴδια D.10.44; μ. πόλεμον ἐπὶ τὴν Λιβύην Plb.1.41.4; τὸν λόγον ἐπί τι D.S.4.7; [τὰς ψυχὰς] εἰς ἕτερον ἐξ ἑτέρου ζῷον Diog.Oen.35. **2.** *lead in a different direction*, τὰς ἐπιθυμίας Pl.*Grg.*517b: abs., σμικρὸν μ. Id.*Lg.*736d; *change the course* or *form* of an argument, Arist.*Top.*101a33, cf. 161a33. **3.** *translate*, D.H.4.1 (Pass.). **-αστέος**, α, ον, *to be altered*, f.l. in Hp.*Acut.*27.

**μεταβιόω**, aor. inf. -βιῶναι, *live after, survive*, *Placit.*5.19.4.

**μεταβλαστάνω**, *grow differently*, Thphr.*HP*2.4.4.

⊛ **μεταβλέπω**, *change one's point of view*, Arat.186. **II.** *look after* or *at*, c. acc., A.R.1.726.

**μετά-βλημα**, ατος, τό, poet. for μεταβολή, Man.4.522. **-βλητέον**, *one must transfer*, τινὰς εἰς ἡδονάς Pl.*R.*413d. **II.** intr., *one must change*, Hp.*Acut.*48; ἐπὶ θάτερα Pl.*Tht.*167a. **-βλητικός** (Dor. -βλᾱτικός [Philol.]21, prob. in Hippod.ap.Stob.4.1.94), ή, όν, *for* or *in the way of exchange*, ἡ [χρῆσις] ἡ μ. Arist.*Pol.*1257a9: ἡ -κή (sc. τέχνη) *exchange, barter*, Pl.*Sph.*223d, Arist.*Pol.*1258b21: τὸ -κόν (sc. γένος) Pl.*Sph.*224d. Adv. -κῶς Poll.4.51. **II.** *able to produce change*, ἀρχή Arist.*Metaph.*1020a5, cf. 1013a32; δύναμις Ph.1.278; κίνησις S.E.*M.*9.195. **2.** *subject to change*, Thphr.*CP*6.10.2; εἰς τἀναντία Arist.*GC*319a20; of animals, *mobile*, opp. μόνιμα, Id.*HA*487b6, cf. *GA*715a26. ⊛ **-βλητός**, ή, όν, *subject to change*, Ph.1.269, Plu.2.718e, S.E.*M.*9.151.

**μεταβοθρεύω**, *move into another trench, transplant*, Hsch.

**μεταβολ-εύς**, έως, ὁ, *one who exchanges* or *barters, trafficker, huckster*, κάπηλος, παλιγκάπηλος, μεταβολεύς D.25.46, cf. Sch.Ar.*Pl.*1156. **II.** *interpreter, paraphraser*, τῶν λέξεων Eust.1347.40. ⊛ **-ή**, ἡ, *change, changing*, μεταβολαὶ ἱστίων Pi.*P.*4.292; ἱματίων μεταβολαί X.*Lac.*2.1. **2.** *exchange, barter*, ἐπὶ μεταβολῇ with a view to *traffic*, Th.6.31: metaph., οὔ τιν' ἀπαλλαγὴν τῶν κακῶν ἀλλὰ μ. μειζόνων Epicur.*Fr.*479. **3.** *turnover* in business, *PSI*5.495.20 (iii B.C.). **4.** *payment by transfer in an account*, *PLond.*3.1129*b*7 (ii A.D.). **II.** (from Med.) *transition, change*, ἀρχὰ κινήσιος καὶ μεταβολᾶς [Philol.]21, cf. Chrysipp.*Stoic.*2.160; μετάστασις καὶ μ. D.2.13; ἐκ μεταβολῆς Men.712, Plb.1.61.7, D.S.13.24; πάλιν ἐκ μ. Aeschin.2.9: freq. in pl., *changes, vicissitudes*, τῶν ὡρέων Hdt.2.77, cf. Arist.*HA*596b23; τῆς τύχης E.*Fr.*554; αἱ μ. κάτω τε καὶ ἄνω γιγνόμεναι Pl.*Phlb.*43b, cf. Antipho 2.4.9; αἱ πλεῖσται μ. μάλιστα τέρπουσιν Hp.*Vict.*1.18; ἦμαρ ⟨ἕν⟩ τοι μ. πολλὰς ἔχει E.*Fr.*549; τῆς γῆς ἡ ἀρίστη αἰεὶ τὰς μ. τῶν οἰκητόρων εἶχεν Th.1.2: c. gen. objecti, *change from* a thing, μεταβολὰ κακῶν E.*HF*735; rarely, *change to*.., ἀπραγμοσύνης μ. Th.6.18: more freq. with Preps., μ. ἐκ φιλοτίμου εἰς φιλοχρήματον Pl.*R.*553d; ἐκ προστάτου ἐπὶ τύραννον ib.565d; ἐκ τοῦ εἶναι ἐπὶ τὸ μὴ εἶναι Id.*Prm.*162c; ἡ ἐπὶ τὸ χεῖρον μ. Diph.104; ἡ ἐναντία μ. *change to* the contrary, Th.2.43; ἅμα τῇ μ. τῇ ἐς Ἕλληνας their *going over* to the Greeks, Hdt.1.57; ἡ πρὸς Ῥωμαίους μ. Plb.9.26.2; μ. μεταβάλλειν Pl.*R.*404a, Arist.*Po.*1449a14: prov., μ. πάντων γλυκύ E.*Or.*234, cf. Arist.*Rh.*1371a28, Antiph.207.5. **2.** *eclipse*, Hdt.1.74; but μ. ἄστρων καὶ ἡλίου *reversal* of motion, Pl.*Plt.*271c. **3.** αἱ μ. τῶν πολιτειῶν *changes* of government, Arist.*Pol.*1292b18; πολιτῶν (v.l. -ειῶν) Th.6.17. **4.** *migration*, [τὰ ζῷα] ποιούμενα τὰς μ. Arist.*HA*597a3: euphemism for *death*, Philostr.*VA*8.31, *Corp.Herm.*11.15, 12.6. **5.** as Military term, *wheeling about*, being a double κλίσις, ἡ εἰς τοὔπισθεν μ. Plb.18.30.4. **6.** of literary style, *variety*, Caecil.Calact.ap.Quint.9.3.38; μ. καὶ ποικίλον D.H.*Pomp.*3: pl., Longin.5, 23.1. **7.** in Music, *modulation*, e.g. of τόνος or γένος, Aristox.*Harm.*p.38 M., Cleonid.*Harm.*13, Bacch.*Harm.*50, Aristid.Quint.1.11, Ptol.*Harm.*2.6. **-ία**, ἡ, = foreg. I. 2, Lxx *Si.*37.12. **-ικός**, ή, όν, *changeable*, τρόπος Plb.38.5.6; of persons, Vett.Val.14.16; *subject to change, mutable*, μέρη Plu.2.373d; φύσις Simp. *in Cael.*114.14. Adv. -κῶς *with a change* of metre, Heph.*Poëm.* p.74 C. **2.** καπηλεῖον μ. *retail* shop (cf. μεταβόλος II), Heraclid.*Pol.*60 (-μελικόν codd.). **3.** φωνήεντα μ. *doubtful* vowels (α ι υ), S.E.*M.*1.100. **-ιμαῖος**, *translaticius*, *Gloss.* **-ος**, ον, *changeable*, Plu.2.428b, Ptol.*Tetr.*96. **II.** as Subst., = μεταβολεύς I, *huckster, retail dealer*, opp. ἔμπορος, *GDI* iv p.876 (Chios, prob. from Erythrae, iv B.C.), cf. *PRev.Laws* 48.3 (iii B.C.), Lxx *Is.*23.2, 3, *PTeb.*116.20 (ii B.C.), Sch.Ar.*Pax*446; τοὶ μ. τοὶ ἐν τοῖς ἰχθύσιν *SIG*1000.21 (Cos, i B.C.): as Adj., ἱματιοπῶλαι μ. *retail* clothes-dealers, *OGI*629.83 (Palmyra, ii A.D.); μ. ἁλιεῖς *Ostr.*1449 (ii A.D.).

**μεταβούλ-ευμα**, ατος, τό, *change of plan*, Sm.*Jb.*21.2. **-εύω**, *alter one's plans, change one's mind*, ἀμφί τινι Od.5.286. **II.** mostly in Med., Hdt.1.156, E.*Or.*1526 (troch.); μ. ἄνω καὶ κάτω Pl.*Epin.*982d; μ. ὥστε μένειν Hdt.8.57: c. μή et inf.. μετὰ δὴ βουλεύεαι στράτευμα μὴ ἄγειν ἐπὶ τὴν Ἑλλάδα Id.7.12: c. gen., *repent of*, μ. τῆς ἀφίξεως Alciphr.2.4.19. ⊛ **-ία**, ἡ, f.l. for μεταιβολία in Simon.37.17. **-ος**, ον, *changing one's mind, changeful*, Ar.*Ach.*632.

**μετάβρασκος**· μέτριος ἑρμηνεύς, Hsch.

**μετάγγελος**, ὁ and ἡ, *one who carries news from one to another, messenger*, epith. of Iris, θεοῖσι μετάγγελος ἀθανάτοισι (al. θεοῖσι μετ' ἄγγελος) Il.15.144; Ἶρις..μετάγγελος ἦλθ' ἀνέμοισιν (al. μετ' ἄ. ἦλθ') 23.199.

⊛ **μεταγγ-ίζω**, fut. -ίσω *Gp.*3.5.2:—*pour from one vessel into another, decant*, Dsc.1.52, Gal.11.215:—Pass., μεταγγισθεῖσα ἡ ψυχή, of the Pythag. metempsychosis, Eust.1090.32. **-ισμός**, ὁ, metaph., *transmigration*, ὁ ἐξ ἀλόγων ζῴων ἢ εἰς ἄλογα μ. Hierocl.*Prov.*p.172 B.

**Μεταγείτν-ια**, τά, *festival in celebration of* μετοικισμός, *SIG*57.20 (Milet., v B.C.), Plu.2.601b. **-ιος**, ὁ, epith. of Apollo at Athens, Lysim.21, Suid. s.v. Μεταγειτνιών:—hence ⊛ **-ιών**, ῶνος, ὁ, second month of the Attic year, Antipho 6.44, Arist.*HA*549a16, Plu.*Publ.*14; also at Delos, *IG*11(2).203*A*32 (iii B.C.), and in Ionic cities, as Priene, *SIG*278.2 (iv B.C.), Miletus, ib.633.75 (ii B.C.); cf. Πεδαγείτνιος. (Derived by Gramm. from μετά, γείτων, because people *changed their neighbours*: gen. sg. written τοῦ Μεταγειτο (abbrev.) *IG*2².1672.34.)

⊛ **μεταγενής**, ές, *born after*, ὁ μεταγενής *the youngest*, Men.154: Comp. -έστερος D.S.12.11, Luc.*Salt.*80; οἱ μεταγενέστεροι *posterity*, D.S.11.14, J.*BJ*2.8.10, Hierocl. *in CA* 4 p.426 M. **2.** *of later time*, μεταγενέστεροι συγγραφεῖς D.H.*Th.*9: hence, in Philos., ταῦτα -έστερα τῶν γενῶν τοῦ ὄντος prob. in Procl. *in Prm.*p.850 S.; also μ. μετὰ ταῦτα τὴν πολυπραγμοσύνην *consequent*, Phld.*Rh.*2.262 S.

**μεταγεννάω**, *restore to life, revive*, οἶνος μ. τὰς ψυχάς J.*AJ*11.3.3:—Pass., *to be born again*, prob. in *PMag.Par.*1.647.

⊛ **μεταγίγνομαι**, later -**γίνομαι** [ῐ], *take place later*, *BGU*1038.22 (ii A.D.); *to be transferred, carried away*, Lxx 2 *Ma.*2.1.

**μεταγιγνώσκω**, Ion. and later **-γῑνώσκω**, fut. -γνώσομαι: aor. μετέγνων:—*find out after*, i.e. *too late*, ἅταν.. μεταγνούς dub. in A. *Supp.*111 (lyr.). II. *change one's mind, repent*, abs., Hdt.1.40,86; μετέγνων, ἔγνων δὲ.. *changed my mind* and determined.., Id.7.15; μεταγνοὺς ἂν ὀρθῶς βουλεύσαιτο Antipho 5.91, cf. Th.4.92, Pl.*Phdr.* 231a, Lys.19.53, D.18.153, etc.; οὐκουν ἔνεστι καὶ μεταγνῶναι πάλιν; S.*Ph.*1270. 2. c. acc. rei, *change one's mind about, repent of*, μετέγνων καὶ τὰ πρόσθ' εἰρημένα E.*Med.*64; μ. τὰ προδεδογμένα *alter* or *repeal* a previous decree, Th.3.40, cf. Luc.*Ner.*4. b. c. dat. rei, μ. τῷ φόνῳ Philostr.*Ep.*16. 3. c. inf., *change one's mind* so as to do something different, τὸ παντότολμον φρονεῖν μετέγνω A.*Ag.*221 (lyr.); ἐν δὲ τῇ ὑστεραίᾳ μετέγνωσαν Κερκυραίοις ξυμμαχίαν μὲν μὴ ποιήσασθαι Th.1.44; μ. ὡς.. *change one's mind and think* that.., X.*Cyr.*5.5.40.

**μετά-γνοια**, ἡ, = μετάνοια, *repentance, remorse*, S.*El.*581. **-γνώμη**, ἡ, *change of mind*: *defection*, App.*BC*5.122. **-γνωσις**, εως, ἡ, *change of mind* or *purpose*, Hdt.1.87, D.*Ep.*1.15, Phld.*Ir.*p.56 W.

**μεταγραμμᾰτ-ίζω**, *transpose the letters of a word*, *Vit.Lyc.*p.5 S. (Pass.). **-ισμός**, ὁ, *transcription in a different orthography*, Gal. 18(2).778.

**μεταγραπτέον**, *one must correct, alter*, μ. τὸ "χρόνον" "χρόνῳ" Plu.2.1036d, cf. Gal.18(1).135. II. Adj. μεταγραπτέος, α, ον, = *transcripticius*, *Gloss.*

**μεταγρᾰφ-εύς**, έως, ὁ, *transcriber, copyist*, Apollon.*Mir.*6, Tz. ad Lyc.354. **-ή**, ἡ, *transcribing*, Aristeas 9(pl.), 10, Jul.*Ep.*107. 2. *borrowing from one person to pay another*, Plu.2.831a (pl.). II. *translation*, τοῦ νόμου J.*AJ*12.2.6. III. *change of text* or *reading*, Str.12.3.22, cf. A.D.*Synt.*156.2. **-ικός**, ή, όν, *of* or *for transcription*, Tz. ad Hes.*Op.*694. **-ω**, *copy, transcribe*, αὖθις μ. πάλιν E.*IA* 108, cf. Luc.*Ind.*4, *SIG*1020.1 (Halic., i B.C.); τὰ μεταγραφόμενα, of hieroglyphics, D.S.3.4; *rewrite, alter* or *correct what one has written*, Th.1.132; esp. of a public document, X.*HG*6.3.19; μεταγράψαι ἀντὶ "τοῦ Σκιαθίου", ὅπως ἂν ᾖ γεγραμμένον.. "τὸν Παλαισκιάθιον" *IG*1².118.28; Μιλτιάδου καὶ Θεμιστοκλέους εἰκόνας εἰς Ῥωμαῖόν τε ἄνδρα καὶ Θρᾷκα μετέγραψαν Paus.1.18.3; μ. νόμον, etc., *tamper with it*, Din.1.42, cf. Isoc.17.32 (Pass.); in a trial, *alter the record*, D.21.85; τἀναντία ταῖς διαθήκαις μεταγραφῆναι Is.4.13. 2. *translate*, ἐς τὸ Ἑλληνικόν Luc.*Hist.Conscr.*21:—Med., τὰς ἐπιστολὰς μεταγραψάμενοι ἐκ τῶν Ἀσσυρίων γραμμάτων *having got* them *translated*, Th.4.50. 3. in book-keeping, *transfer* to another account, *PHib.*1.111.14 (iii B.C.).

⊕ **μετάγω** [ᾰ], fut. -άξω D.S.20.3: pf. μεταγείοχα *PRyl.*67.5 (ii B.C.):—*convey from one place to another, transfer*, τινὰ εἰς Βαβυλῶνα LXX 1*Es.*1.45, cf. Aristeas 12 (Pass.); τὴν ἐκκλησίαν εἰς Σ κυῶνα Plb.5.1.9; τὸν πόλεμον εἰς τὴν Λιβύην D.S. l.c.; ναόν *SIG*587.6 (Peparethus, ii B.C.); τὰ δικαστήρια ἀπὸ τῆς βουλῆς ἐπὶ τοὺς ἱππέας D.C.*Fr.*83.7; *escort*, τινα *SIG*588.51 (Milet., ii B.C.): Medic., *divert*, τὰ ῥεύματα Gal.17(1).965: metaph., τοὺς πολίτας εἰς σωφρονεστέραν βίου τάξιν μ. Plu.2.225f, cf. *SIG*704*E* 12 (Delph., ii B.C.), Epict.*Ench.*33.3; ψυχὴν ἐπ' εὐφροσύνην *AP*10.77 (Pall.); *seduce*, τινὰς ἐς τὸ ἁβροδίαιτον Hdn.3.8.5. 2. *translate*, εἰς ἑτέραν γλῶσσαν LXX *Si.Prol.* (Pass.). 3. *derive* a metaphor, ἀπό τινος Phld.*Rh.*1.179 S. 4. Pass., *to be borrowed*, μετῆκται ἀπὸ τῶν ἐν γεωμετρίᾳ τὸ ὄνομα Iamb. *in Nic.*p.58 P. II. intr., *go by a different route, change one's course*, X.*Cyr.*7.4.8.

**μετᾰγωγ-εύς**, έως, ὁ, name of a bandage, Heliod.ap.Orib.48.33 tit. **-ή**, ἡ, *removal, transference*, τῆς ὕλης Sor.2.42; τινὸς εἰς Αἴγυπτον Aristeas 23, J.*AJ*12.2.3. 2. *change, transfer*, εἰς τοὐναντίον Phld.*Lib.*p.11 O.: ἐκ.. εἰς.. D.H.*Th.*48; *wheeling, manœuvring*, Ascl.*Tact.*7.5 (pl.): Rhet., *transposition, rearrangement*, πραγμάτων μεταγωγαί D.H.*Is.*15. **-ός**, ή, όν, *shifting*, τινος Sch.Od.5.260, 10.32.

**μεταδαίνυμαι**, fut. -δαίσομαι (v. infr.), *share the feast*, σός γε πατὴρ μεταδαίνυται ἡμῖν Il.22.498, cf. Od.18.48; *partake of*, c. gen. rei, ἵνα δὴ.. μεταδαίσομαι ἱρῶν Il.23.207: abs., Q.S.2.157.

**μεταδειπνέω**, *dine* or *sup after*, Hp.*Acut.*32.

**μεταδετέον**, *one must untie*, X.*Eq.*4.4.

**μεταδεῦσαν**· μετάνοιαν, Hsch.

**μεταδέχομαι**, Pass., *to be participated in*, ὑπὸ οὐσίας Procl. *in Prm.* 851 S. (dub. l.).

**μεταδήμιος**, ον, (δῆμος) *in the midst of* or *among the people*, μή τι κακὸν μεταδήμιον εἴη no harm be *among the people*, Od.13.46; *in the country*, οὐ γὰρ ἔθ' Ἥφαιστος μ. 8.293; οἶνος μ., = ἐπιχώριος, D.P. 744.

**μεταδῐαιτάω**, *change one's way of life*, εἰς δίαιταν Μηδικὴν μ. ἑαυτόν Luc.*DMort.*12.3:—Pass., μεταδιαιτηθεὶς LXX 4*Ma.*8.8.

⊕ **μεταδια-τᾰγή**, ἡ, *transfer of an obligation*, *POxy.*899.40 (ii/iii A.D.). **-τάσσω**, *alter ordinances*, *OGI*383.196 (Nemrud Dagh, i B.C.). II. *transfer an obligation*, *POxy.*899.32 (ii/iii A.D.). ⊕ **-τίθεμαι**, *alter a will*, ib.105.3 (ii A.D.), etc.

**μεταδῐδάσκω**, *teach new things, show a better way*, D.H.9.3, Anon. ap.Suid.: c. acc., *convert*, Gal.8.657; πόλιν λόγῳ μεταδιδάξαι Philostr. *VA*1.15: c. dupl. acc., μ. τινὰ ἑτέραν ὄρχησιν Id.*Im.*2.11:—Pass., like μεταμανθάνω, *learn differently, learn something new*, Muson.*Fr.* 10 p.56 H., Plu.2.784b; μ. τὴν διάλεκτον τὴν Δωρίδα Paus.4.27.11; also, *change one's mind* for the worse, D.S.13.28: more freq. for the better, Id.21.21, al.

⊕ **μεταδίδωμι** [δῐ], fut. -δώσω, *give part of, give a share*, c. gen. rei, τοῦ μεταδοῦν (poet. aor. 2 inf.) Thgn.104; μ. τινί τινος Id.925 (prob. l.), Hdt.1.143, Ar.*Ach.*961; γῆς (sc. αὐτοῖσι) Hdt.4.145; τῆς ἀρχῆς (sc. αὐτοῖσι) Id.7.150; τῷ πλήθει τῆς πολιτείας Arist.*Pol.*1306ᵃ25, cf. Pl.*Men.*89e, Isoc.13.10, etc.; τοῖς μηδὲν ἀδικοῦσιν ἐξ ἴσου τῆς πολιτείας Lys.25.3; τὸ ἄλλῳ τῆς γεννητικῆς.. δυνάμεως μεταδεδωκός Procl. *Inst.*56. 2. c. acc. of the part given, μ. τὸ τριτημόριόν τινι Hdt.9.34, cf. 8.5, Ar.*V.*917; ἀρχῆς μηδ' ὁτιοῦν μ. τοῖς ἡττηθεῖσιν Pl.*Lg.*715a; μ. τὸ μέρος X.*An.*7.8.11; μ. πυρούς *distribute*, ib.4.5.5. 3. intr., μ. τινὶ ὑπέρ, περί τινος, *communicate* with one about.., Plb.29.27.4, 38.8.1; ὅτι.. *POxy.*1153.6 (i A.D.):—Pass., *to be communicated, transmitted*, of notices, memoranda, etc., ib.1472.6 (ii A.D.), etc.; of diseases, Hp.*Ep.*19 (*Hermes* 53.64,65).

⊕ **μεταδιεράω**, *strain, filter*, *POxy.*1631.17 (iii A.D.).

**μεταδιοικ-έω**, *transfer* property, in Pass., *PTeb.*61(*a*).30 (ii B.C.). **-ησις**, εως, ἡ, *transference*, *BMus.Inscr.*4.481*.405.

**μεταδίομαι** [ῐ], *pursue*, μετά με δρόμοισι διόμενοι A.*Supp.*819 (lyr.).

**μεταδιορθ-όω**, *set right*, *IPE*1².34.5 (Olbia). **-ωσις**, εως, ἡ, *correcting oneself*, as a figure of speech, Donat. ad Ter.*Ad.*392, *Phorm.* 232.

**μεταδιορισμός**, ὁ, *change which produces distinction*, Dam.*Pr.* 230.

**μεταδιωκ-τέον**, *one must pursue*, Pl.*Ti.*64b, Them.*Or.*22.272b. **-τος**, ον, *pursued, overtaken*, Hdt.3.63. II. *to be pursued*, Iamb. *Comm.Math.*7. **-ω**, fut. -ξω Plot.2.9.15, Jul.*Gal.*89a:—*follow closely after, pursue*, Hdt.3.4,62, X.*Cyr.*4.3.3; μ. τὴν αὐτοῦ φύσιν Pl. *Plt.*310d; τιμωρίαν Id.*Lg.*866e; τέρψεις D.S.2.23; τὸ ἀκριβὲς ἐν τῷ λόγῳ Alex.Aphr.*in Top.*437.19: abs., X.*HG*4.5.12, *Cyr.*7.3.7. 2. *pursue, investigate*, τὰς αἰτίας πρώτας Pl.*Ti.*46e; τὴν τῶν μύθων ἰδέαν ib.59c:—Pass., Id.*Sph.*225e.

**μεταδίωξις** [δῐ], εως, ἡ, *pursuit*, τῆς ἀληθείας Nicom.*Ar.*1.1: censured as σκληρόν by Poll.5.165.

**μεταδοκέω**, *change one's opinion*, used impers., δείσασα μή σφι μεταδόξῃ in fear lest *they should change their mind*, Hdt.5.92.δ', cf. *IG*12(2).526*d*5 (Eresus, iv B.C.); ἐπείτε οὕτω μετέδοξε Hdt.4.98; ἂν μεταδόξῃ ποτέ D.20.34: c. acc. et inf., μετέδοξέ σοι ταῦτα βελτίω εἶναι *you changed your mind and thought that*.., Luc.*Apol.*3: abs. in part., μεταδόξαν αὐτοῖς μὴ ἐκεῖσε πλεῖν D.52.20, cf. D.H.8.10:—Pass., μεταδεδογμένον μοι μὴ στρατεύεσθαι *since I have changed my mind and resolved* not to march, Hdt.7.13.

**μεταδοξάζω**, *change one's opinion*, Pl.*R.*413c; πολλάκις ἀμφότερα μ. Id.*Sph.*265d.

**μεταδόρπιος**, ον, (δόρπον) *in the middle of supper, during supper* (as Eust. takes it, cf. μεταδήμιος, μεταίχμιος, μεταμάζιος), οὐ τέρπομ' ὀδυρόμενος μεταδόρπιος Od.4.194. 2. *after supper*, i.e. *at one's wine*, ὄχημ' ἀοιδᾶν μ. Pi.*Fr.*124.2; νυκτερινὴν ἐπίκωμος ἰὼν μεταδόρπιον (Adv.) ὥρην *AP*12.250 (Strat.); τὰ μ. *dessert*, Pl.*Criti.*115c.

**μετα-δόσιμον**, τό, *certificate, notice* served, *PTeb.*316.12 (i A.D.), *POxy.*1648.32 (ii A.D.). 2. Adj. **-δόσιμος**, η, ον, of disease, *infectious*, Archig.ap.Aët.13.120. **-δοσις**, εως, ἡ, *giving a share, imparting*, Hp.*Jusj.*; σίτων καὶ ποτῶν X.*Cyr.*8.2.2; μ. γίνεσθαι τῷ πλήθει τοῦ πολιτεύματος Arist.*Pol.*1321ᵃ26, etc. 2. *exchange*, Id.*EN* 1133ᵃ2; ποιεῖσθαι τὰς μ. Id.*Pol.*1257ᵃ24, cf. 1280ᵇ20. 3. *distribution* of benefits, Plu.*Cleom.*32 (pl.). 4. *communication*, Plot.5.1.12, Procl.*Inst.*56; esp. *communication* by word of mouth or in writing, τῆς προστάξεως A.D.*Synt.*260.16; *notification*, *POxy.*2134.42 (ii A.D.), 1276.19 (iii A.D.). 5. of disease, *infection*, Aret.*SD*2.13, *CD*2.13; μ. λοιμική Paul.Aeg.2.43. II. *thesis given, subject for discussion*, Plu.2.634a. **-δοτέον**, *one must give a share*, τινὶ ἀρετῆς Pl. *Alc.*1.134c, cf. X.*Cyr.*7.5.79. **-δότης**, ου, ὁ, *one who imparts generously*, παντός Phld.*Oec.*p.53 J. (pl.). **-δοτικός**, ή, όν, *disposed to impart, giving freely*, Arist.*APr.*70ᵇ27, Aristeas 226, Phld. *Oec.*p.54 J., Vett.Val.19.2; κοινωνικὸς μ. Iamb.*Protr.*21.ιθ': c. gen., μ. τῶν ἀγαθῶν D.S.1.70; ἰσχύος Corn.*ND*31: τὸ -κόν M.Ant. 1.3.

**μεταδουλόω**, prob. f.l. for κατα-, in Pass., Sever.*Clyst.*27.

⊕ **μετάδουπος**, ον, *falling at haphazard, indifferent*, ἡμέραι Hes.*Op.* 823.

**μεταδρομ-άδην** [μᾰ], Adv. *running after, following close upon*, Il. 5.80, A.R.1.755, Opp.*H.*4.509 (with v.l. -τροπάδην). **-ή**, ἡ, *pursuit, chase*, esp. of hounds, X.*Cyn.*3.7 (pl.); μ. Ἐρινύων E.*IT*941 (pl.). 2. *running to and fro*, of hunted hares, Plu.2.971d (pl.). **-ος**, ον, *running after, pursuing, taking vengeance for*, μ. πανουργημάτων κύνες S.*El.*1387 (lyr.).

⊕ **Μετάδως**, ἡ, (μεταδίδωμι) *Beneficence*, formed on analogy of αἰδώς by Cerc.4.47.

⊕ **μέταζε**, Adv., (μετά) = μεταξύ, to be read in Hes.*Op.*394, cf. Hdn. Gr.2.951, Sch.Il.3.29, Sch.D.T.p.278 H.; but τὰ μέταζε· μετὰ ταῦτα, Δωριεῖς, Hsch.

**μεταζεύγνῡμι**, *unyoke and put to another carriage*, ἵππους X.*Cyr.* 6.3.21.

**μεταζήτησις**, εως, ἡ, *seeking after*, τινος *PMag.Par.*1.1428.

**μετάθεσις**, εως, ἡ, (μετατίθημι) *change of position, transposition*, Arist.*Metaph.*1024ᵃ4; μεταθέσεις ἐξ ἕδρας ἀτόμων Epicur.*Fr.*61; ἡ τῶν ῥημάτων μ. D.24.84, cf. D.S.1.23; τοῦ ἀναβαθμοῦ *PSI*5.546 (iii B.C.); τοῦ ἐμβρύου Sor.2.60; *couching* of a cataract, Gal.10. 990. 2. generally, *change*, θεὸς οὐδεμίαν ἐπιδεχόμενος μ. Arist.*Mu.* 400ᵇ29; μ. ἐκ τῆς οἰκείας φύσεως Phld.*Rh.*1.216 S.; νόμου μ. *Ep.Hebr.* 7.12; esp. *change of sides* or *opinions*, ἐπὶ τὸ βέλτιον Plb.1.35.7, cf. Porph.*Abst.*1.2, etc. (hence, *amendment*, τῶν ἡμαρτημένων Plb.5.11.

5); ἐκ μεταθέσεως Id.30.20.2; *going over*, πρός τινα Id.5.86.8. 3. *exchange, barter*, Id.10.1.8 (pl.). 4. Gramm., *change* of a letter, A.D.*Pron.*51.5, al., *EM*795.34; also, *metathesis, transposition* of letters, as κραδίη for καρδία, Trypho *Pass.*4, Apollon.*Lex.* s. v. ἀγλαά. 5. *plagiarism*, opp. μίμησις, Demetr.*Eloc.*112. II. *power* or *right of changing sides*, Th.5.29. **-θετέον**, *one must transpose*, Pl.*Lg.*894d; *one must make a change*, Sor.1.46, Gal.17(2).403; *one must transfer*, Agath.5.24. II. Adj. -θετέος, α, ον, *to be transferred*, Plu.*Nob.*19. **-θετος**, ον, *changed*: *changeable*, τύχη Plb.15.6.8 (sed leg. εὐμεταθ-).

**μεταθέω**, fut. -θεύσομαι, *run after*, X.*Cyn.*6.22; *pursue*, τινα Jul. *Or.*5.177b; [τινὰ] ταῖς ἐπιθυμίαις by working on his desires, Clearch. 37: freq. metaph., ὥσπερ αἱ σκύλακες εὖ μεταθεῖς καὶ ἰχνεύεις τὰ λεχθέντα Pl.*Prm.*128c; τὰ τῆς ἀληθεστάτης πολιτείας ἴχνη Id.*Plt.*301e, cf. *Sph.*226b; αἰτίαν Iamb.*Protr.*4. II. *hunt* or *range over*, τὰ ὄρη X.*Cyn.*4.9: abs., *hunt about, range*, ib.6.25, al. 2. *run hither and thither*, ἑκασταχόσε Plu.*Pyrrh.*16, cf. App.*Mith.*74, al.; ἀνιχνευούσας μεταθεῖν, of bees, Arist.*HA*624$^a$28.

⊛**μεταθύω**, *appease by sacrifice*, ἱλαξάσθω τὸν θεὸν καὶ μεταθυσάτω *Schwyzer* 321.4 (Delph., v B. C.).

⊛**μεταιβολία**, ἡ, *change of mind*, prob. in Simon.37.17.

**μετᾱΐγδην**, Adv., (ἀΐσσω) *rushing after*, A.R.2.95.

**μετᾱΐζω**, poet. for μεθίζω, *seat oneself with* or *beside*, Od.16.362.

**μεταιονάω** (cf. αἰονάω), dub. in Anon.Lond.27.53.

⊛**μεταίρω**, Aeol. (also in Trag.) **πεδ-**, *lift up and remove, shift*, ἄγαλμα ἐκ βάθρων E.*IT*1157; πεδαίρειν κῶλον, πόδα, Id.*HF*819 (lyr.), 872 (troch.); ἐκ τόπων νέους πεδαίρουσα Id.*Ph.*1027 (lyr.); [ἀναθέματα] *OGI*573.15 (Cilicia, i A. D.):—Pass., Plu.*Alex.*76, Diog.*Ep.*37.4. 2. *repeal*, ψήφισμα μ. D.19.174. II. intr., *depart*, ἐκεῖθεν *Ev.Matt.*13.53, cf. 19.1.

**μεταΐσσω**, *rush after, rush upon*, Hom., always in pres. or aor. part. with another Verb, κτεῖνε μεταΐσσων Il.16.398; ἠὲ μεταΐξας.. ἕλοιτο Od.17.236, cf. Il.21.564; ἠὲ μεταΐξας θάνατον τεύξειεν ἑκάστῃ Od.20.11. II. μ. τινά *follow closely in* another's *steps*, Pi.*N.*5.43. [ᾰ in Hom.]

**μεταιτ-έω**, *demand one's share of*, c. gen. rei, τῆς βασιληΐης μ. Hdt. 4.146, cf. 7.150; also μέρος τινὸς μ. Ar.*V.*972. 2. abs., μ. παρά τινος D.19.222, cf. Luc.*Nec.*17. II. *beg of, ask alms of*, c. acc. pers., Ar.*Eq.*775. III. *beg, solicit*, τὴν ἐφήμερον τροφήν Luc. *Cyn.*2. ⊛**-ης**, ου, ὁ, *beggar*, Ph.2.516, Luc.*Nec.*15 (s.v.l.), Artem. 3.53. **-ησις**, εως, ἡ, gloss on ἐπητύς, Sch.Od.21.306.

**μεταίτιος**, ον, also α, ον A.*Ch.*100, S.*Tr.*447: c. gen. rei, *being the joint cause of, accessory to*, τοῦ φόνου Hdt.2.100, 4.202, cf. A.*Ch.* 134; τοῦ πολέμου, τοῦ μηδισμοῦ, Hdt.7.156, 9.88; τῆσδε βουλῆς A. *Ch.*100; τοῦδε πάθους S.*Tr.*260, cf. 447; τούτων οὐ μ. πέλει, ἀλλ'.. παναίτιος A.*Eu.*199; κακουχίας μ. Pl.*R.*615b: c. dat. pers. added, θεοὺς.. τοὺς ἐμοὶ μεταιτίους νόστου *who were accessory* to my return, A.*Ag.*811: c. dat. et inf., ἥ μοι μητρὶ μὲν θανεῖν μόνη μεταίτιος (for τοῦ θανεῖν) S.*Tr.*1234; πλείστοις μεταίτιος εἶ.. ἀπολωλέναι X.*HG*2.3.32.—In Att. Prose συναίτιος is preferred.

**μεταίφνιος**, ον, = ἐξαπίνης, Hsch.

**μετ-αιχμεῖ**· μοχθεῖ, Hsch. ⊛**-αίχμιος**, ον, Aeol. (also in Trag.) **πεδ-**, (αἰχμή) *between two armies*, φόνοι Lyc.1435; *debatable*, of territory, J.*BJ*5.1.4:—but usu. Subst. **μεταίχμιον**, τό, *space between two armies*, Hdt.6.77,112; ἐς μέσον μ. E.*Ph.*1361: pl., ib.1279; ἐν μεταιχμίοις δορός Id.*Heracl.*803; *disputed frontier, debatable land*, Sol. ap.Arist.*Ath.*12.5, Hdt.8.140.β': metaph., ἐν μεταιχμίῳ σκότου in *the border-land between* light and darkness, A.*Ch.*63 (lyr.): generally, *interspace*, Arist.*PA*676$^a$2; of Time, οὐδὲν ἔχειν μ. ἀνδρῶν no *interval* of manhood, Luc.*Am.*21; τὸ μ. Ἀφροδίτης καὶ Ἡλίου Nicom. *Harm.*3. 2. *what is mid-way between*, c. gen., ἀνὴρ γυνή τε χὤτι τῶν μεταίχμιον A.*Th.*197; πεδαίχμιοι λαμπάδες *hanging in mid-air*, Id.*Ch.*589 (lyr.): neut. as Adv., ζωῆς καὶ θανάτοιο μ. *AP*9.597 (Cometas).

**μεταιωρέομαι**, gloss on ἀνεπτέρωμαι, Sch.Ar.*Av.*433.

**μετακαθ-έζομαι**, Med., *change one's seat*, μετεκαθέζετο ἐπὶ τὸν ἑξῆς θρόνον Luc.*Icar.*26. **-ίζω**, *shift one's position*, Sch.Il.13.281, Sch.Ar.*V.*397. 2. metaph., *shift one's ground* in argument, S.E. *M.*1.215; *change sides, pass over*, εἴς or πρός τινα, J.*AJ*18.6.6, 19.1.10. **-οπλίζω**, *arm differently*, Plb.3.87.3.

**μετακαινίζω**, *model anew*, *AP*7.411 (Diosc.).

**μετακᾰλέω**, *recall*, Th.8.11: esp. metaph., τὴν ψυχὴν ἀπὸ τῆς ὀργῆς ἐπὶ.. Aeschin.2.159, cf. Plb.30.2.4, Paul.Aeg.3.71:—Med., τινὰς ἀπὸ τῆς ἀποστάσεως D.S.16.10. 2. simply, *summon*, Philostr.*VA*1.15; ἐς κοινωνίαν μετακληθῆναι Id.*Her.*2.14; ψυχαῖς ταῖς εἰς χωρία θεῶν καὶ τοὺς ἐγγὺς ἀστρωντόπους καὶ ἱεροὺς δαίμονας μετακεκλημέναις Herm. ap.Stob.1.49.44; *call in* a midwife, doctor, Sor.1.4, Gal.10.4; ὁ ἰατρὸς μετακληθεὶς *being called in*, Luc.*Peregr.*44:—Med., *summon*, πανταχόθεν E.*Ep.*4.4, cf. *Act.Ap.*7.14, *POxy.*33$^v$ii 2 (ii A.D.); *invoke*, τὴν σελήνην v.l. in Sch.Theoc.2.10. II. *call* or *name differently*, *Arch.Pap.*3.419 (Pass.).

**μετακάρπιον**, τό, (καρπός B) *bones forming the palm of the hand*, Gal.*UP*2.4, al., Poll.2.143, Heliod.ap.Orib.49.15.3.

⊛**μετακατα-σκευάζω**, *repair, refashion*, $IG2^2$.840.14,27 (Act. and Pass.). **-σκευή**, ἡ, *repair*, ib.24. **-τροπή**, Dor. **-τροπά**, ἡ, section of the νόμος κιθαρῳδικός, Poll.4.66. **-χέω**, *pour water over afterwards*, Hp.*Acut.*65 (Pass.). **-ψύχομαι** [ῡ], Pass., *become cold afterwards*, Id.*Coac.*528.

**μετάκειμαι**, fut. -κείσομαι, used as Pass. of μετατίθημι, *to be transposed*, Pl.*Cra.*394b, Arist.*PA*660$^b$31; *to be changed*, μετάκειται τὸ ἔθος D.H.2.14, cf. Str.3.4.20. 2. ἡ μεταφορὰ μετάκειται ἀπρεπῶς the metaphor *is in bad taste*, Demetr.*Eloc.*188.

**μετακεν-όω**, *pour from one vessel into another*, εἰς ἕτερον χῶνον *PLeid.X.*84, Orib.*Fr.*75:—hence **-ωτέον**, εἰς ἕτερον ἀγγεῖον *Gp.*7. 15.1.

**μετακεντρίζω**, *transplant*, metaph., πόθον πρὸς τὸν ἀληθῆ θεὸν Anon. *Prog.* in Rh.1.643 W.

**μετα-κεράννυμι**, *mix by pouring from one vessel into another*, ἐκ τοῦ κυρτιδίου εἰς τὸν λουτῆρα v.l. for μετεράσας in Dsc.1.52, as also in Plu.2.801c. II. *change one's nature*, ἐκ τοῦ θανατώδους ἐς τὸ ἠπιώτερον Paus.9.28.4. **-κερᾶς**, ὁ, ἡ, τό, *intermixed*, esp. of water, *lukewarm*, ἡ μὲν τὸ θερμόν, ἡ δ' ἑτέρα τὸ μ. Alex.137, cf. Philyll.32, Amphis 7. **-κέρασμα**, ατος, τό, *mixture* of cold and hot water, Hp.*Acut.*65; μ. ψυχροῦ καὶ θερμοῦ Plu.2.951e.

⊛**μετακιάθω** [ᾰθ], Ep. Verb, only impf. or aor. μετεκίαθον, *follow after*, ἱππῆες δ' ὀλίγον μ. Il.11.52, cf. 18.532: c. acc., *chase*, Τρῶας καὶ Λυκίους μετεκίαθε 16.685; τὸν δὲ κύνες μ. 18.581. II. *visit*, ἀλλ' ὁ μὲν Αἰθίοπας μ. Od.1.22, cf. Call.*Dian.*46; *go to seek*, A.R.3.802; simply, *come to*, κρήνην Id.1.1221. III. ἀλλ' ὅτε πᾶν πεδίον μετεκίαθον *had passed through* it, Il.11.714. IV. intr., *come next*, A.R. 1.139.

⊛**μετακῑν-έω**, *shift, remove*, τινὰ ἐκ τῆς τάξιος Hdt.9.74; τι *IG*5(1). 1390.186 (Andania, i B. C.):—Med., *go from one place to another*, Hdt. 9.51; μεταβάλλον καὶ -ούμενον γίγνεται πᾶν Pl.*Lg.*894a:—Pass., Hdt.1.51, Arist.*GC*315$^b$14. 2. *change, alter*, μ. τὴν πάτριον πολιτείαν D.23.205, cf. X.*Lac.*15.1 (Pass.); ῥᾷον ἔθος μετακινῆσαι φύσεως Arist.*EN*1152$^a$30; ἡ τομὴ μετεκινήθη the time of cutting *was altered*, Thphr.*HP*4.11.5. **-ημα**, ατος, τό, *movement, displacement*, τῶν ὄψεων Hp.*Prorrh.*2.19 (pl.), cf. Al.*Ps.*43(44).15. ⊛**-ησις**, εως, ἡ, *shifting*: *motion* in space, e.g. of rotation about an axis, κατὰ πᾶσαν μ., ἐν πάσῃ μ., Autol.1, Aristarch.Sam.1; *dislocation*, σφονδύλων Gal. 8.269. 2. generally, *change*, Hp.*Insomn.*90, Thphr.*HP*2.2.12; μετακινήσεις τοῦ κόσμου Arist.*Pr.*892$^a$27; ἡ ἐς τὸ βαρβαρικώτερον μ. Arr.*An.*4.8.4. ⊛**-ητέος**, α, ον, *to be removed*, Luc.*Cont.*5. ⊛**-ητός**, ή, όν, *to be disturbed*, ὁμολογία Th.5.21.

**μετακῑόνιον**, τό, *space between columns, intercolumniation*, $IG1^2$. 373.252, $2^2$.1668.36.

**μετακιρνάω**, = μετακεράννυμι, in Med., Lxx *Wi.*16.21.

**μετακλαίω**, *weep afterwards* or *too late*, ἦ τέ μιν οἴω πολλὰ μετακλαύσεσθαι Il.11.764. II. *lament afterwards*, τῆς παλαιᾶς διαίτης ἑαυτούς Ph.1.209:—Med., τὸν ἐμὸν βίον E.*Hec.*214 (lyr.).

**μετακλάω**, = συγκλάω, Sm.*Ps.*74(75).11.

**μετα-κλείω**, *call by a new name*, A.R.2.296:—also **-κλῄζω**, poet. aor. μετακλῄϊσσαν Euph.176.

**μετακληρουχέω**, *transfer to another* κληρουχία, *PTeb.*61(*a*).107 (ii B. C.), al. (Pass.).

**μετά-κλησις**, εως, ἡ, *summoning*, J.*AJ*17.3.3, App.*BC*3.71; *calling to* a person, ib.5.90 (pl.). 2. *recalling*, J.*BJ*1.31.1, App.*BC* 3.12. **-κλητέος**, α, ον, *to be summoned*, *Gloss.* **-κλητος**, ον, *summoned*, A.D.*Synt.*144.11, Hld.9.26, Agath.1.20.

**μετα-κλίνω** [ῑ], *shift to the other side*, ψυχή, μετάκλινε σεαυτήν Ph. 1.268; τινὰς ἐπὶ τὴν ἀλήθειαν ib.465:—Pass., πολέμοιο μετακλινθέντος Il.11.509; *change about*, Aret.*SD*2.1; *vary in direction*, of muscles, Gal.2.278. II. intr., *shift, move*, Ph.1.299 (s.v.l.); *lean*, ἐς τὰ δεξιὰ Philostr.*Im.*1.28. **-κλῐσις**, εως, ἡ, *change of position*, Archig. ap.Aët.8.73, Aret.*SD*2.1 (pl.): in Tactics, ῥοπαὶ καὶ -κλίσεις J.*BJ* 6.1.7. II. Gramm., = μετάληψις, Eust.15.29.

**μετακλύζω**, *cleanse afterwards by a clyster*, Hp.*Nat.Mul.*7,33.

**μετακοιμ-άομαι**, f.l. for κατα-, Sch.Od.11.322 codd. (= Pherecyd. 148 J.). **-ίζομαι**, Pass., *change to a state of sleep, to be lulled to sleep*, μετακοιμισθὲν μένος ἄτης A.*Ch.*1076.

**μετάκοινος**, ον, *sharing in common, partaking*, ξυνδαίτωρ A.*Eu.* 351 (lyr.); παντὶ δόμῳ μ. ib.964 (lyr.); πατρὶ Id.*Supp.*1038 (lyr.).

**μετακοίνωνος**, ον, *having a share in* a thing, Hsch.

**μετακόκκω**· ἡμέραι μεθ' ἑορτῶν ἑορτῇ οὐκ ἔστι, Hsch.

**μετᾰκολουθέω**, *pursue*, τῇ σοφίᾳ Iamb.*VP*18.83.

⊛**μετακομ-ῐδή**, ἡ, *transporting, conveying*, *Gloss.*: pl., Gal.18(2). 503. ⊛**-ίζω**, *transport*, κατασκευὴν ὡς αὑτοὺς *Hell.Oxy.*12.4; εἰς ἀμείνω τινὰ τόπον Pl.*Lg.*904e (Pass.); ἐπιστολὴν πρός τινα *PHib.*1. 82.8 (iii B. C.): metaph., of a person, εἰς τοὺς ἐκείνων μετακεκομίσθαι νόμους J.*AJ*20.2.3:—Med., *cause to be carried over*, ἱερὰ πατρῷα Lycurg. 56. **-ισις**, εως, ἡ, *transporting*, Sch.D.S.2.16. **-ιστέος**, α, ον, *to be transported*, Plu.2.710f.

**μετακόνδῠλοι**, οἱ, *the last phalanges* (*including knuckles*) *of the fingers*, Ruf.*Onom.*84. 2. *the first knuckles and phalanges*, Sor. *Fasc.*51 (sg.): pl., = τὸ μεταξὺ τῶν κονδύλων, Hsch.:—neut. pl. **-κόνδῠλα**, τά, Poll.2.145.

**μετακόπτω**, *stamp, coin anew*, Polyaen.6.9.1 (Pass.).

**μετακοσμ-έω**, *rearrange*: hence, *modify*, Epicur.*Nat.*67, 102 G.:—more freq. in Pass., Hp.*Fract.*2, Meliss.7; πρὸς τὸ βέλτιον Gal.*UP* 15.1; *to be changed in aspect*, μετακοσμεῖται πρὸς τὸ φῶς ἡ πτέρωσις Luc.*Dom.*11. II. metaph., μ. τινὰς ἐπὶ τὸ βέλτιον J.*AJ*1.8. 1. **-ησις**, εως, ἡ, *new arrangement, change of condition*, Pl.*Lg.* 892a; μ. νεανική.. περὶ τὰ ζῷα Phld.*D.*3.12; ἡ τῶν ἐδεστῶν τάξις καὶ μ. Plu.2.733f, cf. Nic.Dam.31 J. 2. generally, *conversion, change of character*, Plu.2.75e. **-ιος**, ον, (κόσμος IV) *between worlds*: Subst. μετακόσμιον, τό, *interspace between the worlds*, Epicur.*Ep.*2 pp.37,38 U.: pl., Id.*Fr.*359, Plu.2.731d, 734c: later as Adj., μ. χώρα

Phld.*Mort.*15. II. metaph., 'abysmal', ὑπερωκεάνιος καὶ μετακόσμιος ἀσέβεια Ph.1.425, cf. 675. III. name of the twelfth τόπος, *Cat.Cod.Astr.*8(4).126.

**μετακρούω**, *push into another position* (sc. τὴν ναῦν): metaph., *change one's opinion*, v.l. in Plu.2.1069c.

**μετακτέον**, *one must bring over*, S.E.*M.*1.35; *one must bring back*, Sor.2.60; *one must remove*, κλυστῆρι Herod.Med. in *Rh.Mus.*58.71.

**μετακτίζω**, *remove a settlement*, εἰς ἕτερον τόπον Str.13.4.17.

**μετακυκλέομαι**, Pass., *have their orbits changed*, of stars, Pl.*Epin.*982d.

**μετα-κυλίνδω**, *roll to another place, roll over*, μετακυλίνδειν αὑτὸν ἀεὶ πρὸς τὸν εὖ πράττοντα τοῖχον Ar.*Ra.*536:—also **-κυλίω** [ῑ], Paul. Aeg.6.74:—Pass., εἰς ἕτερα πάθη Gal.19.535, cf. Phlp. *in de An.*115.2.

**μετακύμιος** [ῠ], ον, (κῦμα) *between the waves*, μ. ἄτας *between two waves* of misery, i.e. *bringing a short lull* or *pause* from misery, E. *Alc.*91 (lyr.); τὸ μ. *space between the waves*, Numen.ap.Eus.*PE*11.22 (pl.), cf. Hsch.

❀ **μετακύνιον** [ῠ], τό, = μεσοκύνιον, *Hippiatr.*117.

**μετακύριον**· φοινικόν, Hsch.

**μεταλαγχάνω**, *have a share allotted one*, c. gen. rei, Pl.*Grg.*447a (cf. Sch. ad loc.), *R.*429a, *Lg.*873c, Plu.*Arist.*6: also with the part allotted added in acc., μετέλαχες τύχας Οἰδιπόδα μέρος E.*Supp.*1078 (lyr.). II. *give a share in*, τινί τινος Ael.*VH*12.43.

❀ **μεταλαμβάνω**, fut. -λήψομαι Th.6.18:—*have* or *get a share of, partake of*, c. gen. rei, λῃτῆς, καμάτου, μιαρίας, Hdt.4.64, Pi.*N.*10.79, Antipho 3.3.12; ἀμείνονος μοίρας Pl.*Phdr.*248e; τροφῆς *Act.Ap.*2.46, etc.:—Med., μεταλαμβάνεσθαί τινος *lay claim to*, τοῦ οὐνόματος Hdt. 4.45. 2. with the part received added in acc., Ἄρεως μοῖραν μ. E. *Ba.*302; τὸ πέμπτον μέρος τῶν ψήφων Pl.*Ap.*36b, D.18.266, etc.; μ. τῶν τῆς ἀρετῆς μορίων οἱ μὲν ἄλλο οἱ δὲ ἄλλο Pl.*Prt.*329e. 3. c. acc. rei, ἣν μὴ μεταλάβῃ τοὐπίπεμπτον Ar.*Fr.*201; δικαστῶν τοσούτων οὐδὲ διακοσίας ψήφους μ. And.1.17. 4. in Platonic Philos., c. gen. rei, *participate in* the universal, ἤτοι ὅλου τοῦ εἴδους ἢ μέρους μ. Pl.*Prm.*131a. 5. c. gen. pers., *have part in, share his society*, X.*Cyr.*7.5.51; *go shares with* another, ὡς ἐμοῦ τι κεκλοφότος ζητεῖς μεταλαβεῖν Ar.*Pl.*370. 6. *receive notice* or *information*, Mitteis*Chr.*31 ii 2 (ii B.C.): c. acc. et inf., *PTeb.*40.7 (ii B.C.), Lxx 2*Ma.*4.21: c. acc. et part., μ. πολιορκοῦντά τινα ib.11.6; μ. διότι.. Aristeas 316:—Pass., *to be cited*, = Lat. *recitari*, ἐκ διπτύχων *SIG*827 *B*1 (Delph., ii A.D.). 7. *understand*, φωνάς Philostr.*VA*1.19. II. *receive in succession* or *afterwards*, [χαλινόν] X.*Eq.*10.6; [ἱμάτιον] θάτερον Eup.159.6; πλοῦτον ἕτερον Philem.201; *occupy* a position *left by the enemy*, Plb.10.40.11, etc.; μ. τὴν ἀρχήν *succeed to* the government, Id.5.40.6, cf. *PTeb.*79.49 (ii B.C.); μ. τὸν λόγον *take up* the discourse, i.e. *answer*, Plb.18.2.2; μ. alone, Id.10.38.1, etc.; οἱ παρά τινος -λημψόμενοι his *successors in title*, *PTeb.*294.18 (ii A.D.), etc.; ἐκ διαδοχῆς μ. τὸ ἱερόν *Stud.Pal.*22.184.95 (ii A.D.). 2. abs., *come after, come on*, ἅμα τῷ μεταλαβεῖν τὸ τῆς νυκτός Plb.15.30.2. III. *take instead, take in exchange, substitute*, πόλεμον ἀντ' εἰρήνης Th.1.120; ἄλλο ὄνομα ἀντὶ τῆς ἡδονῆς Pl.*Prt.*355c; διαναπαύσωμεν αὐτὸν μεταλαβόντες αὐτοῦ τὸν συγγυμναστήν; Id.*Plt.*257c; τὰ ὄργανα τἀλλήλων Id.*R.*434a, cf. b; μ. τὰ ἐπιτηδεύματα ἐς τὸ ὁμοῖον *adopt new* customs so as to resemble others, Th.6.18, cf. Pl.*Prt.*356d; ἱμάτια, ἐσθῆτας μ., X.*Cyr.*4.5.4, Plb.3.78.3; μ. παλτόν *take another* javelin, X.*Eq.*12.13: c. inf., ἀντὶ τοῦ αἰεὶ φυλάσσεσθαι.. [τὸ] ἀντεπιβουλεῦσαι μ. Th.6.87. IV. Pass., *to be changed*, Sor.2.9, Olymp. *in Mete.*36.19. 2. Medic., of humours, blood, *to be transferred, conveyed*, ὑπὸ δηχθέντος Ruf.*Fr.*118, cf. Sor.2.7. 3. Gramm., *to be changed, altered*, εἰς.. A.D.*Synt.*107.2; also, of words, *have their construction altered*, εἰς.. Id.*Pron.*15.11, al.; but μ. ἐκ.. *to be used in place of*, Id.*Synt.*195.14, al. V. *take words in another sense*, τὰ πράγματα τοῖς ὀνόμασι μ. Hld.9.9, cf. Them. *in de An.*18.35; *parody*, Ath.8.336f (Pass.). 2. *translate, interpret*, Ph.1.480 (Pass.). VI. in the Logic of Arist., τὸ μεταλαμβανόμενον *proposition substituted* for the original thesis in hypothetical reasoning, *APr.*41ᵃ39.

**μεταλγ-έω**, *feel remorse at, rue*, μ. τὸ δίκαιον ἔρξαι (nisi leg. ἔρξας) A.*Supp.*405 codd. (lyr.). **-ής**, ές, *bringing sorrow in its train*, prob. l., ib.111 (lyr.).

**μεταλδήσκω**, *change in growing*, μεταλδήσκοντας ὀδόντας ἀνδράσι τευχηστῆσι δέμας *growing into* armed men, A.R.3.414.

**μεταλήγω**, Ep. μεταλλήγω, *leave off, cease from*, c. gen., μεταλλήξαντι χόλοιο Il.9.157, cf. *h.Cer.*339: abs., in Ep. impf. μεταλλήγεσκεν, A.R.3.951.

**μετα-ληπτέον**, *one must have a share of*, τῷ ἑνὶ μ. οὐσίας Pl.*Prm.*163d: abs., Iamb.*Protr.*21.ιθ'. II. *one must take instead*, τι ἀντί τινος Arist.*APr.*48ᵃ27. III. pl. μεταληπτέα, *one must resume*, τοῦ προτέρου λόγου Agath.3.1. **-ληπτικός**, ή, όν, *capable of partaking of*, c. gen., Porph.*Chr.*39; ἀρσενικοῦ γένους Eust.626.31; τὸ μ. *capability of receiving form*, Platonic name for ὕλη, Arist.*Ph.*209ᵇ12, *Placit.*1.19.1. II. *reversed*, '*translated*', κίνησις Gal.*UP*7.14; τάσις, ἔντασις, Id.10.443, 18(2).506. III. *concerning* or *involving* μετάληψις II.4. Adv. -κῶς Trypho *Trop.*5, Heraclit.*All.*26, Sch.Ar.*Pl.*18. 2. *involving* μετάληψις II. 5, προβλήματα Syrian. *in Hermog.*2.153R.; τρόποι Aps.p.249H. ❀ **-ληψις**, εως, ἡ, *participation*, Pl.*Prm.*131a; λόγων in philosophy, Id.*R.*539d; γένεσις μ. οὐσίας Id.*Def.*411a; γίνεσθαι κατὰ τὴν μ. [τοῦ εἴδους] Arist.*GC*335ᵇ14, cf. *Metaph.*1072ᵇ20, etc.; *partaking* of food, 1*Ep.Ti.*4.3. 2. *concurrence*, *POxy.*1273.39 (iii A.D.), etc. 3. Gramm., τὸ "λέγων" μ. ἐνεστῶτος καὶ παρατατικοῦ *is shared by*.., A.D.*Adv.*124.1. II. *alternation*, τῶν λόγων Pl.*Tht.*173b; αἱ μ. τοῦ σχήματος Plb.9.20.2; ἐκ μεταλήψεως Id.2.33.4. 2. *succession*, μ. τῆς ἀρχῆς Id.31.13.3. 3. *taking* one thing *instead of* another, ἡ ἀντὶ τοῦ μείζονος ἐλάττονος μ. Arist.*Rh.*1369ᵇ25. 4. Rhet., *use of one word for another*, as of Ἥφαιστος for πῦρ, Quint.8.6.37, Trypho *Trop.*5, etc.; *transference* of meaning, Eust.79.12. 5. *objection, counterplea*, Sch.Pl.*Euthphr.*4d; esp. *concurrence coupled with objection*, Syrian. *in Hermog.*2.153R., Corn. *Rh.*p.391H. 6. συλλογισμοὶ κατὰ μετάληψιν hypothetical syllogisms involving the *substitution* of a proposition for the original thesis, Arist.*APr.*45ᵇ17; cf. μεταλαμβάνω VI. 7. Gramm., *change of construction*, A.D.*Synt.*210.3; *change in dialect*, ib.335.1; *change of name*, Demetr.Lac.*Herc.*1014.60. 8. *translation, rendering*, Eust. ad D.P.180; ἡ εἰς τὸ Ἑλληνικὸν μ. Id.ib.294. 9. *transference*, αἱ ἐς νεφροὺς καὶ κύστιας -λήψιες Aret.*SD*1.9. 10. κατὰ μετάληψιν κατατεῖναι, of *reflex* tension over a pulley (cf. μεταληπτικός II), Heliod.ap.Orib.48.9.25.

**μεταλισχευτέον**, *one must transplant*, *Gp.*9.5.11.

**μεταλλ-αγή**, ἡ, *change*, Epich.170.14, Hp.*Aph.*3.1 (pl.); ἡ μ. τῶν σκελέων *alternation* of the legs in walking, Id.*Art.*58; μ. τῆς ἡμέρης *eclipse*, Hdt.1.74; ἐν μεταλλαγᾷ πολυμηχάνου ἀνδρός by *receiving* a crafty man for thy master *instead* [of me], S.*Ph.*1134; μεταλλαγαῖς εἰς ἄλληλα Pl.*Ti.*61c. 2. c. gen. objecti, μ. πολέμου *change from* war, X.*HG*7.4.10, cf. E.*HF*765, 766 (lyr.); μ. τοῦ βίου, i.e. death, Phld. *Acad.Ind.*p.93M., Plu.2.101f; μ. alone, *decease*, ἡ τοῦ Καρνεάδου μ. Phld.l.c., cf. D.S.18.9, D.C.57.4; βασιλέων μεταλλαγαί 'the Deaths of Kings', title of work by Anaximenes, Ath.12.531d; of Alexander the Great, *Marm.Par.*109. 3. *change for the worse, ruin*, εἰς μ. ἀγαγεῖν Men.*Pk.*29. II. *exchange, interchange*, τῶν ἐπιστημῶν Pl. *Tht.*199c. **-ακτέον**, *one must change*, Ph.*Bel.*93.36; τὰς πτώσεις Sch.E.*Hec.*846. **-ακτήρ**, ῆρος, ὁ, *one that changes*, μ. πουλύπουν χροός Ion Trag.36. **-ακτός**, όν, *changed, altered*, δαίμων A.*Th.*706 (lyr.). II. *to be changed* or *altered*, Pi.*Fr.*220. **-αξις**, εως, ἡ, = μεταλλαγή, X.*Cyn.*4.4, Poll.5.61, [Longin.]*Rh.*p.191H. (pl.).

**μεταλλάρχης**, ου, ὁ, *overseer of mines*, *OGI*660 (Egypt, i A.D.), Paul. Al.*N.*3.

**μεταλλάσσω**, Att. -ττω, pf. μετήλλαχα and irreg. μετήλλαγα (v. infr.):—Pass., irreg. aor. 2 inf. μεταλλάγειν *Supp.Epigr.*3.674 *A* 24 (Rhodes, ii B.C.):—*change, alter*, θέσμια Hdt.1.59; τὰν ἀνθρώπου ζόαν ἆται.. μεταλλάσσουσι S.*Fr.*592.6; πότμος.. μ. φύσιν ib.871.2; μεταβολὴν βίου μ. Pl.*Lg.*775c; οὐ γὰρ τὸν τρόπον, ἀλλὰ τὸν τόπον μετήλλαξεν Aeschin.3.78; μετήλλαξαν τὴν ἀλήθειαν ἐν τῷ ψεύδει *Ep.Rom.*1.25; πόνου μεταλλαχθέντος οἱ πόνοι γλυκεῖς S.*Fr.*374; τὰς τύχας ἑκατέρων μετήλλαξαν *interchanged* them, Isoc.4.59. II. *exchange*, 1. *take in exchange, adopt, assume*, ὀρνίθων μεταλλάξας φύσιν Ar.*Av.*117; μ. τόπον *go into a new* country, Pl.*Lg.*760c; μ. χώραν ἑτέραν ἐξ ἑτέρας Id.*Prm.*138c; ἑτέραν μ. τινὰ χώραν Lycurg. 86; μ. διάφορα βρώματα to have varieties of food, Antiph.246:—Med., μεταλλάσσεσθαι χιτῶνα Lys.*Fr.*21; τὴν τύχην Din.1.92. 2. *exchange by leaving, quit*, μ. τὸν βίον Isoc.6.17, 9.15, *OGI*56.55 (Canopus, iii B.C.), *UPZ*19.14, al. (ii B.C.); τὸ ζῆν μ. νόσῳ Phld.*Acad.Ind.* p.96M.: μ. alone, Pl.*Ax.*367c, Sotion p.185W., *Abh.Berl.Akad.* 1925(5).23 (Cyrene, i B.C./i A.D.); οἱ μετηλλαχότες *the dead*, Pl.*Ax.* 369b, cf. *Supp.Epigr.*3.367.39 (Boeot., ii B.C.), *BGU*1148.8 (i B.C.), etc.; Dor. μεταλλαχώς *Test.Epict.*1.10; μεταλλαγότων (sic) *IG*5(1).1433.37; also οἱ μεταλλάξαντες ib.2².1323.10; ἐξ ἀνθρώπων D.S. 18.56 (edict of Polyperchon, 319 B.C.). III. intr., *undergo a change, change*, Epich.170.15, Hdt.2.77, E.*Fr.*262, Arist.*HA*578ᵇ10: with neut. Pron., τοσοῦτο μετήλλαξε κατὰ τὸν βίον Phld.*Acad.Ind.* p.49M.: c. gen., *change from*, Th.8.70. IV. *substitute, transfer*, τινὰς εἰς τήν τινων χώραν Pl.*Ti.*19a.

**μετάλλ-ᾱτος**, Dor. for *μετάλλητος, *to be searched out*, Pi.*P.*4.164. **-άω**, *search carefully, inquire diligently*, ἐμοὶ οὐ φίλον ἐστὶ μεταλλῆσαι καὶ ἐρέσθαι Od.14.378; οὐκέτι μέμνηται.., οὐδὲ μεταλλᾷ 15.23. 2. c. acc. pers., *inquire of, question*, σε.. οὔτ' εἴρομαι οὔτε μεταλλῶ Il.1.553, cf. Od.3.69, 16.287; but ἀντεφθέγξατο.. μετάλλασέν τέ νιν the voice *sought* him *out*, Pi.*O.*6.62. 3. c. acc. objecti, *inquire about, ask after*, μή τι σὺ ταῦτα διείρεο μηδὲ μετάλλα Il.1.550, cf. 5.516; ἕταροι δὲ κατέκταθεν, οὓς σὺ μεταλλᾷς 13.780, cf. 10.125, Od.19.190; ἕκαστα μ. 14.128, cf. 16.465: also with Preps., μεταλλῆσαι.. ἀμφὶ πόσει 17.554; ἀμφ' ἑτάροιο μ. τὰ ἕκαστα A.R.4.1471; θεῶν πέρι τοῖα μ. *APl.*4.183. 4. c. dupl. acc., *ask* one *about* a thing, *ask* him *a question*, τοῦτο δέ τοι ἐρέω, ὅ μ' ἀνείρεαι ἠδὲ μεταλλᾷς Il.3.177; ἔπος ἄλλο μ. καὶ ἐρέσθαι Νέστορα Od.3.243. (Poet. word, also in late Prose, *POxy.*237 vii 40 (ii A.D.), Them.*Or.*22.266c: expld. by Gramm. as *search after other things* (μετὰ ἄλλα), Eust.148.10, etc., but this is very dub.) **-εία**, ἡ, *searching for metals* and the like, *mining*, Pl.*Criti.*114e, *Lg.*842d (pl.), Str.3.2.9, al.: in pl., concrete, *mines*, Id.3.2.3. 2. *mining operations* in a siege, D.S.16.74. 3. *underground channel*, Pl.*Lg.*761c. 4. metaph., μεγαλόδωρος ἡ μ. τοῦ ἀληθοῦς Max.Tyr.17.2. **-εῖον**, τό, in pl., *minerals*, σίδηρος καὶ χαλκὸς καὶ πάντα τὰ μ. Pl.*Lg.*678d. **-εύς**, έως, ὁ, = μεταλλευτής, Lys.*Fr.*89S., Pl.*Lg.*678d, *IG*2.3260*b*: in pl., Max.Tyr.6.2 (cj.), 17.2; title of plays by Pherecrates and Nicomachus. II. a kind of *ant*, Hsch. **-ευσις**, εως, ἡ, v.l. for μεταλλεία, Palaeph.9: in pl., *mining operations*, Ph.*Bel.*91.19. **-ευτής**, οῦ, ὁ, *one who searches for metals* or *water, miner*, Str.9.2.18, 15.1.30, Man.4.259. 2. *metallurgist*, Procl.*Par.Ptol.*250 (pl.). **-ευτικός**, ή, όν, *skilled in searching for metals*: ἡ -κή (sc. τέχνη) *the art of mining*, Arist.*Pol.*1258ᵇ31, *Oec.*

1343ᵃ27; μ. ἐργασία *PSI*8.962ᴮ.28 (ii A. D.). **II.** *of or consisting of mines*, κτῆμα Pl.*Lg*.847d. **-ευτός**, ή, όν, *to be got by mining*, τὰ μ., opp. τὰ ὀρυκτά, Arist.*Mete*.378ᵃ21, cf. Gal.12.166. ❋ **-εύω**, *get by mining*, χαλκόν Lxx *De*.8.9; χρυσοῖο γενέθλην D.P.1114:—Pass., *to be got by mining*, of metals, Pl.*Plt*.288d, Arist.*Mete*.378ᵃ27, *Pol*.1258ᵇ32. **2.** abs., *mine*, οἱ μεταλλεύοντες Ph.*Bel*.99.13, D.S.5.37, Luc.*Cont*.11; Λαμψακηνοῖς μ. *work in mines* for the L., Polyaen.2.1.26 (-ηνοί codd., i. e. *condemn to labour in mines*): c. acc. cogn., πᾶν μεταλλεύων γνύθος Lyc.485. **3.** *carry on mining operations*, of besiegers, D.S.18.70: also c. acc. cogn., μ. τὰς ὑπονόμους σήραγγας D.H.4.44, cf. Polyaen.7.11.5. **4.** *undermine*, τείχη J.*AJ*17.10.3. **5.** *explore*, *AP*6.302 (Leon.), Nic.*Th*.672; μ. τὴν ἔρευναν Porph.*Marc*.26. **II.** = μεταλλάσσω, *pervert*, ῥεμβασμὸς ἐπιθυμίας μ. νοῦν ἄκακον Lxx *Wi*.4.12:—Pass., *to be converted*, εἰς πάντα ib.16.25. ❋ **-ίζομαι**, *to be condemned to hard labour in mines*, *Cod.Just*.11.41.7. **-ικός**, ή, όν, *of* or *for mines*, νόμος D.37.35; δίκαι ib.37, Arist.*Ath*.59.5; ἐργασίαι D.S.5.36; σκεῦος Hsch. s. v. ξοῖς: -κός, ὁ, *miner*, *PLond*.1.324.6 (ii A. D.): -κή (sc. τέχνη), ἡ, *art of mining*, Phld.*Oec*.p.64 J., Alex. Aphr. *in Metaph*.353.18. **II.** *possessing a knowledge of metals*, Ptol.*Tetr*.13, Procl.*Par.Ptol*.20. **2.** *metallic*, φάρμακα Gal.12.208; τὰ μ. Dsc.*Praef*.1, Plu.2.663c, Meges ap.Orib.44.24.2; μ. τάλαντα, of the heavy Egyptian talents, Wilcken *Chr*.321.18 (ii A. D.). **-ίτης** [ῑ], ου, ὁ, fem. -ῖτις, ιδος, *containing minerals*, γῆ Hsch.

**μεταλλοι-όω**, *change*, Aristeas 17 (Pass.), Ph.1.241, Herm.ap. Stob.1.49.69 (Pass.), Syn.Alch.p.59 B., St.Byz. s. v. Ἀζανοί (Pass.). **-ωσις**, εως, ἡ, *change*, Plot.3.6.11.

❋ **μέταλλον**, τό, *mine*, *quarry*, ἁλὸς μέταλλον salt-*pit*, salt-*mine*, Hdt.4.185; μ. τετμημένον Hyp.*Eux*.35; μ. παλαιὸν ἀνασάξιμον *IG* 2².1582.56: mostly in pl., χρύσεα καὶ ἀργύρεα μέταλλα gold and silver *mines*, Hdt.3.57; τὰ ἀργύρεια μ., at Laurium, Th.2.55; μέταλλα (alone) *silver mines*, X.*Vect*.4.4; μαρμάρου μ. marble *quarries*, Str.9.1.23. **2.** *mine* in siege-operations, πολιορκεῖν διὰ τῶν μ. Plb.16.11.2, al. **3.** metaph., *work*, οὐδ' ἐν τοῖς ἀργυρείοις [ἐστί] μοι μ. Alciphr.1.36. **II.** later, *mineral*, *metal*, *Sammelb*.4313 (i/ii A. D.), Ruf.ap.Orib.5.3.21, Nonn.*D*.11.26, Agath.5.9, *AP*7.363. (On the etym. cf. μεταλλάω.)

**μεταλλουργ-εῖον**, τό, *mine*, D.S.5.38. **-έω**, *work mines*, ib. 36. **2.** *dig from a mine*, Dsc.5.74 (Pass.). **-ός**, ὁ, *miner*, D.S. 5.37, Dsc.5.74.

**μετάλμενος**, aor. part. of μεθάλλομαι.

**μετα-λογίζομαι**, *change one's mind*, Sch.E.*Hec*.857. **-λόγιον**, τό, *secondary list*, *POxy*.515.7 (ii A. D.).

**μεταλωφέω**, *cease*, A.R.1.1161.

**μεταμάζιος**, ον, (μαζός) *between the breasts*, ἔβαλε στῆθος μεταμάζιον Il.5.19; τὸ μ. *space between the breasts*, *Anacreont*.16.30.

**μεταμάθησις** [μᾰ], εως, ἡ, = ἡ ἐκ ψευδῶν δοξῶν εἰς ἀληθεῖς μεταβολή, Phlp. *in Ph*.796.7.

**μεταμαίομαι**, *search after*, *chase*, ἄγραν Pi.*N*.3.81.

**μεταμανθάνω**, fut. -μαθήσομαι Paus.4.34.8, Luc.*Herm*.84:—*learn differently*, μ. γλῶσσαν *unlearn one* language *and learn* another *instead*, Hdt.1.57, cf. Paus. l. c.; μ. ὕμνον *learn a new* strain, A.*Ag*.709 (lyr.). **2.** *unlearn*, τὴν ἐλευθερίαν Aeschin.3.157; τοῦ μεταμανθάνοντος (sc. ψευδῆ δόξαν) Pl.*R*.413a. **3.** abs., *learn better*, Ar.*Pl*.924; εἰ γέρων ἄνθρωπος μεταμαθήσει Luc. l. c.; opp. μανθάνειν ἐξ ἀρχῆς, Arist.*Pol*.1289ᵃ4.

**μετ-ᾰμείβω**, Dor. **πεδ-**, *exchange*, *change*, ἐσλὸν πήματος good *for* ill, Pi.*O*.12.12; [οἱ ἐχῖνοι] μ. τὰς ὀπὰς Arist.*HA*612ᵇ6. **2.** *change to another form*, ἐκ βοὸς.. μετάμειβε γυναῖκα Mosch.2.52; μ. φρένα Nonn.*D*.4.182. **3.** *remove*, τινὰ Λαμνόθεν dub. cj. in Pi.*P*.1.52; γᾶν τέκνων τέκνοις μ. *hand down* land to children's children, E.*HF* 796 (lyr.). **II.** Med., *change one's condition*, ἐκ προτέρων μεταμειψάμενοι καμάτων *having escaped* from.., Pi.*P*.3.96: abs., μεταμειβόμενοι ἐναλλάξ *in turns*, Id.*N*.10.55. **2.** c. acc., μεταμείβεσθαί τινί τι *to change* one thing *for* another, E.*Ph*.831 (lyr.). **-άμειψις** [ᾰ], εως, ἡ, *exchange*: *alteration*, Sch.rec.A.*Pr*.669.

**μεταμέλ-ει**, impf. μετέμελε: fut. -μελήσει: aor. μετεμέλησε: (μέλω): **I.** impers., *it repents* me, *rues* me:—Constr.: **1.** c. dat. pers. et gen. rei, ὑμῖν μεταμελησάτω τῶν πεπραγμένων Lys.30.30, cf. Pl.*Phdr*.231a, X.*Cyr*.8.3.32. **2.** more freq. c. dat. rei in part. agreeing with the dat. pers., μετεμέλησέ οἱ τὸν Ἑλλήσποντον μαστιγώσαντι *it repented him of* having scourged it, Hdt.7.54, cf. 1.130, 3.140, Antipho 5.91; οὔτε μοι μεταμέλει οὕτως ἀπολογησαμένῳ I do not *regret* having thus defended myself, Pl.*Ap*.38e; also μ. μοι ὅτι.. X.*Cyr*.5.3.6. **3.** abs., μ. τινί *it repents* one, Ar.*Pl*.358, Antipho 5.94, Lys.16.2: also without a dat., ξυνέβη ὑμῖν πεισθῆναι μὲν ἀκεραίοις μεταμέλειν δὲ κακουμένοις *to repent* when in distress, Th.2.61; μεταλαμβάνειν ταὐτὰ καὶ μεταμέλειν ἐν ταῖς πράξεσιν Pl.*Prt*.356d. **4.** part. neut. μεταμέλον abs., *since it repented* him, τῶν ἀνηλωμένων αὐτοῖς μ. Isoc. 18.60, cf. Pl.*Phd*.114a. **II.** seldom with nom., *cause repentance* or *sorrow*, τῷ Ἀρίστωνι τὸ εἰρημένον μετέμελε Hdt.6.63; τοῖσι.. ἡγεομένοισι τὰ πεπρηγμένα μετέμελε οὐδέν Id.9.1; ὡς αὐτοῖσι μεταμελῇ πόνος A.*Eu*.771 (nowh. else in Trag.); οἶμαι δέ σοι ταῦτα μεταμελήσειν Ar.*Nu*.1114.—Cf. μεταμέλομαι. **-εια**, Ion. -ίη Ps.-Hdt.*Vit. Hom*.19: ἡ:—*change of purpose*, *regret*, *repentance*, μεταμέλειαν λαμβάνει E.*Fr*.1080.3; μεταμελείας A. Th.1.34; ἐπί τισι, περί τινος, Democr.43, Th.3.37; μόνη σιωπῇ μ. οὐ φέρει Men.1105; ἐμπιμπλάναι τινὰ μεταμελείας Pl.*Lg*.727c; μεταμελείας μεστή Id.*R*.577e; μ. τοῦ πεπραγμένου γίγνεται Id.*Lg*.866e; τὸ ἐν μ. Arist.*EN*1110ᵇ19; ἐκ μεταμελείας Plb.1.39.14; αὕτη σε ἡ μ. ἔχει X.*Cyr*.5.3.7, cf. Polystr. p.9 W. (pl.), Phld.*Ir*.p.43 W. (pl.). **-έτη**, gloss on μεταδήα, Hsch. **-ητικός**, ή, όν, *full of regrets*, *always repenting*, Arist.*EN* 1150ᵃ21, Ptol.*Tetr*.155. **-ητός**, ή, όν, *repented of*, Hsch.s.v. πεδάγρετον.

**μεταμελλησμός**, ὁ, = *cunctatio*, *Gloss.*

**μεταμέλ-ομαι**, rare exc. in pres. and impf.: fut. -μελήσομαι Phld.*Rh*.2.16 S., also -μεληθήσομαι Lxx *Ps*.109(110).4, Sch.E.*Ph*. 899: aor. -εμελήθην Plb.8.23.2, D.S.19.75, later -ήσθην *PThead*. 51.15 (iv A. D.); also Ep. μετεμέμβλετο prob. in Panyas. in *Et.Gen*. s. v. μῦθος (*Coll.Alex*.p.249 Powell): pf. -μεμέλημαι Lxx 1*Ma*.11.10, Phld.*Vit*.p.34 J.:—*feel repentance*, *regret*:—Constr.: **1.** c. part., μετεμέλοντο οὐ δεξάμενοι *they repented that* they had not.., Th.4.27, cf. 7.50; μ. ὅτι.. Id.5.14; ὁ μεταμελόμενος Arist.*EN*1110ᵇ23. **2.** μεταμέλεσθαί τινι *repent at* a thing, D.S.15.9; ἐπί τινι Id. 19.75; τινων Phalar.*Ep*.43. **3.** abs., *change one's purpose* or *line of conduct*, X.*Cyr*.4.6.5, Plb.4.50.6. **II.** causal in fut. part., τὸ μεταμελησόμενον *that which will cause regret*, *matter for future repentance*, X.*Mem*.2.6.23. **III.** = μεταμέλει I. 1, μεταμέλεσθαι αὐτοῖς περὶ ὧν ἂν συμβουλεύσωνται Pl.*Demod*.382d.:—the form **μεταμελέομαι**, censured by Thom.Mag.p.123 R., occurs in Hp.*Ep*.27. ❋ **-ος**, ὁ, *repentance*, *regret*, Th.7.55, Conon 23.3, Themist.*Ep*.4.1, J.*AJ*19.4.4, Chor.p.214 B.; ἀποθανὼν ὁ δίκαιος ἔλιπε μετάμελον Lxx *Pr*.11.3. **II.** Adj. μετάμελος, ον, *repenting*, πόλις ταῖς διαδιδομέναις φήμαις μετάμελος οὖσα D.S.25.11.

**μεταμέλπομαι**, *sing* or *dance among*, τισι *h.Ap*.197.

**μεταμήθεια**, ἡ, = μετάνοια, Hsch. **μεταμίξ**, Adv. *mixedly*, Id.

**μεταμίσγω**, *mix among*, Od.18.310, Hp.*Morb*.2.45: fut. μεταμείξω, κτήματα.. τοῖσιν Ὀδυσσῆος μεταμείξομεν Od.22.221.

**μεταμισθόω**, *sublet*, *PTeb*.105.31 (ii B. C.), *POxy*.101.48 (ii A. D.):—Pass., *PTeb*.61(*b*).35 (ii B. C.).

**μεταμορφ-όω**, *transform*, Gal.19.479; ἑαυτὸν εἴς τι Ael.*VH*1.1; *disguise*, ἑαυτόν App.*BC*4.41:—mostly in Pass., *to be transformed*, *Ep.Rom*.12.2, Plu.2.52d, Luc.*Asin*.11; εἰς θηρίων ἰδέαν D.S.4.81; εἰς Ἀπόλλωνα Ph.2.559; εἰς ἰχθύν Ath.8.334c; ἀπὸ δόξης εἰς δόξαν 2*Ep.Cor*.3.18; *to be transfigured*, *Ev.Matt*.17.2, etc. **-ωσις**, εως, ἡ, *transformation*, Str.1.2.11 (pl.), Hierocl.p.21 A., Luc.*Salt*.57, *Halc*.1 tit., Gal.5.193, App.*BC*4.42, Ant.Diog.13 (pl.); τούτοις (sc. φυτοῖς) ἐμφύεται ψυχὴ κατὰ τὴν μ. Porph.*Abst*.1.6; μεταμορφώσεων συναγωγή, title of work by Antoninus Liberalis.

**μεταμοσχ-εύω**, *transplant*, Hsch.: Subst. **-ευσις**, εως, ἡ, *Gloss.*

**μεταμπίσχω**, *clothe in a new dress*, εἱμαρμένη -ίσχουσα τὰς ψυχὰς Plu.*Fr.inc*.146.α':—more freq. in Med., *put on a different dress*, δουλείαν -ισχόμενος *putting on the new dress of* slavery, Pl.*R*.569c; μ. τὸν βίον Procop.*Arc*.16; ψυχὴν Aen.Gaz.*Thphr*.p.10 B.: abs., *change one's dress*, ἐὰν μεταμπίσχηται Aristid.2.207 J.; cf. sq.

**μεταμῡθεύομαι**, Pass., *be fabulously identified with*, εἰς τὸν ἄνεμον Sch.D.P.425.

**μεταμφι-άζω** (later -έζω Plu.2.342e, Luc.*Nec*.16: fut. -έσω Max. Tyr.21.1), *change the dress* of another, *strip off his dress*, τινα Plu. and Luc. ll. cc.; τὰ τοῦ πλησίον Max.Tyr. l. c.: c. dupl. acc., τὸ λαμπρὸν σχῆμά μ. τινά Hld.2.21: metaph., *change*, τι εἴς τι *AP*6.165 (Phal.):—Med., *take off one's own dress*, τὴν βασιλικὴν ἐσθῆτα μεταμφιασαμένη v.l. in Phylarch.30 J. (cf. sq.); πορφυρίδα μεταμφιάσομαι Luc.*Herm*.86 codd.; ἀποδυσάμενος τὸν Πυθαγόραν τίνα μετημφιάσω μετ' αὐτόν; what body *didst thou assume* after him? Id.*Gall*. 19; μ. τὴν τύχην, τὸν βίον, Vett.Val.131.8, Procop.*Arc*.17. **-έννῡμι** (also -εννύω Plu.2.528b), = foreg., metaph., D.L.7.25:—Med., *take off one's own* dress, Phylarch.30 J. (cf. foreg.); *put on another dress*, Plu.*Nic*.3; μ. τὴν Ῥωμαίαν στολήν Hdn.5.5.5; ψυχὴ μ. πολλὰ σώματα D.L.3.67; τινι *change clothes with*.., Theopomp.Hist.89a: metaph., κυνῶν μ. βίον Phld.*Sto*.339.8.

**μετᾰμώλιος**, ον, dub. l. for sq. **II.** = ἐμπόλεμος, Hsch.

**μετᾰμώνιος**, ον, poet. Adj. *vain*, *idle*, μ. νήματα *vainly-woven*, Od.2.98; μεταμώνια βάζεις talkest *idly*, 18.332; τὰ δὲ πάντα θεοὶ μ. θεῖεν may the gods give all that *to the winds*, Il.4.363; ψεύδη μ. Pi.*O*.12.6; μ. θηρεύω Id.*P*.3.23; τὰ δ' οὐκ ἄρ' ἔμελλε θεὸς μ. θήσειν Theoc.22.181.—Used by Hom. only in neut. pl.: the etym. is dub., cf. μωνιή, μωνιόν; but later Poets apptly. connected the word with ἄνεμος (as if for μετανεμώνιος); κονία μεταμώνιος ἀέρθη *borne by the wind*, *on high*, Simon.16; ἐς κόρακας βαδιεῖ μεταμώνιος Ar.*Pax*117, ubi v. Sch.:—μεταμώλιος is v.l. in several passages; cf. ἀνεμώλιος.

**μεταναγιγνώσκομαι**, Pass., *repent of*, c. gen., Αἴας μετανεγνώσθη θυμοῦ (Herm. for θυμῶν).. μεγάλων τε νεικέων S.*Aj*.717 (lyr.).

**μεταναιετ-άω**, *dwell with*, τισι to be read metri gr. for ναναίεται in *h.Cer*.87. **-ης**, ου, ὁ, *one who dwells with*, Hes.*Th*.401.

**μετανα-πείθω**, *change by persuasion*, in Pass., Hsch. s. v. μετανεγνά(σ)θη. **-στάσις**, εως, ἡ, *migration*, in pl., Hp.*Aër*.20, Th.1.2, 2.16, X.*Mem*.3.5.12, Str.3.4.19: sg., of the soul, Ph.1.91: metaph., μεταναστάσεις τῆς γνώμης Procop.*Arc*.22. **-στάτος**, ον, *devastated by migrations*, ἡ Ἑλλὰς οὐχ ὑπ' ἀνθρώπων μόνον γινομένη μ. Ocell.3.5. **II.** *having departed*, πατέρων μετανάστατος ψυχή Ph.1.513.

❋ **μεταναστ-εύω**, *remove*, Lxx *Ps*.51(52).5, Ph.1.299:—Med., *depart*, *flee*, Lxx *Ps*.10(11).1. **2.** intr. in Act., = Med., ib.61(62).6, Str. *Chr*.7.5. **-ης**, ου, ὁ, (μεταναστῆναι, cf. ὑπερανάστης) *one who has left his home*, *wanderer*, *migrant*, commonly as a term of reproach, ἀτίμητος μ. Il.9.648; μοῦνοι οὐ μετανάσται Ἑλλήνων, of the Athenians, Hdt.7.161; *fugitive*, *POxy*.487.18 (ii A. D.), *PTeb*.439 (ii A. D.); μ. γενόμενοι ὑπὸ ἐθνῶν Prisc.p.341 D. (cf. μετανίσταντο ibid.): c. gen., ἀρετῆς μ. *from* virtue, Ph.1.415, cf. 477; πάτρης μ. Man.2.420. **II.**

*wandering*, of *the planets*, opp. the fixed stars, Arat.457:—hence fem. **-νάστις**, ψυχὴ σώματος μ. a *fugitive* from.., Ph.2.462; also **-νάστρια**, σκοπέλων μ. πέρδιξ AP7.204 (Agath.). **-ιος**, ον, *wandering*, Nonn.D.1.110; Νύμφαι AP9.814.

**μεταναφέρω**, in Pass., *to be diverted from their proper use*, of monies, OGI483.52 (Pergam., ii A.D.).

⊕ **μετανέομαι**, = μετανίσομαι II, εὐνήν Musae.205, Nonn.D.14.89.

**μετανέρχομαι**, *to be transported*, POxy.1049.1 (ii A.D.).

**μετανθέω**, *change its colour*, χλαμὺς κατὰ τὴν ἶριν μ. Philostr.Im.1.10, cf. Aristaenet.1.11.

**μετανιπτρίς**, ίδος, ἡ, *cup drunk after washing the hands* at the end of meals, δέξαι τηνδὶ μ. τῆς Ὑγιείας Call.Com.6, cf. Antiph.149; μ. τῆς Ὑγιείας ἔγχεον Nicostr.Com.3; μ. μεστὴν Διὸς Σωτῆρος Diph.69:—also **-νιπτρον**, τό, δαίμονος ἀγαθοῦ μ. Antiph.137.

⊕ **μετανίσομαι** [ῑ], *pass over*, Ἠέλιος μετενίσετο βουλυτόνδε Il.16.779, Od.9.58: c. acc., *pass into, enter*, Καρκίνον ἠέλιος μ. AP9.384.13. 2. of a river, *flow into* another, A.R.4.628. II. c. acc., *pursue*, E.Tr.131 (anap.); *win, get possession of*, [πλοῦτον] Pi.P.5.8; *go in quest of*, A.R.1.1245, cf. E.Hyps.Fr.(3) i iii 37 (lyr., -νεισεται Pap.).

**μετανίστημι**, *remove from his* or *their country*, Plb.3.5.5; εἰς ἄλλας πόλεις Id.9.26.7. 2. generally, *remove*, i.e. *avert*, τὰ χείριστα Phld.D.1.19. II. Pass., c. aor. 2 et pf. Act., *remove, migrate*, Th.1.12, 3.114, S.OC175 (anap.), Ph.1.514, POxy.44.9 (i A.D.); ἐς χῶρον Hdt.9.51, cf. D.S.4.85; ἐκ τῶν ἄνω τόπων Id.1.37; πρός τινας Ph.2.25; μ. Πελοποννήσου *emigrate from*.., Conon 47.1.

**μετανο-έω**, *perceive afterwards* or *too late*, opp. προνοέω, Epich. [280]; opp. προβουλεύομαι, Democr.66; *concur subsequently*, τισι BGU747 i 11 (ii A.D.). 2. *change one's mind* or *purpose*, Pl.Euthd.279c, Men.Epit.72; μ. μὴ οὔτε..τῶν χαλεπῶν ἔργων ᾖ τὸ..ἄρχειν *change one's opinion and think* that it is not.., X.Cyr.1.1.3. 3. *repent*, Antipho 2.4.12; ἐν τοῖς ἀνηκέστοις Id.5.91: freq. in Lxx and NT, Si.48.15, al.; ἀπὸ τῆς κακίας Act.Ap.8.22; ἐκ τῶν ἔργων Apoc.9.20; ἐπὶ τῇ ἀκαθαρσίᾳ 2Ep.Cor.12.21, cf. OGI751.9 (Amblada, ii B.C.); ἐπί τινι Luc.Salt.84, etc.; περί τινων Plu.Galb.6; τοῖς πεπραγμένοις Id.Agis 19: c. part., μ. γενόμενος Ἕλλην Luc.Am.36. 4. c. acc., *repent of*, τὴν ἄφιξιν J.BJ4.4.5. **-ημα**, ατος, τό, *ultimate concept*, Dam.Pr.117. **-ητικός**, ή, όν, *given to repentance*, Max.Tyr.11.3.

**μετάνοια**, ἡ, *change of mind* or *heart, repentance, regret*, Batr.70, Th.3.36, Philem.198, Plb.4.66.7, LxxPr.14.15, Aristeas 188, Plu.2.712c (pl.), etc.; ἀνίατος γὰρ τῶν τοιούτων μ. Antipho 2.4.12; γαμεῖν δ' ὁ μέλλων εἰς μ. ἔρχεται Men.Mon.91; ἡ εἰς τὸν θεὸν μ. Act.Ap.20.21; μ. ἀπὸ νεκρῶν ἔργων Ep.Hebr.6.1. II. Rhet., *afterthought, correction*, Rutil.1.16.

**μεταντλέω**, *draw from one vessel into another*, εἰς ἀγγεῖα Gp.9.19.8: metaph., of Τύχη, AP9.180 (Pall.).

**μέταξ-α**, ης, ἡ, *raw silk*, Procop.Arc.25, Lyd.Mag.2.4, etc. (The etym. is unknown: an earlier Latin form *mataxa* in Lucil.1192, Vitr.7.3.2 in the sense of 'floss', 'tow'.) ⊕ **-άβλαττα**, ἡ, *purple silk*, Edict.Diocl.24.1a, 13. ⊕ **-άριος**, ὁ, *silk-merchant*, Just.Nov.App.5. **-ιον**, τό, Dim. of μέταξα, Sch.E.Hec.447. **-ον**, τό, = μέταξα, Ps.-Callisth.3.7.

⊕ **μεταξύ** (late form **μετοξύ** PLond.2.177.11 (i A.D.), etc.), Adv., (μετά, ξύν) prop. *in the midst*: hence, I. as Adv., 1. of Place, *betwixt, between*, once in Hom., Il.1.156, cf. h.Merc.159, etc.: with Art., τὸ μ. Hdt.2.8, Ar.Av.551; ἐν τούτῳ τῷ μ. Th.4.25; νεάτης τε καὶ ὑπάτης καὶ μέσης καὶ εἰ ἄλλα ἄττα μ. τυγχάνει ὄντα Pl.R.443d; αὐχένα μ. τιθέντες Id.Ti.69e: metaph., φίλος ἢ ἐχθρὸς ἢ μ. Arist.Rh.1376[a]30. 2. of Time, *between-whiles, meanwhile*, Hdt.4.155, S.Fr.225, Pl.Ly.207d, etc.; τὰ μ. the *intervening* events, Isoc.12.201: freq. c. pres. part., μ. ὀρύσσων ἐπαύσατο *in the midst* of his digging, Hdt.2.158; ἐπελαυνόντων ..μ. Id.4.129; μ. θύων Ar.Ra.1242; μ. πίνων Eup.351.5; μ. πορευομένους X.Cyr.8.8.11, cf. Pl.Ly.207b, etc.; ἐξαναστάντες μ. δειπνοῦντες *in the middle of* supper, D.18.169; ἀπαγχομένη μ. κατεκλίθη (κατεκωλύθη Blass), i.e. *in the interval* between this and reviving, And.1.125: freq. with Verbs of speaking, λέγοντα μ. *in the middle of* my discourse, Pl.Ap.40b, cf. Euthd.275e, R.336b: without part., μ. ὑπολαβεῖν *to interrupt*, X.An.3.1.26; μ. τὸν λόγον καταλύομεν Pl.Grg.505c; μ. διαλῦσαι τὴν συνουσίαν Id.Prt.336e; ἐν τῷ μ. (sc. χρόνῳ) X.Smp.1.14: with χρόνῳ, D.30.17. b. in late writers, like μετά (Adv.), *after, afterwards*, τὸ μ. σάββατον the *next* Sabbath, Act.Ap.13.42; οἱ μ. τούτων βασιλεῖς the kings *who followed* them, J.BJ5.4.2; οἱ μ. τούτων, = Lat. *posteri eorum*, IG14.1913. 3. of Qualities, τὰ μ. *intermediate*, i.e. neither good nor bad, Pl.Grg.468a. 4. of Degree, ὅσον τὸ μ. how great is *the difference*, Timocl.22.1. 5. Gramm., the *neuter gender*, Arist.SE166[b]12, Po.1458[a]17. II. as Prep. c. gen., *between*, Hdt.1.6, 7.85, Th.1.118, 4.42, etc.; μ. σοφίας καὶ ἀμαθίας Pl.Smp.202a; μ. τούτοιν ἀμφοῖν ἐν μέσῳ ὂν Id.R.583c; αἱ μ. τῶν λόγων διηγήσεις the explanations *between* the speeches, Id.Tht.143c; but μ. τῶν λόγων *if I may interrupt* the argument, Id.Phdr.230a; μ. τῶν βασιλέων *among* kings, Plu.2.177c; *between* parties to an agreement, τιμὴ ἡ συμφωνηθεῖσα μ. τινῶν BGU316.15 (iv A.D.); τὰ μ. σύμφωνα the terms agreed *between the parties*, POxy.914.8 (v A.D.): sts. one of the extremes is omitted, ἄνωθεν τῶν Θυεστείων ῥακῶν μ. τῶν Ἰνοῦς Ar.Ach.434; ἢ ἐναντίοις οὖσιν ἢ μ. Arist.GC319[b]12; ἦν συμφέρον ὡς πλεῖστον τὸν μ. χρόνον γενέσθαι τῶν ὅρκων D.18.26. b. μ. θύρας *in the opening of* the door, Sor.1.119. 2. of Time, ὁ μ. τῆς δίκης τε καὶ τοῦ θανάτου [χρόνος] Pl.Phd.58c, cf. E.Hec.437; τὰ μ. τούτου *meanwhile*, S.OC291: as a Prep., it may either precede or follow its case, but more freq. precedes, cf. Pl.Phd.71a and b.

**μεταξῠλογία**, ἡ, *use of digressions*, Theon Prog.4 (pl.), Men.Prot. p.28 D., Olymp. in Mete.41.23.

**μεταξύτης** [ῠ], ητος, ἡ, *middle position*, A.D.Conj.221.5. 2. *mean*, = μεσότης, Theol.Ar.50 (pl.). II. in Music, *interval*, διάστημά ἐστι δυοῖν φθόγγων μ. Nicom.Harm.12, cf. 6 (pl.), S.E.M.5.78 (pl.). 2. generally, *interval*, Cat.Cod.Astr.5(1).192.

**μεταξωτός**, ή, όν, (μέταξα) *of silk*, ὕφασμα Hdn.Epim.125.

**μεταπᾰθῶς**, Adv., = συμπαθῶς, POxy.237 vii 23 (ii A.D.).

**μεταπαιδ-ᾰγωγέω**, f.l. for παραπαιδ- in Luc.Nigr.12. **-εύω**, *educate differently*, Lxx 4Ma.2.7 (Pass.), Luc.Anach.17:—Pass., of a substance, *acquire a fresh tendency*, Pall. in Hp.2.104 D. **-ιά**, ἡ, *play, sport*, τῶν ἐφήβων πρὸς ἀλλήλους OGI764.27 (Pergam., ii B.C.).

**μεταπαιφάσσομαι**, *rush, dart to and fro*, A.R.3.1266.

**μεταπαρα-δίδωμι**, *hand down*, τῷ μεθ' ἑαυτὸν ἱερεῖ τι BCH44.79 d2 (Lagina); (καθ)άπερ μυστήρια Iamb.VP32.226; *transfer*, IG14.759.22 (Naples), PMag.Par.1.501: Astrol., *yield up* the χρονοκρατορία, Vett.Val.163.25. **-δοσις**, εως, ἡ, *handing over* of funds, IGRom.4.948.10 (Chios). **-λαμβάνω**, *receive a thing from another*, οἱ παρ' ἐμοῦ -λημψόμενοι my *successors in* t tle, PAmh.2.68.22 (i A.D.), cf. IG4²(1).88.19 (Epid., ii A.D.), PMag.Par.1.525, Vett.Val.219.3; *take over* an office, BGU1192.8 (i B.C.).

**μεταπαραλλάσσω**, *change about, interchange*, in Pass., Hero Geom.3.25.

**μεταπαρατίθημι**, *transfer* in an account, prob. in PFlor.92.6 (i A.D.).

**μετα-παύομαι**, *rest between-whiles*, μεταπαυόμενοι δὲ μάχοντο Il.17.373. II. c. gen., *cease from*, ὅθι λαβρὸν ὕδωρ -παύεται ἅλμης Opp.H.1.115. **-παυσωλή**, ἡ, *rest between-whiles*, πολέμοιο *from* war, Il.19.201.

**μεταπείθω**, *change a man's persuasion*, Ar.Ach.626, Lys.9.7, D.18.228:—Pass., *to be persuaded to change*, Pl.R.413b, X.HG7.1.14, Isoc.3.47, D.Prooem.28.

**μεταπειράομαι**, *try in a different way*, Ar.Ec.217.

**μεταπείρω**, *pierce through again*, Antyll.(?)ap.Orib.45.18.7, Sor.2.62.

**μεταπειστός**, όν, *open to persuasion*, Pl.Ti.51e; μ. ὑπὸ λόγου Id.Def.414c.

**μετα-πεμπτέος**, α, ον, *to be sent for*, Th.6.25. **-πεμπτος**, ον, *sent for*, Hdt.8.67, Th.6.29, X.An.1.4.3, Phld.Mus.p.86 K., etc.; μ. δικαστήρια, of the federal *circuit*-courts of the Lycian league, OGI556.14 (i B.C.), IGRom.3.680.7 (i A.D.). **-πέμπω**, *send after* or *for*, Ἀγαμέμνονος πέμψαντος..μέτα *having sent for* thee, E.Hec.504; παρ' Εὐχαρίδου τρεῖς ἀγλιθας μετέπεμψα Ar.V.680. II. mostly in Med., μεταπέμπεσθαί τινα *summon*, Hdt.1.41, al., Ar.Ach.1087, al., Antipho 1.15, etc.; of things, *send for*, σῖτον OGI56.17 (Canopus, iii B.C.), etc.: Th. uses Act. and Med. indifferently, cf. 1.112, 4.30, 6.52, with 2.29, 5.82:—Pass., μεταπεμφθῆναι *to be sent for*, D.28.14, cf. Pl.Prt.319b; ἐξ Ἀθηνῶν μεταπεπέμφθαι Phld.Mus.p.28 K. **-πεμψις**, εως, ἡ, *a sending for, summons*, Pl.Ep.338b, Str.12.3.24, Nic.Dam.130.30 J. (pl.), Plu.Alex.33.

**μεταπεσσεύω**, Att. **-πεττεύω**, *move as in the game of draughts*, τινα dub. in Pl.Com.124:—Pass., Pl.Min.316c.

**μεταπέταμαι** or **-πέτομαι**, *fly to another place, fly away*, ἀπὸ..εἰς..Luc.Hist.Conscr.50.

**μεταπήγνυμι**, *transfer to another* place, in Med., πρὸς τὰ δένδρα τὴν καλιάν *transfer its* nest to the trees *instead*, D.Chr.72.14.

**μεταπηδ-άω**, *leap from one place to another, hop* or *spring about*, ἀπ' ἄλλου πρὸς ἕτερον ἀκρεμόνα Agatharch.51, cf. Luc.Gall.1, Syr.D.36, Gal.UP10.12: metaph., S.E.M.9.97. II. *leap among*, τισι App.Hann.23. **-ησις**, εως, ἡ, *leaping from one place to another*, Plu.2.739c.

**μετα-πίνω** [ῑ], *drink after*, Hp.Acut.56, in Pass., opp. προπίνομαι. **-πῑπίσκω**, causal of foreg., *give to drink afterwards*, Id.Morb.2.65.

⊕ **μεταπιπράσκω**, *sell after* or *again*, Phryn.PSp.88 B.

⊕ **μεταπίπτω**, used as Pass. of μεταβάλλω, *fall differently, undergo a change*, a. in form, Heraclit.88, Meliss.8, Pl.Cra.440a, etc.; πολλαχῶς μ. Diog.Apoll.2; μ. τὸ εἶδος Hdt.6.61; μ. εἰς ἄλλο εἶδος Pl.Cra.440b; ἐκ γυναικὸς ἐς ὄρνεον Luc.Philops.2: Gramm., τὸ ᾱ μ. εἰς τὸ ō A.D.Adv.188.25; *fall into disrepair*, PSI4.444.3 (iii B.C.). b. in mind, *change one's opinion suddenly*, τὸν ὁμόθεν πεφυκότα στέργων μετέπεσον E.IA502; ἐξ ἐχθίστου μ. Ar.Av.627: abs., Isoc.9.50, Plb.5.49.7, PRyl.118.4 (i B.C.); also μ. εἰς τἀναντία τῆς γνώμης Plb.21.7.7. 2. of place, *migrate, be transferred*, Arist.Mete.360[b]18, al.; of votes, εἰ τριάκοντα μόναι μετέπεσον τῶν ψήφων Pl.Ap.36a, cf. Aeschin.3.252; but ὀστράκου μεταπεσόντος *on the fall* of the sherd *with the other side uppermost*, prov., of a sudden change (borrowed from the game ὀστρακίνδα), Pl.Phdr.241b, cf. Sch. 3. of conditions, circumstances, etc., μεταπίπτοντος δαίμονος E.Alc.913 (anap.); μ. ἄνω κάτω Pl.Grg.493a; τοὐναντίον μεταπέπτωκεν Id.Tht.162d; τὰ μὲν [πάθη] ταχὺ μεταπίπτειν εἴθισται D.26.18; τὸ τῆς τύχης γὰρ ῥεῦμα μ. ταχύ Men.Georg.Fr.2; freq. of political changes, *undergo revolution*, Th.8.68, Pl.Ep.325a; μετεπεπτώκει τὰ πράγματα *a revolution had taken place*, Lys.20.14; ἡ Ῥωμαίων δυναστεία μετέπεσεν εἰς μοναρχίαν Hdn.1.1.4; also ἀρχὴ -πεσοῦσα εἰς ἄνδρα ἐξ ἀσήμου γένους Id.2.3.1: generally, *change for the worse*, ἐξ εὐπορίης εἰς πενίην Democr.101; εἰς δουλείαν Lycurg.50; ἐξ εὐτυχίας εἰς δυστυχίαν Arist.Po.1453[a]2; also, *for the better*, μ. ἐκ τοῦ κακῶς πράττειν Lycurg.60;

μεταπέσοι βελτίονα E.*Ion* 412; τοῦ πυκνὰ μεταπίπτοντος κριτηρίου Epicur.*Fr.*230; of a person, *to be variable*, μ. καὶ μεταρριπίζεσθαι Arr. *Epict.*1.4.19. b. μεταπίπτοντες λόγοι fallacies *due to a change* in meaning of terms, ib.1.7.1; συλλογισμοὶ μ. ib.2.17.27. II. c. gen. rei, *fall from, fail of..*, εἰ ἡ γνῶσις τοῦ γνῶσις εἶναι μὴ μεταπίπτει Pl. *Cra.*440a. III. of property, *to be transferred*, εἴς τινα ἐξ ὀνόματός τινος *Stud.Pal.*4.114.14 (ii A.D.).

**μετά-πλᾰσις**, εως, ἡ, = sq., Eust.58.35. **-πλασμός**, ὁ, in Gramm., *metaplasm*, the formation of cases of Nouns or tenses of Verbs from a non-existent nom. or pres., A.D.*Adv.*183.22 (pl.), Choerob.*in Theod.* 1.377, Arc.129.9. **-πλάσσω**, Att. **-ττω**, *mould differently, remodel*, Pl.*Ti.*92b, Iamb.*Myst.*3.28; τι εἴς τι Pl.*Ti.*5ca (so in Med., *AP*9.708 (Phil.)); βίον μ. ἄλλοι ἄλλως Melinno ap.Stob.3.7.12. 2. *counterfeit*, τὸ θεῖον νόμισμα Ph.1.220. II. Gramm., in Pass., *to be formed by metaplasm*, A.D.*Adv.*184.11, Arc.129.6, Eust.58.38. **-πλαστικός**, ή, όν, *changed in form*, of forms used by Poets, Festus p.138 L.

**μεταπλέω**, *change one's sailing, sail on another tack*, *An.Ox.*3.219; Ion. **-πλώω** Opp.*H.*3.427.

**μεταπλόμενοι**, οἱ, *the transformed, the deified*, Hsch.

**μετάπλοος**, contr. **-πλους**, ὁ, = *prospera navigatio*, dub. in *Gloss.*

**μετα-πνέω**, *recover breath*, καμάτοιο from.., Opp.*H.*5.314. **-πνοή**, ἡ, *recovering of breath*, gloss on μετάψυξις, Hsch.

⊛ **μεταποι-έω**, *alter the make of* a thing, *remodel*, νόμους D.18.121; πάντα ἐς τοὺς τρόπους τοὺς παραπλησίους μ. Hp.*Fract.*26; εἰς γάμον ἀπὸ τῆς θυσίας μ. τὴν εὐωχίαν Hld.5.29, cf. Porph.*Antr.*36: abs., μεταποίησον *re-compose* the verse, Sol.20.3:—Pass., -ποιεῖσθαι εἰς τὸ δέον A.D.*Synt.*199.18. II. Med., *lay claim to, pretend to*, c. gen. rei, e.g. ξυνέσεως, ἀρετῆς τι, Th.1.140, 2.51; τέχνης Pl.*Plt.*289e; οὐδέν σφι μετεὸν μεταποιεῦνται (sc. τοῦ ἐμπορίου) Hdt.2.178. **-ή**, ἡ, *change* of ownership, *POxy.*318 (i A.D.). **-ησις**, εως, ἡ, *claiming*, ἀρετῆς J.*AJ*3.2.4; τῶν διπλῶν *IG*14.1054; *acquisition*, Ph.2.419. II. *changing, alteration*, Apollon.ap.Gal.12.653, Antyll.ap. Orib.7.7.7: also in Rhet., Hermog.*Inv.*4.3. **-ητέον**, *one must alter*, ἐπὶ τὸ χρηστότερον Philum.ap.Aët.9.33.

**μεταποίνιος**, ον, *punishing afterwards*, δίκη Suid. s.v. ποινή.

**μεταπομπή**, ἡ, = μετάπεμψις, Pl.*Ep.*348d, Ael.*VH*13.34.

**μεταπόντιος**, ον, *in the midst of the sea*, Hsch.

**μεταπορεύ-δην**, Adv. *pursuing*, Hsch. ⊛ **-ομαι**, *go after, follow up*, ἔχθραν Lys.31.2; *pursue, punish*, τοὺς ἀποστήσαντας Plb.1.88.9; ἀσέβειαν Id.2.58.11, cf. J.*AJ*6.13.4. 2. *seek after, canvass for*, ἀρχήν Plb.10.4.2, cf. Πολέμων 1.30 (Demetrias). 3. *change*, βουλήν, ἤθη, Procop.*Goth.*4.34, *Aed.*6.2; ῥεῖθρον, of a river, ib.2.10. II. *go from one place to another, migrate*, Pl.*Lg.*904c, *PPetr.*3 p.129 (iii B.C.), *PRev.Laws* 44.10 (iii B.C.).

**μεταποροποι-έω**, = μετασυγκρίνω, Dsc.4.153. **-ησις**, εως, ἡ, = μετασύγκρισις, Gal.10.268.

**μεταποτέον**, (μεταπίνω) *one must drink afterwards*, Hp.*Acut.*63.

⊛ **μετά-πρᾱσις**, εως, ἡ, *re-sale*, Str.5.3.7. **-πράτης** [ᾱ], ου, ὁ, *one who re-sells*, Sch.Ptol.*Tetr.*151, Suid. s.v. μετάβολοι.

**μεταπρεπ-ής**, ές, *distinguished among*, c. dat. pl., δόμον.. μεταπρεπέ' ἀθανάτοισι Il.18.370. ⊛ **-ω**, *distinguish oneself* or *be distinguished among*, c. dat. pl., [ταῦρος] βόεσσι μ. Il.2.481, etc.: freq. (esp. in Il.) of heroes, μ. ἡρώεσσιν ib.579; Τρώεσσι 13.175; ἱππεῦσι 11.720, cf. Hes.*Th.*92 (tm.); συμποσίοισι μ. Phalaec.ap.Ath.10.440d; ἐν πάντεσσι Orph.*A.*806: c. dat. modi, ἔγχεϊ Τρωσὶ μεταπρέπω I *am distinguished among* the Trojans *by* the spear, Il.16.835, cf. 596, Hes.*Th.*377: so c. inf., μετέπρεπε Μυρμιδόνεσσιν ἔγχεϊ μάρνασθαι Il. 16.194, cf. Od.18.2 (tm.): c. acc., μ. ἠϊθέοισιν εἶδος A.R.2.784.

**μεταπτοιέω**, *flee cowering to another place, seek refuge*, A.*Supp.*332.

**μετά-πτωσις**, εως, ἡ, *change*, Pl.*Lg.*895b, etc.; τῶν πραγμάτων Arist.*MM*$1207^{b}$12; τὸ κατὰ μετάπτωσιν ἐνόχλημα Epicur.*Fr.*154; ὁ βίος ἀδήλους τὰς μ. ἔχει Men.*Mon.*581; εἰς ἄλληλα Str.17.1.36: pl., *OGI*335.128 (Pergam.); -σεις λημμάτων, λόγων, Arr.*Epict.*1.7.20, 3.2.17; εἰ..εἰς μ. ἔσται ὁ ἀγρός if it shall be *transferred*, *CIG*3702 (Mysia); ἡ ἐκ τύχης ἄνω καὶ κάτω μ. Ael.*VH*2.29. II. *change of party*, πρός τινας Plb.3.99.3; *change of opinion*, τοῦ πλήθους Phld.*Rh.* 2.17 S. (pl.). III. Gramm., *inflexion*, μ. εἰς ἀριθμόν, πτῶσιν, A.D. *Adv.*181.2: generally, *change*, μ. τοῦ ō εἰς τὸ ᾱ Trypho ib.174.4; ἐκ -πτώσεως A.D.*Synt.*50.20. **-πτωτικός**, ή, όν, *liable to change*: of the quantity of vowels, *common*, D.H.*Comp.*14. 2. of persons, *fickle*, M.Ant.11.10. **-πτωτος**, η, ον, = foreg., ἐνέργειαι ἐν ὀλίγῳ μ. Plu.2.447a, cf. M.Ant.5.10. Adv. -τως Arr.*Epict.*2.22.8.

**μεταπύργ-ιον**, τό, = μεσοπύργιον, *space between two towers, curtain*, Th.3.22, Lys.*Fr.*97 S., *IG*$2^{2}$.463.49, $2^{2}$.1658, al., Ph.*Bel.*80.11, J.*BJ* 3.5.2 (pl.). **-ίς**, ίδος, ἡ, = foreg., Ph.*Bel.*81.23 (s.v.l.).

**μεταπωλέω**, = μεταπιπράσκω, *PLond.*2.856.13 (i A.D.), *SIG*884.20 (Thisbe, iii A.D.):—Pass., *GDI*2562.15 (Delph.).

**μεταρδεύω**, *divert* a stream, metaph., Heraclit.*All.*18.

⊛ **μετᾰρίθμιος**, ον, *counted among*, ἀθανάτοισιν *h.Hom.*26.6, cf. A.R. 1.205; in tmesi, v. ἀρίθμιος II.

**μεταρράπτω**, gloss on ἐπικαττύω, Phryn.*PS* p.69 B.

**μεταρρευματ-ίζω**, *divert a flux*, εἰς τὰ ἐκτός [Gal.]14.744. **-ισμός**, ὁ, *change in flux*, Orib.*Fr.*54.

**μετά-ρρευσις**, εως, ἡ, = μετάρροια, Alex.Aphr.*in Mete.*115.19. **-ρρέω**, fut. μεταρρυήσομαι Gal.7.573:—*flow differently*: *change to and fro, ebb and flow*, ὥσπερ Εὔριπος Arist.*EN*$1167^{b}$7, cf. Aret.*SD*2.1. 2. *change from one side to the other*, as from right to left, Pl.*Tht.*193d: metaph., *change sides, transfer one's allegiance* or *affections*, μ. πᾶν τὸ ἔθνος εἰς αὐτόν J.*BJ*1.4.5; τὰ πράγματα μ. εἰς Μιθριδάτην Posidon.36 J.:—Pass., μεταρρυῆναι εἰς παῖδα Philostr.*VA*3.38, cf. *VS* 2.3.

**μεταρριζόω**, *uproot*, Nonn.*D.*21.106.

**μεταρρῑπίζω**, *fan into flame*, Nonn.*D.*2.408. II. *blow about*, in Pass., μ. ἅμα τισί Arr.*Epict.*1.4.19.

**μεταρρίπτω**, *toss from side to side*, ἑωυτόν Hp.*Epid.*7.10, cf. Thphr.*Ign.*53. 2. *turn upside down*, πάντα μεταρρίπτει θεός Simon. 62 (= *Com.Adesp.*383); τὰ καλῶς πεπηγότα μ. D.25.90. II. *bring over*, ἀπὸ τῆς Φιλίππου συμμαχίας πρὸς τὴν Ῥωμαίων Plb.18. 13.8, cf. 30.7.2, al.; μ. τὴν διάνοιαν ἐπί.. *turn* one's mind to.., Phld. *Vit.*p.17 J.

**μετάρροια**, ἡ, *change of stream, reflux*, τοῦ πνεύματος Arist.*Mete.* $367^{a}$28: pl., Plu.2.433f, Gal.16.540; also of light, Plot.4.5.7.

**μεταρρυθμ-έω**, = sq., dub. l. in Procop.*Goth.*4.2. ⊛ **-ίζω**, *change the form* or *fashion of* a thing, *remodel*, τὰ γράμματα Hdt.5.58; πόρον A.*Pers.*747; τὴν λέξιν Arist.*Ph.*$185^{b}$28; τὸ ἀμφίβολον τῆς προαιρέσεως εἰς βεβαιότητα Hierocl.*in CA* 2 p.422 M., cf. 19 p.460 M.:—Pass., *have one's form changed*, Pl.*Ti.*46a, Arist.*Cael.*$306^{b}$13. 2. esp. *reform, amend*, X.*Oec.*11.2,3, Arist.*EN*$1179^{b}$16, Epicur.*Nat.*82 G.; *cure*, τινὰ τῶν ἁμαρτημάτων Philostr.*VA*1.13:—Pass., οὐδὲ μετερρύθμισθέ πω ib.6.11. II. *make in a different form*, Pl.*Ti.*91d (Pass.). **-ῐσις**, εως, ἡ, *alteration*, prob. in Tz. ad Hes.*Op.* 42. **-ιστέον**, *one must alter, correct*, Sever.*Clyst.*42. **-όω**, = μεταρρυθμίζω, pf. part. Pass. μετερρυθμωμένα, Hsch.; cf. μεταρυσμόω.

**μετάρρῠσις**, εως, ἡ, (μεταρρέω) = μετάρροια, Gal.16.56, 17(2).441, Alex.Aphr.*in Mete.*69.28, *Quaest.*99.2.

**μεταρσιο-λεσχέω**, = μετεωρολογέω, Sch.Ar.*Nu.*319. **-λέσχης**, ου, ὁ, = μετεωρολέσχης, Pl.*Sis.*389a. **-λεσχία**, ἡ, = μετεωρολογία, Plu.*Per.*5. **-λογικός**, ή, όν, = μετεωρολογικός: τὰ μ., title of work by Theophrastus, D.L.5.44.

**μετάρσιος**, Dor. **πεδάρσιος**, ον, also α, ον Hdt.7.188, E.*IT*27: (μεταίρω):—Ion., poet., and in late Prose, as D.S.3.51, Ocell.3.1, J. *AJ*6.9.4, Porph.ap.Eus.*PE*3.9, for μετέωρος, *raised from the ground, high in air*, ἐσπᾶτο γὰρ πέδονδε καὶ μ. S.*Tr.*786; μετάρσιοι χολαὶ διεσπείροντο melted *into air*, Id.*Ant.*1009; λόγοι π. θρῴσκουσι are scattered *to the winds*, A.*Ch.*846; ὑπὲρ πυρᾶς μ. ληφθεῖσ' E. l.c.; μετάρσιον πλευρὰν ἔπαιρε Id.*Hec.*499; μ. ἀναπτόμενος Ar.*Av.*1382; ναῦς ἄρμεν' ἔχοισα μ. having her sails *hoisted*, Theoc.13.68; τὰ μ., = μετέωρα, *the sky, heavens*, Thphr.*Ign.*3; but defined as τὰ μεταξὺ τοῦ αἰθέρος καὶ τῆς γῆς, opp. τὰ μετέωρα (= τὰ ἐν οὐρανῷ), Ach.Tat.*Intr. Arat.*32; πῦρ μ., opp. αἴθριον, D.H.16.1; τὰ μ. also, *birds of the air*, J. l.c., cf. Porph. l.c. 2. *on the high seas*, ὅσας δὲ τῶν νεῶν μεταρσίας ἔλαβε [ὁ ἄνεμος] Hdt. l.c.; νῆσος μ. a *floating* island, Hecat.305 J. 3. *in suspense*, ὅσσα Νεῖκος ἔρυκε μετάρσιον Emp.35.9. II. metaph., *high above this world*, διὰ μούσας καὶ μ. ᾖξα E.*Alc.*963 (lyr.); μ. ὕμνος *IG*3.770: in bad sense, *puffed up, elated*, μ. τὴν ψυχὴν τηρεῖν Vett.Val.340.13; ἡ πάρος ἀγλαΐῃσι μ. *AP*5.272.1 (Agath.). 2. of things, *airy, empty*, κόμποι E.*Andr.*1220 (lyr.). III. in Medic., of the breath, = μετέωρος I.2, πνεῦμα Hp.*Mul.*2.130; πνοὰς θερμὰς πνέω μετάρσι', οὐ βέβαια (neut. pl. as Adv.) E.*HF*1093. 2. of the face, *puffed up, swollen*, Hp.*Mul.*2.110.

**μεταρσιόω**, *lift up*, τὰς ὑστέρας Hp.*Mul.*2.138:—Pass., νέφος μεταρσιωθέν Hdt.8.65.

⊛ **μέταρσις**, εως, ἡ, *transplantation*, Thphr.*CP*1.4.2: ὀμμάτων μετάρσεσι is f.l. in Gal.*Parv.Pil.*2.

**μεταρυσμόω** (ῥυσμός Ion., = ῥυθμός), = μεταρρυθμόω, ἡ διδαχὴ μεταρυσμοῖ τὸν ἄνθρωπον Democr.33.

**μετ-αρχή**, Dor. **-ά**, ἡ, part of the νόμος κιθαρῳδικός, Poll.4. 66. **-άρχιος**, ὁ, name of month in Crete, *Hemerolog.Flor.*

**μετασεύομαι**, Ep. aor. μετέσσῡτο (v. infr.):—Pass., *go with* or *after*, πολλαὶ δὲ μετεσσεύοντο γεραιαί Il.6.296; *rush towards* or *after*, Ἀθηναίη δὲ μετέσσυτο 21.423: c. acc., μετέσσυτο ποιμένα λαῶν 23. 389. II. *rush back*, πέλαγόσδε A.R.4.1270.

**μετασκαίρω**, *prance among* or *after*, Arat.282.

**μετασκάπτω**, *transplant*, Hsch. s.v. μεταβοθρεύοντες.

**μετασκευ-άζω**, *put into another dress* (σκευή), *change the fashion of, transform*, σαυτήν Ar.*Ec.*499; τὰ ἅρματα εἰς τὸν αὐτὸν τρόπον X.*Cyr.* 6.2.8; μ. νόμον *amend*, Din.1.42; *put into a fresh shape*, τὰς λέξεις D.H.*Comp.*6. II. Med., *exchange one's equipment with another*, App.*Pun.*8; μ. εἰς τοὺς ὁπλίτας Jul.*Or.*2.60a. 2. *pack up so as to change one's quarters*, τὰ αὑτοῦ παρά τινα X.Eph.5.13: abs., *shift oneself*, ἐκ..εἰς.. Luc.*Tox.*57, cf. Ach.Tat.3.1. 3. *clothe oneself differently*, οἰκετικαῖς ἐσθήσεσιν μ. *disguise oneself* in.., Polyaen.6.49: pf. Pass., πόθεν μετεσκεύασθε; Philostr.*Her.Prooem.*1. **-αστικός**, ή, όν, *tending to refashion* or *reshape* material, of arts, D.L.3.100. **-ή**, ἡ, *alteration, modification*, D.H.*Comp.*6; *refashioning*, τῶν πόρων Cass.*Pr.*69. **-ωρέομαι**, *alter*, τοὔνομα Pl.*Plt.*276c.

**μετασκηνόω**, *shift an encampment*, D.S.14.32, J.*AJ*3.5.1: metaph., τὸ κοινὸν πάντων ἄγαλμα μ. παρ' ἑτέρους Him.*Ecl.*13.13.

**μετασοβέω**, *drive by scaring*, Phot., Suid.

**μετασπάω**, *draw over from one side to another*, πειρᾷ μετασπᾶν σκληρὰ μαλθακῶς λέγων S.*OC*774.

**μετασπεύδω**, *hasten after*, abs., J.*AJ*6.2.2.

**μετασπόμενος, μετασπών**, v. μεθέπω.

**μέτασσαι**, αἱ, = μεταγενεῖς, of lambs, χωρὶς μὲν πρόγονοι, χωρὶς δὲ μέτασσαι, χωρὶς δ' αὖθ' ἕρσαι, i.e. the early-born, *those born later*, and the freshlings or late-born, Od.9.221:—also neut. **τὰ μέτασσα** *thereafter*, *h.Merc.*125, cf. *An.Ox.*1.280. (From μετά, *after*; cf. ἔπισσαι.)

**μετά-σταλσις**, εως, ἡ, *summoning*, dub. in *Gloss.* ⊛ **-στᾰσις**,

εως, ἡ, (μεθίστημι) *removing, removal*, πόνων S.*Ichn.*217; κακοῦ And. 2.8; μετάστασιν ἴσχειν admit of *removal*, of disease, Hp.*Aph.*5.7. 2. Rhet., *removal of the scene* to some hypothetical condition, Quint. 3.6.53. b. *shifting* of blame, Hermog.*Stat.*2,6 (sg. and pl.). II. (μεθίσταμαι) *removal, migration*, of Place, μ. ἐξ οἰκείας εἰς ἀλλοτρίαν Pl.*Ti.*82a; εἰς τὴν γείτονα πόλιν Id.*Lg.*877a; being something short of banishment, μ. τῶν πολιτῶν Id.*Ep.*356e; μεταστάσεις ποιούντων ἐπ' ἄλλον τόπον Epicur.*Ep.*2 p.38 U.; μ. ἐπὶ τάδε καὶ ἐπ' ἐκεῖνα τοῦ βουλευτηρίου *vote, division* in the Senate, D.C.41.2; ἡλίου μ. its fabled *change of course*, E.*IT*816. b. *departure* from life, τοῦ βίου μεταστάσεις Id.*Fr.*554; ἡ ἐκ τοῦ βίου μ. Plb.30.2.5; μ. alone, *death*, Simon.32, J.*AJ*17.4.1. c. on the Stage, *exit* of the chorus, Poll. 4.108. d. Medic., *transference* of the seat of disease, Hp.*Aff.* 12, Gal.17(2).790, Aret.*SA*1.7; but, *dislocation*, Gal.8.246. 2. *change*, μορφῆς, γνώμης, E.*Hec.*1266, *Andr.*1003; μετάστασιν διδόναι (sc. θυμῷ) to allow *a change* to one's wrath, i.e. suffer it to cease, S. *Ant.*718; τοῦ φρονεῖν μ. Alex.292. 3. *change of political constitution*, πολιτείας μ. Pl.*Lg.*856c; πρώτη μ. τῶν ἐξ ἀρχῆς Arist.*Ath.*41.2; at Athens, the *Revolution* of 404 B.C., Lys.30.10. b. *counter-revolution*, ἐκ στάσεως μ. Th.4.74. **-στᾰτέον**, *one must alter*, Isoc. 5.132. **-στᾰτικός**, ή, όν, *connected with* μετάστασις I. 2, στάσις Hermog.*Stat.*6; of the phrase εἰ δέ, Sch.Th.3.65. Adv. -κῶς Aps. p.276 H., Sch.Aristid.p.289 D. **-στᾰτος**, ον, *removed*, ὑπὸ καθαρμῶν Hp.*Morb.Sacr.*1.

❋ **μεταστείχω**, *go in quest of*, τινα E.*Hec.*509, *Supp.*90. II. abs., *depart*, in aor. 2 μετέστιχε, A.R.3.451.

**μεταστέλλω**, *call back, restore*, πνεῦμα Antyll.ap.Orib.6.21.4. 2. Med., *send for, summon*, τινα J.*AJ*17.13.3, Luc.*Alex.*55, *Cont.*12, *PSI*4.449.11 (iv A.D.):—Pass., μετεσταλμένοι J.*AJ*7.9.2.

**μεταστένω**, *lament afterwards*, ἄτην δὲ μετέστενον Od.4.261; μὴ μεταστένειν πόνον (Sch.; πόνων codd.) A.*Eu.*59; τῆς παλαιᾶς διαίτης ἑαυτούς Ph.1.209. II. Med., *lament after* or *next*, σὸν ἄλγος E. *Med.*996 (lyr.).

**μεταστήθιον**, τό, part of the *palm* of the hand, *Cat.Cod.Astr.*7. 238.

**μεταστοιχεί** or -ί, Adv. *all in a row*, στὰν δὲ μ., of chariots ready to start in a race, Il.23.358; of runners, ib.757.

**μεταστοιχειόω**, *change the elementary nature of* a thing, μ. γῆν *transform* earth into water, of Xerxes, Ph.1.674:—Pass., δράκων εἰς βακτηρίαν μ. Id.2.93.

**μεταστολίζομαι**, *change one's costume*, Sch.Ar.*Ra.*524.

**μεταστονᾰχίζομαι**, *sigh* or *lament afterwards*, Hes.*Sc.*92.

**μεταστρᾰτεύομαι**, Med., of troops, *go over to another general*, ἐς τὸν Σύλλαν App.*Mith.*51.

**μεταστρᾰτοπεδεύω**, *shift one's ground* or *camp*, Plb.3.112.2, D.S. 14.32, Plu.2.228d:—Med., X.*Cyr.*3.3.23; πρὸς τὸ ἄστυ Id.*Ages.*2. 18; εἰς τὸν ἕτερον χάρακα D.H.9.6 (Act. as v.l.).

**μετα-στρεπτέον**, *one must retort*, τὴν ἄγνοιαν εἰς τὸν ἐρωτῶντα Arist. *SE*181$^a$18. **-στρεπτικός**, ή, όν, *fit for turning another way, fit for directing*, ἐπί τι Pl.*R.*525a. **-στρέφω**, aor. Pass. -εστρέφθην Il.8.258, al., -εστράφην [ᾰ] Hdt.3.121, etc.:—*turn about, turn round*, τῷ κε Ποσειδάων.. αἶψα μεταστρέψειε νόον Il.15.52; εἴ κεν Ἀχιλλεὺς ἐκ χόλου.. μεταστρέψῃ φίλον ἦτορ 10.107; τὸ πρόσωπον πρός τι Pl.*Smp.*190e:—Med., μεταστρέφεσθαι πρὸς τὸ μαλθακώτερον Ar.*Ra.*538 (lyr.):—Pass., *turn oneself about, turn about*, whether to face the enemy, στῆ δὲ μεταστρεφθείς Il.11.595, 15.591, cf. Hdt.7.211; or to flee, τῷ δὲ μεταστρεφθέντι μεταφρένῳ ἐν δόρυ πῆξεν Il.8.258; simply, *turn round*, Hdt.3.121, Pl.*Phd.*116d, etc.; *turn about* (to see if any one follows), Ar.*Lys.*125, D.21.221; *recur*, ἐπὶ τὰ προειρημένα Pl.*Cra.*428d. 2. *turn round, retort*, αἰτίας D.41.13. 3. *twist* or *turn all ways*, πάντα μεταστρέφοντα λόγον βασανίζειν Pl.*Tht.*191c; λόγους ἄνω καὶ κάτω μ. Id.*Phdr.*272b; *turn upside down*, ἅπαντα μ. τύχη Philem.111:—Pass., τἄνω κάτω ὁ βίος μεταστραφείς Men.5. 4. *misrepresent*, [δικαιοσύνης καὶ ἀδικίας] τὴν δύναμιν Pl.*R.*367a: generally, *change, alter*, τὸ δίκαιον οὐκ ἔστι μεταστρέψαι Arist.*Rh.*1376$^b$21, cf. 1412$^a$33; *invert*, τὰ τοῦ Ξενοφάνους ib.1377$^a$23:—Pass., ὁρᾷς γὰρ τἄμ' ὅσῳ μετεστράφη how my fortunes *are changed*, E.*Ba.*1329; τὸ ψήφισμ' ὅπως μεταστραφείη Ar.*Ach.*537. 5. ἀντὶ τοῦ ἰῶτα ἦτα μ. *use* one *for* another, Pl.*Cra.* 418c. II. intr., *turn another way, change one's ways*, ἦ τι μεταστρέψεις; Il.15.203: aor. part. μεταστρέψας *contrariwise*, Pl.*Grg.*457a (pl.), *R.*587d. 2. *turn so as to punish* or *avenge*, of the gods, μή τι μεταστρέψωσιν ἀγασσάμενοι κακὰ ἔργα Od.2.67 (unless trans., *turn back* (upon the sinners), cf. μετάτροπος 2). 3. c. gen., *care for, regard*, E.*Hipp.*1226. **-στροφάδην** [ᾰ], Adv. *backwards*, Agath. 5.19. **-στροφή**, ἡ, *turning from* one thing *to another*, ἀπό τινος ἐπί τι Pl.*R.*525c, 532b. II. *turn* of events, Lxx 3*Ki.*12. 15. **-στρωφάω**, = μεταστρέφω, Procl.*H.*1.16:—Med., Orph.*L.* 739.

**μεταστύλιον** [ῡ], τό, *intercolumniation*, *IG*2$^2$.1668.63, *Milet.*7 p.56: pl., *IG*11(2).199*A*73 (Delos, iii B.C.); *spaces between pilasters*, *Rev. Phil.*43.186, 199; *colonnade*, D.C.68.25.

**μεταστῠφελίζω**, *strike rudely*, Nonn.*D.*17.164.

**μετασυγ-κρίνω** [ῑ], *alter the state of the pores*, a term of the Methodic school of medicine, Thessal.ap.Gal.10.250, Sor.2.28, Dsc.5.6, etc.:—hence Subst. **-κρίσις**, εως, ἡ, Id.3.35, Sor.2.16, Gal.10.268: Adj. **-κρῐτικός**, ή, όν, δύναμις Dsc.4.153, Sor.2.15, Gal.12.571. Adv. -κῶς v.l. in Ps.-Dsc.2.166.

**μετασυν-εθίζομαι**, Pass., *have the custom changed*, Posidon.ap. Gal.5.400. **-τάσσω**, *alter the arrangement of* a treatise, Vett.Val. 157.30. **-τίθημι**, *alter the arrangement of* a sentence, Demetr. *Eloc.*59, 249. II. Pass., *to be put together*, Simp. *in Cael.*636.14.

**μετασύρω** [ῠ], Gramm., *alter in form*, Eust.32.42.

**μετασυσχηματίζομαι**, Pass., *to be altered in form*, Hsch. s.v. ἀλλοίωσις.

**μετασφαιρισμός**, ὁ, *movement of a ball*, Antyll.ap.Orib.6.32.4.

**μετάσχεσις**, εως, ἡ, = μέθεξις, *participation*, τῆς δυάδος *in* the nature of the dyad, Pl.*Phd.*101c.

**μετασχημᾰτ-ίζω**, *change the form of* a person or thing, Pl.*Lg.* 903e, Arist.*GC*335$^b$26; τὸ σῶμα τῆς ταπεινώσεως *Ep.Phil.*3.21; of a building, *Sammelb.*5174.10 (vi A.D.):—Med., with Att. fut. -ιοῦμαι, *change one's form*, Demetr.Lac.*Herc.*1012.12; *disguise oneself*, J.*AJ*8.11.1:—Pass., *to be changed in form*, Pl.*Lg.*906c, Arist. *Cael.*298$^b$31, *GA*747$^a$15, D.S.2.57; of grammatical change, A.D. *Pron.*68.5, al. II. μ. τι εἰς ἐμαυτόν *transfer as in a figure*, 1*Ep.Cor.* 4.6. III. *change the posture of*, Sor.2.62 (Pass.), al. IV. of stars and planets, in Pass., *change* their *configuration*, πρὸς ἀλλήλους Adam.*Vent.*47. **-ῐσις**, εως, ἡ, *change of form*, Arist.*Ph.*190$^b$5, *Cael.* 305$^b$29, *Sens.*446$^b$6. **-ισμός**, ὁ, = foreg., Thphr.*CP*2.16.4. Plu. 2.687b tit.: in pl., Str.1.3.3, Dsc.1 *Praef.*7, A.D.*Synt.*230.3, Iamb. *Myst.*7.3. 2. *change of position* or *posture*, Sor.2.21 (pl.). **-ιστέον**, *one must change the attitude of*, τὸν ἀγκῶνα Antyll.ap.Orib.7.12.2.

**μετασχιστής**, οῦ, ὁ, dub. sens. in *Ostr.*1 (Syene).

**μετασωματόομαι**, *to be changed in substance*, Zos.Alch.p.108 B.

**μετά-ταξις**, εως, ἡ, *change in the order of battle*, Plb.12.25$^F$.3 (pl.). ❋**-τάσσω**, Att. -ττω, *transpose*, Arist.*Metaph.*1038$^a$30, cf. Dam.*Pr.*112 (dub. l.):—Med., *adjourn* a trial, μ. εἰς αὔριον ἀκοῦσαι Wilcken *Chr.*14.17 (i A.D.):—Pass., Arist.*GC*327$^a$19. II. Med., *change one's order of battle*, X.*Cyr.*6.1.43; παρ' Ἀθηναίους -τάξασθαι *go over and join* them, Th.1.95; μ. πρός τινα J.*AJ*5.1.17.

**μετατεύχω**, *refashion*, αὐτὸς ἑαυτὸν εἰς μάχιμον μ. Eust.612.10.

❋ **μετατίθημι**, fut. -θήσω:—Med., fut. -θήσομαι D.19.341: I. *place among*, τῷ κ' οὔ τι τόσον κέλαδον μετέθηκε (v.l. μεθέηκεν) then he *would* not *have caused* so much noise *among* us, Od.18.402. II. *place differently*, 1. in local sense, *transpose, change the place of*, τὰ αἰδοῖα εἰς τὸ πρόσθεν Pl.*Smp.*191b; εἰς βελτίω τόπον Id.*Lg.*903d; μ. τὰς θύρας *PSI*5.546.5 (iii B.C.); μετέθηκεν αὐτὸν (sc. τὸν Ἐνώχ) ὁ θεός Lxx *Ge.*5.24:—Pass., Arist.*Int.*20$^b$10; *to be transferred*, *OGI*338.20 (Pergam., ii B.C.), *Act.Ap.*7.16, etc. 2. in Logic, μ. τὸ συμπέρασμα *alter* a conclusion to its contrary, Arist.*APr.*59$^b$1. 3. *change, alter*, of a treaty, μεταθεῖναι ὅπῃ ἂν δοκῇ ἀμφοτέροις Foed.ap. Th.5.18; τὸ νυνδὴ ῥηθέν Pl.*Plt.*297e, cf. X.*Mem.*3.14.6; μ. τινὰ ἐς πτηνὴν φύσιν *AP*11.367 (Jul.); ἐπὶ ὑὸς τὰς ἐπωνυμίας μ. *change* their names *and call them* after swine, Hdt.5.68; *substitute*, προφάσεις ἀντὶ τῶν ἀληθῶν ψευδεῖς μ. D.18.225, cf. Pl.*Lg.*683b (Pass.); *correct*, τοὺς ἠγνοηκότας Plb.1.67.5; but, *pervert*, μετέθηκεν αὐτὸν ἡ γυνὴ αὐτοῦ Lxx 3*Ki.*20(21).25. 4. Med., *change what is one's own* or *for oneself*, μ. τὰ εἰρημένα X.*Mem.*4.2.18; νόμους ib.4.4.14; τὴν δόξαν D.18.229; τὸν τρόπον Id.19.341; τοὔνομα Arist.*Fr.*549; ὀνόματα *change the use of* words, Epicur.*Nat.*95 G. (also in Act., *Nat.*28.5); [τὸ νόμισμα] Arist. *Pol.*1257$^b$11: abs., *change one's opinion, retract*, Pl.*R.*345b, etc.; μεταθέσθω let him *change his mind*, Men.*Pk.*48; also in political sense, *change sides*, μεταθέσθαι πρὸς τὴν Ῥωμαίων αἵρεσιν Plb.24.9.6; Dionysius of Heraclea, who went over from the Stoics to the Cyrenaics, was called μεταθέμενος, *turn-coat*, D.L.7.37, 166; μ. ἀπὸ τῶν πατρίων Lxx 2*Ma.*7.24; ἐξ ἀδικίας Corn.*ND*11. b. τὴν γνώμην μετατίθεσθαι *change to* or *adopt a new* opinion, Hdt.7.18 (but τῆς γνώμης μ. *change from*.., App.*BC*3.29); μετέθου λύσσαν ἄρτι σωφρονῶν *thou hast changed to* madness, E.*Or.*254; μ. τὸ ὄνομα τὸ νῦν ἀπὸ τῶν αἰγῶν *adopted* their present name, Paus.7.26.3. c. μ. [τὸν φόβον] *transfer* one's fear, D.18.177; τῇ μισθαρνίᾳ ταῦτα μετατιθέμενος τὰ ὀνόματα *transferring*.., ib.284. d. c. inf., μ. ἀντὶ τοῦ ἀπλήστως.. ἔχοντος βίου τὸν κοσμίως.. ἔχοντα βίον ἑλέσθαι *change one's mind and determine* to choose.., Pl.*Grg.*493c. e. c. dupl. acc., τὸ κείνων κακὸν τῶδε κέρδος μ. *turning* their misdeeds *into* his gain, S.*Ph.*515 (lyr.). 5. Pass., *to be changed, alter*, μετετέθην εὐβουλίᾳ E.*IA* 388 (troch.); μ. ἐς Ῥωμαίους *pass over*, App.*Hisp.*17; μ. ἀπὸ τοῦ καλέσαντος ὑμᾶς *are turned away* from.., *Ep.Gal.*1.6.

**μετατίκτω**, *bring forth afterwards*, A.*Ag.*759 (lyr., tm.).

**μετατρᾰγῳδία**, ἡ, *piece played after tragedies*, of the Satyric drama, Acro ad Hor.*Sat.*1.10.66.

**μετατρέπω**, Aeol. **πεδατρέπω** Alc.*Supp.*28.10:—*overthrow*, l.c. 2. *turn back* or *away*, μοῖραν -τράπεῖν (aor. 2 inf.) Pi.*Fr.*177; μετὰ δ' ὑμέας ἔτραπεν αἶσα A.R.3.261; οὐ μετέτρεψέ σε πρωτότοκος ἀποπνέων Lxx 4*Ma.*15.18. 3. *change*, νόημα *AP*9.114 (Parmen.):—Pass., ὁ γέλως ὑμῶν εἰς πένθος -τραπήτω v.l. in *Ep.Jac.*4.9; μετατραπεὶς τῇ διανοίᾳ Aristeas 99 (μετατραπεὶς seems to be corrupt in Plu.2. 154e). II. Med., *turn oneself round, turn round*, θάμβησεν δ' Ἀχιλεύς, μετὰ δ' ἐτράπετ' Il.1.199, etc. 2. Med. with aor. 2 Pass. μετετράπην, *look back to, care for, show regard for*, c. gen., Τρώων, τῶν οὔ τι μετατρέπῃ οὐδ' ἀλεγίζεις 1.160, cf. 12.238; σχέτλιος, οὐδὲ μετατρέπεται φιλότητος 9.630: c. acc., οὐ μετετράπη τὸν λογισμόν Lxx 4*Ma.*7.12.—Not in Prose before Aristeas.

**μετατρέφω**, *bring up among*, in Pass., τισι A.R.1.198, 2.1234.

**μετατρέχω**, fut. -θρέξομαι: aor. -έδρᾰμον:—*run and fetch*, βούλει Διοπείθη μεταδράμω; Phryn.Com.9; οὔκουν παρ' Ἀθηναίων μεταθρέξει; you *run and get* it from the A., Ar.*Pax* 261; *run after, seek*, τι Ph.1.576, al. II. *change one's abode*, πρὸς τὴν ἀνδρωνῖτιν ἑστίαν ib.365.

**μετατροπ-ᾰλίζομαι**, Pass., *turn about*, οὔ τι μετατροπαλίζεο φεύγων Il.20.190. **-εύω**, gloss on προμαλχατεύω, Hsch. **-ή**, ἡ, (μετατρέπω II. 2) *retribution*, ἔτι σε μετατροπὰ τῶνδ' ἔπεισιν ἔργων E.*Andr.* 492 (lyr.). II. *change*, σώματος γένεσις καὶ μ. Plu.2.720b, cf. Vett. Val.81.3 (pl.), Nech.ap.eund.125.21, Greg.Cor.*Trop.Prooem.*; ἐπὶ τὰ βελτίονα μ. λαμβάνειν Hippod.ap.Stob.4.34.71. III. *overthrow*, βασιλέων μετατροπαί Herm.ap.eund.1.21.9 (prob.). **-ία**, ἡ, *turn of fortune, reverse*, Pi.*P.*10.21 (pl.). **-(ι)άζομαι**, = μεταστρέφομαι, Hsch. ❀ **-ος**, ον, *turning about, returning*, μ. ἐκ βυθοῦ ἔρρων *AP* 7.506.5 (Leon.), cf. Call.*Del.*99; μ. αὖραι *veering* winds, E.*El.*1147 (lyr.); πολέμου μ. αὔρα Ar.*Pax*945 (lyr.). 2. *turning round upon*, δαίμων μ. ἐπί τινι A.*Pers.*943 (lyr.); μετάτροπα ἔργα deeds *that turn upon their author* or *are visited with vengeance*, Hes.*Th.*89.

**μετατροχαζόντως**, Adv., gloss on μεταδρομάδην, Hsch.

**μετατρωπάομαι**, poet. for μετατρέπομαι, A.R.3.297.

**μετατρωχάω**, poet. for μετατρέχω, Rhian.1.17.

**μετατῡπ-όω**, *transform*, αἰσχρὸν ἀντὶ καλοῦ χαρακτῆρος Ph.2.360:—Pass. (cf. sq. II), Eust.75.5. **-ωσις**, εως, ἡ, *transformation*, Ammon. *Diff.*p.91 V. II. *conversion* of a compound word into two simple ones, as ἀκρόπολις into ἄκρα πόλις, Eust.626.49, cf. 75.4. III. defined as λέξις ἐνηλλαγμένα στοιχεῖα ἔχουσα (as ὑπαί for ὑπό), Trypho *Trop.*2.16.

❀ **μεταυγάζω**, Dor. **πεδαυγ-**, *look keenly after, look about for*, τινα Pi. *N.*10.61. II. *shine, glitter*, ἱστία μεταυγάζοντα Philostr.*Im.* 1.19.

**μεταυδάω**, *speak among*, and so *address*, in Hom. always c. dat. pl., ἀθανάτοισι Od.1.31; ἔπεα Τρώεσσι Il.8.496; ἔπε' Ἀργείοισι 2.109, cf. 18.139, al., and always in 3 sg. impf. μετηύδα, exc. 1 sg. μετηύδων Od.12.153,270; τοῖον ἔπος πάντεσσι μετηύδα A.R.2.773. II. later c. acc. pers., *accost, address*, ib.54, Mosch.4.61.

**μεταῦθις**, Ion. **μεταῦτις**, Adv. *afterwards, thereupon*, A.*Eu.*478, 498 (lyr.), Hdt.1.62.

**μέταυλος**, ον, Att. for μέσαυλος (q.v.).

❀ **μεταύριον**, Adv., ἡ μ. (sc. ἡμέρα) *the day after to-morrow*, *Gloss.*

❀ **μεταυτίκα** [ῐ], Adv. *just after, presently after*, Hdt.2.161, 5.112.

**μεταῦτις**, Ion. for μεταῦθις.

**μεταυχένιος**, ον, *behind the neck*: τὰ μ. *back of the shoulders*, Poll. 2.177.

❀ **μεταφέρω**, fut. μετοίσω S.*Ph.*962: aor. μετήνεγκα D.18.108, part. -ενεγκών ib.225: pf. μετενήνοχα Pl.*Criti.*112a, and Pass. -ενήνεγμαι Id.*Prt.*339a:—*carry across, transfer*, τι εἴς τι Id.*Ti.*73e; ἐκ τῶν ἀπόρων εἰς τοὺς εὐπόρους τὰς τριηραρχίας D.18.108; ἀπὸ τούτου ἐφ' ἕτερον δικαστήριον Lex ap.eund.21.94; τὴν ἀδικίαν εἰς τὸν αὐτοῦ νόμον Id.24.76; ἐπὶ μὴ προσήκοντα πράγματα τοὺς λόγους Id.20.113; *divert* funds to other uses, *SIG*577.65 (Milet., iii/ii B.C.); μ. κέντρ᾽ ι πώλοις *apply* the goad to the horses *in turn*, E.*Ph.*178 (lyr.); μ. ἐπ' ἀνθρώπους τὰς μηχανάς X.*Cyr.*1.6.39; *shift*, μ. τὰ σκεύη Thphr.*Char.*10.6; μ. τι ἐπὶ τἀληθές *translate* it into reality, Pl.*Ti.*26c; μ. [τὰ ὀνόματα] εἰς τὴν αὑτῶν φωνήν *translate* them into their own language, Id.*Criti.*113a; τὸ τῶν λητουργιῶν ὄνομ' ἐπὶ τὸ τῶν ἱερῶν μ. D.20.126; of officials, *transfer* to another post, *BGU*15.11 (Pass., ii A.D.); *transfer* a sum in an account, *PRev.Laws* 16.10, al. (iii B.C.):—Med., *bring over with one*, ἐξ Αἰγίνης Ἀθήναζε μετενεγκαμένη τὴν πορνείαν Theopomp.Hist.244; μετηνέγκαντο τὰ σημεῖα ὡς τοὺς ἑτέρους D.H.9. 6:—Pass., *to be transferred*, εἰς ποίησιν Pl.*Prt.*339a; μ. ἐνθένδε ἐκεῖσε Jul.*Or.*3.122b. 2. *change, alter*, εἰ καὶ πάλιν γνώμην μετοίσεις S. *Ph.*962; μ. τοὺς χρόνους D.18.225; τὴν ἀξίωσιν μ. *change, confound*, Aeschin.3.220; of Poets, μ. ταὔτ' ἄνω τε καὶ κάτω Xenarch.7.2:—Pass., μετενήνεκται ὑμῖν τὰ τῆς πόλεως δίκαια Aeschin.3.193; κύνες πυκνὰ μεταφερόμεναι *doubling and casting about*, X.*Cyn.*4.5. 3. Rhet., *transfer* a word *to a new sense, use it in a changed sense*: and abs., *employ metaphor*, Arist.*EN*1167$^a$10:—Pass., εὖ μετενήνεκται Id. *Rh.*1405$^b$6, cf. μεταφορά II; ἀφ' ἑτέρων πραγμάτων μ. τὰς ὀνομασίας Phld.*Rh.*1.167 S. 4. μ. τοὔνομα ἐπὶ τὸν λόγον *transfer* the word to its literal meaning, re-interpret it etymologically, Arist.*Top.* 112$^a$32.

**μεταφέψω**, *boil gently, simmer*, Herod.Med.ap.Orib.8.3.1.

**μετάφημι**, *speak among* persons, whether in addressing one or more of them, or as their spokesman, Hom. (only 3 sg. impf. μετέφη), c. dat. pl., τῇσιν (sc. δμῳαῖς) μ. Od.18.312; πάντεσσι θεοῖσι Il.19. 100: elsewh. Hom. always joins it with τοῖς or τοῖσι, whether a single person is addressed, as in Il.2.411, 4.153, 19.55, or more than one, as in Od.8.132:—μετέφη c. acc. pers. is f.l. in Il.2.795.

**μεταφημίζω**, *change the name*, Man.2.136:—Med., *call by a new name*, Rhian.25.5.

**μεταφοιτάω**, *pass from one to another*, παρ' ἀλλήλων μ. Str.16.4. 25.

**μεταφορ-ά**, ἡ, *transference*, Nicom.Com.1.35; of ownership, *BGU* 1127.37 (i B.C.). 2. *transport, haulage*, Hero *Bel.*102.11 (pl.); οἴνου *POxy.*729.24 (ii A.D.). 3. *change, phase* of the moon, Plu. 2.923c. II. Rhet., *transference* of a word *to a new sense, metaphor*, Isoc.9.9 (pl.), Arist.*Po.*1457$^b$6, *Rh.*1410$^b$36, Epicur.*Nat.*28.5, Plu.*Cic.*40, Demetr.*Eloc.*78 (pl.), etc. ❀ **-έω**, = μεταφέρω I, Pherecyd. 16(*a*) J. (Pass.), Hdt.1.64, 2.125. **-ητός**, όν, *portable*, ἔστι τὸ ἀγγεῖον τόπος μ. Arist.*Ph.*209$^b$29. **-ικός**, ή, όν, *apt at metaphors*, Id.*Po.*1459$^a$6, *Fr.*70. II. *metaphorical*, Phld.*Po.*2.55, Porph. *in Cat.*58.37. Adv. **-κῶς** Phld.*Mus.*p.30 K., *Placit.*1.19.1, Erot. s. v. νεφέλαι, etc.

**μετα-φράζω**, *paraphrase*, D.H.*Th.*45, Theon *Prog.*1, Hdn.*Fig.* p.95 S. 2. *translate*, J.*AJ*8.5.3, Plu.*Cat.Ma.*19, *Cic.*40. II. Med., *consider after*, ταῦτα μεταφρασόμεσθα καὶ αὖτις Il.1.140. **-φρᾰσις**, εως, ἡ, *paraphrasing, paraphrase*, Plu.*Dem.*8, 2.347f (pl.), Suid. s. v. Μαριανός, etc. **-φραστής**, οῦ, ὁ, *translator*, Tz.*H.*9.370. **-φραστικός**, ή, όν, *paraphrastic*, λόγος Eust.691.20.

**μετάφρενον**, τό, prop. *part behind the midriff* (μετὰ τὰς φρένας), *broad of the back*: hence, generally, *back*, μεταφρένῳ ἐν δόρυ πῆξεν ὤμων μεσσηγύς Il.5.40, cf. 56, al.; μ. ἠδὲ καὶ ὤμω πλῆξεν 2.265; μ. ἠδὲ καὶ ὤμους (of a woman) Od.8.528, cf. Hp.*Acut.*66; in pl., of a single person, Il.12.428; ὤμους καὶ μετάφρενα, of a woman, Archil.29, cf. Hld.10.32.—Ep. word, used by Pl.*Prt.*352a, Arist. *Phgn.*810$^b$25, Luc.*DMeretr.*4.2. II. = τὸ μεταξὺ τοῦ νώτου καὶ ὀσφύος κατὰ τὴν τῶν φρενῶν πρόσφυσιν Ruf.*Onom.*99.

**μεταφρίσσω**, *get a chill*, Hp.*Coac.*110 (= φρίσσω in *Prorrh.*1.136).

**μεταφύομαι**, Med., c. aor. 2 Act. -έφῡν: pf. πέφῡκα:—*become by change*, ἀλλοῖοι μετέφυν Emp.108.1, cf. Hierocl. *in CA*20p.462 M.; ἀνδρῶν ὅσοι δειλοὶ [ἦσαν] γυναῖκες μετεφύοντο ἐν τῇ δευτέρᾳ γενέσει Pl. *Ti.*90e; Εὔφορβος γεγονέναι μεταφῦναί τε Ἴων ἐκ Τρωός Philostr.*Her.* 17. 2. *grow after*, οἱ μεταφύντες (sc. ὀδόντες) Hp.*Carn.*12 (-φύοντες codd., v.l. -φυέοντες, fort. -φυέντες).

**μεταφῠτ-εία**, ἡ, *transplanting*, Thphr.*HP*2.6.3, 7.5.3. 2. perh., *substitution of a different form of cultivation*, *Ostr.Bodl.*189 (ii B.C.). **-ευσις**, εως, ἡ, = foreg. I, *Gp.*3.2.1. **-ευτέον**, *one must transplant*, ib.5.13.3. ❀ **-εύω**, *transplant*, Thphr.*HP*2.6.3, Philem. 147, Sor.1.87 (Pass.); μεταφυτεόντες is f.l. in Hp.*Aër.*12. 2. μ. χώραν, = *pastino, repastino*, *Gloss.*

**μεταφωνέω**, *speak among*, only in impf. (v. μετεῖπον), c. dat. pl., Μυρμιδόνεσσιν Il.18.323, cf. 9.52, al.: abs., A.R.2.1178. 2. c. acc. pers., *accost*, Id.1.702.

**μεταφωτίζομαι**, Pass., *undergo a change of illumination*, Ptol. *Alm.*3.1.

**μεταχάζομαι**, *shrink from*, c. gen., μεταχάσσεαι ἀμήτοιο A.R.3. 436.

**μεταχᾰρακτηρ-ίζω**, *change the orthography*, Sch.A Il.14.241. **-ισμός**, ὁ, *change of form* or *type*, Ammon.*Diff.*pp.13, 91 V.

**μεταχᾰράσσω**, *grave anew, remodel*, γῆρας μ. τὴν ἀνδρίαν εἰς τἀπρεπές Men.552; τὸ θεῖον νόμισμα Ph.1.220; ἰατρικήν Id.2.560:—Pass., Id.1.589, al.

❀ **μεταχάσκω**, *yawn after*, ἑνὸς χανόντος μετακέχηνεν ἅτερος prob. cj. for μετέσχηκεν in Apostol.7.20 (*Journ.Philol.*4.320).

**μεταχειμάζω**, of weather, *to be stormy afterwards*, Veget.*Mil.* 4.40.

**μεταχειρ-έομαι**, = μεταχειρίζομαι, Hp.*Decent.*6. **-ημα**, ατος, τό, *treatment, handling* of a topic, Sch.Aristid.p.288 D. (s. v.l.). ❀ **-ίζω**, aor. -εχείρισα Hdt.3.142, etc.: but more freq. in Med. **-ίζομαι**: Att. fut. -ιοῦμαι Lys.24.10, Pl.*R.*410b: aor. -εχειρισάμην Ar.*Eq.* 345, etc., rarely -εχειρίσθην Pl.*Phdr.*277c: pf. -κεχείρισμαι (v. infr. 6):—*take in hand, handle*, σκῆπτρον E.*Fr.*912.7 (anap.), cf. Phld. *Rh.*1.225 S.:—Med., Hdt.2.121.α', Pl.*Phdr.*240e: always c. acc. (the gen. in Id.*R.*417a belongs only to ἅπτεσθαι, and in Id.*Prm.* 130d ὧν ⟨τι⟩ shd. be read). 2. *have in hand, administer*, [χρήματα] Hdt.3.142:—Med., Πηνελόπης ἱστὸν μεταχειριζομένης Pl.*Phd.* 84a, cf. Luc.*Ind.*29; τὰς μεγίστας ἀρχὰς μ. Pl.*Ti.*20a. 3. *manage, conduct*, τὰ περὶ τὰς ναῦς, τὸν πόλεμον, τὰ δημόσια, Th.1.13, 4.18, 6. 16; πρᾶγμα ὀξέως μ. ib.12:—Med., μεταχειρίσασθαι πρᾶγμα Ar.*Eq.* 345; ῥώμης ἕνεκα σιτία καὶ πόνους Pl.*R.*410b; ὁ νοῦς τὸ σῶμα μ. *governs* it, X.*Mem.*1.4.17. 4. *practise, pursue* an art, study, etc., μεταχειρίζεσθαι μουσικήν, φιλοσοφίαν, παιδείαν, Pl.*Plt.*268b, *R.*497d, *Lg.*670e, cf. *Men.*81a, X.*Vect.*5.4, etc. 5. c. acc. pers., *deal with*, τὸν ἑαυτῶν φονέα -όμενοι Antipho 1.20: usu. with Adv. added, *handle, treat*, χαλεπῶς τινας μ. Th.7.87:—Med., τινὰς ὠμῶς μεταχειρίζεσθαι D.24.171 (so ὡς ἀλυπότατα μ. πάθος Lys.24.10); *treat*, of physicians, Pl.*R.*408d. b. *dispatch, kill*, Hadr.Rh.p.45 H. 6. *prepare* a poultice, Lycus ap.Orib.9.42.1 (Pass.). **-ιος**, ον, pl. -ιοι, *in the hand*, Lat. *in manu*, i.e. *slaves*, *CIG*3344 (Smyrna) = *Epigr.Gr.*313, where Kaibel emends to μετὰ χείρεσι. **-ῐσις**, εως, ἡ, *handling, treatment*, ποιήσεώς τε καὶ πεζοῦ λόγου D.H.*Rh.*4.1 (-ησις codd.); ἁπάντων πραγμάτων Gal.18(2).407. 2. *mode of preparing*, ἐπιπλάσματος Lycus ap.Orib.9.34.1. **-ισμός**, ὁ, = foreg., τῆς κριθῆς Corn.*ND*28; [καταπλάσματος] Lycus ap.Orib.9. 25.5. **-ιστέος**, α, ον, *to be treated*, τρίψεσι Philostr.*Gym.*50. II. -τέον, *one must take in hand, treat*, ἀμπέλους *Gp.*7.18 tit., cf. Philum. ap.Aët.9.25: metaph., Arist.*Rh.Al.*1445$^b$36. **-ιστικός**, ή, όν, *treating of*, τῶν ἀριθμητῶν Hero *Deff.*135.5. **-όω** and Med. **-όομαι**, = *aggredior*, *Gloss.*

**μετα-χεύομαι**, Med., *pour back into oneself, suck back*, Opp.*H.*1. 572. ❀ **-χέω**, *pour from one vessel into another*, Dsc.5.72, J.*AJ*9.4. 2 (prob.), Archig.ap.Orib.8.46.16, *Gp.*7.4.2:—Pass., ib.2.7.4.

❀ **μεταχθόνιος**, α, ον, *to land*, μιν πλημμυρὶς.. μεταχθονίην ἐκόμισσεν A.R.4.1269.

**μετάχοιρον**, τό, *after-pig*, i.e. *the smallest, weakest of the litter*, Arist.*HA*573$^b$5, *GA*749$^a$1:—μετάχοιρα shd. be restored for μετάχοιροι in Poll.1.251.

**μεταχρημᾰτίζω**, *call by a different title*, τὴν δόσιν D.S.33.17; πόλιν Diog.*Ep.*43.

**μετα-χρονέω**, *succeed in time*, opp. πρωτοχρονέω, συγχρονέω, Diog. Oen.26. ❀ **-χρόνιος**, ον, poet. α, ον, (χρόνος) prop., = μετάχρονος, *happening afterwards*, Tryph.1; of an oracle *post eventum*, Luc.*Alex.* 28; *delayed*, Gal.19.522. II. = μετέωρος, *high in air*, μεταχρόνιαι

γὰρ ἴαλλον [Ἅρπυιαι] Hes.*Th.*269, cf. A.R.2.300, al., *Pae.Oxy.*660. 13, Nonn.*D.*20.289, 42.1: μεταχθόνιος is suggested in Sch.A.R.2. 587; but Gramm. recognize this use of μεταχρόνιος, Hsch. s. v. μεταίσιον (leg. μετάρσιον), Apollon.*Lex.*, *EM*581.41, Suid. **-χρονος,** ον, *out of date, anachronistic*, πράγματα μ. [ὀρχεῖσθαι] Luc.*Salt.*80.

**μετάχῦσις,** εως, ἡ, *transfusion*, Gal.7.542, al.

**μεταχρώννῡμι,** *change the colour of* a thing, Suid.

**μεταχωρ-έω,** *go to another place, remove*, τόπων μετά ποι χωρεῖτ' ἐκ τῶνδε A.*Pr.*1060 (anap.); μ. εἰς [χώραν] X.*HG*3.4.26; τὸ ᾠὸν μ. κάτω Arist.*GA*754ᵇ29; of the foetus in the womb, *change its place*, Hp. *Septim.*4; of birds of passage, *migrate*, ἐς τὴν Λιβύην Ar.*Av.*710; of men, *emigrate*, Th.2.72; *withdraw* from a conference, ἐκ τῶν λόγων Id.5.112; *go over* to another party, Plu.*Demetr.*29; μ. εἰς τἀναντία, of syllables, D.H.*Comp.*11; *change*, εἰς φύσιν τινός Ael.*NA*9. 43. **-ησις,** εως, ἡ, *departure, withdrawal*, εἰς τοὺς θεοὺς Arr.*Fr.* 134 J. II. *change of direction*, in pl., Procl.*Hyp.*1.27: generally, *change*, τοῦ δ εἰς ζ Eust.1259.61.

**μεταψαίρω,** *brush against*, ποδὶ πέτρον E.*Ph.*1390.

**μεταψᾰλάσσω,** *remove, put elsewhere*, Hsch. **μεταψέφω·** μεταβουλεύομαι, Id.; also μεταψέφειν· μεταμελεῖσθαι, Id.

**μεταψηφίζω,** *transfer by decree*, App.*BC*4.57 (Pass.).

**μετάψυξις,** εως, ἡ, *recovery of breath* (μεταπνοή), Hsch. (Voss for μετάμιξις).

**μετεγ-γράφω** [ᾰ], *place upon a new register*, Ar.*Eq.*1370 (fut. 2 Pass. μετεγγραφήσεται); *re-register*, τὸν ἐωνημένον Thphr.*Fr.*97.3; ἑαυτὸν εἰς τοὺς ἄνδρας Sch.Pi.*O.*9.134. 2. *rewrite*, prob. f.l. for μεταγρ- in Luc.*Hist.Conscr.*5. **-γυος,** ὁ, *fellow-surety*, *POxy.* 266.10 (i A.D.). **-κεντρίζω,** *bud on another tree*, in Pass., *Gp.*4. 8.5. **-κλίνω** [ῑ], in Pass., *change inclination simultaneously with*, Cleom.1.5. **-χέω,** *pour from one vessel into another*, *EM*149.41.

**μετείθη,** Ion. for μεθείθη, 3 sg. aor. 1 Pass. of μεθίημι.

⊛ **μέτειμι** (εἰμί *sum*), *to be among*, c. dat. pl., ἄνδρεσσι μετέμμεναι Il. 18.91; ὄφρ' ἂν ζωοῖσιν μετέω 22.388; οἷς ὁ γέρων μετέησιν 3.109; εἰ λαοῖσι μετείη Xenoph.2.15: abs., οὐ γὰρ παυσωλή γε μετέσσεται no *interval* of rest *will be mine*, Il.2.386. II. impers., μέτεστί μοί τινος I *have a share in* or *claim to* a thing, Hdt.1.171, etc.; τί τοὐδε σοὶ μ. πράγματος; A.*Eu.*575; κἀμοὶ πόλεως μ. S.*OT*630, cf. *Ant.*1072, Ar.*Av.*1666, 1668; πᾶσι μετεῖναι τῶν ἀρχῶν Arist.*Pol.*1292ᵃ3: so part. neut. used abs., οὐδὲν μᾶλλον Αἰολεῦσι μετεὸν τῆς χώρης since they *had* no more *share* in the land, Hdt.5.94, cf. Th.1.28, Pl.*Lg.*900e, etc. 2. sts. the share is added in nom., ὁκόσον δέ μοι μέρος [τῆς γῆς τῆσδε] μετῆν Hdt.6.107, cf. E.*IT*1299, Pl.*Prm.*163d; μέτεστι κατὰ τοὺς νόμους πᾶσι τὸ ἴσον (v. ἴσος II.2), Th.2.37, Foed.ap.eund. 5.47; ἐμοὶ τούτων οὐδὲν μ. Pl.*Ap.*19c. 3. with inf. as subj., πᾶσι μέτεστι γινώσκειν Heraclit.116; τούτῳ τι μετέσται ψεῦδος ἀγαπᾶν..; *will it be part* of his nature to love falsehood? Pl.*R.*490b, cf. 606b.

⊛ **μέτειμι** (εἶμι *ibo*), Att. fut. of μετέρχομαι (q.v.); Dor. inf. μετίμεν *Foed.Delph.Pell.*2 A 25: impf. μετῄειν: Ep. aor. part. (but v. εἴσομαι II) μετεισάμενος (v. infr.):—*go between* or *among*, μετεισάμενος κρατερὰς ὄτρυνε φάλαγγας Il.13.90; μετεισάμενος Τρώων ἐκέδασσε φάλαγγας 17.285. II. *go after* or *behind, follow*, abs., ἴθ', ἐγὼ δὲ μέτειμι 6. 341; Ἄρης πόλεμόνδε μέτεισι 13.298; τοῦ μὲν ὑφηγουμένου, τῶν δὲ μετιόντων X.*HG*4.5.8, etc. 2. c. acc., *follow*, ταὐτὸν ἴχνος Pl.*Phdr.* 276d. b. *go to seek* or *fetch, go in quest of*, μετῄισαν ἄξοντες Hdt.3. 28; τὸν παῖδα εὗρον οἱ μετιόντες ib.15; ἐν ᾧ δὲ τούτους μετῄισαν ib.19; εἰ γάρ μ' ἀπώσῃ, ..μέτει πάλιν S.*El.*430; μετῇσαν στρώματα Ar. *Eq.*605, cf. *Ach.*728; μ. τινὰ..ἐκ.. Id.*Pax*274; τὰ ἐπιτήδεια ἐκ Σηστοῦ μετιόντας X.*HG*2.1.25: metaph., *search after, pursue*, τέχνην Pl.*Phdr.*263b, Arist.*Sens.*436ᵃ21; ἑκάστας [τὰς ἀρχὰς] ᾗ πεφύκασιν Id.*EN*1098ᵇ4; μ. περί τινος Id.*Rh.Al.*1432ᵇ3, al.; περί τι Id.*Metaph.* 1044ᵇ4; μ. τὸν λόγον Pl.*Men.*74d, *Sph.*252b: abs., *pursue a question*, οἱ οὕτω μετιόντες Arist.*APo.*91ᵇ24, cf. Pl.*Smp.*210a, etc. c. Trag., *pursue with vengeance*, εἰ μὴ μέτειμι τοῦ πατρὸς [φόνου] τοὺς αἰτίους A. *Ch.*273, cf. *Ag.*1666 (troch.), S.*El.*478 (lyr.); also in Th., τιμωρίαις τοὺς ἀδικοῦντας μ. 4.62; μ. δίκας τινά (δίκας acc. cogn.) *execute* judgement *upon* one, A.*Eu.*231; τὸν διδάσκαλον δίκην μέτειμι E.*Ba.*346; ἄποινα μέτεισι Διόνυσός σε ib.517. d. *pursue, go about*, δόλῳ μέτειμι.. φόνον Id.*Med.*391. e. *canvass for* an office, μ. ὑπατείαν, Lat. *ambire consulatum*, Plu.*Publ.*11; ἀρχὴν Id.*Cic.*1. f. μ. θυσίῃσι [τοὺς ἀνέμους] *approach* them with sacrifices, Hdt.7.178: c. acc. et inf., ἕνα ἕκαστον μετῄεσαν μὴ ἐπιτρέπειν *besought* each one not.., Th.8.73; also ἕκαστον μετιόντες ὅπως ἀποστήσωσιν Id.3.70 (unless ἀ. goes with ἔπρασσον). III. *pass by*, A.R.2.688. 2. *pass over*, πρός τινα Hdn.5.4.6. 3. *recur, return*, ἐκεῖσε ὅθεν ἀπέσχισάς με τοῦ λόγου μέτειμι Ar.*Nu.*1408, cf. Ach.Tat.6.2.

**μετεῖπον,** Ep. **μετέειπον,** aor. 2 of μεταφωνέω, *speak among, address*, c. dat. pl.; freq. in Hom., mostly in phrases, ὅ σφιν ἐϋφρονέων ἀγορήσατο καὶ μετέειπεν Il.1.253, al.; τοῖσι δὲ καὶ μετέειπε 2.336, al., cf. Hes.*Th.*643: abs., mostly with ὀψέ, Il.7.94, Od.7.155, etc.—Hom. always uses 3 sg. Ep. μετέειπε, exc. once 1 sg. μετέειπον, Od.19.140.

**μετείς,** Ion. aor. 2 part. of μεθίημι.

**μετεισάμενος,** Ep. aor. 1 part. Med. of μέτειμι (εἶμι *ibo*).

**μετεισ-βαίνω,** *go into another* ship, Hld.5.27. **-δύνω** [ῡ], εἰς ἄλλο ὄστρακον *change and slip into another* shell, Arist.*HA*548ᵃ 16. **-έρχομαι,** *pass into*, Phot. s. v. ἐριγάζειν.

**μετείω,** Ep. subj. pres. of μέτειμι (εἰμί *sum*).

**μετεκ-βαίνω,** *go from one into another*, μετεκβαίνεσκε (Ion. impf.) ἐκ τοῦ ἅρματος ἐς ἁρμάμαξαν Hdt.7.41, cf. 100; εἰς πλοῖον Antipho 5. 21. 2. in speaking, *pass on*, μ. εἰς ἕτερόν τινα λόγον Pl.*Lg.*642b, cf. 935a. 3. c. acc., μ. φθόγγον *pass from one* note *to another*, *AP* 12.187 (Strat.). **-βᾰσις,** εως, ἡ, *outcome, result* of a combination, Adam.*Vent.*32. **-βῐβάζω,** *transfer to another* ship, D.C.48. 47, v.l. in Th.8.74. **-βολή,** = μεταβολή, Cratin.427. **-γονοι,** οἱ, *children's children*, Sch.Aristid.p.651 D. **-δέχομαι,** *take up*, D.P.74. **-δίδωμι,** in Med., *betroth a second time*, Plu.*Comp.Lyc. Num.*3. **-δυμα,** ατος, τό, in pl., *changes of clothing*, metaph., τύφου μ. Socr.ap.Stob.3.4.59. **-δύομαι,** Med., *pull off one's own clothes and put on others*, μ. τὴν βασιλικὴν ἐσθῆτα J.*AJ*6.14.2: metaph., ἐπιείκειαν μ. ib.6.12.7; μ. τὴν αὐτῶν φύσιν Plu.*Num.*15.

**μετεκέχειρον,** Elean **-εκέχηρον,** τό, *interval between two Olympic truces*, *SIG*1021.1 (Olympia, i B.C.), etc.

**μετέκκλιτος** (v.l. **-κλητος**), ον, [δίκη] f.l. for μετ' ἔκκλητον in Lyd. *Mag.*2.15.

**μετεκ-πνέω,** *breathe forth amid*, ψυχὴν ῥοθίοισι Opp.*H.*2.164. **-φώνητος,** ον, *consonant*, dub. in Phld.*Po.Herc.*994.34.

**μετελαύνω,** *drive to fresh pasture*, πρόβατα Philostr.*VA*8.22.

**μετελέγχω,** *confute*, f.l. for μετ' ἐλέγχων in Iamb.*VP*32.218.

**μετ-έλευσις,** εως, ἡ, *sequence, succession*, χρόνων Vett.Val.219. 11. II. Medic., *change of treatment*, Sor.2.15, 29. **-ελευστέον,** *one must punish*, Luc.*Fug.*22.

**μετεμ-βαίνω,** *go on board another* ship, Plu.*Ant.*66; εἰς λῃστρικὸν Id.*Luc.*13. **-βᾰσις,** εως, ἡ, *transition*, ἐκ τῶν ζῳδίων Vett.Val.336. 20 (pl.). **-βῐβάζω,** *put on board another* ship, ἐς ἄλλην ναῦν μ. Th.8. 74 (v.l. μετεκ-); ἐρέτας μ. *change* the crew, Polyaen.5.41. **-μεναι,** Ep. inf. of μέτειμι (εἰμί *sum*). **-πίπτω,** *fall into a new* position, Phlp. *in Ph.*547.14; read by Simp. and Phlp. in Arist.*Ph.*211ᵇ18. **-φὕτος,** ον, *engrafted afresh*, *AP*9.4 (Cyllen.). **-ψῡχοομαι,** Pass., of the soul, *to pass from one body into another*, Olymp.*in Phd.*p.55 N., al. **-ψύχωσις** [ῡ], εως, ἡ, *transmigration of souls*, D.S.10.6, Gal. 4.763, Alex.Aphr.*de An.*27.18, Porph.*Abst.*4.16, Herm.ap.Stob.1. 49.69 tit., Sallust.20 (pl.), Hieronym.*Ep.*124.4, Procl.*in R.*2.340 K., *Theol.Ar.*40 (pl.), Olymp.*in Phd.*p.54 N., Sch.Iamb.*Protr.*14, Sch. E.*Hipp.*736; *non μ. sed* παλιγγενεσίαν *esse dicit* (Pythagoras), Serv. ad Verg.*A.*3.68.

**μετεν-δύνω,** *put on other clothes*, μετένδυνε τὴν λευκὴν ἐσθῆτα Them. *Or.*13.178d. **-δύω,** causal in aor. 1, *put other* clothes *on* a person, θοἰμάτιον τὸ Ἑλληνικὸν περισπάσας αὐτοῦ βαρβαρικὸν μετενέδυσα Luc.*Bis Acc.*34: metaph., τὸν Μαιάνδριον τὴν τυραννίδα μετενέδυσε *invested* him with.., Id.*Nec.*16. II. Med. μετενδύομαι, c. aor. Act. μετενέδῡν, Str.17.1.43:—*put on other clothes*, τὴν ἐσθῆτα l.c., cf. J.*Vit.*28, *AJ*20.6.1; τὰς στολὰς D.C.46.39, cf. Max.Tyr.4.2: metaph., of souls *assuming new bodies*, μ. ἐς γυναικέα σκάνεα Ti.Locr. 104d. **-εκτέον,** (μεταφέρω) *one must refer*, δεῦρο Str.13.1.64; *one must transfer*, Sor.2.46, al. **-ηνεγμένως,** Adv., (μεταφέρω) *metaphorically*, Porph.*in Cat.*67.28. **-νέπω,** *speak among*, τισι A.R. 3.1168, Mosch.2.101.

**μετενσωμᾰτ-όομαι,** Pass., *to be put into another body*, of the soul, Plot.1.1.12, 4.3.9, Hierocl.*Prov.*p.461 B. **-ωσις,** εως, ἡ, *transmigration* of the soul, Hippol.*Haer.*1.3.2, Plot.2.9.6 (pl.), 4.3.9, Olymp.*in Phd.*p.54 N.; τῶν ψυχῶν Herm.*in Phdr.*p.61 A., Hierocl. *Prov.*p.172 B.

**μετέν-ταλμα,** ατος, τό, = Lat. *translatio mandati*, *Cod.Just.*2.12. 27.2. **-τίθημι,** *put into another place*:—Med., aor. 2 μετενεθέμην, τὸν γόμον *shift* a ship's cargo, D.56.25.

**μετεξ-αιρέομαι,** Med., = foreg., τὸν γόμον μ. D.56.24; *put ashore for transshipment*, *PCair.Zen.*93.12 (iii B.C.). **-ανίσταμαι,** Pass., *move from one place to another*, Luc.*Symp.*13. **-αντλέω,** *draw off again*, θάλασσαν ὀργάνοις Callix.1. **-άρτῠσις,** εως, ἡ, = ἐξάρτυσις, Ph.*Bel.*58.2 (s.v.l.). **-εράω,** *transfer* from one vessel to another, τὰ σκόρδα ἐκ..πλοίου εἰς τὴν θαλαμηγόν *PSI*4.332.9 (iii B.C.). ⊛ **-έτεροι,** αι, α, Ion. Pron., = ἔνιοι, *some among many, certain*, Hdt.1.63, 95, 199, al., Hp.*Fract.*11, al.; χρῆσις μετεξετέρη *a certain amount of* use, Id.*Art.*52. (μετ' ἐξετέρην shd. be written divisim in Nic.*Th.*588.)

⊛ **μέτεπειτα,** Adv. *afterwards, thereafter*, Il.14.310, Od.10.519, al., Hdt.1.25, 3.36, 7.7, 197: rare in early Prose, ὁ μ. χρόνος Pl.*Ep.*353c, cf. Arist.*EN*1175ᵃ9; later, *OGI*177.14 (Egypt, i B.C.), LXX *Ju.*9.5, 3*Ma.*3.24, *Ep.Hebr.*12.17.

**μετεπι-γρᾰφή,** ἡ, *transfer by registration of title, conveyance*, *PTeb.* 113.4 (ii B.C.), *PLond.*2.182 (i A.D.). ⊛ **-γράφω** [ᾰ], *put a new inscription on*, εἰκὼν μετεπιγεγραμμένη Plu.2.839d. II. *transfer by registration of title, convey*, *BGU*328.6 (ii A.D.):—Med., *POxy.* 273.21 (i A.D.):—Pass., *PTeb.*73.8 (ii B.C.). 2. *transfer* persons *to another category*, ib.124.37 (ii B.C., Pass.). **-δεσις,** εως, ἡ, *readjustment of a bandage*, Hp.*Fract.*10, 16 (both pl.). **-δέω,** *readjust a bandage*, ib.26, al.

**μετερ-ᾰσις,** εως, ἡ, *transfusion*, αἵματος Sor.2.4. **-άω,** *pour from one vessel into another*, Dsc.1.52, 5.18, Plu.2.801c (prob.), Crito ap.Gal.12.490:—Pass., τὸ μετερώμενον ὕδωρ prob. in Plu.2.52b.

**μέτερρος,** Aeol. for μέτριος, *Lyr.Adesp.*66, cf. *EM*587.12.

⊛ **μετέρχομαι,** Aeol. and Dor. **πεδέρχομαι,** Pi.*N.*7.74, Theoc.29.25: fut. μετελεύσομαι Il.6.280 (in Att. the impf. and fut. are borrowed from μέτειμι, q.v.):—*come* or *go among*, c. dat. pl., Od.1.134, 6.222: freq. abs. in part., μετελθών *if he came among them*, Il.4.539, etc.; of a leader, στίχας.. Ἄρης ὄτρυνε μετελθών *having gone between* the ranks, 5.461, cf. 13.351. 2. *go among* with hostile purpose, *attack*, λέων ἀγέληφι μετελθών 16.487: with a double construction, βουσὶ μετέρχεται ἢ ὀΐεσσιν ἠὲ μετ' ἀγροτέρας ἐλάφους Od.6.132. II. *go to another place*, πόλινδε μετέρχεο Il.6.86; μ. εἰς τὸ ἱερὸν D.*Ep.*2.20; εἰς

θεοὺς μ., i. e. *die*, *OGI*56.55 (Canopus, iii B.C.); *migrate, change one's abode*, Hp.*Aër*.18, *PRev.Laws*44.11 (iii B.C.); of a slave, *to be transferred*, *PCair.Zen*.355.51 (iii B.C.). III. *follow, come after*, εἰ πόνος ἦν, τὸ τερπνὸν πλέον πεδέρχεται Pi. l. c. IV. *go to seek, go in quest of*, c. acc. pers., Πάριν μετελεύσομαι Il.6.280, cf. Archil.44, etc.: also c. acc. rei, πατρὸς κλέος εὐρὺ μετέρχομαι I *go to seek* tidings of my father, Od.3.83: generally, *seek*, E.*El*.582, etc.; τὴν ἐλευθερίαν Th. 1.124; ἀσκήσει τὸ ἀνδρεῖον μ. Id.2.39; τὸ πάγχρυσον δέρας Πελίᾳ μ. E.*Med*.6; ἰατρόν τινι μ. Ar.*Ec*.363. 2. in hostile sense, *pursue*, Il.5.456, 21.422: metaph., Ὀροίτεα τίσιες μετῆλθον Hdt.3.126; ἡ Πυθίη μ. αὐτὸν τοισίδε τοῖσι ἔπεσι Id.6.86.γʹ; Προμηθέα κλοπῆς δίκη μετῆλθεν Pl.*Prt*.322a; in legal sense, *prosecute*, μ. φονέα Antipho 1. 10: *punish*, τινὰς ταῖς ἐσχάταις τιμωρίαις μ. Lycurg.116: c. acc. rei, *seek to avenge*, ὑβρισθέντας γάμους E.*IT*14: c. dupl. acc. pers. et rei, *visit* a crime *upon*.., μ. ἁρπαγὰς Ἑλένης Ἰλίου πόλιν Id.*Cyc*.280, cf. *Or*.423; τόνδ' ἐγὼ μετῆλθον ἐνδίκως μόρον τὸν μητρός A.*Ch*.996(988): later c. gen., J.*AJ*1.4.2, Longus 1.12. 3. of things, *go after, attend to*, ἔργα μετερχόμενος Od.16.314; μετέρχεο ἔργα γάμοιο Il.5. 429; *prosecute, pursue* a business, πρᾶγμα Ar.*Lys*.268; τὰ ἐγκλήματα Th.1.34; τὸν λόγον Pl.*Phd*.88d, etc.; μ. ἄλλων πημάτων κακὰς ὁδοὺς *narrate* them, E.*Ion*930; μ. ἴχνος Pl.*Tht*.187e. 4. *claim* at law, προῖκα ὀφείλεσθαι Mitteis *Chr*.88.20 (ii A.D.); οἱ μετερχόμενοι the *claimants*, *PGnom*.35 (ii A.D.). 5. *approach with prayer* or *sacrifice*, θεὸν εὐχαῖσιν E.*Ba*.713; χρυσὸν θυσίῃσι μεγάλῃσι ἱλασκόμενοι μετέρχονται Hdt.4.7: with inf. added, ἐγώ σε μ. τῶν θεῶν εἰπεῖν τὠληθές I *beseech* you by the gods to speak the truth, Id.6.68, cf. 69; πὲρρ ἀπαλῶ στύματός σε πεδέρχομαι ὀμνάσθην Theoc.29.25. 6. *court, woo* a woman, Pi.*I*.7(6).7. V. *go over*, εἰς Γίτανα Plb.27. 16.5; of an army, πρὸς τὸν Ἀντωνῖνον μ. Hdn.5.5.1; παντάπασιν εἰς ὕδατος πόσιν ἐξ οἴνου μετῆλθεν Gal.6.243. 2. of honours, *pass, descend*, εἰς τοὺς παῖδάς τινος *IG*12(9).906.20 (Chalcis, iii A.D.).

**μετέσσυτο**, v. μετασεύομαι.

**μετεσχηματισμένως**, Adv. *by transformation*, Porph. *in Cat*.69.28.

**μετευάδεν**, f.l. for μέγ' εὔαδεν in Q.S.5.127.

**μετευθύνω**, *set in order*, *PLond*.5.1674.20 (vi A.D.).

**μετεύχομαι**, *change one's wish*, οἶσθ' ὡς μετεύξῃ; E.*Med*.600.

**μετεχομένως**, Adv. *by participation* (cf. sq. II), Procl.*Inst*.23.

**μετέχω**, Aeol. **πεδέχω** Alc.59, Sapph.68.2; inf. πεδέχην Ead. *Supp*.5.22: fut. μεθέξω Th.8.86, later μεθέξομαι (3 sg. misspelt μεθέξετε) *IG*3.1427: pf. μετέσχηκα Hdt.3.80:—*partake of, share in*:—Constr.: 1. mostly c. gen. rei only, κακοτάτων, βρόδων, Alc. l. c., Sapph.68.2; ἀγαθῶν, κακῶν, βίου, Thgn.82, 354, cf. A.*Pr*.333; τῆς τοῦ Μάγου ὕβριος Hdt. l. c.; μ. τοῦ λόγου *to be in* the secret, Id.1.127; τοῦ ἔργου And.1.62: c. gen. pers., μ. τῶν πεντακισχιλίων *to be members* of the 5,000, Th. l. c.; μ. τῆς πόλεως, τῆς πολιτείας, Lys.6.48, 30.15; ἐκκλησίας Arist.*Pol*.1282a29; also ἐκ τοῦ ἑνὸς ἄρτου μ. 1*Ep.Cor*.10. 17: with dat. pers. added, μ. τινός τινι *partake of* something *in common with* another, οὐ οἱ μ. θράσεος Pi.*P*.2.83; πόνων μ. Ἡρακλέει E. *Heracl*.8; τῶν αὐτῶν ἔργων Ἐρατοσθένει μ. Lys.12.58; μ. ἱερῶν καὶ θυσιῶν τισι X.*HG*2.4.20; μ. τῶν ἴσων τισὶ Id.*Cyr*.2.1.15, cf. Pl.*Lg*.805d; κινδύνων Plb.3.16.3; also ξὺν σοὶ μετεῖχον τῶν ἴσων S.*El*.1168. 2. freq. the part or share is added, τοῦ πεδίου οὐκ ἐλαχίστην μοῖραν μ. Hdt.1.204; μ. τάφου μέρος A.*Ag*.507, cf. Ar.*Pl*.226, Lys.31.5; πλεῖστόν σου μέρος μεθέξομεν X.*Cyr*.7.5.54. 3. c. acc. rei, μ. τὸ ἴσον (sc. μέρος) τῶν ἀγαθῶν τινι ib.7.2.28, cf. E.*Fr*.787; μ. τὰς ἴσας πληγὰς ἐμοὶ Ar.*Pl*.1144; μ. τινὶ τὴν μερίδα *PPetr*.3p.67 (iii B.C.). 4. rarely c. acc. only, ἀκερδῆ χάριν μ. S.*OC*1484 (lyr.). 5. c. dat. rei only in a corrupt passage, τῇ.. κατὰ τὴν χώραν.. οἰκήσει μετεῖχον Th.2.16. 6. μ. περὶ ἔργων καὶ τεχνῶν *have some knowledge* respecting.., Arist.*Pol*. 1282a11. 7. abs., *to be a partner*, *PRev.Laws*14.11 (iii B.C.); οἱ μετέχοντες the *partners, accomplices*, Hdt.8.132. II. in Platonic Philos., *participate in* a universal, Arist.*Metaph*.990b31, 1037b19; τὰ μετέχοντα, opp. αἱ ἰδέαι, ib.991a3:—Pass., μετέχονται (sc. αἱ ἰδέαι) *are participated in*, ib.990b30, cf. S.E.*M*.4.16, Procl. *in Prm*.p.650S., etc. III. in Aristotelian Logic, *share in*, viz. admit the definition of, τὰ μὲν εἴδη μετέχει τῶν γενῶν, τὰ δὲ γένη τῶν εἰδῶν οὔ Arist.*Top*. 121a12, cf. 123a8, 143b14.

**μετεωρ-έω**, = μετεωρίζομαι, ηὐξήθη καὶ μετεωρεῖν ἤρξατο Ph.1.130. **-ία**, ἡ, *forgetfulness*, Suet.*Claud*.39, M.Ant.ap.Front.*Ep. ad M.Caes*. 4.7. **-ίδιον**, τό, *provisional conveyance* of property, *PAmh*.2. 136.12 (iii A.D.), *POxy*.117.5 (ii/iii A.D.). **-ίζω**, *raise to a height*, τὸ ἔρυμα Th.4.90; τὸ ἐμβριθὲς ἄγειν ἄνω -ίζουσα Pl.*Phdr*.246d; τὰ σκέλη *lift* the legs, X.*Eq*.10.4; ἑαυτὸν ib.11.7, cf. *Cyn*.10.13; of a dolphin, δελφινίσκον μ. τῷ νώτῳ *lifts* or *buoys* it *up* on his back, Arist. *HA*631a18, cf. 602b27; τοὺς πόδας μ., of quadrupeds, Id.*IA*711b19; τὸ πνεῦμα μ. *cause one to pant* (cf. μετάρσιος III), Id.*Pr*.885a33; ναῦν μ. εἰς τὸ πέλαγος *put* it *out to sea*, Philostr.*VA*6.12 (also abs., πλεῖν -ίζουσα ἐς τὸ πέλαγος Id.*Her*.8.3):—Med., τοὺς δελφῖνας μετεωρίζου *heave up your* dolphins (v. δελφίς II), Ar.*Eq*.762:—Pass., *to be raised up*, Pl.*Ti*.63c; *to be suspended*, σχοινίοις *POxy*.904.6 (v A.D.); of smoke or dust, *rise*, X.*Cyr*.6.3.5; of wind, Ar.*Nu*.404; of water vapour, Hp.*Aër*.8, Arist.*Mete*.346b28, al.; of ships, μετεωρισθεὶς ἐν τῷ πελάγει *keeping out* on the *high* sea, Th.8.16; *rise up*, as from bed, Hp.*Fract*.15; of wind *rising* from the stomach, Id.*Coac*.613; μετεωριζόμενος *suffering from flatulence*, Id.*Epid*.4.41. 2. intr., *attain considerable height*, Thphr.*HP*4.2.4. II. metaph., *buoy up, elevate*, esp. with false hopes, μ. καὶ φυσήσας ὑμᾶς D.13.12, cf. Hegem. ap.Ath.15.698d, Plb.25.3.4; τοὺς Ἀθηναίους δι' ἐπιστολῶν Posidon. 36J.; παραθαρρύνας καὶ μετεωρίσας Plu.*Dem*.18; *unsettle* a man's mind, Plb.5.70.10:—Pass., *to be elevated*, ὑπὸ λόγων ὁ νοῦς -ίζεται Ar. *Av*.1447; μετεωρισθεὶς καὶ περιχαρὴς γενόμενος ἐπί τινι Plb.3.70.1; μεμετεωρισμένοι ταῖς νίκαις D.S.11.32; also, *to be anxious*, *POxy*. 1679.16 (iii A.D.), perh. in this sense *Ev.Luc*.12.29. **-ισις**, εως, ἡ, *lifting up*, Plu.2.951c (pl.). II. = μετεωρισμός II. 2, D.C.*Fr*.12. 9. **-ισμα**, ατος, τό, = sq. II. 2, Metrod.*Herc*.831.5 (pl.). II. gloss on φρύαγμα, Hsch. ⊛**-ισμός**, ὁ, = μετεώρισις I, Hp.*Prog*.9 (pl.); τῶν ποδῶν Arist.*IA*711b23; τοῦ ὅλου σώματος ib.713a23; *rising to the surface*, of roots, Thphr.*CP*1.3.5. II. *being raised up*: hence, *swelling*, Hp.*Art*.50. 2. μ. γνώμης *mental trouble* or *disturbance*, Id.*Acut*. (*Sp*.)14 (γνώμης is prob. interpol.), cf. Vett.Val.185.20 (pl.); *wild thinking, vain imagining*, Metrod.*Herc*.831.4, 12 (pl.). 3. *delay, procrastination*, *PMasp*.32.55 (vi A.D.). **-ιστής**, οῦ, ὁ, *prancer*, of a horse, Hsch. (explaining the Aeol. form πεδαοριστής). **-ιστικός**, ή, όν, *disturbing* to the mind, Vett.Val. in *Cat.Cod.Astr*.8(1).168.

**μετεωρο-θήρας**, ου, ὁ, *one that hunts high in air*, epith. of a hawk, Arist.*HA*620a30 (pl.): metaph., of philosophers, Ph.1.674 (pl.). **-κοπέω**, *prate about high things*, Ar.*Pax*92 (anap.). **-κόπος**, ὁ, *one who prates about high things*, Cerc.4.45. **-λεσχέω**, satirically for μετεωρολογέω, Ph.1.581, Plu.2.400e. ⊛**-λέσχης**, ου, ὁ, *star-gazer, visionary*, Pl.*R*.489c, Plu.*Nic*.23, Luc.*Icar*.5: also in good sense, οἱ περὶ ἀστρονομίαν μ. Ph.1.645. **-λογέω**, *talk of high things*, esp. the heavenly bodies or natural phenomena, Pl.*Cra*.404c, Luc.*Nec*. 21. **-λογία**, ἡ, *discussion of* τὰ μετέωρα, ἀδολεσχία καὶ μ. Pl.*Phdr*. 270a; *meteorology*, Arist.*Mete*.338a26, Ph.1.371: in bad sense, ib. 486. **-λογικός**, ή, όν, *skilled in meteorology*, Pl.*Ti*.91d: τὰ μ., title of treatise on meteorology by Aristotle; ἡ μ. θεωρία Ph.1.371. **-λόγος**, ὁ, *one who talks of the heavenly bodies, astronomer*, Gorg.*Hel*.13, Pl. *Cra*.396c, Arist.*Mete*.354a29: satirically, E.*Fr*.913.2 (anap.); μ. καὶ ἀδολέσχαι Pl.*Cra*.401b. 2. *astrologer*, Procop.*Pers*.2.22. II. Adj. ος, ον, *of* or *belonging to astronomers*, etc., Hp.*Aër*.2. **-ποιέω**, *lift up, raise*, f.l. in Id.*Art*.69. **-πολέω**, v.l. for -πορέω, Pl.*Phdr*. 246c; *haunt the air*, of birds, Ph.1.506. II. metaph., *busy oneself with high things*, ib.101; of the soul, Him.*Or*.14.12; μ. μετὰ τῶν θεῶν Iamb.*Myst*.5.15. **-πόλος**, ον, *busying oneself with high things*, Ph. 1.588. **-πορέω**, *travel through air*, Pl.*Phdr*.246c (v.l. -πολεῖ), Ael. *NA*3.45; of 'levitation', Philostr.*VA*3.15. **-πορία**, ἡ, *travelling through air*, Eust.636.38.

⊛**μετέωρος**, ον, Ep. **μετήορος** (q.v.), (ἀείρω) *raised from off the ground*, τάφον ἑωυτῇ κατεσκευάσατο μ. Hdt.1.187; σκέλεα δὲ.. κατακρέμαται μ. Id.4.72; μ. ἐξεκόμισαν τὰς ἁμάξας X.*An*.1.5.8; πῆχυς μ. an arm *hanging* (without support from a bandage), Hp.*Fract*.7; μ. αἰωρηθῆναι, of a man, Id.*Art*.70: freq. of anatomical structures, *unsupported*, Gal.2.469, al.; τὰ μ. οἰκήματα, opp. τὰ ὑπόγαια, Hdt.2.148; -ότερος.. τῶν σαύρων *raised higher than*.., *above*.., of the chamaeleon, Arist.*HA*503a21; of *high* ground, τῶν χωρίων τὰ -ότατα Th.4.32; ἀπὸ τοῦ μ. ib.128, cf. D.55.29 (Comp.); χωρία νέμεσθαι -ότερα, opp. ἑλώδη, Arist.*HA*596b4; τὰ -ότατα μέρη Protagorid.4; κατὰ τὸ μ. τοῦ ποταμοῦ *as one looks up* the river, Paus.8.30.2. 2. *on the surface*, ἀπὸ τοῦ -οτάτου *IG*2².1668.8: hence, *prominent*, of eyes, X.*Cyn*.4.1; of roots, *running along the ground*, opp. βαθύρριζος, Thphr.*HP*3.10. 3, *CP*1.3.4, 5.9.8; ἀλγήματα μ. *superficial* pains, Hp.*Aph*.6.7; τομαὶ Id.*Loc.Hom*.13; πνεῦμα μ. *shallow*, not deep, Id.*Epid*.3.1.ζʹ, Gal.7. 946; -ότερον ἆσθμα *more rapid* breathing, Phld.*Ir*.p.27 W.; also μ. ὀχετοί *open, surface* drains, Arist.*Ath*.50.2, *OGI*483.62 (Pergam., ii B.C.). II. = μετάρσιος, *in mid-air, high in air*, ἀνακινῆσαί τινα μ. Hdt.4.94; ἀραί τινα μ. Ar.*Eq*.1362; μ. αἴρεσθαι Id.*Pax*80; Ἀήρ, ὃς ἔχεις τὴν γῆν μ. *poised on high*, Id.*Nu*.264; ἀφικνεῖ μ. ὑπ' αὔρας Cratin. 207; τὰ μ. χωρία the regions *of air*, Ar.*Av*.818, cf. 690; κρεμασθεὶς καὶ βλέπων μ. looking *into mid-air*, Pl.*Tht*.175d; of birds, μ. ἀεὶ μένειν ἀδύνατον Arist.*IA*714a21; of fish, μ. πέτεσθαι Id.*HA*535b28; μ. νεῖν swim *near the surface*, ib.602b22; τὰ μ. *things in the heaven above, astronomical phenomena*, Hp.*VM*1; οὐ γὰρ ἄν ποτε ἐξηῦρον ὀρθῶς τὰ μ. πράγματα, says Socrates, Ar.*Nu*.228, cf. 1284; τὰ μ. φροντιστής, of Socrates, Pl.*Ap*.18b; ἀλαζονεύεται περὶ τῶν μ. Eup.146b; τὰ μ. καὶ τὰ ὑπὸ γῆς Pl.*Ap*.23d, cf. Epicur.*Ep*.1 p.27 U., etc.: Comp., οἶσθα -ότερόν τι τῶν θεῶν; X.*Smp*.6.7. Adv. -ως Philostr.*VA*4.21. 2. *on the high sea*, of ships, καθορῶσι τὰς.. ναῦς μ. Th.1.48; αἱ δὲ μ. ὥρμουν Id.4.26; μίαν ναῦν ἀπολλύασι μ. Id.8.10; of persons, ὅσοι μὴ μ. ἑάλωσαν Id.7.71; μ. πλεῖν Str.2.3.4. 3. of a horse, *high-stepping*, πομπικῷ καὶ μ. καὶ λαμπρῷ ἵππῳ X.*Eq*.11.1. 4. generally, *unsettled, fermenting, undigested*, μ. καὶ ἄπεπτα καὶ ἄκρητα Hp.*VM*19; *inflated*, ὑποχόνδρια Id.*Aph*.4.73. III. metaph., of the mind, *buoyed up, in suspense*, Ἑλλὰς ἅπασα μετέωρος ἦν Th.2.8; μετεώρῳ ⟨τῇ⟩ πόλει κινδυνεύειν Id.6.10; μ. ταῖς διανοίαις Plb.3.107.6, etc.; μ. ταῖς ἐπιβολαῖς ἐπὶ πόλεμον *eager* for.., Id.5.101.2; πρὸς ἐλπίδας Id.5. 62.1; ἐπί τινος or τινι, Luc.*Dem.Enc*.28, *Merc.Cond*.15; μ. πορεύῃ εἰς Ἀθήνας Arr.*Epict*.3.24.75, cf. Jul.*Or*.3.122d; *haughty, puffed up*, Plb.3.82.2, Lxx 2*Ki*.22.28; γαῦρος καὶ μ. Luc.*Nigr*.5; μετέωρε 'proud one', *AP*5.20 (Rufin.); of style, *inflated*, opp. ὑψηλός (sublime), Longin.3.2: also in good sense, τὸ μ. καὶ πομπικόν (cf. II. 3) *elevation of style*, D.H.*Is*.19. 2. of conditions, *uncertain*, τῶν πραγμάτων ὄντων μ. D.19.122; ὁπηνίκα ἂν τὰ τῆς βασιλείας μ. ᾖ Hdn. 2.12.4; *unsettled*, χρόνος μ. καὶ κινδυνώδης Heph.Astr.2.28, cf. 33. Adv. -ρως, ἔχειν Plu.*Cim*.13. 3. of contracts, transactions, suits, etc., *in suspense, pending*, δικαστήριον τὸ διαλῦσον τὰ μ. συμβόλαια *Supp.Epigr*.1.363.9 (Samos, iii B.C.); μ. οἰκονομίαι *POxy*.238.1 (i A.D.), cf. *PFay*.116.12 (ii A.D.); δίκη Jul.*Mis*.368a; μετέωρα, τά, *unfinished business*, *PRyl*.144.10 (i A.D.). 4. *unsecured*, of debts,

οἱ τὰ μ. ἐγγυώμενοι *SIG*364.42,46 (Ephesus, iii B.C.). **5.** of persons, *thoughtless, absent-minded*, 'distrait', Cic.*Att*.15.14.4, 16.5.3 (Comp.), Gal.15.910; *fickle*, κοῦφοί τε καὶ μ. Ti.Locr.104e. Adv. -ρως Vett.Val.166.4.

**μετεωρο-σκοπικός**, ή, όν, *of* or *for a* μετεωροσκόπος: ἡ -κή (sc. τέχνη) Procl.*in Euc*.p.42 F.; ὄργανον μ., = sq., Ptol.*Geog*.1.3.3. **-σκόπιον**, τό, *an instrument for taking celestial observations*, ib.1.3.4; -σκοπεῖον, Procl.*Hyp*.6.2. **-σκόπος**, ὁ, *star-gazer*, Pl.*R*.488e. **II.** -σκόπον, τό, = foreg., Simp.*in Cael*.548.30. **-σοφιστής**, οῦ, ὁ, *astronomical sophist*, Ar.*Nu*.360.

**μετεωροσύνη**, ἡ, poet. for μετεωρία, Man.4.436.

**μετεωρότης**, ητος, ἡ, *sublimity*, Corn.*ND*20.

**μετεωρο-φανής**, ές, *appearing in the air*, Ph.Byz.*Mir*.6. **-φέναξ**, ακος, ὁ, *astronomical quack*, Ar.*Nu*.333. **-φρονέω**, *think of high things*, Sch.Ar.*Eq*.821.

⊛ **μετῆλαι**, αἱ, *rods* on either side of a chariot, Poll.1.243:—also **μετιτῆλαι**, Hsch.

⊛ **μέτηλυς**, υδος, ὁ, ἡ, (μετέρχομαι, μετήλυθον) *one who passes from one place to another, foreign settler*, *PFlor*.322.20, al. (iii A.D.), D.P. 689; μετήλυδες Ὠκεανοῖο, of cranes, Tryph.352. **II.** as Adj., μ. ὀμφητήρ Id.133; *changing*, μετήλυδα ταρσὸν ἀμείβων, of a dancer, Nonn.*D*.10.241, 12.365.

**μέτην**· μέσην, μετουσίαν, Hsch.

**μετηνέμιος**, ον, (ἄνεμος) *swift as wind*, πῶλος *APl*.4.62.

**μετήορος**, ον, (ἀείρω) Ep. form of μετέωρος, *lifted off the ground, hanging*, τὰ δέ κ' αὖτε μ. πάντα γένοιτο Il.8.26; [ἅρματα] ἀΐξασκε μ. leapt *high into air*, 23.369; μετήορα δ' αἶψ' ἀνάειρε *h.Merc*.135; ἵππος.. μ. αὐχένα χαίταις with *high-raised* mane, A.R.4.1366; κεράων τὸ μ. the *upper* horn, Arat.794: Dor. **πεδάοροι** (so Stanley for πεδάμαροι) A.*Ch*.590 (lyr.). **II.** metaph., *wavering, inconstant, thoughtless*, μετήορα θρυλίζειν *h.Merc*.488.

**μετήσεσθαι**, Ion. fut. inf. Med. of μεθίημι. **μετιεῖ**, v. μεθίημι.

**μετίσχω**, = μετέχω, c. gen. rei, φόνου Hdt.5.92.γ', cf. Pl.*Ti*.58e, *R*.411d.

**μετιτέον**, *one must pass on*, ἐπί τινα D.L.6.105, cf. Ruf.*Anat*.18, Gal.9.275, Jul.*Or*.2.52b, Arg.D.22.§7, Iamb.*in Nic*.p.91 P.; μ. ἐφ' ἕτερον βίον Alciphr.3.13. **II.** *one must go in search of* a thing, *inquire*, Arist.*Metaph*.1041ᵃ10; περί τινος Id.*Top*.128ᵇ10.

**μετιτῆλαι**, v. μετῆλαι.

**μετοιακίζομαι**, Pass., *have one's course changed*, ὁ ὑφ' ἡδονῆς δεῦρο κἀκεῖ μετοιακιζόμενος Plu.2.34a.

⊛ **μετοικ-εσία**, ἡ, = μετοικία I, esp. of the *captivity* of the Jews, Lxx 4*Ki*.24.16; ἡ μ. Βαβυλῶνος *Ev.Matt*.1.11; also πλεόνων μ. 'the land o' the leal', *AP*7.731 (Leon.). **-έσιον**, τό, = foreg., Hsch. **-έτης**, ου, ὁ, *one who dwells in the middle*, Id. ⊛ **-έω**, Locr. **μεταϝοικέω** *IG*9(1).333.6:—*change one's abode, remove to* a place, c. acc. loci, E.*Hipp*. 837 (lyr.): c. dat. loci, *settle in*, Pi.*P*.9.83. **II.** abs., *to be a settler, reside in a foreign city*, *IG*l.c., etc.; τοὺς μετοικοῦντας ξένους E.*Supp*. 892; opp. πολιτεύεσθαι, Lys.12.20; μ. γῆς A.*Supp*.609; μ. ἐν τῇ πόλει Lys.5.2; ἐν Μιλήτῳ ἔτη πέντε *SIG*633.60 (Milet., ii B.C.); ταύτῃ Ar.*Av*.1319 (lyr.); Ἀθήνησι D.49.26; παρ' ἑτέροις Isoc.*Ep*.8.4. **-ησις**, εως, ἡ, = sq. I, μ. τοῦ τόπου τοῦ ἐνθένδε εἰς ἄλλον τόπον Pl.*Ap*.40c; τὴν μ. τὴν ἐνθένδε ἐκεῖσε Id.*Phd*.117c, cf. *Cat.Cod. Astr*.7.110. **2.** metaph., of the *transmigration* of souls, τὴν ἀρίστην μ. τὴν τοῦ ἀνθρώπου.. λέοντα γίνεσθαι Ael.*NA*12.7. **II.** = sq. II, Pl.*Lg*.850a. **-ία**, ἡ, *change of abode, removal, migration*, Th.1.2 (pl.); of the Jewish *captivity*, Lxx *Je*.20.4. **II.** *settlement* or *residence in a foreign city*, A.*Eu*.1018 (lyr.), Pl.*Lg*.850c; μ. ἡ ἄνω *sojourn* in the upper world, S.*Ant*.890. **2.** *status and rights of a* μέτοικος, Lys.6.49. **-ίζω**, *lead settlers to another abode*, Arist.*Oec*. 1352ᵃ33, *OGI*264.7 (Pergam.), *Act.Ap*.7.4; σφᾶς αὐτοὺς εἰς Ῥώμην Plu.*Rom*.17: metaph., τὰς φρένας μ. Melanth.Trag.1:—Pass., Aristeas 4:—Med., Μυτιλήνη σῶμα μετῳκίσατο *IG*12(2).443 (Mytil.); also, *go to another country, emigrate*, Ar.*Ec*.754, App.*Pun*.84: metaph., τὸν κλόνον εἰς ὃν ἡ ψυχὴ μετῳκίσατο Ph.1.232. **2.** later intr. in Act., *SIG*880.45 (iii A.D.). **-ικός**, ή, όν, *consisting of* μέτοικοι, Hyp.*Fr*. 149; *in the condition of a* μ., ἄνθρωπος Plu.*Alc*.5; συντελεῖν εἰς τὸ μ., v.l. for μετοίκιον, Luc.*Bis Acc*.9. **II.** metaph., *having a part in*, τινος Id.*Lex*.25. ⊛ **-ιον**, τό, *tax paid by the* μέτοικοι at Athens, Eub.87, Men.35, Is.*Fr*.45; μ. κατατιθέναι pay *it*, Lys.31.9; μ. τέθηκεν D.29.3; τελεῖν Pl.*Lg*.850b, etc.; προσφέρειν X.*Vect*.2.1; καταβάλλειν Luc. *Deor.Conc*.3; *similar tax paid by freedmen*, Aristomen.16. **II.** μετοίκια, τά, = συνοίκια (q.v.), Plu.*Thes*.24. **-ιος** Ζεύς, Zeus as *Protector of the* μέτοικοι, Phryn.*PS*p.88 B. **-ισις**, εως, ἡ, *removal*, pl., μ. καὶ μεταναστάσεις Olymp.*in Mete*.115.28. **-ισμός**, ὁ, *emigration*, Plu.*Publ*.22, *Agis*11. **-ιστέον**, *one must transfer*, Id.2.746c. **-ιστής**, οῦ, ὁ, *emigrant*, Id.*Comp.Thes.Rom*.4.

⊛ **μετοικο-δομέω**, *build differently*, Plu.*Caes*.51; *build elsewhere*, τὰς νεοσσιάς Arr.*Epict*.3.24.6. **-νομέω**, *make changes in administration*, *BMus.Inscr*.481*.316 (Ephesus).

⊛ **μέτοικος**, ὁ, ἡ, *settler from abroad, alien resident in a foreign city, denizen*, A.*Th*.548, *Supp*.994, Hdt.4.151, etc.; esp. at Athens, Th. 2.13, And.1.15, etc.; ξένος λόγῳ μ., opp. ἐγγενής, S.*OT*452, cf. Ar. *Ach*.508, *Eq*.347, *SIG*799.25 (Cyzic., i A.D.); μ. γῆς *one who has settled in* a country, A.*Pers*.319; μ. δόμων, χώρας, Id.*Ch*.971 (lyr.), S.*OC*934; ἐν τῇ τῶν πλησίον And.1.144; βροτοῖς οὔτε ⟨νεκρὸς⟩ νεκροῖσιν μέτοικος, οὐ ζῶσιν, οὐ θανοῦσιν *whose home is* neither *with* the living nor the dead, S.*Ant*.852 (lyr.): metaph., of birds, as *sojourners* in the heavens, A.*Ag*.57 (anap.). **2.** *occupant of the same house with* another, *Sammelb*.5837 (ii A.D.).

**μετοικοφύλαξ** [ῠ], ακος, ὁ, *overseer and guardian of the* μέτοικοι, X.*Vect*.2.7.

**μετοιστέον**, *one must transfer*, διαφορὰν ἐπὶ τὸ σῶμα Plu.2.656d.

**μετοίχομαι**, *go after, go in quest of*, τούσδε μετοιχόμενος Il.10.111; κῆρυξ δὲ μετῴχετο θεῖον ἀοιδόν Od.8.47: c. acc. rei, = μετέρχομαι IV.3, καθαρμόν E.*IT*1332. **2.** with hostile intent, *rush upon, pursue*, ὁ δ' Ἄβαντα μετῴχετο Il.5.148. **3.** *go among* or *through*, ἀνὰ ἄστυ Od.8.7 (or in signf. 1). **4.** *follow behind*, τίς τοι.. μετοιχομένη φάος οἴσει; 19.24.

**μετοιωνίζομαι**, *effect an auspicious change in, procure happier omens for*, τὰς τῆς πόλεως πράξεις Din.1.29; τὴν τύχην ib.92.

**μετοκλάζω**, *keep changing from one leg to the other*, of a coward squatting in ambush, Il.13.281: metaph., πρὸς ἀμφοτέρους τοῖς προσποιήμασι μ. D.S.38/9.13; of a bird, *AP*9.209.

**μετοκωχή**, ἡ, = μετοχή, Hsch.

**μετολισθαίνω**, *slip away*, metaph., of a friend, Tz.*H*.8.839.

**μετονομ-άζω**, *call by a new name*, ἐκ τῶν αἰγέων.. αἰγίδας.. μετωνόμασαν *called* them *by a new name*—αἰγίδες, Hdt.4.189; τὰς φυλὰς μετωνόμασε (sc. Cleisthenes) Id.5.69, cf. Phld.*Mus*.p.50 K.:—Pass., *take* or *receive a new name*, ἀντὶ Λυδῶν μετονομασθῆναι ἐπὶ τοῦ βασιλέος Hdt.1.94; Βάττος μετωνομάσθη *took the name of* B., Id.4.155; καταφρόνησιν ἢ.. ὄνομα ἀφροσύνη μετωνόμασται Th.1.122; καινῶς μετωνομασμένον *new-fangled*, Pl.*Tht*.180a. **-ασία**, ἡ, *change of name*: in pl., title of work by Nicanor, Ath.7.296d.

**μετόνυχον**, τό, *the last joint of the fingers*, *Cat.Cod.Astr*.7.238.

**μετοξύ**, v. μεταξύ.

**μετόπη**, ἡ, in Doric Architecture, *metope*, i.e. *interstice between two beam-ends* (ὀπαί), which had the triglyphs carved upon them, *panel between two* ὀπαί, Vitr.4.2.4, al. (*metoph-*, *methoph-* codd.); cf. μεθόπιον.

**μετόπιν**, Adv., = μετόπισθε, S.*Ph*.1189 (lyr.), A.R.4.1764.

**μετόπισθε**, before a vowel or metri gr. **-θεν**, sts. elided μετόπισθ', Od.22.345: Adv. (freq. in Ep., esp. Il.), **1.** of Place, *behind, in the rear*, Il.6.68; μ. λελειμμένοι left *behind* in Troy, 24.687; *in the second rank*, 17.261. **2.** of Time, *after, afterwards*, freq. in Hom., Il.1.82, al.; ἀμαυροτέρη γενεὴ μ. λέλειπται Hes.*Op*.284; ἡ πρόσθ' ἢ μετόπισθεν E.*Fr*.446.5 (anap.). **II.** Prep. c. gen., *behind*, Il.9.504, Od.9.539.

**μέτοποι**· ἄνδρες, Hsch.

**μετοπωρ-ίζω**, *to be like autumn*, Ph.1.13: mentioned as rare by Poll.1.62. **-ινός**, ή, όν (later **μεθοπωρινός** (q.v.)), *autumnal*, νύκτες Th.7.87; ὁ μ. χρόνος X.*Oec*.17.2; ἄμεινον τὸ μ. μέλι Arist.*HA* 553ᵇ27; μ. ἰσημερία Id.*Mete*.364ᵇ2, cf. Hp.*Aër*.11; μ. τροπαί Adam. *Vent*.41: neut. as Adv., μετοπωρινὸν ὀμβρήσαντος Hes.*Op*.415. **-ον**, τό (later **μεθόπωρον** (q.v.)), = φθινόπωρον, *late autumn*, Hp.*Aër*.6; τοῦ ἔτους πρὸς μετόπωρον ἤδη ὄντος Th.7.79: coupled with ἔαρ, θέρος, χειμών, Arist.*GA*784ᵃ19: metaph., τὸ μ. τοῦ κάλλους Philostr.*Ep*. 51.

**μετορμίζω**, Ion. for μεθορμίζω.

⊛ **μετόρχιον**, τό, (ὄρχος) *space between rows of vines* or *fruit-trees*, Ar. *Pax*568, *Fr*.120.

⊛ **μετουσί-α**, ἡ, *participation, partnership, communion*, μ. ἑορτῆς Ar. *Ra*.446; μετουσίαν δεῖ τῶν τρόπων τὸ σῶμ' ἔχειν Id.*Th*.152; σοὶ δὲ ἀρετῆς.. τίς μ.; D.18.128; πεδίων μ. *enjoyment, means of using*, X.*Cyr*.8.5.23; τῶν δικαίων D.15.29; τὰς τῆς ἰσηγορίας καὶ τὰς τῆς ἐλευθερίας ἡμῶν μετουσίας ἀφαιρεῖσθαι Id.21.124, cf. *SIG*426.24 (Teos, iii B.C.), *IG*12(3).1296.23 (Thera, ii B.C.), *OGI*229.77. **II.** in Philos., = μέθεξις, *participation* in the universal by the particular, κατὰ μετοχήν τε καὶ μ. Polyxenus ap.Alex.Aphr.*in Metaph*.84.18; ὁ μὲν αἰσχρός, ὁ δὲ αἰσχίων εἴδους τοῦ αὐτοῦ μετουσίᾳ Plot.6.1.9, cf. 5.3.15, Procl.*in Prm*.p.557 S. **-αστικός**, ή, όν, *denoting participation*: τὸ μ., in Gramm., *derivative adjective*, D.T.636.15; e.g. κέδρινος, αἱματόεις, *EM*30.11, 34.52. ⊛ **-ος**, ον, *inferior to Being*, opp. ὑπερούσιος, Phlp.*in de An*.504.21.

**μετουσῶ**· περιβλέπω, ἀφορῶ, ἀποβλέπω, Hsch.

**μετοχέτ-ευσις**, εως, ἡ, *conveyance in a duct* or *channel*, ἡ ἐς τὸ ἕντερον τῶν ὑγρῶν μ. Aret.*SA*2.5; 'derivation' (opp. ἀντίσπασις), Gal. 1.382, Id.ap.Orib.8.18 tit. **2.** Astrol., *transference of nature* when a planet passes from conjunction with another into conjunction with a third, Porph.*in Ptol*.188. ⊛ **-εύω**, *convey in a channel, divert*, ποταμὸν ἐς τὸ πεδίον App.*Hisp*.78, cf. Tz.*H*.1.823: metaph., *divert*, Lxx 4*Ma*.1.29 (cj.), Iamb.*Myst*.4.12; νοήματα εἰς τὸν ἐρώμενον Herm. *in Phdr*.p.165 A.:—Med., φορὰν εἰς βαναύσους τέχνας μετοχετευσάμενοι Ph.1.637:—Pass., ἐς ἡδονὰς ἀπὸ τῶν καλῶν μ. Hdn.1.3.1.

⊛ **μετοχ-ή**, ἡ, (μετέχω) *sharing, participation*, Hdt.1.144, Pl.*Ep*.345a, *AP*9.316.9 (Leon.); περὶ μετοχῆς τοῦ παραδείσου their *shares* in the orchard, *PCair.Zen*.369.2 (iii B.C.); παρουσία καὶ μ. Plu.2.945f; τίς μ. δικαιοσύνῃ καὶ ἀνομίᾳ; 2*Ep.Cor*.6.14; κατὰ μετοχήν in virtue of *participation* in something else, Arist.*Metaph*.1030ᵃ13, Ph.1.47; κατὰ μετοχήν τε καὶ μετουσίαν τῆς ἰδέας Polyxenus ap. Alex. Aphr. *in Metaph*.84.17; μ. καὶ θείων καὶ ἀνθρωπίνων πάντων *GDI*5040.13, cf. 5042.8 (Hierapytna). **2.** Astrol., *joint possession* or *occupation* by two planets, Antioch.Astr. in *Cat.Cod.Astr*.8(3).107, 115, Porph.*in Ptol*.190. **3.** *partaking* of food, τῇ τῶν ζῴων μετοχῇ Iamb.*VP*24.108 codd. (dub.l.). **4.** *partnership*, *PRev.Laws*14.10 (pl., iii B.C.), etc. **II.** Gramm., *participle*, D.T.634.5, D.H.*Comp*.2, Plu.2.1011c, A.D.*Synt*.15.20, al., Poll.7.9, Eust.138.16. **III.** *compactness*,

LxxPs.121(122).3. **-ικός**, ή, όν, *relating to a partnership*, *PStrassb.* 116.10 (i A.D.). II. *participial*, ὄνομα, σύνταξις, D.H.*Amm.*2.12, A.D.*Synt.*84.23, cf. Eust.32.33, 138.15. Adv. -κῶς Apollon.*Lex.* s.v. τέθηπα.

**μετοχλίζω**, *remove by a lever, hoist* a heavy body *out of the way*, οὔ κέν τις.., οὐδὲ μάλ' ἡβῶν, ῥεῖα μετοχλίσσειεν Od.23.188; οὐδέ κ' ὀχῆα ῥεῖα μετοχλίσσειε θυράων *would* he easily *push back* the bolt of the doors, Il.24.567, cf. Lyc.627, *AP*9.81 (Crin.); ἡ γῆ -ίζουσα [τὸν Ἀνταῖον] Philostr.*Im.*2.21.

**μετοχμάζω**, *carry elsewhither*, Nonn.*D.*1.48.

**μέτοχος**, ον, *sharing in, partaking of*, c. gen., [τῆς συμφορῆς] τὸ πλεῦν μέτοχος Hdt.3.52; μ. ἐλπίδων, τέχνης, E.*Ion*698 (lyr.), Pl.*Phdr.* 262d; τοῦ βίου, of a wife, Diod.Com.3.5; δίκης Arist.*Mu.*401b 29. II. Subst., *partner, accomplice in*, τοῦ φόνου E.*HF*721, Antipho 3.3.11: abs., Th.8.92; *partner* in business, *PHib.*1.109.3 (iii B.C.), *PCair.Zen.*176.102 (iii B.C.), *Ostr.Bodl.*192, 251 (ii B.C.), *Ev. Luc.*5.7, etc. 2. *member of a board* of officials, freq. in phrase ὁ δεῖνα καὶ μέτοχοι πράκτορες, ἐπιτηρηταί, ἀγορανόμοι, τραπεζῖται, etc., *PFlor.*358.5 (ii A.D.), *PSI*2.160.4 (ii A.D.), *PStrassb.*52.17 (ii A.D.), *POxy.*96.4 (ii A.D.), etc. 3. *joint owner* of a house, *CPHerm.*119 *A* iv 20 (iii A.D.). III. θεῶν μέτοχοι, of the demigods, Arist.*Fr.* 640.20, cf. *IG*14.2117 (Rome).

***μετρ-έω**, Heraclean 1 pl. impf. ἐμετρίωμες *Tab.Heracl.*2.45: pres. part. Pass. μετριώμεναι ib.1.22, 28: (μέτρον):—*measure*: I. of Space, *measure*, i.e. *pass over, traverse*, πέλαγος μέγα μετρήσαντες Od.3.179; προτέρω μετρεῖν (sc. θάλασσαν) *to sail* farther, A.R.2.915, cf. 4.1779:—in Med., ἅλα μετρήσασθαι Mosch.2.157; μετρούμενον ἴχνη τὰ κείνου *measuring* them *with the eyes*, S.*Aj.*5:—Pass., *to be measured*, A.*Ch.*209; *to be measured round*, D.P.197. II. of Time, μακροὶ.. ἂν μετρηθεῖεν χρόνοι S.*OT*561. III. of Number, Size, Worth, etc., 1. *count*, Alc.142; ἐπ' ᾐόνι κύματα μ. Theoc. 16.60, cf. *AP*4.3b.10 (s.v.l., Agath.). 2. *measure*, χώρην ὀργυιῇσι, σταδίοισι, etc., Hdt.2.6; χώρας κατὰ παρασάγγας Id.6.42; τῇ γαστρὶ μ. τὴν εὐδαιμονίαν *measure* happiness by sensual enjoyments, D.18. 296; μ. πορφύρᾳ τὸ εὔδαιμον Luc.*Nigr.*15, etc.; ὁπηνίκ' ἂν εἴκοσι ποδῶν μετροῦντι τὸ στοιχεῖον ᾖ when you *measure* it, Eub.119.7, cf. 9; ἀριθμεῖν τἀγαθὰ καὶ μετρεῖν Pl.*R.*348a; μ. καὶ ἀριθμεῖν καὶ ἱστάναι ib.602d: —Pass., Πόντος.. καὶ Ἑλλήσποντος οὕτω μοι μεμετρέαται Hdt.4.86; μετρεῖσθαι πρὸς ἄλληλα Pl.*Plt.*284d, etc. b. Math., of magnitudes or numbers, *measure*, Arist.*Cael.*273b12, Euc.7 *Def.*14, Eratosth.ap. Nicom.*Ar.*1.13 (Act. and Pass.), etc.; μετρηθῆναι κοινῷ μέτρῳ πρός.. to be commensurable with, ibid. 3. *measure out*, τἄλφιτ' ἐν ἀγορᾷ Ar.*Eq.*1009, cf. *Ach.*548 (Pass.); πώλοισι χόρτον μ. E.*Rh.*772; μέτρησον εἰρήνης τί μοι Ar.*Ach.*1021; μετρεῖν τὴν ἴσην *give measure* for measure, Paus.2.18.2; ἢ μετάδος ἢ μέτρησον ἢ τιμὴν λαβέ *lend by measure*, Theopomp.Com.26:—Med., *to have measured out to oneself*, in buying or borrowing, εὖ μετρεῖσθαι παρὰ γείτονος *get* good *measure* from one's neighbour, Hes.*Op.*349; τὰ ἄλφιτα καθ' ἡμίεκτον μετρούμενοι D.34.37, cf. Herod.6.5, *SIG*976.61 (Samos, ii B.C.), Plu. *Caes.*48. 4. *deliver, pay*, of corn and other measurable commodities, σῖτόν τινι D.46.20, *PHib.*1.39.3 (iii B.C.); ἔλαιον ib.131 (iii B.C.):—Med., *receive in payment*, ib.103 (iii B.C.), etc. IV. *moderate*, of pain, Pall.*in Hp.*12.273 C. **-ήδην**, Adv. *by measure*, Nic.*Al.*45 (v.l. -ηδόν). ***-ηδόν**, Adv. *in regular order*, Nonn.*D.* 7.115. **-ημα**, ατος, τό, *measured distance*, E.*Ion*1138; *measurement*, λίθοι..ὧν μ. στερεὸν πόδες ἑπτακόσιοι *Supp.Epigr.*4.446.11 (Didyma, ii B.C.). 2. *measure, allowance, dole*, E.*IT*954; soldier's *rations*, Plb.6.38.3, *OGI*229.106 (Smyrna, ii B.C.), *PLond.* 1.23.26 (ii B.C.); *pay*, Plb.9.27.11: in pl., *deliveries in kind*, *POxy.* 1221.4 (iii/iv A.D.): sg., *amount so delivered*, *PCair.Zen.*223.5 (iii B.C.); μ. θησαυροῦ *Ostr.Bodl.* v D9 (i A.D.), al. **-ημάτιον**, τό, Dim. of foreg. 2, of *payments in kind*, Möller *Pap.Berl.Mus.*12 (ii/iii A.D.). **-ησις**, εως, ἡ, *measurement*, χώρης Hdt.4.99, cf. X. *Mem.*4.7.2, Pl.*Plt.*285a, etc.: pl., Id.*Lg.*819c. 2. *measuring out, dole* of corn, *SIG*976.58 (Samos, ii B.C.); *delivery in kind*, *PAmh.*2.87.21 (ii A.D.), etc. **-ητέον**, *one must measure*, Pl. *R.*531a. ***-ητής**, οῦ, ὁ, *measurer*, Id.*Just.*373a; μετρηταὶ στρατοπέδων, = Lat. *metatores castrorum*, J.*BJ*5.2.1. II. a liquid measure, = ἀμφορεύς, Philyll.7, D.42.20, Sosith.2.8 (s.v.l.), *IG*12(3). 436.13 (Thera, iv B.C.), Arist.*HA*596a7, Hero *Mens.*9, etc.; of the Hebrew *bath*, Lxx 3 *Ki.*18.32, al., *Ev.Jo.*2.6. **-ητιαῖος**, α, ον, *holding a* μετρητής, κεράμιον *BCH*8.219 (Caryanda). **-ητικός**, ή, όν, *skilled in measuring*, Pl.*Just.*373d; of numbers, *capable of measuring*, i.e. *dividing*, c. gen., Iamb.*in Nic.*p.36 P. II. *concerned with measurement*:—κή (sc. τέχνη), ἡ, *mensuration*, μ. μήκους καὶ ἐπιπέδου καὶ βάθους Pl.*Lg.*817e, cf. *Prt.*357d, al. Adv. -κῶς Poll.4.166. **-ητίς**, ίδος, ἡ, = μετρητής II, *IG*12(7).62.21 (Amorgos, iv B.C.). **-ητός**, ή, όν, *measurable*, opp. ἄμετρος, Pl.*Lg.*820c; μ. πρὸς ἄλληλα ib.819e, *Plt.*284b; πένθος οὐ μ. E.*Ba.*1244. II. *measured*, μετρητὸν πίνειν Plu.2.156e, cf. Nonn.*D.*3.64. III. *to be measured*, οὐ χοίνικι μ. ἡ τροφή Iamb.*Protr.*21.ιη'.

***μετρι-άζω**, *to be moderate, keep measure*, S.*Ph.*1183 (lyr.), Th.1.76, Arist.*Pol.*1298a40; τινι *in* a thing, ib.1314b33: with Preps., μ. ἐν ταῖς εὐπραξίαις D.20.162; περὶ τὰ τοιαῦτα Pl.*Lg.*784e; περὶ τὸ δίκαιον D.H.13.13; πρὸς λύπην Pl.*R.*603e; ἐπί τινι Luc.*Im.*21; μ. ἐν τῷ προθύμῳ *show* but *moderate* zeal, Hdn.8.3.5: c. gen., μ. τῶν παθῶν Hierocl.*in CA*10 p.436 M. 2. of disease, *remit, abate*, opp. παροξύνεσθαι, Gal.16.711. 3. of persons, *to be 'only middling', to be unwell*, Men.1037, Lxx *Ne.*2.2, Poet. *de herb.*3. 4. οἱ μετριάζοντες, = οἱ μέτριον τὸ αἰδοῖον ἔχοντες, Arist.*GA*718a24. 5. *jest*, Sch.Ar.*V.* 64. II. trans., *moderate, regulate, control*, ὅρκοις μ. ψυχὴν νέαν Pl. *Lg.*692b; [τὴν βασιλείαν] Arist.*Pol.*1313a26; τι ἡμῖν ἀπὸ τοῦ ἐκφορίου *reduce* our rent, *PCair.Zen.*433.12 (iii B.C.); τὴν τιμωρίαν Ph.1. 41. **-ακός**, ή, όν, *of moderate amount*, ὕπαρξις *PLond.*1.77.20 (vi A.D.). **-ασμός**, ὁ, *jesting*, κατὰ μετριασμόν *in jest*, Suid. s.v. ἀκρισία. **-άω**, v. μετριόω. **-εύομαι**, gloss on λαγαρίττομαι, Hsch. **-κός**, ή, όν, *metrical*, ῥυθμοί Arist.*Rh.*1409a7; οἱ μ. those *learned in metres*, Id.*PA*660a8; opp. οἱ ῥυθμικοί, D.H.*Comp.*17: τὰ -κά and ἡ -κή (sc. τέχνη) *prosody*, Arist.*Po.*1456b34, 38. II. *by measure*, opp. σταθμικός (by weight), Gal.13.417, etc. III. = μετριακός, *PLond.*5.1234.48 (vi A.D.).

**μετριο-λογέομαι**, *speak moderately*, i.e. *disparagingly*, Eust.1689. 50. **-λόγος**, ον, *speaking moderately*, Antipho Soph.103. **-παγής**, ές, *moderately thick*, γάλα Sor.1.91. **-πάθεια** [πᾰ], ἡ, *restraint over the passions*, Ph.1.113, Plu.2.102d, App.*Pun.*52, 57, Alex.Aphr.*in Top.* 239.6, Porph.*Sent.*32:—written **-πᾰθία**, Phld.*Rh.*2.272 S. **-πᾰθέω**, *feel moderately, bear reasonably with*, τοῖς ἀγνοοῦσι καὶ πλανωμένοις *Ep. Hebr.*5.2: abs., Ph.1.113, 2.37, 45, J.*AJ*12.3.2, S.E.*P.*3.235. **-πᾰθής**, ές, *moderating one's passions*, a Peripatetic word, opp. Stoic ἀπαθής, D.L.5.31, cf. Aristeas 256, Ph.2.315 (Sup.); τὸ μ. D.H.8.61. Adv. -θῶς, ζῆν Phld.*Po.*5.13; χρῆσθαι ταῖς εὐπραξίαις App.*Pun.*51; διατίθεσθαι S.E.*M.*11.161. **-πότης**, ου, ὁ, *moderate in drinking*, X.*Ap.*19: Sup. μετριοποτίστατος Poll.6.20.

***μέτριος**, α, ον, also ος, ον Pl.*Ti.*59d; Aeol. **μέτερρος** *Lyr.Adesp.*66 (but μέτριος Sapph.*Oxy.*1231.5): (μέτρον):—*within measure, moderate*, and so, I. of Size, μ. ἄνδρες men *of average height*, Hdt.2. 32; μ. πῆχυς the *common* cubit, Id.1.178; ἰσχὰς μ. a *fair-sized* fig, Diocl.*Fr.*140; of Time, μ. μῆκος λόγων the *proper* length of speech, Pl.*Prt.*338b; μ. χρόνος ἀκμῆς a *fair average* time of maturity, Id.*R.* 460e. II. of Number, [ἱππεῖς] μ. *a reasonable number of*.., X. *Cyr.*2.4.14. III. mostly of Degree, *moderate*, ἔργα Hes.*Op.*306; μ. νῦν ἔπος εὔχου A.*Supp.*1059 (lyr.); μ. χάρις E.*IA*554 (lyr.); σῖτος -ώτατος X.*Lac.*1.3; τὸ μ. *the mean*, S.*OC*1212 (lyr.), cf. Pl.*Lg.*719e, *Plt.*284e; ὁμολογεῖται τὸ μ. ἄριστον καὶ τὸ μέσον Arist.*Pol.*1295b4; περαιτέρω τοῦ μ. X.*Mem.*3.13.5; πέρα τοῦ μ. Thphr.*CP*6.1.4; ἐνδοτέρω τοῦ μ. Plu.2.656f; τὰ μ. E.*Med.*125 (anap.); εἴη γ' ἐμοὶ μέτρια Id.*Ion*632; τὰ μ. κεκτῆσθαι X.*Mem.*2.6.22; μ. καὶ δίκαια Ar.*Nu.* 1137; μ. φιλία a friendship *not too great*, E.*Hipp.*253 (anap.); μετρίων λέκτρων μετρίων δὲ γάμων..κῦρσαι θνητοῖσιν ἄριστον Id.*Fr.*503 (anap.); μ. ἐσθῆτι χρῆσθαι *simple* dress, Th.1.6; μετρίᾳ φυλακῇ *not in strict* custody, Id.4.30; βίος μ. καὶ βέβαιος Pl.*R.*466b; μ. σχῆμα *modest* apparel, Id.*Grg.*511e; μ. οὐσίαν κεκτῆσθαι Arist.*Pol.*1292b 26; οἱ μ. *respectable people*, D.18.10; later, *poor*, μ. καὶ δυστυχεῖς *POxy.*120.7 (iv A.D.), etc.: with inf., ὅσον οἰόμεθα μέτριον εἶναι πιεῖν *just sufficient*, Pl.*Phd.*117b. 2. *tolerable*, οἷς μὴ μ. αἰὼν S.*Ph.*179 (lyr.); ἀπὸ τῶν μ. ἐπ' ἀμήχανον ἄλγος Id.*El.*140 (lyr.); μ. ἄχθος E.*Alc.*884 (anap.); κακά Id.*Tr.*722; ναύταις μ. χειμὼν φέρειν ib. 688; μετρίων δεομένῳ making a *moderate* request, Hdt.4.84; τυχεῖν τῶν μετρίων Lys.9.4; τὰ μ. *tolerable* terms, Decr.ap.D.18.165; ἐπὶ μετρίοις Th.4.22; μηδὲν μ. λέγειν nothing *tolerably accurate*, Pl.*Tht.* 181b; -ωτάτη ἡ δημοκρατία *least intolerable*, Arist.*Pol.*1289b4, cf. Men.532.17 (Sup.). 3. of Persons, *moderate* in desires and the like, *temperate*, Ar.*Pl.*245; -ώτεροι ἐς τὰ πολιτικά Th.6.89; μ. πρὸς τὰς ἡδονάς Pl.*Lg.*816b; σώφρων καὶ μ. πρὸς τὴν καθ' ἡμέραν δίαιταν Aeschin.3.170; ἐν τῷ σίτῳ X.*Cyr.*5.2.17; of Love, μάκαρες οἳ μ. θεοῦ (sc. Ἀφροδίτης) μετέσχον E.*IA*543 (lyr.), cf. *Fr.*967 (lyr.); εἰ δ' ἦσθα μ. τἄλλα γ' ἡδίστη θεῶν πέφυκας Id.*Hel.*1105; also, *moderate, fair*, Thgn.615, Pl.*R.*396c, etc.; a favourite word in democratic states, μ. καὶ φιλάνθρωπος D.21.185; σαυτὸν -ώτερον παρέχειν ib.134; μ. πρὸς τοὺς ὑπηκόους *mild* towards.., Th.1.77. 4. *proportionate, fitting*, μισθὸς σώφροσι μ. Pl.*Ti.*18b; μ. λόγοι X.*Smp.*8.3. 5. *enjoying 'middling' health* (cf. μετριάζω I. 3), *Cat.Cod.Astr.*8(1).182.

B. Adv. μετρίως *moderately, within due limits*, ἀπηγήσασθαι Hdt.2.161; *in due measure, neither exaggerating nor depreciating*, εἰπεῖν Th.2.35; λέγειν Pl.*R.*518b; μ. περὶ αὐτῶν διαλεχθέντες Isoc.12. 171; μ. ἔχειν to be *in due proportion*, neither too much nor too little, Pl.*Tht.*191d; μ. ἔχειν βίου to be *moderately well* off, Hdt.1.32; μ. φιλοσοφίας ἔχειν Pl.*Euthd.*305d: Comp. μετριώτερον (infr. 3), also -ωτέρως Arist.*HA*587a1: Sup. -ώτατα Th.6.88, etc. 2. *enough*, μ. κεχόρευται Ar.*Nu.*1511 (anap.); μ. πρὸς τὴν ἐμὴν ἀνάγκην εἰρημένα Id.*Ec.* 969; *moderately, pretty well*, ἐν οἰκουμένῃ καὶ μ. πολιτείᾳ Pl.*Lg.*936b; σωφρονοῦσι καὶ μ. D.6.19; μ. [λέγειν] Men.*Pk.*262; ἀποδέξασθαι μ. Pl. *Tht.*161b. 3. *modestly, temperately*, χαίρειν E.*IA*921, cf. *HF*709; ἀποκρίνασθαι X.*An.*2.3.20; μ. βεβιωκὼς Lys.16.3 (but μ. διάγειν to be *moderately* off, X.*Hier.*1.8); πενθεῖν μ. Antiph.53.1; φέρειν Plb.3.85. 9; *on fair terms*, μ. ξυναλλαγῆναι Th.4.19, cf. 20: Comp. -ώτερον, πρός τινας φρονεῖν X.*Cyr.*4.3.7. 4. μ. ἔχειν *to be in 'middling' health*, *PLips.*108.6 (ii/iii A.D.). II. neut. μέτριον and μέτρια as Adv., μέτριον ἔχειν Pl.*Lg.*846c (sed leg. μέτρον); μέτρια βασανισθεὶς Id.*Sph.*237b: also with Art., τὸ μέτριον ἀποκοιμηθῆναι X.*Cyr.*2.4.26; τὰ μέτρια διαφέρεσθαι Th.4.19, cf. 8.84.

**μετριόσιτος**, ον, *moderate in eating*, Poll.6.28, 34.

**μετριοσύνη**, ἡ, *poverty*, *PMasp.*20 *B* 14 (vi A.D.), etc.

***μετριό-της**, ητος, ἡ, *moderation*, Th.1.38, Pl.*R.*560d, Philyll.7, Plb.1.88.3; μ. τέρψιος Democr.191; ἡ τῆς φωνῆς μ. Isoc.15.296; ἡ τοῦ βίου μ. Aeschin.3.218, cf. Arist.*Pol.*1315b2 (pl.); μ. τῶν σίτων (leg. συσσίτων) *moderation in (of)*.., X.*Cyr.*5.2.17; μ. περί τι, ἔν τινι, Pl.*Def.*411e, 412b: pl., *middle course*, Isoc.2.33, 4.11. 2. the

*right amount* or *degree* of anything, Hp.*Off*.3, *Fract*.5: pl., *Liq*. 1. II. *middle condition, modest circumstances* or *ability*, POxy. 1121.10 (iii A.D.), *PMasp*.305.11 (vi A.D.), etc. III. *graceful proportions, elegance*, Arist.*Pol*.1309$^b$27, Aesop.204*b*. **-φῐλής**, ές, *loving equity*, *PRyl*.114.3 (iii A.D.). **-φρονέω**, *think modestly, be moderate*, Sch.Il.8.175, Hsch. s.v. μετριάζει. **-φροσύνη**, ἡ, *modesty*, Simp. *in Epict*.p.66 D.

**μετριόω** or **μετριάω**, implied by the form μετριῶ (s.v.l.), Theognost.*Can*.146; but ἐμετρίωμες, μετριώμεναι are forms of μετρέω (q.v.).

**μετρο-ειδής**, ές, *like metre, metrical*, Demetr.*Eloc*.181,182. **-κροτος**, ον, *wrought in metre*, γραφαί Tz. ad Lyc.497. **-λογία**, ἡ, *theory of ratios*, Phld.*Acad.Ind*.p.16 M.

**μέτρον**, τό, *that by which anything is measured*: 1. *measure, rule*, μέτρ' ἐν χερσὶν ἔχοντες Il.12.422; ἐν μέτροισι ταμὼν δόνακας *h.Merc*.47; πάντ' ἄνδρα πάντων χρημάτων μ. εἶναι is *a measure* of all things, Pl.*Tht*.183c, cf. Protag.ap.Arist.*Metaph*.1053$^a$36; μ. αὐτῷ οὐχ ἡ ψυχή, ἀλλ' ὁ νόμος X.*Cyr*.1.3.18. b. Math., *measure, divisor*, Eratosth.ap.Nicom.*Ar*.1.13, etc. 2. *measure of content*, whether solid or liquid, δῶκεν μέθυ, χίλια μ. Il.7.471; εἴκοσι δ' ἔστω μ... ἀλφίτου Od.2.355; ὕδατος ἀνὰ εἴκοσι μ. χεῦε 9.209, cf. Il.23.268,741, Hes.*Op*.350,600, etc.; at Samos, of the μέδιμνος, *SIG*976.55 (ii B.C.); in Egypt, of the ἀρτάβη, μ. δοχικόν *PTeb*.11.6 (ii B.C.); also of smaller units, as μ. ἑξαχοίνικον ib.105.40 (ii B.C.); μέτροις καὶ σταθμοῖς *by measure* and weight, Decr.ap.And.1.83; in the widest sense, either *weight* or *measure*, Φείδωνος τοῦ τὰ μ. ποιήσαντος Πελοποννησίοισι Hdt.6.127; μ. οἰνηρά, σιτηρά, Arist.*EN*1135$^a$2; Κιλικίῳ μ. μετρεῖν *OGI*579.2 (Cilicia). 3. *any space measured* or *measurable, length, size*, in pl., *dimensions*, μέτρα κελεύθου *the length* of the way, Od.4.389; μέτρα θαλάσσης Hes.*Op*.648, Orac.ap.Hdt.1.47; μορφῆς μέτρα bodily *dimensions*, E.*Alc*.1063; τὰ μ. τοῦ λίθου its *distances* from a given point in given directions, its *position*, Hdt.2.121.α', cf. Pl.*Lg*.843e, Plu.*Sol*.23; ἄστρων μέτρα S.*Fr*.432.8; ἀπέχει.. θαλάσσης μέτρον ἑξήκοντα σταδίους Th.8.95; τῷ Ἴστρῳ ἐκ τῶν ἴσων μ. ὁρμᾶται [ὁ Νεῖλος] starts from the same *distances* as (i.e. the position corresponding to the source of) the Ister, Hdt.2.33; εἰδέναι τὴν ἑαυτοῦ χώραν μέτρῳ καὶ τόπῳ X.*Cyr*.8.5.3; ἐντὸς τῶν μ. τετμημένον μέταλλον Hyp.*Eux*.35; later of Time, *duration*, μέτρα βίοιο ἄρκια *APl*.4.333 (Antiphil.); ἐτέων μέτρα, ὡράων μέτρον, *AP*7.334, 9.481; μέτρα ἐνιαυτῶν, νυκτός, Arat.464,731; χρονικὰ μ. Simp. *in de An*.299.37. b. *limit, goal*, ὅρμου μ. the *goal* which is the mooring-place, Od.13.101; ἥβης μ. ἱκέσθαι the *term* which is puberty, Il.11.225, Hes.*Op*.132; but, ἥβης μ. ἔχειν *full measure* of youthful vigour, ib.438, Thgn.1119; σοφίης, γνωμοσύνης μ. Sol.13.52, 16.2. 4. *due measure* or *limit, proportion*, μέτρα φυλάσσεσθαι Hes.*Op*.694; χρὴ κατ' αὐτὸν παντὸς ὁρᾶν μέτρον Pi.*P*.2.34; μέτρα μὲν γνώμᾳ διώκων, μέτρα δὲ καὶ κατέχων Id.*I*.6(5).71; κατὰ μέτρον Hes.*Op*.720; πίνειν ὑπὲρ μέτρον Thgn.498; προστιθεὶς μ. A.*Ch*.797 (lyr.); τί μ. κακότατος ἔφυ; S.*El*.236 (lyr.); μ. ἔχει have *a moderating power*, Pl.*Lg*.836a; πλέον πίνειν τοῦ μέτρου Id.*R*.621a; μ. ἔχειν Id.*Lg*.957a; μέτρῳ, = μετρίως, καταβαίνειν Pi.*P*.8.78; οὐδεὶς τῷ μ. τὸ πίνειν ἔστεργε Alciphr.3.32. 5. τίς ἱππείοις ἐν ἔντεσσιν μέτρα.. ἐπέθηκ' *checks*, i.e. bits, Pi.*O*.13.20. II. *metre*, Ar.*Nu*.638,641, etc.; opp. μέλος (music) and ῥυθμός (time), Pl.*Grg*.502c, etc.; λόγους ψιλοὺς εἰς μέτρα τιθέντες putting into *verse*, Id.*Lg*.669d; τὰ ἐν μέτρῳ πεποιημένα ἔπη X.*Mem*.1.2.21. 2. pl., *verses*, Pl.*Ly*.205a. (I.-E. **mētro-m* from **mēd-tro-m* 'measuring instrument', cf. Goth. *mitan* 'measure'.)

⊕**μετρο-νόμοι**, οἱ, *inspectors of weights and measures*, Din.*Fr*.18.7, Arist.*Ath*.51.2. **-ποιέω**, *make by measure*, Herm.ap.Stob.49.69 (Pass.). II. *make verses*, Oenom.ap.Eus.*PE*5.33. **-ποιΐα**, ἡ, *metrical composition*, Longin.*Proll.Heph*.p.86 C. **-σύνθετος**, ον, *composed in metre*, Tz.*H*.7.650.

⊕**μέττα**, Cret. for μέσ(σ)α, *Leg.Gort*.9.48.

**μέττον**· μεῖζον, Hsch. **μέττος**, v. μέσος. **μεττρία**, = εὔθυνα, Id.; cf. μαστρεία.

⊕**μετωνῠμ-ία**, ἡ, (μετά, ὄνομα) *change of name*: in Rhet., *the use of one word for another, metonymy*, Cic.*Orat*.27.93, Ps.-Plu.*Vit.Hom*.23, Quint.8.6.23. **-ικός**, ή, όν, *of* or *like metonymy*, τρόπος *EM*460.44. Adv. **-κῶς** Artem.5.87, Hsch. s.v. Ἥφαιστος. **-ος**, ον, *connected with a change of name*, cj. in Democr.26.

**μετωπ-ᾱδόν**, Adv., = sq., πρῴρῃσι μ. ἐγχρίμπτονται, of ships, Opp.*C*.2.65. ⊕**-ηδόν**, Adv. *with front foremost*; of ships, *forming a close front, in line*, Hdt.7.100; opp. ἐπὶ κέρως (in column), Th.2.90; μ. ποιεῖσθαι τὴν ἔφοδον Plb.11.22.10, cf. Ph.2.354, Plu.*Lys*.10. **-ιαῖος**, α, ον, *on* or *of the forehead*, of a bandage, Heliod.ap.Orib.48.26.1, Sor.*Fasc*.4, Gal.18(1).786. **-ίας**, ου, ὁ, *having a broad* or *high forehead*, *PPetr*.3p.10 (iii B.C.), Poll.2.43, Rhetor. in *Cat.Cod.Astr*.7.198, *Gloss*. **-ίδιος**, ον, = μετωπιαῖος, ἱδρώς Hp.*Mul*.2.171 (cj. for -ιδαῖος; v.l. περιμετωπίδιος); πλέγμα *AP*9.543 (Phil.). **-ικός**, ή, όν, = foreg., Heliod.ap.Orib.48.27.2. **-ιον**, τό, = μέτωπον, *forehead*, Il.11.95, 16.739. 2. *façade*, ναοῦ *SIG*282 ii 20 (Priene, iv B.C.). 3. *margin* of a book, Gal.17(1).634, Hdn.*Epim*.2, 159. 4. *bandage for the forehead*, Gal.18(1).803. II. *aromatic Egyptian ointment containing* μέτωπον III, Dsc.1.59; *containing oil of bitter almonds*, Apollon.ap.Ath.15.688f, cf. Gal.19.71, Paul.Aeg.7.20. 2. = ἀμυγδάλινον ἔλαιον, Dsc.1.33, *Gloss*.; cf. νετώπιον. **-ίς**, ίδος, ἡ, *head-bandage*, Hsch. ⊕**-ον**, τό, also **-ος**, ὁ, *Gloss*. (s.v.l.): (μετά, ὤψ):—prop. *the space between the eyes* (Arist.*HA*491$^b$12), *brow, forehead*, ὁ δὲ προσιόντα [ἤλασεν] μέτωπον ῥινὸς ὕπερ πυμάτης Il.13.615, etc.; στίγματα ἔχων ἐν τῷ μ. *IG*4²(1).121.48 (Epid., iv B.C.); χαλάσας τὸ μ. Ar.*V*.655; mostly of men, but of a horse in Il.23.454, cf. S.*El*.727; of a boar, X.*Cyr*.1.4.8; of a dog, Id.*Cyn*.4.1: in pl., of a single person, Od.6.107, E.*Hel*.1568, etc.; τὰ μέτωπ' ἀνέσπασεν Ar.*Eq*.631. 2. metaph., γαίας μ., of Etna, Pi.*P*.1.30. II. *front, face* of anything, as a wall or building, Hdt.1.178, 2.124; τεῖχος ὡς ἐπὶ δέκα σταδίους.. μ. ἕκαστον measuring 10 stades on each *face*, Id.9.15, cf. *IG*2².463.66, 7.4255.19, *BCH*20.324.65 (Lebad.); τὰ μ. τῶν κλιμακτήρων vertical *faces* of the steps, *IG*2².244.80; *wall* extending inwards between two doors, ib.1657.3, 1668.23,59 (dub. sens. in 1².372.30); *front* or *front-line* of an army, fleet, etc., A.*Pers*.720, etc.; εἰς μ. στῆναι to stand in *line*, X.*Cyr*.2.4.2; ἐπὶ μετώπου διιέναι, opp. ἐπὶ κέρως or κέρας (in column), ib.2.4.3; ἐν μετώπῳ καθιστάναι, παρατάξασθαι, ib.2.4.4, *HG*2.1.23. 2. *margin* of a book, Gal.15.624, 17(1).80, Marin.*Procl*.25. III. = χαλβάνη, or *the reed* or *wood which yields it*, Dsc.1.59, 3.83. 2. v.l. for νέτωπον (q.v.).

**μετωπο-σκόπος**, ον, *observing the forehead, judging of men by their foreheads*, Plin.*HN*35.88, Suet.*Tit*.2. **-σώφρων**, ον, gen. ονος, *with modest countenance*, A.*Supp*.198 (cj. Pors.).

⊕**μέχρῐ**, and **μέχρῐς**, Adv. *as far as*, so used chiefly in Prose and before a Prep., μέχρι πρός.. Pl.*Ti*.25b, *Criti*.118a; μ. εἰς X.*An*.6.4.26; ἐς γόνυ μ. χιτῶνα ζώννυσθαι Call.*Dian*.11: before Advs. of Place or Time, μ. ἐνταῦθα Pl.*Sph*.222a, al.; μ. δεῦρο τοῦ λόγου Id.*Smp*.217e; μ. ὅποι.. Id.*Grg*.487c; μ. ὅπου.. Call.*Del*.169; οὕτω μέχρι πόρρω D.18.163; μ. τότε Th.8.24; μ. τὰ νῦν Pl.*Lg*.686b; μ. νῦν (v.l. τοῦ νῦν) D.S.17.110; μ. καὶ νῦν Str.16.2.13; μέχρι πότε χηρεύομεν; Ach.Tat.4.1. II. Prep. c. gen., *even to, as far as*, 1. of Place, μέχρι θαλάσσης Il.13.143; μ. τοῦ γούνατος Hdt.2.80; μ. τῆς πόλεως Th.6.96, cf. X.*An*.1.7.6, al.: rarely following its case, ὀμφαλοῦ μ. Pl.*Lg*.925a, cf. *Supp.Epigr*.3.400.5 (Delph., iii B.C.). 2. of Time, τέο μέχρις; i.e. τίνος μέχρι χρόνου; how *long*? Il.24.128; μέχρις τεῦ; Callin.1.1: in Prose, μέχρι τούτου Hdt.1.4; μέχρι οὗ, μέχρι ὅσου, Pl.*Mx*.245a, Hdt.8.3, al.; μ. τοσούτου, ἕως ἄν.. Th.1.90; μ. τούτου, ..μέχρις ἂν ῥηθῶσιν Din.1.91, cf. Pl.*Phd*.81d: with the Art., τὸ μ. ἐμεῦ *up to* my time, Hdt.3.10, 5.115; μ. τῆς ἐκείνου ζόης *till the end of* his life, Id.3.160; μ. ἡμερέων ἑπτά Id.6.12; μέχρι Πυθίων Th.5.1; μέχρι ἡλίου δύνοντος *IG*1².188.4. 3. of Measure or Degree, μ. τοῦ δικαίου *so far as* consists with right, Th.3.82; μ. τοῦ δυνατοῦ Pl.*R*.498e; μ. ὑγιείας, μ. ἡδονῆς, ib.559a, *Grg*.500b; μ. θανάτου *Ep.Phil*.2.8. 4. with Numbers to express a round sum, *up to, about, nearly*, μ. δώδεκα X.*Smp*.2.8, etc.: sts. without altering the case of the Subst., τοὺς μ. τριάκοντα ἔτη γεγονότας Aeschin.2.133; but πίνειν ..τοὺς μ. ἐτῶν τριάκοντα Apollod.Car.5.19; μ. τινὸς πλήθους *up to* a certain number, Aen.Tact.15.3: hence, *just short of*, μ. κόρου μετρεῖσθαι J.*BJ*2.8.5. 5. in Hdt., μέχρι οὗ is sts. used like the simple μέχρι, μέχρι οὗ ὀκτὼ πύργων 1.181; μέχρι οὗ τροπέων τῶν θερινέων 2.19; μ. ὅτευ πληθώρης ἀγορῆς ib.173. III. as a Conj., *until*, c. ind., μέχρι.. ὁρμὴ ἐνέπεσε Th.4.4, cf. Pl.*Smp*.220d; μ. σκότος ἐγένετο X.*An*.4.2.4; μέχρι ἂν c. subj., ib.1.4.13, 2.3.24; μέχρις ἂν ἥλιος δύῃ *IG*12(5).647.17 (Ceos); μέχρις κε μένῃ Call.*Sos*.5.4: rarely without ἄν, μ. τοῦτο ἴδωμεν Hdt.4.119; μ. πλοῦς γένηται Th.1.137; μ. οὔ τι δόξῃ Id.3.28; μέχρι τέκῃ Call.*Sos*.5.5; μέχρις οὗ εἴπῃ Herod.2.43; μ. καταντήσωμεν *Ep.Eph*.4.13; μέχρις ἵνα ψαύσειε Call.*Dian*.28 (s.v.l.): c. inf., μ. σβεσθῆναι τὸ πῦρ App.*Hisp*.75; μέχρις ἧῶ δῖαν ἱκέσθαι Q.S.1.830; also μέχρι ἂν ἔξιν λαβεῖν Ceb.35. 2. *as long as, whilst*, c. ind., Th.3.10,98, Plb.1.62.4; μ. ἄν c. subj., μέχρις ἂν ζῶσιν πονεῖν Men.633; μέχρις ἂν ἐνδημῶσιν οἱ πρέσβεις Aen.Tact.10.11, cf. Epict.*Ench*.11; Dor. μέχρι κα ζώῃ *GDI*1807.7 (ii B.C.), al.—The -ι is elided in *IG*1².115.15, *Supp.Epigr*. l.c.—Cf. ἄχρι throughout and sub fin.

**μέχριπερ** or **μέχρι περ**, Conj., *so long as*, μ. περ ἡ τοῦ θεοῦ φύσις.. ἐξήρκει Pl.*Criti*.120e; μ. περ ἂν c. subj., Id.*Sph*.259a, al. 2. *until*, μ. ἐς ἀνθρώπων ἀπῆλθεν Luc.*Cyn*.13.

⊕**μή**, Elean μά [ᾱ] *SIG*9.5 (Olympia, vi B.C.). (Cf. Skt. *mā*, Arm. *mi* [from I.-E. *mē*], negative used in prohibitions):—*not*, the negative of the *will* and *thought*, as οὐ of *fact* and *statement*; μή rejects, οὐ denies; μή is relative, οὐ absolute; μή subjective, οὐ objective. (A few examples of μηδέ and μηδείς have been included.)

A. in INDEPENDENT sentences, used in expressions of *will* or *wish, command, entreaty, warning*, 1. with pres. imper., 2 pers., μή μ' ἐρέθιζε Il.1.32, al.; 3 pers., μή μευ πειράτω 9.345, etc.: rarely with aor. imper., μή.. ἔνθεο τιμῇ 4.410, cf. Od.24.248; in Att., μὴ ψεῦσον, ὦ Ζεῦ, τῆς.. ἐλπίδος Ar.*Th*.870; 3 pers., μή τις ἀκουσάτω Od.16.301, cf. Pi.*O*.8.55, *P*.5.23, A.*Th*.1041, S.*Aj* 1180; μηδεὶς νομισάτω, προσδοκησάτω, X.*Cyr*.7.5.73, Pl.*Ap*.17c: with pf. imper. 3 pers., μή τις ὀπίσσω τετράφθω Il.12.272; or 2 pers. when pf. = pres., μὴ κεκράγετε Ar.*V*.415. 2. with subj. (usu. 2 pers. of aor.), in prohibitions, μὴ δή με.. ἐάσῃς Il.5.684, cf. A.*Pr*.583 (lyr.), al.; μή τοί με κρύψῃς τοῦτο ib.625, cf. S.*Ph*.470; μὴ φθονήσῃς Pl.*Prt*.320c: coupled with pres. imper., μὴ βοηθήσητε τῷ πεπονθότι δεινά, μὴ εὐορκεῖτε D.21.211; 3 pers., μή.. γένηται Il.4.37, cf. Od.22.213; μὴ ματεύσῃ θεὸς γενέσθαι Pi.*O*.5.24: rarely, if ever, with 2 pers. pres. subj., μὴ κάμνῃς E.*IA* 1143 (leg. κάμῃς); 3 pers., μή τις οἴηται, = μὴ οἰώμεθα, Pl.*Lg*.861e: also with the hortative subj. used to supply the 1 pers. of the imper., pres. μὴ ἴομεν (= ἴωμεν) Il.12.216, etc.; μὴ διώκωμεν Hdt.8.109, etc.: aor. μὴ πάθωμεν X.*Cyr*.1.5.11, etc.: rarely with 1 sg., μή σε.. κιχείω Il.1.26, cf. 21.475, 22.123, S.*OC*174 (anap.). b. with pres. or aor. subj. in a warning or statement of fear, μή.. γένησθε *take care you do*

*not become*, Il.5.487; μὴ..ὑφαίνῃσιν *I fear..may prove to be weaving*, Od.5.356; αἷμα μὴ σοῖς ἐξομόρξωμαι πέπλοις E.*HF*1399: in Att. Prose, to make a polite suggestion of apprehension or hesitation, *perhaps*, μὴ ἀγροικότερον ᾖ τὸ ἀληθὲς εἰπεῖν Pl.*Grg.*462e, cf. *Tht.* 188d, Arist.*Pol.*1291a8, al.: in later Greek the ind. is found, μὴ ἡ ἔννοια ἡμῶν..ἀντιλαμβάνεται Dam.*Pr.*27. **3.** with fut. ind., a dub. usage (νεμεσήσετ' is subj. in Il.15.115), μηδεμίαν ἄδειαν δώσετε Lys.29.13; μὴ βουλήσεσθε (Pap. βούλη[σθ]ε) D.23.117; cf. μαλακὸν ἐνδώσετε μηδέν Ar.*Pl.*488. **4.** with past tenses of ind. to express an unfulfilled wish, μὴ ὄφελες λίσσεσθαι Il.9.698, cf. Od. 11.548; μή ποτ' ὤφελον λιπεῖν τὴν Σκῦρον S.*Ph.*969; εἴθε μή ποτ' εἰδόμαν Id.*OT*1217 (lyr.), cf. E.*IA*70, *Cyc.*186, X.*Cyr.*4.6.3. **5.** with opt. to express a negative wish, with pres., ἃ μὴ κραίνοι τύχη A.*Th.*426, cf. *Eu.*938 (lyr.): more freq. with aor., μὴ σέ γ' ἐν ἀμφιάλῳ Ἰθάκῃ βασιλῆα Κρονίων ποιήσειεν Od.1.386, cf. 403, 11. 613. **6.** in oaths and asseverations, ἴστω Ζεὺς.., μὴ μὲν τοῖς ἵπποισιν ἀνὴρ ἐποχήσεται ἄλλος Il.10.330; ἴστω νῦν τόδε Γαῖα.., μὴ.. Ποσειδάων..πημαίνει Τρῶας 15.41; μὰ τὴν Ἀφροδίτην.., μὴ ἐγώ σ' ἀφήσω Ar.*Ec.*1000, cf. *Av.*195, *Lys.*917. **7.** c. inf., when used as imper., μὴ δή μοι ἀπόπροθεν ἰσχέμεν ἵππους Il.17.501; μὴ πρὶν ἐπ' ἠέλιον δῦναι 2.413; οἷς μὴ πελάζειν A.*Pr.*712. **8.** freq. without a Verb, εἰ χρή, θανοῦμαι. Answ. μὴ σύ γε (sc. θάνῃς) S.*OC*1441; ἄπελθε νῦν. Answ. μὴ (sc. γενέσθω) ἀλλά *nay but*, Ar.*Ach.*458; in curt expressions, μὴ τριβὰς ἔτι (sc. ποιεῖσθε) S.*Ant.*577; μή μοι σύ *none of that* to me! E.*Med.*964; μή μοι πρόφασιν *no* excuses! Ar.*Ach.*345; μή μοί γε μύθους Id.*V.*1179.

**B.** in DEPENDENT clauses: **1.** with Final Conjs., ἵνα μή Il.19. 348, etc.; ὅπως μή D.27.5, al.; ὡς μή Il.8.37, A.*Pr.*53, al.; ὄφρα μή Il. 1.118, al.: with ὅπως ἄν and ὡς ἄν, *that so*, ὅπως ἄν..μηδέ Ar.*V.*178, Pl.*Grg.*481a; ὡς ἂν μή Od.4.749, Hdt.1.5; but **b.** μή alone, = ἵνα μή, *lest*, ἀπόστιχε μή τι νοήσῃ Ἥρη Il.1.522, cf. 587; λίσσεσθαι.., μή οἱ..χολώσαιτο φρένα κούρη Od.6.147: fut. ind. and aor. subj. in consecutive clauses, Ar.*Ec.*495 (lyr., dub. l.). **2.** in the protasis of conditional sentences, v. εἰ (for the exceptions v. οὐ), and with temporal conjunctions used conditionally, v. ἐπειδάν, ὅταν, ὅτε, etc. **b.** ὅτι μή *except*, ὅτι μὴ Χῖοι μοῦνοι Hdt.1.18, cf. Th.4.26; ὅτι μὴ πᾶσα ἀνάγκη Pl.*Phd.*67a; ὅσον μή ib.83a; ὅσα μὴ ἀποβαίνοντες *provided only that* they did *not* disembark, Th.4.16. **3.** in later Gr., with causal Conjs., ὁ μὴ πιστεύων ἤδη κέκριται, ὅτι μὴ πεπίστευκεν *Ev.Jo.*3.18, cf. Luc.*DMort.*21.2, *DDeor.*2.1; ἐπεὶ μή Id.*Hist.Conscr.*3, etc.: also after ὅτι and ὡς *that*, ὅτι μὴ ἐστὶν ἐπίπεδος οὕτως ἂν καταμάθοιμεν Cleom.1.8, cf. Luc.*Hist.Conscr.*29, *DDeor.*20.10. **4.** in relat. clauses, which imply a condition or generality, ὃς δὲ μὴ εἰδέ κω τὴν καννάβιδα *whoever*.., Hdt.4.74; ὃ μὴ κελεύσει (fort. κελεύσαι) Ζεύς *such a thing as*.., A.*Eu.*618, cf. 661, 899; λέγονθ' ἃ μὴ δεῖ *such things as* one ought *not*, S.*Ph.*583; λόγοις τοιούτοις οἷς σὺ μὴ τέρψῃ κλύων Id.*Ant.*691; ὅπου μὴ ἠθέλησεν Antipho1.7: freq. with subj., ᾧ μὴ ἄλλοι ἀοσσητῆρες ἔωσιν Od.4.165, al.: with ἄν, S.*OT*281: with opt., ἃ μὴ σαφῶς εἰδείη X.*Cyr.*1.6.19, etc.: less freq. with opt. and ἄν, Pl.*Phlb.*20a, *Lg.*839a; γένοιτο δ' ἂν ἐν ᾗ μή τι ἂν προσδοκήσειεν χώρᾳ ib.872d. **5.** c. inf., **a.** regularly from Homer on, exc. after Verbs of saying and thinking (but v. infr. c): after ὥστε or ὡς, ὥστε μὴ φρονεῖν A.*Pers.*725 (troch.), etc. (for exceptions v. οὐ): always when the inf. takes the Art., τὸ μὴ προμαθεῖν Pi.*O.*8.60; τὸ μὴ ἀμελεῖν μάθε A. *Eu.*86, cf. 749, *Pr.*624; λείπομαι ἐν τῷ μὴ δύνασθαι S.*OC*496. **b.** by an apparent pleonasm after Verbs of negative result signifying to *forbid*, *deny*, and the like, ὁ δ' ἀναίνετο μηδὲν ἑλέσθαι Il.18.500 (without μή ib.450); ἀντιδικεῖν Lys.6.12 (μηδέν); ἀντιλέγειν Th.5.49, Is.4. 15 (μηδέ); ἀπαγορεύειν Antipho5.34, And.4.9; ἀπειπεῖν Ar.*Av.*557, D.33.19, etc.; ἀπαυδᾶν Ar.*Eq.*1072; ἀπείργειν E.*Hel.*1559, al. (without μή S.*Aj.*70); ἀπιστεῖν Th.4.40; ἀπεγνωκέναι Lys.1.34; ἀποστερεῖσθαι Antipho2.4.1 (μηδέ); ἀποτρέπεσθαι Id.5.32 (μηδέν); ἀρνεῖσθαι, ἔξαρνος εἶναι, Ar.*Eq.*572, Hdt.3.67; ἐναντιωθῆναι Pl.*Ap.*32b; σχεῖν Hdt.1.158; παύειν (where the part. is more freq.) Ar.*Ach.*634; κωλῦσαι E.*Ph.*1269; ἐπάρατον ἦν μὴ οἰκεῖν Th.2.17: in these cases the Art. freq. precedes μή, τὸ δὲ μὴ λεηλατῆσαι..ἔσχε τόδε Hdt.5.101; ἐξομῇ τὸ μὴ εἰδέναι; S.*Ant.*535; εἴργειν τὸ μή..Th.3.1, etc.; also ἀπέφυγε τὰ σφῶν τὸ μὴ πίτνειν κακῶς S.*OC*1740 (lyr.): with Art. in gen., ἔχειν τοῦ μή..X.*An.*3.5.11; ἐμποδὼν γίγνεσθαι τοῦ μή..Id.*Cyr.*2.4.23. **c.** after Verbs of saying and thinking which involve an action of will, as in those signifying to *swear*, *aver*, *believe*, and the like; so after ὄμνυμι, Il.9.133, Od.5.179, Hdt.1.165, 2.179, Ar.*V.*1047, etc.; μαρτυρῶ Lys.7.11, D.45.15, etc.; ὁμολογῶ Pl.*Prt.*336b, *Smp.*202b, cf. *Phd.* 93d, etc.; ἐγγυῶμαι Pi.*O.*11(10).18, Pl.*Prt.*336d; πέπεισμαι Id.*Ap.* 37a, etc.; πιστεύω And.1.2, X.*An.*1.9.8, etc.: occasionally with other Verbs, φημί Id.*Mem.*1.2.39, Pl.*Tht.*155a; λέγω, προλέγω, Th. 5.49, 1.139; πάντες ἐροῦσι μή..X.*Cyr.*7.1.18; νομίζω ib.7.5.59, Th.6. 102; ἡγοῦμαι Pl.*Ap.*27d: very freq. in later Gr., *Ev.Matt.*2.12, Luc. *Peregr.*44, etc. **6.** with the part., when it can be resolved into a conditional clause, μὴ ἐνείκας, = εἰ μὴ ἤνεικε, Hdt.4.64; μὴ θέλων, = εἰ μὴ θέλεις, A.*Pr.*504; μὴ δολώσαντος θεοῦ, = εἰ μὴ ἐδόλωσε, Id.*Ag.* 273; μὴ δρῶν, = εἰ μὴ δρῴην, S.*OT*77, etc.: in a general or characteristic sense, δίδασκέ με ὡς μὴ εἰδότα, = *ut qui nihil sciam*, Id.*OC*1155, cf. *Ant.*1063, 1064; τίς πρὸς ἀνδρὸς μὴ βλέποντος ἄρκεσις; *one who* sees *not*, Id.*OC*73: in this signf. freq. with the Art., ὁ μὴ λεύσσων Id.*Tr.* 828 (lyr.); ὁ μὴ δουλεύσας Pl.*Lg.*762e; τῷ μὴ εἰργασμένῳ Antipho5. 65; τὸν..μὴ φροντίσαντα Lycurg.27, cf. 45, etc.: with causal significance, μὴ παρὼν θαυμάζεται S.*OT*289, etc.; ἄθλια πάσχω μὴ..μόνον βιαζόμενος Antipho2.2.4; ἑτέρας μηδεμιᾶς ὁμολογουμένης εἶναι Is.5.16; μηδενὸς ἐμποδὼν ὄντος D.3.8: very freq. in later Greek, *POxy.*38.16 (i A.D.), Luc.*DMeretr.*12.4, etc.: occasionally after Verbs of knowing and showing, S.*Ph.*79, *OC*656, 797, 1122, E.*Tr.*970, Th.1.76, 2. 17. **7.** with Substs., Adjs., and Advbs. used generically, with or without Art., τὰ μὴ δίκαια A.*Eu.*432; δίκαια καὶ μὴ δίκαια Id.*Ch.*78 (lyr.); τὸ μὴ 'νδικον S.*OT*682 (lyr.); τὸ μὴ καλόν Id.*Ant.*370 (lyr.); ἡ μὴ 'μπειρία, = τὸ μὴ ἔχειν ἐμπειρίαν, *want of* experience, Ar.*Ec.*115; ἡ μὴ ἐπιτροπή Pl.*Lg.*966c; δῆμον καὶ μὴ δῆμον ib.759b; ὁ μὴ ἰατρός Id. *Grg.*459b; νίκης μὴ κακῆς A.*Eu.*903, cf. *Th.*411; τῷ φρονοῦντι μὴ καλῶς Id.*Pr.*1012, cf. *Ag.*349, 927. **8.** after Verbs expressing *fear* or *apprehension* (cf. μὴ οὐ): **a.** when the thing feared is fut., mostly with subj.: with pres. subj., δεινῶς ἀθυμῶ μὴ βλέπων ὁ μάντις ᾖ *shall prove to be*.., S.*OT*747, cf. *Ant.*1113; ὅρα μὴ κυβεύῃς Pl.*Prt.*314a: more freq. with aor., δείδοικα..μή σε παρείπῃ Il.1.555, cf. 9.244, 13.745: with pf., *shall prove to have been*, δέδοικα μὴ περαιτέρω πεπραγμέν' ᾖ μοι S.*Tr.*663, cf. *Ph.*494, Hdt.3.119, 4.140, etc.: less freq. with fut. ind., X.*Cyr.*2.3.6, Ar.*Ec.*488, Pl.*Phlb.*13a: with opt. according to the sequence of moods and tenses: pres. opt., S.*Tr.*482, X.*An.*1. 10.9: aor., Od.11.634, etc.: pf., X.*Cyr.*1.3.10: with fut. opt. in oratio obliqua, Id.*HG*6.4.27, *Mem.*1.2.7, Pl.*Euthphr.*15d: with opt. and ἄν, S.*Tr.*631, X.*Vect.*4.41. **b.** when the action is pres. or past, the ind. is used, εἰσόρα μὴ σκῆψιν οὐκ οὖσαν τίθης S.*El.*584, cf. E.*Ion*1523, Ar.*Nu.*493, Pl.*La.*196c; ὅρα μὴ παίζων ἔλεγεν Id.*Tht.* 145b, cf. E.*Hel.*119; φοβούμεθα μὴ ἀμφοτέρων ἡμαρτήκαμεν Th.3.53, cf. E.*Or.*209, Pl.*Ly.*218d; δείδω μὴ δὴ πάντα θεὰ νημερτέα εἶπεν Od. 5.300. **c.** with ind. and subj. in consecutive clauses, E.*Ph.*93.

**C.** in QUESTIONS: **I.** direct questions, **1.** with ind., where a neg. answer is anticipated (but more generally in A.*Ag.*683 (lyr.), S.*OC*1502, *Tr.*316, Pl.*Grg.*488b), in Hom. only ἦ μή..; Od.6.200, 9.405; μή σοι δοκοῦμεν..; A.*Pers.*344, cf. *Pr.*249, 959, etc.: in Trag. and Att. freq. ἆρα μή; Id.*Th.*208, S.*El.*446, Pl.*R.*405a: for questions in which μή (μηδέ) follows οὐ, v. οὐ μή. **b.** in other questions, τί μὴ ποιήσω; what am I *not* to do? S.*El.*1276 (lyr.); τί μή; why *not?* Id.*Aj.*668 (s.v.l.); cf. μήν. **2.** with subj., when the speaker deliberates about a neg. action, μὴ οὕτω φῶμεν; Pl.*R.*335c, cf. 337b, 417b; ὁ τοιοῦτος μὴ δῷ δίκην; D.21.35; πῶς μὴ φῶμεν; Pl.*Tht.* 161e: with opt. and ἄν, πῶς ἄν τις μὴ θυμῷ λέγοι; how can a man *help being* excited when he speaks? Id.*Lg.*887c, cf. *Grg.*510d, X. *Mem.*3.1.10. **II.** indirect questions, freq. with Verbs implying *fear* and *apprehension* (cf. B.8), ὄφρα ἴδωμεν μὴ τοὶ κοιμήσωνται Il.10. 98, cf. 101, Od.21.395; περισκοπῶ μή πού τις..ἐγχρίμπτει S.*El.*898, cf. Th.2.13, etc.; also σκοπεῖσθαι πῶς ἂν μή..Isoc.5.8, cf. 15.6; later in simple indirect questions, ἐπυνθάνετο μὴ ἔγνω Ant.Lib.23.5. **2.** in questions introduced by εἰ, ἤρετό με..εἰ μὴ μέμνημαι Aeschin.2. 36 (εἰ οὐκ in same sense, 1.84): in the second part of a disjunctive question, εἰ..ἢ (or εἴτε) μή.., εἴτε..εἴτε μή.., A.*Eu.*468, 612, And.1.7, Pl.*Ap.*18a, *R.*457d, X.*Cyr.*2.1.7; εἴτε..εἴτε μή.., εἰ..ἢ οὔ, εἰ..ἢ μή without difference of meaning between μή and οὐ, Is.8.9; so also, τοὺς νόμους καταμανθάνειν εἰ καλῶς κεῖνται ἢ μή, ..τοὺς λόγους, εἰ ὀρθῶς διδάσκουσι τὸ πρᾶγμα ἢ οὔ Antipho5.14.

**D.** POSITION of μή. When the neg. extends its power over the whole clause, μή prop. precedes the Verb. When its force is limited to single words, it precedes those words. But Poets sts. put μή after the Verb, ὄλοιο μή πω S.*Ph.*961; φράσῃς..μὴ πέρα ib.332, cf. *OC*1522. **2.** μή is sts. repeated, μή, μὴ καλέσῃς Ar.*V.*1418, cf. S. *Aj.*190, *OC*210 (both lyr.).

**E.** PROSODY: in Trag. μή may be joined by synizesis with a following ει or ου, μὴ οὐ, μὴ εἰδέναι, S.*OT*13, 221, *Tr.*321, etc.: initial ε after μή is cut off by aphaeresis, μὴ 'πόθουν Id.*Aj.*962; μὴ 'μβαίνῃς Id.*OC*400; μὴ 'γώ Id.*Ph.*910: in Prose, μὴ 'κ *IG*1².115.11: μή folld. by α is sts. written μά..(v. μὴ ἀλλά, etc.); sts. separately, μὴ ἀδικεῖν A.*Eu.*85, etc.

**F.** μή in COMPOSITION, or joined with other Particles, as μὴ ἀλλά, μὴ γάρ, μὴ οὐ, μὴ ὅπως or ὅτι, μή ποτε, etc., will be found in alphabetical order.

**μὴ ἀλλά**, an elliptic phrase for μὴ γένοιτο, ἀλλά.., or μὴ λέγε τοῦτο, ἀλλά..: only used in answers, *nay but*.., *not so, but*.., σὲ δὲ ταῦτ' ἀρέσκει; Answ. μάλλα πλεῖν ἢ μαίνομαι Ar.*Ra.*103, cf. 611, 745, 751, Pl.*Alc.*1.114e, *Men.*75b; μὴ οὕτως, ἀλλ'..Id.*Prt.*318b; μηδαμῶς.., ἀλλὰ..Id.*Grg.*497b, *Phdr.*234e.

**μὴ γάρ**, an elliptic phrase, freq. in emphatic denial, or in assenting to a denial or prohibition, etc., *certainly not*, where Verb in imper. or opt. must be supplied from the context, μὴ λεγέτω τὸ ὄνομα .. Answ. μὴ γὰρ [λεγέτω] Pl.*Tht.*177e, cf. *Sph.*255b: not in a reply, μὴ γὰρ δὴ δίναν γ' Εὐρώτα (sc. ἔλθοιμι) E.*Tr.*210 (lyr.): in parenthesis, where it may be translated *much less* (cf. μὴ ὅτι), Aeschin.2.158; μὴ γὰρ τῆς πόλεώς γε μηδ' ἐμοῦ D.18.200.

**μηγενη**, *stabilitas*, *Gloss.* (dub.).

⊛ **μηδᾰμ-ά** (prop. neut. pl., v. μηδαμός), Adv. of μηδαμός, of Time, = μηδέποτε, and of Manner, *not at all*, freq. in Hdt. with another μή, or compd. of μή, μὴ μὲν γενέσθαι μηδαμὰ μέζονας ἀνθρώπους τῶν νῦν 1.68; μηδαμὰ μηδέν *never* anything, 7.50; ὄψιν, τὴν μηδαμὰ ὤφελον ἰδεῖν 3. 65; τόδ' ἴσθι μηδάμ' ἡμέρᾳ μιᾷ πλῆθος τοσουτάριθμον..θανεῖν A.*Pers.* 431, cf. *Pr.*526 (lyr.), S.*OC*517 (lyr.), 1104, 1698 (lyr.); ἀκοῦσαι μηδὲν ὑπ' ἐμοῦ μηδαμὰ κακὸν τὸ λοιπόν Ar.*Th.*1162; μηδαμὰ κάθοδον εἶναι ἐς Ἀλικαρνησσόν *SIG*45.39 (Halic., v B.C.): with tmesis, οὐ γὰρ μή ποτε τοῦτο δαμ' ᾖ prob. in Parm.7.1 (*Journ.Philol.*21.73). **-εῖ**, Dor. Adv. *nowhere*, *Schwyzer*323 C34 (Delph., iv B.C.). **-ῆ**, Adv., = μηδαμοῦ, μ. χάλα A.*Pr.*58; = μηδαμά, μὴ φύγητε μ. S.*Ph.*789; μὴ προσ-

παίζοντας μηδαμῇ μηδαμῶς οἰκέταις Pl.*Lg.*778a; τοὺς μηδαμῇ μηδαμῶς τοῦ πράγματος ἐγγύς D.45.38. **-ινός**, ή, όν, *good for nothing*, Hsch. s. v. οὐθένεια. **-όθεν**, Adv. of μηδαμός, *from no place*, X.*Cyr.* 8.7.14; μ. ἄλλοθεν *from no other place*, Pl.*Phd.*70e, *GDI* iv p.876 (Chios, iv B.C.), etc.; μηδεὶς μ., Lat. *nullius filius*, D.21.148. **-όθι**, Adv. *nowhere*, γῆς Plu.2.360a, Luc.*Herm.*31. **-οῖ**, Adv. *nowhither*, prob. to be read for μηδαμοῦ or -μῇ in S.*Ph.*256, X.*Lac.* 3.4. **-ός**, ή, όν, for μηδὲ ἁμός, *not even one*, i.e. *not any one, no one*, only in pl. μηδαμοί, *none*, Hdt.1.143, 144, 2.91, etc.: for neut. pl. v. μηδαμά. **-όσε**, Adv. *nowhither*, μ. ἄλλοσε Pl.*R.* 499a. **-οῦ**, Adv. *nowhere*, Th.1.35, Pl.*Lg.*958d; μ. ἄλλοθι Id.*Phd.* 68a: c. gen., μ. τῶν ὄντων, Lat. *nusquam gentium*, Id.*Prm.*162c: metaph., ὅπου τὸ χαίρειν μ. νομίζεται is *of no account*, A.*Eu.*423, cf. 624, S.*Aj.*1007; μηδαμοῦ παρά τισιν εἶναι X.*Mem.*1.2.52: as two words, μηδὲ ἁμοῦ *IG*1$^2$.16.11 (v B.C.). **-ῶς**, Adv. of μηδαμός, = μηδαμῇ, Hdt.4.83, A.*Pr.*339, S.*OC*278; μ. ἄλλως Pl.*Lg.*838d: in replies, as a strong neg., Id.*Prt.*334d, Men.*Sam.*217.

**μηδάτερος** [ᾰ], α, ον, Dor. for μηδέτερος, *Leg.Gort.*1.22, *SIG*56.24 (Argos, v B.C.), *Foed.Delph.Pell.*1 A 4 (iii B.C.).

⊕**μηδέ**, (μή, δέ) neg. Particle (cf. οὐδέ): A. as Conj., *and not* (Ep. also, *but not*), *nor*, connecting two whole clauses, used with the same constructions as μή, μή τι σὺ ταῦτα.. διείρεο μηδὲ μετάλλα Il.1.550, etc.: without a neg. preceding, 4.302, etc.; τεκνοῦσθαι, μηδ' ἄπαιδα θνήσκειν A.*Ag.*754 (lyr.), cf. *Eu.*714, *Supp.*409; ὕδατος, μελίσσης, μηδὲ προσφέρειν μέθυ S.*OC*481, cf. Th.7.77. 2. in μηδέ.. μηδέ.. the first μ. may belong to μηδέ A, e.g. Il.4.303 sq., or to μηδέ B, e.g. Pl.*R.*391c; μήτε.. μηδέ Pi.*I.*2.45, Pl.*Prt.*327d; but μήτε cannot follow μηδέ:—for μηδέ after οὐδέ, v. οὐ A. II. 3.

B. as Adv., joined with a single word or phrase, *not even, not either*, Il.21.375, Od.4.710, etc.; repeated emphatically, μηδ' ὅντινα γαστέρι μήτηρ κοῦρον ἐόντα φέροι μηδ' ὃς φύγοι let *not* the babe unborn —*no let not even* it escape, Il.6.58; τὸ μήποτ' αὖθις μηδ' ἀναστῆναι A. *Ag.*569:—for μηδέ τι v. μήτις.

**μηδεῖα**, Aeol. fem. of μηδείς (q.v.), unless, = Μήδεια, Sapph.162.

**Μήδειοι**, οἱ, = Μῆδοι, Pi.*P.*1.78, Call. in *PSI*9.1092.46.

⊕**μηδείς**, μηδεμία, μηδέν (i.e. μηδὲ εἷς, μηδὲ μία, μηδὲ ἕν): fem. μηδὲ ἴα or μηδεΐα (or -ία) *IG*12(2).6.12 (Mytil.):—*not one, not even one, nobody* (in neut. *nothing*), once in Hom. (who elsewh. uses μή τις, v. μήτις), ἀναίνετο μηδὲν ἑλέσθαι Il.18.500; μή πως.. μηδὲν ἀνύσσῃς Hes.*Op.*395; μηδὲν ἄγαν Pi.*Fr.*216, etc.: rare in pl. (μηδαμοί being used in Ion.), μηδένες ἄλλοι X.*HG*5.4.20; μηδένας Pl.*Euthd.*303c. 2. μηδὲ εἷς (so written) is found in Att. Inscrr., as *IG*1$^2$.114.41, 2$^2$.487.9 (μηδ' hενί ib.1$^2$.73.6), but is used esp. in an emphatic sense, *not even one*, μηδὲ ἕν Ar.*Pl.*37: freq. with an intervening Particle or Prep., μηδ' ἂν ἕνα Pl.*Cra.*414d; μηδ' ἐν ἑνὶ χρόνῳ Id.*Prm.*156c; μηδ' ἐξ ἑνός Id.*Phdr.*245d; μηδ' ἐφ' ἑνί Id.*R.*553d; μηδὲ περὶ ἑνός Id.*Tht.*171c; μηδ' ὑφ' ἑνός, μηδ' ὑπὸ μιᾶς, Id.*Smp.*222d, *Alc.*1.122a; μηδὲ ὑφ' ἑνός *IG*1$^2$.32.8. II. *nobody, naught, good for naught*, κἄμ' ἴσον τῷ μ. S.*OC*918: pl., οὐ γὰρ ἠξίου τοὺς μηδένας Id.*Aj.*1114; μηδέν or τὸ μηδέν as Subst., *naught, nothing*, κεἰ τὸ μ. ἐξερῶ Id.*Ant.*234; μ. λέγειν to say *what is naught*, X.*Cyr.*8.3.20, etc.; ἡ ἡμετέρη εὐδαιμονίη.. ἀπέρριπται ἐς τὸ μ. Hdt.1.32; τοῦ μηδενὸς ἀξίη Id.6.137; ἐπὶ μηδὲν ἔρχεσθαι S.*El.*1000; ἐς τὸ μ. ἥκειν E.*Hec.*622; of persons, τὸ μ. *a good-for-nothing*, τὸ μ. εἶναι, of a eunuch, Hdt.8.106; τοιγὰρ σὺ δέξαι μ' ἐς τὸ σὸν στέγος, τὴν μηδὲν ἐς τὸ μ. S.*El.*1166; κἂν τὸ μ. ὦ Id. *Tr.*1107; τὸ μ. ὄντας Id.*Aj.*1275; ὁ μ. ὢν ib.767; ὅτ' οὐδὲν ὢν τοῦ μηδὲν ἀντέστης ὕπερ ib.1231, cf. 1094, E.*Hec.*843, etc.; ἧττον αὐτοῖς ἔνι ἢ τὸ μ., i.e. it is a mere impossibility, Pl.*Tht.*180a; also μ. εἶναι without the Art., Luc.*Rh.Pr.*2. III. neut. μηδέν as Adv., *not at all, by no means*, μηδὲν ἐγκέλευ' ἄγαν A.*Pr.*72, cf. 344; μ. διαφέρειν πλὴν ὀνόματι Pl.*Plt.*280a, etc.: with an Adv., μ. αἰνικτηρίως A.*Pr.* 949: freq. with Comp., μ. μᾶλλον, ἧσσον, etc., S.*Aj.*280, 1329, etc.—When other negatives, also derived from μή, are used with it, they do not destroy, but strengthen the negation, μηδέποτε μηδὲν αἰσχρὸν ποιήσας ἔλπιζε λήσειν *never* hope to escape, when you have done *anything* base, Isoc.1.16; cf. μηθείς.

**μηδέ-ποθι**, Adv. *nowhere*, *IG*5(2).6.34 (Tegea). **-ποτε**, Dor. **-ποκα** ib.2$^2$.1126.11 (Amphict. Delph., iv B.C.): Adv.:—*never*, with pres. and past tenses, as well as fut., Ar.*Pl.*1000, Pl.*Prt.*313b. II. μηδέ ποτε *and never*, Hes.*Op.*717, 744, A.*Pr.*1073 (anap.). **-πω**, Adv. *nor as yet, not as yet*, Id.*Pr.*741, *Pers.*435, etc. ⊕**-πώποτε**, Adv. *never yet*, D.18.271.

**Μηδεσικάστη**, ἡ, fem. pr. n., prop. *adorned with prudence*, from μήδεσι (dat. pl. of μῆδος) and κέκασμαι, Il.13.173.

⊕**μηδέτερ-ος** or **μηδ' ἕτερος**, α, ον, Dor. **μηδάτερος** (q.v.), *neither of the two*, Th.4.118, Pl.*R.*470a, etc.; also divisim, οἱ μηδὲ μεθ' ἑτέρων Th.2.67, cf. 72; μηδὲ καθ' ἕτερα Id.7.59. Adv. μηδετέρως *in neither way*, Arist.*Po.*1460$^b$35; μ. ἔχοντες *being indifferent* (neither friends nor foes), ib.1453$^b$19. **-ωθεν**, Adv. *from neither side*, Corn.*ND*17, Lib.*Decl.*1.9. **-ωσε**, Adv. *to neither side*, Hp.*Superf.*4, Th.4.118, Paus.2.1.4.

**μὴ δή**, *lest*.., Il.16.81, etc.; but **μὴ δῆτα**, *nay do not*.., A.*Pr.*1075, S.*OT*830, 1153, etc.

**Μηδ-ίζω**, *side with the Medes*, Hdt.4.144, Th.3.62, X.*HG*3.1.6, D. 59.95. ⊕**-ικός**, ή, όν, *Median*: τὰ Μηδικά (sc. πράγματα) *the Median affairs*, esp. *the war with the Medes*, the name given by Gr. historians to the great Persian war, Th.1.14, Arist.*Pol.*1303$^b$33, etc.; ὁ Μ. πόλεμος Th.1.90, 95; Μ. ἐσθής, i.e. *silken* garments, Procop.*Pers.*1.20: Comp. τὰ -ώτερα Philostr.*VA*1.25. Adv. Comp. -ώτερον, κατεσκευασμένος ib.3.26. II. Μηδικὴ πόα, *lucerne, Medicago sativa*, Ar.*Eq.* 606; Μ. alone, Thphr.*HP*8.7.7, Dsc.2.147 (by some written μηδίκη, Hdn.Gr.1.316, Eust.1967.27, cf. D.S.3.43 codd.). 2. μηδική, ἡ, = ἑλένιον, Dsc.1.28, Plin.*HN*14.108. III. μῆλον Μηδικόν, v. μῆλον (B). IV. ὀπὸς Μηδικός a form of silphium juice, prob. *assafoetida*, Dsc.3.80, Philum.*Ven.*3.2. V. Μηδικόν, τό, perh. a tomb *in Persian style*, *JHS*22.124.

**μήδιον**, τό, a plant, *Campanula lingulata*, Dsc.4.18:—written **μήδειον**, Zopyr.ap.Orib.14.16.2, etc.; cf. sq.

**μήδιος**· μαλακός, καὶ βοτάνης εἶδος, καὶ λίθος τις Μηδιάτης, Hsch.

**Μηδ-ίς** (sc. γυνή), ἴδος, ἡ, *Median woman*, Hdt.1.91. **-ισμός**, ὁ, *leaning towards the Medes, Medism*, Id.4.165, 8.92, Th.1.95, 135, D.23.205. **-ιστί**, Adv. *in Median fashion*, Str.11.3.3. **-οκτόνος**, ον, *Mede-slaying*, *APl.*4.62.

**μηδόλως**, Adv., for μηδ' ὅλως, *not at all*, Cerc.17.21, Gal.*Protr.*1, etc.

⊕**μήδομαι**, Il.2.360, etc.: impf. ἐμήδετο *h.Merc.*46; Ep. μήδετο (v. infr.): fut. μήσομαι S.*Tr.*973 (lyr.), E.*HF*1075 (lyr.); Ep. 2 sg. μήσεαι Od.11.474: aor. ἐμήσατο, μήσατο (v. infr.), also μῆστο Hsch.: pf. μέμηδα cj. for μέμηλα *h.Merc.*437: (μέδω, μῆδος):—*to be minded, intend*, αὐτός τ' εὖ μήδεο *resolve* well thyself, Il.2.360; ἅσσ' ἂν ἐμοί περ αὐτῇ μηδοίμην what *counsels I should take* for myself, Od.5.189. 2. c. acc. rei, *plan and do cunningly* or *skilfully, plot, contrive*, in Ep. mostly in bad sense, σφιν κακὰ μήδετο μητίετα Ζεύς Il.7.478; μοι Ζεὺς μήσατο λυγρὸν ὄλεθρον Od.24.96; Αἴγισθος ἐμήσατο λ. ὄ. 3. 194; φρεσὶ μήδετο θέσκελα ἔργα Hes.*Sc.*34; πατρὸς μεγάλ' ἀνδράσι μηδομένοιο Id.*Fr.*96.85: also c. acc. pers. et rei, κακὰ μήσατ' Ἀχαιούς he *wrought* them mischief, Il.10.52, cf. 22.395, 23.24, Od.24.426: in Lyr. and Trag. (usu. lyr.), μέγα ἔργον μ. Pi.*N.*10.64; δίκας ἀδίκοισι B.17.42; πρὸς κακοῖς κακὰ μήσεται E.*HF*1075, cf. *Ph.*799, A. *Ch.*605; ἐπ' ἀνδρὶ τοῦτ' ἐμήσατο στύγος ib.991, cf. S.*Ph.*1114. 3. after Hom., simply, *contrive, invent*, ἄρτια Pi.*O.*6.94; τέχνας καὶ πόρους A.*Pr.*477; ἄφθιτα Ar.*Av.*689 (lyr.); ὅσια καὶ νόμιμα Id.*Th.* 676 (lyr.); ὑμὶν κῦδος.. ἐμήσατο Χῖος ἀοιδός Theoc.22.218; τί δὲ μήσωμαι; what shall I *attempt*? A.*Th.*1062, cf. S.*Tr.*973; τί σοι μήσομαι; E.*Hipp.*592; *make skilfully*, μέλισσα μέλι μηδομένα Simon.47: c. acc. et inf., *contrive that* a thing *should be*, ἄπιστον ἐμήσατο πιστὸν ἔμμεναι Pi.*O.*1.31. II. *take care, keep watch*, ib.106, so prob. in Hes.*Fr.*96.76.—Poet. word, used twice by Ar. (lyr.), Trag. only in lyr. exc. A.*Pr.* l.c., and in late Prose, Luc.*Astr.*6, 21.

**μηδοπόθεν**, Adv. *nowhence*, *SIG*484.4 (Delph., iii B.C.).

**μηδοπότερος**, α, ον, = μηδέτερος, *AP*3.12 tit.

⊕**μῆδος** (A), εος, τό, (μέδω) poet. Noun, only in pl. μήδεα, *counsels, plans, arts*, mostly with collat. notion of *prudence* or *cunning*, δόλους καὶ μ. πυκνά Il.3.202; βουλαί.. μ. τ' ἀνδρῶν 2.340; πεπνυμένα μ. εἰδώς 7.278, Od.2.38; πυκινὰ φρεσὶ μ. ἔχοντες Il.24.674; θεοῖς ἐναλίγκια μ. ἔχοντα Od.13.89; μάχης μ. *plans* of fight, Il.15.467, 16.120; μ. πατρός Hes.*Th.*398; μήδεσιν ἁμοῖς Pi.*P.*4.27, cf. 10.11; ἐπικότοισι μήδεσι A. *Pr.*601 (lyr.); σός τε πόθος σά τε μ. longing for thee and thy *counsels*, Od.11.202.

**μῆδος** (B), εος, τό, Ep. Noun, only pl. μήδεα, *genitals*, Od.18.67, 87, 22.476, Androm.ap.Gal.14.41; μ. φωτός Od.6.129, cf. Call.*Fr.* 50P.; v. μέζεα. (In late Prose, Ant.Lib.17.6.) 2. *urine*, λαγόνων ἀπὸ μήδεα χεύη Opp.*C.*4.441.

⊕**Μῆδος**, ὁ, *Mede, Median*: hence, *Persian*, Hdt.5.77, etc.

**μηδοστισοῦν**, better written μηδ' ὅστις οὖν, *no one whatever*; **μηδοτιοῦν**, better μηδ' ὁτιοῦν, *nothing whatever*, Thgn.64, Pl.*Plt.* 300c.

**μηδοσύνη**, ἡ, *counsel, prudence*, Simm.25.1, Phot.

**μηδοτίη** [ῑ], Boeot. for μηδ' ὁποία (dat. sg. fem.), *Schwyzer* 503$^a$ adn.

**Μηδοφόνος**, ον, = Μηδοκτόνος, *AP*7.243 (Loll. Bass.), *IG*2.2719, 3.116.

**μηθᾰμ-ά**, later form for μηδαμά, *IG*4$^2$(1).74.8 (Epid., iii B.C.). **-όθεν**, later form for μηδαμόθεν, ib.12(5).526.3 (Ceos, iii B.C.). **-οῦ**, later form for μηδαμοῦ, μ. φαίνεσθαι 'to be *nowhere*', i.e. *of no account*, *SIG* 1261.19 (Tab. Defix.): written in Pl.*Phd.*68b in *PPetr.*1 p.18. **-ῶς**, later form for μηδαμῶς, *UPZ*79.8 (ii B.C.).

⊕**μηθείς**, fem. μηθεμία only in *PPetr.*2 p.42 (iii B.C.); neut. μηθέν:— = μηδείς, μηδέν, freq. in Inscrr. and Pap. from iv B.C., *IG*2$^2$.43.37, al., Men.*Epit.*145, *Pk.*129, *PPetr.*1 p.80, *PCair.Zen.*18.7, al. (iii B.C.), etc.: but rarely after the Christian era, once in *NT*, *Act.Ap.*27.32, cf. *POxy.*495.17 (ii A.D.).

⊕**μηθέτερος**, α, ον, = μηδέτερος, Arist.*Cael.*282$^b$11.

**μηθίδη**, ἡ, an Egyptian plant, Plu.2.359b (dub. l.).

**μῆκα**· κέρατα, Hsch.

**μηκ-άζω**, = sq., Nic.*Al.*214. **-άομαι**, pres. only late, Procop. *Goth.*2.17, cf. Phryn.*PS*p.59 B., Sch.Od.9.124: poet. aor. part. μᾰκών (v. infr.): pf. part. μεμηκώς: fem. μεμᾰκυῖα: impf., formed from pf., ἐμέμηκον Od.9.439:—*bleat*, of sheep, μυρίαι ἑστήκασιν.., ἀζηχὲς μεμακυῖαι Il.4.435; θήλειαι δ' ἐμέμηκον ἀνήμελκτοι περὶ σηκούς Od.9.439 (used by Hom. of goats only in the Subst. μηκάς); of a hunted fawn or hare, *scream, shriek*, ὁ δέ τε προθέῃσι μεμηκώς Il.10.362: part. μακών only in the phrase, κὰδ δ' ἔπεσ' ἐν κονίῃσι μακών fell *shrieking* to earth, of a wounded horse, stag, or boar, 16.469, Od. 10.163, 19.454; of a man, 18.98.—Onomatopoeic word. **-άς**, άδος, ἡ, *bleating one*, in Hom. always of goats, in pl., μ. αἶγες Il.11.383, Od.9.124, 244, al., cf. Antiph.1.52.8; also μ. ἄρνες E.*Cyc.*189. II. as Subst., = αἴξ, S.*Fr.*509, *AP*9.123 (⟨Leon.⟩); λευκὴ μ. Luc.*D*

*Meretr.*7.1: pl., Theoc.1.87, 5.100. **-ασμός**, ὁ, *bleating*, τραγοῦ, αἰγῶν, Plu.*Sull.*27, Poll.5.87.

**μηκεδᾰνός**, ή, όν, (μῆκος) *long*, *AP*11.345, Nonn.*D.*9.260, al.

**μηκέτι**, Adv., (formed from μή, ἔτι, with κ inserted on a false analogy with οὐκέτι) *no more, no longer, no further*, Il.13.292, Hes.*Op.* 174, Pi.*O.*1.5, A.*Ch.*805(lyr.), *IG*1².75.29, etc.

**μηκ-ή**, ἡ, = μηκασμός, μ. ἐλάφου Ael.*NA*7.46, cf. Sch.Il.4.435, Sch. Od.9.124. **-ηθμός**, ὁ, = foreg., Opp.*C.*2.359. **-ητικός**, ή, όν, *bleating*, Sch.Il.11.383, 23.31.

**μηκικός**, ή, όν, (μῆκος) *in longitude*, μετάβασις, θέσις, Procl.*Hyp.*5. 6,9.

**μήκιστος**, η, ον, Dor. **μάκιστος** [ᾱ], the only form used by Trag.: irreg. Sup. of μακρός (formed from μῆκος, as αἴσχιστος from αἶσχος), *tallest*, τὸν δὴ μήκιστον καὶ κάρτιστον κτάνον ἄνδρα Il.7.155, cf. Od.11. 309. 2. *greatest*, μάκιστον σέλας A.*Fr.*281.1; μείζονα [πηδήματα] τῶν μακίστων S.*OT*1301 (anap.); τὰ μάκιστ' ἐμῶν κακῶν E.*Hipp.*818 (lyr.); τὸ μήκιστον τεράων A.R.4.1364. 3. *longest*, in point of Time, ἐπὶ τὸ μήκιστον ἀνθρωπίνου αἰῶνος X.*Ages.*10.4: neut. μήκιστον as Adv., *for a very long time* or *in the highest degree*, *h.Cer.*258 (s.v.l.); ὅτι δύνᾳ μάκιστον.. ἐξιδοῦ see to it *as far as possible*, S.*Ph.*851 (lyr.); τί νύ μοι μήκιστα γένηται; what is to become of me *at last?* Od.5. 299,465; τὸ μ. *at longest*, Luc.*Herm.*50; ἐπὶ μ. *for the longest time*, Id.*Demon.*1. 4. *farthest*, X.*Cyr.*4.5.28, A.R.1.82; μ. ἀφέστηκεν τοῦ πείθειν Phld.*Rh.*1.270S.

⊕ **μηκόθεν**, Adv., (μῆκος) *from afar*, στᾶσα ἔφη Aesop.243; μ. βλέπειν Paul.Aeg.5.42.

**μηκοποιέω**, *lengthen*, Eust.32.5.

**μῆκος**, Dor. **μᾶκος** Archyt.1: εος, τό:—*length*, of a club, τόσσον ἔην μῆκος, τόσσον πάχος so large was it *in length*, so large in thickness, Od. 9.324; φιλότης ἴση μ. τε πλάτος τε Emp.17.20, cf. Hdt.1.181, etc.; ἐς μῆκος Id.2.155; εἰς τὸ μῆκος Lxx *Ge.*12.6; ἐν μήκει καὶ πλάτει καὶ βάθει Pl.*Sph.*235d, cf. Gorg.3, Arist.*Ph.*209ᵃ5; ἐπὶ μῆκος *lengthwise*, ἐπὶ μ. ἔκτασις Id.*HA*504ᵃ15, al.; κατὰ μῆκος Id.*Mete.*387ᵃ2; μ. ὁδοῦ A.*Fr.* 378, Hdt.1.72, etc.; πλοῦ Th.6.34; μᾶκος ἔδικε threw *a long distance*, Pi.*O.*10(11).72: pl., μήκη καὶ βάθη καὶ πλάτη Pl.*Plt.*284e, cf. Iamb.*Comm.Math.*26; τὰ μεγάλα μ. great *lengths*, Pl.*Prt.*356d. b. *height*, of a wall, Ar.*Av.*1130; of persons, *stature*, Od.20.71; μῆκος *in height*, 11.312; εἰς μ. αὐξάνεσθαι X.*Lac.*2.6. c. generally, μήκει *in linear measurement*, Pl.*Tht.*147d, cf. 148a; *linearity*, *one-dimensional magnitude*, opp. ἐπίπεδον, βάθος, Id.*Lg.*817e: in Arith., *in the first power*, *Theol.Ar.*3, 4. 2. of Time, μ. χρόνου A.*Pr.*1020; ἐν μ. χρόνου S.*Tr.*69; ἐν χρόνου τινὸς μήκεσιν ἀπλέτοις Pl.*Lg.*683a; μ. λόγου, μ. τῶν λόγων, a *long* speech, A.*Eu.*201, S.*OC*1139; ἐν μήκει λόγων διελθεῖν Th.4.62; μῆκος *at length*, εἰπέ μοι μὴ μ., ἀλλὰ σύντομα S. *Ant.*446. 3. of Size or Degree, *greatness, magnitude*, ὄλβου Emp. 119; μῆκος *in greatness*, ἔοικεν ἄλλη μ. οὐδὲν ἡδονῇ S.*Ant.*303. 4. *longitude*, Str.1.4.5, Cleom.2.1, Ptol.*Alm.*2.12, Vett.Val.260.5, etc. 5. in Prosody, *length*, opp. βραχύτης, Arist.*Po.*1456ᵇ32, D.H.*Comp.*15: pl., μήκη καὶ βραχύτητας προσῆπτε Pl.*R.*400b. 6. *first line of phalanx*, Ascl.*Tact.*2.5. (From same Root as μακρός. Hence μήκιστος, Sup. of μακρός.)

**μή κοτε**, Ion. for μή ποτε, v. μήποτε II.

**μηκότης**, ητος, ἡ, = μῆκος, Gal.19.478.

**μηκύν-σις**, εως, ἡ, *lengthening*, in prosody, Sch.D.T.p.49 H. **-τέον**, *one must prolong*, Socr.*Ep.*30.5, Iamb.*in Nic.*p.25 P. **-τικός**, ή, όν, *fit for lengthening*, A.D.*Adv.*166.26; τῆς φύσεως τῶν στοιχείων (viz. η, ω) οὔσης μ. Sch.Heph.p.95 C. **-ω**, Dor. **μᾱκ-** Pi. (v. infr.): fut. -ῠνῶ Th.4.17, Ion. -ῠνέω Hdt.2.35: aor. ἐμήκῡνα Id.3.60:—Med., v. infr. 7:—Pass., pf. μεμήκυσμαι Phld. (v. infr.), Eust. ad D.P.64:—*lengthen, prolong*, Hp.*Aph.*1.12; τὸ μέτωπον τῆς τάξεως X.*Eq.Mag.*4. 9; τὰς ὁδοὺς Id.*Mem.*3.13.5; μηκυνθέν τε καὶ σχὸν πλάτος Pl.*Plt.*282e; of Time, μ. χρόνον, βίον, E.*HF*87, 143:—Pass., νοσεύματα μηκυνθέντα Hp.*Aër.*7; ἐμηκύνετο ὁ πόλεμος Th.1.102. 2. *delay, put off*, τέλος Pi. *P.*4.286. 3. μ. λόγον, λόγους, *spin out* a speech, *speak at length*, Hdt. 2.35, S.*El.*1484; τέκν' εἰ φανέντ' ἄελπτα μηκύνω λόγον Id.*OC*1120; τὴν ἀπολογίαν Isoc.11.44; λόγους μακροτέρους Th.4.17: without λόγον, *to be lengthy* or *tedious*, Hdt.3.60, Ar.*Lys.*1132, Pl.*R.*437a, D.H. *Comp.*23; μ. περί τινος *enlarge* upon.., Demetr.*Eloc.*71: acc. objecti, μ. τὰ περὶ τῆς πόλεως, τὴν ὠφελίαν, *talk at length about, dwell upon*.., Th.2.42,43:—Pass., *to be expounded at length*, αὖθις ταῦτα μηκυνθήσεται Epicur.*Nat.*14.5; μεμηκυσμένον σύγγραμμα Phld.*Po.*5. 26; *to be continually repeated*, D.H.*Comp.*12; *to be dwelt upon*, Demetr.*Eloc.*137. 4. μ. βοήν *raise a loud* cry, S.*OC*489. 5. Gramm., *lengthen* a syllable, Str.10.5.8:—Pass., D.H.*Comp.*15, Plu.2.275f, A.D.*Adv.*146.18; φωνῆεν μηκυνόμενον a vowel *capable of being scanned long*, as αιυ, Heph.1.4. 6. Arith., *multiply by a fresh factor*, *Theol.Ar.*24, 48. 7. Med., ἐμακύναντο κολοσσόν *reared a tall* statue, *AP*6.171.

**μηκυσμός**, ὁ, *lengthening*, esp. of vowels, Eust.81.6.

⊕ **μήκων**, Dor., Arc. **μάκ-**, Theoc.7.157, *IG*5(2).514.16 (Lycosura, ii B.C.): ωνος, ἡ (ὁ Arist. (v. infr. II. 2), Polem.Hist.88, Polyaen.8. 6.1):—*poppy*, esp. *opium poppy*, *Papaver somniferum*, μήκων δ' ἑτέρωσε κάρη βάλεν ἐνὶ κήπῳ Il.8.306, cf. Ar.*Av.*160, Thphr.*HP*1.12.2 (s. v.l.), Theoc.l.c.; μάκωνσι λευκαῖς *IG*l.c.; μ. ἥμερος, κηπευτή, Dsc. 4.64, Gal.6.548; μ. Ἡρακλεία *frothy poppy*, *Silene venosa*, Thphr.*HP* 9.12.5; μ. ἀφρώδης Dsc.4.66; μ. κερατῖτις *horned poppy*, *Glaucium flavum*, Thphr.*HP*9.12.3, Dsc.4.65 (but = λεοντοπέταλον, Ps.-Dsc. 3.96); μ. μέλαινα *corn poppy*, *Papaver Rhoeas*, Thphr.*HP*9.11.9, Dsc. 4.64 (μέλας Ps.-Dsc.ibid.); μ. ῥοιάς *P. hybridum*, Thphr.*HP*9.12.4, Dsc.4.63; μ. ἀγρία, = μ. μέλαινα, ib.64; μ. ἀγριωτέρα *windrose*, *Papaver argemone*, ibid. 2. a single *poppy-seed*, Archim.*Aren.*2.4; collectively, μ. ἁδρά Hp.*Mul.*2.192; μ. μεμελιτωμένη Th.4.26; ὀπὸς μήκωνος *opium*, Asclep.ap.Gal.14.138, etc. 3. *poppy-head*, Thphr. *HP*4.8.10: as an architectural ornament, Paus.5.20.5. II. *quasi-liver* of testaceous animals (ὀστρακηρά), Arist.*HA*530ᵃ15, 547ᵃ16. 2. *ink-bag of the cuttle-fish*, Id.*Fr.*334 (masc.), Ael.*NA* ap. Suid. III. *a metallic sand*, Poll.7.100. IV. *the part of the ear at the root under the lobe*, Id.2.86. V. μ. ἀφρώδης, = πέπλος, *spurge*, Dsc.4.167; so μ. alone, as a purgative, freq. in Hp., *Mul.*2.124, 192, al., *Morb.*3.16; ὀπὸς μήκωνος *Mul.*2.201; μ. alone, = τιθυμαλλίς, Dsc.4.164. (Etym. dub.; OHG. *māgo*, Germ. *mohn*, OSlav. *makŭ* are prob. borrowed.)

**μηκων-άριον**, τό, Dim. of foreg., Androm.ap.Gal.14.130. **-ειος**, α, ον, *flavoured with opium*, ἄρτοι Philostr.*Gym.*44. II. **-ειον**, τό, *opium*, S.E.*P.*1.81, Sch.Nic.*Al.*434. 2. v. μηκώνιον. **-ικός**, ή, όν, *poppy-like*, σπέρματα Thphr.*HP*9.20.1. 2. *of the poppy kind*, prob. in ib.1.11.2. **-ιον**, τό, = μήκων V, Hp.*Acut.*(*Sp.*)72, *Fist.* 7. 2. *opium*, Phld.*Mort.*9. 3. = τιθύμαλλος, Thphr.*HP*9.8. 2. II. *discharge from the bowels of new-born children*, Arist.*HA* 587ᵃ31, Gal.19.176: also written -ειον, Sor.1.81. ⊕ **-ίς**, Dor. **μᾱκ-**, ίδος, ἡ, *wild lettuce*, *Lactuca scariola*, Nic.*Th.*630, *Inscr.Prien.*171, *BGU*1118.13; in full, μ. θρίδαξ Gal.13.173. 2. a form of *spurge*, Hp.*Int.*7. II. as Adj., = μηκώνειος, μακωνίδες ἄρτοι Alcm.74 B. **-ῖτις**, ίτιδος, ἡ, = πέπλος, *spurge*, Gal.19.22. II. *like a poppy*, name of *a precious stone*, Plin.*HN*37.173.

**μηκωνο-ειδής**, ές, *like a poppy*, Suid. **-φόρος** (sc. γῆ), ἡ, *opium-bearing* land, *Sammelb.*4369ᵇ50 (iii B.C.), *PLond.ined.*2361ʳ (iii B.C.).

**μηλάνθεμον**, τό, = ἀνθεμίς, *Dyer's camomile*, *Anthemis tinctoria*, Dsc.3.137.

**μηλάνθη**, ἡ, = μηλολόνθη, Herod.9a.2. II. *apple-blossom*, Philostr.*Im.*1.28.

**μηλάπιον**, τό, kind of *apple*, Archig.ap.Gal.13.173, Plin.*HN*15. 51.

**μηλάτης**, ου, ὁ, *shepherd*, Eust.877.50, Zonar.; μηλάταν τὸν ποιμένα Βοιωτοί, and **μηλόται**· ποιμένες, Hsch.

**μηλάτων** [ᾰ], metaplast. gen. pl. for μήλων, *sheep*, Lyc.106.

⊕ **μηλᾰφάω**, (μήλη) *probe* (cf. ψηλαφάω), Sophr. in *Cod.Paris.*ap. Cohn *Zu den Parömiographen* 82, Hsch., *EM*818.21, Eust.1394.30.

⊕ **μηλέα**, ἡ, (μῆλον B) *apple-tree*, *Pyrus malus*, μηλέαι ἀγλαόκαρποι Od.7.115, cf. Thphr.*HP*3.3.1, *CP*2.11.6, Androt.ap.Ath.3.82c, etc.; μ. ἐαρινή is a variety, Thphr.*HP*2.1.3, *PCair.Zen.*486.2 (iii B.C.); μ. Ἀρμενική *apricot*, *Prunus Armeniaca*, Gal.6.76; μ. γλυκεῖα *jenneting*, *Pyrus praecox*, Thphr.*HP*4.13.2; μηλείη in Nic.*Al.*230, Nonn.*D.*12. 275; ἡ Περσικὴ μ. *citron*, *Citrus Medica*, Thphr.*HP*1.11.4, *CP*1.11.1 (but, *peach*, *Prunus persica*, in Gal.12.76); also called ἡ Μηδικὴ μ. Thphr.*CP*1.18.5, cf. *HP*1.13.4; μ. Κυδωνία *quince*, *malus Punica*, Dsc.1.115. [Disyll. in Od.24.340.]

**μηλεανορεῖ** (fort. -αγορεῖ)· δημηγορεῖ, Hsch.

**μήλειος**, ον, also α, ον, (μῆλον A) *of* or *belonging to a sheep*, στέαρ Hp.*Nat.Mul.*32; κρέα Hdt.1.119; μ. φόνος slaughter *of sheep*, E.*El.* 92; γάλα Id.*Cyc.*218. II. (μῆλον B) *of the apple*, σπέρματα, στύπος, Nic.*Al.*238, A.R.4.1401.

**μήλη**, ἡ, *probe*, Hp.*VC*10, *AP*11.126, etc. 2. = σμίλη, τῇ μ. τέμνων τοὺς ὑμένας Gal.8.55, cf. 11.300.

**Μηλιάδες**, only in Dor. form **Μᾱλ-**, αἱ, (μῆλον B) *nymphs of the fruit-trees*, Poll.9.122,127; but Μ. νύμφαι nymphs *of Malis*, S.*Ph.* 725 (lyr.).

**Μηλιάς**, v. Μήλιος II, μηλίς (C).

**μηλῐανθμός**, ὁ, = μήλων ἰαυθμός, *sheepfold*, Lyc.96.

**Μηλῐεύς**, *inhabitant of Malis* (Μηλίς), Ion. pl. Μηλιέες Hdt.7.132, etc.; early Att. Μηλιῆς Th.3.92, etc.; later the Dor. form Μᾱλ- was used, Arist.*Pol.*1297ᵇ14, D.S.17.57: as Adj., Μηλιεὺς κόλπος *the Sinus Maliacus*, Hdt.4.33: **Μηλῐακός**, ή, όν, Th.3.96, etc.; fem. **Μηλὶς** λίμνα, = Μηλιεὺς κόλπος, S.*Tr.*636 (lyr.); Μ. γῆ, χώρη, Hdt.7. 198, 8.31; cf. Μηλιάδες.

**μηλίζω**, (μῆλον B) *to be of a quince-yellow*, Dsc.1.120, Archig.ap. Orib.44.26.1, Gal.12.150.

**μηλῐνο-ειδής**, ές, *of a quince-yellow*, Thphr.*HP*6.2.8, 7.3.1. **-εις**, εσσα, εν, = foreg., Nic.*Th.*173.

⊕ **μήλῐνος**, η, ον, Aeol., Boeot. **μάλινος**, (μῆλον B) *of an apple-tree*, ὕσδων μ. Sapph.4. II. *made of apples* or *quinces*, μύρον μ. Thphr. *Od.*26, cf. Dsc.1.45. 2. *of a quince-yellow*, ἄνθος Thphr.*HP*9.18. 1; ἐσθῆτες, καρυωτοί, Ath.12.539e, D.S.2.53, cf. Dsc.3.137; χιτῶνα μάλινον *Schwyzer* 462*B*34 (Tanagra, iii B.C.).

**Μήλιος**, α, ον, Dor. **Μάλ-** *IG*5(1).1*B*1 (Sparta, v B.C.), 12(3). 1097, al. (Melos):—*from the island of Melos*, *Melian*, Thgn.672, Th.3. 91, etc.; λιμὸς Μ., prov. of famine, because of the extremities to which the island was reduced at its siege, Ar.*Av.*186. II. ἡ Μηλία, with or without γῆ, *a greyish aluminous earth*, which painters mixed with mineral colours, to give them consistency, Dsc.5.159 (γῆ μηλίνη (μιλ- codd.) in *Gloss.*); also Μηλιάς Hp.*Ulc.*14, Thphr.*Lap.* 62, Plu.2.436c: used as a styptic, στυπτηρίη Μηλίη Hp.*Steril.*225: written -εία Id.*Ulc.*11,18; corrupted to μηθεία Orib.*inc.*24.2.

**μηλίς** (A), ίδος, ἡ, (μῆλον B) = μηλέα, Ibyc.1; Dor. **μᾱλίς** Theoc. 8.79.

**μηλίς** (B), ίδος, ἡ, *a distemper of asses*, prob. *glanders*, Arist.*HA* 605ᵃ16.

**μηλίς** (C), ίδος, ἡ, *yellow pigment*, Plu.2.58d; cf. Μηλιάς, Μήλιος II.

⊕ **Μηλίς**, ίδος, ἡ, v. Μηλιεύς.

**μηλίσκον**, τό, Dim. of μῆλον B.II.5, *IG*11(2).162*B*32 (Delos, iii B.C., pl.).

**μηλίτης** [ῑ], ου, ὁ, (μῆλον B) οἶνος μ. *apple* or *quince* wine, Plu.2.648e, Dsc.5.20. II. (μῆλον A) μ. ἀριθμοί arithmetical problems *about a number of sheep*, Sch.Pl.*Chrm*.165e, cf. Hero *Deff*.135.5.

**μηλιωτός**, v. σμιλιωτός.

**μηλόβαι**· μηλοβάται, ποιμένες, Hsch. (post μηλοφόροι).

**μηλο-βᾰτέω**, *tup sheep*, Opp.*C*.1.388. **-βᾰφής**, ές, *coloured a quince-yellow*, [λίθοι] Ph.Byz.*Mir*.2. **-βολέω**, *pelt with apples*, Sch.Ar.*Nu*.993. **-βοσις**, ἡ, fem. pr. n., *Sheep-feeder*, *h.Cer*.420. **-βοσκός**, όν, *sheep-feeding*, δώματα E.*Hyps.Fr*.5(3).24. **-βοτέω**, *graze sheep*, Hsch. **-βοτήρ**, ῆρος, ὁ, *shepherd*, Il.18.529, *h.Merc*.286. **-βότης**, ου, ὁ, Dor. **-τας**, = foreg., Pi.*I*.1.48, E.*Cyc*.53(lyr.). **-βοτος**, ον, *grazed by sheep*, epith. of pastoral districts, Pi.*P*.12.2, B.5.66, A.*Supp*.548(lyr.); χώραν μ. ἀνιέναι turn a district *into a sheep-walk*, i.e. lay it waste, Isoc.14.31, cf. Ph.2.473, D.L.6.87; ἐπηράσατο εἰς ἀεὶ μηλόβοτον εἶναι (sc. τὴν Καρχηδόνα) App.*BC*1.24, cf. *AP*9.103 (Mund.): metaph., μ. γυναίοις τὴν ἀρχὴν ἀνῆκεν Philostr.*VA*5.27, cf. *VS*1.21.4. **-γενής**, Dor. **μᾱλ-**, ές, *sheep-born*, πῶϋ μ. a flock *of sheep*, Philox.3.7. **-δᾰΐκτας**, α, ὁ, *sheep-slaying*, λέων B.8.6. **-δόκος**, ον, *sheep-receiving*, i.e. in sacrifice, Πυθών Pi.*P*.3.27. **-δροπῆες**, Aeol. **μᾱλ-**, οἱ, *apple-gatherers*, Sapph.93. **-δωράκινον**, τό, = Lat. *duracinum*, *Gloss*. **-ειδής**, ές, = μηλινοειδής, Dsc.4.68 codd., Gal.13.509. **-θύτης** [ῠ], ου, ὁ, *where sheep are sacrificed*, Πυθών B.7.39, cf. E.*Alc*.121 (lyr., dub. l.); βωμὸς μ. a *sacrificial* altar, Id.*IT*1116(lyr.). **-καρπον**, τό, = ἀριστολόχεια στρογγύλη, Ps.-Dsc.3.4. **-κίτριον**, τό, *citron*, Gal.13.290. **-κόμος**, Dor. **μᾱλ-**, ον, *sheep-protecting*, βόαυλα *Hymn.Is*.164. **-κοπικός**, ή, όν, *for pulping fruit*, λίθοι *PSI*3.237.9 (v/vi A.D.); unless μυλοκοπικός is meant. **-κτόνος**, ον, *sheep-killing*, Hsch. s.v. οἰσφάγῳ σιδήρῳ. **-κῠδώνιον**, τό, *quince*, Aët.16.65.

⊛ **μηλολόνθη**, ἡ, *cockchafer*, Ar.*Nu*.764, Artem.2.22; ἔχει ἐν ἐλύτρῳ τὰ πτερά Arist.*HA*$490^{a}15$, $532^{a}23$; τὸ πτερὸν ἔχει ἐν κολεῷ ib.$531^{b}25$: **μηλολάνθη**, Poll.9.122,124:—Dim. **μηλολόνθιον**, τό, Sch.Ar.*V*.1332.

**μηλο-μᾰχία**, ἡ, *pelting match with apples*, Chares 9 J. **-μελι**, ιτος, τό, *honey flavoured with quince*, Dsc.5.21, Colum.12.47, Artem.1.60.

**μῆλον** (A), τό, *sheep* or *goat*, ἢ βοῦν ἠέ τι μῆλον Od.12.301 (cf. 299); μῆλον, ζατρεφέων αἰγῶν ὅς τις φαίνηται ἄριστος 14.105; elsewh. Hom. uses the pl. (to distinguish the gender, an Adj. is added, ἄρσενα μ. *rams, wethers*, Od.9.438; ἔνορχα μ. Il.23.147) to denote *sheep* or *goats*, ἔνθα δὲ πολλὰ μῆλ', ὄϊές τε καὶ αἶγες, ἰαύεσκον Od.9.184; ὡς δὲ λέων μήλοισιν.. ἐπελθών, αἴγεσιν ἢ ὀΐεσσι Il.10.485: generally, *small cattle*, opp. βόες, βόες καὶ ἴφια μ. 9.406, cf. Hes.*Op*.786,795, etc.; μ. καὶ βοῶν ἀγέλας Pi.*P*.4.148; μ. καὶ ποίμνας S.*Aj*.1061: abs., of *sheep*, ἄργυφα μ. Od.10.85; μήλων εὐπόκοις νομεύμασιν A.*Ag*.1416; of Europa's *bull*, Simon.28; so μυκηθμοῖσι καὶ βρυχήμασιν.. μήλων *of herds*, A.*Fr*.158: generally, *beasts*, opp. men, γαῖαν ἀνθρώποισι καὶ εὔφρονα μήλοις Pi.*O*.7.63; esp. of *sacrificial beasts*, ib.80, A.*Ag*.1057, etc.; also of *beasts of chase*, S.*Fr*.1069:—Lyc.106 has metaplast. gen. pl. μηλάτων. (Not found in Prose, exc. Hdt.ap.Sch.Il.4.476. The Dor. form is **μῆλον** (not μᾶλον), Pi.*P*.4.148, 9.64, al.; also in pr. nn., Εὔμηλος *IG*12(3).540 (Thera), etc.; Boeot. **μεῖλον** in Πισίμειλος ib.7.3193.12 (Orchom., iii B.C.), etc.: cf. OIr. *mīl* '(small) animal', Dutch *maal* 'young cow'.)

**μῆλον** (B), τό, Dor. and Aeol. **μᾶλον**, *apple* or (generally) any *tree-fruit*, Il.9.542, Od.7.120, Hes.*Th*.215, 335 (whereas in Id.*Op*. only μῆλον (A) is found), Hdt.1.195, 2.92, 7.41; χνοῦς ὥσπερ μήλοισιν ἐπήνθει Ar.*Nu*.978; χρύσια μ. Theoc.29.37; μ. ἄγριον *crab*, *Pyrus acerba*, Dsc.1.115.4; μ. Ἀρμενιακόν *apricot*, *Prunus armeniaca*, Id.1.115.5, Gal.6.594 (μ. ἐαρινά *PCair.Zen*.33.13 (iii B.C.)); μ. Ἠπειρωτικόν *rose-apple*, Dsc.1.115.4; μ. Κυδώνιον *quince*, Hp.*Vict*.2.55, Dsc.1.115.1, Gal.6.563, *SIG*1171.15 (Lebena); μ. Μηδικόν *citron*, *Citrus medica*, Dsc.1.115.5 (μ. κίτριον Gal.12.77); μ. Περσικόν *peach*, *Prunus persica*, Id.6.592; τῶν Ποντικῶν ἐκείνων ἃ καλοῦσι μῆλα, of a kind of gourd, ib.563. 2. *seed-vessel* of the rose, Thphr.*HP*6.6.6. II. pl., metaph., of a *girl's breasts*, Ar.*Lys*.155, *Ec*.903, Theoc.27.50. 2. *cheeks*, *PPetr*.3 p.2, al. (iii B.C.), *AP*9.556 (Zon.), Ruf.*Onom*.46, Luc.*Im*.6, *Arch.Pap*.4.271 (iii A.D.): in sg., μ. ἀριστερόν *BGU*998.4 (ii B.C.), etc.: but in Theoc.14.38, τὰ σὰ δάκρυα μᾶλα ῥέοντι thy tears run *like apples*, i.e. *big round tears and sweet withal*. 3. *swellings under the eye*, Hsch. s.v. κύλα. 4. *tonsils*, Ruf.*Onom*.64. 5. *cups shaped like apples*, *IG*11(2).161*B*41, al. (Delos, iii B.C.). (Cf. Lat. *mālum*, perh. borrowed from Gr.)

**μηλο-νομεύς**, έως, ὁ, = sq., *AP*9.452. **-νόμης**, ου, ὁ, Dor. **-μας**, *shepherd* or *goatherd*, *herdsman*, E.*Alc*.573(lyr.). **-νομιαῖος**, α, ον, = ἐννόμιος, Hsch. ⊛**-νόμος**, ον, *tending goats* or *sheep*, Σάκαι μ. the *nomad* Sacae, Choeril.3: as Subst., = μηλονόμης, E.*Cyc*.660 (lyr.). ⊛**-πάρειος** [ᾰ], Aeol. **μᾱλοπάραυος**, ον, *apple-cheeked*, Theoc.26.1. **-πέπων**, ονος, ὁ, *melon*, *Cucumis melo*, Gal.6.566, Antyll.ap.Orib.10.20.4, Mich.*in PN*81.8. **-πλᾰκοῦς**, οῦντος, ὁ, *quince-cake*, Gal.6.603:—hence Dim. **-ούντιον**, τό, Paul.Aeg.3.37.

**μηλός**, = ἥσυχος, ἥμερος, χαῦνος, *EM*584.18.

⊛ **μηλο-σκόπος** κορυφή, the top of a hill *from which sheep* or *goats* (μῆλα) *may be watched*, *h.Hom*.19.11. ⊛**-σόη**, ἡ, *sheep-track* (Rhod.), Hsch.; cf. μαλοσόα. **-σπορος**, ον, *set with fruit-trees*, ἀκτά E.*Hipp*.742(lyr.). **-σσόος**, ον, *sheep-protecting*, *AP*6.334 (Leon.). **-σφᾰγέω**, *slay sheep*, ἱερὰ μ. *offer sheep* in sacrifice, S.*El*.280: abs., μ. δαιμόνων ἐπ' ἐσχάραις E.*Fr*.628: generally, *offer sacrifice*, βουθύτοις ἐπ' ἐσχάραις Ar.*Av*.1232, cf. Porph.*Abst*.1.57; μ. εἰς ἀσπίδα Ar.*Lys*.189 (hence perh. to be read in A.*Th*.43 for ταυροσφ–): comically, *offer*, οἴνου σταμνίον Ar.*Lys*.196. **-σφᾰγία**, ἡ, *sacrifice of sheep*, Hsch. (pl.). **-τρόφος**, ον, *sheep-feeding*, Ἀσίη Archil.26; Ἀσίς A.*Pers*.763; Ἀρκαδία B.10.95; Λιβύη Orac.ap.Hdt.4.155.

**μηλοῦχος**, ὁ, (μῆλον B.II) *girdle that confines the breasts*, *AP*6.211 (Leon.).

**μηλο-φόνος**, ον, *sheep-slaying*, ἆται A.*Ag*.730 (lyr.), cf. Opp.*C*.3.263. **-φορέω**, Dor. **μᾱλ-**, *carry apples*, Theoc.*Ep*.2. **-φορία**, ἡ, *office of the* μηλοφόροι, Clearch.5. ⊛**-φόρος**, Dor. **μᾱλ-**, ον, *bearing apples*, καρπός E.*HF*396 (lyr.); epith. of Demeter at Megara (said to be from μῆλον A), Paus.1.44.3; and so Μαλοφόρος alone at Selinus, *IG*14.268 (v B.C.); οἱ μ. the king of Persia's body-guard, *because they had gold* or *silver apples* at the butt-end of their spears, Hsch. **-φύλαξ** [ῠ], ἄκος, ὁ, ἡ, *one who watches sheep*, *APl*.4.233; or *apples*, Sch.E.*Hipp*.742. **-φυλλον**, τό, = μυριόφυλλον, Ps.-Dsc.4.114. **-χρους**, ουν, = μήλινος II.2, ὀφθαλμοί *Hippiatr*.38.

⊛ **μήλοψ**, οπος, ὁ, ἡ, (μῆλον B, ὄψ) *looking like an apple*, *yellow*, μήλοπα καρπόν, i.e. the *ripe* corn, Od.7.104.

⊛ **μηλόω**, (μήλη) *probe* a wound, Hp.*Morb*.1.6, Ar.*Fr*.614:—Med., *sound* the bladder, Ruf.*Ren.Ves*.12: metaph., *probe* a matter, Cic.*Att*.12.51.2. II. in Med., *dye* wool, Eust.1394.33.

**μηλώδης**, ες, = μήλινος II.2, Gal.*Nat.Fac*.3.7, cf. *An.Ox*.1.280, *EM*584.13.

⊛ **μήλωθρον**, τό, = ἄμπελος λευκή, Thphr.*HP*3.18.11, 6.1.4, Dsc.4.182. II. *dyed wool*, Eust.1394.32.

**μηλών**, ῶνος, ὁ, *orchard*, f.l. for καμηλών (cj.) in *EM*130.29, Arc.13.3.

**Μήλων**, ὁ, epith. of Heracles, to whom μῆλα were sacrificed, Poll.1.31, Hsch.

⊛ **μηλώσιος**, ὁ, epith. of Zeus as *guardian of sheep*, *IG*9(1).702 (Corc.), 12(5).48 (Naxos).

**μήλωσις**, εως, ἡ, *probing*, Hp.*Fract*.31 (pl.), Sor.1.17; *use of the probe*, Hp.*VC*10.

**μηλωτή**, ἡ, (μῆλον A) *sheepskin*, *any rough woolly skin*, Philem.25, *PTeb*.38.22 (ii B.C.), Lxx 3*Ki*.19.13, *Ep.Hebr*.11.37, *OGI*629.32 (ii A.D.), A.D.*Synt*.191.9, Sch.Ar.*V*.670. II. (μήλη) = sq., Erot. s.v. κάτοπτρον.

**μηλωτ-ίς**, ίδος, ἡ, *probe*, Dsc.*Eup*.1.75, Antyll.ap.Orib.44.22.2, Erot. s.v. μήλη, Gal.2.574; cf. foreg. II. **-ρίδιον**, τό, Dim. of sq., Aët.16.108. **-ρίς**, ίδος, ἡ, *instrument for probing*, esp. for cleaning the ears, Antyll.ap.Orib.44.23.53, Gal.19.85; wrongly supposed to be a compound of μηλόω, οὖς, Id.13.407.

⊛ **μήμη**, ἡ, *grandmother*, *Milet*.7 p.67.

**μημωτά**· ψεκτά, Hsch. (leg. μωμητά).

⊛ **μήν**, Dor. (Epich.78, etc.), Aeol. (Sapph.*Supp*.23.5, etc.), and old Ep. **μάν** (in Hom. always folld. by a vowel exc. Il.5.895, 765, whereas μήν is folld. by a consonant exc. in Il.19.45; original μάν has prob. been changed to μέν exc. when the metre prevented), a Particle used to strengthen asseverations, *verily*, *truly*; a synonym of μέν but stronger, and like it always following the word which begins the clause, ὧδε γὰρ ἐξερέω, καὶ μ. τετελεσμένον ἔσται and so *verily*.., Il.23.410; ἴστε μὰν.. ye know *doubtless*, Pi.*I*.4(3).35: freq. with imper., ἄγε μ. on *then*, Il.1.302; ἄγρει μάν 5.765; ἄναγε μάν A.*Ch*.963 (lyr.); ἕπεο μάν S.*OC*182 (lyr.). II. after other Particles, 1. **ἦ μήν**, *now verily*, *full surely*, ἦ μὴν καὶ πόνος ἐστίν Il.2.291, cf. *h.Ap*.87, Hes.*Sc*.101; ἦ μάν Il.2.370, 13.354, Sapph. l c., Pi.*P*.4.40, al. (εἶ μάν *IG*5(1).1390.27 (Andania, i B.C.)): strengthd., ἦ δὴ μάν Il.17.538: freq. later in strong protestations or oaths, c. inf., ὄμνυσι δ' ἦ μὴν λαπάξειν A.*Th*.531, cf. S.*Tr*.1186, X.*An*.2.3.26: in negation, ἦ μ. μή.. Th.8.81, etc. (but also ὀμνύω μὴ μὰν φρονησεῖν *SIG*527.36 (Crete, iii B.C.)): in Prose also to begin an independent clause, ὀμνύω.., ἦ μ. ἐγὼ ἐθυόμην X.*An*.6.1.31; καὶ νὴ τὸν κύνα, ..ἦ μ. ἐγὼ ἔπαθόν τι τοιοῦτον Pl.*Ap*.22a. 2. **καὶ μήν**, sts. simply to add an asseveration, v. sub init., cf. Pi.*N*.2.13, etc.; καὶ δὴ μάν Theoc.7.120: freq. to introduce something new or deserving special attention, καὶ μὴν Τάνταλον εἰσεῖδον Od.11.582, cf. 593, A.*Pr*.459, *Pers*.406, etc.; esp. in dramatic Poets to mark the entrance of a person on the stage, *here comes*.., Id.*Th*.372, E.*El*.339; also ὅδε μ. Αἵμων S.*Ant*.626 (anap.), etc.; of new facts, *and besides*, *nay more*, καὶ μήν..γε A.*Pr*.982, cf. Ar.*Pax*369, X.*Smp*.4.15, etc.; in Orators to introduce new arguments, καὶ μήν..γε Pl.*Tht*.153b, D.21.56; to introduce a counter-argument, Ar.*Nu*.1185, Pl.*Grg*.452c; καὶ μὴν καί D.27.30, etc.: also in answers, to denote approbation or assent, ἀλλ' ἢν ἐφῇς μοι..λέξαιμ' ἂν ὀρθῶς. Answ. καὶ μ. ἐφίημι *well*, I allow it, S.*El*.556; μὴ νῦν διάτριβ', ἀλλ' ἄνυε πράττων.. Answ. καὶ μ. βαδίζω Ar.*Pl*.413 (v.l.), cf. *Ra*.895, E.*Hec*.317; so καὶ μ...γε Pl.*R*.426e, etc. 3. **ἀλλὰ μήν**, yet *truly*, Id.*Pers*.233, etc.; ἀλλὰ μάν Ar.*Ach*.765; ἀλλὰ μήν..γε Id.*Ra*.258; to allege something not disputed, Pl.*Tht*.187a: rarely separated, ἀλλ' ἐστὶ μ. οἰκητός S.*OC*28; ἀλλ' οὐδ' ἐγὼ μ... E.*Hec*.401: more strongly, ὅμως μ. Pl.*Plt*.297d. 4. **ναὶ μήν**, *above all*, Emp.76.2. 5. **οὐ μήν**, *of a truth* not, Il.24.52, A.*Ag*.1068, etc.: elsewh. in Hom. οὐ μάν, Il.12.318, etc.; μὴ μάν (Att. μὴ μήν) *oh* do not, 8.512, 15.476, etc.; ἀλλ' οὐ μάν 17.41; ἀλλ' οὐ μάν..γε S.*OC*153 (lyr.); οὐδὲ μάν Pi.*P*.4.87. 6. **ὡς μήν**, = ἦ μήν, ὀμμνύω Δία..ὡς μ. κρινεῖν τὰ ἀντιλεγόμενα *Delph*.3(1).362 i 40. III. after interrogatives, τί μ.; *well*, what of it? A.*Eu*.203, Pl.*Tht*.145e, etc.; τί μ. οὔ *well*, why not? E.*Rh*.706 (lyr.); πῶς μ.; *well, but how*..? X.*Cyr*.1.6.28; τίνος μ. ἕνεκα; ibid.; ποῦ μ.; to express surprise, Pl.*Tht*.142a; ἀλλὰ πότε μήν; X.*Smp*.4.23. IV. with adversative force, esp. after a neg., so that

it is equivalent to μέντοι, νῦν ἐμὲ μὲν στυγέει.., ἔσται μὰν ὅτ' ἄν.. Il. 8.370–373; οὐ μὴν ἄτιμοι.. τεθνήξομεν A.Ag.1279; ἀνάγκη μὲν καὶ ταῦτ' ἐπίστασθαι.., οὐδὲν μ. κωλύει κτλ. Pl.Phdr.268e, cf. Grg.493c, R.529e, etc.; χαλεπῶς ἔχει ὑπὸ τραυμάτων, μᾶλλον μ. αὐτὸν αἱρεῖ τὸ νόσημα Id.Tht.142b; expressed more strongly by γε μ., Pi.P.7.18, A.Th.1067 (anap.), S.OC587, X.Cyr.6.1.7, etc.; also οὐ μ...γε A. Pr.270, Th.538; οὐδὲ μ. ib.809, Ch.189; οὐ μ. οὐδέ *nor yet indeed*, Th. 1.3,82, etc.; οὐ μὰν οὐδέ Il.4.512; ἀλλ' οὐ μὰν οὐδέ 23.441:—on οὐ μὴν ἀλλά, v. ἀλλά II. 5.

* μήν, ὁ, v. μείς. II. Μήν, an Anatolian divinity, IG2[2].1365,1366, etc.; nom. sg. Μείς Supp.Epigr.4.647.2, 648.3 (Lydia).

**μην-ἀγυρτέω**, v.l. for μητραγυρτέω in D.H.2.19 (ap.Eus.PE2.8). * **-ἀγύρτης**, ου, ὁ, *a priest of Rhea, who made rounds of begging visits* (cf. μητραγύρτης), Ph.2.316, Cels.ap.Orig.Cels.1.9 (v.l.), Poll.7.188 (v.l.), Aesop.290, Hsch., Phot., Suid.; title of plays by Antiphanes (as v.l.) and Menander.

**μηναῖος**, α, ον, *lunar*, Orac.ap.Lyd.Mens.3.8.

**μηνάνθος**, ὁ, *dwarf water-lily, Limnanthemum nymphoides*, Thphr. HP4.10.1.

**μηνάς**, άδος, ἡ, = sq., E.Rh.534 (lyr.).

**μήνη**, ἡ, *moon*, Il.19.374, Emp.42.3, A.Pr.797, E.Fr.1009: rare in Prose, Pythag.ap.Iamb.Protr.21.ιζ'; as a goddess, h.Hom.32.1, Pi.O.3.20. II. f.l. in Ar.Av.1115; cf. μείς I.3 b. III. Alch., *silver*, Ps.-Democr.p.48 B.

**μηνιάζω**, = μηνιάω, Et.Gud.d. s.v. ἐνεκότουν.

* **μηνιαῖος**, α, ον (ος, ον Antyll.ap.Orib.9.3.1), *monthly*, ἀπόκρυψις Placit.2.29.5; περίοδος Str.3.5.8, Gal.7.500; φορά IG2[2].1368.46; διαγραφή PRyl.2.206(b) (iii A.D.); τὰ μ. the *menses* of women, Placit.5. 18.2, Ph.2.305; μ. κάθαρσις Alex.Aphr.Pr.2.57. 2. ὧραι μ. 'seasons' (quarters) *of the month*, Antyll. l.c. II. *a month old*, Lxx Nu.3.15, al.; μ. ὕδωρ Hp.Mul.2.188. III. *a month long*, νύξ Ant.Diog.9; χρόνος Gem.1.8, cf. Cleom.1.7; παραλλαγή, παράλλαγμα, Gem.8.22,19.

**μηνίαμα**, ατος, τό, = μήνιμα, Lxx Si.40.5.

* **μηνιάρχης**, ου, ὁ, *monthly prefect*, POxy.84.6 (iv A.D.), etc.:—also **-αρχος**, ὁ, ib.53.3 (iv A.D.).

**Μηνιασταί**, οἱ, *worshippers of* Μήν, IG12(1).917 (Rhodes).

**μηνιαστεία**, ἡ, *monthly service*, PFlor.322.168 (iii A.D.).

**μηνιάω**, = μηνίω, Lxx Si.10.6, D.H.Rh.9.16, Ph.2.31, Ael.NA6. 17: Ep. 3 pl. pres. μηνιόωσιν A.R.2.247; πρός τι Charito 1.2.

**μηνίγγιον**, τό, Dim. of μῆνιγξ, Gloss.

**μηνιγγό-τρωτος**, ον, *having an injury to the dura mater*, Gal. in Berl. Sitzb.1901.1263. **-φύλαξ** [ῠ], ἄκος, ὁ, a metallic *protector* to prevent injury to the μῆνιγξ in operations on the skull, Cels.8.3, Heliod.ap. Orib.44.11.2, Gal.2.686, Alex.Trall.1.14; also used of a *dressing*, Heliod.ap.Orib.46.19.4.

**μῆνιγξ**, ιγγος, ἡ, *membrane*, Hp.Carn.3; of the *membrane* of the eye, Emp.84.7 (pl.), Arist.GA781[a]20; *drum of the ear*, Id.Pr.961[a]38; esp. *membrane enclosing the brain, dura mater*, Hp.VC1, Arist. HA495[a]8, 514[a]17, Gal.2.708, etc.: in pl., ib.716, Q.S.5.327, 12. 406. II. *scum* on milk, Hsch.

* **μηνιεῖος**, α, ον, = μηνιαῖος, Eudox.Ars15.17; μηνιεῖα, τά, *monthly rations*, UPZ112 ii 6, viii 11 (ii B.C.); μηνιεῖος (sc. λόγος) τοῦ λοιπογραφομένου σίτου PGoodsp.Cair.7.7 (ii B.C.).

**μηνίζω**, = μηνίω, An.Ox.2.440.

**μηνιθμός**, ὁ, *wrath*, Il.16.62,202,282.

**μήνῐμα**, ατος, τό, *cause of wrath*, μή τοί τι θεῶν μ. γένωμαι Il.22.358, Od.11.73; παλαιῶν Ἄρεος ἐκ μηνιμάτων E.Ph.934, cf. Trag.Adesp. in PLit.Lond.79. 2. *guilt*, esp. *blood-guiltiness*, παλαιὰ μ. *guilt* that cleaves to a family from the sins of their forefathers, Pl.Phdr.244d, cf. Hierocl. in CA11 p.445 M.; μ. τῶν ἀλιτηρίων προστρίβεσθαί τινι Antipho 4.2.8. II. *wrath*, Ach.Tat.5.27: in pl., ib.25; μηνίματα τῆς γῆς Philostr.VA6.11, cf. 41.

**μήνιον**, τό, = γλυκυσίδη, Ps.-Dsc.3.140.

* **μῆνις**, Dor. and Aeol. μᾶν-, ἡ, gen. μήνιος Pl.R.390e, later μήνιδος Ael.Fr.80, Them.Or.22.265d, Jul.Or.2.50b, AP9.168 (Pall.):—*wrath*; from Hom. downwds. freq. of the *wrath* of the gods, Il.5.34, al., A. Ag.701 (lyr.), Pl.Lg.880e, Men.585; μῆνιν ἔχειν ἀπὸ θεοῦ Vett.Val. 184.3; μ. χθονίων Pi.P.4.159; also of the dead worshipped as heroes, τοῖσι μ. κατέσκηψε Ταλθυβίου Hdt.7.134, cf. 137; μ. τῶν τετελευτηκότων Pl.Hp.Ma.282a; of injured parents, A.Ag.155 (lyr.), Ch. 294; of suppliants, Id.Eu.234, cf. E.Heracl.762 (lyr.): but also, generally, of the *wrath* of Achilles, Il.1.1, al., cf. Alc.Supp.10.7; of the *revengeful temper* of a people, Hes.Sc.21, Hdt.7.229: c. gen. objecti, ὅτου .. μ. τοσήνδε πράγματος στήσας ἔχεις S.OT699: in pl., Αἰήταο μήνιες A.R.4.1205.

**μηνίσκος**, ὁ, Dim. of μείς, *lunar crescent*, Corn.ND34. II. *any crescent-shaped body*, esp. 1. *covering to protect the head of statues*, Ar.Av.1114. 2. Geom., *crescent-shaped figure, lune*, used in finding areas, Arist.APr.69[a]33, SE171[b]15, 172[a]3, Hero Deff.36; ὁ διὰ τῶν μ. τετραγωνισμός Simp. in Ph.55.26. 3. *crescent-shaped line of battle*, Plb.3.115.5. 4. *neck-ornament*, IG11(2).147 B10 (Delos, iv B.C.), Lxx Is.3.19, Jd.8.21, PRyl.125.17 (i A.D.). 5. = *olla*, Gloss.

* **μηνιτής**, οῦ, ὁ, *wrathful man*, Arr.Epict.4.5.18 (-ντής Schweigh.).

**μηνίω**, Dor. μᾶν-, fut. -ῑσω AP9.79 (Leon.), -ιῶ Lxx Je.3.12, al.: aor. ἐμήνισα: (μῆνις):—*cherish wrath, be wroth against*, c. dat. pers., μήνι' Ἀχαιοῖσιν Il.1.422; Ἀγαμέμνονι μήνιε δίῳ 18.257; Ἀθηναῖοι ὑμῖν μηνίουσι Hdt.9.7.β', cf. 5.84, 7.229: c. gen. rei, ἱρῶν μηνίσας *because of*.., Il.5.178; πατρὶ μηνίσας φόνου S.Ant.1177; ἔργου ἕκατι τοῦδε μ. Id.Tr.274; θεοῖς.. μηνίουσιν ἐς γένος Id.OC965: c. acc. cogn., οὐδ' ἃ μηνίεις φράσας ib.1274: in Hom. mostly abs., and of heroes, μῆνι' Ἀχιλλεύς Il.12.10, etc.: rarely of common men, ὁ ξεῖνος δ' εἴ περ μάλα μηνίει Od.17.14: Med. in act. sense, οὐδεὶς.. δαιμόνων μηνίεται A.Eu. 101.—Poet., Hdt., Arist. (only with ref. to Homer, Rh.1401[b]18, APo.97[b]20), and in later Prose, Lxx (v. supr.), D.S.15.49, Plu.2. 775e, D.C.72.9, etc.; cf. μηνιάω. [In aor. ῑ always: in pres. and impf., Hom. uses ῑ in μήνῑεν Il.2.769, and A. l.c. in μηνῑεται; elsewh. Hom. has μηνῐει, ἐμήνῐε, μήνῐε; E. has μᾶνῑω in lyr., prob. in Hipp. 1146; μηνίων in Rh.494.]

**μηνο-γένειον**, τό, = γλυκυσίδη, Ps.-Dsc.3.140. **-ειδής**, ές, (μείς, μήνη) *crescent-shaped*, Hdt.1.75, Th.2.76, etc.; τομαί Arch.Pap.4.271 (iii A.D.); τάξις, φάλαγξ, X.An.5.2.13, Plu.Fab.16; μηνοειδὲς ποιήσαντες τῶν νεῶν having formed them in a *crescent*, Hdt.8.16; of the sun *when partially eclipsed*, Th.2.28, X.HG4.3.10; of the *crescent* moon, Gem.9.7, Plu.2.157b, Vett.Val.106.31; μ. γωνία *lune-like* angle, Procl. in Euc.p.190.8, al. Adv. -δῶς Antyll.ap.Orib.44.23.39, Philostr. VA3.11, Longus 2.25. **-ρηκτος**, ον, = *continosus*, Gloss. (dub.).

**μήν-ῡμα**, ατος, τό, *information laid*, Th.6.61, PSI6.684.19 (iv/v A.D.): in pl., Th.6.29, Men.Epit.206. II. *indication*, χρόνου Aenesid.ap.S.E.M.10.217, cf. Clearch.45 (pl.), D.H.1.59 (pl.), Ph.2.304 (pl.), Hierocl. in CA1 p.419 M. III. θεῶν μηνύματα *evocations*, Orph. H.86.16, cf. Man.4.556. IV. αἰπολικὸν μήνυμα a *site pointed out* by goatherds, AP9.101 (Alph.). **-ῡσις**, εως, ἡ, *laying of information*, IG1[2].66.16, And.1.23, Pl.Lg.932d, Men.Pk.46, PSI6.684.17 (iv/v A.D.). **-ῡτέον**, *one must disclose, declare*, Ph.2.170, al., Archig. ap.Aët.12.1. **-ῡτήρ**, ῆρος, ὁ, *informer, guide*, A.Eu.245; *one who shows, reveals*, μ. ἁγίων λέκτρων Orph H.41.7. * **-ῡτής**, οῦ, Dor. **μᾱνῡτάς**, ᾶ, ὁ, *bringing to light*, μ. χρόνος E.Hipp.1051. II. Subst., *one who brings information*, τοῖς μέλλουσιν ἀποθανεῖσθαι μ. γενέσθαι Lys.12.32, cf. Jul.Or.5.167b: mostly in legal sense, *informer*, Th.1. 132, etc.; as epith. of Heracles, Vit.Soph.; ἀδικήματος Antipho 2.2. 5; μ. κατά τινος Id.5.24, And.1.19, Lys.13.2; κατὰ σαυτοῦ μ. ἐπὶ τοῖς συμβᾶσι γεγονώς D.18.284; τῶν ἀποκτεινάντων Antipho 2.4.3; of a woman, Cratin.428. **-ῡτικός**, ή, όν, *containing information, incriminating*, γράμμα οὐδὲν τῶν μ. D.C.78.21. II. *significative, indicative*, φωναί τινος μ. S.E.P.1.187, cf. Ph.1.57, Alex.Aphr. in Metaph.197.13; κρίσεως Gal.18(2).299; αἴσθησις μ. τοῦ πάθους Plot. 4.4.17. **-ῡτρίζομαι**, Pass., *to be reported by a claimant for a* μήνυτρον, c. inf., PCair.Zen.15[v].3,28 (iii B.C.); gloss on μηνύομαι, Hsch. **-ῡτρον**, τό, *reward for information*, h.Merc.264,364, PCair. Zen.489.9 (iii B.C.): in Att. only pl. μήνυτρα, Th.6.27, Phryn.Com.58, prob. in S.Ichn.81, etc.; μήνυτρα κεκηρυγμένα *reward* offered, And.1. 40. **-ῡτωρ** [ῡ], Dor. μᾱν-, ορος, ὁ, = μηνυτήρ, AP11.177 (Lucill.). * **-ύω** (v. fin.), Dor. μᾱν- B.Fr.10, SIG417.7 (Delph., iii B.C.): fut. -ύσω Hdt.2.121.γ', etc.: aor. ἐμήνῡσα h.Merc.264, And.1.26, etc.: pf. μεμήνῡκα ib.22, Pl.Ti.48b, Men.Pk.28:—**Pass.**, pf. μεμήνῡται And.1.10, Th.1.20: aor. ἐμηνύθην E.Ion1563, Pl.Criti.108e: fut. μηνυθήσομαι Gal.UP5.15:—*disclose what is secret, reveal*: generally, *make known, declare*, μ. τινί τι h.Merc.254, Pi.N.9.4, Hdt.1.23; τι S.OT102, 1384, etc.; τί μηνύεις νέον; E.Ba.1029; τὸ πρᾶγμ' οὐ μεμήνυκ' Men. l.c.; τοὺς ἑτερογνάθους μ. ἡ πέδη *indicates, betrays* them, X.Eq.3.5; Λυδία λίθος μανύει χρυσόν B. l.c.:—Pass., κατὰ τὸ μεμηνυμένον Phld.Acad. Ind.p.81 M. 2. c. acc. et part., πρὸς τὸν βασιλέα μ. τινὰ ἔχοντα *show* that he has, Hdt.2.121.γ'; ἐξ ἐπιβουλῆς ἀποθανόντα τινὰ μ. Antipho 2.1.5; γεγονὼς ἐμηνύθη πόλεμος Pl.Criti. l.c.: the part. is sts. omitted, τόδ' ἔργον.. σε μηνύει κακόν (sc. ὄντα) E.Hipp.1077: c. acc. et inf., [ποιηταὶ] ταῦτα οὕτως ἔχειν μ. Pl.R.366b; also ἡ ἐπιστήμη μ. ὡς .. ἑπομένης τῆς ψυχῆς *gives indication* of the soul as following, Id.Cra. 412a. 3. folld. by an interrog. or Conj., μήνυσον αὐτοῖς τίς ἐστιν Id.Ap.24d; ἀλλά μοι μηνύσατε εἰ.. *inform* me whether.., Ar.Ach. 206; μ. ὅτι.. Arist.EN1101[b]29. 4. abs., ὡς ὁ ἔμπροσθεν μεμήνυκεν ἡμῖν λόγος Pl.Phdr.277c, cf. Phlb.19b. II. at Athens, *inform, lay information against* another, κατά τινος And.1.20, Lys.6.23; τινας Docum.ap.And.1.13; ταῦτα And.ibid.; περὶ τῶν μυστηρίων ib.19; μ. τι κατά τινος Th.6.60; μ. τοῖς ἄρχουσίν τι Pl.Lg.730d; πρός τινας D. 24.11: abs., ὁ μηνύσας OGI665.29 (Egypt, i A.D.): impers. in Pass., μηνύεται *information is laid*, Th.6.28; ὑποτοπήσαντες.. Ἱππίᾳ μεμηνῦσθαι Id.1.20, cf. 6.57, And.1.10; ὧν πέρι ἄλλων ἐμεμήνυντο Th.6.61:—Pass., also of persons, *to be informed against, denounced*, τῶν μετ' αὐτοῦ μεμηνυμένων ib.53, cf. X.HG3.3.10; πρᾶγμα μηνυθὲν E.Ion 1563; μηνυθέντος τοῦ ἐπιβουλεύματος Th.4.89. [ῡ always in fut., aor., and pf.; and in Att. so in pres. and impf.; ῠ in Ep. and Lyr. in pres. and impf., h.Merc.254, Pi.N. l.c., O.6.52, P.1.93, I.8(7).60, B. l.c., but ῡ, h.Merc.373, B.9.14, and later.]

**μῆον**, ου, τό, *bald money, spignel, Meum athamanticum*, Dsc.1.3, Plin.HN20.253; μ. Κρητικόν Zopyr.ap.Gal.14.150, cf. μεῖον (c).

**μὴ ὅπως** and **μὴ ὅτι**, elliptic phrases, μὴ [λέγε] or μὴ [ὑπολάβητε] ὅπως or ὅτι.. (as οὐχ ὅπως for οὐ λέγω ὅπως), stronger than οὐχ ὅπως, *not to speak of.., let alone..*, I. folld. by other Conjs., 1. μὴ ὅπως or μὴ ὅτι, *not only not*, folld. by ἀλλ' οὐδέ, as μὴ ὅπως ὀρχεῖσθαι.., ἀλλ' οὐδ' ὀρθοῦσθαι ἐδύνασθε X.Cyr.1.3.10; οὐκ ἂν.. ἐργαζοίμεθα μὴ ὅτι τὴν τούτων, ἀλλ' οὐδ' ἂν τὴν ἡμετέραν ib.3.2.21, cf. D.30. 20,21. 2. μὴ ὅτι folld. by ἀλλά and a neg. or suggested neg., as μὴ ὅτι ἰδιώτην τινά, ἀλλὰ τὸν μέγαν βασιλέα Pl.Ap.40d, cf. Prt.319d, etc.; μὴ ὅτι θεός, ἀλλὰ καὶ ἄνθρωποι οὐ φιλοῦσι X.Cyr.7.2.17. II. in second clause, the first being usu. neg. or suggesting a neg., οὐδὲ ἀναπνεῖν, μὴ ὅτι λέγειν τι δυνησόμεθα Id.Smp.2.26, cf. Pl.Phdr.240e, Tht.161d: after a question expecting a neg. answer, δοκεῖ σοι

*ῥάδιον εἶναι διδάξαι ὁτιοῦν πρᾶγμα, μὴ ὅτι τοσοῦτον;* Id.*Cra.*427e; [*ἁρμονίαι*] *ἄχρηστοι καὶ γυναιξίν, μὴ ὅτι ἀνδράσι* Id.*R.*398e: more strongly *μὴ ὅτι γε δή..* D.54.17 codd.; *μὴ ὅτι γε τοσούτου χρόνου ἐπιγεγονότος* *UPZ*59.23 (ii B.C.).

**μὴ οὐ** is used of an apprehended neg.: **I.** with finite forms of the Verb, after Verbs expressing *fear* or *apprehension* (cf. *μή* B. 8): **a.** mostly with subj., *δείδω μὴ οὔ τίς τοι ὑπόσχηται τόδε ἔργον* Il.10.39, cf. Hdt.6.9, Th.3.53,57, Pl.*Men.*89d, etc.: after hist. tenses, with opt., *ἠθύμησάν τινες ἐννοούμενοι μὴ οὐκ ἔχοιεν ὁπόθεν λαμβάνοιεν* X.*An.*3.5.3, etc.: with fut. opt. representing fut. ind. in orat. obliq., *μὴ οὐκ ὀρθῶς αὐτὸ ποιήσοις* Pl.*Euthphr.*15d. **b.** with ind., *ὁρᾶτε μὴ οὐκ ἐμοὶ μάλιστα τῶν πολιτῶν προσήκει* And.1.103, cf. Pl.*La.*196c, *Alc.*2.139d. **2.** without introductory Verb, with subj., *μή νύ τοι οὐ χραίσμῃ* Il.1.28, cf. 566, E.*Tr.*982; also to suggest hesitation, *perhaps* (cf. *μή* B. 9), *μὴ οὐ τοῦτο ᾖ τὸ χρηστήριον* Hdt.5.79, cf. Pl.*Phd.*67b, *Smp.*194c, 214c, etc.: also with ind., *μὴ τοῦτο οὐ καλῶς ὡμολογήσαμεν* Id.*Men.*89c. **3.** *μή* is sts. doubled, irregularly, for *μὴ οὐ*, *ἐθαύμαζε δ' εἴ τις..φοβοῖτο, μὴ ὁ γενόμενος καλὸς κἀγαθὸς..μὴ τὴν μεγίστην χάριν ἔχοι* X.*Mem.*1.2.7, cf. Th.2.13. **II.** after a neg. expressed or implied: **1.** c. inf., **a.** after Verbs of *hindering, denying, avoiding, needing*, when these Verbs are themselves negatived or questioned, *οὐκέτι ἀνεβάλλοντο μὴ οὐ τὸ πᾶν μηχανήσασθαι they no longer hesitated to try every expedient*, Hdt.6.88, cf. 8.100,119; *τί δῆτα μέλλεις μὴ οὐ γεγωνίσκειν;* A.*Pr.*627, cf. S.*Aj.*540, Ar.*Ach.*320, X.*Cyr.*1.4.2, 4.3.8, Pl.*Euthd.*304c, D.24.24; *οὐκ ἀνατίθεμαι μὴ οὐ καλῶς λέγεσθαι* Pl.*Men.*89d, cf. *Phd.*87a; *πολλοῦ δέω μὴ οὐ δύο γε φεύγειν* Id.*Euthd.*297b; *τίνος ἐνδέομεν μὴ οὐ πανσυδίᾳ χωρεῖν;* E.*Tr.*797 (anap.); after *ὥστε*, Hdt.8.57: with the Art., *οὐκ ἐναντιώσομαι τὸ μὴ οὐ γεγωνεῖν πᾶν* A.*Pr.*787, cf. 918, S.*OT*283, E.*Ph.*1176; *αὐτὴν οὐ μισοῦντ' ἐκείνην τὴν πόλιν τὸ μὴ οὐ μεγάλην εἶναι* Ar.*Av.*37; *τοῖς θεοῖς οὐδὲν ἂν ἔχοιμεν μέμψασθαι τὸ μὴ οὐχί..* X.*Cyr.*7.5.42, cf. Pl.*Phlb.*13a, etc.; cf. *μή* B. 5b. **b.** after Verbs and phrases signifying *impossibility, impropriety, reluctance*, when not negatived, *ἄνδρα δ' οὐκ ἔστι μὴ οὐ κακὸν ἔμμεναι* Simon.5.10; *δεινὸν ἐδόκεε εἶναι μὴ οὐ λαβεῖν* Hdt.1.187; *ἔστι οὐδεμία μηχανὴ μὴ οὐκ ἀπολωλέναι* Id.2.181, cf. 3.51, 7.5; *οὐδεὶς ἂν τολμήσειεν μὴ οὐ χρῆσθαι τῷ νόμῳ* Antipho 5.87, cf. Th.8.60; *αἰσχύνη ἦν μὴ οὐ συσπουδάζειν* X.*An.*2.3.11; *αἰσχρόν ἐστι μὴ οὐκ ἄλλας πληγὰς ἐμβάλλειν τῷ υἱεῖ* Id.*Lac.*6.2; *οὐδεὶς οἷός τ' ἐστὶν ἄλλως λέγων μὴ οὐ* (*nemo potest non*) *καταγέλαστος εἶναι* Pl.*Grg.*509a: after an implied neg., *μὴ οὐχὶ παντὶ τρόπῳ ἐλέγχειν μαλθακοῦ εἶναι ἀνδρός* Id.*Phd.*85c; *μόνῃ τῇ μορφῇ μὴ οὐχὶ πρόβατα εἶναι διαφερόντων* Luc.*Alex.*15; after *ὥστε*, E.*Fr.*1068, X.*Ath.*3.8; *μή* and *μὴ οὐκ* in consecutive clauses, Id.*Ap.*34: with the Art., *οὐκ ἀνέξομαι τὸ μὴ οὐ..τιμᾶν* A.*Eu.*914; *οὐδείς γέ μ' ἂν πείσειεν..τὸ μὴ οὐ..* Ar.*Ra.*68, cf. X.*HG*5.2.36. **2.** less freq. c. part. after a neg. expressed or implied, *οὔκων δίκαιον* [*ἀνδριάντα*] *ἱστάναι..μὴ οὐκ ὑπερβαλλόμενον τοῖσι ἔργοισι* Hdt.2.110, cf. 6.9,106; *δυσάλγητος γὰρ ἂν εἴην τοιάνδε μὴ οὐ κατοικτείρων ἕδραν* S.*OT*13, cf. 221, *OC*360, Isoc.10.47 (dub. l.), Pl.*Ly.*212d, Philem.213.5: hence **3.** = *εἰ μή*, *except*, *πόλεις..χαλεπαὶ λαβεῖν, μὴ οὐ χρόνῳ καὶ πολιορκίᾳ* D.19.123. **III.** in questions expecting an affirmative answer, Lxx *Jd.*14.3, 1*Ep.Cor.*9.4, Aesop.404.

**μήποθεν,** *necunde*, *Gloss.*

**μὴ πολλάκις,** *lest perchance*, Th.2.13, Pl.*Prt.*361c, *R.*424c, al.

⊛ **μήποτε** or **μή ποτε,** Ion. **μή κοτε** (v. infr. II): **I.** as Adv. *never, on no account*, after *ὡς*, A.*Pr.*205, *Eu.*882; after *εἰ*, Id.*Ch.*182, etc.: c. inf., Id.*Eu.*977, *Supp.*617; esp. in oaths, *never*, *ὀμοῦμαι, μή ποτε τῆς εὐνῆς ἐπιβήμεναι* Il.9.133,275; *ἐπεκέκλετ' Ἐρινῦς, μή ποτε..ἐφέσσεσθαι* ib.455; in aposiopesis, *ἦ μήποτ' ἄρ'..* Men.*Sam.*97: in orat. obliq., Hes.*Op.*86. **2.** in prohibition or warning, with aor. subj., *μή ποτε καὶ σὺ..ὀλέσσῃς* Od.19.81, etc.: with inf. for imper., 11.441. **3.** in later Gr., *perhaps*, Arist.*EN*1172$^a$33, Lxx *Ge.*24.5, Aristeas 15, Ph.1.13, Arr.*Epict.*3.22.80, Plu.2.106d, A.D.*Pron.*18.4. **II.** as Conj., *lest ever*, *αἰσχυνόμενοι φάτιν ἀνδρῶν.., μή ποτέ τις εἴπῃσι* Od.21.324, al.; *οὐδαμὰ ἐλπίσας μή κοτε ἄρα..ἐλάσῃ* Hdt.1.77, cf. 8.53.

**μή που,** *lest perchance*, Od.4.775, S.*El.*898, etc.

**μήπω** or **μή πω,** **I.** as Adv. *not yet*, Od.22.431, etc.; *ἀλλὰ μήπω τοῦτο* (sc. *σκοπεῖτε*) D.21.90: in expostulation, *μή πώ τι μεθίετε* Il.4.234, 17.422, etc.; *μήπω γε nay, not yet*, A.*Pr.*631: folld. by *πρίν*, Il.18.134, S.*Ph.*961, 1409 (anap.): c. opt. precantis, *μήπω μανείη* E.*Hec.*1278; *μήπω νοῦ τοσόνδ' εἴην κενή* S.*El.*403. **II.** as Conj., *lest yet*, *κελόμην ἐπιβαινέμεν.., μή πώ τις..λάθηται* Od.9.102 (v. l.).

**μὴ πώποτε,** of past time, *never yet*, S.*Ant.*1094; of future time, *ὤμοσα μ. ἐξειπεῖν* *AP*12.179 (Strat.).

**μήπως** or **μή πως,** *lest in any way*, and after Verbs of fearing, *lest perchance*, freq. in Hom., written divisim, *μή πως* Od.4.396, etc.; *οὐδέ τι ἴδμεν, μή πως..μενοινήσωσι that* they will *not..*, Il.10.101.

**μῆρα,** *τά*, old pl. of *μηρός* 2, = *μηρία*, Il.1.464, al., B.*Fr.*3.4, Ar.*Pax* 1088; *Ποσειδάωνι..πόλλ' ἐπὶ μῆρ' ἔθεμεν* Od.3.179.

**μηρία,** *τά* (sg. *μηρίον* only in Posidon.16 J.); in Hom. and Ar. also **μῆρα** (q. v.): *thigh-bones*, *ἐκ μηρία τάμνον..κατά τε κνίσῃ ἐκάλυψαν, δίπτυχα ποιήσαντες* Od.3.456; *ἐπὶ μηρία θέντες Ἀπόλλωνι* 21.267, cf. foreg.; *εἴ ποτέ τοι κατὰ πίονα μηρί'* (i. e. *thigh-bones in their fat*) *ἔκηα* Il.1.40, cf. Od.4.764, al.; *πιανθέντα βοῶν ὅ γε μ. καίει* Theoc.17.126; but *δημὸν καὶ μ. ἔκηα* Il.8.240; *ἀγλαὰ μ.* Hes.*Op.*337, Thgn.1145; *κηκὶς μηρίων* S.*Ant.*1008; *τῶν μηρίων ἡ κνῖσα* Ar.*Av.*193, cf. 1517.—On the distinction between *μηρία* and *μηροί*, cf. Apollon.*Lex.* s. v. *μηρία*, Ammon.*Diff.*p.161 V., etc. **II.** = *μηροί*, *thighs*, *φῦμα μηρίων μεταξύ* Archil.136, cf. Bion 1.84; *βρέφους* Sor.1.100.

**μηριαῖος,** *α, ον*, (*μηρός*) *of* or *belonging to the thigh*, *μυελός* *Hippiatr.*12; *ὀστᾶ* Sch.Il.1.40: Subst., *αἱ μ.* the *thighs*, of the horse, X.*Eq.*11.4; of the dog, Id.*Cyn.*4.1.

**μῆριγξ,** *ιγγος, ἡ*, *bristle*, Hsch.; cf. *σμῆριγξ*.

**μηρίζω,** (*μηρός*) *strike on the thigh*, Com. word coined on analogy of *γαστρίζω*, D.L.7.172.

**μήριθμος·** *δέλτος*, ἢ **μήρινθος,** Hsch.

**μήρινθος,** *ἡ*, gen. *ου*; metapl. acc. sg. *μήρινθα*, as if from *μήριυς* (cf. *ἕλμινς, πείρινς*), Orph.*A.*597:—*cord, line, string*, *ἐκ δὲ τρήρωνα πέλειαν λεπτῇ μηρίνθῳ δῆσεν ποδός* Il.23.854, cf. 869; *μήρινθον ἐπισπασάμενοι* Arist.*Mu.*398$^b$17; *γραμματεῖον μηρίνθῳ δεδεμένον* Ach.Tat.8.12: metaph., *εἰ μὴ μηρίνθους ἡ φιλοσοφία περιτέθεικεν* Plu.2.333c; *fishing-line*, Theoc.21.12: hence prov., *αὕτη μὲν ἡ μ. οὐδὲν ἔσπασε* this *line* caught nothing, i. e. it was of no avail, Ar.*Th.*928, cf. Luc.*Herm.*28; cf. *σμήρινθος*. (Hsch. has *μηρινθίᾳ· σπάρτῳ* (post *μήρυγμα*).)

⊛ **Μηριόνης,** *ου, ὁ*, pr. n. in Hom. **II.** with a play on *μηροί*, *pudenda muliebria*, *AP*5.35 (Rufin.).

**μηρίς,** *ίδος, ἡ*, = *τριπόλιον*, Ps.-Dsc.4.132.

**μήρισμα·** *κάταγμα, ἢ σπάσμα ἐρίου*, Hsch.; found in Hero *Aut.*11.3 codd. (**μήρυσμα** is cj. in both places).

**μηρο-καυτέω,** *burn thigh-bones as a sacrifice*, Phryn.*PS* p.88 B. **-κήλη,** *ἡ*, *femoral hernia*, Antyll.ap.Orib.50.64. **-ρᾰφής,** *ές*, f. l. for *μηροτραφής* in Eust. ad D.P.1153.

⊛ **μηρός,** *ὁ*, *thigh*, *φάσγανον ὀξὺ ἐρυσσάμενος παρὰ μηροῦ* drawing his sword from *his thigh*, where it hung, Il.1.190, cf. Od.11.231, al.; *μηρὼ πληξάμενος*, in sign of vehement agitation, Il.16.125; *ἐπαίσατο τὸν μηρόν* X.*Cyr.*7.3.6; *τύπτειν* Plb.15.27.11; *τὸν μ. ἀλοῆσαι* Plu.*TG*2; *ἐπὶ μηρόν τινος beside* it, Lxx 4*Ki.*16.14: in pl., Alc.*Supp.*11.6, A.*Fr.*135, 136. **2.** *thigh-bone*, *κατ' ἰσχίον, ἔνθα τε μηρὸς ἰσχίῳ ἐνστρέφεται* Il.5.305, cf. Hp.*Art.*57, Gal.18(2).472; esp. of *thigh-bones with flesh* offered in sacrifice, *μηροὺς ἐξέταμον* Il.1.460, al. (cf. *μηρία*); *καταρρυεῖς μ. καλυπτῆς ἐξέκειντο πιμελῆς* S.*Ant.*1011; *θεοῖσι μηρὸν θύετε* Eub.130; *τίθεσο τὼ μηρὼ λαβών* Ar.*Pax*1039. **3.** generally, *leg-bones*, *κάμηλος ἐν τοῖσι ὀπισθίοισι σκέλεσι ἔχει τέσσερας μηροὺς καὶ γούνατα τέσσερα* Hdt.3.103. (Cf. OIr. *mīr* 'piece', Lat. *membrum*, from *mēmsro-*, Skt. *māṃsám* 'meat'.)

**μηρο-τρᾰφής,** *ές*, *thigh-bred*, of Dionysus, *AP*11.329 (Nicarch.), Str.15.1.7, Eust. ad D.P.1153:—also **-τρεφής,** *ές*, Orph.*H.*52.3. **-τῠπής,** *ές*, *striking the thigh*, *κέντρον* *AP*9.274 (Phil.).

**μήρυγμα,** v. *μήρυμα*.

⊛ **μηρυκ-άζω,** *chew the cud*, Arist.*HA*507$^a$36, 632$^b$1; *τὰ μηρυκάζοντα ruminants*, ib.522$^b$8, Thphr.*HP*3.10.2; of fishes, Arist.*HA* 632$^b$8. **-άομαι** (**μᾱρ-** Jul.*Gal.*314d), = foreg., Lxx *Le.*11.26, Ph.1.320, Plu.*Rom.*4: metaph. of the mind, *ruminate*, Ph.1.321, Porph.*Chr.*23. **-ίζω,** = foreg., Gal.18(1).358. **-ισμός,** *ὁ*, *chewing the cud*, *μηρυκισμὸν μηρυκᾶσθαι* Lxx *Le.*11.26; also of a fish, Lyd.*Mag.*3.63: **μᾱρ-** *Gloss.*

⊛ **μήρ-ῡμα,** *ατος, τό*, *that which is drawn out*: *strand* of gut, Ph.*Bel.*65.33; *skein* of such strands, Hero *Bel.*81.14; *thread*, Poll.7.29; *μηρύματα λίθων*, of fibrous stone, Plu.2.434a; of bitumen, J.*BJ*4.8.4; of ship's cordage, Plu.*Cic.*47; *μ. ἐρίου* Dem.Ophth.ap.Aët.7.53; *kink* in a string, Hero *Aut.*2.11. **II.** a serpent's *coil* or *trail*, *δολιχῷ μ. γαστρός* Nic.*Th.*160, 265 (*μηρύγματι* codd., cf. Hsch., Cyr.). **-ῡμάτιον,** *τό*, Dim. of foreg., Hero *Aut.*6.2.

⊛ **μήρυξ,** *υκος, ὁ*, *a ruminating fish*, *Scarus cretensis*, Arist.*HA*632$^b$10.

⊛ **μηρύομαι** [ῡ], Dor. **μᾱρ-** Theoc. (v. infr.): aor. *ἐμηρῡσάμην*:—*draw up, furl*, *ἱστία μηρύσαντο* Od.12.170, cf. A.R.4.889; *ναῦται δ' ἐμηρύσαντο νηὸς ἰσχάδα drew up* the anchor, S.*Fr.*761; *μηρύεσθαι ἀπὸ βυθῶν* Opp.*C.*1.50; *μ. πείσματα, σχοίνους*, *AP*10.2 (Antip. Sid.); *wind up* the strands of a torsion-engine, Hero *Bel.*98.10, *AP*10.5 (Thyill.); *draw out* phlegm, Aret.*SA*1.5. **2.** in weaving, *κρόκα ἐν στήμονι μηρύσασθαι weave* the woof into the warp, Hes.*Op.*538. **b.** *wind off* thread, Lxx *Pr.*31.13, Luc.*Herm.*47. **3.** in Med., *μαρύεται περὶ χείλη κισσός* ivy *draws itself, winds* round the edge, Theoc.1.29. **II.** Act. is found in pf., *περὶ τὸν τένοντα δυσκρίτους φλέβας μεμήρυκεν* has *twined*, Hp.*Oss.*16.

**μήρυσμα,** *ατος, τό*, = *μήρυμα*, v. *μήρισμα*.

**μής,** *ὁ*, v. *μείς*. **μῆστο·** *ἐβουλεύσατο*, Hsch.; cf. *μήδομαι*.

**μήστωρ,** *ωρος* (once *ορος*, v. infr. II), *ὁ*, (*μήδομαι*) *adviser, counsellor*, *ὕπατος μήστωρ*, of Zeus, Il.8.22, 17.339; *θεόφιν μήστωρ ἀτάλαντος*, of Priam, 7.366; Patroclus, 17.477, Od.3.110; Neleus, 3.409; *Ἀθηναῖοι μήστωρες ἀϋτῆς authors* of the battle-din, Il.4.328; *μήστωρα φόβοιο*, of Diomedes, 6.278; of Patroclus, 23.16; *μήστωρε φ.*, of the horses of Aeneas, 5.272, 8.108. **2.** in Ion. Prose, *skilled assistant* to a surgeon, Hp.*Mochl.*38. **II.** as Adj., *μήστορι σιδάρῳ* Tim.*Pers.*143.

⊛ **μήτε,** *and not*, mostly doubled, *μήτε..μήτε..* *neither.. nor..*, Hom., etc.; *μήτε.., μήτ' οὖν..* A.*Ag.*358 (anap.), 472 (lyr.); *μηδέ τῳ ἐκφάσθαι, μήτ' ἀνδρῶν μήτε γυναικῶν* Od.13.308; *μήτε.., μηδέ*, v. *μηδέ*; *μήτε.., τε.. both not.., and..*, Il.13.230, Hdt.1.63, E.*Heracl.*454, Lys.12.72; also *μήτε.., δέ..* S.*OC*421, Pl.*Lg.*627e; *μή.., μήτε..* S.*OC*496 codd., E.*IA*978 codd. **2.** *μήτε* is perh. sts. omitted in the former of two clauses, *ἑκόντα μήτ' ἄκοντα* S.*Ph.*771 (v.l.), cf. *Ant.*267.

**μήτειρα,** *ἡ*, = *μήτηρ*, v.l. for *δμήτειρα*, Il.14.259 (Zenod. and Ar. Byz.).

⊛ **μήτηρ,** Dor. **μάτηρ,** *ἡ*: though parox. in nom., it follows *πατήρ* in

the accent of the obliq. cases, gen. μητερος contr. μητρός, dat. μητέρι, μητρί, both forms being found in Hom., but the longer forms rarely in Trag. exc. lyr., as ματέρος A.*Supp.*539; ματέρι S.*OC*1481; μητέρος in iambics, E.*HF*843, *Or.*580, *Rh.*393: acc. always μητέρα, μητέρας: voc. μῆτερ:—*mother*, Il.1.351, etc.; of animals, *dam*, 17.4, Od.10.414; of a *mother-bird*, Il.2.313; of *queen* bees, Arist.*HA*553ᵃ29, etc.; ἀπὸ ματρὸς φίλας, ἐκ ματρός, from one's *mother's womb*, Pi.*P.*5.114, A.*Ch.* 422 (lyr.): in pl., *mother and grandmother*, Plu.*Agis*9; as an address to elderly women, ὦ μῆτερ D.S.17.37, cf. Theoc.15.60, etc.: in titles, μ. πατρίδος, = *Mater Patriae*, D.C.58.2; μ. τῶν ἀηττήτων στρατοπέδων, = *Mater invictorum castrorum*, of Julia Domna, *BGU*362 xi 16 (iii A.D.). **2.** of lands, μ. μήλων, θηρῶν, *mother* of flocks, of game, Il. 2.696, 8.47, etc.; freq. of Earth, γῆ πάντων μ. Hes.*Op.*563; πὰρ μέσον ὀμφαλὸν εὐδένδροιο.. ματέρος Pi.*P.*4.74; γῆ μήτηρ A.*Th.*16, etc.; ὦ γαῖα μῆτερ E.*Hipp.*601; ἡ Μήτηρ, = Δημήτηρ, τῇ Μητρὶ καὶ τῇ Κούρῃ ὁρτὴν ἄγουσι Hdt.8.65; also of Rhea, Pi.*P.*3.78; ὦ Πάν.., Ματρὸς μεγάλας ὀπαδέ Id.*Fr.*95, cf. E.*Hel.*1355 (lyr.); μ. ὀρεία Ar.*Av.*746 (lyr.); Γαλλαὶ μητρὸς ὀρείης φιλόθυρσοι δρομάδες *Lyr.Adesp.*121; Μ. θεῶν *SIG*1044.8 (Halic., iv B.C.); as title of Isis, *PPetr.*3 p.2 (cf. p.xi) (iii B.C.). **3.** freq. of one's native land, μᾶτερ ἐμά, Θήβα Pi.*I.*1.1, cf. *P.*8.98, A.*Th.*416, Isoc.4.25; and so, like μητρόπολις, Pi.*O.*9.20, cf. 6.100; ἡ Σκῦρος ἀνδρῶν ἀλκίμων μ. S.*Ph.*326. **II.** poet., the *origin* or *source* of events, μ. ἀέθλων, of Olympia, Pi.*O.*8.1; πειθαρχία γάρ τῆς εὐπραξίας μ. A.*Th.*225; ἡ γνώμη κακῶν μ. S.*Ph.*1361; of night, as *the mother* of day, A.*Ag.*265; the grape of wine, Id.*Pers.*614, cf. E. *Alc.*757; ματέρ' οἰνάνθας ὀπώραν Pi.*N.*5.6; Aphrodite of the Loves, Id.*Fr.*122.4; φάτις ὦ μᾶτερ αἰσχύνας ἐμᾶς, of a rumour, S.*Aj.*174 (lyr.): also in Prose, γεωργίαν τῶν ἄλλων τεχνῶν μητέρα X.*Oec.*5.17; πολιτειῶν μητέρες δύο (sc. μοναρχία and δημοκρατία) Pl.*Lg.*693d. (Cf. Lat. *mater*, OE. *módor*, etc.)

**μήτι**, neut. of μήτις (q.v.). **μήτι**, contr. dat. of μῆτις (q.v.).

**μητιάω**, Ep. 3 pl. μητιόωσι and part. μητιόων, -όωσα, Hom. (v. infr.): impf. μητιάασκον A.R.4.7:—**Med.**, 3 pl. impf. μητιόωντο Il.12. 17; 2 pl. imper. μητιάασθε Hom. (v. infr.); inf. μητιάασθαι (συμ-) Il.10.197: fut. μητιάσομαι only in Corn.*ND*7: (μῆτις):—*meditate, deliberate*, καθήατο μητιόωντες βουλάς Il.20.153; ἅσσα τε μητιόωσι μετὰ σφίσιν 10.208; βουλήν, ἥ ῥα θεοῖσιν ἐφήνδανε μητιόωσι 7.45:—Med., μητιάασθε, ἠέ.., ἦε.. *consider among you* whether.., or.., 22.174. **2.** c. acc. objecti, *plan, devise*, νόστον Ὀδυσσῆϊ.. μητιόωσα Od.6.14: c. inf., δὴ τότε μητιόωντο.. τεῖχος ἀμαλδῦναι Il.12.17; in bad sense, Ἕκτορι.. κακὰ μητιόωντι 18.312; θεοὶ κακὰ μητιόωντες Od. 1.234; δόλον ἐπί τινι A.R. l. c.

✻**μητίετα** [ῐ], ὁ, Ep. for μητιέτης, *counsellor*, freq. in Hom., as epith. of Ζεύς, *all-wise*, Il.1.175, al. [μητιετᾰ, though in Hom. ᾱ always by position; later μητιέτης Corn.*ND*20; acc. μητιέτην, of a man, *IG*5 (2).156 (Tegea).]

**μητίζομαι**, v. μητίομαι.

**μήτιμα**, ατος, τό, = μῆτις, Hsch. s. v. μήτεα (pl.).

**μητιόεις**, εσσα, εν, (μῆτις) *wise in counsel*, epith. of Zeus, = μητίετα, *h.Ap.*344, Hes.*Op.*51, 769, etc.; φάρμακα μητιόεντα *wise*, i. e. *well-chosen, helpful* remedies, Od.4.227; μ. δόλος Alex.Aet.3.18.

**μητίομαι**, (μῆτις) Pi.*P.*2.92 (s. v.l.): fut. -ίσομαι: aor. ἐμητισάμην:— = μητιάω II, *devise, contrive*, μητίσομαι ἔχθεα λυγρά Il.3.416; τοσσάδε μέρμερ' ἐπ' ἤματι μητίσασθαι 10.48; μέγα ἔργον ἐμητίσαντο Od.12.373; οἱ θάνατον μητίσομαι Il.15.349; σχέτλι' ἔργα βορᾶς μητίσασθαι Emp.139; πρώτιστον Ἔρωτα θεῶν μητίσατο Parm.13; φράζεο.. ὥς κεν ἐγὼ μητίσομ' ἀρωγήν A.R.3.1026: c. dupl. acc., ὅν ἂν κακὰ μητισαίμην Od.18.27. [ῑ in fut. and aor., and late Act. μήτῑον Orph.*A.* 1333; ῐ in μητίομαι Pi. l. c.]

**μῆτις**, ἡ, gen. ιος Pi.*N.*3.9; acc. pl. μήτιας *h.Ven.*249; also gen. ιδος A.*Supp.*61 (lyr.); acc. pl. ιδας Id.*Ch.*626 (lyr.); dat. μήτιδι Orac. ap.Hdt.7.141; Ep. μήτι for μήτιϊ, Hom. (v. infr.); pl. μητίεσσι Pi. *O.*1.9; acc. μῆτιν Il.2.407, S.*Ant.*158 (lyr.):—*wisdom, skill, craft*, Διὶ μῆτιν ἀτάλαντος (cf. μητίετα) Il. l. c., al.; βροτείη μ. Emp.2.9; τὰν Διὸς γὰρ οὐχ ὁρῶ μῆτιν, ὅπᾳ φύγοιμ' ἄν A.*Pr.*906 (lyr.); μήτι.. καὶ κέρδεσιν Od.13.299; μήτι.. μέγ' ἀμείνων ἠὲ βίηφι Il.23.315; μῆτιν ἀλώπηξ a fox *for craft*, Pi.*I.*4(3).47; of a poet's *craft*, Id.*N.* l. c. **II.** *counsel, plan, undertaking*, ὑφαίνειν μῆτιν Il.7.324, cf. Od.4.678, etc.: pl., σοφῶν μητίεσσι Pi.*O.* l. c.; γυναικοβούλους μήτιδας A.*Ch.* l. c.—Poet. word. (Cf. Skt. *mimāti*, pf. part. Pass. *mitá-* 'measure', Lat. *metior*, OE. *mǽþ* 'measure'.)

**μήτις** or **μή τις**, ὁ, ἡ, neut. μήτι, gen. μήτινος: (τίς) old Gr. and Cret. for μηδείς, Il.12.272, al., *Schwyzer*175 (Gortyn), *Leg.Gort.*5.13, al.; Cret. dat. sg. μηδιμὶ *IG*2².1130.4:—hence **1.** μήτι or μή τι, Adv., with imper., and inf. used imperatively, Il.1.550, 5.130, etc.: with opt. to express a wish, ὄλοιντο μή τι πάντες S.*Tr.*383. **2.** after Verbs of fear or doubt, Il.11.470, Od.2.67, etc. **3.** in direct questions, μή τί σοι δοκῶ ταρβεῖν; *do I..?* (i. e. I do not), A.*Pr.*959, cf. 249, Lxx *Ge.*20.9, *Ev.Marc.*4.21. **4.** μή τί γε *let alone, much less*, οὐδὲ στρατιώτης οὗτός γε οὐδενός ἐστιν ἄξιος, μή τί γε τῶν ἄλλων ἡγεμών D.21.148, cf. 19.137; later, *not to mention*, οὐκ οἴδατε ὅτι ἀγγέλους κρινοῦμεν; μήτι γε βιωτικά 1*Ep.Cor.*6.3: with a word between, ὡς.. δώσοντι δίκην, μή τι ποιήσαντί γε D.8.27; also μή τι δὴ Plb.12.8. 6; μή τί γε δή, οὐκ ἔνι οὐδὲ τοῖς φίλοις.., μή τί γε δὴ τοῖς θεοῖς D.2.23; also μητιγοῦν Ael.*VH*12.9; μή τι δή γε Phld.*Rh.*1.261 S., al.

**μήτοι** or **μή τοι**, stronger form of μή, with imper. and subj., μή τοι δοκεῖτε A.*Pr.*436, cf. S.*OC*1407, 1439, *Ant.*544, etc.; in an oath, c. inf., A.*Eu.*765: in Pl. folld. by γε, *at least not*, *R.*352c, 388b. **2.** after Verbs implying negation, ὅς σ' ἐπεῖχ' ἀεὶ μή τοι.. αἰσχύνειν φίλους S.*El.*518.

**μῆτος**, εος, τό, = μῆτις, Hsch. (pl.).

**μήτρα** (A), Ion. -τρη, ἡ, (μήτηρ) *womb*, Hp.*Prorrh.*2.24, Hdt.3. 108 (dub. l.), Pl.*Ti.*91d, etc.: also in pl., Hp.*Loc.Hom.*47, *Vict.*1.30, Hdt. l. c.: *the cervix including the orifice of the womb*, Arist.*HA*510ᵇ 14. **2.** a swine's *matrix*, reckoned a great dainty, μήτρας τόμοις Telecl.1.14; μήτραν.. πωλοῦσιν, ἥδιστον κρέας Antiph.220; ὑπὲρ μήτρας.. ἀποθανεῖν Alex.193, cf. Plu.2.733e, Ath.3.96f. **3.** metaph., *source, origin*, D.L.7.46; μῆτραι τῆς ψυχῆς Ph.1.441. **II.** *core, heart-wood* of trees, Thphr.*HP*1.6.1. **b.** *diseased condition* of the wood, 'soft-wood', ib.2.7.3. **III.** *queen-wasp*, opp. ἐργάται, Arist. *HA*627ᵇ32, al. **IV.** μ. χελωνίων, χελωνίοις, *bolts* for locks, *BGU* 1028.20, 26 (ii A.D.); μ. θύρας, = *repagulum*, *Gloss.*

**μήτρα** (B), ἡ, in pl., *register of house-property*, at Tarsus and Soli, Arist. in *POxy.*1802.58; sg., = κλῆρος, at Tarsus and Soli, Clitarch. ap.Hsch. (Cf. Skt. *mātrā* 'measure' and ἐρεσιμήτρη.)

**μητρ-ᾰγυρτέω**, *to be a* μητραγύρτης, Antiph.159.8, D.H.2.19. **-ἀγύρτης**, ου, ὁ, *begging priest of Cybele*: nickname of Callias (ὁ Δᾳδοῦχος), Arist.*Rh.*1405ᵃ20; of Ptolemy Philopator, Plu.*Cleom.*36; title of play by Antiphanes. **-ἀδελφος** [ᾰδ], Dor. **ματρᾰδελφεός**, Pi.*P.*8.35: ὁ and ἡ:—*mother's brother* or *sister, uncle* or *aunt*, *BGU* 1158.3, Poll.3.22. **-άζω**, *take after one's mother*, *Gloss.* **-ᾰλοίας**, ου, ὁ, (ἀλοιάω) *striking one's mother*: hence, *matricide*, A.*Eu.*153 (lyr.), 210, Lys.10.8, Pl.*Phd.*114a, etc.:—also written **μητρολῴας** or **-λώας**, 1*Ep.Ti.*1.9, *Gloss.* **-ανοίκτης**, ου, ὁ, *instrument for opening the womb*, *Hermes*38.282. **-άριον**, τό, Dim. of μήτηρ, Lat. *matercula*, *Gloss.* **-εγχύτης** [ῠ], ου, ὁ, *syringe for injections into the womb*, Antyll.ap.Orib.10.28.1, Sor.2.41, Gal.10.328.

**μήτρη**, ἡ, Ion. for μήτρα.

**μήτρ-ια**, = *materna*, *Gloss.* **-ιάζω**, *worship the Mother of the gods*, Poll.3.11.

✻**μητρίδιος** [ῐ], α, ον, *having a* μήτρα: hence, *fruitful, filled with seed*, μ. ἀκαλῆφαι Ar.*Lys.*549 (cf. Sch.).

**μητρίζω**, *to be possessed by the Mother of the gods*, Iamb.*Myst.*3.9, 10.

**μητρικός**, ή, όν, *of a mother*, τιμή Arist.*EN*1165ᵃ27; κτῆσις Poll.3. 11; [χρυσοῦς] τύπος μ. πρὸς ξύλῳ *Inscr.Délos* 399*B* 142 (ii B.C.); τὰ μ. *PStrassb.*122.4 (ii A.D.); μέρη πατρικὰ καὶ μ. *BGU*302.20 (ii A.D.); μ. τόπος a region of the zodiac, Vett.Val.101.8. Adv. -κῶς D.H. *Rh.*9.4.

**μητρίς** (sc. γῆ), ίδος, ἡ, *one's mother country* (cf. πατρίς), Cret. word in Pl.*R.*575d, Plu.2.792e, cf. Pherecr.220; μ. δέ τοι, οὐ πατρίς ἐστιν Epigr.ap.Paus.10.24.2.

**μητρο-γᾰμία**, ἡ, *incest with one's mother*, Sch.Ptol.*Tetr.*166. **-γάμος** [ᾰ], ὁ, *one guilty of such incest*, Arg.Man. post Max.p.98 L. **-δίδακτος** [ῐ], ον, *taught by one's mother*: nickname of Aristippus, Str. 17.3.22, D.L.2.83. **-δοκος**, Dor. ματρ-, ον, *received by the mother*, γοναί Pi.*N.*7.84.

**μητρόθεν**, Dor. **ματρόθεν** (also -θε Pi.*I.*3.17), Adv., (μήτηρ) *from the mother, by the mother's side*, Id.*O.*7.24; καταλέξει ἑωυτὸν μ. Hdt. 1.173, cf. *PMag.Par.*1.316; τὰ μ. Κρῆσσα Hdt.7.99. **2.** *from one's mother*, μ. δεδεγμένη A.*Ch.*750, cf. Ar.*Ach.*478. **3.** *from one's mother's womb*, φυγόντα μ. σκότον A.*Th.*664, cf. *Ch.*607 (lyr.): with the force of a gen., ἢ ματρόθεν.. λέκτρ' ἐπλήσω; S.*OC*527 (lyr.).—Poet. word, used by Hdt., and in later Prose, Luc.*Tox.*51, *Alex.*11, *Arch.Pap.*2.444 (ii A.D.), D.C.49.23.

✻**μητρο-κᾰσιγνήτη**, Dor. ματρο-, ἡ, = κασιγνήτη ὁμομητρία, *uterine sister*, A.*Eu.*962. **-κοίτης**, ου, ὁ, *incestuous person*, Hippon. 14. **-κολωνεία**, ἡ, *mother-colony*, i. e. *colonial metropolis*, of Palmyra, *OGI*646.11 (iii A.D.). **-κτονέω**, *kill one's mother*, A.*Eu.*202, al., E.*Or.*887, Arist.*EN*1110ᵃ29. **-κτονία**, ἡ, *matricide*, Asclep.Tragil. 29 J., Plu.2.18a, 810f. **-κτόνος**, ον, *killing one's mother, matricidal*, μ. φίτυμα, of Orestes, A.*Ag.*1281; μ. χεῖρες Id.*Eu.*102; μ. μίασμα the stain *of a mother's murder*, ib.281; μ. κηλίς, αἷμα, E.*IT*1200, *Or.* 1649. **2.** Subst., *matricide*, A.*Eu.*493 (lyr.), E.*El.*975, Pl.*Lg.*869b; ἔσχατος Αἰνεαδῶν μ. ἡγεμονεύσει, of Nero, D.C.61.16. ✻**-κωμία**, ἡ, *mother-village, the chief village of a district*, *OGI*609.4 (Syria), 769.9 (ibid.), *Princeton Exp.Inscr.* III A.797² (iv A.D.). **-ληπτος**, ον, *possessed by the Mother of the gods*, Herm. in *Phdr.*p.105 A. **-λῴας**, v. μητραλοίας. **-μᾰνία**, ἡ, *hysteria*, Cass.Fel.79. **-μήτωρ**, Dor. **ματρομάτωρ**, ορος, ἡ, *mother's mother, grandmother*, Pi.*O.*6. 84, Ael.*NA*11.16. **-μιξία**, ἡ, *incest with one's mother*, S.E.*M.*11. 191. **-μίξιον**, τό, = foreg., Sch.A.*Th.*778. **-ξενος** (Dor. **ματρό-** Hsch.), ὁ, *bastard*, Poll.3.21.—Rhod. word, acc. to Sch.E. *Alc.*989. ✻**-πάτωρ** [ᾰ], ορος, ὁ, *mother's father, grandfather*, Il. 11.224, Hdt.1.75, 3.51, etc. ✻**-πολις**, Dor. **ματρό-**, poet. **μητρόπτολις**, *Epigr.Gr.*537.4 (Tomi), 842a 1 (Cyrene), *Syria* 7.209 (Damascus), Nonn.*D.*13.166: εως, ἡ:—*mother-state*, as related to her colonies, of Athens in relation to the Ionians, Hdt.7.51, Th.6.82; of Doris in relation to the Peloponn. Dorians, Hdt.8.31, Th.1.107, 3.92; of Meroe in relation to the Ethiopians, Hdt.2.29; of Thera, μεγαλᾶν πολίων μ. Pi.*P.*4.20; μ. Λοκρῶν Ὀπόεις Simon.93; of the Attic Salamis, as the μ. of the Cyprian, A.*Pers.*895 (lyr.); of Corinth, as the μ. of Corcyra, Th.1.24; of Rome, Gal.14.296. **2.** metaph., ἐστὶ μ. τοῦ ψυχροῦ [ὁ ἐγκέφαλος] Hp.*Carn.*4; ἡ ἱστορία μ. τῆς φιλοσοφίας D.S.1.2, cf. Chrysipp.*Stoic.*3.199; γεωμετρία ἀρχὴ καὶ μ. τῶν ἄλλων (sc. μαθημάτων) Ph.ap.Plu.2.718e. **II.** *one's mother-city, mother-country, home*, Pi.*N.*5.8, S.*OC*707 (lyr.), *Ant.*1122 (lyr.). **2.** ἀ σά

ματρόπολις thy *mother's city*, Isyll.59. III. *capital city*, X.*An*.5.2.3, 5.4.15; ἡ μ. τῆς Ἀσίας, of Ephesus, *OGI*496.6, *IG*3.485; ἡ μ. τῆς Ἰωνίας, of Miletus, ib.480. b. in Egypt, *chief town* of a νομός, *PRev.Laws*48.16 (iii B.C.), *BGU*326 ii 10 (ii A.D.), etc. ⊛ **-πολίτης** [ῑ], ου, ὁ, *citizen of a* μητρόπολις, Aristodem.17.1: in Egypt, *PRyl.*216 (ii/iii A.D.). 2. *citizen of Metropolis*, *CIG*4472.4 (Laodicea ad mare). II. *metropolitan bishop*, Just.*Nov*.6.2, *Cat.Cod.Astr.*8(1).249. ⊛ **-πολιτικός**, ή, όν, *belonging to a* μητροπολίτης I. 1, in neut. pl., of taxes, *CPHerm*.120. II. *of a* μητροπολίτης II, δίκαιον Just.*Nov*.131.4, *Cod.Just*.1.5.12.22. **-πόλος**, Dor. ματρο-, ον, *tending mothers*, epith. of Eileithyia, Pi.*P*.3.9. II. αἱ μ., = μέλισσαι II. 2, Hsch. **-ρραίστης**, ου, ὁ, *matricide*, Suid. **-ρριπτος**, Dor. ματρό-, ον, *thrown down by one's mother*, of Hephaestus, Dosiad.*Ara* 8. **-τύπτης**, ου, ὁ, = μητραλοίας, Hsch. s. v. ἀλοία. **-φθόρος**, ον, *defiling one's mother*, *AP*9.498, Agath.2.31. **-φόνος**, ον, *murdering one's mother*, ἀντίποιν' ὡς τίνης ματροφόνου δύας (Casaub. for μητροφόνας) A.*Eu*.268 (lyr.). 2. as Subst., *matricide*, ib.257 (lyr.). II. *slayer of a mother*, Nonn.*D*.43.147, al. **-φόντης**, ου, ὁ, = foreg., E.*Or*.479, 1587, *Andr*.999, Arist.*Rh*.1405ᵇ22.

⊛ **μητρυι-ά**, Dor. ματρ-, ᾶς, Ion. **μητρυιή**, ῆς, ἡ, Aeol. **ματροία** *IG* 12(2).257.6 (Lesbos):—*stepmother*, Il.13.697, Pi.*P*.4.162, E.*Alc*.305, Pl.*Lg*.930b, etc. 2. metaph., from the proverbial unkindness of stepmothers, Is.12.5; ἐδικαίευ εἶναι καὶ τῷ ἔργῳ μ., i.e. not only in name, but in reality, Hdt.4.154; ἀλλότε μητρυιὴ πέλει ἡμέρη, ἄλλοτε μήτηρ, of unlucky and lucky days, Hes.*Op*.825; μ. νεῶν, of a dangerous coast, A.*Pr*.727; τρεφόμενοι οὐχ ὑπὸ μητρυιᾶς ἀλλ' ὑπὸ μητρὸς τῆς χώρας (sc. τῆς Ἀττικῆς) Pl.*Mx*.237b, cf. Plu.2.201e. (Cf. Arm. *mauru* 'stepmother', OE. *mōdrie* 'mother's sister'.) **-άζω**, *to be a stepmother, act as one*, *Gloss*. **-ογάμος** [ᾰ], ὁ, *one who marries his stepmother*, Arg.Man. post Max.p.98 L. **-ός**, ὁ, *stepfather*, Theopomp.Com.12, Hyp.*Fr*.140. **-ώδης**, ες, *step-motherly*: τὸ μ. *a stepmother's treatment, unkindness*, Plu.2.143a.

**μητρωακός**, ή, όν, = μητρῷος II, ἀγιστεῖαι Marin.*Procl*.19; μ. μέτρον, of the galliambic, Heph.12.

**μητρῴζω**, *celebrate the festival of Cybele*, Theognost.*Can*.142.

**μητρώϊος**, α, ον, Ep. and Ion. = μητρῷος, Od.19.410, Hdt.3.53.

**μήτρων**, Dor. μάτρ-, ωνος, ὁ, = μήτρως, *Epigr.Gr*.322.5 (Sardis), 371.3 (Cotiaeum), *BCH*11.471 (Lydia).

**μητρωνῠμικός**, ή, όν, (ὄνομα) *named after one's mother*, *EM*166.11. Adv. -κῶς Sch.Pi.*P*.3.118.

⊛ **μητρῷος**, Dor. ματρ-, α, ον, contr. for μητρώϊος (q. v.), *of a mother*, αἷμα A.*Eu*.230; τὰ πατρῷα καὶ μ. πήματα S.*OC*1196; μ. δέμας, periphr. for τὴν μητέρα, A.*Eu*.84; οἱ πατρῷοι καὶ μ. θεοί X.*Cyn*.1.15, cf. *IG*3.235; μ. τροφή, γάλα, Sor.1.86, 87; μ. κληρονομία *PSI*1.66.2 (v A.D.); τὰ μ. *PMasp*.6 ii 91 (vi A.D.). 2. τὸ μ. μόριον, = μήτρα, Hp.*Epid*.6.5.8. II. Μητρῷον (sc. ἱερόν), τό, *temple of Demeter*, Clitodem.1: more freq. *temple of Cybele*, esp. at Athens, where it was the depository of the state archives, D.19.129, Aeschin.3.187, Chamael.ap. Ath.9.407c, *IG*2².463.28. 2. Μητρῷα (sc. ἱερά), τά, *the worship of Cybele*, D.H.*Dem*.22, Plu.2.407c, *IG*12(7).237.64 (Amorgos). b. Μητρῷα, τά, *music played in her honour*, Duris 16 J.; in full, τὰ Μ. μέλη D.H.2.19; τὸ Μ. αὔλημα Paus.10.30.9. 3. Μητρῷος, ὁ (sc. μήν), month in Bithynia, *Hemerolog.Flor.*

⊛ **μήτρως**, Dor. ματρ-, ὁ, gen. ωος and ω *JRS*16.58 (Eumeneia) (Att. acc. to Suid.), acc. ωα and ων; pl. always of the third declen.:—*maternal uncle*, Il.2.662, 16.717, Hdt.4.80, etc.: dat. μάτρωϊ Pi.*I*.7(6).24. 2. generally, *relation by the mother's side*, μάτρωες ἄνδρες Id.*O*.6.77, cf. *N*.10.37, E.*HF*43. 3. = μητροπάτωρ, Pi.*O*.9.63.

**μητρῳσμός**, Dor. ματρ-, ὁ, (μητρῴζω) *celebration of the festival of Cybele*, Phint.ap.Stob.4.23.61, 61a (both pl.).

**μηχᾰν-άομαι**, fut. -ήσομαι A.*Th*.1043, Pl.*Lg*.965e: aor. ἐμηχανησάμην ib.904b, etc.: pf. μεμηχάνημαι (v. infr. B): used by Hom. only in Ep. forms, μηχανάασθε Od.20.370, μηχανόωνται 3.207, al., -ωντο 22.432, al. (subj. -άᾳται Hes.*Op*.241); opt. -όῳτο Od.16.196; inf. -άασθαι 3.213, 16.93: the Ion. form ἐμηχανέοντο is found in codd. of Hdt.8.7 (ἐμηχανῶντο shd. be read for -έατο in 5.63, and μηχανῴατο for -οίατο in 6.46): (μηχανή):—*make by art, construct, build*, τείχεα μηχανόωντο Il.8.177; πλοῖα Hdt.1.94, cf. Th.4.47; of any work requiring skill or art, μ. λαγὸν *prepare* a hare, Hdt.1.123; μ. σκιάς X.*Cyr*.8.8.17: generally, *prepare, make ready*, τάφον καὶ κατασκαφάς τινι A.*Th*.1043; ψυχῆς κόμιστρα τῇδε Id.*Ag*.965; ἐσβάσεις E.*IT*101. 2. more freq. *contrive, devise*, by art or cunning, freq. in bad sense, ἀτάσθαλα, κακά, ἀεικέα μηχανόωνται, Od.3.207, 17.499, 22.432; θάνατόν τινος Antipho 1.3; but in good sense, γέλωτα μ. τοῖς συνοῦσι X.*Cyr*.2.2.12; τισὶ μ. δύναμιν εἰς σωτηρίαν Pl.*Prt*.320e; simply, *bring about, effect*, Hdt.2.21; πόσα σε δέοι ἂν μηχανᾶσθαι τοῦ δοκεῖν ἕνεκα X.*Cyr*.1.6.22:—Constr.: μ. τί τινι *contrive* something *against* a person, Od.3.207; πατρὶ θάνατον Antipho 1.9; πᾶν ἐπί τινι Hdt.4.154, cf. 6.88, etc.; τι εἴς τινα ib.121, E.*Ph*.1614; ἐπί τινα X.*Mem*.2.3.10: abs., *form designs or plots*, πολλοὶ ἐπ' αὐτῷ μηχανόωνται Od.4.822; μ. τι ἐπί τινι *for* a purpose, Hdt.1.60; πρός τι X.*Cyr*.8.2.26; ἐκ τῶν ἐσθλῶν αἰσχρὰ μ. E.*Hipp*.331: in Prose freq. folld. by ὅπως, *how* or *in order that*, μ. ὅπως τι ἔσται Hdt.2.121.γ', Pl.*Ap*.39a, etc.; πᾶσαν μηχανὴν μ. ὅπως.. Id.*R*.460c: c. acc. et inf., *contrive that* a thing may be, ib.519e. II. Med., *procure for oneself*, S.*Ph*.295, X.*Cyr*.3.2.15.

B. Act. μηχανάω used by Hom. only in Ep. part., ἀτάσθαλα μηχανόωντας *contriving* dire effects, Od.18.143, cf. A.R.3.583; inf. μηχανᾶν S.*Aj*.1037: pf. μεμηχάνημαι in pass. sense, Hdt.1.98, 2.95, S.*Tr*.586, X.*Cyr*.8.3.1, Isoc.3.6; λόγοι πρὸς τὸ φενακίζειν ὑμᾶς μεμηχανημένοι D.22.35 (but also in act. sense, Pl.*Grg*.459d, *Lg*.904b, X.*Hier*.11.4, Is.11.36, etc.): plpf. in pass. sense impers., οὕτως ἐμεμηχάνητο αὐτοῖς Antipho 5.55: aor. ἐμηχανήθην in pass. sense, Epicur.*Nat*.2.2, D.H.12.14, J.*AJ*18.2.4.

⊛ **μηχᾰν-άριος**, ὁ, *engineer*, esp. for irrigation machines, *BGU*325.7 (iii A.D.):—written **-άρις**, *Sammelb*.5124.147 (ii A.D.); **μηκαν(ά-ρ)ιος**, ib.6915. ⊛ **-εύομαι**, = μηχανάομαι, v.l. in X.*Cyr*.4.5.49: used as Pass. by D.H.*Is*.16 codd., Lxx 2*Ch*.26.15, v.l. ib.3*Ma*.6.22. ⊛ **-εύς**, έως, ὁ, *contriver*, epith. of Zeus at Argos, Paus.2.22.2; cf. Μαχανεύς. ⊛ **-ή**, Dor. **μᾱχᾰνά**, ἡ, (μῆχος): I. *contrivance*, esp. *machine* for lifting weights and the like, *crane*, Hdt.2.125, *IG*11(2).161 *A* 69, al. (Delos, iii B.C.); μ. τετράκωλος, δίκωλος, *Rev.Phil*.44.251 (Didyma, ii B.C.); μ. λιθαγωγός Poll.10.148; ἰχθυβόλῳ μ., of Poseidon's trident, A.*Th*.132 (lyr.); λαοπόροις μ., of Xerxes' bridge of boats, Id.*Pers*.114 (lyr.), cf. 722; freq. of irrigation machines, *POxy*.985 (i A.D.), etc.; also of oil-presses, Wilcken *Chr*.176.10 (i/ii A.D.), etc. 2. *engine* of war, μηχανὰς προσάγειν Th.2.76, etc.; ἑλεῖν μηχαναῖς Id.4.13. 3. *theatrical machine* by which gods, etc., were made to appear in the air, Pl.*Cra*.425d, *Clit*.407a; αἴρειν μ. Antiph.191.15, Alex.126.19: hence, prov. of anything sudden and unexpected, ἀπὸ μηχανῆς θεὸς ἐπεφάνης Men.227; ὥσπερ ἀπὸ μ. D.40.59, cf. Arist.*Po*.1454ᵇ1. 4. *area of land irrigated by a machine*, *POxy*.1830.13 (vi A.D.), *PLond*.5.1765 (vi A.D.), *PSI*1.77.14 (vi A.D.). II. *any artificial means* or *contrivance* for doing a thing, ἤτοι κλήρῳ.., ἢ ἄλλῃ τινὶ μ. Hdt.3.83; εἴ τίς ἐστι μ., ἴθι καὶ πειρῶ Id.8.57, etc.; esp. in pl. μηχαναί, *shifts, devices, wiles*, Hes.*Th*.146; πάντα σοφίσματα καὶ πάσας μ. ἐπεποιήκεε ἐς αὐτοὺς Δαρεῖος Hdt.3.152; μηχαναῖς Διός *by the arts* of Zeus, A.*Ag*.677; χερὸς..ἐκτίνοντα μηχανάς acts of violence, ib.1582; Ὀρέστην μηχαναῖσι μὲν θανόντα, νῦν δὲ μηχαναῖς σεσωσμένον S.*El*.1228; κρατεῖ μαχαναῖς.. θηρός Id.*Ant*.349 (lyr.); σοφιστῶν μ. Pl.*Lg*.908d: prov., μηχαναὶ Σισύφου Ar.*Ach*.391:—Phrases: πάσας προσφέροντε μ. E.*IT*112; μηχανὴν προσοιστέον Ar.*Th*.1132; πᾶσαν σπουδὴν καὶ μ. προσφερόμενος Plb.1.18.11; ἐπεισήγαγον μ. Id.29.25.1; μηχανὰς εὑρήσομεν, ὥστε ἀπαλλάξαι A.*Eu*.82; πλέκειν E.*Andr*.66; πορίζεσθαι Pl.*Smp*.191b; ἐκπορίζειν Ar.*V*.365; ζητεῖν ib.149; ἀντλεῖν μαχανάν exhaust *one's resources*, Pi.*P*.3.62; κατ' ἐμὰν μ. ib.109: c. gen. objecti, ἔξευρε μ. τιν' Ἀδμήτῳ κακῶν *contrivance against* ills, E.*Alc*.221 (lyr.); but μ. σωτηρίας *a way, means of procuring* or *providing* safety, A.*Th*.209; μυρίων οὐσῶν μ. ἀπαλλαγῆς X.*Cyr*.5.1.12; οὐδεμία μ. [ἐστι] ὅκως οὐ c. fut. ind., Hdt.2.160; μὴ οὐ c. inf., ib.181, 3.51; τὸ μὴ οὐ (prob.) Id.1.209; τίς μ. μὴ οὐχὶ..; Pl.*Phd*.72d. 2. freq. in adverb. phrases, μηδεμιῇ μ. by no *means* whatsoever, by no *contrivance*, Hdt.7.51, etc.; οὓς οὐδεμιῇ μ. δεῖ τιτρώσκειν Hp.*Art*.11; so μήτε τέχνῃ μήτε μ. μηδεμιᾷ Foed.ap.Th.5.18, cf. *IG*1².39.23; opp. πάσῃ τέχνῃ καὶ μ. Lys.19.53; πάσῃ μ. Ar.*Lys*.300 (lyr.); τρόπῳ ἢ μ. ᾑτινιοῦν Lex ap.D.21.113. **-ημα**, ατος, τό, = foreg., *machine*, Hp.*Art*.42; *mechanical device*, Arist.*Mech*.848ᵃ36; esp. *engine of war*, used in sieges, mostly in pl., D.18.87, Plb.1.48.2, Plu.*Marc*.14, etc. II. *subtle contrivance*, freq. in Trag., as A.*Pr*.469, 989; of the robe in which Agamemnon was entangled, Id.*Ch*.981; λόγου μ. ποικίλον S.*OC*762; τὰ Ἥρας μ. E.*HF*855; οὐδενὶ μηχανήματι οὐδ' ἀπάτῃ Antipho 5.22; τὰ πρὸς τοὺς πολεμίους μ. X.*Cyr*.1.6.38; πρὸς τὸ μέγεθος τῆς ἀρχῆς ib.8.6.17; μ. εἰς τὸ πείθεσθαι τοῖς νόμοις Id.*Lac*.8.5; δεῖ μηχανήματός τινος ὅπως τὰ..χρήμαθ' ἕξω Ar.*Ec*.872. **-ησις**, Dor. **μᾱχᾰνᾱσις** Metop.ap.Stob.3.1.120: εως, ἡ:— = μηχανή, Hp.*Art*.72, Dexipp.12 J.; μ. σιτοποιική Plb.1.22.7. **-ητέον**, *one must contrive*, μ. ὅπως ἄν.. Pl.*Grg*.481a, cf. *Lg*.798e, X.*Eq.Mag*.5.11. **-ητής**, οῦ, ὁ, *deviser of engines of war*, of Artemon, Sch.Ar.*Ach*.850. **-ητικός**, ή, όν, = μηχανικός I. 1, X.*HG*3.1.8 (v.l. μηχανικός): c. gen. rei, μ. τοῦ πολλοὺς φαίνεσθαι τοὺς ὀλίγους ἱππέας Id.*Eq.Mag*.5.2. **-ητός**, ή, όν, *contrived by art*, κεραυνοί, στήλη, Tz.*H*.3.42, 6.611. ⊛ **-ικός**, ή, όν, *resourceful, inventive*, X.*Mem*.4.3.1, v.l. in Id.*HG*3.1.8. Adv. -κῶς D.S.18.27. 2. c. gen. rei, τῶν ἐπιτηδείων -ώτερος X.*Lac*.2.7. II. *of* or *for machines, mechanical*, ὄργανα μ. Arist.*Pol*.1336ᵃ11; αἱ..κινήσεις αἱ μ. Id.*Mech*.848ᵃ14; μ. ἀποδείξεις *in mechanics*, Id.*APo*.76ᵃ24: μηχανικά, τά, *the science of mechanics*, title of work ascribed to Aristotle: ἡ -κή (sc. τέχνη) Id.*Metaph*.1078ᵃ16, *AP*9.807; μ. ποίημα Sotad.15.6; μ. ἔργα *PFlor*.152.4 (iii A.D.): Subst. μηχανικός, ὁ, *engineer*, Plu.*Per*.27, *Sammelb*.310. Adv. -κῶς Callix.2. **-ῖτις**, v. Μαχανῖτις. **-ιώτης**, ου, ὁ, *contriver*, *h.Merc*.436.

**μηχᾰνο-γράφος**, ὁ, *writer on military engineering*, Tz.*H*.2.152. **-δίφης** [ῑ], ου, ὁ, (διφάω) *inventing artifices* or *machines*, Ar.*Pax* 790. **-εις**, εσσα, εν, *ingenious*, σοφόν τι τὸ μ. τέχνας S.*Ant*.365 (lyr.). **-πᾰνουργία**, ἡ, *fraud*, *PMasp*.5.16 (vi A.D.). **-ποιέω**, *use machines*, Hp.*Fract*.15:—Med., ib.20:—Pass., ib.30. **-ποίημα**, ατος, τό, *mechanical construction*, Sallust.8. ⊛ **-ποιΐα**, ἡ, *construction of engines of war*, Ath.Mech.10.9. ⊛ **-ποιός**, ὁ, *maker of engines* or *machines, engineer*, Pl.*Grg*.512b, X.*Cyr*.6.1.22, *Ostr.Bodl*.i 304 (ii B.C.), Sallust.8. 2. *machinist* of the theatre, Ar.*Pax* 174, *Fr*.188. 3. metaph., μ. τῆς ὅλης ὑποθέσεως Jul.*Or*.2.59b. II. Adj. μ. πλῆθος multitude *of siege-engines*, Memn.37. **-ρρᾰφέω**, *form crafty plans*, A.*Ch*.221. **-ρράφος** [ρᾰ], ον, *forming crafty plans*, S.*OT*387: c. gen., μ. κακῶν *crafty schemers* of ill, E.*Andr*.447, cf. 1116. **-στάσιον** [στᾰ], τό, *base of an irrigation machine*, *Sammelb*.4481.10 (v A.D.). **-σφαιροποιΐα**, ἡ, *construction of artificial spheres*, Theo Sm.p.180 H. **-τευχέω**, = μηχανοποιέω, Tz.*H*.3.59.

**μηχᾰν-ουργία**, ἡ, = μηχανοποιία, Ath.Mech.31.13. ⊛ **-ουργός**, ὁ, *architect*, τοῦ δόμου *APl.*5.382.

**μηχᾰνοφόρος**, ον, *for conveying military machines*, ἅμαξαι, νῆες, Plu.*Ant.*38, Arr.*An.*2.22.6.

**μηχάνωμα**, ατος, τό, = μηχάνημα, Thphr.*Ign.*59, Sm.*Le.*8.7:—Dor. **μᾱχάνωμα**, *crane*, *SIG*241 *A* 12 (pl.), al.

**μῆχαρ**, τό, = μῆχος, A.*Pr.*606, *Ag.*199, *Supp.*394, 594 (all lyr.), Lyc.568.

**μήχι**, related to μή as οὐχί to οὐ, ναίχι to ναί, Eub.23.

**μῆχος**, εος, τό, *means, expedient, remedy*, Il.2.342, Od.12.392, Hdt. 2.181, 4.151; κακῶν E.*Andr.*536 (lyr.); νόσῳ Theoc.2.95: c. inf., οὐδὲν ἔσται μ. ὠφελεῖν πάτραν Lyc.1459. (Cf. Goth. *mag* 'can'; if μηχανή (Dor. μᾱχ-) is cogn., μᾶχος must be read in Theoc. l.c. with some codd.)

**μία**, fem. of εἷς (q.v.).

**μῐαιγᾰμία**, ἡ, *unlawful wedlock*, in pl., Suid.

⊛ **μῐαίνω**, fut. μιᾰνῶ Antipho 2.2.11; 3 sg. μιᾰνεῖ *Berl.Sitzb.*1927.158 (Cyrene), Lxx *Is.*30.22, al.: aor. ἐμίηνα Il.4.141, Hp.*Flat.*14, App. *BC*2.104, ἐμίᾱνα Pi.*N.*3.16, S.*Fr.*104, E.*Hel.*1000, *IA* [1595], Lxx *Ge.* 34.5, al.; part. μιάνας Sol.32.3: pf. μεμίαγκα Plu.*TG*21:—Med., aor. ἐμιήνατο Nonn.*D.*45.288:—Pass., fut. μιανθήσομαι Pl.*R.*621c: aor. ἐμιάνθην, Ep. μιάνθην (v. infr.): pf. μεμίασμαι (v. infr.), μεμίαμμαι Lxx *Nu.*5.14, al., D.C.51.22; 3 sg. μεμίανται Porph.*Abst.*4.16 (but 3 pl., Phalar.*Ep.*121.2); inf. μεμιάνθαι D.S.36.13, but μεμιάσθαι Horap.1.44: Cyrenaic aor. 2 Pass. ἐμίᾱν in 3 sg. subj. μιᾷ *Berl.Sitzb.* 1927.160, al.: fut. Pass. μιᾱσέω in 3 sg. ind. μιᾱσεῖ ib.164:—*stain, dye*, ὡς δ' ὅτε τίς τ' ἐλέφαντα γυνὴ φοίνικι μιήνῃ Il.4.141; ὥσπερ ἔβενος περίδρομος ἐλέφαντα τὸν βραχίονα μιαίνων Hld.10.15. **2.** *stain, sully*, μιάνθησαν ἔθειραι αἵματι καὶ κονίῃσι Il.16.795, cf. 23.732; μιάνθην αἵματι μηροί 4.146; αἵματι πεσεῖ μιανθεὶς S.*OC*1374, cf. A.*Ag.*209 (lyr.); τοὺς θεῶν βωμοὺς αἵματι μ. Pl.*Lg.*782c; μ. βωμὸν εὐγενεῖ φόνῳ E.*IA* l.c.; βορβόρῳ . . ὕδωρ μιαίνων λαμπρὸν A.*Eu.*695. **3.** freq. of moral pollution, *taint, defile*, Pi. l.c., etc.; κλέος Sol. l.c., E.*Hel.* l.c.; τὸ καλῶς πεφυκὸς οὐδεὶς ἂν μιάνειεν λόγος S.*Fr.*104; ἐνὶ πόνῳ πολλὰ καὶ λαμπρὰ ἔργα μιῆναι App.*BC*2.104; εὔφημον ἦμαρ κακαγγέλῳ γλώσσῃ μ. A.*Ag.*637; μιαίνων εὐσέβειαν Ἄρης Id.*Th.*344 (lyr.); τὴν δίκην Id.*Ag.*1669; τὰ ἱερά, τὸ θεῖον, Pl.*Lg.*868b, *Ti.*69d; οἶκον θόρυβος μιαίνει Porph.*Abst.*4.12; θεοὺς μιαίνειν οὔ τις ἀνθρώπων σθένει S.*Ant.*1044; τὴν ἁγνείαν τῶν θεῶν Antipho 2.2.12, cf. 2.1.10; *dishonour* a woman, Lxx *Ge.*34.5, al.:—Pass., *incur defilement*, A.*Supp.*366, E.*Or.*75, *Berl.Sitzb.* ll.cc., etc.; τὴν ψυχὴν Pl.*R.*621c; τῆς ἄλλης [γῆς] αὐτῷ μεμιασμένης Th.2.102; ἡ ψυχὴ μεμιασμένη καὶ ἀκάθαρτος Pl.*Phd.*81b; μιανθέντες τῷ τῆς ἀσεβείας μολυσμῷ Aristeas 66; of ritual defilement in funeral rites, *IG* 12(5).593.25 (Iulis).

**μῐαιφον-έω**, *commit murder*, E.*IA*1364, Plu.*Mar.*44. **2.** c. acc., *murder*, Isoc.12.181, Pl.*R.*565e, 571d, Luc.*DMort.*12.3. ⊛ **-ία**, ἡ, *bloodthirstiness*, D.25.84, D.S.17.5, Plu.*Art.*30; *murder*, Id.2.994a: pl., τυραννικαὶ μ. ib.457b. ⊛ **-ος**, ον, (parox.) *bloodthirsty, murderous*, in Il. always epith. of Ares, 5.31, 455, 844, al.: coupled with θρασύχειρ, B.*Scol.Oxy.Fr.*5.1; μ. μύσος pollution *of murder*, E.*Andr.*335: c. gen., μ. τέκνων *murderess* of thy children, Id.*Med.*1346: Comp. -ώτερος Hdt.5.92.α', E.*Med.*266: Sup. -ώτατος Id.*Tr.*881. Adv. **-νως** Memn. 1.4: Sup. -ώτατα D.C.79.3.

**μίαν-σις**, εως, ἡ, *pollution*, Lxx *Le.*13.44, Porph.*Abst.*4.20. **-της**, ου, ὁ, = μιάστωρ 1, *EM*785.37. **-τός**, ή, όν, *stained, defiled*, *Gloss.*

**μῐᾰρία**, ἡ, *brutality*, X.*HG*7.3.6, Is.5.11, D.29.4. **II.** *defilement*, esp. *bloodguiltiness*, Antipho 2.3.1, 3.3.12; τὴν αὐτοῦ μ. εἰς ὑμᾶς αὐτοὺς ἐκτρέψαι Id.2.3.9:—condemned by Phryn.323.

**μῐᾰρόγλωσσος**, ον, *foul-mouthed*, *AP*7.377 (Eryc.).

⊛ **μῐᾰρός**, ά, όν, (μιαίνω) *stained* with blood, περὶ δ' αἷμα νένιπται, οὐδέ ποθι μιαρός Il.24.420. **2.** *defiled with blood*, Κιθαιρών E.*Ba.*1384 (anap.); μ. ἡμέραι certain days in the month Anthesterion, on which expiatory libations (χοαί) were offered to the dead, Hsch.; at Rome, ἡμέρα μ., = *dies nefastus*, D.C.51.19; μιαρά, τά, *actions resulting in ritual impurity*, *Berl.Sitzb.*1927.157 (Cyrene). **3.** generally, *defiled, polluted*, μ. καὶ ἄναγνος Antipho 2.1.10, cf. Pl.*Lg.*716e; of animals, *unclean*, ὗν δὲ Αἰγύπτιοι μιαρὸν ἥγηνται θηρίον εἶναι Hdt.2.47; θάλασσα ὕδωρ -ώτατον Heraclit.61. **4.** in moral sense, *abominable, foul*, ὦ μ. ἦθος S.*Ant.*746; *repulsive* to the moral sense, Arist.*Po.*$1452^{b}$36, al.: freq. in Ar. as a term of reproach, *blackguard*, μ. κεφαλή *Ach.* 285, cf. 282; μιαρώτατος ib.182; μ. φωνή *coarse, brutal* voice, *Eq.* 218, cf. S.*Tr.*987 (anap.); μιαρώτατος περὶ τὸν δῆμον Ar.*Eq.*831; μ. τε καὶ ὀλιγαρχικούς Pl.*R.*562d. Adv. -ρῶς Ar.*Eq.*800; οὕτω φανερῶς καὶ μ. D.21.69. **5.** ὦ μιαρέ *you rogue*, in a coaxing sense, Pl. *Phdr.*236e, al. **6.** = μάχλος, γύναικες μιαρώταται Alc.39. **7.** physically *ugly*, γυναῖκα ὀφθῆναι μ. X.Eph.3.12.

**μῐᾰρότης**, ητος, ἡ, *foulness*, *An.Ox.*2.440.

**μῐᾰρο-φᾰγέω**, *eat abominable meats*, and **-φᾰγία**, ἡ, *eating of abominable meats*, Lxx 4*Ma.*5.27.

**μί-ασμα** [ῐ], ατος, τό, (μιαίνω) *stain, defilement*, esp. by murder or other crime, *taint of guilt*, A.*Eu.*169 (lyr.), 281, etc.; οὐκ ἔστι γῆρας τοῦδε τοῦ μ. Id.*Th*682; μ. φεύγων αἵματος E.*Hipp.*35; μ. τῶν φυτευσάντων λαβεῖν S.*OT*1012; οὐ προσῆκον μίασμα εἰς οἴκους εἰσάγεσθαι Antipho 4.1.3; μ. τινὸς ἐπεξέρχεσθαι Id.4.3.6; τὸ μ. εἰς αὑτὸν δέχεσθαι Pl.*Lg.*871b: in pl., A.*Ag.*1420, *Ch.*1017; αἱμάτων μιάσμασι χρανθεῖσα γαῖα Id.*Supp.*265, etc. **II.** *that which defiles, pollution*, of persons, χώρας μ. καὶ θεῶν ἐγχωρίων Id.*Ag.*1645; πατροκτόνον μ. καὶ θεῶν στύγος, of Clytaemnestra, Id.*Ch.*1028· μ. χώρας ἐλαύνειν S.*OT*97; ὡς μ. τοῦδ' ἡμὶν ὄντος ib.241: in Prose more generally, πνεῦμα μεμιασμένον νοσηροῖσι μιάσμασι Hp.*Flat.*5. **-ασμός**, ὁ, = μίανσις, Lxx *Wi.*14.26, 2*Ep.Pet.*2.10, Plu.2.393c, Porph.*Abst.*4.20 (pl.), Iamb.*Myst.* 3.31 (pl.). **2.** *scandal, crime*, Gal.*Anim.Pass.*4 (pl.). **-άστωρ**, ορος, ὁ, (μιαίνω) *crime-stained wretch who pollutes others*, A.*Ch.*944, S.*OT*353, *El.*275; μ. Ἑλλάδος E.*Or.*1584: in later Prose, Jul.*Or.* 2.58d. **II.** *avenger* of such guilt (cf. ἀλάστωρ), A.*Eu.*177 (unless in signf. 1), S.*El.*603, E.*Med.*1371.

**μίαχος**· μίασμα, ἀσέβημα, κτλ., Hsch.; also, = τὸ δυσῶδες, Id. **μιαχρός**, ά, όν, = καθαρός, Id.

⊛ **μίγα** [ῐ], Adv. *mixed, blent with*, κωκυτῷ Pi.*P.*4.113; μ. θηλυτέρῃσιν A.R.4.1345; μ. τῷδε σὺν ἀνδρί *together* with . ., *Epigr.Gr.*386 (Apamea Cibotus).

**μῐγάδην** [ᾰ], Adv., = foreg., Nic.*Al.*277, 349.

**μῐγάδις**, Adv., = foreg., Theognost.*Can.*163.

**μῐγάζομαι**, Ep. for μείγνυμαι, μιγαζομένους φιλότητι Od.8.271, cf. Orph.*A.*343.

**μῐγάς**, άδος, ὁ and ἡ, *mixed pell-mell*, μιγάσιν Ἕλλησιν βαρβάροις θ' ὁμοῦ E.*Ba.*18, cf. 1356; ἐκ πολλῶν ἐθνῶν μιγάδες συλλεγέντες Isoc.4. 24, etc.; πολλοὶ δ' ἔπιπτον μιγάδες E.*Andr.*1142: c. dat., Θρήϊξιν μιγάδες Σκύθαι A.R.4.320: as fem., μ. λοιβαί Id.3.1210. **2.** = μιξοβάρβαρος, D.Chr.53.6.

**μίγ-δᾰ**, Adv. *promiscuously, confusedly*, Od.24.77, *h.Cer.*426, Alc. 70: c. dat., μίγδ' ἄλλοισι θεοῖσι *among* the gods, Il.8.437. ⊛ **-δην**, Adv., = foreg., *h.Merc.*494, A.R.3.1381, Orph.*Fr.*223.

**μιγδηράζειν**· ὑβρίζειν, Hsch.

⊛ **μῐγής**, ές, = μικτός, Nic.*Fr.*68.4.

⊛ **μίγμα**, ατος, τό, (μείγνυμι) *mixture, compound*, Emp. and Anaxag. ap.Arist.*Ph.*$187^{a}$33, cf. *Metaph* $1012^{a}$28. **2.** μίγματα, τά, of drugs, Plu.2.80a, Dsc.5.44, Apollon.ap.Gal.12.655; μ. σμύρνης καὶ ἀλόης *Ev.Jo.*19.39; of pigments, D.H.*Is.*4, *Comp.*21; of condiments, Plu. 2.997a; of amalgams, Zos.Alch.p.197 B. (In codd. sts. μῖγμα, for which **μεῖγμα** (formed like χεῦμα) shd. perh. be restored in Emp. and Anaxag.ap.Arist., but μίγμα (formed like χύμα) may be retained in later texts.)

**μιγμᾰτοπώλης**, ου, ὁ, *apothecary*, Gal.13.68.

**μιγμός**, οῦ, ὁ, = μίγμα, D.L.7.158.

**Μίδας** [ῐ], gen. ου or α, Ion. **Μίδης**, εω, ὁ, *Midas*, proverbial for his wealth, εἰ . . πλουτοίη . . Μίδεω καὶ Κινύρεω μάλιον Tyrt.12.6, cf. Hom.*Epigr.*3; ἐὰν . . πλουτῇ Κινύρα τε καὶ Μίδα μᾶλλον Pl.*Lg.*660e, cf. *R.*408b; ὑπὲρ . . τὸν Μίδα πλοῦτον Luc.*Merc.Cond.*20; his ass's ears alluded to in Ar.*Pl.*287, etc. **II.** *the luckiest throw* of the dice, which (with the Greeks) was when the numbers were all different, = Ἡρακλῆς, Eub.58. **III.** *a destructive insect in beans*, Thphr.*CP* 4.15.4.

⊛ **μιεῖν**· ἐσθίειν, Hsch.

**μῐερός**, ά, όν, late form of μιαρός, Call.*Hec.*1.4.7, *Epigr.Gr.*336.4 (Alexandria Troas).

**μιηφόνος**, ον, = μιαιφόνος, Archil.48.

**Μιθρᾰδάτης** [δᾱ], ου, ὁ, *Mithradates*, *PPetr.*3 pp.170, 172 (iii B.C.), *OGI*345.6 (i B.C.), etc.:—also **Μιθριδ-**, *IG*7.303.80 (Oropus, iii B.C.), *PStrassb.*115.12 (ii B.C.), etc.; **Μιθροδ-**, *PGurob* 22.2 (iii B.C.); **Μειριδ-**, *PAvrom.*1 *A* 29, *B* 31; **Μιραδ-**, ib.2 *A* 12, *B* 17 (i B.C.):—hence Adj. **Μιθραδάτειος**, α, ον, πόλεμος App.*Mith.*121; **Μ.** φάρμακα ib.111, cf. Gal.14.2; **Μιθριδάτειος** ἀντίδοτος Dsc.*Ther.*3; **Μιθριδάτιον**, τό, *dog's-tooth violet, Erythronium Dens canis*, Plin.*HN*25.6.2 (also, = σκόρδιον, ibid., Ps.-Dsc.3.111); **Μιθραδατισμός**, ὁ, *siding with M.*, Str.13.1.66.

**Μιθραῖον**, τό, *shrine of Mithras*, *PGurob* 22.10 (iii B.C.).

**Μιθράκανα**, τά, *festival of Mithras*, *Rev.Ét.Gr.*2.18 (Amorium), cf. Str.11.14.9 (v.l. Μιθρακηνοῖς).

**Μίθρας**, ου, ὁ, *Mithras*, X.*Cyr.*7.5.53, Str.15.3.13, *IG*14.996, al., Porph.*Antr.*6, etc.

**Μιθριακός**, ή, όν, *of Mithras*, μυστήριον Zos.Alch.p.114 B.

**μίθρος ἢ μίθρους**· συζευγνυμένους, Hsch. **μίκαι**· λάχανα, ὄμβρια, Id. **μίκας**· μικρολόγος, Id.

⊛ **μῑκῐχιζόμενος**, Lacon. **μικκιχιδδόμενος**, in athletic contests at Sparta, *boy under age*, *IG*5(1).285, al.; ἀπὸ μικιχιζομένων μέχρι μελλειρονείας ib.296: **μικιζόμενος** is expld. as *a male child in his third year*, Λέξεις Ἡροδότου in Stein Hdt. ii p.465 (Berol.1871).

**μικκοπρεπής**, ές, Dor. form of μικροπρεπής, *POxy.*410.73.

⊛ **μικκός**, ά, όν, Dor. and Boeot. for μικρός, Ar.*Ach.*909, Archyt.1, Theoc.5.66, 8.64, Call.*Cer.*111; also (ή, όν) Ion., αἱ μικκαὶ σφαῖραι Hp. *Art.*3 (cod. Apollon.Cit.); ἐλαίου μίκκον (sic) Id.*Nat.Mul.*93 (v.l.), cf. 100 (v.l.), Call.*Fr.*179, *Iamb.*1.382, Herod.6.59, *AP*5.120 (Phld.), Ael.Dion.*Fr.*187; found in Epicur.*Fr.*560, Müller-Bees *Inschriften der jüdischen Katakombe* p.51 (ii/iii A.D.), *PLond.*2.239.16 (iv A.D.), *Sammelb.*5747; cf. μικός.

**μικκότρωγος**, ον, *eating little*, name of a parasite in Plaut.*Stich.* 242.

**μικκύλος** [ῠ], Dim. of μικρός, Mosch.1.13.

**μίκλας**· αἶγας, Hsch.

⊛ **μῑκός**, ή, όν, = μικρός, μικκός, Hp.*Nat.Mul.*47 (v.l.), *IG*$2^{2}$.47.12 (iv B.C.), 1407.10 (iv B.C.), *Trag.Adesp.*31 (= *Stoic.*2.57), *PFay.*127.12, 13 (ii A.D.), *POxy.*1655.9, 2153.18 (both iii A.D.).

**μικρ-ᾰδῐκητής**, οῦ, ὁ, *doing petty wrongs*, Arist.*Rh.*$1391^{a}$29. **-αίτιος**, ον, *complaining of trifles, easily provoked*, Demetr.Lac.*Herc.*1055. 24, Luc.*Fug.*19, Charito 6.6; *amor* μ. *semper* Plin.*Ep.*2.2.1. **-ασπις** or **σμίκρ-**, ιδος, ὁ, ἡ, *with small shield*, Pl.*Criti.*119b. **-αῦλαξ**,

ἄκος, ὁ, ἡ, *with small furrows*: χῶρος μ. *a little* field, *AP*6.36 (Phil.). **-έμπορος**, ὁ, *pedlar, huckster*, Babr.111.1, Aesop.322b.

**μικρο-βᾰσῐλεία**, ἡ, *small kingdom*, Eust.76.40, 1952.42. **-βᾰσῐλεύς**, έως, ὁ, = μικρὸς βασιλεύς, Id.81.35, etc. **-βοτρυς**, gloss on μικρόρρωξ, Hsch. **-βωλος**, ον, *in small lumps*, σμύρνα Dsc.1.64. **-γένειος**, ον, *with small chin*, Polem.*Phgn.*35. **-γενυς**, υ, gen. υος, *with small jaws*, Adam.2.23. **-γλάφῠρος** [ᾰ], ον, *refined, neat*, Arist.*Phgn.*808a30. **-γνωμοσύνη**, ἡ, *narrow-mindedness*, Poll.4.13. **-γρᾰφέω**, *write with a short vowel*, Sch.rec.A.*Pers.*297, Hdn.*Epim.*200 (both Pass.). **-γρᾰφία**, ἡ, *writing with a short vowel*, Eust.410.47. **-δοσία**, ἡ, *giving small presents, stinginess*, Plb.5.90.5. **-δουλος**, ὁ, *little slave*, Arr.*Epict.*4.1.55. **-θαύμαστος**, ον, *admiring trifles*, Sch.Ar.*Eq.*677. **-θεν**, Adv. *from childhood up*, *POxy.*1216.5 (ii/iii A.D.). **-θῡμία**, ἡ, *faint-heartedness*, *Placit.* 5.13.1. **-θῡμος**, ον, *mean-spirited, narrow-minded*, D.H.11.12. **-καμπής**, ές, *with a small bend, much bent*, Antyll.(?)ap.Orib. 45.18.5, Paul.Aeg.6.18. **-καρπία**, ἡ, *bearing of small fruit*, Thphr. *CP*6.18.8, Str.2.1.16. **-καρπος**, ον, *bearing small fruit*, Thphr. *CP*2.10.2. **-κενόσπουδος**, ον, *busy with foolish trifles*, Phld.*Herc.* 1457.9. **-κέφᾰλος**, ον, *small-headed*, Arist.*Pr.*955b6: Comp., Id.*Phgn.*809b5: Sup., Id.*Pr.*955b5. **-κίνδῡνος**, ον, *exposing oneself to danger for trifles*, opp. μεγαλοκίνδυνος, Id.*EN*1124b7. **-κλέπτης**, ου, ὁ, *petty thief*, Sch.Ar.*V.*962. **-κοίλιος**, ον, *with small ventricle*, Arist.*PA*667a32. 2. *with small internal canal*, Mnesith. ap.Orib.21.7.6. **-κομψος**, ον, *finicking, affected*, D.H.*Comp.* 4. **-λεγής**, ές, coined as opp. of τανηλεγής by Eust.1436.12. **-ληψία**, ἡ, *acceptance of small presents*, Plb.5.90.5. **-λογέομαι**, *to be* μικρολόγος, esp. *examine minutely*, Cratin.429, X.*HG*3.1.26; *split hairs*, οὐ μικρολογησόμενος οὐδὲ περὶ τῶν ὀνομάτων μαχούμενος Lys.33.3: c. inf., μικρολογούμενοι παθεῖν App.*Pun.*79:—later in Act., D.H. *Dem.*21; *use trivial language*, Demetr.*Eloc.*56. 2. *deal meanly* or *shabbily*, πρὸς τοὺς θεούς (in sacrifice) Luc.*Nav.*28; περὶ τοὺς θεούς Plu.2.179f; πρὸς τοὺς φίλους Hierocl.*in CA* 7 p.429 M. **-λογητέον**, *one must be niggardly*, ἔν τινι Plu.2.822a. ❀**-λογία** or **σμικρ-** (v. μικρός), ἡ, *meanness, stinginess*, Thphr.*Char.*10, Plb.31.27.16. II. *pettiness*, Pl.*R.*486a, Arist.*Metaph.*995a10, Plot.1.4.7; *hair-splitting*, Isoc.13.8, etc.: pl., *meticulous arguments, 'logic-chopping'*, Pl.*Hp.Ma.* 304b; *minutiae*, in Art, D.H.*Comp.*25. 2. *disparagement, depreciating language*, Isoc.15.2. **-λόγος** or **σμικρ-**, ον, *counting trifles, careful about trifles*; and so, 1. *caring about petty expenses, penurious*, D.59.36, Thphr.*Char.*10.1, Hyp.*Fr.*255, etc.; σὺ δὲ μ. ἄρ' οὐ θέλων καινὰς πρίασθαι (sc. ἐμβάδας) Men.109.4. 2. *cavilling about trifles, captious*, μ. καὶ μεμψίμοιρος Isoc.12.8; μ. καὶ μικρολύπους Plu. 2.171b; *petty*, Pl.*Smp.*210d. Adv. -γως Plu.2.730b. **-λῡπος**, ον, *vexed at trifles*, ib.129c, 171b, Heph.Astr.1.1; μ. ἤθη Plu.*Phoc.* 2. **-μεγέθης**, ες, *small in size*, Xenocr.ap.Orib.2.58.95, Sor.1.33, Heph.Astr.1.1. **-μελής**, ές, *small-limbed*, Arist.*Phgn.*808a 29. **-μέρεια**, ἡ, *a consisting of small parts*, Id. *de An.*405a11, *Mete.* 348a9, *Pr.*967b7. **-μερής** or **σμικρ-**, ές, (μέρος) *consisting of small parts*, Pl.*Ti.*60e (Comp.), 78b (Comp.), Arist.*Metaph.*989a1 (Sup.), *Cael.*303b27, Ptol.*Alm.*2.10 (Comp.). Adv. σμικρομερῶς *to a slight extent*, *PMasp.*2.6 (vi A.D.). **-μετρέω**, *give short measure*, Sch. Ar.*Pl.*436. **-μισθος**, ον, *receiving small pay*, Procop.*Goth.*4.25 (s. v.l., fort. μακρο-).

**μικρ-όμμᾰτος**, ον, *small-eyed*, Arist.*Phgn.*808a30.

**μικρό-μυρτος**, ον, *with small berries*, of myrtle, Thphr.*CP*6.18. 5. **-νησος**, ἡ, *small island*, Eust.1619.8. **-πλεον**, Adv. *a little more*, *BGU*316.3 (iv A.D.):—also **-πλους**, ζήσας μικρόπλους ἔτη κβ' *IG*14.2560; ζ. μ. ἐτῶν ἑξήκοντα ib.2300. **-πνοος**, ουν, (πνοή) *short breathing*, Hp.*Epid.*2.3.7. **-ποιέω**, *lower the tone of* writing, Longin.41.1. **-ποιός**, όν, *making small, diminishing*, Id.43.6. **-πολῖτεία**, ἡ, *citizenship in a petty state*, Stob.3.39. 29. **-πολίτης** [ῑ], ου, ὁ, *citizen of a petty state*, Ar.*Eq.*817, X.*HG* 2.2.10, Aeschin.2.120, D.Chr.34.46. **-πολῖτικός**, ή, όν, *belonging to a petty state*, Ar.*Fr.*819. **-πόνηρος**, ον, *wicked in small things*, Arist.*Pol.*1295b10. **-πους**, ουν, gen. ποδος, *small-footed*, Eust. 1502.26. **-πρέπεια**, ἡ, *meanness, shabbiness*, Arist.*Rh.*1366b19, *EN*1107b20, 1122a30, Jul.*Mis.*339b, Hierocl.*in CA*17 p.459 M. II. *triviality*, Demetr.*Eloc.*83. **-πρεπής**, ές, (πρέπω) *petty, mean, shabby*, opp. μεγαλοπρεπής, Arist.*EN*1123a27; ἡ ἀκριβολογία μικροπρεπές ib.1122b8; μικροπρεπὲς ἡ ἀκρίβεια Demetr.*Eloc.*53, cf. 60, Charond.ap.Stob.4.2.24, Phalar.*Ep.*118 (Comp.); μ. [βίος] Plu.2.8a. Adv. -πῶς Posidon.ap.Gal.5.471, Sch.E.*Ph.*111. **-πρόσωπος**, ον, *small-faced*, Arist.*Phgn.*808a30. **-πτερα**, f.l. for μικρὰ πτερά, *Gloss.* **-πτέρυξ**, ῠγος, ὁ, ἡ, *with small wings*, Sch.Pi.*P.* 4.29. **-πύρηνος** [ῡ], ον, *with small kernels*, Thphr.*CP*1.16.2 (Comp.). **-ρραξ**, ᾶγος, ὁ, ἡ, *with small berries*, of the currant-grape, Dsc.5.2. **-ρρῑν**, ῖνος, ὁ, ἡ, *small-nosed*, Suid. s. v. κολοβόρριν.

**μικρορροπύγιος** [ῡ], ον, *with small rump*, Arist.*HA*504a34.

**μικρόρρωξ**, ωγος, ὁ, ἡ, = μικρόρραξ, Hsch.

❀**μικρός** and **σμῑκρός**, ά, όν, Dor., Ion. **μικκός** (q.v.): **σμικρός** is corroborated by metre in Il.17.757, Hes.*Op.*361, and might be restored in Il.5.801, Od.3.296 (μικρός codd.); it is prob. the only form in Hdt. (μικρός 2.74 codd.): freq. in Lyr. and prob. always in Trag. (exc. where metre requires μικρός, as S.*Aj.*161 (anap., Comp.)); most freq. in Pl.; but in Th., also Ar. and other Com., μικρός prevails, σμικρός being found Th.4.13, 7.75, 8.81, Ar.*Ach.*523, *V.*5; Att. Inscrr. have σμικρός *IG*1².313.111, al., μικρός ib.369.10, al.:—*small, little*, 1. in Size, μ. ἔην δέμας Il.5.801; μ. λίθος Od.3.296; κίρκον, ὅ τε σμικρῇσι φόνον φέρει ὀρνίθεσσιν Il.17.757; σμ. ἄστεα Hdt.1.5; μεγάθεϊ σμικροί Id.2.74: with Dims., μ. πολίχνιον, γήδιον, παιδάρια, Isoc.5.145, X. *Cyr.*8.3.38, *Ages.*1.21: as a Com. exaggeration, δικαστηρίδιον μ. πάνυ Ar.*V.*803; σκαλαθυρμάτι' ἄττα μ. Id.*Nu.*630, etc.: c. inf., μικροὶ δ' ὁρᾶν Id.*Pax*821: as a term of reproach, Κλειγένης ὁ μικρός Id.*Ra.*709, cf. Pl.*Prt.*323d, Arist.*EN*1123b7, Alex.98.7; Ἀμύντας ὁ μ. Arist. *Pol.*1311b3; οἱ ἐν μικρῷ μεγάλοι *short but stoutly built*, Philostr.*Gym.* 36; ὁ μ. δάκτυλος *SIG*1172.4 (Lebena). 2. in Quantity, σμικρὸν ἐπὶ σμικρῷ καταθεῖναι Hes.*Op.*361; μέλιτος μικρόν Ar.*V.*878; μ. ὄψον, ἀργυρίδιον, X.*Mem.*3.14.1, Ar.*Pl.*240, cf. Antiph.44. 3. in Amount or Importance, *petty, trivial, slight*, σμ. πρόφασις Thgn.323; ἔπος, ἔγκλημα, ῥοπή, etc., S.*OC*443, *Tr.*361, *OT*961, etc.; ἐκ σμικροῦ λόγου on some *slight* pretext, Id.*OC*620; ἐν σμικρῷ λόγῳ παρῆκεν as of *small* account, ib.569; αἰτίας μικρᾶς πέρι E.*Andr.*387, etc.; οὐδὲ μικρόν, = οὐδὲ γρῦ, D.19.37; of persons, of *small* account, opp. μέγας, σμ. ἐν σμικροῖς, μέγας ἐν μεγάλοις Pi.*P.*3.107; ἄριστ' ἂν καὶ μέγας ὀρθοῖθ' ὑπὸ μικροτέρων S.*Aj.*161 (anap.), etc.; σμ. τίθησί με Id.*OC*958; βίος ὁ μ., = μέτριος, E.*Fr.*504; τίνος σμικροτάτου μεταβαλόντος, σμικρότατος τὴν δύναμιν, Pl.*R.*473b; of the mind, οὐ σμικρὸν φρονεῖ S.*Aj.*1120; of style, *mean*, [Φίλιστος] μικρὸς ταῖς ἐκφράσεσιν D.H.*Vett.Cens.*3.2; of festivals, *of lesser importance*, Ἀλίεια τὰ μεγάλα καὶ τὰ μ. *SIG*1067.14 (Cedreae). II. of Time, *short*, Pi.*O.*12.12, Ar.*Pl.*126, etc.; εἰς μ. χρόνον Pl.*R.*498d; ἐν μικρῷ (sc. χρόνῳ) *shortly*, X.*Cyn.*5.32, *Eq.* 8.7; πρὸ μικροῦ Poll.1.72; ἔτι μικρὸν καὶ καταλιθοβολήσουσί με Lxx *Ex.*17.4. 2. of Age, *young*, Ostr.*Bodl.*i 237 (ii B.C.), etc. III. Adverbial usages, 1. regul. Adv. σμικρῶς, *but little*, Pl.*Criti.*107d; μικρῶς *by a little*, prob. in Archim.*Stom.*1: Sup. σμικρότατα X.*Mem.* 3.11.12. 2. σμικροῦ or μικροῦ *within a little, almost*, Id.*Cyr.*1.4.8, D.18.151, etc.; in full, μικροῦ δεῖν, v. δεῖ II, δέω (B) I; μικροῦ τινος ἀπελείφθη τοῦ μή.. Ach.Tat.7.13; but μικροῦ πρίασθαι *for a little, cheap*, X.*Mem.*2.10.4. 3. σμικρῷ *by a little*, with Comp., Pl.*Plt.* 262c, etc.; also σμικρῷ πρόσθεν *a little* before, Id.*Lg.*719b, etc.; μικρῷ ἄνωθεν D.44.6. 4. μικρόν *a little*, σμικρὸν ὑπολείπεσθαι, σμ. τι παρακλίνειν, X.*An.*5.4.22, Pl.*Cra.*410a; of Time, X.*An.*3.1.11, etc.; repeated, μικρὸν μικρόν Antiph.10: pl., of Degree, σμικρὰ γεωμετρίας ἔμπειροι Pl.*R.*527a, etc.; σμίκρ' ἄττα διατρίψαντες Id.*Prt.*316a; μικρὰ διακινήσω σε περὶ τοῦ πράγματος Sosip.1.22; περιπάτησον μικρὰ μετ' ἐμοῦ Men.*Sam.*243, cf. Plu.*Luc.*31. 5. with Preps., a. ἐπὶ σμικρόν *but a little*, S.*El.*414, Antipho 6.18, Hdt.4.129. b. κατὰ μικρόν *into small pieces*, X.*An.*7.3.22; so κατὰ μικρὰ γενομένης τῆς δυνάμεως ib. 5.6.32; also, *little by little*, κατὰ μικρὸν ἀεί Ar.*V.*702, cf. *Nu.*741; opp. συλλήβδην, Pl.*R.*344a; καὶ κατὰ σμ. or μ. *ever so little*, Id.*Sph.*241c, Isoc.3.10, D.2.22. c. παρὰ μικρόν *within a little*, παρὰ μ. ἐλθεῖν c. inf., to be *within an ace* of doing, E.*Heracl.*295 (anap.), cf. Isoc.7. 6, etc.; παρὰ μ. ἦλθον ἀποθανεῖν Id.17.42; τὸ παρὰ μ. ὥσπερ οὐδὲν ἀπέχειν δοκεῖ Arist.*Ph.*197a30; but τὸ παρὰ μ. σῴζεσθαι to be *only just* saved, Id.*Rh.*1371b11, cf. Simp.*in Ph.*344.10; *gradual, imperceptible* change, Arist.*Pol.*1303a20; οὐδὲ παρὰ μ. ἦν κρεῖττον c. inf., Plb.12.20.7; [ἡ τύχη] παρὰ μ. εἰς ἑκάτερα ποιεῖ μεγάλας ῥοπάς Id.15. 6.8, cf. Isoc.4.59; but also παρὰ μ. ποιεῖσθαι, ἡγεῖσθαι, to think *little* of.., D.61.51, Isoc.5.79. d. μετὰ μικρόν *a little* after, *Ev.Matt.*26. 73. IV. besides regul. Comp. and Sup. μικρότερος, -ότατος (Ar. *Eq.*789, D.*Prooem.*48, etc.), there are the irreg. ἐλάσσων, ἐλάχιστος, from ἐλαχύς, and μείων, μεῖστος, also μειότερος; v. μείων. [ῑ by nature; ῐ only in late Poetry, Epigr.ap.Phleg.*Fr.*36.17 J.] (Perh. cf. Lat. *mīca, mīcidus*, OHG. *smāhi*, ONorse *smár* 'little'.)

**μικρό-σαρκος**, ον, *with little flesh*, Xenocr.ap.Orib.2.58.81. **-σῑτία**, ἡ, *an eating little, spare diet*, Alex.197. **-σῑτος**, ον, *eating little*, Hsch. and Suid. s. v. σικχός. **-σκελής**, ές, *short-legged*, Arist.*PA* 684a10. **-σοφος**, ον, *wise in small matters*, D.S.26.1. **-σπερμος**, ον, *with small seeds*, Thphr.*HP*8.3.5 (Comp.). **-σπλαγχνος**, ον, *with small viscera*, Gal.5.318: Sup., Mnesith.ap.Orib.21.7. 6. **-στᾰχυς**, υ, *with small ear*, Thphr.*HP*8.4.3. **-στηθος**, ον, *narrow-chested*, Mnesith.ap.Orib.21.7.6 (Sup.). **-στομος**, ον, *with a small mouth* or *orifice*, ἄγγος Hp.*Morb.*4.57; ζῷα Arist.*HA* 502a8; of the womb, Sor.2.56. ❀**-σφαιρον**, τό, name of the smallest lump of Indian μαλάβαθρον, *Peripl.M.Rubr.*65. **-σφυκτέω**, *have a weak pulse*, Herod.Med. in *Rh.Mus.*58.83, Gal.7.194. **-σφυκτος**, ον, *with a weak pulse*, Dsc.5.9, Gal.9.831. **-σφυξία**, ἡ, *weakness of pulse*, Id.7.137, Paul.Aeg.3.34. **-τεχνία**, ἡ, *pettiness in art*, Sch.D.T.p.110 H.

**μικρότης** or **σμικρ-** (v. μικρός), ητος, ἡ, *smallness*, first in Anaxag.1, cf. Arist.*Metaph.*1056b29; διὰ σμικρότητα ἀόρατα Pl.*Ti.*43a, cf. Isoc. 4.27; of voice, Arist.*de An.*422b30; ἀνέμων Thphr.*Vent.*1: pl., μεγέθη καὶ μ. Plu.2.687e. 2. *meanness, pettiness*, of rank, Isoc.4.93, Arist.*Pol.*1302b4; of matters, Id.*Rh.*1393a9; of language, *triviality*, Longin.43.1.

**μικρο-τοκιστής**, οῦ, ὁ (in Lat. form), *small money-lender*, *CIL*9. 823 (Luceria). **-τοπος**, ον, *with a small opening*, ὀφθαλμοί Herod. Med. in *Rh.Mus.*58.86. **-τράπεζος** [ᾰ], ον, *keeping a mean, shabby table*, Antiph.172.1. **-τράχηλος** [ᾰ], ον, *with small cervix*, of the womb, Sor.2.56. **-τρῐχος**, ον, (θρίξ) *short-haired*, Arist.*HA* 498b17. **-φάγος** [ᾰ], ον, *eating little*, Suid. s. v. ματιολοιχός.

❀**μικρ-όφθαλμος** or **σμικρ-**, ον, *small-eyed*, Hp.*Epid.*6.7.1, Procl. *Par.Ptol.*203, *BGU*364.6 (vi A.D.).

**μικρο-φῐλοτῑμία**, ἡ, *petty ambition*, Thphr.*Char.*23 tit. **-φῐλότῑμος**, ον, *seeking petty distinctions*, ib.23.2. **-φροσύνη**, ἡ, *littleness of mind*, σοφιστικὴ μ. Plu.2.351a, cf. Poll.4.13. **-φρων**, ονος, ὁ, ἡ,

(φρήν) *small-minded*, D.C.61.5, Max.Tyr.41.5 (σμ-). Adv. -φρόνως Poll.4.15. **-φυής**, ές, *of low growth, short*, Sch.Ar.*Av*.439, Porph. *Antr*.28. Adv. -φυῶς, ὑποκορίσαι Eust.1196.11. **-φυΐα**, ἡ, *low stature, low growth*, Str.17.2.1. **-φυλλος**, ον, *with small leaves*, ποίη, παρθένιον τὸ μ., Hp.*Ulc*.14 (**σμικρόφυλλον**, τό, Id.ap.Gal.19.128). **-φωνία**, ἡ, *weakness of voice*, Arist.*GA*787a3. ⊛ **-φωνος**, ον, *weak-voiced*, Alex.26, Arist.*GA*787a4, Gal.2.656. II. of letters, *weak-sounding*, D.H.*Comp*.14. **-χαρής**, ές, (χαίρω) *easily pleased*: τὰ μ. *paltry pleasantries*, Longin.4.4; τὰ κατάρρυθμα μικροχαρῆ Id.41.1; ἡδοναὶ ἀγεννεῖς καὶ μ. Antip.*Stoic*.3.255, cf. Phld.*Po*.5.25. **-χωρος**, ον, *with little land* or *soil*, Str.3.4.19. **-ψυχέω**, *swoon, faint*, = λιποψυχέω, Arist.*Pr*.890b11. ⊛ **-ψυχία**, ἡ, *littleness of soul, meanness of spirit*, Isoc.5.79, D.18.279, 19.193, Arist.*EN*1125a33, Men. *Georg.Fr*.3, Cic.*Att*.9.11.4, Longin.4.7. **-ψυχος**, ον, *mean-spirited*, Isoc.4.172 (Comp.), D.18.269, Arist.*EN*1123b10. Adv. -χως Procop.Gaz.*Ep*.59.

**μικρ-ύνω** or **σμικρ-**, *belittle*, Demetr.*Eloc*.236. 2. *make small, lessen*, Dsc.*Eup*.1.154, Gal.18(1).77. 3. *write with a short vowel*, σμικρυνθέντος τοῦ ο Eust.68.1, cf. Zonar. s.v. ἔρον. **-ώνυμος**, ον, (ὄνομα) in Comp., *named by a smaller number*, πολύγωνος Iamb.*in Nic*.p.71 P.

**μικτέον**, (μείγνυμι) *one must mix*, Pl.*Ti*.48a codd. (leg. **μεικτέον**).

**μικτός**, ή, όν, *mixed, blended*, Ar.*Th*.1114, Pl.*Phlb*.22d, etc.; opp. ἁπλοῦς, Id.*R*.547e; μ. ἐκ τούτων *compounded* of these, Id.*Lg*.837b, cf. D.H.*Dem*.41. Adv. -τῶς Str.1.2.27, Gal.9.703. 2. *motley*, *POxy*.1153.14 (i A.D.). (In early texts **μεικτός** (which is written in *PCair.Zen*.292.25, al. (iii B.C.)) shd. prob. be restored, v. μείγνυμι.)

**μικτότης**, ητος, ἡ, *compoundedness*, opp. ἁπλότης, Dam.*Pr*.65.

**μικτόχροος**, ον, *party-coloured*, Archim.*Bov*.13, 21.

⊛ **μικύθ-ειος** [ῠ], α, ον, Adj. of pr. n. Μίκυθος, σκάφια *Inscr.Délos* 443 *B b*69 (ii B.C.). **-ινον**· τὸ μικρὸν καὶ νήπιον, Hsch. **-ος**, η, ον, Dim. of μικκός, as pr. n. [ῑ, *AP*6.355 (Leon.).]

⊛ **μῖλαξ**, ᾰκος, ἡ, Att. for σμῖλαξ; v. σμῖλαξ IV. II. = μέλλαξ, Hermipp.33.

⊛ **Μιλήσιος**, α, ον, *Milesian*, Hdt.1.17, etc.; Μιλήσιοι, οἱ, *the Milesians*, Id.5.28, etc.: prov., πάλαι ποτ' ἦσαν ἄλκιμοι M. Anacr.85; Μιλησίη (sc. χώρα), ἡ, Hdt.5.29:—also **Μιλησιακός**, ή, όν, Plu.*Crass*.32, etc.; -κά, τά, title of work by Aristides:—pecul. fem. **Μιλησίς**, ίδος, παρθενικαί Parth.*Fr*.29.6.

**Μιλησιουργής**, ές, (ἔργον) *of Milesian work*, κλίνη Critias 35 D., cf. *IG*1².330.3,7, 11(2).287*B*135 (Delos, iii B.C.); ἡδυπότιον ib.2².1534.246.

⊛ **Μίλητος** [ῑ], Aeol. **Μίλλᾱτος** Theoc.28.21: ἡ:—*Miletus*, Il.2.868, Hdt.5.28, etc.

**μιλι-άζω**, *measure by miles and mark by milestones*, in Pass., Plb.34.11.8. **-αρήσιον**, τό, = Lat. *milliarense*, a small coin, Just.*Nov*.105.2.α', al.; **-αρίσιον** Olymp.Alch.p.76 B., Aët.3.100. ⊛ **-άριον** [ῑλᾰ], τό, *a high copper vessel*, pointed at the top and furnished with winding tubes, to boil water in, *AP*11.244, Ath.3.98c, Hero*Spir*.2.34; gloss on ἱπνολέβης, Sch.Luc.*Lex*.8. II. *milestone*, Lyd.*Mens*.4.49. **-ασμός**, ὁ, *measuring by miles and marking by milestones*, Str.6.2.1. ⊛ **-ον**, τό, *a Roman mile*, Plb.34.11.8, Str.3.1.9, *Ev. Matt*.5.41, Plu.*CG*7:—also **μείλιον** (q.v.).

⊛ **μιλλός**, ή, όν, = βραδύς, Hsch.:—hence **μιλλότης**, ἡ, prob. for μιλώτις in Hsch. s.v. νωχέλεια.

**μῖλος**, ἡ, = σμῖλαξ, *yew*, *Taxus baccata*, Cratin.98, Thphr.*HP*3.4.2, 5.7.6. II. *flower of the yew*, Poll.6.106 (dub. l.).

**μιλτ-άριον**, τό, Dim. of μίλτος III, μ. Τυφῶνος *PMag.Par*.1.2221. **-εῖον**, τό, *vessel for storing* μίλτος, *AP*6.205 (Leon.). **-ειος**, α, ον, *of* μίλτος, μ. στάγμα the *red* mark made by the carpenter's line, ib.6.103 (Phil.). **-εύς**, έως, ὁ, *ruddleman*, *IG*4²(1).143 (Epid., vi B.C.); perh. a pr. n. **-ηλιφής**, ές, (ἀλείφω) *painted with* μίλτος, *painted red*, of ships, Hdt.3.58; Com. of Athenians caught by the ruddled rope (cf. μιλτόω), Pl.Com.6 D. **-ῖνος**, η, ον, *of* μίλτος, γραμμή Plu.2.1081b, cf. Cleom.2.1; τὸ μ., = μίλτος I, Plu.2.287d. **-ίτης** [ῑτ], ου, ὁ, fem. ῖτις, *of the nature of* μίλτος, Plin.*HN*36.147.

**μιλτο-κάρηνος** [ᾰ], ον, *red-headed*, Opp.*H*.5.273. **-λογέω**, *test* the surfaces of stones *with a straight-edge smeared with* μίλτος, *IG*7.3073.120, al. (Lebad.); μ. τὴν ἐργασίαν *Inscr.Délos* 507 (iii B.C.). ⊛ **-πάρηος**, ον, (παρειά) *red-cheeked*, epith. of ships, which had their bows painted red, Il.2.637, Od.9.125: Com., τρίγλη μ. Macho ap.Ath.3.135b; also of a stone, Orph.*L*.615; of plains, Opp.*C*.3.509. ⊛ **-πρεπτος**, ον, *bright-red*, A.*Fr*.116. ⊛ **-πρωρος**, ον, gloss on μιλτοπάρηος, Apollon.*Lex*., Hsch.

⊛ **μίλτος**, ἡ, *red earth, red ochre, ruddle*, Hdt.4.191, 7.69, Ar.*Ec*.378, Diocl.Com.9, 10, *IG*2².1672.16, al., 4²(1).115.19 (Epid., iv/iii B.C.), Dsc.5.96, *POxy*.2144.6 (iii A.D.), etc. 2. *red lead*, Plin.*HN*33.115; μ. Λημνίς Nic.*Th*.864. II. = ἐρυσίβη, Paus.Gr.*Fr*.257. III. magical term for *blood*, μ. περιστερᾶς *PMag.Lond*.121.222; μ. Τυφῶνος *PMag.Leid.V*.3.25.

**μιλτο-φοριών**, ῶνος, ὁ, name of month at Amorgos, *IG*12(7).67.37 (Amorgos). **-φυρής**, ές, *daubed with red*, σχοῖνος *AP*6.103 (Phil.). **-χρως**, χρωτος, *red*, σκέλη Ezek.*Exag*.259.

⊛ **μιλτ-όω**, (μίλτος) *cover with ruddle*, πλίνθους *Supp.Epigr*.4.453.21 (Didyma, ii B.C.); σχοινίον Poll.8.104; τοῖχον S.E.*M*.10.126; glossed by πλύνω, Hsch.:—Med. or Pass., *cover oneself* or *be covered with ruddle*, Hdt.4.194; μεμιλτωμένη τῇ χειρί S.E. l.c.; σχοινίον μεμιλτωμένον the rope *covered with ruddle* with which they drove loiterers out of the Agora to the Pnyx, Ar.*Ach*.22, cf. Poll. l.c. **-ώδης**, ες, *red as* μίλτος, Eub.98.6, Str.16.4.20, Dsc.5.99, Luc.*Syr.D*.8. II. *producing* μίλτος, ὄρος Str.16.4.5. **-ωρυχία**, ἡ, μίλτος*-mine*, Amips.15. **-ωρύχος**, ον, (ὀρύσσω) *digging for* μίλτος, Poll.7.100. **-ωτός**, ή, όν, *coated with* μίλτος, Eust.1885.21.

**μιλφ-ός**, ὁ, *one who suffers from* μίλφωσις, Vett.Val.110.16, *Gloss*. II. **μίλφοι**, οἱ, = sq., Dsc.1.109, *Eup*.1.45, Gal.12.725, al. **-ωσις**, εως, ἡ, *falling off of the eyelashes*, ib.789.

⊛ **μιμαικύλον**, τό, *fruit of* κόμαρος, Crates Com.40, Amphis 38, Theopomp.Com.67, Thphr.*CP*2.8.2, Scyl.108, Porph.*Abst*.2.7; but **μεμαίκυλον**, Thphr.*HP*3.16.4, Poll.7.144, Gal.6.621:—also **μεμαίκυλος**, ἡ, ibid.; **μιμάκυλος**, Hsch.

**Μιμαλλών**, όνος, ἡ, mostly in pl., Macedon., = Βάκχαι, Str.10.3.10, Plu.*Alex*.2.

**μιμάξασα**· χρεμετίσασα, Hsch.; cf. μιμιχμός. **μίμαρ**· ἀναιδές, Id.

⊛ **μίμαρκυς** [ῐ], ἡ, *hare-soup* or *jugged hare*, with the blood of the animal in it, Ar.*Ach*.1112, Pherecr.221, Diph.1.

**Μίμας** [ῑ], αντος, ὁ, a promontory in Ionia, Od.3.172:—hence **Μιμαντοβάτης** [βᾰ], ου, ὁ, title of an official at Erythrae, *IGRom*.4.1543.

**μιμάς**, άδος, ἡ, *actress of* μῖμοι, Ael.*Fr*.123, *IG*14.2342 (Aquileia), *AP*9.139 tit.

**μίμαστα**· ἄγρια λάχανα, Hsch.

**μιμ-αυλέω**, *to be a* μίμαυλος, Hsch. ⊛ **-αυλος**, ὁ, *mimic actor*, accompanied on the flute, Ath.10.452f. **-εία**, ἡ, *farce*, metaph. in Ph.2.598 (v.l. μιμία). ⊛ **-έομαι**, fut. -ήσομαι: aor. ἐμιμησάμην Pi.*P*.12.21, etc.: pf. μεμίμημαι (v. infr.):—*imitate, represent, portray*, ἔργα Γιγάντων Batr.7; φωνάς *h.Ap*.163; γόον Pi.*P*.12.21; γλώσσης αὐτὴν A.*Ch*.564; τὴν τοῦ παιδὸς ὄρχησιν X.*Smp*.2.21; τινα Thgn.370, Hdt.4.166, Th.2.37, E.*El*.1037, etc.; μ. τινά τι one *in* a thing, Hdt.5.67; τινὰ κατὰ τὰ αἰδοῖα dub. in Id.2.104; κατὰ φωνὴν ἢ κατὰ σχῆμα Pl.*R*.393c; [ὀρθὴν πολιτείαν] ἐπὶ τὰ καλλίω, ἐπὶ τὰ αἰσχίονα μεμιμημένας, Id.*Plt*.293e; ἐπὶ τὸ σεμνόν Id.*Lg*.814e; ἡδοναὶ μεμιμημέναι τὰς ἀληθεῖς ἐπὶ τὰ γελοιότερα Id.*Phlb*.40c: c. acc. cogn., μιμήσεις πονηρὰς μ. τινά *imitate* him in what is bad, Id.*Lg*.705c, cf. Ar.*Nu*.1430, *Pl*.306; τὰ πλεῖστα μ. τὴν Κρητικὴν πολιτείαν Arist.*Pol*.1271b22: pf. part. μεμιμημένος, in act. sense, στύλοισι φοίνικας μεμιμημένοισι pillars *made to represent* palms, Hdt.2.169, cf. Pl.*Cra*.414b: in pass. sense, *made exactly like, portrayed*, γραφῇ Hdt.2.78,86, cf. Arist.*Rh*.1371b6: pres. part. in pass. sense, Pl.*R*.604e: fut. part. μιμηθησόμενον ib.599a: aor. part. μιμηθέν Id.*Lg*.668b. II. of the arts, *represent, express by means of imitation*, of an actor, Id.*R*.605c, cf. Ar.*Pl*.291 (lyr.); of painting and music, Pl.*Plt*.306d; τὴν τῶν μελῶν μίμησιν τὴν εὖ καὶ τὴν κακῶς μεμιμημένην Id.*Lg*.812c; of poetry, Arist.*Po*.1447a17, al.; of μῖμοι, *represent, act*, τι X.*Smp*.2.21.—Neither μῖμος, μιμέομαι, nor any derivs. occur in Il. or Od.:—Trag. use only pres. and fut. **-ηλάζω**, = foreg., ἀγαθὸν κακῷ μ. Ph.1.557 (s.v.l.); -άζοντες καὶ παρακόπτοντες τὸ δόκιμον νόμισμα ib.610 (-ίζοντες codd.), cf. Hsch. ⊛ **-ηλός**, ή, όν, *imitative*, τέχνη Luc.*JTr*.33; γραφίς Man.6.525; [πίθηκος] μ. πρὸς τὸ χεῖρον Gal.*UP*3.16: c. gen., μ. ἁπάντων τεχνιτῶν Luc.*Im*.17 (Sup.); βιότου *AP*9.280 (Apollonid.). II. Pass., *imitated, copied*, εἰκών *portrait*, Plu.*Ages*.2. Adv. -λῶς Eust.6.7, Suid. s.v. δρᾶμα. ⊛ **-ημα**, ατος, τό, *anything imitated, counterfeit, copy*, A.*Fr*.364; μίμημ' ἔχεις Ἑλένης E.*Hel*.74; μ. χειρὸς Ἀττικῆς, of certain loaves, Antiph.176.6: freq. in Pl., *Ti*.48e, al.; θεοῦ μ. λαχόντες Cleanth.1.4; αὐτοφυὲς μ. λύρας, of the ἀκρίς, *AP*7.195 (Mel.); ἄνθρωπος μ. θεοῦ Muson.*Fr*.17 p.90 H. 2. *artistic representation*, Pl.*Lg*.669e, 796b (pl.). **-ησις**, εως, ἡ, *imitation*, Ar.*Th*.156, Th.1.95, Pl.*Grg*.511a, etc.; κατὰ σὴν μ. to imitate you, Ar.*Ra*.109; *reproduction* of a model, Dionys.ap.Syrian.*in Hermog*.1.3 R. II. *representation by means of art*, Pl.*Sph*.265b, *R*.598b, al.; esp. of dramatic poetry, Arist.*Po*.1447a22, al. 2. *representation, portrait*, πυγμαίου ἀνδρὸς μ. Hdt.3.37, cf. Hp.*Vict*.1.21. **-ητέος**, α, ον, *to be imitated*, X.*Mem*.3.10.8, etc. II. **μιμητέον**, *one must imitate*, E.*Hipp*.114, Pl.*R*.396b; τινά τι X.*Mem*.1.7.2. **-ητής**, οῦ, ὁ, *imitator*, τινων ib.1.6.3, cf. Hp.*Vict*.1.22, 1*Ep.Cor*.4.16; οἱ μ. τῶν γραμμάτων *forgers*, Lib.*Ep*.115.4. II. *artist* (cf. μίμησις II), Pl.*R*.602a, al.; esp. *one who impersonates* characters, as an actor or poet, Arist.*Pr*.918b28, *Po*.1460a8. 2. coupled with γόης, *mere actor, impostor*, Pl.*R*.598d, cf. *Plt*.303c, *Sph*.235a. **-ητικός**, ή, όν, *able to imitate*, Porph.*Abst*.3.4; esp. of the arts (including music and poetry), *imitative*, Pl.*Lg*.668a, Arist.*Po*.1451a30, etc.; μ. ποιητής Pl.*R*.605a sq.; ἡ φωνὴ πάντων -ώτατον τῶν μορίων Arist.*Rh*.1404a22: ἡ -κή (with or without τέχνη) Pl.*Sph*.265a, *R*.598b; ἡ ἐν ἑξαμέτροις μ. Arist.*Po*.1449b21. Adv. -κῶς Plu.2.18b, Gal.8.155, Ath.11.505b; μ. ζῆν Procl.*in R*.1.60 K.: Comp. -ώτερον Ptol.*Harm*.3.3. **-ητός**, ή, όν, *to be imitated* or *copied*, X.*Mem*.3.10.4, etc. **-ήτωρ**, ορος, ὁ, poet. for μιμητής, Man.4.75. **-ία**, ἡ, v. μιμεία. **-ίαμβοι** [ῐα], οἱ, *μῖμοι written in iambics*, title of poems by Herodas, cf. Plin.*Ep*.6.21.4, Gell.20.9.2. **-ικός**, ή, όν, *of the nature of* μῖμοι, Demetr.*Eloc*.151 (Comp.), Cic. *de Or*.2.59.239, *Orat*.26.88. II. *for stage performances*, θύραι, Ἑλληνικά 1.19 (Gytheum, i A.D.).

**μιμιχμός**, ὁ, *neighing of horses*, Hsch.; cf. μιμάξασα.

**μιμν-άζω**, Ep. form of μίμνω, *wait, stay*, Il.2.392, 10.549, A.R.1.226, *AP*4.4 (Agath.): impf. μίμναζε Opp.*H*.5.463. II. trans., *await, expect*, c. acc., *h.Hom*.9.6.

**Μιμνέρμειον**, τό, *gymnasium named after Mimnermus*, *BMus.Inscr*.1030 (Smyrna).

❀ **μιμνήσκω** (not -ῄσκω, v. infr.), fut. μνήσω: aor. ἔμνησα: causal Verb, formed in pres. and impf. from μέμνημαι as πιπράσκω from πέπραμαι:—*remind, put in mind*, μνήσει δέ σε καὶ θεὸς αὐτός Od.12.38; τινος *of* a thing, ἐπεί μ' ἔμνησας ὀϊζύος 3.103; τῶν σ' αὖτις μνήσω Il.15.31, cf. 1.407; μηδέ με τούτων μίμνησκ' Od.14.169, cf. Thgn.1123, Theoc.15.36. II. ἔμνασεν ἑστίαν πατρῴαν..νικῶν *recalled* it *to memory, made* it *famous*, Pi.*P*.11.13.—Act. is mostly Ep., used once in Trag. (lyr.), E.*Alc*.878: compds. with ἀνα- or ὑπο- were preferred in Prose.

B. Med. and Pass. **μιμνήσκομαι**, imper. -ήσκεο Il.22.268: Ep. impf. μιμνήσκοντο 13.722 (the pres. only in later Prose, Pl.*Ax*.368a, D.H.1.13, Plu.2.653b; μέμνημαι serving as pres. in early writers): other tenses are formed from the stem μνη- (v. μνάομαι): fut. μνήσομαι Od.7.192, Sapph.32; μνησθήσομαι Hdt.6.19, E.*Med*.933, etc.; also μεμνήσομαι Il.22.390, Od.19.581, Hdt.8.62, E.*Hipp*.1461, Pl.*Phlb*.31b, etc.: aor. ἐμνησάμην, inf. μνήσασθαι Od.4.331, Tyrt.12.1, Hdt.7.39; rare in Trag., as S.*OT*564; Ep. μνησάσκετο Il.11.566; Trag. also ἐμνήσθην (used by Hom. only in Od.4.118), S.*El*.373, etc.; Aeol. ἐμνάσθην Sapph *Supp*.4.11: pf. μέμνημαι, Aeol. μέμναιμαι Alc. *Supp*.28.6, in Att. always in pres. sense, as also freq. in Hom.; 2 sg. μέμνηαι Il.21.442, μέμνῃ 15.18; imper. μέμνησο, Dor. μέμνᾶσο Epich. 250, etc., Ion. μέμνεο Hdt.5.105; subj. μέμνωμαι -ώμεθα Od.14.168, S.*OT*49; Ion. -εώμεθα Archil.(?) in *PLit.Lond*.54.4; opt. μεμνῄμην Il.24.745, -ῇτο Ar.*Pl*.991 (μεμνῇο, -ῇτο shd. prob. be read for -ῷο or -οῖο, -ῷτο in X.*An*.1.7.5, *Cyr*.1.6.3, and μεμνοῖτο is dub. in Crates Com.50); Ep. 3 sg. μεμνέῳτο Il.23.361; Dor. 3 pl. μεμναίατο Pi. *Fr*.94; inf. μεμνῆσθαι; Aeol. imper. μέμναισο Sapph.*Supp*.23.8; part. μεμνημένος: plpf. ἐμεμνήμην Isoc.12.35; Ion. 3 pl. ἐμεμνέατο Hdt.2.104:—*remind oneself of* a thing, *call to mind*:—Constr.: sts. c. acc., *remember*, Τυδέα δ' οὐ μέμνημαι Il.6.222, cf. 9.527, Od.14.168, S.*OT*1057, Pl.*Lg*.633d, D.44.7; esp. with relat. clause following, μ. τὸν στόλον ὡς ἔπρηξε Hdt.7.18; μέμνησο δ' ἀμφίβληστρον ὡς ἐκαίνισας A.*Ch*.492; μ. τὸν Εὐφραῖον, οἷ' ἔπαθεν D.9.61; also μέμνησο ἐκεῖνο, ὅτι.. X.*Cyr*.2.4.25; μεμνώμεθα ταῦτα περὶ ἀμφοῖν, ὅτι.. Pl. *Phlb*.31a: more freq. c. gen., φίλου μεμνήσομ' ἑταίρου Il.22.390; τοῦ ποτε μεμνήσεσθαι ὀΐομαι Od.19.581; οὐδὲ παῖδος οὐδὲ φίλων τοκήων οὐδὲν ἐμνάσθη Sapph.*Supp*. l.c., cf. Hdt.8.62, E.*Hipp*.1461, etc.; also μεμνημένος ἀμφ' Ὀδυσῆϊ Od.4.151; ἀμφὶ Διώνυσον..μνήσομαι *h.Hom*.7.2; περὶ πομπῆς μνησόμεθα Od.7.192:—Pass., *to be remembered* (not in early Prose), τὰ παραπτώματα οὐ μνησθήσεται LXX *Ez*.18.22; αἱ ἐλεημοσύναι σου ἐμνήσθησαν *Act.Ap*.10.31, cf. *Apoc*.16.19. 2. c. inf., μέμνηντο γὰρ αἰεὶ ἀλλήλοις.. ἀλεξέμεναι Il.17.364; μέμνησο δ' εἴκειν A.*Supp*.202; μέμνησο δάκνειν, διαβάλλειν Ar.*Eq*.495; μεμνήσθω ἀγαθὸς ἀνὴρ εἶναι X.*An*.3.2.39; μέμνησθέ μοι μὴ θορυβεῖν Pl.*Ap*.27b. 3. after Hom., c. part., θνατὰ μεμνάσθω περιστέλλων μέλη *let him remember that* he clothes, Pi.*N*.11.15; μέμνημαι κλύων I *remember* hearing, A.*Ag*.830; μεμνήμεθα ἐλθόντες E.*Hec*.244; μ. ἀκούσας X.*Cyr*.1.6.3, etc.: folld. by a relat., μέμνησ', ὅπως εὖ μοι στομώσεις αὐτόν Ar.*Nu*.1107. 4. abs., ἀφ' οὗ Ἕλληνες μέμνηνται Th.2.8, cf. 5.66: pf. part. μεμνημένος in commands, ὧδέ τις.. μεμνημένος ἀνδρὶ μαχέσθω let him fight *with good heed, let him remember* to fight, Il.19.153, cf. 5.263, Hes.*Op*.422, etc. II. *make mention of*, c. gen., τῶν νῦν μοι μνῆσαι Od.4.331; Μοῦσαι, μνησαίαθ' ὅσοι ὑπὸ Ἴλιον ἦλθον (i.e. τῶν, ὅσοι) Il.2.492; also μνήσασθαι περί τινος Hdt.7.39: freq. in aor. Pass. μνησθῆναι, Od.4.118, S.*Ph*.310; μνησθῆναι περί τινος Hdt. 1.36, cf. 9.45; περί τινος ἔς τινα Th.8.47, cf. 1.10,37, etc.; μνησθεὶς ὑπὲρ τῆς εἰρήνης D.18.21; μ. τινὸς πρός τινα Lys.1.19: later c. dat. pers., *recall to* one's *memory, remind*, ἐμνήσθην σοι καὶ παρόντι περί.. *PLille* 12.1 (iii B.C.), cf. *PCair.Zen*.122.7, al. (iii B.C.): rarely c. acc., ταῦτα καὶ μακάρων ἐμέμναντ' ἀγοραί Pi.*I*.8(7).29: abs., αἰεν μεμναμένῳ εἰ φιλέεις με *mentioning* your name to see if.., Theoc.3.28. III. *give heed to*, πατρὸς καὶ μητέρος Od.18.267; μ. βρώμης *give heed to* food, 10.177; ὡς μεμνέῳτο δρόμου (v.l. δρόμους) that *he might give heed to* the running, Il.23.361; μ. χάρμης, δαιτός, σίτου, 4.222, Od.20.246, Il.24.129; μεμνᾶσθαι πολέμου τε καὶ μάχας B.17.58; ἀοιδᾶς Pi.*Fr*.94. (Aeol. **μιμναίσκω** (not μιμνάσκω) Hdn.Gr.2.79,178; but Ep., Ion., Att. **μιμνήσκω** without ι, *PCair.Zen*.15ᵛ.35 (iii B.C., ὑπο-), *Inscr. Magn*.16.27 (early ii B.C., [ἀνα-]), *SIG*704*E*18 (Delph., late ii B.C., ὑπο-), Did. in *An.Ox*.1.196; cogn. with Lat. *memini*, etc.)

**μίμνω**, ἔμιμνον, Poet. redupl. pres. and impf. of μένω; Ep. dat. pl. part. μιμνόντεσσι Il.2.296; later Ep. impf. μίμνασκον Orph.*L*.108:—*stay, stand fast*, in battle, Il.13.713, 15.727, etc. 2. *tarry*, μετόπισθε μιμνέτω, ὥς κε κτλ. 6.69, etc. 3. of things, *remain*, σόα μ. Od. 13.364:—Med., κλέος.. μίμνεται ἀθάνατον *Epigr.Gr*.265 (Crete). 4. of things, *remain, be left* for one, ἐμοὶ δὲ μ. σχισμός A.*Ag*.1149, cf. 154 (lyr.). II. c. acc., *await*, esp. an enemy's attack, οὐδ' ἄρα μιν μίμνον Il.5.94, etc.; of time, ἠῶ δῖαν ἔμιμνεν 9.662, etc.; πλόον ὡραῖον Hes. *Op*.630. 2. impers., μίμνει δὲ μίμνοντος ἐν θρόνῳ Διὸς παθεῖν τὸν ἔρξαντα *it awaits* him to suffer, A.*Ag*.1563 (lyr.).

**μῑμο-βίος**, ὁ, *actor*, Man.4.280. -**γράφος** [ᾰ], ον, *writer of mimes*, Phld.*Po*.2.72, 5.9, Gal.2.631; Σώφρων ὁ μ. D.L.3.18. -**λογέομαι**, Pass., *to be recited like mimes*, Str.5.3.6. -**λόγος**, ὁ, *actor, reciter of mimes*, *Ath.Mitt*.26.4 (Athens, iii B.C.), Gal.17(2).150. 2. *composer, writer of mimes*, Ph.2.345 (pl.), J.*Vit*.3, *AP*7.556 (Theod.). II. as Adj., metaph., *mocking*, ἠχώ μ. *APl*.4.155 (Euod.).

**μιμορτοβία**· ναῦς ἣ ἄνθρωποι βεβήκασιν, Hsch.

**μῖμος**, ου, ὁ, *imitator, mimic*, A.*Fr*.57.9 (anap.). 2. esp. *actor, mime*, μ. γελοίων D.2.19, cf. *POxy*.519.3 (ii A.D.), etc.; μίμοις γυναιξὶ Plu.*Sull*.36; τετράπουν μῖμον ἔχων ἐπιγαίου θηρός, i.e. *imitating* or *acting* a four-footed beast, E.*Rh*.256 (lyr.). II. a form of drama, *mime, character-sketch*, Arist.*Po*.1447ᵇ10, *Fr*.72; μ. ἀνδρεῖοι, γυναικεῖοι, Suid. s.v. Σώφρων, cf. Demetr.Lac.*Herc*.1014.61, Plu.2.712e. 2. metaph., μ. ὁ βίος Cleobul.ap.Fulg.*Myth*.2.14.

**μῑμώ**, gen. όος, οῦς, ἡ, *ape*, Suid. s.v. πίθηκος.

**μῑμῳδός**, ὁ, *singer of* μῖμοι, Plu.*Sull*.2, Vett.Val.4.17.

❀ **μιν** [ῐ], *him, her, it*, Ep. and Ion. acc. sg. of the 3rd pers. Pron. (v. ἵ) in all genders, = Dor. νιν (q.v.), both forms in codd. Pi. (μιν *N*.5.38, *Pae*.2.73, al.), and in B. (μιν only 10.111), only νιν in Trag. (μιν f.l. in A.*Eu*.631, al.), neither in Att. Prose:—μὶν αὐτόν *himself* (emphatic), Il.21.245,318, etc. (αὐτήν μιν 11.117); αὐτόν μιν reflexive, = ἑαυτόν, Od.4.244; μιν alone is sts. reflex., Hdt.1.11,45, al.; so αὐτόν (αὐτήν) μ. Id.1.24, 2.100; μ. alone not reflex., Id.2.100, al., Hippon.52, etc. II. 3rd pers. pl. doubtful in Hom., since it refers to δώματα by a sense-construction, Od.10.212, 17.268: in later Ep. certainly pl., as A.R.2.8. (Always enclitic, A.D.*Pron*.39.12.)

**μίνδαξ**, ἄκος, ἡ, a kind of *Persian incense*, Amphis 27.

**μίνδις**, ιος, ἡ, *society of trustees for the care of a tomb*, Petersen-Luschan *Reisen in Lykien* p.22 n.27 (Cyaneae), *TAM* 2(1).62 (Telmessus):—hence **μενδῖται**, οἱ, *members of such a society*, ib.40 (ibid.).

❀ **μίνθᾰ** (Thphr.*HP*2.4.1, al.) and **μίνθη** (Hp.*Vict*.2.54, Dsc.3.34 (v.l. -α), *Gloss*.), ἡ, *mint, Mentha viridis*, Hippon.81, Cratin.129, Thphr.*HP*1.c., *CP*2.16.4sq., etc.:—also **μίνθος**, ἡ, ib.2.16.2, Plu.2.732b:—Dim. **μινθάριον**, τό, = *nepeta*, *Gloss*.; also **μινθίν** (i.e. -ίον), τό, ib.

❀ **μινθόβαψ**, v. πλινθόβαψ.

❀ **μίνθ-ος**, ὁ, *human ordure*, Mnesim.4.63. -**όω**, *besmear with dung*, Ar.*Ra*.1075, *Pl*.313. II. *renounce utterly, abominate*, Archestr.*Fr*.9.1, Damox.2.15.

❀ **μίνθωνος**, dub. sens. (ἀπὸ τῆς μίνθης) in Phld.*Vit*.p.37 J.

**μίνιον**, τό, a substance similar to κιννάβαρι, but distd. from it, Dsc. 5.94.

**Μῐνύαι** [ῠ], οἱ, *Minyans*, a race of heroes in Orchomenos, Pi.*O*.14.4, Hdt.1.146; used of the Argonauts, Pi.*P*.4.69, A.R.1.229, Orph. *A*.375, al.: in sg. as a hero or god, Ἑρμῇ καὶ Μινύᾳ *IG*7.3218 (Orchom.):—Adj. **Μῐνύειος** [ῠ], α, ον, *Minyan*, Ὀρχομενὸς Μ. Il.2.511, Od.11.284; Ep. **Μῐνυήϊος** Il.11.722, Hes.*Fr*.144.4:—fem. **Μῐνυηΐς**, ίδος, ἡ, A.R.1.233.

**μῐνυανθής**, ές, *blooming a short time*, Max.76; τὸ μ., = τριπέτηλον, τρίφυλλον, *treacle clover, Psoralea bituminosa*, Nic.*Th*.522, Gal.12.144.

❀ **μινύζηον**· ὀλιγόβιον, Hsch.

**μῐνῠθ-έω**, = μινύθω, *reduce*, fut. μινυθήσω Hp.*Mochl*.40: aor. inf. μινυθῆσαι Id.*Off*.17, *Liqu*.1 (-ίσαι codd.): pf. μεμινυθήκασι Id.*Mochl*.5; the form ἐμινύθη, in codd. of Id.*Art*.53, *Off*.24, is corrupt for ἐμινύθεε or -ύθει. -**ημα**, ατος, τό, *that which is lessened*, ibid. (pl.). -**ησις**, εως, ἡ, *wasting*, σαρκῶν Id.*Mochl*.11: in pl., τῶν σαρκῶν αἱ μ. Id.*Art*.58; μυελῶν μ. *Theol.Ar*.45. 2. *waning*, σελήνης ib.15. 3. *weakening*, πνεύματος Hp.*Hum*.5. -**ῐκός**, ή, όν, *reducing*, μαλάγματα Cael.Aur.*TP*1.39. ❀ -**ω**, only pres. and Ion. impf. μινύθεσκον, *lessen, curtail*, Ζεὺς δ' ἀρετὴν ἄνδρεσσιν ὀφέλλει τε μινύθει τε Il.20.242, cf. 15.492,493, Hes.*Op*.6. 2. *diminish in number*, τοὺς [σύας] μινύθεσκον ἔδοντες Od.14.17. II. intr., *become smaller* or *less, decrease*, μινύθουσι δὲ οἶκοι ἐν σέλαϊ μεγάλῳ Il.17.738; μινύθει δέ τε ἔργ' ἀνθρώπων 16.392, cf. Hes.*Op*.409; μινύθουσι δὲ οἶκοι, from want of heirs, ib.244; μινύθει δέ τοι ἦτορ ἑταίρων Od.4.374; μ. κραδίη Thgn.361; ἀρετᾶς οὐ μινύθει (fort. μινύνθη) ἅμα σώματι φέγγος B.3.90; μ. αἱ σάρκες *shrink, waste*, Hp.*Art*.53, *Mochl*.19: used by Trag. only in lyr., A.*Th*.920, *Eu*.374, S.*OC*686; τὰς νύκτας ἔφασκον τῶ θέρεος μινύθειν Theoc.21.23. (Cf. Skt. *minóti, mināti* 'diminish', 'violate', 'damage', Lat. *minuo*, etc.; cf. μείων.) ❀ -**ώδης**, ες, *weak*, πνεῦμα Hp.*Epid*.3.17.γ', cf. *Mul*.2.133.

❀ **μίνυνθ-ᾰ** [ῐ], Adv. *a short time*, in Hom. mostly in phrase, μ. περ οὔ τι μάλα δήν Il.1.416, Od.22.473; μ. δέ οἱ γένεθ' ὁρμή but *short-lived* was his effort, Il.4.466; οὐ πολλὸν ἐπὶ χρόνον, ἀλλὰ μ. Od.15.494; μ. δὲ γίγνεται ἥβης καρπός Mimn.2.7; μ. δέ μοι ψυχὰ γλυκεῖα B.5.151; τὴν δ' οὔτι μ. περ εὔνασεν ὕπνος A.R.4.1060. -**άδιος** [ᾰ], α, ον, *short-lived*, μ. γὰρ ἔμελλεν ἔσσεσθαι Il.15.612, cf. Od.19.328; μ. νοῦσος, ὕπνος, A.R.2.856, 3.690; μαζοί Tryph.603: Comp. -ώτερος, ἄλγος Il.22.54. II. later, *small*, μ. γαίης Emp.85; μινυνθαδία· ἡ σελήνη, Hsch.

**μῐνυνθάνω** [ᾰ], = μινύθω I, μινυνθάνει ἀγλαὸν ἥβην *PMich*.11.7.

**μινύον**· τὸ βλίτον λάχανον, ἢ κινάβαρ(ι), Hsch. **μινυός**, = μικρός, Eust.273.2. **μίνυρες**· κλῖναι, μάντες, Hsch.

**μῐνύρ-ιγμα** [ῠ], ατος, τό, some kind of eatable, Philox.2.28 (pl.). -**ίζω**, mostly pres. and impf.: aor. 1, Plu.2.56f: (μινυρός):—*complain in a low tone, whimper, whine*, μή μοι.. παρεζόμενος μινύριζε Il.5.889; περὶ δὲ δμωαὶ μινύριζον Od.4.719. 2. *sing in a low tone, warble, hum*, Ar.*Av*.1414, Pl.*R*.411a; μ. μέλη Ar.*V*.219; opp. λελη-κέναι, Arist.*HA*618ᵇ31; of the voice of the ὑπαέτος, ib.619ᵃ3. -**ισμα**, ατος, τό, *warbling*, Theoc.*Ep*.4.11, S.E.*M*.6.32. -**ισμός**, ὁ, *moaning, warbling*, Sch.Ar.*Th*.106. -**ίστρια**, ἡ, *warbler*, ἀηδών *IG*14.1934*f*5. ❀ -**ομαι** [ῡ], = μινυρίζω, of the nightingale, *warble*, S.*OC*671 (lyr.); *hum a tune*, A.*Ag*.16; μινυρομένη τι πρὸς ἐμαυτὴν μέλος Ar.*Ec*.880. -**ός** [ῠ], ά, όν, *complaining in a low tone, whining, whimpering*, μ. ὑπερσοφιστής Phryn.Com.69; of young birds, *twittering, chirping*, Theoc.13.12; μινυρὰ θρέεσθαι, = μινυρίζειν, A.*Ag*.1165 (lyr.). II. = μικρός, Hsch.

⊛ **μῐνῠ-ώριος**, ον, (ὥρα) *short-lived*, τέκνα *AP*9.362.26:—also⊛**-ωρος**, ον, ib.7.481 (Philet.), Tryph.646, cf. Musae.305.

**μίνω**, Arc. for μένω (q.v.).

⊛ **Μίνως** [ī, but also ĭ Pl.Com.15 D.], ὁ, *Minos*, Hom., etc.; gen. Μίνωος Od.11.322, 17.523; acc. Μίνωα Il.13.450, Od.11.568; also gen. Μίνω Hdt.1.173; acc. Μίνων Il.14.322, Hdt.7.171, Μίνω A.*Ch.*618 (lyr.), Pl.*Lg.*630d, A.R.3.1107; dat. Μίνῳ Pl.*Grg.*524a:—Adj.⊛**Μῑνώϊος**, α, ον, Att. -ῷος, *h.Ap.*393, etc.; Μινῷος, ὁ (sc. μήν), name of fictitious month, Luc.*VH*2.13; Μινῴα, ἡ, a kind of grape, Hsch.:—fem. **Μῑνωΐς**, ΐδος, A.R.2.299; νύμφη, i.e. Ariadne, Call. in *PSI*9.1092.59.

**μίξ**, Adv., = μίγα, μίγδα, Nic.*Th.*615.

**μιξ-**, compd. words so beginning shd. perh. be written **μειξ-**; the evidence is indecisive; Inscrr. prove that Μειξ- is correct in pr. nn.

**μιξ-αίθρια**, τά, or **-αίθριαι**, αἱ, *alternation of fair and foul weather*, Hp.*Epid.*1.4. **-άνθρωπος**, ον, *half man half brute*, Them.*Or.*23.284a, Lib.*Or.*59.30. **-αρχᾱγέτας**, ου, ὁ, Arg. name of Castor, as being *a tribe-hero* (ἀρχαγέτας) *only in union with* his brother, Plu.2.296f. **-έλληνες**, οἱ, *half Greeks half barbarians, mongrel Greeks*, Hellanic.71(*a*) J., *IPE*1².32*B*17 (Olbia, iii B.C.), Plb.1.67.7: sg. μιξέλλην Hld.9.24, Porph.ap.Eus.*PE*3.11. **-ερῐφαρνογενής**, ές, *of kid and lamb mixed together*, χορδά Philox.2.34. **-ίαμβος** [ῐα], ον, *mixed with satires, satiric*, Hsch. **-ίας**, ου, ὁ, *one who mixes* or *mingles*, Suid. **-ιμος**, ον, *alloyed*, Id. s.v. ὑπόχαλκον.

**μίξις**, εως, ἡ, *mixing, mingling*, μ. τε διάλλαξίς τε μιγέντων Emp.8.3, cf. Pl.*Phlb.*47d, al., Arist.*GA*327ᵃ30, etc.; τινὶ πρός τι Pl.*Sph.*260b; πάσας μ. μείγνυσθαι Id.*R.*620d. II. *intercourse* with others, esp. *sexual intercourse* or *commerce*, Hdt.1.203, al.; [γυναικῶν] ἐπίκοινον τὴν μ. ποιεῖσθαι Id.4.172; ὄνων πρὸς ἵππους Anacr.35; ἄρρενος πρὸς ἄρρεν, θήλεος πρὸς θῆλυ μ. Plu.2.990d; ἡ τῶν παίδων μ. *union* for the sake of.., Pl.*Lg.*773d. (In codd. sts. μῖξις, for which **μεῖξις** shd. prob. be restd. in Prose:—with μεῖξις: μίξις, cf. φεῦξις: φύξις.)

**μιξο-βάρβᾰρος**, ον, *half barbarian half Greek*, E.*Ph.*138, X.*HG*2.1.15, Pl.*Mx.*245d. ⊛ **-βόας**, ου, ὁ, *mingled with shouts*, διθύραμβος A.*Fr.*355 (lyr.). **-γενής**, ές, *of mixed descent*, ἔθνος *Peripl.M.Eux.*9.

**μιξοδία**, Ion. -ίη, ἡ, *a place where several ways meet*, μιξοδίαι ἁλός, of the straits of Messene, A.R.4.921:—also **μίξοδος**, **μισγοδία**, Hsch.

**μιξο-θάλασσος** [θᾰ], ον, *having intercourse with the sea*, like fishermen and sailors, Orac.ap.X.Eph.1.6. **-θηλυς**, υ, *partly female*, Philoch.23; τὴν φωνὴν μ. Philostr.*VS*2.30. **-θηρ**, θηρος, ὁ, *half-beast*, φῶτες μ. E.*Ion*1161, cf. Lyc.650, D.H.*Th.*6. **-θηρος**, ον, = foreg., Them.*Or.*23.284a. **-θριξ**, τρῐχος, ὁ, ἡ, *having mixed hair*, Eust.937.37. **-θροος**, ον, *with mingled cries*, A.*Th.*331.

**μιξ-οιφία**, ἡ, *sexual intercourse*, Hsch.

**μιξό-λευκος**, ον, *mixed with white*, Luc.*Bis Acc.*8. **-λύδιος** [ῠ], ον, *half-Lydian*, of the Mysian dialect, μιξολύδιον..πως καὶ μιξοφρύγιον Xanth.8. II. in Music, *mixolydian*, τόνος Aristox.*Harm.*2 p.37 M., Bacch.*Harm.*46; ἁρμονία Plu.2.1136c; εἶδος τοῦ διὰ πασῶν Cleonid.9. **-λῡδιστί**, Adv. *in the mixolydian mode*, Pl.*R.*398e, Arist.*Pol.*1340ᵇ1. **-μβροτος**, ον, for μιξόβροτος, *half-human*, βοτὸν A.*Supp.*568 (lyr.). **-νόμος**, ον, *feeding promiscuously*, ἔριφος Simon.172. **-πάρθενος**, ον, *half-maiden*, of Echidna, Hdt.4.9; of the Sphinx, E.*Ph.*1023. **-πόλιος**, *half-grey, grizzled*, *Gloss.*, prob. in *Sammelb.*5825.1 (Byz.). **-πῡος**, ον, (πῦον) *mixed with foul matter*, Hp.*Epid.*1.10, Ruf.*Ren.Ves.*2.6. **-φρύγιος** [ῠ], ον, *half-Phrygian*, of dialect, Xanth.8; ποικίλαι Str.13.4.13.

**μίξ-οφρυς**, υ, *having eyebrows that meet*, Cratin.430.

**μιξο-φυής**, ές, *of mixed nature*, Sch.E.*Ph.*813. **-χλωρος**, ον, *yellowish*, of the complexion, Hp.*Prorrh.*2.11.

**μιργάβωρ**, = λυκόφως, Hsch. (-άβωρ = ἠώς; μιργ- perh. cogn. with Lith. *mirgėti* 'glimmer', OE. *mirce* 'murky'.) **μιργῶσαι**· πηλῶσαι, Id. (Cf. foreg.) **μίρεα**· λάχανα, Id. **μίρκα**· εὐανθής, ποικίλη ἄνθεσι, Id. ⊛ **μίρμα**· ἐπὶ τοῦ κακοπινοῦς καὶ ῥυπαροῦ καὶ πονηροῦ, Id. **μίρον**· ὅταν ἀπονυστάζῃ τις, λέγουσι Ταραντῖνοι, Id.

**μιρράνης**, a Persian title, Procop.*Pers.*1.13.

**μίρτουλον**· μύσος, μίασμα, Hsch. **μιρύκεον**· σχοῖνον, Id.

**μῑσ-ᾰγᾰθία**, ἡ, *hatred of good* or *goodness*, Plu.*Phoc.*27. **-ᾰδελφία**, ἡ, *hatred of one's brother*, Id.2.478c. **-άδελφος** [ᾰ], ον, *hating one's brother*, D.H.3.21, Ph.1.671, Plu.2.482c. **-ᾰθήναιος**, ον, *hating the Athenians*, Lycurg.39: Sup. -ότατος D.23.202. **-ᾰλάζων**, ον, gen. ονος, *hating boasters*, Luc.*Pisc.*20. **-ᾰλέξανδρος**, ον, *hating Alexander*, Aeschin.3.73, Plu.2.344b. **-ᾰλήθης**, ες, *hating truth*, Tz.*H.*10.873; on the accent v. Hdn.Gr.1.80. **-αλληλία**, ἡ, *mutual hatred*, Tz.*Ep.post H.* **-άλληλος**, ον, *hating one another*, Ph.1.412; μ. βίος life *of mutual hate*, D.H.5.66. **-άμπελος**, ον, *hating the vine*, *App.Anth.*4.20. **-ανδρία**, ἡ, *hatred of men*, Sch.E.*Andr.*228. **-ανδρος**, ον, *hating men*, Poll.3.48.

**μῑσανθρωπ-έω**, *to be a misanthrope*, D.L.1.107, 9.3: c. acc., μ. πάντα Heraclit.*Ep.*7.1. **-ία**, ἡ, *hatred of mankind*, Pl.*Phd.*89d, D.18.112, Phld.*Ir.*p.59 W. ⊛ **-ος**, ον, *hating mankind*, Phryn.Com.3, Pl.*Phd.*89d, *Lg.*791d, *Com.Adesp.*143: Sup., -οτάτη παροιμία Ath.4.186f; Τίμων ὁ μ. Cic.*Tusc.*4.11.25, Olymp.*Vit.Pl.*p.4 W.

**μῑσ-απόδημος**, ον, *hating travel*, Poll.6.172. **-αργῠρία**, ἡ, *hatred* or *contempt of money*, D.S.15.88. **-άρετος** [ᾰ], ον, *hating virtue*, Ph.1.410, al., Lxx 4*Ma.*11.4.

**μίσασθαι**, = μιτώσασθαι, Pl.Com.267.

**μισγάγκεια**, ἡ, (μίσγω, ἄγκος) *meeting of glens, meeting of the waters*, ὡς δ' ὅτε..ποταμοὶ..ἐς μισγάγκειαν συμβάλλετον..ὕδωρ Il.4.453: metaph., Gal.*Nat.Fac.*1.2, Alex.Aphr.*Pr.*1.46; ποιητικὴ μ. Pl.*Phlb.*62d, Dam.*Pr.*113; μ. κακῶν Id.ap.Suid. s.v. Εὐπείθιον.

**μισγοδία**, v. μιξοδία. **μισγόλας**· θόρυβος, Hsch. **μισγόνομος** γῆ, *public pasture*-land, Id. **μίσγω**, v. μείγνυμι; cf. προσμίσγω.

**μῑσ-έλλην**, ηνος, ὁ, *hater of the Greeks*, X.*Ages.*2.31, Plu.*Alc.*24, Man.4.561. **-εργος**, ον, *hating work, lazy*, Poll.6.172. **-ερως**, ωτος, *hating love*, Hdn.*Epim.*206. **-εταιρία**, ἡ, *hatred of one's comrades*, Poll.3.64. **-έταιρος**, ον, *hating one's comrades*, Id.6.172.

**μίσευμα** [ῐ], ατος, τό, = ἡμίσευμα, *Supp.Epigr.*2.705.29 (Perga, perh. i A.D.).

**μῑσ-έω**, pf. μεμίσηκα Pl.*Phlb.*44c:—**Pass.**, fut. Med. in pass. sense μισήσομαι E.*Tr.*664, *Ion*597, 611, Philostr.*VA*6.13, later μισηθήσομαι Lxx *Si.*21.28, Aristid.2.426 J., D.C.52.39: aor. ἐμισήθην Hdt.2.119, etc.: pf. μεμίσημαι Isoc.5.137, Hdn.8.5.8: (μῖσος):—*hate*, once in Hom., c. acc. et inf., μίσησεν δ' ἄρα μιν δηΐων κυσὶ κύρμα γενέσθαι Zeus *hated* (*would not suffer*) that he should become a prey.., Il.17.272; μισῶ φίλοισιν ὕστερον βοηδρομεῖν E.*Rh.*333; οὐ μισοῦντ' ἐκείνην τὴν πόλιν, τὸ μὴ οὐ μεγάλην εἶναι not *hating* that city, as not being.., Ar.*Av.*36; μισῶ λακωνίζειν I *hate* Laconizing, Eup.351.1: but mostly c. acc., ὑβρίζοντα μισεῖν Pi.*P.*4.284; μισοῦντ' ἐμίσει S.*Aj.*1134, etc.; θεῖον μισεῖ μῖσος..μεMen.*Epit.*216; μ. τινὰ μῖσος ἐξαίσιον Aristaenet.1.22; ὁ μισεῖς μηδενὶ ποιήσῃς Lxx *To.*4.15:—Pass., *to be hated*, Hdt. l. c., etc.; ὦ πολλὰ μισηθεῖσα χειρωναξία A.*Pr.*45, cf. S.*Aj.*818; μισεῖσθαι ὑπ' αὐτῶν Th.8.83; μισηθεὶς ἔσχατον μῖσος Plu.*Crass.*6. **-ηδονία**, Dor. **μισᾱδ-**, ἡ, *hatred of pleasure*, Theag.ap.Stob.3.1.117. ⊛ **-ηθρον**, τό, *charm for producing hatred* (opp. φίλτρον), Luc.*DMeretr.*4.5. **-ήλιος**, ον, *hating the sun* or *light*, *Gloss.* **-ημα**, ατος, τό, *object of hate*, of persons, ὦ δύσθεον μ. S.*El.*289: c. gen. pers., σωφρόνων μισήματα A.*Th.*186; μισήματ' ἀνδρῶν καὶ θεῶν 'Ολυμπίων Id.*Eu.*73: c. dat., μ. πᾶσιν E.*Hipp.*407. **-ήνερως**, ωτος, ὁ, = ἐρωτομανής, Poll.6.189 (μίσερως cod. F, v. *Philol.*6.10). **-ητέος**, α, ον, *to be hated*, X.*Smp.*8.20. II. μισητέον, *one must hate*, Hp.*Decent.*2, Luc.*Fug.*30, Themist.*Ep.*4.8. **-ητής**, οῦ, ὁ, *hater*, *Gloss.* **-ητία**, ἡ, *lust, lewdness*, Ar.*Pl.*989, Procop.*Arc.*9, *Aed.*1.9. 2. generally, *greed*, Ar.*Av.*1620, cf. Sch. ad ll. **-ητίζω**, = μισέω, Hsch. **-ητικός**, ή, όν, *inclined to hate*, Arr.*Epict.*1.18.9. ⊛ **-ητός**, ή, όν, *hateful*, A.*Ag.*1228, X.*Mem.*2.6.21, 3.10.5. Adv. -τῶς, ἔχειν πρός τινα Zonar. II. **μίσητος**, η, ον, *lustful, lewd*, Cratin.316:—hence **μισήτη**, ἡ, *prostitute*, Archil.184 (but the distn. of accent is not allowed by Hdn.Gr.1.342). 2. generally, *insatiate*, Hsch., Phot. **-ητρον**, τό, = μίσηθρον, 1*Enoch* 9.8 (pl.), Gal.12.251, Sch.E.*Ph.*1260.

**μισθαπο-δοσία**, ἡ, *payment of wages, recompense*, *Ep.Hebr.*2.2, 10.35. ⊛ **-δότης**, ου, ὁ, *one who pays wages, rewarder*, ib.11.6.

**μισθαποχή**, ἡ, *contract for hire with payment in advance*, *BGU*409.10 (iv A.D.), *PGen.*70.15 (iv A.D.). II. *receipt for wages*, *PKlein.Form.*324.6 (vi A.D.).

**μισθάριον** [ᾰ], τό, Dim. of μισθός, *small fee*, Ar.*V.*300, Eup.432, Men.303, *AP*11.154 (Lucill.): pl., *wretched fees*, Hp.*Praec.*7, cf. *PTeb.*413.13 (ii/iii A.D.).

**μισθαρν-έω**, pf. μεμισθάρνηκα Aeschin.1.154:—*work* or *serve for hire*, ὅσοι μισθαρνοῦντες ἤνυσαν τάδε S.*Ant.*302, cf. Hp.*Ep.*11, Pl.*R.*346b, D.18.49; τῶν βαναύσων καὶ μισθαρνούντων Arist.*Pol.*1296ᵇ29; οἱ μισθαρνοῦντες τῶν ῥητόρων Phld.*Rh.*2.56 S.; ὁ -αρνῶν ὄχλος Plu.*Cat.Mi.*44; μ. παρά τινος *receive pay* from.., D.18.236; esp. of prostitution, τῷ σώματι μ. *quaestum corpore facere*, Id.59.20, cf. Aeschin. l. c., *PMagd.*14.3 (iii B.C.). **-ης**, ου, ὁ, *hired workman*, Phot. (oxyt., Hsch., Suid.). **-ητικός**, ή, όν, *of* or *for hired work, mercenary*: ἡ -κή (sc. τέχνη) Pl.*R.*346b,d; μισθαρνευτικόν is f.l. in Id.*Sph.*222d. **-ία**, ἡ, *wage-earning*, D.18.50, 284, Luc.*Fug.*17; a branch of μεταβλητική, Arist.*Pol.*1258ᵇ25. **-ικός**, ή, όν, *of* or *for hired work, mercenary*, ἐργασίαι, τέχναι, ib.1337ᵇ13, *EE*1215ᵃ31. **-ισσα**, ἡ, fem. of sq., Hdn.*Epim.*57. **-ος**, ὁ, (μισθός, ἄρνυμαι) *wage-earner*, Poll.4.48, Hsch. s.v. πελάται.

**μισθαρχίδης**, ου, ὁ, *Son of a Placeman*, Com. patronym. in Ar.*Ach.*597; cf. σπουδαρχίδης.

**μίσθιος**, α, ον, *salaried, hired*, Plu.*Lyc.*16, *AP*6.283; λινύφος μ. *Sammelb.*4299.14 (iii A.D.). II. Subst. μίσθιος, ὁ, *hired labourer, servant*, Lxx *Le.*19.13 (v.l.), *PCair.Zen.*378.14 (pl., iii B.C.), *Supp.Epigr.*2.569.28, 4.447.45 (Didyma, ii B.C.), *Ev.Luc.*15.17, *PAmh.*2.92.19 (unless = *tenant*) (ii A.D.): in pl., *mercenaries*, J.*BJ*5.2.1.

**μισθο-δοσία**, ἡ, *payment of wages*, Th.8.83, X.*An.*2.5.22 (pl.), etc.; τῶν ξένων D.S.16.73. ⊛ **-δοτέω**, *pay wages*, abs., X.*HG*4.8.21; τινι Id.*An.*7.1.13, D.23.142: c. acc., *furnish with pay*, Id.15.32, Decr.ap.eund.18.115; τοὺς παιδευτὰς *SIG*672.42 (Delph., ii B.C.):—Pass., *receive pay*, τὰ προσοφειλόμενα Plb.1.66.3, etc. **-δότης**, ου, ὁ, *paymaster*, Pl.*R.*463b, X.*An.*1.3.9, Aeschin.3.218, Plb.6.21.5, etc. **-δουλία**, ἡ, *hired service*, Hsch. s.v. θητεῖαι. **-δουλος**, ὁ, *hired slave*, Anon. in *An.Ox.*2.362. **-δωρος**, ον, *giving wages* or *pay*, Eubulid.1. **-καρπία**, ἡ, *leased usufruct*, *PLips.*10 ii 9 (iii A.D.).

**μισθ-ομολογία**, ἡ, *contract of letting*, *PLips.*18.22.

**μισθο-πιπράσκω**, *sell under long lease*, pf. inf. μεμισθοπεπρακέναι *POxy.*2136.4, 14 (iii A.D.). **-ποιέομαι**, *derive rent* or *hire from*,

c. acc., *SIG*1000.18 (Cos, i B.C.). **-πρᾶσία**, ἡ, *sale under long lease*, *BGU*1157.8 (i B.C.), *PLond*.3.1164(*b*).6 (iii A.D.).

**μισθός**, ὁ, *hire*, μισθῷ ἔπι ῥητῷ for fixed *wages*, Il.21.445; μισθοῖο τέλος the end *of our hired service*, ib.450; μισθὸς..εἰρημένος ἄρκιος ἔστω Hes.*Op*.370; θητεύειν ἐπὶ μισθῷ παρά τινι Hdt.8.137, cf. 5.65; πείθειν ἐπὶ μ. Id.8.4; μισθοῦ ἕνεκα ὑπηρετεῖν X.*An*.2.5.14: gen. μισθοῦ *for hire*, S.*Tr*.560, Th.4.124, 7.25, D.19.94; μ. στρατεύεσθαι Plb.3.109.6; μισθὸν δοῦναι, διδόναι, πορίζειν, E.*Andr*.609, *HF*19, Ar.*Eq*.1019; ὡς ἐς ἑξήκοντα ναῦς μηνὸς μισθόν as a month's *pay*, Th.6.8; μισθοὺς μεγάλους ἔφερον Thgn.434, cf. Ar.*Ach*.66; μ. λαβεῖν Hdt.8.117, E.*IT*593, Th.8.83; δέχεσθαι X.*Ap*.16; φέρεσθαι Id.*Oec*.1.4; μ. πράττεσθαι exact it, Pi.*O*.10(11).29, Pl.*Prt*.325b; μ. αἰτεῖν Id.*R*.345e; *hire*, μ. ὄνων, πλοίου, *PAmh*.2.126.11,37. b. esp. at Athens, *pay*, *allowance* for public service, μ. δικαστικός Sch.Ar.*V*.299; μ. ἐκκλησιαστικός Luc.*Dem.Enc*.25; ὁ τῆς πρυτανείας μ. *pay* received during the prytany, Aeschin.1.123. 2. physician's *fee*, μ. ἄρνυσθαι Arist.*Pol*.1287$^a$36. II. generally, *recompense*, *reward*, Il.10.304, etc.; ἀρετῆς μ. Pl.*R*.363d, cf. *Ev.Matt*.5.12, etc. 2. in bad sense, *requital*, A.*Ag*.1261, S.*Ant*.221; μ. ἀνδρὶ δυσσεβεῖ E.*Hipp*.1050. (Cf. Avest. *mīžda*-, Goth. *mizdō*, OSlav. *mĭzda* 'pay', OE. *meord*, *méd* 'meed'.)

**μισθουργός**, ὁ, *hired workman*, Hsch. s.v. λάτρις.

**μισθοφορ-ά**, ἡ, *receipt of wages* or *wages received*, *hire*, *pay*, esp. of soldiers, Ar.*Eq*.807, Th.6.24, 8.45, Lys.27.1, Isoc.*Ep*.2.9, D.3.34, etc.; ἐπὶ τᾶ μισθοφόρα (dat.) *IG*11(4).1064*b*4 (Aeol., found at Delos; unless neut. pl.); of the dicasts, Arist.*Ath*.27.4: pl., D.S.17.64: generally, ἐπὶ μισθοφορᾷ *PLond*.2.328.19 (ii A.D.), *BGU*762.20 (ii A.D.). **-έω**, *receive wages* or *pay*, esp. in the public service, *serve for hire*, Ar.*Av*.584, *V*.683, X.*Oec*.1.4, etc.; δημοτικὸν τὸ μισθοφορεῖν πάντας Arist.*Pol*.1317$^b$35; παρά τινος Luc.*Apol*.11: c. acc. rei, *receive as pay*, τρεῖς δραχμάς Ar.*Ach*.602; τὰ δημόσια μ. χρήματα Id.*Ec*.206; μ. ἄλφιτα Id.*Pax*477; μ. τὰ τούτων *receive pay* from their purse, Lys.27.11. b. freq. of mercenary soldiers, *IG*1$^2$.99.22, Ar.*Av*.1367, etc.; μ. τισί X.*Cyr*.8.8.20; παρά τινι ib.3.2.25, D.23.149; μ. ἐν τοῖς ἀδυνάτοις, as if he were a pauper, Aeschin.1.103; μ. ἐν τῷ ξενικῷ κεναῖς χώραις, i.e. to *draw pay* without filling up the vacancies, Id.3.146. 2. *bring in rent* or *profit*, οἰκία -φοροῦσα, ἀνδράποδα -φοροῦντα, Is.8.35; εἴ τῳ ζεῦγός ἐστιν ἢ ἀνδράποδον -φοροῦν X.*Ath*.1.17:—Pass., *to be let for hire*, Id.*Vect*.3.5. II. causal, *engage for pay*, *take into service*, στρατιὰν ἐπί τινα Phalar.*Ep*.186.2. **-ητέον**, *one must receive pay*, Th.8.65, where ἄλλους is used instead of ἄλλοις, as if it had been μισθοφορεῖν δεῖ. ⊛ **-ία**, ἡ, *service for wages*, *service as a mercenary*, D.49.49, D.S.16.61. II. = μισθοφορά, *IG*2$^2$.145.9 (iv B.C.), Pl.*Grg*.515e (s.v.l.), v.l. in X.*An*.7.1.3. **-ικός**, ή, όν, *mercenary*, δυνάμεις Plb.1.67.4; τὸ μ., = οἱ μισθοφόροι, Plu.*Art*.4; also, *the pay of mercenaries*, J.*AJ*12.2.3; μ. γῆ land *assigned to* μισθοφόροι, prob. in *PLond*.3.604*B*248 (i A.D.). Adv. -κῶς Poll.4.51. **-ος**, ον, *serving for hire* or *pay*, μ. ἄνθρωποι D.23.123; δικαστήρια Arist.*Pol*.1274$^a$9, *Ath*.27.3; ἀνὴρ μ. ἐν λόγοις a *mercenary* in argument, Pl.*Tht*.165d; μ. στρατιῶται Archestr.*Fr*.61; μ. κληροῦχος *PPetr*.3 p.286 (iii B.C.); μ. ἱππεῖς *PGrenf*.2.31.5 (ii B.C.); θανάτου μ. Antiph.266. 2. μ. τριήρεις galleys *manned with mercenaries*, Ar.*Eq*.555. II. Subst. μισθοφόροι, οἱ, *mercenaries*, Th.1.35, al., X.*HG*5.4.45, etc.

**μισθ-όω**, *let out for hire*, *farm out*, in pres. and impf., *offer to let*, τινί τι Ar.*Lys*.958, Lys.7.10, D.50.52; μισθοῖ αὑτὸν Ὀλυνθίοις *offers* his services *for pay* to them, Id.23.150, cf. 149; ἑαυτὸν ἐπί τι for a purpose, Id.18.21; μ. τὸ τέμενος *IG*1$^2$.94.5; οἶκον Lys.32.23, D.27.15, 28.15; τοὺς οἴκους τῶν ὀρφανῶν Arist.*Ath*.56.7: c. inf., μ. τὸν νηὸν τριηκοσίων ταλάντων ἐξεργάσασθαι *farm out* the building of it for 300 talents, Hdt.2.180; ὅσου τὴν τριηραρχίαν ἦσαν μεμισθωκότες D.21.80. II. Med., fut. μισθώσομαι Ar.*V*.52: aor. ἐμισθωσάμην: pf. μεμίσθωμαι (v. infr.):—*have let to one*, *hire*, c. acc. pers. vel rei, πλοῖον, μισθωτούς, ἐπικουρικόν, Hdt.1.24, Ar.*Av*.1152, Th.4.52; οἰκίαν ἣν ᾤκει μεμισθωμένος Is.6.39; τίνα τῶν πολιτῶν ἑταιρεῖν μεμίσθωμαι; D.45.79; τῆς οἰκίας ἧς ἐμεμίσθωτο Lys.3.11; μισθωσάμενός τινος τὴν οἰκίαν D.27.58; μ. τι παρά τινος Hdt.1.68; τοὺς μεμισθωμένους παρ' ἐμοῦ τὸ χωρίον Lys.17.8; μ. τινὰ ταλάντου *engage* his services at a talent, Hdt.3.131; ὀλίγου at a low price, Arist.*Pol*.1259$^a$13: c. inf., μ. νηὸν ἐξοικοδομῆσαι *contract* for the building of the temple, Hdt.5.62; μ. γράψαι ψάφισμα Maiuri *Nuova Silloge* 432 (Cos); μισθοῦσθαί τινα c. inf., *hire* him to do a thing, Hdt.9.34; μισθοῦ σαυτὸν ἀμφορεαφορεῖν Ar.*Fr*.299, cf. D.18.33; μ. ὑπέρ τινος *make a contract* for a thing, Id.53.21; ὁ μισθωσάμενος the *contractor*, Is.11.34. III. Pass., aor. ἐμισθώθην: pf. μεμίσθωμαι (v. infr.):—*to be hired for pay*, Μαρδονίῳ μεμισθωμένος οὐκ ὀλίγου *hired* by him at no small price, Hdt.9.38; ἐπί τινι for a thing, X.*An*.1.3.1; ἐκ τοῦ μισθωθῆναι from the *hire*, D.27.58; of a house, *to be let on contract*, Id.28.1; of a mercenary, μισθωθεὶς ὑπό τινος Id.23.149. **-ωμα**, ατος, τό, *price agreed on in hiring*, *contract-price*, Hdt.2.180, etc.: pl., *IG*1$^2$.347.43, al. (v B.C.), 2$^2$.334.28 (iv B.C.); a courtesan's *price*, Macho ap.Ath.13.581a; τῶν ἀκροαμάτων τὰ μ. Phylarch.66 J.; τὰ παρά τινος μ. Alciphr.1.37. 2. *contract*, μισθοῦσι μισθώματα farm out *contracts*, Arist.*Ath*.47.2, cf. D.19.125; ἀπὸ μισθωμάτων θύειν by *contract*, Isoc.7.29 (but expld. as from the proceeds of *rents* by Did.ap.Harp.). 3. *rent*, *IG*12(7).55.15 (Amorgos, iv/iii B.C.), *Tab.Heracl*.1.128. II. *that which is let for hire*, *hired house*, *Act.Ap*.28.30. **-ωμάτιον**, τό, Dim. of foreg., Alciphr.1.36 (pl.). **-ωσῖμαῖος**, α, ον, *hired*, *mercenary*, *Gloss*. ⊛ **-ώσιμος**, ον, *that can be hired* or *had for pay*, Alex.257.3; μισθοῦσθαι τὰ μ. become lessee of *state-property*, Lex ap.D.24.40. **-ωσις**, εως, ἡ, *letting for hire*, Pl.*Sph*.219d, D.36.7, 27.59; αἱ μ. τῶν τεμενῶν Arist.*Ath*.47.4, cf. Pl.*Lg*.759e. b. *lease*, *PCair.Zen*.334.5 (iii B.C.), *PFay*.96 (ii A.D.); μ. ἁπλῆ, δισσὴ γραφεῖσα, *POxy*.1037.20 (v A.D.), 913.20 (v A.D.). II. *rent*, ὁπόσην ἂν ἄλφῃ μ. τὸ τέμενος *IG*1$^2$.94.15; μ. φέρειν D.36.51; μ. ἀποδιδόναι Lex ap. eund.43.58, cf. Arist.*Ath*.2.2; ὀφείλειν μισθώσεις τεμενῶν D.57.63; σιτικὴ μ. *PAmh*.2.31.6 (ii B.C.). III. *payment of wages* earned by slaves to their master, D.28.12; of soldiers' pay, Lys.19.43. IV. *income* from an estate, μ. φέρειν, λαμβάνειν, Is.5.35,36. V. *farming out by contract*, *PLille* 1$^v$.3 (iii B.C.). **-ωτεύω**, = μισθοφορέω, dub. in Lycurg.*Fr*.86. **-ωτήριον**, τό, *hiring place*, Hsch. s.v. ὄψ' ἦλθες. 2. *society of* μισθωτοί, *Jahresh*.26 *Beibl*.13 (Ephesus, ii A.D.). **-ωτής**, οῦ, ὁ, *one who pays rent*, *tenant*, Is.6.36, D.36.35, *SIG*966.32 (Athens, iv B.C.), *PTeb*.86.19 (ii B.C.), etc. 2. *contractor*, *farmer*, *IG*1$^2$.374.99; χειρωναξίας *BGU*617.2; *tax-farmer*, οἱ μ. τοῦ ἀποστολίου *OGI*674 (i A.D.), etc. 3. *hircr*, dub. in Plu.2.632d. **-ωτικός**, ή, όν, *of* or *for letting out*: ἡ μισθωτική, = μισθαρνητική, *mercenary trade*, Pl.*R*.346b; *connected with letting*, τράπεζα *PLond*.3.932.2 (iii A.D.). Adv. -κῶς Eust.1695.36. II. Subst. μισθωτικόν, τό, *contribution* in money or kind *made by a tenant*, *PFlor*.85.16 (i A.D.), *PAmh*.2.88.26 (ii A.D.). **-ωτός**, ή, όν, *hired*, ἐπίκουροι Hdt.3.45, Pl.*R*.419; ἄνθρωποι Phld.*Mus*.p.67 K. II. Subst., *hireling*, *hired servant*, Ar.*Av*.1152, Pl.*Lg*.918b, *IG*2$^2$.1672.28, *Ev.Marc*.1.20, etc.: freq. of soldiers, *mercenaries*, Hdt.1.61, Th.5.6; of a spy or agent, D.18.38; μ. Φιλίππου ib.52; καλὸς κἀγαθὸς καὶ δίκαιος μ. ἐκείνῳ Id.19.110. **-ώτρια**, ἡ, fem. of μισθωτής, Phryn.Com.74.

**μίσιππος** [μῑ], ον, *horse-hating*, Poll.1.198, 6.172.

**μίσκαιος**· κῆπος, Hsch. **μίσκει**· ἄρχεται, Id. **μίσκελλος** οἶνος, ὁ, *a common red wine*, Id. (Cf. Lat. *miscella*, name of a grape, Varro *RR*1.54.)

⊛ **μῑσο-βάρβᾰρος**, ον, *hating foreigners*, Pl.*Mx*.245c, Luc.*Dem.Enc*.6. **-βᾰσῐλεύς**, έως, ὁ, *king-hater*, Plu.2.147a. **-γελως**, ὁ, ἡ, *laughter-hating*, Alex.Aet.7. **-γόης**, ου, ὁ, *hating fraud* or *jugglery*, Luc.*Pisc*.20. **-γύναιος** [ῠ], ον, *hating women*, Ph.2.312, Ptol.*Tetr*.159, Vett.Val.17.11, Alciphr.1.34: τὸ μ. Dam.*Pr*.388. **-γύνης** [ῠ], ου, ὁ, *woman-hater*, title of play by Menander, cf. Str.7.3.4; of Euripides, Hieronym.ap.Ath.13.557e; title of Heracles in Phocis, Plu.2.403f. **-γῠνία**, ἡ, *hatred of women*, Antip.*Stoic*.3.255, *Stoic*.3.103. **-γῠνος**, ον, = μισογύναιος, title of play by Atilius, Cic.*Tusc*.4.11.25, cf. Theognost.*Can*.88. **-δᾰνειστής**, οῦ, ὁ, *hater of usurers*, Choerob.*in Theod*.1.186, *EM*435.28. **-δημία**, ἡ, *hatred of democracy*, And.4.8, Lys.26.21. ⊛ **-δημος**, ον, *hating the commons* or *democracy*, Ar.*V*.474, *Fr*.108, And.4.16, X.*HG*2.3.47 (Sup.), Lycurg.39. **-δημότης**, ου, ὁ, *hater of the commons*, D.H.7.42 (sed leg. -δημοτάτοις). **-δῐκος**, ον, (δίκη) *hating lawsuits*, Sch.Ar.*Av*.109,110. **-δοξος**, ον, *hating glory*, Hsch. **-δουλος**, ον, *hating slaves*: ἡ μ. βοτάνη, = ὤκιμον, *Gp*.11.28.1, *Gloss*. **-θεος**, ον, *hating the gods*, *godless*, A.*Ag*.1090 (lyr.), Luc.*Tim*.35. **-θηρος**, ον, *hating the chase*: τὸ μ. X.*Cyn*.3.9. **-ῐ́διος** [ῐδ], ον, *hating one's own family*, Ptol.*Tetr*.161, Vett.Val.11.2.

**μισ-οίκειος**, ον, = foreg., Ptol.*Tetr*.164, *Cat.Cod.Astr*.2.173. **-οινία**, ἡ, *hatred of wine*, Stob.2.7.10$^e$. **-οινος**, ον, *hating wine*, Hp.*Steril*.215.

**μῑσο-καῖσαρ**, ᾰρος, ὁ, *hating Caesar*, Plu.*Cat.Mi*.65, *Brut*.8. **-κᾰκέω**, = *maleodo* (prob. *mala* or *malos odi*), *Gloss*. **-κᾰλήμερος**, ον, *curmudgeonly*, Donat. ad Ter.*Adelph*.839, 840. **-κᾰλος**, ον, *hating the good*, Ph.2.4, Ptol.*Tetr*.159, Hsch.; μ. φθόνος Ph.1.464. **-κύκλωψ**, ωπος, ὁ, *hater of the Cyclops*, Eust.1643.22. **-λάκων** [ᾰ], ωνος, ὁ, *Laconian-hater*, Ar.*V*.1165. **-λάμᾰχος** [λᾱ], ον, *hating Lamachus*, Id.*Pax*304. **-λεκτρος**, ον, *hating marriage*, Hld.3.9. **-λογέω**, *hate argument*, *letters*, etc., Poll.4.15. **-λογία**, ἡ, *hatred of argument*, Pl.*Phd*.89d, Plu.2.864d. II. *hatred of speaking*, Hierocl.*in CA*12 p.446 M. **-λογος**, ον, *hating argument* or *discussion*, Pl.*Phd*.89d, *R*.411d, Gal.10.108; opp. φιλόλογος, Pl.*La*.188c. **-νεικος**, ον, *hating strife*, cj. for μεσωνικ- in Vett.Val.14.22 (Comp.). **-νοθος**, ον, *hating bastards*, *APl*.4.94 (Arch.). **-νυμφος**, ον, *hating marriage*, Lyc.356. **-ξενία**, ἡ, *hatred of strangers* or *guests*, Lxx *Wi*.19.13. **-ξενος**, ον, *hostile to strangers*, βίος, νόμιμα, of the Jews, D.S.40.3, 34.1, cf. J.*AJ*1.11.1. **-πᾰθές**, τό, = ὠκιμοειδές, Ps.-Dsc.4.28. **-παις**, ὁ, ἡ, gen. παιδος, *hating one's children*, Luc.*Abd*.18. **-πάρθενος**, ον, *hating maidens*, Ps.-Plu.*Fluv*.23.2. **-πατρις**, ιδος, ὁ, ἡ, *hater of one's country*, Arr.*Epict*.3.20.6. **-πάτωρ** [ᾰ], ορος, ὁ, ἡ, (πατήρ) *hating one's father*, D.H.4.28. **-πέρσης**, ου, ὁ, *enemy to the Persians*, X.*Ages*.7.7. **-ποιέω**, *hate*, Aq.*Ps*.80(81).16. **-ποιός**, όν, *hating*, Sm.*Ps*.80(81).16. **-πόλεμος**, ον, *hating war*, Sch.Ar.*Pax*661. **-πολις**, εως, ὁ, ἡ, *hating the commonwealth*, Ar.*V*.411 (lyr.), Arist.*Rh.Al*.1442$^a$13. **-πολίτης** [ῑ], ου, ὁ, *citizen-hater*, Ptol.*Tetr*.159. **-πονέω**, *hate work*, Pl.*R*.535d. **-πονηρέω**, *hate the wicked* or *wickedness*, Lys.30.35, *UPZ*2.25 (ii B.C.), Plb.9.39.6, Lxx 2*Ma*.4.49, D.S.13.2; μ. τισὶν ὑπὲρ ὧν ἠδίκησαν J.*AJ*13.10.2, cf. *Vit*.27. ⊛ **-πονηρία**, ἡ, *hatred of evil*, Hp.*Praec*.7, Arist.*VV*1250$^b$24, Lxx 2*Ma*.3.1, *BGU*1208.8 (i A.D.), Ph.2.136, Diotog.ap.Stob.4.7.62, Plu.*Tim*.5, etc.; ὑπὸ τῶν Ἑλλήνων -πονηρίας ἀξιοῦσθαι D.S.16.23. 2. *hatred because of wickedness*, πρός τινα, κατά τινος, J.*AJ*12.3.1, 17.5.5; ἐπὶ τοῖς πεπραγμένοις Id.*Vit*.60. ⊛ **-πόνηρος**, ον, *hating knaves and knavery*, D.21.218, Aeschin.1.92, Lxx *Es*.8.13, Phld.*Ir*.p.74 W., *SIG*780.31 (Epist. Augusti), Ph.2.267, al.; τὸ μ. Plb.32.6.6; epith. of God,

*Tab.Defix.Aud.*271.36 (Hadrumetum, iii A. D.). Adv. -ρως *PMagd.* 14.8 (iii B.C.), Plb.30.32.5, Ps.-Plu.*Fluv.*11.3, etc.; simply, *with hostile sentiments*, Plu.2.313f. **-πονία**, ἡ, *hatred of work*, Ph.1.255, Gal.16.324, Luc.*Astr.*2. **-πονος**, ον, *hating work* or *trouble*, D.C. 72.2. **-πόρπαξ**, ᾶκος, ὁ, ἡ, *hating the shield-handle* (πόρπαξ), i.e. *hating war*, Ar.*Pax* 662, in Com.Sup. μισοπορπακίστατος. **-ποσειδων**, ωνος, ὁ, *hating Poseidon*, Hdn.Gr.2.727. **-πράγμων**, ον, gen. ονος, *hating business*, Dam.*Isid.*296. **-πρόβᾰτος**, ον, *hating cattle*, Archyt.ap.Stob.4.5.61. **-προσήγορος**, ον, = ἀπροσήγορος, Poll.5. 138. Adv. -ως ib.139. **-πτωχος**, ον, *hating the poor*, of the gout, Luc.*Epigr.*47. **-πώγων**, ωνος, ὁ, *beard-hater*, i.e. *hater of bearded philosophers*, name of a satire by the emperor Julian. **-ρήτωρ**, ορος, ὁ, ἡ, *hater of orators*, Choerob.*in Theod.*2.44,53. **-ρώμαιος**, ον, *Roman-hater*, Plu.*Ant.*54.

**μῖσος**, εος, τό, *hate, hatred*: I. Pass., *hate borne* one, A.*Ag.* 1413, etc.; μ. ἐμποιεῖν Pl.*R.*351d; μ. ἔχειν πρός τινος incur a man's *hatred*, Id.*Lg.*691d; μ. φέρεσθαι And.2.9. 2. Act., *hate felt against* another, *grudge*, τὸ Τροίας μ. ἀναφέρων πατρί E.*Or.*432, cf. Th.4.128; μῖσος ἐντέτηκέ μοι S.*El.*1311, cf. Pl.*Mx.*245d; ἔχθρα καὶ μ. ἀλλήλων X.*Mem.*3.5.17; μισεῖν τινα μῖσος ἐξαίσιον Aristaenet.1. 22. II. of persons, *hateful object*, = μίσημα, A.*Ag.*1411 (lyr.), S.*Ant.*760; esp. in addresses, ὦ μῖσος Id.*Ph.*991, E.*Med.*1323.

**μῖσό-σοφος**, ον, *hating wisdom*, opp. φιλόσοφος, Pl.*R.*456a. **-στρᾰτιώτης**, ου, ὁ, *the soldier's enemy*, Poll.1.179. **-σύλλας**, ου, ὁ, *enemy of Sulla*, Plu.*Sert.*4. **-σώμᾰτος**, ον, *hating the body*, Ptol. *Tetr.*158. **-τεκνία**, ἡ, *hatred of one's children*, Ph.2.451, Plu.2.4f, *Dem.*22. **-τεκνος**, ον, *hating one's children*, Aeschin.3.78, Ptol. *Tetr.*158; Sup., J.*BJ*1.30.3. **-τύραννος** [ῠ], ον, *tyrant-hater*, Hdt. 6.121,123, Aeschin.3.92, Plu.*Tim.*3. **-τῦφος**, ον, *hating humbug*, Luc.*Pisc.*20. **-φᾰής**, ές, *hating the light*, κόσμος Procl.*in Ti.*3. 325 D. **-φίλιππος** [φῐ], ον, *hating Philip*, Aeschin.2.14. **-φῐλόλογος**, ον, *hating literature*, Ath.13.610d. **-φῐλος**, ον, *hating friends*, Arist.*Rh.Al.*1442$^a$13, *An.Ox.*2.290. **-χρηστος**, ον, *hating the better sort*, opp. μισόδημος, X.*HG*2.3.47, cf. D.H.8.6; τὸ μ. στόμα τῆς κωμῳδίας Phld.*Piet.*p.93 G. **-ψευδής**, ές, (ψεῦδος) *hating lies*, Luc.*Pisc.*20. **-ψηφιστής**, οῦ, ὁ, *hater of calculators*, name of a mime by Philistion, Suid. s.v. Φιλιστίων (nisi leg. μιμο-).

**μισσυνή**· ἡ ὀξύτης παρὰ Χαλδαίοις, Hsch.

**μιστυλάομαι, μιστύλη**, v. μυστιλ-.

**μίστυλλον**, τό, *piece of meat*, Strato Com.1.42.

**μιστύλλω**, *cut up*, in Hom. always of cutting up meat before roasting, μίστυλλόν τ' ἄρα τἆλλα καὶ ἀμφ' ὀβελοῖσιν ἔπειραν Il.1.465, cf. 9. 210, al.; εὗσέ τε μίστυλλέν τε Od.14.75; μιστύλλουσι δρόμον Φαεθοντίδος αἴγλης, metaph., of a sun-dial, *AP*9.782 (Paul.Sil.): pres. part., Ar.*Fr.*409, Clidem.17: aor. 1 ἐμίστῠλα Semon.24: part. fem. μιστύλασα Lyc.154: Med. ἐμιστύλαντο [ῠ] Nonn.*D.*21.115.

**μίσυ**, υος and εως, τό, *a copper ore found in Cyprus*, Hp.*Mul.*1.103, Gal.12.241, 15.32, Dsc.5.100, cf. 74. II. *truffle, Tuber aestivum*, growing near Cyrene, Thphr.*Fr.*167.

**μίσυβρῐς** [μῑ], ιος, ὁ, ἡ, *hating insolence*, Lxx 3*Ma.*6.9.

**μισυοί**, οἱ, *those who are half-white and half-black*, Hsch.

**μίσχος**, ὁ, *stalk* of leaves or fruit, Thphr.*HP*1.1.7, 3.5.5, Porph. *Gaur.*3.3, etc. 2. *husk, shell*, Poll.6.94 (in form μίσκος), cf. Hsch. II. in Thessaly, a kind of *spade* or *hoe*, Thphr.*CP*3.20.8.

**μῐτ-άριον**, τό, Dim. of μίτος, Sch.E.*Hec.*905. **-ηρός**, ά, όν, *woven*, ib.924. **-ινοι**, *licinae*, *Gloss.* **-ίσασθαι**, *liciare*, ib. **-ίσκος**, *mitiscus*, ib.

**μῐτο-εργός**, όν, *working the thread*, *AP*6.289 (Leon.). ⊛ **-ομαι**, Med., *ply the woof* in weaving, *AP*6.285 (Nicarch.): metaph., φθόγγον μιτώσασθαι let one's voice *sound like a string*, ib.7.195 (Mel.); also, of Fate, Μοῖρα οὕτω ἐμιτώσατο *IG*12(9).1240.15 (Aedepsus). **-ρρᾰφής**, ές, *composed of threads*, ἀμφίβληστρον *AP*6.185 (Zos.).

**μίτος** [ῐ], ὁ, *thread of the warp*, Il.23.762, *AP*6.174 (Antip.), Sor. 1.80; ἀγαθὶς μίτου, of Ariadne's *clue*, Pherecyd.148 J., cf. Vett.Val. 276.33, Procop.Gaz.*Ecphr.*p.158 B.; of a spider's *web*, *AP*6.39 (Arch.), cf. E.*Fr.*369.1 (lyr.); κατὰ μίτον *thread by thread*, i.e. *in detail*, or *in their due order, in an unbroken series, continuously*, κατὰ μίτον τὰ πράγματ' ἐκλογίζομαι each thing *in due order*, Pherecr.146.7; βίβλοι τετταράκοντα καθαπερανεὶ κατὰ μίτον (κατάμικτον codd.) ἐξυφασμέναι *in a continuous series*, Plb.3.32.2; *ut mihi* κατὰ μίτον *scriberet*, Cic.*Att.*14.16.3; cf. κατάμιτον. 2. *thread of destiny*, Lyc.584, Man.1.7 prov., ἀπὸ λεπτοῦ μ. τὸ ζῆν ἤρτηται, Suid.: freq. in epitaphs, οὐδὲ.. μοιρῶν μίτον ἔκφυγεν *Epigr.Gr.*324.5 (Cnidus); μοίρης ἐκτελέσασα μίτον *IG*4.627 (Argos); μοῖρα.. ζωῆς κλῶσε μίτοισι χρόνον ib.12(8).609.5 (Thasos), cf. 3.1337. II. *string of a lyre*, Philostr. Jun.*Im.*6, *AP*5.221 (Agath.), etc. III. in Orphic language, *seed*, Orph.*Fr.*33.

⊛ **μίτρα**, Ep. and Ion. **μίτρη**, ἡ, a piece of armour, apparently a metal guard worn round the waist, Il.4.137, 187, 216, 5.857. 2. in later Poets, = ζώνη, *maiden's girdle*, Theoc.27.54 [μίτραν cj., μικρὰν codd.], Call.*Aet.*3.1.45, Mosch.2.73, etc.; μ. λῦσαι A.R.1.288; λύσασθαι, ἀναλύεσθαι, Call.*Jov.*21, *Del.*222; παρθένον ἧς ἀπέλυσε μίτρην *Epigr.Gr.*319; also, = στρόφιον, τὴν μ. ἣ μαστοὺς ἐφίλησε Call.*Epigr.* 39, cf. A.R.3.867, etc. 3. *girdle worn by wrestlers*, *AP*15.44. 4. *surgical bandage*, Q.S.4.213. II. *headband, snood*, μ. Λυδία νεανίδων.. ἄγαλμα Alcm.23.67, cf. E.*Ba.*833, *Hec.*924 (lyr.), Ar.*Th.* 257. 2. *victor's chaplet* at the games, Pi.*O.*9.84 (pl.), *I.*5(4).62: metaph., Λυδία μίτρα καναχηδὰ πεποικιλμένα, of an ode in the Lydian mode, Id.*N.*8.15. 3. *headband* as badge of rank at the Ptolemaic court, *Arch.Pap.*1.220. 4. *oriental head-dress*, perh. a kind of *turban*, Hdt.1.195, 7.90, Duris 14 J., etc.; as a mark of effeminacy, Ar.*Th.*941; *diadem*, Call.*Del.*166. 5. *head-dress* of the priest of Heracles at Cos, Plu.2.304c; of the Jewish high-priest, Lxx *Ex.*29. 6, al. III. = ἐπιδιδυμίς, Hp.ap.Gal.19.123 (where μήτρη). [ῐ by nature, E. ll. cc., etc.; ῑ by position in Hom.]

**Μίτρα**, ης, ἡ, the Persian Aphrodite, Hdt.1.131 (by confusion with Μίθρας).

**μιτράγχουσα**, ἡ, *headband of gold plates*, Hsch. **μιτραῖον** (μιτρεόν cod.)· ποικίλον, Id.

**μιτρανάδεσμος**, ὁ, *headband*, Steph. *in Rh.*313.16.

**μιτρηδόν**, Adv., prob. f.l. for μετρηδόν in Nonn.*D.*48.340.

**μιτρη-φορέω**, *wear a* μίτρα, Arr.*Ind.*7.9. **-φόρος**, ον, *wearing a* μίτρα, Hdt.7.62, Diog.Ath.1.1, Phoen.1.24, D.S.4.4.

**μιτρίον**, τό, Dim. of μίτρα, *Gloss.*

**μιτρό-δετος**, ον, *bound with a* μίτρα, κόμη *AP*6.165 (Phal.). **-φορέω**, = μιτρηφορέω, Ar.*Th.*163. ⊛ **-φόρος**, ον, = μιτρηφόρος, Plu. 2.672a. **-χίτων** [ῐ], ωνος, ὁ, ἡ, *with girded tunic*, Ath.12.523d.

**μιτρ-όω**, *surround as with a girdle*, Nonn.*D.*16.275:—Med., βρέφος .. ἐμιτρώσαντο χορείαις ib.14.28. II. Med., *wear a* μίτρα, Διονυσιακὸν τὸ μιτροῦσθαι Str.15.1.58; μ. τὰς κόμας Id.15.1.71; μιτρωσάμενοι τὰ μέτωπα Id.3.3.7. **-ώδης**, ες, *like a headband*, *An.Ox.* 3.351.

**μίττος**· τάξις, σειρά, τόνος, Hsch.; cf. μίτος, κατάμιττα.

**Μῐτῠλήνη**, ἡ, v. Μυτιλήνη.

⊛ **μίτῠλος** [ῐ] or **μύτῐλος** [ῡ], η, ον (Hdn.Gr.1.162, 2.927), *hornless*, αἶξ Theoc.8.86. II. μίτυλον· ἔσχατον, νήπιον (Laced.), Hsch.

**μίτυς**, υος, ἡ, a substance used by bees; a sort of *propolis*, Arist. *HA*624$^a$14.

**μιτώδης**, ες, *like threads, of threads*, βρόχος μ. σινδόνος a halter *of threads of linen*, S.*Ant.*1222.

**μιχέω**, v. ὀμιχέω.

⊛ **μιχθᾰλόεις**, εσσα, εν, read by Antim. for ἀμιχθαλόεις in Il.24.753 (Sch. T ad loc.), v.l. in Coluth.208.

**μιχωκεῖ**· ἠχεῖ, Hsch.

⊛ **μνᾶ**, ἡ, gen. μνᾶς, nom. pl. μναῖ, etc., always contracted in Att., as *IG*1$^2$.10.3, 2$^2$.1627.299, etc.; Ion. nom. pl. μνέαι *Schwyzer* 707 (Ephesus, vi B.C.), Hdt.2.168, 6.79; acc. pl. μνέας *Schwyzer* l.c., Hdt.2.149, 180, al., μνέ[ας] *IG*12(5).123b (Paros); but acc. sg. μνῆν Herod.2.51; gen. μνῆς Id.7.91; gen. pl. μνέων Id.2.22; nom. pl. μνέες f.l. for μνέαι in Luc.*Syr.D.*48:—*mina*, I. as *a weight*, = 100 drachmae, D.22.76, etc., cf. Poll.9.59, 86. II. as *a sum of money*, also = 100 drachmae, Antipho 5.63, etc. (Semitic word, cf. Hebr. *māneh*.)

**μναάδας**· τὰς ἀμελγομένας αἶγας, Hsch. (leg. μηκάδας).

⊛ **μνᾱαῖος**, α, ον, *of the weight of a* μνᾶ, λίθοι X.*Eq.*4.4, *Eq.Mag.*1.16, v.l. in D.S.19.109; *on which a mina is staked*, τρῆμα Amips.20:—also **μνᾱϊαῖος**, α, ον, Arist.*Cael.*311$^b$4, Ph.*Bel.*69.12, al., Plb.13.2.3, D.S. l.c.: written **μναγιαῖος**, *PLond.ined.*2199 (iv A. D.); μναϊαῖον, τό, = μνᾶ, *POxy.*265.18 (i A.D.); μ. [δίκαι] suits *where a mina is at stake*, *IG*9(1).333.12 (Locr.):—also **μναϊεῖον**, τό, gold coin worth a mina of silver, *PCair.Zen.*22.1, 13 (iii B.C.), *PLille* 15.1 (iii B.C.), *UPZ* 121.10 (ii B.C.): written **-ῖηον**, *BGU*1532 (Ptol.), *POxy.*259.17 (i A.D.): for **μναῖαι** (folld. by αἱ) and **μναίας**, Arist.*HA*547$^a$9, Gal.6. 605, μναϊαῖαι, μναϊαίας shd. perh. be read.

**μνᾱδάριον**, τό, Dim. of μνᾶ, Diph.21.

**μνᾶμα, μναμεῖον, μναμοσύνα**, Dor. for μνημ-.

**Μναμόνα**, = Μνημοσύνη, Ar.*Lys.*1248.

**μναμοσύρειν**· τὸ ἐπιτηρεῖν ἢ μεμνῆσθαί τισι, Hsch. ⊛ **μνανόοι**· μοῦσαι, μνηστῆρες, Id. (extra ordinem, fort. μνακόοι).

⊛ **μνάομαι**, contr. **μνῶμαι**, used by Hom. sts. (only in Od.) in the contr. forms μνᾶται, μνώμεθα, μνῶνται, μνάσθω, μνᾶσθαι, μνώμενος; cf. impf. μνᾶτο Hes.*Fr.*96.1: sts. in these contr. forms lengthd. again, as 2 sg. pres. μνάᾳ, inf. μνάασθαι [μνᾱ-], part. μνωόμενος; Ion. μνώμενος Hdt.1.96 (v.l. μνεώμενος), 205: 3 pl. impf. μνώοντο, Hom. (v. infr.); imper. μνώεο A.R.1.896, al.; opt. μνώοιο Max.74; Ion. impf. μνάσκετο Od.20.290: only pres. and impf., exc. aor. μνήσατο (in signf. II. 1) Eup.413. I. *to be mindful of*, c. gen., οὐ πολέμοιο ἐμνώοντ' Il.2.686; μνῶοντ' ὀλοοῖο φόβοιο 11.71; μνωόμενος προτέρης ἁρπακτύος Call.*Ap.*95: abs., μνωομένῳ *when I remember him*, Od.4. 106, cf. 15.400; also, *turn one's mind* to a thing, φύγαδε μνώοντο ἕκαστος Il.16.697. II. *woo for one's bride, court* (not in Il.), c. acc., μήτ' αὐτὸν κτείνειν μήτε μνάασθαι ἄκοιτιν, of Aegisthus, Od. 1.39; τὴν πάντες μνώοντο 11.287: with no acc. expressed, 16.77, 19.529. 2. after Hom., *sue for, solicit* a favour, office, etc., μνώμενος ἀρχὴν Hdt.1.96; μνώμενον βασιληίην ib.205; φιλοτιμίαν μνώμενοι ἢ στάσιν Pi.*Fr.*210; εὔνοιαν ἑαυτῷ παρὰ τῶν στρατιωτῶν μ. Hdn.7.9.11; πᾶσαν ἑαυτῷ πόλιν πατρίδα μ. Hld.3.14.—Ep., Ion., and late Prose; once in Com. (v. supr.). (For signf. I cf. μιμνήσκω; in signf. II perh. from μνᾱ- = βνᾱ-, i.e. $g^u$nā-, cf. γυνή.)

**μνάριον**· τὸ κάλ(λ)υντρον (Boeot.), Hsch.

**μναρός**, = μαλακός, ἡδύς, Cratin.431.

**μνᾱσῐδωρέω**, Dor. for μνησιδωρέω (q.v.).

**μνασίον**, τό, corn-measure in Cyprus, Hsch.:—also **μνασίς**, έως, ἡ, *Et.Gud.*396.10.

⊛ **μνάσιον**, also **μναύσιον**, τό, *earth-almond, Cyperus esculentus*, Thphr.*HP*4.8.2 and 6.

**μναστήρ, μνάστειρα, μνᾶστις**, v. μνηστ-. **μνέα**, v. μνᾶ.

⊛ **μνεία**, ἡ, = μνήμη, *remembrance*, βίου δὲ τοῦ παρόντος οὐ μνείαν ἔχεις S.*El.*392, cf. E.*Ph.*464, Pl.*Lg.*798b; κατά γε τὴν ἐμὴν μ. dub. in Ael. *VH*6.1; μνείας χάριν, freq. in late epitaphs, *IG*3.3112, al. II. *mention*, περί τινος μνείαν ποιεῖσθαι And.1.100, cf. Aeschin.1.160; περί τινος πρός τινα Pl.*Prt.*317e; τὴν μνείαν περί τινος ἀποδιδόναι Arist.*PA*658ᵇ13; ὅτι καὶ μνείας ἄξιον Id.*Pol.*1274ᵇ17; μ. τινῶν ποιεῖσθαι ἐπὶ τῶν προσευχῶν *Ep.Rom.*1.2, al., cf. *Epigr.Gr.*983.3 (i B.C.); *reminder*, τινος Pl.*Phdr.*254a; *commemoration*, αἱ μ. τῶν ἁγίων v.l. in *Ep.Rom.*12.13.

⊛ **μνῆμα**, Dor. and Aeol. **μνᾶμα**, ατος, τό, (μνάομαι, μιμνήσκω) *memorial, remembrance, record* of a person or thing, c. gen., μνῆμ' Ἑλένης χειρῶν Od.15.126; μ. ξείνοιο φίλοιο 21.40; τάφου μ. Il.23.619; μνᾶμα κακοζοΐας Sapph.120; μ. κάλλιστον ἀέθλων Pi.*O.*3.15 (of the crown of olive); Νικοκλέος μνᾶμα κελαδῆσαι Id.*I.*8(7).68; τῆς σῆς πορείας μ. A.*Pr.*841; λυγρᾶς μνήματα Τροίας, of the sufferings of the Greeks, S.*Aj.*1210 (lyr.); μ... διὰ χειρὸς ἔχων, i.e. the dead body of his son, Id.*Ant.*1258 (anap.). 2. *mound* or *building* in honour of the dead, *monument, tomb*, Hdt.7.167, Epigr.ib.228, *IG*1².906, etc.; ἐν τοῖς δημοσίοις μνήμασιν κειμένους D.18.208; *coffin*, E.*Or.*1053. 3. *memorial* dedicated to a god, Simon.138; μνάματα ναυμαχίας Id.134, cf. Epigr.ap.D.S.11.14: generally, *monument*, *SIG*2*B* (Sigeum, vi B.C.). II. = μνήμη, *memory*, μ. ἔχουσ' ἀγαθῶν Thgn.112.

**μνημ-άδιον**, τό, Dim. of foreg., *small monument* or *tomb*, *JHS*18.308 (Mopsuestia). **-άτιον**, τό, = foreg., name of a play by Diphilus, Ath.3.124d; by Epigenes, Id.11.472e. **-ᾰτίτης** λόγος [ῑ], *funeral* oration, Choerob. in *An.Ox.*2.169, Eust.1673.45. **-ᾰτο-φῠλᾰκία**, ἡ, *guardianship of cemeteries*, *Sammelb.*6025.5 (Alexandria, ii A.D.). **-άφιον**, τό, = μνημάτιον, *IG*14.2090.4 (iii A.D.), cf. *Rev. Ét.Gr.*19.278 (Aphrodisias, in form -φιν), *MAMA*1.133 (Laodicea Combusta, -ειον). ⊛ **-εῖον**, Dor. **μνᾱμεῖον**, Ion. **μνημήϊον**, τό, *memorial, remembrance, record* of a person or thing, μνημήϊα καταλιπέσθαι Hdt.2.126,135; λόγων φερτάτων μ. Pi.*P.*5.49, cf. A.*Th.*49, etc.; μνημεῖα ὅρκων *a record* of the oaths, E.*Supp.*1204; μνημεῖα κακῶν τε κἀγαθῶν ἀΐδια Th.2.41; μνημεῖα τῆς δαπάνης *visible memorials*, Arist.*Pol.*1321ᵃ40; ἐνομίζομεν τὰς συμφορὰς ἱκανὰ μ. τῇ πόλει καταλελεῖφθαι, ὥστε μηδ' ἄν.. ἐπιθυμεῖν Lys.34.1; τὰ παίδων μαθήματα θαυμαστὸν ἔχει τι μ. the lessons of childhood cling strangely to the memory, Pl.*Ti.*26b; μνημεῖα καταλειφθῆναι τῶν μελλόντων ἔσεσθαι to be left behind *as reminders* of things to come, Id.*Phdr.*233a. 2. of one dead, Simon.106 (pl.); μνημεῖ' Ὀρέστου.. προσθεῖναι S.*El.*933; of an urn containing the ashes of the dead, ib.1126; τύμβον χῶσον κἀπίθες μνημεῖά μοι E.*IT*702; τάφων τε καὶ τῶν ἄλλων μ. Pl.*R.*414a; *tomb*, Lxx *Jo.*13.6, *Ev.Jo.*5.28, *SIG*1234, etc.: generally, *monument*, Th.1.138, Pl.*Criti.*120c (pl.), X.*HG*2.4.17, *IG*14.1932 (ii A.D.), etc.

**μνήμενος**, *remembering*, Od.15.400, as cited by Arist.*Rh.*1370ᵇ5.

⊛ **μνήμ-η**, Dor. **μνάμα**, ἡ, (μνάομαι) *remembrance, memory* of a person or thing, abs. or c. gen., κακῶν μ. γίνεται οὐδεμία Thgn.798; οὔτ' ἀγαθῶν μνήμην εἰδότες οὔτε κακῶν Id.1114; τῶν ἐμῶν μνάμα ποκ' ἐσσεῖται πόνων Epich.254; λείπεσθαι ἀθάνατον μ. (sc. ἑαυτοῦ) Hdt.4.144; μ. ἔχειν τινός S.*OT*1246, *OC*509, etc.; τάφου μ. τίθεσθαι E.*Ph.*1585; οἱ ἄνθρωποι πρὸς ἃ ἔπασχον τὴν μ. ἐποιοῦντο made their *recollections* suit their sufferings, Th.2.54; μνήμην πεποίηκεν has made [him] *remembered*, Arist.*Rh.*1414ᵃ6: pl., ἀγήρατοι μνῆμαι Lys.2.79; of the dead, μακαρίας μνήμης, θείας μνήμης, *IG*7.175 (Megara), Just.*Nov.*43 *Praef.*, etc.; κρατίστης μνήμης Wilcken *Chr.*26.30 (ii A.D.); μνήμης ἀρίστης *IG*7.2808.6 (Hyettus, iii A.D.). 2. *memory* as a power of the mind, Simon.146, etc.; μνήμην ἁπάντων μουσομήτορ' ἐργάνην A.*Pr.*461; proper to animals, opp. ἀνάμνησις, of man, Pl. *Phlb.*34c, cf. μνημονεύω I. 2; εἰπεῖν τι μνήμης ἄπο from *memory*, S.*OT* 1131; ἐν μνήμῃ λαβεῖν Pl.*Ti.*26b; φυλάξαι τῇ μ. Id.*Lg.*783c; εἰς μ. ἀναληπτέον ib.864b; ἐφ' ὅσον μ. ἀνθρώπων ἐφικνεῖται X.*Cyr.*5.5.8; φέρειν ἐν μ. Men.*Mon.*435: pl., αἱ πολλαὶ μ. τοῦ αὐτοῦ πράγματος μιᾶς ἐμπειρίας δύναμιν ἀποτελοῦσιν all the *memories, acts of memory*, Arist. *Metaph.*980ᵇ29, cf. *APo.*100ᵃ5; *powers of memory*, Id.*Rh.*1362ᵇ24 (s.v.l.). 3. *memorial, record*, κυπαρίττινας μνήμας εἰς τὸν ἔπειτα χρόνον καταγεγραμμένας Pl.*Lg.*741c; μνῆμαι ἐν μέτροις καὶ ἄνευ μέτρων *inscriptions*, Arist.*Rh.*1361ᵃ34; μ. μυθολόγος mythological *record, history*, Call.*Aet.*3.1.55, cf. Gal.*Sect.Intr.*2. II. *mention, notice* of a thing, μ. ποιεῖσθαί τινος Hdt.1.15, etc.; μ. ποιήσασθαι περὶ or ὑπέρ τινος, Plb.2.7.12, 2.71.1; ἡ ὑπὲρ τῶν δικαίων μ. D.S.15.52; μ. ἔχειν τινός Hdt.1.14, etc. (cf. supr. I); μ. ἐπασκέειν Id.2.77. III. μνήμη βασίλειος the imperial *cabinet* or *archives*, τῆς β. μ. προεστώς, = Lat. *a memoria*, Hdn.4.8.4, cf. D.C.76.14 (prob.). IV. = μνῆμα, *tomb*, *AJP*48.18 (Rome). **-ήϊον**, τό, Ion. for μνημεῖον. II. **μνημήϊος**, ον, *bearing record*, στήλη *Supp.Epigr.*1.456 (Phrygia). **-ίσκομαι**, = μιμνήσκομαι, *PHamb.*37.4 (ii A.D.).

⊛ **μνημοδόχος**, ὁ, *recorder*, *CIG*4316*f* (Arycanda).

**μνημον-εῖον** or **-ιον**, τό, *registry*, *PRein.*18.8 (ii B.C.), *POxy.*1282.22 (i A.D.), etc. **-ειος**, ον, *of the memory*, ζητήματα μ. questions *for exercising the memory*, Theodect.Soph.ap.Poll.6.108. **-ευμα**, ατος, τό, *memory sign, mnemonic token*, Arist.*Mem.*450ᵇ27, 451ᵃ2. 2. *thing remembered* or *to be remembered*, Plu.2.786e, Luc. *Salt.*44. 3. *remembrance* or *record* of the past, τὰ Σωκρατικὰ μ. Phld.*Vit.*p.41 J.; *memorial*, τῆς πρόσθε θοίνης Moschio Trag.6.33; *reminder, means of remembering*, τόπου Men.*Pk.*366. **-ευσις**, εως, ἡ, *remembrance*, J.*AJ*19.3.2 (pl.). **-ευτέον**, *one must remember*, Pl.*R.*441d, Epicur.*Ep.*3 p.62 U., Gal.13.287. ⊛ **-ευτικός**, ή, όν, *of* or *for reminding*, Plot.4.3.29; *given to reminding*, ἐν λόγῳ μ. Asp. in *EN*113.15. II. *with a good memory*, Ptol.*Tetr.*155. III. μ. αἱρέσεις *depending on records of observation*, Gal.*Sect.Intr.*1. **-ευτός**, ή, όν, *that can be remembered*: τὰ μ. *objects of memory*, Arist.*Rh.*1367ᵃ24, 1370ᵇ1, *Mem.*449ᵇ9, 450ᵃ24. ⊛ **-εύω**, pf. ἐμνημόνευκα Pl.*Phd.*103b (ἀπ-), J.*Ap.*1.1; μεμνημόνευκα Ruf.ap.Orib.44.17.2:—**Pass.**, fut. μνημονευθήσομαι Isoc.12.128; also μνημονεύσομαι in pass. sense (v. infr. B): aor. ἐμνημονεύθην ib.192: pf. ἐμνημόνευμαι (δι-) Pl. *Criti.*117e:—**Med.**, aor. ἐμνημονευσάμην Gal.15.50: (μνήμων):— *call to mind, remember, think of*, c. acc., Hdt.1.36, A.*Pers.*783, S.*Ph.*121, *Fr.*1120.9, Epicur.*Ep.*2 p.55 U., etc.: c. gen., Phld.*Piet.*94, Plu. *Oth.*1, etc.: c. inf., *remember* to do, Ar.*Ec.*264; μ. ὅτι.. Pl.*R.*480a; εἰ.. D.1.11; ὡς.. Lxx 2*Ma.*10.6. 2. abs., μ. γὰρ καλῶς Cratin. 122, cf. Pl.*Grg.*499e, Men.*Pk.*142; opp. ἀναμιμνήσκεσθαι, as animal instinct from human faculty, Arist.*Mem.*453ᵃ6. II. *call to* another's *mind, mention, say*, c. acc., ἀληθῆ -εύεις Pl.*Lg.*646b, etc.; μ. τινί τινος *make mention of* a thing *to* another, Phalar.*Ep.*2: c. gen., *make mention of*, τοῦ ἔθνους ἐν ταῖς ἱστορίαις J. l.c., cf. Plu.*Them.*32, etc.; μ. ἀδελφῶν Lxx 1*Ma.*12.11. III. *serve as* μνήμων II. 3, *SIG* 45.11 (Halic., v B.C.); μ. ἁγναῖς θεαῖς *IG*14.204 (Acrae), cf. 9(1).689 (Corc.).

B. Pass., *to be remembered, had in memory*, μνημονεύσεται χάρις E.*Heracl.*334, cf. *OGI*666.22 (i A.D.); τὰ ἐκ τοῦ πρὶν χρόνου μνημονευόμενα Th.1.23; τὴν δόξαν τὴν εἰς ἅπαντα τὸν χρόνον μνημονευθησομένην Isoc.12.128; τὸν ἅπαντα χρόνον μνημονευθήσεται D.18.231; οἱ μνημονευόμενοι ἄνθρωποι X.*Mem.*4.8.2: c. inf., ἐμνημονεύετο γενέσθαι Th.2.47: c. part., πόλεμος.. εὖ πολεμηθεὶς μ. Pl.*R.*600a. **-έω**, = foreg., *Gloss.* ⊛ **-ικός**, ή, όν, *of* or *for remembrance* or *memory*, τὸ μ., = μνήμη, *memory*, X.*Oec.*9.11, cf. Arist.*Top.*159ᵇ29; also τὸ μ. τέχνημα *artificial memory*, '*memoria technica*', Pl.*Hp.Mi.* 368d; τὸ μ. alone, X.*Smp.*4.62, Pl.*Hp.Ma.*285e; invented by Simonides, acc. to *Marm.Par.*70; τὰ μ. Arist.*de An.*427ᵇ19, cf. [Cic.] *ad Herenn.*3.17.30; τὸ μ. παράγγελμα rules *for such a memory*, Arist.*Insomn.*458ᵇ21; μ. ἁμάρτημα Cic.*Att.*13.44.2, 14.5.1. 2. *for record* or *reminder*, συγγραφή *BGU*1132.7 (i B.C.). II. of persons, *having a good memory*, Cratin.154, Ar.*Nu.*483, Pl.*Phdr.*274e (Comp.), Aeschin.2.43; τὸ θῆλυ -ώτερον Arist.*HA*608ᵇ13: Sup. -ώτατος D.18.313; opp. ἀναμνηστικός, Arist.*Mem.*449ᵇ6. III. Adv. -κῶς *from a well-stored memory, accurately and fully*, X.*Cyr.*5.3.46, Pl.*Plt.*257b, Aeschin.2.48, D.59.110, Ruf.*Interrog.*2; συνθεῖναί τι μ. S.E.*M.*7.347.

⊛ **μνημόριον**, τό, *memorial, tomb*, Keil-Premerstein *Zweiter Bericht* No.174 (iv A.D.).

⊛ **μνημοσύνη**, Dor. and Aeol. **μνᾱμοσύνα**, ἡ, *remembrance, memory*, μ. τις ἔπειτα πυρὸς.. γενέσθω let us be mindful of fire, Il.8.181; οὐ μ. σέθεν ἔσσετ' Sapph.68; μ. ἀνεγείρειν Pi.*O.*8.74; μ. καὶ τόνος ἀμφ' ἀρετῆς Xenoph.1.20, cf. Critias 6.12 D.:—in Att. only as pr. n. II. as pr. n. *Mnemosyne*, mother of the Muses, *h.Merc.*429, Hes.*Th.*54, E.*HF*679 (lyr.), Pl.*Tht.*191d, *BCH*50.403 (Thespiae); Μ. Διὸς εὐνέτις, ἣ τέκε Μούσας *Epigr.Gr.*789; cf. Μναμόνα, Μνημώ.

⊛ **μνημόσῠνον**, τό, *remembrance, memorial* of a thing, μνημόσυνον ἑωυτοῦ λιπέσθαι Hdt.1.185, 4.166; μνημόσυνον λιπέσθαι Id.1.186, 2.101; μνημόσυνα ἀποδέξασθαι ib.148, al.: rare in early Att. Prose, Th. 5.11; μ. στοργῆς *AP*12.68 (Mel.); εἰς μ. τινός *Ev.Matt.*26.13, cf. *Act. Ap.*10.4. 2. *memorandum, reminder*, μνημόσυνα γράψομαι Ar.*V.* 538; τουτὶ.. ἔστω τὸ μ. μοι ib.559. 3. *mark, scar*, μ. ὑποκαταλιπεῖν Hp.*Prorrh.*2.20.

**μνημύει**· σκυθρωπάζει, and **μνήμυκεν**· ὑποπτήσσει, δυσχεραίνει, Hsch.

**Μνημώ**, οῦς, ἡ, = Μνημοσύνη, Orph.*Fr.*203.

⊛ **μνήμων**, Dor. **μνάμων**, ὁ, ἡ, μνῆμον, τό, gen. ονος, (μνάομαι) *mindful*, καὶ γὰρ μ. εἰμί I *remember* it well, Od.21.95; μνήμοσιν δέλτοις φρενῶν A.*Pr.*789: c. gen., *mindful of, giving heed to*, φόρτου τε μνήμων Od.8.163; κακῶν μνήμονες A.*Eu.*383 (lyr.). 2. *ever-mindful, unforgetting*, Ἐρινύες Id.*Pr.*516, cf. S.*Aj.*1390; μῆνις A.*Ag.*155 (lyr.). 3. *having a good memory*, Ar.*Nu.*414, 484, Pl.*Tht.*144a; οὐ πάνυ εἰμὶ μ. I have not a good memory, Id.*Men.*71c: prov., μισέω μνάμονα συμπόταν *Lyr.Adesp.*141, etc. II. Act., *reminding*: hence, 1. *counsellor*, '*mentor*', Eust.1697.55. 2. among the Dorians of Sicily, ὁ μνάμων, = ἐπίσταθμος συμποσίου, Lat. *magister convivii*, Plu. 2.612d. 3. μνήμονες, οἱ, title of magistrates, *recorders*, Arist.*Pol.* 1321ᵇ39, *SIG*45.8 (Halic., v B.C.), *Leg.Gort.*11.16: in sg., *registrar* of titles or conveyances, *BGU*177.6 (i A.D.), *PLond.*2.299.20 (ii A.D.). III. Adv. μνημόνως Ael.*NA*13.22.

**μνησῐ-δωρέω**, Dor. **μνᾱσ-**, *offer public thanksgiving*, Orac.ap.D. 21.52, cf. 43.66. **-θεος**, ον, *remembering God*, freq. as pr. n., cf. Pl.*Cra.*394e. II. = ἄρκευθος, Ps.-Dsc.1.75. 2. = βούφθαλμον, Id.3.139.

**μνησῐκᾰκ-έω**, *remember past injuries, bear malice*, Hdt.8.29, Ar. *Lys.*590, *Pl.*1146, etc.; πόλλ' ἂν ἐχόντων -κακῆσαί τισι τῶν πραχθέντων D.18.96; esp. in party politics, Lys.18.19, etc.; μηδὲν or μὴ μ. *pass an act of amnesty*, Th.4.74, X.*HG*2.4.43, Decr.ap.And.1.79, D. 23.193, etc.:—Constr.: c. gen. rei, Antipho 2.1.6: c. dat. pers., Th.8.73, Lys.30.9; ὁ -κακῶν αὐτὸς αὑτῷ And.1.95: c. dat. pers. et gen. rei, μ. τινί τινος *bear* one *a grudge for* a thing, X.*An.*2.4.1; ἔδοξε μὴ -κακεῖν ἀλλήλοις τῶν γεγενημένων And.1.81; also οὐ -ήσω τῶν παροιχομένων ἕνεκα *IG*1².90.15; μ. περί τινος Isoc.14.14: later c. acc. rei, κακίαν ἕκαστος τοῦ ἀδελφοῦ μὴ -κακείτω Lxx *Za.*7.10: c. acc. pers., dub. l. in X.Eph.2.9. II. μ. τὴν ἡλικίαν *cast* his age *in his teeth*, Ar.*Nu.*999. **-ητικός**, ή, όν, = μνησίκακος, δύναμις Arr.*Epict.*

4.5.12. **-ία**, ἡ, *remembrance of wrongs*, Ph.2.78, J.*AJ*16.9.3, Plu.2.860a. ⊛ **-ος**, ον, *bearing malice, revengeful*, Arist.*EN*1125ᵃ3, *Rh*.1381ᵇ4, Lxx*Pr*.12.28.

**μνήσιος**, ον, *of memory* (formed like κτήσιος), Theognost.*Can*.58.

**μνησῐ-πήμων**, ον, gen. ονος, *reminding of misery*: μ. πόνος *the painful memory* of woe, A.*Ag*.180 (lyr.). **-στέφᾰνος**, ον, *wooing crowns*, ἀγών Pi.*Fr*.19. **-τοκος**, ον, *philoprogenitive*, Hp.*Mul*.1.6 (s. v. l.). **-χάρη** [ᾰ], ἡ, (χαίρω) *gaiety*, Hsch.

**μνήσκομαι**, shortd. for μιμνήσκομαι, Anacr.94.4.

**μνηστ-εία**, ἡ, *wooing, courtship*, Antip.*Stoic*.3.254, J.*AJ*17.1.2 (pl.), Plu.*Cat.Mi*.30, Luc.*DDeor*.20.14; πλεῖν ἐπὶ μνηστείᾳ τῶν ἴσων J.*AJ*18.7.1: f.l. for ἀμνηστία in Pl.*Mx*.239c. ⊛ **-ειρα**, Dor. **μνάστ-**, ἡ, fem. of μνηστήρ, *bride*, *AP*5.275 (Agath.). II. Adj. *mindful of*, Ἀφροδίτας μνάστειραν ὀπώραν Pi.*I*.2.5. **-έον**, (μιμνήσκομαι) *one must mention*, τινος D.H.*Rh*.2.5, Eust.1722.46. 2. *one must remember*, ὅτι Hp.*Liqu*.2. **-ευμα**, ατος, τό, *courtship, wooing*, in pl., ἄλλης ἐκπόνει μνηστεύματα γυναικός set about *wooing* another wife, E.*Hel*.1514; ὢ κακὰ μ. oh baneful *spousals*, Id.*Ph*. 580. **-ευσις**, εως, ἡ, *espousal*, *AB*107. **-ευτικός**, ή, όν, *of* or *for courtship* or *espousal*, *Gloss*. ⊛ **-εύω**, Dor. μναστ-, aor. ἐμνήστευσα: pf. μεμνήστευκα D.S.18.23:—**Med.**, fut. μνηστεύσομαι Palaeph.29: pf. μεμνήστευμαι Luc. (v. infr.), in Pass. sense, *Ev.Luc*.1.27, 2.5 (v.l. ἐμν-):—*court, seek in marriage*, c. acc., ἀγαθήν τε γυναῖκα καὶ ἀφνειοῖο θύγατρα μνηστεύειν Od.18.277; τὴν πλεῖστοι.. μνήστευον Hes.*Fr*.33.2; ἐμνήστευσε τὴν γυναῖκα λαβεῖν X.*HG*6.4.37; μ. γάμους E.*IA*847, cf. Pl.*Lg*.773b; *woo and win, espouse*, Thgn.1112, Theoc.18.6:—Med., *court for oneself*, Περσεφόνης γάμον Apollod.2.5.12, cf. J.*AJ*4.8.23, Palaeph. l. c.: censured by Luc.*Sol*.9, but used by him, *Merc.Cond*. 23, *Tox*.37; ὁ τὴν κόρην μεμνηστευμένος Id.*Asin*.26; -ευσαμένου μου τῷ.. υἱῷ.. τὴν.. θυγατέρα *PFlor*.36.4 (iv A. D.):—Pass., of the woman, μναστευθεῖσ' ἐξ Ἑλλάνων E.*IT*208 (lyr.), cf. Isoc.10.39. II. *promise in marriage, betroth*, τινά τινι E.*El*.313; γάμον μνηστεύειν (with or without τινι) *to bring about* a marriage *for* another, help him to a wife, Call.*Dian*.265, A.R.2.511:—Pass., τῇ μεμνηστευμένῃ αὐτῷ γυναικί his *betrothed* wife, *Ev.Luc*.2.5. b. metaph., τοσόνδε κίνδυνον αὐτῷ ὁ ὄλεθρος τῶν ἀδελφῶν μ. J.*AJ*17.1.1; ἡδονήν [τινι] μ. τῷ κάλλει Jul.*Ep*.180; ἡμῖν τοῦ μέλους τὸ ἐνδόσιμον μ. ib.186. III. generally, *sue, canvass for* a thing, c. acc., χειροτονίαν Isoc.8.15: c. inf., μνηστευόμενος ἄρχειν ἑκόντων Plu.*Caes*.58:—also in Med., μ. πόλεμον, διαλλαγάς, J.*BJ*2.17.3, *AJ*5.7.4. IV. λόγον μ. τινί *pass off* a speech upon a person, *hawk* it to him, Socr.*Ep*.30.13. ⊛ **-ήρ**, Dor. **μναστ-**, ῆρος, ὁ, Ep. dat. pl. μνηστήρεσσι, *wooer, suitor*, freq. in Od. of the suitors of Penelope, 1.91, al., cf. Pi.*P*.9.106, Th.1.9, S.*Tr*. 9, 15: c. gen., παιδὸς τῆς ἐμῆς μ. Hdt.6.130; γάμων μ. A.*Pr*.740: metaph., μ. ἀγώνων, πολέμου, στεφάνων, Pi.*P*.12.24, *N*.1.16, *Fr*.19; καλοῖς ἔργοις ὧν μνηστῆρα τὸν κίνδυνον εἶναι J.*AJ*17.6.2. II. Μναστήρ, ὁ, a month at Messene, *IG*5(1).1447 (iii/ii B. C.).

**μνηστηρο-κτονία**, ἡ, *slaughter of the suitors*, Eust.1393.54 sq. **-κτόνος**, ον, *suitor-slaying*, πατὴρ Οἰνόμαος Sch.Il.1.38. ⊛ **-φονία**, ἡ, name of the twenty-second Book of the Odyssey, Str.1.2.11, Ath.5.192d, Plu.1.294c, Longin.9.14.

**μνηστής**, corrupt in Philox.2.15 (fort. νήστις).

**μνῆστις**, Dor. and Aeol. **μνᾶστ-**, ιος, ἡ, *remembrance, recollection, heed*, οὐδέ τις ἡμῖν δόρπου μνῆστις ἔην Od.13.280; ἔστι παρέντων μνᾶστιν ἐπιθέσθαι Alcm.64; ἀλλ' ἴσχε κἀμοῦ μ. S.*Aj*.520, cf. 1269; ὅτου ..ἀπορρεῖ μ. ib.523; μνᾶστίν τινος παρέχειν τινί Theoc.28.23; οὕτω δὴ Γέλωνος μνῆστις γέγονε then you bethought yourselves of Gelon, Hdt.7.158. II. *memory, fame*, Simon.4.3.

⊛ **μνηστός**, ή, όν, (μνάομαι) *wooed and won, wedded*, ἄλοχοι Il.6.246, cf. Od.1.36, etc.; μνηστή, abs., A.R.1.780. II. *memorable, to be remembered*, ψυχή *Sammelb*.6138.

**μνήστρια**, ἡ, fem. of μνηστήρ, = προμνήστρια, Poll.3.31.

⊛ **μνῆστρον**, τό, *betrothal, marriage*, *Cod.Just*.1.17.3.α', Charis. p.34 K.

**μνηστύς**, ύος, ἡ, Ion. for μνηστεία, *wooing, courting, asking in marriage*, παύσεσθαι.. μνηστύος ἀργαλέης Od.2.199; μή πως.. καταισχύνητέ τε δαῖτα καὶ μνηστύν [ῡ] 16.294.

**μνήστωρ**, ορος, ὁ, *mindful of*, τινος A.*Th*.180 (lyr.).

**μνητοί**· δοῦλοι, Hsch. **μνηῷ**· μισθῷ, Id.

⊛ **μνῐᾰρός**, ά, όν, *mossy*, πλαταμῶνες Opp.*H*.2.167. 2. *soft as moss*, τάπης *AP*6.250 (Antiphil.).

**μνίειν**· ἐσθίειν, Hsch., cf. Gal.19.123.

**μνϊόεις**, εσσα, εν, = μνιαρός, μ. βυθοῖο τάρφεα A.R.4.1237.

⊛ **μνίον**, τό, *seaweed*, Lyc.398, Agatharch.44, 83, Str.16.4.7, Ael.*NA* 13.3, etc. [ῐ, Numen.ap.Ath.7.295c; ῑ, Nic.*Al*.396.]

⊛ **μνιός**, = ἁπαλός, Euph.156, cf. Hsch. s. v. μνοῖον.

**μνιώδης**, ες, = μνιαρός, Nic.*Al*.497.

**μνοΐα** or **μνωΐα**, contr. **μνῴα**, ἡ, *a class of serfs* or *vassals*, in Crete, *Scol*.28.5, Sosicr.Hist.6, Str.12.3.4, Hsch.:—hence **μνοΐτης**, also **μνωΐτης**, contr. **μνῴτης**, ου, ὁ, *Cretan serf*, Hermon ap.Ath.6.267c, Poll.3.83. (Cogn. with δμώς, cf. μεσόμνη for μεσόδμη.)

⊛ **μνόος**, contr. **μνοῦς**, ὁ, *fine, soft down*, as on young birds, Ar.*Fr*. 258, Hp.*Mul*.1.61, *AP*5.120 (Phld.). II. *a sweetmeat*, Ephipp. 13.5 (codd. Ath., s. v. l.).

**μνούδιον**, τό, Dim. of foreg. I, *Gloss*.

**μνοῦνες**· οἱ μηροί, Hsch. **μνωΐα, μνωΐτης**, v. μνοΐα. **μνωόμενος, μνώοντο**, v. μνάομαι. **μνώσκει**· μίσγεται, ἔρχεται, Id. **μνῶται**· κινεῖται ἢ κτείνεται, Erot. (dub. l.).

**μογγάς**, άδος, ἡ, a *wild* kind of *dance*, Ath.14.629d (v.l. μιγγάς).

⊛ **μογγός**, όν, *with a hoarse, hollow voice*, *PLond*.3.653.16 (iv A. D.), *Hippiatr*.14: Comp., μογγοτέρα φωνή Paul.Aeg.3.24.

**μογ-είω**, = μογέω, Dorian acc. to Hsch. (leg. μογίοντι). ⊛ **-ερός**, ά, όν, also ός, όν Nic.*Al*.419 (v.l. for σμυγερός): poet. Adj. used by Trag. in anap. and lyr. (μόγος, cf. σμογερός): I. of persons, *toiling, distressed, wretched*, A.*Pr*.565, *Th*.827, E.*Tr*.783, 790, Ar.*Ach*. 1207; so μ. οἶκοι S.*El*.93. Adv. -ρῶς Man.1.146. II. of things, *toilsome, grievous*, κάματοι v.l. in *AP*7.508 (Emp. or Simon.); ἄχεα E.*Med*.205; ἀκοαί ear *trouble*, Marc.Sid.86. ⊛ **-έω**, Il.11.636, al. (part.); Lacon. 1 pl. μογίομες Ar.*Lys*.1002: Ep. impf. μογέεσκον Nonn.*D*.1.312, al., *AP*9.442 (Agath.): Ep. aor. μόγησα Il.9.492, al.: Ep. pf. part. μεμογηώς Nic.*Th*.830, *Al*.529: (μόγος):—poet. Verb, *toil, suffer*, in Hom. usu. with a cogn. acc., ὅσσα γε.. θεῶν ἰότητι μόγησα Od.7.214; μάλα πόλλ' ἔπαθον καὶ πολλ' ἐμόγησα Il.9.492; πολλὰ μογήσας 2.690, etc.; τῷ ἔπ' ἄλγεα πολλὰ μογήσῃ for whom he *suffers* .., Od.16.19, cf. Il.1.162; ὅσα.. ἐμόγησεν ἀμφ' ἐμοί Od.4.152; εἵνεκ' ἐμεῖο πολέας ἐμόγησεν ἀέθλους ib.170, cf. Hes.*Th*.997, Thgn.71: abs. in part., ἐξ ἔργων μογέοντες *tired* after work, Od.24.388: hence nearly = μόγις, *with pain* or *trouble, hardly*, μογέων ἀποκινήσασκε Il. 11.636; θέσαν μογέοντες 12.29. 2. in Trag., *suffer pain, be distressed*, συμπονήσατε τῷ νῦν μογοῦντι A.*Pr*.277; μὴ παίσας μογῇς Id. *Ag*.1624; μογοῦντα πλευρά *in* the side, E.*Alc*.849: c. dat., δυστοκίαις μ. Call.*Del*.242 (-τοκέες codd.); κέντρῳ Nic.*Th*.830: metaph., χαλκοῖο πάλαι μεμογηότος ἄνθην having *lost* its sheen, Id.*Al*.529. II. trans., *labour at*, ὁ λιθουργὸς.. ἐμόγησε κόρας Posidipp.ap.Tz.*H*.7. 662.

⊛ **μογῐλάλος** [ᾰ], ον, (μόγις, λαλέω) *having an impediment in one's speech*, Lxx*Is*.35.6, *Ev.Marc*.7.32, Ptol.*Tetr*.150, Vett.Val.73.12, Aët. 8.38.

⊛ **μόγῐς**, Aeol. **μύγις** Jo.Gramm.*Comp*.3.10: Adv., (μόγος) *with toil and pain*, i. e. *hardly, scarcely*, Il.9.355, Od.3.119, Hdt.1.116, *Ev. Luc*.9.39, etc.; μ. ἀνεκτοί Lys.22.10; μ. παρειποῦσ' A.*Pr*.131 (lyr.); μ. πολλῷ πόνῳ Id.*Pers*.509; τὸν μ. Ἀττικόν Pl.Com.31; πάνυ μ. Pl. *Prt*.360d; μ. πως Id.*Chrm*.155e; μ. καὶ κατ' ὀλίγον Charito 1.8; βίᾳ καὶ μ. Pl.*Phd*.108b.—Cf. the post-Hom. μόλις: μόγις is rare in Att. Prose, exc. in Pl., where it is commoner than μόλις; both forms in codd. of Th. [ῐ metri gr., Il.22.412.]

**μογῐσ-αψ-εδάφα** [δᾰ], ἡ, (ἅπτομαι, ἔδαφος) *hardly touching the ground*, epith. of the gout, Luc.*Trag*.200.

**μογξοῦντες**· πυρέσσοντες, πονοῦντες, and **μόξοντι**· πυρέσσοντι, πονοῦντι, Hsch.

⊛ **μόγος**, ὁ, *toil*, ἱδρῶ θ', ὃν ἴδρωσα μόγῳ Il.4.27; ἀέθλους ἐξανύσαντα μόγῳ *IG*3.900; μόγῳ πολλῷ κάμηλον ἐξειλκύσαμεν Alciphr.1.17. 2. *trouble, distress*, S.*OC*1744 (lyr.). (Cf. Lith. *smagùs* 'heavy': the initial *s* is preserved in σμογερός, σμυγερός.)

**μογοσ-τοκία**, ἡ, *painful child-birth*, Man.1.337. **-τόκος**, ον, goddess *of birth-pangs*, epith. of Eileithyiai (or -yia), Il.11.270, 16. 187, 19.103; of Artemis, Theoc.27.30. 2. μ. ὠδῖνες *hard travail*, Lyc.829. 3. *suffering hard travail*, metaph., ἵππος, of the Wooden Horse, Tryph.386. 4. *bringing the pangs of travail*, ὥρα Nonn.*D*. 41.133; ἄσθμα κεραυνοῦ ib.1.2.

**μόδα**· στρώματα, Hsch.

**μοδίολος**, ὁ, Dim. of Lat. *modius*, *nave of a wheel*, *Edict.Diocl. Geronthr*.15.3.

⊛ **μόδιος**, ὁ, = Lat. *modius*, a dry measure, = ⅙ μέδιμνος, for which it is f.l. in Din.1.43, cf. *OGI*533.30 (i B. C.), Plu.*Demetr*.33. 2. *vessel of this capacity*, *Ev.Matt*.5.15. II. a measure of length, = 200 ὀργυιαί, Hero *Geom*.4.12.

**μοδισμός**, ὁ, *measuring by modii*, Hero *Geom*.4.12, Tz. ad Hes.*Op*. 347.

**μόδος**, ὁ, v.l. for μάδος, Hp.*Acut*.(*Sp*.)38.

**μοεύων**· ψέγων, Hsch.

**μόθαξ**, ᾰκος, ὁ, = μόθων I. 1, Phylarch.43 J., Plu.*Cleom*.8, Ael.*VH* 12.43.

**μόθος**, ὁ, *battle-din*, καὶ εἰ μόθου ἔστ' ἀκόρητος Il.7.117, etc.; κατὰ μόθον Hes.*Sc*.158; οἶδα δ' ἐπαΐξαι μόθον ἵππων Il.7.240; δυσμενέων μόθον οὐ τρέσεν *IG*3.713; generally, *fight*, between animals, Nic.*Th*. 191: in pl., Antim.*Eleg*.17, Semon.(?) in *PLit.Lond*.53ᵛ.14.

**μόθουρα**, ἡ, *loom of an oar*, Hsch.

**μόθων**, ωνος, ὁ, at Sparta, *children of Helots*, brought up as foster-brothers of the young Spartans, Sch.Ar.*Pl*.279; expld. as τὸν οἰκογενῆ δοῦλον, *EM*590.14; cf. μόθαξ. 2. in Att., *presumptuous, impudent fellow*, Ar.*Pl*.279; invoked as the *god of impudence*, Id.*Eq*. 635. II. *a licentious dance*, E.*Ba*.1060 (dub. cj.), Ar.*Eq*.697, cf. Sch.Ar.*Pl*.279; φορτικὸν ὄρχημα καὶ ναυτικόν Poll.4.101. 2. *a tune for the flute*, Trypho ap.Ath.14.618c.

**μοθων-ία**, ἡ, *impudence*, Hsch., Suid. **-ικός**, ή, όν, *like a μόθων*, Ion ap.Plu.*Per*.5.

**μοιμυάω**, *compress the lips* or *make grimaces* in sign of displeasure, Hsch., Phot., v.l. for μοιμυλλᾶν in Poll.2.90; hence restored for τί μοι μυᾶτε; in Ar.*Lys*.126.

**μοιμύλλω**, = θηλάζω, ἐσθίω, Hsch.; = μοιμυάω, *Com.Adesp*.1080, Hsch., Phot.; hence restored (= *eat*) in Hippon.80.

**μοιόν**, τό, = αἰδοῖον, Hdn.Gr.1.376. **μοῖος**· σκυθρωπός, Hsch.

⊛ **μοῖρα**, ας (Ion. μοίρης, acc. μοίραν, gen. ης), (μείρομαι) *part*, opp. whole, τριτάτη μ. [νυκτός] Il.10.253; [ἐσθλῶν] τριτάτην.. μ. Od.4.97; μενέτω τριτάτῃ ἐνὶ μ. Il.15.195. 2. *portion* of land, of a country, etc., χώρης ὀλίγην ἔτι μοῖραν ἔχοντες 16.68; μ. πατρῴας γῆς διαιρετόν S.*Tr*.163; ἡ Περσέων μ. Hdt.1.75; [ἐς] δυώδεκα μοίρας δασάμενοι

Αἴγυπτον Id.2.147; Πελοποννήσουτῶν πέντε τὰς δύο μοίρας Th.1.10. **3.** *division* of a people, Hdt.1.146; of an army, Hdn.6.6.3; in codd. of X., freq. f.l. for μόρα. **4.** political *party*, τὸν δῆμον πρὸς τὴν ἑωυτοῦ μ. προσεθήκατο Hdt.5.69; τριῶν δὲ μ. ἡ 'ν μέσῳ σῴζει πόλεις E.*Supp.* 244. **5.** *degree*, in the astron. and geog. sense, Hipparch.1.7.11, Gem.1.6, Cleom.2.5, etc.: *division* of the zodiac, Arat.716, cf. 560 (pl.), Procl.*Hyp.*3.52. **II.** *lot, portion* or *share* which falls to one, esp. in the distribution of booty, ἴση μ. Il.9.318; μ. καὶ γέρας ἐσθλὸν ἔχων Od.11.534; of a meal, μοίρας ἔνεμον 8.470, cf. 14.448, etc.; μ. ἔχειν γαίης Hes.*Th.*413; σπλάγχνων μ. Ar.*Pax* 1105 (hex.); τὴν τοῦ πατρὸς μοῖραν λαγχάνειν one's *inheritance, patrimony*, Lexap.D.43.51, cf. *AP*11.382.22 (Agath.). **2.** generally, *part, lot*, οὐδ' αἰδοῦς μ. ἔχουσιν have no *part* in shame, Od.20.171; εὐθυμίης μείζω μ. μεθέξει Democr.258, cf. 263; ἐν παντὶ παντὸς μ. ἔνεστι Anaxag.11, cf. 6; μ. ἔχειν ἀχέων A.*Th.*945 (lyr.); μ. Ἀφροδίτας Id.*Supp.*1041 (lyr.); ἔχουσι μ. οὐκ εὐπέμπελον *an office*, Id.*Eu.*476; τέσσαρας μ. ἔχον ἐμοί filling *the place of* four *relations* to me, Id.*Ch.*238; μ. ἡδονῆς πορεῖν Id.*Pr.*631; κατὰ τὴν ἰδίαν ἑκάστου μ., *pro virili parte*, Lycurg.64; οὐκ ἐλαχίστην συμβάλλεσθαι μ. πρός τι Plu.2.9f, cf. Arist.*Ath.*19.4. **III.** one's *portion in life, lot, destiny*, ἐπὶ γάρ τοι ἑκάστῳ μοῖραν ἔθηκαν ἀθάνατοι Od.19.592, etc.; μ. βροτῶν A.*Eu.*105; mostly of *ill fortune*, but also of good, e.g. opp. ἀμμορίη, Od.20.76; ἡ πεπρωμένη μ. Hdt.1.91; ἐξιστορῆσαι μ. A.*Th.*506, cf. *Ag.*1314, etc.; μ. (sc. ἐστι) c. inf., 'tis *one's fate*, οὐ γάρ τοι πρὶν μ. φίλους ἰδέειν Od.4.475; οὐ γάρ πώ τοι μ. θανεῖν Il.7.52, cf. 15.117: c. acc. et inf., εἰ μ.... δαμῆναι πάντας ὁμῶς 17.421, cf. 16.434; ἔσχε μοῖρ' Ἀχιλλέα θανεῖν S.*Ph.*331; ὡς αὐτὸν ἥξοι μ. πρὸς παιδὸς θανεῖν Id.*OT*713; εἴ μοι ξυνείη φέροντι μοῖρα ib.863 (lyr.); μ. βιότοιο one's *portion* or *measure* of life, Il.4.170 (as v.l. for πότμον); ὑπὲρ μοῖραν (v. μόρος) Il.20.336; ἀγαθῇ μοίρᾳ by good *luck*, E.*Ion*153 (lyr.); θείᾳ μοίρᾳ by divine *providence*, X.*Mem.*2.3.18; κατά τινα θείαν μ. Arist.*EN*1099$^b$10, cf. Pl.*Men.*99e, *Ap.*33c; opp. παρὰ μοῖραν Διός Alc.*Supp.*14.10. **2.** like μόρος, *man's appointed doom*, i.e. *death*, Il.6.488, Od.11.560; in full, θάνατος καὶ μ. Il.17.672, etc.; μ. ὀλοή.. θανάτοιο Od.2.100; θανάτου μ. A.*Pers.*917, *Ag.*1462 (both anap.); πρὸ μοίρας before the *appointed time*, S.*Fr.*686, Isoc.11.8; ἐξέπλησε μ. τὴν ἑωυτοῦ Hdt.4.164, 3.142, cf. 1.91; τῇ σεωυτοῦ μ. περιέεις ib.121; also, *the cause of death*, Od.21.24. **IV.** *that which is meet and right*, in Hom. mostly in phrase κατὰ μοῖραν *in order, rightly*, Il.16.367; κατὰ μ. ἔειπες 1.286, al.; ἐν μοίρῃ πάντα δίῖκεο 19.186, cf. Od.22.54, Pl.*Lg.*775c, 958d; opp. παρὰ μοῖραν Od.14.509; ἔχει μ. it is *meet and right*, E.*Hipp.*988. **2.** *respect, esteem*, οὐκ ἔστιν ὅτῳ μείζονα μ. νείμαιμ' ἢ σοί A.*Pr.*294 (anap.), cf. S.*Tr.*1239; ἐν οὐδεμιῇ μοίρῃ μεγάλῃ ἄγειν τινά hold one in no great *respect*, Hdt.2.172; ἐν μείζονι μ. εἶναι Pl.*Cri.*51b; ἀτιμοτάτη ἐνὶ μ. Theoc.14.49; μεγάλην μ. καὶ τιμὴν ἔχει Pl.*Cra.*398b; κατατιθέναι τι ἐν μοίραις ἐλάττοσι Id.*Lg.*923b; τοὺς θεοὺς μοίραις ποεῖσθε μηδαμῶς S.*OC*278 is prob. corrupt. **V.** c. gen. almost periphr., ἐν τῇ τοῦ ἀγαθοῦ μοίρᾳ ἐκεῖνό ἐστι is *a* good, *of the order of* the good, Pl.*Phlb.*54c; ἄγειν ἢ φέρειν ἐν πολεμίου μ. *as if* an enemy, D.23.61; νόστοιο μ. for νόστος, Pi.*P.*4.196; ὡς ἐν παιδιᾶς μοίρᾳ *playfully*, Pl.*Lg.*656b; ὡς ἐν φαρμάκου μ. Plu.2.6e; ὥσπερ ἐν προσθήκης μ. Luc.*Zeux.*2; μέτοχος εἶναι τῆς τοῦ ἀγαθοῦ μοίρας, i.e. τοῦ ἀγαθοῦ, Pl.*Phlb.*60b; ἡ φιλοσόφου μ. Id.*Ep.*329b; ἡ τελειότης τἀγαθοῦ μ. τίς ἐστιν Procl.*Inst.*25; θείας μ. μετέχειν, i.e. τοῦ θείου, Pl.*Prt.*322a, cf. *Phdr.*230a; τὸ ἐμπλήκτως ὀξὺ ἀνδρὸς μοίρᾳ προσετέθη was accounted manly, Th.3.82.

**B. Μοῖρα**, as pr. n., *the goddess of fate*, Hom. always (exc. Il. 24.49) in sg., Il.24.209, al., cf. Orph.*Fr.*33, etc.: three first in Hes. *Th.*905, etc.; as the goddess of death, Il.4.517, 18.119: generally of evil, 5.613; ἐγὼ δ' οὐκ αἴτιός εἰμι ἀλλὰ Ζεὺς καὶ Μ. καὶ ἠεροφοῖτις Ἐρινύς 19.87: with epithets, Μ. κραταιή, ὀλοή, 5.629, 21.83; κακή 13.602; δυσώνυμος 12.116:—Trag. use sts. sg, A.*Ag.*130, *Ch.*910, etc.: sts. pl., Id.*Pr.*516, 895, *Ch.*306, etc.; of the Furies, Id.*Eu.*172: later as objects of worship, *SIG*1044.8 (Halic., iv/iii B.C.).—In the phrases θεοῦ μ. Od.11.292, μ. θεῶν 3.269, μοῖρα is Appellat., = *destiny*.

⊛**μοιρ-ᾱγέτης**, ου, Ion. **-ηγέτης**, εω, Dor. **-ᾱγέτας**, α, ὁ, *guide of fate*, of Zeus, as presiding over the Μοῖραι, *IG*1².80.12, Paus.5.15.5, 8.37.1; of Apollo, Id.10.24.4; δαίμονες μ. Alciphr.1.20, cf. Iamb.*Myst.*8.8; πολέων μ. A.R.1.1127 (pl.). **-άδιος**, = μοιρίδιος (q.v.). **-άζω**, = μοιράω, Anon. in *Rh.*230.7 (Pass.). ⊛**-αῖος**, α, ον, *of destiny*, μίτοι Man.5.8, cf. Alciphr.1.20; μ. τριάς, of the Fates, Procl.*Theol.Plat.*6.23. **-άς**, άδος, ἡ, v.l. for μοιρίς (q.v.). ⊛**-άω**, (μοῖρα) *share, divide, distribute*, κρέα Luc.*Prom.*6:—Med., *divide among themselves*, ἐμοιράσαντο.. κτήματα A.*Th.*907 (lyr.):—Med., also, *have assigned one, receive for one's lot*, c. acc., εἰ δέ κεν ἄλλως ἀνέρα μοιρήσαιο Naumach.ap.Stob.4.23.7: c. gen., ὅσα ψυχῆς μεμοίραται Ph.2.400, cf. Phalar.*Ep.*104; οὐ μεμοιραμένα ἐγκλίσεως ῥήματα non-enclitics, A.D.*Adv.*131.24:—Pass., *to be assigned*, τεθνάναι μεμοίραται ἡμῖν (like εἵμαρται, v. μείρομαι) Alciphr.1.25; τὰ μεμοιραμένα Hp.*Ep.*26, Luc.*Deor.Conc.*13. **II.** Med., ἐμοιρήσαντο χαίτας *divided*, i.e. *tore their* hair, A.R.4.1533. **III.** Pass., *melt*, ἐνὶ φλογὶ μοιρηθεῖσα χαλβάνη, v.l. for ζωγρηθεῖσα, Nic.*Th.*51. **-ηγενής**, ές, (γενέσθαι) *favoured by* Μοῖρα *at one's birth, child of Destiny*, Il.3.182. **-ηγέτης**, εω, ὁ, Ion. for μοιραγέτης. **-ιαῖος**, α, ον, (μοῖρα I.5) *amounting to a degree*, Ptol. *Geog.*2.1.9, Procl.*Hyp.*3.11. **-ίδιος**, α, ον, also ος, ον Pi. (v. infr.): (μοῖρα):—*destined, doomed*, μ. ἦμαρ, etc., the day *of doom*, Pi.*P.*4.255; σύν τινι μοιριδίῳ παλάμᾳ Id.*O.*9.26; μοιρίδιον ἦν Id.*P.*1.55: twice in S. (lyr.), μοιριδία τίσις *OC*228 (μοιραδία cod. Laur.); ἁ μοιριδία τις δύνασις δεινά *Ant.*951; μ. θάνατος Epigr.ap.Plu.2.109d; "μ. χρέος" εἶναι λέγεται τὸ ζῆν Plu.2.106f; ἐν ταὐτῷ φέγγει μ. E.*Epigr.*2.4 (-αδίῳ codd.); μ. μελέτη *AP*11.25 (Apollonid.); μ. κλωστῆρες *IG*3.1339. Adv. **-ίως**, ἔπεσεν ἐπὶ τὴν.. εἱμαρμένην ib.12(7).53.11 (Amorgos). (Poet. and late Prose, τὰ μ. Nic.Dam.57 J.) **II.** *determining one's destiny*, ἀστέρες Orph.*H.*7.6. **-ικός**, ή, όν, (μοῖρα I.5) *by degrees*, Ptol.*Tetr.*125, Vett.Val.20.5, al. Adv. **-κῶς** Id.28.22, Paul. Al.*H.*2; opp. ζῳδιακῶς, *PMich.* in *Class.Phil.*22.13. **-ίς**, ίδος, ἡ, *divided*, μ. λίτρα *a half* λίτρα, Nic.*Al.*329 (v.l. μοιράς).

**μοιρο-γνωμόνιον**, τό, (μοῖρα I.5, γνώμων) *pointer* on a dial in the διόπτρα, Hero *Dioptr.*34, al. **-γρᾰφία**, ἡ, (μοῖρα I.5) *tabulation of degrees*, Ptol.*Tetr.*47, Paul.Al.*H.*1. **-δοκέω**, v. μοιρολογχέω. **-θεσία**, ἡ, (μοῖρα I.5) *determination of degrees*, Ptol.*Tetr.*131, Heph.Astr.2.11. **-κραντος**, ον, (κραίνω) *ordained by destiny, fated*, ἆμαρ, θεσμός, A.*Ch.*611 (lyr.), *Eu.*392 (lyr.). **-λογέω**, *tell a man his fate*, μοιρολογῆσαι ἑαυτόν Ps.-Callisth.1.14. **-λόγος**, ον, *prophetic*, *Gloss.* **-λογχέω**, *receive a portion*, Antipho *Fr.*20 (with vv.ll. -λαχεῖν, -δοκεῖν). **-λόγχος**, ὁ, (λέλογχα) *partaker*, Poll.8.136 (pl., μοιρίλογχοι Hsch.). **-νόμος**, ον, (νέμω) *dispensing fate*, Aristid.*Or.*48(24).31. **-φόρητος**, ον, *borne by fate*, gloss on κηρεσσιφόρητος, Sch.D Il.8.527, *EM*511.31.

**Μοῖσα**, v. Μοῦσα. **Μοισαῖος**, v. Μούσειος.

**μοῖτος**, ὁ, Sicilian for χάρις, *thanks, favour*, μοῖτον ἀντὶ μοίτου *like* for *like*, Sophr.168, cj. in Luc.*Im.*12, cf. Hsch. (Prob. borrowed from Italic *moitos, cf. Lat. *mutuus*.)

**μοιχ-άγρια**, τά, (ἄγρα) *fine imposed on one taken in adultery*, μοιχάγρι' ὀφέλλει Od.8.332. **-άζω**, = μοιχάω, Anon.ap.Suid. **-αινα**, ἡ, = μοιχάς, Tz.ad Lyc.1108. **-αίνω**, = μοιχεύω, Vett.Val.118.5. **-ᾰλίς**, ίδος (also acc. μοιχαλίν Lxx *Ho.*3.1), ἡ, = μοιχάς, *Ep.Rom.*7.3, Hld.8.9, *Cat.Cod.Astr.*8(1).264, etc.; in religious sense, *unfaithful to God*, *Ep.Jac.*4.4: so as Adj., *adulterous*, γενεά *Ev.Matt.*12.39, etc. **II.** = μοιχεία, 2*Ep.Pet.*2.14. **-ᾰλώσια**, τά, = μοιχάγρια, Sch.Od.8.332. **-άς**, άδος, ἡ, fem. of μοιχός, Aeschin.Socr.20 D., *Placit.*1.7.10 (v.l. μοιχαλίδος), Vett.Val.104.11; μ. εὐνή Tz.*H.*4.349. ⊛ **-άω**, = μοιχεύω I: metaph., μοιχᾶν τὴν θάλατταν *have dalliance with* the sea, applied by Callicratidas to Conon, X.*HG*1.6.15:—Pass., *commit adultery*, of a man, *Ev.Matt.*5.32; of a woman, *Ev. Marc.*10.12: metaph., *to be unfaithful to God*, Lxx *Je.*3.8, *Ez.*23.37. **2.** *falsify*, Ael.*NA*7.39. **-εία**, ἡ, *adultery*, And.4.10, Lys.1.36, Pl.*R.*443a (pl.); μοιχείας γραφαί Phot., Suid. s.v. πέμπτη φθίνοντος. **-ευτής**, οῦ, ὁ, *adulterer*, Man.4.305. **-ευτός**, ή, όν, *adulterous*, ib.350. **-εύτρια**, ἡ, *adulteress*, Pl.*Smp.*191e, Plu.2.60f. **-εύω**, *commit adultery with* a woman, *debauch* her, c. acc., Ar.*Av.*558, Lys.1.15, Pl.*R.*360b:—Pass., of the woman, Ar.*Pax*980 (anap.); μοιχευθῆναί τινι Arist.*HA*586$^a$3; μεμοιχεῦσθαι ὑπ' ἀλλήλων, of birds, ib.619$^a$10. **2.** metaph., *worship idolatrously*, τὸ ξύλον καὶ τὸν λίθον Lxx *Je.*3.9. **II.** intr., *commit adultery*, Xenoph.11.3; ἐμοίχευσάς τι Ar.*Nu.*1076, cf. X.*Mem.*2.1.5, Arist.*EN*1129$^b$21. **III.** metaph., in fut. Med. (in pass. sense), οὐ μοιχεύσεταί μου τὰ φιλήματα her kisses *shall not be adulterously stolen* from me, Ach.Tat.4.8. **-ή**, ἡ, rare form for μοιχάς, Ar.Byz.ap.Eust.1761.24. **-ίδιος** [ῐ], α, ον, = sq., Ael.*NA*12.16. **II.** *begotten in adultery*, Hecat.369 J., Hdt.1.137, Hyp.*Fr.*42, Ph.1.598, Luc.*DDeor.*22.1. **-ικός**, ή, όν, *adulterous*, λέκτρα Ps.-Phoc.178; ᾠδαί Ath.15.697b; of persons, Plu.2.18e; μ. διαβολαί accusations *of adultery*, Luc.*Cal.*14. **-ιος**, α, ον, = foreg., λέκτρα *AP*5.301.7 (Agath.). **-ίς**, ίδος, ἡ, rare fem. of μοιχός, Ar.Byz.ap.Eust.1761.24.

**μοιχο-ληπτία**, ἡ, Att. for -*ληψία, *taking in adultery*, Phryn.*PS* p.35 B. **-ληπτα**, τά, gloss on μοιχάγρια, Sch.D Od.8.332.

**μοιχός**, ὁ, *adulterer, paramour*, Hippon.74, S.*Fr.*[1127.6], Ar.*Pl.*168, Pl.*Smp.*191d, etc.: prov., θύραν, δι' ἧς γαλῆ καὶ μ. οὐκ εἰσέρχεται Apollod.Car.6; ὅρκοι μοιχῶν Philonid.7; κεκαρμένος μοιχὸν μιᾷ μαχαίρᾳ having the head close shaven with a razor, as was done by way of punishment to persons taken in adultery, Ar.*Ach.*849. **II.** generally, *paramour*, of a sodomite, *POxy.*1160.26 (iii/iv A.D.). (Cf. ὀμείχω.) **III.** *idolatrous person*, *Ep.Jac.*4.4.

**μοιχοσύνη**, ἡ, poet. for μοιχεία, Man.4.394.

**μοιχό-τροπος**, ον, *of the disposition* or *manners of an adulterer*, Ar.*Th.*392. **-τύπη** [ῠ], ἡ, *adulteress*, formed like χαμαιτύπη, Hsch.

**μοιχώδης**, ες, = μοιχικός, *Com.Adesp.*19.5 D., Ptol.*Tetr.*184.

**μοκκώνωσις** (sic)· περιφρονεῖς, Blaes.3; cf. μακκοάω.

**μοκλός**, v. μοχλός.

**μοκρότον**, τό, a kind of *frankincense*, *Peripl.M.Rubr.*9, 10.

**μόκρων**, = ὀξύς (Erythr.), Hsch.

**μολάχη**, ἡ, = μαλάχη, *Epigr.Gr.*1135 (Naples, vase).

**μολβίς**, ίδος, ἡ, *weight of seven minae*, Hsch. **μόλγης**, ητος, ὁ, = μοχθηρός, Crates Gramm.ap.Sch.Ar.*Eq.*959; cf. μολγός II.

**μόλγῐνος**, η, ον, *made of ox-hide*, φυσητῆρες Theodorid.ap.Poll.10.187.

**μολγός**, ὁ, Tarentine word for βόειος ἀσκός, Poll.10.187: μ. γενέσθαι δεῖ σε, = ἀσκὸν δεδάρθαι (v. ἀσκός 5 fin.), Ar.*Eq.*963; μολγὸν αἰνεῖν (ἀνεῖν), = ἀσκὸν δείρειν, dub. cj. in Ar.*Frr.*101, 694. **II.** = μόλγης, Suid. **III.** = ἀκόλουθος (fem.), Blaes.4. **IV.** μολγῶ· νέφος, Hsch.

**μολεῖν**, aor. 2 inf. of βλώσκω (q.v.); hence a late pres. **μολέω**, Sch.Od.17.219, etc.

**μολεύω**, *cut off and transplant the suckers* or *shoots of trees* (αὐτομολίαι, *stolones*), Lex Att.ap.Poll.7.146; cf. μολούω, μωλύω.

**μόλησις**, εως, ἡ, (μολεῖν) *coming*, Apollon.*Lex.* s.v. μολίονε.

**μολῐβ-αχθής**, ές, *heavy with lead, leaded*, στάθμη *AP*6.103 (Phil.). **-δαινα, -δεος, -δικός, -δος, -δοτήξ, -δουργός, -δοχόος**, v. μόλυβδος,

etc. **-ινος**, η, ον, = μολύβδινος, Paul.Aeg.6.25. **-ιον**, τό, Dim. of μόλιβος, *leaden tube*, Antyll.ap.Orib.10.19.5: **-ίδιον**, Hero *Aut.*30.3. **-οειδής**, ές, gloss on μολοβρός, Sch.Nic.*Th.* 662. **-όομαι**, = μολυβδόομαι, pf. inf. Pass. μεμολιβῶσθαι Aristeas 90. ⊛**-ος**, ὁ, Ep. form of μόλυβδος (q.v.), *lead*, once in Hom., μόλιβος ὣς ἐτράπετ' αἰχμή Il.11.237, cf. Call.*Aet.*3.1.30: also fem., *AP* 9.723 (Antip. Sid.); also found in *PTeb.*121.52 (i B.C., pl.), *PLond.* 3.1177.301 (ii A.D.), *Ostr.Bodl.*iii 310 (prob. iii A.D.), and codd. of Ph.*Bel.*80.7, 90.9, Ael.*NA*14.25, etc.

**μολϊβοσφιγγής**, ές, *fastened* or *bound with lead*, Opp.*C.*1.155.

⊛**μολϊβουργός**, ὁ, = μολυβδουργός, Procl.*Par.Ptol.*251.

**μολϊβοῦς**, ῆ, οῦν, *leaden*, Ph.*Bel.*95.14, Str.16.2.13; στέγαι D.S. 2.10; βάρη Apollod.*Poliorc.*158.8; κεραμίς Ath.14.621a; σφαῖρα S.E.*M.*10.160.

⊛**μόλϊς**, Adv., post-Hom. synonym of μόγις, prevailing in Trag., Com., and Att. prose, though in Pl. and later prose μόγις was preferred (in A. the Laur. Ms. gives each form twice, the same Ms. of S. μόλις always); μ. μέν, ἀλλ' ὅμως ἠνεσχόμην Ar.*Nu.*1363, cf. S.*Ant.* 290, 1105, *El.*575, *Ph.*329; ζῶντι καὶ μάλα μ. nay, *only just* alive, Pl. *Tht.*142b (cod. W μόγις); μ. καὶ ἠρέμα πάσχειν *scarcely at all*.., Arist.*Metaph.*1010ᵃ31 (cod. Aᵇ μόγις); ἢ ὅλως οὐκ ἔστιν ἢ μ. Id.*Ph.* 217ᵇ32; μ. πάνυ Eub.30; πάνυ μ. Philem.88.8: with a neg., οὐ μ. *not scarcely*, i.e. *quite, utterly*, ἀπώλεσας οὐ μ. A.*Ag.*1082; θυραῖος ἔστω πόλεμος, οὐ μ. παρών Id.*Eu.*864 (where Sch. explains οὐ μ. by οὐ μακράν, but the sense is dub.); θέλουσαν οὐ μ. καλεῖς E.*Hel.*334 (lyr.).

**μολίσκω**, = βλώσκω, pres. of aor. ἔμολον, μολεῖν, *EM*201.25, Sch. Il.11.173, etc.

⊛**Μολίων** [ῑ], ονος, ὁ, *Molion*, pr. n. in Il.11.709 (dual), Pi.*O.*10(11). 34 (pl.): prob. a Patron., but Hsch. expl. μολίονες by μαχηταί.

**μολόβρ-ιον**, τό, *the young of the wild swine*, Ael.*NA*7.47; also **κολόβριον** Ar.Byz.ap.Eust.1817.19. ⊛**-ίτης** [ῑ] ὗς, = foreg., Hippon. 77. ⊛**-ός**, ὁ, *greedy fellow*, applied to a beggar, Od.17.219, 18.26, cf. Lyc.775: also as Adj., μολοβρὴ κεφαλή the head of a plant *that rests upon the ground*, Nic.*Th.*662 (variously expld. by Sch.Od. and Sch.Nic.).

**μολόθουρος**, ἡ, *an evergreen plant*, expld. as = ἀσφόδελος and ὁλόσχοινος, Euph.133, Nic.*Al.*147.

**μολοσσίαμβος** [ῐ] (sc. πούς), ὁ, the foot – – – ᴗ –, Diom.p.481 K.

**μολοσσοπυρρῖχος** (sc. πούς), ὁ, the foot – – – ᴗ ᴗ, Diom.p.481 K.

**Μολοσσός**, Att. **-ττός**, όν, *Molossian*, ὄργανον Simon.31; γάπεδα A.*Pr.*829, cf. Hdt.1.146, al.:—fem. **Μολοσσίς**, Att. **-ττίς**, ίδος, Poll. 5.39; ἡ Μολοσσίς (sc. γῆ) *Molossia*, Plu.2.297b: also **Μολοσσία**, ἡ, Pi.*N.*7.38; **Μολοσσικός**, Att. **-ττικός**, ή, όν, χεῖρες S.*Fr.*795; κύων Μ. a kind of wolf-dog used by shepherds, Ar.*Th.*416. II. μολοσσός, ὁ, in Metric, the foot – – –, D.H.*Comp.*17, Heph.3.2, 11.2.

**μολοσσοσπόνδειος** (sc. πούς), ὁ, the foot – – – – –, Diom.p.482 K.

**μολοῦμαι**, fut. of βλώσκω.

⊛**μολουρίς**, ίδος, ἡ, *locust*, Nic.*Th.*416; cf. μελουρίς, μολυρίς.

⊛**μόλουρος**, ὁ, a kind of *serpent*, Nic.*Th.*491.

**μολούω**, inf. -ειν· ἐγκόπτειν τὰς παραφυάδας, Hsch.; cf. μολεύω.

**μόλοφθος**· ἐγκρυφίας, Hsch.

⊛**μολόχ-η**, ἡ, = μαλάχη, Epich.153, Antiph.158, Ph.*Bel.*89.10, *SIG*1172.8 (Lebena). ⊛**-ϊνος**, η, ον, *made of mallow-fibre*, μολόχινα (sc. ἱμάτια), τά, *Peripl.M.Rubr.*6; μ. ὀθόνιον, σινδόνες, ib.49, 48; μαφόρια *Sammelb.*7033.39 (v A.D.), cf. Isid.*Etym.*19.22.12; μ. ἔμπλαστρος Androm.ap.Gal.13.490. **-ιον**, τό, = μαλάχιον (q.v.). **-ῖτις** λίθος, ἡ, a kind of *precious stone*, Plin.*HN*37.114. **-ος**, ὁ, = μαλάχη, *Edict.Diocl.*6.5 (pl., v.l. μολόχαι).

⊛**μολπ-άζω**, *sing of*, τινα Ar.*Ra.*380 (lyr.), Hermesian.7.77. **-αῖος**, ον, *tuneful*, ἀοιδάν Erinn.6.7. ⊛**-αρχέω**, *lead the song and dance*, *IG* 12(7).415 (Amorgos). ⊛**-αστής**, οῦ, Dor. **-τάς**, ὁ, *minstrel, dancer*, *AP*6.155 (Theodorid.). **-άστρια**, ἡ, fem. of foreg., prob. in Hsch. **-εύω**, *to be a* μολπός (q.v.), *Jahresh.*5 *Beibl.*66 (Ephesus). **-ή**, ἡ, (μέλπω) *dance* or *rhythmic movement with song*, Od. 6.101, Il.18.606. 2. more freq. *song*, 1.472; μολπῆς τε γλυκερῆς καὶ ἀμύμονος ὀρχηθμοῖο 13.637; μολπή τ' ὀρχηστύς τε Od.1.152, cf. Hes.*Th.*69, Sapph.*Supp.*25.5, Pi.*O.*10.84, 6.97 (pl.), A.*Ag.*106 (lyr.), etc.: Com. in lyr., μολπὰ κλαγγά Mnesim.4.57 (anap.): metaph., οὐ μ. σύριγγος ἔχων *the note*, S.*Ph.*212 (lyr.): also in late Prose, as Luc.*Salt.*23. **-ηδόν**, Adv. *like a song*, A.*Pers.*389. **-ῆτις**, Dor. **-ᾶτις**, ιδος, ἡ, *she who sings and dances*, metaph., κερκίδα τὰν ἱστῶν μολπάτιδα *AP*6.288 (Leon.). **-ικοί**, οἱ, = μολποί, *Milet.*7 p.68.

⊛**μολποδώρα**, ας, ἡ, *bestower of* μολπή, title of Aphrodite in Cyprus, *Schwyzer*682.6.

⊛**μολποί**, οἱ, guild of musicians at Miletus, *SIG*57 (v B.C.), 272 (iv B.C.).

**μόλσον**· σελίνου καυλός, καὶ ἄνθος, οἱ δὲ τὴν ὑποφυάδα, Hsch. **μόλσος**· ὁ δῆμος (Aeol.), Id.; but, = δήμιος, Hdn.Gr.1.207. **μολτύους**· τὰ κοκκύμηλα, Hsch.

**μολῠβᾶς**, ᾶτος, ὁ, *lead-worker*, *POxy.*1517.12 (iii A.D.).

**μολύβδ-αινα**, ἡ, *piece of lead*, used as *the sink* of a fishing-line, Il.24.80. 2. *bullet*, μ. χερμαδία Luc.*Lex.*5. 3. *plumb* in a mason's line, Poll.7.125, 10.147. II. a metallic substance, prob. *sulphuret of lead, galena*, Hp.*Mul.*2.188, Arist.*GA*735ᵇ16, Dsc.5.85, Plin.*HN*34.173. III. a plant, *Plumbago europaea*, ib. 25.155. **-άνθρωπος**, ὁ, *'lead-man'*, symbol in Alchemy, Zos. Alch.p.117 B.; cf. ἀργυράνθρωπος. **-εος**, α, ον, contr. **-οῦς**, ῆ, οῦν, *leaden*, δελφίς Pherecr.12, cf. Thphr.*Od.*41, *IG*2².1013.43, *PCair. Zen.*89.4 (iii B.C.), Ph.*Bel.*99.23 (-λιβδ- codd.), etc. **-ιάω**, *look lead-coloured* or *pale*, ὑπὸ νόσου *Com.Adesp.*1082. **-ίζω**, *to be leaden in colour*, Olymp.Alch.p.71 B. **-ικός**, ή, όν, *leaden*, *Gloss.* **-ῐνος**, η, ον, *leaden, of lead*, Cratin.318, Eup.171; μ. ἴχνος *leaden* sole, Hp.*Art.*62 (prob. l.); ὑποδημάτιον ibid.; μ. κανών, of a flexible architectural instrument, Arist.*EN*1137ᵇ30; μ. σηκώματα Plb. 8.5.9; μ. κεραμίδες Moschio ap.Ath.5.207b; πῖλος Gal.19.701. ⊛**-ιον**, τό, *leaden weight*, Hp.*Art.*14. II. *sound* for the uterus, Id.*Mul.*1. 11, al. **-ίς**, ίδος, ἡ, = μολύβδαινα, *leaden weight* or *sink* of a net, μ. ὥστε δίκτυον κατέσπασεν S.*Fr.*840, cf. Pl.*R.*519b, Hierocl. *in CA*8 p.432 M.; *piece of lead*, *IG*2².1627.322 (pl.). 2. *leaden ball* or *sling-bullet*, X.*An.*3.3.17, Arist.*Cael.*289ᵃ25, Plb.27.11.6. 3. *plummet*, Call.*Fr.*159. 4. *weight* of seven minae, Hsch. **-ῖτις**, ιδος, ἡ, ἄμμος a kind of sand from which λιθάργυρος is obtained, Dsc.5.87, Plin.*HN*33.106.

⊛**μολυβδό-δετος**, ον, *fastened with lead*, ἐσχάραι Poll.6.88. **-ειδής**, ές, *like lead*, Hp.*Int.*32, Dsc.5.83, Aret.*SA*2.7. **-κόπος**, ὁ, ἡ, *one who inscribes* curses *on leaden plates*, *Tab.Defix.*100ᴬ13. **-κρᾰτευταί**, οἱ, = μολύβδινοι κρατευταί (v. κρατευταί 1), Demioprat.ap.Poll.10.96 (nisi leg. μολύβδου κ., v. κρατευταί 3).

⊛**μόλυβδος**, ὁ (ἡ, v. infr. III. 2), *lead*, Simon.64 (dub.), Hdt.3.56, Th. 1.93, *IG*1².371.12, 2².1666.30, al., *PCair.Zen.*386ʳ (iii B.C.), etc.; τηκτὸς μ. E.*Andr.*267, etc. II. *plumbago*, used as a test of gold, Thgn.417, 1105, Arist.*Mete.*349ᵃ2. 2. *circular piece of lead for drawing ruled lines*, *AP*6.67 (Jul. Aeg.). III. = μολύβδιον II, Hp.*Mul.* 2.132, al. 2. μ., ἡ, = μολυβδίς ?, Ammon.*Diff.*p.120 V.—Acc. to *EM*590.8, μόλυβδος and μόλιβος, with their respective derivs., are the correct forms, and this is corroborated by the earlier Inscrr. and Pap.; but later Inscrr., Pap., and codd. show much variation in spelling in derivs.; cf. βόλιμος, περιβολιβόω. (Prob. a foreign word like the cogn. Lat. *plumbum.*)

**μολυβδοτήξ**, ῆκος, ὁ, *melter of lead*, Theognost.*Can.*40: **μολιβδοτήξ**, Hdn.Gr. ap. Choerob.*in Theod.*1.291: **μολιβδότηξ**, Anon.ap. eund.ibid.

**μολυβδουργός**, ὁ, *lead-worker*, Apollod.*Poliorc.*153.7 (μολιβδ-), Ptol.*Tetr.*180, *Gloss.* (μολιβδ-).

**μολυβδο-φᾰνής**, ές, *lead-coloured*, χρῶμα Alex.Mynd.ap.Ath.9. 391b. **-χαλκος**, ον, *alloy of lead and copper*, Zos.Alch.p.157 B. ⊛**-χοέω**, *melt lead, work as a plumber*, Poll.7.108. 2. c. acc., *fix with molten lead*, e.g. a statue on its pedestal, τὼ πόδε μ. περὶ τὰ σφυρά Ar.*Ec.*1110, cf. *IG*2².1672.176 (Athens), 7.3073.179, al. (Lebad.). **-χοΐα**, ἡ, *work in molten lead*, ib.171. **-χοΐζω**, Att. fut. -ιῶ, = μολυβδοχοέω 2, *IG*2².1670.5 (iv B.C.). **-χόος**, ὁ, *lead-smelter*, *Gloss.* (μολιβδ-). **-χροος**, ον, contr. **-χρους**, ουν, *lead-coloured*, Dsc.5.85, Alex.Trall.*Febr.*2. **-χρως**, ωτος, ὁ, ἡ, = foreg., Gal.1. 343. ⊛**-ω**, only in Pass., *melt like lead*, Dsc.5.84. 2. *to be loaded with lead*, of dice, Arist.*Pr.*913ᵃ36; of a net, Hsch. s. v. ἀποσταδόν.

**μολυβδ-ώδης**, ες, = μολυβδοειδής, Hp.*Prog.*2 (interpol.), Dsc.5.81; τὸ τῆς χροιᾶς μ. Gal.11.282. **-ωμα**, ατος, τό, *lead-work*, Moschio ap.Ath.5.208a. **-ωσις**, εως, ἡ, *leading* or *soldering with lead*, *Gloss.* (μολιβδ-).

**μολῠβίς**, ίδος, ἡ, gloss on μολύβδαινα, Hsch.

**μολῠβοειδής**, gloss on μολυβρός, Hsch.

**μόλῠβ-ος**, ὁ, = μόλιβος, Lxx *Ez.*27.12, *Peripl.M.Rubr.*49. **-ουργός**, ὁ, = μολυβδουργός, *POxy.*135.8 (vi A.D.). **-οῦς**, ῆ, οῦν, contr. for μολύβεος, which is not in use, *leaden*, κεραμίς Hegesand.12; δοῖδυξ Dsc.5.81.

**μολυβρός**, ά, όν, *lead-coloured*, Hsch.

**μόλυμμα**, ατος, τό, = μόλυσμα, *Gloss.*

**μολυνή**, ἡ, = πυγή, Hsch.

**μολῠνοπραγμονέομαι**, Pass., *get into dirty quarrels*, Ar.*Ach.*382. (Com. word, imitated from πολυπραγμονέω.)

**μόλυν-σις**, εως, ἡ, *defilement, pollution*, Lxx *Je.*51(44).4, Sch.Il.11. 709, Sch.Iamb.*Comm.Math.*p.101 F. II. v. μώλυσις. **-τός**, ή, όν, *apt to make dirty*, Olymp.*in Mete.*320.15.

**μολύνω**, fut. -ῠνῶ Lxx *Ca.*5.3: aor. ἐμόλῡνα ib.*Ge.*37.31: pf. μεμόλυγκα Choerob.*in Theod.*2.68:—Pass., fut. μολυνθήσομαι Lxx *Za.*14. 2: aor. 1 ἐμολύνθην ib.*Si.*22.13: pf. μεμόλυσμαι ib.1*Es.*8.83, Epict. *Ench.*33, J.*AJ*3.6.1, μεμόλυμμαι Lxx *Is.*65.4, Choerob. *in Theod.*2. 186:—*stain, sully, defile*, τὴν ὑπήνην Ar.*Eq.*1286; ἑαυτοὺς τῷ πηλῷ Arist.*HA*571ᵇ18, cf. Theoc.20.10; simply, *sprinkle*, ἀλεύρῳ Sotad. Com.1.24; *make a beast of*, τινας (of Circe) Ar.*Pl.*310; *defile, debauch*, παῖδα Theoc.5.87: metaph., χεῖρας ἁρπαγῇ J.*Vit.*47:—Pass., *become vile, disgrace oneself*, Isoc.5.81; μετὰ γυναικῶν *Apoc.*14.4; ὥσπερ θηρίον ὕειον ἐν ἀμαθίᾳ μολύνεσθαι *wallow* in ignorance, Pl.*R.*535e; ὁ μολυνόμενος ὑπὸ τοῦ ὕψου Muson.*Fr.*18ᴮp.101 H.; ἡ συνείδησις αὐτῶν μολύνεται 1*Ep.Cor.*8.7. 2. *stain, dye*, χιτωνίσκον αἵματι J.*AJ*2.3.4:—Pass., ἔρια μεμολυσμένα ἄνθεσι ib.3.6.1. II. v. μωλύω.

**μολυρίς**, ίδος, ἡ, = ἀκρίς, Suid.; cf. μολουρίς.

**μολυρόν**· νωθρόν, κτλ., Hsch. (cf. μωλυρόν).

**μόλυς**, dub. sense in Hdn.Gr.2.938 (fort. μῶλυς).

**μόλ-υσμα**, ατος, τό, *spot, taint*, Hierocl. *in CA*26 p.478 M., Sch.rec. A.*Pers.*576. **-υσμᾰτώδης**, ες, *tainted, polluted*, Herm. *in Phdr.*p.107 A., Procl. ad Hes.*Op.*751. **-υσμός**, ὁ, *defilement, pollution*, Lxx *Je.*23.15, Aristeas 166, Str.17.2.4, 2*Ep.Cor.*7.1, J.*Ap.*1.32 (pl.), Plu. 2.779c (pl.), Iamb.*Myst.*5.4.

⊛**μόλυχνον**· δυσταλέον, Hsch. **μομβρῶ**, = μορμώ, Id., Suid. (μολυβρῶ codd.). **μομμώ**, = foreg., Hsch.

**μομφή**, ἡ, poet. form of μέμψις (also in Pl.*Ep.*323b), *blame, reproof,* Pi.*N.*8.39; μομφῆς ἄτερ τέθνηκεν A.*Th.*1015; *cause of complaint,* μομφὰν ἔχειν τινί Pi.*I.*4(3).36; ἔν σοι μομφὴν ἔχω in one thing I *blame* thee, E.*Or.*1069; μομφὰς ὑπὸ σπλάγχνοις ἔχειν Id.*Alc.*1009; πρός τινα μ. ἔχειν *Ep.Col.*3.13: c. gen., μ. ἔχων ξυνοῦ δορός S.*Aj.*180 (lyr.); ὧν ἕνεκα μ. ἔχει Ar.*Pax*664.

⊛**μόμφος**, ὁ, = foreg., E.*Fr.*633, *IG*5(2).262.34 (Mantinea, v B.C.):—so **μόμφις**, dub. in Telecl.63 (cf. μέμφειραν· τὴν μέμψιν, Τηλεκλείδης, Phot.); cf. **μόμψεις**· δύσκλεια, Hsch.

**μον-άγκων**, ωνος, ὁ, *one-armed* engine to throw projectiles, Ph.*Bel.* 91.36 (pl.), Apollod.*Poliorc.*188.6 (pl.), al. **-αγρία**, ἡ, *solitary field, farm,* Ph.2.4, Alciphr.2.2:—also **-άγριον**, τό, Ph.2.474 codd., v.l. in ib.4, *Jahresh.*23 *Beibl.*93 (Pamphylia). **-ᾰδελφία**, ἡ, *possession of only one brother, Cat.Cod.Astr.*6.70.

**μον-άδην**, Adv., (μόνος) *solitary-wise, only,* A.D.*Adv.*198.4, *EM* 367.9. **-ᾰδιαῖος**, α, ον, *of unit magnitude,* διαστήματα Hero *Metr.* 2 *Praef.* **-ᾰδικός**, ή, όν, *consisting of abstract units,* μ. τοὺς ἀριθμοὺς πάντες τιθέασι, πλὴν τῶν Πυθαγορείων Arist.*Metaph.*1080ᵇ30; μ. ἀριθμός *abstract* number, Id.*EN*1131ᵃ30, cf. *Metaph.*1092ᵇ20. Adv. -κῶς Ph.2.19, Plu.2.744e. II. *solitary,* opp. ἀγελαῖος, ζῷα Arist.*HA* 488ᵃ1, 623ᵇ10. III. *unique, individual,* φύσις, of the κόσμος, Ph. 1.7. 2. *unitary, monadic,* Procl.*Inst.*108, Dam.*Pr.*54. IV. Gramm., *having a single form,* μ. κατὰ τριγένειαν *having one termination* for all three genders, A.D.*Adv.*141.24, cf. *Pron.*11.29; μ. ἐγκλιτικαί, of σφε and μιν, Id.*Synt.*169.20; τὸ μ. *indeclinability,* ib.33. 25. **-ᾰδισμός**, ὁ, *formation of monads,* τὰ γεννώμενα κατὰ -ισμόν Dam.*Pr.*193. **-ᾰδιστί**, Adv. *in units,* Nicom.*Ar.*2.8. **-ᾰδόν**, Ion. **μουνᾰδόν**, Adv., = μονάδην, Opp.*H.*1.444. ⊛**-άζω**, *to be alone,* *AP*5.65 (Rufin.); *live in solitude,* στρουθίον μονάζον ἐπὶ δώματι LXX *Ps.*101(102).7, cf. Iamb.*VP*3.14; μ. ἐν ταῖς ἐρημίαις ib.35.253. 2. Gramm., of words, *to be a solitary instance,* Hdn.Gr.2.913. b. *have a special force,* A.D.*Synt.*191.2. c. *to be used alone,* μ. ἐκτὸς συνδέσμου ib.265.19. 3. trans., *individualize,* Eust.349.35:—Pass., *to be made one,* τῇ συμφυΐᾳ Id.1321.28. II. ἡ μονὰς ἑαυτὴν μονάσασα unity *multiplied into* itself, Iamb.*inNic.*p.60P.

**μόναιπος**, v. μόναπος.

**μον-άκανθος** [ᾰκ], ον, *with one prickle,* Arist.*Fr.*307. **-αλκής**· ἐξέχουσα, ἀνδρωδεστάτη, Hsch. **-άλῠσις** [ᾰ], εως, ἡ, *single chain,* Poll.10.167. **-αμπῠκία**, ἡ, = μονάμπυξ, abstract for concrete, Pi. *O.*5.7. **-άμπυξ**, ῡκος, ὁ, ἡ, of horses, *having one frontlet,* μονάμπυκες πῶλοι horses *that run single, race-*horses, opp. chariots, E. *Alc.*428; μονάμπυκες alone, Id.*Supp.*586, 680; of a bull, *having no yoke-fellow,* μονάμπυκος (-ον codd.) ψήχων δέρην Id.*Hel.*1567. **-ανδρέω**, *to have but one husband,* Anon.ap.Suid. **-ανδρος**, ἡ, *having but one husband, IG*12(3).912 (Thera), 14.191 (Syracuse).

⊛**μονάξ**, v. μουνάξ.

**μοναξία**, ἡ, *solitariness,* Sch.E.*Hec.*1017, Eust.22.12.

**μόναπος**, ὁ, Paeonian name for βόνασος or βόλινθος, Arist.*HA*630ᵃ 20:—written **μόναιπος**, Id.*Mir.*830ᵃ7; cf. μόνωψ, μόνωτος II.

**μονάριος**, ὁ, *keeper of a* μονή, *PLond.*1914.19 (iv A.D.).

**μοναρτᾰβία**, ἡ, *tax of 1 artaba, PRyl.*202.3 (i A.D.), *POxy.*1459.11 (iii A.D.).

**μοναρχ-εία**, ἡ, poet. for μοναρχία, *Hymn.Is.*6. **-έω**, Ion. μουν-, *to be sovereign,* Pi.*P.*4.165, Pl.*R.*576b; ἐπὶ τούτου μουναρχέοντος in this *king's* time, Hdt.5.61, cf. 46; κατὰ νόμους μ. Pl.*Plt.*301b: c. gen., ἑκόντων μ. Arist.*Pol.*1295ᵃ16:—Pass., μοναρχεῖται πᾶς οἶκος ib.1255ᵇ 19. II. *hold the office of* μόναρχος at Cos, *SIG*805.6, Sor.*Vit. Hippocr.* **-ης**, ου, ὁ, = μόναρχος, dub.l. in Jul.*Or.*2.85c. ⊛**-ία**, Ion. **μουναρχίη**, ἡ, *monarchy, government by a single ruler,* Alc.*Oxy.* 1789*Fr.*12, A.*Th.*883 (lyr., pl.), Hdt.3.82; λαβὼν χώρας παντελῆ μ. S.*Ant.*1163, etc.; καὶ γὰρ κατέστησ' αὐτὸν (sc. τὸν δῆμον) εἰς μοναρχίαν E.*Supp.*352; ὦ μισόδημε καὶ μοναρχίας ἐραστά Ar.*V.*474; including βασιλική and τυραννική, Pl.*Plt.*291e: in pl., οἱ ἐν ταῖς μ. ὄντες Isoc.2.5, cf. Arist.*Pol.*1311ᵃ24, 1279ᵃ33, *Rh.*1365ᵇ37; of the Roman Dictator, Plu.*Caes.*37; *supreme command,* of a general, X.*An.*6. 1.31. **-ια**, τά, festival at Calymna, *SIG*1210.3. **-ικός**, ή, όν, *monarchical,* πολιτεία Pl.*Lg.*756e; τὸ μ., = μοναρχία, ib.693e; [πολιτεία] ἔχουσα μοναρχικὸν οὐδέν Arist.*Pol.*1266ᵃ6; ἐξουσία -κωτέρα Plb.10.26.2. 2. of persons, *inclined to monarchy,* App.*BC* 5.54. Adv. Comp. -κώτερον Plu.*Num.*2. **-ος**, Ion. μούν-, ὁ, *monarch, sole ruler,* first in Thgn.52 (in Ion. form, as Hdt.3.82, 5. 46), cf. Sol.9.3, etc.; τραχὺς μ. A.*Pr.*326; μονάρχους καταλύειν Th. 1.122; δῆμος, ἅτε μ. ὤν as *sole ruler,* Arist.*Pol.*1292ᵃ15; γῆς τῆσδε μ. Ar.*Eq.*1330. 2. *princelet, dynast, OGI*54.16 (Adule, iii B.C.): generally, *leader, general,* E.*Rh.*31 (lyr.). 3. = Lat. *dictator,* Plu. *Cam.*18. II. title of magistrate at Cos, *SIG*1012.13, etc. b. name of month at Cos, dub. in *BMus.Inscr.*339. III. as Adj., σκᾶπτον μ. the *royal* sceptre, Pi.*P.*4.152.

⊛**μον-άς**, Ion. **μουνάς** (*AP*9.482 (Agath.)), άδος, ἡ, special fem. of μόνος, *solitary,* ἐρημία E.*Ba.*609 (troch.); αἰών Id.*Ph.*1520 (lyr.); of a woman, *alone, by oneself,* Id.*Andr.*855 (lyr.): as masc., of a man, A. *Pers.*734 (troch.). II. as Subst. μονάς, ἡ, *unit,* Pl.*Phd.*101c, 105c, Arist.*Metaph.*1089ᵇ35, etc.; *monad,* Procl.*Inst.*64, *in Alc.*p.51C. (pl.), Dam.*Pr.*199, al.: in Pythag. philosophy, to denote *fire,* Plu.*Num.* 11. 2. Ion., = οἴνη, *ace* on a die, Poll.7.204. 3. as a measure of length, = δάκτυλος, Hero *Geom.*4.2; εἰς μονάδας ἀγαγεῖν reduce to *units* (of weight, here *drachmae*), Ph.*Bel.*51.24; διεξασμένη κατὰ μονάδας, of alum, Dsc.5.106. **-ασμός**, ὁ, *solitary life, solitude,* Eust.636.36.

⊛**μοναστήριος**, α, ον, *monastic,* οἶκος Men.Prot.p.15 D. II. μοναστήριον, τό, *hermit's cell,* Ph.2.475. 2. *monastery,* Procop.*Arc.* 17, al., Just.*Nov.*3.2, *PSI*8.933.2 (vi A.D.).

**μον-αστρᾰβής**, ές, (ἀστράβη) *with one pack-saddle,* ὄχος Trag. *Adesp.*239.

⊛**μονάστρια**, ἡ, *nun,* Just.*Nov.*123.36, al.

**μονάτωρ**, ορος, ὁ, = μονάμπυξ, Sch.Ar.*Pax*900, cf. Hsch. s. v. κέλης.

⊛**μον-αυλέω**, (αὐλός) *play a solo on the flute,* Plu.*Caes.*52. ⊛**-αυλία** (A), ἡ, (αὐλός) *solo on the flute,* Poll.4.82. **-αυλία** (B), ἡ, (αὐλή) *living alone, celibacy,* Pl.*Lg.*721d, Ph.2.327. **-αυλικός**, ή, όν, *solitary,* prob. in Arist.*EE*1242ᵃ25. ⊛**-αύλιον**, τό, *solo instrument,* Posidon.2 J. ⊛**-αυλος**, ὁ, (αὐλός) *player on the single flute,* Hedyl. ap.Ath.4.176c. 2. μόναυλος (sc. κάλαμος), ὁ, *flute,* S.*Fr.*241, Anaxandr.18, cf. 51, Arar.13. II. as Adj. Pass., *played on a single flute,* μόναυλον μέλος Sopat.2.

**μονᾰχ-ῇ**, Adv., prop. dat. sg. fem. of μοναχός, *in one way only,* opp. διχῇ, Pl.*Lg.*720e, etc.; ᾗπερ μοναχῇ in which way *only,* X.*An.*4.4. 18. **-ή**, ἡ, a kind of ὀθόνιον, *Peripl.M.Rubr.*6, 14. **-ικός**, ή, όν, *of* or *for a* μοναχός, ἄσκησις Just.*Nov.*5 *Praef.*; σχῆμα *PSI*8.932.13 (vi A.D.). **-όθεν**, Adv. *from one side only,* Suid. s.v. παραγωγή. ⊛**-ός**, ή, όν, (μόνος) *unique,* Arist.*Metaph.*1040ᵃ29; στερεὰ μ. a *single* set of solids, ib.1076ᵇ29; ὅσα μ. ἔχει συμφωνίαν Epicur.*Ep.*2 p.36 U.; τὰ σπλάγχνα ἔχειν μ. D.S.2.58, cf. Apollod.*Poliorc.*181.10; μ. τέκνα *only* children, Ptol.*Tetr.*190; τὰ μ. *individual cases,* Phld.*Sign.*14, al.; τὸ μ. *uniqueness,* Plot.6.8.7. Adv. -χῶς Epicur.*Ep.*1 p.30 U. 2. *solitary, deserted,* μοναχῷ ἐνὶ rure Κρεβέννου Aus.*Ep.*8.23. 3. of legal documents, *executed in a single copy, BGU*13.16 (iii A.D.), etc. Adv. -χῶς *Sammelb.*5810.20 (iv A.D.). II. Subst., *monk, AP*11.384 (Pall.), Procop.*Pers.*1.7. **-οῦ**, Adv. *in one place only,* μ. ἐνταῦθα Pl.*Smp.*184e, cf. 212a: c. gen., μ. τῆς Οἴτης Thphr.*HP*9.10.2; ὁ μὲν αἰσθητὸς κόσμος μ., ὁ δὲ νοητὸς πανταχοῦ Plot.5.9.13. **-ουσα**, ἡ, fem. of μοναχός II, *Zeitschr.d.deutschen Palästinavereins*44.98 (Jerusalem, vi A.D.). **-όω**, *make single,* Aq.*Ps.*85(86).11. **-ῶς**, Adv. *in one way only,* opp. πολλαχῶς, Arist.*EN*1106ᵇ31, *Pol.*1308ᵇ 38. 2. *in a uniform way,* Id.*HA*584ᵃ34.

**μον-ειμοφορέω**, *wear one garment,* Suid., Zonar. **-έντερον**, τό, = κόλον II, *Hippiatr.*36. **-ερέτης**, Ion. μουν-, ου, ὁ, *one who rows singly, AP*7.637 (Antip.).

⊛**μονή**, ἡ, (μένω) *abiding, tarrying,* E.*Tr.*1129, *HF*957, Ar.*Av.*418 (lyr.), X.*An.*5.1.5, etc.; opp. ἔξοδος, Hdt.1.94; opp. φορά, Pl.*Cra.* 437b; opp. κίνησις, Arist.*Ph.*205ᵃ17; τὴν μονὴν ποιεῖσθαι make *delay, tarry,* Th.1.131; μὴ λαμβάνειν μονὴν μηδὲ στάσιν Plb.4.41.4; μ. τις καὶ στάσις τῆς φωνῆς Aristox.*Harm.*p.12 M.: pl., Arist.*Ph.*230ᵃ20; κινήσεις ἢ μοναί Id.*de An.*408ᵇ18; μονὰς ποιεῖσθαι Str.1.3.12; *persistence, continuance,* τοῦ αἰσθήματος Arist.*APo.*99ᵇ36. 2. *permanence,* τῆς γῆς Epicur.*Nat.*11.10, cf. Dam.*Pr.*36. 3. Gramm., *preservation,* τοῦ ν A.D.*Pron.*50.25. II. *stopping-place, station,* Paus.10. 31.7; *apartment, Ev.Jo.*14.2, 23; *quarters, billets, OGI*527.5 (Hierapolis). 2. *monastery,* Just.*Nov.*133.1, etc. III. *appearance* in a court of law, *PHib.*93.2, 111.31 (iii B.C.).

**μον-ήλᾰτος**, ον, (ἐλαύνω) *hammered out of one piece,* Hld.9.15. **-ημέριον**, τό, *spectacle lasting for one day, AP*9.581 (in lemmate), Just.*Nov.* 105.1. **-ήμερος**, ον, *staying one day,* καταλύτης LXX *Wi.*5.14. 2. *living one day,* ζῷον Ael.*NA*5.43. 3. *lasting one day,* κόλασις *Supp. Epigr.*4.648.22 (Lydia, ii A.D.). ⊛**-ήρης**, ες, *solitary,* Hp.*Ep.*12, Heraclid.ap.D.L.1.25, Arist.*Fr.*314, 319, Lyc.75, Nic.*Al.*400, Plb. 21.43.13, Babr.132.1; μ. βίος, δίαιτα, Muson.*Fr.*14 p.76 H., Luc.*Tim.* 42. 2. Gramm., of words, *singular, peculiar* in form, etc.; περὶ μονήρους λέξεως, title of work by Hdn.Gr. II. of a ship, *with one man to each oar,* Poll.1.82, Procop.*Goth.*4.22, *Vand.*1.11.

**μονθυλεύω**, **-ευσις**, **-ευτός**, v. ὀνθυλ-.

⊛**μονία** (A), Ion. **-ίη**, ἡ, (μένω) *changelessness,* Emp.27.4. 2. *steadfastness,* Tyrt.1.15 Diehl; μανία derived from this word or from sq. acc. to Cael.Aur.*TP*1.145.

⊛**μονία** (B), Ion. **-ίη**, ἡ, (μόνος) *solitude, celibacy,* Max.71.

**μονίας**, ου, ὁ, *solitary,* Ael.*NA*1.46, 7.47; βίος Eust.1409.61.

**μονικῶς**, Adv., dub. sens. in Phld.*Hom.*p.14 O.

**μόνῐμος**, ον, also η, ον *AP*12.224 (Strat.): (μονή, μένω):—*staying in one's place, stable,* Hp.*Art.*62; μ. οὐδένα χρόνον ib.14; *stationary,* ζῷα μ. κατὰ τόπον Arist.*de An.*410ᵇ19; ζῷα μ. Id.*HA*487ᵇ6; ἡ τῶν φυτῶν φύσις μ. Id.*PA*656ᵃ1; ἄστρα μ. *fixed* stars, Poll.4.156; οἶνος μ. wine *which will keep, PGrenf.*2.24.14 (ii B.C.); μ. σφυγμός *steady* pulse, Gal.9.351. Adv. -μως Arist.*HA*596ᵃ14, Gal.17(1). 508. 2. of persons, *steady, steadfast,* S.*OT*1322 (lyr.); ἐν πολέμῳ Pl.*R.*537d, cf. X.*Cyr.*8.5.11 (Sup.), Pl.*Lg.*706c. 3. freq. of things, conditions, and the like, *lasting, stable,* ὁ μέγας ὄλβος οὐ μ. E.*Or.*340 (lyr.); of political institutions, Th.8.89, Arist.*Pol.*1273ᵇ20, 1297ᵃ7 (Comp.); μ. πόλεις Pl.*Plt.*302a: coupled with ἀμετάπτωτος, Id.*Ti.* 29b; with βέβαιος, Id.*Smp.*184b; τὸ μ. *permanence,* Plot.6.1.11: Comp., Dam.*Pr.*77. Adv. -μως Iamb.*Myst.*1.5, Procl.*Inst.*154. II. μόνιμον, τό, *fixed abode,* LXX *Je.*38(31).17.

**μονῐμότης**, ητος, ἡ, *constancy, steadfastness,* Procl. *in Alc.*p.60C.

**μονιός**, όν, but Ep. μούνιος Hdn.Gr.1.118:—*solitary,* of male beasts which have been driven from the herd: hence, *savage, ferocious,* μ. δάκος Call.*Dian.*84; μούνιος ἐκ θάμνοιο λύκος *AP*7.289 (Antip. Thess.), cf. Luc.*Ep.Sat.*34. 2. Subst., *solitary wild boar* (ὗς ἄγριος ὁ μὴ τοῖς ἄλλοις συναγελαζόμενος Hsch.), v.l. for ὗς ἄγριος in Aesop.407; μ. ἄγριος LXX *Ps.*79(80).13 (v.l.).

**μόνιππος**, ὁ, *single horse, riding-horse*, opp. chariot-horse, X.*Cyr.* 6.4.1, Pl.*Lg.*834c, *GDI*4833 (Cyrene), cf. Paus.Gr.*Fr.*259. II. as Adj., μ. ἱππεῖς Poll.1.141.

**μόννος**, ὁ, v. μάννος.

**μονο-βαίας**, ὁ, *thief*, Hsch. (leg. -βάτας). **-βάλᾰνος** [βᾰ] κλείς, a key *with one ward* (v. βάλανος II.4), Sch.Ar.*Th.*430. **-βάμων** [ᾱ], ον, gen. ονος, *walking alone*, E.*Hyps.Fr.*3(1).38 (lyr.). 2. μέτρον μ. metre *of but one foot*, Simm.26.9. **-βας**, ὁ, = μονοβαίας, Hsch. **-βᾰφος**, ον, *single-dyed*, *Edict.Diocl.*29.35, al. **-βιβλος**, ὁ, or **-βιβλον**, τό, *single book* or *volume*, Prop.1 tit., Gal.1.410, Ammon.*Vit.Arist.*p.11 W., Lyd.*Mag.*1.28, Suid. s.v. Φιλάγριος. **-βολέω**, *undertake sowing without assistance*, *PLond.*1.131ʳ.290,312 (i A.D.). **-βολος**, ον, *in one piece*, opp. δίβολος, ξύλα *IG*2².1672.307, al.: gloss on μονόδροπον, Sch.Pi.*P.*5.56; on αὐτόγυον, Hsch. s.h.v.:—Subst. **-βολον**, τό, *anchor*, *PLond.*3.1264ᵇ9 (iii A.D.). **-γᾰμέω**, *to be the husband of one wife*, *Cat.Cod.Astr.*2.209. **-γᾰμία**, ἡ, *monogamy*, Antig.Nic. ap.Heph.Astr.2.18. **-γάμμᾰτος**, ον, *written with one* γ, Eust.1873.41. ✱**-γᾰμος**, ὁ, *one who marries but once*, Ptol.*Tetr.*183, Vett.Val.120.8. **-γένεια**, Ion. μουνο-, ἡ, fem. of sq., A.R.3.847, Orph.*H.*29.2. II. Subst., *uniqueness*, Phld.*Sign.*20. **-γενής**, ές, Ep. and Ion. μουνο-, (γένος) *the only member of a kin* or *kind*: hence, generally, *only, single*, παῖς Hes.*Op.*376, Hdt.7.221, cf. *Ev.Jo.*1.14, Ant.Lib.32.1; of Hecate, Hes.*Th.*426. 2. *unique*, of τὸ ὄν, Parm. 8.4; εἷς ὅδε μ. οὐρανὸς γεγονώς Pl.*Ti.*31b, cf. Procl.*Inst.*22; θεὸς ὁ μ. *Sammelb.*4324.15. 3. μ. αἷμα *one and the same* blood, dub. l. in E. *Hel.*1685. 4. Gramm., *having one form for all genders*, A.D.*Adv.* 145.18. 5. name of the foot – – – ⏑, Heph.3.3. II. Adv. -νῶς, φέρεται μ. ἐν ἑνὶ τόπῳ grows *only* in one place, *Peripl.M.Rubr.*56, cf. 11. 2. *in a unique manner*, Aët.15.13,14. **-γέρων**, οντος, ὁ, *misanthropic old man*, *Com.Adesp.*1083. **-γληνος**, Ep. μουνό-, ον, *one-eyed*, Call.*Dian.*53, *AP*7.748 (Antip. Sid.). **-γνωμέω**, *to be self-willed, wayward*, Procl.*Par.Ptol.*222 (leg. -γνωμονέω). **-γνωμονέω**, *to be opinionated*, Phld.*Oec.*p.72 J.; cf. foreg. **-γνωμονικός**, ή, όν, *self-willed*, Procl.*Par.Ptol.*222,235. **-γνωμοσύνη**, ἡ, *waywardness*, *Cat.Cod.Astr.*2.161. **-γνώμων**, ον, gen. ονος, *self-willed, wayward*, Ptol.*Tetr.*158 (Comp., 168), Vett.Val.12.4. II. *invested with supreme authority*, D.H.2.12, 5.71. **-γόνᾰτος**, ον, *made from a single joint*, of a reed-pen, *Edict.Diocl.*18.12. **-γονος**, Ep. μουνό-, η, ον, *only-born*, κούρη μουνογόνη, of Persephone, Opp.*H.*3.489 codd.; Δήμητρι καὶ Μουνογόνῃ *IG*9(2).305 (Tricca, ii B.C.); μουνογόναν τὸ ἕν [μανύει] *Supp.Epigr.*4.634 (Sardes, i B.C.). **-γράμμᾰτος**, ον, *consisting of one letter*, συλλαβή D.H.*Comp.*15, A.D.*Adv.*121.23. ✱**-γραμμος**, ον, *drawn with single lines, outlined*, Epicur.ap.Cic.*ND*2.23 (p.234 U.). **-γράφος** [ᾰ], ὁ, *notary*, *PMagd.*12.5 (iii B.C.), *UPZ*62.17 (ii B.C.), *PLond.*1.3.29 (ii B.C.), etc. **-γυιος**, ον, = μονομελής, Simp.*in Cael.*587.26. **-δάκτῠλος**, ον, *one-toed*, Luc.*VH*1.23. **-δᾱμιουργοί**· οἱ τὰς δίκας δικάζοντες, Hsch. **-δέρκτης**, ου, Dor. -τᾶς, ὁ, *one-eyed*, E.*Cyc.*78 (lyr.). **-δερμος**, ον, gloss on μονόλοπος, Hsch. **-δέσμη**, ἡ, *single truss* of hay, *BGU*528 (ii A.D.). ✱**-δεσμία**, ἡ, a tax of uncertain nature, *Sammelb.*1441, *PSI*6.693 (ii A.D.), *PAmh.*2.121.7 (ii/iii A.D.), etc. **-δοξέω**, *possess fame alone*, Simp.*in Epict.*p.86 D. **-δουπος**, ον, *uniform in sound*, Simm. 26.12.

**μον-όδους**, οντος, ὁ, ἡ, *one-toothed*, A.*Pr.*796.

✱**μονο-δραχμία**, ἡ, *tax of 1 drachma*, *PLond.*3.1157ʳ.6, *POxy.*1442.3 (both iii A.D., abbrev.). ✱**-δραχμος**, ον, *of one drachma*, *PRyl.*221.19 (iii A.D.), al. **-δροπος**, ον, *plucked from one stem*: hence metaph., *cut from one block*, of a statue, φυτόν Pi.*P.*5.42. **-είδεια**, ἡ, *uniformity*, S.E.*M.*1.117. II. *singularity*, ib.226. **-ειδής**, ές, *one in kind, simple*, Pl.*R.*612a, *Phd.*78d, *Smp.*211b, etc.; κτήσεις τῶν μ. Phld.*Oec.*p.72 J.; opp. δίσωμος, of ζῴδια, Ptol.*Tetr.*119; *unique*, Pl.*Ti.*59b, Dam.*Pr.*151: Comp., Thphr.*HP*8.5.1; τὸ μ. *uniformity*, Plb.9.1.2. Adv. -δῶς Ptol.*Tetr.*120, S.E.*M.*6.44, Iamb. *Myst.*1.3, etc.; *in single kinds, severally*, εἴτε πάντα εἴτε μ. Epicur. *Ep.*2 p.51 U. **-είλητος**, ον, *simple*, of a figure in stereometry, Hero*Stereom.*1.77. **-είμων**, ον, (εἷμα) = μονοχίτων, Phot. **-ζῠγής**, ές, = sq., σάνδαλον *APl.*4.308 (Eugenes). ✱**-ζυξ**, ῠγος, *yoked alone*: hence, *single, solitary*, A.*Pers.*139 (lyr.). II. ξύλα μ., opp. τετράγωνα, = μονόξυλα, *IG*12(9).907 (Chalcis, iv A.D.). **-ζωνος**, ον, *girt up alone*, i.e. *journeying alone*, Suid., etc. II. μονόζωνοι, οἱ, men *with a* ζώνη *only, light-armed*, Lxx 4*Ki.*5.2, al., Hsch. **-ζωος**, ον, *living alone, solitary*, Quint.*Ps.*67(68).7. **-ζωστος**, ον, = μονόζωνος I, Hermesian.7.7. **-ήμερος**, ον, = μονήμερος, *in one day*, Batr.303. II. *curing in one day*, of remedies, Gal.12.712, al., Aët.7.103; *requiring one day*, of alchemical operations, Zos. Alch.p.140 B. III. σκευὴ ἄγουσα (sc. δαίμονας) μονοημέρους *on the selfsame day*, *PMag.Par.*1.2442.

**μονόθεν**, Adv. *alone, singly*, μοῦνος μουνόθεν Hdt.1.116 (v.l. μουνωθέντα). II. *on one side only*, Sch.Arat.8.

✱**μονο-θρηνέω**, *mourn in solitude*, Hsch. s.v. μονῳδεῖ. **-θῠρος**, ον, *with one leaf*, θύρα *IG*2².1627.419; θυρώματα ib.4²(1).110*A*32, 118.73 (Epid., iv/iii and iii B.C.); of non-spiral shell-fish, *univalve*, opp. δίθυρος, Arist.*HA*528ᵃ13. II. *with only one opening*, Porph. *Antr.*31.

**μον-οίκητος**, ον, *dwelling alone, solitary*, E.*Hyps.Fr.*5(3).17, Lyc. 960. **-οικος**, ὁ, epith. of Heracles in Southern Gaul, Str.4.6.3.

**μονο-κάλᾰμος**, ον, *with a single stalk* or *stem*, Thphr.*HP*8.4.3, 8.9.2. II. *with a single reed* or *pipe*, Ath.4.184a. **-καμπτος**, ον, *with one bend*, δάκτυλος (toe) Arist.*HA*494ᵃ15. **-καυλος**, ον, *with but one stem* or *stalk*, Thphr.*HP*7.8.2, 4.6.8 (Comp.), Dsc.3.91. **-κέλης**, Ion. μουνο-, ητος, ὁ, *single horse, riding-horse*, Epigr.ap.Paus.8.42.9. **-κένταυρος**, ὁ, *man with ox's head*, *Gloss.* ✱**-κερως**, ων, gen. ω Plu.*Per.*6:—*with but one horn*, Arist.*HA*499ᵇ19, Orph.*Fr.* 273: pl. -κέρατα, Arist.*HA*499ᵇ18, *PA*663ᵃ22:—poet. μουνόκερος, ον, Archil.181. II. Subst. μονόκερως, ωτος, ὁ, *wild ox*, Lxx *Ps.* 21(22).21, 28(29).6. **-κέφᾰλος**, ον, *one-headed*, σκόρδον Dsc.2.152; σφῦρα Hsch. s.v. ῥαιστήρ. **-κλᾰδος**, ὁ, *single branch* (i.e. not chopped up into logs), *POxy.*1188.20 (i A.D.). **-κλαυτος** θρῆνος, ὁ, a lament *made by one only*, A.*Th.*1069 (anap.). **-κληρονόμος**, ἡ, *sole heiress*, Sch.Ar.*V.*581, *Av.*1652. **-κλῖνον**, τό, *bed for one only*, i.e. *coffin*, *AP*9.570 (Phld.). **-κλῐτος**, ον, *indeclinable*, Hdn. *Epim.*191; τὸ μ. *EM*314.23. **-κλωνος**, ον, *with a single stem*, Dsc. 4.5, dub. l. in Thphr.*HP*9.18.8, cf. *PMag.Par.*1.808:—also **-κλων**, ib. 2689. **-κνημος**, ον, *showing one shin*, name of picture by Apelles, Petron.83. **-κοίλιος**, ον, *with a single stomach*, Arist.*HA*495ᵇ31, *PA* 676ᵃ12, ᵇ3, Mnesith.ap.Orib.21.7.8. **-κοιτέω**, *sleep alone*, Ar.*Lys.* 592. **-κοιτος**, ον, *sleeping alone*, Sch.Lyc.960. II. *for one sleeper*, κλινίδιον Hsch. s.v. σκιμπόδιον (-κοίτιον cod.). **-κοκκος**, ον, *with a single grain*, of pearls, *Gloss.*; also of onions, ibid. **-κόνδῠλος**, ον, *with but one joint*, δάκτυλος (thumb) Arist.*HA*493ᵇ29. **-κόντιον**, τό, a kind of *spear* or *javelin*, Just.*Nov.*85.4. **-κότῠλος**, ον, *with but one row of arms* or *suckers*, Arist.*HA*525ᵃ17, *PA*685ᵇ13. **-κρήπῖς**, ῖδος, ὁ, ἡ, *with but one sandal*, Pi.*P.*4.75, *APl.*4.127, Lyc.1310. ✱**-κροτος** ναῦς, a vessel *with one squad of rowers*, opp. δίκροτος, X.*HG*2.1.28, cf. *Arch.Pap.*8.197, Str.7.7.6. Ael.*Tact.*[4]. **-κρουνον**, τό, *jug with a single spout*, Haussoullier *Milet* p.199. **-κυκλος**, ον, *with the top made in one piece*, τράπεζα Demioprat ap.Poll.10.81. 2. as Subst., *one-wheeled cart, wheelbarrow*, or perh. *cart with solid wheels* (cf. μονόστροφος II), ὑπερτερία-κύκλου *IG*1².313.115, al. **-κωλος**, Ion. μουνό-, ον, *with but one leg*, of a fabulous race of men, Plin *HN*7.23, Gell. 9.4. 2. *with one stem*, ἄπιος Thphr.*CP*2.15.5; φύλλον Id.*HP*9.18.8 (dub.). 3. *of one story*, οἰκήματα Hdt.1.179. 4. Subst., a bandage, *for one limb*, Sor.*Fasc.*57. 5. of periods, *consisting of one clause*, Arist.*Rh.*1409ᵇ17; also λόγος μ. Plu.2.7b, D.H.*Dem.*42; ὑπόθεσις Id.*Th.*6. 6. generally, *of one kind, one-sided*, ἔχει τὴν φύσιν μ., of nations, Arist.*Pol.*1327ᵇ35. **-κωπος**, ον, *with one oar*: poet., *with one ship*, E.*Hel.*1128 (lyr.). **-λέκῐθος**, ον, *with one yolk*, Sch. E.*Or.*465. **-λεχής**, Ion. μουνο-, ές, = μονόκοιτος, διαζυγίη *AP* 5.8 (Rufin.); κοῖται ib.12.226 (Strat.). **-λέων**, Ion. μουνο-, οντος, ὁ, *solitary*, i.e. *singularly fierce, lion*, *AP*6.221 (Leon.). **-λήκῠθος**, ον, = αὐτολήκυθος II, Posidipp.ap.Ath.10.414e. **-λήμμᾰτος**, ον, *with but one premiss*, λόγοι Chrysipp. and Antip.*Stoic.*2.84; συλλογισμοί Alex.Aphr.*in Top.*8.17, al. **-λῐθος**, Ion. μουνό-, ον, *made out of one stone*, στέγη Hdt.2.175; ὀβελίσκοι D.S.1.46; κίονες Str.9.5.16. **-λῖνον**, τό, *necklace of a single string of pearls*, Capitolin.*Vit. Maximini Jun.*1.8. **-λοπος**, ον, *with but one coat* or *layer*, φλοιός Thphr.*HP*1.5.2; = μονόφυλλος, μονόδερμος, Phot., cf. Hsch. **-λῠκος**, ὁ, *solitary*, i.e. *singularly fierce, wolf*, applied by Demosthenes to Alexander, Plu.*Dem.*23, cf. Ael.*NA*7.47. II. as Adj., λύκος μ. Arat. 1124 [with 2nd syll. long]. **-λωπος**, ον, *with but one garment*, Zonar. **-μαζος**, ον, *with but one breast*, Eust.402.37. ✱**-μαλλος**, ον, *of pure wool* (sc. χιτών), *POxy.*109.2 (iii/iv A.D.), cf. *Gloss.* **-μάτωρ**, v. μονομήτωρ.

**μονομᾰχ-εῖον**, v. μονομάχιον. **-έω**, Ion. μουνο-, fut. -ήσω Men. *Sam.*225: (μονομάχος):—*fight in single combat*, E.*Ph.*1220; τινι with one, Hdt.9.26, Pl.*Cra.*391e, etc.; πρός τινα Plb.35.5.1. II. μοῦνοι Ἑλλήνων μουνομαχήσαντες τῷ Πέρσῃ *having fought single-handed* with the Persians, of the Athenians at Marathon, Hdt.9.27; δυοῖσι οὐκ ἂν μουνομαχέοιμι Id.7.104. III. *fight as a gladiator*, Posidipp.22, Luc.*Tox.*58, Hdn.1.17.2, D.C.75.16. **-ημα**, ατος, τό, *single combat*, Eust.387.5. ✱**-ης**, ου, ὁ, = μονομάχος, S.E.*P.*1.156. **-ία**, Ion. μουνομᾰχίη, ἡ, *single combat*, Hdt.5.1,8, 6.92; ἡ μ., name for part of Il.3, Arist.*Fr.*149. II. *gladiatorial show*, Plb.31.28.5 (pl.), *OGI*529.15 (pl., ii A.D.). **-ικός**, ή, όν, *of* or *in single combat*, μ. φιλοτιμία Plb.1.45.9. II. *gladiatorial*, φάρμακον Aët.15.13; χρήματα D.C.72.19. **-ιον**, τό, = μονομαχία, Luc. *DMeretr.*13.5, App.*Hisp.*53, etc.: in codd. sts. written μονομαχεῖον, as Ath.5.191a (cod. A). ✱**-ος**, ον, (μάχομαι) *fighting in single combat*, μ. προστάται A.*Th.*798; μονομάχον ἐπὶ φρέν' ἠλθέτην E.*Ph.*1300 (lyr.); μονομάχου δι' ἀσπίδος, i.e. in single combat, Id.*Heracl.*819; μονομάχῳ δορί Id.*Ph.*1325; μονομάχου πάλης ἀγῶνα Ar.*Fr.*558. II. μονομάχος, ὁ, *gladiator*, freq. in pl., Str.5.1.7, Nic.Dam.78 J., J.*AJ* 14.10.6, *IG*7.106.7 (Megara), *OGI*533.5 (Galatia, i A.D.), Arr.*Epict.* 3.16.4, Luc.*Demon.*57, Hdn.1.15.8, etc.

**μονομᾰχο-τροφεῖον**, τό, = Lat. *ludus gladiatorius*, Suid. **-τρόφος**, ὁ, *trainer of gladiators*, Lat. *lanista*, *Gloss.*

**μονο-μελής**, Ion. μουνο-, ές, *consisting of a single limb*, γυῖα Emp. 58. **-μερής**, ές, (μέρος) *consisting of one part, single*, opp. πολυμερής, φιλοσοφία S.E.*M.*7.2. 2. *for one side*, of a bandage, Gal.18(1).794. II. ἐκ τοῦ μ. *after hearing only one side*, Luc.*Cal.*6; τὰ μ. *ex parte* applications, Lyd.*Mag.*3.15; μ. μαρτυρίαι Just.*Nov.*90.9. Adv. -μερῶς *in a one-sided manner*, Vett.Val.136.2. **-μετρος**, ον, *composed in one metre*, D.H.*Comp.*26. **-μηλον**, τό, name of an *eye-salve*, Aët.7.103. **-μήτωρ**, Dor. **-μάτωρ** [ᾱ], ορος, ὁ, ἡ, *bereft of a mother*, E.*Ph.*1517 (lyr.).

**μονόμισσα**, τά, *midday adjournment, interval*, Lyd.*Mag.*3.15 (fort. *manumissa*).

**μονόμμᾰτος**, ον, *one-eyed*, A.ap.Str.7.3.6, Cratin.149, *AP*11.12 (Alc.); Κύκλωπες Str.1.2.10.

**μονο-μοιρία**, ἡ, Astrol., *distribution of the planets to each degree of the zodiac*, S.E.*M*.5.15, Vett.Val.202.35, Paul.Al.*C*.4, *Cat.Cod.Astr.* 8(1).243 (pl.). **-μοιριαῖος**, α, ον, *graduated by single degrees*, ἀστρόλαβος Phlp. in *Rh.Mus.*6(1839).131. **-μοιρος**, ον, gloss on αὐτόμοιρος, Hsch. **-μοσχος**, ον, *with but one stem*, Dsc.4.185.

**μον-όμφαλος**, ον, *with a single boss*, *IG*2.1661, 1665.

**μονο-ναύτης**, ου, ὁ, *lonely voyager*, Eust.1536.2:—Adj. **-ναυτικός**, ή, όν, οἰκία Id.1535.62.

**μονονουχί**, v. μόνος B. II. 3.

**μονο-νῠχί**, Ion. **μουν-**, Adv. *in a single night*, *APl.*4.92. **-ξοος**, ον, *singly cleft*, opp. δίξοος, τετράξοος, Thphr.*HP*5.1.10. ⊛ **-ξῠλος**, ον, *made from a solid trunk*, πλοῖα *canoes*, X.*An.*5.4.11; μονόξυλα (sc. πλοῖα) Hp.*Aër.*15, Arist.*HA*$533^{b}$11, Str.3.2.3, cf. Pl.*Lg.*956a; τροχιλίαι Heliod.ap.Orib.49.8.9; *in one block*, φοῖνιξ *BGU*603.20 (ii A. D.); μ. τράπεζαι Str.17.3.4: Subst. μονόξυλον, τό, *single block* or *trunk*, *PMag. Par.*1.2386. **-πάθεια** [πᾰ], ἡ, *suffering in one part of the body only*, Alex.Aphr.*Pr.*1.143 (pl.). **-παις**, παιδος, ὁ, ἡ, *only child*, E.*Alc.* 906 (lyr.), *Sammelb.*5873. II. *having one child*, *IG*12(9).293 (Eretria, iv/iii B. C.). ⊛ **-πάλη**, Dor. **-πάλα** [πᾰ], ἡ, *simple wrestling* (opp. παγκράτιον), B.11.8, *SIG*274(4).3 (Delph., iv B. C.). **-πάλης**, Ion. **μουνο-** [ᾰ], ου, ὁ, *one who conquers in wrestling only* (or *in single bouts*), Epigr.ap.Paus.6.4.6. **-πάτωρ** [ᾰ], ορος, ὁ, *only father*, Iamb.*Myst.*8.2. **-πέδῑλος**, ον, *having but one shoe*, Sch.Lyc. 1310. **-πείρας**, ου, ὁ, *hunting singly*, λύκοι μ. *solitary* wolves, opp. those which hunt in packs, Arist.*HA*$594^{a}$30, Men.1038. ⊛ **-πελμος**, ον, *with a single sole*, *AP*6.294 (Phan.), *Edict.Diocl.*9.16. **πεπλος**, ον, *with but one robe*, i.e. *wearing the tunic only* (v. ἄπεπλος), like a Dorian maiden, E.*Hec.*933 (lyr.). **-πηρος**, ον, *with one scrip*, or *with a scrip only*, Theognost.*Can.*93, *EM*670.57. **-πλευρος**, ον, *with one front*, of a column on the march, Arr.*Tact.*28.4,5. **-πλοια**, ἡ, *single* or *solitary voyage*, Eust.1535.61. **-ποδία**, ἡ, *measurement by single feet*, not by syzygies (διποδίαι), τὸ δακτυλικὸν βαίνει κατὰ μονοποδίαν Sch.Heph.p.138 C., cf. Sch.Ar.*Nu.*275, al. **-ποιος**, ον, *of single nature* or *quality*, S.E.*P.*1.94. **-πους**, Ion. **μουνό-**, ὁ, ἡ, **-πουν**, τό, gen. ποδος, *one-footed*, *AP*9.233 (Eryc.), Man.1.137; μ. τράπεζα Poll.10.69. **-πραγμᾰτέω**, *to be engaged in one thing*, opp. πολυπραγματέω, Arist.*Pol.*$1299^{a}$39. **-προσωπέω**, Gramm., *have but one person*, A.D.*Pron.*6.18. ⊛ **-πρόσωπος**, ον, *with one face*, Artem.2.37; *adorned with one face*, σκάφιον *IG*11(4).1308 (Delos, ii B. C.). 2. *with only one front* decorated, *PSI*5.547.29 (iii B. C.). II. *with one person* or *character*, μ. ποίησις *monologue*, D.L.9.112: Gramm., μ. ἀντωνυμία a pronoun *having reference to one person*, opp. a possessive pronoun, Draco ap.A.D.*Pron.*17.2; but also, a pronoun *having one person*, e. g. ἐκεῖνος (opp. ἵ, which has corresponding first and second persons), Hdn.Gr.1.474, Sch.D.T.p.82 H. Adv. **-πως** *in monologue form*, Tz. ad Lyc.p.4 S., *Proll.Hes.*p.11 G. **-πτερος**, ον, of a circular temple, *with a row of columns only*, and no cella (cf. πτερόν III. 9), Vitr.4.8.1. **-πτύχιος** [ῠ], ον, *folding once*, τράπεζα *PMasp.* 6 ii 47 (vi A. D.). **-πτῠχος**, ον, *univalve*, ὄστρεον Thom.Mag.p.221 R. **-πτωτος**, ον, *with but one case*, A.D.*Synt.*29.1, Porph. *in Cat.* 62.4. **-πύθμενος**, ον, *with one bottom*, Eust.869.31. **-πύργιον**, τό, *fortress with one tower only*, Procop.*Aed.*4.6 (pl.). **-πωλέω**, *enjoy a monopoly*, Plb.34.10.14. ⊛ **-πωλία**, ἡ, *exclusive sale, monopoly*, Arist.*Pol.*$1259^{a}$21, Str.17.1.13. ⊛ **-πώλιον**, τό, *right of monopoly*, Hyp.*Fr.*43, *PSI*6.619.10 (iii B. C.), D.S.5.10, Procop.*Pers.*2.15. 2. *trade mart enjoying a monopoly*, Memn.21. ⊛ **-πωλος**, ον, *driving her steeds alone*, Ἀώς E.*Or.*1004 (lyr.). **-⟨ρ⟩ρήξ**, ῆγος, ὁ, ἡ, *torn off*, Hsch. **-ρριζος**, ον, *with a single root*, Thphr.*HP* 1.6.6, 7.2.7 (Sup.); of teeth, *with a single fang*, Gal.2.753. **-ρρυθμος**, ον, *of solitary kind*, μ. δόμοι houses *dwelt in by one only*, A.*Supp.* 961.

⊛ **μον-ορύχης** [ῠ], ου, ὁ, *digging with one point*, ὄρυξ *AP*6.297 (Phan.). **-ορχις**, εως, ὁ, *with one testicle*, Lxx *Le.*21.20, Plu.2.917d; acc. pl. μονόρχεις *Hippiatr.*14 (v. l. -χας, cf. ἐνόρχης).

⊛ **μόνος**, η, ον, Ep. and Ion **μοῦνος**, the only form used by Hom. (as in all derivs. exc. μονόω), Hes., and Hdt., also by Pi.*P.*9.27, *I.*5(4).12, B.3.80, al., by S. both in iamb. and lyr., by A. only in compd. μουνώψ, by E. only in μούναρχος: Dor. **μῶνος** Theoc.2.64, 20.45:—*alone, solitary*, μοῦνος ἐὼν πολέσιν μετὰ Καδμείοισιν Il.4.388; ἢ ὅ γε μοῦνος ἐών Od.3.217; μούνω ἄνευθ' ἄλλων 16.239: joined with ἐρῆμος, S. *Ant.*887, *Ph.*470; μόνοι γὰρ ἐσμέν Luc.*JTr.*21; ἄνθρωπος πρεσβύτης καὶ μ. *BGU*180.23 (ii A. D.); φυγὴ μόνου πρὸς μόνον Plot.6.9.11. 2. c. gen., σοῦ μόνος *bereft of* thee, *without* thee, S.*Aj.*511; also μοῦνος ἀπ' ἄλλων *h.Merc.*193, S.*Ph.*183 (lyr.); ἑτάρων ἄπο μ. A.R.3.908. II. *only*, μοῦνον Λαέρτην Ἀρκείσιος υἱὸν ἔτικτε, μοῦνον δ' αὖτ' Ὀδυσῆα πατὴρ τέκεν Od.16.118, cf. Il.9.482; μόνης γὰρ σοῦ κλύων ἀνέξεται A.*Pers.* 838, cf. 632 (anap.), *Pr.*425 (lyr.), etc.; χοίνικος μόνας ἁλῶν for a gallon of salt *only*, Ar.*Ach.*814; *single*, οὐκ ἄρα μοῦνον ἔην Ἐρίδων γένος, ἀλλὰ.. δύω Hes.*Op.*11, cf. S.*OT*1280; εἷς μοῦνος or μόνος, Hdt.1.38, S. *OT*63: once in Hom., μία μούνη Od.23.227: joined with αὐτός, αὐτῷ μόνῳ Pl.*Ly.*211c; αὐτοὶ καθ' αὑτοὺς μόνοι Id.*Plt.*307e. 2. c. gen., μοῦνος ποταμῶν *alone* of rivers, Hdt.2.25, cf. 29; μ. θεῶν γὰρ Θάνατος οὐ δώρων ἐρᾷ A.*Fr.*161; μ. τῶν ἄλλων ποιητῶν Lycurg.102; but μοῦνος πάντων ἀνθρώπων he *and no other* of all men, Hdt.1.25; ἀνδρῶν γε μοῦνος he *and no other*, S.*OC*1250, cf. *El.*531; ὦ μόνα ὦ φίλα γυναικῶν E.*Alc.*460 (lyr.). 3. freq. repeated in the same clause, ξυμπεσὼν μόνος μόνοις S.*Aj.*467; Ἕκτορος μόνος μόνου.. ἐναντίος ib.1283; σὺν τέκνοις μόνη μόνοις E.*Med.*513; μόνος μόνῳ D.18.137. 4. expressing rhetorically pre-eminence in an action or quality, μόνα κατέχεσθαι ποιεῖ are *unique* for causing possession, Pl.*Smp.*215c, cf. 222a, S.*OC*261, *OT*299, Isoc.14.57; [ἐπέδειξε] σαφέστατα μόνος ἀνθρώπων Lys.24.9. III. Sup. μονώτατος *one above all others*, Ar. *Eq.*352, *Pl.*182, Lycurg.89, Theoc.15.137, Phld.*Rh.*1.350 S. IV. *made in one piece*, τάπης *Edict.Diocl.*19.23.

B. Adv. **μόνως**, *on one condition only*, folld. by εἰ, Th.8.81, X. *Mem.*1.5.5, *Cyr.*2.2.23; *in one way only*, Them. *in Ph.*29.22, al.; *in a unique manner*, Dam.*Pr.*98: later, simply, *only*, Phld.*Oec.*p.53 J., Ph. 1.559, *AP*12.254 (Strat.), Iamb.*Myst.*4.7, Procl. *in Prm.*p.479 S. II. neut. as Adv., μόνον *alone, only*, οὐχ ἅπαξ μ. A.*Pr.*211, etc.: freq. with imper., μ. φύλαξαι Id.*Supp.*1012; ἀποκρίνου μ. Pl.*Grg.*494d; so μ. Κράτος συγγένοιτό σοι A.*Ch.*244; μὴ 'μὲ καταπίῃς μ. E.*Cyc.*219, etc.; ἐὰν μ. if *only*, Arist.*Pol.*$1292^{a}$3; οὐσίαν.., οὐ χωριστὴν μ. *only* not separable, Id.*Metaph.*$1025^{b}$28. 2. οὐ μόνον.., ἀλλὰ καί.. Ar. *Eq.*1282, X.*Cyr.*1.6.17, etc.; οὐ μ., ἀλλὰ.. S.*Ph.*555: μόνον is sts. omitted, μὴ τοὺς ἐγγύς, ἀλλὰ καὶ τοὺς ἄπωθεν Th.4.92, cf. E.*Hipp.*359, *Ph.*1480 (lyr.). 3. μόνον οὐ *all but, well nigh*, Ar.*V.*516, D.19.220, etc.; μόνον οὐκ ἐπὶ ταῖς κεφαλαῖς περιφέρουσι Pl.*R.*600d: in codd. freq. written μονονού, Plb.3.109.2, etc.; μονονουχί D.1.2, Plb.3.102. 4. III. κατὰ μόνας *alone*, Th.1.32,37, Is.7.38, Arist.*Pol.*$1281^{b}$34, etc. IV. μόνῃ, = μόνον, Plu.2.583d codd. (Prob. from *μόνϝος.)

**μονο-σάνδᾰλος**, ον, *with but one sandal*, Apollod.1.9.16. **-σίλλη**· ὁ ἐν ταῖς ὕασι λαμπρὸς ἀστήρ, Hsch. **-σιρος**, ὁ, name of an Egyptian breed of poultry, *Gp.*14.7.30. **-σῑτέω**, *eat but one meal in the day*, Hp.*VM*10, *Acut.*11, Pl.Com.207, X.*Cyr.*8.8.9, Phylarch. 13 J. II. *eat alone*, Alex.269.1. **-σῑτία**, Ion. **-ίη**, ἡ, *eating but one meal a day*, Hp.*Epid.*2.2.1, Gal.10.544, Philum.ap. Orib.45.29.55. **-σκελής**, ές, *on one leg*, μ. ἑστάναι Str.15.1. 61. **-σκηπτρος**, ον, *wielding the sceptre alone*, μονοσκήπτροισιν ἐν θρόνοις on throne *monarchic*, A.*Supp.*374 (lyr.). **-σκορδον**, τό, *garlic growing by itself*, *PMag.Par.*1.2211. **-στᾰλής**, ές, = μονόστολος, Hsch. ⊛ **-στεγος**, ον, (στέγη) *of one story*, στοά D.H. 3.68; ὕψος Str.17.1.37; οἰκίδιον *BGU*889.8 (ii A. D.). **-στελέχης**, ες, *with one stalk* or *stem*, Thphr.*HP*1.3.1, al.

**μον-όστεος**, ον, *consisting of one bone*, κρανίον Arist.*HA*$516^{a}$16; αὐχήν Id.*PA*$686^{a}$21.

**μονο-στέφᾰνος**, ον, *having won a single contest*, *CPHerm.*74.5 (iii A. D.). **-στῐβής**, ές, (στείβω) *walking alone, unattended*, A.*Ch.* 768. **-στῐχος**, ον, *consisting of one verse*, ἐπίγραμμα *AP*11.312 (Lucill.), Luc.*Demon.*44; μονόστιχα *single verses*, Plu.*Pomp.*27. **-στοιχος** κριθή, *one-rowed* barley, Ath.Med.ap.Orib.1.11.2. **-στολος**, ον, *going alone*, Lyc.690: generally, *alone, single*, δόρυ E.*Ph.*742; λείπομαι φίλας μονόστολος ματρός Id.*Alc.*407 (lyr.). **-στομος**, ον, *with one opening*, of a fistula, Heliod. ap.Orib. 44.23.68, Paul.Aeg.6. 77. II. *one-edged*, Sch.Il.23.851, Hsch. s. v. σάγαρις, Suid. s. v. ἡμιπέλεκκα. **-στόρθυγξ**, υγγος, ὁ, ἡ, *carved out of a single block*, Πρίηπος *AP*6.22 (Zon.). **-στροφικός**, ή, όν, = sq., Heph.*Poëm.* 4.1,2; μ. περίοδος, εἴσθεσις, Sch.Ar.*Ach.*836, *Eq.*621. Adv. **-κῶς** Heph.p.62 C. **-στροφος**, ον, *consisting of a single strophe*, στροφή Sch.Tricl.E.*Ph.*239. Adv. -φως ibid. II. ἅμαξα μ. either a cart *with solid wheels*, or *wheelbarrow*, Thphr.*HP*5.7.6; cf. μονόκυκλος 2. III. *of one turn*, ἕλιξ Speus.ap.Procl. *in Euc.*pp.180.187 F., Papp.1110.2. **-συλλᾰβέω**, *to be a monosyllable*, A.D.*Pron.*40. 30. **-συλλᾰβία**, ἡ, *being monosyllabic*, Id.*Adv.*156.12, Theognost. *Can.*134.12. **-συλλᾰβικός**, ή, όν, = sq., *An.Ox.*1.324. **-σύλλᾰβος**, ον, *of one syllable*, of words, D.T.641.16, D.H.*Comp.*17, A.D.*Pron.* 27.2, al. Adv. -βως Sch.Ar.*Pl.*143, al. II. *dealing in monosyllables*, of grammarians, Herodic.ap.Ath.5.222a; πᾶς δεσπότης δούλῳ μ. Demetr.*Eloc.*7. **-σύστᾰτος**, ον, of an art, *existing only while it is being practised*, e. g. dancing, Sch.D.T.p.445 H. **-σχημᾰτέω**, *to be in simple aspect*, Critodem. in *Cat. Cod. Astr.* 8(4). 201. **-σχημάτιστος** [ᾰ], ον, *of but one form*, A.D.*Adv.*131. 5. **-σχημος**, ον, *employing one figure*, Phoeb.*Fig.*1.1; τὸ μ. ibid. **-σχῐδής**, ές, *with one track*, of a fistula, Heliod.ap.Orib.44. 23.67. **-τεκνος**, ον, *with but one child*, E.*HF*1021 (lyr.), Paul.Al. *O.*2.

**μονότης**, ητος, ἡ, *unity*, Sm.*Ps.*21(22).21, 34(35).17, Iamb.*Myst.* 8.2. II. *uniqueness*, Alex.Aphr. *in Metaph.*416.36, Dam.*Pr.*58.

**μονο-τοκέω**, *bear but one at a time*, Arist.*GA*$772^{b}$1, prob. in *Cat. Cod.Astr.*1.166. II. *have an only child*, Vett.Val.122.32. **-τοκία**, ἡ, *bearing but one at a time*, Arist.*GA*$770^{b}$29. **-τόκος**, Ep. **μουνο-**, ον, *bearing but one at a time*, Arist.*HA*$576^{a}$1, *GA*$772^{b}$2. II. = μονότεκνος, ζῷα Plu.2.93f, cf. Call.*Ap.*54, Nonn.*D.*6.31. III. proparox., μ. κούρη an *only* child, ib.58. **-τομον**, τό, sine expl., *Gloss.* **-τονέω**, *to be obstinate*, Eust.1393.4. **-τονία**, ἡ, *sameness of tone, monotony*, Quint.*Inst.*11.3.45. **-τονος**, ον, (τόνος II. 2) *of one tone* in music, *uniform, monotonous*. Adv. -νως Longin.34. 2. II. metaph., *obstinate*, Ptol.*Tetr.*163; *steady*, Heph.Astr.1.1; expld. by μόνος ὤν, ὑπάρχων, μονομάχος, Hsch. **-τράπεζος** [ᾰ], ον, *at a solitary* or *separate table*, ξένια E.*IT*949. **-τρίγλῠφος**, ον, *with single triglyphs*, Vitr.4.3.7. **-τροπέω**, *live alone*, Tz.*H.*9. 332. **-τροπία**, ἡ, *solitariness*, *Cat.Cod.Astr.*2.160. **-τροπος**, ον, *living alone, solitary*, νεανίας E.*Andr.*281 (lyr.), cf. Lxx *Ps.*67(68). 6: title of plays by Phrynichus, Anaxilas, and Ophelio; ἄφιλοι καὶ ἄμικτοι καὶ μ. Plu.2.479c; μ. βίος Phld.*Ir.*p.49 W., Ph.1.551, Plu. *Pel.*3; μ. λῃστής J.*BJ*2.21.1; μ. ζῷα Gal.*UP*1.2. II. *of one kind*, ἁπλαῖ καὶ μ. ἡδοναί Plu.2.662a; μ. λέξις, opp. ποικίλη, D.H.

*Rh.*1.8. Adv. -πως J.*BJ*5.10.4. **-τροφέω**, *eat once a day*, Str.3.3.6. **-τροφία**, ἡ, *rearing singly*, opp. κοινὴ ἐπιμέλεια, Pl.*Plt.* 261d. **-τροχος**, ὁ, *wheelbarrow*, *Gloss.*

**μόνουα**· τὰ λεπτὰ λέπαδνα, Hsch. **μονουάλος**, name of a star in Leo, Id.

**μονούᾱτος**, ον, *one-eared*, *with one handle*, *AP*5.134.

**μονόϋλος**, ον, (ὕλη) *consisting of one matter*, [φύσις] Zos.Alch. p.112B. 2. *entirely solid*, opp. ὀπώδες, Sever.*Clyst.*42.

**μονουχία**, ἡ, *solitary life*, Suid.

**μονο-φᾰγέω**, = μονοσιτέω II, Antiph.298. **-φᾰγία**, ἡ, *eating alone*, a form of gluttony, Lxx 4*Ma.*1.27. **-φάγος** [ᾰ], ον, (φαγεῖν) *eating alone*, Amips.24, Lxx 4*Ma.*2.7, cf. Plu.2.301d: irreg. Sup. μονοφαγίστατος Ar.*V.*923. **-φᾰλαγγία**, ἡ, *army marching in one phalanx*, Arr.*Tact.*28.6. **-φαντος**, ον, *visible alone*, Hsch.

**μον-όφθαλμος**, Ion. **μουν-**, ον, *one-eyed*, Hdt.3.116, 4.27, Str.2.1.9, *Ev.Matt.*18.9: rejected by Phryn.112; expld. as *one who has one eye*, like the Cyclops, opp. ἑτερόφθαλμος, *one who has lost an eye*, Ammon.*Diff.*p.60V.

**μονό-φθογγος**, ἡ, *monophthong*, *single vowel*, opp. δίφθογγος, Theodos.*Can.*p.68H. **-φθόρους**· μονοφόρους, ὄνους, Hsch. **-φῐλής**, ές, *sole friend*, Sch.Juv.3.121. **-φορβος**, ον, *grazing alone*, Hsch. **-φόρος**, v. -φθόρους. **-φρουρος**, ον, *watching alone*, γαίας μονόφρουρον ἕρκος A.*Ag.*257 (lyr.). **-φρων**, ον, gen. ονος, (φρήν) *single in one's opinion*, ib.757 (lyr.). **-φυής**, Ion. **μουνο-**, ές, *single*, ὀδόντες Hdt.9.83; of bodily organs, τὰ μὲν μ. καθάπερ καρδία καὶ πλεύμων, τὰ δὲ διφυῆ καθάπερ νεφροί Arist.*PA*669b13; ἧπαρ Id.*HA*493a19; opp. πολυσχιδής, Id.*PA*673b17 (Comp.); of trees or herbs, *with a single stem*, Thphr.*HP*2.6.9, Dsc.4.114; of mountains, *with a single summit*, Str.12.8.11. **-φυλλος**, ον, *one-leaved*, Thphr.*HP*1.13.2. **-φῦλος**, ον, *of one tribe*, *race*, or *kind*, Opp.*C.*1.399. **-φωνος**, ον, *with but one voice* or *tone*, of deaf-mutes, Hp.*Carn.*18. **-χάλῑνος** [ᾰ], ον, *with but one bridle*, Sch.Pi.*O.*5.15. **-χειρ**, χειρος, ὁ, ἡ, *with but one hand*, Nicom.*Ar.*1.15. **-χέρια**, *mamillares*, *Gloss.* **-χηλος**, Dor. **-χᾱλος**, ον, *solid-hoofed*, E.*IA*225 (lyr.). **-χίτων** [ῐ], ωνος, ὁ, ἡ, *wearing only the tunic*, Pythaen.6, Arist.*Ath.*25.3, Plb.14.11.2, D.S.17.35, Plu.*Sull.*25, Luc.*Sat.*11. II. *with a single coat*, of veins, Anon. Lond.28.29, Gal.2.816. **-χορδίζω**, *measure intervals by means of the monochord*, Pythag.ap.Aristid.Quint.3.2. ⊛ **-χορδος**, ον, (χορδή) *with* or *of but one string*, κανών Ptol.*Harm.*1.8 tit.: μονόχορδον, τό, *monochord*, Poll.4.60, Nicom.*Harm.*4, Iamb.*VP*26.119. **-χροιος**, ον, v.l. for μονόχροος in Xenocr.ap.Orib.2.58.109. **-χρονέω**, in Prosody, *occupy one time-unit*, *AB*1150. **-χρονος**, ον, in Prosody, *occupying one time-unit*, λέξις Arc.139.20; στοιχεῖα Sch.D.T.p.142H. 2. *having only one quantity*, opp. δίχρονος I, Longin.*Proll.Heph.* 1.10, Sch.D.T.p.127H. II. *momentary*, εὐδαιμονία Aristipp.ap.Ath. 12.544a. **-χροος**, ον, contr. **-χρους**, ουν, also **-χρως**, ων, *of one colour*, freq. in Arist., neut. sg. μονόχρουν *HA*558a26, -χρων *GA*749a25, 786a28: in pl. always μονόχροα, *HA*489b15, Thphr.*HP*1.13.1: gen. -όων Arist.*HA*519a5. **-χρώμᾰτος**, ον, = foreg., Diph.Siph. ap.Ath.3.90d, Dsc.2.61; of paintings, Plin.*HN*35.15. **-χρωμος**, ον, v.l. for μονόχροος, Arist.*GA*755a4. **-χωρος**, ον, *isolated*, of a piece in draughts, *Gloss.* II. ⊛ **-χωρον**, τό, measure of wine, etc., in Egypt, *PFay.*220 (ii A.D.), *Sammelb.*4425 vii 26 (ii A.D.), *PFlor.*76 (iii A.D.). **-ψηφος**, Dor. **-ψᾱφος**, ον, *voting alone*, μονόψαφον κατασχοῖσα ξίφος keeping her sword *solitary of purpose*, of Hypermnestra, Pi.*N.*10.6; μονοψήφοισι νεύμασιν, of Zeus, A.*Supp.*373 (lyr.).

⊛ **μονόω**, Ep. and Ion. **μουνόω**, Od.16.117, Hdt. (v. infr.); but **μον-** in Il.11.470: (μόνος):—*make single* or *solitary*, ἡμετέρην γενεὴν μούνωσε Κρονίων *made* our race *single*, i.e. *allowed but one son* in each generation, Od.16.117; μ. τὸν Φίλιππον *leave* him *isolated*, Plb.5.16.10; *get alone*, τινὰ ἐν σπήλυγγι *AP*9.451; *strip of predicates*, *make unique*, [θεόν] Plot.6.8.15. II. more freq. in Pass., *to be left alone*, *forsaken*, ἐνὶ Τρώεσσι μονωθείς Il. l.c.; μουνωθέντα παρ' οἴεσιν ἢ παρὰ βουσίν Od.15.386; ἐμουνοῦντο *they were left each man by himself*, Hdt. 8.123; μουνωθέντα *taken apart*, *without witnesses* (v.l. for μουνόθεν), Id.1.116; γυνὴ μονωθεῖσ' οὐδέν A.*Supp.*749; of animals when hunted, X.*Cyn.*9.9; when *left solitary*, Arist.*HA*578b33; of the soul, *to be separated* from the body, Diog.Oen.36; of things, *to be taken alone*, Arist.*EN*1096b17; *to be isolated* in thought, Dam.*Pr.*195. 2. c. gen. pers., μεμουνωμένοι συμμάχων *deserted* by allies, Hdt.1.102, cf. 6.15, 7.139; μονωθεὶς δάμαρτος, σοῦ μονούμενος, E.*Alc.*296, 380; δεσποτῶν μονούμενος Id.*Rh.*871; μονωθεῖσ' ἀπὸ πατρός Id.*IA*669; μονωθεὶς μετ' ὀλίγων Th.6.101: abs., μεμονωμένων εἰ κρατήσειαν Id.2.81, cf. 5.40, 58. b. c. gen. rei, μεμονωμένοι τῆς τῶν ἱππέων βοηθείας *bereft of..*, D.S.19.43; μονούμενος τῶν ἀγαθῶν *separated from..*, Pl.*Lg.* 710b; μονωθεῖσαι φρονήσεως *without..*, Id.*Ti.*46e; μονωθεὶς ἐκ τῆς εἱρκτῆς, i.e. *set free* from.., Id.*Ax.*370d.

**μονόωρος**, ον, *within the space of one hour*, ἄγειν [τινὰς] μ. *PMag. Par.*1.2624, cf. 2450.

**μονῳδέω**, *sing a monody* or *solo*, Ar.*Pax* 1012, *Th.*1077 (both anap.): c. acc., βούλει μονῳδήσωμεν αὐτοῖς ἕν γέ τι; Cratin.10D., cf. Luc.*Hist.Conscr.*1.

**μονώδης**, ες, *solitary*, Arist.*Fr.*171.

**μονῳδ-ία**, ἡ, *monody*, *solo*, opp. the song of the chorus, Ar.*Ra.*849 (pl.), al., Philostr.*VA*4.21; opp. χορῳδία, Pl.*Lg.*764d. II. *monody*, *lament*, Him.*Or.*23.1: pl., ib.8. **-ικός**, ή, όν, *of* or *for a* μονῳδία, γυμνάσματα Sch.Ar.*Ra.*974. **-ιον**, τό, Dim. of μονῳδία, Diom. p.492K. **-ός**, όν, *singing alone*, *not in chorus*: ὁ μ., *writer of a funeral ode* or *of a drama* (like Lycophron's Cassandra) *to be spoken by a single person*, Tz.ad Lyc.pp.1, 4S.

**μον-ώνῠχος**, ον, = μῶνυξ, *Gp.*16.1.12: pl. μονώνυχα, τά, of animals, Ph.2.353, Gal.18(1).359. **-ωσις**, εως, ἡ, *solitariness*, *singleness*, Pl.*Ti.*31b, Ph.1.559; ἡ ἀπ' αὐτοῦ μ. *separation* from.., Plu.*Them.*10, cf. Porph.*Abst.*4.20. **-ώτης**, ου, ὁ, *solitary*, Arist.*EN*1099b4, 1170a5, *Fr.*668; βίος μ. a *solitary* life, Id.*EN*1097b9, Max.Tyr.21.7: fem. **-ῶτις**, φωνή Arist.*HA*625b9. **-ωτικός**, ή, όν, *left alone*, *solitary*, βίος Ph.1.549; ζῷα ib.150. **-ωτος**, ον, = μονούατος, Polem.Hist.60, *BCH*35.286 (Delos, ii B.C.):—Dim. **-ώτιον**, *victine* (sic), *Gloss.* II. = μόναπος, Antig.*Mir.*53 cod. **-ώψ**, ῶπος (on the accent cf. Hdn.Gr.1.247), Ion. **μουνώψ**, ὁ, ἡ, *one-eyed*, of the Cyclopes, E.*Cyc.*21, 648; μουνῶπα στρατόν, of the Arimaspi, A.*Pr.* 804: neut. pl. μονῶπα Call.*Fr.*28.2P. 2. μόνωψ, ὁ, *bandage for one eye*, Heliod.ap.Orib.48.41 tit.

**μόνωψ**, ωπος, ὁ, = μόναπος, Ael.*NA*7.3. II. v. foreg. 2.

**μόρα**, ἡ, (μείρομαι (A), ἔμμορε) *a division* of the Spartan army, varying in strength, at first six in number, X.*HG*2.4.31, *Lac.*11.4, Ephor. 210J., Arist.*Fr.*540, etc.

**μοράζομαι**, *to be composed*, *consist*, [ὁ κόσμος] γᾶς μεμόρακται πυρός τε κτλ. Ti.Locr.95a.

**μοργᾶται**· παρῶπται, Hsch. **μοργεύω**, *carry straw in a wicker cart*, Poll.7.116.

**μοργία**, ἡ, *gluttony*, Hsch. (pl.). (Perh. Aeol. for μαργία.) ⊛ **μόργιον**, τό, *a land measure*, = πλέθρον, Id.: a kind of *vine*, Id.

**μόργνῡμι**, = ὀμόργνυμι, only aor. 1 Med. μόρξαντο, μορξάμενοι, Q.S. 4.270, 374.

⊛ **μόργος**, ὁ, *body of a wicker cart*, used for carrying straw and chaff, Poll.7.116. II. *leathern vessel*, Hsch. **μοργυίων**· σπαργάνων, Id. **μοργυλλεῖ**· χρονουλκεῖ, Id.

**μορέα**, Ep. **-έη**, ἡ, (μόρον) *mulberry-tree*, *Morus nigra*, Nic.*Al.*69, *Fr.*75, Gal.11.631.

⊛ **μορέω**, (μόρος) *make with pain and toil*, ὃν ἀπάτωρ..μόρησε Dosiad. *Ara*8, cf. *EM*584.31 (sed leg. μόγησε); πυρὸς μεμορημένος αὐγαῖς, i.e. *boiled* over a fire, Nic.*Al.*229 (unless from μείρομαι (A), q.v.).

**μορία** (A), ἡ, mostly in pl. **μορίαι** (with or without ἐλαῖαι), *the sacred olives* in the Academy, Ar.*Nu.*1005, Anaxandr.19, Arist.*Ath.* 60.2: generally, of *olives that grew in the precincts of temples*, opp. ἴδιαι, Lys.7.5, 7: sg., ib.26: variously expld. by Sch.Ar. l.c.

**μορία** (B), ἡ, = μωρία, θρέμμα μορίης *AP*11.305 (Pall.).

**μορι-ασμός**, ὁ, *dividing into fractional parts*, Ptol.*Alm.*1.10. **-αστικά**, τά, title of treatise *on fractions* by Diophantus, Sch.Iamb. *in Nic.*p.127P.

**μορίδες**· μάντεις, Hsch. **μορίδιος**, gloss on μορόεις, Sch.Nic. *Al.*134. **μορίες**· μερῖται, κοινωνοί, Hsch.

**μόρῐμος**, ον, poet. for μόρσιμος, μόριμον δέ οἵ ἐστ' ἀλέασθαι Il.20.302; μ. υἱός Pi.*O.*2.38; λάχος A.*Ch.*361 (lyr.).

**μόρινος**, η, ον, *mulberry-coloured*, *CPR*27.8 (ii A.D.).

⊛ **μόριον**, τό, prop. Dim. of μόρος, *piece*, *portion*, Hdt.7.23, Pl.*R.*525e, etc.; of *quarters* of the world, Hdt.2.16; *parts* of a country, Th.7.58; of an army, Id.2.39; ψυχῆς μ. E.*Andr.*541 (anap.); βραχεῖ μορίῳ τῆς δαπάνης Th.8.46; ἐν βραχεῖ μ. ἡμέρας Id.1.85, cf. 141; ψαμάθου μ. βραχύ *AP*7.404.7 (Zon.). II. *constituent part*, *member* (opp. μέρος, a mere part), μ. ἀρετῆς, πολιτικῆς, Pl.*Lg.*696b, *Grg.*463d; εἰς ἃ τὸ εἶδος διαιρεθείη ἄν..λέγεται μόρια τούτου Arist.*Metaph.*1023b18; τέχναι καὶ ἐπιστῆμαι κατὰ μόριον γινόμεναι, opp. περὶ γένος ἕν τι τέλειαι, Id.*Pol.*1288b11. 2. esp. of *the members* or *parts* of the body, Id.*HA*488b29; περὶ ζῴων μορίων, title of the treatise *de partibus animalium*: in pl., esp. *parts* or *genitals*, male and female, ἀνδρεῖα μόρια Luc.*Vit.Auct.*6; τὰ γεννητικὰ μ. D.S.1.85; τὰ μόρια Plu.2.797f: less freq. in sg., μ. ἀνδρὸς γόνιμον ib.323b, cf. Gal.12.431; μ. γυναικεῖον Luc.*DMort.*28.2. 3. of persons, *member* of a council, etc., Arist.*Pol.*1282a37. III. Gramm., *part* of speech, D.H.*Comp.*6, A.D.*Pron.*36.21, al.; in full, μ. λέξεως D.H. *Comp.*17; μ. λόγου Plu.2.731e. 2. *prefix* or *suffix*, opp. μέρος (*part* of a word), Corn.*ND*13, *EM*141.47, 809.9. IV. Arith., *fraction with* 1 *for numerator*, Dioph.1 p.6T.; also, *fraction in general*, Id.5.20, al.; *denominator* of a fraction, Id.1.23, al., Hero *Stereom.*2.16; μορίου or ἐν μορίῳ c. gen., *divided by..*, Dioph.3.19, 1.25.

**Μόριος**, ὁ, epith. of Zeus as guardian of μορίαι, S.*OC*705 (lyr.).

⊛ **μόριος**, α, ον, *of burial*, γᾶ *AP*7.477 (Tymn.).

**μοριότμητος**, ον, *castrated*, Anon.post Max.p.98L.

**μοριφόν**· σκοτεινόν, μέλαν, Hsch. **μόρμη**· χαλεπή, ἐκπληκτική, Id. **μορμίλλων**, v. μερμίλλων. **μόρμοι**· φόβοι κενοί, Id.

⊛ **μορμο-λῠκεῖον**, τό, *bogey*, *hobgoblin*, Ar.*Th.*417 (pl.), Pl.*Phd.*77e, Socr.ap.Arr.*Epict.*2.1.15 (pl.), Gal.*Protr.*10. 2. μ. κωμῳδικόν comic *mask*, Ar.*Fr.*31, cf. 131. **-λύκη**, Dor. **-λύκα** [ῡ], ἡ, = foreg. 1, Sophr. 9, Str.1.2.8:—also **-λῠκία**, ἡ, Philostr.*VA*4.25 (s.v.l.). ⊛ **-λύττομαι**, only pres. and impf. (exc. aor. 1 part. μορμολυξάμενος Gal.10.106): (μορμώ):—*frighten*, *scare*, Ar.*Av.*1245, Pl.*Cri.*46c, Ph.2.468; μ. τοὺς φίλους X.*Smp.*4.27. II. *fear*, *be afraid of*, τὸν θάνατον Pl.*Ax.* 364b.—Act. μορμολύττω is f.l. in Crates Com.8.

**μόρμορος**· φόβος, Hsch.; cf. μέρμερος. **μορμορύζω**, = μορμολύττομαι, Phot.

**μορμορωπός**, όν, *hideous to behold*, Ar.*Ra.*925; v. μορμυρωπός.

⊛ **μόρμυλος**, ὁ, = μορμύρος, Dorio ap.Ath.7.313e; μορμύλος Opp.*H.* 1.100 codd.

**μορμύνω**, = μορμολύττομαι, Hsch. **μορμυραία**· φόβος, Id.

**μορμῡρίζω**, = μορμύρω, Hsch., Suid.

**μορμύρος** [ῠ], ὁ, a sea-fish, *Pagellus mormyrus*, Arist.*HA*570ᵇ20 (proparox.), Archestr.*Fr.* 52 (proparox.), *AP*6.304(Phan.), Artem. 2.14 (proparox. as v.l.), cj. in Opp.*H.*1.100; cf. *μόρμυλος*.

⊛ **μορμύρω** [ῠ], of water, *roar and boil*, [ποταμὸν] ἀφρῷ μορμύροντα ἰδών Il.5.599, cf. 21.325; ῥόος Ὠκεανοῖο ἀφρῷ μορμύρων 18.403, cf. A.R. 1.543, etc.: in late Prose, Ael.*NA*14.26:—Med., = Act., D.P.82. 2. metaph., θυμῷ μ. Man.5.118. (Onomatopoeic word.)

**μορμῡρωπός**, όν, *with fixed, lidless eye, like the* μορμύρος, v.l. in Ar. *Ra.*925 (for μορμορωπός) and in Artem.2.36 (ap.Suid., μορμύρων and μορμυρώδης codd. Artem.).

**μορμύσσομαι**, = μορμολύττομαι I, Call.*Dian.*70, *Del.*297: also aor. 1 part. Act. μορμύξαντες *JRS*17.52 (Phrygia, iv A.D.).

**Μορμώ**, όος, contr. οῦς, also **Μορμών**, όνος, ἡ, *she-monster, bogey*, dub. in Erinn. in *PSI*9.1090.51+11 (p.xii); used by nurses to frighten children, Luc.*Philops.*2: generally, *bugbear*, ἀπένεγκέ μου τὴν μορμόνα Ar.*Ach.*582; οὐδὲν δεόμεθ᾽..τῆς σῆς μορμόνος Id.*Pax*474 (both times of Lamachus' helmet and crest); φοβεῖσθαι τοὺς πελταστάς, ὥσπερ μορμόνας (-ῶνας codd.) παιδάρια X.*HG*4.4.17. II. as an exclamation to frighten children with, *boh!*, μορμώ, δάκνει ἵππος Theoc.15.40; μορμὼ τοῦ θράσους *a fig* for his courage!, Ar.*Eq.*693. (Perh. cogn. with Lat. *formido*, where *f* is due to dissimilation, cf. μορφή, μύρμηξ.)

⊛ **μορμωτός**, ή, όν, (as if from *μορμόω) *frightful*, Lyc.342.

**μορνάμενος**· μαχόμενος, Hsch. (Aeol. for μαρνάμενος.)

⊛ **μορόεις**, εσσα, εν, epith. of ear-rings, ἕρματα.. τρίγληνα μορόεντα Il.14.183, Od.18.298; expld. by Hsch., and Eust.976.40, as *wrought with much pains* (cf. μορέω), in which sense it is used of τεύχη, Q.S. 1.152; by Apollon.*Lex.* as ἀθάνατα, μόρου μὴ μετέχοντα; perh. from μόρον, *clustering like mulberries*. II. (μόρος) *fatal, deadly*, ποτόν Nic.*Al.*130, 136; μορόεντος ἐλαίης, dub. sens., Id.*Al.*455.

**μόρον**, τό, *black mulberry*, Epich.207; πεπαίτερος μόρων A.*Fr.*264, cf. S.*Fr.*395, Euryphо ap.Gal.17(1).888, Archig.ap.Aët.9.35, Philum. ib.33. 2. *blackberry*, μ. τοῦ βάτου Hp.*Mul.*2.112, cf. A.*Fr.*116; μ. τὸ βατῶδες Phanias ap.Ath.2.51e.

**μόροξος**, ὁ, = μόροχθος, Gal.12.198, Aët.2.16.

**μοροπονέω**, = κακοπαθέω, Hsch.

**μόρος**, ὁ, (μείρομαι A) = μοῖρα III.1, *fate, destiny*, poet. and Ion. Prose: c. inf., μόρος [ἐστὶν] ὀλέσθαι 'tis my *doom* to die, Il.19.421; ὑπὲρ μόρον beyond *destiny*, of those who by their own fault add to their destined share of misery, 20.30, Od.1.34, etc. (to be written divisim, cf. μοῖρα; but cf. ὑπέρμορα, ὑπερμόρως). II. *doom, death*, ὅτε μιν μόρος αἰνὸς ἱκάνοι Il.18.465, cf. Pi.*P.*3.58, etc.; νῦν δ᾽..ἦλθέ ποθεν σωτήρ, ἢ μόρον εἴπω; A.*Ch.*1074 (anap.); in Hdt. always of a *violent death*, τοιούτῳ μόρῳ ἐχρήσατο 1.117; κακὸς μόρος, θάνατός τε μόρος τε, Il.21.133, Od.9.61, etc.; μόρῳ ἀνοσίῳ, αἰσχίστῳ, Hdt.3.65, 9.17, etc.; μ. λευγαλέῳ S.*Fr.*785: also in pl., Heraclit.20, 25, S.*Ant.*1313, 1329 (lyr.). 2. *corpse*, αἱματηφόρους μόρους A.*Th.*420 (lyr.); νέος νέῳ ξὺν μόρῳ ἔθανες S.*Ant.*1266 (lyr.), cf. *AP*7.404 (Zon.). III. a *measure* of land in Locris, *Berl.Sitzb.*1927.8 (v B.C.); at Mytilene, *IG*12(2).74*B*3. IV. Μόρος personified, Hes.*Th.*211 (never in Trag., cf. τόνδε Μοῖρ᾽ ἐπορσύνει μόρον A.*Ch.*911).

**μόροττον**, τό, *basket* made of bark, used in festivals of Demeter, Hsch.

**μόροχθος**, ὁ, a sort of *pipe-clay*, Dsc.5.134.

**μόρρια**, τά, Paus.8.18.5:—also **μούρρινα**, Arr.*Epict.*3.9.21; **μορρίνη** or **μουρρίνη**, *Peripl.M.Rubr.*6, 48:—name of an Oriental material used for cups and vases, perh. *agate*; also a glass imitation, cf. Plin.*HN*36.198, 37.18.

**μόρσῐμος**, ον, (μόρος) poet. Adj., used also by Hdt., *appointed by fate, destined*, ἡ δέ κ᾽ ἔπειτα γήμαιθ᾽ ὅς κε πλεῖστα πόροι καὶ μόρσιμος ἔλθοι Od.16.392; οὐδ᾽ ἄρ᾽ Ὀδυσσῆϊ..μόρσιμον ἦεν..Διὸς υἱὸν ἀποκτάμεν Il.5.674; μ. ἐστι θεῷ..δαμῆναι 19.417, cf. Hdt.3.154; ᾧ θανεῖν οὐ μ. A.*Pr.*933; σοὶ μὲν γαμεῖσθαι μ. γαμεῖν δ᾽ ἐμοί Id.*Fr.*13; τὸ μόρσιμον *destiny, doom*, Pi.*P.*12.30, A.*Th.*263, 282, S.*Ant.*236, *Fr.*953; τὰ μόρσιμα Sol.13.55. II. *foredoomed to die*, οὔ τοι μόρσιμός εἰμι Il. 22.13; μόρσιμον ἦμαρ the day *of doom*, 15.613, Od.10.175; so μ. αἰών one's *appointed* time, Pi.*O.*2.10, A.*Supp.*46 (lyr.).

⊛ **μορτή**, ἡ, (μείρομαι A) *part, portion*, esp. the portion of a *métayer* in the proceeds of an estate, Poll.7.151, Eust.1854.31: acc. sg. μορτάν Hsch.

**μορτοβάτη**, ἡ, *trodden by the dead*, μ. ναῦς, of Charon's boat, Hsch.

⊛ **μορτός**, ή, όν, = βροτός (q.v.), *mortal*, Call.*Fr.*271.

**μορύσσω**, Ep. Verb, = μολύνω, *soil, defile*, in pf. part. Pass. μεμορυγμένα (v.l. μεμορυχμένα in Od. and Nic.), [εἵματα] καπνῷ Od.13.435; Ὀδυσῆα μ. αἵματι Q.S.5.450; μέλαν κυάνοιο..μ. ἄνθος black *mixed* with blue, Opp.*C.*3.39; μ. ἀφρῷ, ὄξει, Nic.*Al.*318, 330. II. = μωλύνω I, μελισσάων καμάτῳ ἔνι παῦρα μορύξαις (aor. opt.) ῥίζεα ib. 144 (cf. Sch.).

⊛ **Μόρῠχος**, ὁ, epith. of Dionysus in Sicily, from μορύσσω, because his face was *smeared* with wine lees at the vintage: prov., μωρότερος Μορύχου Sophr.94. II. as Adj. only in Adv. Comp. μορυχώτερον *more obscurely*, v.l. in Arist.*Metaph.*987ᵃ10, cf. Alex.Aphr. ad loc.

⊛ **μορφ-άζω**, *gesticulate*, X.*Smp.*6.4; *make grimaces*, μωκᾶσθαι καὶ μορφάζειν Phld.*Vit.*p.38J., cf. Ael.*NA*1.29. **-ασμός**, ὁ, *gesticulation*: hence, name of a *dance* in imitation of animals, Ath.14.629f, Poll.4.103.

**Μορφεύς**, έως, ὁ, *Morpheus*, son of Sleep, god of dreams, so called because of the *forms* he calls up before the sleeper, Ov.*Met.*11.635.

**μορφ-ή**, ἡ, *form, shape*, twice in Hom. (not in Hes.), σοὶ δ᾽ ἔπι μὲν μορφὴ ἐπέων thou hast *comeliness* of words, Od.11.367 (cf. Eust. ad loc.); so prob. ἄλλος μὲν..εἶδος ἀκιδνότερος πέλει ἀνήρ, ἀλλὰ θεὸς μορφὴν ἔπεσι στέφει God adds a crown of *shapeliness* to his words, Od.8.170: freq. later, μορφὰς δύο ὀνομάζειν Parm.8.53; μορφὴν ἀλλάξαντα Emp.137.1; μορφὰν βραχύς Pi.*I.*4(3).53; μορφῆς μέτρα *shape* and size, E.*Alc.*1063: periphr., μορφῆς φύσις A.*Supp.*496; μορφῆς σχῆμα, τύπωμα, E.*Ion*992, *Ph.*162; τὴν αὐτὴν τοῦ σχήματος μορφήν Arist.*PA*640ᵇ34; καὶ Γαῖα, πολλῶν ὀνομάτων μ. μία A.*Pr.*212; ὀνειράτων ἀλίγκιοι μορφαῖσιν ib.449; νυκτέρων φαντασμάτων ἔχουσι μορφάς Id.*Fr.*312; προὔπεμψεν ἀντὶ φιλτάτης μ. σποδόν S.*El.*1159; of plants, Thphr.*HP*1.1.12(pl.); esp. with ref. to *beauty of form*, ὑπέρφατον μορφᾷ Pi.*O.*9.65; οἷς ποτιστάξῃ χάρις εὐκλέα μ. ib.6.76, cf. *IG*4²(1).121.119 (Epid., iv B.C.), Lxx *To.*1.13, Vett.Val.1.6, etc.; σῶμα μορφῆς ἐμῆς *OGI*383.41 (Commagene, i B.C.); μορφῆς εἰκόνας ib.27; χαρακτῆρα μορφῆς ἐμῆς ib.60. 2. generally, *form, fashion, appearance*, A.*Pr.*78, S.*Tr.*699, *El.*199 (lyr.); *outward form*, opp. εἶδος, ἑκατέρῳ τῷ εἴδεος μ. Philol.5; ἀλλάττοντα τὸ αὐτοῦ εἶδος εἰς πολλὰς μορφάς Pl.*R.*380d; μ. θεῶν X.*Mem.*4.3.13, cf. *Ep.Phil.*2.6, Dam.*Pr.*304; ἡρώων εἴδεα καὶ μορφὰς A.R.4.1193; κατά τε μορφὰς καὶ φωνάς *gesticulations* and cries, D.H.14.9; τὴν μ. μελάγχρους, τῇ μ. μελίχροας, in *complexion*, Ptol.*Tetr.*143, 144. 3. *kind, sort*, E.*Ion*382, 1068 (lyr.), Pl.*R.*397c, etc. (Possibly cogn. with Lat. *forma* for *morgʷhmā*, with *f* by dissimilation, cf. μύρμηξ.) **-ήεις**, εσσα, εν, *formed*, λίθου of stone, *IG*3.716; esp. *well-formed, shapely*, ἰδεῖν μορφάεις Pi.*I.*7(6).22; cj. in Melanipp.1.

**μόρφνος**, ὁ, epith. of an eagle, dub. sens., Il.24.316, Hes.*Sc.*134: taken to be a Subst. by Arist.*HA*618ᵇ25, Lyc.838; described as a vulture by Suid. (On the accent v. Hdn.Gr.1.173.)

**μορφο-ειδής**, ές, *of the nature of shape*, σχηματισμός Epicur.*Nat.* 2.8. II. *like the* human *form*, Plu.2.335d; μ. τοῦ σώματος ὁμοιότητες ib.735a. **-ποιέω**, = μορφόω, in Pass., Herm.ap.Stob.1.11. 2. **-σκόπος**, ον, *observing forms* or *figures*, Artem.2.69.

**μορφ-όω**, *give shape* or *form to*, γυναικῶν σώματα μορφώσαντες καὶ ὁπλίσαντες ὡς ἐς ἄνδρας μάλιστα Aen.Tact.40.4, cf. Arat.375:—Pass., *receive shape* or *form*, Thphr.*CP*5.6.7, Plu.2.1013c, etc.; ἄχρις οὗ μορφωθῇ Χριστὸς ἐν ὑμῖν *Ep.Gal.*4.19. **-ύνω**, *adorn*, Hsch. **-ώ**, όος, contr. οῦς, ἡ, name of Aphrodite at Lacedaemon, perh. *the Shapely*, Paus.3.15.8. II. = μορφή, Archyt.ap.Stob.1.41.2. ⊛ **-ωμα**, ατος, τό, *form, shape*, Epicur.*Fr.*310; ἅπαξ ἑκάστῳ κατθανὼν μ. A.*Ag.*873; ὀνείρων προσφερεῖς μορφώμασι ib.1218; βροτείοις ἐμφερεῖς μ. Id.*Eu.*412: pl. for sg., κύκνου μορφώματ᾽ ὄρνιθος λαβών E.*Hel.*19: also in late Prose, Aq.*Ge.*31.19, al., Ptol.*Tetr.*26, Heph.Astr.1.20. **-ωσις**, εως, ἡ, *shaping, bringing into shape*, σχηματισμὸς καὶ μ. τῶν δένδρων Thphr.*CP*3.7.4, cf. Gal.4.640, Ptol.*Tetr.*27, Heph.Astr.1.3. II. *form, semblance*, *Ep.Rom.*2.20, 2*Ep.Ti.*3.5. **-ωτικός**, ή, όν, *giving shape, formative*, δύναμις Gal.4.642, cf. Dexipp.*in Cat.*48.5, etc.; ἡ φαντασία νόησις μ. Procl. *in R.*1.235, cf. 74, 121 K.; εἰκόνες μ. Id. *in Prm.*p.780 S. Adv. **-κῶς** Id. *in R.*1.40 K.; [ἡ φαντασία] μ. [θεοῦ] μετέχει Anon.*Incred.*21. **-ώτρια**, ἡ, fem. as if from *μορφωτήρ, συῶν μ. *changing men into* swine, E.*Tr.*437.

**μοσπνεῦσαι**· ῥινηλατῆσαι, Hsch. **μοσποί**· θυσίαι, Id. **μοσπώλια**, τά, dub. sens., perh. = μώστια, *BGU*1523.6 (Ptol.).

⊛ **μόσσυν**, ῡνος, ὁ, *wooden house* or *tower*, ξύλινοι μ. Aen.Tact.33.3; ὁ βασιλεὺς [τῶν Μοσσυνοίκων] ὁ ἐν τῷ μόσσυνι X.*An.*5.4.26; σὺν τοῖς μοσσύνοις (as if from μόσσυνος, nisi leg. τοῖν μοσσύνοιν) ibid.; [οἱ Μοσσύνοικοι] οἰκοῦσιν ἐπὶ ξυλίνοις..πύργοις.., μόσσυνας αὐτὰ καλοῦντες D.H.1.26, cf. Str.12.3.18. 2. *palisade*, Lyc.433. 3. prob. *slip* for shipbuilding, Id.1432. [μόσσῡνας proved by the metre in A.R. 2.1017, Call.*Aet.Oxy.*2080.70, Lyc. ll. cc.: freq. written μόσυν in codd.]

**μοσσύνειν**· μασᾶσθαι βραδέως, Hsch.

**Μοσσῡνικός**, ή, όν, *made by the* Μοσσύνοικοι, μαζονομεῖα Ar.*Fr.* 417.

**Μοσσύνοικοι** [ῠ], οἱ, a tribe on the south shore of the Euxine who lived in μόσσυνες (q.v.), Hecat.204 J., Hdt.3.94, 7.78, Arist.*Mir.*835ᵃ9, A.R.2.1016, etc.

**μόσυλον**, τό, native name for the best kind of *cinnamon*, resembling **μοσυλῖτις**, ἡ, which is a kind of *cassia*, Dsc.1.14, cf. Gal.14. 257.

**Μόσυχλος**, ὁ, *Mosychlos*, a volcano in Lemnos, Nic.*Th.*472: Adj. **Μοσυχλαῖος**, α, ον, Μοσυχλαίῃ φλογὶ ἶσον Eratosth.17.2.

⊛ **μοσχανοσῖτος**· ὁ ἀπεχόμενος· καὶ χόρτος ὁ ἤδη καρπὸν ἔχων, Hsch.

**μοσχ-άριον**, τό, Dim. of μόσχος (B), *little calf*, *PSI*6.602.4 (iii B.C.), Lxx *Ge.*18.7, al., Arr.*Epict.*3.22.6. **-άς**, άδος, ἡ, *heifer*, *Gloss.* II. *layer, sucker*, μοσχάδες ἐλεῶν *Jahresh.*23*Beibl.*93 (Pamphylia). **-εία**, ἡ, *planting of a sucker* or *layer*, Ph.Byz.*Mir.*1.3, Sch.Theoc.1.48:—written μοσχέα, *Ostr.*1302 (pl.). **-ειος**, ον, *of a calf*, κρέα μόσχεια *veal*, X.*An.*4.5.31; μόσχεια alone, *AP*9.377 (Pall.); μ. αἷμα ib.6. 263 (Leon.); κυνοῦχος μ. *calf-skin* bag, X.*Cyn.*2.9; μόσχειον, τό, *calf-skin*, Id.*Eq.*12.7; in full, μ. δέρμα *PCair.Zen.*61.4 (iii B.C.), Plb.6.23.3. ⊛ **-έλαιον**, τό, *oil scented with musk*, Paul.Aeg.7.20 (pl.). **-ευμα**, ατος, τό, *sucker taken off and planted, offset*, Thphr. *HP*2.2.5, *CP*3.11.5, *PCair.Zen.*33.4, al. (iii B.C.), Lxx *Wi.*4.3, Ph.1. 398, *PLond.ined.*2316*A*. **-ευματική** ῥάβδος, *malleolaris*, *Gloss.* **-ευσις**, εως, ἡ, *propagation of plants by suckers*, *Gp.*11.3 tit. **-εύω**, *plant a sucker*, Thphr.*CP*1.2.1, 3.5.1, etc.; τὸ μεμοσχευμένον ib.3.5.3, cf. *Com.Adesp.*182, *PSI*5.499.7 (iii B.C.): metaph., μ. τοὺς τοιούτους ἐν [τοῖς δικαστηρίοις] D.25.48; μοσχευομένη κατὰ τοῦ δήμου τυραννὶς καθ᾽ ὅλης τῆς πόλεως -εύεται D.H.7.46. II. *train as a calf*, Philostr.*VA*6.30. **-ῆ** (sc. δορά), ἡ, *calf-skin*, Anaxandr.

65. **-ηδόν,** Adv., (μόσχος B) *like a calf,* Nic.*Al.*357. **-ίας,** ου, ὁ, *like a calf*: used of any *young animal, leveret,* etc., Poll.5.74; *three-year-old ram,* Eust.1627.15. **-ίδιον** [ῐ], τό, Dim. of μόσχος (A), *young shoot, sucker* or *layer,* συκίδων Ar.*Ach.*996, Ael.*Ep.*4. **-ίναι·** οἱ σκιρτητικοί, Hsch. **-ίνδα·** τὸ ἑξῆς, καὶ ἀνελλιπῶς, Id. ⊛ **-ινος,** η, ον, *of calf-skin, POxy.*1923.25 (v/vi A.D.). ⊛ **-ίον,** τό, Dim. of μόσχος (B), *young calf,* Ephipp.15.12, Theoc.4.4,44, *PGoodsp.Cair.* 30ii 10(ii A.D.). ⊛ **-ιος,** α, ον, (μόσχος B) *of a calf,* θρίξ E.*El.*811 codd.; κρέας *PLond.*3.1159.20(ii A.D.). **-ίτης** [ῑ], ου, ὁ, = ὀσμύλος, Sch.Opp.*H.*1.307.

⊛ **μοσχο-θύτης** [ῠ], ου, ὁ, *slaughterer of calves, Gloss.* **-μάγειρος** [ᾰ], ὁ, *calf-butcher, POxy.*1764.6 (iii A.D.). **-ποιέω,** *make a calf, Act.Ap.*7.41.

⊛ **μόσχος** (A), ὁ, *young shoot* or *twig,* δίδη μόσχοισι λύγοισι (v. λύγος) Il.11.105, cf. Thphr.*CP*5.9.1; ὁ μ. τῶν φύλλων *leaf-stalk, petiole,* Dsc. 2.179, cf. 4.15,34.

⊛ **μόσχος** (B), ὁ, ἡ, *calf, young bull,* which form the god Apis was believed to assume, Hdt.3.28, cf.2.41, *PCair.Zen.*78.6 (iii B.C.), *Sammelb.*6279.7(iii B.C.): as fem., *heifer, young cow,* μόσχους ἀμέλγειν E.*Cyc.*389, cf. *Ba.*736; πεζαὶ μ., = ἑταῖραι, Eup.169; ᾄδειν ἐπὶ μόσχῳ for the prize of a *calf* (nisi leg. ἐπὶ Μόσχῳ), Ar.*Ach.*13. 2. metaph., *boy,* E.*IA* 1623: as fem., *girl, maid,* Id.*Hec.*526, *Andr.*711, etc. 3. *any young animal,* Id.*IT*163, *Ba.*1185 (both lyr.); even of birds, μ. χελιδόνος Achae.47. 4. μ. θαλάσσιος *seal, Edict.Diocl.*8.37.

**μόσχος** (C), ὁ, *musk,* Aët.1.131, Alex.Trall.12; interpol. in Dsc. *Eup.*1.145 (om. Wellmann). (Borrowed from Pers. *mušk.*)

**μοσχο-σφρᾱγιστής,** οῦ, ὁ, *one who picks out and seals calves for sacrifice,* Chaerem.ap.Porph.*Abst.*4.7, *PGnom.*201 (ii A.D.), *BGU*250. 9 (ii A.D.), etc. **-ταυρος,** ὁ, *bull-calf,* Al.*Le.*4.3. **-τομέα,** ἡ, (μόσχος A) *osier-bed, IG*9(1).61.34 (Daulis, ii A.D.). **-τόμος,** ον, *slaughtering calves,* i.e. *sacrificer,* Lat. *victimarius, Gloss.* **-τρόφια,** τά, *farms for calf-breeding, PTeb.ined.*703.69. ⊛ **-τρόφος,** ον, *rearing calves, PSI*6.600 (iii B.C.), Hsch. s.v. τιθηνός: as Subst., *PSI*4. 409.2 (iii B.C.), *PCair.Zen.*326.6 (iii B.C.). **-φάγος** [ᾰ], ον, *eating calves,* Διόνυσος Sch.Ar.*Ra.*360; οἱ **Μ.,** name of a tribe, *Peripl.M. Rubr.*2,3.

**μότα,** τά, = Σαρδιαναὶ βάλανοι, Dsc.1.106 codd.; cf. ἄμωτον.

**μοτ-άριον,** τό, Dim. of μοτός, Gal.19.107, *EM*592.2. **-ημα,** ατος, τό, *store of linen, PRyl.*153.30 (ii A.D.). ⊛ **-ός,** ὁ, *tent, tampon, lint pledget* for dressing wounds, Hp.*VC*14: dat. pl. μοτοῖς Dsc.3.82, μότοις Heliod.ap.Orib.44.11.11: Ep. gen. pl. μοτάων (as if from **μοτή**) Q.S.4.212: neut. pl. **μότα,** τά, Call.*Fr.*7.40P., Hsch. II. *drainage tube,* μ. κασσιτέρινος κοῖλος Hp.*Morb.*2.47; also μ. στερεός ib.59.

**μοτο-φῠλάκιον** [ᾰ], τό, *bandage for keeping lint in place,* Leonid.ap. Aët.15.12, Antyll.ap.Orib.44.23.74. 2. μ. φάρμακον *applied by means of a bandage,* Paul.Aeg.6.34,62. **-φύλαξ** [ῠ], ακος, ὁ, = foreg. 1, Leonid.ap.Aët.15.5, Heliod.ap.Orib.44.11.11.

⊛ **μοτόω,** fut. -ώσω LXX *Ho.*6.2(1):—*plug a wound with lint,* Hp.*VC* 13, Hsch.

**μοτρογένειος,** ον, *with a thin straggling beard,* Hsch.

**μοττίας·** ᾧ στρέφουσι τῶν ῥυτήρων τὸν ἄξονα, Hsch. **μοττοῖ·** τιτρώσκει, ταράττει, Id. **μοττοφαγία,** a sacrifice in Cyprus, Id. **μόττυες·** οἱ ἔκλυτοι καὶ παρειμένοι, Id. **μοττωνῆσαι·** τῇ πτέρνῃ τύψαι, Id.

**μοτ-ώ,** ἡ, a kind of *cinnamon, Peripl.M.Rubr.*12,13, Gal.14.72. **-ώδης,** ες, *like* μοτώ, Id.12.606.

**μότ-ωμα,** ατος, τό, *lint dressing* for a wound, Hp.*Epid.*6.7.2. II. *tow,* used in soldering, *PLond.*3.1177.295 (ii A.D.). **-ωσις,** εως, ἡ, *dressing with lint,* Hp.*Art.*40, Aq.*Is.*1.6.

⊛ **μουγκρίζω,** *slobber,* or perh. *snarl,* Anon.*in Rh.*216.28.

**μουία,** ἡ, Lacon. for μυῖα, *maggot,* Hsch. **μουκήζειν·** μέμφεσθαι τοῖς χείλεσι, Id. **μούκηρος, μουκηρόβατος,** v. μύκηρος.

**μουκτηριᾷ** (-τυριᾷ cod.)· σκαρδαμύττει, Hsch.

**μουλ-άριον,** τό, Dim. of sq., *Gloss.* ⊛ **-η,** ἡ, = Lat. *mula, mule, PMag. Lond.*121.927, *PLips.*97 xxi 20 (iv A.D.), Alex.Trall.1.15. ⊛ **-ίων,** ωνος, ὁ, = Lat. *mulio, muleteer, Edict.Diocl.*7.19, *Stud.Pal.*20.85 (iv A.D.):—Adj. **-ωνικός,** ἡ, όν, κάλικαι *Edict.Diocl.*9.5a.

⊛ **μουνᾰδόν,** Adv., (μοῦνος) = μόνον, Opp.*C.*4.40.

⊛ **μουνάξ,** Adv., (μοῦνος) *singly,* ὀρχήσασθαι Od.8.371; μ. κτεινομένων *in single combat,* 11.417.

**μουναρχέω, -ία,** etc., v. μοναρχέω, -ία, etc.

**μουνιᾰδικόν,** τό, = βουνιάς, prob. in *Edict.Diocl.*6.16.

**μουνιάς,** άδος, ἡ, = Lat. *napus, Gloss.*

**μουνο-γενής, -γονος, -λιθος, -μήτωρ, -τόκος, μουνόω,** etc., v. μονο-.

**μουνο-έτις,** ἡ, *one year old,* prob. in *BMus.Inscr.*1048 (= *Epigr.Gr.* 431) (Antioch).

⊛ **Μουνῠχία,** ἡ, *Munychia,* a harbour in Piraeus, Hdt.8.76, Th.2.13, Arist.*Ath.*19.2, Str.9.1.15:—also **Μουνίχιον,** τό, Sch.Call.*Dian.*259; **Μουνύχιος** λιμήν Sch.E.*Hipp.*759: **Μουνύχιος,** ὁ, *inhabitant of the place,* St.Byz. II. epith. of Artemis, who was worshipped there, Call.*Dian.*259, cf. D.18.107. (In this group Att. Inscrr. almost always have **Μουνιχ-,** e.g. *IG*1².310.27, 2².1604.72,98, exc. **Μουνυχιών** ib.471.6 (late iv B.C.), 3.77.26.)

**Μουνῠχί-αζε,** Adv. *to Munychia,* Lys.13.29. **-āθεν,** Adv. *from Munychia,* St.Byz. **-āσι,** Adv. *at Munychia,* Th.8.92, Lys. 13.32. **-ών,** ῶνος, ὁ, *Munychion,* the tenth Attic month, Ar.*Av.* 1047, Aeschin.2.91.

**μουνώψ,** v. μονώψ. **μοῦρκορ·** μυχός (Lacon.), Hsch. **μούρρινα,** τά, and **μουρρίνη,** ἡ, v. μόρρια.

**μούρσινος,** η, ον, perh. = μόρινος, *mulberry-coloured,* or μύρσινος, *myrtle-coloured, POxy.*531.15 (ii A.D.).

⊛ **Μοῦσα,** ης, ἡ, Aeol. **Μοῖσα** Sapph.84, *IG*4²(1).130.16, etc.; Dor. **Μῶσα** Alcm.1, etc.; Lacon. **Μῶα** (for Μῶσα) Ar.*Lys.*1298, cf. *An. Ox.*1.277:—*Muse,* Ὀλυμπιάδες Μ., Διὸς αἰγιόχοιο θυγατέρες Il.2.491, cf. Hes.*Th.*25, etc.; nine in number, first in Od.24.60; named in Hes.*Th.*75 sqq. II. μοῦσα, as Appellat., *music, song,* μ. στυγερά A.*Eu.*308 (anap.); εὔφαμος Id.*Supp.*695 (lyr.); καναχὰν . . θείας ἀντίλυρον μούσας S.*Tr.*643 (lyr.); Αἰακῷ μοῖσαν φέρειν Pi.*N.*3.28; τίς ἥδε μοῦσα; what *strain* is this? E.*Ion*757; ἄλυρος μ. Id.*Ph.*1028 (lyr.); διὰ μούσας ἧξα Id.*Alc.*962 (lyr.): in Prose, ᾄδειν ἀδόκιμον μ. Pl.*Lg.* 829d: in pl., μοῦσαι Σφιγγός, of the Sphinx's riddle, E.*Ph.*50; esp. *liberal arts, accomplishments,* τὰς μούσας ἀφανίζων Ar.*Nu.*972; ἀπαίδευτον τῶν περὶ τὰς νυμφικὰς μ. Pl.*Lg.*775b: also in sg., τῆς ἀληθινῆς μ. ἠμεληκέναι Id.*R.*548b; κοινωνεῖν μούσης ib.411c. 2. αὕτη ἡ Σωκράτους μ. that was Socrates's *way,* Gal.*UP*1.9.

**Μουσᾱγέτᾱς,** α, ὁ, Dor. for Μουσηγέτης (v. infr.), *leader of the Muses,* epith. of Apollo, Pi.*Fr.*116; ὁ μ. καὶ ἀρχαγέτας τᾶς ποιητικᾶς θεός *SIG*699.1 (Delph., ii B.C.):—in Att. form **Μουσηγέτης,** Pl.*Lg.* 653c, D.S.1.18, Jul.*Or.*4.132a, al.; voc. **Μουσηγέτᾰ,** *IG*12(5).893 (Tenos); also epith. of Heracles, in dat. **Μουσαγήτῃ,** ib.14.101* (perh. spurious). [ᾱ prop., as in Pi.: but ᾰ in Orph.*H.*34.6 codd.]

**Μουσᾰϊσταί,** οἱ, guild of *worshippers of the Muses, IG*12(1).680 (Ialysus).

**μούσαξ·** ὁ ὑπὸ τοῦ βοαγοῦ τρεφόμενος, Hsch. (Lacon. for μόθαξ.)

**μουσάριον,** τό, name of an *eye-salve,* Alex.Trall.2.

⊛ **Μούσαρχος,** Dor. **Μώσαρχος,** ὁ, *leader of the Muses,* epith. of Apollo, Terp.3 (= *Carm.Pop.*49 Diehl).

⊛ **Μουσεῖον,** τό, *shrine of the Muses, seat* or *haunt of the Muses,* Aeschin.1.10: hence, 2. *home of music* or *poetry,* μουσεῖα θρηνήμασι ξυνῳδά *choirs* chiming in with dirges, E.*Hel.*174 (lyr.); ἀηδόνων μ. *choir* of nightingales, Id.*Fr.*88; parodied χελιδόνων μουσεῖα Ar.*Ra.* 93; τὸ Νυμφῶν νᾶμά τε καὶ μ. λόγων Pl.*Phdr.*278b (but μουσεῖα λόγων, οἷον διπλασιολογία κτλ. *gallery* of tropes, ib.267b): generally, *school of art* or *letters,* τὸ τῆς Ἑλλάδος μ., of Athens, Ath.5.187d, cf. Plu.2. 736d; τὸ τῆς φύσεως μ., a phrase of Alcidamas censured by Arist. *Rh.*1406ᵃ25. 3. *a Museum,* i.e. *a philosophical school and library,* such as that of Plato at Athens, D.L.4.1, etc.; at Alexandria, Str.17. 1.8, *BMus.Inscr.*1076 (Antinoe), etc.; περιπατοῦν Μ. 'a walking *library*', of Longinus, Eun.*VS* p.456 B. II. *the Museum,* a hill at Athens, Paus.1.25.8. III. as the title of a book, Alcid.ap.Stob. 4.52.22. IV. Μουσεῖα, τά, *festival of the Muses,* Paus.9.31.2: sg., Ath.14.629a; τὰ Μ. θῦσαι Phld.*Acad.Ind.*p.41 M.

**Μούσειος,** ον, Aeol. **Μοισαῖος,** α, ον, (Μοῦσα) *of* or *belonging to the Muses,* ἕδρα E.*Ba.*410 (lyr.); Μοισαῖον ἅρμα the car *of Poesy,* Pi.*I.*8 (7).67; λίθος **Μ.** a monument *of song,* Id.*N.*8.47. II. *musical,* κέλαδος *AP*9.372.

**Μουσηγέτης,** v. Μουσαγέτας.

**μουσ-ιάζω,** = μουσίζω, Phld.*Lib.*p.40 O. **-ιάριος,** ὁ, *mosaic-worker,* μ. κεντητής prob. in *Edict.Diocl.*7.6. **-ίδδει** (-ιαδδεῖ cod.)· λαλεῖ, ὁμιλεῖ, Hsch. (perh. Lacon. for μυθίζει). **-ίζω,** *sing* or *play,* Dor. **-ίσδω** Theoc.8.38, 11.81:—Med. in act. sense, ἄχαριν κέλαδον μουσιζόμενος E.*Cyc.*489 (anap.). ⊛ **-ῐκεύομαι,** = foreg., Duris 80 J. 2. *cultivate a taste for music,* S.E.*M.*6.29.

**μουσική** (sc. τέχνη), ἡ, *any art over which the Muses presided,* esp. *poetry sung to music,* Pi.*O.*1.15, Hdt.6.129; μουσικῆς ἀγών Th.3.104, cf. *IG*1².84.16, etc.; ποίησις ἡ κατὰ μουσικήν Pl.*Smp.*196e, cf. 205c; τίς ἡ τέχνη, ἧς τὸ κιθαρίζειν καὶ τὸ ᾄδειν καὶ τὸ ἐμβαίνειν ὀρθῶς; Answ. μουσικήν μοι δοκεῖς λέγειν Id.*Alc.*1.108d. 2. = ἀγὼν μουσικῆς, *IG* 12(9).189.8 (Eretria, iv B.C.). II. generally, *art* or *letters,* μουσικῇ καὶ πάσῃ φιλοσοφίᾳ προσχρώμενος Pl.*Ti.*88c, cf. *Phd.*61a, *Prt.*340a; μουσική, γράμματα, γυμναστική, as three branches of education, Id. *R.*403c, cf. X.*Lac.*2.1; with γραφική added, Arist.*Pol.*1337ᵇ24; ἐν μουσικῇ καὶ γυμναστικῇ παιδεύειν Pl.*Cri.*50d: metaph., εὑρὼν ἀκριβῆ μ. ἐν ἀσπίδι E.*Supp.*926.

⊛ **μουσῐκός,** ή, όν, Dor. **μωσικός,** ά, όν Theag.ap.Stob.3.1.118:—*musical,* ἀγῶνες μ. καὶ γυμνικοί Ar.*Pl.*1163, cf. Th.3.104; χοροί τε καὶ ἀγῶνες μ. Pl.*Lg.*828c; τὰ μουσικά *music,* X.*Cyr.*1.6.38, *Sammelb.* 6319.54 (Ptol.), *SIG*578.18 (Teos, ii B.C.). Adv. -κῶς Pl.*Alc.*1.108d, etc.; cf. foreg. II. of persons, *skilled in music, musical,* X.l.c., etc.; ποιητικοὶ καὶ μ. ἄνδρες Pl.*Lg.*802b; κύκνος καὶ ἄλλα ζῷα μ. Id.*R.*620a; περὶ αὐλοὺς -ώτατοι Ath.4.176e; *lyric poet,* opp. epic, Pl.*Phdr.*243a (but opp. μελοποιός, Phld.*Mus.*p.96 K.); μ., οἱ, professional *musicians, OGI*383.162 (Commagene, i B.C.), *PFlor.*74.6 (ii A.D.); μουσικὸς καὶ μελῶν ποιητής *SIG*662.6 (Delos, ii B.C.). 2. generally, *votary of the Muses, man of letters and accomplishments, scholar,* opp. ἀμαθής, Ar.*Eq.*191; ἀνὴρ σοφὸς καὶ μ. Id.*V.*1244; ἀνδρὸς φιλοσόφου ἢ φιλοκάλου ἢ μ. Pl.*Phdr.*248d, al.; πόλις -ωτάτη *most full of liberal arts,* Isoc.*Ep.*8.4; ἡ τῶν νέων οὐσία μουσικωτάτη Pl.*Lg.*729a: c. inf., παρ' ὄχλῳ -ώτεροι λέγειν *more accomplished in* speaking before a mob, E.*Hipp.*989. III. of things, *elegant, delicate,* βρώματα Diox.1; ἥδιον οὐδέν, οὐδὲ -ώτερον Philem.23; *harmonious, fitting,* τροφὴ μέση καὶ μ., τὸν Δώριον τρόπον τῆς τύχης ὡς ἀληθῶς ἡρμοσμένη Dam.*Isid.*50. Adv. -κῶς *harmoniously, suitably,* οἱ λόγοι οὐ πάνυ μ. λέγονται Pl.*Prt.*333a; μ. ἐρᾶν Id.*R.*403a; ὀρθῶς καὶ μ. Id.*Lg.*816b; εὐρύθμως καὶ μ. εἰπεῖν Isoc.13.16; μ. ἅλας δοῦναι, ὄψον σκευάσαι, Euphro

11.10, Nicom.Com.1.9: Comp. -ωτέρως, λέγειν Arist.*Rh.*1395ᵇ29: Sup. -ώτατα Ar.*Ra.*873.

**μουσικτάς,** = μουσικός II, Hsch.

**μουσίσδω,** Dor. for μουσίζω.

⊛ **μούσμων,** ονος, ὁ, a Sardinian animal, perh. the *moufle*, Str.5.2.7.

**μουσό-δομος,** ον, *built by song*, of the walls of Thebes, *AP*9.250 (Honest.). **-δόνημα,** ατος, τό, (δονέω) *poetic frenzy*, Eup.245 (pl.). **-εργός,** v. μουσουργός. **-κόλαξ,** ᾰκος, ὁ, *courtier of the Muses*, D.H.7.9. **-ληπτέομαι,** Pass., *to be possessed by the Muse*, Aristid. 2.13 J. ap.Phot.*Bibl.*p.411 B. (om. codd. Aristid.). **-ληπτος,** ον, *Muse-inspired*, Phld.*Mus.*p.86 K., Plu.*Marc.*17, 2.452b. **-μᾰνέω,** *to be music-mad*, Luc.*Ner.*6, Ath.4.183e; prob. in this sense in S.*Fr.* 245 (lyr.; unless μουσομανεῖ is dat. of sq.). **-μᾰνής,** ές, *devoted to melody*, τέττιξ *AP*10.16 (Theaet.). **2.** v. foreg. **-μᾰνία,** ἡ, *devotion to the Muses*, Plu.2.706c (pl.). **-μαντις** ὄρνις, bird *of prophetic song*, Ar.*Av.*276, cf. A.*Fr.*60. **-μήτωρ,** ορος, ἡ, *the mother of Muses and all arts*, epith. of Memory, Id.*Pr.*461. **-πᾰλαιο-λύμας** [ῡ], α, ὁ, *corrupter of the old music*, Tim.*Pers.*229. **-πάτακτος** [πᾰ], ον, *smitten by the Muses*, 'moonstruck', Cic.*QF*2.8.1. **-πλαστος,** ον, *ornamented*, λάρναξ *IG*14.1347. **-πνοος,** ον, contr. πνους, πνουν, *breathing melody*, στόματα, of Hesiod, Anon.ap.Procl.*Proll. Hes.*p.4 G. ⊛ **-ποιέω,** *write poetry*, c. acc. cogn., νόμων οὓς Θαμύρας μ. S.*Fr.*245 (lyr.). **II.** *sing of*, τινας Ar.*Nu.*334. **-ποιός,** όν, *making poetry, poet*, of Hipponax, Theoc.*Ep.*19, cf. E.*Tr.*1189; *poetess*, of Sappho, Hdt.2.135. **II.** *singing* or *playing*, μ. μέριμνα E.*Hipp.*1428. ⊛ **-πόλος,** ον, *serving the Muses, poetic*, οἰκία Sapph. 136 (s.v.l.); μ. στοναχά *a tuneful* lament, E.*Ph.*1499 (lyr.); χεῖρες, στέφανος, *AP*9.270 (Marc. Arg.), 12.257 (Mel.); μουσοπόλε θήρ, addressed to Pan, Castorio 2.5. **II.** Subst., *bard, minstrel*, E.*Alc.* 445 (lyr., pl.), *Rev.Phil.*36.67 (Iconium, ii A.D.), *Not.Scav.*1912.327 (Ostia). **-πρόσωπος,** ον, *musical-looking*, *AP*9.570 (Phld.). **-ρρῠτος,** ον, *flowing with music*, i.e. *gifted with poetic talent*, *TAM*2(1). 49 (Telmessus). **-τέχνης,** ου, Dor. **-νᾱς,** ὁ, *musician*, *IG*12(7). 449 (Amorgos, ii B.C.). **-τρᾰφής,** ές, *reared by the Muses*, Eust. 124.25.

**μουσουργ-έω,** = μουσοποιέω, Poll.4.57, Philostr.Jun.*Im.*6. ⊛ **-ία,** ἡ, *singing, making poetry*, Luc.*Vit.Auct.*3, *Corp.Herm.*18.6. **-ικός,** ή, όν, *of* or *for a musician*, Poll.4.57. **-ός,** όν, Ion. **μουσοεργός** Hp.*Nat.Puer.*13, *cultivating music*: Subst., *singing girl*, Hp.l.c., X.*Cyr.*4.6.11, Theopomp.Hist.111(a), *Com.Adesp.*15.18 D.; ὀρχηστρίδες καὶ μ. Luc.*Am.*10, cf. Hippoloch.ap.Ath.4.129a: also masc., *musician*, J.*AJ*15.2.5, *Corp.Herm.*18.1, S.E.*P.*1.54.

**μουσό-φθαρτος,** ον, *slain by the Muses*, Lyc.832. **-φῐλής,** ές, *loving the Muses*, ἑταρος *AP*11.44 (Phld.). **-φίλητος** [ῐ], ον, *dear to the Muses*, Corinn.23. **-χᾰρής,** ές, *delighting in the Muses* or *in poetry*, βίοτος *AP*9.411 (Maec.); ⊛**μουσόχορος** is prob. f.l. for -χαρής in *Cat.Cod.Astr.*8(4).214. **-ω,** *furnish with power of song*, ὅσα φύσις μεμούσωκε, of birds, Ph.1.80. **2.** *adorn with mosaic*, *Ath.Mitt.*8.328 (Tralles). **II.** mostly Pass., *to be trained in the ways of the Muses, to be educated* or *accomplished*, οὐ μεμούσωμαι κακῶς Ar.*Lys.*1127; τὸ μεμουσῶσθαι ἐπαινοῦσιν Phld.*Mus.*p.77 K., cf. Ph.2. 387; πολυγράμματος ὢν καὶ μεμουσωμένος Plu.2.1121f; τὸ Κίμωνος ὑγρὸν καὶ μεμουσωμένον ἐν ταῖς περιφοραῖς his easy and *polished* manners, Id.*Per.*5; μουσωθεὶς φωνὴν *taught to utter* it, Ael.*NA*16.3. **2.** *to be set to music*, τὰ δι' ᾠδῆς . . μουσωθέντα κρούματα D.H.*Dem.*40, cf. *Cat.Cod.Astr.*8(3).188; *to be filled with melody*, μεμούσωται τὰ περὶ τὴν θάλατταν ὑπ' ᾠδῆς τῶν πετρῶν Philostr.*Her.*10.7.

**μουστάκιον,** τό, Dim. of *μούσταξ (= μύσταξ), *An.Ox.*3.76. **II.** in pl., = Lat. *mustacea*, a sort of *cake*, Chrysipp.Tyan.ap.Ath.14. 647d.

**μουστάριον,** τό, a measure of wine, *PFlor.*65.18 (vi A.D.).

**μουστόπιττα,** ἡ, = οἰνοῦττα, Sch.Ar.*Pl.*1122.

**μοῦστος,** ὁ, = Lat. *mustum*, *new wine*, *PStrassb.*1.7 (v A.D.), etc.

**μούσχανον·** τὸ βλαστόν, Hsch.

**μουσῳδός,** όν, (ᾠδή) *singing, making music*, Man.5.143.

**μούσωνες·** οἱ κορυφαῖοι τῶν μαγείρων, καὶ οἱ τεχνῖται, Hsch.

**μοχθ-έω,** *to be weary* or *worn with toil, to be sore distressed*, ἀλλά μιν οἴω κήδεσι μοχθήσειν Il.10.106; χείμωνι μόχθεντες (prob.) μεγάλῳ μάλα Alc.18.5; ὄμβροις ἡλίου τε καύμασι S.*OC*351; πόνοις E.*Ion*135 (lyr.): abs., *work hard, labour*, κάματός ἐστι τοῖς αὐτοῖς μοχθεῖν καὶ ἄρχεσθαι Heraclit.84, cf. E.*Fr.*461, Ar.*Pl.*556, Th.2.39, etc.; χρημάτων ὕπερ E.*Fr.*580.5; ἐπὶ χρηστοῖς (sc. τέκνοις) Id.*Med.*1104 (anap.): c. acc. cogn., μ. μόχθους *undergo* hardships, Id.*Hel.*1446; *execute painful* tasks, μ. πόνους Id.*Ion* 103 (anap.); πολλὰ δὴ καὶ θερμὰ χερσὶ καὶ νώτοισι μ. S.*Tr.*1047; πολλὰ μ. Ar.*Pl.*281; πολλὰ περὶ τὴν στρατιὰν ἐμοχθησάτην X.*An.*6.6.31; τάδε, ταῦτα μ., E.*El.*64, Ar.*Pl.*518, etc.; ἀνήνυτα μ. Epicur.*Fr.*470; μαθήματα μ. *toil at* learning, E.*Hec.*815; μ. ἄπαντ' ἐν οἰκίᾳ Pherecr.10. **2.** c. acc. objecti, τέκνα . . ἀμόχθησα the children *over* whom I *toiled*, E.*HF*281; μ. πόδα σὸν θεραπεύμασιν, = θεραπεύειν, Id.*Ph.*1549 (lyr.).—Cf. μόχθος. **-ήεις,** εσσα, εν, = μοχθηρός, Nic.*Al.*617. **-ημα,** ατος, τό, always in pl., *toils, hardships*, A.*Pr.*464, S.*OC*1616; τεκτόνων μ. E.*Ion*1129. **-ηρία,** ἡ, *bad condition*, σκήνεος Democr.187; σώματος Pl.*R.*609e. **2.** of a person, *lack of skill, incapacity*, τοῦ ἰατροῦ Antipho 4.2.4; τῶν κυβερνητῶν Pl. *Plt.*302a. **II.** mostly in moral sense, *wickedness, depravity*, Ar. *Pl.*109, 159, Pl.*Lg.*734d, etc.; τὰς μ. τῆς ἠλιθιότητος τῆς ἐμῆς Cratin. 188; ἀρεταὶ καὶ μοχθηρίαι Arist.*EN*1129ᵇ24: with a political connotation, τὰ πρῶτα τῆς ἐκεῖ μ. chief *of the rascaldom* (i.e. of the Radical party) up there (on earth), Ar.*Ra.*425. **-ηρόομαι,** Pass., *to be troublesome*, Aq.*Jb.*6.25. **-ηρός,** ά, όν, also ός, όν E.*Fr.*875: (μοχθέω):—*suffering hardship, in sore distress, wretched*, of persons, A.*Th.*257; ὦ πόλλ' ἐγὼ μ. S.*Ph.*254; ὦ μόχθηρε σύ *poor wretch!* Ar. *Ach.*165, *Ra.*1175; ὦ μόχθηρε Pl.*Phdr.*268e; of conditions, μοχθηρῆς ἐούσης τῆς ζόης Hdt.7.46; μοχθηρὰ τλῆναι suffer *hardships*, A.*Ch.*752. Adv., σῶμα μοχθηρῶς διακείμενον in a *bad* way, Pl.*Grg.* 504e; ζῆν μ. ib.505a; μ. ἔχειν Arist.*Pol.*1254ᵇ1: Comp., μοχθηροτέρως ἔχειν Pl.*R.*343e: Sup. -ότατα, διακείμενοι Id.*Erx.*406. **2.** *in bad condition*, βοῦς Ar.*Eq.*316; ἱμάτιον Cratin.207; μοχθηρότερα ἀποδιδόντες ἢ παρέλαβον τὰ ἱμάτια Pl.*Men.*91e; καταλαβὼν μοχθηρὰ τὰ πράγματα finding trade *in a bad state*, D.34.8; μ. ἐλπίδας ἔχειν Din. 1.107; μ. τραγῳδία Arist.*Metaph.*1090ᵇ20; ὕδατα Id.*Pr.*872ᵃ10; χρόα Id.*HA*616ᵇ12; ἀγωγή *PTeb.*24.57 (ii B.C.); of persons, *inferior*, μ. (v.l. πονηρ-) ἰατρός Antipho 4.2.4; also, of appearance, μοχθηρὸς τὴν ἰδέαν *ugly*, And.1.100; of arguments, *unsound, fallacious*, S.E.*P.*2.111; of persons, *mistaken*, Anon.Lond.27.24: so in Adv. -ρῶς, κρίνομεν S.E.*M.*7.210. **II.** most freq. of persons, in moral sense, *knavish, rascally*, Th.8.73, etc.; ἐκ χρηστῶν καὶ γενναίων μοχθηροτάτους ἀπέδειξας Ar.*Ra.*1011, cf. Pl.*Men.*91e; τοὺς τρόπους μ. Ar.*Pl.*1003; of acts, etc., μ. τι πράσσειν *Trag.Adesp.*510; ὑφοψία μ. *OGI*315.58 (Pessinus, ii B.C.); ῥῆμα μ. *SIG*1175.5 (Piraeus, iv/iii B.C.); μοχθηρότερα λεγόντων X.*HG*1.4.13 (v.l. -ότερον Adv. Comp.).—Some Gramm. write μόχθηρος, πόνηρος in signf. I, μοχθηρός, πονηρός in signf. II, Ammon.*Diff.*p.94 V., Arc.71.16, but Hdn.Gr.1.197 (ap.Eust.341.14) argues that like other Adjs. in -ρος these words ought to be oxyt. in both senses. In the voc. the best codd. always give μόχθηρε, Ar.*Ach.* 165, *Ra.*1175, *Pl.*391; cf. πονηρός. **-ητέον,** *one must labour*, S.*Fr.* 1120.10; μέτρῳ μ. E.*HF*1251. **-ίζω,** = μοχθέω, περὶ χρήμασι μ. *toil* for money, Pi.*Fr.*123.6; ἕλκεϊ μοχθίζοντα . . ὕδρου *suffering* from the wound . ., Il.2.723; δαίμονι δειλῷ μ. Thgn.164; φθειρσὶ μ. Archil.137; ἐτώσια μ. Theoc.1.38, 7.48; μόχθους μ. Mosch.4.44: abs., Orph.*A.* 1071. ⊛ **-ος,** ὁ, = Homeric μόγος, *toil, hardship, distress*, ἀμφὶ δ' ἀέθλῳ δῆριν ἔχειν καὶ μ. Hes.*Sc.*306; μόχθων ἀμπνοά, ἀμοιβά, Pi.*O.*8.7, *N.*5. 48: freq. in Trag., A.*Ch.*921, S.*Ph.*480, etc.: also in pl., *toils, troubles, hardships*, A.*Pr.*541 (lyr.), etc.; of the *labours* of Heracles, S.*Tr.*1101, 1170; μ. τέκνων *for* them, E.*Med.*1261 (lyr.); μόχθον ἀμφὶ πράγμασι Epigr.ap.Aeschin.3.184; Ἀπελλείου μ. γραφίδος, of a picture, *APl.*4. 178 (Antip. Sid.).—Rare in early Prose (not in Pl. or Oratt.), cf. μ. καὶ ταλαιπωρίη Democr.223; ἐλευθέριοι μ. X.*Smp.*2.4; διὰ μόχθων Id.*Cyr.*1.6.25: freq. in Lxx, *Ex.*18.8, al.; κόπος καὶ μ. 1*Ep.Thess.*2.9; μ. implies *hardship*, πόνος *work* (but μ. is said to be Cret. for πόνος *AB*1096). **-όω,** *weary*, Aq.*Is.*7.13. **-ώδης,** ες, *laborious*, Vett.Val.104.9.

⊛**μοχλ-εία,** ἡ, = sq. I, Arist.*Ph.*259ᵇ20, *Supp.Epigr.*2.569.19 (Didyma, ii B.C.), Dexipp.*Fr.*27 J. (written μοχλίαις), Orib.49.4.72; μ. τῶν ὀδόντων *extraction* of teeth, Gal.18(2).592; [ὀστῶν] *reduction* of dislocations, Id.19.461: metaph., *dislodgement* of chronic disease, esp. by exercise, μοχλείας δεῖσθαι Antyll.ap.Orib.6.1.1, Gal.17(1). 839; πρὸς ἀνάμνησιν δέονται τῆς μ. [αἱ ψυχαί] Plu.*Fr.*7.19, cf. Olymp.*in Grg.*p.279 J. **-ευσις,** εως, ἡ, *moving by a lever, setting joints by leverage*, Hp.*Fract.*13, 31, *Art.*74. **2.** *removal, dislodgement, extirpation*, τῆς ῥίζης τοῦ κακοῦ Aret.*CD*1.2. **-ευτής,** οῦ, ὁ, *one who heaves by a lever*: hence Com. γῆς καὶ θαλάσσης μ. *he who makes* earth and sea *to heave*, Ar.*Nu.*567; ὦ καινῶν ἐπῶν . . μοχλευτά *O thou who heavest up* new words, ib.1397. **-ευτικός,** ή, όν, *of* or *by means of leverage*, τρόπος, ἐνέργημα, Orib.49.2.7, 49.12. 8; μοχλευτικόν τι καὶ κινητικὸν τῶν ἐμμόνων νοσημάτων *capable of dislodging*, Antyll.ap.eund.6.23.12; μ. ἐργαλεῖον Sch.E.*Ph.* 1155. **-εύω,** (μοχλός) *prise up, heave*, or *wrench* by a lever, [στέγην] Hdt.2.175; θύρετρα, πέτρους, E.*HF*999, *Cyc.*240; πέτρας Pl.Com. 67; θύρας Antiph.195.6; μόχλευσιν μοχλῷ μ. Hp.*Art.*74:—Pass., Arist.*Mech.*853ᵃ38. **2.** metaph., Porph.*Chr.*55:—in Med., *contrive*, 'engineer', μηδὲν μ. κατά τινων ἄδικον J.*AJ*5.1.16:—Pass., of disease, *to be dislodged, removed*, Aret.*CD*1.2. **-έω,** Ion. for foreg., στήλας τε προβλῆτας ἐμόχλεον *they strove to heave* them *up with levers*, Il.12.259. **-ία,** v. μοχλεία. **-ικός,** ή, όν, *concerning leverage*: τὸ μ. *a treatise* (by Hippocrates) *on setting joints by leverage* (*or otherwise*): τὰ μ. *levers*, Id.*Mochl.*42 (s.v.l.); also, title of work *on levers*, Ph.*Bel.*59.18. **-ίον,** τό, Dim. of μοχλός, *Com. Adesp.*1084, Luc.*Somn.*13, *PKlein.Form.*950 (v/vi A.D.). **-ίσκος,** ὁ, Dim. of μοχλός, Hp.*Art.*67, Ar.*Fr.*481, Paul.Aeg.6.107.

**μοχλο-ειδής,** ές, *like a lever*, ξύλον Apollon.Cit.1. **-λῖθος,** ὁ, gloss on θυρεός, Sch.Od.9.240.

**μοχλός** (Ion. **μοκλός** Anacr.88), ὁ, *bar, lever, crowbar*, used for moving ships, μοχλοῖσιν δ' ἄρα τήν γε κατείρυσεν Od.5.261; or heavy weights, μοχλοῖς καὶ μηχαναῖσιν ἀνελκύσαι Ar.*Pax*307; for forcing doors and gates, E.*Or.*1474 (lyr.), cf. *Ba.*348, 1104, etc.; ὑποβαλόντες τοὺς μ. ὑπὸ τὰς πύλας Ar.*Lys.*428, cf. Arist.*Mech.*847ᵇ11, al. **II.** *any bar* or *stake*, as in Od.9.332 the stake which Odysseus runs into the Cyclops' eye, cf. E.*Cyc.*633. **III.** wooden or iron *bar* or *bolt* placed across gates on the inside and secured by the βάλανος, τοῦ μοχλοῦ διακοπέντος Th.4.111, cf. 2.4, *IG*1².313.126; μοχλοὺς ἐπιβάλλειν Ar.*Th.*415; τὸν μ. ἐμβάλλειν X.*An.*7.1.12, cf. Ar.*Lys.*246; μοχλοῖς καὶ κλῄθροισι τὰ προπύλαια πακτοῦν ib.264; τὴν πόλιν . . ἀπεκλῄσατε τοῖσι μ. ib.487; πύλας μοχλοῖς χαλᾶτε by [drawing back] *the bars*, A.*Ch.*879; κλῇθρα λύσαντες μοχλοῖς E.*IT*99 (more naturally κλῄθρων μοχλοὺς λύσαντες, as in Ar.*Lys.*310 κἂν μὴ . . τοὺς μοχλοὺς χαλῶσιν): metaph., μέγας σοι τοῦδ' ἐγὼ φόβου μ. *a bar* or *defence against* fear, S.*Fr.*760.

**μοχλόω**, (μοχλός) *bolt, bar*, μόχλωσον τὴν θύραν Ar.*Fr.*369.

**μοχοῖ·** ἐντός (Paphian), Hsch. (Cypr. loc. of μυχός.)

**Μοψοπία**, ἡ, old name of *Attica*, Call.*Fr.*351, Str.9.1.18: **Μοψόπιοι**, οἱ, *the Athenians*, *APl.*4.118 (Paul. Sil.):—Adj. **Μοψόπειος**, α, ον, *Attic*, Lyc.1340.

**μόψος·** κηλὶς ἡ ἐν τοῖς ἱματίοις (Cypr.), Hsch. **μόων·** μόθων, Id.

***μῦ**, τό, name of the letter μ, *IG*2.4321.24 (iv B.C.), Epigr.ap.Ath. 10.454f, Hellad.ap.Phot.*Bibl.*p.530 B., etc. 2. μῦ or μὺ μῦ, to represent *a muttering sound* made with the lips, μυ λαλεῖν *to mutter*, Hippon.80 (dub. l.); to imitate the sound of *sobbing*, μὺ μῦ, μὺ μῦ Ar.*Eq.*10.

**μῦα**, v. μυῖα.

***μῦ-άγρα**, ἡ, (μῦς) *mouse-trap*, *AP*9.410 (Tull. Sab.), Poll.7.41:—also **μύαγρον**, τό, *Gloss.* II. = ἀσπάραγος πετραῖος, Ps.-Dsc.2.125. **-αγρος**, ὁ, *mouser*, a kind of snake. Nic.*Th.*490. II. = μελάμπυρος, Dsc.4.116, Plin.*HN*27.106. III. = μυάγρα II, Ps.-Dsc. 2.125. **-άκανθος** [ᾰκ], ὁ, = κεντρομυρσίνη, Thphr.*HP*6.5.1, Orph. *Fr.*49.61. II. = ἀσπάραγος πετραῖος, Dsc.2.125:—Adj. **μῠακάνθινος**, η, ον, Gal.11.841, Orib.3.4.1.

***μυάκιον**, τό, Dim. of μύαξ, Aët.12.55, *Gloss.*

**μυᾰλός, μυᾰλόω**, later spellings for μυελ-, blamed by Phryn.282.

**μύαξ**, ᾰκος, ὁ, = μῦς II, *sea-mussel*, Xenocr.ap.Orib.2.58.90, Dsc. 2.5, Plin.*HN*32.95; also of its *shell*, Dsc.1.32,33. II. = μύστρον 2, Crito ap.Gal.14.105; μ. χαλκοῦς Id.12.892. (Cf. Lat. *mūrex.*)

**μῡάω**, (μύω) *compress the lips* in sign of displeasure, τί μοι μυᾶτε; Ar.*Lys.*126 codd., Sch., Suid.; μυᾶτε· σκαρδαμύττετε, Hsch.; cf. μοιμυάω.

**μῡγᾰλῆ** (uncontr. **μῡγᾰλέη** Nic.*Th.*816), ἡ, (μῦς, γαλέη) *shrew-mouse, field-mouse*, Hdt.2.67, Sannyr.8, Cephisod.7, Anaxandr.39. 14, Arist.*HA*604b19, Lxx *Le.*11.30, Dsc.2.68 (v.l. μυογ-), Philum. *Ven.*33, Iamb.*Myst.*5.8.—On the accent v. Hdn.Gr.2.911.

**μύγᾰλος** [ῠ], ὁ, = foreg., *PMag.Lond.*121.2445,2592.

***μύγματα·** καταξέσματα, Hsch.

**μυγμός**, ὁ, *utterance of the sound* μὺ μῦ, *moaning, whimpering* (v. μύζω), ascribed to the sleeping Furies in A.*Eu.*117,120; of wounded men or dogs, D.S.17.11,92; μ. ἀνθρώπινος, of the κυνοκέφαλος, Id.3. 35; μ. βρεφῶν, = Lat. *vagitus*, *Gloss.*; of the noise of the fish γλάνις, Arist.*HA*621a29. II. *utterance of the sound* μ, D.T.631.18 (pl.), D.H.*Comp.*14, Praxiph.ap.Demetr.*Eloc.*57 (pl.), S.E.*M.*1.102.

**μῠδάζομαι**, = μυσάττομαι, ἐμυδάξατο f.l. for ἐμυσάξατο, Nic.*Al.*482.

**μῠδαίνω**, (μύδος A) *wet, soak*, φάρμακα μυδήνας A.R.3.1247, cf. 1042, Lyc.1008; also, = σήπω, Hsch. [ῡ in διαμυδαίνω.]

***μῠδᾰλέος**, α, ον, *wet, dripping*, αἵματι Il.11.54; δάκρυσι Hes.*Sc.* 270, S.*El.*166 (lyr.): abs., Hes.*Op.*556, Antim.90, *Hymn.Is.*27. II. *mouldy*, ὀδμή A.R.2.191. [ῠ, but ῡ metri gr. in dactylic verses.]

**μῠδᾰλόεις**, εσσα, εν, = foreg., μ. ὄμματα κλαυθμῷ *AP*12.226 (Strat.).

***μῠδ-άω**, (μύδος A) *to be damp, dripping*, φόνου μυδώσας σταγόνας S. *OT*1278; μυδῶσα κηκίς Id.*Ant.*1008; φόνῳ μυδόωντες (v.l. -όεντες) ὀδόντες Nic.*Th.*308; μύροις μ. *AP*5.198 (Hedyl.); μυδόωσα ἀπὸ χροὸς ἔρρεε λάχνη A.R.4.1531; of ulcers, Hp.*Ulc.*10; [θυρεοὶ] ὑπὸ τῶν ὄμβρων.. μυδῶντες Plb.6.25.7; of the eyelids (v. sq.), Dsc.1.71,72. II. *to be damp, clammy* from decay, σὰρξ μυδῶσα Hp.*VC*15; of a corpse, S.*Ant.*410. **-ησις**, εως, ἡ, *dampness, clamminess*, Aret.*CD*1.4; esp. of the eyelids, *purulent blepharitis*, αἱ ἐν ὀφθαλμοῖς μ. τῶν βλεφάρων Dsc.1.7, cf. Gal.14.770; also, μυδήσεις οὔλων, prob. *pyorrhoea*, Dsc.1.24. II. *putrefaction*, Diog.Oen.16.

**μύδιον**, τό, *small boat*, D.S.31.38 (pl.), Fest. s. v. *myoparo*, *CIL*8. 27790 (Althiburos). II. *small forceps*, Heliod.ap.Orib.46.10.4, Philum.*Ven.*2.6, Aët.7.64:—also **μυδιόσκελλον**, τό, Id.8.27.

**μῠδόεις**, εσσα, εν, = μυδαλέος, Nic.*Th.*308 (v.l.), 362.

**μύδος** [ῠ] (A), ὁ, *damp: clamminess, decay*, Nic.*Al.*248. (Cf. Lett. *mudēt* 'become mouldy', Engl. *smut.*)

**μύδος** (B), ον, (μύω) = μυνδός, Hsch.

**μυδρίᾱσις**, εως, Ion. **-ίησις**, ιος, ἡ, *dilatation of the pupil*, Cels.6. 6.37, Gal.10.171, Cael.Aur.*TP*2.6, Aët.7.54; prob. in same sense in Aret.*SD*1.7.

**μυδρο-κτῠπέω**, *forge red-hot iron*, A.*Pr.*368. **-κτύπος** [ῠ], ον, *forging red-hot iron*, μ. μίμημα in the manner of a smith *smiting iron*, E.*HF*992.

**μύδρος**, ὁ, *anvil* of stone or metal, A.*Fr.*307 (reading μύδρος); τύπτεσθαι μύδρος, i. e. as hard as an *anvil*, Antiph.195.3; also the *red-hot mass of iron* on the anvil, Call.*Dian.*49, Nic.*Al.*50; μύδρους αἴρειν χεροῖν hold *red-hot iron* in the hands, as an ordeal, S.*Ant.*264; μύδρον σιδήρεον κατεπόντωσαν Hdt.1.165, cf. Arist.*Ath.*23.5, *IG*1$^2$.682 (prob.), Call.*Fr.*209; Πακτώλιος μ. *lump* [of gold] from Pactolus, Lyc.272; μ. διάπυρος a red-hot *mass of stone or metal*, of the sun, Anaxag.ap.D.L.2.8, cf. 15, Archel. in *Placit.*2.13.6, Ph.1.623; ἀστέρος μ. Critias 25.35 D.; μ. διάπυροι the stones thrown out by Aetna, Arist.*Mu.*395b23, cf. Str.6.2.8; also, of *red-hot stones* or *pieces of metal*, thrown into a liquid to vaporize it, Hp.*Mul.*2.134: generally, a *stone*, Orph.*A.*896; ὁ ἀὴρ διάπυρος καὶ μ. γενόμενος dub. in Hp. *Flat.*8; μύδρος κίων παχὺς ἄξυστος (sine interpr.) *Gloss.* (Not in Hom. exc. in a spurious line read by some after Il.15.21.) (Cf. σμύδρος.)

**μῠδών**, ῶνος, ὁ, *fungous flesh in an ulcer*, Poll.4.191. II. μύδωνος is prob. f.l. in D.Chr.47.18 (μυλῶνος Casaubon).

**μύειος** [ῡ], ον, (μῦς) *of, belonging to mice*, *An.Ox.*2.286.

**μυελαυξής**, ές, *increasing the marrow*, τροφή Hsch.

**μυέλῐνος**, η, ον, *soft as marrow, fat*, πυγή *AP*12.37 (Diosc.).

**μυελόεις**, εσσα, εν, *full of marrow*, σάρκας τε καὶ ὀστέα μυελόεντα Od.9.293; *fat, rich*, ὄστρεα μ. Matro ap.Ath.4.135a; of chicken broth, Nic.*Al.*59.

**μυελόθεν**, = Lat. *medullitus*, *Gloss.*

**μυελόομαι**, Pass., *to be full of marrow*, ὁλοκαυτώματα μεμυελωμένα Lxx *Ps.*65(66).15.

**μυελοποιός**, όν, *making marrow*, i.e. *strengthening*, Sch.D Od. 2.290.

***μυελός**, ὁ, *marrow*, μυελὸς αὖτε σφονδυλίων ἔκπαλθ' Il.20.482, cf. Pl.*Ti.*73b sq., 91b, Thphr.*HP*1.2.6, etc.: pl., Ti.Locr.100b; *brain*, S.*Tr.*781, Gal.*UP*8.4; μ. ῥαχίτης spinal *cord*, Hp.*Coac.*499; μ. νωτιαῖος Diocl.*Fr.*141. 2. *fat*, χηνὸς μ. Hp.*Nat.Mul.*109, al. 3. *marrow* as good food, ἐπὶ γούνασι πατρὸς μυελὸν οἶον ἔδεσκε Il.22. 501 (but ἄλφιτα μ. ἀνδρῶν, as becoming or making *marrow*, Od.2. 290, cf. 20.108): metaph., φάγεσθε τὸν μ. τῆς γῆς Lxx *Ge.*45.18. 4. metaph., νεαρὸς μ. A.*Ag.*76 (anap.); πρὸς ἄκρον μ. ψυχῆς *marrow, inmost part*, E.*Hipp.*255 (anap.); Τρινακρίας μ., of Syracuse, Theoc. 28.18. 5. generally, *soft, marrow-like meat*, Alex.186.10. [ῠ always in Hom.: ῡ always in Att.; so also in the deriv. words.]

**μυελοτρεφής**, ές, *breeding marrow*, Tim.*Fr.*24.

**μυελώδης**, ες, *like marrow*, ὑγρότης Arist.*HA*517a3.

***μυέω**, (μύω, q. v.) *initiate into the mysteries*, μυῶν.. ἄλλους ξένους And.1.132, cf. *IG*1$^2$.6.113; ἐκ τοῦ μυεῖν καὶ ἐποπτεύειν Pl.*Ep.*333e, cf. D.59.21; ἐμύησε καὶ μυεῖ τοὺς Ἕλληνας Plu.2.607b: c. acc. cogn., ξένους ἐμύει θεοὺς J.*Ap.*2.37:—more freq. in Pass., *to be initiated*, ὁ βουλόμενος μυεῖται Hdt.8.65; ὅσοι μεμυήμεθα Ar.*Ra.*456; οἱ μεμυημένοι ib.158, And.1.28; δεῖ γάρ μυηθῆναί με πρὶν τεθνηκέναι Ar.*Pax* 375; μυηθῆναι ἀφ' ἑστίας, v. ἑστία; τοῦ ἀφ' ἑστίας μυουμένου prob. in *IG*1$^2$.6.108; μυηθεῖσαν ἀφ' ἑστίας *SIG*853 (Eleusis, i A.D.); θεοπρόποι ἦλθον.., οἵτινες μυηθέντες ἐνεβάτευσαν *OGI*530.15 (Notium, ii A.D.): c. acc. cogn., *to be initiated in* a thing, τὰ μυστήρια μυεῦνται Heraclit. 14; ὅστις τὰ Καβείρων ὄργια μεμύηται in the mysteries of the Cabiri, Hdt.2.51; τὰ μεγάλα (sc. μυστήρια) μεμύησαι, πρὶν τὰ σμικρά Pl. *Grg.*497c; τὰ ἐρωτικὰ μυηθῆναι Id.*Smp.*209e, cf. *Phdr.*250c; τὰ λεοντικὰ μ. Porph.*Antr.*15: also c. dat., ἐμυήθην θεοῖς Theophil.1.4; μυεῖσθαι γάμῳ Alciphr.1.4. II. generally, *teach, instruct*, c. inf., ἐμύησάς τινα ἰδεῖν *AP*7.385 (Phil.); ἀλλά μ' ἀνὴρ ἐμύησ' Ἑλικωνίδα (sc. εἶναι) ib.9.162:—Pass., μεμύημαι καὶ χορτάζεσθαι καὶ πεινᾶν *Ep.Phil.* 4.12; κυβερνᾶν μυηθήσομαι Alciphr.2.4.21.

**μυζ-άω**, *suck*, pres. part. μυζῶσαι Gal.7.130, cf. Paul.Aeg.6.41:—pres. **μυζέω**, Suid., Eust.1821.52: aor. part. μυζήσας Gal.4.550, 19.2, Anon.ap.Suid., Opp.*H.*2.407; cf. ἐκμυζάω, μύζω (B). **-ησις**, εως, ἡ, *sucking*, Gal.7.130. **-ητής**, οῦ, ὁ, *caterpillar*, Sm.*Ps.*77(78). 46.

**μύζουρις**, ἡ, (οὐρά) = *fellatrix*, *Com.Adesp.*1352.

**μύζω** (A), fut. μύξω D.L.10.118: aor. ἔμυξα Men.81:—*make the sound* μὺ μῦ, *mutter, moan*, A.*Eu.*118; μ. οἰκτισμὸν *make a* piteous *moaning*, ib.189: hence to denote displeasure, *murmur, growl*, Ar.*Th.*231; of the noise made by the dolphin, Arist.*HA*535b32; *rumble*, ἐπὶ τοῖσι σπλάγχνοισι μύζει Hp.*Morb.*2.55: impers., ἔμυζεν ἐν τῇ γαστρί Id.*Epid.*5.6: pf., μεμυζότε μυδαλέω τε Antim.90.

***μύζω** (B), = μυζάω, [τοὺς καλάμους] λαβόντα εἰς τὸ στόμα μύζειν X. *An.*4.5.27.

**μυήλα·** σάρξ τις ἐπαίρουσα τὴν γαστέρα, Hsch. (cf. μύλη IV).

**μύησις** [ῡ], εως, ἡ, *initiation*, Androt.34, *OGI*764.7 (Pergam., ii B.C.), Herm. in *Phdr.*p.158 A., etc.: in pl., Ph.1.156, Plu.2.169d, *SIG* 1267.27 (Ios, iii A.D.), Iamb.*VP*17.74.

**μυηφόνον**, τό, = σκίλλα, Phan.Hist.27.

**μύθα·** φωνή (Cypr.), Hsch.

**μῡθ-ᾰρεύομαι**, = μυθέομαι, Dius ap.Stob.4.21.17. **-άριον**, τό, Dim. of μῦθος, Str.13.1.69, Cleom.2.1, Porph.*Chr.*54; τὰ Αἰσώπεια μ. Plu.2.14e. **-αρχοι·** οἱ προεστῶτες τῶν στάσεων, Hsch.; cf. μῦθος III. **-έομαι**, Ep. 2 sg. μυθεῖαι (for μυθέεαι) Od.8.180, μυθέαι 2.202: 3 pl. Ion. impf. μυθέσκοντο Il.18.289: fut. μυθήσομαι 2.488, S.*Aj.*865: Ep. aor. μυθήσατο Il.17.200: (μῦθος): I. *speak*, abs., Il.7.76, 8.40, etc.; μειλίχως μυθεύμενος Semon.7.18; *converse*, ἀλλήλοισιν A.R.1.458: c. acc. et inf., *say that..*, Il.21.462: c. inf., *order*, A.*Pr.*664, prob. (for μυθεύομαι) in Perict.ap.Stob.4.28.19: c. acc., *tell, recount*, πληθὺν δ' οὐκ ἂν ἐγὼ μυθήσομαι οὐδ' ὀνομήνω Il.2.488, cf. Od.11.517; οὕς κεν ἐῢ γνοίην καί τ' οὔνομα μυθησαίμην Il.3.235; *tell of*, Σκύλλην Od.12.223; κήδεα 11.376: c. acc. cogn., *speak, utter*, μῦθον μ. *explain* the reason, 3.140; κερτομίας, ὀνείδεα μυθήσασθαι, Il. 20.202,246; ἀληθέα 6.382; ἐτήτυμα Hes.*Op.*10; μέγα Theoc.10.20; νημερτέα Il.6.376; νημερτέως Od.19.269; τὰ δ' ἄλλ' ἐν Ἅιδου τοῖς κάτω μυθήσομαι S. l. c.: c. dupl. acc., *call* so and so, πόλιν μ. πολύχρυσον Il.18.289: folld. by relat. or interrog. clause, τόν τοι μυθήσομαι, οἷος ἔην Od.19.245, cf. Pi.*P.*4.298. II. *say over to oneself, con over, consider*, dub. in Od.13.191: in full, προτὶ ὃν μυθήσατο θυμόν Il.17.200; πάντα Ζεὺς μυθεῖται Democr.30.—Used in Ep. and Trag.; never in Com. or Att. Prose.—Act. **μυθέω** in Democr.297 as v.l. for μυθοπλαστέω; μυθεῦσαι (i.e. μυθοῦσαι) dub. in E.*IA*789 (lyr.); μυθήσας· εἰπών, Phot. **-ευμα**, ατος, τό, *story*, D.H. 4.3, Plu.*Mar.*11, Man.4.447 (pl.); *plot* of a play, Arist.*Po.*1460a 29. **-εύω**, pf. μεμύθευκα Phld.*Mus.*p.24 K.: later form of μυθέομαι, E.*HF*77; ἅπαντα μυθεύσασα Ezek.*Exag.*34: c. acc. et inf., Phld. l. c., al.:—Pass., *to be spoken of*, E.*Ion* 196 (lyr.); ὡς μεμύθευται βροτοῖς as *is related* by mortals, *as the story goes*, ib.265. II.

*relate fabulously*, Str.1.2.35; πράξεις μεμύθευκε Socr.*Ep.*30.9: c. acc. et inf., Arist.*Mir.*836ᵇ1:—Pass., τὰ μυθευόμενα λιθοῦσθαι Id.*PA*641ᵃ 20; μυθεύονται κατασχεῖν τὴν νῆσον Str.14.2.8, cf. D.C.51.26: without inf., Palaeph.4. **-έω**, v. μυθέομαι. **-ηγορέω**, *tell stories*, in Pass., Procl.*Proll.Hes.*p.5 G. **-ήρια**, τά, *traditions*, a word coined to explain μυστήρια, *EM*595.48. **-ητῆρες**· στασιασταί, Hsch.; cf. μυθιήτης. **-ητής**, οῦ, ὁ, *relater of* μῦθοι, Antig.*Mir.*120. **-ιάζομαι**, *recount fables*, Babr.*Prooem.*ii. **-ίαμβοι** [ῐ], οἱ, the name given to a collection of Fables, such as those of Babr., ib. **-ίδιον**, τό, Dim. of μῦθος, Luc.*Philops.*2. ⊛ **-ίζω**, = μυθέομαι, Dor. μυθίσδω Theoc. 10.58, 20.11; Lacon. μυσίδδω Ar.*Lys.*94, 1076: aor. μυσίξαι ib.981:—Med., ψεύδεα κατὰ πάντων μ. Perict.ap.Stob.4.28.19, cf. Orph.*A.* 191. **-ῑήτης**, ου, ὁ, in pl., = στασιασταί, στασιῶται, Anacr.16 (cf. μυθητῆρες, μύθαρχοι, μῦθος III); in sg., οὐ μ., οὐ δικασπόλος κεῖνος (sc. Νῖνος) Phoen.1.7. **-ικός**, ή, όν, *mythic, legendary*, μ. τις ὕμνος Pl.*Phdr.*265c; οἱ μ. χρόνοι D.H.1.2; τὰ μ. *books of legends*, title of treatise by Neanthes, Ath.13.572e. Adv. -κῶς Arist.*Metaph.*1000ᵃ 18, 1074ᵇ4, *Cael.*284ᵃ23; opp. ἀληθῶς, Phld.*Rh.* 2.53S.: Comp. -ωτέρως or -ώτερον, Sch.Lyc.18, Tz.*H.*2.823. **-ίσδω**, Dor. for μυθίζω. **-ιστορία**, ἡ, *fabulous history*, Capitol.*Macrin.*1. **-ιστορικός**, ή, όν, *containing fabulous history*, *volumina* Vopisc.*Firm.*1.

**μῡθο-γρᾰφέω**, *write fabulous accounts*, c. acc., τὰ περί τι μ. Str.3.4. 4, cf. Jul.*Or.*7.216d. **-γρᾰφία**, ἡ, *writing of fables*, Str.1.2.35, 8.3.9 (pl.). **-γρᾰφος** [ᾰ], ὁ, *writer of legends*, Plb.4.40.2, Phld. *Rh.*2.187S., D.H.1.13, D.S.4.7, Plu.*Thes.*1; Ἀπόλλωνος καὶ Μουσῶν μ. *IG*12(7).273 (Amorgos). **-ειδῶς**, Adv., = μυθωδῶς, Procl.*in R.* 1.15 K. **-λέσχης**, ου, ὁ, *mythologist*, Eust.768.29.

**μῡθολογ-εύω**, *tell word for word*, τινί τι Od.12.450; εἰρημένα μ. ib.453: generally, *relate*, Ps.-Phoc.68, prob. rest. in Sapph.*Supp.* 7.4. ⊛ **-έω**, *tell mythic tales*, such as those of Homer, Isoc.6.24, Pl.*R.*392b, Longin.34.2; πολλὰ τοιαῦτα μ. Pl.*Grg.*493d: folld. by a Relat., μ. ὡς.. X.*Smp.*8.28; μ. ὅτι.. Hp.*Art.*53. 2. c. acc., *tell as a legend* or *mythic tale*, μ. τοὺς πολέμους τῶν ἡμιθέων Isoc.2.49: c. inf., of an animal, ὃν.. μυθολογοῦσι γενέσθαι ἐκ πυρκαϊᾶς which *they fable, fabulously report* to derive its birth, Arist.*HA*609ᵇ10; καθάπερ καὶ τὸν Μίδαν.. μυθολογοῦσι (sc. ἀπολέσθαι) Id.*Pol.*1257ᵇ16, cf. 1274ᵃ 39:—Pass., οἷαι μυθολογοῦνται παλαιαὶ γενέσθαι φύσεις such as they *are fabled* to have been, Pl.*R.*588c, cf. Arist.*HA*617ᵃ5: impers., μυθολογεῖται.. τοὺς Ἀργοναύτας τὸν Ἡρακλέα καταλιπεῖν *the legend goes* that.., Id.*Pol.*1284ᵃ22; μ. περὶ τῆς ζωῆς ὡς ὃν μακρόβιον Id. *HA*578ᵇ23: abs., *become mythical*, D.60.9, etc.; τὰ μυθολογούμενα *fabulous tales*, Arist.*HA*578ᵇ24, cf. Pl.*R.*378e. II. *invent like a mythical tale*, μ. πολιτείαν *frame an imaginary* constitution, ib. 501e. III. *tell stories, converse*, περί τινος Id.*Phd.*61e, *Phdr.* 276e. IV. *relate*, generally with a notion of exaggeration, [Αἴσωπος] ἐμυθολόγησεν ὡς.. Arist.*Mete.*356ᵇ12, cf. Nymphod.12; τὰ τῶν Ἑλλήνων καλὰ Polydeuces ap. Philostr.*VS*2.12.2. **-ημα**, ατος, τό, *mythical narrative* or *description*, Pl.*Phdr.*229c, *Lg.*663e, Plu.*Thes.* 14, D.C.50.12. **-ητέον**, *one must tell as a legend*, Γιγαντομαχίας Pl.*R.*378c. **-ία**, ἡ, *romance, fiction*, ib.394b, al.; οἱ λόγοι καὶ αἱ μ. Id.*Hp.Ma.*298a. 2. *legend*, Corn.*ND*8. II. *story-telling*, Pl. *Lg.*752a, Plu.2.133e (pl.). **-ικός**, ή, όν, *poetical, inventive*, Pl.*Phd.* 61b. ⊛ **-ος**, ὁ, *teller of legends, romancer*, joined with ποιητής, Id. *R.*392d, cf. 398b, *Lg.*664d, Thphr.*HP*4.13.2, Lxx *Ba.*3.23; used of Hdt. by Arist.*GA*756ᵇ6. II. Adj. *mythological*, μνήμη Call.*Aet.* 3.1.55. 2. *prating*, Man.4.445.

**μῡθόομαι**, = μυθέομαι I, A.*Ag.*1368 codd. (leg. θυμοῦσθαι).

**μῡθο-πλάνος** [ᾰ], ον, *fabulous, fictitious*, λόγοι Zos.Alch.p.232 B. (fort. -πλαστος). **-πλαστέω**, *invent*, ψεύδεα Democr.297 (cf. μυθέομαι):—Pass., Tz.*H.*10.41. **-πλάστης**, ου, ὁ, *coiner of legends*, Lyc.764, Ph.1.405 (pl.). **-πλόκος**, ον, *weaving fables*, of Eros, Sapph.125 (proparox.).

**μῡθοποι-έω**, *relate a fable, invent*, τὰ καθ' Ἅιδου D.S.1.92, cf. 4. 35. **-ημα**, ατος, τό, *fabulous narrative*, Plu.2.17a, Ael.*NA*7. 29. **-ησις**, εως, ἡ, = sq., S.E.*M.*9.192. **-ία**, ἡ, *making of fables, invention*, Str.1.1.19, al., D.S.1.96, Ph.1.177 (pl.), Corn.*ND* 17 (pl.), Plu.2.348a. **-ός**, ὁ, *composer of fiction*, Pl.*R.*377b, Luc. *Herm.*73; *fabulist*, Jul.*Or.*7.227b.

⊛ **μῦθος**, ὁ, *word, speech*, freq. in Hom. and other Poets, in sg. and pl., ἔπος καὶ μῦθος Od.11.561; opp. ἔργον, μύθων τε ῥητῆρ' ἔμεναι πρηκτῆρά τε ἔργων Il.9.443, cf. 19.242; esp. *mere word*, μύθοισιν, opp. ἔγχεϊ, 18.252; ἔργῳ κοὐκέτι μύθῳ A.*Pr.*1080 (anap.), etc.:—in special relations: 2. *public speech*, μ. ἄνδρεσσι μελήσει Od.1.358; μύθοισιν σκολιοῖς Hes.*Op.*194; μύθου ἐπισχεσίη the submission of a *plea*, Od.21.71; πρὶν ἂν ἀμφοῖν μ. ἀκούσῃς, οὐκ ἂν δικάσαις Ar.*V.*725; μύθοισι κεκάσθαι to be skilled in *speech*, Od.7.157. 3. *conversation*, mostly in pl., 4.214, 239, etc. 4. *thing said, fact, matter*, μῦθον δέ τοι οὐκ ἐπικεύσω ib.744; τὸν ὄντα μ. E.*El.*346; *threat, command*, ἠπείλησεν μῦθον Il.1.388, cf. 25, 16.83; *charge, mission*, 9.625; *counsel, advice*, 7.358. 5. *thing thought, unspoken word, purpose, design*, 1.545 (pl.); μύθων οὓς μνηστῆρες ἐνὶ φρεσὶ βυσσοδόμευον Od.4.676, cf. 777; ἔχετ' ἐν φρεσὶ μῦθον 15.445; ἔχε σιγῇ μ., ἐπίτρεψον δὲ θεοῖσι 19.502, cf. 11.442; *matter*, θεοῖσι μῦθον ἐπιτρέψαι 22. 289; μῦθον μυθείσθην, τοῦ εἵνεκα λαὸν ἄγειραν the *reason* why.., 3. 140. 6. *saying*, κατὰ τὸν ἡμέτερον μ. Pl.*Epin.*980a; οὐκ ἐμὸς ὁ μ. ἀλλ'.. E.*Fr.*484, cf. Pl.*Smp.*177a, Call.*Lav.Pall.*56, Ph.1.601, Plu. 2.661a; *saw, proverb*, τριγέρων μ. τάδε φωνεῖ A.*Ch.*314 (anap.). 7. *talk* of men, *rumour*, ἀγγελίαν.. τὰν ὁ μέγας μ. ἀέξει S.*Aj.*226 (lyr.), cf. 188 (lyr., pl.), E.*IA*72; *report, message*, S.*Tr.*67 (pl.), E.*Ion* 1340. II. *tale, story, narrative*, Od.3.94, 4.324, S.*Ant.*11, etc.: in Hom. like the later λόγος, without distinction of true or false, μ. παιδὸς *of* or *about* him, Od.11.492: so in Trag., ἀκούσει μῦθον ἐν βραχεῖ λόγῳ (χρόνῳ cod. M.) A.*Pers.*713; μύθων τῶν Λιβυστικῶν Id.*Fr.*139.1: in Prose, τὸν εἰκότα μ. the likely *story*, likelihood, Pl.*Ti.*29d: prov., μ. ἀπώλετο, either of a *story* which never comes to an end, or of one told to those who do not listen, Cratin.59, Crates Com.21, Pl.*Tht.* 164d, cf. *R.*621b, *Lg.*645b, *Phlb.*14a; μ. ἐσώθη 'that's the end of the *story*', Phot. 2. *fiction* (opp. λόγος, *historic truth*), Pi.*O.*1.29 (pl.), *N.*7.23 (pl.), Pl.*Phd.*61b, *Prt.*320c, 324d, etc. 3. generally, *fiction*, μ. ἴδιοι Phld.*Po.*5.5; *legend, myth*, Hdt.2.45, Pl.*R.*330d, *Lg.* 636c, etc.; ὁ περὶ θεῶν μ. Epicur.*Ep.*3p.65 U.; τοὺς μ. τοὺς ἐπιχωρίους γέγραφεν *SIG*382.7 (Delos, iii B.C.). 4. *professed work of fiction, children's story, fable*, Pl.*R.*377a; of Aesop's *fables*, Arist. *Mete.*356ᵇ11. 5. *plot* of a comedy or tragedy, Id.*Po.*1449ᵇ5, 1450ᵃ 4, 1451ᵃ16. III. = στάσις, Panyas. in *Coll.Alex.*p.249, v.l. in Batr. 135; cf. μυθιήτης.

**μῡθουργ-έω**, = μυθοποιέω, Sch.Lyc.17 (Pass.). **-ημα**, ατος, τό, = μυθοποίημα, ibid. **-ία**, ἡ, = μυθοποιία, Tz.*H.*8.519, Poet.ap.Sch. Opp.*H.*1.619.

**μῡθ-ύδριον**, τό, Dim. of μῦθος, Tz.*H.*4.434. **-ώδης**, ες, *legendary, fabulous*, λόγοι μ., opp. ἀληθινοί, Pl.*R.*522a, cf. D.23.65, etc.; τὸ μ. *the domain of fable*, Th.1.21; τὸ μὴ μ. αὐτῶν their non-*fabulous* character, ib.22; τὰ μ. καὶ παιδαριώδη Arist.*Metaph.*995ᵃ4: Comp. -έστερος Antig.*Mir.*1, Str.4.4.6: Sup. -έστατος Isoc.2.48, Plb.34. 11.20, Phld.*Po.*5.4. Adv. -δῶς Aristeas 168, D.S.4.6. **-ωδικός**, ή, όν, *connected with mythology*, Eust. ad D.P.62. **-ῳδός**, ὁ, *singer of mythic tales*, cj. for μυδῴδας (acc. pl.) in *Cat.Cod.Astr.*8(4).211.

**μυῖα**, Att. **μυῖα** Thphr.*HP*3.7.5, Phot.: ἡ:—*fly*, Il.2.469, 4.131, Simon.32, etc.; *carrion fly, bluebottle*, Il.19.25, 31; *gall-insect*, Thphr. l. c.: prov., μυίης θάρσος, of excessive boldness, Il.17.570; ἐάν τις.. ὥσπερ μ. προσπτῆται X.*Mem.*3.11.5; δειπνεῖν ἄκλητος μ. *a fly* for coming to dinner uninvited, Antiph.195.7; ἐλέφαντα ἐκ μυίας ποιεῖν 'to make a mountain out of a molehill', Luc.*Musc.Enc.*12; μυῖα στρατιῶτις, μ. κύων, ibid.; δραίνω μυῖ' ὅσον Herod.1.15. II. χαλκῆ μυῖα a game like *blindman's-buff*, Id.9a, Poll.9.123; cf. μυῖνδα. III. used by peasants of *bees*, Eust.257.6. (Cf. Lith. *musìa* 'fly', Lat. *musca*, etc.)

**μυία**· κοινά, ἀναιδῆ, Hsch.

⊛ **μυίαγρος**, ὁ, *fly-catcher*, name of an Elean god, Plin.*HN*10.75 (prob.); ἥρως μ., in Arcadia, Paus.8.26.7.

**μῡΐδιον**, τό, Dim. of μῦς, *little mouse*, Arr.*Epict.*1.23.4, M.Ant. 7.3.

**μυῑκός**, ή, όν, *of* or *belonging to a fly*, *Gloss.*

**μυῖνδα** παίζειν, *play at* χαλκῆ μυῖα, Poll.9.110, 113, Hsch.

**μύϊνος** [ῠ], η, ον, *mouse-coloured*, *EM*790.4, Phot. s. v. φαιόν.

**μυιο-ειδής**, ές, *like a fly*, Cass.*Pr.*19. **-θήρας**, ου, ὁ, *fly-hunter*, Hsch. s. v. μύαγρος, Suid. s. v. μυίαγρος. **-κέφᾰλον**, τό, a complaint in the eyes, in which the uvea protrudes *like a fly's head*, Gal. 14.768, Paul.Aeg.3.22: **μυοκέφᾰλον**, Gal.19.434, Aët.7.35, Alex. Trall.2; κολλύριον τοῦ Ζωΐλου πρὸς μυοκεφάλους (sic) Gal.12. 771. **-πτερον**, τό, = θλάσπι, Ps.-Dsc.2.156. **-σόβη**, ἡ, *fly-flap*, Men.503, Anaxipp.7, Ael.*NA*15.14, cf. Poll.10.94; of a *long beard*, *AP*11.156 (Ammian.):—also **μυοσόβη** (q. v.). **-σόβιον**, τό, Dim. of foreg., *Gloss.* **-σόβος**, ον, *flapping away flies*, *AP*9. 764 (Paul. Sil.).

**μῡΐσκη**, ἡ, Dim. of μῦς II, *small sea-mussel*, Diph.Siph.ap.Ath. 3.90d, Xenocr.ap.Orib.2.58.92: **μῡΐσκος**, ὁ, Marc.Sid.38, Plin.*HN* 32.149.

**μυῖτις**, ιδος, ἡ, = θλάσπι, Ps.-Dsc.2.156.

**μυιώδης**, ες, = μυίαγρος, at Elis, Plin.*HN*29.106.

**μυιών**, v. μυών.

**μῡκάμων** [ᾱ], ονος, ὁ, Dor. for *μυκήμων, *bellowing*, Ἅιδης *Hymn. Is.*42.

⊛ **μῡκάομαι**, fut. -ήσομαι *AP*9.730 (Demetr. Bith.), Luc.*Phal.*1.11: aor. ἐμυκησάμην Ar.*Nu.*292, Theoc.16.37: used by Hom. once in pres. part., Od.10.413, elsewh. in Ep. aor. μύκον [ῠ], Ep. pf. μέμῡκα (also in A.*Supp.*352 (lyr.)): plpf. ἐμεμύκειν or μεμύκειν Od.12.395: Ep. iterat. μύκεσκε only in *EM*624.40:—prop. of oxen, *low, bellow*, ὁ δὲ μακρὰ μεμυκὼς [ὁ ταῦρος] Il.18.580; μεμυκὼς ἠΰτε ταῦρος 21.237; πόριες.. μυκώμεναι Od.10.413, cf. A. l. c., E.*Ba.*738; of a calf, Theoc. l. c.; of Heracles in agony, E.*HF*870 (troch.: so comically, ἔβλεψεν δριμὺ κἀμυκᾶτο Ar.*Ra.*562); οἷον μυκτὴρ μυκᾶται Id.*V.*1488; μάτηρ κεφαλὰν μυκήσατο παιδὸς ἑλοῖσα Theoc.26.20; ὥσπερ λέων μ. *Apoc.*10.3. 2. of things, πύλαι μύκον οὐρανοῦ Il.5.749; μέγα δ' ἀμφὶ πύλαι μύκον 12.460; of a shield, μέγα δ' ἀμφὶ σάκος μύκε δουρὸς ἀκωκῇ *rang*, 20.260; of meat, ἀμφ' ὀβελοῖσι μεμύκει *bellowed* upon the spits (a portent), Od.12.395; μέμυκε δὲ γαῖα καὶ ὕλη Hes.*Op.*508; βροντῆς μυκησαμένης Ar.*Nu.*292; κόχλον ἑλὼν μυκήσατο κοῖλον Theoc.22.75:—rare in Prose, Pl.*R.*396b, 615e, Arist.*Mete.*368ᵃ25.—An aor. Act., [τυμπάνου] βαρὺ μυκήσαντος *AP*6.220.11 (Diosc.). (Onomatopoeic word.)

**μυκαρίς**· νυκτερίς, Hsch.

**μῡκή** (on the accent v. Hdn.Gr.1.313), ἡ, = μύκησις, A.R.4.1285 (pl.), prob. in Aristias 6 (pl.: μύκαισι codd. Ath.).

**μύκη** [ῠ], ὁ or ἡ, = μύκης (q. v.). II. μύκη· ἡ θήκη, Suid.

**μῡκ-ηδόν**, Adv. *with bellowings*, Poet. in *POxy.*864.22. **-ηθμός**, ὁ, *lowing, bellowing*, of oxen, Il.18.575, Od.12.265, A.R.3.1297, etc.; but μυκηθμοῖσι.. μήλων *with bleatings* of sheep, A.*Fr.*158; ὁ μ. τῆς γῆς *rumbling*, Luc.*Peregr.*39. ⊛ **-ημα**, ατος, τό, = foreg., βοῶν μυκή-

ματα E.*Ba*.691, cf. Call.*Del*.310, A.R.1.1269, etc.; μ. λεαίνας Theoc. 26.21; *roar* of thunder, A.*Pr*.1062 (anap.):—rare in Prose, of a vase, Arist.*Pr*.938ᵃ10; of the earth, Id.*Mu*.396ᵃ13, D.C.68.24; of winds in a cave, Corn.*ND*22.

**Μυκήνη**, ἡ, and **Μυκῆναι**, αἱ, *Mycene, Mycenae*: Hom. uses both sg. (Il.4.52, Od.3.304, al.), and pl. (only in Il.2.569, 4.376); the pl. prevails in Att., Th.1.10, etc.:—Adj. **Μυκηναῖος**, α, ον, *Mycenaean*, Il.15.638, etc.: Dor. Subst. **Μυκᾱνεύς**, έως, ὁ, *a Mycenaean*, *SIG*31 (Delph., v B.C.):—fem. Adj. **Μυκηνίς**, ίδος, Critias 16.12 D.: Adv. **Μυκήνηθεν**, *from Mycene*, Il.9.44: Dor. **Μυκᾱνέᾱθεν** *IG*4.492 (Mycenae, vi B.C.).

**μύκηρος**, ὁ, = ἀμυγδάλη, *almond*, Lacon. and Tenian word, Seleuc. ap.Ath.2.52c: Lacon. also **μούκηρος** Pamphil.ib.53b:—hence **μουκηρόβατος** (leg. -βαγός, i.e. -ϝᾱγός, from ἄγνυμι), ὁ, = καρυοκατάκτης, Id.ibid.; written **μουκηρόβας** in Hsch.

⊕ **μύκης** [ῡ], ητος (but Ion. gen. -εω Archil.47, acc. -ην Hecat.22 J. (-ῆν codd.), Nic.*Fr*.72.7; Dor. and Att. nom. pl. μύκαι Epich.155, Thphr.*Sign*.42, Diocl.*Fr*.119; acc. pl. μύκας *PSI*6.620.31 (iii B.C.), censured by Phryn.178; dat. pl. τοῖς μύκαις Diph.Siph.ap.Ath.2.62c), ὁ, *mushroom* or other *fungus*, Epich. l.c., Antiph.188, 226.4, 227.11, Ephipp.27, Polioch.2.4, Thphr.*HP*1.1.11, *PSI* l.c., Nic.*Al*.525, Dsc. 4.82, Paus.2.16.3. II. *any knobbed round body*, shaped like a mushroom, 1. *chape* or *cap at the end of a scabbard*, Hecat. l.c., Hdt.3.64, Paus. l.c. 2. *membrum virile*, Archil. l.c., Hsch. 3. *fleshy excrescence*, such as forms on wounds, Hp.*Morb*.2.50, Gal.17(1).703. b. *excrescence* on trees, Thphr.*HP*4.14.3. 4. *stump of an olive* cut down, *IG*2.1055.43. 5. *snuff of a lamp-wick*, Ar.*V*.262, Thphr.*Sign*. l.c., Arat.976, Call.*Fr*.47, *AP*5.262 (Agath.). 6. μύκαι οἷς τὰ ἱμάτια βάπτουσι, dub. sens. in Zopyr.ap.Orib.14.62.1.—Fem. only in Epich. l.c. (where however οἵαν αἱ μύκαι is prob. cj.) and Thphr.*Sign*. l.c. (Prob. cogn. with μύξα A.)

**μύκ-ησις** [ῡ], εως, ἡ, = μυκηθμός, Arist.*Pr*.938ᵃ10, Sch.A.R.4.1285 (pl.). **-ητής**, οῦ, Dor. **μῡκᾱτάς**, ᾶ, ὁ, *bellower*, of oxen, Theoc. 8.6; of Poseidon, Corn.*ND*22. **-ητίας** σεισμός, ὁ, an earthquake *accompanied with roaring underground*, Arist.*Mu*.396ᵃ11 (but perh. rather **μυκῆται**, as Stob.). **-ητικός**, ή, όν, *bellowing*, Corn.*ND* 22, S.E.*M*.11.38.

**μυκήτῐνος**, η, ον, *made of mushrooms*, Luc.*VH*1.16.

**μυκήτωρ**, ορος, ὁ, poet. for μυκητής, Nonn.*D*.3.237.

⊕ **μύκλα**, ἡ, and ⊕**μύκλος**, ὁ, *black stripe* on the neck and feet of the ass, acc. to Hsch.; or *a fold on its neck*, acc. to *EM*594.18; of the *ass* itself, *PTeb*.409.7 (i A.D., μοικ-). II. **μύκλοι**, οἱ, *lewd, lustful* persons, Hsch., cf. Archil.183, Lyc.771; μ. κάνθων, of the ass, Id. 816; cf. μυχλός.

**μυκληρόν**· συνεχές, ἀχανές, Hsch. **μύκον**, v. μυκάομαι.

**Μύκονος** [ῠ], ἡ, *Myconus*, one of the Cyclades, Hdt.6.118, etc.; the people were said to be all bald, Lucil.1211, Str.10.5.9: whence (acc. to Donat. ad Ter.*Hec*.440) the proverb μία Μύκονος '*it's all one, all alike*', Plu.2.616b, Them.*Or*.21.250c, Zen.5.17 (with a different expl.), prob. cj. in Luc.*DMort*.1.3; πάνθ' ὑπὸ μίαν Μύκονον Str. l.c. (with a third expl., cf. Eust. ad D.P.525): Adj. **Μυκόνιος**, α, ον, prov. Μ. γείτων, of a bad neighbour, Zen.5.21 (Μηκώνιος codd., Μυκώνιος Phot., Suid.), cf. Cratin.328, *Com.Adesp*.439; also ἡ λεγομένη Μυκόνιος ἀγροικία Jul.*Mis* 349d.

**μῠκόομαι**, (μύκης II. 3) *become fungous*, of ulcers, ἐμυκώθη Hp.*Mul*. 1.40 codd. and Gal.19.97; cf. μυλόομαι.

**μῦκος**· μιαρός, and **μυκός**· ἄφωνος, κτλ., Hsch.

**μυκτήρ**, ῆρος, ὁ, (μύσσομαι) *nostril*, φλέγει δὲ μ., of the fire-breathing bull of Aeetes, S.*Fr*.336, cf. Ar.*V*.1488, etc.: freq. in pl., μυκτῆρσιν ἐρευνᾶν Emp.101, cf. Hp.*Art*.37, *Acut*.(*Sp*.)23, Sophr.135, Hdt.3.87, Ar.*Ra*.893, X.*Smp*.5.6, Antiph.217.6, Ph.1.249, al.: dat. pl. μυκτήρεσσιν, in a prescription, *POxy*.1088.32 (i A.D.): metaph., of a lamp-*nozzle*, Ar.*Ec*.5. 2. from the use of the nose to express ridicule, *sneerer*, of Socrates, Timo 25; in the abstract, *sarcasm, raillery*, μ. πολιτικώτατος Longin.34.2, cf. Plu.2.860e; μ. Ἀττικός Luc. *Prom.Es*1; κεράσας μυκτῆρι φρόνημα *AP*9.188. II. an elephant's *trunk*, Arist.*HA*497ᵇ26, *PA*659ᵃ12; also, the *funnel* of the cuttle-fish, Id.*HA*541ᵇ15.

**μυκτηρι-άζω, -ασμός, -αστής**, = μυκτηρίζω, -ισμός, -ιστής, *Gloss*.

**μυκτηρ-ίζω**, *turn up the nose, sneer at*, Lys.*Fr*.323 S., Lxx *Pr*.1.30, al., S.E.*M*.1.217:—Pass., *to be mocked*, Lxx *Je*.20.7: hence, *to be outwitted*, *Ep.Gal*.6.7. II. *bleed at the nose*, Hp.*Epid*.7.123. **-ισμα**, ατος, τό, *turning up the nose, sneering*, Hsch. s.v. ἀποσκώμματα. **-ισμός**, ὁ, = foreg., Lxx *Ps*.34(35).16, al., Anon. *Oxy*.2086 *Fr*.1ʳ14; *sarcasm*, Quint.*Inst*.8.6.59: pl., Phld.*Herc*.1457.9. 2. *cheating*, Men.1039. **-ιστής**, οῦ, ὁ, *sneerer, mocker*, Ath.5.182a, 187b. **-όθεν**, Adv. *out of the nose*, *AP*10.75 (Pall.).

**μυκτηρόκομπος**, ον, *sounding from the nostril*, πνεύματα A.*Th*. 464.

**μύκωμα** [ῡ], ατος, τό, = μύκημα, *PMag.Par*.1.657.

**μύκων**· σωρός, θημών, Hsch. **μυλαβρίς**, v. μυλακρίς.

**μυλαικά**, τά, name of a species of figs, Ath.3.78a.

⊕ **μῠλ-αῖος**, ον, *working in a mill*, χείρ *AP*9.418 (Antip.). II. μυλαῖον, τό, = μύλη I, *Sammelb*.5246.4 (i B.C.), *PRyl*.167.10 (i A.D.), etc. ⊕ **-ακρὶς** λᾶας, ἡ, *millstone*, Alex.Aet.3.31. II. **μῠλακρίς**, ίδος, ἡ, *cockroach* found in mills and bakehouses, Ar.*Fr*.583:—written **μῠλαβρίς** in Pl.Com.73 (ap.Phot.): both forms in Poll.7.180. **-ακρος**, ὁ, *millstone*, Alcm.23.31. II. μύλακροι· γομφίοι ὀδόντες, Hsch. **-αλγία**, ἡ, *toothache*, Dsc.3.78 (pl.), Gal.12.867. **-αξ**, ἄκος, ὁ, *millstone, any large round stone*, Il.12.161, *AP*9.418 (Antip.), 546 (Antiphil.), Opp.*C*.3.137. **-άριον**, τό, Dim. of μύλη I, of a spell used in grinding salt, *PMag.Par*.1.3087.

⊕ **μυλάσασθαι**· τὸ σῶμα ἢ τὴν κεφαλὴν σμήξασθαι (Cypr.), Hsch.

**μῠλ-εργάτης**, ου, Dor. **-τᾱς**, ὁ, *miller*, *AP*7.394 (Phil.). **-εύς**, έως, ὁ, epith. of Zeus, *guardian of mills*, Lyc.435. **-η**, ἡ, *mill*: in Hom., *hand-mill* turned by women, αἱ μὲν ἀλετρεύουσι μύλης ἔπι μήλοπα καρπόν Od.7.104; γυνὴ.. ἀλετρὶς πλησίον, ἔνθ' ἄρα οἱ μύλαι ἥατο 20.106; μύλην στρέφειν, περιάγειν, περιφέρειν, περιελαύνειν, Poll.7.180; μηδὲ μύλαν (Dor.) ἐνεῖμεν μηδὲ ὅλμον *IG*2².1126.24 (Amphict. Delph., iv B.C.): Cret. acc. pl. μύλανς *Schwyzer* 180.6. II. *nether millstone* (the upper being ὄνος), Ar.*V*.648: pl., αἱ μύλαι Arist.*Mete*.383ᵇ7, cf. Pherecr.10. III. *knee-pan*, Hp.*Off*.9, *Com.Adesp*.450, Arist.*HA* 494ᵃ5, Paus.1.35.5. IV. *hard formation* in a woman's womb, Hp.*Mul*.1.71, 2.178, Arist.*GA*775ᵇ25. V. pl., *molars*, Lxx *Jb*. 29.17, Anon.Lond.24.24, Gal.*UP*9.15: sg., of an ass's *tooth*, *PMag. Lond*.125.22, al. VI. = μῶλυ, Gal.12.80: root of λάπαθον, Aët. 1.251. (Cf. Lat. *molo*, Goth. *malan* 'grind', etc.) ⊕ **-ηβόρος**, ον, *millstone-eating*, μυὸς οἷα μυληβόρου Nic.*Th*.446 (οἷ' ἀμυληβόρου cj. Schneid.). **-ηθρίς**, ίδος, ἡ, = μυλακρίς II, Poll.7.19. **-ήκορον**, τό, (κόρος C) *broom for cleaning a mill*, Fest. s.v. *molucrum*, Poll.6.94: hence generally, *broom*, Archipp.22. **-ητικὴ** ἔμπλαστρος, remedy *for toothache*, Gal.12.877. **-ήφᾰτος**, ον, (θείνω) *bruised in a mill*, εἴκοσι.. μέτρα μυληφάτου ἀλφίτου ἀκτῆς Od. 2.355, cf. A.R.1.1073, Lyc.578. **-ιαῖοι** ὀδόντες, οἱ, = μύλαι V, Ruf. ap.Orib.49.27.2. **-ίας**, ου, masc. Adj. *of* or *for a mill*, λίθος μ. *millstone*, Pl.*Hp.Ma*.292d, cf. Arist.*Mete*.383ᵇ12; also, rock *for millstones*, Str.6.2.3, 10.5.16. **-ιάω**, (μύλη V) *gnash* or *grind the teeth*, only in Ep. part., λυγρὸν μυλιόωντες (with ῡ metri gr.), Hes.*Op*. 530 (μαλκιόωντες, i.e. μαλκίοντες, Crates Gramm.). **-ικός**, ή, όν, (μύλη I) *for a mill*, λίθος *Ev.Luc*.17.2. II. (μύλη V) *of* or *for the grinders*, ἡ μ. (sc. ἔμπλαστρος) remedy *for toothache*, Gal.12.869, 877. **-ινος**, η, ον, *made of millstone*, σορός *CIG*3371 (Smyrna); παραστάς *SIG*996.15 (ibid.). **-ιος**, α, ον, = μυλίας, λίθος Procop. *Aed*.2.6.7, 8.18. ⊕ **-ίτης** [ῑ], ου, ὁ, = μυλίας, λίθος Gal.10.958, 19.118, Procop.*Aed*.2.5.4. II. *molar tooth*, Gal.14.722.

**μυλλαίνω**, (μυλλός A) *distort the mouth, make mouths* or *mock at*, Phot. s.v. σιλλαίνει. **μυλλάς**, άδος, ἡ, (μύλλω) *prostitute*, Id. (μυλάς cod.), Suid. (v.l. μυλάς). **μυλλάω**, = μυλλαίνω, in pf. μεμύλληκε, Hsch. **μύλλη**· λεία, Id.; cf. μυμεῖ. **μυλλίζω**, = μυλλαίνω, Phot. and Suid. s.v. σιλλαίνει.

**μύλλον**, τό, *lip*, Poll.2.90.

⊕ **μυλλός** (A), ή, όν, *awry, crooked*, Hsch. (parox.); *squint-eyed*, Eust.906.54.

**μυλλός** (B), ὁ, cake in the shape of *pudenda muliebria*, Heraclid. Syrac.ap.Ath.14.647a.

**μύλλος**, ὁ, an edible sea-fish, prob. *Sciaena umbra*, Ar.*Fr*.414, Ephipp.12.4; brought salted from the Black Sea, Gal.6.729, 747; a similar fish found in the Danube, Ael.*NA*14.23; cf. μύλος II, πλατίστακος.

**μύλλω**, (μύλη) = βινέω, Theoc.4.58; used ἐπὶ μίξεως οὐ σεμνῆς acc. to Eust.1885.27.

**μῠλόδους**, οντος, ὁ, *grinder*, Eust.1885.27.

**μῠλο-ειδής**, ές, *like a millstone*, βαλὼν μυλοειδέϊ πέτρῳ Il.7.270, cf. Batr.213a. Adv. -δῶς, περιδινεῖσθαι *Placit*.2.2.4. ⊕ **-εις**, εσσα, εν, *made of a millstone*, στέρνον θυείης Nic.*Th*.91; μ. λίθος Nonn.*D*.5.45. **-εργής**, ές, *worked in a mill, ground*, Nic.*Al*.550.

**μύλοικος**, ὁ, a kind of beetle or cockroach, Plin.*HN*29.141.

**μῠλό-κλαστος**, ον, gloss on μυλήφατος, Hsch. **-κόπον**, τό, = Lat. *acisculus, marculus*, *Gloss*. ⊕ **-κόπος**, ὁ, *millstone-worker*, *PTeb*.278.12 (i A.D.), *Gloss*., prob. in *Sammelb*.7199.29 (ii A.D.); = ὀνοκόπος, Poll.7.20. II. = μύλλος, Sch.Opp.*H*.1.130:—also Dim. **-κόπιον**, τό, ibid.

**μῠλόομαι**, Pass., (μύλη) *to be hardened, cicatrized*, of wounds, f.l. for ἐμυκώθη in Hp.*Mul*.1.40, as read by Erot. (ἐμυλώθη· ἐτυλώθη); μυλοῦνται is prob. cj. for μολοῦνται in Hp.*Coac*.501.

⊕ **μύλος** [ῠ], ὁ, = μύλη, *mill*, Lxx *Ex*.11.5, Plu.2.549d, 830d; μ. καβαλλαρικὸς ἐν λίθοις, μ. ὀνικός, μ. ὑδραλετικός, *Edict.Diocl*.15.52, 53, 54. 2. *millstone*, *PCair.Zen*.355.84 (dub., iii B.C.), *AP*11.253 (Lucill.); γυνὴ ἔρριψε κλάσμα μύλου Lxx 2*Ki*.11.21; μ. ὀνικὸς *Ev. Matt*.18.6, *Ev.Marc*.9.42; μύλους σφυρηλάτους ἀργυροῦς Str.4.1.13: metaph., ὀψὲ θεῶν ἀλέουσι μύλοι, ἀλέουσι δὲ λεπτά *App.Prov*.4.48: generally, *stone*, Hp.*Steril*.241. 3. *grinder, molar*, Artem.1.31. II. poet. for μύλλος (q.v.), Opp.*H*.1.130. III. = μύλη IV, Sor.2.36, Erot. s.v. ἐμυλώθη, Hsch.

**μῠλ-ουργός**, όν, *making millstones*, *Gloss*. **-ώδης**, ες, = μυλοειδής, Hsch., Suid. s.v. μύλακες. **-ωθρέω**, *grind*, Men.*Pk*.87; interpol. in Suid. s.v. Πυθέας. **-ωθριαῖος**, α, ον, *in the shape of a millstone*, καλυπτῆρες *Inscr.Délos* 456 *A* 4 (ii B.C.). ⊕ **-ωθρικός**, ή, όν, *fit for a miller*, σκεύη Plu.2.159c. II. -κόν, τό, *tax on milling*, *IG*2.860. **-ωθρίς**, ίδος, fem. of μυλωθρός, *maid of the mill*, title of play by Eubulus, Ath.11.494e. **-ωθρον**, τό, = μυλών, Phot. ⊕ **-ωθρός**, ὁ, (μύλη) *miller* who keeps slaves to work his mill, Din.1.23, D.53.14, Arist.*Ath*.51.3, *IG*2.3566, Poll.7.180: fem., = μυλωθρίς, Sch.Ar. *Pax* 258, Hsch. s.v. ἀλετρίς. **-ών**, ῶνος, ὁ, *mill-house*, Th.6.22, *Inscr.Délos* 445.22 (ii B.C.); εἰς μ. καταβαλεῖν to condemn [a slave] to work the *mill*, E.*Cyc*.240; εἰς μ. ἐμπεσεῖν Lys.1.18; ἐν τῷ μ. εἶναι D.45.33, cf. Din.1.23; μ. καὶ πέδαι Men.*Her*.3; ἄξιοι δεσμωτηρίου καὶ μυλῶνος Ph.1.623; Κηφισόδοτος τὰς τριήρεις ἐκάλει μυλῶνας ποικίλους

painted *mills*, Arist.*Rh.*1411$^a$24. (Sts. parox. in codd., as Arist. l. c., Ph. l. c., Luc.*Vit.Auct.*27, Poll.7.19, but cf. Hdn.Gr.1.30.)

**μῠλων-άρχης**, ου, ὁ, *master of a mill*, *PSI*8.884 (iv A.D.), *PMasp.* 142.3 (vi A.D.), Sch.Ar.*Eq.*253. **-ικός**, ὁ, *miller*, spelt μυλονικός in *PLond.*2.335.7 (ii A.D.), *Sammelb.*7199.43 (ii A.D.). ⊛**-ιον**, τό, Dim. of μυλών, *Gloss.*

**μῠλωρός**, ὁ, = μυλωθρός, Poll.7.19, Aesop.174$^b$, Theognost.*Can.* 72.

**μυλώτατον**· προσηνές, Hsch. (Fort. ⟨αἱ⟩μυλώτατον.)

⊛**μῦμα**, ατος, τό, *meat chopped up with blood, cheese, honey, vinegar, and savoury herbs*, Epaenet.ap.Ath.14.662d.

**μῦμαρ**, τό, Aeol. for μῶμαρ, μῶμος, Hsch. **μῡμᾰρίζω**, Aeol. for μωμάομαι, Id. **μυμεῖ**· λεία, Id.; cf. μύλλη.

⊛**μῡνάομαι**, (μύνη) in Aeol. pres. part. μυνάμενος [ᾰ], *diverting*, ἄλλοι τὸ νόημμα Alc.89.

⊛**μυναρός**· σιωπηλός, Hsch.

**μυνδάν**, fabulous stone found in the Tigris, Ps.-Plu.*Fluv.*24.2.

⊛**μυνδός**, όν, *dumb*, S.*Fr.*1072, Lyc.1375; μυνδότεροι νεπόδων Call. *Fr.*260.

**μύνη** [ῡ], ἡ, *excuse, pretence*, μὴ μύνῃσι παρέλκετε do not put it off *by excuses*, Od.21.111.

**μυννάκ-ια**, τά, a sort of *shoe*, from Μύννακος their maker, Poll.7. 89. **-όομαι**, *wear* μυννάκια, Hsch.

**μυντιζόμενος**· μυωπάζων, παρακαμμύων, Hsch.

**μύξᾰ** (A), ἡ, (μύσσομαι) *discharge from the nose*, = Att. κόρυζα, Hes.*Sc.*267 (pl.), Hippon.60, Hp.*Vict.*3.70 (pl.): generally, *mucus, mucous discharge*, Id.*Prorrh.*2.23, *Aph.*5.45; *synovial fluid*, Id.*Loc. Hom.*7; *slime* of certain fish, Arist.*HA*621$^b$8; of snails, Gal.12. 322. II. = μυκτήρ, Ar.*Fr.*820: pl., S.*Fr.*89. 2. *lamp-wick*, Arat.976, Call.*Epigr.*56, *PGrenf.*2.111.25 (v/vi A.D.).

**μύξᾰ** (B), ἡ, *sebesten, Cordia Myxa*, Dsc.*Eup.*2.69, Aët.5.118.

**μυξάζω**, *to be mucous*, Sch.Pl.*R.*343a.

**μυξάριον**, τό, Dim. of μύξα (A) 1, M.Ant.4.48. 2. Dim. of μύξα (B), Aët.5.118, Hsch. (μυωξάρια cod.); interpol. in D.S.1.34.

**μυξάω**, = μυξάζω, Sch.Luc.*Hist.Conscr.*31.

**μυξέα**, ἡ, *tree bearing* μύξα (B), *CPHerm.*7 ii 17, 28.15 (iii A.D.).

**μυξητήρ**, ῆρος, ὁ, = μυξωτήρ, in pl., Gal.19.401,418.

**μυξῖνος**, ὁ, *slime-fish*, a sort of κεστρεύς, Hices.ap.Ath.7.306e.

**μυξίον**, τό, Dim. of μύξα (B), Paul.Aeg.2.53.

**μυξο-ποιός**, όν, *producing mucus*, Hp.*Art.*40, Aret.*SD*2.4. **-ρροος**, ον, *running at the nose*, Hp.*Morb.Sacr.*5, Ruf.ap.Orib.*inc.* 20.17.

**μύξος**, ὁ, = μύξων, Ath.7.306f (quoting Arist.*HA*543$^b$15). II. = μυωξός, Suid.

**μυξώδης**, ες, *like mucus, abounding in it*, Hp.*Art.*40, cf. 8 (Comp.); δεσμὸς μ. a *pulpy* band of connexion, ib.45; μ. ὑγρότητες, γλισχρότης, Arist.*GA*761$^b$33, *HA*517$^b$28; μ. ὑγρασία Thphr.*HP*3.13.2; μ. ῥίζαι, σάρξ, Dsc.3.17, Gal.1.579.

**μύξων**, ωνος, ὁ, a kind of *grey mullet, Mugil saliens* or *M. auratus*, Arist.*HA*570$^b$2, 543$^b$15 (cf. μύξος).

**μυξωτῆρες**, οἱ, *nostrils*, Hdt.2.86, Dsc.1.54, S.E.*P.*1.127: rare in sg., Hp.*Morb.*2.19 (s. v. l.), Dsc.*Eup.*1.7, Antyll.ap.Orib.8.13.4.

**μῡο-βατρᾰχομᾰχία**, ἡ, = βατραχομυομαχία, v.l. in Batr. tit., Suid. s. v. Ὅμηρος. **-βρωτος**, ον, *devoured by mice*, *POsl.*52.5 (ii A.D.). **-γαλῆ**, v.l. for μυγαλῆ in Dsc.2.68. **-δόχος**, Ion. **-δόκος**, ον, *harbouring mice*, γρῶναι Nic.*Th.*795. [ῡ metri gr.] II. Subst. μυοδόχος, ὁ, *mouse-hole*, prob. in Thphr.*HP*5.4.5. **-δρέπανον**· εἶδος λίθου εὐτελοῦς, Hsch. **-θήρας**, ου, ὁ, *mouse-catching snake*, Arist. *HA*612$^b$3, Sch.Nic.*Th.*490. **-θηρᾱτής**, οῦ, ὁ, *mouse-catcher*, *PLond.*1.125.44 (iv A.D.). **-θηρευτής**, οῦ, ὁ, = foreg., *POxy.*299.2 (i A.D.). **-θηρεύω**, *catch mice*, ib.3. **-θηρέω**, = foreg., Str.3.4. 18. **-θηρος**, = ἀσπάραγος πετραῖος, Ps.-Dsc.2.125. **-κέφᾰλον**, v. μυιοκέφαλον. **-κτόνος**, ον, (κτείνω) *of mouse-killing*, τρόπαιον Batr.159. II. Subst. μυοκτόνος, ὁ, = μυοφόνον, Nic.*Al.*36, 305. **-λόγος**, ὁ, = μυοθήρας, *Gloss.* **-μᾰχία**, ἡ, (μάχη) *battle of mice*, Plu.*Ages.*15. **-πάρων** [ᾰ], ωνος, ὁ, *light pirate boat*, Id.*Ant.* 35, App.*Mith.*92; Lat. *myoparo*, Cic.*Verr.*2.1.34.86, Gell.10.25.5, *CIL*8.27790 (Althiburos). **-πτερον**, τό, = θλάσπι, Ps.-Dsc.2.156 (v.l.). **-σόβη**, ἡ, = μυιοσόβη (q. v.), *IG*11(2).287*B*71 (Delos, iii B.C.), *Inscr.Délos*442*B*33 (ibid., ii B.C.).

⊛**μυοσωτίς**, ίδος, ἡ, also **μυὸς ὦτα**, *madwort, Asperugo procumbens*, Dsc.2.183. II. = ἀλσίνη, Dsc.-Dsc.4.86; also **μυόσωτον**, ibid., and **μυὸς ὦτα**, Dsc.4.86.

**Μῠο-τρῶκται**, οἱ, *Mouse-eaters*, name of a tribe, Porph.*Chr.* 69. **-τρωτος**, ον, (μῦς IV) *hurt in the muscles*, Dsc.1.58.

**μυουρ-ία**, ἡ, *quality of being* μύουρος 2, of a hexameter, Eust.900. 7. **-ίζω**, *taper*, τὰ ἄκρα μυουρίζειν τὰ τοῦ μήκους ἑκατέρωθεν Str. 2.5.14; εἰδομένη πλατάνοιο μυουρίζοντι πετήλῳ D.P.404 (= κατὰ μυὸς οὐρὰν στενουμένῳ Eust. ad loc.); of hellebore root, Aët.3.126; of a dog's tail, ἀπὸ τῆς ἐκφύσεως μυουρίζουσαν ὅλην *Gp.*19.2.1, cf. 5.8.2. 2. of the pulse, *die away gradually*, Ruf.*Syn.Puls.*8.1, Gal. 8.480,524, 9.322. II. Pass., *taper*, πυραμίδες -ιζόμεναι εἰς ὀξεῖαν κορυφήν Nicom.*Ar.*2.13, cf. 14; [σῦριγξ] μεμυουρισμένη κατὰ τὸ βάθος Antyll.ap.Orib.44.23.61. **-ισμός**, ὁ, = μυουρία, Eust.900.10 (in form μειουρισμός). ⊛**-ος** (A), ον, (μῦς, οὐρά) *tapering* (lit. *mouse-tailed*), of a non-carnivorous fish's στόμα (snout), Arist.*PA*662$^a$32, 697$^a$1; of the αἱμόρροος II, ἐπ' εὖρος τέτρυται μύουρος ἀπὸ φλογέοιο καρήνου Nic.*Th.*287, cf. 225; ἐξ εὐρείας τῆς κεφαλῆς μείουρος κάτεισιν ἔστε ἐπὶ τὴν οὐράν Ael.*NA*15.13· εἰς (ἐπὶ) μείουρον ἄγεσθαι *taper* towards the tail, Philum.*Ven.*21.1, 27.1; ἐν τῷ μειούρῳ τῆς οὐρᾶς the *tapering part* of a horse's tail, *Hippiatr.*55; τὸ μείουρον (sc. τοῦ σπέρματος) πρὸς τὴν γῆν ἄγοντας *Gp.*10.57.8, cf. 10.63.4; κάμαξ μύουρος Apollod.*Poliorc.*172.9 (v.l. μεί-), 182.6, cf. Ph.*Bel.*51.8 (μύ-), 83.20 (μεί-); πύργον. . ἐς μύουρον ἀνιόντα Paus.10.16.1; αἱ πρὸς ὄμμα τε καὶ ὀρθογώνιοι στοαὶ πόρρωθεν μείουροι φαίνονται Hero *Deff.*135.9 (v.l. μύ-); μετρεῖ τὰ μείουρα ὡς κώνους κολούρους, i.e. roughly, ib.8; σφὴν μείουρος Id.*Stereom.*1.28; λίθος μείουρος ib.2.17 (v.l. μύ-), 59; ξύλον μύουρον Id.*Mens.*8 (as Subst. μείουρος, ὁ, *tapering prism*, Id.*Deff.*133. 2, *Geom.*3.24); ἐκφύσεις κατὰ τὸ ἄκρον μείουροι Diocl.*Fr.*27; μείουρος σχηματισμὸς [τῶν δακτύλων], i.e. with the tips pressed together, Sor.2.60; μύουρον σχῆμα Str.2.5.6, Apollod.*Poliorc.*181.3; μερίς, τμῆμα, γραμμή, Str.11.11.7. Adv., συνηγμένων μειούρως τῶν δακτύλων Paul.Aeg.6.74. 2. στίχοι μείουροι 'tapering' hexameters, in which the first syllable of one of the last two feet is short instead of long, Ath.14.632e, cf. Sch.Heph.p.290 C., Eust.900.7. 3. of the pulse, *dying away gradually*, Gal.8.480,524, 9.314. Adv. -ρως ibid. 4. of an epic poem with only a single μῦθος, ὥστε. . βραχέως δεικνύμενον μύουρον φαίνεσθαι it seems *too short*, Arist.*Po.*1462$^b$6; of periods, Id.*Rh.*1409$^b$18. (In this group of words codd. freq. vary between μυ- and μει-; both μυουρία and μειουρία are recognized by Eust. l. c.: μυ- prob. became μει- by phonetic change, cf. ἐρρηγεῖα, κώδεια, etc.: μῡ- Nic.*Th.*225, D.P. l. c., but μῠ- Nic.*Th.*287.)

**μύουρος** (B), ἡ, a plant, *mouse-tail*, Orib.*Fr.*52, Alex.Trall.8.2. II. = σάμψυχον, Ps.-Dsc.3.39.

**μῠοφόνον**, τό, *wolf's bane, Aconitum Anthora*, Thphr.*HP*6.1.4, 6. 2.9; cf. μυηφόνον. **μυοχάνη**, v. μυριοχαύνη.

**μῠό-χοδον**, τό, (χέζω) *mouse-dung*, only in pl., Thphr.*HP*5.4.5 (masc., sed leg. μυοδόχον), Dsc.2.80, Heraclid.ap.Gal.12.402, Sor.ap. eund.12.416. **-χοδος** γέρων, old *mouse-dung*, an abusive name in Men.430; cf. μυόχοδον· οὐδενὸς ἄξιον, Phot. **-χροος**, ον, contr. -χρους, ουν, *mouse-coloured*, *PFay.*92.12 (ii A.D.), *PLond.*2.195.12 (i A.D.). **-χρωμος**, ον, = foreg., *POxy.*1707.6 (iii A.D.).

**μυόω**, (μῦς IV) *make muscular*, σῶμα Antyll.ap.Orib.6.33.6:— mostly Pass., *to be* or *become muscular*, γυναῖκες μεμυωμέναι Ruf.ap. Aët.16.50; στῆθος μεμυωμένον *Hippiatr.*14: hence, *hard*, σπλῆνες μεμυωμένοι Hp.*Aër.*7. II. μεμυωμένων· μεμυκότων, Hsch.

**μύραινα**, ἡ, (μῦρος) *sea-eel* or *murry, Muraena helena*, Epich.72, Sophr.103, etc.: coupled with ἔχιδνα as *a sea-serpent*, A.*Ch.*1002, Ar.*Ra.*475; cf. σμύραινα. [μῠ, Epich. l. c.]

**μῠρ-άκανθος** [ᾰκ], = ἠρύγγιον, Ps.-Dsc.3.21. **-άκοπον**, τό, *sweet cordial* or *unguent mixed with myrrh*, Asclep ap.Gal.13.1009: wrongly spelt μυρόκοπον Alex.Trall.7.8. **-άλειπτρον** [ᾰ], τό, *box of unguents*, f. l. for μύρα, νίτρα in Paus.Gr.*Fr.*171. **-ᾰλοιφέω**, *rub with sweet oils*, Poll.7.177:—Med., μ. τὰ καίρια Eust.974. 56. **-ᾰλοιφή**, ἡ, *rubbing with sweet oils*, Poll.7.177. **-ᾰλοιφία**, ἡ, = foreg., Plu.2.662a, Ach.Tat.2.38, *Cat.Cod.Astr.*2.177. **-άπιον**, τό, = sq., Cels.4.26 (pl.). **-απίδιον**, τό, *scented pear*, *Gp.*10.76.11 (pl.). ⊛**-άφιον**, τό, Dim. of μύρον, Arr.*Epict.*4.9.7.

**μύργμα**· ψῆγμα, Hsch.

**μῠρεψ-εῖον**, τό, *unguent-factory*, *Hippiatr.*38. **-έω**, *boil* or *prepare unguents*, Aesop.322$^b$. **-ητήριον**, τό, *ointment-pot*, Aq.*Jb.*41. 23. **-ία**, ἡ, *preparation of unguents*, Arist.*Insomn.*460$^a$27. ⊛**-ικός**, ή, όν, *of* or *for unguents, aromatic*, κάλαμος Plb.5.45.10; μύρον Lxx *Ex.*30.25; οἶνος ib.*Ca.*8.2; μ. βάλανος *zakkum*, the fruit of *Balanites aegyptiaca*, Dsc.4.157: ἡ -κή (with or without τέχνη) Lys.*Fr.*1.2, Arist.*EN*1153$^a$26, Phld.*Rh.*1.116 S. **-ιον**, τό, *prepared unguent*, Sm.*Is.*57.9. ⊛**-ός**, ὁ, (μύρον, ἕψω) *one who boils and prepares unguents, perfumer*, Critias 68 D., Arist.*MM*1206$^a$27, Thphr.*HP*4.2.6, *CP*6.14.11: fem. in Lxx 1*Ki.*8.13, J.*AJ*6.3.5.

**μυρηεν**· λυπρόν, θρηνῶδες, Hsch.

⊛**μῡρηρός**, ά, όν, *of sweet oil*, τεύχη A.*Fr.*180.5; λήκυθος Ar.*Fr.* 205.

**μῡρῐᾰγωγ-έω**, *carry* 10,000 *measures*, Din.*Fr.*89.23. ⊛**-ός**, όν, *carrying* 10,000 *measures*, σκάφη Ph.1.333; μ. (sc. ναῦς), ἡ, *ship of* 10,000 *measures' burden*, *PPetr.*3 p.104 (iii B.C., dub.), Str.3.3.1: condemned by Poll.1.82.

**μῡρίαθλος** [ῐ], poet. **-άεθλος** [ᾰ], ον, *hero of myriad contests*, Orac. ap.D.Chr.31.97.

**μῡρῐάκις** [ᾰ], Adv., (μυρίος) *ten thousand times, numberless times*, Ar.*Nu.*738, *Ra.*63, Pl.*Lg.*677d, Arist.*Metaph.*1007$^a$16.

**μῡρῐάκισμῡριοστός**, ή, όν, 100,000,000*th*, ἀριθμοί Archim.*Aren.* 3.3.

**μῡρῐ-άμφορος**, ον, *holding* 10,000 *measures* (ἀμφορεῖς): Com. metaph., ῥῆμα μ. Ar.*Pax*521. **-ανδρος**, ον, *containing* 10,000 *men* or *inhabitants*, πόλεις Isoc.12.257, cf. Pl.*Ep.*337c, Arist.*Pol.*1267$^b$31, D.S.11.49, al.; πλῆθος Ph.1.81; θέατρον Luc.*Nigr.*18. **-αντοπλάσιος** [πλᾰ], ον, = μυριοπλάσιος, *PMasp.*151.257 (vi A.D.).

**μυριάομαι**, = μύρομαι, Sch.Il.1.2 (cod. A, μύρεσθαι cod. T, etc.).

**μῡρῐ-άρουρος** [ᾰ], ὁ, *having* 10,000 ἄρουραι, *PPetr.*2 p.138 (iii B.C.). **-άρχης**, ου, ὁ, *commander of* 10,000 *men*, Hdt.7.81. **-αρχος**, ὁ, = foreg., X.*Cyr.*3.3.11, etc. ⊛**-άς**, άδος, ἡ, Att. gen. pl. μυριαδῶν Hdn. Gr.1.428:—*number of* 10,000, *myriad*, Simon.91, Hdt.2.30, Archim. *Aren.*3.2, etc.; μ. πρώτη 10,000 and μ. δευτέρα 10,000 *times* 10,000, Dioph.5.8: freq. of *countless numbers*, E.*Ph.*830 (lyr.), etc.; μυριάδες ἐτῶν Phld.*Piet.*93; of money (sc. δραχμῶν), Ar.*Eq.*829 (anap.), Plu. *Cat.Mi.*44; of corn (sc. μεδίμνων), Hdt.3.91, D.20.32; also (sc. ἀρταβῶν), *POxy.*1259.4 (iii A.D.). II. as Adj., φύστις μ. ἀνδρῶν A.*Pers.*927 (lyr.: sed leg. ταρφύς τις μ.); μ. πόλεις E.*Rh.*913

(lyr.). **-αστός,** ή, όν, *ten thousandth*:—Subst. **-ασταὶ τρεῖς,** = $\frac{3}{10000}$, *SIG*1011 (iii/ii B.C., prob.). **2.** μυριαστόν, Adv. *for the 10,000th time*, *PLips.*40 ii 20 (iv/v A.D.). **-ἄχοῦ,** Adv. *in ten thousand places* or *passages*, Phld.*D.*3 *Fr.*2, Zonae.*Fig.*10, Eust.47.29, 76.19.

**μῠρίδιον** [ρῐ], τό, Dim. of μύρον, Ar.*Fr.*521.

**μῡρῐ-έλικτος,** ον, *with countless coils*, ὄφις Eun.*Hist* p.256 D. **-ετής,** ές, *of* 10,000 *years*: *of countless years*, χρόνος A.*Pr.*94 (anap.), Pl.*Epin.*987a; βίος Arist.*GA*745$^a$33; of a man, *AP*9.242 (Antiphil.).

**μῠρίζω,** *rub with ointment* or *unguent*, *anoint*, Ar.*Lys.*938, Alc. Com.23; μύροισιν μ. Ar.*Pl.*529:—Med., *anoint oneself*, Antiph.148.5, Men.518.15; ἐξ ἀλαβάστου Alex.62.1:—Pass., μεμυρισμένοι τὸ σῶμα Hdt.1.195, cf. Antiph.190.2, Arist.*Mir.*832$^a$4; μυρίζεσθαι τὴν κεφαλήν Plu.2.142a. **II.** in Pass. also, μ. τινί *to be fragrant with*.., Hld.10.26. (Cf. σμυρίζω.)

**Μῠρῑκαῖος,** ὁ, epith. of Apollo in Lesbos, Sch.Nic.*Th.*613.

**μυρικᾶς,** v. μύρκος.

**μῠρίκ-η** [on the quantity v. infr.], ἡ, *tamarisk* (in Greece, *Tamarix tetrandra*; in Egypt, *Tamarix articulata*), θῆκεν ἀνὰ μυρίκην [ῐ] Il. 10.466; μυρίκης ἐριθηλέας ὄζους ib.467; δόρυ..κεκλιμένον μυρίκησιν 21.18, cf. *h.Merc.*81, Nic.*Th.*612; but πτελέαι τε καὶ ἰτέαι ἠδὲ μυρῖκαι Il.21.350, cf. Theoc.1.13, 5.101, and Lat. *myrīca*; ἐκ μυρίκης πεποιημένη θύρη Hdt.2.96; μυρίκης κλῶνα Alc.119: pl., *PCair.Zen.*383.16 (iii B.C.). **-ίνεος** [ρῑ] θάμνος, ὁ, *tamarisk* bush, *AP*6.298 (Leon.). **-ῖνος** [ρῑ], η, ον, ὄζος *tamarisk* bough, Il.6.39; κόμη, ξύλον, *PPetr.*3 pp.125, 143 (iii B.C.); ξύλα *PCair.Zen.*176.44 (iii B.C.). **-ώδης,** ες, *like the tamarisk*, Thphr.*HP*4.6.7 (Comp.).

**μῠρ-ίνη,** freq. f.l. for μυρρίνη. **-ίνης** [ῐ] (sc. οἶνος), ὁ, also written μυρρίνης, *sweet wine*, Diph.17.10, Posidipp.34, Ael.*VH*12.31: prob. wine flavoured with μύρον, Philippid.39.

**μυρίνινος,** f.l. for σμύρνινος, Lxx *Es.*2.12.

**μύρινος,** ὁ, a sea-fish, Arist.*HA*602$^a$1 (v.l. μαρῖνος).

**μυριξ** (μυριζ cod.), =*genesta*, *Gloss.* (i.e. μυρίκη).

**μῡρῐό-βοιος,** ον, *with ten thousand oxen*, *AP*9.237 (Eryc.). **-γένεσις,** εως, ἡ, *the signs which rise with Pisces*, Firm.3.1.2, 8.1.10. **-δοξος,** ον, *of infinite renown*, Man.4.175.

**μῡρῐ-όδους,** οντος, ὁ, ἡ, *having immense teeth*, ἐλέφας *AP*9.285 (Phil.).

**μῡρῐό-καρπος,** ον, *with countless fruit*, φυλλάς S.*OC*676 (lyr.). **-κρᾶνος,** ον, *many-headed*, κύων E.*HF*419 (lyr.). **-λεκτος,** ον, *said ten thousand times*, X.*HG*5.2.17, Longin.*Rh.*p.190 H., Poll.6.206, Aristaenet.2.20. **-μέγας,** ὁ, *infinitely great*, Ἑρμῆς Zos.Alch. p.230 B. **-μορφος,** ον, *of countless shapes*, of Dionysus, *AP*9.524.13; of Apollo, ib.525.13; of Isis, *APl.*4.264. **II.** μυριόμορφον, τό, = Ἀχίλλειος, Ps.-Dsc.4.36. **-μοχθος,** ον, *of countless labours*, of Heracles, *APl.*4.91. **-ναυς,** αος, ὁ, ἡ, *with countless ships*, ἄρης *AP*7.237 (Alph.). **-νεκρος,** ον, *where tens of thousands die*, μάχαι Plu.*Alex.*1.

**μῡρῐοντ-ἄδικός,** ή, όν, *of the number* 10,000: μ. διπλοῦς, τριπλοῦς, etc. (sc. ἀριθμός), a *unit of the second* (*third*, etc.) *order of myriads* (= $10{,}000^2$, $10{,}000^3$, etc.), Theo Sm. *in Ptol.*p.64 H. **-άκις,** Adv., = μυριάκις, formed after ἑκατοντάκις, Hsch. **-ἄπλἄσίων,** ον, gen. ονος, 10,000 *times as great*, c. gen., Sch.Papp.1182.4. **-αρχος,** ὁ, = μυρίαρχος, A.*Pers.*314, f.l. ib.993 (lyr.); v. μυριοταγός.

**μῡρῐο-πάλαι** [ᾰ], Adv. *time out of mind*, Eust.725.40; cf. τρισμυριοπάλαι. **-πλάσιος** [ᾰ], ον, = sq. II, c. gen., X.*Oec.*8.22, Arist. *EN*1150$^a$8: abs., τὸ ἅρμα τοῦ θεοῦ μ. Lxx *Ps.*67(68).17. Adv. -ίως ib.*Si.*23.19. **-πλᾰσίων,** ον, gen. ονος, *ten thousand fold*, Archim. *Aren.*2.1, al. **II.** *infinitely more than*, used like a Comp. c. gen., Cleom.2.1, al. **-πλεθρος,** ον, *of immense extent*, ἀγροί cj. for sq. in Plb. 36.16.8, cf. D.S.32.16. **-πληθής,** ές, *infinite in number*, *countless*, E.*IA*571 (lyr.), Anaxandr.41.9 (anap.); στρατός Hld.9.3. **-πους,** ὁ, ἡ, πουν, τό, gen. ποδος, *ten-thousand-footed*, *many-footed*, σκώληξ Tz.*H.*13.561, Sch.Nic.*Th.*805. **II.** *having sides ten thousand feet long*, τρίγωνον Thphr.*CP*6.2.4.

❀**μῡρίος** [ῐ], α, ον (ος, ον *APl.*4.40 (Crin.)), *numberless*, *countless*, *infinite*, prop. of Number, and commonly in pl., as mostly in Hom., Il.2.468, al.: also in sg. with collective Nouns, χέραδος μυρίον 21.320; λόγχη E.*Ph.*441; χαλκός Pi.*N.*10.45; χρυσός Theoc.16.22: strengthd., μάλα μυρίοι Od.17.422, 19.78; πολλάκις μυρίοι Pl.*Tht.* 175a; μυρίαι ἐπὶ μυρίαις πόλεις Id.*Lg.*676b, cf. *Tht.*155c, D.H.*Rh.* 7.4. **2.** in Poets also, of Size, *measureless*, *immense*, *infinite*, μυρίος ὦνος Od.15.452; πένθος, ἄχος μ., Il.18.88, 20.282; μυρία ἄλγεα, κήδεα, 1.2, 24.639; μ. παντᾷ κέλευθος a *boundless* course, Pi.*I.*4(3).1, cf. B. 5.31; πάρεστι μ. κέλευθος μελέων Id.18.1; μ. παντᾷ φάτις Id.8.48; μ. μόχθοι, ἄχθος, A.*Pr.*541 (lyr.), S.*Ph.*1168 (lyr.); χάρις E.*Alc.*544; κλέος Theoc.*Ep.*21.2; μ. εὐφροσύνη *APl.* l.c. (Crin.): in Ion. Prose, ὄψις μυρίη *all kinds of* sights, Hdt.2.136; μ. κακότης, εὐδαιμονίη, Id. 6.67; θῶμα Id.2.148: sts. in Pl., μ. πενία, διαφορότης, ἐρημία, *Ap.*23c, *Phlb.*13a, *Lg.*677e: so in later Prose, μ. ἀχλύς Jul.*Or.*7.232a. **3.** of Time, μ. χρόνος Pi.*I.*5(4).28, S.*OC*397, 617. **4.** neut. pl. μυρία as Adv., *immensely*, *incessantly*, ἔκλαυσεν μ. *AP*7.374 (Marc. Arg.), cf. 12.169 (Diosc.). **b.** dat. as Adv., μυρίῳ σοφώτερος *infinitely* wiser, E.*Andr.*701; μυρίῳ βέλτιον, μυρίῳ κάλλιον, Pl.*R.*520c, *Ti.* 33b; μυρίῳ πρὸς εὐδαιμονίαν διαφέρειν to differ *infinitely*, Id.*Plt.*272c; but μυρίον διαφέρειν Id.*Tht.*166d. **II.** as a definite numeral, in pl. **μύριοι,** αι, α, *ten thousand*, first in Hes., τρὶς μ. *Op.*252, cf. Hdt.3.95, *IG*1$^2$.63.37, etc.: sg. in military phrases, ἵππος μ. 10,000 horse, A.*Pers.*302, Hdt.1.27, 7.41; ἀσπὶς μ. X.*An.*1.7.10: rarely with other words, κατὰ μυρίαν δεσμὴν *by the* 10,000 *bundles*, *PPetr.*3 p.101 (iii B.C.), cf. *PSI*4.393.11 (iii B.C.); οἱ Μύριοι *the Ten Thousand*, an assembly of the Arcadians, X.*HG*7.1.38, *IG*5(2).1.4 (Tegea, iv B.C.); οἱ Μ. ἐν Μεγάλῃ πόλει D.19.11. **III.** in late Greek, Adv. μυρίως Alex.Trall.5.4, Tz.*H.*13.521:—acc. to Gramm., μυρίος (parox.) is the *indefinite*, μύριος (proparox.) the *definite number*, μύριος ὁ ὡρισμένος ἀριθμός, μυρίος ἀόριστος Hdn.Gr.1.125, cf. Suid., Eust.907.8, etc.; but this distn. is not observed in codd.

**μῡρῐοστ-ημόριον,** τό, 10,000*th part*, Arist.*Sens.*445$^b$31. **-ός,** ή, όν, 10,000*th*, μέρος, μοῖρα, Ar.*Lys.*355, *Th.*555; μ. ἔτος 10,000 years ago, Pl.*Lg.*656e; μ. ἔ. γενόμενα ἢ ἐσόμενα Arist.*Rh.*1386$^a$29, cf. *Ph.*218$^a$28. **-ύς,** ύος, ἡ, *body of ten thousand*, X.*Cyr.*6.3.20.

**μῡρῐο-τᾱγός,** ὁ, *leader of a countless host*, prob. in A.*Pers.*993 (lyr.). ❀**-τευχής,** ές, *with ten thousand armed men*, Ἀτρεΐδας E.*IT* 142 (lyr.). **-της,** ητος, ἡ, = μυριάς, Lxx *Wi.*12.22. **-τῑμος,** ον, = πολύτιμος, Cyr. **-τρητος,** ον, *with numberless holes*, ἄγγεα μ. *honeycombs*, Ps.-Phoc.174.

**μῡρῐ-όφθαλμος,** ον, *with countless eyes*, Eust.1504.54.

**μῡρῐό-φῐλος,** ον, *with numberless friends*, Them.*Or.*22.270a. **-φόρος,** ον, *carrying* 10,000 *measures*, to designate a merchant-ship of large tonnage, Th.7.25, Ctes.*Fr.*57.6, Ph.1.28, 2.514, Poll.1.82, 4.165, Them.*Or.*16.212a. **-φορτος,** ον, = foreg., *AP*10.23 (Autom.). **-φυλλον,** τό, a water-plant, prob. *Myriophyllum spicatum*, *water-milfoil*, Dsc.4.114, Gal.12.81. **-φῦλος,** ον, *of ten thousand kinds*, Opp.*H.*1.626. **-φωνος,** ον, *with ten thousand voices*, *APl.*5.362. **-χαύνη,** ἡ, an *infinitely affected* woman, Hp. *Epid.*2.1.12 (μηριοχάνη Erot.; μυοχάνη is f.l. in Gal.19.142).

**μῠρί-πνοος,** ον, contr. **-πνους,** ουν, = μυρόπνοος, Archyt.Amph.1, *AP*9.6 (Pall.).

**μῠρ-ίς,** ίδος, ἡ, (μύρον) *box for unguents*, Poll.7.177. **II.** v. μυρρίς. **-ισμα,** ατος, τό, *ointment*, ibid. (pl.), *Cat.Cod.Astr.*8(1).249 (pl.). **-ισμός,** ὁ, *an anointing*, Antig.Car.ap.Ath.12.547f, Lxx *Ju.*16.8. **-ιστικός,** ή, όν, *fragrant*, κάρυον Aët.1.131: μυριστικά, τά, *Cat.Cod.Astr.*5(3).89.

❀**μῡρῐ-ώνῠμος,** ον, *of countless names*, Ἶσις Plu.2.372f, *OGI*695 (Philae). **-ωπός,** όν, (ὤψ) *with countless eyes*, of Argus, A.*Pr.*568 (lyr.).

❀**μύρκος,** ον, Syrac. word for ἄφωνος, *dumb*, Hsch.:—also **μυρικᾶς,** Id. **μύρμαξ,** v. μύρμηξ. **μυρμέαι·** νύσσειν, Id.

❀**μύρμη,** ἡ, = μορμύρος, Epich.62.

**μυρμηδών,** όνος, ἡ, *ant's nest*, Hsch.: Dor. for *ant*, Id., *Gloss.*

**μυρμηκ-άνθρωποι,** οἱ, *ant-men*, title of play by Pherecrates, Ath. 6.229a. **-ειον,** τό, a species of φαλάγγιον, Nic.*Th.*747, cf. Plin. *HN*29.87. **-ιά** or **-ία,** ἡ, *ant-hill*, Dinol.12 (nisi leg. -ιᾶν), Arist. *HA*534$^b$23, Thphr.*Sign.*22. **II.** metaph., **1.** *throng of people*, as in a crowded lecture-room, Hsch.; also μ. ἀγαθῶν *Com.Adesp.* 828. **2.** ᾄδων (sic Fritzsche pro ἄγων) ἐκτραπέλους μυρμηκιάς *trills* and *arpeggios*, Pherecr.145.23; cf. μύρμηξ I. 2. **III.** *wart*, differing from ἀκροχορδών, which has a neck, whereas μυρμηκία spreads under the skin, also the *irritation* caused thereby, which was compared to the creeping of ants, Hp.*Liqu.*4, Ph.2.225, Dsc.1.68, Heliod. ap.Orib.45.14.1, Poll.4.195. **2.** similar disease in a horse, *Hippiatr.*82. **-ια,** τά, = foreg. III. 1, Cels.5.28.14. **-ίας** λίθος, ὁ, a precious stone *with wart-like lumps upon it*, Plin.*HN*37.174. **II.** μ. χρυσός gold *dug by* μύρμηκες II, Hld.10.26. **-ίᾱσις,** ἡ, *irritation of the skin*, Archig.ap.Philum.*Ven.*14.2; also, = νάρκη, Hsch. s.h.v. **-ιάω,** *to be afflicted with warts*, Lxx *Le.*22.22. Cf. μυρμηκιά I. ❀**-ίζω,** *feel as though ants were running under the finger*, i.e. *to be quick and feeble*, of the pulse, Gal.8.553, al., Ruf.*Syn.Puls.* 8.11. **II.** *have a feeling of irritation*, *itch*, Aët.12.48. **-ιον,** τό, a species of spider, Philum.*Ven.*15.1. **-ῖτις** (sc. λίθος), ιδος, ἡ, a precious stone *having the fossilized impression* (or *form*) *of a creeping ant*, Plin.*HN*37.187.

**μυρμηκό-βῐος,** ον, *living an ant's life*, τὸ τῆς διαίτης μ. Eust.77.3. **-ειδής,** ές, *like an ant*, Hsch. s.v. σίφων; μ. ὁρᾶσθαι Cass *Pr.* 19. ❀**-λέων,** οντος, ὁ, *ant-lion*, Lxx *Jb.*4.11. **-τρώγλη,** *formicaria*, *Gloss.*

**μυρμηκ-τέττιξ,** ῑγος, ὁ, *ant-and-grasshopper*, Tz.*H.*11.135. **-ώδης,** ες, = μυρμηκοειδής, Plu.2.458c; φιλοπλουτία ib.525e. **-ώεις,** εσσα, εν, *full of warts*, κάρηνα Marc.Sid.97.

❀**μύρμηξ,** ηκος, Dor. **μύρμαξ,** ἀκος, ὁ, *ant*, Hes.*Frr.*14.5, 76.4, Theoc.9.31, 15.45, 17.107, etc.: metaph., ναῦται θαλάσσης μύρμηκες Aeschrio 2. **2.** μύρμηκος ἀτραποί, = μυρμηκιά II. 2, Ar.*Th.* 100. **II.** fabulous animal in India, Hdt.3.102; οἱ χρυσωρύχοι μ. Str.2.1.9; λέουσι τοῖς καλουμένοις μύρμηξιν Id.16.4.15, cf. Agatharch.69, Ael.*NA*3.4. **III.** *hidden rock* in the sea, Lyc.878; esp. on the Thessalian coast between Sciathus and Magnesia, Hdt. 7.183; off Smyrna, Plin.*HN*5.119 (pl.). **IV.** a sort of *gauntlet* or *cestus* with metal studs or nails *like warts* (μυρμηκίαι) on it, Poll.3.150. (Cf. βόρμαξ, ὅρμικας, Skt. *vamrás*, Avest. *maoiriš*, OIr. *moirb*, OSlav. *mravĭji*, ONorse *maurr*, Engl. (*pis-*)*mire*, Lat. *formica*: I.-E. forms perh. *momro-*, *momrĭ-*, *memro-* 'ant'.)

❀**μύρμος,** ὁ, = μύρμηξ I, Lyc.176. **II.** = μύρμηξ III, Id.890. **III.** = φόβος, Hsch.

**μυρμύλλων,** v. μερμίλλων. **μυρμύρω,** = μορμύρω, Hsch.

**μῠροβᾰλάν-ινος** [ᾰν], η, ον, *made of* μυροβάλανος, ἔλαιον Aët.3.157; ἄλευρον Paul.Aeg.4.4. **-ος,** ἡ, = βάλανος μυρεψική, Dsc.1.109, J.*BJ*4.8.3, Cels.6.2, Aret.*CA*2.6, Philum.ap.Orib.45.29.59, *Ostr.* 297 (ii A.D.), *PLond.*1.119.80, etc.

**μῠρο-βᾰφία,** ἡ, *dipping in perfume*, *Cat.Cod.Astr.*5(1).189 (pl.).

**-βοστρῠχόεις**, εσσα, εν, *with perfumed locks*, *Epic.Alex.Adesp.*9 iii 9. **-βόστρῠχος**, ον, = foreg., *AP*5.146 (Mel.). **-βρᾰχής** or **-βρεχής**, ές, (βρέχω) *wet with unguent*, κόμη Lxx 3*Ma.*4.6, cf. Suet. *Aug.*86:—also **-βροχος**, ον, Ps.-Callisth.3.16. **-εις**, εσσα, εν, *anointed*, βόστρυχος *AP*6.234 (Eryc.); μοιχευταί Man.4.305. **-θήκη**, ἡ, *box of unguent*, *POxy.*1026.21 (v A.D.), *BGU*717.14, *EM*55.37, etc. **-θήκιον**, τό, Dim. of foreg., Cic.*Att.*2.1.1, *PMasp.*6 ii 90 (vi A.D.). **-κοπον**, v. μυράκοπον. **-λωτος**, ὁ, *scented lotus*, Phot. and Suid. s. v. λωτός.

**μύρομαι**, v. μύρω.

**μῠρομήλινον** (sc. ἔλαιον), τό, *quince-oil*, Alex.Trall.7.5.

**μύρον** [ῠ], τό, *sweet oil, unguent, perfume*, Archil.31 (pl.), Alc.36, Sapph.*Supp.*23.18, Anacr.9, A.*Fr.*14 (pl.), Hdt.3.22; μύρον ἑψῆσαι Ar.*Lys.*946; ὄζω μύρου Id.*Ec.*524; μ. κατὰ τῆς κεφαλῆς καταχέαι Pl. *R.*398a; mixed with wine, Ael.*VH*12.31; various kinds in Dsc.1.42 sqq., Ath.15.688e sqq.; μ. Μενδήσιον, ἠθητόν, *PCair.Zen.*89.3, 436.1 (iii B.C.): prov., τὸ ἐπὶ τῇ φακῇ μ. *sweet oil* on lentils, i.e. 'a jewel of gold in a swine's snout', Cic.*Att.*1.19.2, cf. Stratt.45, Sopat.14, title of Menippean Satire by Varro. 2. place where unguents were sold, *perfume-market*, τὰ μειράκια.. τἀν τῷ μ. Ar.*Eq.*1375, cf. Polyzel.11; οἱ δ' ἐν τῷ μ. λαλεῖτε Pherecr.2; ἵσταται πρὸς τῷ μ. Eup.209. 3. metaph., *anything graceful* or *charming*, *AP* 5.89.

**μῠρο-πισσόκηρος**, ὁ, *ointment of scented oil, pitch, and wax*, Gal. 12.423. ⊛**-πνοος**, ον, contr. **-πνους**, ουν, *breathing sweet unguents*, Πειθώ *AP*12.95 (Mel.), cf. 5.15 (Marc. Arg.), Ph.Tars.ap.Gal.13.268. **-ποιητής**, οῦ, ὁ, *perfumer*, *Cat.Cod.Astr.*8(4).137. **-ποιός**, ὁ, = foreg., Anacr.30, Parmen.ap.Ath.13.608a, Phld.*Mus.* p.86 K. **-πόλος** or **μυρόπωλος**, ον, *busy about scented oils* or, *selling unguents*, alternative forms in *EM*595.31. **-πωλέω**, *deal in scented oils*, Pherecr.64, Ar.*Fr.*821. **-πώλης**, ου, ὁ, *dealer in unguents* or *scented oils*, *perfumer*, Lys.*Fr.*1.5, X.*Smp.*2.4, Antiph.35, Theopomp.Com.1, *PRyl.*420 (ii A.D.), Judeich *Altertümer von Hierapolis* No. 262. **-πωλικός**, ή, όν, *of a perfumer*, ἐργασία *PFay.*93.6 (ii A.D.). **-πώλιον** (in codd. sts. -εῖον), τό, *perfumer's shop*, Lys.24.20, D.25.52, 34.13, Hyp.*Ath.*6, Phld.*Ir.* p.47 W. **-πωλις**, ιδος, ἡ, fem. of μυροπώλης, Ar.*Ec.*841, *AP*5.180.10 (Asclep.). **-πωλος**, v. μυροπόλος. **-ροδον**, τό, an Indian tree, Ctes.*Fr.*57.28. **-ρραντος**, ον, *wet with unguent*, πρόθυρον *AP*5.197 (Mel.).

⊛**μῦρος**, ὁ, a kind of sea-eel, Dorio ap.Ath.7.312f; cf. σμῦρος.

**μῠρο-σταγής**, ές, *dripping with unguent*, Anon.ap.Suid. s. v. ἀναδούμενος. **-στάφῠλον** [ᾰ], τό, *vine with sweet-smelling grapes*, *Gp.*4.9. **-φεγγής**, ές, *shining with unguent*, φανίον *AP*12.83 (Mel.). **-φόρος**, ον, *bearing unguents*, Poll.10.119. **-χριστος**, ον, *anointed with unguent*, E.*Cyc.*501 (lyr.). **-χροος**, ον, *with anointed skin*, *AP*9.570 (Phld.).

**μῠρόω**, rarer form for μυρίζω, in Pass., Ar.*Ec.*1117 (v.l.), Megasth. ap.Str.15.1.58, Ath.1.9e.

**μύρρα**, ἡ, Aeol. for σμύρνα (q.v.), Sapph.163 = p.78 Lobel; in Att. Prose, Thphr.*HP*7.6.3, cf. Gal.19.123. (Bab. *murru.*) II. = μυρρίς, Dsc.4.115, Plin.*HN*24.154.

**μυρρῐν-άκανθος** [ᾰκ], ὁ, = μυρσίνη ἀγρία, *Gloss.* **-άω**, *long for myrtle-wreaths*, which were the badges of certain offices, hence comically for ἀρχοντιάω, Sch.Ar.*V.*857, Hsch. **-η**, ἡ, v. μυρσίνη. **-ης** οἶνος, v. μυρίνης. **-ίτης** [ῑτ], ου, ὁ, = μυρσινίτης, dub. cj. in Ael.*VH* 12.31. **-ος**, η, ον, Att. for μύρσινος.

**Μυρρῐνοῦς**, οῦντος, ὁ, name of a deme of Attica, Str.9.1.22: **Μυρρινούσιος**, ὁ, *an inhabitant of it*, *IG*1².335.42, Aeschin.1.98, etc.:—but **Μυρρινοῦττα**, ἡ, another deme, *IG*2.872, 2².896.45, al.

**μυρρῐνών**, ῶνος, ὁ, v. μυρσινών.

**μυρρίς**, ίδος, ἡ, *sweet cicely*, *Myrrhis odorata*, Dsc.4.115: **μυρίς**, Thphr.*CP*6.9.3.

**μυρρίτης** [ῑ], ου, ὁ, (μύρρα) *stone of the colour of myrtle-juice*, Plin. *HN*37.174.

**μυρσεών**, ῶνος, ὁ, = *murtetum*, *Gloss.*

**μυρσῐν-ᾶτον** ἔλαιον, oil *flavoured with myrtle-juice*, Aët.1.120, Alex. Trall.8.1: μυρσινᾶτον, τό, name of a plaster, Aët.15.42. **-έλαιον**, τό, *myrtle oil*, Dsc.1.39 tit. **-η** [ῐ], Att. **μυρρίνη** *IG*1².313.150, 2².949.18, 1235.14, Thphr.*HP*1.14.4, etc.: ἡ:—*myrtle*, *Myrtus communis*, Archil.29, Lysipp.9, Alex.98.25, Arist.*HA*627b18; μυρσίνας στέφανος Pi.*I.*8(7).74, cf. *IG* ll. cc.; μυρσίνης φόβη E.*Alc.*172. 2. μ. ἀγρία *Butcher's broom*, *Ruscus aculeatus*, Dsc.4.144. II. *myrtle-branch*, Hdt.1.132, 8.99, al., Apolloph.5.2. 2. *myrtle-wreath*, Pherecr.108.25, Ar.*V.*861, *Nu.*1364, etc.; cf. σκόλιον. 3. in pl., *the myrtle-wreath-market*, ἐν ταῖς μ. Id.*Th.*448. III. v. μύρσινος II. 2. **-ινος**, η, ον, = μύρρινος, *of myrtle*, Dsc.1.39, Aët.15.42. ⊛**-ίτης** [ῑτ] οἶνος, ὁ, *wine flavoured with myrtle*, Dsc.5.29. II. Subst. μ., ὁ, a precious stone, Plin.*HN*37.174. 2. *myrtle spurge*, *Euphorbia Myrsinites*, Dsc.4.164.5.

**μυρσῐνοειδής**, ές, *myrtle-like*, ὄζοι *h.Merc.*81, cf. Gal.12.31. II. Medic., *shaped like a myrtle leaf*, of an incision, Antyll.ap.Orib.44.23.47, Aët.15.5. Adv. **-δῶς** Heliod.ap.Orib.44.8.24, Gal.10.886, *Hippiatr.*16. III. μυρσινοειδές, τό, = κληματίς, Dsc.4.7.

**μύρσῐν-ος**, Att. **μύρρῐνος**, η, ον, = μύρτινος, *of myrtle*, [μύρον] Thphr.*Od.*27; ὄζος Call.*Dian.*202; ἔλαιον Androm.ap.Gal.13.687, al., cf. *PPetr.*2 p.114 (iii B.C.). II. Subst. μύρρινος, ὁ, = μυρσίνη I. 1, Thphr.*HP*1.3.3, al. 2. μυρσίνη (with or without σμίλη), ἡ, *convex scalpel*, Gal.2.477, al. 3. μύρρινον, τό, *upper part of membrum virile*, Ar.*Eq.*964. **-ών**, Att. **μυρρινών**, ῶνος, ὁ, *myrtle-grove*, Id.*Ra.*156, Aesop.194, Philostr.*Im.*2.1.

⊛**μύρσος**, ὁ, *basket*, μ. ὠτώεντα Call.*Fr.anon.*102, cf. Hsch.

**μυρτάκανθος** [ᾰκ], ὁ, = μυρσίνη ἀγρία, Dsc.4.144.

**μυρτᾰλίς**, ίδος, ἡ, Lacon. for ὀξυμυρρίνη, Hsch.

**μυρτὰς ὄγχνη**, a kind of *pear-tree*, *Pyrus cordata*, Nic.*Th.*513 (ὄχνης codd.). II. μυρτάς, άδος, ἡ, = μυρτίδανον II, Gal.12.82.

**μυρτεών**, ῶνος, ὁ, = *murtetum*, *Gloss.* **μύρτη**, ἡ, = *murta*, ib. **μυρτήνη**, v. μυρτίνη. **μυρτία**, ἡ, = μύρτος, Hsch.

**μυρτῐδᾰνον**, τό, *a myrtle-like plant*, Hp.*Mul.*1.34. II. *warty excrescence on the stem of the myrtle*, like the kermes berries on the holm-oak, Dsc.1.112, Plin.*HN*23.164. III. *seed of the Persian pepper-tree*, Hp.*Mul.*2.205, Gal.19.106. 2. an Indian or Persian fruit used as pepper, Diosc.Gloss.ap.Gal. l. c.

**μυρτίλωψ**· ζῷόν τι, Hsch.

**μυρτίνη** [ῑ], ἡ, a sort of *olive*, Nic.*Al.*88: **μυρτήνη**, Hsch. II. = μυρτάς I, Nic.*Al.*355.

**μύρτ-ῐνος**, η, ον, *of myrtle*, στέφανος Eub.99; [μύρον] Thphr.*Od.* 28. **-ίς**, ίδος, ἡ, = μύρτον I, Diph.79 (pl.), Plb.12.2.3 (pl.), *Gp.*11.8 tit. (pl.). II. = μυρτίδανον II, Orib.*Eup.*2.1. **-ίτης** [ῑ], ὁ, a species of τιθύμαλλος, = μυρσινίτης II. 2, Thphr.*HP*9.11.9, Crateuas ap.Sch. Nic.*Th.*617, Ps.-Dsc.4.18 (p.311 W.). 2. μ. οἶνος, = μυρσινίτης I, Dsc.5.28, Heras ap.Gal.13.297, *CIL*4.5593 (-είτης); μ. alone, *IG Rom.*1.515 (Italy), cf. Artem.1.66.

**μυρτομῐγής**, ές, *mixed with myrtle-berries*, *Gp.*4.4.

⊛**μύρτον**, τό, *myrtle-berry*, Pherecr.148, Ar.*Av.*160, 1100, Pl.*R.* 372c, Theopomp.Com.67, Antiph.179.4, Thphr.*HP*1.12.1, *Char.*11.4, etc. 2. = μυρσίνη, Archil.164. II. *pudenda muliebria*, Ar. *Lys.*1004, Ruf.*Onom.*111, Poll.2.174.

**μυρτο-πέτᾰλον**, τό, = πολύγονον ἄρρεν, Ps.-Dsc.4.4, Plin.*HN*27.113. **-πώλης**, ου, ὁ, *seller of myrtle-berries*, *Sammelb.*727 (i B.C.).

**μύρτος**, ἡ, *myrtle*, *Myrtus communis*, Simon.10 (pl.), *Scol.*11, *IG* 5(2).514.14 (Lycosura, ii B.C.), etc. II. *twig* or *spray of myrtle*, Pi.*I.*4(3).70; στέφανος μύρτων Ar.*Ra.*330 (lyr.). III. = μύρτον I, *Gp.*11.8. 2. = μύρτον II, Hsch.

**μυρτό-σπληνον**, τό, = μυοσωτίς, Ps.-Dsc.4.86 codd. **-χειλα**, τά, *labia majora pudendorum*, Ruf.*Onom.*112:—also **-χειλίδες**, αἱ, Poll.2.174.

**μύρτων**, ωνος, ὁ, (μύρτον II) nickname of *a debauchee*, Luc.*Lex.*12.

**μυρτωτή**, ἡ, a kind of vase *patterned with myrtle-sprays*, *AJA*31. 349.

⊛**μύρω** [ῡ], Ep. Verb, Act. only impf., *flow, trickle*, δάκρυσι μῦρον they *trickled* with tears, of poisoned arrows, Hes.*Sc.*132. II. elsewh. always in Med. **μύρομαι** (in early Ep. only pres. and impf.), *melt into tears, shed tears*, πολέες δ' ἀμφ' αὐτὸν ἑταῖροι μύρονθ' Il.19.6; κλαίοντέ τε μυρομένω τε 22.427; γοόωσά τε μυρομένη τε 6.373, cf. Od.19.119; ἐλεὸν μύρετο Hes.*Op.*206: aor. 1 opt. 2 sg. μύρηαι Theoc.16.31. 2. later, of a river, *flow*, ῥείθροισι.. μύρεται Σῖνις Lyc.982, cf. A.R.2.372; αἵματι μ. *trickle* with blood, Id.4.666. 3. c. acc., *weep for, bewail*, Bion 1.68: aor. 1 inf. μύρασθαι and 3 sg. ἐμύρατο (s. v. l.), Mosch.3.73, 90.

**μῡρῳδέω**, = foreg. II. 3, Hsch. (μυραδεῖ cod.).

**μῡρ-ώδης**, ες, *like unguent*, Sch.Luc.*Lex.*8. **-ωμα**, ατος, τό, *ointment spread for use*, Ar.*Ec.*1117, cf. Eust.1295.20.

⊛**μῦς**, ὁ (even of the female, Philem.126; ὁ θῆλυς [μ.] Ael.*NA*12.10); gen. μυός Cratin.53, Alc.Com.22; acc. μῦν Arcesil.1 D.; voc. μῦ *AP*11.391 (Lucill.); nom. pl. μύες [ῠ] Ar.*Ach.*762, Anaxandr.41.61 (anap.), μῦες dub. in Epich.44, also μῦς Antiph.193, Herod.3.76; acc. pl. μύας [ῠ] Epich.42.5, Posidipp.14, μῦς Hdt.2.141, Philyll.13; dat. pl. μυσί Hdn.Gr.2.642, μυσί(ν) Batr.174, 178, al.:—*mouse* or *rat*, Batr. 173, etc.: sg. in collect. sense, οὐδὲ τὸμ μῦν ἑτοιμάζονται θηρεύειν *PCair.Zen.*300.17 (iii B.C.); μ. ἀρουραῖος literally the *field-mouse*, but prob. *hamster*, *Cricetus vulgaris*, Hdt. l. c.; prov., μ. πίττης γεύεται, of one who tempted by some apparent good finds himself in inextricable difficulties, 'burn one's fingers', 'catch a Tartar', D. 50.26; μῦς.. γεύμεθα πίσσας Theoc.14.51; ὅκως χώρης οἱ μῦς ὁμοίως τὸν σίδηρον τρώγουσιν, i.e. for lack of food, Herod. l. c., cf. Antig. Car.ap.St.Byz. s. v. Γύαρος; κατὰ μυὸς ὄλεθρον, of a lingering death, Philem.211, Men.219, cf. Herod.5.68 (s. v. l.), Ael.*NA*12.10; μ. λευκός a *lewd* person, Philem.126. 2. *jerboa*, *Dipus aegyptiacus*, Hdt. 4.192, Arist.*HA*581a3, al. II. a shell-fish, *mussel*, A.*Fr.*34, Philyll. l. c., Arist.*HA*547b11 (s. v. l.), al., prob. in *PCair.Zen.*82.11 (iii B.C.). III. a large kind of *whale*, Arist.*HA*519a23 (s. v. l.); but μ. θαλάττιος *file-fish*, *Balistes capriscus*, = Lat. *mus marinus*, Ael. *NA*9.41, cf. Diph.Siph.ap.Ath.8.355f, Marc.Sid.30, Opp.*H.*1.174; μ. θ. prob. sea-water *mussel*, Heraclid.Tar.ap.Ath.3.120d. IV. *muscle* of the body, Hp. *de Arte* 10, Arist.*Pr.*885a37, Theoc.22.48, etc. V. *gag* (as if from μύω), Herod.3.85. VI. μυὸς ὦτα, v. μυοσωτίς. (Cf. Skt. *mū́s*, Lat. *mūs*, OHG., OE., ONorse *mūs*; the signf. *muscle* (IV supr.) belongs also to OHG., OE., ONorse *mūs*, Dutch *muis*, and to the Dim., Lat. *musculus*, cf. OSlav. *myšica* 'arm' (lit. 'little mouse'); cf. σμῦς.)

⊛**μύσ-αγμα** [ῠ], ατος, τό, = μύσος, A.*Supp.*995. **-άζω**, = μυσάττομαι, Aq.1*Ki.*25.26. **-ακτέον**, *one must abominate*, f. l. in Antyll. or Heliod.ap.Orib.50.3.9 (leg. ἐναίμως ἀκτέον).

⊛**μυσάλμαι**· πολὺ πεινῶντες καὶ ἐσθίοντες, Hsch.

**μῠσᾰρ-ία**, ἡ, *loathsomeness*, Sm.*Ez.*16.58. **-ός**, ά, όν, (μύσος) *foul, dirty*: hence, *loathsome, abominable*, αἷμα μητρός E.*Or.*1624, cf. Lxx *Le.*18.23 (v. l. μυσερός); μ. μηδέν Hdt.2.37: Sup., -ώταται πρά-

ξεις Phld.*Sto.*339.2. 2. of persons, *defiled, polluted*, E.*Med.*1393 (anap.), *El.*1350 (anap.), Ar.*Lys.*340, Theoc.2.20. Adv. -ρῶς f.l. for μυστικῶς in Zos.4.3.

⊛ **μῠσάρχης**, ου, ὁ, (μύσος) *the originator of a foul deed*, Lxx 2*Ma.*5.24.

**μῠσᾰρωπός**, όν, *foul-looking*, Man.4.316.

**μῠσ-άττομαι**, fut. μυσαχθήσομαι Luc.*DMeretr.*11.3: aor. ἐμυσάχθην E.*Med.*1149, Luc.*Somn.*8: also aor. 1 part. Med. μυσαξάμενος Ph.2.301: (μύσος):—*feel disgust at, loathe*, c. acc., Hp.*Morb.*2.48, E. l. c., X.*Cyr.*1.3.5; ὡς ἐπὶ τέρατι Luc.*Prom.Es*4. **-αχθής**, ές, poet. for μυσαρός, Nic.*Th.*361, *AP*9.253 (Phil.). ⊛ **-αχνός**, ή, όν, *polluted, defiled*, Hsch.: in fem., *prostitute*, Archil.184.

⊛ **μύσᾰχος**, τό, = μύσος, dub. in *SIG*47.28 (Locr., v B.C., perh. pr. n.).

**μῠσερός**, ά, όν, late form of μυσαρός, Man.4.269, *EM*535.32, v.l. in Lxx *Le.*18.23.

**μυσή**, ἡ, = μυσόν, Arr.*Fr.*59 J.

**μυσημίεκτον**, τό, *half a* ἡμίεκτον, Hsch.

**μῠσητός**, ή, όν, (μύσος) = μυσαρός, *Gloss.*

**μυσία**, ἡ, title of Demeter derived from sq. I, Corn.*ND*28.

**μῠσιάω**, = κεκορῆσθαι, Corn.*ND*28. II. (μύζω A) *breathe hard*, esp. during copulation, Hsch. (μύσειαν cod.). III. = σιλλαίνω, Id.

**μῠσίδδω**, Lacon. for μυθίζω (q. v.).

**μυσικαρφί**, Adv. expld. by μεμυκότως καὶ ξηρῶς, Cratin.267; but perh. rather from pr. n. **Μυσίκαρφος**, cf. Apolloph.8.

**μυσίνη**· ὁ κατοικίδιος πυλών, Hsch.

⊛ **Μύσιος** [ῡ], α, ον, *Mysian*: βόα τὸ Μύσιον (sc. θρήνημα) A.*Pers.*1054 (lyr.).

**μύσις** [ῠ], εως, Ion. ιος, ἡ, (μύω) *closing*, ὑστέρης Aret.*SD*2.1, cf. Dsc.1.32 (pl.); στομίων, στομάχου, πόρων, Gal.6.218, 7.249, 10.602.

**μυσκέλενδρα**, τά, *mouse-dung*, Dsc.*Eup.*2.118, Poll.5.91, Hsch.: sg., Phot. (μυσικ- cod.): Att. word, acc. to Moer.p.264 P.

**μυσκλίον**, τό, = μύσκλον, Orib.*Syn.*6.43, Paul.Aeg.2.53.

**μύσκλοι**· σκολιοί, Hsch. II. = οἱ πυθμένες τῶν ξηρῶν σύκων, Id. **μύσκλον**, τό, = μύξα (B), Orib.*Syn.*6.43. **μύσκος**, ὁ, Dim. of μῦς, for μυΐσκος, Hdn.Gr.1.148. II. μύσκος· μίασμα, κῆδος, Hsch.

**μύσον**· τὴν ἀξίνην (Mysian), Hsch. (leg. ὀξύην): **μυσόν**, τό, Mysian word, = ὀξύη, Arr.*Fr.*59 J., Str.*Chr.*12.56.

**μύσος** [ῠ], εος, τό, *uncleanness, defilement*, Emp.128.9, A.*Ch.*650 (lyr.), *Eu.*839 (lyr.), S.*OT*138, E.*HF*1155, Hp.*Morb.Sacr.*1: and in later Prose, as D.S.1.21, *SIG*985.38 (Philadelphia, i A.D.), Porph.*Abst.*2.11, Dam.*Isid.*108, Sch.Luc.*JTr.*8.

**μῡσός**, ή, όν, = μυσαρός, Hsch.

**Μῡσός**, ὁ, *Mysian*, A.*Pers.*52 (anap.), etc.: proverbially feeble and effeminate, whence prov. Μυσῶν λεία, i. e. *a prey to all*, of anything that can be plundered with impunity, Stratt.35, D.18.72, Arist.*Rh.*1372ᵇ33; ὁ Μυσῶν ἔσχατος the most worthless of men, Magn.5, cf. Philem.77, Men.55; τῶν λεγομένων Μ. ὁ ἔσχατος Pl.*Tht.*209b; εἴ σοι Μυσόν γε ἥδιον καλεῖν Id.*Grg.*521b, cf. E.*Fr.*704.

**μῠσόω**, *pollute*, Aq., Sm., Thd.1*Ki.*25.33.

**μύσπαλα**, *mousetrap*, Hsch. **μυσπαλοίματα**· τὰ κατάλοιπα τῶν ἀλουμένων, Id. **μύσπαν**· μύξαν, οἱ δὲ τὸ μυὸς τρόπον ἀναστρέφεσθαι, Id. **μυσπίην**· μυχοισμόν (fort. μοιχισμόν), μύσαγμα, Id.

⊛ **μυσπολέω**, (μῦς) *run about like a mouse*, Ar.*V.*140, with a play on μυστιπολεύω.

**μύσσομαι**, fut. μύξομαι Epic. in *Arch.Pap.*7.5:—*blow the nose*, μύσσονται δὲ οὐδέν Hp.*Vict.*3.70:—Act. (dub. in Hsch.) is only found in compds. ἀπο-, προ-μύττω. (Cf. μυκτήρ, μύξα (A); Skt. *muñcáti* 'let go', Lat. *e-mungo.*)

**μυσσοτόν**· πάθος περὶ τὴν ὄψιν, Hsch. **μυσσωτά**· γέλοια, Id. **μυσσωτεύματα**· ἀρτύματα, Id.; cf. μυττωτεύω. **μυσ-σ⟨ωτ⟩ότριβον**· ἀλετρίβανον, Id.

**μυστᾰγωγ-έω**, *initiate*, c. acc. pers., Porph.*Abst.*2.53, Ach.Tat.2.19, *SIG*900.49 (Panamara, iv A.D.): c. dupl. acc., τινά τι Ps.-Luc. *Philopatr.*22; opp. μυεῖσθαι, Plu.2.795e: abs., Alciphr.1.19, Porph.*Antr.*6:—Pass., Vett.Val.172.31. 2. *celebrate sacred rites*, Paus. Dam.p.156 D. II. metaph., *act as a guide* or *cicerone*, Str.17.1.38, Alciphr.3.31. ⊛ **-ία**, ἡ, *initiation into the mysteries*, Plu.*Alc.*34, Vett. Val.359.22, Jul.*Or.*5.172d. II. *mystical doctrine*, Iamb.*Myst.*1.1; ἡ Χαλδαίων μ. Dam.*Pr.*131, cf. Procl.*in Prm.*p.779 S. (μυσταγορίας codd.). III. *divine worship*, Just.*Nov.*58. **-ός**, όν, (μύστης, ἄγω) *introducing* or *initiating into mysteries*, *IG*5(1).1390.149 (Andania, i B.C.), Plu.*Alc.*34, etc. 2. generally, *teacher, guide*, βίου Men.550, cf. Him.*Or.*15.3. 3. in Sicily, = περιηγητής, *cicerone*, esp. at temples, Cic.*Verr.*4.59.132. 4. *Christian priest*, Men.Prot. p.111 D., Just.*Nov.*137.1.

**μυστάδης**· εἶδός τι, καὶ φατρία μάντεων, Hsch.

⊛ **μύσταξ**, ᾰκος, ὁ, Dor. and Lacon. for μάσταξ, and always masc., whereas μάσταξ is fem.:—*upper lip* or *moustache*, Stratt.65, Eub.113, Theoc.14.4, Lxx 2*Ki.*19.24(25); the Spartan Ephors on coming into office issued an edict, κείρεσθαι τὸν μύστακα καὶ προσέχειν τοῖς νόμοις, Arist.*Fr.*539.

**μυσταπάγη**, ἡ, *mousetrap*, Hsch.

⊛ **μυστάρχης**, ου, ὁ, *chief of* μύσται, *CIG*3662 (Cyzicus), 3803.10 (Bithynia).

**μυστέα**, ἡ, a kind of game, Hsch.

**μυστηλᾰσία**, ἡ, *driving of initiates*, Ἐλευσινάδε Philicus in *Stud. Ital.*9.45 (pl.).

**μυστηρι-άζω**, *initio*, *Gloss.* ⊛ **-ακός**, ή, όν, = μυστηρικός, Ptol. *Tetr.*163, Sch.Ar.*Pl.*27 (Sup.). ⊛ **-άρχης**, ου, ὁ, = μυστάρχης, *CIG*3666.6 (Cyzicus, dub.). **-ασμός**, ὁ, *initiation*, Eust.1854.46, al. **-κός**, ή, όν, *of* or *for mysteries*, χοιρία Ar.*Ach.*747. ⊛ **-ον**, τό, (μύστης, μυέω) *mystery* or *secret rite*: mostly in pl., τὰ μ. *the mysteries*, first in Heraclit.14, cf. Hdt.2.51 (of *the mysteries* of the Cabiri in Samothrace), etc.; esp. those of Demeter at Eleusis, A.*Fr.*479, S.*Fr.*804, E.*Supp.*173, Ar.*Ra.*887, etc.; μυστηρίοις τοῖς μείζοσιν, τοῖς ὀλείζοσιν μ., *IG*1².6.93,96; but usu., τὰ μεγάλα, τὰ μικρὰ μ., Sch.Ar. *Pl.*846, cf. *IG*1².313.144, 2².1672.4, Pl.*Grg.*497c, etc.; πρὸ τῶν μεγάλων μ. τὰ μικρὰ παραδοτέον Iamb.*Protr.*2; ἀπιέναι πρὸ τῶν μ., i. e. before you have reached the heart of the matter, Pl.*Men.*76e; τὰ τῆς θεοῦ (sc. Μεγάλης Μητρὸς) μ. *OGI*540.21 (Pessinus, i A.D.); οἱ θεοὶ οἷς τὰ μ. ἐπιτελεῖται *IG*5(1).1390.2 (Andania, i B.C.); τὰ μ. ποιεῖν And.1.11, Lys.14.42, cf. Th.6.28 (Pass.); μ. ἐρεῖν And. l. c.: later in sg., *PMag.Leid.W.*3.42 (ii/iii A.D.). 2. *mystic implements* and *ornaments*, σεμνὰ στεμμάτων μυστήρια E.*Supp.*470; esp. *properties*, such as were carried to Eleusis at the celebration of the mysteries, ὄνος ἄγω μυστήρια, prov. of an over-loaded beast, Ar.*Ra.*159. b. later, *object used in magical rites, talisman*, δότε πνεῦμα τῷ ὑπ' ἐμοῦ κατεσκευασμένῳ μ. *PMag.Leid.V.*10.19 (iii/iv A.D.). 3. metaph., ὕπνος, τὰ μικρὰ τοῦ θανάτου μ. Mnesim.11; τῆς Ῥωμαίων ἀρχῆς σεμνὸν μ., of the military *sacramentum*, Hdn.8.7.4: generally, *mystery, secret*, Pl.*Tht.*156a; μυστήριόν σου μὴ κατείπῃς τῷ φίλῳ Men.695, cf. Lxx *Si.*27.16, *To.*12.7; προσήγγειλε τὰ μ. τοῖς πολεμίοις ib.2*Ma.*13.21; μυστήρια βίου Sor.1.3; τοὐμὸν τὸ μ. [the remedy] is my *secret*, Aret.*CD*2.7: hence, of a medicine, Gal.13.96, Alex.Trall. 5.4. 4. *secret revealed by God*, i. e. *religious* or *mystical truth*, *Corp. Herm.*1.16, etc.; τὰ μ. τῆς βασιλείας τῶν οὐρανῶν *Ev.Matt.*13.11; πνεύματι λαλεῖν μυστήρια 1*Ep.Cor.*14.2; τὸ μ. τῆς ἀνομίας the *mystery* of iniquity, 2*Ep.Thess.*2.7; τὸν Ἀντιπάτρου βίον οὐκ ἂν ἁμάρτοι τις εἰπὼν κακίας μ. J.*BJ*1.24.1; esp. of the Gospel or parts of it, τὸ μ. τοῦ εὐαγγελίου *Ep.Eph.*6.19, cf. 3.9, *Ep.Col.*1.26, al.; *symbol*, τὸ μ. τῶν ἑπτὰ ἀστέρων *Apoc.*1.20, cf. 17.7. 5. σύνηθές τι μ. some vulgar *superstition*, Sor.1.4. II. Dionysius the tyrant called *mouse-holes* μυστήρια (μῦς, τηρεῖν), Ath.3.98d.

**μυστηρίς**, ίδος, pecul. fem. of μυστηρικός, τελεταί *AP*7.9 (Damag.).

**μυστηρι-ώδης**, ες, *like mysteries*, τελεταί Plu.2.10e, cf. 996b; διαπράττεσθαι τὰ μ. πράγματα (euphem.) Steph.*in Hp.*1.100 D.; of a remedy, Alex.Trall.1.15. **-ωδία**, ἡ, *mysticism*, Sch.Luc.*Lex.*7. **-ῶτις**, ιδος, ἡ, *of* or *for the mysteries*: μ. σπονδαί an armistice *during the Eleusinian mysteries*, Aeschin.2.133,138; ἡμέραι *IG*2².1338.9; μ. τελεταί Alciphr.2.3.16; ὧραι Philostr.*VA*5.6.

⊛ **μύστης**, ου, ὁ, (μυέω) *one initiated*, Heraclit.14, *AP*9.147 (Antag. or Simon.), Arist.*Ath.*56.4, etc.; τοῖς μύστησιν καὶ τοῖς ἐπόπτησιν *IG*1².6.49; ὁ τῶν μ. κῆρυξ X.*HG*2.4.20; τὰ μυστῶν ὄργια E.*HF*613: c. gen., Διὸς Ἰδαίου μύστης Id.*Fr.*472.10 (anap.), cf. *IG*3.700; λύχνον μύστην σῶν θέτο παννυχίδων *AP*6.162 (Mel.); μ. ἀποκρύφων Vett.Val. 7.30, al.: as Adj., μ. χοροί Ar.*Ra.*370; μ. λύχνος *AP*7.219 (Pomp. Jun.). 2. a name of Dionysus, Paus.8.54.5; of Apollo, Artem. 2.70.

**μυστικός**, ή, όν, *connected with the mysteries*, τέλος A.*Fr.*387; μ. Ἴακχος the *mystic* chant Iacchus, Hdt.8.65; χοῖροι Ar.*Ach.*764; αὔρα τις εἰσέπνευσε -ωτάτη Id.*Ra.*314; βίοτος μ. *IG*3.172.6; μ. λόγοι Phld.*Ir.*p.46 W.; τὰ μ. *the mysteries*, Th.6.28,60; ἡ -κή (sc. παράδοσις) *mystical doctrine*, Procl.*in Prm.*p.779 S., cf. eund.*in Ti.*3.12 D.; τὸ θεῖον καὶ μ. Dam.*Pr.*213; οἱ μ., = μύσται, Str.17.1.29: Comp. -ώτερος Luc.*Salt.*59: Sup. -ώτατος Ar.*Ra.* l. c., Dam.*Pr.*111. Adv. -κῶς, δικάζειν Poll.8.123 (fort. μυστικῶν *in cases relating to the mysteries*); *mystically*, μ. καὶ τελεστικῶς Hermog.*Id.*1.6, cf. D.S.5.77, Porph. *Antr.*4. II. *private, secret*, Cic.*Att.*4.2.7 (Comp.). Adv. -κῶς Str. 10.3.9, Lxx 3*Ma.*3.10, Vett.Val.46.11: Comp. -ώτερον, *scribere* Cic. *Att.*6.4.3.

**μυστῐλ-άομαι**, *sop bread in soup* or *gravy and eat it*, ὦ πλεῖστα... μεμυστιλημένοι.. ἐπ' ὀλιγίστοις ἀλφίτοις Ar.*Pl.*627; ἐμυστιλᾶτο τοῦ ζωμοῦ Luc.*Lex.*5: metaph., ἀμφοῖν χεροῖν μυστιλᾶται τῶν δημοσίων *he scoops up* public money, Ar.*Eq.*827 (anap.):—as Pass., μυστίλας μεμυστιλημένας *scooped out*, ib.1168. **-άριον**, τό, Dim. of sq., Poll. 6.87. ⊛ **-η**, ἡ, *piece of bread scooped out as a spoon*, to sup soup or gravy with, Ar.*Eq.*1168, Pherecr.108.5, Aret.*CA*1.4, Ath.3.126a, Poll.6.87.—The forms μιστύλη or μιστυλλάομαι and μιστυλλάομαι, which occur in codd., are no doubt due to confusion with μιστύλλω.

**μύστιξ**· ἅμα τῷ σκότει, Hsch.

**μυστῐπόλ-ευτος**, ον, *solemnized mystically*, Orph.*H.*76.7. **-εύω**, *solemnize mysteries*, μ. γαμήλια θεσμά Musae.142: abs., Orph.*H.*42.6. ⊛ **-ος**, ον, (μύστης, τελέω) *solemnizing mysteries, performing a mystic rite*, *IG*14.1018, *Rev.Ét.Anc.*31.311 (Thrace); μ. αἵματα *IG*14.1020; δαΐδες ib.3.172.8.

⊛ **μυστίς**, ῐδος, fem. of μύστης, *IG*3.914, Porph.*Antr.*18: usu. metaph., *initiate* or *initiator*, μ. νάματος ἡ Κύπρις *Anacreont.*4.12; πενίης μύστι, λάγυνε *AP*9.229 (Marc. Arg.); μ. τῆς τοῦ θεοῦ ἐπιστήμης, of Σοφία, Lxx *Wi.*8.4; [ψυχὴ] τῶν τελείων μ. τελετῶν Ph.1.173.

**μυστο-γράφος** [ᾰ], ὁ, *confidential clerk*, Lyd.*Mag.*3.18. ⊛ **-δόκος**, ον, (μύστης, δέχομαι) *receiving the mysteries* or *the initiated*, μ. δόμος, i. e. Eleusis, Ar.*Nu.*303 (lyr.). **-δότης**, ου, ὁ, = μυσταγωγός, Mesom.*Mus.*7.

⊛ **μυστρίον**, τό, Dim. of μύστρον, Antyll.ap.Orib.8.6.9, Hero *Geom.*23.64, Eust.1368.51. II. = μυστίλη, Sch.Ar.*Pl.*627.

**μυστριοπώλης**, ου, ὁ, *dealer in small spoons*, Nicopho 19 (anap.).

**μυστροθήκη**, ἡ, *spoon-case*, *PCornell*33.13 (iii A.D.).

⊛**μύστρον**, τό, = μυστίλη, Nic.*Fr.*68.8, cf. Ath.3.126a. **2.** *spoon*, Hippoloch.ap.eund.4.129c, Dsc.3.22, *POxy.*921.25 (iii A.D.), etc.; μύστρου πλῆθος *spoon*ful, as a dose, Archig.ap.Orib.8.2.28, Herod. Med.ap.eund.8.3.2; μ. alone, as a measure, Gal.13.57, 19.770, *Hippiatr.Append.*p.446.

**μύστρος**, ὁ, = foreg., Poll.6.87, Hero *Geom.*23.64.

**μυσφόνον**, τό, *mousetrap*, Hsch. **μύσχαι**· αἱ μυχαί, Id. **μύσχης**· εὖρος, ὡς Ἀμφίλοχος, Id. **μύσχλης**· μύλος, Id. **μύσχον**· τὸ ἀνδρεῖον καὶ γυναικεῖον μόριον, Id.

**μυσώδης**, ες, *abominable*, Plu.*Tim.*5.

**μυσωτός**, ὁ, = μυττωτός, Call.*Fr.*282.

⊛**μῦτᾰκισμός**, ὁ, *fondness for the letter* μῦ, Diom.p.453K., Donat. p.393K., Serv. in eund. p.445K., Mart.Cap.5.514, *Gloss.*, etc. (*moet-*, *moyt-*, *mot-*, *myot-*, etc., codd.)

⊛**μύτης**, ου, ὁ, = μυττός, Hsch. **μυτικίζειν**· κολάζειν, Id.

**Μῠτῐλήνη**, ἡ, *Mytilene*, the chief city of Lesbos, Hecat.140J., etc.; Lesb. Μυτιλήνα *IG*12(2).1.7:—hence **Μῠτῐληναῖοι**, οἱ, *Mytileneans*, ib.1².60.1,17: freq. written corruptly Μιτυλήνη, Μιτυληναῖοι.

**μύτιλος**, η, ον, v. μίτυλος.

⊛**μύτις**, ιδος, ἡ, *that part of molluscs which answers to the liver*, Arist. *HA*524ᵇ15, *PA*681ᵇ20, Plu.2.978a. **II.** *snout*, Eust.950.2. **III.** = μυττίς, Hp.ap.Gal.19.123.

⊛**μύττακες**· μύκαι, Σικελοί· Ἴωνες πώγωνα, Hsch. **μυττάλυτα**· μεγάλα (-λου cod.), Id. **μυττάξασα**· στενάξασα, Id. **μυττηκάζειν**· στένειν, Id. **μύττηξ**, a bird, Id. **μυττιλανός**· ἀπόπληκτος, Id. **μυττίς**, ἡ, *the ink of the cuttle-fish*, Id.; cf. μύτις.

**μυττός**, όν, *dumb*, Hsch. **II.** = γυναικεῖον αἰδοῖον, Id.

**μύττω**, Att. for μύσσω.

**μυττωτεύω**, *hash up*, *make mincemeat of*, τινα Ar.*V.*63.

⊛**μυττωτός** (Ion. **μυσσωτός**, only Hp.*Loc.Hom.*47, cf. μυσωτός), ὁ, *savoury dish of cheese*, *honey*, *garlic*, etc., mashed up into a sort of paste, Hippon.35.2, Anan.5.8, Hp. l. c., *Epid.*2.6.28, Eup.179, Ar. *Ach.*174, *Eq.*771, Thphr.*HP*7.4.11 (pl.), Dsc.2.152, Aret.*SD*2.9.

**μῠχαίτατος**, η, ον, irreg. Sup. of μύχιος, Arist.*Mu.*393ᵃ32, St.Byz. s.v. Ἄλωρος: Comp. **μυχαίτερος** Hdn.*Epim.*166; formed like μεσαίτατος, παλαίτατος.

**μυχάλμη**· βυθὸς θαλάσσης, Phot.

**μύχαλος** [ῠ], = μύχατος, Τάρταρα Trag. in *PGrenf.*2.6*Fr.*1.7; f.l. in E.*Hel.*189 (lyr.).

**μῠχάς**, άδος, ἡ, = μυχός, *Lyr.Adesp.Oxy.*15ii4.

⊛**μύχᾰτος** [ῠ], η, ον, irreg. Sup. of μύχιος, A.R.1.170, Call.*Dian.*68, Ps.-Phoc.164, *AP*9.632; ἔντοσθεν μυχάτοιο δόμου *Klio*15.48 (Delph., iii B.C.).

**μῠχέστατος**, η, ον, irreg. Sup. of μύχιος, Phot.

⊛**μῠχή**, ἡ, = μυχός, f.l. in Suid. **II.** = ἀμυχή, Gal.17(1).963.

⊛**μυχθ-ίζω**, (μύζω A) *make a noise by closing the mouth and forcing the breath through the nostrils*, *snort*, esp. from passion, A.*Fr.*461. **2.** *make mouths*, *sneer*, χείλεσι μυχθίζοισα Theoc.20.13; σιμὰ σεσηρὼς μυχθίζεις *AP*5.178 (Mel.); μ. καὶ διαψιθυρίζω Plb.15.26.8. **-ισμός**, ὁ, *snorting*, Hp.*Coac.*509; νεκρῶν E.*Rh.*789. **II.** *mocking*, *jeering*, Aq.*Ps.*122(123).4. **-ώδης**, ες, *like one snorting*, πνεύματα μ. *hard-drawn* breath, Hp.*Coac.*529.

**μύχιος** [ῠ], α, ον (also μύχιος, ον Arist.*Mu.*395ᵇ31), (μυχός) *inward*, *inmost*, Hes.*Op.*523, v.l. in *Th.*991; μυχία Προποντὶς *embayed*, A.*Pers.* 876 (lyr.); πνοιαί A.R.2.742; μύχιόν τι ὑποκρώζειν Luc.*DMort.*6. 4. **II.** οἱ μ. θεοί, = Lat. *Penates*, D.H.1.67; also θεοὶ μ. coupled with Aphrodite μυχία, Ael.*NA*10.34; Μύχιος and Μυχία divinities at Hiera, *IG*12(2).484.13.—To this Adj. belong various irreg. Sups. (formed from the Subst. μυχός), μυχοίτατος, -αίτατος, -έστατος, -ώτατος, and μύχατος (qq. v.).

**μυχλός**· σκολιός, ὀχευτής, κτλ., Hsch.: Phocian word for *stallion-ass*, Id.; cf. μύκλα.

**μυχμός**, ὁ, (μύζω A) = μυγμός, *moaning*, *groaning*, Od.24.416.

**μῠχ-όθεν**, Adv. *from the inmost part of the house*, *from the women's chambers*, A.*Ag.*96 (anap.), *Ch.*35 (lyr.). **-οῖ**, only in Cypr. form **μοχοῖ** (q. v.). **-οίτατος**, η, ον, irreg. Sup. of μύχιος, ἷζε μυχοίτατος *in the farthest corner* he used to sit, Od.21.146. **-όνδε**, Adv. *to the far corner*, μεγάροιο ib.22.270. **II.** *inwards*, Emp. 100.23.

**μῠχόνοος**, ον, contr. **-νους**, ουν, *deep-souled*, *reserved*, Phot.

**μῠχόομαι**, *to be concealed in a nook*, Sch.Opp.*H.*4.182.

**μῠχό-πεδον**, τό, *the depth of the earth*, *the abyss*, Phot. **-πόντιον**, τό, name of a cave on the coast of the Black Sea, Amm.Marc.22. 8.17. **-ρήμων**, ον, gen. ονος, *speaking from the depths of the soul*, Phot.

⊛**μῠχός**, ὁ, heterocl. pl. μυχά Call.*Del.*142, D.P.117,128, etc.:—*innermost part*, *nook*, *corner*, μυχῷ δόμου ὑψηλοῖο Il.22.440; μ. σπείους γλαφυροῖο Od.5.226; μ. ἄντρου θεσπεσίοιο 13.363; μυχῷ Ἄργεος *in a recess* or *in the farthest nook* of Argos-land, of Mycenae, 3.263; of Ephyre, Il.6.152, cf. Pi.*N.*6.26; Τάρταρά τ' ἠερόεντα μυχῷ χθονὸς Hes.*Th.*119; τῆλε μυχῷ νήσων ἱεράων ib.1015; ἐν μυχῷ τῆς θήκης Hdt.3.16; μ. μαντεῖος Pi.*P.*5.68; κελαινὸς Ἅιδος μ. γᾶς A.*Pr.*433 (lyr.): in pl., Κορίνθου ἐν μυχοῖς Pi.*N.*10.42; μυχοὶ χθονός or γῆς the infernal realms, E.*Supp.*926, *Tr.*952, etc.; μαντικοὶ μυχοί A.*Eu.*180; διὰ μυχῶν βλέπουσ' ἀεὶ ψυχή a soul that sees *in darkness*, i.e. is full of deceit, S.*Ph.*1013. **2.** *inmost part of a house*, ἐς μυχὸν ἐξ οὐδοῖο Od.7.96; μυχοῦ ἀφέρκτος A.*Ch.*446 (lyr.; nisi leg. μυχῷ); τὸ φάρμακον.. ἐν μυχοῖς σῴζειν S.*Tr.*686; οὐ γὰρ ἐν μ. ἔτι no longer *hidden within the house* (for the doors were thrown open, cf. Sch.), Id.*Ant.*1293, cf. E.*Tr.*299. **b.** *store-chamber*, Xenoph.2.22, Pi.*I.* 1.56; ὧν μ. πλουτεῖ Phoen.2.18. **c.** *granary*, *Tab.Heracl.*1.139. **3.** *creek* running far inland, Hdt.2.11, 4.21; ἐς μυχοὺς ἁλός Pi.*P.*6.12; πόντιος μ., i.e. the Adriatic, A.*Pr.*839; ἐν τῷ κοίλῳ καὶ μ. τοῦ λιμένος Th.7.52; ἐν τοῖς ἄγκεσι καὶ μ. τῶν ὀρέων X.*An.*4.1.7; ἐν τῷ μ. τοῦ Ἀδρίου Arist.*Mir.*836ᵃ24.

**μύχ-ουρος** [ῠ], ὁ, (οὖρος) *warder of the interior*, Lyc.373. **-ώδης**, ες, *full of recesses*, *cavernous*, E.*Ion*494 (lyr.). **-ώτατος**, irreg. Sup. of μύχιος, Sch.A.R.2.397.

⊛**μύω**, fut. μύσω [ῡ] Lyc.988: aor. ἔμυσα, Ep. 3 pl. μύσαν: pf. μέμῡκα: [ῡ in pres., Call.*Dian.*95, Nic.*Fr.*74.56: ῠ in aor., Il.24.637, S.*Ant.* 421, E.*Med.*1183, exc. in later writers, as *AP*7.630 (Antiphil.), 9.558 (Eryc.): ῡ in pf., Il.24.420, *App.Anth.*4.39 (Leon.)]: **I.** intr., *close*, *be shut*, of the eyes, οὐ γάρ πω μύσαν ὄσσε ὑπὸ βλεφάροισιν Il.24.637; ἐκ μύσαντος ὄμματος from *closed* eye, E. l. c.; of the mouth or any opening, τὰ τῶν διεξόδων στόματα ἢ τὸ πτερὸν ὁρμᾷ συναναινόμενα μύσαντα Pl.*Phdr.*251d; χεῖλος ἔμυσε *AP*7.630 (Antiphil.); μεμυκὼς χείλεα σιγῇ ib.15.40 (Cometas); τρηχὺς.. μέμυκε πόρος ib.10.5 (Thyill.); of bivalve fish, opp. κεχηνέναι, Ath.3.93f; of flowers, κρόκος εἴαρι μύων Nic. l. c.; but also, *wither*, ἀστάχυσιν μεμυκόσιν ἐξ αὐχμοῦ καὶ ἀνομβρίας Ph.2.383: metaph., τῷ λιμῷ μαραινόμενοι καὶ μεμυκότες J.*BJ*6. 5.1. **2.** of persons or animals, *shut the eyes*, μύω τε καὶ δέδορκα S.*Fr.*774; φαίνεται καὶ μύουσιν ὁράματα Arist.*de An.*428ᵃ16; οὐ μύοντα λαγωόν Call.*Dian.*95; μύσας as a preliminary to going through what is painful, παρέχειν μύσαντα εὖ καὶ ἀνδρείως Pl.*Grg.*480c, cf. S. *Ant.*421, Ar.*V.*988, Antiph.3: metaph., μύσας τῷ λογισμῷ Plu.*Pomp.* 60. **3.** metaph., *to be lulled to rest*, *abate*, of pain, ἀνατέτροφας ὅ τι καὶ μύσῃ S.*Tr.*1009 (lyr.); of storms, *AP*7.293 (Isid. Aeg.). **II.** trans., *close*, *shut*, κανθούς ib.221; ὕπνος ἔμυσε κόρας ib.9.558 (Eryc.); τοὺς ὀφθαλμούς πως μ. Alex.Aphr.*Pr.*1.105; περὶ δὲ πᾶν ὄμμα μύομεν Dam.*Pr.*6.

**μυ-ώδης**, ες, *mouse-like*, τὸ δακεῖν μ. Plu.2.458c. **II.** (μῦς IV) *muscular*, D.S.5.39, Ruf.*Onom.*96, Plu.2.733b, Arr.*Cyn.*6.2. **-ών** [ῡ], ῶνος, ὁ, (μῦς IV) *cluster of muscles*, *muscle*, πρυμνὸν σκέλος, ἔνθα πάχιστος μυὼν ἀνθρώπου πέλεται Il.16.315, cf. 324 (pl.), A.R.4.1520, Theoc.25.149. **-ωνιά**, ἡ, (μῦς I) prob. = μυωξία, as a term of reproach for *a lewd woman*, Epicr.9.4. **-ωξάρια**, τά, f.l. for μυξάρια (q.v.), Hsch. ⊛**-ωξία**, ἡ, *mouse-hole*, also a term of reproach, Id., Suid.; cf. μυωνιά. **-ωξός**, ὁ, *dormouse*, Opp.*C.*2.574.

⊛**μυωπ-άζω**, *blink* the eyes, as shortsighted persons do: hence, *to be shortsighted*, metaph., 2*Ep.Pet.*1.9. **-η**· ῥάμνος, Hsch. **-ία**, ἡ, = μυωξία, Arist.*HA*580ᵇ25, Ael.*VH*1.11. **II.** = μυωπίασις, Aët. 7.47 tit. **-ίας**, ὁ, *shortsighted person*, Poll.2.61, Paul.Aeg.3. 22. **-ίασις**, ἡ, *short sight*, Gal.19.436. **-ίζω**, (μύωψ II.2) *spur*, *prick with a spur*, ἵππον X.*Eq.*10.1,2, Palaeph.52: metaph., *spur on*, ἑαυτόν Plb.20.12.2; of athletes, γυμναστέοι συντόνως μυωπιζόμενοι cj. in Philostr.*Gym.*42; *to be stimulated*, μ. τὴν ὄψιν Alex. Aphr.*in Sens.*58.17. **II.** Pass., (μύωψ II.1) *to be teased by flies*, of a horse, X.*Eq.*4.5, *Eq.Mag.*1.16; βοῦς μυωπισθεὶς Aristaenet.2. 18: metaph., τοῖς τοῦ πάθους κέντροις J.*AJ*7.8.1. **-ός**, όν, = μύωψ I, X.*Cyn.*3.2,3.

**μυωτόν**, τό, *small arrow-head* (in Egypt), Paul.Aeg.6.88 (pl.).

**μυωτός** (A), ή, όν, either *made of mouse-skin*, or *embroidered with figures of mice*, χιτών (among the Armenians) Poll.7.60.

**μυωτός** (B), ή, όν, (μῦς IV) *furnished with muscles*, σάρκες Clearch. 72.

⊛**μύωψ**, ωπος, ὁ, ἡ, (μύω, ὤψ) *closing* or *contracting the eyes*, as shortsighted people do, and so, *shortsighted*, Arist.*Rh.*1413ᵃ4, *Pr.*959ᵃ3, ᵇ38, Alex.Aphr.*Pr.*1.74. **II.** as Subst. **μύωψ** [ῠ, but ῡ Nic.*Th.*417, 736], ωπος, ὁ, *horse-fly*, *gadfly*, *Tabanus*, ὀξυστόμῳ μύωπι A.*Pr.*675; βοηλάτην μ. Id.*Supp.*307, cf. Pl.*Ap.*30e, Arist.*HA*528ᵇ31, 552ᵃ29, al. **2.** *goad*, *spur*, X.*Eq.*8.5; ἐν τοῖς μύωψι περιπατεῖν to walk in *spurs*, Thphr.*Char.*21.8; προσθεῖναι τοὺς μ. Plb.11.18.4, cf. *AP*5. 202 (Asclep.); *ox-goad*, βουσόος μ. Cerc.8.2, cf. Call.*Fr.*46, A.R.3. 277. **3.** metaph., *stimulant*, *incentive*, Luc.*Cal.*14, *Am.*2; τινος to a thing, ῥόμβον θιάσοιο μ. *AP*6.165 (Phal.); τὸν μύωπα ἐμβαλεῖν τινι Ach.Tat.7.4. **4.** a plant growing in the Achelous, Ps.-Plu. *Fluv.*22.5. **5.** *the little finger*, Sch.Opp.*H.*3.254.

**μῶ**, = ζητῶ, coined as etym. of many words, *EM*84.47, al. **II.** = μῦ I, Democr.19, *BCH*29.483 (Delos, iii B.C.).

**Μῶᾰ**, Lacon. for Μοῦσα (q.v.), esp. in sense of *musical contest*, *IG* 5(1).256, al. (Sparta).

**μῶδα**· ἄλφιτα σίτου, Hsch. (Perh. f.l. for Lat. *mola*). **μωδεῖ**· λαλεῖ, ᾄδει, Id. (Perh. for Lacon. μωΐδδει = μουσίζει.) **μῶδιξ**, ἡ, = σμῶδιξ, Id. **μωδύνει**· θάλπει, μωραίνει, ἐκλύει, Id. (leg. μωλύει). **μῶδυξ**· ἀπαίδευτος, Id. (leg. μῶλυξ).

**μωδῶν**, name of a stone found in the Tigris, Arist.*Mir.*846ᵃ32; cf. μυνδάν.

⊛**μώϊον**, τό, Egyptian word for a *receptacle*, *box* or *jar*, *PHib.*1.49.8, *PPetr.*3p.186 (iii B.C.); χαλκωμάτων *PSI*4.428.78 (iii B.C.); prob. also a measure of capacity, ἀχύρου μώϊα μα *Ostr.Bodl.*i231 (ii B.C.): pl. written μώεια *PCair.Zen.*167.7 (iii B.C.); sg. written μούειον *POxy.*146.3 (vi A.D.); cf. μώσιον.

**μωκ-άομαι**, (μῶκος) *mimic*, and so, *ridicule*, Ael.*NA*1.29, Alciphr. 1.33, 3.27: abs., μωκώμενος *in jest*, opp. πεποιθώς, Epicur.*Ep.*3p.63 U., cf. Phld.*Vit.*p.38J.; μωκωμένη διάλεκτος Agatharch.21; προσφορὰ μεμωκημένη (v.l. μεμωμ-) offering *made in mockery*, LXX *Si.*31 (34).18:—Pass., ib.*Je.*28(51).18.—Act. only in Cyr. (Said to be formed from the sound made by a camel, κάμηλος μωκᾶται Anon. *de*

voc.animal. in Stud.Ital.1.93; = *mugio*, Gloss.) **-εύω**, = foreg., Zonar. **-ημα**, ατος, τό, *mockery*, LxxSi.31(34).18 (pl., v.l. μωμ-). **-ία**, ἡ, = foreg., Ael.VH3.19. **-ίζω**, *mock*, Suid.

®**μῶκος**, ὁ, *mockery*, Anon.ap.Ath.5.187a, Simp.inEpict.p.58D.(pl.); cj. in Epich.148.

**μωκός**, ὁ, *mocker*, Arist.HA491$^{b}$17, EM593.7: as Adj., φίλος μ. LxxSi.36(33).6.

**μῶλαξ**, ακος, Lydian name for *wine*, Hsch.

**μώλεια**, τά, an Arcadian festival, Sch.A.R.1.164.

**μωλέω**, Cret. **μωλίω**, *contend, bring an action at law*, αἴ κα μωλῇ, αἰ δέ κ' ἀνφὶ δώλῳ μωλίωντι, Leg.Gort.1.14,17; τὰ μωλιόμενα *the pleadings*, ib.5.44, al.; μωλιομένας τᾶδ δίκας *while* the case *is being pleaded*, ib.1.48:—Hsch. has μ(ω)λεῖ· μάχεται, πικρανθήσεται, and μωλήσεται· μαχήσεται.

**μῶλος**, ὁ, *toil and moil* of war, μῶλος Ἄρηος Il.2.401, etc.: also without Ἄρηος, 17.397, 18.188, Hes.Sc.257: once in Od., ξείνου καὶ Ἴρου μῶλος *struggle between* Irus and the stranger, 18.233; εὖτ' ἂν Ἄρης μῶλον συνάγῃ Archil.3.

**μῶλυ**, τό, *moly*, a fabulous herb, Od.10.305, cf. Com.Adesp.641; cf. μῶλυς II. II. in later writers, *garlic, Allium nigrum*, Thphr.HP 9.15.7, Dsc.3.47; cf. μώλυζα. 2. a kind of πήγανον ἄγριον growing in Cappadocia, ib.46. 3. = ἠρύγγιον, Ps.-Dsc.3.21. 4. = στρύχνον ὑπνωτικόν, Plin.HN21.180. (Cf. Skt. *mūlam* 'root', *mūlakarma* 'magical use of roots'.)

**μώλυγερ**· τὰ ἄνοζα ξύλα, Hsch. (Prob. Lacon. for *μώλυγες.)

**μώλυζα**, ἡ, (μῶλυ II) a *head* of garlic, σκορόδων Hp.Nat.Mul.85; σκορόδου Id.Mul.1.78.

**μωλύνω**, v. μωλύω.

**μῶλυξ**, ῦκος, ὁ (Zacynth.), and **μωλυρός**, ά, όν, = sq., Hsch.

**μῶλυς**, υ, gen. υος, *soft, weak, feeble*, μ. ἐπιστείβων, of a serpent, Nic.Th.32, cf. Sch. 2. metaph., *weak in intellect, dull*, Demetr. Lac.Herc.1014.58, Hsch. (who also has Comp.), cf. S.Fr.693; also μωλύτερον φαίνεσθαι τὸν λόγον Socr.Ep.30.14. II. μῶλυς ῥίζα, = μῶλυ I, Lyc.679.

**μώλ-ῠσις**, εως, ἡ, *imperfect boiling, parboiling, scalding, simmering*, opp. ἕψησις, Arist.Mete.381$^{a}$12, al.; ἀπεψία τις ἡ μ. ἐστι Id.GA776$^{a}$8; of rapidly growing cereals, ὥσπερ τὰ ἐπὶ τὸ ζέον ἐμβαλλόμενα τῶν ἑψομένων, οὐδεμίαν.. οὐδὲ κἀκεῖνα λαμβάνει μ., i.e. they 'cook' too suddenly, without 'simmering', Thphr.CP4.9.6. (Written **μώλυσις** and **μώλυνσις** in some codd. of Arist.Mete.379$^{a}$2, $^{b}$14, 381$^{a}$12,22; **μόλυνσις** in nearly all codd. of Id.Mete.381$^{b}$14, GA l.c., Thphr. l.c.; cf. μωλύω.) **-ῠτής**, οῦ, ὁ, perh. *parboiler, simmerer*, metaph., ἐπέων Timo41. ®**-ῠτική**· φοβερά, Hsch. **-ῠτός**, ή, όν, *putrefied*, μέλη prob. l. in Man.4.254.

**μωλύω** or **μωλύνω**, *boil imperfectly, parboil, scald, simmer*, πάσχει ὅπερ ἐν τοῖς ἑψομένοις τὰ μωλυνόμενα Arist.GA776$^{a}$1 (μολυν- codd.); σκληρότερα μὲν τὰ μεμωλυσμένα γίγνεται τῶν ἑφθῶν Id.Mete.381$^{a}$21 (v.l. μεμολ-); of a herb, μωλυθεῖσα πυρὶ σμαλερῷ Poet.deherb.101, cf. 138; of *half-roasted* meat, [κρέα] πρὸς ὀλίγον τῷ πυρὶ μεμωλυσμένα Hld.2.19 (μεμολ- codd.). II. of ulcers, *'go off the boil', fail to come to a head, subside, fade away*, σκληρὰ καὶ ἄπεπτα πάντα ἐμωλύνθη Hp. Epid.7.3 (v.l. ἐμολ-); συνελειαίνετο (v.l. ἐπεχλιαίνετο) ταῦτα, καὶ ἐμωλύνθη (v.l. κατεμωλύθη) καὶ οὐκ ἀπεπύησεν ib.2.2.6 (= ἠφανίσθη καὶ κατὰ βραχὺ ἀπεμαράνθη· οὕτως γὰρ καλεῖ τὸ τῆς ὀξείας κινήσεως καὶ μεταβολῆς παυσάμενον καὶ ἀποψυχθέν, Gal.17(1).328); μωλυόμενα· κατὰ βραχὺ ἀπομαραινόμενα, Hp.ap.Gal.19.124; μεμωλυσμένους (-μολ- codd.)· ἔνιοι μὲν τοὺς κατεψυγμένους, ἔνιοι δὲ τοὺς ἐσκιρρωμένους καὶ λιθώδεις ᾠήθησαν, Gal.19.121; of certain diseases, κατὰ τὴν ἀρχὴν ὑποβρύχιά τε καὶ μωλυνόμενα (μολ- codd.) φαίνεται latent and *'simmering'*, Id.9.898; cf. μεμολυσμένως. 2. *relax*, μεμωλυσμένη· παρειμένη, Hsch. s.v. μῶλυς; μωλύεται· γηράσκει, Id.; μωλύειν· τὸ ἐκλύειν καὶ διέλκειν καὶ μαραίνειν, Phryn.PSp.89B.; μωλύων κρέας· τὸ ἠρέμα διαχεόμενον καὶ μὴ συνεστός, ibid.; δι' οὗ μωλύονται αἱ ὁρμαὶ καὶ τὰ πάθη, as expl. of μῶλυ, Cleanth.ap.Apollon.Lex. s.v. μῶλυ. III. also of ulcers, *become septic*, ἢν ἕλκος γένηται.., καὶ μὴ ταχὺ ὑγιανθῇ ἀλλὰ μωλυνθῇ (μολυνθῇ codd., quod fort. legend.) Hp.Steril.213. IV. f.l. for μολεύειν (q.v.) in Thphr.HP2.2.2. (μωλ- confirmed by the metre in Poet.deherb. ll. cc., and by Cleanth. l.c.; prob. derived from μῶλυς, cf. Demetr.Lac.Herc.1014.58.)

**μωλωπ-ίζω**, *beat and bruise severely*, τινα Aq.Ca.5.7:—Pass., μεμωλωπισμένος *marked with stripes*, Plu.2.126c. II. *resemble mosquito bites*, Herod.Med.ap.Act.5.129. **-ικός**, ή, όν, *suitable for weals*, Gal.19.139.

**μώλωψ**, ωπος, ὁ, *mark of a stripe, weal, bruise*, Hyp.Fr.200, Arist. Pr.889$^{b}$10, LxxIs.53.5, D.H.16.5, Plu.2.565b, etc.; of an eruption resembling mosquito bites, Herod.Med.ap.Aët.5.129; *blood-clot*, Paul.Aeg.6.8 (pl.); πορφύρεοι μώλωπες, satirically of kings, Daphit. ap.Str.14.1.39.

**μῶμαι**, Med., 3 sg. μῶται Epich.117; 3 pl. μῶνται Euph.157; imper. μῶσο Epich.[288] (corr. Ahrens), prob. in Hsch.; 3 sg. opt. μῷτο Diotog.ap.Stob.3.1.100; inf. μῶσθαι Thgn.771, Pl.Cra.406a, Jul. Or.7.219a; part. μώμενος A.Ch.45,441 (both lyr.), S.Tr.1136, OC836 (lyr.): aor. ἐμώσατο Hsch.:—*seek after, covet*, c. acc., Thgn. l.c., etc.; τὸ ἀκριβές Diotog. l.c.; τὸ λανθάνον Jul. l.c.: c. inf. or abs., A. ll. cc. II. *meditate* or *purpose*, c. acc., S. ll. cc. (Non-thematic mō-, prob. cogn. with Lat. *mōs* 'will', 'caprice'; cf. μαίομαι.)

**μωμ-αίνω**, = sq., Hdn.Epim.88. **-άομαι**, Ion. -έομαι, 3 pl. -εῦνται Thgn.369, cf. 169; inf. -έεσθαι Hp.deArte1: fut. -ήσομαι Il.3.412, Thgn.1079; Dor. μωμάσομαι Simon.5.5: aor. ἐμωμησάμην A.Ag.277; Dor. poet. μωμάσατο Theoc.9.24: (μῶμος):—*find fault with, blame, criticize*, c. acc., Il. l.c., Thgn.169, 369, Simon. l.c., A. l.c., Ar.Av.171, Call.Dian.222:—poet., Ion. (Democr.48, Eus.Mynd. 1), and later Prose, Luc.Hist.Conscr.33, al.: aor. μωμηθῆναι in pass. sense, 2Ep.Cor.6.3; v. μωκάομαι.

**μῶμαρ**, τό, poet. for μῶμος, Lyc.1134.

**μωμ-εύω**, = μωμάομαι, Od.6.274, Hes.Op.756. **-ηλός**, ή, όν, *blameworthy*, Hdn.Epim.88. **-ημα**, ατος, τό, *blame*, v.l. for μώκημα, LxxSi.31(34).18. **-ησις**, εως, ἡ, *blame, censure*, Sch.Il. 2.199. **-ητέον**, *one must censure*, Erot. **-ητής**, οῦ, ὁ, *censurer*, Hp.deArte8. **-ητικός**, ή, όν, *censorious*, Phld.Ir.p.57W., Ptol. Tetr.160, Vett.Val.16.22. **-ητός**, ή, όν, *to be blamed*, A.Th. 508, Luc.Alex.3. 2. *bringing disgrace*, ἀστήρ Cat.Cod.Astr.2. 163. **-ιμος**, ον, *blameful*, τὸ μ. Stoic.2.62.

**μῶμος**, ὁ, *blame, reproach, disgrace*, μῶμον ἀνάψαι to set a *brand* upon one, Od.2.86, cf. Semon.7.84,105, Pi.O.6.74, P.1.82; βροτῶν μ. πάντεσσι.. ἐστὶν ἐπ' ἔργοις B.12.202, cf. APl.4.84; οὐ γὰρ ἔσθ' ὅπως σπουδῆς δικαίας μ. ἅψεταί ποτε S.Fr.257: also in later Prose, as Lxx Si.11.31, Cic.Att.5.20.6, Plu.2.820a, Luc.Herm.20. 2. *blemish*, LxxLe.24.19, al., 2Ep.Pet.2.13. II. personified, *Momus*, first in Hes.Th.214, cf. Pl.R.487a, Babr.59.6.

**μωμοσκόπος**, ον, *looking for blemishes* in sacrificial victims, Ph.1. 320.

**μῶν**, Adv., contr. for μὴ οὖν, μῶν χαραδριὸν περνᾷς· Hippon.52: freq. in Trag., Com., and Pl.; usu. in questions to which a neg. answer is suggested, *surely not?* μῶν ἄλγος ἴσχεις; you are *not* in pain, *are you?* S.Ph.734, cf. E.Hec.676,754, Hel.1198, Achae.9, Ar. Lys.69, Pl.Prt.310d.—Its origin from μὴ οὖν was forgotten, hence μῶν οὖν..; in A.Ch.177, E.Andr.82; μῶν οὖν δῆτα..; Ar.Pl.845: sts. also μῶν μή..; Pl.Phd.84c, R.505c; also μῶν οὐ..; suggesting an affirm. answer, A.Supp.417, S.OC1729 (lyr.), Pl.Sph.234a, etc.

®**μωνιή**· ὀλιγωρία, Hsch. **μωνιόν**· μάταιον, ἀχρεῖον, Id.

**μῶνος**, α, ον, Dor. for μοῦνος, μόνος.

**μῶνυξ**, ῠχος, ὁ, ἡ, τό, *with a single*, i.e. *uncloven, hoof*, epith. of the horse, freq. in Il., 5.236, al.; once in Od., 15.46, cf. Sol.23, E.Ph. 793 (lyr., dub. l.), Stud.Pont.3.16 (ii/i B.C.); also μ. ὗες Arist.HA 499$^{b}$13; τὰ μ. [τῶν ζῴων] Hp.Art.8; τετραπόδων ὅσα μ. Porph.Abst. 4.7; [γένει] τῷ καλουμένῳ μώνυχι Pl.Plt.265d. (From *sm-* (weak form of *sem-*, cf. εἷς) and ὄνυξ (ὀ- lengthd. in composition).)

**μώνῠχος**, ον, = foreg., ὗς Antig.Mir.66.

**μωρ-αίνω**, fut. -ᾰνῶ E.Med.614: aor. ἐμώρᾱνα A.Pers.719 (troch.): —Pass., v. infr. II: (μωρός):—*to be silly, foolish, drivel*, E. l.c., X. Mem.1.1.11, Phld.Mus.p.103K., Luc.Nav.45, etc.; *play the fool*, Arist.EN1148$^{b}$2: c. acc. cogn., πεῖραν μ. *make a mad* attempt, A. l.c.; οὐδεὶς.. ταῦτα μωραίνει *indulges in* these *follies*, E.Fr.282.22: euphem. of illicit love, γυναῖκα μωραίνουσαν Id.Andr.674. II. causal, *make foolish, convict of folly*, ἡ βουλὴ αὐτῶν μωρανθήσεται Lxx Is.19.11; ἐμωράνθην σφόδρα ib.2Ki.24.10, cf. 1Ep.Cor.1.20:—Pass., *to become foolish, be stupefied*, [αἶγες] ἑστᾶσιν ὥσπερ μεμωραμμέναι Arist. HA610$^{b}$30 (sed cf. μωρόομαι); *to become insipid*, ἐὰν τὸ ἅλας μωρανθῇ Ev.Matt.5.13. **-ανσις**, εως, ἡ, = μωρία, Sch.rec.A.Th.756. **-εύω**, = μωραίνω, LxxIs.44.25. **-ία**, Ion. -ίη, ἡ, (μωρός) *folly*, Hdt.1. 146; μωρίας πλέως S.Aj.1150, cf. 745; μωρίην ἐπιφέρειν τισί to impute *folly* to them, Hdt.1.131; μωρίαν ὀφλισκάνειν to be charged with it, S. Ant.470; ἐδόκει μ. εἶναι ταῦτα Th.5.41; μωρίᾳ φιλονικεῖν *foolishly*, Id. 4.64; τῆς μ. *what folly!* Ar.Nu.818, Ec.787; εἰς τοῦτ' ἀφῖχθε μωρίας D.9.54; πολλὴ μ. τοῦ διανοήματος Pl.Lg.818d; of illicit love, E.Hipp. 644, Ion545.

**μωρίαι**· ἵπποι καὶ βοῦς (Arc.), Hsch.

**μωρίζω**, *to be foolish*, Gal.12.965.

®**μώριος**, ἡ, = μανδραγόρας ἄρρην, Dsc.4.75.2, Plin.HN25.148. 2. = στρύχνον ὑπνωτικόν, Dsc.4.75.7, Plin.HN21.180. 3. a plant used in philtres, Hsch.

**μωρίων**, ωνος, ὁ, *fool*, or pr. n. Μωρίων, Arc.17 cod. Oxon. (Cf. Lat. *morio*.)

**μωρο-βλάπτης**, ου, ὁ, *pestilent fool*, Anon. in Script.Physiogn. ii p.126 Foerster. **-κᾰκοήθης**, ες, *both knave and fool*, Procop.Arc. 6. **-κᾰκος**, ον, = foreg., Ptol.Tetr.167. **-κᾰλος**, ον, f.l. for foreg., ib.158. **-κλέπτης**, ου, ὁ, *stupid thief*, Aesop.38, Hsch. s.v. Λυδός.

**μωρολογ-έω**, *talk in a silly way*, Plu.2.175d; ὁπόσοι τάδε μ. Archestr. Fr.23.18. **-ημα**, ατος, τό, *silly tale*, Epicur.Fr.228 (pl.). **-ία**, ἡ, *silly talk*, Arist.HA492$^{b}$2, Ep.Eph.5.4, Plu.2.504b, S.E.M.1.174. **-ος** (parox.), ον, *speaking foolishly*, Arist.Phgn.810$^{b}$15, Man.4.446.

**μωρονοέω**, *think foolishly*, Cat.Cod.Astr.8(1).184.

**μωρόομαι**, Pass., (μωρός) *become dull* or *sluggish*, ἐμωρώθη ἡ καρδίη *was stupefied*, Hp.Virg.1; [αἶγες] ἑστᾶσιν ὥσπερ μεμωρωμέναι as if *stupefied*, v.l. in Arist.HA610$^{b}$30 (cf. μωραίνω); μεμωρωμένα *imbecility*, Hp.Prorrh.1.92; μεμωρῶσθαι περί τι prob. l. in Corn.ND25.

**μωρο-ποιέω**, *deal foolishly*, Astramps.Orac.97.10:—also in Med., Plb.29.9.1. **-ποιός**, όν, *dealing foolishly*, Hsch. s.v. ἠλεός. **-πόνηρος**, ον, *stupidly wicked*, Adam.2.58, Polem.Phgn.68.

®**μωρός**, ά, όν, Att. μῶρος Hdn.Gr.1.192: μῶρος as fem., E.Med.61, but acc. μώραν Herod.5.17 (s.v.l.):—*dull, sluggish*, of the nerves, Hp.Genit.2; χειμῶνος ἀρχομένου μ. γίνονται οἱ ἐργάται [τῶν σφηκῶν] Arist.HA628$^{a}$6. 2. of persons, *dull, stupid*, μωροῦ φωτὸς ἅδε βουλά Simon.57.6, cf. S.Ant.220, 470, Isoc.5.94, LxxSi.18.18, al., Ev.Matt.7.26, etc.: Comp. in prov., μωρότερος Μορύχου Sophr.74: Sup., X.An.3.2.22. b. in a religious sense, λαὸς μ. καὶ ἀκάρ-

διος LXX *Je.*5.21, al. 3. of things, δέδοικα μῶρον πυραύστου μόρον A.*Fr.*288; μῶρόν ἐστι τοὐγχείρημά σου S.*OT*540; τὸ μ. *folly*, E.*Hipp.* 966; τὸ μ. τοῦ θεοῦ σοφώτερον τῶν ἀνθρώπων ἐστί 1*Ep.Cor.*1.25; μῶρα φρονεῖν, φωνεῖν, δρᾶν, S.*Aj.*594, *OT*433, *Ant.*469; μῶρα.. μῶρος λέγει E.*Ba.*369, cf. LXX *Is.*32.6; μ. βουλεύεσθαι Ar.*Ec.*474. b. μ. ἀνάγκη *blind* necessity, Epicur.*Nat.*101 G. 4. of taste, *insipid, flat, Com. Adesp.*596, Diocl.*Fr.*138, Dsc.4.19. II. Adv. -ρως X.*An.*7.6. 21. (Cf. Skt. *mūrás* 'idiot'.)

**μωρό-σοφος**, ον, *foolishly wise, sapient fool*, Luc.*Alex.*40. **-σῦκον**, τό, = συκόμωρον, Cels.3.18. **-φρων**, ονος, ὁ, ἡ, (φρήν) *dull-witted*, Man.4.283.

**μώρτα**· σῖτος, Hsch.

**μώρωσις**, εως, Ion. ιος, ἡ, *dullness, sluggishness*, Hp.*Virg.*1; *extreme dementia*, Id.*Prorrh.*1.32, Gal.16.696.

**Μῶσα**, Dor. for Μοῦσα.

**μῶσις**, εως, ἡ, (μῶμαι) *searching*, Corn.*ND*28: as etym. of Μοῦσα, ib.14.

**μώστιον**, τό, = μώϊον, *Sammelb.*6801.29 (iii B.C.), *PGrenf.*1.14.5 (ii B.C.), *BGU*1523 (Ptol.).

**μωτάπει**· ἰάσεται, Hsch. (cf. μοτ[τ]ώσει· ἰάσεται δι' ὀθονίων, Id.). **μώχεται**· φθονεῖ, Id. **μῶχος**, ὁ, = μῶκος, *Gloss.* ❀ **μώψ**· ὁ μὴ ὀξυδορκῶν, καθαροὺς δὲ ἔχων τοὺς ὀφθαλμούς, Hsch.

# N

**N** **ν, νῦ**, τό, indecl., fourteenth (later thirteenth) letter of Greek alphabet; as numeral, ν' = 50, but ͵ν = 50,000.

**νᾶας**, Dor. acc. pl. of ναῦς (q.v.).

**ναβαισατρεῦ**, barbarous word in Ar.*Av.*1615 (expld. as a term of commendation); v.l. βαβακατρεῦ.

❀ **νάβλα**, ἡ, *a musical instrument of ten* or (acc. to J.*AJ*7.12.3) *of twelve strings*, cj. in S.*Fr.*849, cf. LXX 1*Ki.*10.5, al.:—also **νάβλας**, α, ὁ, Sopat.16, Philem.44, Str.10.3.17; cf. ναῦλον I. (Semitic word, cf. Hebr. *nēbel*; Phoenician, acc. to Ath.4.175b.). II. dub. sens. in acc. τὸν νάβλα, *OGI*175.9 (Egypt, ii B.C.).

**ναβλ-ίζω**, = ψάλλω, *Gloss.* **-ιστής**, οῦ, ὁ, *player on the* νάβλα, Euph.*Fr.Hist.*8. **-ιστοκτῠπεύς**, έως, ὁ, = foreg., Man.4.185.

**ναβοῦς**, ὁ, *camelopard*, *IG*14.1302 (Praeneste). (Ethiopian, acc. to Plin.*HN*8.69.)

**νᾰγεύς**, έως, ὁ, (νάσσω) *pestle*, Tz. ad Hes.*Op.*421.

**νάγμα**, ατος, τό, *anything piled up*, as a stone wall, J.*BJ*1.21.7.

❀ **νάερρα**· δέσποινα, Hsch. **ναέτειρα** (ναιτ- cod.)· οἰκοδέσποινα, Id.

**νᾰετήρ**, ῆρος, ὁ, = sq., *AP*7.409 (Antip. Thess.), D.P.455, etc.

**νᾰέτης**, ου, Dor. **νᾰέτας**, α, ὁ, *inhabitant*, Simon.57, Ephipp.5.1 (anap.), *AP*9.535, Limen.41, *IG*5(2).474 (Megalopolis): as fem., *AP* 6.207.10 (Arch.).

**ναέτωρ**, = νάτωρ, Hsch.

❀ **νᾱεύω**, (ναός) *take sanctuary in a temple*, *Leg.Gort.*1.39.

**ναηλεῖς**· πρόσφατοι (Thess.), Hsch.; cf. νεαλής. **ναθμός**, ὁ, *reef*, Id. II. *upright threads in a loom*, Id. **νάθραξ**, = νάρθηξ, Id.

❀ **ναί**, Adv., used to express strong affirmation, *yea, verily*, in Hom. mostly folld. by δή, ν. δὴ ταῦτά γε πάντα.. κατὰ μοῖραν ἔειπες Il.1.286, al.; ν. μήν Emp.76.2; ν. μάν Theoc.27.27; ν. μέν A.R. 2.151; ν. μέντοι Luc.*Astr.*14: used alone, σὲ κρίνω, ν. σέ *yea* thee, S.*El.*1445; ἀποκρίνασθαι ν. ἢ οὔ Arist.*Top.*158ᵃ16, etc.; τὸ ε̄ οὐκ ἔστι χαρακτηριστικὸν.., τὸ δὲ ᾱ ναί Choerob. *in Theod.*2.85. 2. freq. in oaths, ν. μά *yea by*.., v. μά; ν. alone, ν. τὰν Κόραν Ar.*V.*1438, cf. E. *Ba.*534 (lyr.); ν. τὸν Ποτιδᾶν Epich.81; ν. τὼ σιώ X.*HG*4.4.10; ν. πρὸς θεῶν ἀρήξατ' E.*Med.*1277. II. in answers, *yes*, τοῦτ' ἐτήτυμον; Answ. ν. A.*Pers.*738 (troch.), cf. S.*El.*845 (lyr.), Pl.*Tht.*193a, *Grg.* 448b, etc.; doubled, Ar.*Nu.*1468, Call.*Fr.*1.56P., *Ev.Matt.*5.37. 2. ν. folld. by ἀλλά, etc., to mark a qualified assent, *yes*, but.., Aeschin. 3.84; ν., κατὰ σχολήν γε ἴσως· οὐ μήν.. Pl.*Sph.*226e, cf. *R.*415e.

**ναΐ**, Dor. poet. dat. of ναῦς.

**Ναΐ-α** [νᾱ], τά, festival of Zeus Νάϊος, at Dodona, *IG*5(2).118.21 (Tegea); written Νᾶα ib.2.1318. **-ᾰκός**, ή, όν, *of the Naiads*, λιμένες *AP*10.21 (Phld.). **-αρχος**, ὁ, perh. *warden of temple of Zeus* Νάϊος, *SIG*1206.7 (Dodona). **-άς**, Ion. **Νηϊάς**, άδος, ἡ, (νάω) *Naiad, river-nymph, spring-nymph*, Od.13.104,356 (pl.): in sg., A.R. 1.626:—also **Ναΐς**, Ion. **Νηΐς**, ΐδος, ἡ, in sg., νηῒς Ἀβαρβαρέη Il.6.22; νύμφη τέκε νηῒς 14.444, cf. Pi.*P.*9.16, E.*Hel.*187 (lyr.): pl. Ναΐδες, Str.10.3.10, Paus.8.4.2, etc.

**ναιδᾶμῶς**, Com. form of ναί, *yes certainly*, opp. οὐδαμῶς or μηδαμῶς, *Com.Adesp.*1086.

❀ **ναΐδιον** [ῐδ], τό, Dim. of ναός, Plb.6.53.4, Str.8.6.21.

❀ **ναιετάω**, in pres. forms, -άω Od.9.23, -άει Hes.*Th.*775, -ῶουσι Il. 4.45; freq. in part. ναιετάων, Od.6.245, al., acc. -άοντα 4.96, etc., fem. -άωσα (v.l. -άουσα) Il.2.648, 3.387, 6.415, Od.1.404, 8.574 (-όωσα Aristarch. ad Il.6.415): Ion. impf. ναιετάασκον Il.2.841, etc.: (ναίω): 1. of persons, *dwell*, freq. in Ep.; τοὶ ἐπὶ χθονὶ ναιετάουσι Od.6.153, cf. Hes.*Th.*564; ᾗ ἔνι ναιετάασκε Od.15.385: c. dat. loci, Λακεδαίμονι ν. Il.3.387; Κρήτῃ Od.17.523; ὑπὸ χθονὶ Hes.*Th.* 621; ὑπὸ ὅροις, ἀμφὶ.. θέμεθλα ναιετάοντες, Pi.*O.*6.78, *P.*4.180. 2. c. acc. loci, *dwell in, inhabit*, Λάρισαν, Ἰθάκην, etc., Il.2.841, Od.9.21, etc.; δώματα Hes.*Th.*816. II. of places, *to be situated, lie*, Il.4. 45, Od.9.23; of buildings, 2.400, al.: hence, *exist*, Ἰθάκης ἔτι ναιεταούσης 1.404.—Ep. and Lyr. word, once in Trag., in part. ναιετῶν cj. Dind. metri gr. in S.*Ant.*1123 (lyr.).

**ναιέτις**, ιδος, ἡ, fem. of *ναιέτης, = ναέτης, Call. in *PSI*9.1092.58.

**ναίκι**, barbarism for ναίχι in Ar.*Th.*1183, 1218.

**ναικισήρης**, ες, *one who sneers* or *carps*, Pherecr.222, Hermipp.90.

**ναικισσορεύω**, *disparage*, Hsch.

**νᾱϊκός**, ή, όν, *of a temple*, εὔθυνοι *GDI*1370 (Dodona).

**ναινεύρη**· νὴ τὸν Ἄρη, Ἀττικοὶ δὲ ποδοκάκη, Hsch. **ναῖον**, v. νάω.

❀ **νάϊος**, α, ον, Dor. for νήϊος.

**Νάϊος** [ᾰ], ὁ, epith. of Zeus at Dodona, *GDI*1567, al., Sch.Il.16. 233:—also **Νᾶος**, *GDI*1563, al.; also at Carthaea, *IG*12(5).551 (cf. p.329).

**ναιός**, = ναός, Clinias ap.Sch.A.R.2.1085, cf. Hsch.

**ναῖρον**, τό, a plant used in perfumery; prob. f.l. for μᾶρον (q.v.) in Thphr.*HP*9.7.3.

❀ **Ναΐς**, v. Ναϊάς.

**ναισιελία**, ἡ, = ἀποπληξία, ἐμβροντησία, Hsch.:—also **ναισήματα**, Id.

**νᾱϊσκ-άριον**, τό, Dim. of ναΐσκος, *PMag.Par.*1.3145, Sch.Aeschin. 1.10, *Gloss.* **-ιον**, τό, = foreg., Ὀσειρίδος *POxy.*521.4 (ii A.D.). II. name of various *bandages*, Sostratus and Apollonius ap.Gal.12.496 Chart. ❀ **-ος** (parox.), ὁ, Dim. of ναός, *shrine*, Str.14.1.4, J.*AJ*8.4.4.

❀ **ναίχῐ** (on the accent v. Hdn.Gr.1.9), Adv., for ναί, like οὐχί for οὐ, μήχι for μή, S.*OT*684, Pl.*Hipparch.*232a, Men.*Sam.*81, Call.*Epigr.* 30.5.

❀ **ναίω**, poet. Verb, Act. (intr.) only in pres. and impf. (Ep. ναίεσκον Il.5.708), fut. and aor. in causal and Med. and Pass. forms, v. infr. II, III: 1. of persons, *dwell, abide*, mostly folld. by a Prep. of Place, ἐν Ὕλῃ, etc., Il.l.c., etc.; ῥοῇς ἔπι Σαγγαρίοιο 16.719; ἐπ' ἄκρων ὀρέων S. *OT*1105 (lyr.); κατὰ πτόλιν Il.2.130; ἀν' οὔρεα Hes.*Th.*130; πὰρ ποταμὸν Il.2.522; ὑπὸ Πλάκῳ 6.396: c. dat. loci, αἰθέρι ναίων 2.412, Hes. *Op.*18, etc.; ν. μετά τινος S.*Ph.*1105 (lyr.): metaph., τὴν σὴν δ' ὁμοῦ ναίουσαν [ὀργήν] Id.*OT*338; τὰν ἀρετὰν ναίειν ἐπὶ πέτραις Simon.58: with Adv., [κακότης] ἐγγύθι ναίει Hes.*Op.*288; ἵνα αἱ Φορκίδες ναίουσι A.*Pr.*794. b. c. acc. loci, *dwell in, inhabit*, οἰκία, δώματα, Od.20. 288, Hes.*Op.*8, cf. Pi.*P.*7.5, al.; ἄλα, πλάκας ὀρέων, E.*Hel.*1584, *Ba.* 719; freq. with place-names, Il.2.615, Alex.22, etc.: metaph., Πειθὼ ναίει καὶ Χάρις υἱὸν Ἀγησίλα dub. in Pi.*Fr.*123.10; of the statues of gods, πρόπυλα ναίουσιν τάδε S.*El.*1375:—Pass., *to be inhabited*, Id.*Fr.* 1125 (in aor. ἐνάσθη), etc.; πολίταις Theoc.16.88; ὑπ' ἀνδράσι A.R.1. 794. 2. of places, *lie, be situated*, once in Hom., νήσων αἳ ναίουσι πέρην ἁλὸς Il.2.626; ὦ κλεινὰ Σαλαμίς, σὺ μέν που ναίεις ἁλίπλακτος S. *Aj.*598 (lyr.). II. causal, in Ep. aor. ἔνασσα or νάσσα, Med. ἐνασσάμην: 1. c. acc. loci, *give one to dwell in*, καί κέ οἱ Ἄργεϊ νάσσα πόλιν I would have *given* him a town in Argos *for his home*, Od.4. 174; *make habitable, build*, νηὸν ἔνασσαν *h.Ap.*298; *settle*, Εὔβοιαν ἕλον καὶ ἔνασσαν Pi.*Pae.*5.36:—in Med., *found*, μυρία δ' ἄστη νάσσατ' ἐποιχόμενος A.R.4.275:—in Pass., of places, like Act. I.2, *to be situated*, πολίων εὖ ναιομενάων Il.3.400, al. 2. c. acc. pers., *let one dwell, settle* him, ἐν Ἄργει ἔνασσεν Ἡρακλέος ἐκγόνους Pi.*P.*5.71:—in Med., νάσσατο κούρην A.R.4.567. III. Med. and Pass. in act. sense, fut. νάσσομαι Id.2.747: Ep. aor. 1 νάσσατο Hes.*Op.*639, Dem.Bith.6, Philet.24; later 3 pl. ναιήσαντο D.P.349: pf. νένασται *IG*14.1389 i 8; part. νενασμένος D.P.264: aor. Pass. ἐνάσθην, πατὴρ ἐμὸς Ἄργεϊ νάσθη my father *settled* at Argos, Il.14.119.—More freq. in Compos. with ἀπό, κατά.

**νάκαφθον**, v. νάρκαφθον.

**νάκη** [ᾰ], ἡ, *woolly* or *hairy skin*, ἂν δὲ νάκην ἕλετ' αἰγὸς Od.14.530; also of sheep, Lyc.1310; αἰγῶν νάκαι καὶ προβάτων Paus.4.11.3. (Cf. OE. *næsc* 'leather'.)

**νᾰκο-δαίμων**, ονος, ὁ, = sq., with a play on κακοδαίμων, Ath.8. 352b. **-δέψης**, ου, ὁ, (δέψω) *currier*, Hp.*Vict.*1.19, Ath.8. 352b. **-κλέψ**, ὁ, ἡ, *fleece-stealer*, Hdn.Gr.1.246.

**νάκολον**· τὸ ἀκάθαρτον, Hsch.

**Νᾱκόρειοι**, οἱ, a guild at Camirus, *IG*12(1).701.12.

❀ **Νᾱκόρειον**, v. νεωκόριον. **νᾱκόρος**, v. νεωκόρος.

**νάκος** [ᾰ], εος, τό, *fleece*, ν. κριοῦ Pi.*P.*4.68, Hdt.2.42, cf. Simon.21, *Berl.Sitzb.*1927.170 (Cyrene), Theoc.5.2, *SIG*560.41 (Epidamnus, found at Magnesia, iii B.C.), Luc.*Am.*34.

**νᾰκο-τιλτέω**, *pluck* or *shear off wool*, Archipp.32. ❀ **-τίλτης**, ου, ὁ, *wool-plucker, shearer*, Philem.14. **-τιλτος**, ον, *with the wool plucked off*, Cratin.41.

❀ **νακτός**, ή, όν, (νάσσω) *close-pressed, solid*, ἄμμου χώμασι νακτῆς Plu. *CG*7; τὰ νακτά *felt*, Hsch. II. dub. sens. in *CRAcad.Inscr.*1930. 213 (Susa, i B.C.).

❀ **νᾰκύριον**, τό, Dim. of νάκος, Hsch.

**νᾶμα**, ατος, τό, (νάω) *anything flowing, running water, stream, spring*, ν. Μναμοσύνας cj. in Simon.45, cf. A.*Pr.*806, S.*Ant.*1130 (lyr.); Κασταλίδος νάματα *Pae.Delph.*1.6; δακρύων θερμὰ ν. S.*Tr.*919; νάματ' ὄσσων E.*HF*625; ν. πυρός Id.*Med.*1187; ν. Βάκχιον Ar.*Ec.*14; μὰ νάματα Antiph.296 (= Timocl.38); ν. θυγατέρων ταύρων, i.e. honey, Ph.Tars.ap.Gal.13.269; φλέγματος, χολῆς ν., Philostr.*Gym.*42: freq. in Pl., as κρηνῶν καὶ ποταμῶν νάματα *Criti.*111d: metaph., λόγων ν. *Ti.*75e. 2. *wooden conduit*, Hsch. II. νάματα· προβολαί, Id.

❀ **ναμαρᾶς**, ᾶ, Semitic word of uncertain meaning, Roussel *Délos Colonie Athénienne* p.424.

**νᾱμᾰσῐπήξ**, ῆγος, ὁ, ἡ, *crystallized by evaporation from water*, ἅλς Aglaïas 22.

**νᾱμᾰτ-ιαῖος**, α, ον, *flowing*, ὕδατα *spring* water, Aeschin.2.115, cf. Thphr.*HP*4.2.9, prob. in Alciphr.3.13. **-ιον**, τό, Dim. of νᾶμα, Thphr.*Ign*.29, Phylarch.65 J. **-ώδης**, ες, *full of springs*, Thphr. *CP*3.6.3.

**νᾱμερτής, νᾱμέρτεια**, Dor. for νημ-. **νᾶν**, Dor. acc. of ναῦς. **νανεῖ**· ἵπταται, and **νανῆσαι**· ἵπτασθαι, Hsch. **νάνίον**, τό, Dim. of νᾶνος, *puppet, doll*, *Gloss*. II. νάνιον· ἀμνίον, σφάγιον, Hsch. **νάνναζον**· παιζόμενον, Id.

**ναννάρ-ιον**, τό, *prodigal*, Hsch.: Ναννάριον, pr. n. of a courtesan, Theophil.11. **-ίς**· κίναιδος, Hsch. **-ιστής**, οῦ, ὁ, *prodigal*, Phot. (ναναρ- cod.).

**νάννας**, ὁ, or **νάννα**, ἡ, *maternal* or *paternal uncle* or *aunt*, Hsch.; cf. νέννος. **νάννη**, ἡ, *maternal aunt*, Id.

**Ναννίον**, name of a courtesan, Amphis 23; cf. ναννάριον.

**νανοκάκα**· διὰ ῥινῶν λαλοῦσα, Hsch.

⊛ **νᾶνος**, ὁ, *dwarf*, Ar.*Fr*.427, Arist.*HA*577$^b$27, Longin.44.5; *one whose limbs are too small for his body*, Arist.*PA*686$^b$10. II. *cheese-cake*, Ath.14.646c. (Freq. written νάννος in codd.; cf. sq.)

**νᾱνοφυής**, ές, *of dwarfish stature*, Ar.*Pax*790 (ναννο- codd.).

**νᾱνώδης**, ες, *dwarfish, ill-proportioned*, Arist.*PA*686$^b$3.

**Ναξιουργής**, ές, *of Naxian work*, κάνθαρος Ar.*Pax*143.

**Νάξος**, ἡ, *Naxos*, *h.Ap*.44, etc.:—Adj. **Νάξιος**, α, ον, *Naxian*: οἱ N. *the Naxians*, Hdt.5.30, etc.; Ναξία ἀκόνα a *Naxian* whetstone, Pi.*I*.6(5).73, Dsc.5.149; N. πέτρη *AP*15.25.4 (Besant.); N. λίθος Phot.; γέρρα Νάξια (v. γέρρον v. 2) Epich.235: **Ναξιακά**, τά, *a work on Naxos*, by Andriscus, Parth.9tit.

**ναξος** (accent unknown), η, ον, *solid*, not hollow, ν. παγχρύσεος.. κολοσσός Epigr.ap.Phot. s.v. Κυψελιδῶν ἀνάθημα (s.v.l.).

**νᾱο-δόμος**, ον, (δέμω) *temple-building*, τέχνη *Epigr.Gr*.409.4 (Arycanda). **-ειδής**, ές, *in the form of a shrine*, παστῆον *SIG*996.23 (Smyrna). **-κόρος**, v. νεωκόρος. ⊛ **-λέκτης**, ου, ὁ, dub. sens. in *PLond*.3.982.2 (iv A.D.). **-ποιέω, -ποιία, -ποϊκός, -ποιός**, v. νεω-ποιέω, -ποιία, -ποϊκός, -ποιός. **-πόλος**, Ion. νηοπ-, ον, *dwelling* or *busied in a temple*, μάντις Pi.*Fr*.51 Schroeder, cf. Man.4.427. II. as Subst., *overseer of a temple*, Hes.*Th*.991.

⊛ **νᾱός**, ὁ, Dor., Thess., etc. form. *Leg.Gort*.1.42, *IG*9(2).517.45 (Larissa, iii B.C.), etc., used also in Trag. (even dialogue) to the exclusion of νεώς, S.*El*.8, E.*Hipp*.31, al., exc. A.*Pers*.810, rare in Att. Prose and Com., Pl.*R*.394a, *Lg*.738c, 814b, Arist.*EN*1174$^a$24, Posidipp.29.1, more freq. in X., *HG*2.3.20, *An*.5.3.9, al., found in Att. Inscrr. from iii B.C., *IG*2$^2$.1314.18, 1315.28, etc., and in Hellenistic and later Gr. (along with νεώς), *SIG*277 (Priene, iv B.C.), 214 (Phanagoria, iv B.C.), 494.3 (Delph., iii B.C.), Lxx 1*Ki*.1.9, al. (νεώς only in 2*Ma*.), *UPZ*6.22 (ii B.C.), Plb.9.30.2 (νεώς 10.4.4), etc.; Ion. **νηός**, always in Hom. and Hdt. (v. infr.), but gen. νε[ῶ] *IG*12(7).1.4 (Amorgos, v B.C.); dat. νειῷ *Michel*832.38 (Samos, iv B.C.); Att. **νεώς** (Attic Inscrr. of v–iii B.C. (v. infr.), once in Trag. (v. supr.), freq. in Prose authors and found in Com. (v. infr.)); declension, nom. νεώς X.*HG*1.6.1; gen. νεώ *IG*1$^2$.4.9, 80.6, Ar.*Pl*.733, *IG*2$^2$.1524.45, *SIG*1219.32 (Gambreum, iii B.C.); dat. νεῴ *IG*1$^2$.6.122, 256.4, Antipho6.39, Alex.40.3, *IG*2$^2$.1504.7; acc. νεών ib.1$^2$.24.13, al., X.*HG*6.5.9, Ar. *Nu*.401, *Pl*.741, Philem.139, f.l. in E.*HF*340, later νεώ *IG*2$^2$.212.35 (iv B.C.), al., Lxx 2*Ma*.6.2, al., D.S.16.58 (v.l. νεών), *SIG*877*A*10 (ii/iii A.D.), v.l. in D.H.4.26, but νεών Aristid.*Or*.27(16).19 (v.l. νεώ), Ach.Tat.3.6 (v.l. νεώ Bast*Epist.Crit*.p.176), etc.: pl. nom. νεῴ X. *HG*6.4.7; acc. νεώς A.*Pers*.810, Isoc.5.117, Plb.10.4.4; dat. νεῴς *IG*1$^2$.384; on the accent v. Hdn.Gr.1.8: Aeol. **ναῦος** Alc.9, *IG*12(2).60.27 (Mytil.); Spartan ναϝός ib.5(1).1564 (pl., found at Delos, v/iv B.C.):—*temple*, Il.1.39, al., Pi.*O*.13.21 (pl.), etc. II. *inmost part of a temple, shrine* containing the image of the god, Hdt.1.183, 6.19, X.*Ap*.15, *UPZ*1.c.; ἐν παντὶ ἱερῷ ὅπου ναός ἐστι *PGnom*.79 (ii A.D.). III. *portable shrine* carried in processions, Hdt.2.63, D.S.1.15, etc. IV. metaph., of Christians, ν. θεοῦ ἐστε 1*Ep.Cor*.3.16; of the body of Christ, *Ev.Jo*.2.19, 21. [νάόν and νᾱῷ Orph.*Fr*.32$^b$iv (Phaestus, ii B.C.); elsewh. ᾱ.] (Perh. fr. νασ-ϝός, cf. ναίω.)

**νᾱός**, Dor. and Att. poet. gen. from ναῦς. **Νᾱος**, v. Ναῖος.

**νᾱουργός**, ὁ, *temple-builder*, ν. τέκτονες *Ephes*.3.75.

**νᾱοφύλαξ** [ῠ], ἄκος, ὁ, (ναός) *keeper, warden of a temple*, E.*IT*1284, Arist.*Pol*.1322$^b$25, *BGU*362 (iii A.D.); cf. ναυφύλαξ II. II. (ναῦς) *master* or *pilot of a ship*, S.*Fr*.143.

**νᾱόω**, *bring into a temple*, τὰν ἀγέλαν *GDI*5100.24 (Crete). II. ναοῖ· ἱκετεύει, Hsch.; cf. ναεύω, ναύω II.

**νᾰπαῖος**, α, ον, *of a wooded vale* or *dell*, ν. ἐν Κιθαιρῶνος πτυχαῖς S.*OT*1026; πλάκες E.*HF*958; ν. θεός a *sylvan* god, Ael.*NA*6.42, cf. 7.2.

**νάπειον** [ᾰ], τό, = νᾶπυ, Nic.*Al*.430.

**νάπη** [ᾰ], ἡ, *woodland vale, dell, glen*, Il.8.558; Ἀπολλωνία ν., of Delphi, Pi.*P*.6.9, cf. *SIG*546*A*11 (Delph., iii B.C.), *GDI*5016.9 (Gortyn); νάπαι κάλλισται pleasant *valleys* about a town, Hdt.4.157; χείμαρρος νάπη a torrent *glen*, E.*Ba*.1093; ἢν ἀπόροις νάπαις ἐντυγχάνωσι X.*Eq.Mag*.4.4, cf. *Cyn*.9.11; ὄρη δάσκια καὶ νάπαι πετρώδεις βρέμονται Ar.*Th*.998 (lyr.), cf. *Av*.740 (lyr.), Pl.*Lg*.761b; cf. νάπος.

**ναπόας, ναποίας, ναποός**, v. νεωποίης.

**νάποινος**· μάταιος, Hsch.

⊛ **νάπος** [ᾰ], εος, τό, post-Homeric form, = νάπη, κοιλόπεδον ν., of Olympia, Pi.*P*.5.39, cf. *I*.8(7).68, S.*OC*157 (lyr.), *Tr*.436, E.*Andr*.284 (lyr.), etc.; of a *grove* or *thicket*, S.*Aj*.892 (lyr.); also, *ravine, gully*, ἐγένοντ' ἐπὶ νάπει μεγάλῳ καὶ δυσπόρῳ X.*An*.6.5.12, cf. 22, *Cyr*.1.6.43.

**ναπτάλιον**, τό, or **-άλιος**, ἡ, = νάφθα, Ph.*Bel*.90.18.

**νᾶπυ**, τό, Att., = σίναπι (cf. Phryn.255, Plin.*HN*19.171; on the accent v. Hdn.Gr.1.354), *mustard*, ν. Κύπριον Eub.19; ν. βλέπειν Ar. *Eq*.631: gen. νάπυος Thphr.*HP*1.12.1: dat. νάπυϊ *IG*4$^2$(1).126.17, 21 (Epid., ii A.D.), Luc.*Asin*.47.

**νᾰπώδης**, ες, *woody*, Eust.277.32, St.Byz. s.v. Βῆσσα.

**ναρδίζω**, *resemble nard*, Dsc.1.11, 12.

**νάρδινος**, η, ον, *of nard*, ν. μύρον oil *of spikenard*, Men.274, Plb.30.26.2; ἔλαιον ν. *Edict.Diocl.Troez*.27, al.; τὰ ν. Antiph.35.

**ναρδίτης** [ῑ] οἶνος, *wine flavoured with spikenard*, Dsc.5.57tit.

**ναρδῖτις** βοτάνη, a variety of νάρδος, Gal.10.911.

**ναρδολῖπής**, ές, (λίπος) *anointed with nard-oil*, *AP*6.254 (Myrin.).

**νάρδον**, τό, = sq., Thphr.*Od*.12, Poll.6.104.

⊛ **νάρδος**, ἡ, *spikenard, Nardostachys Jatamansi*, Thphr.*HP*9.7.2, Nic.*Th*.604, Lxx *Ca*.1.12, *Ev.Marc*.14.3; ν. Ἰνδική Dsc.1.7, etc.; νάρδου στάχυς Gal.12.84, al.; cf. sq. 2. ν. Κελτική *Celtic nard, Valeriana celtica*, Dsc.1.8, cf. Plin.*HN*14.107. 3. ν. ὀρεινή or ὀρεία *mountain nard, Valeriana Dioscoridis*, Dsc.1.9 (cf. Thphr.*HP*9.7.4). 4. ν. Συριακή *Syrian nard, Cymbopogon Iwarancusa*, Dsc.1.7, cf. Plin.*HN*12.45. 5. νάρδου ῥίζα *ginger grass, Cymbopogon Schoenanthus*, Arr.*An*.6.22, cf. 7.20. 6. ν. ἀγρία, = ἄσαρον, Dsc.1.10; = φοῦ, ib.11. II. *oil of spikenard*, *PSI*6.628.7 (iii B.C.), *AP*6.250 (Antiphil.), Aret.*CD*2.2, etc.; ν. Βαβυλωνιακή Alex.308. (Semitic word, cf. Bab. *lardu*.)

**ναρδόστᾰχυς**, υος, ὁ, = foreg., Dsc.2.16, Gal.6.339.

**ναρδοφόρος**, ον, *bearing nard*, λίμναι Dsc.2.8.

**ναρεῖ**· τηρεῖ, Hsch. (cf. ναρούς). **νάρειν**· κύειν, κρύπτειν, ζητεῖν, κνίσκεσθαι, ἀμέλγεσθαι, Id. **νάρη**· ἡ ἄφρων καὶ μωρά, Id.

**ναρθηκ-ία**, ἡ, a plant allied to νάρθηξ, Thphr.*HP*6.1.4, 6.2.7. ⊛ **-ιάω**, *beat with a* νάρθηξ or *rod*, Hsch. **-ίζω**, *splint a broken limb* (orig. *with pieces of* νάρθηξ), τὸ σφυρόν Sch.Ar.*Ach*.1176, cf. Heraclas ap. Orib.48.2.2, Paul.Aeg.6.106. 2. *splint* planks *together with laths*, in Pass., Apollod.*Poliorc*.159.4. **-ινος**, η, ον, *made of* νάρθηξ, Arist.*Aud*.803$^a$41. ⊛ **-ιον**, τό, *small splint*, Antyll.ap.Orib.44.23.74. 2. *small rod used* in ἐπίκρουσις 1, Gal.10.998. II. = ἀσφόδελος, Ps.-Dsc.2.169. **-ισμα**, ατος, τό, *splint*, Apollod.*Poliorc*.159.13. **-ισμός**, ὁ, prob. = ἐπίκρουσις 1, Dsc.*Eup*.1.233. 2. *splinting* of planks *with laths*, Apollod.*Poliorc*.160.6.

**ναρθηκο-ειδής**, ές, *like the* νάρθηξ, Dsc.3.81. **-πλήρωτος**, ον, *filling the hollow of the* νάρθηξ, πυρὸς πηγή A.*Pr*.109. **-φανής**, ές, *looking like* νάρθηξ, Archig.ap.Orib.8.2.3. ⊛ **-φόρος**, ον, *carrying a wand of* νάρθηξ, like the Βάκχαι (cf. θυρσοφόρος), Plu.2.1107f; of Dionysus, Orph.*H*.42.1; prov., πολλοὶ τοι ν., παῦροι δέ τε Βάκχοι, i.e. there are many officials, but few inspired, Zen.5.77, cf. Pl.*Phd*.69c, Orph.*Fr*.5. 2. *rod-bearer*, X.*Cyr*.2.3.18.

**ναρθηκώδης**, ες, *like a* νάρθηξ, Thphr.*HP*1.6.10, *Gp*.5.8.2.

⊛ **νάρθηξ**, ηκος, ὁ, *giant fennel, Ferula communis*, Thphr.*HP*1.2.7, Dsc.3.77, etc.; κλέψας.. πυρὸς τηλέσκοπον αὐγὴν ἐν κοίλῳ ν., of Prometheus, Hes.*Th*.567, cf. *Op*.52; of the stalk used as a θύρσος, E.*Ba*.147 (lyr.), al.; as a schoolmaster's *cane*, X.*Cyr*.2.3.20, cf. Arist.*Pr*.948$^a$10; as a *splint* for a broken limb, Hp.*Off*.12, Gal.10.437; *single-stick* for military exercises, Onos.10.4. II. *casket* for unguents, etc., Luc.*Ind*.29; ἡ ἐκ τοῦ ν. διόρθωσις, of Aristotle's recension of Homer, carried by Alexander in a ν., Str.13.1.27, Plu.*Alex*.8. 2. title of medical works by Heras, Cratippus, and Soranus, Gal.12.398, 959, Aët.8.45. III. *fore-court* of a church, *EM*597.48.

**νάρκα**, ἡ, = νάρκη 1, Men.498, Sor.2.17, M.Ant.10.9.

**νάρκαφθον** or **νάσκαφθον**, τό, *a fragrant Indian bark*, used as a spice, etc. (perh. the same as λάκαφθον), Dsc.1.23:—written **ναόκαφθον** and **νάκαφθον** in most codd. of Paul.Aeg.7.3; **νάκαφθον** in one cod. of Id.7.22.4 (v.l. λάκαφθον).

**ναρκ-άω**, fut. -ήσω Lxx *Da*.11.6:—*grow stiff* or *numb*, χεὶρ νάρκησε Il.8.328; τὴν ψυχὴν καὶ τὸ στόμα ναρκῶ Pl.*Men*.80b; ψυχῆς ναρκώσης Democr.290; τὸ ἡσυχάζον ναρκᾷ Epicur.*Sent.Vat*.11; τὸ νεῦρον ὃ ἐνάρκησεν Lxx *Ge*.32.32(33); χεὶρ νεναρκηκυῖα J.*AJ*8.8.5; of the numbness caused by the fish νάρκη, Arist.*HA*620$^b$19, cf. Pl.*Men*.84b; ναρκῶ, ναὶ τὸν Πᾶνα Theoc.27.51. **-η**, ἡ, *numbness, deadness*, caused by palsy, frost, fright, etc., Hp.*VM*22, *Aph*.5.25; ν. κατὰ τῆς χειρὸς καταχεῖται Ar.*V*.713, cf. Arist.*HA*515$^b$20, *Pr*.867$^b$29, 954$^a$23 (pl.). II. *torpedo, electric ray*, which *benumbs* any one who touches it, Antiph.132.2, Anaxandr.41.52, etc.; ἡ πλατεῖα ν. ἡ θαλαττία Pl.*Men*.80a, cf. Arist.*HA*620$^b$19; ν. ποταμία the Egyptian *electric eel, Malapterurus electricus*, *PMag.Osl*.1.284, cf. Ath.7.312b: in metapl. acc. νάρκᾰ Opp.*C*.3.55. **-ησις**, *torpor*, *Gloss*.

⊛ **ναρκίον**· ἀσκόν, Hsch.; cf. λαρκίον.

**ναρκίσσ-ῖνος**, η, ον, *made of narcissus*, Cratin.344, Dsc.1.53. II. *of the colour of* νάρκισσος, *PRyl*.154.8 (i A.D.). ⊛ **-ίτης** [ῑ], ου, ὁ, *like the narcissus*, [λίθος] D.P.1031, Plin.*HN*37.188. ⊛ **-ος**, ὁ, rarely ἡ, Theoc.1.133:—*narcissus*, of various species, *h.Cer*.8, 428, S.*OC*683 (lyr.), Mosch.2.65; *pheasant's eye, Narcissus poeticus*, Thphr.*HP*6.8.1, Dsc.4.158; *autumn narcissus, N. serotinus*, Thphr.*HP*6.6.9; *Narcissus Tazetta, polyanthus narcissus*, Dsc.l.c. (this prob. in S. l.c.). (Connected with νάρκη, because of its *narcotic* properties, acc. to Plu.2.647b.)

**ναρκ-όω**, *benumb, deaden*, ὀδύνην ναρκοῖ Hp.*Liqu*.6; νεναρκωμένοι ib.1: c. acc. pers., Phld.*Rh*.1.380S., cf. Hp.*Epid*.6.2.1. **-ώδης**, ες, *numb, torpid*, Id.*Art*.48 (Comp.), Dsc.3.101; τὸ ν. νεῦρον, in the elbow, Hp.*Mochl*.1, cf. *Prorrh*.1.139, *Art*.19; βαρύτητες ν. Plu.2.

647b; πόνος ν. Gal.8.70; *sluggish*, ὁρμαί Phld.*D*.1.13. Ion. Adv. -ωδέως Hp.*Prorrh*.1.120, *Mul*.2.145. **-ωσις**, εως, ἡ, *a benumbing*, γνώμης Id.*Aph*.5.16. **-ωτικός**, ή, όν, *benumbing, narcotic*, φάρμακα Gal.10.862, al., Eust.1493.5.

**νάρναξ**· κιβωτός, Hsch. (cf. λάρναξ).

**νᾱρός**, ά, όν, (νάω) *flowing, liquid*, Δίρκη A.*Fr*.347; ναρὰ καὶ κρηναῖα ποτά S.*Fr*.621; cf. νηρός.

**ναρούς**· τοὺς φύλακας, Hsch. (Perh. Dor. contr. from νάορ(F)-, cf. ναρεῖ, ναυρός.)

**νάρτη**, ἡ, plant used in perfumery, Thphr.*HP*9.7.3.

**νάρφη**, ἡ, a fancy loaf, = μασιτρίς, Hsch. **νᾶς**, ἡ, Dor. for ναῦς. **νάσθη**, v. ναίω. **νᾱσιώτας**, α, ὁ, Aeol. and Dor. for νησιώτης. **νάσκαφθον**, τό, v. νάρκαφθον.

**ναςμός**, ὁ, (νάω) *flowing*: *stream, spring*, E.*Hipp*.225 (anap.), 653; φοινισσομένην αἵματι.. νασμῷ μελαναυγεῖ Id.*Hec*.153 (anap.); εὐδρόσοισι Κασταλίας ν. Aristonous 1.43.

**νασμώδης**, ες, = ναματώδης, Hsch. **νάσσα, νάσσατο**, v. ναίω. **νᾶσσα**, Boeot. for νῆσσα, νῆττα.

**νάσσω**, Att. νάττω, fut. νάξω Hsch.: aor. ἔναξα (v. infr.): pf. Pass. νένασμαι and νέναγμαι (v. infr.):—*press, squeeze close, stamp down*, γαῖαν ἔναξε Od.21.122; οἱ παῖδες ἔναττον εἰς τὰς σπυρίδας Hippoloch. ap.Ath.4.130b:—Pass., *to be piled up*, ἡ κόπρος ἡ νεναγμένη Hp.*Nat. Puer*.24; ἐν δὲ [τῇ στιβάδι] νέναστται..δέρματα Theoc.9.9: c. gen., κλῖναι σισυρῶν νεναγμέναι (νενασμ- codd.) *piled up* with..., Ar.*Ec*. 840. II. *stuff quite full*, νάττω τὸν θύλακον Epict.*Fr*.23:—Pass., πᾶσα οἰκία ὁπλιτῶν νένακτο *was crammed with*.., J.*BJ*1. 17.6.

**ναστήρ**, ῆρος, ὁ, (ναίω) *inhabitant*, Zonar.

**νάστης**, ου, ὁ, = foreg., Hsch.

**ναστίσκος**, ὁ, Dim. of ναστός 1.3, Pherecr.130.7.

**ναστοκόπος**, ον, *cutting up cakes*, Pl.Com.246.

**ναστός**, ή, όν, (νάσσω) *close-pressed, firm*, Hp.*Gland*.16; κάλαμος, i.e. *archer's reed, Arundo Plinii*, Dsc.1.85; of a tumour, Aët.15. 8; σφυγμός Archig.ap.Gal.8.931: Comp., Id.ib.509. 2. *solid*, opp. κενός, Democr.ap.Arist.*Fr*.208, cf. Ph.1.330, Simp. *in Cael*. 295.5. 3. ναστός (sc. πλακοῦς), ὁ, *well-kneaded cake*, esp. used in sacrifice, *cheese-cake*, Pherecr.108.5, Ar.*Av*.567, *Pl*.1142, Metag.6. 3. II. c. gen., *filled full of*, πόλις ναστὴ ἀνδρῶν J.*BJ*6.9.4.

**ναστότης**, ητος, ἡ, *solidity, absence of void*, Alex.Aphr. *in Metaph*. 35.27, Simp. *in Cael*.609.18, *in de An*.64.3, Phlp. *in Ph*.506.6.

**ναστο-φᾰγέω**, *eat cakes*, Poll.6.75, Hsch. **-φάγος** [φᾰ], ον, *eating cakes*, Poll.6.75.

**νατῆρες**· ὑπηρέται, ἢ κεραμίδες, Hsch. **ναττᾰρέον**· πολύρρουν, Id. (leg. νᾶτορ· ῥέων, πολύρρους).

**νάτωρ** [ᾱ], ορος, ὁ, (νάω) *flowing*, Ἴναχε, νᾶτορ παῖ..Ὠκεανοῦ S.*Fr*. 270 (anap.), cf. foreg. and ναέτωρ.

**ναυᾱγ-έω**, Ion. ναυηγ-, pf. νεναυάγηκα Hdt.7.236 (-ηγ-), Eub.76: (ναῦς, ἄγνυμι):—*suffer shipwreck*, Hdt. l. c., X.*Cyr*.3.1.24, D.34.10, etc.: metaph., of chariots, Id.61.29; of an earthen vessel, A.*Fr*. 180; of persons, ν. ἐν τοῖς ἰδίοις Thphr.ap.D.L.5.55, cf. Phld.*Vit*. p.33 J.; ἐν τῷ βίῳ Ceb.24.2; περὶ τὴν πίστιν 1*Ep.Ti*.1.19; χῶ μὲν ἐναυάγει γαίης ἔπι *AP*5.208 (Posidipp. or Asclep.); ναυαγεῖ συμπόσια μὴ τυχόντα παιδαγωγίας ὀρθῆς Plu.2.622b. **-ησμός**, ὁ, = sq., Hdn. *Epim*.180. **-ία**, Ion. ναυηγίη, ἡ, *shipwreck*, Hdt.7.190, 192, al., E.*Hel*.1070, etc.; ναυαγίᾳ χρῆσθαι, περιπίπτειν, Luc.*VH*2.35, *Tox*.2: in pl., Pi.*I*.1.36 (s. v. l.); ἐν χειμῶνι καὶ ναυαγίαις Ar.*Th*.873. **-ιον**, Ion. ναυήγιον, τό, *piece of wreckage*, Men.536.9, Arist.*Pr*.932ᵃ1: mostly in pl., A.*Pers*.420, Hdt.7.191, 8.12, al., Lys.2.38, Th.1.50, etc.; πολλοὺς ἀριθμοὺς ἄγνυται ναυαγίων, i.e. is shivered into a thousand pieces, E.*Hel*.410: metaph., ν. ἱππικά *wreck* of an overturned chariot, S.*El*.730, 1444; ἀνδρῶν δαιτυμόνων ν. the *wreck* of a feast, Choeril.9; τὰ ν. τῆς πόλεως Demad.ap.Plu.2.803a; ν. οἴκων ib. 517f. II. later, = ναυαγία, ναυαγίῳ περιπεσεῖν Str.4.1.7. **-ός**, όν, Ion. ναυηγός (also in late Prose, Alciphr.1.18), *shipwrecked*, Hdt.4.103, E.*Hel*.408, Philem.213.3; ναυαγοὺς ἀναιρεῖσθαι pick up *shipwrecked men*, X.*HG*1.7.4; ν. τάφος, i.e. a watery grave, *AP*7.76 (Diosc.); ν. μόρος ib.9.84 (Antiphan.). 2. Act., *causing shipwreck*, ἄνεμοι ib.105. II. (ἄγω) = ναύαρχος, Euph.158.

**ναυαρχ-έω**, *command a fleet*, Hdt.7.161, X.*An*.5.1.4, *IG*12(8).183 (Samothrace), Phld.*Rh*.2.209 S.: c. gen., ν. [πλοίων] Philipp.ap.D.18. 77. II. in the cult of Isis, *preside at the festival of the ship* (πλοιαφέσια), Ἀρχ.Δελτ.1.152, al. (Eretria). **-ης**, ου, ὁ, = ναύαρχος, Lyd.*Mag*. 1.27. **-ία**, ἡ, *command of a fleet*, Th.8.20, 33; *period of such command*, X.*HG*1.5.1: pl., Arist.*Pol*.1322ᵇ3. II. *naval supremacy*, ib.1274ᵃ12. III. *fleet*, Lyc.733. **-ίς** (sc. ναῦς), ίδος, ἡ, *admiral's flagship*, Plb.1.51.1, D.S.11.27, Plu.*Alc*.27, Longus 2.28; ν. τριήρης D.S.20.7. II. *mistress of a fleet*, epith. of cities, e.g. Laodicea ad Mare, *IG*3.479; of Tripolis, ib.622; of Tyre, ib.14.830. **-ος**, ὁ, *commander of a fleet, admiral*, A.*Pers*.363, Hdt.7.59, 8.42, Eub.67. 11, *IG*12(3).103.12 (pl., Nisyros); οὔτε στρατηγοὺς οὔτε ν. S.*Aj*. 1232; esp. *the Spartan admiral-in-chief*, Th.4.11, 8.6, 20, 23, X.*An*. 1.4.2, etc.; used of an inferior naval officer, Decr.ap.D.18.73; *nauarchorum coetus circiter provincias Orientis*, *Cod.Just*.11.2.4. II. as Adj., ἐπὶ ναυάρχῳ σώματι..τῷ βασιλείῳ A.*Ch*.723 (anap.).

**ναυβᾰρέω**, *weigh down a ship*, Ph.2.465.

**ναυβᾰτ-έω**, *serve as* ναυβάτης in the cult of Isis (cf. ναυαρχέω II), *CIG*2955 (Ephesus). **-ης**, ου, ὁ, (βαίνω) *seafarer, seaman*, Hdt.1. 143, A.*Pers*.1011 (lyr.), S.*Ph*.301, 540, Th.1.121, *Rev.Bibl*.14.290 (Megiste), etc. II. as Adj., ν. στρατὸς A.*Ag*.987 (lyr.); ὁπλισμοὶ ib.405 (lyr.); ν. στόλος S.*Ph*.270; ν. λεώς E.*IA*294 (lyr.); ν. ἀνήρ collective for ναυβάται, A.*Pers*.375.

**ναύβιον**, τό, *cubic measure* in Egypt, with side = two royal cubits (in Roman times, three cubits), used with application to earth as a unit of labour, in pl., *PLille* 1ʳ.11, Wilcken *Chr*.385.8, *PPetr*.3 pp.80, 290, *Ostr.Bodl*.i 244 (all iii B.C.), *Arch.Pap*.6.132 (i A.D.), *POxy*.669. 11 (iii A.D.):—written **ναούια** ib.1053 (vi/vii A.D.). 2. in sg., tax paid by landholders in lieu of digging so many ναύβια, *PTeb*.5.15 (ii B.C.); ν. κατοίκων, ἐναφεσίων, *BGU*662 (ii A.D.), *PTeb*.352 (ii A.D.). 3. perh. another tax, *Ostr*.1396 (i A.D.), *Ostr.Bodl*.iii 84 (i A.D.).

**Ναυδαμηνός**, ὁ, epith. of Zeus at Sinope, *AJP*9.303.

**ναύδετον**, τό, (δέω A) *ship's cable*, E.*Tr*.811 (lyr.).

**ναυ-ηγέτης**, ου, ὁ, = ναύαρχος, Lyc.873. **-ηγέω, -ηγία, -ήγιον, -ηγός**, Ion. for ναυαγ-.

**ναύκλαρος**, = ναύκραρος, Hsch.

**ναυκληρ-έω**, *to be a shipowner*, Ar.*Av*.598, X.*Lac*.7.1, Lys.6.49; Ἐρασικλῆς μαρτυρεῖ κυβερνᾶν τὴν ναῦν ἣν Ὑβλήσιος ἐναυκλήρει Test.ap. D.35.20: c. gen., φορτηγὸν ἧς ἐναυκλήρει Ῥωμαῖος ἀνήρ Plu.*Pomp*. 73. 2. metaph., ν. πόλιν *manage, govern*, A.*Th*.652, S.*Ant*. 994. II. *to be manager of a tenement-house* (v. ναύκληρος II), ν. συνοικίαν ἐν Πειραιεῖ Is.6.19, cf. Alex.138. **-ημα**, ατος, τό, *voyage*, Tz.*H*.9.60 (pl.). **-ία**, ἡ, *life and calling of a* ναύκληρος, *ship-owning*, Lys.6.19, Pl.*Lg*.643e, Arist.*Pol*.1258ᵇ22, etc.: in pl., And.1.137, Vett.Val.73.6. 2. poet., *voyage*, S.*Fr*.143, E.*Alc*. 112 (lyr.). 3. *adventure, enterprise*, Id.*Med*.527. II. *ship*, Id. *Hel*.1519, Plu.2.87a. **-ικός**, ή, όν, *of* or *for a* ναύκληρος, Luc. *DMeretr*.2.2; ν. δίαιτα Moschio ap.Ath.5.207c; ν. ἄνθρωποι *Peripl. M.Rubr*.21; τὰ -κά, = ναυκληρία, Pl.*Lg*.842d. **-ιον**, τό, *ship of a* ναύκληρος, in pl., *property in ships*, D.23.211, Plu.2.234f: sg., *POxy*. 87.7 (iv A.D.). II. = ναύσταθμος, E.*Rh*.233 (lyr., pl.).

**ναυκληρο-κῠβερνήτης**, ου, ὁ, *pilot of a* ναυκλήριον, Wilcken *Chr*.434. 4 (iv A.D.), etc. **-μάχῐμος** [μᾰ], ὁ, *sailor in the fleet* of the Ptolemies, *PTeb*.5.46 (ii B.C.), *UPZ*110.22 (ii B.C.).

**ναύκληρ-ος**, ὁ, *shipowner and merchant* (opp. ἔμπορος, q. v.), *IG*1². 127.34, 128.4, Hdt.1.5, 4.152, S.*Ph*.128, 547, E.*Fr*.417, Ar.*Av*.595, Th.1.137, X.*Mem*.3.9.11. 2. *skipper, sailing-master*, *OGI*344.4 (Delos, ii B.C.), *Act.Ap*.27.11, *POxy*.63.4 (ii/iii A.D.). 3. generally, *captain, commander*, A.*Supp*.177: as Adj., ν. πλάτη S.*Fr*.430; ν. χείρ *the master's* hand, of a charioteer, E.*Hipp*.1224; ν. πόλις Philostr.*VS*2.26.2. II. at Athens, *one who rented and sub-let tenement-houses*, Sannyr.6, Hyp.*Fr*.37, Diph.37, cf. Hsch., Poll.1. 75. 2. = ναύκραρος, Id.8.108 (s. v. l.); cf. ναύκλαρος. **-ώσιμος**, ον, *to be sub-let* to lodgers, στέγαι Hsch.

**ναυκόρος**, v. νεωκόρος.

**ναυκρᾰρ-ία** [κρᾱ], τά, *registry of the* ναύκραροι, Ammon.*Diff*. p.94 V.; ναυκραρεῖα in Thom.Mag.p.246 R. **-ία**, ἡ, *naucrary* (v. ναύκραρος), Arist.*Ath*.8.3, Clidem.8, Phot. **-ικός**, ή, όν, *of* or *for a* ναύκραρος or ναυκραρία, ἀργύριον Lex Solonis ap.Arist.*Ath*.8.3, cf. Harp.s.v. ναυκραρικά. **-ος**, ὁ, in early Athens, *the chief official of a division* (ναυκραρία) *of the citizens* for financial and administrative purposes, Lex Solonis ap.Arist.*Ath*.8.3, etc.; οἱ πρυτάνιες τῶν ν. Hdt. 5.71; [Κλεισθένης] κατέστησε δημάρχους τὴν αὐτὴν ἔχοντας ἐπιμέλειαν τοῖς πρότερον ν. Arist.*Ath*.21.5; cf. ναύκληρος II. 2, ναύκλαρος. (-κραρος prob. = 'chief', cf. pr. n. [Λ]ακραρίδας *IG*7.1931: from -κρᾱσρος, cf. κάρα.)

**ναυκρᾰτ-έω**, *have the command of the sea*, Th.7.60:—Pass., *to be mastered at sea*, X.*HG*6.2.8. **-ής**, ές, *master* or *mistress of the sea*, ναυκρατέες τῆς θαλάσσης Hdt.5.36. **-ης** (parox.), ου, ὁ, *holding a ship fast*: name of a fish, τὴν ἐχενηΐδα ναυκράτην ἔγραψέ τις Eust.1490.19, cf. Cyran.31. **-ητικός**, ή, όν, *of* or *for victory at sea*, σημεῖον D.C.51.21. **-ία**, ἡ, *naval victory*, And.*Fr*.3, D.C. 49.7, etc.

**Ναύκρᾰτις**, ιος or εως, ἡ, *Naucratis* in Egypt, Hdt.2.97; **Ναυκρατίτης** [ῑ], ου, ὁ, *a Naucratite*, Call.*Epigr*.40, Str.17.1.33; στέφανος N., = σάμψυχος, Anacr.83:—Adj. **Ναυκρατῑτικός**, ή, όν, D.24.11.

**ναυκράτωρ** [ᾰ], ορος, ὁ, ἡ, = ναυκρατής, Hdt.6.9, Th.5.97, 109. II. *master of a ship*, S.*Ph*.1072.

**ναῦλα**, ἡ, later form for νάβλα, Aq.*Ps*.32(33).2, Sm.*Ps*.91(92).4.

**ναυλαῖον**, τό, = ναῦλον Ib, *Sammelb*.4425 iv 32 (ii A.D.).

**ναῦλλον**, τό, = ναῦλον Ia, *IG*11(2).165.55, al. (Delos, iii B.C.), Sch. Ar.*Ra*.272:—also **ναῦλλος**, ὁ, Sch.Ar. l. c.; acc. ναῦλλον (gender indeterminate) *IG*2².1128.13.

**ναυλοδόκος**, ὁ, *receiver of freights*, *Ostr*.1477 (ii A.D.).

**ναῦλον**, τό, later form for νάβλα, Hsch.s.v. νάβλας. II. v. sq.

**ναῦλος**, ὁ, Ar. (v. infr.), *IG*2².1672.126, 159, *SIG*1262.6 (Smyrna, i A.D.), *Com.Adesp*.286; also ἡ, acc. to Sch.Ar.*Ra*.272; and ναῦλον, τό (v. infr.), cf. ναῦλλον:—*passage-money, fare* or *freight*, ἔκβαιν', ἀπόδος τὸν ν., says Charon, Ar.*Ra*.270; τῆς πόλεως ναῦλον τελούσης τοῖς ἄγουσι τοὺς λίθους *IPE*1².32 *B* 50 (Olbia, iii B.C.); ναῦλον συνθέσθαι to agree upon one's *fare*, X.*An*.5.1.12; τὸ ν. τῶν ξύλων παρασχεῖν D.49.26, cf. *IG* ll. cc.; τὸ ν. ἀποστερεῖν Din.1.56; παραπόλλυμι τὸ ν. Arisipp.ap. Plu.2.439e; ἔδωκε τὸ ν. αὐτοῦ Lxx *Jn*.1.3; λαλῶν τὰ ν. Diph.43.21; ἔδωκα αὐτῷ τὰ ν. *Sammelb*.3553; τὸ δὲ ν. διωρθωσάμεθα ὑπὲρ αὐτῶν *PCair.Zen*.52.13 (iii B.C.); συνέβη ναῦλον ἡμῖν προσάγεσθαι τοῦ..πλοίου we were charged for the *hire* of the boat, ib.368.27 (iii B.C.). b. ν. πλοίου name of a tax paid for the use of state-provided boats, *BGU* 645.16 (ii A.D.), *PSI*8.960.15 (iv A.D.); ἀποδιαγράφειν τὸ συναχθησόμενον ν. ἐπὶ τὴν βασιλικὴν τράπεζαν *PTheb.Bank* 12.7 (ii B.C.), cf.

*Sammelb.*6954. II. *freight, cargo* of ships, τὸ ν. σφετερίζεσθαι D.32.2. III. *rent* of a tenement, Poll.1.75. IV. ναῦλα, τά, = ἐφόδια, Hsch. (ascribed to Aeschylus by Cyr. in cod. Laur.57.39).

**ναυλοχ-έω,** *lie in a harbour* or *creek*, esp. *lie in wait* in order to sally out on passing ships, abs. in Hdt.7.189,192,8.6, E.*IA*249 (lyr.):—Med., ναυλοχεῖσθαί τινι D.H.1.44 (s.v.l.). 2. c. acc., *lie in wait for*, Th.7.4. **-ία,** ἡ, *anchorage*, esp. of pirates, App.*Mith.*92. ®**-ιον,** τό, = ναύλοχος II, Ar.*Fr.*78. ®**-ος,** ον, *affording a safe anchorage*, epith. of a harbour, λιμένες δ' ἔνι ν. αὐτῇ Od.4.846; ν. ἐς λιμένα 10.141; ν. λιπὼν ἕδρας S.*Aj.*460; ὦ ν. καὶ πετραῖα θερμὰ λουτρά ye hot springs *by the haven* and from the rock (unless ναύλοχα is Subst.), Id.*Tr.*633 (lyr.); Ἀχαιῶν ναύλοχοι περιπτυχαί E.*Hec.*1015: Sup. ναυλοχώτατος λιμήν Ph.1.181, cf. 352. II. Subst., *station for ships, haven*, Suid.: also neut. pl. ναύλοχα Plu.2.984b; cf. supr.

**ναυλ-όω,** (ναῦλος) *let one's ship for hire*, Plu.2.707c, *OGI*572.42 (Myra), *PLond.*3.948.1 (iii A.D.):—Med., *hire a ship*, Plb.31.12.11, Ath.12.521a, *PFlor.*305.4 (iv A.D.). **-ώσιμος,** ον, *for hire*, πλοῖον *POxy.*276.7 (i A.D.); κτήνη, ὄνοι, *PRein.*54.4 (iii/iv A.D.), *PFlor.*238.7 (iii A.D.). ®**-ωτικός,** ή, όν, *for chartering of ships*: -κή (sc. συγγραφή), ἡ, *POxy.*643 (ii A.D.).

**ναῦμα,** = πολύγονον, Hsch.

**ναυμᾰχ-έω,** *fight by sea*, Hdt.7.143, al.; τινι *with* one, Id.2.161; ἐναντία τῇ πόλει And.1.101; πρός τινας X.*HG*2.1.14; περὶ πατρίδος Hdt.8.57; ν. τὴν περὶ τῶν κρεῶν, i.e. *to be in the battle* of Arginusae (v. κρέας 2), Ar.*Ra.*191; μὰ τοὺς ἐν Σαλαμῖνι ναυμαχήσαντας D.18.208, cf. Pl.*Mx.*241b,d. 2. metaph., *do battle with*, κακοῖς τοσούτοις Ar.*V.*479. **-ησείω,** Desiderat. of ναυμαχέω, *wish to fight by sea*, Th.8.79. **-ητέον,** *one must fight by sea*, Arist.*Rh.*1376ᵃ2. ®**-ία,** Ion. -ίη, ἡ, *sea-fight*, Hdt.6.14, al., Th.1.13, etc.; ν. ποιέεσθαι Hdt.8.49; ναυμαχίῃ κρατήσας, ἑσσωθέντες, Id.3.39, 6.92; ναυμαχίᾳ νικᾶν X.*HG*1.6.2; ναυμαχίας νενικήκατε ib.1.1.28; ναυμαχίαν ἀπώσασθαί τινα *in a sea-fight*, Th.1.32; πολλὰς ν. νεναυμαχηκὼς Lys.7.41; τὴν περὶ Σαλαμῖνα ν. τῶν Ἑλλήνων πρὸς τοὺς βαρβάρους Pl.*Lg.*707b. **-ος,** ον (proparox.), *of* or *for a sea-fight*, ξυστὰ ν. pikes *for sea-battles*, Il.15.389, cf. 677; δόρατα ν. Hdt.7.89, cf. D.Chr.11.117, Opp.*H.*5.301, *C.*2.62. II. parox. ναυμάχος, Act., *fighting at sea*, *AP*7.741 (Crin.), Ath.4.154f, *IG*3.1202.146 (iii A.D.).

**ναῦον,** τό, perh. an Egyptian measure of length, *PCair.Zen.*383 (iii B.C.).

**ναῦος,** v. ναός.

**Ναύπακτος,** ἡ, (ναῦς, πήγνυμι) *Naupactus*, on the north of the gulf of Corinth, Th.2.91:—Adj. **Ναυπάκτιος,** α, ον, A.*Supp.*262, etc.

**ναυπηγ-εῖον,** τό, *shipyard*, D.S.19.58; cf. ναυπήγιον. ®**-έω,** *to be a shipbuilder, build ships*, Ar.*Pl.*513, Pl.*Alc.*1.107c:—more freq. in Med., πλοῖα, νέας ναυπηγέεσθαι, *build oneself* ships, *get* them *built*, Hdt.2.96, 6.46, cf. Pl. l. c.; ἐπί τινι against others, Hdt.1.27; ἐναυπηγοῦντο νεῶν στόλον Th.1.31; τριήρεις ἐναυπηγησάμεθα And.3.5, cf. Th.6.90, D.17.28: pf. νεναυπήγημαι in med. sense, D.S.20.16:—Pass., of ships, *to be built*, Th.1.13 (v.l. ἐνναυπηγηθῆναι); ὁπόσα ἂν οἰκοδομηθῇ ἢ ναυπηγηθῇ X.*Vect.*4.35, cf. *HG*1.3.17, Plu.2.321d. II. metaph. in Med., *contrive*, '*engineer*', τὰ πάντα νεναυπηγημένη ἐπὶ ταῖς Ῥωμαίων τύχαις J.*AJ*19.2.4. **-ής,** ές, *shipbuilding*, τέχναι Man.4.323. **-ήσῐμος,** ον, also η, ον Pl.*Lg.*705c, Str.14.5.3:—*useful in shipbuilding*, of timber, ἴδη Hdt.5.23; ξύλα Th.4.108, 7.25, X.*HG*5.2.16, *SIG*135.10 (Olynthus, iv B.C.); ὕλη Pl. l. c., Str. l. c.; χώρα Philostr.*Her.*19.20. **-ησις,** εως, ἡ, = sq., *Sammelb.*6994.30 (iii B.C.), Asp.*in EN*143.13, Hsch. s. v. ξυλοδωνίη. **-ία,** Ion. -ίη, ἡ, *shipbuilding*, Hdt.1.27; ν. ἁρμόζειν to practise *shipbuilding*, E.*Cyc.*460; ναυπηγίαν τριηρῶν παρασκευάζεσθαι Th.4.108, cf. D.S.19.58. **-ικός,** ή, όν, *for shipbuilding*, πέλεκυς Luc.*DMort.*10.9: ἡ -κή (with or without τέχνη), *art of shipbuilding*, Arist.*EN*1094ᵃ8, Gal.*Thras.*5: Subst., τὸ -κόν Plu.2.571f; *contract for building a ship*, *PLond.*3.1164*h*14 (iii A.D.). ®**-ιον,** τό, *shipbuilder's yard, dockyard*, Ar.*Av.*1157, *Inscr.Délos* 363.41, 365.20 (iii B.C.). ®**-ός,** ὁ, (πήγνυμι) *shipbuilder, shipwright*, Th.1.13, Pl.*R.*333c, al., *PPetr.*2 p.61 (iii B.C.), *PCair.Zen.*270.8 (iii B.C.):—written ναϝπηγός *IG*1².672; ναπηγός ib.428.

**Ναυπλία,** Ion. -ίη, ἡ, *Nauplia* in Argolis, Hdt.6.76, etc.; **Ναυπλιεύς,** έως, ὁ, *a Nauplian*, Str.8.6.14:—Adj. **Ναύπλιος,** α, ον, E.*Or.*369; or -ίειος, ib.54.

®**ναύπλιος,** ὁ, a kind of *shell-fish*, *Peripl.M.Rubr.*17; f.l. for ναυτίλος, Artem.2.14.

**ναύποδα·** μακρόποδα, Hsch. (false division of ταναύποδα).

**ναύ-πορος,** ον, = ναυσίπορος, *ship-frequented*, ἀκταί A.*Eu.*10; λίμνης στόμα A.R.4.1546. II. parox. ναυπόρος, = ναυσιπόρος II. 2, πλάτη E.*Tr.*877. **-πρηστις,** ιδος, ἡ, (πίμπρημι) Adj. *burning ships*, *EM* 598.43. **-πρύτᾰνις** [ῠ], ιος, ὁ, *ruling ships* or *the sea*, δαίμων Pi.*Pae.*6.130.

**ναῦρα ἢ ναυρόν·** ὄγκος, Hsch. **ναυρίζειν·** καταμωκᾶσθαι, Id.

**ναυρός,** ὁ, *temple-guard*, *IG*14.401 (Messana). (Cf. νεωρούς: prob. from ναός and -hoρϝο- (ἐρύω B), cf. θυρωρός, etc.)

®**ναῦς,** ἡ, (v. infr.) *ship*, Hom., etc. (but rare in non-literary Hellenistic Greek, once in *NT*, *Act.Ap.*27.41, πλοῖον being generally used); ἐν νήεσσι or ἐν νηυσίν *at the ships*, i.e. in the camp formed by the ships drawn up on shore, Il.2.688, 11.659; νῆες μακραί *ships* of war, built long and taper for speed, Th.1.41, etc.; opp. νῆες στρογγύλαι round-built merchant-*ships*, Hdt.1.163, etc.; νέες alone, = τριήρεις, opp. πεντηκόντεροι, Id.8.1; νῆες κεναί, i.e. without fighting men in them, D.3.5; ναῦς μακρά collective for μακραί, A.*Pers.*380.—Att. declens. **ναῦς,** νεώς, νηΐ, ναῦν, dual gen. and dat. νεοῖν, pl. νῆες, νεῶν (νηῶν is v.l. in Lys.13.15), ναυσί, ναῦς; in later writers, nom. pl. ναῦς, acc. pl. νῆας, D.S.13.13, Plb.5.2.4, etc., cf. Phryn.147:—Ep. **νηῦς,** νηός, νηΐ, νῆα, pl. νῆες, νηῶν, νηυσί or νήεσσι, νῆας (but also gen. and acc. sg. νεός, νέα [the latter as monosyll. in Od.9.283], pl. νέες, νεῶν, νέεσσι, νέας); Ep. gen. and dat. pl. ναῦφι, -φιν, Il.2.794, 16.281, Od.14.498; in late Ep., nom. νῆυς dub. l. in Mosch.2.104, cf. *EM*440.17; acc. sg. and pl. νηῦν, νηῦς, A.R.1.1358, Herod.2.3, Dem. Bith.4.6: Hdn.Gr.1.401, 2.675,553 also gives νεῦς, νεΐ (v.l. in Hdt. 7.184), and νευσί (Hp.*Ep.*27, *Sammelb.*5829):—Ion. **νηῦς,** νεός, νηΐ, νέα, pl. νέες, νεῶν, νηυσί (νηυσίν Epigr. in *IG*12(8).683 (Thasos, vi/v B.C.)), νέας (but νηός Archil.(?) in *PLit.Lond.*54; νηός is freq. in codd. of Hdt., νηῶν 7.160):—Dor. **ναῦς** (νᾶς Hdn.Gr.1.400), νᾱός Pi.*P.*4.185, al., νᾱΐ Id.*O.*13.54, al. (νᾶ perh. to be read in Alcm.23 iii 27), νᾶυν Pi.*P.*4.245, *Fr.*234 (νᾶν Hdn.Gr.1.328, νᾶα B.16.89); pl. νᾶες Pi.*O.*12.4, al., ναῶν Id.*P.*1.74, ναυσί, ναυσίν, Id.*N.*7.29, *P.*3.68 (νάεσσι ib.4.56), νᾶας f.l. in Theoc.22.17:—Aeol. sg. gen. νᾶος, dat. νᾶϊ, pl. dat. νάεσσι, Alc.19,18,79, gen. νάων Id.*Supp.*12.9, Sapph.*Supp.*5.2:—Trag. commonly use Dor. forms in lyr., Att. in dialogue (but sts. ναός, ναῶν, A.*Th.*62, *Pers.*340, etc.); the Ep. forms νηός S.*Fr.*761, νηῶν E.*IT*1485, νῆας A.*Supp.*744 (lyr.), νηυσίν Id.*Pers.*370 (cod. M) are prob. corrupt. (Cf. Skt. *naús*, Lat. *nāvis*, etc.)

**ναῦθλον,** τό, = ναῦλον, *IG*4.823.12 (Troezen), Hsch.

**ναυσθλόω,** *carry by sea*, ἐκ γᾶς E.*Tr.*162 (lyr.); ἐς γῆν πατρίδα ναυσθλώσων νεκρόν Id.*Supp.*1037:—Med., *take with one by sea*, ναυσθλοῦσθε παῖδα Id.*IT*1487:—Pass., *go by sea*, ναυσθλοῦμαι Id.*Tr.*677; πελάγεσιν ναυσθλούμενος Id.*Hel.*1210; οὐ ναυσθλώσομαι Ar.*Pax* 126. II. Pass., *to be visited by ships*, γῆ ναυσθλωθήσεται Lyc.1415.

**ναυσία,** Ion. -ίη, v. ναυτία.

**ναυσι-ᾰσις** [ῐ], εως, ἡ, *squeamishness*, Hsch. **-άω,** = ναυτιάω, pf. νεναυσίακα *BGU*1097.4 (i A.D.). **-βάτης** [ᾰ], ου, ὁ, = ναυβάτης, *Lyr.Alex.Adesp.*33.7, Man.1.323, Hsch. s.v. βαρυδάνιν. **-βῐος,** ον, *living by the sea*, Alciphr.1.12 (pr. n.). **-δρομος,** ον, *ship-speeding*, οὖρος Orph.*H.*74.10. **-κλειτός,** ή, όν, *famed for ships, famous by sea*, κούρη ναυσικλειτοῖο Δύμαντος Od.6.22, cf. *h.Ap.*31, 219. **-κλῠτός,** όν, = foreg., Φαίηκες, Φοίνικες, Od.7.39, 15.415; fem. ναυσικλυτάν Pi.*N.*5.9. **-όεις,** εσσα, εν, *feeling nausea* or *disgust*, Nic.*Al.*83 (v.l. ναυτ-), 482. **-πέδη,** ἡ, *anchor*, Luc.*Lex.*15. **-πέρᾱτος,** Ion. **νηυσιπέρητος,** ον, *navigable*, Hdt.1.189, 193, 5.52, Arist.*Mete.*351ᵃ18, D.H.3.44. **-ποδες,** οἱ, *ship-footed*, of islanders, Hsch., Eust.1515.27. **-πομπος,** ον, *ship-wafting*, αὔρα E.*Ph.*1712 (lyr.). **-πορος,** ον, *traversed by ships, navigable*, of a river, X.*An.*2.2.3, Arist.*Mir.*846ᵇ31, Hld.10.5, Philostr.*VA*3.1. II. parox. ναυσιπόρος, ον, Act., *passing in a ship, seafaring*, στρατιά E.*Rh.*48 (lyr.). 2. *causing a ship to pass*, πλᾶται ν. *ship-speeding* oars, Id.*IA*172 (lyr.). **-στονος** ὕβρις, the *lamentable* loss *of the ships*, Pi.*P.*1.72. **-φθόρος,** ον, *ship-destroying*, αὖραι Tim.*Pers.*144. **-φόρητος,** ον, *carried by ship, seafaring*, ἄνδρες Pi.*P.*1.33. **-ωσις,** εως, ἡ, = ναυσίασις, *vomiting*: hence φλεβῶν ν. *gushing of blood* from the veins, Hp.*Fract.*11 (pl.).

**ναυσοίκητος,** ον, *occupied by ships*, Sch.Opp.*H.*5.461.

**ναῦσσον,** τό, name of a tax, *SIG*4.6 (Cyzicus, vi B.C.), 1000.1 (Cos, i B.C.).—In *SIG*4 -σσ- is written T.

**ναύ-σταθμον,** τό, (σταθμός) *harbour, anchorage, roadstead*, Th.3.6, E.*Rh.*602 (pl.):—more freq. **-σταθμος,** ὁ, Plb.5.19.6, D.S.27.12, Plu.*Nic.*16, etc.; hence of *ships assembled in a roadstead*, Id.*Arist.*22, *Lys.*5.

**ναύστης,** ου, ὁ, = ναύτης, *Sammelb.*1207.

**ναυστιλεία,** ἡ, late form, = ναυτιλία, *PGrenf.*2.80.16, 2.81.16 (v A.D.).

**ναυστολ-έω,** fut. -ήσω E.*Supp.*474: pf. νεναυστόληκα (συν-) S.*Ph.*550: I. trans., *carry* or *convey by sea*, δάμαρτα E.*Or.*741 (troch.): metaph., ἴδια ν. ἐπικώμια *providing* matter for their own praise, Pi.*N.*6.32, cf. Luc.*Lex.*2:—Pass., with fut. Med. -ήσομαι, *go by sea*. E.*Tr.*1048; τὰ ναυστολούμενα Id.*Fr.*492.6; τηλικοῦτον πέλαγος ναυστοληθείς D.S.4.13. 2. *guide, steer*, metaph., κυμάτων ἅτερ πόλιν σὴν ναυστολήσεις E.*Supp.* l. c.; τὼ πτέρυγε ποῖ ναυστολεῖς; whither *pliest thou* thy wings? Ar.*Av.*1229; ὁ ναυστολῶν . . εἰμ' ἐγὼ τὰς συμφορὰς the enterprise is mine, E.*IT*599. II. intr., *go by ship, sail*, ἐξ Ἰλίου S.*Ph.*245; πρὸς οἴκους ἀπ' Ἰλίου E.*Tr.*77: metaph., διὰ πόνων ἐναυστόλουν Id.*Fr.*821.2. III. c. acc. loci, *approach by sea*, ἵπποισιν ἢ κύμβαισι ν. χθόνα; S.*Fr.*127 (by zeugma), cf. E.*Med.*682, *Hipp.*36, *Cyc.*106.—Poet. and later Prose. **-ημα,** ατος, τό, in pl., = sq., πόντου ναυστολήμαθ' E.*Supp.*209. **-ία,** ἡ, *going by sea, naval expedition*, Id.*Andr.*795 (lyr.), Str.16.2.23.

**ναυστο-λογέω,** *take as a passenger*, metaph. of Ἀχέρων, *CIL*8.21445 (Caesarea Mauret.). ®**-λόγος,** ὁ, = *navis dispositor*, *Gloss.*: also, in pl., *pilotage dues*, ib.

®**ναύστολος,** ον, *dispatched* or *equipped as a ship, crossing the water*, A.*Th.*858.

**ναυτ-εία,** ἡ, *naval affairs*, σύλληψις τῶν εἰς τὴν ν. *OGI*90.17 (Rosetta, ii B.C.), cf. *PRev.Laws*85.6 (iii B.C.). ®**-ης,** ου, ὁ, (ναῦς) *seaman, sailor*, Il.19.375, Sapph.*Supp.*9.8, Pi.*P.*4.188, Pl.*Plt.*302a, etc.: as Adj., ν. ὅμιλος E.*Hec.*921 (lyr.); *by sea*, opp. πεζός (by land), A.*Pers.*719 (troch.). II. *passenger by sea*, ναύτην ἄγειν τινά S.*Ph.*901: metaph., συμποσίου ναῦται *mates* in the drinking bout, Dionys.Eleg.5. **-ία,** Ion. **ναυσίη** Semon.7.54, ἡ:—*seasickness*, or generally, *nausea*, Arist.*PA*664ᵇ13 (pl.), Aret.*SA*1.5, 2.2, Alciphr.2.4, Jul.*Or.*6.190d: pl., Porph.*Gaur.*8.1. 2. generally, *disgust*, Semon. l.c. **-ιασμός,**

ὁ, = foreg., *Hippiatr.*130. **-ιάω,** mostly in pres. and impf. (aor., Luc.*Tox.*19, Gal.16.665, Phryn.172: fut., Aristo *Stoic.*1.89):—*suffer from seasickness* or *nausea*, Ar.*Th.*882, Pl.*Tht.*191a, *Lg.*639b, Arist.*Pr.*868$^a$6, D.*Fr.*30, Plu.*Per.*33; ταῦτα δ' ἐστὶ πλεῖν ἢ ναυτιᾶν *Com.Adesp.*637; ἐναυτίων Luc.*Nec.*4. 2. generally, *to be disgusted*, Demetr.*Eloc.*15, Phryn. l.c. **-ιεύς,** derivative of ναύτης, sine expl., *EM*63.55. ⊛**-ικός,** ή, όν, *of* or *for a ship, seafaring, naval*, ὁ ν. στρατός Hdt.7.100,203, etc.; opp. ὁ πεζός, Id.8.1; ν. λεώς A.*Pers.*383; στόλος S.*Ph.*561; ν. ἐρείπια wrecks *of ships*, A.*Ag.*660; ἑδώλια S.*Aj.*1277; σκάφη ib.1278; ν. πόλεμος And.4.12; ν. ἀστρολογία Arist.*APo.*79$^a$1; ἔγγαια καὶ ναυτικά *property on* land and *sea*, *PEleph.*1.13 (iv B.C.); ν. ἀναρχία *among the seamen*, E.*Hec.*607; τὸ ν. *crew*, Hp.*Ep.*14; but usu. *navy, fleet*, Hdt.7.97,160, Ar.*Eq.*1063, Th.1.36, etc.; ἡ -κή Hdt.7.161. 2. of persons, *skilled in seamanship, nautical*, ναυτικοὶ ἐγένοντο became *a naval power*, Th.1.18, cf. 7.21; ναυτικός, ὁ, = ναύτης, *POxy.*929.8 (ii/iii A.D.). 3. ἡ -κή (sc. τέχνη) *navigation, seamanship*, Hdt.8.1, etc.; τὰ -κά Pl.*Alc.*1.124e: τὰ -κά, also, *naval affairs, sea-power*, Th.4.75, X.*HG*1.6.4. II. **ναυτικόν, τό,** perh. *pilot's fee*, *POxy.*522.15 (ii A.D.); but usu. b. *money borrowed* or *lent on bottomry*, in full, ν. χρήματα Lys.32.7: mostly in pl., ν. ἐκδεδομένα ib.6; ναυτικὸν ἀνελέσθαι to take *it* up, borrow *it*, D.50.17; ναυτικοῖς ἐργάζεσθαι Id.33.4: in sg., X.*Vect.*3.9; also ν. τόκος D.L.6.99. Adv. -κῶς, δανείζειν Id.7.13.

**ναυτῖλ-έῳ,** dat. sg., perh. Coan form of Ναυτίλῳ, *The Sailor*, as place-name, *SIG*1000.11 (Cos, i B.C.). **-ία,** Ion. **-ίη,** ἡ, *sailing, seamanship*, Od.8.253, Hes.*Op.*618, Pl.*R.*527d, al. 2. *voyage*, Hdt.4.145, Hp.*Aph.*4.14: and in pl., ναυτιλίῃσι μακρῇσι ἐπιθέσθαι Hdt.1.1, cf. 163; ναυτιλίῃσι χρέεσθαι Id.2.43, cf. Pi.*N.*3.22, *I.*4(3).57. 3. *ship*, πολύσκαλμος ν. *AP*7.295.4 (Leon.).

**ναυτίλλομαι,** only pres. and impf. (exc. aor. subj. ναυτίλεται [ῐ] Od.4.672 (prob.), inf. ναυτίλασθαι [ῐ] D.C.56.3):—*sail, go by sea*, ναυτίλεται εἵνεκα πατρός Od. l.c., cf. 14.246, Hdt.1.163, 2.5, al., S.*Ant.*717, E.*Fr.*793; ν. τὴν [θάλασσαν] *sail on, navigate*, Hdt.1.202; ναυτιλίαν ναυτίλλεσθαι Pl.*R.*551c. 2. of the nautilus, κενῷ [τῷ ὀστράκῳ] ν. Arist.*HA*622$^b$9. 3. metaph., of water-fowl, Philostr.*Im.*1.9.

**ναυτίλος** [ῐ], ὁ, poet. for ναύτης, *seaman, sailor*, Hdt.2.43, A.*Pr.*468, S.*Aj.*1146: rare in Com., Nausicr.1.2, 2.10. 2. as Adj. ναυτίλος, ον, *of a ship*, ν. σέλματα A.*Ag.*1442; ν. πλάτη E.*Fr.*846. II. the *paper nautilus, Argonauta argo*, a cephalopod mollusc fabled to sail by spreading its membranous arms, Arist.*HA*525$^a$21, 622$^b$5, cf. Call.*Epigr.*6.3, Opp.*H.*1.340, Ael.*NA*9.34.

**ναυτῖλοφθόρος,** ον, *bane of sailors*, Lyc.650.

**ναυτίς,** ίδος, ἡ, fem. of ναύτης, γυναῖκες Theopomp.Com.79.

⊛**ναυτιώδης,** ες, (ναυτία) *nauseous, sickening*, Dsc.1.40, Antyll.ap.Orib.4.11.6, Plu.2.127a, 128d; τὸ ν. Gal.6.678. 2. *disposed to nausea*, διάθεσις Id.13.122,156. Adv. -δῶς, ἔχειν Herod.Med.ap.Orib.5.27.22.

**ναυτο-δίκαι** [ῐ], οἱ, at Athens, *judges of the admiralty-court*, *IG*1$^2$.41.4, Lys.17.5, Luc.*DMeretr.*2.2: they also took cognizance of γραφαὶ ξενίας, Cratin.233, cf. Ar.*Fr.*225. **-κράτωρ** [ᾰ], ορος, = ναυκράτωρ, *BCH*46.331 (Teos), v.l. in Th.5.97,109. **-λογέω,** *take on board passengers* or *cargo*, *PLond.*3.1164*h*19 (iii A.D.): metaph., Κύπριν ν. *AP*9.415 (Antiphil.). ⊛**-λόγος,** ον, *collecting seamen*, Str.8.6.15. **-παίδιον,** τό, *sailor boy*, Hp.*Epid.*2.1.12.

**ναύτρια,** ἡ, fem. of ναύτης, as if from *ναυτήρ, Ar.*Fr.*825.

**ναυ-φάγος** [ᾰ], ον, *ship-devouring, wrecking*, Lyc.1095. **-φαρκτος,** v. ναύφρακτος. **-φθορία,** ἡ, *shipwreck, loss of ships*, *AP*7.73 (Tull.Gem.): pl., Man.1.324. **-φθορος,** ον, *shipwrecked*, ν. στολή, πέπλοι, the garb *of shipwrecked men*, E.*Hel.*1382, 1539. **-φρακτος,** Att. **-φαρκτος** Phot. (ναύφ[....]ος *IG*1$^2$.296.30), ον: (φράσσω):—*ship-fenced*, Ἰάνων ν. Ἄρης, of the Greeks at Salamis, A.*Pers.*951 (lyr.); so ν. ὅμιλος ib.1029 (lyr.); στράτευμα E.*IA*1259; στρατός Ar.*Eq.*567; ναύφαρκτον βλέπειν to look like a *ship of war*, Id.*Ach.*95. ⊛**-φῠλᾰκέω,** *guard a ship*, Eust.1562.36. ⊛**-φύλαξ** [ῠ], ὁ, *one who keeps watch on board ship*, Ar.*Fr.*372. II. = ναοφύλαξ I, *IG*4$^2$(1).402 (pl., Epid., ii A.D.).

**ναύω,** Aeol. for νάω (q.v.), Hsch. II. = ἱκετεύω, Id., Phot. **ναυών,** ῶνος, ὁ, (ναῦς) = νεών, νεώριον, Hsch.

⊛**νάφθᾰ,** ἡ (τό, Eust.700.56), *naphtha* (Persian *naft*), Dsc.1.73, D.C.36.3$^a$:—also **νάφθας,** ὁ, Str.16.1.15; acc. νάφθαν Lxx *Da.*3.64; gen. νάφθα Str. l.c., Plu.*Alex.*35.

**ναφρόν,** τό, *linen thread*, Hsch. **ναχαδόν·** σαθρόν, Id. **ναχειλές,** = foreg., Id.

**νάω,** only pres. and impf., Att. contr. νᾷ S.*Fr.*5, part. νῶντας Phot.:—*flow*, ἐν δὲ κρήνη νάει Od.6.292; καὶ φρείατα μακρὰ νάουσιν Il.21.197; ὄφρ' ἂν ὕδωρ τε νάῃ Epigr.ap.Pl.*Phdr.*264d; οἴνῳ Ἀχελῷος ἆρα νᾷ S. l.c.; ὕδατι νᾶε *was running with* .., A.R.1.1146; νᾶεν φόνῳ Call.*Dian.*224:—Pass., *to be watered*, νᾱομένοισι τόποις Nic.*Fr.*74.58. [ᾰ in Hom. and presupposed by νᾷ, νῶντας, cf. ἀέναος: ᾱ v.l. in Od.9.222, always in late Ep. exc. Euph.23; ναῖον (so Aristarch. and some codd.) δ' ὀρῷ ἄγγεα πάντα is prob. correct in Od. l.c., cf. ἔναιεν ἐν ἅλμῃ (with pun on ναίω *dwell*) Matro *Conv.*77, and ναιομένοισι (νεομ- codd.) shd. perh. be read in Nic. l.c.] (Cf. ἔννυθεν, ναύω, νόα, Skt. *snaúti* (pf. part. Pass. *snutás*) 'drip', MIr. *snuadh* 'river', etc.: νάω [ᾰ] from *snăw-ω*, ναίω and νάω [ᾱ] from *snăw-yω*.)

**ναώριον,** v. νεώριον. **νέα,** Ion. acc. of ναῦς. II. v. νειός.

**νεάγγελτος,** ον, *newly* or *lately told*, φάτις A.*Ch.*736.

**νεᾱγενής,** f.l. for νεογενής in E.*IA*1623 (unless scanned as trisyll.).

⊛**νεάζω,** impf. ἐνέαζον Agath.5.15: aor. 1 inf. νεάσαι *AP*11.256 (Lucill.), elsewh. only pres.: (νέος):—intr., *to be young* or *new*, τὸ νεάζον *youth*, S.*Tr.*144; νεάζων *thinking* or *acting like a youth*, E.*Ph.*713; ν. τῷ τρόπῳ Men.749: metaph., *to be full of youthful spirit*, φιλεῖ δὲ τίκτειν ὕβρις παλαιὰ νεάζουσαν ὕβριν A.*Ag.*764 (lyr.), cf. *Supp.*105 (lyr.); νεάζειν ἀρχόμενος Alciphr.1.28. 2. *to be the younger of two*, ὁ μὲν νεάζων S.*OC*374. 3. *grow* or *be young again*, *AP* l.c.; ὅπως γηράσκων νεάζῃ τοῖς ἀγαθοῖς Epicur.*Ep.*3 p.59 U. II. Pass., *to be renewed*, στέμμα.. ἐκ πατρὸς παιδὶ νεαζόμενον *AP*15.6. III. = νεάω, Hsch. s.h.v. IV. νεάζομεν· ἀφικνούμεθα, Id.

**νέαιρα,** v. νείαιρα.

**Νέαιρα,** ἡ, *Neaera*, daughter of Oceanus:—hence Ν[ε]αιρήϊδες ἵπποι, Hsch.

**νε-αίρετος,** ον, *newly taken*, θήρ A.*Ag.*1063; πόλις ib.1065; βούβαλις Id.*Fr.*330. **-άκης,** v. νεήκης. **-ᾰκόνητος,** ον, *newly-whetted*, νεακόνητον αἷμα χειροῖν ἔχων S.*El.*1394 (lyr.); cf. αἷμα II fin. **-αλδής,** ές, (ἀλδεῖν) *newly grown* or *produced*, Opp.*H.*1.692. **-άλεστος** [ᾰ], ον, *newly-ground*, Sch.Nic.*Al.*410. **-αλής,** ές, *newly caught*, Suid., Hsch., Ammon.*Diff.*p.95 V. 2. *fresh, not tired*, of persons and animals, ἕως νεαλής ἐστιν αὐτὴν τὴν ἀκμήν Ar.*Fr.*361; ἵπποι νεαλεῖς, opp. ἀπειρηκότες, X.*Cyr.*8.6.17; -έστεροι ὄντες Pl.*Plt.*265b; freq. of soldiers, ἀκμαῖοι καὶ ν. Plb.3.73.5, cf. 10.14.3; ἀήττητοι καὶ ν. Plu.*Ant.*39 (hence of *reserve* troops, App.*BC*1.58); ν. καὶ πρόθυμος Plu.2.669a; -έστερος ἐπεισελθεῖν Luc.*Merc.Cond.*26, cf. *Alex.*16. 3. (νέος, ἅλς A) *freshly salted*, opp. τεταριχευμένος, D.25.61 (metaph.); τυρός Archig.ap.Gal.12.808; κρέας Gal.6.528; of a dead body, Luc.*Nec.*15; νεαλὲς γάλα Nic.*Al.*364 (νεαρόν cod. opt.). II. *young*, = νεαρός, μόσχος ib.358. [ᾰ only in Nic. ll. cc.] **-άλωτος** [ᾰ], ον, *newly caught*, Hdt.9.120 (v.l. νεοάλωτος). **-άματα,** τά, = *culta nova*, *Gloss.* **-ᾰμελγής,** ές, *newly milked*, Paul.Aeg.4.1. **-ᾱμέρα,** ἡ, Aeol., = νουμηνία, *IG*12(2).81.1 (Mytil.), *Milet.*3 No.152.37 (ii B.C.; νεναμέρα lapis). **-άν,** ᾶνος, ὁ, = νέος, A.D.*Adv.*160.8 (νεᾶν codd.), Suid. s.v. νεᾶνις, Eust.335.15; cf. ξυνάν. **-ανδρος,** ον: ἀλκῇ ν. in battle *a young warrior*, Lyc.1345. **-ᾱνεία,** ἡ, *spirited, audacious act*, Ph.1.258, 2.128, cf. Hdn.*Epim.*265, Suid.; contr. fr. νεανιεία (q.v.). **-ανθής,** ές, *new-blown*, Nic.*Al.*609; αἶνος *IG*3.716.16.

⊛**νεᾱν-ίας,** ου, Ep. and Ion. **νεηνίης,** εω, ὁ, dat. pl. νεανίοις *IG*9(2).205.25 (Phthiotis, iii B.C.): (νεάν):—*young man*, Hom. (only in Od.) always with ἀνήρ, νεηνίῃ ἀνδρὶ ἐοικώς Od.10.278; ἄνδρες κοιμήσαντο νεηνίαι 14.524; παῖδες νεηνίαι Hdt.1.61, cf. 7.99; ν. γαμβρός Pi.*O.*7.4; τέκτονες κώμων ν. Id.*N.*3.5: without a Subst. in Hdt.1.37,43, S.*OC*335, *El.*750, E.*Alc.*698, X.*Mem.*3.1.2, etc. 2. freq. with the sense of *a youth* in character, i.e. either in good sense, *impetuous, active*, E.*Ion* 1041, cf. Ar.*V.*1333, X.*Cyr.*1.3.6, D.18.313; or in bad sense, *hot-headed, wilful, headstrong*, E.*Supp.*580; ἓν μὲν τοίνυν τοῦτο.. πολίτευμα τοῦ νεανίου τούτου D.18.136, cf. Pl.*Sph.*239d. II. as masc. Adj., *youthful*, νεανίαι τὰς ὄψεις Lys.10.29. 2. of things, etc., *new, young, fresh*, νεανίαις ὤμοισι E.*Hel.*1562; ν. θώρακα καὶ βραχίονα Id.*HF*1095; ἄρτος Ar.*Lys.*1207; ν. λόγοι *rash, wilful* words, E.*Alc.*679. [νεανιῶν is trisyll. in Ar.*V.*1069; cf. νεανικός.] **-ιεία,** ἡ, *youthful spirit*, Ph.2.306; cf. νεανεία. **-ίευμα,** ατος, τό, *youthful*, i.e. *spirited* or (in bad sense) *wanton*, *act* or *word*, Pl.*R.*390a, Luc.*Herm.*33, etc.; of an argument, *bold attempt*, Simp.*in Ph.*1169.9. **-ῐεύομαι** (Act. only in Hsch.), fut. -εύσομαι D.19.242: aor. ἐνεανιευσάμην Id.21.69:—Pass. (v. infr.):—*to be a youth*, Ph.1.303, Poll.2.20. II. more freq., *act like a hot-headed youth, wilfully* or *wantonly, swagger*, Ar.*Fr.*827, Lys *Fr.*324 S.; ν. εἰς τοὺς πολίτας *behave so* towards.., Isoc.20.17, cf. Hyp.*Eux.*27; ἐν τοῖς λόγοις Pl.*Grg.*482c; νεανιευσάμενος εἰπεῖν *with youthful insolence*, Plu.*Cic.*1:—Pass., ἐφ' ἅπασι τοῖς ἑαυτῷ νενεανιευμένοις to all his *wanton acts*, D.21.18; τὰ ἐν τῇ βουλῇ νεανιευθέντα Plu.*Mar.*29. 2. *make youthful*, i.e. *bold, promises*, c. Adj. neut., ν. τοιοῦτον, ὡς.. D.19.194; οὐδ' ἐνεανιεύσατο τοιοῦτον οὐδέν Id.21.69; μέχρι τοῦ λόγου ν. Luc.*Bis Acc.*21: c. inf., *undertake with youthful spirit*, Plu.*Dem.*3. **-ίζω,** = foreg., Id.*Flam.*20, Poll.4.136. **-ῐκέω,** *to be youthful*, Eup.109. **-ῐκός,** ή, όν, (νεάν) *youthful*, ῥώμη Ar.*V.*1067: mostly of youthful qualities: hence, 1. *fresh, active, vigorous, fine*, νεανικώτατε Id.*Eq.*611; κρέας ν. a *fine large* piece, Id.*Pl.*1137; λοπάς Alex.188.2; of trees, Thphr.*HP*5.1.11 (Comp.); -ώτερα ἀγαθά *more splendid*, Pl.*R.*363c. 2. *high-spirited, impetuous, gay*, τὸ νεανικώτατον the *most dashing* feat, Ar.*V.*1205; ἀρχὴ καλὴ καὶ ν. Pl.*R.*563e; γενναῖον καὶ ν. ἔρωτα Id.*Ly.*204e; ν. τε καὶ μεγαλοπρεπεῖς τὰς διανοίας Id.*R.*503c; μέγα καὶ ν. φρόνημα D.3.32; οὐ γὰρ ἡγεῖτο λαμπρὸν οὐδὲ ν. Id.21.131, cf. 201. 3. in bad sense, *headstrong, insolent*, τὸ ν. τοῦ λόγου Pl.*Grg.*508d; ἢ σοῦ τις -ώτερος ib.509a; δημοκρατία ἡ -ωτάτη Arist.*Pol.*1296$^a$4. 4. of things, *vehement, mighty*, ψῦξις -ωτάτη Hp.*VM*16; αἱμορραγία Id.*Prorrh.*1.134; φόβος E.*Hipp.*1204; βούλευμα Id.*Fr.*185.6: freq. in later Prose, ἐπιθυμία ν. Arist.*EN*1148$^a$21; βροντή Id.*HA*602$^b$23; νόσημα ib.602$^b$29; χειμών Thphr.*Ign.*17. II. Adv. -κῶς *in a youthful manner*, ἐστείλαμεν ἑαυτοὺς ν. X.Eph.5.1. 2. *vigorously*, Ar.*Pax* 898; ν. βοηθεῖν τινι Pl.*Tht.*168c; βιαίως καὶ ν. Dsc.1.56; of things, Ph.*Bel.*78.29: Comp. -κωτέρως, ἀγαθός Phld.*Rh.*2.272 S. 3. *violently, wantonly*, τύπτειν, τωθάζειν, Ar.*V.*1307, 1362; ν. ἀκόλαστος Phld.*Acad.Ind.*p.47 M. 4. *excessively*, ν. τρομώδεα Hp.*Prorrh.*1.9; ν. προσπεφυκέναι to be *firmly* attached to.., Arist.*HA*53[illegible]$^a$15. [νεανικήν is trisyll. in Ar.*V.*1067; cf. νεανίας.] ⊛**-ῐκότης,** ητος, ἡ, *youthfulness*, Sext.*Ps.*9.1.

**νεᾶνις**, Ep. and Ion. **νεῆνις** (contr. **νῆνις** Anacr.14.3, *CIG*7629 (vase), Kretschmer *Griech.Vaseninschr.*p.144, *EM*448.29), ῐδος, ἡ, acc. -ιδα *A.Pr.*704, -ιν E.*Cyc.*179:—*girl, maiden*, Il.18.418, Pi.*P.*9.31, A.l.c., *Eu.*958(lyr.), S.*Ant.*784(lyr.), E.l.c., al., A.R.1.843, *Lyr. Alex.Adesp.*26; of a young married woman, E.*Andr.*192; παρθενικὴ ν. Od.7.20. **II.** as Adj., *youthful*, χεῖρες, ἧβαι, E.*Ba.*745, *Ion*477(lyr.). **2.** *new*, βίβλος *AP*4.3ᵇ75 (Agath.).—Poet. word, but freq. in Lxx, *Ex.*2.8, al.

**νεᾶνισκ-άριον**, τό, Dim. of νεανίσκος, Arr.*Epict.*2.16.29. **-αρχέω**, *hold office of* νεανισκάρχης, *IG*3.765, 1098. ⊛ **-άρχης**, ου, ὁ, *official in charge of* ἔφηβοι, ib.1162.8, *Delph.*3(1).238, *IPE*2.440, al. (Tanais), *Supp.Epigr.*2.620 (Teos), *BSA*29.23 (Sparta, ii A.D.), *Philol.*11.293 (Smyrna). **-εύματα**, τά, = Lat. *Juvenalia*, D.C.61.19, 67.14. **-εύομαι**, only pres., *to be in one's youth*, Eup.29, Posidipp.9; ν. ἐν τοῖς ἐφήβοις X.*Cyr.*1.2.15, Plu.2.12b. ⊛ **-ος**, Ion. νεην-, ὁ, (νεάν) *youth, young man*, *IG*1².374.162, al., Hdt.4.72, 112, Pl.*Smp.*211d, Arist.*Pol.*1303ᵇ21, Anon.Hist.(*FGrH*160)p.887J., etc.; ν. τὸ εἶδος (nisi leg. νεανικός) X.*HG*3.3.5; in Hdt.3.53 the same youth is called both νεηνίης and νεηνίσκος; but in Antipho 3.4.6 and 8 the same person is called ν. and μειράκιον, and the eldest son of Socrates is called νεανίσκος X.*Mem.*2.2.1, but μειράκιον Pl.*Ap.*34d; ἔν τε παισὶ καὶ ν. καὶ ἐν ἀνδράσι Id.*R.*413e; παῖς εἴκοσι ἔτεα, νεηνίσκος εἴκοσι, νεηνίης εἴκοσι, γέρων εἴκοσι Pythag.ap.D.L.8.10, cf. Hp.*Hebd.*5: more freq. than νεανίας in later Gr., Wilcken *Chr.*3014 (iii/ii B.C.), Plb.1.36.12, *Ev.Matt.*19.20, etc. **2.** ὁ ἐμὸς ν. my *young man*, i.e. *servant*, Luc.*Alex.*53; perh. also, *PCair.Zen.*18.6 (iii B.C.), *Ev.Marc.*14.51: pl., dub. sens., *PCair.Zen.*153 (iii B.C., written νενίσκοις). **-ύδριον**, τό, = νεανισκάριον, Theognost.*Can.*126.

**νέανσις**, v. νέασις.

**νέαξ** (Ion. **νέηξ** Call.*Fr.*78), ᾶκος, ὁ, = νεανίας, Nicopho 10, cf. Poll.2.11.

⊛ **νεᾰοιδός**, όν, *singing youthfully*, *AP*7.13 (Leon. or Mel.).

**νέαον**· ἀγκυροβόλιον, Hsch.

**Νεάπολις** [ᾰ], εως, ἡ, *new city*, pr. n. of several cities, *Neapolis*: at first in two words, Νέα πόλις, gen. Νέης πόλιος Hdt.2.91, cf. Th.7.50; later in one, Νεάπολις, gen. Νεαπόλεως Str.2.5.40, dat. Νεαπόλει Id.1.2.13: hence **Νεοπολίτης** [ῑ], ου, ὁ, *IG*1².191.31, al., later ⊛ **Νεᾱπολίτης** *Tab.Heracl.*1.187, Lyc.736, Plb.1.20.14, etc., cf. Pl.ap. Poll.9.26.

**νεᾰρο-ηχής**, ές, *sounding new*, διάλεξις Philostr.*VS*2.8.2. **-πάστος**, ον, = *praesalsus*, prob. in *Gloss.* **-ποιέω**, *make new, refresh*, Plu.2.702c:—in Med., *freshen up*, τὴν τῆς ὕλης σύστασιν Herm.ap. Stob.1.49.44. **II.** Medic., *freshen* the edges of an ulcer by removing granulations, ν. ἕλκος, κοιλώματα, Antyll.ap.Orib.44.23.4, Ruf. ap.eund.8.24.48. **2.** *renew, repeat*, Sor.2.41 (Pass.), Aët.15.2 (Act.). ⊛ **-πρεπής**, ές, *possessing youthful charm*, metaph., of style, Aristid.*Rh.*2p.551S.; *becoming* or *natural in youth*, Procl.*in Alc.*pp.23, 47C.; τὸ ν. τῶν ἠθῶν Id.*in Cra.*p.1P., cf. Olymp.*in Phlb.* p.249S.

**νεᾰρός**, ά, όν, poet. for νέος (also in later Prose, v. infr.), *youthful*, παῖδες Il.2.289, cf. Pi.*P.*10.25, etc.; τὸ ἦθος νεαρός, opp. νέος τὴν ἡλικίαν, Arist.*EN*1095ᵃ7; νεαροί *youths*, A.*Ag.*359, 1504 (both anap.); ν. ἥβη Ar.*Fr.*467; = νεαλής, ν. στρατός Hdn.3.7.5; τὸ ν. *youthful spirit*, X.*Cyr.*1.4.3; λόγος ν. καὶ θεατρικός Plu.2.802e; σχηματισμοὶ πολὺ τὸ ν. ἔχοντες D.H.*Comp.*23. **2.** of things, *new*, ὕμνοι Hes.*Fr.*265; νεαρὰ ἐξευρεῖν Pi.*N.*8.20; *fresh*, μυελός A.*Ag.*76 (anap.); σώματα X.*Cyn.*9.10; ν. δέλεαρ, opp. σαπρόν, Arist.*HA*534ᵇ4; τροφή Id.*PA* 675ᵇ29; ν. τυρός, ὄστρεα, Dsc.2.71, Ath.1.7d; -ώτεροι κλῶνες Gal.12.283; καππάρεως ὅτι -ωτάτης *PCair.Zen.*488 (iii B.C.). **3.** of events, *recent*, ξυντυχίαι S.*Ant.*157 (anap.); of a letter, D.L.1.112. **4.** αἱ νεαραί (sc. διατάξεις) title of the *novellae* of Justinian; ἡ θεία καὶ ν. διάταξις *PGrenf.*1.62.13 (vi A.D.). **II.** Adv. -ρῶς *youthfully, rawly*, Luc.*Hist.Conscr.*50: Comp., διειλεγμένον -ωτέρως *with more spirit*, Isoc.12.229. [νεᾱ- by synizesis, as one long syll., Pi. ll. cc.; cf. νηρός.]

**νεᾰροφόρος**, ον, *newly-bearing*, *Gloss.*

**νεᾰρ-ῳδός**, όν, = νεαοιδός, *IG*7.1773 (Thesp.). **-ωσις**, εως, ἡ, *rejuvenation*, Poet. in *PIand.*78.13.

**νέας**, Ion. acc. pl. from ναῦς. **νεάς**, *novella*, *Gloss.*

**νε-άσῐμος** [ᾰ], ον, *to be ploughed up*, of fallow land, *Gloss.* ⊛ **-ᾱσις**, εως, ἡ, (νεάω) *breaking-up of fallow land*, ν. θερινή Thphr.*CP*3.20.7 (νέανσις codd.). **-ασμός**, ὁ, = foreg., *Gp.*2.23.6, 3.3.10.

**νεασπάτωτος** [σπᾰ], ον, Boeot. for νεοκάττυτος, *newly-soled*, Stratt. 47.8.

⊛ **νεάτη** [ᾰ] (sc. χορδή), ἡ, Dor. **νεάτα** Philol.6:—*the lowest of the three strings* which formed the framework of the musical scale (opp. μέση, ὑπάτη), but *the highest* in pitch, Cratin.134, Pl.*R.*443d:—contr. **νήτη** Arist.*Ph.*224ᵇ34, *Metaph.*1018ᵇ28, 1057ᵃ23, Alex.Eph. ap.Theon.Sm.p.140H., etc.: in pl., ἐπὶ τὰς νήτας.. ἀναβαίνειν, in declamation, Antyll.ap.Orib.6.10.23. (Orig. fem. of νέατος (A).)

⊛ **νέᾰτος** (A), Ep. **νείᾰτος**, η, ον, poet. Sup., *uttermost, lowest*, Hom. (who uses the νει- form exc. in Il.11.712, 9.153, 295), always of Space, *the lowest part of*.., ν. ἀνθερεών, κενεών, ὦμος, Il.5.293, 857, 15.341; *extreme, outermost*, ὄρχος Od.7.127; ἀστράγαλος Il.14.466; ν. πείρατα γαίης 8.478; ὑπαὶ πόδα ν. Ἴδης the *lowest* slope of Ida, 2.824; ἐκ ν. πυθμένος εἰς κορυφήν Sol.13.10; πόδες ν. the feet, Orac. ap.Hdt.7.140; νείατον Ἰνίον A.R.3.763, cf. 2.166: c. gen., ν. ἄλλων Il.6.295; πόλις νεάτη Πύλου *on the border* of Pylos, 11.712; πᾶσαι δ' ἐγγὺς ἁλὸς νέαται Πύλου ἠμαθόεντος 9.153, 295 (wrongly expld. ap.Sch. as 3 pl. pres. ind. (like κέαται) of ναίω, *to be situated*):—rare in Prose, τὰς νεάτας πλευράς Hp.*Int.*27, and cf. νεάτη; contr. **νῆτος**· ἔσχατος, Hsch.; Arc. **νήατος** *Schwyzer* 664.10 (Orchom. Arc., iv B.C.). (The orig. form may be νήατος; with νείατος, νέατος, cf. εἵαται, ἕαται (v. ἧμαι), εἵως, ἕως, etc.; cf. νήϊστος, νείαιρα, νειόθεν, νειόθι.)

⊛ **νέᾰτος** (B), η, ον, poet. (post-Hom.) Sup. of νέος, *latest, last*, ν. γέννημα S.*Ant.*627 (anap.); τὰν ν. ὁδὸν στείχουσαν, ν. δὲ φέγγος λεύσσουσαν ib.807 (lyr.); τίς ἄρα νέατος.. λήξει; i.e. ὥστε νέατος γενέσθαι, Id.*Aj.*1185 (lyr.): neut. νέατον as Adv., *for the last time*, E.*Tr.*201 (lyr.).

**νεᾶτός**, ὁ, *breaking-up of fallow land*, X.*Oec.*7.20.

**νεαύξητος**, ον, gloss on νεαλδής, Sch.Opp.*H.*1.692.

**νεάω**, (νειός) *plough up*, of fallow land, ἣν νεᾶν βούλησθε.. τοὺς ἀγρούς Ar.*Nu.*1117: metaph., τὰν μέσαν νεῶν ἄρουραν (in music) Pratin.Lyr.5: abs., Eup.13, Thphr.*CP*3.20.7: aor. 1 subj. νεάσωσι ib.3.20.8:—Pass., νεωμένη (sc. γῆ) *land ploughed up*, after lying fallow, Hes.*Op.*462.

**νεβλάραι** (fort. νεβλᾶραι)· περαίνειν, Hsch.; νεβλάρεται Ar.*Fr.*241 (ap.Phot., -τοι cod.).

**νέβ⟨λ⟩εστα**· ⟨τὰ⟩ περιτάλματα τῶν ἱερῶν (Sicel), Hsch.

**νέβραξ**, ᾱκος, ὁ, *cockerel*, Hsch.

⊛ **νέβρ-ειος**, ον, *of a fawn*, ὀστέα, αὐλοί, Call.*Dian.*244, *APl.*4.305 (Antip.). **-ῆ**, contr. for νεβρέη (sc. δορά), ἡ, = νεβρίς, *fawnskin*, Orph.*Fr.*238.8; ν. παρδαλέη Id.*A.*449. **-ίας**, ου, ὁ, *dappled like a fawn*, γαλεός Arist.*HA*565ᵃ26, cf. Hsch. s.v. λάδας. **-ίδιον** [ῐδ], τό, Dim. of νεβρίς, Artem.4.72.

**νεβρῐδό-πεπλος**, ον, *clad in fawnskin*, of Dionysus and the Bacchae, *AP*9.524.14. **-στολος**, ον, = foreg., Orph.*H.*52.10.

⊛ **νεβρ-ίζω**, *wear a fawnskin at the feast of Dionysus*, or, as trans., *robe in fawnskins* (Phot. gives both explanations), D.18.259. **-ινος**, η, ον, *of a fawn*, δορά S.*Ichn.*219. **-ίς**, ἡ, gen. ῐδος [ῐ] E.*Ba.*136 (lyr.; late ῑδος D.P.703, 946), νεβρίδα E.*Ba.*24, Thesp.1, νεβρίσι E.*Ba.*249, νεβρίδας ib.696:—*fawnskin*, esp. as the dress of Dionysus and the Bacchae, ll. cc. **-ισμός**, ὁ, *wearing of a* νεβρίς, Arignote ap. Harp. ⊛ **-ίτης** [ῑ], ου, ὁ, *like a fawnskin*, ν. λίθος, a precious stone, Orph.*L.*748:—also **-ῖτις**, ιδος, ἡ, Plin.*HN*37.175.

**νεβρόγονος** κνήμη, the bone *of a fawn's leg*, i.e. a flute, Cleobulina 3 (dub. l.).

**νεβρόομαι**, Pass., *to be changed into a fawn*, Nonn.*D.*10.60.

⊛ **νεβρός**, ὁ, *young of the deer, fawn*, Il.8.248, Od.4.336, etc.; πέδιλα νεβρῶν *fawnskin brogues*, Hdt.7.75; a type of cowardice, Il.4.243, 21.29; prov., ὁ ν. τὸν λέοντα (sc. αἱρεῖ), of anything strange, Luc.*DMort.*8.1:—also fem., Il.4.243, E.*Ba.*866 (lyr.), *Trag.Adesp.*419.

⊛ **νεβρο-τόκος**, ον, *bringing forth fawns*, Nic.*Th.*142. **-φανής**, ές, *fawn-like*, Nonn.*D.*5.363. ⊛ **-φόνος**, ον, *preying on fawns*, ν. [ἀετός], = πύγαργος, Arist.*HA*618ᵇ20. **-χίτων** [ῐ], ὁ, ἡ, gen. ωνος, *clad in a* νεβρίς, Simm.15.

**νεβρώδης**, ες, *fawn-like*, of Dionysus, *AP*9.524.14.

**νεδίας**· τὰς αἰθυίας, Hsch. **νέες, νέεσσι**, v. ναῦς. **νεϜόστατος**, v. νεόστατος. **νέη** (sc. ἡμέρα), ἡ, v. νέος. **νέηαι**, v. νέομαι.

**νεη-γενής**, ές, Ion. for νεᾱγενής, *new-born, just born*, Od.4.336. **-θᾰλής**, ές, = νεοθαλής, *fresh-blown, young*, E.*Ion* 112 (lyr.).

**νε-ήκης** (on the accent v. Hdn.Gr.1.82), Dor. **νεάκης** Hsch. (-κίς cod.), ες: (ἀκή A):—*newly whetted* or *sharpened*, Il.13.391. **-ηκονής**, ές, (ἀκόνη) = foreg., S.*Aj.*820. **-ηλαίη**, ἡ, Ion. for νεολαία, Hsch. (νέηλαι cod.). **-ηλάτης** [ᾰ], ου, ὁ, (ναῦς) *rower*, Id. **-ήλᾰτος**, ον, (νέος, ἐλαύνω III) *newly-forged*, Id. **II.** (cf. ἐλατήρ III, ἔλατρον) *freshly rolled out*: νεήλατα, τά, *new* cakes, D.18.260 (expld. by Harp. fr. ἀλέω A). **-ηλῐφής**, ές, (ἀλείφω) *fresh-plastered*, οἰκίαι Arist.*Pr.*899ᵇ18. **-ηλῠς**, ῠδος, ὁ, ἡ, (ἤλυθον) *newcomer*, Il.10.434, Hdt.1.118, Pl.*Lg.*879d. ⊛ **-ήμελκτος**, η, ον, *newly milked*, Nic.*Al.*311.

**νεηνίης, νεῆνις, νεηνίσκος**, Ion. for νεᾱν-: so **νέηξ** for νέαξ.

⊛ **νεή-τομος**, ον, *cut* or *castrated when young*, *AP*6.234 (Eryc.). **-φᾰτος**, ον, poet. for νεόφατος, *newly revealed*, ὅσσα *h.Merc.*443.

**νεί**, Boeot. for νή, Ar.*Ach.*867, 905; also Arc., *IG*5(2).343.42 (Orchom.).

**νεῖαι**, v. νέομαι.

**νείαιρᾰ**, acc. sg. -ᾰν Il.16.465, Hp.*Mul.*1.64, 2.137, *Nat.Mul.*5, 6, al. (codd. opt.), Call.*Fr.*106 codd., Nic.*Al.*270; dat. -ῃ Il. (v. infr.):—fem. Adj. (formed like γέραιρα) with comp. sense, *lower*, νειαίρῃ δ' ἐν γαστρί *in the lower part of* the belly, Il.5.539, 616, cf. Hp. ll. cc.; νείαιραν σάρκα Nic. l.c.:—also **νέαιρα**, νέαιραν γνάθον Simon. 244. **II.** Subst., ἡ νείαιρα the *abdomen*, βάρος ἐν νειαίρῃ Hp.*Coac.*579, cf. Call. l.c.; cf. νειρός (A). (Cogn. with νέατος (A): orig. perh. *νήαιρα, whence νέαιρα (lengthd. to νείαιρα in text of Hom.), contr. *νῆρα, whence νεῖρα.)

⊛ **νειάτιος** [ᾰ], η, ον, later form for νείατος, νέατος (A), Man.6.738.

**νείᾰτος**, v. νέατος (A).

**νεικ-είω**, = νεικέω (q.v.). ⊛ **-έσσιος**· πολέμιος, Hsch. **-εστήρ**, ῆρος, ὁ, *wrangler*: c. gen., *one who wrangles with*, ἐσθλῶν ν. Hes.*Op.*716. **-έω**, fut. -έσω Il.10.115: aor. ἐνείκεσα, Ep. νείκεσσα or νείκεσα, 3.38, 10.158: also pres. **νεικείω** 2.277, etc.; subj. νεικείῃσι, νεικείῃ, 1.579, Hes.*Op.*332; part. νεικείουσα Theoc.1.35: impf. νείκειον Od.22.26: iterat. νεικείεσκον Il.4.241: (νεῖκος):—*quarrel, wrangle with* one, μή μοι ὀπίσσω νεικείῃ Od.17.189; ἔριδος πέρι θυμοβόροιο νεικεῦσ' ἀλλήλῃσι *quarrel* one *with* another, Il.20.254; ἐνείκεον εἵνεκα ποινῆς 18.498: c. acc. cogn., νείκεα.. νεικεῖν ἀλλήλοισιν ἐναντίον 20.252; νεικέσκομεν οἴω, we two alone *strove with him*, is prob. corrupt

in Od.11.512 (νικάσκομεν Aristarch.): abs. in part. νεικέων Hdt.9.55. II. trans., *chide, rail at, upbraid*, c. acc. pers., Il.1.521, al.; Ἀγαμέμνονα ν. μύθῳ 2.224; αἰσχροῖς, ὀνειδείοις, χολωτοῖσιν ἐπέεσσιν, 3.38, 21.480, Od.22.225, etc.; ὅς νείκεσσε θεάς.., τὴν δ' ᾔνησ' [Paris] *insulted* the goddesses (Hera and Athena), but praised the other (Aphrodite), Il.24.29.—Ep. Verb, used twice by Hdt., 8.125, 9.55; not in Att.: in later Prose, LxxPr.10.12, al. -η, ἡ, = νεῖκος, ν. ἀμφὶ Μολιονιδᾶν Epigr.ap.Paus.5.2.5: personified, = Ἔρις, v.l. for Νίκης in Timo 21; prob. in A.Ag.1378, E.Or.1679, Poet.ap.D.Chr. 32.82, cf. EM276.3. -ητήρ, ὁ, v.l. for νεικεστήρ, Hes.Op.716.

**νεικλητήρ**· λικμητήρ (Megar.), Hsch. * **νεῖκλον**, τό, = λίκνον, Id.; cf. νίκλον.

**νεῖκος**, εος, τό, *quarrel, strife, feud*, ν... ὄρωρεν Ἕκτορος ἀμφὶ νέκυι Il.24.107; ν. πρός τινα Hdt.8.87; ν. κρεσσόνων ἀποθέσθαι Pi.O.10(11).39, cf. N.6.51; τὸ ν. εὖ θέσθαι S.OT633; τὸ ν. ἐγκαλῶν imputing the blame of the *quarrel*, ib.702; ν. θέσθαι Call.Iamb.1.202. 2. *strife of words, railing, abuse*, νεῖκος ἄριστε Il.23.483; νείκει ὀνειδίζων 7.95; ἐς νείκεα ἀπικέσθαι Hdt.9.55. 3. *strife at law, dispute before a judge*, κρίνων ν. πολλὰ δικαζομένων αἰζηῶν Od.12.440, cf. Il.18.497; *challenge* to authority, Hdt.3.62. 4. also in Hom. not seldom for *battle, fight*, ν. ὁμοίιον Il.4.444, al.; ν. πολέμοιο 13.271; ν. ὁμοίιου πολέμοιο Od.18.264; ἔριδος μέγα ν. Il.17.384; ν. φυλόπιδος 20.140; πόλεμος καὶ ν. 12.361; ἔριδες καὶ νείκεα 2.376; πόνος καὶ ν. 12.348; νείκεα καὶ δῆριν Hes.Op.33; πόλεμος καὶ ν. Ar.V.867 (anap.), cf. X. Cyn.1.17; νείκεα νεικεῖν Il.20.251; of *hostilities* between whole nations, νεῖκος πρὸς Καρχηδονίους Hdt.7.158, cf. 225. 5. in the philosophy of Emp., the *separative principle* in the κόσμος, opp. Φιλότης, 17.8, al., cf. Pl.Sph.242a, Arist.Metaph.985ᵃ24, etc. (Mostly poet., found in Hdt. and OGI335.119 (Pergam., ii B.C.).) II. v. νῖκος.

**Νειλαιεύς**, έως, ὁ, = sq., AP9.353 (Leon. Alex.).

**Νειλαῖος**, α, ον, *from the Nile*, Μοῦσα AP6.321 (Leon. Alex.), v.l. for Νειλῷος in Ath.7.312a: Νειλαῖα, τά, *festival of the Nile*, BGU362 xvii (iii A.D.).

* **Νειλεῖον**, τό, *temple of* Νείλεως or Νειλεύς (Νηλεύς) (founder of Miletus), IG1².94.27 (written Νελ-).

**Νειλο-βροχέω**, in Pass., *to be inundated by the Nile*, POxy.1502ᵛ.6 (iii A.D.). -**βροχος**, ον, *inundated by the Nile* (i.e. not artificially irrigated), PRyl.208.30 (ii A.D.), etc. -**γενής**, ές, *Nile-born*, AP9.355 (Leon. Alex.), Epigr.Gr.982 (Philae). -**θερής**, ές, *burnt by the Nile*, i.e. by the sun and air of Egypt, παρειά A.Supp.71 (anap.; εἰλοθερής Emperius). * -**κάλάμη** [λᾰ], ἡ, *bulrush*, PMag.Lond.121.490, BGU633.20 (iii A.D.). * -**μέτριον**, τό, *Nilometer*, a rod graduated to show the rise and fall of the Nile, Str.17.1.48, Hld.9.22, POxy.43ᵛvi (iii A.D.):—Adj. -**μετρικός**, ή, όν, *used in the graduation of the Nilometer*, πῆχυς ib.669.36 (iii A.D.). * -**ρῦτος**, ον, (ῥέω) *watered by the Nile*, προβολή AP9.350 (Leon. Alex.).

**Νεῖλος**, ὁ, *Nile*, Hes.Th.338, etc.

**Νειλοσκοπεῖον**, τό, = Νειλομέτριον, D.S.1.36.

**Νειλ-ῶτις**, ῖδος, ἡ, *situated on the Nile*, πυραμίδες AP9.710. -**ῷος**, α, ον, = Νειλαῖος, Luc.Nav.15, PMasp.2ii21 (vi A.D.); τὰ Νειλῷα *festival on the inundation of the Nile*, Hld.9.9. -**ώτης**, ου, ὁ, *in* or *on the Nile*, Ath.7.309a: fem., Νειλῶτις χθών the land *of the Nile*, A.Pr.814.

**νεῖμεν, νεῖμαν, νεῖμον**, Ion. aor. of νέμω.

**νει-όθεν**, Ion. Adv. (cf. νέατος A) *from the bottom*, ἀνεστενάχιζε ν. ἐκ κραδίης he heaved a sigh *from the bottom* of his heart, Il.10.10; [ἐλάτην] ν. ἔλλαβε χερσίν A.R.1.1197: c. gen., Arat.234; ν. ἐξεμέσαι Cerc.4.55; [βλ?]ύσε ν. Epic. in Arch.Pap.7.10:—also νειόθε, ν. δ' ἐξανέηκεν..πηγὴν Supp.Epigr.4.467.25 (Didyma, iii A.D.); in late Prose, ν. δρᾶν *heartily*, Luc.Peregr.7. Cf. νεόθεν II. -**όθι**, Ion. Adv. (cf. νέατος A) *at the bottom*, δάκεν δέ ἑ ν. θυμόν it stung him *to his* heart's *core*, Hes.Th.567: c. gen., ν. λίμνης Il.21.317. 2. *under, beneath*, opp. ὑψόθι, A.R.2.355; *in stooping posture*, Id.3.706: c. gen., ν. γαίης Id.1.63, cf. Arat.89. [ι is rarely elided, as in Nic.Al.520.]

* **νειο-κόρος**, ὁ, ἡ, Ion. for νεωκόρος, AP6.356 (Pancrat.). -**ποιέω**, *take a green crop off* a field, by which it is freshened and prepared for corn, X.Oec.11.16.

* **νειός**, ἡ, also **νεός** X. (v. infr.), SIG963.8 (Amorgos, iv B.C.), *fallow-land*, νειοῖο βαθείης Il.10.353; ν. τρίπολος a thrice-ploughed *fallow*, 18.541, Od.5.127, Hes.Th.971, cf. Call.Dian.175, etc.; μὴ καρπίζεσθαι τὴν γῆν ἀλλὰ νειὸν ποιεῖν *rejuvenate* it, Thphr.CP4.8.1, cf. 4.8.3, HP8.7.2; νειὸν ἄρουραν Hes.Op.463; of a mare, ἕνα ἐνιαυτὸν..ἀνάγκη διαλείπειν καὶ ποιεῖν ὥσπερ νειόν Arist.HA577ᵃ2. 2. *ploughing and sowing* of land *to reinvigorate* it, νειὸς ἀμείνων ἡ χειμέριος τῆς ἐαρινῆς Thphr.HP8.6.3; ἡ ἀρίστη νειὸς ἀπὸ τῶν κυάμων prob. cj. ib.8.7.2; εἰς νειὸν ἀροῦν Gp.3.6.7, 3.11.8; τῷ σπόρῳ νεὸν δεῖ ὑπεργάζεσθαι X.Oec.16.10, cf. SIG l.c.:—also νέα, ἡ, Thphr.CP3.20.7, IG 2².334.17; also παρασκάψει τὴν γῆν νειάν SIG963.46. (Cf. OSlav. *njiva* 'field'.)

**νεῖος** (A), η, ον, Ion. for νέος, A.R.1.125, Hsch.

**νεῖος** (B), α, ον, (ναῦς) Att. for νήϊος, IG2².1610.27, 1629.1000, 1003, al. (in neut. pl. as Subst.), Theognost.Can.121.

**νειότατον**· κατώτατον, Hsch.

**νειοτομεύς**, έως, ὁ, *one who breaks up a fallow*, AP6.41 (Agath.).

**νειόφατον**· νεόκρατον, Hsch. **νεῖρα**, v. sq. 2 and νείαιρα.

**νειρός** (A), ά, όν, *lowest*, ἐν χθονὸς νειροῖς μυχοῖς Lyc.896 (v.l. νηροῖς), cf. Hsch. s.vv. νειρόν, νηρόν. 2. Subst. νειρή, ἡ, = νείαιρα II, Id. s.v. νειρὴ κοίλη (s.v.l.), but acc. sg. νεῖραν as Adj., νεῖραν ἐς πλευρὰν prob. cj. in E.Rh.794 (νείαιραν, νείεραν codd.); dat. sg. νείρᾳ prob. in A.Ag.1479 (lyr.; νείρει codd.); cf. νείαιρα.

**νειρός** (B), ά, όν, *strong, vehement*, Hsch.

**νείσσομαι** or **νείσομαι**, v. νίσσομαι.

**νείφω**, fut. νείψω Epic.ap.Plu.2.949b: aor. ἔνειψα (κατ-) Ar.Ach. 138:—Pass. (v. infr.), aor. ἐνείφθην (κατ-) D.H.12.8:—*snow*, sts. person., ὄτε ὤρετο Ζεὺς νειφέμεν (Ep. inf.) Il.12.280; ὅταν νείφῃ ὁ θεός X.Cyn.8.1; ἔνειφεν ὁ Ζεύς Babr.45; imper. νεῖφε (sc. Ζεῦ) AP 5.63 (Asclep.); ὁπόταν σχολάζῃς, νεῖψον Pherecr.20: metaph., χρυσῷ νείφων *falling in a shower of* gold, Pi.I.7(6).5. 2. impers., νείφει *it snows*, Ar.Ach.1141, cf. V.773; νειφέτω ἀλφίτοις *let it snow* with barley-meal, Nicopho 13. 3. Med. = Act., νιφάδος νειφομένας when the snow *is falling*, A.Th.213 (lyr.); also ὑρίχους νειφομένους σύκων ὁμοῦ τε μύρτων Ar.Fr.569.5. 4. Pass., *to be snowed on*, Hdt.4.31, Ar.Ach.1075, X.HG2.4.3, Plb.16.12.3; χιόνι πολλῇ νείφεται D.S.5.25: metaph., πολιῷ γήραϊ νειφόμενος AP6.198 (Antip. Thess.); Παναθηναίοισιν ἐλαίου νειφόμενον δώροις Inscr.Cos 58.10. II. *rain*, Nonn.D.22.283:—Pass., *to be rained on*, τῶν ὑπὲρ Μέμφιν μηδὲ νειφομένων παράπαν Ph.2.99. III. trans., θεὸς ν. τροφὰς ἀπ' οὐρανοῦ Il.1.617:—Pass., τὸ νειφόμενον, i.e. manna, Id.2.114. [νίφω, ἔνιψα, etc. (μακρὰ ἡ πρώτη συλλαβή Phot.) freq. in codd., but the true early spelling is νείφω, ἔνειψα, etc., Inscr.Cos l.c., Hdn.Gr.2.430,554, sts. in codd., as Nicophol.c.; νιφ- is correct in derivs., which have short ι.] (I.-E. *sneigʷh-* and *snigʷh-*, cf. Lat. *nix, nivis, ninguit*, Lith. *sniẽga* 'it snows', Goth. *snaiws* 'snow', etc.)

**νεκάς**, άδος, ἡ, (νέκυς) *heap of slain*, ἐν αἰνῇσιν νεκάδεσσιν Il.5.886, cf. Ps.-Luc.Philopatr.10. II. simply, = τάξις, in pl., *ranks*, Call. Fr.231. III. in pl., the *dead*, ἄναξ νεκάδων Ἀϊδωνεύς AP15.40.43 (Cometas), cf. EM600.9.

**νεκρ-άγγελος**, ον, *messenger of the dead*, Luc.Peregr.41. -**ᾱγωγέω**, *conduct the dead*, of Hermes, Id.Cont.2. -**ᾱγωγός**, όν, *conducting the dead*, Epigr.Gr.258 = Sammelb.5629 (Alexandria, iii B.C.). -**ᾰκᾰδήμεια**, ἡ, *school of the dead*, Luc.VH2.23. -**επάρτης**, ου, ὁ, *remover of corpses*, Cat.Cod.Astr.8(3).110, 8(4).215, prob. l. ib.7.117. -**ηγός**, όν, *for conveyance of corpses*, πλοῖον PHamb.74.3 (ii A.D.). -**ία**, ἡ, *cemetery*, Mitteis Chr.31 i 20 (pl., ii B.C.), UPZ19.16 (ii B.C.), Sammelb.5216.5 (pl., i B.C.). -**ικός**, ή, όν, *of* or *for the dead*, Luc.DDeor.24.1; νεκρικά, τά, *inheritances, legacies*, Vett.Val. 37.15, al. 2. *deathlike*, χείλη Luc.DMeretr.1.2. Adv. -κῶς Id. Peregr.33, Philops.32. -**ῑμαῖος**, α, ον, = θνησιμαῖος, of animals, Aq.De.14.8, Sch.Ar.Av.538, OGI629.158 (Palmyra, ii A.D.), Erot. and Hsch. s.v. κενέβρεια; also of a human being, τὸ ν. Lxx 3Ki.13.25.

**νεκρο-άρτης**, ου, ὁ, = νεκρεπάρτης, AJP34.448 (Egypt). -**βαρής**, ές, *laden with the dead*, ἄκατος APl.4.273 (Crin.). -**βαστάξ**, άγος, ὁ, ἡ (on the accent v. Hdn.Gr.1.43, 2.740), *bearing the dead*, EM270.30. -**βόρος**, ον, *corpse-devouring*, Cyran.17. -**δέγμων**, ον, gen. ονος, *receiving the dead*, Ἅιδης A.Pr.153 (lyr.). -**δερκής**, ές, *looking like the dead*, Man.4.555 (s.v.l.). -**δόκος**, ον, = νεκροδέγμων, *receiving the dead*, κλιντήρ AP7.634 (Antiphil.). -**δότης**, ου, ὁ, = *uspinio* (fort. *vespillo*), Gloss. -**δοχεῖον**, τό, *burial-place, mausoleum*, Luc.Cont.22. -**δόχος**, ον, = νεκροδέγμων, Eust.1903.63. -**θάπτης**, ου, ὁ, *grave-digger*, Antioch.Astr. in Cat.Cod.Astr.7.117, Sch.Ar.Nu.844, Gloss. -**θήκη**, ἡ, *coffin* or *urn*, E.Fr.472.17 (anap.); *place for a coffin* or *urn*, prob. in Rev. Bibl.39.532 (pl., Palmyra, ii A.D.). -**καύστης**, ου, ὁ, *one who burns corpses*, Gloss. -**κομίζω**, *take care of the dead*, Eust.1080.51. -**κορίνθια**, τά, *vases dug out of the tombs of Corinth*, Str.8.6.23. -**κόσμος**, ον, *laying corpses out for burial*, Plu.2.994e (fort. -κόμοις). -**μαντεία**, ἡ, gloss on νεκυομαντεία, *necromancy*, Hsch. -**μαντεῖον**, τό, = νεκυομαντεῖον, Id. s.v. νεκύωρον. -**μαντις**, εως, ὁ, ἡ, *necromancer*, Lyc.682. -**νώμης**, ου, ὁ, *corpse-bearer*, Man.4.192. -**πέρνας**, ου, ὁ, *one who sells corpses*, i.e. Achilles, Lyc.276. * -**ποιός**, όν, *killing*, Sch.Ar.Pl.263, EM541.55. -**πολις**, εως, ἡ, *city of the dead*, a name given to a suburb of Alexandria, Str.17.1.10 and 14. -**πομπός**, όν, *conducting the dead*, of Charon, E.Alc.441 (lyr.); of Hermes, Luc.DDeor.24.1.

**νεκρορύκτης**, ου, ὁ, *body-snatcher*, Phleg.Fr.36.1 J. (pl.).

**νεκρός**, ὁ (of a woman, Diph.129), *corpse*, Hom., etc.: as Subst., in early writers always of mankind, νεκροὺς συλήσετε τεθνηῶτας Il. 6.71; ν. ἔρυον κατατεθνηῶτας 18.540: freq. of those killed in battle, τοὺς ν. ὑποσπόνδους ἀνείλοντο Th.4.44, etc.: in sg., νεκρῷ ἐούσῃ Μελίσσῃ Hdt.5.92.η'; κεῖται ν. περὶ νεκρῷ S.Ant.1240, etc.; Πατρόκλῳ ν. ὄντι Pl.R.391b: the Art. is freq. omitted even of a particular corpse, esp. when a gen. is added, ν. γυναικός, ἀνθρώπου, Hdt.2.89,90, cf. A. Ag.659, Th.1018; later, of a fish, ν. ἰχθύος M.Ant.6.13: neut. pl. νεκρά, τά, Plu.2.773d: metaph., νεκρὰ καὶ καπνός M.Ant.12.33. 2. *dying person*, μυχθισμὸς νεκρῶν E.Rh.789; ν. ἀσπαίροντες Antipho 2.4.5; ν. ἀποθνῄσκοντες Th.2.52. 3. metaph., ὁ υἱός μου ν. ἦν καὶ ἀνέζησε Ev.Luc.15.24; ὄνομα ἔχεις ὅτι ζῇς καὶ ν. εἶ Apoc.3.1; ν. τῇ ἁμαρτίᾳ Ep.Rom.6.11. 4. in pl., *the dead*, as dwellers in the nether world, κλυτὰ ἔθνεα νεκρῶν Od.10.526, cf. 11.34, etc.; ἐν νεκροῖς Lxx Ps.87(88).5; ἐκ νεκρῶν ἐγείραι Ev.Jo.12.1; ἡ ἀνάστασις ἡ ἐκ ν. Ev.Luc.20.35: metaph., ζωὴ ἐκ ν. Ep.Rom.11.15. II. as Adj. νεκρός, ά, όν, *dead*, first in Pi., ν. ἵππος Fr.203; ν. σώματα Mitteis Chr.31 ii 22 (ii B.C.), Ach.Tat.3.5, cf. Nic.Dam.58 J., Plu.2.685b, X. Eph.5.1, POxy.51.8 (ii A.D.), BGU1024 vii 26 (iv/v A.D.) (but also τὰ τῶν ν. σώματα Pl.Lg.959b; σῶμα..νεκροῦ E.Hec.679); ν. χελώνη Luc.DDeor.7.4: Comp. -ότερος AP11.135 (Lucill.). 2. *inanimate, inorganic*, opp. ἔμψυχος, Plot.3.6.6; οὐχὶ ν., ὥσπερ λίθον ἢ ξύλον,

ἀλλὰ ζῶν Id.4.7.9; οὐρανὸς.. ὂν πρὸ ψυχῆς σῶμα ν., γῆ καὶ ὕδωρ Id. 5.1.2; ἡ ν. θάλασσα the *Dead Sea*, Paus.5.7.4, Gal.11.690, Orph.*A.* 1082. 3. metaph., ν. πλοῦτος Philostr.*VS*2.1.1.

**νεκρο-στολέω,** *ferry the dead*, of Charon, Luc.*Cont.*24. **-στόλος,** ον, *layer-out of corpses*, Artem.4.56 (pl.). **-συλία,** ἡ, *robbery of the dead*, Pl.*R.*469e. **-τᾰγος,** ὁ, *judge of the dead*, of Minos, Lyc. 1399. **-τᾰφέω,** *bury the dead*, Tz.*H.*4.154. **-τάφη** [ᾰ], ἡ, = νεκροταφίς, *PGrenf.*2.75.1 (iv A.D.). **-τᾰφικός,** ή, όν, *pertaining to burial*, κηδεία ib.68.6 (iii A.D.). **-τᾰφίς,** ίδος, ἡ, fem. of sq., ib.76.2 (iv A.D.). **-τάφος** [ᾰ], ὁ, = νεκροθάπτης, *PRyl.*65.3 (i B.C.), *Ostr.Bodl.* iv 51 (i A.D.), *PGrenf.*2.73.7 (iii A.D.), *AJP*54.439 (Egypt), *Cat.Cod. Astr.*7.117, Man.4.192. **-φᾰγέω,** *eat corpses* or *carrion*, Str.17. 3.5. **-φάγος** [ᾰ], ον, *eating corpses* or *carrion*, ὄρνιθες D.C.47. 40. **-φορέω,** *bear as a dead body to the burial*: metaph., of soul bearing body, Ph.2.540, cf. 1.100. **-φόριον,** τό, *sandapila*, Gloss. ❀**-φόρος,** ον, *burying corpses*, *burying the dead*, Plu.*Cat.Ma.* 9, Gloss. **-φύλαξ** [ῠ], ᾰκος, ὁ, *guardian of the dead*, Ph.1.417, Vett.Val.68.14, *Cat.Cod.Astr.*8(4).139. **-χρως,** χρωτος, ὁ, ἡ, gloss on ἐνερόχρωτες, *EM*340.10. **-ψῡχος,** ον, *spiritless*, *Cat.Cod.Astr.* 8(4).139, Vett.Val.68.17.

**νεκρ-όω,** *make dead*, *mortify*, μόριόν τι Gal.11.265:—Pass., νενεκρῶσθαι τὸ μόριον Id.18(1).156: metaph., τὰ δόγματα..δύναται νεκρωθῆναι M.Ant.7.2; οὐ ψυχὴ κυρίως, ἀλλὰ νενεκρωμένη τις Simp.*in Ph.* 1066.27; *to be dead*, νεκρωθεὶς *IG*14.1976; νενεκρωμένος, of the body of Abraham, *Ep.Rom.*4.19. II. metaph., *mortify*, νεκρώσατε τὰ μέλη *Ep.Col.*3.5. ❀**-ώδης,** ες, *corpse-like*, Luc.*Ep.Sat.*28, Aret. *SA*2.11; ν. πρόσωπον, 'facies Hippocratica', Gal.9.917: esp. *mortified*, Id.18(1).156. **-ωμα,** ατος, τό, *lifeless*, *inorganic body*, ἄτομα ὅσα νεκρώματα Simp.*in de An.*318.9. **-ών,** ῶνος, ὁ, *burial-place*, *IG* 5(2).176 (Tegea, ii B.C.), *AP*7.610 (Pall.). **-ώσιμα,** τά, = νεκύσια, Gloss. **-ωσις,** εως, ἡ, *mortification*, Aret.*SA*2.10, Gal.18(1).156; μήτρας *Ep.Rom.*4.19: metaph., νεκροὺς ὁρῶν νέκρωσιν ἕξεις πραγμάτων Astramps.*Onir.*p.6 R. II. *death*, τὴν ν. τοῦ Ἰησοῦ ἐν τῷ σώματι περιφέροντες 2*Ep.Cor.*4.10. **-ωτικός,** ή, όν, *causing mortification*, δύναμις Gal.11.752.

**νέκτᾰρ,** ἄρος, τό, *nectar*, the specific nourishment of the gods; ἀμβροσία (q.v.) and ν. are differentiated in early Ep. as food and drink, Od. 5.93, *h.Cer.*49, *h.Ap.*10, cf. Pl.*Phdr.*247e: but conversely, ν. ἔδμεναι Alcm.100, cf. Anaxandr.57; κέρασσε δὲ ν. ἐρυθρόν Od. l.c.; Ἥβη ν. ἐῳνοχόει Il.4.3; νέκταρος ἀπορρώξ, of choice wine, Od.9. 359; ν. ἀμβροσίην τε στάξον Il.19.347, cf. 38, Pi.*P.*9.63. 2. later, of *wine*, Call.*Fr.*115, Nic.*Al.*44, Eudem.Med.ap.Gal.14.185. b. called σαρράν and χαλβάνη, 1 *Enoch* 31.1. II. metaph., ν. μελισσᾶν, i.e. honey, E.*Ba.*143 (lyr.); αἰθερίου πτηναὶ νέκταρος ἐργάτιδες *AP*9.404 (Antiphil.), cf. 6.239 (Apollonid.); also, of *perfumed unguent*, ib.6.275 (Noss.); of an ode, ν. χυτόν, Μοισᾶν δόσιν Pi.*O.*7.7, cf. *Parth.*2.76, *AP*4.1.36 (Mel.); ν. ἐναρμόνιον ib.7.29 (Antip. Sid.).

**νεκτάρας·** μάστιγξ, Hsch.

❀**νεκτάρεος** [ᾰ], έα, Ion. έη, εον, *nectarous*, in Hom. of garments, i.e. *fragrant*, ν. ἑανός, χιτών, Il.3.385, 18.25; ν. σπονδαί Pi.*I.*6(5).37; κύλιξ *AP*6.248 (Marc. Arg.); Βρομίου νεκτάρεαι προπόσεις *BMus. Inscr.*1036 (Caria); τὸ ν. πόμα Luc.*Herm.*60: neut. as Adv., νεκτάρεον μείδησε A.R.3.1009.

❀**νεκτάρθη·** ἐθυμώθη, Hsch.

**νεκτάρ-ιον** [ᾰ], τό, = ἑλένιον, Dsc.1.28. II. name of a medicine, Gal.13.282; of various eye salves, Id.12.750, 773. **-ίτης** [ῑ] οἶνος, ὁ, wine *flavoured with* νεκτάριον, Dsc.5.56, Plin.*HN*14.108.

**νεκτᾰρο-ειδής,** ές, *like nectar*, πόμα *IGRom.*4.682 (Phrygia, ii A.D.). **-σταγής,** ές, (στάζω) *dropping nectar*, Ar.*Fr.*579, Eub.124.

**νεκταροῦσιν·** ἐλαφρίζουσιν, Hsch.

**νεκτᾰρώδης,** ες, *like nectar*, *Gp.*5.2.10.

**νεκῠ-ᾰγωγή,** ἡ, *calling up of spirits*, *necromancy*, *PMag.Par.*1. 222. **-ᾰγωγός,** όν, = νεκραγωγός, of Hermes, *Tab.Defix.Aud.* 242.10 (Carthage, iii A.D.). **-άμβᾰτος,** ον, (ἀναβαίνω) of Charon's boat, *embarked in by the dead*, Epic.ap.Paus.10.28.2. ❀**-δαίμων,** ονος, ὁ, *ghost of a dead man*, *PMag.Par.*1.368, al., *Tab.Defix.Aud.* 234.1 (Carthage, ii/iii A.D.).

❀**νεκύδᾰλος** or **-αλλος,** ὁ, (νέκυς) *the nympha of the silkworm*, Arist. *HA*551ᵇ12, Ath.8.352f.

**νεκῠ-ηγός,** όν, (ἄγω) = νεκραγωγός, *AP*7.68 (Arch.), Epigr. in *Berl. Sitzb.*1894.908 (Avdjilar). **-ηδόν,** Adv. *corpse-like*, Euph.88, Sch. D.T.p.276 H. **-ηπόλος,** ον, *having to do with the dead*, Man.1.330.

❀**νέκυια,** ἡ, (νέκυς) a magical *rite by which ghosts were called up and questioned* about the future, Plu.2.17b (pl.); νεκυίᾳ χρήσασθαι Hdn. 4.12.4; name for the eleventh Book of the Odyssey, D.S.4.39, Plu. 2.740e. II. *funeral ceremony*, τῶν ἀμφὶ τὴν ν. τε καὶ τὰς διαθήκας καλινδουμένων Luc.*Nigr.*30. III. *rabble*, used contemptuously of Caesar's entourage, Cic.*Att.*9.18.2, cf. Attic.ap.eund.*Att.*9.10. 7. IV. = φλόμος, so called because used in necromancy, Cyran. 30 (written νεκύα).

**νεκυ-ῐκός,** ή, όν, *of the dead*, μαντεῖαι Cyran.30. **-ῐσμός,** ὁ, = νέκυια I, Man.4.213.

**νεκῠο-δαίμων,** ονος, ὁ, *god of the dead*, *Sammelb.*4947 (iii A.D.), *Rev.Phil.*1930.249. ❀**-μαντεία,** ἡ, sub-title of Luc.*Menipp.*; also of the eleventh Book of the Odyssey, Hermog.*Prog.*2, Eust.1670. 23: pl. -τίαι, = *defixiones*, Gloss. ❀**-μαντεῖον,** Ion. -ήιον, τό, *oracle of the dead*, where ghosts were called up, Hdt.5.92.η', Cic.*Tusc.*1. 16.37, D.S.4.22, Plu.*Cim.*6, Paus.9.30.6: in pl., *PMag.Lond.*121. 285. **-μαντικός,** ή, όν, *of* or *for evocation of the dead*, ψυχαγωγίαι Eust.1615.4. **-μαντις,** εως, ὁ, ἡ, = νεκρόμαντις, Str.16.2.39, Ptol.*Tetr.* 181, Artem.2.69. **-πομπός** (sc. λίμνη), ἡ, name of a mythical lake, Sch.Od.p.5 Buttm. (cf. Jo.Malal.p.121). **-στόλος,** ον, *ferrying the dead* over the Styx, of Charon, *AP*7.63, 530 (Antip. Thess.); also ν. Αἶσα Man.4.405. 2. *bearing the dead*, of a bier, *AP*7.634 (Antiphil.).

**νέκυς** (Lacon. νέκυρ Hsch.), ῠος, ὁ, poet. dat. νέκυϊ Il.16.526, etc.; Ep. dat. pl. νεκύεσσι Od.11.491, νέκυσσι ib.569, 22.401, 23.45; acc. pl. νέκῡς Il.7.420, 18.180, Od.24.417, E.*Fr.*176.4; also νέκυας Il.7. 418, al.:—*corpse*, freq. in Il., less freq. in Od.; in Il.4.492, 493, νέκυς and νεκρός are used of the same dead person; ν. ἀνδρός Hdt.1. 140, cf. 3.16, 24, S.*Ant.*26, E.*Or.*1585; ν. τεθνηώς, κατατεθνηώς, Il. 18.173, 16.526; νέκυες κατατεθνηῶτες, κτάμενοι, καταφθίμενοι, Od.10. 530, 23.45, 11.491; ἀνδρὸς Πέρσεω ὁ ν. Hdt.1.140, cf. 3.16; ὁ κατθανὼν ν. S.*Ant.*515; *dead person*, νεκύων σώματα E.*Supp.*62 (lyr.). 2. in pl., *spirits of the dead*, freq. in Od.11, less freq. in Il.; νεκύων ἀμενηνὰ κάρηνα Od.11.29, cf. Il.15.251; πεδ' ἀμαύρων ν. Sapph.68. II. as Adj. *dead*, post-Hom., ἐχθρὸν ὧδ' αἰδῆ νέκυν; S.*Aj.*1356; κίχλαι αἱ νέκυες *AP*11.96 (Nicarch.); cf. however Il.24.35, 423.—Poet. word, used also by Hdt., in *IG*2².1672.119 (iv B.C.), in Cretan, Kohler-Ziebarth *Stadtrecht von Gortyn* p.35, and in late Prose, Plu.*Crass.*19, Hdn.4.8.5. [ῠ of nom. and acc. sg. in Hom., Il.4.492, 22.386, etc.; ῡ Simon.114.5, E.*Supp.*70 (lyr.), *Or.*1585, and in later Poets, A.R. 4.480, Bion 1.71, *AP*7.1 (Alc. Mess.).] (Cf. Avest. *nasu-* 'corpse', Skt. *náśyati* 'perish', 'disappear', Lat. *necare.*)

**νεκύσια** (sc. ἱερά), τά, *festival of the dead*, *PLond.ined.*2309ʳ.21 (iii B.C.), *Bull.Soc.Arch.Alex.*7.67 (iii B.C.), Artem.4.81, Eust.1615.2.

**Νεκύσιος,** ὁ, the eleventh month in Crete, *SIG*712.56 (ii B.C.), *Hemerolog.Flor.*

❀**νεκυσσόος,** ον, *rousing the dead to life*, Nonn.*D.*44.204.

**νεκῠώριον** or **νεκύωρον,** τό, (ὥρα) = νεκρομαντεῖον, Hsch.

**νεκυώτατον·** νεώτατον, προσφατώτατον, Hsch.

❀**Νεμέα,** Ion. -έη, Ep. -είη (Hes.*Th.*329, *Epic.Alex.Adesp.*8.1), ἡ, (νέμος) *wooded district* between Argos and Corinth, Pi.*O.*9.87: freq. in locative Νεμέᾳ, ib.7.82, etc.; Dor. contr. Νεμῇ *SIG*36 *B*19 (Olympia, v B.C.), etc.:—Adj. **Νέμειος,** α, ον, *Nemean*, τὸν Ν. θῆρα E.*HF* 153; ὁ Ζεὺς ὁ Ν. Th.3.96; **Νέμεος,** Theoc.25.169; τοῦ Ν. λέοντος Luc.*Philops.*8; **Νεμειαῖος,** Hes.*Th.*327; **Νεμεαῖος,** Pi.*N.*2.4. etc.; ❀**Νεμεακός,** Sch.Pi.*N.*1.7; **Νεμεήτης** Ζεύς, St.Byz.; **Νεμειήτης,** Max. 102, 346:—poet. fem. Adj. ❀**Νεμεάς,** άδος, Pi.*N.*3.2:—Adv. **Νεμέαθεν,** poet. -ηθε, *from Nemea*, Call.*Fr.*103. II. ❀**Νέμεα** (sc. ἱερά), τά, *the Nemean games*, Pi.*Ol.*13.34, *SIG*82.4 (Delph., iv B.C.), *IG*2².365, etc.; **Νέμεια,** ib.1².606, 3.129, etc. III. **Νέμειον** (sc. ἱερόν), τό, *temple of Nemean Zeus*, in Locris, Plu.2.162c.

❀**νεμέθω,** Ep. for νέμω, νεμέθων Nic.*Th.*430:—in Med., once in Hom., νεμέθοντο, of doves, *were feeding*, Il.11.635, cf. *AP*14.4, Keil-Premerstein *Erster Bericht* p.9 (Troketta).

**νεμενίαν·** νουμηνίαν, Hsch.; cf. νεμονηΐα.

**Νεμεονίκης** [ῑ], ου, ὁ, *victor in the Nemean games*, Sch.Pi.*N.*7. 118, *CIG*4359 (Pamphylia).

**νεμεσάω,** used by Hom. and Hes. in contr. forms νεμεσῶ, -ῶσι (v. infr.); Ep. 3sg. νεμεσσᾷ Hes.*Op.*756; imper. νεμέσσα Od.23. 213; impf. ἐνεμέσων Plu.*Sull.*6; Ep. ἐνεμέσσα Il.13.16, Ep. 3 sg. νεμέσασκε 11.543 (as cited by Arist.*Rh.*1387ᵃ35): fut. -ήσω Arist. ib.12: aor. ἐνεμέσησα D.45.71, etc.; poet. νεμέσησα Od.21.285; Dor. -ᾱσα Pi.*I.*1.3:—**Med.** and **Pass.**, Ep. νεμεσσῶμαι Il.13.119: fut. νεμεσήσομαι 10.129: Ep. aor. opt. νεμεσσήσαιτο Od.1.228: more freq. aor. Pass. νεμεσσήθη 1.119, 3 pl. -θεν Il.2.223, etc.:—*feel just resentment*, *to be wroth at undeserved good* or *bad fortune* (cf. νέμεσις), freq. of the gods, νεμέσησε δὲ πότνια Ἥρη Il.8.198; τῷ δὲ θεοὶ νεμεσῶσι Hes.*Op.*741, etc., cf. Arist.*Rh.*1386ᵇ16; also of men, sts. abs., μὴ νεμέσα Il.10.145; τὸ νεμεσᾶν, opp. τὸ φθονεῖν, Cic.*Att.* 5.19.3; ν. τινί *to be wroth with* a person or *at* a thing, Il.24.53, etc.: rarely in Prose, Pl.*Lg.*927c, D.20.161: c. part., οὐ νεμεσῶ Ἀγαμέμνονι..ὀτρύνοντι if he incites, Il.4.413; νεμεσᾷ ὁ θεός, ὅταν.. Pl.*Min.*319a: c. dat. pers. et acc. rei, μὴ νῦν μοι τόδε χώεο μηδὲ νεμέσσα Od.23.213, cf. Hes.*Op.*756, Arist.*Rh.*1384ᵇ4; ν. ἐπί τινι ib. 1387ᵃ6, Onos.4.2: c. dat. pers. et gen. rei, Luc.*Scyth.*9, Porph.*Abst.* 2.7:—Pass., ἐνεμεσήθη (sc. by the gods) Plu.*Cat.Mi.*38. 2. *grudge*, τὰς εὐπραγίας ἡ τύχη τισὶ ἐνεμέσησε J.*BJ*1.22.1:—Pass., εἰ νεμεσηθείην τῆς ἐπιβολῆς ib.6.1.6. II. Med. and Pass., prop. *to be displeased with oneself*, νεμεσσᾶται δ' ἐνὶ θυμῷ..ἐπεσβολίας ἀναφαίνειν *is indignant*, *ashamed at the thought of*.., *rejects it as unseemly*, Od.4. 158; *feel shame*, νεμεσσήθητε καὶ αὐτοί, ἄλλους τ' αἰδέσθητε 2.64; νεμεσσήθητε δὲ θυμῷ Il.16.544; πᾶσιν δὲ νεμεσσηθεῖσα μετηύδα 15. 103. 2. Med. in act. sense, freq. in Hom., c. dat. pers., εἴ πέρ μοι νεμεσήσεαι Il.10.115, cf. 129: c. part., νεμεσσήσαιτό κεν..ὁρόων Od. 1.228: c. inf., νεμεσσῶμαί γε μὲν οὐδὲν κλαίειν 4.195: c. acc. et inf., οὔ σε νεμεσσῶμαι κεχολῶσθαι 18.227: c. acc. rei, νεμεσσᾶται κακὰ ἔργα *is wroth at* evil deeds, 14.284.—Poet. Verb, never in Trag., rare in good Prose (v. supr.).

**Νεμέσ-εια,** v. Νεμέσια. **-εῖον,** τό, *temple of Nemesis*, St.Byz. s.v. Ἰσεῖον, Theognost.*Can.*129; written -ῆον *Bull.Soc.Arch.Alex.* No.4 p.50.

**νεμεσ-ητικός,** ή, όν, *disposed to indignation at any one's undeserved good* or *ill fortune*, Arist.*EN*1108ᵇ3, *Rh.*1387ᵇ4. **-ητός,** ή, όν, in Hom. always **νεμεσσητός,** exc. Il.11.649:—*causing indignation* or *wrath*, *worthy of it*, νεμεσσητὸν δέ κεν εἴη 3.410, etc.: c. inf., οὔ τι νεμεσσητὸν κεχολῶσθαι 9.523, Od.22.59; οὔτοι νεμεσητὸν S.*Ph.*1193 (lyr.), cf. Pl.*Euthd.*282b; οὐ ν. τὸ διαμαρτάνειν Phld.*Sto.*339.12; ν.

ἰδεῖν Tyrt.10.26; ψεῦδος δὲ . . ν. κατὰ φύσιν Pl.Lg.943e; νεμεσητὸν ἐὰν . . it is matter for indignation that . ., Arist.Rh.1387$^a$32, cf. IPE I$^2$. 34.17 (Olbia). 2. retributive, ἔπαθε πρᾶγμα ν. retribution, Plu. Ages.22; so νεμεσητὰ παθεῖν Id.Per.37; πάθος ν. ἔπαθε Id.Pomp.38; τὸ ν. ἀφοσιούμενος ib.42. b. deserving retribution, Nic.Dam.68. 9J. II. Act., prone to wrath, αἰδοῖος νεμεσητός Il.11.649; Κύπρι νεμεσσατά Theoc.1.101.

**Νεμέσια** (sc. ἱερά), τά, festival of Nemesis, also held in honour of the dead, D.41.11 (v. l. -εια), Ἑλληνικά 3.154 (Rhamnus, iii B.C.).

**νεμεσίζομαι**, Ep. Verb, only pres. and impf., feel righteous indignation, Ζεῦ πάτερ, οὐ νεμεσίζῃ ὁρῶν τάδε καρτερὰ ἔργα; Il.5.872, cf. Od. 2.138: c. dat. pers., Ἥρῃ δ' οὔ τι τόσον νεμεσίζομαι Il.8.407: c. dat. pers. et acc. rei, οὐ νεμεσίζῃ Ἄρῃ τάδε καρτερὰ ἔργα; 5.757: c. acc. et inf., to be angry or amazed that . ., οὐ νεμεσίζομ' Ἀχαιοὺς ἀσχαλάαν 2.296; νεμεσιζέσθω δ' ἐνὶ θυμῷ Πάτροκλον . . μέλπηθρα γενέσθαι 17.254. II. stand in awe of, θεούς Od.1.263.

**νεμέσιον**, τό, = ὠκιμοειδές, Ps.-Dsc.4.28.

**Νεμέσιον**, τό, = Νεμεσεῖον, IG 2$^2$.1310, Ἑλληνικά 3.154 (Rhamnus, iii B.C.).

⊛ **νέμεσις**, εως, ἡ, Ep. dat. νεμέσσι Il.6.335: (νέμω):—prop., like νέμησις, distribution of what is due; but in usage always retribution, esp. righteous anger aroused by injustice, not used of the gods in Hom.; ν. δέ μοι ἐξ ἀνθρώπων ἔσσεται Od.2.136, cf. 22.40, Il.6.351; αἰδῶ καὶ νέμεσιν (where αἰ. is subjective, ν. objective) 13.122 (the two personified, Hes.Op.200): c. gen. obj., Τρώων χόλῳ οὐδὲ νεμέσσι Il.6.335; esp. in phrase οὐ νέμεσις it is no cause for anger that . ., c. inf., οὐ γάρ τις ν. φυγέειν κακόν 14.80: c. acc. et inf., 3.156; πενθεῖν οὐ χρή· ν. γάρ S.OC1753 (anap.); τίς τάδε ν. στυγεῖ; A.Th.235 (lyr.); later, of the wrath of the gods, ἐκ θεοῦ ν. Hdt.1.34; θεῶν ν. S.Ph.518 (lyr.), 602, cf. OGI383.115 (Nemrud Dagh, i B.C.); also ἡ ἐκ τοῦ νόμου ν. Ael.VH6.10; indignation at undeserved good fortune, ν. μεσότης φθόνου καὶ ἐπιχαιρεκακίας Arist.EN1108$^b$35.

B. Νέμεσις, εως, ἡ, as pr. n., voc. Νέμεσι S.El.792:—Nemesis, the impersonation of divine Retribution, coupled with Αἰδώς, Hes. Op.200 (v. supr.), cf. Th.223; ὑπέρδικος N. Pi P.10.44; Ἀδράστεια καὶ N. SIG$^2$940.16 (Cos): in Trag. and later writers freq. avenger of the dead, A.Fr.266, etc.; ἔστι γὰρ ἐν φθιμένοις N. μέγα Epigr.Gr.367. 9; Νέμεσι τοῦ θανόντος S.l.c.: in pl., κάλλους εἰσί τινες Νεμέσεις; AP11.326 (Autom.); two were worshipped at Smyrna, Paus.7.5.2, cf. CIG2663 (Halic.), IGRom.4.1431.5 (Smyrna), AP12.193 (Strat.), Supp.Epigr.4.277 (Panamara). 2. Astrol., name of the seventh κλῆρος (τοῦ Κρόνου) Paul.Al.K.3, Rhetor.in Cat.Cod.Astr.1.160,168, cf. Vett.Val.2.22.

C. Pythag. name for five, Theol.Ar.31.

**νεμεσίτης** [ῑ] λίθος, ὁ, Nemesis-stone, a stone with magical properties, Cyran.30.

**νεμέτωρ**, ορος, ὁ, dispenser of justice, avenger, Ζεύς A.Th.485 (lyr.).

⊛ **νεμήϊος**, ὁ, epith. of Zeus, Archyt.ap.Stob.4.1.138 (expld. as from νέμω).

**νέμ-ησις**, εως, ἡ, (νέμω) distribution, τοῦ χωρίου Is.9.17; τῶν κοινῶν Phld.Rh.2.125S.; οὐσίας Poll.8.135; βασιλείας J.AJ17.11.1; χρημάτων Hld.1.19, cf. Charito 3.7. II. (νέμω A.II) land in occupation, area, territory, Μουνιχίας IG1$^2$.894, cf. 462 (prob.). 2. (νέμω B.I.2c) spreading, Aret.CA1.9. **-ητέον**, one must assign, τί τινι Adrast.ap.Theon.Sm.p.65H. ⊛ **-ητής**, οῦ, ὁ, = νεμέτωρ, Poll.8. 136. **-ητός**, ή, όν, dub. sens., τὸν ν. ἀγῶνα τῶν Ὁμολωΐων IG7.3196. 23 (Orchom. Boeot.). ⊛ **-ήτρια**, ἡ, fem. of νεμητής, ib.14.956B5.

**νεμονηΐα**, ἡ, = νουμηνία, SIG527.146 (Crete, iii B.C.).

⊛ **νέμος**, εος, τό, (νέμω B) wooded pasture, glade, ἐν νέμεϊ σκιερῷ Il.11. 480, AP7.55 (Alc.), cf. S.Aj.413 (lyr.), IG9(2).205.8 (Phthiotis, iii B.C.), BCH49.100 (Delph.).

⊛ **νέμω**, fut. νεμῶ S.Aj.513, (ἀπο-) Pl.Phlb.65b, later νεμήσω Longus 2.23: aor. ἔνειμα, Ep. νεῖμα Il.3.274: pf. νενέμηκα (δια-) X.Cyr.4.5. 45:—Med., νέμομαι, fut. νεμοῦμαι Th.4.64, D.21.203; Ion. νεμέομαι (ἀνα-) Hdt.1.173; later νεμήσομαι D.H.8.71, Plu.Crass.14, etc.: aor. ἐνειμάμην Th.8.21, etc. (ἐνεμησάμην is f.l. in Clearch.10, Hp.Oss.18 (ὑπο-)):—Pass., fut. νεμηθήσομαι Plu.Agis14 (also νεμήσομαι in pass. sense (δια-) App.BC4.3): aor. ἐνεμήθην Pl.Lg.849c, D.36.38 (also in med. sense (κατ-) Plu.Per.34, Ath.15.677e): pf. νενέμημαι Pl.Prm. 144d, etc. (also in med. sense, D.47.35).—Hom. uses of the Act., only pres., impf., and aor.; of the Med., pres. and impf.

A. deal out, dispense, freq. in Hom., esp. of meat and drink, μοίρας, κύπελλα, κρέα, μέθυ ν., Od.8.470, 10.357, Il.9.217, Od.7.179, cf. IG1$^2$. 10.3, al.; οἱ γεωνόμοι νειμάντων τὴν γῆν ib.45.7: then generally, distribute, of the gods, Ζεὺς . . νέμει ὄλβον . . ἀνθρώποισιν Od.6.188; Ζεὺς τά τε καὶ τὰ νέμει Pi.I.5(4).52, cf. P.5.55; θεῶν τὰ ἴσα νεμόντων Hdt.6.11, 109; Ζεὺς νέμων εἰκότως ἄδικα μὲν κακοῖς, ὅσια δ' ἐννόμοις A.Supp.403 (lyr.); [Διὶ] τὸν ὑπεραλγῆ χόλον ν. leave vengeance to Zeus, S.El.176 (lyr.); of men, ν. δευτερεῖά τινι Hdt.1.32; τρίτον μέρος τῶν σκύλων τισί Th.3.114; μοῖραν ν. τινὶ pay one due honour, respect, A.Pr.294 (lyr.); μητρὸς τιμὰς ν. respect her privileges, Id.Eu.624 (but πρόσω ν. τιμάς extend one's privileges, ib.747); Λύκῳ κῆπον Εὐβοίας νέμει S.Fr.24; Πολυκράτης μητέρα νέμει P. allots a mother (to you), prov. in Duris63J.; εἰ πατρὸς νέμοι τιν' ὥραν τοῦ καλῶς πράσσειν δοκεῖν S. Tr.57; τὸ σὸν γέρας τιμὴν ἐμοὶ ν. Id.Ph.1062; ἐκείνῳ . . αἰτίαν νέμει Id.Aj.28; ν. αἵρεσιν give one a choice, ib.265; ναύταις οὐκέθ' ὁδὸν νέμει affords, vouchsafes, E.Hipp.745 (lyr.); τὸ πιστὸν τῆς ἀληθείας ν. observe it, S.Tr.398; τῷ . . ὄχλῳ πλέον ν. E.Hec.868; μήτε οἴκτῳ πλέον ν. μήτ' ἐπιεικείᾳ Th.3.48; τὸ ἧσσον ἀδικίᾳ E.Supp.380 (lyr.); τῷ φθόνῳ πλέον μέρος ib.241; τὸ πλεῖστον ἡμέρας τούτῳ μέρος Id.Fr.183; ἔλασσόν τινι Antipho 5.10; χάριν τινί Ar.Av.384; πενίᾳ καὶ πλούτῳ τιμὴν ν. Pl.Lg.696a; of judges, κολαστὴν . . θάνατον ν. ib.863a; συγγνώμην τισί Gal.6.753: c. inf., νεῖμεν ἐμοὶ τέρψιν ὁμιλεῖν S.Aj.1201 (lyr.):—Pass., νέμεται ἐπὶ τοὺς Ἕλληνας is freely bestowed upon them, Hdt.9.7.α'; κρέα νενεμημένα portions of meat, X.An.7.3.21; πλεῖστα μέρη ἡ οὐσία νενεμημένη distributed into . ., Pl.Prm. 144d. 2. pay out, distribute a bandage, in Act. and Pass., Hp. Off.8,22, Fract.4,16, Sor.Fasc.4, al. 3. allot, distribute in groups, πρὸς τὴν λῆξιν ἑκάστην Arist.Ath.30.3, cf. 31.3 (Pass.); νεῖμαι τινας ἐς τὰς φυλὰς δέκαχα IG2$^2$.1.33:—Pass., ἐκ τῆς φυλῆς ἑκάστης νενεμημέναι τριττύες τρεῖς Arist.Ath.8.3, cf. 63.4. II. Med., distribute among themselves: hence, have and hold as one's portion, possess, πατρώϊα πάντα νέμεσθαι Od.20.336: mostly of land, τεμένεα, τέμενος, 11.185, Il.12.313; ἔργα 2.751, Hes.Op.119; πρὸς τὸν ἀδελφὸν ἐνειμάμην (sc. οὐσίαν) Lys.16.10, cf. 19.46; τἄλλα νεμομένη administering . ., Hdt.4.165; τὰ μέταλλα, τὰ ἐμπόρια, Id.7.112, Th. 1.100; [τὰ λήμματα] ἃ νέμεσθε which you enjoy, D.3.33: abs., ἔμ' οἴεσθ' ὑμῖν εἰσοίσειν ὑμᾶς δὲ νεμεῖσθαι; that you shall reap the fruit, Id.21.203. 2. reap the fruit of: hence, dwell in, inhabit, ἄλσεα νέμεσθαι Il.20.8; freq. with names of places, spread over, occupy a country, Ἰθάκην, Τρίην νέμεσθαι, Od.2.167, Il.2.496; ἀγρούς Pi.P.4.150; τὸ πρὸς τὴν ἠῶ Hdt.4.19, etc.; νεμόμενοι τὰ αὑτῶν . . ὅσον ἀποζῆν Th.1.2. b. generally, enjoy, προσόδους BGU256.9 (ii A.D.), etc. c. of cities, to be situated upon, τὸν Ἄθων Hdt.7.23, cf. 123:—Pass., ἄχρι τῆς ὁδοῦ τῆσδε τὸ ἄστυ τῇδε νενέμηται IG1$^2$.893; cf. νέμησις II.1. 3. in Pi., of Time, spend, pass, αἰῶνα, ἀμέραν, O.2.66, N.10. 56: abs., live, ἡσυχᾷ νεμόμενος P.11.55. III. from Pi. onwards, Act. is found in sense of Med., hold, possess, ἕδος Ὀλύμπου ν. O.2.12; ἔνδον ν. πλοῦτον κρυφαῖον I.1.67; inhabit, γῆν ν. Hdt.4.191; χωρίον κοινῇ ν. Th.5.42; πόλιν S.OC879 (lyr.); ὅτι πλείστους ν. ἄνδρας to have as many husbands as possible, Str.11.13.11: abs., hold land, occupy, dwell, ν. περὶ τὴν λίμνην Hdt.4.188:—Pass., of places, to be inhabited, πάντα ὑπὸ βαρβάροισι νέμεται Id.7.158: abs., of a country, maintain itself, be constituted, Th.1.5,6. 2. hold sway over, manage, πόλιν Hdt. 1.59, 5.29; τὰς Ἀθήνας ib.71, etc.; λαόν Pi.O.13.27; πάντα A.Pr.526 (lyr.); ἀστραπᾶν κράτη ν. S.OT201 (lyr.); κράτη καὶ θρόνους ib.237, cf. Aj.1016; σύνοδον OGI50.3 (Ptolemais, iii B.C.); τὸν μέγαν Πακτωλὸν εὔχρυσον νέμεις S.Ph.393 (lyr.); οἴακα ν. wield, manage it, A.Ag. 802 (anap.); ἀσπίδ' εὔκυκλον ν. Id.Th.590; ἰσχὺν ν. ἐπὶ σκήπτροις support oneself on staves, Id.Ag.75 (anap.); ν. γλῶσσαν use the tongue, ib.685 (lyr.); ν. πόδα Pi.N.6.15: abs., hold sway, ὃς Συρακόσσαισι ν. Id.P.3.70. 3. hold, consider as . ., σὲ νέμω θεόν S.El.150 (lyr.), cf. 598, Tr.483, Aj.1331 (so in Pass., οὐδέ μοι ἐμμελέως τὸ Πιττάκειον νέμεται seems not to me fitly said, Simon.5.9): in Prose, προστάτην νέμειν τινά register as one's patron, Isoc.8.53, Hyp.Fr.21, Arist.Pol.1275$^a$12; ἡγεμόνα ν. τινά Agatharch.Fr.Hist.17J.; ἀθλητῶν τοὺς μὴ νενεμημένους ἢ σεσωμασκηκότας unproved athletes, Plb. 6.47.8. IV. call over, recite, S.Fr.144; = ἀναγινώσκω, Hsch.

B. of herdsmen, pasture, graze their flocks, drive to pasture, abs., ἐπῆλθε νέμων Od.9.233; [χώραν] ἱκανὴν νέμειν τε καὶ ἀροῦν both for pasture and tillage, Pl.R.373d: c. acc., ὁ μὲν ἵππους νέμων, ὁ δὲ βοῦς Hdt.8.137; μῆλα E.Cyc.28, etc.; κτήνη πληγῇ ν. drive them afield with blows, Pl.Criti.109c, cf. Heraclit.11 (Pass.). 2. more freq. in Med., of cattle, feed, graze, Il.5.777, 15.631, Od.13.407, Hdt. 8.115, etc.: c. acc. loci, range over, ὡς λέαινα . . δρύοχα νεμομένα E.El. 1163 (lyr.); κολοιοὶ ταπεινὰ ν. Pi.N.3.82: c. acc. cogn., feed on, νέμεαι . . ἄνθεα ποίης Od.9.449; νομάς Hdt.1.78; χλόην E.Ba.735; τὰ λευκὰ σήσαμα Ar.Av.159; of men, eat, S.Ph.709 (lyr.). b. metaph., of fire, consume, devour, Il.23.177, Hdt.5.101; also τὸ ψεῦδος . . νέμεται τὴν ψυχήν Plu.2.165a. c. Medic., abs., of ulcers, spread, ἐνέμετο πρόσω Hdt.3.133, cf. Thphr.HP9.9.5; of gangrene, prob. in D.S.17.103; of thrush, Asclep.ap.Gal.12.995; ἐπὶ μᾶλλον ν. Aret.CA1.9; ἐς τὸ ἔσω ν. ibid.; of a swelling, ὄγκος νεμόμενος Philum.Ven.17.1. II. c. acc. loci, ὄρη νέμειν graze the hills [with cattle], X.Cyr.3.2.20:—Pass., [τὸ ὄρος] νέμεται αἰξὶ καὶ βουσί Id.An. 4.6.17. 2. metaph., πυρὶ νέμειν πόλιν waste a city by fire, give it to the flames, Hdt.6.33:—Pass., πυρὶ χθὼν νέμοιτο were being devoured, wasted by fire, Il.2.780; πυρὶ νέμεται . . ἡ φάλαγξ Plu.Alex. 18. (Cf. OHG. neman 'take', Avest. nəmah- 'loan', Lith. nuoma 'rent', 'usury'.)

**νεναμένην**· ἠροτριαμένην, Hsch.

**νένασμαι**, pf. Pass. of ναίω (only poet.); also (in Prose) of νάσσω. **νενασμένως**· ἐπιεικῶς, Hsch. **νενέαται**, Ion. 3 pl. pf. Pass. of νέω, to heap. **νενηφότως**, Adv. soberly, Thom.Mag.p.245R.

**νενίηλος** [ῐ], ον, foolish, silly: or weak-eyed, purblind, Call.Jov. 63, cf. Hsch.

**νένιπται**, v. νίζω. **νεννάζει**· κακολογεῖ, Hsch. (leg. δεννάζει).

⊛ **νέννος**, ὁ, mother's or father's brother, uncle, Eust.971.26; but, mother's brother, Poll.3.22, cf. IG12(3).1628 (Thera), cj. in Epigr.ap. Plu.2.1033e; or (in poetry), mother's father, Poll.3.16 (v.l. νόννος, q.v.); cf. νάννας, νίννη.

**νενομισμένως**, Adv. in the established manner, Callistr.Stat.6.

**νενός**· εὐήθης, Hsch. **νένοφεν**· νενέφωται, Phot.; v. συννέφω. **νένωμαι, νενωμένος**, v. νοέω. **νέξας**· τὰ στρώματα, Hsch.

**νεο-αλδής**, ές, = νεαλδής, v.l. for νεοαρδής, Il.21.346, ap.Hsch. **-άλης**, ές, freshly salted, τυρός Dsc.2.71; cf. νεαλής. **-άλωτος** [ᾰ], ον, v.l. for νεάλωτος, Hdt.9.120. **-αρδής**, ές, newly, freshly watered, ἀλωή Il.21.346; cf. νεοαλδής. **-αυξής**, ές, = νεαύξητος,

Hsch. s.v. νεοθρόποις :—also **-αύξητος**, ον, Apollon.*Lex.* s.v. νεοαρδέα. **-βδαλτος**, ον, *newly milked*, γάλα Nic.*Th.*606, Ruf.*Fr.*59, Paul.Aeg.1.72. **-βλαστής**, ές, = sq., Opp.*H.*1.735. ⊛ **-βλαστος**, ον, *sprouting afresh*, Thphr.*HP*1.8.5, Nic.*Al.*484. **-βορος**, ον, *lately, newly devoured*, Hsch. **-βροχοι**· ἔγκυοι, Id. **-βρώς**, ῶτος, ὁ, ἡ, *having just eaten*, Hp.*Acut.*19. **-γάλαξ** [γᾰ], ακτος, ὁ, ἡ, *just beginning to suck*, Hdn.Gr.1.352. **-γᾰμής**, ές, = νεόγαμος, Phot. **-γᾰμητή**, ἡ, *nova nupta*, *Gloss.* **-γᾰμος**, ον, *newly married*, of husband or wife, Hdt.1.36,37, D.H.8.56; ν. νύμφη, κόρη, A.*Ag.*1179, E.*Med.*324; ν. λέκτρα ib.1348. II. *married early*, Ptol.*Tetr.*183. **-γενής**, ές, *new-born*, A.*Ch.*530, Pl.*Tht.*160e, al., X.*Cyn.*10.23; ποίμνη Antiph.52.4, cf. 1.5. 2. *newly produced*, κηρία Alciphr.3.23. **-γέννητος**, ον, gloss on νεογιλός, Phot. **-γηλής**, ές, acc. sg. νεογηλέα, νεβρόν v.l. for νεοθηλέα in Anacr.51 ap.Sch. Pi.*O.*3.52; fort. νεογιλέα from **νεογῑλής**, ές, = sq. **-γῑλός**, ή, όν, *new-born, young*, σκύλαξ Od.12.86; βρέφος Is.*Fr.*12, Theoc. 17.58; ἔριφος Alciphr.1.27; ὀδοὺς ν. one of *the first set of* teeth, Opp.*C.*1.199; βίου χρόνος ν. life *short as childhood*, Luc.*Halc.*3. (In Od. l.c. glossed νεογνῆς, ..νεωστὶ γεννηθείσης by Hsch.; also γάλακτι τρεφομένης by Sch.Od.; spelling and etym. are doubtful, perh. cf. Lith. *žindù* 'suckle'.) **-γλᾰγής**, ές, = νεογάλαξ, πῶλοι Max.517. II. *newly yielding milk*, μαζοί Nonn.*D.*48. 764. **-γλῠφής**, ές, *newly carved*, μηροί Tryph.332. **-γνός**, ή, όν, = νεόγονος, παῖς *h.Cer.*141, cf. *h.Merc.*406, Hdt.2.2, Hp.*Aph.*3.24, A.*Ag.*1163 codd.(lyr.), E.*Ion* 31: in Att. Prose, X.*Oec.*7.21: freq. of young beasts, ποίμνης νεογνὸν θρέμμα E.*El.*495; τὰ νεογνά X.*Cyn.*5. 14, Arist.*PA*665ᵇ7. **-γονος**, ον, = νεογενής, E.*Ion* 1001, *Cyc.*206, *Lyr.Alex.Adesp.*36.8. **-γραπτος**, ον, *newly painted*, θάλαμος Theoc.18.3. **-γρᾰφος**, ον, *newly written*, ἔρνεα *AP*4.1.55 (Mel.). **-γυιος**, ον, *with young limbs*, φῶτες Pi.*N.*9.24; ἥβα Id. *Fr.*123.9. ⊛ **-γύνης** [ῠ], ου, ὁ, *just-wived*, Amips.34. **-δάκρῡτος**, ον, *weeping afresh*, Hsch. s.v. νεοστάλυγες. **-δάμαστος** [δᾰ], ον, = νεόδμητος, Phot. s.v. νεόδμητον, Sch.Lyc.65. **-δᾱμώδης**, ες, a Spartan word, *lately made one of the people* (δᾶμος = δῆμος), *newly enfranchised*, δύναται δὲ τὸ ν. ἐλεύθερον ἤδη εἶναι Th.7.58: applied to Helots freed by the state in reward for service in war, Εἵλωσι καὶ ν. καὶ τοῖς περιοίκοις X.*HG*3.3.6, cf. 5.2.24, Myro 1 J. **-δάρτης**· ἔδεσμά τι ἀβυρτακῶδες, Hsch. **-δαρτος**, ον, *newly stripped off*, δέρματα Od.4.437, Arist.*Pr.*889ᵇ10, cf. Od.22.363; ῥινός Epic. in *Arch. Pap.*7.3; ἀσκός Aen.Tact.32.3. 2. *newly flayed*, βόες X.*An.*4.5. 14. **-δίδακτος** [ῐ], ον, of dramas, poems, etc., *newly produced*, διθύραμβοι Luc.*Tim.*46. **-δμής**, ῆτος, ὁ, ἡ, = sq., *newly tamed*, πῶλος *h.Ap.*231; ν. γάμοι a *newly formed* marriage, E.*Med.*1366. ⊛ **-δμητος** (A), ον, (δαμάω) *newly tamed*: metaph., of young wives, *new-wedded*, κόρη ib.623; γυναῖκες Q.S.3.405. 2. *newly killed*, E.*Rh.*887 (lyr., v.l. νεόκμητον), Lyc.65. 3. *born of recent defeat*, ἀνάγκη Q.S.5.161. ⊛ **-δμητος** (B), Dor. **-δμᾱτος**, ον, (δέμω) *new-built*, Pi. *I.*4(3).62, *IG*14.2508 (Nemausus), App.*Mith.*40. **-δορος**, ον, = νεόδαρτος 1, Thphr.*HP*9.5.3, J.*BJ*3.7.10. **-δουπής**, ές, *newly fallen* or *dead*, παρθενικαί Nic.*Fr.*74.63. **-δρεπής**, ές, = sq., Ael.*NA*4. 10, Aret.*CA*1.1. **-δρεπτος**, ον, *fresh-plucked* or *broken*, κλάδοι A. *Supp.*334, cf. Nic.*Th.*863; ν. βωμοὶ *wreathed with fresh-plucked leaves*, Theoc.26.8. **-δρομος**, ον, *just having run*, νεοδρόμῳ λαβὼν θήρῃ, i.e. νεοθήρευτον λαβών, Babr.106.15. **-δροπος**, ον, = νεόδρεπτος, κλάδοι A.*Supp.*354.

**νεοεία**, ἡ, = νεοίη, Sch.Il.23.604.

**νεο-ειδής**, ές, *fresh* or *youthful in form*, Poll.2.10. **-εργής**, ές, *just made* or *newly wrought*, Hsch. **-ζευκτος**, ον, = νεόζυγος, *newly-married*, *AP*9.514, Nonn.*D.*2.594. ⊛ **-ζῠγής**, ές, = sq., πῶλος A.*Pr.*1009; νεοζυγέεσσι φαλάροισιν Tryph.155: metaph., νεοζυγέων ὑμεναίων Nonn.*D.*48.237. **-ζῠγος**, ον, *newly-yoked*: metaph., *newly-married*, νύμφη E.*Med.*804. **-ζυξ**, ῠγος, ὁ, ἡ, = foreg., πῶλος Id. *Fr.*821. 2. metaph., *newly-married*, A.R.4.1191. **-ηλής**, ές, (ἀλέω A) *fresh-ground*, v.l. for νεοθηλής, Nic.*Al.*412. **-ῆλιξ**, ῐκος, ὁ, ἡ, *young in years*, Orph.*H.*87.7.

**Νεοήνια**, τά, festival of Dionysus, Hsch. (leg. νεοίνια).

**νεο-θάλαμος**· καπνός, Hsch. **-θαλής**, v. νεοθηλής. **-θᾰνής**, ές, (θανεῖν) *just dead*, Agath.2.31, Suid. **-θαπτος**, ον, *newly buried*, Sch.Lyc.1097.

**νεόθεν**, Adv. *newly, lately*, S.*OC*1447 (lyr.). II. = νειόθεν, Nic. *Al.*211, 411.

**νεο-θηγής**, ές, = sq., A.R.3.1388, *APl.*4.124. ⊛ **-θηκτος**, ον, *newly whetted*, Suid. s.v. νεόσμηκτος. **-θηλής**, Dor. **-θᾱλής**, ές, (θάλλω) *fresh-budding* or *sprouting*, νεοθηλέα ποίην Il.14.347, cf. Hes.*Th.*576; ν. ὕλης *h.Merc.*82. 2. of animals, *new-born*, νεβρός, μόσχος, Anacr.51, *AP*9.274 (Phil.), cf. Gal.4.718. 3. metaph., *fresh*, εὐφροσύνη *h.Hom.*30.13; ν. αὔξεται νικαφορία grows *with youthful vigour*, Pi.*N.*9.48; αἰσχύνα E.*IA*188 (lyr.). II. (θηλή) *just giving milk*, μαζός Opp.*C.*1.437. [νεοθᾰλής is also cited by Theognost. *Can.*136.] **-θηλος**, ον, = foreg. II, A.*Eu.*450. **-θήξ**, ῆγος, Aeol. ἄγος, ὁ, ἡ, = νεοθηγής, σίδαρος Sapph.119, *AP*7.181 (Andronic.), cf. Archestr.*Fr.*31. **-θήρᾱτος**, ον, *newly caught*, Gal.14.307. **-θήρευτος**, ον, = foreg., ἰχθύς Zen.2.14, cf. Aët.12.67. **-θλῑβής**, ές, = sq., πῶμα *AP*7.457 (Aristo); γλεῦκος Heraclit.*All.*35. **-θλιπτος**, ον, *newly pressed* or *squeezed*, γλεῦκος Nic.*Al.*299, cf. Dsc.5.32. **-θνής**, ῆτος, ὁ, ἡ, = νεοθανής, Pl.*Lg.*865e. **-θρεπτος**, ον, *newly grown*, A.R.3.1400, prob. in Diotog.ap.Stob.4.1.96. II. *fresh-curdled*, of cheese, Hsch. **-θριξ**, ὁ, ἡ, gen. τριχος, *with young hair*, παρειά Nonn.*D.*3.414. **-θρόποις**· νεοαυξέσιν, νεωστὶ ὁρμῶσιν, Hsch.

⊛ **νεοίη**, ἡ, Ep. for νεότης, *youthful passion*, νόον νίκησε νεοίη Il.23. 604.

**νέοικος**, ον, *newly housed, a new denizen*, Epich.12. II. *newly built*, ἕδρα Pi.*O.*5.8.

**νεο-κάθαρτος** [κᾰ], ον, *newly cleaned*, Suid. s.v. νεόσμηκτος. **-καθίδρῡτος**, ον, gloss on νεόκτιστος, Hsch. ⊛ **-καισαρεών**, ῶνος, ὁ (sc. μήν), month at Tira, *IGRom.*4.1665. **-κατάγρᾰφος**, ον, *newly enlisted*, App.*Hisp.*78. **-κατασκεύαστος**, ον, *newly made*, Sch.Ar. *V.*646, Sch.A.R.1.775, Sch.S.*Tr.*1277. **-κατάστᾰτος**, ον, *newly settled*, ἄνθρωποι Th.3.93; βίος D.Chr.30.27. **-κατάχριστος**, ον, *just smeared*, Dsc.4.43. **-κάτοικος**, ον, = νέοικος 1, Eup. 300. **-κάττῡτος**, ον, *freshly sewn*, Stratt.47.8. **-καυστος**, ον, *newly burnt*, Arist.*Pr.*906ᵇ22 :—also **-καυτος**, ον, Thphr.*CP*6.17.7; ἱερά *OGI*229.48 (Smyrna, iii B.C.). **-κέντητος**, ον, *newly planted*, of vines, Hero *Geom.*23.68. **-κηδής**, ές, *whose grief is fresh*, θυμός Hes.*Th.*98. **-κίνησις** [ῑ], εως, ἡ, gloss on νεόχμωσις, Hsch., *EM* 600.48. **-κλᾰδής**, ές, *with new branches*, Hdn.Gr.2.683. ⊛ **-κλωστος**, ον, *fresh-spun*, τελαμών Theoc.24.44; χιτών Nonn.*D.*48. 691. ⊛ **-κμής**, ῆτος, ὁ, ἡ, = sq., Nic.*Th.*707. 2. metaph., of troops, *fresh, with unimpaired strength*, Aen.Tact.16.14, 38. 1. ⊛ **-κμητος**, ον, (κάμνω) *newly wrought*, Nic.*Th.*498. II. *just slain*, v.l. for νεόδμητος, E.*Rh.*887 (lyr.). **-κονίᾱτος**, ον, *newly whitewashed*, τεῖχος Gal.17(1).528. **-κοπος**, ον, *newly cut out, new*, Eup.20. **-κοπτος**, ον, (κόπτω) *fresh-chiselled*, μύλη Ar.*V.* 648. **-κοτος**, ον, *new and strange, unheard of*, A.*Pers.*257 (lyr.), *Th.*803; for the termination cf. ἀλλόκοτος. **-κουρος**, ον, *newly shorn*, πρόβατα *PMasp.*141 iii *a* 2, al. (vi A.D.). ⊛ **-κουφον**, τό, *new cask*, *PKlein.Form.*968 (iv A.D.). **-κράς**, ᾶτος, ὁ, ἡ, (κεράννυμι) *newly mixed*, σπονδαί A.*Fr.*323; ν. (sc. οἶνος), ὁ, Eratosth.ap.Ath. 11.482b; ν. τις ποιείτω Pl.Com.69.8. II. metaph., *newly made*, νεοκρᾶτα φίλον κομίσειεν A.*Ch.*344 (anap.). **-κρᾱτος**, ον, = foreg., Poll.6.24, Hsch.

**Νεόκρητες**, οἱ, *Cretan recruits*, Plb.5.3.1, al.

**νεό-κρῐτος**, ον, *newly distinguished*, B.7 *Fr.* (p.475 J.). **-κροτος**, ον, *greeted with fresh applause*, νίκα Id.5.48. **-κτητος**, ον, *newly gained*, App.*Mith.*16, D.C.49.44. **-κτιστος**, ον, also η, ον Pi. *N.*9.2 :—*newly founded* or *built*, Pi. l.c., *P.*4.206, Hdt.5.24, Th.3.100, Cic.*Att.*6.2.3; *newly created*, Lxx *Wi.*11.18 :—also ⊛ **-κτῐτος**, ον, B. 16.126, Nonn.*D.*18.294. **-κτονος**, ον, (κτείνω) *lately* or *just killed*, Pi.*N.*8.30.

**νεολαία**, ἡ, (λεώς, λαός) *a band of youths, the youth* of a nation, A. *Pers.*669, *Supp.*687; θῆλυς ν., of a band of maidens, Theoc.18.24: as Adj., ν. χεὶρ γυναικῶν E.*Alc.*103.—Dor. word, used by Trag. only in lyr., also in Ar.*Fr.*67 and in late Prose, Luc.*Phal.*1.3, Hld.8.16, Hdn.4.9.4, Alciphr.1.6, Herm.*in Phdr.*p.101 A.

**νεο-λαμπής**, ές, *shining anew*, Man.4.510. **-λεκτος**, ον, (λέγω (B) 1. 2) *newly enlisted, recruit*, Nic.Dam.130.31 J., Jul.*Or.*1.18b, Wilcken *Chr.*469.3 (iv A.D.), Hsch. **-λεξία**, ἡ, *tirocinium*, *Gloss.* **-ληπτος**, ον, *newly taken* or *subdued*, App.*BC*2.48. **-λουτος**, ον, *just bathed*, Hp.*Superf.*29 :—Ep. **νεόλλουτος** *h.Merc.*241. **-λῠτος**, ον, *resolved in a new fashion*, μέλεα *Lyr.Adesp.*112 = *Trag.Adesp.*136 (prob. referring to the pyrrhic metre of the line, but perh. with a play on μέλος 'limb', with ref. to Pentheus; cf. νεόχυτος). **-λώφητος**, ον, *having just left off*, Hsch., Phot.

**νέομαι**, contr. **νεῦμαι**, Il.18.136: **νείομαι** v.l. in 23.76; 2 and 3 sg. contr. νεῖαι, νεῖται, Od.11.114, 14.152, etc.; 1 pl. νεύμεθα Theoc.18. 56, A.R.2.1153; 2 pl. νέεσθε Id.3.306, νεῖσθε E.*Alc.*737; imper. νεῖο *AP*7.472*b* (Leon.); subj. 2 sg. νέηαι Il.1.32; 1 pl. νεώμεθα 2.236; opt. νεοίμην 14.335; inf. νέεσθαι 2.84, al., contr. νεῖσθαι Od.15.88, Pi.*P.* 4.247, S.*Ant.*33; part. νεόμενος E.*El.*722 (lyr.), νεύμενος Call.*Hec.*1. 1.6, *AP*9.96 (Antip. Thess.): Ep. impf. νεόμην Theoc.25.207, νέοντο Il.5.907 :—*go* or *come* (mostly with fut. sense, to which the inf. is the most freq. exception), πάλιν ν. *go back*, freq. *return*, πάλιν οἴκονδε ν. Il. 6.189, Od.6.110; οὐ νέοντ' ἄνευ στεφάνων Pi.*N.*4.77; in Hom. always of persons, exc. ποταμοὺς δ' ἔτρεψε νέεσθαι κὰρ ῥόον Il.12.32; ἄνεμοι.. ἔβαν οἴκονδε νέεσθαι 23.229: metaph., of the path of song, μακρά μοι νεῖσθαι κατ' ἀμαξιτόν Pi.*P.*4.247 :—Constr.: mostly folld. by εἰς, πρός, ἐπί c. acc., ἐς πατρίδα γαῖαν Il.18.101; πρὸς δῶμα 14.335; ἐφ' ἡμέτερα Od.15.88; also by ὑπό c. acc., ὑπὸ ζόφον Il.23.51; by ἐπί c. dat., 22. 392: c. acc. only, 7.335.—Ep. Verb, rare in Trag. (v. supr.): once in early Prose, dub. l. in X.*Cyr.*4.1.11: in late Prose, Dam.*Pr.*81.—The Act. forms νέουσα *h.Cer.*395, Dor. 3 pl. fut. νησοῦντι Sophr.101, are corrupt. (From νεσ-ομαι, cf. νόστος, Skt. *násate* 'take as companion'.)

**νεο-μάλακτος** [μᾰ], ον, *fresh-kneaded*, Sch.Theoc.4.34. **-μηνι** σελήνῃ, τῇ, at the *new* moon, v.l. in Arat.471. **-μηνία**, ἡ, v. νουμηνία. **-μορφοτύπωτος** [ῠ], ον, *in a newfangled shape*, Man.4. 305. **-μυστος**, ον, *newly initiated*, Orph.*H.*43.10. **-νυμφος**, ον, *newly married*, Sostrat.ap.Stob.4.20.70, *Supp.Epigr.*3.216 (ii/i B.C.), *IG*12(5).472 (Oliaros, i A.D.), Plu.2.310e, f.l. for νεόψηφος in Suet. *Ner.*39. **-ξαντος**, ον, (ξαίνω) *newly carded*, Hp.*Superf.*8. **-ξεστος**, ον, *newly polished* or *carved*, τέχνη Tryph.255. **-πᾰγής**, ές, (πήγνυμι) *newly fixed*: *lately become solid*, ἰλύς Plu.2.602d; σάρξ Gal.18(1).363, Aët.9.36; τυρός Gal.6.768; σύστασις Sor.1.46. 2. *newly built*, τεῖχος J.*BJ*3.7.20. **-πᾰθής**, ές, = νεοπενθής 1, A.*Eu.*514 (lyr.). **-πένης**, ητος, ὁ, ἡ, *lately become poor*, *Com.Adesp.*1087 (v.l. **-πεινής**, glossed ὁ νεωστὶ πεινῶν). **-πενθής**, ές, *in new sorrow, fresh-mourning*, νεοπενθέα θυμὸν ἔχουσαι Od.11.39. II. Pass., *lately mourned*, νεοπενθὴς ᾤχετ' ἐς Ἀίδα *IG*12(7).447.6 (Amorgos), cf. 14.1663. **-πέπειρος**, ον, *just ripe*, Phot. **-πεπτος**, ον, (πέσσω) *newly baked*,

ἄρτοι Aret.*CA*2.3. **—πευθής**, ές, *late-learnt*, prob. for νεοπαθῆ, Hsch., for νεοπεφθῆ, Phot. **—πηγής**, ές, *lately built* or *made*, Ῥώμη *AP*9.808 (Cyrus); γυῖα Orac.ap.Eus.*PE*4.9:—also **—πηκτος**, ον, *fresh-curdled*, τυρός Batr.38; *newly burnt*, κεραμίς Hp.*Mul.*2. 206; *newly built*, θάλαμοι Hld.6.11. **—πηθής**· αἰχμάλωτος, Hsch. (—θείς cod.). **—πλαστής**, ές, *newly formed*, σάρξ Philum.ap.Orib. 45.29.20. **—πλεκής**, ές, *new-plaited*, κάλαθος Nic.*Al.*96:—also **—πλεκτος**, ον, σπυρίδες Id.*Fr.*74.21. **—πλουτοπόνηρος**, ον, *wicked from new-gotten wealth*, Cratin.208. **—πλουτος**, ον, *newly become rich*, opp. ἀρχαιόπλουτος (q.v.): hence, *vainglorious, upstart*, D.17. 23, cf. Arg.D.17, Arist.*Rh.*1387$^a$23; οἰκέτης ν. Luc.*Hist.Conscr.*20; ἀπελεύθερος ν. Plu.2.634c; ν. δεῖπνα Id.*Luc.*40: hence, by a comic metaph., ν. τρύξ, of a low *upstart*, Ar.*V.*1309. **—πλῠνής**, ές, = sq., Poll.1.25. **—πλῠτος**, ον, *newly washen*, νεόπλυτα εἵματ' ἔχοντες Od.6.64, cf. Hdt.2.37, *Mus.Belg.*16.71 (Athens, ii A.D.), v.l. in Anacr.21.6. **—πνευστος**, ον, (πνέω) *newly revived*, Nonn.*D.*25. 550. **—ποδες**, οἱ, *young offshoots of vines*, *Gp.*4.3.6. **—ποιέω**, *renovate, make young again*, Herm.ap.Stob.1.41.8, Arg.E.*Med.* 2. = νεάω, Poll.1.221. II. (νεώς) = νεωποιέω (q.v.). **—ποίης**, = νεωποίης (q.v.). **—ποίητος**, ον, *newly made, renewed*, Id.9. 18. **—ποίκῐλος**, ον, gloss on νεοσίγαλος, Sch.Pi.*O.*3.8:—also **—ποίκιλτος**, ον, ibid. **—ποιός**, ὁ, *one who ploughs up fallow land*, Poll. 1.221. **—ποκος**, ον, *newly shorn*, μαλλός S.*OC*475. **—πολις**, εως, ἡ, *new city*, of Abdera, Pi.*Pae.*2.28. **—πολίτης** [ῑ], ου, ὁ, *newly enfranchised citizen*, Arist.*Ath.*21.4, D.S.14.7, Ath.4.138a, App.*BC* 1.49:—fem. **—πολῖτις**, ιδος, as Adj., ν. πόλεις ib.76. 2. Νεοπολίτης, v. Νεάπολις. **—πότιστος**, ον, *newly watered*, Hsch. s.v. νεοαρδέα. **—ποτος**, ον, (πίνω) *having lately drunk*, Hp.*Acut.* 65. **—πρᾱγέω**, = καινοτομέω, Hdn.*Epim.*63. **—πρεπής**, ές, (πρέπω) *befitting the young, youthful*, λόγος Pl.*Lg.*892d. 2. *like a youth, extravagant*, ν. καὶ περίεργος, opp. εὐτελὴς καὶ ἀφελής, Plu. *TG*2, cf. 2. 334c (Comp.). **—πριστος**, ον, (πρίω) *fresh-sawn*, ἐλέφας Od.8.404.

* **Νεοπτόλεμος**, ὁ, surname of Pyrrhus, son of Achilles, *New-warrior*, because *he came late to Troy*, Il.19.327, Od.11.506: [scanned as quadrisyll. Νεŏπτ-, S.*Ph.*4,241, E.*Andr.*14, *Tr.*1126]:—Adj. **Νεοπτολέμειος**, ον, τίσις Paus.4.17.4.

**νεό-πτολις**, εως, ἡ, poet. for νεόπολις, πόλις ν. *new-founded* city, A. *Eu.*687. **—πτορθής**, ές, *with new branches*, Hdn.Gr.1.79:—also **—πτορθος**, ον, as etym. **—πτραι**· υἱῶν θυγατέρες, Hsch. **—πῡρίητος**, ον, *just come out of a vapour-bath*, Hp.*Superf.*29, *Nat.Mul.*6.

**νέοργος**, ον, (ὀργάω) *freshened, invigorated*, γῆ Thphr.*CP*3.13.3 (Sup.).

**νεο-ρρᾰγής**, ές, (ῥήγνυμι) *newly rent* or *burst*, Aret.*SD*2. 9. **—ρραντος**, ον, (ῥαίνω) *newly sprinkled*, ν. ξίφος *a fresh-reeking* sword, S.*Aj.*30, 828; δάκρυα ν. *newly shed*, Aristid. *Or.*24(44). 44. **—ρρᾰφής**, ές, (ῥάπτω) *newly sewn*, Longus 4.14. **—ρρῠτος**, ον, (ῥέω) *fresh-flowing*, πηγαὶ γάλακτος S.*El.*894; δάκρυα Νυμφᾶν Tim.*Fr.*7; κάλλεα κηροῦ *AP*9.363.15 (Mel.); αἷμα Nonn.*D.*43. 134. **—ρρῡτος**, ον, (ἐρύω A) *newly drawn*, ξίφος A.*Ag.*1351. **—ρρύφητος** [ῠ], ον, *having lately taken liquid nourishment*, Hp.*Acut.*65.

* **νέορτος**, ον, (ὄρνυμι) *newly arisen*, τί δ' ἐστίν, ὦ παῖ Λαΐου, ν. αὖ; S. *OC*1507; of persons, *new*, ἃ ν. ἅδε νύμφα Id.*Tr.*894 (lyr.); also, *youthful* (expld. by ἔφηβος, Phot.), τὰν ν. Ἑρμιόναν S.*Fr.*872 (lyr., νεοργόν or —ουργόν codd. Plu.).

* **νέος**, **νέα**, Ion. **νέη**, **νέον**; Ion. **νεῖος** (q.v.): [fem. νέας as monosyll., A.*Th.*327 (lyr.); contr. fem. νῆ Xenoph.42 (= Ar.*Fr.*9), Eugaeon(?) 1]: I. *young, youthful* (of children, youths, and of men at least as old as 30, v. X.*Mem.*1.2.35), ν. παῖς Od.4.665; κοῦροι ν. Il.13.95; ν. ἀνήρ 23.589: alone, νέοι *youths*, 1.463, Hes.*Sc.*281, etc.: later mostly with Art., οἱ νέοι Ar.*Nu.*1059, etc.: prov., ὁ ν. ἔσται ν. 'boys will be boys', Lib.*Ep.*910.3; οἱ ν., corporately organized, *SIG*831.8 (Pergam., ii A.D.), etc.; opp. ἔφηβοι, παῖδες, ib.589.38 (Magn. Mae., ii B.C.): opp. γέρων, ἡμὲν νέοι ἠδὲ γέροντες Il.2.789, etc.; ἢ ν. ἠὲ παλαιός 14.108, cf. Od.1.395, etc.; opp. γεραίτερος, 3.24; opp. προγενέστερος, 2.29; opp. γεραιός, X.*Lac.*1.7; εὐθὺς ἐκ νέου ἐθίζειν *from youth upwards*, Pl.*Grg.*510d, etc.; ἐκ νέων παίδων Id.*Lg.*887d; ἐκ νέων ἐθίζεσθαι Arist.*EN*1103$^b$24; ἐκ νέας (sc. ψυχῆς) Pl.*R.*409a; τὸ ν., = νεότης, *youth* (in the abstract), S.*OC*1229 (lyr.), E.*Ion*545: also in concrete sense, τὸ ν. ἅπαν all *young creatures*, Pl.*Lg.*653d; οὐ δύναται τὸ ν. ἡσυχάζειν Arist.*Pol.*1340$^b$29; σκιρτητικὸν τὸ ν. Corn. *ND*20; also, of *minors*, νέου ὄντος ἔτι Th.1.107; cf. νεώτερος. b. rarely of animals and plants, ὄρπηκες, ἔρνος, Il.21.38, Od.6.163; οἱ ν. τῶν νεβρῶν X.*Cyn.*9.8. 2. *suited to a youth, youthful*, ἄεθλοι Pi.*O.*2.43; ν. θράσος A.*Pers.*744 (troch.); ν. φροντὶς *youthful* spirits, E.*Med.*48; νέαις ταῖς διανοίαις χρωμένους Lys.24.16; of persons, ἄφρων νέος τε E.*IA*489, cf. Pl.*R.*378a; ν. τε καὶ ὀξὺς Id.*Grg.*463e (but διαφέρει οὐδὲν ν. τὴν ἡλικίαν ἢ τὸ ἦθος νεαρός Arist.*EN*1095$^a$ 6). II. *new, fresh*, ν. θάλαμος Il.17.36; ν. ἄλγος 6.462; νέῳ.. κόλλοπι Od.21.407 (this sense elsewh. in Hom. only in Adv. νέον, v. infr.); λίνον Alc.15 (dub.); πόνοι.. νέοι παλαιοῖσι συμμιγεῖς κακοῖς A.*Th.*740 (lyr.), etc.; οἶνος ν. Ar.*Pax*916; ἐν τοῖς μουσικοῖς τὰ ν. [μέλη] εὐδοκιμεῖ X.*Cyr.*1.6.38; ἡ ν. (sc. σελήνη) the *new* moon, esp. in phrase ἕνη καὶ νέα, v. ἕνος 2; but μηνὸς τῇ ν. (sc. ἡμέρᾳ) *on the first day* of the month, Pl.*Lg.*849b; ν. ἦμαρ A.R.4.1479: in this sense rarely of persons, ὁ ν. ταγὸς μακάρων A.*Pr.*96 (anap.), cf. Ar. *Pl.*960; οἱ ν. θεοί A.*Eu.*721; cf. νεώτερος. 2. of events, etc., *new*, with collat. notion of *unexpected, strange, untoward, evil*, τί ν.; Id.*Ag.*85 (anap.); προσδοκῶ τι γὰρ ν. E.*Supp.*99; μῶν τι βουλεύῃ ν.; S.*Ph.*1229, cf. 554, E.*Hipp.*794, *Ba.*362. Th.5.50. etc.: ἀπροσδοκήτους καὶ ν. λόγους A.*Supp.*712; καινὰ ν. τ' ἄχη Id.*Pers.*665 (lyr.): this sense is more common in Comp., v. νεώτερος. III. neut. νέον as Adv. of Time, *lately, just now*, opp. both to distant past and present, παῖδα ν. γεγαῶτα Od.19.400, cf. Il.3.394; ν. κρατεῖν A.*Pr.* 35, 955, etc.: also used Adverbially with the Art., καὶ τὸ πάλαι (v.l. παλαιόν) καὶ τὸ ν. Hdt.9.26: in Prose νεωστί (q.v.): rarely Comp. Adv. νεωτέρως, Pl.*Lg.*907c: Sup. νεώτατα *most recently*, Th.1.7; also ἐκ νέας, Ion. αὖτις ἐκ νέης, *anew, afresh*, Hdt.1.60, 5.116. IV. the degrees of Comp. are νεώτερος, νεώτατος, v. νεώτερος: νεαίτερος is corrupt for νεαίρετος in A.*Fr.*330. (νέϝος (in νεϝόστατος, q.v.), cf. Skt. *návas*, Lat. *novus*, etc.)

**νεός** (sc. γῆ), v. νειός. **νεός**, Ion. gen. of ναῦς.

**νεο-σίγᾱλος** [ῑ], ον, (σιγαλόεις) *new and sparkling, with all the gloss on*, metaph., τρόπος Pi.*O.*3.4. **—σκᾰφής**, ές, *newly dug*, Lyc.1097, Sch.E.*Ph.*1664. **—σκύλευτος** [ῡ], ον, *newly taken as booty*, ἔντεα *AP*7.430 (Diosc.). **—σμηκτος**, ον, (σμήχω) *newly cleaned*, θώρηκες Il.13.342; μάχαιρα Euph.132; κάλαμος *AP*6.227 (Crin.); χαλκός Plu. *Aem.*32. **—σπᾰδής**, ές, (σπάω) = νεοσπάς, ν. ξίφος *newly drawn from a wound, bloody*, A.*Eu.*42. **—σπάρακτος** [ᾰ], ον, *newly torn*, Sch.Ar.*Eq.*344. **—σπάς**, άδος, ὁ, ἡ, *newly torn away, fresh-plucked*, θαλλοί S.*Ant.*1201, cf. *Fr.*502. **—σπειστος**, ον, *newly poured as an offering*, f.l. in Nonn.*D.*19.177. **—σπορος**, ον, *newly sown*, κῦμα A.*Eu.*659.

**νεοσσ-εία**, ἡ, only in Att. form **νεοττεία**, *nest-building*, Arist.*HA* 560$^b$23. II. = ἐκλέπισις, Suid. **—ευσις**, Att. **νεόττ-**, εως, ἡ, = foreg. I, Arist.*HA*559$^a$3 (pl.). **—εύω**, Att. **νεοττ-**, Ion. and Hellenistic **νοσσεύω**, *hatch*, ἐνεόττευσεν γένος Ar.*Av.*699. 2. *build a nest*, Arist.*HA*559$^a$4, etc.; μελιττῶν ἐν τῷ στήθει τοῦ λέοντος νενοσσευκότων J.*AJ*5.8.6: metaph., [σοφία] θεμέλιον αἰῶνος ἐνόσσευσε Lxx *Si.*1.15:—Pass., ὅσα ἦν νενοσσευμένα ὀρνίθων γένεα as many as *had their nests*, Hdt.1.159. **—ιά**, Ion. **—ιή**, Att. **νεοττιά**, later **νοσσιά**, Ion. **—ιή**, ἡ, *nest of young birds*, Id.3.111, Ar.*Av.*642, Pl.*R.*548a, Thphr.*CP* 4.5.7 (in the form νοσσιῶν); νεοττιὰς ποιεῖσθαι, νεοττιὰν ποιεῖν, Arist. *HA*613$^b$6, 618$^a$8. 2. *brood of young birds*, Lycurg.132, Dsc.*Eup.* 1.21, *Ev.Luc.*13.34; ν. χελιδόνων Men.*Pk.*278: metaph., ν. τέκνων *Com.Adesp.*873 (= *Trag.Adesp.*189). 3. *lair*, ἐφ' ἧς ἀλώπηξ νοσσιὴν πεποίηται Herod.7.72. 4. *beehive*, Lxx*4Ma.*14.19. **—ίον**, Att. **νεοττ-** (later **νοσσίον** Lyr. in *Philol.*80.336), τό, Dim. of νεοσσός, *nestling, chick*, Arist.*HA*536$^a$30: metaph., τοῦ πατρὸς ν. 'chip of the old block', Ar.*Av.*767, cf. Thphr.*Char.*2.6. 2. *yolk* of an egg, Men.42 (prob.), Diph.121, Hsch. **—ίς**, Att. **νεοττ-**, later **νοσσίς**, ίδος, ἡ, = foreg. I, Arist.*HA*559$^b$23; Παφίης νοσσίς, of a *girl*, *AP*9.567 (Antip.): freq. as pr. n. in Com. 2. νοσσίδες, αἱ, name of a kind of *shoe*, Herod.7.57.

**νεοσσο-κόμος**, Att. **νεοττ-**, ον, *rearing chickens*, καλιή *AP*7.210 (Antip.). **—ποιέω**, later **νοσσο-**, = νεοσσεύω, Lxx*Is.*13.22:—also in Med., Aesop.5: metaph., ταῦτα (sc. πλοῦτος καὶ πολυτέλεια) ἐν τοῖς βίοις —ποιεῖται Longin.44.7. **—ποιία**, Att. **νεοττ-**, ἡ, *hatching*, Dsc.2.56. **—πῶλις**, ιδος, ἡ, *seller of young birds*, Herod.6.99 (prob. νοσσο-).

**νεοσσός**, Att. **νεοττ-**, ὁ, (νέος) *young bird, nestling, chick*, Il.2.311, 9.323, S.*Ant.*425, Ar.*Av.*835, *Ev.Luc.*2.24, etc.; ἀπτῆνες ν. Plu.2. 48a. 2. *any young animal*, as a young crocodile, Hdt.2.68; of young children, A.*Ch.*256, 501, E.*Alc.*403 (lyr.), al., Pl.*Lg.*776a: fem., ἣν νεοττὸς καὶ νέα (sc. Lais) Epicr.3.15: in pl., *young bees*, X. *Oec.*7.34, Arist.*HA*624$^a$22; Ἄρεως ν., of the cock, Ar.*Av.*835 (also ironically, of a person, Pl.Com.104): collective, ἵππου ν. the horse's *brood*, A.*Ag.*825. 3. *yolk of an egg*, Arist.*HA*565$^a$3, Orac.ap. Chrysipp.*Stoic.*2.344; cf. νεοττίον.—The disyll. form **νοσσός** is cited in *AB*109 from A.*Fr.*113 and occurs in S.*Oxy.*2081(*b*) *Fr.*3: this and cogn. forms (commonly found in later Gr.) are condemned as ἀδόκιμα by Phryn.182.

**νεοσσο-τροφεῖον**, Att. **νεοττ-**, τό, *chicken-coop*, Colum.8.15. **—τροφέω**, Att. **νεοττ-**, later **νοσσ-**, *rear young birds*, *AP*9.346 (Leon. Alex.):—Pass., *to be reared as in the nest*, of a child, Ar.*Nu.* 999, cf. Ph.2.200. **—τροφία**, Att. **νεοττ-**, *rearing of young birds*, M.Ant.9.9 (pl.), *Gp.*14.7.14, Al.*Jb.*39.16.

**νεό-σσῦτος**, ον, = νέορτος, Hsch.; ἰχώρ Nonn.*D.*29.268; ὄγκος ἀΐνης ib.4.10. **—στᾰθής**, ές, (ἵστημι) *newly settled*, δῆμος Plu.2. 321d. **—στάλυξ**, υγος, ὁ, ἡ, = νεοδάκρυτος, Hsch. **—στᾰσίη**, dub. l. in A.R.3.76 (leg. ἐνεο-), cf. Hsch. **—στατος**, Cypr. **νεϝόστατος**, = νεώτατος, *latest, last*, τᾶν ἐπαγομενᾶν ν. *Inscr.Cypr.*134 H. **—στεπτος**, ον, *fresh-crowned*, Opp.*H.*1.198. **—στεφής**, ές, = foreg., *BMus.Inscr.*1143 (ii/iii A.D.). II. = νεόκρατος, Hsch.; cf. ἐπιστεφής. **—στράτευτος** [ᾰ], ον, *recruit*, App.*BC*2.74. **—στρᾰτος**, ον, = foreg., τείρων (Lat. *tiro*) *PMon.*2.2 (vi A.D.). **—στροφος**, ον, *newly twisted*, νευρή Il.15.469. **—σύλλεκτος**, ον, = sq., D.H.8.13, 11.23, J.*BJ*1.17.1, Plu.*Caes.*25. **—σύλλογος**, ον, *newly collected*, i.e. *incurred*, ἔρανοι Hyp.*Ath.*11; *newly levied*, στρατόπεδα Plb.3.70. 10, cf. Polyaen.3.11.8. **—σύστᾰτος**, ον, *recently formed*, i.e. *recent*, of disease, Crito ap.Gal.12.830; *sudden*, κατάρρους Herod.Med.ap. Orib.10.17.2. II. *having newly joined a sect, proselyte*, J.*BJ*2.8. 9. * **—σφᾰγής**, ές, *fresh-slaughtered*, S.*Tr.*1130, *Aj.*898, E.*Hec.*894; νεοσφαγῆ που τόνδε προσλεύσσων φόνον S.*Aj.*546. **—σφάδαστος** [σφᾰ], ον, *newly struggling*, Id.*Fr.*349. **—σφακτος**, ον, *newly shed*, ν. αἷμα Arist.*HA*581$^b$2. **—σφάξ**, ᾶγος, ὁ, ἡ, *newly slaughtered*, Nic.*Fr.* 68.1. **—σχῐδής**, ές, *just split* or *cloven*, ὄρος Nonn.*D.*45.307. **—τᾰφής**, ές, of a *newly-built tomb*, Sch.Lyc.1097 (ed. Bachm.). **—τελής**, ές, *newly initiated*, Pl.*Phdr.*250e (glossed νεωστὶ τετελεσμένος Tim.*Lex.*,

ν. τετελειωμένος Phot., Suid.), Luc.*DMeretr.*11.2; ψυχή Him.*Or.*14.12; ἦθος Id.*Ecl.*10.6. **–τερπής**, ές, *new and charming*, Opp.*H.* 3.352, etc.: neut. as Adv., *with new delight*, Id.*C.*2.584. **–τευκτος**, ον, *newly wrought*, κασσίτερος Il.21.592; εἰκών *Epigr.Gr.*311 (Smyrna). **–τευχής**, ές, = foreg., δίφροι Il.5.194; μοῦσα Tim.*Pers.*216; κισσύβιον Theoc.1.28.

⊛ **νεότης**, Dor. **–τας**, ητος, ἡ, (νέος) *youth*, ἐκ νεότητος.. ἐς γῆρας Il. 14.86, cf. *Ev.Marc.*10.20, etc.; ἀτέμβονται νεότητος Il.23.445; ἐρατὴν γὰρ ἀπωλέσαμεν νεότητα, i.e. we died young, Simon.89, cf. E.*HF*637 (lyr.), *Fr.*149; ἐν νεότατι, ἐπὶ νεότητος, in one's *youth*, Sapph.*Supp.* 12.3, Ar.*V.*1199, cf. *Ach.*214: in pl., αἱ ν. ἄφρονες *AP*9.359 (Posidipp. or Pl.Com. or Crates); αἱ ν. ῥωμαλέαι ib.360 (Metrod.). 2. *youthful spirit, impetuosity*, Hdt.7.13: in bad sense, *youthful folly, insolence*, ἀκολασίᾳ καὶ ν. Pl.*Ap.*26e; ν. καὶ ἄνοια And.2.7. II. collective, = νεολαία, *body of youth*, esp. of military or athletic age, Pi.*I.*8(7).75, Hdt.4.3, 9.12, Th.2.8, 20, etc. III. in Crete, **νεότας**, ᾶ, acc. νεότα, gen. νεότας, *board of officials representing the* νέοι (cf. νέος I. 1), *GDI*5012.6, *SIG*525.9 (Gortyn, iii B.C.).

**νεοτήσιος**, ον, *youthful*, ὥρη Ps.-Phoc.213; σκίρτημα Antipho Soph.49.

⊛ **νεό-τικτος**, ον, *newly brought forth*, A.*Fr.*451H. **–τμητος**, Dor. **–τμᾱτος**, ον, *newly cut off, divided*, Pl.*Ti.*80d, Theoc.7.134, A.R. 3.857, Dsc.2.70. **–τοκος**, ον, *new-born*: metaph., *fresh, recent*, πάθος Aret.*CD*1.5. II. parox. **νεοτόκος**, ον, Act., *having just brought forth*, E.*Ba.*701, Aret.*CA*2.3; λύκαινα νεοτόκος σπαργῶσα τοὺς μαστούς D.H.1.79, Plu.2.320d. **–τομος**, ον, *fresh-cut*, ὄνυχος ἄλοκι νεοτόμῳ A.*Ch.*25 (lyr.); ν. πλήγματα *newly inflicted*, S. *Ant.*1283. II. *freshly cut off*, ἕλιξ E.*Ba.*1170 (lyr.). **–τρεφής**, ές, *newly reared*, κόροι Id.*Heracl.*92 (lyr.), cf. Nonn.*D.*10. 178. **–τρητος**, ον, = νεότρωτος, *fresh*, τραύματα interpol. in Dsc. 1.106. ⊛ **–τρῑβής**, ές, *freshly ground*, πυροῖο ἄχθος Ps.-Phoc. 167. 2. *freshly extracted*, ἔλαιον Sor.1.46, al. **–τροφος**, ον, = νεοτρεφής, A.*Ag.*724 (lyr.), Cratin.326. **–τρωτος**, ον, (τιτρώσκω) *lately wounded* or *hurt*, Hp.*Fract.*28; ν. ἕλκη, τὰ ν. τῶν ἑλκῶν, *fresh* sores, Id.*Liqu.*4, Dsc.4.114 (v.l.), cf. Gal.10.257.

**νεοττεία**, etc., v. νεοσσ–.

**νεότῡρος**, ὁ, *new cheese*, Alex.Trall.*Febr.*4.

**νε-ουργέω**, *invent new things*, f.l. in Alciphr.3.51. **–ουργής**, ές, = sq., Plu.*Aem.*5, Alciphr.3.57, Jul.*Or.*2.71c. **–ουργός** (A), όν, *newmade, new*, ἱμάτιον Pl.*R.*495e; φοινικίδες Plu.*Aem.*18. **–ουργός** (B), ὁ, (ναῦς) *shipbuilder*, Poll.1.84. **–ούτᾰτος**, ον, (οὐτάω) *lately wounded*, ἄλλον.. νεούτατον, ἄλλον ἄουτον Il.18.536, cf. 13.539, Hes. *Sc.*253. **–ούτητος**, ον, = foreg., Nonn.*D.*17.351, al.

**νεο-ῠ́φαντος** [ῠ], ον, *newly woven*, Eust.1572.4. **–φάντης**, ου, ὁ, *newly initiated*, μύστης Orph.*H.*4.9. **–φᾰτος**, ον, *lately slain*, Hsch. **–φεγγής**, ές, *shining anew*, μήνη, αἴγλη, Man.2.489, Nonn. *D.*22.350. **–φθαρτος**, ον, *newly ruined* or *killed*, Hsch. s.v. νεόφθιτος. **–φθίμενος** [ῐ], η, ον, = foreg., Nonn.*D.*25.274, al. **–φθῐτος**, ον, = foreg., *Trag.Adesp.*240. 2. *newly violated*, Hsch. **–φοιτος**, ον, *having just arrived, newcomer*, Coluth.390. II. Pass., *newly trodden*, ἠέρα *AP*7.699. **–φονος**, ον, *lately killed*: ν. αἷμα *freshshed*, E.*El.*1172. **–φρων**, ονος, ὁ, ἡ, (φρήν) *childish in spirit*, dub. l. in Panyas.12.11 (leg. ἐνεό–): freq. as pr. n. **–φυής**, ές, *new-grown, shooting up anew*, Poll.1.231. **–φύρᾱτος** [ῠ], ον, *newly kneaded*, Sch.Theoc.4.34. ⊛ **–φυτεῖον**, τό, *young plantation, nursery-ground*, *Gloss.* **–φῠτος**, ον, *newly planted*, Ar.*Fr.*828; ἀμπελών *PCair.Zen.* 236.4 (iii B.C.); κτῆμα *POxy.*909.16 (iii A.D.): neut. pl. νεόφυτα, τά, *young plants*, Lxx *Ps.*143(144).12, cf. *PRyl.*138.9 (i A.D.; νεώ– Pap.), etc. II. metaph., *new convert, neophyte*, 1*Ep.Ti.*3.6. **–χάρακτος** [χᾰ], ον, *newly imprinted*, ἴχνος S.*Aj.*6.

**νεοχμ-έω**, = νεοχμόω, in Pass., Procop.*Arc.*30 codd., Suid. s.v. νεοχμός. **–ία**, Ion. **–ίη**, ἡ, = νεοχμωσις, Hsch. **–ίζω**, = νεοχμόω, Id. (Pass.). ⊛ **–ός**, όν, = νέος, *new*, always of things (exc. S.*Ant.*156 (anap.)), μέλος ν. ἄρχε Alcm.1; νεοχμοῖς δὲ δὴ νόμοις Ζεὺς.. κρατύνει A.*Pr.*150 (lyr.); κακόν Id.*Pers.*693, E.*Hipp.*866 (lyr.); τί φροιμιάζῃ ν.; Id.*IT*1162, cf. *Tr.*260 (lyr.); μῦθοι ib.231 (anap.): rare in Com. (only in lyr.), ν. ἄθυρμα Cratin.145; τέρας Ar.*Ra.*1372, *Th.*701: also in Ion. (never in Att.) Prose, *fresh*, ν. ποιέειν τὸ φάρμακον Hp.*Mul.*2. 133. Adv. **–μῶς** ib.1.16. II. *drastic*, ν. τι ποιέειν, i.e. mutiny, Hdt. 9.99, 104; οὐδενὶ ν. ἀρεσκόμενος D.C.38.3. [νεοχμ–, A.*Pers.* l.c., E.*Tr.* 231, *Ba.*216, etc.] **–όω**, *make innovations*, esp. political, mostly with neut. Pron. or Adj., μηδὲν ἄλλο ν. κατά τινας Hdt.4.201, cf. 5. 19; πολλὰ ἐνεόχμωσε *caused* many *changes*, Th.1.12, cf. D.H.1.89, 5. 74. II. *inaugurate*, ἅπερ αὐτὸς νεοχμοῖ Arist.*Mu.*401ᵃ13. 2. Medic., *produce a complication*, Lycus ap.Orib.8.26.2. **–ωσις**, εως, ἡ, *innovation*, Hsch.: in pl., *strange phenomena*, Arist.*Mu.*397ᵃ 20. 2. *renovation*, δυνάμιος Aret.*CA*2.3; *renewal*, ἐπιπλασμάτων ib.1.10.

**νεό-χρηστος**, ον, dub. in Diotog.ap.Stob.4.1.96 (leg. νεόθρεπτα). **–χριστος**, ον, *newly plastered*, D.S.38.4, App.*BC*1.74. **–χρύσεος** [ῡ], ον, *new and golden*, Philod.Scarph.123. **–χῠτος**, ον, (χέω) *flowing in new fashion*, ν. μέλεα v.l. for νεόλυτα (q.v.) in *Lyr.Adesp.* 112 (= *Trag.Adesp.*136). **–ψηφος**, ον, *calculated in a fresh way*, prob. for νεόνυμφον in Suet.*Ner.*39.

**νεόω**, (νέος) *renovate, change*, νέωσον αἶνον A.*Supp.*534 (lyr.):—Med., τάφους ἐνεώσατο *had* them *restored*, *IG*14.1721:—Pass., Hsch. 2. = νεάω, Poll.1.221: c. acc. cogn., νεώσατε ἑαυτοῖς νεώματα Lxx *Je.*4.3. II. *restore* a MS. reading in a corrupt passage, Demetr.Lac.*Herc.*1012.26.

**νέπετος**, ὁ, = καλαμίνθη, Lat. word in Gal.14.43; cf. νέπιτα· ἡ καλαμίνθη, Hsch. (Lat. *nepeta*.)

⊛ **νέπους**, ποδος, ὁ, once in Hom. in pl., νέποδες καλῆς Ἁλοσύδνης, of seals, prob. *children* of H., Od.4.404, cf. Eust.1502.36: so in later Poets, ἀθάνατοι δὲ καλεῦνται ἑοὶ νέποδες Theoc.17.25; γοργοφόνοι νέποδες Cleon Sic.ap.*EM*389.28; ὁ Κεῖος Ὑλλίχου νέπους Call.*Fr.*77, cf. A.R.4.1745: also expld. from νε– (for νη– privat.), πούς, *the footless ones*, Apion ap.Apollon.*Lex.*, and from νέω (A), = νηξί-ποδες, *web-footed*, ibid., *Et.Gud.*405.49: hence in later Poets, of *fish*, θαλασσαίων μυνδότεροι νεπόδων Call.*Fr.*260, cf. Nic.*Al.*468, 485, *AP* 6.11 (Satyr.), 11.60 (Paul. Sil.); ἑκαστά τε φῦλα νεπούδων is f.l. in *h.Ap.*78.

**νέρθε, νέρθεν**, v. ἔνερθε.

**νέρτατος**, η, ον, = ἐνέρτατος, *lowest*, Hsch.

**νερτέριος**, α, ον, *underground*, Orph.*A.*1372, *AP*9.459, etc.; οἱ ν. ib.7.601 (Jul. Aeg.).

**νερτερο-δρόμος**, ὁ, *courier of the dead*, Luc.*Peregr.*41. **–μορφος**, ον, *shaped like the dead*, Man.4.555.

**νέρτερος**, α, ον, also ος, ον E.*Ph.*1020 (lyr.):— = ἐνέρτερος, *lower, nether*, Comp. without Posit. in use (cf. νέρθε, ἔνερθε), νερτέρᾳ προσήμενος κώπῃ A.*Ag.*1617; τὰ δ' ὑπέρτερα νέρτερα θήσει Ar.*Lys.* 772. 2. mostly as Posit., *belonging to the lower world*, ὁ ν. θεός S.*OC*1548; ν. θεοί A.*Pers.*622, S.*Ant.*602 (lyr.), etc.; νέρτεροι alone, *the dead*, A.*Pers.*619, etc.; ν. πλάκες, χθών, δώματα, the world *below*, S.*OC*1576 (lyr.), E.*Alc.*47 (s.v.l.), 1073; ν. κώπα, of Charon's boat, ib.459 (lyr.).

**νέρτος**, ὁ, a bird, Ar.*Av.*303; expld. by ἱέραξ, Hsch.

**Νερώνεια** (sc. ἱερά), τά, *festival of Nero*, D.C.61.21, al.:—Adj. ⊛ **Νερωνιανός**, ή, όν, Plu.*Galb.*17.

**νέρωπα**· λαμπρόν, Hsch. (i.e. νώροπα).

**νεστορίς**, ίδος, ἡ, a kind of *cup*, Ath.11.487f.

**Νέστωρ**, ορος, ὁ, *Nestor*, Il.1.247, etc.:—Adj. **Νεστόρεος**, η, ον, 2. 54, al.; **Νεστόρειος**, α, ον, ἅρμα Pi.*P.*6.32; μέλος E.*Fr.*899; σκύφος Luc.*Herm.*12.

**νέτωπον**, τό, *oil of bitter almonds*, Hp.*Mul.*1.37, *Epid.*5.66, al. (μέτωπον is v.l. in *Loc.Hom.*12, al.):—also **νετώπιον**, Hsch. (cf. μετώπιον II); cf. νίωπον.

⊛ **νεῦμα**, ατος, τό, (νεύω) *nod, sign*, Th.1.134; νεύματος ἕνεκα χαλεπαίνειν for *a mere nod*, X.*An.*5.8.20; ν. χειρός Onos.26.1. 2. *expression of will, command*, μονοψήφοισι νεύμασι A.*Supp.*373 (lyr.); ἀπὸ νεύματος προστάττειν τινί Plb.21.38.4; *approval, sanction*, ἀετὸς φέρων ἐκ Διὸς ταῖς εὐχαῖς ν. Philostr.*Her.*12ᵃ.1, cf. *IG*3.636; *control*, ὑποτάττειν Παλαιστίνην τῷ ν. τινός Chor.p.28 B. II. *quarter of the heavens*, D.P.517. 2. generally, *direction*, Heliod.ap.Orib.49.4. 39, *PMag.Par.*1.178.

**νεῦμαι**, v. νέομαι.

**νευμάτιον**, τό, Dim. of νεῦμα I. 1, Arr.*Epict.*4.13.22.

**νεύμενος**, v. νέομαι.

⊛ **νευρά**, Ion. **–ρή**, ἡ, Ep. gen. sg. **νευρῆφι(ν)** Il.8.309, 15.313, 21. 113:—*string* or *cord of sinew*, in Ep. usu. *bowstring*, ν. εὐστρεφής, νεόστροφος, Il.15.463, 469; βαρύφθογγος Pi.*I.*6(5).34, cf. S.*Ph.*1005, E.*Ba.*784, X.*An.*4.2.28, etc.: made from νεῦρον, Arist.*HA*540ᵃ19; μύες ἐβοήθησαν διατραγόντες τὰς ν. Id.*Rh.*1401ᵇ16. 2. *harpstring*, Poll.4.62. 3. *strand* of a torsion-engine, *IG*2².554.15. 4. *withe*, Lxx *Jd.*16.7. 5. wrongly taken by some, = νεῦρον, Il.8.328. (Cogn. with νεῦρον.)

**νευράς**, άδος, ἡ, Ion. name for ποτίρριον, Dsc.3.15, Plin.*HN*27. 122. II. = δορύκνιον, ib.21.179.

**νευρ-ειή**, ἡ, poet. for νευρά, Theoc.25.213. **–ένδετος**, ον, *strung*, κιθάρη Man.5.163. **–επέντᾰτος**, ον, *stretched on the bowstring*, prob. in Tim.*Pers.*31. **–ή, –ῆφι, –ῆφιν**, v. νευρά. **–ικός**, ή, όν, *suffering from contraction of the tendons*, ν. καὶ ἀρθριτικοί Antyll. ap.Orib.9.11.2, cf. Gal.8.420. 2. of the disease itself, ν. διάθεσις *OGI*331.11 (Pergam., ii B.C.). 3. Adv. **–κῶς** *like a tendon*, Ruf. *Syn.Puls.*7. **–ῐνος**, η, ον, *made of sinew*, χορδή Arist.*GA*787ᵇ17; λύρα ν. τρίχορδος D.S.1.16; κράνη ν. Str.3.3.6. II. *made* or *consisting of fibres*, Pl.*Plt.*279e. **–ιον**, τό, Dim. of νεῦρον, Hp.*Mochl.* 1, Gal.2.400. II. Dim. of νευρά, *AP*11.352.11 (Agath.). ⊛ **–ίτης** [ῑ] λίθος, ὁ, *sinew-like* stone, Orph.*L.*748 codd. (fort. leg. νεβρ–).

**νευρο-βάτης** [ᾰ], ου, ὁ, *rope-dancer*, Rhetor. in *Cat.Cod.Astr.*8(4). 213, *Et.Gud.*345.52: in Lat. form, Vopisc.*Carin.*19, Firm.*Math.*8. 17.4. **–ειδής**, ές, *like sinews*: τὸ ν., = λειμώνιον, Dsc.4.16, Plin.*HN* 20.72. **–θλαστος**, ον, *bruised in the sinews*, Gal.13.576, Orib.*Fr.* 88. **–καυλος**, ον, *with fibrous stem*, Thphr.*HP*7.2.8. **–κοίλιος**, ον, dub. sens. in Hp.*Loc.Hom.*5 (fort. ἐρυκοίλιοι). **–κοπέω**, *hamstring, hough*, Lxx *Ge.*49.6, *PCair.Zen.*462.4 (iii B.C.), Plb.31. 2.11, Str.16.4.10:—Pass., D.S.3.26. **–λάλος** [ᾰ], ον, *with sounding strings*, χορδή *AP*9.410 (Tull. Sab.). **–μῆτραι**, αἱ, = ψόαι, Clearch.72, Ruf.*Onom.*189, 192.

⊛ **νεῦρον**, τό, *sinew, tendon*, once in Hom., in pl., of the *tendons* at the feet, περὶ δ' ἔγχεος αἰχμῇ νεῦρα διεσχίσθη Il.16.316, cf. Hp.*Art.* 11, etc.; τὰ ν. οἷα ἐπιτείνεσθαι καὶ ἀνίεσθαι Pl.*Phd.*98c; ν. ἐξ ἰνῶν [γίγνεται] Id.*Ti.*82c; σάρκες καὶ ν. ibid.; σύγκειταί μου τὸ σῶμα ἐξ ὀστῶν καὶ ν. Id.*Phd.*98c, cf. Arist.*HA*515ᵃ27, al.: used adjectivally, ib.540ᵃ18 (s.v.l.). b. ν. ἔναιμον *vein*, Hp.*Liqu.*2, cf. Ruf. *Onom.*208. 2. metaph., in pl., *nerves, sinews*, τὰ ν. τῆς τραγῳδίας, of the lyric odes, Ar.*Ra.*862; ὑποτέτμηται τὰ ν. τῶν πραγμάτων Aeschin.3.166; ἕως ἐκτέμῃ ὥσπερ ν. ἐκ τῆς ψυχῆς Pl.*R.*411b; ἐκτ. τὰ ν. [οἴνου] Plu.2.692c; also πόλις ἥτις μὴ νεῦρ' ἐπὶ τοὺς ἀδικοῦντας

ἔχει D.19.283: less freq. in sg., τὸ ν. ὑποκόπτοντες τῆς δυνάμεως J.*BJ* 5.1.4; χρήματα ν. πολέμου App.*BC*4.99. **II.** *cord made of sinew*, e.g. bowstring, Il.4.122; string fastening the head of the arrow to the shaft, ib.151; also δέρματα συρράπτειν νεύρῳ βοὸς Hes.*Op.*544; *cord of a sling*, X.*An.*3.4.17, Q.S.11.112; *bowstring*, Ach.Tat.3.8. **2.** = νευρά 3, Plb.4.56.3, App.*Mith.*107. **3.** *string* of a lyre, *AP*9.584.9, Luc.*DMar.*1.4. **III.** in pl., *fibres* of plants, Pl.*Plt.* 280c. **IV.** *nerves*, as organs of sensation, first in Erasistr.ap. Gal.5.602; ν. πρακτικά, αἰσθητικά, etc., Ruf.*Onom.*211; ν. κινητικά, προαιρετικά, Gal.2.613,739; ν. ἀκουστικόν Alex.Aphr.*Pr.*1.71, cf. Gal.2.831, Plot.4.3.23. **V.** *penis*, Pl.Com.173.19, Gal.8.442. (Cf. Skt. *snāvan-*, Avest. *snāvarə*, 'sinew', 'bond'.)

**νευρό-νοσος**, ον, *diseased in the sinews*, Man.4.501. **-πᾰχυς**, υ, *with a thick sinewy coat*, of a vein, Hp.*Oss.*15. **-πλεκής**, ές, *plaited with sinews*, *AP*6.107 (Phil.). **-ποιητικός**, ή, όν, *making sinews*, Gal.*Nat.Fac.*1.6. **-ρᾰφέω** or **-ρρᾰφέω**, *stitch* or *mend shoes*, Pl.*Euthd.*294b, X.*Cyr.*8.2.5. **-ρᾰφία** or **-ρρᾰφία**, ἡ, *cobblery*, Gal.*Thras.*5. **-ρᾰφικός** or **-ρρᾰφικός**, ή, όν, *of* or *for shoe-mending*, *cobbling*, Poll.7.154. **-ρράφος** [ᾰ], ὁ, (νεῦρον II, ῥάπτω) *one who stitches with sinews*, *mender of shoes*, *cobbler*, Ar.*Eq.*739, Pl.*R.*421a, etc. **II.** *one who makes strings for the lyre*, Lycurg. *Fr.*100. **-σπᾰδής**, ές, (νεῦρον II, σπάω) *drawn by the string*, ν. ἄτρακτος the arrow *drawn and just ready to fly*, S.*Ph.*290. **-σπασμα**, ατος, τό, = νευρόσπαστον, in pl., *EM*454.17, Phot. s.v. θραύματα.

⊛ **νευροσπαστ-έω**, *put in motion by strings*, of puppets, D.S.34.34, M.Ant.7.3 (Pass.): esp. metaph., *draw as by a string*, Phld.*Hom.* p.62 O.; ἡ φαντασία σύρει ἡμᾶς καὶ ν. πρὸς αὐτήν Porph.ap.Stob.2.8.40, cf. Ph.1.28; καθ' ὁρμὴν -σπαστεῖσθαι M.Ant.6.16. **II.** Pass., *to be caught by drawing a string*, of birds, Ath.9.391a. **-ης**, ου, ὁ, *puppet-show man*, *IG*11(2).133.80 (Delos, ii B.C.), Arist.*Mu.*398$^{b}$16, Ath.1.19e. **-ία**, ἡ, *motion by means of strings*, metaph., M.Ant.6.28, 7.29. **-ικός**, ή, όν, *connected with puppet-shows*: ἡ -κὴ τέχνη Eust.457.38: also metaph., Alex.Aphr.*de An.*105.33. ⊛ **-ος**, ον, (σπάω) *drawn by strings*, ἀγάλματα ν. puppets *moved by strings*, Hdt.2.48; τὰ νευρόσπαστα *puppets*, X.*Smp.*4.55, Luc.*Syr.D.*16, etc.

**νευρο-στάται**, οἱ, dub. sens., Poll.7.154. **-στρόφος**, ὁ, *tightener of the strings* of a musical instrument, Porph.*Gaur.*12.1. **-τενής**, ές, *stretched by sinews*, παγὶς ν. a snare *of gut*, *AP*6.109 (Antip.). **-τομέω**, *cut the sinews*, Agathin.ap.Orib.10.7.9 (Pass.). **-τόμος**, ον, *cutting sinews*, Man.5.221. ⊛ **-τονον**, τό, *strand* of gut in a torsion-engine, f.l. in Hero *Bel.*83.4. **-τρωτος**, ον, *wounded in the sinews* or *tendons*, Dsc.1.58, Androm.ap.Gal.13.419, Gal.13.563, Alex.Aphr.*Pr.*1.50. **-χᾰρής**, ές, *delighting in the bowstring* or *in the lyre*, epith. of Apollo, *AP*9.525.14 (prob. for νεβροχαρῆ). **-χονδρώδης**, ες, *neuro-cartilaginous*, σῶμα Gal.*UP* 6.19, cf. 2.619.

**νευρ-όω**, *strain the sinews*, *nerve*, πάθος καὶ τοὺς ἀσθενεστάτους ν. Ph. 2.48:—Pass., σῶμα νεότητι καὶ ἀκμῇ νευρούμενον Alciphr.3.49. **2.** in Pass., *to be supplied with nerves*, *innervated*, παρά.. Gal.8.236; ἀπὸ.., ἐκ.., Id.*UP*9.15, 16.5. **II.** νενεύρωται, sens. obsc. (cf. νεῦρον V), but metaph., ν. ἥδε ξυμφορά Ar.*Lys.*1078. **-ώδης**, ες, = νευροειδής, *sinewy*, Hp.*VM*22 (Comp.); τένοντες Id.*Art.*30; κεφαλή Pl.*Ti.*75b; φλέψ Arist.*HA*497$^{a}$14, al.; μέρη Thphr.*Lass.*3 (Sup.); τόποι D.S. 2.56; ὀχετοί Aret.*SD*2.3; *muscular*, *strong*, Dicaearch.Hist.*Fr.*10 M.; τὸ ν. the *sinewy parts*, Antyll.ap.Orib.6.27.3, Gal.1.320, Orib. 5.29.7. **II.** τὸ ν. the *nervous system*, Gal.19.538.

**νεῦσις** (A), εως, ἡ, (νεύω) *inclination*, *tendency* of physical forces to or from a centre, Ti.Locr.100d. **2.** νεύσεις, αἱ, title of work by Apollonius of Perga, problems where a straight line has to be drawn through a point so as to intercept a given length between two lines or curves, Papp.670.4. **3.** *downward tendency*, *gravitation*, Plu. 2.1122c, prob. in Alex.Aphr.*Pr.*1.131. **4.** *tendency*, *inclination*, Plot.1.1.12. **5.** in Neo-Platonic philosophy, *declension* in the scale of Being, esp. of the Soul, ν. ἡ πρὸς σῶμα καὶ ὕλην Id.1.6.5; ν. εἰς or πρὸς τὴν γένεσιν, Hierocl.*in CA*26 p.479 M., Porph.*Antr.*11; ἡ πρὸς τὸ χεῖρον ν. Jul.*Or.*5.166d.

**νεῦσις** (B), εως, ἡ, (νέω A) *swimming*, Arist.*PA*639$^{b}$2, 694$^{b}$9, al.

**νευστ-άζω**, (νεύω) *nod*, νευστάζων κόρυθι βριαρῇ Il.20.162; ὀφρύσι νευστάζων, of one *making signs*, Od.12.194; ἧσται νευστάζων κεφαλῇ μεθύοντι ἐοικώς, of one fainting, 18.240, cf. 154, Theoc.25.260; ἐς χθόνα ν. Bion *Fr.*7.3; of an animal *lowering* its horns, Opp.*C.*2. 467. **-έον**, (νέω A) *one must swim*, Pl.*R.*453d. **-ήρ**, ῆρος, ὁ, (νέω A) *swimmer*, *sailor*, Hsch. (νευτήρ cod., fort. (ἀρ)νευτήρ). **-ικός** (A), ή, όν, (νέω A) *able to swim*, ζῷον Pl.*Sph.*220a; ν. μέρος animal family *that swims*, ib.221e; νευστικὸν μόνον ἰχθύς Arist.*HA*487$^{b}$22; τὰ νευστικά ib.489$^{b}$23. **-ικός** (B), ή, όν, (νεύω) *inclining*, *declining*, τὸ περὶ τὴν γῆν ν. Ph.2.513. **-ός**, ή, όν, (νέω A) = κολυμβάς, Luc. *Lex.*13.

⊛ **νεύω**, Il.13.133, etc.: fut. νεύσω Od.16.283, etc.: aor. ἔνευσα, Ep. νεῦσα (v. infr.): pf. νένευκα E.*IA*1581, etc. (fut. Med. νεύσομαι only in compds.):—*incline in any direction*: **1.** *nod*, *beckon*, as a sign, νεύσω μέν τοι ἐγὼ κεφαλῇ Od.16.283; νεῦσ' Αἴας Φοίνικι Il.9.223, cf. Od.17.330; νεῦσαν ἐς ἀλλήλους *h.Hom.*7.9; ὅρκος βέβαιός ἐστιν ἂν νεύσω μόνον Alex.91, cf. 178.3; *beckon* with the hand, δεξιᾷ δέ μοι ἔνευσε Ezek.*Exag.*73: c. inf., *beckon* to one to do a thing, in token of command, νεανίαις ἔνευσε παρθένον λαβεῖν E.*Hec.*545. **2.** *nod* or *bow in token of assent*, ἐπὶ γλεφάροις ν. Pi.*I.*8(7).50; νεῦσον, Κρονίων Id.*P.*1.71; νεῦσον, τέκνον, πείσθητι S.*Ph.*484, cf. Ar.*Pax* 883: c. acc. et inf., *grant*, *assure*, *promise that...*, νεῦσε δέ οἱ λαὸν σόον ἔμμεναι Il.8.246: c. inf. fut., Pi.*O.*7.67: c. inf. aor., *AP*6.244 (Crin.): c. acc. rei, *grant*, *promise*, νεῦσε δέ οἱ κούρην *h.Cer.*445, cf. 463; νεύσατε τὰν ἀδόκητον χάριν S.*OC*248 (lyr.), cf. E.*Alc.*978 (lyr.). **3.** generally, *nod*, *bend forward*, of warriors, Il.13. 133; νεῦον τὸ αἰδοῖον Hdt.2.48; λόφος καθύπερθεν ἔνευεν Il.3.337, cf. Alc.15.3, etc.; στάχυες νεύοιεν ἔραζε Hes.*Op.*473, etc.; ν. κάτω *stoop*, E.*El.*839; ν. ἐς τὴν γῆν Ar.*V.*1110, cf. Theoc.22.90: c. acc., οὕτω νῦν μνηστῆρες..νεύοιεν κεφαλὰς δεδμημένοι Od.18.237; ἐς πέδον κάρα νεῦσαι φόβῳ S.*Ant.*270, cf. 441. **4.** *incline*, *slope*, ν. ἀπό τινος εἴς τι *incline* towards, Th.4.100; εἰς τὸ αὐτὸ ν. *tend* to the same point, Pl.*Lg.*945d; πρὸς τὸ λυπῆσαν, πρὸς τοῖς ῥήμασιν, Alex.Aphr. *Pr.*1.48,78; of countries, etc., *slope*, ν. εἰς δύσεις, πρὸς τὸ πέλαγος, Plb.1.42.6, 1.73.5, etc.; of buildings, etc., *look*, *face*, εἰς νότον, etc., *PLond.*3.978 (iv A.D.), etc.; μηδαμοῦ ν. *to be in equilibrium*, Plb.6.10. 7; ταῖς πρῴραις ἔξω νεύοντα τὰ σκάφη Id.1.26.12: Geom., of straight lines, *verge*, *tend* to a point (i.e. to pass through it when produced), Arist.*APo.*76$^{b}$9, Apollon.Perg.1.2, etc.: metaph., *to be inclined*, ἄλλως ν. Theoc.7.109; ν. εἰς ὀργάν, εἰς ἔλεον, *APl.*4.136 (Antiphil.); ἐπὶ χάριν Phalar.*Ep.*78; πρὸς γαστέρα Ath.14.659a; πρὸς θῆλυ *Trag. Adesp.*355. **II.** metaph., *decline*, *fall away*, ἐκ..τῶν ποτε λαμπρῶν νεύει βίοτος, νεύει δὲ τύχα E.*Fr.*153: in Neo-Platonic philosophy, *decline*, *sink* in the scale of Being, Plot.2.9.4, etc. **III.** νεύει· ἐπανέρχεται ἢ μᾶλλον φεύγει, Hsch. **IV.** Pass., only pf. part. νενευμένος *inclined*, Teucer in *Cat.Cod.Astr.*7.202. (Cf. Skt. *návate* 'turn round', Lat. *nuo*.)

⊛ **νεφέλη**, ἡ, (νέφος) *cloud*, *mass of clouds* (distd. from ὀμίχλη, *mist* or *fog*, Arist.*Mete.*346$^{b}$33), Il.15.20, Hes.*Th.*745, etc.; ν. κυανέη, πορφυρέη, Od.12.75, Il.17.551; ἐριβρόμον νεφέλας στρατός Pi.*P.*6.11; νεφέλαι πόκοις ἐρίων ὅμοιαι Thphr.*Sign.*13.—Mostly poet., but found in X.*An.*1.8.8, Arist., Thphr. ll. cc., and in late Prose, Plu.2.777e, Philostr.*Ep.*24. **2.** metaph., νεφέλη δέ μιν ἀμφεκάλυψε κυανέη, of death, Il.20.417; τὸν δ' ἄχεος νεφέλη ἐκάλυψε μέλαινα *a cloud* of sorrow, 17.591, cf. S.*Ant.*528 (anap.); πολέμου ν. Simon.89; φόνου ν. Pi.*N.* 9.38, cf. *I.*7(6).27; Κενταύρου φονίᾳ νεφέλᾳ, i.e. with his blood, S. *Tr.*831 (lyr.); κελαινῶπις ν., of sleep, Pi.*P.*1.7. **II.** of *clouds* in urine, Hp.*Prog.*12, Gal.6.252. **2.** = νεφέλιον II.2, Hp.*Prorrh.*2. 20. **3.** *cloud* on a mirror, Arist.*Insomn.*459$^{b}$30. **III.** *fine bird-net*, in pl., Ar.*Av.*194,528 (anap.), Call.*Aet.*3.1.37, Gal.*UP*1.2, Ath.1.25d: in sg., *AP*6.11 (Satyr.), 109 (Antip.), 185 (Zos.). **IV.** Alchem., *sublimate*, Ps.-Democr.Alch.p.50 B.

⊛ **νεφελη-γερέτᾰ**, Ep. for -της, ὁ, (ἀγείρω) used by Hom. only in nom. and in gen. νεφεληγερέταο, *cloud-gatherer*, of Zeus, Il.1.511, al.; acc., ἀέρα νεφεληγερέτην Emp.149. **-γερής**, έος, ὁ, = foreg., Q.S. 4.80. **-δόν**, Adv. *in the manner of clouds*, Nonn.*D.*15.1.

**νεφελ-ίζω**, *wrap in clouds*, in Pass., Sch.Il.15.153. **-ιον**, τό, Dim. of νεφέλη, Arist.*Mete.*367$^{b}$9, Thphr.*Sign.*11,20. **2.** Astron., *nebula*, Ptol.*Alm.*7.5, al., Vett.Val.110.12. **II.** of *clouds* in urine, Hp.*Coac.*571, etc. **2.** *cloud-like opacity* on the eye, Dsc.2.151, Gal.19.534. **3.** *white speck* on the nails, Poll.2.146.

⊛ **νεφελο-ειδής**, ές, *cloud-like*, συστροφαί, of nebulae or star-clusters, Gem.3.4, Ptol.*Tetr.*149; ἀστήρ Hipparch.2.5.15; also of urine, *cloudy*, Hp.*Acut.*(*Sp.*)17. **-κένταυρος**, ὁ, *cloud-centaur*, Luc.*VH* 1.16: partly as *sprung from Ixion and the cloud*, partly as a fantastic shape such as the clouds assume. **-κοκκῡγία**, ἡ, (κόκκυξ) *Cloud-cuckoo-town*, built by the birds in Ar.*Av.*819, al., a satire on Athens. **-κοκκῡγιεύς**, έως, ὁ, *Cloud-cuckoo-town-man*, ib.878, 1035. **-μῐγής**, ές, *mingled with cloud*, πῦρ *Placit.*3.3.4. **-ομαι**, Pass., *to be clouded over*, Eust.127.21. **-στάσια** [στᾰ], τά, (νεφέλη III, ἵστημι) *place where nets are set to catch birds*, Id.1928. 37. **-φόρος**, ον, *bringing clouds*, Lyd.*Mag.*3.32.

**νεφελ-ώδης**, ες, *cloudy*, *bringing clouds*, ὁ νότος Arist.*Pr.*942$^{a}$ 37; κόνις Polyaen.4.6.13. **II.** *clouded*, of the eye, Gal.10. 1019. **-ωτός**, ή, όν, *clouded*: *made of clouds*, Luc.*VH*1.19.

**νεφο-ειδής**, ές, = νεφελοειδής, Epicur.*Ep.*2 p.51 U., *AP*9.396 (Paul. Sil.). ⊛ **-ομαι**, Pass., *to be clouded over*, Nic.Dam.68 J., Ph.2.21, Adam.*Vent.*35, Porph.*Antr.*27: metaph., νενεφωμένα βουλεύοντες Man.4.518. **-ποίητος**, ον, *made of clouds*, Dam.*Isid.*69.

⊛ **νέφος**, εος, τό, *cloud*, *mass of clouds*, Il.4.275, al.; σμικροῦ νέφους ἐκπνεύσας μέγας χειμὼν S.*Aj.*1148; ν. ὄμβριον Ar.*Nu.*288 (lyr.); ν. καὶ ὁμίχλη Pl.*Ti.*49c; τὸν κίνδυνον παρελθεῖν ὥσπερ ν. D.18.188. **2.** metaph. (cf. νεφέλη I.2), θανάτου δὲ μέλαν ν. ἀμφεκάλυψεν Il.16.350, cf. Od.4.180, B.12.64; λάθας ν. Pi.*O.*7.45; σκότου ν., of blindness, S.*OT*1314 (lyr.); ν. οἰμωγῆς, στεναγμῶν, E.*Med.*107 (anap.), *HF* 1140; ὀφρύων ν. *a cloud upon* the brow, Id.*Hipp.*172 (anap.); ὑπὸ τοῦ μετώπου οἷον ν. ἐπανεστηκός Arist.*Phgn.*809$^{b}$22; διασκεδᾶτε τὸ προσὸν νῦν ν. ἐπὶ τοῦ προσώπου Anaxandr.58. **II.** metaph., also, *a cloud of men*, etc., ν. πεζῶν, Τρώων, Il.4.274, 16.66; ψαρῶν, κολοιῶν, 17.755; ν. τοσοῦτον ἀνθρώπων Hdt.8.109; πενεστάων ν. Timo 39; μαρτύρων *Ep. Hebr.*12.1; πολέμοιο ν. *the cloud* of battle, *thick* of the fight, Il.17.243, cf. Ar.*Pax* 1090: applied by Pi.*N.*10.9 to a single hero: used by Prose writers for poet. νεφέλη (q.v.). (Cf. Skt. *nábhas* 'fog', 'cloud', Slav. *nebo* 'heaven', Lat. *nebula*.)

**νέφρ-ησις**, εως, ἡ, *pain in the kidneys*, dub. in *Gloss.* **-ιαῖος**, α, ον, (νεφρός) *of the kidneys*, στέαρ Dsc.2.76; τὸ ν. (to be read for νεφρίδιον) Hp.*Mul.*2.164. **-ικός**, ή, όν, f.l. for νεφριτικός, Dsc. 1.6. **-ίον**, τό, Dim. of νεφρός, *POxy.*1081 9 (ii/iii A.D.). **II.** = ἐλαφόβοσκον, Ps.-Dsc.3.69 (nisi leg. νέβρειον). **-ίτης** [ῑ], ὁ,

fem. **νεφρῖτις,** ἡ, = *νεφριαῖος, σφόνδυλος,* i.e. the first vertebra of the sacrum, Poll.2.179; *νόσον νεφρῖτιν* Th.7.15; *φθίσις ν.* Hp.*Int.*15: also as Subst. *νεφρῖτις* (sc. *νόσος*), ἡ, Id.*Coac.*502: in pl., Id.*Aph.*3.31, Dsc.1.14. **-ῑτῐκός,** ή, όν, *of the kidneys, νοσήματα* Hp.*Art.*41; *τὰ ν.* Id.*Aph.*6.6. II. *affected with νεφρῖτις,* Dsc.1.15, Apollon. ap.Gal.13.326, Gal.*Nat.Fac.*1.13. III. of remedies, *suitable for such cases,* Alex.Trall.11.2.

**νεφροειδής,** ές, *like a kidney,* Arist.*HA*508$^a$30.

⊛ **νεφρ-ός,** ὁ, in pl., *kidneys,* Diog.Apoll.6, Hp.*Aph.*4.78, Pl.*Ti.*91a, etc.: in dual, Ar.*Ra.*475: rarely in sg., Id.*Lys.*962, Euphro 1.25: euphem. for *ὄρχεις,* Philippid.5.4: metaph., Lxx *Ps.*15(16).7. (Cf. OHG. *nioro* 'kidney', Praenest. *nefrones,* Lanuv. *nebrundines* 'kidneys', 'testicles'.) **-ώδης,** ες, = *νεφροειδής,* Arist.*PA*670$^b$13.

**νεφ-ύδριον,** τό, Dim. of *νέφος,* Olymp.*in Mete.*215.25. **-ώδης,** ες, = *νεφοειδής,* like a cloud, Str.3.2.7. II. *cloudy, bringing clouds, ὁ νότος* Arist.*Pr.*942$^a$35. 2. of the voice, *husky,* Id.*Aud.*800$^a$14. ⊛ **-ωσις,** εως, ἡ, (*νεφόομαι*) *overclouding,* Ph.1.27, Hld.9.9 codd. (pl.), Al.*Jb.*3.5.

**Νεφώτης,** ου, ὁ, epith. of Zeus in Egypt, prob. = *Nefr-hotep, OGI* 676 (ii A.D.).

⊛ **νέω** (A), *νεῖ* Pl.*R.*453d, *νέομεν* Pi.*Fr.*218 codd. Ath.; inf. *νεῖν* Epich.53, Th.7.30; part. *νέων* Od.5.344, Pl.*R.*529c: impf. *ἔνεον* Ar.*Eq.*321; Ep. *ἔννεον* Il.21.11; poet. *νέον* Alc.143: fut. *νεύσομαι* Hsch., *νευσοῦμαι* v.l. in X.*An.*4.3.12: aor. *ἔνευσα* (δι–) Pl.*Prm.*137a, (ἐξ–) E.*Hipp.*470, Th.2.90: pf. *νένευκα* (δια–) Pl.*R.*441c:—*swim, χείρεσσι νέων* Od.5.344; *ἶξε νέων* ib.442; *νέειν οὐκ ἐπιστάμενοι* Hdt. 8.89, cf. 6.44; *οὔτε ἐπιστ. νεῖν* Th.7.30; *νεῖν οὐκ ἴσαντι* Epich. l.c. 2. metaph., of shoes that are too large, *ἔνεον ἐν ταῖς ἐμβάσιν* *was floating* in my shoes, as if they were boats, Ar.*Eq.*321; *νεῖν ἐξ ὑπτίας,* v. *ὕπτιος* II. fin. (Prob. cogn. with *νάω,* Lat. *nare*)

⊛ **νέω** (B), fut. *νήσω*: aor. 1 *ἔνησα*:—**Pass.,** aor. *ἐνήθην*: pf. *νένησμαι* (ἐπι–) Ps.-Luc.*Philopatr.*14:—*spin,* Hom. only aor. Med., *ἅσσα οἱ κατὰ Κλῶθες νήσαντο* the happenings which they *spun out* to him, Od. 7.198; of a spider, *νῇ νήματα* Hes.*Op.*777; *στήμονα μακρὸν ἔνησα* Batr.183; *πέπλους τε νῆσαι* S.*Fr.*439; *στήμονα νήσω* Ar.*Lys.*519; *νῶσαι μαλθακωτάτην κρόκην* Eup.319; *τὰ νηθέντα* Pl.*Plt.*282e: 3 pl. *νῶσι* occurs in Ael.*NA*7.12 (as if from *νάω*), cf. Poll.7.32, 10.125, *EM*344.1; and Hsch. cites *νῶντα· νήθοντα*; in Eup. l.c. Meineke restores *νῆσαι* for *νῶσαι.* (Cf. Lat. *neo* 'spin', OHG. *nāan* 'sew', etc.)

**νέω** (C), fut. *νήσω* Suid.: aor. *ἔνησα* (v. infr.):—**Med.,** fut. (in pass. sense) *νήσομαι* Hsch. (v. infr.): aor. *ἐνησάμην* Polyaen.8.65:—**Pass.,** aor. *ἐνήσθην* Arr.*An.*7.3.2, Porph.*Abst.*2.54, also *ἐνήθην* (ἐπ–) prob. in Hdn.4.2.10: pf. *νένημαι* *IG*2$^2$.1522.23 (iv B.C.), X. (v. infr.), perh. also *νένησμαι* (v. infr.); Ion. 3 pl. *νενέαται* (συν–) Hdt.2.135; 3 sg. plpf. *ἐνένηστο* Ael.*VH*5.6: pres. only in compds. *ἐπι–, περι-νέω* (qq.v.):—*heap, pile up, πυρὴν νῆσαι pile* a funeral pyre, Hdt. 1.50, cf. Ar.*Lys.*269, Th.2.52, Porph. l.c. (Pass.); *νήσαντες ξύλα* E. *HF*243; *ἀμφορῆς νενησμένοι* Ar.*Nu.*1203; *ἄρτοι νενημένοι* X.*An.*5. 4.27; *νῶντος,* glossed *σωρεύοντος,* Phot. II. in Pass., *to be stuffed,* c. gen., *νενημένην χοῖρον πολλῆς φορίνης* Herod.4.15; cf. *νησόμεθα· κορεσθησόμεθα,* Hsch. (Contr. from *νηέω,* q.v.)

⊛ **νέω** (D), Dor. Adv., in the phrase *ἐς νέω,* = *εἰς νέωτα, next year, Riv.Fil.*56.266 (Cyrene, dub.), v.l. in Theoc.15.143 (cf. *Riv.Fil.*56. 413); *εἰς νέων* dub. in *BGU*958c13 (iii A.D.).

**νεώ,** Att. gen. and later acc. of *νεώς* (*ναός*).

⊛ **νεωκορ-έω,** *to be a νεωκόρος, serve, tend,* in Pass., *Ἑστία.. ὑπὸ παρθένων νεωκορεῖται* Corn.*ND*28, cf. *BMus.Inscr.*481*.153 (Ephesus, ii A.D.). 2. ironically, *sweep clean, clean out, plunder a temple,* Pl. *R.*574d. 3. *honour with a temple, τὸν αὐτῶν σύμμαχον* (sc. *θεόν*) J.*BJ*5.9.4. II. metaph., *keep clean and pure, νεωκορεῖν ἔρωτα cherish* love *in a pure heart* (as in a temple), Luc.*Am.*48. **-ία,** Ion. **-ίη,** ἡ, *office of a νεωκόρος,* Ph.1.695, Plu.2.351e, *IG*14.1026, Man. 4.430 (pl.): written **νεοκορεία** in *IGRom.*3.584 (Sidyma). ⊛ **-ιον,** τό, *sacristy, IG*11(2).144*B*17 (Delos, iv B.C.), 2$^2$.1672.181, al., *BCH* 35.243 (pl., Delos, ii B.C.), *IPE*2.342.4 (Phanagoria): Dor. **νᾱκορεῖον** *IG*4$^2$(1).109 ii 127 (Epid., iii B.C.). ⊛ **-ος,** ὁ, Dor. **νᾱοκόρος** *GDI* 2116.14, al. (Delph., ii B.C.), Hsch.: contr. **νᾱκόρος** *PMagd.*35.7 (iii B.C., prob. Dor.), *GDI*1912.9, al. (Delph., ii B.C.), 5087 (Crete): as fem., *IG*4$^2$(1).393, al. (Epid., ii A.D.); **ναυκόρος,** ἡ, Buresch *Aus Lydien* p.58: poet. **νηοκόρος** *AP*9.22 (Phil.):—*warden of a temple,* as a sacred officer, *τοῖς ἱεροῖς ν. γίγνεσθαι* Pl.*Lg.*759a; *ἱερέας τε καὶ ν.* ib.953a; *παρὰ Μεγαβύξῳ τῷ τῆς Ἀρτέμιδος ν.* X.*An.*5.3.6, cf. *Inscr. Prien.*231 (iv B.C.); *βωμοῖο ν. AP*11.324 (Autom.); *ν. τοῦ μεγάλου Σαράπιδος POxy.*100.2 (ii A.D.). 2. *sacristan,* Herod.4.41,45, Paus.10.12.5; *ἐνβόλιον ἔχων ν.* in a list of silver articles, *IG*7.3498.25 (Oropus). II. title assumed by Asiatic cities in Imperial times, when they had built a temple in honour of their patron-god or the Emperor, as Ephesus, *ν. Ἀρτέμιδος Act.Ap.*19.35; also as Adj., *τῷ ν. Ἐφεσίων δήμῳ OGI*481.3 (ii A.D.), cf. *BMus.Inscr.*481*.4 (Ephesus, ii A.D.); *δὶς ν. τῶν Σεβαστῶν,* of Ephesus, *OGI*496.7 (ii A.D.); of Smyrna, *IGRom.*4.1419. (Prob. derived from *κορέω, sweep,* the orig. sense being prob. *temple-sweeper,* cf. E.*Ion* 115, 121, 795 (where the word does not occur), *νεωκορέω* I.2, II, Ph.2.236, Hsch.; but Suid. expl. it *ὁ τὸν νεὼν κοσμῶν.., ἀλλ' οὐχ ὁ σαίρων.*)

⊛ **νεωλκ-έω,** *haul a ship up on land,* Thphr.*HP*5.7.2, Plb.1.29.3; *τὰ σκάφη* D.S.20.47: abs., Aristonym.ap.Stob.4.33.29:—Pass., *νενεωλκημένα* [*πλοῖα*] Ath.8.350b, cf. Alciphr.1.1: metaph., of a corpse, *τὸ –ημένον ἐν τῇ κλίνῃ* Phld.*Mort.*28. **-ία,** ἡ, *hauling up a ship into dock,* Aen.Tact.17.1, Arist.*Ph.*253$^b$18, Thphr.*HP*5.7.2 (pl.), *IG*2$^2$. 1028.37 (pl.): metaph., *σῶμα ὥσπερ ἐν ν. τῇ σχολῇ τεθεραπευμένον* Plu.2.136a. ⊛ **-ιον,** τό, *dry dock,* in pl., App.*BC*5.100, Hsch. s.v. *νεῶνας* (*νεόλκια* cod.). **-ός,** ὁ, (*ναῦς, ἕλκω*) *one who hauls up a ship into dock,* Arist.*Ph.*250$^a$18, *SIG*1000.22 (Cos, i B.C.), Poll.7.190, 10. 148.

⊛ **νέωμα,** ατος, τό, (*νεόω*) *fallow land just broken up,* Lxx *Je.*4.3 (pl.).

**νεών,** ῶνος, ὁ, (*ναῦς*) = *νεώριον,* Hsch. (pl.); Ion., acc. to Phot.

**νεώνητος,** ον, *newly bought,* of slaves, Ar.*Eq.*2, Timocl.7.2, Ph.2. 73, cf. Ar.*Pl.*769; *κύνες* Aristo *Stoic.*1.88; *ἀγρός* App.*BC*4.41.

**νεωνία,** ἡ, a kind of *olive,* Hsch.

⊛ **νεω-ποιεῖον,** τό, *office of the νεωποῖαι, Supp.Epigr.*2.568 (Didyma, ii B.C.). **-ποιέω,** serve as *νεωποίης,* Poll.1.11, *Supp.Epigr.*1.371 (Samos, ii A.D.):—also **νεοποιέω,** *OGI*485.8 (Magn. Mae.), *Ephes.*2 No.47: Dor. **νᾱοποιέω** *SIG*241.6 (Delph., iv B.C.), *IG*7.3073.6 (Lebad.). **-ποίης,** ου, ὁ, *official in charge of the temple-fabric, οἱ ν. τῶν θεῶν SIG*46.6 (Halic., v B.C.), cf. 353.1 (Ephesus, iv B.C.), etc.:—also **-πόης,** *Inscr.Prien.*195.4 (iii/ii B.C.), 174.31 (ii B.C.); **νεοποίης,** *Supp.Epigr.*1.395 (Samos, i A.D.), *Ephes.*2 No.83: Dor. **νᾱποίας** *SIG* 1023.33, al. (Cos); **νᾱπόας** *IGRom.*4.1097, 1098, *SIG*793 (ibid., i A.D.). **-ποιία,** ἡ, *office of νεωποίης, Inscr.Prien.*174.29 (ii B.C.; *–ποΐα*): Dor. **νᾱοποιία** *SIG*241.5 (Delph., iv B.C.). **-ποιικός,** ή, όν, *relating to νεωποῖαι,* in Dor. form **νᾱοποϊκός,** *νόμος IG*7.3073.88 (Lebad.). ⊛ **-ποίιον,** τό, in Dor. form **ναοποίιον,** = *νεωποιία, SIG* 479.7 (Delph., iii B.C.). ⊛ **-ποιός,** ὁ, = *νεωποίης, IG*2$^2$.1678*bA*14:—Dor. **νᾱοποιός** Arist.*Rh.*1374$^b$27, *SIG*236*B*, al. (Delph., iv B.C.), *IG* 7.3073.4, al. (Lebad.); also in Att. Inscrr. from late iv B.C., ib.2$^2$.1678 *aA*16,20. II. (*ναῦς*) *building ships,* Poll.1.84.

**νεωρέω,** *to be overseer of a dockyard,* Eust.1562.37, Hsch., Phot.

⊛ **νεώρης,** ες (on the accent v. Hdn.Gr.1.72), (*ὄρνυμι*) *new, fresh, νεώρη βόστρυχον τετμημένον* a lock of hair *just cut off,* S.*El.*901; *εἰληφότας φόβον νεώρη* Id.*OC*730; *ν. ψόφος* Id.*Ichn.*154; *ἄλλο νεῶρες πῆμα* Philet.1.

⊛ **νεώρ-ιον,** τό, (*νεωρός*) *dockyard, IG*1$^2$.57.53, al., Ar.*Ach.*918, Th.2. 93, 3.74, etc.: in pl., E.*Hel.*1530, Ar.*Av.*1540, Th.3.92, Lys.12.99, 13.46, Pl.*Criti.*115c, etc. **-ιοφύλαξ** [ῠ], ἄκος, ὁ, gloss on *νεωρός,* Hsch. **-ίς,** ίδος, ἡ, = *νεώριον,* Str.1.3.20 (sed leg. *νεωρίων*). **-ός,** ὁ, (*ναῦς, οὖρος*) *superintendent of a dockyard,* Hsch.: pl., *IG*1$^2$.74.11.

⊛ **νέωρος,** ον, = *νεώρης,* Hdn.Gr.1.200, Hsch., Phot.

**νε-ώροφος,** ον, (*ὀροφή*) *newly roofed, οἶκος IG*11(2).163*A*10, al. (Delos, iii B.C.). **-ωρῠχής,** ές, (*νέος, ὀρύσσω*) *newly dug,* Nic.*Th.* 940.

**νεώς,** ώ, ὁ, v. *ναός.*

**νεώσοικος,** ὁ, (*ναῦς, οἶκος*) *dock,* Ar.*Ach.*96: mostly in pl., *ship-sheds, slips,* in which ships might be built, repaired, or laid up in winter, Hdt.3.45, Cratin.197, And.3.7, Th.7.25,64, Lys.30.22, *IG*2$^2$. 505.14: divisim, *ἐν Πειραιεῖ νεὼς εἰσιν οἶκοι* Paus.1.29.16.

**νεώσσω,** Att. **-ττω,** (*νέος*) = *νεόω, νεωτερίζω,* Hdn.Gr.1.447, Hsch.

**νεωστί,** Adv. of *νέος,* for *νέως, lately, just now,* Hdt.1.196, 2.15,49, al., S.*El.*1049, Th.4.108, Pl.*Grg.*503c, Antiph.58.4, etc.

⊛ **νέωτα,** Adv. *next year,* Semon.1.9; elsewh. only *εἰς* (*ἐς*) *ν.* X.*Cyr.* 7.2.13, 8.6.15, Thphr.*Char.*3.4; *ἀεὶ γεωργὸς εἰς ν. πλούσιος* Philem. 82; *τὰ μὲν νῦν, τὰ δ' εἰς ν.* Thphr.*HP*9.11.9; *ὁ εἰς ν. καρπός* Id.*CP*3. 16.2; *ταγοὺς τοὺς ἐν ν.* prob. in *Schwyzer* 323*A*12 (Delph., v/iv B.C.); cf. *νέω* (D).

**νεώτατος,** η, ον, Sup. of *νέος.*

**νεωτερ-ίζω,** Att. fut. *–ιῶ* Th.4.51: (*νεώτερος* II):—*make innovations, περὶ γυμναστικὴν καὶ μουσικήν* Pl.*R.*424b; *ἐν ταῖς παιδιαῖς* Id.*Lg.*798c; of climatic change, *ν. ἐς τὴν ἀσθένειαν change* [health] into sickness, Th.7.87. 2. freq. with an implication of violence, *use forcible measures, μὴ σφῶν πέρι ν. μηδέν* Id.1.58; *ἔς τινάς τι ν.* Id.4.51; *ἐς οὐδένα οὐδὲν ἐνεωτέριζον* Id.2.3, cf. X.*HG*2.1.5, D.23.133; *ν. περί τινα* Isoc.*Ep.*7.9:—also in Med., *take the law into one's own hands, POxy.* 237 vi 3 (ii A.D.). II. esp. *attempt political changes, make revolutionary movements, τοῖς ἀτυχοῦσι νεωτερίζειν συμφέρει* Antipho 2.4.9; *ἀπὸ μόνης ν. τῆς ἀσπίδος* Critias 37 D.; *πρὸς τοὺς ξυμμάχους νεωτερίζοντας* Th.1.97, cf. 102; *ν. ἔργῳ* Id.3.66; *νεωτερίζειν ἐβούλετο ἐς τὸ πλῆθος* Lys.20.16; *τὸ νεωτερίζον* the *revolutionary party,* J.*BJ Prooem.* 2; *νεωτερίσαι τὴν πολιτείαν revolutionize* the state, Th.1.115:—Pass., *ἐνεωτερίζετο τὰ περὶ τὴν ὀλιγαρχίαν* Id.8.73, cf. 4.76. **-ικός,** ή, όν, *natural to a youth, youthful, ἀγωγή* Plb.10.21.7; *αὐθάδεια* J.*AJ*16. 11.8; *ἐπιθυμίαι* 2*Ep.Ti.*2.22; *ἁμαρτήματα* Vett.Val.118.3. Adv. **-κῶς** Plu.*Dio*4. II. *modern in style, κάτοπτρον POxy.*1449.56 (iii A.D.). **-ῐσις,** εως, ἡ, *revolution,* Heph.Astr.1.21. **-ισμα,** ατος, τό, *change, ἀέρος* Ph.ap.Eus.*PE*8.11. **-ισμός,** ὁ, *attempt to change*; esp. in bad sense, *innovation, revolutionary movement,* Pl.*R.*422a, 555d, D.17.15, etc.: pl., Pl.*Lg.*758c; *ἔφορος ἐπὶ τῶν ν.,* title of official at Sparta, *BSA*27.234 (ii A.D.). 2. generally, *change,* as of diet, Sabin.ap.Gal.17(1).562. **-ιστής,** οῦ, ὁ, *innovator,* D.H.5.75, J. *Vit.*27, Plu.*Cim.*17. **-ιστικός,** ή, όν, *given to innovation,* esp. in language, *ῥήτωρ* Poll.4.36.

**νεωτεροποι-έω,** *make innovations,* D.H.6.75; *try experiments,* Hp.*Aph.*1.20: c. acc., *revolutionize, τὰ κατὰ τὴν Ἰουδαίαν* J.*AJ*14.11. 3:—Pass., *ὅταν μή τι –ηθῇ* Hp.*Epid.*2.1.4. II. = *νεαροποιέω* (q.v.), *ν. τοὺς ἡλκωμένους τόπους* Gal.10.257. ⊛ **-ία,** ἡ, *revolutionary spirit,* Th.1.102; *revolution,* Nic.Dam.130.20 J., J.*AJ*14.15.6, al. **-ός,** όν, *innovating, revolutionary,* Th.1.70, Arist.*Pol.*1266$^b$14; *φύσει Ἕλληνες ν.* Iamb.*Myst.*7.5; *τὸ ν. τινός* Ael.*VH*12.16.

⊛ **νεώτερος,** α, ον, Comp. of *νέος,* of persons, *younger, γενεῆφι ν.* Il.

21.439; ὧν φύσει ν. S.*OC*1295; *too young*, Od.21.132; *a minor*, Th. 3.26; οἱ ν. *men of military age*, Id.5.50; τὸ πρεσβύτερόν τε καὶ τὸ ν. ib.64: c. gen., οἱ ν. τῶν πεπραγμένων those who are *too young to remember* the events, D.18.50; οἱ ν. the *new school*, of poets, Cic.*Att.*7.2.1; of poets later than Homer, Sch.Il.16.574, 24.257. 2. Sup., γενεῇ δὲ νεώτατος ἔσκον ἁπάντων Il.7.153, etc.; ἡ ν. δημοκρατία, opp. ἡ πατρία δ., Arist.*Pol.*1305ᵃ29. II. of events, *newer, more recent*, νεώτερον κακόν Pi.*P.*4.155; *of recent origin*, Δημόκριτος μουσικήν φησι ν. εἶναι Phld.*Mus.*p.108K.: metaph., *later, worse*, ν. βούλευμα S.*Ph.* 560; νεώτερον πρήσσειν contrive *calamity, injury*, Hdt.5.106: freq. with τι, ἤν τι καταλαμβάνῃ ν. τὸν πεζὸν [στρατόν] Id.8.21; δέδοικα μή τι δρᾷ ν. Ar.*Ec.*338, cf. Pi.*Fr.*107.6, Theoc.24.40; μή τι ν. ἀγγέλλεις; Pl.*Prt.*310b; νεώτερόν τι ποιεῖν ἔς τινα Th.1.132; κατὰ τὴν Ἑλλάδα Hdt.8.142; περὶ πόλιν Ἑλλάδα Id.5.93; νεώτερα βουλεύειν περί τινος Id.1.210; μηδὲν νεώτερον ποιεῖν περὶ ἀνδρῶν Th.2.6. 2. freq. of rebellion or violent revolution, ν. τι ποιέειν Hdt.5.35, etc.; ν. πρήγματα πρήξειν ib.19; νεωτέρων πραγμάτων ἐπιθυμεῖν Isoc.7.59, X.*HG*5.2.9, etc.

**νεω-τευκτικά**, τά, *concerning temple-building*, as title of a book, Suid. s. v. Ὀρφεύς (νεο- codd.). **-φύλαξ** [ῠ], ἄκος, ὁ, Att. for ναοφύλαξ, *Gloss.*

**νεώχερμος**· γῆ νεωστὶ εἰργασμένη, Hsch. (Cf. χερμάζω.)

✱ **νη-**, neg. Prefix used in poet. words, combining with short α, ε or ο, as in νηλεής, νήριθμος, νήκεστος, νήνεμος, νηπελέω, νῆστις, νωδός, νώδυνος, or before consonants, as in νηκερδής, νήκερως, νηπαθής, νηπενθής, νήποινος. (Cf. Lat. *nĕ*-; η arises from I.-E. contraction and is used by analogy in combination with consonants.)

✱ **νή**, Particle of strong affirmation, with acc. of the divinity invoked, once in Trag., ν. τὼ Λαπέρσα, ν. τὸν Εὐρώταν τρίτον, ν. τοὺς ἐν Ἄργει καὶ κατὰ Σπάρτην θεούς S.*Fr.*957; freq. in Com. and Prose, esp. in the phrase νὴ Δία, Ar.*Eq.*319, *Th.*240, etc.; with the Art., ν. τὸν Δία Id.*Pl.*202, Antiph.179.3, etc.; with the names of other gods, usu. c. Art., ν. τὴν Δήμητρα Pherecr.24; ν. τὴν Ἀθηνᾶν Ar.*Pax* 218; ν. τὸν Ἀπόλλω Id.*Ec.*160; ν. τὴν Ἄρτεμιν ib.90; ν. τὸν Ποσειδῶ Id.*Nu.*83, Eup.265; ν. τὼ θεώ (Demeter and Cora) Ar.*Lys.*51, Men.*Georg.*24 (a woman's oath, acc. to Phryn.171; ν. τὼ σιώ (of the Dioscuri) used by a Spartan, Plu.2.234f); ν. τὴν Ἥραν Pl.*Phdr.*230b; ν. τὴν Ἑστίαν Antiph.185; ν. τὴν Ἀφροδίτην Ar.*Ec.*189, Nicostr.Com.35; ν. τὸν κύνα, v. κύων 1 fin.; ν. τοὺς θεούς Ar.*Pl.*74, Pl.*R.*531a, al.; ν. θεούς Hp. *Ep.*17; ν. τόν alone, Ph.2.271. II. ν. (τὸν) Δία is also used, 1. in answering questions, X.*Cyr.*1.3.6, Pl.*Prt.*312a, etc.: in a supposed answer from antagonists, folld. by γάρ, D.8.16. 2. in introducing objections or contentions supposed to come from antagonists, folld. by γάρ, Id.19.285; folld. by ἀλλά, Id.18.117, 19.272; preceded by ἀλλά, X.*HG*7.3.10, *Mem.*1.2.9, D.24.125, al. 3. to add force by way of climax, ἄλλως τε μέντοι ν. Δία πάντως καὶ.. Pl.*Ap.*35d, cf. X.*HG*1.7.21. 4. in adjurations, Ar.*Av.*661, *Ra.* 164.

**νῆ**, contr. for νέα, v. νέος.

**νῆα, νῆας**, v. ναῦς: **νῆαδε**, Adv. *to the ship*, Od.13.19; μετὰ νῆαδε A.R.4.1768.

**νηάς**, άδος, ἡ, a gigantic animal, whose fossil remains were found in Samos, Euph.ap.Ael.*NA*17.28: prov., μεῖζον βοᾷ τῶν νηάδων ibid.

**νήατος**, v. νέατος (A).

**νηγάτεος** [ᾰ], η, ον, Ep. Adj. of doubtful meaning and derivation, perh. *newly made*, χιτών, κρήδεμνον, Il.2.43, 14.185; φᾶρος *h.Ap.* 122; καλύβαι A.R.1.775.

**νήγρετος**, ον, (νη-, ἐγείρω) *unwaking*, νήγρετος ὕπνος *sound* sleep, Od.13.80, *h.Ven.*177; of death, εὕδομες εὖ μάλα μακρὸν ἀτέρμονα ν. ὕπνον Mosch.3.104: in late Prose, Aret.*SD*2.13: neut. as Adv., νήγρετον *without waking*, ν. εὕδειν Od.13.74; ν. ὑπνοῦν, of death, *AP* 7.305 (Adaeus).

**νήδυια**, ων, τά, *bowels, entrails*, Il.17.524, A.R.2.113, Nic.*Al.* 381.

**νηδύμιος** [ῠ], η, ον, = sq., Opp.*H.*3.412.

**νήδῠμος**, ον, = ἥδυμος (q.v.), from which it arises through false division in the Homeric text, in Hom. always epith. of ὕπνος, Il. 2.2, al., also *h.Ven.*171. II. in later Poets, not confined to ὕπνος, *sweet, delightful*, δονάκων Μοῦσα ν. *h.Pan.*16; ν. Ὀρφεύς *APl.* 4.217; ν. ὕδωρ Nonn.*D.*48.602; ἄνθος ib.12.176. (Derived by Aristarch. from νη-, δύνω.)

✱ **νηδύς**, ύος, ἡ, *any of the cavities* in the body, Hp.*deArte*10: hence, 1. *stomach*, Od.9.296, Hes.*Th.*487, S.*OC*1263, etc. 2. *belly, paunch*, Il.13.290, Hdt.2.47. 3. *bowels*, A.*Ch.*757, Hp. *Aër.*19, etc.; ἐξελεῖν τὴν νηδὺν Hdt.2.87; as the seat of thirst, τέγξας ἄδιψον νηδύν E.*Cyc.*574; ἄρδη τε νηδύν Id.*Supp.*207. 4. *womb*, Il.24.496, Hes.*Th.*460, A.*Eu.*665, etc.; also of Zeus when in travail of Athena, Hes.*Th.*890, 899; of Dionysus, E.*Ba.*527 (lyr.). 5. metaph., ν. νάρθηκος Nic.*Al.*272; λέβητος Orph.*L.*276.—Acc. νηδύα for νηδύν in Q.S.1.616; dat. pl. νηδύσι Nic.*Th.*467. [ῠ in trisyll. cases, also νηδὺς A.*Ch.* l.c., Call.*Dian.*160, νηδὺν E.*Andr.*356, *Cyc.* 574: but νηδῡν *AP*9.519 (Alc.), Nic.*Al.*416, Orph. l.c.]

**νῆες, νήεσσι**, v. ναῦς.

**νη-έω**, Dor. **νᾱέω**, older form of νέω (C), *heap, pile up*, ἐπ' αὐτῶν νήησαν ξύλα πολλά Od.19.64; of a funeral pile, μενοεικέα νήεον ὕλην Il.23.139; περὶ δὲ δρατὰ σώματα νήει ib.169; πῦρ τ' εὖ νηῆσαι Od.15. 322; also ἐπ' ἀπήνης νήεον.. ἀπερείσι' ἄποινα *heaped* a huge ransom, Il.24.276; νήεον αὐτόθι βωμόν *piled* it *up*, A.R.1.403:—in Med., πυρὰν ναήσατ' B.3.33: fut. νηήσεται in pass. sense, Opp.*H.*2. 216. II. *pile, load*, νηήσας εὖ νῆας Il.9.358:—in Med., νῆα ἅλις χρυσοῦ.. νηησάσθω *let him pile his* ship with gold enough, ib.137, cf. 279. [Sts. corrupted to νηνέω, q.v.] **-ησις**, εως, ἡ, *a heaping, piling up*, Sch.A.R.1.403.

**νηθίς**, ίδος, ἡ, *spinster*, cj. in Sch.Il.6.491.

**νήθουσα**, ἡ, apptly. name of a *plant*, *PMag.Par.*1.2307.

**νήθω**, *spin*, Cratin.96, Pl.*Plt.*289c, LXX *Ex.*35.25, *AP*11.110 (Nicarch.), Corn.*ND*13, Gal.*UP*1.3 (but said not to be Att., Poll.7. 32, *AB*109): Ion. impf. νήθεσκες *AP*14.134. (Formed from νέω (B), as πλήθω from πλη-, πίμπλημι.)

**Νηϊάς**, άδος, ἡ, Ion. for Ναϊάς.

✱ **νήϊος**, η, ον, Dor. **νᾱ̈ιος**, α, ον (as always in Trag., cf. δάϊος, γάϊος), also ος, ον A.*Pers.*279, 336: (ναῦς):—*of* or *for a ship*, δόρυ ν. *ship*-timber, Od.9.384, etc.: without δόρυ, Il.3.62, 13.391; ν. ξύλα Hes.*Op.*808; ν. δοῦρα A.R.2.79; νήϊα alone, *oars*, Nic.*Th.*814; ἄνδρες νάϊοι A.*Supp.*719; στόλος νάϊος *the ship's* course, ib.2 (anap.); ναΐοισιν ἐμβολαῖς Id.*Pers.* ll. cc.; γένος ναΐας ἀρωγὸν τέχνας, i.e. the seamen, S.*Aj.*357 (lyr.); ναΐα ἀπήνη, νάϊον ὄχημα, i.e. a ship, E.*Med.* 1122, *IT*409 (lyr.).

**Νηΐς**, ΐδος, ἡ, Ion. for Ναΐς.

✱ **νῆϊς** (A), ϊδος, ὁ, ἡ, acc. νήϊδα Il.7.198, A.R.3.32, but νῆϊν Call. *Aet.*1.1.33, A.R.3.130: (νη-, ἰδεῖν, εἰδέναι):—*unknowing of, unpractised in* a thing, οὐ νῆϊς ἀέθλων Od.8.179: abs., Il. l.c.; ν. ἔτι χρυσέας Κύπριδος B.5.174, cf. Call.*Aet.*3.1.49; ναυτιλίης.. νῆϊν ἔχεις βίον ib. 1.1.33, cf. Id.*Aet.Oxy.*2079.2; ν. πατρός *fatherless*, Q.S.5.506: Comp. νηϊδέστερος Hsch. II. (νη-, ἴς) *powerless, feeble*, Id., Suid.

**νῆϊς** (B), ϊδος, ἡ, = νηάς, Heraclid.*Pol.*30, Phot.

**νήϊστος**, η, ον, Sup., = νήατος (v. νέατος A), in form νήϊστα· ἔσχατα, κατώτατα, Hsch.: hence perh. the name of the πύλαι Νήϊσται at Thebes, πύλαισι Νηΐστῃσι (v.l. νηΐτῃσι [-τισι, -ταισι]) A.*Th.*460, cf. Stat.*Theb.*8.354; Νηΐταις πύλαις E.*Ph.*1104 codd. (νήϊι, ταῖς πύλαις Hsch.: perh. Νηΐτταις πύλαις with -ττ- from -στ-).

**νηΐτης** [ῑ], ου, ὁ, *of* or *belonging to a ship, consisting of ships*, ν. στρατός a fleet, Th.2.24, 4.85; στόλος A.R.4.239, etc.

**νη-κερδής**, ές, *without gain, unprofitable*, νηκερδέα βουλὴν Il.17. 469; ἔπος νηκερδὲς ἔειπες Od.14.509. **-κερως**, ων, *not horned*, Ep. nom. pl. νήκεροι, Hes.*Op.*529. ✱ **-κεστος**, ον, (νη-, ἀκέομαι) *incurable*, neut. as Adv., *incurably*, ὅς κε.. νήκεστον ἀασθῇ ib. 283. **-κηδής**, ές, *careless*, f.l. in Epic.ap.Pl.*Smp.*197c. **-κουστέω**, (νη-, ἀκούω) *give no heed to, disobey*, c. gen., οὐδ' Ἐνοσίχθων νηκούστησε θεᾶς Il.20.14. **-κουστος**, ον, (νη-, ἀκουστός) *deaf, not hearing*, Emp.137.3. II. *unheard, unknown*, Arat.173.

**νήκ-της**, ου, ὁ, (νήχω) *swimmer*, Poll.1.97; ἐχθρὸν ἀεὶ νήκτῃσι prob. in Philosteph.Hist.17. **-τικός**, ή, όν, *able to swim*, S.E.*M.*9.171; also ν. τέχνη ibid. **-τός**, ή, όν, *swimming*, opp. χερσαῖος, Arist. *Mu.*398ᵇ31, cf. Plu.2.636e; ν. πλῆθος ἰχθύων Vett.Val.344.15, cf. *AP* 6.4 (Leon.); of a shield, ib.9.115; in air as well as water, Ph.1.14; τὸ πτηνὸν καὶ πεζὸν καὶ νηκτόν Gal.18(1).207; but τὸ ν. *power of swimming*, *Anacreont.*24.5. **-τρίς**, ίδος, ἡ, fem. of νήκτης, ν. ἐλαία Poll. 6.45; cf. κολυμβάς. **-τωρ**, ορος, ὁ, = νήκτης, Man.4.397.

**νηλεγής**, ές, = ἀνηλεγής, *reckless*, ἦτορ Alcm.26 (dub. l.). Adv. -έως Hsch.

**νηλεής**, ές, v. νηλής; cf. ἀνηλεής.

✱ **νηλεῖτις**, ιδος, (νη-, ἀλείτης, ἀλιταίνω) fem. Adj. *guiltless, unoffending*, γυναῖκας.., αἵ τέ σ' ἀτιμάζουσι καὶ αἳ νηλείτιδές εἰσι Od.16.317, 19. 498, cf. 22.418. (νηλιτέες, νηλητέες are vv. ll.; Aristarch. interpr. ἁμαρτωλοί, πολυαμάρτητοι, from νη- intens.)

**νηλεό-θῡμος**, ον, *of ruthless spirit*, μοῖρα *IG*3.1326, *BKT*5(1).87; Χάρων *IG*14.1648, cf. 2012 (Sulp. Max.). **-ποινος**, ον, *punishing ruthlessly*, epith. of the Κῆρες, Hes.*Th.*217.

✱ **Νηλεύς**, έως, ὁ, *Neleus*, father of Nestor, Il.11.683, al.:—Adj. **Νηλήϊος**, υἱός 2.20:—Patron. **Νηλεΐδης**, ου, Ep. ᾱο, ὁ, 23.652; Ep. **Νηληϊάδης**, εω or ᾱο, 8.100, al.: in fem. **Νηληΐς**, ΐδος, A.R.1. 120. II. **Νηλεύς**, έως, ὁ, = Νείλεως, founder of Miletus, *IG*1².94.4 (written Νελ-), Call.*Dian.*226: hence **Νειλεΐδης**, and **Νειληϊάδης**, ου, Ep. ᾱο, ὁ, Alex.Aet.3.26, 1; cf. Νειλεῖον.

**νήλευστος**, ον, (νη-, λεύσσω) *invisible*, Theoc.*Syrinx* 20.

✱ **νηλής**, ές, Ep. neut. νηλεές; Ep. also **νηλειής**, ές, Hes.*Th.*770, *h.Ven.*245, A.R.4.476: (νη-, ἔλεος):—poet. Adj. (in Prose sts. ἀνηλεής, q.v.) *pitiless, ruthless*, Il.9.632; νηλέϊ χαλκῷ with *ruthless* blade, 3.292, al.; νηλέϊ δεσμῷ 10.443; ν. θυμὸν ἔχοντες a *resolute* or *dogged* spirit, 19.229; νηλέϊ ὕπνῳ *relentless* sleep, which has exposed the sleeper to ill, Od.12.372; ν. ἦμαρ, i.e. the day of death, Il.11. 484, Od.9.17, etc.; ν. ἦτορ Il.9.497; νηλέα νόον Φάλαριν Pi.*P.*1.95; νηλεεῖ νόῳ Id.*Fr.*177; ν. σὺ καὶ θράσους πλέως A.*Pr.*42; ν... ὅστις ἰκτῆρας ἐκθύει E.*Cyc.*369 (lyr.). Adv. -εῶς A.*Pr.*242; Ep. -ειῶς A.R. 2.626, *IG*5(1).733 (Sparta). II. Pass., *unpitied*, ἔκειτο νηλεὴς.. σῶμα S.*Ant.*1197; νηλέα δὲ γένεθλα.. κεῖται Id.*OT*180 (lyr.).

**νηλί-πεζος**, ον, *barefooted*, Hsch. ✱ **-πους** [ῐ], ὁ, ἡ, gen. ποδος, *unshod, barefooted*, ἄσιτος ν. τ' ἀλωμένη S.*OC*349 codd., cf. Max.Tyr. 30.6: **νηλῐπος**, ον, A.R.3.646, Lyc.635, prob. l. for νήλυπος in Lyd. *Mag.*1.42; cf. ἀνήλιπος. (Deriv. by Sch.Theoc.4.56 from νη-, ἦλιψ *without shoe.*)

**νῆλος**· ἔριον· ἄμεινον λῆνος, Hsch.

✱ **νῆμα**, ατος, τό, (νέω B) *that which is spun, thread, yarn*, Od.4.134, E. *Or.*1433 (lyr.), Pl.*Plt.*282e: pl., Od.2.98, 19.143; *thread of a* spider's *web*, Hes.*Op.*777; of the Fates, Μοιράων νῆμ' ἄλλυτον Phanocl.2, cf. *IG*14.1188.11; οὔπω πεπλήρωται τὸ ν. αὐτοῦ his *destiny*, Luc.*Philops.* 25; νήματα σηρικά silk *sutures*, Gal.10.942.

✱ **νημᾰτ-ικός**, ή, όν, *woven*, ὅπλον, of a band of plaited rope or web-

bing, Ath.Mech.34.7. **-ώδης**, ες, *fibrous, in filaments*, Plu.2.434a.

**νημέρτ-εια**, ἡ, *truth*; Dor. **νᾱμέρτεια**, used by S.*Tr*.173 in trim. ⁕ **-ής**, ές, Dor. **νᾱμερτής** (the only form used by Trag., A.*Pers*.246), (νη-, ἁμαρτάνω) *unerring, infallible*, γέρων ἅλιος ν., of Proteus, Od.4.349, etc.; ν. τε καὶ ἤπιος, of Nereus, Hes.*Th*.235; εἰπεῖν ν. βουλήν *a sure* decree, i.e. one *that will infallibly be put in force*, Od.1.86, 5.30; νημερτέα εἰπεῖν or μυθήσασθαι to speak *sure truths*, 3.19, Il.6.376; ἦ μάλα τοῦτο ἔπος ν. ἔειπες 3.204; πάντα ναμερτῆ λόγον A.l.c.(troch.); μῦθος, βάξις, A.R.4.810,1184: Sup. -έστατος Lyc.223: more freq. as Adv., νημερτὲς ἐνίσπες Od.22.166; τῶν γε νόον ν. ἀνέγνω 21.205; νημερτὲς ὑπόσχεο Il.1.514: Ion. Adv. νημερτέως as trisyll., Od.5.98.

**νημηθής**, ές, *thoughtless*, Ramsay *Studies in the Eastern Rom. Prov.* p.123 (Phrygia).

**νηνεμ-έω**, *to be still*, of the bowels, dub. l. in Hp.*Mul*.2.113 (νηπελεῖ Gal. ad loc.); of the weather, v.l. for ἀνην- in Str.7.3.18. ⁕ **-ία**, Ion. -ίη, ἡ, *stillness in the air, calm*, νηνεμίης *in a calm*, Il.5.523; γαλήνη ἔπλετο νηνεμίη there was a calm, *a ceasing of all winds* (the generic and specific words being in appos.), Od.5.392, 12.169; ἦν μὲν δὴ ν. Hdt.7.218; ἐξ αἰθρίης τε καὶ ν. ib.188; opp. μέγα πνεῦμα, Pl.*Phd*.77e; νηνεμίῃ *in calm weather*, Arat.1033, A.R.3.970: in pl., νηνεμίαι τε καὶ γαλῆναι Pl.*Tht*.153c; ἐν νηνεμίῃσι γαλήνης Timo 64: c. gen., ν. ἀνέμων Epic.ap.Pl.*Smp*.197c(s.v.l.). **-ος**, ον, (νη-, ἄνεμος) *without wind, calm*, αἰθήρ Il.8.556, Ar.*Th*.43(anap.); γαλάνα A.*Ag*.740 (lyr.); πέλαγος E.*Hel*.1456 (lyr.); αἴθρη Ar.*Av*.778 (lyr.); νηνέμους ἔσχεν αἰθὴρ δρόμους Limen.8; ἐν νηνέμοις in *windless* places, Thphr.*HP*1.8.1: Comp., διὰ τὸ -ώτερον εἶναι Arist.*Mete*.373ᵃ24(s.v.l.). 2. metaph., ν. ἔστησ' ὄχλον E.*Hec*.533; ν. ἔχειν τὴν ψυχήν Plu.2.589d. **-όω**, *make calm*, Hsch. (Pass.).

**νηνέω** (prob. a corruption of νηέω), *heap*, v.l. in Il.23.139: also in compds. ἐπι-, παρα-νηνέω.

**νηνία**, ἡ, *public eulogy* on great men, sometimes accompanied by the flute: hence, *lament, dirge*, only in Lat. *nenia*, a Gr. word acc. to Cic.*Legg*.2.24.62; cf. sq.

⁕ **νηνίατον**, τό, a Phrygian tune for the flute, Hippon.129.

**νῆνις**, v. νεᾶνις. **νηνίται**· νέοι, Hsch. **νηνυρίζοντα**· θρηνοῦντα, λαλοῦντα, Id. **νηξίπους**, ὁ, ἡ, πουν, τό, gen. ποδος, *webfooted*, gloss on νέποδες, Id.

**νῆξις**, εως, ἡ, (νήχω) *swimming*, Batr.68, Antyll.ap.Orib.6.27: pl., Batr.149, Plu.2.1091c, Sor.1.56.

**νηο-βάτης** [ᾰ], ου, ὁ, poet. for ναυβάτης, *AP*7.668(Leon.). **-κόρος**, ον, (νηός) poet. for νεωκόρος, ib.9.22 (Phil.). **-πόλος**, v. ναοπόλος. **-πορέω**, poet. for *ναυπορέω, *go by sea*, *AP*7.675 (Leon.).

**νηός**, ὁ, Ion. for ναός, *temple*. II. **νηός**, Ion. gen. of ναῦς.

**νηοσόος**, poet. **νηοσσόος**, ον, *protecting ships*, Ἄρτεμις, Ἀπόλλων, A.R.1.570, 2.927.

**νηοῦχος**· φύλαξ πλοίου, Hsch.

**νηο-φθόρος**, ον, *destroying ships*, Nonn.*D*.39.122. **-φόρος**, ον, *bearing ships*, νῶτα *AP*10.16.8 (Theaet.).

**νήοχος**, ον, *guiding ships*, πηδάλια *AP*7.636 (Crin.).

⁕ **νη-πᾰθής**, ές, = νηπενθής, Opp.*C*.2.417. **-παυστος**, ον, (νη-, παύω) = ἄπαυστος: neut. as Adv., νήπαυστον αἰάζουσα Lyc.972.

**νηπεδᾰνός**, ή, όν, = ἠπεδανός, Opp.*C*.3.409; cf. νήδυμος, ἥδυμος.

**νη-πεκτής**, ές, *with hair uncombed, dishevelled*, Hsch. **-πεκτος**, ον, *with uncarded wool*, κώεα νηπέκτων οἴων *Epic.Alex.Adesp*.2.30. **-πελέω**, *to be powerless*, Hp.ap.Gal.19.124: hence restored in Id.*Mul*.2.113; cf. κακηπελέων, εὐηπελής. **-πενθής**, ές, (πένθος) *banishing pain and sorrow*, epith. of Apollo, *AP*9.525.14; φάρμακον ν., an Egyptian drug, Od.4.221, cf. Thphr.*HP*9.15.1. II. *free from sorrow*: Adv. -έως Protag.9. **-πευθής**, ές, *unsearchable*, Orac.ap.Macr.*Sat*.1.18.20.

**νηπῐ-άας**, v. νηπιέη. ⁕ **-άζω**, *to be as a babe, childish*, Erinn. in *PSI*9.1090.55 + 15 p.xii), Hp.*Ep*.17, 1*Ep.Cor*.14.20, Porph.*Gaur*.12.4. **-ᾰχεύω**, *to be childish, play like a child*, Il.22.502:—Med., *Rh.Mus*.1879.195 (Rome). **-ᾰχος**, ον, Ep. Dim. of νήπιος, *childish, infantine*, Il.2.338, 6.408, 16.262, *Lyr.Alex.Adesp*.36.13 (Mesom.(?)); Ἔρως Bion *Fr*.7.2; νηπίαχα φρονέων Opp.*H*.5.403; of animals, Id.*C*.1.444, al.: as Subst. νηπίαχος, ὁ, *child*, *IG*12(7).445 (Amorgos), Opp.*C*.3.211. **-άχω** [ᾰ], = νηπιαχεύω, A.R.4.868, Mosch.4.22, Opp.*C*.2.343. **-ᾰχώδης**, ες, *childish*, *Gloss*. **-έη**, ἡ, Ep. form for *νηπιίη, (νήπιος) *childhood, childishness*, οἶνον ἀποβλύζων ἐν νηπιέῃ ἀλεγεινῇ Il.9.491: in pl., οὐδέ τί σε χρὴ νηπιάας (for *νηπιίας) ὀχέειν Od.1.297; ἐπεὶ..ποιήσῃ ἀθύρματα νηπιέῃσιν *in childish fashion*, Il.15.363; ἡγήσατο νηπιέῃσι led them *in his folly*, Od.24.469. **-εος**, α, ον, = νήπιος, χεῖρα... νηπιέην Opp.*H*.3.585. **-εύομαι**, = νηπιαχεύω, Sch.D Il.22.503.

**νηπῐοκτόνος**, ον, *slaying children*, διάταγμα Lxx *Wi*.11.7.

⁕ **νήπῐος**, α (Sor.1.7, al.), Ion. η, ον, also ος, ον Lyc.638:—*infant, child*, freq. in Hom., νήπιον, οὔ πω εἰδόθ' ὁμοιίου πολέμοιο Il.9.440; νήπια τέκνα 2.136, etc.; βρέφος ἔτ' ὄντα ν. E.*Ion* 1399, cf. *Andr*.755, etc.; νηπίους ἔτι Id.*Heracl*.956; τὸ ν. Pl.*Ax*.366d; ἁρμόττουσα τοῖς ν. [πλαταγή] Arist.*Pol*.1340ᵇ30; ἐκ νηπίου from *a child*, from *infancy*, [τὸ ἡδὺ] ἐκ ν. ἡμῖν συντέθραπται Id.*EN*1105ᵃ2; ἐκ νηπίων Plb.4.20.8; ἐκ ν. ἡλικίας *PFlor*.36.5 (iv A.D.); *infant* in law, *minor*, ἐφ' ὅσον ὁ κληρονόμος ν. ἐστιν *Ep.Gal*.4.1; of children up to puberty, αἱ τῶν ν. ἐκλάμψιες Hp.*Epid*.6.1.4 (cf. Herophil.ap.Gal.17(1).826); but of the foetus in its early stage, Hp.*Aph*.4.1 (cf. Gal.17(1).653). 2. less freq. of animals, Il.2.311, 11.113; νήπια alone, *the young* of an animal, 17.134. 3. of plants, Thphr.*HP*8.1.7. II. metaph., 1. of the understanding, *childish, silly*, Od.13.237; μέγα ν. Il.16.46, cf. Od.9.44; simply, *without foresight, blind*, Il.22.445; ἀνὴρ ν. Heraclit.79, cf. Emp.11.1, Pi.*P*.3.82, A.*Pr*.443, Democr.76, etc.; ν. ὃς..γονέων ἐπιλάθεται S.*El*.145 (lyr.); οὔτε πρὶν νήπιον, νῦν τ'..μέγαν no *child* before and now full-grown (i.e. in mind), Id.*OT* 652 (lyr.); of words, νήπια βάζεις Pi.*Fr*.157; ἀντιτείνειν νήπι' ἀντὶ νηπίων E.*Med*.891; μηδὲν εἴπῃς ν. Ar.*Nu*.105. 2. of bodily strength, *like that of a child*, βίη δέ τε ν. αὐτῶν Il.11.561.

**νηπῐό-της**, ητος, ἡ, *childhood, infancy*, Arist.*Pr*.896ᵇ6. II. *childishness*, Pl.*Lg*.808e, J.*AJ*1.19.3, 2.9.7; ν. φρενῶν Luc.*Halc*.3. **-τροφέω**, *nurse, tend children*, Sor.1.88. **-φροσύνη**, ἡ, *childishness, thoughtlessness*, Eust.1418.60(pl.). **-φρων**, ονος, ὁ, ἡ, *of childish mind, silly*, Str.1.2.8.

**νήπλεκτος**, ον, *with unbraided hair*, Bion 1.21.

**νήπλῠτος**, ον, *unwashed*, cj. in Anacr.21.6.

**νήποδες**· ἰχθύες, Hsch.; cf. νέπους.

**νηποινεί**, Adv. of sq., *with impunity*, esp. in phrase νηποινεὶ τεθνάναι, *SIG*194.10 (Amphipolis, iv B.C.), Lexap.And.1.95, Lexap.D.23.60, cf. Pl.*Lg*.874c; ν. ἀποκτείνειν (v.l. νήποινα) X.*Hier*.3.3.

**νήποινος**, ον, (νη-, ποινή) *unavenged, without compensation*, Hom. (only in Od.), νήποινοί κεν ὄλοισθε 1.380, 2.145; ἀλλότριον βίοτον νήποινον ἔδουσιν 1.160; ἀνδρὸς ἑνὸς βίοτον νήποινον ὀλέσθαι ib.377, cf. 18.280; also νήποινα (as Adv.) ἀποκτείνειν (v.l. for νηποινεί) X.*Hier*.3.3. II. φυτῶν νάποινος (νή- codd.), like ἄμοιρος, *without share of, unblest with* fruitful trees, Pi.*P*.9.58.

**νήπους** ἢ **νήποδες**· ἀνυποδέτους, Hsch. (leg. νη⟨λί⟩π-).

**νήπ-της**, ου, ὁ, (νήφω) *sober, discreet*, Plb.10.3.1, D.S.30.3, 33.21ᵃ, Onos.1.1, Ptol.*Tetr*.160. **-τικός**, ή, όν, *sober*, *Com.Adesp*.1088 (Sup.), Plu.2.709b, Vett.Val.242.18; **-κωτάτην**· νήφειν ποιοῦσαν, Hsch. Adv. -κῶς Vett.Val.179.6, al.

**νηπῠθής**, ές, = νηπευθής, Hsch.

**νήπυστος**, ον, *not heard, not learnt*, Nonn.*D*.11.199.

**νηπύτα**· βοητά· κῆρυξ μικρόφωνος, Hsch.; cf. ἠπύτα.

⁕ **νηπῡτί-α**, ἡ, *infancy*, ἐξέτι νηπυτίης A.R.4.791. **-εύομαι**, *play child's tricks*, *AP*11.140 (Lucill.). ⁕ **-ος**, ὁ, Ep. Dim. of νήπιος, *little child*, μηκέτι ταῦτα λεγώμεθα νηπύτιοι ὣς Il.13.292; νηπύτιον ὣς 20.200; once in Ar., ν. γὰρ ἔστ' ἔτι *Nu*.868. II. as Adj., *childish*, ἐπέεσσί γε νηπυτίοισιν Il.20.211; *foolish*, [βροτοί] Orph.*L*.6.

⁕ **νηρείτης** or **νηρίτης** [ῑ], ου, ὁ, name for several kinds of *sea-snails*, Arist.*HA*530ᵃ12, 535ᵃ19, 547ᵇ23, *PA*679ᵇ20.

**Νηρ-εύς**, έως, Ion. ῆος, ὁ, *Nereus*, *h.Ap*.319, Hes.*Th*.240, Alc.*Supp*.8.7, etc. 2. *sea*, Λίβυς, Ἄραψ Ν., Nonn.*D*.25.51, 32.194. **-ειος**, α, ον, Adj. *of Nereus*, Νήρεια τέκνα, i.e. fishes, Euphro 8.2; cf. νηρός. 2. **Νήρειον**, τό, = δελφίνιον, Ps.-Dsc.3.73:—also **Νηρειάδιον**, ibid.

**Νηρηΐς** or **Νηρεΐς**, ΐδος, ἡ, *daughter of Nereus, sea-nymph* (opp. Ναΐς, *spring-nymph*): mostly in pl. Νηρηΐδες, Il.18.38, Pi.*P*.11.2; title of play by Anaxandrides, Ath.11.482c; Νηρεΐδες Alc.*Supp*.8.11, Pi.*I*.(6)5.6, Q.S.2.436, title of play by Aeschylus; Att. Νηρῇδες A.*Fr*.174, S.*OC*719 (lyr.), E.*Andr*.1267, etc.; they were fifty in number, Hes.*Th*.264, Pi.*I*.6(5).6; their names are given, Il.18.39sqq., Hes.*Th*.243 sqq.: rare in sg., gen. Νηρῇδος S.*Fr*.546, Alc.Com.4.

⁕ **νήριθμος**, ον, = ἀνάριθμος, *countless*, Theoc.25.57, Lyc.415.

**νήριον**, τό, *oleander, Nerium Oleander*, = ῥοδόδενδρον, Dsc.4.81, dub. in *CIG*3641 b 20 (Lampsacus).

**νηρίπη**· σεμνή, Hsch.

⁕ **νῆρις**, ιος, ἡ, = βράθυ, Nic.*Th*.531. II. f.l. for πυρῖτις, Dsc.1.9. III. *hollow rock, cavern*, Hsch. (pl.).

**νηρίται**· μεγάλοι, Hsch. **νηρίτης**, v. νηρείτης. **νηρῑτόμῡθος**, ον, = πολύμυθος, Id.

⁕ **νήρῑτος**, ον, = νήριθμος, *countless, immense*, ν. ὕλη Hes.*Op*.511: hence as pr. n. of mountain in Ithaca, Νήριτον εἰνοσίφυλλον Il.2.632, Od.9.22; ν. ταύρων ἴχνια A.R.3.1288.

⁕ **νηρῑτοτρόφος**, ον, (νηρίτης) *breeding sea-snails*, νῆσοι A.*Fr*.285.

**νηρῑτόφυλλος**, ον, = πολύφυλλος, Hsch.

**νηρός**, ά, όν, of fish, = νεαρός, *fresh*, *PCair.Zen*.616 (iii B.C.), Xenocr.ap.Orib.2.58.63; cf. ἡμίνηρος. II. νηρόν, τό, or νηρός, ὁ, *water*, *OGI*201.21 (Nubia, vi A.D.), cf. Phryn.29; acc. sg. written τὸν νιρόν *PSI*3.165.3 (vi A.D.); cf. Mod.Gr. νερό. 2. f.l. for νειρός in Lyc.896, glossed κάθυγρος, Suid. s.v. νηρίτης (interpol.), but ταπεινός, Hsch.

**νῆς**, Adv., = ἔνης (v. ἕνος B), Hsch.: Dor. **νᾶς** (prob.), Id.

⁕ **νησαῖος**, α, Ion. η, ον, *insular*, χώρα, πόλις, E.*Tr*.188 (lyr.), *Ion* 1583; ὄρνιθες Arat.982; πορθμός *AP*9.242 (Antiphil.).

**νησεύομαι**, *form alluvial deposits*, *EM*25.48.

**Νησιάδεια**, τά, festival at Delos, *Inscr.Délos* 366 *A* 134 (iii B.C.):—sg. -ειον, τό, name of a fund, ib.290.139 (iii B.C.).

**νησι-άζω**, = νησίζω I, Str.1.3.18, Ph.1.622; ἄκρα νησιάζουσα *peninsular*, *Stad*.202. **-αρχέω**, *to be governor of an island* or *group of islands*, *CIG*3655.7 (Cyzicus). **-άρχης**, ου, ὁ, *governor of an island* or *islands*, Antiph.190.14, Plu.2.823d. **-αρχος**, ὁ, = foreg., *IG*11(4).559 (Delos, iii B.C.), 1126 (ii B.C.), *Inscr.Délos* 442 *B* 71 (ii B.C.); of Tiberius at Capreae, D.C.58.5. ⁕ **-άς**, άδος, ἡ, = νησίς, in pl., D.P.570 (s.v.l.).

⁕ **νησίγδα**, a kind of dish, Philem.52.

**νησ-ίδιον**, τό, Dim. of νῆσος, *islet*, Th.6.2, Arist.*Mir*.832ᵃ24, Str.2.5.30. **-ίζω**, *to be* or *form an island*, Plb.3.42.7, 5.46.9. II.

*to be peninsular*, Peripl.M.Eux.58. **-ίον**, τό, Dim. of νῆσος, *islet*, Str.2.5.23, 3.3.1.

**νῆσις** (A), εως, ἡ, (νέω B) *spinning*, Pl.R.620e.

**νῆσις** (B), εως, ἡ, (νέω C) *accumulation*, Hp.Loc.Hom.20 codd. (fort. ἴνησις).

❀ **νησ-ίς**, ῖδος, ἡ, Dim. of νῆσος, *islet*, Hdt.8.76,95, Th.8.14, Plb. 16.2.8, Str.1.3.18, Plu.Oth.10. [ῑ Call.Fr.524, Lyc.599, AP6.89 (Maec.), 9.413 (Antiphil.), D.P.479, etc.] ❀ **-ίτης** [ῑ], ου, ὁ, (νῆσος) *of, from*, or *belonging to an island*, St.Byz.:—Dor. fem. **νᾱσῖτις**, ιδος, γῆ PEleph.20.48 (iii B.C.); σπιλάς AP7.2 (Antip. Sid.).

❀ **νησιώτ-ης**, Dor. **νᾱσιώτᾱς**, ου, ὁ, fem. -ῶτις, ιδος, *islander*, Pi.P. 10.47, Hdt.1.27.143, Ar.Pax 298, Th.5.97, etc. 2. metaph., of a *swimmer*, Tim.Pers.44. II. as Adj., *insular*, λαὸς νασιώτας Pi.P. 9.55; ν. βίος E.Heracl.84; νησιώτιδες πόλεις *insular* cities, Hdt.7.22; νησιῶτις πέτρα an *island* rock, A.Pers.390; ἑστία S.Tr.658 (lyr.): also with a neut. Subst., νησιώτῃ μειρακίῳ Luc.Dom.3. 2. epith. of Apollo in Locris, BCH46.446; of Dionysus, Ath.Mitt.29.169 (Pergam.). ❀ **-ικός**, ή, όν, *of* or *from an island*, ἔθνεα Hdt.7.80; δόμοι E.Andr.1261; ὄνομα νησιωτικὸν Σαλαμῖνα θέμενον having given it the *island* name of Salamis, Id.Hel.149; ν. ξενύδρια Men.462.3; τὸ ν. *insular situation*, Th.7.57; κλητὴρ ν. a summoner *of the islanders*, Ar.Av.1422.

**νησο-βάσίλεια** [ῐ], ἡ, *queen of the islands*, of Aphrodite, Cat.Cod. Astr.1.173. **-ειδής**, ές, *like an island*, Str.3.1.7. **-μᾰχία**, ἡ, *island-fight*, Luc.VH1.42.

**νησόομαι**, Pass., (νῆσος) *become an island*, App.(?) Gall.(post Fr. 21).

**νησο-ποιέω**, *insulate*, Oenom.ap.Eus.PE5.26:—Pass., Ptol.Geog. 4.7.7. **-πολις**, εως, ἡ, *island-city*, Isid.Char.1.

**νῆσορ**· νεοττός, Hsch.

❀ **νῆσος**, Dor. **νᾶσος**, ἡ, *island*, Il.2.721, etc.; ἐν τᾷ μεγάλᾳ Δωρίδι νάσῳ Πέλοπος, i.e. the Peloponnese, S.OC696; μακάρων νῆσοι, v. μάκαρ; αἱ ν. *the islands* of the Archipelago, Ar.Eq.1319, X.HG4.8.1; καὶ πῶς γυνή.. νῆσον ἀμφιέννυται; Anaxil.35 (cf. περίνησος): heterocl. gen. pl. νησάων Call.Del.66. 2. *land flooded* by the Nile, PHib. 1.90.7 (iii B.C.), etc.; opp. ἤπειρος, PGiss.60 (ii A.D.); νῆσοι ποταμοφόρητοι POxy.1445.13 (ii A.D.); so of *alluvial land* in Tab.Heracl. 1.38.

**νησοφύλαξ** [ῠ], ἄκος, ὁ, *island-guard*, D.S.3.39.

**νῆσσα**, v. νῆττα.

**νησσίον**, τό, Dim. of νῆσσα, PLond.ined.2181 (vi/vii A.D.).

**νησσοτροφεῖον**, τό, *place where ducks are kept*, Varro RR 3.11.1, Colum.8.15.1.

**νηστ-εία**, ἡ, *fast*, νηστεῖαι καὶ ὁρταί Hdt.4.186, cf. Lxx Is.1.13, Str. 16.2.40, Act.Ap.27.9; νηστείην φέρειν Hp.Aph.1.13; νηστείας ὄζειν (cf. νῆστις I. 2) Arist.Pr.908b12; at Athens, name for the third day of the Thesmophoria, Ath.7.307f, Alciphr.3.39, cf. PCair.Zen.350.5 (iii B.C.). **-ειρα**, ἡ, fem. of νήστης I, as Adj., Nic.Al.130, f.l. in Id.Th.862. **-εύω**, *fast*, Ar.Av.1519, Th.949, Ev.Matt.6.16, etc.; νηστεύσαντες, opp. ἐδηδοκότες, Arist.PA676a1. 2. c. gen., *abstain from*, κακότητος Emp.144. **-ης**, ου, ὁ, *one who is fasting, on an empty stomach*, Semon.38, Arist.Fr.232, Matro Conv.10; ταῦτα νήστῃ δίδου πιεῖν POxy.1088.44 (i A.D.), cf. SIG1171.9 (Lebena), PLit.Lond. 171 (iii A.D.). II. = *staminarius*, Gloss. **-ικός**, ή, όν, (νέω B) *of* or *for spinning*: νηστική (sc. τέχνη), ἡ, *the art of spinning*, Pl. Plt.282a. II. (νῆστις) *for use on fastdays*, γάρον Aët.16.131 (141). **-ῖμος**, ον, *of abstinence*, ἑβδομάδες PFlor.384.55 (i A.D.).

❀ **νῆστις**, gen. ιος or ιδος, ὁ and ἡ (v. infr.); also dat. νήστει Hp. Acut.60: pl. νήστεις Antiph.138, D.H.Rh.9.16: (νη-, ἔδω):—*not eating, fasting*, of persons, ἀνώγοιμι πτολεμίζειν υἷας Ἀχαιῶν νήστιας, ἀκμήνους Il.19.207; νήστιες ἄχρι.. κνέφαος Od.18.370, cf. Diocl.Fr.43, Ev.Matt.15.32, etc.; νήστισιν ἐπιθέντες οἱ πολέμιοι Onos.12.1: c. gen., νῆστις βορᾶς E.IT973: metaph., νῆστιν ἀνὰ.. ψάμμαν over the *hungry* sand, A.Pr.573 (lyr.). 2. with an abstract Subst., freq. in A., νῆστιν νόσον *famine*, Ag.1016 (lyr.); ν. λιμός Ch.250; νήστισιν αἰκίαις the pains *of hunger*, Pr.599 (lyr.); νήστιδες δύαι Ag.1621; also νῆστις ὀσμή the bad breath *of one fasting*, Phryn.PSp.91B. 3. Act., *causing hunger, starving*, πνοαὶ νήστιδες A.Ag.193 (lyr.). II. as Subst., νῆστις, ἡ, acc. νῆστιν Ar.Fr.318.3, 506.4, Eub.110. 1. the *intestinum jejunum*, from its always being found empty, Hp.Carn. 19, Ar.Fr.506.4, Eub.63.5 (anap.), cf. Arist.PA675b33. 2. ν. κεστρεύς, fish so called because its stomach was always found empty, Ar.Fr.156, etc.: hence in Com., of 'empty bellies', ἐγὼ δὲ κεστρεὺς νῆστις οἴκαδ' ἀποτρέχω Alex.256, etc., cf. Ath.7.307d. 3. Νῆστις, ἡ, = ὕδωρ, Emp.6.3, cf. Alex.322.

**νηστο-ποσία**, ἡ, *drinking on an empty stomach*, Herod.Med.ap. Orib.5.27.12. **-ποτέω**, *drink fasting*, in Pass., ib.16.

**νηστός**, ή, όν, (νέω B), *spun*, Lxx Ex.31.4.

**νησύδριον**, τό, Dim. of νῆσος, X.HG6.1.12, Isoc.5.145, etc.

**νήσυρις**, = σφονδύλιον, Ps.-Dsc.3.76.

**νήτεα**· ἀνήνυτα, Hsch. **νήτη**, ἡ, v. νεάτη.

**νήτῑτος**, ον, (νη-, τίνω) *unavenged*, IG14.1389 ii 33.

**νητοειδής**, ές, *akin to the* νήτη, Nic.Harm.11; τόνος -έστερος ib.5.

**νητός**, ή, όν, (νέω C) *heaped, piled up*, ὅθι νητὸς χρυσὸς καὶ χαλκὸς ἔκειτο Od.2.338.

**νητρεκής**, ές, = ἀτρεκής. Adv. -κῶς, = ἀτρεκῶς, Lyc.1.

**νῆτρον**, τό, (νέω B) *spindle*, Suid.

**νῆττα**, Ep. and Ion. **νῆσσα** Hdt.2.77, Arat.918, Boeot. **νᾶσσα** Ar. Ach.875, ἡ:—*duck*, Hdt. l.c., Ar.Av.566, etc.; νῆττα ἀργυρᾶ IG2². 1436.53. (From ə̥-tyā, cf. Skt. ātis 'water-fowl', Lat. anas, anat-is, Lith. ántis 'duck', etc.)

**νηττ-άριον** [ᾰ], τό, Dim. of foreg., *duckling*, used as a term of endearment, Ar.Pl.1011, Men.1041. **-ίον**, τό, = foreg., Nicostr. Com.6.

**νηττο-φόνος**, ὁ, *duck-killer*, a kind of eagle, *Aquila naevia*, Arist. HA618b25. **-φύλαξ** [ῠ], ἄκος, ὁ, *duck-watcher*, Gloss.

**νηῦς**, ἡ, v. ναῦς. **νηυσιπέρητος**, ον, v. ναυσιπέρατος.

**νήϋτμος**, ον, (νη-, ἀϋτμή) *breathless*, Hes.Th.795.

**νηφαίνω**, = νήφω, etym. of νηφαντός, Eust.1306.51.

**νηφᾰλ-έος**, α, ον, = νηφάλιος, Hdn.Gr.2.908, al.; = σώφρων, Suid., cf. Max.Tyr.9.3, Agath.2.3, Sch.Il.23.398 (Sup.). Adv. -έως *sanely*, ξυντελέσαι δόμον Aret.SD1.6. **-εότης**, ητος, ἡ, = sq., Gloss. **-έωσις**, εως, ἡ, *sobriety*, Et.Gud.409.58. ❀ **-ιεύς**, έως, ὁ, = νηφάλιος, AP9. 525.14. **-ιεύω**, *make a libation without wine*, Poll.6.26. **-ίζω**, *purify by a libation without wine*, Hsch. (Pass.). **-ιμος**, ον, = sq., Orac.ap.Phleg.Fr.36.10 J. ❀ **-ιος**, α, ον, also ος, ον 1Ep.Ti.3.11, Plu. 2.657c (νήφω):—of drink, *unmixed with wine*, ν. μειλίγματα offerings of water, milk, and honey to the Eumenides, A.Eu.107; to the Muses and Nymphs, κρατὴρ νηφάλιος Plu.2.156d; νηφάλιαι εὐχωλαί, θυσίαι, A.R.4.712, Polem.Hist.42; ν. βωμοί IG2.1651 (iv B.C.); νηφάλια καὶ μελίσπονδα θύειν Plu.2.464c, 672b; τῷ Διονύσῳ πολλάκις ν. θύομεν ib. 132e (prov. of a frugal meal); ν. σπείσω Κύπριδι AP5.225 (Paul. Sil.); ν. ξύλα wood *other than vine twigs*, burned in sacrifices, esp. the twigs of the herb θύμος, Philoch.31, Crates Hist.5; ν. πόπανον *with no wine in it*, IG3.77.18. II. *sober*. ν. μέθη Ph.1.16, 2.447; βαθὺ ἡ σιγὴ καὶ νηφάλιον, ἡ δὲ μέθη λάλον Plu.2.504a; of persons, 1Ep.Ti.3.2,11, Ep.Tit.2.2, J.AJ13.12.2. Adv. -ίως, ν. ἔχειν Poll.6.26. **-ισμός**, ὁ, metaph., *soberness*, Suid. **-ος**, = νηφάλιος, Orac.ap.Phleg.Fr. 36.10 J.

**νηφαν-τικός**, ή, όν, *sobering*, Pl.Phlb.61c. II. = νηφάλιος, ζῷον, of the bee, Porph.Antr.19. **-τός**, ή, όν, = νηφάλιος, Eust.1306.52, misquoting Ath.10.423b.

**νήφρων**, ονος, ὁ, ἡ, *foolish*, Claudian.Gig.2.23.

❀ **νήφω**, Dor. **νάφω** (v. infr. II), used by early writers only in pres., mostly in part.: later impf. ἔνηφον Chor. in Rev.Phil.1877.67: aor. ἔνηψα 1Ep.Pet.4.7, Orac.ap.Ael.Fr.103, J.AJ11.3.3, Procl. in Prm. p.741 S., (ἐξ-) Aret.SD1.5, (ἀν-) Nic.Dam.4 J.:—*to be sober, drink no wine*, οὔτε τι γὰρ ν. οὔτε λίην μεθύω Thgn.478; νήφειν Archil.4, Pl. Smp.213e, al.: part. νήφων as Adj., = νηφάλιος, Hdt.1.133, Ar.Lys. 1228; ὑμῖν ἀντέκυρσα.. νήφων ἀοίνοις S.OC100; ὑπ' ἐχθροῦ νήφοντος ὑβριζόμην D.21.74; τὸ τοὺς μεθύοντας.. πλείω ζημίαν ἀποτίνειν τῶν ν. Lex Pittaci ap.Arist.Pol.1274b20; μεθύοντα.. παρὰ νηφόντων λόγους παραβάλλειν Pl.Smp.214c; ν. θεός, i.e. water, Id.Lg.773d: prov., τὸ ἐν τῇ καρδίᾳ τοῦ νήφοντος ἐπὶ τῆς γλώττης τοῦ μεθύοντος Plu.2.503f; [Ἀναξαγόρας] οἷον ν. ἐφάνη παρ' εἰκῇ λέγοντας Arist. Metaph.984b17; νήφων μεθύοντα ὑπὸ τῆς Ἀφροδίτης θεᾶται X.Smp.8. 21; τὸ νῆφον ὑπὸ τοῦ πάθους βυθίζεται Alciphr.1.13. II. metaph., *to be self-controlled*, Pl.Lg.918d; *to be sober and wary*, νᾶφε καὶ μέμνασ' ἀπιστεῖν Epich.[250]; γρηγορῶμεν καὶ νήφωμεν 1Ep.Thess.5. 6; νήψατε εἰς προσευχάς 1Ep.Pet. l.c.; νήφων καὶ πεφροντικώς Plu. 2.80b; ν. καὶ φροντιστής Gal.17(1).991; προμηθής τε καὶ ν. Hdn.2. 15.1; καρδίη νήφοντος Poet.ap.Longin.34.4; ν. λογισμός Epicur.Ep. 3p.64 U. 2. ν. ἐκ κακοῦ *recover oneself* from.., Ach.Tat.1.13; ἐγερθέντων καὶ νηψάντων ἀπὸ τῆς πτώσεως Procl. l.c.

**νήφων**, ονος, ὁ, ἡ, *sober*: nom. pl. νήφονες (expld. by νήφοντες) Hsch.: dat. νήφοσι Thgn.481, 627.

**νηχᾰλέος**, α, ον, = νηκτός, φύσις Xenocr.ap.Orib.2.58.1, cf. 12.

**νηχεῖον**, τό, *swimming-place*, Gloss.

**νήχι**, Adv., (νή) = ναίχι, Hsch.

**νήχῠτος**, ον, (νη-, χέω) *full-flowing*, ὕδωρ Philet.21, A.R.3.530; ἅλμη Id.4.1367; εὐρώς Call.Fr.313; ἱδρώς Nic.Al.587; ἀήρ Q.S.1. 417; ν. ὄρπηξ a *juicy* sapling, Nic.Th.33. (Prob. formed on the supposition that νη- had an intens. force.)

**νήχω**, Dor. **νάχω** (προσ-, q. v.):—*swim*, νηχέμεναι μεμαώς Od.5. 375; νῆχε ib.399; νῆχον πάλιν 7.280; νῆχον ἐπ' ἄκρον ὕδωρ Hes.Sc. 317; νήχει Nic.Al.590:—mostly Med. **νήχομαι**, part. νηχόμενος Od. 7.276, 14.352, Hes.Sc.211; inf. νήχεσθαι Democr.172: poet. impf. νήχοντο Titanomach.4 (cj. for -οντες): fut. νήξομαι Od.5.364, Timo 32: aor. ἐνήξατο Lyc.76; part. νηξαμένη AP9.36 (Secund.): the Med. forms alone used in later Prose, Plb.3.84.9, 5.48.9, Plu.2. 1063b, Luc.Dom.1, Ael.NA3.11, and in compds. (fut. νήξω f.l. in Ael.NA9.25).

**νῆψις**, εως, ἡ, (νήφω) *sobriety*, Plb.16.21.4, Str.7.3.11, Ph.1.377, etc.

**νηῶν**, Ion. gen. pl. of ναῦς.

**νηωποιεῖον**, τό, = νεωποιεῖον, Milet.7.60.

**νιβατισμός**, ὁ, *a Phrygian dance*, Ath.14.629d, Hsch.

**νίγλα**· τρόπαια (Pers.), Hsch.

**νιγλᾰρ-εύω**, = τερετίζω, Eup.110. **-ος**, ὁ, *whistle* (the sound), Ar.Ach.554 (pl.): in pl., *trills, quavers*, Pherecr.145.27, prob. in Phryn.Com.69, cf. Hsch., Phot. s.v. νιγλαρεύων.

**νίδες**· αἰδοῖα ἢ ὀρχίδια παιδίων, Phot.; Sicel word, acc. to Suid.; νιίδες Hsch.

❀ **νίζω**, Epich.[273]; imper. νίζε Il.11.830; inf. νίζειν Od.19.374; part. νίζων Il.7.425, E.IT1338: Ep. impf. νίζον Od.1.112, Il.11.846:—the pres. νίπτω, analogically formed from νίψω ἔνιψα, first in Men. Mon.543, cf. Luc.Epigr.19, Arr.Epict.1.19.5, Ev.Jo.13.5, Plu.Thes. 10, though Hp. uses Med. νίπτομαι Mul.1.57 (but δια-νιζέσθω ib.84,

περι-νιζέσθω ib.2.158): fut. νίψω Od.19.376, E.*IT*255: aor. ἔνιψα Id. *Sthen.Prol.*25; Ep. νίψα Od.19.505:—Med., νίζομαι Hp. (v. supr.): impf. νίζετο Od.6.224: fut. νίψομαι (v. ἀπο-, ἐκ-νίζω), late νιφήσομαι Lxx *Le.*15.12: aor. ἐνιψάμην; Ep. 3 sg. νίψατο Il.16.230: pf. νένιμμαι (v. infr.): aor. Pass. ἐνίφθην (κατ-) Hp.*Prorrh.*2.23:—*wash the hands* or *feet* (v. sub fin.), νίζε δ' ἄρ' ἄσσον ἰοῦσα ἄναχθ' ἑόν Od.19.392; αὐτὰρ ἐπεὶ νίψεν ib.505, cf. 358; τῷ σε πόδας νίψω ib.376, cf. Orac.ap.Hdt.6.19; ἃ δὲ χεὶρ τὰν χεῖρα νίζει Epich. l. c.:—Med., νίψατο δ' αὐτὸς χεῖρας Il.16.230, cf. Hes.*Op.*739; νίψασθαι, abs., *to wash one's hands*, Od.1.138, etc.; χεῖρας νίψασθαι ἁλός [with water] *from* the sea, 2.261 (v. infr. II); νίψασθαι λίμνης πόδα Hes.*Fr.*122; οὔρῳ νιψάμενος τοὺς ὀφθαλμούς Hdt.2.111. 2. generally, *purge, cleanse*, νίψαι καθαρμῷ S.*OT*1228, cf. E.*IT*1191. II. *wash off*, ἐπεὶ σφιν κῦμα θαλάσσης ἱδρῶ.. νίψεν ἀπὸ χρωτὸς Il.10.575; ἀπ' αὐτοῦ δ' αἷμα κελαινὸν νίζ' ὕδατι λιαρῷ 11.830,846; φόνον ἐμῆς ἔνιψε χειρός E.*Sthen.* l. c.:—Pass., αἷμα νένιπται Il.24.419:—Med., ἐκ ποταμοῦ χρόα νίζετο ἅλμην *he washed* the brine *off his* skin [with water] from the river, Od.6.224.—Commonly used of *washing part* of the person, while λούομαι is used of *bathing*, πλύνω of *washing clothes*, etc.; but νίζω is sts. used of things, σπόγγοισι.. τραπέζας νίζον Od.1.112; [δέπας] ἔνιψ' ὕδατος καλῇσι ῥοῇσι Il.16.229; ὕδατι νίζειν.. πλίνθον Theoc.16.62.—Att. Prose writers use the word only in compds., v. ἀπο-, ἐναπο-, ἐκ-νίζω. (Cf. OIr. *nigid*, Skt. *nénekti* 'wash', *niktá-* 'washed', Gr. ἀ-νιπτό-ποδες, χέρνιβα, I.-E. *nigᵘ*-.)

**νῑκ-άδιον**, τό, Dim. of νίκη, *small figure of Victory* (spelt νεικ-), *CIG*4558 (Acre), *OGI*426.5 (Haurân, i A.D.). **-ᾱθρον**, τό, *thank-offering for victory*, *IG*5(1).267 (Sparta). ❋**-αῖος**, α, ον, (νίκη) *of or belonging to victory*, θεός J.*AJ*3.2.5; Ζεὺς N., = *Juppiter Victor*, D.C. 47.40; ἐλπίς Nonn.*D.*18.169; Παλλὰς ν., as *the giver of victory*, ib. 37.623: νικαίην, Ion. for νίκην, Phot., Suid. **-αξῶ**, Dor. fut. of νικάω.

❋ **νικάριον**, τό, name of an *eye-salve*, Alex.Trall.2.

❋ **νίκαστρον**· νικητήριον, Phot.; **νίκεστρον**, Hsch.

**νῑκᾱτήρ**, v. νικητήρ.

**Νῑκᾱτόρειον**, τό, *tomb and temple of Seleucus I*, App.*Syr.*63.

**νῑκάτωρ** [ᾱ], ορος, ὁ, Dor. for νικήτωρ, *conqueror*, cult-name of Seleucus I and Demetrius, kings of Syria, *OGI*233, Plu.*Arist.*6 (pl.), etc.; Σέλευκος Ζεὺς Νικάτωρ *OGI*245.11. II. in pl. ν., οἱ, *the ever-victorious*, epith. of the royal Macedonian bodyguard, Liv.43.19.

**νικαφορία, -φόρος**, Dor. for νικηφ-.

❋ **νῑκάω**, Ion. νικέω Democr.249, Herod.1.51, also *GDI*1413.16 (Aetol.), *SIG*265.4 (Delph., iv B.C.), v. l. in *Apoc.*2.7; Aeol. νίκημι Theoc.7.40, *AP*7.743 (Antip.); also in impf. νίκη cj. in Pi.*N.*5.5, cf. Theoc.6.46: Ep. impf. 1 pl. νικάσκομεν Od.11.512: fut. -ήσω, later -ήσομαι Hierocl.*Facet.*205; Dor. 2 sg. νικαξῇ v. l. in Theoc.21.32: pf. νενίκηκα, etc.: (νίκη): I. abs., *conquer, prevail* in battle, in the games, or in any contest, Il.3.439, etc.; ὁ νικήσας the *conqueror*, ib. 138, X.*Smp.*5.9, etc.; ὁ νικηθείς the *conquered*, Il.23.656,663; ἐνίκησα καὶ δεύτερος καὶ τέταρτος ἐγενόμην *I won the first prize* [at Olympia], etc., Th.6.16, cf. Isoc.16.33: pres. freq. in sense, *to be* (or *be proclaimed*) *conqueror*, Pi.*O.*9.112, 13.30, cf. X.*Cyr.*8.2.27, *An.*2.1.1; νικᾶν πᾶσι τοῖς κριταῖς or ἐνὶ κριτῇ in their opinion, Ar.*Av.*445, 447; πολὺ ν. *win* a decisive *victory*, Th.7.34, etc.; τὰ πάντα ν. X.*An.* l. c.: freq. c. dat. modi, πυγμῇ *in* boxing, Il.23.669; ναυμαχίῃ Hdt.7.10.β'; ἵππῳ Id. 6.122; μάχῃ E.*Ph.*1143, etc.; ἵππῳ ἢ συνωρίδι ἢ ζεύγει Pl.*Ap.*36d; λαμπάδι And.4.42, etc.: c. acc. cogn. in same sense, πάντα ἐνίκα he *won* all the bouts, Il.4.389, 5.807; τὰ κοῦφα, τὰ μείζονα ν., E.*Alc.*1029, 1031; τῶν παλαισμάτων ἓν ν. Pl.*Phdr.*256b; ἅρμα ν. Pi.*I.*4(3).25; παγκράτιον Th.5.49; ναυμαχίαν, μάχας, Id.7.66, Isoc.12.257, etc.: freq. ν. Ὀλύμπια *to be conqueror* in the Olympian games, Th.1.126; τὠλύμπια Timocl.8.17; τὰ Παναθήναια Pl.*Ion* 530b; ν. Ὀλυμπιάδα Hdt.9.33 (also ν. Ὀλυμπίασιν Pl.*Ap.*36d; ἐν Πυθίοισι Pi.*N.*2.9): c. dat. et acc., τὰ Πύθια τῷ τεθρίππῳ ν. D.59.33; πολλοὺς ἀγῶνας οὐ παγκρατίῳ μόνον, κτλ., Plu.2.811d; Ὀλυμπίασι παῖδας στάδιον ν. *conquer* in the boys' race in the stadium at Olympia, D.58.66: c. dupl. acc., Πύθια ν. ἄνδρας Diog.Cyn.ap.D.L.6.33: also in Att. Inscrr. c. gen., Λεωντὶς ἀνδρῶν ἐνίκα *IG*2.1291, al.: generally c. acc. cogn., νίκην ν. *win* a victory, E.*Supp.*1060, Pl.*R.*465d, etc. (cf. infr. II); also ν. τρίποδα *win* it, Simon.147. 2. *prevail, be superior*, μύθοισιν, ἔγχεϊ, Il.18.252; δόλοισι Od.3.121; κάλλει ἐνίκα (sc. κρητήρ) Il.23.742; πᾶσαν ἀρετὴν νενικηκώς Pl.*Lg.*964c: c. part., εὐεργετῶν ν. X.*Ages.*9.7. 3. of opinions, etc., βουλὴ κακὴ νίκησεν the evil counsel *prevailed*, Od. 10.46; τὰ χερείονα νικᾷ Il.1.576, Od.18.404; ἐνίκα ἡ γνώμη Hdt.5.36, cf. Th.2.12, etc.; ἡ νικῶσα βουλή E.*Med.*912; ἐκ τῆς νικώσης [γνώμης] according to *the prevailing opinion, vote of the majority*, X.*An.*6.1.18, 6.2.12; ταῦτ' ἐνίκα S.*Ant.*274; νικᾷ πάσαισι ταῖς ψήφοις ὁ νόμος *is carried*, Pl.*Lg.*801a; σὺν ψάφῳ τᾷ νικεούσᾳ *SIG*265.4 (Delph., iv B.C.): freq. of orators, νικᾷ.. ὁ κακὸς ἐν πλήθει λέγων E.*Or.*944; ν. γνώμῃσι Hdt.3.82 (so γνώμῃ, v. l. γνώμην, Id.1.61, cf. Ar.*V.*594): freq. impers., ἐνίκα (sc. ἡ γνώμη) *it was resolved*, c. inf., ἐνίκα μὴ ἐκλιπεῖν τὴν πόλιν *it was carried* not.., Hdt.6.101; τέλος γε μέντοι δεῦρ' ἐνίκησεν μολεῖν S.*Ant.*233, etc.; ἐνίκησε.. λοιμὸν εἰρῆσθαι *it was the prevailing opinion that*.., Th.2.54; ἐν δημοκρατίᾳ νικᾷ ζῆν *it is preferable*.., Pl.*Plt.*303b. 4. c. inf., *succeed* in.., ἐνίκησε σκορπίσαι *Psalm. Solom.*4.13. 5. as law-term, ν. τὴν δίκην *win* one's cause, E.*El.*955, cf. Ar.*V.*581; simply νικᾶν *GDI*5011.11 (Gortyn), Arist.*Ath.*42.1, *Rh.Al.*1433ᵃ6, *PHal.*1.58 (iii B.C.), etc.; νικήσεις ἐν τῷ κρίνεσθαί σε *Ep.Rom.*3.4:—Pass., c. gen., αἴ κα νικαθῇ τῶν ἐνεχύρων *Schwyzer* 177.9 (Crete, v B.C.); v. infr. II. II. c. acc., *conquer, vanquish*, Ἕκτορα Il.7.192, etc.: freq. c. dat. modi, μάχῃ ν. Ἀχαιούς 16.79; ἀγορῇ ν. υἷας Ἀχαιῶν 2.370; πόδεσσι δὲ πάντας ἐνίκα 20.410; κάλλει ἐνίκων φῦλα γυναικῶν 9.130; πάντα ν. ἄνδρα.. κακοῖσιν *surpass* him in miseries, E.*Hec.*659; ν. τινὰ ἔν τινι Pl.*Smp.*213e, etc.; μὴ φῦναι τὸν ἅπαντα νικᾷ λόγον *excels* the whole account, S.*OC*1224 (lyr.); νίκα ἐν τῷ ἀγαθῷ τὸ κακόν *Ep.Rom.*12.21: c. acc. cogn., μάχην ν. τινά Isoc. 8.58, Aeschin.3.181, etc.:—Pass., ἔστιν ἃ τῶν ἄθλων δὶς ἕκαστος ἐνικήθη X.*HG*4.5.2: c. part., ν. ἀλεξόμενός τινα Id.*An.*1.9.11, etc. b. as law-term (cf. I. 5), νίκης τήν μιν ἐγὼ νίκησα Od.11.545:—Pass., ἢ δέ κα νικαθῇ *Leg.Gort.*1.23, al.; also of objects in dispute, damages, etc., *recover*, ib.1.28, al.:—Pass., *to be assigned, adjudicated*, ib.1.55. 2. generally, *overpower*, esp. of passions, etc., νόον νίκησε νεοίη Il.23.604; μὴ φόβος σε νικάτω φρένας A.*Eu.*88, cf. 133; [φύσις] νικᾷ τῷ ἥσσονι τὸ μεῖζον τῆς ἐλπίδος Democr.176; βαρεῖαν ἡδονὴν νικᾶτέ με grievous is the pleasure ye *win prevailing over* me, S.*OC*1204: c. inf., μηδ' ἡ βία σε.. νικησάτω τοσόνδε μισεῖν let not violence *prevail on* thee to.., Id.*Aj.*1334: with gen. of comparison, νικᾷ γὰρ ἀρετή με τῆς ἔχθρας πολύ *weighs with* me *more than* enmity, from the compar. force in νικᾷ, ib.1357 codd. 3. Pass., *to be vanquished*, Hom. only in part. νικηθείς (v. supr. I. 1); νικᾶσθαι ὕπνῳ, κέρδεσιν, A.*Ag.*291, 342; ἡδονῇ S.*El.*1272; συμφορᾷ E.*Med.*1195; also ὑπὸ τοῦ κακοῦ Th.2.51; πρὸς ἱμέρου S.*Fr.*932.4, etc.: sts. c. gen., ἱμέρου νικώμενος A.*Supp.*1005; αὐτῆς ⟨τε⟩ τῆς δίκης.. αὐτοῦ τε τοῦ ἀληθοῦς νικᾶσθαι Antipho 5.87: freq. of persons, νικᾶσθαί τινος, with gen. of comparison, *to be inferior, yield to*, S.*Aj.*1353, E.*Med.*315, *Cyc.*454; ξείνων νενίκανται θύραι the doors *give way to* the guests, Pi.*N.*9.2; ἢν τοῦτο νικηθῇς ἐμοῦ Ar.*Nu.*1087.

❋ **νίκ-η** [ῑ], ἡ, *victory*, ν. φαίνεται Μενελάου *victory* clearly belongs to M., Il.3.457, cf. Alc.80, etc.; μάχης ν. Il.7.26, 8.171; ν. πολέμου Pl.*Lg.*641a, cf. c; ἡ ἐν τῷ πολέμῳ ν. ib.647b: freq. of *victory in the games*, Ἰσθμία ν. Pi.*I.*2.13; ν. παγκρατίου or ἀπὸ π., ib.7(6).22, 6(5).60: c. gen. objecti, ν. ἀντιπάλων *victory over*.., Ar.*Eq.*521; ἡ τῶν ἡδονῶν ν. Pl.*Lg.*840c: c. gen. rei, τῶν πολεμικῶν ν. X.*Mem.*3.4.5; ν. δοῦναί τινι Il.16.845, etc.; ν. καὶ κράτος S.*El.*85; νίκην νικᾶν τινα, v. νικάω I. 1, II. 1b. 2. later, generally, *mastery, ascendancy*, etc., in all relations, νίκην διασῴζεσθαι to keep the *fruits of victory*, X.*Cyr.*4.2.26, cf. 4.1.15. 3. *success* in a lawsuit, Od.11.544; in the concrete, *damages*, etc., *recovered*, *Leg.Gort.*9.31. II. pr. n., *Nike*, the goddess of victory, Hes.*Th.*384, cf. Pi.*I.*2.26, etc.; Νίκη Ἀθάνα Πολιάς S.*Ph.*134, cf. E.*Ion* 457 (lyr.), 1529. 2. Astrol., name of sixth κλῆρος, Paul.Al.*K.*3, *Cat.Cod.Astr.*1.160. **-ήεις**, Dor. **-άεις** [ᾱ], εσσα, εν, *conquering*, *AP* 7.428.5 (Mel.). ❋ **-ημα**, ατος, τό, Dor. **-ᾱμα** *IPE*I².352.26 (Chersonesus), *BCH*27.219 (Crete):—*prize of victory, victory*, *Delph.*3(1).483, Plb.1.87.10, 16.14.5, D.S.4.33, D.H.3.27, Plu.*Lyc.*22. **-ητέον**, *one must conquer*, E.*Ba.*953. **-ητήρ**, in Dor. form **-ᾱτήρ**, ῆρος, ὁ, *winner*, τᾶς ἀγέλας *SIG*527.152 (Dreros, iii B.C.): pl., νικατῆρες· οἱ ἀκμαιότατοι ἐν ταῖς τάξεσιν, Hsch. **-ητήριος**, ον, *belonging to a conqueror* or *to victory*, δόξα ν. the glory *of victory*, Antiph.263; ν. φίλημα a kiss *as the conqueror's reward*, X.*Smp.*6.1; ἆθλα ν. Pl.*Lg.*832e. II. as Subst. νικητήριον (sc. ἆθλον), τό, *prize of victory*, Ζεῦ, σὸν τὸ ν. Ar.*Eq.*1253; τὸν βοῦν ἔλαβε τὸ ν. X.*Cyr.*8.3.33, cf. *HG*6.2.28; ν. ἁμίλλης *Inscr.Délos* 464.10 (ii B.C.): mostly in pl., τῷ καλλικοτταβοῦντι νικητήρια τίθημι S.*Fr.*537; ν. λαβών E.*Alc.*1028; τὰ ν. οἴσεσθαι, φέρεσθαι, κομίζεσθαι, to win the *prize*, Pl.*Euthd.*305d, *Phdr.*245b, *R.*612d; τὰ ν. τοῦ κιθαρῳδοῦ *IG*2².1388.37. 2. νικητήρια (sc. ἱερά), τά, *festival of victory*, ν. ἑστιᾶν to celebrate *this festival* by a banquet, X.*Cyr.*8.4.1, Plu.*Phoc.*20; ποιεῖν D.C.67.9. 3. also in pl., *decisive proof*, Hp. *Septim.*4. ❋ **-ητής**, οῦ, ὁ, *winner* in games, *CIG*5035 (Nubia, iii A.D.); *conqueror*, Eust.157.1; of the Emperor Julian, *SIG*906*B* (Magn. Mae., iv A.D.). ❋ **-ητικός**, ή, όν, *likely to conquer, conducing to victory*, X.*Mem.*3.4.11; ὑπόθεσις Plb.24.9.4 (Comp.); ὅπλον ν. *OGI*90.39 (Rosetta, ii B.C.); τὸ -ώτατον the *most likely way to conquer*, Plu.*Comp. Phil.Flam.*2. Adv. -κῶς Eust.1006.28. II. Subst. νικητικόν, τό, *charm for victory*, esp. in horse-racing, *PMag.Lond.*121.390, *POxy.*1478.1 (iii/iv A.D.); ν. δικαστηρίων *PMag.Osl.*1.35: pl., *PMag.Leid. W.*8.29. **-ήτρια**, ἡ, fem. of *νικητήρ, *conqueress*, *Gloss.* **-ήτωρ**, ορος, *victorious*: τὸ τῶν Ν. στρατόπεδον, = *Legio Victrix*, D.C.55.23.

**νῑκηφορ-έω**, *carry off as a prize*, δάκρυα ν. *win* naught but tears, E.*Ba.*1147. **-ία**, Dor. **νικᾱφ-**, ἡ, *victory*, freq. in Pi., both sg. and pl., *P.*1.59, *O.*10(11).59 (pl.). II. **Νικηφόρια**, Dor. **Νικᾱφ-**, τά, *festival of* Athena Νικηφόρος, *SIG*629.24 (Pergam., ii B.C.). ❋**-ος**, Dor. **νικᾱφ-**, ον, (φέρω) *bringing victory*, δίκη A.*Ch.*148. II. (φέρομαι) *bearing off the prize, victorious*, Pi.*O.*1.116; ν. ἀγλαΐα the glory *of victory*, ib.13.14; πρᾶγμα ν. A.*Eu.*477; κράτος S.*Tr.*186; δίκη E.*Ph.*781; ἄγρα Id.*Ba.*1200; θεός or θεοὶ ν., applied to the Ptolemies, *OGI*89.3 (iii B.C.), *PTeb.*43.28 (ii B.C.); epith. of Athena, Eros, etc., *SIG*629.6 (Pergam., ii B.C.), *IG*11(4).1304 (Delos, ii B.C.), etc.: c. gen., X.*Mem.*3.4.5.

**νῑκίδιον**, τό, *small figure of victory*, *Annuario*6/7.405 (Artemis Pergaea).

**νῑκό-βουλος**, ον, *prevailing in the council*, Ar.*Eq.*615. **-λάεια**, τά, festival at Delos, *Inscr.Délos* 320*B*63 (iii B.C.). **-λᾱος**, ὁ, a kind of *date* named after Nicolaus of Damascus, Plu.2.723d, Ath.14.652a, *PMag.Par.*1.3202, *PMag.Berol.*1.244. **-μάχᾱς** [μᾰ], α, ὁ, *conqueror in the fight*, S.*Fr.*887 (lyr.). **-ποιός**, όν, *causing victory*, Aq.*Ps.*4.1, al.

❋ **νῖκος**, εος, τό, later form for νίκη, Lxx *1Es.*3.9, *BGU*1002.14 (i B.C.), *IG*12(5).764.2 (Andros, prob. i A.D.; written **νεῖκος**), *Ev. Matt.*12.20, Vett.Val.358.5, Orph.*A.*587, *APl.*5.381, read by Aristarch. in Il.12.276; εἰς νῖκος *for ever*, Lxx *2Ki.*2.26, al.

**νῑκοτέλεια**, ἡ, *celebration of victory*, *Stud.Pal.*1.76.648 (pl., i A.D.).

**νικύρτας**, = δουλέκδουλος, Hsch. (cf. Hippon.49.5).

**νίμμα**, ατος, τό, *water for washing*, νίμματα ἐπέχειν Dromo 2, censured by Phryn.170. 2. νίμματα προσώπου *cosmetics*, Crito ap. Gal.12.448; but νίμμα προσώπου *washing* of the face, Orib.*Fr.*82.

**νιμμός**, ὁ, = ἡ κάθαρσις, Zonar.

⊛ **νῖν**, Dor. enclit. acc. of 3 pers. Pron., like Ep. and Ion. μιν, for αὐτόν, αὐτήν, *him. her* (but never used reflexively), *h.Ven.*280, Alcm. 23.44, Thgn.364, Epich.21, Sophr.35, etc.; also in Dor. Inscrr., *IG*4[2](1).121.12, al. (Epid., iv B.C.), *Abh.Berl.Akad.*1925(5).21 (Cyrene, iv B.C.); αὐτόν νιν *IG*4[2](1).122.47 (Epid.): seldom for αὐτό, *it*, as in Pi. *P.*4.242, A.*Ch.*542, S.*Tr.*145: less freq. in pl., for αὐτούς, B.8.15, Pi.*Fr.*7, S.*OT*868 (lyr.), E.*Supp.*1140 (lyr.); for αὐτάς, S.*OC*43, 1123, *Ant.*577; νιν αὐτάς E.*Ba.*32; for αὐτά, S.*El.*436, 624. 2. for dat. αὐτῷ, Pi.*P.*4.36, *N.*1.66 (nisi leg. ἰν, i.e. ϝιν).

**νίννη**, ἡ, perh. *grandmother* or *mother-in-law*, Demitsas Μακεδ. No.416 (Thessalonica, ii A.D.); also **νίνη** ib.No.415 (ibid.); cf. νέννος.

⊛ **ννίον**, *pupus*, *Gloss.*

**νίννος**, ὁ, *nag*, Hsch.; Lat. Dim. *ninnium*, Plaut.*Poen.*371.

**νίνον**, τό, = ἑλένιον, Paul.Aeg.6.88.

**νιπτήρ**, ῆρος, ὁ, (νίζω) *washing-vessel, basin*, *Ev.Jo.*13.5.

**νίπτρον**, τό, (νίζω) *water for washing*, Poll.10.78: mostly in pl., A.*Fr.*225, E.*Ion*1174, *Hel.*1384, *AP*12.68 (Mel.); παῖδες ν. ἔδοσαν κατὰ χειρῶν Philox.2.39. II. **Νίπτρα**, τά, the *Bath Scene*, title of play by Sophocles on the recognition of Odysseus by his nurse; also applied to Od.19, Arist.*Po.*1460[a]26, and to the *Bath Scene* in that book, ib.1454[b]30.

**νίπτω**, v. νίζω. **νίρνος**· φθείρ (Achaean), ἢ **νίρμος**, Hsch. **νίρον**· μέγα, Id. **νιρός**, v. νηρός II.

**νίσσομαι** or **νίσομαι** [ῑ], Il.23.76, νίσσει (v.l. νίσῃ) E.*Cyc.*43 (lyr.), νίσεται Pi.*O.*3.34, νισσόμεθα Od.10.42, νίσεσθε E.*Ph.*1234, νίσονται Hes.*Op.*237, E.*Hel.*1483 (lyr.); part. νισόμενος Il.13.186, 15.577, Od. 4.701, 5.19: impf. νίσσετο A.R.2.824, νίσοντο Il.12.119, 18.566: later pres. subj. νίσηται Man.3.412: aor. κατ-ενίσατο Hermesian.7.65:—*go, come*, ll.cc.: with Preps. of motion, ἐκ πεδίου Il.12.119; ἐπ' ἀνθρώπους Pi.*O.*3.10; ἐς ἑορτάν ib.34; ποτὶ Ἰσθμόν Id.*N.*5.37; πόλεμόνδε, οἴκαδε, Il.15.577, Od.4.701; ἐπὶ νηῶν ν. *go* by sea, Hes. l.c.; οὐρανόθεν ν. *coming down* from heaven, *AP*6.265 (Noss.): c. acc. loci, χθόνα ν. E.*Ph.*1234; ν. σκοπέλους Id.*Cyc.*l.c.; of birds, Id.*Hel.*1483 (lyr.); of fishes, Sophr.101 (v. infr.): mainly Ep. and Lyr., used by E., once in trim. (*Ph.*l.c.).—Freq. spelt νείσσ-, νείσ- in codd., νεισ- also in Papyri of Call.*Fr.*1.45 P., Theoc.7.25, but νίσομαι Hdn.Gr.2. 554, νισόμενος *IG*12(1).202 (Astypalaea, iv/iii B.C.), 12(8).441.2 (Thasos, ii/i B.C.), ἐπι-νίσεται *Pae.Delph.*6; imper. νίσεο Epigr. in *Rev.Phil.*19.178 (i A.D.); and the Act. form νισοῦντι (νησοῦντι codd.) Sophr. l.c.:—later Gramm. (*EM*606.12, Eust.1288.56) wrongly dist. νίσσομαι pres., νίσομαι fut. (Perh. redupl. *ni-ns-ομαι* from νέ(σ)ομαι.)

**νίτρ-ασμα**, ατος, τό, *soap*, Sor.1.82. **-έλαιον**, τό, *emulsion of soda and oil*, Zos.Alch.p.147 B., Olymp.Alch.p.91 B. **-ία**, ἡ, *soda-pit*, *PPetr.*3 p.60 (iii B.C.), Str.17.1.23. **-ική**, ἡ, tax *on soda*, *PPetr.*3 p.294 (iii B.C.), *Ostr.Bodl.*i 36 (iii B.C.), *PTeb.*40.5 (ii B.C.), etc.: also **-κά**, τά, *PPetr.*3 p.302 (iii B.C.). **-ῖτις**, ιδος, ἡ, *producing* νίτρον, λίμνη Str.11.14.8. **-ιώτης** νομός, name of a district in Egypt where νίτρον was found, Id.17.1.23. ⊛ **-ον**, τό, in Hdt. and Att. **λίτρον** (q.v.), *sodium carbonate*, Sapph.165, Hp.*Aër.*7, Arist. *Mete.*383[b]12, *IG*9(1).691 (Corc., iii B.C.), *PCair.Zen.*304.7 (iii B.C.), *PTeb.*182 (ii B.C.), Gal.13.265; ν. ἐρυθρόν Hp.*Nat.Mul.*32, cf. *Mul.* 1.98; ν. θαλάσσιον, i.e. from the Egyptian lakes, *Hippiatr.*130; as an ἄρτυμα, Antiph.142.2; mixed with oil as a soap, Alciphr.3.61, Lib.*Decl.*26.19. (Cf. Egypt. *ntrj* 'natron'.)

⊛ **νιτρο-πηγικός**, ή, όν, *made of congealed* νίτρον, Alex.Trall. 12. **-ποιός**, όν, *producing* νίτρον, γῆ Sch.Ar.*Ra.*725.

**νιτρ-όω**, *cleanse with* νίτρον, Sor.1.83 (Pass.). ⊛ **-ώδης**, ες (Att. **λιτρώδης** Pl.*Ti.*65e), *like* νίτρον, δύναμις Arist.*Pr.*936[a]2; *impregnated with* ν., τὰ ν. Thphr.*CP*2.5.1, *Od.*65. 2. *alkaline*, of mineral springs, Gal.11.387. II. epith. of Nymphs, Νύμφαις νιτρώδεσι *IG*14.892. **-ωδία**, ἡ, *alkalinity*, Ruf.ap.Aët.3.165. **-ωμα**, ατος, τό, *lye*, *PHolm.*3.22, Hsch. s.v. χαλέρυπον. 2. *scurf, dandruff*, *Gloss.*

**νίφα** [ῐ], τήν, *snow*, acc. from nom. νίψ, which is not found (cf. λίβα, λίπα), Hes.*Op.*535.

**νῐφ-αργής**, ές, *snow-white*, Orph.*A.*669 (sed leg. νιφ(ετ)αργέσιν): **νίφαργος**, Hsch. **-άς**, άδος, ἡ, *snowflake*, Hom. (only in Il.), mostly in pl., ὥς τε νιφάδες χιόνος πίπτωσι θαμειαὶ ἤματι χειμερίῳ Il. 12.278; βρέχε.. χρυσέαις νιφάδεσσι, a legendary statement of the wealth of Rhodes, Pi.*O.*7.34; ἔπεα νιφάδεσσιν ἐοικότα χειμερίῃσιν Il. 3.222, cf. Luc.*Dem.Enc.*5: sg. in collect. sense, *snowstorm*, νιφὰς ἠὲ χάλαζα Il.15.170; [πάγος] βρέχετο πολλᾷ νιφάδι was wrapt as in deep *snow*, Pi.*O.*10(11).51. 2. generally, *shower*, πετρῶν A.*Fr.*199.7, cf. *Th.*212 (lyr.), E.*Andr.*1129; τραχεῖα ν. πολέμοιο *storm* or *sleet* of war, Pi.*I.*4(3).17; ὀμβρία ν., of rain, Lyc.876; πληγῶν νιφάδες Lib.*Ep.*112.6. II. as fem. Adj., = νιφόεσσα, πέτρα S.*OC*1060 (lyr.). ⊛ **-ετός**, ὁ, *falling snow, snowstorm*, ὄμβρον.. ἠὲ χάλαζαν ἢ νιφετόν Il.10.7; οὐ νιφετός, οὔτ' ἂρ χειμὼν πολὺς οὔτε ποτ' ὄμβρος Od. 4.566, cf. Pi.*Fr.*107.11, Hdt.4.50, 8.98, Arist.*Mete.*349[a]9, etc.: pl., *OGI*199.7 (Adule). 2. *rain*, Nonn.*D.*6.267, 8.260. 3. metaph., ν. λημμάτων Lib.*Or.*57.48. **-ετώδης**, ες, *snowy*, [ἄνεμος] Arist. *Mete.*364[b]21; ἡμέρα, νύξ, Plb.3.72.3, Plu.*Crass.*10; ἀέρες Str.4.5.2.

**νῐφο-βλής**, ῆτος, ὁ, ἡ, = νιφόβολος, Ἄλπεις *AP*9.561 (Phil.). **-βλητος**, ον, = foreg., ὄρη Opp.*C.*1.429; ἄκρα ib.3.314. **-βολία**, ἡ, *snowstorm*, Eust.905.3. **-βολος**, ον, *snowclad*, δειράσι ν. Παρνασοῦ E.*Ph.*206 (lyr.); ν. πεδία Ar.*Av.*952; ν. ἀναβολαί, a burlesque on the bombast of dithyrambic poets, ib.1385; πέτραι Ἑλικωνίδες Limen.3; ὄρεα Simm.26.19; ὄρη Plu.*Sert.*17. ⊛ **-εις**, εσσα, εν, *snowy, snowclad*, Κρήτης ὄρεα νιφόεντα Od.19.338; κατ' Οὐλύμπου ν. Il.18.616; ν. Ὀλύμπου Hes.*Th.*117; ὤρανος ν. Alc.17; ν. Αἴτνα Pi.*P.*1.20; Παρνασός S.*OT*473 (lyr.); σκόπελος Ar.*Nu.*273. II. *snow-white*, Ἑλένη (v.l. σελήνη) Ion Trag.46. **-κτῠπος**, ον, *rattling with snow* or *sleet*, Castorio 2. ⊛ **-στῐβής**, ές, *piled with snow*, νιφοστιβεῖς χειμῶνες S.*Aj.*670.

**νίφω**, v. νείφω.

**νίψις**, εως, ἡ, (νίζω) *washing*, ποδῶν Plu.*Pomp.*73.

**νίψω**, **νίψαι**, **νίψασθαι**, v. νίζω. **νίωπον**, τό, = νέτωπον, *oil of bitter almonds*, Hp.ap.Erot.

**νόα**· πηγή (Lacon.), Hsch. (Cf. νέω A.) II. **νόα**, v. νοῦς.

**νόαρ**, τό, (νοέω) *phantasm, spectre*, Theognost.*Can.*80.

**νοαρέως**, v. νοήρης.

**νοαρός**, dub. sens. in Comp. νοαρώτερον ἔχραο νύμφην Diosc. in *PLit.Lond.*100C15.

**νοβακκίζειν**· τὸ ὀρχούμενον τοῖς δακτύλοις ἐπιψοφεῖν· σεισμὸς Νιόβη, Phot. (cf. Nauck *TGF*p.51).

⊛ **νο-ερός**, ά, όν, *intellectual*, ψυχαὶ ἀναθυμιώμεναι νοεραὶ ἀεὶ γίνονται Heraclit.12, cf. Pl.*Alc.*1.133c (v.l., Comp.); ζῷον ἔμψυχον ν. τε καὶ λογικόν, of the κόσμος, Zeno *Stoic.*1.32, cf. Ti.Locr.99e; αἰσθητικώτερον καὶ -ώτερον τὸ λεπτότερον [αἷμα] Arist.*PA*648[a]3; ν. τόπος Id.*Pr.* 954[a]35; πνεῦμα ν. *Placit.*1.7.19; νοεραὶ φρένες Nic.*Al.*543; [θεὸν] νοερώτερον ἠὲ νόημα Timo 60; opp. ἀσύνετος, S.E.*M.*7.325, cf. Onos. 1.7; epith. of Apollo, *AP*9.525.14: Sup., Plot.6.6.8. Adv. **-ρῶς** *in the spiritual sense* or *world*, ἴθι εἰς Χάρραν ν. Ph.1.629, cf. Iamb.*Myst.* 1.21, Procl.*Inst.*139; f.l. for νοερῷ in Herm.ap.Stob.1.49.44. ⊛ **-έω**, Aeol. νόημι (q.v.): Ep. aor. 1 νόησα Il.8.91; Ion. ἔνωσα (ἐν-) Hdt. 1.86: pf. νενόηκα, Ion. νένωκα (ἐν-) Id.3.6; imper. νενόηθι Hilgard *Excerpta e libris Herodiani* 30:—Med., Ep. aor. νοήσατο Il.10.501; part. νοησάμενος Alc.*Supp.*7.6, νωσάμενος Thgn.1298, Theoc.25.263, Call.*Fr.*345, etc.:—Pass. (mostly in med. sense), fut. νοηθήσομαι S.E.*P.*2.175, Gal.*UP*17.1: aor. ἐνοήθην Pl.*Lg.*692c; also Ion. (ἐπ-) Hdt.3.122, 6.115: pf. νενόημαι, Ion. νένωμαι Anacr.10, Hdt 9. 53, S.*Fr.*182, Aëthlius 4: 3sg. plpf. ἐνένωτο (in med. sense) Hdt.1.77. Hdn.Gr.2.253 cites νοῦνται from Democr. (v. infr.) and pf. Pass. νένοται.—The compds. with ἀπό, διά, ἐν, ἐπί, μετά, πρό are used chiefly in Med.:—*perceive by the eyes, observe* (οἱ ἀρχαῖοι τὸ ν. σωματικὸν.. ὑπολαμβάνουσιν Arist.*de An.*427[a]26), Il.3.396; ὀξὺ ν. ib.374, Hes. *Th.*838, etc.; ὀφθαλμοῖσιν, ἐν ὀφθαλμοῖσι ν., Il.15.422, 24.294. 2. *perceive by the mind, apprehend*, τὸν δὲ ἰδὼν ἐνόησε 11.599; οὐ.. ἴδον οὐδ' ἐνόησα Od.13.318, cf. Il.10.550, 24.337, etc.; ἡ δ' οὔτ' ἀθρῆσαι δύνατ' ἀντίη οὔτε νοῆσαι Od.19.478; ἢ λάθετ' ἢ οὐκ ἐνόησεν or did not *take notice*, Il.9.537, cf. 5.665; νοέεις δὲ καὶ αὐτός thou thyself *art aware of* it, Od.21.257; θυμῷ νοέω καὶ οἶδα ἕκαστα 18.228; ν. τῇ καρδίᾳ Lxx *Is.*44.18; πρὸ ὃ τοῦ ἐνόησεν one *perceives* before the other, Il.10.224: abs., [θεὸς] οὖλος ὁρᾷ, οὖλος δὲ νοεῖ, οὖλος δέ τ' ἀκούει Xenoph.24; ταὐτὸν δ' ἐστὶ νοεῖν τε καὶ οὕνεκέν ἐστι νόημα Parm.8.34: freq. in Philos., of *thought*, μάλιστα ἔοικεν ἴδιον [ψυχῆς] τὸ ν. Arist.*de An.* 403[a]8; ἔοικε δὴ τὸ ζῆν εἶναι κυρίως τὸ αἰσθάνεσθαι ἢ ν. Id.*EN*1170[a]19, cf. 1166[a]22; καλῶς ν. καὶ λέγειν καὶ πράττειν X.*Cyn.*1.18: also with part. added, ὡς ἐνόησεν ἔμ' ἥμενον Od.10.375; of a future event, νοέω κακὸν ὔμμιν ἐρχόμενον 20.367: c. inf., οὐκ ἐνόησα ἄψορρον καταβῆναι 11.62; πίστει νοοῦμεν κατηρτίσθαι τοὺς αἰῶνας *Ep.Hebr.*11.3: folld. by ὡς.., Od.22.32, cf. Pl.*Epin.*977c; νόει θ' ᾗ δῆλον ἕκαστον Emp.4. 13:—Med., νωσάμενος Thgn.1298; νοούμενος S.*OT*1487:—Pass., *to be apprehended by thought*, τὰς ἰδέας νοεῖσθαι μὲν ὁρᾶσθαι δ' οὔ Pl.*R.* 507b; τὰ νοούμενα, opp. τὰ αἰσθητά, ib.508c; τὰ ἀόρατα τοῖς ποιήμασι νοούμενα *Ep.Rom.*1.20. 3. *think, consider, reflect*, φρεσὶ ν. "ἔνθ' εἴην ἢ ἔνθα" Il.15.81; μετὰ φρεσὶ σῇσι νόησον Αἰνείαν, ἤ κέν μιν ἐρύσσεαι ἤ κεν ἐάσῃς 20.311; οὐδ' ἐνόησε κατὰ φρένα καὶ κατὰ θυμὸν ὡς.. ib.264; ἐπ' ἀμφότερα ν. *look* to both sides, Hdt.8.22: c. acc. cogn., ἄλλα νοέειν *to be* otherwise *minded*, Id.7.168: also εἰπὲ δ' ᾗ νοεῖς S.*Tr.*1135, cf.*El.*1435: part. νοέων, έουσα, *wary, discreet*, Il.1.577; τὴν μέν κεν ἐπαινέσσειε νοήσας Hes.*Op.*12, cf. Od.15.170; τὰ νοέων λέγει what he says *advisedly*, Hdt.8.102; νοῶν καὶ φρονῶν *sane* and in his right mind, in wills, *Test.Epict.*1.1, *PPetr.*3 p.4 (iii B.C.), etc.:—in Med., φρενὶ θεία νοῦνται Democr.129; ὑψηλὰ νενωμένος Anacr. 10. 4. *consider, deem, presume* to be so and so, ὡς μηκέτ' ὄντα κεῖνον.. νόει S.*Ph.*415; τόδε γὰρ νοῶ κράτιστον ib.1176; δεῖ ν. συνεχῆ τὰ ἔνοπτρα Arist.*Mete.*373[a]19: c. inf., δεῖ νοῆσαι τὸ μὲν ὑγρὸν εἶναι ib. 340[b]24, etc.; cf. νοητέον. II. *think out, devise, conceive*, τοῦτό γ' ἐναίσιμον οὐκ ἐνόησε Od.2.122; ἔνθ' αὖτ' ἄλλ' ἐνόησε θεά ib.382; ἄλλα μὲν αὐτὸς ἐνὶ φρεσὶ σῇσι νοήσεις, ἄλλα δὲ καὶ δαίμων ὑποθήσεται 3.26; οὐ γάρ τις νόον ἄλλος ἀμείνονα τοῦδε νοήσει Il.9.104: freq. with neut. pl. Adj., πεπνυμένα πάντα νοῆσαι Od.18.230; ἀνδρῶν πλεῖστα νοησάμενος *most cunning* of men, of Sisyphus, Alc.*Supp.*7.6; ὀρθὰ ν. Hdt. 8.3:—Pass., ἐνθύμημα νενοημένον οὐκ ἀτόπως D.H.*Th.*37. 2. *purpose, intend*, ἐσθλά τινι Hes.*Op.*286; κακόν τινι Hdt.3.81, cf. X.*Hier.* 1.15. III. c. inf., *to be minded, intend*, οὐδ' ἐνόησε ἐξερύσαι δόρυ *bethought himself*, Il.5.665; νοέω φρεσὶ τιμήσασθαι 22.235; νοέω δὲ καὶ αὐτὸς Ἕκτορά τοι λῦσαι 24.560; ἢ γὰρ νοεῖς θάπτειν σφε; S.*Ant.*44, cf. 770, *El.*389, etc.:—Med., once in Hom., μάστιγα.. νοήσατο χερσὶν ἑλέσθαι he *thought with himself* to take the scourge, Il.10.501; ἐνέ-

νωτο στρατεύειν he *was minded* to march, Hdt.1.77, cf. 7.206, 9.53. IV. of words, *bear a certain sense, mean*, πυθοίμεθ' ἂν τὸν χρησμὸν ὅ τι νοεῖ Ar.*Pl.*55, cf. *Nu.*1186, Pl.*Cra.*407e; [εἰ] τοῦτο..νοεῖ αὐτῷ if this *means* for him that.., Id.*R.*335e; also ἐπιδεῖξαι ἐθέλω τὸ νυνί μοι συμβεβηκὸς τί ποτε νοεῖ Id.*Ap.*40a; τὸ νοούμενον the *sense, meaning*, Phld.*Po.Herc.*991.4, al.—Not in Th. or Oratt. ⊛ **-ημα**, ατος, τό, Ion. **νῶμα** Emp.110.10 (but νόημα 105.3): (νοέω):—*that which is perceived, perception, thought*, τῶν νέες ὠκεῖαι, ὡς εἰ πτερὸν ἠὲ νόημα Od.7.36 (cf. ὀξύτερον νοήματος Lib.*Or.*59.148; ἅμα νοήματι 'in the twinkling of an eye', Epicur.*Ep.*1 p.11 U.: hence ἡ ἅμα ν. περίοδος *lightning* survey, ib.p.32 U., cf. Phld.*Mort.*37, Plu.*Alex.*35); ν. φρενός Ar.*Nu.*704(lyr.). 2. *thought, purpose, idea, design*, τοιοῦτον ἐνὶ στήθεσσι νόημα Od.13.330; Ζεὺς..ἐνὶ φρεσὶν ὧδε νόημα ποίησ' 14.273; νοήματα..ἐκτελέει Il.10.104, cf. Alc.77, Pi.*P.*6.29; σοφώτατα νοήματα Id.*O.*7.72; οὐκ οἶδ' ὄττι θέω· δίχα μοι τὰ ν. Sapph.36; ἐκτὸς τῶν ἐωθότων ν. στῆσαί τινα Hdt.3.80; τὸ μὲν ν. τῆς θεοῦ, τὸ δὲ κλέμμ' ἐμόν Ar.*Eq.*1203, cf. *Nu.*743. 3. in Philos., *thought, concept*, opp. sensation, sense-presentation, Parm.8.34, etc.; φύσει διῄρηται τά τε ν. καὶ τὰ αἰσθήματα Arist.*Fr.*87; σύνθεσίς τις νοημάτων Id.*de An.*430$^{a}$28; *discursive thinking*, as the function of διάνοια, Herm.ap.Stob.2.8.31. 4. Rhet., *thought* as expressed in literary form, D.H.*Amm.*2.24, Longin.12.1. II. *understanding, mind*, παρέπλαγξεν δὲ νόημα Od.20.346, cf. Il.19.218, Thgn.435, Emp.110.10; αἷμα γὰρ ἀνθρώποις περικάρδιόν ἐστι ν. Id.105.3; θεὸς..οὔ τι δέμας θνητοῖσιν ὁμοίιος οὐδὲ ν. Xenoph.23.2. **-ημᾰτίζω**, *form concepts*, Eust.1545.7. **-ημᾰτικός**, ή, όν, *rational*, later form for νοητικός, Hsch. s.v. δράστης; λόγος Herm.ap.Stob.2.8.31; οὐσία cj. ibid.; θεοί Id.ap.Stob.1.41.11 (s.v.l.). **-ημάτιον**, τό, Dim. of νόημα 1.4, Arr.*Epict.*3.23.31. **-ημι**, Aeol. for νοέω, Jo.Gramm.*Comp.*3.40. **-ήμων**, ον, gen. ονος, *thoughtful, intelligent*, ἐπεὶ οὔ τι νοήμονες οὐδὲ δίκαιοι Od.2.282, 3.133, cf. Eus.Mynd.20; of philosophers, Luc.*Philops.*34; νοήμονα τέκτονα χαλκοῦ *Epigr.Gr.*907.5 (Sinope). II. *in one's right mind*, opp. παραφρονέων, Hdt.3.34. **-ήρης**, ες, *skilful*, ἔργον Herod.7.3. Adv. Dor. νοᾰρέως, = νουνεχόντως, Hsch. **-ησις**, Ion. **νῶσις** Timo 44.2: εως, ἡ:—*intelligence, understanding*, opp. αἴσθησις, Diog.Apoll.3, al., Pl.*Ti.*28a, etc.; νοήσει καὶ οὐκ ὄμμασι Id.*R.*529b; superior to διάνοια, ib.511d; including ἐπιστήμη and διάνοια, ib.534a; ὁ νοῦς εἷς καὶ συνεχὴς ὥσπερ ἡ ν. Arist.*de An.*407$^{a}$7; ν. νοήσεως Id.*Metaph.*1074$^{b}$34: pl., *processes of thought*, Id.*de An.*407$^{a}$24, *Pr.*917$^{a}$39, Timo l.c. II. concrete, *idea, concept*, ἡ κοινὴ τοῦ θεοῦ ν. Epicur.*Ep.*3 p.59 U.

**νοητάρχης**, ου, ὁ, *ruler of the world of Intelligence*, Iamb.*Myst.*8.2.

**νο-ητέον**, *one must conceive*, θεὸν δὲ ποῖον, εἰπέ μοι, ν.; E.*Fr.*1129, cf. Gal.6.405. **-ητικός**, ή, όν, *intellectual*, opp. αἰσθητικός, τὸ ν. Arist.*de An.*402$^{b}$16; τὰ ν. μόρια Id.*EN*1139$^{b}$12; ἡ ν. ψυχή, opp. ἡ αἰσθητική, Id.*GA*736$^{b}$14, *de An.*429$^{a}$28. Adv. -κῶς Porph.*Gaur.*17.6. **-ητός**, ή, όν, hyperdor. **νοᾱτός** Ti.Locr.95a:—*falling within the province of* νοῦς, *mental*, opp. φατός, ὁρατός, Parm.8.8, Pl.*R.*509d, al.; ν. καὶ ἀσώματα εἴδη Id.*Sph.*246b; ν. ζῷα Id.*Ti.*30c; ν. κόσμος Ph.1.5, etc.; opp. αἰσθητός, Arist.*EN*1174$^{b}$34, Phld.*Piet.*81, Plu.2.1114d, D.L.3.10. Adv. -τῶς, opp. αἰσθητῶς, Plot.4.8.6, cf. Ph.1.467, Iamb.*Myst.*8.6. II. = νοητικός, Orac.ap.Lyd.*Mens.*1.11. Adv. -τῶς *carefully*, Lxx *Pr.*23.1.

**νοθᾱγενής**, ές, Dor. and poet. for *νοθηγενής, *baseborn*, E.*Ion* 592, *Andr.*912, 942.

**νοθ-εία**, ἡ, *birth out of wedlock* or *by a marriage with an inferior*, Plu.*Them.*1, *Aem.*8, *Comp.Ages.Pomp.*1. II. *spuriousness*, τινὲς νοθείαν τοῦ πρώτου βιβλίου κατεψηφίσαντο Olymp.*in Mete.*4.16. **-εῖος**, α, ον, *of* or *belonging to a* νόθος: τὰ ν. (sc. χρήματα) *inheritance of a* νόθος, Lys.*Fr.*140 S., cf. Ar.*Av.*1656 (ap.Sch.). **-ευσις**, εως, ἡ, *adulteration*, interpol. in Suid. s.v. νοθεύειν. **-ευτής**, οῦ, ὁ, *one who adulterates*, Ptol.*Tetr.*159. ⊛ **-εύω**, *corrupt*, γυναῖκα Zeno *Stoic.*1.58; συνοικοῦσαν ἄλλῳ J.*AJ*4.8.23; γάμον τινός Ph.2.48; ἕτερος ἕτερον νοθεύων ὀδυνᾷ Lxx *Wi.*14.24: metaph., ν. τὴν ἐπιστήμην λόγοις κεκαλλωπισμένοις Vett.Val.238.22. 2. *adulterate*, Max.Tyr.37.4:—Pass., νενοθευμένος τῇ ὕλῃ διὰ τὸ σωματικόν Plu.2.373b; νοθευθῆναι Luc.*Deor.Conc.*7. II. Medic., [πυρετὸς] ὅστις ἂν [τὸ εἶδος] νοθεύσῃ *departs from the normal* type, Gal.7.339; of persons, ν. τὰ τοῦ μέτρου τῶν γυμνασίων γνωρίσματα Id.6.130, cf. 10.601 (Pass.). III. *consider spurious*, τὸ "Ἴλιον αἰπύ" ν. Ἀρίσταρχος St.Byz. s.v. Ἴλιον:—Pass., D.L.2.124, Marcellin.*Vit.Thuc.*43, etc. **-ισμοί**, οἱ, *illecebrae, Gloss.*

**νοθο-γέννητος**, ον, *of spurious origin*, Hsch. **-καλλοσύνη**, ἡ, *counterfeit charms*, *AP*11.370 (Maced.).

⊛ **νόθ-ος**, η, ον, also ος, ον (Call.*Fr.*279), *bastard, baseborn*, i.e. born of a slave or concubine, freq. in Il. (never in Od.), ν. υἱός Il.2.727, etc.; παῖδες ν. Hdt.8.103, Pl.*Ap.*27d; opp. γνήσιος, Il.11.102, Ar.*Av.*1650; ὅδ', εἰ ν. τις, γνησίοις ἴσον σθένει S.*Fr.*87; νόθοι καὶ οὐχ υἱοί ἐστε *Ep.Hebr.*12.8: fem., κούρη νόθη Il.13.173. 2. at Athens, *child of a citizen father and an alien mother*, D.23.213, etc.; νόθος πρὸς μητρός Plu.*Them.*1. 3. pl., in Egypt, a class of *temple-attendants*, Wilcken *Chr.*66 (iii B.C.). 4. of animals, *cross-bred*, πρόβατα *PHib.*1.32.15 (iii B.C.). II. generally, *spurious, counterfeit, supposititious*, of persons and things, λογισμῷ τινι ν. Pl.*Ti.*52b, cf. Dam.*Pr.*26; ν. παιδείᾳ Pl.*Lg.*741a; ν. ἡδοναί Id.*R.*587c; ἀοιδαί Call. l.c.; νόθον ἧπαρ ὁ σπλήν Arist.*PA*669$^{b}$28; αἱ ν. πλευραί the *false* ribs, Paus.1.35.6, Gal.*UP*4.9, Aret.*SA*2.6; ν. πυρετός Gal.11.30; ν. σάλπιγξ, of a serpent's hiss, Nonn.*D.*35.214; ν. φέγγος, of the moon, opp. γνήσιον, of the sun, Ph.1.628; ν. ἱματισμός *meretricious*, *Peripl.M. Rubr.*39, 49. Adv. -θως *insincerely, disingenuously*, Lxx 3 *Ma.*3.17, cf. Hsch. 2. of literary works, *spurious*, Porph.*Plot.*16. **-όω**, *counterfeit*, in Pass., τὸν κολακείᾳ -ούμενον ἔπαινον Ph.1.401.

**νοίδιον**, τό, Dim. of νόος, νοῦς, Ar.*Eq.*100 (pl.); = νοημάτιον, Philostr.*VS*2.10.1 (pl.).

**νομάδ-ην** [ᾰ], Adv., cited as parallel to ἐπιτροχάδην, Sch.Il.3.213. **-ία**, ἡ, (νομάς) *pasturage, steppe*, in pl., *Peripl.M.Rubr.*20:—Adj. **-ιαῖος**, α, ον, θρέμματα ibid. **-ικός**, ή, όν, *of* or *for a herdsman's life, pastoral*, βίος Arist.*Pol.*1256$^{b}$1, Dicaearch.ap.Porph.*Abst.*4.2; ν. διασκευή Plb.8.29.7; γένη Scymn.81; also of flying insects, *roving, wandering*, ὁ βίος ν. Arist.*PA*682$^{b}$7. Adv. -κῶς *like nomads*, Str.2.1.17; ν. καὶ Σκυθικῶς Id.11.8.7. II. as pr. n., *Numidian*, ἱππεῖς Plb.1.19.2; ἀλεκτρυών Luc.*Nav.*23. **-ίτης** [ῑ], ου, ὁ, *nomad, pastoral*, βίος Suid.

**νομᾰδόστοιχος**, ον, *going in a row from pasture*, Hsch., Phot.

**νομ-άζω**, *graze*, Nic.*Th.*950:—Med., Id.*Al.*345. **-αῖος**, α, ον, = νομαδικός, χίμαρος *AP*6.157 (Theodorid.); ἀλάλαγμα ν. a *shepherd's* cry, Call.*Fr.*310; *growing in pastures*, ἕρπυλλον Nic.*Th.*67. ⊛ **-αιος**, α, ον, (νόμος) Ion. and later Gr. for νόμιμος, *customary*: νόμαια, τά, *customs, usages*, ξεινικὰ ν. Hdt.1.135; Ἑλληνικὰ ν. Id.2.91, al., cf. Max.Tyr.38.3; λίθων λευκῶν νομαίων *Inscr.Délos* 290.206 (iii B.C.): sg., Hdt.2.49. 2. *prescribed by law*, ἐκκλησία *SIG*589.4 (Magn. Mae., ii B.C.), cf. *GDI*5699 (Samos); ν. ἐπαραί ib.5653 c 10 (Chios).

**νομαλέως**· ἀδιαλείπτως, Hsch. **νομάριον**· σκεῦος τραγικόν, Id.

**νομαρχ-έω**, *hold office of* νομάρχης, *PTeb.*72.205 (ii B.C.), *PAmh.*2.101.1 (iii A.D.). **-ης**, ου, ὁ, *governor of a region* or *province*, Hdt.4.66, Arr.*An.*5.8.3, *Ind.*12.7. II. esp. in Egypt, *governor of a* νομός II.2, Hdt.2.177, Arist.*Oec.*1352$^{a}$10, D.S.1.73, Arr.*An.*3.5.4; later, of a district financial officer, *PRev.Laws* 37.3, al. (iii B.C.), *Sammelb.*6314, al. (iii B.C.), *PSI*4.361.21 (iii B.C.), *PTeb.*108 *Intr.* (i B.C.), *PSI*8.901.11 (i A.D.), *BGU*1605 (ii A.D.), etc.; ν. τοῦ Ἀρσινοΐτου *PPetr.*3 p.205 (iii B.C.); of an official of the town of Antinoöpolis, *POxy.*1463.1 (iii A.D.), etc. **-ία**, ἡ, *province* or *district of a* νομάρχης, *PPetr.*3 p.78, al. (iii B.C.), prob. in D.S.19.85; ἡ τῆς ν. τράπεζα *PTeb.*350.4 (i A.D.); ὁ τῆς ν. λόγος Meyer *Ostr.*42 (iii A.D.). **-ικός**, ή, όν, *levied on a* νομαρχία, of taxes, λογιστήριον τῶν ν. *Sammelb.*5021; ν. λόγος *BGU*915.16 (i A.D.). **-ος**, ὁ, = νομάρχης II, Arist.*Oec.*1353$^{a}$6.

⊛ **νομ-άς**, άδος, ὁ, ἡ, (νομός) *roaming about for pasture*: οἱ νομάδες *pastoral tribes*, Choeril.3, Hdt.1.15, 125, 4.187, 7.85, Arist.*Pol.*1256$^{a}$31; στρατηγὸς νομάδων *OGI*616.3 (Arabia); ν. Σκύθαι Pi.*Fr.*105, A.*Pr.*709; Ἰνδαί Id.*Supp.*284; of the Cyclopes, E.*Cyc.*120. 2. metaph., of a prostitute, Ph.2.327. 3. pr. n., *Numidian*, Plb.1.19.3, al.: hence νομάδες ὄρνεις *guinea-fowl*, Ptol.Euerg.2(*a*) J.; νομάς alone, Artem.ap.Ath.14.663e; ν. λίθος *Numidian* marble, Luc.*Hipp.*6. II. fem. Adj. *roaming, grazing*, ἵπποι S.*Tr.*271; ἔλαφος Id.*Fr.*89; ἐπ' ἀκταῖς νομάδα..ἀλιάετον E.*Fr.*636; δάμαλις ν. calf *of the pastures*, i.e. fatted, Lxx 1 *Ki.*28.24; ν. περιστεραί *wild* doves, Gal.6.435, cf. 12.302; of Oedipus *exposed, turned adrift* on Cithaeron, S.*OT*1350 (lyr.); of irrigation-channels, κρῆναι Κηφισοῦ νομάδες ῥεέθρων Id.*OC*687 (unless *distributing*, cf. νέμω). 2. *pastoral*, βίος Scymn.832. 3. ν. τράπεζα *game* diet, Him.*Or.*25.3. 4. νομάσιν αὐγαῖς is dub. l. in Tim.*Pers.*89. **-εισφορά**, ἡ, *proposal of a law*, Tz.*H.*11.129. **-ευμα**, ατος, τό, *flock, herd*, εὐπόκοις νομεύμασιν A.*Ag.*1416. **-εύς**, έως, Ep. ῆος, ὁ, (νέμω) *herdsman*, κύνες τ' ἄνδρες τε νομῆες Il.17.65; δύω δ' ἅμ' ἕποντο νομῆες, opp. the chief herdsman, Od.17.214, cf. 16.3, 17.246: generic term including the special αἰπόλος, βουκόλος, ποιμήν, συβώτης, cf. Pl.*Tht.*174d, *R.*370d; βοῶν ἀγέλης ν. X.*Mem.*1.2.32; ν. προβάτων Arist.*EN*1161$^{a}$14. II. *dealer out, distributor*, ἀγαθῶν Pl.*Lg.*931d, cf. *Min.*317d, 321b. III. pl., = ἐγκοίλια, *ribs* of a ship, Hdt.1.194, 2.96, cf. Hsch.; also, = σχοῖνοι ἀρμένων, Id. ⊛ **-ευτικός**, ή, όν, *pastoral*, ν. ἐπιστήμη, ν. τέχναι, Pl.*Plt.*267b,d; νομευτική alone, Ael.*NA*9.54. II. *skilled in grazing*, ib.14.16. ⊛ **-εύω**, *put to graze, drive afield*, in Act., of the shepherd, καλλίτριχα μῆλα νομεύων Od.9.336; ἐνόμευε νομὸν κάτα πίονα μῆλα ib.217; ἀγέλην ν. Pl.*Plt.*265d:—Pass., metaph., of ἀνθρώπων ἀγέλαι, ib.295e. 2. βουσὶ νομοὺς ν. *eat down* the pastures with oxen, Lat. *depascere*, *h.Merc.*492. 3. abs., *to be a shepherd, tend flocks*, Theoc.20.35. II. later, = νωμάω, *direct, manage*, Nonn.*D.*7.110. ⊛ **-ή**, ἡ, (νέμω) *pasturage*, ἀμφίβιον..ἔδωκε ν. βατράχοισι Κρονίων Batr.59; νομὰς νέμειν Hdt.1.110; νομὰς νέμεσθαι ib.78, cf. Pl.*Lg.*679a, Arist.*HA*575$^{b}$4, etc.; ποιμνίων νομαί S.*OT*761: in concrete sense, νομαὶ βοσκημάτων *herds*, X.*An.*3.5.2. 2. *food from pasturing*, Pl.*Criti.*111c, etc.; αἷμα, ν. σαρκῶν Id.*Ti.*80e; ἡ προσήκουσα ψυχῆς ν. Id.*Phdr.*248b; ν. τῶν μελιττῶν τὸ θύμον Arist.*HA*626$^{b}$20, cf. *PCair.Zen.*520.10 (iii B.C.). 3. *feeding, grazing*, of herds, νομὴν ποιεῖσθαι, = νέμεσθαι, Arist.*HA*596$^{a}$14. b. metaph., *spreading*, ν. πυρός Plb.1.48.5, Plu.*Alex.*35; freq. of sores, etc., ν. ποιεῖσθαι *spread*, Plb.1.81.6; ὡς γάγγραινα, ν. ἕξει 2 *Ep.Ti.*2.17, cf. Asclep.ap.Gal.12.995; ἵσταται ἡ ν., of baldness, Id.ib.411; νομαί *spreading ulcers*, Hp.*Prorrh.*2.13, cf. Gal.13.860, al.; ν. σαρκὸς θηριώδεις Plu.2.165e. II. *division, distribution*, Hdt.2.52 (pl.), Pl.*Prt.*321c, al.; of an inheritance, D.36.12; ἡ πατρῴα (v.l. πατρῴων) ν. Arist.*Pol.*1303$^{b}$34; διεφθαρκὼς νομῇ χρημάτων τὸν δῆμον by *largess* of money, Aeschin.2.76, cf. *IG*5(1).1346 (Lacon.): in pl., = Lat. *donativa*, Hdn.3.8.9, 5.5.8, 6.8.8. 2. *paying out* or *distribution* in bandaging, Heliod.ap.Orib.48.25.1, Gal.18(2).741. III. in Law, = Lat. *possessio*, Wilcken *Chr.*41 iii 20 (iii A.D.); μακρᾶς ν. παραγραφή, = *longae posses-*

sionis praescriptio, MitteisChr.374i3 (iii A.D.); ν. ἄδικος, = injusta possessio, PTeb.286.7 (ii A.D.); ἐπὶ νομῆς πέμπειν, = in possessionem mittere, Just.Nov.53.4.1. IV. ἐν χειρῶν νομαῖς, = ἐν χειρῶν νόμῳ (cf. νόμος I. 1 e), SIG700.29 (Maced., ii B.C.). -ήματα· δικαιώματα, Hsch. (leg. νόμιμα· τὰ δικαιώματα). -ία, ἡ, lawfulness, opp. ἀνομία, nonce-word in PMag.Osl.1.141. ※ -ίζω, fut. νομιῶ Ar.Av.571, Th.4.87, etc.; Ion. 1 pl. νομιοῦμεν Hdt.2.17; later νομίσω Longus 1.1 codd., Procop.Gaz.Ep.12: aor. ἐνόμισα, poet. νόμισα Pi.I.5(4).2: pf. νενόμικα Axionic.6.8:—Pass., fut. νομισθήσομαι Pl.Sph.240e, etc.: fut. Med. νομιοῦμαι in pass. sense, Hp.Morb.Sacr.1: aor. ἐνομίσθην (v. infr. I. 1, 2): pf. νενόμισμαι, 3 pl. νενομίδαται D.C.51.23; Dor. inf. -ίχθαι Sthenid.ap.Stob.4.7.63: plpf. 3 sg. ἐνενόμιστο Ar.Nu.962: (νόμος):—use customarily, practise, ἐν τόδε ἴδιον νενομίκασι Hdt.1.173; ν. γλῶσσαν to have a language in common use, ib.142; φωνήν Id.2.42; οὔτε ἀσπίδα οὔτε δόρυ Id.5.97; πανήγυριν, πληγὴν ἐν τῇ ὁρτῇ, Id.2.63; ταῦτα . . Ἕλληνες ἀπ' Αἰγυπτίων νενομίκασι have adopted these customs from the Egyptians, ib.51, cf. 4.27; ἱπποτροφίας ἐν Πανελλάνων νόμῳ Pi.I.2.38; ἀργυροστερῆ βίον A.Ch.1003(989); ν. θειότατον νόμον Gorg.Fr.6D.; ν. ἐκκλησίαν have a regular popular assembly, Arist.Pol.1275$^{b}$7; ἀγορᾶς κατασκευὴν ν. (cj. for ὀνομάζουσιν) ib.1331$^{a}$32; δραχμὰς ἂν Τροζάνιοι νομίζοντι IG4$^{2}$(1).77.16 (Epid., ii B.C.):—freq. in Pass., to be customary, οὕτω τοῦτο νομίσδεται Alc.Supp.24; ὅπου τὸ χαίρειν μηδαμοῦ νομίζεται A.Eu.423; σωφροσύνη 'νενόμιστο was the fashion, Ar.Nu.962: impers., εἰκῇ νομίζεται Xenoph.2.13; ὡς νομίζεται as is the custom, A.Eu.32, E.Alc.99 (lyr.), etc.; οἷάπερ ν. A.Ag.1046; οἷα τοῖς κάτω νομίζεται S.El.327, cf. 691; ᾗ νομίζεται Id.OC 1603: part. νομιζόμενος customary, γέρα τὰ ν. Th.1.25; εὐχαὶ αἱ ν. Id.6.32; εἰς τὸν ν. χρόνον IG1$^{2}$.19.15; τὰ ν. customs, usages, Hdt.1.35, 5.42, Ar.Pl.1185; τὰ ν. μυστήρια Heraclit.14; τὰ ἱερὰ τὰ ν. Antipho5.82; συντελέσαι τὰ ν. τοῖς θεοῖς IG1$^{2}$.22.4, cf. 54.16; τὰ τοῖς θεοῖς ν. X.Cyr.4.5.14; freq. of funeral rites, τὰ ν. ποιεῖν Aeschin.1.13, cf. Isoc.19.33; ἐπειδὴ τὰ ν. αὐτῷ φέροιτο D.18.243: also aor. part., τό τοι νομισθὲν τῆς ἀληθείας κρατεῖ S.Fr.86; τὰ ν. E.Ba.71 (lyr.): pf. part., τὰ νενομισμένα τοῖς κατοιχομένοις PRyl.153.6 (ii A.D.), cf. SIG1109.34 (ii A.D.). 2. of a legislator, enact, ἐνόμισεν ἐνὶ ἱματίῳ δι' ἔτους προσεθίζεσθαι X.Lac.2.4, cf. 12.7, Cyr.8.5.3: c. acc., Id.Lac.1.7:—Pass., D.C.37.20; τὰ νομισθέντα ὑπὸ Μάρκου Id.78.22; cf. νομιστέος I. 3. c. dat., make common use of, use, φωνῇ Hdt.4.117; ὑσί ib.63; νομίζουσι Αἰγύπτιοι οὐδ' ἥρωσι οὐδέν, i.e. practise no such worship, Id.2.50; ἀγῶσι καὶ θυσίαις Th.2.38; εὐσεβείᾳ Id.3.82; οὔτε τούτοις χρῆται οὔθ' οἷς ἡ ἄλλη Ἑλλὰς ν. Id.1.77; esp. use as current coin, ἐν Βυζαντίοις, ὅπου σιδαρέοισι νομίσμασιν νομίζουσι Pl.Com.96 (dub. l.); ἐν Λακεδαίμονι σιδηρῷ σταθμῷ νομίζουσι Pl.Erx.400b:—hence in Pass., to be struck, ἀργύριον νενομισμένον ἐς Τιβέριον, i.e. with the head of Tiberius, Philostr.VA1.15. 4. c. inf., to be accustomed to do, νομίζουσι Διὶ θυσίας ἔρδειν Hdt.1.131, cf. 133, 202, 3.15, etc.:—Pass., νενόμισται τὰ σχέτλια ἔργα Λήμνια καλέεσθαι Id.6.138; γυμνοὺς εἰσιέναι νομίζεται it is customary for them . . , Ar.Nu.498, cf. 1420, Th.2.15, X.HG2.4.36. II. own, acknowledge, consider as, ὡς δούλους ν. τινάς Hdt.2.1; τὸν προέχοντα ἔτεσι ν. ὡς πατέρα Pl.Lg.879c: ὡς is freq. omitted, ὄμμα γὰρ δόμων νομίζω δεσπότου παρουσίαν A.Pers.169; τοὺς κακοὺς χρηστοὺς ν. S.OT610, cf. Ant.183, El.1317; τοὺς αὐτοὺς φίλους νομιῶ καὶ ἐχθροὺς IG1$^{2}$.71.20; νομίσαι χρὴ ταῦτα μυστήρια Ar.Nu.143; θεὸν ν. τινά believe in one as a god, σὺ Ἔρωτα οὐ θεὸν νομίζεις Pl.Smp.202d; θεὰν οὐ τὴν Ἀναίδειαν, ἀλλὰ τὴν Αἰδῶ ν. X.Smp.8.35; ν. τούτους [θεούς] believe in these [as gods], Hdt.4.59; οὓς ἡ πόλις ν. θεοὺς οὐ νομίζων X.Mem.1.1.1, Ap.10, Pl.Ap.24b; τοὺς ἀρχαίους οὐ ν. Id.Euthphr.3b; but ν. θεοὺς εἶναι believe that there are gods, Id.Ap.26c, Lg.886a (cf. infr. 4): without εἶναι, δίκην καὶ θεοὺς μόνον ν. [ἄνθρωπος] Id.Mx.237d; τὸ παράπαν θεοὺς οὐδαμῶς ν. to be an atheist, Id.Lg.885c, cf. 908c, Ap.18c, Prt.322a; θεοὺς ν. οὐδαμοῦ A.Pers.497:—Pass., to be deemed, reputed, considered, οἷς τὸ πέλειν τε καὶ οὐκ εἶναι ταὐτὸν νενόμισται Parm.6.8; Ἕλληνες ἤρξαντο νομισθῆναι Hdt.2.51; οἱ νομιζόμενοι μὲν υἱεῖς, μὴ ὄντες δέ . . D.40.47; ἡ -ομένη (v.l. ὀνομαζ-) πολιτεία Arist.Pol.1293$^{b}$22. 2. esteem, hold in honour, χρυσὸν . . περιώσιον ἄλλων Pi.I.5(4).2; οὔτε θεοὺς οὔτε ἀνθρώπους ν. Lys.12.9:—Pass., to be esteemed, Pl.Grg.466b. 3. c. acc. rei, hold, believe, ταὐτὰ περί τινος Id.Phdr.258c, etc.; ἐποίει ἄλλα παρ' ἃ ἐνόμισεν Id.Min.320b; ἀκοῇ ν., opp. πείρᾳ αἰσθάνεσθαι, Th.4.81. 4. c. acc. et inf., deem, hold, believe that . . , πότερα νομίζεις δυστυχεῖν ἐμέ; S.OC800, cf. OT549, X.HG3.4.11; θεὸν νομίζουσι εἶναι τὸ πῦρ Hdt.3.16: c. fut. inf., expect that . . , S.OT551: aor. inf. is sts. found in codd. referring to fut., ἐνόμισαν ἐπιθέμενοι ῥᾳδίως κρατῆσαι Th.2.3 (κρατήσειν in same phrase, Aen.Tact.2.3), cf. Th.3.24, Lys.13.6; in S.Aj.1082 the aor. inf. may be gnomic. 5. c. part., νομίσωμεν ἐκγενησόμενον Th.7.68; νόμιζε . . ἄνδρα ἀγαθὸν ἀποκτείνων X.An.6.6.24; νόμιζε ταῦτα δεδογμένα Pl.R450a, cf. D.14.9 (s.v.l.). 6. with ὡς, Th.3.88. 7. Pass., with gen. of the person in possession, τοῦ θεῶν νομίζεται; whose sanctuary is it held to be? S.OC38; οὐ τοῦ κρατοῦντος ἡ πόλις ν.; Id.Ant.738. 8. abs., νομίζοντα λέγειν to speak with full belief, Pl.Phdr.257d (nisi leg. ὀνειδίζοντα). 9. frequent, μυχὸν ν. A.Ch.801 (lyr., dub. l.). ※ -ικάριος, ὁ, = νομικός II. 2, POxy.1131.3 (v A.D.), etc. -ικεῖος, ὁ, = foreg., Cat.Cod.Astr.1.95. ※ -ικός, ή, όν, relating to laws, αἴτια, title of work by Democritus; resting on law, ἤθη Pl.Lg.625a; conventional, ν. δίκαιον, opp. φυσικόν, Arist.EN1134$^{b}$20; ν. φιλία, opp. ἠθική, ib.1162$^{b}$23. Adv. -κῶς after the manner of law, i.e. in a broad, general way, Id.Pol.1341$^{b}$31. 2. forensic, μάχαι Ep.Tit.3.9; ἀγῶνες, opp. λογικοί, ἠθικοί, Philostr.VS1.22.1; relating to points of law (opp. matters of fact), στάσις, ζήτημα, Hermog.Stat.2,3; ν. ὀνόματα law-terms, Id.Meth.2; τὰ ν. law matters, Phld.Rh.1.37S., Plu.Cic.26. Adv. -κῶς by legal process, Id.2.533b. II. learned in the law, Alex.39, Pl.Min.317e (Sup.); doctor of the Jewish law, Ev.Matt.22.35, al. 2. lawyer, notary, Plu.Cic.26, Gal.Libr.Ord.5, BGU326ii22 (ii A.D.). 3. legal adviser, assessor of a magistrate, MitteisChr.372iii18 (ii A.D.), etc.; ν. ἄριστος CIG2787 (Aphrodisias, cf. BGU361iii2 (ii A.D.), etc. ※ -ιμος, η, ον, also ος, ον Isoc.2.22, Arist.Mu.400$^{b}$24:—conformable to custom, usage, or law, ν. ὅρκος Lexap.And.1.98; ν. ἔρωτες Gorg.Fr.6D.; ἔργα δίκαια καὶ ν. Democr.174; legitimate, ν. παῖδες E.Ph.815 (lyr.): hence, customary, prescriptive, φῶς ib.345 (lyr.), etc.; οἱ ν. θεοί Pl.Lg.954a; ἡ ἐπίδεσις ἡ ν. Hp.Art.14; νόμιμόν [ἐστί] τινι ποιεῖν τι X.Cyr.8.8.8; ν. τινὰ δεδέσθαι Id.Mem.1.2.49. 2. observant of law, Choeril.3, Antipho2.2.12, Archyt.ap.Stob.4.5.61; ν. καὶ κόσμιοι Pl.Grg.504d; ν. πόλις Isoc.l.c. II. νόμιμα, τά, usages, customs, ἄλλα ἄλλοισιν νόμιμα, σφετέραν δ' αἰνεῖ δίκαν ἕκαστος Pi.Fr.215, cf. A.Th.334 (lyr.), Hdt.2.79; ν. Δωρικά, Χαλκιδικά, Th.6.4,5; τὰ κοινὰ τῶν Ἑλλήνων ν. Id.3.59; almost, = νόμοι, ἄγραπτα ν. S.Ant.455; ν. θεῶν E.Supp.19; τὰ εἰωθότα ν. Pl.Phdr.265a; ἄγραφα ν. Id.Lg.793a, D.23.70; τὰ περὶ τοὺς θεοὺς ν., τὸ πρὸς τοὺς πολεμίους ν., X.Mem.4.6.4, Cyr.1.6.34; ν. βαρβαρικά, title of treatise by Aristotle: rare in sg., τὸ πάντων ν. Emp.135.1. 2. legal rights, ν. καὶ φιλάνθρωπα BGU1074.2 (i A.D.); process of law, τοῖς ν. χρῆσθαι MitteisChr.88i12 (ii A.D.); ἄνευ νομίμων ἀπωθεῖσθαι to be illegally ejected, PFay.124.18 (ii A.D.); εἴργεσθαι τῶν ν., i.e. ἱερῶν καὶ ἀγορᾶς, of persons accused of murder, Antipho6.34, Arist.Ath.57.2. 3. funeral rites (cf. νομίζω I. 1), Din.2.8; τιμᾶν τινας ἐσθήμασί τε καὶ τοῖς ἄλλοις ν. Th.3.58. III. Adv. -μως Antipho5.14; κοσμίως καὶ ν. Pl.Smp.182a; ν. ἀποθανεῖν in a natural way, Lys.Fr.53.4; οἱ ν. ἀθλοῦντες, πεπαιδευμένοι, professional athletes, physicians, Gal.6.488, 17(1).26, cf. 8.171: Comp. -ώτερον X.Mem.3.5.20: Sup. -ώτατα D.C.78.13. -ιμότης, ητος, ἡ, observance of law, Iamb.VP16.69, 33.229.

※ νόμιος (A), α, ον, AP6.73 (Maced.), Man.5.161: (νομεύς):—of shepherds, ν. θεός the pastoral god, i.e. Pan, h.Pan.5, AP6.96 (Eryc.); of Apollo, as shepherd of Admetus, Call.Ap.47, cf. Theoc.25.21, A.R.4.1218 (but also, god of Law (cf. sq.), Rendic.Linc.1925.419 (Cyrene, i B.C., dedic. by νομοφύλακες)); of Aristaeus, Pi.P.9.65; of Hermes, Ar.Th.977 (lyr.), Corn.ND16; of Dionysus, AP9.524.14; of Zeus, Archyt.ap.Stob.4.1.138 (expld. fr. νέμω); of the Nymphs, Orph.H.51.12; N. ὄρη, in Arcadia, Paus.8.3.11; ν. μέλος A.R.1.578; τὸ ν. Clearch.37; ν. φορβάς Epic.in BKT5(1).112. 2. νόμιον, τό, pasture-dues, PStrassb.21.14 (ii A.D.).

νόμιος (B), ον, = νόμιμος, in neut. pl., IG9(1).334.15 (Locr.); ὅρκος ὁ νόμιος ib.45. II. v. foreg. I.

νομίουρος, ὁ, watcher of pastures, Arc.73.1.

νόμ-ισις, εως, ἡ, (νομίζω) belief, opinion, ἡ ἀνθρωπεία τῶν ἐς τὸ θεῖον νόμισις the established belief about the Deity, Th.5.105; παρρησία τῆς ν. D.C.37.17. ※ -ισμα, ατος, τό, anything sanctioned by current or established usage, custom, Ἑλληνικὸν ν. A.Th.269, cf. E.IT1471; institution, οὐδὲν γὰρ ἀνθρώποισιν οἷον ἄργυρος κακὸν ν. ἔβλαστε S.Ant.296; θεοὶ ἡμῖν ν. οὐκ ἔστι Ar.Nu.248, with a play on signf. II (do not pass current with us). II. esp. current coin, ν. κόψαι or κόψασθαι, coin money, Hdt.3.56, 4.166; τἀρχαῖον ν. Ar.Ra.720; ν. σύμβολον τῆς ἀλλαγῆς ἕνεκα Pl.R.371b, cf. Arist.EN1133$^{b}$11, Pol.1257$^{a}$11, D.L.6.20; τάλαντα νομίσματος And.3.8; ν. ἡμεδαποῦ IG1$^{2}$.91.4; τὸ ἐπιχώριον ν. PCair.Zen.21.12 (iii B.C.): pl. νομίσματα pieces of money, coins, Hdn.1.9.7. III. full legal measure, τοῦ χοῶς ἡ τῶν κοτυλῶν τὸ ν. διαλυμαίνεται Ar.Th.348. -ισμάτιον, τό, Dim. of νόμισμα, Poll.9.72,92, Sch.Ar.V.213; as name of a coin, Sammelb.6259 (v/vi A.D.), al.

νομισμᾰτο-πώλης, ου, ὁ, money-changer, Poll.7.170. -πωλικός, ή, όν, of or for a money-changer's trade: ἡ -κή (sc. τέχνη) Pl.Sph.223b.

νομ-ιστέος, α, ον, to be enacted (νομίζω I. 2), Pl.R.608b. II. νομιστέον, one must account, deem, Id.Sph.230d, Men.550, LxxEp.Je.40, Porph.Abst.1.12, etc. -ιστεύομαι, Pass., to be current, παρά τισι Plb.18.34.7, cf. S.E.M.1.178. ※ -ιστί or -εί, Adv. conventionally, opp. κατ' ἀλήθειαν, Diog.Oen.6, cf. Gal.1.417. -ιστός, ή, όν, customary, Orac.ap.Phleg.Fr.36.10J. II. conventional, ν. πάντα καὶ πρός τι S.E.P.3.232.

νομῐτεύομαι, = νομίζω I. 3, μέτροις οἷς ἡ πόλις ν. OGI579 (Cilicia); ἀστραγάλοις ν. Phld.Sto.339.14. II. Pass., = νομιστεύομαι, OGI339.44 (Sestos, ii B.C.), PFlor.1.6 (ii A.D.), etc.

νομο-αίολος, ον, (νόμος II) of varied melody, dub. in Telest.2. -γρᾰφέω, draft written laws, D.S.16.70, SIG344.54 (Teos, Epist. Antigoni), 684.18 (Dyme, ii B.C.). -γρᾰφία, ἡ, legislation, Call.Aet.Oxy.2080.93 (of Rhadamanthys), Str.6.1.8; drafting of laws, SIG563.17 (Teos, iii B.C., pl.). II. duties of a νομογράφος II, PTeb.397.34 (ii A.D.). -γρᾰφικός, ή, όν, drawn up by a νομογράφος II, ἐπιστολή BGU1135.7 (i B.C.). -γρᾰφος [ᾰ], ὁ, one who drafts laws, Pl.Phdr.278e, IG4.679.23 (Hermione), 4$^{2}$(1).73.2 (Epid., iii B.C.), 5(1).7 (Sparta), (2).433 (Megalopolis). II. notary, PHamb.4.15 (i A.D.), POxy.34i9 (ii A.D.), etc.; ν. ἀγορᾶς BGU888.4 (ii A.D.). -δείκτης, ου, Dor. -τας, ὁ, one who explains laws, legal adviser, IG5(1).1390.114 (Andania, i B.C.), BSA26.166 (Sparta), IGRom.4.468.19 (Pergam.), Plu.TG9. -δῐδάκτης, ου, ὁ, = sq., Id.Cat.Ma.20, Artem.2.29. -δῐδάσκᾰλος, ὁ, teacher of the law, Ev.Luc.5.17, al. -δίφας [ῑ], ου, ὁ, searcher into law,

*Gloss.* **-δότης**, ου, ὁ, *lawgiver*, Sm.*Ps.*75(76).12. **-θεσία**, ἡ, *legislation*, Pl.*R.*427b, *Lg.*684e: pl., Arist.*Rh.*1354$^b$2, Wilcken *Chr.* 6.11 (v A.D.). II. *code of laws*, Lys.30.35, *Com.Adesp.*110.2, Lxx 2*Ma.*6.23, Plu.2.240b. 2. metaph., of the *order* of nature, Vett. Val.344.1, Luc.*Am.*22. 3. pl., *arbitrary principles*, Epicur.*Ep.*2 p.36 U. **-θέσμως**, Adv. *lawfully*, Lxx *Pr.*31.27(26).

※ **νομοθετ-έω**, pf. νενομοθέτηκα Alex.126.13:—*frame laws*, Lys.15.9, Pl.*R.*534d, etc.; Λακεδαιμονίοις X.*Ap.*15; ταῖς μοναρχίαις Isoc.2.8; περί τινος Id.11.40; περὶ τινων Arist.*Pol.*1294$^a$37; ὑπὲρ ὅλου τοῦ ἐμπορίου D.56.48:—Med., *frame laws for oneself*, Pl.*R.*398b, *Tht.*177e, etc.:—Pass., of a state, *to be furnished with laws, have a code of laws*, Id. *Lg.*701d, 962e, cf. *Ep.Hebr.*7.11. II. *ordain by law*, τι Pl.*Lg.*628d, *R.*417b; ἐναντία τῷ ὅρκῳ τοῦ δήμου ν. And.4.3: c. inf., *enact*, τῶν ζῴων ἐστὶν ἃ σέβεσθαι ἐνομοθέτησε Isoc.11.26, cf. *POxy.*1119.16 (iii A.D.):—in Med., Pl.*Lg.*736c:—Pass., *to be ordained by law*, *Ep.Hebr.*8.6; τὰ καλῶς νενομοθετημένα ἡμῖν ὑπὸ τῶν βασιλέων *OGI*329.13 (Aegina, ii B.C.), cf. Luc.*Pr.Im.*18: impers., περὶ ταῦτα οὕτω σφι νενομοθέτηται *it has been so ordained by law*, Hdt.2.41; ν. καλὸν [εἶναι] τὸ χαρίζεσθαι Pl.*Smp.*182b; ἦν νενομοθετημένον Arist.*Pol.*1319$^a$11. ※ **-ημα**, ατος, τό, *law, ordinance*, Pl.*Plt.*295e, *R.*427b, etc. II. in pl., *conventions*, Hp. *de Arte* 2. ※ **-ης**, ου, ὁ, *lawgiver*, Antipho 5.15, Th.8.97, Pl. *R.*429c, *Ep.Jac.*4.12, etc. II. in pl., at Athens, a committee charged with the revision of the laws, Decr.ap.And.1.83, *IG*2$^2$.140.8, D.3.10, Lex ap.eund.24.21, etc. **-ησις**, εως, ἡ, f.l. for νουθέτησις, Pl.*Lg.*701b. **-ητέος**, α, ον, *to be settled by law*, Id.*R.*459e. II. νομοθετητέον, *one must make laws*, Id.*Lg.*747d; ν. τῷ νομοθέτῃ Arist. *Pol.*1283$^b$37. 2. trans., *one must enact*, ib.1336$^b$20. **-ικός**, ή, όν, *relating to legislation, legislative*, Pl.*Lg.*657a: ἡ -κή (sc. τέχνη) *legislation*, Pl.*Grg.*464c, 520b, al. Adv. -κῶς *Cod.Just.*1.4.34.14, Just.*Nov.*4.3 *Intr.*, Poll.4.26. II. of persons, *fitted for* or *skilled in legislation*, Arist.*EN*1180$^b$24; ἄνδρες Jul.*Caes.*320b. **-ις**, ιδος, ἡ, fem. of νομοθέτης, coined as expl. of θεσμοθέτις, Corn.*ND* 28.

**νομο-θήκη**, ἡ, poet. for νομοθεσία, Timo 9.4. **-ἵστωρ**, ορος, ὁ, ἡ, *learned in the laws*, Hsch. ※ **-μᾰθής**, ές, = foreg., Id. s.v. νομοΐστορες, *Gloss.* **-μᾰχέω**, *fight with laws*, coined on analogy of ναυμαχέω, Lollianus ap.Philostr.*VS*1.23.2.

**νομόνδε**, Adv., (νομός) *to pasture*, Il.18.575, Od.9.438.

**νομο-ποιέω**, *make laws*, Hsch. s.v. νομοθετεῖ. **-ποιός**, όν, (νόμος II) *composing music*, D.L.2.104. **-ρήτωρ**, ορος, ὁ, = ψηφισματοπώλης, Sch.Ar.*Av.*1038.

※ **νομός**, ὁ, (νέμω) *place of pasturage*, Il.2.475, Od.9.217, etc.; ν. ὕλης a woodland *pasture*, 10.159; ν. Περιδάϊος *pasture* of Ida, Pi.*Pae.*4.51. 2. *herbage, pasture*, *h.Merc.*198: generally, *food*, Hes.*Op.*526; ἐπέτονθ'.. ἐπὶ νομόν Ar.*Av.*1287, cf. 239 (lyr.). 3. metaph., ἐπέων πολὺς ν. ἔνθα καὶ ἔνθα a wide *range* for words (but expld. by Sch. as = νέμησις, *apportionment*), Il.20.249; πάντη.. νόμος (νομοὶ Barnes) βεβλήαται ᾠδῆς *h.Ap.*20; but, ἐπέων ν. *expenditure* of words, Hes. *Op.*403. II. *habitation*, Pi.*O.*7.33, S.*OC*1061 (lyr.), etc.; νομὸν ἐν θαλάσσῃ ἔχειν to have their *dwelling-place*, Hdt.5.92.α'; δενδρέων ν. Διόνυσος αὐξάνοι Pi.*Fr.*153. 2. *district, sphere of command, province*, Hdt.5.102, etc.; *satrapy*, Id.1.192, 3.90; of the *regions* of Scythia, Id.4.62, 66; esp. of the *districts* of Egypt, Id.2.4, al., D.S. 1.54, Str.17.1.22, etc.

**νόμος**, ὁ, (νέμω) *that which is in habitual practice, use* or *possession*, not in Hom. (cf. J.*Ap.*2.15), though read by Zenod. in Od.1.3. I. *usage, custom*, [Μοῦσαι] μέλπονται πάντων τε νόμους καὶ ἤθεα κεδνά Hes.*Th.*66; ν. ἀρχαῖος ἄριστος Id.*Fr.*221; ἔνθα ν. (sc. ἐστί) c. inf., where it is *the custom*.., Alc.*Supp.*25.5; ν. πάντων βασιλεύς *custom* is lord of all, Pi.*Fr.*169.1; ν. δεσπότης Hdt.7.104, Pl. *Lg.*715d; ν. τύραννος τῶν ἀνθρώπων Id.*Prt.*337d; ἴησις ὀθονίοισι κατὰ τὸν ν. τὸν ἀρθριτικόν Hp.*Art.*18; ὡς νόμος Id.*Mochl.*37: hence, *law, ordinance*, τόνδε..ν. διέταξε Κρονίων..θηρσὶ..ἐσθέμεν ἀλλήλους Hes. *Op.*276; τρέφονται πάντες οἱ ἀνθρώπειοι ν. ὑπὸ τοῦ θείου Heraclit. 114; ἄφθογγον εἶναι τὸν παλαμναῖον ν. [ἐστί] A.*Eu.*448; ν. κάλλιστον ἐξευρόντα, πειθαρχεῖν πατρί S.*Tr.*1177; ν. κοινός, = ὀρθὸς λόγος, Zeno *Stoic.*1.43: pl., ἔργων..ὧν νόμοι πρόκεινται ὑψίποδες S.*OT*865 (lyr.); νεοχμοῖς ν. Ζεὺς κρατύνει A.*Pr.*150 (lyr.). b. in *VT*, of the *law* of God, ἐν τῷ νόμῳ Κυρίου τὸ θέλημα αὐτοῦ Lxx *Ps.*1.2, al., cf. *Is.*2.3; νόμον ὃν ἐνετείλατο ὑμῖν Μωϋσῆς ib.*De.*33.4; so in *NT*, ὁ ν. Μωϋσέως *Ev.Luc.*2.22, etc.; but also ὁ ν. τοῦ Χριστοῦ *Ep.Gal.*6.2; ὁ ν. τοῦ Πνεύματος τῆς ζωῆς, opp. ὁ ν. τῆς ἁμαρτίας καὶ τοῦ θανάτου, *Ep.Rom.*8.2; ν. τέλειος ὁ τῆς ἐλευθερίας *Ep.Jac.*1.25. c. with Preps., κατὰ νόμον according to *custom* or *law*, Hes.*Th.*417, Hdt.1.61, etc.; κὰν νόμον Pi.*O.*8.78; οἱ κατὰ ν. ὄντες θεοί the *established* deities, Pl.*Lg.*904a; κατὰ νόμους A.*Supp.*241; παρὰ νόμον contrary to.., Id.*Eu.*171 (lyr.); παρὰ τοὺς τῆς φύσεως ν. Pl.*Ti.*83e; ἐν Πανελλάνων νόμῳ Pi.*I.*2.38; ἐν Ἀδραστείῳ νόμῳ by *the law* of Adrastus, i.e. at the Nemean games, Id. *N.*10.28: esp. in dat. νόμῳ *by custom, conventionally*, opp. φύσει, Hdt. 4.39, Philol.9, Arist.*EN*1094$^b$16, etc.; ν. γλυκύ, ν. πικρόν, Democr.9; εἰ μή τις λέγοι ν. δρᾶν καὶ τὰς λεγομένας ποιότητας μὴ ἐν τοῖς ὑποκειμένοις εἶναι Plot.4.4.29; ὅσον νόμου χάριν just for *form's* sake, Diph.43.14, Arist.*Metaph.*1076$^a$27. d. *statute, ordinance made by authority*, [Σόλων] νόμους ἔθηκεν ἄλλους, τοῖς δὲ Δράκοντος θεσμοῖς ἐπαύσαντο χρώμενοι πλὴν τῶν φονικῶν Id.*Ath.*7.1 (but τὸν Δράκοντος ν. τὸν περὶ τοῦ φόνου *IG*1$^2$.115.5), etc.; νόμον τιθέναι, τίθεσθαι, v. τίθημι; βασιλικὸς ν. *OGI*483.1 (Pergam., ii A.D.), *Ep.Jac.*2.8: freq. of *general laws*, opp. ψηφίσματα (special decrees), Pl.*Tht.*173d, etc.; ὅταν τὰ ψηφίσματα κύρια ᾖ ἀλλὰ μὴ ὁ ν. Arist.*Pol.*1292$^a$7: generally, *law*, ἄνευ ὀρέξεως νοῦς ὁ ν. ἐστίν ib.1287$^a$32; ἄγραφος ν. Lex ap.And.1.85, etc.; opp. γεγραμμένος, Arist.*Rh.*1373$^b$6; ν. ἴδιος, opp. κοινός, ib.4; ὁ ν. freq. as subject, οἱ ν. διδόασι τιμωρίας D.18.12; ὧν ὁ ν. ἀγορεύει *Inscr.Magn.* 92b16 (ii B.C.); μὴ ὁ ν. κρίνει τὸν ἄνθρωπον ἐὰν μὴ ἀκούσῃ πρῶτον; *Ev.Jo.*7.51. e. c. gen. rei, οὗτός τοι πεδίων πέλεται ν. Hes.*Op.*388; Ὑλλίδος στάθμας ἐν νόμοις Pi.*P.*1.62; τὸν φαρμάκων δίδαξε μαλακόχειρα ν. Id.*N.*3.55; ν. ἐμβολῆς καὶ διορθώσιος Hp.*Mochl.*38; ὁ ν. τοῦ κριοῦ, τοῦ ἀνδρός, τῶν ἐρανιστῶν, Lxx *Le.*6.31(7.1), *Ep.Rom.*7.2, *SIG* 1198.14 (Arcesine, iii B.C.); ἐς χειρῶν νόμον ἀπικέσθαι to come *to blows, into action*, Hdt.9.48; ἐν χειρῶν νόμῳ ἀπόλλυσθαι, περιπεσεῖν, die *in action*, Id.8.89, Plb.1.57.8; μεταλλάξαι τὸν βίον ἐν χ. ν. Id.3.63.5, cf. 3.116.9; Ἀσδρούβας.. ἐν χ. ν. κατέστρεψε τὸν βίον Id.11.2.1; τοὺς μὲν ἐν χ. ν. διέφθειρε Id.1.82.2; τοὺς ἐν χ. ν. τὰς πολιτείας καταλύοντας by 'direct *action*', Aeschin.1.5; but κτεῖναι ἐν ταῖς πολεμικαῖς ἐξόδοις ἐν χειρὸς νόμῳ *under martial law*, Arist.*Pol.*1285$^a$10; τῷ τοῦ πολέμου νόμῳ κτησάμενος Aeschin.2.33. 2. Νόμος personified, οἱ θεοὶ σθένουσι χὠ κείνων κρατῶν N. E.*Hec.*800, cf. Orph.*Fr.*105, 160. II. *melody, strain*, οἶδα δ' ὀρνίχων νόμως πάντων Alcm.67; ν. ἵππιος Pi.*O.*1.101; Ἀπόλλων ἀγεῖτο παντοίων ν. Id.*N.*5.25; ν. πολεμικοί Th.5.69; ἐπηλάλαξαν Ἀραὶ τὸν ὀξὺν ν. A.*Th.*952 (lyr.); κρεκτοὶ ν. S.*Fr.*463, cf. *AP*9.584: metaph., τοὺς Ἅιδου ν. S.*Fr.*861. 2. esp. a type of early *melody* created by Terpander for the lyre as an accompaniment to Epic texts, ν. ὄρθιος Hdt.1.24; ν. Βοιώτιος S.*Fr.*966; ν. κιθαρῳδικοί Ar.*Ra.*1282, cf. Pl.*Lg.*700d, Arist.*Po.*1447$^b$26, *Pr.*918$^b$13, etc.; also for the flute, ν. αὐλῳδικός Plu.2.1132d; without sung text, ν. αὐλητικός ib.1133d, cf. 138b, Poll.4.79; later, *composition including both words and melody*, e.g. Tim.*Pers.* III. = νοῦμμος (q.v.), Epich.136, Sophr.162, *Inscr.Délos* 407.21 (ii B.C.); ν. σηστέρτιοι, = Lat. *nummi sestertii*, *Inscr.Prien.*41.13 (ii B.C.). IV. Archit., *course* of masonry, *IG*12(2).11.17 (Mytil.).

**νομοφῠλᾰκ-έω**, *preserve the laws*, Arist.*Ath.*8.4; *serve as* νομοφύλαξ I, *SIG*282.18 (Priene, iv B.C.), *Dialex.*7.6, *Abh.Berl.Akad.*1925 (5).7 (Cyrene, iii B.C.), *BSA*26.166 (Sparta, ii A.D.), Lib.*Decl.*43.7: irreg. form νομοφυλάξαντα (as if fr. *νομοφυλάσσω), *IGRom.*4.1637.10 (Philadelphia). **-ία**, ἡ, *preservation of the laws*, Pl.*Lg.*961a; *office of* νομοφύλαξ I, Arist.*Pol.*1322$^b$39, *PCair.Zen.*37.9 (iii B.C.). **-ικός**, ή, όν, *observant of law*, γένος Hierocl. *in CA*11 p.440 M.; ν. ἐπιστήμη ibid. **-ιον** (-εῖον Suid.), τό, *office of the* νομοφύλακες, Poll.8.102, Hsch. s.v. Χαρώνιον. **-ίς**, ίδος, *containing the law*, κιβωτός Ph. 1.584. II. epith. of Aphrodite at Cyrene, *Rendic.Linc.*1925.420 (i B.C.).

**νομοφύλαξ** [ῠ], ᾰκος, ὁ (ἡ Lxx 4*Ma.*15.32), *guardian of the laws*, title of officials appointed to watch over the laws and their observance, Pl.*Lg.*755a, 770c, etc.; οἱ ν. ἀριστοκρατικόν Arist.*Pol.*1323$^a$8, cf. Cic.*Legg.*3.20.46; at Athens, Philoch.141b, etc.; at Sparta, Paus.3.11.2, *IG*5(1).31, al.; at Thasos, *BCH*52.55 (iv/iii B.C.); at Alexandria, *PHal.*1.42 (iii B.C.), prob. in Mitteis *Chr.*369 i 33 (iii B.C.); at Priene, *SIG*282.17 (iv B.C.); at Cyrene, *Abh.Berl.Akad.* 1925(5).7 (iii B.C.). 2. *observer of the law*, σὺ ἡ ν. Lxx l.c. II. minor official under control of village elders, with police and fiscal duties, *PAmh.*2.108.8, *BGU*759.20, *PRyl.*122.7, *POxy.*1440.7 (all ii A.D.).

**νομ-ώδης**, ες, (νομή I.3b) *like a spreading ulcer*, ἕλκος Alex.Aphr. *Pr.*1.92, cf. Gal.13.860; σηπεδών Id.10.702. 2. *full of shreds* as from such sores, διαχωρήματα Id.14.754. **-ῳδός**, ὁ, *one who chants* or *proclaims the law*, Str.12.2.9. ※ **-ώνης**, ου, Boeot. **-ώνας**, ὁ, *official who leases public pasture*, *IG*7.3171.43 (Orchom. Boeot.).

※ **νόννος**, ὁ, = πατήρ (cf. νέννος), τοῦ νόνου (sic) ἀδελφοὶ ὁμοπάτριοι Cumont *Fouilles de Doura-Europos* 310.

**νοο-γάστωρ**, ορος, ὁ, ἡ, *living by one's wits*, Tz.*H.*10.774. **-ειδής**, ές, *having the form of Intelligence, of intelligible character*, Plot.5.1.3, 5.3.8, Procl. *in Ti.*1.247, 407 D. **-πλαγκτος**, ον, = sq. I, Nonn.*D.* 9.255. **-πλᾰνής**, ές, *wandering in mind, deranged*, ib.4.197. II. Act., *distracting the mind*, ib.29.69. **-πληκτος**, ον, *palsying the mind*, μέθη *AP*6.71 (Paul. Sil.). **-πλήξ**, ῆγος, ὁ, ἡ, = foreg., ἀτασθαλίαι Tryph.275. **-ποιός**, όν, *creating Intelligence*, δύναμις Plot.6.8.18, cf. Procl. *in Ti.*1.311 D., *in Prm.* p.543 S., Dam.*Pr.*90.

※ **νόος**, νόου, ὁ, Att. contr. **νοῦς**, gen. νοῦ: Hom. uses the contr. form once, in nom., Od.10.240, cf. Hes.*Fr.*205 (Hdt. never): Trag. use contr. form, exc. in A.*Ch.*742 (iamb.), S.*Ph.*1209 (lyr.): Aeol. gen. νῶ Alc.*Supp.*9.1; acc. νῶν Sapph.ib.25.2; νόον Ead.70 (s.v.l.): heterocl. forms are found in *NT* and later writers, gen. νοός *Ep. Rom.*7.23, Lxx 4*Ma.*1.35; dat. νοΐ 1*Ep.Cor.*1.10, [Aristid.]*Or.*35(9).26; nom. pl. νόες Ph.1.86, Plot.6.7.17, Dam.*Pr.*96; acc. pl. νόας Plu. *Fr.*7.27, Iamb.*Myst.*1.15, Ammon. *in Int.*243.3 (v.l.), Dam.*Pr.*103: Att. pl. νοῖ, acc. νοῦς, gen. νόων ib.122, dat. νοῖς ibid., is rare in early writers, as Ar.*Fr.*471, but freq. in later philosophy: 1. *mind*, as employed in perceiving and thinking, *sense, wit*, οὐ λῆθε Διὸς πυκινὸν ν. Il.15.461; ν. πολυκερδέα Od.13.255; ν. ὁρῇ καὶ ν. ἀκούει, τἆλλα κωφὰ καὶ τυφλά Epich.249, cf. S.*OT*371; νόῳ *prudently*, Od.6.320; παρὲκ νόον *senselessly*, Il.20.133; σὺν νόῳ *wisely*, Hdt.8.86, 138; ξὺν νῷ with play on ξυνῷ, Heraclit.114 (νόῳ codd. Stob.); ξὺν νῷ ἑλομένῳ Pl. *R.*619b; οὐδενὶ ξὺν νῷ Id.*Cri.*48c; μηδενὶ ξὺν νῷ Ar.*Nu.*580; τοῦ νοῦ χωρὶς S.*OT*550; τοῦ ν. κενός Id.*OC*931; νόῳ λαβεῖν τι to apprehend it, Hdt.3.51; νόῳ σχεῖν, ἔχειν, *recall, remember*, Id.5.92.η', Pl.*R.*490a; κοινὸς ν. Phld.*Rh.*1.37 S., Arr.*Epict.*3.6.8; ἀγαθὸς ν., σπουδαῖος ν., Phld.*Rh.*2.61, 1.252 S. 2. νοῦν ἔχειν in two senses, a. to have *sense*, be *sensible*, S.*Tr.*553, *El.*1013, 1465, Ar.*Ra.*535, etc.; ὁ νοῦς ὅδ' αὐτὸς ν. ἔχων οὐ τυγχάνει E.*IA*1139; so ν. ὀλίγον κεκτημένος

Ar.*Ec.*747; σμικρὸν νοῦ κεκτῆσθαι Pl.*Lg.*887e; impers., τὸ γὰρ περισσὰ πράσσειν οὐκ ἔχει ν. οὐδένα S.*Ant.*68, cf. Pl.*Ti.*68b; cf. νουνεχόντως. b. νοῦν or τὸν ν. ἔχειν to have *one's mind* directed to something, ἄλλοσ' ὄμμα, θητέρᾳ δὲ ν. ἔχειν S.*Tr.*272, cf. Sapph.*Supp.*25.2; τὸν ν. πρὸς αὐτὸν οὐκ ἔχων, ἐκεῖσε δέ E.*Ph.*1418; δεῦρο ν. ἔχε Id.*Or.* 1181; οἴκοι τὸν ν. ἔχειν Id.*Ion* 251; ποῦ τὸν ν. ἔχεις; Ar.*Ec.*156; τὸν ν. ἔχειν πρός τινα or τι (like προσέχειν τὸν ν.) Th.7.19, Pl.*Grg.*504d; πρός τινι Id.*Prt.*324a, etc.; περί τινος Id.*R.*534b; ἐν πέρδιξιν *AP*7.206 (Damoch.): conversely, ἐπὶ νοῦν ἐλθεῖν τινι to *occur* to one, D.H.3.15, Arr.*An.*7.24.3. 3. *mind*, more widely, as employed in feeling, deciding, etc., *heart*, χαῖρε νόῳ Od.8.78; κεῦθε νόῳ Il.1.363; [χόλος] οἰδάνει νόον 9.554; ἐνὶ στήθεσσιν ἀτάρβητος ν. ἐστί 3.63; ν. ἔμπεδος, ἀκήλητος, ἀπηνής, 11.813, Od.10.329, 18.381; ν. εὐμενής, ἄγναμπτος, etc., Pi.*P.*8.18, A.*Pr.*164 (lyr.), etc.; πολλῶν ἀνθρώπων νόον ἔγνω Od.1.3; ἐκ παντὸς νόου with all his *heart and soul*, Hdt.8.97; τῷ νῷ.. κἀπὸ τῆς γλώσσης in *heart* as well as tongue, S.*OC* 936: freq. in phrase κατὰ νόον according to one's *mind*, Hdt.1.117, 7.104; εἰ τάδ' ἔχει κατὰ νοῦν κείνῳ S.*OC* 1768 (anap.); πράξειας κατὰ ν. τὸν ἐμόν Id.*Fr.*469 (anap.); κατὰ ν. πράξας Ar.*Eq.*549; χωρεῖ κατὰ ν. Id.*Pax* 940, cf. Pl.*Euthphr.*3e. 4. *mind, resolve, purpose*, ἀγαθῷ νόῳ, i.e. kindly, Hdt.1.60; τί σοι ἐν νόῳ ἐστὶ ποιέειν; what do you *intend* to do? ib.109; ἡμῖν ἐν ν. ἐγένετο εἰπεῖν Id.9.46; ἐν ν. ἔχειν c. fut. inf., *to intend*.., Id.1.10 (v.l.): c. pres. inf., ib. 27, Pl.*R.*344d; ποιέειν τι ἐπὶ νόον τινί to put into his *mind* to do.., Hdt.1.27; ἐπὶ νόον τρέπειν τινί.. Id.3.21; ταύτῃ ⟨δ⟩ ν. ἔφερε Id.9.120. 5. *reason, intellect*, νόου φρενί Xenoph.25, cf. Parm.16.2, etc.; θεῖος ν. Democr.112, cf. Id.ap.Arist.*de An.*404a28; opp. δόξα, Pl.*Ti.*51d, cf. Arist.*de An.*428a5. b. *Mind* as the active principle of the Universe, Anaxag.12, etc.; Θαλῆς νοῦν τοῦ κόσμου τὸν θεόν *Placit.*1.7.11; ἡ τοῦ κόσμου γένεσις ἐξ ἀνάγκης καὶ νοῦ συστάσεως Pl.*Ti.*48a, cf. *Sph.*249a, *Phlb.*30c, Arist.*Metaph.*1072b20, *de An.*430a17, Zeno *Stoic.*1.28, Plot.5.1.4. II. *act of mind, thought*, ἡμῖν δ' οὔ τις τοῦδε νόος καὶ μῆτις ἀμείνων Il.15.509; οὐ γάρ τις νόον ἄλλος ἀμείνονα τοῦδε νοήσει 9.104; οὐ γὰρ δὴ τοῦτον μὲν ἐβούλευσας νόον αὐτή Od.5.23. 2. *purpose, design*, νόον τελεῖν τινι Il.23.149; σάφα οἶσθ' οἷος ν. Ἀτρεΐωνος 2.192. III. *sense, meaning* of a word, etc., οὗτος ὁ νόος τοῦ ῥήματος Hdt.7.162, cf. Ar.*Ra.*1439, Plb.5.83.4, Phld.*Rh.*1.106 S., etc.; ὁ νόος τῆς θυσίης cj. for νόμος in Hdt.1.216; *meaning* of a work of art, Philostr.*VA* 4.28; πολὺς ν. ἐν ὀλίγῃ λέξει συνέσταλται Plu.2.510e; πρὸς τὸν αὐτὸν νοῦν to the same *effect*, Str.15.3.7; πρὸς νοῦν οὐδὲν λέγοντες to the *point*, Phld.*Mus.*p.96 K.; οὐδὲ νοῦν ἔχον *senseless*, Id.*Po.*5.29. IV. Pythag. name for μονάς, *Theol.Ar.*6. (Etym. dub.; the pr. n. ΠολυνόϝΑ *IG*9(1).870 hardly proves νόϝος.)

**νοοσφᾰλής**, ές, (σφάλλω) = νοοπλανής II, Nonn.*D.*17.277.

**νοότης**, ητος, ἡ, *intellectuality*, τῆς νοότητος ὡς ἁπλουστέρας οὔσης τοῦ νοῦ καὶ οἷον ἕξεως τοῦ νοεῖν Procl.*in Prm.*p.863 S., cf. Dam.*Pr.*58.

**νοόω**, *convert into pure Intelligence*, in Pass., νοῦς γενομένη [ἡ ψυχὴ] αὐτὴ θεωρεῖ οἷον νοωθεῖσα Plot.6.7.35, cf. 6.8.5; ἡ νοῦς ἐστιν ἢ νενόωται Procl.*in Prm.*p.491 S.; τὸ δὲ ἔννουν ψυχή ἐστι νενοωμένη Dam.*Pr.*100.

**νορβά**· καλή, Hsch. **νορβεῖ**· ἐνταμεῖται, Id. **νορειά**, v. νόρρος. **νορθακινοί**· ἀσθενεῖς, Id. **νόρρος**· ἄνθος μήλινον λωτοῦ, Id.: also a tree growing by the sea (also called νορειά), Id. **νορύειν**· γῆν ὀρύειν (sic), Id.

⊛ **νορύη**, ἡ, a plant, = στρύχνον, τιθύμαλλος, Thphr.ap.Phot., cf. Hdn. Gr.1.306.

**νοσ-άζω**, (νόσος) *to be ill*, Gal.15.302:—also in Med., opp. ὑγιάζομαι, Arist.*Ph.*229b3. 2. causal, *produce sickness*, τὰ νοσάζοντα αἴτια Gal.1.208, cf. 140. ⊛ **-ἀκερός**, ά, όν, *liable to sickness, sickly*, Arist.*Pol.*1279a15, *PA*670b7.—Vulgar word, acc. to Poll.3.105. **-ανσις**, εως, ἡ, (as if from *νοσαίνω) *falling sick*, opp. ὑγίανσις, Arist.*Ph.*230a22, Plot.6.3.22 and 23; v.l. for νόσωσις, Arist.*Ph.*229a26. **-ερός**, ά, όν, = νοσηρός, of symptoms, Hp.*Aph.*7.67; ν. κῶλον E.*Or.*1016 (anap.); ν. κοῖτα a bed *of sickness*, Id.*Hipp.*131 (lyr.), cf. 179 (anap.); ν. χειμών Arist.*Pr.*861b22; νοσερά, opp. ὑγιεινά, Polystr.p.3 W., cf. Alex.Aphr.*in Top.*71.2; *unhealthy*, of persons, Ph.1.198 (Sup.). Adv. -ρῶς, ἔχειν Arist.*Pol.*1320b36. **-ερότης**, ητος, ἡ, *infirmitas*, dub. in *Gloss.* **-ευμα**, ατος, τό, *sickness*, Hp.*Aër.*7 (pl.). **-εύομαι**, Pass., *to be sickly*, [ἔμβρυα] νενοσευμένα Id.*Septim.*2. ⊛ **-έω** (no Ion. form **νουσέω** is found), *to be sick, ail*, whether in body or mind, Hdt.1.105, etc.; τῆς πόλεως.. οὔπω νενοσηκυίας not yet *having suffered from the plague*, Th.2.31; νενοσηκὸς αἷμα *diseased*, Arist.*HA*521a18; νόσῳ ν. A.*Pr.*386: c. acc. cogn., νοῦσον νοσεῖν Hdt.3.33, cf. E.*Andr.*220; τελευταίαν νόσον ν. Antipho 1.30; τι τῶν ἀπορρήτων κακῶν E.*Hipp.*293: c. acc. partis, νοσεῖν κῶλον S.*Ph.*41; ν. ὀφθαλμούς Pl.*Grg.*496a; νεφρούς Arist.*PA*671b11, etc.; τὸ νοσοῦν, = νόσος, S.*Ph.*675, Pl.*Smp.*186b: freq. in aor. νοσῆσαι, *fall sick*, Hdt.1.19, Th.1.138, Arist.*Rh.*1392a11, Luc.*Macr.*22, etc.; of things, γῆ νοσεῖ X.*Ath.*2.6; of plants, Thphr.*CP*5.9.9:—Pass., ἡμέραι αἱ νοσούμεναι days *on which one is ill*, Hp.*Septim.*7. 2. of passion, ν. μάταν *to be mad*, S.*Aj.*635 (lyr.); θολερῷ χειμῶνι νοσήσας ib.207 (anap.); ἐξ ἀλαστόρων ν. Id.*Tr.*1235; νοσῶν alone, opp. σώφρων, ib.435; ν. τὰς φρένας Cratin.329; ν. περὶ δόξαν *to have a morbid craving* for fame, Plu.2.546f; ψυχῆς νοσούσης ἐστὶ φάρμακον λόγος Men.*Mon.*550. 3. generally, *suffer*, νοσεῖ τὰ τῶν θεῶν E.*Tr.*27; τοῖσιν οἰκείοις κακοῖς S.*OC*766; ἀπαιδίᾳ E.*Ion* 620; πονηρίᾳ X.*Mem.*3.5.18; ἐκεῖ νοσοῦμεν ὅτι.. E.*Hel.*581: c. acc. cogn., τόδ' ἄλγος S.*Ph.*1326; esp. of states, *suffer* from faction and the like, ἡ Μίλητος νοσήσασα στάσι Hdt.5.28; νοσεῖ πόλις S.*Ant.*1015, cf. Pl.*Mx.*243e; νοσοῦσι καὶ τεταραγμένοις D.2.14; νοσοῦντας ἐν αὑτοῖς Id.9.50; ἀπόλωλε καὶ νενόσηκεν ἡ Ἑλλάς ib.39; αἱ δὲ πόλεις ἐνόσουν Id.18.45; τὰ πράγματα νοσοῦντα Arist.*Ath.*6.4; νοσῶν γάμος Ael.*NA*8.20.

**νοσηλ-εία**, ἡ, *care of the sick, nursing*, J.*AJ*4.8.33, Plu.*Lyc.*10, Gal.5.48, D.C.76.7. II. *sickness which needs tending*, Lysimach.ap.J.*Ap.*1.34, Plu.2.110c (pl.), 788f, Sor.1.79 (pl.). 2. *matter discharged* from a sore, S.*Ph.*39. ⊛ **-εύω**, *tend a sick person*, τινα Isoc.19.25, Anaxil.19, Phylarch.61 J., Babr.13.8; οἱ νοσηλεύοντες *physicians*, *IGRom.*1.1228 (Egypt). II. Pass., *need medical attendance*, *to be sick*, J.*BJ*4.1.9, App.*BC*2.28, Gal.8.291, Asp.*in EN*26.17; ν. τρυφηλῶς Jul.*Or.*6.181d. **-ιος**, α, ον, *of* or *for sickness*: νοσήλια (sc. σιτία), τά, *food for sick persons*, Opp.*H.*1.301. ⊛ **-ός**, ή, όν, *morbid*, ὑγρόν Hp.*Loc.Hom.*10; *diseased*, v.l. for νοσηρός (q.v.). Adv. Comp. -ότερον *with a sickly tendency*, Id.*Epid.*6.6.8, *Aph.*6.2 (v.l. νοσηρ-).

**νόσ-ημα**, Ion. **νούσ-**, ατος, τό, (νοσέω) *disease*, Hp.*Flat.*1, S.*Ph.*755, E.*El.*656, Th.2.49,53, etc.; τὰ περὶ τὸ σῶμα ν. Isoc.8.39; νοσήμασι περιπίπτειν X.*Cyr.*6.2.27; νοσήματα τῶν σπερμάτων Thphr.*HP* 8.10.1; [τῶν φυτῶν] ib.4.14.1. 2. metaph., of *passion, vice*, etc., ἔνεστι γάρ πως τοῦτο τῇ τυραννίδι ν. A.*Pr.*227; ν. γὰρ αἴσχιστον εἶναί φημι συνθέτους λόγους ib.685; νοσοῖμ' ἄν, εἰ ν. τοὺς ἐχθροὺς στυγεῖν ib.978; of love, S.*Fr.*149.1; τὸ ν. τῆς ἀδικίας Pl.*Grg.*480b, cf. Chrysipp.*Stoic.*3.103. b. of any *grievous affliction*, S.*OT*1293; esp. of *disorder* in a state, τυραννίδα.. ἔσχατον πόλεως ν. Pl.*R.*544c, cf. D.19.259, etc. **-ημᾰτικός**, ή, όν, *morbid, diseased*, Arist.*GA*725a11; ν. τὰ περὶ τὴν κεφαλήν Id.*Pr.*881b8; τὰ ν. Id.*HA*521a28; ν. τῷ σώματι Plu.2.245c. Adv. -κῶς Thphr.*CP*6.10.5. ⊛ **-ημάτιον**, τό, Dim. of νόσημα, Ar.*Fr.*90. **-ημᾰτώδης**, ες, = νοσώδης, Arist.*GA*727b28, *EN*1149a6, Ptol.*Tetr.*188. Adv. νοσηματωδῶς, ἔχειν Arist.*EN*1148b33. **-ήμη**, ἡ, = νόσημα, Theognost.*Can.*112 (-ίμη cod.). **-ηρός**, ά, όν, *diseased*, ὀστέον νοσηρότερον (v.l. νοσηλ-) Hp.*Art.*50; *unhealthy*, χωρία X.*Cyr.*1.6.16; *unwholesome*, ὕδωρ Plu.2.974c, cf. Hp.*Oct.*12. Adv. Comp. -ότερον v.l. for νοσηλ- (q.v.). **-ητήριος**, α, ον, *unhealthy*, Hsch. s.v. κηρέσιον. **-ηφόρος**, ον, *disease-bringing*, Marc.Sid.58. **-ίζω**, *make sick*, Arist.*Pr.*859a15.

**Νόσιος**, ὁ, *Healer*, title of Zeus, *Schwyzer* 725.9 (Milet., vi/v B.C.).

**νοσο-βᾰρής**, v. νουσο-. **-γνωμονικός**, ή, όν, *skilled in judging of diseases by their symptoms*: ἡ -κή (sc. τέχνη), the physician's art, *diagnostic*, Pl.ap.D.L.3.85. **-εργός**, όν, *causing sickness*, Poet.*de herb.*39. **-θῡμος**, ον, *sick at heart*, Man.4.540. ⊛ **-κομεῖον**, τό, *infirmary, hospital*, *Cod.Just.*1.2.15.1, Suid.: late word for ξενών, acc. to Sch.Poll.1.79. ⊛ **-κομέω**, *tend the sick*, D.S.14.71, D.L.4.54, Iamb.*VP*30.184:—Pass., *to be under medical treatment*, D.S.37.27. **-κομία**, ἡ, *care of the sick*, Arr.*Epict.*3.22.70 (pl.), Iamb.*Protr.*21.κβ' (pl.), Sch.S.*Ph.*39. **-κόμος**, ὁ, *sick-nurse, hospital superintendent*, Poll.3.12, *Cod.Just.*1.3.41.13, Just.*Nov.*7.1. **-λογέω**, *explain a disease*, τὸ αἴτιον οὕτως -λογεῖ Meno *Iatr.*11.40. **-λύτης**, v. νουσο-. **-μελής**, v. νουσο-. **-ποιέω**, *cause sickness*, Hp.*Acut.*35, Arist.*Pr.*865b25, Alex.Aphr.*in Top.*4.27, f.l. in Plu.2.918d. 2. ν. [τινά] *infect* one with a disease, Ceb.19; ν. τὰς ψυχὰς τῶν ἀρίστων D.S.12.12:—Pass., Herophil.ap.Sor.2.3. **-ποιός**, όν, *causing sickness*, Diph.Siph.ap.Ath.3.80e; ν. αἴτια Gal.1.158. 2. metaph., *causing disturbances*, D.H.8.90.

⊛ **νόσος**, Ep. and Ion. (not Dor., cf. *Berl.Sitzb.*1927.156 (Cyrene)) **νοῦσος**, ἡ, *sickness, disease, plague*, νοῦσον ἀνὰ στρατὸν ὦρσε κακήν (sc. Apollo), ὀλέκοντο δὲ λαοί Il.1.10; νοῦσόν γ' οὔ πως ἔστι Διὸς μεγάλου ἀλέασθαι Od.9.411; δολιχῇ ν. 11.172; νοῦσοι ἀργαλέαι Hes.*Op.*92:—Phrases: ἐς ν. πεσεῖν A.*Pr.*473; ἐς ν. ἐμπίπτειν Antipho 1.20; νόσον ἐμπεπτωκέναι τοῖς κτήνεσιν X.*Cyr.*8.3.41; μοι ν. ἐπήλυθεν Od.11.200; νόσῳ ληφθέντι S.*Tr.*445; κάμνειν νόσον, ὑπὸ νόσου, v. κάμνω; ἀσθενεῖν ταύτην τὴν νόσον Isoc.19.24; ἐκ τῆς νούσου ἀνέστη Hdt.1.22; θήλεα ν. ib.105, cf. Hdn.4.12.2; ἱερὰ νόσος, v. ἱερός IV. 8: ν. defined, Gal.7.43. II. generally, *distress, anguish*, Hes.*Th.*527, S.*OC*544 (lyr.), etc. 2. *disease of mind*, esp. caused by madness, passion, vice, etc., ν. φρενῶν A.*Pers.*750 (troch.); θεία ν., i.e. *madness*, S.*Aj.*185 (lyr.); μανιάσιν ν. ib.59; λυσσώδη ν. ib.452; of love, Id.*Tr.*491; Ἀφροδίτας ν. E.*Hipp.*767 (lyr.); ἀκόλαστον ἔσχε γλῶσσαν, αἰσχίστην ν. Id.*Or.*10; τῆς μεγίστης ν., ἀνοίας Pl.*Lg.*691d; ν. καὶ στάσιν οὐ ταὐτὸν νενόμικας; Id.*Sph.*228a. 3. *plague, bane, mischief*, e.g. a whirlwind is θεία ν. S.*Ant.*421, cf. 1141 (lyr.); of the trident of Poseidon, A.*Pr.*924 (s.v.l.); πεντεσύριγγος ν., of the pillory, Polyeuct.ap.Arist.*Rh.*1411a23; κτείνειν τινὰ ὡς νόσον πόλεως Pl.*Prt.*322d.

**νοσο-τροφία**, ἡ, *nursing of disease*, Pl.*R.*407b; ἡ τοῦ σώματος ν. ib.496c, cf. Ael.*VH*4.15. ⊛ **-τῡφέω**, (τῦφος) *to be ostentatious in sickness*, Jul.*Or.*6.181d.

**νοσσάκιον**, τό, Dim. of sq., *PMag.Leid.V.*1.35,36.

**νόσσαξ**, ακος, ὁ, (νοσσός) *chick, cockerel*, Dsc.2.49.

⊛ **νοσσὰς ὄρνις**, ἡ, *fowl*, Panyas.26.

**νοσσεύω, νοσσιά, νοσσίον, νοσσίς, νοσσοποιέω, νοσσός, νοσσοτροφέω**, v. νεοσσ-.

**νοστ-έω**, *go* or *come home, return*, ν. ἐς πατρίδα γαῖαν Od.1.290, Epic.ap.Plu.2.297b; ν. οἴκαδε, οἰκόνδε, ὅνδε δόμονδε, Il.4.103, 5.687, Od.1.83: c. acc., ν. Ἄργος, οἶκον, S.*OC*1386, E.*IT*534: pleon., ὀπίσω ν. Hdt.3.26; ν. πάλιν Ar.*Av.*1270: c. dat. modi, ν. κεινῇσι χερσί Hdt.1.73:—Med., νοστήσατο πάτρην Q.S.1.269. 2. abs., *return safe*, Il.10.247; *return*, ἢ εὖ ἦε κακῶς νοστήσομεν 2.253; κάλλιον ἂν.. ἐνόστησ' ἀντιπάλων Pi.*N.*11.26, etc. 3. *go* or *come*, κεῖσε Od.4.619; δεῦρο E.*Hel.*474; γῆν τήνδε ib.891; εἰς ἐκκλησίαν Ar.*Ach.*

29. 4. c. acc. cogn., ὑπὸ γῆς νοστήσαντι πορείαν Pl.*Ep.*335c. II. (cf. νόστος II, νόστιμος II) ἐνόστησε τὸ ὕδωρ the water *became drinkable*, Paus.7.2.11. -ίζω, Elean inf. νοστίττην, *propose recall from exile*, *Schwyzer* 424.7 (iv B.C.). -ῐμος, ον, (νόστος) *belonging to a return* (not in Il.), ν. ἦμαρ the day *of return*, i.e. *the return* itself, Od.1.9, 168, 3.233, etc.; ν. φάος A.*Pers.*261; ν. σωτηρία ib.797; ν. ἦτορ *AP* 5.231 (Paul. Sil.). 2. *able* or *likely to return*, ἐπεί ῥ' ἔτι ν. ἐστι Od.4.806; ἀπόλωλε καὶ οὐκέτι ν. ἐστι 19.85, cf. A.*Ag.*618; ν. κινεῖν πόδα, v. πούς. II. (νόστος II) of plants and fruit, *yielding a high return, productive*, Thphr.*CP*4.13.2 (Comp. and Sup.); φέρε δ' ἀγρόθι νόστιμα πάντα all things *in abundance*, Call.*Cer.*136; τὸ ν. τῶν καρπῶν S.E.*M.* 7.17. 2. *succulent, nutritious*, τροφή Sor.1.54 (Comp.); of fish, Aët. 9.30 (Sup.); τὸ λιπαρὸν καὶ ν. Plu.2.684d; τὸ -ώτατον ὁ καπνὸς παραλαβὼν ἐς τὸν οὐρανὸν οἴχεται Luc.*Luct.*19. 3. *wholesome*, ὕδωρ J.*BJ* 4.8.3 (Comp.); γένοιτο αὐτῷ.. τὰ ν. ἄνοστα *BCH*51.148 (Tab. Defix., Cyprus); *palatable*, Phld.*D.*3.13, Hsch. s. v. ἔσμιον:—in this sense expld. διὰ τὸ ἡδὺ τοῦ Ὁμηρικοῦ νόστου Eust.1383.40. 4. τὸ ν., of resin obtained from galbanum, starch from wheat, the *valuable* part, Dsc.3.83, 2.101; so τὸ ἰλυῶδες καὶ ν. Id.5.75. III. metaph., τὸ ν. [τοῦ λεγομένου] the *substance, kernel*, M.Ant.2.15. 2. in literary criticism, *succulent*, εἴ τι ν. τῆς ποιήσεως, τῆς ἱστορίας, Eust.ad D.P. *Prooem.*pp.70, 71: generally, ὅπερ ἦν -ώτατον ἐν σοὶ ἀπανθισάμενος Luc.*Merc.Cond.*39. -ος, ὁ, (νέομαι) *return home*, Hom., esp. in Od., νόστοιο τέλος γλυκεροῖο 22.323; ν. μελιηδέα 11.100, al.: freq. c. gen. pers., Ἀχαιῶν ν. 1.326, al.: c. gen. objecti, ὤλεσε.. νόστον Ἀχαιΐδος lost his *chance of returning to* Greece, 23.68; γῆς πατρῴας ν. E.*IT*1066; ἐπ' εὐρέα νῶτα θαλάσσης Od.3.142; ν. ἐς δόμους S.*OC* 1409: in pl., νόστοι ἐκ πολέμων A.*Pers.*861 (lyr.); ὤμοι ἐμῶν ν. S.*Aj.* 900 (lyr.); οἰκτρὰ νόστοις αὐδά Id.*El.*193 (lyr.): generally, *return*, νῆας ἔπι Il.10.509. 2. generally, *travel, journey*, ἐπιμαίεο νόστου γαίης Φαιήκων *to* the land of the P., Od.5.344; ἐπὶ φορβῆς ν. *journey* after (i.e. in search of) food, S.*Ph.*43; ν. πρὸς Ἴλιον, Ἰλίου πύργους ἔπι, E. *IA*966, 1261. 3. as pr. n. Νόστοι, *the homeward journeys* of the Greek heroes after the taking of Troy, title of Cyclic Epic, Paus.10. 28.7, etc.; of a work by Anticlides, Ath.11.466c. II. *yield* or *produce* of grain when ground, Trypho ap.Ath.14.618d; = γεῦσις, *Gloss.*, cf. Hsch.

⊛ **νόσφῐ**, before a vowel or metri gr. -φῐν, though ι may also be elided, as Il.20.7. I. Adv. of Place, *aloof, apart, aside* (cf. ἀπονόσφι), νόσφιν ἀειράσας after carrying the corpse *aside*, Il.24.583; ν. ἰδὼν having looked *aside*, Od.17.304; νόσφιν ἀπό.. *aloof from*, Il.5.322, 15.244, Hes.*Th.*57; ν. ἄτερ.. Id.*Sc.*15; ν. ἤ.. *besides, except*, Theoc. 25.197; ν. μέν.. ν. δέ *separately*, Coluth.105. 2. *aside, secretly*, ν. ἀκούων Il.17.408. II. as Prep., c. gen., *aloof* or *away from, far from*, ν. πολέμοιο, φίλων, 6.443, 14.256; ν. πόληος Od.16.383, etc.; ν. νόσων πενίας τε B.1.60. 2. *without, apart from, unaided by*, mostly of persons, ν. δεσποίνης Od.14.9; ν. Ἀχαιῶν Il.5.803; οὔτε κακὸς ν. δαίμονος οὔτ' ἀγαθός Thgn.166; ν. ἡγητῶν A.*Supp.*239; of things, ν. ἄτερ τε κακῶν καὶ ἄτερ.. πόνοιο Hes.*Op.*91; ν. ἄτερ τε πόνων καὶ ὀϊζύος ib.113; οὔτ' εἰπεῖν ἐστί τι ν. πόθων *AP*12.18 (Alph.). 3. of mind or disposition, τοί κεν Ἀχαιῶν ν. βουλεύωσ' *apart from*, i.e. *differently from*, the (rest of the) Achaeans, Il.2.347; ν. Δήμητρος *without* her *knowledge and consent*, *h.Cer.*4; ν. ἐμεῖο ib.72. 4. *beside, except*, ν. Ποσειδάωνος Od.1.20; νόσφ' Ὠκεανοῖο Il.20.7; ν. Νότου Hes.*Th.* 870.—Ep. and Lyr. word, once in A., l.c., never in S. or E.

**νοσφ-ίδιος**, α, ον, *clandestine*, Hes.*Fr.*187. -ῐδόν, Adv. *by stealth*, Eust.894.50. -ίζω, Att. fut. νοσφιῶ S.*Ph.*1427, E.*Alc.*43: aor. 1 ἐνόσφισα Pi.*N.*6.62, etc.:—Med., fut. νοσφίσομαι *IG*12(7).515. 93 (Amorgos, ii B.C.); Ep. νοσφίσσομαι A.R.4.1108: aor. ἐνοσφισάμην, Ep. νοσφισάμην, νοσφισσάμην (v. infr.): pf. νενόσφισμαι *PCair. Zen.*484.4 (iii B.C.), Str.2.3.4, Plu.*Luc.*37:—Pass., aor. ἐνοσφίσθην Od.11.73, etc.: I. Hom. only Med. and Pass., *turn away, shrink back*, νοσφισθείς ibid., Thgn.94; νοσφίσατ' Od.11.425: metaph., ψεῦδός κεν φαῖμεν καὶ νοσφιζοίμεθα μᾶλλον Il.2.81, 24.222. 2. c. gen., *turn away from*, τίφθ' οὕτω πατρὸς νοσφίζεαι; Od.23.98. 3. c. acc., *forsake, abandon*, παῖδά τ' ἐμὴν νοσφισσαμένην θάλαμόν τε πόσιν τε 4.263; elsewh. in Hom. of places, Κρήτης ὄρεα νιφόεντα νοσφισάμην ib.19.339; νοσφισσαμένη τόδε δῶμα ib.579, 21.77, 104; νοσφισθεῖσα θεῶν ἀγορήν *h.Cer.*92; ὅρκον ἐνοσφίσθης Archil.96; εἴ σε νοσφίζομαι if I *forsake* thee, S.*OT*693 (lyr.). II. after Hom. (ἀπονοσφίσσειεν first in *h.Cer.*158) in Act., *set apart, separate, remove*, τινὰ ἐκ δόμων E.*Hel.*641 (lyr.); βρέφος ματέρος ἀποπρό Id.*IA*1286 (lyr.); τινὰ ἀπό τινος Lyc.1331; τινα A.R.2.793: metaph., ν. τινὰ βίου *separate* him from life, i.e. *kill* him, S.*Ph.*1427; τῷ νύ μ'.. ἐκ βιότοιο νοσφίσατ' (imper.) ἐσσυμένως Q.S.13.282; ν. τινά alone, A.*Ch.*438 (lyr.), *Eu.*211; ν. τινὰ ἐρωμανίης *AP*5.292 (Paul. Sil.). 2. *deprive, rob*, τινά τι one *of* a thing, Pi.*N.*6.62; also ν. τινά τινος A.*Ch.*620 (lyr.), E.*Alc.*43; τοὺς θανόντας νοσφίσας ὧν χρὴν λαχεῖν Id.*Supp.*539; γέροντ' ἄπαιδα νοσφίσας, i.e. ὥστε ἄπαιδα εἶναι, Id.*Andr.*1207 (lyr.). 3. Med., *put aside for oneself, appropriate, purloin*, νοσφίσασθαι ὁπόσα ἂν βουλώμεθα X.*Cyr.*4.2.42, cf. *SIG*993.21 (Calauria, iii B.C.), Plb.10. 16.6, Ἑλληνικά 1.18 (Gytheum, i A.D.): in pf. Pass., νενοσφισμένος πολλά Str. l. c., cf. Plu. l. c.: ν. ἀπὸ τῶν ἀμφιτάπων, ἀπὸ τοῦ ἀναθέματος, ἀπὸ τῆς τιμῆς, *appropriate part of*.., *PCair.Zen.* l. c., Lxx *Jo.*7.1, *Act.Ap.*5.2; ἐκ τοῦ χρήματος Ath.6.234a: abs., *PPetr.*3p.162 (iii B.C.), *Ep.Tit.*2.10. III. Med. in act. sense, *deprive, rob*, σφ' ἀδελφὸς χρημάτων νοσφίζεται E.*Supp.*153, cf. A.R.4.1108. 2. in later poets, *remove*, τοὺς.. ἀπὸ Ξάνθοιο.. πνοιαὶ νοσφίσσαντο D.P.684; νοσφίσατ' ἐκ θυμοῖο καὶ ἤθεος ἐκ βιότοιο Q.S.10.79.—Rare in Att. Prose. -ισμός, ὁ, *absence*, ἤλγει τὸν ν. τῆς ὠμότητος J.*BJ*5.10. 4. II. *appropriating, stealing*, Plb.32.5.8; *peculation*, Ph.2.336, Plu.2.843f: pl., Vett.Val.40.29. -ιστής, οῦ, ὁ, *peculator*, χρημάτων ἀλλοτρίων Id.48.26, cf. *Cat.Cod.Astr.*2.194; τῶν δημοσίων Sch.Luc. *JTr.*48, cf. Sch.Ar.*V.*832.

**νοσ-ώδης**, ες, *sickly, ailing*, Hp.*Aph.*7.67 (Comp.); τὰ ν., opp. τὰ ὑγιεινά, Pl.*R.*438e; of persons, ib.406a; ν. σῶμα, βίος, ib.556e, *Lg.* 734d; τὸ ν. *sickly condition*, Plu.2.662f. II. Act., *unwholesome, pestilential*, ἀήρ Hp.*Aër.*6; θέρος Arist.*Pr.*859$^b$22; χωρίον Isoc.19. 22; τόποι Arist.*Top.*115$^b$20; of plants, Thphr.*HP*7.9.4; τὸ ν. Pl. *Cri.*47d: metaph., *baneful*, νοσῶδες τοῦτο τοῖς ἀμείνοσιν E.*Supp.*423; δράκων στίλβει νοσώδεις ἀστραπάς Id.*Or.*480. Adv. -ωδῶς Gal.9.393, 408: correctly used only in Comp. acc. to Poll.3.105. -ωσις, εως, ἡ, v. νόσανσις.

**νοτάπηλι-ώτης**, ου, ὁ, *south-east wind*, Ptol.*Tetr.*60, Vett.Val.145. 15, *PMag.Par.*1.1647. -ωτικός, ή, όν, *south-easterly*, Str.*Chr.* 11.9, Ptol.*Tetr.*40, Vett.Val.8.24.

**νοτ-ερός**, ά, όν, (νότος) *damp, moist*, δρόσος Simon.183.9; βλέφαρον, ὕδωρ, E.*Alc.*598, *Ion*149 (both lyr.); ἀνεμώνη *AP*5.73 (Rufin.); χειμὼν ν. a storm *of rain*, Th.3.21; πνεῦμα Porph.*Antr.*11 (Comp.); τόπος Thphr.*HP*5.9.8, cf. Epicur.*Ep.*2p.50U.; χωρία Onos.8.2; τὸ ν. *moisture*, Pl.*Ti.*60c. -έω, *to be wet* or *damp, drip*, μύροισι Call.*Epigr.*52; [ζῶναι] ὕδατι νοτέουσαι Eratosth.16.10; νοτέων ἱδρώς, νοτέουσαν ἐλαίην, Nic.*Al.*24, 494. ⊛ -ία, ἡ, *damp, moisture*, νοτίαι εἰαριναί spring *showers*, Il.8.307: abs., *wet weather*, Arist. *HA*551$^a$3, Thphr.*HP*7.14.1. II. ν. φυσική natural *moisture* of the body, Paul.Aeg.6.24. III. a *meteorite* supposed to fall in wet weather, Plin.*HN*37.176. -ιαῖος, α, ον, *southern*, οἱ ν. τῶν ἀνθρώπων Herm.ap.Stob.1.49.45; τὸ ν. Phlp.*in Ph.*894. 19. -ιάω, = νοτέω, Arist.*Pr.*928$^a$14. -ίζω, *moisten, water*, A. *Fr.*44, Ar.*Th.*857:—Pass., *to be wetted* or *wet*, Heraclit.126, Pl.*Ti.* 74c, A.R.1.1005, *AP*7.26 (Antip. Sid.), Str.4.4.1; *perspire*, Gal.18 (2).6, al.; νενοτισμένα οἴνῳ εἴρια Hp.*Fract.*29; νενοτισμένα χεῖτε δάκρυα *wet* tears, *AP*12.92 (Mel.); νενοτ. γῆ Arist.*Mu.*394$^b$14. II. intr., *to be wet*, νοτιζούσης τῆς γῆς Id.*Mete.*361$^b$2; [ὁ νότος] νοτίζειν ποιεῖ τὸ θέρος Id.*Pr.*942$^a$14. 2. = οὐρέω, Heliod.ap.Orib.50.9. 12. 3. *perspire*, Agathin.ap.eund.10.7.22. -ινος, η, ον, = sq. II, *PRyl.*157.5 (ii A.D.), *POxy.*729.9 (ii A.D.), etc. II. = sq. I, κατάστασις Aët.8.31. ⊛ -ιος, α, ον, also ος, ον A.*Pr.*402 (lyr.), Str.2.1.22, etc.:—*moist, damp, rainy*, ν. ἱδρώς *damp* sweat, Il.11.811, 23.715; ν. θέρος Pi.*Fr.*107.13; ἔαρ Hp.*Aph.*3.11, cf. Arist.*Pr.*860$^a$36; παγαί A. l. c.; ὑψοῦ δ' ἐν νοτίῳ τήν γ' ὅρμισαν [ναῦν] well out in *the water*, opp. the beach, Od.4.785, 8.55; ν. δῖναι ἅλμας E.*Hipp.*150 (lyr.): Comp., Str.4.4.1. 2. *bringing rain*, ἀστέρες Arat.238, cf. 490 (both Comp.). II. *to the south, southern*, ν. θάλασσα Hdt.4.13, 6.31; esp. of the Indian Ocean, Id.3.17, cf. 2.11, 158; τὸ τεῖχος τὸ ν., at Athens, And.3.7; ν. ἀήτης a *south* wind, A.R.4.1538; νότια (with or without πνεύματα) *southerly* winds, Arist.*Mete.*364$^a$19, *Pol.*1290$^a$ 14; νοτίοις *during southerly winds*, Id.*HA*574$^a$1; νότια πνεῖ Thphr. *CP*1.13.5; ἐὰν ᾖ νότια Id.*HP*4.14.9; ὁ ν. ἀὴρ Arist.*Mete.*377$^b$27; τὰ ν. ὕδατα *southerly* rains, ib.358$^a$28; ν. [ὕδωρ] water *from southern slopes*, Id.*HA*596$^a$28; ν. Ἰχθῦς, the constellation *Piscis Australis*, Eudox.ap.Hipparch.2.1.21 (νότειος Ἰ. *PLond.*1.130.148 (i/ii A.D.)): Comp. -ώτερος Porph.*Antr.*21: Sup. -ώτατος Str.13.1.68. ⊛ -ίς, ίδος, ἡ, *moisture*, A.*Fr.*481, E.*Ph.*646 (lyr.), Pl.*Ti.*60d, Thphr.*CP* 5.6.1, etc.; ποντία ν. E.*Hec.*1259; of perspiration, Arist.*Pr.*866$^a$21, Gal.10.541. -ισμός, ὁ, *wetting*, Dam.*Isid.*92. II. *moisture*, Sor.1.118. -ιώδης, ες, = νοτώδης, *moist*, Alex.Aphr.*Pr.*2.13; φαντασία Gal.17(1).874. ⊛ -όθεν, Adv. *from the south*, Pl.ap.D.L. 3.41, Thphr.*Sign.*11, 21: c. gen., prob. l. in *IG*1$^2$.4.9.

**νοτολῐβῠκός**, ή, όν, *south-westerly*, Str.*Chr.*11.14, Ptol.*Tetr.*41.

**νοτόνδε**, Adv. *southward*, Aq.*Ge.*12.9.

⊛ **νότος**, ὁ, *south wind* (opp. Βορέας, Arist.*Mete.*363$^b$15, cf. Od.5.331), εὖτ' ὄρεος κορυφῇσι Ν. κατέχευεν ὀμίχλην Il.3.10; ὅ τε ν. καὶ ὁ λίψ, ἀνέμων ὑετιώτατοι Hdt.2.25 (but ὁ ν. οὐκ ἀρχόμενος ἀλλὰ λήγων ὑέτιος Arist.*Pr.* 942$^a$29); ἐτέγχθη κρᾶτ'.. πληγῇσι νότου S.*Ph.*1457 (anap.); χειμερίῳ νότῳ Id.*Ant.*335 (lyr.); ὑγρὸς καὶ βαρὺς Arist.*HA*597$^b$11; ὑδατωδέστερος Id.*Pr.*943$^a$5; ὅταν μὲν ἐλάττων ᾖ, αἴθριός ἐστιν, ὅταν δὲ μέγας, νεφώδης ib.942$^a$34; καυματώδης Id.*Mete.*364$^b$23: in pl., Id.*HA*612$^b$ 6. 2. N. personified as god of the South wind, Hes.*Th.*380, 870. II. *south* or *south-west quarter*, πρὸς μεσαμβρίης τε καὶ νότου Hdt.2.8; πρὸς νότον κεῖται τῆς Λήμνου Id.6.139; τῆς δὲ γῆς τὸ πρὸς ν. S.*Fr.*24.6; τὸ πρὸς ν. τῆς πόλεως Th.3.6; βλέπειν πρὸς ν. *IG*2$^2$.1227. 18; ὁ τοῖχος ὁ πρὸς ν. ib.1$^2$.372.51; πρὸς νότον ἀνέμου ib.56; βασίλισσα νότου *Ev.Matt.*12.42; ἀπὸ νότου c. gen., to the *south* of, *PTeb.* 164.17 (ii B.C.), etc.; later ἐκ νότου c. gen., *PStrassb.*29.8 (iii A.D.), etc.: gen. νότου *to the south*, *PTeb.*105.13 (ii B.C.), etc.

**νότυλος** σφυγμός, '*moist*' (?) pulse, term invented by Archigenes, Gal.8.662.

**νοτώδης**, ες, = νοτιώδης, Hp.*Morb.Sacr.*13.

**νου-βυστικός**, ή, όν, (νοῦς, βύω) *chock-full of sense, shrewd*, πρᾶγμα ν. a *clever* thing, Ar.*Ec.*441. Adv. -κῶς Id.*V.*1294, Cratin.Jun.7. 5. -θεσία, Ion. -ίη, ἡ, = νουθέτησις, Ar.*Ra.*1009, Hp.*Ep.*17, *AP* 11.32 (Honest.), Plu.*Lyc.*25, Diog.Oen.33, Aret.*CA*1.2.

**νουθετ-εία**, ἡ, = foreg., Phld.*Hom.*p.12O., *Lib.*p.31O., Pl.(?)ap. Poll.9.139 (perh. to be read in E.*HF*1256 (pl.)):—also -ία, ἡ, Phryn. *PS*p.35B. ⊛ -έω, (τίθημι) *put in mind*: hence, *admonish, warn, rebuke*, c. acc. pers., Hdt.2.173; παραινεῖν ν. τε τὸν κακῶς πράσσοντα A. *Pr.*266; οὐδὲ νουθετεῖν ἔξεστί σε S.*El.*595; κᾆτα νουθετεῖς ἐμέ Id.*Ph.*

1283; Ἔρωτα *Lyr.Alex.Adesp.*8(*a*): c. acc. rei, ν. τάδε S.*El.*1025, cf. Ar.*V.*732(lyr.); *advise concerning*, μηχανήματα E.*HF*855(troch.): c. dupl. acc., τοιαῦτ' ἄνολβον ἄνδρ' ἐνουθέτει S.*Aj.*1156; ἅπερ με νουθετεῖς E.*Supp.*337, cf. *Or.*299; ν. τινὰ ὡς.. X.*Cyr.*8.2.15:—Pass., S.*OC*1193, E.*Med.*29, etc.; πρὶν ὑπὸ σοῦ ταῦτα νουθετηθῆναι Pl.*Hp.Ma.*301c. 2. metaph., *chastise*, ν. τινὰ κονδύλοις, πληγαῖς, Ar.*V.*254, Pl.*Lg.*879d:—Pass., coupled with κολάζεσθαι, Id.*Grg.*478e. **-ημα**, ατος, τό, *admonition, warning*, A.*Pers.*830 (pl.), E.*Fr.*962 (pl.), Pl.*Grg.*525c (pl.), etc.; τἀμὰ νουθετήματα given [by you] to me, S.*El.*343. **-ησις**, εως, ἡ, *admonition, warning*, Eup.66; διδαχὴ καὶ ν. Pl.*R.*399b, Epicur.*Nat.*72G.; ῥάβδου ν. Pl.*Lg.*700c, etc. **-ησμός**, ὁ, = foreg., Men.1042, censured by Poll.9.139 and Phot. (-ισμός in both Gramm.). **-ητέος**, α, ον, *to be admonished*, E.*Ba.*1256, *Ion* 436. 2. νουθετητέον, *one must warn*, Arist.*Pol.*1260$^{b}$6. **-ητής**, οῦ, ὁ, *monitor*, Ph.2.519: as Adj., ν. λόγος Id.1.171. **-ητικός**, ή, όν, *monitory, didactic*, λόγοι Pl.*Lg.*740e, Phld.*Po.*5*Fr.*1; τὸ ν. εἶδος τῆς παιδείας Pl.*Sph.*230a. **-ία**, v. νουθετεία. **-ικός**, ή, όν, = νουθετητικός, λόγοι X.*Mem.*1.2.21; τὸ ν. Demetr.*Eloc.*298. **-ισμός**, v. νουθετησμός.

⊛ **νοῦθος**, ὁ, *tramp* of feet, ν. δὲ ποδῶν ὑπόδουπος ὀρώρει Hes.*Fr.*48.

⊛ **νουμην-ία**, ἡ, Att. contr. for νεομηνία (which occurs in Pi.*N.*4.35, Hdt.6.57 (pl.), *PMag.Leid.W.*1.28, 9.43 (pl.), Gal.14.298):—also **νευμηνία**, *SIG*1106.19 (Cos, iv/iii B.C.); **νεμονηΐα**, *GDI*5015.28, al. (Crete); **νομενία**, *PCair.Zen.*167.5 (iii B.C.):—*new moon: the first of the month*, Pi.l.c., Antipho *Fr.*58 (pl.), Ar.*Eq.*43, *Ach.*999 (pl.), etc.; ν. κατὰ σελήνην to denote the *true* or *natural new moon*, as opp. to the νουμηνία of the calendars, Th.2.28; also ἡ κατὰ θεὸν ν. *PMag.Par.*1.787, 2389; ν. τοῦ ἔτους, of the spring equinox, Ptol.*Tetr.*91. **-ιαστής**, οῦ, ὁ, *one who celebrates the new moon*, Lys.*Fr.*53. ⊛ **-ιος**, ον, Att. contr. for νεομήνιος, *used at the new moon*, ἄρτοι Luc.*Lex.*6. II. as Subst., perh. a kind of *curlew*: prov., ξυνῆλθεν ἀτταγᾶς τε καὶ ν. 'birds of a feather flock together', D.L.9.114.

⊛ **νοῦμμος**, ὁ, Western Dor. = νόμος, *current coin*. esp. of the Tarentine stater, Arist.*Fr.*590. 2. = λίτρα, the silver equivalent of the bronze pound, ib.589. 3. = Lat. *nummus* (sc. *sestertius*), Plu.*Sull.*1.

**νουνέχ-εια**, ἡ, *good sense, discretion*, Plb.4.82.3, Andronic.*Pass.* p.578 M., *Stoic.*3.64. **-ής**, ές, (ἔχω) *with understanding, sensible, discreet*, Ps.-E.*Fr.*1132.48, Plb.6.48.8 (Sup.); λογισμός Id.3.105.9, cf. Ptol.*Tetr.*164; τὸ νουνεχές, = foreg., Anon.ap.Suid. s.v. ἀνεῖτο. Adv. -χῶς Arist.*Rh.Al.*1436$^{b}$33, Plb.1.83.3, al., Agatharch.63, *Ev.Marc.*12.34, Gal.10.267. ⊛ **-όντως**, Adv. of νουνεχής, as if from Adj. νουνέχων (i.e. νοῦν ἔχων), *sensibly*, Isoc.5.7 (divisim), Men.1043 (Pl. has ἐχόντως νοῦν, *Lg.*686e).

**νοῦς**, ὁ, v. νόος.

**νουσαχθής**, ές, *affected with disease*, Opp.*H.*1.298.

**νούσημα**, Ion. for νόσημα.

**νουσο-βᾰρής**, ές, *caused by grievous disease*, θάνατος *Supp.Epigr.* 2.479 (Olbia). **-λύτης** [ῠ], ου, ὁ, *freeing from illness*, Παιάν *Epigr. Gr.*1026. **-μελής**, ές, *with diseased limbs*, Man.4.476.

**νοῦσος**, ἡ, Ion. for νόσος.

**νουσοφόρος**, ον, Ion. for νοσοφόρος, γῆρας *AP*6.27 (Theaet.).

**νοχελές**, v. νωχελής.

**νυ**, v. νῦν II. II. **νῦ**, τό, indecl., the letter ν, Achae.33.3, Pl.*Cra.*414c, *IG*2.4321.21 (iv B.C.), *BCH*29.483 (Delos), *BGU*153.16 (ii A.D.). (Cf. Hebr. *nūn*.)

**νύγ-δην**, Adv. *by pricking*, A.D.*Adv.*198.9. **-μα** or **νύχμα** (Nic. *Th.*271, al. codd. opt.), ατος, τό, *prick*, Nic.ll.cc., Aret.*SD*2.7, Tryph.365. 2. *lesion of a* νεῦρον, opp. ἕλκος (of flesh) and κάταγμα (of bone), Gal.13.651,883, cf. Steph. *in Hp.*2.439 D. II. pl., νύγματα *solicitations* of the senses, Epicur.*Fr.*413. **-μᾰτικός**, ή, όν, *suitable for* νύγματα I. 2, ἔμπλαστρος Androm.ap.Gal.13. 650. **-μᾰτώδης**, ες, *punctuated*, of heart-beats, Arist.*Pr.*947$^{b}$31. 2. *pricking*, πόνος Archig.ap.Gal.8.92, cf. Aret.*SA*1.10. Adv. -δῶς Gal.19.7. ⊛ **-μή**, ἡ, = sq., Plu.*Ant.*86. 2. *dot*, in punctuation, Dosith.p.380 K. **-μός**, ὁ, *pricking sensation, irritation*, Ruf. ap.Orib.8.24.62: in pl., of gout, Luc.*Ocyp.*30. II. metaph., of the *prickings* of conscience, τῶν παρανομημάτων ν. εἰς τὴν ψυχὴν λαμβάνειν D.S.13.58; but also, = νύγμα II, ὑπὸ νυγμῶν καὶ γαργαλισμῶν τῆς αἰσθήσεως Plu.*Phil.*9. **-ω**, = νύσσω, Hsch.

**νῦθός**, ή, όν, *dumb*, Hsch. II. *dark*, Id.:—also **νῦθώδης**, ες, Id.

**νυκταίετος**, ὁ, = ἐρῳδιός, Hsch.

**νυκταιροδύτειρα** [δῠ], ἡ, *she that rises and sets by night*, of the moon, *PMag.Par.*1.2546.

**νυκτᾰλός**, ή, όν, f.l. in D.L.6.77 codd. Suid., for νυσταλέος (or -λος).

**νυκτᾰλ-ωπάω**, = νυστάζω, Eust.1392.35. **-ωπίασις**, εως, ἡ, *night-blindness*, Orib.*Eup.*4.18.3. **-ωπιάω**, *suffer from night-blindness*, Gal.12.802. **-ωπικός**, ή, όν, in neut. pl. -ικά, τά, *attacks of night-blindness*, Hp.*Epid.*6.7.1. ⊛ **-ωψ**, ωπος, ὁ, ἡ, (νύξ, ὤψ) = ὁ τῆς νυκτὸς ὁρῶν, i.e. *suffering from day-blindness*, Id.*Prorrh.*2.33, cf. Gal.19.435, 14.776; ἐν οἰκίᾳ τυφλῶν καὶ ὁ ν. ὀξυδερκής Prov.ap.Jo. Sic. in Rh.6.293 W.; but also, 2. = ὁ τῆς νυκτὸς ἀλαός, *night-blind*, Gal.19.124, cf. Plin.*HN*8.203, Aët.7.48, etc. 3. ν. *ubi homo neque matutino tempore videt neque vespertino*, Ulp. in *Dig.*20.1.10. 4. II. as Subst., *incapacity to see except in bright light, night-blindness*, Hp.*Epid.*6.7.1, Arist.*GA*780$^{a}$16 (pl.), Gal.10.84, Id.ap. Orib.*Syn.*8.48.1. 2. *day-blindness*, Dem.Ophth.ap.Simon.Jan. s.v. *nictilopa*.

**νυκτ-αυγής**, ές, *shining by night*, *Cat.Cod.Astr.*1.173. **-εγερσία**, ἡ, *waking by night*, Ph.1.155 (pl.): with reference to Il.10, Str.9.5.18, Ps.-Plu.*Vit.Hom.*209, Arg. ii E.*Rh.*; cf. νυκτηγρεσία. **-εγερτέω**, *watch by night*, Plu.*Caes.*40.

**νυκτελεῖν**· ἐν νυκτὶ τελεῖν, Hsch.

**νυκτέλιος**, ον, (νύξ) *nightly*, epith. of Dionysus, from his *nightly festivals*, *AP*9.524.14, Plu.2.389a, Paus.1.40.6. 2. νυκτέλιον, τό, *night-festival*, Ἴσιδος *POxy.*525 (ii A.D.): in pl., *festival of* Dionysus Νυκτέλιος, Plu.2.291a.

**νυκτέπαρχος**, ὁ, = Lat. *praefectus vigilum*, Just.*Nov.*13.1 *Intr.*

**νυκτερεία**, ἡ, *hunting by night, taking game asleep*, Pl.*Lg.*824.

**νυκτέρεια**, τά, = foreg., Eun.*VS*p.485 B.

**νυκτερείσιος**, ον, (νύξ, ἐρείδω) Com. Adj. formed like νυκτερήσιος, sens. obsc., ἔργα Ar.*Th.*204.

**νυκτερέτης**, ου, ὁ, *one who rows* or *fishes by night*, *AP*6.11 (Satyr.).

**νυκτέρ-ευμα**, ατος, τό, *night-quarters*, Plb.12.4.9. **-ευτής**, οῦ, ὁ, *one who hunts* or *fishes by night*, Pl.*Lg.*824. **-ευτικός**, ή, όν, *fit for hunting by night*, κύνες X.*Mem.*3.11.8. ⊛ **-εύω**, (νύκτερος) *pass the night*, Id.*Cyr.*4.2.22; ν. ἀθλίως Timocl.16.1; of troops, *bivouac*, X.*An.*4.4.11; ἐν τοῖς ὅπλοις ν. ib.6.4.27:—so in Med., *pass a sleepless night*, Timachid.ap.Ath.15.699e. **-ήσιος**, ον, *nightly*, Luc.*Alex.* 53 (v.l. -εισ-, -ισ-), S.E.*M.*10.188. **-ῑνεία**, ἡ, *office of commander of the night-watch*, *Supp.Epigr.*4.515.9 (Ephesus, i A.D., written -ῆα). **-ῑνός**, ή, όν, (νύξ) *by night, nightly*, φυλακή Ar.*V.*2; ξύνοδοι Id.*Eq.*477; ἀείσματα Eup.139; πυρετός Hp.*Epid.*1.5; στρατηγός (= νυκτοστράτηγος) Str.17.1.12, *CIG*2930 (Tralles); φρίξ *POxy.*924. 4 (iv A.D.); ἀναχώρησις Th.4.128; σύλλογος Pl.*Lg.*909a, cf. Arist. *HA*592$^{b}$8; φέγγος Aen.Tact.10.25; ν. σύσσημα Id.4.5; ν. γενέσθαι to happen *by night*, Ar.*Ach.*1162; -ώτατόν τι τολμᾶν *at dead of night*, Luc.*Icar.*21. 2. Astrol., *potent by night*, Ptol.*Tetr.*20. 3. Subst., νυκτερινός, ὁ, a kind of musical composition for the flute, used in Dionysiac worship, *BCH*50.235 (Thasos, iii B.C.). **-ιος**, α, ον, also ος, ον Luc.*Peregr.*28:— = foreg., Orph.*H.*49.3; γλαῦξ Arat. 999; ἔργον *AP*9.403 (Maec.).

**νυκτερίρεμβος**, v. νυκτίρεμβος.

**νυκτερ-ίς**, ίδος, ἡ, *bat*, Od.12.433, 24.6, Hdt.2.76, etc.; applied to a person, Χαιρεφῶν ἡ ν. Ar.*Av.*1564 (lyr.). II. a fish, = καλλιώνυμος, Opp.*H.*2.205. III. a plant, = μύρον Ἑλένης, Aët.12. 1. **-ῖτις**, ιδος, ἡ, = ἀναγαλλὶς ἡ κυανῆ, Ps.-Dsc.2.178. **-όβῐος**, ον, *feeding by night*, ζῷα Arist.*HA*488$^{a}$25. **-οειδής**, v.l. for νυκτοειδής, S.E.*M.*10.184.

**νύκτερος**, ον, = νυκτερινός, μήνη A.*Pr.*797; ὀνείρατα Id.*Pers.*176; ἄστρων.. νυκτέρων ὁμήγυριν Id.*Ag.*4; ναυκληρία S.*Fr.*143; δεῖμα Id. *El.*410; ν. ἀπελωβήθη *by night*, Id.*Aj.*217 (anap.); φύλακες E.*Rh.*87: also in late Prose, ν. κοίτη Luc.*Am.*39: neut. as Adv., νύκτερον ἀείδουσα Arat.1023.

**νυκτερο-φεγγής**, ές, *shining by night*, μήνη Man.3.393. **-φοιτος**, ον, = νυκτίφοιτος, Orph.*H.*36.6.

**νυκτερωπός**, όν, (ὤψ) *appearing by night*, δόκημα νυκτερωπὸν ὀνείρων E.*HF*112 (lyr.), cf. Plu.2.1066c.

**νυκτ-ηγορέω**, *debate* or *plan by night*, E.*Rh.*89:—in Pass., A.*Th.* 29. **-ηγορία**, ἡ, *nightly speech, debate by night*, E.*Rh.*19 (anap.), Arist.*Fr.*159, Lib.*Decl.*26.23. ⊛ **-ηγρεσία**, ἡ, written -εγρεσία, = *excubiae*, *Gloss.*; *nyctegresia*, Fest. s.v. *egretus*. **-ηγρετέω**, = νυκτεγερτέω, Them.*Or.*21.260b, Aristaenet.2.13, Sch.B Il.18. 495. **-ήγρετον**, τό, Oriental plant, said to be luminous at night, Plin.*HN*21.62. **-ῆμαρ**, Adv. *day and night*, *PLond.*3.981.12 (iv A.D.). **-ήμερον**, τό, = νυχθήμερον, *Gloss.* **-ηρεφής**, ές, *covered by night, murky, gloomy*, A.*Ag.*460 (lyr.).

**νυκτῐ-βάτης** [ᾰ], ου, Dor. **-βάτᾱς**, *walking by night*, *Lyr.Alex. Adesp.*19.7. **-βαῦ**, indecl., = νυκτικόραξ, *PMag.Berol.*1.223; but gen. -βαοῦτος *PMag.Osl.*1.264. **-βῖος**, ον, = νυκτερόβιος, Hsch., Phot. ⊛ **-βόας**, ου, ὁ, = στρίγλος, Hsch. (νυκτοβόα cod.). **-βόη**, *calling by night*, epith. of the moon, *PMag.Par.*1.2808. **-βρομος**, ον, *sounding by night*, σῦριγξ E.*Rh.*552 (lyr.). **-γᾰμος**, ον, *wedding by night, secretly*, Musae.7. **-γενέτωρ**, ορος, ὁ, *father of night*, of Ἔρως, *PMag.Par.*1.1795. **-διέξοδος**, ον, of stars, *rising above the horizon after sunset and setting below it before sunrise* (so that their whole course above the horizon is visible), Ptol. *Phas.*pp.9, 10 H.: wrongly expld. by Gem.14.12 of stars *setting before sunset and rising after sunrise*. **-δρόμος**, ον, *running by night*, Orph.*H.*9.2, cf. Hymn. in *Sammelb.*4127 (Talmis). **-κλέπτης**, ου, ὁ, *thief of the night*, *AP*11.176 (Lucill.). **-κόραξ**, ᾰκος, ὁ, = ὦτος, *long-eared owl*, Arist.*HA*592$^{b}$9, 597$^{b}$23, 619$^{b}$18, LXX *Ps.*101(102). 6, al., Str.17.2.4, Zopyr.ap.Orib.14.45.4, Gal.12.801, Ant.Lib.15.4; ν. ᾄδει θανατηφόρον *AP*11.186 (Nicarch.). **-κρῠφής**, ές, *hidden by night*, Arist.*Metaph.*1040$^{a}$31. **-λαθραιοφάγος** [φᾰ], ον, *eating secretly by night*, Epigr.ap.Hegesand.1. ⊛ **-λάλος** [ᾰ], ον, *nightly-sounding*, κιθάρη *AP*7.29 (Antip. Sid.). **-λαμπής**, ές, (λάμπω) epith. of the ark of Danae, δούρατι νυκτιλαμπεῖ dub.l. in Simon.37. 8. **-λόχος**, ον, *lying in wait by night*, Theognost.*Can.*84, Hsch. **-μᾰνής**, ές, *raging by night*, Ἀπαρκίας *Ath.Mitt.*12.262 (Erythrae). **-μέδουσα**, ἡ, *ruling by night*, of the moon, *Cat.Cod. Astr.*1.173. **-νόμος**, ον, *feeding by night*, Arist.*HA*616$^{b}$25, Plu. 2.286b, etc.

**νύκτιος**, α, ον, (νύξ) *of the night*, θήρ *AP*6.221 (Leon.).

⊛ **νυκτῐ-πᾰταιπλάγιος** [πλᾰ], ον, *nightly-roaming-to-and-fro*, Epigr. ap.Hegesand.1. **-πήδηκες**, οἱ, (πηδάω) a sort of *slippers*, Herod. 7.59, Poll.7.94. ⊛ **-πλαγκτος**, ον, *causing to wander by night*,

*rousing from bed*, πόνος A.*Ag*.330; δείματα Id.*Ch*.524; κελεύματα ib. 751; ν. εὐνὴ *restless, uneasy* bed, Id.*Ag*.12. **-πλᾰνής**, ές, =sq., νυκτιπλανῆ τελέθουσαν Opp.*C*.3.268 (vv. ll. νυκτιπλανῆτιν τ. (sic), νυκτιπλάνητον ἐοῦσαν). **-πλᾰνος**, ον, *roaming by night*, Orac.ap. Luc.*Alex*.54. **-πλοέω**, *navigate by night*: hence, metaph., *to be exact*, Chrysipp.ap.Zen.5.32. **-πλοια**, ἡ, *voyage by night*, Str.16.2. 24. **-πόλευτος**, ον, =sq., Orph.*H*.79.7. **-πόλος**, ον, (πολέω) *roaming by night*, Βάκχαι E.*Ion*718 (lyr.); ἔφοδοι, of Persephone, ib.1049 (lyr.); epith. of Zagreus, Id.*Fr*.472.11 (anap.); of Artemis, Corn.*ND* 34: as Subst., coupled with Μάγοι, Βάκχοι, Λῆναι, Heraclit.14. **-πόρος**, ον, *prowling by night*, λύκαινα Opp.*C*.1.441, cf. 3.268: as pr. n. of a river, Luc.*VH*2.33. **-ρεμβος**, ον, *strolling, wandering about by night*, Vett.Val.16.11: wrongly spelt νυκτερίρεμβος in Ptol.*Tetr*. 161. **-σεμνος**, ον, *solemnized by night*, δεῖπνα A.*Eu*.108. **-φαής**, ές, *shining by night*, φῶς Parm.14, cf. Orph.*H*.54.10. ✱**-φᾰνής**, ές, = foreg., Μήνη Herm.ap.Stob.1.5.14, cf. *PMag.Par*.1.1794. **-φαντος**, ον, *appearing by night*, ὀνείρατα A.*Pr*.657 (cod. Med., cf. sq.): generally, *nightly*, νυκτίφαντον πρόπολον Ἐνοδίας E.*Hel*.570. **-φοιτος**, ον, *night-roaming*, v.l. for foreg. in A.*Pr*.657; ν. δείματα Lyc.225 (perh. to be read in A.); θεός, of Artemis, Ant.Lib.15.2. **-φόρος**, ον, *bringing darkness*, ἀφροσύνη Ph.1.335. **-φρούρητος**, ον, *watching by night*, θράσος A.*Pr*.861. **-χᾰρής**, ές, *rejoicing in the night*, *PMag.Par*.1.1795. **-χόρευτος**, ον, *belonging to nightly dances*, Nonn.*D*.12.391.

**νυκτό-βας**, gloss on γλαῦξ, Hsch. **-βᾰτία**, ἡ, *night-walking*, in pl., Hp.*Vict*.3.68. **-βίος**, ον, paraphr. of νυκτίρεμβος, Procl.*Par. Ptol*.226. **-βόα**, v. νυκτιβόας. **-γρᾰφία**, ἡ, *writing by night*, Plu.2.634a, 803c (pl.). **-δρόμα** (voc.), *running by night*, epith. of a demon in *Rev.Phil*.1930.249 (Egypt, Tab. Defix.). **-δρομία**, ἡ, *running by night*, Hp.*Vict*.3.68 (v.l. κυνο-). **-δρόμος**, ον, =*noctivago*, *Gloss*. **-ειδής**, ές, *like night*, of fog, Hp.*Aër*.8; χρόνος ἐστὶν ἡμεροειδὲς καὶ ν. φάντασμα Epicur.*Fr*.294 (p.353 U.); σκότος Iamb. *Protr*.21.κθ΄. **-θήρας**, ου, ὁ, *one who hunts by night*, X.*Mem*. 4.7.4. **-λάλημα** [λᾰ], ατος, τό, *spell for making a woman talk in her sleep*, *PMag.Lond*.121.411. **-μαντις**, εως, ὁ, ἡ, *one who prophesies by night*, Poll.7.188. **-μᾰχέω**, *fight by night*, Plu.*Cam*. 36, App.*BC*5.35, etc.: metaph., ν. τῇ παρθένῳ ἐρωτικῶς Aristaenet.1. 10. **-μᾰχία**, Ion. -ίη, ἡ, *night-battle*, Hdt.1.74, Th.7.44, Chor. p.30 B. **-περιπλάνητος** [ᾰ], ον, *roaming about by night*, Ar.*Ach*. 264 (lyr.). **-πλᾰνής**, ές, =νυκτιπλανής, Man.1.311. ✱**-πλοέω**, *sail by night*, Hipparch.1.7.1 (prob. for πυκνο-). **-πλοϊκός**, ή, όν, *given to sailing by night*, Str.*Chr*.16.28. **-πορέω**, *go* or *travel by night*, X.*Cyr*.5.1.20, Str.15.2.6, etc. **-πορία**, ἡ, *night-march*, Plb. 5.7.3, D.S.18.40, Plu.*Alex*.22. **-πότιον**, τό, *night-cup*, Sm.1*Ki*. 26.11. **-στράτηγος** [ᾰ], ὁ, *commander of the night-watch*, *POxy*. 933.24 (ii A.D.), *PLips*.39.3 (iv A.D.).

**νυκτ-ουργός**, όν, *working by night*: τὸ ν. Plu.2.376e. **-οῦρος**, ὁ, =νυκτοφύλαξ, name of the planet *Saturn*, ib.941c.

**νυκτο-φᾰής**, =νυκτιφαής, dub. in Nonn.*D*.44.218. **-φαίνουσα**, ἡ, =*Nocticula*, i.e. *Noctiluca*, *Gloss*. **-φάνεια** [φᾰ], ἡ, *shining by night*, epith. of the moon, *PMag.Par*.1.2523. **-φῠλᾰκέω**, *guard, watch by night*, ν. τὰ ἔξω X.*Cyr*.4.5.3; ν. νυκτοφυλακάς *Supp. Epigr*.4.535.18 (Ephesus, ii/iii A.D.):—impers. in Pass., Aen.Tact. 22.1. II. ὁ -κῶν, =Lat. *praefectus vigilum*, D.C.52.33. **-φῠλᾰκή**, ἡ, =sq., v. foreg. **-φῠλᾰκία**, ἡ, *night-watch*, *PCair.Zen*.329.6 (iii B.C.), *Gloss*. ✱**-φύλαξ** [φῠ], ᾰκος, ὁ, *night-watchman, guard*, X.*An*.7. 2.18, 7.3.34, Onos.10.10 tit., Luc.*Peregr*.27; in Egyptian towns, Ph. 2.534, *PIand*.33.8 (ii A.D.), *Theb.Ostr*.139; at Rome, =Lat. *vigiles*, J.*BJ*4.11.4, D.C.58.9; also, =*praefectus vigilum*, Id.52.24. ✱**-φῠλάξια**, τά, *guard-house*, *IG*11(2).145.30 (Delos, iv B.C.), al.

**νυκτ-ώδης**, ες, contr. for νυκτοειδής, Eust.1951.57. **-ῷον**, τό, (Νύξ) *temple of Night*, Luc.*VH*2.33. **-ωπός**, όν, (ὤψ) =νυκτερωπός, λαθοσύνα E.*IT*1279 (lyr.). **-ωρ**, Adv., (νύξ) *by night*, Hes.*Op*.177, Archil.46, S.*Aj*.47, Ar.*Nu*.175, *Th*.258, Antipho 5.26,44, Lys.1.14, 3.6, Pl.*Grg*.471b, *PHal*.1.194 (iii B.C.), etc.:—the only Adv. of this form, Hdn.Gr.2.952.

**νυκχάζω**, =νύσσω, Hsch.

**νύμφᾰ**, poet. voc. for νύμφη; but **νύμφᾱ**, Dor. for νύμφη.

✱**νυμφᾰ-γενής**, ές, *nymph-born*, Telest.1.5; of Pan, as *reared by Nymphs*, Euph.109. **-γέτης**, ου, ὁ, *leader of the Nymphs*, epith. of Poseidon, Corn.*ND*22; of Pan, *IG*4²(1).130.15 (Epid.); cf. νυμφηγέτης.

**νυμφᾰγωγ-έω**, pf. νενυμφαγώγηκα Plb.25.4.10:—*lead the bride to the bridegroom's house*, ν. τινί τινα Plb. l.c.; τὰς τῶν πολιτῶν θυγατέρας οἱ τύραννοι μετὰ μαστίγων -οῦσιν D.H.11.41; γάμους ν. *promote* a marriage, Plu.*Sol*.20. II. of the bridegroom, *lead home* a bride, Charito 2.1. **-ία**, ἡ, *bridal procession*, Plb.25.4.8, Plu.2. 329e. ✱**-ός**, όν, *leader of the bride*, E.*IA*610; esp. *one who leads her from her home to the bridegroom's house*, Luc.*DDeor*.20.16; esp. in case of a second marriage, Poll.3.41, Eust.652.45: metaph., of the Argo, as bearing Medea, ν. τρόπιν Lyc.1025. 2. generally, *friend*, Lxx *Ge*.21.22, *Jd*.14.20. II. *one who negotiates a marriage for another*, Plu.2.329f. Cf. νυμφευτής.

**νυμφ-αία**, ἡ, =μαδωναΐς, *yellow water-lily, Nuphar luteum*, Thphr. *HP*9.13.1, Dsc.3.132. 2. *white water-lily, Nymphaea alba*, ibid. II. pr. n., a name of Ariadne, *BMus.Cat.Vases* iii p.234. ✱**-αῖος**, α, ον, (νύμφη) *of* or *sacred to the Nymphs*, σκοπιαί E.*El*.447 (lyr.); νᾶμα *AP*14.71; δρύες Tryph.324; νυμφαία λιβάς *pure spring* water, prob. l. in Antiph.52.13. II. νυμφαῖον, τό, *sanctuary of the Nymphs*, *IG* 11(2).144*A*91 (Delos, iv B.C.), *CIG*4616 (Syria, ii A.D.), Plu.*Alex*.7, etc.: Boeot. νυνφῆον *Schwyzer*485.6 (Thespiae, iii B.C.); esp. *fountain with architectural background*, Philostr.*VA*8.12. III. ν. πτέρις, =θηλυπτερίς, Dsc.4.185; =δρυοπτερίς, Ps.-Dsc.4.187. [νυμφαῖον is doubtful in E.*IT*216 (lyr.): fort. νύμφαν.] **-άς**, άδος, ἡ, pecul. fem. of foreg., πύλαι Paus.1.44.3. **-άσματα**, τά, *bride's ornaments*, Orac.ap.Phleg.*Fr*.36.10 J.cod. ✱**-εῖος**, α, ον, also ος, ον E.*IA*131 (lyr.), *AP*7.188 (Thall.):—*bridal, nuptial*, λέχη Simon. 124B; εὐνά Pi.*N*.5.30, cf. E. l.c.; παστάς *AP*l. c., cf. *Supp.Epigr*. 2.874 (Egypt): hence as Subst. 1. νυμφεῖον (sc. δῶμα), Ep. νυμφήϊον Call.*Del*.118: τό:—*bridechamber*, S.*Ant*.891, 1205: in pl., Id. *Tr*.920. 2. νυμφεῖα (sc. ἱερά), Ep. νυμφήϊα Mosch.2.159: τά:—*nuptial rites, marriage*, S.*Tr*.7; but 3. νυμφεῖα τοῦ σαυτοῦ τέκνου thine own son's *bride*, Id.*Ant*.568. **-ευμα**, ατος, τό, *marriage, espousal*, in pl., τὰ μητρὸς ν. Id.*OT*980, cf. E.*IT*365, al. II. in sg., *the person married*, καλὸν ν. τινί 'a good *match* for him', Id.*Tr*. 420. **-ευσις**, εως, ἡ, *bridal, marriage*, Lxx *Ca*.3.11. **-ευτήρ**, ῆρος, ὁ, =νυμφευτής II, Opp.*C*.1.265, 3.356. **-ευτήριος**, α, ον, *nuptial*, τὰ ν., =νύμφευμα, E.*Tr*.252. **-ευτής**, οῦ, ὁ, *groomsman*, =παρανύμφιος, Poll.3.40. 2. metaph., of a herdsman, Pl.*Plt*. 268a. II. *bridegroom, husband*, E.*Ion*913 (lyr.). **-εύτρια**, ἡ, *she who escorts the bride, bridesmaid*, Ar.*Ach*.1056, Plu.*Lyc*.15. 2. =προμνήστρια, Lib.*Decl*.26.13. II. *bride*, Phot. **-εύω**, *give in marriage* to one, *betroth*, Pi.*N*.3.56, E.*Alc*.317, *IA*461,885 (troch.):—in Med., νυμφευομένη, epith. of Hera, Paus.9.2.7. 2. *marry*, of the woman, c. dat., S.*Ant*.654,816 (lyr.); of the man, c. acc., E.*Med*. 625, *Ion*819, Isoc.10.59; ν. λέχη Eub.67.1: abs., of both parties, νυμφεύετ', εὖ πράσσοιτε E.*Med*.313. II. Pass., with fut. Med. νυμφεύσομαι Id.*Tr*.1139, *Supp*.455 (but aor. Med. in act. sense, ἐνυμφευσάμην Id.*Hipp*.561 (lyr.)): aor. Pass. ἐνυμφεύθην Id.*Med*.1336, *Ion* 1371:—*to be given in marriage, marry*, of the woman, E. ll. cc.; νυμφεύεσθαι νυμφεύματα Id.*IT*364; νυμφεύεσθαί τινι *to be wedded* to a man, Id.*Andr*.403; παρά τινι Id.*Med*.1336; ν. ἔκ τινος *to be wedded* by him, Id.*Ba*.28: metaph., ψυχῶν εἰς γένεσιν νυμφευομένων Porph. *Antr*.19. III. Med., of the man, *take to wife*, νυμφεύου δέμας Ἠλέκτρας E.*El*.1340 (anap.). ✱**-η**, ἡ (Ep. voc. νύμφᾰ Il.3.130, Od.4.743 (Aeol. acc. to Choerob. *in Theod*.1.304)); later also as nom., *AP*14.43; but Dor. **νύμφᾱ**, *young wife, bride*, Il.18.492, Hdt. 4.172; ν. ἄγεσθαι Ar.*Pl*.529; Ἀελίοιο Pi.*O*.7.14; opp. νυμφίος, Pl. *Lg*.783e; opp. παρθένος, Praxill.5, *Com.Adesp*.1215; always relatively young, as Iris calls Helen, or as Eurycleia calls Penelope, νύμφα φίλη Il.3.130, Od.4.743, cf. E.*Med*.150, *Andr*.140 (both lyr.). 2. *marriageable maiden*, Il.9.560, Hes.*Th*.298. 3. *daughter-in-law*, Lxx 1*Ki*.4.19, *Ev.Matt*.10.35. 4. *young girl*, πενταέτης ν. *IG*14.2040.2. II. *Nymph* or goddess of lower rank, θεαὶ Νύμφαι Il.24.616, cf. Hes.*Th*.130, *Fr*.171.5, al., *IG*12(8).358 (Thasos, v B.C.); N. κοῦραι Διὸς αἰγιόχοιο Od.6.105; N. ἅλιαι S.*Ph*.1470 (anap.; cf. Ναΐς, Νηρηΐς); N. Ὀρεστιάδες, Ὀρειάδες, Il.6.420, Bion 1.19, cf. Ar.*Av*.1098 (lyr.); N. Μελίαι Hes.*Th*.187, cf. Ἀδρυάδες, Ἁμαδρυάδες, Δρυάδες; N. ὑάδες, ὑδριάδες, Id.*Fr*.180, Porph.*Antr*.18; N. λειμωνιάδες, πετραῖαι, S.*Ph*.1454 (anap.), E.*El*.805. 2. esp. of *springs*, ὀνομάζεσθαι τὰς πηγὰς N. Ath.11.465a, cf. Lib.*Or*.11.28: hence, poetically, *water*, *AP*9.258 (Antiphan.), 331 (Mel.), cf. Plu.2.147f. 3. in mystical theology, Ζεὺς ἄμβροτος ἔπλετο ν. Orph.*Fr*.21a4. b. applied to souls seeking birth, Porph.*Antr*.18; cf. νυμφεύω. III. *doll, puppet*, *AP*6.274 (Pers.), Jul.*Caes*.332d. IV. *young bee* or *wasp*, in the pupa stage, Arist.*HA*551ᵇ2, 555ᵃ3. b. *winged male of the ant*, Hsch. V. kind of *mollusc*, Speusipp.ap.Ath.3. 105b. VI. *point of the ploughshare*, Poll.1.252, Procl. ad Hes.*Op*. 425. VII. *hollow between the under-lip and chin*, Ruf.*Onom*.42, Poll.2.90, Hsch. b. depression on the shoulder of horses, *Hippiatr*. 26. VIII. *opening rosebud*, Phot. IX. *clitoris*, Ruf.*Onom*.112, Gal.*UP*15.3. X. *niche*, Callix.2. **-ηγέτης**, εω, ὁ, =νυμφαγέτης (q.v.), Ἀπόλλων *IG*12(8).358 (Thasos, v B.C.). ✱**-ιάω**, *to be in a frenzy*, a disease of mares, Arist.*HA*604ᵇ10. **-ίδες**, αἱ, *wedding-shoes*, Hsch. **-ίδιος** [ῐ], α, ον, also ος, ον E.*Alc*.885 (lyr.):—*bridal*, λέκτρων ἅμιλλα, εὐναί, Id.*Hipp*.1140 (lyr.), *Alc*. l.c.; ᾠδαί Ar.*Av*. 1729 (lyr.); θάλαμοι A.R.1.1031, cf. *IG*12(8).441.1 (Thasos). ✱**-ικός**, ή, όν, = foreg., A.*Ch*.71 (lyr.), S.*OT*1242, E.*Med*.378; ν. ἱμάτιον, κλίνη, δᾶδες, Plu.2.755a, Luc.*Herod*.5, Poll.3.43; τὰ ν. Pl.*Lg*.783d. Adv. -κῶς Ach.Tat.3.7. II. *of the Nymphs*, οἶκοι S.*Ichn*.149; μῆλα *AP*7.703 (Myrin.). III. -κά, τά, dub. sens. in *POxy*.1740. 9 (iii/iv A.D.). ✱**-ίος**, ὁ, *bridegroom*, παιδὸς ὀδύρεται ὀστέα καίων νυμφίου Il.23.223; τὸν μὲν ἄκουρον ἐόντα βάλ'.. νυμφίον ἐν μεγάρῳ μίαν οἴην παῖδα λιπόντα Od.7.65; ἁρμόζων κόρᾳ ν. ἄνδρα Pi.*P*.9.118, etc.; ζῆτε νυμφίων βίον Ar.*Av*.161; opp. νύμφη, Pl.*Lg*.783e: in pl., τοῖς νεωστὶ νυμφίοις to the *bridal* pair, E.*Med*.366, cf. A.*Th*.757 (lyr.); νυμφίοισι παρθένοις occurs in Ps.-E.*IA*741. 2. *son-in-law*, Lxx *Jd*. 15.6. II. as Adj. νύμφιος, α, ον, *bridal*, τράπεζα νυμφία Pi.*P*.3.16; λέκτρα *Epigr.Gr*.373 (Aezani).

**νυμφό-βας**, ὁ, *nymphas iniens*, Achae.52. **-γενής**, ές, =νυμφαγενής, Epigr.ap.Arist.*Mir*.843ᵇ31, *APl*.1.8 (Alc.). **-γέννητος**, ον, = foreg., S.*Ichn*.35. **-κλαυτος**, ον, Ἐρινύς, i.e. *a bride bringing woe* as vengeance, A.*Ag*.749 (lyr.). **-κομέω**, *adorn as a bride*, τὸ γέρας *APl*.4.147 (Antiphil.). 2. *make ripe for marriage*, ἐπεὶ δέ μ' ἀκμῆς ἄνθος ἐνυμφοκόμει *Supp.Epigr*.1.570.6 (Egypt, Augustan). II. intr., *dress oneself as a bride*, E.*Med*.985 (lyr.). ✱**-κόμος**, ον, (κομέω) *dressing a bride*, ἡ ν. *bridesmaid*, Hsch.: generally, *bridal*, γάμος E. *IA*1087 (lyr.); θάλαμοι *IG*12(8).600 (Thasos); στολίδες *Sammelb*.

6178.3; πάλη Nonn.*D*.48.183. **-ληπτος**, ον, *caught by nymphs*: hence, *raptured, frenzied*, *IG*1².788, Pl.*Phdr.*238d, Arist.*EE*1214ᵃ23, Plu.*Arist.*11. **-πόνος**, ον, *busied with the bride*, title of a poem by Sophron, Ath.8.362c. **-στολέω**, *escort the bride* or *bridegroom*, Ph.1.529, 2.36, Ach.Tat.1.18, al., *AP*9.203 (Phot. or Leo Phil.):—Med., of the bridegroom, Ph.1.323:—Pass., Str.6.1.8 (-ισθείσας codd.). **-στολικῶς**, Adv. *like one escorting a bride*, Sch.E.*Hec.* 388. **-στόλος**, ον, *escorting the bride*, J.*AJ*5.8.6: generally, *bridal*, ἄστρον ἐρώτων Musae.10. **-τερεῖς**· ἄρχοντές τινες, Hsch. (-τήρεις Meineke). **-τῑμος**, ον, *honouring the bride*: μέλος ν. *bridal* song, A.*Ag.*705 (lyr.). **-τομέω**, *remove the clitoris*, Aët.16.116 (Pass.). **-τομία**, ἡ, *removal of the clitoris*, Philum.ap.Aët.16.115 tit., Paul.Aeg.6.70tit. **-τροφέω**, *bring up for marriage*, τὰς θυγατέρας Them.*Or.*34p.467 D. **-φόρος**, ον, dub. sens. in *POxy.*434.

**νυμφ-ώδης**, ες, *of marriageable age*, *Sammelb.*6178.4 (dub.). **-ών**, ῶνος, ὁ, *bridechamber*, Lxx *To.*6.14, *Ev.Matt.*9.15, D.Chr.7.145, Hld.7.8, *PLond.*3.964.19 (ii/iii A.D.). II. temple of Dionysus, Demeter, and Persephone, Paus.2.11.3. III. a kind of νυμφαία, Ps.-Dsc.3.132.

**νῦν** (for νυν, νυ, v. infr. II), Adv. *now*, both of the *present moment*, and of the *present time* generally, οἳ ν. βροτοί εἰσιν mortals *of our day*, Il.1.272; so in Ion. and Att., οἱ ν. [ἄνθρωποι] men *of the present day*, Hdt.1.68; οἵ γε ν. Pi.*O.*1.105, B.5.4, cf. Arist.*Metaph.*1069ᵃ26; ὁ ν. τρόπος, τὸ ν. βαρβαρικόν, Th.1.6; Βοιωτοὶ οἱ ν. ib.12; ὁ ν. παρὼν χρόνος S.*Tr.*174, al., Pl.*Prm.*141e; ἡμέρα ἡ ν. S.*OT*351; νὺξ ἡ ν. Id.*Ant.*16; ἡ ν. ὁδός Id.*El.*1295; τὸ ν. *the present*, Arist.*Ph.*218ᵃ6, al.; ἀπὸ τοῦ ν. Pl.*Prm.*152c, Lxx *Ge.*46.30, etc.; ἀπὸ ν. *AP*5.40 (Rufin.); ἕως τοῦ ν. Lxx *Ge.*46.34; μέχρι ν. (v.l. μ. τοῦ ν.) D.S.17.110; τὰ ν. simply, = ν., Hdt.7.104, E.*Heracl.*641, etc.; τό περ ν. Pi. *N.*7.101; τὰ δὲ ν. S.*OC*133 (lyr.); τὸ ν. εἶναι Pl.*R.*506e, X.*Cyr.*5.3.42, Arist.*Ath.*31.2; τὸ ν. ἔχον *Act.Ap.*24.25. 2. of the immediate past, *just now, but now*, ν. Μενέλαος ἐνίκησεν Il.3.439, cf. 13.772, Od.1.43, S.*OC*84, X.*Cyr.*4.5.48; ν. γοῦν ἐπεχείρησας Pl.*R.*341c; ἡλίκα ν. ἐτραγῴδει D.18.13. 3. of the future, *presently*, ν. αὖτ' ἐγχείῃ πειρήσομαι Il.5.279, cf. 20.307, Od.1.200; ν. φεύξομαι, τόθ' ἁγνὸς ὤν E.*El.*975; cf. νῦν δή, νυνί. 4. sts. opp. to what might have been under other circumstances, *as it is* (or *was*), *as the case stands* (or *stood*), *as a matter of fact*, ν. δ' ὁ μὲν ὣς ἀπόλωλε Od.1.166; εἰ μὲν ὑπώπτευον, οὐκ ἂν . . ἐποιούμην· ν. δὲ κτλ. Th.4.126, cf. 1.122, 3.113, Pl. *Cra.*384b, D.18.195, etc.; καὶ ν. even *so*, X.*An.*7.4.24, 7.7.17. 5. coupled with other Particles, τὰ ν. γε S.*Ph.*245, etc.; ν. γε μάν Pi. *P.*1.50; ν. δή, v. h.v.: with other expressions of Time, ν. . . σήμερον, ν. ἤμερη ἥδε, Il.7.29, 13.828; ν. ἤδη *henceforth*, S.*Ant.*801 (anap.), etc.; ν. . . ἄρτι *but now*, Pl.*Cra.*396c. II. enclit. (but see below) νυν, νυ. [νυ only Ep., Boeot., and Cypr. (also Arc. in ὄνυ, q.v.); νῦν twice in Hom., Il.10.105, 23.485: ῡ in Trag. (ῠ A.*Th.*242, 246, S.*Ant.*705, E.*Or.*1678, etc.; ῠ S.*Tr.*92, E.*Andr.*91, etc.), ῠ in Com. (Ar.*V.*1381, *Pl.*975, al.), exc. Cratin.144, Ar.*Th.*105 (lyr., citing Agatho), and perh. *Nu.*141; both quantities in τοίνυν, q.v.] 1. rarely of Time, *now*, perh. so used in Il.10.105, cf. Parm.19.1, Pi. *P.*11.44, al., Epich.170.6. 2. in Ep. mostly as a particle of emphasis, ἧκε δ' ἐπ' Ἀργείοισι κακὸν βέλος· οἱ δέ νυ λαοὶ θνῆσκον Il.1.382, etc.: freq. coupled with other Particles or Conjs., ἦ ῥά ν. 4.93; καί νύ κεν 3.373; οὔ ν., μή νύ τοι, 10.165, 1.28; ἐπεί νύ τοι ib.416; ὥς νύ περ 2.258. 3. in commands or entreaties, μή ν. μοι νεμεσήσετ' 15.115: freq. with other Advbs., δεῦρό ν. come *now!* 23.485; ἐνταῦθά ν. ὕβριζε A.*Pr.*82, cf. Ar.*Th.*1001, *V.*149, *Pl.*724; εἶά ν. Id. *Pax*467, *V.*430, *Pl.*316: freq. with imper., φέρε ν. ib.789; ἄγε ν. Id. *Pax*1056, *V.*381; σπεῦδέ ν. Id.*Pl.*414; σίγα ν. S.*Aj.*87, Cratin.l.c.; περίδου ν. Ar.*Nu.*644, cf. X.*Cyr.*5.3.21, etc.; ὕφαινέ ν. B.18.8; so in Boeot., ν. ἔνθω *IG*7.3172.88 (Orchom.); also in Cypr. with opt. in commands, δυϝάνοι ν., δώκοι ν., *Inscr.Cypr.*135.6, 16 H. (Idalion). 4. in questions, τίς ν.; τί ν.; who, what, why *now?* Il.5.373, 1.414, 4.31; ἦ νυ . . ; Od.6.125. [In signf. I always perispom. In signf. II perispom. exc. when short, Hdn.Gr.2.39, al.; enclit. when short, sts. in codd., as Il.23.485 (Pap. in *Journ.Philol.*21.304, etc.; oxyt. when = δή, Tyrannio ap.Hdn.Gr.2.27; καθ' ὁμαλισμὸν or κατ' ἔγκλισιν when = δή, Sch.Ar.*Pl.*414, Sch.A.R.1.664). In codd. usu. perispom. in both senses, A.*Pr.*82, *Th.*242, 246, S.*Ant.*705, *El.*324, Ar.*Pl.*414, *V.*758, 922, etc.; even νὺν is written νῦν in codd. vett. Pi. *passim*, also in S.*Aj.*87, *Tr.*92, etc.; hence νυν may freq. be restored where the sense requires it. The accent of τοίνῦν perh. shows that both νὺν and νῦν could be enclitic.—Position: in signf. I νῦν can occupy any position; in signf. II it prefers (like other enclitics, but also like ἄν, δέ, γάρ, etc.) the second place in the sentence, e.g. πρός νύν σε πατρός S.*Ph.*468, cf. *OC*1333; ἀπό νύν με λείπετ' ἤδη Id.*Ph.*1177 (lyr.); μετά νυν δός E.*Supp.*56 (lyr.); νυ (always enclitic) precedes other enclitics and allows only δέ to precede.] (Cf. Skt. *nú*, *nū́*, *nūnám*, OE. *nū* 'now', etc.)

**νύναμαι** [ῠ], Cret. for δύναμαι, *Leg.Gort.*8.20, 12.32.

**νῠνᾰτός**, ά, όν, Cret. for δυνατός, *GDI*4992 aiii 3, al.

**νῦν δή**, stronger form of νῦν, with pres., *now, even now*, Pl.*Grg.* 462b, al., *Com.Adesp.*597, etc. 2. with past tenses, *just now*, ἃ ν. δ. ἐγὼ ἔλεγον Pl.*Prt.*329c, cf. *Phd.*61e, *Grg.*448a. 3. with fut., *now, without further delay*, ν. δ. σὺ δηλώσεις X.*Cyr.*4.1.23. II. ν. δ. μὲν . . , ν. δὲ . . , E.*Hipp.*233 (anap.), Pl.*Lg.*683e.

**νυνί**, Att. form of νῦν, strengthd. by -ῑ demonstr., *now, at this moment*, mostly of *the present*, *IG*1².98.3, etc.: freq. in Com., Ar. *Ach.*325, *Ra.*290, Pherecr.41, Men.*Her.*27, etc.: less freq. with past tenses, ὧν ν. διέβαλλε D.18.14; ν. συνεληλύθαμεν Isoc.6.7; ν. ἐβουλήθη Is.1.20; ν. βοηθήσαντες συγκατετάττοντο *IG*2².237.11 (iv B.C.): also with fut., ν. δὲ πειράσομαι Aeschin.2.25, cf. Isoc.18.35: c. aor. imper., ν. μεταγνώτω Th.4.92: rarely in the sense, *as the case stands* (cf. νῦν I.4), D.21.129, Lycurg.*Fr.*31.—Never in Trag. (E.*Supp.*306 is corrupt): Com. also have νυνμενί, for νυνὶ μέν, Ar. *Av.*448; νυνδί, for νυνὶ δέ, Id.*Eq.*1357, Antiph.190.16; cf. νυνγαρί, for νυνὶ γάρ, Eust.45.3.

**νύννιον**, τό, and **νύννιος**, ὁ, *lullaby*, Hsch.

**νύξ**, νυκτός, ἡ, *night*: either generally, *night-season* (opp. day), or *a night*, ν. ἀμβροσίη Il.24.363; ν. ἄμβροτος Od.11.330; but ν. ὀλοή ib.19, Il.16.567, cf. infr. II. 3, III; νυκτός *by night*, as Adv., Od. 13.278, etc.; οὔτε ν. οὔτ' ἐξ ἡμέρας S.*El.*780; νυκτὸς ἔτι *while it was* still *night*, Hdt.9.10; also τῆς νυκτός Alex.78.3, 148; ν. τῆσδε S. *Aj.*21; ἄκρας ν. at dead of *night*, ib.285 (but ἄκρῃ νυκτί at *night*-fall, Arat.775, ἀκρόθι νυκτός on the verge of dawn, Id.308); ἀωρὶ νυκτός, τῶν νυκτῶν, v. ἀωρί: in pl., τῶν νυκτῶν *at nights*, Ar.*Ec.*668: rarely, νυκτί Hdt.7.12; ν. τῇδε S.*El.*644; νύκτα *the night* long, νύκτα φυλάσσειν to watch *the night* through, Il.10.312, Od.5.466: pl., νύκτας ἰαύειν Il.9.325, Od.5.154, etc.; δύω νύκτας, τρεῖς ν., ib.388, 17.515: in Att., ὅλην τὴν ν. Pherecr.177, Amphis 20.4; τὴν νύχθ' ὅλην Eub.3; τὰς νύκτας Diph.32.14; ὅλας γε καὶ πάσας τὰς ν. X.*Smp.*4.54; νύκτας τε καὶ ἦμαρ Il.5.490; νύκτας τε καὶ ἡμέρας Pl.*Tht.*151a; οὔτε νύκτ' οὐθ' ἡμέραν E.*Ba.*187; τὴν νύχθ' ὅλην τήν θ' ἡμέραν Eub.53.1; νύκτα ἡμέραν ποιούμενος ἀπόστειλον (κατάπεμψον), i.e. without delay, *PCair.Zen.*314.7, *PSI*5.514.3 (both iii B.C.); μέσαι νύκτες *midnight*, Sapph.52, Pl.*R.*621b; περὶ μ. νύκτας X.*An.*7.8.12; ἐν μέσῳ νυκτῶν Id.*Cyr.*5.3.52; πρῳΐτερον μέσων νυκτῶν Th.8.101; ἔξω μέσων ν. D.54.26. 2. freq. with Preps., ἀνὰ νύκτα by *night*, Il.14.80; ἀνὰ πᾶσαν ν. all *night* through, Paus.1.32.4; διὰ νύκτα Od.19.66, etc.; εἰς νύκτα, εἰς τὴν ν., towards *night*, X.*Cyn.*11.4, *HG*4.6.7; ἐν νυττί (νυκτί), opp. πεδ' ἀμέραν, *Leg.Gort.*2.14, *SIG*527.40 (Dreros, iii B.C.); κατὰ νύκτα Ar.*Fr.* 561 (lyr.); ὑπὸ νύκτα towards *nightfall*, Th.4.67, X.*Ages.*2.19; μετὰ νύκτας by *night*, Pi.*N.*6.6; μεθ' ἡμέραν καὶ διὰ νυκτός all through *the night*, Pl.*Criti.*117e; ἐκ νυκτός after *nightfall*, X.*Cyr.*1.4.2, Lxx *Is.* 26.9, etc.; ἐκ πολλῆς ἔτι νυκτός D.H.6.67; ἐκ νυκτῶν Thgn.460, A. *Ch.*287, E.*Rh.*13, 17 (both anap.); ἐκ νυκτὸς εἰς νύκτα Pl.*Ax.*368b; πόρρω τῶν νυκτῶν far into *the night*, Id.*Smp.*217d, *Prt.*310c; ἐπὶ νυκτί by *night*, Il.8.529; ἐφ' ἡμέρῃ αἱ δ' ἐπὶ νυκτί Hes.*Op.*102; ἐν νυκτί A. *Ag.*653, X.*Smp.*1.9, etc.; ὀψίᾳ ἐν ν. Pi.*I.*4(3).36; ἐν ν. τῇ νῦν S.*Ant.* 16; νύκτεσσιν ἔν θ' ἁμέραις Pi.*P.*4.130. 3. in pl., *watches* of the night, ib.256; three such, παροίχωκεν δὲ πλέων νὺξ τῶν δύο μοιράων, τριτάτη δ' ἔτι μοῖρα λέλειπται Il.10.252; τρίχα νυκτὸς ἔην, for τρίτον μέρος τῆς νυκτὸς ἦν, it was the third watch, i.e. next before morning, Od.12.312. II. metaph. of darkness, νυκτὶ καλύψαι Il.5.23, cf. Od. 20.351, etc. 2. metaph. of death, ἀμφὶ δὲ ὄσσε κελαινὴ ν. ἐκάλυψε Il.5.310, al.; ν. Ἅιδης τε S.*Aj.*660. 3. in Comparisons, of anything dark and direful, νυκτὶ ἐοικώς like *night*, of Apollo in his wrath, Il.1.47, cf. 12.463, Od.11.606; τάδε νυκτὶ ἐΐσκει what is here he likens *to night*, 20.362; ὀλεθρία ν., of a great calamity, S.*OC* 1684 (lyr.). III. Νύξ as pr. n., *the goddess of Night*, Il.14.259, Hes.*Op.*17, *Th.*123, 211; N. ὀλοή ib.224. IV. *the night-* or *evening-quarter of heaven, the West*, πρὸς νυκτός ib.275. (Cf. Lat. *nox*, Lith. *naktìs*, Goth. *nahts*, etc.)

**νύξις**, εως, ἡ, *pricking, stabbing*, Aret.*SA*2.9, Gal.1.239; *stinging*, ν. σκορπίου θαλασσίου Dsc.2.81; *impact*, ἀέρα κατὰ νύξιν ἢ ψαῦσιν ἀπὸ τοῦ φωτὸς ἐξηλιοῦσθαι Plu.2.930f.

**νυός**, ἡ, *daughter-in-law*, Il.22.65, Od.3.451, *h.Ven.*136; *daughter-by-marriage* of the race of which the husband is a son, Il.3.49. II. *bride, wife*, Theoc.18.15; cj. in *AP*12.53.5 (Mel.):—ἐνυός is f.l. in Poll.3.32. (I.-E. *snusós*, cf. Skt. *snuṣā́*, OHG. *snur*, Lat. *nurus*, etc.)

**νυρίζει**· νύσσει, ξύει, and **νυρῶν**· νύσσων, ξύων, Hsch., cf. Suid.

**Νῦσα**, ης, ἡ, *Nysa*, name of several mountains sacred to Dionysus, *h.Hom.*26.5, etc.:—Adj. **Νύσιος** [ῡ], α, ον, *h.Cer.*17, S.*Aj.*699 codd. (lyr.) (ν., ὁ, = κισσός, Ps.-Dsc.2.179); **Νῡσήϊος**, Ar.*Ra.*215 (lyr.):—fem. **Νῡσαΐς**, ΐδος, Str.12.8.17; **Νῡσαῖοι**, οἱ, *inhabitants of N.*, Id.15.1.8. II. **νύσα**, ἡ, = δένδρον, Pherecyd.178 J.

**νῦσος**, = χωλός, Syrac. word, Nonn.*D.*9.22, *EM*280.16.

**νύσσα**, ης, ἡ, in a race-course, 1. = καμπτήρ, *turning-post*, Il.23.332, 344; ἐν νύσσῃ ἐγχριμφθήτω, of the near horse, ib.338, cf. Theoc.24.119: metaph., *turning-point* of the recurrent nerve, Gal. *UP*16.4. 2. *starting-* and *winning-post*, τοῖσι δ' ἀπὸ νύσσης τέτατο δρόμος Il.23.758, Od.8.121: metaph., ν. ἀοιδῆς ἰθύνειν Opp.*H.*3.11.

**νυσσητᾶς**, ὁ, Pythag. name for 9, *Theol.Ar.*58 (dub. l.).

**νύσσω**, Att. νύττω, Pass., pf. νένυγμαι Gal.10.221: aor. 1 ἐνύχθην D.L.2.109, Gal.10.390: aor. 2 ἐνύγην [ῠ], 3 sg. opt. νυγείη ib.401; part. νυγείς Chrysipp.*Stoic.*2.233, Gal.13.565, *App.Anth.*3.129.6 (D.L.):—*touch with a sharp point, prick, stab, pierce*, ἔγχεϊ νύξε Il.5.579; χείρεσσι . . ἀσπίδα νύσσων 16.704; χθόνα . . ἵπποι νύσσοντες χηλῇσι *dinting* the earth with their hoofs, Hes.*Sc.*62; ἀγκῶνι νύξας *having nudged* him with the elbow, Od.14.485, cf. Theoc.21.50, Plu.2.79e, etc.; γνωμιδίῳ γνώμην ν. *prick* it (and see what is in it), Ar.*Nu.*321; λέοντα ν. 'beard the lion in his den', Diogenian.1.52. 2. metaph., *sting*, Phld.*Lib.*p.64 O.; νύξας ὁ λόγος Luc.*Herm.*71, cf. Porph.*Abst.* 1.49. II. *impinge upon*, esp. of sense-impressions, Plot.4.5.1, 6.6.12:—Pass., Chrysipp.l.c., Alex.Aphr.*de An.*130.15. 2. Pass., of the νεῦρα, *suffer lesion* (νύγμα I. 2), Gal. ll. cc.

**νύστ-αγμα**, ατος, τό, *nap, short sleep*, Lxx *Jb.*33.15. **-αγμός**, ὁ, *drowsiness*, Hp.*VM*10, Lxx *Ps.*131(132).4, al.: in pl., Porph.*Abst.*1.

28. -άζω, fut. -άξω LXX *Is.*5.27: aor. ἐνύσταξα Thphr.*Char.*7.8, LXX 2*Ki.*4.6, al.; ἐνύστασα Dionys.Com.2.43, *AP*12.135 (Asclep.):—mostly pres., *to be half asleep, doze*, νυστάζοντα οὐδένα ἂν ἴδοις X.*Cyr.* 8.3.43; ὥσπερ οἱ νυστάζοντες ἐγειρόμενοι Pl.*Ap.*31a; ὀφθαλμοὶ πλέοντες ὥσπερ τῶν νυσταζόντων Hp.*Epid.*7.17; οὐχὶ νυστάζειν ἔτι ὥρα 'στίν Ar.*Av.*639, cf. Xenarch.2.1, *Com.Adesp.*185; νυστάζοντος δικαστοῦ Pl.*R.*405c: metaph., ν. τε καὶ ἀπορεῖ Id.*Ion* 533a; τὸν νυστάζοντα καὶ ἀμαθῆ φύσει Id.*Lg.*747b; ἔν τινι *in* a thing, Plu.2.675b. 2. *hang the head*, ἐδάκρυσεν καὶ ἐνύσταξε *AP*l. c. (Cf. Lith. *snústi* (stem *snūd-*) 'grow drowsy'.) -ακτής, οῦ, ὁ, *drowsy*, ὕπνος Ar.*V.* 12, Alciphr.3.46. -ακτικῶς, Adv. *in a drowsy way*, Gal.19. 91. -ᾰλέος, α, ον, *drowsy*, Aret.*SD*2.6, Hsch. -ᾰλος, ον, *drowsy*, γερόντιον *Com.Adesp.*875 (-λέον Kock), cf. D.L.6.77:—written νυσταλογερόντιον in *EM*609.38. -αξις, εως, ἡ, *drowsiness*, Hsch. s. v. νῶκαρ.

**νύττω**, Att. for νύσσω. **νύχᾰ** [ῠ], Adv., = νύκτωρ, Hsch.

**νῠχ-αῖος**, α, ον, = νύχιος, Theognost.*Can.*52. -αυγής, ές, *shining by night*, Orph.*H.*3.7, 71.8. -εγρεσία, ἡ, = νυκτηγρεσία, *AP*5. 263 (Paul. Sil.). -(ε)ία, ἡ, = νύχευμα, Hsch. -ειος, α, ον, = νύχιος, Orph.*H.*9.6 (νυχία codd.). -ευμα, ατος, τό, *nightly watch*, ποῦ νυχευμάτων χάρις; E.*Supp.*1136 (lyr., dub. l.). -εύω, fut. -εύσω Nic.*Fr.*74.8:—*watch the night through, pass the night*, δάκρυσι ν. E.*El.*181 (lyr.), cf. *Rh.*520, *Hyps.Fr.*10, 11.13 (lyr.); Νύμφῃσιν *with* them, Nic. l. c.

**νῠχηβόρος**, ον, *devouring by night*, v.l. for μυλ-, μυχ-, Nic.*Th.* 446.

**νυχθ-ημερήσιος**, α, ον, = sq., Tz. ad Hes.*Op.*412. -ημερινός, ή, όν, = sq., διάστημα Cleom.1.6. -ήμερος, α, ον, *lasting a day and night*, δρόμοι *Peripl.M.Rubr.*15; πλοῦς Scymn.957. II. as Subst. -ήμερον, τό, *a night and a day*, the space of 24 hours, 2*Ep.Cor.*11.25, Gal.7.508, Cleom.1.6, Ptol.*Alm.*3.9, Herm.ap.Stob.1.21.9, *Gp.*5.8. 8, etc.

⊛ **νύχιος** [ῠ], α, ον, also ος, ον E.*IT*1273 (lyr.), Tim.*Fr.*11, parodied by Macho ap.Ath.8.341d:—*nightly*, i. e. 1. of persons, *doing a* thing *by night*, ν. καταλέξεται Hes.*Op.*523 (v.l.), cf. *Th.*991, A.*Ag.* 588, etc.; ἀνὴρ δ' ἐκτέταται ν. *as in nightly sleep*, S.*Ph.*857 (lyr.). 2. *belonging to night*, ν. φθέγματα Id.*Ant.*1147 (lyr.); ἐνοπαί, γόοι, E.*IT* 1277, *El.*141 (both lyr.): in late Prose, ν. θεός Dam.*Pr.*273. 3. of places, *dark as night, gloomy*, νυχίαν πλάκα A.*Pers.*953 (lyr.); δι' ἅλα ν. E.*Med.*211 (lyr.); ἄντρα Id.*Andr.*1224 (lyr.); ὑπὸ μέλαθρα νύχια, i.e. into the nether world, Id.*Hel.*177 (lyr.); χάος Ar.*Av.* 698: in later Prose, τὸ τῶν ἄντρων ν. Porph.*Antr.*9.

**νύχμα**, τό, = νύγμα (q.v.). II. = ὄνειδος, Hsch.; cf. νῶχμα.

⊛ **νύχος**, εος, τό, = νύξ, S.E.*M.*1.243, Hsch., Phot., etc.

**νώ**, v. ἐγώ III. II. **νῷ**, dat. of νοῦς.

**νώγᾰλ-α**, τά, *dainties, sweetmeats*, eaten after dinner, *dessert*, like τρωγάλια, Antiph.65, Ephipp.24. ⊛ -έος· λαμπρός, Zonar. Adv. -έως Id. -ευμα, ατος, τό, in pl., = νώγαλα, Arar.8. -εύω, *munch dainties* or *sweetmeats*, Suid. -ίζω, = foreg., Alex.275: pf. Pass. ἐνωγάλισται in Eub.15.7 is f.l. for νενωγ—. -ισμα, ατος, τό, in pl., = νώγαλα, Poll.6.62.

**νωδογέρων**, οντος, ὁ, *toothless old man*, *Com.Adesp.*1090.

**νωδός**, ή, όν, (neg. Particle *n*(ĕ)-, ὀδούς) *toothless*, Ar.*Ach.*715, *Pl.*266, Phryn.Com.79, Eub.146, Arist.*Metaph.*1068[a]7, Phoen.5.3 (dub. l.), Theoc.9.21.

**νωδότης**, ητος, ἡ, *toothlessness*, Porph. *in Cat.*137.3.

**νωδῠν-ία**, ἡ, *relief from pain*, τέκτονα νωδυνίας Pi.*P.*3.6, cf. Theoc. 17.63. -ος, ον, (*n*(ĕ)-, ὀδύνη) = ἀνώδυνος (q.v.), *painless*, νώδυνον κάματον τιθέναι Pi.*N.*8.50. II. Act., *soothing pain*, φύλλον τι ν. S.*Ph.*44.

**νῶε**, v. ἐγώ III.

**νώθ-εια**, ἡ, *slowness, sluggishness*, Pl.*Phdr.*235d, *Tht.*195c, Luc. *Ind.*22, Babr.95.70, Poll.3.122, Ael.*NA*16.21. ⊛-ής, ές, *sluggish, slothful*, ὄνος Il.11.559; ν. κῶλον E.*HF*819; ἵππος -έστερος Pl.*Ap.* 30e; ν. κίνησις Arist.*HA*503[b]8; τὰ γόνατα νωθής Luc.*Luct.*16; of fire, *dull*, opp. ὀξύς, Thphr.*HP*5.9.3 (Comp.); of earth, opp. water, etc., Pl.*Ti.*86a (Sup.). 2. of the understanding, *dull, stupid*, κατεφαίνετο εἶναι -έστερος (sc. ὁ παῖς) Hdt.3.53; νωθὴς τὸν νόον Hp. *Ep.*17, cf. A.*Pr.*62, Pl.*Plt.*310e (Comp.). II. neut. νωθές as Adv., Poll.4.81: Sup. -έστατα D.C.59.4. -ουρίς, ίδος, ἡ, = βαλλωτή, Ps.-Dsc.3.103. -ουρος, ον, (οὐρά I. 2) *frigidus in venerem*, *Com.Adesp.*1352.

**νωθρ-άς**, άδος, ἡ, = βαλλωτή, Ps.-Dsc.3.103. -εία, ἡ, *sluggishness, torpor, indolence*, Erot. s.v. βλακεύειν, Aristid.Quint.2.3, v.l. in Poll.3.122. -επιθέτης, ου, ὁ, *slow to begin*, Arist.*Phgn.*813[a] 3. -εύω, *to be sluggish* or *torpid*, Poll.1.159, Aq.*Jd.*19.8:—also in Med., of persons, Hyp.*Lyc.Fr.*5; νενωθρευμένοι Hp.*Coac.*600; of tumours, νενωθρευμένα *accompanied by torpor*, ib.60. 2. *to be poorly, indisposed*, *PGiss.*17.6 (ii A. D.):—Med., *PSI*6.717.5 (ii A. D.). -ία, Ion. -ίη, = νωθρεία, Hp.*Prorrh.*1.141, *Coac.*205, Herod.4.53, Ptol. *Tetr.*141; *indisposition*, *PAmh.*2.78.15 (ii A. D.). -ιάω, = νωθρεύομαι I, Dsc.*Alex.Praef.*

**νωθρο-κάρδιος**, ον, *slow of heart*, LXX *Pr.*12.8, Hsch. -ποιός, όν, *making sluggish*, Eust.1395.31.

**νωθρ-ός**, ά, όν, = νωθής, Hp.*VM*10, *Prorrh.*1.102, 117, etc.; ν. σφυγμοί Id.*Coac.*136, Aret.*SA*2.9; καταφορὴ ν. falling into a *heavy* sleep, Hp.*Epid.*3.6, cf. Nic.*Th.*165; ν. κινήσεις Arist.*PA*696[b]6; ν. σύνεσις Demetr.Lac.*Herc.*1014.58; τῇ κινήσει ν. Arist.*HA*622[b]32; ν. ὁδίτης Call.*Fr.*275; νωθρότερος τὴν ἀκοήν Hld.5.1. Adv. -ρῶς Archyt.1; *leisurely, gradually*, Hp.*Aph.*2.7: neut. as Adv., ὄμμασι νωθρὰ βλέπουσα *AP*5.54 (Diosc.). 2. of the mind, ν. καὶ λήθης γέμοντες Pl. *Tht.*144b, cf. Amips.16 (Comp.); στόματα Anaxipp.1.44 (Comp.); ν. καὶ μωροί Arist.*Pr.*954[a]31; ἡσύχιος καὶ ν. Plb.31.23.11; νωθραῖς ἐλπίσιν Babr.16.7. Adv. ἀγεννῶς καὶ νωθρῶς Plb.3.90.6. II. Act., *making sluggish*, νότοι Hp.*Aph.*3.5, cf. S.E.*M.*6.48. -ότης, ητος, ἡ, = νωθρεία, Hp.*Prorrh.*1.13, 70, Arist.*Rh.*1390[b]30; ἡ ἐκ τοῦ γήρως ν. LXX 3*Ma.*4.5: pl., Gal.8.161. -ώδης, ες, *accompanied by torpor*, ῥίγεα Hp.*Coac.*14.

**νωθώδης**, ες, of persons, *lethargic*, Aret.*SD*2.5.

**νῶϊ**, v. ἐγώ III.

**νωΐτερος** [ῐ], α, ον, *of* or *from us two*, Il.15.39, Od.12.185; = ἡμέτερος, Euph.9.9.

⊛ **νῶκαρ**, ᾰρος, τό, *lethargy, coma*, Nic.*Th.*189, Hsch.; expld. by στέρησις τῆς ψυχῆς, Hdn.Gr.2.770. II. as Adj., *slothful, sleepy*, Suid.

**νωκᾰρώδης**, ες, = foreg. II, Diph.18.7.

**νωκελίς**, ίδος, ἡ, = νωχελίς, Ps.-Dsc.3.103.

⊛ **νωλεμές**, Adv. *without pause, unceasingly*, ν. αἰεί Il.9.317, 17.385, Od.16.191, etc.; οἱ δ' αἰεὶ . . ν. ἐγχρίμπτοντο Il.17.413: without αἰεί, μάχην ἀλίαστον ἔχουσι ν. 14.58; later, *firmly*, ν. ἐρρίζωθεν A.R.2. 605:—also **νωλεμέως**, πόνον τ' ἐχέμεν καὶ ὀϊζὺν ν. Il.13.3; ν. ἐχέμεν *persevere*, 5.492; but ν. κτείνοντο they were murdered *without pause*, i.e. one after the other, Od.11.413.—Ep. word, used by Tyrt.5.5, 12.17.

**νῶμα**, v. νόημα. II. pl., *owner's marks, brands*, on cattle, Hsch. (fort. γνώματα). 2. = θρέμματα, Id.

⊛ **νωμ-άω**, Iterat. impf. νώμασκε Mosch.4.108:—Med., v. infr.: (νέμω A. I. 1):—*deal out, distribute*, esp. food and drink at festivals, Il.1. 471, Od.3.340, etc.; ν. φιάλαισιν ἀμπέλου παῖδα *pour* wine into *the several* cups, Pi.*N.*9.51; ν. προπόσεις Critias 1.7 D. II. (νέμω A. III. 2) *direct, guide*, 1. of weapons, implements, etc., *handle, wield*, ἐν παλάμῃσι πελώριον ἔγχος ἐνώμα Il.5.594; οἶδ' ἐπὶ δεξιά, οἶδ' ἐπ' ἀριστερὰ νωμῆσαι βῶν 7.238; σκῆπτρον δ' οὔτ' ὀπίσω οὔτε προπρηνὲς ἐνώμα 3.218; ἄλεισον . . μετὰ χερσὶν ἐνώμα Od.22.10; ἀεὶ γὰρ πόδα νηὸς ἐνώμων *managed* the sheet, 10.32; νηὸς . . οἰήϊα νωμᾷς 12.218; ἀνία χερσὶ ν. Pi.*I.*1.15; *drive*, ν. δίφρους Id.*P.*4.18; ν. κύλικα Theophil.2.5:—Med., νωμήσασθαι σάκος Q.S.3.439. b. metaph., ἐν πρύμνῃ πόλεως οἴακα νωμῶν A.*Th.*3; νώμα δικαίῳ πηδαλίῳ στρατόν Pi.*P.*1.86; πᾶν ἐπὶ τέρμα ν. A.*Ag.*781 (lyr.); νωμᾶτ' ὠκεανόν, νωμᾶθ' ἅλα, δένδρεά τ' αὔτως Orph.*H.*38.8, etc.: abs., *to be the guiding power*, S.*Fr.*941.11. 2. of the limbs of the human body, *ply*, γούνατ' ἐν. Il.10.358; ὄμμα Parm.1.35; φυγᾷ πόδα ν. S.*OT*468 (lyr.); ν. ὀφρύν *move* the brow, A.*Ch.*288; πτερὸν αἰθέρι ν. *AP*9.339 (Arch.); πῆδα . . παμφυὲς νωμῶν δέμας *IG*4[2](1).130.19 (Epid.). 3. metaph., of the mind, *turn over*, ἐνὶ φρεσὶ κέρδε' ἐνώμας thou didst use *to turn* wiles *over* in the mind, Od.18.216; κέρδεα νωμῶν 20.257; *ply nimbly*, ἐν στήθεσσι νόον πολυκερδέα νωμᾷν 13.255. 4. *observe*, νωμῶντες . . σῖτα ἀναιρεομένους *observing* them in the act of foraging, Hdt.4.128; of soothsayers, ἐν ὠσὶ ν. καὶ φρεσὶν . . χρηστηρίους ὄρνιθας A.*Th.*25; ὦ πάντα νωμῶν, Τειρεσία S.*OT*300, cf. E.*Ph.*1256; τὸ νωμᾶν καὶ τὸ σκοπεῖν ταὐτόν Pl.*Cra.*411d; so prob. in *h.Cer.*373 ἀμφὶ ἓ νωμήσας *peering* round him. III. Med., = νέμομαι, *possess, occupy*, χώραν, νῆσον, *Supp.Epigr.*2.511.56, al. (Crete, ii B. C.).—Poet. word, exc. in Hdt. and Pl. ll. cc. and in signf. III. -ήσιμος, ον, f.l. for λωβήσιμος, Nic.*Fr.*73.3. -ησις, εως, ἡ, *observation*, σκέψιν καὶ ν. Pl.*Cra.*411d. II. *motion*, Suid. -ήτωρ, ορος, ὁ, *one who distributes*, Doroth.ap.Heph.Astr.3.30, Man.6.357. II. *one who guides, moves*, etc., Nonn.*D.*12.20, 48.165.

**νῷν**, Att. for νῶϊν, v. ἐγώ III.

**νωνῠμ-ία**, ἡ, *namelessness*, Hsch., *CR*10.420 (Phrygia). ⊛ -ος, in Ep. also **νώνυμνος** (so in a metrical epitaph, *BCH*36.230 (Rhodes, iii B. C.)), ον, (*n*(ĕ)-, ὄνυμα, ὄνομα) *nameless, inglorious*, νωνύμνους ἀπολέσθαι ἀπ' Ἄργεος Il.12.70; γενεήν γε θεοὶ νώνυμνον ὀπίσσω θῆκαν Od. 1.222, cf. 14.182, Hes.*Op.*154, Pi.*O.*10(11).51, A.*Pers.*1003 (lyr.), S.*El.*1084 (lyr.), *Lyr.Adesp.*123 B. 2. *unnamed*, i.e. *lacking* ὄνομα, Democr.26. II. Act., *not naming*, Call.*Aet.Oxy.*2080.57 (nisi leg. οὐδεμιῇ . . νωνυμνί (or -νεί), *without being named*): c. gen., Σαπφοῦς νώνυμος *without naming* Sappho, i.e. *without knowledge of* her, *AP*7.17 (Tull. Laur.).

⊛ **νωπέομαι**, *to be downcast*, Ion Hist.1, Phot. s. v. νενώπηται (Hsch. also has ἐνώπηται (sic)).

**νωρεῖ**· ἐνεργεῖ, Hsch. **νώρεμνος**· μέγας, πολύς, Id.; but also, κατώτατος, ἀσθενής, ἔσχατος, πλατύς, Id.

**νῶροψ**, οπος, ὁ, ἡ, Ep. epith. of χαλκός, *flashing*, Il.2.578, al.; later, simply, *bright*, ν. πέπλῳ Nonn.*D.*32.14.

**νωσάμενος, νώσασθαι**, v. νοέω. **νῶσις**, v. νόησις.

**νωτᾰγωγ-έω**, *carry on the back*, Clearch.ap.Ath.6.258b. -ός, όν, *carrying burdens*, of animals, *Hippiatr.*25.

**νωτ-αῖος**, α, ον, poet. = νωτιαῖος, Nic.*Th.*317. -άκμων, ονος, ὁ, ἡ, *with mailed back*, Batr.294. -άρης, ες, (αἴρω) *carrying on the back*, Suid. -εύς, έως, ὁ, *beast of burden*, Poll.2.180, Hsch. ⊛ -ηγός, όν, (ἄγω) = νωταγωγός, ἵπποι *Peripl.M.Rubr.*24. ⊛ -ιαῖος, α, ον, *spinal*, ν. ἄρθρα the *spinal* vertebrae, E.*El.*841; ν. μυελός Hp.*Aph.* 5.18, Pl.*Ti.*74a; ὁ ν., without μυελός, Hp.*Art.*45; ν. ἄκανθα Diog. Apoll.6. 2. λεπὶς ν. *back-plate*, Ph.*Bel.*63.46. -ιάς, άδος, ἡ, fem. Adj., = foreg., φθίσις Hp.*Morb.*2.51. -ῐδᾰνός, ὁ, a kind of γαλεός I, Arist.*Fr.*310; called ἐπινωτιδεύς by Epaenet.ap.Ath.7. 294d. -ίζω, only in aor. exc. in compd. ἀπο-, *turn one's back*,

οἱ δὲ . . πρὸς φυγὴν ἐνώτισαν *turned their backs and fled*, E.*Andr.*1141: c. acc. cogn., παλίσσυτον δράμημα νωτίσαι S.*OT*193: abs., νωτίσας θυέτω *IPE*2.342 (Phanagoria). II. *cover the back of*, βρέφος E.*Ph.*654 (lyr.). III. *skim the surface of*, πόντον νωτίσαι A.*Ag.*286. IV. Med., νωτίσασθαι *carry on the back*, Hsch. **-ιος**, ον, collat. form of νωτιαῖος, Philox.2.28 (s. v. l.); ν. σπόνδυλοι Ti.Locr. 100a. **-ισμα**, ατος, τό, (νωτίζω II) *that which covers the back*, e.g. wings, *Trag.Adesp.*541.

**νωτο-βᾰτέω**, *mount the back*, sens. obsc., *AP*12.238 (Pass., Strat.). II. *walk over the ridge of*, τύμβους ib.7.175 (Antiphil.). **-γραπτος**, ον, *having markings on the back*, Arist.*Fr.*297, Eust.1960.20. **-κοπέω**, *break* an animal's *back*, *slaughter* it, Thd.*Ex.*13.13, *Is.*66.3.

* **νῶτον**, τό, or **νῶτος**, ὁ, pl. always νῶτα, τά in early writers (οἱ νῶτοι Lxx 3*Ki.*7.19(33)): the gender of the sg. is undetermined in Hom. and Hes.; neut. in Pi.*P.*1.28, 4.83, E.*Cyc.*237, 643, Ar.*Eq.*289, *Pax* 747, Antiph.132.6 (anap.), and always in Att. acc. to Phryn.257, etc.: acc. νῶτον is masc. in Hp.*Prorrh.*2.30,40, X.*Eq.*3.3 (as cited by Hdn.Gr.1.215), Arist.*HA*512$^b$17, 544$^a$6, Ephor.224 J.:—*back*, both of men and animals: sg., of a man, Il.5.147, 13.289, etc.; of a boar, φρίσσει νῶτον ib.473; ν. . . ὄϊος καὶ πίονος αἰγός 9.207; of horses, ἐπὶ νῶτον ἕσαι 2.765; of an eagle, Pi.*P.*1.9: pl. freq. used in Poets in sense of sg., δράκων ἐπὶ νῶτα δαφοινός Il.2.308, cf. Od.6.225, etc.: sts. in Ep. of the *chine* of an animal served as food, νῶτα βοὸς . . πίονα ib.4.65; νώτοισιν δ' Ὀδυσῆα διηνεκέεσσι γέραιρεν 14.437, cf. Il.7.321; of men in battle, τὰ νῶτα ἐντρέψαι to turn *the back*, i.e. flee, Hdt.7.211; νῶτον ἐπιστρέψαι Orac.ib.141; σὺ μὴ δῷς ν. μηδενί *PTeb.*21.8 (ii B.C.); δοτέον τὰ ν. Plu.2.787f; δεῖξαι νῶτα Id.*Marc.*12 (this phrase also of the winner in a race, *AP*9.557 (Antip. Thess.)); πίπτειν ἐπὶ νώτῳ A.*Supp.*91 (lyr.); κατὰ νώτου *in rear*, κατὰ νώτου γενέσθαι τινός Hdt.1.9, 10; τὸ στρατόπεδον κατὰ ν. λαβεῖν ib.75; κατὰ ν. βοηθεῖν Th.1.62, etc.; κατὰ νῶτα Theoc.22.84; *back* of the finger, Procop.Gaz.*Ecphr.*168.11. II. metaph., *any wide surface*, esp. of the sea, ἐπ' εὐρέα νῶτα θαλάσσης Il.2.159, Od.3.142, cf. Hes.*Th.*762; ἐν νώτοισι ποντίας ἁλός E.*Hel.*129; πόντου 'πὶ νώτοις ib.774; also of the land, σχίζε ν. γᾶς Pi.*P.*4.228, cf. 26; χθονὸς ν. E.*IT*46; of the sky, ἀστεροειδέα ν. αἰθέρος Id.*Fr.*114 ap.Ar.*Th.*1067 (lyr.); ἐπὶ τῷ τοῦ οὐρανοῦ ν. Pl.*Phdr.*247c; but ἕσπερα ν. the *evening*, i.e. *western*, *sky*, E.*El.*731 (lyr.). 2. *ridge* of a hill or rock, Pi.*O.*7.87, E.*Hipp.*128 (lyr.); of a tomb, Id.*Hel.*842, etc.; of a chariot, Id.*Tr.*572 (anap.); of a saw, *AP*6.204 (Leon.). 3. *nave* of a wheel, Lxx l.c. 4. *back* of a page, Gal.15.624; τὰ κατὰ νώτου *POxy.*1725.9 (iii A.D.). (Perh. cf. Lat. *nătēs*.)

**νωτοπλήξ**, ῆγος, ὁ, ἡ, *with scourged back*, = μαστιγίας, of slaves, Ar.*Fr.*830, Pherecr.89.

**νῶτος**, v. νῶτον. **νωτοστροφέω**, *turn the back*, *Gloss.*

**νωτοφορ-έω**, *carry on the back*, D.S.2.54: abs., Id.17.105, Vett.Val.77.14. **-ία**, ἡ, *carrying on the back*, D.S.2.54. **-ος**, ον, *carrying on the back*, ὄνοι *PCair.Zen.*215.6 (iii B.C.); ὑποζύγια ib.292.283 (iii B.C.); ἄνδρες Lxx 2*Ch.*2.18(17); κτήνη ν. beasts *of burden*, *OGI*200.14 (Axum, iv A.D.). II. Subst. νωτοφόρος, ὁ, *carrier*, *porter*, *PPetr.*3 p.139 (iii B.C.), Lxx 2*Ch.*34.13, *PTeb.*115.7 (ii B.C.). 2. neut. νωτοφόρον, τό, *beast of burden*, X.*Cyr.*6.2.34 (but v. ἡμίονος as cited by Poll.2.180, cf. *PCair.Zen.*8.13 (iii B.C.)), D.C.56.20.

**νωφαιόν**· ἀφανές, Hsch. **νωφαλή(ς)**· νωθρός, Id. **νωφρύς**, = βαλλωτή, Ps.-Dsc.3.103. **νωχαλίζει**· βραδύνει, Hsch. **νωχᾰλός**, ή, όν, = νωχελής, Id. (νοχ- cod.): Comp. -έστερος, ψυχή Androcyd. ap.Clem.Al.*Strom.*7.6.33.

**νωχελ-εύομαι**, *to be slothful*, Aq.*Pr.*18.9, al.; *malinger*, dub. in *BGU*380.11 (iii A.D.). * **-ής**, ές, *slow-moving*, *sluggish*, *dull*, αἰεί ποτ' ἐστὲ νωχελεῖς καὶ μέλλετε S.*Fr.*142.19; τὸ δυσκίνητον καὶ ν. Diocl.*Fr.*141, cf. Herm.ap.Stob.1.49.3, Vett.Val.68.12; Κρόνου ν. δύναμις Porph.ap.Eus.*PE*3.11; πλευρὰ νωχελῆ νόσῳ E.*Or.*800 (troch.); ν. βάρος Nic.*Th.*162; νωχελέες καὶ ἀνώνυμοι Arat.391; ἄνθρωποι -έστατοι Phld.*Ir.*p.64 W.; ἔκλαμψις -εστέρα *Placit.*3.3.12 (v.l. νωθεστέρα). II. Subst. νωχελές, τό, *abortion*, Hp.*Mul.*1.78 (νοχ- codd.). **-ία**, Ep. -ίη, ἡ, *laziness*, *sluggishness*, βραδυτῆτί τε νωχελίῃ τε Il.19.411, cf. Orph.*Fr.*286, Vett.Val.2.6 (pl.), Iamb.*VP*15.65:—also **νωχέλεια**, Orib.*Fr.*58, Hsch. **-ίς**, ίδος, ἡ, = βαλλωτή, Ps.-Dsc.3.103.

**νῶχμα**· ὄνειδος, Hsch.; cf. νύχμα. **νώψ**, νῶπος, ὁ, ἡ, (η(ε)-, *ὄπτομαι) *purblind*, Id.

# Ξ

Ξ ξ, ξεῖ (q. v.), τό, indecl., fifteenth (later fourteenth) letter of most of the Eastern Greek alphabets, including the Ionic (later general Gr.) alphabet; not used in Western Greek alphabets or in the native Attic alphabet; in form and serial position (*IG*14.2420) it corresponds to the Semitic *samech* (a form of *s*), but has acquired the new value *ks*; as numeral ξ' = 60, but ,ξ = 60,000.

* **ξαίνω**, fut. ξᾰνῶ Ar.*Av.*827: aor. ἔξηνα E.*Or.*12:—Pass., aor. ἐξάνθην (v. infr.): pf. ἔξασμαι (κατ-) Hp.*Ulc.*24, (ἀν-) Gal.ap.Orib.51.57.3, ἔξαμμαι Thphr.*CP*3.23.2, *Gp.*3.1.7, (κατ-) D.S.17.71:—*scratch*, *comb*, esp. of wool, *card*, εἰρία τε ξαίνειν Od.22.423; στέμματα ξ., of Fate, E. l. c.: abs., *dress wool*, *Trag.Adesp.*9, Ar.*Lys.*536, *Ec.*89, 92, Pl.*Sph.*226b, etc.: c. gen. partit., τῶν ἐρίων ξ. Ar.*Fr.*717, Crates Theb.3: metaph., ξ. εὔνοιαν εἰς καλαθίσκον Ar.*Lys.*579; ξ. εἰς πῦρ, prov. of labour in vain, Pl.*Lg.*780c. 2. of cloth, *full*, *dress* it, ξ. τὸν πέπλον Ar.*Av.* l.c. II. metaph., *thresh*, ἡνίκ' ἂν ξανθῇ στάχυς dub. in A.*Fr.*304.7 (leg. ἡνίκ' ἐξανθῇ); *fret*, *mangle*, of waves, ξανθὲν ὑπὸ σπιλάδι *AP*6.223 (Antip.), cf. 23; ὕδωρ ξαινόμενον *fretted* into foam, A.R.4.1266; of bodies, *mangle*, *lacerate*, ξαινόμενος περὶ τῇ γῇ D.H.3.30; esp. of flogging, ξ. τὸ σῶμα μάστιξι ibid.; ῥάβδοις ἔξαινον τὰ σώματα Plu.*Publ.*6, cf. Ach.Tat.6.20 (Pass.): c. acc. cogn., ξ. κατὰ τοῦ νώτου πολλὰς (sc. πληγάς) D.19.197; μελεϊστί ξ. Philostr.*Her.*19.18; also ξαίνουσα παρειὰς δάκρυσιν *AP*7.464 (Antip.); of the throat, in Pass., *to be irritated*, *sore*, Antyll.ap.Orib.10.34.8; of the mind, *fret*, *worry*, ξαίνεσθαι τὴν ψυχὴν φροντίδι J.*AJ*1.1.4.

**ξάμμα**, ατος, τό, = ξάσμα, Hsch. s. v. πεῖκος.

**ξᾰνάω**, fut. -ήσω Suid.:—*grow weary with carding wool*: hence, generally, *work hard*, *grow weary*, ξανῆσαι S.*Fr.*498; νεύρων ξανάᾳ κεχαλασμένα δεσμά Nic.*Th.*383.

**ξάνδαρος**, ὁ, a fabulous sea-monster of the Atlantic, Hsch.

**Ξανδικός**, ὁ (sc. μήν), name of a month in the Macedonian calendar, *PCair.Zen.* 3.43, al. (iii B.C.), *IGRom.*4.661.33 (Acmonia, i A.D.), etc.:—written **Ξανθικός**, D.S.18.56, Lxx 2*Ma.*11.30, Suid., etc.; also **Ξανθικά**, τά, festival held in this month, Hsch.

**ξάνθη**, ἡ, *a pale-coloured stone*, Thphr.*Lap.*37.

**Ξανθίας**, ου, ὁ, *Xanthias*, typical name of a slave in Greek comedy (from his yellow wig), Ar.*Ach.*243, *Av.*656, *V.*1, *Ra.*1, cf. Aeschin.2.157. II. *a throw of the dice*, Hsch., cf. Eub.59.

* **ξανθίζω**, (ξανθός) *make yellow* or *brown*, by roasting or frying, Ar.*Ach.*1047, cj. in Philem.79.6; ἐξανθισμέναι *with hair dyed yellow*, Ar.*Lys.*43 (v.l. for ἐξηνθισμέναι), cf. *Com.Adesp.*289; dub. in D.H.7.9; τὴν τρίχα -όμενος Duris 10 J. II. intr., *to be yellow*, Lxx *Le.*13.30; τρίχες -ουσαι Alciphr.*Fr.*5.4.

**Ξανθικός**, ὁ, v. Ξανδικός.

**ξάνθ-ιον**, τό, a plant used for dyeing the hair yellow, *Xanthium Strumarium*, *broad-leaved burweed*, Dsc.4.136, Gal.12.87. II. = ξυρίς, Ps.-Dsc.4.22. **-ῐσις**, εως, ἡ, *dyeing yellow*, Gal.12.446. **-ισμα**, ατος, τό, *that which is dyed yellow*, κόμης ξανθίσματα *dyed* hair, E.*Fr.*322, cf. *AP*5.259 (Paul. Sil.). **-ισμός**, ὁ, = ξάνθισις, Archig.ap.Gal.12.445.

**ξανθό-γεως**, ων, *of yellow soil*, Luc.*Syr.D.*8. * **-δερκής**, ές, *with fiery eyes*, of a dragon, B.8.12. **-ειδής**, ές, *yellow in appearance*, Heph.Astr.1.1. **-θριξ**, ὁ, ἡ, gen. τριχος, *yellow-haired*, Sol.22 (v.l. πυρρό-), Theoc.18.1; ξ. ἄνθος Aglaïas 13; of a horse, *chestnut*, B.5.37. **-κάρηνος** [κᾰ], ον, *with yellow head*, of Dionysus, *AP*9.524.15. **-κάρῡον** [κᾰ], τό, *clove*, Aët.8.29. **-κόμης**, ου, ὁ, = ξανθόθριξ, Hes.*Fr.*135.5, Pi.*N.*9.17, Theoc.17.103 (v.l. -κομος, as also in Opp.*C.*2.165, 3.24). **-λευκος**, ον, *pale yellow*, Gal.17(1).835. **-λοφος**, ον, gloss on φοινικόλοφος, *EM*797.39, Hsch. (ξανθοῦ λόφου cod.), Suid. **-μήλινος**, ον, *greenish-yellow*, Zos.Alch.p.243 B.

* **ξανθός**, ή, όν, *yellow*, of various shades, freq. with a tinge of red, *brown*, *auburn*, λαμπρὸν ἐρυθρῷ λευκῷ τε μειγνύμενον Pl.*Ti.*68b; ἔστι δὲ τὸ ξ. ἐν τῇ ἴριδι χρῶμα μεταξὺ τοῦ τε φοινικοῦ καὶ πρασίνου χρώματος Arist.*Mete.*375$^a$11; ξανθὸν ἐρεύθεσθαι *AP*12.97 (Antip.): in Ep. mostly used of *fair*, *golden* hair, ξ. κόμη, χαίτη, of Achilles, Il.1.197, 23.141; ξ. τρίχες, of Odysseus, Od.13.399, 431; κάρη ξ. Μενέλαος (but usu. ξ. Μ. alone) 15.133; also of women, ξ. Ἀγαμήδη Il.11.740; Ἀριάδνη Hes.*Th.*947 (but ξ. Δημήτηρ *golden* corn, Il.5.500, etc.); so later, of Helen, Sapph.*Supp.*13.5; of Athena and the Graces, Pi.*N.*10.7, 5.54; of Harmonia, E.*Med.*834 (lyr.) (but in later Gr. of complexion, Cleom.2.1); of dyed hair, τὴν γυναῖκα τὴν σώφρον' οὐ δεῖ τὰς τρίχας ξ. ποιεῖν Men.610; also of horses, *bay*, ἵππων ξ. κάρηνα Il.9.407, cf. 11.680; ξ. πῶλοι Alc.*Supp.*8.14, S.*El.*705; βοῶν ξανθὰς ἀγέλας Pi.*P.*4.149; ξ. λέων Id.*Fr.*237; πώλου δίκην, ἤ τις . . θέρος θερισθῇ ξανθὸν αὐχένων ἄπο S.*Fr.*659.4, etc. 2. after Hom. of all kinds of objects, ἄρτοι ξ. Xenoph.1.9; ξανθῶν σπονδὰς μελιτῶν v.l. in Emp.128.7; ἴων ξ. ἀκτῖνες Pi.*O.*6.55; ξ. νεφέλα, of gold, ib.7.49; μέλι Simon.47; φλὸξ B.*Fr.*3.4; ἀκτῖνες πυρὸς Sopat.13; ἐλαία A.*Pers.*617; of wine, ξ. Ἀφροδισία λάταξ S.*Fr.*277 (lyr.); of a roast pigeon, Ar.*Ach.*1106; ξανθαῖσιν αὔραις ἀγάλλεται exults in its *yellow* fragrance, of a fried fish, Antiph.217.22: in Medic., freq. of bile, Hp.*VM*19, etc.: Comp. -ότερος Pl.*R.*617a: Sup. -ότατος, βόστρυχοι Pherecr.189. II. Ξάνθος, parox., as pr. n., 1. a stream of the Troad, so called by gods, by men Scamander, Il.20.74, etc. 2. a horse of Achilles, *Bayard*, the other being Βαλίος, *Piebald*, 16.149. 3. name of a man, D.H.1.28, etc. 4. fem., a city of Lycia, Hdt.1.176, etc.

**ξανθότης**, ητος, ἡ, *yellowness*, esp. of hair, Str.7.1.2.

**ξανθο-τρῐχέω**, *have yellow hair*, Str.6.1.13. **-φαής**, ές, *golden-gleaming*, Jo.Gaz.*Ecphr.*1.58. **-φυής**, ές, *yellow by nature*, ἕλικες *AP*12.10 (Strat.); Δηώ, ἵππος, Nonn.*D.*6.113, 37.122. **-χίτων** [ῐ], ωνος, ὁ, ἡ, *with yellow coat*, ῥοιή *AP*6.102 (Phil.). **-χλοος**, gloss on φοινικόχλοος, Hsch. (-χλοις cod.). **-χολικός**, ή, όν, *containing* or *consisting of yellow bile*, αἷμα Gal.19.648 (Comp.); χυμός Alex.Trall.1.16. **-χολος**, ον, *suffering from jaundice*, Ruf.*Fr.*80, Aët.3.66, dub. in Sch.Il.1.197. **-χροος**, ον, (χρόα, χρώς) *with yellow skin*, δέμας Mosch.2.84: heterocl. acc. ξανθόχροα Nonn.*D.*11.180. **-χρως**, ωτος, ὁ, ἡ, = foreg., *brown*, of fried fish, Nausicr.2.7.

**ξανθ-όω**, *dye yellow*, Ps.-Democr.Alch.p.52 B.:—Pass., *become yellow*, Dsc.1.68. **-ύνομαι**, Pass., *become brown*, Thphr.*HP*3.15.6. **-ωπός**, όν, (ὤψ) *golden-looking*, χροιή Opp.*C.*2.382; χρώς Nonn.*D.*18.113. **-ωσις**, εως, ἡ, = ξάνθισις, Ps.-Democr.Alch.p.54 B.

**ξάν-ιον,** τό, *card for combing wool*, Poll.5.96, *AB*284, Hsch. II. = ἐπίξηνον, Poll.6.90, 10.101. **-σις,** εως, ἡ, *wool-carding*, *Gloss.* **-της,** ου, ὁ, *wool-carder*, Pl.*Plt.*281a. **-τικός,** ή, όν, *of* or *for wool-carding*: ἡ -κή (sc. τέχνη), *wool-carding*, ib.281a, al.; τὸ -κόν ib.282b. **-τρια,** ἡ, fem. of ξάντης, = *putatrix*, *Gloss.*: Ξάντριαι, name of a play by Aeschylus.

**ξάσμα,** ατος, τό, *carded wool*, S.*Fr.*1073.

**ξατράπης,** v. σατράπης.

**ξεῖ,** τό, indecl., name of the letter ξ, Calliasap.Ath.10.453d, *BCH* 29.483 (Delos), Phld.*Po.*2.3: later **ξῖ** Luc.*Jud.Voc.*9, Sch.D.T.p.489 H., etc.; **ξῦ** (by assimilation to νῦ), f.l. in Luc. l.c. and *AP*9.385.14 (Steph. Gramm.).

**ξεινᾰπάτης, ξείνη, ξείνηθεν,** Ion. for ξεν-.

**ξεινήϊον,** τό, (ξεῖνος) only found in Ion. and Ep. form, *host's gift* to a guest, in full δῶρα ξεινήϊα Od.24.273; ἀντὶ ποδὸς ξεινήϊον, ironically, 22.290; also, *provision made for a guest*, ξεινήϊα πολλὰ φαγόντε 4.33: more generally, *gifts of* (*guest-*)*friendship*, ἀλλήλοισι πόρον ξεινήϊα καλά Il.6.218.

**ξεινίζω, ξεινίη, ξεινικός, ξείνιον, ξείνιος,** v. ξεν-.

**ξεινο-βάκχη,** ἡ, *mad for love of the stranger*, of Medea, Lyc. 175. **-δοκέω, -δόκος, -κτονέω,** Ion. for ξεν-.

**ξεῖνος, ξεινοσύνη, ξεινόω,** v. ξεν-. ⊛ **ξείρης, ξειρίς,** v. ξυρίς.

**ξέλεγνον,** τό, dub. sens. (perh. *writing-tablet*), *POxy.*1297.18 (iv A.D.).

**ξενᾱγ-έτης,** ου, ὁ, *one who takes charge of guests*, Δελφοὶ ξ. the *hospitable* Delphians, Pi.*N.*7.43. **-έω,** *to be a leader of mercenaries*, ξ. ξενικοῦ X.*HG*4.3.15, cf. 4.3.17, D.23.139, Arr.*Fr.*99 J. II. *guide strangers, show them the sights*, ἄριστά σοι ἐξενάγηται your *work as a guide has been done* excellently, Pl.*Phdr.*230c; ξεναγούμενος *one seeing the sights*, ibid.; ξενάγησόν με νέηλυν ὄντα Luc.*DMort.*18.1, cf. *Cont.*1: metaph., generally, *guide, direct*, Alciphr.1.26; ξ. τινὰ πρὸς τὰς Μούσας Them.*Or.*9.123b, cf. Ph.2.330:—Pass., ὑπὸ σοφίας ξ. Id. 1.630. III. Med., *receive hospitality*, Procop.*Goth.*3.9:—so in Pass., ib.4.22. **-ησις,** εως, ἡ, = Lat. *conscriptio*, υἱῶν App.*BC* 5.74. **-ία,** ἡ, *office of* ξεναγός, *command of a body of mercenaries*, Id.*Hisp.*44. 2. = σύνταγμα, Ael.*Tact.*9.4, Arr.*Tact.*10.3. b. *force of two* ψιλαγίαι, Ael.*Tact.*16.3, Arr.*Tact.*14.4, prob. in Ascl. *Tact.*6.3. II. *guiding of strangers*, Hld.7.13. **-ός,** ὁ, (ξένος, ἄγω) *commander of mercenary troops*, Th.2.75 (ubi v. Sch.), X.*HG* 4.2.19, *PCair.Zen.*374.5 (iii B.C.), *SIG*556 *D* 3 (Delph., iii B.C.), etc. (Dor. form (Cretan acc. to *AB*284) adopted in Att. like other military terms.) 2. *commander of a* ξεναγία I. 2, Ael.*Tact.*9.4, Arr.*Tact.*10.3. II. *cicerone, guide*, Plu.2.567a, Hld.7.14 (v.l. -αγωγός).

**ξεν-ᾰγωγέω,** = ξεναγέω, Hsch. **-ᾰγωγός,** όν, later form for ξεναγός II, f.l. in Th.2.75 and Plu.*Ages.*36. ⊛ **-ᾰπάτης** [πᾰ], ου, ὁ, poet. **ξειν-,** (ἀπατάω) *one who cheats strangers*, Pi.*O.*10(11). 34. 2. *one who betrays his host*, Ibyc.*Oxy.*1790 i 10, E.*Med.*1392 (anap.). II. *a treacherous breeze* within a harbour, while another is blowing at sea, *AB*109. **-ᾰπᾰτία,** ἡ, *cheating of guests*, Pl. *Ep.*350c. **-αρκής,** ές, (ἀρκέω) *aiding strangers*, Pi.*N.*4.12. **-εών,** ῶνος, ὁ, = ξενών, *guest-chamber*, *Delph.*3(1).358; *almshouse, hospital*, *PMasp.*151.183 (vi A.D.). ⊛ **-η,** ἡ, fem. of ξένος: 1. (sc. γυνή) *foreign woman*, A.*Ag.*950, etc. 2. (sc. γῆ) *foreign country*, ἐν ξένᾳ S.*Ph.*135 (lyr.); ἐπὶ ξένης X.*Lac.*14.4; ἐπὶ ξ. καταβιοῦν Phld.*Rh.*2. 146 S., cf. Plu.2.576c, etc. ⊛ **-ηδόχος,** ον, = ξενοδόκος, Men.*Mon.* 402. **-ηθεν,** Ion. **ξείν-,** Adv. *from abroad*, Opp.*H.*4.153. **-ήκουστος,** ον, *foreign*, of words, Hdn.*Epim.*3. **-ηλᾰσία,** ἡ, at Sparta, *expulsion of foreigners*, X.*Lac.*14.4: mostly in pl., Th.1.144, 2.39, Pl. *Prt.*342c, *Lg.*950b, Arist.*Pol.*1272$^{b}$17. ⊛ **-ηλᾰτέω,** *banish foreigners*, in Pass., Ar.*Av.*1013, Plb.9.29.4, D.S.40.3. ⊛ **-ία,** ἡ, Ep. **ξενίη** Od.24.286; Ion. **ξεινίη** (v.l. ξεινηΐη) Hdt. (v. infr.): (ξένος):— *hospitality shown to a guest, entertainment*, δώροισιν ἀμειψάμενος.. καὶ ξενίῃ ἀγαθῇ Od.24.286; μείξεσθαι ξενίῃ ἠδ' ἀγλαὰ δῶρα διδώσειν ib.314; κατὰ ξεινίην *hospitii causa*, Hdt.2.182; ἐπὶ ξενίαν ἐλθεῖν to come *as a guest*, Pi.*N.*10.49; but, ἐπὶ ξενίαν καλεῖν, παρακαλεῖν, also ἐπὶ ξενίᾳ καλεῖσθαι, καλεῖν, prob. only as f.l. for ἐπὶ ξένια, v. ξένιος I. 2: in pl., Id.*O.*4.17; ξενίαι καὶ φιλότητες And.1.145; ἑτοίμαζέ μοι ξ. *Ep.Philem.*22. 2. *friendly relation between* two states, or between a person and a foreign state, ξεινίην τινὶ συντίθεσθαι, Lat. *hospitium facere cum aliquo*, Hdt.1.27, 3.39; ξ. τοῖσι Ἀκανθίοισι προεῖπε Id.7.116; ἐποιήσαντο ὅρκια ξεινίης πέρι καὶ συμμαχίης Id.1.69; διαλύσασθαι τὴν ξ. Id.4.154; τὰς παλαιὰς ξ. ἀνανεώσασθαι Isoc.4.43; κατὰ τὴν ξ. because of their *friendly relations*, Th.8.6; διὰ τὴν ξ. Plu.2. 816a; πρὸς ξ. τᾶς σᾶς by thy *friendship with us*, S.*OC*515 (lyr.); ξ. τινός *with* him, D.18.51; φιλίαν καὶ ξ. ib.284. 3. *status of an alien*, opp. that of a citizen, γραφὴ ξενίας indictment *of an alien for usurping civic rights*, Id.*Ep.*3.29; ξενίας φεύγειν (sc. γραφήν) to be so indicted, Ar.*V.*718; ἀγωνίσασθαι Lys.13.60; ἁλίσκεσθαι D. 24.131; ξενίας γράψασθαί τινα Id.40.41. II. *guest-chamber*, *PSI* 1.50.16 (iv/v A.D.); perh. *lodging*, *Act.Ap.*28.23. **-ιᾱγός,** ὁ, = ξεναγός, *Sammelb.*6801.32 (s.v.l., iii B.C.). **-ίδιον,** τό, *guest-house*, *PTeb.*335.17 (iii A.D.). ⊛ **-ίζω,** Ion. and Ep. **ξεινίζω,** fut. -ιῶ, later -ίσω *Gp.*12.13.12: Ep. aor. ἐξείνισσα, ξείνισσα, -ισα (v. infr.): (ξένος):—*receive* or *entertain as a guest*, ξείνους Od.3.355; τὸν μὲν ἐγὼ.. εὖ ἐξείνισσα 19.194; ἐννῆμαρ ξείνισσε Il.6.174; ξείνισσ' ἐνὶ μεγάροισιν ib.217; ξ. τινὰ ἐν δόμοις E.*Alc.*1013, etc.; ξ. [τινὰ] σίτοισι S.*Fr.*666; ξ. τινὰ πολλοῖς ἀγαθοῖς *to present with* hospitable gifts, X.*Cyr.*5.3.2; ὑμᾶς ἐν πόλει ξενίσωμεν ὧν.. εἴχομεν *with* or *on* what we had, Ar.*Lys.*1184: metaph., ὃν.. Ἄρης οὐκ ἐξένισεν, i.e. who fell not in battle, S.*El.*96 (anap.):—Pass., *to be entertained as a guest*, Ar.*Ach.*73; ξενισθεὶς μὴ ἀντιξενίσαι Phld.*Vit.*p.30 J.; ὑπό τινος Hdt.1.30, X.*HG*3.1.24, etc.; παρά τινι D.S.14.30, *Act.Ap.*10. 6, 21.16; πρός τινα Philem.109: metaph., λαχάνοισιν, ὥσπερ χῆνες, ἐξενισμένοι Theopomp.Com.13. II. *surprise, astonish by some strange sight*, ξενίζουσαν καὶ καταπληκτικὴν πρόσοψιν Plb.3.114.4; ξ. τὴν ἀκοήν, of strange words, Hld.6.14; ξ. καὶ ταράττειν *Gp.*2.48.2; ξ. [τὴν τῶν πολλῶν συνήθειαν] *do violence to* the ordinary use of language, Simp. *in Cael.*679.28:—Pass., *to be astonished*, S.*Ichn.*137; τινι Plb.1.23.5, 3.68.9, 1*Ep.Pet.*4.12; διὰ τὸ παράδοξον Plb.1.49.7; ἐπί τινι Id.2.27.4, D.S.31.2; κατά τι Plb.1.33.1; μὴ συντρεχόντων ὑμῶν 1*Ep.Pet.*4.4; εἰ.. M.Ant.8.15, cf. Vett.Val.302.17; πῶς.. *PStrassb.* 35.6 (v A.D.); *to be puzzled, unable to comprehend*, Ael.*Tact.*1.6; of fresh leeches, *to be unaccustomed* to the skin, Antyll.ap.Orib.7.21. 1. 2. *make strange*, of plants and animals, i.e. *stunt their growth and distort* them, *Gp.*9.5.3 (Pass.); τῷ πλήθει ξενιζομένη ἡ φύσις being *altered in character*, Alex.Aphr.*Pr.*1.80, cf. *Hippiatr.*15. III. intr., *to be a stranger, speak with a foreign accent*, D.57.18; τὸ ξενίζον τῆς λέξεως D.S.12.53, cf. Luc.*Hist.Conscr.*45. 2. *to be strange* or *unusual*, of diseases, Gal.17(1).162; ξ. τῷ σχήματι Luc.*Anach.*16; τῷ τρίβωνι Id.*Merc.Cond.*24; θάνατος.. τῇ τόλμῃ ξενίζων Id.*Hist. Conscr.*25.

**ξενικόκουφον,** τό, *foreign cask*, *POxy.*2153.5 (iii A.D., pl.).

⊛ **ξεν-ικός,** ή, όν, also ός, όν E.*Ion* 722 (lyr.); Ion. **ξεινικός** Hdt.1. 77:—*of* or *for a stranger, of foreign kind*, opp. ἀστικός, A.*Supp.*618; ξ. ἱκτῆρες E.*Cyc.*370 (lyr.); ξενικά *taxes paid by aliens* at Athens, ξ. τελεῖν D.57.34; σύσσιτοι ξ., opp. πολιτικοί, Arist.*Pol.*1314$^{a}$10; -ωτέρας.. γενομένης τῆς βοηθείας *more connected with*, or *dependent upon, foreigners*, ib.1257$^{a}$31; τὸ ξ. *the class of aliens*, ib.1278$^{a}$7; also τὸ ξ. (sc. δικαστήριον) the court *in which aliens sued* or *were sued*, ib.1300$^{b}$ 24, cf. *SIG*306.24 (Tegea, iv B.C.), *PHal.*1.164 (iii B.C.); ξ. χαλκός *foreign* money, *PStrassb.*103.8 (iii B.C.); ξ. ἀργύριον *IG*1$^{2}$.313.57, 2$^{2}$. 1436.56; ξ. νόμισμα Pl.*Lg.*742b; ξ. ἐμπόριον *PTeb.*5.33 (ii B.C.); τὰ ξ. *alien* property, *IG*9(1).333.3 (Oeanthea, v B.C.); ξ. βοσκήματα, τὰ ξ. τῶν σπερμάτων, Thphr.*HP*9.20.3, 8.8.1, cf. Pl.*R.*497b. b. *concerning the status of an alien*, δίκα (cf. ξενία I. 3) *SIG*526.25 (Crete, iii B.C.). c. in Thessaly, ξ. λύτρωσις manumission *which confers non-citizen status*, *IG*9(2).28: freq. ξενικῇ alone, ἀπελευθεροῦσθαι ξ. ib.14, al. 2. of *foreign* troops, etc., νῆες ξ. ships *furnished by the allies*, Th.7.42; but usu. of hired troops, ξ. στρατός Hdt.1.77; τὸ ξ., = οἱ ξένοι, *a body of mercenaries*, Ar.*Pl.*173, Th.[8.25], X.*An.*1.2.1, etc.; ξενικὸν τρέφειν D.4.24. 3. rarely = ξένιος, *hospitable*, ὁ ξ. θεός *protector of guests*, Pl.*Lg.*879e; ἡ ξ. τράπεζα Aeschin.3.224, cf. Dosiad.Hist.1; ἡ ξενική (sc. φιλία) friendship *between host and guest*, Arist.*EN*1156$^{a}$31. Adv. -κῶς *hospitably*, Theopomp.Hist.225. II. *foreign, strange*, νόμαια, ἱρά, Hdt.1.135, 172; τὸ ξ., of laws, *their foreign origin* or *character*, Pl.*Lg.*702c; ξ. λόγοι Ar.*Ach.*634; ξ. ὀνόματα *non-Attic* names, Pl.*Cra.*401c; οἶνος ξ. Alex.290, Diph.32.27; δίκαιον τοὺς ξένους πίνειν ξενικόν Alex.230; γλῶσσα, λίθος, *PGiss.*99. 9 (ii/iii A.D.), *POxy.*1449.46 (iii A.D.); ἀγνωστότερα καὶ -ώτερα Arist. *Metaph.*995$^{a}$3; of style, *unfamiliar*, i.e. *abounding in unusual words and phrases*, ξ. λέξις Id.*Rh.*1406$^{a}$15; τὸ ξ. ib.1405$^{a}$8, cf. *Po.*1458$^{a}$22. Adv. -κῶς *in non-Attic fashion*, Pl.*Cra.*407b. ⊛ **-ιος,** α, ον, Ion. **ξείνιος** (as always in Hdt., and mostly in Hom., but ξένιος when the ult. is long, as in Od.14.158, 389, 15.514, al.):—*belonging to friendship and hospitality, hospitable*, Ζεὺς ξ. as *protector of the rights of hospitality*, Ζεὺς ἐπιτιμήτωρ ἱκετάων τε ξείνων τε, ξείνιος, ὃς ξείνοισιν ἅμ' αἰδοίοισιν ὀπηδεῖ (cf. ξένος II) Od.9.271; Ζηνὸς.. ἐδείσατε μῆνιν ξεινίου Il.13.625, cf. A.*Ag.*61, 362 (both anap.), al.; ὦ Ζεῦ ξένιε Cratin.111; also Ἀπόλλων ξ. *CIG*2214*e* (Chios); ξ. τράπεζα *the guests'* table, Od.14.158, 17.155, Pi.*I.*2.39, etc.; ξ. κοίτα his *guest's* adultery, Id.*P.*3.32; ξ. τινί *bound* to one *by ties of hospitality*, Hdt.5.63 codd. 2. ξείνια, Att. ξένια (cf. ξεινήϊον), τά, *friendly gifts*, given to the guest by his host, esp. meat and drink, ξείνιά τ' εὖ παρέθηκεν, ἅ τε ξείνοις θέμις ἐστίν Il.11.779, cf. 18.387, Od.5.91, etc.; εἴ μοι ξ. δοίη 9.229, cf. 19.185 (less freq. in sg., ἵνα τοι δῶ ξείνιον 9.356, cf. 20.296, Pi.*P.*4.35, *SIG*662.32 (Delos, ii B.C.)); ξένια.. παρέσχε δαῖτα *as a friendly gift*, A.*Ag.*1590; βοῦν ξένια ἔπεμψαν X.*HG*7.2.3, cf. *PCair.Zen.*75.6 (iii B.C.); ξ. δοῦναι E.*Cyc.*301; ξ. λήψῃ ib.342; δέξασθαι Lys.18.12; ἐπὶ ξείνια καλέειν to invite one *to meat*, Hdt. 2.107, 5.18, cf. *IG*1$^{2}$.19.14, 108, X.*HG*6.4.20, *Vect.*3.4, D.7.20, etc. (ἐπὶ ξενίαν and ἐπὶ ξενίᾳ freq. as f.l., X.*Vect.* l.c., D. l.c., D.S.8. 25, 13.83, D.H.1.40, Philostr.*VA*3.33, etc.); ἐπὶ ξείνια παραλαβεῖν τινα Hdt.4.154; ξ. προθεῖναι, προθέσθαι, Id.7.29, 135; ἐπαγγείλασθαι καταγωγὴν καὶ ξ. Id.6.35; ξενίοις δέχεσθαί τινα X.*An.*5.5.24: freq. of presents sent by peaceful inhabitants to an army, ib.5.5.2, 14, 25, al.; of *provisions* supplied to a king or official on a visit, Theopomp.Hist.22(*d*), *PPetr.*2 p.25 (iii B.C.), *PGrenf.*2.14(*b*).9 (iii B.C.), etc.; also of *tribute*, Lxx 2*Ki.*8.2, *OGI*132.11 (Egypt, ii B.C.); of *honoraria* to artists, *SIG*689.10 (Delph., ii B.C.): metaph., θάνατος ξένιά σοι γενήσεται E.*Hel.*480. II. *foreign*, ἐπὶ ξενίας (sc. γῆς) Antipho 2.2.9, Pl.*Cra.*429e, cf. *Ath.Mitt.*25.427; ἐν ξενίῃ *Epigr.Gr.* 1041.8. 2. ξ. κόσμος, in Crete, magistrate who tried suits *with aliens*, *GDI*4981.4, al. **-ίς,** ίδος, ἡ, *road leading abroad*, *SIG*636.24 (Delph., ii B.C.). **-ῐσις,** εως, ἡ, (ξενίζω) *entertainment of a guest* or *stranger*, ξ. ποιεῖσθαί τινων Th.6.46. **-ισμός,** ὁ, = foreg., Pl. *Ly.*205c, Luc.*Salt.*45, etc.; τὸν ξ. ποιεῖν τῷ Ἡρακλεῖ *SIG*1106.61 (Cos, iv/iii B.C.); καλέσαι τινὰς ἐπὶ ξενισμόν *BCH*49.306 (Teos): in

pl., Plu.*Demetr.*12, etc. II. *strangeness, novelty*, Plb.15.17.1, D.S.3.33. 2. *injurious effect of change*, ξενισμοὶ ὑδάτων Dsc.2.152: but, generally, *change*, τῶν ξενισμοῦ καὶ μεταποιήσεως χρῃζόντων Antyll.ap.Orib.7.7.7; μέγας ὁ ξ. τοῦ σώματος Gal.17(2).28; ξενισμὸν ἐμποιεῖν Sor.1.116; ξ. στομάχου Ruf.ap.Orib.7.26.152. **-ιστής**, οῦ, ὁ, = ξένος I, Sch.Pi.*P.*4.52.

**ξενῑτ-εία**, ἡ, *living abroad*, Lxx *Wi.*18.3, Aristeas 249, Ptol.*Tetr.* 111, Vett.Val.63.29 (pl.), Luc.*Patr.Enc.*8. 2. *life of a mercenary in foreign service*, Democr.246, *PSI*1.76.8 (vi A.D.). **-ευτής**, οῦ, ὁ, *one who lives abroad*, Rhetor. in *Cat.Cod.Astr.*8(4).148,166 (pl.). **-εύω**, *live abroad*, Timae.139, Nic.Dam.102 J., Str.14.5.13, Luc.*Patr.Enc.*8: ξ. πρός τινας Aristeas 257; *live in exile*, J.*AJ*16.11.8. II. Med., *to be a mercenary in foreign service*, Isoc.5.122, *Ep.*2.19; ἐγὼ ξενιτευόμενος ἐστρατευόμην Antiph.96.

**ξενο-δαΐκτης**, ου, Dor. **-τας**, ὁ, *one who murders guests* or *strangers*, Pi.*Parth.Fr.*13.30; **ξεινο-** prob. cj. in E.*HF*391 (lyr.). **-δαίτης**, ου, Dor. **-τας**, ὁ, (δαίς) *one that devours guests* or *strangers*, of the Cyclops, Id.*Cyc.*658 (lyr.). **-δίκαι** [ῐ], οἱ, *judges who tried suits concerning aliens*, at Athens, prob. in *IG*1².343.89, 342.38; at Oeanthea, ib.9(1).333.10; at Troezen, ib.2².46*a A* 27; in Phocis, ib.9(1).32 (ii B.C.): sg. only late, = *praetor peregrinus*, Lyd.*Mag.*1.38 (-δόκης codd.). ⊛**-δοκέω**, Ion. **ξεινο-**, *entertain guests* or *strangers*, Hdt.6.127, E.*Alc.*552, *AP*10.16 (Theaet.), etc.:—later **-δοχέω**, 1*Ep.Ti.*5.10, Max.Tyr.32.9, *Cod.Just.*1.3.45.1b. II. *testify*, Pi.*Fr.*311:—Med., Hsch. ⊛**-δόκος**, Ion. and Ep. **ξεινοδόκος**, ὁ, *one who receives strangers, host*, ἵν' δμῶς τερπώμεθα πάντες ξεινοδόκοι καὶ ξεῖνος Od. 8.543; ξεῖνος μιμνήσκεται ἤματα πάντα ἀνδρὸς ξεινοδόκου 15.55, cf. Il.3.354, Od.8.210, Theoc.16.27, Jul.*Or.*2.96a, *AP*10.15 (Paul. Sil.):—later **-δόχος**, Ph.2.17, al.; *head of a* ξενοδοχεῖον, Just.*Nov.*7.1, al. II. *witness*, Simon.84.7, cf. Hsch.—The forms ξενοδόχος, -δοχέω, -δοχία are condemned by Moer.p.271 P., Thom.Mag.p.251 R.; cf. ξενηδόκος. **-δοχεῖον**, τό, *place for strangers to lodge in, inn*, Jul.*Ep.*84a, *Cod.Just.*1.2.15.1, Just.*Nov.*120.1 *Intr.*, *PSI*4.284.2, Suid., etc. **-δοχέω**, v. ξενοδοκέω. **-δοχία**, ἡ, *entertainment of a stranger*, X.*Oec.*9.10 (pl.), Thphr.*Char.*23.9 (pl.). **-δόχος**, v. ξενοδόκος. **-δώτης**, ου, ὁ, dub. sens., epith. of Dionysus, *AP*9.524.15. **-εις**, εσσα, εν, *full of strangers*, E.*IT*1281 (lyr.). **-θάνατος** [θᾰ], ον, *dying abroad*, Critodem. in *Cat.Cod.Astr.*8(4).201. **-θυτέω**, *sacrifice strangers*, Str.7.3.6. **-κᾱδής**, ές, *caring for strangers*, Pi.*Pae.Oxy.*841 *Fr.*131. **-κλείδειον**, τό, *fund derived from Xenoclides*, *Inscr.Délos* 320 *B* 78 (iii B.C.). **-κρᾰτέομαι**, Pass., *to be in the power of mercenary troops*, Aen.Tact.12.4. ⊛**-κρίται** [ῐ], οἱ, = ξενοδίκαι, *IGRom.*3.681 (Patara): sg., title of official at Sparta, *BSA*26.163 (ii A.D.). **-κτονέω**, Ion. **ξεινο-**, *slay guests* or *strangers*, Hdt.2.115, E.*Hec.*1247, D.S.4.18. **-κτονία**, ἡ, *murder of strangers*, Id.1.88, D.H.1.41 (pl.). II. *murder of a guest*, Plu. 2.319d; *of a host*, Id.*Dio*54. **-κτόνος**, ον, *slaying guests* or *strangers*, E.*IT*53, Aeschin.3.224; ξ. ἵπποι Scymn.669, cf. Plu.*Mar.* 8. ⊛**-κυστᾰπάτη** [πᾱ], ἡ, *intrigue with strange women*, *AP*11.7 (Nicandr. or Nicarch.).

**ξενολογ-έω**, *enlist foreign troops*, esp. *mercenaries*, Isoc.5.96, D.40.36, Plb.3.27.4, Lxx 1*Ma.*4.35; ξ. ἐκ τᾶς Ἀσίας εἰς ἴδιον πόλεμον *SIG* 581.82 (Crete, ii B.C.); ξ. πλῆθος μισθοφόρων Plb.1.9.6:—Med., *OGI* 270.12 (Crete, iii B.C.):—Pass., Plb.14.7.5, al., *CIG*2623 (Citium), J.*AJ*13.4.9. 2. metaph., ξ. ἔλεον παρά τινων *raise a contribution of* pity, D.S.34/5.2.39. **-ία**, ἡ, *recruitment of mercenaries*, Arist. *Oec.*1353ᵇ11, Plb.15.25.16, D.S.18.61. **-ιον**, τό, *army of mercenaries*, Plb.29.23.6, 31.17.1, *SIG*581.40 (Crete, ii B.C.), *OGI*437.67, 71 (Pergam., i B.C.). **-ος** (parox.), ον, *enlisting mercenaries*, Plb.1.32.1, 5.63.9, D.S.14.62, Plu.*Dio*23; title of a comedy by Menander.

**ξενο-μᾰνέω**, *have a rage for foreign fashions*, Plu.2.527f. **-πάθεια** [πᾰ], ἡ, *strange feelings, malaise*, Sor.1.111, al. ⊛**-πᾰθέω**, *have a strange feeling*, Plu.*Phil.*12; δυσανασχετεῖν καὶ ξ. Id.2.607e; ἀδημονεῖν καὶ ξ. ib.601c, cf. Sor.1.81. **-ποικιλόπτερος**, ον, *with strange, motley plumage*, κολοιός Tz.*H.*2.842. **-πολίτης** [ῑ], ου, ὁ, *pertaining to an alien*, νόμος Id. in Rh.3.670 W. **-πρεπής**, ές, *strange, out of the way*, Hp.*Fract.*1, D.H.*Dem.*34, Aret.*SD*2.13 (Comp.). Adv. **-πῶς** Steph. in *Hp.*2.288 D. **-πρόσωπος**, ον, only in Adv. **-πως**, *with reference to a person other than oneself*, Sch.Aristid.p.430 D.

⊛ **ξένος**, ὁ, Ep. and Ion. **ξεῖνος** (also freq. in Pi., *N.*7.61, al., used by Trag. metri gr. even in trim., mostly in voc., S.*OC*33, al., E.*IT*798 codd., *El.*247), Aeol. **ξέννος** Hdn.Gr.2.302; scanned ‒ ‿ and written ξεῖνος in Theoc.28.6, 30.17: Aeol. Sup. ξεννότατος Sch.Tz. in *An.Ox.* 3.356.18 (sed v. fin.). I. *guest-friend*, applied to persons and states bound by a treaty or tie of hospitality, Od.1.313, etc.; ξεῖνοι δὲ.. εὐχόμεθ' εἶναι ἐκ πατέρων φιλότητος 15.196; ξ. πατρώϊός ἐσσι παλαιός Il.6.215; ξ. δ' ἀλλήλων πατρώϊοι εὐχόμεθ' εἶναι Od.1.187; φησὶ δ' Ὀδυσσῆος ξεῖνος πατρώϊος εἶναι 17.522; later freq. coupled with φίλος, Πλούταρχος ὁ τούτου ξένος καὶ φίλος D.21.110, cf. 18.46, X.*An.*2.1.5, Lys. 19.19; βασιλέως πατρικὸς ξ. Pl.*Men.*78d. 2. of parties giving or receiving hospitality, Od.8.145, etc.; mostly of the *guest*, opp. the host, ξεινοδόκοι καὶ ξεῖνος ib.543, etc.; ἁ ξένα *the visitor*, Theoc.2.154; of *guests* at a club, opp. σύνδειπνοι, *PTeb.*118.4 (ii B.C.): less freq. of the *host*, Il.15.532, A.R.1.208, *Ep.Rom.*16.23, etc.: c. dat., ξεῖνός τινι Hdt.1.20,22, cf. Th.2.13, X.*An.*1.1.10, etc.; also ξ. τινός ib. 2.4.15. II. *stranger*, esp. *wanderer, refugee* (under the protection of Ζεὺς ξένιος), sts. coupled with ἱκέτης, Ζεὺς ἐπιτιμήτωρ ἱκετάων τε ξείνων τε ξείνιος Od.9.270, cf. 8.546; with πτωχός, πρὸς γὰρ Διός εἰσιν ἅπαντες ξεῖνοί τε πτωχοί τε 6.208. III. generally, *stranger, foreigner*, opp. ἔνδημος, Hes.*Op.*225; opp. ἀστός, Pi.*O.*7.90, S.*OC*13, And.4.10, etc.; πολιατᾶν καὶ ξ. Pi.*I.*1.51, cf. A.*Th.*924 (lyr.), Pl.*Grg.* 473d, etc.; opp. ἐπιχώριος, Id.*Men.*94d: coupled with μέτοικος, Th. 4.90, cf. *IG*1².39.53; with ἔπηλυς, Luc.*Herm.*24; opp. a member of the family, *PMasp.*169.10 (vi A.D.), etc. b. as a term of address to any *stranger*, ὦ ξένε E.*Ion*247, Mosch.1.5, etc.; ὦ ξένη Pl.*Smp.* 204c. 2. = βάρβαρος, at Sparta, Hdt.9.11,55. IV. *hireling*, Od.14.102; esp. *mercenary soldier*, *IG*1².949.89, X.*An.*1.1.10, D.18.152, etc.; ξ. ναυβάται Th.1.121: rarely simply, *ally*, X.*Lac.* 12.3.

B. as Adj. **ξένος**, η, ον (also ος, ον E.*Supp.*94), Ion. **ξεῖνος**, η, ον, *foreign*, not in Hom. (in the phrases ξεῖνε πάτερ Od.7.28, ἄνθρωποι ξεῖνοι Il.24.202, both words are Subst.); freq. in later writers, ξεῖνα γαῖα Pi.*P.*4.118 codd.; ξένης ἐπὶ χθονός S.*OC*1256; γᾶς ἐπὶ ξένας ib. 1705 (lyr., cf. ξένη); ἐν ξένῃσι χερσί by *foreign* hands, Id.*El.*1141; ξ. δόμοι, πόλις, etc., E.*Ph.*339 (lyr.), 369, etc.; of *alien* property, ξ. ἄρουραι *PMasp.*295.22 (vi A.D.). II. c. gen. rei, *strange to* a thing, *unacquainted with, ignorant of* it, ξ. τοῦ λόγου S.*OT*219, cf. *AP*4.3ᵃ.37 (Agath.); ξ. τῶν διαθηκῶν τῆς ἐπαγγελίας *Ep.Eph.*2.12, cf. *BGU*405.12 (iv A.D.). Adv. ξένως, ἔχω τῆς ἐνθάδε λέξεως I am *a stranger to* the mode of speech, Pl.*Ap.*17d; ἔχειν τῆς διαλέκτου Them. *Or.*21.253c. III. *strange, unusual*, λόγοι A.*Pr.*688 (lyr.); τιμωρίαι Ti.Locr.104d; ποιεῖν ξένην τὴν διάλεκτον Arist.*Rh.*1404ᵇ11, cf. 1415ᵃ7; οὐδὲν ξ. ἐν τῷ παντὶ ἀποτελεῖται Epicur.*Fr.*266; τοῖς νέοις ποιεῖν ξένα τὰ φαῦλα Arist.*Pol.*1336ᵇ34; ξένα ταῖς ὄψεσι D.S.3.15; ὡς ξένου συμβαίνοντος 1*Ep.Pet.*4.12; διδαχαὶ ποικίλαι καὶ ξ. *Ep.Hebr.*13.9; ξ. δαιμόνια *Act.Ap.*17.18: Sup., πράξεων ὡς -οτάτων Phld.*Herc.*1251.5; ξ. αὐτῷ δοκεῖ τὸ πρᾶγμα Luc.*Cont.*13, etc. Adv. ξένως, λαλεῖν Phld.*Po.*5.12. 2. τοῦ πνεύματος.. φύσις ὡς -ωτάτη air as *fresh* as possible, Hp.*Nat.Hom.*9. (From ξένϝος, cf. πρόξενϝος *IG*9(1).867, Ξενϝάρης ib.869, Ξενϝοκλῆς, Ξένϝων, ib.4.315,348: hence it is improb. that the Aeol. form was ξέννος.)

**ξενοσσόος**, Ion. **ξειν-**, ον, *saving strangers*, Nonn.*D.*3.178.

**ξενό-στᾰσις**, εως, ἡ, *lodging for guests* or *strangers*, S.*OC*90; πανδόκος ξ. Id.*Fr.*274. **-στομος**, ον, = ξενόφωνος, Phld.*Po.*2.41. **-σύνη**, Ep. **ξειν-**, ἡ, *hospitality*, Od.21.35. **-τάφιον** [ᾰ], τό, gloss on πολυάνδριον, Suid. **-τῑμος**, ον, *honouring strangers*, A.*Eu.*547 (lyr.). **-τροπος**, ον, gloss on ἑτερότροπος, Sch.Opp.*H.* 1.379. **-τροφέω**, *maintain mercenary troops*, Th.7.48, Isoc.8.46, Aen.Tact.13.1, D.11.18, Lxx 2*Ma.*10.14, Plu.2.214d; ξ. μεγάλας δυνάμεις D.S.1.67:—Pass., Aen.Tact.13.4. **-τροφία**, ἡ, *maintenance of mercenaries*, Hyp.*Fr.*256, Aen.Tact.13 tit. **-φονέω**, *murder one's host*, E.*IT*1021. **-φονία**, ἡ, *murder of strangers*, Isoc.11.36 (v.l. -κτονία). **-φόνος**, poet. **ξεινο-**, ον, *murdering strangers*, ἄνδρες Pl.*Ep.*336d; μάχαιρα Nonn.*D.*9.41. II. ξ. τιμαί honour paid *to murderers of strangers*, E.*IT*776. **-φυής**, ές, *strange of shape* or *nature*, Tz.*H.*8.579,636. **-φύλαξ** [ῠ], ᾰκος, ὁ, in pl., *magistrates charged with the protection of foreigners*, *Rev.Ét. Gr.*42.35 (Chios).

**Ξενοφῶν**, ῶντος, ὁ, *Xenophon*: hence Adj. **-φώντειος**, α, ον, *of* or *by X.*, λόγοι D.Chr.18.18.

**ξενοφων-έω**, *speak* or *sound strangely, use out-of-the-way words*, Dexipp. in *Cat.*6.17, Sophon. in *de An.*47.12:—Pass., *to be disconcerted by strange expressions*, Olymp.Alch.p.86 B.; so intr. in Act., Sch.Il. 23.403. **-ία**, ἡ, *strange language*, Poll.2.113, Greg.Cor.*Trop.* 27. **-ος**, ον, *speaking* or *sounding strange*, rejected by Poll.2.113.

⊛ **ξεν-όω**, Ion. **ξεινόω**, (ξένος) *make one's friend and guest, entertain*, in Med., ξενοῦμαι A.*Supp.*927, cf. A.R.1.849: fut. ξενώσεται Lyc. 92. II. mostly in Pass., with fut. Med. ξενώσομαι S.*Ph.*303: pf. ἐξένωμαι: aor. ἐξενώθην (ἐξενώθησαν Ἀττικῶς· ἐξενίσθησαν Ἑλληνικῶς Moer.p.167 P.): 1. *enter into a treaty of hospitality with* one, πόλιες ἀλλήλῃσι ἐξεινώθησαν Hdt.6.21, cf. Pl.*Lg.*642e, X.*Ages.*8.5; βασιλεῦσιν ἐξενωμένος Lys.6.48: abs., X.*HG*4.1.34. 2. *take up* one's *abode with* one *as a guest, to be entertained*, Θήβᾳ ξενωθεὶς Pi.*P.*4.299, cf. A.*Ch.*702, S. l. c., etc.; ξενωθεὶς τοῖσδ' ἐν.. δόμοις E.*Alc.*68; ξενοῦνται τῷ Ξενοφῶντι, [παρ'] Ἑλλάδι, X.*An.*7.8.6,8; ξενωθεὶς ὑπὸ τᾶς βωλᾶς *IG*12(1).383 (Rhodes). 3. *reside abroad*, δαρὸν ἐξενωμένον S.*Tr.*65, cf. E.*Ion*820; *go into banishment*, Id.*Hipp.* 1085. III. later, in Act., *deprive one of a thing*, [τινά] τινος Hld.6.7. **-ύδριον**, τό, = ξενύλλιον, Men.462.3. **-υει**· λήγει, Hsch. **-ύλλιον**, τό, Dim. of ξένος, Plu.2.229e, 240d. ⊛ **-ών**, ῶνος, ὁ, *guest-chamber*, in pl., E.*Alc.*543, 547; ξενῶνας οἷγε *Com. Adesp.*1211, cf. D.S.13.83, J.*BJ*5.4.4: sg., Pl.*Ti.*20c; = ξενοδοχεῖον, *OGI*609.21 (Syria, iii A.D.), Just.*Nov.*59.3; cf. ξενεών. ⊛ **-ωσις**, εως, ἡ, (ξενόω) *entertainment of a guest*, E.*HF*965.

**ξερίας**, cj. for ὀξερίας (q.v.).

**ξερόν**, τό, *terra firma*, once in Hom., ποτὶ ξερὸν ἠπείροιο Od.5.402; ποτὶ ξερὸν ἔλθ' ἀπὸ πέτρας to the *mainland*, *AP*6.304 (Phan.), cf. A.R.3.322; ἐπὶ ξερόν Nic.*Th.*704. (Cogn. with σχερός rather than with ξηρός.)

**ξέσ-ις**, εως, ἡ, *planing*, Thphr.*HP*5.6.4. **-μα**, ατος, τό, (ξέω) *that which is smoothed* or *carved*: hence, = ξόανον, *AP*9.328 (pl., Damostr.); v.l. for ξύσμα in Dsc.2.134. II. *abrasion*, in pl., Jul. *Caes.*309c. III. pl., *shavings, filings*, M.Ant.8.50, S.E.*P.*1.129. **-μός**, ὁ, in pl., = ξέσμα II, Hsch. s.v. σπαράγμασι.

**ξέσσε**, v. ξέω.

**ξεστασία**, ἡ, dub. sens. in *Sammelb.*1160.10.

**ξέστ-ης**, ου, ὁ, formed from Lat. *sextarius*, a Roman measure nearly = 1 *pint*, *IG*7.3498.54 (Oropus), J.*AJ*9.4.4, *AP*11.298, Gal.13.435,

Damocr.ap.eund.13.989, *IG*4²(1).93 (Epid., iii/iv A.D.), Phlp. *in APr.* 27.19. II. *pitcher, cup, Ev.Marc.*7.4, *POxy.*921.23 (iii A.D.), Harp.Astr. in *Cat.Cod.Astr.*8(3).139. **-ιαῖος**, α, ον, *of a* ξέστης, μέτρον Gal.13.435, cf. Phlp. *in Mete.*24.24.

**ξεστίζω**, *polish, PMasp.*6 ii 25 (Pass., vi A.D.).

**ξεστίον**, τό, = ξέστης I, *Ostr.Bodl.* iii 357, Orib.*Fr.*28, Aët.6.28: written ξεστίν *Arch.Anz.*38/39.154 (Antioch). II. = ξέστης II, Aët.1.138.

**ξεστός**, ή, όν, (ξέω) *hewn, shaved, planed*, of timber or objects made of it, ξ. οὐδός, τράπεζα, ἐλάται, ἐφόλκαιον, Od.18.33, 17.93, 12.172, 14.350; ἵππος 4.272; ὀϊστός Hes.*Sc.*133; ἄκοντες B.17.49; λόχος Ἀργείων, of the wooden horse, E.*Tr.*534 (lyr.); *carved*, ξόανα prob. in Orac.ap.Phleg.*Fr.*36.10 J. 2. of stone, *hewn*, ἐπὶ ξεστοῖσι λίθοις Il.18.504, cf. Od.3.406; λίθου ξεστοῦ καὶ ζῴων ἐγγεγλυμμένων Hdt.2.124; ἁρπάξαντες ἄγαλμ' Ἀΐδα, ξ. πέτρον, ἔμβαλον στέρνῳ Πολυδεύκεος Pi.*N.*10.67; of buildings, *built of hewn stone*, ξ. αἴθουσαι Il.6.243; ξ. ἀγυιαί E.*HF*782 (lyr.); ξ. τύμβος, τάφος, Id.*Alc.*836, *Hel.*986; τοῖχος Lxx *Si.*22.17, J.*AJ*15.11.5. 3. of horn, *polished*, Od.19.566; of an elephant's ears, *smooth*, Opp.*C.*2.520.

**ξεστουργία**, ή, *process of hewing*, λίθων D.S.1.63.

**ξέστριξ** κριθή, *six rowed* barley (Cnid.), Hsch.

❀ **ξέω**, impf. ἔξεον Od.23.199: fut. ξέσω Paul.Aeg.3.22.12: aor. ἔξεσα Sophr.110; Ep. ξέσσα Od.5.245, ξέσα Simon.185 A: pf. ἔξεκα Choerob. *in Theod.*2.80:—Pass., Hsch. s.v. σπαρασσόμεθα: aor. inf. ξεσθῆναι *Gp.*10.65.6, (κατ-) Plu.2.953b: pf. ἔξεσμαι Ar.*Fr.*728, (ἀπ-) Hp.*Nat.Mul.*109: plpf. ἔξεστο Hld.5.14:—*shave* or *plane* timber, ξέσσε δ' ἐπισταμένως καὶ ἐπὶ στάθμην ἴθυνεν Od.5.245, cf. 17.341, 21.44; οἱ ξέοντες Pl.*Thg.*124b. 2. *carve* wood, *shape by carving*, λέχος ἔξεον, ὄφρ' ἐτέλεσσα Od.23.199; τίς νιν ξέσε; Σκόπας Simon. l.c.:—Pass., Hld. l.c. 3. *whittle, pare*, in grafting, *Gp.*4.12.14. II. *scrape smooth, polish*, τοὺς ὄνυχας Philostr.*VS*2.5.2; τὸ βλέφαρον ξέσομεν διὰ κισήρεως Paul.Aeg. l.c.; τὸ ὀστοῦν Id.6.2; στήμων ἐξεσμένος *smoothed* thread, Ar. l.c. 2. *roughen by scraping*, προτετραχυμμένης (καὶ οἷον) ἐξεσμένης τῆς ὑστέρας Sor.1.36; *irritate*, ἔντερα Aret.*SD*2.9. 3. = ξαίνω, *flog*, τοὺς ἐν δικαστηρίῳ ξεσθέντας καὶ ξύλοις τυφθέντας Orib.*Fr.*90; τοὺς ἐν δικαστηρίῳ μαστιγωθέντας καὶ ξεσθέντας Aët.15.37.

**ξηνός**, ὁ, = κορμός (i.e. ἐπίξηνον), Suid.

❀ **ξηραίνω**, fut. -ᾰνῶ E.*Cyc.*575: aor. ἐξήρᾱνα Th.1.109, Hp.*Epid.*2.3.2, but ἐξήρηνα Id.*Hum.*1, *Mul.*2.112, Aret.*CD*1.3:—Pass., fut. ξηρανθήσομαι Gal.1.516, etc., but Med. ξηρᾰνοῦμαι in same sense, Hp.*Aff.*25, Arist.*Mete.*356ᵇ25: aor. ἐξηράνθην Il.21.345, Hp.*Epid.*5.30, Pl.*Phlb.*31e: pf. ἐξήρασμαι Hp.*Vict.*2.66, *Loc.Hom.*29, Antiph.217.13; ἐξήραμμαι Thphr.*CP*5.14.6, *Ev.Marc.*3.1, *POxy.*1188.19 (i A.D.), Sch.Ar.*Pl.*1082; inf. ἀπ-εξηράνθαι Hp.*Mul.*1.17; part. ἐξηρᾱμένος only late, Sch.Porph.*Abst.*2.6: (ξηρός):—*parch, dry up*, ξηρανεῖ σ' ὁ Βάκχιος E. l.c.; of the sun, X.*Mem.*4.3.8, etc.; τὸ σῶμα πρὸς ἀέρα ξ. Jul.*Or.*6.203b; *make costive*, τὴν κοιλίην Hp.*Aph.*3.17, cf. 2.20 (Pass.):—Pass., *to be* or *become dry, parched*, ἐξηράνθη πεδίον Il. l.c., cf. Pl.*Ti.*88d, etc.; *to be withered*, ἐξηράνθη ἡ συκῆ *Ev.Matt.*21.19, cf. Demetr.Lac.*Herc.*1012.12, *POxy.* l.c. 2. *drain dry*, ξηράνας τὴν διώρυχα Th.1.109. 3. metaph., κακουχεῖ αὐτὸν καὶ ξ. Teles p.34 H. b. Pass., of a paralytic, *Ev.Marc.*9.18.

**ξηρ-ᾰλοιφέω**, (ἀλείφω) *rub dry with oil*, of wrestlers, Lex Solonis ap.Plu.*Sol.*1 (cf. Aeschin.1.138), S.*Fr.*494, Plu.2.152d, Philostr.*Gym.*58, D.C.77.11; opp. χυτλοῦσθαι, Gal.11.532. **-ᾰλοιφία**, ή, *rubbing dry with oil*, Eust.764.13, Suid. **-αμπέλῐνος**, η, ον, *of the colour of withered vine-leaves, bright red, scarlet*, [vestes] *xerampelinae* Juv.6.519; δίπλακες ξ. Lyd.*Mag.*1.17; χλαμύδες ξ. Suid. s.v. ἀτραβατικάς. **-ανσις**, εως, ή, *drying up*, Gal.6.226, 16.415, Heph.Astr.1.22 (pl.). **-αντέον**, *one must dry*, Dsc.5.88, Gal.10.104, *Gp.*3.8. **-αντικός**, ή, όν, *causing to dry up*, c. gen., πνεύμονος Hp.*Acut.*16, 22: abs., ξ. [χυλός] Thphr.*CP*6.1.3; ξ. δίαιτα Diocl.*Fr.*141, cf. Arist.*Pr.*925ᵃ34 (Comp.); ξ. δύναμις Dsc.1.13. Adv. -κῶς *by drying*, Herod.Med.ap.Orib.5.28.23. **-ᾰσία**, Ion. -ίη, ή, *desiccation*, Hp.*Morb.*1.18, Antiph.231.7, Arist.*Mete.*384ᵃ11; *keeping dry*, Thphr.*HP*7.2.2; *drying* of hay, *PTeb.*441 (i A.D.), etc. 2. *dryness*, τοῦ περιέχοντος Str.2.3.7; τοῦ καυλοῦ Dsc.2.142, cf. Lxx *Jd.*6.37; ξηρασίαν λαμβάνειν become *dry*, Agatharch.34. 3. *drought, Gp.*1.8.13 (pl.). ❀ **-ασις**, *siccitas*, *Gloss.* **-ασμός**, gloss on αὐασμός, Erot. **-άφιον**, τό, = ξηρίον, Leonid.ap.Aët.14.13, Orib.*Fr.*84, Paul.Aeg.3.3 (freq. written ξυρ- in codd.). **-ιγγοι**· ποταμοὶ ἀεὶ ῥέοντες, Hsch. **-ίον**, τό, *desiccative powder* for putting on wounds, *POxy.*1142.7 (iii A.D.), Aët.6.65, al., Alex.Trall.1.15; κριθαὶ ξηρίον ἐπιπασσόμεναι τοῖς ἕλκεσι Alex.Aphr.*Pr.*1.150. **-ις**, *ardeola*, *Gloss.* (prob. κεῖρις).

**ξηρο-βᾰλᾰνιστέον**, *one must insert a desiccant suppository*, Orib.*Fr.*60. **-βατικός**, ή, όν, *walking on dry ground*, of land-animals, opp. ἔνυδρος, Pl.*Plt.*264d: of birds, Arist.*HA*559ᵃ20. **-βηξ**, βηχος, ὁ, *dry cough*, Cass.Fel.34 (pl.). **-δερμος**, ον, *dry-skinned*, Aët.1.107. **-κᾰκοζηλία**, ή, *tasteless aridity*, Demetr.*Eloc.*239. **-καρπος**, ον, *bearing dry fruit*, Thphr.*CP*2.8.1 (Comp.). **-καρυόφυλλον**, v. ξυλοκαρυόφυλλον. **-κέφᾰλος**, ον, *dry-headed*, Alex.Aphr.*Pr.*1.2. **-κόλλα**· σύνθεσίς τις παρὰ τοῖς χρυσουργοῖς, Hsch. II. (written *exiricolla*, etc.) = ξυλοκόλλα, *Gloss.* **-κολλούριον**, τό, *dry*, i.e. *thick, eye-salve*, Gal.12.725, Alex.Trall.2. **-κοπτον**, τό, *mortar*, Hsch. s.v. ἴ(γ)δη (Rhod.). **-λογία**, ή, *gathering of dry brushwood*, *Sammelb.*5126.25 (iii A.D.). **-λουσία**, ή, *taking a dry bath*, i.e. in hot sand, Cass.Fel.76. **-λουτρέω**, *take a dry bath*, i.e. roll in hot sand, Hsch. (ξηραλ- cod.). **-μῠρον**, τό, *dry perfume*, i.e. *in cake* or *powder*, *PFay.*331 (ii A.D.), Aët.16.127(118). II. = *rosmarinum*, *Gloss.* **-νομικός**, ή, όν, *feeding on dry land*, f.l. in Ath.3.99b (misquoting Pl.*Plt.*264d). **-ποιέω**, *make dry, dry up*, v.l. in Dsc.5.103 (Pass.). **-ποιός**, όν, *drying up, parching*, δίψα (as gloss on πολυκαγκέα) Eust.871.3; gloss on καρφαλέος, Sch.Nic.*Th.*691. **-πόταμος**, *torrens*, *Gloss.* **-πῡρία**, ή, Medic., *application of dry heat*, Aët.16.29, Sch.Nic.*Al.*586, *Gloss.* **-πῡρίτᾱς** [ῑ] ἄρτος, ὁ, (πυρός) = αὐτόπυρος, Ameriasap.Ath.3.114c.

❀ **ξηρός**, ά, όν, *dry*, opp. ὑγρός, of a dried-up river, Hdt.5.45; χειμάρρους ξηροὺς ὕδατος Arr.*An.*4.3.2; ἠὴρ ξ. Hdt.2.26; ξ. ἄνεμος Ar.*Nu.*404; ξηροῖς ἀκλαύτοις ὄμμασιν A.*Th.*696; ὀμμάτων ξ. κόραι E.*Or.*389; μέτρα ξ. τε καὶ ὑγρά *dry* and liquid measures, Pl.*Lg.*746d; ὕλη αὔη καὶ ξ. ib.761d; ξ. γάλα, i.e. *ripe* cheese, Eust.1001.51 (cf. περίξηρος); so τυρὸς ξ., opp. τυρὸς χλωρός, Antiph.133.7, cf. Philox.3.8; ἐν ξηροῖσιν ἐκτρέφειν on *solid* food, i.e. cereals, E.*Ba.*277; καρπὸς ξ., i.e. cereal, opp. κ. ξύλινος, produce of trees, i.e. fruit, wine, or oil, Pl.*Criti.*115b; ξ. χόρτος *hay*, *PPetr.*3 p.181 (iii B.C.); φοῖνιξ ξ. *dried* dates, *PSI*1.33.14 (ii A.D.); ξ. καρποί, opp. οἶνος, ἔλαιον, Arr.*Epict.*2.23.5; ξ. πυρίαι applications of *dry* heat, Hp.*Acut.*21, Archig.ap.Gal.12.621; cf. ξηροπυρία. Adv. ξηρῶς *by the use of dry powder*, Hp.*Epid.*6.3.13 (s.v.l.). 2. of bodily condition, *withered, lean*, δέμας E.*El.*239; ξηρὸς ὕπαὶ δείους Theoc.24.61; ξ. κοιλίη *costive*, Hp.*Aph.*2.20. 3. of the voice, cf. ξηρόφωνος. II. *fasting*: hence, generally, *austere*, τρόποι Ar.*V.*1452 (lyr.); of persons, Antiph.16; *harsh*, opp. ἡδύς, E.*Andr.*784 (lyr.). 2. metaph., of style, πραγματεία ἀτερπὴς καὶ ξ. Epicur.*Fr.*505 (p.358 U.); τὸ ξ. *aridity*, Demetr.*Eloc.*238; of critics, ξηροὶ Καλλιμάχου πρόκυνες *AP*11.322 (Antiphan.). III. as Subst. ἡ ξηρά (sc. γῆ), *dry land*, opp. ὑγρά, X.*Oec.*19.7 (also Comp. ξηροτέρα γῆ ib.6), cf. *Ev.Matt.*23.15, etc.; τὸ ξηρόν Hdt.2.68; ναῦς ἐπὶ τοῦ ξηροῦ ποιεῖν to leave the ships *aground*, Th.1.109; ναῦς ἐς τὸ ξ. ἐξωθεῖν Id.8.105; τὸ ξ. τοῦ ποταμοῦ *the part* of its bed *left dry*, X.*Cyr.*7.5.18: for Theoc.1.51 v. ἀκράτιστος. 2. ξηρά, ή, in a bath-house, *room for dry heat*, *POxy.*2145.12 (ii A.D.).

**ξηρό-σαρκος**, ον, *dry of flesh*, Diocl.*Fr.*135. **-σμύρνη**, ή, *dry myrrh*, Alex.Trall.12 fin. **-τήγᾰνον**, τό, Syrac. for τήγανον, Hegesand.38.

**ξηρότης**, ητος, ή, *dryness*, Pl.*R.*335d, X.*Oec.*19.11; ἡ ξ. τῶν νεῶν the *dryness*, i.e. *soundness*, of their timbers, Th.7.12. 2. *drought*, Plu.2.687f (pl.). II. *drying* or *becoming dry*, τὸ τάχος τῆς ξ. Arist.*Mete.*361ᵇ22. III. metaph., of character, *austerity*, Phld.*Acad.Ind.*p.51 M.; of style, *aridity*, Longin.3.3.

**ξηρο-τρῐβέω**, *rub dry*, Agathin.ap.Orib.10.7.19. **-τρῐβία**, ή, *dry rubbing*, Arist.*Pr.*966ᵇ1 (pl.), Gal.6.417. **-τροφικόν**, τό, *rearing of land-animals*, Pl.*Plt.*264d,e. **-φαγέω**, *eat dry food*, *AP*11.205 (Lucill.), Dsc.*Eup.*2.65, Sor.1.49. **-φᾰγία**, ή, *eating of dry food*, Chrysipp.Tyan.ap.Ath.3.113b, Gal.14.751; *herbs eaten raw*, *Gloss.*

**ξηροφθαλμία**, ή, *inflammation of the eyelids, blepharitis sicca*, with redness and smarting, Dsc.*Eup.*1.46, *PMed.Strassb.*p.6 K., Cels.6.6, Erot. s.v. κνιπότης, Gal.12.731, Aët.7.77.

**ξηρό-φλοιος**, ον, *with dry bark*, *Gp.*9.16.2. **-φορτον**, τό, *weight* of a cargo of fruit *after drying*, *OGI*629.164 (Palmyra, ii A.D.). **-φρυκτον**, τό, = ξηρόμυρον, Aët.16.126(117). **-φωνος**, ον, *with a husky voice*, Sch.D Il.13.41; τὸ ξ., of the twang of a bowstring, Eust.1914.42. **-χειμάρρους**, ὁ, *dry watercourse*, Hero *Geom.*4.13.

**ξηρώδης**, ες, *dryish, looking dry*, *EM*557.27.

**ξῑ**, v. ξεῖ. **ξίμβρα**, ή, Aeol. for ῥοιά, Hsch.

**ξῑπομάκαιρα** [μᾰ], barbarism in Ar.*Th.*1127, for ξιφομάχαιρα.

**ξιρίς**, = ξυρίς, Dsc.4.22:—also **ξίρις**, v. ξυρίς.

**ξίφαι**· τὰ ἐν ταῖς ῥυκάναις δρέπανα ἢ σιδήρια, Hsch.

**ξιφήν**, ῆνος, ὁ, *sword-bearer*, Suid.

❀ **ξιφ-ήρης**, ες, *armed with a sword, sword in hand*, E.*Or.*1272, 1346, al.: also in later Prose, Phld.*Rh.*2.89 S. (dub.), Ap.Ty.*Ep.*36, Hdn.7.5.3, Iamb.*VP*25.113, Malch.p.410 D.

❀ **ξῐφη-φορέω**, *wear a sword*, Ph.1.282, Hdn.7.11.4. **-φορία**, ή, *wearing of a sword*, Suid. **-φόρος**, ον, *bearing a sword, sword in hand*, E.*Or.*1504, al.; ξ. ἀγῶνες A.*Ch.*584, E.*HF*812 (lyr.); βρόχοι ib.730; χεῖρες Antiph.217.19, cf. Callistr.*Stat.*13: as Subst., *swordsman*, Hdn.7.10.7. II. = ξιφίας II, Sch.Arat.1091.

**ξῐφ-ίας**, ου, ὁ, (ξίφος) *sword fish*, Arist.*HA*505ᵃ18, *Fr.*325, Archestr.*Fr.*40; cf. σκιφίας. II. a kind of *comet* (from the shape), Plin.*HN* 2.89. **-ίδιον**, τό, Dim. of ξίφος, *dagger*, Ar.*Lys.*53, Th.3.22, *POxy.*936.9 (iii A.D.), etc. 2. = σπαργάνιον, Ps.-Dsc.4.21. **-ίζω**, *dance the sword-dance*, Cratin.219. **-ίνδα**, Adv. *sword-game*, Theognost.*Can.*164. **-ιον** or **-ίον**, τό, *corn-flag, Gladiolus segetum*, Thphr.*HP*6.8.1, Dsc.4.20. **-ιος** (-ιός cod. Hsch.), ὁ, = ξιφίας, Hsch. 2. a fish like the ἰουλίς, Cyran.3. 3. a stone, ibid. 4. a bird, = κίρκος, ibid. **-ισμα**, ατος, τό, = sq., Choerob. in *An.Ox.*2.242, cf. Hsch. (pl.). **-ισμός**, ὁ, *sword-dance*, Ath.14.629f; *sword-play*, D.C.47.44. **-ιστήρ**, ῆρος, ὁ, *sword-belt*, *PCair.Zen*35.2 (iii B.C.), Plu.*Pomp.*42, Hld.9.23. **-ιστής**, οῦ, ὁ, = foreg., Hsch. **-ιστύς**, ύος, ή, = μαχαιρομαχία, *sword-play*, Id.

**ξῐφο-δήλητος**, ον, *slain by the sword*, ξ. θάνατος, ἀγῶνες, death *by the sword*, A.*Ag.*1528, *Ch.*729 (both anap.). **-δρέπᾰνον**, τό, *sickle shaped sword, scimitar*, Ph.*Bel.*99.51, *POxy.*1241 vi 22; = ἅρπη, Hsch. **-ειδής**, ές, *sword-shaped*, Thphr.*HP*7.13.1, Str.3.5.

10; ὀστοῦν Gal.2.496; χόνδρος the *ensiform* cartilage, Id.*UP*6.3, al. **-θήκη,** ἡ, *scabbard*, Hsch., *Gloss.* **-κτονέω,** *slay with the sword*, Suid. **-κτόνος,** ον, *slaying with the sword*, χέρες S.*Aj.*10; δίωγμα E.*Hel.*354 (lyr.). **-μάχαιρα** [μᾰ], ἡ, *sabre*, Theopomp. Com.25, 7.2, *IG*1$^{2}$.282.118, 2$^{2}$.1380. **-ποιός,** ὁ, *sword-maker*, *Gloss.*

⊛ **ξίφος** [ῐ], Aeol. **σκίφος** (q.v.), εος, τό, *sword*, ξ. μέγα, ὀξύ, Il.1.194, 4.530, etc., cf. A.*Pr.*863, Hdt.3.64, X.*An.*2.2.9, etc.; ξ. ἄμφηκες Il.21.118, Od.16.80; ξ. ἀργυρόηλον χάλκεον Il.19.372; ξ. σὺν κολεῷ.. καὶ ἐϋτμήτῳ τελαμῶνι 7.303: used by Hom. as equivalent of ἄορ and φάσγανον, Od.11.48 (cf. 24, 82), 10.294 (cf. 321); cf. μάχαιρα. 2. *power of life and death*, Lat. *jus gladii*, Philostr.*VA*4.42. II. *sword-shaped bone* in the cuttle-fish (τευθίς), Arist.*HA*524$^{b}$24, *PA*654$^{a}$21, Opp.*H.*3.558; also in the ξιφίας, Arist.*Fr.*325. III. = ξιφίον, Thphr.*HP*7.13.1.

**ξῐφ-ουλκία,** ἡ, *drawing of a sword*, Plu.*Arist.*18 (pl.), *Pomp.*69 (pl.). **-ουλκός,** όν, (ἕλκω) *drawing a sword*, χείρ A.*Eu.*592. **-ουργός,** ὁ, *sword-cutler*, Ar.*Pax*547.

**ξῐφύδριον,** τό, Dim. of ξίφος, only used = τελλίνη, Xenocr.ap.Orib. 2.58.116, Hsch.; cf. σκιφύδριον.

**ξοᾰν-ηφόρος,** ὁ, *image-bearer*: Ξοανηφόροι, title of a play by Sophocles. **-ιον,** τό, Dim. of sq., *IG*12(3).248.16 (Anaphe, ii B.C.). **-ον,** τό, (ξέω) *image carved* of wood, E.*Ion*1403, X.*An.*5.3.12: then, generally, *image, statue*, esp. of a god, Acus.28 J., E.*IT*1359, *Tr.*525 (lyr.), 1074 (lyr.), *BMus.Inscr.*1012 (Chalcedon, i B.C./i A.D.), Paus.8.17.2, al., Porph.*Abst.*2.56; also of a representation on a scarab, *PMag.Leid.V.*9.22. II. *musical instrument*, ξόαν' ἡδυμελῆ S.*Fr.*238 (anap.).

**ξοᾰνοποιία,** ἡ, *carving of images*, Str.16.2.35.

**ξοᾰνουργία,** ἡ, = foreg., Luc.*Syr.D.*34.

**ξο-ΐδιον,** τό, Dim. of sq., *PTeb.*406.19 (iii A.D.). ⊛ **-ΐς,** ΐδος, ἡ, *chisel*, *IG*2$^{2}$.463.40, 11(2).199*A*87 (Delos, iii B.C.), *Supp.Epigr.*4.447.40 (Didyma, ii B.C.), etc.; ξ. χαρακτή toothed *chisel*, *IG*7.3073.104 (Lebad.); ξ. ἀρτίστομος (q.v.), ib.148; ξ. ἡμιτριβής *Inscr.Délos*507; ποιμενικῆς αὐτομαθοῦς ξ. *APl.*4.86.

**ξοός,** ὁ, = ξυσμός, ὁλκός, Hsch.

**ξουθόπτερος,** ον, *with nimble* (or perh. *humming*) *wings*, μέλισσα(ι) E.*HF*487, *Fr.*467.4, *Lyr.Alex.Adesp.*7.13.

⊛ **ξουθός,** ή, όν, *rapidly moving to and fro, nimble*, φεύγετε τῆς ξουθῆς δειλότεροι κεμάδος Herodic.ap.Ath.5.222a; κόμαι.. ξουθοῖσιν ἀνέμοις ἐνετρύφων φορούμεναι in the *rustling* breezes, Chaerem.1.7; ξ. ἀλκυόνες *AP*9.333 (Mnasalc.); ξ. πτέρυγες *rustling, whirring* wings of the Dioscuri, *h.Hom.*33.13; *whirring* or *steadily-beating* wings of the eagle, B.5.17; ξουθὰν ἐκ πτερύγων ἁδὺ κρέκουσα μέλος, of the cricket, *AP*7.192 (Mnasalc.). 2. *chirruping* or *trilling* larynx of the nightingale, ἐλθὲ διὰ ξουθᾶν γενύων ἐλελιζομένα θρήνοις ἐμοῖς ξυνεργός E.*Hel.*1111 (lyr.); ἐλελιζομένη διεροῖς μέλεσιν γένυος ξουθῆς Ar.*Av.*214 (anap.); δι' ἐμῆς γένυος ξουθῆς μελέων Πανὶ νόμους ἱεροὺς ἀναφαίνω ib.744 (lyr.); of the nightingale itself, *trilling*, οἷά τις ξουθὰ.. Ἴτυν Ἴτυν στένουσ'.. ἀηδών A.*Ag.*1142 (lyr.); ὦ φίλη, ὦ ξουθή, ὦ φίλτατον ὀρνέων πάντων Ar.*Av.*676 (lyr.), cf. Theoc.*Ep.*4.11; of song-birds in general, ξ. λιγύφωνα ὄρνεα *Lyr.Alex.Adesp.*7.1; ξ. χελιδών *twittering* swallow, Babr.118.1. 3. of the bee, either *nimble*, or *humming* (cf. ξουθόπτερος), S.*Fr.*398.5, E.*IT*165 (anap.), 635, Pl.*Epigr.*32.6, Antiph.52.7, Theoc.7.142, *AP*9.226.1 (Zon.), v.l. in *APl.*4.305.3 (Antip.). 4. of the sound produced by a trilling larynx or vibrating wing, ξουθὸν μέλος (of a song-bird) *chirruping* note, Opp.*H.*4.123; οὔρεσι καὶ σκιεραῖς ξουθὰ λαλεῦντα νάπαις, of the τέττιξ, *AP*9.373.4. 5. ξ. ἱππαλεκτρυών perh. *nimble* horse-cock, A.*Fr.*134, parodied in Ar.*Pax*1177, *Av.*800, *Ra.*932. II. *golden yellow*, ξουθῶν τε σπονδὰς μελιτῶν Emp.128.7 (ap.Porph.*Abst.*2.21; ξανθῶν ap.Ath.12.510d); ξουθὸς μὲν πρόπαν εἶδος, of a species of wolf, Opp.*C.*3.297 (ξανθὸς one cod.); but ξουθὸν ἀπ' ἀνέρος αἷμα πάσασθαι *red* blood, Opp.*H.*2.452 (v.l. ξανθὸν ὑπ').

**ξοῦθρος,** ὁ, = στροῦθος, Cyran.92.

**Ξουσαριασταί,** οἱ, a guild at Rhodes, *IG*12(1).963 (dub.).

**ξῦ,** v. ξεῖ.

**ξυγγ-,** for all words so beginning, v. συγγ-.

**ξυζανει,** dub. sens. in *Supp.Epigr.*2.510 (Gortyn, vi B.C.).

**ξῠήλη,** Dor. **ξυάλη** (Hsch., Suid.), ἡ, (ξύω) *whittle, curved knife* used in shaping a javelin, X.*Cyr.*6.2.32; ξ. Λακωνική, as a weapon, Id.*An.*4.7.16, cf. 4.8.25.

**ξῠλάβιον** [ᾰ], τό, for ξῠλο-λάβιον, *fire-tongs*, Sch.Opp.*H.*2.342.

⊛ **ξῠλᾱλόη,** ἡ, = ἀγάλοχον, Aët.1.131; scanned ⏑ – ⏑ – by Heraclit. Gramm. in *An.Ox.*3.277.

**ξῠλᾰμ-άω,** *plant* or *sow*, usu. of green crops or fodder (opp. σπείρω of cereals), mostly c. dat., ξ. χόρτῳ, χλωροῖς, *POxy.*499.15 (ii A.D.), *PSI*4.315.10 (ii A.D.); ἀράκῳ *POxy.*1629.10 (i B.C.); but also ξ. κριθήν *PFlor.*85.21 (i A.D.). ⊛ **-ή,** ἡ, *sowing, planting*, χόρτου, λινοκαλάμης, ib.41.12 (ii A.D.), *POxy.*102.11 (iv A.D.). **-ησις,** εως, ἡ, = foreg., *PHamb.*27.6 (iii B.C.), *PLond.*3.1171$^{r}$.37 (i A.D.). ⊛ **-ητής,** οῦ, ὁ, *sower*, *PMich.Zen.*32.25 (iii B.C.).

**ξῠλ-άνηθον** [ᾰ], τό, a kind of *dill*, Gal.14.732. **-άριον** [ᾰ], τό, Dim. of ξύλον, *small piece of wood, twig*, Lxx 3*Ki.*17.12, Dsc.1.70, Gal.12.422; *log*, ξ. ἐρίκινον *BGU*824.12 (i A.D.), cf. *POxy.*1292.12 (i A.D.), etc. **-άφιον,** τό, = foreg., Eust.492.37. **-εία,** ἡ, *felling and carrying of wood*, Plb.21.39.12, *BGU*1123.9 (i B.C.), J.*BJ*6.2.7; *supply of wood*, Str.5.2.5. II. *timber*, Plb.3.42.3. 2. *wood-work*, Id.10.27.10, Callix.1, Hdn.8.4.8. **-εύς,** έως, ὁ, *woodcutter*, of a sacrificial attendant, *SIG*1021.31 (Olympia, i B.C.), Paus.5.13.2, 5.15.10, Hsch. **-εύω,** *cut wood*, *SIG*685.82 (Crete, ii B.C.), *IPE*1$^{2}$.403*B* (Chersonesus, iii/ii B.C.):—Med., δρυὸς πεσούσης πᾶς ἀνὴρ ξυλεύεται Men.*Mon.*123, cf. Hsch.; cf. ξυλλείομαι. **-ηβόρος,** ον, *eating wood*, Id. (-ιβ- cod.). **-ηγέω,** (ἄγω) *import timber*, D.19.114. ⊛ **-ηγός,** όν, (ἄγω) *for carrying wood*, σκάφη *BGU*1157.8 (i B.C.), cf. Poll.7.130. **-ηρός,** ά, όν, *appertaining to timber*, σταθμοί *SIG*975.2 (Delos, iii B.C.). II. ξυληρά, ἡ, *timber-market*, *PTeb.*316.95 (i A.D.). **-ήφιον,** τό, Dim. of ξύλον, *piece of wood, stick*, Hp.*Steril.*230, Alex.98.24, Plb.6.34.9, D.S.4.76:—misspelt ξυλίφιον D.S. l.c. (v.l.), Thom.Mag.p.253 R.; ξυλύφιον v.l. in Suid. s.vv. Διοκλῆς, ὀξύβαφον; ξυλήριον *EM*611.23. **-ίζομαι,** Med., *gather wood*, X.*An.*2.4.11; ἐκ τοῦ παραδείσου Plu.*Art.*25; ξυλισάμενος ὀλίγα κομμάτια Alciphr.1.1. ⊛ **-ικός,** ή, όν, (ξύλον) *of wood, wooden, like wood*, Arist.*PA*674$^{a}$29; καρπὸς ξ., = ξύλινος (v. sq.), *PSI*5.528.46 (iii B.C.), Artem.2.37; ξ. ὕλη *timber*, *IG*12(3).324 (Thera), *Gloss.*; ξ. παρασκευή *OGI*510.7 (Ephesus, ii A.D.); ξυλική, ἡ, *timber-monopoly*, *PTeb.*8.26 (iii/ii B.C.); ξυλικόν, *lignarium, pulpitum*, *Gloss.* ⊛ **-ῐνος,** η, ον, *of wood, wooden*, τεῖχος Pi.*P.*3.38; δόμος, οἰκίαι, B.3.49, Hdt.4.108, etc.; ὁ ξ. καρπός produce *of trees*, i.e. fruit, wine, or oil, opp. ξηρός (q.v.), Pl.*Criti.*115b, cf. *OGI*55.13 (Telmessus, iii B.C.), Str.15.1.20: pl., ξ. καρποί, opp. σιτικοί, Id.5.4.2, cf. D.S.3.63, Ath.3.78d; opp. ὁ Δημήτριος, *IG*2$^{2}$.2492.19; ξύλιναι ὧναι, opp. σιτηραί, *SIG*$^{2}$554.17 (Magn. Mae., ii B.C.); τομὰ ἁ ξυλίνα cutting *of timber*, *IG*4$^{2}$(1).76.9 (Epid., ii B.C.). 2. metaph., *wooden*, νοῦς *AP*11.275 (Apollon. Gramm.), cf. 255 (Pall.). 3. ξύλινον, τό, *writing-tablet*, ξ. πύξινον *PGrenf.*1.14.12 (ii B.C.). II. *of cotton*, Lxx *Si.*22.16, Plin.*HN*19.14. ⊛ **-ιον,** τό, *block of wood*, *POxy.*901.10 (iv A.D.). **-ισμός,** ὁ, = ξυλεία I, Str.12.2.7, D.H.5.41. **-ιστής,** οῦ, ὁ, = ξυλεύς, Sch.Pl.*Smp.*208d. **-ίτης** [ῑ], ου, ὁ, *like wood*: name of a fish, Hsch. II. ξυλῖτις (sc. γῆ), ἡ, *timber-bearing land*, *PPetr.*3 p.223 (iii B.C.), *PCair.Zen.*387.9 (iii B.C.), *PLille*5.20 (iii B.C.); later ξ. χέρσος, opp. σπόριμος, *PLond.*2.267.99 (ii A.D.), *BGU*703.5 (ii A.D.).

**ξυλλ-,** for words so beginning, v. συλλ-.

⊛ **ξυλλείομαι,** Boeot. for ξυλεύομαι, dub. in *Supp.Epigr.*2.185 (cf. p.152) (v B.C.).

**ξύλλομαι,** = συλάω, *plunder*, *SIG*56.3 (Argos, v B.C.).

**ξῠλο-βάλσᾰμον,** τό, *balsam-wood*, Str.16.2.41, Dsc.1.19, Plin.*HN*12.118, Gal.10.466, *Gp.*7.13.4. **-βολον,** τό, = ξυλοθήκη, *Gloss.* ⊛ **-γλῠκον,** τό, *siliqua*, ib. ⊛ **-γλύφος** [γλῠ], ον, gloss on στυπογλύφος, Hsch. **-γρᾰφέομαι,** Pass., *to be written upon wood*, *Test.Epict.*8.24, 30. **-δωνίη** (leg. -δομίη)· τεκτοσύνη, ναυπήγησις, κωπηλασία, κυβέρνησις, Hsch. **-ειδής,** ές, *like wood*, λόφος τὸ χρῶμα ξ. Clytus 1; *dry*, Androm.ap.Gal.14.42; cf. ξυλώδης. II. *wooden*, θυρίδες *PSI*5.547.15, al. (iii B.C.). **-εργός,** ὁ, = ξυλουργός, *Supp.Epigr.*4.105 (Rome, i A.D.). **-θήκη,** ἡ, *wood-house*, Moschio ap. Ath.5.208a. **-κάνθηλα,** τά, = sq., *Gloss.* **-κανθήλια,** τά, *wooden pack-saddle*, Hsch. s.v. σώρακον: sg. **-κανθήλιον,** *Gloss.* **-κάρπᾰσον,** τό, *wood of flax*, Gal.19.738. **-κάρῠον** [ᾰ], τό, = sq., Aët.16.146. **-κᾰρῠόφυλλον,** τό, *clove*, Id.1.131 (written ξηρο-). **-κᾰσία,** ἡ, an inferior kind of *cassia*, Gal.19.738, *Edict.Diocl.*32.53, Aët.16.130. **-κατασκεύαστος,** ον, *made of wood*, Sch. Lyc.361. **-κέρᾱτον,** τό, *Ceratonia Siliqua*, Alex.Trall.9.3, Steph. *in Hp.*1.211 D., cf. *Gloss.* **-κερκος,** ὁ, a gate at Constantinople, *AP*9.690 tit. **-κιννάμωμον** [ᾰ], τό, *wood of cinnamon*, Dsc.1.14, Plin.*HN*12.91, Gal.13.185, *Gp.*8.22.2. **-κοκκον,** τό, = κεράτιον II, Aët.9.32. **-κόλλα,** ἡ, *glue for wood*, Dsc.3.87, Orib.*Syn.*2.56. ⊛ **-κοπέω,** *cut wood, make a clearance*, *PLille*5.24 (iii B.C.). II. *beat with a stick, cudgel*, of the Roman *fustuarium*, Plb.6.37.1 (Pass.), 6.38.1: generally, Arr.*Epict.*3.7.33:—Pass., ib.4.4.37, *POxy.*706.13 (ii A.D.). **-κοπία,** ἡ, *wood-cutting*, *PLille*5.49 (iii B.C.), *PSI*4.323, al. (iii B.C.). II. = Lat. *fustuarium*, Plb.6.37.2. **-κόπος,** ον, (κόπτω) *hewing, felling wood*, πέλεκυς X.*Cyr.*6.2.36 (v.l. ξυλοτόμος). b. Subst. -κόπος, ὁ, *wood-feller*, Lxx *Jo.*9.27(21), Str.16.4.11. 2. *pecking wood*, of the birds κελεός and κνιπολόγος, Arist.*HA*593$^{a}$9, 14. **-κράμβη,** ἡ, *tree-cabbage*, *Hippiatr.*48 (s.v.l.). **-κύμβη,** ἡ, nickname of an ill-favoured woman, *Com.Adesp.*1091. **-κυστίς,** ίδος, ἡ, *salvia*, *Gloss.* (dub.). **-λεπής,** ές, *with woody shell*, καρπός Sch.Nic.*Al.*108. **-λογεία,** ἡ, *gathering of wood*, *POxy.*729.33 (ii A.D.). **-λυχνοῦχος,** ὁ, *wooden lampstand*, Alex.344. **-λωτος,** ὁ, = πεντέφυλλον, Dsc.4.42, *Gloss.* **-μακερ,** τό, indecl., *nutmeg*, Alex.Trall.9.2. **-μετρέω,** *measure by* ξύλα (v. ξύλον V), i.e. *measure the amount of earth excavated*, Wilcken *Chr.*389.27 (ii A.D.). **-μέτρης,** ου, ὁ, *official charged with the measuring of earth excavated*, *PLond.*5.1648.8, 13 (iv A.D.). **-μῐγής,** ές, *mixed with wood*, Str.12.7.3. **-μοχλον,** τό, *wooden bolt*, *POxy.*1923.21 (v/vi A.D.). **-μυρσίνη,** ἡ, = μυρσίνη ἀγρία, v.l. in Dsc.4.144.

⊛ **ξύλον** [ῠ], τό (pl. spelt ξύλεα *Abh.Berl.Akad.*1928(6).32 (Cos, v B.C.)), *wood* cut and ready for use, *firewood, timber*, etc., Hom., mostly in pl., Il.8.507, 547, Od.14.418; ξ. νήϊα ship-*timber*, Hes.*Op.*808; ξ. ναυπηγήσιμα Th.7.25, X.*An.*6.4.4, Pl.*Lg.*706b, D.17.28; ξ. τετράγωνα *logs* cut square, Hdt.1.186, cf. Pl.*Prt.*325d, Arist.*EN*1109$^{b}$7. 2. in pl., also, *the wood-market*, ἐπὶ ξύλα ἰέναι Ar.*Fr.*403. II. in sg., *piece of wood, log, beam, post*, once in Hom., ξ. αὖον.. ἢ δρυὸς ἢ πεύκης Il.23.327; ξ. σύκινον *spoon made of* fig *wood*, Pl.*Hp.Ma.*291c; *peg* or *lever*, Arist.*MA*701$^{b}$9; *perch*, ἐπὶ ξύλου καθεύδειν Ar.*Nu.*1431: by poet. periphr., Ἀργοῦς ξύλον A.*Fr.*20; ἵπποιο κακὸν ξ., of the Trojan horse, *AP*9.152 (Agath.): hence

anything made of wood, as, 2. *cudgel, club,* Hdt.2.63, 4.180, Ar.*Lys.*357, *PHal.*1.187 (iii B.C.); μετὰ ξύλων εἰσπηδῆσαι *PTeb.*304.10 (ii A.D.); ξύλοις συντρίψειν Luc.*Demon.*50; of the *club* of Heracles, Plu.*Lyc.*30. 3. *an instrument of punishment,* a. *wooden collar,* put on the neck of the prisoner, ξύλῳ φιμοῦν τὸν αὐχένα Ar.*Nu.*592; ἐς τετρημένον ξ. ἐγκαθαρμόσαι..τὸν αὐχένα Id.*Lys.*680; or, b. *stocks,* in which the feet were confined, Hdt.9.37, 6.75, Ar.*Eq.*367, D.18.129; ξ. ἐφέλκειν Polyzel.3; ἐν τῷ ξ. δεδέσθαι Lys.10.16 (v. ποδοκάκκη), cf. *Act.Ap.*16.24, *OGI*483.181 (Pergam., ii A.D.): also in pl., ἔδησεν ἐν τοῖς ξ. And.1.45. c. πεντεσύριγγον ξύλον (v. sub voc.) was a combination of both, with holes for the neck, arms, and legs, Ar.*Eq.*1049. d. *gallows,* κρεμάσαι τινὰ ἐπὶ ξύλου Lxx *De.*21.22; ξ. δίδυμον ib.*Jo.*8.29: prov., ἐξ ἀξίου τοῦ ξύλου κἂν ἀπάγξασθαι, i.e. if one must be hanged, at least let it be on a noble tree, *App.Prov.*2.67, cf. Ar.*Ra.*736; in *NT,* of the *cross, Act.Ap.*5.30, 10.39. e. *stake* on which criminals were impaled, Alex.222.10. 4. *bench, table,* esp. *money-changer's table,* D.45.33. 5. πρῶτον ξύλον front *bench* in the Athenian theatre, Ar.*Ach.*25, *V.*90, cf. Sch. ad locc.: hence οὐπὶ τῶν ξύλων the official who had to take care of the *seats,* Hermipp.9 (according to Meineke). 6. the Hippocratic *bench,* Hp.*Fract.*13, *Art.*72. III. of live wood, *tree,* [ὄρος] δασὺ πολλοῖς καὶ παντοδαποῖς καὶ μεγάλοις ξύλοις X.*An.*6.4.5, cf. Call.*Cer.*41, Agatharch.55, Lxx *Ca.*2.3, al.: opp. σάρξ, Thphr.*HP*1.2.6, al.; τῷ ξ. τοῦ δένδρου ἀνάλογον τὴν λεγομένην εἶναι γῆν Plot.6.7.11; τὸ ξ. τῆς ἀμπέλου E.*Cyc.*572; εἴρια ἀπὸ ξύλου, of cotton, Hdt.3.47; εἵματα ἀπὸ ξύλων πεποιημένα Id.7.65, cf. Poll.7.75. IV. of persons, *blockhead, APl.*4.187; of a stubborn person, σίδηρός τις ἢ ξ. πρὸς τὰς δεήσεις Ach.Tat.5.22. V. *a measure of length,* = 3 (also $2\frac{2}{3}$) cubits, the side of the ναύβιον, Hero *Geom.*23.4, 11, *POxy.*669.11, 28 (iii A.D.), 1053 (vi/vii A.D.).

**ξῠλο-ναΐσκιον,** τό, *wooden shrine, POxy.*521 (ii A.D.). **-ξεσις,** εως, ἡ, *carving,* prob. in *Supp.Epigr.*4.270 (Panamara, i B.C.). **-πᾰγής,** ές, *built on piles,* Str.5.1.7. ⊛**-πάκτων,** ωνος, ὁ, *boat for conveying timber, BGU*812 i 2 (ii/iii A.D.). ⊛**-πέδη,** ἡ, *log of wood tied to the feet,* Aq.*Jb.*13.27, 33.11. **-πέτᾰλον,** τό, = πεντεφυλλον, Dsc.4.42. **-πόδης,** ου, ὁ, *with wooden feet,* Hdn.*Epim.*212. **-ποιός,** όν, *for carpentry,* ἐργαστήριον *BGU*1053.49 (i B.C.). **-πριστικὸς πῆχυς,** *sawyer's* cubit, Hero *Geom.*23.6. **-πύλιον** [πῡ], τό, *wooden gateway, SIG*88.24, 26 (Athens, v B.C.). **-πῡρία,** ἡ, perh. *sharpening to a point with fire,* Anon. *in Rh.*236.8. **-πώλης,** ου, ὁ, *timber-merchant, IG*2².1673.17, *PLond.*3.1177.186 (ii A.D.), Hsch. s. v. συρμιστήρ. **-πωλικός,** ή, όν, *of a timber-merchant,* ἐργαστήριον *BGU* 1151.40 (i B.C.). **-πώλιον,** τό, *lignarium, Gloss.* ⊛**-σπόγγιον,** τό, *sponge on a stick, Hippiatr.*69, 100. **-στεγής,** ές, *covered with wood,* prob. in *POxy.*2146.13 (iii A.D.). **-στομος,** ον, *wooden-* (i.e. *hard-*)*mouthed,* of horses, prob. cj. in *Hippiatr.*115 (-σωμοι codd.). **-σχίστης,** ου, ὁ, *one who splits wood,* Ptol.*Tetr.*179. ⊛**-τομία,** ἡ, *woodcutting, POxy.*1631.9 (iii A.D.). **-τόμος,** ὁ, *woodcutter, Sammelb.*4874: as Adj., πέλεκυς ξ. v.l. in X.*Cyr.*6.2.36. **-τρόφος,** ον, *producing timber,* ὄρη Str.*Chr.*4.21. **-τρώκτης,** ου, ὁ, *eating wood,* σκώληξ Suid. s. v. τερηδών.

**ξῠλουργ-έω,** Ion. -οργέω, *work wood,* Hdt.3.113. **-ής,** ές, *made of wood,* διάφραγμα Lyd.*Mag.*3.37. **-ία,** ἡ, *working of wood, carpentry,* A.*Pr.*451, *IG*1².347.35. **-ικός,** ή, όν, *of* or *for carpentry,* E.*Fr.*988: ἡ -κή (sc. τέχνη), = ξυλουργία, Pl.*Phlb.*56b. **-ός,** ὁ, *carpenter, joiner, IG*1².373.235, Poll.7.101; cf. ξυλοεργός.

**ξῠλο-φάγος** [ᾰ], ον, *eating wood,* σκώληξ Str.12.7.3; cj. for ὑλο- in Ant.Lib.22.5. **-φᾰνής,** ές, *showing wood:* τὸ ξ. τοῦ κατασκευάσματος the *exposed wooden* structure, D.S.20.96. II. *resembling wood,* Archig.ap.Orib.8.2.2. ⊛**-φθόρον,** τό, an insect *that destroys wood,* Arist.*HA*557ᵇ13 codd. (fort. -φόρον *that carries wood*). **-φορέω,** *carry wood,* of a slave or mule, Men.*Her.*52, *PSI*6.667.2 (iii B.C.), Str.14.2.24. 2. *carry a stick,* as the Cynics did, Luc.*Pisc.*24. II. *produce timber,* Str.*Chr.*2.2. **-φορία,** ἡ, *wood-carrying,* Lys.*Fr.*325 S. II. *wood-offering,* Lxx *Ne.*10.34(35). **-φόριος,** ον, *belonging to a wood-offering,* ἡ τῶν ξυλοφορίων ἑορτή the Jewish *feast of Tabernacles,* J.*BJ*2.17.6. **-φόρος,** ον, *carrying wood,* θεράποντες ξ. Dosiad.Hist.1: as Subst., *wood-porter,* Epicur.*Fr.*172, Aq.*De.*29.11(10). II. Subst., *wood-offerer,* Lxx *Ne.*13.31. **-φρακτος,** ον, *fenced with wood,* ξ. γέφυρα, = *pons sublicius,* D.H.3.55, 5.24, 9.68. ⊛**-χάρτια,** τά, *wooden tablets for writing,* Eust.1913.41.

**ξῠλοχ-ίζομαι,** Dor. **-ίσδομαι,** = ξυλίζομαι, ἐρείκας Theoc.5.65. **-ος,** ἡ, *thicket, copse,* ξύλοχον κάτα βοσκομενάων Il.5.162; βαθείης ἐκ ξυλόχοιο 11.415, 21.573; ἐν ξυλόχῳ..λέοντος in his *lair,* Od.4.335, cf. 19.445; κραναῇ κείμεθ' ἐνὶ ξ. *AP*7.445 (Pers.): also in late Prose, Palaeph.14: pl., *Stud.Pont.*3.16 (Amisus, ii/i B.C.), Coluth.42, *Anacreont.*29.5.

⊛**ξῠλ-όω,** *turn into wood:*—Pass., *become wood,* Thphr.*HP*1.2.7: metaph., of persons suffering from tetanus, οἱονεὶ ξ. Herod.Med. in *Rh.Mus.*58.90. II. *make of wood,* γαῦλον *IG*11(2).203 *A* 53 (Delos, iii B.C.), cf. 12(3).1270.15 (Syme, ii/i B.C.), Lxx 2*Ch.*3.5:—Pass., ib. *Ez.*41.16; ναὸς ἐξυλωμένος *SIG*996.18 (Smyrna, i A.D.). **-ώδης,** ες, *woody, hard as wood,* Hp.*Vict.*2.65, Arist.*Mete.*387ᵃ32, Thphr.*HP*6.2.2 (Sup.), 7.9.3, Plu.2.953d; *of the nature of wood,* Corn.*ND*19. II. *of the colour of wood, brown,* Thphr.*HP*7.3.2. **-ωμα,** ατος, τό, *piece of woodwork, IG*11(2).163 *A* 20, 29 (Delos, iii B.C.), 12(2).14.9 (Mytil.; ξύλομα lapis). **-ωμάτιον,** τό, Dim. of foreg., ib.11(2).199 *B* 51 (Delos, iii B.C.). **-ών,** ῶνος, ὁ, *place for wood, wood-house,* ib.159 *A* 56, al. (ib., iii B.C.), *Inscr.Delos* 399 *A* 85 (ii B.C.), *Gloss.* **-ωνία,** ἡ, *purchase of wood, IG*12(5).606.6 (Ceos). **-ώροφον,** τό, *wooden roof,* ib.12(3).1102 (Melos). **-ωσις,** εως, ἡ, *woodwork of a building,* ἡ ξ. τῶν οἰκιῶν Th.2.14; στοιῆς *Milet.*3.32 (iii B.C.), J.*AJ*3.6.5.

**ξυμμ-,** for words so beginning, v. συμμ-. **ξύν,** v. σύν: for compds. of ξυν-, v. συν-. **ξυνάν, ξυνάων,** v. ξυνήων.

**ξῠνεείκοσι,** Ep. for συνείκοσι, *twenty together,* Od.14.98.

**ξυνέων,** v. ξυνήων.

**ξύνηβος·** συμπότης, Phot.: ξυνήβιος (sic)· συμπότης, συνῆλιξ, Hsch.

**ξῡνήϊος,** η, ον, Ep. and Ion. (ξύνειος is not found), *common:* neut. pl. ξυνήϊα, τά, *common stock,* Il.1.124, 23.809.

**ξύνημα,** ατος, τό, *javelin-throwing* on horseback while on the wheel, Celtic word, Arr.*Tact.*42.4.

⊛ **ξῡνήων,** ονος, ὁ, Dor. **ξυνάων** [ᾱ], **ξυνάν;** Ion. **ξυνέων;** Att. **ξυνών:**— *joint-owner, partner,* c. gen., κακῶν ἔργων Hes.*Th.*595; ἔργων ἀργαλέων ib.601; ἑλκέων ξυνάονες, i.e. *afflicted by* sores, Pi.*P.*3.48: abs., ξυνάν *friend,* Id.*N.*5.27; ξυνών S.*Fr.*1074; παρθένου σέβας ἤμειψα, παίδων δ' ἐζύγην ξυνάονι prob. in A.*Fr.*99.6; δυοῖν ζευχθεῖσα φίλοις ξυνάοσι τέκνων, i.e. having married two husbands, *Epigr.Gr.*241ᵃ3 (Smyrna). II. as Adj., ἅλα ξυνέωνα the salt *on the common table,* Alex.Aet.3.15.

**ξύνιε, ξυνίει, ξύνιον,** v. συνίημι.

**ξῡνοδοτήρ,** ῆρος, ὁ, *bounteous giver,* epith. of Apollo, *AP*9.525.15.

**ξῡνός,** ή, όν, = κοινός, *common, public, general,* ξ. κακόν Il.16.262; γαῖα δ' ἔτι ξ. πάντων 15.193; ξ. Ἐνυάλιος, i.e. war *hath an even hand,* 18.309; ξ. ἀνθρώποις Ἄρης Archil.62; also of Apollo and Dionysus, *AP*9.524.15, 525.15; ξυναὶ γὰρ τότε δαῖτες ἔσαν ξυνοὶ δὲ θόωκοι Hes.*Fr.*82; ξ. δ' ἐσθλὸν τοῦτο πόληΐ τε παντί τε δήμῳ Tyrt.12.15; ξ. Ἑλλήνων τε καὶ βαρβάρων λόγος Hdt.4.12; ξ. πᾶσι ἀγαθόν Id.7.53; ξ. δόρυ S.*Aj.*180 (lyr.); τὸ ξ. *state, government* (cf. κοινός), *SIG*37 *A* 3 (Teos, v B.C.); ξυνὰ δ' ἐλπίζω λέγειν *for the common good,* A.*Th.*76; ἐν ξυνῷ *in common,* Pi.*P.*9.93: dat. ξυνῇ as Adv., = κοινῇ, A.*Supp.*367, A.R.2.802, Call.*Dian.*36; also neut. pl., ξύν' ἀλέγειν Pi.*I.*8(7).51; χάρις ξύν' ἀπόκειται cj. in S.*OC*1752 (anap.): regul. Adv. ξυνῶς *Epigr.Gr.*520.6.—Ep. (κοινός first in Hes.), Ion. (Heraclit.113, Hdt., v. supr.), and Lyr.; twice in A. (trim.), twice in S. (lyr.); not in E. or Att. Prose.

**ξῡνό-φρων,** ονος, ὁ, ἡ, *friendly-minded,* of Apollo, *AP*9.525.15. **-χᾰρής,** ές, *rejoicing with all alike,* of Apollo, ibid.

⊛**ξῡν-όω,** *cause to participate,* τινὰ ἀνίῃ Nonn.*D.*17.220:—Med., = κοινοῦσθαι, Nearch.ap.Arr.*Ind.*20.4, Man.2.493. **-ών,** v. ξυνήων. **-ωνία,** ἡ, = κοινωνία, *partnership, fellowship,* ἀλώπηξ καἰετὸς ξυνωνίην ἔμειξαν Archil.86. **-ωνός,** ὁ, = κοινωνός, Theognost.*Can.*68.

**ξυνωρίς,** ίδος, ἡ, v. συνωρίς. **ξῠόεσσαν·** εὖ ἐξεσμένην, Hsch.

**ξῠράφιον,** τό, Dim. of ξυρόν, Sch.Ar.*Ach.*849; *surgical knife,* Gal.14.786.

**ξῠρ-έω,** Trag. and Att. (v. infr.); **ξῠράω,** Plu.2.180b, Artem.1.22 (also in pres. Med., D.S.1.84, Palaeph.32, and pres. Pass., Luc.*Cyn.*14); both forms in cod. of Hdt.; cf. ξύρω: fut. -ήσω Lxx *De.*21.12: aor. ἐξύρησα Hp.*Aff.*4, Hdt.5.35, etc.:—**Med.,** fut. ξυρήσομαι Lxx *Ez.*44.20, J.*BJ*2.15.1, Hsch. s. v. πριαμωθήσομαι: aor. ἐξυρησάμην Lxx *Nu.*6.19, al., Luc.*DMeretr.*12.5:—**Pass.,** fut. -ηθήσομαι Lxx *Le.*13.33: pf. ἐξύρημαι (v. infr.): (ξυρόν):—*shave,* ξυροῦντες (v.l. -ῶντες) τῶν παιδίων τὴν κεφαλήν Hdt.2.65: c. dupl. acc., ξυρήσας μιν τὰς τρίχας Id.5.35: prov. of danger or pain, ξυρεῖ γὰρ ἐν χρῷ *it shaves* close, 'touches the quick', S.*Aj.*786; ξυρεῖν ἐπιχειρεῖν λέοντα, of a dangerous undertaking, 'beard the lion', Pl.*R.*341c:—Med. and Pass., *shave oneself* or *have oneself shaved,* ξυρεῦνται (v.l. -ῶνται) Hdt.2.36; ἐξυρημένος ibid., Ar.*Th.*191; ξυρούμενον Alex.264: also c. acc., ξυρεῦνται (v.l. -ῶνται) πᾶν τὸ σῶμα they *shave their* whole body or *have* it *shaved,* Hdt.2.37; τὰς ὀφρύας, τὴν κεφαλήν, ib.66; ἐξυρημένος τὴν κεφαλὴν *with* one's head *shaved,* Luc.*Merc.Cond.*1. **-ήκης,** ες, (ἀκή A) *keen as a razor,* X.*Cyn.*10.3. II. Pass., *close-shaven,* κάρα E.*Ph.*[372], *El.*335; κουρᾷ ξυρήκει with *close* tonsure, Id.*Alc.*427. 2. = sq., Ael.Dion.*Fr.*265, cf. Phot., Suid. **-ήσιμος,** ον, *fit for shaving,* Ael.Dion.*Fr.*265. ⊛**-ησις,** εως, ἡ, *shaving,* Asclep.ap. Gal.12.413, Plu.2.352c (pl.), Archig.ap.Aët.6.28, Alex.Aphr.*Pr.*2.36; *baldness,* Lxx *Is.*22.12. **-ησμός,** ὁ, = foreg., Hdn.*Epim.*180. **-ητής,** οῦ, ὁ, *barber, BGU*630ᵛ10 (ii/iii A.D.). **-ίας,** ου, ὁ, *shaveling,* Poll.4.133, Hsch. s. v. πριαμωθήσομαι. **-ίζω,** = ξυρέω, Sch.Nic.*Al.*410:—**Med.,** fut. inf. -ιεῖσθαι, f.l. for ξυρεῖσθαι, Alciphr.3.66. **-ιον,** τό, Dim. of ξυρόν, Daimach.4 J. (pl.).

⊛ **ξῠρίς,** ίδος, ἡ, *gladwyn, Iris foetidissima,* Dsc.4.22, Plin.*HN*21.143, Gal.12.87:—also written **ξίρις,** Thphr.*HP*9.8.7, Choerob. in *An.Ox.*2.242; **ξειρίς,** Hsch.; **ξείρης,** Ar.*Fr.*831; cf. **ξιρίς.** II. pl., a kind of *shoe,* Phot.

**ξύρισμα** [ῠ], ατος, τό, *shaving,* βοστρύχων Tz.*H.*2.537.

**ξυρμενέσθαι·** ἀδιακρίτως λαλεῖν καὶ καυχᾶσθαι (Att.), Hsch.

**ξῠρο-δόκη,** ἡ, *razor-case,* Ar.*Th.*220: written ξυροδόχη in Poll.10.140. **-θήκη,** ἡ, v.l. for foreg., Id.2.32.

**ξῠρόν,** τό, *razor,* E.*El.*241, Ar.*Ec.*65, *Th.*219, Nic.*Al.*411, Plu.*Art.*29, etc.: prov., ἐπὶ ξυροῦ ἵσταται ἀκμῆς.., ὄλεθρος ἠὲ βιῶναι death or life is balanced on a *razor's* edge, Il.10.173: freq. in later authors, to express a delicately balanced likelihood of failure or success, ἀκμᾶς ἑστακυῖαν ἐπὶ ξυροῦ Ἑλλάδα Simon.97; ἐπὶ ξ. γὰρ ἀκμῆς ἔχεται ἡμῖν τὰ πρήγματα Hdt.6.11; κίνδυνος ἐπὶ ξ. ἵσταται ἀκμῆς Thgn.557;

βεβῶς . . ἐπὶ ξ. τύχης S.*Ant.*996; ἔβητ' ἐπὶ ξ.; E.*HF*630; ἐπὶ ξ. εἶναι Theoc.22.6; ἐπὶ ξ. ἑστηκέναι Luc.*JTr.*3.

**ξυρόν·** τομόν, ἰσχνόν, ὀξύ, Hsch.

**ξῠροποιός,** ὁ, *razor-maker*, *Gloss.*

**ξῠρός,** ὁ, = ξυρόν, Archipp.45, Alciphr.3.66, v.l. in *AP*11.288 (Pall.); ξ. εἰς ἀκόνην, prov. of lucky meetings, Suid.

**ξῠρουργός,** όν, *tonsorial*: ξ. ἀνθρωπάριον Zos.Alch.p.116 B.

**ξῠροφορέω,** *carry a razor*, Ar.*Th.*218.

**ξυρρ-,** for words so beginning, v. συρρ-; cf. ξύν.

**ξύρω** [ῡ], collat. form for ξυρέω: impf. ἔξῡρον Luc.*Pseudol.*27: aor. part. ξύρας Hp.*Morb.*3.1, Tz.*H.*9.231:—Med., *have oneself shaved*, ξύρεσθαι τὸν πώγωνα Chrysipp.*Stoic.*3.198; τὰς κεφαλάς Plu.2.352c (dub.l.): aor. 1, τὴν κ. ξυράμενος ib.336e, cf. Luc.*Syr.D.*53, 55, Alciphr. 3.43.

**ξύστλος** [ῠ], ον, *shaven*, *smooth*, Sophr.55.

**ξῠσ-ις,** εως, ἡ, (ξύω) *ulceration*, *erosion*, τοῦ ἐντέρου Hp.*Acut.*60. b. *excoriation*, Aret.*CD*1.3. 2. *scraping*, *filing*, Hp.*VC*14, cf. Gal. 14.781, Ammon.*in Int.*23.21, *PMed.* in *Arch.Pap.*4.270; *polishing*, *EM*611.20. (ξύσσις is f.l. in codd.). **-μα,** ατος, τό, *filings*, *shavings*, Hp.*Aph.*7.68, *Inscr.Délos* 442 *B* 96 (ii B.C.): in pl., ξύσματα ξύλων Apollod.*Poliorc.*145.13; ξ. ἐλέφαντος Orib.14.62.1. b. *lint*, Erot. s. v. ἄχνη ὀθονίου. c. in pl., *shreds* of flesh, Hp.*Acut.*59; ἐντέρων Gal.8.382, 18(1).730, cf. Dsc.4.176. 2. in pl., *particles*, *motes* in the sunbeam, ψυχὴν εἶναι τὰ ἐν τῷ ἀέρι ξ. Arist.*de An.*404ᵃ 3, cf. *Pr.*913ᵃ9. II. *that which is scratched* on a thing: hence ξύσματα = γράμματα, Hsch. **-μάλιον,** τό, *erosive plaster*, Cyran. 40. **-μάτιον,** τό, Dim. of ξῦσμα I. 1c, Hp.*Epid.*7.84. 2. ξ. ὀθόνης *strip* of linen, Aët.8.27. **-μᾰτώδης,** ες, *full of* ξύσματα I. 1c, διαχωρήματα Hp.*Prog.*11, cf. *Acut.*52 (Comp.), *Coac.*621, Aret. *SD*2.9. **-μή,** ἡ, in pl., *scratchings*, i.e. critical marks in a Ms., *AP*9.206 (Eupith.); γράμματα λέγεται διὰ τὸ γραμμαῖς καὶ ξυσμαῖς τυποῦσθαι D.T.630.28 (v.l. -οῖς ap.Sch.). II. *scab*, as a term of abuse, Sophr.53. **-μός,** ὁ, *itching*, *irritation*, ξυσμοὶ τοῦ σώματος ὅλου Hp.*Aph.*3.31; ξ. ἐν τῷ πλεύμονι Id.*Loc.Hom.*14.

**ξυσσ-,** for words so beginning, v. συσσ-; cf. ξύν.

⊛ **ξυστάδες·** αἱ πυκναὶ ἄμπελοι, Hsch.

⊛ **ξυστάλλιον,** τό, Dim. of ξύστρον II, *IG*11(2).203*B*76 (Delos, iii B.C.).

**ξυσταρχ-έω,** *hold the office of* ξυστάρχης, *Rev.Arch.*1916(1).338 (Sinope), *PLond.*3.1178.58 (ii A.D.). ⊛ **-ης,** ου, ὁ, (ξυστός) *president of an athletic association*, ὃν βασιλῆς . . στῆσαν ἀεθλοθέτην ξυστάρχην *IG* 3.1171, cf. *POxy.*1050.7 (ii/iii A.D.), *Sammelb.*5725, etc.; διὰ βίου ξ. *IGRom.*4.1215 (Smyrna), *IG*14.1102, al. **-ία,** ἡ, *office of* ξυστάρχης, τυχόντα τῆς διὰ γένους ξ. *SIG*1073.9 (Olympia, ii A.D.): in pl., *IG Rom.*4.1419*b*1, *Delph.*3(1).466.6.

⊛ **ξυστ-ήρ,** ῆρος, ὁ, *scraper*, *rasp*, *file*, Hp.*VC*14, Gal.10.445; *polishing instrument*, = λίστρον, Sch.D *Od.*22.455, Hsch. s. v. λίστρον; *graving tool*, *AP*6.205 (Leon.), Daimach.4 J., Plu.2.350e; ξ. λεῖος *Inscr.Délos* 504 (iii B.C.); ξ. ἱερός *IG*7.3498.11 (Oropus, iii/ii B.C.). II. part of the external ear, Gal.14.701. III. a kind of *eye-salve*, Aët.7. 115. **-ηρίδιον,** τό, Dim. of foreg., Phryn.*PS* p.88 B. **-ήριος,** ον, *of* or *for scraping*: τὸ ξ., dentist's *instrument for scaling* teeth, Paul.Aeg.6.28.

**ξυστῐδωτός** (sc. χιτών), ὁ, (ξυστίς II) *garment with ornament in strigil form* (〰), *IG*2².1514.11.

**ξυστικός,** ή, όν, *of* or *for scraping*: ἡ -κή *the art of polishing*, Sch. D.T.p.110 H. 2. *corrosive*, χυμός Phylotim.ap.Ath.3.81b, Gal. *Nat.Fac.*2.9; ξυστικὸν ἔχει τῶν ἐντέρων Alex.Trall.*Febr.*1; of plasters, Orib.*Fr.*88. II. (ξυστός) *taking exercise in a xystus*: hence, *athlete*, *xysticorum certationes* Suet.*Aug.*45; ἀνὴρ ξ. Gal.13.1023; ξ. ἀθληταί *BCH*28.22; ξ. σύνοδος *Athletic* Association, ἡ ἱερὰ θυμελικὴ καὶ ξ. σ. *OGI*713.3 (Alexandria, iii A.D.); ἡ ἱερὰ ξ. περιπολιστικὴ οἰκουμενικὴ σύνοδος *IG*14.956*B*19, cf. *PLond.*3.1178.2 (ii A.D.), etc.

⊛ **ξυστίς,** ίδος, ἡ, *robe of rich and soft material reaching to the feet*, worn by women of quality, Ar.*Lys.*1190 (lyr.), Antiph.99, Eub.90. 3, Theoc.2.74; τρύφημα παρυφές, ξυστίδα Ar.*Fr.*320; ταῖς ξ. ταῖς χρυσοπάστοις Eub.135; ξ. μαλακάς Plu.2.406d; worn by great men (esp. by victorious charioteers in their chariots) as a robe of state, Ar.*Nu.*70, cf. Pl.*R.*420e; by Trag. heroes, Cratin.268, Duris 14, 70 J., cf. Harp. s. v., *AB*284:—Hsch. and Tim.*Lex.*, who say it was also used by Com., prob. refer to the use of the women's ξ. on the Com. stage. II. = ξύστρα, στλεγγίς, Epich.97, Diph.52. (Perh. from ξυστός, ή, όν, as epith. of cloth, orig. *garment made of cut* (*shorn*, *clipped*) *fabric*, such as fustian, plush, velvet, etc.; cf. ξύω IV, ξυστός 3: for the semantic relation between ξυστίς and ξυστόν (pole, spear, etc.), and ξύω, cf. ONorse *skrúð* 'some kind of textile fabric', *skrúð-klæði* 'suit of fine stuff', Engl. *shroud* 'loppings of a tree, branch, bough', both cogn. with *shred*.)

**ξυστοβόλος,** ον, *spear-darting*, of Dionysus, *AP*9.524.15.

**ξυσ-τόν,** τό, (ξύω, lit. *shaved*, sc. δόρυ) *shaft*, *pole*, e.g. spear-*shaft*, ξ. χαλκήρες Il.11.260; μακροῖσι ξ. 13.497, cf. 15.677; opp. λόγχαι (the head), Hdt.1.52, cf. Plu.*Rom.*20. 2. *spear*, E.*Hec.*920 (lyr.); a horseman's *lance*, X.*Cyr.*4.5.58, cf. 7.1.33, Plu.*Aem.*16: pl. ξυστοί Jul.*Or.*2.60a codd. 3. v. ξυστός. **-τός,** ή, όν, (ξύω) *shaved*, *whittled* with a knife or plane, ἀκόντια Hdt.2.71 (nisi del. ἀκόντια); κάμαξ Ar.*Fr.*404; βέλος Antiph.112; δόρατα Arr.*Tact.*40.4. 2. *scraped*, *shredded*, *grated*, τυρός Antiph.113.18; μοτός pledget *of lint*, Gal.14. 795; ἰὸς ὁ ξ. *collected by scraping*, Dsc.5.79; μέτρον ξ. with the top *raked off*, not heaped up, *PFay.*84.7 (ii A.D.). 3. *trimmed*, *cropped* with scissors, μαχαίρᾳ ξύστ' ἔχων τριχώματα Ephipp.14.6. ⊛ **-τός,** ὁ (in full ξυστὸς δρόμος Aristias 5), also **ξυστόν,** τό, *BCH*23.566 (Delph., iii B.C.), *Inscr.Délos* 409*A* 13 (ii B.C.):—*walking-place* in the grounds of a private residence, X.*Oec.*11.15; in a gymnasium, Plu.2.133d, *OGI*764.42 (Pergam.); name of a gymnasium at Elis containing trees and racing-tracks, Paus.6.23.1; open-air *walks* among trees and statuary, Vitr.5.11.5; τὰ τῶν ξ. ἄλση Philostr.*VA*8. 26. 2. *covered colonnade* in a gymnasium, for winter exercise, Vitr. l. c., *Inscr.Délos* l. c. II. *meeting of athletes* from various places to compete in sports, ἀρχιερεὺς τοῦ σύμπαντος ξ. *IG*14.1102, al., cf. 5(1).669 (Sparta); opp. ξυστικὴ σύνοδος, *Inscr.Olymp.*436. (Expld. by Paus. l. c. as a *clearing*, from the action of Heracles in *clearing out* (ἀναξύειν) the thorn-bushes from the ξ. at Elis; perh. orig. 'raked (ground)'.)

**ξυστο-φορέω,** *carry a lance*, in Pass. (cf. δορυφορέω), Alc.*Oxy.*1789 *Fr.*1 i8. **-φόρος,** ον, *lance-bearing*, of horsemen, X.*Cyr.*7.5.41, 8.3.16, Plb.5.53.2, D.S.19.27, Ascl.*Tact.*2.12, Arr.*Tact.*4.4, Plu. *Flam.*17.

⊛ **ξύσ-τρα,** ἡ, *scraper* used after bathing, Hp.*Nat.Mul.*42, Diph.52, *PCair.Zen.*488.1 (iii B.C.), *OGI*339.77 (Sestos, ii B.C.), *PLond.*3.402 ii25 (ii B.C.), Agathin.ap.Orib.10.7.2: later word for στλεγγίς, acc. to Luc.*Lex.*5, Hellad.ap. Phot.*Bibl.*p.533 B., Poll.3.154, Phryn. 266. II. = ὠτεγχύτης, Archig.ap.Gal.12.620. **-τρεία,** ἡ, *set of graving-tools*, *PFay.*347 (ii A.D.). **-τρίον,** τό, Dim. of ξύστρα, *PLond.*2.191.8 (ii A.D.). 2. *small raspatory* at the end of a forceps, Paul.Aeg.6.25. **-τρίς,** ίδος, ἡ, = ξύστρα, Hsch. s. v. στελγίς.

**ξυστρο-ειδής,** ές, *shaped like a* ξύστρα, Erot. s. v. ἄμβην; γωνία Procl.*in Euc.*pp.127, 238 F. ⊛ **-λήκῠθος,** ὁ, *slave who carried his master's* ξυστρίς *and* λήκυθος *to and from the bath*, Hsch.

**ξῦστρον,** τό, *scythe* fixed to chariots, D.S.17.53. II. = ξυστήρ, *BSA*27.228 (Sparta, ii A.D.): condemned by Thom.Mag.p.252 R.

**ξυστρο-ποιός,** όν, *making* ξῦστραι, *Gloss.*; perh. to be read in Dexipp.*in Cat.*12.7. **-φύλαξ** [φῠ], ἄκος, ὁ, *place* or *box for keeping* ξῦστραι *in*, Artem.1.64.

**ξυστρ-όω,** *channel*, *flute*, in Pass., [κίονες] ἐξυστρωμένοι *Ath.Mitt.* 14.109 (Mylasa). ⊛ **-ωτός,** όν, *fluted*, of pillars, Aq., Thd.3*Ki.*6. 18, *PLond.*3.755 *B*3 (iv A.D.); *chamfered*, πυραμίς Hero *Stereom.*2. 66.1.

**ξύφος,** τό, (ξύω) coined as etym. of ξίφος, *EM*611.8.

**ξύω,** Ep. impf. ξῦον Od.22.456: aor. ἔξῡσα Il.14.179, Hp.*VC*14 (ἐγ-ξύσῃ [ῡ] is prob. f.l. for -ξέσῃ in E.*Fr.*298 codd. Stob., and so δι-έξῡσεν for -έξεσεν in Nonn.*D.*39.321):—Med., aor. ἐξῡσάμην X.*Cyr.* 6.2.32:—Pass., Sophr.150: aor. ἐξύσθην Arist.*HA*570ᵃ9, Thphr. *CP*5.6.13: pf. ἔξυσμαι Gal.13.544, (περι-) Hp.*Mul.*2.192:—*scratch*, *scrape*, λίστροισιν δάπεδον ξῦον they *scraped* the floor with rakes, Od. l.c.; *scratch*, prov. τὸν ξύοντα ἀντιξύειν 'claw me, claw thee', Sophr.149; γέροντα κωνείῳ ξύοντα τὴν γῆν *scratching* a diagram *on* the earth, Call.*Iamb.*1.122; τῷ δακτύλῳ [τὴν γῆν] Sch.Ar.*Ach.*31; γράψαι τὸ ξῦσαι παρὰ τοῖς παλαιοῖς (i. e. in Hom., cf. γράφω I. 1) D.T. 630.28: metaph., ξῦσαι ἀπὸ γῆρας ὀλοιόν *scrape* off, get rid of, sad old age, *h.Ven.*224; πᾶσαν ἠόνα ξύων *scouring* the whole coast, of a fisherman, Babr.6.1; = ἐπιξύω, *graze*, of stars which touch the horizon but do not set, Euc.*Phaen.Prooem.*p.2 H.:—Med., *scratch oneself*, ξυόμενοι ἥδονται Democr.127; ξυόμενοι πρὸς τὰ δένδρα ἐκθλίβουσι τοὺς ὄρχεις Arist.*HA*578ᵇ4, cf. *Pr.*953ᵇ37; τὴν κεφαλὴν ξύστρᾳ ξ. Luc. *Lex.*5:—Pass., τοῦ πηλοῦ ξυσθέντος *being scraped up*, Arist.*HA*570ᵃ9; of land, *to be eroded*, *scoured away*, by water, ξυσθείσης καὶ ἀφανισθείσης γῆς *POxy.*1911.193 (vi A.D.). II. *shred*, ξύων τὴν σάρκα [τοῦ χαραδριοῦ] ἐν οἴνῳ διδόναι πίνειν prob. in Hp.*Int.*37; [τιθύμαλλον] ἐν οἴνῳ ξύοντα πίνειν Thphr.*HP*9.11.2. III. *shape by whittling*, *shaving*, or *planing*, κώπας ib.5.1.7:—Med., παλτὸν ξύσασθαι *whittle oneself* a javelin, X.l.c. IV. *shear the nap of* cloth, ἑανὸν ἕσαθ', ὅν οἱ Ἀθήνη ἔξυσ' ἀσκήσασα Il.14.179; cf. ξυστός 3, ξυστίς I.

# O

**O o,** sixteenth (later fifteenth) letter in Gr. alphabet: as numeral ο' = 70, but ͵ο = 70,000. The name of the letter was οὖ, Pl.*Cra.* 414c, al., Callias ap.Ath.10.453d, Neoptol.ap.eund.10.454f, *AP*9.385 (Steph. Gramm.): this name was in Plato's time pronounced like the letter itself, Pl.*Cra.*393d; ο scanned long, Achae.33.4; τὸ ō (v.l. οὖ) στοιχεῖον Suid. s. v. Φιλοξένου γραμμάτιον; later called **ὃ μικρόν** (Hdn.*Epim.*209, Theognost.*Can.*13), *little* or *short o*, opp. **ὦ** μέγα *great* or *long o*.

⊛ **ὁ, ἡ, τό,** is, when thus written, A. demonstr. Pronoun. B. in Att., definite or prepositive Article. C. in Ep., the so-called postpositive Article, = relative Pronoun, ὅς, ἥ, ὅ.—The nom. masc. and fem. sg. and pl., ὁ, ἡ, οἱ, αἱ, have no accent in codd. and most printed books, exc. when used as the relative; but ὁ, ἡ, οἱ, αἱ differ only in writing from ὃ, ἣ, οἳ, αἳ; the nom. forms of the article are said by Hdn.Gr.1.474 to be oxytone, and by A.D.*Pron.*8.7 not to be enclitic. The forms τῶν, τοῖς, ταῖς were barytone (i. e. τὼν, τοὶς, ταὶς) in Aeol. acc. to Aristarch.ap.A.D.*Synt.*51.26. For οἱ, αἱ some dialects (not Cypr., cf. *Inscr.Cypr.*135.30 H., nor Cret., cf. *Leg.Gort.* 5.28, nor Lesbian, cf. Alc.81, Sapph.*Supp.*5.1) and Hom. have τοί, ταί (though οἱ, αἱ are also found in Hom.): other Homeric forms

are gen. sg. τοῖο, gen. and dat. dual τοῖιν Od.18.34, al.: gen. pl. fem. τάων [ᾱ], dat. τοῖσι, τῇς and τῇσι, never ταῖσι or ταῖς in Hom.—In Dor. and all other dialects exc. Att. and Ion. the fem. forms preserve the old ᾱ instead of changing it to η, hence Dor. etc. ἁ, τάν, τᾶς; the gen. pl. τάων contracts in many dialects to τᾶν; the gen. sg. is in many places τῶ, acc. pl. τώς, but Cret., etc., τόνς (*Leg.Gort.*7.7, al.) or τός (ib.3.50, al.); in Lesbian Aeol. the acc. pl. forms are τοὶς, ταὶς, *IG*12(2).645*A*13, *B*62; dat. pl. τοῖς, ταῖς (or τοὶς, ταὶς, v. supr.), ib.645*A*8, ib.1.6; ταῖσι as demonstr., Sapph. 16. The Att. Poets also used the Ion. and Ep. forms τοῖσι, ταῖσι; and in Trag. we find τοὶ μέν.., τοὶ δέ.., for οἱ μέν.., οἱ δέ.., not only in lyr., as A.*Pers.*584, *Th.*295,298; οἱ μέν..τοὶ δ' S.*Aj.*1404 (anap.); but even in a trimeter, A.*Pers.*424. In Att. the dual has usu. only one gender, τὼ θεώ (for τὰ θεά) And.1.113 sq.; τὼ πόλεε Foed.ap. Th.5.23; τὼ ἡμέρα X.*Cyr.*1.2.11; τὼ χεῖρε Id.*Mem.*2.3.18; τοῖν χεροῖν Pl.*Tht.*155e; τοῖν γενεσέοιν Id.*Phd.*71e; τοῖν πολέοιν Isoc.4.75 (τά S.*Ant.*769, Ar.*Eq.*424, 484, ταῖν Lys.19.17, Is.5.16, etc. have been corrected); in Arc. the form τοῖς functions as gen. dual fem., μεσακόθεν τοῖς κράναιυν *Schwyzer*664.8 (Orchom., iv B.C.):—in Elean and Boeot. ὁ, ἡ (ἁ), τό, with the addition of -ί, = ὅδε, ἥδε, τόδε, nom. pl. masc. τυί *the following* men, *Schwyzer*485.14 (Thespiae, iii B.C.), al., cf. infr. VIII. 5. (With ὁ, ἁ, cf. Skt. demonstr. pron. *sa*, *sā*, Goth. *sa*, *sō*, ONorse *sá*, *sú*, Old Lat. acc. *sum*, *sam* (Enn.):—with τό [from *τόδ] cf. Skt. *tat* (*tad*), Lat. *is-tud*, Goth. *þata*:—with τοί cf. Skt. *te*, Lith. *tie*, OE. *þá*, etc.:—with τάων cf. Skt. *tāsām*, Lat. *is-tarum*:—the origin of the relative ὅς, ἥ, ὅ (q.v.) is different.)

A. ὁ, ἡ, τό, DEMONSTR. PRONOUN, *that*, the oldest and in Hom. the commonest sense: freq. also in Hdt.(1.86, 5.35, al.). and sts. in Trag. (mostly in lyr., A.*Supp.*1047, etc.; in trimeters, Id.*Th.*197, *Ag.*7, *Eu.*174; τῶν γάρ.., τῆς γάρ.., Id.*Supp.*358, S.*OT*1082; seldom in Att. Prose, exc. in special phrases, v. infr. VI, VII): **I.** joined with a Subst., to call attention to it, ὁ Τυδεΐδης *he*—Tydeus' *famous* son, Il. 11.660; τὸν Χρύσην *that venerable man* Chryses, 1.11: and so with Appellat., Νέστωρ ὁ γέρων N.—*that* aged man, 7.324; αἰετοῦ..τοῦ θηρητῆρος the eagle, *that which is called* hunter, 21.252, al.; also to define and give emphasis, τιμῆς τῆς Πριάμου for honour, *namely that* of Priam, 20.181; οἴχετ' ἀνὴρ ὤριστος a man is gone, *and he* the best, 11.288, cf. 13.433, al.: sts. with words between the Pron. and Noun, αὐτὰρ ὁ αὖτε Πέλοψ 2.105; τὸν Ἕκτορι μῦθον ἐνίσπες 11.186, cf. 703, al.:—different from this are cases like Il.1.409 αἴ κέν πως ἐθέλῃσιν ἐπὶ Τρώεσσιν ἀρῆξαι, τοὺς δὲ κατὰ πρύμνας τε καὶ ἀμφ' ἅλα ἔλσαι Ἀχαιούς if he would help the Trojans, but drive *those* back to the ships—*I mean* the Achaeans, where Ἀχ. is only added to explain τούς, cf. 1.472, 4.20, 329, al. **II.** freq. without a Subst., *he*, *she*, *it*, ὁ γὰρ ἦλθε Il.1.12, al. **III.** placed after its Noun, before the Relat. Prons., ἐφάμην σὲ περὶ φρένας ἔμμεναι ἄλλων, τῶν ὅσσοι Λυκίην ναιετάουσι far above the rest, *above those to wit* who, etc., Il.17.172; οἵ' οὔ πώ τιν' ἀκούομεν οὐδὲ παλαιῶν, τάων αἳ πάρος ἦσαν..Ἀχαιαί such as we have not heard tell of yet even among the women of old, *those women to wit* who.., Od.2.119, cf. Il.5.332; θάλαμον τὸν ἀφίκετο, τόν ποτε τέκτων ξέσσεν Od.21.43, cf. 1.116, 10.74:—for the Att. usage v. infr. **IV.** before a Possessive Pron. its demonstr. force is sts. very manifest, φθίσει σε τὸ σὸν μένος *that* spirit of thine, Il.6.407, cf. 11.608; but in 15.58, 16.40, and elsewh. it is merely the Art. **V.** for cases in which the Homeric usage approaches most nearly to the Attic, v. infr. B. init. **VI.** ὁ μέν.., ὁ δέ.. without a Subst., in all cases, genders, and numbers, Hom., etc.: sts. in Opposition, where ὁ μέν prop. refers to *the former*, ὁ δέ to *the latter*; more rarely ὁ μέν *the latter*, ὁ δέ *the former*, Pl.*Prt.*359e, Isoc.2.32,34: sts. in Partition, *the one*.., *the other*.., etc.—The Noun with it is regularly in gen. pl., being divided by the ὁ μέν.., ὁ δέ.., into parts, ἠΐθεοι καὶ παρθένοι.., τῶν δ' αἱ μὲν λεπτὰς ὀθόνας ἔχον, οἱ δὲ χιτῶνας εἵατο Il.18.595; τῶν πόλεων αἱ μὲν τυραννοῦνται, αἱ δὲ δημοκρατοῦνται, αἱ δὲ ἀριστοκρατοῦνται Pl.*R.*338d, etc.: but freq. the Noun is in the same case, by a kind of apposition, ἴδον υἷε Δάρητος, τὸν μὲν ἀλευάμενον τὸν δὲ κτάμενον Il.5.28, cf. Od.12.73, etc.: so in Trag. and Att., S.*Ant.*22, etc.; πηγὴ ἡ μὲν εἰς αὐτὸν ἔδυ, ἡ δὲ ἔξω ἀπορρεῖ Pl.*Phdr.*255c; if the Noun be collective, it is in the gen. sg., ὁ μὲν πεπραμένος ἦν τοῦ σίτου, ὁ δὲ ἔνδον ἀποκείμενος D.42.6: sts. a Noun is added in apposition with ὁ μέν or ὁ δέ, ὁ μὲν οὖτασ' Ἀτύμνιον ὀξέϊ δουρὶ Ἀντίλοχος.., Μάρις δὲ.. Il.16.317–19, cf. 116; τοὺς μὲν τὰ δίκαια ποιεῖν ἠνάγκασα, τοὺς πλουσίους, τοὺς δὲ πένητας κτλ. D.18.102, cf. Pl.*Grg.*501a, etc. **2.** when a neg. accompanies ὁ δέ, it follows δέ, e.g. τὰς γοῦν Ἀθήνας οἶδα τὸν δὲ χῶρον οὔ S.*OC*24; τὸν φιλόσοφον σοφίας ἐπιθυμητὴν εἶναι, οὐ τῆς μὲν τῆς δ' οὔ, ἀλλὰ πάσης Pl.*R.*475b; οὐ πάσας χρὴ τὰς δόξας τιμᾶν, ἀλλὰ τὰς μὲν τὰς δ' οὔ· οὐδὲ πάντων, ἀλλὰ τῶν μὲν τῶν δ' οὔ Id.*Cri.*47a, etc. **3.** ὁ μέν τις.., ὁ δέ τις.. is used in Prose, when the Noun to which ὁ refers is left indefinite, ἔλεγον ὁ μέν τις τὴν σοφίαν, ὁ δὲ τὴν καρτερίαν.., ὁ δέ τις καὶ τὸ κάλλος X.*Cyr.*3.1.41; νόμους..τοὺς μὲν ὀρθῶς τιθέασιν τοὺς δέ τινας οὐκ ὀρθῶς Pl.*R.*339c, cf. *Phlb.*13c. **4.** on τὸ μέν.., τὸ δέ.., or τὰ μέν.., τὰ δέ.., v. infr. VIII. 4. **5.** ὁ μέν is freq. used without a corresponding ὁ δέ, οἱ μὲν ἄρ' ἐσκίδναντο.., Μυρμιδόνας δ' οὐκ εἴα ἀποσκίδνασθαι Il.23.3, cf. 24.722, Th.8.12, etc.: also folld. by ἀλλά, ἡ μὲν γάρ μ' ἐκέλευε.., ἀλλ' ἐγὼ οὐκ ἔθελον Od.7.304; by ἄλλος δέ, Il.6.147, etc.; τὸν μὲν.., ἕτερον δέ Ar.*Av.*843, etc.; ὁ μέν.., ὃς δέ.. Thgn.205 (v. l. οὐδέ): less freq. ὁ δέ in the latter clause without ὁ μέν preceding, τῇ ῥα παραδραμέτην φεύγων, ὁ δ' ὄπισθε διώκων (for ὁ μὲν φεύγων) Il.22.157; σφραγῖδε.. χρυσοῦν ἔχουσα τὸν δακτύλιον, ἡ δ' ἑτέρα ἀργυροῦν *IG*2[2].1388.45, cf. μέν D. III; γεωργὸς μὲν εἷς, ὁ δὲ οἰκοδόμος, ἄλλος δέ τις ὑφαντής Pl.*R.*369d, cf. *Tht.*181d. **6.** ὁ δέ following μέν sts. refers to the subject of the preceding clause, τοῦ μὲν ἅμαρθ', ὁ δὲ Λεῦκον..βεβλήκει Il. 4.491; τὴν μὲν γενομένην αὐτοῖσι αἰτίην οὐ μάλα ἐξέφαινε, ὁ δὲ ἔλεγέ σφι Hdt.6.3, cf. 1.66, 6.9, 133, 7.6: rare in Att. Prose, ἐπεψήφιζεν αὐτὸς ἔφορος ὤν· ὁ δὲ οὐκ ἔφη διαγιγνώσκειν τὴν βοήν Th.1.87; ἔμενον ὡς κατέχοντες τὸ ἄκρον· οἱ δ' οὐ κατεῖχον X.*An.*4.2.6: this is different from ὁ δέ in apodosi, v. infr. 7; also from passages in which both clauses have a common verb, v. ὅ γε II. **7.** ὁ δέ is freq. used simply in continuing a narrative, Il.1.43, etc.; also used by Hom. in apodosi after a relat., v. ὅδε III. 3. **8.** the opposition may be expressed otherwise than by μέν and δέ, οὔθ' ὁ..οὔθ' ὁ Il.15.417; ἢ τοῖσιν ἢ τοῖς A.*Supp.*439; οὔτε τοῖς οὔτε τοῖς Pl.*Lg.*701e. **VII.** the following usages prevailed in Att. Prose, **1.** in dialogue, after καί, it was usual to say in nom. sg. masc. καὶ ὅς; in the other cases the usual forms of the Art. were used (v. ὅς A. II. 1 and cf. Skt. *sas*, alternat. form of *sa*); so, in acc., καὶ τὸν εἰπεῖν Pl.*Smp.*174a, cf. X.*Cyr.*1.3.9, etc.; also in Hdt., καὶ τὴν φράσαι 6.61, al. **2.** ὁ καὶ ὁ *such and such*, τῇ καὶ τῇ ἀτιμίᾳ Pl.*Lg.*721b: but mostly in acc., καί μοι κάλει τὸν καὶ τόν Lys.1.23, cf. Pl.*Lg.*784d; τὰ καὶ τὰ πεπονθώς D.21.141, cf. 9.68; τὸ καὶ τό Id.18.243; ἀνάγκη ἄρα τὸ καὶ τό it must then be *so and so*, Arist.*Rh.*1401[a]4, cf. 1413[a]22; but τὰ καὶ τά *now one thing, now another*, of good and bad, τὸν δ' ἀγαθὸν τολμᾶν χρὴ τά τε καὶ τὰ φέρειν Thgn.398, cf. Pi.*P.*5.55, 7.20, al.; τῶν τε καὶ τῶν καιρόν Id.*O.*2.53; so πάντα τοῦ μετρίου μεταβαλλόμενα ἐπὶ τὰ καὶ ἐπὶ τά, of excess and defect, Hp.*Acut.*46; cf. A. VI. 8. **VIII.** abs. usages of single cases, **1.** fem. dat. τῇ, of Place, *there*, *on that spot*, *here*, *this way*, *that way*, Il.5.752, 858, al.: folld. by ᾗ, 13.52, etc.: also in Prose, τὸ μὲν τῇ, τὸ δὲ τῇ X.*Ath.*2.12. **b.** with a notion of motion towards, *that way*, *in that direction*, Il.10.531, 11.149, 12.124: τῇ ἴμεν ᾗ.. 15.46; δελφῖνες τῇ καὶ τῇ ἐθύνεον ἰχθυάοντες Hes.*Sc.*210:—only poet. **c.** of Manner, τῇ περ τελευτήσεσθαι ἔμελλεν *in this way*, *thus*, Od.8.510. **d.** repeated, τῇ μέν.., τῇ δέ.., *in one way*.., *in another*.., or *partly*.., *partly*.., E.*Or.*356, Pl.*Smp.*211a, etc.: without μέν, τῇ μᾶλλον, τῇ δ' ἧσσον Parm.8.48. **e.** relat., *where*, *by which way*, only Ep., as Il.12.118, Od.4.229. **2.** neut. dat. τῷ, *therefore*, *on this account*, freq. in Hom., Il.1.418, 2.254, al. (v. infr.): also in Trag., A.*Pr.*239, S.*OT*510 (lyr.); in Prose, τῷ τοι.. Pl.*Tht.*179d, *Sph.*230b. **b.** *thus*, *so*, Il.2.373, 13.57, etc.: it may also, esp. when εἰ precedes, be translated, *then*, *if this be so*, *on this condition*, Od.1.239, 3.224, 258, al., Theoc.29.11.—In Hom. the true form is prob. τῶ, as in cod. A, or τώ, cf. A.D.*Adv.*199.2. **3.** neut. acc. τό, *wherefore*, Il.3.176, Od.8.332, al., S.*Ph.*142 (lyr.); also τὸ δέ abs., but *the fact is*.., Pl.*Ap.*23a, *Men.*97c, *Phd.*109d, *Tht.*157b, *R.*340d, *Lg.*967a; even when the τό refers to what precedes, the contrast may lie not in the thing referred to, but in another part of the sentence (cf. supr. VI. 6), τὸ δ' ἐπὶ κακουργίᾳ.. ἐπετήδευσαν Th.1.37; τὸ δὲ..ἡμῖν μᾶλλον περιέσται Id.2.89; φασὶ δέ τινες αὐτὸν καὶ τῶν ἑπτὰ σοφῶν γεγονέναι· τὸ δὲ οὐκ ἦν but he was not, Nic.Dam.58 J. **4.** τὸ μέν.., τὸ δέ.., *partly*.., *partly*.., or *on the one hand*.., *on the other*.., Th.7.36, etc., cf. Od.2.46; more freq. τὰ μέν.., τὰ δέ.., Hdt.1.173, S.*Tr.*534, etc.; also τὰ μέν τι.., τὰ δέ τι.. X.*An.*4.1.14; τὸ μέν τι.., τὸ δέ τι.. Luc.*Macr.*14; τὰ μέν.., τὸ δὲ πλέον.. Th.1.90: sts. without τὸ μέν.. in the first clause, τὸ δέ τι Id.1.107, 7.48: rarely of Time, τὰ μὲν πολλὰ.., τέλος δέ several *times*.. and finally, Hdt.3.85. **5.** of Time, sts. *that* time, sts. *this* (present) time, συνμαχία κ' ἔα ἑκατὸν ϝέτεα, ἄρχοι δέ κα τοΐ (where it is possible, but not necessary, to supply ϝέτος) *SIG*9.3 (Olympia, vi B.C.): so with Preps., ἐκ τοῦ, Ep. τοῖο, from *that* time, Il.1.493, 15.601. **b.** πρὸ τοῦ, sts. written προτοῦ, *before this*, *aforetime*, Hdt.1.103, 122, 5.55, A.*Ag.*1204, Ar.*Nu.*5, etc.; ἐν τῷ πρὸ τοῦ χρόνῳ Th.1.32, cf. A.*Eu.*462; τὸ πρὸ τοῦ D.S.20.59. **c.** in Thess. Prose, ὑππρὸ τᾶς *yesterday*, τὰ ψαφίσματα τό τε ὑππρὸ τᾶς γενόμενον καὶ τὸ τᾶμον the decree which was passed *yesterday* (lit. before *this* [day]), and to-day's, *IG*9(2).517.43 (Larissa, iii B.C.). **6.** ἐν τοῖς is freq. used in Prose with Superlatives, ἐν τοῖσι θειότατον a *most* marvellous thing, Hdt.7.137; ἐν τοῖς πρῶτοι the *very* first, Th.1.6, etc.; ἐν τοῖσι πρῶτος (πρώτοις codd.) Pherecr.145.4; [Ζεὺς] Ἔρωτά τε καὶ Ἀνάγκην ἐν τοῖς πρῶτα ἐγέννησεν first *of all*, Aristid.*Or.*43(1).16, cf. 37(2).2: when used with fem. Nouns, ἐν τοῖς remained without change of gender, ἐν τοῖς πλεῖσται δὴ νῆες the greatest number of ships, Th.3.17; ἐν τοῖς πρώτη ἐγένετο (sc. ἡ στάσις) ib.82: also with Advbs., ἐν τοῖς μάλιστα Id.8.90, Pl.*Cri.*52a, Plu.2.74e, 421d, 723e, *Brut.*6, 11, al., Paus.1.16.3, etc.; ἐν τοῖς χαλεπώτατα Th.7.71; τὴν Αἴγυπτον ἐν τοῖς μάλιστα μελάγγειον οὖσαν Plu.2.364c: in late Prose, also with Positives, ἐν τοῖς παράδοξον Aristid.*Or.*48(24).47 codd.; with πάνυ, ἐν τοῖς πάνυ D.H.1.19, cf. 66 (ἐν ταῖς πάνυ f.l. 4.14,15).

B. ὁ, ἡ, τό, THE DEFINITE ARTICLE, *the*, to specify individuals: rare in this signf. in the earliest Gr., becoming commoner later. In Hom. the demonstr. force can generally be traced, v. supr. A. I, but the definite Art. must be recognized in places like Il.1.167, 7.412, 9.309, 12.289, Od.19.372: also when joined to an Adj. to make it a Subst., αἰὲν ἀποκτείνων τὸν ὀπίστατον *the hindmost man*, Il.11.178; τὸν ἄριστον 17.80; τὸν δύστηνον 22.59; τὸν προὔχοντα 23.325; τῷ πρώτῳ.., τῷ δευτέρῳ.., etc., ib.265 sq.; also in τῶν ἄλλων 2.674, al.: with Advs., τὸ πρίν 24.543, al.; τὸ πάρος περ 17.720; τὸ πρόσθεν 23.583; also τὸ τρίτον ib.733; τὰ πρῶτα 1.6, al.; τὸ μὲν ἄλλο for *the* rest, 23.454; ἀνδρῶν τῶν τότε 9.559.—The true Art., however, is first fully established in fifth-cent. Att., whilst the demonstr. usage

disappears, exc. in a few cases, v. A. VI–VIII.—Chief usages, esp. in Att. I. not only with common Appellats., Adjs., and Parts., to specify them as present to sense or mind, but also freq. where we use the Possessive Pron., τὸ κέαρ ηὐφράνθην Ar.*Ach.*5; τὴν κεφαλὴν κατεάγην *my* head was broken, And.1.61, etc.; τοὺς φίλους ποιούμεθα we make *our* friends, S.*Ant.*190; τὰς πόλεις ἔκτιζον they began founding *their* cities, Th.1.12; οὐχ ὑπὲρ τὴν οὐσίαν ποιούμενοι τοὺς παῖδας Pl.*R.*372b. b. omitted with pr. nn. and freq. with Appellats. which require no specification, as θεός, βασιλεύς, v. θεός I. 1, βασιλεύς III; ἐμ πόλει in *the* Acropolis, *IG*1².4.1, al.: but added to pr. nn., when attention is to be called to the previous mention of the person, as Th.(3.70) speaks first of Πειθίας and then refers to him repeatedly as ὁ Π.; cf. Θράσυλος in Id.8.104, with ὁ Θ. ib.105; or when the person spoken of is to be specially distinguished, Ζεύς, ὅστις ὁ Ζεύς whoever *this* Zeus is, E.*Fr.*480; and therefore properly omitted when a special designation follows, as Σωκράτης ὁ φιλόσοφος: seldom in Trag. with pr. nn., save to give pecul. emphasis, like Lat. *ille*, ὁ Λάϊος, ὁ Φοῖβος, S.*OT*729, *El.*35, etc.: later, however, the usage became very common (the Homeric usage of ὁ with a pr. n. is different, v. A. I). c. Aristotle says Σωκράτης meaning the historical Socrates, as in *SE*183b7, *PA*642a28, al., but ὁ Σωκράτης when he means the Platonic Socrates, as *Pol.*1261a6, al.: so with other pr. nn., *EN*1145a21, 1146a21, al. d. for Σαῦλος ὁ καὶ Παῦλος, etc., v. καί B. 2. 2. in a generic sense, where the individual is treated as a type, οἷς ὁ γέρων μετέησιν.. λεύσσει Il.3.109; πονηρὸν ὁ συκοφάντης D.18.242, etc. b. freq. with abstract Nouns, ἥ τε ἐλπὶς καὶ ὁ ἔρως Th.3.45, etc. 3. of outstanding members of a class, ὁ γεωγράφος, ὁ κωμικός, ὁ ποιητής, ὁ τεχνικός, v. γεωγράφος, κωμικός, ποιητής, τεχνικός. 4. with infs., which thereby become Substs., τὸ εἴργειν prevention, Pl.*Grg.*505b; τὸ φρονεῖν good sense, S.*Ant.*1348 (anap.), etc.: when the subject is expressed it is put between the Art. and the inf., τὸ θεοὺς εἶναι *the* existence of gods, Pl.*Phd.* 62b; τὸ μηδένα εἶναι ὄλβιον *the fact* or *statement* that no one is happy, Hdt.1.86. 5. in neut. before any word or expression which itself is made the object of thought, τὸ ἄνθρωπος *the word* or *notion* man; τὸ λέγω *the word* λέγω; τὸ μηδὲν ἄγαν *the sentiment* 'ne quid nimis', E.*Hipp.*265 (lyr.); τὸ τῇ αὐτῇ *the phrase* τῇ αὐτῇ, Pl.*Men.*72e: and so before whole clauses, ἡ δόξα.. περὶ τοῦ οὕστινας δεῖ ἄρχειν the opinion about *the question* 'who ought to rule', Id.*R.*431e; τὸ ἐὰν μένητε παρ' ἐμοί, ἀποδώσω *the phrase* 'I will give back, if..', X.*Cyr.* 5.1.21, cf. Pl.*R.*327c, etc.; τοὺς τοῦ τί πρακτέον λογισμούς D.23. 148; τὸ ὀλίγοι *the term* few, Arist.*Pol.*1283b11. 6. before relat. clauses, when the Art. serves to combine the whole relat. clause into one notion, τῇ ἣ φῂς σὺ σκληρότητι *the* harshness you speak of, Pl.*Cra.*435a; τὸν ἥμερον καρπόν.., καὶ τὸν ὅσος ξύλινος (i.e. καὶ τὸν καρπὸν ὅσος ἂν ᾖ ξύλινος) Id.*Criti.*115b; τῶν ὅσοι ἄν.. ἀγαθοὶ κριθῶσιν Id.*R.*469b; ἐκ γῆς καὶ πυρὸς μείξαντες καὶ τῶν ὅσα πυρὶ καὶ γῇ κεράννυνται Id.*Prt.*320d, cf. Hyp.*Lyc.*2; ταύτην τε τὴν αἰτίαν καὶ τὴν ὅθεν ἡ κίνησις Arist.*Metaph.*987a8; τὸν ὃς ἔφη Lys.23.8: hence the relat., by attraction, freq. follows the case of the Art., τοῖς οἵοις ἡμῖν τε καὶ ὑμῖν, i.e. τοῖς οὖσιν οἷοι ἡμεῖς καὶ ὑμεῖς, X.*HG*2.3.25, etc. 7. before Prons., a. before the pers. Prons., giving them greater emphasis, but only in acc., τὸν ἐμέ Pl.*Tht.*166a, *Phlb.*20b; τὸν.. σὲ καὶ ἐμέ ib.59b; τὸν αὑτόν Id.*Phdr.*258a; on ὁ αὐτός, v. αὐτός III. b. before the interrog. Pron. (both τίς and ποῖος), referring to something before, which needs to be more distinctly specified, A.*Pr.*251, Ar.*Pax*696; also τὰ τί; because οἷα went before, ib.693. Of τίς only the neut. is thus used (v. supr.): ποῖος is thus used not only in neut. pl., τὰ ποῖα; E.*Ph.*707; but also in the other genders, ὁ ποῖος; ib. 1704; τῆς ποίας μερίδος; D.18.64; τοῖς ποίοις..; Arist.*Ph.*227b1. c. with τοιοῦτος, τοιόσδε, τηλικοῦτος, etc., the Art. either makes the Pron. into a Subst., ὁ τοιοῦτος *that sort of person*, X.*Mem.*4.2.21, etc.; or subjoins it to a Subst. which already has an Art., τὴν ἀπολογίαν τὴν τοιαύτην D.41.13. 8. before ἅπας, Pi.*N.*1.69, Hdt.3.64, 7.153 (s.v.l.), S.*OC*1224 (lyr.), D.18.231, etc.; also τὸν ἕνα, τὸν ἕνα τοῦτον, Arist.*Pol.*1287b8, 1288a19: on its usage with ἕκαστος, v. sub voc.; and on οἱ ἄλλοι, οἱ πολλοί, etc., v. ἄλλος II. 6, πολύς II. 3, etc. 9. the Art. with the Comp. is rare, if ἤ follows, S.*Ant.*313, *OC*796. II. elliptic expressions: 1. before the gen. of a pr. n.. to express descent, *son* or *daughter*, Θουκυδίδης ὁ Ὀλόρου (sc. υἱός) Th.4.104; Ἑλένη ἡ τοῦ Διός (sc. θυγάτηρ) E.*Hel.*470: also to denote other relationships, e.g. *brother*, Lys.32.24, Alciphr.2.2. 10; ἡ Σμικυθίωνος Μελιστίχη M. *the wife* of S., Ar.*Ec.*46; Κλέαρχος καὶ οἱ ἐκείνου Cl. and his *men*, X.*An.*1.2.15; ὁ τοῦ Ἀντιγένεος *the slave* of A., Hp.*Hum.*20. 2. generally, before a gen. it indicates a wider relation, as τὸ τῶν νεῶν, τὸ τῶν Ἑρμῶν, *the matter of* the ships, *the affair of* the Hermae, Th.4.23, 6.60; τὰ τοῦ Ἀρριβαίου πράσσειν to promote *the interests* of Arrhibaeus, Id.4.83, cf. 6.89, etc.; τὸ τῆς τύχης, = ἡ τύχη, Id.4.18; τὰ τῆς τύχης *accidents, chance events*, ib.55; τὰ γὰρ φθιτῶν τοῖς δρῶσι κόσμος performance of *the rites due to* the dead befits the living, E.*Supp.*78 (lyr.); τὰ τῶν θεῶν *that which is destined* by the gods, S.*Tr.*498 (lyr.): hence with neut. of Possessive Pron., τὸ ἐμόν, τὸ σόν, *what regards* me or thee, my or thy business or interests, S.*Aj.*124, *El.*251, etc.: and with gen. of 3 pers., τὸ τῆσδε E.*Hipp.*48. But τὸ τινος is freq. also, *a man's word* or *saying*, as τὸ τοῦ Σόλωνος Hdt.1.86; τὸ τοῦ Ὁμήρου *as* Homer says, Pl.*Tht.*183e; also τά τινος so-and-so's *house*, Ar.*V.*1432, D.54.7, Theoc.2.76, Herod.5.52, *Ev.Luc.*2.49. 3. very freq. with cases governed by Preps., αἱ ἐκ τῆς Ζακύνθου νῆες *the* ships from Zacynthus, Th.4.13; οἱ ἀμφί τινα, οἱ περί τινα, such an one and his followers, v. ἀμφί C. I. 3, περί C. I. 2; also τὰ ἐπὶ Θρᾴκης *the* Thrace-ward *district*, Th.1.59, al.; τὰ ἀπὸ τοῦ καταστρώματος *matters* on deck, Id.7.70; τὰ ἀπ' Ἀλκιβιάδου *the proposals* of Alcibiades, Id.8.48; τὰ ἀπὸ τῆς τύχης *the incidents* of fortune, Id.2.87, etc. 4. on μὰ τόν, μὰ τήν, etc., v. μά IV. 5. in elliptical phrases, ἐπορευόμην τὴν ἔξω τείχους (sc. ὁδόν) Pl.*Ly.*203a; ἡ ἐπὶ θανάτῳ (sc. στολή, δέσις), v. θάνατος; κατὰ τὴν ἐμήν (sc. γνώμην), v. ἐμός II. 4; ἡ αὔριον (sc. ἡμέρα), v. αὔριον: ἡ Λυδιστί (sc. ἁρμονία) Arist.*Pol.*1342b32, etc.: freq. with Advs., which thus take an adj. sense, as ὁ, ἡ, τὸ νῦν, v. νῦν; ὁ οἴκαδε πλοῦς Th.1.52; οἱ τότε, οἱ ἔπειτα (sc. ἄνθρωποι), ib.9, 10, etc.; but τό stands abs. with Advs. of time and place, when one cannot (as in the preceding instances) supply a Subst., as κἀκεῖσε καὶ τὸ δεῦρο E.*Ph.*266, cf. [315] (lyr.); ὁ μὲν τὸ κεῖθεν, ὁ δὲ τὸ κεῖθεν Id.*Or.*1412 (lyr.): rarely abs. in gen., ἰέναι τοῦ πρόσω to go forward, X.*An.*1.3.1; τοῦ προσωτάτω δραμεῖν S.*Aj.*731.

C. as RELATIVE PRONOUN in many dialects; both in nom. sg. masc. ὅ, as κλῦθί μοι, ὃ χθιζὸς θεὸς ἤλυθες Od.2.262, cf. 1.300, al.; Ἔρως, ὃ κατ' ὀμμάτων στάζεις πόθον E.*Hipp.*526 (lyr.); Ἄδωνις, ὃ κὴν Ἀχέροντι φιλεῖται Theoc.15.86; ὃ ἐξορύξῃ *he who* banishes him, *Schwyzer*679.12.25 (Cyprus); and in the forms beginning with τ, esp. in Hom. (Od.4.160, al.), Hdt.1.7, al.: also in Ion. Poets, ἐν τῷ κάθημαι Archil.87.3, cf. Semon.7.3, Anacr.86 (prob.), Herod.2.64, al.: freq. in Trag., τῆς S.*OC*1258, *Tr.*381, 728, E.*Alc.*883 (anap.); τῷ S.*Ph.*14; τήν Id.*OC*747, *Tr.*47, *El.*1144; τό Id.*OT*1427; τῶν ib. 1379, *Ant.*1086.—Never in Com. or Att. Prose:—Ep. gen. sg. τεῦ Il.18.192 (s.v.l.).

D. CRASIS OF ARTICLE: a. Att. ὁ, ἡ, τό, with ᾰ make ᾱ, as ἀνήρ, ἀλήθεια, τἀγαθόν, τἄτιον; so οἱ, αἱ, τά, as ἄνδρες, τἀγαθά; also τοῦ, τῷ, as τἀγαθοῦ, τἀγαθῷ: ὁ, τό, οἱ, before ε gives ου, οὑξ, οὑπί, οὑμός, τοὔργον, οὑπιχώριοι, etc.; also τοῦ, as τοὐμοῦ, τοὐπιόντος; but ἅτερος, θἄτερον (– ∪ ∪), Ion. οὕτερος, τοὔτερον (v. ἕτερος), Att. fem. ἡτέρα, dat. θητέρᾳ (v. ἕτερος); τῷ loses the iota, τὠμῷ, τὠπιόντι: ὁ, τό, before ο gives ου, as Οὑδυσσεύς, Οὑλύμπιος, τοὔνομα: ὁ, τό, etc., before αυ gives ᾱυ, αὑτός, ταὐτό, ταὐτῷ (freq. written ἁτός, etc. in Inscrr. and Pap.); so τὰ αὐτά = ταὐτά, αἱ αὐταί = αὑταί: ἡ before εὐ gives ηὐ, as ηὐλάβεια: τῇ before ἡ gives θη, as θἠμέρᾳ: τὸ before ὑ gives θου, as θοὔδωρ for τὸ ὕδωρ. b. other dialects: in their treatment of crasis these follow the local laws of contraction, hence, e.g., Dor. ὡξ from ὁ ἐξ Theoc.1.65, ὤλαφος from ὁ ἔλαφος ib.135; Ion. ὡσυμνήτης from ὁ αἰσ– *SIG*57.45 (Milet., V B.C.); ὡυτή from ἡ αὐτή Heraclit.60, etc.

ὅ, relat. Pron. masc. for ὅς, v. ὁ, ἡ, τό C. II. ὅ, neut. of relat. Pron. ὅς. III. ὃ ὃ ὅ, Interj., Ar.*Th.*1191.

ὀ-, insep. Prefix, v. α- II.

ὅ γε, ἥ γε, τό γε, the demonstr. Pron. ὁ, ἡ, τό, made slightly (if at all) more emphatic by the addition of γε, *he, she, it*: I. Τεῦκρον ..καὶ Λήϊτον.., τοὺς ὅ γ' ἐποτρύνων Il.13.94; πάντες ἄρ' οἵ γ' ἔθελον 7.169; κεῖνος ὅ γε.. ἧσται there *he* sitteth, 19.344; with a Subst., ὅ γ' ἥρως *he* the hero, 5.327; τόν γε ἄνακτα ib.794. II. in one clause of a disjunctive sentence, either the former, πατὴρ δ' ἐμὸς.. ζώει ὅ γ' ἢ τέθνηκε Od.2.132, cf. 3.90, 4.821; or the latter, ἤ τινας ἐκ Πύλου ἄξει.., ἢ ὅ γε καὶ Σπάρτηθεν 2.327; so λάθοι ἂν ἤτοι μανεὶς ἢ ὅ γε ἀπόπληκτος γενόμενος Hdt.2.173: so also in an adversative clause, Θέτις δ' οὐ λήθετ' ἐφετμέων.., ἀλλ' ἥ γ' ἀνεδύσετο Il.1.496, cf. 11. 226. III. after ὥς (*thus*), ib.136, al. IV. Adverbial usages: 1. dat. τῇ γε, *there, at that point*, 6.435. 2. acc. neut. τό γε, *on that account*, 5.827, Od.17.401.

ὀᾶ, Interj., *woe, woe!*, c. gen., A.*Pers.*117, 122 (both lyr.).

*ὄα (A), ἡ, *service-tree*, *Sorbus domestica*, Thphr., etc.: ὄα in Hsch., but codd. of Thphr. have ὄη in *HP*2.2.10; ὄα in 2.7.7; οἴη in 3.12.9, 3.15.4, *CP*3.1.4; οὖα in *HP*3.6.5. II. its fruit was ὄον, τό, *sorb-apple*, or *service-berry*, which was split and pickled for use, Pl.*Smp.* 190d, Dsc.1.120:—in Pl. l.c. codd. have ᾠά, ὠά, and in Dsc. οὖα, which latter form also occurs in Hp.*Vict.*2.55, Thphr.*HP*3.2.1, *CP* 2.8.2; ὄη τὸ δένδρον, ἧς ὁ καρπὸς ὄα καλεῖται, ὑπὸ δὲ τῶν πολλῶν οὖα Gal.12.87.

ὄα (B) or ὀά, ἡ, = ᾤα, *hem* or *border*, A.*Fr.*280A, Ar.*Fr.*228; σινδόνας.. αἳ ὄας ἔχουσιν prob. in *CIG*2860 ii 7 (Didyma), cf. Poll.7.62, Ael.Dion.*Fr.*266. II. *sheep-skin*, v. ᾤα.

ὀάννες· ἔνεδραι, Hsch. (θράννες· ἕδραι cj. Schmidt). ὄαοι· μόνοι, Id. (Fort. οἶϝοι.)

ὄαρ, ὄαρος, ἡ, *wife*, in gen. pl., ὀάρων ἕνεκα σφετεράων Il.9.327: contr. dat. pl., ἀμυνέμεναι ὤρεσσι 5.486: acc. pl., ὄαρας· γάμους, οἱ δὲ γυναῖκας, Hsch.

ὀαρ-ίζω (ὄαρος), Ep. Verb, used only in pres. and impf., *converse* or *chat with* (Luc.*Par.*43), c. dat. pers., ὅθι ἡ ὀάριζε γυναικί Il.6.516; τῷ ὀαριζέμεναι (v. δρῦς) 22.127; μετ' ἀθανάτοις ὀαρίζειν h.*Merc.*170: c. acc. cogn., ὀάρους ὀαρίζει h.*Hom.*23.3: contr. impf., ὠρίζεσκον φιλότητι h.*Merc.*58. *-ισμα, ατος, τό, *familiar converse*, in pl., Opp. *C.*4.23. -ισμός, ὁ, = foreg., in pl., Hes.*Op.*789; εὐναῖοι ὀ. Call. *Fr.*118: in sg., Q.S.7.316. -ιστής, οῦ, ὁ, *familiar friend*, Μίνως.. Διὸς μεγάλου ὀαριστής Od.19.179, cited by Pl.*Min.*319d; Πυθαγόρην ..σεμνηγορίης ὀ. Timo 57. -ιστύς, ύος, ἡ, Ep., = ὀαρισμός, *familiar converse, fond discourse*, Il.14.216; title of Theoc.27: generally, ἡ γὰρ πολέμου ὀ. such is war's *intercourse*, Il.17.228. II. as concrete, προμάχων ὀ. *the company* of out-fighters, 13.291. -οι, = γυναῖκες, Hsch. (formed from gen. ὀάρων Il.9.327). -ος, ὁ, = ὀαριστύς, mostly in pl., Θέμιστι.. ὀάρους ὀαρίζει h.*Hom.*23.3; ἐμοὺς

ὀάρους καὶ μήτιας *h.Ven.*249; παρθένιοι ὀ. Hes.*Th.*205; ὀ. νυμφᾶν Call.*Lav.Pall.*66: generally, *converse, discourse*, Emp.21.1; οἱ γὰρ ὀ. λόγοι εἰσί Pl.*Min.*319e; *lectures*, Call.*Fr.*9ᶜ P. 2. *song, ditty*, Pi.*P.*4.137; ψάγιος ὀ. an oblique, i.e. biassed, *song*, Id.*N.*7.69: pl., Id.*P.*1.98, *N.*3.11: in later Poets mostly of lovers, ὀ. εὐναῖοι *AP*9.362.16; Κυπρίδιοι ib.10.68 (Agath.), Musae.132, etc.

**Ὄασις**, εως, ἡ, name of cities in the Libyan desert, Hdt.3.26, Olymp.Hist.p.494 D.; cf. Αὔασις:—hence **Ὀασῖται**, οἱ, Ptol.*Geog.* 4.5.25: Adj. **Ὀασιτικός**, ή, όν, *PSI*4.433.6 (iii B.C.).

**ὀβάλλω**, *thrust through*, ὠβάλλετο· διωθεῖτο, Hsch.: perh. from ὀβ(ι)-νω; cf. ὀβελός.

❀**ὄβδη**, ἡ, = ὄψις, μούσῃσι γὰρ ἦλθον ἐς ὄβδην (or ἐσόβδην as Schn.) Call.*Fr.*522; ἐσόβδην and ὄβδην are cited by A.D.*Adv.*198.7; ποιεῖσθαι τὴν ἀπογραφὴν εἰσόβδην, = *palam, in propatulo*, *CIG*(add.)3641*b* 42 (Lampsacus).

❀**ὀβελ-εία**, ἡ, an unknown iron object, in pl., *IG*2².1631.409,1672.310: sg., in a list of cups, etc., prob. in ib.1695.14,15. **-ία**, ἡ, perh. *a tax of an obol*, *SIG*1000.3 (Cos, i B.C.). **-ιαῖος**, α, ον, *sagittal*, of a suture of the skull, ῥαφή Gal.14.720; of an incision, *straight*, διαίρεσις Paul.Aeg.6.8. **-ίας** ἄρτος, ὁ, roll or loaf *baked* or *toasted on a spit*, Hp.*Vict.*2.42, Ar.*Fr.*103, Ph.2.273, cf. Moer.p.287 P.; without ἄρτος, Pherecr.55, Nicopho 15:—also **ὀβέλιος**, *CIG*3597*b* (Ilium); and **ὀβελίτης** (q.v.). But in *AB*111 we have ὀβολίας ἄρτους· τοὺς ὀβολοῦ πωλουμένους, Ἀριστοφάνης Πελαργοῖς (*Fr.*440).—Ath.3.111b writes it ὀβελίας and gives both interpretations. **-ιαφόρος**, ον, *carrying* ὀβελίαι, Poll.6.75: in pl., title of play by Ephippus. **-ίζω**, *mark with a critical obelus* (ὀβελός II), Cic.*Fam.*9.10.1, Hermog.*Id.*2.3:—Pass., ibid. **-ισκολύχνιον**, τό, *spit used as a lampholder* (by soldiers), Theopomp.Com.7, Arist.*Pol.*1299ᵇ10, *PA* 683ᵃ25. ❀**-ίσκος**, ὁ, Dim. of ὀβελός I, *small spit, skewer*, Ar.*Ach.* 1007, *Nu.*178, *V.*354, *Av.*388,672, Sotad.Com.1.10, X.*HG*3.3.7, Arist.*Pol.*1324ᵇ19, *PEleph.*5.2 (iii B.C.), etc. 2. pl., *spits* used as money, Plu.*Lys.*17, *Fab.*27; cf. ὀβολός fin. 3. *nail*, *IG*1².313.141 (prob.), 11(2).148.70 (Delos, iii B.C., pl.). 4. = *subula*, *Gloss.* 5. window *bar*, ib. (pl.). II. *anything shaped like a spit*: the *blade* of a two-edged sword, Plb.6.23.7; *the iron head* of the Roman pilum, D.H.5.46. III. *obelisk*, D.S.1.46, Str.17.1.27, Plin.*HN*36.64. IV. *drainage-conduit*, οἱ ἐν τοῖς τείχεσιν ὀ. D.S.19.45, cf. *IG* 9(1).692.14 (Corc., ii B.C.); so perh. περὶ τοῦ πιλῶνος (= πυλῶνος) καὶ τοὐβιλίσκου (= τοῦ ὀβελίσκου) *PLond.*2.391.2 (vi A.D.); cf. ὀβολίσκος I. **-ισμός**, ὁ, *marking with the obelus* (cf. ὀβελός II), Sch.Ar.*Pl.* 797. **-ίτης** [ῑ], ὁ, = ὀβελίας, Poll.1.248, cf. Hsch. s.v. ἀκροβολίδες. ❀**-ός**, Dor. **ὀδελός**, ὁ, *spit*, ἀμφ' ὀβελοῖσιν ἔπειραν Il.1.465, al., cf. Hdt.2.41,135, E.*Cyc.*303; αἱματίου ὀβελὸς τρικώλιος *SIG*1025.53 (Cos); ὀδελοί Epich.79; κρῆς . . ἂν τὸν ὀδελὸν ἀμπεπαρμένον Megar. in Ar.*Ach.*796; τὸ θερμὸν τοῦ ὀ., prov. of taking a thing by the wrong end, S.*Fr.*814. 2. ὀ. λίθινος *pointed square pillar, obelisk*, Hdt.2.111,170, Jul.*Ep.*59. 3. = ὀβολός, *IG*1².6.95, al., *Milet.*7.59:—so in Dor. form **ὀδελός**, *Leg.Gort.*2.14, *GDI*5011.5 (Crete, iv B.C.), ib. 2561*D*27, al. (Delph., iv B.C.), etc.: Thess. **ὀβελλός** *IG*9(2).1229.20. II. *horizontal line*, — (representation of an arrow acc. to Isid.*Etym.*1.21.3), used as a critical mark to point out that a passage was spurious, Gal.15.110, Luc.*Pr.Im.*24, Sch.Il.i p.xliii Dind.; with an asterisk to denote misplaced lines, ibid.; but with one point below and one above, ÷, ὀ. περιεστιγμένος, in texts of Plato, denoted τὰς εἰκαίους ἀθετήσεις, D.L.3.66.

**ὀβολ-ιαῖος**, α, ον, *of the weight of an obol*, Arist.*HA*522ᵃ31, Gal.13.101; *worth an obol*, i.e. *petty*, κέρδη Theano *Ep.*6.2. ❀**-ίσκος**, ὁ, perh. = ὀβελίσκος IV, *PSI*6.698.16 (iv A.D.). II. part of a ship's tackle, *PLond.*3.1164*h* 11 (iii A.D.). **-ισμός**, ὁ, *charge* for freightage, *PSI*9.1048.17 (iii A.D.).

**ὀβολολογέω**, *collect obols*, Phryn.*PS*p.96 B.

❀**ὀβολός**, ὁ, *obol*, used both as a weight and coin, at Athens, = $\frac{1}{6}$ of a δραχμή, rather more than three halfpence, *IG*1².140.5, al., freq. in Ar., *Nu.*118, al.; πολὺ or μικρὸν τοῦ ὀ. a thing of which you get much or little for an obol, i.e. *worthless* or *valuable*, Antiph.135, Eup.185, cf. Ar.*Eq.*945; ἐν τοῖν δυοῖν ὀβολοῖν θεωρεῖν 'to sit in the cheap seats', D.18.28. II. as a weight, Gal.13.295, etc. (ὀβολός, ὀβελός, ὀβελλός, ὀδελός are different dialect forms of a word for 'spit' or 'nail', nails being used in early times as money, six of them making a handful (δραχμή), cf. Plu.*Lys.*17.)

**ὀβολο-στατέω**, *weigh obols*: hence, *practise petty usury*, Lys.*Fr.* 60, Luc.*Nec.*2. **-στάτηρ**, ῆρος, ὁ, = sq., Hdn.Gr.1.48. **-στάτης** [ᾰ], ου, ὁ, (ἵστημι) *weigher of obols*, i.e. *petty usurer*, Ar.*Nu.*1155, Hyp.*Fr.*154, Antiph.168, Philostr.*VA*8.7, Onos.1.20; but ἐκ τῶν πλουσίων τριάκοντα ἡρέθησαν ὀ., ὅ ἐστι δανεισταὶ ἐπὶ ὀβολῷ τὴν μνᾶν δανείζοντες Sch.Aeschin.1.39: perh. from στῆσαι, = δανεῖσαι; cf. στάσιμος and Hsch. s.vv. ὀβολοστάτης, ἱστάνειν:—fem. **-στάτις**, Pl. *Ax.*367b, Poll.3.112: hence **-στατική** (sc. τέχνη), ἡ, *the trade of a petty usurer*, and generally, *usury*, Arist.*Pol.*1258ᵇ2.

**ὄβρια**, v. ὀβρίκαλα.

**Ὀβριάρεως** [ᾰ], ὁ, Hes.*Th.*617,734; v. Βριάρεως.

❀**ὀβρίκαλα** [ῐ], τά, *the young* of animals, A.*Ag.*143 (lyr.):—a form **ὄβρια**, τά, is cited from A.(*Fr.*48) and E.(*Fr.*616) by Ael.*NA*7.47. (Perh. cf. ὄμβρος (leg. ὄμβριον?)· χοιρίδιον, Hsch. and Arc. slave's name Ὀμβρίας coupled with Χοιροθύων in *IG*5(2).429.)

**ὀβρῐμό-γυιος**, ον, *strong-limbed*, Opp.*H.*5.316, Orph.*Fr.*168.23. **-δερκής**, ές, *with mighty glance*, of Athena, B.15.20. **-δυνάστης**, ου, ὁ, *powerful potentate*, *PMag.Par.*1.1365 (pl.). **-εργός**, όν, *doing strong deeds*, but always in bad sense, *doing deeds of violence* or *wrong*, esp. against the gods, σχέτλιος, ὀ. Il.5.403; ἀτάσθαλον, ὀ. 22.418, cf. Hes.*Th.*996, Callin.3. **-θῡμος**, ον, *strong of spirit*, Hes.*Th.*140, *h.Hom.*8.2: written ὀμβρ-, Orph.*Fr.*169.12. **-παις**, ὁ, ἡ, gen. παιδος, *having mighty children*, Nonn.*D.*10.277. **-πάτηρ**· ἰσχυρὸν πατέρα ἔχων, Hsch. **-πάτρη**, ἡ, *daughter of a mighty sire*, epith. of Athena, Il.5.747, al., Hes.*Th.*587, Sol.4.3: **-πάτρα**, Ar.*Eq.*1178:—also **-πάτρις**, Corn.*ND*21 (s. v. l.).

**ὄβρῐμος**, ον, also α, ον E.*Or.*1454 (lyr.):—*strong, mighty*, epith. of Ares, Il.5.845, al.; of Achilles, 19.408; of Hector, 8.473; also of things, ὀ. ἔγχος 3.357, etc.; ἄχθος Od.9.233; θυρεός, λίθος, ib.241, 305; ὕδωρ Il.4.453; ἐβρόντησε ὄβριμον he thundered *mightily*, Hes.*Th.* 839; ὀ. ἔργα deeds *of might*, Tyrt.11.27.—Ep. word, rare in Trag., ἄνδρες ὀ. A.*Th.*794; μῖσος ὀ. Id.*Ag.*1411 (lyr.); Ἰδαία μᾶτερ ὀ. E.l.c.—The form ὄμβριμος is a freq. f.l., as in Il.5.845, al., Pi.*O.*4.8, *P.*9.27, A.*Th.*l.c. (Cf. βριμός· μέγας, χαλεπός, Hsch., to which ὄβριμος may be related as Ὀβριμώ [ῑ] Lyc.698 to Βριμώ, Ὀβριαρεύς to Βριαρεύς, *EM* 346.41, and Ὀβριάρεως to Βριάρεως; cf. also βρίμη, βριμάομαι, βριαρός.)

**ὀβρῐμόσπορος**, ον, *with mighty offspring*, of Γῆ, B.18.32.

**ὄβρυζ-α**, ἡ, *assaying of gold*, Just.*Edict.*11. ❀**-ιακός**, ή, όν, = sq., *Stud.Pal.*20.146.9 (v/vi A.D.). ❀**-ος**, η, ον, *pure*, of gold, χρυσοῦ νόμισμα ὀβρ(υζον) *PLips.*63.11 (iv A.D.), cf. *PKlein.Form.*393 (vi A.D.), al.; χρυσίον Sch.Th.2.13, etc. (Cf. Lat. *obrussa.*)

**ὀγάστριος**, ον, = ὁμογάστριος, v.l. in Lyc.452; **ὀγάστωρ**· ὁμογάστωρ, Hsch.

**ὀγδο-ᾰδῐκός**, ή, όν, *belonging to the number eight*, *Theol.Ar.*55; *belonging to the eighth heaven*, *Corp.Herm.*1.26. **-αῖος**, α, ον, *on the eighth day*, Plb.5.52.3, al., Plu.2.288c, Gal.9.869, etc. II. of fever, *recurring on the eighth day, octavan*, Id.7.505. **-άς**, άδος, ἡ, *the number eight*, Plu.2.744b; *group of eight*, ἐτέων δισσὰς -άδας *IG* 3.1308; *the eighth heaven*, Basilid.ap.Hippol.*Haer.*7.27: pr. n. of a deity, *PMag.Leid.W.*17.5, cf. 16.46. **-ατικός**, ή, όν, *of the Ogdoad*, *Corp.Herm.*1.26 codd.: f.l. for -αδικός (q. v.). **-ᾰτος**, η, ον, poet. for ὄγδοος, as τρίτατος for τρίτος, *the eighth*, Il.19.246, Od.3.306, Emp. 68; ὀ. δεκάς *Rev.Phil.*22.357; ἡ ὀγδοάτη (sc. ἡμέρα) *the eighth day, octave*, Hes.*Op.*772, 790 (καθ' ὀγδοάδην δεκάδα prob. in *Jahresh.*23 *Beibl.*402 (Egypt)). ❀**-διον**· θυσία παρὰ Ἀθηναίοις τελουμένη Θησεῖ, Hsch. ❀**-ήκοντα**, οἱ, αἱ, τά, indecl., *eighty*, Th.5.47, etc.: Ion. and Dor. **ὀγδώκοντα** Il.2.568, Hdt.1.163, Theoc.4.34; **ὀδώκοντα** *Ostr.* 323.6 (ii B.C.).

**ὀγδοηκοντά-δραχμος**, ον, *amounting to eighty* δραχμαί, *IG*7.3498.45, al. (Oropus, written ὀγδοιη-). **-λῐθος**, ὁ, title of work by Orpheus, Suid. s. v. Ὀρφεύς. **-πηχυς**, υ, *eighty cubits long*, Callix.2.

**ὀγδοηκοντ-άρουρος** [ᾰ], ον, *having tenure of eighty* ἄρουραι, *PTeb.* 63.40 (ii B.C.), etc.

**ὀγδοηκοντα-τάλαντος** [ᾰλ], ον, *possessed of eighty talents*, Lys.26.22. **-τέσσἄρες**, α, *eighty-four*, *Ev.Luc.*2.37.

❀**ὀγδοηκοντούτης**, ες, (ἔτος) *eighty years old*, App.*BC*4.25, Gal.6.360, Luc.*Herm.*77:—fem. **-οῦτις**, D.C.61.19: Ion. **ὀγδωκοντάέτης**, ες, Sol.20.4, Simon.146; **ὀγδωκοντούτης**, *App.Anth.*2.642 (Perinthus); **ὀγδωκον[τέτης]**, *IG*9(1).875 (Corc., ii B.C., metr.).

**ὀγδοηκοστ-αῖος**, α, ον, *on the eightieth day*, Hp.*Art.*69. **-ός**, ή, όν, *eightieth*, Id.*Epid.*1.3, Th.1.12, etc.

**ὀγδοη-μόριον**, τό, *eighth part*, *Inscr.Délos* 504*A* 12 (iii B.C.), *Theol. Ar.*4, Mnesith.Cyz.ap.Orib.*Inc.*15.12:—also **-μορον**, τό, *IG*11(2).203*A* 59,71 (Delos, iii B.C.), *PSI*6.595.7 (iii B.C.).

**ὀγδοιο-, ὀγδοιη-**, alternative spellings of ὀγδοο-, ὀγδοη-, e.g. *IG* 2².347.2, 501.5, 7.3498.45 (Oropus), *PPetr.*1 pp.54,57 (iii B.C.).

❀**ὄγδοος**, η, ον, *eighth*, Il.7.223, etc.; ὀγδόη (sc. ἡμέρα), ὀγδόη τῆς πρυτανείας *IG*1².374.416; ὀγδόη Πυανεψιῶνος Plu.*Thes.*36. [ὄγδοον as disyll., Od.7.261 = 14.287 (s. v. l.): ὄγδος late spelling in *Ostr.*922, etc.]

**ὀγδώκοντα, ὀγδωκονταέτης, ὀγδωκοντούτης**, v. ὀγδοηκ-.

**Ὄγκᾱ**, ἡ, name of Athena at Thebes, A.*Th.*164 (lyr.), 487,501: hence **Ὀγκαίη** πύλη at Thebes, said to be named from the lowing (ὀγκηθμός) of Athena in the form of an ox, Nonn.*D.*5.70.

**ὀγκᾰλέω**, Aeol. for ἀνακαλέω, Sapph.*Supp.*20c.5 (ὀνκ- Pap.).

❀**ὀγκάομαι**, *bray*, of the ass, Theopomp.Com.4, Arist.*HA*609ᵃ33, Call.*Aet.Oxy.*2079.31, Luc.*DMar.*1.4.

**ὄγκη**· γωνία, μέγεθος, Hsch.

**ὀγκ-ηθμός**, ὁ, *braying*, of the ass, Luc.*Asin.*15, *Gloss.* II. *lowing*, of the ox, Nonn.*D.*5.71. **-ημα**, ατος, τό, = foreg. II, *Gloss.* **-ηρός**, ά, όν, (ὄγκος B) *bulky, swollen*, ὀστέα Hp.*Fract.*24 (Comp.); ὀ. εἰς τὸ ἄνω Id.*Art.*13 (Comp.). II. metaph., *stately, pompous*, ὄνομα Demetr.*Eloc.*176; τῆς βασιλείας ὀγκηρότερον διάγειν X.*HG*3.4.8; ἐν τραγῳδίᾳ, πράγματι ὀγκηρῷ φύσει Longin.3.1; τὸ ὀ. *bombast*, Arist.*EN*1127ᵇ24: irreg. Comp. ὀγκότερος (formed from ὄγκος) Id.*Pr.*966ᵃ2: Sup. ὀγκότατος *AP*12.187 (Strat.). **-ησις**, εως, ἡ, = ὀγκηθμός I, Corn.*ND*21, Ael.*NA*5.50. **-ητής**, οῦ, ὁ, *brayer*, ὄνος *AP*9.301 (Secund.), cf. Epigr.ap.Gal.*Protr.*13. **-ηστικός**, ή, όν, *given to braying*, Sch.Nic.*Th.*357.

**ὀγκία**, v. οὐγκία. **ὀγκίαι**· θημῶνες, χώματα, σιδηροθήκη, Hsch.

**ὄγκῑνος**, ὁ, *hook*, Lat. *uncīnus*, Poll.1.137, Sch.Ar.*Pl.*431.

**ὄγκιον** or **ὀγκίον**, τό, (ὄγκος A. I) *case* or *casket for arrows and other implements*, ὄγκιον, ἔνθα σίδηρος κεῖτο πολὺς καὶ χαλκὸς Od.21.61, cf. Hermipp.16.

**ὀγκο-ειδής**, ές, = ὀγκώδης (A), Herm. *in Phdr.*p.110 A. (Comp.). **-λογέω**, *speak in a hollow voice*, = γογγύζω, Hsch. **-πελεθίαν**·

πέλεθον οὖσαν, Id. **-ποιέω**, = ὀγκόω, Sch.Hermog. in Rh.7.953 W., *Gloss.*

**ὄγκος** (A), ὁ, *barb* of an arrow, in pl., *the barbed points*, νεῦρόν τε καὶ ὄγκους Il.4.151, cf. 214; ὄγκοι τοῦ βέλους Philostr.*Im.*2.23: sg., Onos.19.3. 2. οἱ τῆς νεὼς ὄ. *brackets*, Moschio ap. Ath.5.208b.

* **ὄγκος** (B), ὁ, *bulk, size, mass* of a body, μελέων ἀριδείκετον ὄ. Emp. 20.1; ἀέρος ὄ. Id.100.13; σφαίρης ἐναλίγκιον ὄγκῳ Parm.8.43: freq. in Pl., μήτε ὄγκῳ μήτε ἀριθμῷ *Tht.*155a; τὸν..ὄ. τοῦ ἀριθμοῦ their total number, *Lg.*737c; τὸν τῶν σαρκῶν ὄ. ib.959c; σμικρᾶς πόλεως ὄ. a city of small *size*, *Plt.*259b; ἔχθρας ὄ. μέγαν *Lg.*843b; θαυμαστὸν ὄ. ἀράμενοι τοῦ μύθου taking on my shoulders a monstrous *great* story, *Plt.*277b, etc.: freq. also in Arist., *the space filled by a body*, opp. τὸ κενόν, *Ph.*203b28, al.; ἴσος τὸν ὄ. *in bulk*, *GC*326b20; ὄγκῳ μικρόν *EN*1178a1, etc. b. flatulent *distentions*, Diocl.*Fr.*43 (pl.). 2. *bulk, mass, body*, ὄ. φρυγάνων *a heap* of faggots, Hdt. 4.62; ὄ. μαλθακός *mass* or *roll* of something soft, Hp.*Art.*26; σμικρὸς ὄ. ἐν σμικρῷ κύτει, of a dead man's ashes, S.*El.*1142; γαστρὸς ὄ., of a child in the womb, E.*Ion*15; ὄ. πλήρης φλεβίων Arist.*HA* 515b1: pl., ὄγκοι *bodies, material substances*, Id.*Metaph.*1085a12, 1089b14; also ὁ ὄ. τῆς φωνῆς the *volume* of the note, Id.*Aud.*804a15. 3. a bushy *top-knot*, Poll.4.133. 4. the human *body*, τῆς χολῆς ἀναχεομένης εἰς τὸν ὄ. Ruf.*Anat.*30, cf. Sor.1.26, Plu.2.653f, Gal.1.272. II. metaph., *bulk, weight, trouble*, βραχεῖ σὺν ὄ. S.*OC* 1341. 2. *weight, dignity, pride*, and in bad sense, *self-importance, pretension*, ὄ. ὀνόματος μητρῷος *pride* in the name of mother, Id.*Tr.* 817; ὄγκον αἴρειν exalt one's *dignity*, Id.*Aj.*129; βραχὺν..μῦθον οὐκ ὄγκου πλέων *of pretension*, Id.*OC*1162; μεῖζον' ὄ. δορὸς ἢ φρενῶν E. *Tr.*1158; ἔχει τιν' ὄ. Ἄργος Ἑλλήνων πάρα Id.*Ph.*717; ἐς ὄ. βλέπειν τύχης Id.*Fr.*81; τοῖς ζῶσι δ' ὄγκος Id.*Rh.*760; ὁ τῶν ὑπεροπτικῶν ὄ. Isoc.1.30; τῷ..γένους ὄγκῳ Pl.*Alc.*1.121b; πραγμάτων ὄ. Epicur. *Fr.*548; τῆς ἀρχῆς τὸ μέγεθος καὶ ὁ ὄ. Plu.*Fab.*4; ὄγκον περιθεῖναί τινι Id.*Per.*4, etc. 3. of style, *loftiness, majesty*, ὄ. τῆς λέξεως Arist. *Rh.*1407b26; ὁ τοῦ ποιήματος ὄ. Id.*Po.*1459b28, cf. Demetr.*Eloc.*36, al.: in bad sense, *bombast*, ὁ Αἰσχύλου ὄ. Plu.2.79b. III. in Philos., *particle, mass, body*, Epicur.*Ep.*1 p.16 U., *Nat.*12 G., Asclep. Bith.ap.S.E.*M.*9.363; so in the physiology of the Methodics, ὄγκοι καὶ πόροι, = *molecules* and pores, Id.ap.Gal.1.499.

**ὄγκος** (C), ον, as Adj.; v. ὀγκηρός fin.

**ὀγκόφωνος**, ον, *hollow-toned*, of a trumpet, Sch.T Il.18.219.

**ὀγκ-όω**, aor. ὤγκωσα: aor. and pf. Pass. ὠγκώθην, ὤγκωμαι (v. infr.): (ὄγκος B):—*raise up, rear*, ἠρίον Alex.Aet.3.33; ὤγκωσεν τάδε σήματα *Epigr.Gr.*233.9 (Chios):—Pass., τάφῳ ὀγκωθῆναι E.*Ion*388; and of the cairn itself, ὠγκώθην *AP*7.651 (Euph.); ὀστέα δ' ὀγκωθεὶς ..ἔδεκτο τάφος *Epigr.Gr.*233.4. 2. *distend*, τὸ πνεῦμα τὰς φλέβας ὀγκοῖ Arist.*Somn.*457a13, cf. *Pr.*936b11:—Pass., γαστὴρ ὠγκώθη *was swollen* by eating, Babr.86.5, cf. 111.19, Antyll.ap.Orib.7.16.3. 3. *endow with bulk* or *extension*, *Corp.Herm.*8.3: pf. part. Pass., Porph. *Sent.*33, Dam.*Pr.*140. II. metaph., *bring to honour and dignity*, βροτοῖς..βίοτον ὀγκώσας μέγαν E.*Andr.*320; *exalt, extol*, Ἄργος ὀγκῶν Id.*Heracl.*195; ὀγκῶσαι τὸ φρόνημα *puff up* one's conceit, Ar.*V.*1024; ὀ. [τινὰ] ματαίως 'boost', Epicur.*Ep.*2 p.41 U.; of style, ὤγκωσε τὴν νόησιν Longin.28.2:—Med., εἰ δὲ ταῦτ' ὀγκωσόμεσθα Ar.*Ra.*703:—Pass., *to be puffed up, swollen, elated*, ὀγκωθεὶς χλιδῇ S.*Fr.*942; δοκήσει δωμάτων ὠγκωμένος E.*El.*381; δῶμα πλούτῳ δυσσεβῶς ὠγκωμένον Id.*Fr.* 825; ὠγκωμένω ἐπὶ τῷ γένει X.*Mem.*1.2.25: with a part., ὀγκούμεθα ὁ μέν τις.., ὁ δὲ..τίμιος κεκλημένος E.*Hec.*623. **-ύλλομαι**, Pass., = ὀγκόομαι, *to be swollen*, κοιλίη -ομένη Hp.*Prorrh.*1.99, *Coac.*606: metaph., *to be puffed up*, Ar.*Pax*465; ἐπὶ τῇ τέχνῃ Ath.9.382b. **-ύλον**· σεμνόν, γαῦρον, Hsch. **-υλόομαι**, Pass., = ὀγκύλλομαι, in pf. part. ὀγκυλωμένην, Hp.(*Prorrh.*1.99)ap.Erot., cf. Suid. * **-ώδης** (A), ες, (ὄγκος B) *swelling, rounded*, πλευρὰ ὀ..πρὸς τὴν γαστέρα -εστέρα, of a horse, X.*Eq.*1.12; μέρος τι ὀ. (sc. τοῦ οἰσοφάγου) Arist.*PA*674b24. 2. *bulky*, σώματα ὀ., of birds, ib.694a11, cf. *GA*749b32 (Comp.). II. metaph., *puffed up*, Pl.*Men.*90a; τὸ ἡρωικὸν..ὀγκωδέστατον τῶν μέτρων *weightiest*, Arist.*Po.*1459b35; ὀ. ποιήματα *bombastic*, Phld. *Po.*5.5; τὸ ὀ. *turgidity*, D.H.*Din.*7, Heraclid.Pont.ap.Ath.4. 624d. **-ώδης** (B), ες, (ὀγκάομαι) *given to braying*, ὄνων -έστερος Ael.*NA*12.34. **-ωμα**, ατος, τό, *swelling*, Gal.16.720, Sch. Ar.*Pax* 540. II. *elbow*, prob. f.l. for ἀγκῶνα, Orib.45.15.1, Eust. 1397.5. **-ωσις**, εως, ἡ, *intumescence*, Arist.*Resp.*480a3, Sor.2. 20. **-ωτικός**, ή, όν, τῶν πραγμάτων dub. l. in *Cat.Cod.Astr.*2.164. 17 (ἐγκοπτικός Kroll). **-ωτός**, ή, όν, *heaped up*, τάφος *AP*9.117 (Stat. Flacc.); κόνις *Epigr.Gr.*234 (Smyrna).

**ὀγμεύω**, *move in a straight line*, prop. of ploughers or mowers, Hsch. s. v. ὄγμος: metaph., c. acc. cogn., στίβον *plough* or *trail one's weary* way, of a lame man, S.*Ph.*163 (anap.); ὤγμευον αὐτῷ *they were marching in file before* him, X.*Cyr.*2.4.20.

**Ὄγμιος**, ὁ, name of Heracles among Celts, Luc.*Herc.*1.

* **ὄγμος**, ὁ, *furrow* in ploughing, τοὶ δὲ στρέψασκον ἀν' ὄγμους Il.18. 546; πίονες ὄγμοι *h.Cer.*455. 2. *swathe* in reaping, ὥς τ' ἀμητῆρες ὄ. ἐλαύνωσιν Il.11.68; δράγματα δ' ἄλλα μετ' ὄ...πῖπτον 18.552, cf. 557; ὄ. ἄγειν ὀρθόν Theoc.10.2. 3. *strip* of cultivated land (written ὦγμος), *PFay.*120.7 (ii A.D.), *BGU*166.7 (ii A.D.). II. metaph., ὅ τε πλήθει μέγας ὄ. [the moon's] vast *orbit* is accomplished, *h.Hom.* 32.11; of the sun, Arat.749; of a hippopotamus, παλίσσυτον ὄ. ἐλαύνων Nic.*Th.*571; ὄ. κακῶν..γήραος, i.e. wrinkled old age, Archil. 116; ὄ. ὀδόντων *row* of teeth, *APl.*4.265, etc.

**ὄγυρον**· ἱμάτιον, οἱ δὲ μάταιον, Hsch.

**ὀγχέω**, written for ὀκχέω in Lyc.64, 1049, v. ὀχέω.

**Ὀγχησμίτης** [ῑ] (sc. ἄνεμος), ου, ὁ, *wind from Onchesmus*, Cic. *Att.*7.2.1.

**ὄγχνη**, ἡ, *pear-tree*, *Pirus communis*, Od.7.115, 11.589, 24.234, Thphr.*HP*2.5.6. II. *pear*, Od.7.120.—Written ὄχνη in Theoc. 1.134 (where acc. pl. ὄχνας), 7.144, Nic.*Th.*513, Ruf.*Ren.Ves.*14.6, and this form is v.l. in Hom.:—Hsch. also has **ὄγχνια**· ἄπιον.

**ὅδα**· φορτία, ἢ ὤνια (ὀδαφορτία, ἰωνία cod.), οἱ δὲ **ὀδάβα**, Hsch. **ὄδαγμα**· βρῶμα, κτλ., Id.

**ὀδαγμός**, ὁ, (ὀδάξομαι) *itching, irritation*, S.*Tr.*770 codd.: ἀδαγμός Phot.

* **ὀδ-ᾱγός**, ὁ, Dor. for ὁδηγός, *Gp.*18.17.8, Phot. * **-αῖος**, α, ον, (ὁδός) = ἐνόδιος, of Hermes, Id. (s. v.l.). II. ὁδαῖα, τά, *that for which a merchant travels, merchandise* (obtained in exchange for his φόρτος or first freight), Od.8.163, 15.445; though a Sch. explains it as = ἐφόδια, Lat. *viaticum*; cf. ὁδάω.

**ὀδακτάζω**, *bite, gnaw*, Call.*Del.*322, A.R.4.1608: **ὀδακτίζω**, D.H. 14.10; cf. ὀδάξω.

**ὀδάξ**, Adv. *by biting with the teeth*, ὀ. ἕλον οὖδας, of men in the agonies of death, Il.11.749, etc.; so ὀ. λαζοίατο γαῖαν 2.418; γαῖαν ὀ. ἑλόντες E.*Ph.*1423; also ὀ. ἐν χείλεσι φύντες *biting the lips* in smothered rage, Od.1.381: so in Com., ἀποδάκνειν ὀ. Cratin.164; διατρώξομαι ὀ. τὸ δίκτυον Ar.*V.*164; ὀ. ἔχεσθαι ib.943; λαβέσθαι Id.*Pl.*690:—if κυνὸς ἄγριον ὀδάξ be correct in Diog.Cyn.ap.D.L.6.79, ὀδάξ must be taken either as *tooth* or as *bite*.

* **ὀδαξ-ησμός**, ὁ, = ὀδαγμός, Hp.*Aph.*3.25, Ph.2.301, Dsc.2.72, Plu. 2.769e, Aret.*CA*1.2, Ael.*NA*1.38, Artem.5.67. (In codd. freq. misspelt -ισμός.) **-ητικός**, ή, όν, *causing to itch*, Poll.2.110. * **-ω**, impf. ὤδαξον X.*Smp.*4.28:—more freq. in Med. ὀδάξομαι, Hp.*Gland.* 12, *Mul.*2.171 (ἀδάξεται codd.), Dsc.*Alex.*2, Aret.*SD*2.5:—**Pass.**, pf. part., μοιχὸς..καρδίαν ὠδαγμένος S.*Fr.*1127: plpf. ὠδάγμην Hsch.: —also **ὀδαξάω**, Thphr.*Sign.*30:—**Med.** ὀδαξάομαι, Hp.*Mul.*1.90, D.S.3.29, Ph.2.332, Dsc.2.124, Ael.*NA*7.35 (ὀδαξέομαι v.l. in Ph. and Dsc. ll. cc.):—Act., *feel pain* or *irritation*, τὸν δεξιὸν [πόδα] Thphr. l. c.; τὸν ὦμον X. l. c.:—Med., *scratch oneself*, D.S. l. c., cj. in Thphr. *Char.*19.4 (ἀδαξ-). II. ὀδάξει· τοῖς ὀδοῦσι δάκνει, Hsch.; *cause irritation*, *AB*340, Suid., Phot. (where ἀδαξῆσαι); ἀδαξῶντα *irritants*, Hp.*Mul.*1.18 codd. opt.: fut. ὀδαξήσεται ib.2.154: pres. ὀδάξεται *is an irritant*, ib.160; ὀδάξονται μυκτῆρας Id.*Gland.*13: c. acc., ὠδάξατο σάρκα *nibbled at* it, *AP*9.86 (Antiphil.). **-ώδης**, ες, = ὀδαξητικός, Aret.*SD*2.9, etc.; ὀ. εἰς ἡδονήν ib.11.

**ὀδαρός**· ὀκνηρός, Hsch. **ὀδασμένος**· ὠνεῖσθαι ἐπειγόμενος, Id. * **ὄδαχα**· καταπύγων (Tarent.), Id.

**ὀδάω**, (ὁδός) *export and sell*: generally, *sell*, βορὰν ὀδῆσαι ναυτίλοις E.*Cyc.*98; ὄδησον ἡμῖν σῖτον ib.133:—Pass., *to be carried away and sold*, ὡς ὀδηθείης μακράν ib.12:—also **ὀδεῖν**· πωλεῖν, Hsch.—Cf. ἐξοδάω.

* **ὅδε, ἥδε, τόδε**, demonstr. Pron., *this*, formed by adding the enclit. -δε to the old demonstr. Pron. ὁ, ἡ, τό, and declined like it through all cases: Ep. dat. pl. τοῖσδεσσι, τοῖσδεσσιν, as well as τοῖσδε, Il.10. 462, Od.2.47, al.; and τοῖσδεσι 10.268, 21.93; τοῖσδεσιν Democr. 175; τοισίδε Hdt.1.32, al.: Aeol. gen. pl. τῶνδεων Alc.126: Arg. gen. pl. τωνδεωνήν (= τῶνδεων + ἦν) *Mnemos.*57.208 (vi B.C.): nom. pl. neut. ταδήν ibid., *IG*4.506.1; ταδή Sch.Ar.*Ach.*744:—ὅδε, like οὗτος, is opp. ἐκεῖνος, to designate what is *nearer* as opp. to what is *more remote*; but ὅδε refers more distinctly to *what is present*, to *what can be seen* or *pointed out*, though this distinction is sts. not observed, e.g. ξύμπας Ἀχαιῶν λαός, ἐν δὲ τοῖσδ' ἐγώ S.*Ph.*1243 (v.l. τοῖς), cf. *Ant.*449, and on the other hand, ἢ τόνδε φράζεις;—τοῦτον, ὅνπερ εἰσορᾷς Id.*OT*1120: the forms ὁδί, ἡδί, etc. [ῑ], are freq. in Com. and Oratt., but are not used in Trag.: the ι may be separated from the ὅδε by the adversative δέ, as τὸν μὲν.., τηνδεδί Ar.*Av.*18, cf. *Ec.* 989. I. of Place, to point out *what is present* or *before one*, Ἕκτορος ἥδε γυνή *this is*, or *here is*, the wife of Hector, Il.6.460: very freq. in Trag., ἀκτὴ μὲν ἥδε Λήμνου S.*Ph.*1, cf. E.*Tr.*4, *Ion* 5, *Hel.*1, *HF* 4, *Ba.*1; in Com., ἐγὼ σιωπῶ τῷδε; Ar.*Ra.*1134, etc.; and in Prose, ὧν Θεόδωρος εἷς ὅδε Pl.*Tht.*164e; of what belongs to *this* world, Id. *Phdr.*250a, *Smp.*211c. 2. with Verbs of action, = *here*, ἀνδρί, ὅστις ὅδε κρατέει who holds sway *here*, Il.5.175; ἔγχος μὲν τόδε κεῖται ἐπὶ χθονός *here* it lies, 20.345, cf. 21.533, Od.1.185, etc.; ἥδ' ἡ κορώνη.. λέγει the crow *here*.., v.l. in Ar.*Av.*23: freq. in Trag., esp. to indicate the entrance of a person on the stage, καὶ μὴν Ἐτεοκλῆς..ὅδε χωρεῖ *here* comes.., E.*Ph.*443, cf. S.*OT*297, 531, 632, *OC*32, 549; f.l. in E.*Heracl.*80. 3. with a pers. Pron., ὅδ' ἐγὼ..ἤλυθον *here* am I come, Od.16.205; ἡμεῖς οἵδε περιφραζώμεθα let us *here*.., 1.76; δῶρα δ' ἐγὼν ὅδε..παρασχέμεν *here* am I [ready] to provide.., Il.19.140: with a pr. n., ὅδ' εἰμ' Ὀρέστης E.*Or.*380: with αὐτός, ὅδ' αὐτὸς ἐγώ Od.21.207, 24.321. 4. also with τίς and other interrog. words, τίς δ' ὅδε Ναυσικάᾳ ἕπεται; who is *this* following her? 6.276, cf. 1.225; τί κακὸν τόδε πάσχετε; what is *this* evil ye are suffering? 20. 351; πρὸς ποῖον ἂν τόνδ'..ἔπλει; S.*Ph.*572, cf. 1204. 5. in Trag. dialogue, ὅδε and ὅδ' ἀνήρ, = ἐγώ, Id.*OT*534, 815, etc.; γυναικὸς τῆσδε, for ἐμοῦ, A.*Ag.*1438; τῆσδέ γε ζώσης ἔτι S.*Tr.*305; so ξὺν τῇδε χερί with *this* hand *of mine*, Id.*Ant.*43, cf. *OT*811. 6. in Arist., τοδί designates a *particular thing*, 'such and such', τοδὶ διὰ τοδὶ αἱρεῖται *EN* 1151a35; τόδε μετὰ τόδε *GA*734a28, cf. b9; Καλλίᾳ κάμνοντι τηνδὶ τὴν νόσον τοδὶ συνήνεγκε *Metaph.*981a8; τόδε τὸ ἐν τῷ ἡμικυκλίῳ *APo.* 71a20; ἥδε ἡ ἰατρική, opp. αὐτὴ ἡ ἰ., *Metaph.*997b30; τόδε τι a *this*, i.e. a fully specified particular, *Cat.*3b10, al., cf. Gal.6.113, 171; τόδε τι καὶ οὐσία Arist.*Metaph.*1060b1; πορευσόμεθα εἰς τήνδε τὴν πόλιν *Ep.*

*Jac.*4.13. II. of Time, to indicate *the immediate present*, ἥδ' ἡμέρα S.*OT*438, etc.: more strongly, κατ' ἦμαρ..τὸ νῦν τόδε Id.*Aj.*753; τοῦδ' αὐτοῦ λυκάβαντος Od.14.161; but νυκτὸς τῆσδε in the night *just* past, S.*Aj.*21; νυκτὶ τῇδε Id.*El.*644; so τῆσδε τῆς ὁδοῦ on *this present* journey, Id.*OT*1478, cf. *Ant.*878 (cj.); also ἀπόλλυμαι τάλας ἔτος τόδ' ἤδη δέκατον now for *these* ten years, Id.*Ph.*312; τῶνδε τῶν ἀσκητῶν athletes *of the present day*, Pl.*R.*403e. 2. ἐς τόδε elliptic c. gen., ἐς τόδ' ἡμέρας E.*Ph.*425; ἐς τόδε ἡλικίης Hdt.7.38; πῶς ἐς τόδ' ἂν τόλμης ἔβη; S.*OT*125. III. in sentences beginning *this is*.., the Engl. *this* is freq. represented by nom. pl. neut. τάδε; ἐπεὶ οὐκ ἔρανος τάδε γ' ἐστίν *this* is not an ἔρανος, Od.1.226; ἆρ' οὐχ ὕβρις τάδ'; is not *this* insolence? S.*OC*883; of persons, Ἀπόλλων τάδ' ἦν *this* was A., Id.*OT*1329 (lyr.); οὐ γὰρ ἔσθ' Ἕκτωρ τάδε E.*Andr.*168; οὐκέτι Τροία τάδε Id.*Tr.*100 (anap.); οὐ τάδε Βρόμιος Id.*Cyc.*63 (lyr.); οὐκ Ἴωνες τάδε εἰσίν Th.6.77; τάδ' οὐχὶ Πελοπόννησος, ἀλλ' Ἰωνία Inscr. ap.Str.9.1.6. 2. to indicate something *immediately to come*, τόδε μοι κρήηνον ἐέλδωρ (which then follows) Il.1.41,504, cf. 455, al.; Ἀθηναίων οἵδε ἀπέθανον *IG*1$^2$.943.2: hence, in historical writers, opp. what goes before (cf. οὗτος C. I.2), ταῦτα μὲν Λακεδαιμόνιοι λέγουσι.., τάδε δὲ ἐγὼ γράφω Hdt.6.53; ταῦτα μὲν δὴ σὺ λέγεις· παρ' ἡμῶν δὲ ἀπάγγελλε τάδε X.*An.*2.1.20, etc.; v. οὗτος B.I.2; opp. ἐκεῖνος, S.*El.*784: rarely applied to different persons in the same sentence, νῦν ὅδε [Laïus] πρὸς τῆς τύχης ὄλωλεν, οὐδὲ τοῦδ' ὕπο [by Oedipus] Id.*OT* 948. 3. as 'antecedent' to a defining Relat., ὃν πόλις στήσειε, τοῦδε χρὴ κλύειν Id.*Ant.*666, cf. *Tr.*23, *Ph.*87, etc.: in Hom., in such cases, the δέ is separate, as ὃς δέ κε μηρίνθοιο τύχῃ.., ὁ δ' οἴσεται ἡμιπέλεκκα Il.23.858, cf. Od.11.148,149, al. (but ὅδε sts. has its deictic force and the relat. clause merely explains, as νήσου τῆσδ' ἐφ' ἧς ναίει S.*Ph.* 613, cf. Il.2.346, X.*An.*7.3.47, etc.). IV. Adverbial usage of some cases: 1. τῇδε, a. of Place, *here, on the spot*, Il.12.345, Od. 6.173, etc.; so τῶν τε ὑπὸ γῆς θεῶν καὶ τῶν τ. Pl.*Lg.*958d. b. of Manner, *thus*, A.*Eu.*45; ὅρα δὲ καὶ τ., ὅτι.. Pl.*Phd.*79e, cf. *R.*433e, etc. 2. acc. neut. τόδε with ἱκάνω, etc., *hither, to this spot*, Il.14. 298, Od.1.409, al.; also δεῦρο τόδε Il.14.309, Od.17.444,524. b. *therefore, on this account*, τόδε χώεο 23.213: so also acc. pl. neut., τάδε γηθήσειε *on this account*, Il.9.77. 3. dat. pl. neut., τοισίδε *in* or *with these words*, τοισίδε ἀμείβεται Hdt.1.120; τοισίδε προέχει *in these respects*, ib.32.

**ὁδεία**, ἡ, *travelling*, Aristeas 106:—written **ὁδία**, *procession*, *PTeb.* 599 (ii A.D.).

⊛**ὀδελονόμος**, ὁ, title of financial official at Troezen, *IG*4.757.42.

**ὀδελός**, v. ὀβελός, ὀβολός.

**ὅδ-ευμα**, ατος, τό, *passage, journey*, Str.17.1.45. **-εύσιμος**, ον, *passable, practicable*, Id.11.7.5, Max.Tyr.39.3, *Gloss.* **-ευσις**, εως, ἡ, *passage through*, τῆς θαλάσσης, τῶν ποταμῶν, *PMag.Leid.V.*10. 13. **-ευτής**, οῦ, ὁ, *wayfarer*, *Gloss.* **-εύω**, *go, travel*, ἐπὶ νῆας Il.11.569; δι' Ἀδραμυττίου X.*An.*7.8.8; διὰ νυκτός *POxy.*2153.21 (iii A.D.); κοινῶς ὁ. τινί Babr.15.2; ἐξ ὑγιείας εἰς νόσον Arist.*Fr.*41, cf. Hp.*Decent.*18: c. acc. cogn., τὴν ἐπὶ Σμύρνης Hippon.15.1; βιότου τρίβον ὁδεύειν *Anacreont.*38.2. 2. c. acc. loci, *travel over*, χθόνα πεζὸς ὁ. A.R.4.1441; ὁ. τὴν ἔρημον Plu.*Eum.*15; μέγαν οὐρανόν *IG* 14.2012*A* 36; εἴκοσι..λυκάβαντας ὁδεύσας *Epigr.Gr.*226.3 (Teos):— Pass., ὁδευομένη (with or without ὁδός) *thoroughfare, highway*, *POxy.* 1537.18 (iii A.D.), *Stud.Pal.*20.117.6 (v A.D.). 3. Pass., of Ravenna, γεφύραις καὶ πορθμείοις ὁδευομένη *provided with thoroughfares* by means of.., Str.5.1.7.

**ὀδέων** (gen. pl.), v. οὐδός.

**ὁδηγ-έω**, *lead* one *upon his way, guide*, c. acc. pers., Ps.-Phoc.24, A.*Pr.*728, *Act.Ap.*8.31, X.Eph.1.9: abs., E.*HF*1402; φύσιος εἰς τὸ ἄριστον -εούσης Hp.*Lex* 2:—Pass., Plu.2.954b, Vett.Val.359.30:— also **-ετέω**, Them.*Or.*11.151c. **-ησις**, εως, ἡ, *guiding*, S.E.*P.*1. 240, Zonar. **-ητήρ**, ῆρος, ὁ, = ὁδηγός, *Epigr.Gr.*779 (Chalcedon), Orph.*H.*41.6. **-ητικός**, ή, όν, *fitted for guiding*, Suid., Eust. 1441.12. **-ήτρια**, fem. of ὁδηγητήρ, Sch.E.*Ph.*1492. **-ία**, ἡ, *guiding*, εἰς τὸ γνῶναι Phlp. *in APo.*368.6; *teaching*, Eust.637.4. ⊛ **-ός**, ὁ, *guide*, Plb.5.5.15, Plu.*Alex.*27; of a goddess, Paus.2.11.2; part of a dirigible χελώνη, Ath.Mech.34.6; ταῖς Ἀριστοτελείοις τέχναις ὁδηγοῖς χρησάμενος D.H.*Amm.*1.12, cf. Phld.*Lib.*p.20 O.: as Adj., ὁδηγὰ πλοῖα *pilot*-boats, *Sammelb.*7173.16 (ii A.D.).

**ὁδηπορία**, ἡ, = ὁδοιπ-, *IG*14.2000.

**ὁδί**, ἡδί, τοδί [ῑ], v. ὅδε.

**ὅδ-ιος**, ον, (ὁδός) *belonging to a way* or *journey*, ὄρνις ὅ. a bird *of omen for the journey* (or *seen by the way*), A.*Ag.*157 (lyr.); ὅ. κράτος αἴσιον ib.104 (lyr.); Ἑρμῆς ὅ. H. *the guardian of roads and travellers*, whose statues stood on the road-side, Hsch. II. ὅδιον, τό, *travelling expenses*, prob. in *Inscr.Magn.*52.39. **-ισμα**, ατος, τό, πολύγομφον ὅ. *a way* compact with bolts, i.e. Xerxes' bridge over the Hellespont, A.*Pers.*71 (lyr.). **-ιστής**, οῦ, ὁ, v.l. for sq. in *h.Merc.* 203. ⊛ **-ίτης** [ῑ], ου, ὁ, *wayfarer, traveller*, Od.7.204, 17.211, S.*Ph.* 147; ἄνθρωπος ὁδίτης Il.16.263; Dor. ὁδίτας Theoc.16.93.

**ὀδμ-ᾰλέος**, α, ον, *strong-smelling, stinking*, Hp.*Morb.*4.56. **-άομαι**, **ὀδμή**, older forms of ὀσμάομαι, ὀσμή (q.v.). **-ήεις**, εσσα, εν, *giving out a smell*, Nic.*Al.*437. **-ηνος**· πολύοσμος, εὔοσμος, Hsch.

**ὁδό**, barbarism for ὁδός, Ar.*Th.*1222.

**ὁδοι-δοκέω**, *waylay*, D.S.34/5.2.43. **-δόκος**, ὁ, *footpad, highwayman*, Plb.13.8.2, Posidon.36 J., D.Chr.4.95. (From *ὁδοῖ, old loc. of ὁδός, and δέκομαι, = δέχομαι, *wait*.) **-πλᾰνέω**, *roam about*, Ar.*Ach.*69; οἶμον ὁ. Nic.*Th.*267. **-πλᾰνής**, ές, *roaming*, *AP*9.427 (Barb.). **-πλᾰνία**, ἡ, *roaming, straying*, Max.55.

⊛ **ὁδοιπορ-έω**, impf. ὡδοιπόρεον, -ουν, Hdt.4.116 (v.l. ὁ-), S.*OT*1027: fut. -ήσω Hp.*Art.*58: pf. ὁδοιπόρηκα Philippid.13: plpf. 3 pl. διοδοιπορήκεσαν Hdt.8.129:—Pass., pf. ὡδοιπόρηται Luc.*Herm.*2:— *walk*, Hdt.4.110, S.*OT*801; ὀρθότεροι -ήσουσι Hp. l.c.; ἐπ' ἄκρων ὁ. *walk* on tiptoe, S.*Aj.*1230; *come*, ὁ ξένος..ὧδ' ὁδοιπορεῖ Id.*OC* 1251: c. acc. cogn., ὁδοιπορεῖν ὁδόν Hdt.4.116; ὁ. τοὺς τόπους *walk over* this ground, S.*OT*1027.—Used in Trag. and Ion. Prose, = Att. βαδίζω; also in later Prose, *Act.Ap.*10.9, Gal.9.500, *PMag. Lond.*121.181, X.Eph.3.2. **-ία**, Ion. **-ίη**, ἡ, *walking*, *h.Merc.*85, Hp.*Fract.*15 (pl.), Hdt.2.29, 8.118; ὁδοιπορίαις καὶ δρόμοις γυμνάζειν X.*Cyr.*1.2.10; τὸ ἄδηλον τῆς ὁ. the uncertainty of the *journey by road*, *POxy.*118$^v$.6 (iii A.D.); *power of walking*, Nonn.*D.*25.552; *journey*, σημαίνειν μέτρον ὁδοιπορίας *IG*2$^2$.2640. ⊛ **-ικός**, ή, όν, *of* or *for a traveller*, ἐσθῆτες Plb.31.14.6; ἵπποι Poll.1.181: τὸ ὁ. (sc. βιβλίον) *guide-book*, Hieronym.*Ep.*8.8, *Gloss.* Adv. **-κῶς** *like a traveller*, ἐσταλμένος Plu.*Arat.*21. **-ινός**, ή, όν, epith. of βήξ, cough *contracted from walking on roads*, *Hippiatr.*22. **-ιον**, τό, *passage-money* paid to a ship-master, or *provisions for the voyage*, Od.15. 506: pl., *Sammelb.*7243.5 (iv A.D.). ⊛ **-ος**, ὁ, *wayfarer, traveller*, Il.24.375, A.*Ag.*901, S.*OT*292, Ar.*Ach.*205, Stratt.61, *IG*4$^2$(1). 121.83 (Epid., iv B.C.). (From ὁδός, πείρω, cf. πεῖρε κέλευθον Od.2. 434.)

**ὀδολκαί**· ὀβολοί (Cret.), Hsch. **ὀδόλυνθοι**· ἐρέβινθοι, Id.

**ὁδόμετρον**, τό, or **ὁδόμετρος**, ὁ, *instrument for measuring distances* by land or sea, Hero *Dioptr.*34, Simp. *in Cael.*549.8, Tz.*H.*11. 603. II. Ὁδόμετρος, name given to Phayllus, *the runner*, Sch.Ar. *Ach.*213.

**ὀδοντ-άγρα**, Ion. -η, ἡ, *forceps for drawing teeth*, Hp.*Medic.*9, Arist. *Mech.*854$^a$17, Plu.2.468c, Sor.2.63, Gal.17(1).911. **-ᾰγωγόν**, τό, = foreg., Erasistr.ap.Cael.Aur.*TP*2.4. **-αλγέω**, *suffer from toothache*, Ctes.*Fr.*57.15, Dsc.*Eup.*1.68. **-αλγία**, ἡ, *toothache*, Id.3.19 (pl.), Poll.2.96, Gal.10.82, al. **-άριον**, τό, *small cog*, Heliod.ap.Orib.49.4.60. **-ᾶς**, ᾶ, ὁ, *dentatus*, *Gloss.* **-ίας**, ου, ὁ, *dentiosus*, ib. **-ίᾱσις**, εως, ἡ, *teething*, Dsc.2.19 (pl.), Sor. 1.118 (sg.). **-ιάω**, *cut teeth*, Gal.12.334, *Gloss.* **-ίζω**, *polish with a tooth*, *PLeid.X.*8 B., al., *PHolm.*4.40 (so, *charta dentata*, Cic. *QF*2.14[15b].1, cf. Plin.*HN*13.81). II. *furnish with teeth*, in Pass., ὠδοντισμένον a *cogged* wheel, Orib.49.4.43; cf. gloss on ἀμφόδοντα in Hp.*Art.*8. **-ικός**, ή, όν, *dental*, σμῆγμα Antyll.ap.Orib. 10.36.4; ἰατρός Gal.*Thras.*24; δύναμις, of a remedy, Id.11.711; διαμασήματα, in teething, Id.12.864. II. *furnished with teeth*, Suid. s.v. θρῖδαξ. **-ίς**, ίδος, ἡ, name of a fish, *PCair.Zen.*616.6,10 (iii B.C.). **-ισμα**, ατος, τό, = sq., Eust.854.14. ⊛ **-ισμός**, ὁ, a mode of playing the flute, in which the *gnashing of the teeth* of the serpent Pytho was imitated, Poll.4.80,84.

**ὀδοντο-βολέω**, *cast teeth*, *Hippiatr.*96. **-ειδής**, ές, *tooth-shaped*, ἀπόφυσις the *odontoid* process, Gal.2.757, cf. 17(1).374. **-κερας**, ᾱτος, τό, *horn-tooth*, i.e. *tusk*, of an elephant, Amynt.ap.*An.Ox.*3. 357. **-κῠνες**, pl., f.l. for κυνόδοντες, Tim.Gaz.ap.Ar.Byz.*Epit.* 142.22. **-μάχης** [ᾰ], ου, ὁ, *fighting with the tusks*, σύες Eust.854. 11. **-ξέστης**, ου, ὁ, *instrument for cleaning the teeth*, Poll.2. 96. **-ξυστήρ**, ῆρος, ὁ, = foreg., *Hermes* 38.282. **-ομαι**, Pass., *to be furnished with teeth*, Poll.2.96, *Gloss.* **-ποιέω**, *cut teeth*, Poll. 2.96. **-πονία**, *dentium labor*, *Gloss.* **-σμηγμα**, ατος, τό, *tooth-powder*, Paul.Aeg.3.26, *Gloss.* **-τριμμα**, ατος, τό, = foreg., Damocr.ap.Gal.12.890, Gal.12.884, *An.Par.*1.394, *Gloss.* ⊛ **-τύραννος** [ῠ], ὁ, a large animal, prob. *crocodile*, in the Indus or Ganges, Ps.-Callisth.3.10. **-φόρος**, ον, *bearing teeth*, κόσμος ὀ. an ornament for horses, *consisting of strings of teeth*, *AP*6.246 (Phld. or Marc. Arg.). **-φῠέω**, *cut teeth*, Hp.*Aph.*3.25, Pl.*Phdr.*251c, Arist.*HA*587$^b$15, al. **-φῠής**, ές, *sprung from the dragon's teeth*, of the Sparti, γέννα E.*Ph.*821 (lyr.). **-φύησις** [ῠ], εως, ἡ, = sq., Sor.1.78. **-φῠΐα**, Ion. -ΐη, ἡ, *teething*, Hp.*Dent.*6, al., Poll.2.96, Jul.*Or.*7.206d, Herm. *in Phdr.*p.161 A., Paul.Aeg.1.9. **-φῠτικός**, ή, όν, *of* or *for teething*, ἡλικία Steph. *in Hp.Aph.*2.373 D. **-φῠτος**, ον, = ὀδοντοφυής, Nonn.*D.*5.2.

**ὀδοντωτός**, ή, όν, *with large teeth*, of a saw, Gal.18(2).331; ξύστρα ὀ. *comb*, Luc.*Lex.*5; *cogged*, of a wheel, Hero *Spir.*2.36, al.

**ὁδοποι-έω**, impf. ὡδοποίουν X.*An.*4.8.8: plpf. with double redupl. ὡδοπεποιήκεσαν Arr.*An.*1.26.1: pf. part. Pass. ὡδοποιημένος X.*HG* 5.4.39, *OGI*175.10 (ii B.C.) (in X.*An.*5.3.1 codd. vary); cf. προοδοποιέω:—*make* or *level a road*, ὁδόν X.*An.*4.8.8, etc.; without ὁδόν, *IG*1$^2$.363.46, 11(2).203*A* 37 (Delos, iii B.C.); *make passable*, τὰ ἄβατα Luc.*Demon.*1: abs., *make a path* or *course for itself*, of a stream, D. 55.11:—Pass., of roads, etc., *to be made fit for use* or *passable*, X.*An.* 5.3.1, *HG* l.c.: impers., τοὺς τόπους..εἰς οὓς ἑκάστοις ὡδοποίηται Pl. *Phd.*112c. 2. metaph., *pave the way*, αὐτὸ τὸ πρᾶγμα ὁ. αὐτοῖς Arist.*Metaph.*984$^a$18. 3. *make systematic*, Id.*Rh.*1354$^a$8 (nisi leg. ὁδῷ ποιεῖν). II. c. dat. pers., *act as pioneer, serve as guide* to another, ὁ. αὐτοῖς (αὐτούς codd.) X.*An.*3.2.24:—Med., *make a way for oneself*, of troops in a forest, D.S.20.23. III. ὁδοποιεῖν, v.l. for ὁδὸν ποιεῖν, *Ev.Marc.*2.23. **-ησις**, εως, ἡ, metaph., *introduction, preparation*, Arist.*Rh.*1414$^b$21. II. *habituation*, Paul. Aeg.6.114. **-ητικός**, ή, όν, *finding a way, practical*, Zeno *Stoic.* 1.20; μέθοδός ἐστιν ἕξις ὁ. μετὰ λόγου Phlp. *in Ph.*6.28, Eustr. *in EN*7. 13; ἐπιστήμη, e.g. ἰατρική, Phlp. *in Cat.*141.21. **-ία**, ἡ, *road-making, the work of a pioneer*, X.*Cyr.*6.2.36, *IG*2$^2$.1673.28, *PGrenf.* 2.14(*b*).6 (iii B.C.), Plu.*CG*7:—written **-ποΐα**, *Supp.Epigr.*4.447.28 (Didyma, ii B.C.). **-ός**, ὁ, *one who opens the way, road-maker*,

*pioneer*, X.*Cyr*.6.2.36, J.*BJ*3.6.2; *road-surveyor*, Aeschin.3.25, Arist. *Ath*.54.1 (pl.); *courier*, *POxy*.1656.1 (iv/v A.D.).

**ὁδός**, v. οὐδός.

**❋ὁδός**, ἡ (οὐδός once in Hom., Od.17.196): I. of Place, *way, road*, Il.12.168, 16.374, *IG*1².878, al.; ἱππηλασίη ὁ. Il.7.340; λαοφόρος 15.682; ὁ. ἁμαξιτός Pi.*N*.6.54; ὁ. ἱερά, to Eleusis, Paus.1.36.3, cf. *IG*1².881; βασιλικὴ ὁ. *PPetr*.3 p.65 (iii B.C.), *PSI*8.917.8 (i A.D.); ποταμοῦ ὁ. *course, channel* of a river, X.*Cyr*.7.5.16; ὁ. ἀκοντίου Antipho 3.4.5: with expression of the direction, ὁδὸς ἐς.. Od. 22.128; ἡ ὁ. ἡ εἰς ἄστυ Pl.*Smp*.173b; ἐπί.. Id.*Phdr*.272c; τὴν εὐθὺς Ἄργους..ὁ. leading straight to Argos, E.*Hipp*.1197; τῆς ἀληθείας ὁ. the way *to truth*, Id.*Fr*.289; cf. νόστος I.1. 2. with Preps., πρὸ ὁδοῦ *further on the way, forwards*, Il.4.382 (cf. φροῦδος); later, = προὔργου, *profitable, useful*, πρὸ ὁ. εἶναι πρός τι to be *helpful* towards.., Arist.*Cael*.292ᵇ9, cf. *Metaph*.1044ᵃ24; πρὸ ὁδοῦ γέγονεν Id.*Pol*.1338ᵃ35, cf. D.*Prooem*.34; κατ' ὁδὸν *by the way*, Hdt.1.41,111; κατὰ τὴν ὁ. along the *road*, Pl.*Smp*.174d, cf. infr. III.3; ἐκ τῆς ὁ. on his *road*, Hdt.1.157 (but ἄνθρωπος ἐξ ὁ. 'the man in the street', Eup.25D.); ἐν ὁδῷ on *a road*, Hdt.1.114; ἐν τῇ ὁ. μέσῃ Id.3.76 (but ἐν ὁ. καθελών Lex ap.D.23.53, expld. by ἐν λόχῳ καὶ ἐνέδρᾳ by Harp. s. v. ὁδός); ὁδοῦ πάρεργον by *the way*, cursorily, Cic.*Att*.5.21.13, 7.1.5, Gal.11.607. 3. ὁδός is freq. omitted, ἐπορευόμην τὴν ἔξω τείχους Pl.*Ly*.203a; ἡ ἐπὶ θανάτου, v. θάνατος; cf. τηνάλλως. II. as an Action, *travelling, journeying*, whether by land or water, *journey, voyage*, Od.2.285, 8.150, etc.; τρίποδας ὁ. στείχει A.*Ag*.80 (anap.); τὰν νέαταν ὁ. στείχουσαν S.*Ant*.807 (lyr.); ὁ. ἄνω κάτω μία καὶ ὡυτή Heraclit. 60; also, *expedition, foray*, ὁδὸν ἐλθέμεναι Il.1.151, cf. A.*Th*.714; τριήκοντα ἡμερέων..ὁ. a thirty days' *journey*, Hdt.1.104, cf. 206; also ὅσον ἐπὶ τρεῖς ἡμέρας ὁδόν Id.3.5 (codd., ὁδοῦ edd.); ἄστρων ὁδοί E. *El*.728 (lyr.): as acc. cogn. with Verb of motion, τὴν ὁ. ἣν Ἑλένην περ ἀνήγαγεν *by* or *in which*.., Il.6.292; οὐρανοῦ τέμνων ὁ..Ἥλιε, metaph. from a ship, E.*Ph*.1 (but in Prose ὁ. τέμνειν is to make a *road*, Th.2.100, Pl.*Lg*.810e); similarly where ὁ. is *road*, μέσην ἔρχευ τὴν ὁ. Thgn.220; ὁ. χωρεῖν Th.3.24; ἰόντες τὴν ἰρὴν ὁ., from Delphi, Hdt.6.34. III. metaph., *way* or *manner*, πολλαὶ δ' ὁ... εὐπραγίας Pi.*O*.8.13; γλώσσης ἀγαθῆς ὁδός A.*Eu*.989 (anap.); θεσπεσία ὁ. *the way* or *course* of divination, Id.*Ag*.1154 (lyr.); μαντικῆς ὁ. S.*OT*311; οἰωνῶν ὁδοῖς Id.*OC*1314; σῶν ὁ. βουλευμάτων E.*Hec*.744; γνώμης Id.*Hipp*.290; λογίων ὁ. their *way, intent*, Ar.*Eq*.1015; εὐτελείας ὁ. Jul.*Or*.6.198d. 2. *a way* of doing, speaking, etc., τῆσδ' ἀφ' ὁδοῦ διζήσιος Parm.1.33, cf. 8.18; τριφασίας ἄλλας ὁ. λόγων *ways* of telling the story, Hdt.1.95, cf. 2.20,22; but τριφασίας ὁ. τρέπεται turns into three *forms*, Id.6.119; ἄδικον ὁ. ἰέναι Th.3.64; ὁ. ἥντιν' ἰών by what *course of action*, Ar.*Pl*.506, cf. *Nu*.75; ἣν ἔχομεν ὁ. λόγων Id.*Pax*733; μία δὴ λείπεται..ὁ. Pl.*Smp*.184b. 3. *method, system*, Id.*Sph*.218d, Arist.*APr*.53ᵃ2, al.; ὁδῷ *methodically, systematically*, Pl.*R*.533b, *Stoic*.2.39, etc.; so καθ' ὁδόν Pl.*R*.435a; τὴν διὰ τοῦ στοιχείου ὁ. ἔχων ἔγραφεν Id.*Tht*.208b (cf. διέξοδον 208a). 4. of *the Christian Faith and its followers*, *Act.Ap*.9.2, 22.4, 24.14. (Root *sed*- 'go', in Skt. *sad*-, *ā-sad*- 'come to', 'reach', OSlav. *choditi* 'go'.)

**ὁδο-σκοπέω**, *watch the roads*, of footpads, Eust.1445.19. **-στρωσία**, ἡ, *paving of roads*, *CIG*4438 (Tarsus), Just.*Nov*.17.4.

**ὁδούρ-εις**· τοὺς ἐν ταῖς ὁδοῖς κακουργοῦντας, Hsch. **-έω**, *keep, watch the road*, Phot. **-ης**· ὁ τῆς ὁδοῦ ἄρχων ἢ κατάρχων, Hsch. **❋-ός**, ὁ or ἡ, *conductor, conductress*, E.*Ion* 1617. II. *waylayer, highwayman*, S.*Fr*.22, E.*Fr*.260.

**❋ὀδούς**, όντος, ὁ, nom. ὀδούς Arist.*EN*1161ᵇ23, Lxx 1*Ki*.14.4, Luc. *Musc.Enc*.3, Paus.5.12.2, Philostr.*VA*2.13, Ach.Tat.7.4; Ion. ὀδών Hdt.6.107 (bis), Hp.*Epid*.4.19,52, cf. Hdn.Gr.2.928:—*tooth*, Il.5.74, al.; ἕρκος ὀδόντων, v. ἕρκος; πρίειν ὀδόντας, v. πρίω; ὁ. ὀξεῖς *incisors*, opp. πλατεῖς, *molars*, Arist.*PA*661ᵇ8, al. 2. metaph., γλυκὺς ὁ. ὁ τοῦ πόθου Luc.*Am*.3; ὁ τῆς λύπης ὁ. the *tooth* of grief, Ach.Tat. l.c. II. *anything pointed* or *sharp, tooth, prong, spike*, etc., Nic. *Th*.85: pl., *teeth* of a saw, Arist.*Ph*.200ᵇ6; of a comb, Antyll.ap. Orib.10.16.2; of a *cog*-wheel, Hero *Spir*.2.36, Theo Sm.p.180 H.; *ploughshare*, Lxx 1*Ki*.13.21; ὁ. πέτρας *peak, pike*, ib.14.4, *Ps*.77.30. III. *second vertebra* of the neck or its apophysis (the odontoid process), so called from its shape, Hp.*Epid*.2.2.24, cf. Poll.2.131, Gal *UP*12.7 (but the *first vertebra* acc. to Hp.ap.Ruf.*Onom*.154). (Old pres. part. of I.-E. *ed*- (alternating with *od*- (cf. Arm. *utem* 'I eat') and *d*-), the root of ἔδω, ἔδ-μεναι, Lat. *edo*, etc.: cf. Skt. acc. *dántam* 'tooth', Lat. *dens*, Goth. *tunþus*, etc.: Aeol. ἔδοντες Procl. *in Cra*.p.39 P., etc.)

**ὁδο-φῠλᾰκέω**, *watch* or *guard the roads*, Phot.s.v. ὁδωρεῖν. **-φύλαξ** [ῠ], ακος, ὁ, *watcher of the roads*, Hdt.7.239. II. = ὁδουρός II, Eust. 1445.20. **-χνοῦς**, *pulveraria, Gloss*. **-ω**, *lead by the right way*, οὗτός σ' ὁδώσει τὴν τρίγωνον ἐς χθόνα A.*Pr*.813; δυστέκμαρτον ἐς τέχνην ὥδωσα θνητούς ib.498: c. inf., τὸν φρονεῖν βροτοὺς ὁδώσαντα *who put* mortals *on the way* to wisdom, Id.*Ag*.176 (lyr.); of things, *direct, ordain*, E.*Ion* 1050 (lyr.):—Pass., *to be on the right way*, τὰ ἀπ' ὑμέων χρηστῶς ὁδοῦται Hdt.4.139.

**ὀδῠν-αίτερος**, α, ον, irreg. Comp. form of ὀδυνηρός or ὀδυνώδης, Hp. *Fract*.17. **-άω**, aor. ὀδυνῆσαι Gal.10.853:—Pass., Phld.*Lib*.p.29 O.; 2 sg. ὀδυνᾶσαι *Ev.Luc*.16.25: fut. ὀδυνηθήσομαι Gal.10.851, but ὀδυνήσομαι Men.325.16, Teles *Fr*.2 p.9 H.: aor. ὠδυνήθην Ar.*Ach*.3:—*cause* one *pain* or *suffering*, τὸ γὰρ ὀρθοῦσθαι γνώμαν ὀδυνᾷ E.*Hipp*.247 (anap.), cf. Ar.*Lys*.164; οὐ τοὐμὸν ὀδυνήσει σε γῆρας Id.*Ec*.928; μηδὲν ὀδύνα τὸν πατέρα Men.659:—Pass., *feel pain, suffer pain*, Democr.159, Hp.*Epid*.4.12, S.*El*.804, Ar.*V*.283, *Ra*.650, Pl.*R*.583d, etc.; ἃ ὠδυνήθην *the pains I suffered*, Ar.*Ach*.3, cf. 9; Ion. pres. **ὀδυνέομαι** Aret.*SD* 2.4. **-η**, ἡ, *pain of body*, ὀδύνῃσι κακῇσι τειρόμενος Od.9.440, cf. 415, 17.567; ἀλεγεινή Il.11.398; ὀδύναι δῦνον μένος Ἀτρεΐδαο ib.268; ὀδύνῃσι πεπαρμένος 5.399; ἀντίτομα στερεᾶν ὀδυνᾶν Pi.*P*.4.221; cf. ἕρμα I.4; στρόφος μ' ἔχει τὴν γαστέρ'..κὠδύνη Ar.*Th*.484, cf. *Pl*.1131: also in Prose, X.*HG*5.4.58 (pl.), Thphr.*HP*9.11.3, etc. 2. *pain of mind, grief, distress*, once in Il., ὁ. Ἡρακλῆος *grief for* him, 15.25: more freq. in Od., always in pl., ὀδύνας τε γόους τε κάλλιπεν 1.242; ὀδύνας ἐμβάλλετε θυμῷ 2.79, al.: after Hom. the pl. was most common in both senses, ὁ. δυσαπάλλακτοι, ἄλληκτοι, S.*Tr*.959, 986 (both lyr.); ὀδύναις πεφυσιγγωμένοι Ar.*Ach*.526; opp. φιλότητες, Antipho Soph.49; σφαδασμῶν τε καὶ ὀδυνῶν Pl.*R*.579e, cf. 574a, al.: but the sg. also occurs, ἐξ ὀλίγης ὁ. μέγα γίνεται ἄλγος Sol.12.59; γλώσσας ὁ. *pain caused by* the tongue, S.*Ph*.1142, cf. 827 (both lyr.), *Tr*.975 (anap.); ὁ. σε εἴληφε X.*Smp*.1.15; ὁ. μ' ἔχει *Lyr.Alex.Adesp*.1.3; μετ' ὀδύνης Men.706; τοῖς νενικημένοις ὀδύνη, = Lat. *vae victis!* Plu.*Cam*.28. (Perh. from ἐδ- ὀδ- 'eat', cf. θυμὸν ἔδων Od.10.379: the Aeolians called τὰς ὀδύνας ἐδύνας acc. to Greg.Cor.p.597 S.) **-ημα**, ατος, τό, *pain*, Hp.*Acut.*(*Sp.*)31 (pl.). **-ηρός**, Dor. **-ᾱρός**, ά, όν, *painful*, ἕλκος Pi.*P*.2.91, cf. Ar.*Ach*.231; -ότατα πάθη Pl.*Grg*.525c; -ότατον τραῦμα Jul.*Gal*.160d. Adv. -ρῶς Arist.*HA*609ᵇ25: Comp. -ότερον Plu.2.837a. 2. *distressing*, γῆρας Mimn.1.5; πᾶς..ὁ. βίος ἀνθρώπων E. *Hipp*.189 (anap.); -ότερος βίοτος Ar.*Pl*.526; ὁ. πλοῦτος E.*Ph*.566, cf. Phld.*Lib* p.15 O.; ὀδυνηρόν ἐστιν c. inf., Men.655.

**ὀδῠνή-φᾰτος**, ον, (θείνω) *killing*, i. e. *stilling, pain*, ὀδυνήφατα φάρμακα πάσσων Il.5.401,900, cf. 11.847, Orph.*L*.345, 753. **-φόρος**, ον, *causing pain*, Corn.*ND*30, Marc.Sid.89.

**ὀδῠνοσπάς**, άδος, ὁ, ἡ, *racked by pain*, γέρων A.*Fr*.361.

**ὀδῠνώδης**, ες, *painful*, in Adv. -δῶς Gal.7.788.

**ὄδυρ-μα**, ατος, τό, *complaint, wailing*, mostly in pl., A.*Ch*.508, S. *Tr*.50, etc.: in sg., E.*Tr*.1226. **-μός**, ὁ, *lamentation*, ὀδυρμοὶ καὶ γόοι A.*Pr*.33; λῆξασ' ὀδυρμῶν πενθίμων τε δακρύων E.*Ph*.1071; θρήνων ὀδυρμοί Id.*Tr*.609; ὀδυρμοὺς καὶ οἴκτους Pl.*R*.387d; θρήνων τε καὶ ὀδυρμῶν ib.398d, al., cf. Call.*Fr*.1.7 P.: c. gen., τῆς τύχης ὁ. *lamentation* for.., Plu.*Demetr*.47. **-ομαι** [ῡ], mostly used in pres. and impf., Ep. impf. ὀδύρετο, ὀδύροντο (without augm.), Ion. ὀδυρέσκετο Hdt.3.119: fut. ὀδῡροῦμαι D.21.186, and prob. l. Isoc.18.35: aor. ὠδῡράμην Id.12.9, Theoc.1.75 (cf. ἀνοδύρομαι); part. ὀδῡράμενος Il. 24.48: aor. Pass. κατ-ωδύρθην Plu.2.117f.—In Trag. the form **δύρομαι** is required by the metre in A.*Pr*.273, *Pers*.582 (lyr.), S.*OT* 1218 (lyr., ὀδ- codd.), E.*Hec*.740, *Med*.159 (lyr., ὀδ- codd.), and prob. in Id.*Andr*.397, v. infr. 4; in Id.*Ph*.1762, Apollod.Com.8, ὀδύρομαι is necessary; elsewh. either form is possible:—*lament, bewail*, a person or thing: 1. c. acc. pers., ὀδυρομένη φίλα τέκνα Il.2.315; Ἕκτορα δάκρυ χέοντες ὀδύροντο 24.714, cf. S.*OC*1439, *Ant*. 693: less freq. c. acc. rei, ὁ δ' ὀδύρετο πατρίδα γαῖαν *mourned for* it, i.e. for the want of it, Od.13.219; so νόστον ὀ. 5.153, 13.379; προπηλακίσεις Pl.*R*.329b; δυστυχίας Isoc.4.169; πάθη D.18.41; οὐκ ὠδύραντο..τὴν προκαταστροφήν Epicur.*Sent*.40. 2. c. gen. pers., *mourn for, for the sake of*.., ὡς δὲ πατὴρ οὗ παιδὸς ὀ. Il.23.222, cf. 22. 424, Od.4.104, etc.; ὑπέρ τινος Pl.*R*.387d; ἐπὶ πᾶσι Arist.*VV*1251ᵇ21. 3. ὀ. τινί *wail* or *lament to* or *before*, ἐξελθὼν λαοῖσιν ὀ. Od.4. 740; ἀλλήλοισιν ὀδύροντο *wail aloud* one to another, Il.2.290. 4. abs., *wail, mourn*, freq. in Hom., in part., -όμενος στεναχίζω Od.9. 13; στοναχῇ τε γόῳ τε ἧσται ὀ. 16.145; ὀ. κατὰ θυμόν 18.203; τί ταῦτ' ὀδύρομαι; why *mourn I* thus? E.*Andr*.397 (where Pors. restores ταῦτα δύρομαι for the caesura); θρηνοῦντός τε μου καὶ ὀδυρομένου Pl. *Ap*.38d, cf. Phld.*Rh*.1.381 S., etc. **-τέον**, *one must bewail*, Jul. *Or*.8.246b. **-της**, ου, ὁ, *complainer*, Arist.*Phgn*.812ᵃ4, 813ᵃ33, Adam.2.22. **-τικός**, ή, όν, *querulous*, of persons, Arist.*Rh*.1390ᵃ22, J.*AJ*15.3.5, Poll.6.202; also ὀδυρτικόν τι ἀναφθέγγεσθαι Plu.2. 751a. Adv. -κῶς Demetr.*Eloc*.28: Comp. -κωτέρως Arist.*Pol*.1340ᵃ42. **-τός**, όν, *mourned for, lamentable*, Plu.2.499f; φωνή *Epigr. Gr*.1003.4: neut. ὀδυρτά, as Adv., *painfully*, Ar.*Ach*.1226.

**Ὀδύσσ-εια**, ἡ, *the Odyssey*, Hdt.4.29, Pl.*R*.393b, Arist.*Rh*.1406ᵇ12, *Po*.1449ᵃ1, al., *AP*7.377:—Adj. **-ειακός**, ή, όν, *of* or *for the Odyssey*, προσῳδία, title of work by Hdn.Gr., Sch.Ar.*Av*.862. **-ειος**, v. Ὀδύσσειος. **❋-εύς**, έως, Ion. -ῆος, ὁ (also **Οὐλιξεύς** Hdn. Gr.1.14, **Οὐλίξης** prob. in Ibyc.ap.Diom.p.321 K., **Ὀλυσεύς**, **Ὀλυσσεύς**, **Ὀλυτεύς**, **Ὀλυττεύς**, **Ὀλισεύς**, **Ὠλυσσεύς** Kretschmer *Gr.Vaseninschr*.pp.146,147, al.; cf. **Ὀλισσεῖδαι**, οἱ, a φάτρα (q.v.) at Thebes and Argos, prob. in *IG*7.3659, *Mnemos*.43.372, 47.164):—*Odysseus*, king of Ithaca, hero of the Odyssey: in Hom. also **Ὀδῠσεύς**; gen. Ὀδῠσεῦς Od.24.398; acc. Ὀδυσσέα (last syll. short before a vowel) 17.301; Ὀδυσσέα (⏑ – –) S.*Aj*.104, Ὀδυσσῆ Pi. *N*.8.26, Ὀδυσσῆα Od.5.149, Ὀδυσῆα 1.74,83, al.: Οὐδυσσεύς, crasis for ὁ Ὀδ., S.*Ph*.572: pl., Ὀδυσσέας E.*Rh*.866.—On the mythic etym. of the name in Hom., v. ὀδύσσομαι:—Adj. **Ὀδύσσειος**, α, ον, Tz. ad Lyc.1030, etc.; **Ὀδύσσεια**, τά, *games in honour of Odysseus*, Schwyzer 434.16 (Magn. Mae., iii B.C.); **Ὀδύσσειον**, τό, *temple of Odysseus*, ib.2; Ep. **Ὀδυσήϊος** Od.18.353.

***ὀδύσσομαι** or ***ὀδυίομαι**, Ep. Verb, only used in aor. I Med. ὀδύσασθαι (aor. Pass. ὀδυσθῆναι Hsch.), and once in pf. Pass. ὀδώδυσται, Od.5.423:—*to be wroth against, hate*, c. dat. pers., τῷ μὲν ἔπειτ' ὀδύσαντο θεοί Il.6.138; esp. as the mythic origin of the name Ὀδυσσεύς, as *hated* by gods and men, τί νύ οἱ τόσον ὠδύσαο, Ζεῦ; Od.1.62; τίπτε τοι ὧδε Ποσειδάων..ὠδύσατ' ἐκπάγλως; 5.340; πολλοῖσιν γὰρ ἔγωγε ὀδυσσάμενος..ἱκάνω..· τῷ δ' Ὀδυσεὺς ὄνομ' ἔστω ἐπώνυμον 19.407–9,

cf. S.*Fr.*965; also Βριάρεω.. πατὴρ ὠδύσατο θυμῷ Hes.*Th.*617: abs., ὀδυσσαμένοιο τεοῖο Il.8.37: later, c. acc., ὠδύσατο Ζῆνα Hom. *Epigr.*6.8; τί.. ἐμὴν ὠδύσσαο νηδύν; *AP*9.117.—Ep. Verb, borrowed once by Sophocles in reference to Odysseus.

**ὄδωδα, ὀδώδει,** v. ὄζω.

**ὀδωδή,** ἡ, *smell, scent, AP*9.610, Plu.2.648a.

**ὀδών,** v. ὀδούς.

**ὀδωτός,** ή, όν, *passable,* γῆν ὀ. ἐποίησε f.l. in D.Chr.3.127; ὀ. θάλασσα Suid. II. *practicable, feasible,* ἐμοὶ οὐχ ὀδωτά S.*OC*495.

**ὀέα·** μηλωτή, Hsch. (Cf. οἶεος.) **ὀείγω,** v. οἴγω.

**ὀειδής,** ές, late spelling of ᾠειδής, *egg-shaped,* Eudox.*Ars*19.15.

**ὄες·** κώδια, Hsch. **ὄεσσι,** Ep. dat. pl. of ὄϊς, οἶς (q.v.). **ὀέσχαι·** μηλωταί, βαῖται, ἤγουν δερμάτιναι, Id. **ὀέτεας·** παρὰ τοῖς βαρβάροις, ὁ καλλίθριξ, Id. (v. οἰέτεας, and cf. ἀετέα, αὐετή, ὑετής, Id.).

※ **ὄζαιν-α,** ἡ, (ὄζω) *a fetid polypus* in the nose, Gal.12.678, Poll.4.204, *POxy.*1088.28. II. *a strong-smelling sea-polypus,* also called ὀσμύλη and βολβίταινα, Call.*Fr.*38. **-ικός,** ή, όν, *having* or *belonging to an* ὄζαινα 1, Ps.-Dsc.4.137. ※ **-ίτης** [ῑ], ου, ὁ, fem. ※ **-ῖτις,** ιτιδος, *smelling like an* ὄζαινα, name of an Indian form of νάρδος, Plin.*HN*12. 42. **-ομαι,** = ὄζω, c. gen., σίτου Sophr.123.

※ **ὀζᾰλέος,** α, ον, (ὄζος) *branching, AP*9.249 (Maec.).

**ὀζειέα·** θεραπεία, Hsch. (Perh. ὀζεία, cf. ἄοζος.)

**ὄζη,** ἡ, (ὄζω) *bad smell,* of bad breath, Cels.3.11. II. *skin of the wild ass,* Suid.

**ὀζήκεις·** οἱ σφριγῶντες, Hsch.

**Ὀζόλαι,** οἱ, *the Ozolae,* a tribe of the Locrians, Hdt.8.32; perh. from the *strong-smelling* sulphur-springs in their country, Str.9.4.8, cf. Antig.*Mir.*117(129); or from their wearing goat-skins, Plu.2. 294f. II. **Ὀζολίς** (sc. γῆ), ίδος, ἡ, *their country,* St.Byz.

**ὄζολις,** ιδος, ἡ, = ὄζαινα II, Arist.*HA*525ᵃ19.

**ὀζομενία,** ἡ, *mephitis, Gloss.*

**ὀζόομαι,** Pass., (ὄζος) *put forth branches* or *knots,* Hp.*Nat.Puer.*22; ὠζωμένον τυφλοῖς ὄζοις Thphr.*CP*3.5.1.

※ **ὄζος,** ὁ, Aeol. **ὔσδος** Sapph.93:—*bough, branch, twig,* Il.1.234, 2. 312, al., Hes.*Th.*30, Pi.*P.*4.263, etc.: prop. the *knot* or *eye* from which a branch or leaf springs, Arist.*Juv.*468ᵇ25, Thphr.*HP*1.1.9, Aret.*SD* 2.9; τυφλοὶ ὄ. unproductive *eyes, mere knots,* Thphr.*HP*1.8.4; σκύταλον κεχαραγμένον ὄζοις Theoc.17.31; σάρκινος ὄ., of the ear, Emp. 99. II. metaph., *offshoot, scion,* ὄ. Ἄρηος, as epith. of famous warriors, Il.2.540, 12.188, al.; τὼ Θησείδα ὄζω Ἀθηνῶν E.*Hec.*123 (anap.); χρυσοῦ ὄ. ἀδάμας ἐκλήθη Pl.*Ti.*59b. (Cf. Goth. *asts,* Germ. *ast*: in the phrase ὄζος Ἄρηος ὄ. perh. means *follower, servant,* cf. ὀζειέα and ἄοζος.)

**ὄζος,** Cret., = ὅσος, *GDI*4975, al. (Gortyn).

**ὀζό-στομος,** ον, *with foul breath, AP*11.427 (Lucill.), M.Ant.5.28, Orib.*Fr.*24. **-χρωτος,** ον, *hircosus, Gloss.*

**ὄζυγες·** ὁμόζυγες, Hsch.

※ **ὄζω,** Dor. **ὄσδω** Theoc.1.149 (cf. also III infr.): impf. ὦζε Crates Com.2 (cj. Pors. for ὦ Ζεῦ): fut. ὀζήσω Ar.*V.*1059; Ion. ὀζέσω Hp. *Superf.*25, *Gp.*12.29.5, Eust.1523.39, *An.Ox.*2.396: aor. ὤζησα Ar.*Fr.* 635; Ion. ὤζεσα Hp.*Superf.*25, Lxx *Ex.*8.14(10): pf. ὤζηκα Phot.; but pf. with pres. sense ὄδωδα Phylarch.10J., *AP*7.30 (Antip. Sid.), Plu.2.916d, Aret.*SA*1.9: plpf. as impf. ὠδώδειν Plu.*Alex.*20; Ep. ὀδώδειν (v. infr.):—*smell,* whether *smell sweet* or *stink,* Hom. only in 3 sg. plpf. with sense of impf., ὀδμὴ κέδρου.. ἀνὰ νῆσον ὀδώδει Od.5.60; ὀδμὴ δ' ἡδεῖα ἀπὸ κρητῆρος ὀδώδει, of wine, 9.210: later c. gen. rei, freq. with neut. Adj. or Adv. added, *smell of* a thing, τόδ' ὄζει θυμάτων A.*Ag.* 1310; ὄζων τρυγός Ar.*Nu.*50; βύρσης κάκιστον ὄζων Id.*Eq.*892, cf. *V.* 38; also ὠδώδει ὑπὸ μύρων ὁ οἶκος Plu.*Alex.*20: metaph., *smell* or *savour* of a thing, Κρονίων ὄζων *smelling of* musty antiquity, Ar.*Nu.* 398, cf. 1007, *Ach.*192, *Lys.*616; καλοκἀγαθίας X.*Smp.*2.4; that from which the smell comes is also in gen., ὄζων κακὸν τῶν μασχαλῶν Ar. *Ach.*852; τοῦ στόματος Pherecr.67: so c. dupl. gen., τῆς κεφαλῆς ὄζω μύρου Ar.*Ec.*524; v. infr. II. II. freq. impers., ὄζει ἀπ' αὐτῆς ὡσεὶ ἴων *there is a smell* from it as of violets, Hdt.3.23; ὄζει ἡδὺ τῆς χροὸς *there is a* sweet *smell* from the skin, Ar.*Pl.*1020; τῆς γῆς ὡς γλυκὺ ὄζει Cratin.Jun.1; ὄζειν ἐδόκει τοῦ ἄρτου καὶ τῆς μάζης κάκιστον there seemed *to be a* most foul *smell* from.., Lys.6.1; οὐκ ὄζει αὐτῶν (sc. τῶν λαγῶν) *no scent* of the hares *remains,* X.*Cyn.*5.1, cf. 7: c. dupl. gen., ἱματίων ὀζήσει δεξιότητος *there will be an odour* of cleverness from your clothes, Ar.*V.*1059, cf. *Pax*529; ἀπὸ στόματος.. ὄζει ἴων, ὄζει δὲ ῥόδων, ὄζει δ' ὑακίνθου Hermipp.82.8; ὄζει ἐκ τοῦ στόματος μελικήρας Pherecr.25. III. Med., κακὸν ὀζόμενος, for ὄζων, Hp.*Loc.Hom.* 12; οἶνος.. ἄνθεος ὀσδόμενος Xenoph.1.6; δριμὺ ὀσδομένου τοῦ σώματος *PSI*4.297.3 (ca. v A.D.). (Cf. Lat. *odor,* Lith. *uodžiu* 'I smell'.)

**ὀζώδης** (A), ες, (ὄζος) *having branches,* opp. ἄοζος, Thphr.*HP*1.5.4, al.; of a form of coral, Dsc.5.122. II. *having knots in it,* of timber, Thphr.*HP*3.10.4 (Comp.), cf. Plin.*HN*16.65.

**ὀζώδης** (B), ες, (ὄζω) = ὀδμώδης, *EM*775.8, Sch.Nic.*Al.*437, Tz.*H.* 8.991.

**ὀζωτός,** ή, όν, (ὀζόομαι) *branching,* Thphr.*HP*1.3.1.

**ὄη,** v. ὄα (A).

**ὅθεν,** relat. Adv. *whence,* ὑπὸ πλατανίστῳ, ὅ. ῥέεν ἀγλαὸν ὕδωρ Il.2. 307; ἐξ Ἐνετῶν, ὅ. ἡμιόνων γένος ib.852; γένος δέ μοι ἔνθεν, ὅ. σοί 4. 58, etc.; πόλεως ὅθεν εἰ *IG*12(5).310.2 (Paros); also, *from whom* or *which,* ὅθεν περ Ὁμηρίδαι ἄρχονται, Διὸς ἐκ προοιμίου Pi.*N.*2.1; τὴν τεκοῦσαν.., ὅθεν περ αὐτὸς ἐσπάρη S.*OT*1498; Φοῖνιξ, ὅθεν περ τοὔνομ' ἡ χώρα φέρει E.*Fr.*819.8: folld. by Particles, ὅθεν περ (v. supr.); ὅθεν δὴ A.*Supp.*15 (anap.); ὅθεν τε Od.4.358. b. in Att. Prose, ὅθεν δὴ *from whatever source, in what manner soever,* Pl.*Phdr.*267d; so ὁθενδήποτε Dosith.p.410K.; also ἄλλοθεν ὁθενοῦν *from any* other *place whatsoever,* Pl.*Lg.*738c. 2. for *where* or *whither,* by attraction, when the antecedent clause contains a notion of place whence, ἐκ δὲ γῆς, ὅ. προὔκειτ' *from* the ground *where* it lay, S.*Tr.*701; ὅ.. ἀπέλιπες, ἀποκρίνου answer [*from* the point] *where* you left off, Pl. *Grg.*497c; διεκομίζοντο.. ὅ. ὑπεξέθεντο παῖδας καὶ γυναῖκας Th.1.89; ὅθεν, = ἐκεῖσε ὅθεν, X.*An.*1.3.17, 7.6.12, etc.; ὅθεν περ, = ἐκεῖθεν ὅθεν περ, *IG*1².78.9, 88.23. II. *whence, for which reason,* σφυρῶν.. κέντρα διαπείρας μέσον, ὅ. νιν Ἑλλὰς ὠνόμαζεν Οἰδίπουν E.*Ph.*27, cf. Antipho Soph.54, Arist.*Ath.*3.2, *IG*2².1011.42, al.; ὅ... ἱδρύσαθ' ἱερόν Alex. 267.4; *for what reason,* Pl.*Prt.*319b; ὅ. ἠνάγκασμαι κατηγορεῖν αὐτῶν, περὶ τούτων πρῶτον εἰπεῖν βούλομαι Lys.22.1.

**ὀθέτη·** ἅμαξα ἡμιονική, Hsch. (Cf. ὄθιζα.) **ὀθεύει·** ἄγει, φροντίζει, Id. (Cf. ὀθρεῖν, and v. sq.) **ὀθέω,** only ὀθέων· φροντίζων, and ὄθεσαν· ἐπεστράφησαν, Id. **ὄθη·** φροντίς, ὥρα, φόβος, λόγος, Id. **ὄθημον·** ὑστερινόν, Id.

※ **ὅθι,** relat. Adv., poet. for οὗ, *where,* Il.2.722, Od.14.73, 397, al.; also ὅ. περ Il.2.861, al., Pi.*Fr.*77: used by Trag. only in lyr., exc. S. *El.*709: rare in Prose, Pl.*Thg.*125a; ὅ. περ Id.*Phd.*108b; found in Arc. Prose, *IG*5(2).16.12 (Tegea, iii B.C.). [In Hom. ι is freq. elided; and so S. l. c. (s. v. l.).]

※ **ὄθιζα·** ἅμαξα ἡμιονική, Hsch. (Cf. ὀθέτη.)

**ὄθλεις,** plants indicating the presence of water, *Gp.*2.4.1.

※ **ὄθμα,** ατος, τό, = ὄμμα, Call.*Aet.Oxy.*2075.37, Nic.*Th.*178, 443, *Hymn.Is.*157. (Aeol. acc. to Hsch.)

**ὄθμισμα,** ατος, τό, dub. sens. in *Sammelb.*6319.61 (Ptol.).

※ **ὀθνεῖος,** α, ον, also ος, ον E.*Alc.*532:—*strange, foreign,* Democr.60, 80, E.*Alc.* l.c., 646, 810, Parth. in *PLit.Lond.*64.6; joined with ἀλλότριος, Pl.*R.*470b,c; opp. οἰκεῖος, Id.*Prt.*316c, cf. Democr. ll. cc.; χρήμασιν τῶν ὀθνείων καὶ Ἀθηναίοισιν ἅπασιν *IG*1².6.54; opp. συγγενής, Democr.90, cf. Arist.*EN*1162ᵃ8, 1160ᵃ6; opp. προσήκοντες, Phld.*Ir.* p.54 W.; ὀ. φίλοι Is.4.18; ἱερὰ.. ὀ. τῇ χώρᾳ Lycurg.25. II. *abnormal,* θερμόν Gal.10.754; ποιότης Id.11.478; ὕψος Sthenid.ap. Stob.4.7.63; ἐργασίη Aret.*SD*1.15.

**ὀθνιότυμβος,** ον, *buried in a foreign land,* Man.4.281.

**ὄθομαι,** only pres. and impf., *take heed,* Hom. only in Il., and always with neg.: abs., οὐκ ἀλεγίζει οὐδ' ὄθεται Il.15.107: c. inf., οὐκ ὄθεται φίλον ἦτορ ἶσον ἐμοὶ φάσθαι ib.166, cf. 182: with part. for inf., ὃς οὐκ ὄθετ' αἴσυλα ῥέζων 5.403: c. gen. pers., *regard,* σέθεν.. οὐκ ἀλεγίζω, οὐδ' ὄθομαι κοτέοντος 1.181; ἐμεῖο οὐκ ὄθεται A.R.3.94, cf. 1.1267. (Cf. ὀθεύει, ὀθέω, ὄθη.)

**ὀθον-είδιον,** τό, Dim. of ὀθόνιον, *POxy.*1679.5 (iii A.D., pl.). **-η,** ἡ, *fine linen,* in Hom. always pl., *fine linen cloths,* Od.7.107; of a woman's dress, ἀργεννῇσι καλυψαμένη ὀθόνῃσιν Il.3.141, cf. 18.595; ὀθόναις ἐσταλμένος Luc.*DMort.*3.2: sg., *a cloth, Act.Ap.*10.11, 11.5, Gal.11.134, 6.795. 2. later, *sails,* πνεύσεται εἰς ὀθόνας *AP*12.53. 8 (Mel.), cf. 10.5 (Thyill.): sg., *sail-cloth, sail,* Luc.*JTr.*46, *VH*2. 37. 3. in pl., of the *membranes* that enclose the pupil of the eye, Emp.84.8. ※ **-ιακός,** ὁ, *dealer in* ὀθόνη, *POxy.*933.33 (ii A.D.), *IG Rom.*4.246 (Alexandria Troas), *PLips.*39.3 (iv A.D.), *Dig.*50.4.18. 12. II. **-κόν,** τό, *tax on cloth,* πραγματευτὴς ὀθονιακοῦ *Sammelb.* 5941.3 (vi A.D.). **-ιηρά,** ἡ, *tax on linen-making, PTeb.ined.*703. 105, *Ostr.*1499. **-ῐνος,** η, ον, *of fine linen,* Luc.*Alex.*12, 15; πρόσωπον Pl.Com.142. ※ **-ιον,** τό, Dim. of ὀθόνη, *linen cloth,* Hp. *Acut.*7, Ar.*Fr.*104, Thphr.*HP*7.3.5, *PSI*6.599 (iii B.C.), Plb.6.23.3, *Ev.Jo.*19.40, etc.: pl., *linen cloths,* βύσσινα ὀ. *OGI*90.18 (Rosetta, ii B.C.), cf. Lxx *Jd.*14.13, Luc.*Philops.*34, etc.; *towels,* Jul.*Or.*6.203b; *linen bandages* or *lint,* for wounds, Hp.*Off.*8, al., Ar.*Ach.*1176. 2. *sail-cloth,* D.47.20, Plb.5.89.2; so perh. in *PPetr.*1 p.79 (iii B.C., pl.).

**ὀθονιο-πλόκος,** ὁ, *linen-weaver, PTeb.*277 (iii A.D.). **-ποιός,** ὁ, = foreg., Dsc.5.134. ※ **-πώλης,** ου, ὁ, *linen-merchant, UPZ*109.13 (i B.C.), v.l. in Dsc.5.134; = *lintearius, Gloss.*

**ὀθόννα,** ἡ, *greater celandine, Chelidonium majus,* Dsc.2.180, Plin. *HN*27.109. 2. *juice of* ὀθόννα 1, Dsc.2.182; also, *the juice of various other plants,* ibid., cf. Zopyr.ap.Orib.14.45.4. 3. an Egyptian stone, Paul.Aeg.7.3.

**ὀθονοποιός,** ὁ, v.l. for ὀθονιοποιός in Dsc.5.134.

※ **ὁθούνεκα,** for ὅτου ἕνεκα (as οὕνεκα for οὗ ἕνεκα), *because,* c. ind., S. *Aj.*123, 553, etc.; ζηλῶ σ' ὁ... A.*Pr.*332. II. = ὡς or ὅτι, *that,* c. ind., S.*El.*47, 617, 1308, *Ph.*634, etc.: rarely c. opt., Id.*OC*944, *OT* 1271.

※ **ὁθούνεκεν,** = foreg., Timo 34.

**ὀθρεῖν·** ἄγειν, Hsch. (Cf. ὀθεύει.) **ὄθριζε·** διελέγετο, Id. (fort. ὀάριζε).

**ὄθριξ,** gen. ὄτρῐχος, poet. for ὁμόθριξ, ὁ, ἡ, *with like hair,* ἵπποι Il. 2.765, prob. l. for ὁμότριχας, Sophr.52.

**ὄθροον·** ὁμόφωνον, σύμφωνον, Hsch.

**Ὄθρυς,** υος, ἡ, Mt. *Othrys* in Thessaly, Hdt.7.129, Str.8.3.32, etc.; cf. ὄθρυν· Κρῆτες τὸ ὄρος, and ὀθρυόεν· τραχύ, ὑλῶδες, δασύ, κρημνῶδες, Hsch.

**οἵ,** = ὅ with Particle -ί, v. ὁ A. ad init., VIII. 5.

**οἴ,** exclam. of pain, grief, pity, astonishment, *ah! woe!* sts. with nom., οἴ 'γώ S.*Aj.*803, *El.*674, 1115: mostly c. dat. (cf. οἴμοι): c. acc., οἴ ἐμὲ δειλήν *AP*9.408 (Apollonid. or Antip.), cf. *IG*14.1971.5: also οἰοί, οἰοιοῖ, A.D.*Adv.*177.4, cf. A.*Eu.*841, *Supp.*876, *Pers.*955 (all lyr.), etc.: Ion. ὀΐ as exclam. of fear, Ar.*Pax*933.

**οἱ,** enclit. **οἱ,** dat sg. of Pron. of 3 pers. masc. and fem.; v. οὗ.

**οἷ**, relat. Adv. *whither*, οἷ μολὼν δώσεις δίκην S.*Ant.*228; οἴκησις οἷ πορεύομαι ib.892, cf. *El.*8; οὐκ ἤκουσας οἷ προβαίνει τὸ πρᾶγμα Ar.*Ach.* 836; οἷ χρὴ βλέπειν Pl.*Lg.*714b; οἷ (i. e. εἰς ἃ) μὲν ἔδει δαπανώμενον.., οἷ δ' οὐδὲν ἔδει ἀναλώσαντα Id.*Virt.*378b; so οἷ δή Id.*Prm.*127c; οἷπερ S.*El.*404, Ar.*Fr.*403: freq. c. gen., οἷ μ' ἀτιμίας ἄγεις *to what a depth* of dishonour, S.*El.*1035; οἷ προελήλυθ' ἀσελγείας D.4.9. 2. with Verbs of ending, οἷ φθίνει τύχα *where*, i. e. *how, in what*, it ends, E. *Hipp.*371; so οἷ τελευτᾷ κακίας *in what* state of vice he ends, Pl.*Smp.* 181e. (Orig. loc. of ὅς.)

**οἰᾰδόν**, Adv., (οἶος) *alone*, Nic.*Th.*148.

**οἰᾰκ-ηδόν**, Adv., (οἴαξ) *in the manner of an* οἴαξ, A.D.*Adv.*205. 4. **-ίζω**, Ion. **οἰηκ-**, *steer*: hence, *govern, guide, manage*, τελαμῶσι σκυτίνοις οἰηκίζοντες [τὰς ἀσπίδας] Hdt.1.171; [ἵππους] *οἰ. guide* them (when swimming), Plb.3.43.4, etc.:—Pass., of horses, ἀπὸ ῥαβδίου -ίζεσθαι Str.17.3.7; of the seasons, Gal.9.914. 2. metaph., τὰ πάντα *οἰ.* Κεραυνός Heraclit.64; τοὺς νέους -οντες ἡδονῇ καὶ λύπῃ Arist.*EN*1172ᵃ21:—Pass., ὁ κοινὸς βίος ὥσπερ ὑπὸ θεῶν τινος -όμενος D.S.18.59. **-ιον**, τό, Dim. of οἴαξ, Eust.1533.48. **-ισμα**, ατος, τό, *steering, governing*, Trag.*Adesp.*287; *regimen, Gloss.* **-ιστής**, οῦ, ὁ, *steersman, pilot*, Suid.

**οἰᾰκο-νομέω**, *steer, guide, govern*, σκάφος Ph.1.601: metaph., τὰ σύμπαντα ib.419. **-νόμος**, ὁ, *helmsman*: metaph., *pilot, ruler*, A.*Pr.*149 (lyr.). **-στροφέω**, *steer, direct*, θυμὸν φακοστρόφουν Id. *Pers.*767. **-στρόφος**, ὁ, = οἰακονόμος, Pi.*I.*4(3).71(89), A.*Th.*62, E.*Med.*523; ἀνάγκης *οἰ.* A.*Pr.*515, etc.

**οἴακωσις** [ᾰ], εως, ἡ, *guiding*, Aq.*Jb.*37.12.

**οἴαξ**, ᾱκος, Ion. **οἴηξ**, ηκος, ὁ, prop. *handle of rudder, tiller* (Poll.1. 89), πηδαλίων οἴακος ἀφέμενος (cf. πηδάλιον) Pl.*Plt.*272e: generally, *helm*, οἴακος εὐθυντῆρος ὑστάτου νεὼς A.*Supp.*717; στρέφειν οἴακα E. *Hel.*1591: pl., οἰάκων φύλαξ ib.1578; οἴακες εὐπρύμνου νεὼς Id.*IT*1357; τὸν οἴακα εἴσω ἄγειν ἢ ἔξω Pl.*Alc.*1.117c. 2. metaph., *helm of government*, ἐν πρύμνῃ πόλεως *οἰ.* νωμῶν A.*Th.*3; πραπίδων *οἰ.* νέμων Id.*Ag.*802 (anap.); χαλινῶν ἔργον οἰάκων θ' ἅμα S.*Fr.*869, cf. E.*Or.* 795; τὸν *οἰ.* στρέφει δαίμων ἑκάστῳ Anaxandr.4; τύχης *οἰ.* *IG*7.3226. 5 (Orchom. Boeot.); = ὡροσκόπος, Paul.Al.*L.*2. II. in Il.24.269, οἴηκες are prob. *rings of the yoke*, through which pass the reins for guiding the mules, cf. ἕστωρ.

**οἴαροι**· γυναῖκες, Suid. (= ὄαροι). **οἰάς**, = βρυωνία, Hp.ap.Erot. (codd. Erot., but f.l. for οἰνάς). **οἰατά**· δυνά (Aeol.), Hsch. **οἰάτειον κρέας**· τὸ προβάτειον, Suid.

**οἰάτης** [ᾱ], ου, ὁ, found only in Ion. and Dor. forms, v. οἰήτης; but II. Οἰᾶτις νομός, a pasture *in the Attic deme* Οἴα, S.*OC*1061 (lyr.); Οἰᾶται, an Arcadian tribe, Paus.8.45.1.

**οἰάω**, (οἶος) in part. οἰῶντα· μονάζοντα, Hsch.

**οἰβοιβοῖ**, exclam., = οἴμοι, Epich.124.3.

**οἶβος**, ὁ, *piece of meat from the back of an ox's neck*, Luc.*Lex.*3.

※ **οἴγω**, Hes.*Op.*819, etc.; later **οἴγνυμι**, *AP*9.356 (Leon.): fut. οἴξω E.*Cyc.*502: aor. ᾦξα Il.24.457; but augm. forms usu. have ὠϊ- in Ep. (v. infr.); part. οἴξας Il. (v. infr.): Ion. pf. Pass. ὤϊκται Herod.4.55: the compd. ἀνοίγνυμι or ἀνοίγω (q. v.) is much commoner, cf. also διοίγνυμι:—*open*, οἴξασα κληῖδι θύρας Il.6.89; τῇσι θύρας ὤϊξε ib.298; οἴγειν κλῇθρα προσπόλοις λέγω E.*HF*332; ξενῶνας οἴξας Id.*Alc.*547, cf. *Com.Adesp.*1211: abs., ᾦξε γέροντι he *opened the door* for the old man, Il.24.457; also [οἶνον].. ὤϊξεν ταμίη she *opened* the wine, Od.3.392; οἶγε πίθον *open* the wine-jar, Hes. l. c.; πρὸς φίλους οἴγειν στόμα A.*Pr.*611:—Pass., πᾶσαι δ' ὠΐγνυντο (v.l. ὠΐγοντο, i. e. ὠείγ-, in *PHib.*21) πύλαι Il.2.809, 8.58; οἰχθέντος Ὠρᾶν θαλάμου Pi.*Fr.*75.14; ἡ θύρη.. ὤϊκται Herod. l. c. (Aeol. inf. ὀείγην *IG*12(2). 6.43 (Mytil.); part. ὀείγων Alc.225 Lobel: prob. ὀ-ϝειγ- and ὀ-ϝῐγ-, cf. Skt. *vēga-* 'quick movement'; cf. ἐπῴχατο, προσοίγνυμι.)

**οἶδα**, v. *εἴδω B.

**οἰδ-αίνω**, *swell*, φρένες οἰδαίνεσκον A.R.3.383; οἰδαίνουσα θάλασσα Arat.909; οἰδήναντος στομάχου Androm.ap.Gal.14.34, cf. Hsch.; σῶμα.. ἐκ νηπιότητος εἰς ἥβην οἰδαῖνον Max.Tyr.16.5. II. οἰδαίνεσθαι· θυμοῦσθαι, καὶ τὰ ὅμοια, Hsch. **-ᾰλέος**, α, ον, *swollen*, οἰδαλέους ἀμφ' ὀδύνῃς πνεύμονας Archil.9.4; χείλη *οἰ.* Nic.*Al.*210: in late Prose, Dsc.*Eup.*1.78, Aret.*SD*1.16, etc.: Comp. -ώτερος Alex. Trall.*Febr.*3. **-άνω** [ᾰ], *cause to swell*, χόλος.. οἰδάνει ἐν στήθεσσι νόον Il.9.554; μέθυ κῆρ οἰδάνει A.R.1.478:—Pass., *to be swollen*, οἰδάνεται κραδίη χόλῳ Il.9.646. II. = οἰδέω, intr., ὁ φῆληξ οἰδάνων Ar.*Pax*1165. **-αξ**, ᾰκος, ὁ, = φῆληξ, Poll.6.81, Choerob. in *An. Ox.*2.248.

**οἶδας**, v. *εἴδω B.

**οἰδ-έω**, rarely **οἰδάω**, Plu.2.734f: impf. ᾤδεον Od.5.455: aor. ᾤδησα Hp.*Epid.*2.1.7, 2.2.3, Pl.*Phdr.*251b: pf. ᾤδηκα, Dor. 3 pl. -αντι Theoc.1.43; cf. ἀνοιδέω:—*swell, become swollen*, ᾤδεε δὲ χρόα πάντα *he had* all his body *swollen*, Od. l. c.; οἰδῶν τὼ πόδε Ar.*Ra.*1192; τοὺς πόδας καὶ γαστέρα Men.544.4; τὰ σφύρ' ᾤδει Anaxil.36; ἔμβρυα οἰδέοντα Hp.*Aër.*7; ᾠδήκαντι κατ' αὐχένα ἶνες Theoc. l. c.; of growing fruits, etc., ὀπώραν ἐντεταμένην καὶ οἰδῶσαν Plu. l. c.; ᾤδησε.. δ τοῦ πτεροῦ καυλός Pl. l. c. II. metaph., οἰδεόντων τῶν πρηγμάτων when affairs *were in a ferment*, Hdt.3.76,127; οἰδεῖ καὶ ὕπουλός ἐστιν [ἡ πόλις], metaph. from a boil or abscess, Pl.*Grg.*518e; τὸν δῆμον οἰδοῦντα καὶ θρασυνόμενον Plu.*Sol.*19; also, of inflated style, οἰδεῖν ὑπὸ κομπασμάτων Ar.*Ra.*940, cf. Plu.*Cic.*26. **-ημα**, ατος, τό, *swelling, tumour*, Hp.*Aph.*4.34, *Epid.*1.13.θ', D.54.11, Plu.*Cor.*15; only of soft and painless tumours, acc. to Gal.17(1).801, 15.770, 17(2).31:—Dim. ※**-ημάτιον**, τό, Hp.*Fract.*5; name of an eye-salve, Aët.7.118. **-ηματώδης**, ες, *swollen*, Gal.6.752, Alex.Trall.*Febr.* 2. **-ησις**, εως, ἡ, *swelling, fermenting*, τῶν θυμουμένων Pl.*Ti.*70c; *puffiness*, διαφέρει *οἰ.* εὐεξίας Phld.*Vit.*p.27 J.; of dropsy, *Hippiatr.* 38. **-ήτης**, ου, ὁ, *tumor, Gloss.*

**οἴδιον**, τό, Dim. of οἶς, Theognost.*Can.*121.

**Οἰδίπους** [ῐ], ὁ, (οἰδέω, πούς) *Oedipus*, i. e. *the swollen-footed* cf. E. *Ph.*27: gen. Οἰδίποδος Apollod.3.6.3 (but in Trag. always Οἰδίπου, as if from Οἰδίπος, which occurs in *AP*7.429 (Alc.)): acc. Οἰδίπουν Trag., later Οἰδίποδα Plu.2.193d, Paus.9.2.4, etc.: voc. Οἰδίπου S.*OT* 405, *OC*557, cf. Choerob.*in Theod.*1.210 H., and Οἰδίπους S.*OC*740, al., Choerob. l. c.:—collat. form **Οἰδιπόδης**, ὁ, gen. Οἰδιπόδαο Il.23. 679, Od.11.271, Hes.*Op.*163; Dor. contr. Οἰδιπόδα Pi.*P.*4.263, and in lyr. passages of Trag., A.*Th.*725, S.*OT*496, *Ant.*380; Ion. Οἰδιπόδεω Hdt.4.149: acc. Οἰδιπόδαν in lyr., A.*Th.*752, S.*OC*222: dat. Οἰδιπόδῃ Thebaïs 2: voc. Οἰδιπόδα S.*OT*1195 (lyr.):—Adj. **Οἰδιπόδειος**, α, ον, or ος, ον, *of Oedipus*, Plu.*Sull.*19, Paus.9.18.5 (ubi vulg. -πόδια): Οἰδιπόδεια (vulg. -ια), τά, *the tale of Oedipus*, Id.9.5.11; or Οἰδιπόδεια, ἡ, Arist.*Fr.*628, *IG*14.1292 ii 11, Sch.E.*Ph.*1760.

**οἰδίσκω**, = οἰδαίνω, *swell, enlarge*, Gal.18(2).97, 8.485, Alex.Aphr. *Pr.*1.9:—Pass., Hp.*Epid.*5.16.

※ **οἶδμα**, ατος, τό, *swelling, swell*, in Hom. only of water, ὁ δ' ἐπέσσυτο οἴδματι θύων, of a river, *with swollen waves*, Il.21.234; of the sea, ὁ δ' ἔστενεν οἴδματι θύων 23.230, cf. Hes.*Th.*109; ἐπ' οἴδματι μάργῳ Emp. 100.7, cf. 24; περιβρυχίοισι περῶν ὑπ' οἴδμασιν S.*Ant.*337 (lyr.); *οἰ.* θαλάσσης *h.Cer.*14; οἶδμ' ἅλιον *h.Ap.*417, Pi.*Fr.*221 (codd. S.E.); γλαυκᾶς ἐπ' οἶδμα λίμνας S.*Fr.*476 (lyr.); ἐς *οἰ.* πόντου E.*Or.*991 (lyr.); *οἰ.* πόντιον Id.*IA*704: hence, generally, *the sea*, S.*Ant.*588 (lyr.); Τύριον, Φρύγιον οἶδμα, E.*Ph.*202, *Hel.*369 (both lyr.), etc.; ἐς οἶδμ' ἁλὸς Id. *Hec.*26; τῶν κατ' οἶδμα παρθένων the Nereids, Id.*Hel.*6; Αἰγαῖον *οἰ.* Id.*IA*1601, cf. *IT*1412, al.; διὰ πόντιον οἶδμα (mock heroic) Antiph. 196.3. II. *οἰ.* νότων *the swelling* of the south-west wind, *AP*9.36 (Secund.).

**οἰδμᾰτόεις**, εσσα, εν, *billowy*, A.*Fr.*69 (lyr.), Opp.*H.*5.273.

**οἴδομαι**, *swell*, as etym. of οἶδμα, Sch.E.*Hec.*26.

**οἰδοποιέω**, *tumefacio, Gloss.*

**οἶδος**, εος, τό, *swelling, tumour*, produced by internal action, Hp. *Fract.*25 (v.l. εἶδος), *VC*17 (Littré for εἰκός), Nic.*Th.*188, 237, 426; *puffiness*, Aret.*SD*1.16.

**οἰέᾰνος**, ον, (οἶος, ἑανός) = οἰοχίτων, A.R.3.646.

**οἴεος**, α, ον, *of* or *from a sheep*, διφθέραι *sheep*-skins, Hdt.5.58; τυροὶ *SIG*1027.13 (Cos): hence ὀέα (q. v.) and οἰίας (with dial. change of -εα- to -ια-)· τῶν προβάτων τὰ σκεπαστήρια δέρματα (*leather coats for sheep, brats*), Hsch. (Skt. *avyáyas*, Adj. from *ávis* = ὄϝις 'sheep'.)

※ **οἰέτεας**, acc. pl., (ἔτος) *of the same age*, Il.2.765, Matro *Fr.*4: metri gr. for ὀέτεας (q. v.) which occurs in Hsch. with a different explanation: ὀέτης is formed like ὄθριξ, ὄζυξ, ὀγάστωρ, etc.

※ **ϝοιζηάζω**, = οἰκειόομαι (quasi οἰκειάζω), *GDI*4966 (Crete).

**ὀϊζ-ύος**, ον, = sq., *sorry, wretched*, ὀΐζυον οὐδὲν ἀρέσκει Theoc.27. 14. ※ **-ῡρός**, Att. **οἰζῡρός** (trisyll.), ά, όν, *woeful, miserable*, in Hom. mostly of persons, Il.1.417, al.; ὀϊζυροῖσι βροτοῖσιν 13.569, cf. Od.4. 197; ᾠζύρ' you *wretch!* Ar.*Av.*1641: less freq. of actions, conditions, etc., *toilsome, dreary*, παύσασθαι ὀϊζυροῦ πολέμοιο Il.3.112; παύσαστ' ὀϊζυροῖο γόοιο Od.8.540; ὀϊζυραὶ νύκτες 11.182, etc.; also, *sorry, wretched, poor*, κώμῃ Hes.*Op.*639; διαίτην ἔχειν ὀϊζυρήν Hdt.9.82. Adv. -ρῶς Q.S.3.363.—Not used by Trag., nor in early Att. Prose. [ὀϊζῡ- in Hom. (v. supr.); οἰζῠ- in Att., Ar.*Nu.*655, *Av.*1641, *V.*1504, 1514, *Lys.*948: Comp. ὀϊζυρώτερος Il.17.446: Sup. ὀϊζυρώτατος Od.5. 105.] **-ύς**, Trag. and later Ion. (Herod.7.39) **οἰζύς**, ύος, ἡ, *woe, misery*, πόνος καὶ ὀ. Il.13.2; κάματος καὶ ὀ. 15.365, cf. Hes.*Op.*177: contr. dat. ὀϊζυῖ for ὀϊζύϊ, Od.7.270: acc. ὀϊζύα for ὀϊζύν first in Q.S.2. 88: Trag. οἰζύς A.*Ag.*756 (lyr.), *Eu.*893, E.*Hec.*949 (lyr.). II. as pr. n., daughter of Night, Hes.*Th.*214. [ῡ in nom. and acc., v. Hes. l. c.; ῠ in other cases.] **-ύω**, aor. ὀΐζῡσα, *wail, mourn*, ἀλλ' αἰεὶ περὶ κεῖνον ὀΐζυε (impers.) Il.3.408. II. c. acc. rei, *suffer*, ἧς εἵνεκ' ὀϊζύομεν κακὰ πολλά 14.89: abs., *to be miserable* or *suffer*, ὀϊζύσας ἐμόγησεν Od.4.152, 23.307. [υ of pres. short in Hom., long in A.R. 4.1324, 1374; in aor. always long.]

※ **οἰζω**, *cry* οἶ, *lament*, A.D.*Adv.*128.10, who also coins **ὀΐζω** to expl. ὀϊζύω.

**οἴη** (A), ἡ, = κώμη, *GDI*5661.46 (Chios, iv B.C.), A.R.2.139, Hsch., Theognost.*Can.*18; cf. οἰήτης.

**οἴη** (B), ἡ, v. ὄα (A).

**οἰήϊον**, τό, Ep. for οἴηξ, οἴαξ, *rudder, helm*, Od.9.483: pl., 12.218, Il.19.43.

**οἰηκίζω**, Ion. for οἰακίζω.

**οἴ-ημα**, ατος, τό, (οἴομαι) *opinion*, D.C.*Fr.*12.8 (pl.). II. *self-conceit*, *οἰ.* καὶ τῦφος Plu.2.39d; *οἰ.* καὶ ἀλαζονεία ib.43b. **-ημᾰτίας**, ου, ὁ, *self-conceited person*, Ptol.*Tetr.*162, Hsch. s. v. δοκησίσοφος, Suid.

**οἴηξ**, ηκος, ὁ, Ion. for οἴαξ.

**οἴ-ησις**, εως, ἡ, (οἴομαι) = δόξα, *opinion, notion*, Pl.*Phd.*92a, *Phdr.* 244c, Arist.*Po.*1461ᵇ3; esp. *false* or *vague notion*, opp. σαφῶς εἰδέναι, Id.*Rh.Al.*1431ᵃ40, cf. Zeno *Stoic.*1.20, etc. II. = οἴημα, *self-conceit*, Heraclit.46, E.*Fr.*643, Bion ap.D.L.4.50, Ph.1.53, al., Chor. in *Rh.Mus.*49.512; *οἰ.* καὶ ὑπερηφανία Phld.*Vit.*p.29 J. **-ησίσοφος** [ῐ], ον, *wise in his own conceit*, Ph.1.125, Procl. *in Cra.*p.67 P. **-ητέον**, *one must suppose*, Arist.*Ph.*207ᵃ15, *EN*1173ᵇ23, 1176ᵇ21.

**οἰήτης**, ου, ὁ, (οἴη A) = κωμήτης, S.*Fr.*134; Dor. gen. pl. οἰατᾶν prob. in Hsch.

**οἰητικός**, ή, όν, *opinionated*, νοῦς Ph.1.160.

**οἰητόν**, = *rebile*, Gloss.

❀ **οἶις**, ιδος, ἡ, poet. for ὄϊς, *sheep*, Theoc.1.9 (in acc. sg. οἴιδα, but οἰΐδα 'sheepskin' [cj. Ahrens] is prob.).

**οἶκα**, ας, ε, Ion. for ἔοικα.

❀ **οἴκ-ἄδε** (Delph. **ϝοίκαδε** *GDI*2561 *C*42), Adv., = οἰκόνδε, *to one's house, home*, or *country, homewards*, freq. in Hom., Il.1.170, Od.2.176, al.: freq. in Pi.(*N*.4.76, al.), Trag. (as A.*Ag*.1337 (anap.)), Com. (as Ar.*Nu*.618), and Att. Prose (as Pl.*R*.328b). II. *to people's houses*, Telecl.1.6. III. = οἴκοι, *at home*, X.*Cyr*.1.3.4, *An*.7.7.57, Luc.*Dem.Enc*.26, Hld.1.22, Phalar.*Ep*.143, etc. **-ἄδις**, Dor. for οἴκαδε, Ar.*Ach*.742, 779, cf. Epich.35.13:—the form **οἴκαδες** noticed by Greg.Cor.p.230S. is prob. an error. **-άριον** [ᾰ], τό, Dim. of οἶκος, Lys.*Fr*.81.

**ϝοικέα**, ἡ, fem. of ϝοικεύς (v. οἰκεύς), *Leg.Gort*.2.8, al.

**οἴκει**, Adv., = οἴκοι, Men.1044.

**οἰκει-άζω**, v. ϝοιζηάζω. **-ἄκός**, ή, όν, Dor. **οἰκηακός** Callicrat.ap.Stob.4.28.16:— = οἰκεῖος III, *one's own*, Palch. in *Cat.Cod. Astr*.1.96, Eust.124.34, Suid., Zonar. II. *concerning one's relatives*, Heph.Astr.2.32; cf. οἰκιακός.

**οἰκειο-ποιέω**, *appropriate, attach*, ἑαυτὰς τῷ Ὁμήρῳ, of cities, Sch. Philostr.*Her*.p.592B.:—Med., *make one's own, attach to oneself*, Candid.ap.Phot.*Bibl*.p.55B., Sch.Th.2.33; *adopt*, υἱόν τινα Ammon. *Vit.Arist*.p.10W. **-πρᾶγία**, ἡ, *minding one's own affairs*, Pl.*R*.434c, Plot.1.2.7, Marin.*Procl*.24.

❀ **οἰκεῖος**, α, ον, also ος, ον E.*Heracl*.634; Ion. **οἰκήϊος**, η, ον: *in* or *of the house*, once in Hes., δούρατ' ἀμάξης οἰκήϊα θέσθαι *Op*.457; λέβης A.*Fr*.1; κῆρυξ S.*Tr*.757; *of* or *for household affairs, domestic* (for οἰκηΐη, v. οἰκία II), τὰ οἰ. *household affairs, property*, Hdt.2.37, S.*Ant*.661; τὰ οἰ. ἀγαθά X.*Oec*.9.18; τὰ οἰ. τὰ αὑτοῦ his *household goods*, Lys.13.41; opp. πολιτικά, Th.2.40; opp. τὰ τῆς πόλεως, Pl.*Ap*.23b. 2. Astrol., οἰ. ζῴδια *domiciliary* signs, Vett.Val.37.21, al. II. of persons, *of the same household, family*, or *kin, related*, ὥς οἱ ἐόντες οἰκήϊοι as being *akin* to him, Hdt.4.65; οἰκεῖον οὕτως οὐδὲν.. ὡς ἀνήρ τε καὶ γυνή *so closely akin*, Men.647; ἀνὴρ οἰ. *kinsman, relative, near friend*, Hdt.1.108; οἱ οἰ. *kinsmen*, opp. οἱ ἀλλότριοι, And.4.15, cf. Th.2.51; opp. ὀθνεῖοι, Pl.*Prt*.316c; οἱ ἑωυτοῦ οἰκηϊότατοι his own *nearest kinsmen*, Hdt.3.65, cf. 5.5, D.18.288; of the tie itself, κατὰ τὸ οἰ. Ἀτρεῖ because of his *relationship* to Atreus, Th.1.9. 2. *friendly*, εἴχομέν ποτε.. τὸν τόπον τοῦτον οἰ. D.4.4; οὓς ἂν ἡγήσαιτο -οτάτους τε καὶ ἑταιροτάτους Pl.*Phd*.89e. III. of things, *belonging to one's house* or *family, one's own* (defined as ὅταν ἐφ' αὑτῷ ᾖ ἀπαλλοτριῶσαι Arist.*Rh*.1361ᵃ21), οἰ. ἄρουραι Pi.*O*.12.19; σταθμοῖς ἐν οἰκείοισι A.*Pr*.398; γῆ, χθών, S.*Aj*.859, *Ant*.1203; οἰκεῖον, ἢ 'ξ ἄλλου τινός; *born in the house*, or..? Id.*OT*1162; αἱ οἰ. πόλεις *their own* cities, X.*HG*3.5.2; ἡ οἰ. (sc. γῆ), Ion. ἡ οἰκηΐη Hdt.1.64; [ἀναθήματα] οἰκήϊα *his own property*, ib.92; πόλεμοι οἰ. wars *in one's own country*, of the Helot war in Laconia, Th.1.118, cf. 4.64; σῖτος οἰ. καὶ οὐκ ἐπακτός *homegrown*, Id.6.20. 2. = ἴδιος, *one's own, personal, private*, οἰκείων κερδέων εἵνεκα Thgn.46; ἐὼν ἐν κακῷ οἰκηΐῳ Hdt.1.45, cf. 153, Antipho 1.13; αἱ χεῖρες -ότεραι τοῦ σιδήρου Id.4.3.3; μηδὲν -οτέρᾳ τῇ ἀπολαύσει with enjoyment not *more our own*, Th.2.38, cf. 7.70; ἀλλοτρίας γῆς πέρι οἰ. κίνδυνον ἔχειν Id.3.13; οἰ. ξύνεσις *mother* wit, Id.1.138; πρὸς οἰκείας χερός by *his own* hand, S.*Ant*.1176, etc.; for A.*Ag*.1220, v. βορά. b. in Stoic Philos., *endeared by nature* to all animals, including man, τὸ πρῶτον οἰ. *what is earliest endeared*, Chrysipp.*Stoic*.3.43, Hierocl. p.7A. IV. *proper to* a thing, *fitting, suitable*, οὔτε.. καλὸν οὐδὲν [οὐδ'] οἰκήϊον Hdt.3.81, cf. D.18.59. 2. c. dat. rei, *belonging to, conformable to the nature of* a thing, προοίμιον οἰ. ἑκάστῳ Pl.*Lg*.772e, cf. *R*.468d, al., and freq. in Arist., as *EN*1098ᵃ29: also c. gen., τὰ αὐτῶν οἰ. Pl.*Phd*.96d; οἰ. τῆς διαλεκτικῆς Arist.*Top*.101ᵇ2, cf. *EN*1096ᵇ31, *Rh*.1360ᵃ22; οἰ. πρός τι Plb.5.105.1. b. of persons, c. gen., *a student of*.., σοφίας Str.17.1.5; *addicted to*, καινοτομίας Iamb.*VP*30.176. 3. *proper, fit*, οἰ. καταγέλως *fit* subject for ridicule, Men.160; οἰ. ὄνομα a word *in its proper, literal sense*, opp. metaphor, Arist.*Rh*.1404ᵇ35.

B. Adv. οἰκείως has the same senses as the Adj., οἰ. φέρε bear it *like your own affair*, Ar.*Th*.197; διαλέγεσθαι οἰ. τινί converse *familiarly* with him, Th.6.57; οἰ. χρῆσθαί τινι *to be on familiar terms*, X.*HG*2.3.16; οἰ. διακεῖσθαί τινι Id.*An*.7.5.16; πρός τι Plb.13.1.2; οἰ. δέχεσθαί τινας D.18.215; οἰ. ἔχειν τινί Id.4.4, etc.: Comp. -ότερον Is.1.49; -οτέρως Arist.*Cat*.7ᵃ16: Sup. -ότατα Plb.5.106.4. II. *properly, naturally*, Ar.*Lys*.1118, X.*Oec*.2.17; opp. ἀλλοτρίως, Epicur.*Ep*.1p.14U. 2. *affectionately, dutifully*, ἔθαψε, περιέστειλεν οἰ. Men.325.12, cf. Th.2.60. 3. *literally, actually*, Gal.*Phil.Hist*.39D. 4. Astrol., οἰ. σχηματίζεσθαι, of a planet, *to be in its domicile*, Vett.Val.58.27, al.

❀ **οἰκειότης**, Ion. **οἰκηϊότης**, ητος, ἡ, *a being* οἰκεῖος (signf. II), *kindred, relationship*, Hdt.6.54, Th.3.86, etc.; *intimacy, friendship*, φιλία καὶ οἰ. Id.4.19, cf. Pl.*Smp*.197d: pl., And.1.118, D.18.35, *SIG*557.35 (iii B.C.). b. metaph., *connexion* of things, Pl.*R*.537c, M.Ant.4.4, etc. 2. *living together as man and wife, domesticity, marriage*, τῆς Ἑλένης Isoc.10.42, cf. Lys.1.6; εἰς οἰκειότητα καὶ παιδοποιίαν ὁρᾷ Chor. in *Hermes*17.215. II. of words and phrases, *proper sense*, opp. μεταφορά, Plu.*Cic*.40, in pl. III. *conformity to nature* or *environment*, Epicur.*Sent*.40, *Frr*.197, 217.

**οἰκειο-τονέομαι**, *have its own accent*, Sch.Il.11.395. **-τοπέω**, prob. = οἰκοδεσποτέω, Doroth.ap.Heph.Astr.3.34. **-φωνος**, ον, *by word of mouth*: in Adv. -νως Ctes.*Fr*.29.9.

❀ **οἰκει-όω**, Ion. **οἰκηϊόω**, *make* οἰκεῖος: I. *make* a person *a kinsman*, τὴν πόλιν ἐς τὴν ξυγγένειαν -οῦντες Th.3.65. II. mostly in Med., 1. c. acc. pers., *make* a person *one's friend*, Hdt.4.148, Pl.*Lg*.738d; *reconcile*, οἰ. ἕνα πρὸς ἕνα Phld.*Rh*.2.222S., cf. Plu.*Oth*.2; οἰ. δῆμον λόγῳ D.H.9.44: abs., *make friends*, Aen.Tact.24.5:—Pass., *to be made friendly*, opp. πολεμοῦσθαι, Th.1.36, cf. Arist.*Pol*.1336ᵇ30. b. in Stoic Philos., *to be endeared by nature*, Chrysipp.*Stoic*.3.43. 2. c. acc. rei, *make* or *claim as one's own, appropriate*, τὴν Ἀσίην οἰκηιεῦνται οἱ Πέρσαι Hdt.1.4; τούτων τὴν ἐξεύρεσιν οὐκ οἰκηϊοῦνται Λυδοί ib.94; Αἰγύπτιοι οἰ. Καμβυσέα *claim* him *as their own*, Id.3.2; ἅπαντα τὰ ἐν πόλει οἰ. Pl.*R*.466c; *entice* bees, Id.*Lg*.843e. 3. Act., *adapt, make fit* or *suitable*, τινί τι Sotad.Com.1.17; τι πρός τι Plb.9.1.2; ὁ οἰκειῶν πρὸς ἀρετὴν λόγος Aristo *Stoic*.1.80, cf. Plot.4.4.44:—Pass., *to be familiarized to*, ταῖς ψυχαῖς Pl.*Prt*.326b; *become familiar with*, Id.*Prm*.128a; οἱ ᾠκειωμένοι φυσιολογίᾳ Epicur.*Ep*.1p.4U. 4. Astrol., in Pass., *to be domiciliarily related*, -ούμενος τῷ ζῳδίῳ, of a planet, *having* the sign *as its domicile*, Vett.Val.264.21. **-ω**, Ep. for οἰκέω (q.v.). **-ωμα**, ατος, τό, in pl., *private* or *family affairs*, Metrod.*Fr*.59. 2. *affinity*, πρός τι Str.6.2.3. 3. *special feature, advantage*, Epicur.*Sent.Vat*.41 (pl.), D.H.*Rh*.7.5. **-ωματικός**, ή, όν, Gramm., *possessive*, of Adjs. such as οὐράνιος, *EM*30.6. **-ωσις**, εως, ἡ, *appropriation*, οἰ. ποιεῖσθαί τινος Th.4.128: pl., *profits*, Vett.Val.202.17. 2. *affinity*, Ph.1.142, al.; *attraction, affection* (cf. οἰκεῖος III. 2b), πρός τινα Diogenian.Epicur.4.55, Ph.1.256, *Stoic*.1.49, al., Asp. in *EN*44.27, cf. Hierocl.p.35A.; ἡ πρὸς τὸ ζῆν οἰ. Plot.4.4.44; *propensity*, εἰς ἡδονήν Gal.5.456; τῆς ψυχῆς, opp. ἀλλοτρίωσις, Plot.3.6.1, 3.8.8, al., Porph.*Sent*.18; *becoming familiar with*, εἰς τοὺς θεούς Iamb.*VP*24.106. **-ωτικός**, ή, όν, *appropriative*, τέχνη οἰ. Pl.*Sph*.223b; τὸ οἰ. πάθος πρὸς ἕκαστα Polystr.*Herc*.346p.79V. 2. *adapting*, οἰ. δύναμις πρὸς τὸ καλόν Plu.2.759e.

**οἰκέσιον**, given as example of termination by Eust.1751.12.

❀ **οἰκετ-εία**, ἡ, *household of slaves*, Str.14.5.2, Luc.*Merc.Cond*.15, *IPE*1².32*B*15 (Olbia), *PTeb*.285.6 (iii A.D.):—later written **οἰκετία**, Epict.*Ench*.33.7. 2. *servitude*, Aristeas 14, al., J.*AJ*8.6.3. 3. *slave population*, Str.5.1.12, *IGRom*.4.1692.54 (Elaea). **-εύω**, = οἰκέω, *inhabit*, E.*Alc*.437 (lyr.). II. οἰκετεύεται· συνοικεῖ, Hsch. ❀ **-ης**, ου, ὁ, (οἶκος) *household slave*, A.*Ch*.737, Hdt.6.137, 7.170, Antipho 1.30, Th.2.4; δημόσιος οἰ. τῆς πόλεως Aeschin.1.54. 2. οἱ οἰκέται also, = οἰκετεία, *household*, A.*Ag*.732 (lyr.), Hdt.8.4, 106, 142, S.*Tr*.908, X.*Cyr*.4.2.2: hence opp. δοῦλοι, Pl.*Lg*.763a, 777a, 853e; διαφέρειν φησὶ Χρύσιππος δοῦλον οἰκέτου, διὰ τὸ τοὺς ἀπελευθέρους μὲν δούλους ἔτι εἶναι, οἰκέτας δὲ τοὺς μὴ τῆς κτήσεως ἀφειμένους *Stoic*.3.86: but freq. synon. with δοῦλος, Arist.*Pol*.1252ᵇ12, al., *PLille*29.2 (iii B.C.), *IG*5(1).1390.77 (Andania, i B.C.); δοῦλος μεῖζον οἰκέτου φρονῶν Men.796. II. as epith. of Apollo, ἱερέως.. Καρνείου Βοικέτα [Β = ϝ] *IG*5(1).497, cf. 589, 608 (Sparta). (Cf. οἰκότης.) **-ία**, ἡ, v. οἰκετεία. **-ικός**, ή, όν, *of* or *for the menials* or *household*, Pl.*Sph*.226b, Arist.*Pol*.1261ᵇ36; τὸ οἰ. the *servants* or *slaves* collectively, Plu.*Sull*.9; οἰ. ἐπιφάνεια Myro 2J.; οἰ. σώματα *IG*12(5).653.25 (Syros), *PGrenf*.1.21.6 (ii B.C.); οἰκία οἰ. *PSI*9.1040.23 (iii A.D.); οἰ. διάθεσις Lxx 3*Ma*.2.28. 2. δέλφαξ οἰ. *home-bred*, Philox.2.28. ❀ **-ις**, ἴδος, ἡ, fem. of οἰκέτης, Hp.*Aër*.21, Lxx *Ex*.21.7; οἰκέτιν τ' ἐφέστιον περιστεράν S.*Fr*.866; οἰ. γυνή E.*El*.104. II. *housewife*, Theoc.18.38.

**οἰκεύς**, έως, Ion. ῆος, ὁ, = οἰκέτης, *inmate of one's house*, μὴ.. φίλους οἰκῆας ἐγείρῃ Il.5.413, cf. 6.366, Od.17.533; but elsewh., as in 4.245, 14.4, al., = *menial, servant*, cf. Sol.ap.Lys.10.19, S.*OT*756, Theoc.25.33; *serf*, *Leg.Gort*.2.8, al. (ϝοικ-).

❀ **οἰκέω**, Ep. **οἰκείω** Hes.*Th*.330, Locr. **ϝοικέω** *IG*9(1).334.29; Aeol. pres. part. οἴκεις Alc.69; Arg. 3 sg. pres. opt. οἰκείη *BCH*33.452: impf. ᾤκεον Il.20.218, al., Att. ᾤκουν, Ion. οἴκεον Hdt.1.57: fut. οἰκήσω E.*IA*1508 (lyr.): aor. ᾤκησα Hdt.1.1: pf. ᾤκηκα S.*El*.1101:—**Pass.** and **Med.**, fut. οἰκήσομαι in med. sense, Men.Rh.p.363S.; but in pass., v. A. II: aor. ᾠκήθην Il.2.668, etc.; ᾠκησάμην Aristid.1.103J.: pf. ᾤκημαι as Med. and Pass., Ion. 3 pl. οἰκέαται, v. A. I. 2, 3: (οἶκος): A. trans., *inhabit*, ὑπωρείας ᾤκεον πολυπιδάκου Ἴδης Il.20.218 (elsewh. in Hom. always intr., v. infr. B); οἰ. τοῦτον τὸν χῶρον Hdt.1.1, cf. 175, etc.; οἰ. δόμους A.*Supp*.961; ἄντρον Id.*Eu*.194: metaph., οἰ. αἰῶνα καὶ μοῖραν *have, enjoy*, E.l.c.:—Pass., *to be inhabited*, οἰκέοιτο πόλις Πριάμοιο Il.4.18; ἐς γῆν.. οἰκουμένην S.*Ph*.221; διὰ τῆς οἰκεομένης through *the inhabited country*, Hdt.2.32; ὁδοιπόρεον ἐς τὴν οἰκεομένην Id.4.110; τὰς ἄλλας πόλιας οἰκεομένας μηδὲν ἧσσον although *inhabited* no less than before, Id.1.170: for ἡ οἰκουμένη, v. sub voce. 2. *colonize, settle in*, τὰς πλείστας τῶν νήσων Th.1.8, cf. 2.27, etc.; πόλιν prob. in E.*Fr*.360.11; νῆσον οἰκῆσαι, i.e. to be deported, *POxy*.1101.24 (iv A.D.): in pf. Pass., *to be settled in, occupy*, τοῖσι τὰς νήσους οἰκημένοισι Ἴωσι Hdt.1.27; αἱ δύο [πόλιες] νήσους οἰκέαται ib.142 (cf. infr. 3). 3. in Pass., *to be settled*, of men or tribes to whom new abodes are assigned, τριχθὰ ᾤκηθεν καταφυλαδόν Il.2.668: Ion. pf. Pass. οἴκημαι, as pres., οἱ ἐν τῇ ἠπείρῳ οἰκημένοι Ἕλληνες *those who have been settled*, i.e. *those who dwell*.., Hdt.1.27; οἱ ἐντὸς Ἅλυος ποταμοῦ οἰ. ib.28, cf. 8.115; also of cities, *to be situated, lie*, παρ' ὃν [ποταμὸν] Νίνος πόλις οἴκητο Id.1.193. II. *manage, direct* a household or a state, S.*OC*1535 (dub. sens.), E.*El*.386, Th.3.37; οἰκεῖ τὴν πόλιν ὁμοίως ὥσπερ τὸν πατρῷον οἶκον Isoc.2.19: metaph., μὴ τὸν ἐμὸν οἴκει νοῦν don't *manage*.., E.*Fr*.144:—Pass., εὖ οἰκούμεναι πόλεις well *governed*, Id.*Hipp*.486; μετρίως, ὀρθῶς, ἄριστα οἰ., Pl.*Lg*.936b, *R*.371c, 520d, etc.; πατρίδος τετυχηκὼς ἢ νόμοις.. μάλιστα οἰκεῖσθαι δοκεῖ D.21.150: fut. οἰκήσεται in pass.

sense, καθ' ὅτι ἄριστα ἡ πόλις οἰκήσεται Th.8.67, cf. Pl.*La.*185a, Aeschin.1.22, D.58.62, Arist.*Pol.*1284b38.
B. intr., *dwell, live*, of persons, families, or tribes, *have their abodes, settlements*, in Hom. and Hdt. generally with ἐν.., ᾤκεον δ' ἐν Πλευρῶνι Il.14.116, cf. Od.9.200,400; οἰκέε ἐν Πίνδῳ Hdt.1.56, cf. A.*Ag.*1234, Ar.*Av.*967 (Orac.), Antipho 5.78; esp. of metics, ἐγ Κολλυτῷ οἰκοῦντι *IG*1².373.60, al.; κατὰ στέγας E.*Ion* 314; ὑπὸ χθονὸς Id.*Fr.*450: after Hom. with dat. (loc.) alone, Σαλαμῖνι *IG*1².1.2 (vi B.C.); οὐρανῷ Pi.*N.*10.58; ναοῖσι E.*Ion* 314; ἐλθόνθ' ἁγνὸν ἐς Θήβης πέδον οἰ. Eub.10; παρὰ κρημνοῖσιν Pi.*P.*3.34; παρὰ ὄχθον E.*IT*1098 (lyr.); οἰ. μετά τινος, = συνοικεῖν τινι, S.*OT*414,990; κέρδη μὲν οἰκήσαντα.. *having fixed my dwelling* [there] with gain to my hosts, Id. *OC*92; τὸ τὴν φροντίδ' ἔξω τῶν κακῶν οἰκεῖν γλυκύ sweet it is for the mind *to keep* free from cares, Id.*OT*1390; ἐπὶ προστάτου οἰ. (v. προστάτης) Lys.31.9. II. of cities, *to be situated*, Hdt.2.166, X.*HG* 7.1.3, 7.5.5; but τὴν πόλιν σποράδην καὶ κατὰ κώμας οἰκοῦσαν *formed* of detached villages, Isoc.10.35, cf. 4.39 (so in Pass., X.*An.*1.4.1). 2. *to be governed* or *administered*, τίς τῶν πόλεων διὰ σὲ βέλτιον ᾤκησεν; Pl.*R.*599d, cf. 462d, 472e, 473a, 543a, al.: freq. hardly distinguishable from the Pass. (supr. A. II); σωφρόνως γε οἰκοῦσα [πόλις] εὖ ἂν οἰκοῖτο a state *administered* by self-control *would be* well *governed*, Id.*Chrm.*162a; ἀρετῆς, ᾗ πόλεις τε καὶ οἶκοι εὖ οἰκοῦσι X.*Mem.*1.2.64; εἰς ὀλίγους, εἰς πλείους οἰκεῖν, *to be governed* in the interest of the few or the many, Th.2.37.

**οἰκ-ήϊος, -ηϊότης, -ηϊόω**, Ion. for οἰκεῖος, etc. ❀ **-ημα**, ατος, τό, *dwelling-place*, ἱερὸν ἔσχον οἰ. ποταμοῦ Pi.*O.*2.9: in pl., *building, house*, Hdt.1.17, 9.13, Paus.10.5.2, etc. 2. *room, chamber*, Hdt.1.164, 179, 2.121.α', 148, Th.1.134, 3.68, Lys.19.31, Pl.*Thg.* 130d, *Prt.*315d, etc.; esp. *bed-chamber*, Hdt.1.9,10, Pl.*Smp.*217d; *dining-room*, Heraclid.Cum.2 (pl.). II. special senses, 1. *brothel*, τὴν θυγατέρα κατίσαι ἐπ' οἰκήματος Hdt.2.121.ε', 126; στῆσαί τινα ἐπ' οἰ. Din.1.23; ἐπ' οἰ. καθῆσθαι Pl.*Chrm.*163b, cf. Aeschin.1.94, Isoc.6.19; cf. τέγος. 2. = οἰκίσκος, *cage* for animals, Hdt.7.119. 3. horse's *stable* or *stall*, *PCair.Zen.*529.5 (iii B.C.). 4. *temple, shrine*, Hdt.8.144. b. *room in a temple*, *IG*1².4.2,14. 5. *prison*, Th.4.47, Lys.*Fr.*75.4, D.32.29, *Act.Ap.*12.7. 6. *storeroom*, D.42.6,19 (pl.). 7. *workshop*, Pl.*Prt.*321d. 8. *story, floor*, X.*Cyr.*6.1.52 (dub. l.). 9. metaph., αἰσθητικὸν οἰ., of man, Secund.*Sent.*7. **-ημᾰτικός**, ή, όν, *of a dwelling-house* or *room*, D.L.5.55. **-ημάτιον**, τό, Dim. of οἴκημα, *IG*2².2496.11, *PCair. Zen.*507.29 (iii B.C.), Arr.*Epict.*1.28.16, Plu.2.145b, *PRyl.*77.30 (ii A.D.), X.Eph.2.10. **-ήσιμος**, ον, *habitable*, Plb.3.55.9, Str.1.4.4, al., Arr.*An.*6.18.1. **-ησις**, εως, ἡ, *the act of dwelling* or *inhabiting*, ἡ κατὰ τὴν χώραν αὐτόνομος οἰ. Th.2.16; ποιέεσθαι οἰ. ὑπὸ γῆν Hdt.3.102; κοινωνεῖν τῆς οἰ. to share in *residence*, Arist.*Pol.* 1275a8; διάθεσιν.. πρὸς οἴκησιν δεδωκώς *Sammelb.*5357.6 (v A.D.); *right of residence*, εἶναι αὐτοῖς.. οἴκησιν Ἀθήνησι *IG*1².110.31. 2. *management, administration*, πόλεως Pl.*Min.*321b. II. *house, dwelling*, Hdt.9.94, A.*Supp.*1009, S.*Ph.*31, Pl.*Prt.*321d, Aeschin.1.124, etc.; ἔγκτησις γᾶς καὶ οἰκήσιος *Delph.*3(1).359 (iii B.C.); *residence* of a satrap, X.*HG*3.2.1; στρατηγικὴ οἰ. Wilcken *Chr.*385.67 (iii B.C.); κατασκαφὴς οἰ. ἀείφρουρος, of the grave, S.*Ant.*892; εἰς τὴν ἀΐδιον οἰ. X.*Ages.*11.16; *lair* of beasts, Id.*Cyn.*13.14, cf. Pl.*Prt.*320e; bird's *nest*, Arist.*HA*614b31: in pl., of the scattered *dwellings* of people not yet collected in cities, Th.6.88, cf. οἰκέω B. II; ἡ περὶ τὰ τῶν πόλεών τε καὶ οἰκήσεων διακόσμησις Pl.*Smp.*209a, cf. *Lg.*681a: but the distn. is not always observed, cf. ib.685a, etc. III. *inhabited district*, διὰ τὸ τὴν οἰ. κεῖσθαι ταύτην πρὸς ἄρκτον Arist.*Mete.*363a3; *inhabited portion of the globe*, Hp.ap.Gal.*Libr.Propr.*6, Gem.5.43, al., Cleom.1.5, Ptol.*Tetr.*76, D.L.4.58, al. IV. *family, household*, *GDI* 1582 (Dodona). **-ητήρ**, ῆρος, ὁ, poet. for οἰκητής, S.*OC*627, restored by Herm. for οἰκιστῆρας (from recc.) in A.*Th.*19. **-ητήριον**, τό, *dwelling-place, habitation*, Democr.171, E.*Or.*1114, Arist.*Mu.*393a 4, cf. *Fr.*482, Str.12.5.3, Plu.*Pomp.*28, *POxy.*281.11 (pl., i A.D.), etc. 2. Astrol., *house*, Thrasyll. in *Cat.Cod.Astr.*8(3).100.7. **-ητήριος**, α, ον, *domestic*, σκευάρια Alc.Com.27. **-ητής**, οῦ, ὁ, *dweller, inhabitant*, S.*OT*1450, Pl.*Phd.*111b: Locr. ϝοικητάς, *colonist*, *IG*9(1).334.47; ἡ πόλις προσδεῖται πλεόνων οἰκητῶν ib.9(2).517.5 (Larissa, iii B.C.). **-ητικός**, ή, όν, *accustomed to a fixed dwelling*, τῶν ζῴων τὰ μὲν οἰ. τὰ δὲ ἄοικα Arist.*HA*488a21. II. *used as* or *suitable for a residence*, οἰκία *PLond.*3.983.2 (iv A.D.), etc. **-ητός**, ή, όν (ός, όν v. infr.), *inhabited*, S.*OC*28, 39; *habitable*, διὰ τοὺς συκοφάντας οὐκ οἰκητόν ἐστιν ἐν τῇ πόλει Thphr.*Char.*26.5; οἰκία οἰκητή Lxx *Le.*25.29; ζώνη Plu.2.896b; οἰκητὸς (as fem.) [αὐλὴ] ἀράχναις μόνον Philostr.*Im.*2.28. **-ήτωρ**, ορος, ὁ, *inhabitant*, A.*Pr.* 353, Hdt.2.103, 4.9,34, 7.153, Th.1.2, Antiph.91, etc.; οἰ. θεοῦ, i.e. dwelling in the temple, E.*Andr.*1089; Ἅιδου οἰ., of one dead, S.*Tr.* 282, cf. *Aj.*396 (lyr.), 517. 2. *colonist*, Th.2.27, 3.92, Plb.3.100.4.
❀**οἰκί-α**, Ion. **οἰκίη**, Cret. and Locr. **ϝοικία**, *Leg.Gort.*5.26, *Berl. Sitzb.*1927.8 (v B.C.), cf. *IG*14.636 (Petelia):—ἡ, *building, house, dwelling*, Hdt.1.17, 114, etc.; ἡ οἰκία ἡ δημοσία *IG*1².94.36; οἰκία ἱερά ib.363.24; κατ' οἰκίαν at *home*, Pl.*La.*180d; ἰδίᾳ καὶ κατ' οἰκίας Id.*Lg.* 788a; ἔτυχεν ἐπὶ τῆς οἰ. was at *home*, X.Eph.5.4: in Com. and Attic Prose much more freq. than οἶκος: sts. opp. οἶκος as *house* to *set of apartments* or *room*, τᾶν οἰκιᾶν τιμὰν κομιζέσθω τῷ οἴκω ἑκάστω δύο μνᾶς *SIG*306.16 (Tegea, iv B.C.), cf. *PTeb.*46.9 (cf. 18) (ii B.C.), 38.14, 15 (ii B.C.), *PFay.*31.11 (ii A.D.). 2. in Att. law, οἶκος was distd. from οἰκία, the former being the *property* left at a person's death, his *estate*, the latter the *dwelling-house* only, as stated by X.*Oec.*1.5, cf. Hdt.7.224, Jul.*Gal.Fr.*12, etc. 3. distd. from συνοικία, as *one's own apartments* from *those let out to lodgers*, Aeschin.1.124. II. *household, domestic establishment*, Pl.*Grg.*520e; δύ' οἰκίας ᾤκει, i.e. he kept two *establishments*, D.39.26, cf. Arist.*Pol.*1265b26; more primitive than the πόλις, ib.1252b17, *EN*1162a18, al.; ὁ ἐπὶ τῆς οἰκίας the *house*-steward, *PCair.Zen.*150.16 (iii B.C.). III. *the household*, i.e. *inmates of the house*, Pl.*Lg.*909b (pl.). IV. *house* or *family from which one is descended*, οἰκίης ἀγαθῆς Hdt.1.107; οἰκίης οὐ φλαυροτέρης ib.99; οἰκίης οὐκ ἐπιφανέος Id.2.172; τῇ Κύρου οἰκίῃ συγγενέες Id.3.2, cf. Pl.*Grg.*472b; ἐκ τῶν μεγίστων οἰ. Eup.117.5, cf. And.1.126, Th.8.6, etc.; περὶ ὀλίγας οἰ. αἱ.. τραγῳδίαι συντίθενται Arist.*Po.*1453a19; ἡ Μακεδόνων οἰ. Plb.2.37.7; ἡ βασιλικὴ οἰ. D.S. 18.57. V. medical *school*, ἐξ οἰκίας Ἡροφίλου Erot.*Praef.*, cf. Gal. 17(2).145. **-ακός**, ή, όν, *of* or *belonging to a house*, οἱ οἰ. *those of one's household*, *Ev.Matt.*10.36, cf. Vett.Val. in *Cat.Cod.Astr.*8(1). 167: sg., *POxy.*294.17 (i A.D.); οἰκιακός μου *Milet.*3.156 (Epist. Claud.); οἰκιακή μου *PGiss.*88.4 (ii A.D.).
**ϝοικιάτας**, v. οἰκιήτης.
❀ **οἰκ-ίδιον** [ῐδ], τό, Dim. of οἰκία, *small house*, Ar.*Nu.*92, Lys.1.9, Men.*Pk.*199, *PHal.*1.183 (iii B.C.), *CIG*2664.8 (Halic.). 2. *tower* on the back of an elephant, in pl., Plb.*Fr.*162B. **-ίδιος** [ῐδ], α, ον, = οἰκεῖος, *domestic*, Opp.*C.*1.473. **-ίζω**, fut. -ιῶ Th.1.100, 6.23: aor. ᾤκισα; Ion. οἴκισα Hdt.5.42; poet. ᾤκισσα Pi.*I.*8(7).22: pf. ᾤκικα (συν-) Str.12.3.10: plpf. ᾠκίκειν App.*Hisp.*100, *BC*2.26:—Med., fut. οἰκιοῦμαι E.*Heracl.*46 (corrupt in X.*HG*1.6.32): aor. ᾠκισάμην (κατ-) Th.2.102, Isoc.19.23:—Pass., fut. οἰκισθήσομαι D.5.10, App. *BC*2.139: aor. ᾠκίσθην Th.6.5, Pl.*Ti.*72d: pf. ᾤκισμαι E.*Hec.*2; Ion. οἴ. Hdt.4.12 (as v.l.): I. c. acc. rei, *found as a colony* or *new settlement*, Ar.*Av.*172, Th.6.4, etc.; ἀπ' ἄλλης πόλεος οἰ. πόλιν E.*Fr.*360. 11 codd. (leg. -ήσῃ):—Pass., Pl.*R.*403b, X.*An.*5.3.7; πόλις οἴκισται ἐν.. v.l. in Hdt.4.12, cf. 2.44. 2. *people* with new settlers, *colonize*, χῶρον, χώρην, Id.5.42, 7.143; νήσους v.l. in Th.1.8: c. gen. pers., τὴν πόλιν.. ξυμμείκτων ἀνθρώπων οἰκίσας *having colonized* it with.., Id.6.4:—Med., ὅπου γῆς πύργον οἰκιούμεθα *we shall make ourselves a* fenced *home*, E.*Heracl.*46, cf. *Tr.*435. II. c. acc. pers., *settle, plant as a colonist* or *inhabitant*, Pi. l.c.; *remove, transplant*, ἐς ἄλλα δώματα, εἰς τήνδε χθόνα, E.*IA*670, *IT*30: metaph., τὸν μὲν ἀφ' ὑψηλῶν βραχὺν ᾤκισε *brought* him from high to low *estate*, Id.*Heracl.*613 (lyr.):—Pass., *settle as a colonist, fix one's habitation* in a place, Τυδεὺς.. ἐν Ἄργει ξεῖνος ὢν οἰκίζεται S.*Fr.*799.4, cf. E.*Hec.*2, Pl.*Phd.*114c, etc. III. intr., = οἰκέω, Herod.3.12, Hsch.; οἰκίδδειν· καθῆσθαι, Id. (οἰκιδεῖν cod.).
❀ **οἰκι-ήτης**, εω, ὁ, Ion. for οἰκέτης, Pherecyd.ap.D.L.1.122, Ant.Lib. 41.2: Locr., Thess., Arc. **ϝοικιάτας**, *IG*9(1).334.44, 9(2).257, 5(2). 262.16 (all v B.C.); οἰκιάτης St.Byz. s. v. οἶκος, *EM*698.11.
**οἰκιμβάζειν**· στραγγεύεσθαι, διατρίβειν, Hsch.; cf. ὀκιμβ–.
❀ **οἰκ-ίον**, τό, in form Dim. of οἶκος, but in meaning not differing from it; in early Gr. always pl., *house, palace*, οἰκία ναίων Il.6.15, al.; *abode* of a deity, Od.12.4, Hes.*Th.*744; of the nether world, Il.20.64; of *palaces* containing several ranges of buildings, Hdt.1.35, 41, 44, 98, 3.53, 140; but also of *private houses*, Id.1.59, v.l. in 7.118, cf. Pherecyd.Syr.2, *SIG*45.25, al. (Halic., v B.C.): so in later Prose, Arr.*Fr.* 103J.; also of *nests* of wasps, Il.12.168, 16.261; of an eagle's *nest*, 12.221: sg. in later Prose, Lxx *2Ma.*8.33, and Poetry, Call.*Fr.*198, *AP*6.203 (Laco or Phil.). **-ισία**, ἡ, *settlement*, *Abh.Berl.Akad.* 1925(5).21 (Cyrene). **-ισις**, εως, ἡ, *colonization*, Th.5.11, 6.4. **-ίσκη**, ἡ, cited by Poll.9.39 from D.48.13 (ubi codd. οἰκίαν). **-ίσκος**, ὁ, Dim. of οἶκος, *small room* or *chamber*, D.18.97, Plu.*Arat.*20, Hdn.7.9.9. 2. *cage*, ὀρνίθειος οἰ. Ar.*Fr.*405, cf. 441, Metag.5, *Inscr.Délos* 422.11 (ii B.C.), Philostr.*VS*1.21.3. ❀ **-ισμός**, ὁ, = οἴκισις, Sol.19.5; πόλεων οἰκισμοί *foundations* of cities, Pl.*Lg.*708d, cf. *Ephes.*2.20 (ii A.D.). **-ιστήρ**, ῆρος, ὁ, poet. for οἰκιστής, Pi.*O.* 7.30, al., Orac.ap.Hdt.4.155, Call.*Ap.*67, *Abh.Berl.Akad.*1925(5).21 (Cyrene); cf. οἰκητήρ. **-ιστής**, οῦ, ὁ, *colonizer, founder of a city*, *IG* 1².15.30, Hdt.4.159, 6.38, Th.1.24, 3.92, 6.3, etc.; also of those who *frame constitutions* or *charters* for a city, Id.3.34, Pl.*R.*379a; οἱ οἰ., = Lat. *triumviri coloniae deducendae*, App.*BC*1.24. **-ιστικός**, ή, όν, *fit for* or *like a colonizer*: in Adv. -κῶς Poll.9.7. **-ῐτιεύς**, ὁ, Com. word for οἰκέτης, with play on Κιτιεύς, Bion ap.Ath.4.162d (ὁ κιτιεὺς cod. A, οἰκετιεύς Kaibel).
**οἰκο-βᾰσῐλικόν**, τό, *meeting-house*, τῆς γερουσίας *BCH*11.100 (Thyatira), cf. *Supp.Epigr.*4.639 (Sardis). **-βῐος**, ον, *living at home, domestic*, Sch.Pi.*N.*8.58 codd. (ὀλιγόβιος cj. Schmidt). **-γένεια**, ἡ, *certificate of origin of an οἰκογενής*, Mitteis *Chr.*372 vi 11 (ii A.D.), *POxy.*1451.26 (ii A.D.), *Sammelb.*6995.7 (ii A.D.), etc. II. *status of an οἰκογενής*, *PGnom.*67 (ii A.D.). **-γενής**, ές, *born in the house, homebred*, of slaves, Pl.*Men.*82b, Satyr.*Vit.Eur.Fr.*39 xii 27, Plb.38. 15.3, *POxy.*48.4 (i A.D.), etc.; σῶμα γυναικεῖον οἰ. *GDI*1842 (Delph.), cf. *IG*9(1).1066 (Amphissa); τὸ γένος οἰ. *GDI*1859, 1897, al.; also οἰ. ὄρτυγες Ar.*Pax*789; ἀλεκτορίδες Arist.*HA*558b20; κύων Plu.2.48cb: metaph., μανία οἰ., opp. ἔπηλυς, ib.758e, cf. Ph.1.479. **-δέγμων**, ονος, ὁ, *one who receives people into his house*, Trag.*Adesp.*594. **-δέκτωρ**, ορος, ὁ, Astrol., *a planet in whose domicile another planet happens to be*, Vett.Val.186.15, Paul.Al.*F.*2, Rhetor. in *Cat.Cod.Astr.*8(4).206, *PMich.* in *Class.Phil.*22.13. **-δεσπόζω**, of a planet, *to be dominant*, Ptol.*Tetr.*121. **-δέσποινα**, ἡ, *mistress of a family*, *SIG*985. 52 (Philadelphia, i B.C.), Phintys ap.Stob.4.23.61, Babr.10.5, Plu. 2.613a. ❀ **-δεσποσύνη**, ἡ, *household rule*, *CIG*2987 (Ephesus), Keil-Premerstein *Erster Bericht* No.170.13, *Supp.Epigr.*4.574 (Notium).

**οἰκοδεσποτ-εία**, ἡ (better -ία), *planetary predominance*, Ptol.*Tetr.* 39,112, Vett.Val.27.26. **-έω**, *to be master of a house* or *head of a family*, 1*Ep.Ti.*5.14. II. Astrol., *predominate*, *POxy.*235.16 (i A.D.), *PLond.*1.130.163 (i/ii A.D.), Plu.2.908c, Ptol.*Tetr.*39, Luc. *Astr.*20, Vett.Val.64.8, Iamb.*Myst.*9.5, etc.; cf. sq. II. ❀ **-ης**, ου, ὁ, *master* or *steward of a house*, Alex.225, *Ev.Matt.*10.25, *PMeyer* 24.2 (vi A.D.): metaph., of God, Arr.*Epict.*3.22.4 (οἰκίας δ. was preferred by the Atticists, as in Pl.*Lg.*954b: so οἴκων δεσπόται X.*Mem.* 2.1.32, cf. Phryn.348). 2. *native ruler*, opp. foreign emperor, J.*Ap.*2.11. II. Astrol., of a planet, *owner of a domicile* or otherwise predominant, Ptol.*Tetr.*97, Porph.ap.Iamb.*Myst.*9.5, Heph. Astr.1.13, *PSI*3.158.80 (iii A.D.). **-ησις**, εως, ἡ, Astrol., *predominance* of a planet, *Cat.Cod.Astr.*8(1).240. ❀ **-ικός**, ή, όν, *fit for a père de famille*, Cic.*Att.*12.44.2. II. Astrol., *predominant*, Ptol.*Tetr.*109.

**οἰκοδίαιτος** [ῐ], ον, *living in the house*, ἀλεκτρυόνες Gal.14.215.

❀ **οἰκοδομ-εύς**, έως, ὁ, nom. pl. -δομεῖς, = οἰκοδόμος, *Ostr.Strassb.*583 (iii B.C.) (s.v.l., perh. οἱ κοδομεῖς). ❀ **-έω**, fut. -ήσω: aor. ᾠκοδόμησα (not οἰκ- in Att.): pf. ᾠκοδόμηκα Pl.*Grg.*514b: but later Att. pf. Pass. οἰκοδομημένοι *IG*2$^2$.1627.398:—*build a house*: generally, *build*, νεὼν καὶ βωμόν ib.1$^2$.24.13; νηόν Hdt.1.21; οἰκίας ib.114; γέφυραν ib.186; πυραμίδας Id.2.101, cf. Telecl.42; [αἱ μέλιτται] οἰ. τὰ κηρία Arist.*HA*623$^b$27: abs., Pl.*Chrm.*161e, 165d:—also in Med., οἰκοδομέεσθαι οἴκημα *build oneself* a house, *have it built*, Hdt.2.121.α', cf. 148; νεωσοίκους And.3.7; τείχη Th.7.11; οἰκίας Pl.*R.*372a, etc.:—Pass., *to be built*, Hdt.2.126,127; τὰ -ούμενα Arist.*GA*730$^b$8. b. generally, *fashion*, καταπέτασμα Lxx 3*Ki.*6.36. 2. metaph., *build* or *found upon*, ἔργα ἐπί τι X.*Cyr.*8.7.15; οἰ. τέχνην ἔπεσιν Ar.*Pax* 749. 3. metaph., *build up, edify*, 1*Ep.Cor.*8.1, 10.23, etc.; οἰ. εἰς τὸν ἕνα 1*Ep.Thess.*5.11: but also in bad sense, οἰκοδομηθήσεται εἰς τὸ ἐσθίειν *will be emboldened*, 1*Ep.Cor.*8.10; cf. ἀνοικοδομέω. ❀ **-ή**, ἡ, = -δόμησις, -δομία, *PCair.Zen.*499.93 (iii B.C.), prov. Lacon.ap.Suid. s.v. ἵππους, Lxx 1*Ch.*26.27, *PGrenf.*1.21.17 (ii B.C.), *OGI*655.2 (i B.C.), D.S.1.46, Eratosth.ap.Str.16.1.15, Str.5.2.5, Plu.*Cam.*32: condemned by Phryn.394: earlier examples, as Arist.*EN*1137$^b$30 (v.l.), Thphr. *HP*3.8.5 codd., are dub. II. = sq., *Ev.Matt.*24.1, Plu.*Luc.*39, *CIG* 4449 (Beroea), al.: metaph., 1*Ep.Cor.*3.9. **-ημα**, ατος, τό, *building, structure*, Hdt.2.121.α',136, Th.5.11, Antipho Soph.24, Pl.*Grg.* 514b, etc. **-ημάτιον**, τό, Dim. of foreg., Arr.*Epict.*2.15.9. **-ησις**, εως, ἡ, *act* or *manner of building*, Th.3.2,21, Pl.*Grg.*455b, Arist.*EN* 1152$^b$14, etc.: pl., ναῶν οἰ. Pl.*R.*394a. II. = οἰκοδόμημα, Id.*Criti.* 117a, *Lg.*778e (both pl.). **-ητέον**, *one must build*, Id.*R.* 424d. **-ητικός**, ή, όν, *fitted for building*: ἡ -κή (sc. τέχνη) *architecture*, Luc.*Cont.*5 (al. -δομική). ❀ **-ητός**, ή, όν, *built*, Str.3.3.7, 8.6.2. **-ία**, ἡ, = -δόμησις I, *IG*1$^2$.338.15 (prob.), Democr.154, Th. 1.93, Pl.*Lg.*804c, *PHal.*1.181 (iii B.C.). II. *building, edifice*, Th. 2.65 (pl.), Pl.*Lg.*758e, 759a, al. **-ικός**, ή, όν, *skilled in building*, Id.*R.*333b, Plot.1.6.3; τὸ -κόν Pl.*Chrm.*170c, Arist.*Ph.*196$^b$26: ἡ -κή (sc. τέχνη) *the art of building, architecture*, Pl.*Chrm.* l.c., *Grg.* 514b, *R.*346d, al.; so τὰ -κά Id.*Grg.*514a (but τὰ -κά *the built parts* of a house, opp. λεπτουργικά and χρηστικά, *SIG*880.65 (ii/iii A.D.)). Adv. -κῶς Poll.7.117. II. *fit for building*, ὕλη Thphr.*HP*5.7.1. **-ιστήριος**, α, ον, = foreg. II, *SIG*135.10 (Olynthus, iv B.C.). ❀ **-ος**, ὁ (parox.), *builder, architect*, Hdt.2.121.α', Ar.*Fr.*180, Pl.*Prt.*319b, *Supp.Epigr.*4.105, etc.

**οἰκο-δοχεύς**, έως, ὁ, = οἰκοδέκτωρ, Vett.Val.102.24. **-θάλής**, gloss on ἀμφιθαλής, Tim.*Lex.*

❀ **οἴκοθεν** (also **οἴκοθε** Chor. in *Rev.Phil.*1877.227), Adv. *from one's house, from home*, ὁ οἰ. ἦγ' ὁ γεραιός Il.11.632; οἰ. ὥρμησαν Th.4.90; οἰ. οἴκαδε *from home* to home, implying security and ease, Pi.*O.*6.99, cf. 7.4, Lib.*Ep.*149; οἰ. ἐκ Κλαζομενῶν Pl.*Prm.*126a; δεῦρο οἰ. Id.*Hp. Ma.*282b; εὐθὺς οἰ. ὑπάρχει παισὶν οὖσιν, i.e. from childhood, Arist. *Pol.*1295$^b$16: freq. without any sense of motion, νόμοι οἱ οἰ., = οἱ πάτριοι, A.*Supp.*390, cf. E.*Ph.*294 (lyr.); οἱ οἰ. φίλοι Id.*Med.*506; τὰ οἰ. *domestic affairs*, Id.*IA*1000; τὸ οἰ. Pi.*P.*8.51; στρατηγοὺς εἵλοντο ἐκ τῶν οἰ. X.*HG*1.4.10; οἰ. τὸν πολέμιον ἔχειν *at home, within*, Pl.*Sph.* 252c; τὸ γένος οἰ., = οἰκογενής, of a slave, *GDI*2307.5 (Delph.). 2. *from one's household stores*, πάντ' ἐθέλω δόμεναι καὶ οἰ. ἄλλ' ἐπιθεῖναι Il.7.364; οἰ. ἄλλο Εὐμήλῳ ἐπιδοῦναι 23.558; εἰ καί νύ κεν οἰ. ἄλλο μεῖζον ἐπαιτήσειας ib.592: metaph., τὸν νοῦν διδάσκαλον οἰ. ἔχουσα χρηστόν having in my *own* mind a wise teacher, E.*Tr.*653; δεῖ μάντιν εἶναι, μὴ μαθοῦσαν οἰ. one must needs be externally inspired with the vision of truth, if one has not learned it *by one's own intellect*, Id.*Med.* 239; πόθεν ἂν λάβοιμι ῥῆμα..; οὐ γὰρ εἶχον οἰ. I have it not *of my own*, Ar.*Pax*522, cf. Lys.4.7; θρασύ μοι τόδ' εἰπεῖν.. ὁδὸν κυρίαν λόγων οἰ. Pi.*N.*7.51; οἰ. μάτευε ib.3.31: with a Subst., = οἰκεῖος, ἀρεταῖσιν οἰ., ἀνορέαις οἰ., by his *own* prowess, valour, Id.*O.*3.44, *I.*4(3).12. 3. *from one's own financial resources, at one's own expense* (cf. ϝοικω), *PEleph.*11.7 (iii B.C.), Wilcken *Chr.*176.17 (i A.D.), etc.; τὰς πολιτείας οἰ. ἐνδόξως ἐκτελεῖν *IG*4.672 (Nauplia), cf. 716 (Hermione); ἀγωνοθετεῖν Παναθηναίων οἰ. *SIG*869.7 (ii A.D.); παρεχέτω οἰ. τὸ θερμόλυχνον ib.1109.151 (ii A.D.). 4. like ἀρχῆθεν, *to begin with, originally*, ψευδεῖς οἰ. δόξας ἔχοντες entertaining false notions *to begin with*, Aeschin.3.59, cf. 60; εἰς ὑπέρχρεων οὐσίαν καὶ οἰ. into an estate *already* overburdened with debt, Is.10.17.

**οἰκό-θετος**, ον, *laid up at home*, i.e. one's own, δύναμις Pi.*Pae.* 1.4. **-θῐ**, Ep. for οἴκοι, Adv. *at home*, ὥς τις.. βέλος καὶ οἰ. πέσσῃ Il.8.513; εἰ τάδε ἔστο περὶ χροὶ οἴκοθ' Ὀδυσσεύς Od.19.237; τοιαῦτα.. οἰ. κεῖται 21.398. **-θουρος**· οἰκουρὸς κύων, Hsch. **-θρεπτος**, ον, *homebred*, Phot. s. v. οἰκογενές.

**οἴκοι**, Adv. (old loc. of οἶκος) *at home, in the house*, οὔ νυ καὶ ὑμῖν οἰ. ἔνεστι γόος..; Il.24.240; οἰ. βέλτερον εἶναι Hes.*Op.*365, etc.; τὰ οἰ. one's *domestic affairs*, X.*Cyr.*6.1.42; *home products*, Pl.*R.*371a; ἡ οἰ. δίαιτα S.*OC*352; ἡ δ' οἰ. (sc. πόλις) *one's own country*, ib.759; αἱ οἰ. τιμαί Isoc.*Ep.*4.7. 2. = οἴκαδε I, Zos.2.27.2.

**οἰκο-κερδής**, ές, *profitable to a house* or *family*, Phryn.*PSp.*96 B. **-κρᾰτέομαι**, Pass., *live under family rule*, i.e. *without civil bonds* or *laws*, Eust.1618.20. **-μᾰχία**, ἡ, *domestic conflict*, Heph. Astr.2.34.

**οἰκόνδε** (better **οἶκον δέ** A.D.*Adv.*177.27), Ep. Adv., = οἴκαδε, Il. 1.606, al., Hes.*Op.*554; οἰκόνδε ἄγειν bring *home*, of a bride, Od.6. 159, cf. 11.410. 2. *to the women's chamber*, 1.360.

**οἰκονομ-έω**, *manage as a house-steward, order, regulate*, θαλάμους πατρός S.*El.*190 (lyr.); τὴν οἰκίαν Pl.*Ly.*209d; τὰ ἴδια X.*Mem.*3.4.12, etc.; τὸν ἴδιον βίον Euphro 4; ταῦτα (i.e. meats) Alex.110.20; ὄχλον *Com.Adesp.*119:—Med., Arist.*Oec.*1343$^a$23: c. dat., ἄνθρωπος.. μεγίστοις -εῖται πράγμασιν Men.531.14. 2. *dispense*, Pl.*Phdr.* 256e; *disburse*, *SIG*667.20 (Athens, ii B.C.). 3. *treat* a substance with another, πυρίτην ὀξάλμῃ Ps.-Democr.Alch.p.44 B.: metaph., of a poet, εἰ τὰ ἄλλα μὴ εὖ οἰ. *treat, handle*, Arist.*Po.*1453$^a$29; so (in Med.) of an artist, οἰ. τὴν ὕλην Luc.*Hist.Conscr.*51:—Pass., τὰ σκέμματα.. ᾠκονομήσθω Phld.*D.*3.8. 4. of public officers, *administer*, Plb.4.26.6, 4.67.9:—Pass., πολιτεία ἀρίστη ἡ ὑπὸ τῶν ἀρίστων -ουμένη Arist.*Pol.*1288$^a$34. II. intr., *to be a house-steward*, *Ev.Luc.*16.2. **-ημα**, ατος, τό, *administration*, πᾶν τὸ πρὸς τὴν διαδοχὴν ἀνῆκον οἰ. *IG*2$^2$.1099 (ii A.D.): pl., *OGI*453.19 (M. Antonius). **-ημένως**, Adv. *with adjustment to a purpose*, Sch.Od.3.296, *An.Par.*3.435. ❀ **-ία**, ἡ, *management of a household* or *family, husbandry, thrift*, Pl.*Ap.*36b, *R.*498a, X.*Oec.*1.1, Arist.*EN*1141$^b$32, *Pol.*1253$^b$ sqq.: pl., Pl.*R.*407b; *households*, Arist.*GA*744$^b$18. 2. generally, *direction, regulation*, Epicur.*Ep.*1 p.29 U.; esp. of a State, *administration*, αἱ κατὰ τὴν πόλιν οἰ. Din.1.97; *principles of government*, Chrysipp.*Stoic.*2.338; τῶν γεγονότων Plb.1.4.3, al.; πολιτικὴ οἰ. Phld.*Rh.* 2.32 S.; ἡ τῆς ἀρχῆς οἰ. Hdn.6.1.1; of a fund, *SIG*577.9 (Milet., iii/ii B.C.). 3. *arrangement*, ἡ περὶ τὸν νοσέοντα οἰ. Hp.*Epid.*6. 2.24; ἡ περὶ τῶν ὠνίων οἰ. *market, fair*, *SIG*695.35 (Magn. Mae.); οἰκονομίαι *proceedings*, *IG*9(1).226 (Drymaea); τίνα οἰκονομίαν προσαγήγοχας what *steps* you have taken, *PCair.Zen.*240.10 (iii B.C.); αὕτη φύσεως οἰ. Plb.6.9.10; of a literary work, *arrangement*, ἡ κατὰ μέρος οἰ. D.S.5.1, cf. D.H.*Pomp.*4, *Comp.*25, Sch.Od.1.328: pl., Plu.2.142a. 4. in Egypt, *office of οἰκονόμος*, *PTeb.*24.62 (ii B.C.), al. 5. *stewardship*, Lxx *Is.*22.19, *Ev.Luc.*16.2. 6. *plan, dispensation*, *Ep.Eph.*1.10, 3.2. 7. in bad sense, *scheming*, M.Ant. 4.51. II. *public revenue* of a state, *BMus.Inscr.*897.14, al. (Halic., iii B.C.). III. *transaction, contract*, or legal *instrument*, *CPR*4.1 (i A.D.), *BGU*457.10 (ii A.D.), etc. IV. magical *operation* or *process*, *PMag.Par.*1.161,292,2009. ❀ **-ικός**, ή, όν, *practised in the management of a household* or *family*, opp. πολιτικός, Pl.*Alc.*1.133e, *Phdr.*248d, X.*Oec.*1.3, Arist.*Pol.*1252$^a$8, etc.: Sup., [κτημάτων] τὸ βέλτιστον καὶ -ώτατον, of man, Phld.*Oec.*p.30 J.: hence, *thrifty, frugal, economical*, X.*Mem.*4.2.39, Phylarch.65 J. (Comp.): ὁ οἰ. title of treatise *on the duties of domestic life*, by Xenophon; and τὰ οἰ. title of treatise *on public finance*, ascribed to Aristotle, cf. X.*Cyr.*8.1.14: ἡ -κή (sc. τέχνη) domestic *economy, husbandry*, Pl.*Plt.*259c, X.*Mem.* 3.4.11, etc.; οἰ. ἀρχή defined as ἡ τέκνων ἀρχὴ καὶ γυναικὸς καὶ τῆς οἰκίας πάσης, Arist.*Pol.*1278$^b$38; applied to *patriarchal rule*, ib.1285$^b$ 32. Adv. -κῶς Ph.2.426, Plu.2.1126a; also in literary sense, *in a well ordered manner*, Sch.Th.1.63. ❀ **-ισσα**, ἡ, perh. *wife of* οἰκονόμος, or *female official in the church*, *JHS*24.283 (v A.D.), *Papers of Amer. Sch. at Athens* 3 p.216 (Tchaundir). ❀ **-ος**, ὁ, ἡ, *one who manages a household*, = οἰκοδεσπότης, X.*Oec.*1.2, Pl.*R.*417a, etc.; *steward of an estate*, Ζήνωνι τῷ οἰ. *PCair.Zen.*48.2 (iii B.C.); *house-steward*, being a slave, *IG*5(1).40,1235, *IGRom.*4.1699, *TAM*2.518 (Pinara), prob. in *BCH*52.413: metaph., οἰ. ἡδονῆς Alcid.ap.Arist.*Rh.*1406$^a$27. 2. generally, *manager, administrator*, opp. τύραννος, Id.*Pol.*1314$^b$7, etc.: hence, b. title of a subordinate state official, *IG*5(2).389. 15 (Lusi, iv/iii B.C.); also of a high financial officer, *Inscr.Prien.*6.30 (iv B.C.), *BMus.Inscr.*448.7 (Ephesus, iv B.C.); under a monarch, *OGI*225.37 (iii B.C.); in Egypt, *PRev.Laws* 3.3, 5.6, al. (iii B.C.), *PTeb.*39.11 (ii B.C.), etc.; in charge of the Serapeum, *UPZ*56.7 (ii B.C., pl.); οἱ Καίσαρος οἰ., = Lat. *procuratores Caesaris*, Luc.*Alex.* 39; θεοῦ οἰ. *minister* of God, *Ep.Tit.*1.7, cf. 1*Ep.Cor.*4.1. II. as fem., *housekeeper, housewife*, Phoc.3.7, Lys.1.7: metaph., A.*Ag.* 155.

**οἰκοπεδ-ικός** πῆχυς, *rectangle measuring* 1 *cubit* (πῆχυς) × 100 *cubits*, Mitteis *Chr.* 31 v 9 (ii B.C.), *PPar.* 15.42 (ii B.C.), *POxy.* 669.9 (iii A.D.). ❀ **-ον**, τό, *site of a house, place on which a house is* or *has been built*, *IG*1$^2$.325.14 (prob.), X.*Vect.*2.6, Aeschin.1.182, Arist.*Pol.*1265$^b$ 24; *building-site*, *BGU*906.21 (i A.D.), Dsc.2.158, etc.; *site* of a city, πόλεως Plb.15.23.10. 2. *the house itself, building*, Th.4.90, Pl.*Lg.* 741c.

**οἰκο-ποιός**, όν, *constituting a house*, οὐδ' ἔνδον οἰ. ἐστί τις τροφή the comforts *of a house*, S.*Ph.*32. II. **-ποιός**, ὁ, *structor*, *Gloss.* **-πορεία**· τὰ κατ' οἰκίαν σκεύη, Suid.

**οἰκόριος**, α, ον, poet. for οἰκούριος.

❀ **οἶκος**, ὁ, *house*, not only of *built houses*, but of *any dwelling-place*, as that of Achilles at Troy (v. κλισία), Il.24.471,572, cf. S.*Aj.*65; of

the Cyclops' *cave*, Od.9.478; of a *tent*, Lxx*Ge*.31.33; *οἶκον ἱκάνεται* is coming *home*, Od.23.7; *εἰς* or *ἐς οἶκον* A.*Eu*.459, S.*Ph*.240; *πρὸς οἶκον* A.*Ag*.867, S.*OT*1491, etc.; *κατ' οἶκον* Id.*El*.929, etc.; *κατ' οἶκον ἐν δόμοις* Id.*Tr*.689; *οἱ κατ' οἶκον* ib.934; *αἱ κατ' οἶκον κακοπραγίαι* Th.2.60; *τᾶν οἴκῳ* A.*Ch*.579; *ἐν οἴκῳ καθεύδειν* Antipho 2.1.4,8; *οἱ ἐν οἴκῳ* *PCair.Zen*.93.10 (iii B.C.); *ἐξ οἴκου ἀποδημεῖν* ib.44.23 (iii B.C.); *ἐπ' οἴκου ἀποχωρῆσαι* go *home*wards, Th.1.87, cf. 30,108, 2.31, etc.; *ἀπ' οἴκου* from *home*, Id.1.99, etc.; cf. *οἰκία*. b. freq. omitted after *εἰς* or *ἐν*, v. *εἰς* I. 4c, *ἐν* A. I. 2. 2. *room, chamber*, Od.1.356, 19.514,598; *οἶ. θερμός* Dsc.2.164; *dining-hall*, *ἑπτάκλινος οἶ.* Phryn. Com.66, X.*Smp*.2.18; *room* in a temple, *IG*4$^{2}$(1).110*A* 27, al. (Epid., pl.): pl. *οἶκοι* freq., = *a single house*, Od.24.417, A.*Pers*.230,524, etc.; *κλαυθμῶν τῶν ἐξ οἴκων domestic* griefs, Id.*Ag*.1554 (anap.); *ἀπ' οἴκων* S.*Aj*.762; *ἐς* or *πρὸς οἴκους*, Id.*Ph*.311,383; *κατ' οἴκους* at *home, within*, Hdt.3.79, S.*Aj*.65, Mnesim.4.52. 3. of public buildings, *meeting-house, hall*, *οἶ.* *Κηρύκων* *IG*2$^{2}$.1672.24; *Δεκελειῶν* ib. 1237.33; of *treasuries* at Delos, *JHS*25.310, al., cf. Hsch. s.v. *θησαυρός*; *ἐγκριτήριοι οἶ.*, v. *ἐγκριτήριος*; *temple*, *IG*4.1580 (Aegina), Hdt.8.143, E.*Ph*.1373, Ar.*Nu*.600; *οἶ. τεμένιος ἱερός* *SIG*987.3, cf. 25 (Chios, iv B.C.); *ἐν τῷ οἴ. τοῦ Ἄμμωνος* *UPZ*79.4 (ii B.C.); *ὁ οἶ. [τοῦ θεοῦ]* *Ev.Matt*.21.13, al.; of a funerary monument, *BCH*2.610 (Cibyra), 18.11 (Magnesia); *ἀΐδιοι οἶ.*, i.e. tombs, D.S.1.51. 4. *cage* for birds, Id.13.82 (s.v.l., *οἰκ⟨ίσκ⟩ῳ* Valck.); *beehive*, *Gp*.15.2.22. 5. Astrol., *domicile* of a planet, *PLond*.1.98$^{r}$.12, al. (i/ii A.D.), Ael.*NA*12.7, Vett.Val.7.25, Man.2.141, Eust.162.2. II. *one's household goods, substance* (cf. *οἴκοθεν* 2), *οἶ. ἐμὸς διόλωλε* Od.2.64; *ἐσθίεταί μοι οἶ.* 4.318; *καὶ οἶ. καὶ κλῆρος ἀκήρατος* Il.15.498; *οἶκον δέ κ' ἐγὼ καὶ κτήματα δοίην* Od.7.314, cf. Hdt.3.53, 7.224, etc.: in Att. law, *estate, inheritance*, *οἶκον κατασχεῖν τινος* And.4.15, cf. Lys.12.93, Is.5.15, D.27.4, etc.; *οἶ. πέντε ταλάντων* Is.7.42; cf. *οἰκία*. III. a reigning *house*, *οἶ. ὁ βασιλέος* Hdt.5.31, cf. 6.9, Th. 1.137, Isoc.3.41; *Ἀγαμεμνονίων οἴκων ὄλεθρον* A.*Ch*.862 (anap.), cf. S.*Ant*.594 (lyr.); also of any *family*, Is.10.4, Lxx*Ge*.7.1, D.H.1.85; *οἶ. Σεβαστός*, = *domus Augusta*, Ph.2.520; *οὐδενὸς οἴκου δεύτερον γενόμενον* *IG*4$^{2}$(1).84.32 (Epid., i A.D.); *τοὺς πρώτους τᾶς πόλιος οἴκους* ib.86.15 (ibid., i A.D.). (Orig. *ϝοῖκος*, cf. *ϝοίκω*, *οἰκία*: cf. Skt. *veśás, viś-* 'house', Lat. *vicus, vicinus*, etc.)

**οἰκός**, v. *ἔοικα*. **οἴκοσε**, Adv., = *οἴκαδε*, A.D.*Adv*.194.10.

**οἰκο-σῑτία**, ἡ, *living at one's own expense*, Poll.6.36. ⊛ **-σῖτος**, ον, *taking one's meals at home*, *οἰ. υἱός* Anaxandr.24, cf. Luc.*Somn*. 1; *οἰ. τοὺς γάμους πεποιηκέναι*, i.e. without inviting guests outside the family, Men.450; *living at one's own expense, unpaid*, *οἰ. ἐκκλησιαστής* Antiph.200; *οὐκ οἰ. τοὺς ἀκροατὰς λαμβάνεις* Men.*Kith.Fr*. 6; *οἰ. νυμφίος* a bridegroom who takes his bride *without* (or *not on account of*) *a portion*, Id.103, cf. Ath.6.247e; *τοὺς διακονοῦντας ἐν τοῖς γάμοις οἰκοσίτους μισθώσασθαι paying for their food out of their wages*, Thphr.*Char*.22.4, cf. *IG*2$^{2}$.1672.62; *πεζοὶ οἰ.*, of militiamen, Plu.*Crass*.19. 2. = *παράσιτος*, Ph.1.344. II. *living in a house*, of a mouse, opp. *ἀρουραῖος*, Babr.108.4; cf. *οἰκότριψ*. III. *devourer of houses*, Ph.1.311. **-σκευή**, ἡ, *household utensils*, *PLond*.5.1708.44 (vi A.D.), *PMasp*.153.20 (vi A.D.), Arc.103, *Gloss*.:—also **-σκευα**, τά, gloss on *ἔπιπλα*, Sch.Patm.D.27.10 (*BCH* 1.149). **-σκοπικόν**, τό, *observation of an omen at home*, *An.Ox*.4.240. **-σόος**, ον, *maintaining the house*, of an economical wife, opp. *οἰκοφθόρος*, Max.98: poet. **οἰκοσσόος** Nonn.*D*. 21.270. **-της**, ου, ὁ, = *οἰκέτης* I. 1, *Tab.Defix*.87*a*5,6 (iii B.C.). ⊛ **-τρᾰφής**, ές, *homebred*, Hellenistic for *οἰκότριψ*, Moer.p.283 P., *Gloss*., v.l. in Poll.3.76. **-τρίβαιος** [ῐ], α, ον, *belonging to an* *οἰκότριψ*, Poll.3.76; corrupted into *οἰκοτρύβλιον* in Hsch. **-τρῐβής**, ές, *ruining a house* or *family*, *δαπάνη* Critias 6.14. ⊛ **-τριψ**, ῐβος, ὁ, *a slave born and bred in the house*, Att. for *οἰκογενής* (*EM*590.15), *οἰ. κλώψ*, of a mouse (cf. *οἰκόσιτος* II), Babr.107.2; as a term of abuse, *ᾠκότριψ Εὐριπίδης the slave* E., Ar.*Th*.426; *οἰκοτρίβων οἰκότριβας* D. 13.24; *μετὰ τῶν οἰ. παίζειν* Ael.*VH*12.15: metaph., *οἰκότριβες ἐν φιλοσοφίᾳ* Phld.*Acad.Ind*.p.19M. ⊛ **-τροφος**, ον, *house-bred*, *δοῦλοι* dub. in *OGI*765.19 (Priene, iv B.C.); *living at home*, dub. in D.Chr. 6.11. **-τύραννος** [ῠ], ὁ, *domestic tyrant*, *AP*10.61 (Pall.).

⊛ **οἰκότως**, Ion. for *ἐοικότως*, *reasonably, probably*, Hdt.2.25, 7.50.

⊛ **οἰκουμέν-η** (sc. *γῆ*), ἡ, *inhabited region*, v. *οἰκέω* A. 1; then *the Greek world*, opp. barbarian lands, D.7.35; *πᾶσα ἡ οἰ.* Id.18.48; in Arist.*Mete*.362$^{b}$26, *ἡ οἰ.*, = *the inhabited world* (including non-Greek lands, as Ethiopia, India, Scythia), as opp. possibly uninhabited regions, cf. Cleom.2.1; in Arist.*Mu*.392$^{b}$26, *ἥδε ἡ οἰ.*, = our *world* (= Asia, Libya, Europe); *οἰκουμέναι worlds*, ib.31; *ἡ φιλία περιχορεύει τὴν οἰ.* Epicur.*Sent.Vat*.52; *σοῦ* (i.e. Ptolemy II or III) *τῆς οἰ. πάσης βασιλεύοντος* *PSI*5.541.7, cf. Lxx 1*Es*.2.3; loosely, *the whole world*, Hyp.*Eux*.33 (prob.), Antiph.179, *PMag.Lond*.121.704, Luc. *Halc*.3, Ath.8.350a: so perh. in some passages cited under II. II. *the Roman world*, *ὁ ἀγαθὸς δαίμων* (etc.) *τῆς οἰ.*, i.e. the Emperor, *OGI*666.4, 668.5, *POxy*.1021.5 (i A.D.), *CIG*2581–2, 4416, *Ev.Luc*.2. 1, *Act.Ap*.17.6, 24.5, *Sammelb*.176.2 (ii A.D.), Gal.10.7, Luc.*Macr*. 7. III. *ἡ οἰ. ἡ μέλλουσα the world* to come, i.e. the kingdom of Christ, *Ep.Hebr*.2.5. ⊛ **-ικός**, ή, όν, *of, from*, or *open to the whole world* (cf. foreg.), *νεικήσας ἀγῶνας ἱεροὺς οἰ.* *IG*3.129 (iii A.D.); *οἰ. συνέδριον τῶν λινουργῶν* *Rev.Arch*.1874.113.

**οἰκουργός**, όν, (*οἶκος, ἔργον*) *working at home*, *Ep.Tit*.2.5 (v.l. *οἰκουρούς*); *οἰκουργὸν καὶ καθέδριον διάγειν βίον* Sor.1.27 (but cf. *οἰκουροκαθέδριος*).

**οἰκουρ-έω**, usu. in pres., *watch* or *keep the house*, *σηκὸν φυλάσσει.. οἰκουρῶν ὄφις watching*, S.*Ph*.1328; *πόλιν οἰ. guarding* it, A.*Ag*.809: generally, *keep safe, guard*, Ar.*Ach*.1060; *keep watch* in a temple, *ὅταν οἰκουρῶσι μύσται* Arist.*Ath*.56.4. II. *keep at home*, as women, S.*OC*343; *οἰ. ἔνδον* Pl.*R*.451d, cf. D.59.86, Plu.*Cam*.11, Luc.*Nigr*. 18; of persons who *stay at home* and avoid military service, Hermipp. 45, Plu.*Per*.11,12, etc. 2. *ἕβδομον οἰ. μῆνα πολιορκοῦντες idle away* seven months in the siege, Id.*Cam*.28. (Impf. *οἰκ-* or *ᾠκ-* acc. to Choerob. *in Theod*.2.50 H.: 2sg. *οἰκούρεις* *Lex.Mess*.p.413.) **-ημα**, ατος, τό, *the watch* or *keeping of a house*, E.*Hipp*.787; *οἰ. τῶνδε τῶν ξένων watch kept* by these strangers (for *οἱ οἰκουροῦντες ξένοι*), S.*Ph*. 868. II. *keeping the house, staying at home*, E.*Heracl*.700. 2. in concrete sense, of persons, *-ήματα φθείρειν* corrupt *the stay-at-homes*, i.e. the women, Id.*Or*.928. **-ία**, ἡ, *housekeeping and its cares*, in pl., *μακρὰς διαντλοῦσ' ἐν δόμοις οἰ.* Id.*HF*1373: sg., Vett.Val. 1.18. II. *keeping-at-home*, esp. of women, Plu.2.271e, *Cor*. 35. **-ικός**, ή, όν, *inclined to keep at home*: *τὸ -κόν*, = *οἰκουρία*, Luc. *Fug*.16. **-ιος**, α, ον, *of* or *for housekeeping*: hence *οἰκούρια* (sc. *δῶρα*), *τά*, *wages, reward for keeping the house*, S.*Tr*.542. II. *keeping within doors*: *οἰκούρια toys to keep children within doors*, to amuse them in their mother's absence, Hsch., Eust.1423.3; *ἑταῖραι οἰκόριαι* (Dor. for *οἰκούριαι*) *female house*-mates, Pi.*P*.9.19.

**οἰκουροκαθέδριος** *βίος*, *home-keeping and sedentary* life, Tz.*H*.1. 287.

⊛ **οἰκουρός**, όν, (*οὖρος* B) *watching* or *keeping the house*, of a watch-dog, Ar.*V*.970; of a cock, Plu.2.998b; *οἰ. ὄφις*, of the sacred serpent in the Acropolis, Ar.*Lys*.759, Phylarch.72 J., Hsch. II. *keeping at home*: as Subst., *οἰκουρός, ἡ*, *mistress of the house, housekeeper*, S.*Fr*. 487, E.*Hec*.1277: as Adj., Id.*HF*45 (masc.); *ἡ θεὸς ἡ καλουμένη οἰ.* *PLond*.1.125$^{v}$.11 (v A.D.); used in praise of a good wife, Ph.2.431, D.C.56.3. 2. contemptuously of a man, *stay-at-home*, opp. one who goes forth to war, *λέοντ' ἄναλκιν.. οἰκουρόν* A.*Ag*.1225, cf. 1626, Din.1.82; *τὸν ὑγρὸν τοῦτον καὶ οἰ.* Plu.2.751a; *δίαιτα οἰ. καὶ ἀργή* Id. *Per*.34.

**οἰκοφθορ-έω**, *squander one's substance*, Pl.*Lg*.929d, 959c:—Pass., *lose one's fortune, be ruined*, *οἰκοφθορημένος* Hdt.5.29, cf. 8.142, 144; *ἐκακώθησαν καὶ οἰκοφθορήθησαν* Id.1.196. **-ία**, ἡ, *a squandering one's substance*, *οἰ. καὶ πενία* Pl.*Phd*.82c. II. *γυναικῶν -ίαι seduction*, Plu.2.12b. **-ος**, ὁ, *one who ruins a house, a prodigal*, E. *Fr*.1055, Pl.*Lg*.689d, Ph.1.311. II. *seducer, adulterer*, *PGrenf*. 1.53.19 (*-φθερ-*, iv A.D.), Suid. s.v. *Ἱλάριος*.

**οἰκο-φόρος**, ον, *bearing one's house*, *ἔθνη* Scymn.854, *Peripl.M.Eux*. 49. **-φῠλᾰκέω**, *watch a house*, of a dog, v.l. in Aesop.176 Chambry. **-φῠλάκιον** [ᾰ], τό, = *οἰκούριον* (v. *οἰκούριος* 2), Eust.1423. 3. **-φύλαξ** [ῠ], ᾰκος, ὁ, ἡ, *house-guard*, A.*Supp*.26 (anap.), *AP* 9.604 (Noss.); = *οἰκουρός*, *BCH*50.529 (Attica, ii A.D.).

**οἰκτ-ειρέω** or **-ηρέω**, v. *οἰκτίρω*. **-είρημα**, ατος, τό, = *οἰκτιρμός*, Lxx*Je*.38(31).3 (s.v.l.). ⊛ **-ίζω** (pres. only in compd. *κατ-*), Att. fut. *οἰκτιῶ* A.*Pr*.68 (*κατ-* S., etc.): aor. *ᾤκτισα* S.*OT*1508: mostly poet., *pity, have pity upon*, c. acc. pers., A. l.c., S. l.c., etc.; *τινὰ τῆς μικροψυχίας* Arist.*Mu*.391$^{a}$22: c. acc. rei, *πάθος οἰκτίσαι* S.*Tr*.855 (lyr.):—Med. in same sense, *ἐπίδοι.. στόλον οἰκτιζομένα with pitying eye*, A.*Supp*.1031 (lyr.), cf. E.*Hec*.720 (as v.l.), Th.2. 51. 2. Med. also, *bewail, lament*, *τι* E.*IT*486, cf. *Hel*.1053: abs., Din.1.110: c. acc. cogn., *οἶκτον οἰκτίζεσθαι utter a wail*, A.*Eu*.515 (lyr.), cf. E.*Tr*.155 (anap.). **-ικός**, ή, όν, *expressive of pity* or *lamentation*, *An.Bachm*.2.290. ⊛ **-ιρμός**, ὁ, *pity, compassion*, Pi. *P*.1.85: pl., *compassionate feelings, mercies*, *Ep.Rom*.12.1, *Ep.Phil*. 2.1, al. **-ιρμοσύνη**, ἡ, = foreg., Tz.*H*.8 No.173 tit. **-ίρμων**, ον, gen. ονος, *merciful*, Gorg.*Pal*.32, Theoc.15.75, *AP*7.359, Lxx*Ex*. 34.6, al., *Ev.Luc*.6.36. **-ίρω** [ῑ] (in codd. freq. *-ειρ-*, but *-ῑρ-* in early Inscrr., *IG*1$^{2}$.971,976,982, v. sub fin.; cf. *κατοικτίρω*): impf. *ᾤκτ(ε)ιρον* Stesich.18: fut. *οἰκτῑρῶ* A.*Fr*.199.6 (*-ερεῖ* codd.): aor. *ᾤκτ(ε)ιρα* Il.11.814, A.*Pr*.354, al.; Ion. *οἴκτ(ε)ιρα* Hdt.3.52:—**Pass.**, only pres. and impf., ibid., X.*Oec*.7.40, S.*El*.1412:—later forms (as if from *οἰκτειρέω*): fut. *οἰκτειρήσω* Sch.Od.4.740, Lxx*Ex*.33.19, *Ep.Rom*.9.15, Lib.*Descr*.30.18: aor. *ᾠκτείρησα* Sch.A.*Pr*.353: aor. Pass. *οἰκτειρηθῆναι* ib.637.—Cf. *οἰκτείρημα*:—*pity, have pity upon*, c. acc. pers., Il.11.814, 16.5, Hdt. l.c., 7.38; *ἐλεῆσαι καὶ οἰ.* Pl.*Euthd*. 288d; *οἰ. τινά τινος pity* one *for* or *because of* a thing, *οἰκτίρω σε θεσφάτου μόρου* A.*Ag*.1321, cf. *Supp*.209; also *οἰ. τινά τινος ἕνεκα* X.*Oec*. 2.7; *ἐπί τινι* ib.4: c. acc. rei, E.*Med*.1233, Ar.*V*.328, Antipho 3.1. 2. 2. c. inf., *οἰ. νιν λιπεῖν* I *am sorry* to leave her, S.*Aj*.652; *οἰ. εἰ.. to be sorry that* it should be, X.*An*.1.4.7. [Aeol. *οἰκτίρρω* Hdn. Gr.2.558: hence *οἰκτῖρω* is prob. from *οἰκτιρ-yω*, and *οἰκτίρετε* [ῐ] in *AP*7.267 (Posidipp.) is an error: but the Att. fut. is *οἰκτερῶ* acc. to Hdn.Gr.2.559.] **-ισμα**, ατος, τό, *lamentation*, E.*Heracl*.158 (pl.). **-ισμός**, ὁ, *lamentation*, A.*Eu*.189, X.*Smp*.1.16, etc. **-ιστος**, η, ον, irreg. Sup. of *οἰκτρός*, *most pitiable, lamentable*, *οἴ... δειλοῖσι βροτοῖσιν* Il.22.76; *θάνον οἰ. θανάτῳ* Od.11.412; *Ἀτθίσιν οἰκτίστη, σὸν φάος, Ἠριγόνη* Call.*Aet*.1.1.4; *οἰ. δὴ κεῖνο ἴδον* Od.12.258; *οἰ. ἔλεγοι* A.R.2.782: neut. pl. *οἴκτιστα* as Adv., Od.22.472: also in late Prose, Onos.42.21, Luc.*Anach*.11. Adv. *-τως* Phalar.*Ep*.96.

**οἶκτος**, ὁ, (*οἴζω*) *pity, compassion*, *οἶ. δ' ἕλε λαὸν ἅπαντα* Od.2. 81, cf. 24.438; *οἶ. τις ἴσχει ἀποκτεῖναι a feeling of pity* prevents him from.., Hdt.5.92.γ', cf. Th.3.40; *οἴκτου πλέως* S.*Ph*.1074; *ἔχειν οἶκτον φρενί* Id.*Aj*.525; *ἐμοὶ γὰρ οἶ. δεινὸς εἰσέβη* Id.*Tr*.298; *ἐμοὶ μὲν οἶ. δεινὸς ἐμπέπτωκέ τις* Id.*Ph*.965; *θνητοὺς.. ἐν οἴκτῳ προθέμενος* A. *Pr*.241; *δι' οἴκτου ἔχειν τινά* E.*Hec*.851; *εἰσῆλθέ μ' οἶ. εἰ..* Id.*Med*. 931: c. gen. objecti, *compassion for..*, *πόθος καὶ οἶ. τῆς πόλιος* Hdt.

1.165, cf. E.*Hec.*519 : in A.*Supp.*486, οἰκτίσας ἰδών (Herm.) shd. be read for οἶκτος εἰσιδών. 2. *lamentation, piteous wailing*, Simon.4. 3; οἶ. οὔτις ἦν διὰ στόμα A.*Th.*51; τόνδε κλύουσαν οἶ. Id.*Ch.*411 (lyr.); οἶκτον [οἰκτρὸν] αἰών Id.*Supp.*59 (lyr.); κλύω τινὸς οἴκτου S.*Tr.*864; οὐκ οἴκτου μέτα Id.*OC*1636: pl., παθόντος οἴκτοις *by the wailings of* the sufferer, A.*Supp.*386 (lyr.); ἄϊον οἴκτους οὓς οἰκτίζη E.*Tr.*155 (anap.); τοὺς ὀδυρμοὺς ἐξαιρήσομεν καὶ τοὺς οἴ. Pl.*R.*387d; οἴκτων λήγετε E.*Ph.*1584, cf. And.1.48, Pl.*Ap.*37a, *Lg.*949b.

**οἰκτοσύνη**, ἡ, = foreg., Hdn.*Epim.*232.

**οἰκτριζόμενος**· ἐλεούμενος, Hsch. (v. οἰκτρογοοῦντας).

**οἰκτρό-βῐος**, ον, *leading a pitiable life*, Paul.Al.*N.*3. **-γοος**, ον, *wailing piteously, piteous*, λόγοι Pl.*Phdr.*267c. **-γοοῦντας**· οἰκτιζομένους, ἐλεουμένους, Hsch. **-κέλευθος**, ον, *going a wretched journey*, Man.4.222. **-λογία**, ἡ, *piteous discourse*, Poll.2.124, 4.22, 33 (pl.). **-μέλαθρος**, ον, *pitifully housed*, Man.4.33. ❋ **-πᾰθής**, ές, *suffering pitiably*, τέκεα *Syria* 5.338 (Sidon).

**οἰκτρός**, ά, όν, of persons, *pitiable*. κοιμήσατο χάλκεον ὕπνον οἰκτρός Il.11.242, cf. A.*Supp.*61 (lyr.), S.*OT*58, etc.: c. gen., οἰκτροὶ τῆς μεταβολῆς *to be pitied for..*, Plu.*Flam.*13. 2. of things, *pitiable, lamentable*, ἕτερα πεπόνθαμεν -ότερα Hdt.7.46; οἰκτρὰ λογοποιοῦντες X.*Cyr.*2.2.13; συμφορὰ οἰ. Pi.*O.*7.77; -ότατος θάνατος Id.*P.*3.42; πημοναί, ἄλγος, A.*Pr.*240, 435 (lyr.), etc.; οἰκτρὰ γὰρ βόσκειν [ἡ κήρ] S.*Ph.*1167 (lyr.); οἰκτρόν [ἐστι] c. inf., A.*Th.*321 (lyr.). 3. in contemptuous sense, οἰ. τέκνα *sorry* fellows, Aus.*Epigr.*57; παιδίσκη Porph.*Chr.*23; οἰ. τραγῳδία *miserable*, Eust.1691.34. II. in act. sense, *wailing piteously, piteous*, -οτάτην δ' ἤκουσα ὄπα Od.11.421, cf. S.*El.*1067 (lyr.); οἰκτρᾶς γόον ὄρνιθος, of the nightingale, Id.*Aj.* 629 (lyr.): neut. pl. as Adv., οἴκτρ' ὀλοφυρομένη Od.4.719, cf. 10.409, al.: regul. Adv. οἰκτρῶς A.*Pers.*688, S.*El.*102 (anap.), al., And.4. 39, Lys.32.10: Comp. -ότερα *AP*10.65 (Pall.): Sup. -ότατα E.*Hel.* 1209.—Besides οἰκτρότερος, οἰκτρότατος, we find Sup. οἴκτιστος (q.v.); οἰκτότερον is f.l. in Hdt.7.46.

**οἰκτρότης**, ητος, ἡ, *piteous condition*, Poll.3.116, Sch.E.*Or.*672.

**οἰκτρό-φωνος**, ον, *with piteous voice*, Sch.Il.17.5. **-χοέω** φωνήν, *pour forth a piteous* strain, Ar.*V.*555.

❋**οἴκυλα**, τά, *a kind of grain*, οἴκυλά τε ζειαί τε Epic. in *Arch.Pap.* 7 p.7.

**ϝοικύπολις**, doubtful Pamphylian word, *GDI*1267.14, al.

**ϝοίκω**, Delph. Adv., = οἴκοθεν, *at one's own expense*, *Schwyzer* 323 C23 (iv B.C.). (Perh. old abl.)

**οἰκῶναξ**, ακτος, ὁ, (ἄναξ) *master of a house*, Hsch. s. v. ἑστιᾶχος.

**οἰκώς**, v. ἔοικα.

**οἰκωφελ-ής**, ές, *beneficial to the house*, only in Adv. -λῶς D.C.56. 7. **-ία**, Ep. -ίη, ἡ (cf. οἶκον ὀφέλλειν Od.15.21), *increase of the household* or *estate, housekeeping*, τοῖος ἔα ἐν πολέμῳ· ἔργον δέ μοι οὐ φίλον ἔσκεν οὐδ' οἰκωφελίη Od.14.223; γυναιξὶν, νόος οἰκωφελίας αἴσιν ἐπάβολος Theoc.28.2, cf. Naumach.ap.Stob.4.23.7.

**οἰλάωμα**· τὸ προστιθέμενον τῇ πλάστιγγι τοῦ ζυγοῦ, ἐὰν μὴ ἰσορρεπῇ, Hsch.

**Ὀϊλεύς**, έως, ὁ, *Oïleus*, Locrian chief, father of Ajax the Less, Il. 2.527. (Orig. prob. ϝιλεύς.)

❋**οἶμα**, ατος, τό, *spring, rush, swoop*, οἶ. λέοντος ἔχων Il.16.752; αἰετοῦ οἴματ' ἔχων 21.252; of a serpent, Q.S.6.201, etc.

**οἶμαι**, shorter form of οἴομαι (q.v.).

❋**οἰμ-άω**, (οἴμη) only fut. and aor., *swoop* or *pounce upon*, οἴμησεν δὲ ἀλεὶς ὥς τ' αἰετός Il.22.308, cf. 311; κίρκος.. οἴμησε μετὰ τρήρωνα πέλειαν *swooped* after a dove, ib.140. 2. abs., *dart along*, θύννοι δ' οἰμήσουσι Orac.ap.Hdt.1.62. ❋ **-η**, ἡ, = οἶμος: metaph., *way of song, song, lay*, οἴμας Μοῦσ' ἐδίδαξε Od.8.481; θεὸς δέ μοι ἐν φρεσὶν οἴμας παντοίας ἐνέφυσεν 22.347; οἴμης τῆς.. κλέος οὐρανὸν εὐρὺν ἵκανε 8.74; οἴ. δῶκε Φοῖβος τέττιγι *power of song*, *Anacreont.*32.14; οἴμῃ θελγόμενος A.R.4.150; Δήλῳ νῦν οἴμης ἀποδάσσομαι Call.*Del.*9; αἰνιγμάτων οἶμαι Lyc.11. **-ηδοκέω**, *waylay*, Theognost.*Can.*22. (Cf. ὁδοιδοκέω.) **-ηλα**· οἰμίηλα, ἀκρόδρυα, Hsch. **-ημα**· ὅρμημα, Id. **-ητεύει**· διαπορεύεται, Theognost.*Can.*22.

❋**οἴμοι**, exclam. of pain, fright, pity, anger, grief, also of surprise, prop. οἴ μοι *ah me! woe's me!* first in Thgn. and Trag. (v. infr.) (in Hom. always ὤ μοι); οἴμ' ὡς τεθνήξεις Ar.*Ach.*590; and Com., οἴμ' ὡς ἥδομαι Id.*Nu.*773: mostly abs., or with a nom., οἴ. ἐγὼ σοῦ μέλεος cj. in S.*Tr.*971 (lyr.); οἴ. δείλαιος Ar.*Eq.*139: ironical, οἴ., καταύδα *oh!* denounce it, S.*Ant.*86: sts. c. gen. causae, οἴ. ἀναλκείης Thgn. 891; οἴ. φρενὸς σῆς E.*Hipp.*1454; οἴ. ταλαίνης συμφορᾶς S.*El.*1179; οἴμοι μοι Ar.*Pax* 257 (really οἰμοιμοῖ acc. to A.D.*Adv.*177.3):—the forms ᾤμοι and ὤμοι are freq. found in codd., as of S.*Tr.* l. c., *Aj.* 980, *OC*202 (lyr.), etc.; ὤμοι is acknowledged by A.D.*Adv.*126.27. (οἴμοι may become οἴμ' by elision in Trag. and Com. before ὡς, οἴμ' ὡς ἔοικας ὀρθὰ μαρτυρεῖν S.*Aj.*354, cf. *Ant.*320, 1270, Ar. ll. cc., Cratin. 183: freq. written οἴμμοι in codd. of Lxx.)

**οἶμος** (οἶμος S.*Ichn.* 168, Call.*Aet.Oxy.*2079.27, Parth.*Fr.*31, *Epigr.Gr.* (v. infr.), Hdn.Gr.1.546, cf. φροίμιον), ὁ, also ἡ (v. infr.), *way, road, path*, Hes.*Op.*290, Pi.*P.*4.248; λευρὸν οἶ. αἰθέρος A.*Pr.* 396; ἁπλῆ οἶ. εἰς Ἅιδου φέρει Id.*Fr.*239; ὀρθὴν παρ' οἶ., ἣ 'πὶ Λάρισαν φέρει E.*Alc.*835; ἐς τὴν παραπλησίην οἶ. ἐμπίπτουσιν Hp. *Decent.*4; τὸν αὐτὸν οἶ. πορευόμενοι Pl.*R.*420b; ἄλλην οἶ. ἐκπορεύεται Men.681; λυγρὴν θ' οἶ. ἔβην *Epigr.Gr.*227 (Teos). 2. *stripe*, οἶμοι κυάνοιο *stripes* or *layers* of cyanos, Il.11.24. 3. *strip of land, tract, country*, Σκύθην ἐς οἶ. A.*Pr.*2. 4. metaph., οἶμος ἀοιδῆς *the course* or *strain* of song, *h.Merc.*451; ἐπέων οἶμον λιγὺν Pi.*O.*9.47, cf. *P.* 2.96, Call.*Jov.*78.

**οἰμ-ωγή**, ἡ, *wailing, lamentation*, κωκυτῷ καὶ οἰμωγῇ Il.22.409; οἰ. τε στοναχῇ τε 24.696; ἅμ' οἰ. τε καὶ εὐχωλὴ πέλεν ἀνδρῶν 4.450, quoted by Ar.*Pax*1276; οἰμωγῇ διαχρέεσθαι Hdt.3.66, cf. 8.99; οἰμωγὴ.. ὁμοῦ κωκύμασιν A.*Pers.*426; πικρᾶς οἰ. S.*Ph.*190 (lyr.); ἐξῴμωξεν οἰ. λυγρὰς Id.*Aj.*317; στεναγμὸν οἰμωγήν θ' ὁμοῦ E.*Heracl.*833; οἰμωγῇ τε καὶ στόνῳ Th.7.71; ἡ οἰ. ἐκ τοῦ Πειραιῶς διὰ τῶν μακρῶν τειχῶν εἰς ἄστυ διῆκεν X.*HG*2.2.3; cf. τήκω. **-ωγμα**, ατος, τό, *cry of lamentation, wail*, A.*Th.*1028, al., E.*Ba.*1112, al.: pl., A.*Ag.*1346, al. **-ωγμός**, ὁ, = οἰμωγή, S.*Fr.*941.5. **-ώζω**, Hom.*Epigr.* 14.20, Tyrt.7, Ar.*Ra.*257, etc.: impf. ᾤμωζον Id.*Lys.*516: fut. οἰμώξομαι Eup.305, Ar.*Pl.*111, X.*HG*2.3.56, etc.; later οἰμώξω Plu. 2.182d, *AP*5.301.2 (Agath.): aor. ᾤμωξα Hom. (v. infr.):—Pass., v. infr. II. (From οἴμοι, as οἴζω from οἴ):—*wail aloud, lament*, ᾤμωξέν τε καὶ ὦ πεπλήγετο μηρώ Il.12.162, etc.; οἰ. σμερδαλέον, ἐλεεινά, 18.35, 22.408; ἦ κε μέγ' οἰμώξειε γέρων ἱππηλάτα Πηλεὺς 7.125, cf. Hdt.7.159; of a wounded man, οἰμώξας πέσεν Od.18.398; γνὺξ δ' ἔριπ' οἰμώξας Il.5.68; στυγνὸν οἰμώξας S.*Ant.*1226: c. acc. cogn., Τελαμῶνος οἰ. μέλη Theopomp.Com.64. 2. in familiar Att., οἴμωζε, as a curse, *plague take you!* Ar.*Ach.*1035; οἰμώζετε Id.*Ra.*257; οἰμώξἄρα σύ Id.*Pl.*876; οἰμώξεσθ' ἄρα Id.*Nu.*217; οἰμώζειν λέγω σοι Id. *Pl.*58, cf. Luc.*Gall.*23; οὐκ οἰμώξεται; Ar.*Ra.*178, cf. X.*HG*2.3.56, Men.*Epit.*428; οἰμώζων καθεδεῖται Ar.*Ach.*840; οἴμωζε μεγάλα Id. *Av.*1503; οἰμώξει μακρά Id.*Pl.*111, Men.*Epit.*528; κολάκων οἰμωζομένων Ar.*V.*1033; πονηροῦ σοφιστοῦ καὶ οἰμωξομένου D.35.40; ἐᾶν οἰμώζειν 'let go hang', *PCair.Zen.*44.8 (iii B.C.). II. trans., *pity, bewail*, c. acc., Tyrt.7, A.*Ch.*8, S.*El.*788, E.*Hipp.*1405, *El.*248:—Pass., οἰμωχθεὶς *bewailed*, Thgn.1204; ᾠμωγμένον κάρα E.*Ba.* 1285. **-ωκτί**, Adv. *piteously*, Zonar. **-ωκτία**, ἡ, v. οἰμωξία. **-ωκτικός**, ή, όν, *inclined to wailing*, Sch.S.*Ph.*203. **-ωκτός**, ή, όν, *pitiable*, Ar.*Ach.*1195 (a gloss, del. Pors.). **-ωξία**, ἡ, = οἰμωγή, Hsch. (prob. οἰμώξειαν, quoted from S.*Aj.*963); οἰμωκτίαν (sic) f.l. in Phot. **-ώσσω**, Att. -ττω, = οἰμώζω, Lib.*Or.*1.39.

**οἰν-αγγεῖον**, τό, *wine-jar*, *PSI*4.428.113 (iii B.C.) (-αγειον Pap.). **-ᾰγωγός**, όν, *carrying wine*, Cratin.370, Pherecr.143.4.

**οἰνᾰδοθήρας**, ου, ὁ, (οἰνάς II) *dove-catcher*, Ael.*NA*4.58.

**Οἰναῖος**, v. Οἰνόη II.

**ϝοίνακες**· βλαστοί, Hsch. (γοίν-).

**οἰνάλμη**, ἡ, *wine mixed with brine*, Sor.1.81.

**οἰνανθ-άριον**, τό, Dim. of sq., *a compound ointment*, Alex.Trall. 7.3, Paul.Aeg.7.21. ❋ **-η**, ἡ, (οἴνη A) *inflorescence of the grape-vine*, Ar.*Ra.*1320, Thphr.*CP*3.14.8, etc.; = ἡ πρώτη ἔκφυσις τῆς σταφυλῆς, Suid.; also, *of the wild vine, Vitis silvestris*, Thphr.*HP*5.9.6, Dsc.1. 46, 5.4, Plin.*HN*12.132, *Gp.*5.51; *bloom on the grape*, metaph., γένυσι φαίνων τέρειναν ματέρ' οἰνάνθας ὀπώραν the time of ripeness which softly brings forth the *grape-bloom*, Pi.*N.*5.6, cf. Chaerem.12 (pl.). II. in Poets, generally, *vine*, χλωρὸν οἰνάνθης δέμας S. *Fr.*255.4, cf. E.*Ph.*231 (lyr.), Ar.*Av.*588; Λεσβίης νέκταρ οἰνάνθης Call.*Fr.*115. III. *Dropwort, Spiraea Filipendula*, a plant with a smell like the vine, Cratin.98, Arist.*HA*549$^b$33, Thphr.*HP*6.8.1, Dsc.3.120, Plin.*HN*21.65. 2. a bird, perh. *wheat-ear, Saxicola oenanthe*, Arist.*HA*633$^a$15. 3. *a salve*, Asclep.ap.Gal.13.540, cf. 10.550. **-ῐνος**, η, ον, *made of the wild-vine flower* (οἰνάνθη I), μύρον Thphr.*Od.*27, Apollon.ap.Ath.15.689a, Gal.11.110; ἔλαιον Dsc.1. 46; οἶνος Id.5.25. ❋ **-ίς**, ίδος, ἡ, = οἰνάνθη II, Ibyc.1.4.

**οἰνᾰρ-έα**, ἡ, *vine-leaf*, Theoc.7.134 (v.l. -οισι). ❋ **-εος**, α, ον, *of vine leaves* or *twigs*, Ibyc.1.6; σποδιή Hp.*Mul.*2.195. **-ίζω**, *strip off vine-leaves*, as is done when the grapes are ripening, Ar.*Pax* 1147, Phan.Hist.37. **-ιον**, τό, Dim. of οἶνος, *weak* or *bad wine*, D.35.32, Alex.275, Diph.60.8, Polioch.2.7, etc.: pl., *POxy.*1672.5 (i A.D.). II. *a little wine*, Diocl.*Fr.*141, Epict.*Ench.*12, Sor.1.64, *AP* 11.189 (Lucill.). III. colloq. for οἶνος, Thphr.*Char.*17.2, *PEleph.* 13.5 (iii B.C.): pl., *PCair.Zen.*373 (iii B.C.), *Ostr.Bodl.* iii 369. IV. = ἄμπελος, Gal.19.125. **-ίς**, ίδος, ἡ, *vine-tendril* or *branch*, = κλῆμα, Hp.*Mul.*2.206. **-ον**, τό, *vine-leaf* or *tendril*, X.*Oec.*19.18, Thphr.*HP*9.13.5, Babr.34.2 (v.l. οἰνάσιν), etc. II. *vine*, Alciphr. 3.22. **-ος**, prob. f.l. for κόμαρος in Thphr.*HP*1.9.3.

❋**οἰνάς**, άδος, ἡ, = οἴνη, *the vine*, Ion Eleg.1.4, *AP*7.193 (Simm.). b. *bryony*, Hp.ap.Erot. (οἴαδος codd.), v.l. in Babr.34.2 (pl.). 2. *wine*, Nic.*Al.*355. 3. pl., = ἀμπελώδεις τόποι, Hsch. II. *a wild pigeon* of the colour οἰνωπός, *the rock-dove, Columba livia*, Arist.*HA* 544$^b$6, 558$^b$23, 593$^a$19, *Fr.*347, Ael.*NA*4.58:—also **οἰνιάς**, Poll.6. 22; but **οἰνιάξ**· εἶδος κόρακος, Hsch. III. Οἰνάδες, αἱ, = Μαινάδες, Opp.*C.*4.235. IV. as Adj., *of wine, vinous*, μεμεθυσμένος οἰνάδι πηγῇ *APl.*1.15; οἰ. ὀπώρη *AP*9.645 (Maced.).

**οἰναχθής**· μέθυσος, μεθύων, Hsch. **ϝοινέες**· κόρακες, Id. (γοιν-).

**οἰν-έλαιον**, τό, *wine mingled with oil*, Dsc.4.150.7, Heliod.ap.Orib. 44.11.11, Gal.13.404, *Hippiatr.*22, Simp. *in Cat.*230.10. ❋ **-έμπορος**, ὁ, *wine-merchant*, Artem.3.8, *PGrenf.*2.61.13 (ii A.D.), *Supp.Epigr.*3. 537 (Thrace, iii A.D., written ὑν-). **-εραστής**, οῦ, ὁ, *lover of wine*, Ael.*VH*2.41.

**οἴνη** (A) (v. οἶνος), ἡ, old name for *the vine*, Hes.*Op.*572, *Sc.*292; Διονύσου οἴνα E.*Ba.*535, cf. *Ph.*229, *Hyps.Fr.*58.4 (all lyr.), Moschio Trag.6.12; βοτρυώδεος οἴνης *Epigr.Gr.*88.5; γάνος οἴνας *IG*3.779.6; ἀδευκέας οἴνας Orph.*Fr.*282: once in Prose, Hecat.15 J. 2. = οἶνος, *wine*, *AP*6.334 (Leon.), Nic.*Th.*622.

**οἴνη** (B), ἡ, *the ace* on dice, Achae.56: Ion. prov., ἢ τρὶς ἓξ ἢ τρεῖς οἶναι Zen.4.23:—also **οἶνος**, ὁ, Poll.7.204 (οἰνός codd.); and **οἰνίζειν**· τὸ μονάζειν κατὰ γλῶσσαν, Hsch. (Cf. OLat. *oinos* = *unus*, Goth. *ains*, OE. *án* 'one'.)

**οἰν-ηγία**, ἡ, *conveyance of wine*, *POxy.*1651.3 (iii A.D.). ⊛ **-ηγός**, ὁ, *wine-carrying*, πλοῖον *PSI*6.568.2 (iii B.C.); οἱ οἰ. *wine-importers*, *OGI*521.22 (v/vi A.D.). ⊛ **-ηρός**, ά, όν, *of* or *belonging to wine*, θεράπων a butler, Anacr.161; λοιβαί E.*IT*164; τρύξ Nic.*Al.*534; σταγόνες *AP*9.406 (Antig. Caryst.); *vinous*, ὑγρότης Arist.*Pr.*873$^{a}$20; *steeped in wine*, σπλῆνες Hp.*Fract.*24; ἰητρείη treatment *by vinous applications*, ib.34. **II.** *containing wine*, κεράμιον Hdt.3.6, Cratin.461; φιάλαι Pi.*N.*10.43; κρωσσοί A.*Fr.*96 (anap.); ὀξύβαφον Cratin.187; τεύχη E.*Ion*1179; ἀγγεῖον Alex 55, cf. *AJA*16.13 (Sardis, 300 B.C.); μέτρα *wine*-measures, Arist.*EN*1135$^{a}$2; οἰνηρά, ἡ, tax *on wine*, *IG*2$^{2}$.1707 (iii B.C.). **III.** of countries, *rich in wine*, Χίος Call.*Fr.*115, cf. *AP*7.457 (Aristo). **-ήρυσις**, εως, ἡ, (ἀρύω) *vessel for drawing wine*, Ar.*Ach.*1067, Ph.1.390.

**οἰνιάς**, άδος, ἡ, and **οἰνιάξ**, v. οἰνάς II.

**οἰνιαστήρια**, τά, v. οἰνιστήρια.

**οἰν-ίδιον**, τό, Dim. of οἶνος, *small wine, poor wine*, Apollod.ap.D.L.10.11. **-ιεῖς**· ὀξεῖς, ταχεῖς, Hsch. **-ίζω** (A), *resemble wine*, τὸ οἰνίζον Thphr.ap.Apollon.*Mir.*43; οἰνίζουσαν τῇ ὀσμῇ Dsc.1.13, cf. Gal.14.13. **II.** Med., *procure wine by barter, buy wine*, οἰνίζοντο.. Ἀχαιοί, ἄλλοι μὲν χαλκῷ ἄλλοι δ' αἴθωνι σιδήρῳ Il.7.472; οἶνον μελίφρονα οἰνίζεσθε σῖτόν τ' ἐκ μεγάρων 8.506, cf. 546: in later Prose, ἐκ Λήμνου οἰ. Max.Tyr.39.1; ἐκ τοῦ ποταμοῦ Luc.*VH*1.9. **-ίζω** (B), v. οἴνη (B). ⊛ **-ικός**, ή, όν, *of* or *for wine*, γένημα *Milet.*3 No.149.41 (ii B.C.), *PTeb.*5.184 (ii B.C.); γόμος *OGI*629.86 (Palmyra, ii A.D.), cf. Hsch. s.v. κάβος, Suid. s.v. κριός. **-ινος**, η, ον, *of wine*. ὄξος *wine*-vinegar, Archestr.*Fr.*23.8. **-ίσκος**, ὁ, Dim. of οἶνος, *'small wine'*, Cratin.183, Eub.131. **-ιστήρια** (sc. ἱερά), τά, festival at which Athenians cut off the μαλλός, κόννος or σκόλλυς of their sons previous to their being enrolled among the ἔφηβοι, at the same time offering *a measure of wine* (οἴνου μέτρον) to Heracles, and drinking part of it to the health of their φράτερες, Eup.135, Hsch., Phot. (**οἰνιαστήρια** in Eust.907.18). **-ιστηρία**, ἡ, *cup* used at this festival, Pamphil.ap.Ath.11.494f:—also **-ίστρια**, Poll.6.22.

**οἰνιψυκτήρ**, v. οἰνοψυκτήρ.

**οἰνοβᾰρ-είων**, ὁ, = οἰνοβαρής, Od.9.374, 10.555:—hence **-έω**, *to be heavy* or *drunken with wine*, Thgn.503. **-ής**, ές, *heavy with wine*, Il.1.225, *AP*7.24 (Simon.), etc.

**οἰνο-βᾰφής**, ές, *dipped in wine, vinous*, λοιβή Nonn.*D.*7.15. **-βλᾰβής**, ές, *addicted to drunkenness*, *Cat.Cod.Astr.*8(4).186. **-βρεχής**, ές, *wine-soaked, drunken*, *AP*7.428.18. ⊛ **-βρώς**, ῶτος, ὁ, ἡ, *eaten with wine*, Nic.*Al.*493. **-γᾰλα**, ακτος, τό, *milk mixed with wine*, Hp.*Mul.*1.80 (v.l. ὀνείῳ γάλακτι), *Epid.*7.82. **-γᾰρον**, τό, γάρον *mixed with wine*, Aët.3.85.

**οἰνογευστ-έω**, *taste wine*, Antiph.83, *Gp.*7.7.1. **-ης**, ου, ὁ, *wine-taster*, Archig.ap.Gal.8.944. **-ικός**, ή, όν, *of* or *for wine-tasting*: ἡ -κή (sc. τέχνη) *the wine-taster's art* or *skill*, S.E.*M.*6.33.

**οἰνό-δεσμον**, gloss on οἰνοπέπηκτον, Hsch. **-δόκος**, ον, *receiving* or *holding wine*, φιάλη Pi.*I.*6(5).40; κύλιξ *AP*6.33 (Maec.): as Subst. c. gen., νέκταρος οἰ. ib.257 (Antiphil.). **-δοσία**, ἡ, *largess of wine*, *IGRom.*3.833a.19 (Cilicia, ii A.D.). **II.** *prescribing of wine*, Herod.Med.ap.Orib.5.27.1. ⊛ **-δοτέω** τινά, *prescribe wine to* one, ibid. **-δότης**, ου, ὁ, *giver of wine*, of Dionysus, E.*HF*682 (lyr.); of a physician, -της ἰατρός Gal.*Thras.*24, cf. *IG*14.666:—also **-δώτης**, of Asclepiades, Anon.Lond.24.30. **-δοχεῖον**, τό, *vessel for wine*, Hero *Spir.*2.21. **-δόχος**, ον, *containing wine*, ibid., *EM*247.2: as Subst., *cupbearer*, Lxx *To.*1.22 (v.l.). **-δώτης**, v. οἰνοδότης. **-ειδής**, ές, *like wine*, Hsch. s.v. οἰνωπόν. **-εις**, εσσα, εν, *of* or *with wine*; v. οἰνοῦττα.

**Οἰνόη**, ἡ, (οἶνος) *Oenoë*, name of two Attic demes, **1.** of the φυλὴ Ἱπποθοωντίς, on the Boeot. frontier near Eleutherae, Hdt.5.74, Th.2.18, Str.8.6.16 (Οἰνώνη codd.). **2.** of the φυλὴ Αἰαντίς, near Marathon; Οἰνόη or Οἰναῖοι τὴν χαράδραν, prov. of self-inflicted ruin, Zen.5.29, Hsch.: loc. pl. **Οἰνόησι** *IG*1$^{2}$.845.5. **II.** Adj. Οἰναῖος, belonging to one of these demes, ib.2$^{2}$.99, 1623.5, 1926.130, etc.; also Οἰνοαῖος *SIG*541 *A* 3 (Delph., iii B.C.).

**οἰνο-ηθητής**, οῦ, ὁ, *one who strains wine*, Parmenio ap.Ath.13.608a. **-θήκη**, ἡ, *wine-cellar*, *Gp.*6.12.4. **II.** *wine cask*, *PFlor.*385.4 (iii A.D.). **-θήρας**, ου, ὁ, a plant *the root of which smells of wine* or *was used to flavour wine*: but in the best Mss. of Thphr.*HP*9.19.1 it is ὀνοθήρας, as in Dsc.4.117 and Gal.12.89; called also **ὀνάγρα**, Gal. l.c., and **ὀνόθουρις** ibid., Aët.15.15; cf. *onothuris*, Plin.*HN*24.167. **-κάπηλος** [ᾰ], ὁ, *wine-retailer*, *PCair.Zen.*236.8 (iii B.C., pl.), S.E.*M.*1.141. **-κάχλη**, f.l. for οἰνομάχλη (q.v.). **-κηκίς**, ῖδος, ἡ, *styptic made of oak-galls boiled in* οἶνος αὐστηρότερος, Gal.12.25. **-κρεον**, τό, *meat preserved in vinegar*, *PSI*9.1073 (iv A.D.), *PKlein.Form.*773 (v A.D.), *PGrenf.*2.99.3 (vi A.D.), etc. **-ληπτος**, ον, *possessed by wine, drunken*, Plu.2.4b. **-λογέω**, *speak of wine*, Ath.2.40f. **-λογία**, ἡ, a tax (perh. = σπονδὴ Διονύσου) which was paid in wine, *Ostr.*711 (Ptolemaic), *Ostr.Bodl.*i 144 (iii B.C.). **-μᾰνής**, ές, *mad for* or *after wine*, Ath.11.464e. **-μάχλη**, ἡ, *lustful with wine*, Theopomp.Com.78. **-μελι**, ιτος, τό, *honey mixed with wine*, a kind of *mead*, Plb.12.2.7, Carnead.ap.D.L.4.64, Posidon.1 J., *Mim.Oxy.*413 iii 161, al., *AP*12.164 (Mel.), Dsc.5.8, Gal.10.356, etc. ⊛ **-μετρέω**, *measure out wine*, πᾶσι *IG*12(5).38.6, 27 (Naxos). **-μήτωρ**, ορος, ἡ, *mother of wine*, ἄμπελος Astyd.6. **-μύρσινον**, τό, *wine in oil of myrtles*, v.l. in Paul.Aeg.7.12.31.

**οἶνον**, τό, in pl., οἶνα· τὰ τῆς ἀμπέλου φύλλα, Hsch.

**οἰνο-παραλημπτής**, οῦ, ὁ, = Lat. *susceptor vinarius*, *POxy.*1141.2 (iii A.D.), *PKlein.Form.*1132 (vi A.D.), etc. **-πεδος**, ον (η, ον Opp.*C.*4.331), *with soil fit to produce wine, abounding in wine*, ἀνὰ γουνὸν ἀλωῆς οἰνοπέδοιο Od.1.193, cf. 11.193; *productive of wine*, -πέδῃσι φυτηκομίῃσι μεμηλώς Opp. l.c. **II.** Subst. **-πεδον**, τό, *vineyard*, τέμενος.., τὸ μὲν ἥμισυ οἰνοπέδοιο Il.9.579, cf. Thgn.892, Theoc.24.130, Plu.2.604c, prob. for οἰκ- in *SIG*1000.8 (Cos):—also **-πέδη**, ἡ, *AP*11.409 (Gaet.). **-πέπαντος**, *ripe for wine-making*, βότρυς ib.6.232 (Crin.). **-πέπηκτον**· οἰνόδεσμον, Hsch.

**οἰνόπη**, ἡ, a kind of ἄμπελος, Poll.6.82, Hsch.

**οἰν-οπίπης** [ῑ], ου, ὁ, (ὀπιπτεύω) *gaping after wine*, Com. word formed after γυναικ-, παιδ-, παρθεν-οπίπης: cited by Sch. and Suid. from Ar.*Th.*393 (ubi οἰνοπότιδας codd.).

**οἰνο-πλάνητος** [ᾰ], ον, *wine-bewildered*, κυλίκων ἅμιλλαι E.*Rh.*363 (lyr.). **-πληθής**, ές, *abounding in wine*, Συρίη Od.15.406. **-πλήξ**, ῆγος, ὁ, ἡ, *wine-stricken, drunken*, *Trag.Adesp.*238, *AP*9.323 (Antip.).

⊛ **οἰνοποι-έω**, pf. οἰνοποίηκα *PCair.Zen.*236.7 (iii B.C.):—*make wine*, *PRev.Laws* 25.4, al. (iii B.C.), Plu.2.653a. **-ητέον**, *one must make wine*, Ath.1.33a. **-ία**, ἡ, *wine-making*, Thphr.*Od.*67, D.S.3.63, Ath.1.26b. **-ός**, όν, *making wine*, ib.27d; ῥίζα prob. in Gal.4.777: Subst., *SIG*414 (Delph., iii B.C.).

**οἰνο-πόρος**, ον, *flowing with wine*, ποταμός Nonn.*D.*40.238. **-ποσία**, ἡ, *drinking of wine*, Hp.*Acut.*37, Arist.*Pr.*871$^{a}$1 (in tit.); οἰνοποσίας ἀγωνία Ael.*VH*2.41, cf. *CIG*3028 (Ephesus), *Supp.Epigr.*4.598.9 (Teos, i B.C.). ⊛ **-ποσίαρχος**, ὁ, = συμποσίαρχος, *BCH*24.386 (Bithynia). ⊛ **-πόσιον**, τό, = -ία, in form -πόσιν *JHS*50.282 (Nicomedia).

**οἰνοποτ-άζω**, *drink wine*, Il.20.84, Od.6.309, 20.262, Anacr.94.1, Phoc.11. ⊛ **-έω**, = foreg., Lxx *Pr.*24.72(31.4), Ath.11.460c, Erot. s.v. θωρῆξαι, Orib.5.31.12: c. acc., ἄμυστιν Call.*Aet.*1.1.12. **-ήρ**, ῆρος, ὁ, *wine-drinker*, ἄνδρας μέτα οἰνοποτῆρας Od.8.456, cf. *AP*5.205.5 (Leon.). ⊛ **-ης**, ου, ὁ, *wine-bibber*, Anacr.97, Call.*Epigr.*37, Plb.20.8.2, Lxx *Pr.*23.20, *Ev.Matt.*11.19:—fem. **-ις**, ιδος, ἡ, Anacr.162, Ar.*Th.*393 (v. οἰνοπίπης).

**οἰνοπράτης** [ᾱ], ου, ὁ, = οἰνοπώλης, *BGU*34 ii 9, *PSI*8.959.11 (iv A.D.), *Rev.Bibl.*29.316 (Caesarea), Tz. ad Hes. p.13 G.

**οἰνόπται**, οἱ, a board of three officials at Athens whose duty it was to provide lamps, wicks, etc. at certain festivals, Eup.205; οἰνόπτης τις, ὁ τὸν οἶνον ἐπιβλέπων Poll.6.21, cf. *IG*2$^{2}$.1357.23; later, *wine-tasters*, οἱ ἔμπειροι οἰνόπται *Gp.*7.7.1. (Perh. lit. *wine-choosers*, v. ἐπιόψομαι.)

**οἰνοπωλ-έω**, *sell wine*, Arist.*Mir.*832$^{b}$22. **-ης**, ου, ὁ, *wine-merchant*, ib.21, Diph.3.6, *PFay.*63.8 (iii A.D.), etc.:—fem. **-πῶλις**, ιδος, Sch.Ar.*Pl.*435, Lib.*Decl.*26.18. ⊛ **-ιον**, τό, *wine-shop*, *An.Ox.*2.356.

**οἰνορρόδινον**, τό, *mixture of wine and oil of roses*, Orib.*Syn.*9.48, v.l. in Paul.Aeg.7.12.

⊛ **οἶνος**, ὁ, *wine*, μέλας οἶ. (cf. οἶνοψ) Od.5.265, 9.196; ἐρυθρός 5.165, 9.163; αἶθοψ Il.1.462, 4.259; ἡδύς Od.2.349, 9.204; ἡδύποτος 15.507; μελιηδής Il.4.346, al.; μελίφρων 6.264; παλαιός Od.2.340, Pi.*O.*9.48, cf. Simon.75; οἴνους παλαιοὺς εὐώδεις X.*An.*4.4.9; εὔφρων Il.3.246; εὐήνωρ Od.4.622; οἶνον ἔμισγον ἐνὶ κρητῆρσι καὶ ὕδωρ 1.110: with Preps., ἐν οἴνῳ over one's *cups*, Ar.*Lys.*1227, Call.*Epigr.*23.8; παρ' οἴνῳ S.*OT*780; παρ' οἶνον Plu.2.143d; μετὰ παιδιᾶς καὶ οἴ. Th.6.28: also in pl., ἡ ἐν τοῖς οἴ. διατριβή Pl.*Lg.*641c, 645c; ἐπ' οἴνοις Pherecr.153.9: pl. also, οἶνοι, *wines*, X. l.c., Pl.*R.*573a, al.; οἶνος δωδεκάδραχμος *wine* at 12 drachmae the cask, D.42.20: prov., οἶ. τῷ φρονεῖν ἐπισκοτεῖ Eub.135; οἶνος καὶ ἀλάθεα (v. ἀλήθεια), *in vino veritas*, Alc.57, Theoc.29.1; οἶνος.. ἀληθής Pl.*Smp.*217e; οἴνῳ τὸν οἶ. ἐξελαύνειν 'to take a hair of the dog that bit you', Antiph.300.1: οἶνος is freq. omitted, πίνειν πολύν (sc. οἶνον) E.*Cyc.*569, Theoc.18.11; esp. with names of places, Θάσιος, Χῖος, etc., Eub.124, 125, 126: resin was used as a preservative, πισσίτης οἶ. Plu.2.676c. **2.** *fermented juice* of other kinds, οἶνος ἐκ κριθέων πεποιημένος barley *wine*, a kind of *beer*, Hdt.2.77; οἶ. φοινικήϊος palm-*wine*, ib.86, cf. 1.193; *lotus-wine*, Id.4.177, etc.; from which drinks grape-*wine* (οἶ. ἀμπέλινος) is expressly distd., Id.2.60. **II.** *the wine-market*, τρέχ' ἐς τὸν οἶ. Ar.*Fr.*299. **III.** name of Dionysus, Orph.*Fr.*216. (ϝοῖνος *Leg.Gort.*10.39, *Inscr.Cypr.*148 H.; cf. Lat. *vinum*.)

**οἰνός**, ὁ, = οἴνη (B) (q.v.).

⊛ **οἰνό-σπονδος**, ον, *offered with wine*, θυσίαι Poll.6.26; τὰ οἰ. (sc. ἱερά) Porph.*Abst.*2.20. **-τόκος**, ον, *producing wine*, βότρυς Nonn.*D.*7.89, 12.24. **-τροπικοί**, οἱ, *wine-blenders*, Gal.8.768. **-τρόποι**, αἱ, *turning water into wine*, epith. of the daughters of Anios, king of Delos, Lyc.580. (Otherwise expld. as *wine-treaders*; cf. τροπέοντο· ἐπάτουν, Hsch.; or demons who *turned wine sour*, cf. S.E.*P.*1.41.) **-τρόφος**, ον, *rearing* or *bearing wine*, *AP*9.375.

**οἰνουργ-έω**, *make* or *prepare wine*, Sch.Pi.*P.*3.177. **-ία**, ἡ, *making of wine*, Poll.7.193.

**οἰνοῦττα**, ἡ, (οἰνόεις) *cake* or *porridge of barley mixed with wine, water, and oil*, eaten by rowers, Ar.*Pl.*1121. **II.** a plant *with intoxicating properties*, Arist.*Fr.*107.

**οἰνο-φᾰγία**, ἡ, *vinous food*, Luc.*VH*1.7. **-φερής**, ές, *inclined to wine*, Hsch. s.v. οἰνόφλυξ.

**οἰνοφλῠγ-έω**, *to be drunken* or *drunk*, Lxx *De.*21.20, Ph.1.361, Poll.6.21. **-ία**, ἡ, *drunkenness*, X.*Oec.*1.22, Antiph.19, Arist.*EN*1114$^{a}$27, Plb.2.19.4 (pl.), 1*Ep.Pet.*4.3. **-ίζω**, = foreg., Thd.*Is.*56.12.

**οἰνό-φλυξ**, ῠγος, ὁ, ἡ, (φλύω) *given to drinking, drunken*, Hp.*Prorrh.*2.2, X.*Ap.*19, Pl.*Erx.*405e, Arist.*Po.*1461$^{a}$15. **-φορεῖον** or

**-φόριον**, τό, = οἰνοφόρον, *Gloss.* **-φορέω**, *produce wine*, Str.15.1.22. **-φόρος**, ον, *holding wine*, κύλιξ Critias6.2 D.; δέρμα *PLond.*2.402$^{v}$.22 (ii B.C.); σκεύη Hdn.8.4.4. II. Subst. -φόρον (sc. σκεῦος or ἀγγεῖον), τό, *wine-jar*, Poll.6.14: *oenophorus* Probus in *Gramm.Lat.*4.211 K. (gender indeterminate in Hor.*Sat.*1.6.109, etc.). III. *wine-producing*, βότρυς Archestr.*Fr.*36.2. **-φύλαξ** [ῠ], ἄκος, ὁ, *an officer who had charge of the municipal wines*, *Michel* 1226 (Cyzic.), *CIG*3663 *A* 14 (ibid.), *JHS*22.206 (ibid.), *Milet.*3 p.177 No.33*e*5. **-φῦτος**, ον, *planted* or *grown with vines*, Str.12.3.36, D.H.1.37:—hence pr. n. **Οἰνόφυτα**, τά, in Boeotia, Th.1.108, etc. II. Act., *planting vines*, Λυαῖος Nonn.*D.*21.174. **-χἄρής**, ές, *merry with wine*, *IG*14.2125; as a nickname, ib.3.1379. **-χάρων** [ᾰ], οντος, ὁ, *Wine-Charon*, Com. epith. of Philip of Macedon (son of Demetrius), because he put poison in his enemies' wine, and so *sent them over the Styx*; including an allusion to his being *fond of wine* (cf. foreg.), *AP*11.12. **-χειριστής**, οῦ, ὁ, *dispenser of wine*, *POxy.*1752.1 (iv A.D.), *PSI*3.191 (vi A.D.), etc. ⊛ **-χίτων** [ῐ], ωνος, ὁ, ἡ, *vine-clad*, οἰνοχίτωνας ἐλαίας Call.*Fr.anon.*211; δρύες -χίτωνες ib.158.

**οἰνοχο-εία**, ἡ, *pouring out of wine*, Suid. **-εύς**, έως, ὁ, = -χόος, Nonn.*D.*10.315. **-εύω**, Od.21.142; part. -εύων 1.143; inf. -εύειν Il.2.127, 20.234: but Hom. forms obl. tenses from ⊛ -χοέω, Ep. 3 sg. impf. οἰνοχόει Od.15.141, ἐῳνοχόει Il.4.3: aor. inf. οἰνοχοῆσαι Od.15.323, Sapph.51.2: later in pres., Pherecr.70.5, X.*Cyr.*1.3.8, Ph.2.479; part. -οοῦσα *IG*2$^{2}$.1514.32, Aeol. -όεισα Sapph.5 (-οεῦσα codd. Ath.): fut. -ήσω X. l.c.:—Med. -οούμενοι Ph.1.353:—*pour out wine for drinking*, abs., Od.15.141,323, etc.; Διὶ οἰ. Il.20.234. 2. c. acc., νέκταρ ἐῳνοχόει she *was pouring out* nectar, 4.3; θεοῖς ἐνδέξια.. οἰνοχόει.. νέκταρ ἀπὸ κρητῆρος ἀφύσσων Il.1.598: metaph., ἄκρατον τοῖς πολίταις ἐλευθερίαν οἰ. Plu.*Per.*7; ὕμνους Dionys.Eleg.4.1:—Pass., οἰνοχοεῖται ἐπινίκια Plu.2.349f. 3. τὴν Κασταλίαν οἰνοχοῆσαι *cause* Castaly *to run with wine*, Philostr.*VA*6.10; κρήνην -ήσας *mixing* spring-water *with wine*, Id.*Im.*1.22. ⊛ **-η**, ἡ, *vessel for* taking wine from the mixing-bowl (κρατήρ) and *pouring* it into the cups, Hes.*Op.*744, Hermipp.65, Eup.361, etc.; φιάλας τε καὶ οἰ. Th.6.46; χρύσεαι οἰ. E.*Tr.*820 (lyr.); ἀργυρᾶ (-αῖ) *IG*1$^{2}$.315.3, 2$^{2}$.1388.30, al.; οἰ. θεῶν σωτήρων *OGI*214.45 (Didyma). II. a kind of *sideboard* to range the wine-cups on, Phryn.*PS* p.95 B. III. *female cupbearer*, Lxx *Ec.*2.8. **-ημα**, ατος, τό, a festival *at which wine was offered*, Ephor. 80 J., Plu.*Phoc.*6, Polyaen.3.11.2. **-ία**, ἡ, = οἰνοχοεία, D.Chr.71.4, Hld.8.1. **-ΐδιον**, τό, Dim. of οἰνοχόη, *IG*11(2).145.50 (Delos, iv B.C.), etc. **-ϊκός**, ή, όν, *of* or *for an* οἰνοχόος, Hld.7.27. ⊛ **-ος**, ὁ, *cupbearer*, Il.2.128, Od.18.418, Hdt.3.34, E.*Cyc.*560, Pl.*R.*562d (metaph.), X.*HG*7.1.38, Critias33 D.; οἰ. θέραπες Ion Eleg.2.2: dat. sg. contr. οἰνοχῷ *PTeb.*122 *Intr.* (i B.C.).

**οἰνό-χρως**, ωτος, ὁ, ἡ, *wine-coloured*, Thphr.*HP*9.13.4; τὴν -χροα τρίχα Sch.E.*Or.*115. **-χῦτος**, ον, *of poured wine*, πῶμα οἰ. draught *of wine*, S.*Ph.*714 (lyr.). II. Act., = οἰνοχόος, Nonn.*D.*13.256, 33.74, al.

⊛ **οἶνοψ**, οπος, ὁ, (ὤψ) *wine-coloured*, Hom. (never in nom.) epith. of the sea, *wine-dark*, Il.23.316, Od.5.132, 2.421; of oxen, *wine-red*, *deep-red*, βόε οἴνοπε Il.13.703, Od.13.32; also οἰ. Βάκχος *AP*6.44; νύμφη οἴνοπα πῆχυν ἀνεῖλκε Tryph.521.

**οἰνοψυκτήρ**, ῆρος, ὁ, *wine-cooler*, *PEleph.*5.3 (iii B.C., οἰνιψ- Pap.).

**οἰν-όω**, *intoxicate*, οἰνῶσαι σῶμα ποτοῖς Critias6.28 D.: elsewh. always Pass. **οἰνόομαι**, *get drunk*, οἰνωθέντες Od.16.292, Aen.Tact.16.5; οἰνωθεὶς S.*Fr.*929, *PLond.*2.411.14 (iv A.D.); οἰνοῦσθαι Plu.2.672a: fut. οἰνωθήσομαι *Stoic.*3.163: mostly in pf. part. ᾠνωμένος, Ion. οἰνωμένος Hdt.5.18; ἄγαν ᾠνωμένος A.*Supp.*409; δείπνοις, ἡνίκ' ἦν ᾠνωμένος S.*Tr.*268; ᾠνωμένας κρατῆρι E.*Ba.*687: codd. of Arist. always give οἰνωμένος, *EN*1147$^{a}$14, 1152$^{a}$15, 1154$^{b}$10, *Rh.*1389$^{a}$19. (The word used in good Att. Prose is μεθύω (q.v.); but in *Stoic.* l.c. οἰ. = *drink wine in moderation*, opp. μεθυσθῆναι, *to be the worse for wine.*) II. Pass., *turn into wine*, Nonn.*D.*11.517. **-ώδης**, ες, *of the nature* or *flavour of wine*, χυμός Arist.*Mete.*387$^{b}$11; ῥοαί Id.*Pr.*922$^{a}$9; of wines, *containing* more or less *vinous strength*, Hp.*Acut.*37, cf. *Mul.*1.52; οἰ. καρποί Thphr.*CP*6.14.4; of grapes in general, Gal.6.578; ὀπῶραι Id.9.249; ἀναπνέων οἰνῶδες Philostr.*Her.*2.8; *wine-coloured*, λίθοι Luc.*Syr.D.*32, cf. Aret.*SD*2.9. **-ών**, ῶνος, ὁ, *wine-cellar*, X.*HG*6.2.6, *IG*2$^{2}$.1013.9, *PSI*4.396.5 (iii B.C.); *wine-shop*, Timae.60, cf. *Gp.*7.7.6. **-ώνης**, ου, ὁ, *wine-merchant*, Phot.

**οἰνῶντα**· μονήρη, Hsch.; cf. οἰῶντα.

⊛ **οἰν-ωπός**, ή, όν, also ός, όν E.*Or.*115:— = οἶνοψ, βότρυς Semon.180, E.*Hyps.Fr.*41.111; οἰ. ἄχνη, i.e. wine, Id.*Or.* l.c.; οἰ. δράκων Id.*IT* 1245 (lyr.); *ruddy-complexioned*, γένυς, of Dionysus, Od.*Ba.*438; of Polydeuces, Theoc.22.34; but, *dark-complexioned*, Hp.*Mul.*2.111; *black mixed with bright light*, Arist.*Col.*792$^{b}$6; ὀφθαλμοί Id.*Phgn.*812$^{b}$6; *dark*, of ivy, prob. in S.*OC*674 (lyr.); of the fruit of the ἀρία, = φελλόδρυς, Thphr.*HP*3.16.3; of the οἰνάς II, Arist.*Fr.*347; ἰχώρ Philum.*Ven.*18.2. **-ωροί**· οἱ ἱεραγωγοὶ Διονύσου, Hsch. **-ωσις**, εως, ἡ, *drunkenness*, not so bad as μέθη, *Stoic.*3.179, cf. Dsc.5.6, Plu.2.503f, 645a, Gal.19.105: pl., D.L.7.183; σύμμετρος οἰ. Corn.*ND* 30. ⊛ **-ωτρον**· χάρακα, ᾗ τὴν ἄμπελον ἱστᾶσι (Dorian), Hsch. ⊛ **-ώψ**, ῶπος, ὁ, ἡ, = οἶνοψ, of Dionysus, S.*OT*211 (lyr.), prob. in E.*Ba.*236; f.l. in S.*OC*674.

**οἶξασα**, v. οἴγω, οἴγνυμι.

**οἷο**, Ep. for οὗ, gen. of Possess. Pron. ὅς, ἥ, ὅν *his, her* (q.v.):

**οἰόπερ**, Ep. for οὗπερ, A.R.1.1325.

**οἰό-βᾰτος**, ον, (οἶος) *lonesome*, ὕλη *APl.*4.231 (Anyt.). **-βίοισι**· μονοβίοις, Hsch. **-βουκόλος**, ον, *herdsman of one heifer*, i.e. of Io, A.*Supp.*304. **-βώτας**, ου, ὁ, *feeding alone*, prop. of cattle, metaph. of Ajax, φρενὸς οἰ., = μονόφρων, S.*Aj.*614 (unless φρενός is to be joined with πένθος). **-γᾰμος**, ον, = μονόγαμος, *AP*5.231 (Paul. Sil.). **-γένεια**, as if fem. of οἰογενής, *an only daughter*, *IG*14.1648; cf. μονογένεια. ⊛ **-ζωνος**, ον, *alone and girt up*, i.e. *lonely wayfarer*, S.*OT*846. **-θεν**, Adv. *from one only*, i.e. *by oneself*, *alone*, οἰ. οἶος Il.7.39,226; without οἶος, Arat.55, A.R.1.270, etc. **-θι**, Adv. *alone*, Arat.376, A.R.2.709, etc.

**οἰοθόρ**· ὁ Προμηθεύς, Hsch.

⊛ **οἰόκερως**, ωτος, ὁ, ἡ, (κέρας) *one-horned*, Opp.*C.*2.96.

⊛ **οἴομαι**, in Hom. always uncontr. **ὀΐομαι** (exc. οἴομαι Od.10.193, οἴοιτο 17.580, 22.12), v. infr.:—the shortd. form **οἶμαι** is the one chiefly used in Trag., οἴομαι only in A.*Ch.*758, S.*OC*28; but οἴομαι is freq. in Ar.(*Eq.*407, al.); Hdt. does not use either form; in Att. Prose codd. vary, but οἶμαι prevails, and was exclusively used in parenthesis (v. infr. IV): impf. ᾠόμην A.*Pr.*270, Ar.*V.*791, etc.; also 1 pers. ᾤμην Id.*Fr.*636, etc.: fut. οἰήσομαι Lys.30.8, Pl.*R.*397a, etc., later οἰηθήσομαι Gal.*Opt.Doctr.*42:—Ep. aor. **ὠϊσάμην** (v. infr.): aor. ὠΐσθην Od.4.453, 16.475; part. ὀϊσθείς Il.9.453; Att. and Ion. aor. ᾠήθην Hp.*VM*14, Antipho 1.8, Th.4.130, Pl.*Tht.*178c, etc.; but rare in Com. and Trag., οἰηθῆς Ar.*Eq.*860, οἰηθείς, -εῖσα, Antiph.194.2, E.*IA*986; also aor. inf. οἰήσασθαι Arat.896:—Act., Ep. pres. **ὀΐω** and **οἴω**, but only in 1 sg. (v. infr.); Lacon. οἰῶ Ar.*Lys.*81, 156, 998, Epil. 3. [In the uncontr. forms, Hom. uses ῑ in ὀΐομαι Il.5.644, ὀΐεαι 1.561, Od.10.380, ὀΐεται 17.586, ὀϊόμεθ' 21.322, 22.165, ὀϊόμενος Il.15.728, Od.2.351, al. (οἰόμενος Call.*Epigr.*8.2), ὠΐετο Od.10.248, ὀΐσατο 1.323, 9.213, 19.390, ὀϊσάμενος 15.443 (but the v.l. ὀΐσσατο, ὀϊσσάμενος in Hom. can be supported by ὀϊσσάμενος A.R.2.1135, cf. *Epic.Alex.Adesp.*2.41, Arat.1006, by ὑποΐζεσθαι (· ὑπονοεῖν) Hsch., and by ὠϊσάμην A.R.1.291, ὠΐσατο [ῐ] Mosch.2.8, etc.); Act. pres. ὀΐω has ῑ when it stands at the end of a line, also in Od.19.215 (in fourth foot), 18.259 (before caesura in third foot); but ῐ in Il.1.558, 13.153, 23.467, etc.; οἴω as disyll. is always at the end, exc. in 15.298, 21.533, 23.310.]:—*forebode*, *presage*, c. acc., κῆρας ὀϊομένῳ Il.13.283; γόον δ' ὠΐετο θυμὸς Od.10.248; *expect*, ἐελδομένοισι μάλ' ἡμῖν, οὐδ' ἔτ' ὀϊομένοισι 24.401; *suspect*, ἤ τι ὀϊσάμενος, ἤ καὶ θεὸς ὣς ἐκέλευσεν 9.339; ἤ τινά που δόλον ἄλλον ὀΐεαι 10.380; *fear*, κατὰ θυμὸν ὀΐσατο, μή ἑ λαβοῦσα οὐλὴν ἀμφράσαιτο 19.390; τῷ ἑπόμην.., ὀϊόμενός περ, ἀνάγκῃ 14.298: abs., αἰεὶ μὲν ὀΐεαι, οὐδέ σε λήθω *thou art* ever *suspecting*, Il.1.561; πατὴρ δ' ἐμὸς αὐτίκ' ὀϊσθεὶς πολλὰ κατηρᾶτο 9.453, cf. Od.15.443: folld. by ὡς, καὐτὸς ὀΐεαι ὥς κεν ἐτύχθη you can *guess* how it would have happened, 3.255, cf. 17.586: c. acc. et fut. inf., ὀΐομαι ἄνδρα χολωσέμεν Il.1.78; ἅ τιν' οὐ πείσεσθαι ὀΐω ib.289, cf. 5.252, 284, al.; τὸ καὶ τελέεσθαι ὀΐω 1.204; ἀλλ' οὐ νῦν ἐρύεσθαι ὀΐομαι 20.195: c. acc. et pres. inf., referring to present time, οὐδέ τι θυμῷ ὠΐσθη δόλον εἶναι Od.4.453, cf. 10.232; ὀΐσατο γὰρ θεὸν εἶναι 1.323; τῶ σ' ὀΐω κείνης τάδε πάσχειν ἐννεσίῃσιν Il.5.894: c. acc. et aor. inf., referring to past time, τῇ σ' ὀΐω κατανεῦσαι 1.558, cf. Od.3.27, al.: the subj. of the inf. must freq. be supplied from the context, διωκέμεναι γὰρ ὀΐω I *fear* [they] are pursuing me, 15.278, cf. 1.201, 12.212, Il.12.66, al.: c. inf. alone, when both Verbs have the same subject, as κιχήσεσθαι δέ σ' ὀΐω I *think* I shall catch you, 6.341; *mean*, *intend*, c. fut. inf., οὐ γὰρ ἔγωγ' ἔτι σοὶ πείσεσθαι ὀΐω 1.296, cf. 170, Od.19.215: c. pres. inf., οὐ γὰρ ὀΐω ἀνδρῶν δυσμενέων ἑκὰς ἱστάμενος πολεμίζειν Il.13.262. II. impersonal, only Od.19.312, ἀλλά μοι ὧδ' ἀνὰ θυμὸν ὀΐεται *there comes a boding* into my heart. III. *think*, *suppose*, *believe*, freq. in Hom., as Il.1.59, 5.644, etc.; οἶμαι βοὴν ἄμικτον ἐν πόλει πρέπειν A.*Ag.*321; οἶμαι γάρ νιν ἱκετεύσειν (ἱκετεύσαι codd.) E.*IA*462; κτήσεσθαι (-ασθαι codd.) Lys.12.19; διαπράξεσθαι (-ξασθαι codd.) Id.13.53; ἤδη γὰρ αὐτοὺς οἴομαι δεδειπνάναι Ar.*Fr.*464; opp. εἰδέναι, Pl.*R.*506c4; οἴονται, ἴσασι δ' οὐδέν Arist.*Rh.*1389$^{b}$17, cf. *APo.*75$^{a}$15: folld. by ὅτι.., Plu.2.90b:—Pass., μάρτυρας δύο παρεχέτω ὀμνύντας οἰόμενον *that he is the putative father*, *Schwyzer*784$^{a}$ (Tenos, iv B.C.). IV. parenthetically, mostly in first person, ἐν πρώτοισιν, ὀΐω, κείσεται among the first, *I ween*, will he be lying, Il.8.536; ἔπειτά γ', ὀΐω, γνώσεαι Od.16.309, cf. Il.13.153, Od.2.255, etc.: in Hom. only in act. form ὀΐω, exc. Od.22.140, and perh. 14.363, cf. A.*Ch.*758; in Att. this parenthetic use is prob. confined to the shorter form οἶμαι, impf. ᾤμην; rarely in other persons than the first, as οὐκ οἴει ἀναγκασθήσεται; Pl.*R.*486c, cf. *Tht.*147b; πόσης οἴεσθε γέμει σωφροσύνης; Id.*Smp.*216d. 2. expressive of modesty or courtesy, to avoid over-great bluntness of assertion, Id.*Grg.*483c, X.*Cyr.*1.3.11, etc.: even between a Prep. and its case, ἐξ οἶμαι τῆς ἀκροτάτης ἐλευθερίας Pl.*R.*564a; ἐν οἶμαι πολλοῖς D.20.3; or between Art. and Subst., οἱ γὰρ οἶμαι βέλτιστοι Id.54.38. V. answering a question, *I think so*, *I should think so*, Ar.*Ach.*919, etc.; νὴ τὸν Ἡρακλέα, οἶμαί γε Id.*Th.*27; οἶμαι ἔγωγε Pl.*Cri.*47d, etc.; οἴεσθαί γε χρή one must *think* so, it would seem so, Id.*Prt.*325c, *Cri.*53d, *Phd.*68b, *Grg.*522a. VI. Att. phrases: 1. πῶς οἴει; *you can't think* how, to add force, like πῶς δοκεῖς; πόθος τὴν καρδίαν ἐπάταξε πῶς οἴει σφόδρα Ar.*Ra.*54. 2. οἴομαι δεῖν I *think* it my duty, *think* fit, hence sts., *intend*, *purpose*, λέγειν οἴεται δεῖν ποιεῖν δεινούς *his object is* to train orators, Pl.*Men.*95c, cf. 86b, *Tht.*207e; βδελυρὸς καὶ ὑβριστὴς ᾤετο δεῖν εἶναι D.21.143; τοὺς ἐχθροὺς ἀμυνόμενοι τεθνάναι δεῖν ᾤοντο Id.60.31, cf. Pl.*Prt.*316c, X.*An.*2.6.26, *Mem.*4.6.3,6; [ὁ ἀκόλαστος] οἰόμενος δεῖν [διώκει τὰ ἡδέα] *intentionally*, Arist.*EN*1152$^{a}$6, cf. 1136$^{b}$8, Pl.*Hipparch.*225b; but οἴομαι δὲ δεῖν οὐδέν *methinks* there is no

need, S.*OC*28; and in Pl.*Alc.*2.144d ἆρ' οὐκ ἀναγκαῖον.. οἰηθῆναι δεῖν.. ἡμᾶς εἰδέναι ἢ τῷ ὄντι εἰδέναι; must we not either *think* we know or really know? (δεῖν being superfluous). **3.** οἴομαι without δεῖν I *mean to, intend*, οὐκ οἴει.. δοῦναι δίκην; Lys.12.26, cf. Pl.*Criti.*62d, *Ly.*200b, *Ep.*324b; οὐ βαλεῖν (v.l. βάλλειν).. ᾠήθη Arist.*EN*1135ᵇ14, cf. 1172ᵃ7.

**Οἶ-ον**, τό, *Oeum*, name of two Attic demes, **1.** Δεκελεικόν, in the φυλὴ Ἱπποθωντίς, *IG*2².1926.127, Harp. **2.** Κεραμεικόν, in the φυλὴ Λεωντίς, *IG*2².1742.84, Harp. **-όθεν**, Adv. *from Oeum*, *IG*2².2086.175, 2103.174.

**οἱονεί**, for οἷον εἰ, *as if*, Antiph.231.6, Men.*Georg.*58, Arist.*HA* 495ᵇ25, *Pr.*923ᵇ33; = οἷον (οἷος v. 2 d), Arist. *deAn.*430ᵇ13; Dor. οἷον αἱ Epich.155; so οἱονπερεί (q.v.); οἱοναυεί, *Gloss.*

**οἰονοϊστική**, ἡ, coined from οἴησις, νοῦς, ἱστορία, as etym. of οἰωνιστική, Pl.*Phdr.*244c.

**οἰονόμος**, ον, (οἶος) *feeding alone*: hence, *lonely*, of places, Simon. 130; ἐπ' οἰονόμοιο (neut.) in *solitude*, *APl.*4.230 (Leon.). **II.** (ὄϊς, οἶς) *sheep-rearing*, Σύροι *BCH*21.599 (Delph., iv B.C.); Ἀπόλλων prob. in Coluth.309: as Subst., *shepherd*, *AP*7.213 (Arch.), *APl.*4.291 (Anyt.).

**οἰόνους**, coined as etym. of οἶνος, Pl.*Cra.*406c.

**οἱόνπερ**, Adv. *just as though, as it were*, Pl.*Ti.*21a, *Lg.*701c, 965d; so **οἱονπερεί**, Id.*Tht.*201e.

**οἱόντε**, v. οἷος III. 2.

**οἰόομαι**, Pass., *to be left alone, forsaken*, Ep. Verb, only in aor., οἰώθη Il.6.1, 11.401; οἰώθησαν Q.S.6.527.

**οἰο-πέδη**, ἡ, perh. (from οἶς) a *woollen bandage for sore feet*, *AP*7.401 (Crin.). **-πέδιλος**, ον, *with but one sandal*, A.R.1.7. **-πολέω**, *roam alone*, E.*Cyc.*74 (lyr.): c. acc. loci, *roam over*, of shepherds, ὄρεος ῥάχιν οἰ. *AP*7.657 (Leon.). **-πόλος**, ον, (οἶος, πέλομαι) of places, *lonely*, ὄρεα Od.11.574; χῶρος, σταθμός, Il.13.473, 19.377; of persons, *solitary, unaccompanied*, δαίμων Pi.*P.*4.28. **II.** (οἶς, -πόλος, cf. αἰπόλος) *tending sheep*, Ἄρτεμις Id.*Dith.*2.19; Ἑρμῆς *h.Merc.*314; Ἀπόλλων v.l. in Coluth.309; θεαί, of the Hesperides, A.R.4.1322, cf. 1413; Πάριν οἰοπόλοισιν ἐφεδριόωντα θοώκοις Coluth.15. (Signf. I is alternatively derived from οἶς, πολέω (as if 'sheep-traversed') in Sch.Il.13.473.)

**οἰόρπατα**, Scyth. for ἀνδροκτόνοι, οἰόρ being = *man*, Hdt.4.110.

**οἶος**, α (Ep. η), ον, Cypr. οἶϝος *Inscr.Cypr.*135.14 H.:—*alone, lonely*, freq. in Hom. and Hes., thrice in Pi., once in A., twice in S. (v. infr.):—Special usages: **1.** defined by the addition of other words, οἰ. ἄνευθ' ἄλλων Il.22.39; οἰ..., νόσφιν δεσποίνης Od.14.450; οὐκ οἰ., ἅμα τῷ γε.. not *alone*, but.., Il.2.822, cf. Od.1.331, al.; οἰ. ἐν ὄρφνᾳ Pi.*O.*1.71, cf. *P.*1.93; οἰ. (prob. cj.) ἐξέβης λαθὼν S.*Fr.*22: neut. οἶον as Adv., γαστέρες οἶον *naught but*.., Hes.*Th.*26; οἶον μὴ.. *only* let not.., A.*Ag.*131 (lyr.); οὐ.. οἶον, ἀλλ'.. not *only*.., but.., *IG*3.171*B*22. **2.** strengthd., εἷς οἶος, μία οἴη, one *alone*, one *only*, Il.4.397, 18.565, al.; dual, δύ' οἴω 24.473, Od.14.94: pl., δύ' οἴους 3.424; δύ' οἶαι 16.245. **3.** sts. c. gen., οἴη γάρ ῥα θεῶν *alone, the only one*, of the gods, Il.11.74; τῶν οἶος ib.693; οἶος θεῶν Pi.*Fr.*93. **4.** with a Prep., οἴη ἐν ἀθανάτοισιν *alone among* the immortals, Il.1.398; οἶος μετὰ τοῖσι Od.3.362: but οἶον ἀπ' ἄλλων *alone from, apart from*, 9.192; οἶον ἀπ' ἀνθρώπων 21.364; πῶς ἂν.. ἀπὸ σεῖο.. λιποίμην οἶ.; Il. 9.438; οἰ. Ἀτρειδῶν δίχα *clam Atridis*, S.*Aj.*750. **II.** *single in its kind, unique, excellent*, ὅς δέ μοι οἰ. ἔην.., Ἕκτορα Il.24.499. (Cf. OPers. *aiva-* 'one': I.-E. *oi-wo-*, akin to *oi-no-*, v. οἴνη (B).)

**οἷος**, οἵα, Ion. οἵη, οἷον, (ὅς) *such as, of what sort*, relat. and indirect interrog. Pron., correl. to direct interrog. ποῖος, indef. ποιός, demonstr. τοῖος: ὅσσος ἔην οἷός τε Il.24.630; ὁσσάτιόν τε καὶ οἷον 5.758: c. acc., οἶδ' ἀρετὴν οἷός ἐσσι *what a man* for valour, 13.275: freq. to be rendered by an Adv., οἷος πολεμόνδε μέτεισι as he rushes into war, ib.298, etc.:—Usage: **I.** οἷος in an independent sentence as an exclam. of astonishment, ὢ πόποι.., οἷον ἔειπες Il.7.455; οἷ. τὸ πῦρ *what* a fire is this! A.*Ag.*1256, cf. *Pers.*733, al.; οἷ. εἰργάσασθε Pl.*R.*450a; οἷ. ἄνδρα λέγεις ἐν κινδύνῳ εἶναι Id.*Tht.* 142b; οἷα ποιεῖς Id.*Euthphr.*15e, etc.: so in neut. as Adv., v. infr. v. 1. **2.** in indirect sentences, S.*OT*624, 1402, 1488, etc.; ὁρᾶτε δὴ ἐν οἵῳ ἐστὲ X.*Cyr.*3.2.12; ὁρῶν ἐν οἵοις ἐσμὲν Id.*An.*3.1.15. **II.** more freq. as relat. to a demonstr. τοῖος, τοιόσδε, τοιοῦτος, or to ὁ, ὅδε, as τῷ ἴκελον, οἷόν ποτε Δαίδαλος ἤσκησεν Il.18.591; θέαμα τοιοῦτον οἷ. καὶ στυγοῦντ' ἐποικτίσαι S.*OT*1296: but the demonstr. Pron. is freq. omitted, οὐ γὰρ ἐμὴ ἲς ἔσθ' οἵη πάρος ἔσκεν Il.11.669, etc.; οἷ. καὶ Πάρις.. ᾔσχυνε *like as* Paris also.., A.*Ag.*399 (lyr.), cf. *Pers.*21, al.: with δή added, τοιόνδ', οἷ. δὴ σύ *such as* you *surely* are, Il.24.376, v. infr. v. 2: with περ added, οἵη περ φύλλων γενεή, τοίη δὲ καὶ ἀνδρῶν *just such as*.., 6.146, cf. A.*Ag.*607, 1046, X.*Cyr.*1.6.19: very freq. with τε added (this οἷός τε must be distd. from οἷός τε c. inf., v. infr. III. 2), οἷός τε πελώριος ἔρχεται Ἄρης Il.7.208, cf. 17.157, Od.7.106, etc.; οἷός που 20.35: οἷός τις, οἷόν τι generalizes a Comparison, *the sort of person who*.., *thing which*.., Il.5.638, Od.9.348; οἶσθα εἰς οἷόν τινα κίνδυνον ἔρχει..; Pl.*Prt.*313a; with attraction of οἷος to the case of its antecedent (which may follow instead of preceding), οἵοις περ σὺ χρώμενοι συμβούλοις D.24.185; and with further attraction of the subject of the relat. clause, οὐ γάρ πω τοίους ἴδον ἀνέρας.., οἷον Πειρίθοον (for οἷος Πειρίθοος) Il.1.263; πρὸς ἄνδρας τολμηρούς, οἵους καὶ Ἀθηναίους Th.7.21, cf. X.*Mem.*2.9.3; περὶ τοῦ τοιούτου.., οἵου τοῦ ἑνός Pl.*Prm.* 161b. **2.** οἷος, οἵα, οἷον freq. introduce an 'indirect exclamation', giving the reason for what precedes, ἄνακτα χόλος λάβεν, οἷον ἄκουσε *because of what* he heard, Il.6.166, cf. Od.17.479; ἐμακάριζον τὴν μητέρα οἵων τέκνων ἐκύρησε Hdt.1.31; ἀγανάκτησιν ἔχει ὑφ' οἵων κακοπαθεῖ Th.2.41; τὴν ἐμαυτοῦ τύχην [ἀπέκλαον], οἵου ἀνδρὸς.. ἐστερημένος εἴην Pl.*Phd.*117c, cf. S.*OT*701. **3.** sts. in Hom. οἷος introduces the reason for saying what is said, ὠκύμορος.. ἔσσεαι, οἷ' ἀγορεύεις Il.18.95, cf. Od.4.611; αἲ γάρ με θυμὸς ἀνείη ὤμ' ἀποταμνόμενον κρέα ἔδμεναι, οἷα ἔοργας Il.22.347. **4.** οἷα δὴ εἴπας saying *so and so*, Hdt.1.86 (cf. ὅσος III. 2): later with other Particles, v. infr. VI. **5.** οὐδὲν οἷον.. there's nothing *like*.., ἀλλ' οὐδὲν οἷ. ἐστ' ἀκοῦσαι τῶν ἐπῶν there's nothing *like* hearing the verses, Ar.*Av.* 966, cf. *Lys.*135; οὐδὲν γὰρ οἷ. ἀκούειν αὐτοῦ τοῦ νόμου D.21.46, cf. Pl.*Grg.*447c, 481b, X.*Oec.*3.14. **6.** never used like Adv. οἷον (infr. v. 1) with an Adj. = *how*, for in Il.11.653, οἶσθα.. οἷ. ἐκεῖνος δεινὸς ἀνήρ = *what manner of man*, namely dread, cf. 15.94, 21.108, Od.19.493, etc. **7.** as indef., *a sort* or *kind of*.., ὁ δ' ἕτερος οἷός ἐστιν οἰκουρὸς μόνον only *a kind of* watch-dog, Ar.*V.*970; so with Adj., ἀφόρητος οἷος.. κρυμὸς *of an* intolerable *kind*, Hdt.4.28; θαυμαστὸς οἷος *of a* wonderful *nature*, Luc.*Zeux.*6; οἷος ἔμπειρος πολέμου *rather* skilled in war, D.2.18; οἷον τετανότριχα *rather* straight-haired, Pl.*Euthphr.*2b; freq. with Sup., χωρίον οἷον χαλεπώτατον country *of a* very difficult *kind*, X.*An.*4.8.2, cf. Ar.*Eq.*978, *Ach.*384, Pl.*Ap.* 23a; ἀνὴρ οἷος κράτιστος Arist.*EN*1165ᵇ27; κόλπος οἷος βαθύτατος Ael.*NA*14.26: in some of these passages with Sup. it is possible to take οἷος as relat., supplying δυνατόν, cf. ξύμμαχος ἔσομαι οἷος ἂν δύνωμαι ἄριστος *IG*1².39.28. **III.** οἷος c. inf. implies fitness or ability for a thing, οὐ γὰρ ἦν ὥρα οἵα τὸ πεδίον ἄρδειν *fit* for watering, X.*An.*2.3.13, cf. Pl.*Grg.*487d; οἷοι φιλεῖν, μισεῖν, etc., D.25.2, etc.: freq. with τοιοῦτος expressed, τοιοῦτός τις οἷ. διαπονεῖσθαι Pl. *Cra.*395a, cf. *R.*415e; τὸ πρᾶγμα μέγα.. καὶ μὴ οἷ. νεωτέρῳ βουλεύσασθαι not *proper* for a young man to advise upon, Th.6.12: without inf., λόγους οἵους εἰς τὰ δικαστήρια Pl.*Euthd.*272a. **b.** οἷός εἰμι I *intend*, ἐβιάζετο.. καὶ οἷος ἦν ἐξευρεῖν τὴν θύραν Lys.*Fr.*159 S., cf. D. 4.9, al., Is.8.21; οἷος ἦν κατεσθίειν was *on the point of* eating, Antig. Car.ap.Ath.7.345d. **2.** more freq. οἷός τε c. inf., *fit* or *able* to do, λιποίμην οἷός τ'.. ἀέθλια κάλ' ἀνελέσθαι Od.21.117 (preceded by τοῖον ib.173), Hdt.1.29, 67, 91; λέγειν οἷός τε κἀγώ Ar.*Eq.*343, cf. Th.3. 16, Isoc.8.69, etc.; *inclined* to.., Plb.3.90.5, J.*AJ*4.6.3: most freq. in neut. sg. and pl., οἷόν τε [ἐστί] it is *possible* to.., Th.1.80, etc.; οἷά τε [ἐστί] Hdt.1.194, etc.; a dat. is sts. added, μὴ οἷόν τε εἶναι ἐμοὶ κωλῦσαι Th.7.14. **3.** without inf., πάνυ προθύμως ὡς οἷός τ' ἦν ἐπήραξεν Pl.*Prt.*314d: but mostly in neut., οἷόν τε [ἐστίν] it is *possible*, Isoc.9.9; οὐχ οἷόν τε ἐστίν Ar.*Nu.*198, etc.: with Sup., καλὸν ὡς οἷόν τε μάλιστα Pl.*Prt.*349e; ὡς οἷόν τε σμικρότατα Id. *Prm.*144b; ὡς οἷόν τε διὰ βραχυτάτων Id.*Grg.*449d: without Sup., φρίττειν.. ποιεῖ ὡς οἷόν τε πάντας Id.*R.*387c (dub. l.); ὡς οἷόν τε sts. *so far as possible*, of what cannot be done completely, D.8.75, Arist. *Pol.*1313ᵃ39, Luc.*Im.*3. **IV.** sts. twice in the same clause, οἷ' ἔργα δράσας οἷα λαγχάνει κακά after *what* deeds *what* sufferings are his! S.*El.*751; ἱερῶν οἵαν οἵων χάριν ἠνύσω *what* thanks *for what* offerings! Id.*Tr.*994, cf. 1045, E.*Alc.*144: so in Prose, X.*Cyr.*4.5. 29, Pl.*Smp.*195a. **V.** as Adv. in neut. sg. οἷον, in Poets and Ion. Prose also pl. οἷα, *how*, οἷον δή νυ θεοὺς βροτοὶ αἰτιόωνται Od.1.32, cf. Il.5.601, 13.633, 15.287: also with Adjs., οἷον ἐερσήεις *how* fresh, 24.419; οἷον δὴ Μενέλαον ὑπέτρεσας *seeing how* thou didst shrink from M., Il.17.587, cf. 21.57. (Regul. Adv. οἵως is rare, as in Hp. *Epid.*6.7.2, f.l. in Ar.*V.*1363; οἵως ὢν οἷ. ἔχεις *in what a state* art thou for such a man! S.*Aj.*923; οἵως τέ σφ' ἐσάωσα A.R.4.786.) **2.** *as, just as*, οἷον ὅτε.. Il.14.295: also neut. pl. οἷα, οἷά τις.. ἀηδών A.*Ag.*1142 (lyr.), cf. S.*Tr.*105 (lyr.), etc.: so οἷά τε in Hom., οἷά τε λῃϊστῆρες Od.3.73, cf. 9.128, Hdt.2.175: strengthd. by Particles, οἷα δὴ Th.8.84, Pl.*Smp.*219e, *R.*467b; οἷα δή που Ael.*NA*1.14: later a double form occurs, οἷον ὡς.. Demetr.*Eloc.*94, Sch.D.T.p.113 H.; οἷον ὥσπερ.. Phryn.*PS* p.80 B., dub. in Plu.2.563f. **b.** *as for instance*, Pl.*Sph.*218e, Arist.*GC*333ᵃ11, etc.; οἷον τί λέγεις; *as for example*, what do you mean? Pl.*Tht.*207a, cf. Od.4.271, where οἷον is Adj. **c.** in numerical estimates, *about*, οἷον δέκα σταδίους Th.4. 90; μῆκος οἷον ἐπὶ δέκα δακτύλους *IG*2².1457.17. **d.** οἷον parenthetically prefixed to any word or phrase, *as it were, so to speak*, οἷον υἱεῖς γνησίους Pl.*Phdr.*278a, cf. *Cra.*396a, Arist.*HA*532ᵃ6, *GA*753ᵃ33; τῶν οἷον προγυμνασμάτων M.Ant.6.20; τοῦ οἷον δόγματος D.L.9.69; τὴν.. οἷον φάτταν the ring-dove *of my parable*, Pl.*Tht.*199b. **e.** οἷον explanatory, *that is to say*, τὸ νῦν ῥηθησόμενον, οἷον.. what I am about to mention, *viz.*, Arist.*PA*639ᵇ6, cf. *GC*333ᵃ11, al.; κατὰ τὸ μέσον, οἷον κατὰ τὴν συμβολὴν τῶν ἐν αὐτοῖς διαγωνίων in the middle, *i.e.* at the intersection of their diagonals, Procl.*Hyp.*3.16, cf. 22, Hsch. s.v. οἰοφάγῳ, al. **3.** like ὡς, ἅτε, with a part., οἷα ἀπροσδοκήτου κακοῦ γενομένου Th.2.5, cf. 8.95, Pl.*Smp.*203b. **4.** οὐχ οἷον or μὴ οἷον, folld. by ἀλλ' οὐδέ or ἀλλὰ μηδέ, *not only not*.., *but not even*.., Plb. 1.20.12, D.S.3.18, Phld.*Rh.*2.249 S., etc. **VI.** strengthd. with various Particles, οἷος δή, v. supr. II. 4: **οἱοσδήποτε**, οἱαδήποτε, οἱονδήποτε, *of such and such a kind*, Arist.*EN*1114ᵇ17; **οἱοσδηποτοῦν**, *of whatever kind*, Hero *Geom.*12.30, al., *BGU*895.28 (ii A.D.), Paul.Aeg. 6.88; **οἱοσδήπως**, *OGI*521.4 (Abydos, v/vi A.D.); **οἱοσδητισοῦν**, ib.515.16 (Mylasa, iii A.D.); **οἱοσοῦν**, Just.*Nov.*30.7.1; **οἱοσποτοῦν**, Arist.*Top.*146ᵇ26; **οἱοστισοῦν**, v.l. in Dsc.2.76.13. [οἷ is found in Il.13.275, Od.7.312; and sts. in Trag., as A.*Ag.*1256, esp. in the form οἷός τε S.*OT*1415, *OC*262, 803, al.]

**ὄϊος, οἰός**, gen. of ὄϊς, οἶς.

**ὄϊος** [ῐ], α, ον, (ὄϊς) *of a sheep*, γάλα ὄ. *ewe*-milk, Hp.*Vict.*2.41; ὄϊον ἔριον Polem.Hist.88; οἰὸς οἰότερον *more sheepish* than a sheep, Sophr.

122 (v. dub.). (In Hp. and Polem.Hist. ll. cc. δεῖος (like βόειος) shd. be read; cf. ὀέα.)

**οἰσταζομένης·** φιλοτιμουμένης, Hsch. **οἰοφάγῳ** σιδήρῳ· οἷον μηλοκτόνῳ, Id.

**οἰό-φρων,** ονος, ὁ, ἡ, (φρήν) *lonely*, οἰ. πέτρα A.*Supp.*795 (lyr.). **-χίτων** [χῐ], ωνος, ὁ, ἡ, *with only a tunic on, lightly clad*, Od.14.489, Nonn.*D.*8.16 (expld. as = προβατοχίτων, *in a sheep-skin tunic*, Hsch.).

**οἰόω,** v. οἰόομαι.

**οἶπερ,** Adv. *whither*, v. οἷ.

**οἰρών,** ῶνος, ὁ, = ἡ χάραξις τῶν ἀρότρων, Eratosth.38 (οἰορῶν and ἀτρότων cod.), cf. Hdn.Gr.1.35; οἰρών· ἡ ἐκ τῆς καταμετρήσεως τῆς γῆς εὐθυωρία, Hsch.; cf. ἰρών.

**ὄϊς** (Il.24.125), ὁ and ἡ, gen. ὄϊος Od.4.764, al.; Ion. dat. ὀΐ [⏑ –] Ar.*Pax*929; acc. ὄϊν Il.24.621, al. (on οἶδα v. οἶς): pl. ὄϊες – ⏑⏑ Od.9.425 (οἴιες cod. Harl.), ⏑⏑ – Il.4.433, al., οἴιες Call.*Ap.*53; gen. ὀΐων Od.9.167, al.; dat. ὀΐεσσι Il.5.137, al., Theoc.5.130, ὄεσσι Il.6.25, al.; also ὄϊεσι, in corrupt form ὄρεσι(· προβάτοις), Hsch.; acc. pl. ὄϊς [ῑ] Il.11.245, al., Hes.*Op.*775 (always before a consonant); Dor. ὄϊς Theoc.8.45, both from ὄϝις, which is found at Argos, *SIG*56.30 (v B.C.); nom. and acc. pl. further contr. to οἶς, Orac.ap.D.21.53; of these contr. forms Hom. has only gen. sg. οἰός Il.12.451, al., gen. pl. οἰῶν 11.696, al.; cf. dat. pl. οἴεσιν Od.15.386; acc. sg. οἶν Theoc.5.99: in Att. οἰ- is always contracted, οἶς Hdn.Gr.1.400, οἶν E.*El.*513, οἰός S.*OC*475, al., οἰΐ Arist.*GA*769b20, but ὀΐ Id.*HA*522b33; pl. οἶες X.*Mem.*3.2.1, al., *IG*2².1358.36; acc. οἶς X.*Cyr.*5.2.5, *HG*6.4.29, *An.*6.2.3; gen. οἰῶν Arist.*HA*596a31, al.; dat. οἰσίν prob. in *IG*1².825.2, οἰσί prob. in *SIG*624.40 (ii B.C.): Cret. forms, nom. sg. οις, acc. οιν, *GDI*4963, but οἶις, οἶιν, ib.4990:—*sheep*, Hom., Hes., etc. (v. supr.) (but rare in Prose, πρόβατον being preferred), both of the *ram* and the *ewe*, though sts. a word is added to mark gender, ὄϊν ἀρνειὸν ῥέζειν θῆλύν τε μέλαιναν Od.10.527, cf. 9.425; ὄϊν.. θῆλυν, ὑπόρρηνον Il.10.215. [Always ῐ, exc. in dat. sg. ὀΐ, acc. pl. ὄϊς: gen. sg. οἰός exceptionally ⏑ – (before a consonant) in Mnesim.4.47: in οἴιες οἰ- may stand metri gr. for ὀ- (cf. πνοιή, ἠγνοίησε, etc.), but for Cret. οἶις, οἶιν some other expl. is needed.] (Arg. ὄϝις *SIG* l.c., cf. Skt. *avis*, Lat. *ovis*, Engl. *ewe*, etc.)

**οἶς,** Delph., = οἷ, *GDI*1685, al.

**οἶσαξ,** ακος, ἡ, = οἰσύα, *Gp.*2.6.24.

**ὀΐσατο, ὀϊσάμενος,** v. οἴομαι. **οἶσε, -έτω, -ετε, οἰσέμεν, -έμεναι,** v. φέρω. **οἶσθα, οἶσθας,** v. *εἴδω B. **ὀϊσθείς,** v. οἴομαι. **οἰσθλά·** ἀγαθά, Hsch.

**οἶσις,** εως, ἡ, (οἴσω, v. φέρω) *moving*, τῆς ψυχῆς Pl.*Cra.*420c (coined to expl. οἴησις).

**οἰσμός,** ὁ, = ἐκφώνησις ἐναποσβεννυμένου πυρός, Zos.Alch.p.216 B. (fort. σισμός).

**οἰσόκαρπον,** τό, *the fruit of the* οἶσος, Sch.Il.11.105, Eust.834.35.

**οἶσος** (Ael.Dion.*Fr.*76) or **οἰσός,** ὁ, *withy, Vitex Agnus-castus*, the twigs of which served for wickerwork, ropes, etc., Thphr.*HP*3.18.1, 6.2.2, etc.: neut. **οἶσον,** = σχοινίον, Hsch.: perh. cf. οὖσον.

**οἰσοφάγος** [ᾰ], ὁ, *gullet*, Hp.*Loc.Hom.*3, Arist.*PA*650a16, 664a31, Gal.*UP*4.1, etc.

**οἴσπη,** ἡ, *sheep-dung*, esp. *the dirt that collects about the hinder parts of sheep* or *goats*, Gal.19.125, Hsch., Suid., v.l. for οἰσύπη in Hdt.4.187.

**οἰσπώτη** (οἰσπωτή acc. to Hdn.Gr.1.343), ἡ, = foreg., Cratin.39, Ar.*Lys.*575, D.C.46.5, Poll.5.91.

**οἰστέος,** α, ον, (φέρω) *to be borne*, S.*OC*1360. II. οἰστέον *one must bear*, E.*Or.*769; βαρὺ μέν, οἰστέον δ' ὅμως Id.*Hel.*268, cf. Men.531.9. 2. *one must get*, κέρδος S.*Ant.*310. 3. *one must pay*, φόρον Isoc.14.10.

**ὀϊστ-ευμα,** ατος, τό, *an arrow from the bow*, Plu.2.225b. **-ευτήρ,** ῆρος, ὁ, = sq., *AP*6.118 (Antip.), Nonn.*D.*7.271; ἐρώτων ib.35.26. **-ευτής,** οῦ, ὁ, *archer*, Call.*Ap.*43. **-εύω,** *shoot arrows*, ὅν τις ὀϊστεύσας ἔβαλεν whom one shot *with an arrow*, Il.4.196, cf. Od.8.216; τόξῳ ὀϊστεύσας 12.84: c. gen. objecti, ἀλλ' ἄγ' ὀΐστευσον Μενελάου Il.4.100: c. acc. cogn., ἀκτῖνας ὀ., etc., Nonn.*D.*41.257, etc. II. trans., *shoot with an arrow*, *AP*5.57 (Arch.); τινὰ βελέμνῳ Nonn.*D.*15.322.

**οἰστικός,** ή, όν, *productive*, ὑγιείας Sch.Pl.*Grg.*450a; καρπῶν Ph.1.589, cf. 110; μεγάλων φόβων Orib.*Fr.*72. Adv. -κῶς, ἔχειν to be *productive*, Iamb.*VP*5.28 (s.v.l.). II. *able to bear*, πόνων Corn.*ND*28; κικουχιῶν Ptol.*Tetr.*145.

**ὀϊστο-βόλος,** ον, *arrow-shooting*, *AP*7.427.10 (Antip.), Nonn.*D.*24.139. **-βρόχιον,** τό, (βρέχω) *shower of arrows*, Eust.770.48. **-δέγμων,** ὁ, ἡ, gen. ονος, *holding arrows*, θησαυρός, i.e. a quiver, A.*Pers.*1020 (lyr.). **-δόκη,** ἡ, *holding arrows*, φαρέτρη A.R.1.1194, cf. Poll.10.142. **-δόχος,** ον, = foreg., ὅπλον Sch.Hes.*Sc.*128. **-θήκη,** ἡ, *quiver*, Poll.10.142. **-κόμος,** ον, *keeping arrows*, φαρέτρη Nonn.*D.*48.360.

**οἰστός,** ή, όν, *that can be borne, endurable*, οἰστὸν ἂν ἦν Th.1.122; πάντα οἰστὰ ἐφαίνετο Id.7.75: Comp., Hld.2.24. Adv. -τῶς Poll.3.131.

**ὀϊστός,** Att. **οἰστός** (E.*Fr.*1063.13, *Med.*634 (lyr.)), ὁ (also ἡ Zeno ap.Arist.*Ph.*239b30), *arrow*, πικρὸς ὀ. Il.4.134, al.; χαλκήρης 13.650; τριγλώχις 5.393; τανυγλώχις 8.297: rare in Att. Prose, πυρφόροις οἰστοῖς Th.2.75, Pl.*Ion*535b, *Lg.*795a, X.*An.*2.1.6: metaph., of a poem, Pi.*O.*2.90, 9.12; ὁ τῆς σοφίας ὀ. Heraclit.*All.*34. II. a plant, *arrow-head, Sagitta sagittifolia*, Mago ap.Plin.*HN*21.111. III. the constellation *Sagitta*, Eudox.ap.Hipparch.1.11.10.

**ὀϊστοῦχος,** ον, (ἔχω) *arrow-holding*, φαρέτρα Hsch., Phot., Eust.1024.62.

**οἰστρ-άω** or **-έω,** the former in Pl. (v. infr.), Arist.*HA*602a26, Men. (v. infr.), the latter in Theoc.6.28, Luc.*Asin.*33: fut. -ήσω *Gp.*17.5.3: aor. οἴστρησα (Elmsl. ᾤστρησα) E.*Ba.*32, cf. Choerob. *in Theod.*2.50 H.; part. οἰστρήσας (v. infr.):—**Pass.** (v. infr.):—*sting*, prop. of the gadfly (οἶστρος): hence, metaph., *sting to madness*, αὐτὰς ἐκ δόμων ᾤστρησα I *drove* them *raging* out of the house, E. l.c.:—Pass., οἰστρηθεὶς *driven mad*, S.*Tr.*653, E.*Ba.*119 (both lyr.); of sexual passion, οἰστρημένος ὑπὸ τοῦ ἔρωτος Iamb.*VP*31.195; εἰς μεῖξιν Ael.*NA*15.9, cf. Luc.*Asin.*33. II. intr., *go mad, rage*, of Io driven by the gadfly, οἰστρήσασα *in frenzy, frantically*, A.*Pr.*836; of Menelaus, καθ' Ἑλλάδ' οἰστρήσας E.*IA*77; of the tunny when attacked by the οἶστρος (I. 2), Arist.*HA*602a26, cf. 598a18: metaph., ἡ ψυχὴ οἰστρᾷ καὶ ὀδυνᾶται Pl.*Phdr.*251d, cf. *R.*573e; τοῖς οἰστρῶσιν Id.*Tht.*179e; οἰστρῶντι πόθῳ Men.312. **-ηδόν,** Adv. *madly*, Opp.*H.*4.142. **-ήεις,** εσσα, εν, *stinging to madness*, Opp.*C.*2.423, Nonn.*D.*5.328. II. Pass., *stung to madness*, ib.21.188, al. **-ηλᾰσία,** ἡ, *mad passion*, Lxx 4*Ma.*2.4, Suid. s.v. Σαρδανάπαλος. **-ηλατεῖται** (-ιλατεῖ cod.)· μαίνεται, Hsch. **-ήλᾰτος,** ον, *driven by a gadfly*, δεῖμα A.*Pr.*580 (lyr.), cf. E.*Oxy.*2078*Fr.*1.15. **-ημα,** ατος, τό, *the smart of a gadfly's sting*, metaph., κέντρων οἰ. S.*OT*1318; -ήματα λύσσης *ravings* of madness, *AP*6.51. **-ησις,** εως, ἡ, *mad passion*, φρενῶν *Corp.Herm.*13.4, cf. Ael.*Fr.*122, *Gp.*17.5.4.

**οἰστρο-βολέω,** *strike with the sting*, τινα, esp. of the dart of love, *AP*9.16 (Mel.). **-γενέτωρ,** ορος, ὁ, *creator of frenzy*, of Ἔρως, *PMag.Par.*1.1777. **-δίνητος** [δῑ], ον, *driven round and round by the gadfly*, A.*Pr.*589. **-δόνητος,** ον, = foreg., Id.*Supp.*573 (lyr.), Ar.*Th.*324 (lyr.):—also **-δονος,** ον, A.*Supp.*16 (anap.). **-μᾰνής,** ές, *mad from the gadfly's sting*: *raging*, Tim.*Pers.*90, Nonn.*D.*1.282. **-μᾰνία,** Ion. -ίη, ἡ, *fury, frenzy*, Hp.*Ep.*17. **-πλάνεια** [πλᾰ], ἡ, *causing the wanderings of madness*, epith. of Hecate, *PMag.Par.*1.2868. **-πλήξ,** πλῆγος, ὁ, ἡ, *stung by a gadfly, driven wild*, of Io, A.*Pr.*681, S.*El.*5; of Bacchantes, E.*Ba.*1229.

**οἶστρος,** ὁ, *gadfly, breese*, prob. *Tabanus bovinus*, an insect which infests cattle, τὰς μέν τ' αἰόλος οἰ. ἐφορμηθεὶς ἐδόνησεν, ὥρῃ ἐν εἰαρινῇ Od.22.300; of the fly that tormented Io, A.*Supp.*541 (lyr.), *Pr.*567 sq. (lyr.) (also called μύωψ, ib.675, *Supp.*308: but the two are distd. by Arist.*HA*490a20, 596b14). 2. *an insect that infests tunny-fish*, prob. *Brachiella thynni*, ib.557a27, 602a28. 3. a small insectivorous bird, perh. *Sylvia trochilus*, ib.592b22. II. metaph., *a sting, anything that drives mad*, κεραυνοῦ οἰ. E.*HF*862; οἴστροις Ἐρινύων Id.*IT*1456: abs., *the smart of pain, agony*, S.*Tr.*1254. 2. *any vehement desire, insane passion*, Hdt.2.93, E.*Hipp.*1300, Pl.*R.*577e, etc.; ὄρεξις μετὰ οἴστρου καὶ ἀδημονίας Epicur.*Fr.*483: c. gen. objecti, κτεάνων *for* wealth, *AP*11.389 (Lucill.): generally, *madness, frenzy*, S.*Ant.*1002, E.*Or.*791: pl., Id.*Ba.*665; μανιάδες οἰ. Id.*IA*548 (lyr.). 3. in good sense, *zeal*, οἰ. εἰς πᾶν ἀγαθὸν ἔργον *PMasp.*3.13 (vi A.D.). III. a throw at dice, Eub.57.5.

**οἰστροφόρος,** ον, *maddening*, Παφίη *AP*5.233 (Paul. Sil.).

**οἰστρώδης,** ες, *raging, frantic*, ἐπιθυμίαι Pl.*Ti.*91b, *Lg.*734a, Epicur.*Sent.Vat.*80; λύσσαι Ti.Locr.102e.

**οἰσύ-α** [ῠ], ἡ, = λύγος, *osier*, Poll.7.176, Suid. II. οἰ. ἀγρία, = ἑλξίνη, Ps.-Dsc.4.85. **-ϊνος** [ῐ], η, ον, *of osier, of wickerwork*, ῥῖπες Od.5.256; ἀσπίδες Th.4.9; ὅπλα X.*HG*2.4.25; ῥάβδος *AP*6.246; κύρτος Opp.*H.*3.372.

**οἴσυλος·** προϊοῦλος, προύνικος, Hsch.

**οἴσυον,** τό, *wickerwork*, dub. l. in Aen.Tact.29.11. 2. ἐν τοῖς οἰ. in *the basket-market*, Lycurg.112.

**οἰσυοπλόκος,** ον, *plaiting osier-twigs*, Poll.7.175.

**οἰσυουργός,** όν, *working in osier-twigs*, Eup.433.

**οἰσύπ-ειον** [ῠ]· ἔριον ῥυπαρὸν προβάτων, = οἰσυπηρόν, Hsch. **-η,** ἡ, also **οἴσῠπος,** ὁ, *the grease extracted from sheep's wool* (οἴσυπος· τὸ ἐκ τῶν οἰσυπηρῶν ἐρίων λίπος Dsc.2.74, cf. Plin.*HN*29.10), οἰσύπη (v.l. οἴσπη, q.v.) προβάτων Hdt.4.187; οἰσύπη αἰγός Hp.*Mul.*2.195; used for medicinal purposes, Dsc. and Plin. ll. cc.:—freq. confused with οἰσπώτη (q.v.). **-ηρός,** ά, όν, *with the grease in it*, ἔρια οἰ. Ar.*Ach.*1177, Dsc.2.74, cf. Archig.ap.Orib.44.26.11: sg., ἔριον οἰ. Gal.10.965. **-ίς,** ίδος, ἡ, *tuft of greasy wool*, Hp.*Ulc.*14. **-όεις,** εσσα, εν, = οἰσυπώδης, only in acc. pl. neut. οἰσυποῦντα ib.24. **-ον,** τό, = λάδανον, Plin.*HN*12.74. **-ος,** ὁ, = οἰσύπη (q.v.). **-ώδης,** ες, *greasy*, of wool, Hp.*Ulc.*12, 17.

**οἴσω,** v. φέρω.

**Οἴτη,** ἡ, Mount *Oeta* in Thessaly, Str.9.4.12:—Adj. **Οἰταῖος,** α, ον, *of Oeta*, S.*Tr.*436, etc.; οἱ Οἰταῖοι Th.3.92, etc.:—also **Οἰταϊκός,** ή, όν, D.L.1.106; Οἰταϊκά, τά, title of work by Nicander, Nic.*Fr.*15–18.

**Οἰτόλῐνος,** ὁ, a name of Λίνος (q.v.), Paus.9.29.8 (Sapph.62 B).

**οἶτος,** ὁ, *fate, doom*, usu. in a bad sense, κακὸς οἰ. Il.8.34, Od.1.350, al.; σὺ δέ κεν κακὸν οἰ. ὄληαι Il.3.417; ἀλκυόνος πολυπενθέος οἰ. ἔχουσα 9.563; καλὰ τὸν οἰ. ἀπότμου παιδὸς ἐνισπες 24.388; κατὰ κόσμον Ἀχαιῶν οἰ. ἀείδεις Od.8.489; Δαναῶν ἰδὲ Ἰλίου οἰ. ἀκούων ib.578; but simply, *lot*, τὸν τῆς μελίσσης οἰ. ἔχειν Democr.227.—Ep. word, used in lyr. by S.*El.*167, E.*IT*1091 (dub. l.). (Prob. from εἶμι *ibo*.)

**Οἰτόσυρος,** ὁ, Scythian name of Apollo, Hdt.4.59 codd.: Γοιτόσυρος Hsch.

**οἰφεῖ** or **οἰφί,** τό, an Egypt. measure, = 4 χοίνικες, Hsch. (οἶφιν

cod.); = Hebr. *ephah*, Lxx *Le.*5.11, al.—Cf. **οἶφνος**· τετραχοίνικον μέτρον, Theognost.*Can.*18; also ἶφι (B).

*** οἴφω**, Dor. = ὀχεύω I, but only of human beings, τὰν Χελιδονίδα Plu.*Pyrrh.*28, cf. *IG*12(3).536 (Thera, vii B.C.), *Leg.Gort.*2.3; οἰφεῖ, as if from οἰφέω, in prov. ἄριστα χωλὸς οἰ., Mimn.15 Diehl, *Com. Adesp.*36, Diogenian.2.2:—hence ***οἰφόλης**, and fem. **οἰφόλις**, *lewd*, *IG*12(5).97 (Naxos), Hsch., Eust.1597.29.

**Οἰχᾰλία**, Ion. -ίη, ἡ, name of several cities, one in Thessaly, Il.2.730; another in Euboea, S.*Tr.*354, cf. Str.9.5.17:—Adj. **Οἰχᾰλιεύς**, έως, Ep. ῆος, ὁ, Il.2.596, 730:—also **Οἰχᾰλιώτης**, St.Byz.:—Ep. Adv. -ίηθεν, *from Oechalia*, Il.2.596.

**οἰχ-έομαι**, = οἴχομαι (q.v.). **-ητέον**, (οἴχομαι) *one must go*, Alciphr.3.42.

**οἰχμή**· δούλη. οἱ δὲ **οἰχμᾶν**, Hsch.

**οἰχνέω**, *go, come*, Il.5.790, 15.640 (in Iterat. οἴχνεσκον, -εσκε); of birds, Od.3.322; *walk*, i.e. *live*, ἀνύμφευτος αἰὲν οἰχνῶ S.*El.*165 (lyr.). II. like οἴχομαι, *to be gone*, τηλωπὸς οἰχνεῖ Id.*Aj.*564; θυραῖος οἰ. Id.*El.*313. III. c. acc. pers., *approach*, Pi.*P.*5.86: c. acc. rei, Id.*Fr.*75.5:—in form **οἰχνεύω**, Id.*Fr.*206 (where ἰχνεύων codd. Plu.*Nic.*1). (Akin to sq.)

*** οἴχομαι**, impf. ᾠχόμην (in Hdt. οἰχόμην), the only tenses used by Hom.: fut. -ήσομαι Ar.*V.*51, *Fr.*150, Pl.*Tht.*203d, etc.: pf. οἴχωκα S.*Aj.*896, Id.*Fr.*241 codd. (ᾤχωκε A.*Pers.*13); pf. part. οἰχωκώς, υῖα, ός Hdt.9.98, 8.108; also ᾤχηκα (παρ-) Il.10.252 (v.l.), D.H.11.5, etc.: plpf. οἰχώκεε Hdt.1.189, etc.; ᾠχήκει Plb.8.27.9:—Med., pf. ᾤχημαι, Ion. οἴχημαι Hdt.4.136 (δι-), Plu.*Cam.*14 (παρ-, but in Hp. *de Arte*9, X.*An.*2.4.1, παροιχόμενος is now restored):—Act., imper. οἶχε (but perh. οἴχε(ο) with elision) Plu.*Pyrrh.*28: pres. **οἰχέομαι**, contr. οἰχεῦμαι, dub. l. in *AP*7.273 (Leon.): I. rarely in a general sense, *go* or *come*, without the idea of departure, and without a perfect sense, ἐννῆμαρ μὲν ἀνὰ στρατὸν ᾤχετο κῆλα θεοῖο Il.1.53, cf. 5.495; more freq. *go, go away, go off*, Il.1.380, 13.38, 23.564, Od.17.104, al.: but usu. οἴχεται in pf. sense, *he has gone, departed*, and ᾤχετο in plpf. sense, *he had gone*, ἤδη..οἴχεται Il.15.223, cf. 14.311; ἐπεὶ οἴχεο νηῒ Πύλονδε Od.16.24, etc.; οἱ πρέσβεις οἱ μετὰ Πλειστίου οἰχόμενοι *IG*1².57.51; τῶν οἰ. Ἑλλάδ' ἐς αἶαν A.*Pers.*1 (anap.); τὸν κήρυκα τὸν παρὰ τοὺς βροτοὺς οἰ. Ar.*Av.*1270: freq. c. part., εἴ πέρ κεν Ἄρης ..οἴχηται φεύγων shall be fled *and gone*, Od.8.356; ᾤχετ' ἀποπτάμενος he had taken flight *and gone*, Il.2.71; ὥς μ' ὄφελ'..οἴχεσθαι προφέρουσα ..θύελλα 6.346, cf. Od.20.64; so οἴχεται πλέων Hdt.4.145; οἴχεται ἀπολιπών *he has gone and* left.., ib.155; so in Att., οἴχεται θανών (v. infr. II); ἣν δηώσαντες οἴχωνται Foed.ap.Th.5.47; οἰ. φέρων Ar.*Lys.*976, etc.; πρεσβεύων ᾤχετο X.*Cyr.*5.1.3; ᾤχετ' εὐθέως ἀπιών D.18.65, cf. Pl.*Smp.*223b, etc.: with an Adj., οἴχεται φροῦδος *he's clean gone*, Ar.*Ach.*210: rarely in the reverse usage, οἰχόμενοι κόμισαν δέπας Il.23.699, cf. 22.223: c. acc. cogn., οἴχεσθαι ὁδόν Od.4.393.—The part. **οἰχόμενος** in Hom. sts. means *absent, away*, Ὀδυσσῆος πόθος αἴνυται οἰχομένοιο Od.14.144; δὴν οἰ. ib.376. II. Special usages: 1. of persons, euphem. for θνήσκω, *to have departed, be gone hence*, εἰς Ἀΐδαο Il.22.213; ψυχὴ κατὰ χθονὸς ᾤχετο 23.101; οἰ. θανών S.*Ph.*414, cf. E.*Hel.*134, etc.; [τὸ γένος] οἰ. πὰν πρόρριζον And.1.146; οἰχήσομαι ἀπιὼν εἰς μακάρων δή τινας εὐδαιμονίας Pl.*Phd.*115d; part. οἰχόμενος for θανών, *departed, dead*, A.*Pers.*546 (anap.), S.*El.*146 (lyr.), etc. b. *to be undone, ruined*, opp. σῴζομαι, ἢ σεσώσμεθα.. ἢ οἰχόμεσθ' ἅμα Id.*Tr.*85, cf. *Aj.*1128; τὸ μὲν ἐπ' ἐμοὶ οἴχομαι, τὸ δ' ἐπὶ σοὶ σέσωσμαι X.*Cyr.*5.4.11; so οἴχωκα or ᾤχωκα *to be gone, undone, ruined*, A.*Pers.*13 (anap.), S.*Aj.*896, etc.; so οἰχομένας πόλεως E.*Tr.*596 (lyr.), cf. *Heracl.*14; τοῦ..διαλυθεῖσαν οἴχεσθαι πολιτείαν Pl.*Lg.*945c. 2. of things, *to be gone, lost, vanished*, πῇ δή τοι μένος οἴχεται; whither is thy spirit *gone*? Il.5.472, cf. 13.220, 24.201; αἰτία οἴχεται *is absent*, Gal.18(2).48; δίψης οἰχομένης Id.15.564, cf. Aret.*CD*.4.

**οἰχῶρος**· οἰκουρός, Hsch.

**οἴω**, Ep. ὀΐω, Lacon. **οἰῶ**, v. οἴομαι.

**ὀΐω**, late Aeol. for ἀΐω, *hear*, *Epigr.Gr.*989.8 (Balbilla).

**οἰων-ίζομαι**, impf. (without augm.) X.*HG*1.4.12, 5.4.17: fut. -ιοῦμαι Lxx *Le.*19.26: aor. opt. οἰωνίσαιτο D.25.80; part. -άμενος Arist.*Pol.*1304ᵃ1:—*take omens from the flight and cries of birds*, οὐδὲν ἄλλο ἔτι -όμενοι X.*Cyr.*1.6.1, cf. Plu.*Rom.*9. II. generally, *divine from omens*, c. acc. et inf., X.*HG* ll. cc., Lxx *Ge.*44.5. 2. c. acc., *regard as an omen*, οἰ. τι σύμπτωμα Arist. l.c., cf. Epin.2.3, Nic. Dam.66.13 J., D.S.8.32, 17.49, Plu.2.825b; ὃν οἰωνίσαιτ' ἄν τις μᾶλλον ἰδὼν ἢ προσειπεῖν βούλοιτο whom one would rather *shun as an ill omen* if one saw him, than speak to, D. l.c., cf. Thphr.*HP* 8.6.2, Str.13.1.42. **-ισις**, εως, ἡ, *appeal to augury*, J.*AJ*18.6.9. **-ισμα**, ατος, τό, *omen from the flight* or *cries of birds*, οἰωνίσματ' οἰωνῶν μαθών E.*Ph.*839, cf. Lxx 1 *Ki.*15.23, *Je.*14.14 (pl.), Hdn.1.14.2, D.C.37.24; οἰ. τῆς ὑγιείας, = *Salutis augurium*, Id.51.20; a *portent, monster*, Gal.2.623. **-ισμός**, ὁ, = foreg., Lxx *Ge.*44.5, al., Plu. *Num.*14. **-ιστήριον**, τό, *place for watching the flight of birds*, D.H.1.86. II. *omen* or *token*, X.*Ap.*12. **-ιστής**, οῦ, ὁ, *one who foretells from the flight and cries of birds*, Il.2.858, 17.218, Hes.*Sc.*185; θεοπρόπος οἰ. Il.13.70: in late Prose, Gal.9.833; = Lat. *augur*, D.H.10.57, D.C.37.27, al. **-ιστικός**, ή, όν, *of* or *for an omen*, ὁ πταρμὸς σημεῖον οἰ. Arist.*HA*492ᵇ7, cf. Gal.15.441: ἡ -κή (sc. τέχνη) *augury*, Pl.*Phdr.*244d, Plu.2.975a.

**οἰωνό-βρωτος**, ον, *to be eaten of birds*, Phld.*Mort.*33, Str.15.3.20 (v.l. -βοτος), Lxx 2 *Ma.*9.15, 3 *Ma.*6.34, Hsch., Suid. **-θέτης**, ου, ὁ, *interpreter of auguries*, S.*OT*484 (lyr.). **-θροος**, ον, *of the cry of birds*, οἰ. γόος *the* wailing *cry of birds*, A.*Ag.*56 (anap.). **-κτόνος**, ον, *killing birds*, χειμών ib.563. **-μαντεία**, ἡ, *augury*, Suid. **-μαντικός**, ή, όν, *of* or *for an augur*, ἐπιστήμη D.H.3.70. **-μαντις**, εως, ὁ and ἡ, *one who takes omens from the flight and cries of birds*, E.*Ph.*767; = Lat. *augur*, D.H.3.69, 72. **-μικτος**, ον, *half-bird-shaped*, μοῖρα Lyc.595. **-πολέω**, *practise augury*, Choerob.*in Theod.*2 p.50 H. **-πολία**, ἡ, = οἰωνομαντεία, Suid. s.v. Πόλλης. **-πόλος**, ὁ, *one busied with the flight and cries of birds, an augur*, Il.1.69, 6.76, A.*Supp.*57 (lyr.); = Lat. *augur*, D.H.2.64, 3.69: as Adj., -πόλον γέρας Pi.*Pae.*4.30.

**οἰωνός**, ὁ, *a large bird, bird of prey*, οἰωνοί, φῆναι ἢ αἰγυπιοὶ γαμψώνυχες Od.16.216; of the eagle, Κρονίωνι.. φίλτατος οἰωνῶν Il.24.293; called οἰωνῶν βασιλεύς by A.*Ag.*114 (lyr.), Pi.*O.*13.21, cf. Ar. *Av.*515; ἀρχὸς οἰ. Pi.*P.*1.14; mentioned as devouring carcasses, Il.1.5, 22.335, cf. S.*Ant.*205, 698, *Aj.*830; οἰωνοὶ ὠμησταί Il.11.453; θῆρές τ' οἰωνοί τε Emp.21.11, 130.2; ὑπ' οἰωνῶν ταφέντα, of corpses devoured by carrion birds, A.*Th.*1025, cf. S.*Ant.*29; as an image of swiftness, οἰωνοῖς ἅμ' ἕπονται Hes.*Th.*268. 2. generally, *birds*, opp. beasts, S.*Fr.*941.11; so in οἰωνοκτόνος. II. *a bird of omen* or *augury*, Il.12.237, Od.15.532, Hes.*Op.*801; τοὺς ἄνωθεν φρονιμωτάτους οἰωνούς S.*El.*1059 (lyr.); οὔτ' ἀπ' οἰωνῶν.., οὔτ' ἐκ θεῶν του γνωτόν Id.*OT*395, cf. 398; οἰ. αἴσιοι X.*Cyr.*3.3.22, cf. Il.12.237, Plu.2.282d: of augurs, καθέζεσθαι ἐπ' οἰωνῶν, ἐπ' οἰωνοῖς καθῆσθαι, Id.*Rom.*22, *Caes.*47; οἱ ἐπ' οἰωνοῖς ἱερεῖς the *augurs*, Id.*Ant.*5. III. *omen, token, presage*, drawn from these birds, Il.2.859, al., cf. E.*Hipp.*873; εἷς οἰ. ἄριστος ἀμύνεσθαι περὶ πάτρης the one best *omen* is to fight for fatherland, Il.12.243; οἰ. ἀγαθοί good *omens*, Hes.*Fr.*134.11; δέκομαι τὸν οἰ. I accept the *omen*, hail it as auspicious, Hdt.9.91; οὗτος οἰ. μέγας E.*Or.*788; δέδοικα..τὸν οἰ. Ar.*Eq.*28; τοῦ ἔκπλου οἰ. ἐδόκει εἶναι Th.6.27; οἰωνὸν θέσθαι or τίθεσθαι take as an *omen*, E.*Ph.*858, Pl.*Alc.*2.151b; εἰς οἰ. τίθεσθαι χρηστόν Plu.*Luc.*36; πρὸς οἰωνοῦ τ. Ath.1.13e; οἰωνόν τινα ποιεῖσθαι Pl.*Lg.*702c; δι' οἰωνοῦ λαμβάνειν, πρὸς οἰωνοῦ λαβεῖν, D.H.2.67, 3.13; οἰωνοῦ χάριν Pl.*Mx.*249b. IV. as Adj., or in apposition, οἰωνὸς θεά the *bird* goddess, Lyc.721. [First syll. short in S.*El.*1059 (lyr.).]

**οἰωνοσκοπ-εῖον**, τό, *place where auguries are taken*, Paus.9.16.1. **-έω**, *take auguries*, E.*Ba.*347; τισι Id.*Ph.*956:—Med., J.*AJ*18.5.3. **-ητικός**, ή, όν, = οἰωνοσκοπικός: -κή, ἡ, Eust.961.43. **-ία**, ἡ, *augury*, D.H.3.47. **-ικός**, ή, όν, *of* or *for augury*, Ptol.*Tetr.*156, Man.4.212; ἡ οἰ. τέχνη D.H.3.70. **-ος**, ὁ, = οἰωνιστής, E.*Supp.*500, *IG*12(8).528 (Thasos), *Epigr.Gr.*391 (Trajanopolis); = Lat. *augur*, D.H.3.70, etc.

**οἰωνοτροφεύς**, έως, *rearing birds*, epith. of a tree in Lyr. in *Philol.*80.333.

**οἰῶντα**· μονάζοντα, Hsch. **οἴως**, Adv., v. οἶος v. 1. **οἰωτός**· χιτὼν ἀπὸ ἐρίων, Id.

*** ὄκᾰ**, Dor. for ὅτε, Ar.*Lys.*1251, *SIG*1 (Abu Simbel, vi B.C.), 241.145 (Delph.), *Berl.Sitzb.*1927.158 (Cyrene), Theoc.1.66; ἔστ' ὄκα· ἐνίοτε παρὰ Ταραντίνοις, Hsch.:—also **ὄκκᾰ** (q.v.).

**ὄκᾳ**, Aeol. Adv., = ὅπῃ, *BpW*1892.514 (Neandreia, dub.).

*** ὀκέλλω**, = κέλλω, Ar.*Ach.*1159: impf. ὤκελλον Hdt.8.84: aor. ὤκειλα Th.4.11: 1. trans. of seamen, *run* [a ship] *aground* or *on shore*, τὰς νέας Hdt. l.c., Th. l.c.; of a wave, E.*IT*1379. 2. πλόον ὀ. *steer* one's course, Nic.*Th.*295: metaph., στίβον ὀ. ib.321. II. intr. of the ship, *run aground*, Th.2.91, X.*An.*7.5.12: metaph., Ar. l.c.; ἄλγημα..ἐς γλουτὸν ἢ ὀσφὺν ὀκέλλει Aret.*SD*2.12, cf. *CA*2.7.—Prose writers use ὀκέλλω, never κέλλω (q.v.).

**ὄκη**, Ion. for ὅπη.

**ὀκιμβάζω**, = κιμβάζω, σκιμβάζω, Hsch., Phot.

**ὄκκᾰ**, Dor. Adv., = ὄκα, ὅτε, Alcm.94, Cerc.7.11, Epigr. in *Berl. Sitzb.*1894.908. (From *ὀδ-κᾰ, cf. Lesb. ὄττι from *ὀδ-τι, etc.)

*** ὄκκᾱ**, Dor. for ὅταν, Epich.165, al., Sophr.46, Ar.*Ach.*762 (Megar.), *IG*5(1).962.26 (Lacon.), 12(1).694.17 (Rhodes, iii B.C.), Archyt.*Fr.*1, Theoc.1.87, 4.21. [ὄκκᾱ Epich.165, Theoc.8.68, 11.22 (ὄκκ' Ar. l.c., ὄκχ' Epich.29, etc., v. κᾱ): ὄκκᾰ Theoc.4.21, *AP*6.353.4, by confusion with foreg.]

*** ὄκκαβος**, ὁ, *bracelet, armlet*, *EM*383.21, Hsch.

**ὄκκον**· ὀφθαλμόν, Id.:—hence **ὄκταλλος** (Boeot.), ὁ, *eye*, Hdn.Gr.2.559, restored in Corinn.*Supp.*2.89.—Cf. ὄπτιλλος. (Derived by various suffixes from root *oqᵘ*- 'see' in ὄψομαι, ὄσσε, ὄσσομαι, ὀφθαλμός, Lat. *oculus*.) **ὀκκῦλαι**· τὸ ὀκλάσαι, καὶ ἐπὶ τῶν πτερ(ν)ῶν καθέζεσθαι, Hsch.

**ὀκλᾰδ-ία**, ἡ, (ὀκλάζω) = ὄκλασις, Suid., perh. to be read in Cael. Aur.*TP*5.133. **-ίας**, ου, ὁ, *folding-chair, camp-stool*, *IG*1².282.119, Ar.*Eq.*1384, 1386, Luc.*Lex.*6; δίφρος ὀ. Paus.1.27.1, Heraclid.Pont. ap.Ath.12.512c. **-ιστί**, Adv., = sq., ὀ. πηδᾶν, of a frog *hopping*, Babr.25.7 (written ὀκλαστὶ in Suid.):—also -ις, Hdn.Gr.1.512. **-όν**, Adv. *with bent hams, in crouching, cowering posture*, A.R.3.122, Nonn.*D.*1.358, al.; cf. ὀκλάξ.

*** ὀκλ-άζω**, fut. -άσω Ph. (v. infr. 2): aor. ὤκλασα S.*OC*196 (lyr.), Plu.2.320d:—Med., Ep. aor. opt. ὀκλάσσαιντο Euph.17:—*crouch down with bent hams, squat* (in Hom. only μετοκλάζω), of a Persian dance, ὤκλαζε καὶ ἐξανίστατο X.*An.*6.1.10 (cf. ὄκλασμα); διπλοῦς ὀκλάζων S.*Ichn.*90; ἐς γόνυ ὀκλάσας δέχεται τῇ σαρίσσῃ τὴν ἐπέλασιν, of a soldier waiting an attack, Luc.*DMort.*27.4, cf. *Philops.*18; *sink down*, of a weary traveller, S. l.c.; of oxen, Mosch.2.99; of horses that *crouch down* to let their rider mount, Plu.2.139b (but of horses that *stumble* and throw their rider, Procop.*Vand.*2.21, al.); of the wolf *crouching down* to let the Twins suck, Plu.2.320d; θρόνος..ὀκλάζων

*folding-seat*, D.Chr.1.78 : c. acc., ὀ. τὰ ὀπίσθια, τοὺς προσθίους, *bend* their *hind-* or *fore-legs*, X.*Eq.*11.3, Ael.*NA*7.4 :—Med., Euph. l.c. **2.** metaph., *sink, slacken, abate*, ἀπειρίᾳ σοφιστικῶν παλαισμάτων ὀκλάσομεν Ph.1.199 ; τόνος ὀκλάζων Gal.11.172 ; ποδῶν δέ οἱ ὤκλασεν ὁρμή Musae.325 ; of the wind, τῆς φορᾶς Hld.5.23, cf. Adam.*Vent.*37 ; ὤκλαζε αὐτοῖς ὁ θυμός ib.7 ; κραδίης ὤκλασεν ὄγκος *AP*5.250(Iren.). **II.** trans., *abate*, ὀκλάσας τὸν πόθον Hld.1.26. **-άξ**, Adv., = ὀκλαδόν, Hp.*Haem.*4 ; ὀ. καθῆσθαι *squat down*, Pherecr.75, cf. A.R.3.1308, Arat.517 (f.l. for ὀκλάς), Sor.1.61, Gal. *UP*3.15, Luc.*Lex.*11. **-άς**, άδος, ἡ, *the bent hams*, Arat.517 (as read by Hipparchus). **-ᾰσις**, εως, ἡ, *crouching with bent hams, squatting*, Hp.*Art.*82, Luc.*Salt.*41. **-ασμα**, ατος, τό, a Persian dance in which the dancer *squatted* from time to time, Ar.*Fr.*344[b].

**ὀκνάδραστον**· πᾶν πρᾶγμα ἄγνωμον, Hsch. (οἰκν- cod., sed post ὀκνείω).

**ὀκν-ᾰλέος**, α, ον, poet. for ὀκνηρός, Nonn.*D.*18.207. Adv. **-έως** Musae.120. ❀ **-έω**, Ep. ὀκνείω Il.5.255 : impf. ὤκνεον 20.155 : fut. -ήσω Isoc.6.72 : aor. ὤκνησα D.18.103, etc. : (ὄκνος) :—*shrink from* doing, *scruple, hesitate* to do a thing, c. inf., ὀκνείω ἵππων ἐπιβαινέμεν Il.5.255 ; ἀρχέμεναι πολέμοιο ὤκνεον 20.155.—In Att. mostly with collat. sense of the feeling which causes the hesitation, and so, **1.** of shame or fear (in a moral sense), ὀκνῶ προδότης καλεῖσθαι I *shrink from* being called, *fear* to be called, S.*Ph.*93, cf. Th.5.61, Lys.*Fr.* 23 ; οἷα ἐγὼ ὀκνῶ πρὸς ὑμᾶς ὀνομάσαι *shrink from* naming, *hesitate* to name, D.2.19, cf. Pl.*Grg.*462e ; τοσαῦθ' ὅσ' ὀκνήσαιμ' ἂν.. εἰπεῖν D.18.103, cf. 24.7, etc. **2.** of pity, σὰς ὀκνῶ θρᾶξαι φρένας A.*Pr.*628, cf. S.*El.*1271. **3.** most commonly of cowardice or indolence, μεμηνότ' ἄνδρα.. ὀκνεῖς ἰδεῖν Id.*Aj.*81, cf. Th.1.120, etc.—The Homeric constr. c. inf. continued most common (v. supr.): rarely c. acc., πῶς τὸ μητρὸς λέκτρον οὐκ ὀκνεῖν με δεῖ; S.*OT*976 ; ὃν μήτ' ὀκνεῖτε Id.*OC*731, cf. X.*Cyr.*2.2.21 ; ἂν ὀκνῇς τὸ μανθάνειν Philem.213.1 ; also ὀ. περί τινος X.*Cyr.*4.5.20 ; ὀ. μή.. Pl.*Phdr.*257c, X.*An.*2.3.9, D.1.18. **II.** freq. also abs., *shrink, hesitate, hang back*, Hdt.7.50, S.*El.*22, 320, Antipho Soph.55, Luc.*Prom.*18, etc. ; of soldiers, Arist.*Pol.*1297[b] 11. **-ηρεύω**, trans., *fill with reluctance*, Al.*Nu.*32.9. **-ηρία**, ἡ, = ὄκνος, Lxx *Ec.*10.18, *PMasp.*158.15 (vi A.D.), *Gloss.* **-ηρός**, ά, όν, *shrinking, timid*, ἐλπίδες -ότεραι Pi.*N.*11.22 ; ἀσθενέας καὶ ὀ. Hp.*Acut.*28 ; -ότερος ἐς τὴν πρᾶξιν Antipho 2.3.5 ; ἐς τὰ πολεμικὰ -ότεροι Th.4.55, cf. 1.142 ; esp. from fear, opp. τολμηρός, D.25.24 ; τὸ θῆλυ -ότερον Arist.*HA*608[b]13. Adv. **-ρῶς** *reluctantly*, X.*An.*7.1.7 ; ὀ. διακεῖσθαι D.10.28 : Comp. -ότερον X.*Cyr.*1.4.6. **2.** *idle, sluggish*, Hierocl.*Facet.*211, al. **II.** of things, *causing fear, vexatious, troublesome*, ἡμῖν μὲν.. ταῦτ' ὀκνηρά S.*OT*834. **-ησις**, εως, ἡ, *reluctance*, Procop.*Vand.*1.22, al. **-ητέον**, *one must shrink, hesitate*, Pl.*Lg.*891d, Arist.*SE*175[b]38, etc. ❀ **-ος**, ὁ, *shrinking, hesitation*, οὔτε τί με δέος ἴσχει ἀκήριον οὔτε τις ὄ. Il.5.817 (answering to κάματος in 811), cf. 13.224 ; οὔτ' ὄκνῳ εἴκων οὔτ' ἀφραδίῃσι νόοιο 10.122, cf. A.*Th.*54, S.*Ant.*243 ; ὄ. τις καὶ μέλλησις Th.7.49 ; ἀμαθία μὲν θράσος, λογισμὸς δὲ ὄ. φέρει Id.2.40, etc. ; τὸν μὲν ὄ. ψόγον, τὸν δὲ πόνον ἔπαινον ἡγουμένη Isoc.1.7 : hence, **2.** simply, *alarm, fear*, A.*Ag.*1009 (lyr.), S.*Ph.*225 : c. gen., τοῦ μάλιστ' ὄ. σ' ἔχει Id.*OC*652 : in pl., ἀναβολαὶ καὶ ὄκνοι Pl.*Lg.*768e, cf. D.18.246 :—Constr. : c. gen., τοῦ πόνου γὰρ οὐκ ὄ. [ἐστί] I *grudge* not labour, S.*Ph.*887, cf. *OC* l.c. : c. inf., παρέσχεν ὄ. μὴ ἐλθεῖν made them *hesitate* to.., Th.3.39 ; ὄ. ἦν ἀνίστασθαι X.*An.*4.4.11 ; ὄ. πρός τι Pl.*Lg.*665d. **II.** Ὄκνος personified, as title of picture by Polygnotus, Paus.10.29.2, Plin.*HN*35.137, cf. D.S.1.97. **III.** ὄ. χαλκοῦς, a seat used by women in Bithynia, Suid. **IV.** = ἀστερίας II. 1, Arist.*HA*617[a]5, Ael.*NA*5.36, Ant.Lib.7.6. **-ώδης**, ες, = ὀκνηρός, πρός τι Dionys.*Av.*1.6.

**ὀκοδαπός, ὀκόθεν, ὀκοῖος, ὀκόσος, ὀκότε, ὀκότερος, ὄκου**, Ion. for ὁποδαπός, etc.

**ὀκορνός**, ὁ, = ἀττέλεβος or πάρνοψ, Hsch., Phot., cf. A.*Fr.*256.

**ὀκρῐ-άζω**, *to be rough* or *angry*, S.*Fr.*1075. **-άομαι**, Pass., (ὄκρις) *to be made rough* or *jagged* : metaph., πανθυμαδὸν ὀκριόωντο they *grew furiously angry* with each other, Od.18.33 ; ὠκριωμένος *enraged*, Lyc.545.

❀ **ὀκρίβας** [ῐ], αντος, ὁ, (ὄκρις, βαίνω) *platform* or *tribune* in the Odeum at Athens, on which the actors appeared at the Proagon, Pl.*Smp.* 194b ; but expld. as τὸ λογεῖον ἐφ' οὗ οἱ τραγῳδοὶ ἠγωνίζοντο, Hsch. **2.** = κόθορνος, Philostr.*VA*6.11, *VS*1.9.1 : in pl., Id.*VA*5.9, Them.*Or.* 26.316d, Luc.*Ner.*9. **II.** generally, like κιλλίβας, **1.** *painter's easel*, Poll.7.129. **2.** *raised seat of the chariot-driver*, Hsch., Phot., Suid. **3.** dub. sens., ὑπερθέντων ὀκρ[ίβαντα] *IG*12(8).261 (Thasos). **III.** *ass* or *wild goat*, Anon.ap.Hsch.

**ὀκρίβατον**· σχῆμα ἡνιόχου, Hsch. (i. e. ὀκρίβας· ὄχημα ἡνιόχου, v. foreg.).

**ὀκριο-ειδής**, ές, *rugged, jagged*, Hp.*Art.*36 (Comp.), Aret.*SD*2.13. **-εις**, εσσα, εν, (ὄκρις) *having many points* or *roughnesses, rugged, jagged*, of unhewn stone, χερμάδιον, λίθος, μάρμαρος, Il.4.518, 8.327, 12.380, 16.735 ; χερμάς A.*Th.*300 (lyr.) ; χθών Id.*Pr.*283 (anap.) ; οὔρεα Nic.*Th.*470 ; also βέλος ὀ. Theoc.25.231 : metaph., of a Satyr's head, Nonn.*D.*14.137. (v. ὀκρυόεις sub fin.)

**ὄκρῐς**, ιος, ἡ, *jagged point* or *prominence, any roughness* on an edge or surface, as of a fractured bone, Hp.*Art.*14. **II.** as Adj. ὀκρίς, ῖδος, ὁ, ἡ, = ὀκριόεις, *rugged*, φάραγξ A.*Pr.*1016. (Cf. Umbr. *ocar* (acc. *ocrem*, etc.) 'arx, mons', OLat. *ocris* = *mons confragosus*.)

**ὀκρῠόεις**, εσσα, εν, = κρυόεις, *chilling, horrible*, πολέμου.. ἐπιδημίου ὀκρυόεντος Il.9.64 ; ἐμεῖο κυνὸς κακομηχάνου ὀκρυοέσσης (Helen loq.) 6.344 ; ὀ. φόβος A.R.2.607 ; ὀ. βᾶρις, of Charon's boat, *AP*7.67 (Leon.) ; ἀταρπιτὸς ὀ. Parm.(?)20 ; ὀκρυόειν ἔδαφος *Eleg.Alex.Adesp.* 1.7. (Freq. confused with ὀκριόεις : ὀκρυόεις may have arisen from an early mistake in the division of words in Hom. (leg. ἐπιδημίοο κρυόεντος, κακομηχάνοο κ.) ; or ὀκ. may be cogn. with Skt. *áśru*, Lith. *ašara* 'tear', and the Adj. would then mean *tearful*.)

❀ **ὀκτά-βλωμος**, ον, *consisting of eight pieces*, ἄρτον τετράτρυφον ὀκτάβλωμον, an obscure conjunction of epithets, Hes.*Op.*442, cf. Philostr. *Im.*2.26. **-γράμμᾰτον** ὄνομα, *consisting of eight letters*, *PMag. Par.*1.783. **-γωνικός**, ή, όν, *octagonal*, Sch.Papp.ap.Archim.2 p.541 H. **-γωνος**, ον, *eight-cornered*, Gem.2.15, Nicom.*Ar.*2.11, Alex. Trall.8.2 : **-γωνον**, τό, *octagon*, Antipho Soph.13. **-δακτῠλιαῖος**, ον, = sq., ξύλον Heliod.ap.Orib.49.4.71, cf. 49.23.4. **-δάκτῠλος**, ον, *eight fingers long* or *broad*, Clearch.73, *PCair.Zen.*483 (iii B.C.) :—older Att. **ὀκτωδάκτῠλος** Ar.*Lys.*109, *Supp.Epigr.*3.137 iii 11 (iv B.C.), *IG*2[2].1627.123, and so in Ion., Hp.*Steril.*221.

**ὀκτάδιον**, τό, *bird-cage*, Hsch.

❀ **ὀκτά-δραχμος**, ον, *worth eight drachmae*, Epigr.ap.Dioph.5.30. **2.** *privileged to pay only eight drachmae as poll-tax*, *Sammelb.* 7440.6, 32 (ii A.D.). **-εδρικόν** (sc. σχῆμα), τό, *of an octahedron*, Olymp.*in Phd.*p.238 N. **-εδρος**, ον, of a solid figure, *eight-sided*, Gal.5.668 : Subst. **-εδρον**, τό, *octahedron*, Arist.*Cael.*307[a]16, Ti.Locr. 98d, Euc.11 *Def.*26, *Placit.*2.6.5. **-ειδος**, ον, *containing eight ingredients*, φάρμακον v.l. in Paul.Aeg.3.78. **-ετηρίς**, ίδος, ἡ, *cycle of eight years*, used at Athens before Meton's time for bringing the lunar and solar years together, 3 months being intercalated to complete the sum of 2,922 days, Eudox.*Ars* 13.12, Str.7.5.5, Gem.8.27 sqq., *Placit.* 2.32.2. ❀ **-έτης**, ες, *eight years old*, Hp.*Epid.*1.10 ; *of eight years*, χρόνος D.S.17.94 :—fem. **-έτις**, ἡ, *IG*4.620, Pl.*Ep.*361d. **-ετία**, ἡ, = ὀκταετηρίς, Theo Sm.p.173 H., Procl.*Par.Ptol.*285 ; but **ὀκτωετία** in Ptol.*Tetr.*205. **-ήμερος**, ον, *eight days old*, *Ep.Phil.*3.5. **-καιεικοσέτης**, ες, *twenty-eight years old*, *App.Anth.*2.246 (Citium). **-κάτιοι**, Dor. for ὀκτακόσιοι, *IG*5(1).1 *A* 16 (Sparta) ; ℎοκτακ. *Tab.Heracl.*2.79. **-κερκις**, ιδος, ὁ, ἡ, *with eight spokes*, *EM* 621.16.

❀ **ὀκτάκις** [ᾰ], Adv. *eight times*, Luc.*Ind.*4, etc. :—also **ὀκτάκι**, *Epigr. Gr.*356.4 (Hadriani), Iamb.*in Nic.*pp.17, 90 P. ; **ὀκτάκιν**, *IG*5(1).213.19, 25 (Sparta).

**ὀκτάκισ-μύριοι** [ῡ], αι, α, *eighty thousand*, D.S.14.47, Luc.*VH*1.13. **-χίλιοι** [ῑ], αι, α, Dor. **-χήλιοι** *Abh.Berl.Akad.*1925(5).25 (Cyrene) :—*eight thousand*, Hdt.9.28, X.*An.*5.5.4, etc. : also in sg., ἵππος ὀκτακισχιλίη, for ὀκτακισχίλιοι ἱππεῖς, '8,000 horse', Hdt.7.85 ; so ὀ. ἀσπίς Id.5.30. **-χῑλιοστός**, ή, όν, *eight-thousandth*, Theo Sm. p.125 H.

**ὀκτά-κλῖνον**, τό, *dining-room of eight couches*, Arist.*Mir.*830[a] 16. **-κνημος**, ον, (κνήμη II) *eight-spoked*, κύκλα Il.5.723. **-κόσιοι**, αι, α, *eight hundred*, Hdt.2.9, Th.1.55, etc. **-κοσιοστός**, ή, όν, *eight-hundredth*, ἔτος D.C.60.29. ❀ **-κότῠλος**, ον, *holding eight cotylae*, ψυκτήρ Ath.5.180a. **-κωλος**, ον, *of eight lines*, στροφή Sch. Ar.*Ach.*565, Heph.*Poëm.*4.

**ὄκταλλος**, ὁ, v. ὄκκον.

**ὀκτά-λοβος** [ᾰ], ον, *possessing eight lobes*, πνεύμων Ar.Byz.*Epit.*77.14. **-λοχία**, ἡ, *force of eight* λόχοι, Ascl.*Tact.*2.9. **-μερής**, ές, *of* or *in eight parts*, D.L.7.110. **-μετρος**, ον, *of eight measures* : **-μετρον**, τό, *octameter*, Sch.Heph.p.132 C. **-μηνιαῖος**, α, ον, *of eight months*, ἀνοχαί D.S.14.38 ; χρόνος *POxy.*1627.9 (iv A.D.) ; *eight months old*, Ar. Byz.*Epit.*77.18. ❀ **-μηνος**, ον, *eight months old, in the eighth month*, Hp.*Alim.*42, X.*Cyn.*7.6, Arist.*HA*545[a]29, etc. ; *of eight months' duration*, *IG*11(2).199*A* 13 (Delos, iii B.C.) ; ὀκτάμηνος as fem., X. l.c., Hp.*Epid.*2.3.17 ; (sc. περίοδος) *PCair.Zen.*327.77 (iii B.C.) ; but ὀκτάμηναι Arist.*HA*583[b]33. **-ξεστος**, ον, *containing eight sextarii*, *POxy.*1896.19 (vi A.D.). ❀ **-ούγκιον**, τό, = Lat. *bes*, *Gloss.* **-πάλαιστος** [πᾰ], ον, *eight palms wide* or *long*, ἀσπίς Ael.*Tact.*12 : so **ὀκτωπάλαιστος**, Ascl.*Tact.*5.1. **-πεδος**, ον, Dor. for ὀκτάπους, *Tab. Heracl.*2.45, al. (in form ℎοκτ-). **-πηχυς**, υ, *eight cubits long*, δοκός *Inscr.Délos* 290.174 (iii B.C.), Callix.2, cf. Lxx 3*Ki.*7.47(10), Plb.5.89.6, Str.3.5.5. **-πλᾰσιάζω**, *multiply by eight*, Gem.8.38, 47 (Pass.). **-πλάσιος** [πλᾰ], α, ον, *eightfold*, Ar.*Eq.*70, Pl.*Ti.* 35c. **-πλεθρος**, ον, *eight plethra long* or *large*, D.H.4.61. **-πλόος**, ον, contr. **-πλοῦς**, οῦν, *eightfold*, *SIG*672.18 (Delph., ii B.C.) : fem. -πλῆ Gal.13.717. **-πόδης**, ου, ὁ, *eight feet long*, Hes.*Op.*425. **II.** *eight-footed*, καρκίνος Nic.*Th.*605. **-πόδιον**, τό, gloss on πουλύποδες, Sch.Opp.*H.*1.306 (pl.). **-πους**, ὁ, ἡ, πουν, τό, gen. ποδος, *eight-footed*, καρκίνοι Batr.298 ; πάγουρος *AP*6.196 (Stat.Flacc.). **II.** Subst., ὀκτάπους, ὁ, *Octopus vulgaris*, Alex.Trall.7.1. **2.** Scythian name for one who possessed two oxen and a cart, Luc.*Scyth.* 1. **-ραβδος**, ον, *with eight spokes*, *EM*621.16.

❀ **ὀκτ-άρουρος** [ᾰ], ὁ, *tenant of eight* ἄρουραι, *PFlor.*18.12 (ii A.D.).

**ὀκτά-ρριζος**, ον, *with eight roots*, ὀκτάρριζα μετώπων φράγματα, of a stag's horns, *with eight points*, *AP*6.110 (Leon. or Mnasalc.). **-ρρῡμος**, ον, of chariots, *with eight poles*, or rather, *so constructed as to be drawn by eight pairs* of horses or oxen, X.*Cyr.*6.1.52.

❀ **ὀκτάς**, άδος, ἡ, *the number eight*, Arist.*Metaph.*1082[a]30. **II.** *body of eight men*, Nic.Dam.60 J.

**ὀκτά-σημος** [ᾰ], ον, in Prosody, *of eight times*, Sch.A.*Th.*103. Adv. **-μως** *in the eight-time measure*, of the dochmius (⏑ – – ⏑ –), Sch.A.*Th.* 128. **-σκελής**, ές, *eight-legged*, ἐπίδεσμος Heliod.ap.Orib.48.21.1, cf. Gal.18(1).774. **-σοῦφος**, ον, *containing eight* σοῦφα (Egypt. measure of capacity), *Sammelb.*1958 (iii A.D.).

**ὀκτασσός**, ἡ, όν, *eightfold*, *POxy.*1638.30 (iii A.D.).

**ὀκτα-στάδιος** [στᾰ], ον, *eight stadia long*, Plb.34.12.4. **-στῦλος**, ον, *with eight columns in front*, of temples, Vitr.3.2.7. **-σφαιρος**, ἡ, *system of eight spheres*, Phlp. *in Ph.*599.10, al.: as neut., Simp. *in Cael.*435.4. **-τευχος** (sc. βίβλος), ἡ, the volume *containing the first eight books of the Old Testament*, Phot.*Bibl.*pp.7,128 B.: title of work by Ostanes, Ph.Bybl.ap.Eus.*PE*1.10. **-τομος**, ον, *divided into eight tomes*, βίβλος Alex.Trall.7.9. **-τονος**, ον, *eight-stretched*, ἕλικες ὀ. *the eight arms* of the *octopus*, *AP*9.14 (Antiphil.). **-τροπος**, ἡ, *the first eight* τόποι *of the* δωδεκάτροπος, Vett.Val.334.20. **-τροχος**, ον, *with eight wheels*, Ath.Mech.18.16. **-τῦπος**, ἡ, = ὀκτάτροπος (q.v.), *Cat.Cod.Astr.*8(3).117.21 (nisi leg. ὀκτάτροπος); cf. *octotropos*, [Manil.]2.969. **-φορος**, Lat. *octaphorus*, v. ὀκτώφορος. ⊛ **-χορδος**, ον, *with eight strings* or *notes*, ἐμμέλεια Plu.2.1029c; συστήματα Aristox.*Harm.*p.96 M., Theo Sm.p.49 H.: **-χορδον**, τό, *octachord*, Nicom.*Harm.*11, *POxy.*667.24. **-χρονος**, ον, *composed of eight time-units*, Procl. *in Prm.*p.990 S. **-χῶς**, Adv. *in eight ways*, *EM*461.15, Simp. *in Cat.*436.19.

**ὀκτήρης** (sc. ναῦς), ἡ, *warship with eight rowers to each oar*, Plb.16.3.2, Plu.*Ant.*61.

⊛ **ὀκτώ**, Boeot. **ὀκτό** *IG*7.3193.6,9 (iii B.C.), Heraclean **ℎοκτώ** *Tab. Heracl.*1.34, Elean **ὀπτώ** *Schwyzer*419.4 (v/iv B.C.): οἱ, αἱ, τά:—indecl., *eight*, Il.2.313, etc.: prov. πάντα ὀ., in reference to the eight spheres, Timoth.ap.Theon.Sm.p.105 H. (Cf. Skt. *aṣṭā́*, *aṣṭáu*, Lat. *octo*, Goth. *ahtau*, etc.)

**ὀκτώ-βιβλος**, ἡ, *a work in eight volumes*, Gal.7.311. ⊛ **-βολοι**, οἱ, *eight obols*, *IG*5(1).1433 (Messene); also ἁ ὀκτώβολος εἰσφορά *tax of eight obols per mina*, ib.1432.3 (i A.D.). **-δάκτῦλος**, ον, v. ὀκταδ-. **-ετία**, ἡ, v. ὀκταετία. **-καίδεκα**, οἱ, αἱ, τά, indecl., *eighteen*, Hdt.2.111, etc.

**ὀκτωκαιδεκά-δραχμος**, ον, *at the price of eighteen drachmae*, πωλεῖν τὰς κριθὰς -μους D.42.20. **-ετηρίς**, ίδος, ἡ, *period of eighteen years*, Ptol.*Alm.*4.3, al. ⊛ **-έτης**, ες, later form of ὀκτωκαιδεκέτης, Luc. *DMort.*27.7, etc.:—fem. **-έτις**, ιδος, Id.*Tox.*24, *DMeretr.*8.2. **-κις**, *eighteen times*, *Theol.Ar.*64:—also **-κι**, Ptol.*Alm.*9.3. **-πεδος**, ον, *eighteen feet long*, ξύλα *IG*$4^2$(1).109 ii 138 (Epid., iii B.C.). **-πηχυς**, υ, *eighteen cubits long*, ξύλον ib.11(2).203 *B* 100 (Delos, iii B.C.); δοκοί D.S.17.105. **-πλάσιος** [πλᾰ], ον, *eighteen-fold*, Aristarch.Sam.7, *Placit.*2.31.2, Plu.2.925c, Procl.*Hyp.*4.107:—also **-πλᾰσίων**, ον, gen. ονος, Archim.*Aren.*1.9.

**ὀκτωκαιδεκάς**, άδος, ἡ, *the number eighteen*, *Theol.Ar.*39.

**ὀκτωκαιδεκάσημος**, ον, *of eighteen times*, in Prosody, Aristid. Quint.1.14, Anon. in *Musici Scriptores* p.414 von Jan.

**ὀκτωκαιδεκᾰτ-αῖος**, α, ον, *on the eighteenth day*, Hp.*Morb.*2.25. **-ος**, η, ον, *eighteenth*, -δεκάτῃ (sc. ἡμέρᾳ) *on the eighteenth day*, Od.5.279, 24.65; ἔτος Plb.1.56.2, etc.; Boeot. **ὀκτοκηδέκατος** *Schwyzer*485.39 (Thespiae, iii B.C.).

⊛ **ὀκτωκαιδεκέτης**, ες (also **-δεχέτης** *Supp.Epigr.*4.190 (Halic., iv B.C.)), *eighteen years old*, D.40.4, Theoc.15.129:—fem. **-έτις**, ιδος, *AP*7.167.

**ὀκτωκαιεικοσαπλᾰσίων**, ον, gen. ονος, *twenty-eight-fold*, *Placit.*2.20.1.

**ὀκτωκαιεικοσίφθογγος**, ον, *of twenty-eight notes*, Nicom.*Exc.*6.

**ὀκτωκαιεικοστός**, ἡ, όν, *twenty-eighth*, Archim.*Aren.*4.6, al.

**ὀκτωκαιτριακοντάμετρος**, ον, *consisting of thirty-eight* μέτρα, Sch. Ar.*Pax* 153.

**ὀκτωκαιτριακόντεδρον**, τό, *solid figure with thirty-eight faces*, Papp. ap.Archim.2 p.537 H.

**ὀκτώ-μηνος**, ον, = ὀκτάμηνος, *EM*767.34:—also **-μηνιαῖος**, α, ον, Ph.1.29, Sch.Arat.455; *born in the eighth month*, βρέφη Alex.Aphr. *Pr.*2.47. **-πάλαιστος**, v. ὀκταπ-. **-πηχυς**, υ, = ὀκτάπηχυς, Philem.212. **-πους**, ουν, = ὀκτάπους, as Subst., = σκορπίος, -πουν ἀνεγείρεις Cratin.77: acc. pl. [ὀκ]τώπους (dub. sens.) prob. in *PCair. Zen.*510 (iii B.C.). II. *eight feet long*, *IG*$1^2$.313.90; *of eight square feet*, χωρίον Pl.*Men.*82e, 83a. **-στάδιος** [ᾰ], ον, = ὀκταστάδιος, Str. 14.2.4. **-φορος**, ον, *borne by eight*, *octophorus lectica* or *octophorus* alone, a litter *carried by eight*, Cic.*Verr.*5.11.27, *QF*2.8.2; *octăphorus*, Mart.6.84.

**ὀκχέω**, v. ὀχέω. **ὄκχη, ὄκχος**, v. ὄχη, ὄχος. **ὄκως**, Ion. for ὅπως.

***ὄκωχα**, old pf. of ἔχω, whence perh. συν-οχωκότε (q.v.) Il.2.218:—hence **ὀκωχ-εύω**, *hold*, S.*Fr.*327 (κωχεύουσι cod. Hsch. who also has ὀκωχεύειν· ἔχειν, συνέχειν): **-ή**, ἡ, *hold, stay*, *EM*596.50: ⊛ **-ιμος**, ον, *bound, under obligation*, *Riv.Fil.*56.263 (Cyrene).

**ὄλα**· τὰ ἐντὸς τῆς σηπίας στρογγύλα, Hsch.; cf. ὀλός. **ὀλαγμεύειν**· ὀλὰς βάλλειν, Phot. **ὀλαεῖ**· ἐνοχλεῖ, καὶ **ὀλαθεῖ** ὁμοίως, Hsch. **ὀλαί**, v. οὐλαί. **ὀλαιμεύς**· ὁ (τὸ cod.) τὰς ὀλὰς βάλλων, Id. **ὀλαιτοί**· σπερμολόγοι, καὶ **ὀλατοί**, Id., cf. Orus ap.*EM*622.9, Phot. **Ϝόλαμος** (written γόλ-)· διωγμός, Hsch. (cf. οὐλαμός).

**ὀλάργῠρος**, ον, *of solid silver*, Ptol.Euerg.9 J., Callix.2; νόμισμα Ph.2.276.

**ὀλάω**, lisping pronunciation of ὁράω, Ar.*V.*45.

**ὀλβάχιον**, τό, Dinol.13:—also **ὀλβάχνιον, ὄλεχον**, *EM*257.53, 621.20; **ὀλβακήϊα**, Hsch.:—said to be Syracusan for ὀλάχνιον, and expld. as τὸ κανοῦν ἐν ᾧ ἀπετίθεντο τὰς οὐλάς. (β = Ϝ.)

**ὀλβ-ήεις**, εσσα, εν, = ὄλβιος, Man.4.100. **-ία**, ἡ, *bliss*, Phot.

**Ὄλβια**, τά, older form for Ἄλπια, *the Alps*, Posidon.48 J.; **Ὄλπια** in *EM*623.1. II. **Ὀλβία**, ἡ, name of several cities, of which the best known was the Milesian colony in Scythia, *SIG*286.15 (iv B.C.), Str.7.3.17, etc.: its citizens being **Ὀλβιοπολῖται**, Hdt.4.18, *SIG* 286.1: hence Adj. **Ὀλβιοπολῑτικός**, ἡ, όν, ib.218.16.

**ὀλβίζω**, fut. -ιῶ E.*Hel.*228: aor. ὤλβισα S.*Fr.*646.1, etc.:—Pass. (v. infr.):—*make happy*, E.*Ph.*1689, *Hel.* l.c. (lyr.); *deem* or *pronounce happy*, A.*Ag.*928, S.*OT*1529, etc.:—Pass., *to be* or *be deemed happy*, τίς δ' οἶκος..ὠλβίσθη ποτέ; Id.*Fr.*942; οἱ τὰ πρῶτ' ὠλβισμένοι E.*IA* 51; μέγα ὀλβισθεὶς Id.*Tr.*1253 (anap.).

**ὀλβιό-βῐος**, *giving a prosperous life*, epith. of Heracles, *Fouilles de l'Inst. Français d'arch. Orientale* 4(2).72 (Egypt). **-γάστωρ**, ορος, ὁ, ἡ, *whose happiness is in his belly, a belly-god*, Amphis 10. **-δαίμων**, ονος, ὁ, ἡ, *of blessed lot*, Il.3.182. **-δωρος**, ον, *bestowing bliss*, χθών (as v.l. for βιόδωρος) E.*Hipp.*749 (lyr.); μέθυ *AP*11.60.9 (Paul. Sil.). ⊛ **-δώτης**, ου, ὁ, *bestower of bliss*, Orph.*H.*34.2:—fem. **-δῶτις**, ιδος, ib.40.2, etc. **-εργός**, όν, *making happy*, epith. of Dionysus, *AP*9.525.16. **-θῡμος**, ον, *heart-gladdening*, ζωή Orph.*H.*19.21. **-μοιρος**, ον, = ὀλβιοδαίμων, ib.26.6. **-πλουτος**, ον, *blest in wealth*, Philox.3.22.

**ὄλβιος**, ον Tz.*H.*1.600, but usu. α, ον, as Pi.*O.*13.4, E.*Alc.*452 (lyr.), *Or.*1338: (ὄλβος): I. of persons, *happy, blest*, esp. with reference to worldly goods, οἶκον..ἔναιον ὄλβιος ἀφνειόν Od.17.420, cf. Il.24.543 (nowhere else in Il.), etc.; εὐδαίμων τε καὶ ὄ. Hes.*Op.*826; χρήμασι ὄ. Hdt.8.75; μέγα ὄλβιος Id.6.24; Πριάμου τοῦ μέγ' ὀλβίου E.*Hec.*493; τοῖς ὀλβίοις A.*Ag.*941; ὄ. δῶμα Pi.*N.*9.3; τὰν ὀλβίαν Κόρινθον Id.*O.*13.4; also of more than mere outward prosperity, Hdt.1.30–2. 2. generally, *happy, blessed*, ὄλβιον ξάνθαν ἐλάτηρα πώλων Alc.*Supp.*8.14; ὄλβιε Ζεῦ A.*Supp.*526 (lyr.); Διὶ ὀ. εὐχαριστήριον *CIG*2017 (Thrac. Chers.), cf. *JHS*25.56 (Cyzic.); ὄ. ὅστις ἰδών κτλ. Pi.*Fr.*137.1, cf. Emp.132, S.*El.*160 (lyr.), etc.: c. gen., ὄλβιαι ὀρχηθμοῦ *AP*9.189; ὄλβιε καὶ ζωῆς, ὄλβιε καὶ θανάτου *Epigr.Gr.*243.15 (Pergam.). II. of things, used by Hom. (only in Od.) always in neut. pl., θεοὶ δέ τοι ὄ. δοῖεν may they give thee *rich gifts*, Od.8.413; φίλα δῶρα, τά μοι θεοὶ..ὄ. ποιήσειαν may they make them *prosperous*, 13.42 (also as Adv., τοῖσιν θεοὶ ὄ. δοῖεν ζώμεναι *happily*, 7.148); so in Hdt., πάντα μεγάλα..καὶ ὄ. 1.30; εἴπας πολλὰ καὶ ὄ. ib.31; ταῦτα τὰ -ώτατά σφι νενόμισται ib.216. Adv. -ίως S.*OC*1720 (lyr.): irreg. Sup. ὄλβιστος, η, ον, Call.*Lav.Pall.*117, *AP*7.164 (Antip. Sid.), 1 (Alc. Mess.), 12.56 (Mel.), etc.: regul. Comp. and Sup. ὀλβιώτερος, ὀλβιώτατος, Hdt.1.32,30,216.—Poet. word, rare in Att. Prose, as Pl.*Prt.*337d (Sup.), Plu.2.58e, and Com., as Ar.*Ec.*1131.

**ὀλβιότα**, v. ὀλβιοδότης.

**ὀλβιό-τῡφος**, ον, *happy in his own conceit*, said of Archytas, Bion ap.D.L.4.52. **-φρων**, ονος, ὁ, ἡ, *leaning towards the rich*, ποδάγρα Luc.*Trag.*194.

**ὀλβιστήρ**, ῆρος, ὁ, *one who makes prosperous*, Dioscorus in *PLit. Lond.*98 ii 7 (pl.).

**ὀλβο-δότειρα**, ἡ, fem. of sq., E.*Ba.*419 (lyr.), Opp.*C.*1.45. **-δοτήρ**, ῆρος, ὁ, *giver of wealth*, cj. Pierson in Them.*Or.*13.178b. **-δότης**, ου, Dor. **-δότας**, α, ὁ, *giver of bliss* or *wealth*, E.*Ba.*573 (lyr.), *Epic.Alex. Adesp.*9 vi 6 (ὀλβιότα Pap.), *Epigr.Gr.*978.10 (Philae), *IG*$4^2$(1).424,425 (Epid., iii A.D.), Orph.*H.*68.8:—fem. **-δότις**, ιδος, ib.27.9. **-θρέμμων**, ον, gen. ονος, *nursed amid wealth*, Κῆρες Pi.*Fr.*277. ⊛ **-θύλᾰκος** [ῡ], ὁ, *money-bag*, Cerc.10. **-μέλαθρος**, ον, *of a wealthy house*, Man.4.504. **-νομέω** βίον, *live a prosperous life*, ib.581.

⊛ **ὄλβος**, ὁ, *happiness, bliss*, esp. *worldly happiness, weal*, ἀλλ' οὔ μοι τοιοῦτον ἐπέκλωσαν θεοὶ ὄ. Od.3.208, cf. 4.208; Ζεὺς δ' αὐτὸς νέμει ὄ. ἀνθρώποισιν 6.188; ὄλβῳ τε πλούτῳ τε Il.16.596, Od.14.206, cf. Emp. 119: freq. in Lyr., as Pi.*O.*6.72, B.3.92, and Trag., as A.*Pers.*164, 252,709, al.; ὁ πρὶν παλαιὸς ὄ. S.*OT*1282, cf. Plu.*Per.*12: rarely in pl., ἐν Διὸς κήποις ἀροῦσθαι..εὐδαίμονας ὄ. S.*Fr.*320 (lyr.).—Poet. word, used by Hdt.1.32,86, X.*Cyr.*1.5.9, 4.2.44 and 46, Ar.*Av.*421, Hp.*Ep.*3,5, Lxx *Si.*30.15. (Perh. cogn. with Lith. *algà* (I.-E. *olgʷā*) 'wage'.)

⊛ **ὀλβοφόρος**, ον, *bringing bliss* or *wealth*, θεοί E.*IA*596 (anap.).

**ὀλέεσθαι, ὀλέεσκε**, v. ὄλλυμι.

**ὀλεθρ-εία** or **-ία**, ἡ, = sq., Lxx *Es.*8.13 (E 21), *3Ma.*4.2. **-ευσις**, εως, ἡ, *destruction*, ib.*Jo.*17.13. **-εύω**, *slay, destroy*, ib.*Ex.*12.23, al., Vett.Val.123.11. **-ιάω**, *to be on the point of death*, Archig.ap.Aët. 9.40. **-ιος**, ον, E.*Hec.*1084 (lyr.), Pl.*Ep.*334d; but α, ον Hdt.6. 112, Lxx *Wi.*18.15, and freq. in Trag. (v. infr.):—*destructive, deadly*, ὀ. ἦμαρ the day *of destruction*, Il.19.294,409, cf. ἐλεύθερον ἦμαρ, etc.; so μανίη πάγχυ ὀ. Hdt. l.c.; ὀ. μόρος A.*Th.*704; ἔξω κομίζων ὀλεθρίου πηλοῦ πόδα Id.*Ch.*697; κότος ὀ. ib.952 (lyr.); ὀλεθρία νύξ S.*OC*1683 (lyr.), etc.; ψῆφος ὀλεθρία a vote *of death*, A.*Th.*198: in S.*Aj.*799, ἔξοδον..ὀλεθρίαν ἐλπίζει φέρειν seems to be = φέρειν εἰς ὄλεθρον: acc. sg. masc. predicatively used, ἀλλά μ' ἁ..θεὸς ὀλέθριον αἰκίζει *fatally*, ib.402 (lyr.):—rare in Prose, as Pl.*R.*389d, Gal.16.522; νόσοι Phld.*Ir.*p.57 W. (Sup.). Adv. -ίως Eust.132.16. 2. c. gen., γάμοι Πάριδος ὀλέθριοι φίλων *bringing ruin* on his friends, A.*Ag.* 1156 (lyr.). 3. c. dat., as Subst., ψύλλοις ὀλέθριον, name of a fluid, Philum.*Ven.*12.4. II. of persons, *in danger of death*, Hp.*Acut.*58; *lost, undone*, S.*Tr.*878. Adv. -ίως, ἔχειν Gal.16.522, al. 2. *rascally, worthless* (cf. ὄλεθρος II nisi hoc leg.), Luc.*DMort.* 2.1 codd., *Hist.Conscr.*38 codd. **-ιώδης**, ες, gloss on λευγαλέη, Hsch. ⊛ **-ος**, ὁ, *ruin, destruction, death*, αἰπὺς ὄ. Il.11.174, al.; λυγρὸς ὄ. 10.174, al.; ὄ. ἀδευκής Od.4.489; οἴκτιστος ὄ. 23.79; ἵνα ψυχῆς ὤκιστος ὄ. Il.22.325; ὀλέθρου πείρατα, like τέλος θανάτοιο, the consummation *of death*, 6.143; ὄ., opp. γένεσις, Parm.8.21,27; οὐκ εἰς ὄλεθρον; as an imprecation, *plague take thee!* S.*OT*430;

χρημάτων ὀλέθρῳ by *destruction* of property, Th.7.27; εἶναι ἐν ὀλέθρῳ Antipho 1.29; ἐπ' ὀλέθρῳ τῶν χρωμένων E.*Ph.*534; ἐκκλησιάζειν ἐπ' ὀλέθρῳ Ar.*Th.*84; οὐκ ἐπὶ δουλείᾳ κολάζοντες οὐδ' ἐπ' ὀλέθρῳ Pl.*R.*471a: pl., Phld.*Rh.*2.140S. II. *that which causes destruction, pest, plague*, Hes.*Th.*326; contemptuously of persons, γεγονὼς κακῶς καὶ ἐὼν ὄ. Hdt.3.142; ὑπὸ γερόντων ὀ. Ar.*Lys.*325; ὄ. ἄνθρωπος Eup. 376, cf. Men.533.13; ὄ. Μακεδών, of Philip, D.9.31; ὄ. γραμματεύς a *pestilent* scribe, of Aeschines, Id.18.127; τὸν βάσκανον, τὸν δ' ὄ. the cheat, the *pest!* Id.21.209; ἀνθρώπους οὐδ' ἐλευθέρους ἀλλ' ὀ. Id.23. 202; πολλοὶ ὄ. καὶ μεγάλοι Pl.*R.*491b. III. *seduction*, Ἑλένης E. *IA* 1382 (troch.).

**ὀλεθροφόρος**, ον, *destruction-bringing*, Lxx 4*Ma.*8.19.

**ὀλεῖ, ὀλεῖται**, v. ὄλλυμι.

**Ὀλεῖαι**, αἱ, female celebrants in ritual at Orchomenos in Boeotia, Plu.2.299e.

**ὀλείζων**, v. ὀλίγος. **ὄλειρ**· ἔλειος μῦς, Hsch. **ὀλέ-κρανον, -κρανίζω**, v. ὠλ-.

**ὀλέκω**, impf. without augm. ὄλεκον Il.11.150; Iterat. ὀλέκεσκον (v.l. ὀλέεσκον) 19.135:—pres. **ὀλέσκω** Phot., Suid.:—*ruin, destroy, kill*, Hom. always in last sense, and mostly of men, οἱ δ' ἀλλήλους ὀλέκουσιν Il.18.172, cf. 15.249, Theoc.22.108, etc.; but in Od.22. 305, of birds which *prey* on smaller birds, οἱ δέ τε τὰς ὀλέκουσιν ἐπάλμενοι: in Philos., τίκτει τ' ὀλέκει τε Emp.17.4:—Pass., *perish, die*, esp. a violent death, ὀλέκοντο δὲ λαοί Il.1.10, cf. 16.17.—Chiefly Ep., used by Trag. only in lyr., once in Act., τί μ' ὀλέκεις; S.*Ant.*1285 (lyr.); twice in Pass., ὀλέκει A.*Pr.*563 (anap.); ὠλεκόμαν S.*Tr.* 1012 (lyr.): later, Lxx *Jb.*10.16:—Pass., ib.17.1.

**ὀλεμεύς**, = ὄλαιτος, Phot.

**ὄλενον**, τό, late form for ὠλένη, Sch.Ar.*Pax* 442.

**ὀλέρημος**, ον, *entirely deserted*, κώμη *PSI* 1.105.10 (ii A.D.).

❀ **ὀλερός**, ά, όν, Att. for θολερός, *impure, turbid*, Gal.19.126, Hsch.

**ὀλέσαι, ὀλέσας, ὀλέσθαι**, v. ὄλλυμι.

**ὀλεσήνωρ**, ορος, ὁ, ἡ, *man-destroying*, epith. of perjury, ὅρκοι Thgn. 399, Nonn.*D.*28.273.

**ὀλεσί-θηρ** [ῐ], ηρος, ὁ, ἡ, *beast-slaying*, ὀλεσίθηρος ὠλένας, of Cadmus, E.*Ph.*664 (lyr.). **-μβροτος**, ον, *man-destroying*, Orph.*L.* 450. **-οικος**, v. ὠλεσίοικος. **-πτολις**, ὁ, ἡ, *city-destroying*, Tryph.453, 683. **-σῐᾰλοκάλᾰμος** [κᾰ], ον, *made of spittle-wasting reed*, epith. of the flute in Pratin.Lyr.1.12 (cj. Bgk. for ὀλοσίαλον κάλαμον).

**ὀλέσσαι, ὀλέσω**, v. ὄλλυμι.

**ὀλεσσῐτύραννος** [ῠ], ον, *destroying tyrants*, *AP* 15.50.

**ὀλετ-ήρ**, ῆρος, ὁ, *destroyer, murderer*, Il.18.114, Alcm.43, Nic.*Th.* 735, etc.:—fem. **ὀλέτειρα**, Batr.117, Euph.3, *AP* 11.424 (Piso). **-ης**, ου, ὁ, = foreg., *Epigr.Gr.*334.15 (Ilium):—fem. **ὀλέτις**, *AP* 3.7 (Inscr. Cyzic.), *PMag.Par.*1.2860.

**ὄλεχθον**· τὸ μαζονόμον, Hsch. **ὄλεχον**, v. ὀλβάχιον. **ὀλή**, ἡ, v. οὐλαί. **ὀλῆαι, ὀλῆται**, v. ὄλλυμι. **ὀληθεῖς**· ὀδυνηθεῖς, Id. **ὀλήθη**· καὶ τὰ ὄμματα, Id.

**ὀλήμερος**, ον, *working the whole day*, ἄνδρες prob. in *BGU* 513.17 (ii A.D.).

**ὀλημιμναῖον**, τό, *weight of* 1½ *minae*, *IG* 14.2417.4.

**ὀληφόρος**, ἡ, *bearer of the* οὐλαί (Att. ὀλαί), ὀ. Ἀθηνᾶς *IG* 3.323.

**ὀλιβάζω, ὀλιβράζω**, = ὀλισθαίνω, Hsch. s. vv. ὀλιβάξαι, ὠλίβραξαν; cf. ὀλισθάζω, ὀλισθράζω. **ὀλιβρός**, ά, όν, = ὀλισθηρός, Id.

**ὀλῐγ-άδελφος** [ᾰ], ον, *having few brothers*, Vett.Val.123.7. **-αιμία**, ἡ, *want of blood*, Arist.*PA* 651ᵇ11. **-αιμος**, ον, *scant of blood*, Hp. *Oss.*13, Arist.*PA* 651ᵇ9, al.; ὀλιγαιμότατον ὁ χαμαιλέων ib.692ᵃ 21. **-αιμότης**, ητος, ἡ, = ὀλιγαιμία, ib.24. **-άκῐς** [ᾰ], Adv. *but few times, seldom*, Hp.*VM* 9, *Epid.*1.26.δ', E.*Or.*393, Th.6.38, Pl. *Phlb.*52c, etc.; ὀ. καὶ ὀλιγαχοῦ Arist.*Rh.*1404ᵇ29:—a form **ὀλιγάκι** is cited in *EM* 172.6. **-άμπελος**, ον, *scant of vines*, νῆσος *AP* 9.413 (Antiphil.). ❀ **-αναφορία**, ἡ, *quickness in rising*, Sch.Ptol. *Tetr.*119. ❀ **-ανάφορος**, ον, *quick in rising*, of a zodiacal sign, Vett. Val.136.7, Heph.Astr.2.11, Ps.-Ptol.*Centil.*52. **-ανδρέω**, *to be scant of men*, D.S.15.63, Plu.*Publ.*11, D.C.49.1. ❀ **-ανδρία**, ἡ, *scantiness of men*, Str.14.1.10, Plu.2.413f, Philostr.*VA* 3.30. **-ανδρος**, ον, *scant of men*, οἶκοι J.*BJ* 4.3.5; βασιλεία Palaeph.31 (32). **-ανθρωπέω**, = ὀλιγανδρέω, Theagen.17; ἐὰν ἱερὰ -ωπῇ *are short of their number of* priests, *PGnom.*85 (ii A.D.):—Med., J.*AJ* 11. 5.8. **-ανθρωπία**, ἡ, = ὀλιγανδρία, Th.1.11, X.*Mem.*2.7.2, etc.: pl., Pl.*Lg.*780b. **-άνθρωπος**, ον, = ὀλίγανδρος, X.*Lac.*1.1 (Sup.), *Oec.*4.8, Gal.14.624. **-ᾱριστία**, ἡ, *scanty meal*, Alexandr.Magn. ap.Plu.*Alex.*22, 2.127b. **-αρκέω**, *to be contented with little*, Aesop. 384, dub. cj. in *Gp.*14.7.25. **-αρκής**, ές, *contented with little*, Luc.*Tim.*57; τὸ ὀ., = sq., ib.54. **-αρκία**, ἡ, *contentment with little*, Suid. **-αρτία**, ἡ, *scarcity of bread*, *EM* 621.47, Suid.

**ὀλῐγαρχ-έω**, *to be a member of an oligarchy*, οἱ -οῦντες Arist.*Pol.* 1300ᵃ8:—Pass., *to be governed by the few, be under an oligarchy*, Th. 5.31, 8.63, 76, Pl.*R.*552b, al. **-ης**, ου, ὁ, *oligarch*, of the *Decemviri*, D.H.11.43. ❀ **-ία**, Ion. -ίη *IG* 12(8).262.3 (Thasos, v B.C.), etc.: ἡ:—*oligarchy, government in the hands of a few families or persons*, Hdt.3.82, 5.92.β', etc.; of the time of the Four Hundred, Th.8.72; or of the Thirty, And.1.99, Pl.*Ap.*32c; ἄκρατος ὀ. Arist.*Pol.*1273ᵇ 37, al., cf. Pl.*R.*550c sq., *Plt.*291e. 2. Ὀλιγαρχία, personified in a statue, Sch.Aeschin.1.39. ❀ **-ικός**, ή, όν, *oligarchical*, ὀ. κόσμος Th.8.72; ξυνωμοσία Id.6.60; δίκαιον, νόμος, Arist.*Pol.*1280ᵃ8, 1281ᵃ 37; πολιτεῖαι ib.1288ᵃ22; [πόλις] ib.1316ᵇ7; τοῦτο -ώτερον ib.1281ᵃ 33. Adv. **-κῶς** Pl.*R.*555a, D.15.33. 2. of persons, *inclined or devoted to oligarchy*, And.4.16, Lys.25.8, Pl.*R.*545a, al.; οἱ ὀ., opp. οἱ δημοκρατικοί, Arist.*Pol.*1280ᵃ27.

**ὀλῐγ-αῦλαξ**, ακος, ὁ, ἡ, *having but little arable land*, *AP* 6.226 (Leon., ὀλιγόλαυξ cod. Pal.; ὀλιγῶλαξ (Dor.) Brunck). **-ᾰχόθεν**, Adv. *from some few parts*, τῆς Λιβύης Hdt.3.96, cf. Arist.*EE* 1221ᵃ24. **-ᾰχοῦ**, Adv. *in a few places*, πάνυ που ὀ. Pl.*Chrm.*160c, cf. Arist.*Rh.*1404ᵇ 29.

**ὄλιγγος**, ὁ, a kind of *locust*, Phot., Suid.

**ὀλῐγ-εκτέω**, *have little*, *Theol.Ar.*29:—Subst. **-εξία**, in pl., Nicom. *Ar.*1.14 (v.l. ὀλιγοεξίαι). **-ήμερος**, ον, *of or lasting a few days*, ζωή Hp.*Art.*63; πυρετοὶ -ήμεροι κτείνοντες Id.*Fract.*11: Comp., Id. *Acut.*17: Sup., Id.*Art.*63. 2. *lasting a short time*, τρῖψις prob. in Antyll.ap.Orib.10.23.16.

**ὀλῐγηπελ-έων**, ουσα (cf. ἀναπελάσας), Ep. part., *having little power, in feeble case, powerless*, κεῖτ' ὀλιγηπελέων Od.5.457; ὀλιγηπελέουσά περ ἔμπης 19.356, cf. Il.15.245; cf. κακηπελέων. **-ής**, ές, *weak, powerless*, *AP* 7.380 (Crin.), Opp.*H.*1.767. **-ία**, Ion. -ίη, ἡ, *weakness, faintness*, Od.5.468; cf. εὐηπελία, κακηπελία.

**ὀλῐγ-ήρης**, ες, = ὀλίγος, θαλάμη Nic.*Th.*284. ❀ **-ήριος**, ον, = foreg., ὀ. σῆμα a *small* tombstone, *AP* 7.656 (Leon.): or perh. compd. of ὀλίγος, ἠρίον. **-ηροσίη**, ἡ, (ἄροσις) *want of arable land*, ib.6.98 (Zon.). **-ησῖπΰος**, ον, (σιπύα) *with little corn*, or *with a small bread-basket*, opp. εὐσίπυος, ib.288 (Leon.), 300 (Id.). **-ινθα**· ὀλίγον, Hsch. (Cf. μίνυνθα.) **-ιστάκις** [ᾰ], Adv. *most seldom*, opp. πλειστάκις, prob. in Gal.18(1).649. **-ιστος**, v. ὀλίγος.

**ὀλῐγό-αιμος**, ον, = ὀλίγαιμος, Alex.Aphr.*Pr.*1.103. **-βαρής**, ές, *light in weight*, Paul.Aeg.3.76. **-βῐος**, ον, *short-lived*, Arist. *HA* 605ᵇ24 (Comp.), Lxx *Jb.*11.2, 14.1, S.E.*M.*1.73. **-βουλος**, ον, *with little discretion*, Adam.2.31. **-γνώμων**, ον, gen. ονος, = ὀλίγωρος, Hsch., Phot. **-γόνᾰτος**, ον, (γόνυ II) *with few joints*, [κάλαμος] Thphr.*HP* 4.11.11. **-γονία**, ἡ, *production of few offspring*, opp. πολυγονία, Pl.*Prt.*321b. **-γονος**, ον, (γονή) *producing few offspring*, ζῷα ὀ., opp. πολύγονα, Hdt.3.108, Arist.*HA* 558ᵇ28; *unprolific*, Vett.Val.5.25; of plants, Thphr.*HP* 8.4.4: Comp. -ώτερος Arist.*HA* 570ᵇ32. ❀ **-γράμμᾰτος**, ον, *composed of few letters*, opp. πολυγράμματος, Phld.*Po.Herc.*994.34. **-δάπᾰνος** [δᾰ], ον, *consuming or spending little*, Suid. s. v. εὐτελής. **-δεής**, ές, *wanting little*, Posidon.59J., M.Ant.5.5; -δεεστέρα εὐδόκησις '*cheaper*' popularity, Plb.16.20.4: Sup., Ph.1.116. **-δεια**, ἡ, *contentment with little*, ib.307, al. **-δενδρος**, ον, *having few trees*, Sch.D.T.p.152 H. **-δίαιτος** [δῐ], ον, *living on little*, Cephisodor.ap.Caryst. 7. **-δουλος**, ον, *having but few slaves*, Str.16.4.26.

❀ **ὀλῐγοδρᾰν-έω**, (δραίνω) in Ep. pres. part. -έων, *able to do little, feeble, powerless*, Il.15.246, 16.843, 22.337 (never in Od.): also in late Prose, -οῦσα ἡ διάνοια Ph.1.460, cf. 2.573, Jul.*Caes.*331b: pres. ind. -οῦσιν Iamb.*Myst.*2.8. **-ής**, ές, *of little might, feeble*, Ar.*Av.*686, Luc.*Trag.*324. **-ία**, ἡ, *weakness, feebleness*, A.*Pr.*548 (anap.).

**ὀλῐγο-δρομέω**, of the moon, *to be retarded*, *Cat.Cod.Astr.*1.102. 7ᵇ. **-δῠνᾰμέω**, *have little power*, Sch.D Il.22.337. **-δύνᾰμος** [ῠ], ον, *ineffectual*, Sch.Opp.*H.*1.623. **-έλαιος**, ον, *producing but little oil*, Thphr.*CP* 6.8.5. **-εξία**, v. ὀλιγεκτέω. **-εργής**, ές, *of little strength*, σῶμα Hp.*Loc.Hom.*43. **-έτης**, ες, *of few years*, χρόνος, ἄνθρωπος, οἶνος, Poll.1.58. **-ετία**, ἡ, *fewness of years, youth*, X.*Cyr.*1.4.3.

**ὀλῐγ-οζος** [ῐ], ον, *with few branches*, Thphr.*HP* 1.8.2.

**ὀλῐγο-θερμία**, ἡ, *possession of little heat*, Mich. *in PN* 132.22. **-θερμος**, ον, *having little heat*, of cold-blooded animals, Arist.*PA* 652ᵇ25, *GA* 718ᵇ37, al.; of the spleen, Id.*PA* 670ᵇ7, etc. **-θῡμέω**, *to be of little courage*, Eust.159.17. **-ῑνος** [ῑν], ον, (ἴς A) *with few fibres*, Thphr.*HP* 5.1.5. **-καιρος**, ον, *brooking no delay*, ἰητρική Hp.*Loc. Hom.*44. **-κάλᾰμος** [κᾰ], ον, *with few reeds or stalks*, Thphr. *CP* 4.11.4 (Comp.). **-καρπέω**, *bear little fruit*, Str.*Chr.*2.3, Ptol. *Tetr.*221. **-καρπος**, ον, *bearing little fruit*, Thphr.*CP* 2.11.10, D.H.1.37, Ath.Med.ap.Orib.*inc.*7.4. **-καυλος**, ον, *with few stalks*, Thphr.*HP* 7.8.2. **-κερως**, ωτος, ὁ, ἡ, *with small horns*, *Gp.*18. 1.3. **-κίνητος** [ῑ], ον, *little-moving*, Porph.ap.Stob.2.8.41, Phlp. *in Cat.*166.9. **-κλᾰδος**, ον, *with few branches*, Thphr.*HP* 1.5. 1. **-κληρος**, ον, gloss on ἄκληρος, Eust.1695.37. **-λᾰλέω**, *prate little*, Id.1278.12. **-μᾰθής**, ές, *having learnt little*, Eustr. *in EN* 256.24. **-μέρεια**, ἡ, *small compass*, τῆς ἀναγραφῆς *PGnom. Prooem.* (dat. written -ίᾳ). **-μετρία**, ἡ, in Prosody, *the having few feet*, Eust.353.39. **-μισθος**, ον, *receiving small wages*, Pl.*Ep.* 348a (Comp.). **-μῡθία**, ἡ, *speaking little*, Democr.274.

**ὀλῐγ-όνειρος**, ον, *with few dreams*, ὕπνοι Iamb.*VP* 25.114.

**ὀλῐγό-ξῠλος**, ον, *with little wood, shrubby*, ῥωπεῖον *AP* 6.226 (Leon.); *bearing little timber*, Str.*Chr.*12.7. **-παιδία**, ἡ, *fewness of children*, Muson.*Fr.*15ᴬ p.77 H. **-παις**, παιδος, ὁ, ἡ, *with few children*, Pl. *Lg.*930a. **-πιστος**, ον, *of little faith*, *Ev.Matt.*8.26, al., Sext.*Sent.* 6. **-πνους**, ουν, *scant of breath*, Hsch. s. v. ἀζαλές. **-ποιέω**, *make few, diminish*, Lxx *Si.*48.2. **-πόλιος**, ον, *with thin grey hair*, Hsch. s. v. σπαρνοπόλιος. **-πονία**, ἡ, *sparingness in labour, idleness*, Plb. 16.28.3. **-πονος**, ον, *working little*, D.H.*Dem.*51. **-ποσία**, ἡ, *moderation in drinking*, Aret.*CD* 1.4, Luc.*Par.*16; but -ποτίη Aret. *CD* 1.2. **-ποτέω**, *drink little*, Arist.*PA* 670ᵇ5, Plu.2.224d. **-πότης**, ου, ὁ, *one who drinks little*, Ath.10.419a, Herod.Med.ap.Orib.5.27. 13. **-ποτος**, ον, *drinking little*, Arist.*HA* 593ᵇ29, al.; ἄδιψα καὶ ὀ. Id.*PA* 669ᵃ34. **-πραγμοσύνη**, ἡ, *a retired life*, Chrysipp.*Stoic.*3. 176. **-πράγμων**, ον, gen. ονος, *averse to business, retiring*, opp. πολυπράγμων, ibid. **-πτερος**, ον, *with few feathers*, Arist.*HA* 486ᵇ

11. **-πύθμην**, ενος, ὁ, ἡ, sine expl., Theognost.*Can.*86. **-πῡρος**, ον, *with few grains of wheat*, Thphr.*CP*4.11.4. **-ρριζος**, ον, *with few roots*, Id.*HP*1.6.3, *Gp.*4.1.12.

❀ **ὀλίγος** [ῐ], η, ον, later **ὀλίος** (q.v.), of Size, *little, small*, freq. in Hom., rarer later, opp. *μέγας, σάκος* Il.14.376; *κῦμα* Od.10.94, etc.; *ὀλίγῃ ὀπί* with *small, low* voice, 14.492; of stature, 9.515; *ὀ. κῶρος* Theoc.1.47; *οὐκ ὀλίγης αἷμα βοὸς κέχυται* Call.*Aet.Oxy.*2080.85; of Space, *ὀ. χῶρος* Il.10.161, etc.; of Time, *χρόνος* 19.157, 23.418, Pi. *N.*7.38, etc.; *ἐν βραχεῖ κὠλίγῳ χρόνῳ* S.*Fr.*646 (cf. IV. 3). **2.** sts. in a sense between that of Size and Quantity, *ὀ. δόσις* Od.6.208; *οὖρα ὀλίγα not copious*, Hp.*Epid.*1.2; *ὑποστάσιες ὀλίγαι slight* sediments, ib.17; *ὀ. καὶ οὐδέν little* or nothing, Pl.*Ap.*23a; *οὐδὲν ἢ ὀ.* Arist.*PA*651$^{b}$17. **3.** of Degree, *ὀ. καὶ μέγας of low* and high *degree*, Callin.1.17. **4.** *weak*, *ἀθυμοτέρη καὶ ὀλιγωτέρη φύσις* Hp.*Virg.* 1. **II.** of Number, *few*, or of Quantity, *little*, not in Hom., freq. in Att., Ar.*Av.*1417, *Eq.*717, etc., but rare in Trag., as *ὀλίγα κακά* A.*Pers.*330.—The governing body in Oligarchies and the oligarchical party in Democracies was called *οἱ ὀ.*, Th.6.38, 8.9, etc.; *ἡ ὑπὸ τῶν ὀ. δυναστεία, αἱ διὰ τῶν ὀ. δυναστεῖαι*, Pl.*Plt.*291d, D.60.25; *ἑνὸς καὶ πλήθους τὸ ὀ. μέσον* Pl.*Plt.*303a. **2.** c. inf., *ὀλίγους.. στρατιῇ τῇ Μήδων συμβαλεῖν too few* to engage.., Hdt.6.109, cf. 7.207; *μὴ.. αἱ σφέτεραι δέκα νῆες ὀλίγαι ἀμύνειν ὦσιν* Th.1.50. **III.** neut. *ὀλίγον* as Adv., *a little, slightly, little*, with Verbs, *ὀ. παρακλίνας* Il.23.424, cf. 11.52, 12.452; *φροντίσας* E.*Cyc.*163; *ὀ. τοῦ ποιήματος προελθών* Pl.*Prt.*339d: also neut. pl., *ἠκροβολίσαντο ὀλίγα* Th.3.73. **2.** with comp. Adjs., *ὀλίγον προγενέστερος* Il.23.789; *ὀ. ἧσσον* Od.15.365; *στιβαρώτερον οὐκ ὀ. περ* 8.187; *φέρτερος οὐκ ὀ. περ* Il.19.217; *ὀ. τι πρότερον*, v.l. for *ὀλίγῳ*, Hdt.4.79, 81, cf. Pl.*Plt.*262b, etc.; *ὀ. ὕστερον* Id.*Grg.*454b, etc.; but *ὀλίγῳ* is more freq. in Prose, Hdt. ll.cc. (with v.l.), 7.113, al., Pl.*Grg.*460c, *R.*327c, etc. **IV.** special Phrases: **1.** *ὀλίγου δεῖν almost* (v. *δεῖ* II); *ὀλίγου ἐδέησε καταλαβεῖν* wanted *but little* of overtaking, Hdt.7.10.γ′: hence *ὀλίγου* alone, *within a little, all but, almost*, *ὀλίγου σεκύνες διεδηλήσαντο* Od.14.37, cf. Ar.*Ach.*348, 381, *Nu.*722, Lys.14.17, Pl.*Prt.*361b, D.19.334, etc.; *ὀ. ἅπαντες* Pl.*Ap.*22b; *ὀ. ἐς χιλίους close upon* 1,000, Th.4.124; *ὀ. ἦλθεν ἑλεῖν* (v. infr. 9) Paus.1.13.6. **2.** *δι' ὀλίγου at a short distance*, E.*Ph.*1098, Th.2.89, 3.21, dub. in A.*Th.*762 (lyr.); for (during) *a short time*, Th.1.77, 2.85, 3.43; within or after *a short time*, Id.6.11, 47, 7.39, etc.; but **b.** *δι' ὀλίγων in few words*, Pl. *Phlb.*31d, etc.; v. infr. VI. 2. **3.** *ἐν ὀλίγῳ* (*χώρῳ* is added in Hdt. 9.70) *in a small space, within small compass*, E.*Supp.*1126 (lyr.); *ἐν ὀ. στρατοπεδευομένοις* Th.4.26; *κυκλωθέντων ἐν ὀ.* ib.96; *εἰς ταὐτὸ πάντα.. ἀθροίσαντ' ἐν ὀ.* D.3.18; also *ἐν ὀ.* (sc. *χρόνῳ*) *for a brief time*, Pi.*P.*8.92; but also, *in a short time, quickly*, *ἔγνων καὶ περὶ τῶν ποιητῶν ἐν ὀ. τοῦτο* Pl.*Ap.*22b, cf. Th.4.55, *Act.Ap.*26.28. **b.** *ἐν ὀλίγοις one among few*, i.e. *exceedingly, remarkably*, *ποταμὸς ἐν ὀ. μέγας* Hdt.4.52; *ἐν ὀλίγοισι Περσέων.. ἀνὴρ δόκιμος* Id.9.41: freq. in later writers, Plu. *Pomp.*10, Hld.3.1; so *σὺν ὀλίγοις*, v. infr. 10. **4.** *ἐξ ὀλίγου at short notice, suddenly*, *ἐξ ὀ. καὶ δι' ὀργῆς* Th.2.11, cf. 61, 4.108, etc. **5.** *ἐς ὀλίγον*, like *παρ' ὀλίγον*, *within a little*, *ἐς ὀ. ἀφίκετο τὸ στράτευμα νικηθῆναι* ib.129. **6.** *ἐπ' ὀλίγον for a short time*, Hp.*Prorrh.*1.26, Plot. 4.4.29, *Gp.*7.12.22, 10.7.10, etc.; *a little at a time*, Hp.*VC*18; *εἴρηται ἐν τῷ [βιβλίῳ] ἐπ' ὀλίγον a little way on, near the beginning*, Gal.15.428. **7.** *κατ' ὀλίγον by little and little*, Th.1.69, Pl.*Ti.*85d, Luc. *Nec.*11, etc.; *ἐκ τοῦ κατ' ὀ.* D.S.15.34, Ath.Med.ap.Orib.1.2.6: but the Adj. freq. takes the gender and number of its Subst., *κατ' ὀλίγους* Hdt.2.93, 8.113; *οὗτοι κατ' ὀλίγους γινόμενοι ἐμάχοντο* fought *few at a time, in small parties*, Id.9.102, cf. Pl.*Tht.*197d; *κατ' ὀλίγον μαχεῖται* (sc. *τὸ πλῆθος αὐτῶν*) Th.4.10. **8.** *μετ' ὀλίγον τούτων shortly after..*, X.*HG*1.1.2. **9.** *παρ' ὀλίγον with little to spare, only just*, *ἀπέφυγες* E.*IT*870 (lyr.); *to within a short distance of*, *παρ' ὀ. ἦλθε.. ἐκπεσεῖν* Plb. 2.55.4, cf. 18.46.12; but **b.** *παρ' ὀ. ποιεῖσθαι* hold of *small* account, X.*An.*6.6.11. **10.** *σὺν ὀλίγοις*, = *ἐν ὀλίγοις*, *ἐπαινεθῆναι* Plu.*Galb.*3; v. supr. IV. 3b. **V.** regul. Adv. *ὀλίγως* is rare, 2*Ep.Pet.*2.18, Aq. *Is.*10.7; *οὐκ ὀ.* *AP*12.205 (Strat.). **VI.** Comparison: **1.** the Comp. is commonly supplied by *μείων, ἥσσων*, or *ἐλάσσων* (qq.v.); the older form *ὀλείζων* (fr. **ὀλειγ-yων*) is found in Hom., *λαοὶ δ' ὑπ' ὀλείζονες ἦσαν* (*ὑπολίζονες* codd.) Il.18.519; so in Att. Inscrr., *IG*1$^{2}$.76.8 (written *ὄλεζον* ib.63.17, al.); *τοῖσι.. ὀλείζοσι μυστηρίοισιν* ib.6.76, cf. 95; *ὀλείζους* is prob. in X.*Ath.*2.1 (*μείζους* codd.); so in Alexandrian Poets, Call.*Jov.*72 (*ὀλίζοσι* codd.), *AP*9.521; *ἐς ὀλίζονας ἀστέρας ἄρκτου* Poet.ap.Theodos. in Hilgard *Exc. ex Hdn.*p.19; also *ὀλίζωνες* Nic.*Th.*123, *ὀλίζωνα* ib.372; *ὀλιζότερος* is found in Id.*Al.* 479, Opp.*C.*3.65, 394, cf. *ὀλιζόω*; *ὀλιγώτερος* is found in Hp.*Virg.*1 (with the sense *weaker*, v. supr. I. 4), S.E.*M.*1.70, App.*Pun.*42, *Mith.*24, Ael.*NA*2.42, 6.51. **2.** Sup. *ὀλίγιστος, η, ον*, always of Number or Quantity, Il.19.223, Hes.*Op.*723, *IG*1$^{2}$.54.7, Ar.*Ra.*115, *Pl.*628, Pl.*R.*473b, al.; *ὀλιγίστου*, Sup. of *ὀλίγου* (cf. IV. 1), *very nearly*, Phot., Hsch. (ubi *ὀλιγωστοῦ*); *ὀλίγιστον* as Adv., *least, very little*, Pl.*R.*587b; *τὸ ὀ. at least*, Id.*Prm.*149a; *ὡς ὀλίγιστα* Id.*Grg.* 510a, *Lg.*953a (v.l. *ὀλιγοστά*); *ἐν ὀλιγίστῳ διασαφῶν* Eust.1262.54; so *δι' ὀλιγίστων* Pl.*Ep.*351d (interpol.). (Aspirated in papyri of ii–iii A.D., as *μεθ' ὀλίγον* *BGU*388.11, cf. 146.10.)

**ὀλῐγο-σαρκος**, ον, *with little flesh*, Luc.*Abd.*29, Gal.14.45, Herod. Med.ap.Orib.10.18.7 (Comp.). **-σθενέω**, *to be faint*, B.5.152. **-σθενής**, ές, *with little strength*, Sch.Opp.*H.*1.623.

**ὀλῐγοσῑτ-έω**, *eat little*, Hp.*Fract.*27, Plu.2.129f. **-ία**, ἡ, *small eating, moderation in food*, Arist.*Pol.*1272$^{a}$22, *Pr.*863$^{b}$24, Thphr.*Lass.* 17, Sor.1.65, etc. **-ος**, ον, *eating little* or *moderately*, Pherecr.1, Phryn.Com.23.

**ὀλῐγό-σπερμος**, ον, *having little seed*, Arist.*GA*725$^{b}$29, Thphr.*HP* 7.4.4 (Comp.). **-σπορος**, ον, = foreg., of persons, Vett.Val.14.23; of a part of the zodiac, Heph.Astr.1.1. **-στάδιος** [ᾰ], α, ον, *of few stadia*, *πορθμός* Eust. ad D.P.64. **-στῐχία**, ἡ, *the consisting of few lines*, *AP*4.2.6 (Phil.). **-στῐχος**, ον, *consisting of few lines*, Call. *Aet.Oxy.*2079.9, D.L.7.165. ❀ **-στός**, ή, όν, *with few companions*, *ὀ. ὁρμᾶν* Beros.ap.J.*AJ*10.11.1, cf. Plu.*Caes.*49, *Ant.*51, etc. **II.** like *ὀλίγιστος*, *ὀ. χρόνον for the smallest space* of time, S.*Ant.*625 codd. (*-ιστον* Bgk., Jebb), v.l. in Arist.*Metaph.*1053$^{a}$9; *ὀλιγωστοῦ* Hsch. (cf. *ὀλίγος* VI. 2). **-συλλᾰβία**, ἡ, *fewness of syllables*, Eust.25.35. ❀**-σύλλᾰβος**, ον, *of few syllables*, D.H.*Comp.*12, Eust.836.17. **-σύνδεσμος**, ον, *sparing of conjunctions*, *ἁρμονία* D.H.*Comp.* 22. **-σώμᾰτος**, ον, *of small body* or *bulk*, Comp. *-ώτερος* Sch.Pl. ap.Plot. *de Pulcr.*p.536 (ed. Creuzer, Heidelb.1814). **-τεκνία**, ἡ, = *ὀλιγοπαιδία*, Ptol.*Tetr.*189. **-τεκνος**, ον, = *ὀλιγόπαις*, Max. Tyr.6.1 (Sup.). **-της**, ητος, ἡ, opp. *πλῆθος* in all senses: **1.** *fewness*, Pl.*Lg.*678c, Arist.*Metaph.*984$^{a}$10, al., Lxx *Ps.*101(102).23, Plu.*Alex.*20; *fewness of rulers*, Arist.*Pol.*1279$^{b}$27. **2.** *smallness, scantiness*, Pl.*R.*591e, *Lg.*745d; of food, Epicur.*Fr.*456. **3.** of Time, *shortness*, Pl.*Tht.*158d. **4.** *feebleness* of voice, Poll.6.145. **-τῑμάω**, *quote less than the true price*, *IG*5(1).1421.14 (Cyparissia).

**ὀλῐγοτοκ-έω**, *bring forth few*, Arist.*GA*772$^{b}$2. **-ία**, ἡ, *the bringing forth of few*, ib.771$^{b}$6. **-ος**, ον, *bringing forth few*, Id.*PA*688$^{a}$32, *GA*753$^{a}$31.

**ὀλῐγότρῐχος**, ον, *having few hairs*, Arist.*HA*498$^{b}$17.

**ὀλῐγοτροφ-ία**, ἡ, *little nourishment*, Gal.6.209, Sor.1.65, Alex. Trall.*Febr.*3. ❀ **-ος**, ον, *giving little nourishment*, Hp.*Prorrh.*2.3, Thphr.*CP*3.13.4, Diph.Siph.ap.Ath.3.120e, Gal.17(2).368: Comp., *-ώτερον γάλα* Sor.1.117. **II.** Act., *taking little nourishment*, Arist.*PA*682$^{a}$21, *Pr.*898$^{b}$21; *abstemious*, of athletes in training, dub. in *Delph.*3(1).474 (iii B.C.).

**ὀλῐγό-ϋδρος**, ον, *scant of water*, Thphr.*HP*6.7.6 (Sup.). **-ῡλος**, ον, *containing little matter*, Eust.1379.43.

**ὀλῐγοϋπν-έω**, *sleep little*, Eust.1649.32. ❀ **-ία**, ἡ, *little* or *short sleep*, Iamb.*VP*16.69, 31.188. **-ος**, ον, *taking little* or *short sleep*, App.*Hisp.*71(74) (Sup.), Gal.10.538.

**ὀλῐγο-φᾰγία**, ἡ, = *ὀλιγοσιτία*, Sch.Ar.*Pax*28. **-φάγος** [ᾰ], ον, = *ὀλιγόσιτος*, Hp.*Vict.*2.49. **-φᾰής**, ές, gloss on *βραχυφεγγίτης*, Suid. **-φῐλία**, ἡ, *fewness of friends*, Antipho *Fr.*75, Arist.*Rh.* 1386$^{a}$10. **-φόρος**, ον, *that can bear but little*, of weak wine, *that will bear but little water*, Hp.*Acut.*56, Gal.6.807, cf. Sch.Ar.*Pl.* 854. **-φρᾰδής**, ές, *little eloquent*, Sch.Pi.*O.*3.81. **-φρων**, ὁ, ἡ, φρον, τό, gen. ονος, *of small understanding*, Ph.2.70, al., Plu.2.504b, Poll.4.14. Adv. *-όνως* ib.15. **-φυλλος**, ον, *having few leaves*, Thphr.*HP*1.10.8. **-φωνος**, ον, *with little tone*, prob. gloss on *ἄφωνα*, Aristid.Quint.1.20. **-χλωρον**, τό, = *κάππαρις*, Ps.-Dsc.2.173. **-χοος**, ον, contr. **-χους**, ουν, *yielding little*, Thphr.*HP*8.4.4; *πρὸς τὴν γονήν*, = *ὀλιγόσπερμος*, Arist.*GA*757$^{a}$21 (Comp.). **-χορδία**, ἡ, *fewness of strings*, Plu.2.1135d, 1137a. **-χορδος**, ον, *with few strings*, ib.b (cj. Volkmann for *τρίχορδα*). **-χρήμᾰτος**, ον, *of* or *with little money*, *παρακαταθήκη* Ph.1.287, al.

**ὀλῐγοχρον-έω**, *take a short time to rise*, Ptol.*Tetr.*132, Heph.Astr. 2.11. ❀ **-ιος**, ον, also α, ον *AP*7.648 (Leon.), Aret.*CA*2.1:—*of short duration, short-lived*, Thgn.1020, Mimn.5.5, Democr.285, Antipho Soph.51, Hdt.1.38, Pl.*Phd.*87c,d, Arist.*Pol.*1315$^{b}$11, etc.; opp. *πολυχρόνιος*, Phld.*Sign.*23. **II.** *within a short time*, *κίνδυνος* (v.l. *θάνατος*) Hp.*Prog.*7. Adv. *-ίως* Gal.18(2).243, Iamb.*Protr.* 20. **-ιότης**, ητος, ἡ, *shortness of time*, Thphr.*CP*2.12.1, Ptol. *Tetr.*10, Heph.Astr.2.11; *shortness of life*, Ptol.*Tetr.*115, Vett.Val. 147.3, Paul.Al.*H.*2. **-ος**, ον, = *ὀλιγοχρόνιος*, M.Ant.5.10 codd. (*-χρόνια* Casaubon).

**ὀλῐγό-χρῡσος**, ον, *having little gold, poor in gold*, Poll.3.109. **-χῡλος**, ον, *with little juice*, Diph.Siph.ap.Ath.3.120e, Dsc.2.182. **-χῡμος**, ον, = foreg., Xenocr.ap.Orib.2.58.78. **-χώρητος**, ον, *small in area*, Anon. *in Rh.*7.16.

**ὀλῐγοψῡχ-έω**, *to be faint*, Isoc.19.39. **II.** *become discouraged*, *PPetr.*2 p.135 (iii B.C.), Lxx *Nu.*21.4, al., *EM*395.31. **2.** *to be worried*, *περὶ τῆς ἐνκατοχῆς μου, περὶ τοῦ ἐνοικίου*, *UPZ*63.1 (ii B.C.), *POxy.*1294.13 (ii/iii A.D.); *ὠλιγοψύχησεν ἕως τοῦ ἀποθανεῖν* Lxx *Jd.* 16.16:—Med., *UPZ*78.10 (ii B.C.); cf. *ὀλοψυχέω*. **-ία**, Ion. *-ίη*, ἡ, = *λιποψυχία*, Hp.*Mul.*1.8, *Epid.*7.47. **II.** *faint-heartedness*, Lxx *Ex.*6.9, *Ps.*54(55).8. **-ος**, ον, *faint-hearted, feeble-minded*, ib.*Is.* 35.4, 54.6, 1*Ep.Thess.*5.14, Artem.3.5.

**ὀλῐγόω**, *lessen, diminish*, *ἐν ἀπειλῇ -ώσεις γῆν* Lxx *Hb.*3.12; *ἔτη ἀσεβῶν -ωθήσεται* ib.*Pr.*10.27; *ὠλιγώθη ἡ ψυχὴ αὐτοῦ* his soul *was grieved*, ib.*Jd.*10.16, al.

**ὀλῐγόωρος**, ον, *lasting a few hours*, *ἡμέρα* Sch.D.P.30.

**ὀλῐγῶλαξ**, v. *ὀλιγαῦλαξ*.

❀ **ὀλῐγωρ-έω**, aor. 1 written *ὠλιώρησα* *IG*12(8).53.5 (Imbros, ii B.C.):—*esteem little* or *lightly, make small account of*, c. gen., X.*Mem.*2.4.3, Pl.*Ap.*28d, *Phd.*68c, etc. **2.** abs., *take no heed*, Th.5.9, 6.91, Isoc. 9.41, etc.; *εἴς τι* Arist.*Rh.*1379$^{b}$28:—Pass., Pl.*La.*180b; *τοῖς οὕτως ὠλιγωρημένοις* D.17.21. **3.** later c. acc., *neglect*, *τὴν ἄμπελον* *PAvrom.*1.25 (i B.C.): c. inf., *intermit, neglect* to do something, Gal.6.243. **-ημα**, ατος, τό, *act of negligence*, Arist.*VV*1251$^{b}$22. **-ησις**, εως, ἡ, = *ὀλιγωρία*, ib.1251$^{a}$5 (pl.), Them.*Or.*10.136a. **-ητέον**,

*one must esteem lightly*, Isoc.*Ep*.9.18, Aristox.*Fr.Hist*.15. **-ία**, Ion. -ίη, ἡ, *an esteeming lightly, contempt*, ὑπό τε ὕβριος καὶ -ίης Hdt. 1.106, cf. 6.137; ἐν ὀλιγωρίᾳ ποιεῖσθαι, = ὀλιγωρεῖν, Th.4.5; ἐς ὀλιγωρίαν τραπέσθαι τινός Id.2.52; ὀ. πρός τι D.54.39; περί τινος Plb. 11.9.2, cf. Arist.*Rh*.1378$^b$10; εἴς τι Id.*Pol*.1315$^a$18: in pl., Isoc.7. 51. 2. *neglect of duty, negligence*, Decret.ap.D.18.74; διακεχυμέναι πρὸς -ίαν διατριβαί Eun.*Hist*.p.257 D. **-ος, ον**, (ὥρα) *little-caring, lightly-esteeming, contemptuous*, of persons, χαλεπός τε καὶ ὀ. Hdt.3.89; οὐδεὶς οὔτε γέρων οὔτε ὀ. οὕτως D.24.208, etc.; σοβαρὸς καὶ ὀ. τρόπος Id.59.37: c. gen., τὴν εἰρήνην, ἧς οὐδεὶς ἂν ἐπιδείξειεν.. ὀλιγωροτέραν τῶν Ἑλλήνων a peace *more regardless* of Hellenic rights, Isoc.12.106. Adv. -ρως *neglectfully, carelessly*, ὀ. καὶ ῥαθύμως φέρειν D.59.111; ὀ. καὶ πάντοθεν λαμβάνειν Arist.*EN*1121$^b$1; ὀ. ἔχειν to be *careless, negligent*, περὶ τὰς ἐπιθυμίας Pl.*Phd*.68c, X.*HG*1.6.20; τινος with regard to.., Lys.26.9, Is.3.37, etc.; περί τινος Arist.*Rh.Al*. 1433$^a$2; ὀ. διακεῖσθαι Lys.1.3; ὀ. διακεῖσθαι πρός τινα or τι Pl.*Alc*. 2.149a, Isoc.15.5; ὀ. ἔχειν πρὸς ἅπασαν αἰσχύνην Aeschin.1.67. II. of things, *scornful*, ὀλίγωρον.. πεποίηκάς τι Nicom.Com.1.2.

**ὀλῐγωφελής**, ές, (ὄφελος) *of little use*, S.E.*M*.1.296: Comp., Herod. Med.ap.Orib.8.3.3.

**ὀλιζότερος**, v. ὀλίγος VI. 1.

**ὀλιζόω**, *make less, diminish*, Orac.ap.Eus.*PE*5.22:—Pass., Hsch.

**ὀλίζω**, *make into a single whole*, Olymp.*in Phd*.p.86 N.

**ὀλίζων**, later spelling of ὀλείζων, v. ὀλίγος VI. 1.

**ὁλικ-ός**, ή, όν, (ὅλος) *universal, general, absolute* (opp. γενικός or μερικός), ὁ. ζωή Olymp.*in Phd*.p.17 N., cf. Procl.*Inst*.60,70, Simp. *in Cat*.58.30, *in de An*.72.13, Dam.*Pr*.56, al. Adv. -ῶς *OGI*669.64 (Egypt, i A.D.), Hsch., cj. in Gal.19.194: Comp. -ώτερον Phlp.*in APo*.121.6. **-ότης**, ητος, ἡ, *universality*, Simp.*in Cat*.113.17.

**ὄλινοι**, οἱ, *sheaves of barley*, also = λῖνος (Cypr.), Hsch. **ὀλινύει**· λήγει, ἀργεῖ, prob. in Id. ( = ἐλινύει).

* **ὀλίος**, later form of ὀλίγος, first in Pl.Com.168, Rhinth.2,8, then in Inscrr. and Pap. from 300 B.C., *PPetr*.2p.2 (iii B.C.), *IG*2$^2$.1227.8 (ii B.C.), etc. II. Ἀπόλλων Ὄλιος, v. οὔλιος.

**ὀλισβοκόλλιξ**, ῑκος, ὁ, *loaf in the shape of an* ὄλισβος, *Com.Adesp*. 1094.

**ὄλισβος**, ὁ, *penis coriaceus*, Cratin.316, Ar.*Lys*.109, *Fr*.320.13.

* **ὀλίσθ-ἄνος**, ον, = ὀλισθηρός: Comp. -ωτέρα Gal.18(2).624:—also **ὀλισθός**, Hdn.Gr.1.147. * **-άνω** (also -αίνω Arist.*Pr*.936$^a$15, 939$^a$26, A.R.1.377, etc., but never in good Att.): fut. ὀλισθήσω Lxx *Pr*. 14.19, Nonn.*D*.36.458: pf. ὠλίσθηκα Hp.*Art*.57,65: plpf. ὠλισθήκειν (v. infr. II. 1): aor. ὠλίσθησα *AP*9.125, Str.*Chr*.4.8 (p.476 Kr.), etc.; 3 pl. ὠλίσθησαν Nic.*Fr*.74.51 (codd. Ath., ὠλίσθηναν cj. Schn.); part. fem. ὀλισθήνασα Id.*Al*.89: but in classical Att. always aor. 2 ὤλισθον, part. ὀλισθών, inf. ὀλισθεῖν (Hom. only in Il., in Ep. 3 sg. ὄλισθε, v. infr.):—*slip, fall upon a slippery path*, ἔνθ' Αἴας μὲν ὄλισθε θέων Il.23. 774; ἐκ δέ οἱ ἧπαρ ὄλισθεν his liver *fell from* him, 20.470; ἐξ ἀντύγων ὤλισθε *he slipped* from.., S.*El*.746; ὀ. τῆς χειρὸς ὁ σίδηρος Arist.*Mech*. 854$^a$19; νηὸς ὀλισθών *AP*9.267 (Phil.); ὀ. εἴσω, ἔξω, of a bone, *slip out of the socket* on one side or the other, Hp.*Fract*.14, 37; θαυμαστὰ γὰρ τὸ τόξον ὡς ὀλισθάνει *slips, loses its force*, S.*Fr*.960: metaph., ὀ. εἰς νοῦσον *AP*7.233 (Apollonid.); ἐς Ἀΐδου *IG*14.1642; in moral sense, *make a slip*, Ar.*Ra*.690; in literary sense, εἰς τερατώδεις ὀ. ἀναπλασμούς Metrod.*Herc*.831.5. 2. *slip* or *glide along*, ὀ. ἐν τῷ λάβδα ἡ γλῶττα Pl.*Cra*.427b; βέλος διὰ σαρκὸς ὄλισθεν Theoc.25.230. II. causal, *sprain by slipping*, ὠλισθήκει τὸν γλουτόν Philostr.*VA*3.39, cf. *Gym*.14. 2. *make to slip*, τὰς διανοίας Lxx *Si*.3.24. **-ήεις**, εσσα, εν, poet. for ὀλισθηρός, *AP*9.443 (Paul. Sil.). **-ημα**, ατος, τό, *slip, fall*, ὑγρὰ -ήματα ὑδάτων Pl.*Ti*.43c; ὀ. γῆς *place where a landslip has occurred*, J.*AJ*15.10.3; so ὀ. without γῆς, *Inscr.Prien*.42.10,42 (ii B.C.); in moral sense, *cause of slipping*, Plu.2.49c. 2. *luxation*, Hp.*Fract*.14, Heliod.ap.Orib.49.9.16, Gal.19.460, etc. **-ηρός**, ά, όν, *slippery*, οἶμος Pi.*P*.2.96 (metaph.); ἂν.. ὀ. ᾖ τὸ χωρίον X.*Eq*.7.15; λίθοι Id.*An*.4.3.6, etc.; of mucilage, Hp.*Acut*.10, 15 (Sup.). II. metaph., *slippery, hard to catch and keep hold of*, Pl.*Sph*.231a (Sup.); τύχη *AP*10.66 (Agath.); τὸ ὀ. τῆς διανοίας αὐτῶν Ps.-Luc.*Philopatr*. 22; ὀ. ἱκεσίη *AP*5.215 (Agath.). 2. *liable to slip*, πόδες *AP*7.542 (Stat. Flacc.); ὀλισθηροὶ εἰς πόδας ib.398 (Antip.): metaph., πρὸς ὀργὴν ὀ. Plu.*Cat.Mi*.1. Adv. -ρῶς, ἔχειν πρός τι Id.2.31c. **-ησις**, εως, ἡ, *slipping and falling*, ib.611a,731f: hence, *dislocation*, τρόπος ὀλισθήσιος Hp.*Fract*.42, *Art*.74. **-ητικός**, ή, όν, *making slippery*, Id.*Superf*.7.

**ὀλισθο-γνωμονέω**, *make a slip in judgement*, Luc.*Lex*.19. * **-ποιέω**, *labefacio*, *Gloss*.

* **ὄλισθος**, ὁ, *slipperiness*, Hp.*Acut*.58, Plb.15.14.2, etc.; ὄλισθον ἔχειν, of ground, etc., to be *slippery*, Luc.*Merc.Cond*.42, cf. *Anach*.2, Praxagorasap.Gal.18(1).7. 2. = ὀλίσθημα, Apollod.*Poliorc*.150.2: metaph., ὀ. γλώσσης Plu.2.510a, cf. Max.Tyr.37.4. 3. metaph., *snare*, μεθύουσι ὀ. οἶνος Poet.ap.Clem.Al.*Paed*.2.2.28. II. *an unknown fish with a slippery skin*, Opp.*H*.1.113.

**ὀλισθός**, v. ὀλίσθανος.

**ὀλισθράζω**, = ὀλισθάνω, Epich.25, Hp.ap.Gal.19.126.

**ὁλκᾰδικός**, ή, όν, *like a ship of burden*, πλοῖον ὀ., = ὁλκάς, Arist.*IA* 710$^a$19.

**ὁλκᾰδοχρίστης**, ου, ὁ, *ship-caulker*, Man.4.342.

**ὁλκ-άζω**, *draw*, ὅλκασον (ὥλκασσον Pap.) τὴν τροφὴν ἐκ τοῦ ὕδατος *PBaden*49 (ii B.C.); cf. ὁλκάζει· ἕλκει, χαλιναγωγεῖ, Hsch. **-αία**, ἡ, v. ὁλκαῖος II. * **-αῖον**, τό, *stern-post* of a ship, A.R.1.1314, Antioch. (?)ap.Poll.6.100; cf. ὁλκεῖον. **-αῖος**, α, ον, (ὁλκή) *drawn along*, *towed*, of a ship (cf. ὁλκάς), Nic.*Th*.268: hence, *trailing, dragging*, σειρή, of a serpent, ib.119; ἀτραπός ib.160; κακά Lyc.216. II. as Subst. **ὁλκαία**, Ion. **ὁλκαίη**, ἡ, *tail*, because it is *trailed along*, Nic. *Th*.123, 225, A.R.4.1614 (v.l. ἀλκαία, which Schn. writes in Nic. ll.cc.). * **-άς**, άδος, ἡ, *ship which is towed*: hence, *trading vessel, merchantman*, Pi.*N*.5.2, Hdt.3.135, 7.25,137, Lys.32.25; ἐν ὁλκάσιν ἢ πλοίοις Th.7.7, cf. X.*Ath*.1.20; ὁ. σιταγωγοί Th.6.44; οἰναγωγοί Pherecr.143.5, cf. Cephisod.10: metaph., of women, *AP*5.160; of Europa's bull, Nonn.*D*.1.66. 2. of stones, *conveyed* to the place of building, *IG*11(2).199*A* 79 (Delos, iii B.C.). 3. ὁλκάς·.. παρ' Ἀλκμᾶνι ἀειδὼν (i.e. ἀηδών, cf. Hsch. s.v. ὁλκάς), Cyr.Coisl.394 (*Rh.Mus*.43.451). * **-εῖον**, τό, *large bowl* or *basin*, *SIG*869.16 (Eleusis), *Inscr.Olymp*.468.6, Epig.6, Philem.17, Men.73, *BCH*35. 286 (Delos, ii B.C.), Πολέμων 1.126 (Demetrias), Plb.30.26.1 (ὁλκίων codd. Ath.), *PSI*4.428.62, Plu.*Alex*.20 (ὁλκίον codd.). II. in Ep. form **ὁλκήϊον**, = ὁλκαῖον, A.R.4.1609. **-εύς**, έως, pl. ὁλκεῖς· οἱ τὰ ἀμφίβληστρα ἐπισπῶνται, Hsch. * **-ή**, ἡ, (ἕλκω) *drawing, trailing, dragging*, e.g. of the hair, A.*Supp*.884; ἡ τῆς γνάψεως ὁ. the *drawing* of the carding instrument in fulling cloth, Pl.*Plt*.282e; ἀπὸ μιᾶς ὁ. by one *haul* or *pull*, Arist.*Mech*.853$^b$1; ἡ ὁ. τοῦ ἀρότρου S.E.*P*.3.15: metaph., τοῖς δεινοῖς περὶ λόγων ὁλκήν skilled in *drawing* words *to a false meaning*, Pl.*Phlb*.57d. 2. *inhalation* (of vapour), Hp.*Mul*.1.55; ὁ. πνεύματος *drawing in* of the breath, Arist.*Spir*.482$^a$15; τοῦ αἵματος *suction* of blood by the cupping-bowl, Anon.*in Rh*. 170.8. 3. *ray, beam*, prob. cj. for ὁλκὸν in *Lyr.Alex.Adesp*.35. 19. II. *a drawing on* or *towards* a thing, παιδεία ἔσθ' ἡ παίδων ὁ. καὶ ἀγωγὴ πρὸς τὸν λόγον Pl.*Lg*.659d. 2. *attraction, force of attraction*, Id.*Ti*.80c; of a magnet, Epicur.*Fr*.293 (pl.), Ph.1.34; ἡ ὁ. τῆς ὁμοιότητος the *attractive force* of similarity, Pl.*Cra*.435c. 3. *tendency*, διανοίας πρὸς τὸ ὄν Ph.1.332. III. *drawing down* of the scale, *weight*, ὁ. ταλάντου χρυσίου Men.383, cf. Arist.*Mir*.833$^b$10, Thphr.*HP*9.16.8, Plb.30.25.16, Lxx 1*Es*.8.62(64), *IG*2$^2$.659.27, 11(2). 128.25 (Delos, iii B.C.), etc.; ὁλκὴν ἄγειν weigh so much, *Michel*836. 30 (Milet.), etc. 2. *the drachma*, as a weight, Dsc.1.30, S.E.*P*. 1.81, Hero *Geom*.23.55, Gal.19.752, Asclep.ap.eund.13.160, Ruf. *Ren.Ves*.1.11. **-ήεις**, εσσα, εν, *drawing the scale, weighty*, Nic. *Th*.651,908. **-ήϊον**, τό, v. ὁλκεῖον. **-ήρης**, ες, = ὁλκαῖος, ib.351,356. **-ῐμος**, ον, *capable of being drawn out, ductile, sticky*, Hp.*Art*.36; μέλι Dsc.2.82; ἔλαιον Plu.2.696c; of a plaster, Gal.13.345. II. Act., *drawing well*, of a cupping instrument, Paul.Aeg.6.41 (Comp.). III. of a kind of pain in liver diseases, '*dragging*', Archig.ap.Gal.8.87,111. **-ίον**, v. ὁλκεῖον. * **-ός**, ή, όν, *drawing to oneself, attractive*, θερμόν τε καὶ ὁ. Arist.*Pr*.931$^a$25; μάθημα ψυχῆς ὁλκὸν ἀπὸ τοῦ γιγνομένου ἐπὶ τὸ ὄν Pl.*R*.521d; ὁλκὸν.. ψυχῆς πρὸς ἀλήθειαν ib.527b; ὁλκοτέρας τὰς ῥίζας ποιεῖν Thphr.*CP*3. 17.3 (ἑλκοτέρας cod. A: ἑλκτικωτέρας Wimmer). II. *trailing*, ὁλκὰ βαίνων Hld.10.30. Adv. Comp. -ότερον *slowly*, Id.3.5. III. *possible*, ὁλκά· δυνατά, Hsch. IV. Pass., *liable to be attracted, having a propensity*, ὁ. διάνοιαι παρθένων πρὸς ἀρετήν Ph.2.229. **-ός**, ὁ, (ἕλκω): I. *machine for hauling* ships *on land, hauling-engine*, prob. a fixed *capstan, windlass*, Hdt.2.154,159, E.*Rh*.146,673; but also of *movable engines* of like kind, for hauling ships across the Isthmus of Corinth, Th.3.15. 2. *strap, rein* (cf. ῥυτήρ), τμητοῖς ὁλκοῖς S.*El*.863 (lyr.). II. *furrow, track, trace*, αἵματι δ' ὁλκοὶ.. πλήθοντο A.R.3.1391; σμίλης ὁλκός *the traces* of a chisel in the wood, Ar.*Th*. 779 (lyr.); ὁ. τοῦ ξύλου *the furrow made by* the wood, X.*Cyn*.9.18; *path, track*, or *orbit* of a star or meteor, A.R.3.141,4.296, Nonn.*D*. 24.90; ἁμάξης ib.1.96; *ditch* or *channel*, A.R.1.375; οἴδματος ὁλκοί the waves, ib.1167; ὁλκοὶ καλλιρόων ὑδάτων *Milet*.1(9).343; *body-coils* of a serpent, Nic.*Th*.266, al., Luc.*Herm*.79; but, *coiling movement* of a serpent, Nic.*Th*.162, al.; cf. ὁ. γλώσσης Id.*Al*.79, 281; of hair, *coil*, ὁλκὸς ἐθείρης, πλοκάμων.. ὁλκοί, Nonn.*D*.3.413, 32.168: generally, of anything drawn, αἵματος ὁλκῷ ib.4.329, al.; *draught* of wine, Antiph. 237.4 (pl.). 2. in periphrases, δάφνης ὁλκοί *drawings*, i.e. laurel-boughs (or brooms made of them) *drawn along*, E.*Ion* 145 (lyr.); τερπνὸς ἀκούεται ὁ. ἁμάξης a chariot *drawn*, D.P.191. 3. *aqueduct*, *Cod.Just*.1.4.26; ὁ. ὑδάτων Lyd.*Mens*.3.23. III. a kind of *spider*, Dsc.2.63. IV. a kind of *grass, mouse-barley*, Plin.*HN* 27.90.

* **ὁλκότης**· τὰ αὐτά, Hsch.

**ὄλλιξ**, ικος, ἡ, *wooden drinking-bowl*, Pamphil.ap.Ath.11.494f.

* **ὄλλῡμι**, S.*Ant*.673, E.*Or*.1303; part. ὀλλύς Il.8.472, fem. pl. ὀλλῦσαι ib.449:—also **ὀλλύω**, Archil.27, *Com.Adesp*.608, (προσαπ-) Hdt.1.207: poet. **ὀλέκω** (q.v.): impf. 3 pl. ὤλλυσαν A.*Pers*.461, S. *OC*394; Ep. ὀλέεσκον Q.S.2.414 (cf. ὀλέκω): fut. ὀλέσω Od.13.399, Hes.*Op*.180; Ep. also ὀλέσσω Il.12.250, Od.2.49; Ion. ὀλέω (ἀπ-) Hdt.1.34, etc.; Att. ὀλῶ, εῖς, εῖ, S.*OT*448, E.*Andr*.856 (lyr.): aor. ὤλεσα Il.22.107, A.*Ag*.1017 (lyr.), etc.; Ep. ὄλεσα, ὄλεσσα, Od.23. 319, 21.284, etc.:—Med. **ὄλλυμαι**, Il.20.21, S.*OT*179 (lyr.): impf. ὠλλύμην Id.*El*.927, E.*Alc*.633: fut. ὀλέομαι, -οῦμαι, 2 pl. ὀλέεσθε Il. 21.133; but 3 sg. ὀλεῖται 2.325: aor. 2 ὠλόμην, 3 sg. ὤλετο 13.772, A. *Eu*.565 (lyr.), etc.; Ion. ὀλέσκετο (ἀπ- Od.11.586); part. ὀλόμενος as Adj., v. οὐλόμενος: pf. ὄλωλα, v. B. III: plpf. ὀλώλειν Il.10.187:— Pass., aor. ὀλεσθῆναι, fut. ὀλεσθήσομαι (ἀπ-), Lxx *Ps*.82(83).17, Gal. 9.728.—The simple Verb only Poet. and later Prose, as Lxx, ἀπόλλυμι being used in Com. and Classical Prose.

A. Act.: I. *destroy, make an end of*, and of living beings, *kill*, νῆάς τ' ὀλέσας καὶ πάντας Ἀχαιοὺς Il.8.498, cf. Od.23.319; γένος ὀλέσσαι.. θανάτῳ Pi.*P*.3.41; γένος ὠλέσατε πρυμνόθεν A.*Th*.1061

(anap.); θανεῖται καὶ θανοῦσ' ὀλεῖ τινα S.*Ant.*751; ὀλεῖ ὀλεῖ με E. *Andr.*856 (lyr.); ἁ φιλοχρηματία Σπάρταν ὀλεῖ, ἄλλο γὰρ οὐδέν Orac. ap.Arist.*Fr.*544; also, of *doing away with* evil, νῆστιν ὤλεσεν νόσον A.*Ag.*1017 (lyr.). II. *lose*, μένος, θυμόν, ψυχήν, ἦτορ ὀλέσαι, *lose life, die*, Il.8.358, 13.763, 5.250; πόνον ὀρταλίχων ὀλέσαντες A.*Ag.*54 (anap.); ἄγραν ὤλεσα Id.*Eu.*148 (lyr.); τᾶς ἀνάνδρου κοίτας ὀλέσασα λέκτρον E.*Med.*436 (lyr.).

B. Med., I. *perish, come to an end*, and of living beings, *die*, esp. a violent death, ἀπ' αἰῶνος νέος ὤλεο Il.24.725; ὤλεθ' ὑπ' Αἰγίσθοιο δόλῳ Od.3.235; δόλοις ὀλούμεθ' A.*Ch.*888; ἤέ τις ὤλετ' ὀλέθρῳ Od. 4.489: c. acc. cogn., κακὸν οἶτον ὄληαι, ὀλέεσθε κακὸν μόρον, Il.3.417, 21. 133; θάνατον *AP*7.745 (Antip. Sid.); ὄλοιο, ὄλοισθε, *may'st thou, may ye perish!* a form of cursing very common in Trag., S.*Ph.*961, 1019, 1285, etc.; so ὀλοίμην Id.*OT*645; ὄλοιτο ib.1349 (lyr.), etc.; ὄλοιντο Id.*Tr.*383:—Hom. has Act. and Med. in emphatic contrast, ὀλλύντων τε καὶ ὀλλυμένων Il.4.451, 8.65, cf. 11.83. II. of things, *to be lost*, μή τί μοι ἐκ μεγάρων κειμήλιον.. ὄληται Od.15.91; ὤλετό μοι νόστος Il.9.413, cf. Od.1.168; κλέος Il.9.415, cf. A.*Supp.*918. III. pf. ὄλωλα (Syrac. ὀλώλω, Hilgard *Exc.ex Hdn.*p.30), *to have perished, to be dead, undone, ruined*, ὄλωλε μάχη ἔνι Il.15.111, al., cf. A.*Pers.* 255, 1016 (lyr.), etc.; τῶν ὀλωλότων of the *dead*, Id.*Ag.*346, cf. 672, 1367, S.*Ant.*174: also of things, *to be in a state of ruin*, ἐσθίεταί μοι οἶκος, ὄλωλε δὲ πίονα ἔργα Od.4.318.

**ὀλμ-ειός**, ὁ, *mortar*, Sch.Ar.*V.*238. **-ίον**, τό, Dim. of ὅλμος, *BGU*1666.12 (i A.D.). **-ισκοειδής**, ές, *shaped like a* ὀλμίσκος, Orib. 49.22.19. **-ίσκος**, ὁ, Dim. of ὅλμος II, *socket of the hinge of a door*, S.E.*M.*10.54, *PLond.*3.1177.232 (ii A.D.). 2. *tooth-socket*, Ruf.*Onom.*55; *the hollows of the molar teeth*, Poll.2.93 (pl.). 3. *frustum of a cone*, *POxy.*470ʳ.35.

**ὀλμο-ειδῶς**, Adv. *in socket* or *mortar-shape*, Dsc.4.170 ap.Orib. (θολοειδῶς codd. Dsc.). **-κοπέω**, *bray in a mortar*, Heras ap.Gal.13.1043, al., Philum.ap.Orib.45.29.70, Alex.Trall.12, Aët.4. 30. **-κόπος**, ὁ, *one who brays in a mortar*, Anon. in Gal. περὶ τῶν καθ' Ἱπποκράτην στοιχείων (Helmreich *Handschriftliche Studien zu Galen*, Ansbach 1910). **-ποιός**, ὁ, *maker of mortars*, Arist.*Pol.* 1275ᵇ28.

*__ὅλμος__ (ὄλμος codd. of Hes. and Hdt., v. infr. II. 1), ὁ, *a round smooth stone* (περιφερὴς λίθος μάρμαρος, Hsch.), χεῖρας ἀπὸ ξίφεϊ τμήξας ἀπό τ' αὐχένα κόψας, ὅλμον δ' ὣς ἔσσευε κυλίνδεσθαι δι' ὁμίλου Il.11. 147 (from which passage it was taken to signify *the human trunk*, Poll.2.162, *EM*460.17). II. later, any *cylindrical* or *bowl-shaped body*: 1. *mortar*, Hes.*Op.*423, Hdt.1.200, *IG*2².1126.24, 12(5). 872.82 (Tenos, iii B.C.), *PLille*9.9 (iii B.C.), etc. 2. *kneading-trough*, Ar.*V.*201, 238. 3. *hollow seat* on which the Pythia prophesied, hence prov., ἐν ὅλμῳ κοιμᾶσθαι Plu.*Prov.*2.14; ἐν ὅ. εὐνάσω Zen.3.63; τοῦ τοίχου τὸ μέρος τοῦ κατὰ τὸν ὅλμον (in the temple of Amphiaraus at Rhamnus), Ἐφ.Ἀρχ.1909.271. b. *support*, καθίσας τὸν ἄνθρωπον ὀκλὰξ ἐπὶ ὅλμων δύο Hp.*Haem.*4. 4. *drinking-vessel*, Menesth.1. 5. *mouthpiece of a flute*, Eup.267, cf. Poll.4.70, and v. ὑφόλμιον II. 6. *dial*, ὅλμου τοῦ λιθίνου ὃς ἐκαλεῖτο Ἑλληνιστὶ [γν]ώμων *PHib.*1.27.26 (iii B.C.). 7. *stone used as a weight*, prov. ὅ. ὑπὲρ κεφαλῆς Lib.*Ep.*473.3.

**ὀλοαί**, v. οὐλαί.

**ὀλο-άργῠρος**, ον, *all of silver*, Ph.1.666. **-βηρον**, τό, *genuine purple dye*, Procop.*Arc.*25: as Adj., *holovera vestimenta, dyed purple through and through*, *Cod.Just.*11.9.4. **-βολάδες**· θῖνες, Hsch. **-βρᾰχυς**, υ, *consisting only of short syllables*, πυρρίχιος *Anecd.Stud.*1.224.

**ὀλόγινον**· ὀζῶδες, συμπεφυκώς, Hsch. (cf. ὀλόπτοον).

**ὁλο-γράμμᾰτος**, ον, *with all its letters, written at full length*, title of work by Menecrates, Gal.13.503. Adv. -τως Id.14.44. **-γρᾰφέω**, *write at full length*, Plu.2.288e. **-γρᾰφία**, ἡ, *will written entirely in the handwriting of the testator*, *Gloss.* **-γρᾰφος**, ον, *written in full*, in Adv. -φως Sch.E.*Andr.*575. II. *written entirely in the same hand*, *PSI*3.223.6 (vi A.D.), *PGrenf.*2.89.6 (vi A.D.). **-γῦρος**, ον, *entirely round, all round*, in Adv. -ρως, μετρεῖσθαι Hero *Geom.*4. 13. **-δάκτῠλος**, ον, (δάκτυλος III) *wholly dactylic*, Eust.836. 17.

**ὀλό-εις**, εσσα, εν, = ὀλοός, only in S.*Tr.*521 (lyr.). **-εργής**, ές, *ruinous, destructive*, Man.6.722. **-εργός**, όν, = foreg., Nic.*Th.* 828, Doroth.ap.Heph.Astr.3.20.

**ὁλο-ήμερος**, ον, *working the whole day*, *BGU*14 iii 2, al. (iii A.D.). II. *lasting the whole day*, in Adv. -ρως Tz. ad Hes.*Op.*566. **-θούριον**, τό, *holothurium*, a kind of zoöphyte, Arist.*HA*487ᵇ15, *PA*681ᵃ17, Plin.*HN*9.154.

**ὀλοθρ-εύω**, *destroy*, v.l. for ὀλεθρεύω in Lxx *Ex.*12.23, al., Ph.1.73 (citing *Ex.* l. c.), *Ep.Hebr.*11.28; cf. ἐξολοθρεύω:—hence **-ευτής**, οῦ, ὁ, *destroyer*, 1*Ep.Cor.*10.10:—fem. **-εύτρια**, gloss on λοιγίστρια, Hsch.: **-ευτικός**, ή, όν, *destructive*, Sch.Od.11.128.

**ὀλοιός**, όν, poet. for ὀλοός (q. v.). *__ὄλοισος__· ὁ ἀπολλύς, Hsch.

**ὀλοίτροχος**, Ep. **ὀλοοίτροχος**, ὁ, *large stone, boulder*, Ἕκτωρ ἀντικρὺ μεμαώς, ὀλοοίτροχος ὣς ἀπὸ πέτρης, ὅν τε κατὰ στεφάνης ποταμὸς χειμάρροος ὤσῃ ῥήξας.. ἔχματα πέτρης Il.13.137; = τὸ κυλινδρικὸν σχῆμα, Democr.162; of the rounded muscles of an athlete's arm, ἔστασαν ἠΰτε πέτροι ὀλοίτροχοι, οὕστε κυλίνδων χειμάρρους ποταμὸς μεγάλαις περιέξεσε δίναις Theoc.22.49; rolled down by besieged people upon their assailants, Hdt.8.52, Orac.ap.eund.5.92.β', X.*An.*4.2.3, Zos. 1.52. (The ancients derived it from ὀλοός 'destructive' or from ὅλος, and disagreed as to the breathing and accent, Sch.Il. l. c.)

**ὁλο-κάθᾰρος** [κᾰ], ον, *completely pure*, Steph. *in Hp.*1.183 D. *__-κάλᾰμος__ [κᾰ], ὁ, *stake made of a single reed*, *BGU*1529.10 (iii B.C.). **-κᾰλος**, ον, *entirely beautiful*, *Sammelb.*343, 1990, 6124, *BCH*27.331.

**ὁλοκαρπ-όομαι**, Pass., *to be offered as a whole burnt-offering*, Lxx *Si.*45.14, 4*Ma.*18.11. **-ος**, ον, *brought as a whole offering*, θυσία Ph.1.668. **-ωμα**, ατος, τό, *whole burnt-offering*, Lxx *Le.*5.10, al. **-ωσις**, εως, ἡ, *presentation of such an offering*, ib.*Ge.*8.20, al.

**ὁλοκαυστ-έω**, = ὁλοκαυτέω, βοῦς τελείους δέκα *Mon.Ant.*23.154 No. 112 (Adanda), cf. *PMag.Par.*1.2396, *PMag.Leid.V.*1.35. **-ησις**, εως, ἡ, = ὁλοκαύτησις, *IPE*2.342 (Phanagoria). **-ος**, ον, = ὁλόκαυτος, Ph.1.468, *PMag.Par.*1.3148, *Gloss.*

*__ὁλοκαυτ-έω__, *bring a burnt-offering, offer whole*, X.*An.*7.8.4: impf. ὠλοκαύτει ib.5:—Pass., ὁλοκαυτεῖται (v.l. -οῦται) J.*AJ*3.9.1:—more usu. **-όω**, ὠλοκαύτωσαν v.l. in X.*Cyr.*8.3.24; ὁλοκαυτῶσαι J.*AJ*1. 13.1, etc. (ὁλοκαυτοῦσιν Plu.2.694b, ὁλοκαυτῶν J.*AJ*3.9.1, may belong to either form). **-ίζω**, = ὁλοκαυτέω, Porph.*Abst.*2.54:—Subst. **-ισμός**, ὁ, = ὁλοκαύτησις, Phot. * **-ος**, ον, *burnt whole*, Call.*Fr.*1.49 P.; τὸ ὁ. Lxx *Le.*6.23(16); ὁ. θυσία Ph.1.668, al. 2. *in full flame*, opp. ἡμίκαυτος, Gal.18(1).225. **-ωμα**, ατος, τό, *burnt-offering*, Lxx *Ex.*10.25, al., J.*AJ*10.4.5. **-ωσις**, εως, ἡ, *sacrifice of a burnt-offering*, Lxx *Ex.*29.25, al., J.*AJ*3.9.1: but **-ησις**, εως, ἡ, *IG*4²(1). 97.2, al. (Epid.); cf. ὁλοκαυστέω, ὁλοκαύστησις.

**ὅλοκες**· αὔλακες, Hsch.

**ὁλοκληρ-έω**, *to be in good health*, *POxy.*1158.3 (iii A.D.), *PMag. Par.*1.136, etc. * **-ία**, ἡ, *completeness* or *soundness in all parts*, τοῦ σώματος, τῶν αἰσθητηρίων, Chrysipp.*Stoic.*3.33, Plu.2.1041f: abs., *Act.Ap.*3.16, Plu.2.1063f, Demetr.*Eloc.*3, *SIG*1142 (Phrygia, i/ii A.D.), *POxy.*123.6 (iii/iv A.D.). * **-ος**, ον, *complete, entire, perfect*, opp. κολοβός, Arist.*HA*585ᵇ36; *uncastrated*, κίχλαι Pl.Com.174.9; τοὺς ἱερέας ὁ. νόμος εἶναι Anaxandr.39.10, cf. Men.233, Luc.*Asin.*33; ὁ. ὑγιής τε Pl.*Ti.*44c; σῶμα Diog.Oen.39; ὁ. μὲν.. ὄντες καὶ ἀπαθεῖς κακῶν.., ὁ. δὲ.. καὶ εὐδαίμονα φάσματα μυούμενοι *perfect, complete*, Pl. *Phdr.*250c; ὁ. καὶ γνήσιον Id.*Lg.*759c; ἐν ὁ. δέρματι Luc.*Philops.*8; also of evils, ὁ. πήρωσις Democr.296; [ἡ ἀνελευθερία] οὐ πᾶσιν ὁ. παραγίνεται Arist.*EN*1121ᵇ19, cf. 1126ᵃ12; simply, *whole, complete*, ἔτεσιν δυσὶν οὐχ ὁλοκλήρ[οι]ς *IG*14.1386; ὁ. βουλευτήριον *BGU*1027. 12 (iv A.D.); ὁ. οἰκία *PLond.*3.930.13, etc.; ὁ. κολλούρια drug-pencils used *as wholes*, for insertion in cavities, Antyll.ap.Orib.10.23.1. Adv. -ρως Erot. s. v. ἀπαρτί, S.E.*P.*3.226, Gal.16.68, Hld.7.8. **-ωσις**, εως, ἡ, *complete recovery*, Serapio in *Cat.Cod.Astr.*1.101.5.

*__ὁλό-κνημος__, ον, *with the whole shin*, σκελὶς ὁ. a ham *containing the whole leg*, Pherecr.108.13. **-κοπος**, ον, *coarsely pounded*, Dsc.5. 55. **-κυκλος**, ον, *full-orbed*, σελήνη Mich. *in PN*82.17. **-κυρος**, ἡ, Pontic for χαμαίπιτυς, Dsc.3.158, Apollod.ap.Ath.15.681d (ὀλόκληρος is f.l. in Paul.Aeg.5.46, ὁλόπυρος in Orib.12 s.v. χαμαίπιτυς). **-κωνῖτις**, ιδος, ἡ, *earth-almond*, *Cyperus esculentus*, Hp. *Mul.*1.78, cf. Gal.19.126; also **ὀροκωνῖτις** (q. v.). * **-λαμπής**, ές, *shining all over*, Ὄλυμπος Arist.*Mu.*400ᵃ8. **-λευκος**, ον, *all white*, τάριχος Antiph.186.3; χλαμύς Philetaer.20; στρόφιον Plu. *Arat.*53; ὄρνιθες Paus.8.17.3; *albino*, Heph.Astr.1.1. **-λῖθος**, ον, *of massive stone*, βασίλειον Str.17.1.42. * **-λῖνος**, ον, *entirely of fine linen*, σουδάριον *PMag.Osl.*1.268.

*__ὄλολοι__, οἱ, = δεισιδαίμονες, Theopomp.Com.61, Men.112.

**ὀλολῠγ-αῖος**, α, ον, *screeching*, νυκτερίς *IG*14.1934. * **-ή**, ἡ, (ὀλολύζω) any *loud cry*, esp. of women invoking a god, αἱ δ' ὀλολυγῇ πᾶσαι Ἀθήνῃ χεῖρας ἀνέσχον Il.6.301, cf. *h.Ven.*19 (pl.), Ar.*Lys.*240; δοκέει ἔμοιγε καὶ ⟨ἡ⟩ ὁ. ἐπὶ ἱροῖσι ἐνταῦθα πρῶτον γενέσθαι Hdt.4.189; θεία μακάρων ὁ. Ar.*Av.*222; κραυγῇ τε καὶ ὁ. χρωμένων, of the alarm given in the attack on Plataea, Th.2.4.—Mostly in good sense, sts. even opp. to a wailing cry, ἀντίμολπον ἧκεν ὀλολυγῆς μέγαν κωκυτόν E.*Med.* 1176; σύν τ' εὐαγορίᾳ σύν τ' εὔγμασι σύν τ' ὀλολυγαῖς Call.*Lav.Pall.* 139. * **-μα**, ατος, τό, *loud cry*, mostly *of joy*, E.*Heracl.*782 (lyr.); Κυβέλης in honour of C., *AP*6.173 (Rhian.). **-μός**, ὁ, *loud cry*, mostly *of joy*, in honour of the gods, ὁ. ἱρὸν.. παιώνισον A.*Th.*268; ὁ. εὐφημοῦντα τῇδε λαμπάδι ἐπορθιάζειν Id.*Ag.*28, cf. 595, E.*Or.*1137, Lxx *Ze.*1.10, *PMag.Lond.*121.323: pl., Epicur.*Fr.*143, 419; *song of triumph*, ἐφυμνῆσαι.. ὁ. ἀνδρὸς θεινομένου A.*Ch.*387 (lyr.); rarely of *lamentation*, *AP*7.182 (Mel.). * **-ών**, όνος, ἡ, *croaking of the male frog*, Arist.*HA*536ᵃ11, Ael.*NA*9.13; *note of water-creatures*, ib.6. 19. II. in Theoc.7.139, Arat.948, an unknown *animal*, evidently named from its note: some take it for *a small owl*, others for *a singing bird*, others again for the *tree-frog*; cf. Eub.104, Thphr.*Sign.*42, *AP*5.291.5 (Agath.).

*__ὀλολύζω__, Od.22.411, etc.: fut. -ύξομαι E.*El.*691, later -ύξω Lxx *Is.*16.7, *Am.*8.3: aor. ὠλόλυξα, Ep. ὀ. (v. infr.):—*cry with a loud voice*, in Hom. esp. of women *crying aloud* to the gods in prayer or thanksgiving, ὣς εἰποῦσ' ὀλόλυξε· θεὰ δέ οἱ ἔκλυεν ἀρῆς Od.4.767, cf. *h.Ap.*445; αἱ δ' ὀλόλυξαν, at a sacrifice, Od.3.450; of a cry of exultation, ἴθυσέν ῥ' ὀλολύξαι 22.408, cf. 411; also of the cries of goddesses, *h.Ap.*119; so later, mostly of women *crying* to the gods, ὀλολύξατε νῦν ἐπὶ μολπαῖς A.*Eu.*1043 (lyr.); ὠλόλυξεν ἐν μέσαις σταθεῖσα Βάκχαις E.*Ba.*689; mostly in sign of joy (cf. ὀλολυγή), ἢν μὲν ἔλθῃ πύστις εὐτυχὴς σέθεν, ὀλολύξεται πᾶν δῶμα Id.*El.*691, cf. Ar.*Eq.*1327, Theoc. 17.64; μὴ φλαῦρον μηδὲν γρύζειν, ἀλλ' ὀ. Ar.*Pax*97; ἐπὶ τῷ μηδένα πώποτε τηλικοῦτ' ὀλολύξαι σεμνυνόμενος D.18.259; ὠλόλυξαν μὲν αἱ γυναῖκες, ἠλάλαξαν δὲ οἱ ἄνδρες Hld.3.5; of nymphs *crying aloud* to Hecate, A.R.3.1218.

**ὀλολυκ-τόλης**, ου, ὁ, *addicted to wailing*, *An.Ox.*4.336. **–τρια**, ἡ, *professional crier at sacrifices*, *SIG*982.25 (Pergam., ii B.C.).

* **ὄλολυς**, ὁ, *effeminate, dissolute person* (ὁ γυναικώδης καὶ κατάθεος καὶ βάκηλος Phot.), Anaxandr.34.4, Men.34. (On the accent, v. Hdn. Gr.2.938.)

**ὀλολύττω**, = ὀλολύζω, Men.1047.

**ὀλο-μάδιστος** [ᾰ], ον, *completely bald*, Cyran.77. **–μαζος**, ον, *whole, entire*, Hero *Stereom.*1.59. **–μέλας**, αινα, αν, *black all over*, αἴλουρος *PMag.Leid.V.*4.2; κριός *PMag.Lond.*121.539.

**ὁλομέλ-εια**, ἡ, Pythag. name for *six*, Anatolius ap. *Theol.Ar.*36: Ion. **οὐλομέλεια** (q.v.). **–έω**, *to be sound, entire*, ζῷα (embryos) –οῦντα Gal.19.177. **–ής**, ές, *whole of limb, not dismembered*, πλεκτάς Diph.34.2; κρέα Posidon.9 J., *IG*12(7).515.49 (Amorgos); ὁλομελῆ alone, Str.15.3.19; ὁ. κρόκος *uniform*, Dsc.1.26.

**ὀλόμενος**, v. οὐλόμενος.

**ὁλο-μερής**, ές, *in entire parts, in large* or *whole pieces*, κρέα D.S.5.28, Dsc.5.75. Adv. –ρῶς Arist. ap. D.L.5.28. **–μεστος**, ον, *solid, without marrow*, of bones, Pall. *in Hp.*12.286 C.

**ὀλόμην, ὄλοντο**, v. ὄλλυμι.

**ὄλονθος**, ον, (ὅλος, ὄνθος) *all over dung*, γνάθος *Com.Adesp.* ap. Eust. 1329.30.

**ὄλονθος**, ὁ, (ἡ Hp.*Mul.*2.113), *edible fruit of the wild fig*, Hes.*Fr.* 160.1, Thphr.*CP*5.1.8, Anon. (ὁ φιλόσοφος) ap. Ath.3.77f, Lxx *Ca.*2. 13; ὀ. χειμερινοί Hp.*Nat.Mul.*33, al. 2. *sterile summer fruit of the cultivated fig*, Gal.12.133. 3. *sterile male inflorescence of the caprifig*, breeding ψῆνες, which fertilize σῦκα, Hdt.1.193.

**ὀλονθο-φορέω**, *bear* ὄλονθοι, Thphr.*HP*3.7.3. **–φόρος**, ον, *bearing* ὄλονθοι, Id.*CP*5.1.8, Anon. (ὁ φιλόσοφος) ap. Ath.3.77f, *PCair. Zen.*33.12 (iii B.C.). (In this group ὀλονθ- is found in good codd. of Hdt.1.193, Hp.*Nat.Mul.*10,17,33, *Mul.*1.78, 2.112,113,117, Ath. l.c., corroborated by *PCair.Zen.* l.c.; ὀλυνθ- elsewhere, as also in ὀλυνθάζω, ὀλύνθη, ὀλυνθηφόρος.)

**ὁλο-νύκτιος**, ον, *the whole night through*: neut. –ιον as Adv., Sch. Lyc.815 (p.261 S.). **–ξηρος**, *wholly dry*, Sm.*Ps.*57(58).10.

**ὁλοοίτροπα**· παρὰ Ῥοδίοις ἑπτὰ πλάσματα εἰς θυσίαν, Hsch. **ὀλοοί-τροχος**, v. ὀλοίτροχος.

**ὁλόομαι**, Pass., *to be constituted a whole*, Dam.*Pr.*276, cf. *EM*821. 37.

* **ὀλοός**, ή, όν, (ὄλλυμι) *destructive, deadly*, ὀλοὴ Κήρ Il.18.535; μοῖρ' ὀλοή 16.849, al.; ὀλοῷ Ἀχιλῆι 24.39; πυρὸς ὀλοοῖο Od.12.68; ὀλοῷ ἐνὶ δεσμῷ 22.200; πόλεμος, μάχης πόνος, Il.3.133, 16.568; λύσσα, γόος, μῆνις, 9.305, 23.10, Od.3.135; γῆραος οὐδός Il.24.487; νύξ 16. 567, al.; ὀ. τύχαι A.*Pr.*553 (lyr.); νιφάς Id.*Th.*213 (lyr.); θηρὸς κέρας Call.*Fr.*249; γηγενέων ἀνδρῶν ὀ. στάχυς A.R.3.1338: c. inf., ὀ. φέρειν ζυγόν, of the wild horse, Opp.*C.*3.261; ὀλοὰ φρονεῖν design *ill*, τινι Il.16.701: Comp. ὀλοώτερος 3.365, 23.439: Sup. –ώτατος (as fem.), ὀδμή Od.4.442: neut. pl. as Adv., ὀλοὰ στένει S.*Tr.*846 (lyr.), cf. *El.* 843 (lyr.).—Rarer collat. forms are **ὀλοιός**, as ὀλοιὴ μοῖρα πέδησεν Il.22.5; ὀλοιῇσι φρεσὶ θύει 1.342; γῆρας ὀλοιόν *h.Ven.*224; **ὀλώϊος**, Hes.*Th.*591; θάρσος ὀλώϊον Nonn.*D.*13.416; **οὐλοός**, A.R.2.85, 3. 1402 (fem. –ός Man.6.464); **ὀλός** (q.v.). II. rare in pass. sense, *destroyed, lost*, ὀλοοὺς ἀπέλειπον A.*Pers.*962 (lyr.).

**ὀλοόφρων**, ονος, ὁ, ἡ, (ὀλοός, φρήν) *meaning mischief, baleful* (so always in Il.), ὕδρος 2.723; λέων 15.630; σῦς κάπρος 17.21; but II. in Od., *crafty, sagacious*, of persons, Ἄτλας 1.52; Αἰήτης 10.137; Μίνως 11.322. (Sense II is derived from sense I, cf. the signf. of δαΐφρων and δεινός; expld. by Cleanth.*Stoic.*1.125 by ὁ ὑπὲρ ὅλων φρονῶν, i.e. ὁλο–.)

**ὁλό-παππος**, ὁ, *a complete* πάππος (a pun on the name Φιλόπαππος), dub. in *MAMA* 1.267 (nr. Laodicea Combusta). **–ποιέω**, *make into a whole*, Simp. *in Ph.*636.38, Dam.*Pr.*159. **–ποιός**, όν, *creating the whole*, Ζεύς ib.245. **–πόρφῠρος**, ον, *all purple*, X.*Cyr.*8.3.13, Lxx *Nu.*4.7, Plu.2.180e. * **–πράσινος** [ᾰ], η, ον, *all green*, Cyran. 278. **–πτερος**, ον, *with whole* (i.e. *undivided*) *wings*, a generic name of insects such as bees, wasps, etc., opp. σχιζόπτερα, Arist. *APo.*96ᵇ39, cf. *PA*692ᵇ13, *IA*709ᵇ30, 713ᵃ4.

**ὁλόπτοον**· συμπεφυκότα, Hsch. (cf. ὀλόγινον).

* **ὀλόπτω**, *pluck out, tear out*, [χαίτην] ὤλοψας βίηφι Call.*Dian.*77; ἐὰν ὠλόψατο χαίταν *AP*7.241 (Antip. Sid.); ὤλοψεν.. βότρυν ἐθείρης cj. in Nonn.*D.*40.104. II. *strip off*, Nic.*Th.*595.

**ὁλο-πῡρῖται** ἄρτοι, = sq., *Ostr.*1305 (i A.D., written –εῖται). * **–πῡ-ρος**, ον, *of unground wheat*, esp. *of wheat boiled whole*, later word for πύανος, Heliod.Hist.3. II. v. ὁλόκυρος. **–ρριζί**, Adv. of sq., Lxx *Es.*3.13. **–ρριζος**, ον, (ῥίζα) *with the entire root*, Thphr.*HP* 3.18.5: metaph., ὁλόρριζοι ἀπώλοντο Lxx *Jb.*4.7.

**ὀλός**, ὁ, = θολός, *the ink of the cuttle-fish*, Hp.*Epid.*4.20 (vulg.), Phryn.*PS* p.19 B., Phot.; prob. read by Gal. in Hp.*Morb.*2.73. 2. metaph., *blood*, *AP*15.25.1 (Besant.*Ara*).

**ὀλός**, ή, όν, = ὀλοός, Hdn.Gr.1.154; only found in voc. ὦ ὀλὲ δαῖ-μον Alcm.55.

* **ὅλος**, η, ον, Ion. **οὖλος**, η, ον, as in Hom. (twice, v. infr.), Xenoph. (v. infr.), Parm.8.4, Hp.*Acut.*14, *Carn.*13, al. (but ὅλος in Hdt.2.126, 4.64, 7.167, 8.113 (cf. ἡμι-ολίας 5.88), Hp.*Epid.*1.7, Herod.3.18, 5.12, 6.7 (but οὖλος 8.56); ὅλως dub. in Thgn.73 codd.):—*whole, entire, complete in all its parts*, of persons and things, ἄρτος οὖλος *a whole* loaf, Od.17.343; μηνὶ δ' ἄρ' οὔλῳ in a *whole* month, 24.118; οὖλος ὁρᾷ, οὖλος δὲ νοεῖ, οὖλος δέ τ' ἀκούει (sc. ὁ θεός) Xenoph.24; ὅλος ἑσπέρας ὀφθαλμός, i.e. the *full* moon, Pi.*O.*3.19; ὁ ὅ. χρόνος ib.2.30; τρεῖς ὅλους ... ἐκμήνους χρόνους S.*OT*1136; ἐπ' ὤμοις ὅλην πόλιν φέρων a *whole* city, E.*Ph.*1131; ἐκπιεῖν ὅλον πίθον Id.*Cyc.*217; ὅλους ἐκ κρι-βάνου βοῦς Ar.*Ach.*85; λαβράκιον ὀπτᾶν ὅ. Antiph.222.3, etc.; πόλεις ὅλαι *whole, entire* cities, Pl.*Grg.*512b; ὅλη ἡ πόλις, the city *as a whole*, Id.*R.*519e; ὅλους ποιητὰς ἐκμανθάνειν learn *whole* poets by heart, Id.*Lg.*811a: it may either precede the Art. or follow the Subst., τῆς ἡμέρας ὅλης in the course of the *whole* day, X.*An.*3.3.11; δι' ὅλης τῆς νυκτός ib.4.2.4; ὅλην τὴν νύκτα or τὴν νύκτα ὅλην, Id.*Cyr.* 7.5.15, Men.67.2, Pl.*Smp.*219c; ὅ. τὸ δέρμα Men.498; ἡ πόλις ὅ. Id. 882, etc.: less freq. between Art. and Subst., τὸν ὅ. ἀμφὶ χρόνον Pi. *O.*2.30; ἡ ὅ. ἀδικία Pl.*R.*344c; τὸ ὅ. πρόσωπον Id.*Prt.*329e; τῇ ὅ. φάλαγγι X.*An.*4.8.11: joined with εἷς, ἡμέρας.. οὐχ ὅλης μιᾶς S.*Ph.* 480; εἶδος ἓν ὅλον Pl.*Ti.*56e; with πᾶς, ὅλην καὶ πᾶσαν τὴν οἰκίαν Id. *Lg.*808a, cf. *R.*486a; πρὸς τῷ διακινδυνεύειν ὅ. καὶ πᾶς ἦν Plb.3.94.10 (so without πᾶς, οὕτως ἔκφρων ἦν καὶ ὅλος πρὸς τῷ λήμματι καὶ τῷ δωρο-δοκήματι, ὥστε.. D.19.127); τὸ ὅ. αὐτοῖς ἦν καὶ τὸ πᾶν Ἀπελλῆς Plb.5. 26.5. 2. *whole*, i.e. *safe and sound*, ὑγιὴς καὶ ὅ. Lys.6.12, cf. Pl. *Men.*77a. 3. *entire, utter*, ὅ. ἁμάρτημα an *utter* blunder, X.*HG*5.3. 7; πλάσμα ὅ. ἐστὶν ἡ διαθήκη *utter* fiction, D.45.29. 4. neut. as Adv., ὅλον or τὸ ὅ. *wholly, entirely*, διαφέρει ὅ. τε καὶ πᾶν Pl.*Alc.*1.109b; διαφέρει ὅ. καὶ τὸ πᾶν Id.*Lg.*944c; ὅλῳ καὶ παντὶ Id.*Phd.*79e; τῷ ὅ. καὶ παντὶ διοίσει Id.*R.*527c; τῷ παντὶ καὶ ὅ. Id.*Lg.*734e; εἰς τὸ ὅ. Id.*Plt.* 302b: with a Prep., κατὰ ὅλον *on the whole, generally*, opp. ἀπολαβὼν μέρος τι, Id.*R.*392d; so κατὰ ὅλου Id.*Men.*77a; δι' ὅλου, καθ' ὅλου (v. διόλου, καθόλου); αἱ κράσεις δι' ὅλων Plu.2.1078c, cf. 1078d: in this signf. also without a Prep., τὸ μὲν ὅ. *generally speaking*, Pl.*Phdr.* 261a, D.44.11; τὸ δ' ὅ. and *in general, in short*, *PTeb.*33.16 (ii B.C.); οὐδὲ Φιλόξενον δλ' ἐξ ὅλων εὗρον I have *entirely failed* to find P., *POxy.* 936.20 (iii A.D.). 5. = πᾶς, *all*, ὅλων στρατηγός S.*Aj.*1105, cf. Men. *Pk.*225, Nonn.*D.*47.482, *AP*5.216 (Paul. Sil.), 7.679 (Sophronius); ὅλη πόλις *every* city, Lxx 1 *Ki.*14.23; πρὸ τῶν ὅ. τὸ προσκύνημά σου ποιῶ before *all things*, *PTeb.*418.4 (iii A.D.); ἀσπάζομαι.. πάντας τοὺς ἐν τῇ οἰκίᾳ ὅ. κατ' ὄνομα *PLond.*2.404.15 (iv A.D.), cf. *PIand.* 13.20 (iv A.D.). II. as Subst., τὸ ὅ. *the universe*, Pl.*Grg.* 508a, *Ly.*214b, etc.; differing from τὸ πᾶν, as implying a definite order, Arist.*Metaph.*1024ᵃ3, cf. Pl.*Tht.*204a sq. (but as not includ-ing void, *Placit.*2.1.7); also ἡ τῶν ὅ. τάξις X.*Cyr.*8.7.22. 2. τὰ ὅ. *one's all*, τὰ ὅ. πεπρακέναι D.18.28; τοῖς ὅ. ἡττᾶσθαι lose *one's all*, be *utterly* ruined, Id.9.64; in full, τοῖς ὅ. πράγμασιν ἐσφαλμένος Plb. 18.33.1, etc.; τοῖς ὅ., = ὅλως, *altogether*, Philipp. ap. D.18.39: with neg., not *at all*, Phld.*Rh.*2.135 S., Aristid.2.274, 304 J.; τοῖς ὅ. ἠφά-νισαν *utterly* destroyed it, *PRyl.*152.14 (i A.D.), cf. Aristid.2.262 J.; κινδυνεύει τῷ ὅ. ἐξαρθῆναι there is a risk of its being *entirely* carried away, *PRyl.*133.19 (i A.D.). III. Adv. ὅλως (Dor. **οὔλως** Pempel. ap. Stob.4.25.52) *wholly, altogether*, ὅ. σοφόν Pl.*R.*568a; ἀλγοῦνθ' ὅ. Id.*Phlb.*36a; ὅ. ψεύδεται he speaks *utter* falsehood, Isoc.15.31, etc. 2. *on the whole, speaking generally, in short*, ὅ. δ' οὐδείς ἐστιν ὅντιν' οὐ πεφενάκικ' ἐκεῖνος D.2.7, cf. 14, al.; διψῆν καὶ πεινῆν καὶ ὅ. τὰς ἐπιθυμίας Pl.*R.*437b, cf. *Cra.*406a; τί οὖν κωλύει πάντα ἀφῃρῆσθαι καὶ ὅ. τὴν πολιτείαν; D.20.3; ὅ. εἰπεῖν Arist.*Ph.*202ᵇ19, etc. 3. freq. with a neg. (first in Thgn.73, s.v.l.), οὐχ ὅ. or ὅ. οὐ not *at all*, ὅ. μὴ διαλέγεσθαι X.*Mem.*1.2.35; ὅ. οὔτ' ἀφελὼν οὔτε προσθεὶς D.3.35; οὔτ' ἐλεῶν οὔθ' ὅ. ἄνθρωπον ἡγούμενος Id.21.101, cf. 46; οὐδὲ εἷς ὅ. Men.65. 9; μὴ ὄντος ὅ. τοῦ Σωκράτους Arist.*Cat.*13ᵇ19; μηδὲ ὅ. εἶναι τοὺς θεούς Luc.*Tim.*10. 4. *actually, really*, καλῶς ποιήσεις ἐλθοῦσα.. πρὸς ἡμᾶς ἵνα ὅ. ἴδωμέν σε *POxy.*1676.31 (iii A.D.); so perh. in 1 *Ep.Cor.*5.1. (ὅλ(ϝ)ος from I.-E. *sólwos, cf. Skt. *sárvas* 'whole', and perh. Lat. *salus, salvus.*)

**ὁλο-σηρῐκοπράτης** [ᾰ], ου, ὁ, in Lat. form *holosericoprata, silk-mercer*, Champollion-Figeac *Chartes Latines* 1 vi 14, al. (vi A.D.). * **–ση-ρικός**, ή, όν, *of silk*, ῥάκος Cyran.120: –κόν, τό, *silk*, Hsch. s.v. Σῆρες, *Edict.Diocl.*22.14, al.:—written **–σειρικός** ib.19.14k, al. **–σίδηρος** [ῐ], ον, *all iron*, μάχαιρα *IG*2².1481 (iv B.C.), cf. Antiph.216, *IG*11(2). 145.37 (Delos, iv B.C.), Plu.*Cam.*40; ὁλοσίδηροι, οἱ, *soldiers wearing coats of mail*, = Lat. *clibanarii*, Lyd.*Mag.*1.46. **–σκιος**, ον, *quite shady*, Str.6.1.9 ap. Eust. ad D.P.364 (παλίνσκιος codd. Str.). **–σκω-ληκόβρωτος**, ον, *entirely eaten by worms*, *POsl.*26.14 (i B.C.). **–σμᾰ-ράγδινος**, ον, *entirely of emerald*, *BCH*32.248. **–σπάς**, άδος, ἡ, *drunk all at one draught*, ὁλοσπάδες S.*Fr.*1076 ap. Phot. (ὁλοσπαδεῖς Hsch.). **–σπόνδειος**, ον, *all of spondees*, Eust.836.16.

**ὀλ-όστεον**, τό, *all-bone*, *Plantago Bellardi*, Dsc.4.11, Plin.*HN*27. 91.

* **ὁλο-στήμων**, ον, gen. ονος, *consisting all of warp-threads*, ταινία Poll.7.32. **–στομος**, ον, *tempered all through*, of an iron ring, *PMag.Par.*1.2961; σίδηρος Cyran.6.

**ὀλοστός**· ὅλος ὡς ἐστίν, Hsch.

**ὁλο-στρόγγῠλος**, ον, *entirely round*, Sch.Opp.*H.*2.370. **–στροφος**, ον, *moving altogether*, Hsch. s.v. ἑλελίστροφε. **–σφαλτος**, ον, *quite defective*, marg. gloss in cod. of *AP*6.269. **–σφίζειν**, gloss on ὀλοφύρειν, Phot.

**ὁλοσφύρ-ᾱτος** [ῠ], Ion. **–ητος**, ον, *made of solid beaten metal*, opp. cast, hollow, *AP*11.174 (Lucill.), cf. Lxx *Si.*50.9, Plin.*HN*33.82, Hsch. s.vv. ὁλόσφυροι, ναστός: condemned by Phryn.180. **–ήλᾰτος**, ον, = foreg., J.*AJ*14.7.1 (v.l. –σφύρητος, v. foreg.). **–ιον**, τό, *piece of beaten metal*, Ammon.*Diff.*p.41 V. **–ος**, ον, = ὁλοσφύρατος, ἀνδριάς Herm. *in Phdr.*p.82 A., cf. Hsch.; interpol. in Phryn.180, v.l. in Artem.2.5.

* **ὁλό-σφῡρος**, ον, *with undivided ankles*, Ar.Byz.*Epit.*1.19.

**ὁλοσχέρ-εια**, ἡ, *general survey* or *estimate*, Str.2.1.24, Corn.*ND* 20; καθ' ὁλοσχέρειαν in *general terms*, διαλέγεσθαι Phld.*Rh.*1.251 S.;

κατὰ ὁλοσχέρειαν, opp. κατὰ μέρη, S.E.*M.*10.53. **2.** *lumpiness, solidity*, Ruf.ap.Orib.8.24.34. ⊛ **-ής**, ές, *whole, entire, complete*, Hp.*Alim.*26, Theoc.25.210; παρατίθημ' ὁλοσχερῆ ἄρνα Diph.90; ἀνήρ [S.]*Fr.*1127.4; νόμισμα *IG*12(7).67*B* (Amorgos); dub. in ib.12(5).593 (Ceos), cf. δολοσχερής. **b.** *in large pieces*, ὁ ἐλλέβορος -έστερος ληφθείς, opp. εἰς πάνυ σμικρὰ τριφθείς, Aristo*Stoic.*1.89, cf. Chrysipp. ib.2.158. **2.** *absolute*, ἐξουσία *BGU*86.24 (ii A.D.); *universal, widespread*, ὁ. κρίσις Plb.1.57.6; φόβοι καὶ θόρυβοι Id.1.73.7; παλίρροια Id.1.82.3; προτέρημα Id.1.18.6; -εστέρα συμπλοκή Id.1.40.11; τὸ -έστερον μέρος Id.3.37.8; -εστέρα σπάνις *IG*4²(1).66.28 (Epid., i A.D.). **3.** *in rough* or *general outline*, τὸ ὁ., as Adv., *roughly*, Thphr.*HP*3.18.5; irreg. Sup. αἱ -ώταται δόξαι Epicur.*Ep.*1 p.3 U., cf. Phld.*Oec.*p.75 J. (Comp.); opp. ἀκριβής, Str.2.1.41, cf. 30; γενικαὶ καὶ ὡσανεὶ ὁλοσχερεῖς διαφοραί Heliod.ap.Orib.49.1.1; ὁλοσχερεῖ λόγῳ Plot.1.6.9; of an emetic (ἀποφορτισμός), *incomplete*, opp. ἀκριβής, Archig.ap.Orib.8.23.2. **4.** -έστερα διαιτήματα *fuller* diet, Gal.19.194. **II.** Adv. -ρῶς, συνθλάσαι pound *coarsely*, Dsc.5.72: Comp. -έστερον, συγκοπέντα Id.2.76.10, cf. Gal.13.1044. **2.** *entirely, altogether, utterly*, Diph.27, *IG*9(2).338.4 (Thessaly, ii B.C.), Plb.1.10.1, Cic.*Att.*6.5.2, etc.; ὁ. καὶ κατὰ κράτος λαβεῖν J.*BJProoem.*8; ὁ. διακεῖσθαι πρός τι to be *quite* bent upon a thing, v.l. in Isoc.5.135; ὁ. οἰκοδομῆσαι build *completely*, LXX 1*Es.*6.27(28). **3.** *roughly, in a general way*, Str.2.1.3, Longin.43.4; opp. ἀκριβῶς, Plot.3.8.9: Comp. -έστερον Gal.2.901.

**ὀλό-σχιστος**, ον, *cut out in one piece*, Pl.*Plt.*279d, 280c. **-σχοινος**, ὁ, *club-rush, Scirpus Holoschoenus*, Thphr.*HP*4.12.1, 9.12.1, Dsc.4.52: used in wicker-work, sts., like flax, soaked for use (βεβρεγμένος), sts. without soaking (ἄβροχος), Ael.*NA*12.43: hence prov., ἀπορράπτειν τὸ Φιλίππου στόμα ὁλοσχοίνῳ ἀβρόχῳ stop Philip's mouth with an unsoaked *rush* (for rushes were soaked to make them tough), i.e. without any trouble, Aeschin.2.21; so ἀποφράξαι ὁλοσχοίνῳ στόμα *AP*10.49 (Pall.).

**ὅλοσχος**, ὁ, *pedicle of the pomegranate* (cf. ὄσχη), Nic.*Th.*870.

⊛ **ὁλο-σώμᾰτος**, ον, *of* or *with the whole body*, στροφή Hld.4.17; εἰκών *full-length* portrait, *JHS*9.248 (Cyprus). **-τελής**, ές, *quite complete*, 1*Ep.Thess.*5.23, *Placit.*5.21.2, Vett.Val.247.8; ἀνεισφορία *IG*7.2713.45 (Acraephia). Adv. -λῶς, gloss on ὁλοσχερῶς, Suid., cf. Nech.ap.Vett.Val.155.3, *Peripl.M.Rubr.*30, Aq.*De.*13.16. **-της**, ητος, ἡ, (ὅλος) *wholeness, entireness*, Arist.*Metaph.*1023b36, S.E.*M.*10.52, Dam.*Pr.*158, Procl.*Inst.*67, etc. **-τίλλω**, *uproot entirely*, καλάμους *PLond.*1.131r.391. **-τμητος**, ον, *cut in large pieces*, δεῖπνα Phryn.*PS*p.94B.

**ὁλότροχος**· περιφερὴς λίθος, Hsch. (Cf. ὀλοίτροχος.) **ὀλουρίδας**· εἶδος κόγχης, Id. **ὀλούροισιν**· ἄνω τῆς θύρας στρόφιγγες, Id. **ὀλούφω**, = ὀλόπτω, Phot.; cf. ὀλουφεῖν· τίλλειν, Hsch., and v. διολούφειν.

**ὁλο-φάκελος** [ᾰ], ὁ, *complete faggot*, *PSI*6.683.33 (ii A.D.). **-φᾰκος**, ὁ, *unbruised lentils*, *PBouriant*13 (i A.D.), *Gp.*20.12.1.

⊛ **ὀλοφλυκτίς**, ίδος, ἡ, *large pimple*, Hp.*Mul.*2.206; *pimple on the tongue*, Myrtil.3.

**ὀλοφρονέω**, for *ὀλοοφρονέω (cf. ὀλοόφρων) *to be crafty, deceitful*, *WienerSitzb.*132(2).24 (Caria).

**ὀλόφρυς**, = κολοίφρυξ, *EM*526.1.

**ὀλοφυγγών**, όνος, ἡ, = ὀλοφλυκτίς, Theoc.9.30 (v.l. -φυγδών as in Hsch.).

**ὀλοφυδνός**, ή, όν, *lamenting*, ἔπος δ' ὀλοφυδνὸν ἔειπε Il.5.683, cf. 23.102, Od.19.362: neut. ὀλοφυδνά as Adv., *AP*7.486 (Anyt.).

**ὁλο-φυής**, ές, *grown as a whole, consisting all of one piece*, Arist.*PA* 693a25; *having the nature of a whole*, Dam.*Pr.*271, cf. 51; cf. οὐλοφυής. **-φῦλος**, ον, = ὁλόκληρος, Suid.

**ὀλοφυρ-μός**, ὁ, *lamentation*, Ar.*V.*390, Th.3.67, 7.71, Pl.*Ax.*368b. **-ομαι** [ῠ], used mostly in pres.: but fut. ὀλοφυροῦνται Lys.29.4 codd. (-ονται edd.): aor. ὠλοφυράμην Id.2.37; Ep. (without augm.) ὀλοφύραο, ὀλοφύρατο, Od.11.418, Il.8.245:—Pass., aor. part. ὀλοφυρθείς in same signf., Th.6.78:—an Aeol. form **ὀλοφύρρω** cited by Hdn.Gr.2.949. **I.** intr., *lament, wail, moan*, freq. in pres. part., Il.5.871, al.: with an Adv., πόλλ' ὀλοφυρόμενοι 24.328; οἰκτρ' ὀλοφυρομένους Od.10.409; αἰν' ὀ. 22.447, cf. Hdt.2.141, Democr.107a; ὀ. κακοῖς Th.6.78: abs., Pl.*R.*329a. **2.** *lament* or *mourn for the ills of others*: hence, *feel pity*, ὀλοφύρεται ἦτορ Il.16.450; ὀ. θυμῷ Od.11.418: c. gen., *have pity upon* one, Δαναῶν Il.8.33, 202; ὀλοφύρεται ἦτορ Ἕκτορος 22.169. **3.** *beg with tears and lamentations*, καί μοι δὸς τὴν χεῖρ', ὀλοφύρομαι 23.75. **4.** c. inf., πῶς ὀλοφύρεαι ἄλκιμος εἶναι; how is it thou *lamentest that* thou must be brave? Od.22.232: c. part., ὀ. τριηραρχοῦντες Lys.29.4. **II.** c. acc., *lament over, bewail*, Od.19.522, S.*El.*148 (lyr.), E.*Rh.*896 (lyr.), Th.2.44; σφᾶς αὐτοὺς Lys.2.37; τὸν μὲν γενόμενον ὀλοφύρονται, ὅσα μιν δεῖ.. ἀναπλῆσαι κακά for all the miseries which he must go through, Hdt.5.4. **2.** *pity*, τινα Il.8.245, Od.4.364, 10.157.—Ep. Verb, rare in Trag., sts. in Att. Prose, cf. ὀλοφυρμός, ὀλόφυρσις. ⊛ **-σις**, εως, ἡ, = ὀλοφυρμός, τὴν ὀ. τινὸς ποιεῖσθαι Th.1.143; τὰς ὀ. τῶν ἀπογιγνομένων *lamentations for*.., Id.2.51, cf. J.*BJProoem.*4, Philostr.*VA* 4.45. **-τέος**, α, ον, *to be lamented*, ἡμέρα ib.26. **-τικός**, ή, όν, *inclined to lamentation, querulous*, Arist.*EN*1125a9. Adv. -κῶς J.*BJ*6.5.3.

⊛ **ὄλοφυς**· οἶκτος, ἔλεος, θρῆνος, Hsch., prob. in Sapph.*Supp.*10.3.

**ὀλόφυτον**, τό, = κάππαρις, Dsc.2.173.

**ὀλοφώϊος**, ον, Ep. Adj. *destructive, deadly*, Hom. only in Od. and in neut. pl., ὀ. δήνεα *pernicious* arts or plots, 10.289; ὀλοφώϊα εἰδώς versed in *pernicious arts*, 4.460, 17.248; πάντα δέ τοι ἐρέω ὀλοφώϊα τοῖο γέροντος ib.410; in later Ep., λύκων ὀ. ἔρνος Theoc.25.185; ὀ. ἰός Nic.*Th.*327. (The notion of *destruction*, necessary in Theoc. and Nic. ll.cc., and assumed by Hsch., is perh. not certain in Hom., where ὀ. may mean simply *deceptive, tricky*: perh. akin to ἐλεφαίρομαι.)

**ὁλό-φωνος**, ον, *full-voiced*, or *vox et praeterea nihil*, of the cock, Cratin.259 (**ὀλόφωνος** *with fatal voice*, cj. Meineke). **-χάλαρος**, v.l. for ὅλος χαλαρός, Gal.*UP*11.15. **-χαλκος**, ον, *all of brass* or *copper*, Sch.E.*Ph.*120. **-χλωρος**, ον, *all green*, interpol. in Dsc.4.126. **-χρόνιος**, α, ον, *all the year through*, Hdn.*Epim.*186. Adv. -ίως Tz.ad Hes.*Op.*31. **-χρονος**, ον, τριετία *three whole years*, *BGU*1027.17 (iv A.D.). ⊛ **-χροος**, ον, contr. -χρους, ουν, *all of one colour*, ζῷα Arist.*GA*785b19. **-χρῡσον**, τό, = ἀείζων τὸ μέγα, Ps.-Dsc.4.88. **-χρῡσος**, ον, *of solid gold*, Antiph.224.5, Call.*Iamb.*1.130, Callix.2, Plu.2.852b: metaph., Phld.*Rh.*1.190S. **-χῡλος**, ον, *entirely sodden*, Eust.1552.34. **-ψῡχέω**, prob. misspelling of ὀλιγο- or ὀλιο- (v. ὀλίγος) ψυχέω, *to be faint-hearted*, ἐμοὶ μελήσι πῶς σοι ἀρεστὰ ἔσται, μὴ ὀλοψυχήσῃς *PLond.ined.*2132 (ii A.D.). **-ψῡχος**, ον, dub. sens. in Phld.*D.*3*Fr.*19 (perh. *consisting entirely of soul*); *with his whole soul*, Eust.1901.43. Adv. -χως Suid. s.v. ἐκτενῶς.

⊛ **ὄλπη**, ἡ, *leathern oil-flask*, esp. used in the wrestling-school, Theoc.2.156, Nic.*Th.*97; Corinth., Byz., and Cypr. word, acc. to Clitarch. ap.Ath.11.495c; λιθάργυρος ὄ. Achae.19; a Cynic's *flask*, *AP*6.293 (Leon.), 7.68 (Arch.). **2.** = πρόχοος, Ion Trag.10 (Thess. in this sense acc. to Clitarch. l. c.).

**Ὄλπια**, τά, v. Ὄλβια.

**ὄλπις**, ιος and ιδος, ἡ, = ὄλπη, Sapph.51.2, Theoc.18.45, Call.*Fr.*181.

**Ὀλυμπ-ία** (sc. χώρα), ἡ, *Olympia*, district round Pisa and the Elean Olympus, where the Olympic games were held, Hdt.2.160, 5.22, etc.; or Pisa itself, Pi.*O.*1.7, etc.:—also **Οὐλυμπία**, ib.3.15. Adv. **Ὀλυμπίᾱσι**, *at Olympia*, *IG*1².606, Ar.*V.*1382, *Lys.*1131, Th.1.143, And.4.25, Pl.*Ap.*36d, D.21.145, etc.:—also **Ὀλυμπίαζε**, *to Olympia*, Th.3.8, And.1.132, 4.26, Thphr.*Lap.*16; Dor. **Ὀλυμπιάνδις** Theognost.*Can.*163; **Ὀλυμπίᾱθεν**, *from Olympia*, St.Byz. **II.** ⊛ **Ὀλύμπια** (sc. ἱερά), τά, *the Olympic games*, or *games in honour of Olympian Zeus*, Hdt.1.59, etc.: mostly without the Art., Ὀλύμπια ἄγειν Id.8.26; Ὀ. ἀναραιρηκώς having won at the Olympic games, Id.6.36; Ὀ. νικᾶν (v. νικάω I.1); Ὀ. δραμεῖν στάδιον Plu.2.179d: also with the Art., ποιεῖν τὰ Ὀ. X.*HG*7.4.28; στέφεσθαι τὰ Ὀ. Luc.*Merc.Cond.*13. **-ιακός**, ή, όν, *Olympian*, ὅρος X.*HG*7.4.14; ἔτος ib.28; ἐκεχειρία Arist.*Fr.*533; νῖκαι Jul.*Or.*2.83b. **-ίας** ἄνεμος, ὁ, *the WNW. wind*, elsewh. Ἀργέστης or Ἰάπυξ, Arist.*Mete.*363b24, *Mu.*394b26, Lyd.*Mens.*4.119. ⊛ **-ιάς**, άδος, ἡ, = fem. of Ὀλύμπιος, *Olympian*, epith. of the Muses, Il.2.491, *h.Merc.*450, Hes.*Th.*25, 52: then, generally, *dweller on Olympus, goddess*, Id.*Fr.*142.2; Ὀ. βασιλείης, of the Argive Hera, Phoronis4; Ὀ. Χάριτες Ar.*Av.*782; ἤ τις Ὀλυμπιάδων θεᾶν, of the nymphs *of* the Mysian *Olympus*, S.*Aj.*881 (lyr.). **2.** Ὀ. ἐλαῖαι olive-crowns *of the Olympic games*, Pi.*N.*1.17. **II.** as Subst., **1.** *the Olympic games*, Hdt.7.206; τῇ Ὀ. νικᾶν Id.6.103; τὸ κλέος.. τᾶν Ὀλυμπιάδων Pi.*O.*1.94, cf. 2.3, al. **2.** (sc. νίκη) *a victory at Olympia*, τοῖσι Λακεδαιμονίοισι Ὀλυμπιάδα προσέβαλε *the glory of an Olympic victory*, Hdt.6.70; Ὀλυμπιάδα ἀνελέσθαι win *a victory in the Olympic games*, ib.103, cf. 125; νικᾶν Ὀ. Id.9.33, cf. Simon.152; later, *any victory* or *triumph*, Philostr.*VA*4.44. **3.** *an Olympiad*, i.e. the space of four years between the celebrations of the Olympic games, Timae.21, cf. *SIG*557.15 (iii B.C.). **-ίᾱσι**, Adv., v. Ὀλυμπία, ἡ: but **Ὀλυμπιάσι** [ᾰ], dat. pl. of Ὀλυμπιάς. ⊛ **-ιεῖον** or **-ίειον**, τό, *temple of Olympian Zeus*, Th.6.64, 65, 70, al.: in codd. freq. wrongly written **Ὀλύμπιον**, as in Pl.*Phdr.*227b, Arist.*Pol.*1313b23; cf. τὸ ἱερὸν Ὀλύμπιον πεντεσυλλάβως, ὡς Ἀσκληπίειον, Phot. **II.** ⊛ **Ὀλυμπίεια**, τά, *his festival*, *IG*2².1496.82 (iv B.C.), 2.1291.6 (iii B.C.):—later **Ὀλυμπεῖα**, ib.3.127 (ii A.D.), al. ⊛ **-ικός**, ή, όν, *of Olympus*, ἐσβολή Hdt.7.172; ὑπώρεια Plu.*Aem.*13. **2.** *of Olympia, Olympic*, ὁ Ὀ. ἀγών the *Olympic* games, Th.1.6, Ar.*Pl.*583; ὁ Ὀ. λόγος title of work by Gorgias (*Fr.*7): **-κός**, ὁ, name of a month in Elis, *Inscr.Olymp.*8.

**Ὀλυμπιο-δρόμος**, ον, *running at the Olympic games*, ἵπποι B.3.3. ⊛ **-νίκη** [ῑ], ἡ, *victory at Olympia*, Id.4.17, Antipho Soph.49 (both pl.). **-νίκης** [ῑ], ου, Dor. **-νίκας**, ᾱ, ὁ, *conqueror in the Olympic games*, Pi.*O.*6.4, al., Hdt.5.47, 71, And.4.33, Pl.*R.*465d, Arist.*Rh.*1365a25. **II.** as Adj., Ὀ. ὕμνος, τεθμός, Pi.*O.*3.3, 7.88. ⊛ **-νῖκος**, ον, *victorious in the Olympic games*, ib.5.21, al.

⊛ **Ὀλύμπιος**, ον, *Olympian, of Olympus, dwelling on Olympus*, epith. of the gods above, Il.1.399, 20.47; οἱ Ὀ. Men.*Sam.*187; esp. of Zeus, who is called simply Ὀλύμπιος in Il.18.79, 22.130, al., Hes.*Op.*474, etc.; so Ζεὺς πατὴρ Ὀ. S.*Tr.*275: in Prose, ὁ Ζεὺς ὁ Ὀ. Th.2.15, *IG* 1².39.35, 2².112.7; μὰ τὸν Δία τὸν Ὀ. Ar.*Nu.*817; Ζεὺς ὁ Ὀ. Th.3.14; ὁ Ὀ. Ζεύς Pl.*R.*583b; τοι Δι Ὀλυνπιοι *SIG*9.6 (Elis, vi B.C.); Ὀ. ἀστήρ Opp.*H.*4.315; ἕδρη *IG*9(1).882.1 (Corc.): applied by Com. to Pericles, Ar.*Ach.*530, cf. Cratin.71, Telecl.17; also Ὀ. δώματα the mansions *of Olympus*, Il.1.18, al., Hes.*Th.*75.

**Ὀλυ[μπι]ών**, ῶνος, ὁ, name of a month at Chalcis, *IG*12(9).900*b* 1.

⊛ **Ὄλυμπος**, ὁ, Ep. also **Οὔλυμπος**, metri gr., Mount *Olympus* (in Thessaly, Hdt.1.56, etc.), conceived to be the seat of the gods, Od.6.42, but distd. from heaven (οὐρανός), Il.15.192 sq., cf. 5.867 sq.; οὐρανὸς Οὔ. τε 5.750 (but = οὐρανός, *sky*, Od.20.103, cf. 113); Κρονίωνα θεῶν ἄτερ ἥμενον ἄλλων ἀκροτάτῃ κορυφῇ πολυδειράδος Οὐ. Il.5.754; ἑκάστῳ (sc. θεῶν) δώματα καλὰ τέτυκτο κατὰ πτύχας Οὐλύμποιο 11.77, cf. 18.186: in Att. = οὐρανός, a form of oath, οὐ τὸν Ὄ. S.*OT*1088

(lyr.), cf. *Ant.*758. II. of other mountains, as in Mysia, Hdt.1.36, S.*Fr.*522, X.*Cyn.*11.1; in Laconia, Plb.2.65.8; in Elis, Str.8.3.31; in Lycia, Id.14.3.8, cf. 14.5.7; in Cyprus, Id.14.6.3. III. Adv. Ὀλυμπόνδε, in Hom. always **Οὔλυμπόνδε**, Il.1.221, al.:—*to, towards Olympus*, Pi.*O.*3.36, etc.; **Οὐλυμπόθεν**, *from O.*, Id.*P.*4.214.

**ὀλυνθ-άζω**, *impregnate the female palm-tree with the pollen of the male* (cf. ἐρινάζω), Thphr.*HP*2.8.4, *CP*2.9.15.—Used by analogy, cf. ὄλονθος. **-η**, ἡ, = ἐρινεός (the tree), Paus.4.20.2. **-ηφόρος**, ον, = ὀλυνθοφόρος, Zen.2.23. **-ος**, v. ὄλονθος.

**ὀλυνθο-φορέω**, **-φόρος**, v. ὀλονθο-φορέω, -φόρος.

**ὄλυνος**· τὸ ἀπότριμμα, καὶ ἀποκάθαρμα, Hsch.

❋ **ὄλῡρ-ᾰ** (on the accent v. Hdn.Gr.1.262), ἡ, mostly in pl. ὄλυραι, = ζειαί (q.v.), Hdt.2.36,77, D.8.45, *PHal.*20.2 (iii B.C.), Lxx*Ex.*9.32, etc.; mentioned as food for horses along with barley (κρῖ), Il.5.196, 8.564. 2. *rice-wheat*, a cultural variety of ζειά 2, Thphr.*HP*8.9.2, Diocl.*Fr.*113, Dsc.2.91. **-ινος**, η, ον, *of* ὄλυρα, πυρὸς ὀλύρινος wheat *mixed with* ὄλυρα, *PSI*5.537.6 (iii B.C.); *made of* ὄλυρα, ἄρτος Gal.6.504. **-ίτης** [ῑ], ου, ὁ, *made of* ὄλυρα, Lxx 3*Ki.*19.6.

**ὀλῠρο-κόπος**, ὁ, *miller who grinds* ὄλυρα, *OGI*729.4 (iii B.C.). **-κρ(ιθον)** or -(**ιθος**), perh. *a mixture of* ὄλυρα *and barley*, *PLond.ined.*2360 (iii B.C.), *PCair.Zen.*292.14, al. (iii B.C.).

**ὄλχον**· ἐνέδραν, Hsch.

**ὀλώδης**, ες, = θολώδης, Hp.ap.Gal.19.126.

**ὀλώϊος**, rare poet. form of ὀλοός (q.v.).

**ὄλωλα, ὀλώλω**, v. ὄλλυμι B. III. **ὅλως**, v. ὅλος III.

**ὅλωσις**, εως, ἡ, *totalization, integration*, *Theol.Ar.*59, Dam.*Pr.*155.

**ὀμ-** in **ὀμμένω**, etc., Aeol. for ἀνα- (q.v.) before labials.

**ὁμᾷ**, Adv., Dor. for ὁμῇ (-ῇ), *Hymn.Is.*138, *IG*12(3).320.5 (Thera), Hsch.; Aeol. ὄ[μ]α *IG*12(2).526b31 (Eresos); ὔμα, ib.29.10,32.11.

**Ὁμᾰγύριος**, epith. of Zeus at Aegium as god *of the assembly*, Paus.7.24.2.

**ὁμάγυρις**, Dor. for ὁμήγυρις (q.v.).

**ὁμάδελφος** [ᾰ], = αὐτάδελφος, Archyt.ap.Simp.*in Cat.*178.25, *BCH* 21.593 (Delph., iv B.C.), Ramsay *Cities and Bishoprics* 2.567 (Acmonia, iv A.D.), Sch.Ar.*Ra.*768.

**ὁμᾰδ-εύω**, (ὅμαδος) *collect*, Hsch., Suid. **-έω**, *make a noise* or *din*, of a number of people all speaking at once, in Od. always of the suitors, 1.365, al. (never in Il.), cf. A.R.2.638, etc. **-ίς**, Adv. *together*, *EM*806.8. ❋ **-ος**, ὁ, *noise, din*, esp. of the confused voices of a number of men (coupled with δοῦπος, the tramp of men), Il.9.573, 23.234, Od.10.556 (nowh. else in Od.); also opp. the sound of flutes and pipes, συρίγγων τ' ἐνοπὴν ὅμαδόν τ' ἀνθρώπων Il.10.13, cf. Pi.*N.*6.38, Philyll.5 (lyr.); ὅ. ἄλυρον ἔλεγον E.*Hel.*185 (lyr.); rarely of a tempest, Il.13.797. II. *noisy throng* or *mob of warriors*, 7.307, 15.689, 17.380: metaph., βίβλων ὅ. Pl.*R.*364e. III. *din of battle*, Hes.*Sc.*155, 257; χάλκεον στονόεντ᾽..ὅμαδον *the din of* brazen war, Pi.*I.*8(7).27.—Ep. and Lyr., never in Trag., exc. in E. l. c. (lyr.), once in Pl. l. c.

**ὁμάζω**, *growl*, of bears and panthers, Zenod.ap.Valck.*Animadv. ad Ammon.*p.174 (ὀγκάζειν cj. in *Stud.Ital.*1.88).

**ὁμαίμ-ιος**, ον, *related by blood*, Pi.*N.*6.16; cf. sq. **-ος**, ον, *of the same blood, related by blood*, Hdt.1.151, 8.144, Cratin.433, Pl.Com.192, etc.; αἷμα A.*Eu.*653; φόνος ὅ. murder *by one near of kin*, ib.212. 2. mostly as Subst., ὅμαιμος, ὁ or ἡ, *brother* or *sister*, Id.*Th.*681, *Eu.*605, etc.; σῆς ὁ. καὶ κασιγνήτης S.*El.*12; τὴν σὴν ὅ. ib.325, cf. *BMus.Inscr.*1036.6 (Caria, ii/i B.C.): Boeot. gen. pl. ὁμήμων Corinn.*Supp.*2.68. **-οσύνη**, ἡ, = sq., *APl.*4.128. **-ότης**, ητος, ἡ, *blood-relationship*, *Gloss.* **-ων**, ον, gen. ονος, = ὅμαιμος, Hdt.5.49, A.*Th.*415: metaph., ἁρπαγαὶ δὲ διαδρομᾶν ὁμαίμονες *near akin to..*, ib.351 (lyr.): Comp. ὁμαιμονέστερος *more near akin*, S.*Ant.*486. 2. as Subst., *brother* or *sister*, Id.*Aj.*1312, *OC*1275. 3. Ζεὺς ὁ., = ὁμόγνιος II, A.*Supp.*402 (lyr.).

**ὁμάϊον**, τό, (ἀΐω) v. ὁμάκοοι.

**ὁμαιχμ-έω**, (αἰχμή) *fight on the same side with* one, Opp.*H.*5.160. **-ία**, Ion. -ίη, ἡ, *union for battle, defensive alliance, league*, Th.1.18, App.*Gall.*15; ὁ. συνθέσθαι τινί form *a league with* one, Hdt.8.140.α'; πρός τινα *against* one, Id.7.145: pl., Anon.ap.Suid. s.v. δυσμικῶν. **-ος**, ον, *fighting together*: as Subst., *ally*, Th.3.58.

**ὁμάκοοι**, οἱ, (ὁμός, ἀκούω) *fellow-hearers, fellow-students* in the Pythagorean school, Iamb.*VP*17.73:—hence **ὁμακοεῖον** or **ὁμακόϊον**, τό, *the school* of Pythagoreans, ib.6.30, Porph.*VP*20, Olymp.*in Alc.* p.132 C.:—also **ὁμάϊον**, Hierocl.*in CA*27 p.484 M., Eust.856.63.

**ὁμαλεῖς**· ὁμοῦ, Hsch. (i.e. ὁμαδίς).

**ὁμᾰλ-εύς**, έως, ὁ, *leveller* of land, *BGU*1527.3 (iii B.C.). **-ής**, ές, *level, even*, of the ground, Pl.*Criti.*118a; τὰ ὁ. *level ground*, X.*Cyn.*2.7, Arist.*Pr.*880b15; in Archit., ὀρθὸν καὶ ὁ. *IG*2².1668.63; πεσεῖν εἰς ὁμαλές fall on *flat ground*, Arist.*Pr.*913b9; of surfaces, *smooth*, νεφροί Id.*PA*671b7; of certain plants, Thphr.*HP*1.5.3; σωροὶ παράλληλοι καὶ ὁ. Plu.*Lyc.*8. 2. *equable, even*, [κίνησις] Arist.*Ph.*228b28, cf. 223b21, al.; of music, Id.*Pr.*918a12; ἀραιότης, παρεκτάσεις, v.l. for ὁμαλός in Epicur.*Ep.*2 pp.49,53 U. 3. of condition, δίαιτα Aristox.*Fr.Hist.*15, cf. Plu.*Lyc.*8. 4. for Adv. ὁμαλῶς v. ὁμαλός. ❋ **-ίζω**, X.*Oec.*18.5, Arist. (v. infr.): fut. -ιῶ Lxx*Is.*45.2, -ίσω Sm.*Jb.*39.10: aor. ὡμάλισα Lxx*Is.*28.25:—Pass., pf. ὡμάλισμαι (v. infr.): aor. ὡμαλίσθην Arist.*Pol.*1266b3: fut. ὁμαλισθήσομαι ib.1265a40: fut. Med. ὁμαλιεῖται in pass. sense, X.*Oec.*18.5: (ὁμαλός):—*make even* or *level*, τὴν γῆν Thphr.*CP*5.9.8, cf. Damox.2.50:—Pass., X. l.c., *IG*2².380.10, *PPetr.*2 p.43 (iii B.C.). 2. *level, equalize*, μᾶλλον δεῖ τὰς ἐπιθυμίας ὁ. ἢ τὰς οὐσίας Arist.*Pol.*1266b30, cf. 1267b5:—Pass., διὰ τῆς κτήσεως ὡμαλισμένης ib.1270a39; ὁμαλισθησομένη εἰς τὸ αὐτὸ πλῆθος ib.1265a40; πόλεις ὡμαλισμέναι ὑπὸ τῶν συμφορῶν Isoc.5.40, cf. 6.65. 3. *reduce to a uniform mass*, τὰ σιτία καὶ τὸ ποτόν Diocl.*Fr.*141. II. intr., *to be* or *remain equal* or *equable, maintain one's level*, Thphr.*CP*5.1.12, Mnesith.ap.Ath.5.357e, Plb.29.26.2, Phld.*Po.*5.9. **-ιξις**, εως, ἡ, *levelling* of sand for athletic contests, *BCH*23.566 (Delph., iii B.C.), *Milet.*7.60 (Didyma). **-ισμός**, ὁ, *levelling*, τῆς γῆς Lxx *Ba.*5.7, cf. Orib.49.12.1. II. καθ' ὁμαλισμὸν ἀναγνωστέον one must read *without a rise of pitch*, of enclitics, Sch.A.*Ag.*937, Sch.Ar.*Pl.*414; ἡ κατὰ ὁ. [ἀπήχησις] ἐν τῇ βαρείᾳ D.T.630.1. **-ιστέον**, *one must level*, *Gp.*18.2.1. **-ιστήρ**, ῆρος, ὁ, *instrument for levelling, strickle*, in pl., *Gloss.* **-ιστρον**, τό, = foreg., Hsch. s.v. λίστρον.

**ὁμᾰλόδερμος**, ον, *smooth-skinned*, Suid. s.v. λειόφλοιον (λειόφυλλον, -φυτον codd.).

❋ **ὁμᾰλ-ός**, ἡ, όν, (ὁμός, ἅμα) of a surface, *even, level*, οἱ δ' ὁμαλὴν ποίησαν Od.9.327: freq. in Prose, opp. τραχύς, X.*An.*4.6.12, cf. *SIG*996.32 (Smyrna), etc.; ἐν τῷ ὁ., ἐς τὸ ὁ., on (to) *level ground*, Th.5.65, X.*An.*4.2.16: Sup. -ώτατον Th.4.31, cf. Hp.*Aër.*13; λεῖον καὶ ὁ... σῶμα ἐποίησε smooth and *even*, Pl.*Ti.*34b. 2. *uniform* in consistency, of a sediment, Hp.*Prog.*12, cf. *Judic.*3, Gal.9.605. 3. of sound, φωνὴ ὁ. καὶ λεία Pl.*Ti.*67b, cf. Arist.*HA*581a19. 4. *even, equable*, κατάστασις δικαία καὶ ὁ. Hp.*Fract.*30; of motion, Arist.*Ph.*223a1, etc.; δίνη Epicur.*Ep.*2 p.53 U.; τὸ ὁ. καὶ σύμμετρον, opp. τὸ ἄκρατον, Pl.*Lg.*773a; τὸ ὁ. *consistency*, of ἦθος, Arist.*Po.*1454a26. Adv. -λῶς, ἀνώμαλος *regularly* irregular, ib.a27. 5. of circumstances, *on a level, equal*, -ώτεραι ἂν αἱ οὐσίαι εἶεν Id.*Pol.*1309a25; ὁ ὁ γάμος marriage *with an equal*, A.*Pr.*901 (lyr.); ὁ. ἔρωτες Theoc.12.10; ἀλλάλοις ὁμαλοί *on a level with* one another, *equal*, Id.15.50, cf. Erinn.4.2; ὁ. βίος *IG*14.463. Adv. -λῶς, ἡ δίαιθ' ὁ. διάκειται is *equable*, Critias 6.25. 6. *not remarkable, middling, average*, ὁ. στρατιώτης *an ordinary sort of* soldier, Theoc.14.56. II. Adv. ὁμαλῶς (cf. supr. I.4,5) *evenly*, ἀλείφειν καὶ περιστέλλειν ὁ. Hp.*Acut.*17; ὁ. βαίνειν march *in an even line*, Th.5.70; ὁ. προϊέναι X.*An.*1.8.14; ὁ. ῥίπτειν, σπείρειν, Id.*Oec.*17.7, 20.3; κινεῖσθαι Arist.*Ph.*238a21, cf. Epicur.*Ep.*2 pp.49, 51 U.; εὐφραίνεσθαι Id.*Sent.Vat.*48. 2. *on terms of equality*, ὁ. βιῶναι Isoc.4.151; πραγμάτων ὁ. πάντων of all *alike*, Plu.*Per.*6; πάντες ὁ. ib.10, etc.; ὁ. πανταχοῦ Damox.2.30.—Cf. ὁμαλής. **-ότης**, ητος, ἡ, *evenness* of surface, τοῦ ἐνόπτρου Arist.*Mete.*377b17, cf. *Metaph.*1043a24; *level ground*, opp. ἀκρόπολις, Id.*Pol.*1330b20. 2. *equability, equilibrium*, Pl.*Ti.*57e; ὁ. ἀποβάλλειν, ἀπολέσαι, lose *equilibrium*, ib.58e. 3. *evenness* of temperature, Arist.*Metaph.*1032b7; of the pulse, Gal.8.457; *regularity* of motion, Procl.*Hyp.*2.23. 4. *equality*, παίδων Pl.*Lg.*773d; ἐξευπορεῖν ὁ. ταῖς οὐσίαις ib.918c, cf. Arist.*Pol.*1309b39. **-υντικός**, ή, όν, *emollient*, δύναμις Gal.6.500. **-ύνω**, = ὁμαλίζω I.1, τὴν κονδύλωσιν Hp.*Haem.*5, cf. Pl.*Ti.*45e; τὴν ἄρουραν Arist.*Pol.*1284a30. II. *bring* the body *to an even temperature*, Id.*Mete.*381a20, cf. *Metaph.*1032b19 (Pass.). 2. *make regular*, τὸ πνεῦμα Antyll.ap.Orib.6.5.1.

**ὁμάξασθαι**· ἐκμάξασθαι, ὁμοιωθῆναι, Hsch. **ὅμαργες**, sine expl., Theognost.*Can.*131; glossed τὸ συμφωνοῦν by Arc.124. **ὁμαρές**· ὁμοῦ, συμφώνως, Hsch. (Prob. ᾰ, from ὁμός and ἀραρίσκω.)

**Ὁμάριος**, epith. of Zeus, Plb.2.39.6, cf. 5.93.10; cf. Ἀμάριος.

**ὅμαρξον**· ἀπόμαξον, Hsch. (cf. ὀμόργνυμι).

**ὁμαρτ-έω**, Il.24.438, E.*Ba.*923; Aeol. imper. ὐμάρτη Theoc.28.3: impf. ὡμάρτουν S.*OC*1647; Ion. -ευν A.R.1.579, Theoc.2.73; Ep. 3 dual ὁμαρτήτην, v. ὁμαρτήδην: fut. -ήσω Hes.*Op.*196, E.*Ph.*1616: aor. ὡμάρτησα Coluth.25; opt. ὁμαρτήσειεν, etc., Od.13.87, al.: aor. 2 ὅμαρτεν Orph.*A.*511: *act together, at the same moment*, τὸν δ' Αἴας καὶ Τεῦκρος ὁμαρτήσανθ' ὁ μὲν ἰῷ βεβλήκει, Αἴας δὲ..νύξεν Il.12.400; ἐξ οἴκου βῆσαν ὁμαρτήσαντες ἅμ' ἄμφω Od.21.188. 2. *accompany*, ἐν νηῒ θοῇ ἢ πεζὸς ὁμαρτέων Il.24.438; οὐδέ κεν ἴρηξ κίρκος ὁμαρτήσειεν *could* not *keep pace, keep up with* the ship, Od.13.87. 3. c. dat., *walk beside, accompany*, τινι Hes.*Op.*196,676, *Th.*201; ὁ. σύν τινι S.*OC*1647; πρός τινα Call.*Cer.*129; also, *pursue, chase*, A.*Eu.*338 (lyr.): abs., Id.*Pr.*678. 4. of things, *attend*, διθύραμβος ὁ. Διονύσῳ Id.*Fr.*355; τῷ γήρᾳ φιλεῖ χὠ νοῦς ὁμαρτεῖν S.*Fr.*260: abs., *supervene*, Hp.*Morb.*2.61, cf. A.*Th.*1027.—Poet. Verb, used once by Hp. l.c.; cf. ἁμαρτέω. **-ῇ**, Adv., v.l. for ἁμαρτῇ (q.v.) in Hom., also found in E.*Hec.*839, *Hipp.*1195, *Heracl.*138, A.R.1.538; ὁμαρτῇ in Hom., Aristarch. acc. to *Lex.Mess.*p.408 and Eust.751.63, but ὁμαρτηι *Ath.Mitt.*17.272 (Athens, ii A.D.). **-ήδην**, Adv. = foreg., *both together*, τὼ δ' ἄρ' ὁμαρτήδην Il.13.584 (Aristarch., ὁμαρτήτην codd.).

❋ **ὁμάς**, άδος, ἡ, *the whole*, πάντες καθ' ὁμάδα all *together*, *Gp.*10.2.3; ἐν ὁμάδι in *one lump sum*, Men.Prot.p.15 D.; but ἐν ὁμάδι τὸ πρᾶγμα διοικούμενον *comprehensively*, Just.*Edict.*13 *Praef.*

**ὁμ-ασπις**, ιδος, ὁ, *fellow-soldier*, *APl.*4.233. **-αστος**, ον, (ἄστυ) *united in one city* (cf. ὁμόπτολις), prob. l. in Herod.2.7. ❋ **-αῦλαξ**, Dor. **-ῶλαξ**, ἄκος, ὁ, ἡ, *with adjoining lands*, A.R.2.396, *AP*7.402 (Antip.). **-αυλία**, ἡ, *a dwelling together*, σύζυγοι ὁ. wedded *unions*, A.*Ch.*599 (lyr.). ❋ **-αυλος**, ον, (αὐλή) *living together, companion*, θεῶν ὅμαυλοι *POxy.*1083 *Fr.*1.8 (Satyric drama), cf. Hsch., Phot. 2. *neighbouring*, τὴν ὅ. χθόνα S.*Fr.*24.5. II. (αὐλός) *playing together on the flute, sounding together in concert*, γῆρας Id.*OT*187 (lyr.).

**ὀμβρ-έω**, *rain*, μετοπωρινὸν ὀμβρήσαντος Ζηνός when the latter rain

of autumn comes, Hes.*Op.*415, cf. A.R.3.1399, Lyc.79. **II.** trans., *rain* or *shower down upon*, ἀγαθὸν ὀ. τινί Ph.1.402; πηγὰς γάλακτος ὀ. ἐν μαστοῖς Id.2.397, cf. Nonn.*D.*2.33. **2.** *bedew, wet*, δακρύοις λάρνακα *AP*7.340. **3.** ὀμβρεῖ· ἀτιμάζει, ὑπερισχύει, αὔξει, πιαίνει, πλήθει, Hsch. **-ηγενής,** ές, *rain-born*, Orph.*H.*80.4. **-ηλός,** = -ηρός, Theognost.*Can.*62. **-ημα,** ατος, τό, *rain-water*, Lxx *Ps.* 77(78).44, Tz.*H.*5.416. **-ηρός,** ά, όν, = ὄμβριος, Hes.*Op.*451:— also -ήρης, ες, Nic.*Th.*406. Adv. -ρῶς Ph.1.129. **-ησις,** εως, ἡ, *a raining*, Sch.Hes.*Th.*138. ⊛ **-ία,** ἡ, *rain*, Sch.Ar.*Nu.*298. **-ίζω,** = ὀμβρέω, Eust.114.5. **-ικός,** ή, όν, *raining*, Vett.Val.11. 19. **-ιμαῖος,** = ὄμβριμος, ὕδωρ Hdn.*Epim.*100. **-ιμόθυμος,** v. ὀβριμόθυμος. ⊛ **-ῐμος,** η, ον, = sq., ὕδωρ *PMag.Lond.*121. 224. **II.** f.l. for ὄβριμος (q.v.). ⊛ **-ιος,** ον, *rainy, of rain*, ὄ. ὕδωρ *rain*-water, Xenoph.30.4, *SIG*56.29 (Argos, v B.C.), Hdt.2.25, Hp.*Aër.*7, etc.; ὕδατα Pi.*O.*10(11).3; χάλαζα S.*OC*1502; νέφος Ar. *Nu.*288; Ζεὺς ὄ., as sender of rain, Lyc.160, cf. Str.15.1.69, Plu.2. 158e.

**ὀμβρο-βλῦτέω,** *swell from rain*, Suid. **-δόκος,** ον, *holding* or *receiving rain*, κρωσσίον *AP*9.272 (Bianor). **-κτύπος** [ῠ], ον, *sounding with rain*, ζάλη A.*Ag.*656. **-ποιός,** όν, *rain-producing*, Sch.D Il.1.397.

**ὄμβρος** (A), ὁ, *storm of rain, thunder-storm*, sent by Zeus, ὅτ' ἐπιβρίσῃ Διὸς ὄ. Il.5.91; χειμάρρους..ὀπαζόμενος Διὸς ὄμβρῳ 11.493; ὡς δ' ὅτ' ἂν ἀστράπτῃ πόσις Ἥρης.., τεύχων ἢ πολὺν ὄ. κτλ. 10.6; of a storm at sea, Alc.*Supp.*26.4; ὄ. λάβρος Hdt.8.12; dist. fr. ὑετός or common rain, Arist.*Mu.*394ᵃ31; but sts., *heavy rain*, Hdt.8.98, S.*Tr.*146, E. *Tr.*78: in pl., *rains*, ὄ. πολλοὶ καὶ λάβροι Hdt.4.50, cf. 2.25, Pi.*P.*4.81, S.*OC*350. **2.** generally, *water*, as an element, μήτε γῆ, μήτ' ὄ. ἱερός, μήτε φῶς Id.*OT*1428, cf. Emp.98.2, 21.5: f.l. for ὄλβος in S. *Ant.*953; ὄ. ἀναγκαῖοι *urine*, Opp.*C.*4.443. **3.** *inundation*, τῶν παρακειμένων ὑδάτων *PTeb.*61(*b*).133 (ii B.C.), al.; ὀχετοὺς ἀγαγεῖν οἳ ἄξουσιν τὸν ὄ. εἰς τὰς ἐξαγωγούς *PCair.Zen.*383.13 (iii B.C.). **II.** metaph., *storm, shower*, ἐν πολυφθόρῳ Διὸς ὄ., of a battle, Pi.*I.*5(4). 49; δέδοικα δ' ὄμβρου κτύπον..τὸν αἱματηρόν A.*Ag.*1533 (lyr.); μέλας ὄ. χάλαζά θ' αἱματοῦσσ' (χαλάζης αἵματος codd.) S.*OT*1279; ὄμβρῳ δακρυόεντι Nonn.*D.*16.345; πυρὸς ὄμβροι Opp.*H.*3.22; ἡδὺς ὄ. ἀοιδῆς *AP*9.364 (Nestor).

**ὄμβρος** (B)· χοιρίδιον, Hsch. (Cf. ὄβρια.)

**ὀμβρο-τόκος,** ον, *rain-producing*, Orph.*H.*21.2, 82.5, Nonn.*D.*6. 85. **-φόρος,** ον, *rain-bringing*, ἄνεμοι A.*Supp.*35 (anap.); παρθένοι (of the clouds) Ar.*Nu.*299; βρονταί Id.*Av.*1750; κορῶναι Luc. *JTr.*31. **-χᾰρής,** ές, *delighting in rain*, Orph.*H.*26.8.

**ὀμβρ-όω,** only Pass. ὀμβροῦται, *imbricitur*, Gloss. **-ώδης,** ες, *rainy*, χωρία Thphr.*HP*8.7.1, cf. Ptol.*Tetr.*94, Vett.Val.6.5.

**ὀμέθνιος,** ον, = ὁμόεθνος, Phot., Suid.

**ὀμείρομαι** or **ὁμ-,** *desire, long for*, v.l. for ἱμείρομαι in best codd. of Lxx *Jb.*3.21 and 1*Ep.Thess.*2.8, cf. Sm.*Ps.*62(63).2, Hsch., Phot.; ὀμειρόμενοι περὶ παιδός *CIG*4000.7 (iv A.D., v. *JHS*38.152). (Etym. unknown; prob. not related to ἱμείρω or to μείρομαι.)

**ὀμεῖται,** v. ὄμνυμι.

**ὄμειχ-μα,** ατος, τό, *urine*, A.*Fr.*435 (pl., ὀμίχματα codd.). **-ω,** *make water*, μηδ' ἄντ' ἠελίοιο τετραμμένος ὀρθὸς ὀμείχειν Hes.*Op.*727, Pythag.ap.D.L.8.17: aor. ὤμειξα, ὤμειξεν αἷμα Hippon.55A. (Misspelt ὀμιχεῖν and ὤμιξεν in codd.; cf. Skt. *méhati*, Lat. *meiere*, etc.)

**ὁμέμπορος,** ὁ, *fellow-traveller, traveller*, Nonn.*D.*27.337 (pl.).

**ὅμερος·** τυφλός, Hsch. (cf. Ὅμηρος).

**ὁμέστιος,** ον, *sharing the same hearth* or *dwelling together with*, ἀθανάτοις ἄλλοισιν ὁ. Emp.147.1; σὺ δ' ὁ. θεοῖς; Ar.*Fr.*655: abs., ὁμεστίων καὶ πατραδελφεῶν *Schwyzer* 323 *C*43 (Delph., iv B.C.); ὁ. καὶ πολῖται Plb.4.33.5; ὁμοτράπεζοι καὶ ὁ. Plu.2.703e (**ὁμοέστιος** here and v.l. in Plb.2.57.7): metaph., Procl. *in Prm.*p.631 S.

**ὁμευν-αῖος,** α, ον, = ὅμευνος, ἄλοχοι Opp.*H.*1.509. **-έτης,** ου, ὁ, = ὅμευνος, E.*Med.*953, *Ion* 894: in late Prose, *Cat.Cod.Astr.*2.203:— fem.⊛ **-έτις,** ιδος, S.*Aj.*501, *Epigr.Gr.*781.8 (Cnidus); and **-ις,** ιδος, Lyc.372; cf. **ὁμευνήτου·** συγκοίτου, ὁμολέκτρου, Hsch. **-ος,** ον, *sleeping together, partner of the bed*, both of the man and woman, Maiist.3, *AP*7.735 (Damag.), Nic.*Th.*131, Man.3.148.

**ὁμέψιος,** ον, (ἑψία) *playing together, playmate*, Νύμφαισιν *AP*9.826, cf. Nonn.*D.*10.193, al.

**ὁμῆ** or **ὁμῇ,** Adv., (ὁμός) poet. for ὁμοῦ, *AP*12.234 (Strat.); cf. ὁμᾶ.

**ὁμηγενής,** ές, *born together, twin*, κοῦροι *Epigr.Gr.*(add.) 228*b*4 (Ephes.).

**ὁμηγερής,** ές, (ὁμός, ἀγείρω) *assembled*, ὁμηγερέεσσι..θεοῖσι Il.15. 84; ἤγερθεν ὁμηγερέες τ' ἐγένοντο they were *all assembled*, 1.57, al.; cf. ὁμηγυρής.

**ὁμήγοροι·** ἰσάγοροι, ἐν ταὐτῷ συνήγοροι, Hsch.

**ὁμηγῠρ-ής,** Dor. **ὁμᾱγῠρής,** ές, v.l. for ὁμηγερής in Il.1.57, 7.415, Pi.*P.*11.8. **-ίζομαι,** *assemble, call together*, πρὶν κεῖνον ὁμηγυρίσασθαι Ἀχαιοὺς εἰς ἀγορήν Od.16.376:—also **ὁμηγύρειν·** τὸ συνάξαι, Hsch. **-ιος,** v. Ὁμαγύριος. **-ις,** Dor. **ὁμάγ-** [ᾰ], ιος, ἡ, (ἄγυρις) *assembly, meeting*, esp. of the gods, θεῶν μεθ' ὁμήγυριν ἄλλων Il.20. 142, *h.Ap.*187, cf. *h.Merc.*332, Hellanic.54 J.; ὁμάγυρις Ζηνός Pi.*I.* 7(6).46; *any assembly, company*, γυναικῶν A.*Ch.*10; ἡλίκων E.*Hipp.* 1180; ἄστρων..νυκτέρων ὁ. A.*Ag.*4.

**ὁμήθ-εια,** poet. -είη, ἡ, *a living together*, in pl., Opp.*C.*4.2, Man.6. 188. ⊛ **-ης,** ες, (ἦθος) = ὁμοήθης, A.R.2.917, 3.118, Call.*Aet.*1.1.5, Nonn.*D.*5.364, Q.S.9.405. **2.** of Places, *accustomed*, λίμνη Nic. *Th.*415.

**ὁμηλῐκ-ία,** Ion. **-ίη,** ἡ, *sameness of age* (so perh. Il.20.465), used as a collective, *those of the same age*, esp. of young persons, ὁμηλικίην ἐρατεινήν Il.3.175; ὃν περὶ πάσης τίεν ὁμηλικίης 5.326, cf. Od. 3.364, Thgn.1018; οἷος -ίην ἐκέκαστο ὄρνιθας γνῶναι Od.2.158, cf. Il.13.431: as subj. of pl. verb, *Supp.Epigr.*1.567.6 (Karanis, iii B.C.). **II.** of one person, = ὁμῆλιξ, ὁμηλικίη δ' ἐμοὶ αὐτῷ but he is *of the same age with* myself, Od.3.49; ὁ. δέ μοί ἐσσι 22.209, cf. 6. 23; of two persons, Il.13.485. **-ος,** ον, *of like age*, τὸ ὁ. Procl. *in Prm.*p.949 S.

⊛ **ὁμῆλιξ,** Aeol. **ὐμᾶλιξ** Theoc.30.20: ἴκος, ὁ, ἡ:—*of the same age*, mostly of young persons, Od.15.197, 16.419, Hes.*Op.*444, 447, Hdt. 1.99, E.*Hipp.*1098, etc.; of things, παραδοχὰς..ὁμήλικας χρόνῳ Id. *Ba.*201. **2.** as Subst., *equal in age, comrade*, νίψον σοῖο ἄνακτος ὁμήλικα (of an elderly man) Od.19.358; δάμαρτος τῆς ἐμῆς ὁ. E.*Alc.* 953. **II.** *of like stature*, Luc.*Pr.Im.*13: neut., ὁμήλικα ζῷα Apollon.*Mir.*17.

**ὁμηλῠσία,** ἡ, *companionship*, Arat.178.

**ὅμηρα,** τά, v. ὅμηρος.

**Ὁμηραπάτη, Ὁμηραπάτης,** v. Ὁμηροπάτης.

**ὁμηρεία,** ἡ, (ὁμηρεύω) *giving of hostages* or *securities*: *a security*, ὁμηρειῶν ἐκδόσεις εἰς ἀλλήλους Pl.*Plt.*310e; ἐς ὁμηρείαν ὑπολιπεῖν τὸν προσοφειλόμενον μισθόν Th.8.45. **2.** *the condition of a hostage*, ἐκκλέπτειν ἐξ ὁμηρείας D.S.19.75; εἰς ὁ. δοῦναι Plb.9.11.4.—In codd. sts. ὁμηρία; also ὁμηρέα *IG*1².116.34.

⊛ **Ὁμήρ-ειον,** τό, *shrine of Homer* in Smyrna, Str.14.1.37; at Delos, *Inscr.Délos* 443*Bb*147 (ii B.C.). **-ειος,** ον, *Homeric*, Hdt.5.67, Ar. *Fr.*222; also η, ον, Ὁμηρείην ἀγλαΐην ἐπέων Alex.Aet.5.6; τὸ Ὁ. *the Homeric phrase*, Hp.*Mochl.*5; οἱ Ὁ., = οἱ Ὁμηρίδαι II, Pl.*Tht.*179e. Adv. -είως Ael.*NA*15.16.

**ὁμηρέταις·** ὁμοψήφοις, ὁμογνώμοσιν, Hsch.; cf. ὁμηρίταις (sic)· ὁμοψήφοις, ἀπὸ τοῦ ὁμοῦ ἐρέσσειν, ὁμογνώμοσιν, Phot.

**ὁμήρ-ευμα,** ατος, τό, *hostage, pledge*, Plu.*Rom.*16 (pl.). **-εύω** (A), *to be* or *serve as a hostage*, Aeschin.3.133, Antiph.117; παρά τινι Aeschin.2.81; ὑπέρ τινος Is.7.8, *IG*12(7).386.20 (Aegiale, iii B.C.): metaph., [οἶνος] πίστιν ἀνθρώποις καὶ φιλίαν -εύει *is the pledge of*.., J. *AJ*2.5.2. **II.** *take as a hostage*, E.*Rh.*434:—Med., *give hostages*, Aen.Tact.10.23 (the sense in E.*Ba.*297 is doubtful). **-εύω** (B), v. Ὅμηρος. **-εύω** (C), *go shares in*, ξυνῇσιν -εύουσι γενέθλαις ἀμφιβίων Opp.*H.*1.421. **-έω,** *meet*, ὡμήρησε δέ μοι..ἄγγελος ὠκύς Od. 16.468; expld. by Harp. as = ἀκολουθεῖν in Theopomp.Hist.278, cf. Arist.*Fr.*76. **2.** metaph., *accord, agree*, φωνῇ ὁμηρεῦσαι (Ion. for -οῦσαι) Hes.*Th.*39.

**Ὁμηρεών,** ῶνος, ὁ, a month at Ios, *IG*12(5).15.

⊛ **ὁμήρης,** ες, = ὅμηρος, c. dat., Nic.*Al.*70; also as v.l. for ὁμαρτῇ ib. 261. (Cf. ὁμαρές.)

**ὁμήρησις,** v. ὁμούρησις.

**Ὁμηρίδδειν** (ὁμηριάδειν cod.)· ψεύδεσθαι, Hsch. (Dor. for Ὁμηρίζω.)

**Ὁμηρ-ίδης,** ου, ὁ, mostly in pl. Ὁμηρίδαι, οἱ, *the Homerids*, a family or guild of poets in Chios, who claimed descent from Homer, Str. 14.1.35, cf. Hellanic.20 J.; of the ῥαψῳδοί, Pi.*N.*2.1. **II.** *imitators* or *admirers of Homer*, Pl.*R.*599e, *Phdr.*252b, *Ion* 530d, Isoc.10. 65. **-ίζω,** *imitate Homer, use Homeric phrases*, Lib.*Descr.*30.8 codd. **II.** *act scenes from Homer*, Artem.4.2. **III.** (ὁμοῦ, μηρός) *indulge unnatural lust*, with an intentional equivoque, Ach.Tat.8.9; cf. sq. II. ⊛ **-ικός,** ή, όν, *Homeric, in the manner of Homer*, Pl.*R.*600b: Comp. -κώτερος Str.1.1.6: Sup. -κώτατος Longin.13.3. Adv. **-κῶς** Strato Com.1.30, Cic.*Att.*1.16.1: Comp. -κώτερον A.D.*Synt.*165. 12. **II.** used equivocally, as foreg. III, *AP*11.218 (Crates). **-ίς,** ίδος, ἡ, Com. feminine of Ὅμηρος, Plu.2.496d. **-ιστής,** οῦ, ὁ, *rhapsode*, Aristocl.Hist.10, *POxy.*519.4 (ii A.D.). **II.** *actor of Homeric scenes*, Artem.4.2; mentioned (without the word) in Ach. Tat.3.20; cf. ὁμηρίζω II.

**Ὁμηρο-κέντρων,** ωνος, ὁ, *patchwork of Homeric tags*, *AP*9.381 tit., etc. **-μαντεῖον,** τό, *divination by means of verses of Homer*, *PMag. Lond.*121.148a. ⊛ **-μάστιξ,** ῖγος, ὁ, *scourge of Homer*, i.e. the Grammarian Zoïlus, from his spiteful criticisms on the Homeric poems, Gal.10.19, Suid.: in pl., generally, of Homeric critics, Eust.1702. 44. **-πάτης** [ᾰ], ου, ὁ, (πατέω) *one who tramples on Homer*, epith. of Xenophanes in Timo 60.1 as quoted by D.L.9.18, but -απάτης codd. S.E.*P.*1.224, which may be nom. masc., *perverter of Homer*, or gen. of Ὁμηραπάτη, *the Homeric fiction*, as expld. by S.E.

⊛ **Ὅμηρος,** ὁ, *Homer*; the name first occurs in Hes.*Fr.*265.1 (dub.), Xenoph.10, 11, Hdt.2.53: ὅμηρος was a Cumaean word for **τυφλός** acc. to Ps.-Hdt.*Vit.Hom.*13, cf. Lyc.422; ὁμηρεύω was Ion. for ἡγοῦμαι *guide the blind*, acc. to Ephor.1 J.; but Ὅμαρος is a Cretan pr. n., *GDI* iv p.1033.

⊛ **ὅμηρος,** ὁ, *pledge, surety, hostage*, ὁμήρους λαμβάνειν Hdt.6.99; ὁ. παῖδας λαβών Id.1.64; τὰ ἑωυτοῦ τέκνα δοὺς ὁ. Id.7.165, cf. Th.7.83; ἐν ὁμήρων λόγῳ ποιεύμενος Hdt.7.222; ἄγεσθαι ὅμηροι to be carried off *as hostages*, Id.8.94, 9.90; τοῖον ὅμηρόν μ' ἀποσυλήσας having robbed me of such *a hostage*, E.*Alc.*870 (anap.); ἔχω γ' ὑμῶν ὁμήρους have *hostages* for you, Ar.*Ach.*327, cf. *Lys.*244; of things, τὴν γῆν ὅμηρον ἔχειν Th.1.82: neut. pl., ὅμηρα δοὺς Lys.12.68, cf. Plb.3.52.5, *OGI* 751.5 (ii B.C.); ὥσπερ..ὁμήρους ἔχομεν τοῦ λόγου τὰ παραδείγματα Pl. *Tht.*202e: neut. pl. even of one person, μὴ πεμψάτω ὅμηρα τῶν Αἰαντείων μηθένα *Schwyzer* 366.17 (Tolophon); ὃς ἦν ὅμηρα Lxx 1*Ma.* 1.10.

**ὁμηρτῆρες** (post ὁμηρέταις)· ἀκόλουθοι, συνήγοροι, Hsch.

**ὁμῑλ-ᾰδόν**, Adv., (ὅμιλος) *in groups* or *bands, in crowds*, Il.12.3, 15.277:—also **ὁμῑληδόν**, Hes.*Sc.*170. II. c. dat., *together with*, A.R.3.596, Opp.*C.*2.199. **-έω**, Aeol. 3 sg. pres. **ὀμίλλει** Alc.61.29 Lobel, *to be in company with, consort with*, μνηστῆρσιν Od.2.21, al., cf. X.*Smp.*2.10, Pl.*R.*500c, etc.: with Preps., ἠὲ μετὰ Τρώεσσιν ὁμιλέοι ἢ μετ' Ἀχαιοῖς Il.5.86, cf. 834; ἐνὶ πρώτοισιν ὁ. 18.194, cf. 535; πὰρ παύροισι.. ὁμιλεῖς *consortest* with few, Od.18.383. 2. abs., μηδ' ἄλλοθ' ὁμιλήσαντες *joining in company*, 4.684; περὶ νεκρὸν ὁ. *throng* about the corpse, Il.16.641, cf. Od.24.19. II. in hostile sense, *join battle with*, ὁμιλέομεν Δαναοῖσιν Il.11.523, cf. Od.1.265; μετὰ τοῖσιν Il.11.502; σὺν Λαπίθαισί σε Κενταύρων ὁμιλῆσαι δορί E.*Andr.*792 (lyr.): abs., *join battle*, εὖτ' ἂν πρῶτον ὁμιλήσωσι φάλαγγες Il.19.158. III. of social intercourse, *hold converse with, be acquainted with, associate with*, τινι Hdt.3.130; κακοῖς ἀνδράσιν A.*Pers.*753 (troch.); ἀλλήλοις, μετ' ἀλλήλων, πρὸς ἀλλήλους, Pl.*Smp.*188d, *Plt.*272c, *Lg.*886c; τούτῳ τῷ τρόπῳ πρὸς τοὺς ἐρωμένους ὁ. Id.*Phdr.*252d; so of political intercourse, εἰθισμένος πρὸς ἡμᾶς ἀπὸ τοῦ ἴσου ὁ. Th.1.77; ἡμῖν ἀπὸ τοῦ ἴσου ὁ. Id.3.11; of scholars, ὁ. τινί *frequent* a teacher's lectures, *be his pupil*, X.*Mem.*1.2.15,39; ὁ. τῇ Ὁμήρου ποιήσει *to be familiar* with it, Luc.*Pr.Im.*26; cf. ὁμιλητής. 2. *to be friends*, οἱ μάλιστά τινι ὁμιλέοντες Hdt.3.99. 3. *speak to, address, harangue*, c. dat., Plb.4.4.7: abs., ὑπερηφάνως ὁ. Id.16.34.6; πρὸς ἵππον Babr.15.2; πρὸς ἀλλήλους *Ev.Luc.*24.14: generally, *speak, converse*, Phld.*Rh.*1.116 S.; κατά τινα διάλεκτον S.E.*M.*9.179; Ἑβραϊστί J.*AJ*11.5.6; ὁ. τινὶ περί τινος *talk* to.., *POxy.*928.5 (ii A.D.):—Pass., pf. part. ὡμιλημένος *used in conversation*, Phld.*Rh.*2.27 S. IV. of marriage or sexual intercourse, γυναιξὶ καὶ παρθένοις ὁ. X.*An.*3.2.25; παιδικοῖς Id.*Mem.*2.1.24, etc.; σὺν τοῖς φιλτάτοις S.*OT*367, cf. 1185; cf. Moer.p.276 P. V. of things or business which one has to do with, *attend to, busy oneself with*, ὁμιλεῖν ἀρχῇ, πολέμῳ, Th.6.55,70; καινοῖς πράγμασιν Ar.*Nu.*1399, cf. ὁμιλία I.4; φιλοσοφίᾳ, γυμναστικῇ, Pl.*R.*496b, 410c; παιδείᾳ *OGI*505.7 (Aezani); ἐμ Μούσαις ib.282.16 (Magn. Mae., iii B.C.); πονηροτάτοις σώμασιν ὁ., of a physician, Pl.*R.*408d; also like χρῆσθαι, *meet with, enjoy*, ὁ. τύχαις *to be in* good fortune, Pi.*N.*1.61; εὐτυχίᾳ ὁ. E.*Or.*354 (lyr.); but also, 2. of the things themselves, πλαγίαις φρένεσσιν ὄλβος οὐ πάντα χρόνον ὁ. does not *consort with* a crooked mind, Pi.*I.*3.6, cf. *P.*7.6; κυλίκων νεῖμεν ἐμοὶ τέρψιν ὁμιλεῖν gave me their delight *to keep me company*, S.*Aj.*1201 (lyr.); πλοῦτος καὶ δειλοῖσιν ἀνθρώπων ὁμιλεῖ B.1.51, cf. E.*El.*940: in physical sense, ὁ. ὁ βραχίων τῷ κοίλῳ τῆς ὠμοπλάτης πλάγιος *fits* obliquely *into*.., Hp.*Art.*1; of a plaster, *to be in contact*, ὁ. τῷ νοσέοντι μέρει Id.*Medic.*3. VI. *deal with* a man, *bear oneself towards* him, καλῶς ὁ. τινί Isoc.*Ep.*4.9; πρός τινα Id.2.24; τῷ δήμῳ πρὸς χάριν Arist.*Ath.*35.3 (so in Pass., συνειθισμένοι ὑπὸ πάντων πρὸς χάριν ὁμιλεῖσθαι Phld.*Lib.*p.62 O.); ταῦτα ἡ ἐμὴ νεότης.. ἐς τὴν Πελοποννησίων δύναμιν.. ὡμίλησε these were the achievements of my youth *in intercourse* with their power, Th.6.17. VII. of place, *come into, enter, visit*, c. dat., διαβάντες τὸν Ἅλυν.. ὡμίλησαν τῇ Φρυγίῃ Hdt.7.26, cf. 214, Pi.*P.*7.8; βαρεῖα χώρᾳ τῇδ' ὁ. heavily *will I visit* this land, A.*Eu.*720; ὁ. παρ' οἰκείαις ἀρούραις Pi.*O.*12.19; ὁ. τοιᾷδε πόλει Eup.292; poet. also ὁ. ἄνθεσιν Simon.47:—Pass., τὰ ὁμιλούμενα τῶν χωρίων *most frequented*, Philostr.*VA*1.16. VIII. ἐκτὸς ὁμιλεῖ (sc. τῶν ξυντρόφων ὀργῶν) he *wanders* from his senses, S.*Aj.*640 (lyr.). **-ηδόν**, v. ὁμιλαδόν. **-ημα**, ατος, τό, *intercourse*, ξενικά τε καὶ ἐπιχώρια ὁ. Pl.*Lg.*730b. II. of a person, κακὸν ὁ. bad *company*, E.*Fr.*219, cf. Luc.*Am.*25. **-ησις**, εως, ἡ, diplomatic *intercourse*, cj. in Th.6.17. **-ητέον**, *one must associate with*, τοῖς ἀνίσοις Arist.*EN*1163$^{b}$13; πρὸς ἀνθρώπους Iamb.*Protr.*20. **-ητής**, οῦ, ὁ, *disciple, scholar*, X.*Mem.*1.2.12.48, Luc.*Tim.*10, Philostr.*VA*1.16, Gal.10.22; τῶν θεῶν Iamb.*Myst.*5.26. 2. *one who has experience*, πόνων, of Heracles, Max.Tyr.3.7. **-ητικός**, ή, όν, *affable, conversable*, Isoc.1.30, *Stoic.*2.160; οἱ ἔξωθεν ὁ. Phld.*Vit.*p.4 J. II. ἕξις ὁ. a *social* habit, Pl.*Def.*415e; τί ὁμιλητικόν..; what *social charm*..? Alciphr.3.44; ὁ. χάρις Charito 1.4; ἡ -κή (sc. τέχνη) *the art of conversation*, Plu.2.629f. **-ητός**, ή, όν, *with whom one may converse* or *consort*, οὐχ ὁ. θράσος A.*Th.*189. II. τὸ ὁ. *conversation, social intercourse*, Herm. *in Phdr.*p.183 A. **-ήτρια**, ἡ, fem. of ὁμιλητής, Philostr.*VA*1.30. **-ία**, Ion. **-ίη**, ἡ, *intercourse, company*, ἔσθ' ὁμιλίας κακῆς κάκιον οὐδέν A.*Th.*599; τὸ ξυγγενές τοι δεινὸν ἥ θ' ὁ. Id.*Pr.*39, etc.; ὁ. τινός *communion* or *intercourse with* one, Hdt.4.174; πρός τινα S.*Ph.*70, Pl.*Smp.*203a, al.; τοὺς ἀξίους δὲ τῆς ἐμῆς ὁ. of my *society*, Ar.*Pl.*776; ἡ σὴ ὁ. Pl.*Hp.Ma.*283d; ὁ. χθονός *intercourse with* a country, E.*Ph.*1408; ἔχειν ἐν θεοῖς ὁ. live among them, Id.*IA*[1622]; ἥκειν εἰς ὁ. τινί S.*OT*1489; ἡ καθ' ὑμᾶς αὐτοὺς πολιτεία καὶ ὁ. public and *private life*, Th.1.68; ἐξ ὁμιλίας by *persuasion*, opp. βίᾳ, D.*Ep.*1.12: also in pl., ἀνθρώπων κακῶν -ίαι Hdt.7.16.α', cf. Epict.*Ench.*33.14, etc.; φθείρουσιν ἤθη χρήσθ' ὁ. κακαί E.*Fr.*1024 (= Men.218); Ἑλληνικαὶ ὁ. *association* with Greeks, Hdt.4.77; ἐνδίκοις ὁ. A.*Eu.*966 (lyr.); αἱ.. συγγενεῖς ὁ. *intercourse* with kinsfolk, E.*Tr.*51; ὁ. κακαῖς χρῆσθαι Pl.*R.*550b; αἱ τῶν ἀνθρώπων ὁ. καὶ αἱ τῶν πραγμάτων Arist.*Pol.*1336$^{b}$32, etc. 2. *sexual intercourse*, Hdt.1.182, X.*Smp.*8.22, *Mem.*3.11.14, etc.; νυμφικαὶ ὁ. E.*Hel.*1400; ὁ. τῶν ἀφροδισίων Arist.*HA*582$^{a}$26; ἡ πρὸς τοὺς ἄρρενας or τῶν ἀρρένων ὁ., Id.*Pol.*1272$^{a}$24, 1269$^{b}$29. 3. *instruction*, X.*Mem.*1.2.6 and 15; *lecture*, Ael.*VH*3.19: in pl., title of work by Critias, Gal.18(2).656. 4. ὁμιλέειν ὁμιλίῃ to be versed in it by *practice*, opp. λόγῳ εἰδέναι, Hp.*Art.*10. 5. ἡ πλείστη ὁ. τοῦ ὀνόματος its commonest *usage*, Epicur.*Ep.*1 p.22 U.; so ὁμιλίαι φωνῆς, αἱ τῶν λέξεων ὁ., Phld.*Rh.*1.288 S., *Oec.*p.59 J.; αἱ κοιναὶ ὁ. common *usage*, S.E.*M.*1.1; τῶν ἰδιωτῶν -ίαι ib.64; ἡ ἀνὰ χεῖρα -ία A.D.*Synt.*37.2; ἡ κοινὴ καλουμένη καὶ ἀνὰ χεῖρα -ία Hermog.*Id.*2.7. II. *association, company*, ἀνδρῶν τῶν ἀρίστων ἐπιλέξαντες ὁμιλίην Hdt.3.81, cf. A.*Eu.*57. 2. in collect. sense, τήνδ' ὁμιλίαν χθονός these *fellow-sojourners* in the land, ib.406; ναὸς κοινόπλους ὁ. ship-*mates*, S.*Aj.*872; ἀδελφῶν ἡ παροῦσ' ὁ. E.*Heracl.*581, cf. *Hipp.*19 (dub. l.). ※**-ος**, Aeol. **ὅμιλλος** *EM*658.55: ὁ: (ὁμός, ἴλη) *any assembled crowd, throng of people*, for a feast, Od.1.225; for a spectacle, Il.18.603, 23.651, cf. Pi.*P.*9.123, al., A.*Pers.*123, al., E.*Cyc.*100, al., Hdt. (v. infr.): rare in Att. Com. and Prose, as Cratin.323, Th.2.65, 4.112; esp. *the mass of the people, the crowd*, opp. the chiefs, προπάροιθεν ὁμίλου Il.3.22; ὅ. Δαναῶν, Τρώων, etc., 19.402, 4.86, al.; ἵππων καὶ ἀνδρῶν ὅ. 10.338; τὸν ψιλὸν ὅ. the *crowd* of irregulars, opp. ὁπλῖται, Th.4.125; *mob*, διδασκάλῳ χρείωνται ὁμίλῳ Heraclit.104; ὁ πολλὸς ὅ. Hdt.1.88, cf. 3.81; τυφλὸν δ' ἔχει ἦτορ ὅ. ἀνδρῶν ὁ πλεῖστος Pi.*N.*7.24; but also ὅ. πολλὸς μὲν Ἕλλην περιοικέει a large Hellenic *population*, Hdt.5.23. b. of inanimate objects, [σῆμα] οὔ τι μεμιγμένον ἐστὶν ὁμίλῳ Od.8.196. 2. *throng* of battle, τὴν ἔξαγ' ὁμίλου Il.5.353, cf. 4.516, etc.; πρώτῳ ἐν ὁ. in the forefront of *battle*, 17.471: generally, *tumult, confusion*, βοῇ καὶ ὁμίλῳ Hdt.9.59; σοφίῃ καὶ μὴ βίῃ καὶ ὁ. Id.3.127.—The word seems not to be used in pl.

**ὁμιχέω**, v. ὀμείχω.

**ὀμιχλ-αίνω**, *become dark*, opp. λευκαίνω, Lyd.*Mens.*4.76. **-η** (ὁμ- Eust.117.33 and v. infr.; a form **-λα** is condemned by Hdn. *Philet.*p.445 P.), ἡ, *mist, fog* (not so thick as νέφος or νεφέλη, Arist. *Mete.*346$^{b}$33, cf. *Mu.*394$^{a}$19), Hom. only in Il.; εὖτ' ὄρεος κορυφῇσι Νότος κατέχευεν ὀμίχλην 3.10; so Thetis rises from the sea, ἠΰτ' ὀμίχλη 1.359; ὁ. καὶ δρόσος Ar.*Nu.*330; κονίης ὀμίχλην Il.13.336; ὁμίχλη ἐγένετο X.*An.*4.2.7, etc.: metaph., ὅσσοις ὁμίχλα προσῇξε πλήρης δακρύων A.*Pr.*145 (lyr.). 2. *cloud-like darkness, gloom*, κατὰ νυκτὸς ὀ. *AP*5.228 (Maced.), cf. Orph.*A.*521, etc. 3. *the steam of cookery*, Mnesim.4.64. (Cf. Lith. *miglà* 'mist'.) **-ήεις**, εσσα, εν, *misty*, Coluth.208 (cj. Herm. for ἀμιχθαλόεντος); βέρεθρον Nonn.*D.*35.276; λαός, of the Cyclopes, ib.28.173.

**ὀμιχλο-ειδής**, ές, *mist-like*, πυκνώματα Epicur.*Ep.*2 p.54 U.:—also **ὀμιχλώδης**, ες, *misty*, Ti.Locr.99c, Thphr.*CP*5.10.3, Plb.3.84.1, Gal.15.382, etc. **-ομαι**, Pass., *become cloud*, *Placit.*3.4.4, Sm.*Ps.*64(65).13.

**ὀμιχλώδης**, v. ὀμιχλοειδής. **ὄμιχμα**, v. ὄμειχμα. **ὀμίχω**, v. ὀμείχω. **ὀμιώμεθα**, v. ὄμνυμι.

※**ὄμμα**, Aeol. **ὄππα** Sapph.2.11: τό:—*eye*, poet. word, rare in Prose (Th.2.11, Pl.*Ti.*45c, al., X.*Cyr.*8.7.26, *Mem.*1.4.6, al., Thphr.*Sens.*50, al., Polystr.*Herc.*346 p.81 V., *BGU*713.9 (i A.D.), *IG*4$^{2}$(1).121.121 (Epid.)): Hom. and Hes. only use pl., κατὰ χθονὸς ὄμματα πήξας Il.3.217; ὕπνον ἐπ' ὄμμασι χεῦε Od.5.492, etc.: sg. in Pi.*N.*10.63 and Trag. (v. infr.):—Phrases: ὀρθοῖς ὄμμασιν ὁρᾶν τινα look *straight* at, S.*OT*1385; ἀναβλέψαι ὀρθ. ὄμμ. X.*HG*7.1.30; ἐξ ὀμμάτων ὀρθῶν S.*OT*528; also οὐκ οἶδ' ὄμμασιν ποίοις βλέπων πατέρα ποτ' ἂν προσεῖδον how I could have looked him in the face, ib.1371, cf. Aeschin.3.121; ὁρᾶν τινα ἐν ὄμμασι S.*Tr.*241; ποῖον ὄ. πατρὶ δηλώσω; Id.*Aj.*462; τέοισί με χρὴ ὄμμασι.. φαίνεσθαι; Hdt.1.37; λαμπρὸς ὄμματι radiant in *look* or *expression*, S.*OT*81; ἄλλοσ' ὄ. θἀτέρᾳ δὲ νοῦν ἔχειν Id.*Tr.*272; προσέσχον ὄ. turned their *eyes* on him, E.*HF*931; ἐς σὸν ἐλθεῖν ὄ. come within *sight* of thee, Id.*Heracl.*887; κατ' ὄμματα before *one's eyes*, S.*Ant.*760; κατ' ὄμμα ἐλθεῖν face to face, E.*Andr.*1064; κατ' ὄμμα στῆναι *in full sight, openly*, ib.1117; opp. νύκτωρ, Id.*Ba.*469; κρατιστεύων κατ' ὄμμα in *eye-sight*, of the Sun, S.*Tr.*102 (lyr.) (but λαμπρὰ καὶ κατ' ὄμμα καὶ φύσιν is dub. in 379); πρευμενοῦς ἀπ' ὄμματος ἰδέσθαι look kindly on, A.*Supp.*210; πεύθομαι δ' ἀπ' ὀμμάτων νόστον Id.*Ag.*988 (lyr.); ὡς ἀπ' ὀμμάτων to judge by *the eye*, S.*OC*15, cf. E.*Med.*216; ἐν ὄμμασι before one's *eyes*, A.*Pers.*604; ἐν τοῖς ὄ. Th.2.11; ἐπ' ὀμμάτων E.*Supp.*1153 (lyr.); so παρ' ὄμμα, εἰ δ' ἦν παρ' ὄμμα θάνατος ib.484; ἐξ ὀμμάτων out of *sight*, Id.*IA*743; ἄπειμ' ἐξ ὀ. Phryn.Trag.21; πρὸ ὀμμάτων τίθεσθαι, ποιεῖν, Arist.*Po.*1455$^{a}$23, *Rh.*1386$^{a}$34; πρὸ ὀ. θέσις Polystr. l. c. 2. metaph., τὸ τῆς ψυχῆς ὄ. Pl.*R.*533d, Iamb.*Protr.*21.κδ'. II. *the eye of heaven*, i.e. *the sun*, ὄ. αἰθέρος Ar.*Nu.*285, cf. E.*IT*194 (anap.); but ὄ. νυκτός is a periphrasis for *night* (v. infr. v), ἕως.. νυκτὸς ὄμμ' ἀφείλετο (sc. τὴν μάχην) A.*Pers.*428; ὅταν δὲ νυκτὸς ὄ. λυγαίας μόλῃ the dark night, E.*IT*110; νυκτὸς ὄ. τῆς μελαμπέπλου Alex.89; cf. ὀφθαλμός III, βλέφαρον II. III. generally, *light*: hence, metaph., *that which brings light*, ὄμμα ξείνοισι *a light* to strangers, Pi.*P.*5.56; ὄ. δόμων νομίζω δεσπότου παρουσίαν A.*Pers.*169; ἄελπτον ὄμμ' ἐμοὶ φήμης ἀνασχὸν τῆσδε S.*Tr.*203. 2. metaph., *anything dear* or *precious, as the apple of an eye*, ὄ. γὰρ πάσης χθονὸς.. ἐξίκοιτ' ἄν A.*Eu.*1025. IV. *face* or human *form*, ὦ δυσθέατον ὄ. S.*Aj.*1004; ἐμπαίει τί μοι ψυχῇ ξύνηθες ὄ. Id.*El.*903; τὸ ἐρωτικὸν ὄ. Pl.*Phdr.*253e: as periphr. of the person, ὄ. πελείας, = πελεία, S.*Aj.*140 (anap.); ὄ. νύμφας, = νύμφα, Id.*Tr.*527 (lyr.); ξύναιμον ὄ., = ξυναίμων, Id.*Aj.*977; ὦ ταυρόμορφον ὄ. Κηφισοῦ, = ὦ ταυρόμορφε Κηφισέ, E.*Ion* 1261; v. supr. II and cf. ὄνομα IV. V. ὄ. τυκτόν *eye-hole* in a helmet, Nonn.*D.*22.62.

**ὀμμάτ-ειος** [ᾰ], ον, *received through the eyes*, πόθος S.*Fr.*801. **-εῖς**· πηρούς, ἢ βλάπτεσθαι, Hsch. **-ιον**, τό, Dim. of ὄμμα, Arist.*Phgn.*807$^{b}$29, al., *AP*5.129 (Maec.).

**ὀμμᾰτο-γράφος** [γρᾰ], ον, *painting* or *staining the eyes*, στίμμις Ion Trag.25. **-ποιός**, όν, *causing to see*, Iamb.*VP*6.31. **-στᾰγεῖς** [πηγαί], founts *of welling tears*, Trag. in *POxy.*213 (dub. l.). **-στερής**, ές, *bereft of eyes*, S.*OC*1260, E.*Ph.*327 (lyr.). II. Act., *depriving*

*of eyes*, φλογμὸς ὀ. φυτῶν heat *that robs* plants *of their eyes* or *buds*, A.*Eu*.940 (lyr.).

**ὀμματουργός**, όν, = ὀμματοποιός, Iamb.*Protr*.21. γ'.

**ὀμμᾰτόφυλλα**, τά, *eyelids*, gloss on Ar.*Pl*.721.

**ὀμμᾰτ-όω**, *furnish with eyes*, [ἀγάλματα] D.S.4.76:—Pass., τὸ σῶμα πρόσω ὠμμάτωται Plu.*Fr.inc*.91. 2. *give sight to*, τὰ ὄμματα Zos. Alch.p.117 B. II. metaph., ὠμμάτωσα γὰρ σαφέστερον [τὸν λόγον] *made* it more clear *to the mind's eye*, A.*Supp*.467:—Pass., φρὴν ὠμματωμένη a mind *quick of sight*, Id.*Ch*.854. **-ωσις**, εως, ἡ, name of a bandage, Sor.*Fasc*.9, 10.

**ὀμναῖσαι, ὀμνάσθην**, v. ἀναμιμνήσκω.

® **ὄμνῦμι**, Pi.*P*.4.166, etc.; imper. ὄμνῦθι Il.23.585, ὄμνῦ S.*Tr*.1185, E.*Med*.746, cf. Orac.ap.Hdt.6.86.γ'; 3 sg. ὀμνύτω *IG*1².134.5; 3 pl. ὀμνύντων Foed.ap.Th.5.47, *IG*1².87.24: impf. ὤμνυν Ar.*Av*.520, *Ec*. 823, D.17.10, etc.: also (from pres. **ὀμνύω**) 3 sg. imper. ὀμνυέτω Il. 19.175; part. ὀμνύουσα Hyp.*Ath*.2: impf. ὤμνυον Il.14.278, Foed. ap.Th.5.19,24, *IG*2².236.14, etc. (for pres. ind. the Trag. and Ar. use only ὄμνυμι, Hdt. and Att. Prose writers also ὀμνύω, which also occurs in Com., Pherecr.143.9, Amphis 42, Diph.101, Antiph.241.1, Alex.160; in Hdt.1.153 ὀμνύντες is restored for the dub. form ὀμοῦντες): fut. ὀμοῦμαι, εῖ, εῖται, Il.1.233, 9.274, Hes.*Op*.194, Ar.*Nu*. 246, *Lys*.193, X.*HG*1.3.11, etc.; Dor. 1 pl. ὀμιώμεθα Ar.*Lys*.183; later fut. ὀμόσω *AP*12.201 (Strat.), Plu.*Cic*.23, etc.: aor. ὤμοσα Od. 4.253, etc.; Ep. ὤμοσσα Il.20.313; Ep. also without augm. ὄμοσα, -οσσα, 19.113, 10.328: pf. ὀμώμοκα E.*Hipp*.612, Ar.*Ra*.1471, etc.: plpf. ὠμωμόκειν X.*HG*5.1.35, D.9.16, 19.318:—**Med.**, Paus.10.26.3, aor. part. ὀμοσάμενος *SIG*531.28 (Dyme, iii B.C.), *IG*5(2).357.11 (Stymphalus), also in compds. ἀντ-, ἀπ-, δι-, ὑπ-:—**Pass.**, fut. ὀμοσθήσομαι And.3.34: aor. ὠμόσθην X.*HG*7.4.10, (ὑπ-) Hyp.*Fr*.202; but ὠμόθην Is.2.40, (ὑπ-) D.48.25: pf. 3 sg. ὀμώμοται A.*Ag*.1284, ὀμώμοσται E.*Rh*.816, Arist.*Rh*.1377ᵃ11; 3 pl. ὀμώμονται Lexap.And. 1.98; part. ὀμωμοσμένος D.7.10, 22.4, Arist.*Rh*.1377ᵇ7 (ὠμοσμένος v.l. in App.*Pun*.83, etc.):—*swear*, c. acc. cogn., ὀμνυέτω δέ τοι ὅρκον Il.19.175, al.; ὅτις κ' ἐπίορκον ὀμόσσῃ 3.279; ἑκὼν ἐπίορκον ὀμόσσας Hes.*Op*.282: c. dat. pers., νῦν μοι ὄμοσσον.. ὅρκον Il.19.108, al.; πρός τινα Od.14.331, 19.288:—Pass., ὀμώμοται γὰρ ὅρκος ἐκ θεῶν A.*Ag*. 1284; ὅρκων ὀμωμοσμένων D.7.10; εἰ ὀμώμοσται οὗτος [ὁ ὅρκος] Arist. *Rh*.1377ᵃ11, cf. ᵇ7. II. *swear to* a thing, *affirm* or *confirm by oath*, 1. folld. by acc., ταῦτα δ' ἐγὼν ἐθέλω ὀμόσαι Il.19.187, cf. S.*OC*1145, X.*Ages*.1.11; ὀ. τὰς σπονδάς Foed.ap.Th.5.47; τὴν εἰρήνην D.18.32, cf. 9.16; θεῶν πίστεις τινί Th.5.30, etc. 2. folld. by fut. inf., *swear that one will*.., Il.21.373, etc., cf. S.*Ph*.623, 941 (pres. inf., D.21.188 codd.): freq. with ἦ μέν, Att. ἦ μήν, preceding the inf., καί μοι ὄμοσσον ἦ μέν μοι.. ἀρήξειν Il.1.76, cf. 10.321, Lys.31.1, X.*HG* 5.3.26, etc.: also by aor. inf. and ἄν, Id.*An*.7.7.40: by pres. inf., *swear that one does*.., S.*Ph*.357: by pf. inf., *swear that one has*.., D.21.119; ὤμνυς μὴ γεγονέναι Magn.6: by aor. inf., *swear that one did*.., ὀμνύουσι μὴ 'κπιεῖν ἀλλ' ἢ μίαν Pherecr.143.9, cf. Hdt.2.179 (aor. inf. is perh. used, without ἄν, in fut. sense, D.23.170 (s.v.l.)): sts. a clause follows in the ind., ὀμνύω.., ἦ μὴν ἐγὼ ἐθυόμην X.*An*. 6.1.31; ὄμνυμί σοι.., οὐκ ἤθελον.. Theoc.*Adon*.22. 3. abs., εἶπον ὀμόσας ἄν I would have *given my word of honour*, Pl.*Smp*. 215d. III. with acc. of the person or thing sworn by, *swear by*, νῦν μοι ὄμοσσον ἀάατον Στυγὸς ὕδωρ Il.14.271; γαιήοχον ἐννοσίγαιον ὄμνυθι 23.585, cf. 15.40, Hdt.5.7, A.*Th*.529, S.*Tr*.1185, etc.; ὀμωμοκὼς τοὺς θεοὺς D.18.217; ὄμνυμι θεοὺς καὶ θεάς folld. by inf., X.*An*.6.6.17, cf. 6.1.31: rarely c. dat., τῷ γὰρ ὄμνυτ'; ἢ σιδαρέοισι; Ar.*Nu*.248: in Prose also with Preps., ὀ. καθ' ἱερῶν τελείων Lex ap.And.1.97, Th.5.47; κατ' ἐξωλείας D.21.119; κατὰ τῆς Πολιάδος Luc.*Symp*.32; εἰς τὸν Οὐιτέλλιον Plu.*Oth*.18; ἐπὶ τῶν ἱερῶν Plb.38. 20.5; ἐν Κυρίῳ Lxx *Jd*.21.7; ἐν τῷ ναῷ *Ev.Matt*.23.16:—Pass., ὀμώμοσται Ζεύς Zeus *has been sworn by, adjured*, E.*Rh*.816, cf. Ar.*Nu*. 1241.

**ὁμο-αιχμία**· ὁμομαχία, Hsch. **-βῐος**, ον, *living together*, Alciphr. 1.12; *sharing the same life*, ψυχαί Olymp.*in Phd*.p.190 N. **-βλαστέω**, *shoot* or *bud at the same time*, prob. for ὁμοιοβλαστάνω in Thphr. *CP*1.11.1. **-βλαστής**, ές, *sprouting at the same time*, ib.5.5. 4. **-βόρος**· ὁμοφάγος, Hsch. (leg. ὠμο-). **-βουλέω**, *deliberate together*, Plu.2.96e. **-βούλιος**, title of Zeus, *Milet*.3 p.325 No. 144. **-βρομος**, gloss on ἄβρομος, Hsch. ® **-βώμιος**, ον, *having a common altar*, Th.3.59. **-βωμος**, ον, = foreg., *IG*2.1442; θεοί, of Demeter and Kore, Hsch. **-γάλακτες** [γᾰ], οἱ, *persons suckled with the same milk, foster-brothers* or *sisters*: hence, like γεννῆται, *clansmen, tribesmen*, Arist.*Pol*.1252ᵇ18, Philoch.91: nom. sg. ὁμογάλακτος in Longus 4.9. (Spelt ὁμογάλακες in Philoch.ap. Sch.Patm.D. in *BCH*1.152, perh. rightly, cf. γάλα.) **-γαμβροι**, οἱ, *sons-in-law of the same person*, Poll.3.32. **-γᾰμος**, ον, *married to the same wife*: Amphitryon calls Zeus ὁ. with himself, E.*HF* 339. II. ὁμόγαμοι, of persons who have married sisters, Id.*Ph*.137 (lyr.). **-γάστριος**, ον, *from the same womb, born of the same mother, uterine*, κασίγνητος ὁ. Il.24.47; ὁ. Ἕκτορος 21.95; ἀδελφή *BGU*405.5 (iv A.D.); νύμφαι Man.6.118; μίασμα Hld.7.5. **-γάστωρ**, ορος, ὁ, ἡ, = foreg., Poll.3.23. **-γένεια**, ἡ, *community of origin*, Str.16.4.27; of plants, *community of genus*, Dsc.1 *Prooem*.3. **-γενής**, ές, *of the same race* or *family*, ζῷα Democr.164, cf. E.*Or*.244, Pl.*Ti*.18d; ὁ. ψυχά E.*Ph*.1291 (lyr.); ὁ. μιάσματα, of bloodshed *in a family*, Id.*Med*.1268 (lyr.): c. gen., ἀνδροκτόνου γυναικὸς ὁ. *Trag.Adesp*.358; ὁ. ἐμός E.*IT* 918; ἀμείνους τῶν ὁ. better than *their fellows*, Phld.*Rh*.1.223 S. 2. in Arist., τὰ ὁμογενῆ *of the same genus*, in regard to animals, *congeners*, *GA*715ᵃ22, al.: generally, *of the same kind* or *general character*, *Cat*. 5ᵇ19, al., Epicur.*Ep*.1 p.14 U., Ti.Locr.99d; opp. ἑτερογενής, Demetr. Lac.*Herc*.1429.2; opp. ἀνομογενής, *Stoic*.2.81: c. gen., μανίας οὐχ ὁμογενῆ τὴν ὀργήν Phld.*Ir*.p.39 W.: c. dat., Epicur.*Sent*.18. II. *sharing one brood with*, S.*OT*1361 (lyr., ὁμολεχής Meineke). **-γλωσσέω**, Att. **-ττέω**, *speak the same tongue*, D.C.41.58. **-γλωσσος**, ον, Att. **-ττος**, *speaking the same tongue*, Hdt.8.144, Phld.*Po*.2.72; τινι *with* one, Hdt.1.57, 171, X.*Cyr*.1.1.5, etc. **-γνήσιος**, ον, = ὁμόγνιος, *POxy*.46.13 (i A.D.), Wilcken *Chr*.217.10 (ii A.D.), etc. **-γνητος**, ον, = ὁμογενής, *brother* or *sister*, Man.6.117, Nonn.*D*.37.192: fem. ὁμογνήτη Orph.*A*.1215: as Adj., ὁμογνήτῳ γενέθλῃ Nonn.*D*.5.197. **-γνιος**, ον, *of the same race, brother* or *sister*, ἡ πατρὸς ὁ. ἐστιν ἐμοῖο A.R.3. 1076, cf. 4.743, etc.; ὁ. πήματα *in the family*, *APl*.4.44: metaph., διὰ τῶν μέσων καὶ οἷον ὁμογνίων εἰδῶν Procl.*in Prm*.p.521 S. II. θεοὶ ὁ. gods *who protect a race* or *family*, S.*OC*1333, Pl.*Lg*.729c; Ζεὺς ὁ. E.*Andr*.921, Ar.*Ra*.750, Pl.*Lg*.881d, etc.

**ὁμόγνουα**· ἡ ἥγνοια, Hsch.

**ὁμογνωμ-ονέω**, *to be of one mind, agree*, Th.2.97, X.*HG*6.3.5, Mitteis *Chr*.28.8 (iii B.C.); ἑαυτῷ Arist.*EN*1166ᵃ13; ὁ. τινί X.*Cyr*.2. 2.24; ὁ. τινί τι *agree with* one *in* a thing, Id.*Mem*.4.3.10; περὶ ἄλλων ἀντιλέγοντας ἑαυτοῖς τοῦθ' -οῦντας ἀεί D.18.162; ταῦτα ἅπαντες -οῦσι ὅτι.. Arist.*MM*1190ᵃ3. II. Philos., *have the same judgements*, Plot.4.7.5. **-οσύνη**, ἡ, *agreement in opinion*, J.*Ap*.2.37, Iamb.ap. Stob.2.33.15. **-ων**, ον, gen. ονος, *of one mind, like-minded*, τινι *with* one, Th.8.92, Lys.28.17, X.*HG*2.3.15, etc.; ὁ. τινὰ λαμβάνειν, ποιεῖν, ποιεῖσθαι, bring *to one's own opinion*, Id.*Cyr*.2.2.24, 5.5.46, *Lac*. 8.1; ὁμογνώμονες τοῦ συνεδρίου πάντες *IG*14.952.28 (Agrigentum). Adv. -νως Lycurg.97.

**ὁμό-γονος**, ον, = ὁμογενής, Pi.*P*.4.146; οἱ ἀπὸ μητρὸς αὐτῷ ὁ. X. *Ages*.4.5: as Subst., *kinsman*, Pl.*Lg*.878d; τὰ ὁ. *animals of the same kind, congeners*, Arist.*HA*610ᵇ13: more generally, τὸ αἰσθητὸν γένος τούτων ἑκάσταις ὁ. Pl.*Tht*.156b. 2. *born at the same time with*, [χρόνος τῷ παντί] Dam.*Pr*.387. **-γραμμος**, ον, *of* or *with the same letters*, Luc.*Herm*.40. **-γραυς**, ᾱος, ἡ, sine expl., Arc.93.2 codd. (ὠμόγραυς Lobeck). **-γρᾰφέω**, *write in the same manner*, Eust.1960.56 (Pass.). ® **-γρᾰφος**, ον, = ὁμόγραμμος, *An.Ox*.3. 234. II. of documents, *identically worded*, *PMasp*.117.20, 118.38 (vi A.D.). **-δαίμων**, ον, gen. ονος, *sharing the same* δαίμων, ψυχαί Olymp.*in Phd*.p.190 N. **-δαις**, δαιτος, ὁ, ἡ, *companion at table*, Choerob.*in Theod*.1.187, 210 H. **-δάλιον**· ἰσοετές, Hsch. (-ιοι· ἰσοέτες cod.). **-δειπνος**, ον, = ὁμόδαις, Poll.6.12. ® **-δελφυς**, υν, = ὁμογάστριος, ον, Call.*Fr*.168 (prob. for -φον, -φιν codd. *EM*), Id. *Fr*.1.73 P.: ὁμόδελφος, *EM*16.11. **-δέμνιος**, ον, *sharing one's bed*, A.*Ag*.1108 (lyr.), Musae.70.

**ὁμοδημ-έω**, *to be of the same people with*, τινι Plu.2.823b. **-ία**, ἡ, *a living with* others, *agreement*, Iamb.*VP*6.32. **-ος**, Dor. **-δᾱμος**, ον, *of the same people* or *race*, γόνος Pi.*O*.9.44; τινι *with* one, Id.*I*.1.30.

**ὁμο-δίαιτα** [ῐ], ἡ, *living in a common establishment*, τὴν ὁ. ἐποιησάμην ἅμα αὐτῷ *PLond.ined*.2231 (vi A.D.). **-δίαιτος**, ον, *living* or *eating with others*, D.H.6.52, Nic.Dam.4 J., Luc.*Demon*.5, Gal.6.598; τινι Ph.2.32, al.; τῇ νόσῳ Luc.*Abd*.5; ὁ. τοῖς πολλοῖς *common* to the generality, Id.*Hist.Conscr*.16. **-διφρος**, ον, *driving in the same chariot*, Nonn.*D*.21.195. **-δογμᾰτέω**, *hold the same opinions*, σοι M.Ant.9.3: abs., metaph., Id.11.8. **-δογμᾰτία**, ἡ, *agreement in opinion, common principle*, *Stoic*.3.27.

**ὁμοδοξ-έω**, *to be of the same opinion, agree perfectly*, τῷ σώματι Pl. *Phd*.83d: abs., c. acc. et inf., Id.*R*.442d; περί τινος Thphr.*Sens*.70, Plb.1.41.5. **-ία**, ἡ, *agreement in opinion, unanimity*, Pl.*R*.433c; opp. ὁμόνοια, Arist.*EN*1167ᵃ23: pl., Pl.*Plt*.310e. **-ος**, ον, *of the same opinion*, *Vit.Philonid*.p.8 C., Luc.*Eun*.2, Porph.*Abst*.3.8, Simp. *in Ph*.1144.30; *belonging to the same school*, of the Epicureans, *IG*2². 1099.24 (ii A.D.).

® **ὁμό-δουλος**, ὁ, ἡ, *fellow-slave*, E.*Hec*.60 (anap.), Pl.*Phdr*.273e, etc., ὁ. τινός Id.*Phd*.85b; τινι X.*HG*4.1.36, etc. 2. metaph., of persons in love with the same woman, *AP*12.81 (Mel.). 3. of lands, *subject to the same charges* or *servitudes*, *PMasp*.169.26 (vi A.D.). **-δουπος**, ον, *sounding together*, Nonn.*D*.39.128.

**ὁμοδρομ-έω**, *run on the same course with*, ἁλίῳ Ti.Locr.97a, cf. Alcid. *Soph*.7, cf. Max.232, *PMich*. in *Class.Phil*.22.11: abs., *keep pace*, Plu. 2.1143f. **-ία**, ἡ, *running together, meeting*, Luc.*Astr*.22. **-ος**, ον, *running the same course with*, τῷ ἡλίῳ Pl.*Epin*.987b, cf. Plu.2. 1029b: c. gen., Nonn.*D*.1.250: abs., πορείη ib.48.318. Adv. -μως Tz.*H*.10.537.

**ὁμο-δῠνᾰμέω**, *to be of the same power*, Paul.Al.*E*.1, Procl.*Par.Ptol*. 39. **-εγκλίτως** [ῐ], Adv. *with the same inflexions*, Eust.1370.61.

**ὁμοεθν-έω**, *to be of the same people* or *race*, D.S.15.39. **-ής**, ές, *of the same people* or *race*, Hdt.1.91, Arist.*Rh*.1384ᵃ11, Plb.1.67.3: less wide than ὁμόφυλος, Id.11.19.3. 2. generally, *of the same kind*, [ζῷα] Arist.*EN*1155ᵃ19; τροφὴ ὁ. Ael.*NA*13.3. **-ία**, ἡ, lit., *descent from the same people* or *race*: then, *connexion and sympathy of parts*, Hp.*Loc.Hom*.1, *Mul*.2.174. **-ος**, ον, = ὁμοεθνής, Hecat.Abd. ap.J.*Ap*.1.22.

**ὁμοείδ-εια** (in codd. sts. -ειδία), ἡ, *sameness of nature* or *form*, Phld.*Rh*.1.260 S., Str.11.11.6, D.H.*Pomp*.6, *Comp*.26, Olymp.*in Phd*.p.111 N.; *similarity*, e.g. of accent, A.D.*Adv*.165.23. II. *consistency* of conduct, Phld.*Mort*.19. **-ής**, ές, *of the same species* or *kind*, whether in regard to natural distinctions, Arist.*Metaph*. 1032ᵃ24, *GA*747ᵇ30, al.; or logical, Id.*Rh*.1405ᵇ36: generally, τὰ ὁ. Epicur.*Sent.Vat*.73, cf. Metrod.*Fr*.17, etc.: c. dat., Polystr.*Herc*.

346 p.86 V. **2.** *of like form*, κρατῆρες Plb.34.11.17; *homogeneous*, Arist.*Ph.*188$^{a}$13 (codd. omnes), *Metaph.*1014$^{a}$30. Adv. -δῶς Phld.*Rh.* 2.244 S., M.Ant.9.35. **3.** generally, *corresponding*, ἡλικίῃ μάλιστα τῇ ὁμοειδέϊ at the *corresponding* season, of dogs going mad θέρεος καὶ ὑπὸ κύνα, Hp.*Ep.*19 (*Hermes* 53.70). **4.** *uniform*, κίνησις Plot.3.7.8; *unaltered*, ἄνθος Dsc.4.58. **5.** of an author, *lacking in variety, monotonous*, D.H.*Pomp.*3, cf. Cic.*Att.*2.6.1.—Cf. ὁμοιοειδής.

**ὁμό-εργος,** ὁ, *fellow-workman*, *POxy.*1943.4 (v A.D.). **-ερκής,** ές, *within the same house* or *prison*, Sol.ap.Poll.6.156, Din.*Fr.*84 S.; ὁ. κίονες, of pillars in mines, like μεσοκρινεῖς, *AB*286:—also **-ειρκτής,** οῦ, ὁ, Phot. **-έστιος,** ον, v. ὁμέστιος. **-έτης,** ους, ὁ, ἡ, *of the same age*, *EM*386.46. **-ζευκτος,** ον, *joining together*, δεσμός Nonn.*D.*22.333. **-ζηλία,** ἡ, *common zeal*, τῆς καλοκἀγαθίας *for..*, Lxx 4*Ma.*13.25. **-ζηλος,** ον, *of like zeal*, Ph.2.458, Nonn.*D.*37.261; τινι *with* one, Ph.1.146. **II.** *cultivating the same literary style*, Anach.ap.S.E.*M.*7.56.

**ὁμοζῠγ-έω,** *to be yoked together*, of a four-in-hand of dolphins, Philostr.*Im.*2.18: c. acc., τὴν εἰρεσίαν οὐχ ὁ. not *to keep* the oars *together*, Hld.2.2. **-ής,** ές, = ὁμόζυγος, νῆες Nonn.*D.*39.134. ⊛ **-ία,** ἡ, *a being yoked together*: in Rhet., *mutual affinity*, of rhythms, D.H.*Comp.*18 (pl.); *rhythmical correspondence*, ib.25. ⊛ **-ος,** ον, *yoked together*, ἵππος Plu.2.1008d: metaph., στοιχεῖον, i.e. consonant, Nonn.*D.*41.381; neut. pl. as Adv., ὁμόζυγα λατρεύοντας Man.4.602. **2.** *in the same row*, Ascl.*Tact.*2.4. **II.** *corresponding*, τὸ ὁ. κῶλον the *corresponding* limb (on the other side), Hp.*Off.*16, cf. Gal.18(1).369; ὁμώνυμα καὶ ὁ. [μέρεα], e.g. eyes, hands, feet, Aret.*SD*1.7.

⊛ **ὁμό-ζυξ,** ὕγος, ὁ, ἡ, = foreg., ἵππος Pl.*Phdr.*256a; ἡ ὁ. the *female*, *An.Par.*1.29; οἱ ὁμόζυγες *their fellows*, Protarch.ap.Arist.*Ph.*197$^{b}$11: metaph., Νικίας ὁμόζυξ Ἀλκιβιάδου Him.*Or.*5.13. **-ζωΐα,** ἡ, *living together*, Olymp.*in Alc.*p.215 C., Procl.*in Prm.*p.538 S. **-ζωνος,** ον, *houses of the same heavenly body*, ζῴδια Vett.Val.269.9, Paul.Al.*E.*3, Rhetor. in *Cat.Cod.Astr.*8(4).124:—whence **-ζωνέω,** Paul.Al. l.c.; **-ζωνία,** ibid., Rhetor. in *Cat.Cod.Astr.*8(4).122. **-ήγορον·** ὅμοιον, Hsch. **-ήθεια,** ἡ, *agreement of habits*, Nic.Dam.139 J., Poll.3.62, Philostr.*VA*2.11. **-ήθης,** ες, *of the same habits* or *character*, Pl.*Grg.*510c, Arist.*EN*1157$^{a}$11: Comp. -έστερος ib.1162$^{a}$12; cf. ὁμήθης. **-ῆλιξ,** ἵκος, ὁ, ἡ, = ὁμῆλιξ, *Epigr.Gr.*75 (Athens, iv/iii B.C.). **-ηχος,** ον, *sounding together*, Hsch. s.v. ὁμορροθοῦντες. **-θάλᾰμος** [θᾰ], ον, *living in the same house*, c. gen., Pi.*P.*11.2. **-θαμνέω,** *grow up with the plant*, M.Ant.11.8. **-θεν,** (ὁμός) *from the same place*, θάμνοι ἐξ ὁ. πεφυῶτες Od.5.477. **II.** without ἐξ, *from the same source*, ὁ. γεγάασι *h.Ven.*135, Hes.*Op.*108, cf. X.*Cyr.*8.7.14; τὸν ὁ. *brother*, E.*Or.*486; so τὸν ὁ. πεφυκότα Id.*IA*501; οἷς ὁ. εἶ, καὶ γονᾷ ξύναιμος S.*El.*156 (lyr.), cf. E.*Fr.*736.4. **III.** *at close quarters, hand to hand*, ὁ. μάχην ποιεῖσθαι, opp. ἀκροβολίζομαι, X.*Cyr.*8.8.22; ὁ. διώκειν follow *close upon*, ib.1.4.23. ⊛ **-θηλος,** ον, = ὁμογάλαξ, Hsch. s.v. ἀγάλακτος. **-θηρος,** ὁ, *partner in the chase*, Call.*Dian.*210. **-θριξ,** ὁ, ἡ, gen. τριχος, *with the same sort of hair*, f.l. for ὄθριξ, Sophr.52 (οὐμόθριξ (i.e. ὁ ὁμόθριξ) cj. for ὠμόθριξ in Lyc.340). ⊛ **-θρονος,** ον, *sharing the same throne*, Ἥρα Pi.*N.*11.2.

**ὁμοθῡμ-ᾰδόν,** Adv. *with one accord*, πάντες ὁ. Pl.*Lg.*805a, etc.; ὁ. ἐκ μιᾶς γνώμης D.10.59; ὁ. ἅπασιν ὑμῖν ἀντιληπτέον Ar.*Pax* 484, cf. *Av.*1015, X.*HG*2.4.17, Lxx *Ex.*19.8, Plb.1.45.4, al., *SIG*742.13 (Ephes., i B.C.), *Act.Ap.*15.25. **-έω,** v.l. for ὁμονοέω, X.*Cyr.*4.2.47. **-ος·** ὁμόφρων, ὁμόψυχος, Hsch.

**ὁμοι-άζω,** (ὅμοιος) *to be like*, interpol. in *Ev.Marc.*14.70, v.l. in *Ev.Matt.*23.27. **II.** trans., *compare, liken*, Diom.p.365 K. **-εδρος,** ον, *having a similar abode*, Herm.ap.Stob.1.49.69. ⊛ **-ιος** (A), ον, Ep. Adj. of uncertain meaning, perh. *distressing* (= κακός acc. to Anon.ap.Apollon.*Lex.*, also expld. as *common to all* or *impartial*, ibid., Hsch., cf. ξυνός), ἀλλά σε γῆρας τείρει ὁ. Il.4.315, cf. *h.Ven.*244; θάνατος Od.3.236; νεῖκος Il.4.444; πόλεμος 9.440, 13.358, 15.670, al. (In place of ὁμοιΐου (⏑ – – –) πολέμοιο ὁμοιΐοο πτολέμοιο shd. be restored.) ⊛ **-ιος** (B), ον, Ep. (not in Hom.) for ὁμοῖος, πατὴρ παίδεσσιν ὁμοίιος *like in mind* or *wish, at one with*, Hes.*Op.*182; δέμας θνητοῖσιν ὁμοίιος Xenoph.23.2; θηκτοῖσιν ὁμοίιος ἦεν ἀκωκαῖς Pancrat.*Oxy.*1085.23; χἀ νὺξ..ἴσα καὶ ὁμοίιος ἀώς night and day are *equal*, Bion *Fr.*15.18.

**ὁμοιο-βᾰρής,** ές, *equally heavy*, Arist.*Cael.*273$^{b}$23. **-βῖος,** ον, *leading a like life*, Id.*PA*662$^{b}$15. **-βίοτος** [ῐ], ον, = foreg., Id.*HA*617$^{a}$11. **-βλαστάνω,** v. ὁμοβλαστέω. **-γένεια,** ἡ, *likeness of race* or *kind*, D.H.3.15. **-γενής,** ές, *akin, of like kind*, Arist.*GA*715$^{b}$9, *Placit.*4.19.2; ἀρεταί D.H.*Pomp.*3. Adv. -νῶς *An.Ox.*4.273. **-γονία,** ἡ, *generation of like offspring*, Herm.ap.Stob.1.49.44. **-γρᾰφέω,** *write alike*, Eust.1428.19 (Pass.). **-γρᾰφος,** ον, *written alike*, A.D.*Conj.*258.14, Eust.1340.30. **II.** Subst., *one who writes like* another, *a forger*, Vett.Val.74.19. **-ειδής,** ές, *of like form, species* or *kind*, τινι Isoc.15.178, Arist.*Cael.*276$^{b}$5, 308$^{b}$8 (v.l. ὁμοειδής), Epicur.*Ep.*1 p.25 U. (v.l. ὁμοειδής); τέρατα ὁμοιοειδῆ κανθάρῳ *POxy.*465.226 (ii A.D.). **-θερμος,** ον, *equally warm*, Tz.*H.*7.712. **-θριξ,** τρῐχος, ὁ, ἡ, *with like hair*, *EM*637.22. **-καρπέω,** v. ὁμοκαρπέω.

**ὁμοιοκατα-ληκτέω,** *have similar terminations*, A.D.*Pron.*55.15. **-ληκτος,** ον, *ending alike*, ib.50.25, al. **-ληκτώδης,** ες, *given to the use of phrases with similar endings*, of the style of Gorgias and Isocrates, *Vit.Isoc.*p.257 W. **-ληξία,** ἡ, *similarity of termination*, Eust.1399.55. **-ληξις,** εως, ἡ, f.l. for foreg., Sch.Od.7.115.

**ὁμοιο-κάταρκτος,** ον, *having a similar beginning*, of words: neut. pl., of the rhetorical figure in which such words are used, prob. in Phld.*Rh.*1.162 S. **-κίνητος** [ῑ], ον, *of similar motion*, Id.*D.*3 *Fr.*37. **-κλῐνής,** ές, *of like slope*: hence, *in the same latitude*, of Byzantium and Sinope, Sch.Iamb.*Comm.Math.*14 p.102 F. **-κρῖθος,** ον, *resembling barley*, Thphr.*HP*8.1.1, 8.9.2. **-λεπτομερής,** ές, *consisting of equally fine parts*, Sch.Ar.*Nu.*230. **-λογία,** ἡ, *uniformity of style*, Quint.8.3.52. **-λογος,** ον, *having a common definition*, Porph.*in Cat.*69.7.

**ὁμοιομέρ-εια,** ἡ, *a having like parts, similarity of composition*, Epicur.*Nat.*14.6, al.; esp. of the doctrine of Anaxagoras (ἐν παντὶ παντὸς μοῖρα ἔνεστι), *nunc et Anaxagorae scrutemur homoeomerian* Lucr.1.830; *rerum h.* ib.834: pl., in concrete sense, of the ἀρχαί in this theory, *Placit.*1.3.5, Plu.*Per.*4, Diog.Oen.5, D.L.2.8, Simp.*in Ph.*460.4: sg. in this signf., ἑκάστη ὁ. ib.9. ⊛ **-ής,** ές, *having parts like each other and the whole*, Arist.*Cael.*302$^{b}$3, *Metaph.*984$^{a}$14, 988$^{a}$28 (but also of the parts themselves, *like each other or the whole*, opp. ἀνομοιομερής, ὅσα διαιρεῖται εἰς ὁμοιομερῆ Id.*HA*486$^{a}$6, cf. *Cael.*302$^{b}$16, 25); μᾶλλον ὁ. τὰ φυτὰ τῶν ζῴων Thphr.*CP*5.2.1; ὁ. ὄγκοι Epicur.*Ep.*1 p.13 U.; τὰ ὁ., οἷον ὕδωρ ἢ πῦρ ἢ χρυσόν Simp.*in Ph.*27.5, cf. Gal.10.48, al.

**ὁμοιό-μετρος,** ον, *of like metre*, Phld.*Po.Herc.*1676.11. **-μορφος,** ον, *of like form*, Epicur.*Ep.*1 p.12 U., Alex.Aphr.*in Sens.*24.19. **-νομος,** ον, *of like laws*, Phint.ap.Stob.4.23.61$^{a}$.

**ὁμοιοπάθ-εια** [πᾰ], ἡ, *sympathetic emotion*, Arist.*MM*1210$^{b}$23, 1211$^{a}$1, Metrod.*Fr.*38 (pl.); cf. ὁμοπάθεια. **II.** *likeness in condition, homogeneousness*, ἡ κοινὴ τῆς φύσεως ὁ. D.S.13.24 (nisi ὁμοπ- leg.), cf. Str.1.1.9. **-έω,** *have similar feelings* or *affections*, τινι Arist.*EN*1095$^{b}$22 (v.l. ὁμοπ-). **II.** of things, *to be subject to the same laws, to be homogeneous*, Str.1.1.9: Medic., *to be affected in sympathy*, Gal.8.756. **-ής,** ές, *having like feelings* or *passions*, τινι Pl.*R.*409b, *Act.Ap.*14.15; *affected in the same way*, Pl.*Ti.*45c, Thphr.*HP*5.7.2; χελῶναι -παθεῖς ταῖς πορθμίσιν Agatharch.47, cf. 32.

**ὁμοιο-παράγωγος** [ᾰγ], ον, *similarly derived*, Eust.1667.33. **-πλᾰτής,** ές, *of like breadth*, Orib.48.58.3. **-ποιός,** όν, *creating likeness*, Dam.*Pr.*342. **-πρεπής,** ές, *assuming a like appearance*, A.*Ag.*793 (anap.). **-πρόσωπος,** ον, *in the same person*, A.D.*Pron.*45.13. **-πρόφορος,** ον, *similar in pronunciation*, Mart.Cap.5.167. **-πτερος,** ον, = ὁμοπτέρυξ, Arist.*HA*487$^{b}$28; expld. by ὁμοιότιμος, Hsch. **-πτωτος,** ον, *with a similar inflexion, in a like case*, Plu.*Demetr.*14, 2.853b, A.D.*Synt.*124.26, al., Quint.9.3.80, S.E.*M.*1.226; τὰ ὁ., of the rhetorical figure in which such words are used, Phld.*Rh.*1.162 S., Rutil.2.13, al. **2.** Astrol., *corresponding*, ζῴδια Vett.Val.19.10. **-πυκνος,** ον, *of similar density*, τῶν ὁ. καὶ ἴσων χαλκῶν ὁ λεπτότερος [ψόφον ὀξύτερον ποιεῖ] Ptol.*Harm.*1.3. **-πῡρος,** ον, *like wheat*, Thphr.*HP*8.1.1, 8.9.2.

**ὁμοιόριστος,** ον, *having a common definition*, Porph.*in Cat.*69.7.

**ὁμοιό-ρροπος,** ον, *of a like tendency*, γυμνάσιον Gal.6.145. **-ρρυθμος,** ον, *of like form*, τὰ ὁ. τῶν νοημάτων (fort. ὀνομάτων) Aristid.2.497 J. **-ρρυσμος,** ον, Ion. for foreg., Hp.*Anat.*1, Pempel.ap.Stob.4.25.52.

⊛ **ὅμοιος** or (as in Hom., Ion., and old Att.) **ὁμοῖος,** α, ον (cf. ἐρῆμος, ἑτοῖμος): later Ep. also **ὁμοίιος** (B, q.v.); Aeol. **ὔμοιος** Theoc.29.20 (Adv. -ως *IG*12(2).69*a*6); Arc. **ὑμοῖος** *Schwyzer* 665*A*15 (Orchom., iv B.C.): (ὁμός):—*like, resembling*, ὡς αἰεὶ τὸν ὁ. ἄγει θεὸς ὡς τὸν ὁ. 'birds of a feather flock together', Od.17.218; ὁ ὅ. τῷ ὁ. Pl.*Grg.*510b; ὁ ὅ. ὡς τὸν ὅ. Arist.*EN*1155$^{a}$34; τὸ ὅ. τῷ ὁ. φίλον ib.1165$^{b}$17, v. infr. 6; ὡς ἐπὶ τῶν ὁ. as in *similar* cases (of persons), *BGU*79.18 (ii A.D.), etc.: Comp. -ότερος *more like*, Pl.*Phd.*79b: Sup. -ότατος *most like*, Hdt.2.92, S.*Ant.*833 (lyr.), etc. **2.** *the same*, ἄμφω γὰρ πέπρωται ὁμοίην γαῖαν ἐρεῦσαι Il.18.329; χρὼς οὐκέθ' ὁ. Od.16.182; hence (sc. ἑαυτῷ), *always the same, unchanging*, αἰεὶ πόδας καὶ χεῖρας ὁμοῖοι Hes.*Op.*114; ὅ. τὴν γνώμην *the same as ever*, Antipho 5.76; γνῶμαι πρὸς τοὺς αὐτοὺς κινδύνους ὁμοῖαι Th.2.89; ἀεὶ ὅ. εἶ, ὦ Ἀπολλόδωρε Pl.*Smp.*173d; ἓν καὶ ὅ. one and *the same*, Id.*Phdr.*271a. **3.** *equal in force, a match for one*, Il.23.632, Hdt.9.96. **4.** of things, *suiting, according with*, πολλά τε καὶ ὅ. ἑαυταῖς Id.*R.*549e; ὅ. τῇ φύσει Ar.*Th.*167. **5.** ὁμοῖον ἡμῖν ἔσται it will be *all the same, all one* to us, Hdt.8.80; σὺ δ' αἰνεῖν εἴτε με ψέγειν θέλεις, ὁμοῖον A.*Ag.*1404, cf. 1239, E.*Supp.*1069; ἐν τῷ ὁ. καθειστήκει Th.2.49. **6.** τὸ ὅ. ἀνταποδιδόναι give '*tit for tat*', Hdt.1.18; so τὴν ὁμοίην (sc. δίκην, χάριν) ἀποδιδόναι τινί Id.4.119, 6.21, 62; τὴν ὁ. φέρεσθαι παρά τινος to have *a like return* made one, ibid.; ἐπ' ἴσῃ καὶ ὁμοίᾳ, v. ἴσος II.2. **7.** ἐν ὁμοίῳ ποιεῖσθαί τι hold a thing *in like esteem*, Id.7.138, 8.109. **8.** ἐκ τοῦ ὁ. *in like fashion, likewise*, Th.6.78, 87; ἐκ τῶν ὁ. *ceteris paribus*, Pl.*Phdr.*243d; *on equal terms, in fair fight*, A.*Ag.*1423; so ἐν τῷ ὁ. στρατεύεσθαι καὶ ὅτε.. as when.., Th.6.21, etc. **II.** *of the same rank* or *station*, Hdt.1.134; γαμεῖν ἐκ τῶν ὁ. Cleobul.ap.Stob.3.1.172, *POxy.*124.2 (iii A.D.), *PSI* 2.120.33 (iv A.D.?): hence οἱ ὅμοιοι, in aristocratic states, *peers, all citizens who had equal right to hold state-offices*, esp. at Sparta, X.*HG*3.3.5, *Lac.*13.1, 7, Arist.*Pol.*1306$^{b}$30; Περσέων ὁμοίους τοῖσι πρώτοισι δυώδεκα Hdt.3.35. **III.** Geom., of figures, *similar*, Euc.6 *Def.*1, 3 *Def.*11, al.; of angles, *similar*, i.e. *equal*, Arist.*Cael.*296$^{b}$20, 297$^{b}$19, 311$^{b}$34, cf. Thales ap.Procl.*in Euc.*1 p.251 F. **2.** of Numbers, *square*, the product of two equal factors, Plot.6.2.21; cf. ἀνόμοιος 2.

**B.** Construction: **1.** abs., freq. in Hom., etc. (v. supr.). **2.** c. dat. of the person or thing which another resembles: so always in Hom., Hes., and usu. in Hdt. and Att. (v. supr.): but sts. c. gen., τοῖσι τούτων ὁμοίοις χύμασι v.l. in Hp.*Art.*12 (Diels *Ztschr.f. vergl.*

*Sprachf*.47.200), v.l. in Hdt.3.37 and Pl.*R*.472d; τουτέων οὐκ ἔστιν ἄλλο ἔθνος ὁμοίας τὰς κεφαλὰς ἔχον οὐδέν (ellipt. as in b. infr.) Hp. *Aër*.14; ὁ λεκτικὸς πῇ μὲν ὅμοιος Ἡροδότου, πῇ δὲ ἐνδεέστερος D.H. *Pomp*.4; ὁμοία ἀνδριάντος Dion.Byz.53; ὅμοιον ἱέρακος Cyran.22, cf. 12. b. ellipt. phrases, κόμαι Χαρίτεσσιν ὁμοῖαι, for κόμαι ταῖς τῶν Χαρίτων ὁμοῖαι, Il.17.51; οὔ τις ὁμοῖα νοήματα Πηνελοπείῃ ᾔδη, for τοῖς τῆς Πηνελοπείης, Od.2.121: also in Prose, ἅρματα ὅ. ἐκείνῳ, for τοῖς ἐκείνου, X.*Cyr*.6.1.50; ὁμοίαν ταῖς δούλαις ἐσθῆτα, for τῇ τῶν δουλῶν, ib.5.1.4; cf. ἴσος I. 1, συγγενής III. 2. 3. c. acc. of that in which a person or thing resembles another, ἀθανάτῃσι φυὴν καὶ εἶδος ὁμοίη Od.6.16, cf. 3.468, Il.5.778; ὀργὴν ὅ. τῷ κάκιστ' αὐδωμένῳ A.*Th*.678, cf. S.*Aj*.1153, etc.: also with Preps., ὁμοῖοι ἐν πολέμῳ Il.12.270; ἐς φύσιν οὐδὲν ὅ. Batr.32; ὅ. τινὶ πρός τι X.*Cyn*.5.29; but οὐδὲν ὅμοιον ἦν μοι πρὸς τοῦτον I had nothing *in common* with him, Is. 8.26. 4. c. inf., θείειν ἀνέμοισιν ὁμοῖοι *like* the winds in running, Il. 10.437; τῷ οὔ πώ τις ὁμοῖος κοσμῆσαι ἵππους *like* him to marshal or in marshalling horses, 2.553, cf. 14.521; ὅμοιοι ἦσαν θαυμάζειν (s.v.l., θαυμάζοντες codd. dett.) X.*An*.3.5.13. b. ὅμοιον εἰπεῖν *approximately*, Men.*Epit*.548. 5. folld. by a Relat., ὁμοίη, οἵην με τὸ πρῶτον ἐν ὀφθαλμοῖσι νόησας *like* as when thou saw'st me first, *h.Ven*. 178; ὅμοιον.., οἷόνπερ τὸ τῶν ποταμῶν X.*HG*4.2.11, cf. *Hier*.7.5, *Cyr*.6.1.37: folld. by ὅσπερ, Id.*An*.5.4.34; by ὥσπερ, ὅ. ἀτμὸς ὥσπερ ἐκ τάφου πρέπει A.*Ag*.1311, cf. X.*Smp*.4.37; by ὥστε, E.*Or*.697; v. infr. c. 6. folld. by καί (= 'as'), γνώμῃσι ἐχρέωντο ὁμοίῃσι καὶ σύ Hdt.7.50, cf. Th.1.120, Pl.*Cri*.48b, *Tht*.154a; οὐδέν τι γενόμενος ἐς Ἀχαιοὺς ὅμοιος [ἢ] καὶ Καλλίστρατος.. Paus.7.16.4; v. καί A. III.

**C.** Adv., freq. in the neut. sg. and pl. ὅμοιον, ὅμοια (older ὁμοῖον, ὁμοῖα) *in like manner with*, c. dat., ὁμοῖα τοῖσι μάλιστα 'second to none', Hdt.3.8, cf. Th.7.29; ὁμοῖα τοῖσι πλουσιωτάτοισι Hdt.3.57; ὅμοιον μουσίσδει..ταῖσιν ἀηδονίσι Theoc.8.37: folld. by a relat. Partic., ὁμοῖον ὥστε.. *even* as, S.*Ant*.587(lyr.); ὅ. ὡς εἰ.. Pl.*Lg*.628d; ὁμοῖα καὶ βοῦς ἐργάτης S.*Fr*.563. 2. *alike*, ὅμοια χέρσον καὶ θάλασσαν ἐκπερῶν A.*Eu*.240. II. regul. Adv. ὁμοίως *in like manner with*, c. dat., Hdt.1.32, al.; τοῖς μάλισθ' ὅ. D.*Ep*.2.24: folld. by a relat. Partic., ὅ. ὡς εἰ.. Hdt.1.155; ὅ. ὥσπερ.. X.*Cyr*.1.4.6; ὅ. καὶ.. Hdt. 7.86, 8.60.β': abs., ὅ. δέ and *in like manner*, *PEleph*.15.1 (iii B.C.), etc. 2. *alike, equally*, Pi.*P*.9.78, Hdt.7.100; Δαναοῖσι Τρωσί θ' ὅ. A.*Ag*.67(anap.); λέγειν..σιγᾶν θ' ὅ. Id.*Eu*.278, etc.; τῷ νῷ θ' ὅ. κἀπὸ τῆς γλώσσης S.*OC*936; ὅ. μὲν.., ὅ. δὲ.. Pl.*Prt*.319d; ὅ. ἀμφοῖν ἀκροάσασθαι D.18.2; ὅ. ἔχειν *to be uniform*, Arist.*Ph*.261$^b$25: prov., οὐδ' ὅκου χώρης οἱ μῦς ὅ. τὸν σίδηρον τρώγουσιν *like any other food*, Herod. 3.76 (but perh. *all alike*, cf. Ar.*Eq*.1296 cod. R, Th.5.15 (s.v.l.), Plu.2.763c): Comp. -ότερον *AP*11.233 (Lucill.): Sup. -ότατα Ar.*Fr*. 281.

**ὁμοιό-σημος**, ον, *of like signification*, A.D.*Conj*.249.13, *EM*48. 29. **-σκελής**, ές, *with similar legs*, τὰ πρόσθια κῶλα τοῖς ὄπισθεν ὅ. γέγονε Gal.*UP*3.1. **-σκευος**, ον, *in like dress* or *array*, Str.17.3. 7. **-στάδιος** [ᾰ], ον, *like a stadium*, τόπος Tz.*H*.8.26. **-στομος**, ον, *with both fronts facing the same way*, Ascl.*Tact*.10.22, 11.3, Ael. *Tact*.37.5, Arr.*Tact*.29.4. Adv. -μως Ascl.*Tact*.11.4. **-σύστᾰτος**, ον, *similarly constituted*, of physical bodies, Ptol.*Harm*.1.3.

**ὁμοιοσχημ-ᾰτος**, ον, = ὁμοιοσχήμων, Thphr.*CP*6.2.4. **-ονέω**, *to be like in form*, Arist.*Pr*.866$^b$34. **-ος**, ον, v. -σχήμων. **-οσύνη**, ἡ, *uniformity*, Id.*SE*168$^a$25. ❋**-ων**, ον, gen. ονος, *of like form*, Democr.(?) ap. *Placit*.4.19.3, Arist.*APr*.27$^b$11, Thphr.*HP*4.2.4, Epicur.*Ep*.1 p.9 U., Id.*Nat.Herc*.1420.3, D.H.*Comp*.26, Ptol.*Tetr*. 104, etc. Adv. -νως Arist.*EE*1217$^b$35. (The form ὁμοιόσχημος, ον, is doubtful: -σχημον neut. sg. in Antyll.ap.Orib.44.23.41, Simp. *in Cat*.430.25 can be referred to masc. -σχήμων; acc. masc. (fem.) -σχήμον' (with elision of α) is prob. in Corn.*ND*17, Phlp.*in Mete*. 20.29; -σχήμων ὄντων in Id.*in Ph*.662.30 is v.l. for -σχημόνων ὄντων.)

**ὁμοιο-τᾰχής**, ές, *moving with equal velocity*, Sch.Arat.19. Adv. -χῶς Arist.*Mu*.392$^a$14 (v.l. ὁμοταχῶς). **-τέλευτος**, ον, *ending alike*: τὸ ὅ. *the like ending of two or more clauses* or *verses*, Id.*Rh*.1410$^b$1, Phld.*Rh*.1.162 S., D.S.12.53 (pl.): -τέλευτα (sc. κῶλα) Demetr.*Eloc*. 26; -τέλευτον διάνοιαν κατακλείειν *end a sentence with* ὁμοιοτέλ., S.E. *M*.2.57. **-τεχνος**, ον, = ὁμότ-, Anon.*in Rh*.114.34. **-της**, ητος, ἡ, *likeness, resemblance*, Democr.164, Pl.*Phd*.109a, al.: pl., ib.82a, *Sph*.231a; ἡ αὐτοῖς ὅ. τῆς διαγωγῆς *mode* of passing life *like* themselves, Id.*Tht*.177a; ὁμοιότητι τετάχθαι κατά τι *correspond to*.., Id. *R*.555a; so ὁμοιότητι εἶναι κατά τι ib.576c; ὁμοιότητι *equally*, Id.*Ti*. 75d: c. dat., *resemblance to*.., Id.*Phdr*.253b, al.; [ὁμοιότητες] γίνονται τοῖς τέκνοις πρὸς τοὺς γεννήσαντας Arist.*Pol*.1262$^a$16, cf. *EN*1108$^b$31; τίνι τῶν ζῴων εἰς ὁμοιότητα; *in likeness* of what animal? Pl.*Ti*.3cc, cf. 81d; καθ' ὁμοιότητα λέγεσθαι, opp. ἁπλῶς, Arist.*EN*1147$^b$34; καθ' ὅ. σημειοῦσθαι, ἡ καθ' ὅ. σημείωσις, Phld.*Sign*.31, 34; ὁ κατὰ τὴν ὅ. τρόπος ib.8; later καθ' ὁμοιότητα c. gen., *in the same way as*, ἀξιῶν ἐνταγῆναι κἀμοῦ τὸν υἱὸν τῇ τῶν ἐφήβων γραφῇ καθ' ὅ. τῶν σὺν αὐτῷ *POxy*.1202.24 (iii A.D.), cf. 237 vi6 (ii A.D.), *BGU*1028.15 (ii A.D.), *PSI*1.107.2 (ii A.D.), *Ep.Hebr*.7.15: without gen., ib.4.15. **-τῖμοι**, gloss on ὁμοιόπτεροι, Hsch. **-τονος**, ον, *of like tone* or *accent*, D.H.*Comp*. 12. Adv. -νως Eust.1400.19. **-τροπία**, ἡ, *similarity*, Str.1.2.10, 10.3.16, 12.7.3. **-τροπος**, ον, *of like manners and life*, Th.3.10, Arist.*HA*487$^b$27, al., Phld.*Ir*.p.30 W.; simply, *similar*, δυνάμεις τῆς φράσεως D.H.*Pomp*.3; αἰτίαι Ph.2.259; of animals, Agatharch. 1. Adv. -πως *in like fashion* or *manner with*, τινι Th.6.20, Arist.*GA* 755$^b$28, al.; τινὶ ὅ. διατεθῆναι Phld.*Rh*.1.153 S.: neut. pl. as Adv., ὁμοιότροπα τῷ νῦν βαρβαρικῷ διαιτᾶσθαι Th.1.6. II. *conformable*, *having similar effects*, of medicines, Hp.*Acut*.23. ❋**-τῠπής**, ές, (τύπος) *of similar form*, λαϊνέους μορφὰς -εῖς τῆς Λητοῦς *TAM*2.174*B* 12 (Sidyma). **-τῠπος**, ον, = foreg., Ptol.*Tetr*.106. **-τύραννος**, v. ὁμοτύραννος.

**ὁμοι-ούσιος**, ον, *of similar substance*, *Gloss*.

**ὁμοιο-φᾰνής**, ές, name of a bandage, Gal.18(1).777. **-φθογγος**, ον, *like-sounding*, *EM*169.10. **-φλοιος**, ον, *with like bark*, Thphr. *CP*1.6.2, 4 (v.l. ὁμόφλ- in 4). **-φόρος**, ον, (φέρω) *bearing alike*, Id. *HP*4.13.5. **-φωνέω**, *sound like*, τινι Eust.1428.19. **-χροια**, ἡ, cj. for ὁμόχροια in Arist.*Mete*.342$^b$20. **-χρονος**, ον, *of equal* or *like duration*: in Prosody, *of equal length*, D.H.*Comp*.12. **-χροος**, ον, contr. -χρους, ουν, *like-coloured*, Phld.*D*.3.8 (dub.), Plot.2.8.1, Alex. Aphr.*de An*.146.11, *Hippiatr*.55. **-χρώμᾰτος**, ον, *of like colour*, Callix.2. **-χωρος**, ον, *belonging to a similar place*, Herm.ap.Stob. 1.49.69.

❋**ὁμοι-όω**, Th.3.82, Pl.*R*.393c: aor. ὡμοίωσα E.*Hel*.33, Isoc.11.8:—Med., Hdt. (v. infr.):—mostly in Pass., fut. ὁμοιωθήσομαι Pl.*Lg*.964d, or in med. form ὁμοιώσομαι Hdt.7.158: aor. ὡμοιώθην Th.5.103, Pl. *R*.510a, Isoc.5.114, etc.; Ep. inf. ὁμοιωθήμεναι (v. infr.): pf. ὡμοίωμαι Pl.*R*.431e:—*make like*, ὁμοιώσασ' ἐμοὶ εἴδωλον ἔμπνουν E.*Hel*.33; πᾶν παντὶ ὅ. Pl.*Phdr*.261e; ἑαυτὸν ἄλλῳ Id.*R*.393c; χοῦν..-ώσαντες τῷ ἄλλῳ χώρῳ Hdt.8.28; τοῖς πεπλασμένοις καὶ τοῖς γεγραμμένοις τὴν τοῦ σώματος φύσιν Isoc.9.75; ἑαυτῷ τι Arist.*GC*324$^a$10; πρὸς τὰ παρόντα τὰς ὀργὰς τῶν πολλῶν ὅ. *makes* them *correspond* to prevailing conditions, Th.3.82:—Pass., *to be made like, become like*, in Hom. only in aor. inf. Pass., ὁμοιωθήμεναι ἄντην Il.1.187, Od.3.120; ὁμοιωθέντ' Ἀφροδίτη Emp.22.5; ὀργὰς πρέπει θεοὺς οὐχ ὁμοιοῦσθαι βροτοῖς E.*Ba*. 1348, cf. *Med*.890; ἐς τὴν εὐβουλίαν..ἄλλοις ὅ. Th.2.97, cf. 5.103, Hdt.7.158; κατὰ τὸ ἦθος ὅ. τοῖς ἐκείνου βουλήμασιν Isoc.5.114. 2. *liken, compare*, in Med., τὰς πάθας τὰς Κύρου τῇσι ἑωυτοῦ -ούμενος Hdt. 1.123:—later in Act., τίνι ὁμοιώσω τὴν γενεὰν ταύτην; *Ev.Matt*.11.16; ἡ πόλις τινὰ Λυκούργῳ κατὰ τὸ ἦθος καὶ τὴν πρᾶξιν ὁμοιοῦσα *BSA*29.35 (Sparta, iv A.D.). II. intr., *to be like*, interpol. in Dsc.3.45. **-ωμα**, ατος, τό, *likeness, image*, Pl.*Phdr*.250a, Arist.*Rh*.1356$^a$31 (v.l. ὁμοία), Epicur.*Ep*.1 p.10 U., *Nat*.11.6: pl., Pl.*Phdr*.250b, *Sph*.266d, al.; ἐξ ὁμοιώματος in accordance with the practice in *similar cases*, by *analogy*, *OGI*669.52 (Egypt, i A.D.). **-ωμᾰτικός**, ή, όν, *denoting resemblance*, ὄνομα D.T.636.12, cf. 637.11. Adv. -κῶς *in a simile*, Sch.Il.5.638. **-ωσις**, εως, ἡ, *a being made like*, θεῷ Pl.*Tht*. 176b. 2. *likeness, resemblance*, Thphr.*Lap*.41; opp. ἀλλοίωσις, Pl.*R*.454c; καθ' ὁμοίωσιν θεοῦ *Ep.Jac*.3.9, cf. Lxx *Ge*.1.26. 3. *establishment of a resemblance*, τῆς ὅ. ἕνεκεν αὐτῆς λαμβάνεσθαι τὰς μεταφοράς Phld.*Rh*.1.177 S. b. Gramm., *comparison*, -ώσεως ἐπιρρήματα D.T.642.6. 4. *simile*, Ps.-Plu.*Vit.Hom*.84, al. 5. Pythag. name for *nine*, *Theol.Ar*.57. **-ωτής**, οῦ, ὁ, *one who likens*, = μιμητής, condemned by Poll.7.126. **-ωτικός**, ή, όν, *assimilative*, Gal.*Nat.Fac*.1.12. 2. *by means of resemblance, on the basis of analogy*, μετάβασις S.E.*M*.11.250: Subst., ἡ -κή (sc. τέχνη) *the art of likening* or *copying*, Poll.7.126. Adv. -κῶς S.E.*M*.3.40, etc. 3. Pythag. epith. of odd numbers and square numbers (cf. ὅμοιος A. III. 2), *Theol.Ar*.57.

**ὁμό-κᾰποι**, οἱ, (κάπη) *eating at the same manger, messmates*, Epimenid.ap.Arist.*Pol*.1252$^b$15 (v.l. ὁμόκαπνοι *at the same smoke* or *fire*, i.e. *dwelling together*). **-καρπέω**, *bear fruit at the same time*, Thphr. *CP*1.11.1 (prob. for ὁμοιοκαρπεῖ). **-κατάληκτος**, ον, *ending alike*, of numbers, Iamb.*in Nic*.p.17 P., al.; cf. ὁμοιοκατάληκτος. **-κάτοικος**, ον, *dwelling together*, gloss on ὁμωρόφιος, Sch.Opp.*H*.5.418. **-κέλευθος**, ον, *going together*, Pl.*Cra*.405d. **-κεντρος**, ον, *concentric with*, γῇ ὅ. τῷ οὐρανῷ Str.2.5.2, cf. Ptol.*Alm*.3.3, Theo Sm.p.166 H. II. *at the same cardinal point*, Vett.Val.60.14, *Cat.Cod.Astr*.8(4). 136. **-κηνσος** (Lat. *census*), = Lat. *contributarius*, Just.*Nov*. 128.7. **-κίνητος** [ῑ], ον, *moved at the same time*, Sch.E.*Ph*. 328. **-κλᾱρος**, Dor. for ὁμόκληρος.

❋**ὁμοκλ-άω**, Ep. impf. 3 pl. ὁμόκλεον (as if from -κλέω, cf. ὁμοκλεῖ· ἀπειλεῖ, βοᾷ, Hsch.) and 3 sg. ὁμόκλᾱ (v. infr.): aor. ὁμόκλησα Hom. (v. infr.), S.*El*.712; Ion. Iterat. ὁμοκλήσασκε (v. infr.):—Ep. Verb, *call* or *shout to*, c. dat., either to *encourage*, ὁμόκλεον ἀλλήλοισι Il.15. 658: once in Trag., ἵπποις ὁμοκλήσαντες S.*El*.712; or (more freq.), to *upbraid, threaten*, δεινὰ ὁμοκλήσας Il.5.439, etc.; ὁμοκλήσας ἔπος ηὔδα 6.54, etc.; μέγα δὲ Τρώεσσιν ὁμόκλα 18.156; ὁ δ' υἱάσιν οἷσιν ὁμόκλα 24.248; μνηστῆρες δ' ἄρα πάντες ὁμόκλεον Od.21.360: also c. dat. modi, ὁμοκλήσασκέ τε μύθῳ Il.2.199; ὁμόκλησάν τ' ἐπέεσσιν 23.363: c. inf., *command loudly, call on* one *to* do, 16.714. (Spir. asp. indicated by κέκλεθ' ὁμοκλήσας Il.20.365 (v.l. κέκλετ' ὁμ-), spir. lenis by ὑπ' ὀμοκλῆς Hes.*Sc*.341, *h.Cer*.88, Call.*Del*.158: the former is perh. due to the mistaken idea of connexion with ὁμός.) **-ή**, ἡ, or **ὁμοκλή** (v. foreg., fin.), *threat, reproof, rebuke*, οἱ δὲ ἄνακτος ὑποδείσαντες ὁ. Il.12.413; χαλεπαὶ δὲ ἀνάκτων εἰσὶν ὁ. Od.17.189; νήκουστος ὁμοκλέων deaf to *reproaches*, Emp.137.3; of the *threatening shouts* of an attacking enemy, μάχῃ ἔνι μεῖναι ὁμοκλήν Il.16.147; of *shouts* addressed to horses, τοὶ δ' ὑπ' ὁμοκλῆς ῥίμφ' ἔφερον θοὸν ἅρμα *h.Cer*.88, Hes.*Sc*.341; of the *sound* of flutes, ἐν αὐλῶν παμφώνοις ὁμοκλαῖς Pi.*I*.5(4).27, cf. A.*Fr*.57.5 (anap.). II. in later Ep., *onset, attack*, βορέαο ὁ. Nic.*Th*.311; of Sirius, Κυνὸς δριμεῖαν ὁ. Opp.*H*.1. 152; of fire, ib.4.14, cf. Q.S.6.614, al., Man.2.374. (Etym. dub.; signf. II perh. arose from misinterpr. of Il.16.147.)

**ὁμο-κληρία**, ἡ, *joint possession*, *Gloss*. **-κληρος**, Dor. **-κλᾱρος**, ον, *having an equal share*; esp. of an inheritance, *coheir*, Pi.*O*.2.49, *N*.9.5. **-κλής**, ὁ, = ὁμόκλητος, poet. acc. ὁμόκλεα Id.*Fr*.102 Bgk.

(=51$^{b}$ Schr.). -κλήτειρα, ἡ, fem. of sq., as Adj., ὁ. βοή Lyc. 1337. -κλητήρ, ῆρος, ὁ, *shouter, threatener*, ὁμοκλητῆρος ἀκούσας Il.12.273, 23.452. -κλητος, ον, *called by the same name*, Nic. *Th.*882, Hsch. -κλῖνος, ον, *reclining on the same couch*, at table, Hdt.9.16. -κοιτία, ἡ, *a sleeping together*, Sch.A.*Ch.*599. -κοιτος, ον, = ὁμόλεκτρος, Hld.6.8, etc.:—fem. -κοιτις, ἡ, to explain ἄκοιτις, Pl.*Cra.*405d. -κραιρος, ον, *with like horns*, Nonn.*D.*1.336, al. -κτῐτος, ον, lit. *built together*: hence, *joint, common*, αὖλις Opp.*H.*4.352. -κτῠπος, ον, *making a like noise*, Nonn.*D.*36.195. -κωμήτης, ου, ὁ, *member of the same village-community*, *PThead.*17.7 (iv A.D.), *PSI*1.43.2 (v A.D.).

**ὁμολγός**, ὁ, = ζόφος, Blaes.4 (ὁμολογῷ cod. Hsch.).

**ὁμο-λείτωρ**, ορος, ὁ, = συλλειτουργός, *IG*2$^{2}$.1369.38 (ii A.D.). **-λεκτρος**, ον, *sharing the same bed*, γυνή E.*Or.*508; but Ζηνὸς ὁμόλεκτρον κάρα, of Tyndareos, as husband of Leda, ib.476: Subst., *wife*, *AP*7.295 (Leon.), *IG*12(5).307 (Paros), *Ath.Mitt.*49.117 (Argos). ❋ **-λεχής**, ές, = foreg., v. ὁμογενής II:—also **ὁμόλεχος**, Apollon.*Lex.* s.v. ἀλόχου, Sch.Th.7.78, and **ὁμόλοχος**, Sch.Pi.*P.*8.9.

**ὁμολιῶν**· ἰσάζων, καταλειαίνων, Hsch.

**ὁμολογά**, ᾶ, Boeot. for ὁμολογία, *IG*7.3171.27, 3172.47 (both iii B.C.).

**ὁμολογ-έω**, S.*Ph.*980 (but very rare in Poets), Hdt. and Att. (v. infr.): fut. -ήσω Hdt.8.144, etc.: aor. ὡμολόγησα Id.9.88, etc.: perf. ὡμολόγηκα And.1.29, etc.:—Med., pres. and aor., Pl. (v. infr.):—Pass., fut. -ήσομαι Hp.*de Arte*4 (v.l.), Pl.*Tht.*171b: aor. ὡμολογήθην Th.8.29, etc.: pf. ὡμολόγημαι Pl. (v. infr.), etc.:—*to be* ὁμόλογος: hence, I. *agree with, say the same thing as*, c. dat., λέγουσι Κορίνθιοι, ὁμολογέουσι δέ σφι Λέσβιοι Hdt.1.23, cf. 171, 2.4; Κυρηναῖοι τὰ περὶ Βάττου οὐδαμῶς -έουσι Θηραίοισι Id.4.154. II. *correspond, agree with*, whether of persons or things, c. dat., [τὸ ἓν] ἑωυτῷ ὁ. Heraclit.51; ὁμολογέουσι ταῦτα τοῖσι Ὀρφικοῖσι Hdt.2.81; αὗται αἱ πόλιες τῇσι πρότερον λεχθείσῃσι ὁμολογέουσι κατὰ γλῶσσαν οὐδέν Id.1.142, cf. 2.18; *have to do with*, ὁμολογέοντας κατ' οἰκηιότητα Περσέϊ οὐδέν Id.6.54; τοῖς λόγοις τοὺς μάρτυρας -οῦντας Antipho6.31; οὐκ ἔφη τοὺς λόγους τοῖς ἔργοις ὁμολογεῖν Th.5.55; ὥστε μηδὲν ὁμολογεῖν τῷ τρόπῳ τῷ ἀλλήλων are utterly unlike, Lys.20.12. b. *to be coordinated*, πρὸς ἓν ἔργον Gal.*UP*1.8: metaph., of a vowel, *agree*, i.e. form a diphthong, Plu.2.737f. c. *to be suitable for*, c. gen., ὁμολογεῖ ὤμου ἡ περὶ τὴν ἑτέρην μασχάλην περιβολή Hp.*Off.*9. 2. *agree to* a thing, *grant, concede*, ὁμολογῶ τάδε S. l. c.: abs., Hdt.8.94; τινί τι Pl.*Smp.*195b; αὐτοῖς ὡμολογηκὼς ταύτην τὴν ὁμολογίαν Id.*Cri.*52a; ὁμολογοῖεν ἂν ἡμῖν οἱ ἄνθρωποι, ἢ οὔ; Id.*Prt.*357a; ὅπως.. τῇ τύχῃ σου χάριτας ὁμολογεῖν δυνηθῶ that I may *avow* my gratitude.., *PRyl.*114.32 (iii A.D.); ὁ. χάριν θεοῖς *acknowledge* gratitude, Luc.*Laps.*15 (ὁ. ἔν τινι *Ev.Matt.*10.32 appears to be an Aramaism; ὁ. ἐφ' ἁμαρτίαις Lxx *Si.*4.26): without acc. rei, ὁμολογῶ σοι I *grant* you, i.e. I *admit* it, Ar.*Pl.*94; parenthetically, ἀφειλόμην, ὁμολογῶ I *allow* it, X.*An.*6.6.17: c. inf., ὁ. Νικίαν ἑορακέναι *allows, confesses that* he has seen.., Eup.181.3; ὁ. σε ἀδικεῖν I *confess* that I am wronging thee, E.*Fr.*265; ὁ. κλέπτειν Ar.*Eq.*296, cf. Antipho2.4.8; ὁ. καπηλεύειν Isoc.2.1; ὁ. οὐκ εἰδέναι *confess* ignorance, Arist.*SE*183$^{b}$8; ὁ. πατάξαι Ar.*V.*1422; ὁμολογοῦσι νοσεῖν μᾶλλον ἢ σωφρονεῖν Pl.*Phdr.*231d; ὁ. ἓν πάντα εἶναι Heraclit.50; ὁ. Μειδίαν ἁπάντων λαμπρότατον γεγενῆσθαι D.21.153, cf. 197; esp. in receipts, ὁ. ἀπέχειν, ἐσχηκέναι, etc., *PHib.*1.97.5 (iii B.C.), *CPR*229.3 (iii A.D.), etc.; in contracts, ὁ. διαλελύσθαι πρὸς ἀλλήλους *PHib.*1.96.5 (iii B.C.), cf. *BGU*1160.3 (i B.C.), etc.; τοῦθ' ὁ. ὡς.. Pl.*Chrm.*163a, cf. *Lg.*896c: also c. Partic., ὁ. τινὰ δίκαια ὄντα Id.*Cri.*49e, 50a; v. infr. c. 3. *agree* or *promise to* do, c. fut. inf., Antipho6.23, And.1.62, Pl.*Smp.*174a, *Phdr.*254b, etc.: c. aor. inf., D.42.12: c. pres. inf., ὡμολόγησαν ἑκατὸν τάλαντα ἐκτείσαντες ἀζήμιοι εἶναι Hdt.6.92: also freq. abs., *promise*, μισθῷ ὁμολογήσαντες (sc. ἀπαλλάξεσθαι) Id.2.86; ὁ ὁμολογῶν the person *who gives an undertaking*, *BGU*297.22 (i A.D.), etc.; *make an agreement, come to terms*, τινί with another, Hdt.6.33, 7.172, al.; ἐπὶ τούτοισι on these terms, Id.1.60, cf. 8.140.β', Th.4.69. b. c. acc., *promise*, τῆς ἐπαγγελίας ἧς (for ἣν) ὡμολόγησεν ὁ θεὸς τῷ Ἀβραάμ *Act.Ap.*7.17; Θεῷ ὑψίστῳ εὐχὴν Αὐρήλιος Ἀσκλάπων, ἣν ὡμολόγησεν ἐν Ῥώμῃ *IGRom.*4.542 (Phrygia).

B. Med., in sense of Act., ὑπεναντίος ὁ τρόπος.. ὁμολογεόμενος Hp.*Vict.*1.11; αὐτοὶ ἑαυτοῖς ὁμολογούμενοι λόγοι Pl.*Ti.*29c; νόμοι σφίσιν αὐτοῖς ὁ. Isoc.2.17, cf. 6.14; τὸ ταὐτὸν καὶ ὁ. Pl.*Lg.*741a; ὡμολογεῖτ' ἂν ἡ κατηγορία τοῖς ἔργοις αὐτοῦ D.18.14; -ούμενος καὶ σύμφωνος κατὰ τὸν βίον Plb.31.25.8; τοῦτο -ήσασθαι ὅτι.. Pl.*Cra.*439b, etc.

C. Pass., *to be agreed upon, allowed* or *granted by common consent*, X.*An.*6.3.9, etc.; πλέον ἀνδρὶ ἑκάστῳ ἢ τρεῖς ὀβολοὶ ὡμολογήθησαν Th.8.29: c. inf., with predicate added, *to be allowed* or *confessed to be* so and so, ἡ ὑπὸ πάντων ὁμολογουμένη ἄριστον εἶναι εἰρήνη Id.4.62; ὁμολογεῖταί γε παρὰ πάντων μέγας θεὸς εἶναι Pl.*Smp.*202b, cf. X.*An.*1.9.20, etc. 2. without inf., ἡ τοῦ οἰκείου.. ἕξις.. δικαιοσύνη ἂν ὁμολογοῖτο *should be allowed* [to be] justice, Pl.*R.*434a; -ούμενοι δοῦλοι And.4.17; τοὺς -ουμένους θεούς those who are *admitted* [to be] gods, Timocl.1.2, cf. Th.6.89. 3. abs., ὁμολογεῖται *it is granted, agreed*, Pl.*Phd.*72a, al.; τὰ ὡμολογημένα *the things granted*, ibid.; ἐξ ὁμολογουμένου, = ὁμολογουμένως, Plb.3.111.7.

**ὁμολόγ-ημα**, ατος, τό, *that which is agreed upon, taken for granted, postulated*, Pl.*Phd.*93d, *Grg.*480b, al. 2. *convention, compact*, νόμος ἐστὶν ὁ. πόλεως κοινόν Arist.*Rh.Al.*1422$^{a}$2, cf. 1424$^{a}$10; in commerce, *agreement* or *contract*, *POxy.*237 iv 6 (ii A.D.), etc. 3. *admission*, ὡς.. Hyp.*Ath.*20. -ησις, εως, ἡ, *confession*, ἥττης D.S.17.68. -ητέον, *one must allow*, Pl.*Ti.*52a, etc. -ητής, *sponsor*, *Gloss.* -ητικός, ή, όν, *of* or *for confessing*: Adv. -κῶς, ὀμνύειν Eust.233.40. ❋ -ία, Ion. -ίη, ἡ, *agreement*, Pl.*Smp.*187b, al.; αἱ τῶν ὀνομάτων ὁ. verbal consistency, Id.*Tht.*164c. 2. *assent, admission, concession*, τῶν ἐπικαλουμένων Isoc.11.44, cf. Pl.*Grg.*461b, al.; κατὰ τὴν ἐμὴν ὁ. by my *admission*, Id.*Prt.*350e; ἡ ὑπέρ τινος ὁ. Id.*Tht.*169e; ἐξ ὁ. διαλέγεσθαι argue from *premises agreed upon* or *granted*, Arist.*Top.*110$^{a}$33. 3. *agreement, compact*, συνθήκη καὶ ὁ. Pl.*Cra.*384d; ἐμμένειν τῇ ὁ. Id.*Tht.*145c, *Lg.*840e: pl., ὁμολογίας παραβαίνειν, διαλύειν, Id.*Tht.*183d, Isoc.4.175; τὰς ὁ. διαφυλάττειν Id.9.44; κατὰ τὰς ὁ. Pl.*R.*443a; παρὰ τὰς ὁ. Id.*Cri.*52d. b. esp. in war, *terms of peace, truce*, or *surrender*, Hdt.8.52; ὁμολογίῃ ἐχρήσαντο, of the conquered, Id.1.150, cf. 4.201; ἐς ὁμολογίην προσεχώρησαν Id.7.156; τὴν ὁ. δέξασθαι Th.6.10; ἐς ὁμολογίην προκαλέεσθαι, of the conquerors, Hdt.3.13; ἡ ὁ. ἡ πρός τινα γενομένη Id.1.61, cf. And.1.120; ὁμολογίᾳ τὴν ἀκρόπολιν παραδοῦναι Th.3.90, cf. 1.107. c. in Law, *contract, agreement*, συγγραφὴ καὶ ὁ. *PEleph.*2.2 (iii B.C.); ὁ. τινὸς πρός τινα *PFay.*91.1 (i A.D.), etc. 4. *vow*, Lxx *Je.*51(44).25 (pl.). 5. in Stoic Philos., *conformity with nature*, *summum.. bonum, cum positum sit in eo quod* ὁμολογίαν *Stoici, nos appellemus convenientiam*, Cic.*Fin.*3.6.21; ψυχὴ πεποιημένη πρὸς ὁμολογίαν παντὸς τοῦ βίου *Stoic.*3.11. -ιον, τό, = foreg., *Zeitschr.d.Savigny-Stiftung* (rom.Abt.) 48.286 (i B.C.). -ος, ον, *agreeing, of one mind*, ὁ. γενέσθαι τινὶ περί τινος *agree* with one on a point, X.*Smp.*8.36; of things, *agreeing, corresponding*, ὁ. τούτοις εἰσὶ καὶ αἱ τιμαί Arist.*EN*1115$^{a}$31; ὁ. πλευραί *correspondent, homologous*, Euc.12.12, cf. *Tab.Heracl.*1.65; τὰς συντάξεις τῶν ὀργάνων ὁμολόγους the construction of all engines is *on similar lines*, Ph.*Bel.*49.10. 2. of persons, *confessing* guilt, ὁ. κατασταθέντες Mitteis *Chr.*31 iii 12 (ii B.C.); ὁ. κακοῦργοι *BGU*372 i 32 (ii A.D.). 3. *agreed to, admitted*, ὁμόλογόν [ἐστι] S.E.*M.*7.75; τὸ ὁ. the *contract* or *compact*, *IG*7.3172.91, cf. 3173.16, *GDI*1749 (Delph.); συνθήκα Αἰτωλοῖς καὶ Ἀκαρνάνοις ὁμόλογος *SIG*421 *A*3 (Thermon, iii B.C.); ὁ. σπόρος *agreed* amount of seed-corn, *BGU*1192.2 (i B.C.); of land or persons, *admittedly liable* to taxation, etc., *PRyl.*209.40 (iii A.D.), Wilcken *Chr.*63 (i A.D.), *PLond.*2.254.137,141, al. (ii A.D.), *BGU*560 (ii A.D.), 618 (iii A.D.), *Cod.Theod.*11.24.6 (v A.D.). II. Adv. -γως *agreeably to, in unison with*, ὁ. ἔχειν τινί Arist.*EN*1139$^{a}$30; ὁ. κεῖσθαι to be *similarly* placed, Id.*PA*665$^{b}$23, al.; also ἐξ ὁμολόγου *by agreement*, Plb.1.67.1, al.; ἐξ ὁμολόγων *IG*9(2).205.3 (Thess., iii B.C.). 2. *confessedly, openly*, Lxx *Ho.*14.5; also ἐξ ὁμολόγου Plb.3.91.10, etc. -ουμένως, Adv., c. dat., *conformably with*, τοῖς εἰρημένοις X.*Ap.*27: abs., Id.*Oec.*1.11. b. in Stoic Philos., ὁ. ζῆν, with or without τῇ φύσει, Zeno *Stoic.*1.45, Cleanth.ib.125, Chrysipp.ib.3.4. 2. *by common consent, confessedly, admittedly*, ὁ. μαχιμώτατοι Th.6.90, cf. And.1.140, Pl.*Smp.*186b, Hyp.*Lyc.*6, etc.; ὁ. ἀγαθοί, ὁ. ἄριστοι, Pl.*La.*186b, *Mx.*243c; ἡ ὁ. ἰητρική Hp.*VM*5.

**ὁμόλοχος**, v. ὁμολεχής.

❋ **Ὁμολῷος**, ὁ, epith. of Zeus in Boeotia and Thessaly, Phot., Suid., etc.: hence, as name of a month, *IG*7.246, al. (Boeot.), 9(1).375 (Naupactus), etc.:—fem. **Ὁμολωΐδες** πύλαι, of Thebes, A.*Th.*570, E.*Ph.*1119, Paus.9.8.5.—Acc. to Ister 10, from **ὅμολος**, Aeol. for ὁμαλός. Cf. Ὁμονῷος.

**ὁμο-μαθής**, ές, *learning with another*, Heliod. *in EN*180.19. **-μαστιγίας**, ου, ὁ, *fellow-knave* (cf. μαστιγίας), of Zeus (i.e. Zeus Δοῦλιος acc. to Sch.), Ar.*Ra.*756. -μάτηρ [ᾰ], ερος, ἡ, = ὁμομήτριος, *GDI*4972 (Crete). -μηλίς, ίδος, ἡ, = ἀμαμηλίς, Aëthlius 2; cj. for ὀρο- in Theoc.5.94. -μήτριος, α, ον, (μήτηρ) *born of the same mother*, ὁ. ἀδελφεός (Att. -φός) Hdt.1.92, 6.38, Pl.*Prt.*315a, etc.:—Dor. fem. ὁμομάτρια Ar.*Ach.*790, cf. *Nu.*1372; ὁμοπάτριοι καὶ ὁμομήτριοι Lys.32.4. ❋ -μήτωρ, ορος, ὁ, ἡ, = foreg., Orph.*Fr.*15, Poll.3.23. -νᾱος, α, ον, *having a common temple*, *IG*4$^{2}$(1).41.2 (Epid., v/iv B.C.), Hsch. s.v. ὁμωχέται. -νεκρος, ον, *companion in death*, Luc.*DMort.*2.1. -νηδύϊος, ον, (νηδύς) = ὁμογάστριος, *EM*625.29, Phot., Suid.

**ὁμονο-εῖον**, τό, *temple of Concord*, D.C.49.18, etc. -έω, *to be of one mind, agree*, opp. στασιάζω, Th.8.75, Lys.2.63, etc.; οὔθ' οἱ τρόποι γὰρ ὁμονοοῦσ' οὔθ' οἱ νόμοι Anaxandr.39.2; -οῦσα ὀλιγαρχία a *united* oligarchy, opp. στασιάζουσα, Arist.*Pol.*1306$^{a}$9; πόλεις -οῦσαι Id.*Rh.Al.*1422$^{b}$35; συγγενείας -ούσης Epicur.*Sent.Vat.*61; ὁμονόεντες (Aeol. part.) πρὸς ἀλλάλοις *IG*12(2).6.30 (Mytil.); ὁ. ὅτι.. *to be agreed* that.., Pl.*Men.*86c: c. neut. Adj., ἐπειδὴ ὁμονοοῦμεν ταῦτα X.*Cyr.*4.2.47; περὶ τῶν ἄλλων ὁ. Isoc.9.53. 2. c. dat., *live in harmony with*, ἀλλήλοις And.1.108; τινι Pl.*R.*352a; ὁ. τινὶ περί τινος *to be of one mind* with him about.., Id.*Alc.*1.126c, cf. Isoc.4.85; περί τι Arist.*EN*1167$^{a}$29: metaph., αὐλὸς ὁμονοεῖ χοροῖς Diog.Trag.1.11; εὐτυχία ὁ. τοῖς κινδύνοις Lys.2.43; of drugs, δεῖ τὰ καθαρτικὰ μιγνύμενα ὁμονοεῖν ἀλλήλοις Gal.16.117; ὁμονοοῦσαι, term applied to the Muses by Epich.222. -ητέον, *one must be in agreement*, Aeschin.*Ep.*11.12. ❋ -ητικός, ή, όν, *conducing to agreement, in harmony*, ψυχή, βίος, Pl.*R.*554e, *Phdr.*256b: Comp., Arist.*Pol.*1330$^{a}$18. Adv. -κῶς, λέγειν Id.*GC*323$^{b}$3; ἔχειν to be *of one mind*, περὶ χρόνου Id.*Ph.*251$^{b}$14; περί τι Pl.*Phdr.*263a; ἔν τισι ὁ. διακεῖσθαι Id.*R.*603c.

**ὁμό-νοια**, ἡ, *oneness of mind, unanimity, concord*, Democr.250, Th.8.93, And.1.140, Lys.18.17, etc.; τὴν πρὸς ἡμᾶς ὁ. Decr.ap.D.18.164; τὴν πρὸς ἀλλήλους Men.584, cf. 809, Zeno *Stoic.*1.61; defined as ἐπιστήμη κοινῶν ἀγαθῶν, *Stoic.*3.160. 2. Pythag. name for 3 and for 9, *Theol.Ar.*16, 57. 3. = ἀργεμώνη, Ps.-Dsc.2.177. II. personified, A.R.2.718, Paus.5.14.9, *IG*3.2239, etc. 2. = Lat. *Concordia*, Plu.*Cam.*42, App.*BC*1.26, D.C.44.4, al. **-νομος**, ον, (νόμος) under the same laws, φιλία Pl.Lg.708c. II. (νομός) feeding together, Ael.NA7.17. **-νοος**, ον, contr. **-νους**, ουν, of one mind, united, Democr.255, Poll.6.155. Adv. -νόως X.Cyr.6.4.15, Ages.1.37, D.L.4.22. **-νυμφος**, ον, allied by marriage, Sch.Od. 19.518.

⊛ **Ὁμονῷος**, ὁ, epith. of Zeus, IGRom.4.256 (Assos, i A.D.). (Written -νωος, by which -νῳος may be intended: not certainly related to Ὁμολώϊος.)

**ὁμό-οικος**, ον, dwelling together, Hsch. s.v. ὁμέστιος. **-ούσιος**, ον, (οὐσία) consubstantial, Plot.4.4.28, 4.7.10, Porph.Abst.1.19, Iamb. Myst.3.21, Syrian. in Metaph.129.3, Simp. in Ph.44.3, etc. **-ουσιότης**, ητος, ἡ, consubstantiality, Hsch. **-πᾱγος**, ον, (Lat. pagus) from the same canton, D.H.4.15.

**ὁμοπάθ-εια** [πᾰ], ἡ, common affection or quality of two things, τινος sympathy with one, Arist.Fr.101, cf. Plot.4.2.1, al. **-έω**, to have the same experience as, πρὸς ἀλλήλους καὶ πρὸς τὸ πᾶν Id.4.9.1; τῷ ὅλῳ Id.4.9.2, cf. Porph.Sent.32: metaph., of a vowel, to be reconciled, Plu.2.737f. **-ής**, ές, of the same feelings or affections, sympathetic, ἕκαστος ἐν ταῖς ἀτυχίαις ἥδιστα πρὸς τοὺς ὁμοπαθεῖς ὀδύρεται Apollod.Com.8, cf. Arist.EN1161$^{a}$26; ὁ. λύπης καὶ ἡδονῆς affected in the same way as others by pain and pleasure, Pl.R.464d; [θάλαττα] Max.Tyr.39.5; χρῆμα ὁ. ἡμῖν Id.15.1.

**ὁμο-παίκτωρ**, ορος, ὁ, playfellow, Sch.Theoc.6.18 (Scaliger for ὅμοιον παίκτορα). **-παις**, παιδος, ὁ, ἡ, twin-brother or sister, Trag.Adesp.243, Poll.3.23. **-πάτηρ** [ᾰ], πάτερος, = sq., GDI4972 (Crete). **-πάτριος**, α, ον, but ος, ον A.Pr.558 (lyr.):—by the same father, ἀδελφεός (Att. -φός) Hdt.5.25, cf. Antipho 1.1, Lys.19.22, Pl.Lg.774e, etc.; τὰν ὁ. Ἡσιόναν A. l.c.; ἀδελφαὶ ὁ. Is.11.2, cf. Supp.Epigr.2.822 (Dura-Europus, i A.D.):—also **-πάτωρ** [ᾰ], ορος, ὁ, ἡ, Pl.Lg.924e, Is.11.1. **-πληθής**, ές, Math., of classes or series containing the same number of individuals or terms, ὁ. εἴδη terms with the same coefficient, Dioph.1 Def.10. **-πλοέω**, sail together or in company, Plb.1.25.1. **-πλοια**, ἡ, a sailing in company, Cic.Att.16.1.3, 4.4. **-πλοκος**, ον, interlaced, Nonn.D.21.332. **-πλοος**, ον, contr. **-πλους**, ουν, sailing together or in company with, τινι Tryph.265; ναῦς ὁ. consort, AP7.635 (Antiphil.). **-πλωτήρ**, ῆρος, ὁ, one who sails in company, Opp.H.1.208. **-πνοια**, ἡ, conspiration, ὁ. τις ἡ σύνταξις καὶ ἡ πρὸς ἄλληλα ἕνωσις Dam.Pr.2. **-ποιός**, όν, having the same effect, Iamb. in Nic.p.97 P. **-πολέω**, trans., move together, πάντα Pl.Cra.405d sq. **-πόλησις**, εως, ἡ, concordant revolution or rotation, Procl. Theol.Plat.6.12 (p.378 P.). **-πολις**, εως, ὁ, ἡ, from or of the same city or state, Plu.2.276b, etc.: poet. **ὁμόπτολις** S.Ant.733. **-πολῑτεία**, ἡ, community of citizenship, Abh.Berl.Akad.1928(6).45 (Cos). **-πολίτης** [ῑ], ου, ὁ, fellow-citizen, Mich. in EN474.18. **-πολος**, ον, of spheres or circles, having the same poles, ὁμοπόλων οὐσῶν τῶν ἑπτὰ σφαιρῶν Procl. in Ti.3.148 D.; ὁ. κύκλοι Id. Hyp.2.1. **-πρᾱγέω**, take part with, τισι J.AJ17.5.5. **-πράγμων**, ονος, ὁ, coadjutor, ib.17.12.1. **-πτερος**, ον, of or with the same plumage, κίρκος A.Supp.224, cf. Pl.Phdr.256e; οἱ ἐμοὶ ὁ. my fellow-birds, birds of my feather, Ar.Av.229: then generally, comrades, fellows, Stratt.78. 2. metaph., of like feather, closely resembling, βόστρυχος ὁ. A.Ch.174, cf. E.El.530; νᾶες ὁ. consort-ships (or, as others, equally swift), A.Pers.559 (lyr., but λινόπτεροι is prob. cj.); ἀπήνα ὁ., i.e. the two brothers, Eteocles and Polynices, E.Ph.328 (lyr.). **-πτολις**, v. ὁμόπολις.

**ὁμορβεῖν**· ἀκολουθεῖν, ὁδοιπορεῖν, Hsch. (Cf. ἀμορβ-.)

**ὁμοργ-άζω**, = ὀμόργνυμι, wipe off, ὠμόργαζε h.Merc.361 (cj. Ilgen for ὠμάρταζε). **-μα**, ατος, τό, that which is wiped off, a spot, AB 432. ⊛ **-νῡμι**, wipe, aor. Act. opt. ὀμόρξαις Nic.Th.558; cf. ὅμαρξον:—Med., δάκρυά τ' ὠμόργνυντο were drying their tears, Od.11.527, cf. 530; χερσὶ παρειάων δάκρυ' ὀμορξαμένη Il.18.124; θᾶκον ὀμόργνυσθαι Pythag.ap.D.L.8.17. (The simple Verb is Ep., but ἀπ-, ἐξ-ομόργνυμι are used also in Att.) (Cf. Skt. mṛjáti 'wipe'.)

**ὁμορ-έω**, Ion. **ὁμουρέω** (also PLond.ined.2850.26 (ii B.C.)), to be ὅμορος, border upon, march with, [οἱ Κελτοὶ] ὁμουρέουσι Κυνησίοισι Hdt.2.33, cf. 7.123, Hecat.163, 204, 207 J., etc.; χωρίοις ὁμορεῖν Plu. 2.292d, etc.: abs., τὰ ὁμοροῦντα τοῦ ἀέρος adjacent portions.., Epicur. Ep.2 p.51 U. (but οἱ -οῦντες neighbours, Sent.40); -οῦσα γῆ PAmh. 2.68.56 (i A.D.), cf. PLond. l.c. II. cohabit, have intercourse with, ὅπως ἄλλοισιν ὁμουρέῃ, of a woman, Perict.ap.Stob.4.28.19. (Written with ρρ, ὁμορροῦντα SIG1044.16 (Halic., iv/iii B.C.).) **-ησις**, εως, ἡ, neighbourhood, juxtaposition, in Ion. form **ὁμούρησις**, Epicur. Ep.1 p.20 U., Nat.22 G.: Astrol. (written ὁμορ(ρ)όησις, v.l. -ωσις), of planets, prob. in Antioch.Astr. in Cat.Cod.Astr.1.159, 8(3).107, 114, Porph. in Ptol.189. **-ιος**, Ion. **ὁμούριος**, ον, = ὅμορος, Call. Fr.185, A.R.2.379, D.P.649, etc.; for Plb.2.39.6, v. Ὁμάριος.

**ὁμορίτας**· ἄρτος ἐκ πυροῦ διηττημένου γεγονώς, Hsch. (Cf. ἀμορβίτης, ἀμορίτης.)

**ὅμορος**, Ep. and Ion. **ὅμουρος**, ον, having the same borders with, marching with, τοῖσι Δωριεῦσι Hdt.1.57; τῇ Λιβύῃ Id.2.65, etc.: abs., Aristeas Epic.3, Th.6.78; χώρα ὅ. D.2.1; ὅ. πόλεμος a war with neighbours, ib.21, 18.241; τὰ ὅ. τῶν πόλεων the suburbs, Lxx Nu.35.5. 2. metaph., bordering on, closely resembling, ὅμοροι ὁ ἀνδρεῖος καὶ ὁ θρασύς Arist.EE1232$^{a}$25; ὅμορος οὖσα τῇ αἰσθητῇ φύσει Plot.4.8.7. 3. as Subst., ὅ. τινῶν their neighbours, Isoc.14.18, cf. Th.2.85; οἱ ὅ. neighbouring people, Id.1.15, etc.; κατὰ τὸ ὅ. διάφοροι because of their neighbourhood, Id.6.88.

**ὁμοροφέω, ὁμορόφιος, ὁμόροφος**, v. ὁμωρ-.

**ὁμορρευστέω**, = ὁμοῦ ῥεῖν, Olymp.Alch.p.104 B.

**ὁμορρο-έω**, Astrol., of signs of the zodiac, rise together with, τῇ Σελήνῃ Serapio in Cat.Cod.Astr.8(4).226. **-ησις**, v. ὁμόρησις.

**ὁμο-ρροθέω**, flow together, Hp.Mul.1.17; row together, Plu.2.94b; haul together, Orph.A.256. 2. metaph., agree, consent, S.Ant. 536, Fr.489 (lyr.); ὁ. τινί agree with.., E.Or.530; πρὸς τὸ μέλος Ael. NA6.32. ⊛ **-ρροθος**, ον, prop. rowing together: hence, side by side, στείχοντες ὁμόρροθοι Theoc.Ep.3.5:—also **-ρρόθιος**, ον, AP7.374 (Marc. Arg.). **-ρροσα**· ἀθρό[ι]α, Hsch. **-ρρυθμία**, Ion. **-ρρυσμίη**, ἡ, resemblance, Hp.Anat.1. **-ρρυθμος**, Ion. **-ρυσμος**, ον, of the same form, like, ibid.

⊛ **ὁμός**, ή, όν, one and the same, common, joint, οὐ γὰρ πάντων ἦεν ὁ. θρόος Il.4.437; ὁ. γένος 13.354; ὁμὴ σορός 23.91, IG14.2469.10; ὁ. τιμή Il.24.57; ὁ. αἶσα 15.209; ὁ. νεῖκος 13.333; ὁ. ὀϊζύς Od.17.563; ὁ. λέχος Il.8.291, Hes.Th.508; ὁμὰ χθών IG14.1721; οὐ καθ' ὁμὰ φρονέοντε not of one mind, Hes.Sc.50; ἱκνεῖσθαι εἰς ὁμόν unite, Parm.8. 47: c. gen., ἑτέρων ἴχνια μὴ καθ' ὁμὰ δίφρον ἐλᾶν Call.Aet.Oxy.2079. 26. (Cf. Skt. samá-, Goth. sama 'the same', cogn. with εἷς.)

**ὁμόσαι, ὀμόσας**, v. ὄμνυμι.

**ὁμόσε**, Adv., (ὁμός) to one and the same place, [ποταμῶν] ὁ. στόματ' ἔτραπε Il.12.24; ὁμόσ' ἦλθε μάχη the battle came to the same spot, i.e. the fight thickened, 13.337; ὁμόσε ἰέναι come to close quarters, close with the enemy, Ar.Ec.863; ἰέναι τοῖς ἐχθροῖς ὁ. Th.2.62; βαδιστέον ὁ. Ar.Ec.876; ὁ. χωρεῖν τινι Id.Lys.451; ὁ. θεῖν, φέρεσθαι, run to meet, X.An.3.4.4, Cyn.10.21; ὁ. ταῖς λόγχαις ἰέναι Id.Smp.2.13. 2. metaph., ὁ. ἰέναι τοῖς ἐρωτήμασιν come to issue with the questions, Pl. Euthd.294d, cf. R.610c; χωρεῖν ὁ. τοῖς λόγοις E.Or.921; ὁ. χωρεῖν πρὸς τὰς τιμωρίας Phld.Herc.1289 p.59 V.; ὁ. βαδιεῖται τῷ Παρμενίδου λόγῳ Arist.Metaph.1089$^{a}$3; φήμῃ Plu.Thes.10; ὁ. χωροῦσι τοῖς ποιηταῖς are at issue with.., Ael.Fr.166; ὁ. τοῖς δεινοῖς χωρεῖν D.H.6.74. 3. ὁ. πορεύεσθαι to be moving towards agreement, D.56.14. II. together with, c. dat., Plb.3.51.4, etc.; ἱερατευκότα τῆς Ἑκάτης ὁ. ὅτε καὶ τοῦ Παναμάρου at the same time as.., BCH12.86; ὁ. ταῖς ἄλλαις εὐεργεσίαις PGiss.4.6 (ii A.D.).

**ὁμό-σημος**, ον, having the same meaning, Theognost.Can.161. **-σίπῡος**, ον, (σιπύη) sharing the same meal-tub, messmate, Charond. ap.Arist.Pol.1252$^{b}$14. **-σῑτέω**, eat with, take one's meals with, μήτε ὁμοσιτῆσαι τοῖσι ἀνδράσι, of women, Hdt.1.146. **-σῑτος**, ον, eating together, μετά τινος Id.7.119, Plu.2.643d. **-σκευος**, ον, equipped in the same way, Th.2.96, 3.95; f.l. for ὁμόσκηνος, X.Cyr. (2.1.25) ap.D.H.Rh.8.11. **-σκηνία**, ἡ, living in the same tent, v.l. in X.Cyr.2.1.26. **-σκηνος**, ὁ, one living in the same tent, messmate, D.H.1.55, 6.74, Men.Prot.p.3 D.; cf. ὁμόσκευος. 2. Adj., πλῆθος ἀνδρῶν -ον Max.Tyr.6.4; living with, θεὸς ὁ. τῷ πλήθει J.AJ3.8.10. **-σκηνόω**, live in the same tent, ἐν τῷ ὁμοσκηνοῦν X.Cyr.2.1.25 (fort. ὁμοῦ σκ-). **-σπλαγχνος**, ον, = ὁμογάστριος, A.Th.890, S.Ant.511. **-σπονδέω**, join one in a treaty, Poll.1.34, Phryn.PS p.95 B. ⊛ **-σπονδος**, ον, sharing in the drink-offering, ὁμοτράπεζός τέ μοι καὶ ὁ. ἐγένεο Hdt.9.16; μήθ' ὁμωρόφιον μήθ' ὁ... εἶναί τισι D.18.287; [πόλις]..ἧς (οἷς codd.) ὁ. καὶ ὁμοτράπεζος..γέγονεν Din.1.24. 2. bound by treaty to, τινι Lxx 3Ma.3. 7. **-σπορος**, ον, sown together: hence, sprung from the same parents or ancestors, kindred, h.Cer.85, Pi.N.5.43, A.Th.932 (lyr.), etc.: as Subst., brother, E.IT611; sister, A.Ch.242, S.Tr.212 (lyr.), E.IT695, Antiph.18. II. ὁ. γυνή a wife common to two (Laïus and Oedipus), S.OT260; also of Oedipus, τοῦ πατρὸς ὁμόσπορος having the same wife with his father, ib.460.

**ὁμόσσαι, ὀμόσσας**, v. ὄμνυμι.

**ὁμό-σσῠτος**, ον, rushing together, Nonn.D.45.217. **-στεγέω**, to be housed under the same roof, SIG1180.6 (Cnidus, ii/i B.C.). **-στιξ**, ιχος, ὁ, (στείχω) walking together, Choerob. in Theod.1.319 H. **-στῐχάω**, walk together with, βόεσσιν Il.15.635 (nisi leg. ὁμοῦ στιχάει). ⊛ **-στοιχος**, ον, in the same line or rank with, τινι Thphr.CP6.6.3, Jul. Or.5.163c, Dam.Pr.312; v.l. for ὁμότοιχος (q.v.) in Plu.2. 503d. **-στολος**, ον, in company with, attendant, Βάκχον..Μαινάδων ὁμόστολον S.OT212 (lyr.); ὁ. ὔμμιν ἕπεσθαι A.R.2.802. II. generally, similar, μορφῆς δ' οὐχ ὁ. φύσις A.Supp.496. **-στοργος**, ον, feeling the same affection, Nonn.D.3.386. **-συγγενέτας**, αο, ὁ, kinsman, IG12(5).307.5.9 (Paros). **-σύγγονος**, ον, kindred, λαός Inscr.Magn.17.47 (hexam.). **-σύζυξ**, ῠγος, ὁ, ἡ, bound together, neut. pl. ὁμοσύζῠγα Philox.2.36. **-σφῡρος**, ον, walking in company, Hsch., Suid. 2. sister, Hsch.; brother, EM625.31. 3. ὁμόσφῡρος (fr. σφῦρα II. 2), = ὁμόχωρος, Hsch. **-σχημονέω**, to be of the same form, τισι cj. in Democr.ap.Thphr.Sens.50. **-σχήμων**, ον, gen. ονος, of the same shape, Thphr.HP4.2.4 (v.l. ὁμοιοσχ-), Sch.Il.23.65. **-σχολος**, ὁ, schoolfellow, Suid. s.v. Τυραννίων. **-τᾰγής**, ές, ranged in the same row or line, Euc.12.12; of lines of vision, ὄψεις Gal.UP10.12, cf. Hero Dioptr.35; parallel, of streets, Orib.9.20.1. 2. coordinate with, τινι Jul.Or.4.144d, cf. Heliod. in EN59.13, Iamb.Comm.Math.14, Procl.Inst.21, 108, Dam. Pr.37. Adv. -γῶς ib.119. **-τάλαντος**, gloss on ἀτάλαντος, EM161.55. ⊛ **-τᾰφος**, ον, buried together, Aeschin.1.149; τινος Plu.2.359b. **-τᾰχής**, ές, of the same velocity, Arist. Cael.289$^{b}$9, Ph.237$^{a}$1, 249$^{a}$8, etc. Adv. -χῶς ib.236$^{b}$35, Procl.Hyp. 3.45, Simp. in Ph.992.24. **-τεγής**, ές, (τέγος) under the same roof, νεώσοικοι IG2$^{2}$.1668.6. **-τελής**, ές, paying the same taxes, Poll.3.56, Hsch.; ὁ. πόλις SIG581.62 (Hierapytna, iii/ii B.C.). **-τέρμων**, ον, gen. ονος, having the same borders, marching with another, μήτε γείτονος μήτε ὁ. Pl.Lg.842e, cf. D.H.1.9, 26, al.; ὁμοτέρμονα νῆσον Σικελίης Nic.Fr.5, cf. Scyl.22; τινι Ath.14.

625f. **–τεχνέω**, *practise the same art*, Hp.*Ep*.17. ❋ **–τεχνος**, *ον*, *practising the same art*, τινι with one, Pl.*La*.187a. II. as Subst., *fellow-workman*, Hdt.2.89, Pl.*Prt*.328a, Xenarch.7.15; ὁ ὁ. τινός Pl. *Chrm*.171c, cf. D.22.58, Aristaenet.1.19; οὐδεὶς τῶν ὁ. μου Alex. 173.7: as title applied to the good physician, Hp.*Praec*.7. 2. neut. ὁμότεχνον, τό, *guild*, τῶν λαναρίων Keil-Premerstein *Zweiter Bericht* No.217 (ii A.D.). **–τηθος**, *ον*, = ὁμότιτθος, condemned by Phot. (–τιθ– cod.).

❋ **ὀμό-της**, *ου*, ὁ, *one who swears*, Theognost.*Can*.45, *EM* 258. 3. **–τικός**, *ή*, *όν*, *of* or *for swearing*, σχῆμα Longin.16.2; ἐπίφθεγμα A.D.*Synt*.52.27: neut. -κόν, τό, as Subst., *oath*, *Stoic*.2.62.

**ὁμο-τῑμία**, ἡ, *sameness of value* or *honour*, Luc.*DMort*.15.1. **–τῑμος**, *ον*, (τιμή) *equally valued* or *honoured*, *held in equal honour*, Il. 15.186; μακάρεσσι *with* them, Theoc.17.16; μακάρων Nonn.*D*.7. 103: c. gen. rei, τῆς στρατηγίας ὁ. *having an equal share in* the command, Plu.*Fab*.9; οἱ "τῶν ὁμοτίμων" καλούμενοι, among the Persians, *chief nobles*, *peers*, X.*Cyr*.2.1.9, cf. 7.5.85: as title at the court of the Ptolemies, οἱ ὁ. τοῖς συγγενέσι *PTeb*.254 (ii B.C.), *PPar*.15.20 (ii B.C.). Adv. -μως Aristaenet.1.3, Phlp.*in APr*.13.20, *in APo*.367.9. 2. *equal in degree*, σηπεδὼν ἐν ἅπασι τοῖς ἀγγείοις Gal.10.745. Adv. -μως Id.2.653, al.; ὁ. οἱ χυμοὶ διασήπονται Id.10.606, cf. Ascl.*in Metaph*. 226.32, Steph.*in Gal*.1.270 D.: c. dat., τοῖς ἰδίοις.. γνωρίσμασι τὰ συνακολουθοῦντα πολλάκις ὁ. γράφων *no less than*.., Gal.9.385. **–τιτθος**, *ον*, *bred by the same nurse*, Din.*Fr*.89.24 S., Phot. **–τοιχος**, *ον*, *having one common wall*, *contiguous*, ὁ. οἰκία Is.6.39; ὁμότοιχος οἰκῶν Pl.*Lg*.844c; ὁ. τῇ βιβλιοθήκῃ οἶκος D.S.1.49. 2. metaph., νόσος γείτων ὁ. ἐρείδει A.*Ag*.1004 (lyr.); λύπη μανίας ὁ. Antiph.295; μανίᾳ ὁ. ἡ ὀργή Plu.2.503d. **–τονέω**, *have the same tension*, Ph.*Bel*.61. 18 (v.l.), Bito 63.1. 2. *have the same pitch with*, τινι Nicom.*Harm*. 12; *have the same accent*, A.D.*Synt*.51.24, al. **–τονος**, *ον*, *having the same tension*, *with equal force*, of fevers, Gal.10.615; *having equal muscular power in every muscle*, Philostr.*Gym*.36. Adv. -νως, of the pulse, Gal.9.84; of traction, Id.13.685. 2. *having the same pitch*, in Music, Nicom.*Harm*.11.5; τὰ λεγόμενα ὁ. (sc. σημεῖα) Gaud.*Harm*.21: neut. sg. ὁ., τό, between βαρύ and ὀξύ, Pl.*Phlb*. 17c. 3. metaph., *equable*, τὸ ὁμαλὲς καὶ ὁ. ἐν τῇ τιμῇ τῆς φιλοσοφίας M.Ant.1.14, cf. Longin.36.4. 4. Adv. -νως *uniformly*, φερομένου τοῦ ἡλίου Arist.*Pr*.911$^{a}$14. II. *having the same accent*, A.D.*Pron*.75.16, al., D.H.*Comp*.11. Adv. -νως, τινι St.Byz. s.v. Παραισός. **–τοξος**, coined by Id. s.v. Ἄβιοι.

**ὁμοτός**, ή, όν, *sworn*, Theognost.*Can*.75.

**ὁμο-τράπεζος** [ᾰ], *ον*, *eating at the same table with* (cf. ὁμόσπονδος), Hdt.9.16; συνέστιος καὶ ὁ. Pl.*Euthphr*.4c; οἱ ὁ. *messmates*, Persian name for certain of the chief courtiers, X.*Cyr*.7.1.30; cf. ὁμότιμος. ❋ **–τρεχής**, *ές*, etym. of ἀτρεκής, Sch.Pi.*P*.8.9. **–τρῐβέω**, in part., -οῦντες λίθοι *fully polished* stones fitting closely together, *IG*7.3073. 164 (Lebad., ii B.C.). **–τρῐχος**, *ον*, = ὁμόθριξ, Poll.6.156, Hsch. s.v. ὁμόπτεροι. **–τροπία**, ἡ, *sameness of character* or *habits*, D.H. 4.28. ❋ **–τροπος**, *ον*, *of the same habits* or *life*, ὁ. τε καὶ ὁμότροφος γίγνεσθαι, of the mind in relation to the body, Pl.*Phd*.83d: as Subst., οἱ ὁ. τινός Aeschin.1.158, cf. Thphr.*Char*.26.7; Δίκα καὶ ὁ. Εἰρήνα v.l. in Pi.*O*.13.7; λέγοιτο δ' ἄν τις Πυρρώνειος ὁ. D.L.9.70. 2. *of like fashion*, ἤθεα ὁ. Hdt.8.144; τὰ ἐν Αἰγύπτῳ.. ὁ. ἂν ἦν τοῖσι Ἕλλησι Id. 2.49, cf. Aen.Tact.19, al. Adv. -πως *in the same manner*, Id.3.3, Arist.*SE*183$^{b}$6. 3. *homogeneous*, Dam.*Pr*.45. **–τροφία**, ἡ, *a being reared together*, J.*AJ*18.6.1. **–τροφος**, *ον*, *reared* or *bred together with*, τινι *h.Ap*.199; τινος *h.Hom*.9.2 (in both places of Artemis and Apollo); Δίκα καὶ ὁ. Εἰρήνα Pi.*O*.13.7 (cf. ὁμότροπος); ὁ. τοῖσι ἀνθρώποισι θηρία, of domestic animals, Hdt.2.66. II. abs., *feeding together*, *having the same diet*, Pl.*Phd*.83d (v. ὁμότροπος). 2. ὁ. πεδία plains *where we fed in common*, Ar.*Av*.329. **–τροχάω**, (τρέχω) *run in company* or *together*, v.l. in Od.15.451 (ap.Eust., for ἁματρ.); Θοῦρος.. Ἑρμῇ -άων Man.6.527. **–τῠπία**, ἡ, *sameness of form*, Philox.Gramm.ap.*EM*234.55. **–τῠπος**, *ον*, *identical in tenor*, *PFlor*.50.116 (iii A.D.), *PLips*.28.23 (iv A.D.), etc. **–τύραννος** [ῠ], *ον*, *fellow-tyrant*, Ph.1.514 (v.l. ὁμοιο–).

**ὁμοῦ** (Aeol. **ὔμοι** Sapph.*Supp*.23.13), Adv., I. prop. of Place, *at the same place*, *together*, μὴ ἐμὰ σῶν ἀπάνευθε τιθήμεναι ὀστέ', Ἀχιλλεῦ, ἀλλ' ὁ. Il.23.84; ὁ. εἶναι, opp. χωρὶς εἶναι, X.*Cyr*.6.1.7, etc.; ὁ. πάντες ἀναμεμιγμένοι S.*El*.715, etc. 2. generally, *together*, *at once*, ὁ. δ' ἔχον ὠκέας ἵππους Il.11.127; ἄμφω ὁ. Od.12.424; παρῆν ὁ. κλύειν πολλὴν βοήν A.*Pers*.401; χρόνος καθαιρεῖ πάντα.. ὁ. Id.*Eu*.286; δυοῖν ὁ. S.*OC*329; εἰ γὰρ Αἰγίσθῳ θ' ὁ. *likewise*, Id.*El*.1416: freq. accompanying two Substs. already connected by καί or τε, like Engl. *both*, εἰ δὴ ὁ. πόλεμός τε δαμᾷ καὶ λοιμὸς Ἀχαιούς Il.1.61; ὁ. γλυφίδας τε λαβὼν καὶ νεῦρα 4.122; χίλι' ὑπέστη, αἶγας ὁ. καὶ ὄϊς a thousand smaller cattle, *both* goats and sheep, 11.245; θυμὸς τείρεθ' ὁ. καμάτῳ τε καὶ ἱδρῷ 17.745, etc.; ἐπήγαγε λιμὸν ὁ. καὶ λοιμόν Hes. *Op*.243; ἐφόνευον ἄνδρας ὁ. καὶ ἵππους X.*Cyr*.3.3.64; οἴκτειρε θῆλυν ἄρσενός θ' ὁ. γόον A.*Ch*.502; πόλιν τε κἀμὲ καί σ' ὁ. στένει S.*OT*64, cf. *El*.667, *Aj*.1079; ὁ. ταράττων τήν τε γῆν καὶ τὴν θάλατταν Ar.*Eq*. 431; ἱππέας τε καὶ ὁπλίτας ὁ. Th.7.30, etc.: repeated, ὁ. μὲν.., ὁ. δέ.. S.*OT*4; cf. ὁμῶς. 3. c. dat., *together with*, *along with*, ὁ. νεφέεσσιν ἰών Il.5.867; κεῖσθαι ὁ. νεκύεσσι 15.118; ὁ. τῇ λίμνῃ Hdt.2. 101; οἰμωγὴ.. ὁ. κωκύμασιν A.*Pers*.426: also with ὁμοῦ following the dat., ὅσσαι μοι ὁ. τράφεν Od.4.723; θεοῖς ὁ., = ξὺν θεοῖς, S.*Aj*.767; οὔ ποτ' εἶμι τοῖς φυτεύσασίν γ' ὁ. will never *meet* them, Id.*OT*1007; τοῖσιν ἐχθίστοισι συνναίειν ὁ. Id.*Tr*.1237, cf. *OT*337, *OC*949, E.*Hel*. 104. II. *close at hand*, ὁρῶ τάλαιναν Εὐρυδίκην ὁ. S.*Ant*.1180, cf. Ar.*Eq*.245, *Pax*513, *Th*.572, X.*Cyr*.3.1.2: also c. dat., *close to*, τοῖς ἐμοῖς πλευροῖς ὁ. κλιθεῖσαν S.*Tr*.1225, cf. X.*HG*3.2.5, Pl.*Thg*.129d; ὁ. τι τῷ (v.l. τοῦ) τίκτειν παρεγένεθ' ἡ κόρη Men.851, cf. ὁ. τι τῷ τίκτειν D.H.1.78; ὁ. τῷ θανάτῳ ὄντας *at* death's *door*, Ael.*NA*4.36; ὁ. ἦν καὶ ἔχειν τὴν πόλιν καὶ τὸ γένος ὅλον μετὰ τῆς πόλεως it was *much the same thing*, Him.*Or*.2.16. 2. rarely c. gen., νεὼς ὁ. στείχειν S.*Ph*.1218; εἶναι ὁ. ἀλλήλων (v.l. -οις) X.*An*.4.6.24; τόπου *CPR*4. 34 (i A.D.); κυμάτω[ν ὁ]μοῦ dub. in Archil.*Supp*.2.11. 3. of amount, *in all*, *in round numbers*, ἀπὸ Σόλωνος ὁ. διακόσι' ἐστὶν ἔτη D.19.251; εἰσὶν ὁ. δισμύριοι Id.25.51, cf. 36.36, Men.140; γίνονται ὁ πυροῦ ἀρτάβαι λ' *CPR*35.12 (iii A.D.).

**ὁμόῡλος** [ῡ], *ον*, (ὕλη) *of the same material*, χορδαί Iamb.*VP*26. 116.

**ὁμοῦμαι**, v. ὄμνυμι.

**ὅμουρα**· σεμίδαλις ἑφθή, μέλι ἔχουσα καὶ σησάμην, Hsch.

❋ **ὁμουργός**, = συνεργός, *mate* of an animal, *POxy*.922.19 (vi A.D.).

**ὁμουρ-έω**, **–ησις**, **–ιος**, **–ος**, Ion. for ὁμορέω, etc.; but **ὁμούρησις**, Att. for ὁμήρησις (a word not found elsewhere), Hsch.

**ὁμο-φάγος**, gloss on ὠμοβόρος, Hsch. **–φεγγής**, *ές*, *shining together*, αἴγλη Nonn.*D*.5.113. **–φήτωρ**, *ορος*, ὁ, gloss on Homeric ἀφήτωρ, Eust.759.64. **–φθογγος**, *ον*, *sounding* or *giving tongue together*, θῆρες Nonn.*D*.1.157, etc. **–φλεγής**, *ές*, *burning together* or *at once*, θάλασσα ib.6.220. **–φλεκτος**, *ον*, = foreg., ib.42.403 (s.v.l.). **–φλοιος**, v. ὁμοιόφλοιος. **–φοιτος**, *ον*, *going by the side of*, τινος Pi.*N*.8.33 (cf. Phld.*Acad.Ind*.p.52 M.), Nonn.*D*.5.122, etc. **–φρᾰδής**, *ές*, *similar-sounding*, ἦχος *EM*221.39. **–φράδμων**, *ον*, gen. *ονος*, *of the same mind*, *Lyr.Adesp*.138.4. **–φρονέω**, pf. ὡμοφρόνηκα Phld.*Mus*.p.86 K.:—*to be of the same mind*, *have the same thoughts*, εἰ δὴ ὁμοφρονέοις Od.9.456; ὁμοφρονέοντε νοήμασιν.., ἀνὴρ ἠδὲ γυνή *in unity* of purposes, 6.183; Ἕλληνας ὁμοφρονέοντας *being all of one mind*, Hdt.9.2; opp. γνώμῃ διενειχθέντας, Id.7.229; of conspirators, X.*HG*7.5.7, Arist.*Ath*.14.3; also πόλεμος ὁμοφρονέων a war *of common consent*, Hdt.8.3: c. dat., οὐ γὰρ ἀλλήλοισι ὁμοφρονέουσι *are* not *agreed* together, ib.75. **–φροσύνη**, ἡ, = ὁμόνοια, *unity of mind and feeling*, ὁμοφροσύνην ὀπάσειαν ἐσθλὴν [θεοί] Od.6. 181, cf. Orph.*A*.353: pl., Od.15.198, A.R.2.716: also in Ion. and later Prose, Democr.186, D.H.9.45, Ocell.4.6, etc. **–φρων**, *ονος*, ὁ, ἡ, = ὁμόνοος, *agreeing*, *united*, ὁμόφρονα θυμὸν ἔχουσιν Il.22.263, cf. Hes.*Th*.60, Thgn.81; ὁμόφρονος εὐνᾶς Pi.*O*.7.6; ὁ. λόγος Ar.*Av*.632 (lyr.). Adv. -όνως Oenom.ap.Eus.*PE*5.33; poet. -ονέως *IG*9(1).235.6 (Locr.). **–φῠής**, *ές*, *of the same growth*, *age*, or *nature*, Pl.*Phd*.86b, *R*.458c; τινι *with* one, ib.439e; ἄμφω -φυέα, of hands and feet, Aret. *SD*2.12. Adv. -ῠῶς Procl.*in Prm*.p.625 S. **–φῠΐα**, ἡ, *sameness of growth*, *age*, or *nature*, Prisc.Lyd.27.19. ❋ **–φῡλία**, ἡ, *sameness of race* or *tribe*, Str.1.2.34, Plu.2.975f. **–φῡλος**, *ον*, *of the same race* or *stock*, *akin* (wider in sense than ὁμοεθνής, q.v.), Hp.*Aër*.12, Th.1.141, etc.; opp. ἀλλόφυλος, Epicur.*Sent*.39; οἱ ὁ. *those of the same race*, X.*Cyr*.5.4.27; φιλία ὁ. friendship *based on kinship*, E.*HF* 1200 (lyr.), Pl.*Mx*.244a; ὁ. Ζεύς Id.*Lg*.843a; θοὐμόφυλον, = ὁμοφυλία, E.*IT*346, Decr.ap.D.18.186; τὸ μὴ ὁ. a city *peopled by different races*, Arist.*Pol*.1303$^{a}$25. 2. generally, *of the same breed* or *kind*, ἀρχαὶ οὐχ ὁ. Philol.6; ὄρνιθες X.*Cyr*.1.6.39; ἀπιέναι πρὸς τὸ ὁ. ib.8.7.20, cf. Arist.*Mu*.396$^{b}$10; [τὸ πῦρ] συγκρίνει τὰ ὁ. *homogeneous matter*, Id.*Cael*.307$^{b}$1, cf. *GC*329$^{b}$28. **–φῠτος**, *ον*, *originating together*, *Theol.Ar*.50. **–φωκτος**, *ον*, (φώζω) *roasted* or *parched together*, Philox.3.15.

**ὁμοφων-έω**, *speak the same language with*, τινι Hdt.1.142: abs., J. *AJ*1.1.4. II. *sound together* or *in unison*, D.C.41.58: c. dat., *sound like*, A.D.*Pron*.7.25, al.; ὁ. τῷ λόγῳ *chimes in* with.., Arist. *EN*1102$^{b}$28; *agree*, πρός τι Them.*Or*.21.258b; περί τινος S.E.*P*.2. 32. III. *proclaim in unison*, Ἑλλὰς δ' ἀρετὰν ὁμοφωνεῖ *Delph*.3(1). 509. **–ία**, ἡ, in Music, *unison* (v. ὁμόφωνος II), Arist.*Pol*.1263$^{b}$35; ᾀδόντων ὁμοφωνία Luc.*Salt*.68. II. *community of language*, D.H. 1.29; τῶν ζῴων Ph.1.405. III. metaph., *agreement*, *concord*, Procl.*in Prm*.p.542 S., Ecphant.ap.Stob.4.7.64. ❋ **–ος**, *ον*, *speaking the same language with*, ἔθνεα οὐκ ὁ. σφίσι (= ἀλλήλοις) Hdt.3.98, cf. Th.4.3, X.*Mem*.4.4.19. II. *of the same sound* or *tone*, *in unison with*, τισι A.*Ag*.158 (lyr.). Adv. -νως *having the same name with*, τινι Str.9.2.29. 2. in Music, *on the same note*, *in unison*, opp. σύμφωνος (in concord), Arist.*Pr*.921$^{a}$7, al., Nicom.*Harm*.11.5, Ptol.*Harm*.1.7. Adv. -νως *with one voice* (*accord*), Plu.*Galb*.5, S.E.*P*.3.239. 3. Gramm., *having the same sound* (e.g. of voc. and nom. πόλις), Hdn. Gr.2.628.

**ὁμο-χοῖνιξ**, *ῑκος*, ὁ, ἡ, *one who shares the same* χοῖνιξ, Plu.2. 643d. **–χορος**, *ον*, *belonging to the same chorus*, τοῦ θεοῦ ib. 768b. **–χροέω**, *to be of the same colour*, *Gp*.19.6.2, Aët.7. 38. **–χροια**, ἡ, *sameness of colour*, X.*Cyn*.5.18, Arist.*Mete*. 342$^{b}$20, *Gp*.18.1.1. II. *even surface of the body*, *skin*, Hdt.1. 74 (acc. ὁμοχροίην or -χροιίην); so ὁμοχροίη, of inner and outer surfaces of skull, Hp.*VC*1; of surface of eye, Id.*Carn*.17: metaph., οὐδὲ ἅπτεται ταῦτα τῆς ὁμοχροίας Pl.*Ax*.369d. **–χρονέω**, *keep time with*, τῇ γλώττῃ τὸ πλῆκτρον ὁμοχρονεῖ Luc.*Im*.14: abs., *keep time*, Id.*Hist.Conscr*.50. **–χρονος**, *ον*, *contemporaneous*, Them.*Or*.9.128a. ❋ **–χροος**, *ον*, contr. **–χρους**, *ουν*, *of one colour*, opp. ποικίλος, Arist.*HA*543$^{a}$25, cf. 525$^{a}$4; *alike in colour*, prob. in Epicur.*Ep*.1 p.11 U., cf. Gal.13.496, *AP*5.300 (Paul.Sil.); *uniform in colour*, Hp.*Mul*.1.40: heterocl. pl. ὁμόχρους (from ὁμόχροες) Archig.ap. Paul.Aeg.4.5. **–χρώμᾰτος**, *ον*, = foreg., D.S.1.88:—also **–χρωμος**, *ον*, *Hippiatr*.14, *AB*220. **–χρως**, ὁ, ἡ, **–χρων**, τό, gen. χρωτος, =

foreg., Arist.*GA*749$^a$22, Thphr.*Sens.*37, *HP*9.4.10, etc. **-χωρος**, ον, *neighbouring*, [ἔθνη] D.C.*Fr.*74.1; οἱ ὁ. Id.38.45.2, al. **-ψηφέω**, *vote together with*, τινι J.*AJ*17.11.1. **-ψηφος**, ον, *voting with*, μὴ τοῖς ἐχθίστοις ὁμόψηφοι γένησθε And.2.28; ὁ. κατά τινων τοῖς τριάκοντα Lys.13.94. II. *having an equal right to vote with*, τοῖσι στρατηγοῖσι Hdt.6.109; μετὰ τῶν σφετέρων Id.7.149. **-ψῡχία**, *unanimitas*, *Gloss.* ⊛**-ψῡχος**, = ὁμόνοος, Lxx 4*Ma.*14.20. Adv. -χως Eun. *VS*p.474B. II. *endowed with the same soul*, Porph.*Abst.*3.16.

**ὁμόω**, *unite*: Pass., ὁμωθῆναι φιλότητι, = φιλότητι μιγῆναι, Il.14.209. II. = ὁμοιόω, in fut. Med., εἶδος ὁμώσεται Nic.*Th.*334.

**ὀμόω**, *swear*, v. ὄμνυμι. **ὄμπαξ**, v. πάξ. **ὄμπη**, v. ὄμπνη.

**ὄμπν-ειος**, f.l. for ὄμπνιος (q.v.). **-η**, ἡ, *food, bread-corn*, Διονύσου ὄμπνη συντίθησιν Sosith.2.11 (cj. Herm. for δαίνυσι τ' ἔμπης, dub.): in pl. ὄμπναι, *cakes of meal and honey, sacrificial cakes*, Call.*Fr.*123, 268; πολυωπέας ὄμπνας *honeycombs*, Nic.*Al.*450 (ὄμπας codd. opt. and Sch.). (The form ὄμπη is found in Nic. l.c., *AB*287, Hsch., Phot., *EM*625.52.) II. ὄμπνη· τροφή, εὐδαιμονία, Hsch. ⊛**-ηρὸν** ὕδωρ· τρόφιμον, Id. **-ιακός**, ή, όν, = sq., *AP*9.707 (Tull. Gem.); ὀμπνικός is f.l. ap.Suid. ⊛**-ιος**, in codd. freq. ὄμπνειος, α, ον, *of* or *relating to corn*, καρπός MoschioTrag.6.10, Eratosth.16.17; στάχυς A.R.4.989, Lyc.621; ἔργον husbandry, Call.*Fr.*183; ὄμπνια..Δήμητρος..δῶρα Orph.*Fr.*280; *nourishing*, Philet. ap.Sch.A.R.4.989: hence, 2. epith. of Demeter, Ὄμπνια, Ὀ. θεσμοφόρος Call.*Aet.Oxy.*2079.10; Ὀ. Δηώ Nonn.*D.*11.213, cf. Hsch. s.v. ὄμπνιος λειμών, prob. in *IG*2$^2$.1352 (ii A.D.): then in late Poets, Καίσαρος ὄμπνια μήτηρ ib.14.1389 i 56, cf. *BCH*11.161 (Lagina). II. *well-fed, flourishing*: hence, *large*, ὀ. νέφος a *huge* cloud, S.*Fr.*246; κτῆσις Lyc.1264. [Ὄμπνια proparox., Hdn.Gr.2.451: formed like πότνια.]

**ὀμπνιόχειρ**· πλουσιόχειρ, πλούσιος, Hsch.

**ὀμφαῖος**, α, ον, (ὀμφή) *prophetic, oracular*, πέτρη Nonn.*D.*9.284, al. II. Ὀμφαίη, ἡ, as a goddess, Emp.123.3.

⊛ **ὀμφᾰκ-ηρός**, ά, όν, (ὄμφαξ) *for holding* ὄμφακες, ἀγγεῖα Philagr.ap. Orib.5.17.8 codd. (Ὀμφακηνά Daremb.), Aët.5.136,137 (ὀμφακηρὰ α' *PLond.*2.239.13 (iv A.D.) must be pl. in spite of the numeral). **-ίας** (sc. οἶνος), ὁ, *wine from unripe grapes*, Gal.ap.Ath.1.26d. II. as masc. Adj., *harsh, austere*, θυμός Ar.*Ach.*352, cf. Plu.2.11d. 2. ὀ. νεκροί *unripe*, i.e. *untimely*, dead, Luc.*Cat.*5. **-ίζω**, *to be unripe*, prop. of grapes, *Gp.*5.43.3, al.; of olives, ib.3.13.5; of other fruits, Dsc.2.159, Philum.ap.Aët.9.33; of oil, Sor.1.46,50. 2. of a vine, *bear sour grapes*, Lxx *Is.*18.5. II. in Med., Σικελὸς ὀμφακίζεται the Sicilian *steals sour grapes*, prov. of one who will steal anything however worthless, Epich.239, cf. Aristaenet.2.7. ⊛**-ῐνος**, η, ον, *made from unripe grapes*, ὀ. οἶνος, = ὀμφακίας, ὀμφακίτης, Hp.*Mul.*2.189 (vulg., ὀμφακίῳ codd. opt.), *PFlor.*140$^v$.7 (iii A.D.); ὀ. ἔλαιον *oil made from unripe olives*, Dsc.1.30, cf. Gal.6.196. 2. ὀμφάκινον (sc. ἱμάτιον), τό, a garment named prob. from its colour, Poll.7.56. **-ιον**, τό, *juice of unripe grapes*, Dsc.5.5, Gal.12.902; also, *oil made from unripe olives*, Hp.*Acut.*(*Sp.*)65, *Mul.*2.189, Plin.*HN*12.130, *PTeb.*273.33 (ii/iii A.D.). II. = ὄμφαξ II.2, Aristaenet.2.7 (τοῦ στέρνου μῆλα being prob. a gloss). **-ιος**, α, ον, = ὀμφάκινος (q.v.), ὀμφακίων (sic) σταφυλάων Dioscorus in *PLit. Lond.*100*B*. **-ίς**, ίδος, ἡ, *cup of the acorn* of Valonia oak, used for tanning, and as an astringent medicine, Paul.Aeg.3.42. **-ισμός**, ὁ, sine expl., Zonar. **-ίτης** [ῑ] (sc. οἶνος), ὁ, = ὀμφακίας, Dsc.5.6; epith. of Dionysus, Ael.*VH*3.41; λίθος, name of a green stone, prob. for ὀμφαρίτης in Gal.12.207:—fem. **-ῖτις**, ιδος, as Adj., *unripe*, ἐλαίη Hp.*Mul.*2.195: as Subst., *Aleppo gall*, gall of *Quercus infectoria*, Dsc.1.107, Gal.8.114.

**ὀμφᾰκό-καρπος**, v.l. for ὀμφαλό-, Dsc.3.90, cf. Gal.11.834. **-μελῐ**, τό, *drink of sour grapes and honey*, Diocl.*Fr.*69, Dsc.5.23, Philagr.ap. Orib.5.19.4. **-μελίτης** [ῑ] οἶνος, = ὀμφακόμελι, Paul.Aeg.3.39. **-ράξ**, ᾶγος, ὁ, ἡ, (ῥάξ) *with sour grapes*, βότρυες *AP*9.561 (Phil.).

**ὀμφᾰκ-ός**, ὁ, = ὄμφαξ I, v.l. in Hp.*Ulc.*17. **-ώδης**, ες, *like unripe grapes*, Id.*Vict.*2.55, Arist.*Mir.*846$^b$1, Thphr.*HP*3.13.6, *Gp.*4.15.4.

⊛ **ὀμφᾰλη-τομία**, ἡ, *cutting of the navel-string, midwifery*, Pl.*Tht.*149e:—also **ὀμφαλοτομία**, Arist.*HA*587$^a$9, Poll.4.208 (v.l.), Sor.1.80. **-τόμος**, ον, *cutting the navel-string*: as Subst. ὀ., ἡ, *midwife*, Ion. word for Att. μαῖα, Hippon.12 Diehl, Hp.*Mul.*1.46: also **ὀμφᾰλοτόμος**, τριγόλας Sophr.66.

**ὀμφᾰλ-ικός**, ή, όν, = ὀμφάλιος, Phan.Hist.29. **-ιον**, τό, Dim. of ὀμφαλός I, *AP*7.506 (Leon.), Arat.207, Nic.*Al.*596, *PMag.Osl.*1.312. II. = ὀμφαλός II.1, Epigr.ap.D.L.8.45. **-ιος**, α, ον, *having a boss, bossy*, ὀ. σάκεος τρύφος *AP*6.84 (Paul. Sil.). **-ίς**, ίδος, *navel-string*, Sor.1.80. **-ιστήρ**, ῆρος, ὁ, *knife to cut the navel-string*, Poll.2.169, 4.208, Hsch.

**ὀμφᾰλο-ειδής**, ές, *like a navel* or *boss*, Eust.1350.5. **-εις**, εσσα, εν, *having a navel* or *boss*, ἀσπίδος -οέσσης of the shield *with a central boss*, Il.6.118, Tyrt.12.25, cf. Ar.*Pax*1274; ζυγὸν -όεν yoke *with a knob on the top*, Il.24.269, cf. ὀμφαλός II.2; οἰμωγὰς -οέσσας Ar.*Pax*1278 (by comic transference from ἀσπίδας ὀ. ib.1274); συκῆς πόσιν -όεσσαν, prob. referring to a peculiar kind of fig (called **ὀμφάλειος** by Phot.), Nic.*Al.*348; ἄρκτον -όεσσαν, because *pointing to the pole* (ὀμφαλός) of the heavens, ib.7. **-καρπος**, ον, *bearing fruit like an* ὀμφαλός, name for ἀπαρίνη, Dsc.3.90.

⊛ **ὀμφᾰλός**, ὁ, *navel*, Il.4.525, 13.568, Hdt.7.60, etc. 2. *umbilical cord*, Hp.*Superf.*8, *Oct.*10, Sor.1.57, Gal.15.387. II. *anything like a navel*, 1. *knob* or *boss*, Il.11.34; esp. in middle of shield, 13.192, etc. 2. *button* or *knob* in the middle of a yoke, 24.273. 3. *plug* or *valve closing outlet of bath*, Timarch.ap.Ath.11.501f; cf. βαλανειόμφαλος. 4. pl., *knobs at ends of stick round which books were rolled*, Luc.*Merc.Cond.*41, *Ind.*7,16, *AP*9.540. III. *centre* or *middle point*: νήσῳ ἐν ἀμφιρύτῃ, ὅθι τ' ὀ. ἐστι θαλάσσης Od.1.50 (only here in Od.); later Delphi (or rather a round stone in the Delphic temple) was called ὀ. as marking the *middle point of Earth*, Pi.*P.*4.74, B.4.4, A.*Eu.*40,166 (lyr.), cf. Pl.*R.*427c, Str.9.3.6, Paus.10.16.3; also of an altar at Megara, Simon.107.9 (= *IG*7.53); ἄστεος ὀ., at Athens, Pi.*Fr.*75.3; νήσου ὀ., of Enna in Sicily, v.l. in Call.*Cer.*15, cf. Cic.*Verr.*4.48.106. 2. *central part of a rose*, containing the seed-vessel, Arist.*Pr.*907$^a$20; of a pomegranate, Hp.*Nat.Mul.*44, Gal.12.649; *knob* on an oak-gall, Thphr.*HP*3.7.5; *button-shaped stalk* of the fig, *Gp.*10.56.2. 3. *centre* of an army, Poll.1.126; prop. the point at which an army is divided into two wings, Ascl.*Tact.*2.6, cf. Arr.*Tact.*8.4, Ael.*Tact.*7.3. 4. *keystone of an arched vault*, Arist.*Mu.*399$^b$30. 5. *vault, tomb*, *MAMA*3.402,712 (Corycus). IV. γῆς ὀ., = κοτυληδών, *navel-wort, Cotyledon Umbilicus*, Ps.-Dsc.4.91. (Cf. Lat. *umbilicus, umbo*, prob. from *ombh-*: Skt. *nā̆bhis*, OE. *nafel* 'navel', apptly. from *nŏbh-*.)

**ὀμφᾰλο-τομητέον**, *one must sever the navel-string*, Sor.1.78. **-τομία, -τόμος**, v. ὀμφαλητ-.

**ὀμφᾰλ-ώδης**, ες, = ὀμφαλοειδής, Arist.*HA*550$^a$21, *GA*752$^b$2. **-ωτός**, ή, όν, *made with a boss*, χρυσίδες Pherecr.128, cf. Plb.6.25.7, interpol. in Poll.1.134.

**ὄμφαξ**, ᾰκος, ἡ (ὁ Plu.2.138e, 648f, *Gp.*4.15.13), *unripe grape* (cf. Dsc.5.5), πάροιθε δέ τ' ὄμφακές εἰσιν ἄνθος ἀφιεῖσαι Od.7.125; ὅτ' ὀ. αἰόλλονται Hes.*Sc.*399: sg. as collective, ὅταν δὲ τεύχῃ Ζεὺς ἀπ' ὄμφακος πικρᾶς οἶνον A.*Ag.*970; so freq. in Hp., *Ulc.*12, *Acut.*(*Sp.*)65, al., cf. Plu.2.648f; εἶτ' ἦμαρ αὔξει μέσσον ὄμφακος τύπον S.*Fr.*255.5; also of other fruits, as olives, Poll.5.67. II. metaph., *young girl not yet ripe for marriage*, *AP*5.19 (Honest.), 12.205 (Strat.), *JRS*18.30 (Tembris); τί τρυγᾷς ὄμφακας ἡλικίης; (epitaph of a boy, addressed to Pluto) *IG*14.769 (Naples). 2. *the unripe hard breasts* of a young girl, ὄμφακα μαζοῦ Tryph.34; but ὄμφακι μαζῷ, as Adj., Nonn.*D.*1.71, 48.957; cf. ὀμφάκιον II. 3. ὄμφακας βλέπειν *look sour grapes*, look *sour* (cf. βλέπω II), *Com.Adesp.*877: hence τὰς ὀφρῦς σχάσασθε καὶ τὰς ὀ. your scornful brows and *sour-grape looks*, Pl.Com.32; cf. ὀμφακίας II. b. prov., ὑγιέστερος ὄμφακος *Com.Adesp.*910. 4. *a gem, used for seals*, Thphr.*Lap.*30. [Always ᾰ, since στόμφᾰκα has been restored by Gaisf. in Ar.*Fr.*624.]

⊛ **ὀμφ-ή**, ἡ, poet. Noun, *voice*, in Hom. always of the gods, ταῦτα θεῶν ἐκ πεύσεται ὀμφῆς Il.20.129; ἐπισπόμενοι θεοῦ ὀμφῇ Od.3.215, 16.96; θεῖη δέ μιν ἀμφέχυτ' ὀ., of the *voice* of the dream sent by Zeus to Agamemnon, Il.2.41; *oracle* delivered from the inner shrine at Pytho, Thgn.808; τρίποδος Philostr.*Im.*2.19; κληροῦν ὀμφάν (v. κληρόω II.2); signified by the flight of birds, ὀ. οἰωνοῖο A.R.3.939: also in pl., κατ' ὀμφὰς τὰς Ἀπόλλωνος S.*OC*102; κατ' ὀμφὴν σήν on hearing thy *message*, ib.550, cf. 1351. 2. *sweet, tuneful voice*, Pi.*Fr.*152; ὀμφαὶ μελέων ib.75.19; ἁδεῖαι..ὀμφαί Id.*N.*10.34, cf. S.*Ichn.*321 (lyr.). 3. generally, *a voice, sound*, ἰΰζειν ὀμφάν A.*Supp.*808 (lyr.); μύθων αὐδαθέντων ὀ. E.*Med.*175 (lyr.). II. ὀμφά· ὀσμή (Lacon.), Hsch., dub. cj. in *Lyr.Adesp.*63; cf. εὔομφος I, ποτόμφει. III. ὀμφαί, αἱ, name of the best kind of nard, τὰς ὀμφὰς ὀνομαζομένας βαρβάρῳ γλώττῃ κτλ. Gal.14.74. (In sense I cogn. with Engl. *song*: in sense II with ONorse *anga* 'give out a sweet scent', *angi* 'scent', *ang* 'pleasant sensation'.) ⊛**-ήεις**, εσσα, εν, *oracular, prophetic*, Nonn.*D.*2.689. **-ητήρ**, ῆρος, ὁ, *soothsayer*, Tryph.133.

**Ὄμφις**, said to be = Εὐεργέτης, title of Osiris, Plu.2.368b.

**ὄμφορα**· ὅσα ἀπὸ τῶν ἱερῶν ἐκφέρεσθαι ὁ νόμος κωλύει, Hsch. **ὀμφύνειν**· αὔξειν, σεμνύνειν, ἐντιμότερον ποιεῖν, Id., cf. Phot. (Cf. ὤμφυναν.) **ὀμῶλαξ**, ᾰκος, ὁ, ἡ, Dor. for ὁμαῦλαξ (q.v.).

**ὄμωμι**, τό, a Persian plant, Plu.2.369e (μῶλυ cj. Bernardakis).

**ὁμωνῠμ-έω**, *have the same name with*, τινι Ath.11.491c: abs., S.E.*M.*5.22. 2. *have the same meaning with*, A.D.*Pron.*105.31. ⊛**-ία**, ἡ, *a having the same name, verbal identity*, Epicur.*Nat.*2.9, *AP*6.100 (Crin.), Plu.2.427e: pl., Str.13.1.21. II. *fraudulent use of an identity of name*, *POxy.*257.44 (i A.D.), 1266.36 (i A.D.). III. of words, *equivocal sense, ambiguity*, παρὰ τὴν ὁ. Arist.*SE*165$^b$30; καθ' ὁμωνυμίαν *equivocally*, Id.*APo.*85$^b$11: pl., ταῖς -ίαις πλανῶνται Phld.*Sign.*36. 2. *an equivocal word*, τῶν ὀνομάτων τῷ μὲν σοφιστῇ ὁμωνυμίαι χρήσιμοι.., τῷ ποιητῇ δὲ συνωνυμίαι (q.v.) Arist.*Rh.*1404$^b$38. **-ιος**, α, ον, = sq., νῆσος [Arist.]*Pepl.*14. **-ος**, ον, (ὁμός, ὄνομα: ὁμόνυμος is a misspelling in Ant.Lib.34.5) *having the same name*, Il.17.720, Pi.*I.*7(6).24, etc.; τινι *with* one, Th.2.68, Pl.*R.*330b, etc.; τὸν ὁ. ἐμαυτῷ my own *namesake*, D.3.21, cf. Isoc.11.10. II. Subst., ὁ. τινός Pi.*Fr.*105, Hdt.3.67, Pl.*Sph.*218b, 234b; ὁ σαυτοῦ ὁ. your *namesake*, Id.*Prt.*311b; ὁ σὸς ὁ. Id.*Tht.*147d; ἡ ὁ. αὐτῆς Luc.*Im.*20. III. *of like kind*, πάντα τὰ ἐκείνοις ὁ. Pl.*Phd.*78e, cf. *Prm.*133d. IV. in the Logic of Arist., τὰ ὁ. are *things having the same name but different natures and definitions, things denoted by equivocal* or *ambiguous words*, *Cat.*1$^a$1, cf. *EN*1096$^b$27. Adv. -μως *equivocally*, ib.1129$^a$30, *de An.*412$^b$14, al., cf. Thphr.*CP*1.22.1.

**ὄμωρος ἄρτος**, a kind of bread, Epich.52, Sophr.27; cf. **ὄμουρα**.

**ὁμωροφ-έω**, *to be under the same roof*, v.l. in Aesop.10 (-οροφ- cod.). **-ιος**, ον, (ὄροφος) *being* or *lodging under the same roof with*, τινι Antipho 5.11, D.18.287, 21.118: abs., Opp.*H* 5.418: ὁμορόφιος is f.l. in codd., e.g. of Str.9.3.5, Gal.14.215. -**ος**, ον, = foreg., Phanod.13 (-ορρόφους, -ωροφίους codd. Ath.), Aesop.10 (-όροφ- codd.), Babr.12.15, etc.

® **ὁμῶς**, Adv. of ὁμός, *equally, likewise, alike*, Il.1.196, 9.605, Od.11.565 (nisi leg. ὅμως), A.*Eu.*388 (lyr.); *in equal parts*, Hes.*Th.*74: accompanying two Substs. joined by καί, like Engl. *both*, πλῆθεν ὁ. ἵππων τε καὶ ἀνδρῶν both of men and horses *alike*, Il.8.214; κάτθαν' ὁ. ὅ τ' ἀεργὸς ἀνὴρ ὅ τε πολλὰ ἐοργώς 9.320, cf. 11.708, Od.10.28, E.*El.* 407; ἔν τε θεοῖς κἀνθρώποις ὁ. Pi.*P.*9.40; τό τ' ἦμαρ καὶ κατ' εὐφρόνην ὁ. A.*Eu.*692; κἀκεῖ κἀνθάδ' ὤν.. ὁ. S.*Aj.*1372. 2. freq. πάντες ὁ. all *together*, all *alike*, Il.17.422, Od.4.775, etc.; πᾶσι..ὁ. Thgn.252; πάντῃ ὁ. Hes.*Th.*366; ἐς τὰ πάνθ' ὁ. A.*Pr.*736. II. c. dat., *like as, equally with*, ἐχθρὸς ὁ. Ἀΐδαο πύλῃσιν Il.9.312; ὁ. Πριάμοιο τέκεσσι τῖον 5.535, cf. 14.72.

**ὅμως**, Conj. (from ὁμῶς, with changed accent), *all the same, nevertheless*, used to limit whole clauses, once in Hom. (unless it is read in Od.11.565), Σαρπήδοντι δ' ἄχος γένετο.., ὅ. δ' οὐ λήθετο χάρμης Il.12.393; ὅ. πιθοῦ μοι S.*OT*1064, cf. *Ant.*519; κοὐκ ἐπίδηλος ὅ. and *yet* not so as to be observed, Thgn.442; νῦν δὲ ὅ. θαρρῶ Pl. *Smp.*193e, etc.: freq. strengthd. by other words, ἀλλ' ὅ. but *still*, but *for all that*, Pi.*P.*1.85, Ar.*V.*1085, etc.; ὅ. μήν (Dor. μάν) Pi.*P.* 2.82, Pl.*Plt.*297d; ὅ. μέντοι Id.*Cri.*54d; ὅ. γε μήν Ar.*Nu.*631, 822; ὅ. γε μέντοι Id.*V.*1344, *Ra.*61: used elliptically, πάντως μὲν οἴσεις οὐδὲν ὑγιές, ἀλλ' ὅ. (sc. οἰστέον) Id.*Ach.*956, cf. E.*Hec.*843, *Ba.*1027 (prob.). II. freq. in apodosi after καὶ εἰ (κεἰ) or καὶ ἐάν (κἄν), κεἰ τὸ μηδὲν ἐξερῶ, φράσω δ' ὅ. S.*Ant.*234, cf. A.*Ch.*933; but ὅ., though it belongs in sense to the apodosis, is freq. closely attached to the protasis, μέμνησ' Ὀρέστου, κεἰ θυραῖός ἐσθ' ὅ., i.e. κεἰ θ. ἐστι, ὅμως μέμνησο, ib.115; λέξον.., κεἰ στένεις ὅ., i.e. κεἰ στένεις, ὅ. λέξον, Id.*Pers.*295; κἂν ἄποπτος ᾖς ὅ., φώνημ' ἀκούω S.*Aj.*15: sts. it even stands in the protasis, ἐρημία με, κεἰ δίκαι' ὅ. λέγω, σμικρὸν τίθησι Id. *OC*957; ἐγὼ μὲν εἴην, κεἰ πέφυχ' ὅ. λάτρις, ἐν τοῖσι γενναίοισιν ἠριθμημένος E.*Hel.*728. 2. the protasis is freq. replaced by a part., ὕστεροι ἀπικόμενοι ἱμείροντο ὅ. Hdt.6.120; κλῦθί μου νοσῶν ὅ. (i.e. εἰ νοσεῖς ὅ. κλῦθι) S.*Tr.*1115: strengthd., πιθοῦ, καίπερ οὐ στέργων ὅ. A. *Th.*712; ἱκνοῦμαι, καὶ γυνή περ οὖσ' ὅ. E.*Or.*680; τάδ' ἔρδω, καὶ τύραννος ὢν ὅ. S.*OC*851; ἐρήσομαι δέ, καὶ κακῶς πάσχουσ' ὅ. E.*Med.*280: sts. it precedes, τόλμα.., ὅ. ἄτλητα πεπονθώς, for καίπερ πεπονθώς, ὅ. τόλμα, Thgn.1029: in Prose, οἱ δὲ..ὅ. ταῦτα πυνθανόμενοι ἀρρώδεον Hdt.8.74; οἱ τετρακόσιοι..ὅ. καὶ τεθορυβημένοι ξυνελέγοντο Th.8.93, cf. Hdt.5.63, X.*Cyr.*8.2.21: exceptionally, ἡ ἰσομοιρία τῶν κακῶν, ἔχουσά τινα ὅμως..κούφισιν, οὐδ' ὣς ῥᾳδία ἐδοξάζετο Th.7.75. 3. where the protasis does not contain a verb, ἀπάλαμόν περ ὅ. (v.l. ὁμῶς) ἐπὶ ἔργον ἐγείρει Hes.*Op.*20; βαρέα δ' οὖν ὅ. φράσον A.*Th.*810; κόλακι, δεινῷ θηρίῳ, ὅ. ἐπέμειξεν ἡ φύσις ἡδονήν Pl.*Phdr.*240b. III. used to break off a speech, *however*.., A.*Eu.*74; to refer to something previously said or to the general situation, *after all, in spite of all*, Th.1.105, 3.28, 80, 7.1.

**ὁμωχέτᾱς**, ὁ (prob. contr. fr. ὁμοεχέτας), *holding* or *dwelling together*, τοὺς ὁμωχέτας δαίμονας *worshipped in the same temple*, Th.4.97 (prob. Boeot.).

**ὀν-**, Aeol., Cypr., etc. for ἀν-.

**ὀνᾱγός**, ὁ, dialect form of Att. *ὀνηγός, *ass-driver*, v.l. in Plaut. *Asin.Prolog.*10; cf. ὄναγρος I.

**ὀνάγρα**, ἡ, *oleander*, *Nerium Oleander*, Dsc.4.117, Paul.Aeg.7.3.

**ὀνάγρ-εια** (sc. κρέα), *asinina*, *Gloss.* -**ῖνος**, η, ον, *like a wild ass*, of the colour of a garment, ὑποζώνη *BGU*717.10 (ii A.D.), cf. Poll.7.56. -**ιον**, τό, Dim. of ὄναγρος I, *PCair.Zen.*75.5 (iii B.C.).

**ὀναγρόβοτος**, ον, *grazed by wild asses*, ὀροπέδια Str.12.6.1.

**ὄναγρον**, τό, = ὀνάγρα, Gal.12.89.

**ὄναγρος**, ὁ, = ὄνος ἄγριος, *the wild ass*, Lxx *Ps.*103(104).11, Str.7.4.8, Babr.67.1, Artem.4.56; θῆλυς ὄ. Opp.*C.*3.216; title of the Greek original of Plautus' *Asinaria*, *Prolog.*10 (v.l. *Onagos*). II. a kind of *catapult*, = μονάγκων, Procop.*Goth.*1.21, Lyd.*Mag.*1.46, Amm. Marc.23.4.7.

**ὀναίνειν**· ἀπήλαυσα, Hsch. **ὄναιον**· ἀρεῖον, Id., cf. *SIG*1165 (Dodona): perh. ὀναῖον, cf. ὄνειος (B).

**ὀνάλ-ομα**, ἁ, Thess., = ἀνάλωμα, *expenditure*, *IG*9(2).517.22 (Larissa, iii B.C.). -**ουμα**, ατος, τό, late Thess. for foreg., ib.461.12 (Crannon), al.

® **ὄνᾰρ**, τό, used only in nom. and acc. sg., the other cases being supplied by ὄνειρος (q.v.):—*dream, vision in sleep*, opp. a waking vision, οὐκ ὄ., ἀλλ' ὕπαρ ἐσθλόν Od.19.547, cf. 20.90; ἡλίῳ δεικνυσι τοὔναρ S.*El.*425; εἶδον ὄ. Ar.*Eq.*1090; ἄκουε δὴ ὄ. ἀντὶ ὀνείρατος *dream* for dream, Pl.*Tht.*201d; ὥστε μηδὲ ὄ. ἰδεῖν, of profound sleep, Id.*Ap.* 40d: prov., τὸ ἐμὸν γ' ἐμοὶ λέγεις ὄ. 'you are telling me what I know already', Id.*R.*563d, cf. Suid. s. v. ταὐτὸν πέπονθα (cf. ὄνειρος I, ὄνειαρ II). 2. prov. of anything fleeting or unreal, ὀλιγοχρόνιον.. ὥσπερ ὄ. Thgn.1020; σε παρέρχεται ὡς ὄ. ἥβη Theoc.27.8; πόθος δέ μοι ὡς ὄ. ἔπτα Bion 1.58: in Prose, ἡ ἐμὴ [σοφία].., ὥσπερ ὄ. οὖσα Pl. *Smp.*175e, cf. *Men.*85c; ὡς ὄ. ἐλευθερίας δρῶντας Plu.*Thes.*32; and without ὡς, σκιᾶς ὄ. ἄνθρωπος Pi.*P.*8.95; ὄ. ἡμερόφαντον ἀλαίνει, of an old man, A.*Ag.*82 (anap.). II. in Trag. and Att. freq. as Adv., *in a dream, in sleep*, ὄ. γὰρ ὑμᾶς νῦν Κλυταιμήστρα καλῶ Id.*Eu.*116; ὄ. διώκεις θῆρα ib.131; ὄ. πνεύσαντα νυκτὸς S.*Fr.*65: freq. in Pl., ὄ. ἐπλουτήσαμεν *Tht.*208b; ὄ. ὀνείρατα διηγεῖσθαι ib.158c, etc.; also οὐδ' ὄ. not even *in a dream*, E.*Fr.*107, Herod.1.11; πολιτικὸς ἀνὴρ οὐδ' ὄ. Cic.*Att.*1.18.6; μηδ' ἰδὼν ὄ. not even *in my dreams*, E.*IT*518, cf. Pl. *Tht.*173d, Mosch.4.18; ἃ μηδ' ὄ. ἤλπισαν D.19.275: hence freq. opp. ὕπαρ, v. ὕπαρ II; κατ' ὄναρ *in a dream*, condemned by Phryn.395, but quoted by him from Polemo, is also found in *Ev.Matt.*1.20, Aristid. *Or.*47(23).21: with sense, *in consequence of a dream*, in *SIG*1147 (Crete, ii/iii A.D.), *Supp.Epigr.*2.405 (Macedonia).

**ὀναρ-ίδιον**, τό, = sq., *PRyl.*239.21 (iii A.D.). ® -**ιον**, τό, Dim. of ὄνος, Diph.89, Macho ap.Ath.13.582c, Arr.*Epict.*2.24.18, *Vit.Aesop.* *Oxy.*2083.19, *POxy.*63.11 (ii/iii A.D.); of a bronze figure, *PGiss.*47.17 (ii A.D.).

® **ὀνᾶς**· δοῦλον, ἀνόητον, ἀχρεῖον, Hsch. II. **ὀνάς**, άδος, ἡ, fem. of ὄνος, Aq., Sm.*Za.*9.9, Al.*Ge.*45.23, *Gloss.*

**ὄνασθαι**, v. ὀνίνημι. **ὄνᾱσις**, **ὀνάτωρ**, Dor. for ὄνησις, ὀνήτωρ. **ὄναται**· ἀτιμάζεται, μέμφεται, Hsch. **ὄνδικος**, Arc. for ἀνάδικος, *IG*5(2).343*B* (Orchom. Arc., iv B.C.).

® **ὄνε**, Thess. for ὅδε, declined like ὁ with addition of -νε, acc. sg. neut. τόνε *IG*9(2).512.28; gen. sg. neut. τοίνεος, acc. pl. neut. τάνε, gen. pl. τουννέουν, ib.517.15, 23, 17.

® **ὄνειαρ**, ᾰτος, τό (later perh. ὄνεαρ disyll., v. infr. I. 4), Ep. word, *that which brings profit, advantage*, Il.22.486, Hes.*Op.*822, etc.; μέγα στιβάδεσσιν ὄνειαρ *boon* for leafy couches, Theoc.13.34. 2. *means of strengthening, refreshment*, Od.4.444, 15.78, Hes.*Op.*41. 3. in pl. ὀνείᾰτα, *food, victuals*, freq. in Hom. (esp. Od.) in the line οἱ δ' ἐπ' ὀνείαθ' ἑτοῖμα προκείμενα χεῖρας ἴαλλον Od.1.149, al.; also of *rich presents*, τοσσάδ' ὀνείατ' ἄγων Il.24.367. 4. of persons, πᾶσιν ὄ., of Hector, 22.433; πῆμα κακὸς γείτων, ὅσσον τ' ἀγαθὸς μέγ' ὄ. Hes. *Op.*346; ἀθανάτοις θνητοῖσί τ' ὄνεαρ καὶ χάρμα τέτυκται, of Demeter, *h.Cer.*269 (cj. Ilgen, for ὄνειαρ). II. for ὄναρ (v. ὄναρ I. 1 fin., ὄνειρος I), *dream*, τοὐμὸν ὄ. ἐμοί Call.*Epigr.*49, cf. *AP*7.42. (The true spelling in early Ion. is prob. ὄνηαρ, which is called Aeol. by Choerob. in *An.Ox.*2.245: hence later Ion. ὀνέαρ: prob. from *ὀνᾱϝαρ, cf. ὀνίνημι.)

**ὀνειδ-είη**, ἡ, poet. for ὄνειδος, μεσάτοισιν ὀνειδείην ἐπέλασσε Nic. *Al.*408. -**ειος**, ον, *reproachful*, ὀνειδείοις ἐπέεσσι with words *of reproach*, Il.1.519, etc.; once in Od., 18.326; ὀ. μῦθος Il.21.393. 2. *dishonourable*, ψωμὸς ὀ., of the fruits of begging, *AP*9.573 (Ammian.). -**είω**, poet. for sq., Thebaïs *Fr.*3. ® -**ίζω**, fut. -ιῶ S. *OT*1423, E.*Tr.*430, Pl.*Ap.*30a: aor. ὠνείδισα (Ep. ὀν-) Il.9.34, etc.: pf. ὠνείδικα Lys.16.15:—**Pass.**, E.*Tr.*936, etc.: fut. Med. ὀνειδιεῖσθε (in pass. sense) S.*OT*1500: aor. ὠνειδίσθην Plb.11.4.10: I. *cast in* one's *teeth, make a reproach* to one, usu. c. acc. rei et dat. pers., ἀλκὴν μέν μοι πρῶτον ὀνείδισας Il.9.34, cf. Od.18.380, Hes.*Op.*718, Hdt. 1.90, 8.106; αἰσχύνομαί σοι τοῦτ' ὀνειδίσαι A.*Ch.*917; ἃ δ' εἰς γάμους μοι βασιλικοὺς ὠνείδισας E.*Med.*547; ὀ. φόνον [τινί] D.21.120; ὄνειδος ὀ. εἴς τινα S.*OC*754, *Ph.*523: with a relat. clause instead of the acc., Ἀγαμέμνονι.. ὀνειδίζων, ὅτι.. Il.2.255, cf. Pl.*Ap.*30a, al.; ὀ. τινί, ὡς.. X.*Mem.*2.9.8, cf. Il.1.211 (without dat.); ὀ. εἰς ἀχαριστίαν τινί, διότι.. Plb.28.4.11: c. inf., εἴ τις τῳ ὀ. φιλοκερδεῖ εἶναι Pl.*Hipparch.* 232c; ὀ. τινὶ τετρῆσθαι τὰ ὦτα D.L.2.50: without dat. pers., ὀνειδιῶν τι τῶν πάρος κακῶν *make a reproach*, S.*OT*1423, cf. 441, Hdt.8. 143:—Pass., *to be made a reproach*, καὶ σχεδὸν δὴ πάντα..οὐκ ὀρθῶς ὀνειδίζεται Pl.*Ti.*86d, cf. Th.1.77. II. without acc. rei, *reproach, upbraid*, 1. c. dat. pers., Lys.27.16, etc.; τισὶ περί τινος Hdt.4. 79; [τινὶ] ἔς τι Id.8.92; without dat. pers., Il.7.95. 2. c. acc. pers., *chide, reproach*, Pl.*Ap.*30e; τοιαῦτ' ὀνειδίζεις με thus *dost thou reproach me*, S.*OC*1002; also ἐπειδὴ..τυφλόν μ' ὠνείδισας (sc. ὄντα) *didst reproach me with* being blind, Id.*OT*412:—Pass., *to be reproached*, ἔκ τινων E.*Tr.*936; εἰς δειλίαν D.S.20.62; τὴν μικροπολιτείαν *with*.., Stob.3.39.29. -**ῖσις**, εως, ἡ, = ὀνειδισμός, Hsch. s.v. ἔλεγξις. -**ισμα**, ατος, τό, *insult, reproach, blame*, Hdt.2.133. -**ισμός**, ὁ, *reproach*, *Ep. Rom.*15.3 (pl.), al., J.*AJ*19.7.1, Plu.*Art.*22; *calumny*, Vett.Val.65.7, 73.10 (both pl.). -**ιστέον**, *one must reproach*, τινι Pl.*Lg.*689c, Ph. 2.305. -**ιστήρ**, ῆρος, ὁ, = sq., *abusive*, λόγοι ὀ. E.*HF*218. -**ιστής**, οῦ, ὁ, *one who reproaches with* a thing, c. gen. rei, ἁμαρτημάτων, εὐεργετημάτων, Arist.*Rh.*1381$^b$2. -**ιστικός**, ή, όν, *reproachful, abusive*, εἴς τι Luc.*Cont.*7; λόγοι D.S.16.93. Adv. -κῶς M.Ant.1.10, Demetr. *Eloc.*289. -**ος**, εος, τό, *reproach, rebuke, censure, blame*, esp. by word, προθέουσιν ὀνείδεα μυθήσασθαι Il.1.291; λέγ' ὀ. 2.222; ὀ. βάζεις Od.17.461; εἶχε ὀ. καὶ ἀτιμίην was *in disgrace*, Hdt.9.71; ὀ. ὀνειδίζειν S.*Ph.*523; ὀ. φέρει it brings *reproach*, Pl.*R.*590c; ὀ. τινὶ περιθεῖναι Antipho 5.18; περιάψειν Lys.21.24; ὡς ἐν ὀνείδει by way of *reproach*, Pl.*Grg.*512c, cf. *R.*431b (without ὡς *Smp.*189e); ὀνείδει ἐνέχεσθαι, συνέχεσθαι, Id.*Lg.*808e, 944e: pl., ὀνείδη κλύειν A.*Pers.*757; κολάζειν ὀνείδεσι *with censures*, Pl.*Lg.*847a; ὀνείδη ἔχει τὰ μέγιστα Id.*R.* 344b; ὀ. ἐπιφέρειν Arist.*EN*1123$^a$32. 2. *matter of reproach, disgrace*, σοὶ γὰρ ἐγὼ..κατηφείη καὶ ὀ. Il.16.498; σοὶ μὲν δὴ..κατηφείη καὶ ὀ., εἰ.. 17.556, cf. Hdt.2.36; ἐμῇ κεφαλῇ κατ' ὀνείδεα χεῦαν Od. 22.463; τέκνοις ὀ. λιπεῖν E.*Heracl.*301; ὀνειδῶν καὶ κακῶν μέστους D. 22.31; ὄνειδός [ἐστι] c. inf., E.*Andr.*410: c. gen., τὸ..πόλεως ὀ. the *disgrace* of the city, A.*Th.*539; αὐτῆς ὀ. S.*OC*984; ὀ. Ἑλλάνων Id.*Aj.* 1191 (lyr.); τὸ Λυσίου ὀ. Pl.*Phdr.*277a; Oedipus calls his daughters τοιαῦτ' ὀνείδη, S.*OT*1494, cf. Ar.*Ach.*855, D.21.132. 3. the statement of Eust.88.15, 647.36 that ὀ. meant originally *any report* of one, *reputation, character*, is not borne out by the passages he cites— ὀ. οὐ καλόν S.*Ph.*477; Θήβαις κάλλιστον ὀ. E.*Ph.*821 (lyr.); καλὸν ὀ. Id.*Med.*514, *IA*305, which are plainly ironical. (Cf. Skt. *nindati*, *nid-* 'insult', Goth. *ga-naitjan* 'slander', Lett. *naids* 'hatred'.)

**Ὀνείλεον**· θυσία Ποσειδῶνος, Hsch.

**ὀνεῖον**, τό, *ass-stable*, Suid.

**ὄνειος** (A), α, ον, *of an ass*, Ar.*Eq.*1399; ὀ. γάλα *ass's* milk, D.ap.

Phylarch.75 J., Arist.*HA*522ᵃ28; ὀ. ἀσκός an *ass's* skin, Plb.8.21.3; τὰς ὀνείας ματτύας a hash *of ass's flesh*, Sophil.4.5: prov., Σκύθης ὄνειον δαῖτα *Com.Adesp.*717. II. Subst. ὀνεία (sc. δορά), ἡ, *ass's skin*, Babr.7.13.

⊛ **ὄνειος** (B), Ion. **ὀνήϊος**, ον, (ὀνίνημι) *useful*, Nic.*Al.*627, Hsch. (in form ὄνια):—written **ὄνιος** in Tz.ad Lyc.621, Suid.: Ion. Sup. ὀνηΐστος, η, ον (ος, ον prob. in Hp.*Flat.*1, v. *Hermes* 46.274), *most useful, serviceable*, Anaxag.4, Pythag.ap.D.L.8.49 (cf. Call.*Iamb.*1.132,200), Heraclit.121, Hp. l. c., Phoen.4, Aret.*CA*1.4, etc.; ὀνήϊστον πονέεσθαι exert yourselves *to the utmost*, A.R.2.335; ὕδρωπος ὀνήϊστα *the most effectual remedy* for the dropsy, Aret.*CD*2.2.

⊛ **ὀνειραιτ-ησία**, ἡ, *obtaining of revelations in a dream*, *PMag.Berol.*1.329 (ὀνειροτ- Pap.). **-ητέω**, *obtain revelations by means of a dream*, *PMag.Par.*1.2077. **-ητόν**, τό, *revelation obtained in a dream*, ib.1.2501, *PMag.Leid.V.*6.15, *PMag.Lond.*121.222,250.

**ὄνειραρ**, v. ὄνειρος.

**ὀνειρ-ᾰτικός**, ή, όν, *in a dream*, φαντάσματα Simp.*in de An.*209.4, 212.14, cf. Porph.*Gaur.*18. **-άτιον**, τό, Dim. of ὄνειρος, Sch. A.R.2.197. **-αυτοπτέω** or **ὀνειραυθοπτέω**, of an incantation, *cause the operator to see a god in dreams*, *PMag.Par.*1.2624 (ὀνειροθαυπτ- Pap.), 3179 (ὀνειραυθοπτ- corrected fr. ὀνειροθαπτ-). **-αυτ-** (or **-αυθ-**)**οπτικός**, ή, όν, *bringing a vision of a god* (cf. foreg.) (sc. πρᾶξις), ib.3173 (ὀνειροθαυπτανη Pap.). **-ειος**, α, ον, *of dreams*, ἐν ὀνειρείῃσι πύλῃσιν Od.4.809; ἐν πύλαις ὀνειρείαις Babr.30.8. **-ήεις**, εσσα, εν, = foreg., Orph.*H.*86.14.

**ὀνειρο-γενής**, ές, *born of a dream*, Hld.9.25. **-γονος**, ον, *accompanied by* ὀνειρωγμός, Cael.Aur.*TP*1.3, 5.7. **-δότης**, ου, ὁ, *giver of dreams*, Perdrizet-Lefèbvre *Les graffites grecs du Memnonion d'Abydos* No.493:—fem. **-δότειρα**, ἡ, cj. for **-δοτιον** in Poet.*de herb.* 42. **-κρῐσία**, ἡ, *interpretation of dreams*, Artem.2.25,70. **-κρίτης** [ῐ], ου, ὁ, *interpreter of dreams*, Thphr.*Char.*16.11, Theoc.21.33, *SIG* 1133 (Delos, ii/i B.C.):—fem. **-κρίτις**, ἡ, *IG*3.162. **-κρῐτικός**, ή, όν, *for interpreting dreams*, πινάκιον Plu.*Arist.*27; τὰ -κά (sc. βιβλία) *a book on the interpretation of dreams*, such as that of Artemidorus: ἡ -κὴ τέχνη Ph.1.673 (without τέχνη 2.58). **-λεκτέω**, *talk in a dream*, Sch.Aristid.p.344 Dind. **-λεσχία**, ἡ, *talking in dreams*, ibid., dub. l. in Suid. **-μαντις**, εως, ὁ, ἡ, *interpreter of dreams*, A. *Ch.*33 (lyr.), Magn.4.

**ὄνειρον**, v. ὄνειρος.

**ὀνειρό-πληκτος**, ον, *scared by a dream*, Hsch., Suid. **-πλήξ**, ῆγος, ὁ, ἡ, = foreg., Ph.2.43, Porph.*Chr.*30. **-ποιουμένη** Ἀθηνᾶ, *appearing in a vision*, Eust.1549.47.

⊛ **ὀνειροπολ-έω**, pf. ὠνειροπόληκα Phld.*Mus.*p.88 K.:—*dream*, Pl.*R.* 534c, *Ti.*52b; ὀ. τι *dream of* a thing, ἵππους Ar.*Nu.*16; ἱππικήν ib.27; πολλὰ τοιαῦτ' ὀνειροπολεῖ ἐν τῇ γνώμῃ builds many such 'castles in the air', D.4.49; ὀ. τάλαντα Luc.*Merc.Cond.*20:—Pass., -πολησθεὶς πλοῦτος Id.*DMort.*5.2. II. *cheat by dreams*, Ar.*Eq.*809. III. Pass., *to be haunted in dreams*, τινι by.., D.S.17.30, cf. 29.25 (abs.). **-ησις**, εως, ἡ, *dreaming*, Cael.Aur.*TP*5.7. **-ία**, ἡ, = foreg., Pl.*Epin.* 985c. **-ικός**, ή, όν, *of* or *for dreaming*: τὸ ὀ. *the art of interpreting dreams*, *Placit.*5.1.1. **-ος** (parox.), ὁ, *interpreter of dreams*, Il.1. 63, 5.149, Hdt.1.128, 5.56, Ph.1.664. II. Adj. *of* or *belonging to dreams*, Orph.*A.*35, 601.

**ὀνειροπομπ-έω**, *send a dream* or *get a dream sent*, *PMag.Lond.*46. 488, *PMag.Par.*1.1869, 2077: c. acc. pers., ib.2451. **-ία**, ἡ, *sending of dreams*, *PMag.Berol.*1.329 (-πομπεῖας Pap.). **-ός**, όν, *sending dreams*, Gal.12.251, *PMag.Leid.V.*4.16; τὸ ὀ. *sending of dreams*, *PMag.Par.*1.2500, 2.163, *PMag.Lond.*121.916, *PMag.Leid. W.*7.45, cf. 8.48.

⊛ **ὄνειρος**, ὁ, or **ὄνειρον**, τό, the masc. form freq. in Hom., also in Pi.*P.*4.163, Hdt.1.34, 7.16.β', E.*IT*569: acc. pl. ὀνείρους Perdrizet-Lefèbvre *Les graffites grecs du Memnonion d'Abydos* No.528: the neut. in Od.4.841, Hdt.7.14,15, A.*Ch.*541, 550, S.*El.*1390 (lyr.), E.*HF*517; and in prov., τοὐμὸν ὄ. ἐμοί 'you are telling me what I know already', Call.*Epigr.*34, Cic.*Att.*6.9.3 (cf. ὄναρ I. 1, ὕπαρ II): the forms ὀνείρου -ῳ -ων -οις leave the gender doubtful: pl. ὄνειρα E. *HF*518, *AP*9.234 (Crin.); but the form ὀνείρατα (as if from ὄνειραρ, *EM*47.53) is more freq. in nom. and acc., Od.20.87, etc.: also gen. ὀνειράτων Hdt.1.120, A.*Pr.*485, al., S.*El.*481 (lyr.): dat. -ασι A.*Pr.* 655, *Pers.*176, S.*OT*981, E.*Alc.*354: gen. sg. -ατος Pl.*Tht.*201d; dat. sg. ἐν τὠνείρατι A.*Ch.*531:—*dream*, Il.2.80, al.; ὄνειρον ὑποκρίνεσθαι, v. ὑποκρίνω B. I. 2; θέρμετε δ' ὕδωρ, ὡς ἂν θεῖον ὄ. ἀποκλύσω Ar.*Ra.*1340. 2. as pr. n. *dream* personified, Il.2.6 sqq.: also in pl., δῆμος ὀνείρων Od.24.12, cf. Hes.*Th.*212. 3. in similes or metaphors, of anything unreal or fleeting, σκιῇ εἴκελον ἢ καὶ ὀ. Od.11. 207, cf. 222; τοῦ ποτε μεμνήσεσθαι ὀΐομαι ἔν περ ὀ. if only in *a dream*, 19.581; σμικρὰ ὀνείρατα λέλειπται *faint and shadowy traces*, Pl.*Lg.* 695c; ὄνειρα ἀφένοιο *dreams* of wealth, *AP*l. c. (Cf. ὄνοιρος.)

**ὀνειρο-τόκος**, ον, *dream-producing*, λέκτρα Nonn.*D.*10.264. **-φαντος**, ον, *appearing in dreams*, δόξαι A.*Ag.*420 (lyr.). **-φοβος**, ον, *terrified by dreams*, Tz.*H.*9.621. **-φρων**, ονος, ὁ, ἡ, *versed in dreams and their interpretations*, E.*Hec.*709.

**ὀνειρ-ωγμός**, ὁ, *effusion during sleep*, Dsc.3.132 (pl.), Ruf.ap.Orib. 6.38.8 (pl.), Gal.4.598, etc. **-ώδης**, ες, *dream-like*, Philostr.*VA*7. 14. **-ωξις**, εως, ἡ, *dreaming, hallucination*, Pl.*Ti.*52b, Ph.1. 698. II. *effusion in sleep*, Sor.[2.46], Porph.*Abst.*4.20, Orib.*Syn.* 9.38. **-ώσσω**, Att. **-ττω**, *dream*, Pl.*Tht.*158b, *R.*476c, al.; περὶ τὸ ὂν ib.533b: c. acc. rei, *dream of*, τὴν τρίτην [οὐσίαν], ἣν ἅπαντες ὀ., λέγει δ' οὐδεὶς Arist.*GC*335ᵇ8, cf. Phld.*Mus.*pp.22,65 K., Luc.*Gall.* 32. II. *have an emission of semen during sleep*, Hp.*Morb.*2.51, Ph.2.231, Philostr.*Gym.*49,52, Sch.Ar.*Nu.*16.

**ὀν-ελάτης** [ᾰ], ου, ὁ, = ὀνηλάτης, *Stud.Pal.*10.251ʳ.6 (vi A.D.), etc. **-ἔλᾰφος**, ὁ, (ὄνος) a kind of *antelope* (cf. τραγέλαφος), Callix. 2. **-εύος**, ὁ, = ὄνος VII. 1, Sch.Th.7.25. **-εύω**, *draw up with a windlass* (ὄνος VII. 1), impf. ὤνευον Th.7.25: generally, *haul up*, τὸν πέπλον.. ἕλκουσ' ὀνεύοντες Stratt.30:—Med., -εσθαι· τείνειν, Erot., Gal.19.126 (v.l. in Hp.*Fract.*15).

**ὀνέω**, v. ὀνίνημι.

**ὀνή**, ἡ, = ὄνησις, *help*, δὸς οὖν τὴν ὀνήν σου *PTeb.*420.24 (iii A.D.).

**ὀνηγός**, ὁ, v. ὀναγός. **ὀνήϊος, ὀνήϊστος**, v. ὄνειος (B).

**ὀνηλ-ᾰσία**, ἡ, *driving of donkeys*, D.Chr.10.19. 2. ὀ. δημοσία *post of* public *donkey-driver*, *POxy.*2131.11 (iii A.D.), cf. *BGU*15 ii 15 (ii A.D.). *PFlor.*2.205, 211 (iii A.D.). **-άσιον** [ᾰ], τό, *provision of stabling for donkeys*, *PRyl.*183(a).2 (i A.D.). **-ᾰτέω**, *drive donkeys*, Ar.*Fr.*833, *BGU*14 iii 20 (iii A.D.). ⊛ **-άτης** [ᾰ], ου, ὁ, (ἐλαύνω) *donkey-driver*, Archipp.44, D.42.7, Crates Theb.ap.D.L.6.92, *PLond.*1.131. 30 (i A.D.), Gal.10.134, etc. ⊛ **-ᾰτικός**, ή, όν, *relating to conveyance by donkey*, φόρετρον *PLond.*2.314.18 (ii A.D.). **-ᾰτος**, ον, *for donkey-driving*: κλείνη ὀ. *donkey-saddle*(?), *Stud.Pal.*20.46.27 (ii/iii A.D.).

**ὀνημάξιον**, τό, (ἅμαξα) *donkey-cart*, *SIG*1106.4 (pl., Cos, iv/iii B.C.).

**ὀνήμενος, ὄνησα, ὀνήσει**, v. ὀνίνημι.

**ὀνήμων**, ον, gen. ονος, = ὀνήσιμος, of Hermes and Aphrodite, *Cat. Cod.Astr.*2.203.

**ὀνησῐ-δώρα**, f.l. for ἀνησιδ-, Plu.2.317a. **-μος**, ον, *useful, profitable, beneficial*, *h.Merc.*30, A.*Eu.*924 (lyr.); πεπονθὼς ὀνήσιμα S.*Ant.*995, cf. *Aj.*665, etc.; *aiding, succouring*, ἔγχος Id.*Tr.*1014 (lyr.). Adv. -μως Pl.*Lg.*747c. **-πολις**, Dor. **ὀνᾱσ-**, εως, ὁ, ἡ, *profitable to the state*, δίκα Simon.5.3.

⊛ **ὄνησις**, εως, Dor., etc. **ὄνᾱσις**, ιος, ἡ, (ὀνίνημι) *use, profit, advantage*, Od.21.402; ὀ. τισί [ἐστί] τι S.*Ant.*616 (lyr.); ἐπ' ὄνασιν ἐμοί for *a delight* to me, Alc.46 (v.l. ἐπόνασιν); εἰς ὀ. ἀνθρώπων S.*Aj.*400 (lyr.); ὄνησιν ἔχειν bring *advantage*, E.*Med.*618, etc.: c. gen., *enjoyment of* a thing, *profit* or *delight from* it, A.*Ag.*350, E.*Hec.*1231; ὄνησιν ἔχειν τινός Pl.*Sph.*230d; ἀπὸ [τῶν βιβλίων] ὀ. ἕξεις *POxy.*531. 12 (ii A.D.); ὀ. εὑρεῖν ἀπό τινος S.*El.*1061 (lyr.); οὐδέ σφιν ἀρχῆς τῆσδε.. ὀ. ἥξει Id.*OC*452; γένοιτό σοι τέκνων ὀ. Philem.156, cf. *SIG*526.40 (Itanos, iii B.C.); βίου ὀ. Herod.7.34; φέρειν ὀ. ἀστοῖς S.*OC*288; τί γὰρ ἡ σὴ δεινότης εἰς ὀ. ἥκει τῇ πατρίδι; D.18.242; φορᾶς ὀ., as etym. of φρόνησις, Pl.*Cra.*411d.

**ὀνησῐφόρος**, ον, *bringing advantage, beneficial*, Hp.*Praec.*14, Alex. 195.5, *Com.Adesp.*109.11, Agatharch.99, Ruf.ap.Orib.8.24.34, Ptol. *Tetr.*157; *remunerative*, ὕμνοι Phld.*Rh.*1.219 S.; μαθήματα Luc.*Vit. Auct.*26. Adv. -ρως Plu.2.71d.

⊛ **ὀνητός**, ή, όν, (ὀνίνημι) *profitable, beneficial*, Suid. II. ὀνητά· μεμπτά, Hsch. (fort. ὀνοστά).

⊛ **ὀνήτωρ**, Dor. **ὀνάτωρ** [ᾱ], ορος, ὁ, = ὀνήσιμος, *beneficial*, τόκος ὀνάτωρ Pi.*O.*10(11).9 (corr. Herm. for θνατῶν), cf. *Trag.Adesp.*405 (cj. Bgk.), Hsch.; name of a plaster, ὀ. εἰς ἅπαντα Androm.ap.Gal.13.840.

**ὀνθολόγος**, ὁ, *dung-gatherer*, cj. Koechly for ἀνθολόγος, Man.4.259.

**ὄνθος**, ὁ, *dung* of animals, Il.23.775,777, A.*Fr.*275, Antig.*Mir.*140: later also fem., like κόπρος, Apollod.2.5.5.

⊛ **ὀνθοφόρος**, ὁ, *dung-carrier*, *Stud.Pal.*20.108.4 (iv A.D.).

**ὀνθύλ-ευσις** [ῠ], εως, ἡ, *the use of forced meat*, Men.462.7 (pl.). **-εύω**, *dress with forced meat* or *stuffing*, in cookery, τὰς τευθίδας.. ὠνθύλευσα Alex.84.5:—mostly in Pass., ὠνθυλευμένος στέατι Σικελικῷ *stuffed*, Diph.119; ἄρνα.. ὠνθυλευμένον Id.90, cf. Alex.37, Sotad. Com.1.15: the collat. form μονθυλεύω is condemned by Phryn.334; μονθύλευσις (in pl., = αἱ περιτταὶ σκευασίαι) occurs in Poll.6.60; μονθυλευτὴ κοιλία Sch.Ar.*Eq.*342; and μεμονθυλευμένος is f.l. in Alex. 273. II. *doctor* wine, Sch.Ar.*Pl.*1064.

**ὀνί**, Arc. for ὅδε, declined like ὁ with addition of -νί, gen. sg. masc. and neut. τωνί *SIG*306.14 (Tegea, iv B.C.), *IG*5(2).6.36 (ibid.); dat. sg. τῳνί *Schwyzer* 664.8 (Orchom., iv B.C.), τοινί *SIG*559.47 (Megalopolis); acc. sg. fem. ταννί *IG*5(2).6.53; gen. sg. fem. τανί (i.e. *τασνί) *SIG*306.9; gen. pl. fem. ταννί ib.51,55; dat. sg. fem. ταινί ib.559.44; dat. pl. fem. ταινί ib.306.55; ταινίν ib.36.

**ὀνία, ὀνίᾱρος** (v.l. **ὀνίατος**), Aeol. for ἀν-, Sapph.1.3 (pl.), Alc.98 (= 10 Lobel).

**ὀνίας**, ου, ὁ, a sea-fish, a kind of *scarus*, perh. *Smaris vulgaris*, Nic. Thyat.ap.Ath.7.320c.

**ὄνιγλιν**· εἶδος οἴνου, Hsch., but Ὀνογλιν Alcm.117 (ap.Ath.1.31d).

**ὀν-ίδιον** [νῐ], τό, Dim. of ὄνος, *little ass*, Ar.*V.*1306. II. v. ὀνίς. ⊛ **-ῐκός**, ή, όν, *of* or *for an ass*: μύλος ὀ., v. μύλος; ὀ. κτήνη, i.e. *asses*, *PGen.*23.4 (i A.D.), *BGU*912.24 (i A.D.); γόμος ὀ. *OGI* 629.30 (Palmyra, ii A.D.).

**ὀνίνημι** [ῐ], ὀνίνης Pl.*Hp.Ma.*301c, ὀνίνησι Il.24.45, Hes.*Th.*429, etc.; inf. ὀνινάναι dub. in Pl.*R.*600d; part. ὀνινάς, ᾶσα Id.*Phlb.*58c (impf. supplied by ὠφέλουν): fut. ὀνήσω Il.8.36, Orac.ap.Hdt.7.141, E.*Andr.*1004, etc.; Dor. 3 sg. ὀνασεῖ Theoc.7.36: aor. ὤνησα Il.9.509, Hdt.9.76, E.*Tr.*933, Pl.*Ap.*27c; Ep. ὄνησα Il.1.503:—Med., ὀνίναμαι Pl.*Grg.*525c: impf. ὠνινάμην Id.*R.*380b: fut. ὀνήσομαι Il.7. 173, S.*Tr.*570, E.*Hel.*935, Pl.*Ap.*30c: aor. 1 ὠνησάμην only in Gal. 2.381 (unless in *AP*7.484 (Diosc.) we accept ὠνάσατο [with ᾰ] for the meaningless ὠνόσατο); ὀνήσω (2 pers. sg.) in Porph.*Marc.*10 is f.l. either for ὠνήσω or for ὤνησο: aor. 2 ὠνήμην Thgn.1380, E.*Alc.*335, Pl.*Men.*84c; imper. ὄνησο Od.19.68; part. ὀνήμενος 2.33 (cf. ἀπ-); also ὠνάμην, ὤνασθε E.*HF*1368, ὤναο Call.*Aet.*3.1.6, and freq. later,

Luc.*DMort.*12.2, etc.; ὤνατο *IG*14.1389 ii 37, ὤναντο D.H.1.23; inf. ὄνασθαι E.*Hipp.*517, Pl.*R.*528a; opt. ὀναίμην, which is freq. (v. infr. II. 2), may belong to either form: in Hom. ὠνάμην is the aor. 1 of ὄνομαι:—Pass. **ὀνέομαι** occurs twice, ὀνεῖται Stob.4.22.62, ὀνούμενοι Ps.-Luc.*Philopatr.*26: aor. inf. ὀνηθῆναι X.*An.*5.5.2; Dor. ὠνάθην Theoc.15.55: I. Act., *profit, benefit, help,* and sts. *gratify, delight,* abs., βουλὴν.. ὑποθησόμεθ' ἥτις ὀνήσει Il.8.36, cf. Hes.*Th.*429, E.*Med.*533, etc.: with neut. Adj. or Adv., ὀ. παῦρα *h.Merc.*577; σμικρὰ ὀνήσει πόλιν E.*Heracl.*705 (anap.), cf. Pl.*Phlb.*58c; μᾶλλον Simon.55, Aret. *CA*1.4: c. acc. pers., Il.5.205, 7.172, Orac.ap.Hdt.7.141, E.*Hipp.*314, Ar.*Lys.*1033, etc.: with neut. Adj., ἄνδρας μέγα σίνεται ἠδ' ὀνίνησι Il.24.45, cf. 9.509, v.l. in X.*An.*3.1.38, etc.; πολλὰ ὀ. τινά Od.14.67; τοσόνδε E.*Tr.*933; εἴ ποτε δή τι Il.1.395: c. dat. modi, εἴ ποτε δή σε ὄνησα ἢ ἔπει ἢ ἔργῳ ib.503: c. part., Ξενοφῶντα ὠνήσατε οὐχ ἑλόμενοι *by* not electing him, X.*An.*6.1.32, cf. Pl.*Smp.*193d, *Hp.Ma.*301c; ὡς ὤνησας ὅτι ἀπεκρίνω Id.*Ap.*27c: c. dupl. acc., σὲ δὲ τοῦτό γε γῆρας ὀνήσει this *benefit* at least *will* thine old age *bestow on* thee, Od.23.24; also οὐδεμίαν ὤνησε κάλλος εἰς πόσιν ξυνάορον *helped* her in her relations with.., E.*Fr.*909.1. II. Med., *have profit* or *advantage, enjoy help* or *support, have enjoyment* or *delight,* Il.6.260, 7.173, Od.14.415, E.*Hipp.*517, etc.: c. part., *have benefit from* being or doing so and so, Thgn.1380, Pl.*Ap.*30c, *R.*380b, *Men.*84c, etc.: but most freq. c. gen., *have advantage from.., have delight* or *enjoyment of..,* δαιτὸς ὄνησο Od.19.68; λέκτρων -ήσομαι E.*Med.*1348; πρὶν σφῷν ὄνασθαι ib.1025, cf. *Alc.*335: freq. with neut. Adj. added, τί σευ ἄλλος ὀνήσεται; what *good will* others *have* of thee, i.e. what good will you have done them? Il.16.31; τοσόνδ' ὀνήσῃ τῶν ἐμῶν.. πορθμῶν S.*Tr.*570, etc.; so ὄνασθαί τι ἀπό τινος Pl.*R.*528a; also ὀ. τοῦτο ὅτι.. Luc.*DMort.*12.2: also with an ironical sense, ὄναιο μέντἄν, εἴ τις ἐκπλύνειέ σε *you'd be the better of it,* if one were to wash you clean, Ar.*Pl.*1062; ἁλσὶν διασμηχθεὶς ὄναιτ' ἂν οὑτοσί *he'd be very nice* if he were rubbed down with salt, Id.*Nu.*1237; so ὠνάθην μεγάλως ὅτι.. *lucky for me* that.., Theoc.15.55; ὤνησο, διότι μὴ ὁ Ζεὺς ἐπήκουσέ σου Luc.*Prom.*20. 2. aor. opt. ὀναίμην, αιο, αιτο, in protestations, wishes, etc., ὄναιο *mayst thou have profit,* i.e. *bless thee..,* E.*Or.*1677, etc.: and c. gen., ὄναιο τῶν φρενῶν *bless thee* for.., Id.*IA*1359; ὄναισθε μύθων Id.*IT*1078, cf. *Hel.*1418; οὕτως ὀναίμην τῶν τέκνων so *may I have profit* of them, in a parenthesis, Ar.*Th.*469; οὕτως ὄναισθε τούτων D.28.20; ὄναιντο βίου Simon.128; μή νυν ὀναίμην, ἀλλ'.. ὀλοίμην *may I* not *see good,* but die, S.*OT*644; ὄναιο τοῦ γενναίου χάριν *bless thee* for thy noble spirit, Id.*OC*1042. 3. aor. part. ὀνήμενος, of those to whom (or of whom) one says ὄναιο (ὄναιτο), *blessed,* ἐσθλός μοι δοκεῖ εἶναι, ὀνήμενος Od.2.33: for this sense of a part. cf. ἐπίτριπτος, οὐλόμενος.

**ὄνιννος,** ὁ, parasite found in sea-weed, perh. *millepede,* Thphr.*HP*4.6.8 codd.

**ὄν-ιον,** τό, Dim. of ὄνος, *BGU*765.3 (ii A.D.). **-ιος,** v. ὄνειος (B). **-ίς,** ἴδος, ἡ, *ass's dung,* Hp.*Nat.Mul.*82, Dsc.2.80, Gal.12.803: also in pl., Ar.*Pax*4, Arist.*HA*552$^{a}$17; ἡμιόνου ὀνίς Hp.*Mul.*2.192 (elsewh. ἡμιονίς): but **ὀνίδια** (ὀνιαῖα Hsch.) is strangely expld. *horse's dung* by Hsch., Phot., Suid. **-ίσκος,** ὁ, Dim. of ὄνος, but only metaph.: I. a sea-fish of the *gadus* or *cod* kind, Dorio ap. Ath.3.118c, Euthyd.ap.eund.7.315f, Gal.6.721. II. prob. *woodlouse* (cf. ὄνος III), Id.12.366, al. III. = ὄνος VII. 1, *windlass, crane,* Hp.*Fract.*13, *Art.*72, Ath.Mech.14.7, Ph.*Bel.*68.5, Hero *Bel.*84.14. IV. ὀνίσκος· τεκτονικὸς πρίων, Hsch.

**ὀνίσκω,** = ὀνίνημι, Ath.2.35c.

**ὀνίστειοι·** νεοσσοί, Hsch.

**ὀνῖτις,** ιδος, ἡ, *pot marjoram, Origanum Onites,* Nic.*Al.*56, Dsc.3.28, Gal.12.91.

**ὄννα,** Aeol. for ὠνή, *sale,* *IG*11(4).1064*b*17, cf. 21 (Delos).

**ὄννις,** Cret. for ὄρνις, *Schwyzer*181 iii 8 (Gortyn).

**ὀνο-βᾰτέω,** *have* a mare *covered by an ass,* τὰς ἵππους X.*Eq.*5.8. II. of the ass, *cover,* Poll.5.92. **-βάτις** [ᾰ], ιδος, ἡ, *riding on an ass,* of an adulteress who was thus punished at Cumae, Plu.2.291e, cf. Hsch. **-βλιτον,** τό, v.l. for βλίτον, Hp.*Mul.*2.196. **-βρῡχίς,** ίδος, ἡ, a leguminous plant, *cock's head, Onobrychis caput-galli,* Dsc.3.153, Gal.12.89. **-γαστρις,** ιος, ἡ, *fat paunch,* *Com.Adesp.*878. **-γλιν,** v. ὄνιγλιν.

**ὀνόγῡρος,** ὁ, = ἀνάγυρος, Nic.*Th.*71, cf. Sch.Nic.*Al.*55. II. ὀνόγυροι· σειροί, Hsch.

**ὀνοδέστεροι·** ἄγνωστοι, Hsch. (fort. οἱ νηϊδέστεροι).

**ὀνο-ειδής,** ές, *of the ass kind,* *EM*220.32. **-θήλεια,** ἡ, *she-ass,* *POxy.*922.24 (vi/vii A.D.), *Gloss.* **-θήρας,** ὁ, and **-θουρις,** ἡ, *oleander, Nerium Oleander,* Thphr.*HP*9.19.1, Dsc.4.117.

**ὄνοιρος,** Aeol. for ὄνειρος, *EM*660.53; voc. Ὄνοιρε Sapph.*Oxy.*1787*Fr.*3 ii 15.

**ὀνο-κάρδιον,** τό, = δίψακος II, Ps.-Dsc.3.11. 2. = χαμαιλέων II, Apul.*Herb.*25. ®**-κένταυρα,** ἡ, or **-κένταυρος,** ὁ, a kind of *tailless ape,* Ael.*NA*17.9. 2. a kind of *demon* haunting wild places, Lxx *Is.*13.22, 34.11, 14. **-κέφᾰλος,** ον, *with the head of an ass,* Cyran.70, Horap.1.23. ®**-κίνδιος,** ὁ, *donkey-driver,* epith. of Peisander in Eup.182; in Hsch. also **-κίνδας.** **-κλεία** (v.l. **-κλεια**), ἡ, = ἄγχουσα, Dsc.4.23. **-κόμος,** ὁ, *one who tends asses,* $IG2^{2}$.10*B*7 (v/iv B.C.). **-κόπος,** ον, *chipping millstones,* Alex.13. **-κρότᾰλος,** ὁ, *pelican,* Plin.*HN*10.131, Mart.11.21.10. **-κτηνοτρόφος,** ὁ, *one who keeps donkeys,* *PTeb.*564 (i A.D.), *PLond.*3.1165.6 (ii A.D.) **-κωλος,** ον, = ὀνοσκελίς, of the hobgoblin Empusa, Sch.Ar.*Ra.*296:—also **-κωλις,** ἡ, Eust.1704.42.

® **ὄνομα,** Aeol. and Dor. **ὄνῠμα** *IG*12(2).68.8 (Lesb.), *GDI*4992*a* iii 7 (Crete), *SIG*1122.8 (Selinus), *Berl.Sitzb.*1927.167 (Cyrene); Lacon. ***ἔνυμα** prob. in pr. nn. Ἐνυμακρατίδας *IG*5(1).213.45, Ἐνυμαντιάδας ib.97.20, 280.2; poet. also (metri gr.) **οὔνομα** (v. infr.), which appears regularly in codd. of Hdt. (along with ὀνομάζω, as 2.50, 4.35, al.), and sts. in other Ion. prose authors (v.l. in Hp.*Prog.*25, etc.), but is prob. not Ionic; Ion. Inscrr. have only ὄνομα, *IG*7.235.39 (Oropus), etc.: Hom. has οὔνομα Od.6.194, 9.355, Il.3.235, οὐνόματ'(α) 17.260, ὄνομα Od.9.16, 364, 366, 19.183, ὄνομ'(α) 4.710 et saep.:—*name* of a person or thing, in Hom. always of a person, exc. ἐρέω δέ τοι οὔνομα λαῶν Od.6.194 and in Od.13.248 (v. infr. II); Οὖτις ἐμοί γ' ὄ. 9.366, cf. 18.5, 19.183, 247; Ἀρήτη δ' ὄνομ' ἐστὶν ἐπώνυμον 7.54, cf. 19.409, Hes.*Th.*144: in Prose ὄνομα is used abs., *by name,* πόλις ὄ. Καιναί X.*An.*2.4.28, etc.: also dat., πόλις Θάψακος ὀνόματι ib.1.4.11 (v.l.); ὀνόματι λέγειν *by name,* Pl.*Ap.*21c; ἐπ' ὀνόματος δηλοῦσθαι Plb.18.45.4, etc.; κατ' ὄνομα by *name,* Strato Com.1.14, *Epigr.Gr.*983.4 (Philae); ἀσπάζου τοὺς φίλους κατ' ὄ. each *by* his *name,* 3*Ep.Jo.*14. 2. ὄ. τίθεσθαι or θέσθαι τινί give one *a name,* Od.19.403, 406, 8.554, A.*Fr.*6, Ar.*Av.*810:—Pass., ὄ. κεῖταί τινι ib.1291; ὄ. ἐστι or κεῖται ἐπί τινι, X.*Mem.*3.14.2, *Cyr.*2.2.12; so ὄ. φέρειν or ἐπιφέρειν ἐπί τι, Arist.*EN*1119$^{a}$33, *HA*572$^{a}$11. 3. ὄνομα καλεῖν τινα call one *by name,* εἴπ' ὄνομ', ὅττι σε κεῖθι κάλεον Od.8.550; καλοῦσί με τοῦτο τὸ ὄ. X.*Oec.*7.3, cf. E.*Ion*259, 800, Pl.*Cra.*393e, etc.:—so in Pass., ὄ. δ' ὠνομάζετο Ἕλενος S.*Ph.*605, cf. *El.*694; ὄ. δημοκρατία κέκληται Th.2.37; τὸ ἐναντίον ὄ. ἀφροσύνη μετωνόμασται Id.1.122; ὄ. ἐν κεκλημένους Σικελιώτας Id.4.64; λεγόμενοι τοὔνομα γεωργικοί Pl.*Lg.*842e; but also ὀνόματί τινα προσαγορεύειν Antipho 6.40; reversely, ὄνομα καλεῖν τινι give *a name* to, Pl.*Plt.*279e, *Cra.*385d; ὄ. καλεῖν ἐπί τινι Id.*Prm.*147d; τύμβῳ δ' ὄ. σῷ κεκλήσεται.. Κυνὸς σῆμα E.*Hec.*1271; τοὔνομα προσηγορεύθη Anaxil.21.3. II. *name, fame,* Ἰθάκης γε καὶ ἐς Τροίην ὄνομ' ἵκει Od.13.248; οὐδὲ θανὼν ὄνομ' ὤλεσας 24.93; ὄ. ἔχειν or σχεῖν ἀπό τινος, Hdt.1.71, Pl.*Hp.Ma.*282a; τὸ μεγα ὄ. τῶν Ἀθηνῶν Th.7.64; τῷ μέλλοντι χρόνῳ καταλιπεῖν ὄ. ὡς.. Id.5.16; τοὔνομά τινος μεῖζον ἀφικνεῖται εἰς τὴν πόλιν X.*An.*6.1.20; ὧν ὀνόματα μεγάλα λέγεται ἐπὶ σοφίᾳ Pl.*Hp.Ma.*281c; ὄ. μέγιστον ἔχειν Th.2.64; ἐν ὀνόματι εἶναι to have *a name,* to be *notable,* Str.9.1.23; οἱ ἐν πράγμασιν ἐπ' ὀνόματος γεγονότες Plb.15.35.1; παράσιτοι δ' ἐπ' ὀνόματος ἐγένοντο *notably,* Ath.6.240c; τῶν δι' ὀνόματος παρασίτων ib.241a. III. *a name and nothing else,* opp. the real person or thing, ἵνα μηδ' ὄνομ' αὐτοῦ ἐν ἀνθρώποισι λίπηται Od.4.710; βοᾶς δ' ἔτι μηδ' ὄνομ' εἴη Theoc.16.97; opp. ἔργον, E.*Or.*454, *Hipp.*502; περὶ ὄ. μάχεσθαι Lys.33.3; ἐκ τῶν ὀ. μᾶλλον ἢ τῶν πραγμάτων σκέψασθαι D.9.15; ὀνόματι διαφέρεσθαι dispute about a *word,* Pl.*Euthd.*285a, *Lg.*644a. 2. *false name, pretence, pretext,* ὀνόματι ἐννόμῳ ξυμμαχίας under the *pretence..,* Th.4.60; μετ' ὀνομάτων καλῶν Id.5.89; χώρα καλῶν ὀ. καὶ προσχημάτων μεστή Pl.*R.*495c, cf. Plb.11.5.4. IV. in periphr. phrases, ὄ. τῆς σωτηρίας, = σωτηρία, E.*IT*905, cf. ὄνομ' ὁμιλίας ἐμῆς (v.l. for ὄμμ') Id.*Or.*1082: with the names of persons, periphr. for the person, ὦ φίλτατον ὄ. Πολυνείκους Id.*Ph.*1702. 2. of persons, ὄχλος ὀνομάτων *Act.Ap.*1.15; ἕτερα ὀ. ἀντ' αὐτοῦ.. πέμψαι Wilcken *Chr.*28.19 (ii A.D.); in Accountancy, both of persons and things (cf. Lat. *nomen*), Hyp.*Ath.*6, 10 (both pl.), *Jahresh.*26 *Beibl.*13 (Ephes., ii A.D., pl.); βαρέσαι τὸ ἐμὸν ὄ. charge my *account,* *POxy.*126.8 (vi A.D.); τὸν τόκον τὸν ὀνόματί μου παραγραφέντα ib.513.22 (ii A.D.); in registers of title-deeds, etc., οἰκίας οὐ κειμένης ἐν ὀνόματι τῆς ἀποδομένης not booked under the *name* of the seller, *PLips.*3 ii 25 (iii A.D.); ὀνόματι ἰδιωτικῆς under the *head* of private land, *PCair.Preis.*47.10 (iv A.D.); δικαιώματα .. ἑκάστῳ ὀνόματι παράκειται *BGU*113.11 (ii A.D.); in tax-receipts, ἔσχον ὀνόματος Σομτοῦς on *account* of S., *Ostr.Bodl.* ii 39 (ii A.D.), cf. *PFay.*85.7 (iii A.D.), etc. V. *phrase, expression,* esp. of technical terms, ὀ. τὰ ἐν τῇ ναυτικῇ X.*Ath.*1.19: generally, D.19.187. VI. Gramm., *word,* opp. ῥῆμα (expression), Pl.*Cra.*399b, cf. *Ap.*17c, *Smp.*198b, 199b, 221e, Isoc.9.9, 11, Arist.*Rh.*1404$^{b}$5, Aeschin.3.72, A.D.*Synt.*12.25, al., Demetr.*Eloc.*23, al.; τὸ ἰλλαίνειν ὄ. the *word* ἰλλαίνειν, Gal.17(1).679. 2. *noun,* opp. ῥῆμα (verb, predicate), Pl.*Tht.*168b, *Sph.*262a,b, cf. Arist.*Po.*1457$^{a}$10, *Int.*16$^{a}$19, al.; as one of five parts of speech, Chrysipp.*Stoic.*2.45; ὄ. κύριον a proper *name,* opp. προσηγορικόν, D.T.636.16, A.D.*Pron.*26.12, al. (so ὄ. alone, Ar.*Nu.*681 sqq., Diog.Bab.*Stoic.*3.213); also of adjectives, S.E.*M.*1.222. (Cf. Goth. *namo,* gen. *namins,* Lat. *nōmen,* Skt. *nāma.*)

® **ὀνομάζω,** impf. ὠνόμαζον A.*Ag.*682 (lyr.), etc.; Ep. ὀν– Il.1.361, al.: fut. ὀνομάσω Pl.*Cra.*423d: aor. ὠνόμασα Od.24.339, etc.: pf. ὠνόμακα Pl.*Sph.*219b:—Pass., fut. -ασθήσομαι Gal.*UP*6.16, al.: aor. ὠνομάσθην and pf. ὠνόμασμαι, Th.1.96, 6.96, etc.; Ep. ὀνόμασται Parm.9.1, etc.; 3 pl. ὠνομάδαται D.C.37.16:—Med., impf. ὠνομάζετο S.*OT*1021.—Aeol. or Dor. fut. 3 sg. ὀνυμάξει (or -εῖ) *Berl.Sitzb.*1927.167 (Cyrene): aor. ὀνύμαξε Pi.*P.*2.44; Med. fut. ὀνυμάξομαι ib.7.5; pres. ὀνυμάζεται Metop.ap.Stob.3.1.116: (ὄνομα):—*speak of by name, call* or *address by name,* of persons, πατρόθεν ἐκ γενεῆς ὀνομάζων ἄνδρα ἕκαστον Il.10.68, cf. 22.415 and ὀνομακλήδην; Πυθοδώρου.., ὃν Ἀθηναῖοι οὐκ ὀνομάζουσιν X.*HG*2.3.1 (interpol.); τοῖς προγόνοις -αζομένοις ἀπομνημονεύεται ὁπόστος ἀφ' Ἡρακλέους ἐγένετο his descent.. is traced by *naming* his ancestors, Id.*Ages.*1.2. 2. of things, *name, specify,* περικλυτὰ δῶρ' ὀνόμαζον Il.18.449; but also, *name* or *promise,* opp. giving, εἰ μὲν.. μὴ δῶρα φέροι, τὰ δ' ὄπισθ' ὀνομάζοι 9.515; εἶναί τι ὀνομάζειν *use the term* 'being', Pl.*Tht.*160b, cf. 166c, 201d; *dedicate,* τράπεζαν τῷ δαίμονι Theopomp.Hist.121:—Pass., λόγοισι.. ὠνόμασται βραχέσι *have been expressed,* S.*OC*294. II. ὀ. τινά τι *call* one something, Pi.*P.*2.44, A.*Ag.*681 (lyr.), Hdt.4.6, Th.1.3, E.*Hel.* 1193; ὄνομα τί σε.. ὠνόμαζεν λεώς; Id.*Herad.*87 (lyr.):—rarely in Med., παῖδά μ' ὠνομάζετο *called* me *his* son, S.*OT*1021:—Pass., ὄνομα δ' ὠνομάζετο Ἕλενος Id.*Ph.*605; τὴν αὐτῆς ἐπωνυμίαν ὀνομαζόμενον Pl.*Phdr.*238a; ἀντὶ γὰρ φίλων καὶ ξένων, ἃ τότ' ὠνομάζοντο D.18. 46. b. *nominate*, ὀνομασθεὶς εἰς δεκαπρωτείαν *POxy.*1257.1, cf. 1204.4 (iii A.D.). 2. εἶναι is freq. added pleon., τὰς ὀνομάζουσι εἶναι Ὑπερόχην καὶ.. whose *names they say are* Hyperoche and.., Hdt.4. 33; σοφιστὴν ὀνομάζουσιν τὸν ἄνδρα εἶναι Pl.*Prt.*311e, cf. *R.*428e (Pass.), X.*Ap.*13, etc.; cf. καλέω II. 3b. III. *name* or *call* with reference to, in accordance with, or after.., τινὰ or τι ἐπί τινι Pl. *R.*493c:—Pass., ἐπί τινος Isoc.12.183; ἔκ τινος S.*OT*1036, X.*Mem.* 4.5.12; ὁ τῆς ἀρίστης μητρὸς ὠνομασμένος S.*Tr.*1105. IV. *utter names* or *words*, ἐς τρὶς ὀνομάσαι "Σόλων" Hdt.1.86; μάλα σεμνῶς ὀνομάζων D.18.35, cf. 122, 21.158:—Pass., φύσις ἐπὶ τοῖς ὀνομάζεται ἀνθρώποισι *the name* φύσις *is given* by men to those things, Emp. 8.4, cf. Parm.9.1; παρανομίαν ἐπὶ τοῖς μὴ ἀνάγκῃ κακοῖς ὀνομασθῆναι *the name* of transgression *is applied*.., Th.4.98; ἀπὸ τούτου τοῦτο ὀνομάζεται (sc. "οὐ φροντὶς Ἱπποκλείδῃ") hence this *saying is used*, Hdt.6.130. V. *make famous*, in Pass., οἱ ὠνομασμένοι persons *of renown*, v.l. for διωνομασμένοι in Isoc.20.19.—Cf. ὀνομαίνω.

⊛ **ὄνομαι**, 2 sg. ὄνοσαι Od.17.378; Ep. 2 pl. οὔνεσθε (Aristarch. ὀνόσασθε, Buttm. and Pap. οὔνοσθε) Il.24.241; 3 pl. ὄνονται Od.21.427, Hdt.2.167; opt. ὄνοιτο Il.13.287: impf. 3 pl. ὤνοντο (κατ-) Hdt.2.172: Ep. fut. ὀνόσσομαι Il.9.55, Od.5.379: aor. ὠνοσάμην Il.14.95; Ep. part. ὀνοσσάμενος 24.439: also Ep. aor. 3 sg. ὤνατο 17.25; and Pass. ὠνόσθην (κατ-) Hdt.2.136; cf. ὀνοστός, ὀνοτός:—*blame, find fault with, treat scornfully*, c. acc., νῦν δέ σευ ὠνοσάμην πάγχυ φρένας Il.14. 95; οὔ τίς τοι τὸν μῦθον ὀνόσσεται 9.55; οὐδέ κεν.. μένος καὶ χεῖρας ὄνοιτο 13.287; ὡς ἂν σὴν ἀρετὴν.. οὔ τις ὄνοιτο Od.8.239: folld. by a relat., ἦ οὔνεσθ' ὅτι μοι.. Ζεὺς ἄλγε' ἔδωκεν; *do ye think it a light thing* that..? (others wrongly refer it to ὀνίνημι, *is it to your profit* that..?), Il.24.241; ἦ ὄνοσαι ὅτι τοι βίοτον κατέδουσιν ἄνακτος; Od.17.378: c. gen., οὐδ' ὥς σε ἔολπα ὀνόσσεσθαι κακότητος for all that, I think *thou wilt* not *quarrel with* thy ill-luck (i.e. *deem it too light*), 5.379: Ep. Verb, once in Hdt. (cf. κατόνομαι), ὀ. τινά *throw a slur upon*, 2. 167.—In *AP*7.484 (Diosc.) v.l. for ὀνίνημι (q.v.).

**ὀνομαίνω**, *h.Ven.*290, Aeol. and Dor. **ὀνῠμαίνω** *GDI*4992*a*ii6 (Gortyn), Ti.Locr.100c (Pass.): Ion. fut. οὐνομανέω Hdt.4.47 (v.l. ὀν-): aor. ὠνόμηνα Is.3.33; Ep. ὀνόμηνα Hom., Hes. (v. infr.); Boeot. ὠνούμηνα Corinn.2 cod. (fort. -ανα):—Ep. and Ion. Verb, = ὀνομάζω, *name* or *call by name*, φίλον τ' ὀνόμηνεν ἑταῖρον Il.10.522, cf. 16.491, etc.; θεοὺς ὀ. ἅπαντας 14.278; of things, *name, recount*, περικλυτὰ δῶρ' ὀνομήνω 9.121; πληθὺν οὐκ ἂν ἐγὼ μυθήσομαι οὐδ' ὀνομήνω 2.488; so πάντα μὲν οὐκ ἄν.. Od.4.240, etc.—Rare in Prose, Hdt. and Is. ll. cc. 2. simply, *utter, speak*, ἴσχεο μηδ' ὀνομήνῃς Od.11.251, cf. *h.Ven.*290; then (cf. ὀνομάζω I. 2) *promise* to do, ὅρκους δέ μοι ὧδ' ὀνόμηνας δώσειν Od.24.341. II. *name, call by a name*, Hes.*Op.*80; καί οἱ τοῦτ' ὀνόμην' ὄνομ' ἔμμεναι Id.*Fr.*116.2: in Dor. Prose, ἁδοναὶ ὀνυμαίνονται Ti.Locr.l.c., etc. III. *nominate, appoint*, καὶ σὸν θεράποντ' ὀνόμηνεν Il.23.90.

**ὀνομα-κλήδην**, Adv., (καλέω) *calling by name, by name*, ἐκ δ' ὀνομακλήδην Od.4.278, v. ἐξονομακλήδην. **-κλήτωρ**, ορος, ὁ, (καλέω) *one who announces guests by name*, Lat. *nomenclator*, Luc.*Merc.Cond.*10, Ath.2.47e. **-κλῠτος**, ον (α, ον Pi.*Pae.*6.123), *of famous name*, Il. 22.51, *h.Merc.*59, Ibyc.10A, Pi. l. c.; κοὐνομάκλυτον in Semon.7.87 should be emended to κὠν-, cf. κὠνομαστόν Phoen.2.11. II. *articulate*, βροτῶν ὀνομάκλυτον αὐδήν Simm.1.13.

⊛ **ὀνομ-ᾰσία**, ἡ, *name*, Hippias I J. (pl.), Pl.*Plt.*275d, Arist.*Top.*148$^b$ 20, al., *SIG*827 v6 (pl., Delph., ii A.D.). 2. *nomination* for office, *POxy.*1642.3 (iii A.D.), 2130.12 (iii A.D.), Jul.*Mis.*368b (pl.). II. *expression, language*, ἑρμηνεία διὰ τῆς ὀ. by means of *language*, Arist. *Po.*1450$^b$14; διά τινος ὀνόματος ἢ ὀνομασίας ἀδιαφόρου κοινότητα Epicur.*Nat.*14.10, cf. Phld.*Rh.*1.208 S., *Po.*2.37 (both pl.), D.H. *Comp.*25, *Dem.*56; κανὼν ὀνομασίας Demetr.*Eloc.*91. **-αστέον**, *one must name*, Pl.*Cra.*387d. ⊛ **-αστής**, οῦ, ὁ, *autumator*, *Gloss.* II. ὀ. τῆς δεκαπρωτείας Κυρίλλου *nominator* of C. for the δεκαπρωτεία, *BGU*96.9 (iii A.D.). ⊛ **-αστί**, Adv. *by name*, ὀ. τινὰς βώσαντες Hdt. 5. 1; λέγειν Id.6.79; ἀνακαλεῖν Th.7.70; διελθεῖν Isoc.9.51; μνησθῆναί τινος D.21.58.—Rare in Poets, as Critias 6.3 D., Call.*Aet.Oxy.*2080. 81:—in form **ὀνῠμαστί** *Berl.Sitzb.*1927.167 (Cyrene). [Written -ῑ in *IG*I$^2$.57.44 (v B.C.), *Berl.Sitzb.* l.c., and this is confirmed by the quantity [ῑ] in Critias and Call. ll. cc.; but -ει *SIG*355.18 (Ilium, iv/iii B.C.), *OGI*218.27 (ibid., iii B.C.).] **-αστικός**, ή, όν, *skilful at naming*, Pl.*Cra.*424a; *of* or *belonging to naming*, hence ἡ τέχνη ἡ ὀνομαστική ib.423d; ἡ -κή alone, ib.425a. II. ἡ -κή (sc. πτῶσις) the *nominative* case, Str.14.1.41, D.T.636.5, A.D.*Synt.*107.4 (pl.). III. τὸ -κόν (sc. βιβλίον) *vocabulary*, arranged acc. to the subjects, and not alphabetically as in a λεξικόν, such as the work of Jul. Pollux: -κά, τά, title of work by Democr.(*Fr.*26$^a$). IV. Adv. -κῶς *by a special name*, Ath.14.646a; *in the nominative case*, Hermog.*Inv.* 4.4. ⊛ **-αστός**, ή, όν, in dialects **ὀνῠμ-** Pi.*P.*1.38 (as pr. n. of a Delphian, *Berl.Sitzb.*1927.158 (Cyrene)):—*named, to be named*, and οὐκ ὀνομαστός *not to be named* or *mentioned*, i.e. *abominable*, Κακοΐλιον οὐκ ὀνομαστήν Od.19.260,597, cf. Hes.*Th.*148. II. *of name* or *note, famous*, Thgn.23, Pi. l. c., Hdt.4.47, Isoc.12.261, Phoen.2.11, etc.: Comp. and Sup., Hdt.6.126, 2.178. 2. of things, *notable*, ὀνομαστὰ πράσσων E.*HF*509.

**ὀνομᾰτ-ίζω**, *dispute about names*, Gal.18(2).870. ⊛ **-ικός**, ή, όν, *consisting of nouns*, opp. ῥηματικός, λέξις D.H.*Amm.*2.4, *Th.*22, Hermog.*Id.*1.6; τὰ ὀ. *nouns substantive*, D.H.*Comp.*2,5,12, al.; -κὴ θέσις as paraphr. for ὄνομα, A.D.*Synt.*313.27; -κὴ ὕπαρξις existence *in name*, opp. οὐσιώδης, ib.82.3. Adv. -κῶς *in noun-form*, D.H. *Amm.*2.2,5, Str.9.5.6, A.D.*Adv.*204.15. **-ιον**, τό, Dim. of ὄνομα, Longin.43.2, Arr.*Epict.*2.23.14: without dim. sense, *POxy.*2131.9 (iii A.D.). **-ισμός**, ὁ, *list of names*, Ἀρχ.Ἐφ.1910.362 (Thess.).

**ὀνομᾰτο-γρᾰφία**, ἡ, *writing of names*, Lxx 1*Es.*6.12, S.E.*M.*11. 67. **-θεσία**, ἡ, *the giving a name, nomenclature*, Eust.39. 23. **-θέσια** (sc. ἱερά), τά, *nominalia* (also *nominalium nuncupatio*), *Gloss.* **-θετέω**, *give a name*, Olymp.*in Cat.*105.16, Eust. 32.6; cj. for νομοθετῆσαι in Arist.*APo.*83$^a$14 (γρ. D). ⊛ **-θέτης**, ου, ὁ, *one who gives a name, namer*, v.l. in recc. for νομοθέτης, Pl.*Chrm.* 175b. **-θετικός**, ή, όν, *prone to name-giving*, Sch.Il.5.60. **-θήρας**, ου, ὁ, *word-hunter*, Ath.3.98a, 14.649b. **-κλήτωρ**, ορος, ὁ, = ὀνομακλήτωρ, *Gloss.* **-λόγος**, ον, *collector of words*, Ath.9.397a. II. *one who tells people's names*, Lat. *nomenclator*, Plu.*Cat.Mi.* 8. **-μάχος** [ᾰ], ον, *fighting about a word, expression*, or *name*, Critol.ap.Clem.Al.*Strom.*2.7.33.1. **-ποιέω**, *coin names*, Arist. *Cat.*7$^a$5, *EN*1108$^a$18, *Top.*104$^b$36, Phld.*Mus.*p.54 K., Ph.1.602, S.E. *M.*1.314, Gal.2.736. **-ποίησις**, εως, ἡ, *the coining of a name* or *word*, Suid. s. v. Ναύσων. **-ποιία**, ἡ, *the coining of a word in imitation of a sound*, Str.14.2.28, Quint.*Inst.*1.5.72: pl., Plu.2. 747d. **-ποιός**, ὁ, *coiner of names*, esp. significant names, Ath. 3.99c, Zos.Alch.p.230 B.

**ὀνομᾰτ-ουργέω**, = ὀνοματοποιέω, Demetr.*Eloc.*95, Procl.*in Cra.*p.6 P. **-ουργία**, ἡ, *the making of names*, ib.p.44 P. **-ουργός**, ὁ, = ὀνοματοποιός, Pl.*Cra.*389a. **-ώδης**, ες, *of the nature of a name*: λόγος ὀ. a *nominal* definition, Arist.*APo.*93$^b$31.

⊛ **ὀνό-πορδον**, τό, *pellitory*, *Parietaria cretica*, Epich.161, Plin.*HN* 27.110, Hsch. **-πρόσωπος**, ον, *ass-faced*, Herm.Trism. in *Rev.Phil.*32.256, Sch.Luc.*Sacr.*14. **-πυξος**, ὁ, *cotton-thistle*, *Onopordon illyricum*, Thphr.*HP*6.4.3, Plin.*HN*21.94. **-ρυγχος**, ἡ, a plant, *bunilla*, *Gloss.*

⊛ **ὄνος**, ὁ and ἡ, *ass*, once in Hom., Il.11.558; then in *IG*I$^2$.40.12, Hdt.4.135, etc., cf. Arist.*HA*580$^b$3; ὄνοι οἱ τὰ κέρεα ἔχοντες, together with a number of fabulous animals, Hdt.4.191,192; ὀ. μονοκέρατος Arist.*HA*499$^b$19, *PA*663$^a$23, cf. Ael.*NA*3.41:—freq. in provs.: 1. ὀ. λύρας (sc. ἀκούων), of one who can make nothing of music, Men. 527, Id.*Mis.*18, cf. Varro ap.Gell.3.16.13, Diogenian.7.33; expld. in Apostol.12.91a, ὀ. λύρας ἤκουε καὶ σάλπιγγος ὗς; ὀ. κάθηται, of one who sits down when caught in the game of ὀστρακίνδα, Poll.9.106, 112; the two provs. combined by Cratin.229 ὄνοι δ' ἀπωτέρω κάθηνται τῆς λύρας, cf. κιθαρίζω. 2. περὶ ὄνου σκιᾶς for an *ass's* shadow, i.e. for a trifle, Ar.*V.*191 (v. Sch.), Pl.*Phdr.*260c; ταῦτα πάντ' ὄνου σκιά S. *Fr.*331. 3. ὄνου πόκαι or πόκες, v. πόκος II; ὄνον κείρεις, of those who attempt the impossible, Zen.5.38. 4. ἀπ' ὄνου καταπεσεῖν, of one who gets into a scrape by his own clumsiness, with a pun on ἀπὸ νοῦ πεσεῖν, Ar.*Nu.*1273, cf. Pl.*Lg.*701d. 5. ὄνος ὕεται *an ass* in the rain, of being unmoved by what is said or done, Cratin.52, cf. Cephisod.1; ὄνῳ τις ἔλεγε μῦθον, ὁ δὲ τὰ ὦτα ἐκίνει Diogenian.7.30; ὀ. εἰς Ἀθήνας Macar.*Prov.*6.31. 6. ὀ. ἄγω μυστήρια, i.e. my part is to carry burdens, Ar.*Ra.*159. 7. ὄνων ὑβριστότερος, of wanton behaviour, X.*An.*5.8.3; κριθῶσης ὄνου S.*Fr.*876. 8. ὦτ' ὄνου λαβεῖν, like Midas, Ar.*Pl.*287. 9. ὀ. εἰς ἄχυρα, of one who gets what he wants, Diogenian.6.91; ὄνου γνάθος, of a glutton, ib. 100. 10. ὀ. ἐν μελίσσαις, of one who has got into a scrape, Crates Com.36; but ὀ. ἐν πιθήκοις, of extreme ugliness, Men.402.8; ὀ. ἐν μύρῳ 'a clown at a feast', Suid. 11. εἰς ὄνους ἀφ' ἵππων, of one who has come down in the world, Lib.*Ep.*34.2, cf. Zen.2.33, etc. II. a fish of the cod family, esp. the *hake*, *Merluccius vulgaris*, Epich. 67, Arist.*HA*599$^b$33, *Fr.*326, Henioch.3.3, Opp.*H.*1.151, etc. III. *wood-louse*, κυλισθεὶς ὥς τις ὀ. ἰσόσπριος S.*Fr.*363, cf. Arist.*HA*557$^a$ 23 (v.l. ὀνίοις), Thphr.*HP*4.3.6, Hsch. s. v. σηνίκη; cf. ὀνίσκος II, ἴουλος IV. IV. *wingless locust*, = τρωξαλλίς, Dsc.2.52. V. ὄνων φάτνη a nebulous appearance between the ὄνοι (two stars in the breast of the Crab), Theoc.22.21, cf. Arat.898, Thphr.*Sign.*23 (ἡ τοῦ ὄνου φάτνη ib.43,51), Ptol.*Tetr.*23. VI. ὄνου πετάλειον, = φύλλον ὀνίτιδος, Nic.*Th.*628. VII. from *the ass as a beast of burden* the name passed to: 1. *windlass*, Hdt.7.36, Hp.*Fract.*31, Arist.*Mech.*853$^b$12. 2. *the upper millstone* which turned round, ὀ. ἀλέτης X.*An.*1.5.5; also ὀ. ἀλετών Alex.13,204, cf. Hsch. s. v. μύλη; perh. simply, *millstone*, Herod.6.83: Phot. says that Aristotle also calls the *fixed nether millstone* ὄνος (but Arist.*Pr.*964$^b$38 says, ὄνου λίθον ἀλοῦντος when *the millstone* is grinding stone, as it does when no grist is in the mill). 3. *beaker, winecup*, Ar.*V.*616, Posidon.2 J. 4. *spindle* or *distaff*, Poll.7.32, 10.125, Hsch. 5. perh. *coping* of a wall, *Inscr.Délos* 372 *A* 158 (iii/ii B.C.). VIII. *ass's load*, as a measure, πυροῦ ὀ. τρεῖς *PFay.*67.2 (i A.D.).

**ὄνοσις**, εως, ἡ, *blame*, Eust.733.61.

**ὀνοσκελίς**, ίδος, ἡ, *she with the ass's legs* (cf. ὀνόκωλος), epith. of the Ἔμπουσα, Sch.Ar.*Ec.*1048.

**ὄνοσμα**, ατος, τό, *stone bugloss*, *Onosma echinoides*, Dsc.3.131, Gal. 12.89, Plin.*HN*27.110.

**ὀνοσσάμενος, ὀνόσσεσθαι**, v. ὄνομαι.

**ὀνοστάσιον** [ᾰ], τό, (ὄνος, στάσις) *ass-stall*, *Gloss.*

**ὀνοστός**, ή, όν, *to be blamed* or *scorned*, δῶρα μὲν οὐκ ἔτ' ὀνοστὰ διδοῖς Il.9.164; οὐδ' ὀνοστὸς ἐν μάχαις Lyc.1235. Adv. -στῶς Eust.1101. 2:—also **ὀνοτός**, Pi.*I.*4(3).50, Call.*Del.*20, A.R.4.91.

**ὀνο-στύππαξ**, ακος, ὁ, *donkey-ropeseller* (cf. στύππαξ), *Com.Adesp.* 94. **-σφἄγία**, ἡ, *sacrifice of asses*, Call.*Fr.*188 (pl.).

※ **ὀνοτ-άζω**, like ὄνομαι, *blame*, *h.Merc.*30; σκολιῶς ὀ. Hes.*Op.*258:—Med., γάμον ὀνοταζόμεναι *abominating* it, A.*Supp.*10 codd. **-αστός**, ἡ, όν, οὐκ ὀ. *not to be made light of*, prob. cj. in *h.Ven.*254. **-ός**, ἡ, όν, v. ὀνοστός.

**ὀνοτρόφος**, ὁ, *donkey-keeper*, *PLips.*97 viii 20, al. (iv A.D.).

**ὄνουρις**, f.l. for ὀνόθουρις in Dsc.4.117.

※ **ὀνο-φορβός**, ὁ, (φέρβω) *ass-keeper*, Hdt.6.68,69. ※ **-φυλλον**, τό, gloss on ὄνου πετάλειον ὀριγάνου, Sch.Nic.*Th.*628. **-χειλές**, έος, τό, *Cretan bugloss, Echium parviflorum*, Ps.-Dsc.4.23 (whence restd. in Thphr.*HP*7.10.3, for ὀνοκίχλης), Plin.*HN*22.51:—also **-χειλος**, ἡ, Aët.1.5, Paul.Aeg.7.3 p.187 H.: **-χηλον**, τό, as if from χηλή, *ass's hoof*, Sch.Nic.*Th.*838 (with v.l. -χειλον); cf. ὀνοκλεία.

※ **ὄντα**, τά, neut. pl. part. of εἰμί (*sum*), *the things which actually exist, the present*, opp. the past and future, E.*Hel.*14; but also, 2. *reality, truth*, opp. that which is not, Pl.*Sph.*263d; *actual objects*, σκιὰς τῶν ὄντων Id.*R.*532c, etc.; v. εἰμί. II. *that which one has, property, fortune* (cf. οὐσία), D.18.102.

**ὀντοποιέω**, *make things to be*, Dam.*Pr.*65.

**ὀντότης**, ητος, ἡ, *reality*, Alex.Aphr. *in Metaph.*641.27, Eustr. *in EN*13.7.

※ **ὄντως**, Adv. part. of εἰμί (*sum*), *really, actually, verily*, with Verbs, E.*HF*610, *Ion* 223 (lyr.), *IA*[1622], Ar.*Nu.*86, *Pl.*286,289, Herod. 4.65, etc.; ὄντως τε καὶ ἀληθῶς really and truly, Pl.*Sph.*263d; ὀ. φιλοσοφεῖν Epicur.*Fr.*220; opp. to ὡς ἔπος εἰπεῖν, Pl.*Lg.*656e; to εἰκότως, Antipho 2.2.10 and 4.10: in Pl. with the part. ὤν, οὖσα, ὄν, to imply *real* existence, *Phdr.*247c,e, *R.*597d: also with Nouns, τὰ ὄντως ἀγαθά Id.*Phdr.*260a; ὅ γε ὄντως φιλομαθής Id.*R.*490a; ὄντως ἑταίρας Antiph.212.6, cf. Men.367, etc.: not used by Th. or Arist., nor in Ion. (ἐόντως is not found); more freq. in the later dialogues of Pl. than in the earlier.

※ **ὄνυ**, Arc. and Cypr. for ὅδε, declined like ὁ with addition of -νυ, nom. sg. masc. ὄνυ *Inscr.Cypr.*141 H., acc. τόνυ ib.140 H., dat. τῷνυ *Schwyzer* 664.11 (Orchom. Arc., iv B.C.), acc. pl. neut. τάνυ *IG*5(2). 3.14 (Tegea, iv B.C.), gen. τῶνυ *SIG*306.59 (ibid., iv B.C.), *IG*5(2). 262.23 (Mantinea, v B.C.), dat. pl. fem. ταῖνυ *SIG*306.30; also, with -νυν for -νυ, acc. sg. fem. τάνυν, acc. pl. masc. τόσνυν, ib.559.48,49 (Megalopolis, found at Magn. Mae., iii B.C.).

※ **ὀνύδιν**, τό, = ὀνάριον, *PGoodsp.Cair.*15.16 (iv A.D.).

**ὄνυμα, ὀνυμάζω, ὀνυμαίνω, ὀνυμαστός**, Aeol. and Dor. for ὀνομ-.

※ **ὄνυξ**, ὔχος, ὁ, Hom. only in Ep. dat. pl. ὀνύχεσσι, and always of the eagle, *talons, claws*, Il.8.248, al.; so of the falcon, Hes.*Op.*204, 205, Ar.*Av.*1180; so of beasts of prey, Pi.*N.*4.63, Hdt.3.108; of the crocodile, Id.2.68; of the Sphinx, E.*El.*471 (lyr.); of human beings, *nail*, Hes.*Sc.*266, Hdt.4.64, etc.; τοὺς ὄνυχας τῶν δακτύλων Ar.*Av.*8; of horses and oxen, *hoof*, X.*Eq.*1.3, *AP*9.64 (Asclep. or Arch.): Arist. speaks of the hoof (ὁπλή) as homologous to the *nail* or *claw* (ὄνυξ), *HA*486$^b$20, *PA*690$^a$9: metaph., πρὸς ὀξὺν γ' ὀ. πετραῖον λίθου E.*Cyc.*401 codd. (leg. στόνυχα):—Special phrases: 1. εἰς ἄκρους τοὺς ὀ. ἀφίκετο (sc. ὁ οἶνος) warmed me to *my fingers' ends*, ib.159; so ἐκ κορυφῆς εἰς ἄκρους ὀ. *AP*9.709 (Phil.), cf. 12.93 (Rhian.); so also ἐξ ὀνύχων from *the fingers' ends*, ib.5.13 (Rufin.), Plu.2.3c; but ἐξ ἁπαλῶν ὀ. from childhood, Horace's *de tenero ungui*, *AP*5.128 (Autom.). 2. ὄνυχας ἐπ' ἄκρους στάς on *tiptoe*, E.*El.*840; ἐπ' ἄκρων ἐβάδιζε τῶν ὀ. Macho ap.Ath.8.349b. 3. ὅταν ἐν ὄνυχι ὁ πηλὸς γένηται, i.e. when the model reaches the *nail* stage, because the sculptor puts the finishing touches to the model with his nail, Polyclit.ap.Plu. 2.636c, cf. Plu.2.86a; so ἡ δι' ὄνυχος δίαιτα *a most careful, close* life, ib. 128e; τὸν Λυσιακὸν χαρακτῆρα ἐκμέμακται εἰς ὄνυχα *ad unguem expressit*, D.H.*Dem.*13; σύμπηξις εἰς ὄνυχα a *nice* fit, Gal.2.737; τὰς γωνίας ἐπ' ὄνυχος συμβεβλημένας ἔχειν Ph.*Bel.*66.37; πρὸς ὄνυχα τὴν προσκαρτέρησιν ποιεῖσθαι Phld.*Rh.*1.11 S.; cf. ὀνυχίζω III, ἐξονυχίζω. 4. ὀδοῦσι καὶ ὄνυξι καὶ πάσῃ μηχανῇ, i.e. in every possible way, Luc. *DMort.*11.4. 5. ἐξ ὀνύχων λέοντα (sc. τεκμαίρεσθαι) to judge by the *claws*, i.e. by a slight but characteristic mark, Alc.113, Apostol. 7.57. II. *anything like a claw*, 1. *fluke* of an anchor, Plu.2. 247e. 2. *an instrument fixed by a surgeon to his finger*, Hp.*Superf.* 7, Gal.19.107. 3. ὀ. σιδηροῦς tool used for scraping the 'figs' of the συκάμινος, Thphr.*HP*4.2.1 (pl.); also for making incisions to extract gum of balsam, ib.9.6.2 (pl.). 4. κλιμακίδοιν τοὺς ὀ., τῶν πλαισίων τοὺς ὀ., dub. sens. in *IG*1$^2$.373.208,212, cf. 372*E*10. III. *anything like the nail*: 1. *the white part at the end of rose-petals* by which they are attached to the stalk, Dsc.1.99. 2. *hypopyon*, an accumulation of pus in the eye resembling a nail-paring, Aët.7.30 tit. (pl.), Paul.Aeg.3.22.23. 3. *part of the liver*, Ruf.*Onom.*180, Sch.Nic.*Th.*560. 4. *veined gem, onyx*, Lxx *Jb.*28.16, Aristeas 66, J.*BJ*5.5.7; Σαρδῷος ὀ. *sardonyx*, Luc.*Syr.D.*32 (cf. σαρδόνυξ); ὀ. σφραγίς *IG*2$^2$.1388.86, cf. 1$^2$.282.128. 5. an aromatic substance, *onycha*, Lxx *Ex.*30.34, Damocr.ap.Gal.13.226, Dsc.2.8, *POxy.*1142. 4 (iii A.D.). 6. = ἀστράγαλος VII, Ps.-Dsc.4.61. 7. *operculum of the* κογχύλιον, Dsc.2.8, Gal.13.320, Orib.5.77.1, Paul.Aeg.7.3; *of the* πορφύρα, Dsc.*Eup.*2.92. 8. a shell-fish, supposed female of σωλήν, prob. *Lithodomus*, Xenocr.ap.Orib.2.58.106 (pl.). 9. ὄνυχες θαλάσσιοι *sea-weed*, Ps.-Democr.Alch.p.42 B. (Cf. Lat. *unguis*, Skt. *nakhás* 'nail', etc.)

**ὀνυρίζεται**· ὀδύρεται, Hsch. (cf. ἐνυρήσεις).

**ὀνῠχ-άλειμμα** [ᾰ], ατος, τό, *ointment of* ὄνυξ III.5, *Hippiatr.*100. **-ιαῖος**, α, ον, *of a nail's breadth*, Eust.ad D.P.*Prooem.*p.73.31 B. ※ **-ίζω**, *pare the nails*, in Med., Jul.*Mis.*339b, Iamb.*VP*28.154: aor. ὠνυχισάμην Lxx 2*Ki.*19.24(25):—Pass., ὠνυχισμένος *with one's nails pared*, Cratin.455. II. ὀ. ὄνυχας *to have the hoof cloven*, Lxx *Le.*11.7, al. III. *examine with the nail, examine closely*, Artem.4*Prooem.*, Jul.*Or.*5.162c: fut. ὀνυχιεῖ· ἐπιμελῶς ἐξετάσει, Hsch.:—Pass., ὀνυχίζεται, expld. by Phot. ἀκριβολογεῖται, Ar.*Fr.*834. IV. *overreach*, ἐν τῇ συνηθείᾳ -ίζεσθαί φαμεν τὸν ἐπὶ βλάβῃ ὑπό τινος ἐξαπατηθέντα Artem.1.22. **-ῐμαῖος**, α, ον, *of the size of nail-parings, diminutive*, *Com.Adesp.*879. **-ῐνος**, η, ον, (ὄνυξ III.4) *made of onyx*, *IG* 11(2).287*B*70 (Delos, iii B.C.), Posidon.25 J., Plu.*Ant.*58, etc. 2. *like onyx*, Plin.*HN*15.55; esp. *onyx-coloured*, of garments, *POxy.*114. 6 (ii/iii A.D.), 1026.10 (v A.D.); πρόβατα *PGen.*68.6 (iv A.D.). II. ὀνύχινον (sc. ἔλαιον), *made of* ὄνυξ III.5, Dsc.1.54.2. **-ιον**, τό, Dim. of ὄνυξ I, *small claw*, Arist.*HA*503$^a$29. 2. pig's *trotters*, *Sammelb.*1941 (iv A.D.), *PLond.*3.1259.37 (iv A.D.). 3. an eye-disease, = ὄνυξ III.2, *PMed.Strassb.*p.6 K.: pl., Aët.7.30. 4. σκόρδων ὀνύχια *cloves* of garlic, Id.11.11. II. (ὄνυξ III.4) a kind of *onyx*, Thphr.*Lap.*31, Lxx *Ex.*28.20: as Adj. ὀνύχιος (sc. λίθος), Suid. ※ **-ισμός**, ὁ, *paring of the nails*, Str.17.3.7. **-ιστήρ**, ῆρος, ὁ, *hoof*, Lxx *Le.*11.3, al. **-ιστήριον**, τό, *nail-knife* or *scissors*, Posidipp.38; = *unguicularium*, *Gloss.* **-ίτης** [ῑ], ου, ὁ, (ὄνυξ III.4) *of the onyx kind*, ὀ. λίθος Dsc.5.74:—also fem. **-ῖτις** λίθος, App.*Mith.* 115, cf. Plin.*HN*34.103.

**ὀνῠχο-γρᾰφέομαι**, Pass., *to be scored with the nail*, Hp.*Epid.*6.6. 4. **-ειδής**, ές, *like a nail*, Dsc.1.64.3. **-πάχος**, ον, *of the thickness of a finger-nail*, Ps.-Democr.Alch.p.48 B. **-τόμον**, τό, *resectorium*, *Gloss.* **-φόρος**, ον, *carrying the nails*, of the last phalanx of the finger, *Cat.Cod.Astr.*7.238.26.

**ὀνῠχόω**, *make like a nail, claw,* or *hook*, τὸ ὠνυχωμένον the *claw-shaped* side of the scalpel, Orib.46.11.18; ὠνύχωται *has horny hoofs*, Sch.Ar.*Ra.*232.

**ὀνώδης**, ες, *ass-like*, of persons, Arist.*Phgn.*812$^a$10, Phld.*Rh.* 1.6 S. (Sup.); ὀ. φιλοπλουτία Plu.2.525e; of colour, ib.362f.

※ **ὄνωνις** or **ὀνωνίς**, ιδος, ἡ, *rest-harrow, Ononis antiquorum*, Thphr. *HP*6.1.3, Dsc.3.131; τρηχεῖαν ὄνωνιν Call.*Fr.anon.*366 (ap.Plu.2. 44e, al., v.l. ἄνωνιν): metaph., ἐς [τὴν] πόλιν ἄξεις τήνδε τὴν ὀνώνιδα this *troublesome weed* (perh. with a play on ὄνος), *Com.Adesp.*438.

**ὀξάλ-ειος** [ᾰ], ον, *sourish*, συκαῖ Apollod.Car.25.3. **-ίς**, ίδος, ἡ, *sour wine*, Hsch. II. *sorrel, Rumex acetosa*, Nic.*Th.*840; = ὀξυλάπαθον μικρόν, Ps.-Dsc.2.114.

**ὀξάλμη**, ἡ, (ὄξος) *sauce made of vinegar and brine*, Cratin.143, Ar.*V.* 331 (anap.), Gal.6.616, al.; mentioned as a natural product of Sicily, Arist.*Mete.*359$^b$15; used medicinally, Apollon.ap.Philum.*Ven.*32. 3:—written **ἐξάλμη**, *UPZ*89.14 (ii B.C.).

**ὀξέα, ὀξεῖνος**, v. ὀξύα, ὀξύϊνος.

**ὀξέλαιον**, τό, *sauce of vinegar and oil*, Xenocr.ap.Orib.2.58.119, Gal.6.728.

**ὀξερίας**, ὁ, = τυρὸς χλωρός (Poll.) or τυρὸς ἀχρεῖος (Hsch.), name of a Sicilian cheese, *Com.Adesp.*880 (fort. ξερίας).

**ὀξηλίς**, ίδος, ἡ, a plant (cf. ὀξαλίς II), Theognost.*Can.*14.

**ὀξ-ηρός**, ά, όν, (ὄξος) *of* or *for vinegar*, ἄγγος S.*Fr.*306; κεράμιον, κέραμος, Ar.*Fr.*723, *AP*12.108 (Dionys.); ἀγγεῖα Sor.1.90. II. *acid*, -ῶν ἐμουμένων Diocl.*Fr.*139; σπλῆνες ὀ. pads *soaked in vinegar*, Hp.*Ulc.*15. **-ίδιον**, τό, Dim. of ὄξος, *PCair.Zen.*527.9 (iii B.C.): written -είδιον in Dieuch.ap.Orib.4.7.21, Suid.: pl. ὀξείδια *Sammelb.* 4425 vii 20 (ii A.D.), *BGU*417.31 (ii/iii A.D.). ※ **-ίζω**, *taste* or *smell like vinegar*, Dsc.1.115.2,5.6, *Gp.*3.7.1 (= interpol. in Dsc.2.96, with -ύσῃ), Archig.ap.Gal.13.218, etc.

**ὀξίνα** (prob. Dor. fem.), *harrow*, Hsch. (Cogn. with ὀξύς, cf. Lith. *ekéti*, Germ. *eggen* 'harrow', Lat. *occa*.)

**ὀξ-ίνης** [ῑ], ου, ὁ, *sharp, sour*, χυμός Plu.2.913b (codd. Wyttenb., ὀξὺν codd. Bernardak.); ὀξίνης (sc. οἶνος), ὁ, *sour wine*, Hermipp.91, Thphr.*HP*9.11.1; ὀ. οἶνος Hp.*Vict.*2.52 (in pl. ὀξῖναι), Thphr.*HP* 9.20.4, Diph.82: distd. from ὄξος, Plu.2.732b, 1047e. 2. metaph., *sour-tempered, tart*, πολίτης Ar.*Eq.*1304; θυμός Id.*V.*1082.—In *Gp.* 6.4.2 and Phryn.*PS*p.92 B., we find ὀξίνος:—also ὀξυνος v.l. in *Gp.* l.c. **-ίς**, ίδος, ἡ, (ὄξος) *vinegar-cruet*, Nicostr.Com.9, Axionic.7, *AJA*31.351 (pl.), *PLond.*2.402 ii 24 (ii B.C.); prop. of earthenware, Sch.Ar.*Ra.*1488: hence ὀξὶς χαλκῆ γέγονε, instead of being κεραμεᾶ, Ar.*Pl.*812; also ὀξίδ' ἀργυρᾶν ἔχει Sopat.19; ὀξὶς ἢ φάλαγξ; (exact sense doubtful) Ar.*V.*1509. 2. a measure, at Athens the same as ὀξύβαφον, but at Cleonae, = κοτύλη, Id.*Fr.*688, Diph.96. II. = ὀξαλίς II, Gal.11.631 (where ὀξύδα). III. in pl., *acidities*, Alex. Trall.*Febr.*1: sg., *acidity*, ib.6. **-ῖτις**, ιδος, fem. Adj. *tasting like vinegar*, στυπτηρία *PHolm.*18.5, 25.39.

**ὀξό-βαφον, -γαρον**, v. ὀξύβαφον, ὀξύγαρον. **-πώλης**, ου, ὁ, *vinegar-merchant*, Poll.7.198, Lib.*Or.*29.30.

**ὄξος**, εος, τό, (ὀξύς) *poor wine, 'vin ordinaire'*, Ar.*Ach.*35; κοτύλας τέτταρας ὄξους Δεκελικοῦ Alex.285, cf. X.*An.*2.3.14, *POxy.*1275.20 (iii A.D.); cf. ὀξίνης I. 2. *vinegar* made therefrom, *IG*1$^2$.334.4, A.*Ag.*322, Hp.*Acut.*61, Gal.11.413, etc.; ὑπώμνυτο ὁ μὲν οἶνος ὀ. αὐτὸν εἶναι γνήσιον, τὸ δ' ὀ. οἶνον αὐτό Eub.65; σφόδρ' ἐστὶν. ὁ βίος οἴνῳ προσφερής· ὅταν ᾖ τὸ λοιπὸν μικρόν, ὀ. γίγνεται Antiph.240; ἐς τὰς ῥῖνας ὀ. ἐγχέων, as a mode of torture, Ar.*Ra.*620. 3. metaph., of a *sour fellow*, χὠνὴρ ὀ. ἅπαν Theoc.15.148.

**ὀξύα** or **ὀξύη** [ῠ] (the latter preferred by Phryn.*PS*p.96 B. and more freq. in texts, as Thphr.*HP*3.3.8, al., but ὀξύα ib.3.10.3, 5.1.2 and 4), ἡ, *beech, Fagus silvatica*, Xanth.8, Thphr *HP*3.3.8, 3.10.1, Dicaearch. 2.2; later, as in Mod. Gr., called **ὀξέα**, Dosith.p.396 K., *Gloss.*, condemned by Phryn. l. c. II. *spear-shaft* made from its wood, *spear*, Archil.186, E.*Heracl.*727. (Prob. cogn. with ONorse *askr* 'ash', Lat. *ornus*, etc.)

**ὀξῠ-άκανθα** [ᾰκ], ἡ, *fiery thorn*, *Cotoneaster Pyracantha*, Dsc.1.93, Gal.6.643:—also **-άκανθος**, Thphr.*HP*1.9.3, 3.3.1, Gal.12.90. **-ἀκουσίλογος** [ῑ], ον, *sharp of hearing*, Lat. *auritus*, *Gloss.* **-αύγεια**, ἡ, *dazzling light*, Ph.*Fr.*73 H. **-βᾰρις** (sc. προσῳδία), ἡ, *circumflex accent*, Ammonius (pupil of Aristarchus) in *Gramm.Lat.*4.531 K.; called **ὀξυβαρεῖα** in Arc.188.4 (spurious passage, only in cod. C). **-βάφιον** [ᾰ], τό, Dim. of sq., Antiph.163.5, *POxy.*1657.7 (iii A.D.); -βάφια τρύλλια *Stud.Pal.*20.67.10 (ii A.D.). **-βᾰφον**, τό, (βάπτω) *small vinegar-saucer*: then, generally, *shallow earthen vessel, saucer*, Hp. *Morb.*2.47, Cratin.187, Ar.*Av.*361, Antiph.163.5 (v.l.), Eub.65, *Inscr. Délos* 407.18 (ii B.C.), etc. 2. pl., a kind of *harmonica* made of saucers of different materials struck with a wooden hammer, Phlp. *in de An.*353.13 (ὀψόβ- codd.), Suid. s. v. Διοκλῆς. II. as a measure, *the fourth part of a* κοτύλη, about ⅛ of a pint, μέλιτος Alex.172.11, cf. Thphr.*HP*9.11.7, al., Nic.*Th.*598, Dsc.3.27. (The form ὀξόβαφον *BGU*781 iii 5 (i A.D.), *PMed.Strassb.*p.7 K., is condemned by Phryn. *PS*p.97 B.) ❋ **-βελής**, ές, *sharp-pointed*, ἆλτο δ' ὀϊστὸς ὀξυβελὴς Il.4.126; ὀ. χαῖται, of the porcupine's bristles, Emp.83.2; ἥλιος Id.40; νῶτα καράβου Opp.*H.*2.346: metaph., πόθος ὀ. ib.4.41: in Prose, of a lancet, τὸ -ές Gal.12.413. II. *shooting sharp-pointed*, and therefore *swift, missiles*, ὀ. [ὄργανα], opp. λιθοβολικά, Ph.*Bel.*54.49; ὀξυβελής, ὁ, with and without καταπέλτης, *an engine for throwing sharp-pointed bolts*, opp. πετροβόλος, D.S.20.85,86; so **ὀξυβελικόν** (sc. ὄργανον), τό, ib.75, etc. **-βλαττα**, ἡ, (ὀξύς II. 2b) in Lat. form *oxyblatta*, *bright purple*, *Cod.Just.*4.40.1. **-βλεπτέω**, *to be sharp-sighted*, Arr.*Epict.*2.11.22. **-βλέπτης**, ου, ὁ, *one who is sharp-sighted*, Hsch. s. v. ἀτρέστοις, *Gloss.* **-βλεψία**, ἡ, *sharpness of sight*, Hsch. s. v. ὀξυωπίαν. **-βόας** and **-βόης**, ου, ὁ, *shrill-screaming*, of birds, A.*Ag.*57; of men, Luc.*JTr.*31; *sharp-buzzing*, of mosquitoes, *AP*5.150 (Mel.). **-βόλος**, ον, = ὀξυβελής II, *IG*2².468 (iv B.C.). **-βουλία**, ἡ, *quickness of counsel*, Sch.B Il.10.204 (better ὀξυλαβία, as Sch.T). ❋ **-βρέχω**, *steep in vinegar*, *Stud.Pal.*20.27.2 (ii/iii A.D.). **-γάλα**, ακτος, τό, *sour milk, whey*, πίνουσι ..ὀ. τῶν προβάτων Ctes.*Fr.*57.22, cf. Str.7.4.6, Plu.*Art.*3, Gal.6.689. **-γᾰλάκτινος**, η, ον, *made of sour milk*, τυρός ib.697, 12.272, cf. 6.518. **-γᾰρον**, τό, *sauce of vinegar and* γάρον, Arr. *Epict.*2.20.30, Gal.6.534, Ath.2.67e, 9.366c:—also **ὀξόγαρον**, *Gloss.*, condemned by Phryn.*PS*p.97 B.

**ὀξύγγιον**, τό, = Lat. *axungia*, *lard*, Dsc.3.90, al., Orib.*Fr.*97, *Gloss.*

**ὀξῠ-γένειος**, ον, *with pointed chin*, Poll.4.145. **-γεννς**, νος, ὁ, *point of the chin*, Id.2.97.

**ὀξύγη**, ἡ, = εἶδος ⟨ἀ⟩κρίδος, Lat. *bufo et cufo*, *Gloss.*

**ὀξῠ-γλῠκυ** (sc. ποτόν), τό, *drink of acidulated honey*, Hp.*Fract.* 11 (in dat. -εῖ), 36 (in acc. -υ), etc.:—so **-γλῠκές**, τό, Gal.18(2).466; **-γλῠκον**, τό, Lat. *dulcacidum*, *Gloss.* **-γλῠκυς**, εια, υ, *sour-sweet*, ῥόα A.*Fr.*363; ὁ τῆς ὀξυγλυκέος ῥοιᾶς χυλός (prob. a special variety) Orib.*Fr.*53. **-γονον**, τό, = μήκων ῥοιάς, cj. in Ps.-Dsc.4.63,64 (-τονον codd., cf. Apul.*Herb.*53, *Gloss.*). **-γοος**, ον, *shrill-wailing*, λιταί A.*Th.*320 (lyr.). ❋ **-γράφος** [ᾰ], ον, *writing fast*, Lxx *Ps.*44 (45).2, Ph.2.363, etc. **-γώνιος**, ον, *acute-angled*, Arist.*Top.*107ᵃ 17, *Cael.*307ᵃ2, Euc.1 *Def.*21, Onos.10.16: neut. as Subst., *acute-angled body*, Epicur.*Ep.*2 p.50 U. (pl.). **-γωνιότης**, ητος, ἡ, *a being acute-angled*, Apollod.*Poliorc.*159.7. **-δερκέω**, prob. f.l. for ὀξυδορκέω, Ph.1.409, 2.480, Hsch. s. v. ἐκ δυοῖν τρία βλέπεις (-δορκ- Suid.). **-δερκής**, ές, *sharp-sighted, quick-sighted*, Luc.*Tim.*25, al.: Comp. -έστερος Id.*Vit.Auct.*26, Hegesand.9; ὄψις Alex.Aphr. *in Top.*262.10: Sup. -έστατος Hdt.2.68, Arist.*Mir.*834ᵇ28. Adv. -κῶς Ph.1.590: Comp. -έστερον ib.229. II. Act., *promoting quickness of sight*, ὕδωρ Diocl.*Fr.*128, cf. Dsc.5.5, Gal.12.263, al. **-δερκία**, ἡ, *sharp-sightedness*, αἰσθήσεων Epicur.*Nat.*28 *Fr.*6, cf. Apollod. 3.10.3, Gal.14.241, Alex.Aphr. *in Top.*258.17, etc.: Ion. **-δερκείη** Democr.119. ❋ **-δερκικός**, ή, όν, *making the sight sharp*, as L. Dind. for ὀξυδερκιῶν in Antyll.ap.Orib.10.23.29 (ὀξυδορκικῶν Dar.); -δερκικοῖς (and -δορκικοῖς) v.l. for -δερκέσι in Dsc.2.163. **-δερκώ**, οῦς, ἡ, epith. of Athena, Paus.2.24.2. **-δορκέω**, *to be quick of sight*, Arist. *Rh.Al.*1421ᵃ22, *Com.Adesp.*359, Str.6.2.1, etc.; v. -δερκέω. **-δορκία**, ἡ, = ὀξυδερκία, Andronic.Rhod.p.572 M., Hippod.ap.Stob.4.39.26, Plot.5.9.1, etc. **-δορκικός**, ή, όν, = ὀξυδερκικός (q. v.), Plu. 2.69a, Gal.11.778. **-δουπος**, ον, *sharp-sounding*, κύμβαλα *AP*6.94 (Phil.). ❋ **-δρόμος**, ον, *swift-running*, Sch.Pi.*O.*13.51. **-έθειρ**, gen. -έθειρος, ὁ, ἡ, *with sharp points*, nom. pl. -έθειρες, ἐχῖνοι Marc.Sid.35; acc. pl. -έθειρας, ἀκάνθας Nonn.*D.*14.368; gen.sg. -έθειρος, ἀκάνθης ib. 22.25. **-έλαιον**, τό, *mixture of oil and vinegar*, Gal.13.397. **-ζύμια** [ῠ], τά, *acid ferments*, Ps.-Democr.ap.Zos.Alch.p.160 B.

**ὀξύζω**, v. ὀξίζω.

**ὀξῠ-ζωμος**, ον, *with a sharp sauce*, Apic.6.9.241. **-η**, v. ὀξύα. **-ηκοΐα**, Dor. **-ᾱκοΐα**, ἡ, *a sharp, quick ear*, Hippod.ap. Stob.4.39.26, Metop.ib.3.1.115, Plu.2.34c, Alex.Aphr. *in Top.*327.14, interpol. in Poll.2.82. **-ήκοος**, ον, *quick of hearing*: *of quick perception, keen*, αἴσθησις Pl.*Ti.*75b; ἰχθύες Arist.*HA*534ᵃ6, cf. A.D.*Synt.*295.23.—In codd. sts. wrongly ὀξύκοος, ὀξυκοΐα: Comp. ὀξυηκοώτερος Luc.*Pr.Im.*20, Porph.*Abst.*3.8: Sup. ὀξυηκοώτατος prob. l. in S.E.*M.*9.65, for ὀξυηκούστατος. **-ηχής**, ές, *sharp-sounding*, of high notes, Philostr.*VS*1.8.1: **-ηχος**, ον, Alex.Aphr. *Pr.*1.97. **-θᾰνᾰσία**, ἡ, *early death*, Heliod.Astr. in *Cat.Cod. Astr.*8(4).238. **-θάνᾰτος** [θᾰ], ον, *dying quickly, shortlived*, Eun. *Hist.*p.269 D., Heliod.Astr. in *Cat.Cod.Astr.*4.154. II. *killing quickly*, Str.17.2.4 (Comp.). **-θηγής**, ές, = sq.: metaph., καιροί v. l. in Gal.19.183. **-θηκτος**, ον, *sharp-edged, sharp-pointed*, φάσγανον, βέλος, E.*Andr.*1150, *El.*1159 (lyr.): gloss on ταναηκής, Sch.Il.*Oxy.* 1087.63. II. of a person, *goaded to passion, infuriated*, S.*Ant.* 1301 (s. v. l.). **-θρήνητος**, ον, gloss on ὀξυγόοις [λιταῖσιν], Sch. A.*Th.*320. **-θριξ**, τρῐχος, ὁ, ἡ, perh. *light-haired* or *bristly-haired*, *Cat.Cod.Astr.*7.198.

**ὀξῠθῠμ-έω**, *to be quick to anger*, E.*Andr.*689. II. Pass., *to be provoked*, ὀξυθυμηθεῖσά μοι Ar.*V.*501, cf. *Th.*466; *to be irritable*, Gal.15. 598. **-ησις**, εως, ἡ, *passionateness*, v.l. in Artem.4.69. **-ία**, ἡ, *vivacity* or *instability of temper*, Hp.*Epid.*2.4.4, E.*Andr.*728, Ruf.ap.Orib.*inc.* 6.5; *excitability*, ἐς γέλωτα Aret.*SD*1.5, cf. Poll.2.231 (v.l.). **-ια**, τά, *refuse deposited at cross-roads near the statues of Hecate*, ὃν χρῆν ἔν τε ταῖς τριόδοις κἀν τοῖς ὀξυθυμίοις προστρόπαιον τῆς πόλεως κάεσθαι τετριγότα should have been burned among the *refuse*, Eup.120; περὶ οὗ πολλῷ ἂν δικαιότερον ἐν τοῖς ὀ. ἡ στήλη σταθείη ἢ ἐν τοῖς ἡμετέροις ἱεροῖς Hyp.*Fr.*79; τῶν ὀ. ἀτιμότερος Poll.5.163, cf. 2.231; = Ἑκαταῖα II, Did.ap.Harp., cf. Phot., Suid.; or perh. *gallows* (so Aristarch.), τίς γὰρ ἂν ἀντὶ ῥαφανῖδος ὀξυθύμι' εἰσορῶν ἔλθοι πρὸς ἡμᾶς; prob. in *Com. Adesp.*400; cf. ἑκάτη. **-ίας**, ου, ὁ, *one who is quick to anger*, Poll. 2.231, 6.124.

**ὀξῠ-θῠμον**, τό, *a kind of thyme*, *PLille* 58 ii 21. iii 10 (iii B.C.). **-θῡμος**, ον, *quick to anger, choleric*, Epich.281, E.*Med.*319, Ar.*V.*406,455, 1105, Arist.*Rh.*1368ᵇ20, Lxx *Pr.*14.17, al.; *sharp to punish*, of the Areopagus, A.*Eu.*705; τὸ ὀξύθυμον, by crasis τοὐξύθυμον, = ὀξυθυμία, E.*Ba.*671, Men.*Georg.Fr.*3.

**ὀξύϊνος**, η, ον, (ὀξύα) *of beech-wood*, Theopomp.Coloph.ap.Ath. 4.183b (οἰσύινον Kaibel), Thphr.*HP*5.7.2, *Inscr.Délos* 290.226 (iii B.C.):—later **ὀξεῖνος**, Apollod.*Poliorc.*176.5, *Gp.*15.2.7, *Gloss.*

**ὀξῠ-καμπής**, ές, *sharply curved*, of hooks, Antyll.ap.Orib.45.18. 13. **-κάρδιος**, ον, = ὀξύθυμος, A.*Th.*907 (lyr.), Ar.*V.*430. **-κάρηνος** [ᾰ], ον, = ὀξυκέφαλος, D.P.642, Nic.*Th.*223, 397. **-κεδρος**, ἡ, *prickly cedar*, *Juniperus Oxycedrus*, Thphr.*HP*3.12.3. **-κέλευθος**, ον, *quick-travelling*, δρόμος Nonn.*D.*5.233 codd. (λοξοκέλευθον Koch, Ludw.). **-κέρᾰτος**, ον, = sq., Sch.rec.A.*Pr.*424, Hsch. s. v. ὀξύπρῳροι. **-κερως**, ωτος, ὁ, ἡ, *with pointed horns*, Opp.*C.*2. 445. **-κέφᾰλος**, ον, *with pointed head*, Poll.2.43, Philum.*Ven.*31. 1, Sch.Ar.*Av.*1295. **-κῑνησία**, ἡ, *quickness of motion*, Ptol.*Tetr.* 19, Porph.ap.Eus.*PE*3.12, Eun.*VS*p.473 B., Lyd.*Mens.*2.9. **-κίνητος** [ῑ], ον, *quickly moving*, Luc.*Abd.*28, *Dips.*5; διάνοια Ph.1.605; of tumours, etc., Cass.*Pr.*1.

**ὀξυκοΐα, ὀξύκοος**, v. ὀξυηκ-.

❋ **ὀξῠ-κόμινα**, τά, in Lat. form *oxycomina*, *olives served in brine* or *vinegar*, Petron.66.7 (cf. *cominia*, pl. = *a kind of olive*, Pallad.*Agric.* 3.18, *oximinum* = *aceto mixto cum cumino*, *Gloss.*). **-κόμμι**, τό, a kind of *gum*, in the form ὀξωκόμη (dat. sg. fem.), *PMag.Osl.*1. 74. **-κομος**, ον, *with pointed hair*, of the porcupine, Opp.*C.*2. 599; of a stag, ib.194; of a pine, *App.Anth.*5.46; *with pointed spines*, of a fish, Marc.Sid.21. **-κόρᾰκος**, ον, (κόραξ II) *with a sharp hook*, σμιλίον Paul.Aeg.6.87. **-κρᾶμα**, ατος, τό, *posca*, *Gloss.* **-κρᾱμᾰτοπώλης**, ου, ὁ, *poscarius*, ib. **-κρᾶτον**, Ion. **-κρητον**, τό, (κεράννυμι) *sour wine mixed with water*, Dsc.2.105, Aret.*CA*1.1, Antyll.ap.Orib.45.18.31, 4.11.14, Erot. s. v. μᾶζα, Gal. 11.439, al., Aët.15.1. **-κύᾰμια** [ᾰ], τά, and **-κύᾰμα**, τά, *fabae acetatae* (*acetosae*), *Gloss.* **-κώκῡτος**, ον, *wailed with shrill cries*, πάθος S.*Ant.*1316. **-λάβεια** [ᾰ], ἡ, *quickness in seizing an opportunity*, Eust.123.46; cf. ὀξυλαβία. **-λᾰβέω**, *seize quickly*: *seize an opportunity*, X.*HG*7.4.27, Men.*Epit.*528, Gal.*Parv.Pil.* 3. **-λάβη** [ᾰ], ἡ, a kind of *tongs*, Suid. s. v. Ἥφαιστος: **-λᾰβος**, ὁ, Sch.Il.18.477, *Gloss.*:—Dim. **-λᾰβίδιον**, τό, *Hermes* 38. 282. **-λᾰβής**, ές, *quick at seizing*, of the eagle, Arist.*HA*619ᵇ 29. **-λᾰβία**, ἡ, *quickness in seizing an opportunity*, Sch.T Il.10. 204, Sch.A.*Th.*97; cf. ὀξυλάβεια. **-λᾰβος**, ον, = -λαβής, Eust. 1753.50. II. cf. ὀξυλάβη. **-λάλος** [ᾰ], ον, *glib of tongue*, Ar. *Ra.*815 (lyr.). **-λάπᾰθον** [λᾰ], τό, *curled dock*, *Rumex crispus*, Dsc.2.114, Gal.6.635, al., Aret.*CA*2.2, etc.: also **-λάπαθος**, ὁ, *Gp.*2. 5.4. **-λίπᾰρος** [ῐ], ον, *composed of vinegar and oil*, τρίμμα Timocl. 3.2; χυμίον Sotad.Com.1.19. **-λίπης** ἄρτος, ὁ, bread *dressed with vinegar and fat*, Gal.10.575. **-λοβέω**, *have sharp ears, hear sharply*, Suid.

**ὄξυλον**· ὅμοιον.., ἰσόξυλον, Hsch.

**ὀξῠ-μάθεια** [μᾰ], ἡ, *quickness at learning*, Str.2.3.5, with v.l. ὀξυμαθία. **-μᾰθής**, ές, *learning quickly*, Phryn.*PS*p.97 B., Suid. s. v. θυμόσοφος. **-μᾶλον Περσικόν**, τό, Lacon. for κοκκύμηλον Περσικόν, *peach*, *Prunus persica*, Ar.Byz.ap.Ath.3.83a, Hsch **-μελής**, ές, *clear-singing*, f.l. in Ar.*Av.*1095 (lyr.). **-μελίκρᾱτον**, Ion. **-κρητον**, τό, *mixture of vinegar and honey*, *oxymel*, Hp.*Loc.Hom.*17:—also **ὀξύμελι**, ιτος, τό, Id.*Acut.*19, 59, Lys.*Fr.*42, Arist.*Pr.*922ᵃ6, cf. Dsc.5.14, Gal.15.677. **-μέριμνος**, ον, *keenly laboured* or *studied*, παλαίσματα Ar.*Ra.*877 (lyr.). **-μήνῑτος**, ον, perh. *bringing down quick anger* (i. e. of the Erinyes), φόνου (-ους codd.) ὀξυμηνίτου A.*Eu.* 472. **-μολπος**, ον, *clear-singing*, Id.*Th.*1028. **-μυρσίνη**, ἡ, = κεντρομυρσίνη, *butcher's broom*, *Ruscus aculeatus*, Dsc.4.144, cf. 1. 11, Androm.ap.Gal.13.842, Gal.6.643; also called χαμαιμυρσίνη, Plin.*HN*15.27, 23.165. **-μωρος**, ον, *pointedly foolish*: τὸ ὀξύμωρον *a witty saying, the more pointed from being paradoxical* or seemingly *absurd*, such as *insaniens sapientia, strenua inertia, splendide mendax*,

Serv. ad Verg. *A*.7.295, etc. **-νιτρον, τό,** *mixture of vinegar and soda,* Paul.Aeg.5.4. **-νοσία, ἡ,** *acute illness,* Cat.Cod.Astr. 1.119 (pl.). **-νους,** νουν, *sharp-witted,* Sch.rec.A.*Pers*.93.

**ὀξυν-τέον,** *one must pronounce with the acute accent,* Sch.Il.15.445. **-τήρ,** ῆρος, ὁ, *sharpener,* δονακήων, i.e. a penknife, *AP*6.64 (Paul. Sil.), cf. Aq.*Jb*.41.22. **-τρα, τά,** *payment for sharpening* tools, σιδήρου *IG*2².1672.121; τῶν Βακχίου σιδηρίων Παρμένοντι ὄξυντρα ib.11(2).203 *A* 58 (Delos, iii B.C.), cf. *Supp.Epigr*.4.447.42,453.49,59 (Didyma, ii B.C.). **-ω** [ῡ], fut. ὀξυνῶ Lxx *Wi*.5.20, (παρ-) D.2.11,54.25: aor. ὤξῡνα S.*Tr*.1176: pf. ὤξυγκα (παρ-) Plb.31.1.3, J.*AJ*11.6.7:—Pass., fut. ὀξυνθήσομαι (παρ-) Hp.*Acut*.(*Sp*.)17: aor. ὠξύνθην Hdt. (v. infr.), etc.: pf. ὤξυμμαι (παρ-) Lys.4.8, D.14.16, (ἀπ-) Plb.18.18.13, etc.; later ὤξυσμαι (ἀπ-, συν-) Id.1.22.7, 6.22.4:—*sharpen, point,* ἔγχος ὀ. σιδήρῳ *Epigr.Gr*.790.5 (Dyme); ἄκρη ἐς μυχὸν ὀξυνθεῖσα D.P.177; of the nose, ῥῖνα ὠξυμμένην Gal.17(1).998. II. metaph., *goad to anger, provoke,* τοὐμὸν ὀξῦναι στόμα S. l. c.:—Pass., ὀξυνθείς Hdt.8.138, cf. Lxx *Ez*.21.9(14). 2. intr., *become acute,* of pain, Aret.*SD*2.11. III. Gramm., = ὀξυτονέω, A.D.*Pron*.28.5 (Pass.), 43.10, al. IV. *make acid,* Gal.6.691:—Pass., *to be* or *become so,* of wine, Arist.*GA*753ᵃ23, Luc.*Sat*.26:—so, intr. in Act., Thphr.*HP* 4.3.4.

**ὀξύ-όδους,** όδοντος, ὁ, ἡ, *with sharp teeth*; in Nonn.*D*.40.484, with a neut. Subst. ❀ **-όεις,** εσσα, εν, (ὀξύη) *with beechen shaft, beechen,* ἔγχεα ὀξυόεντα Il.5.568, cf. 50, etc.; δουρὶ μετάλμενος ὀξυόεντι 14.443, cf. Eust.1951.2, Hsch.: the deriv. from ὀξύς is less probable. **-όστρᾰκος,** ον, *with a sharp shell,* Luc.*Lex*.13. **-πᾰγής,** ές, *sharp-pointed,* στάλικες *AP*6.109 (Antip.); ὄνυξ Nonn.*D*.14.385; *prickly,* κάραβος Opp.*H*.1.261. **-παιδερώτινος,** in Lat. form *oxypaederotinus, bright pink, Hist.Aug.Aurelian*.46. **-παραύδητος,** ον, *wildly screaming,* Tim.*Pers*.76. **-παροπτάω,** *concoct too fast,* χυμόν Gal.19.649. ❀ **-πεινος,** ον, *ravenously hungry, ravenous, greedy,* of the eagle, Arist.*HA*619ᵇ29; of persons, Antiph.276, Eub.10.4: metaph., πρὸς τοὺς λόγους ὀ. Plu.2.512f, cf. Cic.*Att*.2.12.2:—later **-πείνης,** ου, ὁ, of one who eats between meals, Anon.*in EN*182.9; τένθης λέγεται ὁ ὀ. καὶ προτένθης Procl.ad Hes.*Op*.522. **-πέπερι,** εως, τό, *mixture of vinegar and pepper,* Xenocr.ap.Orib.2.58.84. ❀ **-πετής,** ές, *flying speedily,* Sch.Od.3.372. **-πετρος,** ον, *with sharp stones,* γῆς ποιὸν εἶδος οἱ γεωργικοὶ φασιν, Hsch. **-πευκής,** ές, *sharp-pointed,* ξίφος A.*Ch*.640 (lyr.). **-πικρος,** ον, *keen, smarting,* Hsch. s. v. ὀξυπευκές; = *acidus, Gloss.* **-πληκτος,** ον, *struck by a sharp blow,* cj. in S.*Ant*.1301. **-πλήξ,** ῆγος, ὁ, ἡ, *accompanying fierce blows,* γόους Id.*Fr*.523. **-ποδέω,** *quicken one's pace, Gloss.* **-ποδητής,** οῦ, ὁ, *one who quickens his pace,* ib. **-ποδία,** ἡ, *quickening of one's pace,* ib. **-πολῠφᾰγία,** ἡ, *quickness of eating and digesting,* ib. (prob.). **-πόριος,** ον (sc. φάρμακον), *a carminative medicine,* Ps.-Gal. 19.717, Aët.5.68; [τροφή] Philum.ap.eund.9.23:—also **-πορος,** ον, Gal.14.751, Orib.*Fr*.46, etc. ❀ **-πόρος,** ον, *with pointed mouth,* ἄγγος Opp.*H*.2.406. II. *quick-passing, active,* of medicines, Dsc.3.51.3. **-πους,** ὁ, ἡ, πουν, τό, *swift-footed,* E.*Or*.1550 (troch.). **-πρῳρος,** ον, *sharp-prowed*: *sharp-pointed,* αἰχμαί A.*Pr*.423 (lyr.); ῥάχις Opp. *H*.3.333: to be written with iota, Achae.ap.*Lex.Mess*.p.408. **-πτέριον,** τό, *hawk, Gloss.* ❀ **-πτερος,** ον, *sharp-* or *swift-winged*: as Subst. ὀ., ὁ, = ὀξύσχοινος, Ps.-Dsc.4.52; but, *hawk,* Clem.Al.*Strom*.5.8.52.1 (in citation of *De*.14.13):—also **-πτερον,** τό, = *falco, Gloss.*; τὰ ὀξύπτερα *swift wings,* Aesop.8. **-πῡγος,** ον, *sharp-rumped, Hippiatr*.14. **-πύθμενος,** ον, *with pointed bottom,* of shell-fish, Xenocr.ap.Orib.2.58.85 (Comp.; -μενοί τε codd.). **-πυκνος,** ον, *in the higher region of the πυκνόν* (q. v.), φθόγγος Cleonid.*Harm*.4,9, Bacch.*Harm*.27, cf. Aristid.Quint.1.6. **-πύνδαξ,** ᾰκος, ὁ, ἡ, = ὀξυπύθμενος, of a cup, Eub.56.4. ❀ **-πώγων,** ον, gen. ωνος, *with a pointed beard,* Heph.Astr.2.2.

**ὀξῠρεγμ-ία,** ἡ, (fr. *ὀξ-ερυγμία, cf. ἐρευγμός) *the sour fumes caused by indigestion, heartburn,* Hp.*Aph*.6.1, Aret.*SA*2.3, Gal.6.344, Aët. 9.43, etc. 2. *the peevishness* or *fretfulness* caused thereby, Ar.*Fr*. 473; cf. κρομμυοξυρεγμία, ὀξωρεγμία. **-ιάω,** *to be troubled with heartburn,* Dsc.3.30, 4.1, Antyll.ap.Orib.6.8.3. **-ιώδης,** ες, *troubled with heartburn,* Hp.*Aph*.6.33, *Acut*.28; *causing heartburn,* φῦσαι Aret.*SD*2.8; ἀπεψία Gal.10.579.

**ὀξῠ-ρεπής,** ές, = ὀξύρροπος, ὀ. δόλῳ with *quick-turning* art, Pi.*O*.9.91; ὀξυρρεπής in Hsch. **-ρρῑν** (*PPetr*.3 p.25 (iii B.C.)) or **-ρρῖς,** ῖνος, ὁ, ἡ, (ῥίς) *with sharp* or *fine nose,* Hp.*Epid*.2.5.1:—also ❀ **-ρρῖνος,** ον, interpol. in Zonar. s. v. Γρυπόν. **-ρρόδῑνον** [ἔλαιον], τό, *rose-oil mixed with vinegar,* Ath.2.67f, Gal.11.559, *Gloss.* **-ρροπία,** ἡ, *quick change,* τῆς ὥρας Vett.Val.299.35. ❀ **-ρροπος,** ον, *turning quickly,* prop. of a delicate balance: metaph., ὀ. πρὸς τὰς ὀργὰς *sudden and quick* to anger, Pl.*Tht*.144a; εἰς ὀργὴν Jul.*Or*.2.65d; νοῦς ὀ. πρὸς τὰς μιαιφονίας Memn.2; also ὀ. θυμός *unstable* temper, Pl.*R*.411b; τὸ ὀ. τῆς νεύσεως *rapidity* or *vehemence,* Longin.18.1; cf. ὀξυρεπής. Adv. -πως D.C.*Fr*.50.3. ❀ **-ρρυγχῑτικόν** (sc. μέτρον), τό, a measure of capacity in Egypt, *PLond*.3.1170ᵛ.79 (iii A.D.), *PGiss*.34.12 (iii A.D.). ❀ **-ρρυγχος,** ον, *sharp-snouted*: metaph., *sharp-pointed,* ῥαφίδες Epich.51; ὁ ὀ. χαρακτήρ, name of a style of handwriting, Phlp.*in APr*.5.9; ὁ ὀ. τύπος Id.*in APo*.1.13, *in de An*.227.15. 2. Subst., ὀ., ὁ, a sharp-snouted Egyptian fish, [Hes.] ap.Ath.3.116b, Str.17.2.4, Ael.*NA*10.46, Ath.7.312b.

**ὀξύς,** ύδος, ἡ, *wood sorrel, Oxalis Acetosella,* Plin.*HN*27.112. 2. = ὀξύσχοινος, *great sea-rush, Juncus acutus,* ib.21.113. 3. = ὀξαλίς, *sorrel, Rumex acetosa,* Gal.11.667.

❀ **ὀξύς,** εῖα, ύ, Ion. fem. ὀξέα Hdt.9.23, al., v.l. in Hp.*Mul*.1.64, al. (in codd. freq. ὀξέη, and so Babr.73.1 metri gr.): ὀξεῖα, poet. for neut. pl. ὀξέα, Hes.*Sc*.348:—*sharp, keen,* whether of a point or an edge, in Hom. and Hes. mostly of weapons or anything made of metal, ἄκων Il.10.335, al.; ἄορ 21.173, Hes.*Sc*.457; βέλος Il.4.185, etc.; also of non-metallic substances, λᾶας 16.739; μοχλός Od.9.382; σκόλοπες Il. 12.56,64; ὀξεῖα κορυφή, of a mountain-peak, Od.12.74; so πάγοι ὀξέες 5.411; λίθος ὀξὺς πεποιημένος *sharpened* so as to serve as a knife, Hdt. 7.69, cf. 3.8; κυρβασίας ἐς ὀξὺ ἀπηγμένας brought to a *point,* Id.7.64; ὄρεα ἐς ὀ. τὰς κορυφὰς ἀ. Id.2.28; τὸ ὀ. the *apex* of a triangle, ib.16; of the heart, Arist.*Resp*.478ᵇ5; τὸ ὀ. τοῦ ᾠοῦ Id.*GA*752ᵇ8; ὀ. γωνία an *acute* angle, Id.*Top*.107ᵃ16, al., Euc.1 *Def*.12, Archim. *Spir*.16; Χρόνος ὀξὺς ὀδόντας Simon.176; ἡ ὀξεῖα, name of a surgical instrument, *Hermes* 38.282, Heliod.ap.Orib.44.23.59; but also, a *pointed splinter* of bone, ib.46.20.5. II. in reference to the senses, 1. of feeling, *sharp, keen,* ὀδύναι Il.11.268; ὀ. ἠέλιος the *piercing* sun, *h.Ap*.374; ὀξειᾶν ἀκτίνων πατήρ, i.e. the Sun, Pi.*O*.7.70; Σείριος ὀξὺς ἐλλάμπων Archil.61; πῦρ ὀ. Anaxipp.1.12; so χιὼν ὀξεῖα Pi.*P*.1.20; so also of grief and the like, ἄχος Il.19.125; μελεδῶναι Od.19.517: and generally, *sharp, severe,* μάχη ὀξέα.. γίνεται *keenly contested,* Hdt.9.23; ὀ. πυρετός Hp.*VM*16 (Sup.); [ἡ νόσος] ὀξεῖα φοιτᾷ καὶ ταχεῖ' ἀπέρχεται S.*Ph*.808; νόσοι, μανίαι, Pi.*O*.8.85, *N*.11.48 (Comp.), cf. Hp.*Acut*. tit., Archig.ap.Gal.9.887; πάθαι Pi.*P*.3.97; ἐπιμομφά Id.*O*.10(11).9, etc. 2. of the sight, ὀξύτατον ὄμμα Id. *N*.10.62; ὄψις.. ὀξυτάτη τῶν διὰ τοῦ σώματος.. αἰσθήσεων Pl.*Phdr*. 250d: freq. in neut. as Adv., ὀξύτατον δέρκεσθαι to be *keenest* of sight, Il.17.675; ὀξύτατα καθορᾶν Pl.*R*.516c; so ὀξὺ νοεῖν notice a thing *sharply,* Il.3.374; ὀξὺ προϊδεῖν Od.5.393; ὀξύτερον βλέπει Ar.*Pl*.1048, *Lys*.1202 (lyr.): prov., ὀξύτερον τοῦ Λυγκέως βλέπειν Id.*Pl*.210, cf. Macar.*Prov*.6.41; also ὀξὺ ἄκουσεν heard *with sharp ear,* Il.17.256, cf. Pl.*Lg*.927b; ὀξεῖαν ἀκοήν.. λόγοις διδοὺς *keen* attention, S.*El*. 30. b. of things that affect the sight, *dazzling, bright,* αὐγὴ Ἠελίου Il.17.372; [Ἠελίου] ὀξύτατον πέλεται φάος εἰσοράασθαι 14.345: hence of colours, Ar.*Pax*1173 (v. φοινικίς 2); αἱ ὀξεῖαι χροιαί Arist. *Phgn*.806ᵇ4; πορφύρα Plu.*Cat.Mi*.6, *PHolm*.20.36; [ἐσθὴς] ὀξυτέρα καὶ τηλαυγεστέρα Ael.*NA*4.46. 3. of sound, *shrill, piercing,* ἀϋτή Il.15.313; ὀξὺ βοήσας 17.89; ὀξὺ δὲ κωκύσασα 18.71; ὀξὺ λεληκώς 22.141; ὀξέα κεκληγώς 17.88, etc.; of whinnying horses, ὀξεῖα χρέμισαν Hes.*Sc*.348; of young pigs, ὀξὺ κεκράγατε Ar.*Ach*.804; of the scream of birds of prey, ὀξέα κλάζων S.*Ant*.112 (anap.); of metals, ἰάχεσκε σάκος ὀξέα καὶ λιγέως Hes.*Sc*.233; also of the wail of the nightingale (cf. ὀξύφωνος), ὄρνιθος ὀ. φθόγγον S.*Ant*.424; so ἐπηλάλαξαν τὸν ὀ. νόμον shrieked their *shrill* song, A.*Th*.952 (lyr.); ὀξὺ μέλος, of the grasshopper, Ar.*Av*.1095 (lyr.). b. of musical tones, in a technical sense, *high-pitched,* opp. βαρύς, φθόγγοι Pl.*Ti*.80a, X. *Cyn*.6.20; ὀξυτάτη χορδή Pl.*Phdr*.268d; φωνὴ ὀξεῖα, βαρεῖα, μέση Arist.*Rh*.1403ᵇ29; τῷ ὀξεῖ ἐν φωνῇ μὲν ἐναντίον τὸ βαρύ, ἐν ὄγκῳ δὲ τὸ ἀμβλὺ Id.*Top*.106ᵃ13. c. in Music, διʼ ὀξειῶν (Dor. -ᾶν) *interval of a fifth,* Philol.6, Arist.*Pr*.920ᵃ24. d. ἡ ὀξεῖα (sc. προσῳδία) the *acute* accent, D.T.630.1, A.D.*Pron*.35.10, al.; τὸν τόνον φυλάσσειν ὀ. ib.60. 1; ὀ. συλλαβή Pl.*Cra*.399b; ὀ. στοιχεῖον S.E.*M*.1.113. 4. of taste, *sharp, pungent, acid,* φακῆ X.*Cyr*.6.2.31; ὄξος Diph.18.1; οἶνος Alex. 141.12; ἐξ ὀξέος καὶ ἁλμυροῦ ξυνθεὶς ζύμωμα Pl.*Ti*.74c. 5. of smell, Arist.*de An*.421ᵃ30; ὀξύτατον ὄζειν τινός Ar.*Ach*.193. III. metaph., of the inner sense, *sharp, keen, hasty,* esp. *quick to anger, passionate,* epith. of Ares, Il.2.440, al.; μένος ὀξὺ *h.Hom*.8.14; καρδίη ὀξυτέρη Thgn.366; θυμὸς ὀ. S.*OC*1193; νέος καὶ ὀ. Pl.*Grg*.463e; οἱ ἀκρόχολοι ὀξεῖς Arist.*EN*1126ᵃ18: so in ὀξύ-θυμος, -κάρδιος, -χολος. 2. *sharp, quick,* δεινοὶ καὶ ὀξεῖς Pl.*Ap*.39b: c. inf., ἐπινοῆσαι ὀ. Th.1.70; γνῶναι.. ὀξύτατοι τὰ ῥηθέντα D.3.15; also εἰς πάντα τὰ μαθήματα ὀξεῖς Pl.*R*.526b; τὰς ἐνθυμήσεις ὀξύς Luc.*Salt*. 81. IV. of motion, *quick, swift,* post-Hom., ὀξυτάτους ἵππους Hdt. 5.9 (v.l. ὠκυτάτους); ἱερακίσκος Ar.*Av*.1112; ὀξυτέρῳ χαλινῷ S.*Ant*. 108 (lyr.); of a report, ὀξεῖα βάξις διῆλθ' Ἀχαιούς Id.*Aj*.998; ὀξεῖαν ἐκβάλλει ῥοήν, of a dying man, Id.*Ant*.1238, cf. A.*Ag*.1389; of a flame, *fierce,* Thphr.*HP*5.9.3; ᾄξας ὀξὺς νότος ὣς S.*Aj*.258 (anap.); τὸ εὔψυχον.. ὀξεῖς ἐνδείκνυνται are *quick* in displaying, Th.4.126; opp. βραδύς, Id.8.96; opp. ῥάθυμος, Arist.*EE*1240ᵃ2; opp. ἡσύχιος, Id. *EN*1116ᵃ9; ὀ. παράγγελμα Onos.10.2; ὀ. καιρός an *urgent* crisis, Id. 6.1, al.; ὁ ὀ. δρόμος the *express* post, *POxy*.900.7 (iv A.D.), 2115.6 (iv A.D.); ὀξεῖς οἱ πόδες αὐτῶν ἐκχέαι αἷμα *Ep.Rom*.3.15: esp. in Adv. (v. infr.). V. regul. Adv. ὀξέως *quickly, soon,* βοηθεῖν, μεταχειρίσαι, Th.6.10,12, etc.; *sharply,* ὁρᾶν, αἰσθάνεσθαι, Pl.*R*.567b, *Phdr*. 263c; poet. ὀξείως *Epigr.Gr*.986.3 (Philae): Comp. ὀξυτέρως Hp. *Epid*.3.17.β'; ὀξυτέρως ἀποθνήσκειν ib.1.2; but, 2. neut. ὀξύ and pl. ὀξέα as Adv., v. supr. II. 2,3: Comp. ὀξύτερον Th.2.8, Pl.*Tht*. 190a: Sup. ὀξύτατον Il.17.675, Pl.*Lg*.741d; or ὀξύτατα Id.*R*.401e, al. (Cf. ὀξίνα, ὄκρις.)

**ὀξῠσιτία,** ἡ, *a disorder in which the food turns acid* on the stomach, like ὀξυρεγμία, Aristid.*Or*.47(23).9.

**ὄξυσμα,** ατος, τό, in pl., *sharpening* of tools, *IG*11(2).158*A*83, al. (Delos, iii B.C.); cf. ὄξυντρα.

**ὀξύ-στερνος,** ον, *sharp-breasted,* of animals as compared with man, Gal.18(1).536. **-στομος,** ον, *sharp-beaked,* of gryphons, A.*Pr*.803; of Io's gadfly, ib.674; of a gnat, Ar.*Av*.244 (lyr.). 2. of a sword, *sharp-edged,* E.*Supp*.1206; of a cupping instrument, *sharp-rimmed,* Antyll.ap.Orib.7.16.15. **-σχοινος,** ὁ, *great sea-rush, Juncus acutus,* Batr.164, Dsc.4.52, Gal.12.136. **-τελής,** ές, *with sharp ends, diamond shaped,* διόπτραι, of open spaces in lattice-work, dub. l. in Lyd.*Mag*.3.37 (fort. **ὀξυτενής,** ές, eodem sensu, cf. Suid.).

**ὀξύτης**, ητος, ἡ, *sharpness, pointedness*, of acute angles, Pl.*Ti.* 61e, cf. 56d. II. of the senses, 1. of sound, *sharpness*, opp. βαρύτης, Id.*Phlb.*17c, *Tht.*163c. 2. of taste, *pungency, acidity*, in pl., Hp.*VM*19, *Acut.*61, cf. Gal.11.656. 3. of sight, Arist.*HA* 492ᵃ4. III. metaph., *sharpness, cleverness*, τῆς ψυχῆς Phld.*Rh.* 2.31 S.; σκέψεως ibid.; διαφέροντα τῇ τέχνῃ τῇ τ' ὀξύτητι Philosteph. Com.1; ὀ. ἐς τὰ πολιτικά Luc.*Im.*17. IV. *quickness*, of motion, action, or occurrence, Critias 37 D., Pl.*Chrm.*160b, *Plt.*306c, al.; ταῖς ὀξύτησι..ἀκολουθεῖν D.24.95; ἡ ὀ. τοῦ καιροῦ the *pressing* occasion, Plu.*Pyrrh.*2, D.S.15.43. V. = ὀξεῖα, ἡ, v. ὀξύς II.3d, A.D.*Adv.* 138.16, cf. Arist.*Po.*1456ᵇ33: pl., Pl.*Cra.*399a.

**ὀξύ-τόμος**, ον, *sharp-cutting, keen*, Pi.*P.*4.263. **-τονέω**, *pronounce with an acute accent*, i.e. on the last syllable, τὴν λέξιν Ath.9. 400b, cf. Ph.1.243, Cleonid.*Harm.*12, A.D.*Synt.*264.4:—Pass., Id. *Pron.*29.3, al., Gal.18(2).518. 2. in Music, *make high-pitched*, τοὺς φθόγγους Nicom.*Harm.*10. **-τόνησις**, εως, ἡ, *a pronouncing with an acute accent*, Eust.60.13. **-τονητέον**, *one must pronounce oxytone*, *AB*457. **-τονος**, ον, *sharp-sounding, piercing*, of sound, ὀ. γόοι S.*El.*243 (lyr.); ὀξυτόνους ᾠδὰς θρηνήσει Id.*Aj.*631 (lyr.); ὀξυτόνου διὰ πνεύματος Id.*Ph.*1093 (lyr.). II. *sung to a high note*, D.H.*Comp.*11; *having the acute accent*, Hermog.*Id.*1.12, A.D.*Pron.* 33.24, al. Adv. -νως ib.29.2, S.E.*M.*1.222, Eust.41.4. III. Subst. -τονον, τό, v. ὀξύγονον. ❋ **-τόρος**, ον, *piercing, pointed*, πίτυς ὀ. the pine *with its sharp spines*, *AP*4.1.16 (Mel.). **-τρίφυλλον** [ῐ], τό, = ὀξύφυλλον, Scrib.Larg.163, Plin.*HN*21.54, *Gloss.* ❋ **-τυρία**, ἡ, *bright Tyrian purple*, *Edict.Diocl.*24.4, al. **-φαγρος**, ὁ, a kind of φάγρος, a sea-fish, v.l. in Opp.*H.*1.140. **-φᾰής**, ές, *keen-sighted*, Nonn.*D.* 7.214, 28.303 (with v.l. **ὀξυφανής**). **-φεγγής**, ές, *bright-beaming*, epith. of ῥόδα, Chaerem.8. **-φθογγος**, ον, = ὀξύφωνος, Ath.14.633f, *AP*6.51. **-φλεγμᾰσία**, Ion. -ίη, ἡ, *violent inflammation*, Hp.*Virg.* 1. **-φοίνῑκον**, τό, = ὀποπάναξ, Ruf.*Fr.*80. **-φρων**, ονος, ὁ, ἡ, *acute, sagacious*, E.*Med.*641 (lyr.); *crafty*, Ptol.*Tetr.*165. **-φυλλος**, ον, *with pointed leaves*, θρίδαξ Dsc.4.23. II. **-φυλλον**, τό, = τρίφυλλον, Id.3.109, Gal.12.144. **-φωνέω**, *to have a shrill voice*, Id.16.607, Herod.Med. in *Rh.Mus.*58.71. 2. *pronounce with an acute accent*, Eust.22.4 (Pass.). **-φωνία**, ἡ, *high pitch of voice*, Hp.*Coac.*252, Arist.*EN*1125ᵃ15; opp. βαρύτης, Id.*GA*788ᵃ3. **-φωνος**, ον, *shrill-voiced, piercing* (cf. ὀξύς II.3), Telest.5; of the nightingale, S.*Tr.*963 (lyr.), Babr.12.3; *with high-pitched voice*, γυναῖκες Alex.Aphr.*Pr.*1. 97: Comp. -ότερος Arist.*HA*538ᵇ13, *GA*787ᵇ9. **-χειρ**, χειρος, ὁ, *quick with the hands, quick to strike, quarrelsome*, Lys.4.8, Men. 1048, Theoc.*Ep.*22.2; ὀ. κοὐκ ἐγκρατής Nicom.Com.1.33. 2. ὀξύχειρι σὺν κτύπῳ with *quick* beating *of the hands* in lamentation, A.*Ch.* 23 (lyr.). **-χειρία**, ἡ, *quickness of hand*, Alex.323; of conjurers, S.E.*M.*2.39; ἀπνευστὶ καὶ -χειρίᾳ δρᾶν τι Ph.2.87. **-χολος**, ον, *quick to anger*, Sol.13.26, S.*Ant.*955 (v.l. for ὀξυχόλως), *AP*9.127; τὸ ὀ. Luc.*Fug.*19. **-ωπέω**, *to be sharp-sighted*, Thphr.*Sens.*8, Ph. 1.392, Alex.Aphr.*in Top.*327.13; ὀ. πρὸς τὴν κατάληψιν Anachars. ap.S.E.*M.*7.55. **-ωπής**, ές, (ὤψ) *sharp-sighted*, ὀφθαλμοὶ -έστατοι Arist.*HA*492ᵃ9; ὁ ἁλιάετος -έστατος ib.620ᵃ2, cf. Luc.*Icar.*14: Comp. -έστερος Ph.1.531, 2.546. Adv., -έστερον βλέπεις Suid. s.v. Λυγκέως; -έστατα δρᾶν Ph.1.338; βλέπειν Herm.ap.Stob.1.49.45. 2. metaph., θέξις -εστέρα Marcellin.*Puls.*19. II. Act., *sharpening the sight*, Dsc.3.45. **-ωπία**, ἡ, *sharp-sightedness*, Arist.*PA*691ᵃ25, *Pr.*876ᵇ25, Dsc.2.56, S.E.*M.*5.81; λογισμοῦ Ph.2.314. **-ωπίας**, ου, ὁ, *one who sees sharply*, Poll.2.51. **-ωπός**, όν, = ὀξυωπής I, Arist.*HA*618ᵇ8, *PA*657ᵇ26. **-ώριος**, ον, (ὄρος) *with sharp angles*, of dressed stone, *IG*7.3073.133 (Lebad., ii B.C.; cf. εὐθύωρος).

**ὀξ-ώδης**, ες, *like vinegar, acid*, Gal.8.34, al., S.E.*P.*1.110, Alex. Aphr.*in Sens.*83.19, al. **-ωρεγμία**, ἡ, = ὀξυρεγμία, Phryn.*PS* p.97 B. **-ωτός**, ή, όν, (as if from ὀξόω) *pickled*, Ar.*Fr.*130.

**ὄοιγα**· φαρέτρα, Hsch. **ὄον**, τό, *the fruit of the service-tree*, v. ὄα (A). **ὅου**, Ep. gen. for οὗ, *of whom*, v. ὅς. **ὅπᾳ**, v. ὅπῃ. **ὀπαδός**, v. ὀπηδός.

**ὀπάζω**, impf. ὤπαζον Il.8.341; Ep. ὀπ- 16.730: Ep. fut. ὀπάσσω Od.8.430, 21.214: aor. ὤπασα Il.13.416, Hes.*Th.*974, Pi.*N.*1.16, and Trag. (v. infr.); Ep. and Lyr. also ὄπασσα, Od.10.204, Pi.*I.*7(6). 38:—Med., aor. ὠπασάμην, Ep. 3 sg. ὀπάσσατο Il.19.238; 2 sg. subj. ὀπάσσεαι 10.238:—Pass., only in pres. (v. fin.):—poet. Verb, perh. causal of ἕπομαι, *make to follow, send with* one, *give as a companion* or *follower*, ἐπεί ῥά οἱ ὤπασα πομπόν Il.13.416; σοὶ γάρ με πατὴρ ἅμα πομπὸν ὄπασσεν 24.461, cf. Od.9.90; ἅμ' ἡγεμόν' ἐσθλὸν ὄπασσον 15.310; ἀρχὸν δὲ μετ' ἀμφοτέροισιν ὄπασσα 10.204; πολὺν δέ μοι ὤπασε λαόν, i.e. made me leader over many, Il.9.483, cf. Pi.*N.*1. 16; ὦ Ζεῦ, γυναικῶν οἷον ὤπασας γένος A.*Th.*256:—Med., *bid* another *follow* one, *take with* one, *take as a companion*, σὺ δὲ χείρον' ὀπάσσεαι Il.10.238; Νέστορος υἷας ὀπάσσατο 19.238; κήρυκά τ' ὀπασσάμενος καὶ ἑταῖρον Od.10.59:—Nic. uses the Med. in act. sense, σκολόπενδρα.. ὀπάζεται ἀνδράσι κῆρα *Th.*813: Hes. never has it in this sense. II. also of things, *make* or *give to be with* a person, then simply, *give, grant*, τούτῳ..Ζεὺς κῦδος ὀπάζει *gives* him glory *to be with* him, Il.8. 141, cf. 17.566; κτήματα, ἀρετήν, κάλλος, ἀοιδήν, φῆμιν, ὀϊζύν, etc., freq. in Hom., Od.21.214, 13.45, Il.6.156, Od.8.498, 24.201, 23.210, al.; πολλὰ γὰρ ὤπασε παιδί *gave* her *as a portion*, Il.22.51: τέλος ἐσθλὸν ὀ. *grant* a happy end, Hes.*Op.*474; ὄλβον, ἄγρην, Id.*Th.* 420, 442; εὐδίαν ἐκ χειμῶνος ὀ. Pi.*I.*7(6).38, al.; "Ὕβρις..πλοῦτον.. ἀλλότριον ὤπασεν B.14.60; πῦρ ἐγώ σφιν ὤπασα A.*Pr.*254, cf. 8, 30, *Pers.*762, *Eu.*530 (lyr.); a few times in E., e.g. *Med.*517, twice in Ar., *Eq.*200 (mock heroic), *Th.*973 (lyr.): with pleon. inf., Πατρόκλῳ..κόμην ὀπάσαιμι φέρεσθαι, like δίδωμι ἔχειν, Il.23.151, cf. Pi.*O.*9.66:—Med., καλάμινθον ὀπάζεο *take to yourself*.., Nic.*Th.*60, cf. 520. 2. *give besides* something else, *add*, ἔργῳ δ' ἔργον ὄπαζε *h.Merc.*120; χάριν ἅμ' ὄπασσον ἀοιδῇ *h.Hom.*24.5; μελέταν ἔργοις ὀ. *devote*, Pi.*I.*6(5).67; ἔργον ὤπασεν πρὸς ἀσπίδι *put* the work of art *on* the shield, A.*Th.*492. III. *press hard, chase*, "Ἕκτωρ ὤπαζε κάρη κομόωντας Ἀχαιούς Il.8.341; χαλεπὸν δέ σε γῆρας ὀπάζει ib.103; πολὺν καθ' ὅμιλον ὀπάζων (sc. αὐτήν) 5.334, cf. 17.462; φόνια δ' ὤπασας λέχε' ἀπὸ γᾶς *didst chase* them *away*, E.*El.*1192 (lyr.):—Pass., ποταμὸς.. ὀπαζόμενος Διὸς ὄμβρῳ a torrent *forced on* by rain, Il.11.493. IV. ὀπασθείς· ἐκ τῶν ὀπίσω δεθείς, καὶ ἐξαγκωνισθείς, Hsch. (but cf. ὀσταθείς Id.). (The relation to ἕπομαι, ὀπαδός, ὀπάων is uncertain.)

**ὀπαῖος**, α, ον, *with a hole* or *opening*, διὰ τῆς ὀπαίας κεραμίδος, = διὰ τῆς καπνοδόκης, through the tile *with a hole in it* (for the smoke to escape), Diph.84, cf. Moer.p.292 P., Poll.2.54:—also **ὀπαῖον**, τό, *IG* 1².374.127–139 (pl.), Plu.*Per.*13; cf. ὀπή.—On the reading ἀν' ὀπαῖα Od.1.320, v. ἀνοπαῖα.

**ὀπάλλιος**, ὁ, *opal*, Orph.*L.*282; *opalus*, Plin.37.80.

**ὀπαστόν**· τὸ ἐφόδιον, Πέρσαι, Hsch. (Perh. OPers. *upastā* 'help', 'aid'.) **ὀπατόν**, *laseratum*, *Gloss.*

**ὄπατρος**, ον, = ὁμοπάτριος, *by the same father*, κασίγνητος καὶ ὄπατρος Il.11.257, 12.371:—also **ὀπάτριος**, ον, Lyc.452.

❋ **ὀπάων** [ᾱ], ονος, ὁ, as in Hom. and Trag.; later Ion. ὀπέων, ωνος, Hdt.9.50, 51, restored by Dind. in 5.111: (v. ὀπάζω fin.):—*comrade* in war, *esquire*, denoting the slight subordination in which one hero stood to another, as Meriones to Idomeneus, Il.8.263, 10.58, etc.; Phoenix to Peleus, 23.360; so, = ὑπασπιστής, Hdt.5.111. 2. generally, *follower, attendant*, B.17.35, Hdt.9.50, 51, A.*Ch.*769, *Supp.* 492, 954, S.*Ant.*1108; ὀ. μήλων a shepherd, Pi.*P.*9.64; of a female, *h.Cer.*440.—Cf. ὀπηδός. II. as Adj., *following*, ὀπάονι ῥιπῇ Opp. *H.*5.489; ὀ. Νύμφην *IG*14.1389 i 52.

❋ **ὀπεάς**, ᾰτος, τό, *awl*, Poll.10.141 (v.l. ὄπεαρ); dat. written ὑπέατι in Hdt.4.70, cf. Hsch. s.v. ὕπεα, and ῥάπτει ὑπητίῳ *rupiat*, *Gloss.*:— Dim. **ὀπήτιον**, τό, Nicoch.9 (dub., ὄπεαρ Kock), Hp.*Epid.*5.45, Lxx *Ex.*21.6, *De.*15.17, *Peripl.M.Rubr.*17; **ὀπητίδιον**, Poll.7.83. (Prob. from same root as ὀπή.)

**ὅπερ**, Ep. for ὥσπερ, Il.7.114.

❋ **ὀπέρ**, = ὑπέρ, *Schwyzer*664.16 (Orchom. Arc., iv B.C.).

**ὀπερδικίω**, = ὑπερδικέω, *Schwyzer*511.5 (Lebad., ii B.C.).

**ὀπευεῖ**· περισκοπεῖ, βλέπει, Hsch. (but cf. ὀπιπεύει Id.). **ὀπέων**, v. ὀπάων.

❋ **ὀπή**, ἡ, *opening, hole*, ὀπὰς γὰρ εἶχεν οὐκ ὀλίγας [τὸ τριβώνιον] Ar. *Pl.*715; a mouse's *hole*, Sannyr.8; of *holes in the earth*, Arist.*HA* 559ᵃ4, al.; in a door, Luc.*Asin.*52; in a rock, Lxx *Ex.*33.22; of an orifice in the body, Poll.5.73; ἡ ὀπὴ τῶν ὤτων Id.2.84 (cod. B). 2. *hole in the roof*, serving as a chimney, = κάπνη, καπνοδόκη, Ar.*V.*317 (lyr.), 350; καὶ δι' ὀπῆς κἀπὶ τέγους Id.*Fr.*11, cf. Xenarch.4.11. II. pl., in Archit., *holes* in the frieze left to receive the beam-ends, Vitr.4. 2.4; later, of *windows, lights in doors*, αἱ ὀ. τῶν τοίχων Ptol.ap.Simp. *in Cael.*710.21; σιδήρια ἐξ ὀπῆς *IG*4.39 (Aegina, v B.C.). III. (ὄψομαι, ὄπωπα) *sight*, τοὶ μήτ' ἀκουὰν μήτ' ὀπὰν πεπαμένοι Cerc.4.22.

**ὅπη**, Ep. ὅππη, both in Hom., v. infr. (better written ὅπῃ A.D. *Adv.*209.27, Eust.174.1); Dor. ὅπᾳ *Leg.Gort.*2.35, etc. (ὅππᾳ *Com. Adesp.*p.126 D.), also ὅπη *Leg.Gort.*1.42, *Berl.Sitzb.*1927.158 (Cyrene), etc., and ὅπει *IG*12(3).248.11 (Anaphe), etc.; Aeol. ὅππα ib. 12(2).645 a 47, Theoc.28.4; but ὅππᾳ prob. in Alc.*Supp.*1 A.4; Ion. ὅκῃ (better ὅκῃ) Hdt. (v. infr.):—Adv., relat. and indirect interrog.: I. of Place, *by which* or *what way, in which* or *what direction* or *part*: sts. nearly = ὅπου, *where*, Il.22.321, Od.9.457; εἰρωτᾶν ὅκῃ εἴη v.l. in Hdt.5.87; ὅππῃ τ' ἰθύσῃ, τῇ τ' εἴκουσι στίχες ἀνδρῶν *to whatever point*.., at that point.., Il.12.48; ὅκῃ ἰθύσειε στρατεύεσθαι Hdt.1.204, cf. 2.146; ἀμηχανῶ..ὅπᾳ τράπωμαι A.*Ag.*1532 (lyr.); ἐμβαλοῦ μ' ὅπῃ θέλεις S.*Ph.*481 codd. II. of Manner, *in what way, how, as*, ὅπῃ νόος ἐστὶν ἑκάστου Il.20.25, cf. Od.1.347: more freq. in Trag. and Att., as A.*Pr.*586, 906 (both lyr.), *Ag.*67 (anap.), al., Th.1.129, Lys. 14.4, etc.: joined with ὅπως, ὅπῃ ἔχει καὶ ὅπως Pl.*R.*612a, cf. *Lg.* 899a, b, etc.; ὅπῃ ἔτυχεν Arist.*GA*743ᵃ21 (v.l. ὅπου); ὅπῃ ἄν, with subj., ὅπῃ ἂν δοκῇ ἀμφοτέροις Foed.ap.Th.5.18; ὅπᾳ κα δικαιότατα Dor.Foed.ap.eund.5.79, cf. 8.56; ἔστιν ὅπῃ *in a way*, Pl.*Prt.*331d; ἔσθ' ὅπῃ..; Id.*R.*486b; οὐκ ἔστιν ὅπῃ Aeschin.3.209 (as v.l.). III. with other Particles, ὅπῃ δή Il.22.185, etc.; ὅπῃ ποτέ *in what possible direction* or *manner*, Pl.*Sph.*230c, *R.*372e; ὅπῃ δή ποτε Id.*Ep.*338a: c. gen., τοὺς ὅπῃ ποτὲ κατοικοῦντας Εὐρώπης Plu.*Per.*17; ὅπῃ οὖν or ὁπηοῦν, *in any direction* or *way whatever*, Pl.*Prt.*353d, *Lg.*652a; ὁπῃγοῦν Id.*Tht.*187d fort. ὁπητιοῦν, cf. *Ap.*35b); ὅπηπερ, ὅπηπερ ἄν, S.*OT*1458 (as v.l.), Pl.*Sph.*251a, *Ti.*45c, etc.; cf. ὁπωστιοῦν.

**ὀπηδ-εύω**, = sq., A.R.4.675, 974. ❋ **-έω**, Dor. ὀπᾱδέω (v. ὀπηδός), used by Hom. only in 3 sg. pres. ὀπηδεῖ, and impf. ὀπήδει (without augm.): inf. ὀπηδεῖν *h.Ap.*530:—*follow, accompany, attend*, τινι Il. 2.184, 24.368, Pi.*P.*4.287; also ἅμα τινί Od.7.165, Hes.*Th.*80, *h.Ap.* l.c.; μετά τινι, v. infr. II. II. of things (cf. ἕπομαι II), ἀνεμώλια γάρ μοι ὀπηδεῖ [τόξα] useless do they *go with* me, Il.5.216; ἀρετήν σὴν.., ἥ τοι ὀπηδεῖ Od.8.237; ἐκ δὲ Διὸς τιμὴ καὶ κῦδος ὀπηδεῖ Il.17.251, cf. Hes.*Op.*142, 313, Thgn.933, etc.; μετ' ἀνδράσι λιμὸς ὀπηδεῖ Hes. *Op.*230; μετ' ἴχνια Κύπριδος ὀ. Call.*Del.*19.—Ep. Verb, rare in Trag., as ὀπαδεῖ A.*Fr.*475; ὀπαδοῦσ' prob. in Id.*Ag.*426 (lyr.), and once in a late Pap., *Sammelb.*4324.11 (Tab. Defix.): ὀπαδός however is used by Trag. **-ησις**, εως, Dor. ὀπάδησις [ᾱ], ιος, ἡ, *a following after, attending, pursuit*, Critoap.Stob.2.8.24. **-ητήρ**· σύνοδος, ἀκόλουθος,

Hsch. ⊛ -ός, ὁ, Dor. ὀπᾱδός, which is also the usual form in Trag. and Prose (v. infr.) (neither form occurs in Hom., though ὀπηδός may be inferred from ὀπηδέω), *attendant* (cf. the Homeric ὀπάων), S.*Tr.* 1264 (anap.), E.*Alc.*136; of body-guards, A.*Supp.*985: c. gen., Πάν, Ματρὸς μεγάλας ὀπαδέ Pi.*Fr.*95; ἀοιδὰ στεφάνων ἀρετᾶν τε.. ὀ. Id.*N.* 3.8; τέκνων ὀ., of a παιδαγωγός, E.*Med.*53; πυκνοστίκτων ὀ. ἐλάφων *pursuing* them, of Artemis, S.*OC*1093 (lyr.); ἀστέρες.. νυκτὸς ὀ. Theoc.2.166; τὴν Ἑκάτην ὀπαδὸν Ἀρτέμιδος εἶναι Phld.*Piet.*91, cf. 33. II. as Adj., c. dat., *following, accompanying, attending*, ἐγὼ Μούσῃσιν ὀπηδός *h.Merc.*450; πτεροῖς ὀπαδοῖς ὕπνου κελεύθοις *following* the ways of sleep (ὀπαδοῦσ' *following* on wing the ways of sleep, cj. Dobree), A.*Ag.*426 (lyr.); σταγόνα σπονδῖτιν, θυέεσσιν ὀπηδόν *AP* 6.190 (Gaet.).—Poet. word, used by Pl.*Phdr.*252c, *Phlb.*63e, and in late Prose, Phld. (v. supr.), Plu.*Alc.*23, Jul.*Or.*4.157a (ὀπηδός Ant. Lib.7.7).

**ὀπήεις**, εσσα, εν, (ὀπή) *with a hole*, δίφρος ὀ., i.e. an obstetric chair, Hp.*Mul.*2.114.

**ὀπηλίκος**, η, ον, relat. and indirect interrog., *however big* (or *small*), *how big*, Pl.*Lg.*737c, Epicur.*Ep.*1 p.16 U.; exclamatory, *how big!* Diocl.*Fr.*145; indef. **ὀπηλικοσοῦν**, Arist.*Cael.*274$^a$14, al., Epicur.*Ep.*1 p.16 U.; **ὀπηλικοσδηποτοῦν**, Hp.*Superf.*27.

⊛ **ὄπημος**, v. ὀπτῆμος.

**ὀπηνίκᾰ**, Dor. **ὀπᾱνίκα**, Adv., relat. and indirect interrog., *at what point of time, at what hour, on what day*, more precise than ὁπότε, S. *OC*434, Th.4.125, Theoc.23.33; though sts. it cannot be distd. from ὁπότε, Pl.*Alc.*1.105d, Jul.*Or.*7.204a, al.; ὁπότε καὶ ὁ. Pl.*Lg.*772d; ὁ. ἄν *at whatever hour* or *time*, S.*Ph.*464; *whenever*, *PGiss.*53.3 (iv A.D.); simply, *when*, Lxx 4*Ma.*2.16. 2. in indirect questions, in answer to a direct question, πηνίκ' ἐστὶν ἄρα τῆς ἡμέρας;—ὀπηνίκα; what time of day is it?—*what time*, do you say? Ar.*Av.* 1499. 3. c. gen., οὐδεὶς οἶδ' ὁ. ἐστὶ τοὐνιαυτοῦ *what time* of year, Id.*Fr.*569.7. II. with conditional or causal force, ὁ. ἐφαίνετο ταῦτα πεποιηκώς *when once* it was seen that.., D.18.14, cf. 21.42.

**ὀπηοῦν, ὅπηπερ, ὅπῃ ποτέ**, v. ὅπῃ III. **ὄπης**, ητος, ὁ, v. ἔρπης II. **ὀπητίδιον, ὀπήτιον**, v. ὄπεας. **ὀπητιοῦν**, Adv., v. ὅπῃ III.

**ὀπίας** (sc. τυρός), ὁ, *cheese made from milk curdled with fig-juice* (ὀπός), Ar.*V.*353 (with a pun on ὀπή); in full, τυρὸς ὀπίας E.*Cyc.*136, cf. Ath.14.658c; v. ὀπίζω.

**ὀπιδνός**, ή, όν, *dreaded, awful*, A.R.2.292 (Sup.).

**ὀπιέλαιος**, ὁ, name of a plant, dub. in *Inscr.Délos* 366*B* 19 (iii B.C.).

**ὀπίζομαι**, Lacon. **ὀπίδδομαι** *IG*5(1).919, Hom. only pres. and impf. 2 and 3 sg.: later also part. (v. infr.), and aor. ὠπίσατο Q.S.2. 618: (ὄπις):—*regard with awe and dread*, Διὸς δ' ὠπίζετο μῆνιν Od.14. 283; τῶν δ' γ' ὀπίζετο μῆνιν Hes.*Sc.*21; σὸν θυμὸν ὀπίζομαι Od.13.148; μητρὸς.. ὠπίζετ' ἐφετμὴν Il.18.216; ἐμὲ δ' οὐδὲν ὀπίζεο νόσφιν ἐόντα 22. 332, cf. *h.Merc.*382: abs. in part., *feel awe* or *reverence*, Pi.*P.*4.86, *I.*3. 5; χάρις ὀπιζομένα *filled with reverence*, Id.*P.*2.17. 2. after Hom., *care for*, c. gen. pers., Thgn.734, 1148, A.R.2.181, Man.6.218:—so later in Act., σώματος.. ὀπίζων *App.Anth.*3.143.—Ep. and Lyr. Verb, never in Trag.

**ὀπίζω**, (ὀπός) *extract juice from*, θριδακίνην Thphr.*HP*7.6.2; τὸν καυλὸν καὶ τὰς ῥίζας ib.9.1.3:—Pass., *to be extracted*, Gal.14.62; *ooze out*, D.S.5.41. II. ὀ. [γάλα] *curdle* milk *with fig-juice* (ὀπός), Arist. *Mete.*384$^a$22; cf. ὀπίας.

**ὄπῑθε** and **ὄπῑθεν**, poet. and late Gr. for ὄπισθε, ὄπισθεν.

⊛ **ὀπῑθόμβροτος**, ον, poet. for ὀπισθόμβροτος, *following a mortal*, ὀ. αὔχημα the glory *that lives after men*, Pi.*P.*1.92.

**Ὀπῖκοί**, οἱ, *the Opici* or *Osci* (*Opsci*, Fest.p.218 L.), an ancient people of Southern Italy, Arist.*Pol.*1329$^b$19, Str.5.4.3:—also **Ὄπικες**, v.l. in Th.6.2; **Ὀπικία**, ἡ, *their country*, ib.4: hence, II. **Ὀπικός**, ή, όν, *barbarous*, *AP*5.131 (Phld.), cf. Juv.3.207: hence **ὀπικίζω**, = βαρβαρίζω, Lyd.*Mens.*1.13, as v.l. for ὀππικίζω; also ὀφφικίζω ibid.: **ὀππικιστής**, *opicus*, Gloss.

**ὀπικός**, ή, όν, *made of opium*, *PTeb.*273.42 (ii/iii A.D.).

**ὄπιον**, τό, Dim. of ὀπός, *poppy-juice, opium*, Diocl.*Fr.*94, Dsc.2. 152, *POxy.*1088.6, al. (i A.D.), Plin.*HN*20.199, Gal.13.269, Alex. Trall.2.1.

**ὀπίουρος**, ὁ, *peg, pin*, Arist.*Pr.*915$^a$11 codd. (leg. ἐπίουρος).

⊛ **ὀπιπᾶ**· ἐξαπατᾶ, ἀπαταιῶν, Hsch.; i.e. ὀπιπᾷ· ἐξαπατᾷ, and ὀπῖπα· ἀπατεών (cf. γυναικοπίπης, παρθενοπίπης, παιδοπίπης, πυρροπίπης).

**ὀπῖπ-ευτήρ**, ῆρος, ὁ, *starer, gaper*, Nonn.*D.*37.270, etc.; also, = παρθενοπίπης, ib.7.193, Man.6.584. ⊛ **-εύω**, *stare at*, with collat. notion of spying, *watch*, ὀπιπεύσεις δὲ γυναῖκας Od.19.67; or of fear, τί δ' ὀπιπεύεις πολέμοιο γεφύρας; Il.4.371, cf. Hes.*Op.*29. II. *watch, spy*, οὐ γάρ σ' ἐθέλω βαλέειν.. λάθρῃ ὀπιπεύσας, ἀλλ' ἀμφαδόν Il.7.243; εὖ μάλ' ὀπιπεύοντα.. βάλλειν Hes.*Op.*806, cf. Musae.101, Orph.*A.*249:—Med., *to be on the alert*, Onos.10.26. III. *seduce*, Man.3.196:—Pass., δολεροῖσιν -ευθεῖσαι ἔπεσσιν Id.6.182. (Redupl. from ὀπ-, cf. ὄπ-ωπα.)

**ὄπῐς**, ῐδος, ἡ, acc. ὄπιν Il. and Hes. (v. infr.), but in Od. and other Poets also ὄπιδα; poet. dat. ὄπι, v. II. 1; acc. ὄπιν by mistake for ὄπα, Maiist.58: I. of the gods, 1. in bad sense, as always in Hom., ὄπις θεῶν *the vengeance* or *visitation* of the gods for transgressing divine laws, θεῶν ὄπιν οὐκ ἀλέγοντες Il.16.388, Hes.*Op.*251; οὐδ' ὄπιδα τρομέουσι θεῶν Od.20.215; οὐδὲ θεῶν ὄπιν αἰδέσατ' οὐδὲ τράπεζαν 21.28; θ. ὄπιν εἰδότες Hes.*Op.*187; ὄπιν ἀθανάτων πεφυλαγμένος εἶναι ib.706, cf. Theoc.25.4: also without θεῶν, *divine vengeance*, οὐκ ὄπιδα φρονέοντες ἐνὶ φρεσίν Od.14.82; τοῖς ὄπιδος.. δέος ἐν φρεσὶ πίπτει ib.88; of the avenging goddesses, κακὴν ὄπιν ἀποδοῦναι Hes.*Th.*222. 2. in good sense, *the care* or *favour* of the gods, θεῶν ὄπιν αἰτεῖν Pi.*P.*8. 71. II. of men, 1. *the awful regard* which men pay to the gods, *religious awe, veneration, obedience*, οὔτε δαιμόνων οὔτε θεῶν ὄπιν ἔχοντας paying no *regard* to.. (cf. ὀπίζομαι), Hdt.9.76, cf. 8.143; so also ὄπι (v.l. ὄπιν) δίκαιον ξένων strict in his *reverence towards* strangers, i.e. in the duties of hospitality (al. ξένον), Pi.*O.*2.6; αἰδεσθεὶς ὄπιδα.. πολιοῖο γενείου maintaining *due reverence for* the hoary beard, Mosch. 4.117. 2. *pious care* or *zeal*, Pi.*I.*5(4).58. (Hence ὀπίζομαι, ὀπιδνός.)

**ὀπῖσαμβώ**, ἡ, (ἀμβαίνω, ἀναβαίνω) *a going backwards*, S.*Fr.*406: metaph. in Chrysipp.*Stoic.*3.202, cf. Ael.Dion.*Fr.*415.

**ὄπισθᾰ**, Aeol. and Dor. for ὄπισθε, A.D.*Adv.*153.18.

**ὀπισθ-άγκωνα**, Adv. *with the arms behind the back*, *PMag.Par.*1. 301 (-αγγωνα Pap.), Tz.ad Lyc.704, Gloss. **-έκτιτος**, ον, gloss on παλίντιτος, Hsch.

⊛ **ὄπισθεν**, in Ion. (Hdt.4.72, al., *SIG*46.65 (Halic., v B.C.), etc.) and late Att. (Luc.*Am.*16, etc.) **ὄπισθε** before a conson., as also in Poets, E.*Cyc.*545, *IT*1333: poet. also **ὄπῑθεν** Il.6.181, al., Pi.*O.*10(11).35, A.*Pers.*1001 (lyr.):—Adv.: I. of Place, *behind, at the back*, opp. πρόσθε, Il.5.595; πρόσθε λέων ὄπιθεν δὲ δράκων μέσση δὲ χίμαιρα 6.181; ὄπισθεν καταλιπεῖν Od.10.209; μένειν Il.9.332, etc.; πέμψει οὖρον ὄ. Od.15.34; ὄπιθεν κομόωντες with long *back*-hair, Il.2.542; ὄπιθεν κομόωσαι ἔθειραι *IG*12(9).1179.9 (Euboea); ὄ. ἕπεσθαι, ἀκολουθεῖν, A. l.c., etc.; οἱ ὄπιθεν *those who are left behind*, e.g. at home, Od.11.66; but also, *those who are in the rear*, X.*Cyr.*2.2.8; εἰ τοὺς ὄ. ἐς τὸ πρόσθεν ἄξομεν shall bring the *rear ranks* to the front (metaph.), S.*Aj.* 1249; αἱ ὄ. ἁψῖδες the *hinder* fellies, Hdt.4.72; τὰ ὄ. the *hinder parts, rear, back*, Il.11.613; οἱ ὄ. ἁρμοί *IG*1$^2$.372.117; εἰς τοὔπισθεν *back, backwards*, E.*Ph.*1410, Pl.*Sph.*261b, etc.; εἰς τ. τοξεύειν, i.e. '*versis sagittis*', like the Parthians, X.*An.*3.3.10: opp. ἐκ τοὔπισθεν Ar.*Ec.*482, cf. Th.7.79, X.*An.*4.1.6; ἐν τῷ ὄ. Pl.*R.*614c, X.*Cyn.*9.8, etc.; ὄ. ποιήσασθαι τὸν ποταμόν place the river *in his rear*, Id.*An.*1.10. 9. 2. Prep. c. gen., *behind*, στῆ δ' ὄπιθεν δίφροιο Il.17.468; ὄπισθε μάχης 13.536; ὄπισθε τῆς θύρης Hdt.1.9; ἔμπροσθέ τε Θερμοπυλέων καὶ ὄ. Id.7.176; ὄ. ἐμοῦ.. εἰσῄει Pl.*Smp.*175a, etc.: sts. after its case, δίφρου ὄπισθεν Il.24.15; ἵμεν φάμας ὄπισθεν *follow* the voice, Pi.*O.* 6.63; γνώμης πατρῴας πάντ' ὄ. ἑστάναι S.*Ant.*640; also τούτοισι δ' ὄ. ἴτω Cratin.30; πνοιαῖς ὄπιθεν Βορέα Pi.*O.*3.31 (s.v.l.). II. of Time, *after, in future, hereafter*, Il.4.362, Od.2.270, 18.168, etc.; either of a thing absolutely future, or of one which follows something else, opp. αὐτίκα, Il.9.519; ὄπιθεν οὐ πολλόν Pi.*O.*10(11).35; πολλοῖς μησὶν ὄ. Theoc.*Ep.*22.8; cf. ὀπίσω II. 1. 2. ἐν τοῖσι ὄ. λόγοισι in the books *yet to come*, in the *following* books, Hdt.5.22, 7. 213; cf. ὀπίσω II. 2: but, in Gramm., of what has gone before, Sch. Od.3.366, Hsch. s.v. Ἴωνες, Sch.Ar.*Ra.*1488; ὁ ὄπιθεν χρόνος the *earlier* time, *PMasp.*158.22 (vi A.D.):—for Comp. ὀπίστερος, Sup. ὀπίστατος, v. sub vocc. (Prob. from *ὄπις 'back', contained in ἀνόπιν, κατόπιν, μετόπιν, ὀπίσω.)

**ὀπισθέναρ**, ἄρος, τό, *the back of the hand*, Poll.2.143, 144, 9.126.

**ὀπισθένη**, *postilena*, Gloss.

**ὀπισθ-ίδιος**, α, ον, = sq., Sophr.50, Call.*Dian.*151, *AP*9.482 (Agath.). ⊛ **-ιος**, α, ον, (cf. πρόσθιος) *hinder, belonging to the hinder part*, *IG*1$^2$.369.12; τὰ ὀ. σκέλεα the *hind*-legs, Hdt.3.103, X.*Eq.*11.2: sg., Arist.*HA*500$^b$30; πόδες Semon.28, Philem.145; τένων ὁ ὀ. the *tendo Achillis*, Hp.*Fract.*11; so ὀπίσθια (sc. μόρια) Arist.*GA*722$^b$29; τὸ ὀ. the *hinder part*, opp. τὸ πρόσθιον, Id.*IA*706$^b$1; also of the *cheek* of animals, Id.*HA*492$^b$23: Subst. fem. ὀπισθία, *hinder part*, Epich. 90; of stars, *following* in the daily movement, Cleom.1.1. Adv. -ίως Lxx 1*Ki.*4.18.

**ὀπισθο-βάμων** [ᾰ], ον, gen. ονος, *walking backwards*, *AP*6.196 (Stat. Flacc.). **-βᾰρής**, ές, *loaded behind*, metaph., τῆς ἀσεβείας ὀπισθοβαρεῖς ἀνάγκαι *OGI*383.120 (Nemrud Dagh, i B.C.), cf. Plot.6.9.4, Simp.*in Epict.*p.35 D. 2. name of an eye-salve, Aët.7.115: as Adj., ἄδηκτον μὲν ὀ. δέ ib.109. **-βάτης** [ᾰ], ου, ὁ, *mounting*, sens. obsc., *AP*12.33 (Mel.). II. *tardy, dragging*, πούς *Trag.Adesp.*25 (lyr.). **-βολος**, ον, *thrown backwards*, Nonn.*D.*2.65, 41.25. **-βρῑθής**, ές, *loaded behind*, ἔγχος A.*Fr.*338. **-γρᾰφος**, ον, *written on the back as well as the front*, of papyrus rolls, Plin.*Ep.*3.5.17, Luc.*Vit. Auct.*9, Ulp. in *Dig.*37.11.4, Gloss. **-δάκτῠλος**, ον, *with fingers bent backwards*, Str.2.1.9. **-δετος**, ον, *bound behind* or *backwards*, Simon.177 (= Simm.3). **-δίωξις** [δῐ], εως, ἡ, = παλίωξις, Jo.Diac.ad Hes.*Sc.*154. ⊛ **-δομος**, ὁ, *back chamber, inner cell* of the old temple of Athena in the Acropolis at Athens, used as the Treasury, *IG*1$^2$. 139.17, al., Ar.*Pl.*1193, D.13.14, 24.136, *IG*2$^2$.1388.73, etc.; Delph. **ὀπισσόδομος** *SIG*246 iii 35 (iv B.C.). II. as Adj., *at the back of a building*, αἱ ὀ. στῆλαι Plb.12.11.2. **-δρομέω**, *run backwards*, Suppl. ad Procl. *in Prm.*p.989 S. **-δρόμος**, ον, *running backwards*, Theognost.*Can.*83. **-κάρπιος**, ον, *bearing its fruit behind* (instead of above) *the leaves*, like some fig-trees, Thphr.*CP*5.2.3. **-κέλευθος**, ον, *following behind*, Nonn.*D.*18.159. **-κεντρος**, ον, *with a sting in the tail*, Epich.66, cf. Arist.*HA*490$^a$17, al. **-κέφᾰλον**, τό, *the back of the head, occiput*, Gloss. **-κόμης**, ου, ὁ, = sq., Poll.2. 28. **-κομος**, ον, *wearing the hair long behind*, Nonn.*D.*13. 420. **-κράνιον** [ᾱ], τό, *the back part of the skull, occiput*, Sever.ap. Aët.7.92, Paul.Aeg.6.2, Gloss. ⊛ **-κρηπίς**, ῖδος, ἡ, a kind of *shoe*, Poll.7.91, Hsch. **-κύφωσις** [ῡ], εως, ἡ, *backward curvature of the spine*, Gal.18(1).493. **-μήριον**, τό, = sq., Melamp.*Palp.*A 142 Diels. **-μηρον**, τό, *the back of the thigh*, Ptol.*Alm.*7.5, al. **-νόμος**, ον, (νέμω) *grazing backwards*, of certain cattle with large horns slanting forwards, Hdt.4.183, cf. Arist.*PA*659a10, Ael.*NA*16.33. **-νῦγής**, *ές*, *pricking from behind*, κέντρα *AP*6.104 (Phil.). **-ποντος**, *ον* (-πονδῦχος cod.), sine expl., Theognost.*Can*.83. ✻ **-πόρος**, *ον*, *following*, Nonn.*D*.27.255, etc. **-πους**, *ὁ*, *ἡ*, *πουν*, *τό*, gen. *ποδος*, *walking behind*, *following*, *attendant*, προσπόλων ὀπισθόπους κῶμος E.*Hipp*.54, cf. 1179, A.*Ch*.713. II. = ὑποστρέψας, *one who has returned*, Hsch.

**ὀπισθ-ορμέω**, *hasten back*, Hsch. **-όρμητος**, *ον*, *hastening back*, Id. s. v. παλίνορσος, etc.

**ὀπισθό-ρροια**, *ἡ*, *flowing back*, Epicur.*Nat*.908.2. **-σφενδόνη**, *ἡ*, *the back part of a ring* (v. σφενδόνη II. 3), Ar.*Fr*.320.4.

**ὀπισθότερος**, *α*, *ον*, = ὀπίστερος, Arat.148.

**ὀπισθο-τίλη** [ῐ], Boeot. **ὀπιτθοτίλᾱ**, *ἡ*, name for the σηπία or cuttle-fish, which *squirts its liquor from behind*, Stratt.47.3, Hsch. **-τονία**, *ἡ*, *a disease in which the body is drawn back and stiffens, tetanic recurvation*, Cael.Aur.*CP*3.61. **-τονικός**, *ή*, *όν*, *subject to* ὀπισθοτονία, Dsc.1.48, Gal.1.156; v.l. for ὀπισθότονος II in Dsc.3.16; -κὸν πάθος Id.5.113. Adv. -κῶς Id.1.59. **-τονος**, *ον*, *drawn backwards*, τόξον Nonn.*D*.7.195. II. ὀπισθότονος, ὁ, = ὀπισθοτονία, Hp.*Epid*.5.75,76, Pl.*Ti*.84e, Aret.*SA*1.6. **-τονώδης**, *ες*, *suffering from* ὀπισθοτονία, Hp.*Prorrh*.1.88; *arising from* ὀ., ῥῖγος Id.*Coac*.23.

**ὀπισθ-ουρητικός**, *ή*, *όν*, *retromingent*, Arist.*HA*500b18, *PA*689a31, al.

**ὀπισθο-φάλακρος** [φᾰ], *ον*, *bald behind*, Tz.*H*.8.433. **-φᾰνής**, *ές*, *seen from behind*, *IG*1².374.165; *showing behind*, Gal.18(1).777; *appearing behind* or *after*, Vett.Val.8.9; epith. of ἔνοπτρα, prob. *reversing the image*, Olymp.*in Mete*.264.18; *looking backwards*, πρόσωπον Lxx *Ge*.9.23. Adv. -νῶς, πορεύεσθαι *backwards*, ibid.; βαδίζειν Phlp.*in Ph*.829.22, al. **-φόρος**, *ον*, *in a backward direction*, Opp.*H*.3.318. **-φῠλᾰκέω**, *guard the rear*, *form the rearguard*, X.*An*.3.3.8, J.*AJ*14.15.8; of the pillar of cloud, Ph.2.109. II. *command it*, X.*An*.2.3.10, etc. **-φῠλᾰκία**, *ἡ*, *the command of the rear*, ib.4.6.19. **-φύλαξ** [ῠ], *ακος*, *ὁ*, *one who guards the rear*: οἱ ὀ. *the rearguard*, ib.4.1.6, Ph.2.121, etc. **-χειμών**, *ῶνος*, *ὁ*, *afterwinter*, *late winter*, in pl., Hp.*Epid*.1.4, Thphr.*CP*2.1.6. **-χειρ**, *χειρος*, *ὁ*, *ἡ*, *with the hands tied behind*, D.C.*Fr*.24.3. **-ψῖλος**, *ον*, *bald behind*, Steph.*in Hp*.2.249 D.

✻ **ὀπισθῦπέρα**, *ἡ*, *brace of a sail*, *PCair.Zen*.756.2 (iii B.C.).

**ὄπισμα**, *ατος*, *τό*, (ὀπίζω) *the juice* of plants, Dsc.5.22, Orib.*Fr*.124. 2. = ὀποβάλσαμον, Aglaïas 23, cf. Sch.

**ὀπισμός**, *ὁ*, (ὀπίζω) *extraction of vegetable juice*, Thphr.*HP*9.8.2, *PCair.Zen*.368.20 (iii B.C.), Dsc.3.22.

**ὀπισσό-δομος**, v. ὀπισθόδομος. **-πόρευτος**, *ον*, *journeying backwards*, neut. as Adv., Tim.*Pers*.196.

**ὄπισσος**· εἰς τοὐπίσω ἐπάνω φέρεσθαι, Hsch. **ὀπίσσω**, v. ὀπίσω.

**ὀπίστατος**, *η*, *ον*, (ὄπισθε) *hindmost* or *last*, αἰὲν ἀποκτείνων τὸν ὀ. Il.8.342, 11.178:—Comp. **ὀπίστερος**, *α*, *ον*, Arat.284, Nonn.*D*.7.189: c. gen., ib.37.436, al.—No posit. occurs.

✻ **ὀπίσω** [ῐ], Ep. **ὀπίσσω**, the former rare in Hom. and only in signf. 1; Aeol. **ὐπίσσω** Sapph.*Supp*.8.9:—Adv.: I. of Place, *backwards*, opp. to πρόσω, Il.12.272; to προπρηνές, 3.218; ἀνεχάζετο τυτθὸν ὀπίσσω 5.443; ἀ. πολλὸν ὀ. 16.710; πάλιν εἶσιν ὀπίσσω Od.11.149: in Prose also, τὸ ὀπίσω, contr. τοὐπίσω, τὸ ὀ. φεύγειν Hdt.1.207, cf. 8.108; ἄναγε εἰς τοὐπίσω Pl.*R*.528a, cf. Th.4.4, Arist.*Fr*.106, etc.; [γνάμ]φθη δ' ὀπίσσω [φάσγα]νον B.12.53; τὰ ὀ. the *hinder parts*, Lxx *Jl*.2.20; τοῦ προπύλου τὸ ὀ. μέρος *SIG*756.17 (Athens, i B.C.); τὴν ὀ. τοῦ προπύλου στέγην ib.12; ἐκ τοῦ ὀ. on the *back* (of the papyrus), *BGU*1002.16 (i B.C.); τἀπίλοιπα ὀ. *PTeb*.58.27 (ii B.C.). 2. *back*, *back again*, of movement, ἀπήνυσαν οἶκαδ' ὀπίσσω Od.7.326; ὀπίσω πάλιν οἴκαδε Pi.*N*.3.62; ἂψ ὀ. Theoc.25.74; ἀπίκοντο ὀ. Hdt.1.62; ὀ. πορευόμενοι ib.75; ὀ. ἀναπλῶσαι ib.78; ἐν τῇ ὀ. κομιδῇ on his way *back*, Id.8.120, cf. 1.111, etc. 3. *back again*, *again*, of action that reverses an action or occurrence, ἀνακτᾶσθαι ὀ. τὴν τυραννίδα ib.61, cf. 68, 2.14; ἀποδόντες ὀ. Id.5.92.γ'; σφραγίζεις λύεις τ' ὀπίσω E.*IA*38 (anap.). 4. c. gen., δεῦτε ὀ. μου come *after* me, follow me, *Ev.Matt*.4.19. II. of Time, *hereafter*, since the future is unseen and was therefore regarded as *behind* us, whereas the past is known and therefore before our eyes, ἡμῖν τεκέεσσί τ' ὀπίσσω πῆμα λίποιτο Il.3.160; Τρῳαὶ δέ μ' ὀπίσσω πᾶσαι μωμήσονται ib.411, cf. Hes.*Op*.741, *Th*.488; ἔς περ ὀπίσσω Od.20.199 (εἰσοπίσω S.*Ph*.1104 (lyr.)); opp. to νῦν, τούτῳ δ' οὔτ' ἂρ νῦν φρένες ἔμπεδοι [εἰσίν], οὔτ' ἄρ' ὀπίσσω ἔσσονται Il.6.352; to προπάροιθε, σεῖο δ', Ἀχιλλεῦ, οὔ τις ἀνὴρ προπάροιθε [ἦν] μακάρτατος, οὔτ' ἄρ' ὀπίσσω [ἔσσεται] Od.11.483; where ὀπίσσω and πρόσσω are opposed, πρόσσω must be the past and ὀπίσσω the *future*, οἶδε νοῆσαι ἅμα πρόσσω καὶ ὀπίσσω Il.1.343; ἅμα πρόσσω καὶ ὀ. λεύσσει 3.109; ὁρᾷ πρόσσω καὶ ὀ. 18.250, Od.24.452; so ὅσσα τ' ἦν ὅσα τ' ἔσθ' ὅσα τ' ἔσται ὀπίσσω Emp.21.9 (ap.Arist.*Metaph*.1000a30); οὔτ' ἐνθάδ' ὁρῶν οὔτ' ὀπίσω neither present nor *future*, S.*OT* 488 (lyr.); τοὐπίσω σκοπεῖν E.*Fr*.49; θνητὸς πεφυκὼς τοὐπίσω πειρῶ βλέπειν Isid.Trag.2; cf. ὄπισθεν II. 1. 2. ἐν τοῖσι ὀ. λόγοις in the books *yet to come*, in the *following* books, Hdt.1.75; cf. ὄπισθεν II. 2.

**ὀπίσωρ**· δυσάρεστος, Hsch.

**ὀπισώτατος**, *η*, *ον*, Sup. Adj. from ὀπίσω, *hindmost*, *Sammelb*.4308.5 (iii B.C.).

**ὀπιτθοτίλα**, v. ὀπισθοτίλη.

**ὀπιτίων**, *ωνος*, *ὁ*, *tuberous root of Bunium ferulaceum*, *earth-nut*, Thphr.*HP*7.13.9.

**ὁπλ-άριον** [ᾰ], *τό*, Dim. of ὅπλον, *IG*11(2).199 *A* 23 (Delos, iii B.C.), *Supp.Epigr*.4.447.44 (Didyma, ii B.C.), Plu.*Flam*.17, *IGRom*.4.1318 (Tamasus, Lydia). **-ασία**, v. ὁπλισία.

**ὁπλέω**, poet. for ὁπλίζω, *make ready*, ἅμαξαν ὥπλεον Od.6.73.

**ὁπλή**, *ἡ*, (ὅπλον) *hoof*, in Hom. always *the solid hoof* of the horse, Il.11.536, 20.501, cf. Ar.*Eq*.605, Porph.*Abst*.3.9: after Hom., like χηλή, *the cloven hoof* of horned cattle, *h.Merc*.77, Hes.*Op*.489, Pi.*P*.4.226, Hdt.2.71, Pl.*R*.586b, Arist.*HA*575b8; τοῦ βοὸς ὁπλὰ *SIG* 1026.19 (Cos, iv/iii B.C.); of swine, Semon.28, Ar.*Ach*.740; of sheep, Arist.*Fr*.253:—distd. from χηλή, Gal.*UP*3.4.

**ὁπλήεις**, *εσσα*, *εν*, (ὁπλή) *hooved*, Poeta ap.D.Chr.32.85.

**Ὅπλητες**, *οἱ*, = ὁπλῖται, name of one of the four old tribes at Athens, Hdt.5.66, E.*Ion*1580, *CIG*3665 ii 32 (Cyzicus); Ὁπλήθων (gen. pl.) *SIG*57.2 (Milet., v B.C.); φυλὴ Ὁπλείτων *Dacia* 1.273 (Tomi); cf. Αἰγικορεῖς.

**ὁπλίας**· Λοκροὶ τοὺς τόπους ἐν οἷς συνελαύνοντες ἀριθμοῦσι τὰ πρόβατα καὶ τὰ βοσκήματα, Hsch.

**ὁπλ-ίζω**, aor. ὥπλισα, Ep. ὅπλισσα (v. infr.): pf. ὥπλικα (παρ-) D.S.4.10: plpf. ὡπλίκει D.C.78.6:—Med., fut. -ίσομαι (ἐφ-) *AP*9.39 (Music.), -ιοῦμαι Sch.Il.13.20: aor. ὡπλισάμην, Ep. ὁπλίσσατο (v.l. ὡπλ-) Od.2.20:—Pass., aor. ὡπλίσθην Hdt.2.152, etc., Ep. 3 pl. ὅπλισθεν Od.23.143: pf. ὥπλισμαι E.*Ba*.733, etc.—Hom. usu. uses the augm., but codd. have ὁπλισάμεσθα Od.4.429, ὅπλισθεν 23.143 (v.l. ὡ-): (ὅπλον, cf. ὁπλέω, ὅπλομαι):—*make* or *get ready*, in Hom. of meats and drink, ἐπὶ δ' ὥπλισσε κυκειῶ Il.11.641; ὅπλισσόν τ' ἤϊα Od.2.289; δαῖθ' ὁ. E.*Ion*852:—Med., δόρπον or δεῖπνον ὁπλίζεσθαι *make oneself* a meal *ready*, Od.2.20, 16.453, Il.11.86; ὡπλίσσατο λύχνον Emp.84.1; ὀ. θυσίαν θεοῖς cause it *to be prepared*, E.*Ion*1124. 2. of chariot-horses, *get ready*, *harness*, *equip*, αὐτὰρ ὅ γ' υἷας ἅμαξαν.. ὁπλίσαι ἠνώγει Il.24.190 (so in Med., *prepare* or *get ready for oneself*, ἐύτριχας ὡπλίσαθ' ἵππους 23.301); ὥπλιζον ἵππους προμετωπιδίοις X.*Cyr*.6.4.1:—Pass., of ships, νῆες.. ὁπλίζονται Od.17.288; of any implements, λαμπὰς διὰ χερῶν ὡπλισμένη *ready for use*, A.*Th*.433; θώρακα.. περιβόλοις ὡπλισμένον *furnished with*, E.*Ion*993. 3. of persons, esp. of soldiers, *equip*, *arm*, Hdt.1.127, E.*Ion*980, etc.; also, *train*, *exercise* soldiers, Hdt.6.12: in Att. Prose, *arm* or *equip as* ὁπλῖται, ὁπλίζειν τὸν δῆμον πρότερον ψιλὸν ὄντα Th.3.27, cf. 6.100 (Pass.), Lys.31.15, etc.:—Med. and Pass., *make oneself ready*, *prepare* or *equip oneself*, *get ready*, ἀλλ' ὅ γ' ἄρ' ἔξω ἰὼν ὡπλίζετο Od.14.526; ὅπλισθεν (for ὡπλίσθησαν) δὲ γυναῖκες the women *got ready* [for dancing], 23.143; Τρῶες.. ἀνὰ πτόλιν ὡπλίζοντο *were arming*, Il.8.55; ἀλλ' ὁπλιζώμεθα θᾶσσον Od.24.495; χαλκῷ ὁπλισθέντας Hdt.2.152; κατάπερ Κόλχοι ὡπλισμένοι Id.7.79; χρωμένους τῷ πλήθει ὡπλισμένῳ Pl.*R*.551e; ὁπλίζου, καρδία E.*Med*.1242: c. inf., τοὶ δ' ὡπλίζοντο.. νέκυάς τ' ἀγέμεν, ἕτεροι δὲ μεθ' ὕλην Il.7.417; βουσφαγεῖν ὡπλίζετο E.*El*.627:—in Med., also c. acc., ὁπλίζεσθαι χέρα *arm* one's hand, Id.*Or*.926 (in Act., Id.*Alc*.35 (anap.)); ὁπλίζεσθαι θράσος *arm oneself with* boldness, S.*El*.996, cf. *AP*5.92, 1*Ep.Pet*.4.1: freq. c. dat. instrum., ὁπλιζώμεσθα φασγάνῳ χέρας E.*Or*.1223, cf. *Ph*.267; θύρσοις διὰ χερῶν ὡπλισμέναι Id.*Ba*.733. **-ικός**, *ή*, *όν*, *pertaining to arms*, Vett.Val.17.3. **-ισία**, *ἡ*, *armoury*, cj. Lobeck for ὀπτασία in *AP*6.210 (Philet.); fort. ὁπλασία, cf. ἐξοπλασία. **-ισις**, *εως*, *ἡ*, *preparing for war*, *equipment*, *accoutrement*, *arming*, ὁπλίσεις ἀνδρῶν Ar.*Ra*.1036; εὐσταλεῖς τῇ ὁ. Th.3.22; περὶ ὅπλισιν [τοῦ δήμου] Arist.*Pol*.1297a16. 2. *armour*, τῆς ὁ. σχέσις Pl.*Ti*.24b, cf. Ephor.54 J. **-ισμα**, *ατος*, *τό*, *armour*, *armament*, E.*IA*253 (lyr., pl.). II. *weapon*, ὅ.. δεινῆς κορύνης Id.*Supp*.714: in pl., Pl.*Plt*.279d. III. *tackle* in ships, Hsch. **-ισμός**, *ὁ*, = ὅπλισις, A.*Ag*.405 (lyr.), D.S.20.49, J.*AJ*7.2.2, Onos.10.9, al. **-ιστέον**, *one must arm*, X.*Eq.Mag*.1.6. **-ιστής** (Dor. -τὰς) κόσμος, *ὁ*, *a warrior-dress*, *AP*7.230 (Eryc.): as Subst., ὁπλιστής *warrior*, Vett.Val.3.8; *armator*, *Gloss*.

**ὁπλῖτ-ἄγωγός**, *όν*, *carrying the heavy-armed*, νῆες ὁ. *troop*-ships, *transports*, Th.6.25,31, 8.30. **-εία**, *ἡ*, *the service of the heavy-armed*, *warfare*, Pl.*Lg*.706c. **-εύω**, *serve as a man-at-arms*, Th.6.91, 8.73, Lys.20.25, X.*An*.5.8.5; οἱ ὁπλιτεύοντες *men now serving*, opp. οἱ ὡπλιτευκότες, Arist.*Pol*.1297b13, cf. 1265b28. **-ης**, *ου*, *ὁ*, (ὅπλον) *heavy-armed*, *armed*, ὁ. δρόμοι races *of men in armour*, opp. the naked race (v. στάδιον II), Pi.*I*.1.23; called ὁ ὁ. or simply ὁπλίτης (Dor., Arc. -τας) in *IG*5(1).1120 (Geronthrae, v B.C.), 5(2).550.26 (Lycaeum, iv B.C.), etc. (= τοῦ ὅπλου δρόμος, Paus.6.13.1), cf. ὁπλιτοδρομέω; ἀνὴρ ὁ. A.*Th*.717, E.*Supp*.585, etc.; ὁ. στρατός *an armed* host, Id.*Heracl*.800; ὁ. κόσμος *warrior*-dress, armour, ib.699. II. mostly as Subst., ὁπλίτης, ὁ, *heavy-armed foot soldier*, *man-at-arms*, who carried a pike (δόρυ) and a large shield (ὅπλον), Ἀθηναίων οἱ στρατηγοὶ καὶ.. οἱ ὁ. *IG*1².116.25; ὁπλῖται, opp. ψιλοί, Hdt.9.30, Th.1.106; opp. γυμνῆτες, Hdt.9.63; opp. ἱππεῖς, Pl.*R*.552a; opp. τοξόται, Id.*Criti*.119b; to be a ὁπλίτης implied the possession of full civic rights, hence οἱ ὁ., opp. οἱ βάναυσοι, Arist.*Pol*.1326a23; and, in oligarchical states, opp. ὁ δῆμος, ib.1305b33. **-ικός**, *ή*, *όν*, *of* or *for a man-at-arms*, μάχη Pl.*R*.374d; αἱ ὁ. τάξεις X.*HG*3.4.16; ὅπλα ib.4.2.7. 2. ἡ -κή (sc. τέχνη) *the art of using heavy arms*, *the soldier's art*, Pl.*R*.333d; so τὸ -κόν Id.*La*.182d; also τὰ -κὰ ἐπιτηδεύειν profess the *art of arms*, ib.183c. II. of persons, *heavy-armed*, τὸ -κόν *the soldiery*, = οἱ ὁπλῖται, opp. τὸ ἄνοπλον, Arist.*Pol*.1289b32, cf. Th.5.6, X.*An*.7.6.26; ἡ ὁ. δύναμις Arist.*Pol*.1321a18. **-ις**, *ιδος*, fem. of ὁπλίτης, χεῖρες Poll.3.150.

✻ **ὁπλῖτο-δρομέω**, *run a race in armour*, Paus.1.23.11. **-δρόμος**, *ον*, *running a race in armour*, *IG*1².531 (dub.), *CIG*2758 iv 2, al.

(Aphrodisias), Poll.3.151, Sch.Pi.*P.*10.22, Sch.Ar.*Ach.*213. **-πάλης** [ᾰ], ου, Dor. **-ας**, ὁ, *heavy-armed warrior*, A.*Fr.Eleg.*5.

**ὁπλο-δῐδακτής**, οῦ, ὁ, *one who teaches the use of arms*, Vett.Val.74.13, *Gloss.* **-δῐδάσκᾰλος**, ὁ, = foreg., ib. **-δοτέω**, *arm*, ἄνδρας Lxx 1*Ma.*14.32. **-δότης**, ου, ὁ, *armidator*, *Gloss.* **-δουπος**, ον, *rattling with armour*, Orph.*H.*65.3, as Piers. for δολόδουπος. ❋ **-θήκη**, ἡ, *armoury*, *SIG*253*T*9 (Delph., iv B.C.), Lxx 2*Ch.*32.27, D.S.17.79, Str.4.1.5, J.*BJ* 2.4.1 (pl.), Plu.2.159e (pl.), *Sull.*14, Ael.*VH*6.12. 2. *shield-case*, *OGI*339.80 (Sestos, ii B.C., pl.). **-κᾰθαρμός**, ὁ, *armilustrium*, *Gloss.* **-κᾰθαρσία**, ἡ, and **-ιον** (sc. ἱερόν), τό, = foreg., ib. **-κτῠπος**, ον, *hoof-resounding*, restored by Seidler in A.*Th.*83 (lyr.). **-λογέω**, *collect arms from*, τινας Lxx 2*Ma.*8.27:—Pass., *to be disarmed*, ὑπό τινος Ph.2.530.

**ὅπλομαι**, poet. for ὁπλίζομαι, *prepare*, δεῖπνον ἄνωχθι ὅπλεσθαι Il.19.172, 23.159; cf. ὁπλίζω I, ὁπλέω. (ὁπλεῖσθαι shd. perh. be restored.)

**ὁπλο-μᾰνέω**, *to be mad on war*, *AP*9.320 (Leon.); περί τινος *show war-madness* in fighting for.., Posidon.48 J. ❋ **-μᾰχέω**, *serve as a man-at-arms*: *practise the use of arms*, Isoc.15.252, Arist.*Ath.*42.3, Plu.*Cam.*37, Gal.6.42, etc. II. *to be a drill-sergeant* (ὁπλομάχος II), *Abh.Berl.Akad.*1925(5).7 (Cyrene), *IG*2².957.47 (ii B.C.), 3.1085 (i A.D.). ❋ **-μάχης** [ᾰ], ου, ὁ, = ὁπλομάχος, Pl.*Euthd.*299c. **-μᾰχητικός**, ή, όν, *of* or *for the use of arms*: ἡ -κή (sc. τέχνη) *the art of using arms*, S.E.*M.*11.197. **-μᾰχία**, ἡ, *fighting with heavy arms*, *the art of using them*, Pl.*Lg.*813e, 833e, X.*An.*2.1.7, Ephor.54 J.; as a form of athletic exercise, *SIG*1061.11 (ii B.C.), *OGI*339.81 (Sestos, ii B.C.), Antyll.ap.Orib.6.36. **-μᾰχικός**, ή, όν, *of* or *for* ὁπλομαχία, ἀγῶνες D.C.59.14; κινήσεις Gal.6.153; -κός, ὁ, ibid.; -κόν, τό, title of work by Democr., *Fr.*28ᶜ. ❋ **-μάχος** [ᾰ], ον, *fighting in heavy arms*, X.*Lac.*11.8, Plb.2.65.11, Lxx *Is.*13.5; -χοι ἄνδρες Alciphr. 1.11. II. Subst. ὁ, ὁ, *one who teaches the use of arms*, *drill-sergeant*, opp. a mere fencing-master, Thphr.*Char.*5.10, Teles p.50 H., *PCair.Zen.*298 (iii B.C.), *SIG*697*E* 11 (Delph., ii B.C.). **-μελέτη**, ἡ, = *armatura*, Lyd.*Mag.*1.46.

❋ **ὅπλον**, τό, *tool*, *implement*, mostly in pl., like ἔντεα, τεύχεα: (prob. from ἕπω A): I. a ship's *tackle*, *tackling*, Hom. (only in Od.), 2.390, al., Hes.*Op.*627; esp. *ropes*, *halyards*, etc., δησάμενοι δ' ἄρα ὅπλα Od.2.430, etc.; in which sense Hom. twice uses the sg., *rope*, 14.346, 21.390: generally, *any ropes*, Hdt.7.25, 9.115, Hp.*Art.*78. II. *tools*, strictly so called, in Hom. esp. of *smiths' tools*, Il.18.409, 412; in full, ὅπλα χαλκήϊα Od.3.433: in sg., ὅπλον ἀρούρης sickle, *AP*6.95 (Antiphil.); ὅπλον γεροντικόν staff, Call.*Epigr.*1.7; δείπνων ὅπλον ἑτοιμότατον, of the wine-flask, *AP*6.248 (Marc. Arg.). III. in pl., also, *implements of war*, *arms* and *armour*, Hom. (only in Il.), αὐτὰρ ἐπεὶ πάνθ' ὅπλα κάμε, of the *arms* of Achilles, 18.614, cf. 19.21; ὅπλοισιν ἔνι δεινοῖσιν ἐδύτην 10.254, 272; so in Pi.*N.*8.27, *IG*1².1.9, E.*Hec.*14, etc.: rarely in sg., *weapon*, οὐδέ τι ἀρήϊον ὅπλον ἐκτέαται Hdt.4.23, cf. 174, E.*HF*161, 570, 942, Pl.*R.*474a, X.*Cyr.*7.4.15; ποτὶ πονηρὸν οὐκ ἄχρηστον ὅπλον ἁ πονηρία [Epich.]275; *piece of armour*, D.S.3.49. 2. *the large shield*, from which the men-at-arms took their name of ὁπλῖται (εἰκόνα γραπτὴν ἐν ὅπλῳ *IG*2².1012.18 (ii B.C.), cf. *IGRom.*4.1302.35 (Cyme, i B.C./i A.D.), Th.7.75, D.S.15.44, 17.18); ὅπλον στύππινον *IG*11(2).203*B*99 (Delos, iii B.C.): metaph., τῆς πενίας ὅπλον ἡ παρρησία Nicostr.Com.29; ὅ. μέγιστον.. ἀρετὴ βροτοῖς Men.*Mon.*433, cf. 619. 3. in pl., also, *heavy arms*, Hdt.9.53; ὅπλων ἐπιστάτης, = ὁπλίτης, opp. κώπης ἄναξ, A.*Pers.*379; ὁ πόλεμος οὐχ ὅπλων τὸ πλέον ἀλλὰ δαπάνης Th.1.83; ὅπλα παραδοῦναι Id.4.69; ὅπλα ἀποβάλλειν Ar.*V.*27, etc. 4. ὅπλα, = ὁπλῖται, *men-at-arms*, πολλῶν μεθ' ὅπλων S.*Ant.*115 (lyr.): and freq. in Prose, ἐξέτασιν ὅπλων ποιεῖσθαι to have a muster *of the men-at-arms*, Th.4.74, etc.; ὁ ἐπὶ τῶν ὅπλων στρατηγός, opp. ὁ ἐπὶ τῆς διοικήσεως, Decr.ap.D.18.38, Decr.ib.115; χειροτονηθεὶς ἐπὶ τὰ ὅ. πρῶτος.. στρατηγός *IG*2².682.44 (iii B.C.); στρατηγεῖν ἐπὶ τὰ ὅ. *SIG*697*E* (Delph., ii B.C.), etc. 5. τὰ ὅ. *the place of arms*, *camp*, ἦλθεν εἰς τὰ ὅ. Lys.13.12, cf. X.*Cyr.*7.2.5, etc.; ἐκ τῶν ὅ. προϊέναι Th.1.111, cf. 3.1. 6. Phrases: ἐνέδυνον (v.l. ἐνέδυντο) τὰ ὅ. Hdt.7.218, etc.; ἐν ὅπλοισι εἶναι or γενέσθαι to be *in arms*, *under arms*, Id.1.13, cf. E.*Ba.*303, Th.6.56; ἐν ὅπλοισι [ἱππομ]άχεντας Sapph.*Supp.*5.19; ἐν ὅπλοις μάχεσθαι Pl.*Grg.*456d; ἡ ἐν τοῖς ὅπλοις μάχη Id.*Lg.*833e; ποιῆσαι ἐξέτασιν ἐν ὅπλοις Decr.ap.Arist.*Ath.*31.2; εἰς τὰ ὅ. παραγγέλλειν X.*An.*1.5.13; ἐφ' ὅπλοις or παρ' ὅπλοις ἧσθαι, E.*Supp.*674, 357; μένειν ἐπὶ τοῖς ὅπλοις X.*Cyr.*7.2.8; for ὅπλα ῥίπτειν, ἀφιέναι, κατατίθεσθαι, v. sub vocc.; for ὅπλα τίθεσθαι, v. τίθημι. IV. of *the arms* possessed by animals for self-defence, [τὸν ἄνθρωπον] οὐκ ἔχοντα ὅπλον πρὸς τὴν ἀλκήν Arist.*PA*687ᵃ25, cf. ᵇ4, al. V. *membrum virile*, Nic.*Fr.*74.30, *APl.*4.242 (Eryc.), Hsch. VI. *a gymnastic exercise*, the last which came on in the games, Artem.1.63.

**ὁπλο-παικτής**, οῦ, ὁ, *juggler with weapons*, Vett.Val.74.13; = *armilusor*, *ventilator*, *Gloss.* (written -πεκτής and -πετής). **-πάροχος**, *insigniarius*, *armiger*, ib. **-πεκτής**, **-πετής**, v. ὁπλοπαικτής. **-ποιέω**, *make* or *use as a weapon*, Lxx *Wi.*5.17. II. *make weapons*, Str.15.3.18. **-ποιητική** (sc. τέχνη), ἡ, = ὁπλοποιική (q.v.), Phlp.*in APr.*8.2. ❋ **-ποιία**, ἡ, *making of arms*, D.S.14.43, Poll.7.154; name of the eighteenth book of the Iliad, Str.1.1.7. **-ποιική** (sc. τέχνη), ἡ, *the art of forging arms*, Pl.*Plt.*280d, Poll.7.209; in both places with v.l. -ποιητική. **-ποιός**, ὁ, *armourer*, D.S.14.43, J.*AJ*6.3.5, Poll.7.154, prob. in *JRS*14.35 (Iconium).

**ὁπλορχηστής**, οῦ, ὁ, *armed dancer*, Ptol.*Tetr.*180.

**ὁπλοσκοπία**, ἡ, *inspection of arms*: *review*, Ph.2.130.

**Ὁπλόσμιος**, ὁ, epith. of Zeus in Arcadia, Arist.*PA*673ᵃ19, *IG*5(2).344.18 (Orchom. Arc., iii B.C.); **Ὁπλοσμία**, ἡ, of Hera in Peloponnesus, Lyc.614; prob. *armed*, *in armour*: **Ὁπλοδμία**, name of a phyle at Mantinea, *IG*5(2).271.10 (iv B.C.).

❋ **ὁπλότερος**, α, ον, Comp. without any Posit. in use, Ep. for νεώτερος, *the younger*, always of persons, Il.4.325, Od.21.370, B.10.71; ὁπλότερος γενεῇ *younger* by birth, Il.2.707, Od.19.184: fem. gen. pl. ὁπλοτεράων Il.14.267, 275: Sup., *youngest*, ὁπλότατος γενεῆφιν 9.58; ὁ. θυγάτηρ Od.7.58, cf. 11.283, Hes.*Th.*946, Pi.*I.*6(5).6, al.: Ar.*Pax* 1270–1 uses the Comp. in mock heroic lines.—The orig. sense was perh. *capable of bearing arms*; and so ὁπλότεροι would be *the serviceable men*, hence, *the young men*, opp. the old men and children, Il.3.108, Hom.*Epigr.*4.5; then simply, *younger* or *youngest*, hence of women, Νέστορος ὁπλοτάτη θυγάτηρ Od.3.465, etc.; then, as *the youngest* are *the last born*, ἄνδρες ὁπλότεροι also means *the latter generations*, *men of later days*, Theoc.16.46; ὁπλοτέρου τ' Ἀχιλῆος ἀκούομεν Εὐρυλόχοιο Euph.80.

**ὁπλ-ουργία**, ἡ, = ὁπλοποιία, Tz. ad Lyc.227 (pl.). **-ουργός**, ὁ, = ὁπλοποιός, Ptol.*Tetr.*180.

**ὁπλο-φάγος** [ᾰ], ον, *nibbling at arms* or *shields*, μύες Eust.34.44. ❋ **-φορέω**, *bear arms*, *be armed*, X.*Cyr.*4.3.18, *AP*9.320 (Leon.), *BCH*32.429 (Delos, ii B.C.), *Jahresh.*26 *Beibl.*61 (Ephesus, iv/vii A.D.). II. Pass., *to be guarded*, c. dat., μυριάσι πεζῶν Plu.*Aem.*27. ❋ **-φόρος**, ον, *bearing arms*: *armed man*, *warrior*, *soldier*, E.*Ph.*789, *IA*190 (both lyr.), X.*Cyr.*5.4.27, Lxx 2*Ch.*14.8(7). II. = δορυφόρος, X.*Hier.*2.8, J.*AJ*6.6.2, al. 2. a magistrate or religious official, *IG*12(8).178 (Samothrace). III. epith. of Pallas, Ἀρχ.Ἐφ.1911.126 (Thessaly; of Ares, *Rev.Bibl.*32.118 (Palestine). **-φῠλάκιον** [ᾰ], τό, *armoury*, *arsenal*, Str.15.1.52. **-φύλαξ** [ῠ], ἄκος, ὁ, ἡ, *one who has the charge of arms*, Ath.12.538b; = *custos armorum*, *IGRom.*4.733, 736 (Eumenia); a name of Heracles at Smyrna, *CIG*3162, *BMus.Cat.Coins Ionia* pp.259, 260. **-χᾰρής**, ές, *delighting in arms*, Orph.*H.*32.6. **-χελώνη**, ἡ, *hard-shelled tortoise*, Tz.*H.*11.609.

**ὁπλωνέω**, *purchase arms*, *SIG*363.11 (Ephesus, iii B.C.).

**ὀπο-βαλσάμινος** [σᾰ], η, ον, *of the balsam-tree*, ξύλα κυπαρίσσινα ἢ ὀ. *PMag.Leid.W.*9.21. **-βάλσᾰμον**, τό, *the juice of the balsam-tree*, *balsam of Mecca*, Thphr.*HP*4.4.14, *CP*6.18.2, J.*AJ*14.4.1, Gal.12.554, *Edict.Diocl.* in *BCH*22.403 (written ὀποπ-, as also in *PMed.Strassb.* p.4 K., *Gloss.*); *the tree itself*, *Balsamodendron Opobalsamum*, J.*AJ*8.6.6, al.

**ὁποδᾰπός**, ή, όν, correlative to ποδαπός in indirect questions, *of what country*, *what countryman*, Hdt.5.13, 9.16 (v.l.), Pl.*Phdr.*275c; of things, δέκ' ὀβολῶν, οὐχὶ προσθεὶς ὁποδαπῶν Diph.66.10.

**ὀποειδής**, ές, *like* ὀπός I. 1, *milky*, Hp.*Epid.*7.25; **ὀπώδης**, *full of* ὀπός I. 1, σῦκα Id.*Vict.*2.55 (Sup.), cf. Arist.*PA*676ᵃ15; *milky*, Thphr.*HP*1.12.2; *acid*, Alex.Trall.2; δένδρα, of spice-bearing trees, Philostr.*VA*2.2.

**ὀπόεις**, εσσα, εν, *juicy*, ἐρινοί Nic.*Al.*319. II. as place name, *Opus*, Il.2.531, *IG*9(1).334.33 (v B.C.); **Ὀπούντιοι**, οἱ, name of a section of the Locrians, Th.1.108, etc.; Locr. **Ὁπούντιοι** *SIG*597*B* 2; also Ὀπόντιοι *IG*9(1).334.39, and uncontr. Ὀποέντιος ib.7.393.2 (Oropus).

**ὁπόθεν**, Ep. **ὁππόθεν**, Ion. **ὁκόθεν** (never -θε, for ὁππόθ' Od.3.89 is for ὁππόθι):—Adv. correl. to πόθεν: 1. chiefly used in indirect questions, opp. ὅποι (q.v.), *whence*, *from what place*, εἴρεαι ὁππόθεν εἰμέν Od.3.80; ἐρέσθαι, ὁππόθεν οὗτος ἀνήρ 1.406, cf. Pi.*P.*9.43, Hdt.2.54; σήμαιν' ὅτου τ' εἶ χὠπόθεν S.*Fr.*104. 2. Relat., ἀπαίροντες.. ὁπόθεν τύχοιεν Th.4.26; ὁπόθεν.. ῥᾴδιον ἦν λαβεῖν, οὐκ ἧγον *to the place from which*, X.*An.*5.2.2; ὁ αὐτὸς τι κερδανεῖ Id.*Mem.*2.6.4; so ὁ. ἂν τύχῃ *from whencesoever*.., Pl.*Tht.*180c; γαμεῖν ὁ. ἂν βούληται Id.*R.*362b, cf. *IG*1².58.12; ἡδέως ζῆν.. ἐὰν ἔχῃ τις ὁ. Philetaer.7.3; ὁ. ἔσοιτο μᾶζα Pl.Com.33; ὁ. ἔτυχεν ἄρχεσθαι at haphazard, Arist.*Po.*1450ᵇ32: also with other Particles, ὁ. ποτέ Pl.*Smp.*173d; ὁ. δήποτε D.Chr.31.54 (corr. Emperius for ὁ. δήποθεν); ὁποθενοῦν Pl.*Grg.*512a, Arist.*Cael.*271ᵃ24; ὁκοθενοῦν Hp.*Ulc.*7; ὁποθενδηποτοῦν J.*AJ*8.4.3.

❋ **ὁπόθι**, Ep. **ὁππόθι** as always in Hom., poet. Adv., correl. to πόθι, ὁππόθι πιότατον πεδίον.., ἔνθα.. τέμενος ἑλέσθαι Il.9.577; ὁπόθι θάνατος ἀπῇ (or ἐπῇ) A.*Supp.*124 (lyr.), as corrected. 2. used in indirect questions, like the Prose ὅπου, σάφα εἰπέμεν ὁππόθ' ὄλωλεν Od.3.89; v. ὅθι.

❋ **ὅποι**, Ion. **ὅκοι**, Dor. **ὅπυι**, **ὅπυς** (qq.v.), Adv. correl. to ποῖ; on its difference from ὅπῃ, v. sub voce: 1. Relat., *to which place*, *whither*, ἐκεῖσ' ὅ. πορευτέον S.*Aj.*690; ἴθ' ὅ. χρῄζεις Ar.*Nu.*891; ὅ. *thither where*, E.*IT*119; πέμψον.. ὅ. προσωτάτω as far as possible, Id.*Andr.*922, cf. X.*An.*6.6.1, etc.; ὅ. ἄν, with subj., *whithersoever*, ἀπιέναι ὅ. ἂν βούλωνται Foed.ap.Th.5.18, cf. Pl.*Ap.*37d, *IG*1².76.31, etc.; ὅ. ἂν ἄλλοσε βούλῃ *whithersoever* else, Pl.*Phdr.*230e; also ὅποιπερ S.*Aj.*810, *OT*1458 (v.l. ὅπηπερ); ὅποι ποτέ Id.*Ph.*780, etc. 2. in indirect questions, *to what place*, *whither*, ἀμηχανεῖν ὅποι τράποιντο A.*Pers.*459; ἂν σκοπῇ.. ὅποι φέρονται Antiph.40.7; ἴστε ὅθεν ἥλιος ἀνίσχει καὶ ὅποι (ὅπου codd. meliores) δύεται X.*An.*5.7.6; μέχρι ὅ. up to what point, Pl.*Grg.*487c: in repeating a question, ποῖ; Answ. ὅποι μ' ἐρωτᾷς; Crobyl.5. b. in pregnant sense with Verbs of rest, διδάξαι.. μ' ὅποι καθέσταμεν (i.e. ὅποι ἐλθόντες) S.*OC*23; τοὺς δὲ σοὺς ὅποι θεοὶ πόνους κατοικτιοῦσιν, οὐκ ἔχω μαθεῖν *at what point* the gods will take pity on (i.e. will end) thy sorrows, ib.383 (v.l. ὅπῃ). c. c. gen., ὅποι γῆς *whither* in the world, ὅποι γῆς.. πεπλάνημαι A.*Pr.*564 (anap.); ὅποι τέτραπται γῆς Ar.*Ach.*209; οὐκ οἶσθ' ὅποι γῆς οὐδ' ὅποι γνώμης φέρῃ S.*El.*922.

**ὁποῖος**, α, ον, Ep. **ὁπποῖος**, η, ον, Hom., but twice ὁποῖος, Od.17.421, 19.77; Ion. **ὁκοῖος**, η, ον, Archil.70, Hdt.2.82, al., *GDI* iv p.883 (Erythrae, iv B.C.); Cret. **ὀτεῖος** (q.v.): correlat. to ποῖος: replaced by οἷος in Att. Inscrr. after 300 B.C.: 1. as Relat., *of what sort* or *quality*, ὁπποῖόν κ' εἴπησθα ἔπος, τοῖόν κ' ἐπακούσαις *as* [is] the word thou hast spoken, such shalt thou hear again, Il.20.250; τοίῳ ὁποῖος ἔοι such *as* he might be, Od.17.421; οὐθ' οἷ' ἔπασχεν οὐθ' ὁποῖ' ἔδρα κακά S.*OT*1272. 2. in indirect questions, Od.1.171, etc.; εὑρεῖν ὁποίοις φαρμάκοις ἰάσιμος A.*Pr.*475: in direct questions only as f.l. in E.*Ph.*878, *Ba.*663: sts. folld. by ποῖος in the same clause, οὐ γὰρ αἰσθάνομαί σου ὁποῖον νόμιμον ἢ ποῖον δίκαιον λέγεις X.*Mem.*4.4.13; οὐκ οἶδα ὁποίᾳ τόλμῃ ἢ ποίοις λόγοις χρώμενος ἐρῶ Pl.*R.*414d. II. with indefinite words added, ὁποῖός τις Th.7.38, X.*An.*2.2.2; ὁκοῖόν τι Hdt.1.158; γιγνομένων ὁποῖοί τινες ἔτυχον Arist.*Pol.*1286ᵇ24; so in Hom., ὁπποῖ' ἄσσα *of what sort*, for ὁποῖά τινα, Od.19.218; ὁποῖ' ἄττα Pl.*Grg.*465a; ὁποιοσοῦν *of what kind soever*, Id.*Tht.*152d, al.; ὁποῖος δή, δήποτε, δηποτοῦν, and οὖν δή, as ὁποία δὴ φλέψ X.*HG*5.4.58; τοὺς ὁποιουσδήποτε..ἐξεπέμπετε στρατηγούς D.18.146: gen., ὁποίου τινὸς οὖν X.*Cyr.*2.4.10: acc. fem., ὁποιαντινοῦν Lys.13.11; ὁποῖόσπερ A.*Ch.*669; ὁποιοσποτοῦν Arist.*Ph.*253ᵇ23; ὁποιοσδητισοῦν Iamb.ap.Simp.*in Ph.*639.30; πόλιν.. οὐδ' ὁποίας ἧττω inferior to *none*, Plb.4.65.3; οὔτ' ἄλλους οὐδ' ὁποίους Theopomp.Hist.217(c); μηδὲ καθ' ὁποῖον τρόπον *SIG*672.14 (Delph., ii B.C.); μηδ' ὀτίη or μηδοτίη, v. μηδοτίη. III. neut. pl. used as Adv., *like as*, S.*OT*915, 1076, E.*Hec.*398. IV. Adv. ὁποίως, *qualiter*, *Gloss.*

**ὀπο-καλπᾰθίζω**, of myrrh, *smell of* ὀποκάλπασον, Gal.14.68. **-κάλπᾰσον**, τό, *Hotai*, an acrid kind of myrrh, *Balsamodendron Playfairii*, ib.56. **-κάρπᾰσον**, τό, = ὀπὸς καρπάσου (v. κάρπασος II), Dsc.*Alex.Praef.*; *opocarpatum*, Plin.*HN*28.158, 32.98. **-κιννάμωμον** [ᾰ], τό, *the juice of the* κιννάμωμον, prob. f.l. in Thphr.*HP*4.4.14. **-πάλσαμον**, v. ὀποβάλσαμον. **-πανάκη**, ἡ, and **-πανάκιον**, τό, = seq., *Gloss.* **-πάναξ** [πᾰ], ἄκος, ὁ, *gum of Opopanax hispidus, Hercules' woundwort*, Heraclid.Tar.ap.Gal.14.186, Dsc.3.48, Gal.12.94, *PGrenf.*1.52.11 (iii A.D.).

**ὀπός**, ὁ, *juice*, distd. from χυλός, χυμός, in that ὀπός is prop. *vegetable juice, the milky juice* which is drawn from a plant by tapping it, ὀπὸν..στάζοντα τομῆς..κάδοις δέχεται S.*Fr.*534 (anap.), cf. Thphr.*HP*9.8.1, etc.; esp. *the acid juice of the fig-tree*, used as rennet (τάμισος) for curdling milk, Il.5.902, Emp.33, Hp.*Morb.*4.52, Menestor ap.Thphr.*HP*1.2.3, Arist.*Mete.*384ᵃ21, 389ᵇ10, *GA*737ᵃ14; generally, *acid juice*, Pl.*Ti.*60b; βλέπειν ὀπόν Ar.*Pax*1184: in pl., Antiph.88.4, cj. in Anaxandr.41.59 (anap.); cf. ὀπίας, ὀποειδής. 2. metaph., ὀπὸς ἥβης *the juicy freshness* of youth, opp. ῥυτίς, *AP*5.257 (Paul. Sil.). II. ὀποῦ καρπός, = σιλφίου σπέρμα, Hp.ap.Gal.19.126; and so prob. in Ar.*Ec.*404, *Pl.*719; but ὀπὸς σιλφίου silphium *juice*, Hp.*Acut.*23, cf. 37, *Acut.(Sp.)*48, Thphr.*HP*6.3.2; so ὀπός alone, Gal.12.90. III. *gravy*, Ath.9.402c. (Perh. cf. Lith. *sakaĩ* (pl.) 'resin', Slav. *sokŭ* 'sap'.)

**ὀπός**, gen. of ὄψ (q.v.).

**ὀποσάγωνον** [ᾰ], τό, *polygon of any number of sides*, Papp.314.19.

**ὀποσάκῐς** [ᾰ], Aeol. **ὀπoσσάκιν** (leg. ὀππόσσακιν) Theoc.30.27:—Adv., (ὁπόσος) *as many times as*.., X.*Cyr.*2.3.23; ὁποσάκις ἂν *so often as ever*, Pl.*Tht.*197d; ὁποσακισοῦν *as many times as you please*, Arist.*Cael.*273ᵃ32.

**ὁποσά-μηνος** [ᾰ], ον, ὁ. οὐκ οἶδα I know not *how many months old*, Hp.*Epid.*4.6. **-πλᾰσιοσοῦν**, *how many-fold soever*, Arist.*Ph.*204ᵇ17, Simp.*in Ph.*949.9. **-πους**, ὁ, ἡ, πουν, τό, gen. ποδος, in indirect questions, *how many feet long*.., Luc.*Gall.*9.

**ὁποσ-άχῆ**, Adv. *in as many ways as*.., X.*Cyn.*6.20. **-άχοῦ**, Adv. *in as many places as*.., Aristid.*Rh.*2 p.542 S. **-άχῶς**, Adv. *in as many ways as*.., ib.1 p.506 S.

**ὁπόσε**, Ep. **ὁππόσε**, poet. for ὅποι, Od.14.139, but f.l. in *h.Ap.*209.

**ὁπόσος**, Ep. **ὁππόσος** Od.14.47, **ὁπόσσος** 22.220, Il.23.238 (also **ὅποσος** 24.7), **ὁπόσσος** also *Berl.Sitzb.*1927.160 (Cyrene), *IG*4²(1).121.109 (Epid., iv B.C.); Ion. **ὁκόσος**; Cret. and Boeot. **ὀπόττος** *Leg. Gort.*4.40, al., *IG*7.522.19 (iii B.C.), etc.: correlat. to πόσος: freq. in *IG*1², but replaced by ὅσος in Att. Inscrr. after 300 B.C.: I. as Relat., like ὅσος, of Number, *as many, as many as*.., ὁπόσα τολύπευσε σὺν αὐτῷ Il.24.7; πᾶσι θεοῖς.., ὁπόσοι τὴν Διὸς αὐλὴν εἰσοιχνεῦσιν A.*Pr.*121 (anap.), cf. 411, *Th.*927 (both lyr.); τοσαῦτα ὁπόσα σοι φίλον Pl.*Lg.*642d; ὁπόσους πλείστους ἐδυνάμην X.*Cyr.*4.5.29, etc.: in Prose freq. ὁ. ἄν with subj., ὁπόσοις ἂν δοκῇ Foed.ap.Th.4.118, cf. Pl.*Sph.*245d, etc. 2. of Quantity, *as much as*, of Size or Space, *as great as*, ὁπόσσον ἐπέσχε *as far as* it spread, Il.23.238; χθόνα.., ὁπόσαν καὶ φθιμένοισιν κατέχειν *as much as* is allowed the dead to occupy, A.*Th.*732 (lyr.); ὁπόσην τῆς χώρας X.*Oec.*4.8: Adverbial in dat., ὁπόσῳ πλέον.., τοσούτῳ πλειόνων κτλ. Pl.*Lg.*649b. 3. with indefinite Particles added, ὁποσοσοῦν *how great* or *much soever*, Th.4.37, 6.56, Pl.*Sph.*245d: Ion. dat. pl., ὁκόσῃσι ὦν Hdt.5.20; so ὁπόσῳ δήποτε D.21.39; ὁποσοιδηποτοῦν Euc.9.12, al.; ὁπόσοσπερ Pl.*Lg.*753b, X.*Oec.*4.5; ὁποσουτινοσοῦν *for however large a price*, Lys.22.15. II. in indirect questions, ὄφρα..εἴπῃς ὁππόσα κήδε' ἀνέτλης Od.14.47; ὁπόσαι ψάμαθοι κλονέονται, καθορᾷς Pi.*P.*9.46; εἰπὲ..ὁκόσοι τοιοῦτοι [εἰσὶ] Hdt.7.234; διαλογισώμεθα..ὁπόσα..πέφανται *how many things* he has been found to be, Pl.*Sph.*231d; ἠρώτων τὸ στράτευμα, ὁπόσον εἴη X.*An.*4.4.17, cf. Pl.*Sis.*388e; ἤρετο ὁπόσου asked *for how much, at what price*, Timocl.11.9. III. = ὅς, Paus.9.31.5.

**ὁποσταῖος**, α, ον, *of what day in serial order*, εἴρει ὁποσταίη μηνὸς περιτέλλεται ἠώς Arat.739.

**ὁποστημόριος**, α, ον, *what fraction*, Eudem.ap.Simp.*in Ph.*973.24.

**ὁπόστος**, η, ον, *in what* or *which place in numerical order*, ὁπόστον μέρος Archyt.1; ὁ. εἰλήχει *what number* he had drawn, Pl.*R.*617e; ὁ. ἐγένετο ἀφ' Ἡρακλέους *how many generations* from.., X.*Ages.*1.2; οὕτως ὁπόστος τὸν ἀριθμόν, κτλ., in a sense determined by *the number of which he is one*, Arist.*Pol.*1262ᵃ3; οὐ πρῶτος, οὐ δεύτερος.., οὐχ ὁποστοσοῦν D.18.310.

**ὁπότᾰν**, i.e. ὁπότ' ἄν, as it is freq. written in codd. (the distn. did not exist for the Greeks): Adv., related to ὅταν as ὁπότε to ὅτε (v. ὁπότε), *whensoever*, used only with subj., Il.15.209, etc. (Hom. uses ὁππότε κεν in the same way, Il.4.40, 229, al.): rarely after past tenses, πολλὰς..ᾔσθου πλαγάς, ὁπόταν..νὺξ ὑπολείφθῃ (for ὁπότε νὺξ ὑπολειφθείη) S.*El.*91 (anap.): never with ind. in early writers, for φθέγξομαι (Il.21.340), ἱμείρεται (Od.1.41) are Ep. aor. subj. forms, and in Od.16.282 θῇσιν is the right reading: never with opt. save in late writers (unless the Mss. can be trusted in Pl.*Alc.*2.146a), for in Il.7.415 ὁππότ' ἄρ' is the reading of the best codd.; in X.*Cyr.*1.3.11 ὁπότε ἥκοι is the right reading. II. *as soon as*, ὁπότ' ἂν τὸ πρῶτον ἴδῃ φάος *h.Ap.*71.

**ὁπότε**, Ep. **ὁππότε**, both in Hom.; Ion. **ὁκότε**; Cyrenaic **ὁπόκᾰ** *Berl.Sitzb.*1927.164; in Dor. Poets **ὁππόκᾰ** Theoc.5.98: Adv. of Time, correlat. to πότε, used much like ὅτε, exc. that the sense is less definite (cf. X.*Cyr.*1.6.3), though the two were freq. used without distinction: I. Relat., with the ind., mostly with reference to the past, *when*, Il.1.399, 3.173, etc.; the ind. ἧστε is omitted, 8.230: in Class. Att. Prose only ὅτε is so used, when referring to a particular time, but later ὁπότε returns, as ὁπότε περιῆν *when* she was alive, *POxy.*243.10 (i A.D.): with the pres. in a simile, ὡς δ' ὁπότε.. ποταμὸς πεδίονδε κάτεισι Il.11.492: with subj., like ὁπόταν, with reference to an indef. number of occasions in the pres. or to the future, ὁππότ' Ἀχαιοὶ Τρώων ἐκπέρσωσ' εὖ ναιόμενον πτολίεθρον 1.163, cf. 13.817, 21.112, Od.14.170, Hes.*Th.*782: sts. in similes, ὡς ὁπότε νέφεα Ζέφυρος στυφελίξῃ Il.11.305, cf. Od.4.335; but ὁπότ' ἄν, Ep. ὁπότε or ὁππότε κεν, is more common with subj., and in Att. Prose ἄν must be used, v. ὁπόταν: Cyrenaic ὁπόκα κα δήληται *Berl.Sitzb.* l.c. 2. with opt.: a. to express an event that occurred often, ὁπότε Κρήτηθεν ἵκοιτο Il.3.233, cf. 10.189, 15.284, Od.11.591, Th.1.90, 2.15, Pl.*Smp.*220a, X.*An.*3.4.28. b. after a verb of waiting, of a time future relatively to the past, ἷζε..δέγμενος ὁππότε ναῦφιν ἀφορμηθεῖεν Il.2.794, cf. 4.334, 7.415, 9.191, 18.524. c. in orat. obliq., S.*Tr.*824 (lyr.), X.*An.*4.6.20; in implied orat. obliq., Od.24.344 (of a past promise); ἀποδοτέον..ὁ. μανεὶς ἀπαιτοῖ we were not [as you remember] to.., Pl.*R.*332a. d. where the principal clause has an opt., μηδ' ἀντιάσειας ἐκείνῳ ὁππότε νοστήσειε Od.18.148, cf. Pl.*R.*396c, X.*Cyr.*1.6.3. II. in indirect questions, with ind., ἦ ῥά τι ἴδμεν..ὁππότε Τηλέμαχος νεῖται; *when* he is to return, Od.4.633; εἰς ὁ. *by what time*, Aeschin.3.99: rarely after a past tense, προσεδέρκετο, δέγμενος αἰεί, ὁππότε δὴ..ἐφήσει (for ἐφείη, v. supr. I. 2b) Od.20.386; εἰς σὲ βλέψαι καὶ τὸν ταμίαν ὁπότ' ἄριστον παραθήσει Ar.*V.*613. III. ὁποτεοῦν *at any time whatever*, Arist.*Metaph.*1049ᵃ1.

B. in causal sense, *because, since*, with ind., Thgn.749 (s.v.l.), Hdt.2.125, Pl.*Lg.*895c, etc.; also ὁπότε γε S.*OC*1699 (lyr.), X.*Cyr.*8.3.7.

**ὁπότερ-ος**, α, ον, Ep. **ὁππότερος**, as always in Hom.; Ion. **ὁκότερος** Hdt.5.119:—correlat. to πότερος, used in sg. of individuals, in pl. of groups, e.g. of two armies, Il.3.299, 5.33: 1. as Relat., *which of two*, ἡμέων δ' ὁπποτέρῳ θάνατος..τέτυκται, τεθναίη Il.3.101: with ἄν, Ep. κε, *whichsoever*, ὁππότερος δέ κε νικήσῃ ib.71; ὁπότερ' ἂν κτίσῃς A.*Supp.*434 (lyr.); ὁπότεροι ἂν κρατῶσιν X.*Cyr.*4.2.37. 2. as indirect interrog., Ζεὺς οἶδε.., ὁπποτέρῳ θανάτοιο τέλος πεπρωμένον ἐστίν Il.3.309, cf. 22.130, 23.487; περὶ τοῦ ὁκότερος ἡμέων πλέω ἀγαθὰ ..ἐργάσεται about the question, *which of* us *two*.., Hdt.8.79; ὥστε μὴ γνῶναι ὁπότερος.. Lys.*Fr.*78.3, cf. Antipho 3.2.6; ἀσαφῶς ὁποτέρων ἀρξάντων, for ἀσαφὲς ὂν ὁπότεροι ἦρξαν, Th.4.20: rarely in direct questions, for πότερος, prob. f.l. in Pl.*Euthd.*271a and *Ly.*212c. 3. as indef., *either of two*, ἐὰν..ὁπότερος αὐτοῖν..πράξῃ Id.*Lg.*868a, cf. *R.*579a, X.*Cyr.*3.2.22, And.3.26, D.16.27; so ὁποτεροσοῦν Pl.*Men.*98d, *Phlb.*14c, al.; ἐξεῖναι δ' ὁποτεροισοῦν Th.5.41, cf. Arist.*Pol.*1319ᵇ9, al.: with οὐδέ, οὐδ' ὁπότερος (or οὐδοπ—) *neither*, Hero *Dioptr.*37. II. Adv. **ὁποτέρως**, *in which of two ways*, as Relat. and indirect interrog., ὁ. ἔσται, ἐν ἀδήλῳ κινδυνεύεται Th.1.78, cf. Lys.26.5, Isoc.12.76, Pl.*R.*348b, etc.; so ὁποτερωσοῦν Arist.*APr.*60ᵃ16, al. 2. also neut. ὁπότερον or -ερα as Adv., mostly in indirect questions, *whether*, folld. by ἢ..ἤ.., as ἐβουλεύοντο ὁκότερα ἢ παραδόντες..ἢ ἐκλιπόντες.., ἄμεινον πρήξουσι Hdt.5.119; by one ἤ, Ar.*Nu.*157: folld. by πότερον..ἤ.., Pl.*Erx.*405c, etc.; also ὁπότερον εἴτε.., εἴτε.. Isoc.12.76, cf. X.*HG*3.5.19. **-ωθε, -θεν**, Ep. ὁπποτ—, Adv. *from which of the two sides* or *directions*, Il.14.59; ὁ. ἂν ᾖ ἡ πληγή Arist.*PA*691ᵇ10; ὁποτερωθενοῦν *on either of the two sides*, Id.*APr.*61ᵃ38. **-ωθι**, Adv. *in whichever of the two places*, Hp.*Superf.*10, X.*Eq.Mag.*4.15. **-ωσε**, Adv. *in which of two directions, to which of two places*, Th.1.63, 5.65; ἐπορεύετο ὁ. βουληθείη Pl.*Smp.*190a. 2. οὐδ' ὁποτέρωσε (or οὐδοπ—) *in neither of two directions*, Dosith.p.410 K.

**ὅπου**, Ion. **ὅκου**, Relat., indirect interrog., and indef. Adv. of Place, correlat. to ποῦ: I. as a Relat., sts. c. gen. loci, τῆς πόλεως ὅπου κάλλιστον στρατοπεδεύσασθαι Pl.*R.*415d, cf. Hdt.2.172; ὅπου βούλοιτο τοῦ δρόμου X.*HG*2.4.27; ἔσθ' ὅπου *in some places*, A.*Eu.*517 (lyr.), *Fr.*302: standing for the Relat. Adj., μέλη, ὅπου (i.e. ἐν οἷς) χελιδὼν ἦν τις ἐμπεποιημένη Ar.*Av.*1301: with other Particles, ὅκου δή *somewhere or other*, Hdt.3.129; ὅπου ἄν *wherever*, with subj., *IG* 1².76.11, etc.; in Trag. the ἄν may be omitted, as ὅπου δ' Ἀπόλλων σκαιὸς ᾖ, τίνες σοφοί; E.*El.*972, etc. (never in Att. Prose): c. gen., ὅπου ἂν τύχῃ τῶν λεγομένων Pl.*Prt.*342e; ὁπουοῦν *anywheresoever*, Id. *Cra.*403c; ὅπουπερ c. opt., *wherever*, X.*Cyr.*3.3.5; ὅπου ποτέ S.*OC* 12; ὁπουδάν, = ὅπου δὲ ἄν, *anywhere*, D.C.*Fr.*109.21; ὁπουδήποτε, = *ubicumque*, Dosith.p.410K.; ὁπουδηποτοῦν *anywheresoever*, J.*Ap.* 2.15. 2. in indirect questions, ὄφρα πύθηαι πατρός, ὅπου κύθε γαῖα Od.3.16, cf. 16.306, S.*OT*924, etc.: with Verbs of motion in pregnant sense, ὅκου ἐτράπετο, οὐκέτι εἶχον εἰπεῖν Hdt.2.119; κεῖνος δ' ὅπου βέβηκεν, οὐδεὶς οἶδε S.*Tr.*40, v.l. in X.*Cyr.*3.1.37, etc.: in many passages editors have in this sense restd. ὅποι, mostly from codd.; in repeating a question, ἡ Λακεδαίμων ποῦ 'στιν; Answ. ὅπου 'στίν; (do you ask) *where* it is? Ar.*Nu.*214: c. gen., εἰδότες ὅκου γῆς εἴη Hdt.4.150, cf. Pl.*R.*403e. II. the strict local sense occasionally passes into, 1. a sense involving Time or Occasion, ὅ. τιν' ἴδῃ Thgn.922, cf. 999, X.*HG*3.3.6; σιγᾶν θ' ὅ. δεῖ καὶ λέγειν τὰ καίρια A.*Ch.*582, cf. *Eu.*277; οὐκ ἔσθ' ὅ. there is no case *in which*, i.e. in no case, S.*OT*448, *Aj.*1069, E.*HF*186, D.3.35: so ἔστιν ὅ.; as a question, Id.18.22. 2. of Cause, *whereas*, Hdt.1.68, 4.195, Antipho 1.7; ὅ. γὰρ ἐγὼ.. ὁμολογῶ D.21.205; ὅκου γε, Lat. *quandoquidem* or *quippe*, Hdt.7.118; ὅπου γε X.*Cyr.*2.3.11, etc.

B. later as a demonstr. Adv., only in the phrase ὅ. μέν.., ὅ. δέ.. *here*... *there*.., Plu.2.427c, S.E.*P.*1.53, etc.

**ὀπόφυλλον**, τό, *the seed of the* σίλφιον, Dsc.*Eup.*1.20, 66, prob. in Dsc.3.80.

**ὅππᾱ, ὅππᾳ**, v. ὅπῃ. **ὀππάτεσσι**, Aeol. for ὄμμασι, Sapph.2.11. **ὅππη**, Ep. for ὅπῃ. ***ὀππῆμος**, Adv., Ep. for ὁπῆμος (= ὁπότε), *when*, Arat.568.

**ὀππικίζω, ὀππικιστής**, v. ὀπικίζω. **ὁππόθεν, ὁππόθῐ, ὁπποῖος**, Ep. for ὁπόθεν, ὁπόθι, ὁποῖος. **ὀππόκα**, Dor. for ὁπότε (q.v.).

**ὀπποποῖ**, an exclamation, S.*Ichn.*191 (lyr.).

**ὁππόσε, ὁππόσος**, Ep. for ὁπόσε, ὁπόσος. **ὁππόταν, ὁππότε, ὁππότερος, ὁπποτέρωθεν**, Ep. for ὁποτ-. **ὅππως**, Ep. for ὅπως.

**ὀπτάζομαι**, Pass., *to be seen*, Lxx*Nu.*14.14:—so **ὀπτάνομαι**, ib. 3*Ki.*8.8, *UPZ*62.32 (ii B.C.), *PTeb.*24.5 (ii B.C.), *Act.Ap.*1.3, [Ar.Byz.] Arg.Ar.*Pl.*4, *PMag.Par.*1.3033, *Corp.Herm.*3.2:—an Act. **ὀπταίνω** in Eust.969.33.

**ὀπτ-ᾰλέος**, α, ον, (ὀπτάω) *roasted, broiled*, κρειῶν πίνακας παρέθηκε ..ὀπταλέων Od.16.50; ὀπταλέα κρέα ἔδμεναι Il.4.345; κρέα.. ὀπταλέα τε καὶ ὠμά Od.12.396; opp. ἑφθός (boiled), Ath.9.380c. **-ᾰνάριος**, *assator, coctarius*, Gloss.

**ὀπτᾰν-εῖον**, τό, v. ὀπτάνιον. **-εύς**, έως, ὁ, (ὀπτάω) *one who roasts*, *PBerol.*ap.Wilcken *Ostr.*i p.693 (iii B.C.), *PTeb.*277 (iii A.D.); *assator*, Gloss. **-ία**, ἡ, = ἀπόβλεψις, Suid. **-ικός**, ή, όν, *for roasting*, *PRyl.*227.24 (iii A.D.). ***-ιον**, τό, *place for roasting, kitchen*, Ar.*Eq.* 1033, *Pax*891, Alex.173.13, Philem.61, etc.; *oven*, *PHolm.*11.18: these and other passages from Com. Poets, together with *IG*2².1672.189, *SIG*1097.28 (both iv B.C.), show that ὀπτάνιον is a real form, but **ὀπτανεῖον**, which is found in codd. of Plu.*Crass.*8, Luc.*Asin.*27, etc., can be defended by the older **ὀπτανήϊον** (v. Hdn.Gr.2.417) and would be a normal derivative from ὀπτανεύς:—mock-heroic gen. pl. ὀπτανιάων for ὀπτανίων, Matro *Conv.*12. II. *firewood for roasting*, Man.ap.J.*Ap.*1.26.

**ὀπτάνομαι**, v. ὀπτάζομαι.

**ὀπτᾰνός**, ή, όν, (ὀπτάω) *roasted*, opp. ἑψανός, ἀπ' ὀβελίσκων ὀπτανά Sotad.Com.1.10, cf. Xenocr.ap.Orib.2.58.151; τὰ ὀ. *meat for roasting*, Arist.*Pr.*927ᵃ21.

**ὀπτᾰσία** (A), ἡ, (ὀπτάζομαι) *vision*, *AP*6.210 codd. (Philet.; v. ὀπλισία), Lxx*Es.*4.17, *Ev.Luc.*1.22; simply, *appearance*, Lxx*Ma.*3.2, *Si.* 43.2.

**ὀπτᾰσία** (B), ἡ, prob. scribal error for ὀπτάνιον, *PHolm.*9.39.

***ὀπτάω**, pf. ὤπτηκα Euphro 1.5: irreg. part. Pass. ὀπτεύμενος Theoc.7.55: Dor. pres. part. ὀπτᾶντες Epich.164: fut. Med. ὀπτήσομαι (in pass. sense) Luc.*Asin.*31: aor. Pass., ὀπτηθῆναι Od.20.27: pf. Pass. ὤπτημαι Ar.*Fr.*627: (ὀπτός (A), q.v.):—*roast, broil*, κρέα ὤπτων Od.3.33, etc.; σπλάγχνα δ' ἄρ' ὀπτήσαντες ἐνώμων 20.252; ὤπτησάν τε περιφραδέως Il.1.466, 2.429: also c. gen. partit., ὀπτῆσαί τε κρεῶν *roast* some meat, Od.15.98; then in Hdt.9.120, Ar.*Av.*1690, X.*Cyr.*8.2.6, etc.; *broil* or *fry* fish, Ar.*Fr.* l.c., Crates Com.17, al.; *fry* an egg, *PLit.Lond.*170 (i A.D.); *toast* cheese, Eub.150.2.—Hence it appears that ὀπτᾶν was used of all kinds of *cooking by means of fire* or *dry heat*, opp. ἕψω (boil in water), which never appears in Hom., whose heroes ate only roast meat, κρέα δὲ μόνον ὤπτων, ἐπεὶ ἑψοντά γ' οὐ πεποίηκεν αὐτῶν οὐδένα Eub.120. 2. *bake* bread, Hdt.2.47; ὅκως ὀπτῷτο v.l. ὀπτῴη) ὁ ἄρτος Id.8.137, cf. X.*An.*5.4.29; ὀπτᾶν πλακοῦντας Ar.*Ra.*507; also of bricks or pottery, *bake, burn*, Hdt.1.179; καλῶς ὠπτημένη [χύτρα] Pl.*Hp.Ma.*288d; ὁ ὀπτώμενος κέραμος Arist. *Mete.*383ᵃ21. 3. *bake, scorch*, of the sun, ἐπεὶ τόκα μ' ἅλιος ὀπτῇ Bion *Fr.*15.12; ἡ γῆ ὀπτᾶται ὑπὸ τοῦ ἡλίου X.*Oec.*16.14. 4. metaph. (as we say), '*roast*' a man, τοῦτον ὀπτᾶν καὶ στρέφειν Ar.*Lys.* 839, cf. Sopat.6.9 (Pass.):—Pass., of the fire of love, ὀπτεύμενον ἐξ Ἀφροδίτας Theoc.7.55, cf. 23.34, *AP*12.92.7 (Mel.): so, prob., in Act., Sapph.115.

**ὀπτέον**, (ὄψομαι) *one must see*, Hld.7.17, Plot.6.7.28.

***ὀπτευτήρ**, ῆρος, ὁ, (ὀπτάω) *forger*, σιδήρου, of Hephaestus, Coluth.54.

**ὀπτ-εύω**, = ὁράω, *see*, Ar.*Av.*1061 (lyr.), A.D.*Synt.*290.18, Max.Tyr. 8.7; but ὀπτευσάμενοι (μόχθους) in Eust. ad D.P.195 is prob. f.l. for ὀττευσάμενοι. **-ήρ**, ῆρος, ὁ, (ὄψ) *one who looks* or *spies, spy, scout*, Od. 14.261, A.*Supp.*185, S.*Aj.*29. II. *one who has seen*, Id.*Ichn.*77; *eyewitness*, Antipho 5.27, X.*Cyr.*4.5.17. ***-ήρια** (sc. δῶρα), τά, *presents made by the bridegroom on seeing the bride without the veil*, = ἀνακαλυπτήρια, θεώρητρα, Poll.2.59, 3.36, Hsch. 2. generally, *presents upon seeing* or *for the sight of* a person, παιδὸς ὀ. E.*Ion*1127, cf. Call. *Dian.*74; προσβάλλων ἀκοαῖς ὀ. θυμοῦ Aspasia ap.Ath.5.219d.

**ὀπτ-ήσιμος**, ον, *for roasting*, Eub.4. **-ησις**, εως, ἡ, *roasting, frying*, σπλάγχνων, opp. κρεῶν ἕψησις, *SIG*57.34 (Milet., v B.C.), cf. Hp.*Aff.*49, Arist.*Mete.*381ᵃ23. 2. *baking*, of bread, J.*AJ*3.10.7, Ath. 3.109c (pl.); of pottery, *BGU*1143.17 (i B.C.), Luc.*Prom.Es* 2. 3. *overheating* of humours, Gal.13.335, 19.580. **-ήτειρα**, ἡ, *one who roasts*, κάμινος Call.*Fr.*475. **-ητέον**, *one must roast*, Dsc.5. 88. **-ητήρια**, τά, gloss on ὠψά, Hsch. (dub. sens.). **-ητός**, ή, όν, *roasted*, Eust.135.17.

**ὀπτ-ίζομαι**, Pass., = ὀπτάζομαι, f.l. in Archyt.ap.Iamb.*Protr.* 4. **-ίκια**, τά, = Lat. *auspicia*, Arr.*Epict.*3.24.117. **-ικός**, ή, όν, *of* or *for sight*: τὰ ὀπτικά *the theory of the laws of sight, optics*, Arist. *Metaph.*1077ᵃ5, etc.; so ἡ ὀπτική (sc. θεωρία) ib.997ᵇ20; -καὶ ἀποδείξεις Id.*APo.*76ᵃ24; -καὶ λόγοι Gal.17(2).214; -κὴ δύναμις Id.8.20. Adv. -κῶς Id.18(1).309.

**ὀπτιλίασις**· ὀφθαλμίασις, Hsch. (ὀπτιαλίασις cod.): **ὀπτιλίας** is prob. cj. for ὁ ἐπὶ τηλείας in Id. s.v. λαμόπτης.

**Ὀπτιλῖτις** or **-ιλλέτις**, ιδος, ἡ, a name of Athena, Plu.*Lyc.*11.

**ὀπτῖλος** [ῐ], ὁ, Dor. for ὀφθαλμός, Metop.ap.Stob.3.1.115, Plu.*Lyc.* 11; **ὀπτίλλος** in *IG*4²(1).121.40 (Epid., iv B.C.), al., Hdn.Gr.1.159, 2.560 (whence the spelling with one λ should prob. be corrected).

**ὀπτίων**, ωνος, ὁ, Lat. *optio, assistant*; esp. in military sense, *adjutant* or *aide-de-camp*, Plu.*Galb.*24, where ὀπίων is f.l., cf. *IGRom.*4. 825 (Hierapolis), 3.1131 (Syria), *Sammelb.*6063 (Nubia). (Plu. wrongly derives it from the Greek ὄψομαι, fut. of ὁράω.)

**ὀπτόπλινθον**, τό, *baked tile*, *PFlor.*378.17 (v A.D., pl.), etc.

**ὀπτός** (A), ή, όν, *roasted, broiled*, σῖτός τε κρέα τ' ὀπτά Od.22.21, cf. 16.443; νῶτα βοὸς.. ὀπτ' ἐν χερσὶν ἑλών 4.66; σάρκες A.*Ag.*1097; ἑφθὰ καὶ ὀπτά boiled meats and *roast*, E.*Cyc.*358 (lyr.), cf. Hdt.2.77, Pl.*R.*404c. 2. *baked*, βοῦν καὶ ἵππον.. ὀπτοὺς ἐν καμίνοισι Hdt.1.133; of bread, Id.2.92; of fish, *PCair.Zen.*66.8 (iii B.C.); also of bricks and pottery, *baked, burned*, Hdt.1.180, 186, X.*An.*2.4.12, *PAmh.*2. 99(a)9 (ii A.D.), etc.; of soil, *parched*, X.*Oec.*16.13: Sup. ὀπτότατος *best dressed* or *done*, Cratin.143. 3. of iron, *forged, tempered*, S. *Ant.*475. 4. *scorched*, τὰ ὑπέρθυρ' ὀπτά Herod.2.65.

**ὀπτός** (B), ή, όν, (ὁράω, ὄψομαι) *visible*, Luc.*Lex.*9, Ath.8.338c.

**ὀπτώ**, v. ὀκτώ.

**ὄπτω**, *see*, A.D.*Adv.*198.7.

**ὀπυάζομαι**, *get married*, in irreg. aor. Pass. subj. 1 pl. ὀπυασθῶμεθα *Lyr.Alex.Adesp.*1.52 (dub. l.).

***ὄπυι**, Dor. for ὅποι, *SIG*56.39 (Argos, v B.C.), *Leg.Gort.*4.15; οὐδ' ὄπυι κα ἕνθῃ no matter *where* he may go, *Berl.Sitzb.*1927.158 (Cyrene).

**ὀπυιητής**, έω, ὁ, *husband*, Herod.4.84.

***ὀπυίω**, Att. ὀπύω Arist.*EN*1148ᵇ32, Moer.p.278 P., also Cerc.17. 41 (Hsch. gives ὀπυόλαι· γεγαμηκότες), used by Hom. only in pres., and in impf. with or without augm.: fut. ὀπύσω [ῡ] Ar.*Ach.*255.—Ep. Verb, used also in Cret. (v. infr.) and later Att. Prose: I. Act., of the man, *marry, take to wife* (= τὸ κατὰ νόμον μίγνυσθαι, Hsch. s.v. βεινεῖν), τὴν Εὐμήλος ὄπυιε Od.4.798, cf. 2.207, Il.16.178; πρεσβυτάτην δ' ὤπυιε 13.429, cf. 18.383; τοῦ γὰρ ὀπυίεις παῖδα Hes.*Sc.*356; δῶκεν ὀπυίειν θυγατέρα ἣν Id.*Th.*819, cf. Pi.*I.*4(3).59, Ar. l.c.; αἱ δέ κα.. ὁ ἐπιβάλλων ἡβίονσαν λείονσαν ὀπυίεθθαι μὴ λῇ ὀπυίεν if.. the man whose right it is does not wish to *marry* her, though she is of marriageable age and willing to *marry*, *Leg.Gort.*7.42: abs., πέντε δέ τοι φίλοι υἷες.., οἱ δύ' ὀπυίοντες, τρεῖς δ' ἠΐθεοι θαλέθοντες two *wedded*, etc., Od.6.63. 2. Pass., of the woman, *to be married*, τόν ῥ' ἐξ Αἰσύμηθεν ὀπυιομένη τέκε μήτηρ Il.8.304, cf. Solon.ap.Plu.*Sol.* 20; αἱ κύσαιτο καὶ τέκοι ϝοικέα μὴ ὀπυιομένα *Leg.Gort.*4.19: c. dat., αἱ δὲ τῷ αὐτῷ αὐτὶν ὀπυίοιτο πρὸ τῶ ἐνιαυτῶ ib.4. II. later, in Act., merely *to have connexion with* a woman, Cerc. l.c., Luc.*Eun.* 12, *Merc.Cond.*41, etc.:—Pass., of the woman, οὐκ ὀπύουσιν ἀλλ' ὀπύονται [γυναῖκες] Arist. l.c., cf. *AP*10.56.7 (Pall.); ἔνθ' ἂν εὕρῃ τὸν ἄρρενα ὑπὸ τῆς θηλείας ὀπυιόμενον D.H.10.2. (ὀπύ(σ) yω, cf. ὀπυσ-τύς and perh. Skt. *pusyati* 'nourish', 'maintain'.)

**ὄπυς**, Dor. Adv., = ὅποι, *IG*4²(1).74.14 (Epid.), *SIG*1166 (Dodona).

**ὀπυστύς**, ύος, ἡ, (ὀπυίω) *marriage*, *GDI*4971.7 (Crete).

**ὄπω**, Dor. Adv., = ὁπόθεν, *Leg.Gort.*5.23, 10.33, *GDI*4998 v 15 (Crete), *IG*9(1).334.9 (Locr., v B.C.).

**ὀπώδης**, ες, v. ὀποειδής.

**ὀπωπ-α**, pf. 2 of ὁράω:—hence late pres. **ὀπωπέω**, Orph.*A.*183, 1022; ὀπωπήσασθαι Euph.107. (Cf. ὄψ.) ***-ή**, ἡ, (ὄπωπα) poet. for ὄψις, *a sight* or *view*, ὅπως ἤντησας ὀπωπῆς Od.3.97. 2. *outward appearance*, μετεβάλλετ' ὀπωπάν Erinn. in *PSI*9.1090.53+13 (p. xii), cf. Nonn.*D.*2.60, al. II. *sight, power of seeing*, ἁμαρτήσεσθαι ὀπωπῆς Od.9.512. 2. *eyeball*, A.R.2.109: pl., ib.445; but, *eyes*, Id. 3.1023, 4.1670, Opp.*C.*3.75. **-ητήρ**, ῆρος, ὁ, = ὀπτήρ, *h.Merc.*15, prob. in *Epigr.Gr.*1032 (Augusta Treverorum). **-ια** (sc. ὀστέα), τά, *bones of the eyes*, Hp.*Oss.*1.

***ὀπώρ-α**, Ion. -η, ἡ: sts. **ὀπώρα**, cf. χεῖμα χὠπώραν, i.e. καὶ ὀπ-, Alcm.76 (χειμάχωι πάραν, etc. codd.); pr. nn. Ὀπωρίς *IG*5(1).1497, *Hopora* *CIL*6.21782; cf. μεθόπωρον, μεθοπωρινός:—*the part of the year between the rising of Sirius and of Arcturus* (i.e. the last days of July, all Aug., and part of Sept.), *the latter part of summer*; Hom.

names θέρος and ὀπώρη together, θέρος τεθαλυῖά τ' ὀπώρη Od.11.192; Σείριος being the star of ὀπώρη, Il.22.27; cf. ὀπωρινός.—In later times it became the name of a definite season, *autumn* (v. ὥρα I. 1 c), but was still used sts. to denote *summer* (autumn being distd. as φθινόπωρον or μετόπωρον), ἀρξάμενος ἀπὸ τοῦ ἠρινοῦ χρόνου πρὸ ὀπώρας X.*HG*3.2.10, cf. Ar.*Av.*709, Arist.*Mete.*348ᵃ1; ἐπ' ὀκτὼ μῆνας Κυρηναίους ὀπώρη ἐπέχει Hdt.4.199; νέας δ' ὀπώρας ἡνίκ' ἂν ξανθῇ στάχυς A.*Fr.*304.7. II. *fruit*, γλαυκῆς ὀπώρας.. ποτοῦ χυθέντος..Βακχίας ἀπ' ἀμπέλου S.*Tr.*703; τέμνεται βλαστουμένη καλῶς ὀ. Id.*Fr.*255.8; σικυούς, βότρυς, ὀπώραν Ar.*Fr.*569.1: so in Prose, X. *HG*2.4.25, Pl.*Lg.*844d, 845c, Arist.*HA*606ᵇ2, 629ᵃ2: in this sense also in pl., Is.11.43; Alcm.(75) even calls *honey* κηρίνα ὀπώρα; ἐαρινὴ ὀπώρα Alciphr.*Fr.*6.10. III. metaph., life's *summer, the time of* youthful *ripeness*, Pi.*I.*2.5; τέρειναν ματέρ' οἰνάνθας ὀπώραν (v. οἰνάνθη) Id.*N.*5.6; *ripe virginity*, A.*Supp.*998, 1015; ὀ. Κύπριδος Chaerem.12. -άριον, τό, *pomarium*, *Gloss.* -εύς, έως, ὁ, epith. of Zeus at Acraephiae, *IG*7.2733. -ιαῖος, α, ον, *autumnal*, τὰ ὀ., = ὀπώρα II, *fruit*, Thphr.*Ign.*41. -ίζω, (ὀπώρα II) *gather fruit*, ὀ. ὀπώραν Pl.*Lg.*844a; σῦκα ib.844e; ἀπὸ συκῆς ὠπώριζε D.L.6.61; *eat fruits*, Arist.*HA*612ᵃ10; *gather in the fruits*, Plu.*Per.*9:—so in Med., *gather in one's fruits*, Theopomp.Hist.89: metaph., τοῖς τὰν ὥραν αὐτῶν βαλλομένοις ὀπωρίξασθαι Diusap Stob.4.21.16. II. *gather fruit off*, ὀπωριεῦντες (Ion. fut. for -ιοῦντες) τοὺς φοίνικας Hdt.4.172, 182. ※ -ικός, ή, όν, *of fruit*: in fem. -κή, ἡ, name of a remedy for dysentery, Plin.*HN*24.129. 2. = ὀπωρινός, *Gp.*4.1.14. -ιμαῖος, α, ον, *of fruit*, εἴδη dub. l. in *PLond.*3.974i3, ii5 (iv A.D.), cf. *Addenda* p.vii). -ιμος, = ὀπωρικός, Anon.ap.Suid. -ινός, ή, όν, *of* ὀπώρα or *late summer*, ἀστέρ' ὀπωρινῷ ἐναλίγκιον, i.e. Sirius, the star whose rising marked the beginning of that season (v. ὀπώρα), Il.5.5; ἦμαρ 16.385; βορέης 21.346, Od.5.328; ὄμβρος Hes.*Op.*674, 677; ὄρχατοι E.*Fr.*896; δέλφαξ Ar.*Fr.*506.1; πυλαία *SIG*239C31, al. (Delph., iv B.C.). [In Hom. the last syll. is always long (by position in Il.21.346), and the penult. is long also, metri gr.: when the ult. is short, the penult. also is short, as in Hes.*Op.*674; in Att. ῑ always; cf. μετοπωρινός.] -ισμός, ὁ, *vintage*, Aq.*De.*7.13.

**ὀπωρο-βᾰσιλίς**, ίδος, ἡ, *queen of fruits*, a fine kind of *fig*, Anon.ap. Ath.3.75d. -θήκη, ἡ, *fruit-room*, Varro *RR*1.59. -κάπηλος [ᾰ], ὁ or ἡ, *fruiterer*, Alciphr.3.60. -λόγος, ον, *plucking fruit*, Opp.*C.*1.125. -πώλης, ου, ὁ, *fruiterer*, *POxy.*980 (iii A.D.), 1133.7 (iv A.D.), Hsch. s.v. ὡραιοπώλης; gen. -πώλη *MAMA*3.359 (Corycus); but ὀπωρώνης was the Att. word acc. to Phryn.181. -τροφέω, *pomifero*, *Gloss.* -φᾰγία, ἡ, *eating of fruit*, Sch.Gal.ap.*Corp. Med.Gr.*5.9(2).198, Steph.*in Hp.*1.54D. -φορέω, *bear fruit*, *AP* 6.252 (Antiphil.). -φόρος, ον, *bearing fruit*, ib.7.321; δένδρα *Gp.*3.13.4; ὀξόβαφα *BGU*781 iii5 (i A.D.). -φυλάκιον [ᾰ], τό, *hut of a garden-watcher*, Lxx *Is.*1.8, cf. Theognost.*Can.*136; = *pomarium*, *Gloss.* -φύλαξ [ῠ], ᾰκος, ὁ, *watcher of fruits*, *garden-watcher*, Arist.*Pr.*938ᵃ16, D.S.4.6, *PRyl.*244 *Intr.* (iii A.D.).

**ὀπωρώνης**, ου, ὁ, = ὀπωροπώλης (q.v.), D.18.262, Aristaenet.2.1, *PLond.*5.1794.6 (v A.D.).

※ **ὅπως**, Ep. also and Aeol. ὅππως, Ion. ὅκως, Dor. ὁπῶς acc. to A.D.*Adv.*173.11: correlat. to ὡς and πῶς. A. ADV. OF MANNER, Relat. *as, in such manner as*, and with interrog. force *how, in what manner*, rarely indef., v. infr. A. V. B. FINAL CONJUNCTION, *in such a manner that, in order that.*

A. ADV. OF MANNER, *how, as*: I. Relat. to ὥς or οὕτως (like ὡς), *in such manner as, as*: 1. with the ordinary Constr. of the Relat.: a. with ind., ἤ τοι νόστον, ὅπως φρεσὶ σῇσι μενοινᾷς, ὥς τοι Ζεὺς τελέσειεν Od.15.111; οὕτως ὅ... S.*Tr.*330; ὧδ' ὅ. Id.*El.*1301; οὕτως ὅ. δύνανται Th.7.67: sts. an analogous word replaces the antec. Adv., με τοῖον ἔθηκεν, ὅπως (for οἷον) ἐθέλει Od.16.208: freq. without any antec. expressed, ἔλθοι ὅ...ἐθέλω (sc. αὐτὸν ἐλθεῖν) 14.172; ἕρξον ὅ. ἐθέλεις Il.4.37, Od.13.145; χρῶ ὅ. βούλει X.*Cyr.*8.3.46; ποίει ὅ. ἄριστόν σοι δοκεῖ εἶναι ib.4.5.50; ὅ. ἔχω *as* I am, *on the spot*, S.*Ph.*819. b. with fut. ind., esp. after Verbs of seeing, providing, taking care.., *in the manner in which, how, that*, οἱ Περσικοὶ νόμοι ἐπιμέλονται ὅπως μὴ τοιοῦτοι ἔσονται οἱ πολῖται X.*Cyr.*1.2.3; ποιέειν ὅκως μηκέτι κεῖνος ἐς Ἕλληνας ἀπίξεται Hdt.5.23; ἐφρόντιζον ὅκως μὴ λείψομαι τῶν πρότερον γενομένων Id.7.8.α'; cf. Pl.*Ap.*29e; ἔπρασσον ὅπως τις βοήθεια ἥξει Th.3.4; τοῦτο μηχανᾶσθαι ὅπως ἀποφεύξεται πᾶν ποιῶν θάνατον Pl.*Ap.*39a; τούτου στοχαζόμενοι, ὅπως..ἔσονται Id.*Grg.*502e (cf. infr. III. 1 b, etc.): this fut. ind. may become opt. after a historical tense, ἐπεμελεῖτο ὅπως μήτε ἄσιτοι μήτε ἄποτοί ποτε ἔσοιντο X.*Cyr.*8.1.43, cf. *HG*7.5.3, *Cyr.*8.1.10, *Oec.*7.5, *Ages.*2.8; and ὅπως is freq. used interchangeably with such forms as δι' ὧν, ὅτῳ τρόπῳ, etc., εἰσηγοῦνται μὴ δι' ὧν..ἀσκήσουσιν, ἀλλ' ὅπως..δόξουσι Isoc.1.4, cf. Th.6.11: this sense easily passes into a final sense, *so that*, τοῦτο ἀπόβαλε οὕτω ὅκως μηκέτι ἥξει Hdt.3.40; οὕτω δ' (sc. ποίει) ὅπως μήτηρ σε μὴ 'πιγνώσεται S.*El.*1296, cf. Ar.*Ra.*905, X.*Cyr.*4.5.25, *HG* 2.4.17; v. infr. B. 2. with ἄν (Ep. κε) and subj. in indefinite sentences, *in whatever way, just as, however*, ὅππως κεν ἐθέλῃσιν Il.20.243 (but ὅπως ἐθέλῃσιν (without κε) Od.1.349, 6.189); οὕτως ὅκως ἂν καὶ δυνώμεθα Hdt.8.143; οὕτως ὅπως ἂν αὐτοὶ βούλωνται X.*Cyr.*1.1.2, cf. *IG*2².1.13 (v B.C.), Pl.*Phd.*116a, *Smp.*174b, etc. b. with opt. after historical tenses, οὕτως ὅ. τύχοιεν Th.8.95; ὅ. βούλοιντο X.*HG* 2.3.13; in a gnomic statement, εἰκῇ κράτιστον ζῆν ὅ. δύναιτό τις S.*OT*979: when ἄν appears with the opt., it belongs to the Verb and not to ὅπως, ὅ. ἄν τις ὀνομάσαι τοῦτο *however* one might think fit to call it, D.13.4. 3. a very common phrase is οὐκ ἔστιν ὅ. (οὐκ ἔσθ' ὅπως) there is no way *in which*.., it cannot be *that*, οὐκ ἔστι ὅκως κοτὲ σοὺς δέξονται λόγους Hdt.7.102, cf. Ar.*Pl.*18, D.18.208, al.; so οὐκ ἔστιν ὅ. οὐ. *fieri non potest quin*, οὐκ ἔσθ' ὅ. οὐ πιστὸν ἐξ ὑμῶν πτερὸν ἐξήγαγ' S.*OC*97, cf. Ar.*Ach.*116, *Eq.*426, *Th.*882, Pl.*Ap.*27e; οὐδαμῶς ὅ. οὐ, in answer, *it must positively be so*, Id.*Tht.*160d; so also οὐκ ἂν γένοιτο τοῦθ' ὅ...οὐ φανῶ S.*OT*1058; οὐ γὰρ γένοιτ' ἄν, ταῦθ' ὅ. οὐχ ὧδ' ἔχειν (anacoluth. for ἔχει or ἕξει) Id.*Aj.*378: so in questions, ἔσθ' ὅ...ἔλθωμεν; Ar.*V.*471 (v.l. -οιμεν); ἔστιν οὖν ὅ. ὁ τοιοῦτος φιλοσοφήσει; Pl.*R.*495a, cf. *Phdr.*262b, *Tht.*154c: so, besides ind. of all tenses, οὐκ ἔσθ' ὅ. may be folld. by opt. with ἄν, οὐ γὰρ ἔσθ' ὅπως μί' ἡμέρα γένοιτ' ἂν ἡμέραι δύο Ar.*Nu.*1181, cf. *V.*212, Isoc.12.156, Pl.*La.*184c: by ind. with ἄν, οὐκ ἔστιν ὅπως ἄν..κατέστησαν Isoc.15.206, cf. D.33.28: ἄν is omitted in οὐκ ἔσθ' ὅπως λέξαιμι A.*Ag.*620, cf. E.*Alc.*52, Ar.*V.*471 (v.l. ἔλθωμεν). 4. in Trag., etc., like ὡς in comparisons, κῦμ' ὅπως A.*Pr.*1001; γύγης ὅπως S.*Tr.*32, cf. 442, 683; ὅπως δρῦν ὑλοτόμοι σχίζουσι κάρα Id.*El.*98 (anap.); ὅπως ἁ πάνδυρτος ἀηδών ib.1076 (lyr.), cf. *Ph.*777, E.*Andr.*1140; ὅκως τις καλλίης κάτω κύπτων Herod.3.41; so in Locr. Prose, ὅπω(ς) ξένον *IG*9(1).334.2 (v B.C.). 5. like ὡς or ὅτι, with Sup. of Advs., ὅ. ἄριστα A.*Ag.*600, *IG*1².44.8, etc.; ὅ. ἀνωτάτω *as* high up *as* possible, Ar.*Pax* 207; in full, οὕτως ὅ. ἥδιστα (sc. ἔχει) S.*Tr.*330. 6. with a gen. added, σοῦσθε ὅ. ποδῶν run *as you are off for* feet, i.e. as quick as you can, A *Supp.*837 (lyr., where however (ἔχετε) shd. prob. be added); v. infr. III. 10. ἔχω (A) B. II. 2 b. 7. sts. of Time, *when*, Τρῶες..ὅπως ἴδον αἷμ' Ὀδυσῆος.., ἐπ' αὐτῷ πάντες ἔβησαν Il.11.459, cf. 12.208, Od.3.373: freq. in Hdt. with opt., *whenever*, ὅκως μὲν εἴη ἐν τῇ γῇ καρπὸς ἁδρός 1.17, cf. 68, 100, 162, 186, 2.13, 174, al.: in Trag. and Com., A.*Pers.*198, S.*El.*749, *Tr.*765, Ar.*Nu.*60: with Sup. of Advs.. ὅ. πρῶτα *as soon as*, Hes.*Th.*156; ὅ. ὤκιστα Thgn.427; ὅ. τάχιστα A.*Pr.*230. 8. of Place, *where*, dub. in Herod.3.75. II. ὅπως is sts. used to introduce the substance of a statement, after Verbs of saying, thinking, or perceiving, *that, how*, λόγῳ ἀνάπεισον ὅκως.. Hdt.1.37; οὐδὲ φήσω ὅκως.. Id.2.49, cf. 3.115, 116; τοῦτ' αὐτὸ μή μοι φράζ', ὅπως οὐκ εἶ κακός S.*OT*548, cf. *Ant.*223, Pl.*Euthd.*296e; after ἐλπίζειν, S.*El.*963, E.*Heracl.*1051; after Verbs of emotion, ἐμοὶ δ' ἄχος.., ὅπως δὴ δηρὸν ἀποίχεται grief is mine, when I think *how*.. (i.e. *that*..), Od.4.109, cf. S.*Ph.*169 (lyr.); after θαυμάζω freq in Att., θαυμάζω ὅ. ποτὲ ἐπείσθησαν Ἀθηναῖοι X.*Mem.*1.1.20, cf. Pl.*Cri.*43a. 2. οὐχ ὅ...ἀλλὰ or ἀλλὰ καὶ.. is *not only not..but*.., and is expld. by an ellipsis of λέγω or ἐρῶ (cf. ὅτι IV), οὐχ ὅ. κωλυταὶ..γενήσεσθε, ἀλλὰ καὶ..δύναμιν προσλαβεῖν περιόψεσθε *not only* will you *not* become.., *but* you will *also*.., Th.1.35, cf. X.*HG*5.4.34, D.6.9; οὐχ ὅ. ὑμῖν τῶν αὑτοῦ τι ἐπέδωκεν, ἀλλὰ τῶν ὑμετέρων πολλὰ ὑφῄρηται Lys.30.26; οὐχ ὅ. τούτων χάριν ἀπέδοσαν, ἀλλ' ἀπολιπόντες ὑμᾶς εἰς τὴν Λακεδαιμονίων συμμαχίαν εἰσῆλθον Isoc.14.27, cf. D.18.131, 53.13; οὐ γὰρ ὅπως.., ἀλλὰ καὶ.. Id.21.11; οὔκουν ὅπως.., ἀλλὰ.. X.*Cyr.*8.2.12; also οὐχ ὅ..., ἀλλ' οὐδέ.., οὐχ ὅ. ἀδικοῦντες, ἀλλ' οὐδ' ἐπιδημοῦντες ἐφυγαδευόμεθα Id.*HG*2.4.14; οὐχ ὅ. τῆς κοινῆς ἐλευθερίας μετέχομεν, ἀλλ' οὐδὲ δουλείας μετρίας τυχεῖν ἠξιώθημεν Isoc.14.5; διμοιρίαν λαμβάνων ἐν ταῖς θοίναις οὐχ ὅπως ἀμφοτέραις ἐχρῆτο, ἀλλὰ διαπέμπων οὐδετέραν αὑτῷ κατέλειπε X.*Ages.*5.1; οὐχ ὅ. ζημιοῦν, ἀλλὰ μηδ' ἀτιμάζειν.. Th.3.42: so sts. μὴ ὅ. (where an imper. must be supplied), μὴ ὅ. ὀρχεῖσθαι ἀλλ' οὐδὲ ὀρθοῦσθαι ἐδύνασθε do *not think that* you could dance = *so far from being able* to dance, X.*Cyr.*1.3.10. b. οὐχ ὅ. rarely follows another clause, *to say nothing of*.., *let alone*.., πεπαύμεθ' ἡμεῖς, οὐχ ὅ. σε παύσομεν S.*El.*796; μηδ' ἐμπίδα, οὐχ ὅπως ταῦρον ἔτι ἄρασθαι δυνάμενος.. *let alone* a bull, Luc.*Cont.*8, cf. *Prom.*8, *Pr.Im.*7, *Pisc.* 31. III. in indirect questions, *how, in what way* or *manner*: 1. with ind., a. ἔσπετε νῦν μοι ὅππως δὴ..πῦρ ἔμπεσε νηυσίν Il.16.113; εἴπ' ἄγε μ'..ὅππως τούσδ' ἵππους λάβετον 10.545; εὖ μοι κατάλεξον ὅπως ἤντησας Od.3.97; ὅπως ἠφανίσθη οὐδὲ λόγῳ εἰκότι δύνανται ἀποφαίνειν Antipho 5.26; Ἀλκιβιάδης ἀνήχθη..ἐπὶ κατασκοπὴν..τοῦ οἴκαδε κατάπλου ὅπως ἡ πόλις πρὸς αὐτὸν ἔχοι X.*HG*1.4.11; οὐδέ τί πω σάφα ἴδμεν ὅπως ἔσται τάδε ἔργα Il.2.252, etc. b. notably fut. after Verbs of deliberation (like the subj., v. infr. 2), φραζώμεθ' ὅπως ἔσται τάδε ἔργα 4.14; φράζευ ὅπως Δαναοῖσιν ἀλεξήσεις κακὸν ἦμαρ (v.l. ἀλεξήσῃς) 9.251, cf. Od.13.376, 386, 19.557, 20.29, 39. 2. with deliberative subj. after Verbs of deliberation, taking care, and the like, λεύσσει ὅπως ὄχ' ἄριστα..γένηται Il.3.110; ἐνόησεν (gnomic aor.) ὅππως κέρδος ἔῃ 10.225; ἀλλ' ἄγεθ' ἡμεῖς οἵδε περιφραζώμεθα πάντες νόστον ὅπως ἔλθῃσι Od.1.77, cf. 13.365; οὐκ οἶδ' ὅπως ..φῶ S.*OT*1367, cf. *Aj.*428, Lys.8.5, Pl.*Men.*91d; ἐπιμελητέον ὅπως τρέφωνται οἱ ἵπποι X.*Eq.Mag.*1.3, cf. *Oec.*7.36, 37, 9.14, 15.1, Pl.*Grg.*515c.—Sts. the fut. and subj. are conjoined without difference of meaning, ἐπράττετο γὰρ.., πρῶτον μὲν ὅπως μὴ περιμείνητε.., δεύτερον δὲ ὅπως ψηφιεῖσθε.., τρίτον δὲ ὅπως μὴ ἔσται Aeschin.3.65, cf. X.*Ages.*7.7, *Mem.*2.2.10.—On ὅπως ἄν (κεν), v. infr. 5. 3. with opt. after tenses of past time, τῶν ἄθλων ὅπως ἀποβήσοιτο ib.1.3.2, etc.: after Verbs of deliberation, being virtually orat. obliq., μερμήριξε..Ἥρη ὅπως ἐξαπάφοιτο (orat. rect. πῶς ἐξαπάφωμαι;) Il.14.160; μερμήριζεν ὅπως ἀπολοίατο πᾶσαι νῆες Od.9.554, cf. 420; οὐ γὰρ εἴχομεν ..ὅπως δρῶντες καλῶς πράξαιμεν S.*Ant.*271; ἐπεμελήθημεν ὅπως ἐξαλειφθείη αὐτῷ τὰ ἁμαρτήματα Lys.6.39, cf. 13.32, X.*Cyr.*6.2.11. 4. with opt. and ἄν freq. expressing a wish, which in orat. rect. would be expressed by πῶς ἄν, σκόπει ὅ. ἂν ἀποθάνοιμεν ἀνδρικώτατα Ar.*Eq.*81 (v.l. ἀποθάνωμεν), cf. *Nu.*760; βουλευόμεθα ὅ. ἂν τὴν ἡγεμονίαν λάβοιεν τῆς Ἑλλάδος X.*HG*7.1.33, cf. *Cyr.*2.1.4; τῶν ἄλλων ἐπιμελεῖται ὅ. ἂν θηρῷεν (v.l. -ῶσιν) ib.1.2.10: the opt. with ἄν and subj. sts. appear in consecutive clauses, Id.*HG*3.2.1. 5. ὅπως ἄν (κεν) with the subj. is used after imper. or inf. used as imper., πείρα ὅπως κεν δὴ σὴν πατρίδα γαῖαν ἵκηαι Od.4.545; φράζεσθαι.., ὅππως κε μνηστῆρας.. κτείνῃς 1.295; σκοπεῖτε.., ὅ. ἂν ὑμῖν πρᾶγος εὖ νικᾷ τόδε A.*Supp.*233, etc.; φύλασσε..ἔπειθ' ὅ. ἂν..ἡ χάρις..ἐξ ἁπλῆς διπλῆ φανῇ S.*Tr.*618, cf. E.*IA*539: in Prose, ἐπιμεληθῆναι ὅ. ἂν.. X.*Cyr.*8.3.6, cf. Pl.*Prt.* 326a; μηχανᾶσθαι Id.*Phdr.*239b, *Grg.*481a, cf. Ar.*Eq.*917. 6. rarely c. inf., ἐπιμελήθητε προθύμως ὅπως διπλάσια..σῖτα καὶ ποτὰ παρασκευασθῆναι X.*Cyr.*4.2.37 (v.l. -εσκευασμένα ᾖ), cf. *Oec.*7.29, *HG*6.2.32; so later ὅπως παρακολουθῆμεν (Dor. inf.) *Supp.Epigr.*1.170.18 (cf. p.138, Delph., ii B.C.); ὅπως..ἔχειν, ὅπως..εἴργεσθαι, D.S.20.4,85; ὅπως πέμπιν *PTeb.*315.30 (ii A.D.). 7. after Verbs of fear and caution, ὅπως and ὅπως μή are used with fut. ind. or aor. subj.:—the readings are freq. uncertain: the following (among others) are made certain either by the metre or the form, a. with fut. ind., δέδοιχ' ὅπως μὴ τεύξομαι Ar.*Eq.*112; παντὶ λόγῳ ἀντιτείνετε εὐλαβούμενοι ὅπως μὴ..οἰχήσομαι Pl.*Phd.*91c; φόβος..ἔστιν..ὅπως μὴ αὖθις διασχισθησόμεθα Id.*Smp.*193a: sts. the preceding Verb is omitted, ὅπως μὴ οὐκ..ἔσομαι Id.*Men.*77a. b. with aor. subj., τὴν θεὸν δ' ὅ. λάθω δέδοικα E.*IT*995; φυλάττου, ὅ. μὴ εἰς τοὐναντίον ἔλθῃς X.*Mem.*3.6.16: rarely with pres., οὐ φοβεῖ ὅ. μὴ ἀνόσιον πρᾶγμα τυγχάνῃς πράττων Pl.*Euthphr.*4e: sts. the preceding Verb is omitted, with aor. subj., ὅκως μή τι ὑμῖν πανώλεθρον κακὸν ἐς τὴν χώρην ἐσβάλωσι Hdt.6.85: with pres. subj., ὅπως μὴ..ᾖ τοῦτο Pl.*Cra.* 430d. c. with opt. representing subj. after a historical tense, X. *Mem.*2.9.3. 8. this Constr. is used in admonitions or commands: in the orig. Constr. a Verb implying caution or circumspection precedes, ὅρα ὅκως μή σευ ἀποστήσονται Πέρσαι Hdt.3.36; ἄθρει.. ὅπως μὴ ἐκδύσεται Ar.*V.*141; τηρώμεσθ' ὅπως μὴ..αἰσθήσεται ib.372: but this came to be omitted, and ὅπως or ὅπως μή with fut. ind. or aor. subj. are exactly = the imper., ἔμβα χὤπως ἀρεῖς Id.*Ra.*378 (lyr.): most freq. with fut. ind., ὅκως λόγον δώσεις τῶν μετεχείρισας χρημάτων, = δίδου λόγον, Hdt.3.142; ὅπως παρέσει μοι, = πάρισθι, Ar.*Av.* 131; ὅπως πετήσει Id.*Pax*77, cf. X.*An.*1.7.3, Lys.1.21, 12.50, Pl.*Grg.* 489a, etc.: rarely with 1 pers., ὁποῖα κισσὸς δρυός, ὅπως τῆσδ' ἕξομαι E.*Hec.*398, cf. Ar.*Ec.*297 (lyr.): very rarely with aor. subj., ὅπως μή τι ἡμᾶς σφήλῃ Pl.*Euthd.*296a codd.; ὅπως μὴ..ἐξαπατήσῃ Id.*Prt.*313c; ὅπως μὴ ποιήσητε D.4.20 codd.—The codd. freq. vary, as between διδάξεις and -ξῃς Ar.*Nu.*824; τιμωρήσονται and -ωνται Th.1.56; πράξομεν and -ωμεν ib.82; θορυβήσει and -σῃ D.13.14, etc.—Since the fut. is frequently, and the aor. (whether 1 or 2) rarely guaranteed by metre or form, the aor. 1 forms shd. prob. be rejected, both in signf. 7 and 8, in cases where codd. vary. 9. as the echo to a preceding πῶς; in dialogue, *A* καὶ πῶς; *B* ὅπως; [do you ask] *how?* Ar. *Eq.*128; *A* πῶς με χρὴ καλεῖν; *B* ὅπως; Id.*Nu.*677, cf. *Pl.*139. 10. with a gen. (v. supr. I.6), οὐκ οἶδα παιδείας ὅπως ἔχει καὶ δικαιοσύνης *in the matter of..*, Pl.*Grg.*470e, cf. *R.*389c. IV. in *direct* questions, *how?* ἔπραξας ὅπως; Jul.*Ep.*82 p.106 B.-C.; cf. ὅστις. V. indef., *anyhow*, τὸ οὐδ' ὅ. the expression '*not at all*', Pl.*Tht.*183b (v.l. οὐδ' οὕτως).

B. FINAL CONJUNCTION, *that, in order that*, the original notion of modality being merged in that of purpose or design, cf. ἵνα, with which it is sts. interchanged, Antipho 1.23 and 24, And.3.14, Lycurg. 119 sq.:—in early Att. Inscrr. only ὅπως ἄν is used, *IG*1$^{2}$.39.19, al.; ὅπως without ἄν only once in cent. iv B.C., ib.2$^{2}$.226.42 (343 B.C.), after which it becomes gradually prevalent: 1. with subj., a. after primary tenses, or after subj. or imper., τὸν δὲ μνηστῆρες.. λοχῶσιν, ὅπως ἀπὸ φῦλον ὄληται Od.14.181, cf. A.*Ch.*873, S.*Ph.*238, *El.*457, X.*Mem.*2.10.2, etc. b. after historical tenses (v. ἵνα B.I.1b), when there is no pf. form, or when the aor. represents the pf., ξυνελέγημεν ἐνθάδε, ὅ. προμελετήσωμεν we were convened, i.e. we have met in assembly, Ar.*Ec.*117; παρήλθομεν.., ὅπως μὴ χεῖρον βουλεύσησθε Th.1.73; also when the occurrence purposed is regarded from the point of view of the person purposing, ἦλθον πρεσβευσόμενοι, ὅπως μὴ σφίσι..τὸ αὐτῶν [ναυτικὸν] ἐμπόδιον γένηται ib.31, cf. 57,65, etc.: sts. the opt. and subj. appear in consecutive clauses, φρυκτοὺς παρεσκευασμένους ἐς αὐτὸ τοῦτο, ὅπως ἀσαφῆ τὰ σημεῖα..ᾖ καὶ μὴ βοηθοῖεν Id.3.22, cf. 6.96, 7.17. 2. with opt. after historical tenses, πὰρ δέ οἱ αὐτὸς ἔστη, ὅπως..κῆρας ἀλάλκοι Il.21.548; more freq. in Od., as 13.319, 14.312, 18.160, 22.472; so in S.*OT*1005, *OC*1305, X.*Cyr.*1.4.25, Pl.*Ti.*77e, etc.: after historical pres., πέμπει τούσδ' ὅπως κτείνοιεν A.*Pers.*450; ἡγεμόνα πέμπει ὅπως ἄγοι X.*An.*4.7.19: after opt., ἔλθοι..ὅ. γένοιτο A.*Eu.*297, cf. S.*Aj.*1221 (lyr.). 3. with ind., a. of historical tenses, where the principal clause expresses an action or obligation unfulfilled, εἴθ' εἶχε φωνὴν ἔμφρον' ἀγγέλου δίκην, ὅ. δίφροντις οὖσα μὴ 'κινυσσόμην A.*Ch.*196, cf. S.*El.* 1134: rare in Prose, ἐδεξάμην ἂν..φράσαι πρὸς ὑμᾶς.., ὅ...προῄδετε And.2.21; τίς οὐκ ἂν..ταῦτα ἐδήλωσεν, ὅ...ταῦτα ἠλέγχθη; D.36.20; οὐκοῦν ἐχρῆν σε Πηγάσου ζεῦξαι πτερόν, ὅ. ἐφαίνου τοῖς θεοῖς τραγικώτερος Ar.*Pax*135; τί..οὐκ ἔρριψ' ἐμαυτὴν..ὅ. ἀπηλλάγην; A.*Pr.* 749. b. of fut., θέλγει, ὅ. Ἰθάκης ἐπιλήσεται (= φραζομένη ὅπως ἐ.) Od.1.57, cf. Il.1.136; [χρὴ] ἀναβιβάζειν ἐπὶ τὸν τροχὸν τοὺς ἀπογραφέντας, ὅ. μὴ πρότερον νὺξ ἔσται And.1.43; ἐμισθώσατο τοῦτον.., ὅ. συνερεῖ D.19.316: sts. fut. ind. and aor. subj. are conjoined, σιγᾶθ', ὅ. μὴ πεύσεταί τις, ὦ τέκνα, γλώσσης χάριν δὲ πάντ' ἀπαγγείλῃ τάδε A. *Ch.*265. II. ὅπως c. subj. is sts. used after Verbs of will and endeavour, instead of the inf., λίσσεσθαι..ὅ. νημερτέα εἴπῃ Od.3.19; αἰτεῖσθαι ὅ. μὴ καταψηφίσησθε Antipho 1.12; δεήσεται.., ὅ. δίκην μὴ δῷ ib.23; ὅ. μὴ ἀποθάνῃ ἠντεβόλει Lys.1.29; παρακελεύεσθε ὑμῖν αὐτοῖς ὅ...ἐξίητε Lycurg.127 (ἔξιτε Rehdantz): with ἄν, δεῖταί μου σφόδρα ὅπως ἂν οἰκουρῇ Ar.*Ach.*1060, cf. Hdt.2.126, 3.44; διεκελεύετο ὅπως ἂν..ἐγγράφωσί με Is.7.27; so δεῖ σ' ὅ. δείξεις (for δεῖξαι), S.*Aj.* 556, may be expld. as ellipsis for δεῖ σ' ὁρᾶν (σκοπεῖν) ὅπως, cf. Id. *Ph.*55; δεῖ σ' ὅπως..μηδὲν διοίσεις.. Cratin.108.

**ὅπως δή**, = ὅπως, *how*, Il.16.113. II. = ὁπωσοῦν, Pl.*Hipparch.* 232b; so **ὅπως δήποτε** D.3.7, 18.261; φύσει ἢ ὅ. Arist.*EN*1114$^{b}$14:—also **ὁπωσδηποτοῦν**, Dsc.*Ther.*3, Eustr.*in EN*23.3.

**ὅπως οὖν** or **ὁπωσοῦν**, *in any way whatever, ever so little*, Th.1. 77, 7.60, Isoc.2.5, etc.; οὐδ' ὁπωσοῦν *in* no *way whatever*, Th.7.49, Isoc.12.2, etc.:—so **ὁπωστιοῦν**, Th.8.71, Pl.*Phdr.*258c; οὐδ' ὁπωστιοῦν Id.*R.*579e, *Phd.*61c, al.; μηδὲ ὁ. Id.*Tht.*179b.

**ὅπως περ**, = ὥσπερ, Hdt.9.120 (ὅκ-), S.*Aj.*1179, *OT*1336 (lyr.), etc.

✻ **ὅπως ποτέ**, *how ever*, D.18.269, D.H.1.11.

**ὁραῖος**, α, ον, *of a boundary*: ὁραία τεκτονική, = *gruma*, *Gloss.*; cf. ὁριαῖος.

**ὅρᾱμ-α**, ατος, τό, *that which is seen, visible object, sight*, Arist.*de An.* 428$^{a}$16, *EN*1173$^{b}$18, al.; *sight, spectacle*, X.*Cyr.*3.3.66; *vision* during sleep, *dream*, Lxx *Ge.*15.1, al., *PGoodsp.Cair.*3.5 (iii B.C.), *UPZ*78.37 (ii B.C.), *SIG*1128 (Delos, ii/i B.C.), *Cat.Cod.Astr.*8(1).249; ἐν τοῖς ὁράμασι τοῦ θεοῦ Aristid.*Or.*42(6).8 codd. (ἰάμασι cj. Keil). II. *device, plan*, τὸ ὅ. Θάλεω (Camer. εὕρημα) Arist.*Pol.*1259$^{a}$31, cf. D. *Prooem.*55.1. **-ᾰτίζομαι**, *look*, Aq.*Ps.*10(11).4. **-ᾰτισμός**, ὁ, *vision*, νυκτός Id.*Jb.*4.13 (pl.). ✻ **-ᾰτιστής**, οῦ, ὁ, *visionary*, Sm. *Is.*56.10.

**ὄραμνος**, ὁ, later form of ὀρόδαμνος, Nic.*Al.*154, *AP*5.291.1 (Agath.).

**ὀρανός**, v. οὐρανός.

✻ **ὀράριον**, τό, = Lat. *orarium, kerchief, scarf*, *Sammelb.*7033.42 (v A.D.).

✻ **ὅρ-ᾱσις**, εως, ἡ, *seeing, the act of sight*, Demad.3, Arist.*EN*1174$^{a}$14, Men.123, etc.; distd. as the ἐνέργεια or *act* from ὄψις (the sense or faculty), Arist.*de An.*426$^{a}$13, cf. 428$^{a}$7; but, *power of sight*, *SIG*1141 (Thrace). 2. pl., *eyes*, τὰς ὁ. ἐκκόπτειν D.S.2.6, cf. D.H.8.45, Plu. 2.88d: metaph., as title of the daughter-goddess of the Sun, ὅρασιν αὐτοῦ (sc. τοῦ Ἡλίου) *OGI*56.56 (Canopus, iii B.C.). II. *a vision*, Lxx *Jl.*2.28, *Act.Ap.*2.17 (pl.). III. *appearance*, ὅμοιος ὁράσει λίθῳ ἰάσπιδι *Apoc.*4.3; ὁ μεταμορφούμενος ἐν ταῖς ὁράσεσιν *PLeid.W.*13. 36. **-ᾱτέον**, *one must see*, *Theol.Ar.*38. **-ᾱτήρ**, ῆρος, ὁ, = sq., Hsch. s.v. ὀπτήρ. **-ᾱτής**, οῦ, ὁ, *beholder*, Lxx *Jb.*34.21, Plu.*Nic.*19. **-ᾱτίζω**, *keep in view, aim at*, οἰκείου σκοποῦ Sever.*Clyst.*p.13 D. ✻ **-ᾱτικός**, ή, όν, *able to see*, τὰ ὄμματα ὁ. τῶν πόρρωθεν Arist.*GA*781$^{a}$1; of persons, Ph.1.336, al.; -κὴ διάνοια Id.2.19: abs., ὁρατικὸν τὸ ὁρᾶν, καὶ ὁρατὸν τὸ δυνατὸν ὁρᾶσθαι Arist.*Metaph.*1049$^{b}$15; τὸ ὁρατικόν *the power of sight*, Id.*GA*716$^{a}$30; ἡ ὁ. δύναμις Plu.2.433d; -κῶν πόνοι pains *in the eyes*, Vett.Val. in *Cat.Cod.Astr.*8(1).168, cf. Nech.ap. Vett.Val.279.33. Adv. -κῶς S.E.*M.*7.355. II. *of* or *for the sight*, θεραπεύματα D.L.8.89. ✻ **-ᾱτός**, ή, όν, *to be seen, visible*, Hp.*Praec.* 14: joined with ἁπτός, Pl.*Ti.*28b, al.; opp. νοητός, Id.*R.*509d, 524c, etc.; cf. ὁρατικός. Adv. -τῶς Aen.Tact.23.4, Plu.2.1029e.

**Ὁράτριος**, epith. of Zeus in Crete, *GDI*5039.11 (ii B.C.), al.

**ὁραυγέομαι**, (ὁράω, αὐγή) *inspect closely*, Aesar.ap.Stob.1.49.27.

✻ **ὁράω**, contr. **ὁρῶ** even in Il.3.234, Ep. **ὁρόω** 5.244, etc.; Aeol. **ὄρημι** (q.v.); Ion. **ὁρέω** Hdt.1.80, etc., 2 sg. ὁρῇς Herod.2.67, al., 3 sg. ὁρῇ Hp.*Carn.*17, *Vid.Ac.*1; inf. ὁρῆν Democr.11, Hp.*Carn.*2 (but 2 sg. ὁρᾷς Archil.87, 3 sg. ὁρᾷ Semon.7.80, cf. κατορᾷ Hdt.2.38; 1 pl. ὁρῶμεν Id.5.40; 3 pl. ὁρῶσι (ἐπ-) Id.1.124; inf. ὁρᾶν ib.33, 2.64): the forms ὁρῇς, ὁρῇ, ὁρῆν (exc. when found in Dor., as *IG*4$^{2}$(1).122.2, 15,47 (Epid., iv B.C.); impf. 3 sg. ἑώρη ib.28,70) seem to imply ὁρή-ω (cf. ὄρημι), but ὁρᾷ, ὁρῶμεν, ὁρῶσι, etc. imply ὁρᾰ-ω: Att. impf. ἑώρων Th.1.51, Ar.*Pl.*713, *Nu.*354, (ἐ-) *SIG*344.110 (Teos, iv B.C.); Ion. 3 sg. ὥρα Hdt.1.11, 3.72, 1 pl. ὡρῶμεν (v.l. ὁρῶμεν) Id.2.131, 2 pl. ὡρᾶτε Id.7.8.β', 3 pl. ὥρων Id.4.3, etc.; Ep. 3 sg. ὅρα Il.16.646, cf. ὄρημι: pf. ἑόρᾱκα, a form required by the metre in many passages, as Ar.*Th.* 32, 33, *Av.*1573, *Pl.*98, 1045, Eup.181.3, Alex.272.1, Men.*Epit.*166, *Pk.*270, Bato 5.11, etc., whereas the metre never requires ἑώρακα; whence ἑόρακα, -άκῃ ought always to be restored in early Att. writers, though ἑώρακα was used in later Gr., *PPetr.*2 p.55 (iii B.C.), *SIG*685.74 (ii B.C.), *UPZ*119.43 (ii B.C.), cf. Theognost.*Can.*150 (ἑώρακε⟨ν⟩ is prob. in Men.5 D.): ἑωρ- in the impf. prob. comes from ἠ-ϝορ- (with a long form of the augment, cf. ἠειδ- (ᾐδ-) in impf. of οἶδα), while ἑορ- in the pf. comes from ϝε-ϝορ-, v. infr.: Ion. pf. ὀρώρηκα Herod.4.77, al., also ὥρηκα ib.40; Dor. pf. part. ὡρακυῖα *IG*4$^{2}$(1).122.6 (Epid., iv B.C.); 1 sg. ὥρακα Baillet *Inscr. des tombeaux des rois* 1210: an aor. 1 ἐσορήσαις only f.l. in Orph.*Fr.*247.16:—**Med.** ὁράομαι, contr. ὁρῶμαι even in Il.13.99; Ep. 2 sg. ὅρηαι Od.14.343 (v. ὄρημι): impf. ἑωρώμην, also ὡρώμην (προ-) *Act.Ap.*2.25, Ep. 3 sg. ὁρᾶτο Il.1.56:—**Pass.**, pf. ἑώραμαι Isoc.15.110, D.54.16: aor. ἑωράθην only in late Prose, D.S.20.6; inf. ὁρᾱθῆναι Arist.*MA*699$^{b}$19, Pl.*Def.*411b, Luc.*Jud.Voc.* 6, etc.: fut. ὁραθήσομαι Gal.*UP*10.12: verb. Adj. ὁρᾱτός, ὁρᾱτέον (qq.v.).—Hom. uses contr. forms, as ὁρῶ, ὁρᾷς, ὁρᾷ, ὅρα, ὁρᾶν, ὁρῶν, ὁρῶμαι, ὁρᾶται, ὁρᾶσθαι, ὁρώμενος, as well as lengthd. Ep. ὁρόω, ὁράᾳς, ὁράασθαι, ὁρόων, 2 pl. opt. ὁρόῳτε Il.4.347, etc.; besides these forms from ὁρα- (ὁρη-) we have II. from root ὀπ- (v. ὄψ) the only fut. in use, ὄψομαι, always in act. sense, Il.24.704, and Att., Ep. 2 sg. ὄψεαι 8.471, Od.24.511: a rare aor. 1 ἐπ-όψατο in Pi.*Fr.*88.6 (for ἐπιώψατο, v. ἐπιόψομαι); subj. ὄψησθε *Ev.Luc.*13.28 (where the v.l. ὄψεσθε may be right): pf. ὄπωπα Il.6.124, Od.21.94, Emp.109, Hdt. 3.37,63, Hp.*Art.*1, *Carn.*17; Trag. and Com., as A.*Eu.*57, S.*Ant.*6, al., Ar.*Lys.*1157,1225, never in Att. Prose: plpf. 3 sg. ὀπώπει Od.21. 123, ὀπώπεε Hdt.5.92.ζ'; ὀπώπεσαν Id.7.125:—Pass., aor. 1 ὤφθην

S.*Ant.*709, E.*Hec.*970, Th.4.73, etc.; opt. (Ion.) ὀφθείησαν Hdt.8.7; part. ὀφθείς, inf. ὀφθῆναι, Id.1.9,10 (for ἐπι-οφθέντας, v. ἐπιόψομαι): fut. ὀφθήσομαι S.*Tr.*452, E.*HF*1155, And.2.10, Lys.3.34: pf. ὦμμαι Is.*Fr.*165, ὦψαι D.18.263, ὦπται A.*Pr.*998, D.24.66; cf. ὀπτέον. III. from ϝιδ- are formed aor. Act. εἶδον, inf. ἰδεῖν: aor. Med. εἰδόμην, inf. ἰδέσθαι: pf. with pres. sense οἶδα *I know*, inf. εἰδέναι: verb. Adj. ἰστέος (for these tenses, v. *εἴδω). (ὀρ- prob. from ϝορ-, as indicated by the impf. and pf. forms; cf. βῶροι (i.e. ϝῶροι), Engl. (*a*)*ware*.)

Senses: I. abs., *see, look*, freq. in Hom.; εἴς τι or εἴς τινα to or at a thing or person, Il.24.633, Od.20.373, al., E.*Fr.*607; εἰς τὸν πράττοντα Arist.*Po.*1460$^{a}$14:—Med., Od.5.439, Hes.*Op.*534, *Fr.*188; but ἔς τινα ὁρᾶν *to be of* so-and-so's *party*, Philostr.*VS*1.18; εἰς τὴν Ἀττάλου καθαίρεσιν εἶδεν *aimed* at.., Zos.6.12; for κατ' αὐτοὺς αἰὲν ὅρα Il.16.646, Τροίην κατὰ πᾶσαν ὁρᾶται 24.291, cf. καθοράω II; ὁρόων ἐπ' ἀπείρονα πόντον *looking* over the sea, 1.350; ὁρᾶν πρός τι *look towards*, ἀκρωτήριον τὸ πρὸς Μέγαρα ὁρῶν Th.2.93, cf. *AP*7.496 (Simon., cj.); πρὸς πλοῦν ὁρᾷ *looks* to sail (i.e. is ready), E.*IA*[1624]; ὁ. ἐπὶ τὴν προδοσίαν D.S.36.3; πρὸς σπονδάς Id.33.1. 2. *have sight*, opp. μὴ ὁρᾶν, to be blind, S.*Aj.*84; ὅσ' ἂν λέγωμεν, πάνθ' ὁρῶντα λέξομεν [though I am blind,] my words *shall have eyes*, i.e. shall be to the purpose, Id.*OC*74; ἐν σκότῳ.. οὓς μὲν οὐκ ἔδει ὀψοίαθ', i.e. should be blind, Id.*OT*1274; ἀμβλύτερον ὁ., opp. ὀξύτερον βλέπειν, Pl.*R.*596a; ἐπὶ σμικρὸν ὁ. *to be* short-*sighted*, Id.*Tht.*174e; ὁ. βραχύ τι Id.*R.*488b. 3. *see* to, *look* to, i.e. *take* or *give heed*, Il.10.239; ὁ. εἰς γλῶσσαν.. ἀνδρός *look* to, *pay heed* to, Sol.11.7, cf. A.*Supp.*104 (lyr.): freq. in imper., like βλέπε, folld. by a dependent clause, ὅρα ὅπως.. Ar.*Ec.*300, cf. Th.5.27; ὅρα εἰ.. *see* whether.., A.*Pr.*997, Pl.*Phd.*118, etc.; also ὅρα μὴ.. S.*Ph.*30, 519, etc.; ὅρα τί ποιεῖς ib.589; πῶς.. ὑπερδικεῖς, ὅρα A.*Eu.*652. 4. ὁρᾷς; ὁρᾶτε; *see'st thou? d'ye see?* parenthetically, esp. in explanations, Ar.*Nu.*355, *Th.*490, etc.; ὡς ὁρᾷς S.*El.*1114, *Tr.*365; also ὁρᾷς; at the beginning of a sentence, Id.*El.*628, E.*Andr.*87; ἀλλ'—ὁρᾷς; but, *do you see..?*, Pl.*Prt.*336b; ὁρᾷς οὖν.. ὅτι Id.*Grg.*475e; οὐχ ὁρᾷς; ironically, D.18.232. 5. c. acc. cogn., like βλέπω II, *look* so and so, δεινὸν ὁρῶν ὄσσοισι Hes.*Sc.*426; ὁρᾶν ἀλκάν Pi.*O.*9.111; ἔαρ ὁρόωσα Νύχεια Theoc.13.45; also ἡδέως ὁρᾶν *look* pleasant, E.*IA*1122: c. acc., κακῶς ὁρᾶν τινα Philostr.*VA*7.42. II. trans., *see* an object, *behold, perceive, observe*, c. acc., freq. in Hom., etc.: pf. ὄπωπα exclusively in this sense, Il.2.799, Od.21.94, etc.; ὀφθαλμοῖσιν or ἐν ὀφθαλμοῖσιν ὁρᾶν *to see with* or *before* the eyes, Il.24.392, Od.8.459, etc.; αἰεὶ τέρμ' ὁρόων always *keeping* it *in sight*, keeping his eye on it, Il.23.323; φίλως χ' ὁρόῳτε καὶ εἰ δέκα πύργοι Ἀχαιῶν.. μαχοίατο, i.e. δέκα πύργους, εἰ μαχοίατο, 4.347; ὁ. τινά *look to* (for aid), D.45.64: in signfs. I and II combined, οὐχ ὁρᾷς ὁρῶν τάδε; A.*Ag.*1623, cf. D.25.89. b. ζώει καὶ ὁρᾷ φάος ἠελίοιο, poet. for ζῆν, like βλέπειν, Il.18.61, Od.4.833, etc.; so φῶς ὁρᾶν S.*OT*375, E.*Or.*1523, *Alc.*691:—in Med., φέγγος ὁρᾶσθαι Id.*Andr.*113 (eleg.); so ὁρᾶν alone, τὰ γὰρ φθιτῶν τοῖς ὁρῶσι κόσμος Id.*Supp.*78 (lyr.). c. folld. by a clause, οὐχ ὁράᾳς οἷος..; Il.21.108; ὁρᾷς ἡμᾶς, ὅσοι ἐσμέν; Pl.*R.*327c; οὐχ ὁρᾷς ὅτι ἥμαρτες; A.*Pr.*261, cf. 325, 951; Διὸς.. οὐχ ὁρῶ μῆτιν ὅπᾳ φύγοιμ' ἄν ib.906 (lyr.); ἴδεσθέ μ' οἷα.. πάσχω ib.92. d. c. part., καπνὸν.. ὁρῶμεν ἀπὸ χθονὸς ἀΐσσοντα *we see* it rising, Od.10.99; ὁρῶν ἐμαυτὸν ὧδε προυσελούμενον *seeing* myself thus insulted, A.*Pr.*438, cf. 70, 384, al.; ὁρῶ σε κρύπτοντα.. *see* you hiding.., E.*Hec.*342; so ὁρῶ μ' ἔργον ἐξειργασμένην I *see that* I have done, S.*Tr.*706; cf. infr. 4b; rarely in reference to the subject, ὁρῶ μὲν ἐξαμαρτάνων (= ὅτι ἐξαμαρτάνω) E.*Med.*350:—so in Med., ἄνδρα διωκόμενον.. ὁρῶμαι Il.22.169, cf. A.*Pr.*896 (lyr.): also c. inf., ἑώρων οὐκέτι οἷόν τε εἶναι.. Th.8.60. e. rarely c. gen., οὐδεὶς Σωκράτους οὐδὲν ἀσεβὲς.. οὔτε πράττοντος εἶδεν οὔτε λέγοντος ἤκουσεν (where the Constr. is suggested by the use of ἤκουσεν) X.*Mem.*1.1.11; μέχρι Βορῆος ἀπαστράψαντος ἴδηαι Arat.430. 2. *see to*, ἴδε πῶμα Od.8.443; *look out for, provide*, τινί τι S.*Aj.*1165 (anap.), Theoc.15.2; πρόβατον εἰς ὁλοκάρπωσιν Lxx *Ge.*22.8. 3. the inf. is used after an Adj., δεινὸς ἰδεῖν Sol.13.6; εὐφεγγὴς ἰδεῖν A.*Pers.*387, cf. 398, *Ch.*174, 176, al. (cf. *εἴδω A.I.1a); ἐχθίστου.. ὁρᾶν most hateful *to behold*, S.*Aj.*818; ὦ πάτερ δύσμοιρ' ὁρᾶν Id.*OC*327; ὁρᾶν στυγνὸς ἦν X.*An.*2.6.9:—Med. or Pass., αἰσχρὸς ὁρᾶσθαι Id.*Cyn.*3.3: with an Adv., μὴ διχορρόπως ἰδεῖν A.*Ag.*349: with a Subst., ἄνδρα τευχηστὴν ἰδεῖν Id.*Th.*644: with a Verb, πρέπουσι.. ἰδεῖν Id.*Supp.*720, cf. S.*OT*792. 4. Med. is used by Poets like Act., Il.13.99, A.*Pers.*179, *Ch.*407 (lyr.), S.*Ant.*594 (lyr.), *Tr.*306, Cratin.138, etc., v. supr. II.1b, c: but in Prose Med. occurs only in compds., as προ-ορῶμαι: for the imper. ἰδοῦ, ἰδού, v. ἰδοῦ. b. no Pass. is used by Hom.; in Att. the Pass. has the sense *to be seen*, A.*Pr.*998, *Eu.*411, etc.: c. part., ὤφθημεν ὄντες ἄθλιοι *was seen* in my wretchedness, E.*IT*933; ὀφθήσεται διώκων *he will prove to be..*, Pl.*Phdr.*239c, cf. *Smp.*178e; τὰ ὁρώμενα *all that is seen, things visible*, like τὰ ὁρατά, Id.*Prm.*130a. III. metaph., of mental sight, *discern, perceive*, S.*El.*945, etc.; so blind Oedipus says, φωνῇ γὰρ ὁρῶ, τὸ φατιζόμενον I *see* by sound, as the saying is, Id.*OC*138 (anap.); ἂν οἴνου.. ὀσμὴν ἴδωσιν Alex.222.4; cf. supr. I.4, δέρκομαι I.2. IV. abs., *see visions*, ὁ ἀληθινῶς ὁρῶν Lxx *Nu.*24.3,15:—Pass., *appear in a vision*, ὤφθη ἄγγελος πρὸς τὴν γυναῖκα ib.*Jd.*13.3. V. *interview*, ἐμνήσθης μοι ἰδεῖν τὸν κεραμέα περὶ τῶν κεραμίων you told me to *see* the potter about the jars, *PCair.Zen.*264 (iii B.C.).

* **ὀρβικλᾶτον**, τό, Lat. *malum orbiculatum*, Diph.Siph.ap.Ath.3.80f, Dsc.1.115.4.

**ὀρβιο-ποιέω**, (ὀρόβιον) *make a preparation of vetch*, *PBouriant*13.3 (i A.D.). **-πωλεῖον**, τό, *vetch-seller's shop*, *POxy.*1323 (vi A.D.). **-πώλης**, ου, ὁ, *vetch-seller*, ib.1432.6 (iii A.D.), 1037.4 (v A.D.), etc. **-πωλία**, ἡ, *the right to sell vetch*, *PBouriant*13.2 (i A.D.).

**ὀρβοπώλης**, ου, ὁ, = ὀρβιοπώλης, *POxy.*1323 (vi A.D.), *PKlein.Form.*31 (vi/vii A.D.).

**ὀργ-άζω**, *soften, knead, temper*, A.*Fr.*451 F; πηλὸν ὀργάζειν χεροῖν S.*Fr.*482, cf. 510, 787; πηλὸν.. ὄργασον Ar.*Av.*839, cf. Eup.248; κλωστῆρσι χειρῶν ὀργάσας κατήνυσε σειραῖα δεσμά S.*Fr.*25; ὀ. λίπεϊ.. θρόνα Nic.*Al.*155; of the action of fire, τὰ ἐντὸς καθάπερ ὀ. Arist.*Pr.*869$^{b}$27:—Med., φύλλα ξηρὰ.. ἐλαίῳ ὀργάσασθαι Hp.*Mul.*2.206, cf. Archil.ap.Phot.p.64 R., Nic.*Th.*652; dub. cj. in Alciphr.3.7:—Pass., ὅταν ὁ κηρὸς μετρίως ὠργασμένος ᾖ *has been* well *kneaded*, Pl.*Tht.*194c (restored from Tim.*Lex.* and Suid. for εἰργ-). Cf. ὀργάω. **-αίνω**, = ὀργίζω, *make angry, enrage*, καὶ γὰρ ἂν πέτρου φύσιν σύ γ' ὀργάνειας S.*OT*335. II. intr., like ὀργίζομαι, *grow* or *be angry*, Id.*Tr.*552; τινι *with* one, E.*Alc.*1106; cf. ὁρμαίνω II.2.

* **ὀργᾰν-άριος**, ὁ, = *fistularius*, *Gloss.* **-η**, v. ὄργανος. * **-ικός**, ή, όν, *serving as organs* or *instruments, instrumental*, esp. of the several parts of the body, Arist.*PA*646$^{b}$26: distd. from τὰ κινητικά, Id.*GA*742$^{b}$10; τὰ ὀ. μέρη Id.*EN*1110$^{a}$16, cf. *PA*661$^{b}$29, *GA*739$^{b}$14, al.; αἱ ὀ. [ἀρεταί], of a slave, Id.*Pol.*1259$^{b}$23; ὀ. καὶ μηχανικαὶ κατασκευαί Plu.2.718f; esp. of war-engines, ἡ ὀ. βία D.S.17.43; ὀ. κατασκευαί Onos.42.3: metaph., ὁ ὀ. εἰς πλήθη λόγος speech which is *brought to bear on* the mob, Plu.*Cat.Mi.*4; of musicians, *practical*, opp. λογικοί (theoretical), Id.2.657e; ἐποιεῖτο ἀκροάσεις λογικάς τε καὶ ὀ. *Supp.Epigr.*2.184.6 (Tanagra, ii B.C.); so of surgeons, τῶν ὀ. οἱ διασημότεροι *PMed.Lond.*155.2.13; ἡ ὀ. (sc. τέχνη) Plu.*Marc.*14; but ὀργανικός, = λογικός, *logical*, Elias *in Porph.*115.17. Adv. **-κῶς** *by way of instruments*, Arist.*EN*1099$^{b}$28; **-κώτερον** *making more use of instruments*, Simp.*in Cael.*504.33; τὸ κινοῦν ὀ. Arist.*de An.*433$^{b}$21. **-ιον**, τό, Dim. of ὄργανον, *AP*5.190 (Mel.), M.Ant.10.38. **-ιστής**, οῦ, ὁ, *waterworks-engineer*, *PLond.*3.1177.72,80 (pl., ii A.D.). 2. *musician, instrumentalist*, Olymp. *in Alc.*p.202 C. **-ίτης** [ῑ], ου, ὁ, *engineer*, *PLond.*1.125.20 (iv A.D.), *PLips.*97 vii 13 (iv A.D.).

**ὀργᾰνο-θεσία**, ἡ, (ὄργανον IV) *drawing up of tables*, κανονικαὶ -θεσίαι Vett.Val.150.23. **-θετέω**, *tabulate*, [ζῴδια] Id.295.24 (Pass.).

* **ὄργανον**, τό, (ἔργον, ἔρδω) *instrument, implement, tool, for making* or *doing* a thing, S.*Tr.*905, cf. ἀθηρόβρωτος; λογχοποιῶν ὄργανα E.*Ba.*1208, cf. *Ion* 1030; πολεμικὰ ὅπλα τε καὶ ὄργανα Pl.*R.*374d, cf. *Lg.*956a; ὄ. without any Adj., *engine of war*, Ctes.*Fr.*81; τὰ ναυτικὰ ὄ. *tackle*, Pl.*Plt.*298d; ὄ. ὅσα περὶ γεωργίαν Id.*R.*370d; ὄνομα ἄρα διδασκαλικόν τί ἐστιν ὄ. Id.*Cra.*388b; ὄργανα χρόνων or χρόνου, of the stars, Id.*Ti.*41e, 42d; ὄ. κυβευτικά Aeschin.1.59; of a person, ἁπάντων ἀεὶ κακῶν ὄ. S.*Aj.*380 (lyr.). 2. *organ of sense* or *apprehension*, τὰ περὶ τὰς αἰσθήσεις ὄ. Pl.*R.*508b; τὸ ὄ. ᾧ καταμανθάνει ἕκαστος ib.518c, cf. *Tht.*185c, al.; δι' ἀμυδρῶν ὀ. θεᾶσθαί τι Id.*Phdr.*250b, cf. *Ti.*45b, Epicur.*Nat.*11.6,7. b. of the body and its different parts, Arist.*PA*642$^{a}$11, 645$^{b}$14, *GA*716$^{a}$24, Phld.*Mus.*pp.71,96 K., Gal.10.47; the hand is called ὄργανον ὀργάνων or ὄ. πρὸ ὀργάνων, Arist.*de An.*432$^{a}$2, *PA*687$^{a}$21; τὰ πορευτικὰ ὄ. the *organs* of locomotion, Id.*GA*732$^{b}$28; ὄ. πρὸς ἐργασίαν τῆς τροφῆς the digestive *organs*, ib.788$^{b}$24; τὸ ὄ. τὸ περὶ τὴν ἀναπνοήν the respiratory *organ*, Id.*PA*664$^{a}$29; τὰ ὄ. τὰ χρήσιμα πρὸς τὴν ὀχείαν Id.*HA*500$^{a}$15; of plants, Id.*de An.*412$^{b}$1, *PA*656$^{a}$2. 3. *musical instrument*, Simon.31, f.l. in A.*Fr.*57.1; ὁ μὲν δι' ὀργάνων ἐκήλει ἀνθρώπους, of Marsyas, Pl.*Smp.*215c; ἄνευ ὀργάνων ψιλοῖς λόγοις ibid., cf. *Plt.*268b; ὄ. πολύχορδα Id.*R.*399c, al.; μετ' ᾠδῆς καί τινων ὀργάνων Phld.*Mus.*p.98 K.; of the pipe, Melanipp.2, Telest.1.2. 4. *surgical instrument*, Hp.*Off.*2, X.*Cyr.*5.3.47, Pl.*Plt.*298c. II. concrete, *work* or *product*, μελίσσης κηρόπλαστον ὄ. S.*Fr.*398.5; λαϊνέοισιν Ἀμφίονος ὀ., of the walls of Thebes, E.*Ph.*115 (lyr.). III. of logic as an *instrument* of philosophy, ἡ λογικὴ πραγματεία ὀργάνου χώραν ἔχει ἐν φιλοσοφίᾳ Alex.Aphr. *in Top.*74.29, cf. Phlp. *in APr.*6.23; πᾶσα τεχνικὴ διδασκαλία ὑπὸ τὸ λογικὸν ὄ. ἀνάγεται Sch.D.T.p.161 H.; but τὸ ὄ. as title of Aristotle's collected logical writings lacks authority. IV. *instrument* or *table of calculations*, εἰσῆλθον εἰς τὸ προκείμενον ὄργανον Vett.Val.20.12. V. ὄ. χλούνιον, = ἠρύγγιον, Ps.-Dsc.3.21.

**ὀργᾰνο-πήκτωρ**, ορος, ὁ, ἡ, = ὀργανοποιός, Man.4.439. **-ποιέω**, *furnish with organs*, c. acc., Syrian. *in Metaph.*186.10. **-ποιία**, ἡ, *instrument-making*, Ti.Locr.101e, Ph.1.29, 2.94, al.; *apparatus*, Heliod.ap.Orib.44.23.43, 49.20.8, 49.22.15; anatomical *structure*, Porph.*Gaur.*13.4. **-ποιικά**, τά, *manufacture of war-engines*, Ph.*Bel.*49.6. **-ποιός**, ὁ, *maker of instruments* or *engines*, D.S.17.43, *IG*14.1717 (Rome), Ptol.*Tetr.*180.

* **ὄργᾰν-ος**, η, ον, *working, forming*, ὀργάνη χείρ E.*Andr.*1014 (s.v.l.): Ὀργάνη as epith. of Athena, *BCH*52.52 (Thasos, v B.C.), *IG*2.1329, Hsch., Phot.; cf. ἐργάνη. **-όω**, in Pass., *to be organized*, πρὸς τὴν τῆς ἀληθείας γνῶσιν S.E.*M.*7.126, cf. Porph.*Abst.*3.8. **-ωσις**, εως, ἡ, *organization, arrangement*, ib.7.

* **ὀργ-άς** (sc. γῆ), άδος, ἡ, *any well-watered, fertile spot of land, meadow-land*, partially wooded, with or without cultivated fields, *IG*1$^{2}$.325.18, E.*Ba.*340, 445, *El.*1162 (lyr.), X.*Cyn.*9.2, *AP*6.41 (Agath.); ὑπ' ὀργάδα τὰν Ἀχέροντος *Hymn.Is.* in *Not.Arch.*4.212. 2. *rich tract of land sacred to the gods*: such a tract between Athens and Megara, sacred to Demeter and Persephone, was specially called ἡ ὀ. or ἱερὰ ὀ., D.13.32, Call.*Fr.*35 P., Plu.*Per.*30, Paus.3.4.2, cf. *IG*2$^{2}$.204.8,16; similarly perh. ὀργή in Herod.4.46 (s.v.l.). **-ασμός**, ὁ, (ὀργάω) *orgasm*, Sch.Hp.*Hum.*3. **-αστήριον**, τό, for ὀργιαστήριον, *a place of* ὄργια, Nic.*Al.*8. **-άω**, mostly in pres.: pf. part.

ὀργηκότες (v.l. ὡρμ-) occurs in J.*AJ*17.9.2: plpf. Pass. ὤργητο in Hsch., v. II fin. I. *to be getting ready to bear, growing ripe* for something, of soil, Thphr.*CP*3.2.6; of trees, συμβαίνει.. τὰ.. δένδρα ὀργᾶν πρὸς τὴν βλάστησιν ib.1.6.2; ὀργᾷ [ἡ σμῖλαξ] πρὸς τὴν ἄνθησιν Plu.2.647f; and of fruit, *swell* as it ripens, ὁ καρπὸς πεπαίνεται καὶ ὀργᾷ Hdt.4.199: so c. inf., ὀργᾷ ἀμᾶσθαι *grows ripe* for cutting, ibid., cf. X.*Oec.*19.19; of a wound, ὀργᾶν φαίνεται appears *turgid*, Hp.*Fract.*28, cf. *Aph.*1.22. II. of men, like σφριγάω, *swell* with lust, *wax wanton, be rampant*, Ar.*Lys.*1113, *Av.* 462 (where the Sch. explains it ἐπιθυμητικῶς ἔχω); ὁ ἐπ' ἀφροδισίοις μαινόμενος..ὀργῶν Poll.6.188; of human beings and animals, *to be in heat, desire sexual intercourse*, ὀργᾶν πρὸς τὴν ὁμιλίαν, ὀχείαν, Arist.*HA*542$^{a}$32, 560$^{b}$13; ὀ. ὀχεύεσθαι ib.500$^{b}$11; πρὸς τὸ γεννᾶν Plu. 2.651c. 2. generally, *to be eager* or *ready, to be excited*, Λακεδαιμονίων ὀργώντων ἔμελλον πειράσεσθαι Th.4.108; ὀργῶντες κρίνειν judge *under the influence of passion*, Id.8.2: c. inf., ὄργα μαθεῖν A. *Ch.*454 (lyr.); ὀργᾶν τεκεῖν Arist.*HA*613$^{b}$28; ἀκοῦσαι ὀργῶ Cratin. 21 D.; of a thing, *to be urgent*, ὤργα τὸ πρᾶγμα A.*Fr.*54 A; ὀ. πρός τι Plu.*Alex.*6, D.Chr.36.26, Marcellin.*Vit.Thuc.*54; ἐπὶ ἐκφύλους συνόδους Ph.2.21; ὀργᾷς ὃς ἱππίαν ἐς ὁδόν dub. cj. in Pi.*P.*6.50: plpf. Pass. in act. sense, ὧν ἀκροᾶσθαι..ὤργητο (restd. from Hsch. and some Mss. for ὥρμητο) Th.2.21. III. ὀργήσας is f.l. for ὀργάσας in Hdt.4.64. ❋ **-εών**, ῶνος (nom. pl. once ὀργεῶναι *IG*2$^{2}$. 2361.18 (iii A.D.)), ὁ, at Athens, *member of a religious association*, Is. 2.14,16, al., Philoch.94, *IG*2$^{2}$.1252 (iv B.C.), etc.: poet., generally, for ἱερεύς, *priest*, A.*Fr.*144:—a poet. form **ὀργειών** (in codd. sts. ὀργιών), ῶνος, ὁ, is used by Antim.*Eleg.Fr.*2, Hermesian.7.19: in acc. with ο for ω, ὀργίονας *h.Ap.*389 codd.:—a gen. pl. ὀργέων Lys. *Fr.*112 S. is prob. f.l. for ὀργεώνων:—a fem. pl. ὀργεῶναι, = ἱέρειαι, in Hsch. (The Att. stem ὀργεών- may come from ὀργηόν- of which acc. pl. ὀργηόνας (or its corruption ὀργειόνας) may be read in *h.Ap.* l.c.: prob. cogn. with ὄργια.) **-εωνικός**, ή, όν, *of* or *for the* ὀργεῶνες, δεῖπνον ὀ. a feast *of the* ὀργεῶνες, Ath.5.186a; ὀ. σύνοδος *IG*2$^{2}$.2361.14 (iii A.D.); τὸ γραμματεῖον τὸ ὀργειωνικόν ib.12(8).19 (Lemnos); θύματα ὀ. *AB*240, Phot.

❋ **ὀργή**, ἡ, *natural impulse* or *propensity* (v. ὀργάω II): hence, *temperament, disposition, mood*, κηφήνεσσι κοθούροις εἴκελος ὀργήν Hes.*Op.* 304, cf. Thgn.98, 214, 964, etc.; ὀργὴν ἄλλοτ' ἀλλοίην ἔχει Semon.7. 11; so μείλιχος, γλυκεῖα ὀργά, Pi.*P.*9.43, *I.*2.35; εὐανθεῖ ἐν ὀργᾷ παρμένων Id.*P.*1.89; ὀργῆς τραχύτης A.*Pr.*80; ὠμή, ἀτέραμνος ὀργή, Id. *Supp.*187, *Pr.*192, etc.; ὀργῆς νοσούσης εἰσὶν ἰατροὶ λόγοι *of 'a mind* diseased', ib.380: so in pl., *h.Cer.*205, Pi.*I.*5(4).34; ὀργαῖς ἀλωπέκων ἴκελοι Id.*P.*2.77; κνωδάλων ἔχοντες ὀργάς A.*Supp.*763; ἀστυνόμοι ὀργαί social *dispositions*, S.*Ant.*356 (lyr., cf. σύντροφος 3); ὀργαὶ ἤπιοι E.*Tr.*53: also in Prose, διεπειρᾶτο αὐτῶν τῆς τε ἀνδραγαθίης καὶ τῆς ὀργῆς Hdt.6.128; οὐ τῇ αὐτῇ ὀ. ἀναπειθομένους τε πολεμεῖν καὶ ἐν τῷ ἔργῳ πράσσοντας Th.1.140; τῇ ὀ... χαλεπῇ ἐχρῆτο ib.130; ἐπιφέρειν ὀργάς τινι suit *one's moods* to another, Id.8.83, cf. Cratin.230; ὁ πόλεμος πρὸς τὰ παρόντα τὰς ὀ. τῶν πολλῶν ὁμοιοῖ Th.3.82; τὴν τῶν πολλῶν..συνιόντων ὀ...σοφίαν ἡγούμενος Pl.*R.*493d. II. *anger, wrath*, ὀργῇ χρῆσθαι to be in a *passion*, Hdt.6.85, S.*OT*1241; ὀργὴν ποιήσασθαι Hdt.3.25; ὀργὴν ποιεῖσθαι εἰ.. Th.4.122; ὀργῇ χάριν δοῦναι S.*OC*855; ὀργῇ εἶξαι, χαρίζεσθαι, E.*Hel.*80, *Fr.*31; ὀργὴν ἔχειν τινί Ar.*Pax*659 (but ὀ. ἔχει *involves* anger, D.10.44); δι' ὀργῆς ἔχειν τινά Th.5.46; ἐν ὀργῇ ἔχειν, ποιεῖσθαί τινα, Id.2.65, D.1.16; οὐ τίθεται ταῦτα παρ' ὑμῖν εἰς..ἣν προσῆκεν ὀ. Id.18.138; εἰς ὀργὴν πεσεῖν E.*Or.*696, etc.; ὀργῇ περιπεπτωκέναι D.*Ep.*2.14; ἀνιέναι τῆς ὀργῆς, ὀργὴν χαλᾶν, remit *one's anger*, be pacified, Ar.*Ra.*700, *V.*727; ὀ. κατέχειν Philem.185; ὀργῆς κρατεῖν Men.574; ὀ. ἐμποιεῖν τινι make one angry, Pl.*Lg.*793e; ὀργῆς τυγχάνειν to be visited with *anger*, D. 21.175, etc.; ὀργὴν ἄκρος quick *to anger*, passionate, Hdt.1.73: in pl., ὀργὰς ἀφιέναι A.*Pr.*317; φαίνειν Id.*Ch.*326 (lyr.), al. 2. Adverbial usages, ὀργῇ *in anger, in a passion*, Hdt.1.61, 114, S.*OT*405, etc.; ὀργᾷ περιόργῳ A.*Ag.*216 (lyr.); δι' ὀργῆς S.*OT*807, Th.2.11; δι' ὀργάν A.*Eu.*981 (lyr.); ἐξ ὀργῆς S.*Ant.*766; κατ' ὀργήν Id.*Tr.*933, etc.; μετ' ὀργῆς Isoc.2.23, Pl.*Ap.*34d; μετὰ τῆς ὀ. D.21.76; πρὸς ὀργήν S. *El.*369, Ar.*Ra.*844, Th.2.65; ὀργῆς χάριν, ὀ. ὕπο, E.*Andr.*688, *IA* 335. 3. c. gen., Πανὸς ὀργαί *visitations of* Pan's *wrath*, Id.*Med.* 1172; but b. c. gen. objecti, ὀργή τινος *anger at* or *because of* a thing, S.*Ph.*1309 (cj.), Lys.12.20; ὀ. τῆς προδοσίας εἶχε τοὺς Ἀθηναίους Plu.*Them.*9; ἀπύρων ἱερῶν ὀργάς A.*Ag.*71 (anap.). 4. v. ὀργάς 2.—Not in Hom., who uses θυμός instead; once in Hes.; freq. in Eleg. and Lyr. and in Ion. and Att. Prose.

**ὄργημα**, ατος, τό, = ὀργή, dub. cj. in Sch.S.*Aj.*913, for ὄρυγμα.

**ὀργητύς** (-γύς cod.), ύος, ἡ, = ὀργή, Hsch.

❋ **ὄργι-α**, ίων, τά, *secret rites, secret worship*, practised by the initiated, a post-Hom. word; used of the worship of Demeter at Eleusis, *h.Cer.*273, 476, Ar.*Ra.*386, *Th.*948; of the *rites* of the Cabeiri and Demeter Achaia, Hdt.2.51, 5.61; of Orpheus, Id.2.81; of Eumolpus, *App.Anth.*1.318; of Cybele, E.*Ba.*78 (lyr.): most freq. of the *rites* of Dionysus, Hdt.2.81, E.*Ba.*34, al., Theoc.26.13. II. generally, *rites, sacrifices*, *SIG*57.4 (Milet., v B.C.), A.*Th.*179 (lyr.), S.*Tr.*765, *Ant.*1013; ὄργια Μουσῶν Ar.*Ra.*356. 2. metaph., *mysteries*, without reference to religion, ἐπιστήμης Hp.*Lex*5; τοῖς τῆς Ἀφροδίτης ὀ. εἰλημμένον Ar.*Lys.*832, cf. Ach.Tat.4.1; τὰ Ἐπικούρου θεόφαντα ὄ. Metrod.38.—The sg. ὄργιον is rare, *Jahresh.*13 *Beibl.*29 No.3 (Erythrae, iv B.C.), Luc.*Syr.D.*16, Orph.*H.*52.5. (Prob. cogn. with ἔρδω, ῥέζω, cf. ἔργον, ὀργεών.) ❋ **-άζω**, *celebrate* ὄργια, E.*Ba.*415 (lyr.), etc.: c. acc., ὀ. τελετήν Pl.*Phdr.*250c; ἱερά Id.*Lg.*910c; θυσίας, πομπάς, χορείας Plu.*Num.*8: c. dat., *pay ritual service to a god* or *goddess*, ταύτῃ Str.10.3.12:—so in Med., ὀργιάζεσθαι δαίμοσι, and in Pass., of the sacred places, *have service done* in them, both in Pl.*Lg.*717b. II. c. acc., *honour* or *worship with* ὄργια, ταύτην v.l. in Str. l.c.; τοὺς μεγάλους θεούς D.H.1.69, cf. Plu.*Cic.*19. 2. ὀ. τινά *initiate into* ὄργια, Ph.2.158, Luc.*Trag.*112. **-άς**, άδος, ἡ, pecul. fem. Adj., *ecstatic and mystic*, Man.4.63. **-ασμός**, ὁ, *celebrating of* ὄργια, Str.10.3.11, Plu.2.169d; οἱ περὶ τὸν Διόνυσον ὀ. Id.*Alex.* 2. **-αστής**, οῦ, ὁ, *one who celebrates* ὄργια, μυστηρίων ὀργιασταί Id.2.417a; τῆς Ἴσιδος App.*BC*4.47; τῆς Ἀκαδημείας ὀ. an *enthusiastic adherent* of the Academy, Plu.2.717d:—fem. ❋**-αστίς**, ίδος, *IG*2.1413, 1414. **-αστικός**, ή, όν, *of* or *for* ὄργια, *exciting*, οὐκ ἔστιν ὁ αὐλὸς ἠθικόν, ἀλλὰ..ὀργιαστικόν Arist.*Pol.*1341$^{a}$22; ὀ. καὶ παθητικά ib.1342$^{b}$3. **-άω**, poet. for ὀργιάζω, Man.4.229, for ὀργάω, Id.1.260, in the Ep. form ὀργιόωντες. 2. *to be fierce*, of lions, Lxx *Is.*5.29 (ὁρμῶσιν cod. A).

❋ **ὀργ-ίζω**, X.*Eq.*9.2: aor. ὤργισα Ar. and Pl. (v. infr.): (ὀργή II):—*make angry, provoke to anger, irritate*, τινα Ar.*V.*223, 404, Pl.*Phdr.* 267c; opp. εὔνουν ποιῆσαι, Arist.*Rh.*1415$^{a}$35. II. more freq. in Pass., Pl.*Phdr.*267d, etc.: fut. Med. (in pass. sense) ὀργιοῦμαι X.*An.*6.1.30, Lys.15.9, Isoc.18.4, etc.; but ὀργισθήσομαι Lys.21. 20, D.59.111: aor. ὠργίσθην Lys.22.2, Pl.*Prt.*346b, etc.: pf. ὤργισμαι E.*Hipp.*1413, Ar.*V.*431, etc.: *grow angry, be wroth*, S.*OT*364, etc.: c. part., τίς γὰρ..οὐκ ἂν ὀργίζοιτ'.. κλύων; ib.339, etc.; τινι *with* a person or thing, E.*Hel.*1646, Th.4.128, Pl.*Ap.*23c, al.; ὑπέρ τινος Th.1.143, Isoc.9.60; ἐπί τινι And.1.30, Lys.28.2, etc.; ἐπί τινος D.21.183; διά τι X.*An.*1.2.26: abs., in part., ἄνθρωπος -όμενος *in a passion*, Antipho 5.72; τὸ -όμενον τῆς γνώμης their *angry* feelings, Th.2.59. Cf. ὀργαίνω. **-ίλος** [ῐ], η, ον, (ὀργή II) *inclined to anger, irascible*, Hp.*Epid.*1.19, X.*Eq.*9.7, D.6.33, Arist.*EN*1108$^{a}$ 7: Comp. -ώτερος Id.*Cat.*10$^{a}$7, Phld.*Ir.*p.74 W., J.*AJ*15.7.4 (v.l. -αίτερος). Adv. -λως, ἔχειν *to be angry*, D.21.215; τινι with one, Id. 45.67; ἐπί τινι Paus.8.25.6; διατίθεσθαι Phld.*Ir.*p.42 W.: neut. as Adv., ὀργίλον βλέπειν Jul.*Or.*3.103b, Lib.*Or.*62.24: Comp. -ώτερον J.*BJ*3.2.3. **-ῐλότης**, ητος, ἡ, *irascibility*, Arist.*EN*1108$^{a}$7, Plu.2. 443d. **-ιον**, τό, v. ὄργια.

❋ **ὀργιοφάντης**, ου, ὁ, *priest, one who initiates others into orgies*, *AP*9. 688, Orph.*H.*6.11.

**ὀργ-ιστέον**, *one must be angry*, D.21.123, Arist.*EN*1109$^{b}$16, M.Ant. 5.22. **-ιστός**, ή, όν, *fit to cause anger*, τῶν ἐπιθυμητῶν καὶ τῶν -τῶν Plot.4.3.28.

**ὀργιών**, v. ὀργεών.

**ὀργογοργονίστρια**, ἡ, epith. of Ἐρινύς, *PMag.Par.*1.1419.

❋ **ὄργυιᾰ**, Att. **ὀργυᾶ**, ᾶς, *IG*2$^{2}$.1672.9; Ion. **ὄργυιᾰ**, ῆς, ἡ (v. infr.): (ὀρέγω):—*the length of the outstretched arms*, about 6 *feet* or 1 *fathom*, ἕστηκε ξύλον..ὅσον τ' ὄργυι' ὑπὲρ αἴης Il.23.327; τοῦ μὲν ὅσον τ' ὄργυιαν ἐγὼν ἀπέκοψα Od.9.325, cf. 10.167, X.*Mem.*2.3.19. 2. more precisely, αἱ ἑκατὸν ὀργυιαὶ δίκαιαί εἰσι στάδιον ἑξάπλεθρον, ἑξαπέδου τῆς ὀργυιῆς μετρεομένης καὶ τετραπήχεος Hdt.2.149, cf. 4.41, 86, *PHal.* 1.98 (iii B.C.), *POxy.*669.39 (iii A.D.). 3. *rod for measuring land*, = $9\frac{1}{4}$ σπιθαμαὶ βασιλικαί, Hero *Geom.*4.11:— poet. also **ὀρόγυια** (q.v.): in compds. -ωρυγ-, v. δεκ-ώρυγος. (Proparox. in nom. and acc. sg., Hom. ll. cc.; oxyt. or perispom. in other cases, cf. Hdn.Gr.2.613, al.; in Ion. the nom. and acc. sg. end in -ᾰ, -ᾰν, as in Att., Hom. ll. cc., the gen. and dat. sg. in -ῆς, -ῇ (acc. ὀργυιήν before consonant in Arat.69, 196, is corrected to ὄργυιαν by Voss); ὀργυιά, -άν in late Gr., Hero l.c., etc.)

❋ **ὀργυι-αῖος**, α, ον, *an* ὄργυια *long* or *wide*, κέρας *AP*6.114 (Simm.). **-όεις**, εσσα, εν, poet. for foreg., Nic.*Th.*216. **-όομαι**, Pass., *to have the arms extended*, πέδαις..ὠργυιωμένη bound with outstretched arms, Lyc.1077; φώσσωνες ὠ. *outspread* sails, Id.26.

**ὄρδειλον**, τό, = τόρδιλον, *hartwort, Tordylium officinale*, Nic.*Th.* 841 (sed leg. τόρδειλον).

**ὄρδ[η]μα**· ἡ τολύπη τῶν ἐρίων, Hsch. **ὄρδικον**· τὸν χιτωνίσκον (Parian word), Id. **ὀρδῠλεύω**, = μοχθέω, Id. s.v. ὠρδυλευσάμην.

**ὀρεᾶνες** or **ὀρειᾶνες**, οἱ, *men*, in the mystic language of the Pythia, Plu.2.406e (Hsch. ὀρείονες· ἄνδρες).

**ὀρέγ-δην**, Adv. *by reaching out*, Sch.Il.2.543, Hsch. s.v. ὀρεκτῇσι μελίῃσι. **-ιάω**, *subo*, *Gloss.* **-μα**, ατος, τό, *stretching out*, τὰ χερὸς ὀ. A.*Ch.*426 (lyr.); προτείνει δὲ χεὶρ ἐκ χερὸς ὀρέγματα (as Herm. from Sch. for ὀρεγόμενα of cod. M) Id.*Ag.*1111 (lyr.); βημάτων ὄρεγμα Id.*Ch.*799 (lyr., but the passage is corrupt); ὄ. ποδός *APl.*4.189 (Nic.): abs., διὰ τὸ μέγεθος τοῦ ὀ. of their *reach* or *stride*, of camels, Arist.*HA*632$^{a}$31; v. ἁμιλλάομαι II. 2. *holding out, offering*, παρηΐδων E.*Ph.*307 (lyr.). II. a measure of length, a subdivision of the σχοῖνος, *Tab.Heracl.*2.33, al. **-μίη**, ἡ, *eructation*, Aret.*SD*1.5 (v.l. ὀρυγ-). **-νυμι**, = ὀρέγω, only in part., χεῖρας ὀρεγνύς Il.1.351, 22. 37; χεῖρας ὀρεγνύμενος *AP*7.506.6 (Leon.), cf. Mosch.2.112.

❋ **ὀρέγω**, Od.17.366, E.*Ph.*1710 (lyr.), etc.; Ion. and later Prose, Hdt. 2.2, Arist.*HA*497$^{b}$27, etc.: impf. ὤρεγον Pi.*P.*4.240, App.*BC*4.126: fut. ὀρέξω Il.13.327, E.*Med.*902: aor. ὤρεξα Il.23.406, Trag. (S.*OC*846, etc.), and sts. in Prose, Pl.*Phd.*117b, X.*An.*7.3.29:—**Med.** and **Pass.**, Il.24.506, Th.2.65, etc.: fut. ὀρέξομαι E.*Hel.*353, Pl.*R.*486a (ἐπ-): aor. ὠρεξάμην Il.23.99, E.*HF*16, etc.: rare in Prose, X.*Mem.*1.2.15; also ὠρέχθην ib.16, *Ages.*1.4, *Smp.*8.35, Hp.*Ep.*17, Epicur.*Sent.*7, *Fr.*187, as well as in E.(*Hel.*1238) (not in Hom.): pf. ὤρεγμαι Hp.*Oss.*18; redupl. 3 pl. ὀρωρέχαται, plpf. -έχατο, Il.16.834, 11.26.—Cf. ὀρέγνυμι, ὀριγνάομαι:—*reach, stretch, stretch out*, χεῖρ' ὀρέγων Od.17.366; εἰς οὐρανόν Il.15.371, Od.9.527; χεῖρας ἐμοὶ ὀρέγοντας, in entreaty, 12.257, cf. Plu.*Cam.*36; μοι..λεχέων ἐκ χεῖρας ὄρεξας Il.24.743; πρός τινα Pi. *P.*4.240, cf. S.*OC*846, etc.; Ὅμηρον.., ἐφ' ὃν πᾶσαι χεῖρ' ὀρέγουσι πόλεις, to claim him, *APl.*4.294. 2. *reach out, hold out, hand, give*, κοτύλην καὶ πύρνον Od.15.312; δέπας Il.24.102; ὁπποτέροισι πατὴρ Ζεὺς κῦδος ὀρέξῃ 5.33, cf. 17.453, Hes.*Th.*433; ἠέ τῳ εὖχος ὀρέξομεν, ἠέ τις ἡμῖν Il.12.328, cf. S.*Ph.*1203 (lyr.); ὁ. πλοῦτόν τινι Pi.*P.*3.110; τέλος ἔμπεδον Id.*N.*7.58; ὤρεξε τὴν κύλικα τῷ Σωκράτει Pl.*Phd.*117b; later βοήθειαν ὀρέξαι τοῖς ἀδικουμένοις *extend* help, *POxy.*902.11 (v A.D.). II. Med. and Pass., 1. abs., *stretch oneself out, stretch forth one's hand*, Od.21.53; ἀνδρὸς..ποτὶ στόμα χεῖρ' ὀρέγεσθαι Il.24.506 (but χεῖρας ὀρεξαμένου *having lent a helping hand, Epigr.Gr.*448.4 (Syria)); ὀρεξαμένη ἀπὸ δίφρου Hes.*Sc.*456; ὠρέξατο χερσὶ φίλῃσι, χειρὶ σκαιῇ, Il.23.99, Hes.*Th.*178; ἔγχει ὀρεξάσθω *let him lunge with* the spear (from the chariot), Il.4.307; πρόσθεν Ἄρης ὠρέξαθ' ὑπὲρ ζυγὸν.. ἔγχεϊ χαλκείῳ 5.851; ποσσὶν ὀρωρέχαται πολεμίζειν, of horses, *they galloped* to the fight, 16.834; ὀρέξατ' ἰών *he stretched himself* as he went, i.e. *made a stride*, 13.20; ὀρωρέχατο προτὶ δειρήν *were stretched out* towards the neck, 11.26; of fish, *rise at the bait*, καί τις τῶν τραφερῶν ὠρέξατο Theoc. 21.44; for A.*Ag.*1111, v. ὄρεγμα I. 1. 2. c. gen., *reach at* or *to* a thing, *grasp at*, οὗ παιδὸς ὀρέξατο he *reached out to* his child, Il.6.466, cf. Od.11.392; in a hostile sense, *aim at, assail, hit*, τοῦ δ' ἀντίθεος Θρασυμήδης ἔφθη ὀρεξάμενος..ὦμον *hit* him first *on* the shoulder, Il.16.322; ib.314, a gen. pers. must be supplied, ἔφθη ὀρεξάμενος πρυμνὸν σκέλος; so in 23.805 ὁππότερός κε φθῇσιν ὀρεξάμενος χρόα καλόν; δηΐων ὀρέγοιτ' ἐγγύθεν ἱστάμενος Tyrt.12.12; also of a suppliant, τί χρῆμα θηρῶσ' ἱκέτις ὠρέχθης ἐμοῦ; E.*Hel.*1238. b. metaph., *reach after, grasp at, yearn for*, γάμων Id.*Ion* 842; τῶν μεγίστων Id.*Fr.*240; ἀπεόντων Democr.202; ζωῆς Id.205: freq. in Att. Prose, Antipho 2.2.12, Th.3.42, Pl.*R.*439b, 485d, etc.; ὁ. τοῦ πρῶτος ἕκαστος γίγνεσθαι Th.2.65: so c. inf., πόλιν ὠρέξατ' οἰκεῖν E.*HF*16; ὁ. τοιοῦτος γενέσθαι Pl. *Prt.*326a; οὐδέποτε ὠρέχθην τοῖς πολλοῖς ἀρέσκειν Epicur.*Fr.*187: also, abs., *yearn, desire*, πάσῃσιν ὀρέξαιτο πραπίδεσσιν Emp.129.4; θυμὸς ὀρέξατο γηθοσύνῃσιν A.R.2.878; ὀρεγόμεθα κατὰ τὴν βούλευσιν Arist.*EN*1113$^a$12; cf. ὀρεκτός, ὄρεξις. 3. c. acc., σῖτόν τ' ὄρεξαι *take* food, E.*Or.*303 (v.l. σίτων); αἰώρημα διὰ δέρης ὀρέξομαι I *will put* the noose on *my* neck, Id.*Hel.*353 (lyr.).

**ὀρειάλωτος** [ᾰ], ον, *wandering on the mountains*, condemned by Thom.Mag.p.267 R.

**ὀρειᾶνες**, οἱ, v. ὀρεᾶνες.

**ὀρει-άρχης**, ου, Dor. **-ας**, ὁ, *mountain-king*, i.e. *Pan*, *AP*6.34 (Rhian.). **-άς**, άδος, ἡ, (ὄρος) pecul. fem. of ὄρειος, *of* or *belonging to mountains*, πέτρα ὀ. *mountain* crag, ib.219.5 (Antip.), cf. *Arch.Pap.*1.219 (Ptol.). II. *Oread, mountain-nymph*, Bion 1.19, Nonn.*D.*6.259, 19.331. **-αυλος**, ον, (αὐλή) *inhabiting the mountains*, Opp.*C.*3.18, *H.*4.309. **-βᾰσία**, ἡ, *wandering on mountains*, in pl., Str.10.3.23, Ael.*NA*3.2, Max.Tyr.34.1. **-βάσια** [ᾰ] (sc. ἱερά), τά, *a festival in which persons traversed the mountains in procession*, Str.12.4.3. **-βᾰτέω**, *traverse mountains*, c. acc., D.S.5.39. II. intr., *roam the mountains*, *AP*10.11 (Satyr.), Plu. *Fab.*7; of horses, Str.3.4.15. **-βάτης** [ᾰ], ου, ὁ, *mountain-ranging*, θήρ S.*Ph.*955; Κύκλωψ E.*Tr.*436; αἶγες, πιθήκη, Ael.*NA*14.16, 6.26; ὄρνις Ar.*Av.*276 codd. (ὀριβ- Brunck); v. οὐριβάτας, ὀρειοβάτης. **-βρεμέτης**, ου, ὁ, written ὀριβρεμέτης, *roaring in the mountains*, Suid., Eust.460.27, cf. *An.Ox.*2.398.

**ὀρείγανον**, τό, v. ὀρίγανον.

**ὀρει-γενής**, ές, *mountain-born*, Nic.*Th.*874. II. = ὀρεινός, σπήλαια Moschio Trag.6.5. **-δρομία**, ἡ, *running on the hills*, *AP*7.413 (Antip.). ❀**-δρόμος**, ον, *running on the hills*, Pi.*Pae.*7.6 (ὀριδρ- Pap.), E.*Ba.*985 (lyr.), *IA*[1593], Nonn.*D.*5.229, 25.194 (v.l. ὀριδρ-). **-θᾰλής**, ές, *blooming on the hills*, Lyc.1423.

**ὀρεικός**, ή, όν, v. ὀρικός.

**ὀρεί-κτῐτος**, ον, *dwelling in the mountains*, σῦς Pi.*Fr.*313. **-λεχής**, ές, *couching on the hills*, λέοντες Emp.127.1. **-μᾰνής**, ές, *frenzied haunter of the heights*, Διόνυσος Tryph.370; μητρὸς ὀ. cj. in Orph. *H.*31.5 (ὀρειομανοῦς codd.). **-νομέω**, *graze* or *live on the hills*, Suid. **-νόμος**, ον, (νέμω B) *feeding on the hills*, δέλφακες Anaxil. 12 (codd. Ath., but ὀρειονόμους is prob. cj.); αἶξ Thphr.*HP*9.18.3; *mountain-ranging*, Κενταύρων γέννα E.*HF*364 (lyr.); ὀ. πλάνη a *roaming o'er the hills*, *AP*6.107 (Phil.).

❀**ὀρεινός**, ή, όν, (ὄρος) *mountainous, hilly*, χώρη Hdt.1.110, cf. 2.34; opp. πεδινός, X.*Cyr.*1.6.43; opp. πεδιάς, J.*BJ*3.3.4; ὀρεινὴν οὖσαν [τὴν Ἀρκαδίαν] Arist.*Mete.*351$^a$3; ἡ ὀρεινή *hill-country*, Id.*HA*556$^a$4, al. II. *of* or *from the mountains, dwelling on the mountains*, οἱ ὀ. Θρᾷκες Th.2.96, X.*An.*7.4.11; of birds, Arist.*HA*592$^b$19; of plants, Thphr.*HP*6.8.3; τὸ ἄγριον καὶ τὸ ὀ. his wild and *mountain nature*, Pl.*Cra.*394e: metaph., ὀ. ἱμάτιον, = ἄκναπτον, *Com.Adesp.* 328. III. in Egypt, *belonging to the edge of the desert*, esp. as epith. of canals, *PTeb.*61(*b*).160, al. (ii B.C.).

**ὀρειοβάτης** [ᾰ], ου, ὁ, = ὀρειβάτης, Sch.S.*OC*1054:—written **ὀρηο-**, *Sammelb.*286.2 (Ptol.); **ὀρεο-**, ib.294 (Ptol.).

**ὀρείοικος**, ον, *mountain-dwelling*, Sch.E.*Or.*1621, *Ph.*683.

**ὀρειομανής**, ές, v. ὀρειμανής.

**ὄρειον**, τό, = πολύγονον θῆλυ, *mare's tail, Hippuris vulgaris*, Plin. *HN*27.115. **ὀρείονες**, v. ὀρεᾶνες.

**ὀρειονόμος**, ον, = ὀρεινόμος, *AP*6.14 (Antip. Sid.), 240 (Phil.); prob. cj. in Anaxil.12; cf. ὀρεινόμος.

❀**ὄρειος**, α, ον, also ος, ον Plu.2.965c, Luc.*Demon.*2, *DDeor.*20.3; Ep. **οὔρειος**:—*of* or *from the mountains, mountain-haunting*, νύμφην οὐρείην *h.Merc.*244, cf. Hes.*Fr.*198, Phoronis 2; this Ep. form is also used by Trag. and Com. in lyr., S.*Ant.*352, E.*IT*127, 1126, *Ph.*806, Ar.*Av.*1098, etc.; but ὄρειος (which is not only Att. but Ion., v. infr.) in trim., as in A.*Ag.*497, S.*Ph.*937; Μήτηρ ὀρεία, of Rhea, Ar.*Av.*746 (lyr.); Ion. gen., Μητρὸς Ὀρέης *IG*12(7).75 (Amorgos); Ion. acc. pl., πέτρας ὀρείας Hippon.35.5: in Prose, ὄρειοί τινες..νομῆς Pl.*Lg.*677b, cf. *Criti.*109d; opp. ἄγροικος, of animals, Arist.*HA*488$^b$2; so ὀρειότερος Opp.*C.*2.22.

**ὀρειοχᾰρής**, ές, *delighting in the hills*, *APl.*4.256.

**ὀρει-πέλαργος**, ὁ, a kind of *vulture* or *eagle*, the same as περκνόπτερος, Arist.*HA*618$^b$34. **-πλαγκτος**, ον, *mountain-roaming*, Νύμφαι Ar.*Th.*326 (lyr.), cf. Opp.*C.*3.224, Nonn.*D.*21.189. (ὀριπλ- freq. in codd.) **-πλᾰνής**, ές, ib.9.291 (in form ὀριπλ-); and **-πλᾰνος**, ον, ib.16.184 (ὀριπλ-, v.l. ὀρειπλ-); = foreg. **-πολέω**, = ὀρεοπολέω, Suid. **-πτελέα**, ἡ, *wych-elm, Ulmus montana*, Thphr. *HP*3.14.1.

**ὄρεις**, v. ὄρημι.

**ὀρείτης**, ου, ὁ, (ὄρος) name of a stone, Orph.*L.*362, 457. 2. a kind of hawk, Ael.*NA*2.43.

**ὀρείτορες**· ἄγριοι, Hsch.

**ὀρει-τρεφής**, ές, *mountain-bred, mountain-fed*, A.R.2.34; ποταμός Tryph.193:—also **-τροφος**, ον, βοτά S.*Ichn.*151, cf. Opp.*H.*1.12. [Both are freq. written ὀριτρ- in codd., and ὀρίτροφος has ῐ in Babr. 106.3.] **-τῠπία**, Ion. **-ίη**, ἡ, *mountain-labour* (v. ὀρειτύπος), Hp. *Epid.*6.3.9. **-τύπος** [ῠ], ον, (τύπτω) *working in the mountains*: ὀρειτύποι, acc. to Gal.17(2).49, were *wood-cutters* and *quarry-men, who brought down materials from the mountains*:—so **ὀρεοτύποι**, Thphr. *HP*3.3.7, 3.12.4, al. (but ὀρει- *CP*5.11.3); **ὀροιτύποι**, Nic.*Th.*5, 377, *AP*7.445 (Pers.), *Eleg.Alex.Adesp.*1.6; cf. also ὀροτύπος. **-φοιτέω**, *roam the mountains*, Sostr.Eleg.ap.Eust.1665.49. **-φοίτης**, ου, ὁ, *mountain-roaming*, Phanocl.3:—so **ὀρείφοιτοι** ποιμένες, ὀρείφοιτα θηρία, Babr.91.2, 95.25; ὀρείφοιτοι Βάκχαι Corn.*ND*30. **-χάλκῐνος**, η, ον, *of orichalc*, στήλη Pl.*Criti.*119c, cf. *IG*2$^2$.1533.24 (iv B.C.). ❀**-χαλκος**, ὁ, Lat. *orichalcum* (which by a false etym. was freq. written *aurichalcum*), *mountain-copper*, i.e. *yellow copper ore, copper* or *brass made from it*, *h.Hom.*6.9, Hes.*Sc.*122, Stesich.88, Ibyc. *Oxy.*1790.42, B.*Fr.*68 Bgk., Pl.*Criti.*114e, Arist.*APo.*92$^b$22, *Mir.*834$^b$25, Philostr.*VA*2.7, 20; a mirror of it, Call.*Lav.Pall.*19; described by Theopomp.Hist.109 as a mixture of ψευδάργυρος and χαλκός. II. as Adj., = foreg., Suid. **-ώδης**, ες, *mountainous*, Eust.1246.28. **-ώτης**, ου, Dor. **-ας**, α, ὁ, = ὀρεσσιβάτης, *AP*9.824 (Eryc.).

**ὀρεκτ-έος**, α, ον, *to be desired*, *Stoic.*3.22. **-έω**, = ὀρέγομαι, Hsch., Suid. **-ιάω**, = ὀρέγομαι, Hsch. **-ικός**, ή, όν, (ὄρεξις) *appetitive*, Arist.*deAn.*433$^b$3, *EE*1233$^a$38, al.; τὸ ὀρεκτικόν the *impulsive* or *conative* faculty, Id.*EN*1102$^b$30; οὐχ ἕτερον τὸ ὀ. καὶ φευκτικόν..ἀλλήλων Id.*deAn.*431$^a$13, al.; ὁ. νοῦς Id.*EN*1139$^b$4. Adv. **-κῶς** Hsch. s.v. θουραῖη; πρὸς τὸ ἀγαθὸν **-κῶς** κινεῖσθαι Arr.*Epict.*3.3.2. 2. *exciting appetite*, οἶνος Dsc.5.6. **-ός**, ή, όν, (ὀρέγω) *stretched out*, ὀ. μελίαι pikes *to be used for thrusting*, Il.2.543; so ὀρεκτὸν δόρυ *pike*, opp. παλτόν (javelin), Str.10.1.12. II. *longed for, desired*, τὸ ὀ. the *object of appetency*, Arist.*deAn.*433$^a$18, cf. *EN*1113$^a$10, al.; τὸ ὀ. κινεῖ οὐ κινούμενον τῷ νοηθῆναι ἢ φαντασθῆναι Id.*deAn.*433$^b$11; opp. ὀρεκτέος, *Stoic.*3.22.

**ὀρεμπόται**, οἱ, (ὄρος, ἐμπίνω) *drainers of the mountains*, epith. of rivers, Orac.ap.Plu.2.406e.

**ὄρεξις**, εως, ἡ, (ὀρέγω) general word for all kinds of *appetency, conation*, including ἐπιθυμία, θυμός, βούλησις, Arist.*deAn.*414$^b$2, cf. 433$^a$13, al., *Stoic.*3.40, Epicur.*Fr.*202, Metrod.*Herc.*831.16, Phld. *Mus.*p.78 K.; opp. φυγή, Arist.*deAn.*431$^a$12; opp. ἔκκλισις, Arr. *Epict.*1.4.1, M.Ant.8.7. 1. c. gen. objecti, *longing* or *yearning after* a thing, *desire for* it, Democr.219, Pl.*Def.*414b, Arist.*EN*1119$^b$7, *deAn.*414$^b$6, al.: more rarely, ὄ. ἐπί τι Plu.2.48c; περί τι Democr. 72. 2. abs., *propension, appetency*, ὄ. βουλευτική Arist.*EN*1113$^a$11; ὄ. διανοητική ib.1139$^b$5; [ἐπιθυμίαι τινὲς] εὐδιάχυτον τὴν ὄ. ἔχουσιν Epicur.*Sent.*26.

**ὀρεο-βαζάγρα**, epith. of Hecate or the Moon-goddess, *Tab.Defix. Aud.*41 A 6 (i/ii A.D.), cf. 38.28, al.; also **-βαρζάγρα** and **-βαρζάγραμ**, *Mélanges Beyrouth* 15.111. **-βάτης**, v. ὀρειοβάτης. **-κομέω**, **-κόμος**, v. ὀρεωκ-. **-μήκης**, ες, *mountain-high*, χιόνες Adam.*Vent.* 40 (ὠρεο- cod.).

**ὀρέοντο**, v. ὄρνυμι.

**ὀρεο-πολέω**, *haunt mountains*, Luc.*DDeor.*20.7. **-πόλος**, ον, *haunting mountains*, *Gloss.* **-σέλῑνον**, τό, *mountain-parsley*, *Athamanta macedonica*, Thphr.*HP*7.6.3, Dsc.3.65, Gal.12.119, Plin. *HN*20.117. **-τύπος** [ῠ], ον, v. ὀρειτύπος. **-φύλαξ** [ῠ], ἄκος, ὁ, *saltuarius*, *Gloss.*; *desert-guard*, *Mim.Oxy.*413.141, *Sammelb.* 4636.28 (iii A.D.), prob. in *OGI*111.16 (ii B.C.).

**ὀρέσ-βῐος**, ον, *living on mountains*, Opp.*C.*3.345; **ὀρεσίβῐος**, Eust. ad D.P.322.

**ὀρεσι**· προβάτοις, Hsch. (v. οἶς).

**ὀρεσί-δρομος**, ον, = ὀρειδρόμος, Nonn.*D.*2.442, 32.134. **-κοίτης**, ου, = ὀρειλεχής, Sch.rec.S.*OT*1100; **ὀρεσίκοιτος**, ον, gloss on ὀρεσκῴοισιν, Hsch. **-νομία**, ἡ, *frequenting of heights*, Sch.Il.8.93. **-οικος**, ον, = ὀρείοικος, Hsch. s.v. ὀρεσκῴοισιν. **-τροφος**, ον, = ὀρείτροφος, in Hom. always epith. of the lion, Il.12.299, Od.6.130, al.; βούτης Nonn.*D.*15.204. **-φοιτος**, ον, = ὀρείφοιτος, Corn.*ND*34.

**ὀρεσκευω**, (ὄρος) *live on mountains*, Nic.*Th.*413.

**ὀρέσκῐος**, ον, = sq., of Dionysus, *AP*9.524.16.

❀**ὀρεσκῷος**, ον, (ὄρος, κεῖμαι) *lying on mountains, mountain-bred, wild*, of the Centaurs, Φῆρες Il.1.268; Κένταυροι Hes.*Fr.*79.5; αἶγες

Od.9.155 :—the Trag. form is **ὀρεσκόος**, ον, A.*Th*.532, E.*Hipp*.1277 (lyr.), *Cyc*.247 ; also in Archil.ap.*Lex.Mess*.p.409.

**ὀρέσσαυλος**, ον, = ὀρείαυλος, *APl*.4.233 (Theaet.), Coluth.107.

**ὀρεσσί-βάτης** [ᾰ], ου, ὁ, poet. for *ὀρεσιβάτης, *mountain-roaming*, Πανὸς ὀρεσσιβάτα (Dor. gen.) S.*OT*1100 (lyr.), cf. *Ant*. 350 (lyr.). **-γονος**, ον, poet. = ὀρειγενής, A.*Fr*.168, Ar.*Ra*.1344, *BMus.Inscr*.902 (Halic., iii B.C.). **-δρόμος**, ον, = ὀρεσιδρόμος, Orph.*A*.21. **-νόμος**, ον, = ὀρεινόμος, Hes.*Sc*.407, Nonn.*D*. 28.25. ❋**-πόλος**, ον, = ὀρεοπόλος, ib.13.137, prob. cj. ib.14. 250. **-φῦτος**, ον, *growing on mountains*, ῥίζα ib.44.272. **-χῦτος**, ον, *pouring from the mountains*, ib.20.337.

**Ὀρέστ-εια**, ἡ, *the tale of Orestes*, a poem by Stesichorus, *Frr*.34 sqq. Bgk.; the collective name of Aeschylus' Agamemnon, Choephoroe, and Eumenides, Ar.*Ra*.1124; cf. Λυκούργεια. **-ειος**, α, ον, *of Orestes*, κακά S.*El*.1117.

**ὀρέσ-τερος**, α, ον, poet. for ὀρεινός, epith. of a snake, Il.22.93; of wolves and lions, Od.10.212 ; ὀρεστέρα παμβῶτι γᾶ S.*Ph*.391 (lyr.); παρθένος E.*Tr*.551 (lyr.); ἀγρευτῆρες Opp.*H*.4.586. (Posit. Adj. formed from ὄρος (τό), opp. ἀγρότερος from ἀγρός.) **-της**, ὁ, = ἐν ὄρεσι διαιτώμενος, Phot.: elsewh. only as pr. n. ❋**Ὀρέστης**, voc. Ὀρέστα, S.*El*.6,15, etc. **-τιάς**, άδος, ἡ, (ὄρος) *of the mountains*, νύμφαι ὀρεστιάδες, = Ὀρειάδες, Il.6.420, *h.Hom*.19.19. II. ὀρεστίας, ου, ὁ, *mountain-wind*, Arist.ap.Ach.Tat.*Intr. Arat*.33, Call.*Fr*.39. **-τιον** or **-ειον**, τό, = ἑλένιον, Dsc.1.28, 5.56, Plin.*HN*14.108.

**ὄρεσφι, -φιν**, Ep. gen. and dat. sg. and pl. of ὄρος.

**ὀρεσχάς**, άδος, ἡ, = ὄσχη, Harp. s. v. ὀσχοφόροι ; = τὸ σὺν τοῖς βότρυσιν ἀφαιρεθὲν κλῆμα, Hsch.

**ὀρεύειν**· φυλάσσειν, Hsch. (cf. οὐρεύω).

❋**ὀρεύς**, Ion. **οὐρεύς**, έως, ὁ (even ὁ θῆλυς ὁ. Arist.*HA*577$^b$22, though τῆς θηλείας follows τοῖς θήλεσιν ib.573$^a$16), *mule*, in Il., as a beast of draught and burden, always in Ion. form, synon. with ἡμίονος, cf. 23.115 with 121, and 24.702 with 716 ; also in Ar.*Ra*.290, etc.; νικᾶν τοῖς ὀρεῦσι win the *mule*-race, Arist.*Rh*.1405$^b$25.—In Att. ἡμίονος is the usual word, though the Adj. ὀρικός is preferred to ἡμιονικός by Moer.p.273 P. II. poet. Adj. for ὀρεινός, Lyc.1111.

**ὀρεχθέω**, Ep.Verb, once in Hom., βόες . . ὀρέχθεον ἀμφὶ σιδήρῳ σφαζόμενοι Il.23.30: expld. by most Gramm. of the death-*rattle* in the throat (as though cogn. with ῥοχθέω) (κατὰ μίμησιν ἤχου τραχέος . . , ἀντὶ τοῦ ἔστενον ἀναιρούμενοι Sch.T ad loc., cf. Eust.1285.60 sq., Apollon. *Lex*., Hsch., etc.); but also as cogn. with ὀρέγομαι, ἀναιρούμενοι ὠρέγοντο ἤτοι ἐξετείνοντο Eust. l. c. (cf. Sch.T, Zonar., etc.), i. e. *they were stretching themselves, struggling*, in the throes of death.—In later Poets it seems freq. to mean *swell up*, esp. of the heart when stirred by emotion, like ὀρίνομαι, πῶς οἴεσθέ μου τὴν καρδίαν ὀρεχθεῖν; Ar.*Nu*. 1368 ; νεάτη δ' ὑπὸ κύστις ὀρεχθεῖ the bladder *swells*, Nic.*Al*.340; σφακέλῳ δέ οἱ ἔνδον ὀρεχθεῖ μαινομένη κραδίη, of a dying whale, Opp. *H*.2.583 ; τῇ δὲ . . δέδεται κέαρ ἔνδοθεν ἄτῃ, οὐδ' ἔχει ἐκφλύξαι τόσσον γόον, ὅσσον ὀρεχθεῖ A.R.1.275 ; καί οἱ ὀρέχθει θυμὸς ἐελδομένῳ στηθέων ἐξ αἷμα κεδάσσαι Id.2.49: in Aristias 6, μύκαισι (μυκαῖσι Schneidewin) δ' ὠρέχθει τὸ λάϊνον πέδον, it must have the sense of ῥοχθέω if μυκαῖσι is accepted ; θάλασσαν ἔα ποτὶ χέρσον ὀρεχθεῖν let the sea *roar* landwards, Theoc.11.43 (cf. βοάω I. 2, ἐρεύγομαι (B)).

**ὀρέω**, v. ὁράω.

**ὀρεω-κομέω**, = ὀρεωπολέω, Poll.7.183 (written ὀρεο-). **-κόμος**, ὁ, (ὀρεύς) *muleteer*, Ar.*Th*.491, *Fr*.633, *IG*2$^2$.10*B*4 (v/iv B.C.), 1673. 18 (iv B.C.), Pl.*Ly*.208b, X.*HG*5.4.42, Hyp.*Lyc*.5.—In codd. freq. misspelt ὀρεοκόμος, as in Pl. l. c., Poll.7.183, Hsch.; the latter also cites a form ὀρειοκόμος, which may be an Ep. spelling of *ὀρη(ϝ)οκόμος, the older form implied by ὀρεωκόμος. **-πολέω**, *tend mules*, and **-πώλης**, ου, ὁ, *mule-dealer*, Suid.

**ὄρηαι**, v. sq.

**ὄρημι**, Aeol. for ὁράω, Sapph.2.11 ; 3 sg. ὄρη Theoc.30.22, cf. Aeol. ἐπόρημι; part. ὄρεις Pittac.ap.D.L.1.81 ; to this athematic stem ὀρη- (not from ὀρα-) prob. belong 2 sg. Med. ὄρηαι Od.14.343 and 2 sg. Act. ποθόρησθα Theoc.6.8 :—but many Dor. forms have η by contr. from άε, as Lacon. inf. ὁρῆν Ar.*Lys*.1077, Syrac. imper. ὅρη Epich.170.12, etc.; v. ὁράω.

**ὀρητός**, ή, όν, Ion. for ὁρατός, Man.2.31,130.

**ὀρῆχον**· τῆς αἱμασιᾶς, Hsch.

**ὀρθαγγελέω**, *announce rightly and truly*, Phryn.*PS*p.92 B.

**ὀρθάγης** or **Ὀρθάγης**, v. Ὀρθάννης.

**ὀρθαγόρας**, ου, ὁ, pun on a pr. n., with an obsc. allusion, Ar.*Ec*. 916.

❋**ὀρθᾰγορίσκος**, ὁ, *sucking-pig*, Lacon. word, Ath.4.139b, 140b, Hsch.; cf. ὀρθραγορίσκος. 2. name of a fish, Apion ap.Plin.*HN* 32.19.

**ὄρθαι**, v. ὄρνυμι.

**ὀρθάκανθος** [ᾰκ], ον, *with straight thorns*, Thphr.*HP*3.18.11.

**ὀρθάμπελος**, ου, ἡ, *a vine growing without props*, Plin.*HN*14.40.

**ὀρθάνθρωπον**, *chelidonium*, *Gloss*.

**Ὀρθάννης**, ου, ὁ, (ὀρθός) a sort of demon with the attributes of Priapus, Pl.Com.174.12, *IG*12(8).52 (Imbros, ii B.C.), Str.13.1.12, cf. Phot. s. v.: written with -νν- in *IG* l. c. and codd. of Pl.Com. and Str., cf. Hdn.Gr.1.70, with -ν- in Phot.; Ὀρηθάνης in Hsch.; Ὀρθαγένης v.l. in Str. l. c.; Ὀρθάγης Lyc.538 (cf. Sch. ad loc.).

**ὄρθαπτον**, τό, *a woollen cloth for wiping the shrines of temples*, Din. ap.Poll.7.69.

❋**ϝορθασία**, ά, epith. of Artemis, *IG*5(2).429 (v B.C.), 5(1).1572 ; v. sq.

❋**Ὀρθεία**, ἡ, epith. of Artemis in Laconia and Arcadia ; at her altar the Spartan boys were whipped, X.*Lac*.2.9, Plu.2.239c :—written **ϝορθεία**, *IG*5(1).252 (Sparta, vi B.C.); **ϝωρθεία**, ib.255.1 (ibid., iv B.C.); **Βωρθεία**, ib.303.9 (ii A.D.); **Βορθέα**, ib.343.4, al.; **Ὀρθεία**, ib.2$^2$.1623.76 (name of a ship), 5(1).602.6 (of the goddess); **Ὀρθία**, codd. X., Plu. ll. cc. :—also **ϝορθασία**, **Ὀρθωσία** (qq. v.).

**ὀρθέσιον**· ὄρθιον, μακρόν, ὀξύ, μέγα, Hsch.

**ὀρθεύω**, (ὀρθός) = ὀρθόω, impf. ὤρθευεν E.*Or*.405.

**ὀρθηλός**, ή, όν, *tall, straight*, κυμβία *IG*11(2).145.49 (Delos, iv/iii B.C.), cf. 154*B*29, 161*B*37, al., Str.12.7.3 :—so **ὀρθηρός**, *BGU*781 i 15, al. (i A.D.).

**ὀρθ-ιάδε**, Adv., (ὄρθιος) *uphill*, X.*Lac*.2.3. ❋**-ιάζω**, *speak in a high tone, speak loud*, ὀ. γόοις *shriek with loud* wailings, A.*Pers*.687, cf. Phld.*Ir*.p.60 W. II. trans., = ὀρθόω, *set upright*, *APl*.4.261.2 (Leon.). 2. ὀρθιάζοντα, gloss on ἐξηνδρωμένον, Hsch., cf. Paul. Aeg.6.70. **-ιαξ**, ᾶκος, ὁ, *the lower part of a mast*, Epich.106 :—also **ὀρθίας**· ἱστὸς νεώς, Hsch.; also, sens. obsc., Id. **-ίασις**, Ion. **-ίησις**, εως, ἡ, *a setting upright, erection*, Aret.*SA*2.12, Sch.E.*Ph*. 1284. **-ίασμα**, ατος, τό, *a high pitch of voice*: in pl., *loud commanding tones*, Ar.*Ach*.1042. ❋**-ιάω**, = ὀρθόω, *Gloss*., Sch.Lyc.538.

**ὀρθιόκωπος**, ον, *rowing upright*, Hsch.

❋**ὄρθιος**, α, ον, Att. also ος, ον Th.5.58 : (ὀρθός) :—*straight up, steep, uphill*, οἶμος Hes.*Op*.290 ; πάγοι S.*Fr*.89 ; πρόσβασις E.*El*.489; ὁδός X.*An*.1.2.21, etc.; ὄρθιον ἑτέραν (sc. ὁδὸν) ἐπορεύοντο Th. l. c.; ὄρθιον πρὸς ὄρθιον ἰέναι march *uphill*, X.*An*.4.6.12, *HG*2.4.15 ; ἡ ἀρετὴ πρὸς ὄρθιον ἄγουσα leading *by a steep path*, Id.*Cyr*.2.2.24 ; πρὸς ὀρθίῳ on *rising ground*, opp. ἐν ἐπιπέδῳ, Id.*HG*6.4.14 ; κατὰ τοῦ ὀ. by a *steep descent*, Arr.*An*.1.1.8 ; τὰ ὄ. the country *from the coast upwards*, τὰ ἐς μεσόγαιαν φέροντα, Hdt.4.101. 2. *upright, standing*, ὄ. ἦν τὰ γέρρα Id.9.102 ; πύργοι E.*Andr*.10 ; esp. of hair, ὀ. στῆσαι τρίχας S.*OC*1624; τριχὸς ὀρθίας πλόκαμος ἵσταται A.*Th*.564 (lyr.), cf. E.*Hel*.632 (lyr.); also ὄ. ἐφιστὰς τὸ οὖς pricking up the ear, Luc.*Tim*.23 ; of animals, *rampant*, Pi.*P*.10.36. II. of the voice, *high-pitched, shrill*, κελεύματα A.*Ch*.751 ; κωκύματα S.*Ant*.1206 ; κηρύγματα Id.*El*.683, *Ichn*.40; ὀρθία σάλπιγγος ἠχώ E.*Tr*.1266 : more freq. the neut. as Adv., ἤϋσε . . ὄρθια she cried *aloud*, Il.11.11 (not found elsewh. in Hom.); ἰάχησε δ' ἄρ' ὄρθια φωνῇ *h.Cer*.20, cf. 432 ; so ὄρθιον ὤρυσαι, φωνεῖν, Pi.*O*.9.109, *N*.10.76 ; ὄρθιον ἀντηλάλαξε . . ἠχώ A.*Pers*.389 ; ἐσήμην' ὄρθιον σάλπιγγι E.*Heracl*.830. 2. νόμος ὄ. a traditional melody *of very high pitch* (cf. Arist.*Pr*.920$^b$20), Hdt.1.24, Ar.*Eq*.1279, etc.: pl., ὀρθίοις ἐν νόμοις A. *Ag*.1153 (lyr.); also ὁ ὄρθιος alone, Ar.*Ach*.16, etc., cf. Sapph.*Supp*. 20c.4 (p.78 Lobel); μελῳδία ὄ. Plu.2.1140f. b. ὄρθιος, ὁ, in Metre, the foot ⏑⏑⏑⏒, Aristid.Quint.1.16, cf. Plu.2.1140f, Bacch.*Harm*. 101. III. in military language, *formed in column*, opp. in line or extended front, ὀ. ποιεῖσθαι τοὺς λόχους X.*Cyr*.3.2.6, cf. *An*.4.8.10 ; προσβάλλειν ὀ. τοῖς λόχοις ib.4.2.11 ; ἄγειν τοὺς λόχους ὀ. bring them up *in column*, ib.4.3.17 ; προῆγεν [αὐτοὺς] ὀ. ἐπὶ τοὺς πολεμίους Plb. 11.23.2, cf. Polyaen.5.16.1. b. of stones in building, *engaged lengthwise* in the wall, i. e. with only the short sides showing, *headers* (opp. stretchers) τιθέντας τοὺς λίθους ὀρθίους ἐν γύψῳ Ph.*Bel*.80. 21. IV. generally, like ὀρθός, *straight*, opp. crooked, φλέψ Hp. *Aph*.5.68, Gal.11.218 ; ἴχνος X.*Cyn*.6.14,15 ; τάφροι Thphr.*CP*3.6. 3 ; opp. πλάγιος, κάλαμοι Aen.Tact.32.2 : metaph., ἤθη ὄ. *straightforwardness*, Plu.*Sull*.1 ; ὄ. καὶ αὐθέκαστος Id.*Cat.Ma*.6. V. ὀρθία (sc. γωνία) *a right angle*, Id.2.373f. 2. -ία, ἡ, *latus rectum* of a conic, Apollon.Perg.1.11, al. 3. ὀ. διάμετρος *conjugate* diameter of a two-branched curve, Id.1 *Def*.1, al. VI. Ὄρθιος, epith. of Asclepius, *IG*4$^2$(1).459 (Epid.).

**ὀρθο-βᾰτέω**, *walk straight*, ἀτραπόν (of a blind man) *AP*9.11 (Phil. or Isid.). **-βολέω**, *shoot straight*, metaph., Phld.*Rh*.2.71, 98 S. **-βολος**, ον, *thrown straight*, Hsch. s. v. ἰθυπτίωνα (-βουλον cod.). **-βουλία**, ἡ, *right counsel*, Adam.1.11. **-βουλος**, ον, *right-counselling, wise*, μῆτις, μαχαναί, Pi.*P*.4.262, 8.75 ; of persons, A.*Pr*.18. **-γνωμονέω**, *think* or *judge rightly*, Ph.1.547. **-γνώμων**, ονος, ὁ, ἡ, *thinking* or *judging rightly*, ψυχή Hp.*Ep*.17 ; ὀ. ἐπιμονή, transl. of 'Rebekah', Ph.1.549. **-γόη**, v. ὀρθρο-. ❋**-γρᾰφέω**, *make an elevation* (cf. sq. II), ὡς ὀρθογραφεῖται as *is shown in the accompanying plan*, Apollod.*Poliorc*.193.1. **-γρᾰφία**, ἡ, *orthography*, A.D.*Adv*.165.15, S.E.*M*.1.92 ; name of works by Herodian, Orus, and other Gramm. II. *the elevation of a building*, opp. the ground-plan, Vitr.1.2.2. ❋**-γράφος** [ᾰ], ὁ, *orthographer*, Suid. s. v. ἀνώγεων. **-γυιον**, τό, = στρύχνον μανικόν, Dsc.4.73. **-γώνιον**, τό, *rectangle*, Arist. *de An*.413$^a$17 ; **-ιος**, ον, *rectangular*, Archyt.ap.Simp. *in Cat*.392.8 ; τρίγωνον Ti.Locr.98a, D.L.8.12 ; κῶνος Archim.*Sph. Cyl*.1 *Prooem*.; ἐξ ὀρθογωνίου by *rectangular measurement*, *PSI*4.320. 12 (i A.D.), *POxy*.2134.15 (ii A.D.). **-δᾱής**, ές, *knowing rightly how* to do a thing, c. inf., A.*Ag*.1022 (lyr.). **-δίκας** [ῐ], Dor. for ὀρθοδίκης, ὁ, *by which justice is upheld*, γᾶς ὀμφαλὸς Pi.*P*.11.9 :—so **-δικος**, ον, Στύξ B.10.9, cf. 13.23, and **-δίκαιος**, A.*Eu*.994 (lyr.). **-δοξαστικός**, ή, όν, *according to right opinion*, βίος Procl.*in Alc*.p.76 C., cf. Id. *in Prm*.p.721 S., etc. Adv. -κῶς Ascl.*in Metaph*.273.7. **-δοξέω**, *have a right opinion*, περί τι Arist.*EN*1151$^a$19, Posidon.ap.Gal.5. 469, Alex.Aphr.*in Top*.265.13. **-δοξία**, ἡ, *right opinion*, Poll. 4.7, Hierocl.*in CA*10 p.435 M., Olymp.*in Phd*.p.113 N. **-δοξος**, ον, *orthodox* in religion, *Cod.Just*.1.5.21, al., *MAMA*1.290 (Phrygia). **-δότειρα** διανοίης, *giver of a right* judgement, Orph.*H*.76.5 (pl.). **-δρομέω**, *run straight forward*, X.*Eq*.7.14, Poll.1.205. **-δωρον**, τό, (δῶρον II) *the length from the wrist to the finger-ends*, = σπιθαμή, Hsch., cf. Poll.2.157. II. = *membrum erectum*, *PLond*.

1821.166. **-έθειρος**, *ον*, = ὀρθόθριξ, Orph.*H*.19.8. **-έπεια**, ἡ, *correctness of diction*, Democr.20a, Pl.*Phdr*.267c, Phld.*Rh*.1.191 S., D.H.*Dem*.26, Quint.1.6.20. **-επέω**, *speak* or *pronounce correctly*, Phld.*Rh*.1.186 S., D.H.1.90. **-θριξ**, *τρῐχος*, ὁ, ἡ, *with hair upstanding* or *making the hair stand on end*, φόβος A.*Ch*.32 (lyr.); φόβαι D.H.7.72. **-κάθεδρος**, *ον*, *sitting upright*, cj. in Paul.Aeg.6.99, for *-ευδον*. **-καθεύδω**, in neut. part. *-κάθευδον σχῆμα*, dub. in Paul.Aeg.6.99 (v. foreg.). **-κάθημαι**, *sit upright*, ib.60. **-κάλᾰμος** [κᾰ], ὁ, *upright stalk*, interpol. in Dsc.4.2. **-κάρηνος** [ᾰ], *ον*, = ὀρθοκέφαλος, v.l. in Orph.*H*.19.8. **-καυλος**, *ον*, *straight-stalked*, Thphr.*HP*7.8.2, 8.3.2. **-κέρᾱτος**, *ον*, = sq., Apollon.*Lex*. and Hsch. s.v. ὀρθοκραιράων. **-κερως**, *ωτος*, ὁ, ἡ, *straight-horned*, βοῦς A.*Fr*.74.2; *upright-horned*, ἔλαφος Epic. in *Arch.Pap*.7 p.4; ὀ. φρίκη horror *which makes the hair stand up like horns*, S.*Fr*.875: Poll.2.31, Hsch., and Phot. explain it by ὀρθόθριξ. **-κέφᾰλος**, *ον*, *with head erect*, Apollon.*Lex*. s.v. ὀρθοκραιράων. **-κοιλος**, v. ὀρθόκωλος. **-κόπος**, ὁ, prob. *stonemason*, *Inscr.Magn*.290. **-κόρῠδος**, ὁ, *a very lark*, nickname of one with a thin bad voice, Alciphr.3.48 (Bergler for ὀρθοκόρυζος). **-κορυς**, *υθος*, ὁ, ἡ, *having an upright crest*, Hsch. **-κραιρος**, *α*, *ον*, *with straight* or *upright horns*, epith. of horned cattle, Il.8.231, Od.12.348; also of galleys, of which the two ends turned up so as to resemble horns, Il.18.3, 19.344; of a mountain range, Πυρήνην *-κραιρον* *AP*14.121.5 (Metrod.).—Hom. has it only in poet. gen. pl. fem. ὀρθοκραιράων. **-κρᾱνος**, *ον*, *having a high head*, τύμβος ὀ. a *high* funeral-mound, S.*Ant*.1203. **-κυλλος**, *ον*, = sq., Gal.18(1).636. **-κωλος**, *ον*, *with limbs fixed in extended position*, ib.623; *ἵπποι τὰ γόνατα ἔχοντες σκληρὰ καὶ ὅμοια τοῖς ὀρθοκοίλοις* (sic) *Hippiatr*.115. **-λεκτέω**, = sq., Ps.-Alex.Aphr.*in Metaph*.783.27. **-λογέω**, *speak correctly*, Plu.2.570e. **-λογία**, ἡ, *correctness of language*, Pl.*Sph*.239b. **-λοξος**, *ον*, of a spiral bandage, *criss-cross*, Asclep.ap.Erot. s.v. σκέπαρνος. **-μαντεία**, ἡ, *true prophecy*, A.*Ag*.1215. **-μαντις**, *εως*, ὁ, ἡ, *a true prophet*, opp. ψευδόμαντις, Pi.*N*.1.61. **-μίλιον**, τό, gloss on τρύβλιον, Suid.

**ὀρθόμφᾰλος**, *ον*, *with an outstanding boss*, πόπανον *IG*2$^2$.1367.13.

**ὀρθο-νόμος**, *ον*, *making right award*, δαίμονες A.*Eu*.963 (lyr.). **-νοτος**, ὁ, v. ὀρθρόνοτος. **-νύσταγμος**, *ον*, *dozing in an upright position*, Pall.*in Hp*.2.119 D. **-πᾰγής**, *ές*, *fixed erect*, κίδαρις Plu.2.340c. **-πᾰγον**, τό, *Steep-hill*, name of a hill near Thurii, Id.*Sull*.17. **-παιία**, ἡ, *hitting while standing*, opp. pummelling while on the ground, *CR*43.210 (Fassiller, Asia Minor). **-πάλη** [ᾰ], ἡ, *wrestling in an upright posture*, opp. κλινοπάλη, Luc.*Lex*.5. **-περιπᾰτητικός**, ή, όν, *walking about erect*, Alex.Aphr.*in Top*.381.25, Ammon.*in Porph*.54.20, Ascl.*in Metaph*.345.28, Phlp.*in APr*.275.20, al. **-πλήξ**, *ῆγος*, ὁ, ἡ, of a horse, *rearing*, Ar.*Fr*.43. **-πλοέω**, *sail prosperously*, *have a fair voyage*: metaph., *to be successful*, Euryph.ap.Stob.4.39.27 (Med.), Clin.ib.3.1.76. **-πλοος**, *ον*, contr. **-πλους**, *ουν*, *sailing prosperously*: metaph., *successful*, Hippod. ap.Stob.4.39.26. ❋ **-πλουμος**, *ον*, (Lat. *pluma*) *embroidered with feathers*, *Sammelb*.7033.39 (v A.D.). ❋ **-πνοια**, ἡ, *breathing only in an upright posture*, *orthopnoea*, a symptom of various diseases, Hp.*Prog*.23, *Acut*.17. ❋ **-πνοϊκός**, ή, όν, *connected with* ὀρθόπνοια, Id.*Coac*.417, 538. **-πνοος**, *ον*, contr. **-πνους**, *ουν*, = foreg., Id.*Mul*.2.126. ❋ **-ποδέω**, *walk straight* or *uprightly*, *Ep.Gal*.2.14. **-πόδης**, *ου*, = ὀρθόπους I, ἐλέφας Nonn.*D*.26.335, 28.72. **-πολις**, *εως*, ὁ, ἡ, *upholding the city*, Pi.*O*.2.7, *BCH*23.302 (Termessus). **-πόρος**, *ον*, *in a straight course*, Orac.ap.Porph.*Plot*.22. **-πους**, ὁ, ἡ, *πουν*, τό, gen. *ποδος*, *upright on their feet*, ὀ. βαίνοντες ἄνις..τιθήνης Nic.*Al*.419. II. *steep*, ὀρθόποδος ὑπὲρ πάγου S.*Ant*.985 (lyr.); cf. ὄρθιος I, Ὀρθόπαγον. **-πρᾱγέω**, *act uprightly*, Democr.181, Arist.*Pol*.1260$^a$26, Phld.*Herc*.1251.13. **-πρᾱγία**, ἡ, *right conduct*, Teles p.22 H., prob. in Phld.*Herc*.1251.12. **-πρίων** [ῑ], *ονος*, ὁ, *instrument for trepanning*, = χοινικίς II, Hp.ap.Gal.19.126. **-πρυμνος**, *ον*, *with upright stern*, Hsch. s.v. ὀρθοκραιράων. **-πτερος**, *ον*, *with high hills* or *with high columns*, S.*Fr*.33. **-πτωσις**, *εως*, ἡ, *nominative case*, Sulp.Vict.*Inst.Or*.19 p.323 Halm. **-πτωτος**, *ον*, *in the nominative case*, Sch.rec.A.*Pers*.135, Sch.E.*Ph*.1288. **-πῡγιάω**, *straighten the back*, *Com.Adesp*.1095. **-πύγιον** [ῡ], τό, = ὀρροπύγιον, Eratosth.*Cat*.25, 41, Vett.Val.10.3, Sch.Arat.276. **-πύθμενος**, *ον*, *with a straight base*, of vases, *BGU*781 iii 1 (i A.D.); for the form cf. ὀξυπύθμενος. **-πῠρεταίνω**, *to be normally feverish*, Gal.19.558. **-ρρημοσύνη**, ἡ, *right use of a word*, Them.*Or*.23.289d.

❋ **ὀρθός**, ή, όν, *straight*, I. in height, *upright*, *standing*, Hom., who commonly joins it with στῆναι, στῆ δ' ὀρθός Il.23.271, al., cf. Hdt.5.111, 9.22 (where it is used of a horse rearing); ὀρθαὶ τρίχες ἔσταν Il.24.359, cf. Hes.*Op*.540; ὀρθῶν ἑσταότων ἀγορή Il.18.246; οἱ δ' ἐν νηΐ μ' ἔδησαν..ὀρθὸν ἐν ἱστοπέδῃ Od.12.179, cf. S.*Aj*.239 (anap.); κυρβασίας..ὀρθὰς εἶχον πεπηγυίας Hdt.7.64; ὀρθὸν αἴρεις κάρα A.*Ch*.496, etc.; ὀρθὸν οὖς ἵστησι pricks up his ear, S.*El*.27, etc.; applied to the *erect* posture of man, Arist.*PA*653$^a$31, al.; ὀ. θηρίον, of man, Philem.3; of buildings, *standing with their walls entire*, [τὸ Πάνακτον] ὀρθὸν παραδοῦναι Th.5.42; ὀρθαὶ κίονες Pi.*P*.4.267, cf. *PLond*.3.755$^v$.2 (iv A.D.); of a *standing* crop, ib.1165.2 (ii A.D.). Adv., ὀρθῶς ἑστῶτες Arist.*PA*689$^b$19. b. Geom., *at right angles to*.., εὐθεῖα πρὸς ἐπίπεδον ὀρθή ἐστιν ὅταν.. Euc.11 *Def*.3. c. Astrol., ὀρθὰ ζῴδια signs *which rise vertically*, opp. πλάγια, Doroth. in *Cat. Cod. Astr*.5(1).240. II. in line, *straight* (opp. σκολιός crooked and πλάγιος aslant), ἀντ' ἠελίου τετραμμένος ὀρθός *straight*, *right* opposite the sun, Hes.*Op*.727; ὀρθὸν εὐθύνοι βέλος A.*Fr*.200; ποιῶν ὀρθὰ πάντα πρὸς κανόνα *IG*7.3073.108 (Lebadea, ii B.C.); ὀ. τρῶμα *longitudinal* to the muscle, opp. ἐπικάρσιος, Hp.*Prorrh*.2.15; ὀρθὸς εἰς ὁδὸν πορεύεται S.*Aj*.1254; εἶμι..ὀ. ὁδόν Thgn.945; ὀ. κέλευθον ἰών Pi.*P*.11.39; ὀρθὴν κελεύεις, i.e. ὀρθὴν ὁδόν με ἰέναι κ., Ar.*Av*.1; so ὀρθὴν ἄνω δίωκε (sc. ὁδόν) Id.*Th*.1223 (but ὀρθήν, = εὐθύς, Hyp.*Fr*.257); δι' ὀρθῆς τήνδε ναυκληρεῖς πόλιν (sc. ὁδοῦ) S.*Ant*.994; εἰς ὀρθὸν τρέχειν Diph.61.5; εἰς ὀρθὸν ἀποδοῦναι *to face the front originally held*, Ascl.*Tact*.10.1; κατ' ὀρθὸν εὐδρομεῖν Men.681; also ὀρθᾷ χερί *straightway*, Pi.*O*.10(11).4; ὀρθῷ ποδί ib.13.72, *Fr*.167; but τιθέναι ὀρθὸν πόδα is prob. *to put the foot out*, as in walking, A.*Eu*.294 (v. κατηρεφής I), cf. E.*Med*.1166. 2. βλέπειν ὀρθά, opp. being blind, S.*OT*419; ὀρθὸν ἀνέβλεψε *recovered his sight*, *IG*14.966 (Rome, ii A.D.); ἐξ ὀμμάτων ὀ... κἀξ ὀρθῆς φρενός S.*OT*528; ὀρθοῖς ὄμμασιν ib.1385; v. ὄμμα I. III. metaph., 1. *right*, *safe*, *prosperous*: a. partly from signf. I, τοὺς δὲ τομαῖς ἔστασεν ὀρθούς *set them up*, *restored*, Pi.*P*.3.53; so ὀρθὸν ἀστάσας (= ἀναστήσας) *IG*4$^2$(1).122.52 (Epid., iv B.C.); ἐς ὀρθὸν ἱστάναι τινά E.*Supp*.1230; ὀρθὰν φυλάσσειν Τένεδον Pi.*N*.11.5; so στάντες τ' ἐς ὀρθὸν καὶ πεσόντες ὕστερον S.*OT*50, cf. Pl.*La*.181b; ταύτης ἔπι (sc. χθονός) πλέοντες ὀρθῆς (the state being represented as a ship) S.*Ant*.190; ἐν ὀρθῷ κεῖσθαι Plb.31.7.1. b. partly from signf. II, κατ' ὀρθὸν ἐξελθεῖν, of prophecies, S.*OT*88, cf. *OC*1424; κατ' ὀρθὸν οὐρίσαι to speed *in prosperous course*, Id.*OT*695 (lyr.). 2. *right*, *true*, *correct*, ἄγγελος, ἀγγελία, νόος, Pi.*O*.6.90, *P*.4.279, 10.68; μάρτυρες A.*Eu*.318 (anap.), etc.; γλῶσσα S.*Fr*.351; ὀρθᾷ φρενί Pi.*O*.8.24; ὄρθ' ἀκούειν to be *rightly*, *truly* called, S.*OT*903 (lyr.); κατὰ τὸ ὀ. δικάζειν Hdt.1.96; ὀ. λόγῳ *strictly speaking*, *in very truth*, Id.2.17, 6.68, etc.: so in Adv., ὀρθῶς λέγειν Id.1.51; ὀ. ἔλεξας S.*Ph*.341; ὀ. φράσαι A.*Ch*.526; εἴρηκας ὀ. S.*El*.1040; ὀ. φρονεῖν A.*Pr*.1000, Archyt.1 (so εἰς ὀρθὸν φ. S.*Fr*.612); ὀ. γνῶναι Antipho 2.2.8; ὀ. ἔχει it is *right*, c. inf., Pl.*Euthphr*.9a; ὀ. ἐνδίκως τ' ἐπώνυμον A.*Th*.405, cf. 829 (anap.): in answers, *rightly*, *exactly*, Pl.*Prt*.359e; ὀ. γε Diph.32.18: Sup., ὀρθότατα καλεόμενος Hdt.4.59; so τὸ ὀρθὸν ἐξείρηκα S.*Tr*.374; φωνεῖν δίκης ἐς ὀρθόν ib.347; κατ' ὀρθόν Pl.*Ti*.44b. 3. *true*, *real*, *genuine*, ὀ. πολιτεῖαι, opp. παρεκβάσεις, Arist.*Pol*.1279$^a$18, etc.; ὀ. μανία *real* madness, Ael.*NA*11.32, cf. Theoc.11.11. Adv. -θῶς *really*, *truly*, τοὺς ὀ. φιλομαθεῖς Pl.*Phd*.67b; ὁ ὀ. κυβερνήτης Id.*R*.341c; τὸν ὀ. συγγενῆ Diph.102. 4. *upright*, *just*, ἐμμένειν ὀ. νόμῳ S.*Aj*.350 (lyr.); τὸ ὀ. *uprightness*, Pl.*R*.540d; ἐπιστήμη ἐνοῦσα καὶ ὀ. λόγος (v. λόγος IV.1) Id.*Phd*.73a; ὁ ὀ. λόγος διὰ πάντων ἐρχόμενος (v. λόγος III.7) Chrysipp.*Stoic*.3.4; ὀ. λόγοι *virtues* on the intellectual side, Phld.*Piet*.8. Adv. ὀρθῶς *rightly*, *justly*, Th.3.56; ὀ. καὶ δικαίως Antipho 1.10, *IG*2$^2$.228.14 (iv B.C.), *IPE*1$^2$.32 *B*73 (Olbia, iii B.C.), etc.; ὀ. καὶ νομίμως Isoc.7.28. 5. of persons, '*straight*', *straightforward*, σμικροὶ καὶ οὐκ ὀρθοὶ τὰς ψυχάς Pl.*Tht*.173a. 6. *on tiptoe*, *full of expectation*, *excited*, ὀρθῆς τῆς πόλεως γενομένης διά τι Isoc.16.7; τὴν Ἑλλάδα ὀρθὴν οὖσαν ἐπί τινι Id.5.70; ὀ. ἦν ἡ πόλις ἐπὶ τοῖς συμβεβηκόσιν Lycurg.39, cf. Hyp.*Fr*.39; ὀ. καὶ μετέωροι ταῖς διανοίαις Plb.28.17.11; ὀ. καὶ περίφοβος ἦν ἡ πόλις Id.3.112.6; ὀ. διὰ τὸν φόβον D.S.16.84; ὀ. καὶ δραστήριος διὰ τὸ θαρρεῖν Plu.*Phil*.12. IV. ἡ ὀρθή, 1. (sc. ὁδός) v. supr. II.1. 2. ὀ. γωνία *right* angle, Pl.*Ti*.55b; so ὀ. alone, Arist.*EN*1098$^a$30, al.; cf. ὄρθιος V.1: τέμνειν πρὸς ὀρθάς to cut *at right angles*, Euc.3.3, al.; εἴ τις δείξειεν ὅτι αἱ ὀρθαὶ οὐ συμπίπτουσι..that *right angles* do not meet (short for 'that two straight lines making, with a third, interior angles equal to two right angles, etc.'), Arist.*APo*.74$^a$13; τὸ δυσὶν ὀρθαῖς *the theorem that the angles of a triangle are together equal to two right angles*, ib.85$^b$5; ὀρθὸς κῶνος, κύλινδρος, a *right* cone, cylinder, Archim.*Sph.Cyl*.1.26, 1.11. 3. (with or without πτῶσις) *nominative*, Lat. *casus rectus*, opp. the oblique cases, D.T.636.3, Str.14.2.28, A.D.*Pron*.39.10, al., S.E.*M*.1.177. V. ὀρθά *active verbs*, opp. ὕπτια (passive) and οὐδέτερα (neuter), Chrysipp.*Stoic*.2.59. VI. ὀ. τόνος *real* or *unmodified* (cf. supr. III.3) accent, opp. ἐγκλινόμενος, A.D.*Pron*.36.10, al.; so ὀρθὴ τάσις ib.54.8, al. (The gloss of Hsch., βορθ-αγορίσκοι, = ὀ., and the dialect forms of Ὀρθεία (q.v.), suggest that the word orig. had ϝ.)

❋ **ὀρθό-σημος**, *ον*, *with vertical stripes*, Δαλματικαί *Edict.Diocl*.29.24, cf. 44. **-σκοπέω**, *see aright*, Asp.*in EN*99.12. **-στάδην** [ᾰ], Adv., (ἵστημι) *standing upright*, A.*Pr*.32, Luc.*Anach*.3, etc.; of invalids *not obliged to keep their bed*, Hp.*Epid*.1.1, 5; ὀ. καθεύδειν, of elephants, Ael.*NA*4.31. **-στάδης**· εἶδος πέμματος, Hsch.; cf. ὀρθοστάτης II. **-στάδιον** [ᾰ], τό, *a loose*, *ungirded tunic*, which hung down *in straight folds* from the neck to the ground (v. στάδιος, στατός), Ar.*Lys*.45, D.C.63.17:—also **-στάδιος** χιτών, Poll.7.49, Eust.1166.55. **-στᾰδόν**, Adv. = ὀρθοστάδην, ὀ. λόγχαις ἐπείγοντες φόνον E.*Fr*.495.6; ἔρνεα ὀ. ἠέξοντο A.R.4.1426. **-στᾰτέω**, *stand upright*, Hp.*Epid*.2.2.24. ❋ **-στάτης** [ᾰ], *ου*, ὁ, (ἵστημι) *upright shaft*, *pillar*, E.*Ion*1134, *HF*980; *building stones laid with their longest edges vertical*, *IG*1$^2$.372.60, al., 2$^2$.1668.19, 4$^2$(1).103.74, al.; *upright beam*, Ph.*Bel*.74.8, Apollod.*Poliorc*.162.14; κλιμάκων ὀρθοστάτας prob. cj. in E.*Supp*.497. 2. *funeral monument with pillars*, *Ath.Mitt*.24.235 (Thyatira); so perh. in E.*Hel*.547. II. a sort of sacrificial bread, Poll.6.73, cf. Thphr.ap.Porph.*Abst*.2.7. III. = *librarius*, *Gloss*. **-στᾰτος**, *ον*, *upstanding*, *upright*, κλίμακες E.*Supp*.497 codd.; but v. foreg. **-στομέω**, *speak straight* or *freely*, Procop.*Goth*.3.33. ❋ **-στρωτοι** τοῖχοι, *upright* walls *cased with marble*, Hierocl.p.54 A. (λιθόστρωτοι cj. Diels). **-σύνη**, ἡ, = ὀρθότης, Democr.40. **-τενής**, *ές*, *stretched out*, *straight*, Opp.*C*.1.189, 408. ❋ **-της**, *ητος*, ἡ, *upright posture*, *erectness*, X.*Mem*.1.4.11; of man, Arist.*PA*658$^a$22, al. 2. *straightness*, opp. κάμψις, ib.654$^b$5. 3. *fixity*, ὀμμάτων Hp.*Coac*.223. II. metaph., *rightness*, *correctness*, τῶν ἐπῶν Ar.*Ra*.1181; λογισμῶν Pl.*Ti*.47c; μουσικῆς Id. *Lg*.655d; λόγων Gorg.*Fr*.6 D.; ἡ τῶν ὀνομάτων ὀ. Pl.*Cra*.422b sq., etc. III. *use of the nominative case* in narrative, Hermog.*Id*.1.3, al. **-τίτθιος**, ον, *with outstanding breasts*, Procop.*Arc*.10, Suid. ❋ **-τομέω**, *cut in a straight line*, τὰς ὁδοὺς Lxx *Pr*.3.6: metaph., ὀ. τὸν λόγον *teach* it *aright*, 2*Ep.Ti*.2.15. **-τονέω**, *pronounce with the unmodified* (e.g. ἡμῶν, opp. ἧμων) *accent*, and Pass., *to be so pronounced*, A.D.*Pron*.35.6, al.:—hence **-τονητέον**, ib.49.19. **-τόνησις**, εως, ἡ, *use of the unmodified accent*, ib.36.6, 55.19. **-τονος**, ον, *with the unmodified accent*, ib.8.9. Adv. -ως ib.46.8. **-τονουμένως**, Adv., (ὀρθοτονέω) *with the unmodified accent*, Hdn. Gr.1.555. **-τρῐχέω**, *to have one's hair up-standing*, Sm.*Ez*.27.35, Thd.*Is*.13.21, *Gloss*. **-τρῐχία**, ἡ, *hair which stands on end*, Dsc. *Ther*.6, *Hippiatr*.89, Gal.19.564. **-τρῐχίᾱσις**, εως, ἡ, *standing up of the hair*, Paul.Aeg.5.8, *Gloss*. **-τρῐχιάω**, = ὀρθοτριχέω, ib. ❋ **-ῠφος** [ῠ], ὁ, *weaver for a special* (*unknown*) *kind of weaving*, *PGrenf*.2.79.3 (iii A.D.). **-φρων**, ονος, ὁ, ἡ, *of excited mind*, S.*Fr*.1077. **-φῠέω**, *grow straight*, dub. in Thphr.*HP*2.6.4. **-φυής**, ές, *of straight growth*, ib.3.8.4, al. **-φῠΐα**, ἡ, *straight growth*, ib.3.8.5. **-χαίτης**, ου, ὁ, *with hair standing on end*, Str.15.1.57; gloss on φριξολόφος, Hsch. **-ψάλακτος** [ψᾰ], ον, *loud*, ὀμφά cj. in S.*Ichn*.321 (lyr.); [ἔριν] ὀρθοψάλακτον ἐν λόγοισιν ἱστάναι ib.249.

❋ **ὀρθόω**, *set straight*, 1. in height, *set upright*, *set up* one fallen or lying down, *raise up*, τὸν δ' αἶψ' ὤρθωσεν Ἀπόλλων Il.7.272; χερσὶ λαβὼν ὤρθωσε 23.695, v. infr. II.1; ὀρθοῦν κάρα, πρόσωπον, E.*Hipp*. 198 (anap.), *Alc*.388 (so in Med., οὔατα ὀρθώσασθαι Q.S.4.511); of buildings, *raise up*, *rebuild*, E.*Tr*.1161; πολὺ τοῦ τείχους X.*HG*4.8.10: generally, *build*, *raise*, Ζηνὸς ὀρθῶσαι βρέτας τρόπαιον E.*Ph*.1250; ἔρυμα λίθοις καὶ ξύλοις Th.6.66:—Pass., *to be set upright*, ἕζετο δ' ὀρθωθείς he sat *upright*, Il.2.42, etc.; ὀρθωθεὶς δ' ἄρ' ἐπ' ἀγκῶνος 10.80; ὠρθοῦθ' ὁ τλήμων ὀρθὸς ἐξ ὀρθῶν δίφρων S.*El*.742; ὀρθούμενοι ἐξιέναι X.*Cyr*. 8.8.10, cf. 1.3.10; simply, *rise from one's seat*, *stand up*, A.*Eu*.708, S. *Ph*.820; *rise up*, ὀρθωθεὶς εὐνῆθεν A.R.2.197. 2. in direction, *make straight*, τὰ διεστραμμένα τῶν ξύλων Arist.*EN*1109$^b$7, cf. X.*Mem*.3.10.15; ὀρθώσατ' ἐκτείνοντες ἄθλιον νέκυν E.*Hipp*.786:—Pass., ἢν τόδ' ὀρθωθῇ βέλος if this dart *go straight*, S.*Ph*.1299; παρὰ στάθμην.. ὀρθοῦται κανών Id.*Fr*.474. II. metaph. (from signf. I.1) *raise up*, *restore to health* or *happiness*, ἐκ κακῶν ἄνδρας ὀρθοῦσιν.. κειμένους Archil.56.2; ψυχῆς τελεότης σκήνεος μοχθηρίην ὀρθοῖ Democr.187; ὧδε ποιήσας ὀρθώσεις σεωυτόν Hdt.3.122, cf. A.*Th*.229 (lyr.), S.*OC*394, etc.; ὀ. βίον Id. *OT*39; ὀ. ὕμνον *raise* it *as a monument of glory*, Pi.*O*.3.3, cf. *I*.1.46; also, *exalt*, *honour*, Σικελίαν, οἶκον, Id.*N*.1.15, *I*.6(5).65; *make famous*, Id.*P*.4.60, cf. Pl.*La*.181a; ὀρθοῦν τὸν ὑπτιάζοντα λόγον *restore* it *to vigour*, Hermog.*Id*.2.1. 2. (from signf. I.2) *guide aright*, γνώμην A.*Ag*.1475 (lyr.); πόλλ' ἁμαρτὼν οὐδὲν ὤρθωσας φρενί Id.*Supp*.915; ὀ. ἀγῶνας, ξυμφοράς, *bring* them *to a happy end*, Id.*Ch*.584, *Eu*.897; τὰ.. πόλεος θεοὶ.. σείσαντες ὤρθωσαν πάλιν S.*Ant*.163; τύχη τέχνην ὤρθωσεν Men.*Mon*.495, cf. 625:—Pass., of actions or persons acting, *succeed*, *prosper*, ἢν ἡ διάβασις μὴ ὀρθωθῇ Hdt.1.208; στρατηγὸς πλεῖστ' ἂν ὀρθοῖτο Th.3.30, cf. 42; ὀρθοῦνται τὰ πλείω ib.37; τὸ -ούμενον *success*, Id.4.18; of persons and places, *to be safe* and *happy*, *flourish*, S. *Ant*.675, Antipho 5.7, Th.2.60; of words and opinions, *to be right*, *be true*, οὕτως ὀρθοῖτ' ἂν ὁ λόγος Hdt.7.103; ὀρθοῦσθαι γνώμην E.*Hipp*. 247 (anap.); ἐν ἀγγέλῳ γὰρ κρυπτὸς ὀρθοῦται λόγος it lies with the messenger to *set right* a secret message, A.*Ch*.773 (κυπτὸς v.l. ap. Sch.Il.15.207, i.e. to *straighten* a crooked message). 3. Pass., ὀρθουμένων *if all goes well*, A.*Eu*.772. III. intr., *use the nominative case* (opp. πλαγιάζω), Hermog.*Id*.1.3,9.

**ὀρθᾰγορίσκος**, = ὀρθαγ-, Pers.*Stoic*.1.102.

❋ **ὀρθρ-εύω**, (ὄρθρος) *lie awake before dawn*, κατ' εὐνάν Theoc.10.58; ὀρθρεύουσαν ψυχὰν ἐκπληχθεῖσα my soul terror-stricken *in the sleepless dawn*, E.*Tr*.182 (lyr.):—Med., γόοισιν ὀρθρευομένα wailing *sleepless in the early dawn*, Id.*Supp*.978 (lyr.), cf. *Fr*.773.25 (lyr.); ὀρθρεύεσθαι καλοῦσιν οἱ Ἀττικοὶ τῷ λύχνῳ προσκεῖσθαι, πρὶν ἡμέραν γενέσθαι Phryn.*PS* p.93 B. **-ία** (sc. ὥρα), ἡ, *morning*: prop. fem. of ὄρθριος, Suid. **-ίδιος** [ρῐ], η, ον, poet. for ὄρθριος, *AP*5.2 (Antip.Thess.). ❋ **-ίζω**, = ὀρθρεύω, Lxx *Ge*.19.27, *Jb*.7.21, al., *Ev.Luc*.21.38. **-ινός**, ή, όν, (ὄρθρος) later form (Phryn.*PS* p.93 B.) for ὄρθριος, Lxx *Wi*.11.22, al.; ὀρθρινὸς οἴχεσθαι *AP*5.176 (Mel.); ὀ. ὧρα ib.7.195 (Id.): neut. pl. as Adv., ὀρθρινὰ παίζειν ib.12.47 (Id.). [ῑ *AP*5.176, 12.47, as in ἠρινός, θερινός, χειμερινός: Arat.948, *AP*6.160 (Antip. Sid.), etc. make ι long, prob. in imitation of ὀπωρινῷ which is a metr. necessity in Hom., v. sub voc.]

**ὀρθροκόκκυξ**, ῡγος, ὁ, *early-crower*, of the cock, dub. in Diph.ap. Eust.1479.45 (om. Kock).

**ὄρθριος**, α, ον, (ὄρθρος) *at daybreak*, *in the morning*, *early*, mostly with Verbs of motion, so as to agree with the person, ἀφίκετο.. ὄρθριος *h.Merc*.143; ὀρθρίη αὖθις ἔσειμι Thgn.863; ὄρθριος παρεῖναι, ἥκειν, Ar.*Ec*.283, Pl.*Prt*.313b; ἤλουν ὄρθριοι τὰ σιτία Pherecr.10. 2. generally, *of the morning*, πόλτος Epich.23; διὰ τὸν ὀ. νόμον the *morning* song, as parody of ὄρθιον, Ar.*Ec*.741; ὄρθριον ᾆσαι (sc. ᾆσμα), of the cock, Id.*Av*.489; δεῖ ὄρθριον εἶναι τὸν σύλλογον Pl.*Lg*. 961b; τὸ ὀ. as Adv., *in the morning*, *early*, Hdt.2.173, Luc.*Gall*.1; or ὄρθριον Ar.*Ec*.377, 526: irreg. Comp. and Sup. ὀρθριαίτερος, -αίτατος, Hdn.*Epim*.166; also ὀρθρίτερον as Adv., *earlier*, *UPZ*62.19 (ii B.C.), *BGU*1201.4 (I A.D.).

**ὀρθριοφοίτης**, ου, ὁ, *early comer* or *goer*, Phot., Suid.

**ὀρθρισμός**, ὁ, *rising early*, Aq.*Pr*.11.27.

**ὀρθρο-βόας**, ου, ὁ, *early caller*, *chanticleer*, Alexarch.ap.Heraclid. Lemb.5, *AP*12.137 (Mel.). **-γόη**, ἡ, Adj. *early-wailing*, ὀρθρογόη Πανδιονὶς ὦρτο χελιδών Hes.*Op*.568, cf. *Stud.Pont*.3.6 (Amisus); ὀρθογόη, ὀρθοβόη are ff. ll. in Hes. l. c. **-λάλος** [ᾰ], ον, *early-twittering*, epith. of the swallow, *AP*6.247 (Phil.). **-νοτος**, ὁ, name for *the S.E. wind* (Εὖρος), Arist.*Fr*.250 (ὀρθόνοτος codd.).

❋ **ὄρθρος**, ὁ, *the time just before* or *about daybreak*, *dawn*, *cock-crow* (ἀπ' ὄρθρου μέχρι περ ἂν ἥλιος ἀνάσχῃ Pl.*Lg*.951d), τάχα δ' ὀ. ἐγίγνετο δημιοεργός *h.Merc*.98; ἐπειδὰν ὀ. ᾖ Ar.*Ach*.256, cf. *Av*.496, etc.; ὄρθρου *at dawn*, Hes.*Op*.577, Sopat.25, Aristopho 10; ὄρθρου γενομένου Hdt.1.198; ἅμα ὄρθρῳ Id.7.188, Th.3.112, etc.; ἐς ὄρθρον Theoc.18.56, cf. X.*Cyn*.6.6; κατ' ὄρθρον Ar.*V*.772; περὶ ὄρθρον Th.6.101 (cf. περίορθρος); πρὸς ὄρθρον towards *dawn*, Ar.*Lys*.1089; πρὸς ὄρθρον γ' ἐστίν Id.*Ec*.20; ὑπ' ὄρθρον Batr.103; ὑπὸ τὸν ὀ. D.C.76.17; τὸν ὀ., abs., *in the morning*, Hdt.4.181; δι' ὄρθρων each *morning early*, E.*El*. 909; ὀ. βαθὺς dim *morning twilight*, ἀλλὰ νῦν ὀ. β. Ar.*V*.216, cf. Pl. *Cri*.43a, Theoc.18.14; τῆς παρελθούσης νυκτὸς.., ἔτι βαθέος ὀ. Pl.*Prt*. 310a, cf. *Ev.Luc*.24.1. II. Ὄρθρος, ὁ, a mythical dog, son of Typhaon and Echidna, that kept the herds of Geryoneus on the island Erytheia, and was there killed by Heracles, Hes.*Th*.309, cf. 293 (v.l. Ὄρθος).

**ὀρθρο-φοιτο-σῡκοφαντο-δῐκο-τᾰλαίπωροι** τρόποι, *early-prowling base-informing sad-litigious plaguy* ways, Ar.*V*.505.

**ὀρθρόω**, dub. l. in Lxx *Ps*.118(119).148.

**ὀρθώνῠμος**, ον, (ὄνομα) *rightly named*, κῆδος (in double sense), A. *Ag*.699 (lyr.).

**ὀρθωσία**, ἡ, = ὄρθωσις, Suid.

**Ὀρθωσία**, Ion. -ίη, ἡ, = Ὀρθία, a name of Artemis, Pi.*O*.3.30, Hdt. 4.87, Lyc.1331, *IG*7.113 (Megara), 12(5).913.11 (Rhodian dedication at Tenos, ii B.C.); cf. ϝορθασία. II. **Ὀρθώσιος**, a name of Poseidon, Ποσειδῶνι Ἀσφαλείῳ καὶ Ὀ. *Inscr.Délos* 440*A*61 (ii B.C.). 2. Ὀ. Ζεύς, = Lat. *Jupiter Stator*, D.H.2.50.

❋ **ὄρθ-ωσις**, εως, ἡ, *making straight*, *direction*, *guiding*, λόγων καὶ ἔργων Plu.2.166e. 2. *use of the nominative case*, Hermog.*Id*. 1.9. 3. *prosperity*, πόλις εὖ ἀγομένη μεγίστη ὀ. ἐστι Democr. 252. **-ωτήρ**, ῆρος, ὁ, *one who sets* or *keeps upright*, *restorer* or *preserver*, Pi.*P*.1.56.

❋ **ὀρία**, ἡ, *boundary*, *IG*$2^2$.2630.

**ὅρια**, τά, v. ὅριον. II. v. ὅρριον.

**ὁριαῖος**, α, ον, *marking the boundary*, λίθος *Gloss*.

**ὁριάριος**, = Lat. *horrearius*, *JHS*34.28 (Lycia).

**ὀρίας** ἄνεμος, ὁ, = ὀρεστίας, Arist.ap.Ach.Tat.*Intr.Arat*.33.

**ὀριαχές**· ὀρίκοιτον, Hsch. (fort. ὀρειλεχές).

**Ὀρί-βακχος** [ῐ], ὁ, *Mountain-Bacchus*, because his orgies were held there, Opp.*C*.1.24. **-βάτης**, v. οὐριβάτης.

**ὀρῑγάν-ίζω**, *to be like* ὀρίγανον, τῇ ὀσμῇ Dsc.1.15; τῇ γεύσει Id.3. 62. **-ίς**, ίδος, ἡ, = μᾶρον, Ps.-Dsc.3.42; but **ὀρίγανις**, εως, Lycus ap.Orib.9.34.4. **-ίτης** [ῑ] οἶνος, ὁ, wine *flavoured with* ὀρίγανον, Dsc.5.51, Philum.ap.Orib.45.29.48. **-ίων**, ὁ, name of a frog, Batr.256. **-οειδές**· τὸ ὕσσωπον, Zonar. ❋ **-όεις**, εσσα, εν, *made of* or *with* ὀρίγανον, Nic.*Th*.65. ❋ **-ον**, τό, Epich.17, Hp. *Vict*.2.54, Ar.*Fr*.130, Antiph.222.4, Amips.35, Thphr.*HP*1.9.4, al.:—also **ὀρίγᾰνος**, ἡ, Ar.*Ec*.1030, Arist.*Pr*.925$^a$29, *HA*612$^a$25, Thphr. *HP*6.1.4, al., Clearch.ap.Ath.3.116e, Dsc.3.27, Gal.12.91, cf. 6.668; ὀρίγανος, ὁ, Ion Eleg.5, Hp.*Epid*.5.54, Anaxandr.50:—an acrid herb, ὀ. Ἡρακλεωτική Dsc., Gal. ll. cc.; = ὀ. λευκή *organy*, *Origanum heracleoticum*, Thphr.*HP*6.2.3; ὀ. μέλαινα *marjoram*, *Origanum viride*, ibid.; ὀρίγανον βλέπειν look *origanum*, i.e. look *sour* or *crabbed*, like νᾶπυ βλ., Ar.*Ra*.603. [In codd. freq. wrongly ὀρείγανον, v. Hdn.Gr.2.410; ἐρίγανον *PTeb*.112 *Intr*. (ii B.C.).]

**ὀριγνάομαι**, fut. -ήσομαι D.C.41.53: aor. ὠριγνήθην Antipho Soph. 21, Isoc.*Ep*.6.9:—*stretch oneself*, like ὀρέγομαι, ἔγχεσιν ἠδ' ἐλάτῃς αὐτοσχεδὸν ὠριγνῶντο *they fought with outstretched* spears, Hes.*Sc*.190. 2. c. gen., *stretch oneself after* a thing, *aim at*, *grasp at*, ὅτε.. θηρῶν ὀριγνῷτο E.*Ba*.1255; ποίας δόξης Isoc. l. c.; τελαμῶνος Theoc.24.44; κερδέων Herod.7.37; χορείας Pl.*Ax*.366a; τοῦ πλείονος Socr.*Ep*.29, D.C. l. c.; *aim at*, *strive*, c. inf., κενῶσαι τελέως Gal.11.363; νικῆσαι Id.10.5. 3. *reach*, *win*, Δήμητρος εὐνῆς D.H.1.61 (v.l. εὐνήν).

**ὀρί-γονος** [ῐ], ον, = ὀρειγενής, πεῦκαι Tim.*Pers*.88. **-δρόμος**, v. ὀρειδρόμος.

❋ **ὁρίζω**, Ion. **οὐρ-** Hdt. (v. infr.): fut. ὁριῶ Arist.*Cat*.5$^b$5, (δι-) Isoc. 4.174: aor. ὥρισα S.*Ant*.452, Pl.*Lg*.864e; Ion. οὔρισα Hdt.3.142: pf. ὥρικα D.26.24, Arist.*Mete*.382$^a$19:—**Med.**, fut. -ιοῦμαι Pl.*Tht*. 190e, *Lg*.737d: aor. ὡρισάμην Id.*Tht*.148a, Epicr.11.18, etc.:—**Pass.**, fut. ὁρισθήσομαι Pl.*Tht*.158d: aor. ὡρίσθην Id.*Chrm*.171a: pf. ὥρισμαι Th.1.71, Pl.*Smp*.182a, etc.; but in med. sense, E.*Hec*.801, D.31.5: (ὅρος):—*divide* or *separate from*, *as a border* or *boundary*, c. acc. et dat., ὁ Νεῖλος ὁ τὴν Ἀσίην οὐρίζων τῇ Λιβύῃ Hdt.2.16: c. acc. et gen., S.*Ph*. 636:—Pass., θύρα βαλανωτῇ ὡρισμένη ἀπὸ τῆς ἀνδρωνίτιδος X.*Oec*. 9.5; or b. with two accs. joined by καί, *separate*, [λίμνη] οὐρίζει τήν τε Σκυθικὴν καὶ τὴν Νευρίδα γῆν Hdt.4.51, cf. 56, 7.123, Arist.*HA*501$^b$16, *OGI*335.112 (Pergam., ii B.C.), Lyc.1289, etc.; ἐὰν.. κύκλος.. ὁρίζῃ τό τε ἀφανὲς καὶ τὸ φανερὸν ἡμισφαίριον Autol.*Sph*.4: hence ὁρίζων κύκλος Id.1.1; v. ὁρίζων. c. *delimit*, χρὴ τὸν νόμον ὁρίζειν πειρᾶσθαι κατὰ μέρη Pl.*Lg*.944a. 2. *bound*, τὴν ἀρχὴν ὥριζεν αὐτῷ ἡ Ἐρυθρὰ θάλαττα X.*Cyr*.8.6.21; τὰ δὲ πρὸς Τριβαλλοὺς.. Τρῆρες ὥριζον Th.2.96; of a line (or surface) as *limiting* a surface (or solid), Arist. *Metaph*.1017$^b$17:—Pass., Εὔβοια.. ὅροις ὑγροῖσιν ὡρισμένη E.*Ion*295: metaph., ὡρίσθω μέχρι τοῦδε so far *let it go and no further*, Th.1.71. 3. *pass between* or *through*, διδύμους πέτρας E.*Med*.433 (lyr.). 4. *part*, *divide*, χειμὼν ἄλλοσ' ἄλλον ὥρισεν Id.*Hel.*128; ὁ. τινὰ ἀπὸ.. *banish* one *from*.., Id.*Hec.*941 (lyr.):—Pass., ματρὸς ἐκ χερῶν ὁ. *depart* from.., Id.*Ion* 1459 (lyr.), but very dub. in Ar.*Ec.*202; cf. ἐξορίζω (A) II, III. II. *mark out by boundaries, mark out*, βωμὸν ἱδρύσατο καὶ τέμενος περὶ αὐτὸν οὔρισε Hdt.3.142, cf. 6.108, S.*Tr.*754, E.*Hel.*1670, *IG*1².76.54, 4²(1).76.19 (Pass., Epid., ii B.C.), etc.; v. infr. IV. 1: metaph., ὁ. τι ἔς τι *limit* one thing according to another, Th.3.82. 2. *trace out as a boundary*, πόρον (of Io tracing out the Bosporus), A.*Supp.*546 (lyr.). III. *ordain, determine, lay down*, αἶσα τόνδε σοὐρίζει (i.e. σοι ὁρίζει) μόρον Id.*Ch.*927 (σοι πορίζει M¹, σ' ὁ. M²); ἡμῖν ὥρισεν σωτηρίαν E.*IT*979; ἐς τήνδε παῖδα ψῆφον ὥρισαν φόνου Id.*Hec.*259; ἡ Δίκη.. ἐν ἀνθρώποισιν ὥρισεν νόμους S.*Ant.*452; [τὸν χρόνον] ὁ νόμος ὁ. Pl.*Lg.*864e; ἀριθμὸς ὁ ὁρίζων τὸ πολὺ καὶ τὸ ὀλίγον X.*An.*7.7.36; τὸ δοῦλον γένος πρὸς τὴν ἐλάσσω μοῖραν ὥρισεν θεός E.*Fr.*218; ὁρίσατέ μοι μέχρι πόσων ἐτῶν δεῖ νομίζειν νέους X.*Mem.*1.2.35: c. inf., ἄνακτες ὥρισαν.. θανεῖν ἐμὴν δέσποιναν οὐ ψήφῳ μιᾷ E.*Ion* 1222, cf. S.*Fr.*24; ὁ. τινὰ θεόν *determine* one *to be* a god, *deify*, *AP*12.158.7 (Mel.); ὁ. θάνατον εἶναι τὴν ζημίαν Lycurg.65, cf. Din.1.61 (Med.); θάνατον ὡρικέναι τὴν ζημίαν D.26.24:—Pass., ὧραι ἑκάστοις εἰσὶν ὡρισμέναι Arist.*HA*542ᵃ19, etc.; ἐπί τισι ὡρισμένοις on certain *definite terms* (cf. ῥητός), Id.*Pol.*1285ᵇ22; ἀρχαὶ ἀριθμῷ ὡρισμέναι *limited, definite*, opp. ἄπειροι, Id.*Metaph.*1002ᵇ18; τόποι ὡ. Id.*Cael.*273ᵃ14; τὸ ὡρισμένον Id *Mete.*369ᵇ29. 2. *define* a thing, Pl.*Chrm.*171a (Pass.), X.*Mem.*4.6.4, al.: more freq. in Med. than Act., v. infr. IV. 3. IV. Med., *mark out for oneself*, τίνα ὅρον ὁρίζῃ what *criterion* do you *assign*, Pl.*Grg.*470b; στήλας ὁ. *set up* stones as *boundary marks*, X.*An.*7.5.13; ὁ. χθόνα *take possession of, take to oneself*, A.*Supp.*256; γαῖα.. ἣν Πέλοψ ὁρίζεται E.*Fr.*696; ὁ. ἑαυτῷ μέρος τῆς οὐσίας Lys.17.6: with inf. added, ἱερὸν ὡρίσαντ' ἔχειν E.*IT*969; ὁρίζεσθαι βωμούς *set up*, S.*Tr.*237 (just like ὁρίζειν ib.754); v. ὕπαστρος. 2. *determine for oneself, get* or *have* a thing *determined*, ἃ ὡρίσω σὺ δίκαια D.19.241, cf. v.l. in Lys.2.19: c. acc. et inf., αὐτὸν πολεμεῖν ὁρίζομαι I *lay it down* that.., D.9.19; τί ποτ' ἄρ' ὡρίσαντο καὶ τίνος γένους εἶναι τὸ φυτόν; Epicr.11.18. 3. *define* a thing, τὴν ἡδονὴν ἀγαθὸν ὁ. Pl.*R.*505c, cf. *Sph.*246b: ὁ. τὰς ἀρετὰς ἀπαθείας τινάς Arist.*EN*1104ᵇ24, al.; ἡδονῇ τε καὶ ἀγαθῷ ὁ. τὸ καλόν Pl.*Grg.*475a; τὸ ζῆν ὁ. δυνάμει αἰσθήσεως Arist.*EN*1170ᵃ16, al.: c. acc. et inf., ὁ. δικαίους εἶναι τοὺς εἰδότας κτλ. X.*Mem.*4.6.6, cf. Pl.*Tht.*190e, etc.:—Pass., *to be defined*, [ἡ αἰδὼς] ὁρίζεται φόβος τις ἀδοξίας Arist.*EN*1128ᵇ11; οἷς αἱ φιλίαι ὁρίζονται ib.1166ᵃ2; τὸ ὁριζόμενον Id.*Top.*141ᵇ24, al. V. intr., *border upon*, πλὴν ὅσον αὐτῆς πρὸς τὴν Ἀσίην οὐρίζει Hdt.4.42. VI. as Att. law-term, δισχιλίων ὡρισμένος τὴν οἰκίαν *having* the house *marked with* ὅροι (cf. ὅρος II) to secure a claim on it for 2,000 drachmas, D.31.5; so χωρίον ὡρισμένον Poll.9.9.

**ὁρίζων** (sc. κύκλος), οντος, ὁ, *separating circle* (cf. ὁρίζω I. 1b), *horizon*, Autol.*Sph.*5, Ti.Locr.97a; ὁ τοῦ ὁρίζοντος κύκλος Arist.*Mete.*363ᵃ27; ὁ ὁ. κύκλος Id.*Cael.*297ᵇ34, al.; ὁ αἰσθητὸς ὁ., opp. ὁ λόγῳ θεωρητός, Gem.5.56,57; οἱ ὁρίζοντες Ti.Locr.97d. 2. Pythag. name for 9, because it *limits*, i.e. *finishes*, the series of units, *Theol. Ar.*57.

**ὁρικάνην**· δεσμωτήριον, οἱ δὲ φραγμόν, οἱ δὲ σαργάνην, ἢ σκῆπτρον, Hsch. (Cf. ὁρκάνη.)

**⊛ ὀρῖκός**, ή, όν, (ὀρεύς) *of* or *for a mule*, ὀ. ζεῦγος a pair *of mules*, Pl.*Ly.*208b, Is.5.43, Aeschin.2.111, 3.76, D.S.2.11, Jul.*Or.*2.72a:—the form ὀρεικός occurs in Thom.Mag.p.253 R. and Suid. (interpol.) and as v.l. in Pl. l.c.

**⊛ ὁρῐκός**, ή, όν, (ὅρος) *akin to definition*, Arist.*Top.*102ᵃ9; ὁ. στάσις *turning on a definition*, Hermog.*Stat.*2, cf. *Inv.*3.2, D.21 Arg.1. Adv. -κῶς Ph.1.297, S.E.*M.*7.426, Hermog.*Stat.*8, D.L.9.71. 2. Astrol., *belonging to a* ὅριον, Vett.Val.143.15. Adv. -κῶς Id.268.4.

**ὀρί-κτιτος**, v. ὀρείκτιτος. **-κτῠπος**, ον, *sounding in* or *on the hills*, Nonn.*D.*14.29, 24.143. **-κυπτεῖν**· τὸ ἀνατείνεσθαι, καὶ ἐπ' ἄκρων ὀνύχων ἵστασθαι, Hsch. (Cf. ὀρκ-.) **-μαλίδες**, αἱ, v. ὀρομαλίδες.

**ὀρινάδες**· τὰ ἀνώτερα, Hsch.

**ὀρίνδης** ἄρτος, ὁ, *bread made of* ὄρυζα, S.*Fr.*609 (ap.Ath.3.110e), Poll.6.73 (who also has **ὀρίνδιον** σπέρμα), Hsch.; **ὀρίνδα** in Phryn. *PS* p.93 B. is perh. corrupt. (Loan-word, cf. Mod.Pers. *birinj, gurinj*, Afghan *vrižě*, Skt. *vrīhi* 'rice': ὄρυζα comes from the same source.)

**ὀρινίαι**· ἀναδενδράδες, Hsch.

**⊛ ὀρινοβάτης** (sc. γαστραφέτης), ου, ὁ, the *mountain* stomach-bow, Bito 64.4.

**ὀρίντης**, ου, ὁ, *exciter*, Theognost.*Can.*43.

**ὀρίνω** [ῑ], aor. ὤρῖνα, Ep. ὄρ- Il.24.760, al.:—**Med.**, aor. ὠρίνατο B.12.112:—**Pass.**, impf. ὠρίνετο Od.18.75: aor. ὠρίνθην, Ep. ὀρ- Il.5.29, al.: (cf. ὄρνυμι):—Ep. Verb (used by Epicr.11.36, Arist.*Pr.*947ᵇ32), *stir, raise*, ὡς δ' ἄνεμοι δύο πόντον ὀρίνετον Il.9.4; [ἀέλλη] πόντον ὀρίνει 11.298, cf. Od.7.273; πάντα δ' ὄρινε ῥέεθρα Il.21.235: mostly metaph., *stir, move, excite*, θυμὸν ὀρίνειν Od.4.366; θυμὸν ἐνὶ στήθεσσιν ὀ. Il.2.142; μνηστῆρας ὀρίνων *driving* them *wild* with fear, Od.24.448; ἦτορ ἐν στήθεσσιν ὄρινε 17.47; ὄρινε δὲ κῆρ Ὀδυσῆος ib.216; also γόον Il.24.760; ὀρυμαγδὸν 21.313; Κύπριν Ps.-Phoc.3; φρένας οἶνος ὀρίνει *AP*15.9 (Cyrus):—Pass., *to be stirred, roused*, Ἴρῳ δὲ κακῶς ὠρίνετο θυμός his heart *was troubled within him*, Od.18.75; ὀρίνθη θυμὸς Il.18.223; Τρῶας ὀρινομένους *driven in flight*, 11.521, cf. 525; ὀρινθέντες *affrighted*, Od.22.23; ὀρινόμενοι Pi.*Fr.*208; οὐδὲν ὀρινθεὶς Epicr.11.36; ὡς πάρος οὐ λαλέεις καὶ ὀρείνομαι *BCH* 51.326 (Athens). II. *incite* one to do, c. acc. et inf., Orph.*L.*59.

**ὁριο-δείκτης**, ου, ὁ, = ὁριστής I, *AB*287, *BGU*426.1 (ii/iii A.D.), *PAmh.*2.83.5 (iii/iv A.D.):—hence **-δεικτέω**, *BGU*983.17 (ii A.D.). **-θετέω**, *set boundaries*, Aq.*De.*19.14, Sm.*Ex.*19.12. **-κράτωρ** [ᾰ], ορος, ὁ, Astrol., *ruler of certain degrees in a zodiacal sign*, Doroth. in *Cat.Cod.Astr.*2.193, Paul.Al.*Q.*4, *S.*4, Sch. Ptol.*Tetr.*p.173.

**⊛ ὅριον**, τό, = ὅρος, Dim. only in form, *boundary, limit*, Hp.*Off.*3, *Schwyzer* 664.4 (Orchom. Arc., iv B.C.), *Epigr.Gr.*978.12 (Philae), *POxy.*2134.18 (ii A.D.): mostly in pl., *boundaries, bounds, frontier*, E.*Tr.*375, D.18.230, *PCair.Zen.*251.3 (iii B.C.), *Supp.Epigr.*3.378 *B* 11 (Delph., ii/i B.C.); ἐπὶ τοῖς ὁ. on *the frontier*, Th.2.12, And.1.45; ὅρια κελεύθου *limits* of a road, i.e. the road itself, S.*Fr.*721 (dub.); μὴ κινείτω γῆς ὅ. μηδεὶς Pl.*Lg.*842e; *territories*, Lxx *Ex.*10.4, al. 2. Astrol., a subdivision of a zodiacal sign, appropriated to a planet, Ptol. *Tetr.*43, S.E.*M.*5.37, *PMag.Lond.*46.48, *PTeb.*277.15, Heph.Astr. 1.1, Man.2.166, 4.265. II. pl., *rules*, e.g. for the use of wine, Hp. *Liqu.*5. III. ὅριον· τείχισμα, φραγμόν, Hsch.; so ὅρια καὶ σταυρώματα Th.6.74 (restd. from Sch.).

**⊛ ὅριος**, ον, (ὅρος) *of boundaries*, Ζεὺς ὅριος *guardian of boundaries and landmarks*, Pl.*Lg.*842e, D.7.39. II. = Lat. *Terminus*, D.H.2.74, Plu.*Num.*16.

**ὀρι-πλαγκτος**, ον, v. ὀρείπλαγκτος. **-πλανής**, ές, and **-πλανος**, ον, v. ὀρειπλ-.

**ὅρισ-ις**, εως, ἡ, = ὁρισμός, Gal.8.698, Hsch. s.v. προθεσμία. **-μα**, Ion. **οὔρ-**, ατος, τό, (ὁρίζω) *boundary, limit*, Hdt.2.17: and in pl., like ὅρια I, Id.4.45, E.*Hec.*16; ὅ. βαρβάρων *against* them, Id *IA*952: prov., Μυσῶν καὶ Φρυγῶν ὁρίσματα, of matters which should be kept apart, *Trag.Adesp.*560. **-μός**, ὁ, *marking out by boundaries, limitation*, οἱ ὁ. τῶν κτήσεων D.H.2.74; ἀκριβὴς.. οὐκ ἔστιν ὁ., ἕως τίνος.. Arist.*EN* 1159ᵃ4; ὁ. τοῦ λυπεῖσθαι Hyp.*Epit.*41; *boundary*, καρπῶν *BGU* 599.3 (ii A.D.), cf. *PAmh.*2.97.11 (ii A.D.). II. *the definition of a thing*, freq. in Arist., *APo.*91ᵃ1, *Top.*139ᵃ26, *Metaph.*1031ᵃ1, al. III. *wager*, Plu.*Alex.*6, *TG*14. IV. *decree*, Lxx *Da.*6.12(13). V. *vow*, ib.*Nu.*30.3, al., cf. Ph.1.77. **-τέον**, *one must determine, define*, Pl. *Lg.*632b, Arist.*Metaph.*1064ᵃ21, etc. **-τής**, οῦ, ὁ, *one who marks the boundaries*: in pl., *officers appointed to settle boundaries*, public or private, *IG*1².94.7, Hyp.*Eux.*16, *Tab.Heracl.*1.2, al., Plu.*TG*21; the chief being called γαμέτρας (γεωμέτρης), *Tab.Heracl.*1.187, cf. Poll.9.9, *AB*287. II. *one who determines*, δικαίων D.15.29, cf. Hermog. *Stat.*8, Plot.5.1.5. **-τικός**, ή, όν, *of* or *for defining*, λόγος Arist.*de An.*413ᵃ14, al.; δύναμις Plu.2.1026d; διδασκαλία Gal.1.307: **-κή**, ἡ, *art of definition*, Ammon. *in APr.*7.32, Elias *in Porph.*3.28. Adv. **-κῶς** *by definition*, Hermog.*Stat.*3, Syrian. *in Metaph.*12.12: Comp. **-κώτερον**, ἐπιδραμεῖν Gal.7.463. 2. *giving definite form to*, c. gen., Olymp. *in Mete.*275.22. II. ἡ ὁριστική (sc. ἔγκλισις), *indicative mood*, D.T.638.7, A.D.*Synt.*31.14; **-κὰ** ῥήματα *indicative* verbs, Id. *Adv.*124.9; **-κὴ** προφορά ib.123.12. Adv. **-κῶς** *in the indicative mood*, Phryn.337, Sch.E.*Hec.*87. **-τός**, ή, όν, *definable*, Arist.*Metaph.*998ᵇ6, Plu.2.720b, A.D.*Pron.*27.18, al. 2. of land, *delimited*, *Abh. Berl.Akad.*1925(5).21 (Cyrene).

**ὀρι-τρεφής**, ές, and **-τροφος**, ον, v. ὀρειτρ-. **-χαλκος**, v. ὀρείχαλκος.

**⊛ ὀριχᾶται**· γλίχεται, ἐπιθυμεῖ, Hsch. **Ὄριψα**· Ἐρινύς, Id. **ὀρκάθους**· ἐφ' ὧν τὰ σῦκα ψύχουσι, Id.

**⊛ ὀρκάνη** [ᾰ], ἡ, = ἑρκάνη, ἕρκος, *enclosure, fence*, ὁ. πυργῶτις A.*Th.*346 (lyr.); *prison*, E.*Ba.*611 (troch., pl.), cf. Sch.Theoc.4.61, *EM*632.25.

**ὁρκᾰπάτης** [πᾰ], ου, ὁ, *oath-breaker*, *AP*5.249 (Paul. Sil.), Phot., Suid.: as Adj., Nonn.*D.*48.544.

**ὄρκη**· ὄψις, Hsch.

**ὀρκῆσι**, barbarism for ὀρχῆται, Ar.*Th.*1179.

**ὁρκ-ιᾰτομέω, -ιᾰτόμος**, v. ὁρκιοτ-. **-ίζω**, Dor. fut. ὁρκιξέω *IG* 2².1126.13 (Delph.):—like ὁρκόω (used with it in D.19.278), *make* one *swear, administer an oath to* a person, τινα; rejected by Phryn.338, but found in X.*Smp.*4.10, D.18.30, 19.278, 23.172, Arist.*Fr.*149, *PCair. Zen.*254.2 (iii B.C.); ὁ. ἐφ' ᾧ ἔσται *SIG*684.25 (Dyme, ii B.C.): c. dupl. acc., ὁ. τινὰς ὅρκον *IG*9(2).1109.52 (Thess., ii/i B.C.), 5(1).1390.1 (Andania, i B.C.); ὁ. τινά, c. inf., Lxx *Ne.*5.12; *adjure*, δαίμονας, c. inf., *PMag.Par.*1.345; ὁ. τινὰ κατὰ τοῦ Θεοῦ Lxx 2*Ch.*36.13, cf. *PMag. Par.*1.289, *PMag.Lond.*121.242; ὁρκίζω σε τὸν Θεόν *Ev.Marc.*5.7, cf. *PMag.Par.*1.3045; οὐρανὸν ὁρκίζω σε Orph.*Fr.*299; ὁ. σε τοῖς Μήδων καὶ Περσῶν δόγμασιν ἵνα.. Lxx *Da.*6.13:—Pass., *to be sworn*, ὡρκισμένοι νόμῳ ἰητρικῷ Hp.*Jusj.*, cf. Plb.38.13.5. **-ιητόμος, -ιηφόρος**, v. ὁρκιοτόμος. **-ικός**, ή, όν, *belonging to, of the nature of, an oath*, *Stoic.*2.58,60, Sch.Il.1.77. **-ίλλομαι**, *swear vain oaths*, Phot., dub. in Hsch. **⊛ -ιον**, τό, = ὅρκος, *oath*, Il.4.158, Hdt.1.29, etc.; ὅρκια δοῦναι take *oaths*, Od.19.302, E.*Supp.*1232 (anap.); ὅ. πορεῖν A.R.2.433; ὅρκια δὲ Ζεὺς ἴστω let Zeus witness our *oath*, Il.7.411. II. mostly in pl., ὅρκια, τά, *the offerings and other things used at a solemn oath* or *treaty*, κήρυκες.. ὅ. πιστὰ θεῶν σύναγον Il.3.269, cf. 245; οἱ ἐννέα ἄρχοντες ὀμνύουσιν ὥσπερ ἐπὶ Ἀκάστου τὰ ὅ. ποιήσειν Arist. *Ath.*3.3; ὅ. παρεχέτω ὁ ἱερωργός *SIG*581.91 (Crete, iii/ii B.C.); then, *that which is sworn to, treaty, solemn agreement*, freq. in Hom. (esp. Il.), οὐκ ἔστι λέουσι καὶ ἀνδράσιν ὅ. πιστά 22.262: freq. in phrase, ὅρκια πιστὰ ταμεῖν 2.124, cf. 3.105, al.; κατόπερ τὰ ὅ. ἔταμον *SIG*45.44 (Halic., v B.C.); ὅ. ἐπιταμνέτω *Schwyzer* 687 *D* 2 (Chios, vii/vi B.C.); ὅ. ποιεῖσθαι *SIG*591.32 (Lampsacus, ii B.C.); ὅ. τελεῖν Il.7.69; φυλάσσειν 3.280; ὅ. δηλήσασθαι or ὑπὲρ ὅ. δηλ. violate *a solemn treaty*, ib. 107, 4.67; ὑπὲρ ὅ. πημῆναι 3.299; κατὰ δ' ὅ. πιστὰ πάτησαν they trampled on *the treaty*, 4.157; σὺν γ' ὅρκι' ἔχευαν ib.269; ψεύσασθαι 7.351; ἀκούεις ὁρκίων ἐμῶν θέμιν A.*Ag.*1431; τὰ ὅ. ἐστί τινι, c. inf., one is bound by *treaty* to do, Th.6.52: Hdt. has sg. also in this sense, κατὰ τὸ ὅ. 1.77; ὅ. ποιέεσθαι πρός τινας ib.141: abs., ib.143, etc.; ὅ. μένει κατὰ χώρην remains as it was, 4.201; ὀμόσαι τὸ ὅ. ἦ μὴν ἐάσειν.. Th.6.72; ὅρκιον ἔταμον *SIG*4.10 (Cyzicus, vi B.C.). 2. *pledge* or *surety resting on oath*, in sg., Pi.*O*.11(10).6, *N*.9.16; ὅ. ἔχειν Lys.20.26: generally, *pledge*, Ar.*Nu*.533 (pl.). (ὅρκιον is neut. of ὅρκιος, with which ἱερόν or ἱερά may be supplied.) ⊛ **-ιος**, ον, rarely α, ον E.*Med*.208 (lyr.):—*belonging to an oath*, i.e. 1. *sworn, bound by oath*, δικαστὰς ὁ. αἱρουμένη (so Casaub.) A.*Eu*.483; ὅ. λέγω I speak *on oath*, S.*Ant*.305, cf. *OC*1637: Comp., ὁρκιωτέραν δ' ἦμην τὰν δῶλαν the slave's *oath shall carry the greater weight*, *Leg.Gort*.2.15. 2. *that which is sworn by*, ὅ. θεοί the gods *invoked at an oath*, who watch over its fulfilment and punish its violation, E.*Ph*.481, cf. *IT*747: in Prose, θεοὶ οἱ ὅ. Th.1.71,78; οἱ ὅ. θ. Aeschin.1.114; esp. Ζεὺς ὅ. S.*Ph*.1324, E.*Hipp*.1025, Arist.*Mir*.845$^{b}$33, Paus.5.24.9 sq., etc.; ὁρκία Θέμις E.*Med*. l. c.; φθιμένων σέβας ὅ. *AP*7.351 (Diosc.); ξίφος ὅ. a sword *sworn by*, E.*Ph*.1677.

**ὁρκιο-τομέω**, = ὅρκια τέμνω, Sch.Il.19.197; ὁρκιᾰτομεῖ (Dor. for ὁρκιητ-) Timocr.3. **-τόμος**, ον, *swearing solemnly at a sacrifice*, in Ion. form **ὁρκιη-** Poll.1.39; Ἴωνες τοὺς ὁρκιοτόμους ὁρκιητόμους (cj. Lobeck for **ὁρκιηφόρους**) φασί A.D.*Adv*.189.9.

**ὅρκ-ισμα**, ατος, τό, *conjuration*, in pl., *Tab.Defix.Aud*.41 *A* 15 (Megara, i/ii A.D.). ⊛ **-ισμός**, ὁ, *administration of an oath*, Lxx *Ge*.21.31, al., Plb.6.33.1; prob. f.l. for ὁρισμός, = *sponsio*, in Plu.*Cat.Ma*.17. **-ιστής**, οῦ, ὁ, v. ὁρκωτής.

**ὅρκμον**· φράγμα, Hsch.

⊛ **ὅρκος**, ὁ, *the object by which one swears*, as the Styx among the gods, Στυγὸς ὕδωρ, ὅς τε μέγιστος ὅ. δεινότατός τε πέλει μακάρεσσι θεοῖσι Il.15.38, cf. 2.755, Hes.*Th*.400,784,805, *h.Cer*.259, Arist.*Metaph*.983$^{b}$31; or as Zeus among mortals, Pi.*P*.4.167; so of things, ὅρκον δ' ἐνοσφίσθης μέγαν, ἅλας τε καὶ τράπεζαν Archil.96; οἷς ἦν μέγιστος ὅ.... κύων, ἔπειτα χήν Cratin.231, cf. *Placit*.1.3.8: hence, 2. *oath*, mostly with epith. μέγας, καρτερός, Hom. (v. infr.), etc.; θεῶν ὅ. *an oath by* the gods, Od.2.377; μακάρων ὅ. 10.299, cf. S.*OT*647, E.*Hipp*.657; ὅ. ἐκ θεῶν μέγας A.*Ag*.1284; ὅ. κατὰ τῶν..ὀφθαλμῶν Aeschin.2.153; ὅ. πλατύς a firm-based *oath*, Emp.30.3; ὅρκον ὀμόσαι swear *an oath*, ὄμοσέν τε τελεύτησέν τε τὸν ὅ. Od.2.378, etc.; ὅ. ἀπώμνυ ib.377, cf. 10.381; ἐπὶ δ' ὅρκον ὀμεῖται Hes.*Op*.194; κατομόσαι E.*IT*790; ὅ. ἐπιορκῆσαι take a false *oath*, Aeschin.1.115, etc.; ὅρκου προστεθέντος when *an oath* is added, S.*Fr*.472, cf. *El*.47; δαίμονι τῷ Πλεισθενιδῶν ὅρκους θεμένη having made a *sworn compact* with.., A.*Ag*.1570 (anap.); ὅ. ἀλλήλοις ποιοῦνται οἱ μὲν ἔφοροι ὑπὲρ τῆς πόλεως, βασιλεὺς δ' ὑπὲρ ἑαυτοῦ X.*Lac*.15.7; ὅρκους συνῆψαν E.*Ph*.1241, etc.; of the person demanding the oath, ὅ. ἑλέσθαι τινός or τινί take *it* of him, i.e. make him swear, Od.4.746, Il.22.119; ὅρκους ἐπελάσαι and προσάγειν τινί lay *oath* upon a man, put him on *his oath*, Hdt.1.146, 6.62,74; τὸν ὅ...ἐπάγειν..'Οποντίοις readminister *the oath*, *IG*9(1).334.12 (Locr., v B.C.); ὅρκους δοὺς καὶ δεξάμενος after tendering *his oath* to them and accepting theirs, Hdt.6.23, cf. *IG*1$^2$.52.18, A.*Eu*.429, Ar.*Ra*.589, D.39.3 and 4; so ὅρκον διδόναι καὶ λαμβάνειν Arist.*Rh*.1377$^{a}$7,8; ἀποδοῦναι take *it* oneself, D.19.318, Aeschin.3.74; ἀπολαμβάνειν administer or tender *it*, D.5.9, 18.25; ὅρκους καὶ πίστιν ἀλλήλοις δότε *swear to* one another, Ar.*Lys*.1185, cf. And.1.107; ὅρκοις καταλαβὼν τὰ τέλη having bound the authorities *by oaths*, Th.4.86; ὅρκοις κατειλημμένους Id.1.9; ὅρκῳ ἐμμένειν abide by it, E.*Med*.754; ὅ. τηρεῖν Democr.239; παραβαίνειν E.*Fr*.286.7, Ar.*Av*.332, D.19.318; ἐκβάντι τῶν ὅ. Pl.*Smp*.183b; ἐκλιπεῖν E.*Supp*.1194; συγχέαι Id.*Hipp*.1063; ἐμπεδοῦν X.*An*.3.2.10: after ὅρκος aor., pres., or fut. inf. may refer to fut. time, ὤμοσα καρτερὸν ὅ., μὴ..ἀναφῆναι Od.4.253; ἐμεῦ δ' ἕλετο μέγαν ὅ., μὴ πρὶν σοὶ ἐρέειν ib.746; ὅρκους ἔδοσαν καὶ ἔλαβον, ἀποδοῦναι.., 'Αθηναίους δὲ μὴ πολεμεῖν.. X.*HG*1.3.9: with Preps., οὐκ αὔτως.., ἀλλὰ σὺν ὅρκῳ Od.14.151; σὺν θεῶν ὅρκῳ X.*Cyr*.2.3.12; εἶπαι ἐπ' ὅρκου say on *oath*, Hdt.9.11; κατὰ τοὺς ὅ. X.*HG*5.4.54; opp. παρ' ὅρκον Pi.*O*.13.83; παρὰ τοὺς ὅ. X.*An*.2.5.41: prov., ὅρκους ἐγὼ γυναικὸς εἰς ὕδωρ γράφω S.*Fr*.811; parodied by Philonid.7 ὅρκους δὲ μοιχῶν εἰς τέφραν..γράφω, cf. Xenarch.6, Men.*Mon*.25. II. Ὅρκος, personified, son of Eris, Hes.*Op*.804; a divinity who punishes the false and perjured, ib.219, *Th*.231, Orac. ap.Hdt.6.86.γ'; Διὸς Ὅ., as servant of Zeus, S.*OC*1767 (anap.). (Cogn. with ἕρκος.)

**ὁρκοῦρος**, ὁ, v. ἑρκοῦρος.

**ὁρκόω**, *make* one *swear*, *bind by oath*, Cratin.366, Ar.*Th*.276, Lys.20.26: folld. by fut. inf., ὁρκώσαντες πίστεσι μεγάλαις μηδὲν μνησικακήσειν Th.4.74; ὁ. τινὰ ἦ μὴν ἐμμενεῖν Is.5.33; ὁ. τινὰς εἴς τινα Plu.*Galb*.10: c. acc. cogn., ὁ. τοὺς στρατιώτας τοὺς μεγίστους ὅρκους Th.8.75, cf. Ar.*Lys*.187:—Pass., *to be bound by oath*, Polem.Hist.83; cf. ὁρκίζω. 2. abs., *administer an oath*, *IG*1$^2$.39.36: c. acc., 'Αθηναίους ib.16, cf. *SIG*45.20 (Halic., v B.C.).

**ὀρκύαλος**, v. ὄρκυνος.

**ὀρκ-ῡνεῖον**, τό, *tunny-fishery* or *place for curing tunnies*, *SIG*46.44 (Halic., v B.C.). **-ῡνος**, ὁ, = ὄρκυς, Dorio and Hices.ap.Ath.7.315c,d, Ael.*NA*1.40, Opp.*H*.3.132, etc.; also **ὀρκύαλος** (v.l. ὄρκυνος), Xenocr.ap.Orib.2.58.140.

**ὀρκύπτω**, *stand on tiptoe and lean forward*, so as to examine a thing, Hsch., Suid. s.v. ὤρκυπτεν.

**ὄρκῡς**, ῡνος, ὁ, acc. ὄρκῡν, *a large kind of tunny*, Anaxandr.41.62, Archestr.*Fr*.34.3, Arist.*HA*543$^{b}$5, etc.; cf. ὄρκυνος.

**ὅρκ-ωμα**, ατος, τό, (ὁρκόω) *oath*, only in A.*Eu*.486, 768 (pl.). ⊛ **-ωμοσία**, ἡ, *swearing*, *oath*, Lxx *Ez*.17.18, *Ep.Hebr*.7.20, Poll.1.38. **-ωμόσια**, τά, *asseverations on oath*, Pl.*Phdr*.241a. II. like ὅρκια, *sacrifice on taking a solemn oath* or *swearing to a treaty*, τὰ τῶν ὁ. καύματα Id.*Criti*.120b, cf. *OGI*229.82 (Smyrna, iii B.C.), *IG*11(2).287*A*67 (sg., Delos, iii B.C.), *SIG*1007.29 (sg., Pergam., ii B.C.). III. sg. ὁρκωμόσιον, τό, name of a place in Athens where a treaty or alliance had been sworn to, Plu.*Thes*.27. **-ωμοτέω**, *take an oath*, Ar.*Fr*.96; τινι to one, A.*Eu*.764; πάσης ὑπὲρ γῆς Δαναϊδῶν ὁρκωμοτῶν E.*Supp*.1190; ἐπί τινι Luc.*Tox*.50; κατὰ σφαγίων Plu.*Pyrrh*.6: folld. by aor. inf., θεοὺς ὁ. τὸ μήτε δρᾶσαι.. *swear by* the gods that they did it not, S.*Ant*.265: by fut. inf., Ἄρη..ὡρκωμότησαν..λαπάξειν ἄστυ *made oath by* Ares that they would.., A.*Th*.46. **-ωμότης**, ου, ὁ, *juror*, *IG*5(2).261.2 (Mantinea, vi B.C.), 9(1).333.16 (Locr., v B.C.), cf. Poll.1.38. 2. = ὁρκωτής (q.v.), *Ostr.Bodl*. i 275 (ii/i B.C.). **-ωμοτικός**, ή, όν, *used in oaths*, ἐπίρρημα Sch.Ar.*Pl*.608, cf. Eust.92.16. Adv. -κῶς Id.53.15. **-ώμοτος**, ον, = ὅρκιος 2, *that which is sworn by*, Lyc.707. **-ωτής**, οῦ, ὁ, *the officer who administers the oath*, *IG*1$^2$.39.17,63.11, Antipho6.14, Cratin.366, X.*HG*6.5.3, *SIG*581.101 (Crete, iii/ii B.C.), Polem.Hist.83, etc.—On the form, Phot. remarks: ὁρκωτάς (-ωντας cod.), οὐχὶ ὁρκιστάς, οὐδὲ ὁρκωμότας λέγουσι; but v. ὁρκωμότης. **-ωτός**, ή, όν, *bound by oath*, Poll.1.39, *Gloss*.

**ὁρμάζω**, late form of ἁρμόζω, *EM*631.49, Aët.16.26 (v.l. ἁρμόζειν).

**ὁρμᾰθ-ίζω**, *string together*, Hsch. s.v. πινακοπώλης, Suid. s.v. μασχαλίσματα. **-ιον**, τό, Dim. of sq., Gal.12.207, Sch.D.T.p.195 H. ⊛ **-ός**, ὁ, (ὅρμος) *string*, *chain*, or *cluster* of things hanging one from the other, as of *beads* or *the links of a chain*, Pl.*Ion* 533e; of bats, Od.24.8; νεοττιῶν Arist.*HA*559$^{a}$8; κριβανωτῶν, ἰσχάδων, Ar.*Pl*.765, *Lys*.647; μελῶν Id.*Ra*.914; ἁμαξῶν X.*Cyr*.6.3.2; ἐνθουσιαζόντων, χορευτῶν, Pl.*Ion* 533e, 536a; γραμματιδίων Thphr.*Char*.6.8; perh. of a *chain* of reasoning, Polystr.p.9 W., cf. Phld.*Rh*.1.186 S., Gal.4.698; ἐρώτων *Anacreont*.13.11. II. ὁ. ψάμμου a *revolving* sand-eddy, Arist. *de An*.419$^{b}$24.

**ὁρμᾱθῶ**, ῇς, ῇ, Dor. aor. 1 Pass. subj. of ὁρμάω, E.*Andr*.859 (lyr.).

⊛ **ὁρμαίνω**, used by Hom. only in pres., impf., and aor. ὥρμηνα Il.21.137, Od.2.156: (ὁρμάω):—poet. Verb, I. in Hom. always, *turn over* or *revolve anxiously in the mind*, *debate*, *ponder*, mostly c. acc., ἧος ὁ ταῦθ' ὥρμαινε κατὰ φρένα καὶ κατὰ θυμόν Il.1.193, etc.: more shortly, κατὰ φρένα 10.507; ἐνὶ φρεσίν Od.4.843, *h.Merc*.66; φρεσίν Il.10.4, Od.3.151; ἀνὰ θυμόν 2.156; θυμῷ A.R.3.451; μετὰ φρεσί ib.18; also ὁρμαίνειν τι alone, *ponder over*, *meditate*, πόλεμον, πλόον, etc., Il.10.28, Od.3.169, etc.; πολλά or ἄλλα δέ οἱ κῆρ ὅρμαινε 7.83, 18.345; ὁρμαίνων τέρας Pi.*O*.8.41. 2. abs., *think*, *muse*, ὣς ὥρμαινε thus he *debated with himself*, Il.21.64, cf. 14.20. 3. folld. by a clause, ἤ.., ἦ.. *debate* whether.., or.., 16.435, Od.4.789, 15.300; ὁ. ὅπως *debate*, *ponder* how a thing is to be done, Il.21.137, 24.680. 4. c. inf., *long*, *desire*, Hom.*Epigr*.4.16, A.R.3.620, Theoc.24.26; ὁ. νᾶας καῦσαι *rushing on to*.., B.12.106. II. after Hom., 1. *set in motion*, *drive forth*, θυμὸν ὁ. *gasp out* one's life, A.*Ag*.1388 (ὀρυγάνει cj. Hermann); *excite*, *urge*, τινὰ πορεύειν Pi.*O*.3.25 (v.l. ὧρμα). 2. intr., *to be eager* or *impatient*, *chafe*, *fret*, [ἵππος] βοὴν σάλπιγγος ὁρμαίνει κλύων A.*Th*.394; κέαρ ὁ. B.*Fr*.16.12; ἄπρηκτον ὁ. Semon.1.7: part. ὁρμαίνων *eagerly*, *quickly*, Pi.*O*.13.84.

**ὁρμανόν**· ἀνεστηκός, χαλεπόν, Hsch.

**ὁρμάστειρα**, ἡ, *one who urges on*, Orph.*H*.32.9 codd. (ὁρμήτειρα Abel).

⊛ **ὁρμάω**, fut. -ήσω Pl.*Lg*.875b: aor. ὥρμησα Il.6.338, Pl.*Ion* 534c; Lacon. imper. ὅρμᾱον, i.e. ὅρμαόν, = ὅρμησον, Ar.*Lys*.1247: pf. ὥρμηκα Pl.*Plt*.265a:—Med. and Pass., Pi.*N*.1.5, A.*Pr*.339, Hdt.1.17, etc.: Ep. impf. ὡρμᾶτο Il.3.142: fut. ὁρμήσομαι Hdt.5.34, X.*Cyr*.7.1.9, ὁρμηθήσομαι Gal.5.85: aor. ὡρμησάμην Il.21.595, v.l. in Hes.*Sc*.127 (ἐφ-), never in Prose, exc. ἐξ- X.*HG*6.5.20 codd.: more freq. in pass. form ὡρμήθην Il.5.12, al., Th.3.98, etc.: pf. ὥρμημαι S.*El*.70, E.*El*.340, Th.6.33, etc.: Ion. 3 pl. pf. and plpf. ὁρμέαται and -έατο (with vv.ll. ὡρμ-) Hdt.5.121, 8.35; in Hom. codd. usu. have the augm., but Aristarch. read ὁρμήθησαν in Il.10.359: (ὁρμή): A. Act., I. causal, *set in motion*, *urge on*, *cheer on*, τινὰ εἰς πόλεμον Il.6.338, Th.1.127; τινὰ ποτὶ κλέος Pi.*O*.10(11).21; τὸ στράτευμα ὁ. ἐπὶ τὰς 'Αθήνας Hdt.8.106, cf. S.*Aj*.174 (lyr.), E.*Or*.352 (anap.); ἡ φύσις ὁρμήσει τινὰ ἐπὶ πλεονεξίαν Pl.*Lg*.875b, cf. *Ion* 534c; [τὰ] ὁρμῶντα [σώματα] Hp.*Epid*.6.8.7; μέριμναν ὁρμήσασ' ἐπ' ἔργον E.*Ph*.1064 (lyr.); ὁ. τινὰ ἐκ χερός *tear* from one's arms, Id.*Hec*.143 (anap.):—Pass., ὁρμηθεὶς θεοῦ ἄρχετο *inspired* by the god he began, Od.8.499; πρὸς θεῶν ὡρμημένος S.*El*.70; ὑπὸ ἔρωτος Pl.*Smp*.181d; ἵπποι..ὁρμηθέντες ὑπὸ πληγῇσιν ἱμάσθλης *urged on* by.., Od.13.82. 2. with a thing as the object, *stir up*, πόλεμον 18.376: c. acc. et inf., τὰς διόδους τῶν πτερῶν..ὥρμησε πτεροφυεῖν Pl.*Phdr*.255d:—Pass., ὡρμάθη πλαγά *was sped*, S.*El*.196 (lyr.). II. more freq. intr., *start*, 1. c. inf., ἴρηξ ὃς ὁρμήσῃ διώκειν ὄρνεον ἄλλο *starts* in chase of.., Il.13.64; ὁσσάκι δ' ὁρμήσειε πυλάων..ἀντίον ἀΐξασθαι whenever he *started* to rush for the gates, 22.194; ὁσσάκι δ' ὁρμήσειε..στῆναι ἐναντίβιον 21.265; ἐξελαύνειν ὁρμῆσαι τὸν στρατόν *began* to lead out.., Hdt.1.76, cf. 7.150; νίκην ὁρμῶντ' ἀλαλάξαι *eager to*.., S.*Ant*.133 (lyr.); ὥρμα ἀντιλαμβάνεσθαι τοῦ λόγου Pl.*R*.336b. 2. c. gen., *rush headlong at* one, Τρώων Il.4.335: more freq. with Preps., ὁ. ἐπί τινα Hes.*Sc*.403, Hdt.1.1, etc.; πύργωμα Καδμείων ἔπι E.*Supp*.1220; εἴς τινας X.*Cyr*.7.1.17; καθ' αὑτούς Id.*An*.5.7.25; also ὁ. ἐς μάχην *hasten* to battle, A.*Pers*.394; εἰς ἀγῶνα E.*Ph*.259 (lyr.); εἰς τὸ διώκειν X.*An*.1.8.25; ἐπὶ ἁρπαγάς Pl.*R*.391d; ἐπὶ τοὺς 'Αθηναίους Th.7.34; ὥρμασε (Dor.) ἐπὶ τὰ βασίλεια τῶν Σκυθᾶν *SIG*709.19 (Chersonesus, ii B.C.): without any sense of hostility, *rush*, τᾶσδ' ἀπὸ πέτρας πηδήσασα πυρὸς ἔσω E.*Supp.*1015 (lyr.); ἐς πατρὸς δόμους Id.*Med.*1178; *set out*, ἀπὸ [τῆς Οἰνόης] Th.2.19; ἐς φυγήν Hdt.7.179, etc.; εἰς τὸ ἐπ' ἐκεῖνα τῆς γῆς Pl.*Phd.*112b; ἐπ' ἄλλον λόγον Antipho 3.4.5; ἐπὶ τὸ σκοπεῖν X.*Mem.*3.7.9; ἐπὶ τραγῳδίαν ὥρμηκε *has turned* to tragedy, Alex.135.14; δηλώσεις..τὴν φύσιν ἐπὶ τί μάλισθ' ὥρμηκε, i.e. what your natural *bent* is, ib.8; φυσικῶς ἐπὶ τὴν ὀργὴν ὁρμᾶν Phld.*Ir.*93 W.; πρὸς τὰς πράξεις Id.*Mus.*p.71 K.; ἐπὶ φιλοσοφίαν Id.*Acad.Ind.*p.64 M.; πρὸς τὰς ὀχείας Arist.*HA* 546ᵃ15: c. acc. cogn., ὁδόν X.*An.*3.1.8; στρατείαν Id.*Cyr.*8.6.20. **3.** abs., *start, begin*, ὥσπερ ὡρμήσαμεν, ἴωμεν Pl.*Prt.*314b, cf. *R.*425c; αἱ μάλιστα ὁρμήσασαι [νῆες] the ships *that were* hottest *in pursuit*, Th.8.34. **B.** Med. and Pass., like the intr. Act., A. II: **1.** c. inf., μὴ φεύγειν ὁρμήσωνται *that they put* not *themselves in motion, set* not *themselves* to flee, Il.8.511; so διώκειν ὁρμήθησαν 10.359, cf. Od.4.282; ὡρμήθη κόρυθα κρατὸς ἀφαρπάξαι *he rushed* to snatch.., Il.13.188, cf. 182; ἦτορ ὡρμᾶτο πτολεμίζειν ἠδὲ μάχεσθαι *was eager* to.., 21.572; μᾶλλον ὅρμητο στρατεύεσθαι *was eager* to march, Hdt.7.1, cf. 19, al., Th.3.45; ὅδε ὁ λόγος ὅρμηται λέγεσθαι this account *has begun* to be given, Hdt.4.16, cf. 6.86.δ' (λέγεσθαι is restored for λέγεται in 3.56); but λόγον, τὸν ὅρμητο λέγειν which *he purposed* to make, Id.5.50. **2.** the object *for* or *after* which one goes is sts. in gen., Il.14.488, 21.595: a case with a Prep., ὡρμήθησαν ἐπ' ἀνδράσιν Od.10.214; ἐπί τινα S.*Aj.*47, etc.; εἴς τινα X.*Cyr.*7.1.9; μετά τινα *after* one, Il.17.605; so ὁ. ἐπὶ τὸ ἱρόν Hdt.8.35; ἐς πύλας A.*Th.*31; πρὸς δόμους E.*Hipp.*1152; ἐπ' ἀλήθειαν Pl.*Sph.*228c; ἐς φυγήν Th.4.14; πρὸς τίσιν S.*OC*1328; πρὸς τὸ κρατεῖν Pl.*R.*581a; [ἡ ποίησις] πρὸς ἡδονὴν ὥρμηται Id.*Grg.*502c; οἱ περὶ λόγον ἢ παιδείαν ὁρμώμενοι persons *keen* about.., Vett.Val.199.5: rarely c. acc. loci, νερτέρας πλάκας S.*OC*1576 (lyr.). **b.** the starting-point is expressed by ἐκ, ὡρμᾶτ' ἐκ θαλάμοιο Il.3.142, cf. 9.178, etc.; or ἀπό, S.*Tr.*156, Pl.*Phd.*101d, etc.; ἀπὸ φιλοσοφίας Phld.*Rh.*1.357 S.; or by a form in -θεν, σέθεν..ὕμνος ὁρμᾶται θέμεν αἶνον Pi.*N.*1.5: in historical Prose, ὁρμᾶσθαι ἐκ.. *start from, begin from*, esp. of the place where one carries on any regular operations, ἐνθεῦτεν ὁρμώμενοι *living there and going out from thence* to do their daily work, Hdt.1.17; of fishers, ἐκ πλοίων ὁρμώμενοι Id.3.98; of a general, *making that place his head-quarters* or *base of operations*, Id.8.133, cf. 5.125, al., Th.1.64, 2.69, al.; ἀπ' ἐλασσόνων ὁρμώμενος *setting out, beginning* with smaller means, ib.65, cf. 1.144; of rivers, ἐκ τῆς Ἴδης ὁ. *rising*.., Pl.*Lg.*682b. **3.** abs., *rush, dart, attack*, Il.5.12, Od.12.126, al., S.*OC*1068 (lyr.); also with ἔγχεϊ, ξιφέεσσι, etc., added, Il.5.855, 17.530, 13.496, al. **b.** generally, *hasten, be eager*, ὁρμώμενον δὲ μηδαμῶς μ' ἀντισπάσῃς A.*Pr.*339, cf. 395; ἀλλ' ἤδε..ὁρμᾶται *comes forth*, Id.*Pers.*151 (anap.); τὸ φέγγος ὁρμάσθω πυρός Id.*Eu.*1029; ὕβρις ἀτάρβητα ὁρμᾶται insolence *goes* fearless *forth*, S.*Aj.*197 (lyr.).

**ὀρμενόεις**, εσσα, εν, *having a long stalk*, Nic.*Th.*840.

**⊕ ὄρμενος** or **ὅρμενος**, ὁ, *shoot, sprout*, or *stem, stalk*, = ἀσφάραγος II, esp. = κραμβοσπάραγον, Diph.Siph.ap.Ath.2.62f, Hsch.: pl. ὅρμενοι Poll.6.61; but also ὅρμενα Posidipp.24, cf. Phryn.*PS*p.67 B., *EM* 161.4; dat. pl., Jul.*Or.*5.176a. (Cf. ὄρμενος, aor. part. Med. of ὄρνυμι.)

**ὁρμέω**, (ὅρμος II) *to be moored, lie at anchor*, of a ship, ἐν Ἐλαιοῦντι Hdt.7.22; πρὸς γῇ ib.188; ἀκταῖσιν E.*Or.*55; ἐν λιμένι Th.1.52; opp. μετέωρος ὁ., Id.4.26; οὗ ναῦς ὁρμεῖ E.*IT*1043; ἐνταῦθα D.35.29; κατὰ τὴν Κύρου σκηνήν X.*An.*1.4.3:—Med., πρόκροσσαι ὁρμέοντο ἐς πόντον *moored themselves, came to anchor*, Hdt.7.188 codd. (ὅρμεον τὸ is prob. cj.). **II.** prov. phrases, ἐπὶ δυοῖν ἀγκύραιν ὁ., etc., v. ἄγκυρα: metaph., ἐπὶ σμικροῖς μέγας ὁ. S.*OC*148 (anap.); ἐπὶ τῆς ἐκείνων ἀρετῆς ὁ. Aristid.1.134 J.; ἐπὶ τῆς ποιητικῆς δυνάμεως Luc.*Dem. Enc.*18.

**⊕ ὁρμ-ή**, ἡ, *rapid motion forwards, onrush, onset, assault*, μόγις δέ μεν ἔκφυγεν ὁρμήν Il.9.355; ἐκ τοῦ αὐτοῦ χωρίου ἡ ὁ. ἔσται the *attack, invasion*, Hdt.1.11; ἡ ἐπὶ βασιλέα ὁ. X.*An.*3.1.10; also of an *impulse* received from another, ἐμὲτ' εἰσορόων καὶ ἐμὴν ποτιδέγμενος ὁ. Il.10.123, cf. Od.2.403. **2.** more freq. of things, πυρὸς ὁ. the *rage* of fire, Il.11.157; ὑπὸ κύματος ὁρμῆς by the *shock* of a wave, Od.5.320; ἔγχεος ὁ. Hes.*Sc.*365; but ἐς ὁρμὴν ἔγχεος ἐλθεῖν within my spear's *cast*, within *reach* of my spear, Il.5.118; ὁ. γονάτων *spring* of knee, i.e. power to spring or leap, Pi.*N.*5.20; ποδὸς ὁ. *speed* of foot, E.*El.*112 (lyr.): pl., of the tides, Ptol.*Tetr.*3. **II.** *impulse* to do a thing, *effort*, μίνυνθα δέ οἱ γένεθ' ὁρμή Il.4.466; μελέη δέ μοι ἔσσεται ὁ. Od.5.416; φιλότητος..ἄμβροτος ὁ. Emp.35.13; πίσιος ὁ. Id.114.3; ἐπεὶ δὲ δαιμονίη τις γίνεται ὁ. Hdt.7.18; μαινομένᾳ σὺν ὁρμᾷ S.*Ant.*135 (lyr.), cf. *Tr.*720; τίς προσήγαγε χρεία; τίς ὁ.; Id.*Ph.*237; οὕτω καθ' ὁρμὴν δρῶσιν, i.e. with so much zeal, ib.566; εἰ..ἄγοι αὐτὸν ὁ. θειοτέρα Pl.*Phdr.*279a: joined with ἐπιθυμία, Id.*Phlb.*35d, Th.3.36; μιᾷ ὁ. with one *impulse*, X.*An.*3.2.9; ἀπὸ μιᾶς ὁ. Th.7.71; ὑπὸ μιᾷ τῇ ὁ. Luc.*Hist.Conscr.*2: c. gen. objecti, *eager desire of* or *for* a thing, Th.7.43, etc.: so with a Prep., ἡ ὁρμή, ἣν ὁρμᾷς ἐπὶ τοὺς λόγους Pl.*Prm.*135d, cf. 130b; ἔχειν ὁρμὴν πρός τι Arist.*MM*1185ᵃ31, al.; ὁ. ἐπέπεσέ τισι, c. inf., Th.4.4; ὁ. παραστῆσαί τισι εἴς τι or c. inf., Plb.2.48.5, Plu.*Cor.*33; ὁ. σχεῖν, c. inf., Id.*Publ.*19. **2.** in Stoic philosophy, *appetition*, including reasoned choice and irrational impulse, *Stoic.*3.40, al. **3.** Pythag. name for 2, Anatolius ap. *Theol. Ar.*8. **III.** *setting oneself in motion, start* on a march, etc., ἐν ὁρμῇ εἶναι to be on *the point of starting*, X.*An.*2.1.3, cf. Arist.*Rh.*1393ᵃ3; ἐπὶ παντὸς ὁρμῇ..πράγματος at the *start* of every undertaking, Pl.*Ti.*27c; ἡ ὁ. [τούτων τῶν ἀνέμων] the *point at which* these winds *start*, Arist.*Mete.*364ᵇ5, cf. Pl.*R.*511b (pl.). (Cf. Skt. *sárati* 'flow'.) **-ηδόν**, Adv. *impetuously*, Herm.ap.Stob.1.49.68. **⊕ -ημα**, ατος, τό, *sudden rush, swoop, onset*, ἀετοῦ Lxx *De.*28.49; of attacking troops, ib.1 *Ma.*4.8, al.; of the fall of a stone, *Apoc.*18.21: pl., *rapid movement*, ὁρμήμασι νηός, = νηῒ ὁρμωμένῃ, Orac.ap.Ael.*NA*13.21. **2.** = ὁρμή, *impulse, incitement, motive*, μηδ'..ἡμῶν τι συνεργὸν μηδ' ὁ. Epicur.*Nat.*98 G., cf. Plu.2.452c; τὸ ὅ. μου my *indignation*, Lxx *Ho.*5.10; θαλάσσης -ήματα, of the tides, Procl.*Par.Ptol.*4. **II.** the earliest ex. is Ἑλένης ὁρμήματά τε στοναχάς τε Il.2.356, 590, where Ἑλένης is taken by Aristarch.ap.Sch.A as the objective gen., the *cares* (as if from ὁρμαίνω) and groans [of the Greeks] *about* Helen, i.e. caused by her; by the χωρίζοντες (ibid.) as the subjective gen., the *searchings of heart* and groans *of* Helen; the former view is more prob., but ὁ. may be from ὁρμάομαι and mean the *rushes, struggles* of war. **-ησις**, εως, ἡ, *rapid motion*, Sch. A.R.4.847. **2.** *eagerness*, ἐπὶ στρατείαν Vett.Val.60.18. **-ήτειρα**, v. ὁρμάστειρα. **-ητέον**, *one must urge*, Ath.Med.ap.Orib.*inc.*23.19. **-ητήριον**, Dor. -ἀτήριον (v. infr.), τό, *stimulant, incentive*, X.*Eq.*10.15 (pl.). **II.** (from Med. ὁρμάομαι) *starting-place, military position, base of operations*, Isoc.4.162, D.19.219 and 326; ὁρμητηρίῳ χρῆσθαι ταύτῃ τῇ πόλει πρὸς τὸν πόλεμον Plb.1.17.5, cf. 5.3.8; of a *naval station*, Str.5.2.5; πόλιν καὶ λιμένας καὶ ὁρματήρια (Dor.) παρέχειν *SIG*581.10 (Crete, iii/ii B.C.); of a wild beast's *lair*, Plu.2.961c: metaph., ὁ. ἐφ' ἡμᾶς εὐφυὲς ἔχοντι τὴν φιλαυτίαν ib.48f; ὁ. τῆς εὑρέσεως *base* for investigation, Gal.4.634, cf. 10.158; πόλις ὁ. ἀκολασίας its *head-quarters*, Lib.*Decl.*25.12. **-ητής**, οῦ, ὁ, *imperious person*, Philostr.Jun.*Im.Prooem.*, *Cat.Cod.Astr.*2.173, 211, 8(1).183. **2.** of a boxer's arm, *ready to strike*, Philostr.*Gym.*35. **-ητίας**, ου, ὁ, = sq., Eust.1819.24. **-ητικός**, ή, όν, *impetuous, impulsive*, ὁ. [δύναμις] *appetite*, Ti.Locr.102e; ὁ. πρός τι *eager* for a thing, Arist. *Pr.*869ᵇ13: Sup., Id.*HA*573ᵃ27: abs., Thphr.*HP*9.18.10 (Comp.); -κὸν [κίνημα] Plu.2.1122c; -κώτερον τὸ σχῆμα τοῦ πυκτεύοντος *more adapted for attack*, Philostr.*Gym.*34. Adv. -κῶς, ἔχειν Ath.9.401c; ὁ. ἔχειν πρός τι *to be eager* for a thing, Arist.*HA*572ᵃ8, Diocl.*Fr.*141, Sor.1.38: Comp. -κώτερον Arist.*HA*597ᵃ29. **II.** *exciting, stimulating*, Demetr.Ix.ap.Ath.3.74b; φαντασία -κή *creating appetition*, *Stoic.*3.40. **-ητός**, ή, όν, *set in motion*, τὸ [τῆς διανοίας] ὁρμητόν *that which is set in motion* by.., M.Ant.9.28.

**ὁρμιά**, ἡ, (ὅρμος) *fishing-line of horse-hair*, Pl.Com.11, Antiph.28, Arist.*HA*621ᵃ15, S.E.*M.*9.3, etc. [ῐ in Babr.6.3 and in ὁρμιατόνος, ὁρμιηβόλος, qq.v.: ῑ metri gr. in dactylic verses, as Theoc.21.11, *AP* 6.4 (Leon.).]

**ὁρμῐᾱτόνος**, ὁ, (ὁρμιά, τείνω) *fisherman*, E.*Hel.*1615.

**ὁρμιευτής**, οῦ, ὁ, *angler*, un-Att. word in Moer.p.42 P., Hsch.

**ὁρμίζω**, Ep. fut. -ίσσω Il.14.77: aor. ὥρμισα Od.4.785, etc.:—Med. and Pass., fut. -ιοῦμαι Th.6.42: aor. ὡρμισάμην Hdt.9.96, Th.2.86, etc.: less freq. ὡρμίσθην (v. infr.): pf. ὥρμισμαι E.*IT*1328: (ὅρμος II):—*bring to a safe anchorage, bring into harbour, moor, anchor*, νῆα Od.3.11, 12.317, cf. Hdt.6.107; ἐπ' ἀγκυρῶν [τριήρεις] Th.7.59; ὑψοῦ δ' ἐν νοτίῳ τήν γ' ὥρμισαν *moored* the ship in the deeper water, Od.4.785, 8.55; ὁρμίσας ἕκαστον ἀσκόν, λίθους ἀρτήσας καὶ ἀφεὶς ὥσπερ ἀγκύρας X.*An.*3.5.10; οἴκαδ' ὁ. πλάτην *bring* the ship *safe* home, E.*Tr.*1155 (v.l.); ὁ. τινὰ εἰς λιμένας, of Zeus, *AP*9.9 (Jul. Polyaen.); *bring to land*, ἀσπίδα..θάλασσα..παρὰ τύμβον..ὥρμισεν ib.115: metaph., ἐν σπαργάνοισι παιδὸς ὁρμίσαι δίκην that she *wrapped* it *safely, put it to rest*, in swathing bands, A.*Ch.*529. **II.** Med. and Pass., *come to anchor, lie at anchor*, Hdt.9.96, Antipho 5.22; Κύπριδος ὁρμισθεῖσα..ἐν λιμένεσσιν Emp.98.3, cf. E.*Or.*242; ἐπὶ τῷ Ῥίῳ, ἔξω [τοῦ Ῥίου] ὡρμίσαντο, Th.2.86; ὡρμίσαντο παρὰ τῇ Χερρονήσῳ X.*An.*6.2.2; πρὸς ταὐτὸν ὁρμισθεὶς πέδον *having come to* a place *and anchored* there, S.*Ph.*546; πρὸς τὴν γῆν ὁρμισθεὶς X.*HG*1.4.18; ὡρμίσαντο εἰς Ἁρμήνην Id.*An.*6.1.15, cf. D.7.15, etc.; ταῖς λοιπαῖς [ναυσὶν] ἐς τὸ νησίδιον ὁρμίζονται Th.8.11. **2.** metaph., *to be in haven*, i.e. *rest in safety*, εἰς λιμένα τὸν τῆς τέχνης Philem.213.9; ὁρμίζεσθαι τὴν τελευταίαν ὅρμισιν, i.e. to die, Ael.*Fr.*79; ἐκ τύχης ὡρμισμένον *dependent on*.., E.*HF*203.

**ὁρμιηβόλος**, ον, *throwing a line*, *AP*6.196 (Stat. Flacc.), 7.693 (Apollonid.). [ῐ possible in the former, certain in the latter.]

**ὅρμικας**· μύρμηξ, Hsch.

**ὅρμῑνον**, τό, a kind of *sage, clary, Salvia Horminum*, Thphr. *HP*8.1.4, Dsc.3.129:—so **ὅρμῑνος**, ὁ, Polem.Hist.88; **ὅρμῑνοι** in Hsch.

**ὅρμ-ισις**, εως, ἡ, (ὁρμίζω) *bringing a ship to anchor*, metaph., Ael. *Fr.*79. **-ίσκιον**, τό, name of a gem, Plin.*HN*37.168. **-ίσκος**, ὁ, Dim. of ὅρμος, *small necklace*, *IG*1².317.6, Chares 3 J., Lxx *Ca.*1.10, *IG*12(8).51.18 (Imbros, ii B.C.), Ph.1.665, Ael.*NA*8.4. **2.** *signet-cord*, Lxx *Ge.*38.18, J.*AJ*1.16.2. **3.** *collar*, Hsch. **-ισμα**, ατος, τό, = ὅρμος II, metaph., Heraclit.*All.*61. **-ιστέον**, *one must moor*, ναῦν ἔκ τινος Socr.ap.Stob.3.1.104, Epict.*Fr.*30, cf. Arr.*An.*6.19.3. **-ιστηρία**, ἡ, *cord* or *chain for holding fast* or *hanging up* a thing, Ph.*Bel.*91.12, D.S.17.44. **-ίστρια**, ἡ, *bringer to safe anchorage*, epith. of Isis, *POxy.*1380.74 (ii A.D.).

**ὁρμοδοτήρ**, ῆρος, ὁ, *harbour-giver*, of Priapus, *AP*10.16 (Theaet.).

**⊕ ὅρμος**, ὁ, (εἴρω A) *cord, chain*, esp. *necklace, collar*, Il.18.401, *h.Ven.*163; of gold and electron, Od.15.460, 18.295, cf. *h.Ven.*88, Hes.*Op.*74; χρυσεόδμητοι ὅρμοι A.*Ch.*617 (lyr.); χρύσεοι E.*El.*177 (lyr.), cf. *IG*1².386.24, Ar.*V.*677; ὁ. Ἐριφύλης *IG*11(2).161 *B*42 (Delos, iii B.C.), cf. Pl.*R.*590a. **2.** generally, *anything strung like a necklace, wreath, chaplet*, Pi.*O.*2.74; στεφάνων ὅρμος *a string* of crowns, i.e. of praises,

Id.*N*.4.17. **3.** a kind of *dance, performed in a ring* by youths and maidens alternately, Luc.*Salt*.11. **4.** ὁρμοί (on the accent v. infr.)· ἱμάντες ὑποδημάτων, Hsch. **II.** *roadstead, anchorage*, esp. *the inner part of a harbour* or *basin, where ships lie*, Il.1.435, A.*Supp*.765, 772, *Ag*.665, *IG*1$^2$.889, 890, etc.; ὅρμον ποιέεσθαι or θέσθαι, = ὁρμίζεσθαι, Hdt.7.193, Theoc.13.30; τοῖσι οὕτω εἶχε ὅρμου those whom the *anchorage* permitted to do so, Hdt.7.188. **2.** metaph., *haven, place of shelter* or *refuge*, E.*Hec*.450 (lyr.); ὅ. ἐλευθερίας *AP*7.388 (Bianor); τὸ γῆρας . . ὅ. τῶν κακῶν Bion ap.D.L.4.48; βίου πλεύσαντα πρὸς ὅρμον having come to the *end* of life, *IG*2.2081; ὅρμον ὁδοιπορίης *to* the journey's *end*, *AP*11.317 (Pall.). **b.** pl., of the *favourite haunts* of game, X.*Cyn*.10.7. **III.** *means of mooring, attachment*, *AP* 9.296 (Apollonid.). (Some Gramm. distd. signf. I from II, making I oxyt. ὁρμός, v. Eust.1788.46, 1967.29.)

**ὁρμο-φῠλᾰκία**, ἡ, *office of* ὁρμοφύλαξ, *Ostr*.262 (ii A.D.), al., *Arch. Pap*.5.177 (Syene, ii A.D.). ⊛**-φύλαξ** [ῠ], ᾰκος, ὁ, *harbour-master*, *PFay*.23 ii 22 (ii A.D.).

**ὀρν-ᾱπέτιον**, τό, Boeot. for ὄρνεον, Ar.*Ach*.913. ⊛**-εάζομαι**, *carry the head high*, like a fowler looking out for birds, *Com.Adesp*. 1202. **-εᾰκός**, ή, όν, *of* or *belonging to birds*, Tz. ad Lyc.598.

**ὀρνεό-βρωτος**, ον, *eaten by birds*, Suid. s.v. οἰωνόβρωτος. **-γλῠφιστί**, Adv. *in the language of bird-hieroglyphs*, *PMag.Leid.W*.2.37, 4.22. **-θηρευτικός**, ή, όν, *skilled in bird-catching*: ἡ -κή (sc. τέχνη) Ath.1.25d. **-θῠσία**, ἡ, *sacrifice of birds*, Paus.Dam.p.160 D. **-μαντις**, εως, ὁ, = Lat. *augur* or *auspex*, Sch.Ar.*Av*.718. **-μῑγής**, ές, *half-bird, half-human*, Tz. ad Lyc.721:—also **-μικτος**, ον, ib. 592. **-μορφος**, ον, *bird-shaped*, Procl *Par.Ptol*.281.

**ὄρνεον**, τό, = ὄρνις, *bird*, Il.13.64, Cratin.108, Ar.*Av*.291, 305, Th. 2.50, Pl.*Phdr*.274c, al., Arist.*GA*756$^a$16, al. **II.** τὰ ὄ. the *bird-market*, Ar.*Av*.13.

**ὀρνεο-πώλης**, ου, ὁ, *dealer in birds*, Sch.Ar.*Av*.14. **-πώλιον**, τό, *place where birds are sold*, ib.13, Hsch. s.v. ὄρνεα. **-σκοπέω**, = ὀρνιθοσκοπέομαι, Hdn.[*Philet*.]p.465 P., Dosith.p.430 K. **-σκοπικός**, ή, όν, *of* or *for augury*, *An.Ox*.4.240, Gal.*Phil.Hist*.105 D. **-σκόπος**, ον, = ὀρνιθοσκόπος, Vett.Val.4.14, Sch.D Il.1.69, prob. l. in Paus.Dam. p.157 D. **-τρόφος**, ον, = ὀρνιθοτρόφος, *Cat.Cod.Astr*.1.166, *BGU* 725.7 (615 A.D.). ⊛**-φοιτος**, ον, *frequented by birds*, *AP*10.11 (Satyr.).

**ὀρν-εώδης**, ες, = ὀρνιθώδης, of a fickle man, Plu.2.44c. **-εώτης**, ου, ὁ, = ὀρνιθευτής, Poll.7.198. ⊛**-ίζω**, *twitter*, Aq.*Is*.38.14.

**ὀρνῑθ-αγρευτής**, οῦ, ὁ, *bird-catcher*, Sch.Ar.*Nu*.731. **-άριον**, τό, Dim. of ὄρνις, *small bird*, Anaxandr.41.63 (anap.), Nicostr.Com.2, Arist.*Mir*.841$^b$18, *PFay*.118.16 (ii A.D.), Arr.*Epict*.2.7.12 (v.l. τὸν ὀ., i.e. *augur*). **-αρχος**, ὁ, *king of birds*, Ar.*Av*.1215. **-ᾶς**, ᾶ, ὁ, *poulterer*, *POxy*.2139 (ii/iii A.D.), 1568.1 (iii A.D.), *Stud.Pal*.20.107.4 (iv A.D.), *PMasp*.166.9 (vi A.D.). **-εία**, ἡ, *observation of the flight* or *cries of birds* for divination, = Lat. *auspicium*, Plb.6.26.4. **2.** = ὀρνιθευτική, Poll.7.139. ⊛**-ειος**, α, ον, also ος, ον Ar.*Av*.865:—*of* or *belonging to a bird*, οἰκίσκος *bird*-cage, Id.*Fr*.405; κρέα ὀ. *fowl's* flesh, *chicken*, Id.*Ra*.510, *Nu*.339, X.*An*.4.5.31, Arist.*EN*1141$^b$20: abs., ὀ., τά, Ar.*Av*.1590, Pherecr.45; ὀ. ζωμός *chicken* soup, Hegesand.15; ᾠὰ ὀρνίθεα (sic) *hen's* eggs, *PCair.Zen*.266 (iii B.C.). **II.** sg. **ὀρνιθεῖον**, τό, *haunt of birds*, Phryn.*PS*p.94 B. [In Arat.274 ὀρνιθέης (trisyll.) κεφαλῆς.] **-ευτής**, οῦ, ὁ, *fowler, bird-catcher*, Ar.*Av*.526 (anap.), Pl.*Lg*.824b, Pl.Com.157. **-ευτικός**, ή, όν, *of* or *for bird-catching*: ἡ -κή (sc. τέχνη) *the art of bird-catching, fowling*, Pl.*Sph*.220b, Porph. *Abst*.1.53, Poll.7.139. **-εύω**, *catch, snare birds*, X.*HG*4.1. 16. **II.** ὀρνιθεύομαι, = οἰωνίζομαι, *observe the flight* or *cries of birds* for divination, D.H.4.13, Hecat.Abd.14. **-ία**, ἡ, *poisoning by bird-dung*, *Hippiatr*.89. **-ιάζω**, *talk bird-language*, Sch.Ar.*Av*. 1677. **-ιᾰκός**, ή, όν, *of* or *for birds*: τὰ ὀρνιθιακά *a history of birds*, a work attributed to D.P., *Proll.Schol*.; also called Ἰξευτικά and attributed to Oppian. **-ίας**, ου, ὁ, in pl., (sc. ἄνεμοι) annual winds in spring, *which brought the birds of passage*, Hp.*Epid*.7.105, Democr.14, Arist.*Mete*.362$^a$23, *Mu*.395$^a$4; βορέαι *PHib*.27.59, cf. Gem.*Calend*.9, Adam.*Vent*.44 (νότοι ib.45): hence in Ar.*Ach*.877, χειμὼν ὀ. a tempest *of birds*, a *fowl*-wind. **II.** -ίας, α, ὁ, *dealer in birds*, Lib.*Arg.D*.19, Tz.*H*.6.56. **-ικός**, ή, όν, *of* or *for birds*, τροφή Luc.*Gall*.5. ⊛**-ιον**, τό, Dim. of ὄρνις, *small bird*, Hdt.2.77, Ar. *Av*.223, Arist.*HA*609$^a$16, al.; esp. *chicken*, Cratin.113; τὰ χοιρίδια τέθνηκε καὶ τὰ μίκρ' ὀ. Stratt.58.

**ὀρνῑθο-βόρος**, ον, *devouring chickens*, of the fox, Cyran.52. **-βοσκεῖον**, τό, in Lat. form *ornithoboscion, aviary, poultry-house*, Varro *RR*3.9.2, etc. **-γᾰλον**, τό, *starflower, Ornithogalum umbellatum*, v.l. for ὄρνιθος γάλα, Dsc.2.144; gen. pl. -γάλων Gal.19.739; nom sg. *ornithogale*, Plin.*HN*21.102. **-γενής**, ές, = ὀρνιθόγονος: τὰ ὀ. the *bird kind*, Artem.1.37. **-γνώμων**, ον, gen. ονος, *knowing in birds*, Ael.*NA* 16.2. **-γονία**, ἡ, *the generation of birds*, a work by Boeus or Boeo, mentioned by Philoch.207, Ant.Lib.3 tit., etc. **-γονος**, ον, *sprung from a bird*, [Ἑλένη] E.*Or*.1385 (lyr.). **-ειδής**, ές, *like a bird*, Adam. 1.4. **-θήρας**, ου, ὁ, *bird catcher, fowler*, Ar.*Av*.62, Arist.*HA*609$^a$15, *PCair.Zen*.398.9 (iii B.C.), Plu.2.80ca, D.Chr.72.16. **-θηρευτής**, οῦ, ὁ, = ὀρνιθευτής, Sch.Ar.*Av*.526. **-θηρέω**, *catch birds*, Telecl. 26 (ὀρνιθοθηρᾶν codd. Poll., wrongly; cf. λαγοθηρέω). **-κάπηλος** [ᾰ], ὁ, *dealer in birds*, Critias 70 D. **-κλέπτης**, ου, ὁ, *bird-stealer*, Herod.6.102. **-κλόος**, v. ὀρνιθοκόος. **-κομεῖον**, τό, *place where birds are kept*, Suid.; v.l. ὀρνιθονομεῖον. **-κόμος**, ον, *keeping poultry*, Procop.*Vand*.1.2: Ὀρνιθοκόμοι a comedy of Anaxilas. **-κόος**, ον, *understanding birds*, *EM*632.18, as etym. of ὀρνιθοκλόος, cf. Phot. ὀρνιθοκλόνοι· ὀρνιθοσκόποι. **-κρίτης** [ῐ], ου, ὁ, *interpreter of the flight* or *cries of birds*, *Gloss*. **-λόγος**, ὁ, v. sq. **-λόχος**, Dor. **ὀρνῑχ-**, ὁ, (λοχάω) *bird-catcher, fowler*, Pi.*I*.1. 48, which passage is cited with ὀρνιθολόχῳ by Plu.2.473a, but with ὀρνιθολόγῳ (wrongly) in ib.406c. **-μᾰνέω**, *to be bird-mad*, Ar.*Av*. 1284, 1344. **-μᾰνής**, ές, *mad after birds, bird-mad*, Chrysipp. *Stoic*.3.130, 167. **-μαντεία**, ἡ, *divination from birds*, Procl. ad Hes.*Op*.824. **-μαντις**, εως, ὁ, = ὀρνεόμαντις, Hsch. s.v. οἰωνοπόλοι. **-νομεῖον**, v. ὀρνιθοκομεῖον. **-ομαι**, Pass., *to be changed into a bird*, Philoch.207. **-παις**, παιδος, ὁ, ἡ, *born of a bird*: *like a bird*, epith. of a Siren, Lyc.731. **-πέδη**, ἡ, *snare for birds*, *AP* 9.396 (Paul. Sil.). **-πρόσωπος**, ον, *bird-faced*, Porph.*Abst*.3. 16. **-πώλης**, ου, ὁ, *dealer in birds*, Poll.7.198:—hence **-πωλεῖον**, ibid.

**ὀρνῑθοσκοπ-έομαι**, Dep., = ὀρνεοσκοπέω, *observe birds, interpret their flight and cries*, Lxx *Le*.19.26. **-ία**, ἡ, = ὀρνιθομαντεία, Phleg. 37 J. **-ος** (parox.), ον, *observing and predicting by the flight and cries of birds*, Lat. *augur, auspex*, Thphr.*Char*.16.11, 19.8, D.H.2.60, Poll.7.188, etc.; θᾶκος ὀ. *an augur's* seat, S.*Ant*.999.

⊛**ὀρνῑθοτροφ-εῖον**, τό, *poultry-house*, Varro *RR*3.5.8. **-έω**, *keep poultry*, *Gp*.14.7.8. **-ία**, ἡ, *keeping of birds*, Plu.*Per*.13 (pl.). ⊛**-ος**, ὁ, *bird-keeper*, D.S.1.74, *Cat.Cod.Astr*.8(4).216 (both pl.).

**ὀρνῑθο-φάγος** [ᾰ], ον, *eating birds*, Arist.*HA*612$^b$14. **-φῠής**, ές, (φυή) *of a bird's nature* or *shape*, Ath.11.491d.

**ὀρνῑθ-ώδης**, ες, = ὀρνιθοειδής, Arist.*PA*659$^b$27, Adam.2.25: Comp. -έστερος Arist.*HA*564$^b$20. **-ών**, ῶνος, ὁ, *poultry-house*, Varro *RR* 3.3.1, *CIG*2694*b*11 (Mylasa), *POxy*.1207.4 (ii A.D.).

**ὄρνιος**, poet. for ὀρνίθειος, *AP*9.377 (Pall.).

⊛**ὄρνις**, ὁ, also ἡ Il.9.323, 14.290, al., freq. in Att., cf. III; gen. ὄρνῑθος; acc. sg. ὄρνῑθα and ὄρνιν, neither in Hom.: pl., nom. and acc. ὄρνῑθες, -θας, but in acc. also ὄρνεις or ὄρνῑς (S.*OT*966, E.*Hipp*.1059, Ar.*Av*.717, 1250, 1610, D.19.245, etc.): also **ὄρνιξ**, *PCair.Zen*.375. 1 (iii B.C.), v.l. in *Ev.Luc*.13.34, called Ion. and Dor. by Phot. (but ὄρνις nom. in Alcm.26.4); acc. ὄρνῑχα Pi.*O*.2.88; gen. ὄρνῑχος Id.*I*. 6(5).53: nom. pl. ὄρνῑχες B.5.22, Theoc.7.47; gen. pl. ὀρνίχων Alcm. 67, *Abh.Berl.Akad*.1925(5).33 (Cyrene, iv B.C.); dat. ὄρνιξι, ὀρνίχεσσι, Pi.*P*.5.112, 4.190 (ὄρνιξι also in *PLond*.1.131$^r$.125, al. (i A.D.)): on the gender and declens., v. Ath.9.373 sq. (Cf. ὄρν-εον, Goth. *ara*, gen. *arins* 'eagle', etc.) [In the trisyll. cases ῑ always: Hom. has ὄρνῑς in Il.9.323, 12.218, but ὄρνῐς ib.24.219; and later Ep. use both ὄρνῑς and ὄρνῐς: in Trag. both quantities are found, ὄρνῐς in A. *Fr*.304.3 (-ῐν), S.*Ant*.1021, *El*.149 (lyr.), *Fr*.654, E.*HF*72, and so Philem.79.10; but ὄρνῑς E.*Ba*.1365, and always in Ar. (*Av*.103, al.), for in ib.168, the words τίς ὄρνῐς οὗτος; are borrowed from Sophocles; ὄρνῑς is said to be Att., *EM*632.8.] **I.** *bird*, including birds of prey and domestic fowls, Hom., etc.; applied to ostriches, X. *An*.1.2.7: freq. added to the specific names, ὄρνισιν ἐοικότες αἰγυπιοῖσιν Il.7.59; λάρῳ ὄρνιθι ἐοικώς Od.5.51; ὄ. ἀηδών, πέρδιξ, S.*Aj*. 629, *Fr*.323; ὄ. ἀλκυών, ὄ. κύκνος, E.*IT*1089 (lyr.), *Hel*.19. **II.** like οἰωνός, *bird of omen*, from the flight or cries of which the augur divined, Hes.*Op*.828; δεξιός, ἀριστερὸς ὄρνις, Il.13.821, Od.20.242, al.; χρηστηρίους ὄρνιθας A.*Th*.26, cf. *Ag*.112, 157 (both lyr.); ὄ. αἴσιος S.*OT*52, cf. Plu.*Fab*.19, Gal.12.314; ὀρνίθων οἰωνίσματα E.*Ph*. 839. **2.** metaph., *omen taken from the flight* or *cries of birds*, Il.10. 277, al.: generally, *omen, presage*, without direct reference to birds, 24. 219, Pi.*P*.4.19; ὄρνιθα δ' οὐ ποιῶ σε τῆς ἐμῆς ὁδοῦ A.*Fr*.95, cf. E.*IA*988, Ar.*Pl*.63, *Av*.719 sqq.; v. ὅδιος. **III.** in Att. ὄρνις, ὁ, is mostly, *cock*, S.*El*.18; κοκκυβόας ὄ. Id.*Fr*.791, cf. Ar.*V*.815; ὄρνις, ἡ, *hen*, Men.167, 168, *PCair.Zen*.266 (iii B.C., pl.); ἀλέκτορα καὶ ὄρνιθα τελέαν cock and *hen*, *TAM*2(1).245.8 (Lycia); in full, ὄ. ἐνοίκιος A.*Eu*.866; θήλεια ὄ. S.*Fr*.477; πότερον ὄ. ἢ ταὧς; Ar.*Av*.102 (with play on this signf. and signf. I); ὁ ὄρνιξ ὁ σιτευτός fatted *fowl*, *PCair.Zen*.375.1; ὀρνίθων φοινικολόφων Theoc.22.72, cf. 24.64, Mosch.3.49; ὄ. οἰκίης Babr.17.1; also, *goose*, Id.123.1. **IV.** in pl. sts., *bird-market*, D.19.245; cf. ὄρνεον II. **V.** Μοισᾶν ὄρνιχες *song-birds*, i.e. *poets*, Theoc.7.47. **VI.** Provs.: διώκει παῖς ποτανὸν ὄρνιν A.*Ag*. 394 (lyr.); ὄ. ὥς τις ἐκ χερῶν ἄφαντος E.*Hipp*.828; ὀρνίθων γάλα 'pigeon's milk', i.e. any marvellous dainty or good fortune, Ar. *V*.508, *Av*.1673, Mnesim.9, Men.936; but ὄρνιθος γάλα *white of egg*, Anaxag.22; also a plant, v. ὀρνιθόγαλον. **VII.** a constellation, later Cygnus, Eudox.ap.Hipparch.1.2.16, Arat.275, Ptol.*Tetr*. 26.

**ὄρνῑτο**, barbarism for ὄρνισι, Ar.*Av*.1679.

**ὀρνῑχολόχος, ὄρνῑχος, -χα**, v. ὀρνιθ-, ὄρνις.

**ὀρνόλη**, ἡ, = *urceolus*, *Gloss*.

⊛**ὄρνῡμι** or **-ύω**, poet. Verb: from the former come imper. ὄρνῠθι, ὄρνῠτε, Il.6.363, Od.10.457, al.; inf. ὀρνύμεναι Il.17.546, ὀρνύμεν 9. 353, al.; and from the latter, pres. ὀρνύει Pi.*O*.13.12, cf. Orph.*L*.222: 3 sg. and pl. impf. ὤρνυε, -νον, Od.21.100, Il.12.142: fut. ὄρσω 21. 335, Pi.*N*.9.8, S.*Ant*.1060: aor. ὦρσα Il.5.629, al., Hes.*Th*.523, A. *Pers*.496; Ion. 3 sg. ὄρσασκε Il.17.423: redupl. aor. 2 ὤρορε 2.146, Od.4.712, etc. (but ὤρορε stands for ὄρωρε, Il.13.78, Od.8.539):— Med. ὄρνῠμαι, used by Hom. in 3 sg. ὄρνυται Il.5.532, al., imper. ὄρνυσθε ib.102, al., part. ὀρνύμενος 20.158, al.: impf. ὠρνύμην, used by Hom. in 3 sg. and pl., ὤρνῠτο Il.3.267, al., ὤρνυντο Od.2.397, al.: fut. 3 sg. ὀρεῖται Il.20.140: aor. 2 ὠρόμην, 3 sg. ὤρετο 12.279, 14.397, also very freq. ὦρτο, 5.590, al.; 3 pl. without augm. ὄροντο Od.3.471 (but v. ὄρομαι), ὀρέοντο Il.2.398, 23.212 (unless this is impf.); imper. ὄρσο or ὄρσεο, 5.109, al., 3.250, al.; Ion. contr. ὄρσευ 4.264, 19.

139; subj. ὄρηται Od.16.98,al.; inf. ὄρθαι Il.8.474; part. ὀρόμενος A.*Th.*87, 115 (both lyr.), ὄρμενος Il.11.326, al., and in lyr. passages of Trag., A.*Ag.*1408 (cf. 429), *Supp.*422, S.*OT*177: to the Med. also belongs the pf. ὄρωρα, used by Hom. only in 3 sg. ὄρωρε (v. supr.), subj. ὀρώρῃ Il.9.610, al.; and plpf. ὀρώρει 2.810, al. (cf. ὄρομαι), also ὠρώρει 18.498, A.*Ag.*653, S.*OC*1622:—Pass., perf. ὀρώρεται, = ὄρωρε, Od. 19.377; subj. ὀρώρηται Il.13.271: 3 pl. aor. ὦρθεν Corinn.*Supp.*1.21. (Cf. Skt. *ṛṇóti* 'rush', aor. 3 sg. *ārta* = ὦρτο, Lat. *orior*; cf. also ἔρσεο, ἔρσῃ, and ἔρετο in Hsch.):—*stir, stir up*; esp. 1. of bodily movement, *urge on, incite*, τινὰ ἐπί τινι Il.5.629, 12.293; οἱ ἐπ' αἰετὸν ὦρσε *let loose* his eagle upon him, Hes.*Th.*523; τινὰ ἀντία τινός Il.20.79; rarely, τινὰ εἰς ἀυάταν Pi.*P.*2.29: c. inf., Ζεὺς ὦρσε μάχεσθαι *urged* them *on* to fight, Il.13 794, cf. 17.273; τὴν.. ῥέξαι θεὸς ὤρορεν ἔργον Od.23. 222; τόλμα μοι γλῶσσαν ὀρνύει λέγειν Pi.*O.*13.12, cf. *P.*4.170, S.*Ant.* 1060:—Med., with pf. ὄρωρα, *move, stir oneself*, εἰς ὅ κε.. μοι φίλα γούνατ' ὀρώρῃ while my limbs *have power to move*, Il.9.610, cf. Od.18.133, etc.: used by Hom. in imper. ὄρσεο, *up! arise!* (like ἄγε and ἴθι) in exhorting, Il.3.250, al.; ὄρσο 5.109, 24.88; ἀλλ' ὄρσευ πόλεμόνδε 4. 264, 19.139: in hostile sense, *rush on, rush furiously*, ὦρτο δ' ἐπ' αὐτοὺς [Ἕκτωρ] 5.590, 11.343; ὦρτο δ' ἐπ' αὐτῷ 21.248; ὤρνυτο χαλκῷ Τυδεΐδης 5.17, etc.; ὄρνυται λαός A.*Th.*89 (lyr.), cf. 419 (lyr.), S.*OC* 1320. 2. *make to arise, call forth*, ἀπ' Ὠκεανοῦ..Ἠριγένειαν ὦρσεν Od.23.348, cf. 7.169; *awaken, arouse* from sleep, ὦρσεν..Ἱπποκόωντα Il.10.518; of animals, *start, chase*, ὦρσαν δὲ Νύμφαι..αἶγας ὀρεσκῴους Od.9.154; ὡς δ' ὅτε νεβρὸν ὄρεσφι κύων..ὄρσας ἐξ εὐνῆς Il.22.190:—Med., *arise, start up*, esp. from bed, Ἠὼς ἐκ λεχέων..ὤρνυθ' 11.2; ὤρνυτ' ἄρ' ἐξ εὐνῆφιν Od.2.2, etc.; ἀπὸ θρόνου ὦρτο φαεινοῦ Il.11.645; ἀπὸ χθονὸς ὤρνυτο *attacked* from.., 5.13: abs., ὀρνυμένοιο ἄνακτος Hes.*Th.*843: c. inf., *rise to do* a thing, *set about* it, οἱ δ' εὕδειν ὤρνυντο Od.2.397 (so c. part., ὄρσο κέων *get thee* to bed, 7.342); ὦρτο..ἴμεν 7.14, cf. Hes.*Sc.* 40; ὦρτο πέτεσθαι Il.13.62, etc.; ὤρετο..Ζεὺς νειφέμεν *started* or *began to*.., 12.279; without inf., ὤρορε θεῖος ἀοιδός Od.8.539. 3. freq. used of things as well as persons, *call forth, excite*, of storms and the like, which the gods call forth, ὄρσας..ἀνέμων..ἀϋτμήν 11.407, cf. Il.14. 254, 21.335; νοῦσον ἀνὰ στρατὸν ὦρσε 1.10, etc.; θεὸς χειμῶν' ἄωρον ὦρσε A.*Pers.*496:—and in Med., *arise*, ὀρώρει δ' οὐρανόθεν νύξ Od.5. 294, al.; φλὸξ ὦρτο Il.8.135; ὅτε τις χειμὼν..ὄροιτο Od.14.522; ὦρτο δὲ κῦμα πνοιῇ ὕπο λιγυρῇ Il.23.214; πῦρ ὄρμενον ἐξαίφνης 17.738, cf. S.*OT*177 (lyr.). b. of human actions, passions, and the like, ὄρσαι πόλεμον Il.4.16; ἔριν Od.3.161; ἐν δὲ κυδοιμὸν ὦρσε κακόν Il.11. 53; ὑφ' ἵμερον ὦρσε γόοιο 23.108, al.; μή μοι γόον ὄρνυθι Od.17.46, cf. 10.457; ἐν φόβον ὦρσε Il.13.362; ἐν μένος ὦρσεν 8.335:—and in Med., φευγόντων δ' οὔτ' ἄρ κλέος ὄρνυται οὔτε τις ἀλκή 5.532; καί μοι μένος ὤρορε 13.78; ὅππῃ οἱ νόος ὄρνυται Od.1.347; ἔριδος μέγα νεῖκος ὀρώρει Il.17.384; τῶν δὲ στόνος ὤρνυτ' ἀεικής 10.483, al.; δοῦρα ὄρμενα πρόσσω the darts *flying* onwards, 11.572; ὀρνυμένων πολέμων Pi.*O.*8. 34; ἀφρὸς ἀπὸ χροὸς ὤρνυτο *started* from the skin, Hes.*Th.*191; ὡς λόγος ἐκ πατέρων ὄρωρεν Alc.71. 4. A.R. uses ὄρωρε nearly as = ἐστί, 1.713, al.; ὀρώρει = ἦν, 2.473, 3.457.—The Verb is mainly used in Ep. and Lyr. poetry; seldom found in Trag. trim., ὄρσω S.*Ant.*1060; ὦρσα A.*Pers.*496; ὄρνυμαι S.*OC*1320; ὀρώρει ib.1622, A.*Ag.*653; prob. never in Com. (Ar.*Ra.*1529 is mock-Epic) or correct Prose.

**ὀρνύφιον**, τό, Dim. of ὄρνις, Thphr.*Fr.*160, Dsc.2.54, 4.79, Ael.*NA* 4.41, 7.47, Orib.*Fr.*118; ὀρνύφιν *PMag.Leid.V.*11.33.

**ὀροβάγχη** or **ὀροβάκχη** (as Hsch. writes it, cf. v.l. in *Gp.*2.42.1), ἡ, *dodder, Cuscuta europaea*, Thphr.*HP*8.8.4, *Gp.*2.43. II. *choke-fitch, Orobanche crenata*, Dsc.2.142, *Gp.*2.42.

**ὀροβάδων**· νεβρῶν, Hsch.

**ὀρόβακχος**, ὁ, pl., ὀρόβακχοι σίδης *fruits* of the pomegranate, Nic. *Th.*869.

**ὀρόβαξ**, ἡ, = γλυκυσίδη, Ps.-Dsc.3.140:—also **ὀροβάδιον**, ibid.

**ὀρόβηθρον**, τό, = ὑποκισθίς, Ps.-Dsc.1.97.

**ὀροβ-ιαῖος**, α, ον, *of the size of the* ὄροβος, Dsc.4.150,164, Orib.*Fr.* 56, Alex.Trall.7.4. **-ίας**, ου, ὁ, name for a kind of ἐρέβινθος, Thphr.*HP*8.5.1 (reading ὀροβίαι οἱ), Gal.11.876, 13.236, Orib.*Eup.*2.1 p.359 R., prob. in Dsc.2.104. 2. a kind of λίβανος, Id.1.68, Plin. *HN*12.62. **-ίζω**, *feed on* ὄροβοι, Hsch. s. v. ὠροβισμένοι. **-ῖνος**, η, ον, *made of* ὄροβος, ἄλευρον Ph.*Bel.*89.18, Dsc.2.108, Gal.14.162, etc. ✱ **-ιον**, τό, Dim. of ὄροβος, Hp.*Dieb.Judic.*9. II. *meal made from* ὄροβοι, Id.*Nat.Mul.*34. III. a kind of χρυσόκολλα, Hsch. IV. *pill the size of an* ὄροβος, Dsc.*Eup.*1.12. **-ίτης** [ῑ], ου, ὁ, *like* or *of the size of the* ὄροβος, λίθος D.S.3.13:—fem. **ὀροβῖτις**, *prepared chrysocolla*, Plin.*HN*33.89.

**ὀροβοειδής**, ές, *like vetch-seed*, of certain urinal deposits, Gal.7.950, al. II. *of the colour of vetch*, [χλαμύς], θωρακεῖον, *PCair.Zen.*92.8, 445.6 (iii B.C.).

✱ **ὄροβος**, ὁ, *bitter vetch, Vicia Ervilia*, Thphr.*HP*2.4.2, al., Dsc.2.108, *Sammelb.*4369$^a$9 (iii B.C.), etc.: freq. in pl., of its seeds, Hp.*VM*8, *Acut.*21, *Vict.*2.45, Heraclit.4 (prob.), D.22.15, Arist.*HA*522$^b$29, Thphr.*HP*8.1.4, D.Chr.6.62, etc. II. = χάλαζα II, Eust.853.55. (Cf. ἐρέβινθος.)

**ὀροβο-φαγέω**, *eat vetch*, Hp.*Epid.*2.4.3 = 6.4.11. **-φόρος**, ον, *bearing vetches*, γῆ *Sammelb.*4369$^b$50 (iii B.C.).

**ὀρογενής**, ές, (ὅρος) *productive of terms* (cf. ὅρος IV. 2), μονὰς ὀ. οὖσα Iamb.*in Nic.*p.57 P.

**ὄρογκοι**, οἱ, *mountains*, D.P.286, Nic.*Al.*42 (expld. by Hsch., Phot., Eust. ad D.P. l.c., as = οἱ τῶν ὀρῶν ὄγκοι: Hsch. adds τινὲς δὲ καὶ τὰ ἐργάσιμα ξύλα.).

**ὀρογλυφέω**, *remove* or *alter marks on boundary stones*, Eust.767.57.

**ὀρόγυια**, ἡ, = ὄργυια, Pi.*P.*4.228, Ar.*Fr.*942; gen. pl. ὀρογυιῶν *IG*2$^2$. 1693.

**ὀροδαμνίς**, ίδος, ἡ, Dim. of ὀρόδαμνος, *sprig, spray*, Theoc.7.138.

**ὀρόδαμνος**, ὁ, *bough, branch*, *AP*9.3 (Pl. or Antip.), Thphr.*HP*9. 16.3, Call.*Fr.*139, Nic.*Th.*863, *Al.*603, etc.:—a shortd. form **ὄραμνος** (q.v.); also **ῥάδαμνος**, Lxx *Jb.*8.16, Suid., Hsch. (who also gives **ῥόδαμνος**), etc.; and **ῥάδᾰμος** [ρᾰ], Nic.*Al.*92.

**ὀροδεμνιάδες** (sc. Νύμφαι), αἱ, *couching on mountains, mountain-nymphs*, Hsch.

**ὀρο-θεσία**, ἡ, *fixing of boundaries*: in pl., *limitations, boundaries*:—*Inscr.Prien.*42.8 and 12 (ii B.C.), *Act.Ap.*17.26 (pl.), *BGU*889.17 (ii A.D.). II. **-θέσια**, τά, Gal.19.349, Hsch., etc.: gloss on οὖροι, *Gloss.Hdt.*ap.Stein *Herodotus* 2 p.468: the sg. ὀροθέσιον (*boundary*) occurs in Petr.Patr.p.433 D. **-θετέω**, *fix boundaries*, *OGI*538. 12 (Galatia, i A.D.), Aq.*De.*19.14, etc. ✱ **-θέτης**, ου, ὁ, = *terminator*, *Gloss.*

**ὀροθύνω**, used by Hom. once in pres., Od.18.407, but chiefly in Ep. impf. 3 sg. ὀρόθυνε(ν), Il.13.351, al.: aor. 1 ὠρόθυνα Lyc.693; imper. ὀρόθυνον Il.21.312:—*stir up, rouse, urge on*, mostly of persons, Il.13.351, etc.; also of things, πάντας δ' ὀρόθυνον ἐναύλους 21.312; πάσας δ' ὀρόθυνεν ἀέλλας Od.5.292: c. inf., *urge* one to do, A.R.1.522, 1275.—Ep. word, used in Pass. by A., στάσις τ' ἐν ἀλλήλοισιν ὠροθύνετο *Pr.* 202; and Herm. restores ὀροθύνεις (for ὀρθεῖς or ὀρθοῖς) in E.*Ba.* 1168 (lyr.).

**ὀροιβάδες**· αἱ αἶγες, Hsch. **ὀροικλάνοι**· ὀξύσχοινοι, Id. **ὀροιτύπος** [ῠ], ον, v. ὀρειτύπος.

**ὀροκάρυον** [ᾰ], τό, *mountain-nut*, a tree which grows near the Black Sea, Str.12.3.12.

✱ **ὄρομαι**, *keep watch*, used only in compd. with ἐπί, which is always separated from the Verb by tmesis, αἰπόλια πλατέ' αἰγῶν..ἐσχατιῇ βόσκοντ', ἐπὶ δ' ἀνέρες ἐσθλοὶ ὄρονται Od.14.104; ἐπὶ δ' ἀνέρες ἐσθλοὶ ὄροντο, οἶνον οἰνοχοεῦντες 3.471 (cf. ὄρνυμι ad init.); ἐπὶ δ' ἀνὴρ ἐσθλὸς ὀρώρει Μηριόνης Il.23.112.—So Sch.Od.14.104 (cf. ὄρει· φυλάσσει, Hsch.) rightly: ἐπὶ..ὄρομαι is related to ἐπίουρος (ἔφορος).

**ὀρομᾱλίδες**, αἱ, (μῆλον B) Dor. for *ὀρομηλίδες, a kind of *wild apples*, Theoc.5.94 (vulg. ὀριμαλίδες).

✱ **Ὀρομπάτας**, α, ὁ, epith. of Zeus at Amathus, *Hermes* 50.158.

✱ **ὄρον**, τό, wooden *implement for pressing grapes*, A.*Fr.*107, Is.*Fr.* 24, Men.172; **ὅρος** in Poll.7.150, 10.130.

**ὀρόντιον**, τό, name of a plant, a remedy for jaundice, Archig.ap. Gal.13.236.

**ὀρο-νύχιον** [ῠ], τό, *night-watch*, Phot. **-πέδιον**, τό, *mountain-plain, table-land*, δι' ὀροπεδίων Str.7.1.5, cf. 11.12.4, 12.6.1: sg. in 15. 1.44.

**ὀρο-ποτέω**, *drink whey*, Hp.*Morb.*2.70, *Int.*16 (with v. l. ὀρρ-). **-ποτίη**, ἡ, Ion. for *-ποσία, *drinking of whey*, Id.*Morb.*2.70 (with v. l. ὀρρ-).

✱ **ὄρος**, εος, τό: gen. pl. ὀρέων (the form proper to Ion. and other dialects) is required by the metre in E.*Ba.*719 (iamb.) and freq. in lyr. verse, as S.*OT*1106, and is alone used in Lxx, *Ge.*8.5, al., cf. *IG*7. 2225.18 (ii B.C.), *Apoc.*6.15; but ὀρῶν (the Att. form) is required in A. *Pr.*719, 811, *Fr.*342, E.*Ba.*791, and occurs in Th.3.24, Pl.*Criti.*111c, *SIG*888.120 (Scaptopara, iii A.D.), etc.: the Ep. and Lyr. forms οὔρεος, οὔρεϊ, οὔρεα, οὔρεσι prob. have οὐρ- metri gr. for ὀρ- (so ὤρεα, ὤρεος metri gr. in Dor., Theoc.1.77, 115, 4.35, *Hymn.Is.*162): the Ion. form is ὀρ-, Od.9.21, al., Anacr.2.5, v. ὄρειος (οὔρεσιν is an Epicism in Semon.14.1, cf. οὔρη at end of a hexam., *IG*12(8).445 6 (Thasos)); ὄρος is found in codd. of Hdt. 1.43, 2.8, 12, 7.176 and should perh. be restd. elsewh.:—*mountain, hill*, ὄρεος κορυφῇσι Il.3.10, al.; οὔρεος ἐν βήσσῃσιν 11.87; ἐν ὄρεσσι 1.235, al.; ἐν οὔρεσιν 24.614, al.; τρέμε δ' οὔρεα μακρά 13.18, etc.; Γαῖα..γείνατο δ' Οὔρεα μακρά, θεῶν χαρίεντας ἐναύλους Hes.*Th.*129. 2. *canton, parish*, ὀ. Ἀργειατᾶν, ὀ. Ὀγχνιάίον, etc., *Mnemos.*42.332 (Argos, iv B.C.). 3. in Egypt, *desert*, *PLeb.* 383.61 (i A.D.); as place of burial, *POxy.*274.27 (i A.D.), *PRyl.*153. 5 (ii A.D.), *PGrenf.*2.77.22 (iii/iv A.D.). 4. part of the foot, = τὸ ἄνω πρὸ τῶν δακτύλων, Poll.2.197. 5. = ἀμίς, Sch.Ar.*Ach.*82.

✱ **ὀρός**, ὁ, *the watery* or *serous part of milk, whey*, ναῖον δ' ὀρῷ ἄγγεα πάντα Od.9.222; ὀρὸν πίνων 17.225, cf. Hp.*Mul.*1.29, *Acut.*2, Arist. *HA*521$^b$27, al., Eust.1626.1, 1818.23. 2. *the watery part* or *serum of the blood*, Pl.*Ti.*83d. 3. *the watery part of wood-tar*, ὀρὸς πίσσης Hp.*Ulc.*12, Thphr.*HP*3.9.2, Paul.Aeg.3.74. 4. σπερματικὸς ὀρός seminal *fluid*, *Placit.*5.23:—the form **ὀρρός** is f.l. in Hp. ll. cc., Arist. l. c., Ruf.*Ren.Ves.*14. etc.; the form **οὐρός** was coined by Nic. *Th.*708. (Cf. Skt. *sarás*, Adj. 'fluid', Lat. *serum*.)

✱ **ὅρος**, Corc. ὅρϝος *IG*9(1).698.1 (written ὄρβος 700.1); Cret. and Arg. **ὦρος** *SIG*685.59, *Mnemos.*42.332; Heracl. **ὅρος** *Tab.Heracl.*1. 53, al., cf. ἄντορος; Ion. **οὖρος** *GDI*5518 and 5493*b*25, Democr.4, Hdt. (v. infr.) (also Theraean *IG*12(3).436); Megarian **ὅρρος** (?) *Berl. Sitzb.*1888.885, cf. ὁμορέω: ὁ:—*boundary, landmark*, ἀμφ' οὔροισι δύ' ἀνέρε δηριάασθον Il.12.421; λίθον.., τόν ῥ' ἄνδρες πρότεροι θέσαν ἔμμεναι οὖρον ἀρούρης 21.405; ἐγὼ δὲ τούτων ὥσπερ ἐν μεταιχμίῳ ὅ. κατέστην Sol.ap.Arist.*Ath.*12.5: the regions separated by the *boundary* are usu. in gen., οὖρος τῆς Μηδικῆς ἀρχῆς καὶ τῆς Λυδικῆς Hdt.1.72, etc.: in dat., οὐδεὶς ὅρος ἐκ θεῶν χρηστοῖς οὐδὲ κακοῖς E.*HF*669 (lyr.): with a single gen., ῥεῖθρον ἠπείροιν ὅρον A.*Pr.*790; γάμου ὅ. *the time within which* one may marry, Pl.*Lg.*785b; οἱ ὅ. τῶν διαστημάτων the *notes which limit* the intervals in the musical scale, Id.*Phlb.*17d, cf. Aristox. *Harm.*pp.49, 56 M.; ὅροι τρεῖς ἁρμονίας.., νεάτης τε καὶ ὑπάτης καὶ μέσης Pl.*R.*443d; ἐς ἑβδομήκοντα ἔτεα οὖρον τῆς ζόης ἀνθρώπῳ προτίθημι I set the *limit* of human life at seventy years, Hdt.1.32, cf. 74, 216; ζωᾶς ὅρον ἡμετέρας B.5.144: abs., εἰς τὸν τόπον.., ἐν οἷς ἂν.. ὅρους θῶνται τῶν ὠνίων wherever (they) appoint *fixed places* for trading, Pl.*Lg.*849e; *decision* of a magistrate, ὅρον δώσω *PThead.*15.20 (iii A.D.); so ὅρον προσγράψαι D.23.40; ὅρους τοῖς βαρβάροις πήξαντες Lycurg.73; εἷς ὅρος παγήσεται Th.4.92; τὸν ὅρον ὑπερβάντες Pl.*R.*373d, etc.: also in pl., *bounds, boundaries*, ἐν οὔροισι χώρης Hdt.4.52, cf. 125; τοὺς Αἰγυπτίων οὔρους Id.2.17; ὑπὸ Κυλλάνας ὅροις Pi.*O.*6.77; γῆς ἐπ' ἐσχάτοις ὅροις A.*Pr.*666; τὸ ἀκόντιον ἔξω τῶν ὅ. τῆς αὐτοῦ πορείας.. ἐξενεχθὲν ἔτρωσεν αὐτόν Antipho 3.2.4; ἐντὸς ὅρων Ἡρακλείων Pl.*Ti.*25c. 2. metaph., ὅροι θεσπεσίας ὁδοῦ A.*Ag.*1154 (lyr.); θῆλυς ὅ. *the boundary* of a woman's mind, v. ἐπινέμω II. 3. II. *memorial stone* or *pillar*, Hdt.1.93: esp. b. *pillar* (whether inscribed or not, cf. Harp.) *set up on mortgaged property*, to serve as a bond or register of the debt, Sol.36; ὅπως..ὅροι τεθεῖεν Is.6.36: with gen. of the amount, τίθησιν ὅρους ἐπὶ μὲν τὴν οἰκίαν δισχιλίων (sc. δραχμῶν), ἐπὶ δὲ τὸ χωρίον ταλάντου D.31.1, cf. 25.69; δανείζειν τοὺς ἱερέας..ἐπὶ χωρίῳ..καὶ ὅρον ἐφιστάναι *IG*2$^2$.1183.29, cf. D. 41.6, Thphr.*Char.*10.9: specimens are *IG*12(7).412 (Amorgos), 2$^2$.2642, al. c. *boundary-stone* marking the limits of temple-lands, ὅ. τοῦ ἱεροῦ ib.1$^2$.858, cf. 860, 2$^2$.2597, al.; ὅρος· μὴ τοιχοδομεῖν ἐντὸς τῶν ὅρων ἰδιώτην ib.7.422 (Orop.), cf. 1785 (Thesp.), etc.; ὅ. κρήνης, λεσχέων δημοσίων, ὁδοῦ, etc., ib.1$^2$.874,888,877, etc.; similarly, ὅ. σήματος ib.903, al., 2$^2$.2568, al.; ὅ. μνημάτων ib.1$^2$.906; ὅ. μνήματος ib.2$^2$.2527, al.; ὅ. θήκης ib.2586, al. III. *standard, measure*, ἣν δ' ἄγαν δοκῶ χρονίζειν.. Answ. τοῦδ' ὅ. τίς ἐστί μοι; E.*IT*1219; ὅροι τῶν ἀγαθῶν καὶ κανόνες D.18.296; *rule, canon*, εἷς ὅρος, μία βροτοῖσίν ἐστιν εὐτυχίας ὁδός B.*Fr.*7; ὅρον πολιτείας ὀλιγαρχικῆς ταξάμενοι πλῆθος χρημάτων Pl.*R.*551a; ἀριστοκρατίας ὅρος ἀρετή, ὀλιγαρχίας πλοῦτος Arist.*Pol.*1294$^a$10; ὁμολογίᾳ θέμενοι ὅρον, εἰς τοῦτο ἀποβλέποντες καὶ ἀναφέροντες τὴν σκέψιν ποιώμεθα Pl.*Phdr.*237d: hence, *end, aim*, ἕν' ὅ. θέμενος παντὶ τρόπῳ μ' ἀνελεῖν D.21.105. IV. in Logic, *term* of a proposition (whether subject or predicate), Arist.*APr.*24$^b$16, *Cael.*282$^a$1, al.; ὅ. μέσος the middle *term*, Id.*EN*1142$^b$24, cf. *APr.*25$^b$33 sq.: hence, b. *definition*, ἔστι ὅ. λόγος ὁ τὸ τί ἦν εἶναι σημαίνων Id.*Top.*101$^b$39, cf. 139$^a$24, al.; defined as ἡ τοῦ ἰδίου ἀπόδοσις Chrysipp.*Stoic.*2.75: in pl., title of pseudo-Platonic work. c. *premiss* of a syllogism, ὅ. κατηγορικοί, στερητικοί, Arist.*APr.*29$^a$21, cf. 31$^b$33, al. 2. Math., *term* of a ratio or proportion, Archyt.2, Arist.*EN*1131$^b$5 sqq., Euc.5*Def.*8, Nicom.*Ar.*1.8. 3. pl., *terms, conditions*, συνθέσθαι πρός τινα ἐπὶ ὅροις, ὥστε..*CPR*19.8 (iv A.D.). 4. Astrol., οἱ τρεῖς ὅ. the three *terms*, used in various calculations, Vett. Val.304.1, al. (Spir. lenis in some dialects which have not lost spir. asper is inferred from absence of a sign for *h* in Corc. ὀρϝος, Arg. ὦρος, Heracl. ὅρος, cf. ἄντορος.)

**Ὀροσάγγαι**, οἱ, Persian word for *the Benefactors of the King*, Hdt. 8.85; *bodyguard*, S.*Fr.*183, cf. 634; ὀρσάγγης in Hsch.

**ὀρόσπιζος**, ὁ, *bluethroat, Cyanecula suecica*, Arist.*HA*592$^b$25.

⊛ **ὀροτύπος** [ῠ], ον, *dashing down a mountain*, ὕδωρ A.*Th.*85 (lyr.).

**ὀρούα**, v. ὀρύα.

**ὀρούματα**· ὁρμήματα, πηδήματα, Hsch.

**ὄρουσις**, εως, ἡ, (ὀρούω) = ὅρμησις, ὁρμή, defined as φορὰ διανοίας ἐπί τι μέλλον, *Stoic.*3.40; prob. cj. in Ph.1.602 for ἔρυσιν.

**ὀρούω**, Pi.*P.*10.61, Democr.228: impf. ὤρουον E.*HF*972: fut. ὀρούσω *h.Ap.*417: aor. ὤρουσα Pi.*O.*9.102, A.*Eu.*113; Ep. ὄρουσα Il. 2.310, Hes.*Sc.*437, part. ὀρούσας Il.11.359, E.*IT*297: (cf. ὄρνυμι):—*dart, rush forward*, Hom., both of men and things (v. infr.): Hom. always joins it with words expressing motion to a place, ἐς δίφρον ὀρούσας Il.11.359; ἐς βυσσὸν ὄρουσεν 24.80; πρός ῥα πλατάνιστον ὄ. 2.310; ἐπ' ἀλλήλοισιν ὄρουσαν 14.401, Hes.*Sc.*412,436, cf. Theoc.6. 13; or motion from a place, αἰχμὴ ἀπὸ χειρὸς ὄρουσεν Il.13.505, al., cf. Hes.*Sc.*437; ἐκ μέσων ἀρκυστάτων ὤρουσεν A.*Eu.*113; ἐκ τάξεων ὤρουσε E.*Ph.*1237; μόσχους ὀρούσας ἐς μέσας Id.*IT*297; ὤρουον ἄλλος ἄλλοσε Id.*HF*972: c. acc. cogn., πήδημ' ὀρούσας A.*Ag.*826; simply, *move*, ὀ. βραδέως Archestr.*Fr.*24.3: metaph., ἀπότομον ὤρουσεν εἰς ἀνάγκαν S.*OT*877 (lyr.); ὡς ὀρούσῃ πρὸς δίκας ἀγῶνα Id.*El.*1441 (lyr.); πρὸς θάνατον ὀρούειν Philem.214. 2. c. gen. objecti, *rush at, strive after*, Pi.*P.*10.61. 3. c. inf., *to be eager* to do, Id.*O.*9.102. 4. generally, *rise, tower*, ἐκ..κεφαλῆς δίδυμον κέρας ἰθὺς ὀρούει Opp.*C.*3. 474.—Poet. Verb, Ep., Lyr., and Trag., once in Ar. (*Fr.*523, in prov., πέρδιξ ὄρουσον '*look sharp*') and once in Philem. l. c.

**ὀροφή**, ἡ, (ἐρέφω) *roof of a house*, or *ceiling of a room*, Od.22.298, *IG*1$^2$.373.246, Hdt.2.148, Pherecr.121, Ar.*Nu.*173, etc.: pleon., καταστέγασμα τῆς ὀ. Hdt.2.155; διελεῖν τὴν ὀ. take off the *tiling*, Th. 4.48; cf. κέραμος II. 2: pl., *woodwork of the roof*, Thphr.*HP*5.3.7. 2. *top* of a beehive, Arist.*HA*624$^a$6. II. Syrian name of a plant, = κροκοδιλιάς, Aët.11.2.

**ὀροφη-φάγος** [ᾰ], ον, *roof-destroying*, πῦρ *AP*9.152 (Agath.). -**φόρος**, ον, *bearing a roof*, ib.631 (Id.); -φόρον· ζῷον πᾶν ὀστρακόδερμον, Hsch.

**ὀροφ-ιαῖος**, α, ον, *of* or *belonging to the* ὀροφή, λίθοι *IG*1$^2$.372. 85. -**ίας**, ου, ὁ, *living under a roof*, μῦς ὀ. the *common* mouse, opp. μ. ἀρουραῖος, Ar.*V.*206; ὀ. ὄφις a *tame house*-snake, Hsch. ⊛ -**ικός**, ή, όν, *of* or *for a roof*, Id. s. v. κουράς, etc. -**ῖνος**, η, ον, *roofed with reeds*, Aen.Tact.32.8; cf. ὀρ(ο)φίνη· καλάμη μελίνης, Hsch. -**ιος**, α, ον, = ὀροφικός, [λίθοι] *Supp.Epigr.*4.446.9 (Didyma, iii B.C.).

**ὀρο-φοιτάω**, = ὀρειφοιτέω, Lxx 4*Ma.*14.15 (v. l. -οῦντα, but perh. ὀροφοφοιτ- shd. be read), Hsch. -**φοίτης**, ου, ὁ, = ὀρειφοίτης, *EM* 461.27.

⊛ **ὄροφ-ος**, ὁ, (ἐρέφω) *reed used for thatching houses*, described as λαχνήεις, Il.24.451: distd. fr. κάλαμος, etc., Arist.*Fr.*268. II. = ὀροφή, *roof*, Orac.ap.Hdt.7.140, A.*Supp.*650 (lyr.), Ar.*Lys.*229, Th. 1.134, Pl.*R.*417a, etc.: pl., ὀρόφους Φοίβου, i.e. his *temple*, E.*Ion*89 (anap.). 2. *cover* of a wagon, Paus.1.19.1. -**όω**, *cover with a roof*, *IG*11(2).199*A* 104 (Delos, iii B.C.), Lxx 3*Ki.*7.7: pf. part. ὠροφωκώς Ph.Byz.*Mir.*1.1; *form into a roof*, τοὺς θυρεοὺς ὑπὲρ τῶν σωμάτων J.*BJ*6.1.3:—Pass., *to be roofed*, δοκοῖς Plu.2.210e; φατνώμασι J.*BJ*5.5.2.

⊛ **ὀροφῠλάκ-έω**, *to be a frontier guard*, *BCH*32.499 (Aphrodisias?). -**ικός**, ή, όν, *of* or *for a frontier-guard*, τέλος *SIG*633.93 (Milet., ii B.C.).

**ὀροφύλαξ** [ῠ], ακος, ὁ, *curator of boundary-stones*, *GDI*5653*A* 15 (Chios, v B.C., prob. in Ion. form οὐρο-). 2. *frontier guard*, *PSI* 4.406.12 (iii B.C.), *SIG*633.89 (Milet., ii B.C.). II. *preserving limits*, τινων Procl.*in Ti.*3.184D.

**ὀροφύλαξ** [ῠ], ακος, ὁ, *mountain-guard*, *JHS*8.236 (Asia Minor), *Papers of Amer. Sch. at Athens* 2 No.156 (ibid.), prob. in *MAMA*1. 123; cf. ὀρεοφύλαξ.

**ὀρόφ-ωμα**, ατος, τό, *roof, ceiling*, Callix.1, Lxx *Ez.*41.26, al., D.S. 2.10, Anon.Vat.10. -**ωσις**, εως, ἡ, *roofing, ceiling*, *IG*11(2).199*A* 106 (Delos, iii B.C.), 11(4).1246 (ibid.). -**ωτός**, ή, όν, *roofed* or *ceiled*, Eust.892.33.

**ὀρόω**, v. ὁράω. **Ὄρπα**· Ἐρινύς, Hsch. (Cf. Ὄριψα.) **ὅρπαξ**· θρασὺς ἄνεμος, Id. (prob. Aeol. for ἅρπαξ). **ὅρπας**· τῆς ἀκρίδος ὁ γόνος (i.e. young locusts, 'hoppers'), ἔνθεν γάρον ποιοῦσιν, Id.

**ὄρπετον**, τό, Aeol. for ἑρπετόν, Sapph.40, Theoc.29.13. (Cf. ἄρπετον.)

**ὅρπη**· σίδηρος, ἐν ᾧ τὸν ἐλέφαντα τύπτουσιν, Hsch. (Perh. cf. ἅρπη II. 2.)

⊛ **ὄρπηξ**, Att. **ὅρπηξ**, ηκος, Aeol. and Dor. **ὅρπαξ**, ακος, ὁ, *sapling, young shoot*, Il.21.38, Pi.*Parth.*2.7, A.R.4.1425, Theoc.7.146, Call. *Iamb.*1.215, *Ap.*1; ὅρπακι βραδίνῳ Sapph.104, cf. 78. 2. anything made of such shoots or trees, *goad* for driving cattle, Hes.*Op.* 468; *lance*, E.*Hipp.*221 (anap.). II. metaph., *scion, descendant*, Orph.*A.*215. [Acc. ὅρπᾰκα is f.l. in *AP*7.200.]

**ὀρρέξας**· θραύσας, ἀνελόμενος, Hsch.

**ὀρρεοπραιποσιτία**, ἡ, *office of the horreorum praepositi*, *IG*7.24.7 (Megara, v A.D.).

**ὀρριδιᾶν**· τὸ ἐπὶ τὰ ἰσχία καὶ τοὺς γλουτοὺς πεσεῖν, Hsch. **ὄρριον**· ὀρίγανον, Id.

**ὄρριον**, τό, *granary*, Lat. *horreum*, *IG*7.24.11 (Megara, v A.D., pl.): written ὅρια (pl.) *Supp.Epigr.*4.106 (Rome, ii A.D.).

**ὀρρόβηλος**· ὀδός, Ἰταλιῶται, Hsch. (Leg. ὀδός 'threshold', cf. οὐδός as gloss on βηλός and βατήρ, Id., *AB*224.)

**ὀρρό-μελι**, ιτος, τό, *whey and honey*, *Gp.*12.22.1 (v.l. οἰνό-). -**ποτέω**, v. ὀροποτέω. -**ποτίη**, ἡ, v. ὀροποτίη.

**ὀρροπύγιον** [ῠ], Ion. **ὀρσοπύγιον** *GDI*5702.35 (Samos, iv B.C.), τό: (ὄρρος):—*rump* of birds, in which the tail-feathers are set, Arist. *HA*504$^a$32, 618$^b$33, al. (with vv. ll. οὐροπ-, ὀροπ-, cf. τουροπ- in Phld. *Rh.*2.189S., but ὀρροπ- is certain in *IG*2$^2$.1498.27 (Athens, iv B.C.)); of the sepia, Arist.*HA*525$^a$12: generally, *tail, rump* of any animal, Ar.*V.*1075, *Nu.*162.

**ὀρροπυγόστικτος**, ον, *having a spotted tail*, Arist.*Fr.*298.

**ὀρρός**, ὁ, v. ὀρός.

**ὄρρος**, ὁ, *end of the os sacrum* (cf. ὀρροπύγιον), Gal.19.127, Sch.Ar. *Pl.*122, Moer.p.284P., Ath.13.565f; but Ammon.(*Diff.*p.27) identifies it with ταῦρος III, cf. Poll.2.173; = τράμις, Ruf.*Onom.*101. 2. generally, *rump*, Ar.*Ra.*222, *Pax*1239, *Lys.*964, etc. (The orig. form was prob. ὄρσος (contained in Ion. ὀρσοπύγιον, v. ὀρροπ-, and perh. in ὀρσοθύρη), cf. OE. *ears*, OHG. *ars*, etc.: akin also to οὐρά.)

⊛ **ὀρρωδ-έω**, Ion. **ἀρρ-**, *dread, shrink from*, c. acc., Hdt.5.35, al., E. *El.*831, Ar.*Eq.*126, 541, al.; τήν τινος μανίαν Pl.*Smp.*213d: c. gen. rei, *fear for* or *because of* a thing, Hdt.1.111; so ὑπέρ τινος Lys.28.7; περί τινος And.2.7; περὶ τῷ ἐμαυτοῦ σώματι Th.6.9; ἀμφὶ θανάτου Aret.*SA*2.2: folld. by a Relat. clause, ἀ. ὅτι.. Hdt.8.70: more freq. ἀ. or ὀ. μή.., Id.1.9,156, Antipho 3.3.4, Pl.*Euthphr.*3a, etc.; ὅπως μὴ .. Hp.*Mul.*1.70: also c. inf., ὀ. θανεῖν E.*Hec.*768; αὐτὸς ὀ. παθεῖν Id. *Fr.*130: abs., Hdt.3.1, 5.98. -**έως**, Adv., = ἐμφόβως, Hsch.

**ὀρρώδης**, ες, (ὄρρος) *pertaining to the rump*, Hp.*Acut.*(*Sp.*)37, cf. Gal.19.127. II. false spelling of ὀρώδης II (q. v.).

**ὀρρωδία**, Ion. **ἀρρωδίη**, ἡ, *terror*, Hdt.7.173, E.*Ph.*1389, etc.; τοὺς Ἕλληνας εἶχε δέος τε καὶ ἀ. Hdt.8.70; ἐν ὀ. ἔχειν τι Th.2.89; ἐστὶ ἀ. τινὶ περί τινος Hdt.9.101; ἐς πᾶσαν ἀ. ἀπίκατο, μὴ.. Id.4.140; ὀ. μοι μή τι βουλεύσῃς κακόν E.*Med.*317.

**ὀρσάγγης**, = ὀροσάγγης, Hsch. **ὄρσ-ας, -ασκε, -εο, -ευ**, v. ὄρνυμι.

**ὀρσί-ᾰλος** [ῐ], ον, *stirring the sea*, of Poseidon, B.15.19. -**βάκχας**, acc. -αν, *inspiring Bacchants*, Διόνυσος Id.18.49. -**γύναικα** [ῠ], τόν, acc. sg., *one who excites women*, Διόνυσον *Lyr.Adesp.*131.—No nom. is found. -**κτῠπος**, ον, *stirring* or *making noise*, ὀ. Ζεύς the *rouser of thunder*, Pi.*O.*10(11).81. -**νεφής**, ές, *cloud-raising*, Id. *N.*5.34. -**πέτης**· ὑψοῦ πετόμενος, Hsch. -**πους**, ποδος, ὁ, ἡ, *raising the foot, swift-footed*, ἔλαφοι *AP*15.27 (Simm.); ὀ. βοή *stirring the feet to flight*, *Trag.Adesp.*245.

**ὀρσίτης**, ου, ὁ, a Cretan dance, Ath.14.629c.

**ὄρσο**, v. ὄρνυμι.

⊛ **ὀρσοδάκνη**, ἡ, *an insect which eats the buds of plants*, perh. *Haltica oleracea*, Arist.*HA*552$^a$30. (The word ὀρσός, *bud*, is not found.)

**ὀρσό-θριξ**, ὁ, ἡ, gen. τριχος, *raising the hair* (cf. ὀρθόθριξ), Theognost.*Can.*97. **-θύρη** [ῠ], ἡ, prob. *a door high up in the wall*, Od. 22.126,333; ἀν' ὀρσοθύρην ἀναβαίη ib.132: sens. obsc., τῆς ὄπισθεν ὀ. Semon.17 [where υ appears to be long]. (θύρα ἐν ὕψει τοῦ τοίχου, Phot., Suid., cf. the second explanation in Hsch.: a form ὀρσορόκα (acc. sg.) given by Apollod.ap.*EM*633.57 sqq. is apptly. corrupt:—ὀρσοθύρη was derived in antiquity from ὀρούω, *EM* l.c., etc.: the true etym. is uncertain, but cf. ὄρρος, ὀρρόβηλος.) **-θώραξ**, sine expl., Theognost.*Can.*97.

**ὀρσολοπ-εύω** or **-έω**, *irritate, provoke*, c. acc., ἤ με βοῶν ἕνεχ' ὧδε χολούμενος ὀρσολοπεύεις; *h.Merc.*308; ὀρσολοπεύει μύθῳ ὀνειδείῳ Max. 107:—Pass., ὀρσολοπεῖται θυμός my heart *is troubled*, A.*Pers.*10 (anap.). ⊛ **-ος**, ον, perh. *eager for the fray, tempestuous*, epith. of Ares, Anacr.70.

**ὀρσός**, Lacon. for ὀρθός, Ar.*Lys.*995. II. ὀρσοί· τῶν ἀρνῶν οἱ ἔσχατοι γενόμενοι, Hsch. (Cf. ἔρση II.)

**ὀρσότης**, ητος, ἡ, = ὁρμή, Critias 41 D.

**ὀρσοτρίαινᾰ** [ῐ], gen. ᾱ, acc. ᾱν, Dor. for **-τριαίνης**, ου, ην, *wielder of the trident*, Pi.*O.*8.48, *P.*2.12, *N.*4.86, *Pae.*9.47.

**ὀρσύδρα**, ἡ, (ὄρνυμι, ὕδωρ) *water-pipe*, Eust.1921.15.

**ὄρσω**, v. ὄρνυμι. **ὀρτάζω**, Ion. for ἑορτάζω.

**ὀρτᾰλ-ίζω**, only in compd. ἀνορταλίζω. **-ίς**, ίδος, ἡ, *fowl*, Nic. *Al.*294. **-ῐχεύς**, έως, ὁ, = sq., ib.228. **-ῐχος**, ὁ, Dim. of ὀρταλίς, *chick*, Theoc.13.12; Boeot. for ἀλεκτρυών, acc. to Stratt.47. 4, cf. Ar.*Ach.*871 et Sch. 2. generally, *young bird*, A.*Ag.*54 (anap.); ὄρνιθες δροσερῶν μητέρες ὀρταλίχων *AP*5.291 (Agath.); ὁ. χελιδόσι Opp.*H.*5.579; *young animal*, S.*Fr.*793 (anap.).

**ὀρτή**, ἡ, Ion. for ἑορτή. **ὀρτός**· βωμός (Cypr.), Hsch.

**Ὀρτῠγία**, Ion. **-ίη**, ἡ, (ὄρτυξ) *Quail-island*, the ancient name of Delos or Rhenaea, Str.10.5.5; also of other places in Greece; in one of these Artemis killed Orion, Od.5.123: hence she is called Ὀρτυγία, S.*Tr.*213 (lyr.). II. part of the city of Syracuse, otherwise called Νᾶσος, the Island, Str.6.2.4.

**ὀρτύγιον** [ῠ], τό, Dim. of ὄρτυξ, Eup.214; ὀρτυγίου ψυχὴν ἔχων Antiph.5.

**ὀρτῠγο-θήρας**, ου, ὁ, *quail-catcher*, Pl.*Euthd.*290d. **-κόμος**, ὁ, *keeper of quails*, Ar.*Fr.*242. **-κομπος**, read by Dionys.Zop. in Ar. *Av.*1299 (Sch. ad 1297).

**ὀρτῠγοκοπ-έω**, *play at* ὀρτυγοκοπία, Plu.2.34d, Poll.9.107. **-ία**, ἡ, *the game of quail-striking*, ibid. **-ικός**, ή, όν, *skilled in the game*, ib.108. ⊛ **-ος**, ον, = foreg., Pl.Com.108, cf. Sch.Ar.*Av.*1297.

**ὀρτῠγο-μᾰνία**, ἡ, *madness after quails*, Chrysipp.*Stoic.*3.167. **-μήτρα**, ἡ, *a bird which migrates with quails*, perh. *corncrake, landrail, Rallus crex*, Cratin.246, Arist.*HA*597ᵇ16, Alex.Mynd.ap.Ath. 9.393a, Lxx *Ex.*16.13, *Nu.*11.31; ludicrously applied to Latona, *the Ortygian mother* (cf. Ὀρτυγία I), Ar.*Av.*870. **-πώλης**, ου, ὁ, *dealer in quails*, Poll.7.136. **-τροφεῖον**, τό, *quail-coop*, Arist.*Pr.* 892ᵃ11. **-τροφέω**, *feed* or *keep quails*, M.Ant.1.6. **-τρόφος**, ὁ, *keeper of quails*, Pl.*Euthd.*290d.

⊛ **ὄρτυξ**, ῠγος, ὁ (also ἡ, Lyc.401: gen. ῠκος Philem.245), *quail, Coturnix vulgaris*, Epich.45, Hdt.2.77, Pl.*Ly.*211e, Ar.*Av.*707,1298, etc.; for its migratory habits, v. Arist.*HA*597ᵃ23,ᵇ5. II. = στελεφοῦρος, Thphr.*HP*7.11.2. (γόρτυξ (i.e. ϝόρτυξ)· ὄρτυξ, Hsch.; cf. Skt. *vártikā, vartakas.*)

**ὀρτῶς**, barbarism for ὀρθῶς, Ar.*Th.*1215.

**ὀρυά**, ἡ, a quarrying tool, perh. *pickaxe*, *PCair.Zen.*759 (iii B.C.).

**ὀρύα**, ἡ, = χορδή, *sausage*, name of a play of Epicharmus, p.110 K.: v.l. ὀρούα in Hsch.: ὄρῦα Aristarch.(?)ap.Hdn.Gr.1.303 (s.v.l.):—hence prob. **ὀρυαῖον**, τό, *POxy.*1742.9 (iv A.D.).

**ὀρυγάνει**· ἐρεύγεται, Hsch. (post ὀρτός); cf. ὀρμαίνω II. 1.

**ὀρυγεύς**, *fossorium, Gloss.*

⊛ **ὀρῠγή**, ἡ, = ὀρυχή, D.H.4.59, Dsc.4.162, Tz.*H.*1.915. 2. pl., *steps*, Cyran.5.

**ὀρύγιον** [ῠ], τό, Dim. of ὄρυξ I, Hsch. s.v. σκαπάνη.

**ὄρυγμα**, ατος, τό, (ὀρύσσω) *excavation, trench, ditch, moat*, Hdt.1. 179, 7.23, Th.1.106, *OGI*483.148 (Pergam., ii A.D.), etc.; *tunnel, mine*, Hdt.3.60; ὀρύσσειν ὀ. ὑπόγαια Id.4.200; *mine*, in sieges, X.*HG*3.1.7, Plb.5.100.2, etc.; also in metal-working, Id.34.10.11; at Athens, = βάραθρον, *pit* into which condemned criminals were thrown, ὁ ἐπὶ τῷ ὀ. the executioner, Din.1.62, cf. Lycurg.121, Poll.8.71. II. = ὄρυξις, Luc.*VH*2.1. (Written **ὄρυμα** *Annuario* 10/12.20 (Crete, iii/ ii B.C.).)

**ὀρυγμάδες**· θόρυβοι, Hsch.

**ὀρυγμίη**, ἡ, v.l. for ὀρεγμίη, Aret.*SD*1.5.

**ὀρυγμός**, ὁ, = ὄρυγμα, *Inscr.Prien.*363.18 (iv B.C.). II. ὄρυγμος· βρυχόμενος, Hsch.

**ὄρυγξ**, v. ὄρυξ.

**ὄρυζ-α**, ἡ, *rice, Oryza sativa*, both the plant and the grain, Str.15.1. 13, Aristobul.ib.18, Dsc.2.95; ὀ. ἑφθή, the food of the Indians, Megasth.28; οἶνος ἐξ ὀρύζης Ael.*NA*13.8:—also **ὄρυζον**, τό, Thphr. *HP*4.4.10. (v. ὀρίνδης.) **-ιον**, τό, Dim. of ὄρυζα, Sch.D.T.p.195 H. **-ίτης** [ῑ] πλακοῦς, ὁ, *rice-cake*, Chrysipp.Tyan.ap.Ath.14.647d.

⊛ **ὀρυζοτροφέω**, *grow rice*, Str.17.3.23.

**ὀρυκ-τέον**, (ὀρύσσω) *one must dig*, Ph.*Bel.*91.19, Ruf.*Fr.*66. **-τή**, ἡ, = ὄρυγμα, Ph.1.626. ⊛ **-τήρ**, ῆρος, ὁ, *miner*, Zeno *Stoic.*1.30 (pl.). ⊛ **-της**, ου, ὁ, *digger*, Aesop.99. II. *ploughshare* (cf. ὄρυξ I) or *implement for digging*, Str.7.4.6, 15.1.18. **-τικός**, ή, όν, *fit for digging* or *mining*, ἐργαλεῖον Suid. s.v. ἄμη (cj. Salm. for τεκτονικόν). ⊛ **-τός**, ή, όν, *dug, formed by digging*, τάφρον ὑπερθορέονται ὀρυκτήν Il.8.179, al., cf. X.*An.*1.7.14; opp. a natural channel, στόματα, opp. ἰθαγενέα, Hdt.2.17; λίμνη ib.149; τάφος E.*Tr.*1153; εἴσοδοι X.*An.*4.5.25; ἀποθῆκαι ὀ. ὑπόγειοι Plu.2.770e. II. *dug out, quarried*, of stone or metal, τὰ ὀ., opp. τὰ μεταλλευτά, Arist.*Mete.*378ᵃ20; ὀ. χρυσός Plb.34.10.10; ἅλες Gal.11.694; ἅλς Dsc.5.109; ἰχθῦς ὀ. fish *taken by digging* in sand, such as sand-eels, Arist.*Mir.*835ᵇ16, Thphr. *Fr.*171.7, cf. Ath.8.331c, Archestr.*Fr.*22. **-τρίς**, ίδος, fem. of ὀρυκτήρ, χελώνη Ath.Mech.19.3, Tz.*H.*11.609.

**ὄρυμα**, v. ὄρυγμα.

**ὀρῡμαγδός**, ὁ, *loud noise, din*, as of a throng of men fighting, working, or running about, freq. in Hom. (esp. in Il., 17.424, al.), cf. Hes. *Sc.*232,401; also of men and dogs, Il.10.185; of horses and men, 17. 741: not used of voices, but only of inarticulate sounds: hence also δρυτόμων ὀ. *the sound* of wood-cutters, 16.633; ὀρυμαγδὸν ἔθηκε, of the *rattling* made by throwing a load of wood on the ground, Od. 9.235, cf. Il.21.313; of the *roar* of a raging river, ῥέων μεγάλῳ ὀρυμαγδῷ ib.256; of the sea, Simon.51; of oars, A.R.4.105.

**ὄρυμος**· βωμός, οἱ δὲ **ὄρυμβος**, Hsch. **ὀρυνθεῖ**· γρυλλίζει, Id.

**ὄρυξ**, ῠγος, ὁ (**ὄρυγξ** Hsch.), *pickaxe* or *any sharp iron tool for digging*, *AP*6.297 (Phan.). II. a kind of *gazelle* or *antelope*, in Egypt and Libya, so called from its *pointed horns, beisa, Oryx leucoryx*, described as μονόκερως, Arist.*HA*499ᵇ20, *PA*663ᵃ23, cf. Callix. 2, Lxx *De.*14.5, Ph.2.353, Plu.2.974f, Opp.*C.*2.446, 4.34, Ael.*NA*7. 8. 2. ὀ. τετράκερως Indian four-horned *antelope, Tetraceros quadricornis*, ib.15.14; also an Indian *gazelle*, ib.13.25. III. a great fish, perh. *narwhal, Monodon monoceros*, or a kind of whale, Str.3.2.7.

**ὄρυξις**, εως, ἡ, *rootling*, Arist.*PA*693ᵃ16; *digging*, τοῦ μετάλλου *IG*4²(1).109 iii 43 (Epid., iii B.C.); τάφρων Plu.*Pomp.*66 (pl.).

**ὀρύομαι**, prob. f.l. for ὠρύομαι, Hsch.

⊛ **ὄρυς**, υος, ὁ, a wild animal in Libya, prob. = ὄρυξ II. 1, Hdt.4.192.

⊛ **ὀρύσσω**, Od.10.305, Att. **-ττω** (late pres. imper. ὄρυγε *IG*12(5).519 (Seriphos)): fut. ὀρύξω Il.7.341: aor. ὤρυξα, Ep. ὄρυξα as always in Hom., Od.11.25, al.: pf. ὀρώρῠχα (κατ-) Pherecr.145.19: plpf. ὀρωρύχειν App.*BC*4.107:—Med., aor. ὠρυξάμην Hdt.1.186, A.R.3.1032, etc.:—Pass., fut. ὀρυχθήσομαι (κατ-) Antipho 3.2.10, also ὀρῠχήσομαι (κατ-) Ar.*Av.*394 (Elmsl.) and ὀρωρύξομαι Suid. s.v. ὤρυσσον (prob.): aor. ὠρύχθην Hdt.1.186, etc.: pf. ὀρώρυγμαι Id.2.158, etc.; in compds., ὥρυγμαι (κατ- Antipho 3.3.12 codd., ὑποκατ- Sophr.3, δι- Luc.*Tim.* 53, etc.): plpf. ὀρωρύγμην Hdt.1.186, Pl.*Criti.*118c, also ὠρωρύγμην (δι-) X.*An.*7.8.14.—An aor. 2 Act. ὤρῠγον occurs in Philostr.*VA*1. 25: Pass. ὠρύγην *OGI*672.7, 673.6 (Egypt, i A.D.), (δι-) Hld.9.7, *Gp.*4. 3.2, (κατ-) f.l. in X.*An.*5.8.11:—*dig*, ὀρύξομεν ἐγγύθι τάφρον Il.7.341; βόθρον ὄρυξα Od.11.25; ἔλυτρον Hdt.1.186; ὀρύγματα Id.4.200; ταῖς ὁπλαῖς εὐνάς Ar.*Eq.*605; ὑπόνομον ἐκ τῆς πόλεως Th.2.76: abs., ὤρυσσον ὑπὸ μαστίγων Hdt.7.22; ἐὰν ὀρύξῃ τις παρὰ τὴν θάλασσαν Arist.*Pr.* 933ᵇ33:—Med., δεξαμενὰς ὀρύξασθαι Hdt.3.9:—Pass., ὀρώρυκται (sc. ἡ διῶρυξ) Id.2.158; τὸ ὀρυχθέν, = τὸ ὄρυγμα, the *trench*, Id.1.186. II. *dig up*, [μῶλυ] Od.10.305; κυκλάμινον Theoc.5.123: Med., λίθους ὠρύξατο *had* stones *dug* or *quarried*, Hdt.1.186:—Pass., ὁ ὀρυσσόμενος χοῦς the soil *that was dug up*, ib.185; ὑπὸ μεταλλείας ὀρύττεσθαι Pl.*Criti.* 114e. III. *dig through*, i.e. *make a canal through* (like διορύσσειν), τὸν ἰσθμὸν ὀ. Orac.ap.Hdt.1.174; τὸ χωρίον ὀρώρυκτο Id.1.186; of moles, *burrow*, either abs., as Arist.*HA*606ᵃ2; or γῆν ὀ., Id.*Mir.*842ᵇ 4. IV. *bury*, ἔγχος.. γαίας ὀρύξας ἔνθα μή τις ὄψεται (where γαίας depends on ἔνθα) S.*Aj.*659, cf. X.*Oec.*19.2. V. of a wrestler, *dig into, gouge* a tender part, τὠφθαλμὼ Ar.*Av.*442, cf. *Pax* 899, Philostr. *VA*8.25; *gouge out*, ὀφθαλμὸν ὤρυττέν τις ὥσπερ ἰχθύος Antiph.119.

**ὀρῠχή**, ἡ, = ὄρυξις, *Inscr.Délos* 365.32 (iii B.C.), *SIG*799 ii 2 (Cyzicus, i A.D.), Luc.*Ner.*1. 2. apptly., = *snout* of a pig, Plu.2.670a (s.v.l.).

**ὀρύχω** [ῠ], = ὀρύσσω, Arat.1086.

**ὀρφᾰκίνης** [ῑ], ου, ὁ, *a young* ὀρφώς, Dorio ap.Ath.7.315b.

**ὀρφᾰν-εία**, ἡ, = ὀρφανία, *UPZ*9.11 (ii B.C.), *PFay.*94.5 (iii A.D.). **-ευμα**, ατος, τό, *orphan state, orphanhood*, E.*HF*546. **-εύω**, *take care of, rear orphans*, τέκνα, παῖδας, Id.*Alc.*165, 297:—Pass., c. fut. Med., *to be an orphan*, ib.535, *Hipp.*847, *Supp.*1132. **-ία**, ἡ, *orphanhood*, Lys.26.12, Pl.*Lg.*926e, al.: in pl., Id.*Cri.*45d. II. *bereavement, want of*.., στεφάνων Pi.*I.*8(7).7. **-ίζω**, *make orphan, make destitute*, πρὸς παίδων, οὓς ὀρφανιεῖς E.*Alc.*276 (anap.); ἀμὸν βίον ὠρφάνισσε (prob. cj., -ισε codd.) ib.397: c. gen., *rob, bereave of* a thing, τινὰ ὕπνου, ζωᾶς, Theoc.*Ep.*5.6, *AP*7.483; βιότου *IG*12(8).441. 8 (Thasos); ὀ. κακὰν γλῶσσαν ὀπὸς *rob* Slander of her voice, Pi.*P.* 4.283:—Pass., *to be bereaved*, τῶν φίλων Gorg.*Hel.*7; ἐκ δυοῖν.. ὠρφανισμένος βίον (βίου codd.) S.*Tr.*942: abs., *to be left in orphanhood*, Pi. *P.*6.22. II. *sweep away*, Ἅιδης.. ἐλπίδας ὠρφάνισεν Epigr.Gr.233. 10 (Chios). **-ῐκός**, ή, όν, *orphaned, fatherless*, παῖς Il.6.432, 11. 394; ἦμαρ ὀ. the day *which makes one an orphan*, i.e. *orphanhood*, 22.490. II. *of* or *for orphans*, τύχη Pl.*Lg.*928a; συμβόλαια ib. 922a; ὀρφανικά, τά, *their property and interests*, Arist.*Pol.*1268ᵃ14, *OGI*266.8 (Pergam., iii B.C.); οἶκος ὀ. Arist.*Ath.*56.6. ⊛ **-ιος**, ον, = foreg., *desolate*, γῆρας *AP*7.466 (Leon.). ⊛ **-ιστής**, οῦ, ὁ, *tender of orphans, guardian*, S.*Aj.*512; -ταί, οἱ, officials at Selymbria, *BCH*36.549.

⊛ **ὀρφᾰνο-δῐκασταί**, in Cretan spelling ὀρπ-, *judges in the affairs of orphans*, *Leg.Gort.*12.23. ⊛ **-ομαι**, Pass., c. gen., *to be destitute of*, ἀκμῆς *AP*6.101 (Phil.). **-πάτωρ** [πᾰ], ορος, ὁ, *father of orphans*, of God, *PMasp.*151.254 (vi A.D.).

**ὀρφᾰνός**, ή, όν, also ός, όν E.*Hec.*149 (anap.):—*orphan, without parents, fatherless*, αἱ δ' ἐλίποντο ὀρφαναὶ Od.20.68; ὀ. τέκνα Hes.*Op.* 330; παῖδά τ' ὀ. λιπεῖν S.*Aj.*653: as Subst., *orphan*, ἐπίκληροι καὶ ὀ. Lys.26.12; ὀρφανοῖς καὶ ὀρφαναῖς Pl.*Lg.*926c; ὀρφανῶν κάκωσις Arist.

*Ath.*56.6, cf. *IG*1².6.124: also in neut., εἰς ὀρφανὰ καὶ ἔρημα ὑβρίζειν Pl.*Lg.*927c; of animals, ὄρνις Ar.*Av.*1361; ὀ. οἶκος, δόμος, S.*Fr.*943, E.*Alc.*657: metaph., *neglected*, ἡ δέλτος ὀρφανὴ κεῖται Herod.3.15; ὀρφανὰ κεῖται σκῦλα Epigr.ap.Paus.1.13.3. II. c. gen., *bereaved* or *bereft of*, 1. of children, ὀ. πατρός *reft* of father, E.*El.*914, 1010; τοῦ πατρὸς ὀ. D.57.70; γονέων Plu.2.293d, etc. 2. of parents, πότμον ὀρφανὸν γενεᾶς childless, Pi.*O.*9.61; ὀ. παιδός, τέκνων, E.*Hec.*149 (anap.), *Fr.*332.6; νεοσσῶν ὀρφανὸν λέχος S.*Ant.*425. 3. generally, ὀ. ἑτάρων Pi.*I.*7(6).10, cf. Pl.*Lg.*730d; νύμφας ἔθηκεν ὀρφανὰς ξυναόρων E.*Or.*1136; ἐπιστήμης Pl.*Alc.*2.147a; κρατός Sosith.2.20; ὀρφανοὶ ὕβριος *free from* insolence, Pi.*I.*4(3).8(26); ψόφον.. Κασταλίας ὀρφανὸν ἀνδρῶν χορεύσιος Id.*Pae.*6.9; ὀ. μαχᾶν, = ἀπόμαχος, Tim.*Pers.*154; ὀρφανὴ βίου, i.e. *poor*, Herod.3.39; ὀ. ἀγκίστρου κάλαμος *AP* 12.42 (Diosc.): Com. metaph., ὀ. ταρίχιον salt-fish *without sauce*, Pherecr.22 (dub. l.). (A shorter form ὀρφο- appears in ὀρφο-βότης (q. v.), ὀρφόω, cf. Lat. *orbus*, Goth. *arbi* 'inheritance'.)

**ὀρφᾰνότης**, ητος, ἡ, *orphanhood*, *BCH*51.399 (Caesarea in Cappadocia).

**ὀρφᾰνοτροφ-εῖον**, τό, *orphanage*, *Cod.Just.*1.2.17.2 (pl.). **-έω**, *bring up orphans*, Sch.E.*Alc.*165. **-ος** (parox.), ον, *bringing up orphans*, Suid. s.v. Ἀκάκιος, *Cod.Just.*1.3.41.12, al.

⊛ **ὀρφᾰνοφύλαξ** [ῠ], ἄκος, ὁ, *one who guards orphans*; esp. at Athens, in pl., *guardians of orphans* who had lost their fathers in war, X. *Vect.*2.7; cf. ὀρφανοδικασταί.

**Ὀρφεῖος**, ὁ (sc. μήν), month at Mytilene(?), *Inscr.Magn.*52.38.

**Ὀρφεοτελεστής**, οῦ, ὁ, *one who initiates into the mysteries of Orpheus*: generally, *hierophant*, Thphr.*Char.*16.12, Phld.*Po.*2.41, Plu. 2.224e.

**ὀρφεύς**, έως, ὁ, = ὀρφός, ὀρφώς, Marc.Sid.33 (pl. ὀρφέες); with a pun on Orpheus, Alex.113.

**Ὀρφεύς**, έως, ὁ, Dor. Ὄρφης Ibyc.10A, Ὀρφήν Hdn.Gr.1.14:— *Orpheus*, Pi.*P.*4.177, Pl.*R.*364e, etc.:—Adj. **Ὀρφεῖος**, α, ον, E.*Alc.* 969(lyr.), Pl.*Lg.*829e; or **Ὀρφικός**, ή, όν, Hdt.2.81; ἐν τοῖς Ὀ. ἔπεσι καλουμένοις Arist.*de An.*410ᵇ28.

**ὄρφιος**, α, ον, *made of* ὀρφώς, ἴσικος Alex.Trall.7.8, 11.6.

**ὀρφίσκος**, ὁ, = κίχλη II, Pancrat.ap.Ath.7.305d.

**ὀρφν-αῖος**, α, ον, *dark*, *murky*, in Hom. always epith. of night, Il. 10.83, al., E.*Or.*1225, etc.; ὀρφναίη (sc. νύξ) A.R.2.670; φανέντος ὀρφναίου πυρός *in the darkness*, A.*Ag.*21. **-η**, Dor. **ὄρφνα**, ἡ, *the darkness* of night, *night*, first in Thgn.1077, and Pi., who has both ἐν ὄρφνᾳ and ἐν ὀρφναισιν, *O.*1.71, *P.*1.23; so δι' ὄρφνας E.*Supp.*994 (lyr., cj. Herm. for δι' ὀρφναίας); χθονὸς μέλαιναν ὄρφνην, of the nether world, Id. *HF*46; ἐνέρων ἐς ὄρφναν ib.353 (lyr.); οὔτε.. ἠοῦς, οὐκ ὄρφνης neither at morn, nor *by night*, *IG*14.2012 *Ca*4 (Rome):—rare in Prose, X. *Lac.*5.7, Ti.Locr.97c,d, Plb.18.19.7, Phint.ap.Stob.4.23.61ᵃ. ⊛ **-ήεις**, εσσα, εν, poet. for ὀρφνός, Q.S.3.657, Man.4.57. ⊛ **-ῖνος**, η, ον, = ὀρφνός, ὀ. χρῶμα a *brownish grey* colour, being mixed of black, red, and white (but with most black), Pl.*Ti.*68c, cf. Duris 31 J.; put by X. between πορφύρεος and φοινίκινος, *Cyr.*8.3.3:—the form **ὄρφνιος** occurs in Arist.*Col.*792ᵃ27, 794ᵇ5, Plu.2.565c, but is prob. corrupt. **-ίς**, ίδος, ἡ, (ὀρφνός) *a dark garment*, dub. l. in Hsch. s.v. ὄρφνινον. ⊛ **-ίτης** [ῑ], ου, ὁ, dub. epith. of τάλαρος, *AP*6.289 (Leon.). **-ός**, ή, όν, *dark*, *dusky*, Nic.*Th.*656: Comp. ὀρφνότερος Id.*Fr.*74.61. **-ώδης**, ες, = foreg., Hp.*Prog.*24, Adam.*Vent.*33; χολή Gal.17(2).129.

⊛ **ὀρφο-βότης**, ου, ὁ, = ὀρφανοτρόφος, and **-βοτία**, ἡ, *the care or education of orphans*, Hsch., who also cites ὤρφωσεν (fr. **ὀρφόω**) for ὠρφάνισεν.

⊛ **ὀρφώς** or **ὀρφῶς** (v. infr.), *great sea-perch*, *Epinephelus gigas*, still called ὀρφός in Greece, Ar.*V.*493, Pl.Com.56, 173.13, Cratin.147, Amips.8, Arist.*HA*543ᵇ1, 591ᵃ11, Numen.ap.Ath.7.315b, cf. 295b, Olymp. *in Grg.*p.360 J.; *orphus rubens*, Plin.*HN*32.152. (Nom. sg. -φώς Arist.*HA*543ᵇ1 (-φός 591ᵃ11): Hdn.Gr.1.224 has ὄρφος κοινῶς, ὀρφῶς δὲ Ἀττικῶς, cf. Hsch.; but Ath.7.315b states that nom. Att. is ὀρφώς, citing Archipp.17; gen. sg. ὀρφῶ Cratin. l. c., acc. -φῶν Pl. Com.173.13, dat. pl. -φῶσι Id.56, Amips. l. c., acc. pl. -φῶς Ar. l. c.)

**ὀρχάμη** [ᾰ], ἡ, *an uncultivated copse*, v. l. in Poll.7.147.

⊛ **ὄρχᾰμος**, ὁ, *leader*, *chief*, early Ep. only in the phrases ὄρχαμος ἀνδρῶν Il.2.837, al., Hes.*Fr.*96.12, ὄρχαμε λαῶν Il.14.102, al.; the former applied to the swineherd Eumaeus, Od.14.22, 121, and the cowherd Philoetius, 20.185, 254.—Ep. word, used once by A., ὀ. στρατοῦ *Pers.*129 (lyr.); ὄρχαμε τ[όξου?] *IG*1².516: in late Poetry without a gen., *AP*11.284 (Pall.).

**ὀρχάς** (A), άδος, fem. Adj. *enclosing*, στέγη S.*Fr.*812; ὀρχάς· περίβολος, αἱμασιά, Hsch.

**ὀρχάς** (B), άδος, ἡ, (ὄρχις) a kind of *olive*, so called from its shape, Nic.*Al.*87, Virg.*G.*2.86; cf. ὄρχις III.

**ὄρχᾰτος**, ὁ, = ὄρχος, *row of trees*, πολλοὶ δὲ φυτῶν ἔσαν ὄρχατοι ἀμφίς Il.14.123; πεπαίνοντ' ὀρχάτους ὀπωρινούς E.*Fr.*896.2; οἴνης ὀρχάτους Moschio Trag.6.12; hence also ὀδόντων ὄ. *AP*11.374 (Maced.); κιόνων Ach.Tat.5.1. 2. as collective Noun, *orchard*, *garden*, ἔκτοσθεν δ' αὐλῆς μέγας ὄρχατος Od.7.112, cf. 24.222, al.; ὀ. ἠνεμόεις *AP*9.314 (Anyt.).

**ὄρχεα**, = ὄσχεος, Gal.19.127; ὀρχέα· ἡ τοῦ ταύρου ὀ(σ)χέα, Hsch.

**ὀρχείδιον**, v. ὀρχίδιον.

⊛ **ὀρχέομαι**, impf. ὠρχούμην: Ep. 3 pl. pres. ὀρχεῦνται, impf. ὠρχεῦντο (v. infr.): fut. ὀρχήσομαι Ar.*Th.*1178, etc.: aor. ὠρχησάμην Anacr. 69, Hdt.6.129; inf. ὀρχήσασθαι Hom. (v. infr.):—Pass., aor. ὠρχήθην Euph.87:—*dance*, ἠΐθεοι καὶ παρθένοι.. ὠρχεῦντ' Il.18.594; Ἅλιον καὶ Λαοδάμαντα κέλευσε μουνὰξ ὀρχήσασθαι Od.8.371, cf. 14.465; πόσσ' ἁπαλοῖσιν ὀρχεῦνται Hes.*Th.*4; ὀ. πρὸς ὅπλα, of the Pyrrhic dance, Demetr.Sceps.ap.Ath.4.155b; ἐν ῥυθμῷ X.*Cyr.*1.3.10; ὀρχεῖσθαι ταῖς χερσί (cf. χειρονομέω) Antiph.113.1: c. acc. loci, δώσω τοι Τεγέην ποσσίκροτον ὀρχήσασθαι *to dance in* or *on*, Orac.ap.Hdt. 1.66, cf. Euph. l. c. (Pass.): also c. acc. cogn., Λακωνικὰ σχημάτια ὀρχεῖσθαι *dance* Laconian steps, Id.6.129; ὀ. τὸ Περσικόν X.*Cyr.*8.4. 12; ὀ. πρὸς τὸν αὐλὸν σχήματα Id.*Smp.*7.5; ὀ. τὸν ὅρμον Luc.*Salt.*11 sq., etc.:—Pass., τῶν ὕμνων οἱ μὲν ὠρχοῦντο οἱ δὲ οὐκ ὠρχοῦντο Ath.14. 631d. 2. *represent by dancing* or *pantomime*, ὀρχεῖσθαι τὴν τοῦ Κρόνου τεκνοφαγίαν, ὀ. τὸν Αἴαντα, Luc.*Salt.*80, 83, cf. *AP*9.248 (Boeth.), 11.254 (Lucill.). II. metaph., *leap*, *bound*, ὀρχεῖται δὲ καρδία φόβῳ A.*Ch.*166, cf. Anaxandr.59; Θεσσαλίη ὠρχήσατο Thessaly *shook*, *trembled*, Call.*Del.*139. III. Act. **ὀρχέω**, *make to dance* (v. Pl.*Cra.*407a), is used by Ion Trag.50, ἐκ τῶν ἀέλπτων μᾶλλον ὤρχησεν φρένας *made* my heart *leap* (so codd. Ath, ὤρχησαι Nauck); but ὀρκῆσι in Ar.*Th.*1179 is a barbarism for ὀρχῆται.

**ὀρχηδόν**, Adv., (ὄρχος) *in a row*, *one after another*, *man by man*, λάξεσθαι Hdt.7.144; wrongly explained as = ἄνδρας καὶ παῖδας, γυναῖκας δὲ οὔ, Sch.Aristid.3.597, 599 D.; also, = ἡβηδόν, Hsch.

**ὀρχ-ηθμός**, ὁ, *dance*, φιλοπαίγμων Od.23.134; μολπῆς τε γλυκερῆς καὶ ἀμύμονος ὀρχηθμοῖο Il.13.637, cf. Od.8.263, Hes.*Sc.*282, v. l. in *h.Ap.* 149; cf. ὀρχησμός. **-ημα**, ατος, τό, *dance*, *dancing*, Simon.31, S. *Aj.*699 (lyr.), X.*Smp.*2.23, Luc.*Salt.*70. **-ηματικός**, ή, όν, *belonging to the dance*, Eust.137.38. **-ησις**, εως, ἡ, *dancing*, *the dance*, Epich. 171; ἐς ὄρχησιν ἀνίστασθαι Hdt.1.202; esp. *pantomimic dancing*, Id. 6.129; δεινὰ ἐποιοῦντο πάσας τὰς ὀ. ἐν ὅπλοις εἶναι X.*An.*6.1.11; ἐκπονεῖν Plb.4.20.12: a part of ἡ γυμναστική, acc. to Pl.*Lg.*795e; ἡ ἐν τοῖς ὅπλοις ὀ. Id.*Cra.*406d; ὀ. ἐνόπλιος, ἐναγώνιος ὀ., Luc.*Salt.*8, 32, *POxy.* 1241 v 27 (ii A.D.), etc.; περὶ Ὀρχήσεως, title of work by Lucian; cf. Ath.1.14d sq., 14.630b sq., Poll.4.95 sq. **-ησμός**, ὁ, = ὀρχηθμός, in pl., A.*Eu.*375 (lyr.), Panyas.14.3, *AP*6.33 (Maec.). **-ηστήρ**, ῆρος, ὁ, = sq., κοῦροι ὀρχηστῆρες Il.18.494, cf. Hes.*Fr.*198.3; ὀρχηστῆρες Ἐνυοῦς Nonn.*D.*28.275; ὀρχηστὴρ πολέμοιο, i. e. *warrior*, ib.304; of fishes taken out of the water, Opp.*C.*1.61. ⊛ **-ηστής**, οῦ, ὁ, *dancer*, Il.16.617, 24.261, *IG*1².785, 919, Epich.171, Pi.*Fr.*148, Pl.*Euthd.* 276d, *OGI*51.45 (Ptolemais, iii B.C.), etc.; later esp. *pantomimic dancer*, αὐτῷ τῷ ῥυθμῷ μιμοῦνται αἱ τῶν ὀ. Arist.*Po.*1447ᵃ27, cf. Luc. *Salt.*67; ὀ. οἱ ἐς τὰς μαχαίρας ὀρούοντες Democr.228. **-ηστικός**, ή, όν, *of* or *fit for dancing*, of the trochaic verse, τετραμέτρῳ ἐχρῶντο διὰ τὸ σατυρικὴν καὶ -ωτέραν εἶναι τὴν ποίησιν Arist.*Po.*1449ᵃ23; ὀ. [μέτρον] ib.1460ᵃ1; ὀ. μέλος Id.*Fr.*583; σχήματα Ath.1.21e; of persons, *good at dancing*, Gal.6.158, Ptol.*Tetr.*64; ἡ -κὴ τέχνη the *art of dancing*, Pl.*Lg.*816a, etc.; εἰς -κὸν συνεκπίπτοντες Longin.41. 1. II. *pantomimic*, Luc.*Salt.*31.—ὀρχηστρικός is perh. f. l. for ὀρχηστικός in Theopomp.Hist.111(*a*).

**ὀρχηστο-δῐδάσκᾰλος**, ὁ, *dancing-master*, X.*Smp.*2.15, 9.3, Luc. *Merc.Cond.*27, etc. **-μᾰνέω**, *to be dancing-mad*, Id.*Salt.*85.

⊛ **ὀρχηστο-πᾰλάριος**, ὁ, *one skilled in* ὀρχηστοπάλη, Firm.8.15. **-πάλη** [ᾰ], ἡ, *a combination of dancing and wrestling*, *CIL*9.1663 (Beneventum); ὀρκιστοπάλη· *hormestapala*, *Gloss.*

**ὀρχήστ-ρα**, ἡ, (ὀρχέομαι) *orchestra*, i. e. in the theatre the *space on which the chorus danced*, Arist.*Pr.*901ᵇ30, *SIG*577.31 (Milet., iii/ii B.C.), etc.: metaph., ὀ. πολέμου Plu.2.193e. 2. *part of the* ἀγορά at Athens, Pl.*Ap.*26e, cf. Tim.*Lex.*, Phot. **-ρια**, ἡ, fem. of ὀρχηστήρ, *dancing girl*, v. l. in Poll.4.95, Hellenistic acc. to Moer.p.279 P. **-ρικός**, v. ὀρχηστικός. **-ριον**, τό, Dim. of ὀρχήστρα, Suid. **-ρίς**, ίδος, ἡ, *dancing girl*, Ar.*Ach.*1093, *Nu.*996, Crates Com.27, Metag.4, Pl.*Prt.*347d: ὀρχηστριάδες, f. l. for -ίδες, Arist. *EE*1246ᵃ35. **-ύς**, ύος, ἡ, Ion. for ὄρχησις, *the dance*, Il.13.731, Od.1.152, E.*Cyc.*171: contr. dat. ὀρχηστυῖ Od.8.253, 17.605, v. l. in *h.Ap.*149. [ῠ in nom. and acc.]

**ὀρχίδιον**, τό, Dim. of ὄρχις, Dsc.4.189; ὀρχείδιον, Suid.

**ὀρχίλος** [ῐ], ὁ, a bird, prob. *wren* (cf. τροχίλος), Ar.*Av.*568, *V.*1513, Arat.1025; a bird of ill omen at weddings, Euph.4; in Arist.*HA*609ᵃ 12, Thphr.*Sign.*39, 53, proparox. ὄρχιλος.

**ὀρχῐπέδ-η**, ἡ, *restraint of the testicles*, i. e. *impotence*, *AP*10.100 (Antiphan.). **-ίζω**, *seize the testicles*, Ar.*Av.*142 (ὠρχιπέδησας codd.), cf. Hsch.; ὀρχιπεδεῖν in Phot. is prob. corrupt. **-ον**, τό, in pl., *testicles*, Ar.*Eq.*772, *Av.*443, *Pl.*956. (From ὄρχις and πέδον, like λακκόπεδον.)

⊛ **ὄρχις**, ιος and εως, ὁ, Att. nom. pl. ὄρχεις, Ion. ὄρχιες, *testicle*, freq. in pl., *testicles*, Hdt.4.109, Hp.*Aër.*4, Eub.63.4 (anap.), etc.; cf. ὄσχις. 2. in females, *ovaries*, Gal.2.810, al. II. plant so called from the form of its root, *salep*, *Orchis papilionacea*, and *O. longicruris*, Thphr. *HP*9.18.3, Dsc.3.126. III. ὄρχις, ἡ, a kind of *olive*, Colum.5.8; cf. ὀρχάς (B). (Cf. Avest. *ərəzi* 'testicles'.)

**ὀρχμαί**· φραγμοί, καλαμῶνες, φάραγγες, σπῆλυγξ, Hsch.: **ὀρχμούς**· λοχμώδεις καὶ ὄρειον χωρίον, οὐκ ἐπεργαζόμενον, *Lex.Rhet.Cant.*p.29 Meier. (Cf. ὀρχάμη.)

⊛ **Ὀρχομενός**, ὁ, also ἡ (Th.1.113, A.R.4.257), the name of several Greek cities, the most famous of which was Ὀρχομενὸς Μινύειος in Boeotia, Il.2.511, etc.:—Adj. **Ὀρχομένιος**, Hp.*Ulc.*7, Hdt.9.16, *SIG* 519.7 (Aegium, iii B.C.), Str.9.2.40:—hence **Ὀρχομενίζω**, *side with the Orchomenians*, Hellanic.81 J. (but perh. not Hellanic.).—The old Boeot. form was **Ἐρχ-**, and this is found in Inscrr. and on coins to the time of Alexander, *SIG*60 (v B.C.), *IG*7.3166, al., *BMus.Cat.Coins Central Greece* p.54: the Arcadian Orchomenians are similarly **Ἐρχομένιοι** *SIG*31.12 (Delph., v B.C.), Ἐρχομίνιοι *IG*5(2).343 (Orchom. Arc., iv B.C.).

**ὄρχος**, ὁ, *a row of vines* or *fruit-trees*, παρὰ νείατον ὄ. Od.7.127, cf.

24.341, Hes.*Sc.*296; ὄρχους ἐπέκειρεν ὀδόντι, of a boar, B.5.108; ἀμπελίδος ὄ. Ar.*Ach.*995; ἡμερίδων ὄρχους *IG*14.1389 ii 23; οὐκ ὀρθῶς τοὺς ὄ. ἐφύτευσεν X.*Oec.*20.3; φυτεύουσι.. αὐτὸ κατ' ὄρχους Thphr.*HP* 4.4.8. **II.** ὀρχός, = ταρσός, *rim of eyelid*, Poll.2.69. (Wrongly derived by Sch.Theoc.1.48 from ὀρύσσω and glossed by βόθρος.)

**ὀρχο-τομέω,** (ὄρχις) *castrate*, in Pass., Alex.Aphr.*Pr.*1.9, *Hippiatr.* 2. **-τομία,** ἡ, *castration*, ib.99.

**ὄρω,** = ὄρνυμι, *raise*, only in part. nom. dual, ἰαχὴν ὀξεῖαν ὄροντε Orph.*L.*113 (cj. for ὀρῶντες).

**ὄρῳ,** Phryg. = ἄνω, Neoptol.ap.Ach.Tat.*Intr.Arat.*5.

**ὀρώδης,** ες, (ὄρος) *mountainous*, *EM*208.4. **II.** (ὀρός) *like whey, serous*, Thphr.*CP*5.9.7, Gal.*UP*14.13, cf. 6.765 K. [Freq. ὀρρ- in codd.]

**ὄρωρα, ὀρώρει, ὀρώρεται,** v. ὄρνυμι, ὄρομαι. **ὀρωρέχαται, ὀρωρέχατο,** v. ὀρέγω. **ὀρώρυχα, ὀρώρυκτο,** v. ὀρύσσω.

❋ **ὅς,** ἥ, ὅ, gen. οὗ, ἧς, οὗ, etc.; dat. pl. οἷς, αἷς, οἷς, etc.: Ep. forms, gen. ὅου (prob. replacing *ὅο) in the phrases ὅου κλέος οὔ ποτ' ὀλεῖται Il.2.325, *h.Ap.*156; ὅου κράτος ἐστὶ μέγιστον Od.1.70 (elsewh. οὗ Il. 7.325, al., never οἷο); fem. ἕης Il.16.208 (perh. imitation of ὅου; elsewh. only ἧς 5.265, al.); dat. pl. οἷς, οἷσι, ἧς, ᾗσι (never αἷς or αἷσι in Hom.):—Pron. used, **A.** as demonstr. by the side of οὗτος, ὅδε, and the Art. ὁ, ἡ, τό: in post-Homeric Gr. this use survived only in a few special phrases. **B.** as a Relat. by the side of the Art. ὅ, ἥ, τό (v. ὁ, ἡ, τό, c):—this demonstr. and Relat. Pron. must not be confounded with the Possess. ὅς, ἥ, ὅ cf. Skt. Relat. *yas, yā, yad*, Lith. *jis, ji* (*he, she*), OSlav. *i, ja, je* (*he, she, it*).)

**A.** Demonstr. Pron., = οὗτος, ὅδε, *this, that*; also, *he, she, it*: **I.** Homeric usage: this form only occurs in the nom. masc. and neut. ὅς, ὅ, and perh. nom. fem. ἥ and nom. pl. οἵ, the other cases being supplied by ὁ, ἡ, τό (ὅ, ἥ, τό); most codd. have ἡ in Il.17.551, Od. 24.255, al., and this (as also οἵ) can be referred equally to either (on the accent v. ὁ, ἡ, τό): with γάρ or καί, ὃς γὰρ δεύτατος ἦλθεν 1.286; ἀλλὰ καὶ ὃς δείδοικε Il.21.198; ὃ γὰρ γέρας ἐστὶ θανόντων Od.24.190, Il.23.9, cf. 12.344: freq. used emphatically in apodosi, mostly with οὐδέ or μηδέ before it, μηδ' ὃν τινα γαστέρι μήτηρ κοῦρον ἐόντα φέροι, μηδ' ὃς φύγοι Il.6.59, cf. 7.160, Od.4.653: after a part., εἰς ἕτερον γάρ τίς τε ἰδών.., ὃς σπεύδει (for ὅστις ἂν ἴδῃ, ὃς σπεύδει) Hes.*Op.*22. **II.** in later Gr. this usage remained in a few forms: **1.** at the beginning of a clause, καὶ ὅς and *he*, Hdt.7.18, X.*Smp.*1.15, Pl. *Phd.*118, *Prt.*310d; καὶ ἥ and *she*, καὶ οἵ and *they*, Hdt.8.56,87, Pl. *Smp.*201e, X.*An.*7.6.4. **2.** ὃς καὶ ὅς *such and such a person*, Hdt.4.68:—here also the Art. supplied the obl. cases. **3.** ἦ δ' ὅς, ἦ δ' ἥ, said *he*, said *she*, v. ἠμί. **4.** in oppositions, where it sts. answers to the Art., Λέριοι κακοί· οὐχ ὁ μέν, ὃς δ' οὔ.. Phoc.1; ὃς μέν.., ὃ δέ.. Mosch.3.76; ὁ μέν.., ὃς δέ.., ὃ δέ.., ὃς δέ.. Bion 1. 81; so τῷ μέν.., ᾧ δέ.., ᾧ δέ.. *AP*6.187 (Alph.); ὃ μέν.., ὃ δέ.., ὃ δέ.. (neut.) *Ev.Matt.*13.8; ἃ μέν.., ἃ δέ.. Heraclit.102, Archyt.ap. Stob.3.1.110; ὧν μέν.., ὧν δέ.. Philem.99; πόλεις ἃς μέν.., ἃς δέ.. D.18.71 (as v.l.): so in Dor. dat. fem. as Adv., ᾇ μέν.., ᾇ δέ.. *Tab. Heracl.*1.81; ἐφ' ὧν μέν.., ἐφ' ὧν δέ.. Arist.*EN*1109ᵃ1: very freq. in late Prose, Arr.*Epict.*3.25.1, etc.: also answering to other Prons., ἑτέρων.., ὧν δέ.. Philem.31.6; ἐφ' ᾧ μέν.., ἐπὶ θατέρῳ δέ.. Arist. *HA*564ᵃ21, etc.

**B.** Relat. Pron., *who, which.*—By the side of the simple Relat., ὅς, ἥ, ὅ (in Hom. also ὁ, ἡ, τό), we find in common use the compd. forms ὅστε, ὅστις and ὅτις, ὅσπερ and ὅπερ, ὅς γε (q.v.).

Usage of the Relat. Pron. (the foll. remarks apply to ὅς γε, ὅσπερ, ὅστε, ὅστις, as well as to ὅς, and to ὁ, ἡ, τό as relat.): **I.** in respect of Concord.—Prop. it agrees in gender and number with the Noun or Pron. in the antec. clause.—But this rule admits of many exceptions: **1.** the Relat. may agree with the gender implied, not expressed, in the antec., φίλον θάλος, ὃν τέκον αὐτή Il.22.87; τέκνων, οὓς ἤγαγε E.*Supp.*12: so after collective Nouns, the Relat. is freq. put in pl. in the gender implied in the Noun, λαόν.., οὕς.. Il.16.369; στρατιάν.. τοιαύτην.., οἵ τινες.., τὸ ναυτικόν, οἵ.., Th.6.91, 3.4; πλήθει, οἵπερ.. Pl.*Phdr.*260a; esp. after the names of countries or cities, Τηλέπυλον Λαιστρυγονίην ἀφίκανεν, οἵ.. (i.e. to Telepylos *of the Laestrygonians, who..*) Od.23.319; τὰς 'Αθήνας, οἵ γε.. Hdt.7.8.β'; Μέγαρα.., οὕς.. Th.6.94: it also may agree with the Noun or Pron. implied in an Adj., Θηβαίας ἐπισκοποῦντ' ἀγυιάς, τάν.. the streets *of Thebes, which..*, S.*Ant.*1137 (lyr.); τοὺς 'Ηρακλείους παῖδας, ὅς.. the children *of Heracles, who..*, E.*HF*157; τῆς ἐμῆς ἐπεισόδου, ὅν.. *of me whom..*, S.*OC*731; τὸν ἡμισύν ἐστ' ἀτελὴς τοῦ χρόνου· εἶθ' ἧς πᾶσι μέτεστι.., where ἧς agrees with ἀτελείας implied in ἀτελής, D.20.8. **2.** when the antec. Noun in sg. implies a class, the Relat. is sts. in pl., ἢ μάλα τις θεὸς ἔνδον, οἵ.. ἔχουσιν (for τις θεῶν, οἵ..) Od.19.40; κῆτος, ἃ μυρία βόσκει..'Αμφιτρίτη *one of the thousands, which..*, 12.97; αὐτουργός, οἵπερ.. *one of those who..*, E.*Or.*920: rare in Prose, ἀνὴρ καλός τε κἀγαθός, ἐν οἷς οὐδαμοῦ σὺ φανήσει γεγονώς D.18.310, cf. Lys.1.32. **3.** reversely, the sg. Relat. may follow a pl. antec., where the relat. clause refers to each individual; but in this case ὅστις or ὃς ἄν is mostly used, ἀνθρώπους τίνυσθον, ὅ τις κ' ἐπίορκον ὀμόσσῃ, for ἀνθρώπων τινά, ὃς κε.., Il.3.279; πάντα.., ὅ τι νοοίης, i.e. anything *which..*, Ar.*Nu.* 1381: rarely ὅς alone, τὰ λίνεα [ὅπλα], τοῦ τάλαντον ὁ πῆχυς εἷλκε a cubit's length *whereof..*, Hdt.7.36. **4.** the Relat. is sts. in the neut., agreeing rather with the notion implied in the antec. than with the Noun itself, διὰ τὴν πλεονεξίαν, ὃ πᾶσα φύσις διώκειν πέφυκεν for profit's sake—*a thing which..* Pl.*R.*359c, cf. *Lg.*849d; τοὺς Φωκέας, ὃ σιωπᾶν εἰκὸς ἦν *a name which..*, D.19.44; γυναῖκας, ἐφ' ὅπερ.. women, for *dealings with whom*, E.*Ba.*454. **5.** with Verbs of naming, the Relat. freq. agrees with the name added as a predicate, rather than with the antec., ξίφος, τὸν ἀκινάκην καλέουσι Hdt.7.54; τὴν ἄκρην, αἳ καλεῦνται Κληΐδες Id.5.108, cf. 2.17,124, etc. **II.** in respect of Construction.—Prop., the Relat. is governed by the Noun or Verb in its own clause.—But it is freq. thrown by attraction into the case of the antec. (prob. not in Hom., ἧς in Il.5.265, cf. 23.649, can be expld. otherwise), ἀπὸ παιδεύσιος, τῆς ἐπεπαίδευτο (for τῇ or τήν) Hdt.4.78; freq. in Att., Th.7.21, etc.: esp. where a Demonstr. Pron. is unexpressed, while the Relat. takes its case, οὐδὲν ὧν λέγω (for οὐδὲν τούτων ἃ λ.) S.*El.*1048, 1220, etc.; ξὺν φπερ εἶχον οἰκετῶν (for ξὺν τούτῳ ὅνπερ) Id.*OC*334; ἀνθ' ὧν ἂν ἐμοὶ δανείσῃς (for ἀντὶ τούτων ἃ..) X.*Cyr.*3.1.34; πρὸς οἷς ἐκτήσαντο (for πρὸς τούτοις ἅ..) Pl.*Grg.* 519a, etc.: the Demonstr. Pron. sts. follows, ἀφ' ὧν ἐγένεσθε ἀγαθοί, ἀπὸ τούτων ὠφελεῖσθαι Th.3.64, cf. D.8.23,26.—This attraction is rare, exc. when the acc. passes into the gen. or dat (v. supr.): sts. nom. is so attracted, οὐδὲν εἰδότες τῶν ἦν (for τούτων ἃ ἦν) Hdt.1.78; ἀφ' ὧν παρεσκεύασται (for ἀπὸ τούτων ἃ π.) Th.7.67: also dat., ὧν ἐγὼ ἐντετύχηκα οὐδείς (for τούτων οἷς..) Pl.*Grg.*509a. **b.** reversely the antec. passes into the case of the Relat., φυλακὰς δ' ἃς εἴρεαι.., οὔτις (for φυλακῶν.. οὔτις) Il.10.416; τὰς στήλας, τὰς ἵστα, αἱ πλεῦνες.. (for τῶν στηλῶν.. αἱ πλεῦνες) Hdt.2.106: so also when the Noun follows the Relat. clause, it may be put in apposition with the Relat., Κύκλωπος κεχόλωται, ὃν ὀφθαλμοῦ ἀλάωσεν, ἀντίθεον Πολύφημον Od.1.69, cf. 4.11, Il.3.123, A.*Th.*553, E.*Hec.*771,986, *Hipp.*101, etc. **2.** the Demonstr. Pron. or the Noun with an Art. is sts. transferred to the Relat. clause, 'Ινδὸν ποταμόν, ὃς κροκοδείλους δεύτερος οὗτος.. παρέχεται the river Indus, *being the second river which..*, Hdt.4.44; σφραγῖδα.., ἣν ἐπὶ δέλτῳ τήνδε κομίζεις E.*IA*156 (anap.); φοβούμεθα δέ γε.. δόξαν.., ὃν δὴ καὶ καλοῦμεν τὸν φόβον ἡμεῖς γε αἰσχύνην Pl.*Lg.*647a. **3.** the Relat. in all cases may govern a partit. gen., ἀθανάτων ὅς τίς σε.. *any one* of the immortals *who..*, Od.15.35, cf. 25, 5.448, etc.; οἱ.. τῶν ἀστῶν Hdt.7.170; οὕς.. βαρβάρων A.*Pers.*475; ᾧ.. τῶν ἡνιόχων Pl. *Phdr.*247b: freq. in neut., ἐς ὃ δυνάμιος to *what a height* of power, Hdt.7.50; οἶσθ' οὖν ὃ κάμνει τοῦ λόγου; *what part* of thy speech, E.*Ion* 363; ᾧπερ τῆς τέχνης ἐπίστευον *in which particular* of their art.., Th. 7.36; τὰ μακρὰ τείχη, ἃ σφῶν.. εἶχον *which portion* of their territory, Id.4.109, etc.: rarely in such forms as ἔξουσι δ' ἣν λάβωσιν ἐν ταφῇ χθονός (for ὃ χθονός) A.*Th.*819 (χθόνα cj. Brunck). **III.** in respect of the Moods which follow the Relat.: **1.** when the Relat. is equivalent to καί + demonstr. (ὅς = *and he..*) any mood may follow which may be found in independent clauses: ἦλθε τὸ ναυτικὸν τὸ τῶν βαρβάρων, ὃ τίς οὐκ ἂν ἰδὼν ἐφοβήθη; Lys.2.34; ὁ δ' εἰς τὸ σῶφρον ἐπ' ἀρετήν τ' ἄγων ἔρως ζηλωτὸς ἀνθρώποισιν· ὧν εἴην ἐγώ E.*Fr.*672; ἐλπίς, ἣ μόνη σωθεῖμεν ἄν Id.*Hel.*815; εἰς καλὸν ἡμῖν Ἄνυτος ὅδε παρεκαθέζετο, ᾧ μεταδῶμεν τῆς σκέψεως *to whom* let us.., Pl.*Men.*89e; ὃν ὑμεῖς.. νομίσατε *which* I would have you think.., Lys.19.61: so the inf. in orat. obliq., ἔτι δὲ.. προσετίθει χρήματα οὐκ ὀλίγα, οἷς χρήσεσθαι αὐτούς (sc. ἔφη) Th.2.13: for the inf. after ἐφ' ᾧ τε, v. ἐπί B. III. 3. **2.** after ὅς, ὅστις, = *whoever*, in collective hypothetical sense (= *if* A + *if* B + *if* C..), the same moods are used as after εἰ: **a.** pres. ind., τῷδ' ἔφες ἀνδρὶ βέλος.. ὅς τις ὅδε κρατέει Il.5.175; κλῦθι, ἄναξ, ὅτις ἐσσί Od.5.445; δουλητήν.., ἥτις ἐστί (as we say) *whatever* it is, Hdt.6.12; ὅ τι ἀνὴρ καὶ γυνή ἐστι πλὴν παιδίων *all that* are man and woman, Id.2.60; Ζεύς, ὅστις ποτ' ἐστίν A.*Ag.*160 (lyr.): also after ὅς, ἐχθρὸς γάρ μοι κεῖνος.. ὃς πενίῃ εἴκων ἀπατήλια βάζει Od.14.157, etc. **b.** subj. with ἄν (κεν) or, in poetry, without ἄν: ξυνίει ἔπος ὅττι κεν εἴπω 19.378: οὐ δηναιὸς ὃς ἀθανάτοισι μάχηται Il.5.407:—in such cases the opt. is used after secondary tenses, Τρῶας ἄμυνε νεῶν, ὅς τις φέροι ἀκάματον πῦρ 15. 731, cf. Hes.*Sc.*480; πάντας ἑξῆς, ὅτῳ ἐντύχοιεν,.. κτείνοντες Th.7.29, cf. Pl.*Ap.*21a, etc. **c.** sts. opt. without ἄν after a primary tense, ὃν πόλις στήσειε, τοῦδε χρὴ κλύειν S.*Ant.*666; after an opt., ἔρδοι τις ἣν ἕκαστος εἰδείη τέχνην Ar.*V.*1431. **IV.** peculiar Idioms: **1.** in Homer and correct writers, when two coordinate Relat. clauses were joined by καί or δέ, the Relat. Pron. was freq. replaced in the second clause by the demonstr. even though the case was changed, ἄνδρα.., ὃς μέγα πάντων 'Αργείων κρατέει καί οἱ πείθονται 'Αχαιοί (for καὶ ᾧ) Il.1.78; ὅου κράτος ἐστὶ μέγιστον..· Θόωσα δέ μιν τέκε νύμφη (for ὃν τέκε) Od.1.70, cf. 14.85, etc.; and this sts. even without the demonstr. being expressed, δοίη δ' ᾧ κ' ἐθέλοι καί οἱ κεχαρισμένος ἔλθοι (for καὶ ὅς οἱ) 2.54, cf. 114; οὓς κεν ἐῢ γνοίην καί τ' οὔνομα μυθησαίμην (for καὶ ὧν) Il.3.235; ᾗ χαλκὸς μὲν ὑπέστρωται, χαλκὸν δ' ἐπίεσται (nom. supplied) Orac.ap.Hdt.1.47; ἃς ἐπιστήμας μὲν προσείπομεν.., δέονται δὲ ὀνόματος ἄλλου Pl.*R.*533d. **2.** the neut. of the Relat. is used in Att. to introduce a clause qualifying the whole of the principal clause which follows: the latter clause is commonly introduced by γάρ, ὅτι, εἰ, ἐπειδή, etc., ὃ δὲ δεινότατόν γ' ἐστὶν ἁπάντων, ὁ Ζεὺς γάρ.. ἕστηκεν κτλ. Ar.*Av.*514, cf. D.19.211, etc.; ὃ δὲ πάντων σχετλιώτατον, εἰ.. βουλεύσομεθα Isoc.6.56; ὃ μὲν πάντων θαυμαστότατον ἀκοῦσαι, ὅτι.. Pl. *R.*491b, cf. *Ap.*18c: also without any Conj., ὃ δὲ πάντων δεινότατόν ἐστι, τοιοῦτος ὢν κτλ. And.4.16; ὃ δ' ἠπάτα σε πλεῖστον.., ηὔχεις κτλ. E.*El.* 938: c. inf., ὃ δὲ πάντων δεινότατον, τὴν ἀδελφὴν ὑποδέξασθαι Lys.19.33 (but ὑποδέξασθαι (δεῖ) is prob. cj.), etc.:—so also the neut. pl. ἅ may mean *with reference to that which*, ἃ δ'.. ἐστί σοι λελεγμένα, πᾶν κέρδος ἡγοῦ.. *as to what* has been said.., E.*Med.*453, cf. Hdt.3.81, S.*OT* 216, Ar.*Eq.*512, etc. **3.** in many instances the Gr. Relat. must be resolved into a Conj. and Pron., θαυμαστὸν ποιεῖς, ὃς ἡμῖν οὐδὲν δίδως (= ὅτι σύ) X.*Mem.*2.7.13, cf. Lys.7.23 codd., Pl.*Smp.*204b, etc.: very freq. in conditional clauses, for εἴ or ἐάν τις, βέλτερον ὅς..

προφύγῃ κακόν, ἠὲ ἁλώῃ Il.14.81, cf. Hes.*Op.*327; συμφορὰ δ', ὃς ἂν τύχῃ κακῆς γυναικός E.*Fr.*1056; τὸ δ' εὐτυχές, οἳ ἂν..λάχωσι κτλ. Th.2.44; τὸ καλῶς ἄρξαι τοῦτ' εἶναι, ὃς ἂν τὴν πατρίδα ὠφελήσῃ Id. 6.14. **4.** the Relat. freq. stands where we should use a final Conj. or the inf., ἄγγελον ἧκαν, ὃς ἀγγείλειε sent a messenger *to* tell.., Od. 15.458; κλητοὺς ὀτρύνομεν, οἵ κε τάχιστα ἔλθωσ' *that they may*.., Il. 9.165: and freq. with fut. ind., πρέσβεις ἄγουσα, οἵπερ φράσουσι (v. l. φράσωσι) *to* tell.., Th.7.25; πέμψον τιν', ὅστις σημανεῖ E.*IT*1209 (troch.), cf. X.*HG*2.3.2, *Mem.*2.1.14: so with fut. opt., ὀργάνου, ᾧ τὴν τροφὴν δέξοιτο Pl.*Ti.*33c: also for ὥστε, after οὕτω, ὧδε, etc., οὐκ ἔστιν οὕτω μῶρος, ὃς θανεῖν ἐρᾷ (for ὥστε ἐρᾶν) S.*Ant.*220, cf. Hdt.4.52, E.*Alc.* 198, Ar.*Ach.*737, etc. **5.** ὅς is freq. used where we should expect οἷος, as μαθὼν ὃς εἶ φύσιν *what* thou art, S.*Aj.*1259, cf. E.*Alc.*640, Pl. *Euthd.*283d, etc. **6.** ὅς is sts. = ὅστις or τίς in indirect clauses, γνώσῃ..ὅς..ἡγεμόνων κακὸς ἠδ' ὅς κ' ἐσθλὸς ἔῃσι Il.2.365 (perh. felt as Relat.); ὃς ἦν ὁ ἀναδέξας, οὐκ ἔχω εἰπεῖν I cannot tell *who* it was that.., Hdt.6.124; γενομένης λέσχης ὃς γένοιτο..ἄριστος Id.9.71 (in 4.131, 6.37, 7.37, τί θέλει (θέλοι) has been conjectured for τὸ of the Mss.); so in Att., ἐγῷδ' ὅς ἐστι, Κλεισθένης ὁ Σιβυρτίου Ar.*Ach.*118, cf. 442, *Av.*804, *Pl.*59, 369, S.*OT*1068, *OC*1171; πέμπει πρὸς τὸν Κῦρον, εἰπὼν ὃς ἦν X.*Cyr.*6.1.46, cf. D.52.7; δηλώσας ὃς ἦν Arist.*Po.* 1452$^{a}$26; γράψας παρ' οὗ κομιούμεθα *PCair.Zen.*150.11 (iii B.C.). **b.** later ὅς = τίς even in direct questions, ἐφ' ὃ πάρει; *Ev.Matt.*26.50; ἣν δοκεῖς; Arr.*Epict.*4.1.120 (both dub.). **7.** in exclamations, ὦ Ἡράκλεις, ἃ πέπονθα Men.*Epit.*146.

**A a.** the Relat. Pron. joined with Particles or Conjs.: **I.** ὅς γε, v. ὅσγε. **II.** ὃς δή, v. δή II. 2; ὃν δήποτε τρόπον in *some* way *or other*, Arist.*Metaph.*1090$^{a}$6; ὁδήποτε, ἁδήποτε, *anything* or *things whatever*, Id.*EN*1167$^{a}$35, 1164$^{a}$25; **ὁσδηποτοῦν**, Euc.*Phaen.*p.10 M., Dsc.5.10, Jul.*Or.*1.18c, *IG*2$^{2}$.1121.30 (iv A.D.); **ὁσδηποτεοῦν**, *IGRom.* 4.915 (Cibyra, i A.D.), *IG*2$^{2}$.1368.133 (ii A.D.); **ὁσδητισοῦν** (in Boeot. form ὁσδειτισῶν), ib.7.3081.5 (Lebad.); **ὁσποτοῦν**, Dicaearch.2. 4. **III.** ὃς καί, v. καί B.6; but καὶ ὅς and *who (which)*, D.23. 68. **2.** Ἀπολλώνιον ὃν καὶ Φᾶβι A., *called also* Ph., Wilcken *Chr.*11 *A*52 (ii B.C.), etc.: for nom. sg. masc. v. καί B.2. **IV.** ὅς κε or κεν, Att. ὃς ἄν, *whosoever, who if any*.., v. ἄν B. I. 2. **2.** ὅς κε is also used so as to contain the antec. in itself, much like εἴ τις, as νεμεσσῶμαί γε μὲν οὐδὲν κλαίειν, ὅς κε θάνῃσι I am not wroth that men should weep *for whoever* be dead, Od.4.196: ὅστις is also used in this way, cf. ὅστις I. **V.** ὅσπερ, ὅστε, ὅστις, v. sub vocc.

**A b.** abs. usages of certain Cases of the Relat. Pron.: **I.** gen. sg. οὗ, of Place, **1.** like ὅπου, *where*, A.*Pers.*486, S.*OC*158 (lyr.), etc.; οὗ δή A.*Pr.*814, v. l. in Pl.*Phdr.*248b, etc.; οὗπερ A.*Th.*1016, S. *Aj.*1237, *OC*77, etc.; also of circumstances, οὗ γὰρ τοιούτων δεῖ, τοιοῦτός εἰμ' ἐγώ Id.*Ph.*1049; εἰ γένοιο οὗ νῦν εἰμί Pl.*Smp.*194a, etc.; ἔστιν οὗ *in some places*, E.*Or.*638; οὗ μέν.., οὗ δέ.. *in some places.., in others*.., Arist.*Oec.*1345$^{b}$34: c. gen., οὐκ εἶδεν οὗ γῆς εἰσέδυ *in what part* of the earth, E.*IA*[1583]; ἐννοεῖς οὗ ἐστὶ..τοῦ ἀναμιμνήσκεσθαι Pl.*Men.*84a; συνιδὼν οὗ κακῶν ἦν Luc.*Tox.*17. **2.** in pregnant phrases, μικρὸν προϊόντες.., οὗ ἡ μάχη ἐγένετο (for ἐκεῖσε οὗ) X.*An.*2. 1.6; so οὗπερ προσβεβοηθήκει Th.2.86, cf. 1.134; ἀπιὼν ἐκ τῆς πόλεως, οὗ κατέφυγε (for οἷ κατέφυγε καὶ οὗ ἦν) X.*Cyr.*5.4.14 (dub. l.); ἐπειδὰν ἱζήσωμεν οὗ ἄγεις Philostr.*Her.Prooem.*13: in later Gr. οὗ was used simply for οἷ, οὗπερ ἂν ἔλθῃ Timo 69, cf. *Ev.Luc.*10.1, etc.: but in early writers this is f. l., as in D.21.74, etc. **II.** dat. fem. ᾗ, Dor. ᾇ, of Place, *where*, or Manner, *as*, v. ᾗ. **III.** old loc. οἷ, as Adv., v. οἷ. **2.** old abl. (?) ὧ, in Dor. (cf. ϝοίκω), τηνῶθε καθεῖλον, ὧ (*whence*) μ' ἐκέλευ καθελεῖν τυ Theoc.3.11; ἐν τᾷ πόλι, ὧ κ' ᾖ, καρῦξαι ἐν τἀγορᾷ *IG*9(1).334.21 (Locr., v B.C.). **IV.** acc. sg. neut. ὅ, very freq. = ὅτι, *that, how that*, λεύσσετε γὰρ τό γε πάντες ὅ μοι γέρας ἔρχεται ἄλλῃ Il.1.120, al.; and so also, *because*, ταρβήσας ὅ οἱ ἄγχι πάγη βέλος 20.283, al. **2.** in Att. ὅ, *for which reason*, E.*Hec.*13, *Ph.*155, 263, Ar.*Ec.*338: also acc. neut. pl. ἅ in this sense, S.*Tr.*137 (lyr.), Isoc.8.122. **3.** *whereas*, Th.2.40, 3.12, *Ep.Rom.*6.10, *Ep. Gal.*2.20. **V.** ἀφ' οὗπερ *from the time that*.., A.*Pers.*177. **VI.** ἐφ' ᾧ, v. ἐπί B. III. 3.

⊛ **ὅς**, ἥ, ὅν (not ὅ, v. Il.1.609, 21.305, Od.11.515), gen. οἷο Il.3. 333, Od.1.330, al., οὗ 23.150, al.; Cret. ϝός *Leg.Gort.*1.18, al., *SIG* 1183; so in Aeol., Sapph.*Supp.*1.6, *Lyr.Adesp.*32, cf. A.D.*Pron.* 107.11:—Possess. Pron.: **I.** of the 3 pers., *his, her*, put either before or after its Noun, ᾧ πενθερῷ, ὃν θυμόν, etc., Il.6.170, 202, etc.; ἧς ἀρχῆς *IG*1$^{2}$.761; πόσιος οὗ, πατέρι ᾧ, Od.23.150, 3.39, etc.: sts. also with Art., τὰ ἃ κῆλα Il.12.280; τὰ ἃ δώματα Od.14.153, etc.; also in Lyr., Pi.*O.*5.8, *P.*6.36 (elsewh. Pi. prefers ἑός), B.5.47: sts. in Trag., λέσχας ἃς A.*Eu.*367 (lyr.); ὧν παίδων S.*OC*1639 (iamb.); ἐκγόνοισιν οἷς E.*Med.*955 (iamb.): with Art., λιτῶν τῶν ὧν A.*Th.* 641; ὅπλων τῶν ὧν S.*Aj.*442; τῶν ὧν τέκνων Id.*Tr.*266, cf. 525 (lyr.); τοῖς οἷσιν αὐτοῦ Id.*OT*1248: so in Cret. Prose, τὰ ϝὰ αὐτᾶς *Leg.Gort.* 2.46; in Thgn.1009, ὧν αὐτοῦ κτεάνων is to be restd. for τῶν.. from *IG*1$^{2}$.499; once in Hdt., γυναῖκα ἥν 1.205; never in Att. Prose. **II.** of the 2 pers., for σός, *thy, thine*, Hes.*Op.*381, *AP*7.539 (Pers.), Mosch.4.77 (dub. in Hom., v. infr.); and **III.** of the 1 pers., for ἐμός, *my, mine*, Od.9.28, 13.320, A.R.4.1015, 1036.—Signfs. II and III were denied for Homer by Aristarch., see esp. A.D.*Pron.*109. 20; in Od.9.28 and 34 he (or at least A.D. l.c.) rendered ἧς γαίης and πατρίδος '*a man's own* fatherland', and athetized Od.13.320: in Il.14.221, 264, 16.36, 19.174, al., φρεσὶ σῇσιν has better Ms. authority than φρεσὶν ᾗσιν; and in Od.15.542, cf. 1.402, δώμασι σοῖσιν than δώμασιν οἷσιν; v. ἑός. (Cogn. with Skt. *svás* 'his (my, thy) own', Slav. stem. *svo-* (used of all 3 persons, as in Skt.): I.-E. *swo-* was related to I.-E. *sewo-*, v. ἑός.)

**ὅσα**, v. ὅσος IV.

**ὁσάγωνος** [ᾰ], ον, *of whatever number of sides*, ἀριθμός Theo Sm. p.40 H.

⊛ **ὁσάκις** [ᾰ], Ep. **ὁσσάκι**, as always in Hom.; also **ὁσσάκις**, *Tab. Heracl.*1.132, Call.*Epigr.*2.2: (ὅσος):—*as many times as, as often as*, Relat. to τοσσάκι, Il.21.265, 22.194, Od.11.585; Att. form in Th.7. 18, Lys.25.9, Pl.*Tht.*143a, X.*Mem.*3.4.3, 1*Ep.Cor.*11.25, etc.:—also **ὁσᾰκισδήποτε**, Dosith.p.409 K.; **ὁσᾰκισοῦν**, Nicom.*Ar.*2.17.

**ὁσᾰ-πλάσιος** [πλᾰ], ον, = sq., Archim.*Sph.Cyl.*1.2, Iamb.*in Nic.* p.97 P. **-πλᾰσίων**, ον, gen. ονος, *as many times as*, Arist.*Pr.*929$^{b}$ 14, Euc.12.13, Archim.*Aequil.*1.6.

**ὁσᾰχῇ**, Adv. *in as many ways as*, only with περ, ὁσαχῇπερ Pl.*Ti.* 43e: **ὁσᾰχοῦ**, Adv. *in as many places as*, D.23.184: **ὁσᾰχοῖ**, Aristid. *Or.*38(7).21 (v. l. -χοῦ): **ὁσᾰχῶς**, Adv., = ὁσαχῇ, Hp.*Decent.*9, Arist. *Metaph.*1017$^{a}$23, *Top.*105$^{a}$34.

**ὅσγε**, ἥγε, ὅγε, (ὅς, γε) *who* or *which*, with emphasis, τό γε μάλιστα ἐν τιμῇ ἄγονται Hdt.2.83, cf. 111, etc.; τῇ γέ μοι φαίνεται εἶναι ἀληθές Id.7.139. **II.** mostly, like Lat. *qui quidem* or *quippe qui*, οἵ γε.. ὑπῆρξαν ἄδικα ποιεῦντες *since it was they who*.., ib.8.β' (cf. ὅς B. I. 1); ἀνδρῶν [σὲ] πρῶτον..κρίνοντες.., ὅς γ' ἐξέλυσας *since it was thou who*.., S.*OT*35, cf. 342, 853, *OC*127, etc.—Never in Hom.

⊛ **ὅσδε**, late form, = ὅδε, *Wiener Denkschr.*44(6).91 (Cilicia), *Rev.Bibl.* 1908.568 (Palestine). **ὅσδω**, v. ὄζω.

⊛ **ὁσημέραι**, Adv. for ὅσαι ἡμέραι, *as many days as are*, i. e. *daily, day by day*, Th.7.27, Ar.*Pl.*1006, Pl.*Lg.*849d, Alex.28, Phld.*Ir.*p.61 W.; δι' ἡμέρας ὁ. all day and *every day*, Hermipp.4; ὁ. ἕως ἄν.. Lex ap. D.24.23: divisim, ὅσαι ἡμέραι Hyp.*Ath.*19, Arist.*Ath.*43.3, Them. *Or.*15.192d (so in Od.14.93, ὅσσαι..νύκτες τε καὶ ἡμέραι ἐκ Διός εἰσιν):—so **ὅσα ἔτη**, *every year*, X.*Ath.*3.4; **ὁσέτη**, Ar.*Th.*624; **ὅσοι μῆνες**, *every month*, D.24.142; **ὅσαι ὧραι**, *every hour*, Them. l. c., etc.

**ὀσθάλη**, ἡ, = φοῖνιξ, dub. in Ps.-Dsc.4.43.

⊛ **ὁσί-α**, Ion. **ὁσίη**, ἡ, (fem. of ὅσιος) *divine law*, οὐδ' ὁσίη κακὰ ῥάπτειν ἀλλήλοισιν *it is* against *the law of God and nature* to.., Od.16.423, cf. 22.412, Pi.*P.*9.36, Call.*Aet.*3.1.5; τοῖσι οὐδὲ κτήνεα ὁσίη θύειν ἐστί those for whom it is not *lawful*, Hdt.2.45; ὅσον..ὁ. ἐστὶ λέγειν ib. 171; ἐκ πάσης ὁ. *h.Merc.*470; ὁσίης πλέον εἰπεῖν more *than law allows*, Emp.4.7; νομίσας πολλὴν ὁ. τοῦ πράγματος holding the thing fully *sanctioned*, Ar.*Pl.*682; οὔτε θεοὺς οὔθ' ὁσίαν οὔτ' ἄλλ' οὐδὲν ἐποιήσατ' ἐμποδών D.21.104; τῶν ἱερῶν ὁσία παντί all may share *lawfully* in the rites, *Berl.Sitzb.*1927.158 (Cyrene): personified Ὁσία, *Righteousness*, E.*Ba.*370 (lyr.). **II.** *the service* or *worship owed by man to God, rites, offerings*, etc., κἀγὼ τῆς ὁσίης ἐπιβήσομαι ἧς περ Ἀπόλλων I will enter into (enjoyment of) the same *worship* as A., *h.Merc.*173; ὡς ὁσίη γένετο *the rites* were established, *h.Ap.*237; ὁσίη κρεάων the *rite* of the flesh-*offering*, *h.Merc.*130: so without a gen., *offering*, λιτῇ προσγελάσαις ὁσίῃ *AP*9.91 (Arch. Jun.). **2.** *funeral rites, last honours paid to the dead*, τὴν ὁ. ἀποπληροῦν Iamb.*VP*30.184. **III.** prov., ὁσίας ἕκατι for *form's* sake, Lat. *dicis causa*, E.*IT*1461; ὁσίας ἕνεκα Eub.110, Ephipp.15.4; so ὁσίᾳ (or Ὁσίᾳ) δίδωμ' ἔπος τόδε E. *IT*1161. (οὐκ ὁσία *Berl.Sitzb.* l. c.) **-εύω**, = ὁσιόω, f. l. in Linus ap.Stob.3.1.70. ⊛ **-ος**, α, ον, also ος, ον Pl.*Lg.*831d, D.H.5.71:—*hallowed*, i. e. *sanctioned* or *allowed by the law of God* or *of nature*, δίκη Thgn.132; θοῖναι A.*Pr.*529 (lyr.); λουτρά S.*Aj.*1405 (anap.); καθαρμοί E.*Ba.*77 (lyr.); μέλος Ar.*Av.*898; οὐχ ὅ. *unhallowed*, ὕβρις E.*Ba.* 374 (lyr.); ἔρως Id.*Hipp.*764 (lyr.); θυσίαι Id.*IT*465 (anap.).—The sense of ὅσιος often depends on its relation on the one hand to δίκαιος (sanctioned by *human* law), on the other to ἱερός (*sacred* to the gods): **1.** opp. δίκαιος, *sanctioned by divine law, hallowed, holy* (μόριον τοῦ δικαίου τὸ ὅ. Pl.*Euthphr.*12d), δικαιότερον καὶ ὁσιώτερον καὶ πρὸς θεῶν καὶ πρὸς ἀνθρώπων Antipho 1.25; τὰ πρὸς τοὺς ἀνθρώπους δίκαια καὶ τὰ πρὸς τοὺς θεοὺς ὅ. Plb.22.10.8: hence, in a common antithesis, τὰ δίκαια καὶ ὅ. *things of* human and *divine ordinance*, Pl. *Plt.*301d, etc., cf. *Euthphr.*6e; also ὅ. καὶ νόμιμα Ar.*Th.*676 (lyr.); οὐ..νόμιμον οὐδ' ὅ. ἂν εἴη Pl.*Lg.*861d; θεοὺς ὅσιόν τι δρᾶν discharge *a duty men owe the gods*, E.*Supp.*40, cf. *Hipp.*1081; τὸ ὅσιον, = εὐσέβεια, Pl.*Euthphr.*5d: in an imprecatory formula, ἀποδοῦσι μὲν αὐτοῖς ὅσια ᾖ, μὴ ἀποδοῦσι δὲ ἀνόσια *SIG*1199 (Cnidus), cf. ἀνοσία II; so ὅ. καὶ ἐλεύθερα ib.1180.6 (ibid.). **2.** opp. ἱερός, *permitted* or *not forbidden by divine law, profane*, ἱερὰ καὶ ὅ. things sacred and *profane*, ἐς ὀλιγωρίαν ἐτράποντο καὶ ἱερῶν καὶ ὁ. ὁμοίως Th.2.52, cf. Pl.*R.*344a, *Lg.*857b, etc.; κοσμεῖν τὴν πόλιν καὶ τοῖς ἱεροῖς καὶ τοῖς ὁ. with sacred and *profane* buildings, Isoc.7.66; τῶν ἱερῶν μὲν χρημάτων τοὺς θεούς, τῶν ὁ. δὲ τὴν πόλιν ἀποστερεῖ D.24.9; ἀργυρίου ὁσίου *IG*1$^{2}$.186. 13; ὁ ταμίας τῶν ὁ. προσόδων *OGI*229.58 (Smyrna, iii B.C.); ὁ ταμίας τῶν ὁ. *Supp.Epigr.*1.366.58 (Samos, iii B.C.); ὅ. χωρίον a *lawful* place (for giving birth to a child), Ar.*Lys.*743; ὅσιόν ἐστι folld. by inf., *it is lawful, not forbidden by any law*, E.*IT*1045, etc.; οὐκ ὅσιόν ἐστι *nefas est*, Hdt.6.81; οὐκ ὅσιον ποιεῦμαι I deem it *impious*, Id.2.170, cf. D.*Ep.*5.3; οὐδὲ ὅσια (sc. ἐστι)..μιαίνειν Pl.*R.*416e; οὐ γάρ σοι θέμις οὐδ' ὅσιον..ἱστάναι κτερίσματα S.*El.*432; ὅσια ποιέειν Hdt.6.86.α'; λέγειν Id.9.79; φωνεῖν S.*Ph.*662; φρονεῖν E.*El.*1203 (lyr.). **II.** of persons, *pious, devout, religious*, ἄνδρες A.*Supp.*27 (anap.), cf. E.*Med.*850 (lyr.), etc.; Παλλάδος ὁ. πόλις Id.*El.*1320 (anap.); ὅ. θιασῶται, μύσται, Ar.*Ra.*327, 336 (both lyr.); ἐμαυτὸν ὅ. καὶ δίκαιον παρέχειν Antipho 2.2.2; ὅσιοι πρὸς οὐ δικαίους ἱστάμεθα Th.5. 104; opp. ἀνόσιος, E.*Or.*547; opp. ἐπίορκος, X.*An.*2.6.25; ὅσιος εἴς τινα, περὶ ξένους, E.*Heracl.*719, *Cyc.*125; πρὸς τοὺς τοκέας Gorg.6. **2.**

**sinless**, *pure*, ἐξ ὁ. στομάτων Emp.4.2; ὁ. ἔστω καὶ εὐαγής Lex Solonis ap.And.1.96: c. gen., ἱερῶν πατρῴων ὅσιος in regard to the sacred rites of his forefathers, A.*Th.*1015; ὅσιος ἀπ' εὐνᾶς E.*Ion* 150 (lyr.); also ὅσιαι χέρες *pure, clean* hands, A.*Ch.*378 (anap.), cf. S.*OC*470. 3. rarely of the gods, *holy*, Orph.*H.*77.2; θεοῖς ὁ. καὶ δικαίοις *CIG*3830 (Cotyaeum), cf. 3594 (Alexandria Troas). 4. title of five special priests at Delphi, Plu.2.292d, 365a. 5. οἱ ὅσιοι 'the *saints*', Lxx *Ps.* 29(30).4, al. III. Adv. ὁσίως Antipho 2.4.12, etc.; ὁ. οὐχ, ὑπ' ἀνάγκας δέ E.*Supp.*63 (lyr.); οὐχ ὁ. Id.*Hipp.*1287 (anap.), cf. Th.2.5 (v.l.); καλῶς καὶ ὁ. Pl.*Phd.*113d; δικαίως καὶ ὁ. Id.*R.*331a; ὁ. καὶ κατὰ νόμον Id.*Lg.*799b; ὁ. ἂν ὑμῖν ἔχοι τοῦτον θύειν.. it would be *right* for you that he should.., X.*Cyr.*8.5.26: c. part., ὁ. ἂν ἔχοι αὐτῷ μὴ δεχομένῳ .. Id.*HG*4.7.2: Comp. -ώτερον E.*IT*1194, etc.: Sup., ὡς -ώτατα διαβιῶναι τὸν βίον Pl.*Men.*81b, etc. (Not in Hom., who has only Subst. ὁσίη, v. ὁσία.) -ότης, ητος, ἡ, *disposition to observe divine law, piety*, Pl.*Prt.*329c, *Euthphr.*14d sq., X.*Cyr.*6.1.47, *SIG*654B10 (Delph., ii B.C.), etc.; πρὸς θεῶν ὁ. *piety towards* them, Plu.*Alc.*34; πρὸς τοὺς θεοὺς Id.2.359f; also, like Lat. *pietas*, ἡ πρὸς γονεῖς ὁ. D.S.7.4; πρὸς τὴν τεκοῦσαν Id.31.27. -ουργῆσαι· ἀποκαρδιουργῆσαι, καὶ τὸ ἐπιλέγειν ἐν ταῖς θυσίαις, ὅταν ἀπάρχωνται τῶν θεῶν αὐτῶν, Hsch. -όω, *make holy*, Med., *keep oneself pure*, E.*Ba.*114, v.l. in 70 (both lyr.):— Pass., *to be purified, hallowed*, ὁσιωθεὶς Id.*Fr.*472.15 (anap.); ὡσιώθησαν αἱ ἡμέραι X.*HG*3.3.1; of the souls of men, Plu.*Rom.*28. 2. abs., *make* things *pure, do what heaven requires*, φυγαῖσι by banishing the murderer, E.*Or.*515; τὸ τὸν κατιόντα ὁσιοῦν καὶ καθαίρεσθαι D.23.73; ὁσιοῦν [τινα] τῇ γῇ *satisfy divine law* by throwing earth, Philostr.*Her.*10.7.

**Ὄσῑρις**, ὁ, *Osiris*, Hdt.2.42, etc.; gen. Ὀσείριδος *IG*11(4).1234 (Delos, ii B.C.), Ὀσίριος Hdt. l.c., *OGI*90.10 (Rosetta, ii B.C.), Ὀσίρεως Man.ap.J.*Ap.*1.26; dat. Ὀσίριδι *IG*2².1367.4, Ὀσίρει *OGI*60.4 (Canopus, iii B.C.): Ὀσίριδος ἀστήρ, = the planet Jupiter, Ach.Tat.*Intr.Arat.*17: **Ὀσῑρίειον**, τό, *temple of O.*, *Sammelb.*5022 (Ptolemaic); later **Ὀσιρεῖον**, Theognost.*Can.*129:—Verb **Ὀσιριάζω**, *to be given to his worship*, Dam.ap.Suid. s.v. Ἀσκληπιόδοτος (-ράζ- codd.):—Adj. **Ὀσῑριακός**, τὰ -κά Plu.2.360f: fem. Adj. **Ὀσῑριάς**, Dam.*Isid.*107; πόα, = ὄσιρις, Aët.1.304.

**ὄσῑρις**, ιδος, ἡ, *poet's cassia, Osyris alba*, Dsc.4.140 (v.l. ὄσυρις), Gal.12.93, Plin.*HN*27.111.

**ὀσιρίτης** [ρῑ], ου, ὁ, Egypt. = κυνοκέφαλιον, Apion ap.Plin.*HN*30.18.

**ὁσί-ωσις**, εως, ἡ, *purification from*, τῶν μιασμάτων D.H.1.88. **-ωτήρ**, ῆρος, ὁ, *consecrator*, the name given at Delphi to *the victim offered when one of the priests called* ὅσιοι *was appointed*, Plu.2.292d.

**ὄσκαλσις**, εως, ἡ, = σκάλσις, Thphr.*HP*2.7.5.

**ὀσκάπτω**· ἀνασκάπτω, Hsch. (Prob. Aeol. = ὀ(ν)σκ-.)

**ὀσμ-άομαι**, older form ὀδμ- (v. ὀσμή), *smell at* a thing, τινος Arist.*HA*541ᵃ25, etc.; τι Gal.17(2).151: abs., *smell, have the sense of smell*, Democr.11 (in form ὀδμ-), Heraclit.98, Arist.*de An.*421ᵃ11, 424ᵇ16, *AP*11.240 (Lucill.); τὰ ὀσμώμενα *the organs of smell*, Gal.*UP*8.4:— Pass., ὀδμᾶσθαι Anon.Lond.33.19. II. metaph., *perceive, remark*, Λάκωνος ὀσμᾶσθαι λόγου S.*Fr.*176 (s.v.l.). -άς, άδος, ἡ, = ὄνοσμα, Dsc.3.131. ⊛ -ή, ἡ, Att. form of the older ὀδμή (v. fin.), *smell, odour*, freq. of *foul smells*, δεινὴ δὲ θεείου γίγνεται ὀδμή Il.14.415; πικρὸν ἀποπνείουσαι ἁλὸς.. ὀδμήν, of seals, Od.4.406; ὀδμὰ.. κατὰ χῶρον κίδναται Pi.*Fr.*129.6; ὀσμὴ βροτείων αἱμάτων A.*Eu.*253; ὀσμὴν ἀπ' αὐτοῦ (sc. τοῦ νεκροῦ).. πεφευγότες S.*Ant.*412; κακὴ ὀσμή Id.*Ph.*891: pl., βυρσῶν ὀσμὰς δεινάς Ar.*Pax*753; ὀσμαὶ οὐκ ἀνεκτοί Th.7.87, etc.; but also of *fragrant odours*, ὡς καλὴν ὀσμὴν ἔχει E.*Cyc.*153, cf. Ar.*Ec.*1124; οἴνου ὀ. Alex.222.4, Philem.98.4: hence, *scent, perfume*, X.*Hier.*1.4, Ach.Tat.2.38; on ὀ. as affecting the sense, cf. Arist.*Sens.*440ᵇ28 sq., *de An.*421ᵃ7 sq., Thphr.*CP*6.1.1 sq. II. *the sense of smell*, = ὄσφρησις, Democr.11, Hsch.—The older form ὀδμή (cf. ὄδωδα, ὄζ-ω, *od-or*) is alone used by Hom., Hdt., and Pi.; it occurs also in A.*Pr.*115 (lyr.), Democr. l.c., and in later Prose, Thphr.*CP*6.14.1, al., Phylarch.63 J., Diocl.*Fr.*129, Anon.Lond.34.38, etc.; but ὀσμή is Att. acc. to Phryn.71; also Ion., Hippon. in *PSI*9.1089.11. -ήρης, ες, *smelling, odorous*, Nic.*Al.*237. ⊛ -ηρός, ά, όν, = foreg., Id.*Fr.*74.57. 2. ὀσμηρός, ὁ, = μηδική, prob. in Ps.-Dsc.2.147. -ησις, εως, ἡ, *a smell*, Aret.*SA*2.11. -ητός, ή, όν, *smelt: that can be smelt*, Thphr.*Sens.*90. -ῖτις, ιδος, ἡ, = καλαμίνθη, Ps.-Dsc.3.35; = θύμβρα, ib.37: βρόμος ὀσμίτης, *mentastrum*, *Gloss.*

**ὀσμύλ-η** [ῠ], ἡ, *a strong-smelling musky octopus, Eledone cirrosa*, Arist.*Fr.*305: -ος (parox.), ὁ, = foreg., Id.ap.Ath.7.318e, Ael.*NA*5.44, Opp.*H.*1.307,310. -ιον, τό, Dim. of foreg., Ar.*Fr.*247, Call.*Fr.*38; = ὄζαινα, Hsch.: prob. to be read (with some codd.) for βομβύλια in Gal.19.89 s.v. βολβίτια. -ος, ὁ, v. ὀσμύλη. II. v.l. for μορμύρος, Arist.*HA*570ᵇ20, cf. Ael.*NA*9.45.

**ὀσμώδης**, ες, = ὀσμήρης, Arist.*Sens.*443ᵃ13: Comp. ὀδμωδέστερα Thphr.*CP*2.16.1: Sup. ὀσμωδέστατα Id.*Sens.*20.

**ὁσονοῦν**, Ion. ὁσονῶν, v. ὅσος III. 3, IV. 6; cf. ὁσοῦν.

⊛ **ὅσος**, Ep. ὅσσος, η, ον, both forms in Hom. and Hes.; ὅσσος also in A.*Pers.*864 (lyr.); and in many dialects, e.g. Lesb., Alc.*Oxy.*1788 *Fr.*15 ii 18 (ὅσσος), Arg., *IG*4.748.5 (Troezen, iv B.C.), Thess., ib. 9(2).517.19, al.; Central Cret. **ὅζος** *GDI*5090 (Lyttos), al., and **ὅττος** ib.5000 (Gortyn): Relat. and indirect interrog. Adj.:—of Size, *as great as, how great*; of Quantity, *as much as, how much*; of Space, *as far as, how far*; of Time, *as long as, how long*; of Number, *as many as, how many*; of Sound, *as loud as, how loud*: correl. with τόσος (τόσσος), τοσόσδε, τοσοῦτος, in sense *as*, τόσσον χρόνον ὅσσον ἄνωγας Il.24.670, cf. Od.19.169; τόσονδ', ὅσον.. S.*El.*286; τοσοῦτον ὄχλον καὶ παρασκευήν, ὅσην.. D.4.35: sts. with πᾶς or ἅπας as antec., χῶρον ἅπαντα ὅσσον.. Il.23.190; ἐκ πασέων, ὅσσαι.. Od.4.723; πάντα μάλ' ὅσσα.. Il.22.115; τοὺς πάντας.., ὅσοι.. A.*Pr.*976, etc.; also ὅσων.. ψαύοιμι, πάντων τῶνδ' ἀεὶ μετειχέτην S.*OT*1464: with ἴσος, just so much *as*, ἐμοὶ δ' ἴσον τῆς χώρας μέτα, ὅσονπερ ὑμῖν Ar.*Ec.*174, cf. D.21.44: freq. without antec., τῆς ἦ τοι φωνὴ μὲν ὅση σκύλακος νεογιλῆς Od.12.86, cf. 10.113, etc.; ἀσπίδες ὅσσαι ἄρισται Il.14.371, cf. 75, 18.512; agreeing with an antec. implied in an Adj., γυναικείας ἀρετῆς, ὅσαι.. the virtue *of all the women, who*.., Th.2.45, cf. ὅς B. I. 1: the Subst. freq. precedes, where we put it in the Relat. clause, οὐδέ τι οἶδε πένθεος (about the woe), ὅσσον ὄρωρε Il.11.658; ὁρᾷς.. τὴν θεῶν ἰσχύν, ὅση [ἐστί]; S.*Aj.*118; ὦ Ζεῦ.., τὸ χρῆμα τῶν κόπων ὅσον! Ar.*Ra.*1278; τὸ χρῆμα τῶν νυκτῶν ὅσον· ἀπέραντον! Id.*Nu.*2: and sts. it is attracted to the case of the antec., εὐτραφέστατον πωμάτων ὅσων ἴησιν (for ὅσα) A.*Th.*309 (lyr.); joined with οἷος, ὅσσος ἔην οἷός τε Il.24.630; so ὅσσοι τε καὶ οἵτινες Od.16.236: repeated in the same clause, τὸ δὲ ὅσον μέτρον ὅσοις [μειγνύμενον] the quantities of the first ingredient and the others, Pl.*Ti.*68b; γαίης ὅσσης ὅσσον ἔχει μόριον *AP*7.740 (Leon.): perh. sts. folld. by a partic. for a finite Verb, ὅσοι συμπαρεπόμενοι (s.v.l.) X.*Eq.*11.12, cf. *HG*6.1.10. 2. with a partit. gen. in the principal clause, Τρώων θάνον ὅσσοι ἄριστοι Il.12.13; ἄριστοι ἵππων, ὅσσοι ἔασιν 5.267; Περσῶν ὅσοιπερ A.*Pers.*441; οὔ τις.. ὀνόσσεται, ὅσσοι Ἀχαιοί of all the Achaeans, Il.9.55; [τῶν στρατειῶν] ὅσαι τε καὶ μὴ ἐπικίνδυνοι which are and which are not.., Pl.*R.*467d; on τῶν ὅσοι, v. ὁ, ἡ, τό A. III. 3. of Time, ὅσαι ἡμέραι, ὅσα ἔτη, etc., v. ὁσημέραι. 4. with τις, in indirect questions, ἰδώμεθα .. ὅσσος τις χρυσὸς.. ἔνεστιν Od.10.45; ὅσον τι δένδρον.. γίνεται Hdt.1.193; ὅσον τι ἐστὶ ib.185; ὅσοι τινὲς ἐόντες.. Id.7.102, etc. 5. with acc. of extent, λίμνη.. μέγαθος, ὅσηπερ ἡ ἐν Δήλῳ in size *as large as* that in Delos, Id.2.170, cf. 175, Pl.*R.*423b. 6. with Adjs. expressing Quantity, etc., both words being put in the same case, [πίθηκοι] ἄφθονοι ὅσοι.. γίνονται, i.e. in amazing numbers, Hdt.4.194; ὄχλος ὑπερφυὴς ὅσος prodigiously large, Ar.*Pl.*750; χρήματα θαυμαστὰ ὅσα Pl.*Hp.Ma.*282c, cf. Luc.*Halc.*5, etc.; ἀπλάτων ὅσων, ἀμύθητα ὅσα, Phld.*Rh.*1.3, 91 S., cf. Corn.*ND*9; ὀλίγους ὅσους τῶν κουφίνων Luc.*Alex.*1; ἐτόλμησαν ἐπιφύεσθαι ἡμεῖν πλεῖστοι ὅσοι *SIG*888.65 (Thrace, iii A.D.); μετὰ ἱδρῶτος θαυμαστοῦ ὅσου Pl.*R.*350d; διὰ μυρίων ὅσων Longin.1.1: freq. in adverbial construction, θαυμαστὸν ὅσον ἐπιδιδόντες Pl.*Tht.*150d; θ. ὅσον διαφέρει Id.*La.*184c; ἀμηχάνῳ δὴ ὅσῳ πλεῖον Id.*R.*588a; τυτθὸν ὅσσον ἄπωθεν Theoc.1.45; βαιὸν ὅσον παραβάς *AP*12.227 (Strat.). 7. with Sup., ὅσας ἂν πλείστας δύνωνται καταστρέφεσθαι τῶν πολίων the most they possibly could.., Hdt.6.44, cf. Th.7.21; also ὅσον τάχος *as* quickly *as possible*, Ar.*Th.*727 (more freq. ὅσον τάχιστα, v. infr. IV. 4); ὅσον σθένος with all possible strength, Theoc.1.42, A.R.2.589. 8. c. inf., *so much as is enough for*.., ὅσον ἀποζῆν *enough to* live off, Th.1.2; ἐλείπετο τῆς νυκτὸς ὅσον.. διελθεῖν τὸ πεδίον X.*An.*4.1.5; εὐδαιμονίας τοσοῦτον, ὅσον δοκεῖν so much *as is enough for* appearance, S.*OT*1191 (lyr.), cf. Th.3.49, Pl.*R.*416e, etc. II. for ὅτι τοσοῦτος (v. οἷος II. 2, 3, ὅς B. IV. 3), Od.4.75, E.*Hel.*74, etc. III. folld. by Particles: 1. ὅσος ἄν (κεν) *how great* (*many*) *soever*, with subj., Il.3.66, etc. 2. ὅσος δή *of such and such a size* or *number* (but in Hom. merely strengthd. for ὅσος, Od.15.487, al.), κήρυγμα ἐποιήσατο.., ζημίην τοῦτον ὀφείλειν, ὅσην δὴ εἴπας naming *such and such an amount*, Hdt.3.52; ἐπέταξε τοῖσι.. ἔθνεσι γυναῖκας.. κατιστάναι, ὅσας δὴ ἐπιτάσσων ordering *such and such a number*, ib.159; παρεσκευάζοντο ἐπὶ μισθῷ ὅσῳ δή for payment *of a certain amount*, Id.1.160; σιτία παρακαταλιπόντες ὅσων δὴ μηνῶν Id.4.151; so ὅσος δή κοτε Id.1.157; ὁσοσδηποτοῦν, in pl., *any number whatsoever*, Euc.9.9, al., Agatharch.34; ὁσοσδηοῦν *however large*, Jul.*Or.*3.119a; ὅσος δή τις D.H.2.45, 4.60. 3. ὁσοσοῦν, Ion. -ῶν, *ever so small*, Hdt.1.199: in pl., *however many*, Arist.*Pol.*1265ᵃ41; v. infr. IV. 6. 4. ὅσοσπερ, *precisely as great as*, τοῦ μὲν χειμῶνός ἐστι [ὁ Ἴστρος] ὅσοσπέρ ἐστι *of its normal size*, Hdt.4.50, cf. 2.170, etc.: in pl., *as many as*, Hes.*Th.*475, A.*Pers.*423, 441; ἔθνεα πάντα ὅσαπερ ἦγε Hdt.4.87; ἅπαντα.., ὅσαπέρ γ' ἔφασκον, κἄτι πολλῷ πλείονα Ar.*V.*806: but ὅσοσπερ can freq. hardly be distd. from ὅσος, v. supr. I. 2, 5, infr. IV. 1, 3, and 7; and this is still more the case with Ep. ὅσος τε (cf. ὅστε), Od.10.113, al. IV. Adverbial usages of ὅσον and ὅσα: 1. *so far as, so much as*, οὐ μέντοι ἐγὼ τόσον αἴτιός εἰμι, ὅσσον οἱ ἄλλοι Il.21.371: c. inf., ὅσον αὔξειν ἢ καθαιρεῖν *so far as* to.., Arist.*Rh.*1376ᵃ34: in parenthesis, c. inf., ὅσον γέ μ' εἰδέναι *as far as* I know, Ar.*Nu.*1252, Pl.*Tht.*145a, cf. D.H.2.59; so μακραίων γ', ὅσ' ἀπεικάσαι cj. in S.*OC*152 (lyr.); ὅσον ἐς Ἑλλάδα γλῶσσαν ἀπὸ Λατίνης μεταβαλεῖν App.*BC*4.11: but more freq. c. ind., ὅσσον ἔγωγε γιγνώσκω Il.13.222, cf. 20.360; so ὅσονπερ ἂν σθένω S.*El.*946; ὅσα γε.. ἦν εἰκάσαι Th.8.46; ὅσον δυνατόν Pl.*Smp.*196d, etc.; ὅσον καθ' ἕν' ἄνδρα *so far as* was in one man's power, D.18.153; ὅσον τὸ σὸν μέρος S.*OT*1509: c. gen., ὅσον γε δυνάμεως παρ' ἐμοί ἐστι Pl.*Cra.*422c, cf. S.*OT*1239; also ὅσα ἐγὼ μέμνημαι X.*Mem.*2.1.21; οἱ πατέρες, ὅσα ἄνθρωποι, οὐκ ἀμαθεῖς ἔσονται Pl.*R.*467c; ὅσα γε τἀνθρώπεια *humanly* speaking, Id.*Cri.*47a. b. *how far, how much*, ἴστε γὰρ ὅσσον ἐμοὶ ἀρετῇ περιβάλλετον ἵπποι Il.23.276; μαθήσεται ὅσον τό τ' ἄρχειν καὶ τὸ δουλεύειν δίχα A.*Pr.*927: with Adjs., *how*, ὅσον or ὅσσον.. ὄνειαρ, Hes.*Op.*41, 346; ὅσ' ἤπειρος πολλὰ τρέφει Id.*Th.*582. 2. *only so far as, only just*, ὅσον ἐς Σκαιάς τε πύλας καὶ φηγὸν ἵκανεν Il.9.354; ὅσον ἐκ Φοινίκης ἐς Κρήτην Hdt.4.45; φιλοσοφίας, ὅσον παιδείας χάριν, μετέχειν Pl.*Grg.*485a, cf. *R.*403d; οὐδὲν ἡδέως ποιεῖ γὰρ οὗτος, ἀλλ' ὅσον νόμου χάριν Diph.43.14, cf. Arist.*Metaph.*1076ᵃ27, al.; ὅσον καὶ ἀπὸ βοῆς ἕνεκα ὠργίζετο, opp. τῷ ἀληθεῖ ἐχαλέπαινον, Th.8.92: so, more fully, ὅσον μοῦνον Hdt.2.20, cf. Th.6.105, Pl.*R*.607a, etc.; or μόνον ὅσον Id.*Lg*.778c; ἐγὼ μέν μιν οὐκ εἶδον εἰ μὴ ὅσον γραφῇ Hdt.2.73, cf. X.*An*.7.3.20; σιτάρια μικρὰ προσφέρων οἴνου θ' ὅσον ὀσμήν Philem.98.3; τί οὐκ ἀπεκοιμήθημεν ὅ. ὅ. στίλην; Ar.*V*.213; ἢ ὅσον ὅσσον στιγμή *AP*7.472 (Leon.), cf. 5.254 (Paul. Sil.); ἐπαναγαγεῖν ὅ. ὅ. *Ev.Luc*.5.3 (cod. D, v.l. ὀλίγον); ὅσον· ὀλίγον, ὅσον ὅσον δέ, ὀλίγον ὀλίγον, Hsch.; παρ' ὅσον ἧττον *a little* less, D.T.631.17 (= παρ' ὀλίγον ἧττον, Sch.); οὐδ' ὅσον *not even*, οὐδ' ὅ. ἀττάραγόν τυ δεδοίκαμες Call.*Epigr*.47.9: abs., *not the least mite*, Id.*Ap*.37, A.R.2.181,190; οὐδέ περ ὅσσον Id.3.519; οὐδ' ὅσον ὅσσον Philet.7; cf. IV. 5. **3.** of size or distance, ὅσον τε *about*, *nearly*, ὅσον τ' ὄργυιαν, ὅσον τε πυγούσιον, Od.9.325, 10.517; ὅσον τ' ἐπὶ ἥμισυ 13.114, cf. Il.10.351; ὅσον τε δέκα στάδια Hdt.9.57; ξύλα ὅσον τε διπήχεα Id.2.96, cf. 78; so ὅσονπερ τρία στάδια Id.9.51; in Att. ὅσον alone, ὅσον δύο πλέθρα Th.7.38; ὅσον δύ' ἢ τρία στάδια Pl.*Phdr*.229c; ὅσον παρασάγγην X.*Cyr*.3.3.28; so of other measurements, ὅσον τριχοίνικον ἄρτον Id.*An*.7.3.23. **4.** with Adjs. of Quality or Degree, mostly with Comp., αἴθ', ὅσον ἥσσων εἰμί, τόσον σέο φέρτερος εἴην Il.16.722, cf. 1.186; ὅσσον βασιλεύτερός εἰμι *so far as*, *inasmuch as* I am a greater king, 9.160: and with Sup., γνώσετ'.., ὅσον εἰμὶ θεῶν κάρτιστος 8.17, cf. 1.516, etc.: with Advs., ὅσον τάχιστα A.*Ch*.772, S.*Ant*.1103, *El*.1433; ὅσον μάλιστα A.*Pr*.524; [ὅσ]α ἐδύνατο μ. Hdt.1.185. **5.** with negs., ὅσον οὐ or ὁσονού *just not*, *all but* (cf. IV. 2), Th.1.36, 5.59, etc.; ὅσον οὐκ ἤδη *almost* immediately, E.*Hec*.141 (anap.), Th.8.96; later ὅσον ἤδη Plb.2.4.4, 8.34.8; ὅσον οὔπω E.*Ba*.1076, Th.4.125, 6.34: ὅσον οὐδέπω with fut., *presently*, *in a minute*, Nicom.*Ar*.1.8, Hld.2.31, al. **b.** οὐχ ὅσον οὐκ ἠμύναντο, ἀλλ' οὐδ' ἐσώθησαν *not only not.., but not even*, Th.4.62. **c.** ὅσον μή *so far as not*, *save* or *except so far as*, καλός τε κἀγαθὸς τὴν φύσιν, ὅσον μὴ ὑβριστής (sic leg.) Pl.*Euthd*.273a; ὅσον γ' ἂν αὐτὸς μὴ ποτιψαύων *so far as I can* without touching.., S.*Tr*.1214; ὅσον μὴ χερσὶ καίνων Id.*OT*347; ὅσα μή Th.1.111, 4.16: sts. with a finite Verb, πείθεσθαι.., ὅσον ἂν μὴ ἀνάγκη ᾖ X.*Oec*.21.4, cf. Pl.*Phd*.83a; cf. ὅ τι II. **6.** ὁσονοῦν, Ion. ὁσονῶν, *ever so little*, εἰ τοίνυν ἐχιδνιζε καὶ ὁσονῶν Hdt.2.22; so ἐφ' ὁσονοῦν Thphr.*HP*6.7.5, Iamb.*in Nic*.p.14 P. **7.** ὅσα and ὅσαπερ, just like ὡς, ὥσπερ, *as*, X.*Cyr*.1.5.12, Luc.*VH*1.24, etc. **V.** ὅσῳ, ὅσῳπερ, *by how much*, freq. with Comp., ὅσῳ πλέον ἥμισυ παντός Hes.*Op*.40; ὅσῳ κρείττω Ar.*Fr*.488.3; ὅσῳ ἂν πλεονάκις εἰσίῃς X.*Cyr*.1.3.14: with Sup., διέδεξε, ὅσῳ ἐστὶ τοῦτο ἄριστον Hdt.3.82, cf. S.*Ant*.59, 1050. **2.** ὅσῳ with Comp. when folld. by another Comp. with τοσούτῳ, *the more.., so much the more..*, X.*Cyr*.7.5.80; ὅ. μᾶλλον πιστεύω, τοσούτῳ μᾶλλον ἀπορῶ Pl.*R*.368b: with τοσούτῳ omitted, Ar.*Nu*.1419, S.*OC*792: sts. a Sup. replaces the Comp., ὅσῳ μάλιστα ἐλεύθεροι.., τοσούτῳ καὶ θρασύτατα Th.8.84, cf. Lys.7.39; ὅσῳ alone, ἑωυτοὺς δὲ γενέσθαι τοσούτῳ..ἀμείνονας, ὅσῳ.. Hdt.6.137, cf. 5.49, 8.13; νιν τῶνδε πλεῖστον ᾤκτισα.., ὅσῳπερ καὶ φρονεῖν οἶδεν μόνη S.*Tr*.313, cf. *OC*743. **VI.** ἐς ὅσον, ἐφ' ὅσον, καθ' ὅσον are freq. used much like ὅσον, εἰς ὅσον σθένω Id.*Ph*.1403 (troch.); ἐφ' ὅσον ἐδύνατο Th.1.4; εἰς ὅσον δύνανται Pl.*R*.607a; καθ' ὅσον δυνατόν Id.*Ti*.51b; ἐφ' ὅσον ἐστὶν δυνατός *as far as* he can, *IG*2$^2$.903.11 (ii B.C.); later of Time, ἐς ὅσον δύναμίς μοι ὑπῆρχεν *as long as..* *POxy*.899.8 (ii/iii A.D.); ἐφ' ὅσον περιῆσαν *as long as* they lived, Mitteis *Chr*.31 i 23 (ii B.C.). **2.** ἐν ὅσῳ *while*, Ar.*Pax*943 (lyr.), Th.8.87. **VII.** no Adv. ὅσως occurs.

**ὅσοσπερ**, v. ὅσος III. 4.

**ὁσοῦν**, = ὁστισοῦν, τρόπῳ τινὶ ἢ παρευρέσει ᾑοῦν *SIG*578.42 (Teos, ii B.C.).

⊛ **ὅσπερ**, ἥπερ, ὅπερ (Ep. **ὅπερ** as masc., Il.7.114, 21.107); gen. οὗπερ, Ep. οἷόπερ A.R.1.1325; in Ion. writers and in Poets the obl. cases are sts. borrowed from the Art., τόπερ Id.3.1098; τοῦπερ A.*Pers*.779; τῇπερ Il.24.603, Hdt.1.30; τοίπερ Od.13.130; τάπερ A.*Ch*.418 (lyr.), Hdt.3.16; τῶνπερ Il.13.638, A.*Ag*.974; on concord and constr. cf. ὅς B. I. 1,2,4, II. 1a,3, IV. 4:—*the very man who*, *the very thing which*; freq. indistinguishable from simple ὅς, cf. ὅσος III. 4: with words intervening between ὅς and περ, ὅς ῥ' ἔβαλέν περ Il.4.524, cf. 13.101, etc. **2.** used after Adjs. of resemblance, ὡυτὸς ὅσπερ Hdt.8.42; ἐκ τῶν ἴσων.., ὧνπερ αὐτὸς ἐξέφυ S.*OT*1499; ὅμοια ἔπραττον ἅπερ ἄν.. X.*An*.5.4.34; ὅρκια τάπερ τε.. *the same as..*, Hdt.1.74. **II.** special uses of cases, **1.** ὅπερ, *wherefore*, D.S.13.18 codd. (s.v.l.); *although*, A.D.*Pron*.103.7. **2.** ἅπερ, *as*, *like*, A.*Ch*.381 (lyr.), *Eu*.131, 660, S.*Aj*.168 (anap., as v.l.), *OT*175 (lyr.), X.*HG*5.1.18, etc.; cf. καθάπερ. **3.** οὗπερ, v. ὅς A b. I. **4.** ᾗπερ, Dor. ᾇπερ, *which way*, *where*, *whither*, Il.6.41, 12.33, X.*An*.6.5.10, etc.; Ion. τῇπερ, ἔθαψαν..τῇπερ ἔπεσε Hdt.1.30; also, *as*, Il.7.286, A.*Ch*.440 (lyr.), Ar.*Ach*.364; ᾗπερ δή Il.9.310; ᾗπερ καί X.*Mem*.3.8.2. **5.** in the Logic of Aristotle, ὅπερ ἐστί, or ὅπερ alone, has two senses: **a.** non-technical, and unemphatic, *what* (a thing) *is*, ἑκάστη οὐσία τοῦθ' ὅ. ἐστίν, οὐ λέγεται μᾶλλον καὶ ἧττον each substance is called *what* it *is* without the difference of more or less, *Cat*.3$^b$36; τὸ διπλάσιον τοῦθ' ὅ. ἐστίν, ἑτέρου λέγεται the double is called *what* it *is* (viz. the double) of something, i.e. is relative, ib.6$^a$39. **b.** expressing identity, οὔτε ἡ χιὼν ὅ. λευκόν snow is not *what* white *is*, i.e. is not identical with white, *Top*.120$^b$23; ὁ λευκὸς ἄνθρωπος οὐκ ἔστιν ὅ. χρῶμα ib.116$^a$27: hence, to indicate the *precise* or *essential* nature of a thing, οὐ γὰρ ἂν φαίη ὅ. κακόν τι εἶναι τὴν ἡδονήν he would not say that pleasure is *essentially* something bad, *EN*1153$^b$6; τὰ μὲν οὐσίαν σημαίνοντα ὅ. ἐκεῖνο ἢ ὅ. ἐκεῖνό τι σημαίνει expressions which show the essence show *precisely what* the thing in question *is* or *precisely* of what kind it *is* (i.e. indicate either its species or its genus), *APo*.83$^a$24; ὅ. ⟨τόδε⟩ τί ἐστι τὸ τί ἦν εἶναι the essence of a thing *is precisely* a 'this', i.e. a fully specified particular, *Metaph*.1030$^a$3; ἡ μὲν [ἐπιστήμη] ὅ. ἀνθρώπου ἐστίν knowledge (that man is an animal) is apprehension that 'animal' is *an element in the essential nature* of man, *APo*.89$^a$35.

**ὄσπρα**· ποικίλα, Hsch.; cf. ὄσπρος.

**ὄσπρ-εον**, τό, later spelling of ὄσπριον, *POxy*.494.10 (ii A.D.), etc., rejected by *EM*635.48. ⊛ **-εύω**, *plant with* ὄσπρια, *IG*2$^2$.1241.23. ⊛ **-ηγοί**, οἱ, *those who carry a cargo of* ὄσπρια, *OGI*521.25 (Abydos, v/vi A.D.). (Contr. fr. ὀσπριηγοί.)

**ὀσπριο-δόχος**, ον, *for holding* ὄσπρια, ἀγγεῖον Eust.976.34. **-θήκη**, ἡ, *a place to keep pulse in*, Gloss.

**ὄσπριον**, τό, *pulse* of all kinds, Hdt.2.37, Alex.266.7, Thphr.*HP*8.1.1, *PPetr*.3 p.261 (iii B.C.), Gal.6.302, etc.: mostly in pl., Hp.*Acut*.(*Sp*.)47, X.*An*.4.4.9, Pl.*Criti*.115b, Orib.*Fr*.142.—Cf. ὄσπρεον, ὄσπρος.

⊛ **ὀσπριο-πώλης**, ου, ὁ, *one who deals in pulse*, *IG*2$^2$.1558.67: fem. -πωλις, ιδος, Sch.Ar.*Pl*.427. **-φᾰγέω**, *eat pulse*, Hp.*Epid*.2.4.3 = 6.4.11.

**ὀσπριώδης**, ες, *like pulse*, Aq.*Le*.2.14, Orib.*Fr*.80.

**ὀσπρολέων**, οντος, ὁ, = ὀροβάγχη, *Gp*.2.42.1.

**ὄσπρος**· ἰδίως τις λέγεται ὡς πισὸς καὶ ἐρέβινθος, Hsch. (cf. ὄσπριον).

⊛ **ὄσσᾰ**, Att. **ὄττα**, ἡ, *a rumour*, which, from its origin being unknown, was held divine, ὄ. ἐκ Διός Od.1.282, 2.216; personified as messenger of Zeus, Il.2.93, Od.24.413. **2.** generally, *voice*, of the Muses, Hes.*Th*.10, 43, 65; of a bull, ib.832. **3.** more generally, *sound*, of the lyre, *h.Merc*.443; *din* of battle, Hes.*Th*.701. **4.** *ominous voice* or *sound*, *prophecy*, *warning*, Pi.*O*.6.62; ὄρνιθος ὄ. A.R.1.1087.—Rare in Prose, κακὴν ὄτταν Pl.*Lg*.800c; ὄτταν ἀγαθήν Ael.*NA*12.1; δι' ὀνειράτων καὶ συμβόλων καὶ δι' ὄττης Porph.*Abst*.2.53. (Hence ὀττεύομαι: ὄσσα prob. fr. *woq*$^u$*-ya*, cf. (ϝ)ἔπος.)

**ὅσσα**, Ion. and Ep. neut. pl. of ὅσος for ὅσα. **ὁσσάκῐ**, Ion. and Ep. for ὁσάκις.

**ὁσσάτιος** [ᾰ], Ep. lengthd. form of ὅσος, Il.5.758, A.R.1.372, etc.; ὁσσάτιός περ, with τόσσος as antec., Nic.*Th*.570.

**ὄσσε**, τώ, prop. neut. dual, *the two eyes*, nom. and acc. freq. in Hom., who however adds the Adj. in the pl., ὄ. φαεινά, αἱματόεντα, Il.13.435, 616 (dual φαεινώ 14.236): and the Verb in the sg., πυρὶ δ' ὄ. δεδήει 12.466; ὀξύτατον κεφαλῆς ἐκ δέρκεται ὄ. 23.477; ἐν δέ οἱ ὄ. δαίεται Od.6.131: later gen. pl. ὄσσων Hes.*Th*.826, A.*Pr*.400 (lyr.), *Supp.Epigr*.3.400.5 (Delph., iii B.C.); dat. ὄσσοις, ὄσσοισι, Hes.*Sc*.145, 426, 430, Sapph.29, A.*Pr*.144 (lyr.), 679, *Ag*.469 (lyr.), S.*Ant*.1231, *Ichn*.47, etc.; Eust.58.28 cites also dat. ὄσσει, and Hsch. gen. pl. ὀσσέων. (Prob. I.-E. *oq*$^u$*-ye*, cf. ὄσσομαι, ὄψομαι.)

**ὀσσεία**, **ὀσσεύομαι**, v. ὀττ-. **ὀσσῆξαι**· ἐπιδεῖξαι, Hsch. **ὀσσητῆρα**· βοηθόν, Id. (i.e. ἀοσσ-).

**ὀσσίχος** [ῐ], η, ον, Dim. of ὅσος, ὅσσος, *as little*, *how little*, Theoc.4.55, Hsch.

⊛ **ὄσσομαι**, (ὄσσε) Ep. Verb, used only in pres. and impf. without augm., pres. (I.-E. *oq*$^u$*-yo-*) corresponding to fut. ὄψομαι (v. ὄψ): Act. ὄσσω only *EM*562.6, 673.11: prop. *see*, *look*, as in A.R.4.318, cf. ὄμμασι λοξὸν ὑποδρὰξ ὀσσομένη Call.*Fr.anon*.63, and in the compd. προτιόσσομαι (q.v.): but mostly, **II.** *see in spirit* or *with the mind's eye*, ὀσσόμενος πατέρ' ἐσθλὸν ἐνὶ φρεσίν Od.1.115, cf. 20.81. **2.** *presage*, *have foreboding of*, κακὰ δ' ὄσσετο θυμός 10.374, cf. 18.154; ὄσσοντο γὰρ ἄλγεα θυμῷ Il.18.224. **3.** by imparting such presages to others, *forebode*, used only of evil, ὡς ὅτε πορφύρῃ πέλαγος μέγα κύματι κωφῷ ὀσσόμενον λιγέων ἀνέμων λαιψηρὰ κέλευθα 14.17; esp. by look or mien, κάκ' ὀσσόμενος *boding* evil *by his looks*, 1.105; of two eagles, ὄσσοντο ὄλεθρον *boded* death, Od.2.152; οὐ μὲν γάρ τοι ἐγὼ κακὸν ὀσσομένη τόδ' ἱκάνω Il.24.172, cf. Hes.*Th*.551.

**ὅσσος**, η, ον, v. ὅσος. **ὀσσῶσθαι**· κληδονίσασθαι, Hsch.

**ὀστάγρα**, ἡ, (ὀστέον) *forceps for extracting splinters of bone*, Sor.2.63, Gal.10.449, Heliod.ap.Orib.44.11.7. **II.** = ὀστεοκόπος, Thphr.*Lass*.2.

**ὀσταθείς**· ἐξαγκωνισθείς, Hsch.: **ὄστασαν**· ἀνέστησαν, Id. (Both prob. Aeol., ὀ(ν)στ- = ἀναστ-.)

⊛ **ὀστᾰκός**, ὁ, = ἀστακός, *lobster*, Aristomen.6, Eun.*Hist*.p.251 D.: as pr. n. Ὄστακος *Inscr.Délos*442 *A* 20 (ii B.C.).

**ὀσταλιόχος**· τόξευμα, Hsch.

**ὀστανα-βολεύς**, έως, ὁ, and **-λᾰβεύς**, έως, ὁ, names of surgical instruments, *Hermes*38.284 (*-boleos* cod.), 282 (-λαβες cod.).

**ὀστᾰρίδιον**, τό, = ὀστάριον, Pall.*in Hp*.12.279 C. (pl.).

**ὀστάριον**, τό, Dim. of ὀστέον, *little bone*, *PTeb*.1.18 (ii/i B.C.), *AP*11.96 (Nicarch.), Damocr.ap.Gal.14.94, Tz.*H*.10.231; *small piece of bone*, Heliod.ap.Orib.46.11.30, Dsc.*Eup*.1.235. **II.** *stone*, *kernel*, of nuts, etc., Id.1.118, Alex.Trall.8.2, Paul.Aeg.6.24.

**ὄστασαν**, v. ὀσταθείς. **ὀσταφίς**, v. ἀσταφίς.

⊛ **ὅστε**, ἥτε, ὅτε (also written divisim), in Hom. also **ὅ τε** as masc., Il.17.757: (ὅς, τε):—*who*, *which*, like the simple ὅς or ὅστις, freq. with a generalizing force (τε is however sts. otiose, as in ὅτε, ὥστε, οἷός τε, ἐπεί τε, etc., v. τε B. 1), Od.14.221, etc.: neut. pl. τά τε Il.5.481, etc.: pl. fem. τάς τε 11.554: used also in Pi.*P*.2.39, al., and lyr. passages of Trag. (A.*Pers*.16, *Ag*.49, *Ch*.615, S.*El*.151, *Tr*.824, E.*Hec*.445), but very rare in trim., A.*Pers*.297, 762, *Eu*.25, 1024; and in Prose only in special forms, such as ἅτε, ἐφ' ᾧτε:—rarely with antec. expressed, θεάων τάων, αἵ τ'.. Il.5.332; τῷ ἴκελος, ὅν τ'.. 24.758; τά τε φρονέων, ἅ τ' ἐγώπερ Od.7.312.—Not to be confounded with ὅς τε, *and who*, Il.2.365, Od.3.185, al. **2.** ἐξ οὗτε *from the* *time when..*, A.*Pers.*762, *Eu.*25; ἀπ' οὗτε *PCair.Zen.*291.3 (iii B.C.). 3. freq. folld. by περ, τά τε στυγέουσι θεοί περ Il.20.65. 4. with ῥα between ὅς and τε, αἴγειρος ὥς, ἥ ῥά τε.. 4.483, cf. 15.411, 19.31, al. II. ὅ τε *in that, because*, 1.244; introducing the reason for making a statement or asking a question, 4.32, al.; so prob. 15.468: for ἅτε, ᾧτε, v. sub vocc.: ᾇτε, Dor. for ᾗτε, *as*, Ar. *Lys.*1308 (lyr.): ἐφ' ᾧτε, v. ἐπί B. III. 3.

**ὀστέϊνος**, η, ον, *made of bone, of bone*, Hdt.4.2, Pl.*Ti.*74a, Arist. *HA*493ᵃ2; cf. ὄστινος, ὀστόϊνος.

**ὀστεο-γενής**, ές, *produced in the bones*: ὀστεογενές, epith. applied to the marrow, Pl.ap.Arist.*Top.*140ᵃ5. **-κόλλος**, ἡ, a herb, = σύμφυτον, *Hippiatr.*66. **-κόπος**, ὁ, *an inflammatory attack, which makes one feel as if one's bones were giving way*, Hp.*Acut.*(*Sp.*)1 (v.l.), Thphr.*Lass.*2, Gal.8.104, al.: in *Com.Adesp.*329, Gal.6.194 **ὀστοκόπος**. **-λογέω**, *treat of bones*, Id.14.690. **-λογία**, Ion. -ίη, ἡ, *extraction of bones*, Hp.*Steril.*249. II. *description of bones*, Ruf. *Oss.*1, Gal.14.720:—but **ὀστολογία**, Id.2.220. **-λόγος**, ον, *extracting bones*: -λόγον, τό, a surgical instrument, Hp.*Mul.*1.70.

**ὀστέον**, τό, Att. contr. **ὀστοῦν**, poet. **ὀστεῦν** *AP*7.480 (Leon.); Aeol. perh. **ὄστιον** Alc.*Oxy.*2081(*d*)*Fr.*5: pl. ὀστέα, Att. contr. ὀστᾶ, late Ep. ὀστά [ᾰ] Opp.*C.*1.268, Epigr.in D.L.1.63, *Epigr.Gr.*517.7 (Edessa); Dor. ὀστία Theoc.2.61; but Trag. and Com. use gen. pl. ὀστέων, A.*Fr.*367 (codd. Poll.), S.*Tr.*769, Ar.*Ach.*1226, and it is so written in E.*Tr.*1177 where metre requires ὀστῶν: and the uncontr. forms generally occur in later Prose, as in Arist. (v. infr.); nom. ὀστέον *PLit.Lond.*167.17 (ii/iii A.D.); dat. pl. ὀστέοις Diog.Oen.39; Ep. gen. pl. ὀστεόφιν (v. infr.):—*bone*, freq. in Hom. (Il.4.460, al.) and Hp.(*VC*1, al.); Hes. only in pl., *Th.*540, al.; λευκ' ὀστέα *the bleached bones of the dead*, Od.1.161, etc.; σάρκας τε καὶ ὀστέα 9.293; πολὺς δ' ἀμφ' ὀστεόφιν θὶς a huge heap *of bones* around, 12.45; ῥινὸν ἀπ' ὀστεόφιν ἐρύσαι 14.134; γυμνοῦσι τὰ ὀστέα τῶν κρεῶν Hdt.4.61; ὀστέων στέγαστρον, of the skin, A.*Fr.*367; ἀρχὴ τῶν ὀστῶν ἡ καλουμένη ῥάχις Arist.*PA*654ᵇ11; esp. of the cranium, Hp.*VC*2, al., cf. Il. 12.185. II. metaph., γῆς ὀστέοισιν ἐγχριμφθεὶς πόδα, i.e. *rocks*, Choeril.Trag.2 (ὀστοῖσιν Nauck). III. *stone* of fruit, ὀστῶν περσείνων *PCair.Zen.*176.168 (iii B.C.), cf. Dsc.*Eup.*1.66, *Gp.*10.13.3, al., Sch.Nic.*Al.*99. [Accent ὀστέον Hdn.Gr.2.943, but ὄστεον Anon.ap. Sch.Il.24.793.] (Cf. Skt. *ásthi*, gen. *asthnás* 'bone', etc.)

**ὀστεώδης**, ες, *bony*, Plu.2.916a.

**ὄστἵνος**, η, ον, (ὀστέον) Att. form of ὀστέϊνος (q.v.) acc. to Poll.2. 232, Phot., found in Arist.*PA*692ᵇ18 codd., Gal.18(1).237; τὰ ὄστινα *bone-pipes*, ὀστίνοις φυσᾶν Ar.*Ach.*863 (spoken by a Boeotian).

⊕ **ὅστις**, ἥτις, ὅ τι (sts. written ὅ,τι to dist. it from ὅτι, *that*): Hom. has also the masc. collat. form ὅτις Od.1.47, al. (also in Critias 2.9 and Ion. and Arc. Prose, *Jahresh.*12.136 (Erythrae), *IG*12(5).22 (Ios), 5(2).343.34 (Orchom. Arc.)) and the neut. ὅττι Od.9.402, al., cf. ὅττι Alc.45.—In some forms only the second part is inflected, viz. gen. ὅτου Th.1.23, al., Ep. ὅττεο Od.1.124, later Ion. ὅτεο *Jahresh.* l.c., contr. ὅττευ Od.17.121, ὅτευ ib.421, Hdt.1.7; Lesb. ὅττω Sapph.*Supp.*5.3: dat. ὅτῳ Th.1.36, al.; perh. also in Ion., Emp. 2.5, Democr.99, Hp.*VC*14; Ep. ὅτεῳ Od.2.114, and as disyll., Il.12. 428, 15.664; so Hdt.1.86, al., Democr.100, Heraclit.15, *SIG*194.21 (Amphipolis, iv B.C.); Arc. ὀτέοι *IG*5(2).262.14 (Mantinea, v B.C.); Ep. acc. ὅτινα Od.8.204, 15.395; Delph. gen. ὅτινος *IG*2².1126.37 (iv B.C.), also *Berl.Sitzb.*1927.167 (Cyrene); Delph. dat. ὅτινι *IG* 2².1126.25; Cret. dat. sg. ὅτιμι *Leg.Gort.*7.51, 8.7, al.: pl., nom. masc. Arg. ὅττινες *Mnemos.*44.65 (iii B.C.); neut. ὅτινα Il.22.450; gen. ὅτεων Od.10.39, Hdt.8.65, Att. ὅτων S.*OT*414, X.*An.*7.6.24 (cj.), *Oec.*3.2 (cj.) (also in Hes.*Fr.*238, Anaxag.12, Hp.*Aër.*21); dat. ὀτέοισι(ν) Il.15.491, Hdt.2.82, Att. ὅτοισι S.*Ant.*1335, Ar.*Eq.*758, ὅτοις S.*Tr.*1119; acc. ὅτινας Il.15.492, Aeol. ὅττινας Sapph.12: in a few forms only the first part is inflected, Cret. gen. sg. ὅτι prob. in *Leg.Gort.*1.5, 2.50, 11.50, al., *GDI*4993ii 10: neut. pl. ἅτι *Leg.Gort.*2. 47, al.: of the forms with double inflexion Hom. has only ὅν τινα Il.2. 188, al., ἥν τινα 3.286, al., οἵ τινες Od.4.94, al., οὕς τινας Il.4.240, al., ἅς τινας Od.8.573; ᾧτινι first in Hes.*Op.*31, ἧστινος A.*Ag.*1358, ᾗ τινι δή Th.8.87, οἷστισι Ar.*Pax* 1279: Att. Inscrr. have ἧστινος ἧτινι along with masc. and neut. ὅτου ὅτῳ, and this rule holds with few exceptions in Trag. and Att. Prose before iv B.C.; ᾡτινιοῦν occurs in Lys.1.37, etc.: ὅτῳ rarely as fem., E.*IT*1071.—For the Ion. and Ep. form **ἅσσα**, Att. ἅττα, v. ἅσσα.—On the concord and construction cf. ὅς B. I. 1, 3, II. 3, III. 2a, b:—Radic. sense, *any one who, anything which, whosoever, whichsoever*; ὡς ἀπόλοιτο καὶ ἄλλος, ὅτις τοιαῦτά γε ῥέζοι Od.1.47; ἀθανάτων ὅς τίς σε φυλάσσει 15.35, etc.: freq. without express antec., χαίρει δέ μιν ὅς τις ἐθείρῃ Il.21.347; ἄσσον ἴτω ὅς τις δέπας οἴσεται 23.667: hence freq. in maxims or sentiments, οὐκ ἔστιν ὅ. πάντ' ἀνὴρ εὐδαιμονεῖ Ar.*Ra.*1217; μακάριος ὅ. οὐσίαν καὶ νοῦν ἔχει Men.114; οὗτος βέλτιστος ἂν εἴη, ὅ.. Lys.3.4, etc.: freq. in such phrases as ὅστις εἶ, ὅστις ἐστί, v. ὅς B. III. 2; ἔστιν ὅ., freq. with a neg., οὐ γὰρ ἔην ὅς τίς σφιν.. ἡγήσαιτο Il.2.687; οὐκ ἔστιν ὅτῳ μείζονα μοῖραν νείμαιμ' ἢ σοί A.*Pr.*293 (anap.), cf. 989, 1070 (anap.), etc.; εἰσὶν οἵτινες S.*Fr.*354.5; οὐδὲν ὅ τι οὐ.. *everything*, Hdt. 5.97, Th.7.87:—in these phrases the case of ὅστις commonly depends on that of οὐδείς; but sts. the reverse, v. οὐδείς I. 2: also joined with Sup., τρόπῳ ὅτῳ ἂν δύνωνται ἰσχυροτάτῳ Foed.ap.Th.5.23; ὅντινα ἀφανέστατον δύναιντο τρόπον Paus.10.1.5: in Trag. and Att. sts. strengthd. by an antec. πᾶς, but only in sg., ἅπας δὲ τραχὺς ὅ. ἂν νέον κρατῇ A.*Pr.*35, cf. Th.8.90 (πάντες ὅσοι being commonly used in pl., not πάντες οἵτινες; but πᾶσιν.. ὅστις ἐρωτᾷ *IG*1².410). II. referring to a definite object, prop. only when a general notion is implied, Πολυκράτεα.., δι' ὅντινα κακῶς ἤκουσε, not *the man through whom*, but *one through whom..*, Hdt.3.120; τελευταῖόν σε προσβλέψαιμι νῦν, ὅστις πέφασμαι φύς τ' ἀφ' ὧν οὐ χρῆν may I see thee now for the last time, I *who am one* born from sinful parentage, S.*OT*1184, cf. A.*Pr.* 38, *Ag.*1065; but in quite definite sense, βωμόν, ὅστις νῦν ἔξω τῆς πόλεώς ἐστι Th.6.3: sts. even with οὗτος or ὅδε as antec., Hdt.1. 167, 2.99, 6.47, E.*Hipp.*943, Theoc.8.87. 2. ἐφ' ὅτῳ, = ἐφ' ᾧτε, D.S.16.4; so ἐφ' ὅτῳ τε *Delph.*3(2).236 (ii B.C.). III. in indirect questions, Hom., etc., εἴπ' ἄγε μοι καὶ τόνδε.., ὅς τις ὅδ' ἐστί Il.3.192, cf. 167, etc.; ἔσπετε νῦν μοι, Μοῦσαι, ὅς τις δὴ κτλ. *who it was that..*, 14.509; ξεῖνος ὅδ', οὐκ οἶδ' ὅς τις Od.8.28: in dialogue, when the person questioned repeats the question asked by τίς, as οὗτος τί ποιεῖς;—ὅ τι ποιῶ; Ar.*Ra.*198; ἀλλὰ τίς γὰρ εἶ;—ὅστις; πολίτης χρηστός Id.*Ach.*595, cf. *Pl.*462, Pl.*Euthphr.*2c, etc. 2. rare and late in direct questions, ὅ τι ἐστὶ τὸ ἐμποδίζον; A.D.*Adv.*140.12; ἀνθ' ὅτου..; = *why?* Jul.*Ep.*82 p.109 B.-C.; cf. ὅπως. IV. limited or made more indefinite by the addition of Particles: 1. ὅστις γε *being one who* (cf. ὅσγε), S.*OT*1335, *OC*810, Ar.*Ra.*1184. 2. ὅστις δή (v. δή IV. 1), freq. used without any distinct relative force, θεῶν ὅτεῳ δή *to some one or other* of the gods, Hdt.1.86; ὅτευ δὴ χρήματος δεησόμενον Id.3.121; ᾗ τινι δὴ γνώμῃ Th.8.87, etc.; also ὅ τι δήκοτε πρήξοντα Hdt.6.134; ὅστις δήποτ' ὢν Pl.*Phdr.*273c; ὡς ἀπετύγχαν' ὁτουδήποτε D.19.167; ὁτῳδήτινι τρόπῳ *PFay.*21.11 (ii A.D.); so b. ὁστισοῦν, ὁτιοῦν *anybody* (*anything*) *whatsoever*, Th.4.16, Pl. *Smp.*198b, etc.; μετὰ ὁτουοῦν τρόπου Th.8.27; ὁτῳοῦν Pl.*Tht.*175a; εἷς ὁστισοῦν *any one person*, Arist.*Pol.*1286ᵃ31: freq. with neg., μηδ' ἂν ὁστισοῦν τυγχάνῃ ὤν Pl.*Euthphr.*5e, cf. *Phd.*78d, etc.; οὐδ' ὁτιοῦν not *the least mite*, nothing *whatsoever*, Ar.*Nu.*344, *Pl.*385; μηδοτιοῦν Thgn.64: rarely, = *whoever* (*whatever*), as subject of a verb, ὁτιοῦν ἔτυχε τῶν ἐπὶ μέρους (v.l. ὅτι ἂν) Arist.*Mu.*391ᵃ22. c. ὁστισδηποτοῦν D.40.8, Aeschin.1.164. d. so also ὅστις alone, Pl.*Hp.Ma.* 282d, etc.: with neg., μηδὲ οἵτινες none *at all*, X.*HG*1.5.9; οὐδ' ἧστινος ἂν ἀσχολίας τὸ πρᾶγμα προσεδεῖτο Plb.9.14.6. 3. ὅστις ποτὲ *whoever*, A.*Ag.*160 (lyr.), cf. Hdt.8.65. 4. ὅστις περ (cf. ὅσπερ), mostly in neut., ὅ τι πέρ ἐστ' ὄφελος Ar.*Ec.*53, cf. Pl.*R.*492e: in masc., D.21.225. 5. ὅστις τε, where τε is otiose as in ὅστε, Il.23.43, al. V. neut. ὅ τι used abs. as a Conj., v. ὅτι. VI. ἐξ ὅτου *from which time*. S.*OC*345, *Tr.*326, Ar.*Nu.*528, X.*Cyr.*8.2.16, etc.; ἐξ ὅτου περ Ar.*Ach.*596; ἀπ' ὅτευ *since..*, Hdt.1.7, cf. *SIG*45.18 (Halic., v B.C.); so ἕως ὅτου *until..*, *Ev.Luc.*13.8. 2. *from what cause*, S. *Tr.*671, E.*Cyc.*639.

**ὀστίτης** [ῑ], ου, ὁ, *in* or *of the bones*, μυελὸς ὀ. Ruf.*Onom.*217.

**ὄστλιγξ**, ιγγος, ἡ, *hair*, esp. *curled hair, lock of hair*, Call.*Fr.*12; cf. ἄστλιγξ. II. *anything curled* or *twisted*, as, 1. *tendril* of vine and other climbing plants, Thphr.*HP*3.18.5. 2. *curling flame*, πυρός A.R.1.1297. 3. of the *arms* of the cuttle-fish, Nic.*Al.* 470.

**ὀστο-δερμία**, ἡ, *skin and bone*, Tz.*H.*10.717 (pl.). **-δέτης**, ου, ὁ, *bonesetter*, Zos.Alch.p.233 B.: -δετική διαγραφή, diagram *for purposes of bonesetting*, ibid. **-ειδής**, ές, *like bones*, Hp.*Loc.Hom.*4 (Comp.), Gal.14.720. **-θηκάριον**, τό, Dim. of sq., Wood *Ephesus Append.*(*Inscrr.fr.Tombs*)14. ⊕ **-θήκη**, ἡ, *receptacle for bones, sarcophagus*, Lyc.367, *Com.Adesp.*329, *IPE* 1².542.3 (Chersonese, i A.D.), *CIG*2728, 2731 (Stratonicea). **-θήκιον**, τό, Dim. of foreg., *Schwyzer*625.1 (Mytil., ii/i B.C.).

**ὀστοινα**, dub. sens. in *PFay.*331 (ii A.D.).

**ὀστόϊνος**, = ὀστέϊνος, Aq.*Ex.*1.9, al.

**ὀστο-κατεάκτης**, ου, ὁ, *ossifrage, lammergeyer*, *Gloss.* **-κλάστης**, ου, ὁ, = foreg., Cyran.98, *Gloss.* **-κόπος**, ὁ, v. ὀστεοκόπος. **-κοπώδης**, ες, *feeling as if one's bones were broken*, ῥῖγος Pall.*Febr.*22.2, cf. Aët.4.38. **-κόραξ**, ακος, ὁ, = ὀστοκατεάκτης, *Gloss.* ⊕ **-λογέω**, *gather bones*, Is.4.19. **-λογία**, ἡ, *gathering up of bones* after the burning of a body, D.S.4.38:—also **-λόγιον**, τό, Lat. *ossilegium*, *Gloss.* II. v. ὀστεολογία. **-λόγος**, ον, (λέγω B) *collecting bones*, Epil.7; Ὀστολόγοι, name of a tragedy by Aeschylus, Ath.15.667c. **-μάχιον** [ᾰ], τό, a game played with fourteen pieces of bone, Aus.*Opusc.*17 *Praef.* **-ποιητικός**, ή, όν, *of* or *for making bone*, δύναμις Gal.*Nat.Fac.*1.6.

**ὀστοῦν**, τό, Att. contr. for ὀστέον (q.v.).

**ὀστο-φᾰγέω**, *eat bones*, Str.16.4.17, Paul.Aeg.3.42, Alex.Trall. 4. **-φᾰνέω**, *show bones*, i.e. *ribs*, *Hippiatr.*38. **-φυής**, ές, *of a b y nature* or *substance*, Batr.296.

**ὀστρᾰκ-ᾶς**, ᾶ, ὁ, *potter*, Hdn.Gr.2.657, *MAMA*3.718 (Corycus). **-εος**, α, ον, = ὀστράκινος, Nic.*Fr.*73.3 (dub. l.), Orph. *A.*322:—also **-ειος**, *PCair.Zen.*82.11 (iii B.C.), Sch. Luc. *Lex.* 7. **-εύς**, έως, ὁ, *potter*, *APl.*4.191 (Nicaen.). **-ηρός**, ά, όν, *of the nature of earthenware*, [ζῷα] ὀ. *testaceous* animals, Arist.*GA* 763ᵃ30, *PA*679ᵇ12, al. **-ίας**, ου, ὁ, *a stone resembling an agate*, Plin.*HN*37.177. **-ίζω**, *banish* (esp. from Athens) *by potsherds*, *ostracize*, Th.1.135, 8.73, And.3.3, Arist.*Ath.*22.6, *Pol.*1284ᵃ21, Sch. Ar.*Eq.*851; also used at Argos, Arist.*Pol.*1302ᵇ18; at Megara and Miletus, Sch.Ar. l.c. **-ίνδα**, Adv. *played with potsherds* or *oyster-shells* (the black and white surfaces being analogous to our 'heads and tails'), [παιδιά] Poll.9.111, Herm. *in Phdr.*p.90 A.: with a play on ὀστρακισμός, ὀ. βλέψαι Ar.*Eq.*855. **-ῐνος**, η, ον, *earthen, made of clay*, of vessels, Hp.*Nat.Mul.*34, al., Pl.Com.114, *AP*7.645 (Crin.), 11.74 (Nicarch.), 2*Ep.Ti.*2.20, 2*Ep.Cor.*4.7, *PLond.* 3.1177.95 (ii A.D.). 2. *like earthenware*, ὀστράκινα τὸ δέρμα, = ὀστρακόδερμα, v.l.

in Luc.Lex.6. -ιον, τό, Dim. of ὄστρακον, Arist.HA594$^{a}$11, Str. 17.3.11, Sch.D.T.p.196 H. 2. shell-fish, Str.17.2.4. -ίς, ίδος, ἡ, pine-cone or pine-seed, Mnesith.ap.Ath.2.57b, cf. Ath.3.126a. II. ἀγαλμάτιόν τι Ἀφροδίτης, Hsch. -ισμός, ὁ, ostracism, Arist.Ath. 22.3, Pol.1284$^{a}$17, al. -ίτης [ῑ], ου, ὁ, = ὀστράκινος, λίθος ὀ. Dsc.5. 146, cf. Plin.HN36.139; also, ostracitis, = ὀστρακίας, ib.37.177. 2. fem. ὀστρακῖτις, ιδος, an inferior variety of καδμεία, Dsc.5.74, Plin.HN 37.151. II. a kind of cake, Ath.14.647f.

**ὀστρᾰκό-δερμος**, ον, with a shell like a potsherd, hard-shelled, καρκίνοι Batr.295; ὀ. ζῷα testaceans or molluscs (excl. cuttle-fishes), opp. μαλακόστρακα, Arist.HA523$^{b}$9, cf. 590$^{a}$19, Thphr.HP4.6.8, Ath.3. 89f, Jul.Or.6.193b; also of certain crabs, Arist.HA601$^{a}$18; of eggs, ib.489$^{b}$14. -εις, εσσα, εν, poet. for ὀστράκινος, δόμος ὀ. AP9.86 (Antiphil.); νῶτα Poet.ap.Suid. s.v. στυφελισμός: contr. ὀστρακοῦς Gal.8.190. -κονία, ἡ, pavement made of crushed potsherds, concrete, Gp.2.27.5.

**ὄστρᾰκον**, τό, earthen vessel, Ar.Ra.1190, Ec.1033, Lys.3.28, 4.6; flower-pot, Thphr.HP6.7.3. 2. fragment of such a vessel, potsherd, IG4$^{2}$(1).121.82 (Epid., iv B.C., pl.), LxxPs.21.16, al., Ostr.1152, etc.; ἱπνοῦ ὄστρακα Hp.Morb.2.47; esp. the potsherd used in voting (v. ὀστρακίζω): hence τοὔστρακον παροίχεται the danger of ostracism is past, Cratin.71; τὰ ὄστρακα, = ὀστρακισμός, Pl.Com.187; τὸ ὄ. ἐπιφέρειν τινί to vote for any one's banishment, Plu.Alc.13, cf. Per. 14. 3. ὀστράκου περιστροφή, of the game ὀστρακίνδα (q.v.), Pl. R.521c; so ὀστράκου μεταπεσόντος 'if heads become tails', Id.Phdr. 241b. 4. earthenware castanet, ἡ τοῖς ὀ. κροτοῦσα [Μοῦσα], of the poetry of Euripides, Ar.Ra.1305. II. the hard shell of snails, mussels, cuttle-fishes, tortoises, etc., h.Merc.33, S.Ichn.303 (dub. l.), Hp.Steril.245, Theoc.9.25, Arist.HA528$^{a}$4, etc.: hence, tortoise-shell or mother-of-pearl, κλιντῆρες ὀστράκοις.. ἐνδεδεμένοι prob. l. in Ph. 1.666; the shell at the base of the constellation Lyra, Ptol.Alm. 7.5. 2. egg-shell, ἀπτῆνα.., ἄρτι γυμνὸν ὀστράκων A.Fr.337, cf. Arist.GA754$^{a}$2.

**ὀστρᾰκό-νωτος**, ον, having the back covered with a hard shell, Teucer ap.Ath.10.455e, Ael.NA9.6. -ποιός, ὁ, potter, Gloss. -ρῖνος, ον, = ὀστρακόδερμος, Opp.H.1.313, 5.589, Luc.Lex.6.

**ὀστρακοῦς**, v. ὀστρακόεις.

**ὀστρᾰκο-φορέω**, vote with ὄστρακα, Sch.Ar.Eq.851. -φορία, ἡ, voting with ὄστρακα, Arist.Ath.43.5, Plu.Alc.13. -χρως, acc. ὀστρακόχροα, with a hard skin or shell, AP6.196 (Stat. Flacc.).

**ὀστρᾰκ-όω**, turn into potsherds, dash to pieces:—Pass., to be dashed in pieces, A.Fr.180.4. II. make the skin hard like shell, ὀ. τὸ δέρμα Arist.Pr.869$^{b}$25:—Pass., become covered with a hard shell, Lyc.89; so of bread baked to a crust, Gal.14.50. III. pave with concrete (cf. ὀστρακοκονία), IG2$^{2}$.463.82 (iv B.C.). -ώδης, ες, like an earthen pot or sherd, testaceous, of crabs, Arist.HA525$^{b}$12, al.; of the shell of the tortoise, ib.600$^{b}$20; of oysters, ib.531$^{a}$17; of the covering of certain eggs, Id.GA733$^{a}$20, HA558$^{a}$28. 2. full of potsherds, τὸ ὄρος τὸ -ῶδες LxxJd.1.35; ὀ. τόπος POxy.941.2 (vi A.D.).

**ὀστρειακός**, ή, όν, of the oyster, σάρξ Zonar.

**ὀστρεΐνος**, η, ον, of or living in a shell, testaceous, Pl.Phlb.21c. II. (ὄστρεον III) purple, in form ὀστρῖνος, POxy.109.5 (iii/iv A.D.).

**ὀστρειογρᾰφής**, ές, purple-painted, Mamerc.ap.Plu.Tim.31.

**ὄστρειον**, τό, v. ὄστρεον.

❀ **ὄστρε-ον** or **ὄστρειον**, τό, oyster; the proper Att. form is ὄστρειον (ὄστρεια.. ἔλεγον οἱ ἀρχαῖοι Ath.3.92e, cf. Moer.p.285 P. (who recommends ὀστρία [ῐ] wrongly), Phot., etc.), and this is required by the metre in the earlier Poets, κόγχοι, μύες, κὤστρεια A.Fr.34; ὄστρεια συμμεμυκότα Epich.42 (ὄστρεα codd. Ath.); πίννῃσι καὶ ὀστρείοισιν ὁμοίη Cratin.8; πίνναι, λεπάδες, μύες, ὄστρεια Anaxandr.41.61 (anap.); while ὄστρεον is used in late Ep., Matro Conv.16, Nic.Fr.83, and is found in Pap., PCair.Zen.82.13 (iii B.C.), POxy.738.5 (i A.D.):—the readings vary in Pl. (v. infr. III), as in Arist., cf. HA490$^{b}$10, 525$^{a}$20: generally, of all bivalves, ib.525$^{a}$20, 528$^{a}$1, Fr.304, Gal.12.345. II. oyster- or bivalve-shell, Arist.HA531$^{b}$5, 590$^{a}$32. III. purple pigment, prob. that produced by the murex, cf. Arist.HA548$^{a}$12; ὄστρεον μόνον ἐπιφέρειν Pl.Cra.424d; ὀστρείῳ ἐναληλιμμένος Id.R.420c: τὰ σώματα ἐκέχριντο ὀστρείῳ Callix.2: ὄστρεα· τὰ κογχύλια, Λάκωνες ἄνθος, Hsch. -ώδης, ες, of the oyster kind, Arist.HA607$^{b}$3, Str. 3.2.7, Aristid.Quint.2.17, Olymp.in Phd.p.143N.:—also **ὀστρειώδης**, hard-shelled, Arist.PA684$^{a}$9.

**ὀστρῖμον**, τό, byre or enclosure for cattle, βόας ὀστρίμου ἐξήλασσεν Antim.41, cf. Lyc.94 (pl.): ὄστριμον· ἐν ᾧ αἱ θεριναὶ μοναὶ τόπος, οἱ δὲ ἔπαυλις, Hsch.

**ὀστρῖνος**, v. ὀστρεΐνος II.

**ὀστρίτης** [ῑ] λίθος, ὁ, a kind of stone, Orph.L.344.

**ὀστρύα** (or ὀστρύη), and **ὄστρυς**, υος, ἡ, hop hornbeam, Ostrya carpinifolia, Thphr.HP3.10.3, cf. 3.3.1, 3.6.1, Plin.HN13.117; also **ὀστρυΐς**, ΐδος, ἡ, Thphr.HP1.8.2.

**ὀστώδης**, ες, like bone, bony, X.Eq.1.8, 5.6, Arist.HA500$^{b}$23, al., Thphr.HP3.18.5; ὀ. μέρη PMed.in Arch.Pap.4.271 (iii A.D.), cf. Porph.Gaur.17.7: Comp. -έστερος Arist.PA654$^{a}$30.

**ὄσυρις**, v. ὄσιρις.

**ὄσφρα**, ἡ, = ὀσμή I, in pl., Ach.Tat.2.38; v. ὀσφραίνομαι.

**ὀσφράδιον**, τό, nosegay, Eust.46.3.

**ὀσφρ-αίνομαι**, fut. ὀσφρήσομαι Ar.Pax 152: aor. 2 ὠσφρόμην Hdt. (v. infr.), Ar.Ach.179; inf. ὀσφρέσθαι Eup.10; part. ὀσφρόμενος Philonid.3 (the aor. 1 form ὤσφραντο in Hdt.1.80, Aristid.2.308 J. seems to be an error of the copyists for ὤσφροντο which is v.l. in Aristid.):—Pass., aor. ὠσφράνθην Hp.Superf.25, Arist.de An.424$^{b}$4, Pr.887$^{a}$10, LxxGe.8.21: fut. ὀσφρανθήσομαι ib.To.6.18, Ps.134(135). 17: the forms ὀσφρᾶται, -ῶνται, etc. only in late writers, as Ph. 1.617 (dub. l.), Paus.9.21.3, Luc.Pisc.48, Anon.Lond.33.30 (f. l. in Antiph.147.6, Philem.79.26): aor. ὠσφρήσαντο Arist.ap.Ael.NA9. 54 (om. Rose), Arat.955, Ael.NA5.49, etc., ὀσφρηθῆναι Anon.Lond. 34.49, ὠσφρήθη Hsch.:—catch scent of, smell, c. gen., Hdt.1.80, Ar.Ra.654, X.Mem.2.1.24, etc.: abs., Pl.Phd.96b, etc.; ἡ αἴσθησις ἡ τοῦ ὀσφραίνεσθαι Arist.Sens.445$^{a}$5: c. acc. only in late writers, ὀ. θρυαλλίδα ἐσβεσμένην Arist.ap.Ael.NA9.54; for in E.Cyc.154 (εἶδες γὰρ αὐτήν;—οὐ μὰ Δί', ἀλλ' ὀσφραίνομαι), αὐτῆς must be supplied, cf. Ar.Ra.489; and in Id.Pl.896, ὀσφραίνει τι; τι is adverbial, at all. 2. metaph., get scent of, τῆς Ἱππίου τυραννίδος Id.Lys.619; τοῦ χρυσίου Luc.Tim.45. II. causal in Act., ὀσφραίνειν τινά τινι make one smell at a thing, Gal.12.795; cf. ἀπ-, προσοσφραίνω. -ανσις, εως, ἡ, = ὄσφρησις, Clearch.ap.Ath.13.611b. -αντέον, one must cause to smell at, κασσίᾳ, etc., Antyll.ap.Orib.10.20.1, etc. -αντήριος, α, ον, able to smell, keen-scented, μυκτῆρες ὀ. Ar. Ra.893. -αντικός, ή, όν, capable of smelling, quick of scent, [κυνίδια] Arist.GA781$^{b}$10; of the vine, sensitive to odours, Thphr.CP2.18. 4. 2. τὸ ὀ. αἰσθητήριον the organ of the sense of smell, Arist.de An. 421$^{b}$32; τὸ ὀσφραντικόν the capacity of smelling, ὁ ἐνεργείᾳ ἡ ὄσφρησις, τοῦτο δυνάμει τὸ ὀ. Id.Sens.438$^{b}$22. -αντός, ή, όν, that can be smelt, Id.de An.421$^{b}$6, Sens.445$^{b}$1 sq., Sor.1.67, Gal.11.54, Porph.Abst.1. 33. -ασία, ἡ, odour, LxxHo.14.7. 2. smelling, Arr.Epict. 1.20.8. -ησις, εως, ἡ, the sense of smell, Pl.Phd.111b (as v.l.), Tht.156b, Arist.de An.421$^{b}$23; τὸ τῆς ὀ. αἰσθητήριον Id.PA658$^{b}$28; ῥινῶν ὀσφρήσιες Opp.C.4.66. 2. the organ of smell, Arist.de An. 425$^{a}$5, Pr.907$^{b}$28, 1Ep.Cor.12.17, PRyl.63.5 (iii A.D.); αἱ ὀ. Hdn.1. 12.2. -ητικός, ή, όν, = ὀσφραντικός, Gal.2.873, D.L.9.80. -ητός, ή, όν, = ὀσφραντός, S.E.M.8.43, P.1.51, Gal.1.363, al., Alex.Aphr.in Sens.86.12.

**ὀσφῠαλγ-έω**, have lumbago, Hp.Coac.154. -ής, ές, suffering from lumbago, γέρων A.Fr.361, cf. Hp.Coac.313. -ία, Ion. -ίη, ἡ, lumbago, ib.606.

**ὀσφύδιον**, τό, Dim. of ὀσφῦς, Theognost.Can.125.

**ὀσφυήξ**, ῆγος, ὁ, ἡ, (ἄγνυμι) having dislocated one's hip, γέρων Poet. ap.Lex.de Spir.p.209 V.

**ὀσφῦς**, ἡ, gen. ὀσφύος: acc. ὀσφῦν, also ὀσφύα AP12.213 (Strat.): —loin or loins, lower part of the back, Epich.80, Hp.Aër.20, Aph.3.23, Arist.HA493$^{a}$22, al.; opp. κῶλα, ὦμοι, A.Pr.497, Hdt.2.40; loin of a victim, SIG57.9 (Milet., v B.C.), 1037.2 (iv/iii B.C.), Pherecr.23.4, Ar.Pax1053, Lys.964, Men.319.12; of wasps, ἔχουσι κέντρον ἐκ τῆς ὀ. Ar.V.225, cf. 740 (anap.); of a horse, X.Eq.1.12; of a fish, Antiph. 132.6 (anap.). 2. Hellenist., metaph., ὁ καρπὸς τῆς ὀ., of a son, Act.Ap.2.30, cf. LxxGe.35.11, al. 3. περιζώννυσθαι or ἀναζώννυσθαι τὴν ὀσφύν gird up one's loins, ib.Je.1.17; βυσσίνῳ ib.Da.10.5, cf. Ev.Luc.12.35. [ῠ in nom. and acc. sg., which are accented ὀσφῦς, ὀσφῦν by Hdn.Gr.2.937; ὀσφύς, -ύν freq. in codd., and this may be admitted for late writers: cf. ὀφρῦς.]

**ὀσχέα, ὄσχεον, ὄσχεος**, v. ὄσχη.

**ὄσχη**, ἡ, scrotum, Hp.Morb.2.61 and 71, al.; but in Arist.HA510$^{a}$ 12, 632$^{a}$16, GA719$^{b}$5, Pr.949$^{a}$16, we find the form **ὀσχέα**: if ὄσχη is contr. from ὀσχέα, it shd. be written ὀσχῆ:—another form **ὄσχεος**, ὁ, is found in Id.HA493$^{a}$33 (v.l. ὀσχέα), Poll.4.203 (v.l. in 2.172), Ruf.Onom.104, Hsch.; also **ὄσχεον**, τό, Poll.2.172 (with vv.ll.), Hsch. II. = ὄσχος, Nic.Al.109, cf. Hsch. [Accent ὀσχεός acc. to Hdn.Gr.2.121.]

**ὄσχιον**, τό, raised margin of the womb, Gal.19.127; cf. ὄσχις.

**ὄσχις**, ιος, ἡ, said to be = ὄσχιον, Hp.Coac.528; but as the reference is to a male in Id.Epid.7.33 Littré's cj. ἰξύας (acc. pl.) should be accepted in both places, as also for ὄρχιας in ib.5.61.

❀ **ὄσχος**, ὁ, v. ὦσχος; for Hp.Mul.2.204, v. ὄχος.

**ὀσχο-φόρια**, τά, -φόριον, τό, -φόροι, οἱ, etc., v. ὠσχ-.

**ὅτα**, Aeol. for ὅτε, like πότα for πότε, Sapph.43, IG12(2).645$^{a}$33 (Nesos, iv B.C.).

**ὅταμπερ**, Relat. Adv., = ὅταν περ, at precisely whatever time, with subj., IG1$^{2}$.40.8, al.

❀ **ὅταν**, for ὅτ' ἄν (ὅτε ἄν) as sts. in codd.: Adv. of Time, whenever, with a conditional force, so as nearly to = ἐάν (v. εἰ B. II), referring to an indef. future (cf. ὅτε A. I. 1 c), Il.1.519, etc.; also of events likely to recur, 2.397, IG1$^{2}$.97.9, etc.: also in Ep. ὅτε κεν Il.1.567, 6.225: strengthd., ὅ. περ S.OC301, Pl.R.565a,d: repeated for rhet. effect, ὅ. ὡς ὑβρίζων, ὅ. ὡς ἐχθρὸς ὑπάρχων, ὅ. κονδύλοις, ὅ. ἐπὶ κόρρης D.21. 72. b. later causal, since, ὅταν.. ᾖ since it is, Arist.Mu.395$^{a}$19, cf. D.Chr.7.105, Porph.Gaur.11.2; in earlier examples the application to the particular case is less directly expressed, καὶ τοῦτο τυφλὸν ὅταν ἐγὼ βλέπω βραχύ this too (viz. my staff) is blind when I am (= when its owner is) short-sighted, E.Ion744, cf. S.Aj.137 (anap.), Pl.Sph.241a, Din.3.9. 2. never with ind. in early authors, exc. in Od.10.410, ὡς δ' ὅταν.. σκαίρουσι (s.v.l.); in 24.88, ὅτε κεν.. ζώννυνταί τε νέοι καὶ ἐπεντύνονται ἄεθλα; and in Il.12.41, ὡς δ' ὅτ' ἂν ἔν τε κύνεσσι καὶ ἀνδράσι.. στρέφεται (ἔναντα κύνεσσι cj. Monro): but freq. in Lxx with impf. ind., as ὅταν εἰσήρχετο Ge.38.9, cf. Plb.4.32.5, Ev. Marc.3.11: also with aor. ind., LxxEx.16.3, Apoc.8.1: with fut. ind., ὅταν ἕξουσι Apollod.Poliorc.187.12; ὅταν ὄψεσθε (v.l. ὄψησθε) Ev.Luc. 13.28: with pres. ind., ὅταν δείκνυται Str.12.3.27 (s.v.l.): generally, ὅταν supersedes ὅτε in Hellenistic Greek. 3. never with opt. in early authors, exc. in orat. obliq., where in orat. recta the subj. with ὅταν would have stood, as perh. A.*Pers.*450 may be expld. (ὅτ' ἐκ νεῶν Elmsl.); ὅτε κεν folld. by ἴκοι, Il.9.525. II. Special usages: to introduce a simile, 10.5, Od.5.394. 2. πρίν γ' ὅ., = πρίν γε ἤ ὅ. (v. ὅτε A. II. 2), 2.374. 3. εἰς ὅτε κεν until *such time as*.., ib.99, 19. 144. 4. ὅ. τάχιστα, Lat. *cum primum*, Ar.*Th.*1205, X.*Cyr.*4.5. 33; ὅ. πρῶτον Pl.*Ly.*211b. [ὅτᾱν only in later Poetry, *Lyr.Alex. Adesp.*37.17.]

⊛ **ὅτε**, also Cypr., *Inscr.Cypr.*135.1 H., Dor. **ὅκα**, Aeol. **ὅτα** (qq. v.), Relat. Adv., formed from the Relat. stem ὁ- and τε (v. τε B), answering to demonstr. τότε and interrog. πότε; prop. of Time, but sts. passing into a causal sense (cf. ὁπότε).

A. of Time, *when, at the time when*, I. Constr.: 1. with ind. to denote single events or actions in past time, with impf. or aor., *when*, Il.1.397,432, etc.: rarely with plpf., 5.392: the Verb is sts. to be repeated from the apodosis, Καλλίξενος δὲ κατελθών, ὅ. καὶ οἱ ἐκ Πειραιῶς (sc. κατῆλθον) X.*HG*1.7.35: freq. in ellipt. phrases, πῇ ἔβαν εὐχωλαί, ὅ. δὴ φάμεν εἶναι ἄριστοι; whither are gone the boasts, [*which we made*] *when* we said..? Il.8.229: so after Verbs of perception and the like, ἦ οὐ μέμνῃ, ὅ. τ' ἐκρέμω..; rememberest thou not [*the time*] *when*..? 15.18, cf. 21.396, Od.24.115, Ar.*V.*354, Th.2.21, etc.; ἄκουσα εὐχομένης ὅτ' ἔφησθα.. Il.1.397, cf. Pl.*Lg.*782c; οὐδ' ἔλαθ' Αἴαντα Ζεύς, ὅ. δὴ Τρώεσσι δίδου..νίκην Il.17.627. b. with pres., of a thing always happening or now going on, 2.471; νῦν, ὅ... σοι ὀξέως ὑπακούω X.*Cyr.*2.4.6; ᾔδεα μὲν γὰρ ὅ...Δαναοῖσιν ἄμυνεν, οἶδα δὲ νῦν ὅ. τοὺς..κυδάνει Il.14.71. c. rarely with fut., of a definite future, Od.18.272. 2. with opt., to denote repeated events or actions in past time, ἔνθα πάρος κοιμᾶθ', ὅ. μιν γλυκὺς ὕπνος ἱκάνοι *whenever, as often as*, Il.1.610, cf. Od.8.87, etc.; ὅ. δὴ Il.3.216. b. sts. of future events which are represented as uncertain, in clauses dependent on a Verb in the opt. or subj., οὐκ ἄν τοι χραίσμῃ κίθαρις.., ὅτ' ἐν κονίῃσι μιγείης 3.55, cf. 18.465, 21.429, A.*Eu.*726. c. ὅ. μή, in early authors always with opt., for εἰ μή, *unless, except, save when*, Il.13.319, Od.16.197, Arist.*Pol.*1277$^{a}$24: used by A.R. with subj., 1.245, 4.409. 3. with subj., only in Ep. and Lyr., Il.4.259, 19.337, 21.323, etc., prob. in A.*Ag.*766 (lyr.). II. Special usages: 1. in Hom. to introduce a simile, ὡς δ' ὅτε *as when*, mostly with subj., Il. 2.147, 4.130,141, 6.506, al.: sts. with ind., 16.364, 21.12: the Verb must freq. be supplied from the context, as in 2.394, 4.462. 2. in the Ep. phrase πρίν γ' ὅτε δή.., ἤ is omitted before ὅτε, 9.488, 12. 437, cf. Od.13.322. III. ὅτε with other Particles, 1. ὅτ' ἄν, ὅτε κεν, v. ὅταν. 2. ὅτε δή and ὅτε δή ῥα, stronger than ὅτε, freq. in Hom. and Hes., ὅτε δή Il.5.65, al., Hes.*Th.*280, al.; ὅτε δή ῥα Il.4.446, al., Hes.*Th.*58, al.; v. infr. IV. 1; so ὅτ' ἄρ' Il.10.540. 3. ὅτε τε (where τε is otiose, v. τε B. 1) 2.471, 10.83, etc. 4. ὅτε περ *even when*, 5.802, 14.319, al., Hdt.5.99, Th.1.8, etc.; ὅτε πέρ τε Il.4.259, 10.7. IV. the proper correl. Adv. is τότε, as ὅ. δὴ.., τότε δὴ.. 10.365; ὅ. δή ῥ'.., δὴ τότε 23.721; ὅ. δὴ.., καὶ τότε δὴ.. 22.208; ὅ. δή ῥα.., καὶ τότ' ἄρ' 24.31: for τότε we sts. have ἔπειτα, 3.221; αὐτίκα δ', 4.210; δὲ.., 5.438; also νῦν..., ὅ... S.*Aj.*710 (lyr.), etc.; μεθύστερον, ὅ... Id.*Tr.*711; ἤματι τῷ, ὅ... Il.2.743, etc.; so in Att., ἦν ποτε χρόνος, ὅ... Pl.*Prt.*320c, cf. *Phd.*75a, Hdt.1.160. 2. elliptical in the phrase ἔστιν ὅ. or ἔσθ' ὅ., *there are times when, sometimes, now and then*, ἔστι ὅ. Id.2.120; ἔστιν ὅ. Pl.*Phd.*62a; ἔσθ' ὅ. S.*Aj.*56 (v. infr. c).

B. ὅτε sts. has a causal sense, *when, seeing that*, mostly with pres. ind., Il.16.433 (v.l. ὅ τε); ὅ. δὴ 20.29; and in Trag. and Att. Prose, as S.*Aj.*1095, *OT*918, Pl.*Smp.*206b, *R.*581e, *Prt.*356c, *Sph.*254b, etc.; so ὅ. γε Hdt.5.92.α': with pf. used as pres., S.*Ph.*428, Ar.*Nu.* 34. 2. sts. where ὥστε would be more usual, οὕτω..πόρρω κλέος ἥκει, ὅ. καὶ βασιλεὺς ἠρώτησεν Id.*Ach.*647.

C. ὁτέ Indef. Adv., *sometimes, now and then*, used like ποτέ at the beginning of each of two corresponding clauses, *now.., now.., sometimes.., sometimes..* (not in early Prose, ὁτὲ μὲν.., ὁτὲ δὲ.. Arist. *Pol.*1290$^{a}$4, al.), ὁτὲ μὲν.., ἄλλοτε.. Il.20.49sq.; ὁτὲ μὲν.., ἄλλοτε δ' αὖ.. 18.599sq.; ὁτὲ μέν τε.., ἄλλοτε δὲ.. 11.64; ὁτὲ μὲν.., ὁτὲ δ' αὖτε.. A.R.1.1270; ὁτὲ μέν τε.., ὅτ' αὖ.. Id.3.1300; ὁτὲ μὲν.., ποτὲ δὲ.. Plb.6.20.8; ὁτὲ μὲν.., ὁτὲ δὲ.., καὶ ἄλλοτε.. D.L.2.106; ὁτὲ μὲν.., πάλιν δὲ.. Arist.*EN*1100$^{a}$28; ἐνίοτε μὲν.., ὁτὲ δὲ.. Id.*Mete.*360$^{b}$ 3; ὁτὲ μὲν.., ἤ.. Id.*Po.*1448$^{a}$21 (s. v. l.): also reversely, ἄλλοτε μὲν.., ὁτὲ δὲ.. Il.11.568; also ὁτὲ δέ in the second clause, without any correlative in the first, 17.178; S. joins ἔσθ' ὅτε.., ὅτ' ἄλλοτ' ἄλλον *Aj.*56; ὁτὲ δέ alone, at the beginning of a clause, X.*Cyn.*5.8 and 20, 9.8 and 20.

**ὅτε**, neut. of ὅστε: also Ion. masc. for ὅστε, v. ὅς, ἥ, ὅ.

⊛ **ὀτεῖος**, α, ον, Cret. for ὁποῖος, but in sense, = ὅστις, *Leg.Gort.*4.52, 5.1, *Schwyzer* 183.5 (iii B.C.):—Boeot. **ὀτῖος** in μηδοτίη (q.v.); cf. τεῖος, τέουτος.

**ὅτεο, ὀτέοισιν, ὅτευ, ὅτεῳ, ὅτεων**, Ep. and Ion. cases of ὅστις.

**ὅτερος**, α, ον, Cret. for ὁπότερος, *Leg.Gort.*9.53, *SIG*525.11 (iii B.C.). (Cf. Skt. *yatarás* 'which of two' (relat.).)

**ὀτῆμος**, f.l. for ὀπῆμος in Herod.3.55.

**ὅ τι** or **ὅτι** (as it is freq. written exc. in I, sts. also **ὅ,τι**), Ep. **ὅττι**, neut. of ὅστις, used as an Adv. like διότι, in indirect questions, *for what, wherefore*, ὅς κ' εἴποι, ὅ τι τόσσον ἐχώσατο Il.1.64, cf. Od.19.464; εἴρετο, ὅ τι οὐ χρᾶται τῇ χειρί Hdt.3.78, cf. 1.111, 2.19,91, al.; ἦν μὴ φράσῃς ὅ τι.. unless you tell me *why*.., Ar.*Pl.*19, cf. 966: sts. with a Prep., εἰρωτώμενος κατ' ὅ τι.. οὕτως ἐπέστειλε Hdt.6.3. II. ὅ τι μή (usu. written ὅτι μή), after a neg. clause, *except*, Il.16.227 (v.l. ὅτε μή); οὐδαμοί.., ὅ τι μὴ Χῖοι μοῦνοι Hdt.1.18; οὐδεὶς ἀνθρώπων, ὅ τι μὴ γυνὴ μούνη ib.181, cf. 143, Th.4.26, etc.: rarely with a different Verb, διέφυγε μὲν οὐδείς, ὅ τι μὴ διέλαθέ τις no one escaped, *save that* one escaped notice, Arr.*An.*1.16.2, etc.: after a question with οὐ, *so far as not*, οὐ..τὴν ἀπὸ τοῦ μανθάνειν [ἡδονήν], ὅ τι μὴ μάθημα τιμὴν φέρει, καπνὸν καὶ φλυαρίαν [ἡγεῖται]; Pl.*R.*581d.—That this phrase belongs to the pronominal ὅ τι is shown by the similar usage of ὅσον, v. ὅσος IV. 5c. 2. so ὅτι ἀλλ' ἤ, = ὅτι μή, Lxx 1*Ki.*30.17, al. III. with a Sup. Adv., ὅττι τάχιστα as quick as possible, Il.4.193, Od.5.112, al.; also ὅ τι τάχος Hdt.9.7.β', S.*Ant.*1321 codd. (lyr., dub. l.), Th.7.42, etc.; ὅ τι μάλιστα Id.5.36, etc.; ὅ τι ἐγγύτατα Id.3.40; ὅ τι ἐλάχιστα Id. 6.23; ὅ τι χρησιμώτατα Id.7.74: also with Adjs., ὅ τι πλείστη ἀπορία Id.4.32; ὅ τι πλεῖστον ναυτικόν, ὅ τι πλεῖστον χρόνον, X.*HG*4.8.6, *Cyr.*6.1.43; ὅ τι πλείστη εὐδαιμονία Pl.*R.*421b; ὅ τι μεγίστη πρόφασις Th.1.126, cf. 7.69; παῖδας ὅ τι χειροτεχνικωτάτους Ar.*V.*1276, etc.—Here also the usage may be compared with that of ὅσος I. 7, IV. 4.

⊛ **ὅτι**, Ep. **ὅττι** (both in Hom.): Conj., to introduce an objective clause, *that*, after Verbs of seeing or knowing, thinking or saying; in Hom. freq. strengthd. ὅτι ῥα, and ὅτι δή:—Usage: I. when ὅτι introduces a statement of fact: a. in Hom. always with ind., the tense following the same rules as in English, ἤγγειλ' ὅττι ῥά οἱ πόσις ἔκτοθι μίμνε πυλάων Il.22.439. b. in Att., ὅτι takes ind. after primary tenses, ind. or opt. after secondary tenses, e.g. ἐνδείκνυμαι ὅτι οὐκ ἔστι σοφός Pl.*Ap.*23b; ᾔσθετο ὅτι τὸ Μένωνος στράτευμα ἤδη ἐν Κιλικίᾳ ἦν X.*An.*1.2.21, cf. 2.2.15, al.; ἔλεγον ὅτι οὐκ ὀρθῶς αἱ σπονδαὶ γένοιντο Th.5.61, cf. Pl.*Phd.*59e, etc.; ἠπείλησ' ὅτι..βαδιοίμην Ar.*Pl.* 88: the ind. is freq. retained in the same tense which the speaker used or would have used, ἠγγέλθη..ὅτι Μέγαρα ἀφέστηκε news came *that* Megara had (lit. has) revolted, Th.1.114; ἀποκρινάμενοι ὅτι πέμψουσι ib.90: sts. opt. and ind. are found in the same sentence, ἔλεγον, ὅτι Κῦρος μὲν τέθνηκεν, Ἀριαῖος δὲ πεφευγὼς..εἴη X.*An.* 2.1.3; Περικλῆς..προηγόρευε..ὅτι Ἀρχίδαμος μέν οἱ ξένος εἴη.., τοὺς δ' ἀγροὺς τοὺς ἑαυτοῦ καὶ οἰκίας.., ἀφίησιν αὐτὰ δημόσια εἶναι Th. 2.13, cf. Pl.*Phd.*61b, etc.: also ὅτι.. and the acc. with inf. are found together, Th.3.25, X.*Cyr.*1.3.13. 2. when ὅτι introduces a conditional sentence, the Constr. after ὅτι is the same as in independent conditional sentences, εἴ τις ἔροιτο, καθ' ὁποίους νόμους δεῖ πολιτεύεσθαι, δῆλον ὅτι ἀποκρίναισθ' ἄν.. it is manifest *that* you would answer.., D.46.12, cf. X.*Mem.*1.6.12. II. ὅτι is freq. inserted pleon. in introducing a quotation (where we use no Conj. and put inverted commas), λόγον τόνδε ἐκφαίνει ὁ Πρωτεύς, λέγων ὅτι ἐγὼ εἰ μὴ περὶ πολλοῦ ἡγεύμην.. Hdt.2.115; καὶ ἐγὼ εἶπον, ὅ. ἡ αὐτή μοι ἀρχὴ ἔστι.. Pl.*Prt.*318a, cf. 356a, 361a, etc.; even where the quotation consists of one word, ib.330c, *Men.*74b,c. 2. ὅ. is also used pleon. with the inf. and acc. (cf. ὡς B. I. 1), εἶπον ὅτι πρῶτον ἐμὲ χρῆναι πειραθῆναι κατ' ἐμαυτόν (which is in fact a mixture of two constrr.) Id.*Lg.* 892d, cf. *Phd.*63c, X.*HG*2.2.2, etc.; but ὅτι has freq. been wrongly inserted by the copyists, as if εἶπεν or λέγουσιν must be followed by it, as in Th.4.37 (om. Pap.), X.*Cyr.*5.4.1, etc. III. ὅτι in Att. freq. represents a whole sentence, esp. in affirm. answers, οὐκοῦν.. τὸ ἀδικεῖν κάκιον ἂν εἴη τοῦ ἀδικεῖσθαι. Answ. δῆλον δὴ ὅτι (i.e. ὅτι κάκιον ἂν εἴη, or ὅτι ταῦτα οὕτως ἔχει) Pl.*Grg.*475c; cf. οἶδ' ὅτι, ἴσθ' ὅτι, οἶσθ' ὅτι, S.*Ant.*276, 758, Pl.*Grg.*486a, etc.: hence arose the practice of using δηλονότι (q.v.) as Adv. 2. what we make the subject of the Verb which follows ὅτι freq. stands in the preceding clause, Λυκάονας δὲ καὶ αὐτοὶ εἴδομεν, ὅτι..καρποῦνται (for εἴδομεν, ὅτι Λυκάονες καρποῦνται) X.*An.*3.2.23, cf. 3.2.29, etc. IV. ὅτι sts. = *with regard to the fact that*, ὅτι..οὔ φησι..ὄνομα εἶναι, ὑποπτεύω αὐτὸν σκώπτειν Pl.*Cra.*384c, cf. *Prt.*330e, etc. V. οὐχ ὅ..., ἀλλὰ or ἀλλὰ καὶ.., οὐχ ὅ. ὁ Κρίτων ἐν ἡσυχίᾳ ἦν, ἀλλὰ οἱ φίλοι αὐτοῦ *not only* Crito.., but his friends, X.*Mem.*2.9.8; more fully, οὐ μόνον ὅ. ἄνδρες, ἀλλὰ καὶ αἱ γυναῖκες Pl.*Smp.*179b: so folld. by ἀλλ' οὐδὲ.., ταύτῃ ἀδύνατα ἐξισοῦσθαι οὐχ ὅ. τὰ ἐν τῇ Εὐρώπῃ, ἀλλ' οὐδ' ἐν τῇ Ἀσίᾳ *not only* the powers in Europe, but.., Th.2.97: οὐχ ὅ., not folld. by a second clause, means *although*, οὐχ ὅ. παίζει καί φησι Pl.*Prt.*336d, cf. *Grg.*450e, *Tht.*157b; cf. ὅπως A. II. 2. 2. for ὅτι μή, v. ὅ τι II.

B. as a causal Particle, *for that, because*, generally after Verbs of feeling, Il.1.56, 14.407, al.; οὐδὲν ἐκπλαγείς, ὅτι..εἶδες Jul.*Or.*1.31a: but without such a Verb, ὃν περὶ πάσης τῖεν ὁμηλικίης, ὅτι οἱ φρεσὶν ἄρτια ᾔδη Il.5.326, cf. 9.76, al.; μάλιστα δ' αὐτοὺς ἐπεκαλέσαντο ὅτι τειχομαχεῖν ἐδόκουν δυνατοὶ εἶναι Th.1.102, cf. And.1.75, Aeschin.3. 231; so ὅτιπερ Th.4.14. b. folld. by τί, ὅτι τί; *why?* (lit. *because why?*) D.23.214; ὅτι τί δή; Ar.*Pl.*136, Luc.*Dem.Enc.*22; ὅτι δὴ τί μάλιστα; Pl.*R.*343a; ὅτι δὴ τί γε; Id.*Chrm.*161c; cf. ὁτιή. 2. *seeing that*, in giving the reason for saying what is said, γλαυκὴ δέ σε τίκτε θάλασσα..ὅτι τοι νόος ἐστὶν ἀπηνής *as is proved by the fact that*.., Il.16.35, cf. 21.488, Od.22.36. [The last syll. is never elided in Att., prob. to avoid confusion with ὅτε: in Hom. ὅτ' (ὅ τ') prob. always represents ὅτε (ὅ τε): there are no examples of ὅττ': hiatus after ὅτι is permitted in Com., Ar.*Lys.*611, *Ach.*516.]

**ὀτιαφόροι**· οἱ τὰς ὀτίδας φέροντες ἐργάται· ὀτὶς δὲ εἶδος ὄρνιθος, *AB* 287.

⊛ **ὁτιή** (better **ὅτι ἤ**, v. infr.), Conj., colloquial form of ὅτι B, *because*, E.*Cyc.*643, Eup.305, Ar.*Eq.*29, 34, 181, 236, etc.: folld. by τί, ὁτιὴ τί; *'cause why?* Id.*Nu.*784; ὁτιὴ τί δή; ib.755. (The accentuation ὅτι ἤ is implied by A.D., who says πρὸς πάντων συμφώνως ἀνεγνώσθη ἐν ὀξείᾳ τάσει τὸ ὅ *Conj.*256.2, cf. *Synt.*307.22; only ὁτιή is found in codd., and Eust. has οἱ Ἀττικοὶ ὀξυτόνως λέγουσι τιὴ καὶ ὁτιὴ 118.36, cf. 45.4; cf. ἤ I. 2.) 2. more rarely, = ὅτι, *that*, Ar.*Eq.*360, *Nu.* 331, *V.*1395, *Av.*1010.

**ὁτιοῦν**, v. ὅστις IV. 2b. **ὅτιπερ**, v. ὅτι B. I a. **ὅτις, ὅτινα, ὅτινας**, Ep. cases of ὅστις. **ὀτίς**, v. ὀτιαφόροι.

⊕ **ὀτλ-εύω**, = sq., A.R.2.1008, Babr.37.3. **-έω**, *suffer, endure*, c. acc., Call.*Fr.*274, A.R.3.769, Lyc.819, etc.: abs., A.R.4.1227. ⊕ **-ημα**, ατος, τό, *distress*, Hsch., Theognost.*Can.*13. ⊕ **-ήμων**, ον, = ἄθλιος, Hsch. (ὀτλήμων· ὁ ἄθλιος, Schmidt).

**ὄτλος**, ὁ, *suffering, distress, arising from* a thing, παιδείας ὄτλον A.*Th.*18; νυμφείων ὄτλον S.*Tr.*7 (as the Sch., though the Ms. gives ὄκνον). (ὄτλος, ὀτλέω, ὀτλήμων seem to be cogn. with τάλας, τλῆναι, τλήμων.)

**ὀτοβ-έω**, *sound loudly*, κοτύλαις A.*Fr.*57.6 (anap.). ⊕ **-ος**, ὁ, *any loud noise*, as *the din* of battle, ὁ. ἄπλητος Hes.*Th.*709; *rattling* of chariots, A.*Th.*151,204 (both lyr.); *crash* of thunder, S.*OC*1479 (lyr.); also of the flute, γλυκὺν αὐλῶν ὄ. Id.*Aj.*1202 (lyr.): pl., ὀ. κροτάλων Antim.*Eleg.Fr.*17.—The freq. Mss. reading ὀττοβέω, ὄττοβος is disproved by the metre. (Onomatop.)

**ὀτόστυλλος**, ὁ, or -ον, τό, a plant, Epich.161.

**ὀτοτοῖ** (not ὀττοτοῖ, as freq. in codd.), an exclamation of pain and grief, *ah! woe!* A.*Pers.*918 (anap.), E.*Or.*1389, al.; doubled, Id.*Andr.*1197, etc.; also lengthd., ὀτοτοτοῖ A.*Pers.*268, al.; ὀτοτοτοτοῖ Id.*Ag.*1072; ὀτοτοτοτοῖ τοτοῖ cj. in S.*El.*1245; ὀττοτοτοτοτοῖ E.*Tr.*1294; ὀττοτοττοτοῖ Id.*Ion*789.—Trag., only in lyr.

**ὀτοτύζω**, *cry* ὀτοτοῖ, *wail aloud*, Ar.*Pax*1011, *Th.*1081, *Schwyzer* 323*C*35 (Delph., iv B.C.): fut. ὀτοτύξομαι Ar.*Lys.*520:—Pass., *to be bewailed*, ὀτοτύζεται.. A.*Ch.*327 (lyr.).

**Ὀτοτύξιοι**, οἱ, Com. pr. n. in Ar.*Av.*1043, *men of Wails*, with a play on Ὀλοφύξιοι (*men of Olophyxus* near Mount Athos).

**ὄτρα**· ἡ τοῦ ἀλέκτορος οὐρά, Hsch.

**ὀτρᾰλέος**, η, ον, (cf. ὀτρύνω) = ὀτρηρός, Opp.*H.*2.273, Q.S.11.107:—used by Hom. and Hes. only in Adv. -έως, *quickly, readily*, Il.3.260, Od.19.100, Hes.*Sc.*410, Sapph.*Supp.*2ca.11, A.R.1.1210.

⊕ **ὄτρεα**· ἡμίονος, Hsch. (Perh. οὐρέα, acc. of οὐρεύς = ὀρεύς: but **ὀτρεύς** ὁ ἡμίονος Theognost.*Can.*13.)

**ὀτρηρός**, ά, όν, (cf. ὀτρύνω) *quick, nimble, busy, ready*, θεράποντε Il.1.321, cf. Od.1.109, 4.23, al., Ar.*Av.*909 (lyr.); ταμίη Il.6.381; ὀτρηρὸν.. τὸ ληδάριον ἔχεις, comically, Ar.*Av.*915; μάζῃ ὀτρηρῇ Matro *Conv.*92. Adv. -ρῶς, = ὀτραλέως, Od.4.735. II. = ὀξύς, *sharp, cutting*, ὀδύναι Opp.*H.*2.529.

**ὄτριχες**, v. ὄθριξ. **ὀτρύγη**· χόρτος, καλάμη, Hsch.

**ὀτρῡγηφάγος** [ᾰ], ον, = τρυγηφάγος, Archil.97.

**ὀτρυν-τήρ**· κῆρυξ, κελευστής, σαλπιγκτήρ, Hsch. **-τικός**, ή, όν, *stirring up, rousing*, Eust.831.29. **-τύς**, ύος, ἡ, *a cheering on, exhortation*, Il.19.234,235, Antim.91. [ῡς, ῠος.] **-ω** [ῡ], Ep. inf. ὀτρυνέμεν Il.4.286: impf. ὤτρυνον Hom. (v. infr.), etc.; Iterat. ὀτρύνεσκον Il.24.24: fut. ὀτρῠνέω Hom. (v. infr.): Ep. aor. ὄτρῡνα Od.17.430:—Med. or Pass., only in pres. and impf. (v. infr.): poet. Verb, the compd. ἐπ-οτρύνω being used in Prose: (v. sub fin.):—*stir up, egg on, encourage*, esp. to battle, to any sudden or violent exertion, τινα Il.5.482, 10.158, etc.; τί με σπεύδοντα καὶ αὐτὸν ὀτρύνεις; 8.294; ὄτρυνε μένος καὶ θυμὸν ἑκάστου 5.470: freq. c. inf., ὀπτῆρας.. ὄτρυνα νέεσθαι Od.17.430; ὀ. τινὰ μάχεσθαι Il.4.294,414, etc.; γήμασθαι Od.19.158, etc.; ἡμέας ὀτρύνων καταπαυέμεν 2.244: without inf., ἤ τιν' ἑταίρων ὀτρυνέεις Τρώεσσιν ἐπίσκοπον (sc. ἰέναι); Il.10.38; ὃν ναῶν Ἕκτωρ ὤτρυνε κατόπταν E.*Rh.*558 (lyr.): with Preps., Ἑρμείαν.. νῆσον ἐς Ὠγυγίην ὀτρύνομεν (sc. ἰέναι) Od.1.85, cf. Il.15.59; σέ γε θυμὸς ὀ. ἐπὶ νῆας 24.289; τὸν δ' ὀ. πόλιν εἴσω Od.15.40; ποτὶ δῶμα 17.75; προτὶ Ἴλιον Il.19.156; πόλινδε Od.15.306; πόλεμόνδε Il.2.589; ποτὶ βουθυσίαν Ἥρας Pi.*N.*10.23: rarely folld. by ὡς, Ὀδυσῆα ὄτρυν', ὡς ἂν πύρνα..ἀγείροι Od.17.362: rarely also c. dat. pers. et inf., ὤτρυνον.. θεραπόντεσσιν φυλάξαι Pi.*P.*4.41:—Med. or Pass., *rouse oneself, bestir oneself, hasten*, c. inf., ἕπεσθαι Od.10.425; ὀτρυνώμεθ' ἀμυνέμεν ἀλλήλοισιν Il.14.369, cf. Od.17.183; ὑμεῖς δ' ὀτρύνεσθαι.., ὥς κ' ἐμὲ.. ἐπιβήσετε πάτρης 7.222:—the Act. in this intr. sense is only f.l. in Il.7.420. 2. less freq. of animals, *urge on, cheer on*, οὐρῆας 23.111; ἵππους τε καὶ ἀνέρας 16.167, etc.; κύνας 18.584. 3. of things, *urge forward, quicken, speed*, πομπὴν ὀτρύνετε Od.7.151, cf. 8.30; τούτῳ δ' ὀτρυνέει Μέντωρ ὁδὸν 2.253; ἀγγελίην ὀτρύνομεν 16.355; μάχην ὤτρυνον Ἀχαιῶν Il.12.277; βοὰν ὤτρυνε λαῶν *roused* the shouts of the people, B.8.35 (s.v.l.).—Ep. Verb, used now and then by Trag., in lyr., A.*Th.*726, E.*Rh.*25,558: in trim., S.*Aj.*60,771, *El.*28, E.*Alc.*755: rare even in later Prose, Arist.*Mu.*399ᵇ11. (Prob. ὀ-τρῠ-ν-yω, with ὀ- prefix (as in ὀ-κέλλω); -τρῠ- perh. cogn. with Skt. *tvárate* 'hasten'.)

**ὅττα**, Att. for ὅσσα.

**ὄττᾰβος**, ὁ, given as a form of κότταβος, *EM*615.57 (cod. Leid.).

**ὀττεία**, ἡ, *divination from ominous sounds*, D.H.8.37; σὺν οἰωνοῖς τε καὶ ὀττείαις Id.9.45; *evil foreboding*, Id.1.38.

**ὅττεο, ὅττευ**, Ep. gen. of ὅστις.

**ὀττεύομαι**, Att. for ὀσσεύομαι (which does not occur), *divine from an ominous voice* or *sound* (ὄσσα), ὀττευομένη δὲ κάθηται she sits *looking for omens*, of a lover, Ar.*Lys.*597; ταῖς τούτων κληδόσι by the cries of children, Plu.2.356e; πρὸς [κόρακος] βοήν Ael.*NA*1.48: generally, *have forebodings of* a thing, τὸ μέλλον Plb.27.16.5; τι περὶ τῶν ὅλων Id.1.11.15: c. (acc. et) inf., *augur that*.., Porph.*Antr.*33, Luc.*Lex.*19. II. *regard as ominous*, τὴν τύχην, τὸ ἔργον, D.H.9.23, 55: hence, *deprecate as ill-omened*, πάντα τῦφον Id.2.19.—The Act. ὀττεύουσιν prob. f.l. in Ael.*NA*3.9 (ὀπυίουσιν cj. Pierson *Moer.*p.279 P.): κληδονίζομαι was the equiv. Hellenic form, acc. to Moer. l. c.

**ὅττι**, Ep. for ὅτι (q.v.); also Ep. for ὅ τι, neut. of ὅστις (q.v.).

**ὄττις**, ἡ, = ὄψις, Hsch.; ὄττιες ἀχλυώδεες Aret.*SD*2.13.

**ὀττοτοῖ**, f.l. for ὀτοτοῖ. **ὅτῳ**, Att. dat. of ὅστις.

**οὗ**, name of the letter ο (omicron), v. O. 2. **οὗ**, Greek transcription of the Latin name of the letter *u*, Jul.*Or.*2.72a.

⊕ **οὐ**, the negative of *fact* and *statement*, as μή of *will* and *thought*; οὐ denies, μή rejects; οὐ is absolute, μή relative; οὐ objective, μή subjective.—The same differences hold for all compds. of οὐ and μή, and some examples of οὐδέ and οὐδείς are included below.—As to the Form, v. infr. G.

A. USAGE. I. as the negative of single words, II. as the negative of the sentence.

I. οὐ adhering to single words so as to form a quasi-compd. with them:—with Verbs: οὐ δίδωμι *withhold*, Il.24.296; οὐκ ἐῶ *prevent*, 2.132, 4.55, al.; οὐκ ἐθέλω *refuse*, 1.112, 3.289, al.; οὔ φημι *deny*, 7.393, 23.668, al. (In most of these uses μή can replace οὐ when the constr. requires it, e.g. εἰ μή φησι ταῦτα ἀληθῆ εἶναι Lycurg.34; but sts. οὐ is retained, εἰ δ' ἂν.. οὐκ ἐθέλωσιν Il.3.289; εἰ δέ κ'.. οὐκ εἰῶσι 20.139; ἐὰν οὐ φάσκῃ Lys.13.76; ἐάντε.. οὐ (v.l. μή) φῆτε ἐάντε φῆτε Pl.*Ap.*25b):—with Participles: οὐκ ἐθέλων Il.4.224,300, 6.165, etc.:—with Adjectives: οὐκ ἀέκοντε 5.366,768, al.; οὐ πολλήν Th.6.7, etc.:—with Adverbs: οὐχ ἥκιστα Id.1.68, etc.: rarely with Verbal Nouns (v. infr. II. 10).—On the use of οὐ in contrasts, v. infr. B. II. as negativing the whole sentence, 1. οὐ is freq. used alone, sts. with the ellipsis of a definite Verb, οὔκ (sc. ἀποκερῶ), ἄν γε ἐμοὶ πείθῃ Pl.*Phd.*89b: sts. as negativing the preceding sentence, Ar.*Pax*850, X.*HG*1.7.19: as a Particle of solemn denial freq. with μά (q.v.) and the acc.; sts. without μά, οὐ τὸν πάντων θεῶν θεὸν πρόμον Ἅλιον S.*OT*660 (lyr.), cf. 1088 (lyr.), *El.*1063 (lyr.), *Ant.*758. 2. with ind. of statement, τὴν δ' ἐγὼ οὐ λύσω Il.1.29, cf. 114,495; οὐ φθίνει Κροίσου φιλόφρων ἀρετά Pi.*P.*1.94; ἔνθα κεν οὔ τιν' ἀδάκρυτόν γ' ἐνόησας Ἀργείων Od.24.61; οὔ κεν.. ἔπαξε Pi.*N.*7.25; οὐκ ἂν ὑπεξέφυγε Il.8.369. 3. with subj. in fut. sense, only in Ep., οὐ γάρ τίς με βίῃ γε ἑκὼν ἀέκοντα δίηται 7.197; οὐκ ἄν τοι χραίσμῃ κίθαρις 3.54, cf. 11.387. 4. with opt. in potential sense (without ἄν or κεν), also Ep., ὃ οὐ δύο γ' ἄνδρε φέροιεν 5.303, 20.286. 5. with opt. and ἄν, κείνοισι δ' ἄν οὔ τις.. μαχέοιτο 1.271, cf. 301, 2.250, Hdt.6.63, A.*Pr.*979, S.*Aj.*155 (anap.), E.*IA*310, Ar.*Ach.*403, etc. 6. in dependent clauses οὐ is used, a. with ὅτι or ὡς, after Verbs of saying, knowing, and showing, ἐκ μέν τοι ἐρέω.. ὡς ἐγὼ οὔ τι ἑκὼν κατερύκομαι Od.4.377, cf. S.*El.*561, D.2.8, etc.: so with ind. or opt. and ἄν, ἀπελογοῦντο ὡς οὐκ ἄν ποτε οὕτω μωροὶ ἦσαν X.*HG*5.4.22, cf. Pl.*R.*330a; ὡς δὲ οὐκ ἂν δικαίως αὐτοὺς δέχοισθε μαθεῖν χρή Th.1.40, cf. X.*Cyr.*1.1.3, etc.: with opt. representing ind. in orat. obliq., ἔλεξε παιδὶ σῷ.. ὡς.. Ἕλληνες οὐ μενοῖεν A.*Pers.*358, cf. S.*Ph.*346, Th.1.38, X.*HG*6.1.1, Pl.*Ap.*22b, etc.: for μή in such sentences, v. μή B. 3. b. in all causal sentences, and in temporal and Relat. sentences unless there is conditional or final meaning, χωσαμένη, ὅ οἱ οὔ τι θαλύσια..ῥέξε Il.9.534; ἄχθεται ὅτι οὐ κάρτα θεραπεύεται Hdt.3.80; διότι οὐκ ἦσαν δίκαι, οὐ δυνατοὶ ἦμεν παρ' αὐτῶν ἃ ὤφειλον πράξασθαι Lys.17.3; μή με κτεῖν', ἐπεὶ οὐχ ὁμογάστριος Ἕκτορός εἰμι Il.21.95, etc.; νῦν δὲ ἐπειδὴ οὐκ ἐθέλεις.., εἶμι Pl.*Prt.*335c; ἐπειδὴ τὸ χωρίον οὐχ ἡλίσκετο Th.1.102; νηπιάχοις οἷς οὔ τι μέλει πολεμήϊα ἔργα Il.2.338, etc.: in causal relative sentences, οἵτινές σε οὐχὶ ἐσώσαμεν Pl.*Cri.*46a; esp. in the combinations, οὐκ ἔστιν ὅστις οὐ.., as οὐκ ἔστ' ἐραστὴς ὅστις οὐκ ἀεὶ φιλεῖ E.*Tr.*1051, cf. *Hec.*298; οὔτις ἔσθ' ὃς οὐ S.*Aj.*725; οὐδεὶς ἐστιν ὅστις οὐ.. Isoc.15.180. c. after ὥστε with ind. or opt. with ἄν, ὥστ' οὐ δυνατόν σ' εἴργειν ἔσται Ar.*V.*354, cf. S.*Aj.*98, *OT*411; οὕτως αὐτοὺς ἀγαπῶμεν.. ὥστε.. οὐκ ἂν ἐθελήσαιμεν Isoc.8.45; οὐκ ἂν ὡρκίζομεν αὐτὸν ὥστε τῆς εἰρήνης ἂν διημαρτήκει καὶ οὐκ ἂν ἀμφότερ' εἶχε D.18.30: ὥστε οὐ with inf. is almost invariably due to orat. obliq., ὥστ' οὐκ αἰσχύνεσθαι (for οὐκ αἰσχύνονται) Id.19.308, cf. Th.5.40, 8.76, Lys.18.6, Is.11.27 (cj. Reiske).—Rarely not in orat. obliq., S.*El.*780, E.*Ph.*1358, *Hel.*108, D.53.2, 9.48. 7. in a conditional clause μή is necessary, except, a. in Hom., when the εἰ clause precedes the apodosis and the verb is indic., εἰ δέ μοι οὐκ ἐπέεσσ' ἐπιπείσεται Il.15.162, cf. 178, 20.129, 24.296, Od.2.274, Il.4.160, Od.12.382, 13.144 (9.410 is an exception). b. when the εἰ clause is really causal, as after Verbs expressing surprise or emotion, μὴ θαυμάσῃς, εἰ πολλὰ τῶν εἰρημένων οὐ πρέπει σοι Isoc.1.44; κατοικτίραι.., εἰ.. οὐδεὶς ἐς ἑκατοστὸν ἔτος περιέσται Hdt.7.46, cf. S.*Aj.*1242; so also δεινὸν γὰρ ἂν εἴη πρῆγμα, εἰ Σάκας μὲν καταστρεψάμενοι δούλους ἔχομεν, Ἕλληνας δὲ οὐ τιμωρησόμεθα Hdt.7.9, cf. And.1.102, Lys.20.8 (prob.), D.8.55; οὐκ αἰσχρόν, εἰ τὸ μὲν Ἀργείων πλῆθος οὐκ ἐφοβήθη τὴν Λακεδαιμονίων ἀρχήν, ὑμεῖς δ' ὄντες Ἀθηναῖοι βάρβαρον ἄνθρωπον.. φοβήσεσθε; Id.15.23, cf. Hdt.5.97, Lys.22.13. c. when οὐ belongs closely to the next word (v. A. I), or is quoted unchanged, εἰ, ὡς νῦν φήσει, οὐ παρεσκευάσατο D.54.29 codd.; εἰ δ' οὐκέτ' ἐστί (sc. ὥσπερ λέγεις), τίνι τρόπῳ διεφθάρη; E.*Ion*347. 8. οὐ is used with inf. in orat. obliq., when it represents the ind. of orat. recta, φαμὲν δέ οἱ οὐ τελέεσθαι Od.4.664, cf. Il.17.174, 21.316, S.*Ph.*1389, etc.; λέγοντες οὐκ εἶναι αὐτόνομοι Th.1.67, cf. Pl.*R.*348c, X.*Cyr.*1.6.18; οἶμαι.. οὐκ ὀλίγον ἔργον αὐτὸ εἶναι Pl.*R.*369b, cf. S.*OT*1051, Th.1.71, etc.; ἡγήσαντο ἡμᾶς οὐ περιόψεσθαι ib.39. (For the occasional use of μή, v. μή B. 5c: sts. we have οὐ and μή in consecutive clauses, οἶμαι σοῦ κάκιον οὐδὲν ἂν τούτων κρατύνειν μηδ' ἐπιθύνειν χερὶ S.*Ph.*1058 sq.; αὐτὸ ἡγοῦμαι οὐ διδακτὸν εἶναι μηδὲ.. παρασκευαστόν Pl.*Prt.*319b.) 9. οὐ is used with the part., when it can be resolved into a finite sentence with οὐ, as after Verbs of knowing and showing, τὸν καθανόνθ' ὁρῶντες οὐ τιμώμενον E.*Hec.*316; κατενόησαν οὐ πολλοὺς τοὺς Θηβαίους ὄντας Th.2.

3; ἔργῳ δηλώσω οὐ παραγενόμενος Antipho 2.4.8, etc.; or into a causal sentence, τῶν βαρβάρων οἱ πολλοὶ ἐν τῇ θαλάσσῃ διεφθάρησαν νέειν οὐκ ἐπιστάμενοι Hdt.8.89; τὴν Μένδην πόλιν ἅτε οὐκ ἀπὸ ξυμβάσεως ἀνοιχθεῖσαν διήρπασαν Th.4.130; or into a concessive sentence, δόξω γυναῖκα καίπερ οὐκ ἔχων ἔχειν E.*Alc.*352, cf. S.*Ph.*377, etc.: regularly with ὡς and part., ὡς οὐχὶ συνδράσουσα νουθετεῖς τάδε Id.*El.*1025, etc.; ἐθορυβεῖτε ὡς οὐ ποιήσοντες ταῦτα Lys.12.73, cf. S.*Ph.*884, *Aj.*682, Hdt.7.99, Th.1.2,5,28,68,90; ὥσπερ οὐ πάντας τούτῳ τῷ τεκμηρίῳ χρωμένους Lycurg.90, cf. Th.8.1, Isoc.4.11:—for exceptions, v. μή B. 6. b. when the part. is used with the Art., μή is generally used, unless there is a distinct reference to a fact, when οὐ is occasionally found, ἡμεῖς δὲ ἀπὸ τῆς οὐκ οὔσης ἔτι [πόλεως] ὁρμώμενοι Th.1.74; τοὺς ἐν τῇ πόλει οὐδὲν εἰδότας Id.4.111; οἱ οὐκ ἐθέλοντες Antipho 6.26; τῶν οὐ βουλομένων And.1.9; τοὺς οὐδὲν ἀδικοῦντας ἀκρίτους ἀπέκτειναν Lys.12.82, cf. τὸν οὐδὲ συμπενθῆσαι τὰς τῆς πατρίδος συμφορὰς τολμήσαντα (preceded by τὸν.. μήτε ὅπλα θέμενον ὑπὲρ τῆς πατρίδος μήτε τὸ σῶμα παρασχόντα κτλ.) Lycurg.43; τὸ οὐχ εὑρημένον Pl.*R.*427e. 10. Adjectives and abstract Substantives with the article commonly take μή (v. μή B. 7), but οὐ is occasionally used, τὰς οὐκ ἀναγκαίας πόσεις X.*Lac.*5.4; τοὺς οὐδένας E.*IA*371; τὸν οὐδέν Id.*Ph.*598 (whereas ὁ μηδείς, τὸ μηδέν is the rule); τὴν τῶν γεφυρῶν οὐ διάλυσιν the *non*-dissolution of the bridges, the fact *of their not* being broken up, Th.1.137; ἡ οὐ περιτείχισις Id.3.95; ἡ τῶν χωρίων οὐκ ἀπόδοσις Id.5.35, cf. E.*Hipp.*196 (anap.); so without the article, ἐν οὐ καιρῷ Id.*Ba.*1287; οὐ πάλης ὕπο ib.455. 11. for οὐ μή, v. sub voc. 12. in questions οὐ ordinarily expects a positive answer, οὔ νυ καὶ ἄλλοι ἔασι..; Il.10.165; οὐχ ὁρᾷς..; *dost* thou *not* see? Od.17.545; οὐκ..ᾐσθόμην; A.*Pr.*956: so as a strong form of imper., οὐκ ἀπαλλάξει; E.*Ion* 524; οὐκ ἀποκτενεῖτε τὸν μιαρὸν τοῦτον ἄνθρωπον; Din.1.18; οὐκ εἶ καταπιὼν Εὐριπίδην; Ar.*Ach.*484; βάλλε, βάλλε folld. by οὐ βαλεῖς; οὐ βαλεῖς; ib.281 and 283, cf. S.*Ant.*885: also with opt. and ἄν, οὐκ ἂν δὴ τόνδ' ἄνδρα μάχης ἐρύσαιο (= ἔρυσαι); Il.5.456; οὐκ ἂν φράσειας (= φράσον); S.*Ph.*1222; but in questions introduced by οὐ δή, οὐ δή που, οὔ που, οὔ τί που, a doubt is implied of the statement involved, and an appeal is made to the hearers, οὐ δή ποθ' ἡμῖν ξυγγενὴς ἥκεις ποθέν; surely you are *not*..? Id.*El.*1202, cf. *Ph.*900; οὔ τί που οὗτος Ἀπόλλων..; Pi.*P.*4.87, cf. S.*Ph.*1233, E.*IA*670, *Hel.*135, *Ion* 1113, Ar.*Ra.*522, 526.

B. Position. οὐ is generally put immediately before the word which it negatives, οὐκ ἐκεῖνον ἐθεώμην.—ἀλλὰ τίνα μήν; ἔφη ὁ Τιγράνης X.*Cyr.*3.1.41; οὐχ αἱ τρίχες ποιοῦσιν αἱ λευκαὶ φρονεῖν Men.639; οὐ διὰ τὸ μὴ ἀκοντίζειν οὐκ ἔβαλον αὐτὸν ἀλλὰ διὰ τὸ μηδενὶ ὑπὸ τὸ ἀκόντιον ὑπελθεῖν Antipho 3.4.6: in Poetry the position is freq. more free, κίνδυνος ἄναλκιν οὐ φῶτα λαμβάνει Pi.*O.*1.81; οὐ ψευδεῖ τέγξω λόγον ib.4.19; κατακρύπτει δ' οὐ κόνις ib.8.79; χρὴ πρὸς θεὸν οὐκ ἐρίζειν Id.*P.*2.88: sts. emphatically at the end of the clause, καὶ τοὶ γὰρ αἰθοίσας ἔχοντες σπέρμ' ἀνέβαν φλογὸς οὔ Id.*O.*7.48; ταρβήσει γὰρ οὔ S.*Aj.*545: in clauses opposed by μέν and δέ the οὐ (or μή) is freq. placed at the end, βούλονται μέν, δύνανται δ' οὔ Th.6.38; οὗτος δ' ἦν καλὸς μέν, μέγας δ' οὔ X.*An.*4.4.3; ἔδοξέ μοι ὁ ἀνὴρ δοκεῖν μὲν εἶναι σοφὸς.., εἶναι δ' οὔ Pl.*Ap.*21c; so τὸ Πέρσας μὲν λέληθε, ἡμέας μέντοι οὔ Hdt.1.139: freq. with ὁ μὲν..ὁ δέ, οὐ πάσας χρὴ τὰς δόξας τιμᾶν, ἀλλὰ τὰς μέν, τὰς δ' οὔ Pl.*Cri.*47a, cf. *Ap.*24e, *R.*475b, etc.; Λέριοι κακοί, οὐχ ὁ μέν, ὃς δ' οὔ Phoc.1: sts. in the first clause after μέν, οἱ δὲ στρατηγοὶ ἐξῆγον μὲν οὔ, συνεκάλεσαν δέ X.*An.*6.4.20, cf. 4.8.2, *Cyr.*1.4.10, Pl.*Phd.*73b; κατώρα πᾶν μὲν οὒ τὸ στρατόπεδον Hdt.7.208.

C. Accumulation. A simple neg. (οὐ or μή) is freq. repeated in composition with Prons., Advbs., or Conjs., as οὐδείς or μηδείς, οὐδέ or μηδέ, οὐδαμῶς or μηδαμῶς, first in Hom., οὔ μιν ὀΐομαι οὐδὲ πεπύσθαι λυγρῆς ἀγγελίης Il.17.641; ἀλλ' οὔ μοι Τρώων τόσσον μέλει ἄλγος ὀπίσσω οὔτ' αὐτῆς Ἑκάβης οὔτε Πριάμοιο ἄνακτος 6.450; οὐκ ἔστιν οὐδὲν κρεῖσσον οἰκείου φίλου E.*Andr.*986: the first neg. may be a compd., καθεύδων οὐδεὶς οὐδενὸς ἄξιος οὐδὲν μᾶλλον τοῦ μὴ ζῶντος Pl.*Lg.*808b; οὐδενὶ οὐδαμῇ οὐδαμῶς οὐδεμίαν κοινωνίαν ἔχει Id.*Prm.*166a (similarly with μή, *Phdr.*236e): or a neg. Adj., ἀδύνατος οὐδὲν ἄλλο πλὴν λέγειν μάτην E.*Andr.*746; οὐ follows the compd. neg., οὐδ' εἰ πάντες ἔλθοιεν Πέρσαι, πλήθει γε οὐχ ὑπερβαλοίμεθ' ἂν τοὺς πολεμίους X.*Cyr.*2.1.8; οὐδ' ἂν ἡ πόλις ἄρα (ὅπερ ἄρτι ἐλέγομεν) ὅλη τοιοῦτον ποιῇ, οὐκ ἐπαινέσῃ Pl.*R.*426b, cf. *Smp.*204a: sts. a confirmative Particle accompanies the first οὐ or οὐδέ, and the neg. is repeated with emphasis, οὐδὲ μὲν οὐδέ μ' ἔασκες Il.19.295; οὐδὲ γὰρ οὐδὲ Δρύαντος υἱὸς..δὴν ἦν 6.130, v. οὐδέ c. II; οὐ μέντοι οὐδὲ αὖ ὡς σύ μοι δοκεῖς οἴεσθαι Pl.*Prt.*332a: so also in Trag. and Att. without any such Particle, οὐ σμικρός, οὐχ, ἁγὼν ὅδε *not* small, *no*, is this struggle, S.*OC*587; θεοῖς τέθνηκεν οὗτος, οὐ κείνοισιν, οὔ Id.*Aj.*970, cf. Ar.*Ra.*28, 1308, X.*Smp.*2.4, Pl.*R.*390c. 2. when the compd. neg. precedes and the simple neg. follows with the Verb, the opposing negs. produce an emphatic positive, οὐδεὶς ἀνθρώπων ἀδικῶν τίσιν οὐκ ἀποτείσει Orac.ap.Hdt.5.56; γλώσσης κρυφαῖον οὐδὲν οὐ διέρχεται S.*Fr.*935 (but prob. f.l.); οὐδεὶς οὐκ ἔπασχέ τι X.*Smp.*1.9. 3. similarly each of two simple negs. may retain its negating force, ὥσπερ οὐ διὰ πρᾳότητα καὶ ἀσχολίαν τὴν ὑμετέραν οὐ δεδωκὼς ὑμῖν δίκην Lys.6.34; ἐγὼ δ' οὐκ οἶμαι..οὐ δεῖν ὑμᾶς ἀμύνεσθαι Id.13.52 (similarly with μή, D.19.77): sts. a combination of a μέν-clause with a δέ-clause containing οὐ is negatived as a whole by a preceding οὐ, e.g. οὐ γὰρ δήπου Κτησιφῶντα μὲν δύναται διώκειν δι' ἐμέ, ἐμὲ δέ, εἴπερ ἐξελέγξειν ἐνόμιζεν, αὐτὸν οὐκ ἂν ἐγράψατο Id.18.13.

D. Pleonasm of οὐ: after Verbs of denying, doubting, and disputing, folld. by ὡς or ὅτι with a finite Verb, οὐ is inserted to show the neg. character of the statement, where in Engl. the neg. is not required, ὡς μὲν οὐκ ἀληθῆ ταῦτ' ἐστὶν οὐκ ἔχετ' ἀντιλέγειν D.8.31, cf. Th.1.77, X.*HG*2.3.16, *Smp.*2.12, Isoc.5.57, etc.; οὐδεὶς ἂν τολμήσειεν ἀντειπεῖν ὡς οὐ τὴν μὲν ἐμπειρίαν μᾶλλον τῶν ἄλλων ἔχομεν Id.6.48, cf. And.4.34, D.16.4, etc.; οὐκ ἂν ἀρνηθεῖεν ἔνιοι ὡς οὐκ εἰσὶ τοιοῦτοι Id.9.54; ἀρνεῖσθαι ὅτι οὐ παρῆν X.*Ath.*2.17; οὐδ' αὐτὸς ὁ Λάμπις ἔξαρνος ἐγένετο ὡς οὐκ εἴη εἰρηκὼς κτλ. D.34.49; ἀμφισβητεῖν ὡς οὐχὶ.. δοτέον δίκην Pl.*Euthphr.*8c, cf. *R.*476d, *Prm.*135a; ἀπιστεῖν ὅτι οὐ.. Id.*Men.*89d; ἀνέλπιστον καταστῆσαί τισιν ὡς οὐκ ἔσται μεταγνῶναι Th.3.46: οὐ is sts. thus used in the second member of a negative comparative sentence, ἥκει ὁ Πέρσης οὐδέν τι μᾶλλον ἐπ' ἡμέας ἢ οὐ καὶ ἐπ' ὑμέας Hdt.4.118, cf. 5.94, 7.16.γ', Th.2.62, 3.36: after πλήν, X.*Lac.*15.6, D.18.45.

E. Omission of οὐ: οὐ is sts. omitted, esp. by Poets, when it may be supplied from the next clause, γῆ δ' οὐδ' ἀὴρ οὐδ' οὐρανὸς ἦν Ar.*Av.*694; σιδήρῳ οὐδ' ἀργύρῳ χρέωνται οὐδέν Hdt.1.215; ῥοδιακὴ οὖς οὐδὲ πυθμένα οὐκ ἔχουσα *Inscr.Délos* 313*a*84 (iii B.C.).

F. in Poetry, if ἤ stands before οὐ, the two sounds coalesce into one syllable, as in ἢ οὐχ Il.5.349, cf. Od.1.298; so, in Att., μὴ οὐ S.*OT*283, etc., and ἐγὼ οὔτε ib.332, ἐγὼ οὐ Ar.*Eq.*340.—This synizesis is general in Ep., universal in Att.

G. Form. οὐ is used before consonants (including the digamma, e.g. before ἕθεν, οἱ, ἑ, Il.1.114, 2.392, 24.214, but not before ὅς Possess., οὐχ ᾧ πατρί Od.13.265, cf. οὐκ ἐπέεσσι Il.15.162, etc.); οὐκ before vowels with spir. lenis, οὐχ before vowels with spir. asper; in our text of Hdt. οὐκ is used before all vowels (prob. because Hdt. had no spir. asper): the Ep. form οὐκί [ῐ] is used by Hom. mostly at the end of a clause and at the close of the verse, ὅς τ' αἴτιος ὅς τε καὶ οὐκί Il.15.137; ἠὲ καὶ οὐκί 2.238, 300, al.; but in the middle of a verse, 20.255; οὐχί [ῐ] is found twice in Hom., Il.15.716, 16.762, and is common in Trag., where it is freq. employed like οὔ emphatic (supr. B), τί δ' οὐχί; A.*Ag.*272, *Fr.*310; πῶς δ' οὐχί; Id.*Supp.*918, Ar.*Pax* 1027; ἐμὸς μὲν οὐχί E.*IA*859: also in Prose, Th.1.120, al., 1*Ep.Cor.*5.12, etc.: the diphthong is genuine and always written ου (ουκ, ουδε, etc.) in early Inscrr., *IG*1$^2$.10.22, etc.; in iv B.C. rarely written οκ, ib.2$^2$.1635.112, 116, 121; οὐ abbreviated ο, Suid. s. v. Φιλοξένου γραμμάτιον.

H. Accentuation. οὐ is oxytone acc. to Hdn.Gr.1.494 (text doubtful in 504): Arist.*SE*166$^b$6, referring to Il.23.328 τὸ μὲν ου (i.e. οὐ = οὗ) καταπύθεται ὄμβρῳ, says λύουσι..τῇ προσῳδίᾳ λέγοντες τὸ ου ὀξύτερον (i.e. οὔ), cf. 178$^b$3. In codd. the word is written oxytone when folld. by a pause (v. supr. B), and is usu. written without any accent in other cases.

I. οὐ in connexion with other Particles will be found in alphabetical order, οὐ γάρ, οὐ μή, etc.—The corresponding forms of μή should be compared.

**οὗ**, gen. of relat. and possess. Prons. ὅς: as Adv. *where*, v. ὅς, ἥ, ὅ A b. 1.

⊛**οὗ, οἷ, ἕ,** A. Forms: gen. ἕο Il.5.343, al., εὗ v.l. in Od.19.446 (ap.A.D.*Pron.*76.15, etc.), al., εἷο Il.4.400, Od.22.19, ἑοῦ A.D.*Pron.*77.10; ἑο enclit., Od.14.461, εὑ Il.14.427, al., Hdt.3.135; ἕθεν is another Ep. form, Il.3.128, al. (used by A.*Supp.*66 (lyr.)), enclit. in Il.9.686, al.; ϝέθεν Alc.11; οὗ ἕθεν together, A.R.1.362, 4.1471; εἷο for ἐμοῦ, Id.2.635: Att. οὗ, but rarely used, S.*OT*1257, Pl.*Smp.*174d, *R.*393e, 614b: Locr. ϝέος dub. in *IG*9(1).334.33 (v B.C.): Boeot. ἑοῦς Corinn.2: Dor. ϝίο (γίο cod.) Hsch.: late Ep. ἑοῖο A.R.1.1032 (v.l. ἑεῖο): dat. οἷ Od.11.433, al., enclit. in 1.17, al. (enclit. οἱ perh. as gen., Il.16.531, Archil.29, Hdt.1.60, 3.15, A.R.3.371, Theoc.25.66, cf. Sch. Il.19.384 and ἐγώ II): Delph. ϝοι *GDI*2561*D*14 (also Aeol., Sapph.111): Att. οἷ Pl.*Smp.*174e, X.*An.*1.1.8, enclit. οἱ A.*Ag.*1147 (lyr.), Th.2.13, al., Antipho 5.93, And.1.38, Pl.*Phlb.*60d, al., X.*Mem.*1.2.32, etc.: ἑοῖ twice in Hom., Il.13.495, Od.4.38; ἑοῖ αὐτῇ used of the 1 pers., A.R.3.99: for ϝίν, ἵν, v. ἵ: Boeot. ἑΐν Corinn.36: acc. ἕ Il.4.497, al., Pi.*O.*9.14, enclit. ἑ Il.1.236, al., never in Trag., Com., Th., Hdt., or X., but found in Pl.*Smp.*175a, al.; ἑέ twice in Hom., Il.20.171, 24.134 (perh. with elision in 14.162, 17.551); ἑ as fem. pl., *h.Ven.*267; ϝhé dub. in *GDI*1267.23 (Pamphylia): for the forms σφε, μιν, νιν, ἵ, σφωέ, σφεῖς, v. sub vocc.

B. Meanings: I. *him, her*, ἐπεί ἑό φημι βίῃ πολὺ φέρτερος εἶναι Il.15.165; ἅλις δέ οἱ· ἀλλὰ ἕκηλος ἐρρέτω· ἐκ γάρ εὑ φρένας εἵλετο μητίετα Ζεύς 9.376–7; περὶ κεῖνον ὀΐζυε καί ἑ φύλασσε 3.408; ἡ δέ οἱ κόμη ὤμους κατεσκίαζε Archil.29, etc.: this use is not found in Prose, exc. in dialects, *IG*4.506 (Argos), 7.2407.7 (Boeot.), *Berl.Sitzb.*1927.169 (Cyrene); ἀπέλαβε τήν οἱ ὁ πατὴρ εἶχε ἀρχήν *his* father, Hdt.3.15, cf. 4.50, al. II. as ἐμέ can be used reflexively (αὐτὰρ ἐγὼν ἐμὲ λύσομαι Il.10.378), so also ἕ (οὗ, οἷ), Ἀχιλῆα, ἕο μέγ' ἀμείνονα φῶτα, ἠτίμησεν Il.2.239; ἡ δ' ἔξοχα λυγρὰ ἰδυῖα οἷ τε κατ' αἶσχος ἔχευε καὶ ἐσσομένῃσιν ὀπίσσω Od.11.433; ἡ δὲ..ἀπὸ ἕο κάββαλεν υἱόν Il.5.343: later this reflex. sense is found only when the Pron. is used in a subordinate clause or construction (esp. acc. c. inf.) and refers to the subject of the principal Verb, e.g. προηγόρευε τοῖς Ἀθηναίοις..ὅτι Ἀρχίδαμος μέν οἱ ξένος εἴη..καὶ μηδεμίαν οἱ ὑποψίαν κατὰ ταῦτα γίγνεσθαι Th.2.13. 2. οὗ ἕ οἷ in combination with αὐτοῦ, αὐτόν, etc. forms a reflex. Pron. used without the foregoing restriction: in Hom. the two words are separate, e.g. πειρήθη δ' ἕο αὐτοῦ ἐν ἔντεσι δῖος Ἀχιλλεύς Il.19.384, cf. 5.64, al.: later they form one word, v. ἑαυτοῦ. [ὅς 'ϝ' ἄξει, i.e. with elision of 'ϝέ, must be read or understood for ὃς ἄξει, Il.24.154, in view of ὅς σ' ἄξει in l. 183, and so prob. in 1.195 (cf. 208), 4.315 (ὥς 'ϝ'), 16.545 (μή 'ϝ'), Od.5.135 (ἠδέ 'ϝ'): so ἔνθα 'ϝ(οι) ἔσαν is conjectured for ἔνθ' ἔσαν οἱ Il.6.289 (cf. ἔνθα οἱ ἦσαν ὕες Od.15.556), also ἀμφὶ δέ ϝ(οι) ὄσσε in Il.5.310: the elided acc. ϝ' is prob. to be recognized in δὸς δέ ϝ' ἐν ἀνθρώποις δόξαν ἔχεν ἀγαθ(ά)ν *IG*14.652 (Metapontum), rather than ϝιν.] (ἕ from *swe, ἑέ from *sewe, cogn. with ὅς (Possess.) and ἑός, qq. v.)

**οὐά** or **οὐᾶ**, Lat. *vah!* exclam. of admiration, or of astonishment, Arr.*Epict.*3.22.34, D.C.63.20; of irony, *Ev.Marc.*15.29.

**οὖα, οὖα**, v. ὄα (A) I, II.

**οὔαδας**, = οὖδας, Orac.ap.Keil-Premerstein *Erster Bericht* p.9 (Troketta).

**οὐαί**, exclam. of pain and anger, *ah! woe!* c. nom., Lxx *Am.*5.18, al.: c. voc., ib.3*Ki.*13.30: c. dat., οὐαί μοι, οὐαί σοι, *woe is* me! *woe to* thee! ib.*Nu.*21.29, Arr.*Epict.*3.19.1, *Mim.Oxy.*413.184: c. acc., οὐαὶ οὐαὶ οὐαὶ τοὺς κατοικοῦντας ἐπὶ τῆς γῆς *Apoc.*8.13. **II. οὐαί**· φυλαί (Cypr.), Hsch. (Cf. Dor. ὠβά.)

**οὐάραι**· ἡμεῖς, οὔαρον δὲ ἔλαιον (Cypr.), Hsch.

**οὐαστής** θρίαμβος, = Lat. *ovatio*, D.H.5.47.

**οὔατα, οὔατος, οὔασι**, v. οὖς.

⊛**οὐάτιον**, τό, Dim. of οὖς, *PMag.Lond.*46.92. (Prob. a misunderstanding of a transcription of Egypt. *wdȝ-t* = *eye*.)

⊛**οὐᾰτό-εις**, εσσα, εν, *long-eared*, θήρ Call.*Aet.Oxy.*2079.31; λαγώς *AP*7.207 (Mel.). 2. *with ears* or *handles*, σκύφος Simon.246; καλαύροπες Antim.61. (Cf. ὠτώεις.) **-κοίτης**, ου, ὁ, = ἐνωτοκοίτης, Nonn.*D.*26.94,99, 30.315.

**οὐ γάρ**, in orat. recta, *for not*, in assigning a negative reason, Il. 22.438, etc.: other Particles are sts. put between, as οὐ μὲν γάρ 5. 402; οὐ γάρ, in assent to a neg., *no indeed*, Pl.*Tht.*152a, etc. **II.** elliptic, in interrog. replies, where *yes* or *well* must be supplied, τούτους ἀγαθοὺς ἐνόμισας;—οὐ γάρ..; *yes* (or *well*), *and aren't they?* Ar. *Pax* 970. 2. in questions, where an affirm. answer is expected, οὐ γὰρ ὁ Παφλαγὼν ἀπέκρυπτε ταύτας; did *not* he keep them hidden? Id.*Eq.*1392, cf. D.22.73, etc.

**οὐ γὰρ ἀλλά**, an ellipt. phrase, used in Att. to express an indignant or impassioned affirmative, οὐ γὰρ ἀλλ' ὑπερβάλλει τάδε this is *indeed* too much! E.*Ba.*785; μὴ σκῶπτέ μ', ὦδέλφ', οὐ γὰρ ἀλλ' ἔχω κακῶς I *really am* unwell! Ar.*Ra.*58, cf. *Ec.*386: also to negate by substituting a still stronger affirmative, ἆρ' οὐ παρεῖναι τὰς γυναῖκας δῆτ' ἐχρῆν; Answ. οὐ γάρ, μὰ Δί', ἀλλὰ πετομένας ἥκειν πάλαι *more than that*, they ought to have come flying long ago, Id.*Lys.*55: = καὶ γάρ, Id.*Nu.*232, *Ra.*192,498, *Eq.*1205, *Supp.*570, Call.*Iamb.*1. 92; οὐ γὰρ μοὐστὶν ἀλλ' ἀκουστέα Ar.*Ra.*1180.

**οὐ γὰρ δή**, *for surely not*, S.*OT*576, *Ant.*46, etc.; so **οὐ γὰρ δή.. γε** D.29.14; **οὐ γὰρ δήπου** Pl.*Prt.*309c; **οὐ γὰρ δήπου..γε** Id.*R.* 509a, prob. in *Smp.*199a.

**οὐ γὰρ οὖν**, = οὐ γάρ strengthd., used in assenting to a neg. propos., *no*,—*certainly not*, Pl.*Prm.*134b.

**οὐ γάρ που..γε**, *for I don't suppose..*, Pl.*Phd.*62d, etc.

**οὐ γάρ τοι**, = οὐ γάρ strengthd., Od.21.172, etc.:—but **οὐ γάρ τοι ἀλλά..γε**, = οὐ γὰρ ἀλλά strengthd., Pl.*Euthd.*286b.

⊛**οὐγγία** or **οὐγκία**, ἡ, Lat. *uncia*, as adopted by the Sicil. Greeks, Arist.*Fr.*510, Gal.13.789, Alex.Aphr.*in Top.*210.7:—written **ὀγκία** in Epich.203, Sophr.151: hence Adj. **οὐγκιαῖος**, α, ον, *of one uncia*, prob. in *SIG*1042.23 (Sunium, ii/iii A. D.): ⊛**οὐγκιασμός**, ὁ, *measurement by unciae*, in pl., Just.*Nov.*107.1.

**οὐδαῖος**, α, ον, and ος, ον, *on the ground*, Orph.*A.*394, etc. **II.** like χθόνιος, *under the earth, infernal*, of Persephone, Lyc.49,698; of Zeus, *AP*14.123 (Metrod.), D.P.789.

**οὐδάλλος**, = οὐδέτερος, Theoc.6.46.

**οὐδᾰμ-ά** [μᾰ], Adv. *never, not at all*, οὐ. σ' οὐδ' ἀπεὼν δηλήσομαι Thgn. 1363, cf. 1372, Archil.*Supp.*3.6, Sapph.77 (οὐδ-), Anacr.50, Emp.17. 6,12, 26.11, A.*Supp.*884; καί νιν ὄμβροι..χιών τ' οὐ. λείπει S.*Ant.*830 (lyr.), cf. 763, *Tr.*323; οὐ. ἐν τὠυτῷ μένουσαν Hdt.1.5, cf. 56, 2.168, 3. 10, al. **-ῇ**, Adv. *nowhere, in no place*, οὐδαμῇ ἐστήρικτο Hes.*Sc.*218, cf. A.*Pers.*385, Telecl.21; οὐ. βίου E.*Fr.*34; οὐ. ἄλλῃ Hdt.2.116; ἄλλῃ οὐ. Id.4.114: c. gen., οὐ. Αἰγύπτου Id.2.43. 2. *in no direction, no way*, Id.1.24,34,56, etc. (Cf. οὐθαμεί.) **-ινός**, η, ον (proparox., cf. Hdn.Gr. 2.26), *worthless, good for nothing*, J.*AJ*17.2.4, 18.7.1, Heph.Astr.3.2, Anon.*in Rh.*186.16, Hsch. **-ινότης**, ητος, ἡ, *worthlessness*, Eust. 201.28. ⊛**-όθεν**, Adv. of οὐδαμός, *from no place, from no side*, X.*An.* 2.4.23; οὐ. προσήκει μοί τινος And.4.34; οὐ. μαθών Pl.*Prt.*319d; οὐ. ἄλλοθεν Id.*Phd.*70d. **-όθι**, Ion. for οὐδαμοῦ, *nowhere, in no place*, Hdt.7.49; οὐ. ἑτέρωθι Id.3.113: c. gen., οὐ. πάσης τῆς Εὐρώπης Id.7. 126. **-οῖ**, Adv. of οὐδαμός, *to no place, no-whither*, restd. for οὐδαμοῦ in Ar.*V.*1188, X.*HG*5.2.8, *An.*6.3.16(14); οὐ γὰρ ἤλθομεν οὐ. τῆς Θρᾴκης D.23.166, cf. Hdn.Gr.1.502.—Cf. μηδαμοῖ. **-ός**, ή, όν, for οὐδὲ ἀμός, *not any one, no one*, like οὐδείς, A.D.*Pron.*57.2: used only in pl. and only by Ion. writers (= Att. οὐδένες), οὐδαμοί, οὐδαμῶν, etc., *none*, Hdt.1.18,24,57, al.; πρήγματα..οὐδαμῶν Ἑλληνικῶν τῶν οὐ πολλὸν μέζω, i.e. much greater than any Greek power, Id.7.145: rarely in fem., οὐδαμὰς ἄλλας Id.4.114.—Cf. μηδαμός. **-όσε**, Adv. of οὐδαμός, = οὐδαμοῖ, Th.5.49, Pl.*Phd.*108a, 109a, D.43.74. **-οῦ**, Adv. of οὐδαμός, = οὐδαμόθι, *nowhere*, answering to ποῦ; *where?* A. *Supp.*329,442, al., Hdt.2.150, al., Th.1.3, etc.: also c. gen., οὐ. γῆς Hdt.7.166; οὐ. μὲν οὖν φρενῶν E.*Hipp.*1012: freq. f.l. for οὐδαμοῖ (q.v.). 2. οὐ. λέγειν τινά to esteem *as naught*, S.*Ant.*183; θεοὺς.. νομίζων οὐ. A.*Pers.*498; οὐ. εἶναι *to be non-existent*, Pl.*Phd.*70a; οὐδαμοῦ ἂν φαίνοιτο *would be 'nowhere', 'not in the running'*, ib.72c, cf. *Grg.*456b, D.18.310, 19.116; δειλοὶ δ' εἰσὶν οὐδὲν οὐ. E.*IT*115; cf. μηδαμοῦ. **II.** of Manner, ἄλλοθι οὐ. *in no* other *way*, Pl.*Smp.* 184e, *Prt.*324e. **-ῶς**, Adv. of οὐδαμός, *in no wise*, Hdt.2.148,173; ἄλλως οὐ. Id.1.123, etc.; οὐδέποτε οὐδαμῇ οὐ. Pl.*Phd.*78d, cf. *Phlb.* 29b: freq. in answers, πότερα γάρ..πρέπει;—οὐ. A.*Pers.*240, cf. 716; so οὐ. γ' Ar.*Nu.*688, *V.*79, etc.; also **οὐθαμῶς**, Thphr.*Metaph.*7, etc.—Cf. μηδαμῶς.

**οὖδας**, τό, gen. οὔδεος, dat. οὔδει Il.5.734, al. (more rarely οὔδεϊ 23. 283, *h.Merc.*284):—poet. Noun, prop. *surface of the earth, ground*, ἄσπετον οὖ. Od.13.395, al.; ὑπ' οὖ. under the *surface*, 9.135; ὀδὰξ ἕλον οὖ. bit *the dust*, of wounded or dying men, Il.11.749, 19.61, Od. 22.269; οὔδει ἐρείσθη he rested *on the ground*, Il.12.192; ἀπ' οὔδεος from *the ground*, ib.448, Od.9.242; οὖδάσδε *to the ground, to earth*, Il. 17.457, Od.10.440: also in Trag., πρὸς οὖδας φορεῖσθαι, πεσεῖν, βεβλῆσθαι, S.*El.*752, E.*Hec.*405, *IT*49, etc.; χθονὸς οὖ. Emp.115.10; πατρῷον οὖ. Ἀργείας χθονὸς A.*Ag.*503. 2. *floor, pavement* in rooms and houses, κραταίπεδον οὖ. Od.23.46; ἐν Διὸς οὔδει on *the floor* of Zeus' abode, Il.24.527; πατρὸς ἐπ' οὔδει 5.734, 8.385: prov., ἐπ' οὔδεϊ φῶτα καθίσσαι to bring a man *to the pavement*, i.e. to strip him of all he has, *h.Merc.*284.

⊛**οὐδέ**, neg. Particle, related to μηδέ as οὐ to μή, partly Conj., partly Adv.: **A.** Conjunction, *but not*, mostly answering to μέν (sts. written divisim), Il.5.138, 24.418; without μέν, 5.21, etc.: sts. the first οὐδέ, *but not*, is folld. by οὐδέ, *nor*, ἄλλοις μὲν πᾶσιν ἑήνδανεν, οὐδέ ποθ' Ἥρῃ, οὐδὲ Ποσειδάων', οὐδὲ γλαυκώπιδι κούρῃ 24.25. **II.** more freq. *and not, nor*: sts. without a neg. preceding, Κίρκη δ' ὡς ἐνόησεν ἔμ' ἥμενον, οὐδ' ἐπὶ σίτῳ χεῖρας ἰάλλοντα Od.10.375; τραχὺς μόναρχος οὐδ' ὑπεύθυνος A.*Pr.*326, cf. 102,259, al.; δεινὸν γάρ, οὐδὲ ῥητόν S.*Ph.*756, cf. 996, *OT*398, 868 (lyr.), Hdt.1.97, etc.: after a neg. compd., ὃν ἠτίμησ' Ἀγαμέμνων, οὐδ' ἀπέλυσε θύγατρα Il.1.95; ἀνήμεροι γὰρ οὐδὲ πρόσπλατοι ξένοις A.*Pr.*716; ἄστιπτος οὐδ' οἰκουμένη S.*Ph.*2; ἄθικτος οὐδ' οἰκητός Id.*OC*39. 2. with a neg. preceding, *nor*, βρώμης δ' οὐχ ἅπτεαι οὐ. ποτῆτος Od.10.379; οὐκέτι σοὶ..μένος ἔμπεδον οὐ. τις ἀλκή 22.226; οὐκ ἔχων βάσιν οὐ. τιν' ἐγχώρων S.*Ph.*692 (lyr.), cf. 681 (lyr.), 905,955, X.*Oec.*20.2, etc.: sts. the preceding neg. is itself οὐδέ, = *and not*, as in Od.22.222; οὐδέ, = *nor* may be repeated any number of times, e.g. three times in S.*OT*1378.—Sts. the neg. follows the whole word-group instead of preceding it, σιδήρῳ δὲ οὐδ' ἀργύρῳ χρέωνται οὐδέν but iron *or* silver use they not at all, Hdt. 1.215; Θεσσαλοῦ μὲν οὐδ' Ἱππάρχου οὐδεὶς παῖς Th.6.55; ἁπλοῦν μὲν οὐ. δίκαιον οὐδὲν ἂν εἰπεῖν ἔχοι D.22.4: but οὐδὲ..οὐδέ never means *neither..nor* (like οὔτε..οὔτε); where this combination occurs, the first οὐδέ is used without reference to the second, e.g. καὶ μὴν οὐδ' ἡ ἐπιτείχισις οὐδὲ τὸ ναυτικὸν ἄξιον φοβηθῆναι and moreover we have *no* reason to fear their fortifications, *nor yet* their navy, Th.1.142. **III.** οὐδέ may also follow οὔτε, by an anacoluth., as in τε..,δέ.. (v. οὔτε II.3); but οὔτε cannot follow οὐδέ.—Cf. μηδέ A. 2.

**B.** Adverb, *not even*, in Hom. mostly with Advbs., οὐδ' ἠβαιόν *not even* a little, *no not* a bit, *not at all*, Il.2.386; οὐ. τυτθόν 1.354; οὐ. μίνυνθα 20.27; so also ἐπεὶ οὔ οἱ ἔνι φρένες οὐδ' ἠβαιαί he has *no* sense, *no not even* a little, 14.141, cf. Od.21.288; τότε μὲν εὖ ζῶντες, νῦν δὲ οὐ. ζῶντες Pl.*R.*329a: freq. in Att., τούτῳ μὲν οὐ. διελέγετο he did *not even* exchange words with him, Lys.3.31, cf. Ar.*Nu.*425; οὐδ', εἰ γέγονεν, οἶδα D.18.70, etc.: in the same sense, οὐ. γ' Pl.*Phd.* 97a,b, 106b; οὐ. γ' αὖ Id.*R.*499a; οὐ. μήν X.*Cyr.*3.3.50, etc.; Ep. οὐ. μέν Il.9.374, etc.: in Att. freq. with εἷς (whence οὐδείς), οὐδ' ἂν εἷς θύσειεν Ar.*Pl.*137: sts. without elision, οὐδὲ εἷς ib.1182, Herod.1.45; οὐκ ἄλλ' οὐ. ἕν Ar.*Pl.*138, cf. *Ra.*927; also οὐ. καθ' ἓν Th.2.87; οὐ. παρ' ἑνός X.*Cyr.*2.3.10, etc.—This οὐδέ freq. follows καί, *and not even*, καὶ οὐδ' αὐτοὶ αὖ μόνον, ἀλλὰ καὶ.. Th.7.56, cf. X.*An.*3.2.4, etc.; also ἀλλ' οὐδέ, most freq. in phrase ἀλλ' οὐδ' ὧς.. Il.7.263, 9.351, etc. **II.** *also not, not..either, nor yet..*, ὁ δίκαιος τοῦ δικαίου δοκεῖ τί σοι ἂν ἐθέλειν πλέον ἔχειν; Answ. οὐδαμῶς..; Qu. τί δέ; τῆς δικαίας πράξεως; Answ. οὐ. τῆς δικαίας Pl.*R.*349b, cf. *Ap.*19d, 21d, X.*Mem.*3.11.4.

**C.** Repetition of οὐδέ and combination with οὐ: **I.** in Relat. as well as antec. clause, ὥσπερ οὐδ' ηὔχετο, οὐδ' ᾤετο Pl.*Alc.*2. 141a, cf. X.*Cyr.*1.6.18. **II.** οὐ γὰρ οὐδέ, as ἀλλ' οὐ γὰρ οὐ. νουθετεῖν ἔξεστί σε S.*El.*595, cf. *Aj.*1242, *OT*287, etc.; οὐ. γὰρ οὐ. Il.5.22, 6.130, Od.8.32, Hdt.4.16, etc.; οὐ. μὲν οὐ. Il.2.703, etc.; οὐ μὰν οὐ. 23.441, etc.; cf. οὐ c.

**οὐδείς**, fem. οὐδεμία (never nom. acc. -μίη, -μίην, since οὐδεμιῇ is prob. in Call.*Aet.Oxy.*2080.56, rarely οὐδ' ἴα Sapph.69, Mosch.4.40), neut. οὐδέν (declined and accentuated like εἷς, μία, ἕν), *not one*, i.e. *no one, none*, used by Hom., Hes., and Pi. (who prefer οὔτις) only in neut. nom. and acc. οὐδέν, exc. in the phrase τὸ ὃν μένος οὐδενὶ εἴκων Il.22. 459, al.; οὐδείς is found in B.*Fr.*28; but all genders and cases are common in all other writers, Hdt.1.32,33, etc.: rare in pl., *no set* of persons or things, And.1.23 (dub. cj.), X.*Lac.*3.1; πρὸς οὐδένας τῶν Ἑλλήνων D.18.23 (v.l.), cf. 19.31, 66.312, 24.214, 27.7; οὐδένων εἰσὶ βελτίους, i.e. οὔ τινων ἄλλων, Id.2.17 (cf. οὐδενὸς βελτίους Pl.*Prt.*324d): dat. pl. οὐδέσιν Paus.3.24.3; for another sense of the pl., v. infr. II. 3.—In Ion. the pl. is usu. οὐδαμοί. 2. οὐ. ὅστις οὐ *every one*, Hdt.3. 72, etc.; οὐδὲν ὅ τι οὐ *every*, Id.5.97; this came to be regarded as one word, so that οὐδείς passed into the same case as ὅστις, οὐδένα ὅντινα οὐ κατέκλασε Pl.*Phd.*117d; οὐδενὸς ὅτου οὐ πάντων ἂν..πατὴρ εἴην Id.*Prt.* 317c, cf. 323b; οὐδενὶ ὅτῳ οὐκ ἀποκρινόμενος Id.*Men.*70c; so οὐ. ὃς οὐχὶ..ὀνειδίζει S.*OT*373; οὐδὲν γάρ..οὔτ' αἰσχρὸν οὔτ' ἄτιμόν ἐσθ', ὁποῖον οὐ..οὐκ ὄπωπ' ἐγώ Id.*Ant.*4. 3. later οὐδὲν ὅ τι without οὐ, = *nothing*, οὐδὲν ὅ τι παρήσω Agath.*Praef.*p.137 D., al. 4. ὅστις οὐδεὶς *not one*, ἐτεθνήκεσαν δὲ αὐτῶν μὲν ἀμφὶ τοὺς τετρακοσίους, Ῥωμαίων δὲ ὅστις οὐδείς Id.5.20. **II.** *naught, good for naught*, ὦ νῦν μὲν οὐ. αὔριον δ' ὑπέρμεγας Ar.*Eq.*158, cf. E.*Fr.*187.5; τὸ μὲν [γένος ἀνδρῶν] οὐδέν

Pi.*N.*6.3: freq. in neut., οὐδὲν εἰδώς knowing *naught*, Thgn.141, E.*Fr.*391; οὐκ ἄρ' ἤστην οὐδὲν ἄλλο πλὴν δάκνειν knew *nothing* save how to.., Ar.*Av.*19; οὐδὲν λέγειν to say *naught*, v. λέγω (B) III. 6; τὸ οὐδ' οὐδέν the absolute *nothing*, Pl.*Tht.*180a. 2. in neut., of persons, οὐδέν εἰμι S.*Ph.*951, etc.; οὐδὲν εἶ Ar.*Ec.*144; πρὸς τὸν οὐδέν E.*Ph.* 598; τὸ μηδὲν εἰς οὐδὲν ῥέπει Id.*Fr.*532.2; ᾧ ἀνεμέσητον..οὐδενὶ εἶναι Pl.*Tht.*175e. 3. in pl., οὐδένες ἐόντες ἐν οὐδαμοῖσι ἐοῦσι Ἕλλησι being *nobodies*, Hdt.9.58; ὄντες οὐδένες E.*Andr.*700, cf. *IA*371; ὁ μηδὲν ὢν κἀξ οὐδένων κεκλήσομαι dub. cj. in Id.*Ion* 594; οὐ γὰρ ἠξίου τοὺς μηδένας S.*Aj.*1114. 4. with Preps., παρ' οὐδὲν εἶναι Id.*OT*983, etc.; παρ' οὐδὲν ἄγειν, θέσθαι, Id.*Ant.*35, E.*IT*732; δι' οὐδενὸς ποιεῖσθαι S.*OC*584; ἐν οὐδενὸς εἶναι μέρει D.2.18. 5. τὸ οὐδέν *naught, zero*, in Arith., Nicom.*Ar.*2.6; used by Democritus as a name for Place, Arist.*Fr.*208. III. neut. οὐδέν as Adv., *not at all, naught*, ἄριστον Ἀχαιῶν οὐ. ἔτισεν Il.1.412, cf. 24.370, Hdt.5.34, Th.8.22, etc.; so οὐδέν τι X.*Mem.*1.2.42, etc.; οὐ. τι πάντως Hdt.5.65: in answers, *nothing, never mind, no matter*, E.*Med.*64, *IT*781, Ar.*Nu.* 694; οὐδέν γε *not at all*, Id.*Av.*1360, etc.; οὐδὲν μᾶλλον, οὐδὲν ἧσσον, οὐδὲν ὕστερος, v. μάλα II. 5, ἥσσων III, ὕστερος A. I. 2. οὐδὲν ἄλλο ἤ, v. ἄλλος III. 2. B. REMARKS: the more emphatic and literal sense, *not even one*, i.e. *none whatever*, belongs to the full form, οὐδὲ εἷς, οὐδὲ μία, οὐδὲ ἕν, which is never elided, even in Com. (v. Ar.*Ra.*927, *Lys.*1045 (lyr.), *Pl.*138,1115), but freq. has a Particle inserted between, cf. οὐδέ B.—Zen. (in *EM*639.17) and others wrongly assume οὐδείς as a compd. not of οὐδέ and εἷς, but of οὐ and δείς (q. v.). (Later οὐθείς, q. v.)

**οὐδέκοτε**, Ion. for οὐδέποτε, Hdt.8.111.

**οὐδεν-άκῐ**, Adv. of οὐδέν, *not once, no times*, Iamb.*in Nic.*p.19 P. **-ία** or **οὐδένεια**, ἡ, *nothingness, worthlessness*, Pl.*Phdr.*235a, *Tht.*176c, Ephor.137 J., Plb.34.14.3, Ph.1.477, Ael.*NA*15.13, etc. (Codd. vary, e.g. in Ph. l. c., οὐδένειαν Pap., -ίαν G, οὐθένειαν cett.)

**οὐδενόσωρος**, ον, (ὥρα) *worth no notice* or *regard*, τείχεα..ἀβλήχρ' οὐδενόσωρα Il.8.178; ὀστέον Opp.*H.*2.478.

**οὐδεν-όω**, (οὐδέν) *bring to naught*, *EM*350.25. **-ωσις**, εως, ἡ, *annihilation*, Thd.*Is.*34.11. **-ωτής**, οῦ, ὁ, *vilifier*, Phld.*Vit.* p.42 J.

**οὐδέ πῃ** or **οὐδέπῃ**, Conj. and Adv. (*and*) *in no wise*, Od.12.433; οὐδέ πῃ ἔστι c. inf., 'tis *in no wise* possible, Il.6.267, *h.Hom.*7.58.

**οὐδέποτε**, in Ion. Prose **οὐδέκοτε**, Dor. **οὐδέποκα** prob. in *IG*2[2]. 1126.5 (cf. μηδέποκα ib.11), etc.:—Conj. and Adv. *and not ever* or *nor ever, not even ever* or *never*, in Hom. mostly with past tenses, Il.1.155, 5.789, al.: but with pres., Od.10.464, Hes.*Th.*759: with fut., Od.2. 203, Hes.*Op.*176; in Att., οὐδέποτε is commonly found with pres. or fut. (or its equivalent, as in οὐδέποτε μὴ λειφθῇ *SIG*800.29 (Lycosura, i A. D.)), οὐδεπώποτε with past tenses, so οὐδέποτε ἐπὶ μέλλοντος.., ἐπὶ δὲ παρῳχημένου τὸ οὐδεπώποτε Phryn.*PS*p.91 B.: but οὐδέποτε occurs with past tenses in *Com.Adesp.*23 (cited by Phryn. l. c.), X.*An.*2.6. 13, *Ages.*11.7, *Oec.*20.22, Aeschin.3.151, Men.653; cf. οὐδέποτε *tam in praeterito quam in futuro, quomodo et nos 'nunquam'*, Priscian.*Inst.* 18.257: in late writers the reference of πω to past time was neglected, v. οὐδεπώποτε, and cf. ἐξ ὧν ἀνάγκη..μηδεπώποτε ἐλευθερίας ἐπιτυγχάνειν D.Chr.14.1; cf. οὐδέπω, οὔποτε, οὔπω, οὐπώποτε, also μηδέποτε, μηπώποτε.—In Hom. οὐδέ ποτε shd. prob. be written divisim: sts. a word is put between, as in Il.6.99.

**οὐδέ πω**, Conj. and Adv. *and not yet, not as yet*, A.*Pr.*322, Pl.*Smp.* 172c, etc.: in Hom., mostly with a word between, οὐδέ τί πω, οὐδ' ἄν πω, etc., always of the past (cf. οὔπω): later with pres., Pl.*Phd.* 106b, etc.; σὺ δὲ οὐδέπω δρᾷς Luc.*Merc.Cond.*21: with fut., ὅσον οὐδέπω συμβήσεσθαι Zos.2.1; cf. οὐδέποτε.

**οὐδεπώποτε**, Conj. and Adv. *and not yet ever, never yet at any time*, usu. of the past, as S.*Ph.*250, And.1.22, Pl.*Prt.*313c: later of the fut., οὐδεπώποτε ἀπολαύσομεν Them.*Or.*26.330a; v. οὐδέποτε.

**οὐδέτερ-ος**, α, ον, *not either, neither of the two*, Hdt.1.51, Ar.*Ra.*1412, Pl.*Phlb.*21e: in pl., when each party is pl., first in Hes.*Th.*638, *Sc.* 171, cf. Hdt.1.76, etc.: divisim, v. ἕτερος I. Adv. οὐδετέρως *in neither of two ways*, Pl.*Lg.*902c: also neut. pl. as Adv., = οὐδετέρως, Id.*Plt.* 258a, *Tht.*184a, etc. II. *neutral*, τῶν μὲν αἱρετῶν οὐσῶν, τῶν δὲ φευκτῶν, τῶν δ' οὐ. Arist.*EN*1175[b]26: so in Medic., of a state which is neither illness nor health, διάθεσις Herophil.ap.Gal.6.388; σῶμα Gal.1.307,311. 2. in Gramm., *neuter*, ἀρσενικῶν καὶ θηλυκῶν καὶ οὐ. D.H.*Amm.*2.10; τὸ οὐ. (sc. γένος) the *neuter* gender, A.D.*Pron.* 6.19. Adv. **-ρως** *in the neuter*, Id.*Synt.*199.20, Gal.9.458, Ath.15.701a; also of Verbs, οὐδετέρα διάθεσις Sch.D.T.p.246 H. **-ωθεν**, Adv. *from neither side*, Lys.17.4 (or οὐδ' ἑ.), Gal.16.157. **-ωθι**, Adv. *in neither place*, Simp.*in Cael.*4.1. **-ωσε**, Adv. *to neither of two sides, neither way*, οὐδ' ἄρα τε προκυλίνδεται οὐ. Il.14.18; οὐ. κλινόμενος Thgn.945; οὐ. ῥέπει Str.2.1.11. (Perh. οὐδ' ἑτέρωσε shd. be written everywhere.)

**οὔδετις**, v. τις.

**οὐ δή**, *certainly not, in sooth not*, Od.20.322, al.; in a question, *surely not..?* 7.239, S.*Ph.*900.

**οὐδήεις**, εσσα, εν, (οὖδας) *terrestrial*, v.l. in Od.5.334, 10.136.

**οὐ δή που** or **οὐ δήπου**, v. δήπου.

**οὐ δῆτα**, *no truly*, A.*Pr.*349, 770, etc.

**οὐδοπότερος**, v. ὁπότερος. **οὐδοποτέρωσε**, v. ὁποτέρωσε. **οὐδοπωσοῦν, οὐδοπωστιοῦν**, v. ὁπωσοῦν.

⊛ **οὐδός** (A), Dor. **ὠδός** *Berl.Sitzb.*1927.170 (Cyrene), Hsch.; Trag. and Att. **ὀδός** S.*OC*57, 1590, *IG*2[2].1668.33, 7.412.7 (Orop.), Lycurg. 40, Hyp.*Dem.Fr.*6, Men.671, *BCH*35.286 (Delos); also at Samos, *Michel*832.30, and Epidaurus, *IG*4[2](1).102.232 and 249, also (later) at Branchidae, *CIG*2885*d*9: gen. pl. **ὀδέων** *IG*4[2](1).109 ii 105, 150 (Epid., iii B. C.): ὁ:—*threshold*, esp. *threshold of a house*, in Hom. χάλκεος οὐδός (as in Hes.*Th.*811), Od.7.83,89; also λάϊνος Il.9.404, Od. 8.80, Parm.1.12; μέλινος Od.17.339; δρύϊνος 21.43; μέγας Hes.*Th.* 749. 2. generally, *threshold, entrance* to any place, ἐπὶ προθύροις Ὀδυσῆος, οὐδοῦ ἐπ' αὐλείου Od.1.104; to the nether world, Il.8.15; χαλκόπους ὀδός S.*OC*57, cf. 1590: in pl., perh. *lintel*, Theoc.23.50 (dub. l., ὀδῶν cod.). 3. metaph., ἐπὶ γήραος οὐδῷ on the *threshold* which is old age, i.e. perh., on the *threshold* that leads from life to death (so οὐδὸς βιότου the *end* of life, Q.S.10.426), Il.22.60, Od.15. 348, Hes.*Op.*331, Hdt.3.14, cf. Pl.*R.*328e; ἐπὶ γήρως ὀδῷ Lycurg., Hyp., and Men. ll. cc.; μέχρι γήραος οὐδοῦ Ps.-Phoc.230; γήραος οὐδὸν ἱκέσθαι Od.23.212, cf. 15.246.—Poet. word, used by Arist. *Metaph.*1042[b]19, Plu.*TG*17, and Luc.*Dom.*18, al., in the form οὐδός, which is Ion., cf. Hp.*Art.*78, *GDI*5601*a* (Ephesus), *IG*11(2).158*A* 69 (Delos, iii B. C.), and is used later as gloss on βηλός, *AB*224 (so ὀδός in 225 and Hsch. s. v. ὀρρόβηλος). (The forms οὐδός ὠδός ὀδός point to *ὀδϝός.)

**οὐδός** (B), ἡ, = ὁδός, *way*, only in Od.17.196.

**οὐδοστισοῦν**, neut. οὐδοτιοῦν, v. ὅστις IV. 2.

**οὐδραία**· ὑδρία, μέτρον τι, Ἀττικοῦ μετρητοῦ ἥμισυ, Hsch. **οὐδραίνει**· περικαθαίρει, Λάκωνες, Id. **οὐδύεται**· ἐρίζει, Id.

**Οὐδυσσεύς**, Att. crasis for ὁ Ὀδυσσεύς, S.*Ph.*572, Ar.*Av.*1561 (lyr.).

⊛ **οὐδών**, ῶνος, ὁ, a kind of *felt shoe*, Poll.10.50: Dim. ⊛ **-ώνιον** *Edict. Diocl.* in *IG*5(1).1406.24 (Asine):—also **οὐδωνάριον**, Charis.1.552 K., *Gloss.*

**οὐένετος**, η, ον, Lat. *venetus*, *of the faction of the Blues* in the chariot races, *Tab.Defix.Aud.*234.5 (Carthage, ii/iii A. D.):—also **οὐενετιανός**, ib.237.6; cf. βένετος, βενετιανός:—also **οὐενέτιος**, ον, στολή D.C. 61.6, 77.10.

⊛ **οὐετερανός**, ὁ, = Lat. *veteranus*, *IGRom.*3.140 (Galatia), etc.; also **οὐετρανός** ib.99,142, etc.; written **βετράνος** in Zonar.

**οὔθα**· σποδός, ὁδός, Hsch. **οὐθαμεῖ**, Dor. Adv. *nowhere*, *IG*4[2](1). 122.22 (Epid., iv B. C.). **οὐθαμῶς**, v. οὐδαμῶς.

**οὖθαρ**, ατος, τό, prop. of animals, *udder*, Od.9.440, Hdt.4.2, Theoc. 8.42,69, etc.; καθιέναι τὸ οὖθαρ Arist.*HA*523[a]1; τὰ οὔθατα distd. from οἱ μαστοί by Plu.2.496c; eaten as a dish, ib.124f; later of women, *breast*, A.*Ch.*532; ὡς οὖθαρ θῆλυς εἰκότως οὐ. φορῷ Telecl. 31. II. metaph., οὐ. ἀρούρης *the richest, most fertile* land, Il.9.141, 283, *h.Cer.*450, Cratin.220; οὐ. ἀγαθῆς χθονός Ar.*Fr.*110; of the vine, ὀπώρη οὔθατος ἐκ βοτρύων ξανθὸν ἀμέλξε γάνος *AP*9.645 (Maced.). (Cf. Skt. *ū́dhar*, gen. *ū́dhnas*, OE. *ūder* 'udder', Lat. *ūber*.)

**οὔθαρα**· ἐπὶ ἀσκοῦ ὁ κατὰ τὸ οὖθαρ τόπος, οἱ δέ, περὶ ὃν στρέφεται ὁ χορός, ἢ ὁ τροχός, Hsch.

**οὐθάτ-ιος** [ᾰ], α, ον, *of the udder*, μαστός *AP*9.430 (Crin.). **-όεις**, εσσα, εν, = foreg., Nic.*Al.*90, Orph.*L.*193: metaph., *fruitful*, Opp.*C.* 2.148.

**οὐθείς**, οὐθέν, later form for οὐδείς, οὐδέν, found in Att. Inscrr. from 378 B. C. onwards along with οὐδείς, which it supersedes entirely from about 325 B. C. to 100 B. C. (forty examples of θ, none of δ); οὐθείς is in a majority in Ptolemaic papyri up to about 130 B. C., after which οὐδείς begins to be common, but does not prevail until i A. D.; the evidence of non-Att. Inscrr. is in general agreement with the foregoing; codd. of Th., Antipho, And., Lys., and Hdt. never have οὐθείς, but the θ forms are freq. in those of Pl., X., Isoc., D., Hyp., Arist., and Thphr., freq. as variants for the δ forms; also in Hellenistic writers, Teles, Plb., etc.; the frequency of θ forms in the uncials of Lxx varies roughly according to the date (known or probable) of the translation of the book in question (though the δ forms are in a large majority in the Lxx as a whole); the θ forms are rare in codd. of Str. and later writers.

**οὐθέτερος**, α, ον, = οὐδέτερος, S.E.*M.*11.186, Iamb.*Protr.*21.κϛ'.

**οὐ θην, οὐ θην δή**, Adv. *surely not, certainly not*, v. θην.

**οὔϊγγον, οὔϊπον, οὔϊτον** (the spelling varies), τό, *Egyptian arum*, *Colocasia antiquorum*, Thphr.*HP*1.1.7, 1.6.9,11; cf. οὔϊτον· τὸ ὑπ' ἐνίων οἰτόν, Hsch.

**οὐΐτουλος**, ὁ, the Lat. *vitulus*, Hellanic.111 J., as root of **Οὐιταλία**, *Italia*.

**οὐκ**, v. οὐ G.

**οὐκ**, Att. crasis for ὁ ἐκ, Arist.*Fr.*675.9 (lyr.).

**οὐκ ἄρα**, Adv. *so not, not then*, οὐκ ἄρα σοί γε πατὴρ ἦν..Πηλεύς Il. 16.33. II. in questions, οὐκ ἄρ' ἔμελλες οὐδὲ θανὼν λήσεσθαι.. χόλου; *so not* even in death wert thou to forget thine anger? Od.11. 553.

**οὐκέτι** or **οὐκ ἔτι**, Adv. *no more, no longer, no further*: and generally, *not now*, opp. οὔπω (not yet), freq. in Hom., Hes., Hdt., and Att.; οὐκέτι πάμπαν Il.13.701; οὐκέτι πάγχυ 19.343; with a word between, οὐ πάμπαν ἔτι 13.7; οὐ γὰρ ἔτι 2.13,141, etc.—Sts. reversely, ἔτ' οὐκ S.*Tr.*161, cf. ἔτ' οὐδέν Id.*Ph.*1217 (lyr.); ἔτ' οὐδείς Ar.*Pl.*1177.

**οὐκί**, Ion. for οὐχί, v. οὐ G.

**οὔκουν**, Ion. **οὔκων**, Adv., (οὐκ, οὖν): I. in direct negation, *certainly not, at any rate..not*, freq. with stress on the word which follows οὖν, οὔκουν Ἀτρεῖδαι τοῦτ' ἔτλησαν εὐφόρως οὕτως ἐνεγκεῖν the Atridae (emphat.) *certainly* did *not* consent.., S.*Ph.*872; οὔκουν μ' ἐν Ἄργει γ' οἷα πράττεις λανθάνει Ar.*Eq.*465; οὔκουν..γε is the neg. of γοῦν, οὔκουν ἔμοιγε χρώμενος διδασκάλῳ A.*Pr.*324, cf. S.*Ant.*321, 993, *Ph.*907, 1389, E.*IA*9, *IT*516, Th.2.43, Pl.*Sph.*241c, *Phdr.*258c, X. *Mem.*4.2.10; οὔκουν ἀπολείψομαί γέ σου.., εἰ τοῦτο λέγεις I will *not* desert (emphat.) you, if that is what you mean, Id.*Cyr.*4.1.23; οὔκουν γ' ἂν οἶμαι.. εἰπεῖν τινα.. Pl.*Phd.*70b; ἐγὼ τοίνυν κινδυνεύω ἐκτὸς τῶν πάντων εἶναι· οὔκουν ἱκανῶς γε ἔχω.. συμβαλέσθαι *at any rate* I can-*not* guess.., Id.*R.*398c, cf. *Lg.*807a, 810e. 2. where οὖν has a resumptive force, οὔκουν ἀπιστεῖν εἰκός *accordingly*, it is *un*reasonable to disbelieve.., Th.1.10 (referring back to οὐκ ἄν τις ἀπιστοίη ibid.); so οὐκ ἂν οὖν νήσων ἐκράτει.. εἰ μή ναυτικὸν εἶχε ib.9; οὔκουν χρή Id.2.11; with inferential force, οὔκουν τοῦτο δεῖ δεικνύναι, ὅτι.., ἀλλ' ὅτι.. *therefore* one ought to prove *not* that.., but that.., Arist.*Ph.*213ᵃ31, cf. Ar.*Ra.*1065; οὔκουν οἶδα so I *don't* know, Pl.*Cra.*384b. II. in impassioned questions, almost = οὐ alone, οὔκουν, Προμηθεῦ, τοῦτο γιγνώσκεις, ὅτι..; A.*Pr.*379, cf. *Eu.*725; οὔκουν ἐγώ σοι ταῦτα προὔλεγον πάλαι; S.*OT*973; οὔκουν τάδ', ὦ παῖ, δεινά; Id.*Ph.*628, cf. E.*IT* 1190, 1196, Ar.*Eq.*820, Lys.10.12, 13, Is.5.34, 11.13, Aeschin.1.85, 2.87, al. (sts., but prob. wrongly, written οὐκοῦν or οὐκ οὖν): sts. separately, οὐ δεινὸν οὖν δῆτ'..; Ar.*Eq.*875: freq. with 2 sg. fut., to express an urgent or impatient imper., οὔκουν ἐπείξη τῷδε δεσμὰ περιβαλεῖν; A.*Pr.*52; οὔκουν μ' ἐάσεις κἀκτὸς εἶ; S.*OT*676, cf. *Ant.*244, Ar.*Ra.*200, *Pl.*71, Pl.*Smp.*175a: also with τις and 3 sg. fut., οὔκουν τις ὡς τάχιστα.. ἀναγκάσει..; S.*OC*897; or opt. with ἄν, οὔκουν ἂν εἴποις..; Id.*Aj.*1051: with neg. repeated, οὔκουν ἐάσεις οὐδ' ὑπ' εὐφήμου βοῆς θῦσαί με; Id.*El.*630. 2. in replies, where the speaker seizes an opening offered by the previous speaker, οὔκουν ὅμαιμος χὠ καταντίον θανών; *well, and* is *not* he who died facing him your brother too? Id.*Ant.*512; οὔκουν γέλως ἥδιστος εἰς ἐχθροὺς γελᾶν; *well, and* is *not* the sweetest laughter to laugh over one's enemies? Id.*Aj.*79; ἴτ' ἐγκονεῖτε, σπεύδεθ', ὡς ὁ καιρὸς οὐχὶ μέλλειν. Answ. οὔκουν ὁρᾷς ὁρμωμένους ἡμᾶς πάλαι προθύμως; Ar.*Pl.*257, cf. 916, 1031, *Ra.*27, 89, 1139, *V.*171. III. in Ion. Prose ὦν (freq. with little meaning) is inserted between οὐκ and a Verb (as elsewh. between a Prep. and a Verb, v. οὖν II. 2), ταῦτα λέγοντες, τοὺς Κροτωνιήτας οὐκ ὦν ἔπειθον Hdt.3.137, cf. 138; οὐκ ὦν δὴ ἔπειθε *however*, he *failed to* persuade her, Id.1.11, cf. 24, 59, al.

**οὐκοῦν**, Dor. **οὐκῶν**, Adv., composed, like οὔκουν, of οὐκ and οὖν, but differing in meaning and accent, cf. A.D.*Conj.*257.18 sqq., Hdn.Gr.1.516, Phryn.*PS* p.98 B. I. in questions, inviting assent to an inference, or to an addition to what has already received assent, οὐκοῦν δοκεῖ σοι..; you think *then, do you not*, that..? X.*Cyr.*2.4.15, *Mem.*1.4.5, cf. 4.2.20, Pl.*Prt.*332b, 360b–d, *Cra.*416c, etc.: with hortatory subj., οὐκοῦν καὶ ἄλλους σε φῶμεν δυνατὸν εἶναι ποιεῖν (sc. ῥήτορας ἀγαθούς); Id.*Grg.*449b: folld. by οὐ when a neg. answer is invited, οὐκοῦν οὐκ ἂν εἴη τὸ μὴ λυπεῖσθαί ποτε ταὐτὸν τῷ χαίρειν; Id.*Phlb.*43d, cf. *Phd.* 105e; οὐκοῦν οὐδ' ἂν εἷς ἀντείποι; D.16.4. II. in affirm. sentences, *surely then*, οὐκοῦν, εἰ ταῦτα ἀληθῆ, πολλὴ ἐλπὶς ἀφικομένῳ οἷ ἐγὼ πορεύομαι Pl.*Phd.*67b: with subj. or imper., οὐκοῦν διδάσκωμεν αὐτόν, ἀλλὰ μὴ λοιδορῶμεν let us teach him, *then*, Id.*La.*195a; οὐκοῦν.. ἱκανῶς ἐχέτω let this *then* suffice, Id.*Phdr.*274b, cf. 278b, Luc.*DMort.*23.3; οὐκοῦν ἂν ἤδη.. λέγοι Ar.*Pax* 43: with a prohibition, οὐκοῦν μὴ.. αὐτομολήσῃς Aeschin.1.159; οὐκοῦν ὑπόλοιπον δουλεύειν slavery, *then*, is the only alternative, D.8.59. 2. in replies, *very well, yes*, ἴωμεν.. Answ. οὐκοῦν ἐπειδὰν πνεῦμα τοὐκ πρῴρας ἀνῇ, τότε στελοῦμεν S.*Ph.*639; ἀμηχάνων ἐρᾷς. Answ. οὐκοῦν, ὅταν δὴ μὴ σθένω, πεπαύσομαι Id.*Ant.*91; ἥξει γὰρ αὐτά, κἂν ἐγὼ σιγῇ στέγω. Answ. οὐκοῦν ἅ γ' ἥξει καὶ σὲ χρὴ λέγειν ἐμοί Id.*OT*342; ἀπόλωλας, ὦ κακόδαιμον. Answ. οὐκοῦν, ἢν λάχω Ar.*Pax* 364; ἴθι δὴ σκεψώμεθα.. Answ. οὐκοῦν χρή *yes*, let us do so, Pl.*Plt.*289d, cf. 287c, *Sph.*254d; *surely*, οὐκοῦν τρύγοιπος ταῦτα πάντ' ἰάσεται Ar.*Pl.*1087; οὐκοῦν κλεινὴ καὶ ἔπαινον ἔχουσ'.. ἀπέρχῃ S.*Ant.*817 (anap.).

**οὔκω**, Ion. for οὔπω. **οὔκων** and **οὐκῶν**, v. οὔκουν and οὐκοῦν. **οὔκως**, Ion. for οὔπως. **οὐλᾰδώνῠμος**, ον, v. οὐλαμώνυμος.

⊕ **οὐλαί**, Att. **ὀλαί**, αἱ, *barley-corns, barley-groats*, which were sprinkled on the head of the victim before the sacrifice (cf. Sch.Ar.*Eq.*1164), Od.3.441, cf. Hdt.1.132, Ar.*Eq.*1167, *Pax* 948, 960, Thphr.*Char.*10.13 (ὀλ-, v.l. οὐλ-), *SIG* 1024.18 (Myconos, iii/ii B.C.); οὐλαὶ κριθῶν Hdt.1.160. (The variation οὐλαί: ὀλαί points to orig. *ὀλϝαί, cf. ὀλβάχνιον: the Arc. form ὀλοαί *IG*5(2).514.15 (Lycosura, ii B.C.) prob. comes from a bye-form *ὀλοϝαί. Perh. cogn. with ἀλέω (A), ἄλυμος III, ὄλυρα.)

**οὐλᾰμ-ηφόρος**, ον, *bringing an army, warlike*, πεῦκαι Lyc.32. **-οεργός**, ὁ, = foreg., epith. of the planet Mars, *Cat.Cod.Astr.*1.173. ⊕ **-ός**, ὁ, *throng of warriors*, esp. in battle, in Hom. always οὐ. ἀνδρῶν, Il.4.251, 273, al. (never in Od.); μελισσαῖος οὐ. *a swarm* of bees, Nic.*Th.*611. II. later as a t.t., *troop* of cavalry, Plb.6.28.3, al., Plu.*Lyc.*23. **-ώνῠμος**, ον, (ὄνομα) *named from the armed throng* (οὐλαμός), epith. of Neoptolemus, Lyc.183 (v.l. οὐλαδωνύμου, which the Sch. explains as epith. of Paris, whose name was derived from πήρα, v. οὐλάς II).

**οὐλαπισμός**, ὁ, = οὐρανίσκος, Zonar.

⊕ **οὐλάς**, άδος, ἡ, pecul. fem. of οὖλος (B), *crisped, crinkled*, χαίτη δρυός, of oak-leaves, Nic.*Al.*260. II. as Subst., = πήρα, θύλακος, πτωχῶν οὐ. ἀεὶ κενεή Call.*Fr.*360 (θυλὰς cj. Ruhnken for οὐλάς, κενεή Hecker for κεναί), cf. Hsch. s. vv. θυλίδες, θυλλίς, οὐλάδες, Phot., Sch.Theoc.1.53; restd. for οὖδας in *AP*7.413 (Antip.).

**οὐλᾰφη-φορεῖ**· νεκροφορεῖ, Hsch.; cf. sq. **-φόρος**, ὁ, *undertaker, corpse-carrier*, Call.*Iamb.*1.234.

**οὔλαφος**· νεκρός, Hsch. **οὖλε**, v. οὔλω. **οὐλέω**, v. οὔλω. **οὐλή**, ἡ, v. οὐλαί.

⊕ **οὐλή**, ἡ, *wound scarred over, scar*, Od.19.391, 393, al. (never in Il.), E.*El.*573, Hp.*Morb.*1.21, *PGrenf.*2.32.5 (ii B.C.), etc.; τὰς οὐ. τῶν τραυμάτων X.*Mem.*3.4.1; ἴχνη τῶν πληγῶν οὐλὰς ἐν τῷ σώματι Pl.*Grg.*524c; ἕλκη.., ὧν ἔτι τὰς οὐ. ἔχει D.53.8; ἐκ τοῦ μὴ ἐν ταῖς οὐ. φύεσθαι τρίχας Arist.*Pr.*877ᵃ2: metaph., ἡ οὐ. τῆς διαβολῆς Plu.2.65d.

**οὐλιαζόεις** ἀτμοί *deadly* vapours, cj. Headlam in A.*Fr.*205.2.

⊕ **οὔλιγξ**, acc. pl. οὔλιγγας, v.l. for ὤλιγγας (ἔλιγγας, ὤριγγας) in Poll.2.67.

**οὔλιμος**· ὀλέθριος, Hsch.

**οὔλιος**, α, ον, (οὖλος C) = ὀλοός, *baleful, deadly*, οὐ. ἀστήρ, of the dog-star, Il.11.62; epith. of Ares, Hes.*Sc.*192, 441, Pi.*O.*9.76; αἰχμαί, θρῆνος, ib.13.23, *P.*12.8: once in Trag., οὐ. πάθος S.*Aj.*932 (lyr.). II. as epith. of Apollo and Artemis, Pherecyd.149 J., cf. Ἀπόλλων Οὔλιος *IG*12(1).834.3 and 845.10 (Lindos), *SIG*765.17 (ibid., i B.C.); Ἀπόλλων Οὔλιος also at Miletus and Delos acc. to Str.14.1.6, who derives the epith. from οὐλείν, Apollo and Artemis being healers: more prob. it is only a special application of sense I. III. = οὖλος (B), *woolly*, χλαμύς only in B.17.53.

**οὐλίριος**, ον, *woolly*, dub. l. in *POxy.*109.17 (iii/iv A.D.).

**οὐλοβάται**· οἱ κολοβοί, Hsch.

**οὐλοβόρος**, ον, (οὖλος C) *with deadly bite*, ἔχιες Nic.*Th.*826 (v.l. λοβόρος).

**οὐλο-δέτης**, ου, ὁ, (οὖλος D) *sheaf of barley*, Eust.1162.33:—also ⊕ **-δετον**, τό, *straw-band for binding sheaves*, ib.30.

**οὐλό-θριξ**, τρῐχος, ὁ, ἡ, (οὖλος B) *with crisp, curly hair*, like negroes, opp. εὐθύθριξ, Hdt.2.104, Arist.*GA*782ᵇ18, *Pr.*963ᵇ10, Str.2.2.3: **-τρῐχος**, ον (censured by Phot.) occurs in Arist.*HA*629ᵇ34 (in Comp.), and is v.l. in *Gp.*16.1.9 (Posit.).

**οὐλόθῡμος**, ον, (οὖλος C) = ὀλοόφρων, Hsch.

**οὐλο-θῠσία**, ἡ, (οὖλος A) *whole* or *perfect sacrifice*, Hsch., dub. in *BMus.Inscr.*1017.21 (Erythrae, iv B.C., cf. *SIG*229). **-θῠτέω**, *offer a whole* or *perfect sacrifice*; or (from οὐλαί), *strew the sacred barley before the sacrifice*, Suid.

⊕ **οὐλο-κάρηνος** [ᾰ], ον, (οὖλος B) *with crisp, curling hair*, Od.19.246. II. (οὖλος A) οὐλόποδ', οὐλοκάρηνα, for ὅλους πόδας, ὅλα κάρηνα (cf. οὐλοκίκιννα), *h.Merc.*137. **-κερως**, ων, gen. ω, (οὖλος B) *with crumpled horns*, Str.2.2.3. **-κέφᾰλος**, ον, = οὐλοκάρηνος I, Pherecr.223, Ptol.*Tetr.*142. ⊕ **-κίκιννα** [κῐκ], poet. for οὖλοι κίκιννοι (cf. οὐλοκάρηνος II), Telesill.ap.Poll.2.23 (Bgk.(8) reads οὐλοκίκιννος). **-κόμης**, ου, ὁ, = sq., Plu.*Arat.*20, Aristid.*Or.*50(26).40. ⊕ **-κομος**, ον, = οὐλόθριξ, Alex.324, Heph.Astr.2.2. **-κρᾶνος**, ον, = οὐλοκάρηνος, Arr.*Ind.*6.9.

**οὐλο-μελής**, ές, (οὖλος A) *sound of limb*, prob. f.l. in Parm.8.4. **-μελίη**, ἡ, Ion. for ὁλομέλεια, *wholeness of limbs*: hence, *the general nature* of a thing, περὶ ἀδένων οὐλομελίης Hp.*Art.*11, *Gland.* 1 and 7, also cited by Gal.*UP*1.8: dat. οὐλομελίῃ, as Adv., = καθόλου, *upon the whole*, Hsch.; so κατὰ οὐλομελίην, opp. κατὰ μέρος, Hp.*Alim.*23.—In Arist.*Metaph.*1093ᵇ4, codd. have τῇ οὐλομελείᾳ τοῦ οὐρανοῦ (leg. ὁλομελείᾳ, as in *Theol.Ar.*36), *to the whole* celestial *system*.

**οὐλόμενον**, τό, = κώνειον I. 1, Ps.-Dsc.4.78.

⊕ **οὐλόμενος**, η, ον, poet. (metri gr.) for ὀλόμενος, aor. part. of ὄλλυμαι, used as a term of abuse, *accursed*, i.e. one of or to whom the word ὄλοιτο (or ὄλοιο) may be used (opp. ὀνήμενος), Il.14.84; ἄλοχος Od.4.92; μῆνις Il.1.2; Ἄτη 19.92; φάρμακον Od.10.394; γαστήρ 15.344; Γῆρας Hes.*Th.*225, etc.; νοῦσος Pi.*P.*4.293; ἔριδες, ὕβρις, Thgn.390, 1174; Νεῖκος Emp.17.19: used by Trag. in lyr., στένω σε τᾶς οὐ. τύχας A.*Pr.*399; πρὸς ἀδελφῶν οὐλόμεν' αἰκίσματα νεκρῶν E.*Ph.*1529; also in trim. in unlengthd. form, ὀλόμενε παίδων, ποῖον εἴρηκας λόγον; *Trag.Adesp.*2 (= S.*Fr.*185). II. *ruined, lost*: hence, *unhappy, wretched*, ἵετε δάκρυ καναχὲς ὀλόμενον ὀλομένῳ δεσπότᾳ A.*Ch.*152; in lit. sense, ἃ πλείστους ἔκανεν Ἑλλάνων δορὶ παρὰ ποταμὸν ὀλομένους E.*Or.*1307; πύργων ὀλομένων (v.l. οὐλ.) Id.*IT*1109; τίς ἄρα μ'.. πατρίδος οὐλομένας ἀπολωτιεῖ; Id.*IA*792 (in the two last passages Erfurdt conjectured ὀλλυμένων, ὀλλυμένας); Aeol. **ὠλόμενος** dub. sens. in Alc.*Oxy.*1788 *Fr.*4.29.

**οὐλομέτ[ριον]**, τό, *a measure of barley-meal*, *SIG*1027.5 (Cos).

**οὖλον**, τό, mostly in pl., οὖλα, τά, *the gums*, A.*Ch.*898, Hp.*Epid.*7.113, *Aph.*3.25, *Morb.*2.11, Pl.*Phdr.*251c, Nic.*Th.*306, etc.: sg., Arist.*HA*493ᵃ1, D.L.7.176.

**οὐλόομαι**, (οὐλή) Pass., *to be scarred over*, Arist.*Pr.*893ᵃ27:—Act., *cause cicatrization*, Thessal. in *Cat.Cod.Astr.*8(3).145.1, cf. Hdn.Gr.1.447.

**οὐλοός**, όν, Ep. for ὀλοός, A.R.2.85, Nic.*Th.*352, Man.6.464.

**οὐλο-ποίησις**, εως, ἡ, (οὖλος B) *making curly*, Gal.12.445. **-ποιός**, όν, in neut. pl. -ποιά, τά, *preparations to make the hair curl*, Paul.Aeg.3.2. **-πους**, ποδος, v. οὐλοκάρηνος II.

**οὐλοπρόσωπος**, ον, (οὐλή) *with scars on the face*, Anatolius in *Cat.Cod.Astr.*8(3).188.6.

**οὖλος** (A), η, ον, old Ep. and Ion. form of ὅλος, *whole, entire*, v. ὅλος.

⊕ **οὖλος** (B), η, ον, *woolly, of thick, fleecy wool*, τάπητες Il.16.224; χλαῖναι Od.4.50, 299, etc.; χλανίδες Hermipp.47.1 (anap.): οὔλη λάχνη Il.10.134; χιτὼν οὔλων ἐρίων Ar.*Ra.*1067; εἱμάτιον *IG*5(1).1390.21 (Andania, i B.C.); οὖλαι κόμαι *crisp, close-curling* hair, Od.6.231, 23.158, cf. Luc.*Im.*5; βόστρυχος οὖλος *AP*6.201 (Marc. Arg.); οὐλότατον τρίχωμα, of the *crisp, woolly* hair of the negro, Hdt.7.70; also of persons, οὔλας ἐθείρας Ἕσπερος Call.*Del.*302; σελίνων οὐλοτέρη, of a girl, *AP*5.120 (Phld.); τοῖς τριχώμασιν οὖλοι D.S.3.8; of sheep, αἱ οὖλαι Arist.*HA*596ᵇ6; ὥσπερ σέλινον οὖλα τὰ σκέλη φορεῖν *Com.Adesp.*208. 2. of plants, *twisted, twined, curly, crinkled*, ἴων κορωνίδες οὖλαι Stesich.29; οὔλης.. σκολιὸν πλέγμα.. ἕλικος, of the vine, Simon.183.

2; σέλινον Hp.*Mul.*2.181; φύλλον Thphr.*HP*9.4.3; θρίδακες *AP*9.412 (Phld.): neut. pl. as Adv., of smoke, *curling*, οὖλα κυλινδόμενον Call. *Fr.*1.41 P. 3. of wood, *compact, tough, close-grained*, Thphr.*HP*3.11.1, 4.2.7, 5.3.7, Ph.*Bel.*66.51; ξύλα οὖλας ἔχοντα συστροφάς Thphr. *HP*5.5.1; δένδρον -ότερον τῇ ὄψει ib.3.9.6; οὐ. ὄστρακον *tough*, Babr. 115.10: hence metaph., like πυκνός, of speech, *compact, concise*, οὖλα καὶ πυκνὰ καὶ συνεστραμμένα φθεγγομένους Plu.2.510e; of dancing, *rapid, in quick tempo*, πόδεσσι οὖλα κατεκροτάλιζον Call.*Dian.* 247, cf. *Jov.*52; of rowing, Id.*Epigr.*6.5; and so perh. οὖλον κεκλήγοντες uttering *quick* (*frequent*) cries, Il.17.756,759, cf. Sch.T and Eust.ad loc.; v. οὖλος (c). (Perh. cogn. with εἴλλω 'pack tightly together'.)

⊛ **οὖλος** (C), η, ον, = ὀλοός, *destructive, baneful, cruel*, epith. of Ares, Il.5.461,717; of Achilles, 21.536; χεῖμα Bion 15.14; στόμιον Nic. *Th.*233; οὖλος Ὄνειρος Il.2.6,8; *cruel*, Ἔρως A.R.3.297,1078. 2. οὖλον κεκλήγοντες, of the *death-cry* of birds flying from the hawk, Il. 17.756,759 (but v. οὖλος (B) 3 fin.); so later οὖλον γεράνων νέφος *AP* 7.543; οὖλον ἀείδειν ib.27 (Antip. Sid.); κυνζηθμὸν κυνὸς οὖλον Nic. *Th.*671.

**οὖλος** (D), ὁ, *corn-sheaf*, = ἴουλος II (q.v.), Hsch.: hence, a cry or song in honour of Demeter, who was herself from this word named **Οὐλώ**, Semus 19, Did.ap.Sch.A.R.1.972.

**οὐ]λόσφαιρα**, ἁ, *a kind of pastille*, *Supp.Epigr.*1.414.4 (Crete, v/iv B.C.).

**οὐλότης**, ητος, ἡ, (οὖλος B) *curliness, woolliness*, τῶν τριχῶν, opp. εὐθύτης, Arist.*GA*782ᵃ3,ᵇ28, *Pr.*909ᵃ30; τῶν σελίνων Philostr.*Im.*2.6; *close-grained texture*, ξύλων Thphr.*CP*6.11.8, cf. *HP*5.2.3, etc.

**οὐλοτριχ-έω**, *to have curly hair*, Str.15.1.13 and 24. **-ος**, ον, v. οὐλόθριξ.

**οὐλο-φόνον**, τό, a plant, = χαμαιλέων μέλας, Dsc.3.9, cf. Nic.*Al.* 280 (v.l.). **-φρων**, ον, gen. ονος, = ὀλοόφρων, restd. by Valck. in A. *Supp.*750 (lyr.) for δουλόφρονες.

⊛ **οὐλοφυής**, ές, (οὖλος A) *rough, raw, undifferentiated*, of lumps of earth (τύποι χθονός), Emp.62.4.

**οὐλόφυλλος**, ον, (οὖλος B) *with curling leaves*, opp. λειόφυλλος, of cabbage, Thphr.*HP*7.4.4.

**οὐλο-χοεῖον** or **-χόϊον**, τό, (οὐλαί) *the vessel in which the sacred barley was kept*, Hsch. **-χύται** [ῠ], αἱ, (οὐλαί, χέω) *barley-groats* or *coarsely-ground barley sprinkled* over the victim and the altar before a sacrifice (τὰς οὐλοχύτας φέρε δεῦρο.—τοῦτο δ' ἐστὶ τί;—κριθαί Strato Com.1.34), οὐλοχύτας ἀνελέσθαι, προβαλέσθαι, Il.1.449,458; ἐν δ' ἔθετ' οὐλοχύτας κανέῳ Od.4.761; χέρνιβά τ' οὐλοχύτας τε κατάρχετο, of the ceremony of sprinkling the barley before sacrifice, 3.445:—also **-χύτα**, τά, Hsch. **-χυτέομαι**, *sprinkle the sacred barley-groats* at a sacrifice, Thphr.ap.Porph.*Abst.*2.6.

**οὐλόω**, v. οὐλόομαι. **Οὐλύμποιο, Οὐλυμπόνδε**, v. Ὄλυμπος.

⊛ **οὔλω**, (οὖλος A) *to be whole* or *sound* (τὸ γὰρ οὔλειν ὑγιαίνειν Str.14.1.6), used by Hom. in imper. οὖλε, as a salutation, *health to thee*, οὖλέ τε καὶ μάλα χαῖρε *health* and joy *be with thee*, Od.24.402, cf. *h.Ap.*466:—a form **οὐλέω** is cited by Hsch. (οὐλείοιεν· ἐν ὑγείᾳ φυλάσσοιεν) and Greg.Cor.p.491 S.

**Οὐλώ**, οῦς, ἡ, = Ἰουλώ, v. οὖλος (D).

**οὔλωμα**, ατος, τό, = οὔλωσις, Suid. s.v. ἐνσκειρωθείς (Ms. cited by Gaisf.).

**οὔλως**, Adv., Dor. for ὅλως, Pempel.ap.Stob.4.25.52.

**οὔλωσις**, εως, ἡ, *cicatrization*, Gal.18(2).598, Eust.1199.46.

**οὐ μά, οὐ μὰ γάρ**, v. μά. **οὐ μάν**, *assuredly not*, prop. Dor., Aeol., etc. for Ion.-Att. οὐ μήν, also used in Hom., who has οὐ μὰν οὐδέ, v. οὐδέ C. II, οὐ μήν.

**οὐ μέν**, without δέ after it, *no truly, nay verily*, Od.3.14, al.

**οὐ μὲν οὖν** or **οὐμενοῦν**, *on the contrary..not..*, introducing a neg. statement in contradiction or correction of a preceding statement or suggestion, Ar.*Pl.*870, *Ra.*556, 1188 οὐδενὸς μὲν οὖν ἄξιον Pl.*Euthd.* 305a; ἐγώ σοι οὐκ ἂν δυναίμην ἀντιλέγειν; Answ. οὐ μὲν οὖν τῇ ἀληθείᾳ δύνασαι ἀντιλέγειν nay it is *not me, but rather* truth, that you cannot gainsay, Id.*Smp.*201c, cf. D.18.140:—so **οὐμενοῦν..γε**, Paus.1.20.1; v. μέν B. II. 2.

**οὐ μέντοι**, *surely not, verily not*, Il.8.294, 21.370. 2. οὐ μέντοι..γε *not however*, Hdt.1.104, Th.1.3,111, Ar.*V.*231, etc.; οὐ μέντοι ἀλλ' ἴσως γε *not but that*, Pl.*Phd.*62b; οὐ μέντοι ἀλλὰ καί..γε Id.*Smp.* 173b. II. in interrog., οὐ μέντοι..; *surely.., is it not so?* where an affirm. answer is expected, Id.*Phdr.*229b, *Prt.*309a, *R.*339b, etc.

**οὐμές**, οὐμίων, Boeot. for ὑμεῖς, ὑμῶν, Corinn.6, 22.

**οὐ μή**, in independent sentences, is used either in Denial or in Prohibition: I. in Denial, 1. with subj., a. chiefly of aor., οὔ τι μὴ ληφθῶ δόλῳ A.*Th.*38, cf. 199, 282, *Ch.*895; οὔ τοί σ' Ἀχαιῶν ..μή τις ὑβρίσῃ S.*Aj.*560, cf. *El.*42,1029, *Ph.*103,381, *OT*329,771, *OC* 450, 1023 (v. infr.); οὔ τι μὴ φύγητε λαιψηρῷ ποδί E.*Hec.*1039, cf. *HF* 718; οὐ γὰρ μὴ ἀπώσηται Hdt.1.199, cf. 7.53; οὐ μήποτε..ἐσβάλωσιν Th.4.95, cf. 5.69; οὐ μή ποθ' ἁλῶ Ar.*Ach.*662, cf. *V.*394; οὐ μή ποτε δέξηται Pl.*Phd.*105d, cf. *Phdr.*260e, *R.*609b; οὐ μὴ κρατηθῶ X.*Cyr.* 5.1.17, cf. 3.2.8 (v.l. δέξονται), *An.*4.8.13; so οὐδεὶς μὴ ποθ' εὕρῃ κατ' ἐμ' οὐδὲν ἐλλειφθέν D.18.246. b. rarely of pres., mostly with Verbs expressing possibility or ability, οὐ μὴ δύνηται (v.l. δυνήσεται) X.*Cyr.* 8.1.5, cf. *An.*2.2.12, *Hier.*11.15; οὐ μὴ οἷός τ' ᾖς Pl.*R.*341b; οὐ γὰρ μὴ δυνατὸς ὦ Id.*Phlb.*48d: in S.*OC*1023, for οὐ μή ποτε..φυγόντες.. ἐπεύχωνται θεοῖς, two Mss. give ἐπεύξωνται, and this has been adopted by most edd.; and in Is.8.24, for οὐ μὴ εἰσίῃς Bekk. restd. οὐ μὴ εἴσει εἰς..:—Note: οὐ μή with subj. prob. arose from the ellipsis of a Verb or phrase expressing fear or apprehension; such words are sts. expressed, οὐ γὰρ ἦν δεινὸν..μὴ ἁλῷ κοτε Hdt.1.84, cf. 7.235, Ar.*Ec.* 650, X.*Mem.*2.1.25, Pl.*Ap.*28b, *Phd.*84b, *Grg.*520d, *R.*465b.—Sts. there is no idea of fear, as in S.*Ph.*103, E.*IT*18; the constr. is freely used after ὅτι, Th.5.69, X.*HG*4.2.3, Pl.*R.*499b; after ὡς, *since*, Ar. *Av.*461; after ὥστε, Pl.*Phdr.*227d. 2. with fut. ind., οὔ σοι μὴ μεθέψομαί ποτε S.*El.*1052, cf. *OC*176 (lyr.); οὐ μή σ' ἐγὼ περιόψομαι Ar. *Ra.*508; οὐ μὴ δέξονται (v.l. δέξωνται) X.*Cyr.*3.2.8: the reading in Id. *HG*1.6.32 is doubtful: in orat. obliq. the opt. is used, ἐθέσπισεν ὡς οὐ μή ποτε πέρσοιεν S.*Ph.*611: or inf., εἶπεν..οὐ μή ποτε..εὖ πράξειν πόλιν E.*Ph.*1590. II. in Prohibition, οὐ μή is used interrogatively with fut. ind. (chiefly of the 2 pers.) so as to express a strong prohibition, οὐ μὴ 'ξεγερεῖς τὸν ὕπνῳ κάτοχον; = μὴ ἐξέγειρε, S.*Tr.*978 (anap.); οὐ μὴ μῦθον ἐς πολλοὺς ἐρεῖς; E.*Supp.*1066, cf. *Andr.*757, *El.*982, *Hipp.* 213 (anap.); οὐ μὴ πρόσει τούτοισιν ἐσκοροδισμένοις; Ar.*Ach.*166, cf. *Nu.*367, *V.*397: when the Mss. give an aor. subj. in such phrases (as οὐ μὴ σκώψῃς μηδὲ ποιήσῃς Id.*Nu.*296) it has generally been changed by edd. into fut. ind.—The prohibition is continued by καί or by μηδέ, οὐ μὴ 'ξεγερεῖς..κἀκκινήσεις; S.*Tr.*978 (anap.); οὐ μὴ προσοίσεις χεῖρα μηδ' ἅψῃ πέπλων; E.*Hipp.*606, cf. Ar.*Nu.*296, *Ra.*298.—The prohibition is changed into a direct command by ἀλλά or δέ, οὐ μὴ λαλήσεις ἀλλ' ἀκολουθήσεις ἐμοί; Id.*Nu.*505, cf. *Ra.*202, 462, 524, E.*Ba.*792; οὐ μὴ προσοίσεις χεῖρα βακχεύσεις δ' ἰών; ib.343, cf. *Med.*1151, *El.*383. 2. later οὐ μὴ ἐμπέσω *let me not* fall, Lxx 2*Ki.*24.14. 3. in questions, οὐ μή, = Lat. *nonne*, ὁ θεὸς οὐ μὴ ποιήσῃ τὴν ἐκδίκησιν τῶν ἐκλεκτῶν αὐτοῦ; *Ev.Luc.*18.7. III. in A.*Th.*250, οὐ σῖγα μηδὲν τῶνδ' ἐρεῖς κατὰ πτόλιν; seems to mean *keep silent and say nothing..*, σῖγα being short for σιγήσει and καί being omitted: similarly, οὐ σῖγ' ἀνέξει, μηδὲ δειλίαν ἀρῇ; *submit silently and do not play the coward*, S.*Aj.*75, cf. *Tr.* 1183, *OT*637, E.*Hipp.*498, *Hel.*437, Pl.*Smp.*175a.

**οὐ μήν**, *not however*, A.*Ag.*1068, etc.; οὐ μὴν οὐδέ *nor on the other hand*, Th.1.3,82, 2.97, X.*Mem.*1.2.5, etc. 2. οὐ μήν..γε after a neg., *no nor even yet*, Ἀφροδίτης γὰρ οὔ μοι φαίνεται, οὐ μὴν Χαρίτων γε Ar.*Pax*41: without a preceding neg., οὐ μὴν ἐρῶ γ' ὡς.. *I cannot, it is true*, say.., Id.*Nu.*53; v. οὐ μάν.

**οὐ μὴν ἀλλά**, *nevertheless, notwithstanding, yet, still*, ἀληθῆ μέν ἐστι τὰ πολλά, οὐ μὴν ἀλλ' ἴσως οὐχ ἡδέ' ἀκούειν D.4.38, cf. 1.4, 2.22; so **οὐ μὴν ἀλλά..γε**, Pl.*Grg.*449b, *Plt.*263b. II. **οὐ μὴν ἀλλὰ καί..**, *not only so, but what is more*, D.37.23, S.E.*M.*5.99.

⊛ **οὖν**, Ion. and Dor. **ὦν** (the latter in Pi.*P.*3.82, al., but οὖν in Hom. (v. infr.), B.18.29,37, Cerc.4.18, al.), Adv. *certainly, in fact*, confirming something, freq. in contrast with something which is not confirmed, in Hom. only in combination with γε (v. γοῦν), γάρ, οὔτε or μήτε, ὡς, ἐπεί, μέν, etc.: 1. *really*, φημὶ γὰρ οὖν κατανεῦσαι..Κρονίωνα for I declare that Zeus did *really* promise.., Il.2.350, cf. Pl.*Prt.*309b; τόφρα γὰρ οὖν ἑπόμεσθα.., ὄφρ' for we followed them up to the *very* point, where.., Il.11.754, cf. 15.232, Od.2.123; εἰ δ' οὖν τις ἀκτὶς ἡλίου νιν ἱστορεῖ..ζῶντα A.*Ag.*676, cf. 1042; ἐλέχθησαν λόγοι ἄπιστοι μὲν ἐνίοισι Ἑλλήνων, ἐλέχθησαν δ' ὦν but they *really* were spoken, Hdt.3.80, cf. 4.5, 6.82; Θηβαῖοι μὲν ταῦτα λέγουσι.., Πλαταιῆς δ' οὐχ ὁμολογοῦσι.., ἐκ δ' οὖν τῆς γῆς ἀνεχώρησαν *at all events* they *did* return, Th.2.5, cf. 1.63, Pl.*Prt.*315e; σωτηρίαν λεπτὴν μὲν.., μόνην δ' οὖν Id.*Lg.*699b; so δ' οὖν after a parenthesis; εἰ δή τις ὑμῶν οὕτως ἔχει,—οὐκ ἀξιῶ μὲν γὰρ ἔγωγε,—εἰ δ' οὖν but if he is so, Id.*Ap.*34d, cf. Hdt.6.76, Th.1.3; so ἀλλ' οὖν..γε but *at all events*, S.*Ant.*84, *Ph.*1305; ἔμπης οὖν ἐπιμεῖναι ἐς αὔριον to stay nevertheless *at least* till to-morrow, Od.11.351; οὖν concessive, *I grant you*, τάχ' οὖν τις ἄκων ἔσχε S.*Ph.*305: in apodosi after εἰ or ἐάν, εἰ καὶ σμικρά, ἀλλ' ὦν ἴση γε ἡ χάρις.. Hdt.3.140, cf. 9.48, E.*Ph.*498, Pl.*Phd.*91b, etc.: after ἐπεί and ὡς, ἀλλ' ἐπεὶ οὖν τὸ πρῶτον ἀνέκραγον but now that I have (emphat.) once spoken up, Od.14.467, cf. 17.226, Il.18.333; Τληπόλεμος δ', ἐπεὶ οὖν τράφ' ἐνὶ μεγάρῳ εὐπήκτῳ, αὐτίκα..κατέκτα *when once*, i.e. as soon as, he had grown up, 2.661, cf. 15.363, 16.394, al.; νεβροί, αἵ τ' ἐπεὶ οὖν ἔκαμον.. ἑστᾶσ' which, *as soon as* they are tired, stand still, 4.244; to indicate that something foreshadowed has *actually* occurred, ἀγορήνδε καλέσσατο λαὸν Ἀχιλλεύς.., οἱ δ' ἐπεὶ οὖν ἤγερθεν 1.57, cf. 3.340, al: sts. οὖν after ἐπεί or ὡς has either no force or approaches signf. II or III, οἱ δ' ἐπεὶ οὖν παύσαντο πόνου Od.16.478, cf. 19.213,251, al.; τὸν δ' ὡς οὖν ἐνόησε Il.3.21, al.; οὔτ' οὖν.., οὔτε.. or οὔτε.., οὔτ' οὖν.. both = *neither..nor*, but preferred according as the first or second clause is to be marked by emphasis, cf. 17.20, Od.2.200, Hdt.9.26, with Od. 11.198 sq., S.*OT*90, 271, etc.; so εἰ.., εἴτ' οὖν.. if.., or if.., E.*Alc.* 140; εἴτ' οὖν, εἴτε μὴ γενήσεται whether it shall be so, or no, Id. *Heracl.*149, cf. A.*Ag.*491, S.*El.*560; ξεῖνος αἴτ' ὦν ἀστός, i.e. αἴτε ξ. αἴτ' ὦν ἀ., Pi.*P.*4.78; and doubled, εἴτ' οὖν ἀληθὲς εἴτ' οὖν ψεῦδος Pl. *Ap.*34e, cf. A.*Ch.*683: so also in parenth. Relat. clauses, ἣ σῖγ', ἀτίμως, ὥσπερ οὖν ἀπώλετο πατήρ *even* as, *just* as, ib.96, cf. 888, E.*Hipp.* 1307 (v.l.); εἰ δ' ἐστίν, ὥσπερ οὖν ἐστι, θεός if he is, as he *in fact* is, a god, Pl.*Phdr.*242e; οὗτος μὲν οἴεταί τι εἰδέναι οὐκ εἰδώς, ἐγὼ δέ, ὥσπερ οὖν οὐκ οἶδα, οὐδὲ οἴομαι Id.*Ap.*21d: for γὰρ οὖν, v. γάρ A. II. 5; for μὲν οὖν, v. μέν B. II. 2. 2. added to indef. Prons. and Advbs., like Lat. *cunque*, ὅστις *whoever*, ὁστισοῦν *whosoever*; ὅπως *how*, ὁπωσοῦν *howsoever*; ἄλλος ὁστισοῦν another, *be he who he may*; so ὁποιοσοῦν, ὁποιοστισοῦν, ὁποσοσοῦν, ὁπωσδηποτοῦν, ὁπητιοῦν, ὁποθενοῦν, etc., v. sub vocc. II. to continue a narrative, *so, then*, καὶ τὰ μὲν οὖν..θῆκαν Od.13.122; ὅτ' οὖν since, *then*,.., S.*Ant.*170, *El.*38, 1318; ζεῖ οὖν ἐν τούτῳ.. Pl.*Phdr.*251c, cf. *Prt.*322b; εὐθὺς οὖν ὁ Κῦρος εἶπεν X.*Cyr.*4.1.22: in Hdt. and Att., μὲν οὖν (q.v.) is very common in this sense; so δ' οὖν A.*Ag.*34, S.*Aj.*114; οὖν is also used alone merely to resume after a parenth. or long protasis, *well, as I was saying,* ὦ Λακεδαιμόνιοι, χρήσαντος τοῦ θεοῦ.., ὑμέας γὰρ πυνθάνομαι προεστάναι..,—ὑμέας ὦν..προσκαλέομαι.. Hdt.1.69, cf. 4.75, Th.2.16, Pl.*Ap.*29d, *Smp.*201d, etc.: Hdt. so uses ὦν after a short protasis, 1.144, etc. 2. ὦν is freq. inserted by Hdt. (sts. without any discernible meaning) between the Prep. and its Verb (but only, it seems, in narrative with the aor., which is always the aor. of habitual action exc. in 2.172), ἐπεὰν δὲ ταῦτα ποιήσωσι, ἀπ' ὦν ἔδωκαν ib.87; καὶ ἔπειτα ἀπ' ὦν ἔδωκαν ib.88: after a part., οἱ δὲ φέροντες ἐς τὴν ἀγορήν, ἀπ' ὦν ἔδοντο ib.39; κατευξάμενοι, κοιλίην μὲν κείνην πᾶσαν ἐξ ὦν εἷλον ib.40; ἥν τις ψαύσῃ.., αὐτοῖσι τοῖσι ἱματίοισι ἀπ' ὦν ἔβαψε ἑωυτόν ib.47; τοῦτον κατ' ὦν κόψας ib.172; so in Hp., δι' οὖν ἐφθάρησαν *Morb.*1.14 (v.l.), al.; also ἐπ' ὦν ἐπίομες οἶνον Epich.124.3: this tmesis is rare in Att., ὥστε γε καὐτόν σε κατ' οὖν ἔβαλεν Ar.*Ra.*1047; but occurs in later writers, Dorieus ap.Phylarch.3 J., *AP*12.226 (Strat.). III. in inferences, *then, therefore,* not in Hom., rare in A., and usu. in questions (v. infr.); in a statement, *Eu.*219; very common from Hdt. downwds.; so καὶ σὺ οὖν you too *therefore,* X.*Cyr.*4.1.20; καὶ γὰρ οὖν Id.*An.*1.9.8; cf. οὐ γὰρ οὖν, τοιγαροῦν: strengthd., δὴ οὖν Pl.*Smp.*191c, etc.; οὖν δὴ Id.*R.*340e: in questions, τίς οὖν ὁ λύσων σ' ἐστίν; A.*Pr.*771, cf. S.*Tr.*1191, Ar.*Pl.*906, 909, etc.; ἆρ' οὖν δή; Pl.*Tht.*146a; τί οὖν δή; S.*Aj.*873 (lyr.), Pl.*Phd.*57a.

**οὑν,** Att. crasis for οἱ ἐν, E.*Med.*819; for ὁ ἐν, Ar.*Th.*1165.

**οὖνει·** δεῦρο, δράμε (Arc.), Hsch.

⊛ **οὕνεκα,** and (usu. before a vowel) **οὕνεκεν** (first in Pi., v. infr.): relat. Conj. for οὗ ἕνεκα, *on account of which, wherefore,* δὸς δ'..ἐμὲ πρήξαντα νέεσθαι, οὕ. δεῦρ' ἱκόμεσθα Od.3.61; ἡ δ' Ἄτη σθεναρή τε καὶ ἀρτίπος, οὕ. πάσας..ὑπεκπροθέει Il.9.505; οὕνεκεν τὸ πεπονημένον εὖ μὴ..κρυπτέτω Pi.*P.*9.93. 2. correlat. to τοὔνεκα, *because,* after τοῦδ' ἕνεκα Il.1.111; after τῷ Od.13.332: but usu. without any antec. expressed, Il.1.11, etc.; οὕνεκ' ἄρα 7.140, 11.79; οὕ. δὴ 3.403, cf. Pi.*N.*9.36, A.*Supp.*639 (lyr.), *Fr.*374, S.*Ph.*586, al.; οὕνεκα πιστὸς ἔφυς *IG*1².1017; οὕνεκεν πλεῖ τὴν θάλασσαν Herod.2.21. 3. like ὅτι, *that,* i.e. *the fact that,* after οἶδα Od.5.216; ἔγνω *h.Ap.*376; ἐνόησε Od.7.300; ἐρέει 16.379, cf. 330, 15.42; τόδε..νεμέσσα 23.214: in Trag., after ἴσθι S.*Ph.*232; ἐννοεῖν Id.*Ant.*63; μαθεῖν Id.*OT*708; αἰσθάνεσθαι Id.*El.*1478; λέγειν E.*IA*102. II. οὕνεκα (in this sense rarely οὕνεκεν, Herod.1.84), as Prep. c. gen., = simple ἕνεκα, εἵνεκα, *on account of, because of,* sts. following its case, Sol.37.5: freq. in Trag., as A.*Pr.*347, *Ag.*823, S.*Ph.*774, *El.*387, al. (S. never uses ἕνεκα); whereas reversely in Call., A.R.4.1523, and even in *h.Ven.*199, εἵνεκα, ἕνεκα (q.v.) are used for οὕνεκα, *because.*—It has been suggested that the Ion. form εἵνεκα shd. be restd. for οὕνεκα, wherever it occurs as a Prep.; εἵνεκα occasionally occurs in Mss., as A.*Supp.*188, Ar.*Pax* 210, *Lys.*74, *Ec.*659: but οὕνεκα as a Prep. freq. occurs in Inscrr., *IG*1².802, 1037, 2.1334.11, etc.; οὕνεκεν χρόνου *in respect of* years, Poet. in *PMich.Zen.*77.9 (iii B.C.).—Poet. word, rare and late in Att. Prose, *IG*2 l.c. (iii A.D.), f.l. in Th.6.56, D.49.36, 53, 59.39.

**οὔνεσθε,** v. ὄνομαι. **οὔνης·** κλέπτης, κλεπτῶν συνηφαρεία (sic), Hsch. **οὔνιος·** εὖνις, δρομεύς, κλέπτης, Id. **οὔνομα, οὐνομάζω,** etc., v. ὄνομα, ὀνομάζω, etc. **οὖνον·** ὑγιές. Κύπριοι δρόμον, Id.

**οὔ νυ,** nearly like οὐ δή, strengthening the negation by an implied conclusion from the foreg., *surely not,* only in Ep., Od.2.60, al.; also to strengthen a negative question, Il.4.242, etc.

**οὖξ,** crasis for ὁ ἐξ. **οὖον,** τό, v. ὄα (A).

**οὔπα,** Dor. for οὔ πῃ, Ar.*Lys.*1157.

**οὔ περ** or **οὔπερ,** strengthd. for οὐ, *not at all,* Il.14.416, al.

**οὗπερ,** Adv., v. ὅς, ἥ, ὅ A b. I.

**οὔ πῃ,** *nowhere,* Il.13.191, 17.643, 23.463, Od.5.410; οὐδέ πῃ, v. sub voc.

**οὑπί,** Att. crasis for ὁ ἐπί, Ar.*Nu.*218.

**οὔπιγγος,** ὁ, *a hymn to Artemis,* Ath.14.619b, Poll.1.38; at Troezen, acc. to Did.ap.Sch.A.R.1.972.

⊛ **Οὖπις,** ιος, ἡ, name of Artemis, Call.*Dian.*204. II. later, epith. of Nemesis, *IG*14.1389ii 2. III. name of a maiden at Delos, Euph.103; cf. Ὦπις.

**οὔ ποθι,** *nowhere,* Il.13.309, A.R.4.1443; οὐδέ ποθι *nor anywhere,* Il.24.420, Od.20.114.

**οὔ ποτε** or **οὔποτε,** Dor. **οὔποκα** Epich.170, Call.*Lav.Pall.*5, 59: Adv.:—*not ever, never,* Hom. and Att. (Ar.*Eq.*1289, Pl.*Phdr.*245c, Lib.*Ep.*1347.2, etc.): joined as well with fut. as with pres. and past tenses, Il.1.234, 10.164, al.: sts. with one or more words between οὐ and ποτέ, Il.1.163, 4.48, etc.

**οὔ που..;** *surely you do not mean that..?* E.*Hel.*135.

**οὑποψ,** Att. crasis for ὁ ἔποψ, Ar.*Av.*226.

**οὔπω** or **οὔ πω,** Ion. **οὔκω,** Adv. *not yet,* opp. οὐκέτι (no longer, no more), usu. with pres. or past (esp. pf., or aor. in pf. sense) tenses, Il.2.799, Od.13.335, Hes.*Op.*521, *Sc.*10, Pl.*Prt.*322b, Men.*Epit.*98, etc.; freq. with another word between, as οὐ γάρ πω Il.1.262, 2.192; so οὔ τί κω Hdt.6.110; οὔτι πω A.*Pers.*179, S.*Aj.*106, *El.*513 (lyr.), *OC*1370; οὐ πέφυκέ πω A.*Pr.*27, cf. *Eu.*590, etc. 2. sts. merely as a stronger form of the neg., *not, not at all,* when it may be used with the pres. or fut., σοὶ δ' οὔ πω..θεοὶ κοτέουσιν Il.14.143, cf. 12.270, Od.2.118, S.*OT*594; οὐ πω τλήσομ'..ὁρᾶσθαι Il.3.306, cf. Od.5.358: with aor., A.*Fr.*241, S.*OT*105.

**οὐ πώποτε** or **οὐπώποτε,** Dor. **οὐπώποκα** Epich.170.1, *never yet at any time,* Hom. and Att., mostly with past tenses; with pres. only Od.12.98; with fut. only in late authors, Men.*Prot.*p.94 D.; with γάρ inserted, οὐ γὰρ πώποτε Il.1.154, 3.442, etc.

**οὔπως** or **οὔ πως,** Ion. **οὔκως** Hdt.1.33:—Adv. *no-how, in no wise, not at all,* giving the greatest possible strength to the negation, Il.4.320, etc.; separated, οὐ μέν πως 2.203, 4.158, etc.

⊛ **οὐρά,** Ion. **οὐρή,** ἡ, (akin to ὄρρος) *tail,* of a lion, οὐρῇ δὲ πλευράς τε καὶ ἰσχία..μαστίεται Il.20.170; of a dog, οὐρῇ μέν ῥ' ὅ γ' ἔσηνε Od.17.302; of the wolves and lions round the house of Circe, οὐρῇσιν μακρῇσι περισσαίνοντες 10.215; of other animals, Hes.*Op.*512, Hdt.2.38, 47, Arist.*PA*689ᵇ30, al.; not used of birds (cf. ὀρροπύγιον), Id.*HA*504ᵃ31. 2. = αἰδοῖον, S.*Fr.*1078, f.l. in Hom.*Epigr.*12. II. of an army marching, *rearguard, rear,* X.*An.*3.4.38, etc.; ἡ οὐ. τοῦ κέρατος *rear-rank,* ib.6.5.5; κατ' οὐράν τινος ἕπεσθαι to follow in his *rear,* Id.*Cyr.*2.3.21, cf. 2.4.3; ὁ κατ' οὐ. *the rear-rank man,* ib.5.3.45; ἐπ' οὐράν *to the rear,* Id.*Ages.*2.2; εἰς οὐράν Ael.*NA*16.33; ἐπ' οὐρᾷ τῶν ἱππέων *in rear,* X.*HG*4.3.4; κατ' οὐρὰν προσπίπτειν to attack *in rear,* Plb.2.67.2. b. *left wing* of a phalanx (opp. κεφαλή), Ael.*Tact.*7.3, Arr.*Tact.*8.3. 2. ῥήματος οὐρή, i.e. its *echo, APl.*4.155 (Euod.). 3. ἑπτὰ κλῶνας ἐλαίας ἄρας, τὰς μὲν ἐξ ὅσον οὐρὰν καὶ κεφαλὴν ἐν καθ' ἕν, i.e. tie together the two *ends* of each twig separately, *PMag.Par.*1.1250.

**οὐρᾰγ-έω,** *to be* οὐραγός, *lead the rear,* App.*Hisp.*86, Suid.: generally, *to be in the rear,* Plb.4.11.6, LXX *Jo.*6.8, D.S.13.18, App.*Hisp.*48. II. τὸ -οῦν ζυγόν the rank *consisting of* οὐραγοί 2, Ascl.*Tact.*10.14. III. metaph., *lag behind,* ἐν ὥρᾳ ἐξεγείρου καὶ μὴ οὐράγει LXX *Si.*35.11. **-ία,** ἡ, *rearguard,* ib.*De.*25.18, Plb.1.19.14, 6.40.6, D.S.15.71. **-ός,** ὁ, (οὐρά, ἄγω) *leader of the rearguard,* X.*An.*4.3.26, *Cyr.*2.3.22, Plb.6.24.2 and 35.6. 2. *rear man in* λόχος, Ascl.*Tact.*2.2, Ael.*Tact.*5.1, Arr.*Tact.*5.4. 3. in cavalry, *rear man in* ῥόμβος, Ascl.*Tact.*7.2. 4. *one of the* ἔκτακτοι *attached to a* τάξις, ib.2.9, Ael.*Tact.*9.4, Arr.*Tact.*10.4; *to a* ἑκατονταρχία *of light-armed troops,* Ascl.*Tact.*6.3.

**οὐρᾰγωγός,** όν, (οὖρον (A), ἄγω) *promoting urine,* πότισμα Sor.1.71.

**οὐρ-άδιον,** τό, Dim. of οὐρά, *Gp.*20.27. **-αία,** ἡ, = οὐρά, Aret.*CD*2.13, Hdn.Gr.1.531, Eust.1758.56; in Babr.110.3, κέρκον οὐραίης is perh. f.l. for οὐραίην. **-αῖος,** α, ον, (οὐρά) *of the tail,* τρίχες ἄκραι οὐραῖαι Il.23.520; ἄκρα οὐ. πτερά A.R.2.571, cf. Euph.51.6, Orib.8.6.15: generally, τὰ οὐ. the *tail* or *hindmost* parts of fish, Hp.*Vict.*3.79; πόδες the *hind*-feet, Theoc.25.269, Arat.352. 2. οὐραῖον, τό, *tail,* Achae.27.3; κυνὸς Men.*Kol.Fr.*7; Ἄρκτος στρέφουσ' οὐραῖα E.*Ion* 1154; in fish, *tail-fin,* S.*Fr.*762, Arist.*HA*490ᵃ4, al., dub. l. in Arat. 363; τὰ οὐ. *hinder part, rear,* Ph.2.109, Luc.*VH*1.35, 2.1. 3. οὐραῖον, τό, = τὸ πέρας τοῦ ὀστέου, of the coccyx, Gal.15.863.

**οὐραῖος,** ὁ, Egypt. word, = βασιλίσκος II, Horap.1.1.

**οὐρακός,** f.l. for οὐρίαχος, Poll.1.90.

**οὐράνη** [ᾰ], ἡ, (οὖρον) *chamber-pot,* A.*Fr.*180.2, S.*Fr.*565. II. = οὐρητήρ, Poll.2.223.

⊛ **Οὐρανία** (Boeot. Ὠρανία *IG*7.1804, also at Epidaurus, ib.4²(1).283), Ep. and Ion. -ίη, ἡ, *Urania,* name of one of the Muses, Hes.*Th.*78; later, she was looked on esp. as the Muse of Astronomy, Cic.*Div.*1.11.17, al. II. epith. of Aphrodite, opp. Ἀ. Πάνδημος, Pl.*Smp.*181c, cf. Pi.*Fr.*122.4, Hdt.1.105; worshipped in Scythia, Id.4.59, *IPE*2.28 (Panticapaeum); in Amorgos, *IG*12(7).57 (iii B.C.). III. the Arabians called *the moon* Ἀλιλάτ, i.e. Οὐρανίη, Hdt.3.8. IV. *a game in which a ball was thrown into the air,* Hsch. V. a plant, = ἶρις, Ps.-Dsc.1.1. VI. Aeol. or Dor. **ὠρανίαφι,** said to be voc., *O* (Muse) *of heaven,* Alcm.59.

**οὐρᾰνιάζω,** *throw* a ball *high in air,* Hsch. s. v. οὐρανίαν.

⊛ **Οὐρᾰνιάς,** άδος, ἡ, [*celebration of*] *games* (cf. Ὀλυμπιάς) *in honour of Urania, IG*5(1).659, 662 (Sparta, dating by No. of Οὐρανιάς).

**Οὐρᾰνίδης,** ου, Dor. -ας, α, ὁ, *son of Uranos,* Hes.*Th.*486; Οὐ. Κρόνος Pi.*P.*3.4; Οὐρανίδαι *the Titans,* Hes.*Th.*502; *the gods,* Pi.*P.*4.194, Cerc.4.39, Call.*Jov.*3, etc.

**οὐρᾰν-ίζω** or **-ίζομαι,** *reach to heaven,* A.*Fr.*436.

⊛ **οὐρᾰν-ιος** [ᾰ], α, ον, also ος, ον E.*Ion* 715, *Ph.*1729 (both lyr.), Pl.*Phdr.*247a (v.l.), *IG*12(2).58*b*4 (Mytil.):—*heavenly, dwelling in heaven,* γέννα A.*Pr.*165 (lyr.); θεοὶ *h.Cer.*55, A.*Ag.*90 (anap.), E.*HF* 758 (lyr.), etc.; οὐράνιαι *the goddesses,* Pi.*P.*2.38 codd.; οὐράνιοι *the gods, IG*5(1).40 (Laconia); of special gods, Θέμις οὐ. Pi.*Fr.*30.1; Ζεύς Hdt.6.56, Call.*Jov.*55, etc.; αἱ οὐ. θεοί, Demeter and Kore, *IG*12(5).655.6 (Syros, nr. Delos); Ἥρα *CIG*7034; Ἔρως ib.3157; v. Οὐρανία. 2. generally, *in* or *of heaven,* ἀστήρ Pi.*P.*3.75; πόλος A.*Pr.*429 (lyr.); οὐ. θεᾶς βρέτας *fallen from heaven,* E.*IT*986; ἀστραπὰ S.*OC*1466 (lyr.); φῶς Id.*Ant.*944 (lyr.); νεφέλαι Ar.*Nu.*316; οὐ. ὕδατα, i.e. rain, Pi.*O.*11(10).2, *Gp.*2.6.10; so τὰ οὐ. alone, = *rains,* Thphr.*HP*4.14.8; οὐ. ἄχος, of a storm, S.*Ant.*418 (where it may be metaph., cf. infr. II); οὐ. σημεῖα X.*Cyr.*1.6.2; τὰ οὐ. *the phenomena of the heavens,* Id.*Mem.*1.1.11; οὐρανιά τε καὶ χθονοστιβῆ S.*OT*301. II. *reaching to heaven, high as heaven,* κίων, of Aetna, Pi.*P.*1.19; ἐλάτης οὐ. ἄκρος κλάδος E.*Ba.*1064; πήδημα Id.*El.*860 (lyr.); σκέλος οὐ. ἐκλακτίζειν, ῥίπτειν, kick up *sky-high,* Ar.*V.*1492, 1530; of sounds, ὁμφὰν οὐ. A.*Supp.*808 (lyr.), cf. Ar.*Ra.*781; ἵππον οὐράνια βρέμοντα E.*Tr.*519 (lyr.): metaph., *mountainous, colossal,* οὐ. ἄχη A.*Pers.*573 (lyr.); ἡμάρτηκεν οὐράνιόν γ' ὅσον Ar.*Ra.*1135. III. *sky-blue,* λίθος κυανωτάτη καὶ -ία ἰδεῖν Philostr.*VA*1.25. IV. οὐράνιον, τό, name of an eye-salve, Orib.ap.Aët.7.106. V. Adv. -ίως *from the point of view of heaven,* opp. γηΐνως, Procl.*Sacr.*p.148 B. **-ίς,** ίδος, ἡ, = fem. of οὐράνιος, τελετά *AP*15.5. **-ίσκος,** ὁ, Dim. of οὐρανός, *a little heaven* or *sky*: hence, I. *vaulted ceiling,* esp. *top of a tent,* *canopy*, Callix.2, Phylarch.41 J., Plu.*Alex.*37, *Phoc.*33. **II.** *roof of the mouth*, Sor.2.62, Gal.*UP*11.10, Ath.7.315d, v.l. in Arist.*Pr.* 963ᵃ2. **III.** a constellation of the southern hemisphere, *Corona Australis*, Sch.Arat.400.

⊛**Οὐρᾰνίωνες,** οἱ, *the heavenly ones, gods*, θεοὶ Οὐ. Il.1.570, etc.; simply Οὐ. 5.373, Hes.*Th.*461,919,929; also the Titans, as *children of Uranos*, Il.5.898: fem., θεαὶ Οὐρανιῶναι *IG*14.1389i5.

**οὐρᾰνο-βάμων** [ᾰ], ονος, ὁ, ἡ, *traversing heaven*, Suid. **-βᾰτέω,** *walk* or *move in heaven*, Vett.Val.241.14. **-γνώμων,** ον, gen. ονος, *skilled in the heavens*, Luc.*Icar.*5, Eust.1337.18. **-γρᾰφία,** Ion. **-ίη,** ἡ, *description of the heavens*, title of a work by Democritus, D.L. 9.48. **-δεικτος,** ον, *showing itself in heaven*, αἴγλη (of the moon) *h.Hom.*32.3. **-δρόμος,** ον, *running along the sky*, *Tab.Defix.Aud.* 41 *B* 5 (Megara, i/ii A.D.). ⊛**-ειδής,** ές, *like the sky*, εἶδος χρώματος Hsch. s.v. κυανόν. ⊛**-εις,** εσσα, εν, *of* or *to heaven*, ἀταρπός Man. 4.273. **II.** ὑπήνη οὐ., = οὐρανός II. 2, *roof of the mouth*, Nic.*Al.* 16. **-θεν** (parox.), Adv. *from heaven, down from heaven*, Od.5.294, Hes.*Th.*761, Lxx 4*Ma.*4.10, *JRS*17.49 (Phrygia, iv A.D.): joined with Preps., ἀπ' οὐ. Il.21.199, Od.11.18, Hes.*Sc.*384; ἐξ οὐ. Il.8.19, 21, 17.548; κατ' οὐ. Orph.*L.*601. **-θεσία,** ἡ, *star-map* (opp. σφαιρογραφία), Sch.Arat.248. **-θῐ,** Adv. *in heaven, in the heavens*, οὐρανόθι πρό Il.3.3, expld. by Sch.A as = ἐν τῷ ὑπὸ τὰ νέφη τόπῳ (like Ἰλιόθι πρό or ἠῶθι πρό); v.l. οὐρανόθεν. **-κάτοικος,** ον, *dwelling in heaven*, *Gloss.* **-κευθμωνοδίαιτος** [ῐ], ον, *dwelling in the recesses of heaven*, *PMag.Par.*1.1351. **-κλῖμαξ,** ἄκος, ἡ, *ladder reaching to heaven*, v.l. in Ph.1.620. **-μήκης,** ες, *high as heaven, shooting up to heaven, exceeding high* or *tall*, ἐλάτη Od.5.239; δένδρεα Hdt.2.138; στήλη Lys.*Fr.*14; λαμπάς A.*Ag.*92 (anap.); Ἄθω οὐρανομήκη (voc.) Xerxis Epist.ap.Plu.2.455d. **2.** metaph., οὐ. φωνή, κλέος, Ar.*Nu.* 357, 459 (lyr.); κακόν Arist.*Rh.*1408ᵇ13; οὐ. ποιεῖν τι to exalt it *to the skies*, Isoc.15.134; οὐ. σημεῖα τῆς εὐνοίας Epicur.*Fr.*183; διαφορά Phld. *Rh.*2.272 S.; ἐλπίδες Eun.*Hist.*p.251 D. **-μίμητος** [ῑ], ον, *imitating heaven*, πολιτεία Ph.*Fr.*15 H. **-νῖκος,** ον, *conquering heaven*, γαμετῶν οὐ. A.*Supp.*165 (lyr.). **-παις,** παιδος, ὁ, ἡ, *child of Uranos*, Orph.*H.*27.13, 79.1. **-πετής,** ές, *fallen from heaven*, δαίμονες Plu.2.830f, cf. 870c. **-πλαγκτος,** ον, *wandering through heaven*, Orph.*H.*21.1, Man.4.623. **-ποιία,** ἡ, *creation of heaven*, D.L.3.77. **-πολις,** εως, ἡ, *celestial city*, of Rome, Ath.1. 20c. **-πολίτης** [ῑ], ου, ὁ, *citizen of heaven*, attributed to Plato by Anon.*Proll.Plat.*10 (Plato vi p.206 H.), cf. Phlp.*in de An.*563.8.

**οὐρᾰν-όροφος,** ον, *with vaulted ceiling* or *canopy*, prob. cj. for -οφόρος in Ath.1.48f; v. sq. II.

⊛**οὐρᾰνός,** ὁ, Dor. and Boeot. **ὠρανός** Alcm.23.16, Theoc.2.147, 5. 144, Corinn.*Supp.*2.79, *Hymn.Is.*19; Aeol. **ὄρανος** (ὀράνω Sapph.37, 64, Alc.34, but ὠράνω Sapph.1.11 (s.v.l.), Alc.17 (s.v.l.), and v. Οὐρανία):—never used in pl. by classical writers, v. I.4: (v. fin.): **I.** *heaven*: in Hom. and Hes., **1.** *vault* or *firmament of heaven, sky*, γαῖα.. ἐγείνατο ἶσον ἑαυτῇ οὐρανὸν ἀστερόενθ', ἵνα μιν περὶ πάντα καλύπτοι Hes.*Th.*127; ἔχει δέ τε κίονας αὐτὸς [Ἄτλας] μακράς, αἳ γαῖάν τε καὶ οὐρανὸν ἀμφὶς ἔχουσι Od.1.54, cf. A.*Pr.*351; χάλκεος Il.17.425; πολύχαλκος 5.504, Od.3.2; σιδήρεος 15.329; wrapped in clouds, Il.15.192, Od.5.303; above the aether, Il.2.458, 17.425, 19.351, cf. Sch.Il.3.3; even Emp. continued to regard it as solid (στερέμνιον), *Placit.*2.11.2 (*Vorsokr.*i p.209); defined as αἰθέρος τὸ ἔσχατον by Zeno *Stoic.*1.33, cf. Ar.*Nu.*95 sqq.; ἠέλιος δὲ οὐρανοῦ ἐξαπόλωλε, of an eclipse, Od.20.357, cf. S.*Aj.*845; ἐν δὲ τὰ τείρεα πάντα, τά τ' οὐρανὸς ἐστεφάνωται Il.18.485; Ἕσπερος, ὃς κάλλιστος ἐν οὐρανῷ ἵσταται ἀστήρ 22.318; οὐρανὸς ἀστερόεις 6.108, al. **2.** *heaven*, as the seat of the gods, outside or above this skyey vault, the portion of Zeus (v. Ὄλυμπος), 15.192, cf. Od.1.67, etc.; οὐ. Οὔλυμπός τε Il.1.497, 8.394; Οὔλυμπός τε καὶ οὐ. 19.128; πύλαι οὐρανοῦ *Heaven*-gate, i.e. a thick cloud, which the Ὧραι lifted and put down like a trap-door, 5.749, 8.393; so, later, οἱ ἐξ οὐρανοῦ the gods of *heaven*, A.*Pr.*897 (lyr.); οἱ ἐν οὐρανῷ θεοί (viz. Sun, etc.) Pl.*R.*508a; εὔχετο, χεῖρ' ὀρέγων εἰς οὐ. ἀστερόεντα Il.15.371, Od.9.527; νὴ τὸν οὐ. Ar.*Pl.*267, 366. **3.** in common language, *sky*, οὐδέ τις ἄλλη φαίνετο γαιάων, ἀλλ' οὐ. ἠδὲ θάλασσα Od.14. 302; σέλας δ' εἰς οὐ. ἵκῃ Il.8.509; κλέος οὐρανὸν ἵκει, κλέος οὐ. εὐρὺν ἱκάνει, renown reaches *to heaven*, ib.192, Od.19.108; so ὀρυμαγδός, κνίση, σκόπελος οὐρανὸν ἷκεν or ἱκάνει, Il.17.425, 1.317, Od.12.73 (cf. οὐράνιος II, οὐρανομήκης): metaph., ὕβρις τε βίη τε σιδήρεον οὐ. ἵκει deeds of violence 'cry *to heaven*', 15.329, 17.565; γῇ τε κοὐρανῷ λέξαι ..τύχας E.*Med.*57, cf. Philem.79.1; πρὸς οὐρανὸν βιβάζειν τι to exalt *to heaven*, S.*OC*381; πρὸς τὸν οὐ. ἥλλοντο leaped up *on high*, X.*Cyr.*1.4. 11; πρὸς τὸν οὐ. βλέπειν Id.*Oec.*19.9. **4.** in Philos., *the heavens, universe*, Pl.*Plt.*269d, *Ti.*32b, Arist.*Cael.*278ᵇ21, *Metaph.*990ᵃ20, al.: pl. in *VT*, οἱ οὐρανοί the *heavens*, Lxx *Ps.*96(97).6, 148.4, al. **5.** *a region of heaven, climate*, Hdt.1.142. **6.** Pythag. name of 10, *Theol.Ar.* 59. **II.** *anything shaped like the vault of heaven*, as, **1.** *vaulted roof* or *ceiling*, Hsch. **2.** *roof of the mouth, palate*, Arist.*HA*492ᵃ 20, *PA*660ᵃ14, Ath.8.344b, *AP*5.104 (Marc. Arg.). **3.** *lid*, Matro *Conv.*12. **4.** *tent, pavilion*, Them.*Or.*13.166b. **III.** pr. n., *Uranos*, son of Erebos and Gaia, Hes.*Th.*127 sq.; but husband of Gaia, parent of Cronos and the Titans (cf. Οὐρανίδης), ib.106, *h.Hom.* 30.17, cf. A.*Pr.*207. (Acc. to Arist.*Mu.*400ᵃ7, from ὅρος and ἄνω, cf. Pl.*Cra.*396c. This must be wrong, but the true etym. is doubtful.)

**οὐρᾰνο-σκόπος,** ον, *observing the heavens*: as Subst., a kind of fish, elsewh. καλλιώνυμος, Diph.Siph.ap.Ath.8.356a, Plin.*HN*32.69, Gal. *UP*3.3. ⊛**-στεγὴς ἆθλος,** the task *of bearing up* or *sustaining the heaven*, A.*Fr.*312; cf. ὑποστενάζω II.

**οὐρᾰν-ουσία,** ἡ, *heavenly element*, *PMag.Lond.*121.831. **-οῦχος,** ον, (ἔχω) *holding heaven*, οὐ. ἀρχά the rule *of heaven*, A.*Ch.*960 (lyr.).

**οὐρᾰνο-φάντωρ,** ορος, ὁ, ἡ, *shining up to heaven*; or *disclosing heaven*, Suid. **-φι(ν)** (parox.), Adv. *in heaven*, A.D.*Adv.*163. 29. **-φοιτάω,** *walk in heaven*, Hsch. **-φοίτης,** ου, ὁ, *walking in heaven*, *Hymn.Mag.*2(2).14, Suid. s.v. οὐρανοβάμονος, etc. **-φοιτος,** ον, *soaring in the sky*, v.l. for ἀνώφοιτος, Ph.2.513. **-φόρος,** ον, = *caelifer*, *Gloss.*; v. οὐρανόροφος.

**οὐρᾰν-όω,** *remove to heaven, deify*, in Pass., Eust.17.34. **-ωσις,** εως, ἡ, *deification*, Id.82.3.

**οὖραξ,** gen. αγος, ἡ, Att. name of *the bird* τέτριξ (q.v.), Arist.*HA* 559ᵃ12.

**οὐρᾰχοειδής,** ές, *like the* οὐραχός I, Sor.1.73.

⊛**οὐρᾰχός,** ὁ, *urachus*, a foetal organ connected with the bladder, Gal.*UP*15.5, Id.4.657, 2.907, Sor.1.57, 80. **II.** *apex* of the heart, Hp.*Cord.*4, cf. Aret.*SA*1.8. **III.** pl., οὐ. τῶν ὀφρύων *outer ends* of the eyebrows, *PMed.* in *Arch.Pap.*4.271 (iii A.D.). **IV.** τοὺς καλουμένους οὐ. τῶν καρπίμων *stems* or *stalks*, Ael.*NA*6.43, cf. Dsc.4. 177. **V.** *point* of a drill or borer, Apollod.*Poliorc.*148.8.

⊛**οὐρβᾶνὸς** στρατηγός, = Lat. *praetor urbanus*, *IGRom.*3.172 (Ancyra).

**οὑργάτης,** Att. crasis for ὁ ἐργάτης, S.*Ant.*252.

**οὔρεα,** τά, poet. nom. and acc. pl. of ὄρος, τό.

**οὐρεῖον,** τό, (οὖρος B) *fortress*, *SIG*527.52 (Crete, iii B.C.); cf. ὠρεῖα, οὐρεύς, οὐρεύω.

**οὔρειος,** η, ον, Ep. for ὄρειος. **II.** (οὖρον A) οὔρειος, α, ον, *for urine*, βῖκος Antisth.ap.Phot.; οὔριομ βῖκον, Hsch.

**οὐρεοφοιτάς,** άδος, fem. Adj. *mountain-haunting*, *AP*11.194 (Lucill.).

**οὐρεσῐ-βώτης,** ου, ὁ, poet. for ὀρεσιβ-, *feeding on the mountains*, θῆρες S.*Ph.*1148 (lyr.). **-οικος,** ον, poet. for ὀρεσίοικος, *AP*6.181 (Arch.). **-φοίτης,** ου, ὁ, *mountain-haunting*, ib.9.524.16, 525.16 codd., etc.:—fem. **-φοῖτις,** ιδος, Orph.*H.*1.8. **-φοιτος,** ον, = ὀρεσίφ-, *AP*5.143 (Mel.), Opp.*H.*5.403, Nonn.*D.*9.76.

⊛**οὐρεύς,** ῆος, ὁ, Ion. for ὀρεύς (q.v.): in Il.1.50, 10.84 it has been taken as, = οὖρος, φύλαξ, *a guard, warder*, cf. Arist.*Po.*1461ᵃ10; but it may well mean *mules* here, as in other places, and the Sch. give both explanations.

**οὐρεύω,** *to be on garrison duty*, *SIG*527.127 (Crete, iii B.C.); cf. ὀρεύειν, ὠρεύειν.

**οὐρέω** (A), impf. ἐούρουν (προσ-) D.54.4; Ion. οὔρεον Hp.*Epid.*1. 26.δ', or οὔρεσκον (v. infr.): fut. οὐρήσω ib.7.85; Att. -ήσομαι Ar. *Pax* 1266: aor. ἐούρησα (ἐν-) Eup.45; Ion. οὔρησα Hp.*Epid.*1.26. ε'; pf. ἐούρηκα (ἐν-) Ar.*Lys.*402: Ion. plpf. οὐρήκειν Hp.*Epid.*6.8. 30:—Pass., Ion. aor. οὐρήθην Id.*Prorrh.*1.92, *Coac.*571: (οὖρον A):—*make water*, Hes.*Op.*729, 758, Hdt.1.133, etc. **2.** c. acc. rei, *pass with the water*, αἷμα Hp.*Aph.*4.80, 81; οὔρεσκεν ὄφεις Ant.Lib.41:— Pass., τὸ οὐρούμενον, = οὔρημα, Hp.*Coac.*584, etc.; οὐρέεται μᾶλλον *is* more *diuretic*, Id.*Vict.*2.46, cf. Ath.1.32f, Orib.*inc.*4.28; οἶνος -εόμενος *diuretic* wine, Aret.*CD*1.4. **3.** Act., *act as diuretic*, Id.*CA*1.10.

**οὐρέω** (B), (οὖρος B) *watch*, Sch.A.R.4.1614, *EM*54.31.

**οὐρη-βόρος,** ον, *devouring its tail*, δράκων Lyd.*Mens.*3.4; cf. οὐροβόρος. **-δόχος,** ον, = οὐροδόχος, Gal.4.686, Alex.Aphr.*Pr.*1.108.

**οὐρ-ήθρα,** Ion. **-θρη,** ἡ, (οὐρέω A) *urethra*, Hp.*Aph.*4.82, Arist.*HA* 493ᵇ4. **II.** *sewage tank*, *IG*4²(1).109iii97 (Epid., iii B.C., pl.). **-ημα,** ατος, τό, = οὖρον, *urine*, Hp.*Nat.Hom.*14. **-ηρός,** ά, όν, *urinary*, ἄγγος Philum.*Ven.*14.5, cf. Aët.6.3, Sch.Ar.*V.*803. **-ησις,** εως, ἡ, *a making water*, Hp.*Aër.*9, *Aph.*4.83, Arist.*Mete.*366ᵇ19, Epicur.*Fr.*177: Ion. pl. οὐρήσιες Hp.*Prorrh.*1.113, *Coac.*582, etc.; λύειν τὴν οὔρησιν Mnesith.ap.Ath.3.121d. **-ητήρ,** ῆρος, ὁ, in earlier writers, = οὐρήθρα, Hp.*Aër.*9, *Coac.*463, Arist.*HA*519ᵇ17, *Pr.* 895ᵇ9. **II.** later, in pl., *the ducts which convey the urine from the kidneys into the bladder*, Gal.19.363, *UP*5.5. **-ητιάω,** Desiderat. of οὐρέω, Ar.*V.*807, Arist.*Pr.*878ᵇ33. **-ητικός,** ή, όν, of persons, *inclined to make water much* or *often*, Hp.*Acut.*(*Sp.*)52 (Sup.); οἱ λίαν οὐ. Arist.*PA*670ᵇ9. **II.** *promoting urine*, v.l. in Hp.*Acut.* 53, cf. Arist.*Pr.*865ᵃ19, al.; οἶνος Ath.1.32c sq.: Comp., Diph.Siph. ap.Ath.9.371b, Dsc.3.137. **2.** *like urine*, ὀσμή Arist.*Pr.*908ᵇ 2. **III.** ἀγγεῖον, πόρος οὐ., = οὐρήθρα, Sor.1.57 (cj.), Gal.*UP*5. 16. **-ητός,** ή, όν, in neut. pl., *diuretics*, Orib.*Eup.*1.9. **-ητρίς,** ίδος, ἡ, *chamber-pot*, Sch.Ar.*V.*803.

**οὐρία,** ἡ, v. οὔριος II. 2.

**οὐρία,** ἡ, *a water-bird*, Alex.Mynd.ap.Ath.9.395e.

**οὐρίᾰχος** [ῐ], ὁ, (οὐρά) *bottom*, ἔγχεος οὐ. *butt-end* of the spear, opp. αἰχμή, Il.13.443, A.R.3.1253, *AP*6.111 (Antip.), Hld.9.15; of an arrow-head, the part fixed in the shaft, *tang*, Paul.Aeg.6.88 (v.l.); apptly. *stem* of a candlestick in Call.*Fr.anon.*50. **2.** *part of an oar*, Poll.1.90 (v.l. οὐρακός).

**οὐρῐβάτας** [βᾰ], ου, ὁ, poet. for ὀρειβάτης, *walking the mountains*, E.*Fr.*773.27 (lyr.), cj. in Id.*El.*170 (lyr.).

**οὐρίζω,** Ion. for ὁρίζω.

**οὐρίζω,** Att. fut. -ιῶ, (οὖρος A) *carry with a fair wind, waft on the way*, of words and prayers, A.*Ch.*317 (lyr.); κατ' ὀρθὸν οὐ. *speed on the way, guide prosperously*, S.*OT*695 (lyr.): an acc. αὐτούς may be supplied in A.*Pers.*602 (but Sch. took it intr. = οὐριοδρομεῖν).

**οὐρίθρεπτος,** η, ον, poet. for ὀρείθρ-, *mountain-bred*, E.*Hec.*205 (lyr.).

**οὐριοδρομέω,** *run with a fair wind*, of a ship, D.S.3.34, Ph.2.571, S.E.*M.*10.56, Antyll.ap.Orib.6.23.3, D.L.1.116, Hld.5.17.

**οὔριον**, τό, (οὖρος Β) *ward, watch*, Hsch. (ὄρ- cod.).

**οὔριος**, α, ον, also ος, ον S.*Ph*.355: (οὖρος Α):—*with a fair wind*, οὔ. πλοῦς a *prosperous* voyage, ib.780, E.*IA*1596; οὔ. δρόμος S.*Aj*.889 (lyr.); πομπή E.*IA*352; of a ship, οὔ. πλάτη S.*Ph*.355; λαῖφος E.*Hel*. 406; νεὼς πτερόν ib.147; ἀφήσω κατὰ κῦμ' ἐμαυτὸν οὔριον Ar.*Eq*.433: neut. pl. as Adv., οὔρια θεῖν to run *before the wind*, Id.*Lys*.550; cf. infr. II. 2. 2. metaph., *prosperous, successful*, πρᾶξις A.*Ch*.814 (lyr.), cf. E.*HF*95; φόνος Id.*Heracl*.822; βίοτος *AP*7.164.10 (Antip. Sid.): neut. pl. οὔρια as Adv., E.*Hel*.1588 (codd., but prob. οὔριοι). II. *prospering, favouring*, πνεῦμα, πνοαί, ib.1663, *Hec*.900, X.*HG*1.6.37; ἐπὶ τοὺς Ἀθηναίους οὔριος ἄνεμος Th.7.53: Com. of bellows, οὐρία ῥιπίδι Ar.*Ach*.669. Adv. Sup. -ώτατα *Stud.*150, 178. 2. οὐρία (sc. πνοή), ἡ, = οὖρος, *a fair wind*, Archil.(?) in *PLit.Lond*.54, etc.; οὐρίᾳ ἐφέντα (sc. ἑαυτόν or τὸ πλοῖον) running before the wind, Pl.*Prt*.338a; ἐξ οὐρίας διαδραμεῖν, πλεῖν, Arist.*Mech*.851$^b$6, Plb.1.47.2; also, ἐξ οὐρίων δραμοῦσαν S.*Aj*.1083; πάντα ἐξ οὐρίων θεῖ Lib.*Ep*.178; ἐν οὐρίῳ πλεῖν Luc. *Lex*.15. III. Ζεὺς οὔριος as *sending fair winds*, i.e. *conducting things to a happy issue*, A.*Supp*.594 (lyr.), *AP*12.53.8 (Mel.), *BMus. Inscr*.1012 (Chalcedon), *OGI*368 (Delos, ii B.C.), etc.; οὔριος.. ἐπίλαμψον ἐμῷ καὶ ἔρωτι καὶ ἱστῷ Κύπρι *AP*5.16 (Gaet.). IV. οὔ. ᾠόν a *wind-egg*, = ὑπηνέμιον, Arist.*GA*753$^a$22, etc.; those laid in spring were called ζεφύρια, those in autumn κυνόσουρα, Id.*HA*560$^a$5 (v.l. οὐρινά).

**οὔριος**, α, ον, (οὖρον Α) *of* or *for urine*, v. οὔρειος.

⊛**οὐριοστάτης** [ᾰ], ου, ὁ, (ἵστημι) *steady and prosperous*, A.*Ch*.821 (lyr.):—a dub. passage.

**οὐριότης**, ητος, ἡ, *success* (v. οὔριος I. 2), τῶν ποιημάτων Sch.Pi.*N*. 6.48.

**οὐριόω**, *give to the winds*, ἐθείρας *AP*9.777 (Phil.).

**οὐρίς**, ίδος, ἡ, = ἀμίς, *EM*642.40.

**οὔρισμα**, ατος, τό, Ion. for ὅρισμα, *boundary-line*, Hdt.2.17, 4.45.

**οὐροβόρος**, ον, (οὐρά) *devouring its tail*, δράκων *PMag.Lond*.121. 587, *PMag.Osl*.1.184, Olymp.Alch.p.80B.; cf. οὐρηβόρος.

**οὐρό-γαλον**, τό, (οὖρον Α) *urine of* γαλῆ, Zos.Alch.p.226B. **-δοχεῖον**, τό, = sq., *Gloss.*:—also **-δόχιον**, ib. **-δόχη**, ἡ, *chamber-pot*, Hsch.; **-δόκη**, X.ap.Phot. **-δόχος**, ον, *holding urine*, Gal. 8.373, 19.363, Sch.Ar.*Ach*.82.

**οὐροειδής**, ές, *like a tail*, οἰκουμένη Agathem.1.2.

**οὖρον** (Α), τό, *urine*, Hdt.2.111, etc.: pl., Hp.*Aph*.4.69,72, Thphr. *Od*.60(62). (Cf. Skt. *vāri* 'water', Lat. *ur-ina*.)

**οὖρον** (Β), τό, *limit, range*, δίσκου οὖρα Il.23.431, cf. δίσκουρα; ὅσσον τ' ἐπὶ οὖρα πέλονται ἡμιόνων, αἱ γάρ τε βοῶν προφερέστεραί εἰσιν ἑλκέμεναι νειοῖο βαθείης πηκτὸν ἄροτρον the *range* of mules, i.e. the breadth of land ploughed in a day by mules, the length of the furrow being fixed, 10.351: so in sg., ὅσσον τ' ἐν νειῷ οὖρον πέλει ἡμιόνοιιν, τόσσον ὑπεκπροθέων Od.8.124; later, simply, *boundaries*, in pl., A.R. 2.795.

**οὐροπύγιον**, v.l. for ὀρροπύγιον (q.v.).

**οὖρος** (Α), ὁ, *fair wind*, ἡμῖν δ' αὖ κατόπισθε νεὸς.. ἵκμενον οὖ. ἵει πλησίστιον Od.11.7, cf. 15.292, Il.1.479, etc.; νηῦς.., ᾗ λιγὺς οὖ. ἐπιπνείῃσιν ὄπισθεν Od.4.357; πέμψω δέ τοι οὖ. ὄπισθεν 5.167; οὖ. ἀπήμονά τε λιαρόν τε ib.268; πομπαῖος Pi.*P*.1.34; πρύμνηθεν οὖ. E.*Tr*.20; πλευστικός Theoc.13.52; Διὸς οὖρος Od.5.176, etc. (rarely of a *rough breeze* or *storm*, Il.14.19, A.R.2.900); ἂψ δὲ θεοὶ οὖ. στρέψαν the gods changed *the wind* again *to a fair one*, Od.4.520: pl., ib.360; later, ἀποπέμπειν κατ' οὖρον send down (i.e. with) the *wind*, speed on its way, Orac.ap.Hdt.4.163: so metaph., ἴτω κατ' οὖρον.. πᾶν τὸ Λαΐου γένος let it be swept before the *wind* to ruin, A.*Th*.690: κατ' οὖρον.. αἴρονται φυγήν Id.*Pers*.481; ταῦτα μὲν ῥεῖτω κατ' οὖρον let them drift with *wind* and stream, S.*Tr*.468; εὔθυνε δαίμονος οὖρον Pi.*O*.13.28; οὖ. ὀφθαλμῶν ἐμῶν αὐτῇ γένοιτ' ἄπωθεν ἑρπούσῃ let *a fair wind* be with her as she goes from my sight, i.e. let her go as quick as may be, S. *Tr*.815; οὖρός [ἐστι] 'tis *a fair time*, Id.*Ph*.855 (lyr.); γένοιτό (ἐγένετό codd.) τις οὖρος ἐκ κακῶν E.*Ion*1509 (lyr.); οὖ. ἐπέων, ὕμνων, Pi.*O*. 9.47 (cj. for οἶμον), *N*.6.29, *P*.4.3 [ῡ].—Rare in Prose, as X.*HG*2.3. 31, Luc.*Tox*.7.

⊛**οὖρος** (Β), ὁ, *watcher, guardian*, οὖρον ἰὼν κατέλειπον ἐπὶ κτεάτεσσι Od.15.89; Νέστωρ.., οὖ. Ἀχαιῶν Il.8.80, 11.840, 15.370, Od.3. 411; οὖ. Αἰακιδᾶν, of Achilles, Pi.*I*.8(7).60; νήσου A.R.4.1643; βουκολίων Opp.*C*.1.375; cf. ἐπίουρος, οὐρεύς. (I.-E. *sorwos* 'guardian', found also as second element in πυλωρός (πυλαουρός), θυρωρός, φρουρός (fr. προ-ὁρ(ϝ)ος), οἰχῶρος (οἰκουρός), etc., Avest. *pasu(š)-haurva*- 'cattle-guarding', epith. of a dog: cogn. with ἐρύω (Β), q.v.: also with ὅρομαι (ἐπί), cf. Avest. *haurvaiti* and *haraiti* 'watches'.)

**οὖρος** (C), ὁ, Ion., etc. for ὅρος (q.v.).

**οὖρος** (D), ὁ, βοῦς οὖρος, Lat. *urus*, *Bos primigenius*, *AP*6.332 (Hadr.).

**οὐρός**, ὁ, *trench* or *channel* for hauling up and launching ships, οὐροὺς ἐξεκάθαιρον Il.2.153, cf. Poll.10.149.

**οὐροτομέω** ἵππον *dock* a horse's *tail*, Anon.ap.Suid.

**οὐροφύλαξ**, ὁ, v. ὀροφύλαξ.

**οὐρώδης**, ες, (οὐρά) *of the tail* or *rump*, τένοντες Hp.*Acut*.(*Sp*.)37 (v.l. for ὀρρ-).

⊛**οὖς** (nom. sg. freq. in *IG*11(2).161*B*126, al. (Delos, iii B.C.), v. sub fin.), τό, gen. ὠτός, dat. ὠτί: pl. nom. ὦτα, gen. ὤτων, dat. ὠσί (ὤτοις condemned by Phryn.186):—Hom. has only acc. sg. and dat. pl. (v. infr.); the other cases he forms as if from οὖας (which is found in Simon.37.14), gen. οὔατος, pl. nom. and acc. οὔατα (also in Epich.21, Hp.*Cord*.8, al., *SIG*1025.62 (Cos, iv/iii B.C.)), dat. οὔασι Il.12.442 (ὠσίν Od.12.200): Hellenistic nom. sg. ὦς *PPetr*.3p.33 (iii B.C.), *PGrenf*.1.12.29, 2.15 ii 1 (ii B.C.), *IG*7.3498.19 (Oropus, ii B.C.), Roussel *Cultes Égyptiens* 217 (Delos, ii B.C.), *PStrassb*.87.14 (ii B.C.): also Dor. ὦς Theoc.11.32; pl. ὤϝαθ' cj. for ὦτά θ' in Alcm.41:—*ear*, Ἀντίφον αὖ παρὰ οὖς ἔλασε ξίφει Il.11.109; [κηρὸν] ἐπ' ὠσὶν ἄλειψ' Od.l.c.; αἲ γὰρ δή μοι ἀπ' οὔατος ὧδε γένοιτο oh may I never hear of such a thing! Il.18.272; αἲ γὰρ ἀπ' οὔατος εἴη 22.454; ἀμφὶ κτύπος οὔατα βάλλει 10. 535; ὀρθὰ ἱστάναι τὰ ὦτα, of horses, Hdt.4.129, cf. S.*El*.27, etc.; ἐν τοῖσι ὠσὶ.. οἰκέει ὁ θυμός Hdt.7.39, cf. 1.8; βοᾷ ἐν ὠσὶ κέλαδος rings in *the ear*, A.*Pers*.605; φθόγγος βάλλει δι' ὤτων S.*Ant*.1188, cf. A.*Ch*.56 (lyr.); δι' ὠτὸς παῦρα ἐννέπειν πρός τινα S.*El*.1437 (lyr.); ὀξὺν δι' ὤτων κέλαδον ἐνσείσας ib.737, cf. *OT*1387; δι' ὤτων ἦν λόγος E.*Med*.1139, cf. *Rh*.294, 566; so ἀμὶν τοῦτο δι' ὠτὸς ἔγεντο Theoc.14.27; λόγους ψιθύρους εἰς ὦτα φέρει S.*Aj*.149 (anap.); εἰς οὖς ἑκάστῳ.. ηὔδα λόγους E.*Andr*.1091, cf. *Hipp*.932; προσκύψας μοι μικρὸν πρὸς τὸ οὖς Pl.*Euthd*. 275e; ἐπ' (ἐς cj. Dawes) οὔατα λάθριος εἶπεν Call.*Ap*.105; reversely, παρέχειν τὰ ὦτα to lend the *ears*, i.e. to attend, Pl.*Cra*.396d, etc.; so ἐπισχέσθαι τὰ ὦτα Id.*Smp*.216a; παραβάλλειν Id.*R*.531a, cf. Call.*Fr*. *anon*.375; τὰ ὦτα ἐξεπετάννυντο Ar.*Eq*.1347; ὦτα χορηγεῖν Plu.2.232f; ἀποκλείειν τὰ ὦτα ib.143f; οἱ ὦτα ἔχοντες those who have *ears* to hear, ib.1112c: metaph., of spies in Persia, X.*Cyr*.8.2.10sq., Luc.*Ind*.23, cf. Arist.*Pol*.1287$^b$30; τὸ τῶν λεγομένων ὤτων καὶ προσαγωγέων γένος Plu.2.522f; τὰ ὦτα ἐπὶ τῶν ὤμων ἔχοντες, of persons who slink away ashamed (hanging their ears like dogs), Pl.*R*.613c: prov., v. λύκος; τεθλασμένος οὔατα πυγμαῖς, of a boxer, Theoc.22.45 (cf. ὠτοκάταξις); ἐπ' ἀμφότερα τὰ ὦτα καθεύδειν sleep *soundly*, Aeschin.Socr.54 D. II. from resemblance to *an ear*, 1. *handle*, esp. of pitchers, cups, etc., οὔατα δ' αὐτοῦ τέσσαρ' ἔσαν Il.11.633, cf. 18.378, Bion ap.Plu.2.536a, *IG*11(2).161*B*126 (Delos, iii B.C.), Hero *Spir*.2.23, Dsc.5.87; [ποτήριον] ὦτα συντεθλασμένον Alex.270.3. 2. in Archit., = παρωτίς 4, *IG*2².372.201, cf. 319.6. 3. οὖς Ἀφροδίτης, a kind of *shell-fish*, Antig.Car.ap.Ath.3.88a; οὖς θαλάττιον, = ἀγρία λεπάς, Arist.*HA*529$^b$ 16. 4. τὰ ὦτα (οὔατα Hp.) τῆς καρδίας the *auricles* of the heart, Hp.*Cord*.8, Gal.*UP*6.15, cf. 2.615 K. 5. name of part of a bandage, Heraclas ap.Orib.48.15 tit. [Written ὄς in *IG*1². ll. cc.] (Cogn. with Lat. *auris*, Lith. *ausis*, OE. *ēar*, etc.; details obscure; nom. sg. οὖς perh. from *ὄ(ϝ)ος (contained in ἀμφώης).)

⊛**οὐσί-α**, Ion. -ίη Hdt.1.92, 6.86.α', *SIG*167.26 (Mylasa, iv B.C.); Dor. ἐσσία, ὠσία (qq.v.): ἡ: (ὀντ-, part. of εἰμί *sum*):—*that which is one's own, one's substance, property*, Hdt. ll. cc., S.*Tr*.911 (s.v.l.), E. *HF*337, *Hel*.1253 (pl., *Fr*.354 (s.v.l.)), Ar.*Ec*.729, Lys.18.17, Pl.*R*. 551b, *SIG* l.c., etc.; opp. τὰ σώματα (civil status), And.1.74; καλῶς.. ἐπεμελήθη τῶν οὐσιῶν ὑπὲρ τοῦ δημάρχου *BSA*24.154 (Attica, iv B.C.); εἰ ἐκεκτήμην οὐ. if I had been a man of *substance*, Lys.24.11; ὑπὲρ τὴν οὐ. δαπανᾶν Diph.32.7; πατρῴαν οὐ. κατεσθίειν Anaxipp.1.32, cf. Critias 45 D.; φανερὰ οὐσία real *property, immovables*, And.1.118; opp. ἀφανής, Lys.32.4; freq. of *estates* in Egypt, *PTeb*.6.23 (ii B.C., pl.), *BGU*650.3 (i A.D.), *OGI*665.30 (i A.D.), etc. II. in Philos., like Ion. φύσις (with which it is interchanged in various uses, e.g. Philol.11, Pl.*R*.359a,b, Arist.*PA*646$^a$25, Thphr.*HP*6.1.1), *stable being, immutable reality*, opp. γένεσις, ὅτιπερ πρὸς γένεσιν οὐσία, τοῦτο πρὸς πίστιν ἀλήθεια Pl.*Ti*.29c, cf. *Sph*.232c; ὧν κίνησις γένεσιν παραλαβοῦσα ἀέναον οὐ. ἐπόρισεν Id.*Lg*.966e; γένεσις μὲν τὸ σπέρμα, οὐ. δὲ τὸ τέλος Arist.*PA*641$^b$32, cf. 640$^a$18, etc.; ὁδὸς εἰς οὐσίαν Id. *Metaph*.1003$^b$7: hence, *being* in the abstract, opp. non-being (τὸ μὴ εἶναι), Pl.*Tht*.185c. 2. *substance, essence*, opp. πάθη ('modes'), Id.*Euthphr*.11a; πάθη οὐσίας Arist.*Metaph*.1003$^b$7; opp. συμβεβηκότα ('accidents'), Id.*APo*.83$^a$24, *PA*643$^a$27; ἡ φύσις [τῆς ψυχῆς] καὶ ἡ οὐ., εἶθ' ὅσα συμβέβηκε περὶ αὐτήν Id.*de An*.402$^a$8. 3. *true nature* of that which is a member of a kind, defined as ὃ τυγχάνει ἕκαστον ὄν Pl.*Phd*.65d; as τὸ ὅ ἐστι ib.92d; as τὸ τί ἐστι Arist.*APo*. 90$^b$30; τὸ εἶναί τε καὶ τὴν οὐ. Pl.*R*.509b; expressed in a formula or definition, ψυχῆς οὐ. τε καὶ λόγον Id.*Phdr*.245e; τὸ τί ἦν εἶναι οὗ ὁ λόγος ὁρισμός, καὶ τοῦτο οὐ. λέγεται Arist.*Metaph*.1017$^b$22; μόνης τῆς οὐ. ἐστὶν ὁ ὁρισμός ib.1031$^a$1. 4. the possession of such a nature, *substantiality*, ἔτι ἐπέκεινα τῆς οὐ. πρεσβείᾳ.. ὑπερέχοντος Pl.*R*. 509b. 5. in the concrete, *the primary real*, the *substratum* underlying all change and process in nature, applied by Arist. to the atoms of Democritus, *Fr*.208; to τὰ ἁπλᾶ σώματα Id.*Cael*.298$^a$29, cf. *Metaph*.1017$^b$10; πᾶσαι αἱ φυσικαὶ οὐ. ἡ σώματα ἢ μετὰ σωμάτων γίγνονται Id.*Cael*.298$^b$3, al.; ταὐτὸν σῶμα καὶ οὐσίαν ὁριζόμενοι Pl. *Sph*.246a; but also, νοητὰ ἄττα καὶ ἀσώματα εἴδη.. τὴν ἀληθινὴν οὐ. ib.b. 6. in Logic, *substance* as the leading category, Arist.*Cat*.1$^b$ 26, *Metaph*.1045$^b$29; αἱ πρῶται οὐ. (individuals), αἱ δεύτεραι οὐ. (species and genera), Id.*Cat*.2$^b$5, 2$^a$15 (but ὁ ἄνθρωπος καὶ ὁ ἵππος.. οὐκ ἔστιν οὐ. ἀλλὰ σύνολόν τι Id.*Metaph*.1035$^b$29, cf. σύνθετος or συνθέτη οὐ. ib. 1043$^a$30, *de An*.412$^a$16); ἡ μὲν ψυχὴ οὐ. ἡ πρώτη, τὸ δὲ σῶμα ὕλη Id.*Metaph*.1037$^a$5; ἡ ψυχὴ οὐ. ὡς εἶδος Id.*de An*.412$^a$19; οὐ. ἐντελέχεια ib.21; [ψυχὴ] οὐ. τοῦ ἐμψύχου Id.*Metaph*.1035$^b$15; of the abstract objects of mathematics, μονὰς οὐ. ἄθετος, στιγμὴ δὲ οὐ. θετός Id.*APo*.87$^a$36. 7. after Pl. and Arist. in various uses, as ἡ ἄποιος οὐ., = ἡ ὕλη, Zeno *Stoic*.1.24; κατὰ οὐσίαν, opp. κατὰ δύναμιν ἢ ἐνέργειαν, Polystr.p.12 W.; πᾶς νοῦς ἀμέριστός ἐστιν οὐ. Procl.*Inst*.171, cf. Plot.2.4.5, 2.6.1, 4.7.8, 6.1.2, al. 8. Pythag. name for 1, *Theol. Ar*.6. III. name of a plaster, Aët.15.15,45. IV. αἱ οὐ. *fire-resisting substances*, Zos.Alch.p.168B.; of the four σώματα (copper, tin, lead, iron), Ps.-Democr.ap.eund.p.167B. V. in Magic, *a material thing by which a connexion is established between the person to be acted upon and the supernatural agent*, e.g. a hair, λαβὼν βελόνην διείρων τὴν οὐ. εἰς αὐτὴν *PMag.Par*.1.2949, cf. *PMag.Osl*.1.73; mould from a tomb, *PMag.Par.*1.435; κυνοκεφάλου οὐ., . κυνὸς οὐ., = κόπρος (cf. 2460), ib.2687, etc. -άζω, *make magically efficacious by applying an* οὐσία v, *PMag.Lond.*121.463. ⊛ -ἀκός, ή, όν, *of* or *pertaining to an estate*, μίσθωσις *OGI*669.11 (i A.D.); μισθωταί *BGU*509.9 (ii A.D.); λόγος ib.14. -άρχης, ου, ὁ, *source of existence, substantiae auctor*, Apul. *Asclep.*19 (p.54 Thomas).

**οὐσίδιον** [σῐ], τό, Dim. of οὐσία I, Nicom.Com.3, Arr.*Epict.*2.2.10.

**οὐσιο-μετρία**, ἡ, f. l. in Herm.ap.Stob.1.49.69 (p.470.15 W.). -**πάτωρ** [ᾰ], ορος, ὁ, *father of existence*, of the Second God, Iamb. *Myst.*8.2. -**ποιός**, όν, *creating substance* or *essence*, Herm. *in Phdr.* p.153 A., Procl.*Inst.*157, Dam.*Pr.*83, Simp. *in Cat.*325.20, etc.

⊛ **οὐσι-ότης**, ητος, ἡ, *the quality of existence*, Dam.*Pr.*58, Elias *in Cat.* 221.1: *substantiality*, *Corp.Herm.*12.1, Herm.ap.Stob.1.41.4. -**όω**, (οὐσία II) *invest with being, existence* or *substance*, Plot.6.1.10, Suppl. ad Procl.*in Prm.*p.1003 S., Dam.*Pr.*80, Phlp. *in GA*7.26, 39.7, Simp. *in Cat.*129.23:—Pass., *to be existent* or *have essence* or *substance*, Porph. *in Cat.*99.7, Id.ap.Stob.3.21.28, Procl. *in Cra.*p.57 P., Syrian. *in Metaph.*7.24, Dam.*Pr.*83 bis, Simp. *in Epict.*p.129 D., etc. -**ώδης**, ες, *essential, substantial, real*, σύγκρισις Epicur.*Nat.*14.1, cf. Aret.*SD* 2.12, Plu.2.1085d, A.D.*Synt.*83.11, Plot.2.6.1; οὐ. νόησις Id.5.3.5: Comp., Id.6.6.8. Adv. -δῶς Hero *Deff.*136.2, Syrian. *in Metaph.*147.31, etc. -**ωσις**, εως, ἡ, *substantification*, Dam.*Pr.*80 bis, Simp. *in Ph.*433.17. -**ώτερα**, prob. f.l. for οὐσιωδέστερα, Procl. *in Prm.* p.619 S. -**ωτικός**, ή, όν, *substantified, substantive*, Dam.*Pr.*83 bis. -**ωτός**, ή, όν, *substantifiable*, ibid.

**οὔσκη**, ἡ, glossed in margin by πῶμα κικκάβου, Zos.Alch.p.222 B.

⊛ **οὖσον**, τό, *ship's tackle, ropes*, Lyc.20 (pl.), Alex.Aet.3.21, pl. prob. in Antim.Col.6 (οἶσον is similarly glossed in Hsch.).

**οὐτάζω**, v. οὐτάω.

**οὐ τἄν**, Att. crasis for οὔ τοι ἄν, S.*OC*1351, etc.

**οὐ τᾶρα**, Att. crasis for οὔ τοι ἄρα, E.*Hel.*85, etc.

**οὐτάω**, 3 sg. οὐτᾷ A.*Ch.*640 (lyr.); Ep. imper. οὔταε Od.22.356: fut. οὐτήσω Nonn.*D.*21.37: aor. οὔτησα Il.11.260; Ion. οὐτήσασκε 22.375:—Pass., aor. part. οὐτηθείς 8.537.—As pres. and impf. Hom. uses **οὐτάζω**, Act. and Pass., Il.20.459, 7.273, al. (so E.*Fr.*176): hence fut. οὐτάσω Id.*Rh.*255 (lyr.): aor. οὔτασα Il.7.258, E.*HF*199: pf. Pass. οὔτασται Il.11.661; part. οὐτασμένος Od.11.536, A.*Ag.*1344.—Also (as if from οὔτημι) 3 sg. Ep. aor. οὖτα Il.4.525, 11.491, 13.561, etc.; inf. οὐτάμεναι 21.68, al., οὐτάμεν 5.132, 821; part. (in pass. sense) οὐτάμενος 11.659, 17.86, Od.11.40, Hes.*Sc.*363; Ion. Iterat. οὔτασκε Il.15.745 (cf. ἀν-, νε-ούτατος):—Ep. Verb, used sts. in Trag. (never by S.), *wound, hurt, hit* with any kind of weapon, οὖτα δὲ δουρί Il.4.525, cf. 11.260, al.; οὐ. ἔγχεϊ 21.402; χαλκῷ 12.427; but prop. opp. βάλλω (q.v.), *wound by striking* or *thrusting*, 11.659, etc.: which is more fully expressed by σχεδὸν οὔτασε, 5.458; αὐτοσχεδὸν οὐτάζοντο 7.273; αὐτοσχεδίην οὐτασμένος Od.11.536: mostly with acc. of pers. or part wounded, c. dupl. acc., Κύπριδα.. οὔτασε χεῖρα Il.5.458; Λειώκριτον οὖτα.. κενεῶνα Od.22.294; also οὐ. τινὰ κατὰ χρόα, κατ' ἰσχίον, κατ' ἀσπίδα, etc., Il.12.427 (Pass.), 11.338, 434, al.: more rarely c. acc. rei, σάκος οὔτασε δουρὶ *pierced* the shield, 7.258, al., cf. Hes.*Sc.*363 (Pass.): c. acc. cogn., ἕλκος, ὅ με βροτὸς οὔτασεν ἀνήρ the wound which a man *struck* me *withal*, Il.5.361: hence κατ' οὐταμένην ὠτειλήν by the wound *inflicted*, 14.518; so also τὸ ξίφος διανταίαν [πληγήν].. οὐτᾷ A.*Ch.*640 (lyr.). 2. sts. generally, *wound*, like βάλλω, πυρί with lightning, E.*Hipp.*684; τοξεύμασιν Id.*HF*199, cf. Opp.*H.*2.372.

⊛ **οὔτε**, Adv., (οὐ, τε) joining neg. clauses, as τε joins posit., but rare in the simple sense *and not*, Il.22.265 (v.l.), Hdt.3.155 (v.l.); οὔτε γὰρ ἐκείνους διδόναι, Lat. *neque enim*, Id.1.3 (prob. f.l. for οὐδέ); and occasionally in later writers, Arist.*Ph.*208ᵃ8, Luc.*Par.*27, 53, etc. II. mostly repeated, οὔτε.., οὔτε.. *neither.., nor..*, Lat. *neque.., neque..*, Hom., etc.—Hom. freq. joins another Particle with the first or second οὔτε, as οὔτ' ἄρ.., οὔτε..; οὔτ' ἄρ.., οὔτ' ἄρ..; οὔτ' ἄρ τε.., οὔτ' ἄρα.. Il.5.89; οὔτ' οὖν, v. οὖν I; οὔτε.. οὖν.., οὔτ' ἄρα.. 20.7; οὔτ' ἄρ.., οὔτε τι.., or οὔτε τι.., οὔτε.., 1.115, Od.1.202; so too οὔτε.., οὔτε μὴν.. X.*Cyr.*4.3.12; οὔτε.., οὔτ' αὖ.., v. infr. 3. 2. freq. used to divide up a general negation into two or more parts, ὡς δ' ἐν ὀνείρῳ οὐ δύναται φεύγοντα διώκειν, οὔτ' ἄρ ὁ τὸν δύναται ὑποφεύγειν οὔθ' ὁ διώκειν Il.22.200; thrice repeated, οὔ μοι Τρώων.. μέλει ἄλγος.., οὔτ' αὐτῆς Ἑκάβης οὔτε Πριάμοιο ἄνακτος οὔτε κασιγνήτων 6.450; οὐκ ἔπειθεν οὔτε τοὺς στρατηγοὺς οὔτε τοὺς στρατιώτας Th.4.4: without a neg. preceding, Il.1.490, 2.202, etc. 3. within one of the two clauses distd. by οὔτε a subordinate part may be introduced by οὐδέ, οὔτε γὰρ ἐκ σκίλλης ῥόδα φύεται οὐδ' ὑάκινθος (οὔθ' codd.), οὐ δέ ποτ' ἐκ δούλης τέκνον ἐλευθέριον Thgn.537; οὔτε.. ἀπέφηνεν οὐδὲ παρέσχηται μάρτυρας, οὔτ' αὖ τὸν ἀριθμὸν.. ἐπανέφερεν D.27.49: sts. after several clauses distd. by οὔτε the last is introduced emphat. by οὐδέ, οὔτε φάρμακα οὔτε καύσεις οὔτε τομαὶ οὐδ' αὖ ἐπῳδαί *nor yet* incantations, Pl.*R.*426b, cf. 499b (so μηδέ after clauses with μήτε, μήτε παιδεία μήτε δικαστήρια μήτε νόμοι μηδὲ ἀνάγκη μηδεμία Id.*Prt.*327d); so οὐδέ (μηδέ) may sts. follow a single οὔτε (μήτε), οὐδέ ποτέ σφιν οὔτε τι πημανθῆναι ἔπι δέος, οὐδ' ἀπολέσθαι *neither* to suffer misery, *nor yet* to die, v.l. in Od.8.563, cf. Pi.*P.*8.83, *I.*2.44, S.*OC*1139, 1141 (s.v.l.), 1297 (cj.), Pl. *Ap.*19d: in many of these places, however, the readings vary, and editors have altered οὐδέ into οὔτε; but this cannot be done in some cases, as οὔτ' ἂν ὑπό γε ἑνὸς.. πάθοι, ἴσως δ' οὐδὲ ὑπὸ πλειόνων Id.*La.*182b: so when οὔτε is folld. by οὐδὲ μέν, Od.13.207; by οὐδὲ μήν, X.*Cyr.*4.5.27; οὐδ' αὖ, v. supr.—But οὔτε (μήτε) cannot be used simply answering to οὐδέ (μηδέ), v. μηδέ A. 2. 4. οὔτε may be folld. by a Posit. clause with τε, οὔτ' αὐτὸς κτενέει, ἀπό τ' ἄλλους πάντας ἐρύξει he *both* will *not* kill *and* will defend, Il.24.156, cf. A.*Pr.*246, 262, Hdt.5.49, X.*An.*7.7.48, etc.: sts. the neg. is added *after* the τε, οὔτ' ἂν.. καρπὸν ἔδωκαν ἄρουραι, δένδρεά τ' οὐκ ἐθέλει.. φέρειν Pi.*N.*11.40, cf. S.*Ant.*763, E.*Hipp.*302; κυάμους δὲ οὔτε τι μάλα σπείρουσι, τούς τε γενομένους οὔτε τρώγουσι οὔτε ἕψοντες πατέονται Hdt.2.37: the combination οὔτε.., καί.. is dub. in E.*IT*591, but is found in later writers, as Luc.*DMeretr.*2.4, Chor. in *Rev.Phil.*1877.218. 5. οὔτε is freq., by anacoluthon, folld. not by a second οὔτε, but by some other Particle, as by οὐδέ, v. supr. 3; by δέ alone, Il.24.368, Hdt.1.108, Pl.*R.*388e, X.*An.*6.3.16. b. in Poets, οὐ sts. follows without any conjunctive Particle, οὐκ ἦν ἀλέξημ' οὐδὲν οὔτε βρώσιμον, οὐ χριστόν, οὔτε πιστόν A.*Pr.*479; οὔτε πληθυνθεὶς δόμους.. ἦσαν, οὐ ξυλουργίαι ib.450, cf. Theoc.15.139 sq.: οὔτε βλάστας.. πατρός, οὐ μητρὸς εἶχον S.*OC* 972, cf. *Ant.*249, E.*Or.*41: so also in the Prose of Hdt., ἐς ποταμὸν οὔτε ἐνουρέουσι οὔτε ἐμπτύουσι, οὐ χεῖρας ἐναπονίζονται, οὐδέ.. 1.138. c. in Poets also οὔτε is sts. replaced by οὐ, οὐ νιφετὸς οὔτ' ἂρ χειμὼν πολὺς οὔτε ποτ' ὄμβρος Od.4.566; οὐ γὰρ ἂν εἰδείης ἀνδρὸς νόον οὔτε γυναικός Thgn.125 (dub. l.), cf. Il.1.115, Od.9.136, A.*Pers.*588 (lyr., s. v. l.), etc. d. the former οὔτε is sts. omitted, ναυσὶ δ' οὔτε πεζὸς ἰών Pi.*P.*10.29; νόσοι δ' οὔτε γῆρας ib.41; Πάρις γὰρ οὔτε συντελὴς πόλις A.*Ag.*532, cf. *Ch.*294; and v. μήτε 2. 6. when οὔτε and μήτε correspond, each retains its proper sense, ἀναιδὴς οὔτ' εἰμὶ μήτε γενοίμην *neither* am I shameless, *nor* may I become so, D.8.68, cf. Aeschin.3.128.

**οὔτερος**, Ion. for ὁ ἕτερος, Hdt.1.34, 134: neut. τοὔτερον ib.32.

**οὐτ-ήσασκε**, v. οὐτάω. -**ησις**, εως, ἡ, (οὐτάω) *a wounding*, Zonar. -**ήτειρα**, ἡ, *she who wounds*, ἔχιδνα *AP*7.172 (Antip. Sid.).

**οὐτῐδᾰνός**, ή, όν, *of no account, worthless*, esp. with regard to strength or courage, in Hom. always of persons, δειλὸς καὶ οὐ. Il.1.293; βέλος ἀνδρὸς ἀναλκίδος, οὐτιδανοῖο 11.390; ἄφρων.. καὶ οὐ. Od.8.209; ὀλίγος τε καὶ οὐ. καὶ ἄκικυς 9.515; οὐτιδανὸς βίην Opp.*H.*2.144. II. Act., *reckless*, γᾶς δόσις οὐτιδανοῖς ἐν ῥυθίοις φορεῖται, of a surging crowd, A.*Th.*361 (lyr.). (Prob. suffix -ανός, and *οὐτιδ, earlier form of οὔτι 'nothing', cf. Lat. *quid*, Skt. *cid.*)

**οὔ τι πη** (or πῃ), Dor. **οὔ τι πα** (or πᾳ), *in no wise*, Hes.*Op.*105, Theoc.1.63.

**οὔ τι που**, *not, I suppose.., surely you do not mean that..*, used in a half interrog. way, Pi.*P.*4.87, S.*Ph.*1233, Ar.*Ra.*522, etc.: in codd. sts. οὔτιπου, in one word.

**οὔ τι πω**, Ion. **οὔ τι κω**, *not at all yet*, v. οὔπω.

⊛ **οὔτις**, neut. οὔτι, declined like τις, (οὐ, τις) *no one* or *nobody*, neut. *nothing*, common in all Poets (Hom. uses it almost exclus. for οὐδείς in masc. and fem., but οὐδείς occurs in B.*Fr.*28 (masc.), and is preferred by Trag. (οὔτις only twice in E., *Fr.*45, 325)), whereas οὐδείς only is used in Prose, exc. in neut. (v. infr.), οὔτις.. Δαναῶν Il.1.88; οὐ. θεῶν A.*Ag.*396 (lyr.), etc.: freq. agreeing with its Subst., οὐ. ἀνήρ S.*El.*188 (lyr.), cf. A.*Pr.*445, *Pers.*414, etc.: in Hom. and Hes. other words may come between, οὐ γάρ τις, οὐ μὲν γάρ τις, Il.6.487, Od.8.552; οὔτε τινά.., οὔτε τις.. Il.13.224: rare in pl., ἐπεὶ οὔτινες ἐγγύθεν εἰσίν Od.6.279; προφήτας οὔτινας A.*Ag.*1099 (lyr.). 2. neut. οὔτι is freq. used as Adv., *by no means, not at all*, Il.1.153, 2.338, etc.: so not only in Trag., but in Hdt., 1.148, 3.36, al., and in Pl., *R.*331a, 351a, al.: strengthd. οὔτι γε, Id.*Phd.*81d; οὔτι μὲν δή Id.*Tht.*186f, etc.; οὔτι μήν S.*El.*817, etc.: also separated, οὐ γάρ τι Il.20.467, S.*Aj.*1111, etc.; οὐ μὲν γάρ τι Il.19.321, etc.; οὐ νύ τι 8.39, etc. 3. τὸ οὔτι *nothing*, S.E.*M.*1.15: pl., τῶν οὐτινῶν ib.17. II. as pr. n. with changed accent **Οὖτις**, ὁ, acc. Οὖτιν, *Nobody, Noman*, a fallacious name assumed by Odysseus (with a punning allusion to μῆτις and μή τις, v. Od.20.20) to deceive Polyphemus, 9.366, 408, cf. E.*Cyc.*549, 672 sq., Ar.*V.*184 sq. 2. name of a fallacy, περὶ τοῦ οὔτιδος, title of work by Chrysippus, D.L.7.198, cf. 82.

**οὐτίς**, ίδος, ἡ, = ὠτίς, ὠτίς, Alcm.146 B, Gal.6.703.

**οὔτοι** or **οὔ τοι**, Adv. *indeed not*, Il.1.298, 515, 3.65, 4.29, Hes.*Op.*759, etc.: in Att. freq. before protestations, οὔτοι μὰ τὴν Δήμητρα Ar.*Pl.*64; οὔτοι.. μὰ τὸν Ἀπόλλω Id.*V.*1366; οὔτοι μὰ τὴν Γῆν Id.*Pax* 188; μὰ τὸν Δί' οὔτοι Id.*Th.*34; μὰ τὸν Δί' οὐ τοίνυν Id.*V.*1141 (cf. τοίνυν); ἀλλ' οὔτοι.. γε S.*El.*137 (lyr.), etc.; οὔτοι δή Pl.*Cri.*43d; οὔτοι δή.. γε Id.*Euthphr.*2a, etc.; οὔτοι μὲν οὖν Id.*Phdr.*271b; οὔτοι πότε *never indeed*, S.*Ant.*522, etc.; οὔτοι ποτέ.. γε Id.*OT*852; cf. οὐ τἄν, οὐ τᾶρα. (οὔτοι is freq. confounded with οὔτι.)

**οὗτος**, αὕτη, τοῦτο, gen. τούτου, ταύτης, τούτου, etc.: the dual fem. never in Att., v. ὁ, ἡ, τό, init.:—demonstr. Pron., *this*, common from Hom. downwds. A. ORIGIN and FORMS: οὗτος, αὕτη, τοῦτο prob. arose from a reduplication of the demonstr. ὁ, ἡ, τό with insertion of -υ- (= Skt. Particle *u*), e.g. ταῦτα fr. τα-υ-τα: Dor. gen. sg. fem. τούτας Philol.11; nom. pl. τοῦτοι, ταῦται A.D.*Synt.*111.23: the former occurs Sophr.24, *GDI*3045 *B*6 (Selinus), *SIG*339.16 Rhodes, iii B.C.), etc., the latter is dub. in Sophr.97, certain in *SIG*241 *B*117 (Delph., iv B.C.): in Boeot. all forms begin with οὑτ-, as gen. sg. neut. οὕτω *Supp.Epigr.*3.359.11 (iii B.C.); acc. sg. fem. οὕταν Corinn. *Supp.*2.80; acc. pl. neut. οὗτα *SIG*1185.20 (Tanagra, iii B.C.), etc.: gen. pl. fem. Att. τούτων, Cret. ταυτᾶν *Leg.Gort.*5.19; neut. ταύτων *Michel*1334.10 (Elis, iv B.C.).—In Ion. sts. written ταότην, ταοτα, *SIG*283.19 (Chios, iv B.C.), 46.7 (Halic., v B.C.), al.—In Att. οὗτος was freq. strengthd. by the demonstr. -ί, οὑτοσί, αὑτηί, τουτί, gen. τουτουί, dat. τουτῳί, acc. τουτονί; pl. nom. οὑτοιί, neut. ταυτί, etc., *this man here*: sts. a Particle is inserted between the Pron. and -ί, as αὑτηγί for αὑτηί γε, Ar.*Ach.*784; τουτογί for τουτί γε, Id.*V.*781,

*Av.*894, al.; ταυταγί for ταυτί γε, Id.*Eq.*492, *Pax*1057, al.; τουτοδί for τουτὶ δέ, Id.*Pl.*227; τουτουμενί for τουτουὶ μέν, Id.*Ra.*965.—In codd. the ν ἐφελκυστικόν is sts. added in the forms οὑτοσίν, οὑτωσίν, and οὑτοσίν is said to be Att. by A.D.*Pron.*59.24, 82.11. [This ι is always long, and a long vowel or diphthong before it becomes short, as αὑτηΐ, τουτῳΐ, οὑτοιΐ, Ar.*Nu.*201, *Pl.*44, *Ach.*40, etc.]

B. Usage in regard to Concord. οὗτος is freq. used as a Pron. Subst.: hence neut. is folld. by gen., κατὰ τοῦτο τῆς ἀκροπόλιος Hdt. 1.84; εἰς τοῦθ' ὕβρεως ἐλήλυθεν D.4.37; εἰς τοῦθ' ἥκεις μανίας Id.36.48; ταῦτα τῶν μαθημάτων Pl.*Euthd.*278b: but quite as freq. as Adj., in which case its Subst. commonly takes the Art., οὗτος ὁ ἀνήρ or ὁ ἀνὴρ οὗτος.—But the Art. is absent, **1.** always in Ep. Poets (exc. Od.18.114), οὗτος ἀνήρ Il.14.471, Od.1.406, etc.: sts. also in Trag., A.*Pers.* 122 (lyr.), 495, S.*Ph.*406, *OC*471, 1177: once in an Inscr., τοπεῖα· τούτων τὰ ἡμίσεα τοπείων *IG*2².1622.135 (iv B.C.). **2.** sts. when the Noun is so specified that the Art. is not needed, ἐς γῆν ταύτην.., ἥντινα νῦν Σκύθαι νέμονται Hdt.4.8; ταύτας ἃς οἱ πατέρες παρέδοσαν μελέτας Th. 1.85, cf. Pl.*R.*449d, etc.; πατὴρ σὸς οὗτος, ὃν θρηνεῖς ἀεί S.*El.*530. **3.** when οὗτος is used in local sense, *here*, v. infr. C. I. 5. **4.** when the Noun with which οὗτος agrees stands as its Predicate, αὕτη γὰρ ἦν σοι πρόφασις S.*Ph.*1034; δικαστοῦ αὕτη ἀρετή [ἐστι] Pl.*Ap.*18a: this exception extends to cases in which the Predicate is not so distinctly separated from the Subject, αἰτίαι μὲν αὗται προυγεγένηντο *these* were the grievances which already existed, Th.1.66; ταύτην φήμην παρέδοσαν *this* was the report which.., Pl.*Phlb.*16c: freq. with a Sup., κίνησις αὕτη μεγίστη δὴ..ἐγένετο *this* was notably the greatest movement which.., Th.1.1, cf. 3.113: with πρῶτος Id.1.55, 98, 6.31, *Ev.Luc.* 2.2. **5.** when 3rd pers. is used for 2nd to express contempt, οὗτος ἀνήρ, οὑτοσὶ ἀνήρ, Pl.*Grg.*467b, 489b, etc. **II.** though οὗτος usu. agrees with the Noun that serves as Predicate, it is not rare to find it in the neut., μανία δὲ καὶ τοῦτ' ἐστί E.*Ba.*305; τοῦτο γάρ εἰσι..εὔθυναι D.19.82, etc.: and in pl., οὐκ ἔστι ταῦτα ἀρχή Aeschin. 3.13; ταῦτ' ἐστὶν ὁ προδότης Id.2.166: so with an explanatory clause added, τοῦτο γάρ ἐστιν ὁ συκοφάντης, αἰτιᾶσθαι μὲν πάντα ἐξελέγξαι δὲ μηδέν D.57.34. **2.** so also with a Noun in apposition, τούτοισιν μὲν ταῦτα μέλει, κίθαρις καὶ ἀοιδή Od.1.159; τούτου τιμῶμαι, ἐν πρυτανείῳ σιτήσεως Pl.*Ap.*36e, cf. E.*Fr.*323.3, etc. **3.** the neut. also may refer to a masc. or fem. Noun, καρπὸν φορέει κυάμῳ ἴσον· τοῦτο ἐπεὰν γένηται πέπον κτλ. Hdt.4.23, cf. X.*An.*1.5.10, etc. **4.** the neut. is also used of classes of persons, μελιτοπῶλαι καὶ τυροπῶλαι· τοῦτο δ' εἰς ἕν ἐστι συγκεκυφός Ar.*Eq.*854, cf. Pl.*Lg.*711a; or of an abstract fact, οὐκ Ἰοφῶν ζῇ;—τοῦτο γάρ τοι καὶ μόνον ἔτ' ἐστὶ λοιπὸν ἀγαθόν Ar.*Ra.*73. **III.** with Prons., **1.** personal, οὗτος σύ, in local sense, v. infr. C. I. 5. **2.** interrog., τί τοῦτ' ἔλεξας; what is *this that*..? S.*Ph.*1173 (lyr.), cf. *Ant.*7; ποίοισι τούτοις; for ποῖά ἐστι ταῦτα οἷς [ἔχεις ἐλπίδα]; Id.*OC*388, cf. *Ant.*1049; Νέστορ' ἔρειο ὅν τινα τοῦτον ἄγει whom he brings *here*, Il.11.612. **3.** with οἷος, Od.20.377, Pl.*Phd.*61c. **4.** possess., πατὴρ σὸς οὗτος *this* father of thine, S.*El.*530, cf. X.*An.*7.3.30. **5.** demonstr., οὗτος ἐκεῖνος, τὸν σὺ ζητέεις, where ἐκεῖνος is the Predicate, Hdt.1.32; τοῦτ' ἔστ' ἐκεῖνο E.*Hel.*622, cf. *Or.*804; αὐτὸ τοῦτο, v. αὐτός I.7; τοῦτον τὸν αὐτὸν ἄνδρα *this* same man, S.*Ph.*128. **b.** exceptionally, Διφίλου οὗτος ὅδ' ἐστὶ τύπος *IG*12(5).300 (Paros). **6.** ἄλλος τις οὗτος ἀνέστη another man *here*, Od.20.380. **IV.** with Numerals, τέθνηκε ταῦτα τρία ἔτη *these* three years, Lys.7.10 codd.; [στρατείαν] ἑνδέκατον μῆνα τουτονὶ ποιεῖται for *these* eleven months, D.8.2, cf. 3.4; τριακοστὴν ταύτην ἡμέραν Men.*Epit.*27; ταύτας τριάκοντα μνᾶς D.27.23, cf. Pl.*Grg.* 463b, etc.

C. Signification and special Idioms: **I.** *this*, to designate *the nearer*, opp. ἐκεῖνος, *that, the more remote*, ταῦτα, like τὰ ἐνταῦθα, *things round and about us, earthly things*, Pl.*Phd.*75e (v.l.); cf. ὅδε init.: but οὗτος sts. indicates that which is not really nearest, but most important, δεῖ..τὸ βέλτιστον ἀεί, μὴ τὸ ῥᾷστον λέγειν· ἐπὶ ἐκεῖνο μὲν γὰρ ἡ φύσις αὐτὴ βαδιεῖται, ἐπὶ τοῦτο δὲ κτλ. D.8.72, cf. 51.3 and 18. **2.** when, of two things, one precedes and the other follows, ὅδε prop. refers to what follows, οὗτος to what precedes, οὐκ ἔστι σοι ταῦτ', ἀλλά σοι τάδ' ἔστι S.*OC*787, cf. ὅδε III. 2: freq., however, where there are not two things, οὗτος refers to what follows, Il. 13.377, Od.2.306, etc.; οὔκουν..τοῦτο γιγνώσκεις, ὅτι..; A.*Pr.*379, etc. **3.** οὗτος is used emphat., generally in contempt, while ἐκεῖνος denotes praise, ὁ πάντ' ἄναλκις οὗτος, i.e. Aegisthus, S.*El.*301; τούτους τοὺς συκοφάντας Pl.*Cri.*45a; so D. *de Coron.* uses οὗτος of Aeschines, ἐκεῖνος of Philip; but οὗτος is used of Philip, D.2.15, 4.3. **b.** of what is familiar, τούτους τοὺς πολυτελεῖς χιτῶνας, of the Persians, X.*An.*1.5.8; οἱ τὰς τελετὰς..οὗτοι καταστήσαντες Pl.*Phd.*69c, cf. *Men.*80a; τὸ θυλακῶδες τοῦτο the *familiar* bag-like thing, Thphr.*HP*3.7.3, cf. 3.18.11, 4.7.1; οἱ τὰς κόρας ταύτας ὠνούμενοι τοῖς παισίν D.Chr.31.153. **4.** in Att. law-language, οὗτος is commonly applied to *the opponent*, whether plaintiff (as in Aeschin. 2.130) or defendant (as in Id.1.1); so, in the political speeches of D., οὗτοι are *the opposite party*, 4.1, 8.7, etc.; but in the forensic speeches, οὗτοι freq. means *the judges, the court*, 21.134, 36.47. **5.** much like an Adv., in local sense (cf. ὅδε init.), τίς δ' οὗτος κατὰ νῆας.. ἔρχεαι; who art thou *here* that comest..? Il.10.82; freq. in Att., τίς οὑτοσί; who's this *here?* Ar.*Ach.*1048; πολλὰ ὁρῶ ταῦτα πρόβατα I see many sheep *here*, X.*An.*3.5.9 (as v.l.): with Pron. of 2 pers., οὗτος σύ *ho* you! you *there!* S.*OT*532, 1121, E.*Hec.*1280, etc.: and then οὗτος alone like a voc., οὗτος, τί ποιεῖς; A.*Supp.*911, cf. S.*Aj.*71, E.*Alc.* 773, Ar.*Eq.*240, *Nu.*220, al.: with a pr. n., ὦ οὗτος, Αἴας S.*Aj.*89; ὦ οὗτος οὗτος, Οἰδίπους Id.*OC*1627, cf. Ar.*V.*1364: with voc., βέντισθ' οὗτος Theoc.5.76:—the fem. is rarer, αὕτη E.*Med.*922; αὕτη σύ Ar.*Th.* 610.—This phrase mostly implies anger, impatience, or scorn. **II.** simply as antec. to ὅς, Od.2.40, S.*OT*1180, etc.: freq. following relat. clause, ἅ γ' ἔλαβες,.. μεθεῖναι ταῦτα Id.*Ph.*1247, cf. 1319, *Ant.* 183, 203, Pl.*Grg.*469c. **III.** = τοιοῦτος, οὗτος ἐγὼ ταχυτᾶτι Pi.*O.* 4.26; σὺ τοίνυν οὗτος εὑρέθης D.18.282, cf. 173. **IV.** after a parenthesis, the Subject, though already named, is freq. emphat. repeated by οὗτος, οὐδὲ γὰρ οὐδὲ Ἀριστέης.., οὐδὲ οὗτος προσωτέρω..ἔφησε ἀπικέσθαι Hdt.4.16, cf. 81 (s.v.l.), 1.146, Pl.*Phd.*107d, etc. **V.** καὶ οὗτος is added to heighten the force of a previous word, ξυνεστῶτες..ναυτικῷ ἀγῶνι, καὶ τούτῳ πρὸς Ἀθηναίους Th.4.55, cf. Hdt.1.147, 6.11, etc.; so οὐδὲ τούτου Aeschin.2.100; v. infr. VIII. 2. **VI.** repeated, where for the second we should merely say *he* or *it*, τοῖσιν τούτου τοῦτον μέλεσιν..κελαδοῦντες Ar.*Ra.*1526, cf. Pl.*La.*200d. **VII.** ταῦτα is used in some special phrases, **1.** ταῦτ', ὦ δέσποτα *yes* Sir (i.e. ἔστι ταῦτα, ταῦτα δράσω, etc.), Ar.*V.*142, *Pax*275, cf. *Eq.*111; so ταῦτα δή Id.*Ach.*815; ταῦτά νυν Id.*V.*1008; so also ἦν ταῦτα *even so, true*, E.*Ph.*417. **2.** ταῦτα μὲν δὴ ὑπάρξει *so* it shall be, Pl.*Phd.*78a. **3.** καὶ ταῦτα μὲν δὴ ταῦτα so much for *that*, freq. in Att., as Pl.*Smp.* 220c. **4.** ταῦτα at end of a formula in epitaphs, etc., prob. short for ταῦτα οὕτως ἔχει or ὁ βίος ταῦτά ἐστιν, e.g. οὐδὶς (= -εὶς) ἀθάνατος· ταῦτα *IG*14.420; Προκόπι ταῦτα ib.1824; χαίρεται (= -τε) ταῦτα ib.1479, etc.: similarly perh. in a letter, ἂμ μὴ πέμψῃς, οὐ μὴ φάγω, οὐ μὴ πείνω. ταῦτα *POxy.*119.15 (ii/iii A.D.). **VIII.** Adverbial usages: **1.** ταῦτα abs., *therefore, that is why*.., Il.11.694; ταῦτ' ἄρα Ar.*Ach.*90, *Nu.* 319, 335, 394, al., X.*Smp.*4.55; ταῦτα δή A.*Pers.*159, Pl.*Smp.*174a; ταῦτ' οὖν S.*Tr.*550, Ar.*V.*1358, etc.; αὐτὰ ταῦτα ἥκω, ἵνα.. Pl.*Prt.* 310e: τοῦτο is rare in this sense, τοῦτ' ἀφικόμην, ὅπως..εὖ πράξαιμί τι S. *OT*1005; αὐτὸ γὰρ τοῦτο *just because of this*, Pl.*Smp.*204a. **b.** πρὸς ταῦτα *so then, therefore*, prop. used in indignant defiance, A.*Pr.*992, 1043, S.*Aj.*971, 1115, 1313, *OT*426, *OC*455, etc. **2.** καὶ ταῦτα, adding a circumstance heightening the force of what has been said, *and that*, ἄνδρα γενναῖον θανεῖν, καὶ ταῦτα πρὸς γυναικός A.*Eu.*627: but mostly with a part., ὅς γ' ἐξέλυσας ἄστυ.., καὶ ταῦθ' ὑφ' ἡμῶν οὐδὲν ἐξειδὼς πλέον S.*OT*37, cf. Ar.*Ra.*704, Pl.*Phdr.*241e, etc.; or with a part. omitted, ἥτις..τὴν τεκοῦσαν ὕβρισεν, καὶ ταῦτα τηλικοῦτος (sc. οὖσα) S.*El.*614; so καὶ ταῦτα μέντοι Pl.*Erx.*400b. **b.** καὶ ταῦτα *anyhow, no matter what happens* (or *happened*), ἐπεχείρησας, οὐδὲν ὢν καὶ ταῦτα you tried, but were no good *anyhow*, i.e. try as you might, Id.*R.* 341c, cf. Diod.Com.3.5. **3.** τοῦτο μέν.., τοῦτο δέ.. *on the one hand.., on the other.., partly.., partly*.., very freq. in Hdt., as 1.161, al.; τοῦτο μέν is sts. answered by δέ only, 4.76, S.*Aj.*670, *OC*440; by δὲ αὖ, Hdt.7.176; by ἔπειτα δέ, S.*Ant.*61; by ἀλλά, D.22.13; by εἶτα, S.*Ph.*1345; by τοῦτ' αὖθις, Id.*Ant.*165. **4.** dat. fem. ταύτῃ, **a.** *on this spot, here*, ταύτῃ μὲν.., τῇδε δ' αὖ.. Id.*Ph.* 1331; ἀλλ' ἐὰν ταύτῃ γε νικᾷ, ταυτῃὶ πεπλήξεται Ar.*Eq.*271, cf. *Th.* 1221. **b.** *in this point, herein*, μηδὲν ταύτῃ γε κομήσῃς Id.*Pl.*572, cf. X.*Hier.*7.12, etc. **c.** *in this way, thus*, A.*Pr.*191, S.*OC*1300, etc.; οὐ..ταῦτ' ἐστί πω ταύτῃ Ar.*Eq.*843; ἀλλ' οὔτι ταύτῃ ταῦτα E. *Med.*365, cf. A.*Pr.*511: antec. to ὥσπερ, Pl.*R.*330c; to ὅπῃ, X.*Cyr.* 8.3.2; οὕτω τε καὶ ταύτῃ γίγνοιτο Pl.*Lg.*681d; καὶ οὕτω καὶ ταύτῃ ἂν ἔχοι ib.714d; ταύτῃ καλεῖσθαι, etc., like οὕτω κ., Sch.Pl.*Smp.* 215b. **5.** ἐκ τούτου or τούτων *thereupon*, X.*HG*2.1.6, *Oec.*2.1; *therefore*, Id.*An.*3.3.5. **6.** ἐν τούτῳ *in that case*, Pl.*R.*440c. **b.** *in the meantime*, Hdt.1.126, Th.3.72, X.*Mem.*2.1.27. **7.** πρὸς τούτοις (-οισι) *besides*, Hdt.2.51, Pl.*Prt.*326a, X.*Mem.*2.4.4, Ar.*Pl.*540.

⊛ **οὕτως**, and before a consonant **οὕτω** (but sts. οὕτως before a consonant, Ar.*Av.*63, Pl.*Grg.*522c, D.23.34, *PPetr.*2 p.20 (iii B.C.), *PTeb.* 124.18 (ii B.C.), etc., and οὕτω before a vowel is found in Ep. Poets and Ion. Prose, v. fin.); in Att. strengthd. οὑτωσί Pl.*Grg.*503d, etc.; οὑτωσίν Hdn.Gr.1.509.2; v. οὗτος A:—Adv. of οὗτος, *in this way* or *manner, so, thus*: οὕτως is antec. to ὡς, Il.4.178, Od.4.148, etc.; in Att. also οὕτως ὥσπερ S.*Tr.*475, etc.; ὥσπερ.., οὕτω καὶ.. X.*Cyr.*1. 4.21; ὡσαύτως, ὥσπερ.., οὕτω καὶ.. Pl.*Ion* 534a; also οὕτως, ὅπως.. S.*Tr.*330, X.*Cyr.*1.1.2; poet. also ὥστε.., οὕτω δὲ.. S.*Tr.*116 (lyr.): οὕτως is freq. left out after ὡς, ὡς ἔδοξεν αὐτοῖς, καὶ ἐποίουν ταῦτα Th. 8.1, cf. Theoc.7.45 sq.—In Prose, the relat. Pron. freq. follows instead of ὥστε, v. infr. III: when two modes are opposed, they are freq. expressed by οὕτω and ἐκείνως, τότε μὲν ἐκείνως, νῦν δ' οὕτω Isoc. 12.172; οὕτω ῥᾷον ἢ 'κείνως Pl.*R.*370a, etc.—Sts. οὕτω or -ως refers to what follows, *thus, as follows*, οὕτω χρὴ ποιεῖν· ἐὰν.. X.*An.*2.2.2; οὑτωσὶ δὲ λογίζεσθε D.18.244; οὕτω πως ὑπείληφα ib.269; οὑτωσί πως folld. by a quotation, Pl.*Ap.*28c; καὶ οὕτως even *so*, even *on this supposition*, Th.1.10; οὐδ' οὕτως Id.2.76, 6.89, Lys.1.14, v.l. in X.*An.*4.8.3: strengthd. οὕτω δή Il.2.158; οὕτω γὰρ δή τοι 15.201; οὕτω δή τι, v. infr. III; also οὕτω που *so* I ween, 2.116, Od.9.262, etc.; οὕτω πῃ Il.24.373; ὡς ὁ μὲν οὕτως ἐστὶ σόος *so in this way* is he saved, Od.19.300:—Phrases: **1.** οὕτω δὴ ἔσται *so* it shall be, ratifying what goes before, 11.348; ἔσσεται οὕτως 16.31, etc.: in Prose οὕτως alone in answers, *even so, just so*, X.*Oec.*1.9; so ἢ οὐχ οὕτως;—οὕτω μὲν οὖν Pl.*R.*551b, etc. **2.** emphat. with the imper., *just, without more ado*, ἔρρ' οὕτως Il.22.498, cf. 21.184, Od. 6.218, 17.447; but, οὕτω νῦν ἀπόπεμπε *as you say*, 5.146. **3.** in wishes or prayers, *so*, i.e. if you grant my prayer, οὕτως ἔρως σοι.. τελεσφόρος γένοιτο E.*Med.*714; οὕτω τί σοι δοίησαν αἱ Μοῦσαι..τοῦτον ..δεῖρον Herod.3.1; also in protestations, *so*, i.e. only if what I say is true, οὕτως ὀναίμην τῶν τέκνων, μισῶ τὸν ἄνδρ' (as in Engl., *so* help me God, *so* mote I thrive, etc.) Ar.*Th.*469, cf. Men.*Epit.*530, Herod.7.

25, Aristaenet.2.13; οὕτω..νομιζοίμην σοφός, ὡς.. Ar.*Nu*.520. 4. in colloquial phrase, beginning a story, οὕτω ποτ' ἦν μῦς καὶ γαλῆ *there* were once on a time.., Id.*V*.1182; οὕτως ἦν νεανίσκος Id.*Lys*.785; ἦν οὕτω δὴ παῖς Pl.*Phdr*.237b. 5. οὕτω with gen., τούτων μὲν οὕτω *so much* for this, A.*Ag*.950; οὕτω καὶ τῶν οἰκονομικῶν (v.l. τῷ -κῷ) *so* also of.., Arist.*Pol*.1253$^{b}$27; ὥσπερ Χαλκὶς..τῆς Εὐβοίας..κεῖται, οὕτω Χερρονήσου..ἡ Καρδιανῶν πόλις as Chalcis in respect of Euboea.., *so* Cardia in respect of the Chersonese, D.23.182; so οὕτως ἔχω τινός or περί τινος, v. ἔχω (A) B. II. 2; also for εἰς τοῦτο, οὕτω δὲ τάρβους..ἀφικόμην E.*Ph*.361 codd. (dub. l.). 6. ὁ οὕτω καλούμενος, ὀνομαζόμενος, the *so*-called.., τῶν Ῥιπαίων οὕτω καλουμένων Ael.*NA*11.1; τοῦ καὶ ὀνομασθέντος οὕτω ῥήτορος Hermog.*Id*.2.11; Ποταμὸς δῆμος οὕτω καλούμενος P., a deme of *that* name, Str.9.1.22. 7. οὕτω, or οὕτω δή, freq. introduces the apodosis after a protasis, ἐπειδὴ περιελήλυθε ὁ πόλεμος.., οὕτω δὴ Γέλωνος μνῆστις γέγονε Hdt.7.158, cf. 150, Th.1.131, 2.12, 19, etc.; esp. after parts., ἐν κλιβάνῳ πνίξαντες, οὕτω τρώγουσι, i.e. ἐπειδὰν πνίξωσιν, οὕτω.., Hdt.2.92, cf. 100; also οὕτω δή Id.7.174; τὰ ἄλλα καταστρεψάμενος, οὕτως..στρατεῦσαι ὕστερον Th.3.96; εἰς τὰ σκληρότατα ἀποβλέποντες, οὕτως ἂν μᾶλλον συννοήσαιμεν Pl.*Phlb*.44e, cf. *Grg*.457d, 507e, *Ap*.29b; so ἔπειτα οὕτως X.*An*.7.1.4: so also after the gen. abs., ὡς..τῶν ἡγεμόνων ὑμῖν μὴ μεμπτῶν γεγενημένων, οὕτω τὴν γνώμην ἔχετε Th.7.15, cf. X.*Cyr*.1.6.11, *An*.1.3.6, etc. II. sts. in a really inferential sense, as we say *so* for *therefore*, S.*Ant*.677; οὕτω δή Pl.*Phd*.61b, etc. III. *to such an extent, so, so much, so very, so excessively*, καλὸς οὕτω Il.3.169; πρυμνόθεν οὕτως *so* entirely, A.*Th*.1061 (anap.), cf. Th.2.47, X.*Cyr*.1.3.8; οὕτως τι Ar.*Av*.63: freq. folld. by ὡς or ὥστε, Hdt.1.32, X.*An*.7.4.3, etc.: sts. the relat. ὅς takes the place of ὥστε, κρήνη οὕτω δή τι ἐοῦσα πικρή, ἣ..κιρνᾷ (i.e. ὥστε κιρνᾶν) Hdt.4.52; οὐκ ἔστιν οὕτω μῶρος ὃς θανεῖν ἐρᾷ S.*Ant*.220; τίς δ' οὕτως ἄνους ὃς..; Ar.*Ach*.736, cf. D.8.44; also δυσχείμερος αὕτη ἡ..χώρη οὕτω δή τί ἐστι, ἔνθα (i.e. ὥστε ἐνταῦθα) τοὺς μὲν ὀκτὼ τῶν μηνῶν ἀφόρητος οἷος γίνεται κρυμός Hdt.4.28: sts. no connecting Particle is used, αἱ [κεφαλαὶ] οὕτω δή τι ἰσχυραί, μόγις ἂν λίθῳ παίσας διαρρήξειας *so excessively* hard, you could scarcely break them, Id.3.12. 2. with Sup. Adj., τῆς οὕτω μεγίστης ἐγχειρήσεως ἀποσφαλείς Zos.5.19. IV. sts., like αὕτως, with a diminishing power, *so, merely so, simply*, in Hom. always μὰψ οὕτω, Il.2.120 (for without μάψ he always uses αὕτως), cf. Hdt.1.5; μὴ διὰ μέθης..ἀλλ' οὕτω πίνοντας πρὸς ἡδονήν Pl.*Smp*.176e, cf. *Grg*.494e, *Phdr*.235c, *Tht*.147c, 158b, Thphr.*Od*.67, etc.; ἐν συνουσίᾳ καὶ διατριβῇ οὕτως ἰδίᾳ D.21.71, cf. 1.20; τοὺς ὀδόντας ... οὕτως ἂν τοῖς δακτύλοις αὐτοῖς..παρατρίβειν, i.e. without a dentifrice, Diocl.*Fr*.141; so οὕτω γε ἀπὸ στόματος Pl.*Tht*.142d; οὕτω ποτέ Id.*Ly*.216c; οὕτω πως D.1.20; also, *off-hand, at once*, Pl.*Grg*.464b, etc.; ἁπλῶς οὕτως Id.*Lg*.633c; ἀλλ' οὕτως ἄπει; *so, without a word more..?* S.*Ph*.1067; ἦ στραφεὶς οὕτως ἴω; Id.*Ant*.315, cf. E.*Heracl*.374 (lyr.); ἐφεξῆς οὑτωσὶ καθεζόμενος D.21.119; ὡς οὕτω γ' ἀκοῦσαι *at first* hearing, Pl.*Euthphr*.3b; so ὥς γε οὑτωσὶ ἀκοῦσαι Id.*Ly*.216a; ἀκούειν μὲν οὕτως ἁπλῶς Id.*Phlb*.12c; οὐ..οὕτως ἄπει, = *impune*, E.*Alc*.680. V. as Hebraism, οὕτως, = *such a person* (*thing*), οὕτως οὐδέποτε εἴδαμεν *Ev.Marc*.2.12, cf. Lxx *Ge*.29.26, *Ev.Matt*.9.33, *Ev.Luc*.2.48, al.

B. Position of οὕτω or οὕτως, mostly *before* the word which it limits, but in Poets sts. *after*, καλὸς οὕτω Il.3.169; οὐδέ τι λίην οὕτω νώνυμός ἐστιν Od.13.239; ἔρημος οὕτω, ἄγαν οὕτω, S.*Ph*.487, 598: rarely at the end of a clause, Od.18.255, Hdt.7.170 (dub. l.): sts. separated from the word which it limits, οὕτως ἔχει τι δεινόν; S.*Ph*.104; οὕτως ἐπὶ δεινὰς ἁρπαγάς Pl.*R*.391d, cf. Th.2.11; οὕτω δ' ἦν ὁ Φίλιππος ἐν φόβῳ.., ὥστε.. D.18.33.

C. Prosody. The last syll. of οὕτω is short before a vowel in Il.3.169, Od.3.315. The ι of οὑτωσί is always long, v. οὗτος init.

**οὑτωτρόπως**, Adv. *thus*, Pall. *in Hp*.2.98 D.

**οὐφέλλαν**· γῆν τὴν εἰς τὰ ἱμάτια (*fuller's earth*), Hsch.

**οὐφίδρωμα**· τοῦ σάγματος ἡ πρὸς τῇ πλευρᾷ διφθέρα, Hsch.

**οὖφις**, Att. crasis for ὁ ὄφις, A.*Ch*.544.

**οὐχ ὅπως, οὐχ ὅτι**, v. ὅπως A. II. 2, ὅτι A. V. **οὐχί**, Att., v. οὐ fin.

**οὑχῖνος**, Att. crasis for ὁ ἐχῖνος, Ar.*V*.1437.

**ὄφ**, exclamation of pain or fear accompanied by a sudden drawing in of breath, Eust.900.27. **ὄφατα**· δεσμοὶ ἀρότρων (Acarnan.), Hsch. **ὀφείδιον, τό**, v. ὀφίδιον.

**ὀφείλ-εια**, ἡ, *indebtedness*, *POxy*.1495.15 (iv A.D., s.v.l.). **-έσιον**, τό, *small debt*, Eust.1751.12. ⊛**-έτης**, ου, ὁ, *debtor*, τινι Pl.*Lg*.736d, etc.; ὀ. εἰμί c. inf., I am *under bond* to.., S.*Aj*.590, cf. *Ep.Rom*.8.12:—fem. **-έτις**, ιδος, E.*Rh*.965. **-έω**, = ὀφείλω, in Pass., *to be due*, τιμωρίη dub. l. in Eus.Mynd.31. II. in Act., *to be bound* to.., c. inf., dub. l. in Id.48. **-ή**, ἡ, *debt*, X.*Vect*.(ap.*EM*644.3), *Ostr.Bodl*.i 311 (iii B.C.), *BGU*1158.18 (i B.C.), 112.11 (i A.D.), al., *Ev.Matt*.18.32. 2. *one's due*, *Ep.Rom*.13.7, 1*Ep.Cor*.7.3. **-ημα**, ατος, τό, *that which is owed, debt*, Th.2.40, etc.; ἀποτίνειν ὀ. Pl.*Lg*.717b; ἀποδοτέον Arist.*EN*1165$^{a}$3: also in Inscrr., *IG*1$^{2}$.57.14, *SIG*306.38 (Tegea, iv B.C.), 1108.11 (Callatis, iii/ii B.C.), etc.; and Pap., *PHib*.1.42.10 (iii B.C.), etc.; cf. ὀφήλωμα. **-ησις**, εως, ἡ, = foreg., *PMagd*.17.12 (iii B.C.). **-όντως**, Adv. part. of ὀφείλω, *as of debt, deservedly*, Hsch. s.v. προσηκόντως. ⊛ **-ω**, impf. ὤφειλον; Ep. **ὀφέλλω** (also Aeol., *IG*12(2).67.7 (Mytil.), and Arc., ib.5(2).343.27 (Orchom. Arc., iv B.C.)), impf. ὤφελλον or ὄφελλον, v. infr. II. 2, 3 (the Att. or Ion. ὀφείλετ', ὄφειλον in Il.11.686, 688, 698, Hes.*Op*.174 is prob. due to the Copyists): fut. ὀφειλήσω X.*Cyr*.7.2.28, D.30.7, also ὀφειλέσω *TAM*2.431, al.: aor. 1 ὠφείλησα Ar.*Av*.115, Th.8.5 (ἐπ-): pf. ὠφείληκα: plpf. -ήκειν D.45.33: aor. 2 ὤφελον (v. infr. II. 2, 3):—**Pass.**, aor. part. ὀφειληθείς Th.3.63. (Cret. **ὀφήλω** *GDI*5015.21, written **ὀπέλο** *Leg.Gort*.10.20, al., Arc. **ὀφέλλω** (v. supr.) and **ὀφήλω** *SIG*306.40 (Tegea, iv B.C.): in early Att. Inscrr. written both ὀφελ- *IG*1$^{2}$.91.8, al., and ὀφειλ- ib.109.9, al.):—*owe, have to pay* or *account for*, τὸ καὶ μοιχάγρι' ὀφέλλει Od.8.332; ὅτι μοι..ζωάγρι' ὀφέλλεις ib.462; χρεῖος, τό ῥά οἱ πᾶς δῆμος ὄφελλεν 21.17; πολέσιν γὰρ Ἐπειοὶ χρεῖος ὄφειλον Il.11.688; ζημίην ὀ. τῷ θεῷ Hdt.3.52, etc.: metaph., μητέρα μοι ζώουσαν ὀφέλλετε Call.*Fr*.126; τί ὀφείλω; what *do I owe?* Ar.*Nu*.21; ὀ. ἀργύριον, χρέα, Id.*Av*.115, *Nu*.117; ὀ. ἢ θεῷ θυσίας ἢ ἀνθρώπῳ χρήματα Pl.*R*.331b; ὀ. τινὶ δρᾶν τι ib.332a: c. dat. only, ὀ. τινί *to be debtor* to another, Ar.*Nu*.1135, *Lys*.581, etc.; τρίτον δὲ χαίρειν, εἶτ' ὀ. μηδενί Philem.163: abs., *to be in debt*, Ar.*Nu*.485, etc.; οἱ ὀφείλοντες *debtors*, Arist.*EN*1167$^{b}$21, Plu.2.832a:—Pass., *to be due*, ἔνθα χρεῖός μοι ὀφέλλεται (v.l. ὀφείλεται) Od.3.367; χρεῖος ὀφείλετο Il.11.686, 698; ἣν..ὀφείληταί τί μοι Ar.*Nu*.484; μισθὸς τοῖς στρατιώταις ὠφείλετο X.*An*.1.2.11, etc.; τὸ ὀφειλόμενον *a debt*, ib.7.7.34; -όμενα ἀποδιδόντες Hdt.5.99, cf. Simon. ap.Pl.*R*.331e. 2. metaph., ὀ. μέλος τινί Pi.*O*.10(11).3; πολλὰ δώμασιν καλά E.*HF*287; ὀ. χάριν, v. χάρις I. 2; Ἀπόλλωνι χαριστήρια X.*Cyr*.7.2.28; τὴν ψυχὴν πᾶσιν Ael.*VH*10.5:—Pass., ὀφείλεταί τινι ἐκ θεῶν κλέος A.*Fr*.315; ὀ. τινὶ εὐεργεσία Th.1.137; ἀντὶ χαρίτων ἔχθραι ὀ. X.*Cyr*.4.5.32; τοῖς μὲν ἐχθροῖς βλάβην ὀ., τοῖς δὲ φίλοις ὠφελίαν Pl.*R*.335e, cf. 332b; τοὐφειλόμενον πράσσουσα Δίκη *what is due*, A.*Ch*.310. 3. as a legal term, *to be bound to render*, εὐθύνας ὤφειλον And.1.73 codd. (f.l. for ὦφλον): hence, like ὀφλισκάνω, *incur* a penalty, ζημίαν Lys.9.10; διπλῆν τὴν βλάβην Id.1.32, cf. E.*Andr*.360; τὴν τοιαύτην δίκην Pl.*Lg*.909a, cf. 774b, d, 844e, D.21.77; ἁμαρτίαν ὀ. Μηνὶ Τυράννῳ *IG*3.74.15 (ii/iii A.D.). 4. in Pass., of persons, *to be due* or *liable to*, θανάτῳ πάντες ὀφειλόμεθα Simon.122, cf. Lxx *Wi*.12.20, *IG*3.1381; but τοιαύταις χερσὶν ὀφειλόμεθα *our help is due*, *AP*9.283 (Crin.). II. c. inf., *to be bound, to be obliged* to do, ὀφέλλετε ταῦτα πένεσθαι *ye are bound, ye ought to..*, Il.19.200, cf. Hdt.1.41, 42, al., E.*Alc*.682, 712, etc.; and of things, *ought* to be, ὁ λόγος οὐκ ἀκριβῶς ὀ. λέγεσθαι Arist.*EN*1104$^{a}$2:—Pass., δράσαντι γάρ τοι καὶ παθεῖν ὀφείλεται A.*Fr*.456; σοὶ τοῦτ' ὀφείλεται παθεῖν *it is* thy *destiny* to.., S.*Ph*.1421, cf. *El*.1173; ὡς πᾶσιν ἡμῖν κατθανεῖν ὀφείλεται E.*Alc*.419, cf. 782, *Or*.1245, Lys.25.11; v. supr. I. 4. 2. in this signf. Ep. impf. ὤφελλον or ὄφελλον and aor. ὤφελον or ὄφελον are used of that which one has not, but *ought to have*, done (*ought* being the pret. of *owe*), ὤφελεν ἀθανάτοισιν εὔχεσθαι Il.23.546; νῦν ὄφελεν πονέεσθαι λισσόμενος 10.117, cf. Od.4.472. 3. these tenses are also used, folld. by pres. or aor. inf., in wishes that something were or had been in present or past, ἀνδρὸς..ὤφελλον ἀμείνονος εἶναι ἄκοιτις I *ought to* be.., *would that* I were..! Il.6.350; τὴν ὄφελ' ἐν νήεσσι κατακτάμεν Ἄρτεμις *would that* Artemis had slain her!, Il.19.59, cf. Od.4.97; τιμήν πέρ μοι ὄφελλεν Ὀλύμπιος ἐγγυαλίξαι Il.1.353: freq. preceded by εἴθε (Ep. αἴθε), ὡς, ὡς δή, which express the wish still more strongly, αἴθ' ὄφελες ἄγονός τ' ἔμεναι ἄγαμός τ' ἀπολέσθαι *O that thou hadst!*, Il.3.40, cf. 1.415, etc.; αἴθ' ὤφελλες..σημαίνειν 14.84; αἴθ' ὤφελλ' ὁ ξεῖνος..ὀλέσθαι Od.18.401; αἴθ' ἅμα πάντες..ὠφέλετε..ἐπὶ νηυσὶ πεφάσθαι Il.24.254: with ὡς, ὡς ὄφελον..ἐλέσθαι *O that I had..!*, 11.380; θανέειν Od.14.274; ὡς πρὶν ὤφελλον ὀλέσθαι Il.24.764, cf. Od.14.68; ὡς ὤφελες αὐτόθ' ὀλέσθαι Il.3.428; ὡς..ὤφελες Od.2.184; ὡς ὄφελεν.. Il.3.173, etc.: strengthd., ὡς δὴ ἔγωγ' ὄφελον.. Od.1.217: also with neg., μὴ ὄφελες λίσσεσθαι.. *would thou hadst never..!*, Il.9.698; ἢ μὴ ὤφελλε γενέσθαι 17.686; τὼ μὴ γείνασθαι ὄφελλον Od.8.312; ὡς μὴ ὤφελλε τεκέσθαι Il.22.481; ὡς δὴ μὴ ὄφελον νικᾶν Od.11.548.—So in Trag. and Att., ὤφελον.. S.*OT*1157; ὤφελες.. Ar.*Th*.865; ὤφελε.. A.*Pr*.48, X.*An*.2.1.4, etc.: also, as in Ep., εἴθ' ὤφελες.. S.*El*.1021; εἴθ' ὤφελ'.. Ar.*Nu*.41, etc.; εἰ γὰρ ὤφελον.. Id.*Ec*.380, Pl.*R*.432c, *Cri*.44d; ὡς ὤφελες.. Ar.*Ra*.955: with neg., μήποτ' ὤφελον S.*Ph*.969, E.*Alc*.880 (anap.), D.18.288; ὡς μήποτ' ὤφελον.. E.*Ion*286; ὡς μηδὲ νῦν ὤφελον D.21.78: without augm. in Hdt., εἶδον..τὸ μὴ ἰδεῖν ὄφελον (v.l. ὤ-) 1.111, cf. 3.65: sts. in Trag. (lyr. and anap.), εἴθ' ὄφελε.. A.*Pers*.915; ὄφελε.. S.*Aj*.1192; μήποτ' ὄφελον.. E.*Med*.1413. (In this signf. ὤφειλον is used in late Ep., ὡς μὴ ὤφειλες ἱκέσθαι Q.S.5.194, but ὤφελλον shd. be read in Hes.*Op*.174 and ὤφελε in E.*IA*1291.) b. with ind., ὤφελε μηδ' ἐγένοντο θοαὶ νέες Call.*Epigr*.19.1, cf. Q.S.10.378, etc. c. ὄφελον (Adv. acc. to A.D.*Adv*.142.9, *EM*643.48) in this signf.: c. acc. et inf., ὤμοι ἐγών, ὄφελόν με..ὀλέσθαι Orph.*A*.1159: even with 2 pers. of Verb, ὄφελον ἐβασιλεύσατε 1*Ep.Cor*.4.8, cf. 2*Ep.Cor*.11.1, *Ep.Gal*.5.12, *Apoc*.3.15, Lxx *Jb*.14.13, Ath.4.156a; ὄφελον δυνήσῃ Luc.*Sol*.1 (as a solecism): with 3 pers., Arr.*Epict*.2.18.15, D.Chr.38.47: with 1 pers. pl., ὄφελον ἀπεθάνομεν Lxx *Ex*.16.3; ὤφελον (sic) εἰ ἐδυνάμεθα πέτασθαι *PGiss*.17.10 (ii A.D.): c. inf., ὄφελομ μὲν ἡ θεὸς..στερῆσαι.. *OGI*315.16 (Pessinus, ii B.C.). III. impers. ὀφείλει, *it behoves*, c. acc. et inf., Pi.*N*.2.6; ὄφελλέ με μήτε..εἰσοράαν κτλ. A.R.3.678: so pers. in part., abs., αἱ ὀφείλουσαι ἱερουργίαι τῶν θεῶν the *due* services of the gods, *PTeb*.294.24 (ii A.D.); κατὰ τὸν ὀφείλοντα καιρόν Sor.1.79. (ὦφλον, ὤφληκα, aor. and pf. of ὀφλισκάνω, were prob. orig. aor. and pf. of ὀφείλω: ὄφελον in signf. II. 3c may be orig. neut. part. of ὤφελε (signf. III) with omission of ἐστί.)

**ὀφελής**, ές, *advantageous*, *POxy*.237 viii 15 (ii A.D.).

**ὀφέλλιμος**, ον, *profitable, beneficial*, Max.135.

**ὀφέλλιον**, = Lat. *ofella*, *Gloss*.

**ὀφέλλω** (A), Ep., Aeol., and Arc. for ὀφείλω (q.v. sub init.).

⊛ **ὀφέλλω** (B), Aeol. aor. ind. 3 sg. ὤφελλε Od.16.174, ὄφελλε(ν) Il.2.420, Theoc.25.120 (unless these are impf.); aor. subj. 3 pl. ὀφέλλωσιν Il.1.510; aor. opt. ὀφέλλειεν 16.651, Od.2.334:—old Ep. Verb, *increase, enlarge, strengthen,* στόνον Il.4.445; πόνον 16.651, Od.2.334; ἀνδρὸς ἐρωήν Il.3.62; δέμας δ' ὤφελλε καὶ ἥβην Od.16.174; ἐς ἀνέμου.. κύματ' ὀφέλλει the force of the wind *raises high* the waves, Il.15.383; μῦθον ὀ. *multiply* words, 16.631; ὕβριν ὀ. *add to* insult, Hes.*Op.*213; πόλεμον καὶ δῆριν ὀ. ib.14, cf. 33; ὄφρ' ἂν 'Αχαιοὶ υἱὸν ἐμὸν τίσωσιν, ὀφέλλωσίν τέ ἑ τιμῇ *advance* him in honour, Il.1.510; οἶκον ὀ. *advance* it, *make* it *thrive,* Od.15.21, Hes.*Op.*495 (hence οἰκωφελίη); πεδίον σὺν θεῶν τιμαῖς ὀ. Pi.*P.*4.260:—Pass., οἶκος ὀφέλλετο it *waxed great, prospered,* Od.14.233; ὀφέλλετο γὰρ μένος ἠΰ ἵππου Il.23.524; λήϊον.. ὀφελλόμενον Διὸς ὄμβρῳ Theoc.17.78; τὰ τῶν θύραθεν.. ὀφέλλεται A.*Th.*193; ἀραγμὸς ἐν πύλαις ὀφέλλεται *increases, waxes louder,* ib.249. (Dialectal word acc. to Pl.*Cra.*417c.)

**ὀφέλλω** (C), *sweep,* τὴν στέγην Hippon.51.

**ὄφελμα** (A), ατος, τό, (ὀφέλλω B) *increase, advantage,* S.*Fr.*1079.

**ὄφελμα** (B), ατος, τό, (ὀφέλλω C) *broom,* Hippon.51, Eust.1887.34, Hsch. (pl.).

**ὀφελμός,** ὁ, = ὄφελμα (A), Keil-Premerstein *Erster Bericht* p.9 (pl.).

⊛ **ὄφελος,** τό, (ὀφέλλω B) only in nom. and acc. sg., *furtherance, advantage, help,* αἴ κ' ὄφελός τι γενώμεθα in case we can be of any *use,* Il.13.236; ὅς τοι πολλ' ὄ. γένετο who was a *help* to thee in many matters, 17.152; οὐδὲν σοί γ' ὄ. not as any *good* to thee, 22.513; ὄ. τί μοι ἔσσῃ h.*Merc.*34; τί δ' ἔστ' ὄ. δειλὸς ἀνήρ; Thgn.102; λέγεις 'Ατρείδαις ὄ. ἢ 'π' ἐμοὶ τόδε; S.*Ph.*1384; τί δῆτ' ἂν εἴης ὄ. ἡμῖν; what *good* could you be to us? Ar.*Pl.*1152, cf. Pl.*R.*505a, etc.; τὸ μέγα ὄ. τῆς πόλεως, Lat. *columen rerum,* ironical in Aeschin.2.24 (quoted from D.): c. inf., τί γὰρ ὄ. σώματί γε κάμνοντι.. σιτία πολλὰ διδόναι; Pl.*Grg.*504e, cf. 513e; τί ζῆν ὄ. ᾧ μή 'στι τὸ ζῆν εἰδέναι; Philem.104. 2. c. gen., φυγὰς ὄ. εἴ τί μοι A.*Supp.*737 (lyr.); τῶν ὄ. ἐστι οὐδέν Hdt.8.68.γ'; οἷσι.. οὐδὲν ὄ. ἐστιν οὔτε χρημάτων οὔτε τῶν ἄλλων οὐδενὸς ἄτερ τῆς ὑγιείης Hp.*Vict.*3.69; τί τῆς εὐμορφίας ὄ.; E.*Fr.*548; ἐλευθερίας οὐδὲν ὄ. And.4.17; ἐάν τι ἡμῶν ὡς νομοθετῶν ὄ. ᾖ Pl.*R.*530c; ἀνὴρ ὅτου τι καὶ σμικρὸν ὄ. ἐστιν Id.*Ap.*28b; γεωργοῦ ἀργοῦ οὐδὲν ὄφελος X.*Cyr.*1.6.18; μαγείρῳ μαχαίρας οὐδὲν ὄ. ἥτις μὴ τέμνει D.25.46; τί δ' ὄ. εὖ λαλοῦντος, ἂν κακῶς φρονῇ; Men.821. 3. ὅ τι πέρ ἐστ' ὄ. ἐν τῇ πόλει all *that is best,* all the best people, Ar.*Ec.*53, cf. Luc.*Herod.*8: c. gen., ὅ τι περ ὄ. τοῦ στρατεύματος *the serviceable part* (or perh. *the flower*) of the army, X.*HG*5.3.6, cf. Theoc.13.18; ὅ τι περ.. ἀπληστίας ὄ. the *flower* (*acme*) of gluttony, Luc.*Tim.*55. 4. c. gen. objecti, *help against* a thing, Nic.*Th.*518.

**ὀφελός,** ὁ, coined as etym. of ὀβελός, Arist.*Fr.*580.

**ὀφέλσιμος,** ον, poet. for ὠφέλιμος, Call.*Ap.*94, Orph.*A.*469, Opp.*H.*3.429.

**ὀφελ-τρεύω,** (ὀφέλλω C) *sweep,* Lyc.1165. **-τρον,** τό, *broom,* Hsch.

**ὀφεό-δηκτος,** ον, *bitten by a serpent,* Eust.330.12:—written **ὀφεώδηκτος,** Tz.*H.*8 No.170 tit. **-πρόσωπος,** ον, *serpent-faced, PMag. Leid.V.*5.19 (so Pap., cf. ὀφιο-).

⊛ **ὀφεώδης,** ες, *snake-like,* Pl.*R.*590b. Adv. **-δῶς** Eust. ad D.P.16.

**ὀφεωπλόκαμος,** ον, *with serpent hair,* Corn.*ND*10 (dub. l.), *PMag. Par.*1.2863 (written ὀφεο-), Eust.716.57.

**ὀφήλωμα,** ατος, τό, Cret. for ὀφείλημα, *GDI*4998 vi 14.

**ὀφθαλμ-ηδόν,** Adv. *like eyes, Gloss.* **-ία,** Ion. **-ίη,** ἡ, *ophthalmia,* a disease of the eyes accompanied by the discharge of humours, Hp.*Aër.*10, *Epid.*1.5 (both pl.), *Vid.Ac.*9 (sg.), Ar.*Pl.*115, X.*Mem.*3.8.3, Pl.*Phdr.*255d, *Alc.*2.139e, etc.; ὀ. ξηραί Hp.*Aër.* l.c.; **-ίαι** ὑγραί ib.3. II. metaph., [φθόνος] ὀ. τίς ἐστιν ψυχῆς Phld.*Vit.* p.21 J. **-ια** (proparox.), τά, *region of the eyes,* Gal.19.429. II. *imitation eyes,* as votive offerings, Roussel *Cultes Égyptiens* p.236 (Delos, ii B.C.). **-ίας,** ου, ὁ, *quick-sight,* a kind of eagle, ἀετὸς ὀ. Lyc.148. II. a kind of fish, Plaut.*Cap.*850. **-ίασις,** gloss on ὀπτιλίασις, Hsch.; = ὀφθαλμία, Plu.*Fr.inc.*149. **-ιάω,** *suffer from ophthalmia,* Hdt.7.229, Hp.*Aph.*6.17, Ar.*Ra.*192, *Fr.*129, X.*HG*2.1.3, Pl.*Alc.*2.139e, Antiph.252.1, etc. II. metaph., of the pain caused by envy *at the sight* of other men's prosperity, *look longingly, jealously,* or *covetously,* of lovers, Hyp.*Fr.*258; ἐπί τινι Anon.ap.Suid., cf. Plu.2.705d (so beautiful women are called ὀφθαλμῶν ἀλγηδόνες, Hdt.5.18); ὀ. περὶ τὸ κάλλος τῆς πόλεως, τῆς χώρας, *feel jealous* or *envious* about or at.., Plb.1.7.2, 2.17.3: c. acc., *look jealously at,* τὸ πλῆθος τῶν προσόδων Id.31.21.1. **-ίδιον** [μῐ], τό, Dim. of ὀφθαλμός, Ar.*Eq.*909. ⊛ **-ίζομαι,** Pass., *to be inoculated* or *engrafted,* of trees, Thphr.*CP*2.14.4 sq. codd.; cf. ἐνοφθαλμίζω. 2. *to be set* with precious stones, etc., Suid. II. *to be ill of ophthalmia,* Plu.2.633d. **-ικός,** ή, όν, *of* or *for the eyes,* φλεγμοναί Dsc.1.12; ὁ ὀ. *ophthalmic surgeon,* στόλου Βρεττανικοῦ Gal.12.786, cf. *UP*10.11, al. **-ιον,** τό, only in pl., v. ὀφθάλμια, τά. **-ῖτις,** ιδος, ἡ, epith. of Athena as *goddess of the Moon,* Paus.3.18.1.

**ὀφθαλμο-βολέω,** *cast the eyes upon* an object, Sch.Il.3.443. **-βόλος,** ον, *casting glances,* opp. ἐπιτευκτικός, Vett.Val.117.18. **-βόρος,** ον, *picking out eyes,* of the heron, Arist.*HA*617$^{a}$9. **-δουλεία,** ἡ, *eye-service, Ep.Eph.*6.6: in pl., *Ep.Col.*3.22. **-ειδής,** ές, *like eyes,* ἄνθη Dsc.3.139. Adv. **-δῶς** Ps.-Dsc.4.58. 2. *visible,* ἔργον Aristox.*Harm.* p.40 M. **-κλέπτης,** ου, ὁ, *stealer of the eye* (viz. Perseus), Tz. ad Lyc.843. **-πονέω,** *suffer from eye-strain,* Anon. *in Rh.*21.21. **-πόνος,** ὁ, *suffering from eye-strain,* Vett.Val.111.2.

⊛ **ὀφθαλμός,** ὁ, (ὄπωπ-α, ὀφ-θῆναι, v. ὄψ B) *eye,* used by Hom. and Hes. mostly in pl.; ὀφθαλμοὶ δ' ὡς εἰ κέρα ἕστασαν.. ἀτρέμας ἐν βλεφάροισι Od.19.211: sg., παίειν τινὰ ἐς τὸν ὀ. Hdt.9.22: the pl. continued most common, but the dual also occurs, as in Ar.*Nu.*362: pl. is used in many phrases, ἐλθέμεν ἐς ὀφθαλμούς τινος before one's *eyes,* Il.24.204; οὐδ' 'Αχιλῆος ὀφθαλμοὺς εἴσειμι ib.463; ὀφθαλμοῖσιν ἰδεῖν, ὁρᾶσθαι, etc., 10.275, Od.4.47, etc.; but ἐν ὀφθαλμοῖσιν ὁρᾶν, νοεῖν, to see before one's *eyes,* 8.459, Il.24.312; ἔχειν ἐν ὀ. to have before one's *eyes,* X.*An.*4.5.29; τὰ ἐν ὀ. what is before one's *eyes,* Pl.*Tht.*174c; τὸ ἐν τοῖς ὀ. δὴ γελοῖον what was ridiculous *to the eye,* Id.*R.*452d; ἐπίπροσθε τῶν ὀ. Id.*Smp.*213a; πρὸ τῶν ὀ. προφαίνεσθαι Aeschin.2.148; ἐπ' ὀφθαλμῶν Luc.*Tox.*20; γενέσθαι τινὶ ἐξ ὀφθαλμῶν to get out of any one's *sight,* Hdt.5.106; ἐξ ὀ. ἀποπέμψασθαι Id.1.120; ἐξ ὀ. ποιεῖν Alciphr.3.20; κατ' ὀφθαλμοὺς λέγειν τινί to tell one *to one's face,* opp. εἰς οὖς, Ar.*Ra.*626; τυράννου κατ' ὀ. κατηγορεῖν to accuse him to his *face,* X.*Hier.*1.14: sg. in the phrase πρὸς ὀφθαλμὸν ἐπιχεῖν, μίσγειν, *by eye, PHolm.*7.23, *PLeid.X.*62; *eyes* were painted on the bows of vessels, βλοσυροῖς κατὰ πρῷραν ὀφθαλμοῖς οἷον βλέπει Philostr.*Im.*1.19, cf. *IG*2².1607.24, Poll.1.86; whence the joke in Ar.*Ach.*97. 2. στέρησις ὀφθαλμῶν temporary loss of *sight,* Gal.17(1).400. II. in sg., *the eye* of a master or ruler, πάντα ἰδὼν Διὸς ὀ. Hes.*Op.*267; Δίκης ὀ. ὃς τὰ πάνθ' ὁρᾷ Men.*Mon.*179; δεσπότου ὀ. X.*Oec.*12.20; ἀκοίμητος ὀ., of God, Secund.*Sent.*3; so a king is called ὀ. οἴκων A.*Ch.*934 (so ὄμμα *Pers.*169); and in Persia ὀφθαλμὸς βασιλέως *the king's eye* was a confidential officer, through whom he beheld his kingdom and subjects, A.*Pers.*979 (lyr.), Hdt.1.114, Ar.*Ach.*92, X.*Cyr.*8.2.10 sq., Arist.*Pol.*1287$^{b}$29, Ph.1.642; cf. οὖς. III. *the eye of heaven,* ἑσπέρας ὀ., νυκτὸς ὀ., of the moon, Pi.*O.*3.20, A.*Th.*390; also οὐράνιος ὀ., of the sun, Secund.*Sent.*5. IV. *the dearest, best,* as the eye is the most precious part of the body, hence of men, ὀ. Σικελίας, στρατιᾶς, Pi.*O.*2.10, 6.16; also, *light, cheer, comfort,* μέγας ⟨γ'⟩ ὀ. οἱ πατρὸς τάφοι S.*OT*987, cf. E.*Andr.*406. V. *eye* or *bud* of a plant or tree, Alcm.43, Ion Eleg.1.6, Hp.*Nat.Puer.*26, X.*Oec.*19.10, Thphr.*HP*1.8.5, etc. VI. *a surgical bandage covering one or both eyes,* Hp.*Off.*7, Heliod.ap.Orib.48.29,30. VII. Archit., in dual, the *disks* forming the centres of the volutes of an Ionic capital, *IG*1².374.291.

**ὀφθαλμό-σοφος,** ον, *skilled in the eyes, an oculist,* Luc.*Lex.*4. **-στατήρ,** ῆρος, ὁ, a surgical instrument, *Hermes* 38.283. **-τεγκτος,** ον, *welling from the eyes,* πλημμυρίς E.*Alc.*184. **-φανής,** ές, *apparent to the eye, visible,* Arist.*Fr.*208; ἀργύριον ὀ. ἐναντίον.. μαρτύρων *PHib.*1.89.8 (iii B.C.); *obvious,* Str.2.1.18; ἔργον Aristox.*Harm.* p.41 M. Adv. **-νῶς** Lxx *Es.*8.13, Ph.1.614, S.E.*M.*9.39, Cleom.2.6.

**ὀφθαλμωρυχ-έω,** *gouge out the eyes,* Phld.*Hom.*p.59 O. **-ος** (parox.), ον, (ὀρύσσω) *tearing out the eyes,* A.*Eu.*186.

**ὀφι-ακός,** ή, όν, *of* or *belonging to serpents*: τὰ ὀφιακά (also τὸ **-κόν**), a work of Nicander, Sch.Nic.*Th.*377, cf. 557, 626. **-ασις,** εως, ἡ, *bald place on the head, of serpentine* or *winding form,* Gal.12.381, 10.1004. 2. *a form of leprosy in which the patient sheds his skin like a snake,* Ps.-Gal.14.757.

**ὀφιδεύειν·** σχολάζειν, διατρίβειν, ὀκνεῖν, Hsch.

**ὀφίδιον,** τό, Dim. of ὄφις, *IG*2².1533.16 (iv B.C.), 1472.17 (iv B.C.), 7.303.71 (Oropus, iii B.C.), 11(2).161 *B*50 (Delos, iii B.C.), Thphr.*HP*9.15.2, Apollon.*Mir.*12: written ὀφείδιον in codd. of Arist.*HA*607$^{a}$30, Str.15.1.45. II. a kind of fish, Plin.*HN*32.149; cf. ὄφις· ποιὸς ἰχθύς, Hsch. (Prob. ὀφῑδιον, contr. fr. ὀφῐ-ίδιον.)

**ὀφῑηβοσίη,** ἡ, *food of serpents,* of the Pythian laurel and the Nemean celery, *Inscr.Cos* 58.5.

**ὀφιῆτις,** ιδος, ἡ, v. ὀφίτης.

**ὀφῐο-βόρος,** ον, *serpent-eating,* Orac.ap.Plu.2.406e. **-γενής,** ές, *serpent-engendered*: οἱ 'Ο., a name of some Asiatic tribes, Crates Gramm. ap.Plin.*HN*7.13, Varro ap.Priscian.*Inst.*10.32, Str.13.1.14, Ael.*NA*12.39, etc. **-γένιον,** τό, = ἐλαφόβοσκον, Ps.-Dsc.3.69. **-δειρος,** ον, *serpent-throated,* Orac.ap.Arist.*Mir.*832$^{a}$21. **-δηκτος,** ον, *bitten by a serpent,* Lxx *Si.*12.13, Gal.14.300, *Hippiatr.*86, Sch.Il.2.722, etc. **-διώκτης,** ου, ὁ, *snake-chaser,* i.e. *-charmer, Gloss.* **-ειδής,** ές, *like a serpent,* Dsc.2.166. **-εις,** εσσα, εν, *abounding in serpents,* Antim.78 [who has ὀφ-, v. ὄφις]; cf. ὀφιοῦσσα. **-θριξ,** τρῐχος, ὁ, ἡ, *snake-haired,* Tz. ad Hes.*Sc.*235. **-κτόνη,** ἡ, *serpent-killer,* a kind of σκολόπενδρα, prob. for -κτένη in Dsc.*Ther.*5. **-κτόνος,** ὁ, *serpent-killer,* Eust.183.12: **-κτόνον,** τό, = ἐλαφόβοσκον, Ps.-Dsc.3.69. **-μάχος** [ᾰ], ον, *fighting with serpents,* γνώμη Ph.1.86: as Subst., a kind of *locust,* and *the ichneumon,* Hsch.:—in the former sense **-μάχης** is found in Lxx *Le.*11.22, Ph.1.39. **-νεος,** η, ον, (ὄφις) *of, belonging to,* or *like a serpent,* Opp.*C.*2.237, 3.436 [where ῐ]. **-νῖκοι,** οἱ, title of a book of comic stories by Κόγχλας, Gal.11.798. **-παίκτης,** ου, ὁ, *snake-charmer,* Lat. *praestigiator,* prob. cj. for ὀψιο-, *Gloss.* ⊛ **-πλόκαμος,** ον, *with snaky curls,* Orph.*H.*69.12. **-πους,** ποδος, ὁ, ἡ, *with serpents for legs,* Luc.*Philops.*22, Suid. **-πρόσωπος,** ον, *with serpent face,* dub. cj. in Sch.Veron.Verg.*A.*7.341. **-σκόροδον,** τό, *wild garlic, Allium scorodoprasum,* Gal.12.126:—also written **-σκορδον,** Dsc.2.152, *Gp.*12.30.7. 2. = κάππαρις, Dsc.2.173. **-σπαρτος,** poet. **-σπᾰτος,** ον, (σπείρω) *sown* or *engendered by serpents, EM*287.13. **-στάφυλον** [ᾰ], τό, = ἄμπελος λευκή, *white bryony,* Dsc.4.182; *ophiostaphyle* in Plin.*HN*13.127, cf. 23.21. 2. = κάππαρις, Dsc.2.173.

**ὀφίουρος,** ον, (οὐρά) *serpent-tailed,* of an Ethiopian bird, Hsch.

**ὀφιοῦσσα,** contr. for ὀφιόεσσα (sc. νῆσος), *Serpent-island,* a name of Cythnos, Arist.*Fr.*522; of Rhodes, Hsch.; of an island SW. of Majorca, Str.3.5.1; of various islands, St.Byz. s. v. Βέσβικος, al. II. a magical plant, Plin.*HN*24.163.

**ὀφιοῦχος,** ὁ, (ἔχω) the constellation *Ophiuchus, Serpentarius,* or *Anguitenens,* Arat.76, Eudox.ap.Hipparch.1.2.7, Ptol.*Tetr.*26, etc.:

—Adj. **ὀφῑούχεος**, ον, Arat.75,521. II. *a δαίμων who interferes with alchemists*, Olymp.Alch.p.86 B.

**ὀφῐο-φάγος** [ᾰ], ον, *serpent-eating*: οἱ Ὀ., name of a people, Plin. *HN*6.169. ❀ **-φόρος**, ον, *serpent-bearing*, *IG*14.872.

❀ **ὄφις**, ὁ, gen. ὄφεως, poet. also ὄφεος E.*Supp.*703, *Ba.*1026,1331; Dor. and Ion. ὄφιος Hes.*Th.*322, Hdt.9.81, Arat.82:—*serpent*, αἰόλος Il.12.208; γλαυκῶπα ποικιλόνωτον ὄφιν Pi.*P.*4.249, cf. A.*Ch.*544, S.*Ph.*1328, Hdt.8.41, Pl.*Phd.*112d, *R.*358b, etc.; ὁ ψυχρὸς ὄ. Theoc.15.58; equiv. to δράκων in Hes.*Th.*322,825: metaph., πτηνὸν ἀργηστὴν ὄφιν, of an arrow, A.*Eu.*181. II. like δράκων, *a serpent-like bracelet*, Men.387, Nicostr.Com.33, Philostr.*Ep.*22; ὄφεις is Att. for ψέλλια acc. to Moer. p.288 P. 2. τρικάρηνος ὄ. ὁ χάλκεος dedicated at Delphi (= *SIG* 31), Hdt.9.81. III. the constellation *Serpens*, Arat.82, Eudox. ap.Hipparch.1.2.18. IV. *a creeping plant*, Hp.*Mul.*2.114. V. a kind of *fish*, v. ὀφίδιον II. VI. *guinea-worm* (elsewh. δρακόντιον), Ruf.*Interrog.*65. VII. = ὀφίασις I, Cels.6.4, Poll.4.192. [The first syll. is sts. made long in the older Poets, αἰόλον ὄφιν Il.12.208, cf. Hippon.49.6; so ὀφιοέσσης Antim.78. It was then pronounced (and perh. written) ὄπφις, ὀπφιοέσσης, v. Eust.Il.l.c.—The ult. of the nom. and acc. ὄφις, ὄφιν is commonly long, as in Hes.*Th.*334, A.*Ch.*928, A.R.2.1269, Mosch.4.22; short only in later Poets, as A.R.4.128, 1398, Arat.578.]

**ὀφίτης** [ῑ], ου, ὁ, *of* or *like a serpent*, ὁ. λίθος *serpentine*, Orph.*L.*463, Dsc.5.143, etc.:—also **ὀφιῆτις** πέτρη, Orph.*L.*341, D.P.1013. II. = ἕρπης, *shingles*, Gal.19.440.

**ὀφιώδης**, ες, = ὀφιοειδής, Arist.*PA*696ᵇ22, *IA*707ᵇ30 (Comp.); πάθος Ph.1.81; ἡδονή ib.82; τὴν λεγομένην ὀφιώδη φλέβα *Hippiatr.* 10. II. = ὀφιόεις, *snaky*, Γοργών Pi.*O.*13.63; νῆσος Str.16.4.6.

**ὀφίων**, ονος, ὁ, *mousmon*, the wild sheep of Sardinia, Plin.*HN*28. 151, 30.146.

**ὀφλανεῖ**, **-ειν**, **ὀφλεῖν**, v. ὀφλισκάνω. **ὀφλάριον**, τό, = Lat. *ofella*, *Gloss.*

**ὄφλ-εμα**, ατος, τό, = sq., prob in *IG*12(5).1080 (Ceos, iii B.C.). **-ημα**, ατος, τό, (ὀφλεῖν) *fine incurred in a lawsuit*, *judgement-debt*, D. 21.99, etc.; ὀφλήματα εἰσπράττειν Is.11.43; ἐκτεῖσαι Arist.*Ath.*63.3, cf. D.39.15, D.S.16.23, etc.; *debt* in general, *POxy.*237 iv 18 (ii A.D.), Luc.*Herm.*80, etc.; ὥσπερ ὄ. κληρονομίας Hdn.5.1.6. **-ησις**, εως, ἡ, *penalty*, Lxx *Ba.*3.8; = ὄφλημα, Phot., Suid.; = χρεώστησις, Hsch. **-ητής**, οῦ, ὁ, *debtor*, *Gloss.*

❀ **ὀφλισκάνω**, S.*Ant.*470, E.*Alc.*1093, Pl.*Tht.*161e: impf. ὠφλίσκανον D.30.2: fut. ὀφλήσω S.*OT*511 (lyr.), E.*Hec.*327, Ar.*Pax*172, Pl. *Phd.*117a: pf. ὤφληκα Ar.*Nu.*34, etc.; Arc. part. dat. pl. ϝοφληκόσι *IG*5(2).262.18 (Mantinea, v B.C.), and 3 pl. ϝοφλέασι prob. in ib.1: aor. ὤφλησα Lys.13.65 codd. (ὦφλεν Sauppe), Aristid.2.143 J., Sopat. in Rh.8.243 W., (προσ-) Alciphr.3.26: in correct writers the aor. is ὦφλον, Hdt.8.26, And.1.73, etc.; inf. ὀφλεῖν Th.5.101, etc.; part. ὀφλών *IG*1².6.31, Th.3.70, etc.: sts. wrongly written ὄφλειν, ὄφλων, as if there were an Att. pres. **ὄφλω**; but this pres., though quoted by Hdn.Gr.1.448, occurs only in late writers as D.Chr.31.142,153 (f.l.): **ὀφλέω** is a still more doubtful form; for in Hsch. ὀφλεῖ shd. be corrected ὄφλει; ὤφλεε in Hdt.8.26 is an error for ὦφλε (which is given by some codd.): pres. **ὀφλίσκω** is cited by Suid.; **ὀφλάνω** by Phot. and Hsch.; and 3 sg. fut. ὀφλανεῖ from Sol. by Sch.Gen.Il.21.282. (From same root as ὀφείλω, q.v.; origin doubtful: ὀφλισκάνω and ὀφλήσω may be recent formations from ὦφλον, ὤφληκα.):—*become a debtor*, prop. of one condemned to pay a fine, *become liable to pay*, ζημίαν E.*Med.*581, etc.; χρήματα Lys.20.14; πέντε τάλαντα Ar.*Pax* 172; χιλίας δραχμάς Pl.*Ap.*36a; τὸ μείωμα εἴκοσι μνᾶς X.*An.*5.8.1; τὴν ἐπωβελίαν Isoc.18.12. 2. δίκην ὀφλεῖν *to be cast in* a suit, *lose* one's cause, δίκας ὤφληκα Ar.*Nu.*34, cf. *Av.*1457; ἥν τις ὄφλῃ παρὰ τοῖς ἄρχουσι δίκην τῳ Id.*Ec.*655; ὀφλεῖν δίαιταν *to lose in* an arbitration, Is.12.12 (prob. cj. for ὤφειλον codd.), D.29.58, etc.; ἐρήμην ὀ. τὴν δίκην *to let* judgement *go against one* by default, Antipho 5.13; ἐξούλας ἢ γραφὰς ἢ ἐπιβολάς And.1.73; κλοπῆς ἕνεκα τὰς εὐθύνας ὀ. Aeschin.3.10. 3. abs., *to be cast*, *to be the losing party*, μέλλων ὀφλήσειν Ar.*Nu.*777; κᾆτ' ὀφλὼν ἀπέρχεται Id.*Ach.*689, cf. Th.3.70, Pl.*Lg.*745a, *PHal.*1.200 (iii B.C.); ὀφλεῖν τῷ δημοσίῳ ἐπί τινι for an offence, D.39.14. 4. c. gen. criminis, ὀφλὼν ἁρπαγῆς τε καὶ κλοπῆς δίκην A.*Ag.*534: without δίκην, ὠφληκὼς φόνου Pl.*Lg.*874b; ὁ. τραύματος ἐκ προνοίας ib.877c; ὀψὲ δδοῦ Id.*Cra.*433a (s.v.l.); ὀ. κλοπῆς, δώρων, And.1.74; ἀστρατείας, ἀποστασίου, D.24.103, 25.65; but also b. c. gen. poenae, θανάτου δίκην ὀ. Pl.*Ap.*39b, *Lg.*856d. c. c. inf., ὦφλεν δύο τριήρεις καινὰς ἀποδοῦναι *IG*2².1623.149. d. c. part., ἄν τις ὄφλῃ φαρμακείαις τισὶ βλάπτων Pl.*Lg.*845e. II. generally, of anything which one *deserves* or *brings on oneself*, αἰσχύνην, βλάβην ὀ., *incur* them, E.*Hel.*67, *Andr.*188; ὀ. γέλωτα to be laughed at, Id.*Med.* 404, Ar.*Nu.*1035; τινι by one, E.*Ba.*854; παρά τινι, πρός τινα, Pl. *Phd.*117a, *Hp.Ma.*282a. 2. δειλίαν ὀ. *incur a charge of* cowardice, *get a character for* cowardice, δειλίην ὦφλε (v.l. ὤφλεε) πρὸς βασιλέος he *drew upon himself the reproach* of cowardice from the king, Hdt.8. 26, cf. E.*Heracl.*985; μώρῳ μωρίαν ὀφλισκάνω S.*Ant.*470, cf. E.*Med.* 1227, etc.; αὐθαδία τοι σκαιότητ' ὀ. S.*Ant.*1028; ἀπ' ἐμᾶς φρενὸς οὔποτ' ὀφλήσει κακίαν Id.*OT*511 (lyr.); ἀμαθίαν ὀφλήσομεν E.*Hec.*327, cf. *Ion* 443; μοχθηρίαν καὶ ἀδικίαν Pl.*Ap.*39b; ἄνοιαν D.1.26; αἰσχύνην Id.2.3.

**ὀφλοί**· ὀφειλέται, ὀφειλαί, Hsch. **ὀφνίς**· ὕννις, ἄροτρον, Id.

❀ **ὄφρᾰ**, used as a Final and Temporal Conj., correlat. to τόφρα, by Ion. and Dor. Poets, and thrice (in the latter sense) in lyr. passages of Trag., A.*Ch.*360, *Eu.*338, S.*El.*225.

A. Final Conj., *that*, *in order that*: I. with subj., 1. after primary tenses and imper., Il.1.524, 4.205, al.; so also ὄ. κε 22.382, etc.; ὄφρ' ἄν Od.17.10, 18.364; ὄ. μή Il.1.118, etc.; ἴομεν, ὄ. κε θᾶσσον ἐγείρομεν ὀξὺν Ἄρηα (where ἴομεν, ἐγείρομεν are Ep. for ἴωμεν, ἐγείρωμεν) 2.440; so ὄ. . . ἱερεύσομεν, for -ωμεν, 6.308, etc.; so also ὄ. . . αἰνέσω Pi.*O.*7.15; ὄ. . . κελαδῆτον Id.*P.*11.9; ὄ. βάσομεν . . ἵκωμαί τε Id.*O.*6.23 (where βάσομεν is prob. aor. subj.); ὄ. μήσεται B.17. 42; but Hom. thrice uses it with fut. ind., ὄφρα καὶ Ἕκτωρ εἴσεται Il.16.242; ὄφρα . . ἔπος ὑποθήσεαι Od.4.163; ὄφρα με μήτηρ ὄψεται 17.6. 2. after past tenses, Il.1.158,444, 5.128, Od.3.15, 6.173, 9.13, Pi.*P.*4.92, A.R.1.16, 3.1307, 4.908. II. with opt. after past tenses, Il.4.300, Od.1.261, etc.: rarely ὄφρα κε or ὄφρ' ἄν with opt., Il.12.26, Od.17.298.

B. Temporal conj.: I. *so long as*, *while*, 1. commonly with impf., ἀνδρῶν . . ἄριστος ἔην Τελαμώνιος Αἴας, ὄφρ' Ἀχιλεὺς μήνιεν Il.2.769, cf. Od.20.136, al.: the correlat. τόφρα or τόφρα δέ . . commonly follows in apodosi, as ὄ. μὲν ἠὼς ἦν καὶ ἀέξετο ἱερὸν ἦμαρ, τόφρα δὲ . . 9.56, cf. Il.4.220, 9.550, 15.343, etc. 2. with subj., and usu. with ἄν, κε or κεν, 6.113, Od.2.124, etc.: also pleon., ὄφρ' ἂν μέν κεν ὁρᾷς, with τόφρα in apodosi, Il.11.202, cf. Od.5.361, 6.259; but τόφρα precedes in Od.2.124: sts. without ἄν, κε or κεν, Il.4.346, Od.15.81, etc.: in Il.24.554 κεῖται (so codd. with v.l. κῆται) is subj. II. *until*: 1. with aor. ind., of a fact in past time, ὄ. καὶ αὐτὼ κατέκταθεν *till at last* they too were slain, Il.5.557, cf. 588, 10. 488, 13.329, Od.5.57, 7.141, etc.; with τόφρα preceding, 4.289. 2. with aor. subj., of an event at an uncertain future time, ἔχει κότον, ὄ. τελέσσῃ he bears malice *till* he shall have satisfied it, Il.1.82, cf. 14. 87, 16.10: but in this case ἄν (κε or κεν) is commonly added, 6.258, 10.444, Od.4.588, etc.; with τόφρα preceding, Il.1.509. 3. with opt., of an event future in relation to past time, νωλεμέως δ' ἐχόμην, ὄφρ' ἐξεμέσειεν Od.12.437, cf. 3.285, Il.10.571. III. used for τόφρα or τέως (cf. ἕως B), *for a while*, only in Il.15.547. IV. ὄ. ποτὶ στόμα Θερμώδοντος *as far as*, *up to*, A.R.2.805.

**ὀφρῠ-άζω**, (ὀφρῦς) *signify* anything *with the eyebrows*, Amips. 36. II. *to be haughty*, *supercilious*, Phryn.*PS*p.93 B., Procop. *Goth.*4.11,28, *Arc.*16, Suid. **-ανασπᾰσίδης**, ου, ὁ, (ἀνασπάω) *one who raises his eyebrows in scorn*, Epigr.ap.Hegesand.2. **-άω**, (ὀφρῦς II) *to have ridges* or *hills*, Κόρινθος ὀφρυᾷ τε καὶ κοιλαίνεται proverb. in Str.8.6.23; cf. ὀφρυόεις.

**ὀφρυγνᾶ**· ὁμοίως [i.e. = ὀφρυάζει] (Boeot.), Hsch.

**ὀφρύδιον** [ῠ], τό, Dim. of ὀφρῦς, Hsch. s. v. ἐπισκύνιον, Theognost. *Can.*125.

❀ **ὀφρύη** [ῠ], ἡ, Ion. for ὀφρῦς II, Hdt.4.181,182,185; also (not ὀφρύα) in E.*Heracl.*394: written ὀφρύγην (acc. sg. = *embankment*) in *PHal.*1.84 (iii B.C.), cf. Hsch.: Dor. **ὀφρύα** *Schwyzer* 89.14 (Argos, iii B.C.).

❀ **ὀφρύκνηστον**· ἐρυθριῶντα, οἱ γὰρ ἐρυθριῶντες κνῶνται τὰς ὀφρῦς, Hsch. (Cf. Lat. *homo fronte perfricta*, one who has rubbed his brow so often that he can blush no more.)

❀ **ὀφρῠό-εις**, εσσα, εν, (ὀφρῦς II) *on the brow* or *edge of a steep rock*, *beetling*, Ἴλιος Il.22.411; of the Acrocorinthus, Orac.ap.Hdt.5.92.β'; μέτωπον Nonn.*D.*15.106; cf. ὀφρυάω. 2. metaph., *majestic*, *solemn*, ὀφρυόεσσα ἀοιδή, of Aeschylus' poetry, *AP*7.39 (Antip. Thess.). **-ομαι**, Pass., *to be supercilious*, Timo 29, S.E.*P.*3.278, Alciphr.3.4; ἀγροικίαν ὠφρυωμένος *full of supercilious* rudeness, Luc. *Am.*2. [ὠφρυωμένος is quadrisyll. in Timo l.c.] **-σκιος**, ον, *shaded by the eyebrows*, ὀφθαλμός Pl.(Com.?)ap.Arist.*Top.*140ᵃ4 (om. Kock).

❀ **ὀφρῦς**, ύος, ἡ, acc. ὀφρῦν, in late Poets ὀφρύα, *AP*12.186 (Strat.), Opp.*C.*4.405, Q.S.4.361: acc. pl. ὀφρύας (in the fourth foot) Od.9. 389; but ὀφρῦς (before caesura) Il.16.740, and so in Att. (v. infr.). [ῡ in nom. and acc., which are accented ὀφρῦς, -ῦν by Hdn.Gr.2.937: the accentuation ὀφρύς, ὀφρύν may be admitted in late writers: compds. have ῠ, εὔοφρυς, λεύκοφρυς, etc.] (Cf. Skt. *bhrūs*, gen. *bhruvas*, Slav. *brŭvĭ*, OE. *brū* 'brow'.):—*brow*, *eyebrow*, τὸν . . ὑπ' ὀφρύος οὖτα Il.14. 493; ἡ ὀ. ἡ δεξιά, ἡ ἀριστερά, Arist.*PA*671ᵇ32, cf. *Pr.*878ᵇ28: elsewh. in pl., ὑπ' ὀφρύσι δάκρυα λεῖβον Il.13.88, al.; ὑπ' ὀ. πῦρ ἀμάρυσσεν Hes. *Th.*827, etc.: freq. of signs, ἐπ' ὀφρύσι νεῦσε Κρονίων, i.e. ἐπένευσε ὀφρύσι, *nodded assent*, Il.1.528, etc.; ἡ δ' ἄρ' ἐπ' ὀ. νεῦσε *nodded* to him to do a thing, Od.16.164; ἀνὰ δ' ὀφρύσι νεῦον ἑκάστῳ *made a sign* not to do, 9.468; ὀφρύσι νευστάζων 12.194: in various phrases expressing emotions, τὰς ὀ. ἀνασπᾶν, in token of grief, τὰς ὀφρῦς ἀνεσπακώς, ὥσπερ τι δεινὸν ἀγγελῶν Ar.*Ach.*1069; ἀνασπάσας τις τὰς ὀφρῦς οἴμοι λαλεῖ Men.556.3; of pride (cf. ὀφρυόομαι), D.19.314; οἱ τὰς ὀφρῦς αἴροντες Men.39; ὀφρῦν ἐπαίρειν E.*Fr.*1040, cf. Amphis 13; τὰς ὀ. ἔχειν ἐπάνω τῆς κορυφῆς Alex.16.6; ὑπὲρ αὐτοὺς τοὺς κροτάφους ὑπεραίρειν Luc.*Am.*54; ὀφρῦς ἔχειν Ar.*Ra.*925; ὀφρῦν ἐφέλκεσθαι *AP*7.440.6 (Leon., interpol.?); ἐρύσσαι ib.5.215 (Agath.); ἀνελκταῖς ὀφρύσι σεμνός Cratin.355: contrariwise, τὰς ὀφρῦς συνάγειν knit *the brows*, *frown*, Ar.*Nu.*582, *Pl.*756, etc.; τὰς ὀ. συνέλκειν Antiph.307; συσπᾶν Luc.*Vit.Auct.*7; κατεσπακώς Alciphr.3.3: on the other hand, καταβαλεῖν, λῦσαι, μεθεῖναι τὰς ὀ. or τὴν ὀ., let down or unknit *the brow*, become calm or cheerful again, E.*Cyc.*167, *Hipp.*290, *IA*648; ὀ. μὴ καθειμένη Zeno *Stoic.*1.58; σχάζεσθαι τὰς ὀ. Pl.Com.32; καθέσθαι Plu. 2.1062f: the brow was also the seat of smiles and joy, ἀγανᾷ χλοαρὸν γελάσσαις ὀφρύϊ Pi.*P.*9.38, cf. *h.Cer.*358; or gravity, στυγνὸν ὀφρύων νέφος E.*Hipp.*[172]; ὁρᾶτε ὡς σπουδαῖαι μὲν αὐτοῦ αἱ ὀφρύες X.*Smp.*8. 3; on their physiognomical character, v. Arist.*HA*491ᵇ14, *Phgn.* 812ᵇ26. 2. ὀφρῦς alone, *scorn*, *pride*, *AP*7.409 (Antip.), 9.43 (Parmen.), 10.122 (Lucill.), etc. II. from likeness of shape, *brow of* *a hill*, *crag*, Il.20.151, Pi.*O*.13.106; *embankment*, ὀ. ἀπότομος Plb. 36.8.3; *overhanging bank* of a river, Id.2.33.7, etc.; ἐπ' ὀφρύων ποταμοῦ *PAmh*.2.68.9 (i A.D.); of the sea, A.R.1.178, etc.; of a ditch, Str.5.3.7 (cf. ὀφρύη); of the *rim* of joint-cavities, Gal.*UP* 1.15, al.; of the woodwork enclosing the bore of a torsion-engine, Ph.*Bel*.57.7: in Archit., *architrave*, Procop.Gaz.p.157 B. III. a plant, Plin.*HN*26.164.

**ὀφρῠ-ώδης**, ες, *projecting*, ὀ. κοιλότητες joint-sockets *with rims*, Gal.*UP*13.2, cf. Heliod.ap.Orib.46.15.2, Gal.2.776, etc. **-ωσις**, εως, ἡ, *rim* of socket of thigh-bone, Paul.Aeg.6.118 (in pl.).

**ὄχᾰ**, Ep. Adv., used by Hom. only as intens. before the Sup. ἄριστος, ὄχ' ἄριστος *far* the best, Il.1.69, al.; cf. ἔξοχα. (Prob. from ἔχω to hold; ὄχα is to ὀχυρός as the old Germ. *fast* very, to *fest* fast, tight.)

**ὀχάν-η** [ᾰ], ἡ, = sq., Plu.*Cleom*.11. **-ον**, τό, (ἔχω A) *holder of a shield*, i.e. *a bar* or *band fastened crosswise on the under side of the shield*, through which the bearer passed his arm, Anacr.91, Hdt.2. 141, Aen.Tact.29.12; invented by the Carians acc. to Hdt.1.171.

**ὀχάομαι**, *leap*, *Trag.Adesp*.250. II. Act., part. ὀχῶν· ὀχευτικῶς ἔχων, Hsch.

**ὀχεά**, Ion. **-εή**, ἡ, = χειά, *cave*, *grot*, Arat.1026, Nic.*Th*.139, Orph. *A*.79: contr. gen. ὀχῆς Arat.956. [Oxyt. acc. to Theognost.*Can*. 102.]

⊛ **ὀχ-εία**, ἡ, (ὀχεύω) *a covering* or *impregnating*, of the male animal, X.*Eq*.5.8, *PCair.Zen*.225.4 (iii B.C.); ὀχείαν δέχεσθαι, προσίεσθαι, ὑπομένειν, of the female, Arist.*GA*748$^{a}$21, al.; ὀχείαν ποιεῖσθαι, of the two, Id.*HA*540$^{a}$2; περὶ τὰς ὀ. in the *breeding* season, Thphr. *Od*.61. 2. *fertilization* of plants, *PRyl*.172.21 (iii A.D., written ὠχ-). II. (ὀχέω) ὀχεία ποντία *holder* of the ship, i.e. *anchor*, *Trag.Adesp*.251 (ap.Hsch., cf. ὀχεῖον II. 2). **-εῖον**, τό, *male animal kept for breeding*, *stallion*, Arist.*HA*572$^{a}$14, *GA*748$^{a}$27, Str. 16.2.10, Plu.*Lyc*.15; *cock*, Arist.*GA*730$^{a}$11; ἵππων ὄνων τ' ὀχεῖα A. *Fr*.194. 2. γείτονας τοῦ ὀχείου Lycurg.*Fr*.26 (expld. conjecturally by Harp. as a place ἐν ᾧ ὀχεῖαι γίνονται κτηνῶν ἢ ὀχήματα μισθοῦται). II. (ὀχέω) = ὄχημα II, ὄχος, Din.*Fr*.64.2. 2. *anchor*, *Trag. Adesp*.251 (ap.Theognost.*Can*.128). **-εῖος**, α, ον, *kept for breeding*, ἵππος Din.*Fr*.64.2:—but **ὀχεός**, sine expl., cited as deriv. of ὀχεύω in Sch.Patm.D. in *BCH*1.142.

**ὄχεσφι, -σφιν**, Ep. dat. pl. of ὄχος.

**ὀχετ-ᾰγωγέω, -ᾰγωγία, -ᾰγωγός**, = ὀχετηγέω, -γία, -γός, Poll.1. 224, Pl.*Lg*.844a (pl.), Poll.1.221. **-άριος**, ὁ, = Lat. *aquilex*, *Gloss*. (pl.). ⊛ **-εία**, ἡ, *conducting* of water *by a conduit*, *irrigation*, Arist.*PA* 668$^{a}$27 (pl.): metaph., ὀ. τῆς τροφῆς Thphr.*CP*3.7.6. **-ευμα**, ατος, τό, = ὀχετός: *duct* or *passage of the nose*, Arist.*HA*492$^{b}$16. **-εύω**, *conduct* water *by a conduit* or *canal*, τὸν ποταμὸν ὀχετεῦσαι Hdt.2.99, cf. *PPetr*.1 p.78 (iii B.C.): metaph., ἐκ στομάτων καθαρὴν ὀχετεύσατε πηγήν Emp.4.2; πῦρ ἐπὶ πῦρ ὀ. εἰς τὸ σῶμα Pl.*Lg*.666a; ἡ φύσις τὸ αἷμα διὰ παντὸς ὠχέτευκε τοῦ σώματος Arist.*PA*668$^{a}$20:—Med., ῥοῦν ὀχετευσάμενος *AP*9.162:—Pass., *to be conducted*, *conveyed*, ὕδωρ ὀχετευόμενον διὰ σωλήνων Hdt.3.60; πρὸς οἶκον ὠχετεύετο φάτις A.*Ag*. 867; ὀχετεύσομαι in pass. sense, Pherecr.130.8. 2. *construct as a conduit*, τίς ὁ ὀχετεύσας τὰς φλέβας; *Corp.Herm*.5.6. **-ηγέω**, *conduct by ditches* or *conduits*, Eust.1379.49. **-ηγία**, ἡ, *irrigation by ditches*, Suid., v.l. in Procop.*Goth*.4.12. **-ηγός**, όν, (ἄγω) *conducting* or *drawing off water by a ditch* or *conduit*, ὡς δ' ὅτ' ἀνὴρ ὀ. ἀπὸ κρήνης μελανύδρου ἂμ φυτὰ καὶ κήπους ὕδατι ῥόον ἡγεμονεύῃ Il.21.257: metaph., πνεῦμα ὀ., of the flute, *AP*9.505.6; ἑῶν ὀ. ἐρώτων, of the Alpheus, ib.362.5, cf. 5.284 (Agath.); ἔρως ὀ. ἀνίης ib.228 (Maced.). **-ιον**, τό, Dim. of ὀχετός, D.L.7.17. **-λον**, τό, = ὄχημα, in pl., Hsch., Phot.

⊛ **ὀχετό-κρᾱνον**, τό, *end* or *issue of an aqueduct*, Hyp.*Fr*.132, *Mnemos*. 42.332 (Argos, iv B.C.):—Dim. **-κράνιον**, τό, *EM*644.48, *AB*287 (expld. by κηλώνειον).

**ὀχετός**, ὁ, (ὄχος, ὀχέω) *means for carrying water*, *water-pipe*, made of leather, Hdt.3.9; when carried underground, sts. of wood, *IG*1$^{2}$. 373.64, 66, 2$^{2}$.1672.305; of stone, ὀ. λίθινος κρυπτός ib.7.4255.5 (Oropus, iv B.C.); material not named, Th.6.100, Pl.*Phd*.112c, etc.; τοὺς προϋπάρχοντας ὀ. κρυπτοὺς ποιεῖν *OGI*483.74 (Pergam.); *conduit*, *channel*, Arist.*Pol*.1303$^{b}$13, al.; ὀ. μετέωροι open *drains*, Id.*Ath*.50.2, *OGI*483.63 (Pergam.); = ἀφεδρών, *Ev.Marc*.7.19 (cod. D). 2. in Anatomy, τῆς ἀρτηρίας ὀχετοί *ducts* leading to the lungs, Pl.*Ti*.70d; οἱ τοῦ αἵματος ὀ. Poll.2.217; of the urinal and intestinal *canals*, Hp. *Art*.48, 50, X.*Mem*.1.4.6; ὥσπερ ἐξ ὀχετῶν (of sweat), Hp.*Epid*.6.3. 1. II. in pl., *streams*, Pi.*O*.5.12; Σιμούντιοι ὀ. E.*Or*.809 (lyr.), *IA* 767 (lyr.). III. metaph., βαθὺς ὀ. ἄτας Pi.*O*.10(11).37; παρεκτρέποντες ὀ. ὥστε μὴ θανεῖν making *a side channel* or *means of escape*, E. *Supp*.1111; ὀχετοὶ βοτρύων Pherecr.130.7, cf. Telecl.1.9; ἐν τοῖς μεριστοῖς ὀ. *currents*, Dam.*Pr*.127, cf. 130, 206. IV. Att. for βόρβορος acc. to Hellad.ap.Phot.p.535 B.

**ὄχευμα**, ατος, τό, *result of* ὀχεία, *the embryo*, Arist.*HA*577$^{a}$26, prob. cj. in Ph.2.506.

**ὀχεύς**, έως, Ep. ῆος, ὁ, (ἔχω) *anything used for holding* or *fastening*: 1. *band* or *strap for fastening the helmet* under the chin, Il.3. 372. 2. pl., *fastenings* or *clasps of the belt*, ὅθι ζωστῆρος ὀχῆες χρύσειοι σύνεχον 4.132, 20.414. 3. *bolt* or *bar* of a door, ἐπικεκλιμένας σανίδας καὶ μακρὸν ὀχῆα 12.121; θυρέων δ' ἀνέκοπτεν ὀχῆας Od.21.47, cf. Parm.1.16, Theoc.24.49; ὀ. θύρας Phld.*Rh*.1.280 S.; *bolts* holding the ἀγκῶνες in place in a war-engine, Ph.*Bel*.72.31; νεῶν..ὀχῆας ships' *rudders*, Opp.*C*.4.59. 4. ὀχῆες τῆς ὑστέρης, = ὄχοι II. 2, Aret.*SD*2.11 (vv.ll. ὄσχιες, ὄχιες). II. = ὄχανον, οἱ ὀ. οἱ σκύτινοι Plb.18.18.4. III. *axle*, σφαίρης ἥ τ' ἀμφὶς ὀχῆος ἀεὶ περιτέλλει Orph.*Fr*.247.25.

**ὄχ-ευσις**, εως, ἡ, = ὀχεία, κυνός J.*AJ*4.8.9, cf. Plu.*Fr*.13.7 (= Sch. Arat.1070). **-ευτής**, οῦ, ὁ, = ὀχεῖον I. 1, *PCair.Zen*.529 (iii B.C.), Hsch.s.v. κήλων; ὀ. ἵππος Dsc.2.79, Gal.6.533, *Hippiatr*.14: metaph., *lewd person*, *lecher*, *AP*11.318 (Phld.), Corn.*ND*27. ⊛ **-ευτικός**, ή, όν, *salacious*, of animals, Arist.*Long*.466$^{b}$7; of birds, Id.*HA*564$^{b}$11 sq.; of human beings, Ptol.*Tetr*.64: Comp., Thphr.*Fr*.183. Adv. -κῶς, ἔχειν Hsch. s.v. ὀχῶν. **-εύτρια**, ἡ, fem. of ὀχευτής, Id. s.v. ψόαν. ⊛ **-εύω**, of male animals, *cover*, τὸ μὲν θῆλυ τίκτειν, τὸ δὲ ἄρρεν ὀχεύειν Pl.*R*.454d, cf. Hdt.3.85:—the Act. being used of the male, the Pass. of the female, ὀχεύει καὶ ὀχεύεται Arist.*HA*575$^{a}$22; so ὠχευμένην Id.*GA*748$^{a}$33:—Med., of both sexes, *copulate*, Hdt.2.64 (of birds), cf. Thphr.*Sign*.25, al. II. c. acc., *mount*, *cover*, τὴν κύνα Pl.*Euthd*.298e, etc. 2. of the groom, *put the horse to* the mare, Arist.*GA*748$^{a}$19.—It seems to have been the generic word for all animals, v. Ath.8.353e; but was not prop. used of mankind, though in Pl.*R*.586a it is used of men like beasts, cf. Ph.2.307, M.Ant.10.19.

**ὀχέω**, impf. ὤχουν prob. in E.*Hel*.277; Ion. Iterat. ὀχέεσκον Od.11. 619: fut. ὀχήσω A.*Pr*.143 (anap.), E.*Or*.802 (troch.): aor. ὤκχησα Call.*Jov*.23 (v. infr.):—**Med. and Pass.**, impf. ὠχέετο Hdt.1.31, -εῖτο X.*Cyr*.7.3.4: fut. ὀχήσομαι Il.24.731: Ep. aor. ὀχήσατο Od.5.54: also aor. ὀχηθῆναι Hp.*Art*.58, Luc.*Lex*.2: Aeol. pres. part. ὀχήμενος *Lyr. Adesp*.51: in Att. Prose, used only in pres. and impf.: Hom. never uses the augm.: [the first syll. is made long in Pi.*O*.2.67, Euph. 9.13, Lyc.64, 1049, where it is written **ὀκχέω** (Pi. and Euph.) or **ὀγχέω** (Lyc.), cf. ὄχος I. 1, ὄφις sub fin.]:—Frequentat. of ἔχω, as φορέω of φέρω (ἔχειν τε καὶ ὀχεῖν Pl.*Cra*.400a), *hold fast*, ἄγκυρα δ' ἥ μου τὰς τύχας ὤχει (sic leg.) μόνη E.*Hel*.277. b. *endure*, *suffer*, ὀχέοντας ὀϊζύν Od.7.211; κακὸν μόρον.., ὅνπερ ἐγὼν ὀχέεσκον 11. 619; ἣν ἄτην ὀχέων 21.302; ἀπροσόρατον ὀκχέοντι πόνον Pi.*O*.2.67; ἄχθος ὀ. Hp.*Fract*.9; τἀγαθὰ μὴ..ὀ. εὐπόρως *bear* prosperity not with moderation, Democr.173. c. *continue*, *keep doing*, νηπιάας ὀχέειν *to keep on with* childish ways, like ἔχειν, ἄγειν, Od.1.297; φρουρὰν ἄζηλον ὀχήσω *will maintain* an unenviable watch, A. l.c. 2. *carry*, χερσὶ λύρην Thgn.534; τινα E.*Or*.802; φιάλην X.*Cyr*.1.3.8; of the legs, *carry* the body, Hp.*Art*.52; so of the soul, Pl.*Cra*. l.c. 3. *let* another *ride*, *mount*, αὐτὸς βαδίζω.., τοῦτον δ' ὀχῶ Ar. *Ra*.23; of a general, *let* the men *ride*, X.*Eq.Mag*.4.1. II. more freq. in Med. and Pass., *to be borne* or *carried*, *have oneself borne*, ὀχήσατο κύμασιν Ἑρμῆς Od.5.54; νηυσὶν ὀχήσονται Il.24.731; ἵπποισιν ὀχεῖτο *h.Ven*.217; so ἐπὶ τῆς ἁμάξης ὀχέεσθαι Hdt.1.31, cf. Ar.*Pl*.1013; ἐπὶ τῶν ἵππων X.*Cyr*.4.5.58; ἐφ' ἅρματος Pl.*Ly*.208a; ἐν [ἁρμαμάξῃ] X.*Cyr*.7.3.4; δελφῖνος περὶ νώτῳ Opp.*H*.5.449; ἐπὶ θατέρου σκέλους ὀχοῦνται τὸ σῶμα *let* their weight *rest on*.., Plu.2.967c: metaph., *to be carried* or *brought to* (ἐπί), Dam.*Pr*.26, cf. 68, 99; ὁ χρόνος..συνθεῖ [τῇ κινήσει] ὡς ἐπὶ φερομένης ὀχούμενος Plot.6.3.22. 2. abs., *drive*, *ride*, *sail*, etc., [ἵπποι] ἀλεγεινοὶ..ὀχέεσθαι difficult *to use in a chariot*, Il.10.403, cf. Ar.*Ra*.25, D.21.171; of a dislocated bone, which *rides* on the edge of another instead of resting in the socket, Hp.*Art*. 51. 3. of a ship, *ride at anchor*, metaph., λεπτή τις ἐλπίς ἐστ' ἐφ' ἧς ὀχούμεθα 'tis but a slender hope on which we *ride at anchor*, Ar.*Eq*.1244; ἐπὶ λεπτῶν ἐλπίδων ὠχεῖσθ' ἄρα Id.*Fr*.150, cf. Pl.*Lg*. 699b; so ἐπ' ἀσθενοῦς ῥώμης E.*Or*.69; but, ἐπὶ τούτου [τοῦ λόγου], ὥσπερ ἐπὶ σχεδίας *buoyed up*, *carried*, Pl.*Phd*.85d; νεὼς ἐκπεσὼν..ἐπ' ἐλπίδος ὀχεῖταί τινος Plu.2.1103e; τὰ ὀχούμενα *floating bodies*, in title of work by Archimedes, Str.1.3.11, cf. 15.1.38, Hero *Spir*.1 *Praef*.; εἰδώλου καλοῦ ἐφ' ὕδατος ὀχουμένου Plot.1.6.8; of Delos, οὗ νᾶσος ὀχεῖται *floats*, Orac.ap.D.H.1.19; cf. ὁρμέω. III. = ὀχεύομαι, Arat.1070. (In signf. I cogn. with ἔχω (A), Skt. *sáhate* 'prevail': in signf. II cogn. with ϝέχω, Lat. *veho*, Skt. *váhati*, etc. 'carry': the similarity of the forms in Gr. has caused some assimilation of the senses.)

⊛ **Ὀχεών**, ῶνος, ὁ, a month at Smyrna, *Ath.Mitt*.12.248.

⊛ **ὀχ-ή**, ἡ, *prop*, *support*, Call.*Fr.anon*.48 (in poet. form ὀκχή, cf. ὄφις). 2. *support*, *food*, Lyc.482, Ath.8.363b. II. ὀχῆς contr. gen., for ὀχεῆς, v. ὀχεά. III. = ὀχεία, Arat.1069. ⊛ **-ημα**, ατος, τό, *anything that bears* or *supports*: hence, Zeus is called γῆς ὄχημα *stay* of earth (γαιήοχος), E.*Tr*.884. II. *carriage*, *chariot*, Hdt.5.21, etc.: prop. *mule-car*, opp. ἅρμα (war-car), Pi.*Fr*.106.6; also ὀ. ἱππικά S.*El*.740; ἁρμάτων ὀχήματα E.*Supp*.662; ὄ. ἵππειον, πωλικόν, Id.*Alc*. 67, *Rh*.621, cf. Tim.*Pers*.205; αὔρα, θεῶν ὄ. *Trag.Adesp*.565; ἔπαρχος ὀχημάτων, = Lat. *praefectus vehiculorum*, *IG*14.1072 (Rome, ii A.D.), cf. *Supp.Epigr*.4.520.12 (Ephes., ii A.D.). 2. of *ships*, mostly with some addition, λινόπτερ' ηὗρε ναυτίλων ὀ. A.*Pr*.468; ὄ. ναός S.*Tr*.656 (lyr.); νάϊον ὄ. E.*IT*410 (lyr.); τὰ ὀ. τά τε πεζὰ καὶ τὰ ἐν τῇ θαλάττῃ Pl. *Hp.Ma*.295d, cf. *Phd*.113d. 3. of animals that are ridden, ὄ. κανθάρου a *riding*-beetle (as we say a *riding*-horse), Ar.*Pax*866; of Arion's dolphin, *App.Anth*.1.3; of a horse, Max.Tyr.14.4. 4. metaph., *vehicle*, *raft*, ὄ. ἀοιδᾶν, as Pi. calls his ode, *Fr*.124.1; ἐπὶ βεβαιοτέρου ὀ., λόγου θείου τινός, διαπορευθῆναι Pl.*Phd*.85d; ὄ. τροφῆς, of water, Hp.*Alim*.55 (but of the *vena cava*, Id.ap.Gal.*UP*4.5); τὸ σιτίον οἷον ὀ. τῷ ὑγρῷ χρώμενον Plu.2.698d; of honey as a *vehicle* for drugs, Gal. 10.300; σῶμα..ψυχῆς λεπτὸν ὄ. Orac.ap.Hierocl.*in CA* 26 p.478 M.; of the supposed *vehicle* consisting of fine and indestructible matter informed by the soul, its spiritual body, Procl.*Inst*.205, cf. Iamb. *Myst*.5.12, Dam.*Pr*.102; ἀχράντῳ ὀ. χρώμεναι τῷ..κάλλει Procl.*in Alc*. p.33 C. **-ημᾰτῐκός**, ή, όν, *of* or *for a vehicle*: -κὴ δύναμις *mounted*, etc., Ascl.*Tact.*1.3; τὸ -κόν, of cavalry, charioteers, and elephant-riders, ib.1.1. **-ημάτιον**, τό, Dim. of ὄχημα, *Gloss.* **-ησις**, εως, ἡ, *a being carried*, Pl.*Ti.*89a (pl.), Arist.*Ph.*243ᵃ17; ἵππων ὀχήσεις *riding*, Pl.*R.*452c, cf. Phld.*Rh.*2.197 S.; τὴν ὄχησιν ἐπὶ τῆς γῆς ποιεῖσθαι, = ὀχεῖσθαι, Str.1.3.12; ἡ ὀ. πλείστη ἐπὶ τοῦ ὑγιέος σκέλεος, of lame people, *the weight is thrown* on the good leg, in walking, Hp.*Art.*52.

**ὀχθᾶσθαι**· ἀπὸ τοῦ ὄχθη, οἱ γὰρ στένοντες ἑαυτοὺς μετεωρίζουσιν, Hsch.

⊛ **ὀχθέω** (pres. only in compd. προσ-οχθέω, q.v.), fut. -ήσω Q.S.3.451: Ep. Verb used by Hom. only in aor.:—*to be sorely angered, vexed in spirit*, ὤχθησαν Il.1.570, 15.101; elsewh. only in part., μέγ' ὀχθήσας προσέφη 1.517, 4.30, etc.; ὀχθήσας δ' ἄρα εἶπε 11.403, al.; ὀχθήσας προσεφώνεε Od.23.182.

**ὄχθη**, ἡ, older form of ὄχθος, *any height* or *rising ground*, natural or artificial, *bank, dyke* by the side of a river, ὑψηλὴν βάλεν ὄχθην Il. 21.171, cf. 172: in sg., also, Plu.*Publ.*16, Arr.*An.*1.14.4, *CPHerm.*95.10 (iii A.D.): mostly in pl., *raised banks of a river*, in full, ποταμοῖο παρ' ὄχθας Il.4.487, 18.533, cf. 3.187; παρ' ὄχθῃσιν ποταμοῖο Od. 6.97; Καφισοῦ παρ' ὄχθαις Pi.*P.*4.46, cf. Xenoph.2.21, A.*Pr.*810, *Th.*392, etc.; ὄχθαι καπέτοιο the *raised banks* of the trench, *dykes*, Il.15.356; also, *heights* beside the sea, ἁλὸς παρ' ὄχθας Od.9.132; ταὶ ὑπὲρ Κύμας ἁλιερκέες ὄ. Pi.*P.*1.18, cf. 12.2; also of *rising banks* at a little distance from a river, X.*An.*4.3.3 and 5: ὄχθη is distd. as *the bank of a river*, from ὄχθος *a hill*, in S.*Ph.*726, 729 (both lyr.); and this distn. generally holds, but in Pi.*P.*1.64 we read ὄχθαις ὑπὸ Ταϋγέτου; and in S.*Ant.*1132 (lyr.), Νυσαίων ὀρέων ὄχθαι; reversely, we have in Sapph.p.44 Lobel, ὄχθοις Ἀχέροντος; in A.*Ag.*1161, Ἀχερουσίους ὄχθους; and in E.*Supp.*655, Ἰσμήνιον πρὸς ὄχθον; in late Prose, τὴν ὄχθαν (sic) τῆς θαλάσσης *sea-shore*, Aët.2.203.—Cf. ὄχθος.

**ὀχθηρός**, ά, όν, *hilly*, Euph.120, D.H.11.26, *APl.*4.256.

**ὄχθ-ησις**, εως, ἡ, (ὀχθέω) *indignation, vexation*, Hsch. **-ίζω**, late form of ὀχθέω, Opp.*H.*5.179, 540; v. προσοχθίζω.

**ὄχθοιβος**, ὁ, *purple stripe down the front of the* χιτών, Ar.*Fr.*320.2, Pherecr.100. II. *neckband*, ὄχθοιβοι χρυσία ἔχοντες *IG*1².387.35, cf. 2².1388.84, 1400.67; ὀ. ὃν ἡ θεὸς ἔχει ἐπὶ τῷ τραχήλῳ ib.1425.309.

**ὄχθος**, ὁ, *eminence, bank, hill*, first in *h.Ap.*17, Sapph.*Supp.*13.11, Pi.*O.*9.3, freq. in Hdt. (9.25, al.), A. (v. infr.), and E., as Ἄρειος ὄ. *IT* 961 of the Areopagus, cf. Hdt.8.52; of a *barrow* or *mound*, A.*Pers.* 647, 659 (both lyr.), *Ch.*4: rarely, like ὄχθη, of a *river's bank*, v. ὄχθη sub fin. (ὄχθῳ ἐφεζόμενοι παρ' Ἕβρον ποταμόν Ar.*Av.*774 need not be taken in this sense).—In A.*Ch.*954, dat. ὄχθει (as if from ὄχθος, εος, τό) is corrupt. II. *tubercle* in leprosy, Aret.*SD*2.13, Ruf.ap. Orib.45.28.3. 2. *tubercle* on plants, Archig.ap.Gal.12.263, Man. 1.54.

**ὀχθοφύλαξ** [ῠ], ἄκος, ὁ, *watchman on a river-bank*, Lat. *riparius*, *Gloss.*

**ὀχθώδης**, ες, *mound-like, hilly*, χωρία D.H.6.33; τόποι Onos. 18. II. *tuberous*, ἐπίφυσις Dsc.1.112, cf. Ruf.ap.Orib.8.24.30, Gal.19.132 (s.v. μυρτίδανον and s.v. πομφοί); τὸ τοῦ δέρματος ὀ. *tubercular* leprosy, Id.12.313; ὀ. ἐπαυξήσεις σαρκῶν Hierocl.p.35 A.

**ὀχί**, = οὐχί, Diog.Oen.8.

**ὀχλᾰγωγ-εύς**, έως, ὁ, = ὀχλαγωγός, Lat. *circulator*, *Gloss.* **-έω**, *court the mob*, Plb.24.7.2; *attract a crowd*, Str.14.2.5, cf. Lxx *Am.* 7.16. **-ία**, ἡ, *fooling of the mob*, Plu.*Pyrrh.*29; *conventus, convicium*, *Gloss.* **-ικός**, ή, όν, *quackish*, Gal.14.305. **-ιον**, τό, *assemblage, mob*, = *comitium*, *Gloss.* **-ός**, ὁ, *mountebank, charlatan, quack*, J.*Ap.*2.1, Gal.14.180, Vett.Val.74.18.

⊛ **ὀχλάζω**, *to be in a tumult*, Aq.*Je.*4.19, al.

**ὀχλ-εύς**, έως, ὁ, = μοχλός, Hsch. **-εύω**, = sq., Id. (Pass.). **-έω**, (ὄχλος) *move, disturb*, ψηφῖδες ἅπασαι ὀχλεῦνται all the pebbles *are rolled* or *swept away* by the water, Il.21.261. II. generally, *trouble, importune*, c. acc., Hdt.5.41; ὀχλεῖς μάτην με A.*Pr.*1001; *disturb* citizens by false alarms, Aen.Tact.6.1: abs., *to be troublesome* or *irksome*, Hp.*Epid.*2.1.3, S.*OT*446, *OGI*262.22 (Baetocaece); ὀ. πρὸς αὐγάς impede the sight, Hp.*Prorrh.*1.147 = *Coac.*191 (v.l.): freq. in Pap., *POxy.*269 ii 4 (i A.D.), etc.:—Pass., *to be troubled*, ὑπέρ τινος Arist.*EN*1167ᵃ10, cf. 1171ᵇ19; ἀσθενείᾳ σώματος Plb.*Fr.*188; ὑπὸ ὑδέρου *Hippiatr.*38; τὴν ἀκοήν Phld.*Po.*2.18; cf. ἐνοχλέω: later c. inf., μὴ ὀχλοῦ δὲ πέμπειν τι ἡμῖν don't *trouble* to.., *POxy.*1481.6 (ii A.D.). III. in Pass., *to be crowded*, ὁδὸς.. ἥτις οὐ πολὺ ὀχλεῖται Ceb.15 (nisi πολυοχλεῖται leg.). **-ημα**, ατος, τό, *annoyance*, S.E. *M.*11.158. ⊛ **-ηρία**, ἡ, *troublesomeness, importunity*, Lxx *Ec.*7.26 (25). **-ηρός**, ά, όν, *troublesome, irksome, importunate*, of persons, Aeschin.1.135, D.*Prooem.*48; ἴσθ' ὀ. ὢν δόμοις Ar.*Ach.*460 (parody); ὀ. ἴσθ' ὤν E.*Hel.*452; τινι *to* one, Id.*Alc.*540, Pl.*Hp.Ma.*295b; of a writer, *offensive*, D.H.*Th.*30. 2. of things, *troublesome, annoying*, Hdt.1.186, Isoc.5.151, etc. Adv. -ρῶς D.H.*Dem.*15: Comp. -οτέρως, ἔχειν Hp.*Epid.*1.19, Phld.*Mus.*p.63 K. II. *turbulent*, συμπόται Pl. *R.*569a. **-ησις**, εως, ἡ, *disturbance, annoyance, distress*, Democr. 212, Epicur.*Nat.*131 G., Plb.15.36.2, Andronic.Rhod.p.570 M., D.H. *Comp.*12, Plu.2.1127d; τὴν ὀ. [τῆς] ἀποδημίας *IG*7.2711.98, cf. 105 (i A.D.), *POxy.*2110.37 (iv A.D.): freq. in pl., Epicur.*Sent.*8, etc.; ἡδοναὶ καὶ ὀ. Phld.*Mus.*p.63 K.; αἱ ἐκ τῶν παθῶν ὀ. Phlp. *in APr.*276. 26; ὀ. σωματική Vett.Val.167.20: pl., of disease, Corn.*ND*33; ὀ. πνεύματος *Hippiatr.*38:—the old Att. word being ὄχλος, cf. Moer. p.289 P. **-ητικός**, ή, όν, = ὀχλικός, Procl.*Par.Ptol.*p.218. ⊛ **-ίζω**, *move by a lever, heave up*, τὸν [λᾶαν] οὔ κε δύ' ἀνέρε.. ἀπ' οὔδεος ὀχλίσσειαν Il.12.448; οὐκ ἂν τόν γε [θυρεὸν] δύω καὶ εἴκοσ' ἅμαξαι.. ἀπ' οὔδεος ὀχλίσσειαν Od.9.242; [νήσους] ἐκ νεάτων ὤχλισσε Call.*Del.*33; νῆα διὲκ πέτρας A.R.4.962, etc.: for Nic.*Al.*226 v. διοχλίζω. II. ὀχλιζομένων· συναγομένων, Hsch. ⊛ **-ικός**, ή, όν, *of* or *suited to a* or *the mob, popular*, ὑποδοχαί Posidon.9 J.; ἑστίασις D.H.2.60; ὀ. θύελλα Phld.*Rh.*1.184 S.; ὀ. ἄνθρωπος Ph.2.537; διάταξις Plu.*Comp.Lyc. Num.*2; ὀ. βωμολοχία Id.*Per.*5; τὸ περὶ τὴν λέξιν ὀχλικόν Id.2.142a; ὀ. ἀηδία Hld.3.6.

**ὀχλοάρεσκος** [ᾰ], ὁ, *mob-flatterer*, Timo 34.3.

**ὀχλοισίαν**· ἱκεσίαν, ἐκκλησίαν, Hsch.

**ὀχλοκοπ-έω**, *court the mob*, Plu.2.796e. **-ικός**, ή, όν, *of* or *suited to an* ὀχλοκόπος: ἡ -κή (sc. τέχνη) the *art of cajoling a mob*, S.E.*M.* 2.50. **-ος** (parox.), ὁ, *mob-courtier*, Plb.3.80.3, Ptol.*Tetr.*159.

**ὀχλο-κρᾰτία**, ἡ, *mob-rule*, the lowest grade of democracy, Plb.6.4.6, 6.57.9, Plu.2.826f, etc.: -κρασία is v.l. in Ph.1.41, Max.Tyr.33. 6. **-λογος**· κατάλογος λαοῦ, Hsch. **-λοίδορος**, ον, *reviling the mob*, Timo 43. **-μανέω**, *to be mad after mob popularity*, Plu.2. 603c. **-ποιέω**, *make a riot*, *Act.Ap.*17.5. **-ποίησις**, εως, ἡ, *creating a riot*, Hsch. s.v. δημαγωγίας. **-πολῑτεία**, ἡ, *a constitution in which the mob rules*, Olymp. *in Grg.*p.251 J. (pl.).

⊛ **ὄχλος**, ὁ, *crowd, throng*, Pi.*P.*4.85, A.*Pers.*42 (anap.), etc.; ἐς ὄχλον ἕρπειν παρθένοισιν οὐ καλόν E.*Or.*108, cf. *Heracl.*44; ὁ ὄ. τῶν στρατιωτῶν the *mass* of the soldiers, X.*Cyr.*6.1.26, cf. Th.6.64, 7.62; μηδένα ὄ. Πελοποννησίων νεῶν Id.2.88; ὄχλῳ in *numbers* (for an army), Id.1.80; ὁ μισθοφόρος ὄ. Id.3.109, cf. 4.56; οἱ τοιοῦτοι ὄ. *undisciplined masses* like these, ib.126; ὄ. μᾶλλον ἢ στρατός Hdn.6.7.1; of *the camp-followers*, X.*An.*3.4.26, 4.3.26, etc. 2. in political sense, *populace, mob*, opp. δῆμος (*people*), Th.7.8, cf. Pl.*Plt.*304d; πρὸς ὄχλον ζῶν Id.*Ax.*368d; οἱ ὁμότιμοι ὤκνουν τὴν τοῦ ὄ. ἰσομοιρίαν X.*Cyr.*2.2.21; δικαστηρίων καὶ τῶν ἄλλων ὄ. and *popular assemblies* (in a contemptuous sense), Pl.*Grg.*455a, cf. *Euthd.*290a: prov., δι' ὄχλου ἤδη τοῦτό γε this is already *in the mouths of the people*, D.H.*Lys.*10, cf. J.*BJ*2.13.1, 4.9. 2. 3. generally, *mass, multitude*, ὄ. τὸν πλεῖστον λόγων A.*Pr.* 827; τὸν πλεῖστον ὄ. τῶν πραχθέντων Isoc.12.192; ἵππων ὄ. E.*IA*191 (lyr.); ἄκριτος ἄστρων ὄ. Critias 19.5 D.; σαρκῶν Pl.*Ti.*75e: in pl., *the masses*, καχεξία τις ὑποδέδυκε τοὺς ὄχλους Diph.24.4, cf. Men.161.1, 466.4; πιθανώτεροι οἱ ἀπαίδευτοι ἐν τοῖς ὄ. Arist.*Rh.*1395ᵇ28. II. *annoyance, trouble*, σχολὴν ὄ. τε μέτριον E.*Ion*635, etc.; ὄχλον παρέχειν to give *trouble*, Hdt.1.86, cf. E.*Med.*337, X.*An.*3.2.27, Pl.*Phd.* 84d; δι' ὄχλου εἶναι, γενέσθαι, to be or become *troublesome*, Ar.*Ec.*888, Th.1.73, Pl.*Alc.*1.103a; μάταιον ὄ. τοὺς λόγους νομίσητε D.18.214; οἱ δὲ ἀντιλέγοντες ὄ. ἄλλως καὶ βασκανία κατεφαίνετο Id.19.24.

**ὀχλο-τερπής**, ές, *delighting the mob*, Poll.4.31, 96. **-χᾰρής**, ές, *courting the mob*, M.Ant.1.16, Man.4.277.

**ὀχλώδης**, ες, *turbulent, unruly*, θηρίον Pl.*R.*590b; *troublesome*, of sores, Hp.*Fract.*11; τὸ ὀ. τῆς παρασκευῆς *troublesomeness*, Th.6. 24. 2. *common, vulgar*, δόξα Plu.*Cat.Ma.*18; θρίαμβος Id.*Luc.* 37.

⊛ **ὄχμα**· πόρπημα, Hsch.

**ὀχμάζω**, *grip fast*, E.*Cyc.*484 (anap.); μέσον τινὰ ὀ. Id.*Or.*265; τὸν λεωργὸν ὀχμάσαι.. ἐν ἀρρήκτοις πέδαις *bind* him *fast*, A.*Pr.*5; τίς ἐν φάραγγί σ' ὤχμασεν; ib.618; ἵππον τ' ὀχμάζει *he makes* the horse *obedient to the bit*, E.*El.*817 (and this, acc. to Sch.A.R.1.743, is the proper sense). II. *bear, carry*, Ἄρεος ὀχμάζουσα.. σάκος A.R.1. 743; *uphold*, φελλοὶ.. δόλον Opp.*H.*3.374.

**ὀχμή**, ἡ, = ὄχανον, Sch.A.*Pr.*618.

**ὀχμός**, ὁ, = ὄγμος, Hsch. II. (ἔχω) *fortress*, Lyc.443.

**ὄχνη**, ἡ, later way of writing ὄγχνη (q.v.).

**ὀχομένιον**, τό, = ἐχομένιον, *POxy.*101.12 (ii A.D.), etc.

⊛ **ὄχος**, ὁ, (ϝέχω) *carriage*, used by Hom. in heterocl. neut. pl. ὄχεα, τά, even of a single *chariot*, ἐξ ὀχέων Il.4.419, etc. (so Pi.*O.*4.13, *P.*9. 11); and in poet. dat. ὄχεσφι, -φιν, σὺν ἵπποισιν καὶ ὄχεσφι Il.4.297, cf. 5.28, 107, etc.: later also in masc. pl., ἐπὶ χρυσέοισιν ὄχοισιν *h.Cer.* 19; ἐπ' εὐκύκλοις ὄχοις, of the Scythian wagons, A.*Pr.*710, cf. E. *Andr.*1019 (lyr.), *Supp.*676, al.: also in sg., Pi.*O.*6.24 (in poet. form **ὄκχος**), A.*Ag.*1070, Hdt.8.124, Critias 2.3: periphr., ἁρμάτων ὄχος or ὄχοι, = ὄχημα, E.*Hipp.*1166, *IT*370, *Ph.*1190; ὄ. ταχυήρης, of a ship, A.*Supp.*32 (anap.). 2. τρόχαλοι ὄχοι the swift or round *bearers* of the chariot, i.e. the wheels, E.*IA*146 (anap.). II. *anything which holds*, λιμένες νηῶν ὄχοι *roadsteads* for ships, *harbours*, Od.5.404, Orph.*A.*1200. 2. νεῦρα τῆς ὑστέρης τὰ καλεόμενα ὄχοι Hp.*Mul.*2.204 (v.l. ὄσχοι); cf. ὀχεύς I. 4. III. perh. = ὀχετός, μισθωτοῖς τοὺς ὀ. ἀνακαθάρασι τοὺς ἐν τῷ ἱερῷ *IG*11(2).203*A*33 (Delos, iii B.C.).

**ὀχός**, όν, (ἔχω) *firm, secure*, Ph.Byz.*Mir.*1.5.

**ὀχρός**· ὀχούμενος, φερόμενος, Hsch. **ὀχρύνει**· βαίνει, Id. **ὀχυρίαι**· αἱ ἀσφάλειαι καὶ οἷον ὀχυρότητες Sch.Patm.D.(*BCH*1.154).

**ὀχῠροποιέομαι**, *fasten, fortify*, Plb.1.18.4:—Act. in Sch.Philostr. *Im.*1.4.

⊛ **ὀχῠρός**, ά, όν, (ἔχω) = ἐχυρός, *firm, lasting, stout*, of wood, Hes.*Op.* 429 (Sup.); of persons, διθρόνου Διόθεν.. τιμῆς ὀχυρὸν ζεῦγος Ἀτρειδαιν A.*Ag.*44 (anap.): but elsewh. A. uses ἐχυρός (q.v.). 2. of places, *strong, secure*, παρθενῶνες E.*IA*738; esp. as military term, of a stronghold or position, *strong*, ὄρος X.*An.*1.2.22; χωρίον ib.1.2.24, Isoc.9. 30 (v.l. ἐχ-); πόλεις Plb.7.15.2; τὰ ὀ. X.*Cyr.*6.1.15, etc. Adv. -ρῶς E.*Med.*124 (anap.), Charito 7.2.

**ὀχῠρότης**, ητος, ἡ, *firmness, strength*, esp. of a stronghold or country, -τητος μετέχειν Aen.Tact.22.2, cf. J.*AJ*3.14.2: pl., Plb.5. 62.6, 7.15.2.

⊛ **ὀχῡρ-όω**, *fortify*, τοὺς λιμένας *IG*2².834.14 (iii B.C.); πόλιν Plb.14.

9.9, J.*AJ*12.7.7; τὰ στόματα τῶν ποταμῶν *OGI*90.25 (Rosetta, ii B.C.); τείχη Lxx *Je.*28(51).53: metaph., τὸν τῆς εὐσεβείας λιμένα ib.4*Ma.*13.7:—Med., in act. sense, X.*Cyr.*5.4.39, Plb.1.18.3:—Pass., τὰ πρόπυλα κλείθροις ὀχυροῦται Pl.*Ax.*371b, cf. *OGI*90.22 (Rosetta, ii B.C.); πρόθυρα τείχεσι..ὠχύρωτο Arist.*Mu.*398ᵃ18. 2. ὠχυρωμένη *besieged*, Lxx *Jo.*6.1. II. metaph., *confirm*, τὸ λεγόμενον Phld.*Rh.*2.98 S. III. *constrain*, τοὺς πονηρούς ib.148 S. **-ωμα**, ατος, τό, *stronghold, fortress, prison*, X.*HG*3.2.3, Lxx *Ge.*39.20, *PPetr.*2 p.34 (iii B.C.), Plb.4.6.3, *PStrassb.*85.23 (ii B.C.): pl., Phld.*Rh.*1.334 S., *OGI*455.14 (Aphrodisias, i B.C.). **-ωμάτιον**, τό, Dim. of foreg., Lxx 1*Ma.*16.15. * **-ωσις**, εως, ἡ, *fortification*, *PLille* 3.21 (iii B.C.), Lxx 1*Ma.*10.11, J.*BJ*7.6.2 (pl.). **-ωτέον**, *one must strengthen*, τὸ στρατόπεδον Plu.*Mar.*18. **-ωτικός**, ή, όν, *serving to strengthen*, τῆς διανοίας S.E.*M.*7.23.

**ὄψ** (A), ἡ, poetic Noun, used in obliq. cases of sg., ὀπός, ὀπί, ὄπα, *voice*, whether in speaking, shouting, lamenting, Ἀτρείδεω ὀπὸς ἔκλυον Il.16.76, cf. 14.150, 18.222, 22.451, etc.; or in singing, Κίρκης..ἀειδούσης ὀπὶ καλῇ Od.10.221, cf. 5.61; ἄειδον ἀμειβόμεναι ὀπὶ καλῇ Il.1.604, cf. Hes.*Th.*41, al., Pi.*N.*7.84, al., B.16.129, A.*Supp.*60 (lyr.), etc.; also of cicadae, ὄπα λειριόεσσαν ἱεῖσι Il.3.152; of lambs, ἀκούουσαι ὄπα ἀρνῶν 4.435; of flutes, αὐλῶν φθεγγομένων ἱμερόεσσαν ὄπα Thgn. 532. II. *word*, ὡς γὰρ ἐγὼν ὄπ' ἄκουσα θεῶν Il.7.53; ἀμείλικτον δ' ὄπ' ἄκουσαν 11.137, cf. 21.98, S.*El.*1068 (lyr.), etc. (Cogn. with ἔπος, εἰπεῖν.)

* **ὄψ** (B), ἡ, gen. ὀπός, (ὄψομαι) = ὄψις, *the eye, face*, Emp.88, Antim.63.

**ὀψάγονος**, ον, = ὀψίγονος, *Stud.Ital.*2(1922).365 (Crete, Epigr., iii/ii B.C.).

**ὀψᾱμάτης** [μᾱ], Dor. for -αμήτης, ὁ, (ὀψέ, ἀμάω) *one who mows till late at even*, Μίλων ὀψαμᾶτα (voc.) Theoc.10.7.

**ὄψᾰνον**, τό, (ὄψομαι) = ὄψις I. 3, A.*Ch.*534.

**ὀψ-άομαι**, (ὄψον) *eat as* ὄψον, τι Plu.2.668b. **-ᾰρίδιον**, τό, Dim. of sq., *POxy.*2148.13 (i A.D.), *Sammelb.*1974 (iii A.D.), *Gp.*20.46.1. * **-άριον**, τό, Dim. of ὄψον, Ar.*Fr.*45, Pl.Com.95, Pherecr.27, Philem.32, *Test.Epict.*6.11, *PPetr.*3 p.327 (iii B.C.), *PCair.Zen.*440.3 (iii B.C.), etc.; λαγύνιον ταριχηροῦ (i.e. -ῶν) ὀψαρίων a jar of pickled *fish*, *BGU*1095.17 (i A.D.), cf. *PRyl.*229.21 (i A.D.), *Ev.Jo.*6.9, al., *OGI*484.12 (Pergam., ii A.D.).

* **ὀψᾰριοπωλ-εῖον**, τό, *fish-shop*, τὰς ἐν τῷ ὀ. μαρμαρίνας τραπέζας *CIG*2930 (Tralles). **-ης**, ου, ὁ, *fishmonger*, *Jahresh.*26 *Beibl.*51 (Ephes., i A.D.), *OGI*484.21 (Pergam., ii A.D.).

**ὀψᾰρότης**, ου, ὁ, (ὀψέ, ἀρόω) *one who ploughs late*, Hes.*Op.*490.

**ὀψαρτ-ῡσία**, ἡ, *art of cookery, cookery-book*, Pl.Com.173.4, Alex. 135.9; *things cooked*, like Fr. *cuisine*, ἀστυκὴ ὀ. Longus 4.16. **-ῡτής**, οῦ, ὁ, *cook*, Hyp.*Fr.*259; ὀψαρτυταὶ καὶ μυροποιοί Phld.*Mus.*p.86 K.; used derisively of a gourmand, Timae.70. **-ῡτικός**, ή, όν, *of* or *for a cook* or *cookery*: ἡ -κή (sc. τέχνη) *the art of cookery*, Timocl.37, S.E.*M.*6.33, Phlp.*in APo.*74.16; ὀ. καὶ μυρεψική Phld.*Mus.*p.45 K.: -κόν, τό (with or without βιβλίον), *cookery-book*, Ath.3.105c, 9.387c, 12.516c; ὀ. λέξεις, γλῶσσαι, Id.1.5b, 9.387d. **-ύω** [ῠ], *dress* or *season food*, Timae.71 (metaph.), Ath.1.18a.

* **ὀψέ**, Aeol. ὄψι (q.v.), Adv. *after a long time, at length, late*, ἔκ τε καὶ ὀ. τελεῖ, opp. αὐτίκα, Il.4.161; ὀ. κακῶς ἔλθοι Od.9.534, etc.; ὀ. διδάσκεσθαι, μανθάνειν, to be *late* in learning, learn *too late*, A.*Ag.*1425, S.*OC*1264; ὀψέ γε φρονεῖς εὖ E.*Or.*99; also ὀ. δή Il.7.399, etc.; ὀ. γοῦν A. l. c.; ὀ. περ Pi.*N.*3.80. b. ὀ. ἀφ' οὗ.. *it is not long* since.., Th.1.14. 2. *late in the day, at even*, Il.21.232, Od.5.272, Th.4.106, etc.; ὀφλεῖν..ὀ. ὁδοῦ incur a penalty for *being out late at night*, Pl.*Cra.*433a (dub.); *late in the season*, Hes.*Op.*485; ὀ. ἦν, ὀ. ἐγίγνετο, it was, it was getting, *late*, X.*An.*2.2.16, 3.4.36; ἡ μάχη ἐτελεύτα ἐς (v.l. ἕως) ὀ. did not end till *late*, Th.3.108; so ἐς ὀψέ Id.8.23; but εἰς ὀ. ψηφίζεσθαι continue voting till *late in the day*, D.57.15. 3. c. gen., ὀ. τῆς ἡμέρας *late* in the day, ἤδη γὰρ τῆς ἡμέρας ὀ. ἦν Th.4.93, cf. X.*HG*2.1.23; τῆς δ' ὥρας ἐγίγνετ' ὀ. D.21.84; ὀ. τῆς ἡλικίας *late* in life, Luc.*Dem.Enc.*14, cf. *Am.*37. 4. as Prep. c. gen., ὀ. τούτων *after* these things, Philostr.*VA*6.10, cf. 4.18; so perh. ὀ. σαββάτων *after* the sabbath day, *Ev.Matt.*28.1.—For the Comp. and Sup. Advbs. v. ὄψιος.

**ὀψείω**, (ὄψομαι) Desiderat. of ὁράω, *wish to see*, c. gen., ἀϋτῆς καὶ πολέμοιο Il.14.37: impf. ὤψεον in Sophr.81.

**ὄψημα**, ατος, τό, = ὄψον, Plu.2.664a (from Pl.*R.*372c, ubi codd. ἑψήματα), Str.7.4.6, Longus 3.5.

**ὀψημέρα**, ἡ, (ὀψέ) *evening*, like ὀψία, *Gloss.*

**ὀψητήρ**, ῆρος, ὁ, prob. = ἑψητήρ, Theodorid.ap.Ath.6.229b.

**ὄψι**, Aeol. for ὀψέ, *Lyr.Adesp.*57.

**ὀψία**, Ion. -ίη (sc. ὥρα), ἡ, *the latter part of day, evening*, opp. ὄρθρος, freq. joined with δείλη (q.v.), μέχρι δείλης ὀψίης Hdt.7.167; περὶ δείλην ὀ. Th.8.26; δείλης ὀ. *late* in the evening, D.57.9; ὀψίας alone, *POxy.*528.5 (ii A.D.).—Cf. ὄψιος.

**ὀψιαίτερος, ὀψιαίτατος**, Att. Comp. and Sup. of ὄψιος.

**ὀψῐανθ-έω**, *bloom late*, Thphr.*HP*6.2.6. **-ής**, ές, *late-blooming*, ib.6.4.4, 6.6.10.

**ὀψιᾰνὸς** λίθος, ὁ, a black stone, perh. *obsidian*, Pliny's *obsiana* (neut. pl.), *HN*36.196, cf. *Peripl.M.Rubr.*5, Orph.*L.*285, Cyran.26: written ὀψειανόν *PLeid.X.*36 B.; [ὀψ]ειανόν dub. in *Supp.Epigr.*2.776 i 15 (Syria, iii A.D.). (Named from its discoverer Obsius, v. Plin. l. c.; *obsidiana* is f.l. ibid.; prob. ᾱ by nature.)

**ὀψιβλαστ-έω**, *sprout* or *shoot late*, Thphr.*HP*6.2.6. **-ής**, ές, *late sprouting* or *shooting*, ib.1.14.3, 6.6.10. **-ος**, ον, = foreg., ib. 3.4.2: Comp. -ότερος Id.*CP*1.10.7.

**ὀψῐγᾰμ-έω**, *marry late*, Vett.Val.119.3. **-ία**, ἡ, *late marriage*, *Cat.Cod.Astr.*8(4).143, Suid. s. v. ὑπεργαμία. **-ίου γραφή**, ἡ, a prosecution *for putting off marriage beyond the appointed age*, Aristo Stoic.1.89, Plu.*Lys.*30. **-ος**, ὁ, ἡ, *late-married*, Vett.Val.118.23, prob. f.l. in Plu.2.493e.

* **ὀψῐ-γενής**, ές, *late-born*, Hsch., Phot.; also **ὀψιγέννητος**, Hsch. **-γονία**, *posteritas*, *Gloss.* * **-γονος**, ον, *late-born*, τί σευ ἄλλος ὀνήσεται ὀψίγονός περ; Il.16.31, cf. Thphr.*Fr.*30.6: mostly in pl., ὀψιγόνων ἀνθρώπων of men *after-born*, Il.3.353, cf. Od.1.302, etc. 2. of a son, *late-born, born in one's old age*, *h.Cer.*165, Arr.*Ind.*9.2; *born late in the season*, ἔριφος Longus 4.6. 3. *later-born*, i.e. *younger*, A.*Supp.*361 (lyr.), Hdt.7.3; *young*, Theoc.24.31. 4. *late in spawning*, of the needle-fish, Arist.*HA*571ᵃ2.

**ὀψιέστερος**, Comp. of ὄψιος (q.v.).

* **ὀψίζω**, (ὀψέ) *do, go*, or *come late*, X.*An.*4.5.5, *HG*6.5.21, Plu.*Lyc.* 12:—Pass., ὀψίζεσθαι ἐν ταῖς ὁδοῖς *to be* in the streets *late at night*, Lys.*Fr.*18, cf. X.*Cyn.*6.4; ὑπὸ θήρας ὀψισθέντες *belated, benighted*, Id.*Lac.*6.4; ὠψίσθημεν τῆς ἀναγωγῆς Hld.5.22.

**ὀψίκαρπ-έω**, *to be late in fruiting*, Thphr.*CP*1.17.9. **-ία**, ἡ, *late fruiting*, Id.*HP*3.2.1. **-ος**, ον, *fruiting late*, ib.6.4.6, al.

**ὀψί-κλωψ**, κλωπος, ὁ, *one who steals at night*, f.l. in Polem.*Phgn.* 2.5. **-κοιτος**, ον, *going late to bed, late-watching*, ὄμματα A.*Ag.* 889.

**ὀψῐμᾰθ-έω**, *learn late*, Luc.*Merc.Cond.*23. * **-ής**, ές, *late in learning, late to learn*, Isoc.10.2, Pl.*Sph.*251b, Epicur.*Fr.*173; ὀψιμαθεῖς *scis quam sint insolentes*, Cic.*Fam.*9.20.2: c. gen., τῶν πλεονεξιῶν X.*Cyr.* 1.6.35; κακῶν Isoc.12.96; τῆς ἀδικίας οἷόν ἐστιν Pl.*R.*409b. II. *vain of late-gotten learning, pedantic*, Thphr.*Char.*27, Timae.70, Luc. *Salt.*33. **-ία**, ἡ, *late-gotten learning*, Thphr.*Char.*27, Plb.12.4ᶜ.1, Plu.2.334c, 634d, Iamb.*VP*31.209, etc.

* **ὀψί-μοθος** [ῐ], ον, *coming late to battle*, Nonn.*D.*28.92 codd. **-μορος**, ον, *dying slowly*, Opp.*H.*1.142.

**ὄψῐμος**, ον, (ὀψέ) poet. for ὄψιος, *late, slow*, τέρας ὄ. *for* (concerned with) *a late time*, Il.2.325: in Prose, *late in the season*, σπόρος X.*Oec.* 17.4, 5, but f.l. for ὄψιος in Thphr.*HP*1.9.7, al.; of crops, Lxx *Ex.*9.32, *PSI*4.433.2 (iii B.C.), *PCair.Zen.*299.2 (iii B.C.); ἐν τοῖς ὀ. τῶν ὑδάτων D.S.1.10; ὑετὸς πρώϊμος καὶ ὄ. *Ep.Jac.*5.7: Comp., καιρὸς -ώτερος *PFay.*133.9 (iii A.D.); *recent*, ποιητική Plu.2.674f. Adv. -μως *PTeb.* 72.361 (ii B.C.), *POxy.*474.24 (ii A.D.), Procl. ad Hes.*Op.*483.

**ὀψίνοος** [ῐ], ον, *late-observing*, i.e. *remiss, inobservant*, of Epimetheus, Pi.*P.*5.28.

**ὀψινός**, ή, όν, = ὄψιος, rejected by Phryn.35, but found in later writers, as *Peripl.M.Rubr.*32, Ptol.*Alm.*8.1, *PMasp.*61.2 (vi A.D.), and mentioned by A.D.*Synt.*111.5, al., Dosith.p.397 K.

**ὀψίον**, τό, Dim. of ὄψον, Them.*Or.*13.173a.

**ὀψιοπαίκτης**, v. ὀφιοπ-.

* **ὄψιος**, α, ον, (ὀψέ) *late*, ὀψία ἐν νυκτί Pi.*I.*4(3).35(53); ὅταν ἔαρ ὄ. γένηται Arist.*HA*553ᵇ20, cf. 627ᵇ20; ὄ. σῦκα, πυροί, etc., Thphr. *HP*2.8.1, 8.4.3, etc.; [ᾠὰ] τὰ μὲν πρώϊα τὰ δ' ὄ. Arist.*HA*543ᵃ10; cf. ὀψία. II. Att. Comp. ὀψιαίτερος, α, ον, *later*, Id.*Mete.*362ᵃ24, al., Thphr.*CP*1.10.5: Sup. ὀψιαίτατος, η, ον, X.*HG*5.4.3: hence ὀψιαίτερον as Adv., Comp. of ὀψέ, Pl.*Cra.*433a, Thphr.*HP*3.2.1, Eub.119.11: Sup. ὀψιαίτατα, opp. πρωϊαίτατα, Pl.*Prt.*326c, X.*HG*4.5.18, etc.: also Comp. ὀψιέστερος as v.l. in Thphr. (*CP*4.8.3, *HP*3.4.6): also shortd. form ὀψιτέρα, ἄλωσις Pi.*Pae.*6.82; ὀψίτερον Plu.2.1119c; ὀψίτατον Poll.1.69; ὀψίτερον τῆς ὥρας *BGU*759.6 (ii A.D.), cf. *PTeb.*230 (ii B.C.).

**ὀψιότης**, ητος, ἡ, *lateness*, opp. πρωϊότης, Thphr.*CP*4.11.9.

**ὀψιπέδων**, ωνος, ὁ, *one who has long been in fetters*, Men.1049 (pl.).

* **ὄψις**, ἡ, gen. εως, Ion. ιος, (ὄπωπα): I. objective, *aspect, appearance* of a person or thing, πατρὸς φίλου ὄψιν ἀτυχθείς Il.6.468; εἰσορόων ὄ. τ' ἀγαθὴν καὶ μῦθον ἀκούων 24.632, cf. S.*Ph.*1412 (anap.); δῶρον, οὐ σπουδαῖον εἰς ὄ. Id.*OC*577; πλείω τὴν ὄ. παρείχετο made the *appearance* greater, Th.6.46; ἀξιόλογον ὄ. παρέχεται τὸ δένδρος *PCair.Zen.* 157.4 (iii B.C.); ὥστε ὄ. καλὴν φαίνεσθαι X.*An.*5.9.9; εἰκάζεσθαι ἀπὸ τῆς φανερᾶς ὄ. Th.1.10; τὴν ὄ. τοῦ σώματος προορᾶν Id.7.44: the acc. is used abs., *in appearance*, τῷ ὄψιν ἐειδόμενος Pi.*N.*10.15; στρογγύλος τὴν ὄ. Hermipp.4; ἀστειότατον τὴν ὄ. Alex.59; καλός τε κἀγαθὸς τὴν ὄ. Pl.*Prm.*127b; ἀπὸ τῆς ὄ. Ἑλληνικός to judge from his *looks*, Antiph. 33.2; so ἐκ τῆς ὄ. *POxy.*37 ii 3 (i A.D.). b. *countenance, face*, E.*Med.*905, Pl.*Phdr.*240d, 254b, etc.; διοίδησις ὅλης ὄ. Herod.Med. in *Rh.Mus.*58.83, cf. Sor.1.44, Philum.ap.Aët.9.7; οὐκ ἄξιον ἀπ' ὄψεως οὔτε φιλεῖν οὔτε μισεῖν οὐδένα by the *face* or *look* merely, Lys.16.19; ἀδήλως τῇ ὄ. πλασάμενος so that nothing could be learnt from his *countenance*, Th.6.58; τίνι δεδούλωταί ποτε; ὄψει Men.541.2: pl., Alex.98.6, Anaxandr.41.38. c. *visual impression* or *image* of an object, Pl.*Tht.*193c. 2. *thing seen, sight*, φοβερὰν ὄ. προσιδέσθαι A.*Pers.*48 (anap.), cf. *Supp.*567 (lyr.); ὁρῶ Πυλάδην.., ἡδεῖαν ὄ. E.*Or.*727, cf. Pl.*Lg.*887d, etc.; ἄλλην ὄ. οἰκοδομημάτων other architectural *sights*, Hdt.2.136; τὰ δὲ χρήματα..ἔστιν ὄψις mere *outside show*, Antiph.33.2; πολλὴν ὄ. παρασχόντα ἔπειτα μηδὲν ὠφελῆσαι Hp.*Art.*44; of scenic representations, Arist.*Po.*1453ᵇ1, al.; ὁ τῆς ὄ. κόσμος ib.1449ᵇ33: pl., ib.1462ᵃ16. 3. *vision, apparition*, Hdt.1.39, etc.; ὄ. ἐν τῷ ὕπνῳ Id.3.30, al.; ὄ. ἐνυπνίου Id.8.54; ὄ. ὀνείρου Id.1.38; ὄ. ἔννυχοι A.*Pr.*645, cf. *Ag.*425 (lyr.), S.*El.*413, E.*Hec.*72 (lyr.), *IG*4²(1).121.11 (Epid., iv B.C.), etc. II. subjective, *power of sight* or *seeing, vision*, ὄψει τινὰ ἰδεῖν, ἐσιδεῖν, Il.20.205, Od.25.94, cf. Heraclit.55, Democr.11, Emp.4.10, Th.7.75, etc.; τῆς ἐμῆς ὄ. Hdt.2.99, 147; τῆς ὄ. στερηθῆναι Id.9.93, etc.; οὐ τὸ δρασθὲν πιστό-

τερον ὄψει λαβόντες ἢ τὸ ἀκουσθέν Th.3.38; οὐ καθορωμένους τῇ ὄ. νυκτὸς οὔσης ib.112. **b.** *act of seeing* or *looking*, ἡ εἰς τὸ ἄνω ὄ. Pl.*Cra.* 396b; *sense of sight*, Arist. *de An.*428$^{a}$6, *Mete.*369$^{b}$9; τὰ διὰ τῆς ὄ., of pleasures, Id.*EN*1118$^{a}$3, etc. **c.** pl., *organs of sight, eyes*, ὄψεις μαρᾶναι to quench *the orbs of sight*, S.*OT*1328, cf. *Ant.*52, Heraclit. 26; τὸ κάλλος πάντων εἷλκε τὰς ὄ. ἐπ' αὐτόν X.*Smp.*1.9; ἀσθενῖ (= -εῖ) τὰς ὄ. *POxy.*911.6 (iii A.D.): so in sg., ἐστερήθη τῆς μιᾶς ὄ. Plb.3.79. 12: sg. in collective sense, *the eyes*, [ἰχθῦς] λευκὴν ἔχοντες τὴν ὄ. Arist. *HA*602$^{a}$11, cf. *PA*656$^{b}$29. **d.** Medic., *iris* of the eye, Hp.*Prorrh.* 2.19 (but *eye-ball* or *eye*, Id.*Prog.*7 (pl.)); also, *pupil*, Ruf.*Onom.* 23. **e.** of the *visual rays* which were supposed to proceed from the eyes, Pl.*Ti.*45c, 46b, Arist.*Mete.*343$^{a}$13, 370$^{a}$19: in other places Arist. controverted this Empedoclean theory, *Sens.*437$^{b}$14. **2.** *view, sight*, ἀπικνέεσθαι ἐς ὄψιν τινί come into one's *sight*, i.e. *presence*, Hdt.1.136; εἰς ὄψιν τινὸς or τινὶ ἥκειν, μολεῖν, ἐλθεῖν, περᾶν, A.*Ch.*215, *Pers.*183, E.*Med.*173 (anap.), *Or.*513; καλέσαι τινὰ ἐς ὄ. Hdt.5.106; ἀποφαίνειν τί τινι ἐς ὄ. Id.4.81; λυπηρὰς τῇ ὄ. ἀχθηδόνας προστιθέμενοι Th.2.37; ἐν ὄ. τοῦ δήμου Plu.*TG*12; κατ' ὄψιν *in person*, ὡς ἐνετειλάμην σοι κατ' ὄ. as I enjoined you *when with you*, *POxy.*1154.4 (i A.D.), cf. 117.3 (ii/iii A.D.), etc. **b.** *dignity, position*, κατὰ τὴν ἐμὴν ὄ. καὶ ὑπόληψιν *PLond.*1.77.59 (vi A.D.); ἡ τῶν γονέων ἡμῶν προτεραία ὄ. *PMasp.*2 iii6 (vi A.D.).

**ὀψισμός**, ὁ, *a being too late*, D.H.4.46.

**ὀψι-σπορέω**, *sow late*, Thphr.*HP*8.1.7. **-σπορος**, ον, *late-sown, to be sown late*, Id.*CP*2.12.4. **-τεκνος**, ον, *late descendant*, Lyc. 1272. **-τέλεστος**, ον, *late of fulfilment*, τέρας ὄψιμον ὀ. Il.2.325, cf. Tryph.48, Nonn.*D.*25.362, al. **-τέλευτος**, f.l. for foreg., ib.5. 206, Sch.Il.21.232.

**ὀψίτερον**, v. ὄψιος sub fin.

**ὀψί-τομος** [ῐ], ον, *cut*, or *to be cut* or *pruned, late*, Thphr.*CP*3.2. 3. **-τῠχος**, ον, *successful after long delay*, Hdn.Gr.2.932, Anub. in *Cat.Cod.Astr.*2.209.28, Paul.Al.*M.*3, Man.5.71; ὀ. εἶ· μὴ ἀγωνία Astramps.*Orac.*15.8. **-φόρος**, ον, *late-bearing*, Thphr.*CP*1.17. 9. **-φῠγος**, ον, *fleeing late*, Hdn.Gr.1.234.

**ὀψίχα**· ὀψέ, Βυζάντιοι, Hsch.

**ὀψο-δαίδᾰλος**, ον, (ὄψον) *skilful in dressing food, a clever cook*, epith. of Archestratus in Ath.3.101b; cf. λογοδαίδαλος. **-δεία**, ἡ, (δέω B) *want of food* or *fish*, Suid. **-δόκη**, ἡ, = sq., Phot. s.v. κέραμον. **-θήκη**, ἡ, *place for keeping victuals in*, Suid. s.v. γύλιος. **-λογία**, ἡ, *cookery*, Ath.7.284e. **-λόγιον**, τό, *sample of imported foodstuff*, prob. in *PLond.*3.856.22 (i A.D.). **-λόγος**, ον, *one who discourses on cookery*, Ath.8.337b.

**ὄψομαι**, v. ὁράω.

**ὀψο-μᾰνής**, ές, *mad after dainties*, Chrysipp.*Stoic.*3.167. **-μᾰνία**, ἡ, *madness after dainties*, Eust. ad D.P.374.

⊛ **ὄψον**, τό, *cooked* or otherwise *prepared food, a made dish*, eaten with bread and wine, ἐν δὲ..σῖτον καὶ οἶνον ἔθηκεν, ὄψα τε Od.3.480; ἐν δέ οἱ ἀσκὸν ἔθηκε..οἴνοιο.., ἐν δὲ καὶ ἦα κωρύκῳ, ἐν δέ οἱ ὄψα τίθει 5. 267, cf.6.77, Il.9.489; παμπόνηρον ὄ. ὁ γέρανος Epich.87; ἄρτον,.. οἶνον.., ὄψον Th.1.138 (taken in signf. 3 by D.S.11.57); ἄρτους,.. ὄψον.., οἶνον Pl.*Grg.*518c; ὄ. ὀπτόν Ar.*Eq.*1106, cf. *Av.*900; ἐσθίουσι ἐπὶ τῷ σίτῳ ὄ. X.*Mem.*3.14.2, cf. 3.14.3; τῷ ὄ. (*cuisine*) τε καὶ τῷ οἴνῳ χαίροντα μᾶλλον ἢ τοῖς φίλοις ib.1.5.4; ὄ. ἕξουσιν, ἅλας τε δηλονότι καὶ ἐλάας καὶ τυρόν, καὶ βολβοὺς καὶ λάχανά γε, οἷα δὴ ἐν ἀγροῖς ἑψήματα, ἑψήσονται Pl.*R.*372c; opp. τραγήματα, Clearch.65; ὄψα..καὶ τραγήματα, ὄψα..καὶ μύρα, Pl.*R.*372e, 373a; Σικελικὴ ποικιλία ὄψου ib. 404d; φακῆν, ἥδιστον ὄψων Ar.*Fr.*23; τὴν ἔγχελυν..ὄψων μέγιστον the greatest of *delicacies*, Anaxandr.39.6; ὄ. δὲ ταὐτὸν ἀεί ποτε πᾶσίν ἐστιν, ὕειον κρέας ἑφθόν (in the Spartan φειδίτια) Dicaearch.Hist.23; εἷς ἄρτος, ὄ. ἰσχάς Philem.85, cf. X.*Cyr.*1.2.8; [τέχνη] ἡ τοῖς ὄ. (*dishes*) τὰ ἡδύσματα (sauces, seasonings) [ἀποδιδοῦσα μαγειρικὴ καλεῖται] Pl. *R.*332d, cf. *Tht.*175e, Plu.2.99d; ὄ. ὀξέα καὶ δριμέα καὶ ἁλμυρά X.*Cyr.* 6.2.31; τοὺς παῖδας διδάσκομεν..τῇ δεξιᾷ λαμβάνειν τοῦ ὄ. τῇ δ' ἀριστερᾷ κρατεῖν τὸν ἄρτον Plu.2.99d: metaph., ὄ. δὲ λόγοι φθονεροῖσι are a *treat* to the envious, Pi.*N.*8.21. **2.** *relish*, κρόμυον, ποτῷ ὄ. Il.11. 630; κολλύραν..καὶ κόνδυλον ὄ. ἐπ' αὐτῇ pudding and knuckle-*sauce*, Ar.*Pax*123: metaph., λιμῷ ὅσαπερ ὄψῳ διαχρῆσθε 'hunger is the best sauce', X.*Cyr.*1.5.12; ἡ ἐπιθυμία τοῦ σίτου ὄ. Id.*Mem.*1.3.5; ὄ. τροφῆς τὸ πεινῆν Socr.ap.Porph.*Abst.*3.26; οἱ πόνοι ὄ. τοῖς ἀγαθοῖς X.*Cyr.* 7.5.80. **3.** at Athens, esp. *fish*, the chief delicacy of the Athenians (πολλῶν ὄντων ὄ. ἐκνενίκηκεν ὁ ἰχθὺς μόνος ἢ μάλιστά γε ὄψον καλεῖσθαι Plu.2.667f, cf. Ath.7.276e); so in Pap., ὄ. as collective, = *fish*, *PCair. Zen.*82.17 (iii B.C.); in Hp.*Mul.*1.37 ὄψα θαλάσσια is v.l. (dub.). **II.** *market-place*, esp. *fishmarket*, εἰς τοὔψον Ar.*Frr.*247, 545, cf. Aeschin. 1.65.

**ὀψο-νομέω**, *to be an* ὀψονόμος, Critias 60 D. **-νόμος**, ὁ, (νέμω) *one who watches the price of fish*, Sophil.2. **-πλύνια**, gloss on σκάφαι, Hsch.

**ὀψοποι-εῖον**, τό, *oven for baking food*, Hsch. s.v. πύρδαλον. **-έω**, *dress food* (esp. *fish*) *nicely*, Alex.24.1, Plu.2.663c, etc.: metaph., ὀ. λόγον *make a dainty* speech, ib.55a:—Med., c. acc. cogn., X.*Mem.*3. 14.5: abs., Id.*HG*7.2.22, D.54.4. **-ημα**, ατος, τό, *a dainty dish*: generally, *food*, Lxx *Ju.*12.1, *Gp.*20.18 tit. **-ητικός**, ή, όν, *of* or *fit for delicate cookery*: ἡ -κή (sc. τέχνη) *the art of cookery*, Arist.*EN* 1153$^{a}$26, *Metaph.*1027$^{a}$4; *for cooking purposes*, μάκτρα *PRyl.*127.34 (i A.D.). **-ία**, ἡ, *cookery*, esp. *fine cookery*, X.*Mem.*3.14.5, Pl. *Grg.*462d; ὁ τὴν ὀ. συγγεγραφὼς τὴν Σικελικήν who wrote the Sicilian *cookery-book*, ib.518b. **-ικός**, ή, όν, = ὀψοποιητικός, ib.465d, X. *Oec.*9.7: ἡ -κή (sc. τέχνη), = ὀψοποιητική, Pl.*Grg.*463b, 465d (here with v.l. -ητική), Arist.*Pol.*1255$^{b}$26 (as v.l. for -ητική); coupled with κομμωτική, Phld.*Rh.*2.183 S. **-ός**, ὁ, *one who cooks food, a cook*, distd. from ἀρτοκόπος or ἀρτοποιός, Hdt.9.82, X.*HG*7.1.38, *Cyr.*5.5.39; from σιτοποιός, ib.8.5.3, Pl.*Grg.*517e; from μάγειρος, Id.*R.*373c, cf. *Tht.*178d; οὐκέτι μάγειρος ὀ. δ' ἐστί που Dionys.Com. 2.9; τὸν ὀ. σκευάσαι χρηστῶς μόνον δεῖ τοὔψον Alex.149.6: metaph., τοὺς εἰωθότας τῶν λόγων ὀ. Chor.*Brum.*14.18.

**ὀψο-ποΐς**, = -ποιός, *IG*5(1).210.60 (Sparta). ⊛ **-πόνος**, ον, *dressing food elaborately*, *AP*6.306. **-πώλης**, ου, ὁ, *victualler*, esp. *fishmonger*, *Gloss.*:—fem. **-πωλις** (sc. ἀγορά), ιδος, *fishmarket*, Clearch. 16, Plu.*Tim.*14; cf. sq. **-πωλία**, ἡ, *fishmarket*, Str.14.2. 21. **-πώλιον**, τό, *fishshop*, Id.17.2.4 (pl.), Lyd.*Mens.*4.138, Suid.

⊛ **ὄψος**, εος, τό, = ὄψον, Lxx *Nu.*11.22.

**ὀψοτράγος** [ᾰ], ὁ, = ὀψοφάγος, dub. in Cerc.6.13.

**ὀψοφᾰγ-έω**, *eat delicacies, live daintily*, Ar.*Nu.*983; ἡ μέλισσα πρὸς σάρκα..οὐθενὸς καθίζει, οὐδ' ὀψοφαγεῖ does not settle on cooked dishes, Arist.*HA*625$^{b}$21. **-ία**, ἡ, *dainty living*, Aeschin.1.42 (pl.), Theopomp.Hist.179, Arist.*EE*1231$^{a}$20, Philostr.*VA*1.9. **II.** *fish-diet*, Zeno *Stoic.*1.66. ⊛ **-ος**, ὁ, *one who eats delicacies*, such as *fish* and other *dainties, epicure, gourmet*, Ar.*Pax*810, Cephisod.9, Antiph. 190.5, Eub.88, Arist.*EN*1118$^{a}$32; ὀ. εἶ καὶ κνισολοιχός Sophil.7, cf. X.*Mem.*3.14.2 sq., Timae.71: epith. of a fish, Opp.*H.*1.141: irreg. Att. Sup. ὀψοφαγίστατος X.*Mem.*3.13.4, Poll.6.37.

⊛ **ὀψοφόρος**, ον, *carrying food*, Matro *Conv.*47, Poll.10.91.

**ὀψῶνα**· τὴν πρὸς τὸ ὀψωνεῖν σπυρίδα, Hsch.

**ὀψων-άτωρ** [ᾱ], ορος, ὁ, *caterer*, Ath.4.171a (from Lat. *obsonator*, cf. *AB*339.14). **-έω**, *buy fish and other dainties*, ὀψωνεῖν ἔοιχ' ἅνθρωπος ἐπὶ τυραννίδι Ar.*V.*495: c. acc., τριχίδας ὀ. Eup.154; καρκίνους Ar.*V.*1506; ὑπογάστρια Antiph.192.1, etc.: generally, *buy victuals, cater*, X.*Mem.*3.14.1: prov., Δελφοῖσι θύσας αὐτὸς ὀψωνεῖ κρέας ap.Plu.2.709a. **-ης**, ου, ὁ, (ὄψον) *one who buys fish* or *victuals, caterer, purveyor*, Ar.*Fr.*503, Alciphr.1.1:—also **-ητής**, Arr.*Epict.*3. 26.21, Tz.*H.*5.534. **-ητικός**, ή, όν, *of* or *for purveying*, τέχνη Ath. 6.228c, 7.313f. **-ία**, ἡ, *purchase of fish, etc., catering*, Critias 60 D., Antiph.184, Alex.186.2; ἔφερε ἕκαστος..πρὸς τούτοις (viz. food) εἰς ὀ. μικρόν τι κομιδῇ νομίσματος (in the Spartan φειδίτια) Plu.*Lyc.*12, cf. Dicaearch.Hist.23. **-ιάζω**, *furnish with provisions*, ὀ. τὰς δυνάμεις *furnish* an army *with supplies* or *pay*, Plb.15.25.11, cf. D.S.33. 22:—Pass., *to be supplied*, *PCair.Zen.*499.42 (iii B.C.), Plb.23.8.4, dub. l. in Str.14.2.5; ἐκ τῶν ἀλλοτρίων χρημάτων D.H.4.19, cf. D.S. 16.22. **-ιασμός**, ὁ, *furnishing with provisions*, Men.1050. **2.** *supplies and pay of an army*, Plb.1.66.7, 1.69.7, D.H.8.68. ⊛ **-ιαστής**, οῦ, ὁ, *caterer*, *PLips.*97 xii 8, al. (iv A.D.). **-ίζομαι**, = ὀψωνιάζομαι, παρὰ βασιλέων *Cat.Cod.Astr.*8(4).137.

**ὀψωνιοδόκος**, ον, *receiving provisions*, σπυρίς Poll.10.92.

**ὀψώνιον**, τό, (ὄψον, ὠνέομαι) *salary*, reckoned in money, τό τε ὀ. καὶ σιτομετρίαν καὶ τὸ ἔλαιον *PCair.Zen.*507.5, cf. 421.6, 483.14, 498.5 (all iii B.C.); ἵνα ἡμῖν ὀ. προστεθῇ καὶ σιτάριον ib.49.4 (iii B.C.); μετρήματα καὶ ὀ. corn- and *money*-payments, *UPZ*14.26 (ii B.C.); φυλακιτῶν *PPetr.*3 p.230 (iii B.C.); of a bank clerk, *PCair.Zen.*342.6 (iii B.C.): distd. from γραμματικόν (bonus on turnover), *PStrassb.*105.4 (iii B.C.); χωρὶς ὀψωνίων, of unsalaried services, *Inscr.Prien.*121.34 (i B.C.). **2.** a policeman's *pay*, *PLille* 25.55 (iii B.C.), *PFay.*302 (ii B.C.), *IG*9(2).1109.27 (Thess., ii/i B.C.); freq. a soldier's *pay*, *PStrassb.*103.16 (iii B.C.), *PTheb.Bank*6.7 (ii B.C.), Plb.6.39.12: so in pl., *pay* of an army, *Rev.Ét.Anc.*33.8 (Theangela, iv/iii B.C.), *OGI* 229.106 (iii B.C.), *SIG*410.19 (iii B.C.), 581.34 (ii/i B.C.), Plb.1.67.1, 3.25.4, Lxx 1*Ma.*3.28, Aristeas 22. **3.** *allowance* paid to a victorious athlete, *PRyl.*153.25 (ii A.D.), *CPHerm.*54.7, al. (iii A.D.); *allowance* or *scholarship* paid to a music-student, προδοῦναί μοι τὸ ὀ. καὶ τὸ κατὰ μῆνα ἀνάλωμα *PCair.Zen.*440.6 (iii B.C.); *allowance* to a son or daughter, *BGU*665 ii 15 (i A.D.), *POxy.*898.31 (ii A.D.); to a slave, distd. from ἱματισμός, *PCair.Zen.*28.6, 100.14 (iii B.C.). **4.** *wages* of labour, τὰ σώματα ἐνοχλεῖ ἡμᾶς τὰ ὀ. ἀπαιτοῦντα ib. 43.2, cf. 27.2, al., *PPetr.*2 p.113 (all iii B.C.), *POxy.*974 (iii A.D.); ἀρτάβην κριθῆς εἰς λόγον ὀψωνίων *PTeb.*420.24 (iii A.D.): metaph., ὀψώνια ἁμαρτίας the *wages* of sin, *Ep.Rom.*6.23. **5.** a magician's *fee*, *PMag.Par.*1.2454. **6.** *gratuity* to tax-farmers, *UPZ*112 v3 (pl.). **7.** = ὄψον I.1 (cf. Lat. *obsonium*), τῶν ἀνηλωμάτων πάντων σίτου καὶ ὀψωνίων ib.91.13 (ii B.C.).—The word is rejected by Phryn. 393. First used by Men.1051 (no context); ᾔτησεν εἰς ὀ. τριώβολον Thugen.2. Glossed ὀψωνία, also (in pl.) κέρδη, χαρίσματα, by Phot.

**ὀψωνιοπώλης**, ου, ὁ, *victualler*, *Gloss.*

# Π

**Π π**, **πεῖ**, *IG*2$^{2}$.2783.23 (iv B.C.), *BCH*29.483 (Delos), Hellad.ap. Phot.p.530B., indecl.: seventeenth (later sixteenth) letter of the Gr. alphabet: as numeral π′ = 80, but ͵π = 80,000.

**πᾷ**, Dor. for πῇ, *how?* Ar.*Ach.*785, *Lys.*171; for ὅπα, *GDI*2171 (Delph.); for ὅπου, Archim.ap.Simp. *in Ph.*1110.5: **πᾳ** for πῃ, *anywhere, anyhow*, Ar.*Lys.*155.

**πα**, apoc. for παρά, πα Δάματρα, π. Δάματρι, *GDI*3536*a*20, 3542.11 (Cnidus).

**πᾶά**, Lacon. for πᾶσα, Ar.*Lys.*995, Hdn.Gr.2.301.

**πᾱγά**, Dor. for πηγή.

**παγαίη**, = κύων (Scyth.), Hsch. **πάγανα**· σφύρα, Id.

**πᾶγᾶν-ικός**, ή, όν, (*pagus*) *civilian*, opp. στρατιωτικός, *PMasp.*2ii 23 (vi A.D.). 2. *unofficial*, *BGU*936.10 (v A.D.). 3. *lay*, opp. μοναχικός, *PFlor.*287.1 (v A.D.). ⊛ -ός, ὁ, *civilian*, *BGU*1043.25 (iii A.D.), etc. 2. *unofficial, private person*, *PLond.*5.1711.32 (vi A.D.), etc. 3. a kind of gladiator, *Rev.Arch.*30(1929).39 (Edessa).

**πᾶγάομαι**, (παγά = πηγή) *wash in a spring*, *GDI*1588 (Dodona).

**πᾶγαρχ-έω**, *hold office of* παγάρχης, *Ath.Mitt.*13.238 (Laodicea Combusta), Just.*Edict.*13.25:—Pass., *to be under a* π., *POxy.*133.8 (vi A.D.). **-ης**, ου, ὁ, = *magister pagi*, Just.*Edict.*13.25, *PMasp.* 3.25 (vi A.D.), etc. ⊛ **-ία**, ἡ, *district under a* π., Just.*Edict.*13.25, etc.; *office of* π., *POxy.*2110.4 (pl., iv A.D.). **-ικός**, ή, όν, *of a* π., ἐξουσία *PMasp.*19.4 (vi A.D.). **-ος**, ὁ, = παγάρχης, ib.68.10 (pl., vi A.D.), etc.

**παγάς**· γῆ τις ὑπὸ τῶν γεωργῶν, Hsch. **πάγασα**· θύρα, καὶ παγασαί, Id.

**Πᾰγᾰσαί**, αἱ, *Pagasae* in Thessaly, the port of Pherae, whence the Argonauts sailed, Hdt.7.193, etc.:—hence ἥρως **Πᾰγᾰσαῖος**, of Jason, *AP*4.3$^b$20 (Agath.): ὁ **Πᾰγᾰσίτης** [ῑ] κόλπος, D.12.5; λιμὴν **Πᾰγᾰσήϊος**, A.R.1.524; ἀκτὴ **Πᾰγᾰσηΐς**, ib.318.

**παγγάς**· πλάνος, Hsch.

**παγ-γέλοιος**, ον, (πᾶς) *thoroughly ridiculous*, Pl.*Phdr.*260c, *R.*522d, Palaeph.26; π. ἐστ' ἰδεῖν Eub.53.6. **-γενεί**, Adv. *with one's whole race*, π. τε καὶ πανδημεί Xanth.10; ἐκριζωθήσεται π. *IG*3.1423, 1424: written παγγενῆ in *EM*647.53, v.l. in Ael.*NA*17.27. **-γενέτης**, ου, *father of all*, Ζεύς Orph.*H.*20.5:—fem. **-γενέτειρα**, *mother of all*, φύσις *AP*12.97 (Antip.). **-γενέτωρ**, ορος, ὁ, = παγγενέτης, Ἥλιος Orph.*Fr.*236. ⊛ **-γεος**, ον, *holding the whole earth*, ἅρμα Id.*H.*59.8; δῆμος, of the Roman people, *Epigr.Gr.*344.10 (ii A.D.). **-γέωργος**, ον, *master-gardener*, metaph., ὁ π. λογισμός Lxx 4*Ma.*1.29. **-γήρως**, ων, *very old*, Tz. ad Lyc.826. **-γλῠκερός**, ά, όν, *sweetest of all*, Ar. *Lys.*970 (anap.). **-γλωσσία**, ἡ, *wordiness, garrulity*, Pi.*O.*2. 87. **-γόνατον**, τό, = βήχιον 1, Ps.-Dsc.3.112. **-γυμνος**, ον, *quite naked*, Eust.1398.59. **-γῠναικί**, Adv. *with all their women*, παμπαιδὶ καὶ π. D.C.41.9.

**παγελός**, = ἀστράγαλος, Hsch. **πάγεν**, v. πήγνυμι.

⊛ **πᾰγερός**, ά, όν, *frosty, cold*, D.Chr.30.11. II. τὸ π. *power of coagulation*, Aret.*CA*2.2: Comp. -ώτερος *more coagulated*, Id.*SA*2.2 (παγετ- codd.).

**πᾰγετ-ός** or **πάγετος** (Hdn.Gr.1.219), ὁ, = πάγος II, *frost*, Pi.*Pae.* 9.17, Hp.*Aër.*7 (pl.), etc.; ὅταν πάχνη ᾖ ἢ παγετὸς X.*Cyn.*5.1. **-ώδης**, ες, *frosty, ice-cold*, S.*Ph.*1082 (lyr.); of water, Hp.*Aër.*7; of air, Arist.*Mu.*392$^b$6; λουτρά Agathin.ap.Orib.10.7.22.

**πᾰγεύς**, έως, ὁ, *pedestal*, Hero *Dioptr.*3.

⊛ **πάγη** [ᾰ], ἡ, (πήγνυμι) *anything that fixes* or *fastens, snare, noose*, ὑπὸ πάγης ἁλόντος Hdt.2.121.ε'; ἐν τῇ π. ἐνέχεσθαι ib.β', cf. Pl.*Lg.* 824a; *fowling-net*, X.*Cyr.*1.6.39. 2. metaph., *trap, snare*, πάγας ἐπραξάμεσθα (leg. ἐφραξάμεσθα) A.*Ag.*822; π. ὑπόπυροι, of the beacons of Nauplius, S.*Fr.*435.

**παγηνός**· ὁ ἐξ ὁδοιπορίας καὶ διωγμοῦ κονιορτός, Hsch.

**πᾰγῐδάμεια** [δᾰ], ἡ, fem. *burster of toils*, perh. to be read in *PMag. Lond.*121.694 (πακ- Pap.).

**πᾰγῐδ-ευμα**, ατος, τό, *snare, enticement*, Aq.*Ec.*7.27(26). **-εύω**, (παγίς) *lay a snare for, entrap*, Lxx 1*Ki.*28.9, *Ev.Matt.*22.15. **-ιον**, τό, Dim. of παγίς, *snare, gin*, prob. in Vett.Val.284.26 (παγνίῳ codd.).

⊛ **πάγῐ-ος** [ᾰ], α, ον, also ος, ον Plot.2.1.4: (πήγνυμι):—*solid*, κηρὸς.. σιδήρου παγιώτερος Luc.*Alex.*21. Adv., εἶναι -ίως to be *solid*, opp. ῥεῖν, Arist.*Cael.*298$^b$30. II. *firm, steadfast*, οὐδὲν π. ἐστι τῶν ἀνθρωπίνων D.C.65.1; π. ἔχειν τὸν λόγον hold it *fast*, Pl.*Epin.*984d, cf. Plot. l.c.; πάγιον ἕστηκε Lib.*Or.*64.47; of persons, συστῆναι παγιώτατοι *steady* in the ranks, D.C.76.12. Adv. -ίως, λέγειν to say *positively, without reservations*, Pl.*R.*434d; π. νοῆσαι ib.479c, *Tht.* 157a; π. διισχυρίζεσθαι Id.*Ti.*49d, cf. Arist.*Rh.*1389$^b$19; *firmly, immovably*, ἑστάναι Dam.*Pr.*266. **-ότης**, ητος, ἡ, *certainty*, Hsch. s.v. εὐστάθεια. **-όω**, *make firm* or *fast*, Elias in *Porph.*118.31:—Pass., *EM*646.45; ἐπαγιώθη *it was resolved*, Men.Prot.p.23D.

⊛ **πᾰγίς**, ίδος, ἡ, (πήγνυμι) = πάγη, *trap*, Batr.117, Call.*Fr.*458, *AP* 6.109 (Antip.); παγίδας ἱστάναι Ar.*Av.*527 (anap.), cf. 194. 2. metaph., *trap, snare*, of women, Amphis 23, Men.689; δουρατέα π., of the Trojan horse, *AP*9.152 (Agath.); τοῖς ἄρτοις.. ἱστᾶσι παγίδας they try to 'raise the wind', Alex.66; of women's ornaments, Ar. *Fr.*666. II. ἄγκυρα νεῶν π. the anchor *which holds* ships *fast*, *AP* 6.5 (Phil.).

**παγίωσις**, εως, ἡ, *making fast*, π. τοῦ ὄντος τὸ ἀεί Olymp.*in Phd.* p.66N.

**παγ-καίνιστος**, ον, *ever renewed, ever fresh*, κηκίς A.*Ag.*960. **-κᾰκος**, ον, *utterly bad*, π. ἦμαρ *most unlucky* day, Hes.*Op.*813; *very noxious*, τὸ ἔλαιον τοῖς φυτοῖς π. Pl.*Prt.*334b. Adv. -κως, ὀλέσθαι A. *Th.*552; δόμοις π. ἔχειν Id.*Ch.*740; π. ἔθεσαν Id.*Pers.*282 codd.; τεθνάναι E.*Med.*1135; π. διακείμενος Python 1.6. 2. of persons, *utterly evil*, Thgn.149, Pl.*Lg.*928e, Arist.*EN*1099$^b$5: Sup., ὦ παγκάκιστε S.*Ant.*742, E.*Med.*465, etc. **-κάκουργος** [ᾰ], ον, *utterly wicked*, Hsch. s.v. παναίγυλος. **-κάλλιστος**, ον, *most beautiful*, π. στέφανος τοῦ ἰδίου γένους *IG*12(7).53.15 (Amorgos). **-κᾰλος**, η, ον, *all* or *very beautiful, good*, or *right*, Ar.*Pl.*1018, Pl.*Smp.*204c, *Phdr.*276e, *Lg.*722c, *Min.*319c; π. ᾠᾷ Theopomp.Com.9, etc. Adv. -λως Hp.*Art.*70, E.*Fr.*285.7; π. ἔχειν Pl.*Phdr.*230c; π. ἐναντιοῦσθαι, θορυβεῖν, Id.*Ap.*31d, *Euthd.*303b, cf. *Cra.*396a, *Euthphr.*7a. **-κάρπεια**, ἡ, *offering of all kinds of fruits*, π. συμμιγής S.*Fr.*398, cf. E.*Fr.* 912.4 (anap.). **-καρπία**, ἡ, = foreg., Anticl.13, Thphr.*HP*9.8.7; π. νηφάλιος *IG*2$^2$.1367. II. at Alexandria, a kind of *sweet cake*, Harp.Mend.ap.Ath.14.648b. **-καρπος**, ον, *of all kinds of fruit*, θύματα S.*El.*635; *rich in every fruit*, φυτά, χθών, Pi.*P.*9.58, *I.*4(3).41; γονὴ π. produce *of all kinds*, Pl.*Ax.*371c: metaph., π. ἀοιδά *AP*4.1.1 (Mel.); πάγκαρπον, τό, as title of a book, Gell.*Praef.*8. 2. *covered with fruit, berried*, δάφνη S.*OT*83. II. as Subst., = χαμαιλέων μέλας, Ps.-Dsc.3.9. **-κατάμικτος**, ον, *mixed of all sorts, hashed up together*, prob. l. in Philox.3.13. **-καταπύγων** [ῡ], ονος, ὁ, ἡ, *utterly lewd*, Ar.*Lys.*137. **-κατάρᾱτος** [ᾰρ], ον, *all-accursed*, ib. 588. **-κευθής**, ές, *all-concealing*, νεκρῶν πλάξ S.*OC*1563 (lyr.). **-κ(λ)άδια** [ᾰδ], τά, (κλάδος) festival at Rhodes at the pruning of vines, Hsch. **-κλαυστος** or **-κλαυτος**, ον, *most lamentable*, ἄλγη, θέρος, A.*Th.*368 (lyr.), *Pers.*822; π. αἰῶνα κοινόν, i.e. death, S.*El.*1085 (lyr.). II. Act., *all-tearful*, Id.*Tr.*652, *Ant.* 831 (both lyr.). **-κλειτος**, ον, *all-renowned*, Castorio 2. **-κλέπτης**, ου, ὁ, *thieve-all*, irreg. voc. πάγκλεπτε Tz.*H.*13.371. **-κληρία**, ἡ, *entire possession, property, estate, inheritance*, A.*Ch.*486, S.*Fr.*915, E. *Ion* 814, *Supp.*14. **-κληρος**, ον, *inherited*, δόμοι Id.*Ion* 1542. **-κοινος**, ον, *common to all*, νοσήματα Hp.*Aër.*2, Gal.17(1).2; π. σοφισταί Poll.4.43: mostly poet., π. χώρα, of Olympia, Pi.*O.*6.63; παγκοίνοις.. Δηοῦς ἐν κόλποις, of Eleusis, S.*Ant.*1120 (lyr.); πληγεὶς θεοῦ μάστιγι παγκοίνῳ, i.e. by death, A.*Th.*608; ἐξ Ἅιδου παγκοίνου λίμνας S.*El.* 138 (lyr.); ἐν ἀπέχθημα π. βροτοῖς one object of hate *common to all* mankind, E.*Tr.*425; π. τέρας Pi.*Pae.*9.10; στάσις π. *all* the band *together*, A.*Ch.*458 (lyr.). Adv. -νως Man.4.506. **-κοίρᾰνος**, ον, *supreme ruler*, θεὰ παγκοίρανε θήρης Opp.*C.*4.21. ⊛ **-κοίτης**, ου, ὁ, *where all must sleep*, π. θάλαμος, i.e. the grave, S.*Ant.*804 (anap.); π. Ἅιδας ib.811 (lyr.). **-κόνῑτος**, ον, *covered with dust*, ἄεθλα conflict *full of toil and dust*, Id.*Tr.*505 (lyr.). **-κόσμιος**, ον, *common to all the world*, μοῖρα Orph.*H.*34.20. **-κοσμος**, ὁ, *an entire world*, βουληθεὶς ὁ νοῦς ἕκαστος π. εἶναι Dam.*Pr.*279. **-κράδη**· ἀπὸ τῆς κράδης τῶν σύκων, Hsch. **-κρᾶνον**, τό, = θαψία, Ps.-Dsc.4.153 (παγκράτιον Wellmann).

**παγκρᾰτ-ευτής**, οῦ, ὁ, = παγκρατιαστής, Ps.-Callisth.1.18. ⊛ **-ής**, ές, (κράτος) *all-powerful*, epith. of Zeus, A.*Th.*255, *Eu.*918 (lyr.), E. *Fr.*431.4; π. ἕδραι his *imperial* throne, A.*Pr.*391; also of Μοῖρα, B.16. 24; of Hera, Id.10.44; of Apollo, E.*Rh.*231 (lyr.); of Athena, Ar.*Th.* 317 (lyr.); ὁ π. Κύριος Lxx 2*Ma.*3.22; τοῖνδε π. φονεὺς their *victorious* slayer, A.*Ag.*1648. 2. of things, π. πῦρ Pi.*N.*4.62; κεραυνός Id. *Dith.*2.15; σέλας S.*Ph.*986; ὕπνος, χρόνος, Id.*Aj.*675, *OC*609; ἀλάθεια B.*Fr.*10. **-ησία**, ἡ, *full power* or *possession*, Ph.2.129. **-ιάζω**, *perform the exercises of the* παγκράτιον, Isoc.15.252, Pl.*Grg.*456d, *Chrm.*159c, etc.: c. acc. cogn., πάντας ἐπαγκρατίασε τοὺς κλήρους *SIG*1073.28 (Olympia, ii A.D.): metaph., of gesticulation, *sway one's arms about like a gymnast*, ἐν τῇ ἐκκλησίᾳ Aeschin.1.26, cf. 33. **-ιαστής**, οῦ, ὁ, *one who practises the* παγκράτιον, Pl.*R.*338c, *Euthd.*271c, *IG*5(1).669 (Sparta), etc.; ἀνὴρ π. *SIG*1073.14 (Olympia, ii A.D.); παῖς π. *IG*1$^2$.846.13; title of plays by Alexis, Philemon, etc. **-ιαστικός**, ή, όν, *of* or *for the* παγκράτιον, ἡ π. τέχνη Pl.*Euthd.* 272a. Adv. -κῶς Poll.3.150, Sch.Pi.*N.*3.27. II. *skilled in the* παγκράτιον, ὁ θλίβειν καὶ κατέχειν δυνάμενος, παλαιστικός· ὁ δ' ὦσαι τῇ πληγῇ, πυκτικός· ὁ δ' ἀμφοτέροις τούτοις, π. Arist.*Rh.*1361$^b$26, cf. Gal. 6.158. **-ιον**, τό, (παγκρατής) '*all-in' contest in boxing and wrestling*, Xenoph.2.5, Pi.*N.*5.52, al., Hdt.9.105, *IG*5(1).658.14 (Sparta), 7.1765 (Thespiae), etc.; π. νικᾶν Th.5.49; π. μάχεσθαι Ar.*V.*1191; ὁ π. ἠσκηκώς Pl.*Lg.*795b. II. *sea daffodil, Pancratium maritimum*, Dsc.2.172, Plin.*HN*27.92. 2. = στοιχάς, Ps.-Dsc.3.26. 3. v. πάγκρανον. ⊛ **-ωρ**, ορος, ὁ, *all-powerful*, *CRAcad.Inscr.*1931.241 (Susa, i A.D.).

**πάγκρεας**, ατος, τό, *sweetbread, pancreas*, Arist.*HA*514$^b$11, Ruf. *Onom.*175, Gal.*UP*5.2. II. nickname given by Timo to the sceptic Pyrrho, Timo 31 (nisi leg. τὸ πᾶν κρέας).

**παγκρότως** ἐρέσσειν, to row *all in time* or *with a great noise*, A.*Supp.* 723.

**παγ-κτησία**, ἡ, *full ownership*, *SIG*364.78 (Ephes., iii B.C.), Ph.2. 392, Aq.*Le.*25.23, Poll.10.12. **-κτητικός**, ή, όν, *of full ownership*, κυρεία *Inscr.Perg.*245 C46. **-κύνιον**, τό, a poisonous seaweed, Ael.*NA*14.24. **-κῡφος**, ον, *quite crooked*, π. ἐλαία the sacred olive-tree in the citadel at Athens, because of its *dwarfed and twisted* shape, Ar.*Fr.*727.

**πάγνιον**, v. παγίδιον.

⊛ **πάγξενος**, ον, *all-hospitable, common to all*, S.*Fr.*378.1.

**παγό-λῠτον** ὕδωρ, water *from thawed ice*, Herod.Med.ap.Orib. 5.30.18, prob. in Democr.ap.Gal.14.131. **-πληξία**, ἡ, *frostbite*, *Hippiatr.*125.

⊛ **πάγος** [ᾰ], ὁ, (πήγνυμι) prop., *that which is fixed* or *firmly set*: I. *crag, rock*, σπιλάδες τε πάγοι τε Od.5.405; π. ὀξέες ib.411: generally, *rocky hill*, Hes.*Sc.*439, Pi.*O.*10(11).49, *I.*2.33; χλοερὸς ὑλώδης π. S.*Ichn.*215; ὁ Ἄρειος (Ion. Ἀρήϊος) π. *the Areopagus* at Athens, Hdt. 8.52, cf. A.*Eu.*685 sq.; Ἄρεος εὔβουλος π. S.*OC*947; Ἀρείοις ἐν π. E. *IT*1470, cf. 961; ἐν κλεινοῖς Ἀθηναίων π. S.*Fr.*323; μαντεῖος, ἀκρονιφὴς π., of Delphi, *Pae.Delph.*7, 16. II. after Hom., = παγετός, *frost*, πάγου χυθέντος S.*Ph.*293; π. φανέντος αἰθρίου Id.*Fr.*149.3; ὄντος π. οἵου δεινοτάτου Pl.*Smp.*220b, etc.: pl., τῶν ὑπαιθρίων π. A.*Ag.*335, cf. S.*Ant.*357 (lyr.), Arist.*HA*523$^a$20, *GA*735$^a$35, etc.: heterocl. dat. pl. πάγεσι Id.*Pr.*907$^a$9: dat. sg. πάγει (v.l. πάγοις) D.S.3.34. 2. *scum on the surface of milk*, Sch.Nic.*Al.*91. 3. *salt*, as formed by the evaporation of sea-water, Lyc.135. 4. *coagulation*, π. αἵματος

Aret.*CA*2.2, cf. *SA*2.7. 5. ἄκριτον πάγος of the confused *mass* outside the universe, Hp.*Hebd.*6; τὸν περιέχοντα πάγον Id.*Vict.*1.10, cf. Paul.Al.*I*.4.

**πᾶγος**, ὁ, = Lat. *pagus*, *district*, Plu.*Num.*16, *PGen.*54.33 (iv A.D.), etc. **πᾱγός**, v. πηγός. **παγούαιρ**· μάρμαρος ἢ μικακύς, Hsch.

⊛ **πάγουρος** [ᾰ], ὁ, *crab*, Ar.*Eq.*606, Xenarch.8.2, Speus.ap.Ath.3.105b, Arist.*HA*525b5, *Gp.*2.18.3, *MAMA*3.672 (Corycus):—applied to Phoenix by Lyc.419.

⊛ **πάγρος**, ὁ, perh. = φάγρος, Hdn.Gr.1.203.

**παγ-χάλεπος** [ᾰ], ον, *very difficult, impracticable*, of persons and things, Antipho 2.2.3, Pl.*Phd.*85c, *Cra.*409d, *Lg.*708d, v.l. in X.*An.* 5.2.20: c. inf., Pl.*Sph.*236d, *Plt.*291c, *Phlb.*16c. Adv. -πως, ἔχειν πρός τινα X.*An.*7.5.16. **-χάλκεος**, ον, *all-brazen*, ἄορ, ῥόπαλον, Od.8.403, 11.575; of a man, οὐδ' εἰ π. εὔχεται εἶναι Il.20.102. **-χαλκεύς** (παστχ- cod.)· πολύτεχνος, Hsch. **-χαλκος**, ον, = παγχάλκεος, κυνέη Od.18.378; ἀσπίς A.*Th.*591; γέννες S.*El.* 195 (lyr.); π. τέλη, of arms to be dedicated to Zeus, Id.*Ant.*143 (anap.); αἰχμή, ὅπλα, E.*Heracl.*276, *Or.*444. **-χαρής**, ές, *gladdening all*, Hermapio ap.Amm.Marc.17.4.22. II. Pass., *much rejoiced*, Astramps.*Onir.*p.5 R. **-χορτος**, ον, *all-satiating*, σῖτα S.*Fr.* 666. **-χρηστος**, ον, *good for all work*, ἄγγος Ar.*Ach.*936; κτῆμα X.*Mem.*2.4.5: -χρηστον, τό, name of various remedies, Gal.12.756, 13.101, Orib.*Fr.*97. **-χριστος**, ον, (χρίω) *thoroughly anointed*: τᾶς πειθοῦς παγχρίστῳ συγκραθείς without a Subst. in a corrupt passage, S.*Tr.*661 (lyr.; Sch. supplies πέπλῳ). **-χρόνιος**, ον, *persisting throughout all time*, Dam.ap.Simp.*in Ph.*776.23. **-χροος**, ον, contr. **-χρους**, ουν, *of all colours*, name of a gem, Plin.*HN*37.178; of the stone ταΐτης, Cyran.38. **-χρύσεος** [ῡ], ον, *all-golden, of pure gold*, θύσανοι Il.2.448; τόξα *h.Hom.*27.5; μῆλα Hes.*Th.*335:—also **-χρύσιος**, ον, Alcm.23.67; **-χρῡσος**, ον, Pi.*O.*7.4; νάκος Id.*P.*4.68; δίφροι S.*El.*510 (lyr.); δέπας E.*Med.*5, etc. **-χρωμα**, *verbena*, and **-χρώματον**, *dracontea*, *Gloss.*

**πάγχῠ**, Adv., (πᾶς, πᾶν) Ep., Ion., and Aeol. for πάνυ, *wholly, entirely*, μάλα π. Il.14.143; π. μάλα 12.165; π. λίην Od.4.825; ἐπὶ π. λάθωνται, λαθέσθαι (where ἐπί belongs to the Verb), Il.10.99, Hes.*Op.* 264; π. δ' εὔμαρες σύνετον πόησαι πάντι τοῦτ' Sapph.*Supp.*5.5; π. δοκέειν or ἐλπίζειν think or hope *fully* that.., Hdt.1.31, 4.135, cf. Pi.*P.*2.82, Epich.99.3, *Epic.Alex.Adesp.*8.3, Eus.Mynd.*Fr.*63.—Rare in Trag., once in A., *Th.*641 (trim.); also once in Ar., *Ra.*1531 (hexam.): in late Prose, App.*BC*2.2, *Syr.*24.

**παγχυρισμός**· πολυσύγκριτος, Hsch.

**πᾱγώδης**, ες, (πάγος) = παγετώδης, Thphr.*CP*2.4.12.

**πᾱδάω**, Dor. for πηδάω, 3 sg. παδῇ Sophr.20; imper. πάδη = πῆδα, Ar.*Lys.*1317.

**παδησχέαι**· σχίζαι, Hsch.

**παδόεις**, εσσα, εν, in fem. Παδόεσσα, as place-name, *πάδος-garden* or *grove*, *Schwyzer*664.18 (Orchom. Arc., iv B.C.).

⊛ **πάδος**, ἡ, prob. = πῆδος II, *Prunus Mahaleb*, Thphr.*HP*4.1.3.

⊛ **πάζιον**, τό, a gem, Hsch., Cyr.

**πᾰθ-αίνω**, (πάθος) *make pathetic*, τὰ μὴ ἔχοντα πάθος Corn.*Rh.*p.388 H.; *fill with emotion*, τοὺς ἀκροωμένους D.H.*Dem.*18, cf. 20, *Th.*23:—Med., aor. ἐπαθηνάμην Luc.*Am.*29; *speak with passionate gestures*, σύ μοι χολὴν κινεῖς παθαινομένη Men.*Epit.*587, cf. D.H.3.73, D.C.51.12; of an orator, D.H.*Lys.*9, Plu.2.447f, Luc.l.c.; of a dancer, *AP*5.128 (Autom.); of a musician, Plu.2.713a:—Pass., *to be subject to passion* or *emotionally affected*, π. κατὰ τὴν αἴσθησιν Porph.*Abst.*1.42, cf. *Sent.* 29, Procl.*Inst.*209. II. in Pass., *to be subject to external influences*, Olymp.*in Mete.*9.28, Simp.*in Cat.*316.12. ⊛ **-εινός**, ή, όν, *suffering, mournful*, Lxx *Jb.*29.25; *sick*, *Ostr.Bodl.*i 354 (ii/i B.C.):—written **παθινός**, *PTeb.*234 (ii B.C.). **-η**, ἡ, *passive state*, Pl.*Ti.*80b; *what is done* or *happens* to a person or thing, opp. πρᾶξις, Id.*Lg.*903b, cf. *Epin.* 983d; τὰς ἐκεῖ..π. *what happened* there, S.*Aj.*295; πᾶσαν τὴν ἑωυτοῦ π. all *that had happened* to him, Hdt.1.122. 2. *suffering, misfortune*, Pi.*P.*3.42,97 (pl.), S.*OC*7, etc.; πάθαι, opp. εὐτυχίαι, Hdt.3.40; ἡ π. τῶν ὀφθαλμῶν blindness, Id.2.111; of *morbid affections*, τὰς π. τὰς ἐν τῷ ὀστέῳ γινομένας Hp.*VC*13; ἡ τοῦ πνίγους π. suffocation, Pl.*Phlb.* 32a, cf. *Lg.*728c, 865e, 866b. ⊛ **-ημα**, ατος, τό, dat. pl. παθημάτοις *Com.Adesp.*283 (Aetol. acc. to Eust.279.42, 1761.36):—*that which befalls one, suffering, misfortune*, S.*Tr.*142, Th.4.48, etc.; τὸ π. τοῦ Χριστοῦ the *passion* of Christ, 2*Ep.Cor.*1.5; of good fortune, χαῖρε παθὼν τὸ π. (deification) Orph.*Fr.*32f: mostly in pl., Hdt.8.136, etc.; παθήμαθ' ἄπαθον S.*OC*361; ἀκούσια π., opp. ἑκούσια καὶ ἐκ προνοίας ἀδικήματα, Antipho 1.27; τὰ δέ μοι π. μαθήματα γέγονε my *sufferings* have been my lessons (cf. πάθος I. 2), Hdt.1.207, cf. Ar.*Th.* 199, Pl.*Smp.*222b. II. *emotion* or *condition, affection*, π. τῆς ψυχῆς εἶναι τὴν σωφροσύνην, οὐ μάθημα X.*Cyr.*3.1.17, cf. Pl.*Phd.*79d; opp. ποίημα, Id.*Sph.*248b; τὸ τῆς ἑτέρας χειρὸς π. Plot.4.9.2; but in early writers mostly in pl., *affections, feelings*, opp. ποιήματα, Pl.*R.*437b; τὰ περὶ τὸ σῶμα π. Id.*Phlb.*33d; ὅσα διὰ τοῦ σώματος π. ἐπὶ τὴν ψυχὴν τείνει Id.*Tht.*186c; π. ἐν τῇ ψυχῇ γιγνόμενα Id.*R.*511d; παθήμασιν ὑπηρετεῖν obey *the feelings*, Arist.*Pol.*1254b24; opp. ἤθη, ἕξεις, Id.*Rh.* 1396b33, cf. *Po.*1449b28. 2. Medic., pl., *troubles, symptoms*, Hp. *VM*2, *Epid.*2.2.24; π. καὶ νοσήματα Pl.*R.*439d, cf. 389c. III. in pl., *incidents, happenings*, τὰ ἐν..'Οδυσσείᾳ π. ib.393b; πάντα εἴδη καὶ π. πολιτειῶν Id.*Lg.*681d. 2. *incidents* or *changes* of material bodies, τὰ οὐράνια π. Id.*Ion* 531c, cf. *Phd.*98a; τὰ τῆς σελήνης π. Arist. *Metaph.*982b16, cf. *Mete.*363a24, 365a12. 3. in Logic, *incidents, properties*, or *accidents*, Pl.*Phdr.*271b, *Prm.*141d, 157b, Arist.*APo.* 76b13, *Cael.*310a20; τὰ π. τὰ αἰσθητά, of colour, etc., Id.*Sens.*445b 4. **-ημᾰτικός**, ή, όν, *liable to* παθήματα, *impressionable*, τὸ π. τῆς ψυχῆς μόριον Jul.*Or.*6.199c. Adv. -κῶς f.l. in S.E.*P.*2.10. **-ησις**, εως, ἡ, *passivity*, opp. ποίησις, Arist.*Ph.*202a23, *de An.*426a9, Plot. 6.1.20. II. *morbid affection, disease*, ὄψεων παθήσεις Antig.*Mir.* 171. ⊛ **-ητικός**, ή, όν, *capable of emotion*, δύναμις Ti.Locr.102e, cf. Porph.*Abst.*2.39, Jul.*Or.*6.183d: c. gen. rei, *capable of feeling*, Arist. *EN*1105b24. 2. *sensuous, impassioned, pathetic*, ἐποποιΐα Id.*Po.* 1459b9; λέξις Id.*Rh.*1408a10; ἐκ τῶν π. λέγειν describe the *symptoms of emotion*, ib.1417a36; τὸ π. *emotional style*, Cic.*Orat.*37. Adv. -κῶς, λέγειν Arist.*Rh.*1408a24; π. εἰρῆσθαι ib.1395a21. II. *receptive, passive*, opp. ποιητικός, Id.*GC*324a7, *Metaph.*1021a15, *Ph.*255a35, al.; π. ποιότητες *affective*, Id.*Cat.*9a28; τὸ π. μόριον (sc. τῆς ψυχῆς) *emotional*, Id.*Pol.*1254b8, cf. *Ph.*202a23, al.; *liable to* πάθη, [ζῷα] Thphr. *CP*1.22.3; τῆς ψυχῆς τὸ φανταστικὸν καὶ π. Zeno *Stoic.*1.56. Adv. -κῶς, σώματα π. κινούμενα *passively, without resistance* or *effort*, Plu.2.1111e; χωρεῖν Iamb.*Myst.*1.18. 2. Gramm., *passive*, ῥήματα D.H.*Amm.* 2.2, cf. 7, A.D.*Synt.*150.19, al. Adv. -κῶς *in the passive*, ib.276. 20. 3. Astrol., π. ζῴδιον, = παθικόν, Vett.Val.113.24. Adv. -κῶς Ptol.*Tetr.*172. 4. π. στέγνωσις *morbid* constriction of the pores, Sor.1.29. ⊛ **-ητός**, ή, όν, *one who has suffered*, Men.*Mon.*457. II. *subject to suffering*, *Act.Ap.*26.23; τὸ θνητὸν καὶ π. Plu.*Pel.*16, cf. *Num.*8. 2. *liable to external influence* or *change*, opp. ἀπαθής, Arist. *Mu.*392a33; π. καὶ μεριστόν Plot.6.4.8; *passive*, opp. δραστήριος, Ph. 1.2; νοῦς ἐστι π. καὶ μεριστός Olymp.*in Phd.*p.101 N.; but ὁ νοῦς ἀπαθής, ἡ δὲ γένεσις π. Dam.*Pr.*414, cf. Ph.1.176. 3. Medic., *diseased, affected*, στεφάνη *PMed.Strassb.*p.8.

⊛ **πᾰθῐκ-εύομαι**, *to be sexually passive*, *AP*11.73 (Nicarch.). ⊛ **-ός**, ή, όν, *remaining passive*: hence Lat. *pathicus*, i.e. *qui muliebria patitur*, Juv.2.99, etc.

**παθιώταρ**· συγγενοῦς, τελευταίου, Hsch.

⊛ **πάθνη**, ἡ, vulgar form of φάτνη, *Gp.*15.4.1, cf. Moer.p.391 P.: misspelt παθμή, Lxx *Jb.*6.5.

**πᾰθο-γνωμονικός**, ή, όν, *indicating a particular disease*, συμπτώματα Gal.17(2).390; συνδρομαί Id.8.14; τηρήσεις Id.18(2).663. **-κράτεια** [κρᾰ], with v.l. **-κρᾰτορία**, ἡ, *government of the passions, self-restraint*, Lxx 4*Ma.*13.5. **-κρᾰτέομαι**, Pass., *to be governed by passion*, ib. 7.20. **-λογέω**, *treat of* or *analyse the passions*, Phld.*Ir.*p.18 W., M.Ant.8.13. 2. *treat of pathology*, Gal.14.691; περί τινος Anon. Lond.20.17. **-λογία**, ἡ, *study of the passions*, *Gloss.* **-λογικός**, ή, όν, *treating of feeling* or *sensation*, τρόπος, opp. αἰτιολογικός, Epicur. *Nat.*143 G.; *treating of the passions*, τόπος Stob.2.7.2; τὸ π. μέρος *the branch of science which treats of disease, pathology*, Gal.14. 689. **-ποιΐα**, ἡ, *excitement of the passions*, Rufin.*Fig.*36. **-ποιός**, όν, *causing bodily disease*, Gal.12.251. 2. = παθητικός II. 3, ζῴδια *Cat.Cod.Astr.*1.147.

⊛ **πάθος** [ᾰ], εος, τό, (πάσχω) *that which happens* to a person or thing, τὰ ἐν τοῖς κατόπτροις τῆς ὄψεως π. Pl.*Tht.*193c; τὰ ἐν τῷ ἀνθρωπίνῳ βίῳ [τῆς ψυχῆς] π. Id.*R.*612a; *incident, accident*, τὰ ἀνθρωπήϊα π. Hdt.5.4; τὸ συντυχὸν π. S.*Aj.*313; οὗ τόδ' ἦν π. where this *incident* took place, Id.*OT*732; ἔξωθεν π. Pl.*R.*381a; *unfortunate accident*, Antipho 3.4. 10. 2. *what one has experienced*, good or bad, *experience*, τὸν πάθει μάθος θέντα κυρίως ἔχειν A.*Ag.*177 (lyr.); τά γ' ἐμὰ π. my *experiences*, Pl.*Phd.*96a; τὸ δρᾶμα τοῦ πάθους πλέον A.*Ag.*533; opp. ἔργα, Pl. *Phdr.*245c, Arist.*Cael.*298a28; opp. πρᾶξις, Pl.*Lg.*876d; ἤθη καὶ π. καὶ πράξεις Arist.*Po.*1447a28. b. in bad sense, *misfortune, calamity*, A.*Pr.*703, Hdt.1.91, Lys.32.10, etc.; οὐλίῳ σὺν πάθει S.*Aj.*932 (lyr.); τὰ τῆς Νιόβης π. Pl.*R.*380a, etc.; ἀνήκεστον π. ἔρδειν to do *an act which is* an irreparable *mischief* to one, Hdt.1.137; μετὰ τῆς θυγατρὸς τὸ π., i.e. her *death*, Id.2.133; π. μέγα πεπονθέναι, of a great *defeat*, Id.3.147, cf. 5.87, al. c. = πάθημα II. 2, Arist.*GA*738a16, 750a30, Gal.10.91. II. of the soul, *emotion, passion* (λέγω δὲ πάθη ..ὅλως οἷς ἕπεται ἡδονὴ ἢ λύπη Arist.*EN*1105b21), σοφίη ψυχὴν παθῶν ἀφαιρεῖται Democr.31; διὰ πάθους Th.3.84; ἐρωτικὸν π. Pl.*Phdr.*265b; π. ποιεῖν to excite *passion*, Arist.*Rh.*1418a12; ἐν π. εἶναι Id.*Pol.*1287b 3; ἐκτὸς τοῦ π. εἶναι to be exempt from *passion*, Teles p.56 H.; ἔξω τῶν π. γίγνεσθαι D.C.60.3; περὶ παθῶν, title of work by Zeno the Stoic, D.L.7.4; in Epicur., *sensation* (including pleasure and pain), ἀκουστικὸν π. *Ep.*1 p.13 U., cf. p.19 U. (pl.); ὡς κανόνι τῷ π. πᾶν ἀγαθὸν κρίνοντες ib.3 p.63 U. III. *state, condition*, τὸ τῆς παντοδαπῆς ἀγνοίας π. Pl.*Sph.*228e, cf. 247c, *Plt.*277d, *Ap.*22c; opp. ἐνέργεια, A.D.*Synt.*12.17; opp. ποίημα, Pl.*Sph.*248d. 2. *incidents* of things, *changes* or *happenings* occurring in them, τὰ οὐράνια π. Pl.*Hp.Ma.* 285c; τὰ περὶ τὸν οὐρανὸν π. Id.*Phd.*96c; τὰ τοῦ οὐρανοῦ π. καὶ μέρη Arist.*Metaph.*986a5; π. τοῦτο, ὃ καλεῖν εἰώθαμεν σεισμόν Id.*Mu.*395b 36. 3. *properties, qualities* of things, opp. οὐσία, Pl.*Euthphr.*11a; π. λέγεται..ποιότης καθ' ἣν ἀλλοιοῦσθαι ἐνδέχεται, οἷον τὸ λευκὸν καὶ τὸ μέλαν, καὶ γλυκὺ καὶ πικρόν, καὶ βαρύτης καὶ κουφότης, κτλ. Arist. *Metaph.*1022b15; τῶν ἀριθμῶν π. ib.985b29; ἀριθμοῖς καὶ γραμμαῖς καὶ τοῖς τούτων π. Iamb.*Comm.Math.*23; γεωμετρία περὶ τὰ συμβεβηκότα πάθη τοῖς μεγέθεσι Arist.*Rh.*1355b31, cf. *APo.*75b1; τῶν φυτῶν τὰ μέρη καὶ τὰ π. Thphr.*HP*1.1.1; αἱ δυνάμεις καὶ τὰ π. ib.8.4.2. IV. Gramm., *modification in form* of words (esp. dialectal), πάθη τῆς λέξεως Arist.*Rh.*1460b12, cf. A.D.*Pron.*38.24, al. 2. in Syntax, *modified construction*, of omission or redundancy, Id.*Synt.*6.15, 267. 8. b. *passivity*, D.T.637.30, A.D.*Synt.*12.17, al. c. in writing, signs other than accents and breathings (ἀπόστροφος, ὑφέν, ὑποδιαστολή), D.T.*Supp.*1 p.107 U. V. Rhet., *emotional style* or *treatment*, τὸ σφοδρὸν καὶ ἐνθουσιαστικὸν π. Longin.8.1; πάθος ποιεῖν Arist.

*Rh.*1418ᵃ12; πράγματα π. ἔχοντα Plu.2.711e, etc.: pl., πάθη διεστῶτα ὕψους Longin.8.2.

⊛ **παι** (accent unknown), a demonstr. Particle in Cypr., *Inscr.Cypr.* 135.4 H., al.

⊛ **Παιάν, ᾶνος, ὁ,** Ep. **Παιήων, ονος,** Att., Ion. **Παιών, ῶνος** (v. sub fin.), Aeol. **Πάων, ονος,** Sapph.*Supp.*20c.5:—*Paean* or *Paeon,* the physician of the gods, Il.5.401,899, cf. Pi.*P.*4.270; Παιήονος γενέθλη, i.e. physicians, Od.4.232. 2. title of Apollo (later as epith., Ἀπόλλωνι Παιᾶνι *BCH*11.94 (Hierocaesarea); ὦ βασιλεῦ Π.. Ἀπόλλον *BMus.Inscr.*1151); ἰὴ Παιήον' ἄειδον *h.Ap.*517, cf. Call.*Hec.*1.1. 10 (in Id.*Ap.* 103 ἰὴ ἰὴ Παιῆον', ἵει βέλος an etym. from ἵημι may be suggested); ἰὴ Παιών *GDI*iv p.884 (Erythrae, iv B.C.); ἰήϊε Παιάν A. *Ag.*146 (lyr.), S.*OT*154 (lyr.); ἰὼ Παιάν Id.*Tr.*221 (lyr.), Ar.*Ach.* 1212; ὦναξ Π. E.*Alc.*220, etc.; τὸν Παίωνά (better Παιῶνά) τε καὶ τὰς Μούσας ἐπικαλούμενος Pl.*Criti.*108c, cf. *Lg.*664c, A.*Ag.*1248; Πάον' ὀνκαλέοντες Sapph. l. c.; also of other gods, Ἀσκληπιὸς Παιών Ar. *Pl.*636, cf. *Pae.Erythr.*1; of Zeus at Rhodes, Hsch.; of Dionysus, Philod.Scarph.5, al., Orph.*H.*52.11; of Helios, ib.8.12; of Pan, ib. 12.11. 3. *physician, healer,* παιὼν γενοῦ τῆσδε μερίμνης A.*Ag.*99 (anap.); παιῶνα κακῶν S.*Ph.*168 (anap.). b. *saviour, deliverer,* ὦ θάνατε Παιάν A.*Fr.*255.1, cf. E.*Hipp.*1373 (anap.). **II. παιάν,** Ep. **παιήων,** Att., Ion. **παιών,** *paean,* i.e. *choral song,* addressed to Apollo or Artemis (the burden being ἰὴ or ἰὼ Παιάν, v. supr. 1. 2), in thanksgiving for deliverance from evil, μολπῇ θεὸν ἱλάσκοντο, καλὸν ἀείδοντες παιήονα Il.1.473; Κρητῶν παιήονες *h.Ap.*518; παιᾶν' ἐπευφήμησεν A.*Fr.*350.4, cf. B.15.8, Procl.ap.Phot.*Bibl.*p.320 B.: hence opp. θρῆνοι, A.*Ch.*343 (anap.), cf. Sch.Ar.*Pl.*636 (but v. infr. 4); addressed to other gods, as to Poseidon after an earthquake, X.*HG*4.7.4. 2. *song of triumph* after victory, prop. to Apollo, Il.22.391 sq.; ἁλώσιμος π. A.*Th.*635, etc.; also, *battle-song,* παιᾶν' ἐφύμνουν σεμνὸν Ἕλληνες Id.*Pers.*393, cf. Lys.2.38, X.*Cyr.*4.1.6; addressed to Ares, Sch.Th.1.50; ἐξάρχειν τὸν π. or τοῦ παιᾶνος, X. *Cyr.*3.3.58, Plu.*Rom.*16; π. ποιεῖσθαι X.*HG*7.4.36. 3. *any solemn song* or *chant,* esp. on beginning an undertaking, Th.7.75 (pl.); π. γαμήλιος Ar.*Th.*1035 (lyr.); τριτόσπονδος π. A. *Ag.* 247 (lyr.); ἔγχει κἀπιβόα τρίτον παιῶνα Pherecr.131.5, cf. Antiph.4, 85.5. 4. by oxymoron, π. Ἐρινύων, π. τοῦ θανόντος, A.*Ag.*645, *Ch.*151; π. στυγνός, of a dirge, E.*Tr.*126 (lyr.); παιᾶνα στενάζειν ib.577; π. τῷ κάτωθεν θεῷ Id.*Alc.*424. **III.** in Prosody, *paeon,* a foot consisting of 3 short and 1 long syll., ‒⏑⏑⏑, ⏑‒⏑⏑, ⏑⏑‒⏑, or ⏑⏑⏑‒, Arist.*Rh.*1409ᵃ2 (in form παιάν; later παιών), Heph.3.3, etc.; also π. διάγυιος, the foot ‒ ⏑ ‒, and π. ἐπιβατός, a foot of 5 long sylls., Aristid.Quint.1.16.—Attic form: Παιών is used of the god in *IG*1².310.229 (v B.C.), and in codd. of Att. Prose and Com.; παιάν is used of the song in *IG*2². 1338.19 (i B.C.), but this may be Hellenistic; codd. have παιών in Pherecr.131.5, Ar.*Th.*1035, Pl.*Ion* 534d, *Lg.*700b, d, *Ep.*348b (prob. also in *Smp.*177a), παιάν in Antiph.4, D.19.338, Aeschin.2.162, and freq. in X., *HG* ll. cc., al. (cf. παιωνίζω); the metrical foot is always παιών; the Ion. forms are παιών, Παιών, *SIG*57.12 (Milet., v B.C.), *GDI*iv p.884 (Erythrae, iv B.C.):—Accentuation: Παιών (the pr. n.) *An.Ox.*1.276; παιών (the song) Theognost.*Can.*38, Eust.138.10, 1109.11, Suid.; παίων is sts. found in codd., and Παίων (the god) is right acc. to Suid. Cf. παιανίζω, -ανισμός, παιωνίζω, -ωνισμός.

**παιᾶν-ίας, ου, ὁ,** *paean-singer, IG*5(1).209, al. (Sparta). **-ίζω,** v. παιωνίζω. **-ικός, ή, όν,** *of* or *like a paean,* ἰδίωμα Ath.15.696c; ᾠδή Eust.137.39. ⊛ **-ις, ιδος, ἡ,** = foreg., ἀοιδαί Pi.*Fr.*139. **-ισμός,** ὁ, v. παιωνισμός. ⊛ **-ισταί, οἱ,** guild of *paean-chanters,* at Rome, *IG*14.1084 (ii A. D.); at the Piraeus, *SIG*1110 (iii A. D.). **-ῖτις, ιδος, ἡ,** name of a *gem,* Plin.*HN*37.180 (prob. l.), Isid.*Etym.* 14.4. 13.

**παιᾶνογράφος** [γρᾰ], ὁ, *writer of paeans,* Apollon.*Mir.*40.

**παιγ-μα, ατος, τό,** *play, sport,* λωτὸς ὅταν..παίγματα βρέμῃ whene'er the pipe sounds its *sportive strains,* E.*Ba.*161 (lyr.); Λύδια π. λύρας *Lyr.Alex.Adesp.*37.15. **II.** 'child's play', τὸ τοιοῦτο π. τῶν λόγων Polystr.p.28 W. **-μός, ὁ,** = foreg., Sch.Il.21.575. **-μοσύνη,** ἡ, poet. = foreg., Stesich.50 (pl.).

**παιγν-ήμων, ον,** gen. **ονος,** *jocular,* Hdn.*Epim.*106. Adv. **-όνως** Eust. 772.38. ⊛**-ία,** Ion. **-ίη, ἡ,** *play, sport, game,* Hdt.1.94, 2.173, Lxx *Jd.*16.27, Phld.*Rh.*2.50 S. **II.** = ἑορτή, Ar.*Lys.*700. **-ιᾰγράφος** [γρᾰ], ὁ, *writer of playful poetry,* Ath.14.638d. **-ιήμων, ον,** gen. **ονος,** = παιγνήμων, Hdt.2.173; τὸ κομψὸν καὶ π. [τοῦ Σωκράτους] Numen.ap.Eus.*PE*14.5. ⊛ **-ιον, τό,** *plaything, toy,* ἄνθρωπον θεοῦ τι παίγνιον εἶναι Pl.*Lg.*803c, cf. *Plt.*288c; τύχης π. Secund.*Sent.*7; πλοῖον ἀνέμων π. ib.17; οἷον π. φεῦγον, of Matter because of its instability, Plot.3.6.7: in pl., Pl.*Lg.*797b, etc.; *dainties,* Ephipp. 24. 2. of persons, *darling, pet,* Anaxandr.9.3: also in pl. (of one person), Ar.*Ec.*922, Plu.*Ant.*59. **II.** in Theoc.15.50, the Egyptians are called κακὰ παίγνια, roguish *cheats,*—unless here it be acc. cogn. (*dirty tricks*) after παίζω. **III.** *game,* Κουρήτων ἐνόπλια π. Pl. *Lg.*796b: metaph., *child's play,* of an easy task, Euphro1.35. 2. *comic performance,* Pl.*Lg.*816e, Ephipp.7, Suet.*Aug.*99. 3. *light poem, AP*6.322 (Leon.), Plb.16.21.12; Ὁμήρου, Κράτητος π., Jul.*Or.* 2.60d, 6.199d; title of poems by Philetas, Stob.2.4.5, al.; applied to those of Theocritus, Ael.*NA*15.19: metaph., of the *merry chirp* of the cicada, *AP*7.196.6 (Mel.). 4. of a prose *trifle,* Gorg.*Hel.* 21. 5. Δημοκρίτου παίγνια *jocular recipes, PMag.Lond.*121. 167. ⊛ **-ιος, ον,** *playful,* εὐστοχίη *AP*7.12.212 (Strat.). **-ιώδης, ες,** = foreg., Plu.*Ages.*2; τὸ π. *playfulness,* X.*HG*2.3.56; τὸ παιγνιωδέστερον Id.*Smp.*2.26.

**παιδαγρέται** (παιλ- cod.)· ἀρχή τις ἐπὶ ἱππέων, Hsch. (i.e. = ἱππαγρέται).

**παιδᾰγωγ-εῖον, τό,** *room in a school-house in which the* παιδαγωγοί *waited for their boys,* D.18.258, *IG*11(2).199 *A* 112 (Delos, iii B.C.). 2. later, *school,* Plu.*Pomp.*6, Them.*Or.*21.258b. **-έω,** pf. πεπαιδαγώγηκα Luc.*Tim.*13:—Pass., fut. παιδαγωγήσομαι in pass. sense, Pl. *Alc.*1.135d: aor. ἐπαιδαγωγήθην Hp.*Art.*52, Pl.*Lg.*641b: pf. πεπαιδαγώγημαι Plu.*Ant.*10:—*attend as a* παιδαγωγός, *lead* or *manage like a child,* γέρων γέροντα παιδαγωγήσω σ' ἐγώ S.*Fr.*695 (= E.*Ba.* 193); ἢ παιδαγωγεῖν γὰρ τὸν ὁπλίτην χρεών; Id.*Heracl.*729:—Pass., of a child, Hp. l. c. 2. generally, *train, guide, educate, moderate,* τινα Pl.*Tht.*167c; τὰς ἐπιθυμίας Muson.*Fr.*7 p.29 H.; τὸ θέατρον.. π. τὰ ἤθη τῶν δρώντων Luc.*Salt.*72, cf. *Tim.*13; *guide* an elephant's trunk, Ael.*NA*2.11:—Pass., συμποσίου ὀρθῶς παιδαγωγηθέντος well *led, managed,* Pl.*Lg.*641b; τὴν παιδαγωγηθεῖσαν οὕτω πόλιν ib.752c; ἂν ὑπὸ τοῦ λόγου παιδαγωγηθῇ τὸ πάθος Plu.2.443d. 3. *attend like a* παιδαγωγός, *wait upon, follow,* Pl.*R.*600e, *Alc.*1.135d. 4. 'lead by the nose', *cajole,* in Pass., ὑπό τινος Hyp.*Ath.*3. **-ημα, ατος, τό,** *plan of educating,* Max.Tyr.37.5. **-ία, ἡ,** *office of a* παιδαγωγός, hence metaph., Pl.*Ti.*89d; *training,* ψυχὰς παιδαγωγίας τυχούσας Id.*R.*491e; *culture* of trees, Plu.2.2e: generally, *attendance* on the sick, E.*Or.* 883. **-ικός, ή, όν,** *suitable to a teacher* or *trainer,* παρρησία M.Ant. 11.6, cf. Plu.2.124d; ἡ -κὴ τῶν νοσημάτων ἰατρική system of medicine which *waits upon* diseases, Pl.*R.*406a; ὁ -κός (sc. λόγος), title of a *treatise on education* by Cleomenes the Cynic, D.L.6.75. Adv. **-κῶς** Plu.2.73a. **-ός, ὁ,** = παιδὸς ἀγωγός, *slave who went with a boy from home to school and back again,* Hdt.8.75, E.*Ion* 725, *El.*287, Antipho 3.3.7, Lys.32.28, Pl.*Ly.*208c: coupled with τίτθη, τροφός, Id.*R.*373c; with ἡγεμών, ib.467d; with διδάσκαλος, X.*Lac.*3.1; of Phoenix, as the π. of Achilles, Pl.*R.*390e, etc.; Fabius is called the π. of Hannibal, *because he always followed him about,* Plu.*Fab.*5: metaph., ὁ νόμος π. εἰς Χριστόν *has guided us* until attainment of faith in Christ, *Ep.Gal.*3.24: generally, *leader,* δημοκρατίας, τυραννίδος, Plu.*Arat.*48, *Galb.*17.

**παιδαλήθριον**· παιδισκάριον, Hsch.

**παιδάρειον,** late spelling of παιδάριον, σῶμα ἀνδρεῖον π. *BCH*17.389 (Delph., written σ. ἀ. παιδάριον *GDI*1904.2 (ibid.)).

⊛**παιδᾰρ-ίδιον, τό,** Dim. of παιδάριον, *Gloss.* **-ιεύομαι,** Dep., *behave childishly,* Aristox.ap.Stob.4.1.49, Hsch. s. v. βλαττοῖ, al. **-ιήματα**· παιδάρια, Id. ⊛ **-ικός, ή, όν,** *for slaves,* of perquisites, *PHamb.*23.33 (vi A. D.). ⊛ **-ιον, τό,** Dim. of παῖς, *little boy,* Ar.*Av.*494, *Pl.*536, etc.; ἐκ παιδαρίου from *a child,* Pl.*Smp.*207d; ἐκ μικροῦ π. D.53.19; π. εἶ you're *a mere boy,* Ar.*Nu.*821; also, *little girl,* Id.*Th.*1203, Hyp.*Fr.*164, Men.428 (in this sense only Att. acc. to Moer.p.321 P.): in pl., *young children,* Ar.*V.*568; π. καὶ γύναια And.1.130, cf. D.19.305. **II.** *young slave,* Ar.*Pl.*823, 843, X.*Ages.* 1.21, *PPetr.*2 p.128 (iii B.C.), etc. **-ιοτρόφος, ὁ,** *one who keeps young slaves,* prob. in Judeich *Altertümer von Hierapolis* 270. ⊛ **-ίσκος, ὁ,** = παιδάριον, Hld.5.14. ⊛ **-ιώδης, ες,** *childish, puerile,* Pl.*Phlb.*14d, Arist.*Pol.*1270ᵇ28, *Metaph.*995ᵃ5, Nicoch.21, Plb.12.4ᴮ.1 (Sup.); τὸ -έστατον *the most puerile style,* Longin.4.1. Adv. **-δῶς** Plb.27.2.10, Phld.*Mus.*p.91 K., Gal.14.224.

**παιδαρτάω, -ησις,** ff. ll. for πεδαρτάω, -ησις (qq. v.).

**παιδδωάν,** v. παίζω.

**παιδεία, ἡ,** *rearing of a child,* A.*Th.*18. 2. *training and teaching, education,* opp. τροφή, Ar.*Nu.*961, Th.2.39 (pl.); π. καὶ τροφή Pl. *Phd.*107d, *Phlb.*55d. 3. its result, *mental culture, learning, education,* ἡ π. εὐτυχοῦσι κόσμος, ἀτυχοῦσι καταφύγιον Democr.180, cf. Pl. *Prt.*327d, *Grg.*470e, *R.*376e, Arist.*Pol.*1338ᵃ30, etc.; τῆς Λακεδαιμονίων π. Pl.*Prt.*343a: in pl., *parts* or *systems of education,* Id.*Lg.* 653c, 804d. 4. *culture* of trees, Thphr.*CP*3.7.4. 5. πλεκτὰν Αἰγύπτου παιδείαν ἐξηρτήσασθε the twisted *handiwork* of Egypt, i.e. (acc. to Sch.) *ropes of papyrus,* E.*Tr.*129 (lyr.). 6. *anything taught* or *learned, art, science,* π. ἱερή, of medicine, *IG*14. 2104. 7. *chastisement,* Lxx *Pr.*22.15, *Ep.Hebr.*12.5. **II.** *youth, childhood,* παιδείης πολυήρατον ἄνθος Thgn.1305, cf. 1348; ἐκ παιδείας φίλος Lys.20.11; so (prob.) στερρὰν παιδείαν E.*IT*206 (lyr.). 2. in collect. sense, *body of youths,* παιδείας λιπαρὴς ὄχλος Luc.*Am.*6.

**παίδειος** or **παιδεῖος** (Hdn.Gr.1.135), **ον,** = παιδικός, *of* or *for a boy,* ὕμνοι π. songs *to the boys they loved,* Pi.*I.*2.3, cf. Ath.13.601a; π. κρέα A.*Ag.*1242, 1593; π. τροφή the care *of rearing children, a mother's* cares, S.*Ant.*918; π. οἰκοδομήματα Pl.*Lg.*643b; μάθημα ib.747b; αἱ π. τιμαί honours *bestowed on children,* ib.810a. **II.** Subst. **παιδεῖον, τό,** *boy's dress,* prob. in *IG*2².1516.8.

**παιδεραστ-εύω,** = sq., Rhetor. in *Cat.Cod.Astr.*8(4).169. **-έω,** *to be a lover of boys,* Pl.*Smp.*192b, Luc.*DDeor.*12.1, al. **-ής, οῦ, ὁ,** *lover of boys,* mostly in bad sense, Ar.*Ach.*265 (lyr.), X.*An.*7.4.7, Pl. *Smp.*192b, Eub.130, etc. **-ία, ἡ,** *love of boys,* Pl.*Smp.*181c. **-ικός, ή, όν,** *of* or *for* παιδεραστία, Luc.*Dom.*4. **-ρια, ἡ,** fem. of παιδεραστής, as title of the Niobe of Sophocles, dub. in Ath.13.601b (Schweigh. for παιδεραστάν).

⊛**παιδέρως, ωτος, ὁ,** = παιδεραστής, Telecl.40. **II.** *holm-oak, Quercus Ilex,* Paus.2.10.6 (in pl. παιδὸς ἔρωτες Nic.*Fr.*74.55). b. = ἄκανθος, Dsc.3.17 (but = ἄκανθα, 4.73). c. *chervil, Anthriscus cerefolium,* Plin.*HN*19.170. 2. a kind of *opal,* ib.37.84, cf. Orph.*L.* 282. 3. *rouge,* Alex.98.18, Duris10J., Alciphr.1.33, 3.11, etc. b. a vegetable dye of purple hue, *PHolm.*23.5, al.:—also **παιδερώτινον, τό,** *PLeid.X.*96.

⊛ **παίδ-ευμα, ατος, τό,** *that which is reared up* or *educated,* i.e.

*nursling, scholar, pupil*, E.*El.*887: [ὑμεῖς] παιδεύματα θεῶν ὄντες Pl.*Ti.* 24d; μῆλα, φυλλάδος Παρνασίας παιδεύματ' E.*Andr.*1100; πόντου παιδεύματα, of fish, Id.*Fr.*27.5 (lyr.): in pl., of a single object, Id.*Hipp.* 11. II. *thing taught, subject of instruction*, S.*Fr.*1120.3, Pl.*Lg.* 747c (pl.), X.*Oec.*7.6, D.60.16 (pl.), Arist.*Pol.*1338ᵃ11 (pl.). 2. *means of instruction*, κακόν τι π. ἦν ἄρ'.. ὁ πλοῦτος E.*Fr.*54. **-ευσις**, εως, ἡ, *process* or *system of education* (παιδείας παράδοσις Pl.*Def.*416a), Hdt.4.78, 6.128, Ar.*Nu.*986, 1043; τροφὴ καὶ π. Pl.*Criti.*110c, *R.*424a; ξενικὴν π. παιδεύειν Id.*Hp.Ma.*284c; τὴν ὑπ' ἀρετῆς Ἡρακλέους π. his *education* by virtue, X.*Mem.*2.1.34; Ἕλληνας καλεῖσθαι τοὺς τῆς π. τῆς ἡμετέρας μετέχοντας Isoc.4.50, cf. 3.57; ἡ περὶ τοὺς λόγους π. *instruction* in rhetoric, Id.11.49: in pl., τροφαὶ καὶ -σεις Pl.*Lg.* 926e. 2. its result, *culture, learning*, Ar.*Th.*175, Antipho Soph. 60, Isoc.9.78, Pl.*Prt.*349a, Arist.*Rh.*1399ᵃ13. 3. *instructing, coaching, priming* of witnesses, ἐκ παιδεύσεως, v.l. for ἐκ παρασκευῆς in D.34. 48. II. *means of educating*, τὴν πόλιν πᾶσαν τῆς Ἑλλάδος παίδευσιν εἶναι is *the school* of Greece, Th.2.41. III. in late Gr., ἡ σή, ἡ ὑμετέρα π., form of address to members of the learned professions, *Stud. Pal.*20.129.13 (v A.D.), *POxy.*1165.2 (vi A.D.), etc. **-ευτέος**, α, ον, *to be educated*, ἐν [μαθήματι] Pl.*R.*526c; τῷ λόγῳ Arist.*Pol.*1334ᵇ8. II. παιδευτέον, *one must educate*, Pl.*R.*377a, 402c. **-ευτήριον**, τό, *school*, D.S.13.27, Str.4.1.5, Longus 2.9, Jul.*Or.*6.182b. **-ευτής**, οῦ, ὁ, *teacher, instructor*, Pl.*R.*493c, al., *IG*2².1011.35. 2. *minister of education*, Pl.*Lg.*811d, al. II. *corrector, chastiser*, *Ep.Hebr.*12.9. **-ευτικός**, ή, όν, *of* or *for teaching*, δυνάμεις Ti.Locr.103e; βίος Str.14.5.4; ἡ -κή (sc. τέχνη) *education*, Pl.*Sph.*231b; π. ἐπιστῆμαι Phld.*Mus.*p.105 K.; τὸ π. Plu.*Lyc.*4; παράδειγμα π. τοῖς εὖ φρονοῦσι Hierocl.*in CA* 11 p.441 M. Adv. -κῶς Ph.1.169: Sup. -ώτατα ib. 319. 2. *skilled in teaching*, ib.438. **-ευτός**, ή, όν, *to be gained by education*, παιδευτὴν εἶναι ἀρετήν Pl.*Prt.*324b. **-εύω**, fut. -σω: aor. ἐπαίδευσα: pf. πεπαίδευκα:—Med., fut. παιδεύσομαι E.*Fr.*1068: aor. ἐπαιδευσάμην Pl.*R.*546b:—Pass., fut. παιδευθήσομαι ib.376c; παιδεύσομαι (in pass. sense) Id.*Cri.*54a: aor. ἐπαιδεύθην S.*OC*562, Pl. *Mx.*236a, etc.: pf. πεπαίδευμαι X.*Cyr.*5.2.17, Pl.*Lg.*920a, etc.: (παῖς):—*bring up* or *rear a child*, λευκὸν αὐτὴν.. ἐπαίδευσεν γάλα S.*Fr.* 648:—Pass., ἐπαιδεύθην ξένος Id.*OC*562; Ἅιδου δ' ἐν δόμοις παιδεύεται E.*Ion*953: but mostly, II. opp. τρέφω or ἐκτρέφω (Pl.*Cri.*54a, al.), *train and teach, educate*, παῖδας, etc., S.*Tr.*451, E.*Supp.*917; τοὺς νέους Pl.*Ap.*24e, etc.; κάκιστον ἡ εὐπετείη παιδεῦσαι τὴν νεότητα Democr. 178; οἱ πεπαιδευμένοι *educated, cultured* persons, opp. ἀμαθεῖς, Id.185; τὴν Ἑλλάδα πεπαίδευκεν.. ὁ ποιητής Pl.*R.*606e; also, of animals, *train*, X.*Eq.*10.6 (Pass.), v. infr.:—Constr.: π. τινά τινι *educate in* or *by*.., παιδείᾳ πεπαιδευμένους Pl.*Lg.*741a; μουσικῇ καὶ γυμναστικῇ π. τινάς Id. *R.*430a; ἔθεσι τοὺς φύλακας ib.522a; π. τινὰ ἐν τοῖς ἔργοις Lys.2.3, etc.; ἐν ἤθεσι, ἐν ἀρετῇ, Isoc.4.82, 12.138; ἐν μουσικῇ καὶ γυμναστικῇ Pl.*Cri.*50e; π. τινὰ εἰς ἀρετήν, εἰς τέχνην τινά, Id.*Grg.*519e, X.*Mem.* 2.1.17 (Pass.); πεπαιδευμένον πρὸς ἀρετήν, πρὸς τὸ μετρίων δεῖσθαι, Pl. *R.*492e, X.*Mem.*1.2.1 (Pass.); πρὸς τὴν πολιτείαν βλέποντας Arist. *Pol.*1260ᵇ15; ἐπ' ἀρετήν X.*Cyn.*13.3 (Pass.); περὶ βύρσας Id.*Ap.*20, etc.: c. dupl. acc., π. τινά τι *teach* one a thing, Antipho 3.2.3, Pl.*R.* 414d; ἀείμνηστον παιδείαν αὐτοὺς ἐπαίδευσε Aeschin.3.148: c. acc. rei only, *teach* a thing, Arist.*Pol.*1337ᵇ23: c. acc. et inf., π. τινὰ κιθαρίζειν Hdt.1.155: with predicative Adj. or Subst., π. τινὰ κακόν S.*OC*919; γυναῖκας σώφρονας π. E.*Andr.*601:—in Pass., c. acc. rei, *to be taught* a thing, παιδεύεσθαι τέχνην Pl.*Lg.*695a, al.; ἀκούσματα Men.*Kith.Fr.*5: c. acc. cogn. (attracted), ἀπὸ παιδεύσιος τῆς ἐπεπαίδευτο Hdt.4.78: c. inf., π. ἄρχειν X.*Mem.*2.1.3; ὄρνιθες ἐπεπαίδευντό σοι.. ὥστε ὑπηρετεῖν Id.*Cyr.*1.6.39 (in later Gr., of things, ἡ ὕλη παιδεύεται φέρεσθαι.. Pall.*in Hp.*2.106 D.); ἐν τοῖς ἀναγκαιοτάτοις π. *to be educated* only in what is indispensable, Th.1.84: esp. in pf. part. Pass. πεπαιδευμένος, *educated, trained, expert*, X.*Cyr.*5.2.17; opp. ἀπαίδευτος, Pl.*Lg.*654d; ἱκανῶς π. ib.b; φαυλοτέρως π. δικασταί ib.876d; opp. δημιουργός, Id.*Amat.*135d; ἰατρὸς ὅ τε δημιουργὸς καὶ ὁ ἀρχιτεκτονικός, καὶ τρίτος ὁ π. περὶ τὴν τέχνην Arist.*Pol.*1282ᵃ4; π. also, *well-bred*, Id.*EN*1128ᵃ21:—Med., *to have* any one *taught, cause* him *to be educated*, E.*Fr.*1068; οὓς ἡγεμόνας πόλεως ἐπαιδεύσασθε *educated* as leaders, Pl.*R.*546b: c. acc. cogn., πολλὰ δ' ἐκεῖνος αὐτὸν ἐπαιδεύσατο Id.*Men.*93d:—also in Act. in this sense, ἐν Ἀρίφρονος ἐπαίδευε *had* him *educated* in the house of Ariphron, Id.*Prt.*320a, cf. *Cri.*50e: c. acc. cogn., Id.*Men.*93e; of animals, *cause to be trained*, Nausicr.2.8 (whereas Med. is sts. used like Act., τροφαὶ αἱ παιδευόμεναι *educating* nurture, i.e. education, E.*IA*561 (lyr.)). 2. abs., *give instruction, teach*, Isoc.15.226. III. *correct, discipline*, τοὐμὸν ἦθος π. νοεῖς S. *Aj.*595; διαίτῃ τὴν ψυχὴν ἐπαίδευσε καὶ τὸ σῶμα X.*Mem.*1.3.5; ὕβρις πεπαιδευμένη *chastened* (i.e. *well-bred*) insolence, Aristotle's definition of εὐτραπελία, *Rh.*1389ᵇ11. 2. *chastise, punish*, Lxx *Ho.*7.12, *Ev.Luc.*23.16, al. **-ήϊος**, η, ον, Ion. for παίδειος, Eus.Hist.p.203 D., Nonn.*D.*9.185, al. II. παιδήϊα, τά, *festival of a φρατρία on the admission of a child*, *Schwyzer* 323 *A* 25 (Delph., v/iv B.C.). **-ία**, Ion. -ίη, ἡ, *childhood*, = παιδεία II. 1; ἐν παιδίῃ καὶ νεότητι Hp.*Prorrh.* 2.42; παιδίας καὶ νηπιότητος χάριν Pl.*Lg.*808e; *childishness*, ib. 864d. **-ιά**, ᾶς, ἡ, (παίζω) *childish play, pastime, amusement*, opp. σπουδή, X.*Smp.*1.1; ἔν τε παιδιαῖς καὶ ἐν σπουδαῖς Pl.*Lg.*647d, cf. Arist.*EN*1176ᵇ9 (pl.); π. μαχητικαί, etc., Id.*Rh.*1370ᵇ35; π. παῖσαι πρός τινα *to play a game* with.., Ar.*Pl.*1056; μετὰ παιδιᾶς *in sport*, Th. 6.28, Pl.*Phlb.*19d; σὺν πολλῷ γέλωτι καὶ παιδιᾷ (v.l. παιγνιᾷ) X.*Cyr.* 2.3.18, cf. 2.3.20; ἐν π. Pl.*Cra.*406c; τοὺς ἐν ταῖς παιδιαῖς νεωτερίζοντας in their *games*, Id.*Lg.*798c; π. καὶ φλυαρία, λῆροι καὶ π., σκώμματα καὶ π., γέλως καὶ π., Id.*Cri.*46d, *Prt.*347d, Plu.2.59b, 456e; παιδιᾷ πεπαῖσθαι to be done *in fun*, Pl.*Phdr.*265c: metaph., ὥστε σοι τὸν νῦν χόλον (ὄχλον Döderl.).. παιδιὰν εἶναι δοκεῖν will seem *mere child's play*, A. *Pr.*316; παιδιᾶς ἕνεκα καὶ ἀναπαύσεως Arist.*Pol.*1339ᵃ16; διαγωγὴ μετὰ παιδιᾶς Id.*EN*1127ᵇ34; *wit, jesting*, ib.1128ᵃ20:—Pl. plays on the words παιδιά and παιδεία, *Lg.*656c. II. in pl., *school holidays*, *SIG* 577.79 (Milet., iii/ii B.C.). **-ιακός**, ή, όν, *of children*, ἐπίκρισις *PSI* 5.450.69 (ii/iii A.D.). **-ικέωρ**· ἐν γυμνασίῳ ὑπηρέτης, Hsch.; cf. παιδισκιωρός. **-ικός**, ή, όν, *of a child*, θρίξ *IG*12(5).173 iii 4 (Paros); χιτών *PTeb.*127 (ii B.C.); ἡλικία Demetr.Lac.*Herc.*1055.10; *for* or *like a child*, whether *boy* or *girl*, but more commonly the former, *boyish*, ἔρως Pl.*R.*608a, cf. S.*Fr.*841; πέος Ar.*Lys.*415; π. χορός the chorus *of boys*, Lys.21.4; π. δῶρον a present *for a child*, Arist.*EN*1123ᵃ15; π. ἁμαρτίαι, φιλίαι, ib.1119ᵃ34, 1165ᵇ26; π. μαθήματα the *elementary* sciences, chiefly geometry, Plb.9.26ᵃ.4; π. μέτρησις Str.2.4.2; παλαίστρα *SIG*577.84 (Milet., iii/ii B.C.); τὸ π. νικᾶν to win *in the boys' games*, *IG*5(1).275, al. (Sparta, also written παιδιχόν, ib.260, al.); π. αὐλός, opp. παρθένιος, Arist.*HA*581ᵇ11. 2. *playful, sportive*, λόγοι X.*Ages.*8.2; opp. σπουδαῖος, Pl.*Cra.*406c. Adv. -κῶς, opp. σπουδαίως, ibid., Id.*Ly.*211a, etc. 3. *puerile*, φθόνος Id.*Phlb.*49a; ἠλίθιον καὶ λίαν π. Arist.*EN*1176ᵇ33. II. *of* or *for a beloved youth*, ὕμνοι π. *love*-songs, B.*Fr.*3.12; π. λόγος a *love*-tale, X.*Cyr.*1.4.27; παιδικά (sc. μέλη), such as the twenty-ninth Idyll of Theoc. III. as Subst. παιδικόν, τό, *boys' gymnasium*, *AJA* 18.329 (i B.C.): but mostly, 2. *darling, favourite, minion*, μηδὲ παλλακὴν μηδὲ π. ἔχειν *PTeb.*104.20 (i B.C.):—elsewh. in pl. (of a single person) παιδικά, ῶν, τά, mostly of a boy, S.*Fr.*153, Pl.*Prt.*315e, etc.; [Ζήνων] π. τοῦ Παρμενίδου his *darling pupil*, Id.*Prm.*127b; π. ὢν καὶ πιστότατος Th.1.132, cf. Pl. *Phdr.*239a: seldom as a real pl., ἐρασταὶ καὶ π. Id.*Smp.*178e, Onos. 24; rarely of a *girl*, Cratin.258, Eup.327: generally, Philostr.*Her.* 2.7. b. metaph., *darling pursuit*, φιλοσοφία τὰ ἐμὰ π. Pl.*Grg.*482a, cf. Max.Tyr.35.1, Lib.*Or.*59.133.

**παιδικῡνηγεσία**, ἡ, or **-έσια**, τά, *boys' hunting*, *BCH*3.328.

**παιδίνορ**· παιδίσκη, Hsch.

**παιδι-όθεν**, Adv. *from a child*, ἐκ π. Lxx *Ge.*47.3, *Ev.Marc.*9.21. **-ον** (parox.), τό, Dim. of παῖς (never in Trag.), *little* or *young child* (up to 7 yrs., acc. to Hp.ap.Ph.1.26), Hdt.1.110, 2.119, Ar.*Pax* 50; τὰ νεωστὶ γεγονότα π. Pl.*Ly.*212e; ἐκ παιδίου from *a child*, Ar. *Eq.*412, X.*Cyr.*1.6.20: prov., τοῦ πατρὸς τὸ π. 'chip of the old block', *Com.Adesp.*672, title of satire by Varro; so τῆς μητρὸς τὸ π. Str.10.3. 15 (with play on Μήτηρ). II. *young slave*, male or female, *IG*1².329. 27, 2².1554.67, 1556.22, Ar.*Ra.*37, *Nu.*132, *Av.*1150 (s.v.l.). III. τὸ παιδίον, a disease of children, prob. *convulsions*, dub. l. in Hp.*Aër.* 3. **-ος**, ὁ, barbarism for foreg., Plu.*Alex.*27. **-ότης**, ητος, ἡ, *childhood*, Aq.*Ps.*109(110).3.

**παιδισκ-άριον**, τό, Dim. of παιδίσκη, Men.338, 402.15, Ph.2.451, Arr.*Epict.*3.25.6, Luc.*DMort.*27.7, Hld.1.11; μουσικὰ π. Posidon.28.4 J. **-εῖος**, α, ον, *for a child*, χλανίσκιον *Jahresh.*16 *Beibl.*53 (iv B.C.). II. Subst. παιδισκεῖον, τό, *brothel*, Ath.10.437f. **-η**, ἡ, Dim. of παῖς (ἡ), *young girl, maiden*, X.*An.*4.3.11, Anaxil.22.26, Men.102, etc.; π. νέα, of a wife, Plu.*Cic.*41. II. *young female slave, bondmaid*, Lys.1.12, 13.67, *PCair.Zen.*142 (iii B.C.), *Ep.Gal.*4. 22: generally, *maidservant*, *Ev.Marc.*14.66; τοὺς παῖδας καὶ τὰς π. *Ev.Luc.*12.45. 2. *prostitute*, Hdt.1.93, Is.6.19, Plu.*Per.*24, *Cat. Ma.*24, etc.; αἱ δημόσιαι π. Ath.10.437e. **-ιωρός**, ὁ, *officer in charge of boys' gymnasium*, *IG*5(1).133 (Sparta). **-ος**, ὁ, Dim. of παῖς (ὁ), *young boy* or *son*, Ar.*Ec.*1146, X.*HG*5.4.32, Herod.3.30, Plb.30.26.9, Luc.*Merc.Cond.*28, D.C.45.2, *PStrassb.*56.23 (iii A.D.).

**παιδιώδης**, ες, (παιδιά) *playful*, Ion Hist.1; *fond of amusement*, Arist.*EN*1150ᵇ16, Aret.*SD*1.6; τὸ π. Plu.2.68a. II. (παιδίον) *puerile*, τὸ π. D.H.*Pomp.*6.

**παιδνός**, ή, όν (also ός, όν E.*IT*1271 (lyr.)), *childish*, A.*Ag.*479; παιδναὶ χέρες, for παιδὸς χ., *AP*7.632 (Diod.). II. *of childish years*, π. ἐών Od.21.21, 24.338, Call.*Jov.*57.

**παιδο-βάτιον**· εἶδος ἀμπέλου, Hsch. **-βόρος**, ον, *child-eating*, μόχθοι π., of Thyestes, A.*Ch.*1068 (anap., Aurat. for παιδόμοροι), cf. Nonn.*D.*21.120. **-βοσκός**, όν, *keeping boys*, Luc.*Lex.*13. **-βρώς**, ῶτος, ὁ, ἡ, *eating children*, Κρόνος Eust.86.13. **-βρωσία**, ἡ, *child-eating*, Dam.*Pr.*377. **-βρωτος** θοίνη, a feast *at which children were eaten*, Lyc.1199. **-γονία**, ἡ, *begetting of children*, Pl.*Smp.* 208e, Hld.10.40; *giving birth to children*, of the mother, Ath.Med.ap. Orib.*inc.*7.3, Sor.1.27. **-γόνια** (sc. ἱερά), τά, a festival *at a child's birth*, D.S.33.13. **-γόνος**, ον, (γονή) *begetting children*, ἰὼ Ζεῦ.. παιδογόνε πρόπος Ἰνάχου *father of a child by* the daughter of Inachus, E. *Supp.*629 (lyr.); *giving birth to children*, Κύπρις *AP*5.53 (Diosc.); φύσις (i.e. *genitalia*) Ps.-Phoc.187. II. *giving generative power, making fruitful*, φάλης Theoc.*Ep.*4.4; π. ὕδωρ a spring *with aphrodisiac properties*, Thphr.*HP*9.18.10. **-δῐδάσκᾰλος**, ὁ, *teacher of boys*, Sch.E.*Or.*1492. **-εις**, εσσα, εν, v. παιδοῦς. **-θεν**, Adv. *from childhood*, Ibyc.1.10, Them.*Or.*25.310d, Ps.-Luc.*Philopatr.*19; ἐκ π. *Sammelb.*5294.8 (iii A.D.). **-κομέω**, *take care of a child*, *AP* 7.623 (Aemil.). **-κομία**, ἡ, *care, education of a child*, Hsch. **-κόμος**, ον, *cherishing children*, Nonn.*D.*5.378. **-κόραξ**, ἄκος, ὁ, *boy-raven*, i.e. *greedy after boys*, θυμός *API*2.42 (Diosc.). **-κόρης**, ου, ὁ, title of Hermes at Metapontum, Hsch. **-κράτωρ** [ᾰ], ορος, ὁ, ἡ, *guardian of boys*, Id. s.v. κουράτωρ. **-κτίζω**, corrupt for παιδοποιέω, Erot. s.v. οὐ παιδοκτίσει. **-κτονέω**, *murder one's children*, E.*HF*1280. **-κτονία**, ἡ, *child-murder*, Ph.2.27, Hierocl.*in CA*14 p.452 M. **-κτόνος**, ον, *slaying one's children*, S.*Ant.*1305, E.*HF* 835: generally, *slaying offspring*, Opp.*H.*5.586.

**παιδ-ολετήρ**, ῆρος, ὁ, *child-slaying*, Suid. :—fem. **-ολέτειρα**, ἡ, *murderess of her children*, E.*Med*.849 (lyr.), *APl*.4.138. **-ολέτις**, ιδος, ἡ, = foreg., *AP*3.3 (Inscr. Cyzic.). **-ολέτρια**, ἡ, = foreg., Hsch. **-ολέτωρ**, ορος, ὁ, ἡ, *child-murdering*, Ἔρις A.*Th*.726 (lyr.), cf. E.*Med*.1393 (anap.); ἀηδονίς Id.*Rh*.550 (lyr.).

**παιδο-λῡμάς**, άδος, ἡ, (λύμη) *destroying her child*, ἁ π. Θεστιάς A.*Ch*.605 (lyr.). ⊕ **-μᾰθής**, ές, *having learnt in childhood*, Hp.*Lex* 2; *precociously quick*, π. πρός τι Antid.2.5; περὶ τὰ πολεμικά Plb.3.71.6; τινος Longin.44.3. **-μᾰθία**, Ion. -ίη, ἡ, *instruction from infancy*, Hp.*Lex* 2,3. **-μᾰνής**, ές, *mad after boys*, *AP* 5.18 (Rufin.), Plu.2.88f; π. ἔρως Alex.Aet.5.5; κραδία *AP*5.207 (Mel.); ἀλιτροσύνη ib.301.8 (Agath.). **-μᾰνία**, ἡ, *mad love of boys*, Plu.2.769b. ⊕ **-νομέω**, *hold office of* παιδονόμος, *Milet*.1(9).336 (ii A.D.), Artem.2.30. **-νομία**, ἡ, *education of children*, Arist.*Pol*.1335$^{b}$4. II. *the office of* παιδονόμος, ib.1322$^{b}$39. **-νομικός**, ή, όν, *concerning* παιδονόμοι, νόμος *SIG*577.54 (Milet., iii/ii B.C.). **-νόμος**, ὁ, (νέμω) *supervisor of education*, mostly in pl., of a board of magistrates, as in Crete, Ephor.149 J.; at Sparta, X.*Lac*. 2.2; at Miletus, *SIG*577.26, al. (iii/ii B.C.); at Ephesus, *BMus.Inscr*. 481*.274 (παιδω- lapis, ii A.D.); in Caria, *CIG*2715.12 (Stratonicea); of a single magistrate, *SIG*694.57 (Pergam., ii B.C.); of a woman, *Milet*.1(7) No.265; παιδονόμος..ἀριστοκρατικόν Arist.*Pol*.1300$^{a}$4, cf. 1336$^{a}$32. **-παις**, παιδος, ὁ, *grandson*, *IG*12(2).168 (Mytil., i B.C.), al.

⊕ **παιδ-οπίπης** [ῑ], ου, ὁ, *spying after boys*, = παιδεραστής, Ath.13.563e.

**παιδοποι-έω**, *beget children*, of the man, Luc.*DDeor*.22.1; ἐκ γυναικός E.*Heracl*.525: pf. Pass., ἐξ ἧσπερ ὁ βάσκανος οὗτος πεπαιδοποίηται *has been begotten*, D.25.80. 2. *bear children*, of the woman, S.*El*.589, Ar.*Ec*.615, Sor.1.29. II. more commonly in Med., fut. -ήσομαι Pl.*R*.449d: aor. ἐπαιδοποιησάμην E.*Or*.1080, Pl.*Lg*.868d, etc.: pf. πεπαιδοποίημαι Aeschin.2.149, D.S.16.6: abs., of the man, E.*Or*.1080, Pl.*R*.449d, X.*Mem*.2.2.4, Men.404.2; ἐκ γυναικός And. 4.23; ἐξ ἑταιρῶν Aeschin.2.177: also c. acc., υἱόν D.S.4.28. 2. f.l. for παῖδα ποιεῖσθαι, *adopt*, Plu.2.1000d. **-ήσιμος**, ον, *fit for begetting children*, gloss on ἀρώσιμοι, Sch.S.*Ant*.569. **-ησις**, εως, ἡ, *child-bearing*, Pl.*Lg*.947d, Vett.Val.123.2. **-ητέον**, *one must beget children*, Arr.*Epict*.3.7.19. **-ία**, ἡ, *procreation of children*, Pl.*R*.423e, Ocell.4.4, Porph.*Marc*.1, etc.: in pl., Pl.*Smp*.192b. II. *adoption*, νομοθέτης ἐγένετο Φιλόλαος περὶ τῆς π. Arist.*Pol*.1274$^{b}$3, cf. Ptol.*Tetr*.174. ⊕ **-ός**, όν, *begetting* or *bearing children*, δάμαρ E.*Andr*.4, cf. J.*AJ*4.8.23; π. ἀδονά E.*Ph*.338 (lyr.). 2. *generative*, σπέρμα Hdt.6.68.

**παιδο-πόρος**, ον, *through which a child passes*, γένεσις *AP*9.311 (Phil.). **-σπορέω**, *beget children*, Pl.*Phdr*.250e, Ph.2.20. **-σπόρος**, ον, *begetting children*, Ar.*Fr*.358.

**παιδοσύνη**, ἡ, poet. for παιδεία, Man.4.378.

**παιδοτόκος**, ον, *favouring child-birth*, Εἰλείθυιαι Orac.ap.Phleg. 37 J.

**παιδοτρῐβ-έω**, *to be a gymnastic trainer*, *IG*2.1224, *SIG*577.25 (Milet., iii/ii B.C.), etc. 2. generally, *train, exercise, educate*, τινα D.25.7; τινὰ ἔν τινι Plu.2.795e: metaph., πεπαιδοτριβηκὼς τυραννίδα *trained up*, Plu.*Comp.Cic.Dem*.4:—Pass., ψυχῆς πεπαιδοτριβημένης Ph.2.265; π. ἐπὶ στρατηγίᾳ παρά τινος Jul.*Caes*.324d. II. = παιδεραστέω, *AP*12.34 (Autom.), 222 (Strat.). **-ης**, ου, ὁ, (τρίβω) *physical trainer, gymnastic master*, Antipho 3.3.6, Pl.*Prt*.312b, *IG*2$^{2}$.665.25, *PHal*.1.261 (iii B.C.), *SIG*697 E 10 (Delph., ii B.C.), etc.; οἱ περὶ τὸ σῶμα, π. καὶ ἰατροί Pl.*Grg*.504a; ἐν παιδοτρίβου at *his* school, Ar.*Eq*. 1238, *Nu*.973; ὁ διὰ βίου π. τῶν ἐφήβων *IG*3.746: metaph., ὁ π. τοῦ τυράννου Jul.*Or*.2.58c. **-ία**, Ion. -ίη, ἡ, *the art of a* παιδοτρίβης, Hp.*Vict*.1.24, Archipp.51. **-ικός**, ή, όν, *of* or *for a* παιδοτρίβης: ἡ -κή (sc. τέχνη) *his art*, Isoc.15.181, Arist.*Pol*.1338$^{b}$7. Adv. -κῶς, λέγειν *like a gymnastic master*, Ar.*Eq*.492.

**παιδότριψ**, ῐβος, ὁ, = παιδοτρίβης, Luc.*Tim*.14; but f.l. for πεδότριψ in Ph.2.446.

**παιδοτροφ-έω**, *rear children*, Ar.*Lys*.956 (anap.), Luc.*DMeretr*.2.1, M.Ant.4.32:—Pass., of plants, *to be reared*, *Gp*.4.3. **-ία**, ἡ, *rearing of children*, Antipho Soph.66, X.*Oec*.7.21, Pl.*R*.465c, D.22.65, 24.172, Men.*Epit*.37, J.*AJ*2.6.2, etc.; of animals, Opp.*C*.3.161. **-ιον**, τό, perh. *feeding-bottle*, *PTeb*.414.20 (ii A.D.). ⊕ **-ος**, ον, *nourishing young life*, Simon.12.4; ἐλάα S.*OC*701 (lyr.). 2. as fem. Subst., *mother*, E.*HF*902 (lyr.). 3. title of Artemis in Messenia, Paus. 4.34.6.

**παιδότρωτος**, ον, *wounded by children*, πάθεα π. wounds and death *at children's hands*, A.*Eu*.496 (lyr.).

⊕ **παιδουργ-έω**, = παιδοποιέω, E.*Ion* 175 (lyr.). ⊕ **-ία**, ἡ, = παιδοποιία, Pl.*Lg*.775c. II. = γυνὴ παιδοποιός (abstract for concrete), *a mother*, S.*OT*1248. **-ός**, όν, = παιδοποιός 2, μόρια Ascl. *in Metaph*.411.3, Olymp. *in Grg*.p.262 J.

**παιδοῦς**, οῦσσα, οῦν, contr. for παιδόεις, όεσσα, όεν, *rich in children*, Call.*Fr*.431. 2. fem. παιδοῦσα, *pregnant*, Hp.*Nat.Mul*.99.

**παιδο-φάγος** [ᾰ], ον, *child-devouring*, ἰχθύς Pi.*Fr*.306. ⊕ **-φῐλέω**, = παιδεραστέω, Thgn.1318, 1345, Sol.25, Call.*Fr*.107, etc.:—Pass., of the boy, Pl.Com.247. ⊕ **-φίλης** [ῐ], ου, ὁ, = παιδεραστής, Thgn. 1357, Telecl.49. **-φῐλος**, ον, *loving children*, fem. παιδοφίλη, epith. of Demeter, Orph.*H*.40.13; Γέλλως παιδοφιλωτέρα, of over-fond mothers, Sapph.47. **-φονεύς**, έως, ὁ, *slayer of children*, Ep. acc. -φονῆα, Q.S.2.322. **-φονία**, ἡ, *murder of one's children*, Plu.2. 727d, al. **-φόνος**, ον, *killing children*, ἀνήρ *the slayer of my children*, Il.24.506, cf. Porph.*Abst*.3.19; λέαινα E.*Med*.1407 (anap.); συμφορὴ π. the accident or calamity *of having killed a son*, Hdt.7.190; π. αἷμα the blood *of slain children*, E.*HF*1201 (lyr.). ⊕ **-φόντης**, ου, ὁ, = παιδοφονεύς, Ph.2.581. **-φορέω**, *waft away a boy*, παιδοφορῶν ἄνεμος *AP*12.52 (Mel.). **-φύλαξ** [ῠ], ἄκος, ὁ, *guardian of boys*, a public officer, *CIG*2715.8 (Stratonicea).

**παίδωσις**, εως, ἡ, *adoption* (Elean word), *Inscr.Olymp*.59.9, al.

⊕ **παίζω**, Dor. **παίσδω** Theoc.15.42: Lacon. pres. part. gen. pl. fem. **παιδδωᾶν** Ar.*Lys*.1313 (lyr.): fut. παιξοῦμαι Syrac. in X.*Smp*. 9.2, παίξομαι Lxx 2*Ki*.6.21, *AP*12.46 (Asclep.), παίξω ib.211 (Strat.), *Anacreont*.41.8: aor. 1 ἔπαισα Hom. (v. infr.), Ar.*Pl*.1055, etc.: pf. πέπαικα Men.923.3: pf. Pass. πέπαισμαι Hdt.4.77 (v.l. πέπλασται), Ar.*Th*.1227; imper. πεπαίσθω Pl.*Euthd*.278d: also aor. ἔπαιξα Crates Com.23, Ctes.*Fr*.29.59, Lxx *Jd*.16.25, Luc.*DDeor*.6.4, etc.: pf. πέπαιχα Plu.*Dem*.9:—Pass., aor. ἐπαίχθην Id.2.123f, Hld.8.6: pf. πέπαιγμαι *Epigr.Gr*.979.3 (Philae); inf. πεπαῖχθαι Timarch.ap. Ath.11.501f; imper. πεπαίχθω Phld.*Mus*.p.106 K., Fronto *Ep.Gr*.5. 86: Hom. uses only pres. and impf., and (in Od.8.251) aor. imper. παίσατε; Trag. only pres.: (παῖς):—prop., *play like a child, sport*, τῇ δέ θ' ἅμα Νύμφαι..ἀγρονόμοι παίζουσι Od.6.106, cf. 7.291 (never in Il.), Hdt.1.114, etc.: metaph., αἰὼν παῖς ἐστι παίζων Heraclit.52. 2. esp. *dance*, παίσατε Od.8.251; δῶμα περιστεναχίζετο ποσσὶν ἀνδρῶν παιζόντων 23.147, cf. Hes.*Sc*.277; π. τε καὶ χορεύειν Ar.*Ra*.409, cf. 390; ἐνόπλια χαλκωθεὶς ἔπαιζεν Pi.*O*.13.86:—Pass., ἀλλὰ πέπαισται μετρίως ἡμῖν, of the chorus, Ar.*Th*.1227. 3. *play* [a game], σφαίρῃ π. Od.6.100; κλεψύδρῃ Emp.100.9; κύβοις ἐπὶ συνθήκαις π. Ctes.l.c.; ἀντ' ἀστραγάλων κονδύλοισι π. Pherecr.43, cf. Antiph.92; π. διὰ γραμμῆς (v. γραμμή III. 2); π. πρὸς κότταβον Pl.Com.46.1; μετά τινων with others, Hdt.1.114: c. acc. cogn., κότταβον ἀγκύλῃ π. Anacr.53 (dub.); σφαῖραν Plu.*Alex*.73; π. παιδιὰν πρός τινα Ar.*Pl*.1055, cf. Pl.*Alc*.1. 110b; κύνα καὶ πόλιν π., of a game similar to our draughts, Cratin. 56: with Advbs., φαινίνδα π. Antiph.283, cf. Crates Com. l.c., etc. 4. *play* on a musical instrument, *h.Ap*.206: c. acc., Πὰν ὁ καλαμόφθογγα παίζων Ar.*Ra*.230; *dance and sing*, Pi.*O*.1.16. 5. *play amorously*, πρὸς ἀλλήλους X.*Smp*.9.2; μετά τινος Lxx *Ge*.26.8; of mares, Arist.*HA*572$^{a}$30. 6. *hunt, pursue game*, π. κατ' ἄλσος S. *El*.567. II. *jest, sport*, Hdt.2.28, 5.4, 9.11; opp. σπουδάζω, X. *Mem*.4.1.1; opp. σπουδῇ λέγω, Id.*Cyr*.8.3.47; παίζετε ταῦτα λέγοντες (opp. σπουδάζετε) Pl.*Euthd*.283b; π. καὶ χλευάζειν Ar.*Ra*.376; π. καὶ γελᾶν Antiph.218.4; πῖνε, παῖζε Amphis 8; π. πρός τινα *make fun* with a person, E.*HF*952, cf. Pl.*Men*.79a, Men.*Pk*.198; π. εἴς τι *play* with a thing, Pl.*Phd*.89b: c. Adj. neut., τοιαῦτα ἔπαιζον σπουδῇ πρὸς ἀλλήλους X.*Cyr*.6.1.6: part. παίζων is freq. abs., *jestingly*, Pl.*Tht*.145b, al.; opp. σπουδάζων, Id.*Lg*.636c, al.:—Pass., ὁ λόγος πέπαισται *has been made up as a jest* (v.l. for πέπλασται), Hdt.4.77; ταῦτα πεπαίσθω ὑμῖν enough of *jest*, Pl.*Euthd*.278d, cf. *Phdr*.278b, Phld. l.c.; πεπαῖχθαι τὴν λέξιν Timarch. l.c.; τοῦτο τὸ παιζόμενον 'as the joke is', Plu. 2.1090f; τὸ Μενεδήμῳ πεπαιγμένον ib.81e; but οἷα πέπαιγμαι, in act. sense, *Epigr.Gr*.979.3 (Philae). 2. c. acc., *play with, make sport of*, Luc.*Nigr*.20, *AP*10.64 (Agath.). 3. Gramm., of words *played upon* or *coined for the joke's sake*, οἱ κωμῳδοὶ παίζειν εἰώθασι τὰ τοιαῦτα Sch.Ar.*Av*.42, cf. 68, etc.

**Παιηόνιος**, α, ον, *healing*, like Παιώνιος, *APl*.4.270 (Magnus):—fem. **Παιηονίς**, ίδος, v.l. for παιωνιάς, *AP*11.382.6 (Agath.).

**Παιηοσύνη**, ἡ, *healing art*, Hsch.

**παιητέον**, (παίω) *one must strike*, Hsch. (παικτέον cod.). II. Adj. παιητέος, α, ον, *to be struck, knocked at*, ἡ θύρα π. Men.*Epit*.535.

**Παιήων**, ονος, ὁ, v. Παιάν.

**παικτέον**, gloss on ἑψιατέον, Suid.; cf. παιητέον.

⊕ **παίκ-της**, ου, ὁ, *dancer* or *player*, *AP*7.422 (Leon.); δειλοὶ καὶ παῖκται καὶ αἰσχρολόγοι Heph.Astr.2.2:—fem. **παίκτειρα**, Orph.*H*. 3.9. **-τικός**, ή, όν, *playful, sportive*, τὸ π. Corn.*ND*27.

⊕ **παῖλλος** [ᾰ], ὁ, *male infant*, *IG*7.700, al. (Tanagra).

**παῖμα**, ατος, τό, Cret., = κόμμα I. 2, Γόρτυνος τὸ π. *Schwyzer* 178 (v B.C.), etc.

**παίνεται**, barbarism for φαίνεται, Ar.*Th*.1114.

**παῖον**· ἀσφαλές, βέβαιον, Hsch. (Perh. a dialectic form of πάγιον.)

**Παίονες**, οἱ, *Paeonians*, a people of Macedonia, Il.2.848, etc.; Παίων στρατός E.*Rh*.540 (lyr.): **Παιονία**, Ion. -ίη, ἡ, *their land*, Il.17. 350, etc.:—Adj.⊕**Παιονικός**, ή, όν, ἔθνη Th.2.96, etc.; pecul. fem. **Παιονίς**, ίδος, Hdt.4.33.—In late writers used for Παννονία, Παννόνιοι, Philostr.*VS*2.1.12, D.C.49.36, *Hippiatr*.124; τὰ **Παιόνια** ἔθνη Philostr.*VS*2.1.11.

**παιονίη**, Ep. for παιωνία, Orph.*A*.918.

**παιόνιος**, η, ον, Ep. for παιώνιος, χείρ *AP*14.55.

**παιπᾰλ-άω**, *to be subtle*, Hsch., Suid. **-εος**, α (Ep. η), ον, dub. sens., [πιπὼ] παιπαλέη Antim.Col.4 P. **-η**, ἡ (redupl. from πάλη (B)) *the finest flour* or *meal*, Ar.*Nu*.262; π. ἀλφίτων Apollon.ap.Gal. 12.502, v.l. in Dsc.3.39: metaph., λέγειν γενήσει..παιπάλη, i.e. a *subtle* talker, Ar.*Nu*.260, cf. sq. and πασπάλη. ⊕ **-ημα**, ατος, τό, *piece of subtlety*: metaph., of men, π. ὅλον Id.*Av*.431, cf. Aeschin.2.40, Luc. *Pseudol*.32; λόγων τι π. καὶ κακὴ γλῶσσα Aeschrio 8.8. ⊕ **-ῖμος**, ον, *subtle, sly*, Theognost.*Can*.10; but only in the vulgar dialect, Sch. D Od.10.97.

**παιπάλλω**· σείω, Hsch.

**παιπᾰλ-όεις**, εσσα, εν, Ep. word, *rugged*, ὄρος Il.13.17; σκοπιά Od.10.97, 148, 194; of mountain-paths, ὁδός Il.12.168, Od.17.204; ἀταρπός Il.17.743; of rocky islands, 13.33, Od.3.170, 4.671, 11.480, al., *h.Ap*.172, A.R.4.1635; βῆσσαι Hes.*Th*.860 (nisi leg. Αἴτνης

-έσσης). -ον, τό, παίπαλά τε κρημνούς τε *steeps* and crags, Call.*Dian.*194, cf. Sch.Ar.*Nu.*260. -ώδης, ες, *of subtle nature*, γυναῖκες *EM*515.7, Suid.

**παῖς**, also **πάϊς** (q.v.), παιδός, ὁ, ἡ, gen. pl. παίδων, Dor. παιδῶν Greg.Cor.p.317 S.; dat. pl. παισί, Ep. παίδεσσι Od.3.381, etc.; in early Ep. freq. disyll. in nom. **πάϊς**, e.g. when forming part of two different feet, Il.2.609, 5.704, etc.; prob. also in the fifth foot, 9.57, 11.389; and before bucolic diaeresis, 2.205, al.; also in Lyr., Sapph.38, 85; and in Boeot., *IG*7.690, al. (Tanagra), cf. πῆς; πάϊ [ᾰῐ] Od.24.192 (παιδ- is never disyll. in oblique cases in Hom.); acc. πάϊν A.R.4.697, *AP*3.8 (Inscr. Cyzic.), 9.125; gen. παϊδός Epigr.ap.Luc.*Symp.*41; dat. παϊδί prob. in Anacr.17: I. in relation to Descent, *child*, whether *son*, Il.2.205, 609, al. (with special reference to the father, opp. τέκνον, q.v.): pl., Th.1.4, etc.; or *daughter*, Il.1.20, 443, 3.175; παῖδες ἄρρενες καὶ θήλειαι Pl.*Lg.*788a; παῖς, opp. κόρα, *Berl.Sitzb.*1927.7 (Locr., v B.C.); of an *adopted son*, ἀλλά σε παῖδα ποιεύμην Il.9.494; παίδων παῖδες, τοί κεν μετόπισθε γένωνται 20.308, cf. Pi.*N.*7.100, *Inscr.Cypr.*135.11 H., etc.; Ἀγήνορος παῖδες ἐκ παίδων E.*Ph.*281; freq. in orators of legal *issue*, Isoc.19.9, Is.7.31, etc.; of animals, A.*Ag.*50 (anap.). 2. metaph., ἀμπέλου π., of wine, Pi.*N.*9.52; χορῶν ἐραστὴς κισσὸς ἐνιαυτοῦ δὲ παῖς Chaerem.5; ὀρείας πέτρας π., of Echo, E.*Hec.*1110; ὅρκου π. ἀνώνυμος, of the *penalty* of perjury, Orac.ap.Hdt.6.86.γ'; ἄναυδοι π. τᾶς ἀμιάντου, of fishes, A.*Pers.*578 (lyr.). 3. periphr., οἱ Λυδῶν παῖδες *sons* of the Lydians, i.e. the Lydians, Hdt.1.27, cf. 5.49; π. Ἑλλήνων A.*Pers.*402; οἱ [Ἀσκληπιοῦ] π., i.e. physicians, Pl.*R.*407e; οἱ ζωγράφων π. painters, Id.*Lg.*769b; παῖδες ῥητόρων orators, Luc.*Anach.*19; π. ἰατρῶν, π. πλαστῶν καὶ γραφέων, Id.*Dips.*5, *Im.*9; cf. υἱός 2. II. in relation to Age, *child, boy* or *girl*, νέος π. Od.4.665; παῖδες νεαροί Il.2.289; σμίκρα π. Sapph.34: with another Subst., π. συφορβός *boy*-swineherd, Il.21.282; παῖδα κόρην γαμεῖν Ar.*Lys.*595; ἐν παισὶ νέοισι π. Pi.*N.*3.72; π. ἔτ' ὢν A.*Ch.*755, cf. Il.11.710; ἔτι π. Pl.*Prt.*310e; παιδὸς μηδὲν βελτίων ib.342e: distd. from παιδίον, μειράκιον, Hp.*Hebd.*5, cf. X.*Smp.*4.17, *Cyr.*8.7.6, 1.2.4; ἐκ παιδὸς *from a child*, Pl.*R.*374c; ἐκ παιδὸς εἰς γῆρας Aeschin.1.180; ἐκ τῶν παίδων εὐθὺς Pl.*Lg.*694d, cf. *R.*386a; ἀκούων τῶν παίδων εὐθὺς Id.*Lg.*642b; εὐθὺς ἐκ παίδων ἐξελθὼν D.21.154; ἡλικίαν ἔχειν τὴν ἄρτι ἐκ π. to be just out of one's *childhood*, X.*HG*5.4.25; ἐκ μικρῶν π. Arist.*Pol.*1336ᵃ14; [Ἡρακλῆς] ἐν παισὶν ὄφεις ἀπέκτεινεν D.C.56.36; ἐν παισὶ (v.l. παιδὶ) ποιμαίνων Hdn.6.8.1; χορηγεῖν παισί (cf. χορηγέω II): prov., τοῦτο κἂν π. γνοίη Pl.*Euthd.*279d; δῆλον τοῦτό γε ἤδη καὶ παιδί Id.*Smp.*204b; παῖδας [τοὺς πρὸ αὐτοῦ] ἀπέφηνε Luc.*Peregr.*11, cf. *Alex.*4; ἔνι τις καὶ ἐν ἡμῖν π., of the superstitious fears of a child, Pl.*Phd.*77e, cf. Porph.*Abst.*1.41. III. in relation to Condition, *slave, servant, man* or *maid* (of all ages), παῖ, παῖ A.*Ch.*653, cf. Ar.*Ach.*395, Epicr.5.2, etc.; παῖ, παιδίον Ar.*Nu.*132: pl., of the crew of a ship, D.33.8. (From *παϝις, cf. παῦρος, Lat. *puer.*)

παισά· πλακούντια παρὰ Κῴοις, Iatrocl.ap.Ath.14.646f.

παισαρ-εύματα· περικόμματα, Hsch. -εύς· παιρέτης, Id. (παιρεύς cod.).

παίσδω, Dor. for παίζω.

παισ-τέον, *one must play*, Pl.Com.46.3. -της, ου, ὁ, *player, executant*, *PGen.*73.5 (ii/iii A.D.). -τικός, ή, όν, *facetious*, γρῖφος πρόβλημά ἐστι π. Clearch.63. -τρα, Ion. -τρη, ἡ, *gambling-hell*, Herod.3.11, 64.

παίταυρα, v. πέταυρα.

**παιφάσσω**, *dart, rush about*, παιφάσσουσα διέσσυτο λαὸν Ἀχαιῶν Il.2.450, cf. A.R.4.1440; περί τινα Procl.*in Alc.*p.136 C.; *quiver*, Opp.*C.*2.250, *H.*2.288. 2. trans., *wave violently*, λαμπάδα Jo.Gaz.*Ecphr.*2.167. (Redupl. form; cf. δια-φάσσειν, Lat. *fax.*)

**παίχνιον**, τό, Ion. for παίγνιον, Call.*Iamb.Fr.*9.390 P.

**παίω**, Boeot. πήω Hdn.Gr.2.949; Att. 2 sg. imper. παῖ X.*Cyn.*6.18 codd.: fut. παίσω E.*El.*688, X.*An.*3.2.19, παιήσω Ar.*Nu.*1125, *Lys.*459: aor. ἔπαισα *Supp.Epigr.*2.509.4, al. (Crete, v B.C.), A.*Pers.*397, X.*An.*5.8.10: pf. πέπαικα LXX *Nu.*22.28, (ὑπερ-) Ar.*Ec.*1118, D.50.34:—Med., impf. ἐπαιόμην Plu.*Pomp.*24: aor. ἐπαισάμην X.*Cyr.*7.3.6:—Pass., aor. ἐπαίσθην A.*Th.*957, *Ch.*184, Luc.*Salt.*10: pf. πέπαισμαι (ἐμ-) Ath.12.543f; but the pass. tenses were mainly supplied by πλήσσω (παίσαντές τε καὶ πληγέντες S.*Ant.*171); and ἐπάταξα (from πατάσσω) was generally used as aor.:—poet. Verb (not in Hom., rare in Att. Prose), *strike, smite*, whether with the hand, or with a rod or other weapon, σκυτάλοισί τινας Hdt.3.137, cf. A.*Ag.*1384, etc.: freq. with acc. omitted, παισθεὶς ἔπαισας Id.*Th.*957; παῖε πᾶς *strike home!*, E.*Rh.*685; παισάτω πᾶς (παῖς codd.), παῖ δή, παῖ δή X.*Cyn.*l.c.; π. τινὰ ἐς τὴν γῆν Hdt.9.107; π. τινὰ μάστιγι S.*Aj.*242 (lyr.), etc.; π. ὑφ' ἧπαρ αὐτήν Id.*Ant.*1315; παίσας πρὸς ἧπαρ φασγάνῳ E.*Or.*1063; π. τινὰ ἐς τὴν γαστέρα Ar.*Nu.*549; εἰς τὰ στέρνα X.*Cyr.*4.6.4; τινὰ ἐς πλευρὰν ξίφει E.*Rh.*794; κατὰ τὸ στέρνον X.*An.*1.8.26; κάρα S.*Aj.*308, cf. *OT*1270; τὸν νῶτόν τινος Alciphr.3.43: c. dupl. acc., π. ῥοπάλῳ τινὰ τὸ νῶτον Ar.*Av.*497: c. acc. cogn., ὀλίγας π. (sc. πληγάς) X.*An.*5.8.12; τί μ' οὐκ ἀνταίαν ἔπαισέν τις (sc. πληγήν); S.*Ant.*1309 (lyr.); π. ἅλμην, of rowers, A.*Pers.*397, E.*IT*1391:—Med., ἐπαίσατο τὸν μηρόν *he smote his* thigh, X.*Cyr.*7.3.6, cf. Plu.*Pomp.*24:—Pass., παιομένους Th.4.47, cf. A.*Pers.*416, Antipho 2.4.4, etc.; πὺξ παιόμενος, opp. ἐγχειριδίῳ πληγείς, Lys.6. b. rarely of missiles, X.*Cyr.*6.4.18:—Pass., τὰ παιόμενα τοῖς κεραυνοῖς Plu.2.665d; of atoms, παίονται καὶ παίουσι τὸν ἅπαντα χρόνον ib.1111e. 2. c. acc. instrumenti, *drive, dash* one thing against another, ναῦς ἐν νηῒ στόλον ἔπαισε *struck* its beak against.., A.*Pers.*409; π. λαιμῶν εἴσω ξίφος E.*Or.*1472 (lyr.); [ναῦς] θάλασσα π. πρὸς χωρία δύσορμα Plu.*Pyrrh.*15: metaph., ἐν δ' ἐμῷ κάρᾳ θεὸς.. μέγα βάρος ἔπαισεν S.*Ant.*1274 (lyr.). 3. *drive away*, τοὺς σφῆκας ἀπὸ τῆς οἰκίας Ar.*V.*456. 4. of sexual intercourse, Id.*Pax*874. 5. *hit hard in speaking*, π. στρογγύλοις τοῖς ῥήμασιν Id.*Ach.*686, cf. Lib.*Or.*63.34. 6. metaph., *quench* one's *thirst*, διψῶντα.. ὀξει παίειν Eub.138 (anap.); cf. πατάσσω II. 2. II. intr., *strike, dash against* or *upon*, λόγοι παίουσ' εἰκῇ πρὸς κύμασιν ἄτης A.*Pr.*885 (anap.); πρὸς τὰς πέτρας π. X.*An.*4.2.3: c. acc., ἔπαισεν ἄφαντον ἕρμα A.*Ag.*1007 (lyr.); λανθάνει στήλην ἄκραν παίσας, of a charioteer, S.*El.*745. (From *παϝιω, cf. Lat. *pavio, pavimentum.*) III. *devour*, παίειν ἐφ' ἁλὶ τὴν μάδδαν Ar.*Ach.*835, cf. Hsch.; perh. to be read in Epich.35.12: it has been doubted whether this is the same word as παίω I, but cf. ἐρείδω II. 2, κόπτω I. 10, σποδέω III, φλάω I. 2.

**Παιών**, **παιών**, v. Παιάν.

**Παιώνειος**, ον, = Παιώνιος, Longin.16.2, Marin.*Procl.*31.

**παιωνία**, ἡ, (Παιών) = γλυκυσίδη, *peony*, Thphr.*HP*9.8.6; π. ἄρρην, θήλεια, = *Paeonia officinalis, corallina*, Ps.-Dsc.3.140; Ep. παιονίη Orph.*A.*918. 2. = χελιδόνιον μέγα, Ps.-Dsc.2.180. II. name of an *antidote*, Orib.*Fr.*82.

**παιωνιάς**, άδος, ἡ, v. Παιώνιος.

**παιων-ίζω**, *chant the paean* or *song of victory*, *SIG*57.8, al. (Milet., v B.C.), *GDI* iv p.884 (Erythrae), Hdt.5.1, Ar.*Eq.*1318, *Pax*555, Th.1.50 (Pass.), X.*An.*6.1.5, D.C.43.37, etc.; π. ἐπὶ ταῖς τῶν Ἑλλήνων συμφοραῖς D.18.287: c. acc. cogn., *sing in triumph*, ὀλολυγμὸν ἱρὸν.. παιώνισον A.*Th.*268 (v.l. παιάνισον). II. *honour with paeans*, τὸν θάνατον μόνοι ἀνθρώπων παιωνίζονται (Med.) Philostr.*VA*5.4:—Pass., οὐδὲ παιωνίζεται (sc. ὁ Θάνατος) A.*Fr.*161.3. (The Att. and Ion. form παιων- is found in most codd. of ll. cc. and of Th.2.91, 4.43, al.; παιαν- in X.*Smp.*2.1, Pl.*Ax.*365b, Plb.3.43.8.) -ικός, ή, όν, *healing*, φάρμακα Gal.19.169; ἐνέργειαι Procl.*in Cra.*p.100 P. II. (Παιάν III) *paeonic*, ῥυθμοποιίαι Plu.2.1143d; κῶλον Demetr.*Eloc.*41, Sch.Ar.*Eq.*303; [μέτρον] Heph.13.1. -ιος, α, ον, *belonging to Paeon* or *medicine, healing*, χείρ, χεῖρες, A.*Supp.*1066 (lyr.), S.*Ph.*1345, Ar.*Ach.*1223; φάρμακα A.*Ag.*848; εὐχαί Id.*Fr.*144: in later Prose, Jul.*Or.*8.240b: c. gen., χρυσὸς ἔρωτος ἀεὶ παιώνιος *AP*9.420 (Antip.):—fem. **παιωνιάς** σοφίη, *healing art, medicine*, ib.11.382.6 (Agath.); also **παιωνὶς** τέχνη, S.E.*M.*1.51; cf. παιώνιος. 2. Subst. **Παιώνιος**, ὁ, *healer*, c. gen., S.*Tr.*1208; Παιωνία, epith. of Athena, Paus.1.2.5, etc. b. **Παιώνιον**, τό, *hospital*, Crates Com.15.3 (also Παιωνεῖον Phot.). c. name of a *pill*, Gal.13.242. d. **Παιώνια**, τά, *festival of Paeon*, Ar.*Ach.*1213. II. κέλαδος οὐ π. un*like a song of victory*, A.*Pers.*605. -ισμός, ὁ, *chanting of the paean*, Th.7.44; later **παιανισμός**, Str.9.3.12, D.H.2.41.

**πακιάλιον**, τό, = φακιάλιον, *Sammelb.*7033.45 (v A.D.), *PMasp.*6 ii 66 (vi A.D.).

πακοτή· ἀποσκότ(..), Hsch.

πακτά, -τίς, -τός, v. πηκτή, -τίς, -τός.

πακτ-εύω (*pactum*), *come to terms*, πρός τινας Petr.Patr.p.431 D. **-ον**, τό, = Lat. *pactum, agreement, lease*, *PLond.*1.113 (vi A.D.), etc.

**πακτοποιός**, ὁ, = πακτωνοποιός, *PMasp.*20.17 (vi A.D.).

**πακτ-όω**, (πακτός) *fasten, close*, Archil.187; δῶμα πάκτου *make fast* the house, S.*Aj.*579; μοχλοῖς καὶ κλῄθροισι τὰ προπύλαια π. Ar.*Lys.*265. 2. *stop up, caulk*, τὰ τετρημένα ῥακίοις Id.*V.*128. 3. *bind fast*, λαίφεα *AP*10.23 (Autom.). -ων, ωνος, ὁ, *light boat* of wicker-work, used on the Nile, Str.17.1.50, *PMag.Lond.*46.69, *BGU*812.3 (ii/iii A.D.), *POxy.*1220.12 (iii A.D.), etc. -ωνίτης [ῑ], ου, ὁ, *ship-wright*, ib.814 (i A.D.). -ωνοποιός, ὁ, = foreg., *PLond.*4.1419, etc. (vi A.D.). -ωσις, εως, ἡ, *fastening, putting together*, *PPetr.*3 p.136 (iii B.C.), Poll.1.84. **-ωτής**, οῦ, ὁ, = πακτωνίτης, Wilcken *Chr.*31.7 (ii A.D.), cf. *PBerol.* in *Arch.Pap.*3.244.

πάλα, ἡ, *nugget* of gold, Str.3.2.8. (Spanish word.) II. πάλα· ζώνη, Hsch.

**πᾰλαγμός**, ὁ, *sprinkling*, παλαγμοῖς αἵματος A.*Fr.*327.

**πᾰλάθ-η** [λᾰ], ἡ, *cake of preserved fruit*, Hdt.4.23, Thphr.*HP*4.2.10, LXX 1 *Ki.*25.18, al., Amynt.ap.Ath.11.500d, Luc.*Pisc.*41, *Vit.Auct.*19. -ιον, τό, Dim. of foreg., Polem.Hist.88; cf. παλάσιον. -ίς, ίδος, ἡ, = foreg., Ph.*Bel.*89.28, Str.2.3.4. -ώδης, ες, *like a* παλάθη, Dsc.1.67.

**πάλαι** [ᾰ], Adv. *long ago*, π. οὔ τι νέον γε Il.9.527; π. κοὐ νεωστί S.*El.*1049; π. πολλὰ ἤδη ἔτη Pl.*Ap.*18b; π. ποτέ *once upon a time*, Ar.*Pl.*1002, Pl.*Criti.*110a: freq. with pres. of an act lasting to the pres., ὁρῶ.. π. I have *long* seen, S.*Aj.*5; ἰχνεύω π. ib.20, cf. *Ph.*589, Pl.*Men.*91a, Ar.*Pl.*257, etc.; but, π. ποτ' ὄντες ye who were *long ago*, Id.*V.*1060: also with pf., τέθνηχ' ὑμῖν π. S.*Ph.*1030, cf. A.*Pr.*998, Ar.*Nu.*556: with impf. of an act lasting to a past time, ἔχεν π. had *long* been holding it, Il.23.871, cf. Eup.11; ἔχεις π. ὧν ἐπεθύμεις Theoc.10.17: with Art., τὸ π. Th.1.5, 7.74, 95, 142, Th.1.5, etc.; ἀπὸ π. *BGU*1036.24 (ii A.D.). 2. like an Adj. with Art. and Noun, οἱ π. φῶτες men *of old*, Pi.*I.*2.1; Κάδμου τοῦ π. νέα τροφή S.*OT*1; τοῦ πρόσθε Κάδμου τοῦ π. τ' Ἀγήνορος ib.268; τὰ καινὰ τοῖς π. τεκμαίρεται ib.916, cf. *Tr.*1165, *El.*1490, etc.; τὰ π. D.19.276 (nisi leg. παλαί'); οἱ π. the *ancients*, opp. οἱ νῦν, Arist.*Metaph.*1069ᵃ29. II. *before*, opp. the present, sts. of time *just past*, ἡμὲν π. ἠδ' ἔτι καὶ νῦν Il.9.105, cf. S.*Ant.*181: hence, *not long ago, just now*, like ἄρτι, οἱ π. λόγοι A.*Pr.*845; ὁ π. λόγος the reason *just* given, Arist.*Pol.*1282ᵃ15, cf. 1282ᵇ7; π. σοὶ ἔλεγον X.*Oec.*19.17, cf. 18.10; but opp. ἄρτι, Pl.*Tht.*142a.

**πᾰλαι-γενής**, ές, *born long ago, full of years*, γεραιὲ παλαιγενές, addressed to Phoenix, Il.17.561; γρηῦς π. Od.22.395; ἄνθρωποι *h.Cer.*113; ὁ π. Κρόνος A.*Pr.*222; ἡ π. μήτηρ..Θέμις ib.873; π. Μοῖραι Id.*Eu.*172(lyr.); παρβασία Id.*Th.*742(lyr.); ἀοιδαί E.*Med.*421; Βάκχιος π. *old* wine, Antiph.237.1; νέκταρ π. Alex.119.2; ἐχθρὸς ἢ π. *long long ago*, A.*Ag.*1637. **-γονος**, ον, = παλαιγενής, Pi.*O.*13.50, 14.3. **-ένδοξος**, ον, *of old renown*, Ph.2.437. **-ετής**, ές, *old in years*, Hsch. (-δέτης cod.). **-θεος**, ἡ, = παλαιὰ θεός, Id., Phot. **-θετος**, ον, *laid up, stored long ago*, κᾶλα Call.*Fr.*66c: generally, *ancient, old*, ὕμνος IonTrag.22.

**πᾰλαιμ-ονέω**, *wrestle, fight*, Pi.*P.*2.61. **-οσύνη**, v. παλαισμοσύνη.

⊛ **Πᾰλαίμων**, ονος, ὁ, *Palaemon*, a sea-god friendly to the shipwrecked, E.*IT*271, Lyc.229; also epith. of Heracles, Id.663, Hsch.:—hence **Πᾰλαιμόνιον**, τό, *temple of Palaemon*, *IG*4.203(Corinth).

**πᾰλαιο-γενής**, ές, = παλαιγενής, Ar.*Nu.*358. **-γονος**, ον, = παλαίγονος, Pl.Com.90, *APl.*4.295. **-δουλος**, ὁ, *slave from of old, hereditary slave*, Ph.2.446,468. **-θέτης**· παλαιοπράγμων, δραστήριος, Hsch. **-κτητος**, *olim comparatus*, *Gloss.* **-λογέω**, *discuss antiquities*, App.*Hisp.*2. **-μάγᾰδις** [μᾰ], ἡ, = μάγαδις II, Ath.4.182d. **-μάτωρ** [μᾱ], ορος, ἡ, *ancient mother*, E.*Supp.*628(lyr.). **-μώλωψ**, ωπος, ὁ, *old rogue*, = Lat. *veterator*, *Gloss.* **-πλουτος**, ον, *full of ancient wealth*, χωρίον Th.8.28, cf. Arist.*Ath.*6.2. **-πράγμων**, gloss on παλαιοθέτης, Hsch. **-ράφιον** [ρᾰ], τό, *cobbler's shop*, *Gloss.* **-ράφος** [ρᾰ], ὁ, *cobbler*, ib.

⊛ **πᾰλαιός**, ά, όν, Aeol. **πάλαος** Eust.28.33, *Epigr.Gr.*992(Balbilla); Boeot. **παληός** *EM*32.6; Lacon. **παλεός** (v. infr.): regul. Comp. and Sup. παλαιότερος Pi.*N.*6.53, Th.1.1 codd., παλαιότατος Pl.*Ti.*83a, etc.: more freq. παλαίτερος, παλαίτατος (from πάλαι), Pi.*P.*10.58, *N.*7.44, Th.1.4, etc. [The penult. is sts. short in Poets, S.*Fr.*956 (s. v. l.), E.*El.*497, Democr.ap.Gal.13.1049; παλεός γα ναὶ τὸν Κάστορα ἄνθρωπος Ar.*Lys.*988; in these places παλεός (a form mentioned by Hdn.Gr.2.909, cf. Theognost.*Can.*50.3, Sch.Ar.*Lys.* l. c., Suid., and corroborated by the Pap. (iv B.C.) of Timotheus (v. παλεομίσημα, παλεονυμφάγονος)) may be retained or restored).]: I. *old in years*, 1. mostly of persons, *aged*, ἢ νέος ἠὲ παλαιός Il.14.108; νέοι ἠδὲ παλαιοί Od.1.395, cf. Epicur.*Ep.*3 p.59 U.; παλαιῷ φωτὶ ἐοικώς Il.14.136; π. γέρων, π. γρηῦς, Od.13.432, 19.346, cf. Ar.*Ach.*676; χρόνῳ π. S.*OC*112; ἐν παλαιτέροισι Pi.*N.*3.73; ἔνθα δὴ παλαίτατοι θάσσουσι E.*Med.*68: in bad sense, *a dotard* (μωρός Hsch., but σκώπτης Suid.), Ar.*Lys.*988. 2. of things, οἶνος Od.2.340; νῆες..νέαι ἠδὲ π. ib.293; τρὺξ π. καὶ σαπρά Ar.*Pl.*1086; [τριήρεις] π. ἀντὶ καινῶν Lys.28.4; ὑποδήματα Pl.*Men.*91d; σπέρματα Thphr.*HP*7.1.6. II. *of old date, ancient*, 1. of persons, ξεῖνος π. an *old* guest-friend, Il.6.215, cf. S.*Tr.*263, E.*Alc.*212; Ἴλου παλαιοῦ Il.11.166; κέρδεα..οἵ' οὔ πώ τιν' ἀκούομεν οὐδὲ παλαιῶν Od.2.118; Μίνως παλαίτατος ὧν ἀκοῇ ἴσμεν Th.1.4; οἱ πάνυ π. ἄνθρωποι Pl.*Cra.*411b; οἱ π. the *ancients*, Th.1.3; π. ἡμερῶν Lxx *Da.*7.9. 2. of things, λέκτρον Od.23.296; παλαιά τε πολλά τε εἰδώς 7.157; καινὰ καὶ π. ἔργα Hdt.9.26; νόμοι A.*Eu.*778(lyr.); κατὰ τὸ νόμιμον τὸ π. καὶ ἀρχαῖον Lys.6.51; κατὰ τὸν π. λόγον Pl.*Grg.*499c; ἡ π. παροιμία Id.*R.*329a; παλαί' ἂν [εἴη], ἐξ ὅτου S.*Ph.*493; παλαιᾷ σύντροφος ἁμερᾷ Id.*Aj.*622(lyr.); of places, A.*Pers.*17(anap.), S.*El.*4, etc.; καιροὶ π. *ancient* times, *PPetr.*2 p.15 (iii B.C.); τὸ π. as Adv., *anciently, formerly*, A.*Pers.*102(lyr.), Hdt.1.171, Pl.*Cra.*401c, etc.; ἐκ παλαιοῦ from *of old*, Hdt.1.157; ἐκ π. ἐχθρὸς ὢν αὐτοῦ Antipho 2.1.5; ἐκ τῶν παλαιῶν Herod.2.102; ἐκ παλαιτέρου from *older time*, Hdt.1.60; ἐκ παλαιτάτου Th.1.18; also εὐθὺς ἀπὸ παλαιοῦ ib.2; ἀρχαῖα καὶ παλαιά joined, D.22.14, cf. Lys. (v. supr.); παλαιὸν δῶρον ἀρχαίου ποτὲ θηρός S.*Tr.*555. 3. of things, also, a. in good sense, *venerable, held in esteem*, like Lat. *antiquus*, ἅπερ μέγιστα καὶ παλαιότατα τοῖς ἀνθρώποις Antipho 6.4. b. in bad sense, *antiquated, obsolete*, κωφὰ καὶ π. ἔπη S.*OT*290. c. π. δρᾶμα a drama *which has been previously acted*, *SIG*1078 lxxxvii (Athens, iv B.C.). III. Adv. παλαιῶς *in an old way*, τὰ καινὰ π. διδάσκειν Socr.*Ep.*30.9: Comp. παλαίτερον *at an earlier time*, D.H.8.57, al.

**πᾰλαιότης**, ητος, ἡ, *age*, π. καὶ πλῆθος ἐτῶν Aeschin.2.42; of seeds, Thphr.*HP*7.1.6. 2. more freq. *antiquity, obsoleteness*, π. γὰρ τῷ λόγῳ γ' ἔνεστί τις E.*Hel.*1056; ὑπὸ παλαιότητος Pl.*Cra.*421d; εἴτε π. εἴτε σαπρότης Id.*R.*609e; π. γράμματος, opp. καινότης πνεύματος, *Ep.Rom.*7.6; in Lit. Crit., D.H.*Rh.*10.19.

**πᾰλαιο-τόκος**, ον, *having brought forth long ago*, Aret.*CA*2.3. **-τροπία**, ἡ, *old-fashionedness*, Eust.531.40. **-τροπος**, ον, *old-fashioned*, χαρακτήρ Iamb.*VP*23.103; βωμοί Nicom.*Ar.*2.16.

⊛ **πᾰλαιουργός**, ὁ, *cobbler*, Poll.7.82.

**πᾰλαιο-φᾰνής**, ές, *appearing old*, οἶνοι *Gp.*7.24.1. **-φρων**, ονος, ὁ, ἡ, *with the wisdom of age*, A.*Eu.*838, *Supp.*593(both lyr.). **-χάρακτος** [χᾰ], ον, *of the old currency*, χρυσός *PLond.ined.*2163(iv A.D.); νομισμάτιον *PMon.*15.2(vi A.D.).

**πᾰλαιόω**, aor. ἐπαλαίωσα Lxx *La.*3.4: pf. πεπαλαίωκα *Ep.Hebr.*8.13: (παλαιός):—*make old*, Lxx *Jb.*9.5, al.:—mostly in Pass., *decay through lapse of time*, οἱ παλαιούμενοι νεκροί Arist.*Mete.*390ᵃ22; κηρὸς παλαιούμενος Id.*HA*557ᵇ6, al.; τὸ..παλαιούμενον Pl.*Smp.*208b, cf. *Ti.*59c; τὸ ἱερὸν πεπαλαιῶσθαι *Sammelb.*5827.11(i B.C.); πεπαλαιωμένον ἔκπτωμα βραχίονος one *which is of long standing*, Hp.*Art.*7; γένος παλαιωθὲν ὑπὸ χρόνου D.H.3.10; πεπαλαιωμένε ἡμερῶν κακῶν Lxx *Su.*52; of wine, *become old*, Thphr.*CP*6.7.5, Gal.14.14, al., Ath.1.33a. II. *abrogate, cancel*, [διαθήκην] *Ep.Hebr.* l. c.

**πᾰλαι-πλούσιος**, ον, = παλαιόπλουτος, Ph.1.233. ⊛ **-πλουτος**, ον, = foreg., *Quarterly of Dept. of Ant. in Palestine* 1.155 (Gaza, iii A.D.).

**πάλαισ-ις** [ᾰ], εως, ἡ, *contest*, Ptol.*Harm.*1.1. **-μα**, ατος, τό, *bout* or *fall in wrestling*, παρὰ ἓν π. ἔδραμε νικᾶν Hdt.9.33; ἓν μὲν τόδ' ἤδη τῶν τριῶν π. A.*Eu.*589, cf. Pl.*Phdr.*256b: in pl., *feats of wrestling*, Pi.*O.*9.13, *P.*8.35, cf. *CR*43.210(Asia Minor). 2. *struggle*, A.*Ag.*63(anap.), *Eu.*776, S.*OT*880(lyr.), E.*Med.*1214; of war, Jul.*Or.*2.66c; παλαίσμαθ' ἡμῶν ὁ βίος E.*Supp.*550. 3. *trick, 'chip' in wrestling*, metaph., Ar.*Ra.*689, cf. 878; π. δικαστηρίου *a trick* of the courts, Aeschin.3.205; σόφισμα..καὶ π. τῶν ἀκουόντων D.H.*Rh.*8.12; ὦ Θετταλὸν π., addressed to a person, Ath.7.308b. 4. in pl., of works of art, *groups of wrestlers*, Philostr.*Im.*2.32. **-μοσύνη**, ἡ, poet. for πάλη, *the wrestler's art*, Il.23.701, Od.8.103,126, Simon.149, *Inscr.Prien.*268c2(ii/i B.C.): **παλαιμοσύνη**, Aristarch.ap.Eust.1587.40, v.l. in Tyrt.12.2.

⊛ **πᾰλαιστᾰγής** οἶνος wine *that has become oily from age*, Nic.*Th.*591.

**πᾰλαιστέον**, v. παλαίω II.

**πᾰλαιστ-έω**, *thrust away with the hand*, Ps.-Luc.*Philopatr.*1, Eust.1415.21; cf. sq. ⊛ **-ή**, ἡ, = παλαστή (q. v.); Aeol. **παλαίστα** Alc.33.6(v. l. παλάσταν).

**πᾰλαιστής** (A), οῦ, ὁ, (παλαίω) *wrestler*, Od.8.246, Hdt.3.137, Pl.*Lg.*819b, *Trag.Adesp.*383.3, etc.; ἄνδρες π. Ar.*Lys.*1083; παῖδες π. *CIG*1969(Thessalonica); σὺν σάκει..π., of soldiers, S.*Fr.*859(lyr.). 2. generally, *rival, adversary*, τοῖον π. νῦν παρασκευάζεται ἐπ' αὐτὸς αὑτῷ A.*Pr.*920; σοφὸς π. κεῖνος, of Odysseus, S.*Ph.*431; λόχος..ἐξηνδρωμένος δεινὸς π. ἦν E.*Supp.*704. 3. *suitor*, A.*Ag.*1206.

**πᾰλαιστής** (B), v. παλαστή.

**πᾰλαιστιαῖος**, α, ον, = παλαστιαῖος, Thphr.*HP*2.7.7, Plb.6.23.3, J.*AJ*8.3.5, Heliod.ap.Orib.49.7.1, S.E.*M.*9.300, etc.

**πᾰλαιστικός**, ή, όν, (παλαίω) *expert in wrestling*, Arist.*Rh.*1361ᵇ24, Luc.*DDeor.*20.14, etc.; ἡ -κή (sc. τέχνη) *the art of wrestling*, Paus.1.39.3, etc. Adv. -κῶς Poll.3.149: Comp. -ώτερον Philostr.*Gym.*25. II. *suited for wrestling*, ἰσχύς Plu.2.130b; στέρνα -ώτερα Philostr.*Gym.*35; cf. παλαιστρικός.

**πᾰλαιστός**, ὁ, = παλαιστή, *IGRom.*1.1290(Elephantine).

**πᾰλαίστρα**, ἡ, (παλαίω) *wrestling-school*, δρόμον καὶ π. ποιησάμενος Hdt.6.126, cf. Hp.*Art.*4: in pl., E.*El.*528, Ar.*Ra.*729, etc.; εἰς παλαίστραν φοιτῆσαι Pl.*Grg.*456d; πέμπουσιν εἰς διδασκάλων μαθησομένους καὶ γράμματα καὶ μουσικὴν καὶ τὰ ἐν παλαίστρᾳ X.*Lac.*2.1. b. Κερκυόνος π., of the spot where Cercyon slew his victims, B.17.26, Paus.1.39.3. II. metaph., *school*, ἡ Ἀλεξάνδρου π. Plu.*Demetr.*5; ἡ Σωκράτους π. Longin.4.4.

⊛ **πᾰλαιστρᾰτιώτης**, ου, ὁ, *veteran*, *IGRom.*1.1489(Moesia), 3.213(Ancyra).

**πᾰλαιστρ-ιαῖος**, α, ον, *suited for a* παλαίστρα, αὐλίδιον Thphr.*Char.*5.9. ⊛ **-ίδιον**, τό, Dim. of παλαίστρα, *PSI*4.418 iii A.D.), cj. in Thphr.*Char.*5.9. **-ικός**, ή, όν, *of* or *for the wrestling-school*, Alex.325; ἐπιστήμη Arist.*Cat.*10ᵇ4. Adv. -κῶς *after the manner of the palaestra*, Sch.Ar.*V.*1206. II. later confounded with παλαιστικός, Plu.2.639f, Sor.*Fasc.*51, Gal.6.158, Hierocl.*in CA*16 p.456 M. **-ίτης** [ῑ], ου, ὁ, *like a* παλαιστής, *athletic*, Call.*Fr.*191, Plu.2.274d; π. θεός god *of the palaestra*, Babr.48.5; of Hermes, *IG*12(5).911.22(Tenos); οἱ π. *those who practised in the palaestra*, *CIG*2627(Cypr.): Medic., π. τρόπος *manipulative* treatment of dislocations, Heliod.ap.Orib.49.1.1.

⊛ **πᾰλαιστροφύλαξ** [ῠ], ᾰκος, ὁ, *superintendent of a wrestling-school*, Hp.*Epid.*6.8.30, *IG*5(2).47(Tegea), *Inscr.Délos* 372 *A* 98(200 B.C.), *OGI*345.22(Delph., i B.C.), *Epigr.Gr.*411, Ael.*VH*8.14; π. τοῦ μεγάλου γυμνασίου *PRyl.*121.3(ii A.D.).

**πᾰλαίστωμα**, ατος, τό, = παλαιστή, Aq.3*Ki.*7.9(46).

**πᾰλαίτερος, πᾰλαίτατος**, v. παλαιός.

⊛ **πᾰλαι-φάμενος** [φᾰ], η, ον, = sq., ἄγνος Call.*Fr.anon.*102. **-φᾰτος**, ον, (φημί) poet. Adj. I. *spoken long ago*, ἦ μάλα δή με π. θέσφαθ' ἱκάνει Od.9.507, cf. Pi.*O.*2.40, S.*OC*454; π. λόγος, ἀραί, A.*Ag.*750(lyr.), *Th.*766(lyr.). II. *spoken of long ago, legendary*, δρῦς π. an oak *of ancient story*, Od.19.163 (vv.ll. παλαίφαγος, παλαίφυτος, cf. Hsch.). 2. *of ancient fame, made known* or *declared of old*, γενεά Pi.*N.*6.31; γένος A.*Supp.*532(lyr.); πρόνοια S.*Tr.*823(lyr.); Δίκη Id.*OC*1381; Ἀχάρναι δὲ παλαίφατον εὐάνορες Acharnae was brave *of old time*, Pi.*N.*2.16. **-χθων**, ονος, ὁ, ἡ, *that has been long in a country, an ancient inhabitant, indigenous*, Ἄρης A.*Th.*104(lyr.); δῆμος Epigr.ap.Aeschin.3.190.

**πᾰλαίω**, Aeol. **πάλαιμι** Hdn.Gr.2.930; Boeot. **παλήω** ib.949: fut. παλαίσω: aor. ἐπάλαισα: (πάλη A):—*wrestle*, οὐ γὰρ πύξ γε μαχήσεαι οὐδὲ παλαίσεις Il.23.621; καί νύ κε τὸ τρίτον..πάλαιον ib.733; παλαίουσ' ἐς τρίς S.*Fr.*941.13; οἱ ἐπιστάμενοι παλαίειν Pl.*Prt.*350e; ἐπάλαισαν κάλλιστα Ἀθηναίων Id.*Men.*94c; τὸν παλαίσαντά ποτ' ἐκεῖνον him once famous *as a wrestler*, D.21.71. 2. π. τινί *wrestle with* one, Φιλομηλείδῃ ἐπάλαισεν Od.4.343, 17.134; λέοντι Pi.*P.*9.27: metaph., *wrestle with* a calamity, ἀάτῃσι Hes.*Op.*413; φόνῳ Pi.*N.*8.27; κακῷ μερμέρῳ E.*Rh.*509; πολλαῖς ζημίαις X.*Oec.*17.2. II. c. acc., *overcome*, λόγον λόγῳ παλαιστέον *An.Ox.*3.216:—Pass., παλαισθεὶς *beaten*, E.*El.*686; οἶνος..παλαίεσθαι βαρύς Id.*Cyc.*678. III. c. inf., *endeavour*, Ach.Tat.3.1.

⊛ **πᾰλαί-ωμα**, ατος, τό, *antiquity*, in pl., Lxx *Jb.*36.28, al. ⊛ **-ωσις**, εως, ἡ, (παλαιόομαι) *keeping for a long time*, esp. of wine, παλαίωσιν δέχεσθαι Str.5.4.3, cf. Plu.2.656b, Ath.1.33b, Xenocr.ap.Orib.2.58.140; of drugs, *maturing*, Hp.*Decent.*10; *dilapidated condition* of a house, *Stud.Pal.*22.131.7(ii A.D.): metaph., διελθεῖν εἰς π. Lxx *Na.*1.15(2.1); μῆνις ὀργὴ εἰς π. ἀποτιθεμένη Andronic.Rhod.p.572 M.

**πᾰλᾰμ-άομαι**, fut. -ήσομαι, Aeol. -άσομαι Alc.72: (παλάμη):—

*manage, execute*, ταῖς χερσὶ τὸ δέον π. X.*Cyr*.4.3.17. II. *manage adroitly*, πρὸς ταῦτα Κλέων παλαμάσθω Ar.*Ach*.659, cf. *Nu*.176, E.*Fr*. 918 (lyr.); τόλμημα παλαμήσασθαι *plan* a daring deed, Ar.*Pax* 94; μηχανὰς Philostr.*VA* 2.33.—Act. only in aor. part. παλαμήσας· τεχνάσας, Hsch. ⊛ -η, ἡ, Ep. gen. and dat. παλάμηφι, -φιν :—poet. Noun, *palm of the hand*: hence, generally, *hand*, esp. as used in grasping, παλάμῃ δ' ἔχε χάλκεον ἔγχος Od.1.104; ἔγχος ὅ οἱ παλάμηφιν ἀρήρει Il.3.338, cf. 1.238, etc.; παλάμᾳ δονέων Pi.*P*.1.44. 2. *hand as used in deeds of violence*, ἔπασχον ὑπ' Ἄρηος παλαμάων by *the hands* of Ares, Il.3.128, cf. 5.558, A.*Supp*.865 (lyr.); Κυπρογενῆας παλάμαισιν Alc.60: hence, *a deed of force*, ῥέξαι παλάμαν S.*Ph*.1206 (lyr.). 3. *hand as used in works of art*, etc., Il.15.411, Hes.*Th*.580, *Sc*.219, 320; ἐργατίναις π. *IG* 12(2).129 (Mytil.). II. metaph., *cunning, art, device*, either in good or bad sense, π. βιότου *a device* for one's livelihood, Thgn.624, cf. Hdt.8.19; esp. of the gods, θεοῦ σὺν παλάμᾳ, θεῶν παλάμαι, παλάμαις Διός, by their *arts*, Pi.*O*.10(11).21, *P*.1.48, *N*. 10.65; ὦ παλάμαι θεῶν S.*Ph*.177 (lyr.); πυκνότατος παλάμαις, of Sisyphus, Pi.*O*.13.52, cf. A.*Pr*.167 (lyr.), etc.; παντοίας πλέκειν παλάμας Ar.*V*.645. III. *piece of handiwork, work of art*, Hsch. (pl.); πυριγενὴς π., i.e. a sword, E.*Or*.820 (lyr.). (Cf. Lat. *palma*, OE. *folm* 'hand'.)

**Πᾰλᾰμήδης**, ὁ, voc. ες Ar.*Ra*.1451; gen. ους E.*Or*.433, etc.; dat. ει Pl.*Ap*.41b, εῖ Q.S.5.198; acc. η Pl.*Ep*.311b, εα E.*IA* 198 (lyr.); but some forms occur of I decl., dat. ῃ Hsch. s.v. ἀκέστρον; acc. ην Pl.*Phdr*.261d: (παλάμη):—*Palamedes*, i.e. *the Inventor*, Ar.*Th*.770, *Ra*.1451, Paus.2.20.3:—hence Adj. **Πᾰλᾰμήδειος**, α, ον, *worthy of Palamedes, ingenious*, βούλευμα Alciphr.3.4; ἀβάκιον *EM* 666.21; also **Πᾰλᾰμηδικός**, ή, όν, Π. τοὐξεύρημα Eup.351.6.

**πᾰλάμημα** [λᾰ], ατος, τό, *device, scheme*, Com.*Adesp*.706, Ael.*NA* 1.32.

**πᾰλᾰμίς**, ίδος, ἡ, = ἀσπάλαξ, Alex.Trall.12. II. = πηλαμύς, Cyran.22. III. παλαμίς· τεχνίτης παρὰ τοῖς Σαλαμινίοις, Hsch.

⊛ **πᾰλαμναῖος**, ὁ, (παλάμη I. 2) *one guilty of violence*: hence, *murderer*, τινος S.*Tr*.1207; *one defiled by blood-guiltiness*, A.*Eu*.448, S. *El*.587, Hyp.*Fr*.85; ὦ παλαμναίη O *miscreant!*, of the fox, Babr.82. 6. 2. as Adj., τῷ π. ξένῳ the *abominable* stranger, Phryn.Com. 58; ἱκεσίαι *a murderer's* supplications, A.R.4.709; ἀσπίς Orph.*L*. 512; π. μόρον ἕξει *a miscreant's* death, prob. in *Supp.Epigr*.1.442 (Lydia). II. = ἀλάστωρ, *avenger of blood*, μὴ παλαμναῖον λάβω E. *IT* 1218, cf. X.*Cyr*.8.7.18 (pl.); in full, δαίμονες π. *avenging* deities, Ti.Locr.105, cf. Plu.*Oth*.1, Jul.*Caes*.336b; Ζεὺς π. Arist.*Mu*.401ᵃ23, cf. Plb.*Fr*.98, Poll.5.131, *EM* 647.43.

**πάλαξις** [πᾰ], εως, ἡ, *laying on of a preliminary coat of paint, priming*, *IG* 4²(1).109 iii 111, 117 (Epid., iii B.C.).

⊛ **πᾰλάσιον**, τό, = παλάθιον, Ar.*Pax* 574 codd. (lyr.; παλάθιον Suid.).

**πᾰλάσσω**, pf. Pass. πεπάλαγμαι, Ep. Verb, *besprinkle, defile*, αἵματί τ' ἐγκεφάλῳ τε παλαξέμεν.. οὖδας Od.13.395:—mostly in Pass., παλάσσετο δ' αἵματι θώρηξ Il.5.100; αἵματι καὶ λύθρῳ πεπαλαγμένον Od.22. 402, cf. Call.*Lav.Pall*.7; πεπάλακτο πόδας καὶ χεῖρας ὕπερθεν Od.22. 406; αἰδοῖα γονῇ πεπαλαγμένος Hes.*Op*.733; νιφετῷ π. ὕδωρ Q.S.12. 410:—in Med., παλάσσετο χεῖρας *he bespattered his* hands, Il.11. 169. 2. Pass., *to be scattered abroad*, ἐγκέφαλος πεπάλακτο ib.98, 12.186. II. Ἀσωπὸς..πεπάλακτο κεραυνῷ *was smitten*, for ἐπεπλήκτο, Call.*Del*.78. III. in pf. Med., *shake*, i.e. *draw* lots from an urn, κλήρῳ νῦν πεπάλαχθε διαμπερές *determine your fate* by lot, Il.7. 171; τοὺς ἄλλους κλήρῳ πεπαλάχθαι ἄνωγον Od.9.331; πεπάλαχθε κατὰ κληῖδας ἐρετμά A.R.1.358.—Aristarch. read πεπάλασθε, πεπαλάσθαι in Hom. (cf. πάλλω).

⊛ **πᾰλαστ-ή**, ἡ, = παλάμη, *palm of the hand*: hence, as a measure of length, *palm, four fingers' breadth*, *IG* 1².372.35, Cratin.133, *IG* 2². 1665.10, 1666 *A* 67,70, al. (iv B.C.), 11(2).287 *A* 95 (Delos, iii B.C.), *CIG* 2860.14 (Delos), cf. Phryn.264, *PLit.Lond*.183:—also **παλαιστή**, Hp.*Nat.Mul*.33, Arist.*HA* 606ᵃ14, *PCair.Zen*.484.11 (iii B.C.), Plb.1.22.4, Hero *Aut*.3.1, *Geom*.4.1, D.S.1.55, etc.; also **παλαιστής**, οῦ, ὁ, Lxx *Ex*.25.23(25), 3*Ki*.7.24, Hero *Deff*.131, *Geom*.4.10, S.E. *M*.9.300; written **παλεστής**, *POxy*.669.27,34 (iii A.D.); cf. παλαιστιαῖος. **-ιαῖος**, α, ον, *a palm long, broad*, or *high*, ὕψος π. Hdt.1. 50, cf. *IG* 2².1675.13, 1693, 2492.44; later παλαιστιαῖος (q.v.).

⊛ **Πᾰλάτιον** [λᾱ], τό, = Lat. *Palatium, the Palatine Hill*, D.H.1.31, etc.:—hence **Πᾰλᾱτῖνος**, η, ον, *Palatine*, Id.2.70.

**πᾰλᾰχή**, ἡ, (παλάσσω III) *anything acquired by lot*, = ἀρχή, λῆξις, μοῖρα, γενεά, Hsch.; ἐκ παλαχῆς, = ἐξ ἀρχῆς, Nic.*Th*.449 (cf. Sch. ad loc.): but παλαχῆθεν· ἐκ γενεᾶς, ἐκ παλαιοῦ, Hsch.

**πᾰλεο-μίσημα** [ῑ], ατος, τό, (παλεός = παλαιός) *ancient object of hate*, Tim.*Pers*.90. **-νυμφάγονος** [φᾰ], ον, *where nymphs were born of old*, ἄντρον ib.120 (-φαιο- Pap.).

**πάλ-ευμα** [πᾰ], ατος, τό, *allurement*, Anon.ap.Bast. ad Greg.Cor. p.1017 S. **-ευτά**· τὰ λίνα οἷς τὰ θηρία ἁλίσκεται, Phot. ⊛ **-ευτής**, οῦ, ὁ, *decoy-bird*, Hsch. **-ευτικόν**· θηρευτικόν, Id. (πατ- cod.). **-εύτρια**, ἡ, fem. of παλευτής, Arist.*HA* 613ᵃ23: as Adj., πελειάδες Ael.*NA* 13. 17: metaph., of courtesans, φιλῳδοὶ κερμάτων π. Eub.84.1:—also **-ευτρίς**, ίδος, ἡ, Phot. ⊛ **-εύω**, *act as decoy birds*, Ar.*Av*.1083, 1087:—Pass., of a bird, *to be decoyed*, Philostr.*Im* 2.33. II. metaph., π. τινά *decoy, entrap*, Plu.2.52b, *Sull*.28, etc.; π. τινὰ τοῖς ἀφροδισίοις Philostr.*VA* 4.25: abs., Ph.1.654.

⊛ **πᾰλέω**, *to be disabled*, εἰ παλήσειε ὁ ναυτικὸς στρατός Hdt.8.21: elsewh. only in Hsch., παλήσειε· διαφθαρείη. ἐπάλησεν· ἐφθάρη. πεπαληκέναι· ἐκπεσεῖν. πεπαλημέναι· βεβλαμμέναι: also in shortd. forms, πεπαλμένος· βεβλαμμένος, Id., Phot.; πεπαλκέναι λέγεται τὸ ἐκπίπτειν τὰ πλοῖα Id.

⊛ **πάλη** [ᾰ] (A), ἡ, *wrestling*, Il.23.635; ἢ πὺξ ἠὲ πάλῃ ἢ καὶ ποσίν Od. 8.206: κρατέων πάλᾳ Pi.*O*.8.20; νικᾶν πυγμὴν καὶ π. E.*Alc*.1031. cf. Hp.*Acut*.(*Sp*.)62, Th.1.6, Pl.*Lg*.795b, Plu.2.638d, Antyll.ap.Orib. 6.28.3; τίνα π. ἐμάνθανες; Ar.*Eq*.1238; παίδων, ἐφήβων νεωτέρων, μέσων, πρεσβυτέρων, ἀνδρῶν π., *SIG* 959 (Chios), cf. *IG* 5(2).549.16,30 (Lycosura, iv B.C.), etc. 2. generally, *fight, battle*, ἅπτειν πάλην τινί A.*Ch*.866 (anap.); π. δορός E.*Heracl*.159.

**πάλη** [ᾰ] (B) (or **παλή** acc. to Sch.Il.10.7, to dist. it from foreg.), ἡ, *the finest meal*, π. ἀλφίτου Hp.*Mul*.1.64, cf. Ruf.*Ren.Ves*.6.7, Archig.ap.Gal.12.791; π. πυρίνη Lycus ap.Orib.9.51.1; νάρθηκος πάλαι Zopyr.ap.eund.14.61.1. 2. *any fine dust*, ἀνέπλησα τὠφθαλμὼ πάλης φυσῶν τὸ πῦρ Pherecr.60, cf. Hsch. (Cf. Lat. *pollen, pulvis*.)

**πάλ-ημα** [πᾰ], ατος, τό, = foreg., π. ὀρόβοιο Nic.*Al*.551. **-ημάτιον**, τό, Dim. of foreg., Ar.*Fr*.682.

**πάλῐ** [ᾰ], later poet. form of πάλιν, Call.*Epigr*.12, *AP* 5.181 (Mel.), *Epigr.Gr*.314 (Smyrna), Orph.*H*.3.10, Scymn.470: also in later Prose, Phld.*Mus*.pp.17,40 K., Anon.Lond.6.36, 18.4, *POxy*.298.27 (i A.D.), cf. Phryn.249.

**πᾰλιγ-γέλως**, ωτος, ὁ, *mutual mockery*, prob. l. in Ph.1.528. ⊛ **-γενεσία**, ἡ, *rebirth, regeneration*, of the world, παλιγγενεσίας ἡγεμόνες, of Noah and his sons, Id.2.144; ἡ ἀνάκτησις καὶ π. τῆς πατρίδος J. *AJ* 11.3.9; *renewal* of a race, *Corp.Herm*.3.3; of persons, *beginning of a new life*, εἰς π. ὁρμᾶν Ph.1.159, cf. Luc.*Musc.Enc*.7: hence of *restoration* after exile, Cic.*Att*.6.6.4; *transmigration, reincarnation* of souls, Plu.2.998c; cf. μετεμψύχωσις fin. 2. in Stoic Philos., *rebirth* of the κόσμος, Chrysipp.*Stoic*.2.191: pl., ib.187, Boeth.*Stoic*. 3.265; so later, ἡ περιοδικὴ π. τῶν ὅλων M.Ant.11.1, cf. Procl.*in Ti*.3.241 D. 3. Medic., *relapse*, Gal.13.83; *regrowth* of a tumour, Antyll.ap.Orib.45.2.7. II. in Roman Law, = *restitutio natalium*, Just.*Nov*.18.11. III. in *NT*., 1. *resurrection*, *Ev.Matt*.19.28. 2. *regeneration* by baptism, διὰ λουτροῦ παλιγγενεσίας *Ep.Tit*.3.5. **-γενής**, ές, *born again*, Nonn.*D*.2.650; *generated anew*, αἰών *PMag.Lond*.121.510. **-γλωσσος**, ον, *contradictory, false*, ἀγγέλων ῥῆσις Pi.*N*.1.58; but ἔρις οὐ π. *unrelenting*, Id.*Parth*.2.63. II. *of strange* or *foreign tongue*, πόλις Id.*I*.6(5). 24. III. = δύσφημος, Com.*Adesp*.1098. **-γναμπτος**, ον, *bent* or *doubled back*, κέλευθοι Tryph.523; written **παλίγναμπτος** in Opp. *C*.2.305, *H*.1.54. **-γνωστος**, gloss on παλινδαές, Hsch. **-γρᾰφία**, ἡ, *revision of a* γραφή III, Jul.Laod. in *Cat.Cod.Astr*.5(1).191. ⊛ **-κάπηλεύω**, *to be a retail dealer*, D.56.7. **-κάπηλος** [κᾰ], ὁ, *retailer of imported produce*, Ar.*Pl*.1156 (ὁ ἀπὸ τοῦ ἐμπόρου ἀγοράζων καὶ πωλῶν Sch.): metaph., π. πονηρίας D.25.46. **-κλαστον**· σκολιόν, αὐστηρόν, δύστροπον, Hsch. **-κλῐνής**, ές, *bent back*, gloss on παλιμπετές, Sch.A.R.4.1315.

**πᾰλιγκοτ-αίνω**, = sq., Hp.*Fract*.11, *Mul*.2.171. **-έω**, of wounds, *grow malignant, fester*, Id.*Fract*.11, 25. **-ησις**, εως, ἡ, *festering*, of a wound, ib.31 (pl.). **-ία**, ἡ, = foreg., Id.*Art*.67 (pl.). **-ος**, ον, *spiteful, malignant, resentful*, ἀλλά τις οὐκ ἔμμι παλιγκότων ὄργαν Sapph.72; κληδόνες π. *injurious, untoward* reports, A.*Ag*.863, 874; π. τύχη the *spitefulness of* fortune, ib.571; πῆμα Pi.*O*.2.20; π. ὄψιν ἰδοῦσα *a dreadful* sight, Mosch.4.92; τὰ π. λέγειν Antipho Soph. 49. 2. of persons, *hostile, malignant*, τινι Ar.*Pax* 390, Euph.51. 12, etc.; πρὸς πάντα π. Theoc.22.58; οἱ παλίγκοτοι *adversaries*, Pi.*N*. 4.96, A.*Supp*.376. Adv., αὐτῷ..-τως συνεφέρετο it fared *ill* with him, Hdt.4.156; φέρειν τὰ συμπίπτοντα μὴ π. to bear accidents not *resentfully*, E.*Fr*.572.2. II. metaph., of wounds or injuries, *growing malignant, festering*, Hp.*Art*.27 (Sup.). III. *steep, rugged*, πάγος τρηχύς τε καὶ π. Archil.87. (Cf. ἀλλόκοτος.)

**πᾰλιγ-κρῐσία**, ἡ, *revision of a* κρίσις II. 1, Jul.Laod. in *Cat.Cod. Astr*.5(1).191 (prob.). **-κτησις**, εως, ἡ, *recovery of possession*, Rhetor ib.7.196 (pl.). ⊛ **-κτιστος**, *redivivus*, *Gloss*. **-κυρτος**, ὁ, *fishing-net*, Plb.*Fr*.65.

**πᾰλίδορκος** [ῐ], ον, *looking back*, cj. in Alcm.145.

**πᾰλίζεσθαι**· σφαιρίζειν, Hsch. (fort. παλλ-).

**πᾰλῐκαμπής**, ές, gloss on παλιμπετές (fort. παλιγκαμπής), Sch.Par. A.R.4.1315.

**Πᾰλῖκοί**, οἱ, a lake near Leontini in Sicily, emitting two jets of volcanic gas, Arist.*Mir*.834ᵇ8, Str.6.2.9, D.S.11.88. II. in Mythol., sons of Zeus, worshipped at Palice, A.*Fr*.6, D.S. l.c.

**πᾰλίλ-ληπτος**, gloss on παλινάγρετος, Hsch. **-λογέω**, *repeat, recapitulate*, ὥς οἱ ἐπαλιλλόγητο [τὸ πρῆγμα] Hdt.1.118, cf. 90, Arist. *Rh.Al*.1433ᵇ31, Phld.*Po*.5.26, Ph.2.358, J.*AJ* 17.5.5, App.*Mith*.14, Simp. *in Ph*.1159.4. **-λογία**, ἡ, *recapitulation*, Arist.*Rh.Al*.1433ᵇ 29: pl., ib.1428ᵃ8. 2. *equivocation*, Thphr.*Char*.1.7 (pl.). **-λογος**, ον, (λέγω B) *collected again*, Il.1.126. **-λῠτος**, ον, *loosed again, unloosed*, Nonn.*D*.35.250, al.

**πᾰλιμ-βάκχειος**, ὁ, *a reversed* Βακχεῖος, Heph.3.2, Aristid.Quint. 1.22, Eust.1551.54:—hence Adj. **-βακχειᾰκός**, ή, όν, Heph.13. 1. **-βᾰλής**, ές, = ὕπτιος, Call.*Fr.anon*.52. **-βᾱμος**, ον, (βαίνω) *walking back*, ἱστῶν παλίμβαμοι ὁδοί, of women working at the loom, since they had to walk to and fro from side to side, Pi.*P*.9.18. **-βῐος**, ον, *living again*, Keil-Premerstein *Erster Bericht* p.9, Hsch., Phot., Suid. **-βλαστής**, ές, *sprouting* or *growing again*, κύων, of the hydra, E.*HF* 1274; καυλοί Thphr.*HP* 7.2.4. **-βληθείς**, εῖσα, έν, *ricochetting*, βέλος Ruf.*Interrog*.60. **-βολία**, ἡ, *change of mind, fickleness*, *AP* 5.301.12 (Agath.), Agath.2.6. ⊛ **-βολος**, ον, *reversed*, γνώμη Sch.Ar.*Nu*.298: hence, *untrustworthy, unstable*, ἤθη π. καὶ ἄπιστα Pl.*Lg.*705a, cf. D.Chr.31.37, Aristaenet.1.28; δολερὸς καὶ π. Plu.*Crass.*21; τὸ π., = παλιμβολία, Aeschin.2.40; of a slave, = παλίμπρατος, Men.445; πέδιλα π. *turned* or *patched* sandals, Nic.*Fr.*85. Adv. -λως Poll.3.132. **-βορέας**, ου, ὁ, *a wind counter to the prevalent north wind*, Thphr.*Vent.*28 (pl.). ®**-βουλία**, f.l. for -βολία, Adam.2.24: ®**-βουλος**, f.l. for -βολος, Id.1.15, Sch.Th.3.37, Eust. 375.1. **-μᾰχέω**, *renew the fight*, Lyd.*Mag.*3.55. **-μεταβολή**, ἡ, *repeated change*, εἰς σώματα Plu.2.998d. **-μήκης**, ες, *as long again, doubly long*, χρόνος A.*Ag.*196 (lyr.). **-παις**, παιδος, ὁ, ἡ, *again a child*, Luc.*Sat.*9. **-παστος**, ον, dub. l., epith. of πέλαγος, Dion.Byz.53. **-πέτεια**, ἡ, *recurrence*, *Theol.Ar.*58. **-πετής**, ές, (πίπτω) *falling back*, Nonn.*D.*3.30; *recurrent*, *Theol.Ar.*57: in early writers only in neut. as Adv., *back again*, ἂψ ἐπὶ νῆας ἔεργε παλιμπετὲς Il.16.395; ὡς.. ἐν νηῒ παλιμπετὲς ἀπονέωνται Od.5.27, cf. Call.*Del.*294, A.R.2.1250, etc. **-πηγα**, τά, (πήγνυμι) *cobbled shoes*, *Com.Adesp.*1099. **-πηξις**, εως, ἡ, *patching up* or *cobbling* of shoes, Thphr.*Char.*22.11. ® **-πισσα**, ἡ, *pitch reboiled, dry pitch*, Dsc.1.72; cf. παλίνπιττα. **-πλαγκτος**, ον, *back-driven*, δρόμοι A.*Pr.*838. **-πλάζομαι**, Pass., only in aor. part. παλιμπλαγχθείς, *foiled, driven back*, Il.1.59, Od.13.5 (better divisim). **-πλᾰνής**, ές, *wandering to and fro*, Μαίανδρος *AP*6.287 (Antip., v.l. πολυ-); βίοτος *Epigr.Gr.*491.5 (Orchom. Boeot.). ® **-πλεκής**, ές, *twined* or *plaited back*, κύρτοι Opp.*H.*4.47. **-πλους**, ὁ, ἡ, -πλουν, τό, *sailing back*, Ael.*NA*3.14. ® **-πλῠτος**, ον, *washed up again, vamped up*: metaph., of a *plagiarist who retouches the works of others* and passes them off for his own, κηφὴν π. *AP*7.708 (Diosc.). **-πλωτος**, ον, Ion. for παλίμπλους, Lyc.1431. **-πνόη**, ἡ, *counter-wind*, Thphr.*Vent.* 26; poet. -πνοίη A.R.1.586 (pl.). ® **-πνοος**, ον, *breathing again*, Nonn.*D.*37.295; poet. **-πνοιος**, η, ον, *eddying*, δῖναι cj. in Opp.*H.*1. 771. **-ποινος**, ον, *retributive*, δίκαι Max.17. II. παλίμποινα, τά, *retribution, repayment*, A.*Ch.*793 (lyr.). **-πόρευτος**, ον, = sq., Tim. *Pers.*186, Lyc.180, 628. **-πορος**, ον, *going back*, φυγή Tim.*Pers.* 174, cf. Opp.*H.*4.529, Nonn.*D.*2.247. ® **-ποτον**, τό, *reversible cup*, *Michel*39.37, 40 (Milet., iii B.C.):—also **-πότης**, ου, ὁ, *Inscr.Délos*442 *B* 205 (ii B.C., pl.). **-πους**, ὁ, ἡ, gen. ποδος, *going back, returning*, Lyc.126, *AP*5.162 (Mel.); π. τύχη περιίσταται J.*BJ*4.1.6. **-πρᾱτέω**, *to be a retailer*, *PRev.Laws*47.16 (iii B.C.). **-πράτης** [πρᾱ], ου, ὁ, = παλιγκάπηλος, Socr.*Ep.*1.1. ® **-πρᾱτος**, ον, *sold again* or *by retail*, of a good-for-nothing slave who passes from hand to hand, Poll.3.125. 2. generally, *good-for-nothing*, Ph.2.523, Poll.4.36; also of things, D.Chr.31.37, Poll.7.12. **-προδοσία**, ἡ, *double treachery*, Plb.5.96.4, D.H.8.32, D.S.15.91, etc. **-προδότης**, ου, ὁ, *traitor to both sides*, Din.*Fr.*89.26, D.S.15.91, App.*BC*5.96. **-πρυμνηδόν**, Adv. *stern-foremost*, E.*IT*1395, from Hsch., who expl. it οἷον παλίμπρυμνον χώρησιν. **-πῡγηδόν**, Adv. *rump foremost*, Arist. *PA*659ᵃ20, Hsch. **-πωλος**, ον, = παλίμπρατος, v.l. in Poll.7.12; esp. of works not completed by the first contractor and given to another, *IG*7.3073.26 (Lebad.), *BCH*20.324 (ibid.). **-φημος**, Dor. **-φᾱμος**, ον, *back-speaking, recanting*, π. ἀοιδά, = παλινῳδία, a song *of recantation*, reproaching the male sex instead of the female, E.*Ion* 1096 (lyr.), cf. *Med.*415 sq. II. = κακόφημος, δύσφημος, λαβροσύναι Tryph.423, cf. Hsch.; π. εὐχαί Ph.2.301; ὄναρ ib.55. **-φοιτος**, ον, *returning*, Max.332, 570, *PMich.* in *Class.Phil.*22.16. **-φρων**, ονος, ὁ, ἡ, *changing one's mind*, Lyc.1349. **-φυής**, ές, *growing again*, of the hydra, Luc.*Am.*2. **-ψηκτρον**, *deleticia* (sc. *charta*), *Gloss.* **-ψηστος**, ον, (ψάω) *scraped again*, βιβλίον π. *palimpsest*, Plu. 2.779c: -ψηστον, τό, as Subst., ib.504d, cf. Catull.22.5, Cic.*Fam.*7. 18.2.

® **πάλῐν** [ᾰ], poet. also **πάλι** (q.v.), Adv. 1. of Place, *back, backwards* (the usual sense in early Ep.), mostly joined with Verbs of going, coming, etc.; π. χώρει Hdt.5.72; π. ἐλεύσεται, κατελθεῖν, ἐπανέλθωμεν, A.*Pr.*854, S.*OC*601, Pl.*Cra.*438a, etc.; κέλευθον ἥνπερ ἦλθες ἐγκόνει π. A.*Pr.*962; δίκα καὶ πάντα π. στρέφεται E.*Med.*412 (lyr.); δεῦρο σωθήσῃ π. Id.*Ph.*725, cf. 1400; δόμεναι π. give *back*, *restore*, Il.1.116, etc.; π. ἀποδοῦναι And.2.23; π. ἀγκαλέσαι to call *back*, A.*Ag.*1021 (lyr.): less freq. c. gen., π. τράπεθ' υἷος ἑοῖο she turned *back from* her son, Il.18.138; δόρυ Ἀχιλλῆος π. ἔτραπεν 20.439, cf. Od.7.143: coupled with other Advbs., π. αὖτις ἔβαινον νηὸς ἐπὶ γλαφυρῆς 14.356, cf. Pi.*O.*1.65; αὖ π. Od.13.125; ἂψ π. Il.18.280; π. εἶσιν ὀπίσσω Od.11.149; π. φέρεσθαι ἐξοπίσω Hes.*Th.* 181; ἄψορρον π. S.*El.*53; π. οἴκαδε, π. οἴκαδ' αὖ, Ar.*Lys.*792, *Ra.*1486; π. αὖ Pl.*Prt.*318e, etc.: with the Art., ἡ π. ὁδός E.*Or.*125. 2. to express *contradiction*, π. ἐρέει *gainsay*, Il.9.56; π. ὅ γε λάζετο μῦθον took *back* his word, *unsaid* it, 4.357; opp. ἀληθέα εἰπεῖν, Od.13.254; μηδέ τῳ δόξῃ π. let no one think *contrariwise*, A.*Th.*1045: in Prose, *contrariwise*, Pl.*Grg.*482d; π. αὖ Id.*R.*507b; αὖ.. π. Id.*Ap.*27d: in this sense sts. c. gen., τὸ π. νεότατος youth's *opposite*, Pi.*O.*10(11). 87; χρόνου τὸ π. *the change* of time, E.*HF*777 (lyr.); cf. ἔμπαλιν. II. of Time, *again, once more*, rare in Hom., Il.2.276, cf. S.*OT*1166, X. *Mem.*1.6.11, etc.: freq. coupled with αὖ, αὖθις (q.v.); π. ἐξ ἀρχῆς Ar.*Pax*997, etc.; π. καὶ π. Str.17.1.3, Plu.2.565d, Ael.*VH*1.4; ἔγχει καὶ π. εἰπέ, π. π. "Ἡλιοδώρας" *AP*5.135 (Mel.): both senses (I and II) are appropriate in Od.16.456, Pl.*Prt.*322b, etc. III. *in turn*, S.*El.*371, Ar.*Ach.*342, Call.*Dian.*87, etc.; π. ὁ Κῦρος ἠρώτα X.*An.* 1.6.7; π. ἀπαιτῶ Pl.*R.*612d; *again*, πρῶτον μέν.. ἔπειτα π. Arist.*Pol.* 1289ᵇ29, etc. (In compos. πάλιν sts. means *doubly*, as in παλιμμήκης, παλίνσκιος.)

**πᾰλῐν-άγγελος**, ον, *bringing messages to and fro*, Hsch., Phot., Suid. **-άγρετος**, ον, (ἀγρέω) *to be taken back* or *recalled*, οὐ π. οὐδ' ἀπατηλόν *irrevocable*, Il.1.526; π. ἀάτη Hes.*Sc.*93; νεότατα δ' ἔχειν π. οὐκ ἔστι Theoc.29.28; π. αἰών, ἀρχή, etc., Nonn.*D.*3.255, 6.175, al.; *recoverable*, of an element, Numen.ap.Eus.*PE*15.17. 2. *retracting his words*, of the philosopher Arcesilaus, Id.ib.14. 5. **-αίρετος**, ον, *removed from office and re-elected*, of public officers, Eup.89, Archipp.14, Nicostr.34. 2. of buildings, *pulled down and rebuilt, patched up*. Pi.*Fr.*84, cf. Harp. s.v., Hsch., etc.; also σιδήρου π. *IG*1².313.131 (Eleusis). 3. παλιναίρετα γεγονότα.. καὶ διεφθαρμένα Pl.*Ti.*82e, expld. by Tim.*Lex.* φευκτά, ἔκβλητα, τὸ ἐναντίον.. αὐτῇ τῇ αἱρέσει πάθος ἐμποιοῦντα. **-αυξής**, ές, *growing again*, *APl.*4.221 (Theaet.), Nonn.*D.*25.542. **-αυτόμολος**, ὁ, *deserting back again, double deserter*, X.*HG*7.3.10. **-δᾱής**, ές, (*δάω) *learnt again*, Hsch.

**πᾰλινδῐκ-έω**, *go to law again, bring a fresh action*, *BGU*613.17 (ii A.D.), Hsch. **-ία**, ἡ, *second action, new trial*, π. διδόναι τινί Hdn.7. 6.4; π. εὑρίσκειν Plu.*Dem.*6; μὴ ἦμεν.. π. *Tab.Heracl.*1.157. **-ος**, ον, *litigious*, Crates Com.51.

**πᾰλιν-δίνητος** [δῐ], ον, *whirling round and round*, θάλασσα *AP*9.73 (Antiphil.); κόσμοιο παλινδίνητον ἀνάγκην ib.1.19 (Claudian.), cf. 9. 505.14. **-δῑνία**, ἡ, *eddying* of water, Hsch. **-δίωξις** [δῐ], εως, ἡ, = παλίωξις, App.*Pun.*46, D.C.74.6. **-δορία**, ἡ, *mending of shoes*: hence in concrete, *mended shoes*, Pl.Com.164, cf. Poll.6.164.

**πᾰλινδρομ-έω**, *run back again*, ἐπὶ τόπον J.*BJ*3.2.3; ἐς ταὐτά Aret. *SD*1.6: abs., Manetho ap.J.*Ap.*1.26; of a ship, Ps.-Hdt.*Vit.Hom.* 19, D.S.20.74, Plu.*Cic.*32: prov., παλινδρομῆσαι μᾶλλον ἢ κακῶς δραμεῖν Luc.*Asin.*18. II. Medic., *go back* without coming to a head, of an abscess, dub. in Hp.*Prog.*18; μὴ -δρομῇ τὸ ἐρυσίπελας ἔσω *strike inwards*, ib.23. b. *recur, relapse*, Id.*Epid.*2.3.18, Aret. *SA*1.7, Luc.*Abd.*32. c. παλινδρομῶν σφυγμός *recurrent, recovering*, Gal.9.510, Marcellin.*Puls.*400. d. of *recurrent* nerves, Gal.8.53, *UP*16.4. III. metaph., π. πρὸς τὰς τῶν Καρχηδονίων ἐλπίδας *fall back* upon.., Plb.7.3.8; γεωμετρία ἐπὶ τὰ αἰσθητὰ -δρομοῦσα Plu.2. 718f. 2. βλασφημία -δρομοῦσα, of abuse which *comes home* to roost, ib.88d. **-ής**, ές, = παλίνδρομος, ἐς ταὐτά Aret.*SA*2.9. **-ησις**, εως, ἡ, = sq., Eust.244.28. **-ία**, Ion. **-ίη**, ἡ, *running back, going backwards*, *AP*6.307 (Phan.), Iamb.*in Nic.*p.76 P.; τοῦ ἡλίου D.L. 7.152; τῆς φύσιος ἡ π. *restoration*, Aret.*CD*1.3; *striking inwards*, of an abscess or eruption, Hp.*Prorrh.*2.7: in pl., *relapses*, Id.*Epid.*4. 42. **-ικός**, ή, όν, *recurring*, of the tide, κίνησις Str.1.3.8. **-ος**, ον, *running back again*, π. ἄπιθι Luc.*Tim.*37; *recurring*, σελήνη π. ἀνάμνησις Secund.*Sent.*6; π. ἔλλαβε πένθος *recurring*, *Epigr.Gr.* 233.7 (Chios); μνᾶς.. παλινδρόμους ἀπολαβεῖν *back again*, D.L.2.65: metaph., *uncertain*, S.E.*P.*2.203.

**πᾰλῐν-εδρος** [ῐ], ον, *coming home to roost*, πτηνῶν γένη π. *PMag. Par.*1.2556. **-εκχῠμενίτας** [ῑτ], α, ὁ, *one who squanders again*, Cerc. 4.12. **-έμπορος**, ὁ, *retail-dealer*, Phot. ® **-ζωος**, *redivivus*, *Gloss.*

**παλίνη**, ἡ, = πάλη (B), *EM*650.3.

**πᾰλῐ-νηνεμία**, ἡ, *returning calm*, *AP*10.102 (Bass.; v.l. πολυν-).

**πᾰλῐν-ίδρῠσις**, εως, ἡ, *sinking, settling down*, Hp.*Hum.*2. **-λῐθηγία**, ἡ, *return of* rejected *blocks* to a quarry, *Supp.Epigr.*4.453.30 (Didyma, ii B.C.). **-νοστος**, ον, *returning*, Nonn.*D.*6.62, al. **-οδέομαι**, *retrace one's path*: hence in Math., *recur*, of numbers, *Theol.Ar.*22. **-οδία**, ἡ, (ὁδός) *retracing one's path*: hence, *recurrence* of numbers, ib.57 (pl.); κατὰ παλινοδίαν ib.59. **-οιωνίαι**· ἐκ δευτέρου μαντεῖαι, Hsch. **-οπτα**· τὰ ἀπὸ τοῦ ἡλίου ἀπεστραμμένα, Hp.ap.Gal.19.127. **-όρμενος**, η, ον, *rushing back*, Il.11.326 (better divisim). **-όρμητος**, ον, (ὁρμάω) = παλίνορσος, Sch.Ar.*Ach.*1178, Sch.S.*OT*193. **-ορσος**, ον, *backwards, back*, ὡς ὅτε τίς τε δράκοντα ἰδὼν παλίνορσος ἀπέστη Il.3.33, cf. Emp.35.1; ἄγε νῆα.. π. ἐς Ἑλλάδα A.R.1.416; π. φορή *retrograde* movement, Aret.*SA*2.5; *recurrent*, ἢν ἡ νοῦσος π. ὀφθῇ Id.*CD*1.5: neut. as Adv., *back again*, *AP*7.608 (Eutolm.): Att. **πᾰλίνορρον**, *with a backward wrench*, Ar.*Ach.*1179. (-ορσος prob. = ὄρρος, cf. παλιμπυγηδόν.) **-ορτος**, ον, (ὄρνυμι) *recurring, inveterate*, μῆνις A.*Ag.*154 (lyr.).

**πᾰλῐ-νοστέω**, *return*, Gal.16.89, Olymp.*in Mete.*112.20. **-νόστιμος**, ον, *returning*, ὁρμή Opp.*H.*1.616, cf. Nonn.*D.*11.413.

**πᾰλίν-ουρος**, ον, (οὖρον) *making water again*, with play on pr. n. Palinurus, Mart.3.78.2. ® **-πιττα**· ἐφθὴ πίττα, Hsch.; cf. παλίμπισσα. **-ρύμη**, v. παλιρρύμη. **-σάγης**· χήρα γυνή, Id. **-σκῐος**, ον, *shaded over again, thick-shaded*, ἐν -σκίῳ Archil.24, Plu.*Num.*10, cf. Is.*Fr.*112; π. ἐλαῖαι Arist.*HA*556ᵃ24; ὗλαι Luc.*Am.* 12; *dark*, χειμὼν S.*Fr.*289:—also **πᾰλίσκιος**, ον, ἄντρον *h.Merc.*6, *h.Hom.*18.6; ἐν -σκίοις Thphr.*HP*1.8.1, cf. *Od.*40; εἰς τὸ π. Max.Tyr. 5.1. **-σκοπιά**, ἡ, *looking back again*, -σκοπιὰν ἔχομεν E.*Or.*1262 (lyr.). ® **-σοος**, ον, *safe again*, Nonn.*D.*25.535 codd. (leg. παλίμπνοον). **-στᾰτέω**, *return from secession*, of the Roman plebs, f.l. for πάλιν ἀστατοῦντος, Lyd.*Mag.*1.38. **-στομέω**, = δυσφημέω, *speak words of ill omen*, A.*Th.*258. **-στρᾰφής**, ές, *reversed*, βήματα S.*Ichn.* 112. **-στρεπτος**, ον, *turned backward*, Κριός Max.80, cf. Nic.*Th.*679 (v.l. παλίστρ-). **-στρόβητος**, ον, *whirled* or *twirled round*, Lyc. 739. **-στροφος**, ον, = παλίνστρεπτος, Opp.*C.*2.99; παλίστρ-, Sch. Ar.*Nu.*298. **-σύλλεκτος**, ον, *gathered again*, Hsch., Phot. s.v. παλίλλογα. **-τῑτος**, ον, (τίνω) *done in requital*, παλίντιτα ἔργα γενέσθαι Od.1.379. II. Act., *requiting*, πνεύματα Emp.111.5. **-τοκία**, ἡ, *demand for repayment of interest*, Plu.2.295d. **-τονος**, ον, *bent backward*, i.e. the opposite way to that in which they were drawn, τόξα, in Hom. of the bow whether strung, Il.8.266, cf. 15.443; or unstrung, 10.459, Od.21.11, cf. S.*Tr.*511 (lyr.); Ἀράβιοι τόξα π. ἐχον μακρά Hdt. 7.69; Σκυθικὰ π. βέλη A.*Ch.*161 (lyr.). 2. *back-stretched*, ἡνίαι Ar.

*Av.*1739. 3. *caused by opposite tensions*, π. ἁρμονίη κόσμου ὅκωσπερ λύρης καὶ τόξου Heraclit.51 (v.l. παλίντροπος). II. παλίντονα, τά, *military engines for throwing stones*, but not pointed missiles, = λιθοβόλα, Ph.*Bel.*91.36, Hero *Bel.*74, 104, etc. **-τρᾰπελία**, ἡ, = παλιντροπία, Poll.3.132. **-τράπελος** [τρᾰ], ον, = παλίντροπος II. 2, Pi.*O.* 2.37. **-τρῐβής**, ές, *rubbed again and again*, of the ass, *obstinate, resisting all blows*, Semon.7.43. 2. *knavish, crafty*, τὰ.. πανοῦργα καὶ π. S.*Ph.*448. **-τριψ**, ῐβος, ὁ, ἡ, = foreg., *Gloss.* **-τροπάομαι**, *return*, ἐπὶ νῆα -τροπάασθαι A.R.4.165; ἂψ δὲ -τροπόωντο ib. 643. **-τροπής**, ές, = παλίντροπος, Nic.*Th.*402. **-τροπία**, ἡ, *turning about*: in pl., *changes of mind*, A.R.3.1157. **-τροπος**, ον, *turned away, averted*, ὄμματα, ὄψις, A.*Ag.*777 (lyr.), *Supp.*173 (lyr.). II. *turning back*, π. ἕρπειν, στρέφεσθαι, S.*Ph.*1222, E.*HF* 1069 (lyr.); π. ἐκ πολέμοιο *AP*9.61; π. κέλευθος Parm.6.9. 2. *changing to the other side, contrary*, πλάστιγξ τοῦ βίου S.*Fr.*576.5 (s.v.l.); π. τῆς ἐλπίδος ἀποβαινούσης πρὸς τὰς ἐξ ἀρχῆς ἐπιβολάς Plb. 14.6.6; π. ταῖς ἐξ ἀρχῆς ἐλπίσιν *exactly contrary* to their original expectations, Id.5.16.9, cf. 9.21.1; π. ποιῆσαι τὴν μάχην D.S.15.85, cf. App.*Mith.*88; π. ποιήσασθαι τὴν δίωξιν Onos.27 (v.l. παλίστροφον); τὸ π. τοῦ δαιμονίου *changeableness*, Id.35.4. III. Act., *turning to flight*, νόημα B.10.54. IV. v. παλίντονος I. 3. **-τῠπής**, ές, *beaten back*, neut. as Adv., A.R.3.1254. **-τῠχής**, ές, *with a reverse of fortune*, τριβὰ βίου A.*Ag.*464 (lyr.).

**πᾰλῐνῳδ-έω**, *recant an ode*: hence, generally, *revoke, recant*, Pl. *Alc.*2.142d, 148b; π. πρὸς τὸ χεῖρον Luc.*Apol.*1. 2. *repeat an ode*: hence, generally, *repeat*, Ph.1.586, S.E.*M.*7.202. **-ητέον**, *one must recant*, Gal.11.224. ❀ **-ία**, ἡ, *palinode, recantation*, first used of an ode by Stesichorus, in which he recanted his attack upon Helen, Isoc.10.64, Pl.*Ep.*319e, *Phdr.*243b. 2. generally, *recantation*, ib.257a, Cic.*Att.*4.5.1, Ph.1.260, Plu.*Alex.*53. **-ικός**, ή, όν, *palinodic*, i.e. *having the form a b b a*, of metrical schemes, Heph. *Poëm.*4; π. ὕμνοι Cratin.6 D.

**πᾰλίνωρος** [ῐ], ον, (ὥρα) *changing and returning with the seasons*, Arat.452. II. παλινώρους· ἄκοντας, Hsch. (παλίνωρον is f.l. for παλίνορρον, Id.).

**πᾰλἴούρ-ῐνος**, η, ον, *made of* παλίουρος, Str.16.4.17. **-ίς**, = *ruta*, *Gloss.* **-ος**, ὁ (Thphr.*HP*1.3.2, Agatharch.34) or ἡ (*AP*9.414 (Tull. Gem.)), *Christ's thorn, Paliurus australis*, E.*Cyc.*394, Theopomp. Hist.129, Theoc.24.89, Dsc.1.92, etc. II. *great jujube, Zizyphus Spina-Christi*, Thphr.*HP*4.3.3, Agatharch.l.c., *BGU*1120.16 (i B.C.), Plin.*HN*13.111. III. = κάδος, ἀντλητήρ, Hsch.

❀ **πᾰλἴουροφόρος** θρῖναξ, ὁ, three-pronged fork *made of the wood of the* παλίουρος I, *AP*6.95 (Antiphil.).

**πᾰλιρ-ροέω**, *ebb and flow*, Str.1.3.8, 3.3.3; ἀέρος -ροοῦντος Thphr. *Vent.*10. 2. *flow back*, of perspiration, Diocl.*Fr.*147. **-ρόθιος**, η, ον, *back-rushing, refluent*, π. δέ μιν αὖτις πλῆξεν [τὸ κῦμα] Od. 5.430; ἠπειρόνδε π. φέρε κῦμα, of the wave caused by the rock thrown by the Cyclops, 9.485; πενίης κῦμα π. Luc.*Epigr.*2.12: generally, = παλίρροος, ναῦς π. Arat.347; τὰ π., = παλίρροια, A.R.1.1170. **-ροθος**, v. παλίρροχθος. **-ροια** (also **-οίᾱ** S.*Fr.*832), Ion. **-οίη**, ἡ, *flowing back, backwater*, δίνας τινὰς.. ἰσχυρὰς καὶ παλιρροίην Hdt.2.28; παλιρροία βυθοῦ, of the tide, S.l.c.; παλιρροίη ἐπινήχεται, of Delos, Call.*Del.*193: in pl., Agathem.5.22. 2. generally, *reflux*, ἡ π. τῆς ὑγρότητος, in the spleen, Arist.*PA*670ᵇ8; τοῦ θερμοῦ Id.*Insomn.*461ᵃ6; ἐς π. ἰέναι Aret.*CA*1.7. 3. metaph., παράδοξος π. τῶν πραγμάτων, of fortune, Plb.1.82.3; ἡ ἐπ' ἀμφότερα τὰ μέρη τῆς τύχης π. D.S.18.59; also of ἀνάμνησις, Ph.1.593. **-ροιβδος**, ον, *dashing back with a roar*, Opp. *H.*5.220 (v.l. **-ροιζος**). **-ροιος**, ον, = sq., of waves, δῖναι Lyc.380, Opp.*H.*1.778. **-ροος**, ον, contr. **-ρους**, ρουν, *back-flowing, refluent*, κλύδων E.*IT*1397; *ebbing and flowing*, metaph., of the breath, ἀήρ Opp.*H.*2.398; ἆσθμα Tryph.76. II. metaph., *recurring, returning upon one's head*, πότμος E.*HF*739 (lyr.), cf. *El.*1155 (lyr.). **-ροπος**, ον, *tottering, bent*, π. γόνυ (of an old man) ib.492. **-ροχθος**, ον, *roaring with ebb and flow*, of Aulis, prob. in A.*Ag.*190 (lyr., restd. metri gr. for παλιρρόθοις). **-ρύμη** or **πᾰλίν-ρύμη** [ῠ], ἡ, *rush backwards, back-flow*, τοῦ σάλου Plu.*Flam.*10; π. τύχης *a reverse of* fortune, Plb.15.7.1, D.S.3.51 (mostly and perh. rightly written divisim in codd.). **-ρῠτος**, ον, = παλίρροος, π. αἷμα *flowing in retribution*, prob. for πολύρρυτον in S.*El.*1420 (lyr.); π. παγαί, of honey, dub. in Philox.3.8 (μελιρρύτοισι Mein.).

**παλίσκιος**, v. παλινσκιος.

**πᾰλίσ-συρτος**, ον, (σύρω) *dragged back*, *Corp.Herm.*10.8 (v.l. -συτος). **-σῠτέω**, *rush quickly back*, of waves, D.S.1.32, 3. 22. **-σῠτος**, ον, (σεύω, ἔσσυμαι) *rushing back*, π. δράμημα *hurried* flight, S.*OT*193 (lyr.); π. στεῖχε E.*Supp.*388; ὁρμῆσαι Plb.15.12.2, cf. παλίσσυρτος; χολή Aret.*SD*1.15; π. φύσις *recovering*, Id.*CA*2.3.

**πᾰλίστρεπτος, παλίστροφος**, v. παλίνστρεπτος, -στροφος.

**πᾰλιτρᾰχηλίζω**, *to be stiff-necked, refractory, contumacious*, *PPetr.*3 p.136 (iii B.C.).

❀ **πᾰλίωξις**, εως, ἡ, (πάλι, ἰωκή) *pursuit in turn*, when fugitives rally and turn on their pursuers, π. δὲ γένηται ἐκ νηῶν [ῑ metri gr.] Il.12.71; ἄν τοι ἔπειτα π. παρὰ νηῶν αἰὲν ἐγὼ τεύχοιμι 15.69, cf. 601; opp. προΐωξις, Hes.*Sc.*154: in late Prose, App.*Mith.*49.

**πάλκος**· πηλός, Hsch.

❀ **πάλλα**, ἡ, *ball* (σφαῖρα ἐκ ποικίλων ναμάτων (fort. νημάτων) πεποιημένη Hsch.), read by Dionysodorus for σφαῖρα in Od.6.115.

**πάλλαγμα**, f.l. in A.*Supp.*296, v. ἐμπάλαγμα.

❀ **Παλλάδιον** [ᾰ], τό, *statue of Pallas*, Hdt.4.189, Ar.*Ach.*547, *Jahresh.*16 *Beibl.*42 (iv B.C.), *IG*2².1388.67, etc.; Π. ἐκάλουν τὰ βαλλόμενα εἰς γῆν ἐκ τοῦ οὐρανοῦ ἀγάλματα Pherecyd.179 J. II. a *court* of the ἐφέται at Athens, ἐπὶ Π. δώσεις δίκην Ar.*Fr.*585, cf. Arist.*Ath.* 57.3, Paus.1.28.8 sq.

**παλλᾰκ-εία** or **-ία**, ἡ, *concubinage*, Is.3.39 (παλλακίδι codd.), Str. 17.1.46, *Peripl.M.Rubr.*49. **-εύω**, *to be a concubine*, esp. for ritual purposes, Str.17.1.46, *BCH*7.276 (Tralles): generally, τῷ Μιθριδάτῃ Str.13.4.3:—more freq. in Med. and Pass., 1. *keep as a concubine*, Hdt.4.155. 2. Pass., *to be a concubine*, Plu.*Them.*26; τινι to one, Id.*Fab.*21, *Art.*26. **-ή**, ἡ, = παλλακίς, πολλὰς κουριδίας γυναῖκας, πολλῷ δὲ πλεῦνας παλλακάς Hdt.1.135, cf. 84, 2.130, al., Ar.*V.*1353, Antipho 1.14, Lex ap.D.23.53, Lys.1.31, Pl.*Ion* 538b, *Lg.*841d, D.59. 122, Lxx *Jd.*19.1, etc.; μηδὲ π. μηδὲ παιδικὸν ἔχειν Mitteis *Chr.*284.4 (ii B.C.). (Prop. *young girl*, Ael.Dion.*Fr.*172; cf. πάλλαξ.) **-ίδιον**, τό, Dim. of παλλακίς, Plu.2.789b. **-ῖνος**, ὁ, *son by a concubine*, Sophr.124. **-ιον** [ᾰ], τό, Dim. of πάλλαξ, Alcm.92 (dub. l.), Pl.Com.206, Ael.Dion.*Fr.*172 (who rejects the form **παλλήκιον**), Hsch. II. = παλλακεία, *Gloss.* ❀ **-ίς** [ᾰ], ίδος, ἡ, *concubine*, opp. lawful wife (ἄκοιτις), Il.9.449, 452; ὠνητὴ π. Od.14.203, cf. Lxx *Jb.* 19.17, Heroph.ap.Sor.2.53 (dub. l.), etc.; π. δούλη *AP*3.3 (Inscr. Cyzic.); ἐκ προγόνων παλλακίδων, of ritual prostitution, *BCH*7.276 (Tralles). **-ός**, ὁ, *minion*, Hsch., Phot.

**Παλλαντιὰς** κόρη, = Παλλάς, *AP*6.247 (Phil.).

**Παλλάντιος** λόφος, ὁ, the *Palatine* hill at Rome, Ael.*VH*12.11, cf. D.H.1.31, Paus.8.43.1.

**πάλλαξ**, ακος [prob. ᾰ], ὁ, *youth*, below the age of an ἔφηβος, Ael. Dion.*Fr.*172: fem., *girl*, Gell.4.3:—also **πάλληξ**, *GDI*5704.7 (Samos, iii/ii B.C.), Ar.Byz.ap.Ammon.p.37 V., Corn.*ND*20, Hsch.

❀ **Παλλάς**, άδος, ἡ, *Pallas*, epith. of Athena, Παλλὰς Ἀθηναίη Il.1.200, etc.; later used alone, = Ἀθήνη, B.5.92, Hdt.5.77, *IG*1².573, etc. 2. *coin bearing the head of Pallas*, Eub.6 (pl.). II. *maiden-priestess*, Str.17.1.46, Eust.1742.37. III. Pythag. name for *five*, *Theol.Ar.* 32. (Commonly deriv. from πάλλω, either as *Brandisher* of the spear, or παρὰ τὸ ἀναπεπάλθαι ἐκ τῆς κεφαλῆς τοῦ Διός, etc., Pl.*Cra.*407a, *EM* 649.52, cf. Eust.84.43, but prob. orig. *virgin, maiden*, cf. sq. and v. παλλακή fin., πάλλαξ.)

**πάλλᾱς**, αντος, ὁ, *youth*, Philistid.1 J.

**παλλάχανον**· κρόμμυον (Ascalon), Hsch.

❀ **Παλλειών**, ῶνος, ὁ, name of month at Magnesia on the Maeander, *Inscr.Magn.*2.3 (iv/iii B.C.).

**πάλλευκος**, ον, *all-white*, A.*Eu.*352 (lyr.); δέρη, πούς, E.*Med.*30, 1164:—written **πάνλευκος**, Orac.ap.Phleg.*Fr.*37 J. (restd. for ζάλευκος from Zos.2.6), Nonn.*D.*7.218.

**παλλήκιον**, v. παλλάκιον.

**Παλλήνη**, ἡ, a peninsula and town of Chalcidice, Hdt.7.123, Th.1. 56, etc.; Maced. **Βαλλήνη** Eust.1618.45 (whence the joke on Βαλλήναδε in Ar.*Ach.*234, v. Sch. ad loc.). II. an Attic deme; **Παλληνεύς**, ὁ, *an inhabitant thereof*, Harp.; fem. **Παλληνὶς** Ἀθηναίη, Hdt.1. 62, cf. *IG*1².310.189; **Παλλήνᾰδε**, *to Pallene*, v. supr. I.

**πάλληξ**, v. πάλλαξ.

**παλλία**, name of a contest, Hsch. (Prob. Lat. *Palilia*.)

**παλλικάριον**, τό (for παλληκ-, cf. παλλήκιον, πάλληξ), *page*, *POxy.* 1863.4.

**παλλιχίαρ**· πεμμάτιόν τι (Lacon.), Hsch.

**παλλυριν** (acc. sg., perh. for -ύριον), perh. name of a disease, *BMus. Cat. Coins Ionia* p.70 (Ephesus):—also written **παλυρριν**, *Num.Chron.*8 (1908).282 (ibid.).

**παλλύτας**· ὄργανον βασανιστήριον, Hsch.

❀ **πάλλω**, impf. ἔπαλλον E.*Hec.*1158; Ep. πάλλον always in Hom. (v. infr.): aor. 1 ἔπηλα S.*El.*710; Ep. πῆλα Il.6.474: Ep. aor. 2 part. πεπᾰλών Hom. only in compd. ἀμπεπαλών:—Med., aor. 1 πήλασθαι Call.*Jov.*64: πεπάλασθε, πεπαλάσθαι (v. παλάσσω) have been attributed to πάλλω; πεπάλεσθε, πεπαλέσθαι are conjectured as more prob. forms:—Pass., pf. πέπαλμαι A.*Ch.*410 (lyr.): aor. 2 ἐπάλην (ἀν-) Str.8.6.21: Ep. aor. πάλτο Il.15.645 (in 13.643, 21.140, ἔπᾱλτο is from ἐφάλλομαι):—*poise, sway* a missile before it is thrown, τὸ μὲν [ἔγχος] οὐ δύνατ' ἄλλος Ἀχαιῶν πάλλειν, ἀλλά μιν οἶος ἐπίστατο πῆλαι Ἀχιλλεύς Il.16.142; [αἰχμήν], ἣν.. πάλλεν δεξιτερῇ 22.320; δοῦρε δύω .. πάλλων 3.19; χερμάδιον.. ὃ οὐ δύο γ' ἄνδρε φέροιεν.., ὁ δέ μιν ῥέα πάλλε καὶ οἶος 5.304; ἄκοντα, λόγχην π., Pi.*N.*3.45, E.*IT*824; κεραυνόν Ar.*Av.*1714. 2. generally, *sway, brandish*, [σάκος] Hes.*Sc.*321; ἰτύν, πέλτας, E.*Ion* 210 (lyr.), *Ba.*783; *toss* a child, πῆλε χερσίν, of Hector and Astyanax, Il.6.474, cf. E.*Hec.*1158; Νὺξ ὄχημ' ἔπαλλεν she *drove it furiously*, Id.*Ion* 1151. 3. κλήρους ἐν κυνέῃ χαλκήρεϊ πάλλον *shook* the lots together in a helmet, Il.3.316, cf. Od.10.206; πάλλεν *shook the lots*, Il.3.324, 7.181; but στάντες δ' ὅθ' αὐτοὺς οἱ.. βραβῆς κλήροις ἔπηλαν καὶ κατέστησαν δίφρους *ranged* them *by casting* lots, S.*El.*710:—Med., *draw lots*, ἔλαχον πολιὴν ἅλα ναιέμεν... ἀλλομένων I obtained the white sea *when we cast lots*, Il.15.191; παλλόμενος κλήρῳ λάχον ἐνθάδ' ἔπεσθαι 24.400, cf. Hdt.3.128:—Pass., κλῆρος οὐκ ἐπάλλετο S.*Ant.*396. II. Pass., *swing, dash oneself*, ἐν ἄντυγι πάλτο *tripped* on the shield-rim, Il.15.645; *quiver, leap*, esp. in fear, ἐν δ' ἐμοὶ αὐτῇ στήθεσι πάλλεται ἦτορ 22.452; πέπαλται μοι φίλον κέαρ A. *Ch.*410; of the person, παλλομένη κραδίην Il.22.461; δείματι παλλόμεναι, -οι, *h.Cer.*293, Orac.ap.Hdt.7.140, etc.; γόνυ πάλλεται γερόντων Ar.*Ra.*345; of dying fish, *quiver, leap*, Hdt.1.141, cf. 9.120; καὶ πέραν πόντοιο πάλλοντ' αἰετοί *fly quivering* even beyond the sea, Pi.*N.*5.21; *vibrate*, of strings, Pl.*Phd.*94c (ψάλλοιτο ap.Stob.); σκιρτητικὸν καὶ παλλόμενον τὸ νέον (etym. of Παλλάς) Corn.*ND*20, cf. Pl.*Cra.* 407a. III. intr., *leap, bound*, E.*El.*435, Ar.*Lys.*1304 (lyr.);

quiver, quake, φρένα δείματι πάλλων S.OT153 (lyr.); dash along, of horses, E.El.477 (lyr.).

**παλλώβητος**, v. πανλ–.

**παλμᾰτίας**, ου, ὁ, (πάλλω) σεισμὸς π. an earthquake with violent shocks, Arist.Mu.396$^a$10.

**πάλμη**· γέρρον (i.e. Lat. parma), Hsch. II. date, POxy.519.18 (ii A.D.).

**παλμικός**, ή, όν, conveyed by palpitation, π. οἰώνισμα, title of a book, Suid. s.v. Ποσειδώνιος.

⊛ **παλμός**, ὁ, quivering motion, πυγῆς Alciphr.1.39; esp. pulsation, throbbing (on π. and σφυγμός cf. Gal.8.716), φλεβῶν Hp.Acut.37; ὑποχονδρίου Id.Epid.1.26.β'; ὑπὸ κροτάφοισι Nic.Al.27, cf. Th.744: abs., palpitation of the heart, a disease, Arist.Resp.479$^b$21; twitching, Gal.7.588. 2. of natural phenomena, vibration, rapid motion, D.S. 3.51, Nonn.D.2.193, al.; of meteors, Plu.Lys.12 codd.; impetus of a projectile, Ath.Mech.37.8. 3. in Epicur., internal vibration of bodies, Ep.1 p.8 U., cf. Id.ap.Placit.1.12.5 (v.l. ἀποπαλμός).

**παλμουλάριος**, ὁ, = Lat. parmularius, M.Ant.1.5.

**πάλμυς**, υδος, ὁ, Lydian word, = βασιλεύς, Hippon.1, 15; epith. of the king of the gods, Zeus, Lyc.691: gen. πάλμυδος (Dind. for παλάμυδος) A.Fr.437: acc. Πάλμυν pr. n. in Il.13.792.

⊛ **παλμώδης**, ες, throbbing, palpitating, of persons, Hp.Prorrh.1.30; ἰδέαι D.S.3.50; π. νόσος Ph.1.166; κινήσεις (opp. σφυγμώδεις) Gal.8.722.

⊛ **πάλος** [ᾰ], ὁ, (πάλλω 1.3) lot cast from a shaken helmet, A.Th. 458. 2. Lyr., Ion., and Trag. generally, = κλῆρος, lot, τόνδε τὸν πάλον λαχόην Sapph.9, cf. A.Th.376; πάλῳ λαχεῖν ib.126, Hdt.4.94, 153, Aen.Tact.20.2; πάλῳ ἀρχὰς ἄρχειν Hdt.3.80; πάλου κύρσαι A. Pers.779; τύχης π. Id.Ag.333; οὓς ἐκλήρωσεν π. E.Ion416, cf. S. Ant.275, dub. in E.IA1151. 3. ballot, vote, A.Eu.742, 753.

**πᾶλος**, ὁ, = Lat. pālus, stake, PLond.2.191.12 (ii A.D.), Aesop.402, Edict.Diocl.14.1, Zos.2.35. II. squad or team of gladiators, CIG 2663 (Halic.), Rev.Arch.30 (1929).40 (Aphrodisias), etc.

**παλός**, v. πηλός.

**πάλσᾰμον**, τό, dial. form of βάλσαμον, Paus.9.28.3.

**πάλσις**, εως, ἡ, rapid motion, vibration, ἀκτίνων Porph.ap.Eus.PE 3.11; in Epicur., = παλμός, internal vibration, Ep.1 p.12 U. 2. brandishing, δοράτων EM394.56; palpitation, τῆς καρδίας Chrysipp. Stoic.2.247.

**παλτάζω**, (παλτόν) throw a dart, in aor. 1 ἐπάλταξα, Hsch.

**παλτάρια**· σεμίδαλις, Phot., Suid.; cf. πολτάριον.

**παλτεύω**, dub. sens., perh. scutch flax, BGU1506.2.

**πάλτο**, v. πάλλω.

⊛ **παλτός**, ή, όν, brandished, hurled, πῦρ S.Ant.131 (lyr.). II. as Subst. **παλτόν**, τό, missile, dart, A.Fr.16; of a light spear used by the Persian cavalry, X.Cyr.4.3.9, 6.2.16, cf. Arr.Fr.158 J.; projectile discharged from a catapult, Id.Tact.43.1.

**πᾰλύνω**, strew, sprinkle, λεύκ' ἄλφιτα πολλὰ πάλυνον (i.e. sprinkled in water, expld. by Sch. ἔμασσον, ἔφυρον) Il.18.560; ἐπὶ δ' ἄλφιτα λευκὰ παλύνειν Od.10.520, cf. 11.28, etc.; τι ἐπί τινι S.Ant.247. II. bestrew, besprinkle, with dat. of the thing sprinkled, παλύνας ἀλφίτου ἀκτῇ Od.14.429:—Pass., ἁ σῦριγξ εὐρῶτι παλύνεται Theoc.4.28. 2. of liquids, κάρην ἱδρῶτι παλῦναι D.P.1049. 3. besmear, ἰξῷ AP10. 11 (Satyr.), cf. A.R.3.1256 (Pass.). III. cover lightly, χιὼν ἐπάλυνεν ἀρούρας Il.10.7; νιφετῷ δ' ἐπαλύνετο πάντα A.R.3.69.

**πᾶμα**, ατος, τό, (πάομαι) property, Schwyzer657.39 (Tegea, iv B.C.), Theoc.Syrinx 12 (v.l. πῆμα): mostly pl., πατρῷα καὶ ματρῷα π. Schwyzer l.c. 6, cf. 27, Besant.Ara 5, AJP26.463 (Argos); of cattle, SIG527.89 (Dreros, iii B.C.).

**πᾱμᾰτοφᾰγέω**, (πᾶμα, φαγεῖν) confiscate, IG9(1).334.41 (Locr., v B.C., Pass.).

**παμβακίς**, ίδος, ἡ, = βαμβάκιον, in pl., AP6.254.6 (Myrin.).

**παμβᾰσῐλ-εία**, ἡ, absolute monarchy, Arist.Pol.1285$^b$36, 1287$^a$ 8. -ειᾰ, ἡ, queen of all, all-powerful queen, Ar.Nu.357, 1150, A.R. 4.382; of Persephone, IG12(5).310.15 (Paros). ⊛ -εύς, έως, ὁ, absolute monarch, Alc.5, LxxSi.50.15(17); of Hadrian, Epigr.Gr. 990.3 (Balbilla).

**παμ-βδελῠρός**, ά, όν, utterly abominable, Ar.Lys.969, Ec.1043. -βίας [ῐ], ου, ὁ, all-subduing, κεραυνός Pi.N.9.24. -βλᾰβής, ές, wholly hurtful, Man.4.31. -βοιώτιος, ὁ (sc. μήν), name of a month in Boeotia, IG7.3321. II. Παμβοιώτια (sc. ἱερά), τά, festival of the United Boeotians, Plb.4.3.5, 9.34.11, IG7.3087 (Lebadea), Str.9. 2.29.

**Παμβοιωτοί**, οἱ, United Boeotians, IG7.2712.49 (Acraeph.).

**πάμ-βορος**, ον, all-devouring, J.AJ5.8.6, Ael.NA1.27 (Sup.). -βότᾰνον, τό, all the herbage, τοῦ ἀγροῦ LxxJb.5.25. -βοτος, ον, all-nourishing, ἄλσος A.Supp.558 (lyr.), cf. Fr.99. -βώτωρ, ορος, ὁ, ἡ, = foreg., Cypr.1.4:—fem. ⊛-βῶτις, ιδος, Γᾶ S.Ph.391 (lyr.). -μᾰκᾰρ, ᾰρος, ὁ, ἡ, all-blissful, Orph.H.19.3, Hsch. ⊛-μᾰκάριστος [ᾰ], ον, = foreg., JHS22.97 (Pisidia), Hsch. s.v. πανόλβιος. -μᾰταιος [μᾰ], ον, all-vain, A.Ag.388 codd. (leg. πᾶν μ.).

**παμμᾰχ-ί** [ῐ], Adv. in which all fight, A.D.Conj.234.9. -ία, ἡ, in pl., contests of all kinds, B.12.76. -ιον, τό, = παγκράτιον, Phot., Suid. -ος, ον, ready or sufficient for every battle, θράσος A.Ag.169 (lyr.); epith. of Athena, Ar.Lys.1321; esp. = παγκρατιαστής, fighting by all means, with all one's resources, Pl.Euthd.271c, Theoc.24. 114, APl.4.52 (Phil.), D.Chr.8.19; τοὺς πέντε προεκαλεσάμην πάμμαχα Sammelb.6222.22 (iii A.D.); so εἰς τὸ πάμμαχον ib.26; ὁ παμμάχων κεραυνός AP7.692 (Antip. or Phil.): metaph., οὐ φαῦλος ἀλλὰ π. ἀγὼν ὁ τῆς πολιτείας calling for all resources, Plu.2.804b; also π. ἀτυχίη incompetence ready for anything, Hp.Praec.13.

**πάμ-μεγᾰς**, άλη, α, very great, immense, Pl.Phdr.273a, Ti.26e, etc.: Sup. παμμέγιστος Ael.VH10.2. -μεγέθης, ες, = foreg., Pl. Prm.164d, Lg.913d, X.Mem.3.6.13, Timocl.8.14, D.19.241, Arist. GA745$^a$34, al., Men.Her.2: neut. as Adv., παμμέγεθες ἀναβοᾶν Aeschin.2.106, cf. Men.Sam.149. -μείλῐχος, ον, exceeding mild, Jo.Gaz.Ecphr.1.75. -μέλᾱς, αινα, ᾰν, all-black, ταῦροι Od.3.6; ὄϊς 11.33; τράγος IG2².1358 (iv B.C.); βόες Ael.NA15.14. -μελεί, Adv. of sq. II, Porph.Chr.94. -μελής, ές, in all kinds of melodies, ὕμνοι Lxx3Ma.7.16. II. with all the limbs, entire, ἱερεῖα Poll.1.29. -μεστος, ον, quite covered with, ὄρος π. τερμίνθων Thphr. HP3.15.3. -μετρος (sc. βίβλος), ἡ, a book of verse in all kinds of metres, D.L.7.31. -μήκης, ες, very long, prolonged, γόοι S.OC 1609; λόγος Pl.Plt.286e; ῥήσεις Id.Phdr.268c; ἐν χρόνοις π. Arist. Mete.351$^b$10: neut. as Adv., πάμμηκες διαφέρει ἔπαινος ἡδονῆς Max. Tyr.7.7. -μηνις νύξ, ἡ, a night lighted by the full moon, Arat. 189. -μηνος, ον, through all months, through the live-long year, S.El. 851 (lyr.). 2. π. σελήνη, = πανσέληνος, ἡ, Plu.2.936a, Doroth.ap. Heph.Astr.3.9; at full moon, ἱκετεῖαι cj. in Philod.Scarph.114 (BCH 49.130). -μήστωρ, ορος, ὁ, ἡ, all-inventive, μοῖρα βροτῶν Lyc.490; Ἄρης Trag.Adesp.129.9 (lyr.); Μοῖρα Orph.Fr.47. -μήτειρα, ἡ, = παμμήτωρ, h.Hom.30.1, AP5.164 (Mel.), v.l. in Orph.Fr.168. 27. -μῆτις, ιδος, ὁ, ἡ, all-knowing, all-planning, θεός Simon. 61. -μήτωρ, ορος, ἡ, mother of all, γῆ A.Pr.90, Ph.1.32, cf. Orph. Fr.168.27; θεᾷ παμμήτορι Ῥείῃ Epigr.Gr.823.4. II. a very mother, γυνὴ τοῦδε π. νεκροῦ S.Ant.1282. -μῐᾰρος [ῐ], ον, all-abominable, Ar.Pax183, Ra.466, Lxx4Ma.10.17 (Sup.). -μῐγής, ές, mixed of all sorts, all-blended, βέλεα A.Pers.269 (lyr.); στρατός Tim.Pers.188; ἔθνη Lxx2Ma.12.13; σύμμαχοι D.S.29.19; βοή Lyc.5. -μῑκρος, ον, very small, Arist.PA665$^b$1, 669$^b$29, Po.1450$^b$37, Gal.18(2). 753. -μικτος, ον, = παμμιγής, ὄχλος A.Pers.53 (anap.); ἐπίκουροι ib.903 (lyr.), cf. Aq.Ps.77(78).45, Vett.Val.15.15. -μορος, ον, all-hapless, S.OC161 (lyr.). -μορφος, ον, assuming all forms, of Proteus, Theol.Ar.7; ἰδέαι Dam.Pr.311. ⊛-μουσος, ον, all-musical, ἁρμονία, χορεία, Ph.1.625, 526; ἀνήρ Calder Philadelphia and Montanism 35. -μύριος [ῡ], ον, all-countless, Ph.1.329. -μῠσᾰρός, ά, όν, = παμμίαρος, Ar.Lys.969.

**πάμνηστος**, ον, all-remembering, πραπίδες Maiist.46.

**παμ-πᾰθής**, ές, wholly passive, Plot.1.8.3; ὕλη Iamb.Myst.3. 29. II. sens. obsc., = παθικός, Man.4.311. III. name of a plaster, Aët.15.15. -παιδί, Adv. with all their children, D.C.41.9; cf. παγγυναικί. -πάλαιος [ᾰλ], ον, very old, Pl.Tht.181b, Arist.Metaph.1074$^b$1, cj. in ib.983$^b$28; opp. καινός, Plu.Cat.Ma.1. -πᾰλιν, Adv. altogether to the contrary, Crates Com.15. -πάμων [ᾱ], ον, gen. ονος, possessing all, Hsch. (cj. for Πάμπανον). -πᾰν, Adv., (πᾶς) wholly, altogether, with Verb, Il.1.422, Od.2.49, Hes.Op.275, 302, Sapph.51.4, Pi.O.2.69, Emp.140: with Adj., π. ὀϊζυρός Od.20.140, cf. E.Med.1091 (anap.); οὐ π. ἀληθέες Call.Jov.60: with Adv., π. ἐτήτυμον Il.13.111: preceded by a neg., οὐδέ τι πάμπαν not at all, by no means, 9.435, cf. 21.338: with the Art., τὸ π. E.Rh.855, Fr.196: rare in early Prose, Hdt.2.45, X. Ages.11.4, Aen.Tact.16.2; τὸ π. Pl.Plt.270e, Ti.41b: freq. in Arist., as Cael.286$^a$6, al. II. as Adj., πάμπαν τὸ λοιπόν IG1².6.117. -πᾰνύ, Adv. strengthd. for πάνυ, dub. in D.C.56.30. -πειθής, ές, all-persuasive, Pi.P.4.184. ⊛-πήδην, Adv., = πάμπαν, entirely, Thgn.615, A.Pers.729 (troch.), Fr.156, S.Aj.916:—also -πηδόν, -ονίς, Theognost.Can.163. ⊛-πησία, ἡ, (πέπαμαι) entire possession, full property, A.Th.817, E.Ion1305, Ar.Ec.868. -πλειστος, η, ον, in large quantity, number, χρήματα Hdn.5.6.5; ἄργυρος Ael.NA10.50; πάμπλειστα δαπανήσας D.C.76.16. -πλείων, ονος, ὁ, ἡ, much greater, ὄγκος τῆς φωνῆς Arist.Aud.804$^a$15. -πλήγδην, Adv. strengthd. for ἐμπλήγδην, Suid. -πληθεί, Adv. with the whole multitude, Ev. Luc.23.18, D.C.75.9. -πληθής, ές, in or with their whole multitude, παμπληθεῖς Ἀρκάδες X.HG6.5.26. II. = πάμπολυς, very numerous, multitudinous, μεταβολαί Pl.Lg.782b, cf. Tht.156b; γεωργίαι D.19. 145; πονηρίαι Id.21.19; χρήματα prob. in D.S.14.13; κραυγαί POxy. 1242.54 (i A.D.): c. gen., παμπληθεῖς Ἀργείων Isoc.12.169: with sg., π. ἂν τὸ γένος ἦν (sc. τῶν ἰχθύων) Arist.HA567$^b$2; π. κεκτήμεθα τὴν οὐσίαν a vast amount of.., Isoc.15.154; πῦρ π. Arist.Mir.833$^a$ 20. III. neut. as Adv., entirely, παμπληθὲς ἀπέσχεν D.19.19, cf. D.C. 55.20. -πληθία, ἡ, multitude, οἰκετῶν S.Fr.373.4. -πληθύς, = παμπληθής II, παμπληθὺν θρήνων γόον Epigr. in Abh.Berl.Akad.1909 (2).62. -πληθύω, to be plentiful, Aq.Jb.36.31. -πληκτος, ον: ἄεθλα π. contests in which blows fall thick, S.Tr.505 (lyr.). -πλήρης, ες, quite full, Arist.GC325$^a$29 (v.l. -πληθές). -πλούσιος, ον, very rich, Pl.Lg.743c, D.C.40.12. -πλουτος, ον, = foreg., ὄλβος S. Fr.646.5; π. ἐν πλούτῳ γενέσθαι Gal.Anim.Pass.9. -ποίκῐλος, ον, all-variegated, of rich and varied work, πέπλοι Od.15.105, cf. Il.6.289; of sacred vases, Pi.N.10.36; νεβρῶν π. στολίδες E.Hel.1359 (lyr.); of persons, π. περὶ πᾶσαν τέχνην καὶ πρᾶξιν Vett.Val.17.16. II. metaph., ὕφασμα, of the universe, Ph.1.651, cf. 654; manifold, ἀλλοιότητας παμποικίλους (παμποικίλας codd.) Pl.Ti.82b. -πολις, εως, ὁ, ἡ, prevailing in all cities, universal, νόμος dub. in S.Ant.614 (lyr., πάμπολύ γ' Heath). ⊛-πολυς, πόλλη (v. infr.), πολυ, very great, large, or numerous, κατάγελως Ar.Eq.320; γῆς πλῆθος Pl.Lg.677e; στράτευμα X.An.2.4.28; τύχη Pl.Lg.640d (but πάμπολλος as fem., Luc.Cyn.1, Ael.VH4.8, A.D.Pron.89.12, Synt.36.27): in pl., very many, Ar.Pax 694, Pl.R.373c, etc. II. neut. πάμπολυ, as Adv., very much, Id. Sph.255d, etc.; cf. foreg. -πόνηρος, ον, thoroughly depraved, Ar.

*Ach.*854, *Nu.*1319, Pl.*R.*489d, D.18.119, Phld.*Rh.*1.344S. 2. of things, *very bad*, ὄψον Epich.87; διάθεσις Phld.*Ir.*p.77 W. 3. Adv. -ρως, ἔχειν to be *very ill*, Luc.*Abd.*14, cf. Jul.*Or.*8.241b. **-πορθής**, ές, *all-destroying*, prob. for παμπρόσθη in A.*Ag.*714(lyr.). **-πόρφῠρος**, ον, *all-purple*, Pi.*O.*6.55. **-πότνια**, ἡ, *all-venerable*, *AP*6.281 (Leon.). ❀ **-πρᾶσία**, ἡ, *unreserved sale of property*, Poll.7.196, al. **-πρεπτος**, ον, *all-conspicuous*, ἕδραι A.*Ag.*117 (lyr.). **-πρόσθη**, v. παμπορθής. **-πρόσωπος**, ον, *all face*, χρῆμα Plot.6.7.15. **-πρύτᾰνις** [ῠ], εως, ὁ, *lord of all*, Ph.1.642. **-πρωτος**, η, ον, *the very first*, *first of all*, Il.7.324, 9.93: neut. πάμπρωτον as Adv., Od.4.577; ἐπεὶ π. εἶδον φέγγος Pi.*P.*4.111: also in pl. -πρωτα, Il.4.97, 17.568: Sup. παμπρώτιστα A.R.4.1693. **-πῦος**, ον, *full of pus*, πτύσιες Hp.*Coac.*373. **-πωρος**, ον, *very miserable*, *Arch.Pap.*1.428 (iv A.D.). **-φάγος** [ᾰ], ον, *all-devouring*, *voracious*, ὁ π. Ἀλκμάν Alcm. 33.4; πῦρ E.*Med.*1187. II. *omnivorous*, ζῷα (opp. ζῳοφάγα, καρποφάγα) Arist.*Pol.*1256ᵃ25, cf. *HA*488ᵃ15, 593ᵇ25; τῶν π., οἷς πάντα ἐσθίειν νόμος Jul.*Or.*6.192d: Comp., τὰ -ώτερα ποικιλώτερα Arist.*GA*786ᵃ34: Sup., -ώτατον πάντων ὁ βοῦς Thphr.*HP*9.15. 4. **-φᾰής**, ές, *all-shining*, *radiant*, of fire, S.*Ph.*728 (lyr.), E.*Tr.* 548 (lyr.); of the sun, Id.*Med.*1251 (lyr.), cf. Ar.*Av.*1709, *IG*12(5). 891.3 (Tenos), etc.; of honey, *bright*, *pure*, A.*Pers.*612. **-φαίνω**, only pres. and impf. (παμφαίνεσκε Eratosth.17), *shine* or *beam brightly*, of burnished metal (cf. παμφανόων), ἧλοι χρύσειοι πάμφαινον Il.11.30; σάκος χαλκῷ παμφαῖνον 14.11; τεύχεσι παμφαίνων, of Achilles, 19.398; of a star, ὅς τε μάλιστα λαμπρὸν παμφαίνῃσι or -ησι (Ep. for παμφαίνει or -ῃ) 5.6; πρῶτον παμφαίνων Hes.*Op.*567; στήθεσι παμφαίνοντες with their breasts *white-gleaming*, i.e. naked, Il. 11.100; ὕπερθε κέρα πάμφαινεν ἰδέσθαι Epic.in *Arch.Pap.*7.3: cited as a recondite word by Phld.*Po.*2.40. (Redupl. form of φαίνω.)

**παμφᾰλάω**, redupl. form like παιφάσσω (cf. παπταλάω, παπταίνω), *gaze in astonishment*, Ion. word, Hippon.131, Anacr.160, Herod.4. 77; πάντοσε παμφαλόωντες Eryc.ap.Sch.A.R.2.127: aor. 1 ἐπαμφάλησα· ἐθαύμασα, Hsch.:—Med., ἄγχι παμφαλώμενος Lyc.1433.

**παμφάλυα**· τὴν πομφόλυγα, Sophr.152.

**παμφαλύζω**, = τρέμω, Hsch.

**παμφᾰνής**, Egypt., = ἀείζων τὸ μέγα, Ps.-Dsc.4.88.

**παμ-φᾰνόων**, gen. ωντος, fem. παμφᾰνόωσα, Ep. part. as if from παμφᾰνάω (cf. παμφανάᾳ· λάμπει, Hsch.), *bright-shining*, *radiant*, of burnished metal, αἴγλη [χαλκοῦ] Il.2.458; τεύχεα 5.295, 18.144; ἠέλιος Od.13.29; αἰθήρ Emp.98.2. **-φάρμᾰκος**, ον, *skilled in all charms* or *drugs*, of Medea, Pi.*P.*4.233. **-φεγγής**, ές, = παμφαής, S.*El.*105 (lyr.). **-φερής**, ές, *all-bearing*, *all-including*, Gal.19. 469. **-φημος**, ον, *all-speaking*, Zonar. **-φθαρτος**, ον, *all-destroying*, μόρος A.*Ch.*296. **-φθερσις**, εως, ἡ, *destroyer of all*, στάσις B.*Fr.*20.2. **-φθογγος**, ον, *with* or *of all sounds*, Hsch.

**πάμφῐ**, Adv., = παντάπασι, Hsch.

❀ **πάμ-φῐλος**, ον, *beloved of all*, ὄλβος prob. in A.*Eu.*536 (lyr.): Sup. -έστατος *PGrenf.*2.92.11 (vi A.D.). **-φλεκτος**, ον, *all-blazing*, βωμοί S.*Ant.*1006; π. πῦρ Id.*El.*1139, Axionic.4.11. **-φόβερος**, α, ον, *very dreadful*, *Tab.Defix.Aud.*38.11 (Alexandria, iii A.D.), *Gloss.* **-φορβος**, η, ον, *all-feeding*, παλάμη *AP*7.698 (Christod.), cf. *Epigr.Gr.*1036 (Nicomedia, dub.), Eust.978.4. **-φορος**, ον, *all-bearing*, *all-productive*, χώρη παμφορωτέρη Hdt.7.8.α', cf. Hp.*Coac.*502, Pl.*Lg.*704c, Thphr.*HP*3.2.6; γαῖα A.*Pers.*618; ἔτος Orph.*Fr.*251; παμφορώτατον κτῆμα ὁ καλεῖται φίλος X.*Mem.*2.4.7. II. *bearing all things with it*, π. χέραδος a *mixed* mass of rubbish, Pi.*P.*6.13: metaph., π. θεωρήματα Pall.*in Hp.*2.114D. **-φρόνιμος**, ον, *wise in all things*, Tz.*H.*6.595 (Sup.). **-φύγδην**, Adv. *in total rout*, Opp.*H.*2.548 (v.l. παμφύρδην). **-φυής**, ές, *combining all natures*, δέμας, of Pan, *IG*4²(1).130.19 (Epid.).

**Παμφῡλία**, ἡ, *Pamphylia*, Th.1.100, Pl.*R.*615c, etc.: **Παμφῡλιάρχης**, ου, ὁ, *President of the Provincial Council of P.*, *BCH*23.302 (Termessus), *IGRom.*3.474 (Balbura).

❀ **πάμ-φῡλος**, ον, (φυλή, φῦλον) *of mingled tribes* or *races*, γένος Pl. *Plt.*291a; πόλις Poll.9.21; π. θῆρες Ar.*Av.*1063. II. Πάμφυλοι, οἱ, one of the three Dorian tribes, Hdt.5.68, *IG*4²(1).71.49 (Epid.), *SIG*1025.8 (Cos), etc.: gen. pl. Παμφυλᾶν *IG*4.598 (Argos); Παμφύλεων *SIG*1027.4 (Cos). III. *Pamphylian*, Hdt.1.28, al., Pl.*R.* 614b, etc. **-φυρτος**, ον, *mixed of all sorts*, γέννημα Ph.1.148, cf. 2.53, Longin.9.7, Opp.*H.*1.779: neut. pl. as Adv., *confusedly*, S. *Ichn.*232. **-φωνος**, ον, *with all tones*, *full-toned* or *many-toned*, ἔντεα αὐλῶν Pi.*O.*7.12; μέλος Id.*P.*12.19; αὐλῶν ὁμοκλαί Id.*I.*5(4). 27; ὑμέναιοι Id.*P.*3.17: generally, *expressive*, χεῖρες *APl.*4.290 (Antip.); π. οἶνος *noisy*, Philox.16. **-ψεκτος**, ον, *much-blamed*, Man.4.316. **-ψέκτωρ**, ορος, ὁ, *one that blames all*, ib.58. **-ψηφεί**, Adv. *with all the votes*, π. νικᾶν *AP*11.239 (Lucill.), cf. Sch.Ar.*Eq.* 525, etc.; Dor. -ψᾱφεί Polus ap.Stob.3.9.51. ❀ **-ψογος**, ον, = παμψέκτωρ, Ptol.*Tetr.*160. **-ψῡχος**, ον, (ψυχή) *in full life*, π. ἀνάσσει, of Amphiaraus, S.*El.*841 (lyr., also expld. by Sch. as 'ruling over all the shades' or 'immortal', = πασῶν ψυχῶν ἀνάσσει, cf. Od.11.483 sq., A.*Ch.*355).

**πᾰμ-ωχέω**, *own*, *possess*, *Tab.Heracl.*1.168:—also **-ωχιῶν**· κεκτημένος, Hsch; and **-ῶχος**, ὁ, Dor. for *παμοῦχος, *owner*, Id.

**πάν**, πανός, ὁ, a kind of *fish*, Ptol.Chenn.ap.Phot.*Bibl.*p.153 B., Suid. s.h.v. (Cf. Egypt. *p-ān* 'Nile perch, *Tilapia nilotica*'.)

**Πάν**, gen. Πᾶνός, dat. Πᾶνί (uncontr. Πάονι *IG*5(2).556 (Melpea, vi B.C.)), ὁ, *Pan*, Πᾶνα δέ μιν καλέεσκον, ὅτι φρένα πᾶσιν ἔτερψεν *h.Hom.* 19.47, cf. 5, Hdt.2.145, 6.105, etc.; ὦ Πὰν Ἀρκαδίας μεδέων Pi.*Fr.*95, cf. Theoc.1.123, etc.; Π. κεροβάτας Ar.*Ra.*230 (lyr.): pl. Πᾶνες Id.*Ec.* 1069, Theoc.4.63, D.S.1.88; dat. pl. Πᾶσιν Id.5.28; Πανὸς γόνος, σπέρμα, in magic, *PMag.Par.*1.2306, 2996; Πανὸς κέρατα, = γλυκυσίδη, Ps.-Dsc.3.140.

**πᾰν-αβρος** [πᾰ], ον, *quite* or *very soft*, Luc.*Rh.Pr.*11. **-ᾰγᾰθία**, ἡ, *perfect goodness*, Theag.ap.Stob.3.1.117. **-άγᾰθος** [ᾰγ], ον, also η, ον, *absolutely good*, Cratin.434, Pl.*Ep.*354e, Simp.*in Epict.*p.76 D. ❀ **-ᾰγής**, ές, *all-hallowed*, Call.*Fr.*1.36 P.; κόρη (Cassandra) D.Chr.11.153; ἱέρειαι Poll.1.35, Hsch. (πανaιεῖς cod.); ἱερωσύνη Jul. *Or.*5.160b (Sup.); ἱερεύς *IG*3.716; = Lat. *sacrosanctus*, of the Rom. *Tribuni Plebis*, D.H.6.89, 8.87, Plu.*Cam.*20. II. *under an* ἄγος, Philonid.5, Man.4.120. **-άγητος** [ᾰγ], ον, *most reverend*, Id.2. 433. **-ᾰγία**, v. παναγιστία. **-άγιος** [ᾰγ], α, ον, *all-holy*, Lxx 4 *Ma.*7. 4. **-ᾰγιστία**, ἡ, = παναγία, dub. sens., Hsch. **-αγνος**, = παναγής I, ὄμμα Callistr.*Stat.*10; κήρυκες Sch.Aeschin.1.20. **-ᾰγορία**, ἡ, = πανήγυρις, *Schwyzer*657.21 (Tegea, iv B.C., pl.). **-ᾰγόρσιος**, ὁ, = πανηγύριος, name of month at Tegea, *IG*5(2).3.30 (iv B.C.). **-άγορσις**, εως, ἡ, = παναγορία, ib.26. **-άγρετος**, ον, *taking all kinds of game*, νευρά *AP*6.75 (Paul. Sil.). **-αγρεύς**, έως, ὁ, *one who catches everything*, παναγρέος ἐλπίδα Μοίρης ib.7.609 (Id.); φυλάκων.. παναγρέα κανθόν ib.5.218 (Id.). **-άγριος**, ον, *quite wild* or *savage*, Opp.*C.*2.45, dub. in Ps.-Phoc.202. **-αγρίς**, ίδος, ἡ, = λεβητάριον, *IG*4.1588.18 (Aegina), Poll.10.165 (v.l. ταν-). **-αγρον**, τό, *fishing-* or *hunting-net*, Opp.*C.*1.150, *H.*3.83. II. *large hen-coop* in which fowls are fattened, Ath.1.22d. **-αγρος**, ον, (ἄγρα) *catching all*, λίνον π., of a large *fishing*-net, Il.5.487; δίκτυον Ath.1.25b: metaph., λίνῳ θανάτοιο π. Tryph.674. **-άγρυπνος**, ον, *all-wakeful*, μέριμνα *AP*7.195 (Mel.). ❀ **-αγυριάρχας**, **-αγύριος**, **-άγυρις**, v. πανηγ-. **-άεθλος**, *passing through all trials*, epith. of martyrs, *PMasp.*162.8 (vi A.D.). **-αεικής**, ές, *cruel*, μοῖραι *Epigr.Gr.*403.1; μόχθος Antioch. Astr. in *Cat.Cod.Astr.*1.112. **-αεργής**, ές, *all-undigested*, δόρπος Nic.*Al.*66. **-άζωστος**, ον, *unarmed*, ὤμοσαν ἀγελάοι π. *SIG*527.11 (Crete, iii B.C.). **-αθέσμιος**, ον, *utterly lawless*, cj. for sq. in Man. 4.56. **-άθεσμος**, ον, = foreg., Opp.*C.*2.438, 3.224. **-άθεστος**, ον, (θέσσασθαι) *quite inexorable*, Hsch. (παναίθετος cod.).

**Πᾰνᾰθήναια** (sc. ἱερά), τά, *Panathenaea*, festival at Athens, Hdt. 5.56; τὰ μεγάλα Π. Th.5.47, Lys.21.1, Isoc.12.17, *IG*1².10.2, 304.6; τὰ μικρὰ Π. Lys.21.2 (also τὰ κατ' ἐνιαυτόν *IG*2².334.32), cf. Ar.*Nu.* 988, And.1.28, etc.; also at Ilium, festival of Athena Ilias, *SIG*355. 18 (iv/iii B.C.).

❀ **Πᾰνᾰθηναϊκός**, ή, όν, *of*, *for*, or *at the Panathenaea*, ἡ Π. πομπή Th. 1.20, etc.; ὁ Π. (sc. λόγος), name of a speech of Isocrates: τὰ π. name of *vases given as prizes at the P.*, Posidon.25 J.

**Πᾰνᾰθήναιος**, ὁ (sc. μήν), month at Ilium, *Supp.Epigr.*4.663.

**Πᾰνᾰθηναΐς**, ΐδος, ἡ, four-year *period between celebrations of the Great Panathenaea*, *IG*3.1202. II. as Adj., Παναθηναῒς σκάφη ship *borne in procession at the Panathenaea*, *SIG*894 (iii A.D.).

**Πᾰνᾰθηναϊσταί**, οἱ, *celebrators of* Παναθήναια, at Teos, *CIG*3073; at Rhodes, *IG*12(1).107, al.

❀ **πᾰν-άθλιος**, α, ον, *all-wretched*, A.*Ch.*695, S.*OC*1110, E.*Hec.*658, Timocl.25: in late Prose, Ph.1.542. **-αιγλήεις**, εσσα, εν, *all-shining*, κῆπος *AP*9.806. **-αίδοιος**, η, ον, *all-revered*, *Epigr.Gr.* 228b (Ephesus). **-αιθος**, η, ον, *all-blazing*, κόρυθες Il.14. 372. **-αίολος**, ον, *shot with many colours*, *glancing*, ζωστήρ 4.186, 215, 10.77; θώρηξ 11.374; σάκος 13.552, Hes.*Sc.*139; *star-spangled*, π. οὐρανός Orph.*H.*4.7, *Fr.*238. II. metaph., *manifold*, βάγματα A.*Pers.*636 (lyr.). **-αισθησία**, ἡ, *full vigour of the senses*, D.L. 10.65 (Meibom for ἀναισθ-). **-αίσῠλος**, ον, *all-impious*, Hsch. (-αιγ- cod.). **-αίσχης**, ες, *utterly ugly*, τὴν ἰδέαν Arist.*EN*1099ᵇ 4, cf. Poll.6.163. **-αισχραμορφία**, ἡ, *absolute ugliness*, Tz.*H.*3. 216. **-αισχρος**, ον, = παναίσχης, D.Chr.31.35, Ptol.*Tetr.*172: Sup., παναισχίστη τέρψις *AP*6.163 (Mel.). Adv. -ρως Plb.4.58.11, Tz.*H.* 6.44. **-αίτιος**, ον, (αἰτία) *cause of all*, Ζεύς A.*Ag.*1486; ἐν π. Dam. *Pr.*37. 2. *to whom all the guilt belongs*, opp. μεταίτιος, A.*Eu.*200.

**Πᾰναιτωλικά**, τά, *meeting and festival of the Aetolian League*, *SIG* 563 (Teos, iii B.C.), *IG*9(1).411:—also **Πᾰναιτώλια**, τά, Poll.6.163:—also in sg., Liv.31.29.

**πᾰν-ακαρπής**, ές, *all-barren*, Nic.*Th.*612. ❀ **-άκεια** [ᾰκ], ἡ, *universal remedy*, *panacea*, Longin.38.5, Ph.1.215, Gal.13.766. 2. name of *a healing herb* or *its juice* (cf. πανακής II), Call.*Ap.*40, etc.; πανακείας ῥίζα Gal.14.156; *Hercules' woundwort*, *Opopanax hispidus*, Thphr.*HP*9.15.7. b. = λιγυστικόν, *Laserpitium garganicum*, Ps.-Dsc.3.51. c. = ἄρκιον, Id.4.106. 3. Pythag. name for *six*, *Theol. Ar.*38. II. personified as daughter of Asclepius, Hp.*Jusj.*, Ar.*Pl.* 702, 730. **-άκειον** [ᾰκ], τό, = foreg. I.2, Nic.*Th.*508. **-ακες**, τό, v. πανακής II. ❀ **-άκη** [ᾰκ], ἡ, = πανάκεια I.2, *APl.*4.273 (Crin.). **-ᾰκηδής**, ές, *free from all care*, σαύρη, of the salamander, prob. in Nic.*Al.* 538. ❀ **-ᾰκήρᾰτος**, ον, *all-uncontaminated*, θεός *Corp.Herm.*18.12; Ἀπόλλων *PMag.Berol.*2.87. **-ᾰκής**, ές, (ἄκος) *all-healing*, π. πάντων φάρμακον ἁ σοφία Call.*Epigr.*47.4, cf. Ph.1.455 (Sup.); ποτάμιον π. πρὸς τὰς τῶν θρεμμάτων νόσους Str.6.3.9; λύπης πανακές Epicur.*Fr.* 154. II. πάνακες, ους, τό, *all-heal*, *Ferulago galbanifera*, Hp.*Mul.* 2.201, Thphr.*HP*9.7.2, etc.; π. Ἀσκληπίειον *Aesculapius' all-heal*, *Echinophora tenuifolia*, ib.9.8.7, 9.11.1; π. Ἡράκλειον, = πανάκεια I.2a, ib.9.11.3, Dsc.3.48; π. Κενταύρειον *centaury*, *Centaurea salonitana*, Plin.*HN*25.33, Sch.Nic.*Th.*564; π. λεπτόφυλλον *feverfew*, *Erythraea Centaurium*, Thphr.*HP*9.11.4; π. Χειρώνειον *elecampane*, *Inula Helenium*, ib.9.11.1; also, = *Chiron's all-heal*, *Hypericum olympicum*, Nic. *Th.*565 (cf. 500), Dsc.3.50, Gal.12.95. **-ακίτης** [ῑ] (sc. οἶνος), ὁ, wine *prepared with* πάνακες, Dsc.5.62. **-άκτειος**, ον, in Nic.*Th.*626, π. κονίλη, expld. by Sch. either as ἡ ἐπὶ πάσῃ ἀκτῇ φυομένη or as a poet. form of πανάκειος; cf. **πάνακτος**· ὀρίγανος, Hsch. **-άλάστωρ**, ορος, ὁ, strengthd. for ἀλάστωρ, *AP*9.269 (Antip. Thess.). **-ἄληθής**, ές, *all true*, π. κακόμαντις Ἐρινύς A.*Th.*722 (lyr.). Adv. -θῶς Id.*Supp.*86 (lyr.). 2. of things, *absolutely true* or *real*, ἡδονή Pl.*R.*583b, cf. Iamb.*Protr.*4 (Sup.). **-ἄλήμων**, ον, gen. ονος, *roving all about*, ψυχή Procl.*H.*3.15. **-αλθής**, ές, *all-healing*, Nic.*Th.*939. **-αλκής**, ές, *all-powerful*, v. l. for παναρκής, A.*Th.*166 (lyr.): Sup., of a poultice, Aët.3.177 (sed cf. παναρκής). **-ἄλουργής**, ές, *all-purple-dyed*, Xenoph.3.3. **-άλωτος** [ἄλ], ον, *all-catching*, ἄτη A.*Ag.*361 (anap.).

**Πᾰνάμᾰρος** [νᾱ], title of Zeus in Caria, *BCH*12.254, al., *Supp. Epigr.*4.263.3, al. (Panamara):—also **Πανήμερος**, ib.288, al.; **Πανημέριος**, ib.304, al. (ibid.): hence **Παναμάρεια**, τά, his festival, *BCH* 11.376, *Supp.Epigr.*4.301.12 (ibid.).

**πᾰν-ἄμείδητος**, ον, *all-unsmiling*, πρόσωπα Opp.*C.*3.141. **-ἄμείλικτος**, ον, *all-implacable*, δράκαινα ib.223. **-ἄμείλῐχος**, ον, *all-unmerciful*, ἦτορ ib.2.203. **-άμερος**, ον, Dor. for πανήμερος. **-άμμορος**, ον, *without any share in*, ἠελίοιο *AP*14.125 (Metrod.).

**Πάνᾱμος** [πᾰ], ὁ, name of a month, at Argos, *Mnemos.*44.51; at Epidaurus, *IG*4²(1).117.9, al.; at Megara, ib.7.188; at Thespiae, ib. 1720:—also written **Πάνεμος** (Boeot.), Plu.*Cam.*19; **Πάνημος**, D. 18.157 (Corinth.), Call.*Epigr.*46, *IG*11(2).203 *A*31 (Delos, iii B.C.), *PCair.Zen.*20.5 (iii B.C.):—hence **Πανάμια**, τά, festival at Thespiae, *Schwyzer*491.11.

**πᾰνάμωμος**, ον, *all-blameless*, Simon.5.17.

**πᾰνάνῠτον**· παντοδύναμον, Phot.; πάντα δυνατόν, Suid.

**πάναξ** [ᾰν], ακος, ὁ, = πάνακες or πανάκεια, Dsc.2.163, 3.51, Ps.-Dsc. 3.48, Philagr.ap.Orib.5.19.12, etc.

**πᾰν-άξιος**, ον, *all-worthy*, Opp.*C.*3.408. **-ἀοίδιμος**, ον, *sung by all*, *APl.*4.71, Dioscorus in *PLit.Lond.*100*C*6. **-ἄπᾰλος** [ᾰπ], ον, *all-tender* or *delicate*, ἀνδρὶ δέμας εἰκυῖα νέῳ.., παναπάλῳ Od.13.223 [πᾱν-, metri gr.]; γυναῖκες Ph.2.432. **-άπαστος**, ον, *without tasting*, ἐδωδῆς Nic.*Al.*592. **-απειθής**, ές, f. l. for -απευθής, Parm. 4.6. **-ἀπείρῐτος**, ον, *all-unbounded*, Opp.*C.*2.517. **-απείρων**, ον, gen. ονος, = foreg., ὦ π. Κρονίων Pi.*Pae.*8.24. **-απενθής**, ές, f. l. for ταλαπενθής, *APl.*4.265. **-απευθής**, ές, *utterly inscrutable*, ἀταρπός Parm.4.6. **-ἀπήμων**, ον, gen. ονος, *all-harmless*, Hes.*Op.* 811; of Apollo, *AP*9.525.17. **-απηρής**, ές, *all-unmutilated*, κεφαλαί Call.*Cer.*126. **-άπιστος**, ον, *all-untrustworthy*, Phld.*Rh.*1.232 S. (Sup.). **-απόπληκτος**, ον, *all-astounded*, Socr.*Ep.*36. **-άπορος**, ον, = πανήπορος (on which Hsch. gives it as a gloss), Ascl. *in Metaph.* 421.29. **-απόστροφος**, ον, *entirely opposite*, οἶμος (of heavenly bodies) Man.6.295. **-άποτμος**, ον, *all hapless*, ὤ μοι ἐγὼ πανάποτμος Il.24.255, cf. 493. **-άπυστος**, ον, *all-unheard of*, Phot., Suid., restd. in Philic. in *Stud.Ital.*9.48. **-άργῠρος**, ον, *all-silver*, κρητήρ Od.9.203, 24.275, Antim.15, cf. S.*Fr.*378.3. **-ἄρείων**, ονος, *all-heroic*, in pl., Dioscorus in *PLit.Lond.*99.9. **-άρετος** [ᾰρ], ον, *model of all virtue*, Phld.*Rh.*2.203 S., Ph.1.451, Luc.*Philops.*6, S.E.*M.*9.152, *IG*14.2098, *CIG*4413 (Iotape); also ἡ π. σου φιλία *PSI* 1.98.3 (vi A.D.). Adv. -τως *CIG*4150 (Amastris). II. πανάρετος, ἡ, *a Book of Fortunes*, Paul.Al.*K.*2. **-ἀρίζηλος**, ἡ, *wholly enviable*, Ἀριάδνη Dioscorus in *PLit.Lond.*99.4.

**πᾰνάριον**, τό, = Lat. *panarium* (Gr. ἀρτοφόριον), S.E.*M.*1.234.

**πᾰν-άριστος** [ᾰρ], ον (fem. -αρίστη *IG*12(7).296 (Amorgos)), *best of all*, Hes. *Op.* 293, Phld. *Rh.* 2.198 S., *AP*11.394, Luc.*Fug.* 30. **-άρκεια**, ἡ, *self-sufficiency*, etym. of πανάκεια 1.3, *Theol. Ar.*38. **-αρκέτας** νόσου, *utter, complete*, dub. in A.*Ch.*70 (lyr.). **-αρκής**, ές, = πανταρκής, θεοί Id.*Th.*166 (lyr.); Ἥλιος the sun *that shines on all alike*, Call.*Fr.*48.1, cf. Suid. s. v.: Sup., of a poultice, Lycus ap.Orib.9.26.1; cf. παναλκής. **-αρμόνιος**, ον, *embracing all modes* or *scales*, in neut. of a style of Music, οὐκ ἄρα πολυχορδίας γε οὐδὲ παναρμονίου ἡμῖν δεήσει ἐν ταῖς ᾠδαῖς τε καὶ μέλεσι Pl.*R.*399c, cf. 404d; [ὄργανα] π. ib.399d; αὐτὰ τὰ π. ibid.; τὸ π. τὸ καινόν Alex.298; π. ὄργανον D.C.74.3. II. metaph., *complex, elaborate*, ποικίλῃ μὲν ποικίλους ψυχῇ καὶ π. διδοὺς λόγους, opp. ἁπλοῦς, Pl.*Phdr.*277c, cf. Iamb.*Myst.*5.21; π. τι χρῆμα ἡ ὄρχησις Luc.*Salt.*72; ψυχαὶ π. διὸ παντοδαπῶς ἔστιν ἀκούειν ἀμφοτέρων, of Homer and Plato, Olymp. *Vit.Pl.*p.4 W. 2. *harmonious*, χορός Ph.2.399; ἀστέρων στρατιά ib.242; συζυγία τῶν τεττάρων δυνάμεων ib.136; ἑβδομάς, ὀγδοάς, ib. 166, Pythag.ap.*Theol.Ar.*54; τετράχορδον, of Diocletian and his associates, Jul.*Caes.*315c; π. ἐρωαί, of the song of the Muses, Orac. ap.Porph.*Plot.*22: neut. as Adv., π. ᾄδειν Philostr.*Im.*2.1. **-αρχαϊκός**, ή, όν, *extremely ancient*, πίναξ Chron.Lind.*B*.88. **-αρχαῖος**, ον, = foreg., γράμματα Poll.5.150. **-αρχος**, ον, *all-powerful, ruling all*, θρόνοι S.*OC*1293. **-άρχων**, οντος, ὁ, *ruler of all*, Ph.2.452 (pl.). **-ασκηθής**, ές, *all-unharmed*, Hsch. **-ασμένως**, Adv. *very readily*, only in Sup. -έστατα Tz.*H.*9.10. **-ασφάλιος** [ᾰλ], ὁ, *giving security*, epith. of Zeus and Poseidon at Mytilene, *Ath.Mitt.*24. 358 (Mytil.).

**πανᾶτις**, v. πηνῖτις.

**πᾰν-ατρεκής**, ές, *all-exact, infallible*, φάτις Keil-Premerstein *Erster Bericht* p.9 (Troketta); μνῆμα *AP*7.594 (Jul.): neut. as Adv., A.R.4. 1382. **-αύγεια**, ἡ, *fount of light*, Ph.1.7. **-αυγής**, ές, *all-bright, radiant*, Orph.*H.*10.3. **-άϋπνος**, ον, *all-sleepless*, Opp.*H.* 2.659. **-ἄφᾰνής**, ές, *all-invisible*, Eratosth.*Cat.*23. **-άφηλιξ**, ῐκος, ὁ, ἡ, *completely severed from companions of his own age*, ἦμαρ ὀρφανικὸν παναφήλικα παῖδα τίθησιν Il.22.490. **-άφθῐτος**, ον, *all-imperishable*, ἦμαρ *AP*7.14 (Antip. Sid.). **-άφθονος**, ον, *all-bountiful*, epith. of Isis, *POxy.*1380.88 (ii A.D.). **-άφυκτος**, ον, *all-inevitable*, βρόχος *AP*9.396 (Paul. Sil.); ζεῦγμα *IG*3.1339. **-άφυλλος**, ον, *all-leafless*, *h.Cer.*452.

**Πᾰνᾰχαιοί**, οἱ, *all the Achaeans*, Il.2.404, al.: fem. **Πᾰνᾰχαιά**, ἡ, epith. of Demeter, Paus.7.24.3; of Artemis, *BCH*25.350 (Delph.):—also **Πᾰνᾰχαιὶς** γῆ, *all Achaea*, A.R.1.243; **Πᾰνᾰχαιίς**, epith. of Athena, Paus.7.20.2.

**πᾰν-άωριος**, ον, *doomed to an untimely end*, ἀλλ' ἕνα παῖδα τέκεν π. Il.24.540; π. ῥυτίς *AP*5.263.5 (Paul. Sil.). **-άωρος**, ον, = foreg., *Epigr.Gr.*313.3 (Smyrna). **-δαής**, ές, *all-knowing*, Δημόκριτος Tz.*H.*4.529. **-δαίδαλος**, ον, *richly carved*, Pi.*Fr.*75.5. **-δαισία**, Ion. -ίη, ἡ, (δαίς) *complete banquet at which no one and nothing fails*, Hdt.5.20, Ar.*Pax*565, Is.*Fr.*100, Plu.2.1102a, *Supp.Epigr.*4.304.6 (Panamara), Alciphr.3.18:—also **-δαίσιον**, τό, Phot., Suid. **-δακέτης**, ου, ὁ, *biting all*, of Cato, Epigr.ap.Plu.*Cat.Ma.*1. **-δάκρῡτος**, ον, *all-tearful*, ὀδύρματα S.*Tr.*50. II. *all-bewept, most miserable*, γένος A.*Th.*654; βιοτά S.*Ph.*689 (lyr.); ἐφαμέρων ἔθνη E.*Or.*976 (lyr.). **-δάλητος** [prob. ᾰ], ον, (δηλέομαι, δάλλει) = ἐπίτριπτος, Hippon.2 (vv. ll. πανδάληκτος, πανδαύληκτος, whence Bgk. proposes **πανδαύχνητος**, = πανδάφνωτος, *all laurel-crowned*). **-δᾰμάτωρ** [μᾰ], ορος, ὁ, (δαμάω) *the all-subduer, all-tamer*, of sleep, Il.24.5, Od.9.373; of time, Simon.4.5, B.12.205, *Epigr.Gr.*1050 (Ephesus); π. δαίμων S.*Ph.* 1467 (anap.); κεραυνός Luc.*Tim.*2, etc.:—pecul. fem. **πανδᾰμάτειρα**, Orph.*H.*10.26, *Epigr.Gr.*434.6 (Petra), *IG*12(5).303 (Paros); πανδαμάτωρ μοῖρα Arist.*Pepl.*43. **-δᾱμεί**, **-δᾱμος**, v. πανδημεί, πάνδημος. **-δειλος**, ον, *all-cowardly, all-miserable*, Emp.141, Opp.*C.*3. 230. **-δείμαντος**, ον, *all-dreaded*, *Lyr.Adesp.*140, dub. in Pi.*Fr.* 189. **-δεινος**, ον, *all-dreadful, terrible*, πάνδεινον ἡ ἀδικία Pl.*R.*610d, cf. 605c; πρᾶγμα D.54.33, cf. Men.*Sam.*212, Ruf.*Fr.*69; πάνδεινα πεπονθέναι Luc.*Prom.*8; πάνδεινόν [ἐστι] it is *outrageous*, D.23.79, cf. *PTeb.*27.34 (ii B.C.), Phld.*Ir.*p.86 W. II. *very able*, c. inf., Pl. *Plt.*290b; ironically, D.19.120. **-δέκτειρα**, ἡ, pecul. fem. of sq., κοιλίη π. Hp.*Ep.*23. **-δέκτης**, ου, ὁ, *all-receiver*: in pl. πανδέκται, οἱ, name of a *Universal Dictionary* or *Encyclopedia*, such as those compiled by Tiro and Dorotheus, Gell.13.9. 2. in pl., also, *the Pandects*, i.e. the law-books of Justinian, *Cod.Just.*1.17.1.12, al.: sg., ὁ π., = *Digesta*, Id.*Const.*Δέδωκεν 1. II. Stoic word for ἐπίρρημα II, Charis.p.190 K.

**Πανδελέτειος**, ον, *knavish like Pandeletus* (cf. Cratin.242), γνῶμαι Ar.*Nu.*924, cf. Sch. ad loc.

**παν-δερκέτης**, ου, ὁ, = sq. II, Ζεῦ π. βροτῶν E.*El.*1177 (lyr.). **-δερκής**, ές, *seen by all*, B.16.70. II. Act., *all-seeing*, *AP*9.525.17, Q.S.2.443, Orph.*Fr.*62. **-δέτης**, ου, ὁ, *secure fastener*, prob. name of a knot, δήσας τινὰ πανδέτην *PMag.Leid.V.*5.23. **-δεχής**, ές, *all-receiving*, Pl.*Ti.*51a; ἀήρ Ph.1.386; σῶμα Ocell.2.3; φύσις Plu.2. 1014d; μήτηρ ἁπάντων Orph.*Fr.*315.3. **-δημεί** or **-μί**, Dor. **πανδᾱμεί** or **-μί** A.*Th.*296, *Eu.*1038 (both lyr.):—Adv. of **πάνδημος**, *with the whole people, in a mass* or *body*, Hdt.6.63, 7.120, al.; π. προπέμπεσθαι ἐπὶ θάνατον Isoc.10.27; π., πανομιλεί A.*Th.* l. c., cf. *Eu.* l. c.; π. θύειν Th.1.126; στρατεῦσαι Id.5.33, cf. 1.73, 90, 4.42, Pl.*Lg.*814a; παρεῖναι And.3.18; ἐξελθεῖν Lys.2.49; τὸν βάρβαρον π. δέκεσθαι Hdt.7. 144, cf. 6.16, 8.40, 72. [-ῑ Trag. (nisi leg. -εί); -ῐ *AP*5.43 (Rufin.); written -ί in *IG*12(2).526 *A*8, *B*2 (Eresus, iv/iii B.C.), Ἀρχ.Δελτ.9 παρ.53 (ibid.); -εί in *BGU*646.20 (ii A.D.).] **-δημία**, ἡ, *the whole people*, π. ἐξάγειν Pl.*Lg.*829b; π. καθιστάναι, of Theseus in Attica, Arist.*Fr.*384, Plu.*Thes.*25; πανδημίᾳ, as Adv., = πανδημεί, A.*Supp.* 607. **-δήμιος**, ον, *of* or *belonging to all the people*, ἦλθε δ' ἐπὶ πτωχὸς π. *public* beggar, Od.18.1; π. ἄγρη a draught *of all kinds of fish*, *AP*9.383.2. **-δημος**, Dor. **πάνδᾱμος**, ον, = πανδήμιος (esp. in Prose), βοῦς S.*Aj.*175 (lyr.); ἀγών E.*Alc.*1026; στέγαι Id.*Ba.*227; π. πόλις, στρατός, *the whole body of* the city, *of* the army, S.*Ant.*7, *Aj.* 844; π. χάρις *general* favour, Alcid.ap.Arist.*Rh.*1406ᵃ26; δόξα Plb. 31.25.8; δεῖπνον *IG*7.2712.79 (Acraeph.); ἀρχή *Sammelb.*5765 (iii/iv A.D.); of diseases, *pandemic*, Gal.17(1).2; epith. of Zeus at Athens, *IG*2².1075. Adv. -μως, = πανδημεί, τοὺς ἀνθρώπους εὐώχησε π. ib.5(2). 268.43 (Mantinea). II. π. Ἔρως *vulgar* love, opp. οὐράνιος, Pl.*Smp.* 180e sq., cf. X.*Smp.*8.9; π. Ἀφροδίτη Pl.*Smp.*181a, *IG*2².659, *SIG* 1014.57 (Erythrae, iii B.C.), Paus.1.22.3, Luc.*DMeretr.*7.1, etc. (also in pl., Dam.*Pr.*97 bis); π. ἐρασταί Pl.*Smp.*181e; π. μουσική *common, vulgar* music, Aristox.*Fr.Hist.*90; ἡ π. λέξις *ordinary* (*common*) speech, Phld.*Rh.*1.165 S.

**Πάνδῖα** (sc. ἱερά), τά, *a festival of Zeus* at Athens, D.21.9, *IG*2². 1172.9.

**πάνδῐκος**, ον, *all-righteous*, φρήν S.*Tr.*294; π. σέβας prob. in A. *Supp.*776 (lyr.). Adv. -κως *most justly*, Id.*Th.*172 (lyr.), 670, *Ch.*241, S.*OC*1306, E.*Rh.*720 (lyr.); *as in duty bound*, S.*Tr.*611, 1247.

**Πανδῑονίδης**, ου, ὁ, *son of Pandion*, used of Pericles, Cratin.56 (s. v. l.). II. fem. **Πανδῑονίς**, ίδος, *daughter of Pandion*, χελιδών Sapph.88, cf. Hes.*Op.*568. 2. one of the Attic tribes, Aeschin.2. 169, Harp.

**παν-δῖος**, ον, *all-divine*, ῥίζα, = χελιδόνιον μέγα, Ps.-Dsc.2.180 (Wellm. Πανδίονος ῥ.): pecul. fem., πανδῖα Σελήνη Max.146; Π. alone, Id.123. **-δόκεια**, ἡ, *hostess*, Hdn.Gr.1.248:—written **-δόκια**, *IG*14.24 (Syracuse). **-δοκεία**, ἡ, *trade of an innkeeper*, Pl.*Lg.*918d, Poll.7.16. **-δοκεῖον** (**-δοκῖον** (sic) Hsch.), τό, *inn*, Ar.*Ra.*550, D. 19.158, Aeschin.2.97, *IG*2².1638.30, Philippid.25.2, *Com.Adesp.*159, Plb.2.15.5:—later **πανδοχεῖον**, Thphr.*Lap.*53 codd., Aen.Tact.10.10 codd., Str.5.3.9, 12.8.17, etc., condemned by Phryn.276. **-δοκεύς**, έως, ὁ, *one who receives all comers, innkeeper*, Pl.*Lg.*918b, Plb.2.15.6, Arr.*Epict.*1.24.14, Plu.2.234e, etc.: metaph., πάσης κακίας π. Pl.*R.*

580a; π. Ἅιδης Lyc.655:—later **πανδοχεύς**, *Ev.Luc.*10.35; of the δεκάς, *all-containing*, Pythag.ap.Procl.*in Ti.*3.107 D.; also Pythag. name for *unity*, *Theol.Ar.*6. **-δόκευσις**, εως, ἡ, = πανδοκεία, Pl. *Lg.*842d (pl.). **-δοκευτής**, οῦ, ὁ, = πανδοκεύς, *BGU*1468.3 (iii/ii B.C., pl.). **-δοκεύτρια**, ἡ, *hostess*, Ar.*Ra.*114, *Pl.*426, Eup.9, D.C.46.6: metaph., φάλαινα π. a sea-monster *ready to take all in*, Ar. *V.*35. **-δοκεύω**, (πάνδοκος) *entertain as a host* or *innkeeper*, Timocr. 1.10, Hdt.4.95, Pl.*Lg.*918e: abs., *keep an inn* or *lodging-house*, Thphr.*Char.*6.5:—Pass., *to be furnished with inns*, ὅσα μέρη -εύεται κατὰ τὴν δίοδον D.H.4.53. **-δοκέω**, = foreg., only metaph., *take upon oneself, assume*, ἅπαντα παιδείας ὅπλον A.*Th.*18. **-δόκισσα**, ἡ, = πανδοκεύτρια, St.Byz. s. v. Καππαδοκία. **-δοκος** or **-δόκος**, ον, (δέχομαι) *all-receiving, common to all*, χέρσος, of Hades, A.*Th.*860; of the sacred places at Elis and Delphi, Pi.*O.*3.17, *P.*8.61; π. ξενίαι Id.*O.*4.17; π. ξενόστασις S.*Fr.*274: c. gen., δόμοι π. ξένων A.*Ch.* 662. **-δοξ**, ὁ, = πανδοκεύς, gen. -δοκος *MAMA*3.576, al. (Corycus); gen. -δοχος ib.459 (ibid.): nom. sg. in Hsch. **-δοξία**, ἡ, *absolute fame, perfect glory*, Pi.*N.*1.11. **-δοσία**, ἡ, *one who gives herself to all*, of a harlot, Anacr.156, *Com.Adesp.*1352. **-δοσις**, εως, ἡ, an unknown article of household equipment, *PLond.*2.191. 6 (ii A.D., pl.). **-δουλος**, ον, *slave to all*, *AP*5.21 (Rufin.), Man.4.602. **-δοῦρα** or **-δούρα**, ἡ, *three-stringed lute* (prob. of Oriental origin), Poll.4.60, Ath.4.183f:—also ⊛ **-δουρος**, ὁ, Euph. (?) ap.Ath.4.183f, *MAMA*3.24 (Seleucia ad Calycadnum) (written **φάνδουρος** and used of the monochord by Nicom.*Harm.* 4):—Dim. **-δούριον**, τό, Hsch. and Phot. s. v. πηκτίς:—also **-δουρίς**, ίδος, ἡ, Hsch., *Gloss.*:—hence **-δουρίζω**, *play the* πανδοῦρα, *Hist.Aug.Elag.*32; **-δουριστής**, οῦ, ὁ, *one who plays it*, Euph.*Fr. Hist.*8, *JRS*18.177 (Jerash). **-δοχεῖον**, **-χεύς**, v. πανδοκεῖον, -κεύς. **-δρόσειον**, τό, *temple of Pandrosos*, daughter of Cecrops and Agraulos, *IG*1².372.45,171, al. ⊛ **-δύναμος** [ῠ], ον, *all-powerful*, Procl.*Theol.Plat.*4.27, *Gloss.* **-δυνάστειρα**, ἡ, fem. Adj. *ruling over all*, ἄνασσα *Tab.Defix.Aud.*38.27 (Alexandria, iii A.D.). ⊛ **-δυρτος**, ον, poet. for πανόδυρτος, *all-plaintive*, αὐδά A.*Pers.* 941 (lyr.); θρῆνοι E.*Hec.*212 (lyr.); ἀηδών S.*El.*1077 (lyr.). ⊛ **-δυσία**, ἡ, *total setting of a star*, *AP*7.273 (Leon.), 395 (Marc. Arg.), 502 (Nicaen.). **-δώρα**, ἡ, *giver of all*, epith. of Earth (cf. πάνδωρος), Ar.*Av.*971, Ph.1.32. II. Pass. as fem. pr. n., *Pandora*, i. e. *the All-endowed* (i. e. by the gods), Hes.*Op.*81. **-δωρος**, ον, *all-bounteous*, epith. of Earth, Hom.*Epigr.*7, Opp.*C.*1.12; *dispenser of all* (whether good or ill), αἶσα B.*Fr.*20.4; Ζεύς Cleanth.1.32. ⊛ **-δώτειρα**, ἡ, *giver of all*, φύσις, Δημήτηρ, Orph.*H.*10.16, 40.3. **-εθνεί**, Adv. *with the whole nation*, ἀπολέσθαι Str.5.1.6:—also **-εθνί**, Lxx *Wi.* 19.8.

**πάνεια**· κεχορτασμένη, Hsch.; cf. πανός.

**πᾰν-είδᾰτος**, ον, *furnished with all sorts of food*, Q.S.1. 88. **-είδεος**, ον, *capable of assuming all forms*, Zos.Alch.p.205 B. **-ειδής**, ές, *of every figure*, of unity (as the base of all figurate numbers), *Theol.Ar.*4. **-εικέλιος**, ον, *like in all points*, Man.2. 494. **-είκελος**, ον, = foreg., Opp.*C.*1.434: c. dat., γάλακτι π. ῥεύματα *AP*9.699, cf. 12.156, *Supp.Epigr.*2.423 (Macedonia): also c. gen., ἰχὼρ π. γάλακτος Orph.*L.*203: neut. as Adv., Call.*Aet.Oxy.* 2079.31.

⊛ **Πάνειος** [ᾱ], ον, = Πανικός: πάνειον, τό, = πανικόν, *panic*, Aen.Tact. 27.1, al. (ὄνομα Πελοποννήσιον καὶ μάλιστα Ἀρκαδικόν, l.c.). II. **Πᾶνεῖον**, τό, *sanctuary of Pan*, Str.9.1.21, 17.1.10, *CIG*4837 (Egypt). III. **Πάνεια**, τά, festival of Pan at Delos, *Inscr.Délos* 312.6, 320*B*58 (iii B.C.).

**πανείπας**· ἀναιδής, Hsch.

**πᾰν-ελεήμων**, ον, gen. ονος, *all-merciful*, Θεός Mitteis*Chr.*361.8 (iv A.D.). **-ελεύθερος**, ον, *entirely free*, *APl.*5.338, *IG*14.400 (Lipara).

**Πᾰνέλλ-ηνες**, οἱ, *all the Hellenes*, Il.2.530, Hes.*Op.*528, Archil.52, Str.8.6.6, Ph.2.477; τὸν Πανελλήνων νόμον σῴζων E.*Supp.*526; οἱ Π. *the Greeks*, Phld.*Mus.*p.78 K., *Piet.*17, *Rh.*2.224 S. II. *League of United Greeks* formed by Hadrian, *IG*7.2712.40, etc.: also in sg., as title of a *Councillor of the League*, ib.5(1).45, al. **-ηνιάς**, άδος, ἡ, *celebration of the* Πανελλήνια (cf. sq. III), *Supp.Epigr.*2.410 (Thessalonica, iii A.D.). ⊛ **-ήνιος** Ζεύς, ὁ, the chief god *of the* Πανέλληνες II, Paus.1.18.9, 1.44.9, 2.29.8; also ἀγὼν Π. his festival, *IG*2².1077. 14; cf. III. II. **Πᾰνελλήνιον**, τό, *his temple*, at Aegina, built by Hadrian as their meeting-place, Paus.2.30.4, D.C.69.16. 2. *body of* Πανέλληνες II; τὸ κοινὸν τοῦ Π. *CIG*3832, cf. 3834. III. τὰ **Πᾰνελλήνια**, *the festival of the United Greeks*, *IG*2².1106, Philostr.*VS* 2.1.5, 2.17, etc.

**πᾰνέλοψ**, ὁ, Dor. and Aeol. for πηνέλοψ, Alc.84, Ibyc.8.

**Πάνεμος**, v. Πάναμος.

**πᾰν-εμφερής**, ές, *absolutely like*, Tz.*H.*8.419. **-ένδοξος**, ον, *all-glorious*, as title of address, *PMasp.*2 iii 24 (vi A.D.). **-έξαλλος**, ον, *quite different*, Hsch. **-έξοχος**, ον, *far above*, Orph.*A.*81, Opp.*C.*1. 477; πάντων π. Man.2.30; ἐν μούσαισι π. *eminent* in poetry, *IG*12(8). 442.3 (Thasos). Adv. -ως *pre-eminently*, *PMasp.*2 i 1 (vi A.D.). ⊛ **-εορτεύω**, *keep high festival*, Puchstein *Epigr.Gr.*p.61 (Egypt). **-έορτος**, ον, *kept as a high festival*, Ph.2.477. ⊛ **-επάρκιος**, ον, *all-sufficient*, Epigr.ap.Suid. s. v. Παλαμήδης. **-επαφροδῑσία**, ἡ, *perfect loveliness*, Eust.1598.5. **-επήκοος**, ον, *giving ear to all*, θεός *MAMA*1.8 (Laodicea Combusta). **-επήρᾰτος**, ον, *all-lovely*, Χαρίτων εἶδος *IG*14.1858. **-επητρῖμος**, ον, *of very close texture*: neut. pl. as Adv., π. χευαμένοιο, of snow, falling *thickly*, Opp.*C.*3. 172. **-επίκλοπος**, ον, *all-treacherous*, ib.2.28. **-επίσκοπος**, ον, *all-surveying*, *AP*7.245 (Gaet.), *MAMA*1.171 (Laodicea Combusta). **-επιστήμων**, ον, gen. ονος, *all-knowing*, Gal.16.324, Sch.Pl.*Phdr.*261d. **-επίφρων**, ον, gen. ονος, *all-remarking*: πανεπίφρονα *cunning arts*, Opp.*C.*1.328. **-επόπτης**, ου, ὁ, *all-observing*, Lxx 2*Ma.*9.5 (v. l. παντεπ-), Dioscorus in *PLit.Lond.*98 ii 11, *PLond.*5.1676.65 (vi A.D.). **-επόρφνιος**, ον, (ἐπί, ὄρφνη) *all night long*, *AP*5.205 (Leon., s. v. l.). **-επόψιος**, ον, *all-observing*, *Hermes*66.327 (Egypt), Nonn.*D.*9.133, 32.94. **-επώπης**, ου, ὁ, = πανεπόπτης, *Ath.Mitt.*24.358 (Mytil.). **-εργέτης**, ου, ὁ, *all-effecting*, Ζεύς A.*Ag.*1486 (lyr.). **-έρημος**, ον, *all-desolate*, Str.17.1.27, Heb. *Je.*2.24, *PFlor.*36.12 (iv A.D.), Luc.*DMort.*27.2. **-έρως**, ἔρωτος, ὁ, gem supposed to remove sterility, Plin.*HN*37.178. **-έσπερος**, ον, *lasting the whole evening*, *AP*7.194 (Mnasalc.). **-έστιος**, ον, (ἑστία) *with all the household*, Plu.*Sol.*24. **-έσχᾰτος**, ον, *last of all*, A.R.4.308. **-ετες**, Adv., (ἔτος) *all the year long*, Pi.*P.*1. 20. **-ετήτῠμος**, ον, *all-true*, Orph.*A.*540. **-ετώσιος**, ον, *all-ineffectual*, ib.1228. **-ευγενής**, ές, *most noble*, Tz.*H.*1.198: Sup., ib. 190. **-ευδαίμων**, ον, gen. ονος, *quite happy*, J.*AJ*8.1.1, Plu.2.1063d, Luc.*Cont.*14. 2. *all-blessed*, as honorary title, βασιλεία *OGI*722.2 (iv A.D.); πόλις (Constantinople) *PMasp.*32.93 (vi A.D.). **-ευέφοδος**, ον, *quite easy of access*, χερρόνησος Plb.4.56.6. **-εύκηλος**, ον, *all-silent*, αἰθήρ A.R.3.1196. **-ευμήχᾰνος**, ον, *very clever*, Tz.*H.*9. 530. **-εύμορφος**, ον, *most beautiful*, ib.2.17, 8.995 (both Sup.). **-ευπρεπής**, ές, *all-comely*, v. l. in D.Chr.11.153: Sup., Tz.*H.*8.518. **-εύρυθμος**, ὁ, perh. the *all round champion* of the ἔφηβοι, *IG*2².2221. 45. **-ευσεβής**, ές, *most holy*, τὸ π. ὑμῶν κράτος (of the Emperor) *PMasp.*19.1 (vi A.D.). **-ευσθενής**, ές, *very strong*, Tz.*H.*2. 569. **-ευτελής**, ές, *very cheap, vile*, Suid. s. v. ἀγοραῖος νοῦς. **-εύτονος**, ον, *very active*, *AP*7.425 (Antip. Sid.). **-ευτῠχία**, Ion. -ίη, ἡ, *all good fortune*, *Epigr.Gr.*443. **-ευφημέω**, in Pass., *to be praised everywhere*, τὸ ἐν πᾶσι -ούμενον ὑμῶν ὕψος *PMasp.*2 i 4 (vi A.D.). ⊛ **-εύφημος**, ον, *all-praiseworthy*, as honorary title, *POxy.*136.6 (vi A.D.), etc. **-εύφρων**, ον, gen. ονος, (εὐφρόνη) = πάννυχος, Cratin. 435. **-ευφυής**, ές, *good-natured*, Tz.*H.*4.854 (Sup.).

**Πᾶνεύω**, (Πάν) *treat after the manner of Pan*, π. γυναῖκας Heraclit. *Incred.*25.

**πᾰν-ευώχητος**, ον, gloss on πάνθοινος, Sch.Opp.*H.*2.221. **-εφθος**, ον, *quite boiled*; of metals, *quite cleansed of dross*, κασσίτερος Hes. *Sc.*208. **-εχθής**, ές, *all-hostile*: *all-hateful*, Orph.*H.*61.11: Sup. πανέχθιστος Lyc.1057. **-έχινος**, ὁ, or **-ον**, τό, dub. sens., ἐν πανεχίνῳ (v. l. πάχει νώτῳ) τῆς ἀσπίδος αὐτοῦ Lxx *Jb.*15.26. **-ηβηδόν**, Adv. *with all the youth*, Tz.*H.*7.995. **-ηγεμών**, όνος, ὁ, *ruler of all*, Ph.1.227. **-ηγῠράζω**, *celebrate a* πανήγυρις, *SIG*344.3 (Teos, iv B.C.).

**πᾰνηγῠρι-αρχέω**, *to be president of a* πανήγυρις, *SIG*869.9 (Eleusis, ii A.D.), *IG*3.716, etc.; πανηγυριαρχήσαντα καὶ ἀγωνοθετήσαντα τῶν μεγάλων Παναθηναίων ib.709. **-άρχης**, Dor. and Aeol. **πᾰνᾱγῠριάρχας**, ου, ὁ, *president of a* πανήγυρις, Plu.2.679b, *IG*5(1).38 (Sparta), *SIG*867.59 (Ephes., ii A.D.), *IG*12(2).244, al. (Mytil.):—also **-αρχος**, ὁ, ib.241 (Mytil.), *Ephes.*3 No.14.

**πᾰνηγῠρ-ίζω**, *celebrate* or *attend a public festival*, πανηγυρίας π. *keep holy-days*, Hdt.2.59; Ὀλύμπια καὶ Κάρνεια π. Plu.2.873e; τὴν τῶν ἐπινικίων ἡμέραν *POxy.*705.35 (iii A.D.): abs., *PSI*4.374.15 (iii B.C.); π. ἐς πόλιν *go* to a city *to attend a festival*, Hdn.1.9.2: metaph., *enjoy oneself*, Alex.219.17, Ael.*VH*13.1. 2. *frequent fairs* or *markets*, App.*Pun.*116. II. later, *make a set speech in a public assembly, deliver a panegyric*, Isoc.5.13, Plu.2.802e. 2. Pass., *sound as at a festival*, of flutes, etc., Heraclit.*All.*9. ⊛ **-ικός**, ή, όν, *of* or *for a public festival* or *assembly*, οἱ ὄχλοι οἱ π. Isoc.12.263; πολυτέλεια, κόσμος, Plu. 2.608f. II. generally, *solemn, festive*, λόγος *festival oration*, such as those pronounced at the Olympic games, *panegyric*, Isoc.5.9, 84, al.; Ἰσοκράτης ἐν τῷ π. in his *Panegyric*, Arist.*Rh.*1408ᵇ15; π. εἶδος [τῆς ῥητορικῆς] Phld.*Rh.*2.251 S.; τὰ π. Plu.2.79b: Comp. -ώτερος, of Isocrates himself, D.H.*Vett.Cens.*5.2; -ώτεραι διηγήσεις Aps.p.257 H. 2. *flattering, false*, π. λῆροι Plu.2.6a; of style, *showy, ostentatious*, opp. ἀληθινός, D.H.*Dem.*8; of persons, *pompous*, γυνὴ σοβαρὰ καὶ π. Plu.*Luc.*6. Adv. -κῶς *showily*, π. κατεσκευασμένος Id.*Cam.* 16, cf. *Ant.*61; opp. στρατιωτικῶς, Posidon.36 J.: Comp. -κώτερον Plb.5.34.3. ⊛ **-ις**, Dor. **πανᾱγ-**, εως, ἡ, (πᾶς, ἄγυρις) *general* or *national assembly*, ἐν πανηγύρει βουλευσόμεσθα A.*Ag.*845; esp. *a festal assembly* in honour of a national god, Δήμητρος ἁγνῆς καὶ Κόρης Archil.120; Ζηνὸς ἀμφὶ πανάγυριν Pi.*O.*9.96; πανηγύριας πανηγυρίζειν, ποιήσασθαι, to hold *such festivals*, keep *holy-days*, Hdt.2.59, 58; συναγαγεῖν Isoc.4.1; διαλύειν X.*Cyr.*6.1.10; ἐς π. θεωρεῖν Ar.*Pax* 342; θεωρίαι ἐς τὰς ἐν τῇ Ἑλλάδι π. Decr.ap.D.18.91; Ὀλυμπίαζε εἰς τὴν τῶν Ἑλλήνων π. ἐπανιών Pl.*Hp.Mi.*363c; in Caria, *PCair.Zen.*341(*a*)11 (iii B.C.); in Egypt, *PHib.*27.76 (iii B.C.), etc.; ἐν ταῖς π. καὶ δείξεσι τῶν σοφιστῶν Phld.*Rh.*2.256 S.; ἁμίλλαις ἱππικαῖς καὶ πανηγύρει προσκαθήμενος Jul.*Or.*1.39c; π. ἐμπορικόν τι πρᾶγμα Str.10.5.4, cf. *CIG*4474.35 (Baetocaece), Prisc.p.277 D. 2. *any assembly*, θεῶν ἅδε πανάγυρις A. *Th.*220 (lyr.); νεοσσῶν, φίλων, E.*Heracl.*239, *HF*1283. 3. metaph., π. ὀφθαλμῶν *feast* for the eyes, Ael.*VH*3.1, cf. Lib.*Or.*59.145; τὸν.. Ἔχετον χρυσὸν ἀποδείξων καὶ π. destined to exhibit E. as gold and a *feast* (by comparison with himself), Eun.*Hist.*p.236 D. b. in bad sense, παίγνιον ὁ βίος καὶ πλάνη καὶ π. Vett.Val.246.2. II. *people assembled*, τῇ π. δέος ἐγένετο μή.. Th.5.50: generally, *crowd, audience*, ὅταν ᾖ π. Thphr.*Char.*6.7. **-ισμός**, ὁ, *celebration of a* πανήγυρις, Lxx *Wi.*15.12, D.H.7.71, etc.; *display, ostentation*, Plu.2.791b, etc. **-ιστήριον**, τό, *place where national festivals are held*, ἐν τοῖς κοινοῖς τῆς Ἑλλάδος π., Ὀλυμπίασι καὶ Ἰσθμοῖ καὶ Νεμέᾳ *IG*5(2).517.16

(Lycosura, i/ii A.D.); ἐν τοῖς π. τῶν Παναχαιῶν ib.4²(1).81.15 (Epid., i A.D.). -ιστής, οῦ, ὁ, *one who attends a πανήγυρις*, Str.17.1.17, Luc.*Herod.*2, *Pseudol.*5, Poll.1.34.

**πᾰν-ήλιος**, ον, *quite sunny*, Ael.*Fr.*67. ⊛ **-ημᾰδόν**, Adv., = sq., Max.182, Orac.ap.Oenom.ap.Eus.*PE*5.22. ⊛ **-ῆμαρ**, Adv. *all day, the livelong day*, Od.13.31. **ημάτιος** [μᾰ], η, ον, late poet. form for πανημέριος, Opp.*H.*1.696. **-ημερεύω**, *spend the whole day* in a thing, *keep* it *up all day long*, θιάσους E.*Rh.*361 (lyr.). **-ημέριος**, Dor. **πᾰνᾱμ-**, α, ον, *all day long*, agreeing with the subjects of Verbs, οἱ δὲ π. μολπῇ θεὸν ἱλάσκοντο Il.1.472, cf. 2.385, Od.12.24, Hes.*Sc.*396, Thgn.1336, Cratin.142; ὅσσον τε πανημερίη.. νηῦς ἤνυσεν *in a whole day's sail*, Od.4.356, cf. 11.11; so σαίρω δάπεδον.. παναμέριος E.*Ion* 122 (lyr.): neut. πανημέριον as Adv., = πανῆμαρ, Il.11.279. 2. *of the whole day*, π. χρόνος the livelong day, E.*Hipp.*369 (lyr.). II. Ζεὺς π., v. Πανάμαρος. **-ήμερος**, ον, = foreg., ἄκλητος ἕρπων δαιταλεὺς π., of Prometheus' eagle, A.*Pr.*1024: neut. πανημερόν (oxyt.) as Adv., Hdt.7.183, Max.107. 2. Ζεὺς π., v. Πανάμαρος. II. πανάμερος is prob. f.l. for πανίμερος in S.*Tr.*660 (lyr.). **-ημος**, v. Πάναμος. **-ήπορος**, ον, *quite in want*, Hsch.; cf. πανάπορος. **-ήρης**, ες, *agreeable to all*, Id. **-θᾰλής**, ές, *giver of all bloom*, Κλειώ B.12.229.

**πανθάνω**, = πάσχω, late form in *EM*98.46, al.

**παν-θαρσής**, ές, *exceeding bold*, Man.2.171. **-θαυμάσιος**, ον, = sq., φάρμακον Aët.15.15. **-θαύμαστος**, ον, *all-wonderful*, Suid. s.v. Ἀβραάμ. **-θέᾱτος**, ον, *beheld by all*, Id. s.v. Πάνθεος. ⊛ **-θειος**, ον, *of* or *common to all gods*, τελετή Orph.*H.*54.7, al. II. Subst. **Πάνθειος**, ὁ, *all-embracing divinity*, *IG*4²(1).549, 550 (Epid.). b. (sc. μήν) a month in Lesbos, etc., *Supp.Epigr.*3.710.3 (ii B.C.), etc. 2. πανθεία, ἡ, name of a plaster, Orib.*Fr.*46. 3. **Πάνθειον** (sc. ἱερόν), τό, *temple* or *place consecrated to all gods*, Arist.*Mir.*834ᵃ12; esp. *the Pantheon* at Rome, D.C.53.27: metaph., τὸ τῶν πλανητῶν π. Arist.*Fr.*18, cf. Ph.1.483. **-θελγής**, ές, *charming all*, Nonn.*D.*31.273. ⊛ **-θέλκτειρα**, ἡ, *charmer of all*, Simon.183.1.

**πανθ-έψης**, ου, ὁ, (ἕψω) *a vessel for cooking*, *Gloss.*

⊛ **Παν-θεών**, ῶνος, ὁ (sc. μήν), name of a month at Naples, *IG*14.759.16. **-θηής**, ές, = πανθέατος, βωμός Ramsay *Studies in the Eastern Rom.Prov.*p.128. **-θηλής**, Dor. **-θᾱλής**, ές, (θάλλω) *luxuriant*, [ἄνθεα] B.12.69; ὕλη *AP*9.282 (Antip. Thess.). **-θηλυς**, εος, ὁ, *quite effeminate*, of Dionysus, *EM*277.3.

**πάνθηρ**, ηρος, ὁ, term applied to various spotted *Felidae*, Hdt.4.192, X.*Cyn.*11.1, Anaxil.12, Arist.*HA*580ᵃ25, Ar.Byz.*Epit.*96.11, Str.16.4.16, Ael.*NA*15.14, Opp.*C.*2.572, prob. in *IG*2².1491.23, 37: pl. πάνθηροι (v.l. -ες) Callix.2.

**πανθήρα**, ἡ, a birdcatcher's *whole* (future) *catch*, Ulp. in *Dig.*19.1.11.18; cf. Lat. *panthera*, = *rete aucupale*, *Gloss.* (*panther*, = *rete quoddam*, Varro *LL*5.100).

**πανθήριον**, *lynx*, *Gloss.*

**πανθηρίσκος**, ὁ, Dim. of πάνθηρ, Hero *Aut.*4.1.

**πάνθηρος**, ον, *supporting all animals*, γῆ Lyd.*Mens.*4.51.

**πανθιωνάριος**, ον, *in the form of the Pantheon*, μυροθήκη *POxy.*1026.21 (v A.D.).

**παν-θοινί** or **-εί**, Adv. *at a high festival*, A.D.*Conj.*234.9, Hdn.*Epim.*255. ⊛ **-θοινία**, ἡ, *a high festival*, Ael.*NA*2.57, 5.54. **-θοινος**, ον (and η, ον, v. infr.), (θοίνη) *feasting high* or *splendidly*, δαῖτα πανθοίνην Babr.95.90; π. τράπεζα Opp.*H.*2.221; παν[θοίν]ην is dub. in Phld.*Po.*2.49. **-θροος**, ον, contr. **-θρους**, ουν, *speaking out freely*, δῆμος Hsch. **-θῡμᾰδόν**, Adv. *most heartily*, Od.18.33. **-θῦος**, ον, = θυσιμικός, ἔτος *SIG*57.30 (Milet., v B.C.). **-θῦτος**, ον, *celebrated with full sacrifices*, θεῶν θέσμια S.*Aj.*712 (lyr.).

**πανία**, ἡ, = πλησμονή, and **πάνια**, τά, = πλήσμια, Dorian words, Dinol.6, Rhinth.1, Blaes.1.

**Πᾶνιάς**, άδος, poet. fem. of Πανικός, Nonn.*D.*7.49.

**Πᾶνιασταί**, οἱ, *worshippers of Pan*, a guild at Rhodes, *IG*12(1).155.75; at Pergamum, *IGRom.*4.1680.

**πᾰνίερος**, ον, *all-holy*, Ph.1.483, al.

**Πᾶνικός**, ή, όν, *of* or *for Pan*, πηγή Luc.*Bacch.*6. II. of fears, *panic, groundless*, π. δεῖμα J.*BJ*5.2.5; πανικόν, τό, *panic*, π. ἐμπεσόντος αὐτοῖς Plb.20.6.12; πανικῷ περιπεσόντες Id.5.96.3: pl. πανικά D.H.5.16; also θόρυβος ὁ καλούμενος π. D.S.14.32; π. τάραχος Plu.*Caes.*43, Onos.41.2, cf. Plu.2.356d, Corn.*ND*27, Polyaen.1.2, Sch.E.*Rh.*36: hence πανικόν, *a canard, startling and baseless rumour*, Cic.*Att.*14.3.1, 16.1.4; cf. πάνειον.

**πᾰνικτός**, όν, dub. sens. in Hermipp.54.

**πᾰν-ίλᾰος** [ῑ], ον, *all-gracious*, Opp.*H.*2.40. ⊛ **-ίμερος** [ῑ], ον, *all-lovely*, prob. in Man.5.78. II. *burning with desire, ardent*, prob. in S.*Tr.*660 (lyr.).

**Πάνιον** [ᾰ] (sc. τέμενος), τό, *temple of Pan*, *IG*4²(1).71.29 (Epid., iii B.C.); (sc. ἄντρον), τό, = Lat. *Lupercal*, *Gloss.*

**πᾶνίον**, τό, Dor. for πηνίον. **πάνιον**, τό, = πλήσμιον, v. πάνια.

⊛ **Πάνιος** [ᾰ], α, ον, = Πανικός, Π. βήσσας A.*Fr.*98; = μανιώδης, δαίμων Hsch.

**πανίουρος**, ὁ, perh. = παλίουρος, *BGU*563.22, *PTeb.*343.5 (both ii A.D.).

**πᾶνίσδομαι**, Dor. for πηνίζομαι.

⊛ **Πᾶνίσκος**, ὁ, Dim. of Πάν, Cic.*ND*3.17.43.

**πανισμός**, ὁ, *panic terror*, Ps.-Plu.*Fluv.*5.2 (leg. παιανισμός).

**πᾰνίσχῡρος**, ον, *very strong* or *firm*, Sch.A.*Th.*255.

**Πανῖτις**, v. Πηνῖτις.

⊛ **πᾰνίχνιον**, τό, *the whole track*, Opp.*C.*1.454 (pl.).

⊛ **Πᾰνίωνες**, οἱ, *the whole body of Ionians*, Eust.1414.36: **Πᾰνιώνιον**, τό, *their place of meeting* at Mycale, and *the common temple* there built, Hdt.1.141, al., *CIG*2909 (Mycale). 2. Πανιώνια (sc. ἱερά), τά, *festival of the United Ionians*, Hdt.1.148. 3. Πανιώνιος, ὁ, epith. of Apollo, *IG*3.175; of Hadrian, *Hermes*4.183 (Ephes.). b. (sc. ἀμφορίσκος), *IG*11(2).154 *A*36 (Delos, iii B.C.).

**Πᾰνιωνικὴ θυσία**, = Πανιώνια, Str.8.7.2.

**πάνλευκος**, v. πάλλευκος.

**πανλῡσῐτελής**, ές, *extremely profitable*, *Inscr.Prien.*112.67 (i B.C.).

**πανλώβητος**, ον, *grievously disfigured, hideous*, Luc.*Tox.*24.

**παν-νέφελος**, ον, *all-cloudy*, Orph.*H.*19.4. **-νεωτερικῶς**, Adv. *quite recently*, in form *paneotericos*, Sch.Bemb.Ter.*Adelph.*765 (*Hermes* 2.397). **-νῑκος**, ον, *all-victorious*, B.10.21.

**πάννος**, ὁ, = Lat. *pannus*, D.C.49.36.

**παννύχ-εύω**, *emaneo*, *Gloss.* **-ίζω**, (παννυχίς) *celebrate a night-festival, keep vigil*, Sapph.*Supp.*17.3, etc.; τῇ θεᾷ Ar.*Ra.*448; π. περὶ τὰ ἀγάλματα Timae.127; π. ἑορτήν Hdn.1.17.6, etc.:—Med., Luc.*DMeretr.*14.1. II. generally, *do* anything *the livelong night*, φλὸξ συνεχὲς π. it lasts all night long, Pi.*I.*4(3).65; παννυχίζων *all night long*, Ar.*Fr.*695 (lyr.): c. acc., π. τὴν νύκτα *spend the livelong* night, Id.*Nu.*1069. **-ικός**, ή, όν, *fit for a παννυχίς*, κορώνη π., of a greedy night-reveller, Posidipp.ap.Ath.10.414d. ⊛ **-ιος**, ον, *all night long*, agreeing with the subjects of Verbs, εὗδον παννύχιοι Il.2.2; π. γάρ μοι.. ψυχὴ ἐφεστήκει 23.105; π. δ' ἄρ' ἔλεκτο σὺν αἰδοίῃ παρακοίτι Hes.*Sc.*46; π. δ' ἄρα τοί γε [οἱ ἄνεμοι].. φλόγ' ἔβαλλον Il.23.217; π. μέν ῥ' ἥ γε [ἡ νηῦς] καὶ ἠῶ πεῖρε κέλευθον Od.2.434; π. χοροί S.*Ant.*153 (lyr.), E.*Ba.*862 (lyr.); τὸ ἑλλύχνιον.. καίεται παννύχιον Hdt.2.62: neut. παννύχιον as Adv., Porph.*Chr.*55: regul. Adv. -ίως *EM*650.48. **-ίς**, ίδος, ἡ, *night-festival, vigil*, Ar.*Ra.*371 (anap.), *IG*2².1199.22, *MAMA*3.50 (Cilicia), etc.; παννυχίδες θεᾶς E.*Hel.*1365 (lyr.); παννυχίδα στήσειν Hdt.4.76; ἀμφιέπειν Critias 1.8 D.; ποιεῖν Pl.*R.*328a, *IG*2².334.30; παννυχίδας ἐπιτελεσθείσας Hdn.3.8.10. II. *watching all night, vigil*, S.*El.*92 (anap.). **-ισμα**, ατος, τό, = sq., ᾗ σελήνης π. Secund.*Sent.*15; σελήνη πλεόντων π. ib.6. **-ισμός**, ὁ, *keeping vigil*, *Gloss.* **-ιστής**, οῦ, ὁ, *one who keeps vigil*, ib. **-ος**, ον, = παννύχιος, ὗε δ' ἄρα Ζεὺς πάννυχος Od.14.458; π. λύχνος παρακαίεται Hdt.2.130, cf. A.*Pers.*382, S.*Ant.*1152 (lyr.). 2. *lasting all the night*, τί πάννυχον ὕπνον ἀωτεῖς; Il.10.159; π. σελάνα E.*Alc.*451 (lyr.); ὄργια *IG*3.713: neut. pl. as Adv., πάννυχα *the livelong night*, S.*Aj.*929 (lyr.), *Supp.Epigr.*1.567.6 (Karanis, iii B.C.).

**πᾰν-όδυρτος**, ον, *most lamentable*, *AP*7.476.9 (Mel.), *Epigr.Gr.*230 (Erythrae), *IG*12(8).445.7 (Thasos); βοή Lxx *3Ma.*4.2, cf. 6.32. **-οιζυς**, υ, gen. υος, *all-unhappy*, ἑστία A.*Ch.*49 (lyr.).

**πᾰνοικ-εσία**, Adv. *with all the household*, Th.2.16, 3.57, Antipho Soph.108, D.H.7.18, *PLond.*2.479.4 (iii A.D.), etc.:—also **-ησίᾳ**, Max.Tyr.19.1, *Sammelb.*6267.18 (iii A.D.), v.l. in Th.3.57. **-ί** or **-εί**, = foreg., Pl.*Erx.*392c, Str.16.4.13, *Act.Ap.*16.34, etc., v.l. in Lxx *Ex.*1.1. (Written -εί in *PGiss.*75.10 (ii A.D.), *POxy.*935.30 (iii A.D.), etc.) **-ία**, ἡ, *whole household*, Lxx *Ge.*50.8, al.; elsewh. in dat. πανοικίᾳ, Ion. -ίῃ, as Adv., *with all the house*, Hdt.7.39, 8.106, 9.109, Philem.50, *Schwyzer*344.18 (Delph., ii B.C.), *BGU*450.27 (ii/iii A.D.). **-ιος**, ον, *with all one's house*, *AJA*16.13 (Sardes, iv/iii B.C.), D.H.1.71, D.S.5.20, Str.4.4.2, Ph.2.9; π. ὑγίεια Epist.Neronis in *SIG*810.15: neut. sg. as Adv., Demetr.Lac.*Herc.*1055.23 (s.v.l.).

**πᾰνοικτιστής**, οῦ, ὁ, *all-merciful*, θεός *PLond.*5.1676.56 (vi A.D.).

**πᾰν-οίμοι**, exclam. *oh utter woe!* οἴμοι, πανοίμοι A.*Ch.*875. **-όλβιος**, ον, *truly happy*, *h.Bacch.*54, Thgn.441; *blessed*, χρῆμα Eun.*Hist.*p.267 D. **-ολβος**, ον, = foreg., A.*Supp.*582 (lyr.).

**Πανόληπτος**, ον, *possessed by Pan*, *Mim.Oxy.*413.173, Herm. *in Phdr.*p.105 A.

**πᾰν-ομιλεί**, Adv. *in whole troops*, A.*Th.*296 (lyr.). **-όμοιος**, Ep. **-ομοίῐος**, ον, *just like*, Phld.*Rh.*1.179 S., Nonn.*D.*16.161, *AP*7.599 (Jul.), 9.482.19 (Agath.). Adv. -ως Hp.*Medic.*10.

⊛ **πᾰνομφ-αῖος**, ὁ, *sender of ominous voices, author of divination*, Ζεύς Il.8.250, Simon.144, Orph.*A.*660; Ἥλιος Q.S.5.626; Ἥρα πανομφαία *EM*768.53. **-ής**, ές, = foreg., ὄνειροι Orac.ap.Porph.ap.Eus.*PE*5.8.

**πᾰνοπλ-ία**, Ion. **-ίη**, ἡ, *suit of armour of a ὁπλίτης*, i.e. shield, helmet, breastplate, greaves, sword, and lance, *IG*1².45.11 (prob.), Th.3.114, Isoc.16.29, *SIG*421.39 (Thermae, iii B.C.), etc.; γυναῖκα σκευάσαντες πανοπλίῃ Hdt.1.60; πανοπλίᾳ παντελεῖ κοσμηθεῖσα Pl.*Lg.*796c; κοσμήσαντες π. Ἑλληνικῇ Hdt.4.180; πανοπλίαν ἕστηκ' ἔχουσα Ar.*Av.*830; π. ἔχων βαδίζεις Id.*Pl.*951: in pl., π. ἐπάργυροι καὶ κατάχρυσοι Onos.1.20: metaph., ἐνδύσασθε τὴν π. τοῦ θεοῦ *Ep.Eph.*6.11. **-ίτης** [ῑ], ου, ὁ, *man in full armour*, v.l. for sq., Tyrt.11.38. **-ος**, ον, *in full armour, with all harness on*, Tyrt. l.c. (-ίοισι codd. vett.); στρατός A.*Th.*59; ὄχλος E.*Ph.*149 (lyr.), cf. 671 (lyr.); τεύχη πάνοπλά τ' ἀμφιβλήματα suits *of full armour*, ib. 779; νικᾶν πάνοπλον in the *heavy-armed contest*, *POxy.*1110.6 (ii A.D.).

**πᾰνοπλότατος**, η, ον, *the very youngest*, A.R.3.244.

**πᾰνόπτης**, ου, ὁ, (ὄψομαι) *all-seeing*, κύκλος ἡλίου A.*Pr.*91, cf. Porph.*Abst.*2.26; of Zeus, A.*Eu.*1045 (lyr.), Orph.*Fr.*170; π. οἰοβουκόλος, of Argus, A.*Supp.*304 (also πανόπτης alone, E.*Ph.*1115, Ar.*Ec.*80, Kretschmer *Griech.Vaseninschr.*p.202); πανόπται, οἱ, title of comedies by Cratin. and Eub.

**πάνοπτος**, ον, (ὄψομαι) *seen of all, fully visible*, Hsch.

**πᾰνόπτρια**, ἡ, fem. of πανόπτης, Phot.

**πανορμιη·** ἐπίθετον Ἀπόλλωνος, Hsch. (fort. ad πάνοπτος spectat).

**πάνορμος** [ᾰ], ον, *always fit for mooring in*, λιμένες Od.13.195. II.

**Πάνορμος**, ὁ, the name of several seaport towns, esp. in Sicily, modern Palermo, Th.6.2, etc.; **Πανορμῖται**, οἱ, *its people*, D.S.22.10; **Πανορμῖτις**, ιδος, ἡ, *its territory*, Plb.1.40.2.

**πανός**, ὁ, Messapian for ἄρτος, Ath.3.111c.

**πᾱνός**, ὁ, *torch*, v. φανός.

**πάνος**· ὁ δίφρος, f.l. for θρᾶνος, Arc.63.

**πᾰν-όσμεος**, ὁ, or **-εον**, τό, *all-scent*, name of a flower, Nic.*Fr*.74.62. ⊛ **-οσπρία**, ἡ, *mixture of all sorts of pulse*, Poll.1.248, Phot.

**πανουκλίζω**, = πηνίζω, Orib.*Fr*.137; cf. *panucula*, *Gloss*.

**πανουλεύς**· ἐξώλης, Hsch.

**πᾰνούργ-ευμα**, ατος, τό, = πανούργημα (for which it is v.l. in Sch. Ar.*Eq*.800, Lxx *Si*.1.6, al.): pl., in good sense, *wonderful feats*, ib.*Ju*.11.8 (v.l. -ήματα). **-εύομαι**, = sq., ib.1*Ki*.23.22:—Pass., *to be falsified* or *adulterated*, Gal.15.105, v.l. for πανουργέομαι in 6.269. ⊛ **-έω**, pf. πεπανούργηκα Ar.*Pl*.368:—*play the knave*, E.*Med*.583, Ar.*Ach*.658, Antipho 5.65: c. acc. cogn., ἃ πανουργεῖς Ar.*Eq*.803, cf. *Pl*.368, 876; ὅσια πανουργήσασα *having dared a* righteous *crime*, S.*Ant*.74; πανουργίας π. περί τι D.35.56. II. Pass., *to be adulterated*, Gal.6.269 (v. foreg.). **-ημα**, ατος, τό, *knavish trick*, *villainy*, S.*El*.1387 (lyr.), Lxx *Si*.1.6 (v.l.); *sophistry*, Gal.5.251; cf. πανούργευμα. ⊛ **-ία**, ἡ, *knavery*, A.*Th*.603, S.*Ph*.927, Lys.22.16, Pl.*Lg*.747c, Arist.*EN*1144$^{a}$27: in pl., *villainies*, S.*Ant*.300, Ar.*Eq*.684, etc. 2. of animals, Arist.*HA*588$^{a}$23 (pl.), 614$^{a}$30. 3. *adulteration* of drugs or honey, Gal.14.27. **-ικὸν ξύλον**, *gallows*-wood, *PMag.Lond*.46.73 (unless an error for *πανιούρινον = παλιούρινον, v. πανίουρος); π. ὅπλα dub. sens. in Ps.-Callisth.2.16 (cod. B). Adv. -κῶς Sch.Ar.*Pl*.1064. **-ιππαρχίδης**, ου, ὁ, *knave-Hipparchides*, Ar.*Ach*.603. ⊛ **-ος** (properisp.), ον, *ready to do anything*, *wicked*, *knavish*, A.*Ch*.384, E.*Alc*.766, Ar.*Eq*.250, 450, al.: Sup., opp. εὐηθέστερος, Lys.3.44: as Subst., *knave*, *rogue*, E.*Hipp*.1400, Ar.*Eq*.249, al.; ὦ πανοῦργε E.*Hec*.1257, Ar.*Ach*.311; τὰ π. *the knavish sort*, S.*Ph*.448; τὸ π., = πανουργία, Id.*El*.1507: Comp. -ότερος Lxx *Pr*.21.11; -έστερος Plu.2.395c: Sup. -ότατος Ar.*Eq*.45, Lys. l. c. 2. Adv. -γως Ar.*Eq*.317, Pl.*Sph*.239c: Sup. -ότατα Ar.*Eq*.56. b. πανούργως κατασκευάζεσθαι to be *adulterated*, Gal.14.54. 3. of animals, as the fox, Arist.*HA*488$^{b}$20, cf. 613$^{b}$23. II. in a less positively bad sense, *cunning*, *clever*, *smart*, π. καὶ δεινός D.1.3, cf. Pl.*Tht*.177a, Arist.*EN*1144$^{a}$28; π. τε καὶ σοφός Pl.*R*.409c; κομψὸς καὶ π. Plu.2.28a: Sup., Plb.5.75.2. Adv. -γως, π. καὶ ὑποκριτικῶς λέγειν τὰ ἔπη Ath.9.407a.

**πᾰν-ούριος**, ον, (οὖρος) *quite fair*, of the wind, Hsch. **-ούσιος**, ον, *constituting universal substance*, Dam.*Pr*.13.

**πᾱνοῦχος** φλόξ, flame *of a torch*, *Trag.Adesp*.160; cf. πᾱνός, φανός.

**πᾰνόψια**, τά, v. πυανέψια.

**πᾰνόψιος**, ον, (ὄψις) *all-seen*, *in the sight of all*, πανόψιον ἔγχος ἑλοῦσα Il.21.397 (v.l. ὑπονόσφιον). II. *all-seeing*, ὄμμα Nonn.*D*.14.169.

⊛ **πάνριζος**, ον, *with all its roots*, γένος *IG*7.2545.28.

**πάνρῠτος**, ον, (ῥέω) *quite liquid*, Orph.*H*.10.23.

**πάνσα**, v. πᾶς.

⊛ **πανσᾰγία**, ἡ, = πανοπλία, πανσαγίᾳ *in full armour*, S.*Ant*.107 (lyr.).

**πανσέβαστος**, ον, *most august*, Mich. *in PN*142.5.

**πανσεληνιάζω**, *to be at the full moon*, Ptol.*Tetr*.149, 169.

**πανσεληνιακός**, ή, όν, *of* or *at the full moon*, συζυγία, σύνδεσμος, Ptol.*Tetr*.92, cf. Vett.Val.21.22, al., Paul.Al.*G*.3.

**πανσέληνος** or **πασσ-** (Arist.*APo*.93$^{a}$37 cod. A), ον, of the moon, *at the full*, ἡ σελήνη ἐτύγχανε οὖσα π. Th.7.50; κύκλος π. *the moon's full* orb, E.*Ion* 1155; τὰς νύκτας τὰς π. Arist.*HA*622$^{b}$27. 2. ἡ πανσέληνος (sc. ὥρα) *the time of full moon*, Hdt.2.47, 6.120, Ar.*Ach*.84; τὰν αὔριον π. (s.v.l.) at to-morrow's *full moon*, S.*OT*1090 (lyr.): without the Art., πανσέληνος A.*Th*.389, And.1.38; ταῖς πανσελήνοις or ἐν ταῖς π. *at the seasons of full moon*, Arist.*HA*544$^{a}$20, 555$^{a}$10, cf. *Stoic*.1.34; πανσέληνον, τό, Apollon.*Mir*.36. II. *round as the full moon*, χρυσίς Hermipp.37 (dub. l.).

**πάνσεμνος**, ον, *all-majestic*, μαθήματα Luc.*Vit.Auct*.26, cf. *Anach*.9.

**πανσεμνοστομέω**, *speak with all dignity*, Tz.*H*.6.47.

**πάνσεπτος**, ον, *most sacred*, *PMasp*.3.7 (vi A.D.), Mich. *in PN*62.3.

**πανσκᾰφία**, ἡ, *digging pits for planting*, *Gp*.5.9.11.

**πάνσκῑος**, ον, *all-shaded*, γῆ *Gp*.3.11.8.

**πάνσκοπος**, ον, *all-seeing*, ὄμμα Δίκης *AP*7.580 (Jul. Aegypt.).

**πάνσμῑκρος**, ον, *very small*, Pl.*Lg*.903c.

**πανσόβητος**, ον, *readily impelled*, Lyd.*Mens*.2.7.

⊛ **πάνσοφος**, ον, *most clever*, π. κρότημα, of Odysseus, S.*Fr*.913; εὕρημα E.*HF*188; τὸ π. ὄνομα A.*Supp*.320; τὸν πάνσοφον ἀριθμὸν εὕρηκ' ἔξοχον σοφισμάτων *Trag.Adesp*.470.3:—also **πάσσοφος**, as in the best codd. of Pl.*Prt*.315e, *Tht*.149d, al., *IG*12(5).891.4 (Tenos). Adv. -φως Pl.Com.(?) 269 (= 1 p.196 Meineke), Steph. *in Hp*.1.92 D.

**πανσπερμηδόν**, Adv. *with all sorts of seeds*, Nic.*Fr*.72.5.

⊛ **πανσπερμία**, ἡ, *mixture of all seeds* (cf. πανοσπρία), Arist.*GA*769$^{a}$29, $^{b}$2, Sosib.20, Luc.*Herm*.61, Alciphr.3.14, *Gp*.15.8.2: metaph., π. μύθων Plu.2.348a. II. of the mixture of elements, in the systems of Anaxagoras and the atomists, ὡς οὖσαν τὴν φύσιν οἷον π. πάντων τῶν στοιχείων Arist.*Cael*.303$^{a}$16, cf. *GC*314$^{a}$29, *Ph*.203$^{a}$21; π. παντὶ θνητῷ γένει μηχανώμενος Pl.*Ti*.73c; παθῶν π. τις ὁ θυμός Plu.2.463a.

**πάνσπερμος**, ον, *composed of all sorts of seeds*, *AP*6.98 (Zon.).

**πανστρᾰτί**, Adv., = sq., Suid.

**πανστρᾰτιᾷ**, Ion. -ιῇ, *with the whole army*, Hdt.1.62, 3.39, 7.203, al., Th.2.5, 6.7, al.: nom. πανστρατιά is not found; gen., πανστρατιᾶς ξένων καὶ ἀστῶν γενομένης Id.4.94.

⊛ **πανσῠδί** or **-δεί**, Adv., (σεύομαι) *with all one's force*, hence = πανστρατιᾷ, π. διεφθάρθαι *utterly*, Th.8.1, cf. Pherecr.31, D.H.5.46: written **πασσυδί** X.*Cyr*.1.4.18, Onos.42.12, v.l. for sq. in X.*HG*4.4.9, *Ages*.2.19.

⊛ **πανσῠδίᾳ**, Ep. -ίῃ, or **πασσ-**, Adv., (σεύομαι) *with all speed*, Il.2.12, 11.709, 725, E.*Tr*.797 (anap.). II. = πανστρατιᾷ, X.*HG*4.4.9, *Ages*.2.19 (cf. foreg.), Aen.Tact.15.9, Q.S.7.432, Tryph.142.

**πανσῠδίην**, Adv. = foreg., *EM*650.55, v.l. in Suid.; also **πασσυδίην**, Hsch. s. v. πασσύριον.

**πάνσυρτος**, ον, (σύρω) *swept together from every side*, πάνσυρτος δεινῶν αἰών (prob. l.) a life of *accumulated* woe, S.*El*.851 (lyr.).

**πανσχήμων**, ον, gen. ονος, *of every*, i.e. *of indeterminate*, *form*, δύο ἀριθμῶν σχέσις π. ἐστίν *Theol.Ar*.8, cf. Iamb. *in Nic*.p.57 P.

**πανσώτειρα**, ἡ, *all-saving*, of Isis, *CIG*(add.)4900 (Egypt).

**πανταᾷ**, v. πάντῃ.

**παντ-άγᾰθον** [ᾰγ], τό, *good-for-all*, name of a plaster, Gal.13.649. **-άγᾰθος** [ᾰγ], ον, *wholly good*, *Supp.Epigr*.6.125 (Cotiaeum). **-αγήρως**, v. παντογήρως. **-άδῐκος**, ον, *all-unrighteous*, πλοῦτος Ph.2.362. **-άδουσα**, ἡ, *star-thistle*, *Centaurea Calcitrapa*, Thphr.*HP*6.5.1 (s.v.l.). **-αεθνής**, ές, *of any nation*, dub. in App.*BC*4.34. **-άθλιος**, α, ον, *most wretched*, κώμη *PMasp*.2.2 (vi A.D.). **-αίολος**, ον, *all-radiant*, Ἥλιος Orph.*Fr*.236. **-ακύριος**, ον, *all-supreme*, dub. in *PMag.Lond*.46.139.

**παντάλᾱς** [τᾰ], αινα, ἄν, *all-wretched*, E.*Andr*.140, *Hec*.667 (both lyr.); παντάλαν' ἄχη A.*Pers*.638 (lyr.).

**παντᾰληθής**, ές, *all-true*, of an oracle, Perdrizet-Lefèbvre *Les graffites grecs du Memnonion d'Abydos* 493, 500.

⊛ **παντάπᾱσι** or (before a vowel) **-ιν**, Adv. *all in all*, *altogether*, *wholly*, πείθεσθαι Hdt.7.152; ἱπποκρατεῖσθαι Th.6.71; ἀπόλλυσθαι, ἄγασθαι, Pl.*Phd*.88a, *Lg*.631a; τὰ δίκαια π. ἀκριβῶ X.*Cyr*.1.3.17: with Adjs., π. ὀλίγοι *very* few *indeed*, Pl.*Plt*.293a; π. ῥᾴδιον Id.*Prt*.328a; π. βλάξ *quite* a simpleton, X.*Cyr*.1.4.12; π. ἔρημος D.21.80: with Advbs., οὐ π. οὕτως ἀλόγως not so *absolutely* without reason, Th.5.104; π. ἀνοήτως Isoc.12.232: with the Art., τὸ π. Th.3.87: with a neg., π. οὐδέν, οὐδὲν π., nothing *at all*, Anaxag.12, Arist.*GC*316$^{a}$27. 2. in affirmative answers, *by all means*, *undoubtedly*, π. μὲν οὖν Pl.*Phdr*.278b, *Sph*.227a; π. γε X.*Mem*.4.5.3.

**παντά-πρωτος**, η, ον, *first of all*, honorary title at Sparta, *IG*5(1).501, al.; π. γυνή ib.535.17. ⊛ **-πώλης**, ου, ὁ, = παντοπώλης, *BCH* 26.201 (Syria).

**παντάρβη**, ἡ, a precious stone, perh. *ruby*, Ctes.*Fr*.57.2, Philostr.*VA*3.46, Hld.8.11.

**πανταρβής**, ές, *fearing all*, Man.2.168, Rhetor. in *Cat.Cod.Astr*.1.145.

**παντ-άρετος** [ᾰρ], η, ον, *wholly virtuous*, παντα[ρέτη]ν γυναῖκα prob. in *Delph*.3(1).553. **-άριστος**, η, ον, *best of all*, honorary title at Sparta, *IG*5(1).530; cf. παντάπρωτος. **-αρκής**, ές, *all-powerful*, βασιλεύς A.*Pers*.855 (lyr.). **-άρχας**, α, ὁ, Dor. for -χης, *lord of all*, Ar.*Av*.1059 (lyr.). **-αρχέω**, *hold every public office*, τῆς Ὀμβειτῶν πόλεως *IGRom*.1.1288 (Egypt, iii A.D.). **-αρχία**, ἡ, *universal sway*, gloss on παντοκρατορία, Suid. **-αρχος**, ον, *all-ruling*, θεῶν S.*OC*1085 (lyr.); ὁ π. *the Almighty*, Ph.1.242; ἡ π., of Isis, *POxy*.1380.137 (ii A.D.). **-άρχων**, οντος, ὁ, *one who has served all offices*, βουλευτὴς π. *TAM*2.349, 382 (Xanthus). **-άσκῑος**, ον, *all-shadowless*, Hsch. **άσπορος**, ον, *quite unsown*, *Sammelb*.7366.52 (ii/iii A.D.). **-αυγής**, ές, *eyeing all*, Man.1.287, 4.122.

**πανταχῇ** (with iota, *IG*2$^{2}$.1666.22, al. (iv B.C.), *PEleph*.3.6, al. (iii B.C.)), Adv. of Place, *everywhere*, Th.1.49, Pl.*Phd*.109b, etc.; π. πάντων ἴσον κρατεῖν v.l. in X.*An*.2.5.7: c. gen. loci, *in every part of*.., τοῦ Ἑλλησπόντου Hdt.7.106; π... ἄστεως ζητῶν νιν E.*Ion* 1107. 2. *on every side*, Hdt.2.124; π. κύκλῳ Th.7.79; διακοσίων ποδῶν π. a *square* of 200 ft., Id.3.68; *in every direction*, *every way*, προσπεύθου π. S.*OC* 122 (lyr.); διασκοπεῖν π. Ar.*Th*.660; μὴ περιπέτεσθε π. κεχηνότες Id.*Av*.165, etc. II. metaph., *in every way*, δηλοῖ οὐ κατ' ἓν μοῦνον, ἀλλὰ π. Hdt.5.78, cf. 3.38, etc.; κακῶς πέπρακται π. E.*Med*.364; οἱ π. ἄριστοι ἄνδρες Pl.*Lg*.918e; π. δρῶντες acting *in every way*, i.e. whatever we do, S.*Ant*.634; π. *in any case*, Id.*Aj*.1369, cf. A.*Pr*.200.

**πανταχόθεν**, Adv. *from all quarters*, *from every side*, ἐκ τῆς Ἀσίης π. Hdt.7.25, cf. Ar.*Lys*.1007, Pl.*Smp*.190e, al.; περιέχεσθαι π. *on all sides*, Hdt.8.80. II. *from every side*, i.e. *in every way*, π. ἡ Ἑλλὰς κατείχετο μή.. Th.1.17; π. καλῶς ὑπάρχον πολεμεῖν ib.124, cf. X.*Mem*.2.1.25; π. βάσκανος D.18.242.

**πανταχόθι**, Adv. = πανταχοῦ, Gal.14.81, *Vict.Att*.16: c. gen., Luc.*DDeor*.9.1.

**πανταχοῖ**, Adv. *in every direction*, *any whither*, ἄγειν τινά Ar.*V*.1004; π. πρεσβεύσομεν (cf. πανταχοῦ), Id.*Lys*.1230; π. μᾶλλον οἴχεται πλέων D.4.24, cf. 8.76.

⊛ **πανταχόσε**, Adv., = foreg., Th.7.42, Pl.*R*.540a, etc.; incorrectly for πανταχοῦ, τοῖς π. δήμοις Plu.*Agis* 14.

**πανταχοῦ**, Adv. *everywhere*, Hdt.3.117 (nisi leg. πενταχοῦ), Th.4.108, etc.; οἱ φρονοῦντες εὖ κρατοῦσι π. S.*Aj*.1252; οὐδαμοῦ καὶ π. E.*IT*568; ἄλλοθι π. Pl.*Chrm*.160a: c. gen., π. τῆς γῆς (v.l. πολλαχοῦ) Id.*Phd*.111a: later with Verbs of Motion, ἐξῆλθε ἡ ἀκοὴ αὐτοῦ π. *Ev.Marc*.1.28: in early writers πανταχοῖ should be restd., as E.*IT*68, Ar.*Lys*.1230. II. *altogether*, *absolutely*, Pl.*R*.503a; οὐ π. ἤσθησαι not *at all*, Id.*Prm*.128b.

**πανταχῶς**, Adv. *in all ways*, *altogether*, Pl.*Prm*.143c, Isoc.15.94.

⊛ **παντεβιπᾶσιν**, = πάντ' ἐπὶ πᾶσιν, dub. in *IG*12(7).117 (Arcesine).

**παντειδήμων**, ονος, ὁ, a *know-all*, Phld.*Vit*.p.32 J.

**παντέλεια**, ἡ, *consummation*, ἡ π. τῆς καταφθορᾶς Plb.1.48.9; π. ἀρετῆς Ph.1.38; πᾶσα πολιτικὰ κοινωνία λύρας παντελήᾳ ποτέοικεν prob. in Hippod.ap.Stob.4.1.94; εἰς ἀσφαλῆ τινα καὶ βεβαίαν π. ἀγαθῶν ἐξικόμενον Plu.2.1061f; εἰς π. διδαχθῆναι, opp. εἰς τύπωσιν, Phld. *Rh.*2.34 S.; τριετηρικὴ π., of the great mysteries, Plu.2.671d, cf. *IG* 3.77. II. παντέλεια was a Pythagorean name of the number *ten*, *Theol.Ar.*63.

**παντέλειος**, ον, later form of παντελής, *in pure perfection*, νοῦς Thphr.*Fr.*53 codd., Porph.*Sent.*22; σοφία Hierocl.*in CA* 1 p.419 M.; ἀπὸ τῶν π. τὰ τέλεια Procl.*Inst.*64; π. ἀριθμός (i.e. ten) Ph.*Fr.*72 H.; δεκὰς ἡ π. Id.1.10; τὰ π. *the consummation* (i.e. *the chief day*) of the Thesmophoria at Syracuse, Heraclid.Syrac.ap.Ath.14.647a. Adv. -είως Erot. s.v. ἀπαρτί.

**παντελειόω**, *consummate, make perfect*, Zos.Alch.p.245 B. (Pass.).

⊛ **παντελής**, ές, *all-complete, absolute*, παντελῆ σάγην ἔχων A.*Ch.*560; μοναρχία S.*Ant.*1163; πανοπλία, ἐλευθερία, μανία, Pl.*Lg.*796c, 698a, D.Chr.38.17; π. δάμαρ *mistress* of the house, S.*OT*930; δήμου π. ψηφίσματα *with full authority*, A.*Supp.*601; π. κήρυγμα S.*Ichn.*13; π. ἐσχάραι *complete tale* of sacrificial hearths, Id.*Ant.*1016. 2. π. δύναμις ἁ τᾶς δεκάδος *perfect*, Philol.ap.Stob.1 *Prooem.*3, cf. Dam. *Pr.*195. II. Act., *all-accomplishing*, Ζεύς A.*Th.*118 (lyr., s.v.l.); χρόνος Id.*Ch.*965 (lyr.); π. εὐεργέτης S.*Ichn.*79. III. Adv. παντελῶς, Ion. -έως, *altogether, utterly*, with Verbs, διῶρυξ π. πεποιημένη Hdt.7.37; λίθινα π. ἐξειργασμένα *IG* 1².372.93; παντελέως εἶχε τὸ οἴκημα it was *quite finished*, Hdt.4.95; π. διώρισε A.*Pr.*440; π. κρανθήσεται ib.911; π. θανεῖν to die *outright*, S.*OT*669; ἐκμεμάθηκα ταῦτα π. Epicr.4, etc.: with Adjs., π. βαθεῖα φάλαγξ X.*HG*2.4.34; π. ἄφρων Men.694; ἄχρηστα π. Philippid.12; π. Βοιώτιοι Alex.237.1; οὐ π. not *at all*, Men.5; *from first to last*, π. ἕως ἂν διεξέλθῃ διὰ πάντων Arist.*Pol.*1298ᵃ16. 2. in answers, *most certainly*, παντελῶς γε Pl. *R.*379c, 485d; π. μὲν οὖν Id.*Prm.*155c, 160b, *R.*401a. 3. later εἰς τὸ παντελές, = παντελῶς, Ph.2.567, *Ev.Luc.*13.11, Ael.*NA*17.27, S.E. *M.*7.30, Jul.*Or.*2.61c; = *for ever*, *Rev.Bibl.*39.544, 546 (Palmyra), *PLond.*3.1164 *f* 11 (iii A.D.), etc.; κατὰ τὸ π. Ph.1.90, al.

**παντ-ενέργητος**, ον, *source of all activity*, τὸ ἓν π. Porph.*Sent.* 36. **-επίθυμος**, ον, = παντορέκτης II, Polem.*Phgn.*30. **-επίσκοπος**, ον, *all-surveying*, πνεῦμα Lxx *Wi.*7.23 (v.l. πανεπ-). **-επόπτης**, ου, ὁ, *all-seeing*, Vett.Val.1.4, al., *JRS* 18.173 (Jerash), Procl.*in Prm.* p.820 S., Sch.Ar.*Ach.*434:—written **-εφόπτης**, *Tab.Defix.Aud.*271. 36 (Hadrumetum, iii A.D.).

**παντερπής**, ές, *all-delighting*, ἰαχὰ αὐλῶν *Lyr.Adesp.*96, cf. Opp.*C.* 3.149.

**παντεύμορφος**, ον, *altogether beautiful*, Tz.*H.*5.949.

**παντευχία**, ἡ, = πανοπλία (for which it is v.l. in Lxx 4 *Ma.*3.12), *complete armour*, Pherecyd.158 J., E.*Heracl.*787; ὅπλων π. ib.720; πολέμιον παντευχίαν enemies *in full array*, Id.*Supp.*1192; παντευχίαν δὲ τοῦ θεοῦ . . λαβεῖν his *panoply*, Aristomen.5; ξὺν, ἐν παντευχίᾳ, *in full armour*, A.*Th.*31, *Fr.*304.3: pl., Phld.*Hom.*p.58 O.

**πάντευχος**, ον, *armed cap-à-pie*, Orac.Chald.ap.Dam.*Pr.*70.

⊛ **πάντεχνος**, ον, *assistant of all arts*, παντέχνου πυρὸς σέλας A.*Pr.*7.

**πάντῃ** (σὺν τῷ ῑ *Lex.Mess.*p.409, and so written in *PEleph.*1.14 (iv B.C.)), Dor. **παντᾷ** Pi.*O.*1.117, 9.24, Ar.*Lys.*169, 180, *Tab.Heracl.* 1.141:—also **παντεῖ**, *Schwyzer* 366 *A* 12 (Tolophon, iii B.C.); Aeol. **πάντᾳ** Sapph.*Oxy.*2076 ii 18: Adv.:—*every way, on every side*, freq. folld. by a Prep., π. ἀνὰ στρατὸν Il.1.384; π. περὶ τεῖχος 12.177, etc.; π. ἀμφὶ νέκυν 23.34; π. φοιτῶντες ἐπ' αἶαν Hes.*Op.*125; ὅσον τε ἐπὶ τη' σταδίους . . π. Hdt.1.126; also π. παπταίνοντι Od.12.233; διασκοπεῖν Ar.*V.*246; ἱρὸν δύο σταδίων π. *on every side*, Hdt.1.181, cf. 2.168; κύκλῳ π. X.*An.*3.1.2. II. *in every way, altogether*, π. συγγίνεσθαι ἀήθεα Emp.22.8; οὐδὲν ἦν π. καλὸν *Trag.Adesp.*26; π. πάντως Pl.*Ti.* 29c, *Prm.*160b, Arist.*EN* 1100ᵇ20; πάντως καὶ π. Pl.*Phlb.*60c; π. καὶ πανταχοῦ *Act.Ap.*24.3; οὐ π. not *quite*, App.*BC* 1.8, Luc.*Tim.*2.

**παντῐβόλος**, ον, *having cut all its teeth*, ἵππος *Supp.Epigr.*6.634; cf. ἄβολος.

**πάν-τῑμος**, ον, *all-honourable*, νίκης π. γέρας S.*El.*687, cf. Orph.*H.* 14.5, etc.; π. ἱερεύς, of the Rom. *pontifex maximus*, D.S.38/9.17; τὸ π. ὕψος ὑμῶν (of the *dux*) *PMasp.*5.9 (iv A.D.).

**παντλήμων**, Dor. **-τλάμων**, ον, gen. ονος, = παντάλας, S.*OT* 1379, *El.*150, E.*Hec.*197 (lyr.).

**παντο-βᾰρής**, ές, *all-overwhelming*, Ἅιδης *IG* 9(1).489 (Thyrrheum, ii B.C.). **-βίης** [ῐ], ου, ὁ, *all-overpowering*, Ἀχέρων *AP* 7.732 (Theodorid.). **-γένεθλος**, ον, *all-generating, father of all*, Ζεύς Orph.*H.* 15.7. II. *of every kind*, πνεύματα ib.58.6. ⊛ **-γενής**, ές, = foreg. 1, Αἰών Sotad.15.1. **-γήρως**, ων, gen. ω, *making all old*, i.e. *subduing all*, ὕπνος S.*Ant.*606 (lyr., v.l. παντ-αγήρως, *never growing old, unaltering*, but both are prob. corrupt). **-γόνος**, ον, *all-generating*, Μοῖραι Orac.ap.Phleg.37 J. (παντο- ap.Zos.2.6). **-δαής**, ές, *all-knowing*, Epigr.ap.D.L.9.43. **-δᾰπῆ**, Adv. *in every direction*, Arist.*PA* 660ᵃ 24. **-δαπής**, ές, late form of -δαπός, Epicur.*Herc.*1413.4, Procl. *in Prm.*p.605 S., *EM* 204.23, 711.48. **-δᾰπία**, ἡ, *abundance of all kinds*, Aq.*Is.*66.11, prob. in Id.*Ps.*49(50).11. **-δᾰπός**, ή, όν, (cf. ἀλλοδαπός) *of every kind, of all sorts, manifold*, ἄνθεα, χροιαί, καρπός, *h.Cer.*402, Sapph.20, A.*Th.*357 (lyr.), etc.; παντοδαπᾶς ἐπὶ γᾶς E. *Hel.*525 (lyr., s.v.l.); π. ἱστορία *miscellaneous*, D.L.5.5; τὸ π. [τῆς λέξεως] Phld.*Rh.*1.198 S.; *of every country*, ποδαπὸς εἶ; Answ. π. Luc.*Vit.Auct.*8: in pl., πολλοὶ καὶ π. Hdt.9.84; παντοδαποὶ τῆς στρατιῆς, = π. στρατιῶται, Id.7.22: contemptuously, δοῦλοι καὶ ξένοι π. And.2.23; πολλὴ καὶ π. ἄγνοια Pl.*Sph.*228e: Comp. -ώτερος Arist. *HA* 525ᵇ3: Sup. -ώτατος Hp.*Aër.*9, Isoc.15.295. Adv. -πῶς *in all kinds of ways*, ἐσθλοὶ μὲν γὰρ ἁπλῶς, π. δὲ κακοί Poet.ap.Arist.*EN* 1106ᵇ35, cf. Pl.*Prm.*130a, etc.; π. ἔχειν Arist.*EN* 1100ᵃ27. 2. παντοδαπὸς γίγνεται *assumes every shape*, Ar.*Ra.*289, Pl.*R.*398a; ὥσπερ ὁ Πρωτεὺς π. γίγνει Id.*Ion* 541e. **-δίαιτος** [ῐ], ον, *all-consuming*, Orph.*H.*66.5. **-δίδακτος** [ῐ], ον, *all-learned*, Πλουτωνίς Orac.ap.Phleg.36 J. **-δότειρα**, ἡ, = πανδώτειρα, Orph.*H.*59. 18. ⊛ **-δύνᾰμος** [ῠ], ον, *all-powerful*, Lxx *Wi.*7.23, Elias *in Porph.*17. 18, Sch.A.*Th.*166; φύσις νοερὰ καὶ π. Plot.5.9.9. ⊛ **-δῠνάστης**, ου, ὁ, = foreg., Orph.*H.*12.4, 45.2. **-επής**, ές, *all-chattering*, Adam. 2.41. **-εργός**, όν, *all-effective*, δύναμις Philol.ap.Stob.1 *Prooem.* 3. **-έρκτης**, ου, ὁ, = παντορέκτης 1, Herod.5.42. ⊛ **-θᾰλής**, ές, *making everything bloom*, Orph.*H.*34.16; ὧραι *IG* 9(2).649 (Larissa). 2. *all-blooming*, *BMus.Inscr.*1067.15 (Memphis).

**πάντοθεν**, Adv., (πᾶς) *from all quarters, from every side*, Il.15.623, S.*OC* 1240 (lyr.), etc.; π. πληθύνομαι A.*Ag.*1370: in Ion. Prose, Hdt.2.138, 7.129: rare in Att. (πανταχόθεν being preferred), Pl. *Criti.*117e; μὴ π. κέρδαινε Men.625, cf. *Mon.*63; οὐ μόνον κατ' εὐθυωρίαν, ἀλλὰ π. Arist.*PA* 656ᵇ29; π. λαμβάνειν Id.*EN* 1121ᵇ32: freq. with Prep., π. ἐκ κευθμῶν Il.13.28; περὶ γὰρ κακὰ π. ἔστη Od. 14.270: c. gen., π. εἰδώλων Arat.455:—the form **πάντοθε** is only v.l. in Hdt.7.225, Theoc.17.97, *AP* 11.85 (Lucill.).—On the accent, v. A.D.*Adv.*192.2.

**πάντοθῐ**, Adv. *everywhere*, Arat.743, *AP* 4.1.48 (Mel.).

**παντοιάς**, άδος, ἡ, *manifold universe*, Orac.Chald.ap.Dam.*Pr.*70.

⊛ **παντοῖος**, α, ον, *of all sorts* or *kinds, manifold*, ἄνεμοι Il.2.397; δόλοι 3.202; ἀρετή 22.268, E.*Med.*845 (lyr.); τέχνη Od.6.234, S.*Aj.*752; φιλότης Od.15.246, S.*El.*134; λῦπαι Id.*OT* 915; λόγοι E.*Hec.*840; τύχαι Arist.*EN* 1100ᵃ5; ἐξυβρίσαι παντοῖα Hdt.3.126; πολλὰ καὶ π. λέγειν Id.9.90, etc. 2. in Prose of persons, παντοῖος γίνεται he takes *all possible shapes*, i.e. *tries every shift*, of persons in danger or difficulty, ib.109: with part., π. ἐγένοντο δεόμενοι Id.7.10.γ'; π. ἐγίνετο (sc. δεομένη) μὴ ἀποδημῆσαι τὸν Πολυκράτεα Id.3.124; π. ἦν δεδιὼς Luc. *DDeor.*21.2; π. γενόμενος ὑπὲρ τοῦ σῶσαι Plu.*Mar.*30; rarely of joy, π. ὑπ' εὐφροσύνης γενόμενοι *they played all sorts of antics* from joy, Luc. *Demon.*6; π. ἦν ὑπ' ἀπορίας Id.*Laps.*1. II. Adv. -ως *in all kinds of ways, variously*, Hdt.7.211; π. ἔχειν Pl.*R.*559d, etc.

**παντο-κράντειραι** (-μάντ- cod.)· Μοῖραι, Hsch. ⊛ **-κράτειρα** [κρᾰ], ἡ, pecul. fem. of παντοκράτωρ, Orph.*H.*10.4, *POxy.*1380.20 (ii A.D.). **-κρᾰτέω**, *to be almighty*, v.l. in Lxx *Za.*8.2. **-κρατορία**, ἡ, *omnipotence*, interpol. in ib.*Si.*19.18. ⊛ **-κράτωρ** [κρᾰ], ορος, ὁ, *almighty*, of Hermes, *Epigr.Gr.*815 (Cret.); Κύριος Lxx 2 *Ki.*5.10, al.; θεός Aristeas 125; ὁ π. alone, *the Almighty*, *Apoc.*1.8.

**παντ-ολέτειρα**, ἡ, *destroyer of all*, Orph.*H.*26.2. **-ολέτωρ**, f.l. for πατρολέτωρ (q.v.).

**παντόλμιος** (sc. τροχίσκος), ὁ, name of a lozenge, Paul.Aeg.4.43, 7.12.

⊛ **πάντολμος**, ον, *all-daring, shameless*, φωτὶ παντόλμῳ φρένας A.*Th.* 671, cf. *Ch.*430 (lyr.); ἔρωτες ib.596 (lyr.); ὠμὰ καὶ π. E.*IA* 913 (troch.), cf. D.H.4.28.

**παντο-λόγος**, ον, *ready to say anything*, Polem.*Phgn.*30. **-μεταβόλος**, ον, *dardanarius*, Gloss. **-μιγής**, ές, *mixed of everything*: hence, *rich in variety of produce*, χωρίον Eun.*Hist.*p.254 D.; χρῆμά τι πρὸς ἅπασαν ἀρετὴν π., of a person, Id.*VS* p.457 B. **-μῖμος**, ον, *pantomimic*, ὀρχηστής Jul.*Mis.*351d; ὄρχησις Suid. s.h.v.: Subst. π., ὁ, *pantomimic actor*, Luc.*Salt.*67. **-μισής**, ές, *all-hateful*, A.*Eu.* 644. **-μορφος**, ον, = πάμμορφος, Θέτις S.*Fr.*618; σπλάγχνων γένη Hp. *Ep.*23 (παντάμ- codd.); of the universe, *Corp.Herm.*11.16: hence, as Subst. π., ὁ, *the Universe*, Ps.-Apul.*Asclep.*19 (cf. 35); as figure-head of a ship, perh. Proteus, *PGrenf.*1.49.20 (iii A.D.). **-μωρος**, ον, *all-foolish*, f.l. for πάνυ βορός, *gluttonous*, Polem.*Phgn.*33. **-νίκης** [ῑ], ου, ὁ, *all-conquering*, D.C.63.10. **-πᾰθής**, ές, *all-suffering*, sens. obsc., *AP* 5.4 (Stat. Flacc.). **-ποιός**, όν, *capable of anything*, Thphr.*Char.*6.2, Ptol.*Tetr.*160. II. *creating universality*, Dam. *Pr.*33. III. *omnipotent*, [θε]ῷ πανθο[ποι]ῷ prob. in *Arch.Anz.*44. 234 (Thrace). **-πόρος**, ον, *all-inventive*, opp. ἄπορος, S.*Ant.*360 (lyr.). **-πράκτης**, ου, ὁ, = πανοῦργος, Ptol.*Tetr.*166.

**παντ-όπτης**, ου, Dor. **παντόπτας**, α, ὁ, = πανόπτης, A.*Supp.*139 (lyr.), *Fr.*192.5 (anap.), S.*OC* 1085 (lyr.), Ar.*Av.*1058 (lyr.).

**παντο-πωλέω**, *to be a general dealer, huckster*, Men.*Pk.*93. **-πώλης**, ου, ὁ, *huckster*, Anaxipp.1.10, *Ostr.*347, 348 (ii B.C.), *Ostr.Bodl.* 195 (ii/i B.C.):—written **πατοπούλης**, *MAMA* 3.249 (Corycus); cf. παντοπώλης. **-πωλία**, ἡ, *dealing in all kinds of wares*, Archipp. 31. **-πώλιον**, τό, *place where all sorts of things are for sale, general market, bazaar*, Pl.*R.*557d, *Sammelb.*6803 iii 11 (iii B.C.), Wilcken *Chr.*415.78, *POxy.*520.1, 2 (both ii A.D.):—written **-πωλεῖον** in Aen. Tact.30.1, Poll.7.16. ⊛ **-πωλις**, ιδος, ἡ, fem. of παντοπώλης, *PRyl.*227.3 (iii A.D.). **-ρέκτης**, ου, ὁ, (ῥέζω) = πανοῦργος, Ἔρως *Anacreont.*10.11, cf. Porph.*Abst.*1.42, Jul.*Or.*6.197b. II. (ὀρέγομαι) *all-desiring*, Adam.1.16, 2.41.

**πάντοσε**, Adv. *every way, in all directions*, π. ἐποίχεσθαι Il.5.508; φοιτᾶν 12.266; παπταίνειν 13.649, etc.; cf. ἐΐσος: in Prose, X.*An.*7. 2.23, *HG* 7.4.4, Arist.*de An.*413ᵃ29: c. gen., π. θειλοπέδων *AP* 9.668. 10 (Marian.).

**παντό-σεμνος**, ον, = πάνσεμνος, A.*Eu.*637. **-σοφος**, ον, = πάνσοφος, Pl.Com.90. **-σώμᾰτος**, ον, *incarnate in all bodies*, θεός *Corp.Herm.*5.10.

⊛ **πάντοτε**, Adv. *always*, Philem.187, Arist.*EN* 1166ᵃ28, Men.*Mon.* 324, 720; twice in Lxx, *Wi.*11.21, 19.18, cf. *BGU* 1123.8 (i B.C.), *Ev. Matt.*26.11, al., *IG* 3.1362, 7.2713, D.Chr.32.37, etc.: condemned by the Atticists, who recommend διαπαντός or ἑκάστοτε, Phryn.82, Moer.p.319 P.

**παντό-τεκνος**, ἡ, *Mother of All*, epith. of Μήτηρ Θεῶν, *IG*2. 2116. **-τεχνής**, ές, = πάντεχνος, Orph.*H*.10.20.

**παντότης**, ητος, ἡ, *all-ness*, i.e. *integrality*, opp. ὁλότης (whole-ness, totality), Dam.*Pr*.158, al., Simp.*in Ph*.785.8; ἡ π. ἡ νοητή Procl.*in Ti*.1.426, cf. ib.390.

**παντο-τῑνάκτης**, ου, ὁ, *All-Shaker*, epith. of Zeus, Orph.*H*.15. 8. **-τολμος**, ον, = πάντολμος, A.*Ag*.221 (lyr.), 1237. **-τρόφος**, ον, = παντρόφος, Id.*Fr*.192.4 (anap.), Lxx *Wi*.16.25.

**παντουργός**, όν, = πανοῦργος, φωτὶ παντουργῷ φρένας S.*Aj*.445, cf. Eust.524.37. II. *creating all*, Dam.*Pr*.57, cf. Eust.29.31.

**παντοῦχος**, ον, *all-containing* or *-embracing*, συναίρεσις Dam.*Pr*.66; ἐνέργεια π. τοῦ ἑνός ib.117.

**παντο-φᾰγία**, ἡ, *indiscriminate eating*, Lxx 4*Ma*.1.27. **-φάρυγξ** [φᾶ], υγγος, ὁ, *glutton*, Eust.1837.39.

**παντ-όφθαλμος**, ον, *all-eyes*, ἴκτιν Ar.*Fr*.628.

**παντο-φόβος**, ον, *all-fearing*, Cael.Aur.*CP*3.12. **-φόρος**, ον, = πάμφορος, χώρα Arist.*Pol*.1326ᵇ28. **-φυής**, ές, *all-producing*, φλέδων Timo 37, cf. Orph.*H*.11.10, Dam.*Pr*.2, al. **-φυρτος**, ον, *mixed all together*, A.*Eu*.554 (lyr.); cf. πάμφυρτος. **-χάρυβδις** [χᾰ], εως, ἡ, *all-devouring gulf* or *whirlpool*, Bgk. for ποντοχ- in Hippon. 85.1. **-χροος**, ον, *of all kinds of colours*, Orph.*H*.43.4.

⊛ **πάν-τρητος**, ον, *all-pierced*: αὐλοῦ πάντρητον *the part* of the flute *in which the holes are*, Plu.2.853e. **-τρομος**, ον, *all-trembling, timid*, πελειάς A.*Th*.294 (lyr.). ⊛ **-τροπος**, ον, *all-routed, tumultuous*, π. φυγᾷ ib.953 (lyr.). II. *assuming all modes of existence*, Dam. *Pr*.13. **-τρόφος**, ον, *all-nurturing*, Γᾶ *AP*7.476 (Mel.). **-τῠχία**, ἡ, *general prosperity*, *GDI*1567.4 (Dodona).

**παντ-ώνια**· παντοδαπά, Hsch. **-ώνῠμος**, ον, *all-celebrated*, *Epigr.Gr*.415 (Egypt).

⊛ **πάντως**, Adv., (πᾶς) *in all ways*, ἄλλως τε π. καί.., i.e. *especially* (*since*).., A.*Pers*.689, *Eu*.726, Pl.*Ap*.35d; σκιδνάμενον πάντῃ π. Parm.2.3; περιφέρεσθαι καὶ π. φέρεσθαι Pl.*Cra*.411b, cf. *Grg*.527a: in Hom. always folld. by οὐ, *in no wise, by no means*, Il.8.450, Od.19.91, al.; πάντως γὰρ οὐ πείσεις νιν A.*Pr*.335, cf. Hdt.5.34, Pl.*Grg*.497b, etc.: without οὐ first in Parm. l. c., A. (v. supr.); ἔδεε πάντως it was *absolutely* necessary, Hdt.1.31; εἰ δὴ δεῖ γε π. Id.7.10.θ'; π. θελῆσαι to wish *at all hazards*, Id.2.42; εἰ π. ἐλεύσονται if they *positively will* go, Id.6.9; π. κου πυνθάνεαι *no doubt*, Id.7.157: with an Adj., π. ἀναρίστητος Alex.233: freq. with πᾶς or its derivs., Th.7.87, Pl.*Criti*.107d, al.; cf. πάντῃ II. II. in strong affirmations, *at all events, at any rate*, A.*Pr*.16, Hdt.5.111, Pl.*Ap*.33d, 1*Ep.Cor*.9.22, etc.; so νηστεύωμεν δὲ π. Ar.*Th*.984 (lyr.); π. κρέ' ἡμῖν ἐστίν Ephipp.15.11; π. γε μήν Ar.*Eq*.232; π. δήπου Id.*Th*.805; *assuredly*, opp. ἴσως, Jul.*Or*.7.222a; παρήγγειλά σοι ὅτι μὴ ἀπέλθῃς.., καὶ ἀπῆλθες π. and you did (emphat.), *Sammelb*.7249.5 (iii/iv A.D.); τάχ' οὖν.. μᾶλλον δὲ π. nay rather *I am sure*, Herod.7.89; π. ὅτι.. *evidently* because.., Dam.*Pr*.96 (but, *it follows that*.., ib.86). 2. c. imper., in command or entreaty, Hdt.1.156, etc.; ἀλλ' ἐμοὶ πείθεσθε π. do *but* obey me, Eup.357; π. παρατίθετε *just* put on the table, Pl.*Smp*.175b; καὶ τὸ ἱερεῖον δὲ π. ἡμῖν ἀπόστειλον *be sure to* send.., *PCair.Zen*.191.14 (iii B.C.). 3. in answers, *by all means, no doubt*, Pl.*R*.574b; πάντως γάρ.. Ar.*Pl*.273; π. δήπου And.1.102, Pl.*Phd*.75e, etc.

**πάνῠ** [ᾰ], Adv., (πᾶς) *altogether*, first in Xenoph.1.18, then in Trag. and Att., mostly in Prose: 1. with Verbs, A.*Ch*.861 (anap.), Pl. *Cra*.386c, *Euthd*.272d, etc.; π. μανθάνω *perfectly*, Ar.*Ra*.65,195; ὡς π. εἰδῆτε X.*An*.6.1.31: with Adjs., *very, exceedingly*, π. πολλοί, ὀλίγοι, μικρός, etc., *very* many or few, *very* small, A.*Ag*.1456 (anap.), Pl. *Ap*.25b, Arist.*HA*542ᵃ5; π. ταρφύς A.*Pers*.926 (anap.); π. πλούσιοι Lys.19.15, etc.: freq. in opposed clauses, οὐ πονηρός, ἀλλὰ καὶ π. χρηστός D.21.83; οὐκ ὀρθῶς, οὐδὲ δικαίως, ἀλλὰ καὶ π. αἰσχρῶς ibid.: after the Adj., ὀλίγοι π., σπάνιος π., X.*An*.4.7.14 (v.l.), 1.9.27, cf. Pl.*Cra*.402a; separated from it, ἐκτὸς π. τινῶν ὀλίγων Id.*R*.605c, cf. *Euthd*.287b: with Nouns in adj. sense, π. εἶναι ὑβριστής Id.*Ap*. 26e: in late writers with Sup., π. φαυλότατος Sch.Ar.*Ra*.1363, cf. Ath.1.22d (π. γάρ ἐστιν ὡρικωτάτη is dub. in Crates Com.40): with Advbs., π. ταχύ Eup.311; ταχὺ π. Ar.*Pl*.57; π. σφόδρα ib.25,745, Pl.*Ap*.25a; σφόδρα π. Aeschin.2.36; π. πολύ *very* much, Pl.*Chrm*. 157d, X.*Cyr*.6.1.41, etc.; μόγις π. Pl.*Ap*.21b; π. μόλις or μόλις π., Philem.88, Eub.30; εὖ π. Theopomp.Com.14, etc.: with adverbial phrases, π. σπουδῇ in *very great* haste, D.20.105; σπουδῇ π. Th.8. 89; π. ἐν τῷ μεγίστῳ κινδύνῳ ib.50; π. ἐξ εἰκότος λόγου Pl.*Euthd*. 305e; ἐν ὀλίγῳ χρόνῳ π. Id.*Hp.Ma*.282e; π. παρὰ πολλοῖς Id.*Euthd*. 305c; π. ἐπὶ σμικροῖς Id.*Ap*.40a; ἀπὸ σμικροῦ π. Ar.*Pl*.377: with part., π. ἀδικῶν if *ever so* criminal, Th.3.44. 2. strengthd., καὶ πάνυ Id.2.11, X.*Mem*.1.3.13, Pl.*Ap*.17c, *Euthd*.276d, *Cra*.400c; δοκεῖ μοι.. καὶ π. οὐδὲ εἶναι ἡ ἐπίκλησις αὕτη I believe this name *actually* did not exist, Th.1.3. 3. οὐ πάνυ not *quite*, οὐ π. τι μανθάνω Pl.*Euthd*. 286e, cf. *Phd*.62a, *Prt*.331e, X.*An*.6.1.26, etc.; ἡ οὐσία οὐδὲ τριῶν ταλάντων π. τι ἦν not *quite* so much.., D.59.7; οὐ π. εὐδαιμονικὸς.., ἔτι δ' ἴσως ἧττον Arist.*EN*1099ᵇ3: sts. with litotes, not *quite*, implying 'not *at all*', ταῦτα νεκρῷ μὲν οἷόν τε ποιεῖν, ζῶντι δὲ οὐ π. Hp.*Art*. 46; εὐφόρως δὲ οὐ π. ἔχει it is not *very* (or not *at all*) easy, ib.77; οὐ π. μοίρας εὐδαιμονίσαι πρώτης *hardly* to be congratulated.., S.*OC*144 (anap.); οὐ π. προσίεμαι X.*Mem*.2.8.5. 4. in affirmative answers, *by all means, no doubt*, Ar.*Pl*.393: mostly with a Particle added, πάνυ γε Pl.*Alc*.1.107e, etc.; καὶ πάνυ γε Id.*Chrm*.154e; π. γε, ἀλλά.. *very well*, but.., D.21.89; πάνυ μὲν οὖν Ar.*Pl*.97, Pl.*Euthphr*. 13d, al.; πάνυ καλῶς *no I thank you*, Ar.*Ra*.512. II. ὁ πάνυ the *real*, the *very* (τοῦ π. Διός Luc.*Icar*.2): hence, the *excellent*, the *famous*, οἱ π. τῶν στρατιωτῶν Th.8.1, D.C.*Fr*.70.6; ὁ π. Περικλῆς X. *Mem*.3.5.1; οἱ π. ἐπ' ἀξιώματος *IG*12(7).407.14 (Amorgos); οἱ π. alone, prob. in Th.8.89 (omitting στρατηγῶν); ἡ π. Luc.*Vit.Auct*. 22.

**πάν-υγρος** [ᾰ], ον, *quite damp* or *wet*, Plu.2.355f, Man.1.87, etc.; τὸ π. Γαληνοῦ, of an application, Aët.15.33; mostly v.l. for πάρυγρος (q.v.). **-υπείροχος**, ον, *pre-eminent, supreme*, θεοί *IG*3.171a, cf. Opp.*C*.1.311, *AP*9.656,741, *IGRom*.4.415 (Pergam., iii A.D.), *MAMA*1.306 (Phrygia), Dioscorus in *PLit.Lond*.98 ii 8: neut. pl. as Advb., Opp.*C*.2.63, al. ⊛ **-υπέρτατος**, η, ον, *highest of all*, μεγέθει π. Arist.*Mu*.397ᵃ15; π. ἐρρίζωνται, of trees, are rooted *highest* on the mountain, A.R.1.1122: hence, *most remote* or *farthest from land*, π. εἰν ἁλὶ κεῖται, of Ithaca, Od.9.25. 2. *supreme*, Call.*Jov*.91, Orph. *H*.19.2, al. **-υπέρφρων**, ον, gen. ονος, *exceeding haughty*, ib. 61.12.

**πάνυσσα**, ἡ, *band, fillet*, Hsch.

**πᾰν-υστάτιος** [τᾰ], α, ον, later for sq., Call.*Lav.Pall*.54, *IG*14. 1937 (Rome). **-ύστᾰτος**, η, ον, *last of all*, Il.23.532,547, Od. 9.452, S.*Tr*.874, E.*Med*.1041: neut. as Adv., *for the very last time*, S.*Aj*.858, E.*Alc*.164: also pl., πανύστατα Id.*HF*457.

⊛ **πᾰν-ῳδός**, όν, *all-tuneful*, ἀχώ *IG*4²(1).130.21 (Epid.). **-ώδῠνος**, ον, *all-grievous*, λιμός App.*BC*5.67. **-ώδῠρος**, ον, *most unhappy*, *Supp.Epigr*.1.572.10 (Egypt). **-ωλεθρί**, Adv. = πανωλεθρίᾳ (which is v.l.), J.*AJ*3.2.5. **-ωλεθρία**, ἡ, *utter destruction*; by early writers used in dat., πανωλεθρίῃ ἀπολόμενοι Hdt.2.120; πανωλεθρίᾳ δὴ (τὸ λεγόμενον).. ἀπώλετο Th.7.87: later in gen., D.C.56.4: nom. pl., Plu.2.1049b. **-ώλεθρος**, ον, (ὄλεθρος) *utterly destroyed*, π. ἐξαπόλλυνται Hdt.6.37 (v.l. -θρως, found also Apollod.3.16.2); πανωλέθρους τὸ πᾶν.. ὀλέσθαι S.*El*.1009; π. πεσεῖν, γενέσθαι, A.*Ch*.934, *Eu*. 552 (lyr.); πόλιν πανώλεθρον ἐκθαμνίσαι Id.*Th*.71; γένος π. ἀναστρέψαι Ar.*Av*.1239; π. ξυναρπάσαι τινά S.*Aj*.839, etc. 2. in moral sense, *utterly abandoned*, τοῖς π. Ἀτρείδαις Id.*Ph*.322; ἡ π. μήτηρ E.*El*.86; οὔτε σὺν πανωλέθροισιν οὔτ' ἄνευ πανωλέθρων Ar.*Lys*. 1039. II. Act., *all-destructive, ruinous*, π. κακόν Hdt.6.85; ἐμβολαὶ A.*Pers*.562 (lyr.); θεός Id.*Supp*.414. **-ώλεια**, ἡ, = πανωλεθρία, *CIG*4224f (Lycia), *Et.Gud*.71.12. **-ώλης**, ες, (ὄλλυμι) = πανώλεθρος I. 1, π. ὄλλυσθαι A.*Th*.552; ἔρρειν π. Id.*Pers*.732; ἤτω ἐξώλης τε καὶ πανώλης, a form of execration, *Wiener Denkschr*.44(6) p.54 (Cilicia). 2. in moral sense, = πανώλεθρος I. 2, S.*OC*1264, *El*.544, E.*El*.60. II. Act., *all-destructive*, συμφοραί S.*OC*1015. **-ωνία**, ἡ, *general sale of wares*, Zos.2.38. ⊛ **-ώνιος**, ον, and Adv. -ίως, *with all saleable products*, *Inscr.Cypr*.135.10,22 H. **-ωπήεις**, εσσα, εν, = πανόψιος, *visible to all*, *APl*.4.166 (Even.). **-ωρος**, ον, *produced in every season*, φέρμα A.*Supp*.690 (lyr.). **-ωφελής**, ές, *all-beneficial*, prob. in Herm.ap.Stob.1.49.44.

⊛ **πάξ**, exclam. to end a discussion, *enough!*, Men.*Epit*.517, Diph.96, Herod.7.114 (misunderstood by Hsch., πάξ· ὑπόδημα εὐυπόδητον); κόγξ· ὁμοίως πάξ is prob. cj. for κόγξ· ὅμπαξ in Hsch.

**πάξαιτο**, v. πήγνυμι.

⊛ **παξαμᾶς**, ᾶ, ὁ, *biscuit* (so called from the baker Paxamos), Gal.14. 537 tit., Suid.:—Dim. **παξαμάδιον**, τό, Gal.14.554, Tz.*H*.2.574; **παξαμάτιον**, *Gloss*.

⊛ ***πάομαι**, fut. πάσομαι [ᾱ] A.*Eu*.177 (lyr.); redupl. πεπάσομαι Pempel.ap.Stob.4.25.52: aor. ἐπᾱσάμην *Leg.Gort*.6.5, al., Thgn.146, A.*Fr*.215, Call.*Cer*.128, Theoc.15.90:—mostly Dor., Arc., and poet. (used by X., v. infr.), *get, acquire*, πασάμενος ἐπίτασσε, i.e. order your own slaves, Theoc. l. c.: chiefly used in pf. πέπᾱμαι, = κέκτημαι, *possess*, Pi.*P*.8.73, *Fr*.105, E.*Ion*675, Ar.*Av*.943 (lyr.), *Leg.Gort*.9.43, *SIG*1164 (Dodona), *Foed.Delph.Pell*.2 A 18, *SIG*306.7 (Tegea, iv B.C.); 3 pl. πέπανται X.*An*.3.3.18; inf. πεπᾶσθαι Sol.13.7, E.*Andr*. 641, Theoc.10.32, Diotog.ap.Stob.4.7.62; part. πεπᾱμένος A.*Ag*. 835, X.*An*.6.1.12 (written πεπεμμένος in error, *IG*4²(1).77.18 (Epid., ii B.C.)): plpf. ἐπεπάμην X.*An*.1.9.19 (dub. l.), *AP*7.67 (Leon.).

**πᾱός**, ὁ, Dor. for πηός:—hence **πᾱόω**, in aor. Pass., *become a* πηός, Alc.*Supp*.23.6 (p.26 Lobel).

**παπᾶ**, v. sq. I ad fin.

**πᾰπαῖ** (not παπαί, Hdn.Gr.2.933), exclam. of suffering, whether mental, as A.*Pers*.1031, or (more freq.) physical, Ar.*Ach*.1214, etc.; doubled, A. l. c., *Ag*.1114; φεῦ παπαῖ, παπαῖ μάλ' αὖθις S.*Ph*.792; also παππαπαππαπαῖ ib.754; παπαῖ, ἀπαππαπαῖ, παπᾶ παπᾶ παπᾶ παπαῖ ib.746. II. of surprise, Hdt.8.26; π., οἷον λέγεις you don't say so!, Pl.*Lg*.704c; also παπαπαπαῖ Ar.*Th*.1191: c. gen., παπαῖ τῶν ἐπαίνων Luc.*Cont*.23; expressing scorn, S.*Fr*.153.

**πᾰπαιάξ**, Com. exaggeration of παπαῖ, ἀππαπαῖ παπαιάξ Ar.*V*.235, cf. Luc.*Fug*.33. II. exclam. of surprise, E.*Cyc*.153, Ar.*Lys*. 924.

**Παπαῖος**, ὁ, Scythian name of Zeus, Hdt.4.59.

**πάπας**, v. πάππας.

**παπάω**, *handle*, *EM*651.1.

⊛ **παπίας**, α, ὁ, *janitor* or *keeper of the Palace*, Tz.*H*.3.839.

⊛ **παππάζω**, (πάππας) *call* any one *papa*, οὐδέ τέ μιν παῖδες ποτὶ γούνασι παππάζουσιν Il.5.408. II. abs., *say papa, prattle like a child*, παππάζεσκες Q.S.3.474.

**παππάξ**, **πᾰπᾰπαππάξ**, sounds to imitate a *crepitus ventris*, Ar. *Nu*.390 sq.

⊛ **πάππας**, ου, ὁ, *papa*, child's word for *father*; mostly in voc., πάππα φίλε Od.6.57; χαῖρε π. φίλτατε Philem.42: in acc., πάππαν καλεῖν Ar.*Pax* 120, *Ec.*645:—nom. **πάπας**, Corn.*ND* 25, *PGiss.*80.3 (ii A.D.); acc. πάπαν *BMus.Inscr.*918 (Halic.); dat. πάπᾳ Epicur. *Herc.*176 p.49 V. (Syracusan, acc. to Eust.565.17, but **πᾶς** (which should prob. be πᾶ, for Eust. adds ὥσπερ καὶ μᾶ μήτηρ) is Syrac. acc. to *EM* 651.7).

**παππασμός**, ὁ, *calling out 'papa'*, Suid.

**παππεπίπαππος**, ὁ, one's *grandfather's grandfather*, Nicopho 22, = Philonid.15.

⊕ **παππίας**, ου, ὁ, Dim. of πάππας, *dear little papa*, a term of endearment, Ar.*V.*297, *Pax* 128, Ephipp.21.

**παππίδιον** [πῐ], τό, = foreg., Ar.*Eq.*1215, *V.*655, Jul.*Caes.*309d, 331b.

**παππίζω**, = παππάζω, *coax* or *wheedle one's father*, Ar.*V.*609, cf. Eust.565.32.

⊕ **παππικός**, ή, όν, *inherited from one's grandfather*, *BGU* 410.23 (ii A.D.).

**παπποκτόνος**, ον, *grandfather-slaying*, Lyc.1034.

**πάππος**, ὁ, *grandfather*, Hdt.3.55, Ar.*Eq.*447, *Nu.*65, And.3.6; π. καὶ πάππου πατήρ Pl.*Lg.*856d; π. ὁ πρὸς μητρὸς ἢ πατρός on the mother's or father's side, ibid., cf. *CIG* 1628, 3332, Poll.3.16: in pl., *grandparents*, *CIG* 2837 *b* (p.1117); also, generally, *ascendants*, *ancestors*, Pl.*Tht.*174e; ἐπὶ πάππους δύο ἢ τρεῖς ἢ πλείους [ὁρίζεσθαι πολίτην] Arist.*Pol.*1275ᵇ24; εἰς τρίτον π. ἀναφέρειν τὸ γένος D.H.4.47; φυσάτω πάππους παρ' ἡμῖν Ar.*Av.*765, with pun on signf. III, cf. Sch. ad loc. 2. a character in Com. dramas, *Pantaloon*, Poll.4.143. II. *down on the seeds* of certain plants, γραίας ἀκάνθης π. S.*Fr.*868; π. ἀπ' ἀκάνθης Eub.107.19: pl., Thphr.*Sign.*37, Arat.921, Dsc.4.96, *Alex.*33; = ἀκανθίς II, Plin.*HN* 25.168. 2. *first down on the chin*, opp. μύσταξ, Ruf.*Onom.*49, Poll.2.80, Eust.1353.57, Suid. III. a small bird in whose nest the cuckoo lays (cf. ὑπολαΐς), Ael.*NA* 3.30, Sch.Ar.*Av.*766.

**παππο-σπέρματα**, τά, *seeds crowned with down*, Thphr.*HP* 7.3.2. **-φόνος**, ον, = παπποκτόνος, Theoc.*Syrinx* 10.

**παππυλιάζω**, v.l. for ποππ- (q. v.).

**παππ-ώδης**, ες, *woolly, downy*, σπέρματα Thphr.*HP* 6.4.11, cf. 6.6.6. ⊕ **-ωνῠμικῶς**, Adv. *called after one's grandfather*, formed like πατρωνυμικῶς, Suid. s. v. Ἀλκείδης. ⊕ **-ῷος**, α, ον, = παππικός, βίος Ar.*Av.*1452; ὄνομα Pl.*La.*179a, etc.; ἔρανος ὁ λεγόμενος π. the so-called *ancestral* fund, i. e. the fund contributed by your grandfathers, Ar.*Lys.*653; τὰν π. προξενίαν *Schwyzer* 334.6 (Delph., ii B.C.).

**πάπραξ**, ακος, ὁ, a Thracian lake-fish, Hdt.5.16.

**παπταίνω**, aor. ἐπάπτηνα (in Hom. always without augm.): Ep. Verb, *look about one with a sharp, searching glance*, πάντοσε παπταίνων, ὥς τ' αἰετός Il.17.674; δεινὸν π., αἰεὶ βαλέοντι ἐοικώς Od.11.608, cf. Il.13.551, etc.; πάντοσε παπταίνοντε, φόνον ποτιδεγμένω αἰεί Od.22.380; πάπταινε καὶ φρόντιζε A.*Pr.*1034; μηκέτι πάπταινε πόρσιον Pi.*O.*1.114: folld. by a relat. clause, πάντοσε παπταίνων, μή τις χρόα χαλκῷ ἐπαύρῃ Il.13.649, cf. A.*Pr.*336; πάπτηνεν δὲ ἕκαστος, ὅπῃ φύγοι αἰπὺν ὄλεθρον *looked about* [to see] how.., Il.16.283; πάπτηνεν.., εἴ τις ἔτ' ἀνδρῶν ζωὸς ὑποκλοπέοιτο Od.22.381: with Preps., ἀμφὶ ἓ παπτήνας Il.4.497, 15.574; μοι ὅσσε Τρωϊκὸν ἂν πεδίον παπταίνετον 23.464; τρέσσε δὲ παπτήνας ἐφ' ὁμίλου 11.546; π... κατὰ στίχας 17.84; πάντῃ π. πρὸς πέτρην Od.12.233; πάντοσε π. ποτὶ τοίχους 22.24; π. μεθ' ὁμήλικας *look wistfully* after his comrades, Hes.*Op.*444; πρὸς αὐγάς Parm.15; εἴσω τῆσδε π. πύλης S.*Aj.*11; ἐς γάμον ἄλλης π. *AP* 7.700 (Diod.): also in later Prose, π. περὶ ἕδρεσιν Onos.3.2; ἐπὶ θάτερα Plu.*Pomp.*71; πρός τινα Id.*Ant.*37. II. c. acc., *look round for, look after*, παπταίνων ἥρωα Μαχάονα Il.4.200; π. Αἴαντα μέγαν 17.115; π. τὰ πόρσω Pi.*P.*3.22; τὰ μακρά Id.*I.*7(6).44; παπτάναις (Aeol. aor. 1 part.) ἀρίγνωτον πέδιλον *having set eyes on..*, Id.*P.*4.95; εἰρεσίαν ἀδάητον ἔτ' ὄθμασι *Hymn.Is.*157; τὸν δ' ἀγρίοις ὄσσοισι π. *glaring at* him, S.*Ant.*1231.

**παπτᾰλάομαι**, = foreg., Lyc.1162.

⊕ **πᾰπῠλιών**, ῶνος, ὁ, = Lat. *papilio*, *tent*, *Sammelb.*1.3 (iii A.D.), *Edict.Diocl.*19.4: also **παπυλεών** Procop.*Pers.*2.21; gen. sg. written παπυλαιῶνος, Suid.

**πᾰπῡρ-εών**, ῶνος, ὁ, = παπυρών, Aq.*Ex.*2.3,5. **-ικός**, ή, όν, *of papyrus*, ἕλος *BGU* 1121.10,18 (i B.C.). **-ινος**, η, ον, *made of papyrus*, [κιβωτός] *Inscr.Délos* 443 *Bb* 138 (ii B.C.); σκάφη *PLeid.V.* 11; βᾶρις Plu.2.358a; σόλια *POxy.*1742.6 (iv A.D.). **-ιον**, τό, Dim. of πάπυρος, Dsc.*Eup.*1.183, *Gp.*4.7.1.

**πᾰπῡροειδής**, ές, *like papyrus*, σκῆπτρον *OGI* 56.63 (Egypt. iii B.C.).

⊕ **πάπῡρος** [ᾰ], ὁ and ἡ, *papyrus*, *Cyperus Papyrus*, Thphr.*HP* 4.8.2, Dsc.1.86, Porph.ap.Eus.*PE* 3.7, etc.; as food, *UPZ* 91.8, 96.40 (ii B.C.). 2. *linen, cord*, etc., *made of it*, *AP* 6.249 (Antip.), *Anacreont.*30.5, Plin.*HN* 13.72, etc. [Prop. ⏑–⏑, as in *Anacreont.* l.c. and Latin poets, but in *AP* l.c., ⏑⏑⏑.]

**πᾰπῡροφάγος** [φᾰ], ον, *eating the root of papyrus*, of the Egyptians, Sch.A.*Supp.*761.

**πᾰπῡρ-ώδης**, ες, *like papyrus*, Gal.19.152, Sch.E.*Or.*147. **-ών**, ῶνος, ὁ, *papyrus-bed*, *IG* 14.1047.

**πάρ**, Elean, = περί, *SIG* 9.4 (Olympia, vi B.C.), etc. II. v. sq.

⊕ **παρά** [ρᾰ], Ep. and Lyr. also **παραί**: shortd. **πάρ**, in Hom., Lyr. (but rarely in Trag., in lyr. passages, A.*Supp.*553, S.*Tr.*636), and in all dialects exc. Att., *GDI* 5434.8 (Paros), *IG* 5(2).3.14 (Tegea, iv B.C.), *Inscr.Magn.*26.28 (Thess.), etc.:—Prep. c. gen., dat., and acc., prop. *beside*: hence,

A. WITH GEN. prop. denoting motion *from the side of, from beside, from*: I. of Place, πὰρ νηῶν ἔλθωμεν Il.13.744; παρὰ ναῦφιν ἐλευσόμεθ' 12.225, etc.; παρ' Ὠκεανοῖο ῥοάων.. ἐπερχομένη Od.22.197; πὰρ νηῶν ἀπώσεται Il.8.533, etc.; δῶρα π. νηὸς ἐνεικέμεν 19.194; φάσγανον ὀξὺ ἐρυσσάμενος π. μηροῦ 1.190, cf. 21.173; σπασσάμενος.. ἄορ παχέος π. μηροῦ 16.473; πλευρὰ παρ' ἀσπίδος ἐξεφάνθη was exposed *beside* the shield, 4.468, cf. A.*Th.*624. II. commonly of Persons, 1. with Verbs of going or coming, bringing, etc., ἦλθε.. πὰρ Διός Il.2.787; παρ' Αἰήταο πλέουσα Od.12.70, etc.; ἀγγελίη ἥκει π. βασιλέος Hdt.8.140.α'; αὐτομολήσαντες π. βασιλέως X.*An.*1.7.13; ἐξεληλυθὼς παρ' Ἀριστάρχου D.21.117; ὁ π. τινὸς ἥκων his messenger, X.*Cyr.*4.5.53; so οἱ π. τινός Th.7.10, *Ev.Marc.*3.21, etc.; ὅστις ἀφικνεῖτο τῶν π. βασιλέως πρὸς αὐτόν X.*An.*1.1.5, etc.; τεύχεα καλὰ φέρουσα παρ' Ἡφαίστοιο *from* his workshop, Il.18.137, cf. 617, etc.; ἀπαγγέλλειν τι π. τινός X.*An.*2.1.20; σὺ δὲ οἰμώζειν αὐτοῖς παρ' ἐμοῦ λέγε Luc.*DMort.*1.2. 2. *issuing from* a person, γίγνεσθαι π. τινός to be born *from*, Pl.*Smp.*179b; λόγος (sc. ἐστί) π. Ἀθηναίων c. acc. et inf., Hdt.8.55: freq. following a Noun, δόξα ἡ π. τῶν ἀνθρώπων glory *from* (*given by*) men, Pl.*Phdr.*232a; ἡ π. τινὸς εὔνοια the favour *from*, i. e. *of*, any one, X.*Mem.*2.2.12; τὸ παρ' ἐμοῦ ἀδίκημα *done by* me, Id.*Cyr.*5.5.13; τὰ π. τινός *all that issues from* any one, as commands, commissions, Id.*An.*2.3.4, etc.; or promises, gifts, presents, Id.*Mem.*3.11.13; τὰ παρ' ἐμοῦ my opinions, Pl.*Smp.*219a; παρ' ἑωυτοῦ διδούς giving *from* oneself, i. e. *from* one's own *means*, Hdt. 2.129, 8.5; παρ' ἑαυτοῦ προσετίθει X.*HG* 6.1.3; νόμον θὲς παρ' ἐμοῦ *by* my *advice*, Pl.*Prt.*322d; αὐτοὶ παρ' αὐτῶν *of* themselves, Id.*Tht.* 150d, cf. *Phdr.*235c. 3. with Verbs of receiving, obtaining, and the like, τυχεῖν τινος π. τινός Od.6.290, 15.158; πὰρ δ' ἄρα μιν Ταφίων πρίατο 14.452; ἀρέομαι πὰρ μὲν Σαλαμῖνος Ἀθαναίων χάριν Pi.*P.*1.76; εὑρέσθαι τι π. τῶν θεῶν Isoc.9.14, cf. *IG* 1².40.10; δέχεσθαι, λαμβάνειν, ἁρπάζειν π. τινός, Th.1.20, X.*Oec.*9.11, Hes.*Th.*914; ἀντιάσαι, αἰτήσασθαι π. τινός, S.*El.*870 (lyr.), X.*HG* 3.1.4; ἀξιοῖ π. τοῦ ἰατροῦ φάρμακον πιὼν ἐξεμέσαι τὸ νόσημα Pl.*R.*406d; κόσμος τοῖς πράξασι γίγνεται π. τῶν ἀκουσάντων Id.*Mx.*236e: without Verb, ὁ καρπὸς ὁ π. τῶν δημάρχων *IG* 1².76.27: with Verbs of learning, etc., μεμαθηκέναι π. τινῶν Hdt.2.104, etc. 4. with Pass. Verbs, πὰρ Διὸς.. μῆνις ἐτύχθη Il.15.122; π. θεῶν ἡ τοιαύτη μανία δίδοται Pl.*Phdr.*245c, etc.; τὰ π. τῶν θεῶν σημαινόμενα, συμβουλευόμενα, X.*Cyr.*1.6.2; τὰ π. τινὸς λεγόμενα ib.6.1.42; τὰ π. τῆς τύχης δωρηθέντα *the presents of..*, Isoc.4.26; με π. σοῦ σοφίας πληρωθήσεσθαι Pl.*Smp.*175e. III. rarely for παρά c. dat., *by, near*, πὰρ ποδός Pi.*P.*10.62, 3.60; παρὰ δὲ κυανέων πελαγέων dub. l. in S.*Ant.*966 (lyr.); τὸν Ῥειτὸν τὸν παρὰ τοῦ ἄστεως *IG* 1².81.5; πολλοὶ παρ' ἀμφοτέρων ἔπιπτον, = ἀμφοτέρωθεν, D.S.19.42. IV. π. τῆς συγχωρήσεώς τινος *without* his consent, *BCH* 46.337 (Teos).

B. WITH DAT. denoting rest *by the side of* any person or thing, answering the question *where?* I. of Places, κατ' ἄρ' ἕζετ'.. πὰρ πυρί, ἔκειτο π. σηκῷ, Od.7.154, 9.319; νέμονται π. πέτρῃ 13.408; ἑστάοτες παρ' ὄχεσφιν Il.8.565; πὰρ ποσὶ μαρναμένων ἐκυλίνδετο *at* their feet, 14.411, etc.; π. θύρῃσι *at* the door, 7.346; π. ῥηγμῖνι θαλάσσης 2.773; δεῖπνον.. εἵλοντο παρ' ὄχθῃσιν ποταμοῖο Od.6.97, cf. Il.4.475, 20.53, etc.; κεῖσθαι παρ' Ἅιδῃ S.*OT* 972; παρ' οἴνῳ *over* wine, ib. 780, etc. II. of persons, *beside*, πὰρ δὲ οἱ αὐτῷ εἷσε Θεοκλύμενον Od.15.285; κεῖτο παρὰ μνηστῇ ἀλόχῳ Il.9.556, cf. 6.246, etc.; παρ' ἀνδράσιν εὐνάζεσθαι Od.5.119; δαίνυσθαι π. τινί 8.243; πὰρ δέ οἱ ἑστήκει stood *by* him, Il.4.367. 2. *at* one's *house* or *place, with* one, μένειν π. τισί 9.427; θητευέμεν ἄλλῳ, ἀνδρὶ παρ' ἀκλήρῳ Od.11.490; φιλέεσθαι π. τινί Il.13.627; παρ' ἑωυτοῖσι *at* their own *house*, Hdt.1.105, cf. 86; παιδευθῆναι π. τινί X.*Cyr.*1.2.15; καταλύειν π. τινί D.18.82 (but παρά τινα καταλῦσαι Th.1.136), etc.: hence οἱ παρ' ἐμοί those *of my household*, X.*Mem.*2.7.4, etc.; τὰ παρ' ἐμοί life *with me*, Id.*An.*1.7.4; οἱ παρ' ἡμῖν ἄνθρωποι our people, Pl.*Phd.*64b; ἡ παρ' ἡμῖν πολιτεία, ὁ παρ' ὑμῖν δῆμος, D.15.19; ὁ παρ' αὐτῷ βίοτος one's *own* life, S.*OT* 612; τὸ παρ' ἡμῖν πῦρ Pl.*Phlb.*29f; ὅσος παρ' ὑμῖν ὁ φθόνος φυλάσσεται S.*OT* 382; τὸ παρ' ἡμῖν σῶμα Pl.*Phlb.*29f; also, *in* one's *hands*, τὰ π. τοῖς Ἑλληνοταμίαις ὄντα *IG* 1².91.6; ἔχειν παρ' ἑωυτῷ Hdt. 1.130, etc.; οὔπω παρ' ἐμοὶ τότ' ἦν λέγειν I had no *right* to speak then, Men.*Epit.*98. 3. *before, in the presence of*, ἤειδε π. μνηστῆρσιν Od. 1.154; *before* a judge, δίκας γίγνεσθαι π. τῷ πολεμάρχῳ *IG* 1².16.9; π. Δαρείῳ κριτῇ Hdt.3.160; π. τῷ βασιλεῖ Id.4.65; παρὰ δικασταῖς Th. 1.73; εἰς κρίσιν καθιστάναι τινὰ π. τισί D.18.13: hence παρ' ἐμοί *in* my *judgement*, Hdt.1.32, cf. S.*Tr.*589, E.*Heracl.*881, 1*Ep.Cor.*3.19; π. τούτῳ μέγα δυνήσεται *with* him, Pl.*Grg.*510e. 4. in quoting authors, παρ' Ἐφόρῳ, παρ' Αἰσχίνῃ, π. Θουκυδίδῃ, *in* Ephorus, etc., Plb. 9.2.4, D.H.*Comp.*9,18. III. Arc., = π. c. gen., *from*, καθὰ εἶχον τὰς ἰντολὰς π. τᾷ ἰδίᾳ πόλι *SIG* 559.9 (Megalop., iii B.C.), cf. 558.10 (Ithaca, iii B.C.).

C. WITH ACCUS. in three main senses, I. *beside, near, by*, II. *along*, III. *past, beyond.*

I. *beside, near, by*: 1. with Verbs of coming, going, etc., *to the side of, to*, ἴτην π. νῆας Il.1.347, cf. 8.220, etc.; βῆ.. π. θῖνα 1.34, cf. 327, etc.; τρέψας πὰρ ποταμόν *to the side of..*, 21.603, cf. 3.187: more freq. of persons, εἶμι παρ' Ἥφαιστον *to the chamber of* H., 18.143, cf. Od.1.285, etc.; ἐσιόντες π. τοὺς φίλους Th.2.51, etc.; φοιτᾶν π. τὸν Σωκράτη Pl.*Phd.*59d; πέμπειν ἀγγέλους, πρέσβεις π. τινά, Hdt. 1.141, Th.1.58, etc.; ἄγειν π. τινά Hdt.1.86; καταφυγὴ π. φίλων τινάς Th.2.17. 2. with Verbs of rest, *beside, near, by*, sts. with ref. to past motion (expressed in such phrases as ἧσο παρ' αὐτὸν ἰοῦσα Il.3.406, cf. 11.577), ἕς ῥα θρόνους ἕζοντο παρ' Ἀτρεΐδην Μενέλαον Od.4.51, cf. 13.372; κεῖται ποταμοῖο παρ' ὄχθας lies *stretched beside..*, Il.4.487, cf. 12.381; παρ' ἔμ' ἵστασο come and stand *by* me, 11.314, cf. 592, 20.49, etc.; π. πυθμέν' ἐλαίης θῆκαν Od.13.122; καταθέτω π. τὰ ἴκρια *IG*1$^{2}$.94.28; κοιμήσαντο π. πρυμνήσια they lay down *by*.., Od.12.32, cf. 3.460; ὁ παρ' ἐμὲ καθήμενος Pl.*Euthd.*271b, cf. *Phd.*89b; ἐκάθητο π. τὴν πύλην, π. τὴν ὁδόν, Lxx *Ge.*19.1, *Ev.Marc.* 10.46; παρ' αὐτὸν τὸν καλέσαντα κατακείμενος δειπνῆσαι Thphr.*Char.* 21.2, cf. Pl.*Smp.*175c; ἐκαθέζετο π. τὸν Λύσιν Id.*Ly.*211a, cf. *R.*328c; στὰς παρ' αὐτόν Id.*Phd.*116c; τέμενος νεμόμεσθα..παρ' ὄχθας Il.12.313, cf. 6.34, *IG*1$^{2}$.943.45; τοῦ Εὐρίπου, παρ' ὃν ᾤκει Aeschin.3.90; κατελείφθη π. τὸν νηόν Hdt.4.87; τὴν παρ' ἐμὲ ἐοῦσαν δύναμιν Id.8.140.α' (v. l. ἐμοί); εἶπεν αὐτῷ μένειν παρ' ἑαυτόν X.*Cyr.*1.4.18, cf. *An.*1.9.31, Ar.*Fr.*451, Is.8.16, Alex.248, Demetr.Com.Nov.1.5, *IG*2$^{2}$.654.23 (iii B.C.), Plb.3.26.1, 11.14.3, 28.14.3; ἡ π. θάλασσαν Μακεδονία Th.2.99, cf. S.*El.*184 (lyr.), *Tr.*636 (lyr.); Καρβασυανδῆς π. Καῦνον *IG*1$^{2}$.204.52; τὸ κουρεῖον τὸ π. τοὺς Ἑρμᾶς Lys.23.3, cf. And.1.62, Is.6.20, 8.35, Aeschin.1.182, 3.88, Lycurg.112; τᾶς παστάδος τᾶς παρ' Ἀπόλλωνα *IG*4$^{2}$(1).109iii 146 (Epid.); παρ' ὄμμα *before* one's eyes. E.*Supp.*484; π. πόδας *on* the spot, Phld.*Ir.*p.78 W., *Rh.*2.2 S.; *immediately thereafter*, Plb.1.7.5, 1.8.2, al. **b.** Dor., Boeot., and Thess., = supr. B. II. 2, *at the house of*.., *with* a person, *IG*7.3171.7 (Orchom. Boeot.), *GDI* 1717 (Delph.); παρ' ἁμὲ πολυτίματος [ὁ σῖτος] Ar.*Ach.*759 (Megar.); τοῖς κατοικέντεσσι πὰρ ἀμμέ *IG*9(2).517.18 (Larissa, iii B.C.); τοῖ πὰρ ἀμμὲ πολιτεύματος ib.13; πεπολιτευκὼρ πὰρ ἁμέ *Schwyzer*425.5 (Elis, iii/ii B.C.): so in Att., θέμενος π. γυναῖκας depositing *with*.., Pl. *R.*465c. **3.** with Verbs of striking, wounding, etc., βάλε στῆθος π. μαζόν Il.4.480, etc.; τὸν δ' ἕτερον..κληῖδα παρ' ὦμον πλῆξε 5.146; τύψε κατὰ κληῖδα παρ' αὐχένα 21.117, cf. 4.525, 8.325, etc.; αἰχμὴ δ' ἐξελύθη παρὰ νείατον ἀνθερεῶνα 5.293, cf. 17.310; δησάμενος τελαμῶνι π. σφυρόν ib.290. **4.** with Verbs of placing, examining, etc., *side by side with* .., ὁ ἔλεγχος π. τὸν ἔλεγχον παραβαλλόμενος Pl.*Grg.*475e, cf. *Hp.Mi.*369c, *Smp.*214c, *R.*348a; ἐξέτασον παρ' ἄλληλα τὰ σοὶ κἀμοὶ βεβιωμένα D.18.265; ἄλλα παρ' ἄλλα τιθέμενα..τῶν χρωμάτων Arist.*Mete.*375$^{a}$24. **b.** Geom., παραβάλλειν π. apply an area *to* (i.e. *along*) a finite straight line, Euc.1.44, Archim.*Aequil.*2.1; π. τὴν δοθεῖσαν αὐτοῦ γραμμὴν παρατείναντα Pl. *Men.*87a; ἡ [εὐθεῖα] παρ' ἣν δύνανται αἱ καταγόμεναι τεταγμένως the line *to* which are applied the squares of the ordinates, etc., Apollon. Perg.*Con.*1.11: hence, **c.** Arith., παραβάλλειν τι π. τι divide *by* .. (v. παραβάλλω A. VII. 2); μερίζω τι π. τι Dioph.4.33; ἐπὶ γ' π. ι' multiply by 3 and divide *by* 10, *PLond.*5.1718.2 (vi A.D.). **5.** Geom., *parallel to*.., Democr.155, Arist.*Top.*158$^{b}$31, Archim.*Sph. Cyl.*1.12, al. **6.** metaph. in Gramm., *like, as a parody of*.., π. τὸ Σοφόκλειον, π. τὰ ἐν Τεύκρῳ Σοφοκλέους, Sch.Ar.*Av.*1240, *Nu.*584. **b.** Gramm., of words which differ *as compared with* other words, π. τὸ τοῦ ἔρωτος ὄνομα σμικρὸν παρηγμένον ἐστίν..[τὸ ἥρως] Pl.*Cra.*398d, cf. 399a, *Lg.*654a: hence, *derived from*.., π. τὸ ἔδαφος, δάπεδον, A.D. *Pron.*31.16; π. τὸ δρῶ δρᾶμα Sch.A.R.2.624; σύγκειται [τὸ αὐθέντης] π. τὸ εἶναι..καὶ π. τὸ αὐτός Phryn.*PS*p.24 B. **7.** generally, of Comparison, *alongside of, compared with*, usu. implying superiority, δοκέοντες π. ταῦτα οὐδ' ἂν τοὺς σοφωτάτους ἀνθρώπων Αἰγυπτίους οὐδὲν ἐπεξευρεῖν Hdt.2.160, cf. 7.20, 103; ἡλίου ἐκλείψεις αἳ πυκνότεραι π. τὰ ἐκ τοῦ πρὶν χρόνου μνημονευόμενα ξυνέβησαν Th.1.23, cf. 4.6; τῶν ἁπάντων ἀπερίοπτοί εἰσι π. τὸ νικᾶν Id.1.41; π. τὰ ἄλλα ζῷα ὥσπερ θεοὶ ἄνθρωποι βιοτεύουσι X.*Mem.*1.4.14; φαίνεται π. τὸ ἀλγεινὸν ἡδὺ καὶ π. τὸ ἡδὺ ἀλγεινὸν ἡ ἡσυχία Pl.*R* 584a, cf. *Phdr.*236d, *La.*183c, al.; εὐδαίμων μᾶλλον π. πάντας *BCH*26.332 (Halae); προετέρει π. πάντας *PSI* 4.422.34 (iii B.C.): sts. implying inferiority or defect, ἠλάττωσας αὐτὸν βραχύ τι παρ' ἀγγέλους a little *lower than* the angels, Lxx *Ps.* 8.6; μιᾷ ἡμέρᾳ ὑστεροῦσι π. τὸν ἥλιον lag one day *behind* the sun, Gem.8.19; so perh. παρ' αὐτόν, ὑπὲρ αὐτόν (has passed the ball?) *short of* him, beyond him, Antiph.234; μέγα τοι ἡμέρα παρ' ἡμέραν γιγνομένη γνώμην ἐξ ὀργῆς μεταστῆσαι one day *compared with* another is important.., a day's delay makes a difference, Antipho 5.72; τί γὰρ παρ' ἦμαρ ἡμέρα τέρπειν ἔχει προσθεῖσα κἀναθεῖσα τοῦ γε κατθανεῖν; what joy has one day *compared with* another to offer, since it only brings us nearer to, or farther from, death (which is neither good nor evil)? S.*Aj.*475; ὃς μὲν κρίνει (prefers) ἡμέραν παρ' ἡμέραν, ὃς δὲ κρίνει (approves) πᾶσαν ἡμέραν *Ep.Rom.*14.5. **8.** with Verbs of estimating, to set *at* so and so much, hence π. = *equivalent to*.., ταρβῶ μὴ..θῆται παρ' οὐδὲν τὰς ἐμὰς ἐπιστολάς set *at* nought, E.*IT*732, cf. A. *Ag.*229 (lyr.); παρ' οὐδὲν ἄγειν S.*Ant.*35; π. μικρὸν ἡγεῖσθαι or ποιεῖσθαί τι hold *of* small *account*, Isoc.5.79, D.61.51; παρ' ὀλίγον ποιεῖσθαί τινα X.*An.*6.6.11; so with εἶναι, etc., παρ' οὐδέν ἐστι are *as* nothing, S.*OT*983, cf. *Ant.*466; παρ' οὐδὲν αὐταῖς ἦν ἂν ὀλλύναι πόσεις E.*Or.*569; οὐ π. μέγα ἔσεσθαι τὸ πταῖσμα Arr.*An.*1.18.6; so perh. π. σμικρὰ κεχώρηκε have turned out *of* little *account*, have *amounted to* little, Hdt.1.120. **b.** in Accountancy, without a verb, π. τὴν καταλλαγὴν *on account of* κ., *PHib.*1.100.4 (iii B.C.). **9.** of correspondence, ὀφείλειν στατῆρα π. στατῆρα stater *for* stater (one to each of two creditors), *BCH*50.214 (Thasos, v B.C.); πληγὴν π. πληγὴν ἑκάτερον Ar.*Ra.*643; συνεῖναι ἑκατέρῳ ἡμέραν παρ' ἡμέραν stayed day *for* day with each, D.59.46; hence of alternation, ποιεῖσθαι ἁγνείας καὶ θυσίας δύο π. δύο, of four priests acting two and two alternately, *BGU*1198.12 (i B.C.); τοῦ καθημερινοῦ ἢ μίαν π. μίαν (sc. ἡμέραν) [πυρετοῦ] quotidian or *tertian* fever, ib.956.3 (iii A.D.): sts. without doubling of the Noun, παρ' ἡμέρην, opp. καθ' ἡμέρην, *tertian*, opp. quotidian, Hp.*Aph.*1.12; καθ' ἡμέραν, παρ' ἡμέραν, π. δύο, π. τρεῖς every day, *every second* day, every third (fourth) day, Arr.*Epict.*2.18.13; π. μίαν every second day, Plb.3.110.4; παρ' ἐνιαυτόν every second year, Plu.*Cleom.*15; παρ' ἔτος year and year about, Arist.*GA*757$^{a}$7; every second year, Paus.8.15.2; π. μέρος by turns (v. μέρος II. 2); ὁ ἀνὰ μέρος παρ' ἓξ μῆνας ὑπὲρ γῆν τε καὶ ὑπὸ γῆν γινόμενος Ἄδωνις Corn. *ND*28; π. μῆνα τρίτον every third month, Arist.*HA*582$^{b}$4, cf. Plu.2. 942e; but π. τρία [ἔτεα] prob. every fourth year, *IG*5(2).422 (Phigalea), cf. Arr.*Epict.* l. c.; ἕνα παρ' ἕνα παραλειπτέον every second one, Nicom.*Ar.*1.18; ἕνα π. δύο (τρεῖς) every third (fourth) one, ibid.; παρὰ δ' ἄλλαν ἄλλα μοῖρα διώκει now one now another, E.*Heracl.* 611. **10.** *precisely at the moment of*, παρ' αὐτὰ τἀδικήματα *flagrante delicto*, D.18.13, 21.26; ἀποδώσω π. τὸν εὔθυνον τὸ καθῆκον *IG*1$^{2}$.188.31; π. τοιοῦτον καιρόν, π. τὰς χρείας, D.20.41, 46; π. τὰ δεινά *in the midst of* danger, Plu.*Ant.*63; π. τὴν πρώτην γένεσιν Jul.*Or.*1.10b; π. τὴν πρώτην (sc. ἐπίθεσιν) *at* the first attack, Hld.9.2; π. γε τὴν πρώτην ὁρμήν Ael.*NA*14.10. **b.** distributively, whether of Time, π. τὰ ἑβδομήκοντα ἔτεα *in each* complete period of seventy years, Hdt.1.32; ἐν ταῖς ὁδοιπορίαις π. στάδια διακόσια..τοῖς ἑκατὸν σταδίοις διήνεγκαν ἀλλήλων X.*Oec.*20.18; πὰρ ϝέτος *each* year, *every* year, *Tab.Heracl.* 1.101; π. τὸν ἐνιαυτὸν ἕκαστον *IG*12(7).5.14 (Amorgos); παρ' ἆμάρ τε καὶ νύκτα day and night, B.*Fr.*7; or more generally, πὰρ τὰν ἐλαίαν *in respect of each* olive plant, *Tab.Heracl.*1.122; παρ' ἡμέραν αἱ ἀμίαι πολὺ ἐπιδήλως αὐξάνονται *from* day *to* day, *per* day, Arist.*HA*571$^{a}$21; τὸ παρ' ἑκάστην βάσιν γινόμενον μικρὸν πολὺ γίνεται π. πολλάς Id.*Pr.* 881$^{b}$26; ἡ παρ' ἡμέραν χάρις D.8.70; τὸ παρ' ἑκάστην ἡμέραν ἡδύ Pl. *Lg.*705a. **c.** παρ' ἆμαρ *on* (this) day, *to-day*, τὸ μὲν πὰρ ἆμαρ, τὸ δέ.. *to*-day and to-morrow, Pi.*P.*11.63; but παρ' ἦμαρ *to*-morrow, S.*OC*1455 (lyr.). **d.** *throughout* a period of time, π. τὴν ζόην Hdt. 7.46; π. τὸν βίον ἅπαντα Pl.*Lg.*733a; π. πάντα τὸν χρόνον D.18.10; also more loosely, *during*, π. τὴν πόσιν *while* they were drinking, Hdt.2. 121.δ'; π. τὸν πότον Aeschin.2.156; π. τὴν κύλικα Plu.*Ant.*24; π. δεῖπνον or π. τὸ δεῖπνον, Id.2.737a, 674f. **II.** *along*, ὄνος παρ' ἄρουραν ἰών Il.11.558; βῆ δὲ θέειν π. τεῖχος 12.352; π. ῥόον Ὠκεανοῖο ἤομεν Od.11. 21; ἔπλεον π. τὴν ἤπειρον Hdt.7.193; π. πᾶσαν τὴν ὁδόν Isoc.4.148; ὀρθὴν παρ' οἶμον..τύμβον κατόψει straight *along* the road, E.*Alc.*835; παρ' ὅλην τὴν φάραγγα Plb.10.30.3; παρ' αὐτὴν τὴν χαράδραν παραπορευομένων ib.9; for παραβάλλειν π., v. supr. C. I. 4b. **2.** *strictly according to, without deviating from*, εἶμι π. στάθμην ὀρθὴν ὁδόν Thgn. 945, cf. S.*Fr.*474.5; ὠμοί τε δούλοις πάντα καὶ π. στάθμην, i.e. too strict, A.*Ag.*1045; π. τὸν λόγον ὃν ἀποφέρουσιν..ἐπιδείξω I will prove to you *strictly according to* the accounts which they themselves submit, D.27.34. **III.** *past, beyond*, παρὰ σκοπιὴν καὶ ἐρινεὸν ἠνεμόεντα.. ἐσσεύοντο Il.22.145, cf. Od.3.172, 24.12; βῆ δὲ π. Κρουνούς *h.Ap.*425; π. τὴν Βαβυλῶνα παριέναι pass *by* Babylon, X.*Cyr.*5.2.29; παρ' αὐτὴν τὴν χύτραν ἄκραν ὁρῶντες looking *over the edge of*.., Ar.*Av.*390. **2.** metaph., *over and above, in addition to*, οὐκ ἔστι π. ταῦτ' ἄλλα Id.*Nu.* 698; π. ταῦτα πάντα ἕτερόν τι Pl.*Phd.*74a, cf. *R.*337d, D.18.139, X.*HG* 1.5.5; ἑκὼν ἐπόνει π. τοὺς ἄλλους *more than* the others, Id.*Ages.*5.3, cf. *Mem.*4.4.1, *Oec.*20.16; ἃ τῷ ῥαψῳδῷ προσήκει καὶ σκοπεῖσθαι καὶ διακρίνειν π. τοὺς ἄλλους ἀνθρώπους Pl.*Ion* 539e. **3.** metaph., *in excess over*, πὰρ δύναμιν *beyond* one's strength, Il.13.787, cf. Th.1.70, Hyp.*Lyc.*16, Arist.*Rh.Al.*1423$^{b}$29; π. τὴν δ. Id.*Po.*1451$^{b}$38. **4.** metaph., *in transgression* or *violation of*, π. μοῖραν Od.14.509; π. μοῖραν Δίος Alc.*Supp.* 14.10; παρ' αἶσαν, παρὰ δίκαν, Pi.*P.*8.13, *O.*2.16, etc.; π. τὸ δίκαιον Th.5.90, etc.; π. τὰς σπονδάς, τὸν νόμον, Id.1.67, X.*HG*1.7.14; π. φύσιν Th.6.17, cf. Pl.*Lg.*747b; π. τὴν στήλην prob. in *IG*1$^{2}$.45.20; π. καιρόν *out of* season, Pi.*O.*8.24, etc.; π. γνώμαν ib.12.10, cf. A.*Supp.*454; π. δόξαν, π. τὸ δοκοῦν ἡμῖν, π. λόγον, Th.3.93, 1.84, Plb.2.38.5; παρ' ἐλπίδα or ἐλπίδας, A.*Ag.*899, S.*Ant.*392, etc.; πὰρ μέλος *out of* tune, Pi.*N.*7.69; π. τὴν ἀξίαν Th.7.77, etc.; π. τὸ εἰωθός, τὸ καθεστηκός, Id. 4.17, 1.98. **5.** π. τοσοῦτον ἦλθε κινδύνου, = παρῆλθε τοσοῦτον κινδύνου, *passed over* so much ground within the sphere of danger, i.e. incurred such imminent peril, Id.3.49, cf. 7.2; in such phrases the tmesis was forgotten, and the acc. came to be governed by παρά, which thus came to mean '*by* such and such a margin', '*with* so much *to spare*', ἐνίκησαν π. πολύ, ἡσσηθέντες π. πολύ, Id.1.29, 2.89, cf. Pl. *Ap.*36a; παρὰ δ' ὀλίγον ἀπέφυγες *only just*, E.*IT*870 (lyr.); παρ' ὀλίγον ἢ διέφευγον ἢ ἀπώλλυντο Th.7.71; δεινότατον π. πολύ *by* far, Ar.*Pl.* 445; παρ' ὅσον *quatenus*, Luc.*Nec.*17, etc.; π. δύο ψήφους ἀπέφυγε *by* two votes, Hyp.*Eux.*28, cf. D.23.205; π. τέτταρας ψήφους μετέσχε τῆς πόλεως Is.3.37; π. τοσοῦτον ἐγένετο αὐτῷ μὴ περιπεσεῖν *by* so much (= little) he missed falling in with.., Th.8.33; π. πέντε ναῦς πλέον ἀνδρὶ ἑκάστῳ ἢ τρεῖς ὀβολοὶ ὡμολογήθησαν ib.29; οὐ π. μικρὸν ἐποίησαν they made no little *difference*, Isoc.4.59. **b.** in phrases like π. τοσοῦτον ἦλθε κινδύνου, τοσοῦτον was sts. understood of the interval *from* danger, etc., and παρά came to mean '*by* so much *short of*' (τὸ π. μικρὸν ὥσπερ οὐδὲν ἀπέχειν δοκεῖ Arist.*Ph.*197$^{a}$29), *within* such and such *a distance of*, so *near to*, τὴν Ἠϊόνα π. νύκτα ἐγένετο (sc. αὐτῷ) λαβεῖν he was *within* one night of taking E., Th.4.106; π. μικρὸν ἦλθον ἀποθανεῖν I came *within* a little *of*.., Isoc.19.22, cf. Plb.1.43.7, Plu.*Caes.* 39; παρ' ἐλάχιστον ἦλθε..ἀφελέσθαι was *within* an ace *of* taking away, Th.8.76; παρ' οὐδὲν μὲν ἦλθον ἀποκτεῖναι (were *within* a mere nothing, *within* an ace *of* killing him), ἐξεκήρυξαν δ' ἐκ πόλεως Aeschin. 3.258, cf. Plu.*Pyrrh.*14, *Alex.*62; π. τοσοῦτον ἦλθε διαφυγεῖν so *near* he came to escaping, Luc.*Cat.*4; παρὰ ἓν πάλαισμα ἔδραμε νικᾶν Ὀλυμπιάδα Hdt.9.33; παρ' οὐδὲν ἐλθόντες τοῦ ἀποβαλεῖν Plb.1.45.14, cf. 2.55.4, D.S.17.42: hence without ἐγένετο or ἐλθεῖν, π. μίαν μονάδα (less) *by* one, i.e. *less* one, Nicom.*Ar.*1.8; τεσσαράκοντα π. μίαν, = 39, 2*Ep.Cor.*11.24; παρ' ἕνα τοσοῦτοι the same number *less* one, Plu. *Publ.*9; σύ μοι παρ' ἕνα ἥκεις ἄγων you have brought me one *too few*, Luc.*Cat.*4; δύναται π. δύο συλλαβὰς εἶναι τὸ καταληκτόν Heph.4.2; τὰ ὁλοκόττινα ηὑρέθησαν π. ἑπτὰ κεράτια seven carats *short*, *PMasp.*70.2

(vi A. D.): πάντες παρ' ἕνα, πάντες παρ' ὀλίγους, all *save* one (a few), Plu.*Cat.Mi.*20, *Ant.*5; ἔτη δύο π. ἡμέρας δύο *IG*5(1).801 (Laconia); of one Μάρκος, θηρίον εἶ π. γράμμα you are a bear (ἄρκος) *all but* a letter, *AP*11.231 (Ammian.); ὡς π. τι καὶ τὰς ὄψεις ἀφανίσαι so that he *all but* (lit. *less* something) lost his sight, Vett.Val.228.6; π. τι βυθίζεσθαι v.l. in *Ev.Luc.*5.7; τὸ π. τοῦτο the figure *less* that, i.e. the remainder or *difference*, *PTeb.*99.10 (ii B. C.), cf. *POxy.*264.4 (i A. D.), *PAmh.*2.148.5 (v A. D.); hence of any *difference* whether of excess or defect, οὐδὲν π. τοῦτο ποιούμενοι τοὺς..Λευκανούς τε καὶ τοὺς..Σαυνίτας making no *difference* between .., Str.6.1.3, cf. 14.5.11, Plu.2.24c. 6. hence of the margin *by* which anything increases or decreases, and so of the cause *according to* which anything comes into existence or varies, τὸ εὖ π. μικρὸν διὰ πολλῶν ἀριθμῶν γίνεται Polyclit.2 (cf. μικρός III. 5c); διαφέρει π. τὰς τῶν παθημάτων ἐναντιώσεις *according to*.., Arist.*HA*486$^b$5; μεταπίπτει π. τὰ κλίματα Gem.5.29, cf. 11.5, al.; π. τὰ πράγματα cj. in Apollod.Car.11. 7. more generally of the margin *by* which an event occurs, i.e. of the necessary and sufficient cause or motive (τὸ μὴ π. τοῦτο γίνεσθαι τότε λέγομεν, ὅταν ἀναιρεθέντος τούτου μηδὲν ἧττον περαίνηται ὁ συλλογισμός Arist.*APr.*65$^b$6, cf. 48$^a$24, al.), κεινὰν π. δίαιταν *just for the sake of* unsatisfying food, Pi.*O.*2.65; ἕκαστος οὐ π. τὴν ἑαυτοῦ ἀμέλειαν οἴεται βλάψειν each thinks that his own negligence will not *suffice to cause* injury, Th.1.141, cf. Isoc.3.48; π. τὴν αὑτοῦ ἁμαρτίαν *all through* his own fault, Antipho 3.4.5, cf. Isoc.6.52, D.4.11, 18.232; πολλὰ..ἐστιν αἴτια τούτων, καὶ οὐ παρ' ἓν οὐδὲ δύ' εἰς τοῦτο τὰ πράγματ' ἀφῖκται not *from* one or two causes *only*, Id.9.2; οὐ π. τοῦτο οὐκ ἔστι *it does* not *follow that* it is not.., 1*Ep.Cor.*12.15; π. τὸ τὴν ἀρίθμησιν ποιήσασθαι ἐξ ἑτοίμου τοὺς ἐργώνας οὐκ ὀλίγα χρήματα περιεποίησε τῇ πόλει *by the simple fact of* prompt payment, *IPE*1$^2$.32*B*35 (Olbia, iii B. C.); οὐδὲν ἂν παρ' ἕνα ἄνθρωπον ἐγένετο τούτων Lycurg.63, cf. Plb.3.103.2, 18.28.6, al.; οὐδεὶς παρ' ἑαυτόν ἐστι βασιλεύς *thanks to* himself *alone*, Aristeas 224; παρ' αὑτὸν ἀτυχεῖ Arr.*Epict.*3.24.2, cf. Phld.*Rh.*2.16 S.; παρ' ἡμᾶς ἡ τῶν ἀγαθῶν ἀπόστασις Hierocl. *in CA*25 p.477 M.; εἶναι π. τοῦτο σωτηρίαν τε πόλει καὶ τοὐναντίον, i.e. *on* this *depends*.., Pl.*Lg.*715d, cf. X.*Eq.Mag.*1.5, D.C.*Fr.*36.5; π. μίαν ἡμέραν καὶ ἓν πρᾶγμα καὶ ἀπόλλυται προκοπὴ καὶ σῴζεται Epict.*Ench.*51.2; π. τὸ Ἑλληνά με εἶναι *just because* I am a Greek, *UPZ*7.13 (ii B. C.); π. τὸ ἀγαπᾶν αὐτὸν αὐτήν LXX *Ge.*29.20, cf. *Ex.*14.11; later more loosely, *because of*.., Phld.*Rh.*1.158 S., Gem.6.24, etc.; οὐδὲν π. σὲ γέγονε it is no fault of yours, *PRyl.*243.6 (ii A.D.), cf. *POxy.*1420.7 (ii A.D.). 8. of a limit of possibility, εἴπερ ἐνεδέχετο π. τοὺς παρόντας καιρούς D.18.239; πεῖσαι τό γε παρ' αὑτόν to persuade (the judges) *so far as in* you *lies*, Arr.*Epict.*2.2.20; οἴμωζε παρ' ἐμέ *as far as* I *am concerned, for all* I *care*, Ar.*Av.*846.

D. POSITION: παρά may follow its Subst. in all three cases, but then becomes by anastrophe πάρα: when the ult. is elided, the practice varies, τῇσι παρ' Il.18.400; but Ἡφαίστοιο πάρ' ib.191.

E. παρά abs., as ADV., *near, together*, Il.1.611, al., E.*IA*201 (lyr.).

F. πάρα (with anastrophe) stands for πάρεστι and πάρεισι, Il.1.174, Hes.*Op.*454, A.*Pers.*167, Hdt.1.42, al., S.*El.*285, Ar.*Ach.*862, etc.

G. IN COMPOS., I. *alongside of, beside*, of rest, παράκειμαι, παράλληλοι, παρέζομαι, πάρειμι (εἰμί), παρίστημι; of motion, παραπλέω, πάρειμι (εἶμι). II. *to the side of, to*, παραδίδωμι, παρέχω. III. *to one side of, by, past*, παρέρχομαι, παροίχομαι, παραπέμπω, παρακμάζω, παρατρέχω. IV. metaph., 1. *aside* or *beyond*, i.e. *amiss, wrong*, παραβαίνω, παράγω, παροράω, παρορκέω, παρακούω, παραγιγνώσκω. 2. of comparison, as in παραβάλλω, παρατίθημι. 3. of alteration or change, as in παραλλάσσω, παραπείθω, παραπλάσσω, παρατεκταίνω, παραυδάω, παράφημι. 4. of a side-issue, παραπόλλυμι. (Cogn. with Goth. *faúr* 'along', Lat. *por-*.)

⊛ **παραβαίνω**, Ep. impf. παρέβασκε (v. infr.): acc. pl. pres. part. παρβεῶντας *Abh.Berl.Akad.*1925(5).21 (Cyrene) is prob. from a by-form *παραβάω: fut. -βήσομαι: pf. -βέβηκα; part. -βεβώς, Ep. -βεβᾱώς: pf. Pass. -βέβασμαι (v. infr. II. 1): aor. 2 παρέβην: aor. Pass. παρεβάθην Th.4.23:—*go by the side of*, and in pf., *stand beside*, twice in Hom., c. dat., of one *standing beside* the warrior in the chariot (cf. παραβάτης), Ἕκτορι παρβεβαώς Il.11.522; of two warriors, παρβεβαῶτε..ἀλλήλοιιν 13.708; also impf. παρέβασκε, of the combatant in the chariot, 11.104; but παρεβεβήκεέ οἱ ἡνίοχος Hdt.7.40. II. *pass beside* or *beyond*, mostly metaph. (lit. π. τὸν ὅρον *PHal.*1.87 (iii B. C.)), in trans. sense: 1. *overstep, transgress*, τὰ νόμιμα Hdt.1.65; δίκην A.*Ag.*789 (anap.); δίκην τὴν δεδικασμένην Antipho 5.87; εἴ τι τούτων παραβαίνοιμι *IG*1$^2$.15.42, cf. 76.57; θεοῦ νόμον E.*Ion* 230 (lyr.); οὐ τοὺς νόμους μόνον, ἀλλὰ καὶ τὸν καιρὸν τῆς ἀναρρήσεως καὶ τὸν τόπον Aeschin.3.204; θεσμούς, ὅρκους, Ar.*Av.*331, 332 (both lyr.), cf. Th.1.78, Lys.9.15; τὰς σπονδάς Ar.*Av.*461: c. acc. pers., π. τινὰ δαιμόνων *sin against* a god, Hdt.6.12, cf. D.H.1.23; οὓς παραβαίνειν αἰσχρόν *disappoint*, Chor.p.80 B. (cf. v): abs., παραβάντες *transgressors*, A.*Ag.*59 (anap.); ὁ παραβαίνων Arist.*Pol.*1325$^b$5:—Pass., *to be transgressed* or *offended against*, σπονδὰς.., ἅς γε ὁ θεὸς..νομίζει παραβεβάσθαι Th.1.123; νόμῳ παραβαθέντι Id.3.67; ἐὰν καὶ ὁτιοῦν παραβαθῇ Id.4.23; παραβεβασμένοις ὅρκοις D.17.12; παραβαινομένων abs., *as offences were committed*, Th.3.45. b. with Prep., π. παρὰ τὴν συγγραφήν *AJA*16.13 (Sardes, iv/iii B. C.). c. c. gen., *go aside from*, τῆς ἀληθείας Arist.*Cael.*271$^b$8. 2. *pass over, omit*, S.*Tr.*499 (lyr.), D.18.211, Aristeas 297. 3. *let pass*, καιρούς Din.1.36. 4. οὔ με παρέβα φάσμα it *escaped* me not, E.*Hec.*704 (lyr.). III. *pass on*, π. εἰς ἀπέχθειαν Plb.38.12.3 (sed leg. προβῆναι). IV. *come forward*, esp. of the Com. parabasis (v. παράβασις), π. πρὸς τὸ θέατρον *step forward* to address the spectators, Ar.*Ach.*629, *Eq.*508, *Pax* 735; also οὐκ ἂν παρέβην εἰς λέξιν τοιάνδ' ἐπῶν Pl.Com.92.2: similarly, metaph., δοκεῖν παραβεβηκέναι τῇ πρώτῃ σκηνῇ Procl. *in Prm.*p.523 S. V. in Med., c. acc. pers., *commit an offence against*, Chor.p.68 B.

**παραβάκτρος**, ον, *near* or *like a staff*, π. θεραπεύμασι with service *as of a staff*, E.*Ph.*1548 (lyr.).

**παράβακχος**, ον, *like a Bacchanal, theatrical*, Plu.*Dem.*9; θειασμός Eun.*VS* p.499 B.

**παραβαλλέταιρος**, ὁ, (παραβάλλω A. VI) *one who betrays his comrade*, Eust.1406.24.

⊛ **παραβάλλω**, fut. -βᾰλῶ: aor. 2 παρέβᾰλον: pf. -βέβληκα:—*throw beside* or *by, throw to* one, as fodder to horses, παρὰ δέ σφισι βάλλετ' ἐδωδήν Il.8.504, cf. 5.369; πὰρ δ' ἔβαλον ζειάς Od.4.41; π. [τοῖς ἵπποις] ἀμβροσίαν Pl.*Phdr.*247e; π. τοὺς ἀνθρώπους τοῖς ὄχλοις Plb.38.17.2; πυρὶ φρύγανα π. *add* fuel to the flame, Arr.*Epict.*2.18.5, cf. 2.18.12:—Pass., παραβληθῆναι [τοῖς θηρίοις] D.C.59.10; τάριχος..ἀπόνως παραβεβλημένον *thrown* carelessly *before people*, Ar.*Fr.*333:—Med., μάζας ἐπὶ κάλαμον παραβαλλόμενοι *ordering* them *to be served up*, Pl.*R.*372b. b. *throw in*, φακέλους ἐς τὸ μεταξύ Th.2.77, cf. 6.99. 2. *hold out to* one *as a bait*, X.*Cyn.*11.2. 3. *cast in one's teeth*, τινί τι Aeschin.3.189; *object, offer in rejoinder*, τῷ πρώτῳ -βληθήσεται τοιοῦτος λόγος Phld.*Ir.*p.95 W. II. *expose*, παρέβαλέν τ' ἐμὲ παρὰ γένος ἀνόσιον *put* me *in* their *power*, Ar.*Av.*333 (lyr.); τῇ τύχῃ..αὑτὸν π. Philippid.6 (v.l. for προ-); ἂν δ' ἀληθινὸν σαυτὸν παραβάλλῃς if *you present, show* yourself.., Posidipp.26:—freq. in Med., *expose oneself* or *what is one's own to hazard* or *danger*, αἰὲν ἐμὴν ψυχὴν παραβαλλόμενος πολεμίζειν *risking* it in war, Il.9.322; π. τὰ τέκνα *risk the lives of one's* children, Hdt.7.10.θʹ; παῖδας Th.2.44; πλείω παραβαλλόμενοι *having* greater *interests at stake*, Id.3.65; οὐκ ἴσα π. X.*Cyr.*2.3.11: pf. Pass. in med. sense, Λακεδαιμονίοις πλεῖστον δὴ παραβεβλημένοι *having risked* far the most upon them, Th.5.113; also τὸν κίνδυνον τῶν σωμάτων παραβαλλομένους Id.3.14; *venture*, πρὸς τὴν θάλατταν ὅταν -βάλωνται Plb.1.37.9; π. καὶ τολμᾶν Id.18.53.2: c. dat., π. τοῖς ὅλοις Id.2.26.6; τῷ βίῳ *IG*12(3).1286.22 (Astypalaea): c. inf., *venture* to do, Plu.*Pel.*8:—Pass., παραβεβλημένον τι εἰπεῖν make an *unguarded* statement, Philostr.*VA*4.42. b. in wagering, *deposit* one's stake, Plu.*Cat.Mi.*44. 2. Pass., c. dat., *to be given up to*, πόρναισι καὶ κύβοισι παραβεβλημένος Ar.*Pl.*243. III. *set beside* or *parallel with*, Arist.*PA*668$^a$17 (Pass.), cf. *Rh.*1419$^b$35; Εὔβοια τῇ ἠπείρῳ παραβεβλημένη *lying parallel with*, Str.9.1.22: hence, 2. *compare* one with another, Isoc.9.34, etc.; τι παρά τι Pl.*Grg.*472c; π. [ἵππον] ἵππῳ *match* one *against* another, X.*Eq.*9.8:—in Med., παραβάλλομαί σοι (sc. ὄρνιθι) θρήνους I *set my* songs *against*.., E.*IT*1094 (lyr.): abs., παραβαλλόμεναι *vying with one another*, Id.*Andr.*289 (lyr.); [ἀφορμὰς] αἷς οὔτε Ἁρμόδιος παραβεβλήσεται Philostr.*VA*5.34:—freq. in Pass., π. τινί Hdt.4.198; πρός τι Hp.*Art.*51, X.*Mem.*2.4.5; παρά τι Pl.*Grg.*475e; ἀπάτα δ' ἀπάταις παραβαλλομένα one piece of treachery *set against* another, S.*OC*231 (lyr.). 3. *bring alongside*, in Med., τὴν ἄκατον παραβάλλου *bring your* boat *alongside, heave to*, Ar.*Eq.*762; ἐφόλκιον Plu.*Pomp.*73; also π. τὼ κωπίω Ar.*Ra.*269: abs., παραβαλοῦ ib.180: metaph., παραβάλλου λοιδορῶν *avast* with your abuse! Plu.2.711d. IV. *throw, turn, bend sideways*, ὄμμα π. θύννου δίκην *cast* it *askance*, A.*Fr.*308; τὸν ὀφθαλμὸν παράβαλλ' ἐς Καρίαν Ar.*Eq.*173; τὠφθαλμὼ παραβάλλεις Id.*Nu.*362 (referred to by Pl.*Smp.*221b); π. τὸ ἕτερον οὖς πλάγιον X.*Cyn.*5.32; π. τὰ ὦτα *apply* one's ears to listen, Pl.*R.*531a; παραβαλὼν τὴν κεφαλήν Id.*Phd.*103a; Ἡρακλεῖ στόμα π. *lend* one's mouth to Heracles, i.e. join in his praise, Pi.*P.*9.87 (v.l. περιβ-); π. τοὺς γομφίους *lay to* one's grinders, Ar.*Pax* 34; π. τὸ θύριον τοῦ λόγου, metaph., *put to* the door.., *close* it, Plu.2.940f. V. *deposit with* one, *entrust to* him, τινί τι Hdt.2.154. VI. in Med., *deceive, betray*, Id.1.108, Th.1.133, Alc.Com.30 (Act. in the same sense, Hsch.; cf. παραβαλλέταιρος). VII. Geom., π. παρά.. *apply* a figure to a finite line, παραλληλόγραμμον π. παρὰ εὐθεῖαν Euc.6.27, cf. Archim.*Aequil.*2.1. 2. since to *apply* an area *xy* to a line of length *x* is to divide *xy* by *x*, π. = *divide*, τι παρά τι Dioph.5.10, al.; cf. παρά C. I. 4c.

B. intr., *come near, approach*, Pl.*Ly.*203b, *PPetr.*3p.102 (iii B. C.), etc.; *enter*, Arist.*Pol.*1331$^a$34; π. ἀλλήλοις *meet* one another, Pl.*R.*556c; f.l. for περιβάλῃ, ib.499b; παρέβαλεν Ἀναξιμένει τῷ ῥήτορι *was a pupil of* A., Plu.2.846f. II. *go by sea, cross over*, παρέβαλε νηυσὶ ἰθὺ Σκιάθου Hdt.7.179, cf. Philipp.ap.D.12.16, Arist.*Mir.*836$^a$29; of ships, ναῦς Πελοποννησίων ἐς Ἰωνίαν π. Th.3.32. III. *come alongside, bring to*, περὶ Ῥόδον παραβαλόντος ναυτικοῦ στόλου Arist.*GA*763$^a$31; παραβαλόντες τῇ πεντήρει *having come alongside of her*, in a sea-fight, Plb.15.2.12, cf. 1.22.9: generally, *come to land*, of quails, Arist.*HA*597$^b$15:—in Med., *put in*, πρός τινας Philostr.*VA*6.16. IV. metaph., *direct one's course towards*, εἰς ἡδονάς Arist.*EN*1153$^b$34. V. Astrol., *to be in the same right ascension as*, c. dat., *Cat.Cod.Astr.*1.113, 5(1).188.

**παραβαπτ-ίζω**, *baptize without authority*, Just.*Nov.*42.3.1. **-ιστής**, οῦ, ὁ, *false dyer*: hence, metaph., *impostor*, Arr.*Epict.*2.9.21. **-ός**, όν, *dyed*, ποικίλματα LXX *Ez.*23.15. **-ω**, *dye at the same time*, Plu.*Phoc.*28 (Pass.).

**παραβαρβᾰρίζω**, *speak barbarously*, Hsch. s.v. ἀσαλγάνας.

**παραβᾰσία**, ἡ, Ep. παραιβασίη, = παράβασις II, Hes.*Th.*220 (pl.), *PLond.*1.113.1 (vi A. D.), etc.: poet. **παρβασία** A.*Th.*743 (lyr.).

**παραβᾰσῐλεύω**, *reign beside, be co-regent*, εἰς τὸν Καίσαρα Eun.*VS* p.476 B. II. *govern ill*, or *commit treason*, Lxx 3*Ma*.6.24.

⊛ **παρά-βᾰσις**, Ep. **παραίβ–**, εως, ἡ, *going aside, escape*, παραίβασις ἔσσετ' ὀλέθρου A.R.4.832; *deviation*, v.l. in Arist.*Pol*.1307ᵇ33, cf. Plu. 2.649b (pl.); *digression*, Str.1.2.2, Longin.12.5 (pl.). 2. of the action of *walking*, π. καὶ παράλλαξις σκελῶν Plu.*Phil*.6. 3. *transition, passage*, Demetr.Lac.*Herc*.1012.31. II. *overstepping*, ὅρων Plu.2.122e; ἔθους Str.12.8.9; τοῦ πατρίου νόμου J.*AJ*18.8.2; τῶν δικαίων παραβάσεις Plu.*Comp.Ages.Pomp*.1: abs., *transgression*, Lxx 4*Ki*.2.24, *Ep.Gal*.3.19, Plu.2.209a,746c, etc.; *error, illusion*, Epicur. *Nat*.11.7; cf. παραβασία. III. *parabasis*, a part of the Old Comedy, *in which the Chorus came forward* (cf. παραβαίνω IV) and addressed the audience in the Poet's name, Plu.2.711f, Heph.*Poëm*.8, Sch.Ar.*Pax* 733, etc. **–βᾰτέον**, *one must overstep, go beyond*, οὐ π. τὰ καλῶς ἔχοντα Aristeas 55. **–βᾰτέω**, *to be a* παραβάτης (q.v.), τινι *to* one, Philostr.Jun.*Im*.11: generally, *sit* or *stand by the driver*, in early Att. form **παραιβ–**, Clidem.24, Arist.*Ath*.14.4. ⊛ **–βάτης** [βᾰ], poet. and early Att. **παραιβάτης** (*IG*1².5, etc.), ου, ὁ, (παραβαίνω I) *one who stands beside*: prop. *the warrior* or *combatant who stands beside the charioteer*, ἂν δ' ἔβαν ἐν δίφροισι παραιβάται ἡνίοχοί τε Il.23.132, cf. D.S.5.29; παραιβάτας ἔστησαν ἐς τάξιν δορός E.*Supp*.677; ἀναλαβεῖν τοὺς παραβάτας X.*Cyr*.7.1.29, etc.; δύο δ' εἰσὶν ἐπὶ τῷ ἅρματι π. πρὸς ἡνιόχῳ Str.15.1.52: = Att. ἀποβάται, acc. to D.H.7.73; fem. **παραιβάτις**, A.R.1.754. 2. light troops (*velites*) who *ran beside* the cavalry, Plu.*Aem*.12. II. (παραβαίνω II.1) *transgressor*, A.*Eu*. 553 (lyr., in poet. form **παρβάτης**), cf. Sm.*Ps*.16(17).4; π. θεῶν Polem.ap.Macr.*Sat*.5.19.29; π. νόμου *Ep.Rom*.2.25. **–βᾰτικός**, ή, όν, in Adv. -κῶς, ἔχειν τινός to be *disposed to transgress*.., Arr.*Epict*. 2.20.14, cf. Asp.*in EN*82.26. II. *belonging to the* παράβασις III, μελύδρια Sch.Ar.*V*.1257. **–βάτις**, poet. **παραιβάτις**, ιδος, ἡ, fem. of παραβάτης (q.v.). II. *woman who follows the reapers, gleaner*, Theoc.3.32. **–βᾰτός**, poet. **παρβᾰτός**, όν, *to be overcome* or *overreached*, Διὸς οὐ παρβατός ἐστιν φρήν A.*Supp*.1048 (lyr.); κράτος παραβατὸν οὐδαμᾶ πέλει S.*Ant*.874 (lyr.).

**παραβᾰφής**, ές, = παραλουργής, Hsch.; **παράβᾰφος**, ον, Phot.

**παραβεβάσθαι**, pf. inf. Pass. of παραβαίνω.

**παραβεβλημένως**, Adv. pf. part. Pass. of παραβάλλω, *recklessly*, Poll.3.136.

**παραβεβυσμένως**, Adv., (παραβύω) gloss on βύζην, Sch.Luc. *Lex*.2.

⊛ **παρα-βῐάζομαι**, *do* a thing *by force against nature* or *law*, Lxx *De*.1. 43; *use violence*, περὶ τῶν τοιούτων Plb.24.8.3. II. c. acc., π. τὸν χάρακα *force* the palisade, Id.21.27.7; π. τινά *constrain, compel* him, Lxx 4*Ki*.2.17, al., *Ev.Luc*.24.29, *Act.Ap*.16.15; of arguments or explanations, τὸ ἀδύνατον π. Epicur.*Ep*.2 p.36 U., *Nat*.107 G.; μύθους π. καὶ διαστρέφειν *to do* them *violence*, Plu.2.19f, cf. *Lyc*.6; *constrain*, c. inf., Onos.19.2 (Pass.):—Act. in Gal.5.287. **–βίας**, ου, ὁ (or **–βίη**, ἡ), *drink made from millet and* κόνυζα, Hecat.154 J. **–βῐασμός**, ὁ, *forcing of nature* or *law*, Plu.2.1097f.

⊛ **παραβῐβάζω**, *put aside, remove*, τὸ ἁμάρτημα Lxx 2*Ki*.12.13. 2. *transgress* a law, Ph.2.539 (Pass., v.l. -βιασθῆναι).

**παραβλάπτω**, *damage incidentally*, X.Eph.4.2, Gal.*UP*13.3 (Pass.), al., Eun.*Hist*.p.246 D.; φρένες -βεβλαμμέναι *EM*322.23. 2. *help to damage*, Vett.Val.56.1.

**παραβλαστ-άνω**, fut. -ήσω, *sprout* or *shoot up beside*, Hp.*Acut*. (*Sp*.)26 (cf. Gal.15.837), Arist.*GA*762ᵃ4: metaph., Pl.*R*.573d. 2. *shoot sideways*, Thphr.*HP*5.1.3; of bulbous plants, *make offsets*, ib. 7.2.2. II. c. acc., *put forth like shoots*, τὰς κακίας Them.*Or*.32. 360b. **–η**, ἡ, *sidegrowth, offshoot*, Thphr.*HP*1.2.6. **–ημα**, ατος, τό, = foreg., ib.4.9.2, Gal.*UP*16.2. **–ησις**, εως, ἡ, = foreg., Thphr.*HP*5.1.8, 4.9.3. **–ητικός**, ή, όν, *inclined to put out offshoots*, ib.1.3.3, 1.5.1, 1.6.5, al. **–ικός**, ή, όν, = foreg., Id.*CP*5.6.3.

**παράβλεμμα**, ατος, τό, *side-glance, sidelong look*, Poll.2.56.

⊛ **παρα-βλέπω**, *look aside, take a side look*, Ar.*Ra*.411; π. θατέρῳ (sc. ὀφθαλμῷ) *look suspiciously* with one eye, Id.*V*.497 (also, *peep out of the corner of* one's eye, Id.*Ec*.498); opp. ἀτενίζω, Arist.*Mete*.343ᵇ13; τῷ ὀφθαλμῷ π. καὶ δεινὸν δέδορκε *looked askance*, Nicostr.ap.Stob. 4.22.102. 2. *see wrong*, Luc.*Nec*.1. II. *overlook*, τί τἀλλότριον.. κακὸν ὀξυδερκεῖς, τὸ δ' ἴδιον παραβλέπεις; *Com.Adesp*.359, cf. Plb.6.46.6. 2. *despise*, Hsch. s.v. ὑπεροψᾷ. **–βλεψις**, εως, ἡ, *looking at askance*, Plu.2.521b.

**παρα-βλήδην**, Adv., (παραβάλλω) *thrown in by the way*, κερτομίοις ἐπέεσσι π. ἀγορεύων speaking *with a side-meaning*, i.e. *maliciously, deceitfully*, Il.4.6, cf. Hsch., and v. παράβολος I, παραβάλλω A. VI; so perh. in Opp.*H*.2.113. 2. *in answer*, A.R.1.835, 2.448, 3.107. II. *parallelwise*, Arat.535. ⊛ **–βλημα**, ατος, τό, *that which is thrown beside* or *before, fodder*, Eust.1406.25. II. *curtain* or *screen used to cover* the sides of ships, X.*HG*2.1.22. III. Geom., *rectangle applied to a straight line*, Archim.*Con.Sph*.25, al. **–βλής**, ῆτος, ὁ, ἡ, *distraught*, Man.6.560; al. παραπλήξ. **–βλητέος**, α, ον, *to be compared*, τινι to one, Plu.*Cim*.3. II. παραβλητέον, *one must compare*, π. καὶ συγκριτέον Muson.*Fr*.8 p.37 H. 2. *one must set before, offer*, Porph. *Abst*.2.35; *one must throw before*, [βοΐ] τροφήν *Gp*.17.19.2. 3. *one must divide*, Nicom.*Ar*.2.27, Theo Sm.p.119 H. **–βλητικός**, ή, όν, *employing comparisons*, Porph. *ad Il*.p.315 S., Hsch. 2. Gramm., *comparative*, Gal. in *Abh.Berl.Akad*.1925(1).37. Adv. -κῶς *comparatively*, Gal.12.814, al.; = παραβλήδην II, Sch.Arat.525. **–βλητός**, ή, όν, *comparable*, Plu.*Aem*.7, Gal.*Nat.Fac*.3.7.

**παραβλύζω**, *spirt out, disgorge*, π. τὸ περιττὸν [τοῦ οἴνου] Anon.ap. Suid.: c. gen. partit., π. τοῦ οἴνου ἐν τῷ ὕπνῳ Philostr.*Im*.1.22; κραιπάλης Eun.*VS*p.462 B.

**παραβλώσκω**, poet. pf. παρμέμβλωκα, *go beside*, esp. for the purpose of protecting, τῷ δ' αὖτε φιλομμειδὴς Ἀφροδίτη αἰεὶ παρμέμβλωκε Il.4.11; ἡ γάρ οἱ αἰεὶ μήτηρ παρμέμβλωκεν 24.73.

**παραβλώψ**, ῶπος, ὁ, ἡ, *looking askance, squinting*, παραβλῶπές τ' ὀφθαλμώ Il.9.503, *AP*11.361 (Autom.); π. ὀφθαλμοί Luc.*Ind*.7; of a person, Ael.*Fr*.325; also π. Λιταί Corn.*ND*12. 2. *blind*, *PLond*. 1821.265. (From παραβλέπω, as κλώψ from κλέπτω.)

**παραβοάω**, *shout beside*, παρὰ τὸ βῆμα D.59.43, cf. Aristid.2.114 J.

**παραβοήθ-εια**, ἡ, *aid, succour*, αἱ τῶν ἔργων π. Pl.*Lg*.778a; αἱ π. *aids in war*, Plb.2.5.2, Onos.6.4; αἱ π. τοῦ χάρακος Ph.*Bel*.85.42. **–έω**, *come to aid*, τινι Th.1.47, Antiph.228.3; πρός τινα against one, Plb.2. 54.10: abs., *come to the rescue*, Ar.*Eq*.257, Th.3.22, X.*HG*1.1.6. 2. *aid on the other hand*, Pl.*R*.572e. **–ημα**, ατος, τό, *aid*: in pl., *devices for strengthening* a perforated beam, Ph.*Bel*.57.37.

**παραβολ-άδην**, poet. **παρβ–**, = παραβλήδην II, A.R.4.936, Arat. 525; π. δύο πὰρ δύο Id.318. ⊛ **–ᾶνοι**, οἱ, in Lat. form *parabalani*, *persons who risk their lives as sick-nurses*, *Cod.Theod*.16.2.42, al.; *parabalanin*, *Cod.Just*.1.3.17,18, al. ⊛ **–εύομαι**, *venture, expose oneself*, π. τῇ ψυχῇ *Ep.Phil*.2.30 (v.l. παραβουλ–): c. acc. cogn., τοὺς ὑπὲρ φιλίας κινδύνους π. *IPE*1².39.28 (Olbia, iii (?) A.D.). ⊛ **–ή**, ἡ, *juxtaposition, comparison*, τῶν βίων Pl.*Phlb*.33b; π. καὶ σύγκρισις Plb.1.2.2; ἐν παραβολῇ by *juxtaposition*, Arist.*Top*.104ᵃ28, cf. 157ᵃ14; ἐκ παραβολῆς Id.*Rh*.1420ᵃ4. 2. *comparison, illustration, analogy*, τὴν π. ἀπρεπῆ πεποιῆσθαι Isoc.12.227; π. δὲ τὰ Σωκρατικά (distd. from λόγος, *apologue*) Arist.*Rh*.1393ᵇ3; ἐκ τῶν θηρίων ποιεῖσθαι τὴν π. Id.*Pol*.1264ᵇ4. 3. *NT, parable*, *Ev.Marc*.12.1, al.; *type*, *Ep. Hebr*.9.9, 11.19. 4. *by-word, proverb*, Lxx *Ez*.18.2, *Ev.Luc*.4. 23; in bad sense, εἰς π. ἐν τοῖς ἔθνεσι Lxx *Ps*.43(44).14, cf. *Wi*.5. 3. 5. *objection* to an argument, Phld.*Rh*.1.5 S. II. *moving side by side*, ἐκ παραβολῆς [νεῶν] μάχεσθαι to fight a sea-fight *broadside to broadside*, Plb.15.2.13, cf. D.S.14.60. III. *sidelong direction, obliquity*, διὰ πολλῶν ἑλιγμῶν καὶ π. Plu.*Arat*.22. IV. *venture*, D.S.27.17, v.l. in Th.1.131. V. Astron., *conjunction*, παραβολαὶ ἀλλήλων Pl.*Ti*.40c, cf. Procl.*in Ti*.3.146 D., Plot.3. 1.5, Iamb.*Myst*.9.4: also f.l. for περιβολή, τοῦ ἡλίου Max.Tyr.17. 9. VI. Math., *division*, opp. multiplication, Dioph.4.22; *quotient*, ib.10: hence, *section produced by division* of a line, Nicom.*Ar*.2. 27. VII. Geom., *application*, π. τῶν χωρίων Pythag.ap.Procl.*in Euc*.p.419 F.; τὰ ἐκ τῆς π. γενηθέντα σημεῖα, of the foci of an ellipse or hyperbola, points found by *application* of an area to the axis, Apollon.Perg.*Con*.3.45, cf. 48. 2. *parabola*, because the square on the ordinate is equal to a rectangle whose height is equal to the abscissa *applied to* the parameter, ib.1.11. VIII. = παράβολον (v. παράβολος III. 1), Arist.*Oec*.1348ᵇ13 (vv.ll. παράβολον, -βόλιον), *OGI*41.5 (Samos, iii B.C., pl.), *PPetr*.3 p.232 (iii B.C., pl.). **–ικός**, ή, όν, *expressive of comparison*, Sch.Il.13.62. **–ιον**, τό, in later Gr., = παράβολον (v. παράβολος III. 1), *IGRom*.4.1211 (Thyatira, i B.C.), Poll.8.63, Phryn.214; π. θεὶς Astramps.*Orac*.69 p.6 H. II. *payment on account*, *PSI*4.324.2, 325.4 (iii B.C.). III. = *sacramentum*, *Gloss*. **–ίσκος**, ὁ, dub. sens., παραβολίσκοι τῆς τετρακύκλου *IG*2².1425.414.

**παραβολοειδής**, ές, *indicating comparison*, ἐπίρρημα Sch.Il.13. 152.

⊛ **παράβολος**, poet. **παραίβ–**, ον, (παραβάλλω): I. (parox.) *with a side-meaning, deceitful*, παραιβόλα κερτομέουσιν *h.Merc*.56. II. *exposing oneself* or *what belongs to one*: hence, 1. of persons, *venturesome, reckless*, Ar.*V*.192; πρὸς κινδύνους παραβολωτάτω App.*BC*2.149; φιλοκίνδυνος καὶ π. ἐν ταῖς μάχαις D.S.19.3. Adv. -λως *desperately, recklessly*, π. πλεῖν Men.643; π. κινδυνεῦσαι, χρῆσθαι τῷ πολέμῳ, διαγωνίσασθαι, Plb.16.5.6, 2.47.3, Plu.*Phil*.5: Comp. -ώτερον Id.*Phoc*.6. 2. of things and actions, *hazardous, perilous*, ἔργον Hdt.9.45; π. καὶ χαλεπὸν πρᾶγμα Isoc.6.49; π. ὁ λόγος ἴσως ἔστ' Men.*Sam*.113; π. καὶ καλὰ ἔργα Plb.18.53.1; -ώτερον ἀγώνισμα Id.1.58.1; πρᾶξις ἀνέλπιστος καὶ -ωτάτη D.S.20.3; ἡ τόλμα καὶ τὸ π. Plb.3.61.6; π. θρασύτης Plu. *Num*.8; θρασὺ καὶ π. *Cat.Cod.Astr*.1.164.13 (-βουλον cod.); also π. ὁδοί, τόποι, *dangerous* roads, etc., Heraclit.*Incred*.21, Plb.5.14.9; τὰ π. *bold metaphors*, Longin.32.4; τὸ π. τῆς ζητήσεως Simp.*in Cael*. 481.19. 3. Adv. -λως *in an extraordinary manner*, ἡ τύχη μεταβιβάσασά τινας π. Plb.1.58.1; π. διασῴζεσθαι App.*Hann*.38. III. παράβολον, τό, as law-term, *deposit made* in lodging an appeal, Arist. *Fr*.456, v.l. in *Oec*.1348ᵇ13; Dor. **πάρβολον**, prob. in *Foed.Delph. Pell*.4 A 10, *IG*12(3).254.25 (Anaphe). 2. *border along the edge* of a garment, ib.2².1514.41.

**παραβόσκω**, *maintain besides*, Ephipp.8.6.

**παραβουκολέω**, *lead astray by fraud, beguile*, Oenom.ap.Eus.*PE* 5.20.

**παρα-βουλεύομαι**, v. παραβολ–. **–βουλος**, v. παράβολος II. 2.

**παραβρᾰβεύω**, *give an unjust judgement*, esp. in an athletic contest, Plu.2.535c:—Pass., *to be the victim of a perversion of justice*, παραβεβραβευμένοι Plb.23.1.12 (v.l. -μένοις κρίμασι, i.e. *perverted*).

**παράβροχον**, *salamen*, *Gloss*.

**παρά-βυσμα**, ατος, τό, *stuffing*, Harp. ⊛ **–βυστος**, ον, *stuffed* or *forced in*, of a self-invited guest, Tim.Com.1, cf. Ath.6.257a; ἐκ παραβύστου καθῆσθαι Plu.2.617f; π. κλίνη a *small* or *supplementary* couch, Poll.3.43, Harp., Hsch., Suid. II. *pushed aside* or *into a corner*: τὸ π. (sc. δικαστήριον), an Athenian law-court *lying in an obscure part of the town* (where οἱ ἕνδεκα held their sittings, Harp.), Timocl.26,

Paus.1.28.8, dub. in Lys.*Fr.*322 S. 2. metaph., ἐν παραβύστῳ *in a hole and corner*, D.24.47, Arist.*Top.*157$^{a}$4, Luc.*Nec.*17, Zos.Alch. p.242 B. ⊛ **-βύω,** *stuff in, insert*, δάκτυλον Hp.*Superf.*5; ῥῆμα Luc. *Lex.*24, cf. *Pisc.*22; π. ἐς τὴν πλευρὰν τὸν ἀκινάκην Id.*Tox.*58:—Med., Id.*DMeretr.*12.1, *AP*11.210 (Lucill.):—Pass., Luc.*Deor.Conc.* 10. II. *stop up*, τὰ ὦτα S.E.*P.*1.50. [ῡ in *AP* l.c.]

⊛ **παραβώμιος,** ον, *beside* or *at the altar*, f.l. in S.*OT*184. 2. π., τό, *hymn sung at an altar*, *Michel* 499.11 (Teos), cf. *Inscr.Perg.*374 *C*10, Ph.2.484 (pl.), Luc.*Syr.D.*42. 3. παραβώμια θύειν *IG*2$^{2}$. 1361.7.

**παραγαύδης,** ου, ὁ, *garment with purple border*, Lyd.*Mag.*1.17, 2.4 (-γώδ- cod.); *paragaudae*, *Cod.Theod.*10.21.1:—Dim. ⊛ **-γαύδιον,** *POxy.*1026.12 (v A.D.); in form **-γαῦδιν,** *Edict.Diocl.*19.29; cf. παρακαυτωδόν.

**παραγγᾰρεία,** ἡ, *extra transport provision*, in pl., *Cod.Theod.*8.5.15, 16.2.10, 16.2.14, *Cod.Just.*1.3.2.3, al.

**παραγγ-ελεύς,** έως, ὁ, *informer, accuser*, *Gloss.* ⊛ **-ελία,** ἡ, *command* or *order* issued to soldiers, X.*HG*2.1.4, *Act.Ap.*16.24; τόπος ἐπιτηδειότατος εἰς π. for giving the *word of command*, Plb.6.27.1: generally, *order* issued by an authority, *PAmh.*2.68.63 (i A.D.), etc. II. *summoning one's partisans* to support one in a suit at law, *exertion of influence*, σπουδὴ καὶ π., συγγνώμη καὶ π., D.19.1, 283. 2. *summons* to appear in court, *POxy.*484.18 (ii A.D.), etc. 3. *canvassing for public office*, Plu.*Crass.*15, App.*BC*1.21, etc. III. *set of rules* or *precepts*, ὑπὸ παραγγελίαν πίπτειν Arist. *EN*1104$^{a}$7; παραδόσεις καὶ π. Phld.*Rh.*1.78 S. (pl.); μεθοδικὴ π. Id. *Po.*2.33; *instruction, precept, advice*, Hp.*Jusj.*, D.S.4.36, 15.10; τὸ τέλος τῆς π. ἐστὶν ἀγάπη 1*Ep.Ti.*1.5; τεχνίτης π. λογικῆς, of *rules* of literary composition, D.S.26.1. ⊛ **-έλλω,** fut. -ελῶ: aor. 2 inf. Pass. παραγγελῆναι *PHamb.*25.9 (iii B.C.):—*pass on* or *transmit* a message, σέλας παραγγείλασα Μακίστου σκοπαῖς (nisi leg. παρηγγάρευσε) A.*Ag.*289, cf. 294, 316; μνήμην παραγγέλλοντες ὧν ἐκύρσατε E.*Supp.*1173. II. *give orders, give the word of command*, esp. of a general, A.*Pers.*469, Hdt.7.147, etc.; π. τινὶ κτείνειν Id.3.147, cf. X.*An.*1.8.3, Pl.*Phd.*116c, etc.: with dat. omitted, Hdt.8.70, etc.; τισὶ ὅπως c. fut., Pl.*R.*415b; π. ὅπως ἂν.. *give orders* to the end that.., Id.*Phd.*59e: c. acc. rei only, *order*, π. παρασκευὴν σίτου *order* corn to be supplied, Hdt.3.25; σιτία Th.7.43: c. acc. cogn., π. παράγγελμα Lys.12.17, Hyp.*Ath.*14; παραγγελίᾳ π. *Act.Ap.*5.28:—Pass., τὰ παραγγελλόμενα *orders*, Th.2.11, Arist.*Pol.*1298$^{a}$18; ἐς τὰ π. ἰέναι Th. 1.121, 3.55; κατὰ τὰ παρηγγελμένα X.*An.*2.2.8; παρηγγέλλετο ἐπ' αὐτὸν στρατεία Aeschin.3.65, cf. 90. 2. *recommend, exhort* (not so strong as κελεύω), π. τινὶ πράσσειν τι S.*Ph.*1178 (lyr.), etc.; τινί τι E. *Heracl.*825; τινί τι περί τινος Th.1.129. 3. *summon* to appear, π. παραγίνεσθαι ἐπὶ τὸ κριτήριον *Sammelb.*3925.3 (ii B.C.). 4. of a physician, *prescribe*, τι Arist.*Pr.*885$^{b}$27. 5. τὰ παρηγγελμένα *the points we have enjoined*, Id.*Top.*153$^{a}$5; τὰ ὑπὸ [λόγου] παραγγελθέντα Id.*Rh. Al.*1420$^{b}$26. III. *encourage, cheer on*, c. acc., ἵππους Thgn.998; π. εἰς ὅπλα *call* to arms, X.*An.*1.5.13. IV. *summon to one's help*, esp. in politics, *summon one's partisans, form a cabal*, D.21.4 (v.l. περιήγγελκεν), cf. *Prooem.*55, Lys.1.41. 2. π. τὴν ἀρχήν *canvass for* office, D.H.11.61, cf. Plu.*Mar.*5, etc.: abs., π. εἰς ὑπατείαν *to be candidate for..*, Id.*Caes.*13, cf. *Cat.Mi.*8; ἐς δημαρχίαν App.*BC*1.21. 3. ἐκ μειρακίων π. εἰς ἄνδρα *claim* one's majority, Poll.2.10. **-ελμα,** ατος, τό, *message transmitted* by beacons, φλογὸς παραγγέλμασιν A. *Ag.*480 (lyr.). II. *order, word of command*, Lys.12.17; παράγγελμα ἐχόντων μὴ χωρίζεσθαι Test.ap.D.21.168; ἀπὸ παραγγέλματος by *word of command*, Th.8.99; ἐκ π. Plb.1.27.8, etc.; διδόναι τὰ παραγγέλματα Id.10.23.9; ἄρχων παντὸς π. Lxx 1*Ki.*22.14. b. *mobilization order*, *PHib.*1.78 (iii B.C.); *mobilization*, μὴ εἶναί σε ἐμ βασιλικῷ π. *PBaden*48.10 (ii B.C.), cf. *Ostr.*1535 (ii B.C.), *PAmh.*2. 50.5 (ii B.C.). 2. *edict* of a Roman governor, Wilcken *Chr.*202 (ii A.D.). III. *instruction, precept*, Democr.208, X.*Cyn.*13.9, Arist. *Insomn.*458$^{b}$21; τὰ δικανικὰ π. Id.*Rh.Al.*1421$^{b}$4; τὰ π. ὡς δεῖ ζῆν Zeno *Stoic.*1.57; π. σοφιστικά Phld.*Rh.*1.89 S.; τὸ π. τῶν τεχνῶν D.H.*Comp.*25; τεχνικὰ π. Longin.2.1; τούτῳ δέδωκεν ὁ Ζεὺς π. *SIG*985.12 (Philadelphia, i A.D.); distd. from τόπος, Thphr.*Fr.* 70. **-ελμᾰτικός,** ή, όν, *concerned with rules, like a manual*, D.H. *Comp.*22. Adv. -κῶς *by way of admonition*, S.E.*P.*1.204. **-ελσις,** εως, ἡ, in war, *transmission of orders*, Th.5.66 (pl.), Pl.*Lg.*942b (pl.); ἀπὸ παραγγέλσεως πορεύεσθαι X.*An.*4.1.5.

**παράγειος,** ον, (γῆ) *haunting the shallow water near the shore*, ζῷα π., opp. πελάγια, Arist.*HA*602$^{a}$16; of sea-plants, Thphr.*HP*4.6.7.

**παραγεμιστή,** ἡ, a local name for the *torpedo*, Eust.261.17.

**παραγένησις,** εως, ἡ, *presence*, Epicur.ap.Eust.111.25.

**παραγεύω,** *give a taste* of a thing, φρονήματος παραγεύειν τὸ θῆλυ *to give* women *a slight taste* of courage, Plu.*Lyc.*14:—Med., fut. -εύσομαι D.C.64.1; *taste slightly*, ποτοῖ Anaxil.10; καινοῦ τινος Antiph.246, cf. J.*AJ*4.8.2.

**παρα-γήρᾱμα,** *cadaver, delirus, silicernium*, *Gloss.* **-γηράω,** *to be the worse for old age, be superannuated*, ὁ δῆμος ὥσπερ παραγεγηρακώς Aeschin.3.251, cf. D.S.9.4, J.*BJ*1.30.3, Poll.2.16.

⊛ **παραγίγνομαι,** Ion. and later Gr. **-γίνομαι** [ῐ], aor. Pass. παρεγενήθην Plb.3.99.2, etc.:—*to be beside, by* or *near*: c. dat. pers. et rei, καί σφιν παρεγίγνετο δαιτί *attended* them *at* the banquet, Od.17.173: c. dat. pers. only, Σοφοκλεῖ π. ἐρωτωμένῳ *was by* him when he was asked, Pl.*R.*329b, cf. Antipho 6.17: c. dat. rei only, π. τῇ μάχῃ *to be present at..*, Pl.*Chrm.*153c; τῇ συνουσίᾳ Id.*Smp.*172c, cf. Hdt.8. 109; also π. ἐν τοῖς ἀγῶσι Isoc.12.52; ἐν τοιοῖσδε λόγοις, ἐν τῇ συνουσίᾳ, Pl.*Prt.*337a, *Smp.*173b: abs., Antipho 2.3.5. 2. π. τινί *come to one's side, stand by, second*, Hes.*Th.*429, 436, Hdt.3.32; μάρτυρες.. τοῖσι θανοῦσιν π. A.*Eu.*319 (anap.); ἐπί τινα against one, Th.2. 95; μάχῃ.. π. τισί *support* them in battle, Id.3.54: abs., Hes.*Th.* 432, Th.6.67; ἄνδρες ἱππῆς -γένεσθε Ar.*Eq.*242; -γενηθεὶς ἐπάγγελτος *SIG*708.21 (Istropolis, ii B.C.). 3. of things, *to be at hand, accrue* to one, πόλεμος ὅθεν καί τις δύναμις παρεγένετο Th.1.15, cf. X.*Mem.* 4.2.2; φόβοι παραγιγνόμενοί τισι Isoc.5.34; ἀρετὴ π. οἷς ἂν π. Pl. *Men.*99e, cf. 86d, Arist.*EN*1099$^{b}$16; ἀπὸ φυσιολογίας Phld.*Rh.*1. 122 S.; of scientific learning, Arist.*APo.*71$^{a}$4; of virtue, ὅτῳ τρόπῳ παραγίγνεται Pl.*Men.*71a. 4. π. ἀπό τινος *to be descended* from.., or perh. *to have a right to attend a sacrifice through descent* from.., *Inscr.Cos*405. II. *come to*, τινι Thgn.139, X.*Cyr.*4.1.14, etc.; π. ἐς κώμην Hdt.1.185; π. ἐς τὠυτό *come to* the same point, Id.2.4; ἐς τὸ δέον Id.1.32; ἐπὶ τὰς ταφάς Aeschin.3.235: abs., *arrive, come up*, παρεγένοντο αἱ νέες Hdt.6.95. 2. *come to maturity*, of corn, Id. 1.193; of the horns of oxen, *to be fully grown*, Id.4.29. 3. *have recourse to*, ἐπὶ τροφὴν καὶ πόμα Gal.15.506; ἐπὶ τὸ τῆς ὄνου γάλα ib. 746.

**παραγιγνώσκω,** later **-γῑνώσκω,** *decide wrongly, commit an error of judgement*, ὑπὲρ τούτων περὶ αὐτοῦ X.*Mem.*1.1.17; π. τοῦ δικαίου Philostr.*VS*2.27.2.

**παραγκᾰλ-ίζομαι,** *take into one's arms*, Poll.2.139. **-ισμα,** ατος, τό, *that which is taken into the arms, darling*, of mistress or wife, S. *Ant.*650, Lyc.113.

**παραγκιστρόομαι,** Pass., *to be furnished with barbs*, βέλη παρηγκιστρωμένα Plu.2.631e, cf. D.S.17.43.

**παραγκων-ίζω,** *set the arms a-kimbo*, Clearch.26, Phot., Suid.:—Med., *push aside with the elbows, elbow out*, τὸν πλησίον Luc.*Tim.*54; ἀλλήλους Id.*Pisc.*34 (v.l.): generally, *elbow out, supplant*, Str.5.3.2; ἐραστάς Alciphr.1.6; *supersede* an antiquated theory, Ael.*Tact.Praef.* 4; *throw aside*, πᾶσαν αἰδῶ Sor.2.25. **-ιστής,** οῦ, ὁ, *one who elbows*, Clearch.26.

**παράγλουτος,** ον, *with spare buttocks*, *Hippiatr.*14.

**παραγλύφω** [ῠ], *counterfeit*, τὰς σφραγῖδας D.S.1.78. II. *cut a notch*, παραγλύψαντα χρὴ τοῦ ὀστέου ἐνέδρην τῷ μοχλῷ ἀσφαλέα ποιῆσαι Hp.*Fract.*31, cf. Gal.2.461, *UP*13.3.

**παραγνᾰθ-ίδιος,** ον, *on* or *for the cheek*, κόσμος ἵππου Eust.1324.39; τὸ π., = sq., Id.67.43. **-ίς,** ίδος, ἡ, *cheekpiece* of a helmet or tiara, *IG*2$^{2}$.1461.16, Str.15.3.15, Eust.601.10. II. *cheek-muscle*, *Hippiatr.*34. III. pl., name of a fish or parts of a fish, *PCair. Zen.*680.31 (iii B.C.).

**παραγνάμπτω,** *pass by*, Coluth.239b.

**παρ-άγνυμι,** *fracture at the side* or *slightly*, pf. παρέᾱγα (intr.), Hp. *Mochl.*40.

**παρᾰγοράζω,** = παροψωνέω, Alex.61.

**παρᾱγορέομαι,** Dor. for παρηγ-.

**παρᾰγόρευσις,** εως, ἡ, *prohibition*, cj. in J.*AJ*18.9.2; = ἄρνησις, Hsch.

⊛ **παράγραμμα,** ατος, τό, *that which one writes beside*: *additional clause*, προσπαραγράφειν π. D.39.9. II. in cipher, *substitute for a letter*, Aen.Tact.31.18.

**παραγραμμᾰτ-εύω,** *alter by changing a letter*: hence, *make an alliterative pun on* a name, Sch.Ar.*Eq.*78; cf. γράμμα II.1c. ⊛ **-ίζω,** = foreg., D.L.3.26. II. *emend* a reading *by change of letters*, Str. 1.2.34. **-ισις,** εως, ἡ, *putting one letter for another*, Tz.*H.*8.125 (pl.). **-ισμός,** ὁ, = foreg., St.Byz. s.v. Τύανα, Sch.Ar.*Eq.*59, Eust. ad D.P.827.

**παραγραμμίζω,** = παραγραμματίζω I, Sch.Ar.*Pax*867: metaph., π. τὰ τῶν θεῶν *makes* the gods *nugatory*, prob. in Epicur.*Fr.*87.

**παρα-γραπτέον,** *one must mark with the* παραγραφή, Sch.Il.14. 153. **-γραπτος,** ον, *limited*, Phld.*Piet.*86.

**παραγρᾰφ-ή,** ἡ, *anything written beside, marginal note* or *sign*, to mark the close of a sentence, Isoc.15.59, Hyp.*Dem.Fr.*(c), Arist.*Rh.* 1409$^{a}$20; to mark that a passage is spurious, Luc.*Pr.Im.*24; in a drama, to indicate the change of persons, Sch.Ar.*Ra.*1479, *Pax* 443; *stage-direction*, cj. in Ath.10.453c. 2. *entry* in a register of debts or liabilities, *PHib.*1.40.14 (iii B.C.), *PTeb.*188 (ii/i B.C.), etc. II. *exception taken* by the defendant *to the admissibility of a suit, special plea, demurrer*, Isoc.18.1, 20, D.35.45, Poll.8.57, 58; π. διδόναι D.34.17; opp. εὐθυδικίᾳ εἰσιέναι, Id.45.6; τὰς π. ἀντιλαγχάνειν Id.37.33: coupled with ὑπωμοσία, Id.21.84 (pl.): metaph., of argument, *counterplea*, Gal.19.170. 2. in Roman Law, μακρᾶς νομῆς π., = *longae possessionis praescriptio*, Mitteis *Chr.*374 (iii A.D.); χρονία π. Just.*Nov.*30.7 *Intr.*; also, = *exceptio*, ib.94.1. III. Rhet., *brief summary* of one subject *before passing on* to another, Sch.Il.16.1, Eust.107.46. IV. *limit*, τοῦ βίου Phld.*Mort.*39; παραγραφαῖς ὁρίζειν τὰς ἐπιμελείας Id.*Oec.*p.75 J. V. (γράφω I.1) *trenching round* vines, *POxy.*1631.11 (iii A.D.), 1692.14 (ii A.D.). **-ικός,** ή, όν, *in the form of a* παραγραφή II.1, κεφάλαιον Hermog.*Inv.*3.5; ἀγών D.32 Arg.; τὸ π. *objection of the defendant to the indictment*, Hermog. *Stat.*3. Adv. -κῶς *by way of* παραγραφή II.1, D.22 Arg.ii.11. **-ίς,** ίδος, ἡ, *writing instrument*, Aq.*Is.*44.13, Poll.4.18, 10.59. ⊛ **-ος** (sc. γραμμή), ἡ, *line* or *stroke drawn in the margin*, with a dot over it, to mark the change of persons in a dialogue, or the corresponding parts of a chorus or parabasis, Heph.*Poëm.*p.73 C., Sch.Ar.*Nu.*518, etc.; = παραγραφή I.1, Harp. **-ω,** *write by the side*, πλησίον π. Ar.*V.*99. b. mostly, *add, subjoin*, esp. a clause to a law, contract, etc., τί βεβούλευται περὶ τῶν σπονδῶν ἐν τῇ στήλῃ παραγράψαι; Id.*Lys.*

513, cf. Pl.*Lg*.785a (Pass.); π. "τῷ δεῖνι ἀποδοῦναι δεῖ" D.52.4; ὑποκάτω π. *add* particulars below, Hyp.*Eux*.30; π. τὸ ὄνομα παρ' ᾧ ἂν κείωνται αἱ συνθῆκαι *IG*2².1176.20. c. *enter* a debt or liability against a person's name, c. acc. pers. et rei, *POxy*.488.32 (ii/iii A.D.), 513.33 (ii A.D.):—more freq. Pass., *have entered against one*, *PTeb*.5.189 (ii B.C.), etc.: with personal subject, παραγέγραμμαι τῷ πράκτορι *PPetr*. 2 p.42 (iii B.C.), cf. *POxy*.513.13 (ii A.D.), etc. 2. *change an entry*, ἄλλου πατρὸς ἑαυτὸν π. *enrol* oneself as the son of *another* father, D.39.31. 3. *interpolate* in a Ms., Gal.7.891, 18(1).151,155. 4. *imitate*, διὰ τούτων τῶν στίχων τὰ εἰρημένα ὑπὸ Ἰβύκου Sch.A.R.3.158. 5. Pass., *to be marked with the* παράγραφος, κατὰ δύο παραγεγραμμένον ᾆσμα Heph.*Poëm*.1. 6. *bring to a close*, λόγον Phld.*Piet*.22. II. Med., with pf. Pass., in various legal phrases: 1. παραγράφεσθαι τὸν νόμον *have* the law *written in parallel columns with* a decree which is charged with illegality, νόμους ἄλλους παραβέβηκεν, οὓς οὐ παραγεγράμμεθα διὰ τὸ πλῆθος D.23.63, cf. 51:—Pass., οἱ παραγεγραμμένοι νόμοι Id.18.111, Aeschin.3.200. 2. π. τινὰ διαιτητήν *have* him *registered* as arbiter, D.40.16. 3. Δημοσθένει τὴν γραφὴν τοῦ φόνου παραγράψασθαι *to bring a false charge*, Test.ap.D.21.107. 4. παραγεγραμμένος μὴ εἰσαγώγιμον εἶναι τὴν δίκην *having demurred to* the admissibility of the suit (v. παραγραφή II. 1), Id.32.1; π. περί τινος Id. 38.1, cf. Isoc.18.2: coupled with ὑπόμνυσθαι, D.47.39,45; ἑαυτὸν -όμενος μόνος ἀγωνίσασθαι τὴν δίκην ἐντολὰς οὐκ ἔχων *calling* himself *inadmissible* as pleader on the ground that he has no orders to plead alone, Philostr.*VS*2.32. 5. *draw a line across, cancel*: metaph., *efface*, τὸ τιμᾶσθαι μετὰ τοῦτο πᾶσαν παρεγράψατο τὴν συμφοράν Aristid. 2.246 J.; ὁ θυμὸς τῇ ῥύμῃ τῆς ὀργῆς -γραφόμενος τὴν φύσιν Callistr. *Stat*.13 (v.l. περι-):—Pass., *to be abolished*, τὰ φιλάνθρωπα παρεγράφη Plb.9.31.5. 6. *reject*, Phot.:—in Pass., Sch.S.*OT*906.

⊛ **παραγράψῐμος**, ον, *exceptionable*, S.E.*M*.7.170.

**παρ-αγρυπνέω**, *watch diligently*, Onos.42.15 (Pass.).

**παράγυμν-ος**, ον, *naked at the side, half-naked*, D.L.2.132. **-όω**, *lay bare at the side, expose*, τι τῆς πλευρᾶς Arr.*Tact*.40.5, cf. D.C.49.6 (Pass.). 2. metaph., *lay bare, disclose*, τὸν πάντα λόγον Hdt.1.126, cf. 8.19, 9.44; τὸ βούλευμα Conon 50:—Pass., παρεγυμνώθη διότι.. Plb.1.80.9.

**παραγύρως**, Adv., gloss on διαμπερές, Hsch. (s.v.l.).

**παραγχῠσία**, poet. -ίη, ἡ, *stagnant pool* left by a receding tide, Man.4.254 (pl.).

**παρ-άγω**, fut. -ξω Phld.*Rh*.1.19S.: pf. παραγέωχα *PTeb*.5.198 (ii B.C.), παραγείοχα *Stud.Pal*.22.3 (ii A.D.):—*lead by* or *past* a place, c. acc. loci, Hdt.4.158, cf. 9.47; πάραγε πτέρυγας fly *past*, E.*Ion* 166 (lyr.); π. θριάμβους App.*Mith*.117, cf. *BC*2.101; of a person, ἐν θριάμβῳ παράγεσθαι Plu.*Caes*.55. 2. in Tactics, *march* the men *up from the side, bring them from column into line*, π. τοὺς ἐπὶ κέρως πορευομένους.. εἰς μέτωπον X.*HG*7.5.22, cf. *Cyr*.2.3.21, *An*.4.6.6; τὰς [τάξεις] εἰς τὰ πλάγια ib.3.4.14; ἔξωθεν τῶν κεράτων ib.3.4.21. 3. *bring round* or *forward*, ἀγκῶνα παρὰ τὸ στῆθος Hp.*Art*.2, cf. 74; *twist round* or *out of place*, Alex.Aphr. *in Sens*.16.19. 4. π. ὑπόχυμα *couch* a cataract, Gal.*Thras*.23. 5. *divert*, ὑδραγωγόν *POxy*.971 (i/ii A.D.). II. *lead aside from the way, mislead*, ἔννυχοι πάραγον κοῖται Pi.*P*.11.25; σοφία παράγοισα μύθοις Id.*N*.7.23; π. τινὰ εἰς ἀρκύστατα A.*Pers*.99 codd. (lyr.); π. ψεύδεσι Pl.*R*.383a; φενακίζειν καὶ π. D.22.34, cf. *PMagd*.12.7 (iii B.C.), *PCair.Zen*.289.20 (iii B.C.):—Pass., φόβῳ παρηγόμην S.*OT*974; λόγοις παράγεσθαι Th.1.91; ἀπάτῃ π. ὑπό τινων ib.34; νέοις παραχθεὶς E.*Supp*.232. 2. *divert from one's course, influence*, Μοίρας Hdt.1.91: c. acc. pers. et gen. rei, *divert from*, [τινὰ] τοῦ τῆς ῥητορικῆς τέλους Phld. l.c.; *induce, lead to* or *into* a thing, ἔς τι E.*IT*478: mostly in bad sense, π. ἐς ἀμπλακίην, ἐς ἀναιδείην, Thgn.404, Archil.78:—Pass., *to be influenced, persuaded*, οἷοι θυσίαις τε καὶ εὐχωλαῖς παράγεσθαι Pl.*R*.365e, cf. *Lg*. 885b, Th.2.64; λόγῳ παραχθέντες X.*Mem*.4.8.5: c. inf., παρηγμένος μισθοῖς εἰργάσθαι τι S.*Ant*.294. 3. of things, *lead aside*: hence, *wrest*, π. τοὺς νόμους ἐπί τι *pervert* the laws to this end, Pl.*R*.550d, cf. Is.11.36; οἱ θεοὶ τῶν πονηρῶν ἀνθρώπων τὴν διάνοιαν π. Lycurg.92; π. τὴν ἀλήθειαν Philostr.*Ep*.35:—Pass., τὰ γράμματα παρῆκται, from age, Paus.6.19.5. 4. *avert*, πειθοῖ καὶ λόγῳ τὴν ἀνάγκην Plu.*Phoc*.2. 5. *change slightly*, of letters in the derivation of words, Pl.*Cra*.398c,d, 400c, Plu.2.354c: freq. in Gramm. in Pass., *to be derived*, ἀπό.. Demetr.Lac.*Herc*.1014.58, D.T.641.4, A.D.*Pron*.34.25; ἐκ.. Id. *Synt*.111.2; παρά c. acc., Id.*Adv*.146.10: c. gen., τὸ μελιτηρὸν τοῦ τηρεῖν [παραχθέν] Id.*Pron*.30.17: generally, *to be formed*, διὰ τοῦ "θεν" Id.*Adv*.184.12; τὴν κτητικὴν διὰ τῆς "οι" π. Id.*Pron*.109.6; *to be inflected*, ἀντωνυμίαι ὡς ὀνόματα εἰς τὰ γένη καὶ τὰς πτώσεις π. ib.111.2, cf. *Synt*.110.8; ὁ ἀνδριὰς οὐ λέγεται ξύλον, ἀλλὰ παράγεται ξύλινος *is called by a modification*, Arist.*Metaph*.1033ᵃ17. III. *bring and set beside* others, *bring forward, introduce*, ἐς μέσον Hdt.3.129; εἰς τὸ μέσον Pl. *Lg*.713b; εἰς ὑμᾶς Antipho 4.1.5; π. εἰς τὸν δῆμον *bring before* the people, Lys.13.32, cf. Th.5.45; εἰς τὸ δικαστήριον *before* the court, D.26.17; παραχθῆναι τὴν γραφήν Antipho 2.3.6; also, *bring forward* as a witness, etc., τὸν ἥκοντα παρήγαγον D.18.170:—Med., μάρτυρα παραγόμενος Pl.*Lg*.836c. b. *introduce* on the stage, *bring in*, Ath. 3.117d, 6.230b, al., D.L.2.28, prob. in Anon. *de Com*.(*CGF* p.7); οἵους οἱ κωμῳδοδιδάσκαλοι π. ἀγροίκους Arist.*EE*1230ᵇ19: hence, *represent, portray*, τοξότας αὐτοὺς παρήγαγον Corn.*ND*32, cf. 14 (Pass.). c. *produce, deliver*, ἐπὶ τὰ χώματα καλαμείαν *PTeb*.5.198 (ii B.C.), cf. 92.8 (ii B.C., Pass.). 2. *bring in*, with a notion of secrecy, ἄνδρας π. ἔσω Hdt.5.20:—Pass., *come in stealthily, slip in*, π. γὰρ ἐνέρων δολιόπους ἀρωγὸς εἴσω στέγας S.*El*.1391 (lyr.); of things, τὸ ὕδωρ ὀρύγμασι καὶ τάφροις εἰς τὸ πεδίον π. Plu.*Cam*.4. IV. *carry on, protract*, τὴν πρᾶξιν D.S.18.65; π. τὸν χρόνον *pass* it, Plu.*Agis* 13, etc.; v. infr. B. III. V. *direct, guide*, κῆτος παραγόμενον εὐπειθῶς Id.2.981a. VI. *produce, create*, Plot.6.8.20, etc.; τὸ παράγον, opp. τὸ παραγόμενον, Procl.*Inst*.7, cf. Dam.*Pr*.32, etc.:—Pass., ἀπὸ τῶν ἀτελεστέρων τελειότερα παράγεται Iamb.*Myst*.3.22, cf. *Gp*.9.1.1. VII. *draw along*, ἄνωθεν κάτω τὰς χεῖρας (in massage), Herod.Med.ap. Orib.6.20.8.

B. intr., *pass by, pass on one's way*, X.*Cyr*.5.4.44, Euphro 10. 15, Plb.5.18.4, etc.; τοῖς παράγουσιν χαίρειν *IPE*2.378 (Phanagoria): also c. acc., *pass by*, μνήματα *Lyr.Alex.Adesp*.37.25; κώμην *PTeb*.17.4 (ii B.C.). 2. *pass away*, Lxx *Ps*.143(144).4, 1*Ep.Cor*.7.31:—in Pass., 1*Ep.Jo*.2.8,17. II. *pass along* the coast, Plb.4.44.3; simply, *go*, εἴσω πάραγε Men.*Epit*.188, cf. 194, *Sam*.80, *Pk*.275. III. *delay* (v. supr. A. IV), παρῆγον ἐφ' ἱκανὸν χρόνον D.S.11.3; ἐξέκρουε καὶ π. Plu.*Rom*.23.

⊛ **παραγωγ-εύς**, έως, ὁ, *introducer*, *IG*7.2428.6 (Thebes, iii B.C., pl.). ⊛ **-ή**, ἡ, *leading by* or *past, carrying across*, X.*An*.5.1. 16. 2. *production* in court, παίδων καὶ γυναικῶν Hermog.*Stat*.3; συμβολαιογράφου ἢ μαρτύρων *Cod.Just*.4.21.16.2. 3. in Tactics, *deploying from column into line*, X.*Lac*.11.6 (pl.), Plb.10.23.5. 4. π. τῶν κωπῶν *sliding motion* of the oars, so that they made no splash in coming out of the water, X.*HG*5.1.8; *drawing along* of the hands in massage, Herod.Med.ap.Orib.6.20.9. 5. in Surgery, *coaptation* in reducing a dislocation, Hp.*Art*.22 (pl.), Orib.49.27.5; in setting a fracture, Gal.10.430. b. *twisting out of place*, Alex.Aphr. *in Sens*. 17.15. 6. *supplying, furnishing*, ἡ π. τοῦ ὑγροῦ τῷ ὕδρωπι Metrod. *Fr*.46 K., cf. *PRyl*.ii pp.255, 421, *BGU*362 viii 9 (iii A.D.). 7. *import-* or *transport-licence*, *PLond*.3.1169.45 (ii A.D.). II. *leading astray, misleading*, τῆς ἀπάτης τῇ π. *by the seduction* of the fraud, deception practised, Hdt.6.62: freq. in Oratt., *false argument, quibble*, D.23.95,219 (pl.); λόγος ταῦτα καὶ π. τοῦ πράγματος *attempt to mislead* as to the facts, Id.30.26; οὐ περιπλοκαὶ οὐδὲ π. Plu.*Fab*.3; ἐπὶ παραγωγῇ Eus.Mynd.63. 2. *misbehaviour*, Phld.*Ir*.p.50 W. (pl.). 3. *variation* of dialect, Hdt.1.142 (pl.). 4. *persuading, turning*, ἡ τῶν θεῶν ὑπ' ἀνθρώπων π. Pl.*R*.364d. III. Gramm., *derivation*, A.D.*Synt*.192.3, *Adv*.146.9 (pl.); π. Ἀττική (ἀγειρέθω from ἄγω) *EM*8.23; *formation*, ἡ π. ἡ διὰ τοῦ "φι" A.D.*Adv*.194.22; *inflexion*, ἡ ἐν τοῖς ὀνόμασι π. Id.*Pron*.18.14. 2. *addition to the end* of a syllable, Id.*Synt*.100.8, *EM*92.30. 3. generally, *derivation, production, creation*, Iamb.*Myst*.3.22, Dam.*Pr*.39. IV. (παράγω B) *coming to land*, Plb.8.5.4. 2. *march in battle-order*, Ascl.*Tact*.10. 1, 11.1, etc.: concrete, *body of troops on the march*, Arr.*Tact*.29.2, Ael.*Tact*.37.2. 3. *deviation, transgression*, Pl.*Lg*.741d, Iamb. *Myst*.10.5. 4. *evasion, delay*, π. καὶ πρόφασιν ἐμβάλλειν Plu.*Sull*. 28; εὐλάβεια καὶ π. Id.*Luc*.29. **-ιάζω**, *levy toll on ships visiting a port*, τινας Plb.3.2.5, 4.44.4 and 46.6. **-ιον**, τό, *toll levied on ships visiting a port*, Philippid.17, *IG*11(2).163 *A* 24 (Delos, iii B.C.), *Milet*.3 No.139.6 (iii B.C.), Plb.4.47.3, Poll.9.30. II. *well, source*, *Cod.Just*.11.43.10. **-ίς**, ίδος, ἡ, *groove, slot*, in a torsion-engine, Ph.*Bel*.76.20. **-ός**, όν, *misleading, deceitful*, ὦ πρόδοτι καὶ παραγωγέ *Com.Adesp*.595. 2. *creative*, Ascl. *in Metaph*.92.5. II. Pass. (proparox.), *easily movable*, ὀστέα Hp.*Fract*.16 (Comp.). 2. *derived from* another word, opp. πρωτότυπος, D.T.634.21, A.D.*Adv*. 146.2; ἔκ τινος Id.*Synt*.200.21, *EM*97.33; τινος Eust.1553.35. Adv. -γως *by a slight change*, Plu.2.316a, Ath.11.480f. b. *formed in parody*, ἔπος Numen.ap.Eus.*PE*14.5.

**παραγών-ιος**, ον, *adjacent to an angle*, *Inscr.Délos* 504 *A* 6 (iii B.C.); λίθος *Rev.Phil*.43.202 (Didyma), *Milet*.7 p.57. **-ίσκος**, ὁ, *a cutting* or *scraping instrument*, v.l. in Lxx *Is*.44.13.

**παραδαίνῠμαι**, aor. 1 -εδαισάμην, *dine with*, τινι Simm.1.2.

**παράδακρυ**, τό, = βούνιον, Ps.-Dsc.4.123.

**παραδακρύω**, *weep beside* or *with*, τινι Luc.*Nav*.2.

**παραδαρθάνω**, only in Ep. aor. 2 παρέδρᾰθον:—*sleep beside*, τῇδε γὰρ αὖ μοι νυκτὶ παρέδραθεν Od.20.88; παραδραθέειν φιλότητι Il.14. 163.

**παράδειγ-μα**, ατος, τό, (παραδείκνυμι) *pattern, model*: of an architect's *model* (or perh. *plan*) of a building, Hdt.5.62, *IG*2².1668.95, 11(2).161 *A* 43,75, 203 *B* 95, al. (Delos, iii B.C.); a sculptor's or painter's *model*, Pl.*Ti*.28c, *R*.500e, *IG*1².374.248, 2².1675.23 (pl.); of the divine *exemplars* after which earthly things are made, ἐν οὐρανῷ ἴσως π. ἀνάκειται Pl.*R*.592b; of the Platonic *ideas*, opp. εἰκών, Arist.*Metaph*. 991ᵃ21, 1013ᵃ27 (later, *copy*, Πλάτων τὸν ὁρατὸν κόσμον γεγονέναι π. τοῦ νοητοῦ κόσμου *Placit*.2.6.4 (v.l. πρὸς π.)). 2. *precedent, example*, παραδείγματα λαβεῖν παρά τινος Pl.*Men*.77b; ἐμὲ π. ποιούμενος Id.*Ap*. 23b; παραδείγμασι χρῆσθαι Th.3.10; π. χρῆσθαί τινι copy one's *example*, And.4.22; τοῖς γεγενημένοις π. χρῆσθαι Lys.25.23; π. ἐξοίσετε Din. 1.107; π. καταλείπεσθαι Lycurg.9; δοῦναι παραδείγματα Pl.*Lg*.876e; ἐπὶ παραδείγματος by way of *example*, Aeschin.1.177; παραδείγματος εἵνεκα Lys.22.20; παραδείγματα ἁμαρτημάτων And.3.32. b. *sample*, παραδείγματα νεκρῶν ξύλινα *samples* of mummies made of wood, Hdt. 2.86, cf. *PSI*5.485 (iii B.C.), *PCair.Zen*.445.9, 665.2 (iii B.C.). 3. *lesson, warning*, ἔχοντες παραδείγματα τῶν ἐκεῖ Ἑλλήνων Th.6.77; τὸ σὸν π. ἔχων S.*OT*1193 (lyr.); τοῖς ἄλλοις ἔσται π. ὕβρεως Ar. *Th*.670 (anap.); π. καθιστάναι Th.3.40; ζῶντά τινα τοῖς λοιποῖς π. ποιῆσαι D.19.101, cf. 343, 21.98; π. τοὺς Σύρους λαβέ Men. 544.1; π. τοῦ μὴ ἀδικεῖν Lys.27.5. 4. *argument, proof from example*, Th.1.2, etc., cf. Arist.*APr*.68ᵇ38, *Rh*.1356ᵇ3, 1402ᵇ14, 1418ᵃ 3, Zeno *Stoic*.1.23; including παραβολή and λόγος, Arist.*Rh*.1393ᵃ

27. 5. in Law, *leading case, precedent*, Wilcken *Chr.* 27.5 (ii A.D.). II. *foil, contrast*, τὰ γὰρ κακὰ π. τοῖς ἐσθλοῖσιν εἴσοψίν τ' ἔχει E.*El.*1085. **-μᾰτάριον**, τό, Dim. of foreg., *small model*, Ph.*Bel.*56.7. ⊛ **-μᾰτίζω**, *make an example of*, τινα Lxx *Nu.*25.4, Plb.2.60.7, 29.19.5 (Pass.); *make a show* or *spectacle of*, *Ev.Matt.*1.19; π. ἑαυτόν Plu.2.520b. II. *show by example*, Eust.153.18 (Pass.). **-μᾰτικός**, ή, όν, *consisting of* or *serving as a model* or *pattern*, μουσική Ph.1.18; opp. εἰκονικός, Dam.*Pr.*73: Comp. **-ώτερος** Procl. *in Alc.*p.38 C.; *serving as examples*, ἐπιχειρήματα Hermog. *Inv.*4.1. Adv. **-κῶς** *by means of examples*, Arist.*Metaph.*995$^{a}$7, S.E. *P.*3.163, Sch.Iamb.*Comm.Math.*18, Dam.*Pr.*270; opp. εἰκονικῶς, Procl.*Inst.*195. **-μάτιον**, τό, Dim. of παράδειγμα, *small model*, Ph.*Bel.*55.20. **-μᾰτισμός**, ὁ, *making an example of, pointing out to public shame*, Plb.15.20.5, 30.8.8, Lxx 3*Ma.*7.14, D.S.34.9, Ptol. *Tetr.*154; esp. of *military reprimand*, Plb.6.38.4. **-μᾰτιστέον**, *one must punish for example's sake*, Id.35.2.10. **-μᾰτώδης**, ες, *characterized by examples*, ῥητορεῖαι Arist.*Rh.*1356$^{b}$20, cf. 1403$^{a}$5.

⊛ **παραδείκ-νῡμι** (also **-ύω** Plb.4.25.3, *BCH*50.252 (Thasos), Phld. *Rh.*1.87 S.), *exhibit side by side*, τὸν χρυσὸν δοκιμάζομεν ἕτερα παραδεικνύοντες Isoc.12.39: abs., *make comparisons*, Pl.*Lg.*829e; *compare*, τινί τι Philostr.*VA*7.1: generally, *indicate, point out*, *PSI*4.353.11 (iii B.C.), etc.; τινὶ τὰ δέοντα Sosip.1.56; π. πόσοι κακῶς ἀπώλοντο Phld.*Lib.*p.34 O.; *point* a moral, D.C.58.22. 2. *exhibit, bring forward*, in Med., D.14.1. 3. *represent*, of a painter, *AP*5.148 (Mel.); *represent* as so and so, π. τινὰς οὐκ ὄντας Plb.3.21.5: folld. by an indirect interrog. clause, π. πότε καὶ πῶς καὶ δι' ἃς αἰτίας γέγονέ τι Id.4.28.4, etc.; ὅτι.. Epin.1.3: in bad sense, *expose, show up*, οἷος ὢν πολίτης διαλάθοι π. Plu.*Lys.*30. 4. *exhibit and hand over*, φόρους τινί X.*HG*2.1.14, cf. 2.3.8; ἐνέχυρα, γῆν, πρόβατα, *PCair.Zen.*18.4, 362.20, 406.2 (iii B.C.). 5. *assign, allot*, as a task, *PPetr.*3 p.103 (iii B.C.): generally, χέρσον *PTeb.*79.19 (ii B.C.):—Pass., ib.16. 6. *demonstrate*, A.D.*Synt.*137.11 (Pass.). **-τέον**, *one must show*, Gal.1.154, Iamb.*Protr.*6.

**παράδειξις**, εως, ἡ, *proof, establishment* of a fact, *PAmh.*2.68.63 (i A.D., pl.), etc. 2. *indication*, Iamb.*Comm.Math.*p.8 F. II. *comparison*, Phot.

**παραδειπν-έομαι**, *go without one's dinner*, Thphr.*Char.*8.13; παραδεδειπνημένος Amphis 31. **-ια**, τά, *side-dishes, dainties*, Porph. *Abst.*3.20. **-ίζω**, *cause to dine*, Lxx 2*Ki.*3.35 (v.l.). **-ις** (proparox.), ιδος, ὁ, ἡ, = παράσιτος, ἀλλοτρίων κτεάνων Eub.139.

**πᾰρᾰδεισ-άριος**, ὁ, *gardener*, Hsch. s.v. ἐρνοκόμων. ⊛ **-ος**, ὁ (also **παράδισος** *SIG*463.8 (Crete, iii B.C.)), *enclosed park* or *pleasure-ground*, Oriental word first used by X., always in reference to the *parks* of the Persian kings and nobles; π. μέγας ἀγρίων θηρίων πλήρης *An.*1.2.7; π. δασὺς παντοίων δένδρων ib.2.4.14; τὰ ἐν π. θηρία *Cyr.*1.3.14; θῆραι.. ἐν περιειργμένοις παραδείσοις *HG*4.1.15, cf. Thphr.*HP* 4.4.1, *AJA*16.13 (Sardes, 300 B.C.), Lxx *Ne.*2.8, Plu.*Art.*25. 2. generally, *garden, orchard*, *PRev.Laws* 33.11 (iii B.C.), *PCair.Zen.*33.3 (iii B.C.), *OGI*90.15 (Rosetta, ii B.C.), Lxx *Ca.*4.13, *Ec.*2.5, *CIG* 2694*b* (Mylasa), *PFay.*55.7 (ii A.D.), etc. 3. *the garden of Eden*, Lxx *Ge.*2.8. b. *Paradise, the abode of the blessed*, *Ev.Luc.*23.43, 2*Ep. Cor.*12.4. c. expl. of μακάρων νῆσοι, Procl. ad Hes *Op.*169. II. *stupid fellow*, *Com.Adesp.*1102. (Persian word, cf. Poll.9.13, Phot., and Avest. *pairidaēza-* 'enclosure'.)

**παραδέκομαι**, v. παραδέχομαι.

**παραδεκ-τέον**, *one must admit*, τι εἰς τὴν πόλιν Pl.*R.*378d; τὴν ἐξήγησιν Steph. *in Hp.*1.248 D. II. παραδεκτέος, α, ον, *to be admitted*, Pl.*R.*595a, *PGnom.*36 (ii A.D.). **-τός**, όν, *accepted*: *acceptable*, Jul.*Ep.*88.

**παραδέρω**, aor. 1 -έδειρα, *excoriate*, βραχίονα Hp.*Foet.Exsect.*1.

⊛ **παραδέχομαι**, Ion. **-δέκομαι**, fut. -ξομαι Pl.*Tht.*155c:—*receive from* another, σῆμα Il.6.178; [Γαῖα] σταγόνας παραδεξαμένη τίκτει θνητούς E.*Fr.*839.4 (anap.); τὰ φερόμενα γράμματα X.*Cyr.*8.6.17, etc.; of children, *receive by inheritance*, σοφώτατα νοήματα Pi.*O.*7.72; τὴν ἀρχήν Hdt.1.102; π. τὸν πόλεμον παρὰ τοῦ πατρός ib.18; but μάχην π. *take up and continue* the battle, Id.9.40; *receive by way of rumour* or *tradition*, π. φήμην Pl.*Lg.*713c; ἀκοήν τινος Id.*Ti.*23d; of magistrates or others, *receive* articles entered in an inventory, etc., *IG*1$^{2}$.91.21, al., *PHib.*1.32.4 (iii B.C.), etc.; of pupils, *receive lessons from* a master, τοὺς μετὰ πόνου.. παραδεχομένους Plu.*Cat.Mi.*1. b. *take over* an office or function, *BGU*1199.3, al. (i B.C.). 2. c. inf., π. τινὶ πράττειν τι *take upon oneself* or *engage* to another to do a thing, D.58.38. 3. *admit*, εἰς τὴν πόλιν Pl.*R.*394d, 399d, 605b; εἰς [τὴν οἰκίαν] D.40.2; εἰς τοὺς ἀγῶνας Aeschin.1.178; *admit to citizenship*, τῶν περιοίκων τινάς Arist.*Pol.*1303$^{a}$7; *admit* as a pupil, Pl.*Euthd.*304b; π. τὸ ἔθνος *admit to friendly relations*, Plb.38.9.8. 4. *admit, allow*, τὴν ἀπαγωγήν Lys.13.86, cf. Pl.*Tht.*155c, *Lg.*935d; π. σκῆψιν Hyp. *Eux.*7; π. τὸν λόγον *accept* the definition, Pl.*Chrm.*162e, cf. Arist. *Cat.*4$^{a}$28; *recognize as correct, agree to*, συντίμησιν *BGU*1119.54 (i B.C.); τὸ δαπανηθέν *PFay.*125.10 (ii A.D.). 5. *signify*, κτῆσιν A.D. *Synt.*171.6. II. in later writers the aor. παρεδέχθην takes also a pass. sense, Luc.*VH*2.21, *Gloss.*; ἀξιῶ παραδεχθῆναί τινα εἰς τοὺς ἐφήβους *to be admitted*, *POxy.*477.24 (ii A.D.); also, *to be credited* as a set-off, *BGU*831.15 (iii A.D.): so fut. -δεχθήσομαι *PAmh.*2.86.13 (i A.D.).

**παραδέω**, *fasten to* or *alongside of*, in Pass., Moschio ap.Ath.5.208b.

⊛ **παραδηλόω**, *intimate, insinuate, hint at*, D.19.22; ὡς.. Plu.*Crass.*18, etc.:—Pass., Hp.*Ep.*12. 2. *inform against*, Plu.*Alex.*49.

**παραδιαζεύγνῡμι**, *join disjunctively*, ἀξίωμα παραδιεζευγμένον a *subdisjunctive* proposition, Gell.16.8.14, cf. Gal.*Inst.Log.*15, al.

**παραδιαζευκτικός**, ή, όν, σύνδεσμος *subdisjunctive*, i.e. disjunctive, with the meaning '*or if you like*', used where either alternative alone and the two together are alike admissible, e.g. ἤ (ἠέ) in ἢ νέος ἠὲ παλαιός (Il.14.108), A.D.*Conj.*219.12, Gal.7.80, cf. Hdn.Gr.1.517, etc. Adv. **-κῶς** Gal.7.537, al.

**παραδῐαιτάομαι**, Pass., *live with*, παρά τινι Phot.; *live by* or *beside*, τῷ Νείλῳ Ael.*NA*2.48.

**παραδιᾱκονέω**, *live with and serve*, τινι Ar.*Av.*838.

**παραδια-στολή**, ἡ, in Rhet., *putting together of dissimilar things*, as a figure, Quint.*Inst.*9.3.65, Rutil.1.4, Isid.*Etym.*2.21.9. **-τάττομαι**, *rearrange, alter*, τὴν τῆς πολιτείας κατάστασιν Hierocl.p.52 A. (παραδιαλλάττοιτο Bentley). **-τῠπόω**, *enact beside*, Just.*Nov.*22.2 *Intr.* **-φέρομαι**, *coast all the way along*, περὶ τὰς νήσους Str.3.2.5.

**παραδιδάσκω**, *produce again*, παλαιὸν δρᾶμα *IG*2$^{2}$.2318.203.

⊛ **παραδίδωμι** (late **-δίδω** (δειδ-) *Tab.Defix.Aud.*156.8 (Rome, iv/v A.D.)), *give, hand over to another, transmit*, [παιδίον] τινί Hdt.1.117; τὰ ἐντεταλμένα, of couriers, Id.8.98; καθάπερ λαμπάδα τὸν βίον π. Pl. *Lg.*776b, etc.; of sentinels, π. τὸν κώδωνα Th.4.135; τὴν ἑωθινὴν φυλακήν Plu.*Arat.*7; τῷ παιδὶ π. τὴν ἀρχήν Hdt.2.159; τὰ πάτρια τεύχεα S.*Ph.*399 (lyr.); of letters to the person addressed, X.*Cyr.*8.6.17; of a purchase to the buyer, Id.*Oec.*20.28; of articles entered in an inventory by magistrates, *IG*1$^{2}$.324.2, etc.; in Astrol., π. τὸ ἔτος Vett.Val.100.30, Paul.Al.*I.*4; of an argument, π. τινὶ τὸν ἑξῆς λόγον Pl.*Criti.*106b; π. τὴν προξενίαν *hand* it *down* to one's posterity, X.*HG*6.3.4; τὴν πόλιν εὐδαιμονεστάτην τοῖς ἐπιγιγνομένοις π. Isoc.8.94, cf. Th.2.36, Pl.*R.*372d; π. τὴν ἀρετήν *transmit, impart* as a teacher, Id.*Men.*93c: c. inf., παῖδάς σφι παρέδωκε τὴν γλῶσσαν ἐκμαθεῖν Hdt.1.73; ἥν ἐμῇ μητρὶ παρέδωκεν τρέφειν E.*Or.*64; π. τινὶ τοὺς νέους διδάσκειν Pl.*Lg.*812a, cf. *Ti.*42d, al. 2. *give* a city or person *into another's hands*, τὴν Σάμον π. Συλοσῶντι Hdt.3.149; ἄλλον ἐς ἄλλην πόλιν π. Id.5.37; esp. as a hostage, or to an enemy, *deliver up, surrender*, ἑωυτὸν Κροίσῳ Id.1.45, cf. 3.13, Th.7.86; τὰς ναῦς And.3.11, etc.: with collat. notion of treachery, *betray*, X.*Cyr.*5.4.51, Paus.1.2.1; π. ὅπλα X.*Cyr.*5.1.28, etc.; τύχῃ αὑτὸν π. *commit* oneself to fortune, Th.5.16; ταῖς ἡδοναῖς ἑαυτὴν [τὴν ψυχήν] Pl.*Phd.*84a; ἑαυτοὺς [ἐπιθυμίαις] ib.82c: without acc., *give way*, ἡδονῇ παραδούς Id.*Phdr.*250e. 3. *give up* to justice, etc., ἥντινα μήτε.. παραδοῦναι ἐξῆν Antipho 6.42; π. τινὰς τῷ δικαστηρίῳ And.1.17; τοῖς ἕνδεκα παρεδόθη Lys.14.17; also π. τινὰ εἰς τὸ δεσμωτήριον D.51.8; δεθέντα εἰς τὸν δῆμον X.*HG*1.7.3 (Pass.); ἐπὶ κρίσει παρεδέδοτο εἰς τὸν δῆμον D.49.9: c. inf., π. τινὰ θανάτῳ ζημιῶσαι Lys.22.2; *give up* a slave *to be examined by torture*, Isoc.17.15, Test.ap.D.45.61:—Pass., ἐγκλήματι π. dub. l. in D.C.62.27: metaph., σιωπῇ καὶ λήθῃ παραδοθείς D.H.*Pomp.*3. 4. *hand down* legends, opinions, etc., *by tradition*, φήμην Pl.*Phlb.*16c; παραδεδομένα καὶ μυθώδη D.23.65; οἱ παραδεδομένοι μῦθοι Arist.*Po.*1451$^{b}$24; ὁ π. τρόπος Id.*Pol.*1313$^{a}$35; οἱ παραδεδομένοι θεοί the *traditional* gods, Din.1.94; ἡ οἰκία.. ἐγκεκωμιασμένη παραδέδοται ἡμῖν Pl.*Chrm.*157e; δόγματι παραδοθῆναι *to be embodied* in a decree, D.C.57.20. b. *teach* doctrine, *Ev.Luc.*1.2, Sor.1.124, M.Ant.1.8, Philum.*Ven.*37.3, Dam.*Pr.*154, 433, Paul.Aeg.6.50:—Pass., ὅταν [τέχνη] παραδιδῶται Arr.*Epict.*2.14.2. II. *grant, bestow*, κῦδός τισι Pi.*P.*2.52: in pres. and impf., *offer, allow*, αἵρεσιν Id.*N.*10.83. 2. c. inf., *allow* one *to*.., Hdt.1.210, 6.103, al.: c. acc. rei, *permit*, ὁ θεὸς τοῦτό γε οὐ παρεδίδου Id.5.67; πληγὴν.. παραδοθεῖσαν εἰσιδών a blow *offered*, i.e. opportunity of striking, E.*Ph.*1393: abs., τοῦ θεοῦ παραδιδόντος if he *permits*, Hdt.7.18; ἢν οἱ θεοὶ παραδιδῶσιν X.*An.*6.6.34; ὅπως ἂν οἱ καιροὶ παραδιδῶσιν Isoc.5.118; τῆς ὥρας παραδιδούσης Plb.21.41.9: less freq. in aor., πότμου παραδόντος Pi.*P.*5.3; ὡς ἂν ὁ δαίμων παραδῷ D.60.19. III. *hazard*, τὰς ψυχὰς ὑπέρ τινος *Act.Ap.*15.26.

**παραδιηγ-έομαι**, *relate incidentally* or *by the way*, Arist.*Rh.*1417$^{a}$2, D.H.*Th.*13. **-ημα**, ατος, τό, *incidental narrative*, Ph.1.533. **-ησις**, εως, ἡ, = foreg., ib.149, Quint.*Inst.*9.2.107 (pl.), Ruf.Rh.p.403 H.: wrongly distd. by some from παρέκβασις, Corn.*Rh.*p.364 H.

**παραδιηθέω**, *percolate through*, Aët.7.112.

**παραδῑνέω**, *distort*, τοὺς ὀφθαλμούς Gal.19.91.

**παραδιοικέω**, *meddle with* another's *government*, Plu.2.817d.

**παραδιορθ-όω**, *alter for the worse*, of stolen verses, Porph.ap.Eus. *PE*10.3. **-ωμα**, ατος, τό, *blundering correction*, Porph. *ad Il.*p.287 S. (pl.). **-ωσις**, εως, ἡ, *marginal correction*, in pl., Plu.2.33b.

⊛ **παραδιώκω**, *reject*, A.D.*Synt.*145.20; = *persequor*, *Gloss.* II. Pass., *to be hurried along*, παραδεδιωγμέναι ἄλογοι (sc. συλλαβαί) D.H. *Comp.*20.

**παρᾱδολεσχέω**, *chatter, gossip incidentally*, Plu.2.639c:—Pass., ταῦτα -ηδολεσχήσθω *let* this *digression be introduced*, Iamb. *in Nic.* p.68 P.

**παραδοξ-άζω**, *make wonderful* or *extraordinary*, Lxx 2*Ma.*3.30; τὰς πληγάς σου *will lay unheard-of* inflictions *upon* thee, ib.*De.*28.59. 2. π. ἀνὰ μέσον τῶν κτηνῶν *put a mark of distinction* between, *separate*, ib.*Ex.*9.4; π. τὴν γῆν ib.8.22. **-ασμός**, ὁ, *object of wonder*, Sm.*Is.*9.6(5). **-ία**, ἡ, *marvellousness*, παραδοξίαν ἔχειν τινά to partake of *the marvellous*, Str.1.2.29; τὸ σπάνιον ποιεῖ τὴν π. Id.11.11.5.

**παραδοξο-γράφος** [γρᾰ], ὁ, *writer on marvels*, Tz.*H.*2.151. **-λογέω**, *tell marvels* or *incredibilities*, Str.13.4.5, D.S.1.69, Gem.16.27, Ph.1.340; *speak in paradox*, Simp. *in Ph.*50.27; περί τινος Arr.*Epict.*2.22.13: folld. by εἰ, ib.4.1.125:—Pass., πολλὰ παραδοξολογεῖται many *marvels are told*, Str.5.4.9; τὰ περὶ τὸν Νεῖλον παραδοξολογούμενα D.S.1.42. **-λογία**, ἡ, *tale of wonder, marvel*, εἰς π. τοῖς μεθ' ἡμᾶς φῦναι Aeschin.3.132, cf. Plb.3.47.6, 3.58.9, prob. in Phld. Po.5.33 (pl.); *love* or *use of paradox*, Plu.2.1071d, Simp.*in Ph.*50. 26. **-λόγος**, ὁ, *narrator of marvels*, Gal.1.55, al., D.L.8. 72. ❋**-νίκης** [ῑ], ου, ὁ, *conquering marvellously*, Plu.*Comp. Cim.Luc.*2; esp. of athletes, = παράδοξος II, *IG*14.747 (Naples, ii A.D.). **-ποιός**, ὁ, *wonder-worker*, Gal.14.641.

❋ **παράδοξος**, ον, *contrary to expectation, incredible*, π. λόγος *a paradox*, Pl.*R.*472a; π. τε καὶ ψεῦδος Id.*Plt.*281a; παράδοξα λέγειν X.*Cyr.*7.2. 16; ἂν παράδοξον εἴπω D.3.10; ἐκ τοῦ παραδόξου καὶ παραλόγου *contrary to all expectation*, Id.25.32, cf. Phld.*Vit.*p.23 J.; πολλὰ ποικίλλει χρόνος π. καὶ θαυμαστά Men.593; π. μοι τὸ πρᾶγμα Thphr.*Char.*1.6; τὸ ἔνδοξον ἐκ τοῦ π. θηρώμενος Plu.*Pomp.*14; παράδοξα Stoical *paradoxes*, Id.2.1060b sq.: Comp., Phld.*Mus.*p.72 K., Plot.4.9.2: Sup., Lxx *Wi.*16.17. Adv. -ξως Aeschin.2.40, Plb.1.21.11, Dsc.4.83: Sup. -ότατα D.C.67.11; -οτάτως Gal.7.876. II. παράδοξος, title of distinguished athletes, musicians, and artists of all kinds, *the Admirable*, *IG*3.1442, 14.916, Arr.*Epict.*2.18.22, *IGRom.*4.468 (Pergam., iii A.D.), *PHamb.*21.3 (iv A.D.), *Rev.Ét.Gr.*42.434 (Delph.), etc.

**παραδοξότης**, ητος, ἡ, *marvellousness*, Them.*Or.*29.344c.

**παρα-δόσῐμος**, ον, *handed down, transmitted, hereditary*, δόξα, φήμη, Plb.6.54.2, 12.5.5, etc.; π. στήλη *commemorative* tablet, Id.12. 10.9; π. ἔχειν τι *handed down by tradition*, D.S.4.56; παραδόσιμα, τά, *temple-property handed down*, *IG*7.303.8 (Orop.). ❋**-δοσις**, εως, ἡ, *handing down, bequeathing, transmission*, τοῦ σκήπτρου Th.1.9; *handing over, transfer*, ἡ π. τῶν χρημάτων Arist.*Pol.*1309a10, cf. Pl. *Lg.*915d; σίτου, etc., *POxy.*1257.3 (iii A.D.), etc.; τῆς βασιλείας Plu. *Comp.Lyc.Num.*1; ἐν παραδόσει παραλαμβάνειν ἀεί, of a reserve fund, *IG*11(2).161 *A* 126 (Delos, iii B.C.). 2. *transmission* of legends, doctrines, etc., *tradition*, διδασκαλία καὶ π. Pl.*Lg.*803a; πραγματεῖαι αἱ ἐκ π. ηὐξημέναι Arist.*SE*184b5; ἐν παραδόσει ἔχειν τι Plb.12.6.1, etc.; *treatment, exposition*, ὅπως πᾶσιν εὐπαρακολούθητος γένηται ἡ π. Hero *Bel.*73.12; ἡ βοτανικὴ π. *the subject* of botany, Dsc.*Praef.*1; παραδόσεις καὶ παραγγελίαι Phld.*Rh.*1.78 S.; σύντομος π. succinct *account*, Ammon.*in Porph.*38.10. b. in military sense, *transmission of orders*, Ael.*Tact.*21.2. 3. *that which is handed down* or *bequeathed*, *tradition, doctrine, teaching*, ἡ π. τῶν πρεσβυτέρων *Ev.Matt.*15.2, *Ev.Marc.*7.3, etc.; αἱ π. τῶν θεῶν καὶ τῶν θείων ἀνδρῶν Dam.*Pr.*265: also in Gramm., Ἑλληνικὴ π. A.D.*Conj.*213.13, cf. 19 (pl.); in textual criticism, defined as ἡ τῶν γραμματικῶν μαρτυρία, *EM*815.18; so παρὰ τὴν π. γράφειν Demetr.Lac.*Herc.*1012.34, cf. *EM*240.4, al. II. *surrender*, πόλεως Th.3.53; ἐκ παραδόσεως, opp. κατὰ κράτος, Plb.9.25.5; *giving up to punishment* or *torture*, Isoc.17.16; π. ἐπὶ θανάτῳ D.H.7.36. 2. Astrol., *handing over*, τῶν χρόνων Vett.Val.141.4. **-δοτέος**, α, ον, *to be handed down*, Pl.*Lg.* 802e. 2. παραδοτέον, *one must hand over*, τινί τι Id.*Alc.*1.132c; πρὸ τῶν μεγάλων μυστηρίων τὰ μικρὰ π. Iamb.*Protr.*2. II. *to be given up*, Pl.*Lg.*715a, Luc.*Cat.*28, etc. 2. παραδοτέα, *one must give up*, οὓς οὐ π. Th.1.86. **-δοτός**, ή, όν, *capable of being taught*, Pl.*Men.*93b, Phld.*Rh.*1.369 S., D.L.4.12.

**παρα-δοχή**, Dor. -δοχά, ἡ, *reception*, Epicur.*Nat.Herc.*908.4; σπέρματος Orib.22.7.1, cf. Plu.2.1056f, Sor.1.55; of mental *apprehension*, Phld.*Sign.*22. 2. *that which has been received, hereditary custom*, πάτριοι π. E.*Ba.*201; *tradition*, Hippod.ap.Stob.4.1.95; κοινὴ π. S.E.*P.*1.146; π. Ἑλληνισμοῦ A.D.*Adv.*168.9. II. *acceptance, approval*, Plb.1.1.1, 1.5.5, etc.; τῶν βλαβερῶν Hierocl.*in CA*18p.459 M. b. *admission, register* of persons admitted, τῶν ἀπὸ τοῦ γυμνασίου *PFlor.*79.24 (i A.D.). 2. Gramm., ἐν π. τοῦ ἄρθρου γενέσθαι *admit* the use of the article, A.D.*Synt.*57.6. 3. *credit* or *rebate allowed* (cf. παραδέχομαι), ἀβρόχου *BGU*571.11 (ii A.D.). **-δοχικός**, ή, όν, *traditional*, μέτρα *PHib.*1.87.13 (iii B.C.). **-δόχιμος**, ον, *hereditary*, ἱερεῖς *PTeb.*298.10 (ii A.D.), etc.

**παραδρᾰθεῖν**, v. παραδαρθάνω. **παραδρᾰμεῖν**, v. παρατρέχω.

**παραδράω**, *to be at hand, serve*, οἷά τε τοῖς ἀγαθοῖσι παραδρώωσι χέρηες (Ep. for -δρῶσι) Od.15.324.

❋ **παραδρομ-άδην**, Adv. *in running* or *passing by*, Orph.*A.*858. **-αξ**, ακος, ὁ, *mantle, wrap*, *POxy.*1346 (ii A.D.). ❋**-ή**, ἡ, *running beside*: hence concretely, π. κολάκων *attendant swarm* of flatterers, Posidon. 7 J.; μετὰ πολλῆς π. with a large *train*, Lxx 2*Ma.*3.28. II. *running by, traversing*, Plu.*Alex.*17; ἐν παραδρομῇ ποιεῖσθαι τὸν λόγον *cursorily*, Arist.*Pol.*1336b24; ἐκ παραδρομῆς Plb.21.34.2. **-ίς**, ίδος, ἡ, *place for taking the air*, *IG*2$^2$.1035.56 (pl.), 12(9).234.34 (Euboea), *Inscr.Perg.*252.32, *PCair.Zen.*764.34,44 (iii B.C.), Vitr.5.11.4, *POxy.*502.19 (ii A.D.), 2146.9 (iii A.D.). **-ος**, ον, *that may be run through*, τὰ π. *spaces for getting through, gaps*, X.*Cyn.*6.9. II. *running alongside*, θίς *Stad.*67.

**παραδρύπτω**, *scratch, scrape at the side*, τὰ λαιὰ παρεδρύφθην τοῦ σώματος Lib.*Decl.*28.12.

**παραδῠναστεύω**, *reign beside* or *with another*, Th.2.97, D.C.53. 19. 2. *have great influence* or *authority with*, c. dat., Id.75.14, Jul. *Mis.*365a.

**παρα-δύνω**, = sq., Arist.*Pr.*925b4. **-δύομαι**, Med. with intr. aor. Act. παρέδυν (v. infr.): pf. παραδέδῡκα Aeschin.3.37:—*creep, slink*, or *steal past*, ταῦτα δ' ἐγὼν αὐτὸς τεχνήσομαι.., στεινωπῷ ἐν ὁδῷ παραδύμεναι Il.23.416; ἐκδρᾶσα παρέδυν Ar.*Ec.*55. 2. *creep* or *steal in*, ἐς τὰν ἀκοάν Archyt.1; ὅτε πρῶτον ἐκεῖνος εἰς Πελοπόννησον παρεδύετο D.18.79; ἡ παρανομία λανθάνει παραδυομένη Pl.*R.*424d, cf. Arist.*Pol.*1307b32; ἃ φυλακτέον ὅπως μὴ λήσει εἰς τὴν πόλιν παραδύντα Pl.*R.*421e, cf. Aeschin. l.c.; π. ἐπί τι D.22.48. **-δῠσις**, εως, ἡ, *creeping in beside, encroachment*, π. κατὰ μικρόν Id.17.27; παραδύσεις διδόναι τισί Plu.2.727a; αἱ τῶν Ἰουδαίων π. J.*BJ*3.7.9; βέλους π. ib. 4.7.4.

**παραδωσείω**, Desiderat. of παραδίδωμι, *to be disposed to deliver up*, Th.4.28 (fort. -δοσ-, cf. συμβασείω).

**παρ-ᾰείδω**, *sing beside* or *to* one, τινι Od.22.348.

**παρ-ᾰείρω**, = παραλύω, *detach*, π. φρένας *unhinge* the mind, Archil. 94, cf. Opp.*H.*4.19 (tm.):—Pass., *hang on one side*, παρηέρθη δὲ κάρη Il.16.341.

**παρ-ᾰέξομαι**, Pass., *grow beside*, λιβάσιν Nic.*Th.*61.

**παρ-ᾰετίς**, ίδος, ἡ, *tile* placed on the raking cornice of a pediment, *IG*11(2).161 *A* 55,80 (Delos, iii B.C.):—also spelt **-αιετίς**, ib.4$^2$(1). 102.100 (Epid., iv B.C.), 2$^2$.1666 *B* 15.

**παραζάω**, v. παραζῶ.

**παρα-ζεύγνυμι** and **-ύω**, aor. 2 Pass. παρεζύγην [ῠ] Epicur.*Fr.*59:—*yoke beside, couple* in marriage, χρηστῷ πονηρὸν λέκτρον E.*Fr.*520; φρουρῷ π. φύλακε σώματος *having set beside* him, Id.*Ion* 22:—Pass., *to be coupled to* another, γυνὴ ἐσθλὴ παραζευχθεῖσα καὶ σῴζει δόμους Id. *Fr.*1055.2, cf. Epicur. l.c.: c. dat., D.*Prooem.*55. 2. generally, *associate*, τί τινι Phld.*Mus.*p.71 K.:—Pass., *to be associated* in a task, *PRyl.*237.4 (iii A.D.); ἡ παρεζευγμένη χωλεία the *associated* lameness, Apollon.Cit.3. **-ζευξις**, εως, ἡ, *yoking beside, coupling*, Plu. 2.1109f (pl.).

❋ **παραζηλ-όω**, *provoke to jealousy*, Lxx 3*Ki.*14.22, *Ep.Rom.*10.19, etc. 2. *fret, be vexed*, ἔν τινι Lxx *Ps.*36(37).1. II. *emulate, imitate*, Suid. s.v. Ἀστυάνασσα. **-ωσις**, εως, ἡ, *emulation*, Ph.2. 422, Sm.*Ez.*8.3.

**παραζητέω**, *inquire into, search amiss*, M.Ant.12.5, Al.*Le.*27.33.

**παρα-ζῠγή**, ἡ, *transport service*, *PTeb.*121.52, al. (i B.C.), *PFay.*47. 5 (i A.D.). **-ζυξ**, ῠγος, ὁ, ἡ, *yoked beside*: metaph., παράζυγες, οἱ, *supernumeraries*, Arist.*Pol.*1265b4.

**παραζῶ**, *live by the side of* or *as an appendage to*, [ψυχὴ] τῷ σώματι παραζῶσα Plu.2.672e. II. abs., *live merely*, without doing anything, οὕτω παρέζων, κοὐκ ἔζων *I was alive*, but lived not, Anaxandr.2. 4; ζῆν, οὐ π. προσῆκε Plu.2.13a.

**παραζωγρᾰφέω**, *paint beside* or *in the same picture*, App.*Mith.*117 (Pass.).

**παρα-ζώνη**, ἡ, *girdle*, Lxx 2*Ki.*18.11. **-ζωνίδιον**, τό, *dagger worn at the girdle*, Posidon.2 J. (pl.). **-ζώνιον**, τό, = foreg., *PGiss.* 47.14 (ii A.D.). **-ζώννυμι** and **-ύω**, *hang at the girdle*, ἀκινάκας Pl.*R.*553c:—Med., *wear at the girdle*, ξίφος D.H.2.70, cf. Plu.*Ant.* 70. II. *gird along the side*, of clouds hanging on a mountain-side, Thphr.*Sign.*51. **-ζωσμα**, ατος, τό, *axle-pin*, *Gloss.* **-ζωστρίς**, ίδος, ἡ, = παραζώνιον, Hsch.

**παραθᾰλασσ-ίδιος**, ον, = sq., Th.6.62, D.C.54.9. **-ιος**, Att. -ττιος, α, ον (also ος, ον Th.4.56), *beside the sea*, τὰς πόλιας τὰς π. Hdt.7.109; τὰς π. κώμας Id.8.23; τὰ π. τῆς Ἑλλάδος Id.3.135; τὰ π. τῶν καρπῶν Id.4.199; ἡ π. (sc. γῆ) X.*HG*4.8.7.

**παραθάλλω**, pf. -τέθηλα, *grow beside*, Ἀλφειῷ cj. for περιτεθ- in Philostr.*Im.*2.6.

**παραθάλπω**, *comfort, cheer*, Sch.Pi.*I.*5(4).14:—Pass., παραθαλπομένα φρένα μύθοις E.*Med.*143 (anap.).

**παραθάπτω**, *bank up at the sides*, *BGU*1121.24 (i B.C.).

**παραθαρσύνω**, Att. -θαρρύνω, fut. -ῠνῶ Plu.*Alc.*26:—*embolden, encourage*, Th.4.115, 8.77, X.*An.*3.1.39, etc.; παραμυθεῖσθαι καὶ π. Pl.*Criti.*108c: c. acc. pers. et inf., Plu. l.c.

**παραθεάομαι**, *inspect side by side, compare*, τι παρά τι Pl.*Ep.*313c; παρατεθεαμένος τούς τε ἀγαθοὺς καὶ τοὺς φαύλους Thphr.*Char.Praef.*2.

**παραθέλγω**, *assuage*, ὀργάς A.*Ag.*71 (anap.).

**παράθεμα**, ατος, τό, *appendage*, π. θυσιαστηρίου δικτυωτόν Lxx *Ex.* 38.24(4). 2. = ἐπίθεμα, Hsch.

**παραθεμιστεύω**, *transgress a law*, Herm.ap.Stob.1.49.45.

**παραθερίζω**, *graze in passing*, in poet. aor. 1 παρέθρισα, A.R.2. 601, Q.S.6.629 (tm.).

**παραθερμαίνω**, *warm, cheer*, οἶνος π. τὴν ψυχήν Ath.5.185c:—Pass., *to be heated*, Arist.*Pr.*876b3: metaph., παραθερμανθείς, of a man, *become quarrelsome* in his cups, Aeschin.2.157; παρατεθέρμανται τῇ καρδίᾳ Lxx *De.*19.6.

❋ **παράθερμος**, ον, *over-hot*, Plu.*Comp.Pel.Marc.*3. 2. metaph., of persons, D.S.24.3; also π. καινουργία *violent* change, Hierocl.p.52 A.

**παρα-θέσιμος**, ον, (cf. sq. III) *that which is deposited, stored*, *PSI*5. 463.13 (ii A.D.). ❋**-θεσις**, εως, ἡ, *juxtaposition*, θέσις καὶ π. Hp. *Off.*3: in Tactics, π. λόχου ἑτέρῳ λόχῳ Arr.*Tact.*7.1; αἱ κατὰ τὰς π. μίξεις, opp. αἱ δι' ὅλων κράσεις, Antip.*Stoic.*3.255, cf. Chrysipp.ib.2. 153,220; opp. ἔγκρασις, κατάκρασις, *Theol.Ar.*9,10; κατὰ παράθεσιν, opp. κατ' ἀλληλουχίαν, ib.4. 2. Gramm., *juxtaposition*, opp. *composition* (σύνθεσις), as in Διόσ-κοροι, opp. Διο-γενής, *EM*278.25, 649.14; also, *addition*, π. προθετικὴ *addition* of prepositions, A.D.*Synt.*333.7, cf. *Pron.*23.12, al. 3. a mode of wrestling, Plu.2.638f (pl.). 4. Pass., *juxtaposition, neighbourhood*, Plb.2.17.3, etc.; κατὰ παράθεσιν Id.4.28.2; ἐκ παραθέσεως on *comparison*, Id.3.62.11, cf. Aret.*SA*2.2, etc.; ἐκ τῆς π. καὶ συγκρίσεως τῶν λέγεσθαι μελλόντων Plb.16.29.5, etc., cf. Chor. in *Rev.Phil.*1.71. II. *dish* or *dinner set before* people, τοὺς διακόνους τοὺς τὰς π. φέροντας Plb.30.26.6, cf. Lxx 2*Ch.* 11.11, Ath.14.664c; ὑγρῶν π. Plb.13.2.2: pl., *supplies*, *PPetr.*3p.133 (iii B.C.). 2. *offering* of food to a god, *PMag.Berol.*1.23, *PMag. Par.*1.2887. III. *storing up*, τῶν χορηγιῶν Plb.3.17.11; οἴνου καὶ ἀκροδρύων D.S.3.73; *store of provisions*, αἱ εἰς τὰ στρατόπεδα π. Plb. 2.15.3; π. πυρῶν, ὕδατος, *IG*12(7).515.77 (Amorgos), Ath.Mech.13.9;

ὅπλων *OGI*90.22 (Rosetta, ii B.C.): gen. παραθέσεως *for storage*, *IG*5(1).870, al. (Sparta); ἐσχηκέναι ἐν παραθέσει on *deposit*, *POxy*.1039.7 (iii A.D.), etc. **IV.** ἡ τῶν ὀνομάτων π. *putting down* or *mention* of names, Plb.3.36.3; τῶν μαρτυριῶν *citation* of instances, D.L.7.180: hence in Gramm., *instance*, A.D.*Synt*.5.13 (pl.), al. **V.** *laying of advice before* others, *suggestion*, αἱ τῶν φίλων π. Plb.9.22.10, al. **-θετέον**, *one must add*, D.H.*Rh*.2.5, Porph.*Abst*.1.13. **2.** *one must place before, furnish, serve*, τροφήν (to the sick), Gal.19.216. **3.** *one must place beside*, σηκῷ σανίδας *Gp*.14.6.3; *one must apply*, Antyll.ap. Orib.10.23.23. **4.** *one must compare*, ὄγκον πρὸς ἄογκον Plot.6.4.5. **-θέτης**, ου, ὁ, *one who serves up dishes*, *Gloss*.

⊕ **παραθέω**, *run beside* or *alongside*, Pl.*La*.183e, X.*HG*7.1.21, etc.; τινι Plu.*Luc*.21; *run along*, τὴν ὄχθην Ael.*NA*6.53; of winds, παρὰ τὰ κοῖλα τῆς Εὐβοίας Thphr.*Vent*.32. **II.** *run to one side of* or *overrun*, τὸ ὀρθόν Pl.*Tht*.171c. **III.** *run beyond, outrun*, τινα X.*An*.4.7.12; *run past*, Id.*Cyn*.6.16,19. **IV.** *touch on cursorily*, Luc.*Hist.Conscr*.57. **V.** *pass on, be transient*, π. καὶ οὐ μένειν Plot.4.6.3.

**παραθεωρ-έω**, *examine* a thing *beside* another, *compare*, πρὸς τοὺς ἄλλους ἐμαυτόν X.*Mem*.4.8.7; τινά τινι Luc.*Herod*.8, cf. *Pr.Im*.7, D.61.45, Plu.2.33a. **2.** *keep in mind, take into account*, ποσαχῶς.. Epicur.*Ep*.1 p.29 U.; τοὺς πολιτικοὺς καιρούς Phld.*Rh*.1.373 S. **II.** *take slight notice of, overlook*, D.H.*Is*.18, etc.:—Pass., *Sammelb*.1161.38 (i B.C.), *Act.Ap*.6.1. **-ησις**, εως, ἡ, *comparative examination*, Plu.2.820a. **-ητέον**, *one must overlook*, Ath. Med.ap.Orib.*inc*.21.10.

**παραθήγω**, *whet, sharpen upon*, ἐγχειριδίου..ἀκόνῃ..παραθηγομένου Hermipp.46 (anap.). **2.** metaph., *exasperate, provoke*, τὰς ὀργάς τινων (v.l. τισι) D.H.8.57; παρατέθηκται ἐξ ἐπιστολῆς Ph.2.575, cf. 543; τὴν ψυχὴν τοῖς καλλίστοις τῶν μελῶν π. *incite*, Plu.2.1145f.

**παρα-θηκαρία**, ἡ, *receipt for an object taken in charge*, *POxy*.144.17 (vi A.D.). ⊕ **-θήκη**, ἡ, *anything entrusted to* one, *deposit*, Hdt.6.86, 9.45, *BGU*1004.15 (iii B.C.), Lxx *Le*.6.2(5.21), Ps.-Phoc.135, *Ostr. Bodl*.i 274 (i B.C.), *SIG*742.51 (Ephesus, i B.C.); of persons, *hostage*, Hdt.6.73.

**παραθηλάζω**, *nurse at the breast as well as* another child, *BGU*1106.30 (i B.C.), etc.

**παραθηλύνω**, *make effeminate*, Lyd.*Mag*.3.64.

**παραθήματα**, *insignia*, *Gloss*.

**παράθηξις**, εως, ἡ, *incitement to*.., ἀρετῆς Mich. *in EN*513.13.

**παραθητεύω**, *serve for hire*, τινι Epic.ap.Plu.2.761e.

**παραθιγγάνω**, aor. 2 -έθιγον, *touch at the side* or *in passing*, Him. *Or*.23.12.

**παρα-θλίβω** [ῑ], *press at the side*, τὸν ὀφθαλμόν S.E.*P*.1.47; *press close*, π. τινὰ ἐν τῇ θύρᾳ Lxx 4*Ki*.6.32; τὴν σάρκα Herod.Med.ap.Orib. 10.18.15:—Pass., Arat.993; παραθλιφθείσης τῆς κόρης Gal.*UP*10.12; τὸ ὕδωρ σῶμά ἐστιν..παρατεθλιμμένον εἰς χύσιν Herm.ap.Stob.1.49.68. **2.** π. τῆς ἀναπνοῆς *shut off part of* the escape of air from a flute, Onos.10.3. **-θλιψις**, εως, ἡ, *pressure at the side*, Gal.18(1).69, Sor.1.119 cod., Cass.*Pr*.28.

**πάρ-αθλον**, τό, *by-contest*, Sch.Pi.*N*.3.42.

**παραθόλιον**, τό, *passage round a* θόλος or *vapour-bath*, *POxy*.896.13 (iv A.D.).

**παράθρᾱνος** (sc. ὁδός), ἡ, *gangway along the seats of the* θρανῖται, Poll.1.88 (v.l. παράθρονος); παράθρανος (fort. -θράνιος)· κώπη τις ἐν ταῖς παραθράνοις (-θρόνοις cod.), Hsch.

**παρά-θραυμα**, ατος, τό, *anything broken off, fragment*, in pl., Ar. *Fr*.366 (v.l. -αυσμ-). **-θραυσις**, εως, ἡ, *breaking off*, Hsch. s.v. ἀγμίεις; cf. περίθραυσις. **-θραύω**, *break, smash*, of ships and pottery, *Dialex*.1 (Pass.). **II.** *break off*, metaph., τὴν εἰρήνην ψηφίσματι πολέμου π. Demad.44; ὀλίγον τοῦ λόγου Gal.4.623, cf. 9.931; *infringe, violate*, τὸ δίκαιον Porph.*Abst*.3.1:—so in Pass., παρατεθραυμένος (v.l. -αυσμένος) Pl.*Lg*.757e.

**παρ-αθρέω**, = παροράω, 2 sg. aor. 1 opt. παραθρήσειας Phot.

**παραθριγκίζω**, *edge as with a cornice, make a row along*, τὸν καυλόν prob. in Thphr.*HP*3.18.12:—hence Subst. **-ισμός**, ὁ, cj. ibid.

**παραθρίζω**, v. παραθερίζω.

⊕ **παραθρῴσκω**, *run* or *leap past*, Oikonomos Ἐπιγραφαὶ τῆς Μακεδονίας p.39 (ii B.C.), D.P.286.

⊕ **παράθυμα**, v. πάρθυμα.

**παραθυμιάω**, *burn* incense *beside, fumigate*, τισι D.S.3.47; ἀσφάλτου π. βραχύ Agatharch.99.

**παρα-θύρα** [ῠ], ἡ, *side-door, wicket*, *Inscr.Perg*.237, 239, *Gloss*. **-θύριον** [ῠ], τό, Dim. of foreg., ib. **-θυρίς**, ίδος, ἡ, *side-window*, *IG*11(2).163 *A* 4 (Delos, iii B.C.). **-θυρος** (sc. θύρα), ἡ, = παραθύρα, *PMich.Zen*.38.11 (iii B.C.), Plu.2.617a. **II.** (sc. λίθος), ὁ, *stone forming part of a side-door*, *Milet*.7 p.56.

**πᾰραί**, poet. for παρά.

⊕ **παραι-βᾰδόν**, Adv. *in going beside* or *near to*, c. gen., ἀτραπιτοῖο prob. in Opp.*C*.1.484. **-βάσιη, -βάσις**, v. παραβασία, παράβασις. **-βᾰτέω, -βάτης, -βάτις**, poet. for παραβ-. **-βολος**, ον, poet. for παράβολος.

**παραιγιάλ-ιος** [ᾰλ], ον, = sq., Xenocr.ap.Orib.2.58.42 (v.l. -λοι). **-ίτης** [λῑ], ου, ὁ, (αἰγιαλός) *haunting the shore*, of certain fish, Clearch.73, St.Byz.:—fem. **-ῖτις**, ἡ, *close inshore*, [θάλασσα] Eust.116.6.

**παραιετίς**, v. παραετίς. **παραΐζω**, v. παρίζω.

**παραίθεναρ**, τό, for *παράθεναρ, *hand from little finger to wrist*, Hsch. (in pl. -θένατα).

⊕ **παραιθύσσω**, poet. aor. -αίθυξα Pi.*O*.10(11).73:—*move* or *stir in passing*, ἄκρα πτερύγων *AP*7.204 (Agath.): metaph., θόρυβον π. *raise* a shout *in applause*, Pi. l. c. **II.** *whizz past*, λαίφεα πτερύγεσσιν A.R.2.1253. **2.** metaph., of words, *fall by chance from* a person's lips, εἴ τι καὶ φλαῦρον π. Pi.*P*.1.87.

**παραικάτια**· αἱ ἐπὶ τοῖς ζεύγεσι τῶν ὁπλιτῶν τάξεις, Hsch.

**παραίν-εμα**, ατος, τό, *advice*, Phld.*Hom*.p.5 O. **-εσις**, εως, ἡ, *exhortation, address*, A.*Eu*.707, Hdt.9.44, Th.2.45, etc.; π. ποιήσασθαι ib.88: c. gen. pers., *advice* or *counsel given by* a person, Hdt.5.11,51: c. gen. rei, *advice given for, of*, or *towards* a thing, αἱ π. τῶν ξυναλλαγῶν Th.4.59; ἐπὶ γνώμης παραινέσει *to recommend* an opinion, Id.1.92; cf. παράκλησις II. **-ετέον**, *praecipiendum*, *Gloss*. ⊕ **-ετήρ**, ῆρος, ὁ, *encourager, adviser*, Ath.1.14b. **-έτης**, ου, ὁ, = foreg.; π. γυναικῶν *seducer*, Vett.Val.14.25. **-ετικός**, ή, όν, *hortatory*, π. καὶ ὑποθετικὸς τόπος Aristo *Stoic*.1.80. Adv. **-κῶς** S.E.*M*.1.271, *Rev. Et.Gr*.28.56 (Egypt). **-έω**, 3 sg. impf. παρῄνει Th.1.139; Ion. παραίνεε Hdt.8.19: fut. -έσω S.*OC*1181, Ar.*Pax* 1245, D.37.11, etc.; -έσομαι Pl.*Mx*.236e: aor. παρῄνεσα S.*Ph*.1434, Ar.*Ra*.1420, Isoc. 12.264; Ion. -αίνεσα Hdt.1.80: pf. παρῄνεκα Isoc.*Ep*.2.1, Luc.*Im*.16:—Pass., aor. παρῃνέθην Hp.*Fract*.8: pf. inf. παρῃνῆσθαι Th.7.69:—*exhort, recommend, advise*, παραίνεσε μὴ φειδομένους κτείνειν πάντα Hdt.1.80; ὧδε παραινέων, πέμψαντα δέεσθαι Id.3.4; π. τινί c. inf., Ar. *Ra*.1132, Pl.*Phdr*.234b; τοῖς ναύταις παραινῶ μὴ ἐκπεπλῆχθαι Th.7.63; π. τινί τι Pi.*P*.6.23, A.*Pr*.309, S.*OC*464, etc.; τι Hdt.1.59, 5.31, etc.; π. τινί *advise* a person, A.*Ch*.903; τοῖς πέλας Th.5.9; ἄλλῳ πονοῦντι ῥᾴδιον παραινέσαι Philem.75.1:—Pass., ὥσπερ πρότερον παρῃνέθη Hp. l. c., cf. Th.7.69. **2.** *advise* or *recommend publicly, propose*, παρῄνει τοιάδε Id.1.139, cf. *IG*1².90.43, etc.; π. περὶ τῶν παρόντων Th.2.13; οὐ π. *advise* not.., c. inf. (cf. οὔ φημι, etc.), ib.18.

**παραινίττομαι**, *indicate enigmatically*, Ath.13.604f; simply, *hint at, suggest, allude to*, Phld.*Piet*.91, Lyd.*Ost*.44.

**παραιολίζω**, fut. -ίξω, *trick*, τινα Lyc.1094, 1380.

**παραίπαιμα**, v. παράπαισμα.

**παραιπεπίθησιν, -θοῦσα**, v. παραπείθω.

**παραίρ-εσις**, εως, ἡ, *taking away from, stripping one of*, τῶν προσόδων Th.1.122; τῆς οὐσίας παραιρέσεις Pl.*R*.573e; τὴν π. ποιοῦνται τῶν ὅπλων Arist.*Pol*.1311ᵃ12. **-έτης**, ου, ὁ, *one that takes away* or *diminishes*, χρόνων Vett.Val.139.7. **2.** *a planet which is out of its proper* αἵρεσις, Paul.Al.*S*.2, Sch.Ptol.*Tetr*.100 (fort. **παραιρετιστής**, formed like συναιρετιστής). **-ετός**, όν, *which may be removed* or *taken away*, πλοῦτος..οὐ π. *Mémoires de la Mission arch. de Perse* 20.91 (Susa). **-έω**, aor. παρεῖλον E.*Hec*.591:—*take away from, withdraw, remove*, τι E. l. c.; λύπας Id.*Hipp*.1105 (lyr.): c. gen. partit., *take away part of*.., *some of*.., φρονήματος Id.*Heracl*.908; τῆς λύπης Hyp.*Epit*.41; τοῦ φρουρίου Th.3.89:—Pass., Hp.*Fract*.33. **2.** π. [ἀρὰν] εἰς παῖδα *thou hast turned aside* the curse on to thy son's head, E.*Hipp*.1316. **II.** Med. with aor. 2 παρειλόμην, later aor. 1 παρειλάμην Lxx *Nu*.11.25, Plb.4.51.6:—*draw off* or *away from, seduce, detach*, X.*Mem*.1.6.1; πόλεις παραιρεῖται οὐδὲν αὐτῷ προσηκούσας Decr. ap.D.18.181, cf. *Ep*.3.31; γυναῖκα παρελέσθαι Arist.*Pol*.1311ᵇ6. **2.** *take away*, τὰ ὅπλα πάντων X.*HG*2.3.20, Arist.*Ath*.37.2; αὐτῆς τὸν βίον παρείλετο Anaxil.22.10, cf. Men.128.8 (Pass., παρῃρημένοι τὰ ὅπλα *having their* arms *taken away*, D.19.81); παραιρεῖσθαι τὴν θρασύτητά τινων *lessen, damp* it, ib.208; π. τοὺς ἐκ δούλου *disfranchise* them, Arist.*Pol*.1278ᵃ32; *remove* privileges, ib.1285ᵇ16; τὰ ἐφόδια παρῃρῆσθαι, in med. sense, *had deprived themselves of*.., Iphicr.ap. eund.*Rh*.1411ᵃ12. **3.** generally, *take away, filch from*, εἴ τινος τοῦ κλήρου ὁ ποταμὸς τι παρέλοιτο Hdt.2.109, cf. E.*IT*25, etc.; γῆν τῶν γεωργῶν *PTeb*.5.146 (ii B.C.): metaph., τῶν ἀγαθῶν ἀνθρώπων τὰς ἐλπίδας Phld.*Piet*.p.94 G.; τὰς ἀγορὰς τοῖς στρατοπέδοις Plb.1.18.9:—Pass., τῆς Περαίας ἐκχωρεῖν ἧς αὐτῶν (sc. τῶν Ῥοδίων) παρῄρηται Id.18.2.3. **4.** c. acc. pers. et gen. rei, *deprive*, τινά τινος Zos.1.7, cf. 23. **-ημα**, ατος, τό, *edge* or *selvage of cloth*: generally, *band, strip*, Th.4.48; prob. for παραίρεμα or πάρερμα in Hp.*Off*.12; expld. by παράρματα ἱματίων, Hsch.

**παραισᾰβάζω**, poet. for *παρασαβάζειν (nisi hoc legend.), *to be inspired by Sabazius*, i.e. Dionysus, Hsch., Phot.

**παραισθ-άνομαι**, *remark* or *hear of by the way*, τινος X.*Cyr*.4.2.30: abs., οὐχὶ παρῄσθευ; Theoc.5.120. **II.** *misperceive, be subject to illusory perceptions*, Pl.*Tht*.157e, Aret.*SD*1.6, Iamb.*Protr*.2. **-ησις**, εως, ἡ, *misperception*, Phld.*Piet*.116.

**παραίσιος**, ον, *of ill omen*, σήματα Il.4.381 (παραίσιμα Hsch.), cf. Call.*Hec*.1.3.4.

**παραΐσσω**, Att. **παρᾴσσω**, *dart past*, Il.5.690; παρήϊξεν κοίλας ἐπὶ νῆας 8.98; παραΐσσοντος 20.414; μύσας παρᾶξον Ar.*V*.988, cf. 837: c. acc., ἵπποι γάρ με παρήϊξαν Il.11.615: in later Prose, Plu.2.774f. [ᾱ in Hom.]

⊕ **παραιτ-έομαι**, *beg of* or *from* another, *ask as a favour of* him, τινά τι Pl.*Ap*.27b, etc.; τι Hdt.1.24,90: with inf. added, ἐν δ' αὐτοὺς παραιτησόμεθα, ἐπίδηλον ἡμῖν..ποιεῖν, ἣν τοῖς ἔπεσι χαίρωσι Ar.*Eq*.37: with inf. for acc., θεοὺς παραιτοῦ τῶν σ' ἔρως ἔχει τυχεῖν A.*Supp*.521; Προμηθέα -εῖται Ἐπιμηθεὺς αὐτὸς νεῖμαι *asks* P. *for permission to*.., Pl.*Prt*.320d, cf. Hdt.4.146: c. acc. cogn., παραίτησιν π. Pl.*Criti*.107a. **2.** παραιτησάμενος βασιλέα *having obtained* the king's *leave*, Hdt.6.24: generally, *intercede with, appeal to* a person, Id.3.132, 5.33; κτεῖν', οὐ παραιτοῦμαί σε E.*Heracl*.1026, cf. Ar.*V*.1257; π. σφέας, ὡς ἄξουσι..*entreating* them and *saying* that.., Hdt.4.158: c. dupl. acc., *beg* one's *pardon for*.., σε παραιτοῦμαι τάδε E.*IA*685: abs., εἴ τις ὑμῶν ἀχθεσθήσεται, παραιτοῦμαι And.3.21, cf. Plb.39.1.6. **3.** c. acc. et inf., *entreat* one *to*.., Hdt.1.90, 6.86.γ', X.*Mem*.2.2.14, etc.; παραιτήσομαι δ' ὑμᾶς μηδὲν ἀχθεσθῆναί μοι D.21.58; π. σε συγγνώμην ἔχειν Men.867: c. gen. pers. et inf., *beg of*.., παραιτήσῃ πατρὸς φυγὰς ἀφεῖναι E.*Med.*1154: c. inf. only, π. μηδὲν τούτων δρᾶν Th.5.63. II. c. acc. rei, *avert by entreaty, deprecate*, τὴν ὀργήν Aeschin.3.198; τὰς ζημίας ὑπέρ τινος Id.2.19, cf. D.21.5; αἰκίαν Plb.1.80.8; τὸν φθόνον Plu.*Pomp.*56; τὸ ἀποθανεῖν *Act.Ap.*25.11: abs., τοῖς.. παραιτουμένοις [πρᾷοί εἰσιν] Arist.*Rh.*1380ᵃ28, cf. *PCair.Zen.*482.14 (iii B.C.). 2. *decline, deprecate*, χάριν Pi.*N.*10.30; τὴν διαίρεσιν τῶν ὀνομάτων Pl.*Prt.*358a; τοὺς πότους Plu.*Them.*3; τοὺς.. γραώδεις μύθους 1*Ep.Ti.*4.7; π. [τὰ ὦτα] *refuse* to hear, Philostr.*Her.*11; *refuse*, βρώσεις Id.*VA*1.8, cf. Porph.*Abst.*4.7: c. inf., παλιλλογεῖν παρῄτηται Sch.Il.1.365; παραιτοῦ φαγεῖν κάπρου κεφαλήν Herm. in *Rev.Phil.*32.252; also τοὺς πολλοὺς χαρακτῆρας παρῃτημένοι εἰσὶν αἱ ἀντωνυμίαι *do not admit*.., A.D.*Synt.*104.16; *reject* a theory, interpretation, or MS. reading, Theo Sm.p.200 H., Iamb.*VP*2.7, Sch.A.R.2.127, Sch.Ar.*Pax*854; *except*, Hdn.Gr.2.929; *reject the use of, avoid*, τὴν λογικήν S.E.*M.*7.15, cf. Ptol.*Tetr.*107, etc. b. *demand exemption from*, τὴν εἰς τὸ μέλλον γεωργίαν *PLond.*3.1231.3 (ii A.D.); ἀρχήν *POxy.*1252ᵛ28 (iii A.D.). 3. c. acc. pers., *ask* him *to excuse* one, *decline* his *invitation*, Plb.5.27.3; παραιτησάμενος Ἔφορον, Lat. *pace Ephori*, Id.5.33.2: abs., *Ev.Luc.*14.18:—Pass., ἔχε με παρῃτημένον ibid. 4. π. γυναῖκα *divorce* her, Plu.2.206a; π. οἰκέτην *dismiss* him, D.L.6.82; π. τινὰ τῆς οἰκίας Luc.*Abd.*19:—Pass., τὴν παραίτησιν ἣ παρὰ τοῦ Καρακάλλου παρῄτητο D.C.78.22. 5. of medicines, *relieve*, ναυσίαν Dsc.3.70; ὀδόντων ἀλγήματα ib.48. III. c. acc. pers., *intercede for, beg off*, esp. from punishment, Hdt.3.119, Plb.4.51.1; π. τινὰ τιμωρίας Plu.*Sull.*31; Θεσσαλοὺς τοῦ Μηδισμοῦ π. *excuse* them *from the charge* of Medism, Id.2.868d; π. περί τινων X.*An.*6.6.29. -ησις, εως, ἡ, *supplication, entreaty*, π. παραιτεῖσθαι Pl.*Criti.*107a; μηδεμία τῆς μονῆς π. γιγνέσθω no *application for leave* to stay, Id.*Lg.*915c; πρόφασιν εἰσδέχεσθαι καὶ π. Plb.16.17.8; *petition*, *POxy.*899ᵛ21 (iii A.D.). II. *deprecating*, Th.1.73; *excuse, apology*, Plb.39.1.5, Jul.*Or.*2.64a (pl.), Chor. in *Rev.Phil.*1.73, etc.; *pardon*, ἁμαρτημάτων Ph.2.296, cf. 223. 2. *declining*, Plu.2.124b; *dismissal*, D.C.78.22. III. *intercession, begging off*, Gorg.*Pal.*37, D.9.37. ❋ -τέος, α, ον, *to be deprecated*, Ph.1.275; *to be declined*, Plu.2.709d; π. οἱ λέγοντες.. *we must reject* the view that.., Iamb.*in Nic.*p.28 P. 2. παραιτητέον, *one must decline*, S.E.*M.*10.118, Ath.10.421a, 11.464a; π. τὸν νοῦν Ph.1.161; *one must avoid*, D.S.21.14, Sor.2.24, etc.; *one must reject*, στίχον Sch.Il.3.230; [τοῦτο] ib.2.8. -τής, οῦ, ὁ, *intercessor*, Ph.1.598, 2.167, Plu.*Sull.*26. -τικός, ή, όν, *deprecatory*, λόγοι ὀργῆς π. words *fit for turning away* wrath, D.H.*Th.*45. -ητός, ή, όν, *to be appeased by entreaty, placable*, θεοὶ τοῖς ἀδικοῦσι Pl.*Lg.*905d, al., cf. Phld.*D.*1.17. II. *to be deprecated*, Plu.2.23a. III. *pardonable*, Ph.2.319.

❋ **παραίτιος**, ον, also α, ον A.*Ch.*910, Plb.5.88.3, Onos.1.8, A.D.*Pron.*43.9:—*being in part the cause*, ἡ Μοῖρα τούτων π. *shared the blame*, A.l.c.; τὸ κακὸν ἀγαθοῦ γίγνεται π. E.*Fr.*174.3; ἀγαθῶν π. Decr.ap.D.18.92; later, practically, = αἴτιος, *Supp.Epigr.*3.468.4 (Thess., i B.C.), Ph.2.92, al., Ocell.4.14; τῶν αἰσχρῶν τὸ θεῖον [οὐκ ἔστι] π. Chrysipp.*Stoic.*2.326. 2. in bad sense, *accessory to* a crime, τῶν δ' ἐγὼ π. A.*Fr.*44.7; π. τοῦ φόνου Paus.4.3.8; π. τινί τινος Plb.18.41.3, cf. *Michel* 56.14, 1015.15 (both Teos, ii B.C.).

**παραι-φάμενος**, η, ον, Ep. part. Med. of παράφημι, *talking over, persuading*, Il.24.771, *h.Cer.*336, Hes.*Th.*90. ❋-φάσίη, ἡ, = sq. 1, Musae.*Fr.Epic.*5, A.R.2.324 (pl.); *comfort*, Nonn.*D.*48.133. 2. π. λιμοῦ *consolation against*.., Poet.ap.Orion. s.v. πεσσοί. ❋-φάσις, εως, ἡ, poet. for παράφασις, *encouragement, persuasion*, ἀγαθὴ δὲ π. ἐστιν ἑταίρου Il.11.793, cf. Aret.*SD*1.1, Nonn.*D.*40.115, Them.*Or.*8.106d. 2. *beguilement*, πόνου *AP*5.284 (Agath.); ἐρώτων *APl.*5.373.—Cf. πάρφασις. -φάσσει· τινάσσει, πηδᾷ, παρακινεῖ καὶ τὰ ὅμοια, Hsch. -φηλούμεθα· παραγόμεθα, Id. -φρονέω, poet. for παραφρονέω, v.l. in Theoc.25.262.

**παραιωρ-έω**, *hang up beside*, τινί τι Nonn.*D.*1.43, etc.:—mostly in Pass., *to be hung* or *hang beside*, ἐγχειρίδια παρὰ τὸν δεξιὸν μηρὸν παραιωρεύμενα ἐκ τῆς ζώνης Hdt.7.61, cf. Achae.19.2; of persons, ξιφίδια παρῃώρηντο *they had* daggers *hung at their side*, Hdn.2.13.10: abs., of a suppliant, *hang upon another*, Plu.*Ant.*77. II. Pass., *take passive exercise*, e.g. in a boat, Aët.9.30. -ησις, εως, ἡ, *suspension*, Thphr.*Metaph.*29; Math., '*suspension*', Arist.*Cael.*306ᵃ21.

**παρακάββαλε**, v. παρακαταβάλλω.

**παρακαθάπτω**, *fasten, hang by the side*, Poll.1.252 (Pass.).

**παρακαθεζόμενος**, -καθεσθείς, v. παρακαθίζω II.

**παρακαθεύδω**, *sleep beside*, of a dog, Ael.*VH*1.13; of persons, *keep watch by*, τινι Lxx *Ju.*10.20.

**παρακάθημαι**, inf. -καθῆσθαι, *to be seated beside* or *near*, τινι Ar.*Ra.*1492, Th.6.13: abs., Pl.*Cri.*43b; οἱ παρακαθήμενοι Id.*Prt.*320c, al.; of *passengers* in a ship, *GDI*3835 (Rhodes). 2. of an army, *encamp beside*, Plb.9.11ᴬ.2. 3. *to be busy about*, τινι *PSI*4.402.10 (iii A.D.).

**παρακαθ-ιδρύω**, in Pass., *to be placed by* or *near*, τῷ θεῷ Plu.*Caes.*9. -ιζάνω, = sq. II. *attend*, σχολαῖς *IG*2².1011.22, 1028.85. -ίζω, pf. παρακεκαθικέναι Arr.*Epict.*2.6.23:—*set beside* or *near*, Pl.*R.*553d; τινὰ ἐπὶ τοῦ βάθρου D.C.73.3; στρατιὰν π. περὶ τὴν πόλιν Palaeph.40: intr., = signf. II, Lxx *Jb.*2.13, D.S.23.9, Arr. l.c., Plu.*Mar.*17. 2. Med. with aor. 1 παρεκαθισάμην, *let* another *sit down beside* one, π. παῖδας καὶ γυναῖκας ἑαυτοῖς Lycurg.141, cf. J.*AJ*19.4.5; also π. τινά *make* him *assessor* or *co-arbiter*, D.33.14. II. mostly Pass. and Med., fut. -καθιζήσομαι Pl.*Ly.*207b: aor. 2 παρεκαθεζόμην Id.*Euthd.*273b, Ar.*Pl.*727; part. παρακαθεζόμενος X.*Cyr.*5.5.7, *Mem.*4.2.8, Pl.*Chrm.*153c, Thphr.*Char.*3.2, Plu.*Art.*26; later -καθεσθείς *Ev.Luc.*10.39, J.*AJ*6.11.9, Gal.14.637:—*seat oneself, sit down beside* or *near* another, ll. cc., Pl.*Tht.*144d. -ίημι, *let down beside*, of the nautilus, ἀντὶ πηδαλίων τῶν πλεκτανῶν παρακαθίησι *lets down* some of its feelers.., Arist.*HA*622ᵇ14; *let drop* or *sink by the side*, τὰς χεῖρας Plu.*Nic.*9; δακτύλιον Id.2.63e: abs., *send out side-roots*, Thphr.*HP*8.2.3:—Med., πηδάλια ζεύγλαισι παρακαθίετο E.*Hel.*1536. 2. intr. (sc. ἑαυτόν), *sink down*, π. τοῖς σώμασι διὰ τὸν κόπον Plb.35.1.4. -ίστημι, also -ιστάνω, J.*AJ*14.15.7:—*set down beside, station* or *establish beside*, στρατιώτας ὥσπερ ἐπόπτας π. D.4.25; πολιτείας ἐναντίας π. Isoc.4.104, cf. *IG*1².46.9; π. ἐπίτροπόν τινι D.S.16.38, cf. *PCair.Zen.*199.7 (iii B.C.), *PRev.Laws* 54.15 (iii B.C.):—Pass., παρακαθεσταμένος τινὶ *being made* his *colleague*, D.S.16.47.

**παρα-καίριος**, ον, *unseasonable, ill-timed*, παρακαίρια ῥέζων Hes.*Op.*329. -καιρος, ον, = foreg., Epich.260, Men.*Mon.*217, Clearch.5, Luc.*Nigr.*31; τὸ π. Lib.*Or.*64.100. Adv. -ρως *immoderately*, Isoc.1.9.

**παρακαίω**, aor. -έκαυσα (v. infr.), *light* or *keep lighted beside*, πῦρ π. τοῖς νοσοῦσι Plu.2.383d; in ceremonies at tombs, *Supp.Epigr.*2.415 (Macedonia):—Pass., πάννυχος λύχνος π. Hdt.2.130. 2. of cautery, *burn partly*, ὅταν φλέβα παρακαύσῃς Hp.*Vid.Ac.*3.

**παρακᾰκόω**, pf. part. Pass. -κεκακωμένος *deranged*, *Gloss.*

❋ **παρακᾰλέω**, Att. fut. -καλῶ, later -καλέσω Lxx *Jb.*7.13, al.:—*call to* one, X.*An.*3.1.32. II. *call in, send for, summon*, Hdt.1.77, Ar.*V.*215, etc.; σύμμαχον π. τινά Hdt.7.158, cf. Th.1.119, Pl.*Phd.*89c, etc.; π. ἑταίρους And.4.14; π. τινὰ ἐς τὸν πόλεμον Hdt.7.205, cf. D.18.24; π. τινὰ σύμβουλον X.*An.*1.6.5; τινὰς εἰς συμβουλήν Pl.*La.*186a; συνήγορον Aeschin.2.184; *invoke* the gods, τοὺς θεούς D.18.8; περὶ τούτου τὸν θεόν (as medical adviser) *IG*4²(1).126.31 (Epid., ii A.D.); τὸν Ἐνυάλιον X.*HG*2.4.17; Διόνυσον εἰς τὴν τελετήν Pl.*Lg.*666b; [τοὺς θεοὺς] π. βοηθοὺς Arr.*Epict.*3.21.12:—Pass., παρακαλούμενος καὶ ἄκλητος, '*vocatus atque non vocatus*', Th.1.118; -κληθέντες ἐς ξυμμαχίαν Id.5.31; παρακαλουμένη ἀμύνειν *being called upon* to ward off, Pl.*Lg.*692e; -κληθεὶς γυμνασιαρχῆσαι *OGI*339.53 (Sestos, ii B.C.). 2. *summon* one's friends *to attend one* in a trial, π. τοὺς φίλους Is.1.7, etc.; π. τινάς *call* them *as witnesses*, Lys.14.28; π. πάντας ἀνθρώπους D.34.29:—Med., dub. in Lycurg.28:—Pass., παρακεκλημένοι *summoned* to attend at a trial, Aeschin.1.173. b. *summon* a defendant into court, in Pass., *PTeb.*297.5 (ii A.D.), Mitteis *Chr.*71.5 (v A.D.). 3. *invite*, ἐπὶ δαῖτα E.*Ba.*1247; εἰς (v.l. ἐπὶ) θήραν X.*Cyr.*4.6.3; ἐπὶ τὸ βῆμα π. *invite* him to mount the tribune, Aeschin.3.72. 4. *appeal to*, τινὰ περὶ γῆς App.*Pun.*136. III. *exhort, encourage*, τάξις τάξιν παρεκάλει A.*Pers.*380, cf. Plb.1.60.5; π. τινὰ εἰς μάχην E.*Ph.*1254; τινὰ ἐπὶ τὰ κάλλιστα ἔργα X.*An.*3.1.24; π. τὴν νόησιν εἰς ἐπίσκεψιν Pl.*R.*523b; πρὸς τὸ μνημονεύειν Isoc.3.12: c. inf., E.*Cyc.*156, X.*An.*5.6.19, Decr.ap.D.18.185:—Pass., Isoc.2.14; παρακέκληται ἡ διάνοια Arist.*EN*1175ᵃ7. 2. *comfort, console*, τοὺς πενθοῦντας Lxx *Si.*48.24:—Pass., *Ev.Matt.*2.18, 5.4. 3. *excite*, τινὰ ἐς φόβον E.*Or.*1583; ἐς δάκρυα Id.*IA*497; *incite*, π. καὶ παροξύνειν ἐπί.. Epicur.*Nat.*54 G.; of things, *foment*, φλόγα X.*Cyr.*7.5.23. IV. *demand, require*, ὁ θάλαμος σκεύη π. Id.*Oec.*9.3:—Pass., τὰ παρακαλούμενα *proposals, demands*, Philipp.ap.D.18.166 sq., Plb.4.29.3. V. *beseech, entreat*, Id.4.82.8, *PTeb.*24.46 (ii B.C.), etc.; π. τινὰ ἵνα.. Aristeas 318, *Ev.Marc.*8.22, Arr.*Epict.*2.7.11, etc.; ὅπως.. *Ev.Matt.*8.34: but ἐρωτῶ καὶ π. for δέομαι is condemned by Hermog.*Meth.*3. VI. Pass., *relent*, πρός, ἐπί τινι, *towards* a person, Lxx *Jd.*21.6, 15, cf. 2*Ki.*24.16. 2. *repent, regret*, παρακέκλημαι ὅτι.. ib.1*Ki.*15.11.

**παρακαλλύνω**, gloss on παρακορέω, Hsch.

**παρακαλπάζω**, *run beside a trotting* horse, π. καὶ καταψήσας Plu.*Alex.*6.

❋ **παρα-κάλυμμα** [κᾰ], ατος, τό, *anything hung up beside* or *before so as to cover* a thing, *covering, curtain*, Plu.*Alex.*51, etc. 2. metaph., *veil, cloak*, τῶν κακῶν Antiph.167; ἀφεγγὲς λήθης π. Lxx *Wi.*17.3; γήρᾳ π. τοῦ χρόνου ποιούμενος J.*AJ*16.8.1; π. τῆς ἡδονῆς τὸ σκότος προθέσθαι Plu.2.654d; *excuse, pretext*, τῇ λύρᾳ π. χρώμενος Id.*Per.*4; ἐχρήσατο τῆς ἀπορίας -καλύμματι Id.2.27e, cf. Ph.2.186. -κᾰλύπτω, *cover by hanging something beside, cloak, disguise*, τῇ μέθῃ τὴν διάνοιαν Plu.*Demetr.*52:—Med., *cover one's face*, Pl.*R.*439e, Plu.*Alc.*34; πρὸς τὸ δεινὸν Id.*Pomp.*60 (Act. in same sense, Id.*Per.*35): metaph., παρακαλυπτομένου τοῦ λόγου *veiling itself*, Pl.*R.*503a, cf. Plu.2.370f; π. τὴν ἀλήθειαν Ph.2.196; *set aside, ignore*, τὸν θεόν ib.189.

**παρακαμμύω**, for παρακαταμύω, *give a side wink at*, Phot. s.v. μυωπιζόμενος.

**παρακάμπτω**, *bend aside*: hence, *avoid, shun*, τὰς ἀπαντήσεις καὶ ὁμιλίας τῶν ἀνθρώπων D.S.5.59.

**παρ-ᾰκανθίζω**, *to be somewhat prickly*, Thphr.*HP*1.10.6, al.

**παρακατα-βαίνω**, fut. -βήσομαι, *dismount*, of mounted infantry, Plb.3.65.9; ἀπὸ τῶν ἵππων Id.3.115.3, etc. 2. *disembark* from a ship, D.S.3.40. II. of a roof, *project at the side*, Ath.Mech.13.6. -βάλλω, *throw down beside*, παρακάββαλον [Ep. for παρακατέβαλον] ἄσπετον ὕλην Il.23.127; ζῶμα δέ οἱ πρῶτον παρακάββαλεν *he put* a waistband *on* him, ib.683. II. *make a claim* to property *together with a deposit* (παρακαταβολή) to be forfeited in case of failure, *IG*5(2).357.58 (Stymphalus), *Foed.Delph.Pell.*4 A 7; esp. at Athens, 1. in a διαδικασία κλήρου, of a claimant by descent, will, etc., as against collateral heirs, οὑτοσὶ παρακατέβαλε τοῦ κλήρου ὡς υἱὸς γνήσιος D.44.42, cf. 43.5; ἑαυτῷ κατὰ δόσιν π. Is.4.10, cf. Poll.8.32, Harp. and Suid. s.v. παρακαταβολὴ καὶ παρακαταβάλλειν. 2.

of a claimant who enters a διαμαρτυρία μὴ ἐπίδικον τὸν κλῆρον εἶναι, Is.6.12. 3. of one who claims property as his own which has been confiscated to the state, Harp., Suid. III. Med., π. ψήφισμα *annex* a decree *to their* manifesto, Plb.4.25.6. **-βάσις,** εως, ἡ, in Law, perh. *rejoinder*, or *appearance of the defendant in court*, Pl.*Lg.*956e. **-βολή,** ἡ, *money deposited in court* by claimants, and forfeited in case of failure, D.49.46, Lex ap.eund.43.16, cf. Suid. s.v. παρακαταβολὴ καὶ παρακαταβάλλειν. II. *the process in which such a deposit was required*, Poll.8.32. III. generally, *court-deposit*, ἐπειδὴ θᾶττον ἀνείλετο τὰς π. D.37.41; δίκας καὶ γραφὰς ἄνευ -βολῆς Isoc.20.2.

**παρακατ-ᾰγωγή,** ἡ, a method of throwing in wrestling, Sch.T Il. 23.730.

**παρακατα-ζεύγνῡμι,** *add besides*, ὄρχησιν καὶ ῥυθμόν Diotog.ap. Stob.4.1.96. **-θάπτω,** Ep. aor. 1 παρκατέθαψα, *bury beside*, Q.S.1.804 (s. v. l.). **-θετέον,** *one must entrust*, τῷ λόγῳ τὸν βίον Socr.ap.Stob. 3.1.73. ⊛ **-θήκη,** ἡ, *deposit* of money or property *entrusted to one's care*, Hdt.5.92.η'; αἱ τῶν χρημάτων π. Isoc.1.22; π. Ἀθηναίας, i.e. deposited in her temple, *IG*2².1407.42; π. ἔχειν ib.1².116.16, Th.2.72, cf. Anaxandr.55.1; π. χρυσίου ἢ ἀργυρίου δεξάμενος Pl.*R.*442e; π. καταθέσθαι παρά τινι Lys.32.16, cf. 5; ἀποδιδόναι to restore it, Arist. *EN*1135ᵇ7; ἀποστερῆσαι to withhold it, Id.*Rh.*1383ᵇ21; ἐν π. δοθῆναι, ἔχειν, Plb.5.74.5, Mitteis *Chr.*372 vi 19 (ii A.D.); αἱ π. τῆς τραπέζης banking *deposits*, D.36.6: metaph., ταῦτ' (sc. τοὺς νόμους) ἔχεθ'.. παρὰ τῶν ἄλλων ὡσπερεὶ π. Id.21.177; οἱ τὴν τῶν νόμων π. ἔχοντες Aeschin.1.187. 2. of persons entrusted to guardians, *ward*, Ἀπόλλωνα παρὰ Ἴσιος π. δεξαμένη Hdt.2.156; of children, D.28.15; of persons under the protection of the state, *sacred trust*, Din.1.9. (Cf. παρκαθήκα.) **-θνήσκω,** *die beside*, aor. παρκάτθανε *AP* 9.735. **-κειμαι,** Pass., *lie beside* or *near*, esp. at meals, τινι X.*Cyr.* 2.2.28, Pl.*Ep.*360b, etc. **-κλίνω** [ῑ], *lay down beside*, *put to bed with*, τινά τινι Aeschin.2.149, Luc.*DDeor.*6.4, Artem.4.61. **-λείπω,** *leave with* one, τινά τινι Th.6.7; *leave as deputy*, D.C.46.37. **-λέχομαι,** Pass., *lie down beside*, *lie* or *sleep with* (Ep. only in non-thematic aor. or impf.), τῇ δ' γε παρκατέλεκτο Il.9.565, cf. 664. **-λογή,** ἡ, in Music, *recitative*, *melodramatic delivery*, Arist.*Pr.*918ᵃ10, Plu. 2.1141a. **-πήγνυμι,** *drive in alongside*, σταυρούς Th.4.90; ξύλα μακρά Thphr.*HP*8.3.2. **-σκευάζω,** gloss on ὀτρύνω, *EM*637.29; v. l. for προκ-, Sch.Pi.*O.*6.1. **-στᾰσις,** εως, ἡ, = παρακαταβολή, *AB*290, Phot., *EM*653.3. ⊛ **-σχεσις,** εως, ἡ, *retention*, τοῦ νομίμου μέρους Just.*Nov.*39 *Praef.* ⊛ **-τίθημι,** *entrust*, υἱόν τινι ἐκτρέφειν Charito 8.4: Ep. aor. παρκατέθηκα dub. in Orph.*A.*312:—elsewh. in Med., with Ep. aor. παρκάτθετο A.R.2.504:—*deposit* one's property *with* another, *entrust* it to his *keeping*, τινί τι Hdt.3.59, X.*HG*6.1.2, Pl. *R.*331e sq., cf. Hyp.*Lyc.*18, etc.; π. νόμους [φύλαξι] Aeschin.1.7; παῖδας διδασκάλοις ib.9; τὸ αὐτοῦ σῶμα τῷ ἵππῳ X.*Eq.*4.1; τῷ δήμῳ ἑαυτόν D.*Ep.*3.27; τὴν διατριβὴν τοῖς φιλοσοφοῦσιν Epicur.*Fr.*217; τοῖς ὑπάτοις τὰ πράγματα Plu.*Cic.*15; π. τινί τι τηρεῖν *Tab.Defix.*100ᵃ7: metaph., of the pledge given by a good citizen to the state, τὰς δικαίας πίστεις π. Din.1.71. II. *expose to risk*, τὰ σώματα -θέμενοι διακινδυνεύειν Aeschin.3.180. III. Med., *trust*, c. dat., τῇ πίστει τινός *BGU*326.16 (ii A.D.). **-χράομαι,** *use beside*, *use for* a purpose, ἡ φύσις π. [τινὶ] πρός τι Arist.*PA*690ᵃ1, cf. 659ᵃ21.

**παρακάτ-ειμι,** (εἶμι *ibo*) *go farther down*, παρακατιὼν εἴρηκε, φησι, *farther down* he says, Steph.*in Hp.*2.327 D., Sopat. in Rh.5.144 W.; π. ὁ λόγος δηλώσει Sch.Od.11.90; ἐξέτεινεν δ καὶ π. συνέστειλε v.l. in Sch. Theoc.1.4. **-εσθίω,** *eat with* something else, Sotad.Com.3. **-έχω,** *keep back*, *detain*, Plb.1.66.5, etc.; *restrain*, τινας Th.8.93; τὴν ὁρμήν τινος, τὸν ἴδιον θυμόν, Plb.5.67.11, 15.4.11; π. τὰς ὠδῖνας *check* them, D.S.4.9; π. τὰ ὑγρά *checks* their *circulation*, Heraclid.Tar.ap.Ath.2. 64f. 2. *retain possession of*, τὸν Ἀκροκόρινθον Plb.18.45.12. II. Pass., *to be detained*, ὑπὸ τοῦ Σαράπιος *UPZ*8.19 (ii B.C.). **-ηγόρημα,** ατος, τό, = παρασύμβαμα, *Stoic.*2.59, Steph.*in Int.*11.16, Ammon.*in Int.*44.26. **-οικίζω,** *make to dwell* or *settle beside*, τοὺς Εἵλωτας ὁμόρους ἡμῖν Isoc.6.28; π. φόβον καὶ φρουράν τισι *make* fear and watching their *companions*, Plu.*Per.*11:—Med., *settle near oneself*, Εἵλωτας Isoc.6.87:—Pass., [τὴν Κόρινθον] παρακατῳκίσθαι πάσαις [θαλάτταις] Aristid.*Or.*46(3).26. **-ορύσσω,** aor. 1 -ώρυξα, *bury* or *plant in the earth beside*, Hp.*Art.*47.

**παρακαττύω** [ῠ], *sew on beside*, *patch up*:—in Med., generally, *put in order*, *set straight*, στιβάδα παρεκαττύετο Ar.*Pl.*663.

**παρακάτω,** *just below*, c. gen., *PMasp.*87.13 (vi A.D.): as Adv., Zos.Alch.p.112 B.

**παρακαυδωτόν,** v. παρακαυτωδόν.

**παρακαυλίζω,** *shoot out at the side*, Thphr.*HP*6.2.8.

**παράκαυσις,** εως, ἡ, *burning for light*, *PPetr.*2 p.73, al. (iii B.C.). II. Medic., *firing* a horse, ib.3 p.178 (iii B.C.). 2. *inflammation*, Gal. 18(2).548.

**παρακαυτωδόν** and **παρακαυδωτόν,** τό, = παραγαύδης, *Sammelb.* 7033.43, 44 (v A.D.).

⊛ **παράκειμαι,** poet. **πάρκειμαι** Pi. (v. infr.): Ep. impf. παρεκέσκετο Od.14.521:—used as Pass. to παρατίθημι, *lie beside* or *before*, ἔτι καὶ παρέκειτο τράπεζα Il.24.476; ὀϊστόν, ὅ οἱ παρέκειτο τραπέζῃ Od.21. 416, cf. Pherecr.108.17, Telecl.1.7, etc.; ἡ παρακειμένη τροφή Arist.*HA*599ᵃ25: generally, *to be at hand*, *available*, οἷα τέκτοσιν ἡμῖν ὕλη παράκειται Pl.*Ti.*69a; *to be adjacent*, c. dat., *PTeb.*74.56 (ii B.C.): metaph., ὑμῖν παράκειται ἐναντίον ἠὲ μάχεσθαι ἢ φεύγειν *the choice is before* you, to fight or flee, Od.22.65; ἔρδειν.. ἀμηχανίη παράκειται Thgn.685; ἅμα παρακεῖσθαι λύπας τε καὶ ἡδονάς *lie side by side*, Pl. *Phlb.*41d: freq. in part., Ἀΐδᾳ παρακείμενος *lying at* death's *door*, S. *Ph.*861 (lyr.); παρκείμενον τέρας the *present* marvel, Pi.*O.*13.73; τὸ παρκείμενον the *present*, Id.*N.*3.75; ἱκανὰ τὰ κακὰ καὶ τὰ παρακείμενα Ar.*Lys.*1048; τὰ π. ὕδατα *PTeb.*61(*b*).132 (ii B.C.); τὰ π., also, *dishes on table*, Amphis 30.6; κλίνην..παρακειμένην τε τὴν τράπεζαν Diod. Com.2.10; ἡ π. πύλη the *nearest* gate, Plb.7.16.5; ἐν μνήμῃ παρακείμενα *things present* in memory, Pl.*Phlb.*19d; *under discussion*, λόγος Phld.*Sign.*16; *obvious*, Id.*Rh.*1.3, 6 S.; *to be closely connected with*, παράκεινται τῇ μαθηματικῇ θεωρίᾳ ἥ τε θεολογικὴ ἐπιστήμη καὶ ἡ φυσική Iamb.*Comm.Math.*28. b. in legal phrases, *to be attached* or *appended*, of documents, *BGU*889.15 (ii A.D.); *to be noted*, *scheduled*, *PTeb.*27.7 (ii B.C.); *to be preserved* in a register or archive, *PSI*5.454.18 (iv A.D.), etc. 2. *press on*, *urge*, c. dat., πυκνότερον ἡμῖν -κείμενοι Lxx 3*Ma.*7.3, cf. Plb.5.34.7. 3. metaph., *lie prostrate*, of absolute subjection, π. πρὸ προσώπου σου Lxx *Ju.*3.3. 4. *to be permissible*, Hp.*Dent.*15. II. in Gramm., etc.: 1. *to be laid down*, *mentioned* in text-books, τὰ σημεῖα οὐ παράκειται Philum.*Ven.*29; simply, *to be cited*, ἐκ τῶν Θεοφράστου Sch.Ar.*Pl.*720. 2. ὁ παρακείμενος (sc. χρόνος) the *perfect* tense, A.D.*Synt.*205.15. 3. ἀντίφρασίς ἐστι λέξις..διὰ τοῦ π. τὸ ἐναντίον παριστῶσα, *ex adjecto*, as when the Furies are called *Eumenides*, Trypho *Trop.*2.15, cf. Ps.-Plu.*Vit.Hom.* 25. 4. of words, *to be joined by juxtaposition* (not composition, cf. παράθεσις I.2), A.D.*Synt.*330.26, al. 5. *to be interpolated*, Gal. 18(1).58.

**παρακειμένως,** Adv. *similarly*, σκύφος π. ἔχων τὰ ὦτα Ath.11.489b, cf. Corn.*ND*32. II. *next*, *following*, τῷ περὶ θεῶν λόγῳ *Placit.*1. 8.1 (dub.); *in the next place*, ib.4.22.3, S.E.*M.*7.227, al. III. *conveniently*, Arr.*Epict.*3.22.90.

**παρακεκᾰλυμμένως,** Adv. *concealedly*, Steph.*in Hp.*1.74 D.

**παρακεκινδῡνευμένως,** Adv. *in a bold dashing style*, Pl.*Lg.*752b.

**παρακεκλῐμένως,** = παρακλιδόν, Sch.A.R.1.757.

**παρακεκόαται·** παρανοεῖ, Hsch.; cf. παρακοάω.

**παρακεκομμένως,** Adv. *briefly*, v.l. for περικ- in Sch.Luc.*Lex.*3.

**παρα-κέλευμα** or **-κέλευσμα,** ατος, τό, *exhortation*, *cheering address*, E.*Supp.*1155 (lyr.); τὸ δεινὸν π. Id.*IT*320; ἐξ ἑνὸς or ἀφ' ἑνὸς π., D.S.15.32, D.H.6.47. 2. *precept*, *maxim*, τὸ τοῦ Φωκυλίδου π. Pl. *R.*407b, cf. *Lg.*688a, al. **-κελεύομαι,** *recommend* an action to one, *prescribe*, σοὶ ἕτερα τοιαῦτα Hdt.1.120, cf. Th.7.63, Lys.28.15, etc.; ταῦτα π. *give* this *advice*, Ar.*V.*530, Pl.*Ap.*31b; π. τινί c. inf., Id. *Smp.*221a, al.; τοῖς συμμάχοις π. μὴ ἀθυμεῖν X.*HG*1.1.24; π. ὅκως μὴ παρήσουσι.. Hdt.8.15, cf. Pl.*Mx.*248d; ὅτι.. X.*HG*1.1.14; π. πρός τινας μὴ ὑπομένειν Aeschin.2.1. II. *exhort*, *encourage*, τινι Isoc. 9.79, Pl.*Phd.*60e, etc.; ὁ Νικίας τοιαῦτα παρακελευσάμενος having *delivered* this *address*, Th.6.69: abs., *encourage one another by shouting*, Hdt.9.102; ἀλλήλοις π. X.*An.*4.2.11; ἐν ἑαυτοῖς π. ὡς.. Th.4. 25. III. Act., Hp.*Decent.*16, Plb.7.16.2, 16.20.8:—Pass., παρακεκέλευστο *orders had been given*, Hdt.8.93; τὰ παρακελευόμενα ὑφ' ἡμῶν Pl.*Ep.*333a; χαίρειν παρεκελεύοντο Philostr.*VA*5.27. **-κέλευσις,** εως, ἡ, *cheering on*, *exhorting*, Th.7.70; διδαχὴν ἅμα τῇ π. ποιεῖσθαι Id. 4.126; ἐκ παρακελεύσεως Id.7.40; π. τοῦ μὴ ποιεῖν δεῖσθαι Phld.*Oec.* p.36 J.; τυφλοῦ π. *advice given* by a blind man, Pl.*Tht.*209e: pl., X. *Cyr.*3.3.50, Isoc.9.31, etc. II. *factious combination* for elections, ἐκ π. ἢ καὶ δεκασμοῦ D.C.53.21. **-κέλευσμα,** v. παρακέλευμα. **-κελευσμᾰτικός,** ή, όν, *hortatory*, δύναμις Eust.1393.4. Adv. -κῶς, ἔχειν Id.1416.40. **-κελευσμός,** ὁ, = παρακέλευσις I, Th. 4.11, Lys.2.38, X.*Cyr.*3.3.59, etc. **-κελευστέον,** *one must encourage*, θαρρεῖν Herod.Med. in *Rh.Mus.*58.100. ⊛ **-κελευστής,** οῦ, ὁ, *one who calls out to* or *encourages*, Gloss. **-κελευστικός,** ή, όν, *calling out to*, *cheering on*, π. λόγος ἐπὶ τὴν ἀρετήν Pl.*Euthd.*283b; π. ἐπίφθεγμα, in battle, Poll.4.86; π. [ἐπίρρημα] A.D.*Adv.*123.12. Adv. -κῶς Sch.Od.8.11. **-κελευστός,** ή, όν, *summoned*, of a *packed* audience, Th.6.13.

**παρακελητίζω,** Att. fut. -ιῶ, *ride by* or *past*, τινα Ar.*Pax*901.

**παρακέλομαι,** *call upon*, τὰς..παρεκέκλετ' ἀοιδαῖς A.R.4.1668.

**παρακενόω,** *empty beside* or *near*, τὸ παρακενωθέν *void*, *vacuum*, *Placit.*4.22.1, 5.15.3.

**παρακεντ-έω,** *pierce* or *poke at the side*, τὴν κάμινον ὀβελίσκοις Thphr. *HP*5.9.4. 2. Medic., *tap*, for dropsy, τοὺς ὑδεριῶντας Gal.*Thras.* 23. b. *couch*, for cataract, Id.*UP*10.1 (Pass.). 3. *embroider*, κέντρων ᾧ παρακεντοῦνται διάφοροι χρόαι Eust.1308.63. 4. *stab*, prob. in D.S.10 *Fr.*18. II. metaph., *stir up*, τὸ πρᾶγμα Bato 7. 6. **-ημα,** ατος, τό, *embroidery*, Eust.1308.64. **-ησις,** εως, ἡ, Medic., *tapping* for dropsy, etc., Gal.18(1).39, Orib.44.13.4. b. *couching* for cataract, Gal.*UP*10.4 (pl.), Simp.*in Cat.*401.8. **-ητήριον,** τό, *instrument for tapping* or *couching*, prob. in Gal.18(2). 672. **-ητής,** οῦ, ὁ, *one who taps* or *couches*, Id.*Thras.*24, Gloss. **-ητικός,** ή, όν, *of tapping* or *couching*, τέχνη Gal.*Thras.* 24.

**παρακένωσις,** εως, ἡ, *evacuation*, Pall.*in Hp.*2.171 D.

**παρακερδαίνω,** *make incidental* or *unjust gain*, Lib.*Decl.*2.7, Heliod.*in EN*81.22.

**παρακερκίς,** ίδος, ἡ, *small bone of the leg*, Poll.2.191. II. *side-bone*, as a pathological condition, *Hippiatr.*51.

⊛ **παρακίναιδος** [ῐ], ὁ, = κίναιδος, f.l. in D.L.4.34.

**παρακινδύν-ευμα** [ῡ], ατος, τό, = sq., Hsch. s.v. ἐκ παραβολῆς. **-ευσις,** εως, ἡ, *desperate venture*, τὴν π. ποιεῖσθαι Th.5.100. **-ευτέον,** *one must make a venture*, D.H.9.57, Jul.*Or.*4.146b; π. εἶναι νομίζων Phld.*Lib.*p.7 O. **-ευτικός,** ή, όν, *venturesome*, *audacious*, λόγος Pl.*Sph.*242b, D.25.43: Sup., Dam.*Pr.*5; of a person, App.*Hann.*

50. Adv. -κῶς, λέγειν Pl.*R*.497e: Comp. -ώτερον Longin.32. 3. **-εύω**, *make a venture*, Hp.*Aër*.23, Ar.*V*.6, And.2.11, Th.4.26, etc.; ἐς Ἰωνίαν π. *venture* to Ionia, Id.3.36. 2. c. acc. rei, *venture*, *risk* a thing, Ar.*Eq*.1054, Pl.*Lg*.967b; παρακινδυνεύων λέγω I *venture* to say, Id.*Tht*.204b; τοιουτονί τι παρακεκινδυνευμένον a *bold*, *venturous* phrase, Ar.*Ra*.99; τὸ θρασὺ καὶ -ευμένον D.H.*Comp*.23, cf. *Is*.13; π. μάχαι *desperate* battles, Id.9.30; π. ἔντευξις Plu.*Caes*.9, etc. 3. c. inf., *to have the hardihood to* .., εἰπεῖν τὰ δίκαια Ar.*Ach*.645, cf. X.*HG*3.5.16; also παρεκινδύνευε .. παραλαμβάνεσθαι *might almost* be used, A.D.*Synt*.16.23:—so in Pass., τὸ -ευόμενον εἶναι ἐπίρρημα ib.237.18, cf. 215.11. 4. in a double construction, τοὺς θεοὺς ἂν ἔδεισας -εύειν μὴ οὐκ ὀρθῶς ποιήσοις Pl.*Euthphr*.15d. **-ος**, ον, *risking dangers*, τὸ π. τῶν ἀνθρώπων *temerity*, *daring character*, Str.17.3.20. Adv. -νως *with great danger*, ὁρμίζεσθαι Id.5.3.5.

⊛ **παρακῑν-έω**, *move aside*, *disturb*, τι Pl.*R*.591e (unless intr., v. infr. II. 2): abs., *raise troubles*, *enter into conspiracies*, D.15.12, Luc.*Rh.Pr*.5; τὸ -κινοῦν μέρος the *revolutionary* element, D.H.7.55. 2. *excite violently*, *madden*, Thphr.*HP*9.19.1:—Pass., *to be distracted*, Arg.S.*Aj*.; εἴς τι *to be violently excited* or *incited* to .., Luc.*Hist. Conscr*.1; ὑπόθερμος καὶ παρακεκινημένος Id.*Cal*.5; later, simply, *urge*, c. inf., *Mantiss.Prov*.2.46. 3. metaph., *stir up*, i.e. *raise a question about*, τὸν Ἀριστοτέλη Plu.2.656c. II. intr., *to be disturbed*, *become turbid*, Thphr.*CP*6.7.6. 2. *shift one's ground*, *change*, Pl.*R*.540a, 591e (cf. I. 1), D.H.3.10. 3. *to be highly excited* or *impassioned*, ἐπὶ τοῖς ὡραίοις X.*Mem*.4.2.35; πρὸς τὰς ἡδονάς Theopomp.Hist.111; μηδὲν παρακινέειν *feel* no sexual *impulse*, Hp.*Aër*.22; of political unrest, *to be in a state of ferment*, π. τὰ τάγματα Plu.*Galb*.13; *to be out of one's senses*, παρακεκινηκὼς ὑφ' ἡλικίας *Com.Adesp*.885; νουθετεῖται .. ὡς παρακινῶν as *out of his senses*, Pl.*Phdr*.249d; τῇ διανοίᾳ παρακεκινηκώς D.S.24.3, cf. 10.14. **-ημα**, ατος, τό, *distortion*, *Hippiatr*.24, Gal.14.780. II. *derivative*, τὰ τοῦ "βάλλειν" π. Eust.1405.32. **-ηματικός**, ή, όν, *exciting*, π. τι καὶ μανιῶδες Ph.2.477. **-ησις**, εως, ἡ, *disturbance*, Phld.*Rh*.2.5S. II. gloss on παρακελευσμός, Sch.Th.4.11. **-ητικός**, ή, όν, *stimulating*, τῆς τοῦ σώματος εὐεξίας Hierocl.*in CA*16p.456M.; πρὸς ἔρωτα Sch.Theoc.11.40: abs., v.l. in Ph.2.477. 2. *deranged*, Plu.*Fr*.3. Adv. -κῶς, ἔχειν *show symptoms of madness*, Id.*Sol*.8.

⊛ **παρακίρναμαι**, Pass., *to be mixed with*, τινι J.*BJ*4.3.7.

**παρακίω** [ῐ], *pass by*, τινα Il.16.263 (tm.).

⊛ **παρακλαίω**, *weep*, *whine beside*, Sch.Ar.*V*.971.

**παρακλάομαι**, Pass., *to be broken off*, f.l. for περι- in Sch.Arat.785.

**παράκλᾰσις**, εως, ἡ, *breaking off*: applied to the circumflex accent, Eust.25.35.

**παρακλαυσίθῠρον** [ῐ], τό, *lover's complaint sung at his mistress's door*, *serenade*, Plu.2.753b.

**παρακλείδιος** κλείς, ἡ, *false key*, Pl.Com.77. II. Subst. παρακλείδιον, τό, *lock*, *POxy*.1269.22 (ii A.D.).

**παρακλείω**, Ion. **-κληΐω**, *shut out*, *exclude*, τινας Hdt.6.60. II. *shut up* in prison, Plb.5.39.3 (dub. l.), Lxx 2*Ma*.4.34.

**παρακλέπτω**, *filch*, Ar.*Pax*414, Luc.*Jud.Voc*.4; τὰ παρακλεπτόμενα Is.11.44. II. *deceive*, Nonn.*D*.37.354.

**παρακληΐω**, v. παρακλείω. **παρακληρόω**, v. παραπληρόω.

**παρά-κλησις**, εως, ἡ, *calling to one's aid*, *summons*, οἱ ἐκ παρακλήσεως συγκαθήμενοι a *packed* party in the assembly, D.18.143. 2. *imploring*, *appealing*, τινος *of* or *on the part of* one, Th.4.61; *deprecation*, συγγνώμης δεῖ καὶ π. Str.13.1.1. 3. *invocation* of gods, Iamb.*Myst*.4.3 (pl.). 4. *demand*, *request*, *PGrenf*.1.32.7 (pl., ii B.C.), etc.; κατὰ -σιν on *demand*, *PLond*.3.1164$^{d}$10 (iii A.D.). II. *exhortation*, *address*, πρὸς τὸν ὄχλον Th.8.92; οὐ π. εὑρόντες, ἀλλὰ παραίνεσιν γράψαντες not *a mere address* to their feelings, but counsel to act rightly, Isoc.1.5; π. τῶν πολιτῶν πρὸς ἀρετήν Aeschin.1.117; τὴν τῆς σωφροσύνης παράκλησιν .. αὐτοὺς παρακέκληκα Id.2.180; ἀξιώσεις καὶ -κλήσεις Plb.1.67.10. III. *consolation*, Lxx *Is*.30.7, *Na*.3.7, *Ep.Hebr*.6.18, Phalar.*Ep*.103.1. **-κλητέος**, α, ον, *to be called upon*, *summoned*, Plu.2.1104a, Luc.*Pseudol*.4. II. παρακλητέον, *one must call on*, θεόν Pl.*Lg*.893b; *summon*, ἑτέρους σοι συμβούλους π. Isoc.*Ep*.7.7, cf. Pl.*Ti*.27d; [τοὺς φίλους] Arist.*EN*1171$^{b}$18. **-κλητεύω**, *act as advocate* or *intercessor*, *Bull.Soc.Roy.des lettres de Lund* 1928/9 iv 16 (Thuria, i B.C./i A.D.), Ph.2.520. **-κλητικός**, ή, όν, *stimulating*, νοήσεως Pl.*R*.523e; τῆς διανοίας ib.524d; *hortatory*, π. τι ᾄδειν Phld.*Mus*.p.18K.; σημαίνειν τὰ π. τοῦ πολέμου D.H.4.17; λόγος π. ὁμονοίας ib.26; π. λόγοι Lxx *Za*.1.13; π. εἰς εὐσέβειαν Iamb.*Protr*.21. II. π. ὁμολογία agreement concluded *on demand* (cf. παράκλησις I. 4), *POxy*.125.11 (vi A.D.), etc. **-κλητος**, ον, *called to one's aid*, in a court of justice: as Subst., *legal assistant*, *advocate*, D.19.1, Lycurg.*Fr*.102, etc. 2. *summoned*, δοῦλοι D.C.46.20, cf. *BGU*601.12 (ii A.D.). II. *intercessor*, Ph.2.520: hence in *NT*, Παράκλητος, of the Holy Spirit, *Ev.Jo*.14.16, cf. 1*Ep.Jo*.2.1. **-κλήτρια**, ἡ, fem. of foreg., Sch.E.*Hec*.100. **-κλήτωρ**, ορος, ὁ, *one who encourages*, *comforter*, παρακλήτορες κακῶν, = κακοὶ π., Lxx *Jb*.16.2. 2. *suppliant*, τινος Sch.E.*Hec*.147; but π. Ζεύς, = ἱκέσιος, ib.345.

**παρα-κλῐδόν**, Adv., (παρακλίνω) *turning aside*, *swerving*, οὐκ ἂν ἔγωγε ἄλλα παρὲξ εἴποιμι π. would not tell you another tale beside the mark and *swerving from the truth*, Od.4.348; ὄσσε π. ἔτραπεν ἄλλῃ she turned her eyes *aside*, *h.Ven*.182; π. πῖπτεν A.R.1.757. II. *leaning against*, τοίχων ἔνθα καὶ ἔνθα π. Orph.*A*.559. **-κλίντωρ**, ορος, ὁ, = παρακλίτης, *AP*9.257 (Apollonid.). ⊛ **-κλίνω** [ῑ], *bend*, *turn aside*, ἧκα παρακλίνας κεφαλήν Od.20.301; π. τοὺς μυκτῆρας πρὸς τὰς λαύρας Ar.*Pax*157; π. τὴν πύλην *set* it *ajar*, Hdt.3.156; π. τῆς αὐλείας *open a bit* of the hall-door, Ar.*Pax*981. 2. metaph., ἄλλῃ παρκλίνωσι δίκας *turn* justice *from her path*, Hes.*Op*.262; π. τὸν νόμον Arist.*Rh.Al*.1444$^{b}$16; of words, σμικρόν τι π. *alter* slightly, Pl.*Cra*.410a, cf. 400c. 3. *lay beside*, τὰς λαγόνας γυναιξί dub. in Lxx *Si*.47.19 (v. παρανακλίνω), cf. Ruf.*Ren.Ves*.1.13:—Med. and Pass., *lie alongside*, Hp.*Art*.54; *lie down beside*, τινι Theoc.2.44, *AP*5.293 (Agath.); *lie side by side*, Arist.*HA*540$^{a}$1; of adjacent lands, Πελοπηΐς ὅση παρακέκλιται Ἰσθμῷ Call.*Del*.72. 4. Med., *turn aside*, Ant.Lib.17.6. II. intr., *turn aside*, Il.23.424 (where however ἵππους may be supplied); παρακλίνασα *having swerved* from her first seeming, A.*Ag*.744 (lyr.). III. *turn aside from*, *avoid*, τὴν ἁφὴν τὴν ἀλλήλων Arist.*GA*745$^{a}$26. **-κλίτης** [ῐ], ου, ὁ, *one who lies beside* at meals, X.*Cyr*.2.2.28.

**παρακλύζω**, *submerge*, Al.*Ps*.123(124).4.

**παρακλύω** [ῠ], = παρακούω IV, *APl*.4.255.

**παρακμ-άζω**, *to be past the prime*, of fruits, etc., X.*Mem*.4.4.23, Thphr.*Od*.34, etc.; παρηκμακότες, of old trees, Id.*HP*9.4.7; of men compared to wine, Alex.45.5: metaph., of beauty, X.*Smp*.4.17, 8.14; πρεσβύτεροι καὶ παρηκμακότες Arist.*Rh*.1389$^{b}$13, cf. *Pol*.1275$^{a}$17; π. τοῖς σώμασι Plu.*Caes*.37; of a state, Plb.6.51.5; of sea-waves, *abate*, Thphr.*Vent*.35; of passion, ἂν δὲ μικρὸν παρακμάσῃ [ὀργή] Men.573, cf. Plu.*Brut*.21. **-αστικός**, ή, όν, *past its prime*, ἡλικία Gal.17(2).643; π. καὶ πρὸς φθορὰν ὁδεῦον Simp.*in Ph*.1335.7. II. *past its climax*, πυρετός Gal.7.337. Adv. -κῶς, ἐλύθη τὸ νόσημα Aët.5.53. **-ή**, ἡ, *point at which the prime is past*, *decay*, Plu.2.453b; σώματος Ph.*Fr*.97H.; φθινοπώρου Sch.Arat.1082; π. τῆς νόσου *abatement*, Plu.*Marc*.24, cf. S.E.*P*.2.238: metaph., of numbers, Iamb.*in Nic*.p.77P.

**παρακνάομαι**, Med., *rub against*, τινι Philostr.*Im*.1.28.

**παρα-κνήμιον**, τό, (κνήμη) *outer shin-bone*, opp. προκνήμιον, Poll.2.190. **-κνημόομαι**, Pass., *go with difficulty*, Hippon.130: Dor. impf. παρεκναμεῦντο Hsch.

**παρακοάω**, = παρανοέω, pf. παρακεκόακε, Hsch., Phot.

**παρᾰκοή**, ἡ, *that which has been heard imperfectly*, *hearsay*, Pl.*Ep*.341b. 2. *misunderstanding*, Gal.4.764, 8.629. II. *defect of hearing*, Id.7.108. III. *unwillingness to hear*, *disobedience*, *contumacy*, *Ep.Rom*.5.19, 2*Ep.Cor*.10.6.

⊛ **παρακοιμ-άομαι**, Pass., *lie* or *keep watch beside*, τῷ βασιλεῖ J.*AJ*7.7.1; τοῖς βασιλείοις Ath.5.189e, cf. Nic.Dam.4J.; οἱ παρακοιμώμενοι the *night-nurses on duty*, Gal.18(1).49. 2. *lie beside*, τινι, in death, *IG*14.1539. **-ημα**, ατος, τό, = παραγκάλισμα, Sch.S.*Ant*.650. **-ησις**, εως, ἡ, *watch*, *Gloss*. **-ητής**, οῦ, ὁ, *guard*, ib. **-ίζω**, *make to lie with*, τινά τινι Alex.Polyh.ap.Eus.*PE*9.21, cf. Artem.4.61, *Cat.Cod.Astr*.2.208 (prob.): hence Subst. **-ιστής**, οῦ, ὁ, in pl., π. τῶν ἰδίων γυναικῶν *panders* to their own wives, Paul.Al.*O*.2.

**παρακοινάομαι**, Med., *communicate*, τινί τι Pi.*P*.4.133.

⊛ **παρα-κοιτέω**, *keep watch* or *ward beside*, τινι Plb.6.33.12: abs., Teles p.50H., *SIG*731.15 (Tomi, i B.C.). **-κοίτης**, ου, ὁ, *one who lies beside*, *bedfellow*, *husband*, Il.6.430, 8.156, Hes.*Th*.928. **-κοιτῐς**, ῐος, ἡ, acc. ῐν (later -κοίτιδα *Supp.Epigr*.1.455.10 (Phrygia, iii A.D.)), fem. of foreg., *wife*, αἰδοίη, θαλερή, ἰφθίμη, κυδρή, Il.21.479, 3.53, Od.23.92, 15.26, etc.; Ep. dat. παρακοίτῑ 3.381, Hes.*Sc*.14, 46. **-κοιτος**, ὁ, = παρακοίτης, D.S.5.32: fem. in Thd.*Da*.5.2.

**παρακολλ-άω**, *glue* or *fasten on*, Hp.*Mochl*.2. II. *unite directly by 'first intention'*, τραύματα Heras ap.Gal.13.794, Antyll.ap.Orib.10.23.6, 50.2.8. **-ημα**, ατος, τό, *that which is glued on*, perh. *ornamental woodwork glued on* furniture, Thphr.*HP*5.7.6. 2. *crimp* or *loop* of string glued to a cylinder, Hero *Aut*.23.7. II. *eye-salve*, Gal.13.643, Severus ap.Aët.7.96. **-ησις**, εως, ἡ, *glueing* or *fastening on*, Hp.*Off*.11. II. *healing* or *closing up* of sinuses, Heras ap.Gal.13.795, Antyll.ap.Orib.45.25.6, Leonid.ap.Aët.15.2. ⊛ **-ητικός**, ή, όν, *healing by 'first intention'*, π. ἀγωγή, opp. συσσάρκωσις, Orib.45.17.11. ⊛ **-ος** χαμεῦνα, *low couch with only one end to it*, *IG*1$^{2}$.330.5 (Poll.10.36). II. *on the same meridian*, Serapio in *Cat.Cod.Astr*.8(4).226, Vett.Val.215.8, 360.18.

**παρᾰκολουθ-έω**, *follow* or *attend closely*, *dog one's steps*, τινι Ar.*Ec*.725; τὸ παρακολουθοῦν εἴδωλον ἑκάστῳ Pl.*Sph*.266c, cf. D.21.14, 69, Philem.124; οὓς σὺ ζῶντας μέν, ὦ κίναδος, κολακεύων παρηκολούθεις D.18.162; πόροι κατὰ πάντα τὸν πλεύμονα παρακολουθοῦντες Arist.*HA*496$^{a}$29; *accrue*, esp. of loss or damage, c. dat., *PSI*3.168.24 (ii B.C.), *PRein*.18.15 (ii B.C.). 2. *make a succession* of growths, Thphr.*HP*6.4.8. II. metaph., *follow closely*, *attend minutely to*, π. τῷ νοσήματι Pl.*R*.406b; π. ἅπασι [τοῖς πονηρεύμασι] *trace accurately* all his knaveries, D.19.257; π. τοῖς πράγμασιν ἐξ ἀρχῆς Id.18.172; π. χρόνοις *follow all* the times and dates, Nicom.Com.1.20, cf. *Ev.Luc*.1.3; τοῖς δικαίοις π. Demad.1; π. ταῖς τιμαῖς (prices) *PMich.Zen*.28.26 (iii B.C.); τῇ Ὁνοράτου κρίσει *POxy*.653.29 (ii A.D.). 2. of an audience, προσέχειν τὸν νοῦν καὶ π. εὐμαθῶς Aeschin.1.116: generally, *follow with the mind*, *understand*, π. τῷ πῶς .. Plb.1.12.7, etc.: as Stoic term, Arr.*Epict*.2.16.33, etc.; παρακολουθεῖν τούτῳ ὅτι .. *understand* that .., ib.2.26.3; simply, π. ὅτι .. Gal.11.554; διότι .. *PPetr*.2p.132 (iii B.C.): c. part., π. ἐλεγχόμενος Arr.*Epict*.4.5.21: c. acc., τίς παρακολουθεῖ ταῦτα; Damox.2.25; π. τὰ ἐψηφισμένα *become acquainted with* .., *GDI*4940.8 (Cret.), cf. *BSA*29.64 (Eretrian, found at Sparta), *IG*11(4).1065*a*17 (Delos), etc.: in later Philosophy, ἑαυτῷ π. *to be conscious*, Plot.1.4.5; esp. *to be* self-*conscious*, νοῦν νοοῦντα μόνον, μὴ παρακολουθοῦντα δὲ ἑαυτῷ ὅτι νοεῖ Id.2.9.1, cf. 4.4.37, Iamb.*Myst*.3.4, 14. 3. of things, πυρετοὶ π. μοι καὶ ἀλγήματα D.54.11, cf. Ruf.ap.Orib.44.17.2; τῷ βίῳ π. *keep company with, keep close to*, of things that benefit, Isoc.15.262; αὐτοῖς π. ἡ ἔχθρα ⟨ἡ⟩ παρὰ Λακεδαιμονίων D.59.98; of rules, *hold good throughout*, δι' ὅλης τῆς ἱππικῆς π. X.*Eq*.8.14. 4. of a logical property, τὸ ἀεὶ παρακολουθοῦν Arist.*Top*.131$^{b}$9; also of the genus, ib.125$^{b}$28, cf. 123$^{a}$19; of notions *inseparably connected* one with another, Id.*Cat*.8$^{a}$33, *Metaph*.1054$^{a}$14; of cause and effect, Id.*APo*.99$^{a}$17; τὸ παρακολουθοῦν τινι *constant attribute*, Phld.*Sign*.8.19, cf. A.D.*Pron*.4.3; *to be proper to*, ταῖς αἰσθηταῖς [ἁρμονίαις] Plot.1.6.3. **-ημα**, ατος, τό, *that which follows*, αἱ σκιαὶ π. τῶν σωμάτων Iamb.*Comm.Math*.8; *accompaniment* or *attendant circumstance*, Demetr.Lac.*Herc*.1012.46, *Placit*.1.22.5, Numen.ap.Porph.ap.Stob.1.49.25, Nicom.*Ar*.1.19, Plot.3.7.10, Hierocl.*in CA*15 p.453 M., Procl.*in Ti*.3.24 D., etc.; *by-product*, Herm.ap.Stob.1.21.9; *logical accident*, A.D.*Synt*.229.13. **-ησις**, εως, ἡ, *following closely, interrelation*, τοῦ αἰτίου καὶ οὗ αἴτιον Arist.*APo*.99$^{a}$30. 2. κατὰ -ησιν *as an incidental result*, Chrysipp.*Stoic*.2.336. II. *following with the mind, understanding*, Plu.2.1144b, Arr.*Epict*.1.6.13, A.D.*Synt*.37.16, M.Ant.3.1; διὰ τὴν τῶν πολλῶν π. Gal.6.817; ῥᾳόνος ἕνεκα π. Nicom.*Harm*.1; διὰ τὸ μὴ ἔχειν -ήσεις, of a mentally defective person, Mitteis *Chr*.96 ii 8 (iv A.D.). 2. *inference*, αἱ πολιτικαὶ ἐκ τῆς ἱστορίας π. Phld.*Rh*.1.122 S. 3. *awareness, consciousness*, Plot.1.4.10 (pl.), 3.9.3, 4.3.26. ⊛ **-ητέον**, *one must follow*, Procl.*in Ti*.1.26 D. ⊛ **-ητικός**, ή, όν, *of* or *for following* or *understanding*, δύναμις Arr.*Epict*.1.6.14, M.Ant.5.9: c. dat., Arr.*Epict*.1.6.17. Adv. -κῶς, εἰδότως καὶ π. *consciously*, M.Ant.6.42, cf. Ptol.*Tetr*.107. 2. -κή, ἡ, *contact*, of orator with audience, Phld.*Rh*.1.52 S.

⊛ **παρακολυμβάω**, *swim beside*, Hero *Aut*.22.5.

**παρακομ-ῐδή**, ἡ, *transportation, conveyance*, τῶν ἐπιτηδείων ἐκ τῆς Εὐβοίας Th.7.28, cf. *PRev.Laws* 48.11 (iii B.C.), etc.; ποιεῖσθαι τὴν π. τῶν ἀναγκαίων Plb.10.10.13; *bringing up*, τοῦ χάρακος Id.18.18.4. II. (from Pass.) *going* or *sailing across, passage, transit*, ἡ π. ἡ ἐς τὴν Σικελίαν Th.5.5, cf. Plb.3.43.3, etc. ⊛ **-ίζω**, fut. -ιῶ *PPetr*.3 p.122 (iii B.C.):—*escort, convoy*, E.*HF*125 (lyr.), X.*HG*1.4.7:—Pass., Plu.*Oth*.16. 2. *carry* or *convey over, transport*, ἐξ Ὑπερβορέων εἰς Δῆλον Arist.*HA*580$^{a}$17; π. ναῦς ἐπὶ τὸ χῶμα D.50.6: generally, *convey, carry*, Hdt.7.147, etc.:—Med., *have* a thing *brought one*, σῖτον X.*HG*5.4.57:—Pass., ib.5.4.61, Plu.*Oth*.3. 3. *obtain, receive* a document, Mitteis *Chr*.227.4 (ii A.D.), etc. II. Pass., *go* or *sail beside, coast along*, τὴν Ἰταλίαν Th.6.44; παρὰ τὴν ἤπειρον D.C.48.27; π. ἐς τὸν.. λιμένα, ἐπὶ Καμαρίνης, Th.4.25, 6.52: abs., Plu.*Luc*.37. 2. *go* or *sail across, pass over*, Plb.1.52.6, etc. **-ιστής**, οῦ, ὁ, *one who transports* or *purveys*, *Gloss*.

**παράκομμα**, ατος, τό, *money with a false stamp*, Ph.2.561, etc.: metaph., *counterfeit*, Id.1.683.

**παράκομος**, ον, *with flowing hair*, Amphis 50.

**παρᾰκονάω**, *sharpen* or *whet*, μάχαιραν *Com.Adesp*.599; τὰ σκληρὰ [ξύλα] π. (sc. τὰ σιδήρια) Thphr.*HP*5.5.1; ὁ λόγχην ἀκονῶν ἐκεῖνος καὶ τὴν ψυχήν τι παρακονᾷ X.*Cyr*.6.2.33:—Pass., αἱ φύσεις ἄλλως κράτισται, νῦν δὲ καὶ παρηκόνηνται Ar.*Ra*.1116 (lyr.):—Med., τὴν ἀκμὴν τῆς μαχαίρας π. Philostr.Jun.*Im*.2. II. generally, *rub against* the cheek, ἐν τῷ ἀσπάζεσθαι Hsch., cf. Phot.

**παρακονί-ᾱσις**, εως, ἡ, *whitewashing*, *Inscr.Délos* 365.48 (iii B.C.). **-άω**, *whitewash*, τοῖχον *IG*11(2).144 *A* 69, al. (iv B.C.), cf. *Inscr.Délos* 403.11 (ii B.C.).

⊛ **παρᾰκοντίζω**, *throw the dart with others*, Luc.*Par*.61.

**παρα-κοπή**, ἡ, metaph., (παρακόπτω II) *infatuation, frenzy*, A.*Ag*.223 (lyr.), *Eu*.329 (lyr.); ἔστιν ὁ γέλως π. τις καὶ ἀπάτη Arist.*Pr*.965$^{a}$14; λύττα καὶ π. D.S.15.7, cf. Dsc.4.68; π. φρενῶν J.*BJ*1.25.4: pl., Demetr.Lac.*Herc*.1012.30, Iamb.*Myst*.3.25. 2. *delirium*, Hp.*Aph*.6.26: in pl., ἐνύπνια καὶ π. Plu.2.1123b. **-κοπος**, ον, metaph., *frenzied, frantic, distraught*, A.*Pr*.581 (lyr.); λῆμα π. E.*Ba*.1000 (lyr.); π. κινήματα τῆς διανοίας Metrod.*Herc*.831.2; π. διὰ μέθην Sor.1.39: c. gen., π. φρενῶν E.*Ba*.33; π. δόξα φρενῶν Tim.*Pers*.77. II. *counterfeit*, παράσημοι καὶ π. χλιδαί Ph.1.261. ⊛ **-κοπτικός**, ή, όν, *frantic, raving*, Antyll.ap.Orib.9.13.7; gloss on παρακρουστικός, Erot., Gal.19.415. ⊛ **-κόπτω**, *strike falsely, counterfeit*, prop. of money, D.S.1.78: generally, *falsify*, Luc.*Lex*.20; κίβδηλα καὶ νόθα καὶ παρακεκομμένα Id.*Ind*.2; opp. δόκιμα and ἀκίβδηλα, Id.*Hist.Conscr*.10, *Herm*.68; ἀνδράρια μοχθηρά, παρακεκομμένα knavish manikins, *base coin*, Ar.*Ach*.517. 2. Med., *cheat* or *swindle out of* a thing, οἵων ἀγαθῶν παρεκόπτου Id.*Eq*.807; simply, *cheat*, τινα ib.859:—Pass., *to be cheated*, παρεκόπην διχοινίκῳ Id.*Nu*.640. II. metaph., *strike* the mind *awry, drive mad, derange*, π. φρένας E.*Hipp*.238; παρακεκομμένος τὸν νοῦν Sch.rec.A.*Pr*.581, cf. Phot. s. v. 2. intr., *to be deranged*, τοῦ νοῦ παρακόπτοντος Hp.*Aff*.10; παρακόψαι τῇ διανοίᾳ *go mad*, Arist.*Mir*.832$^{b}$17: abs., παρακόψας *in a fit of madness*, D.L.4.44, cf. D.S.5.50: so in pres., παρακόπτων Plu.2.963e, 1123f; -κόψας *wrongheadedly*, Phld.*Oec*.p.10 J. III. *cut in pieces*, μέλη -κεκομμένα Plb.10.15.5; *cut pieces off* (sc. τῆς πυέλου), Arr.*An*.6.29.9. IV. *cut across* a neck of land, ἐπικαρσίᾳ τάφρῳ J.*BJ*4.1.1.

**παρακορέω**, *sweep clean*, Pl.Com.69.3, Philyll.3.

**παράκοσμος**, ον, *unseemly*. Adv. -μως J.*AJ*1.6.3.

**παρακοτέω**, *to be angry besides*, Phot.; cf. **παρακοττεῖ**· παραφρονεῖ, Hsch. (nisi leg. -κόπτει vel -κόττει (Cret.)).

**παράκουσ-ις** [ᾰκ], εως, ἡ, *defect of hearing*, Gal.7.56, al. II. *mishearing*, Mich.*in PN*64.32. **-μα**, ατος, τό, *thing heard amiss, false notion*, Pl.*Ep*.338d (pl.), etc.; *false story* or *report*, Str.7.5.9 (pl.); ἐκ παρακούσματος or -των D.H.9.22, J.*Ap*.1.8; *equivocation*, Περιπατητικῶν π. Jul.*Caes*.330c. II. in pl., *defects of hearing*, Gal.7.108. **-μάτιον**, τό, Dim. of foreg., Plu.2.354a. **-τέον**, *one must disobey*, τινος Muson.*Fr*.16 p.82 H.

**παρακουφίζω**, *relieve tension*, Sor.1.77.

⊛ **παρᾰκούω**, *hear beside*, esp. *hear accidentally, hear talk of*, Δημοκήδεος τὴν τέχνην Hdt.3.129; ἀξίων λόγου πραγμάτων Pl.*Ep*.339e; παρακήκοα νῦν ὅτι τίκτει *AP*5.74 (Rufin.). II. *eavesdrop, overhear from*, δεσποτῶν ἅττ' ἂν λαλῶσι Ar.*Ra*.750; τι παρά τινος Pl.*Euthd*.300d; π. τινός *overhear* him, Luc.*Merc.Cond*.37; π. τὸν λόγον *Ev.Marc*.5.36. III. *hear imperfectly* or *wrongly, misunderstand*, ἀκούειν τι τοῦ λόγου, παρακούειν δέ Arist.*EN*1149$^{a}$26, cf. Pl.*Prt*.330e, *Tht*.195a, Phld.*Mus*.p.102 K., Ceb.3, Luc.*Anach*.31; ἑκουσίως π. D.S.30.8. IV. *hear carelessly, take no heed of*, τῆς παραγγειλάσης φύσεως Epicur.*Fr*.200; τῶν γραφομένων Plb.24.9.1, cf. Luc.*Salt*.6, etc.; τῶν ἐντολῶν Lxx *To*.3.4; τῶν λεγομένων Plb.7.12.9 (but τὰ λεγόμενα Lxx *Es*.3.3). 2. c. gen. pers., *PHib*.1.170 (iii B.C.), Plb.2.8.3, 3.15.2, *Ev.Matt*.18.17:—Pass., *to be disregarded*, Plb.5.35.5; περί τινος Id.30.20.2, prob. cj. in 23.3.3. 3. *disobey*, τοῦ θεοῦ J.*AJ*1.10.4: abs., Lxx *Is*.65.12, J.*AJ*1.1.4, Luc.*Sat*.10:—Pass., J.*AJ*6.7.4. 4. *pretend not to hear*, Plu.*Phil*.16, Luc *Jud.Voc*.2.

**παρακρᾰτ-έω**, *detain, keep waiting*, τινα App.*Hisp*.35; *restrain*, Arr.*Epict*.3.7.28; τρίχας ῥεούσας π. *prevent* the hair *from falling off*, Dsc.4.134; *retain*, τὰ ἐν τῇ γαστρί Ruf.*Anat*.42:—Pass., *to be held in check*, M.Ant.11.20, Apollod.*Poliorc*.183.1. 2. *compress, squeeze*, Dsc.*Eup*.1.8 (Pass.). II. *hold out to*, ἀμίδα τινί Arr.*Epict*.1.2.8. **-ητέον**, *one must keep up* (a hernia), Orib.*Fr*.85.

⊛ **παρακρέμᾰμαι**, Pass., *hang beside*, Luc.*Asin*.23: metaph., *to be dependent*, τὰ παρακρεμάμενα μέρη the *dependencies* of an empire, Plb.5.35.10.

⊛ **παρακρεμάννῡμι**, *hang beside*, χεῖρα παρακρεμάσας *letting* the hand *hang down*, Il.13.597.

**παράκρημνος**, ον, *steep at the side, on the edge of a precipice*, ὁδός, ἀτραπός, Str.9.1.4, D.S.11.8; *precipitous*, χωρία Plu.*Phil*.18; *with steep banks*, ῥεῖθρον Id.*Brut*.51.

**παρα-κρίνω** [ῑ], *judge falsely*, Hsch. s. v. παραβραβεύων. II. Pass., *to be drawn up in line opposite*, Plu.*Ant*.39; πεζὸς παρακεκριμένος παρὰ τὸν αἰγιαλόν the land force *drawn up along* the shore, Hdt.9.98; παρεκρίθησαν διαταχθέντες Id.8.70, cf. Plu.*Cat.Mi*.13. **-κρῑτής**, οῦ, ὁ, *one who judges falsely*, *EM*435.44.

**παρακρο-άομαι**, = παρακούω IV. 3, *disobey*, J.*AJ*18.8.5. **-ᾱσις**, εως, ἡ, *disobedience*, ib.18.8.2.

**παρακροκίζω**, *to be somewhat saffron-coloured*, Dsc.5.127.

**παρακροτέω**, *pat, clap* one, εἰς τὸν ὦμον Luc.*Anach*.1. 2. *encourage*, τινα D.H.7.46, J.*BJ*1.19.5, 1.31.5:—Pass., ib.3.10.2.

**παρά-κρουσις**, εως, ἡ, *striking falsely, false note, discord*, Plu.2.826e (pl.). 2. metaph., *cheating, deception*, D.23.175; φενακισμὸς καὶ π. Id.24.194. b. *fallacy*, Arist.*Pol*.1263$^{b}$30, cf. *SE*175$^{b}$1 (pl.). 3. *delirium*, Hp.*Prorrh*.1.19 (pl.); *insanity*, Id.*Ep*.11. II. *checking*, τοῦ θερμοῦ Arist.*Pr*.872$^{b}$29 (nisi leg. κατά-). **-κρουσῐχοίνῐκος**, ον, *striking off too much from the top of the measure* (cf. παρακρούω VII), *Com.Adesp*.1104. **-κρουσμα**, ατος, τό, *fallacy*, Simp.*in Cat*.135.28. **-κρουστικός**, ή, όν, = παρακοπτικός, Hp.*Prorrh*.1.11; πυρετός Ruf.ap.Orib.45.30.59; ἀγρυπνίαι Gal.7.467. II. *deceitful*, Poll.4.21. Adv. -κῶς ib.51. **-κρουστος**· μωρός, Hsch. **-κρούω**, *strike aside*, οὐκ ἄν σε παρακρούοι ἡ παροῦσα συμφορά will not *put* you *out, bias* your *judgement*, Pl.*Cri*.47a:—Pass., *to be led astray, go wrong*, ἄθρει.. πῇ παρακρουόμεθα Id.*Ly*.215c; ἐφενακίσθητε καὶ παρεκρούσθητε D.23.107; μὴ παρακρουσθῆτε *be* not *diverted from the point*, Id.21.160; ὑπό τινος by one, Aeschin.1.170; περί τινος about a thing, Plb.23.3.3 (s.v.l.); τὰ σφάλματα, ἃ αὐτὸς ὑφ' ἑαυτοῦ.. παρεκέκρουστο the faults into which *he had been misled*, Pl.*Tht*.168a. 2. Med., *mislead, deceive, cheat*, esp. by fallacies, π. καὶ παραλογίζεσθαι Isoc.12.243; τὰς δόξας τῶν ἀκροωμένων π. ib.271, cf. Pl.*Cra*.393c, D.2.5, 18.276, Din.1.40, Arist.*Pol*.1297$^{a}$10, *Metaph*.1025$^{a}$6, Men.*Epit*.329, *PSI*4.442.24 (iii B.C.), etc.; τηλικουτονὶ πρᾶγμα π. τοὺς δικαστάς D.43.39: pf. Pass. παρακέκρου(σ)μαι in sense of Med., Id.6.23, Luc.*Tim*.57. 3. Med., metaph., *crack*, φυλάττου μὴ πεσὼν σαυτὸν παρακρούσῃ Phryn.Com.58. II. *strike away, parry*, Them.*Or*.32.359b:—but usu. Med., π. ταῖς μαχαίραις τοὺς κοντούς Plu.*Luc*.28, cf. *Sull*.18; *shun, avoid*, τὸν θρίαμβον Id.2.198b. III. παρακεκροῦσθαι τῶν φρενῶν *to be driven from* one's senses, *Com.Adesp*.705:—so also intr. in Act., πάντα παρέκρουσε Hp.*Epid*.1.26.α'. IV. ἡ ὀθόνη παρακέκρουσται *is ready hoisted*, Luc.*Cat*.1 (s.v.l.). V. perh. *strike* a horse *sideways*, *IG*1$^{2}$.374.166. VI. of a wrestler, *make a feint*, *EM*652.48. VII. of a seller, *strike off too much from the top of the measure* (from which signf. I. 2 is said to be derived), Harp.; cf. παρακρουσιχοίνικος.

**παρα-κρύπτω**, *hide one's sympathies, dissimulate*, D.S.18.9:—Med., *hide oneself*, D.L.2.131. **-κρυψις**, εως, ἡ, *concealment, suppression*, ψηφισμάτων Phld.*Rh*.1.276 S. (prob.).

**παρακρώζω**, *croak beside*, v.l. for περικράζω in Dionys.*Av*.1.9 (*An.Par*.1.25).

**παρακταῖος**, η, ον, *on the shore* or *bank*, Opp.*H*.4.316.

**παρακτάομαι**, *get over and above*, ξεινικοὺς νόμους Hdt.4.80.

**παρακτέον**, (παράγω) *one must have recourse to*, ταῦτα Aët.5.96.

**παράκτης**, ου, ὁ, (παράγω) *one who leads hounds*, Hsch.

**παρακτίδιος**, ον, = παράκτιος, κῦμα *AP*9.371.

**παρακτικός**, ή, όν, (παράγω) *productive*, πᾶν τὸ π. ἄλλου κρεῖττόν ἐστι τῆς τοῦ παραγομένου φύσεως Procl.*Inst.*7, cf. Dam.*Pr.*32, Ascl.*in Metaph.*35.13; π. δύναμις prob. in Procl. *in Prm.*p.893 S.

**παράκτιος**, α, ον (ος, ον *AP*6.167 (Agath.)), *on the sea-side*, κέλευθος, ὁδός, A *Pr.*836, S.*Fr.*905; λειμῶνες Id.*Aj.*654; πλάξ Phryn.Trag.5.3; παράκτιοι δραμεῖσθε E.*IT*1424: in Prose, οἱ π. *IG*5(2).268.24 (Mantinea, i B.C.); also later, Agath.2.16, al.

**παρακῡέω**, *to be spuriously pregnant*, dub. rest. in $IG4^2$(1).122.26 (Epid.).

**παράκυκλος**, ὁ, *part of a chariot-wheel*, Poll.10.53.

**παρακῡμάτιος**, ον, (κῦμα I. 3) *with a wavy border*, χιτωνίσκος $IG2^2$. 1514.46.

**παρακῡνάγχη**, ἡ, *a form of* κυνάγχη, Anon.ap.Gal.17(2).706; the name is rejected by Gal.8.248.

**παρα-κυπτικός**, ή, όν, *fit for peeping through*, θυρίδες *Cod.Just.*8.10. 12.2. **-κύπτω**, poet. **παρκύπτω**, *stoop sideways*, of the attitude of a bad harp-player, Ar.*Ach.*16; *lean over* a railing, *POxy.*475.23 (ii A.D.). II. *stoop for the purpose of looking*, and so, **1.** *look sideways* at, *cast a careless glance* on a thing, παρακύψαντ' ἐπὶ τὸν τῆς πόλεως πόλεμον D.4.24. **2.** *peep out of* a door or window, ἐκ θυρίδος Ar.*Th.*797, cf. 799, *V.*178; π. ὥσπερ γαλῆ Id.*Ec.*924; of girls *peeping after a lover*, Id.*Pax*982, 985, Theoc.3.7; διὰ τῶν θυρίδων LXX *Ca.*2.9; π. τὸν ἐραστὴν ἰδεῖν so as to see him, Plu.2.766d: metaph., σωτηρία παρέκυψε a hope of safety *peeped out*, Ar.*Ec.*202; ὀδόντων παρακυψάντων, of the first teeth, Sor.1.118: folld. by an interrog. clause, *peep out and see*, π. τίς ἄνεμος πνεῖ Arr.*Epict.*1.1.16:—Pass., θυρίδες παρακυπτόμεναι prob. *out of which people look*, LXX 3*Ki.*6. 9(4). **3.** of persons outside a place, *peep in, look in*, εἰς οἰκίαν ib.*Si.* 21.23; παρέκυψεν εἰς τὸ μνημεῖον *Ev.Jo.*20.11; παρακύψας βλέπει ib. 5, *Ev.Luc.*24.12; ὁ παρακύψας εἰς νόμον τέλειον *Ep.Jac.*1.25; π. εἰς τὰ ὑμέτερα Luc.*Pisc.*30, cf. 1*Ep.Pet.*1.12; of a thing, *appear in*, ἐς ἀρχὸν Hp.*Fist.*3. **4.** *meddle with*, πράγματι *PLips.*29.10 (iii A.D.).

⊛ **παρακῡρόω**, *annul*, Sm.*Jb.*40.3(8).

**παρακύρω** [ῡ], = παρατυγχάνω, Q.S.11.423.

**παράκυψις**, εως, ἡ, *stooping to one side, peeping in*, Sm.3*Ki.*7.4(41): prov. ὄνου π., of those who bring frivolous actions, Men.246, cf. Zen. 5.39.

**παρακωμῳδέω**, *satirize incidentally*, Ath.12.525a.

**παρακωχή**, v. παροκωχή.

**παραλαγχάνω**, pf. -είληχα, *obtain as one's portion*, Sch.Ar.*Av.* 569.

**παραλᾰλ-έω**, *talk at random*, Men.923.4, LXX *Ps.*43(44).17. D.C. 69.4. **-ία**, ἡ, *consolation*, θάνατος πενήτων π. Secund.*Sent.*19 (s.v.l.).

**παραλαμβάνω** (Cret. **παλλαμβάνω** *Riv. Fil.* 58.472 (Gortyn, iii B.C.)), fut. -λήψομαι, Ion. -λάμψομαι Hdt.2.120:—*receive from* another, esp. of persons succeeding to an office, etc., [τὴν βασιληΐην] Hdt.l.c., cf. Th.1.9; τὴν βασιλείαν παρὰ τοῦ πατρὸς *OGI*90.1 (Rosetta, ii B.C.); τοῖς παραλαμβάνουσι (sc. τὴν βασιλείαν) *the successors*, Arist.*Pol.*1285ᵇ8; π. τὴν ἀρχὴν Pl.*Lg.*698e; τῆς πόλεως τὰ πράγματα Ar.*Ec.*107; τὴν ἐπιμέλειάν τινος Aeschin.1.143; τὴν τριηραρχίαν D.47.32; π. πόλιν ἀνάστατον And.1.108, cf. Th.1.9, etc.; νόμον ὄντα παραλαβόντες, opp. θέντες, Id.5.105, cf. Isoc.8.102; of inherited rites or customs, Hdt.2. 51; of persons succeeding *by inheritance*, E.*Ion*814, Lys.10.5, etc.; οἱ μὴ κτησάμενοι ἀλλὰ -λαβόντες τὴν οὐσίαν Arist.*EN*1120ᵇ12; παρὰ τοῦ πατρὸς πολλὴν οὐσίαν π. D.21.157; opp. ἐπικτᾶσθαι, Pl.*R.*330a; π. ἀρὰς *inherit* curses, E.*Ph.*1611; of officers, *receive* things as stated in an inventory from their predecessors, $IG1^2$.301.5, al.; τὰ μὲν παρειληφότα τὰ δ' αὐτὸν εὑρηκότα Isoc.15.208: Astrol., *take over*, [χρονοκρατορίαν] Vett.Val.171.16: generally, *receive*, ἔρια παραλαβοῦσα ἱμάτιον ἀποδεῖξαι X.*Oec.*7.6; of cargo, *POxy.*276.13 (i A.D.), etc. **2.** *take upon oneself, undertake*, πρᾶγμά τι Ar.*Eq.*345; τὰ παραλαμβανόμενα *undertakings*, Hdt.1.38; *take to oneself, admit, employ*, π. ἐν ταῖς μάχαις τὸν θυμὸν Plu.2.988e:—Pass., π. πρὸς τὴν σύστασιν τῆς ψυχῆς ib.1027d. **3.** *take in pledge*, Hdt.3.136; *take by force* or *treachery, seize*, οὐδὲν ἐδυνέατο π. τῆς ἐσόδου Id.7.211; ναῦς παραλαβόντες Th.1.19, 4.16, And.3.39; π. τὰ πράγματα *get control of* affairs, Plu.*Alc.*26:—in Med., *lay hold of*, ἄκρων τῶν χειρῶν Paus.6.4.1 (s.v.l.). **4.** *receive by hearing* or *report, ascertain*, παρὰ τῶν Αἰγυπτίων Hdt.2.19; π. ἀληθείην Id.1.55; π. ἀκοῇ Id.2.148; π. τὰ περὶ Ἀλκμέωνα Th.2.102; τι περί τινος Plb.12.22.5; *receive by way of lesson*, σοφίαν παρά τινος Pl.*La.*197d:—Pass., *to be received, accepted*, τὰ παρειλημμένα *the received* or *traditionary doctrines*, Arist.*Mete.*365ᵃ16; οἱ π. μῦθοι Id.*Po.*1453ᵇ22; [λόγοι] ἔνιοι π. ὡς Ἀριστογείτονος Plu.2. 850e. **5.** *take, receive*, or *use* as a substitute or equivalent, τὸν ἀριθμὸν ἀντὶ τοῦ νοῦ π. *Placit.*4.2.3:—Pass., "ὑμέτερον" ἀντὶ τοῦ "ὑμεῖς" παρείληπται D.H.*Amm.*2.14. **b.** Gramm. and Medic., simply, *use, employ*, D.H.*Comp.*25; εἰς λόγον A.D.*Synt.*250.3; θλῖψιν, βοηθήματα, Antyll.ap.Orib.8.6.37, 8.10.1 (Pass.):—freq. in Pass., *to be found, used*, D.H.*Comp.*14, 17, A.D.*Synt.*83.2, al.; π. ἐκ κοινοῦ, δεικτικῶς, ib.123.1, *Pron.*10.17. **c.** *admit*, ἡ ὅλη ὑπόθεσις τὸ ἓν εἶναι παρελάμβανεν Dam.*Pr.*417. **6.** *take up, catch up*, τὸ οὔνομα τοῦτο Hdt. 1.122, cf. 126; τὸν λόγον Plb.33.18.9; π. ἐπὶ βραχὺ *give a résumé of*, Id.6.58.1. **7.** *compare*, Porph. *in Cat.*97.8 (Pass.). **8.** Pass., *to be derived*, ἔκ τινος v.l. in A.D.*Pron.*32.16. **II.** c. acc. pers., *take to oneself, associate with oneself*, as a wife or mistress, Hdt.4.155; as an adopted son, Id.1.113; as a partner, auxiliary, or ally, ib.76, 7.150, Th.1.111, etc.; παραλαμβάνων ἄλλος ἄλλον ἐπ' ἄλλου.. χρείᾳ Pl.*R.* 369b; συμβούλους π. Arist.*EN*1112ᵇ10; *get control of*, Pl.*Ap.*18b, *R.* 460b, 541a, *Alc.*1.121e; μάρτυρας π. *call in* witnesses, D.47.67: c. inf., τὴν αἴσθησιν ὑπουργεῖν Jul.*Or.*8.248a. **2.** *invite*, ἐπὶ ξείνια Hdt.4. 154; παραληφθεὶς ἐπὶ δεῖπνον Alciphr.3.46; ἐφ' ἑστίασιν παρειλημμένος Plu.2.40b; παραληφθεὶς εἰς τὸ συσσίτιον Id.*Lyc.*20: abs., Id.2.461d; παραληφθῆναι πρός τινα Parmenisc.ap.Ath.4.156e. **3.** *receive, take over* in succession, Hdt.4.203; Λυκοῦργος π. τοὺς Σπαρτιάτας οἴκοι σκηνοῦντας X.*Lac.*5.2. **4.** *take prisoner*, Plb.3.69.2 (Pass.). **5.** of the dead, παραλημφθεὶς ὑπὸ θεῶν καταχθονίων *IG*14.1702.

**παραλάμπω**, *glimmer*, *Placit.*2.18.1.

⊛ **παράλαμψις**, εως, ἡ, *shining spot on the cornea*, prob. for παράληψις in Hp.*Prorrh.*2.20, cf. Gal.19.127.

**παραλανθάνω**, *escape the notice of*, τινα Pl.*Hp.Ma.*298b, Isoc.10. 14, 11.48, D.46.17: abs., *lie hid, concealed*, ἐν ταῖς ψάμμοις f.l. in Hdn. 4.15.2.

**παράλασσις**, ιος, ἡ, name of a *garment*, *Michel*832.19 (Samos, iv B.C.).

**παραλᾰχᾰνίζω**, *defraud in the matter of vegetables*, *Com.Adesp.* 1108.

**παραλε-αίνω**, *smooth, polish*, in Med., Clearch.9. **-αντικός**, ή, όν, *emollient, lenitive*, Diph.Siph.ap.Ath.2.62c.

⊛ **παραλέγω**, *pluck out superfluous hair*, Hsch.:—Pass., παραλέλεξαι *you have had your eyebrows plucked*, Ar.*Ec.*904 (lyr.); παραλελέχθαι τὰς τρίχας Poll.2.35. **II.** Med., παραλέγεσθαι τὴν γῆν *sail* or *coast along*, Hanno *Peripl.*11, D.S.14.55, *Peripl.M.Rubr.*60; τὴν Ἰταλίαν D.S.13. 3; τὴν Κρήτην *Act.Ap.*27.8, 13: abs., Str.13.1.22. **III.** *speak beside* the purpose, *wander in one's talk, rave*, πολλὰ π. Hp.*Epid.*1.18, 26.δ':—Med., παραλεξάμενος *speaking beside the point*, Phld.*Rh.*1.101 S. **2.** *speak incidentally*, μῦθον Plu.2.653e:—Pass., *to be cited*, ἐπὶ παραδείγματος Aen.Tact.4.7. **3.** *add* to what one has said, *BGU* 665 ii 15 (i A.D.).

⊛ **παραλειπ-τέον**, *one must pass over*, οὐ π. ὡς.. X.*Ages.*8.3; οὐ π. τὰ περὶ τῆς πόλεως Isoc.*Ep.*2.14; οὐ π. περί τινος D.S.5.83. **-τικός**, ή, όν, *passing over, designedly omitting*, μέθοδος π. Hermog.*Id.*2. 6. **-τός**, όν, *to be passed over*, κώθων Chrysipp.(?)ap.Ath.1. 8d. **-ω**, fut. -ψω X.*HG*4.6.4: pf. -λέλοιπα Isoc.4.171:—Pass., pf. -λέλειμμαι ib.74:—*leave on one side, leave remaining*, ll.cc.:—Pass., ὅσα παρελέλειπτο Th.3.26; τοῖς ἐχθροῖς παραλείπεται *is reserved* for enemies, D.21.118. **II.** *leave to* another, λόγον τινὶ π. *leave* him time for speaking, οὐδενὶ τῶν ἄλλων -λιπὼν λόγον Aeschin.3.71; *permit, allow*, π. τινὶ ποιεῖν τι Plu.*Arat.*28. **III.** *leave on one side, pass over*, in an invitation, in a will, etc., τινα Ar.*Ec.*1145, Lys.31. 21, etc.; τὸ πρὸς ἀλλήλους ἀγωνίζεσθαι D.18.16; as dogs a hare, X. *Cyn.*3.6, etc. **2.** *neglect*, E.*Tr.*43, Ar.*Ra.*1494, *Av.*456 (Pass.); τι τῶν τεταγμένων X.*Cyr.*8.6.16; opportunities, duties, etc., D.2. 23, *PHib.*1.82.21 (iii B.C.), etc.:—Pass., τὰ παραλειπόμενα *omissions, deficiencies*, Pl.*R.*401e, cf. *Lg.*772c, Arist.*Pol.*1329ᵇ34; εἴ τις παραλείπεται [πρόσοδος] if the revenue *is insufficient*, Id.*Rh.*1359ᵇ25, cf. X. *Mem.*3.6.5. **3.** *pass over, leave untold, omit*, E.*Hel.*773, And.1.8, Pl.*Smp.*188e, al.; πολλὰ -λιπόντι ἀτοπίας Th.2.51; μυρία τοίνυν ἕτερ' εἰπεῖν ἔχων.. παραλείπω D.18.138; περί τινος π. D.S.5.26; πλείω τὰ παραλελειμμένα τῶν εἰρημένων Isoc.10.67, 6.68; *omit* from a schedule, Lys.17.4; τὰ παραλειπόμενα *events omitted* from the Books of Kings, title of the Books of Chronicles: abs., *make an omission*, Arist.*EN*1137ᵇ21. **4.** *cease* doing, ἀδικοῦντες οὐ παραλείπουσι Ath. 6.234b.

**παρᾰλείφω**, *bedaub with ointment*, τὰ βλέφαρα Ar.*Ec.*406; σιάλῳ π. τινά Arist.*Rh.*1407ᵃ8.

**παράλειψις**, εως, ἡ, *neglect, disregard*, τῶν καθηκόντων Plu.2. 33a. **2.** *omission*, κατὰ παράλειψιν τοῦ ῡ with the *omission* of.., Ath.11.490f; κατὰ π. τοῦ "εὐκαίρως" Plu.2.1037e; opp. παραδοχή, Hierocl. *in CA*19 p.461 M. **3.** a rhetorical figure, in which a fact is *designedly passed over*, so that attention may be specially called to it, Arist.*Rh.Al.*1434ᵃ25, 1438ᵇ6, Demetr.*Eloc.*263, Fronto *Ep.*1.2, Hermog.*Id.*2.6; κατὰ παράλειψιν Id.*Inv.*2.5.

**παραλεκτέον**, (παραλέγω II) *one must coast along*, Str.13.1.22.

**παράλευκος**, ον, *partly white*, Arist.*HA*524ᵃ6, Str.4.4.6.

**παραλέχομαι** (pres. not found), Med., *lie beside* or *with*, of intercourse with a woman, ὁ δέ οἱ παρελέξατο λάθρῃ Il.2.515, cf. 20.224, etc.; of the woman, *lie down beside*, τῷ δὲ Βρισηῒς παρελέξατο 24.676; παραλέξομαι ἐν φιλότητι 14.237; πὰρ δ' Ἑλένη.. ἐλέξατο Od.4.305: Ep. aor. παρέλεκτο *h.Ven.*167: Com., τυρῷ καὶ μίνθῃ π. καὶ ἐλαίῳ Cratin. 129 (dub.).

**παραλήγω**, *to be next to the end*, ἡ παραλήγουσα (sc. συλλαβή) *the penultima*, A.D.*Synt.*255.5, etc.; π. τῷ ῑ *to have* ι *in the penultima*, Hdn.Gr.2.926; ἴαμβος παραλήγων *in the last foot but one*, Heph.5.1:—also in Med., τῷ ῑ -λήγεσθαι A.D.*Adv.*175.20, cf. Hdn.Gr.2.927, Hermog.*Id.*1.6.

**παράλημμα**, ατος, τό, *treatment*, Sor.1.42.

**παράληξις**, εως, ἡ, *penultima*, Hdn.Gr.2.949, *EM*397.28. **2.** *antepenultima*, Eust.30.42.

**παραληπ-τέον**, (παραλαμβάνω) *one must take to oneself*, [γυναῖκα] Antip.*Stoic.*3.257; *one must provide oneself with*, μάρτυρας D.34.30. **2.** *one must apply* remedies, etc., Sor.2.10, Gal.12.519, Philum.ap. Orib.45.29.15; τὸ τοῦ λύχνου φέγγος π. Herod.Med. in *Rh.Mus.*58. 71. **II.** Adj. -ληπτέος, α, ον, *to be applied* or *employed*, π. ὁ κλυστήρ Ruf.*Fr.*80; π. ἁλτῆρες Philostr.*Gym.*55. ⊛ **-τής**, later -λημπτής, οῦ, ὁ, *receiver* of dues, *Peripl.M.Rubr.*19, *OGI*202.4 (Egypt, i B.C./i A.D.), *BGU*381.1 (ii/iii A.D.); π. σίτου *receiver* of soldiers' allowances, *Ostr.*1135, al. (iii A.D.). ⊛ **-τικός**, ή, όν, later -λημπτικός, *used for calculating dues*, μέτρον *POxy.*101.41 (ii A.D.), etc. **-τός**, ἡ, όν, *to be received*, opp. παραδοτός, ἄλλῳ παρ' ἄλλου Pl.*Men.*93b. II. *deserving of inclusion*, Chrysipp.*Stoic.*3.17. **-τωρ**, ορος, ὁ, *inheritor*, Herm.ap.Stob.1.49.44. II. (in form -λήμπτωρ) = παραληπτής, dub. in *PRein.*42.12 (i/ii A.D.).

**παραληρ-έω**, *talk nonsense, rave*, Hp.*Epid.*1.26.ι', Ar.*Eq.*531, *Ra.*594, Isoc.12.23, Pl.*Tht.*169a; ἀκοῦσαι.., κἂν δοκῇ τις παραληρεῖν D.*Prooem.*4; φαίνεται..ἄττα καὶ τοῖς παραληροῦσιν even *to crazy persons*, Arist.*Rh.*1356$^{b}$35. **-ημα**, ατος, τό, *piece of absurdity*, of a person, D.C.59.26. **-ησις**, εως, ἡ, *raving, delirium*, Hp.*Epid.*7.5. **-ος**, ον, *raving, delirious*, ib.1.2, Ph.1.387, etc. II. as Subst., = παραλήρησις, Hp.*Epid.*3.17.ζ', Suid. s.v. λῆρος.

⊛ **παράληψις**, later **-λημψις**, εως, ἡ, *receiving from another, succession to*, ἡ π. τῆς ἀρχῆς Plb.2.3.1; τῆς βασιλείας *OGI*90.45 (Rosetta, ii B.C.), Phld.*Piet.*94, D.S.15.95; τῆς οὐσίας Ath.5.218c; τῶν πόλεων D.C.36.18; opp. παράδοσις, *SIG*880.71 (Pizus, iii A.D.): Astrol., *taking over*, [τῆς χρονοκρατορίας] Vett.Val.168.18 (pl.): generally, *receiving*, τὴν παρὰ τῶν μελιττῶν τοῦ καρποῦ π. Porph.*Abst.*2.13. b. *receipt* of dues, customs, etc., ἡ π. τῶν ἐκφορίων *PAmh.*2.35.15 (ii B.C.); ἐλαίου *Sammelb.*4425 vii 7 (ii A.D.). c. *appropriation, filching*, Plb.2.46.2. 2. μετὰ θείας π. with a *calling in* of, *appeal* to the gods, Arist.*Rh.Al.*1432$^{a}$33. 3. *tradition, doctrine*, τεχνική τις π. Arr.*Epict.*2.11.2; ἑκάστου σχήματος π. Iamb.*VP*5.22. 4. *use, employment*, τῶν δεινοτάτων θυμάτων Porph.*Abst.*2.7; καθαρμῶν Hierocl.*in CA*26 p.478 M.; ἀμφορέων Porph.*Antr.*3: Medic., *application*, ἀλειμμάτων Alex.Trall.1.15, cf. Archig.ap.Aët.12.1. Cf. παράλαμψις.

**παραλῐθάζω**, *grow stony* or *hard*, Thphr.*HP*3.8.3.

**παράλιμνος**, ον, *lying by lakes* or *marshes*, Plu.2.951f.

**παραλιμπάνω**, collat. form of παραλείπω, Arist.*Pr.*951$^{a}$33, Aristox.*Harm.*p.35 M., Chrysipp.*Stoic.*3.200, Hermog.*Inv.*2.5, *OGI*519.18 (Aragueni, iii A.D.), Olymp.*in Grg.*p.242 J.

**παράλιον**, τό, v. παράλιος IV. II. = μήκων κερατῖτις, Dsc.4.65.

⊛ **παράλιος**, α, ον or ος, ον (v. infr.), = πάραλος, *by the sea*, παραλία ψάμμα A.*Pr.*573 (lyr.); γῆ, πόλις παραλία, E.*Ion* 1592, *Rh.*700 (lyr.); ὄρνιθες παράλιοι S.*Aj.*1065; τὰ π. τῆς Λακωνικῆς Plu.2.213a; νησιῶται καὶ π. ib.965c; of maritime plants, esp. *sea-spurge, Euphorbia Paralias*, Thphr.*HP*9.11.7, Dsc.4.164.6; of πιτύουσα, ib.165. II. ἡ **παρᾰλία**, Ion. **-ίη** (sc. γῆ or χώρα), *seacoast, seaboard*, τῆς Θρηΐκης τὴν π. Hdt.7.185; of Epidaurus, Arist.*Rh.*1411$^{a}$11. 2. esp. of *the maritime district* or *seaboard of Attica*, between Hymettus, Brauron, and Sunium, Hdt.5.81; παραλία [γῆ] Th.2.56; ἡ χώρα ἡ π. *IG*2.1195; ἡ π. Plb.3.39.3, Str.9.1.21; also ἡ παράλιος D.S.3.15, al. III. οἱ Παράλιοι, = οἱ Πάραλοι, Plu.2.805e. IV. Παράλιον, τό, *sanctuary of the hero* Πάραλος, *Rev.Ét.Gr.*44.294 (Attica, iv B.C.), D.49.25, Phot., *AB*294. [πᾱρᾰλίη, metri gr., A.R.4.1560, D.P.253.]

**παρᾰλίσκομαι**, Pass., *to be put under restraint*, Hsch. s.v. παραλούς.

**παρᾰλῐταίνω**, aor. -ήλῐτον, *do amiss, sin*, ἦ μέγα δή τι παρήλιτον A.R.3.891; ὅσσα οἱ..παρήλιτε cj. in Q.S.13.400. 2. c. acc. pers., ἦ ῥα θεοὺς..παρήλιτες *didst sin against* them, A.R.2.246.

**παρᾰλίτης** [ῑ], ου, ὁ, *one of the crew of the* Πάραλος, Hsch.

⊛ **παραλλ-ᾰγή**, ἡ, *passing from hand to hand, transmission*, πυρὸς παραλλαγαί A.*Ag.*490; *change of position, movement*, τὸ τάχος τῆς π., of the sun's apparent motion, Str.17.3.10. b. Astrol., of a heavenly body, *passing beyond* the degree occupied by another, Antioch.Astr. in *Cat.Cod.Astr.*8(3).113. 2. *alternation*, μυῶν παραλλαγαὶ καὶ νεύρων their *alternate movements*, Hp.*Art.*30; παραλλαγὰς τοῖς ποσὶν ἐποίουν, of dancers, Critias 36. 3. *distortion* of the vertebrae, Hp.*Art.*48; *contortion, twisting*, of wood, Thphr.*HP*5.1.12 (pl.). 4. *interchange*, διανοίας πρὸς αἴσθησιν π. *interchange* of intellect and sense, putting one for the other, Pl.*Tht.*196c; π. προσώπων, πτώσεως, A.D.*Pron.*110.3, *Synt.*214.9. II. *difference between* things, ποιεῖν τινα π. εὐοσμίας καὶ ἀοσμίας Thphr.*HP*6.6.5; μεγάλας τὰς π. ποιεῖσθαι περί τι Plb.6.7.5; μεγάλην ἔχειν π. D.S.5.37, cf. Plot.3.1.5; ἡ π. βραχεῖα Phld.*Po.*2.5; ἡ π. ἡ [τοῦ ἀνθρώπου] πρὸς τὰ ἄλογα Arr.*Epict.*2.8.3; κάλλους πρὸς αἶσχος ib.2.23.32. III. *variety, variation*, Thphr.*HP*2.3.2; μεγεθῶν Epicur.*Ep.*1 p.15 U. (pl.), al., cf. Chrysipp.*Stoic.*3.182, *Ep.Jac.*1.17, Cleom.1.7; γραμμῶν καὶ γωνιῶν *Theol.Ar.*63; *change* of meaning, παραλλαγῶν κατὰ σύμβολον γινομένων Chrysipp.*Stoic.*2.258, cf. 3.33. IV. *frenzy, madness*, ἐν π. γενέσθαι Lxx 4*Ki.*9.20; π. ψυχῆς *perturbation* of soul, Iamb.*VP*25.111. **-αγμα**, ατος, τό, *alternation*, παραλλάγματα *overlapping ends* of broken bones, Hp.*Art.*16. II. *difference, variation*, Epicur.*Nat.Herc.*908.1, al., Str.2.1.35 (pl.), Plu.*Num.*18; π. μηνιαῖον Gem.8.19, al.; *departure from the normal*, Metrod.*Herc.*831.5,7. **-ακτικός**, ή, όν, *for determining parallax*, ὄργανον Ptol.*Alm.*5.12, Procl.*Hyp.*4.49. **-ακτός**, όν, *liable to change*, κόσμοι D.L.9.19. **-άξ**, Adv. *alternately, in turn*, S.*Aj.*1087; ἀνάπαλιν καὶ π. Ti.Locr.95c; [ἀναπνεῖν καὶ ἐκπνεῖν] π. Arist.*Resp.*471$^{a}$11; τῶν ἀετῶν θάτερον τῶν ἐκγόνων ἁλιαίετος γίνεται π. Id.*Mir.*835$^{a}$1; of the production of leaves, Thphr.*HP*6.2.8. 2. *in alternating rows*, νῆσοι..π. καὶ οὐ κατὰ στοῖχον κείμεναι Th.2.102. II. π. εἶναι, = παραλλάσσειν II.1, ἐν τῇ γῇ π. εἰσιν οἱ πόροι Arist.*Mete.*385$^{b}$25. III. *side by side*, Hermog.*Meth.*5. **-αξις**, εως, ἡ, *alternation*: *overlapping* of broken bones, Hp.*Fract.*15 (pl.); ἡ π. τοῦ ὀστέου ib.35; π. ἔχειν πρὸς ἄλληλα καὶ συμπλοκήν Thphr.*Sens.*66. 2. *alternating motion*, τῶν σκελῶν Plu.*Phil.*6; ἡ δεῦρο κἀκεῖ π. τῆς κεφαλῆς Id.2.977b. II. *change, deviation, mutation*, Pl.*Ti.*22d, cf. *Plt.*269e, *Placit.*1.7.33 (pl.); διαστροφὴ μεγάλη καὶ π. τῆς γωνίας Plu.2.930a; παραλλάξιες φρενῶν mental *aberrations*, Hp.*Acut.*(*Sp.*)1. III. *change of position*, τῶν γωνιῶν Arist.*Cael.*287$^{a}$18; ἡ τοῦ ἡλίου π. D.C.76.13. 2. Astron., *parallax*, Ptol.*Alm.*5.11, 9.1, Procl.*Hyp.*4.53, al. b. φάσις defined as ἡ μετὰ τὴν κρύψιν τοῦ ἡλίου πρώτη..ἐξ αὐτοῦ π. Phlp.*in Mete.*76.30. **-άσσω**, Att. **-ττω**, pf. παρήλλᾰχα Arist.*Pr.*872$^{b}$11, Plu.*Cim.*1, Arr.*Epict.*3.21.23:—*cause to alternate*, π. τοὺς ὀδόντας *make the alternate* teeth of the saw *stand contrary ways*, Thphr.*HP*5.6.3; π. τὰς ἀρχάς *make* the ends [of the bandages] *overlap* or *cross*, Hp.*Fract.*29; παραλλάξας *having transposed* [the two], Pl.*Tht.*193c; π. τῶν αἰσθήσεων τὰ σημεῖα *transpose, interchange* the impressions received from the senses, ib.194d; ἐὰν παραλλάξῃ τὴν τομὴν *transposes* the caesura, Heph.15.18:—Pass., *overlap*, of the ends of broken bones, Hp.*Fract.*31; ὀδόντες παρηλλαγμένοι (in persons with hollow palate) Id.*Epid.*6.1.2. 2. *change, alter*, ὀλίγα π. Hdt.2.49; μίαν μόνον συλλαβὴν π. Aeschin.3.192, cf. Arist.*Top.*119$^{a}$15; esp. *alter for the worse*, π. φρένας χρηστάς S.*Ant.*298; *twist*, τὸν λόγον Chrysipp.*Stoic.*2.258:—freq. in Pass., *to be altered*, πολὺ παρηλλάχθαι τὴν ἔξοδον πρὸς τὸν εἰθισμένον καιρόν Plb.5.56.11, etc.; τὸ κίνημα παρηλλαγμένον τῆς συνηθείας Id.7.17.7: hence παρηλλαγμένος, η, ον, *strange, extraordinary*, Id.2.29.1, 3.55.1; παρηλλαγμένους τοῖς μεγέθεσιν ὄφεις D.S.17.90; ὑποδήματα π. *peculi:r* footwear, Satyr.1. 3. of Place, *pass by* or *beyond*, ἐνέδραν X.*HG*5.1.12, Plb.5.14.3, etc.; ὅταν τὸ ὕδωρ παραλλάξῃ τὸ χωρίον D.55.17; *elude, avoid*, Plu.*Cam.*25; so Astrol., τὴν διάμετρον ἀκτῖνα π. Vett.Val.142.5; also, *get rid of*, διακρούσασθαι καὶ π. τὸ πάθος Plu.*Caes.*41. 4. *go beyond, surpass*, τῷ τάχει π. τὰ ἄστρα Arist.*Mete.*342$^{a}$33; *exceed* in point of time, τὴν παιδικὴν ἡλικίαν Plu.*Alc.*7, *Cim.*1: c. acc. pers. et gen. rei, γραμμέων συνθέσιος οὐδείς κώ με παρήλλαξεν [Democr.]299. II. intr., *deviate from one another*, of two tunnels or the like, which start from opposite directions, and, instead of meeting, *miss each other*, ὀλίγον τι π. τῆς χώρης Hdt.2.11; of bones, ἄρθρον παραλλάξαν *displaced*, Hp.*Art.*17; πόροι παραλλάττοντες *deviating, not in line*, opp. κατάλληλοι, Arist.*Pr.*905$^{b}$8, cf. 890$^{b}$39. 2. *alternate*, Id.*APr.*42$^{b}$15. 3. *differ* or *vary from*, τῶν πολλῶν..δικαίων Pl.*Lg.*957b; πολύ τι τῶν ἄλλων Thphr.*HP*4.10.5; τῶν προκειμένων Hdn.Gr.2.948; παραλλάξουσιν ἀλλήλων κατὰ παρρησίαν Phld.*Lib.*p.43 O.; π. ἀπό τινος Arr.*Epict.*3.21.23: abs., *differ, vary*, ὀλίγον παραλλάσσοντες Hdt.7.73; ἡ χρεία π. μικρόν Arist.*Pol.*1254$^{b}$24; μήκη παραλλάττοντα Epicur.*Ep.*2 p.43 U.; μικρὸν ταῖς γλώτταις Str.4.1.1; π. κατὰ τὰς ὀσμὰς καὶ τοὺς χυλούς Thphr.*HP*1.12.3; τοσοῦτον τῆς δόξης παραλλαττούσης Isoc.9.25; τὸ παρηλλαχός the *changeable*, Chrysipp.*Stoic.*3.129; also, of persons, οἱ παρηλλαχότες those *whose character has changed*, ib.125. b. impers., οὐ σμικρὸν παραλλάττει οὕτως ἔχον ἢ ἄλλως *it makes* no small *difference*, Pl.*Tht.*169e. 4. π. τοῦ σκοποῦ *go aside from* the mark, ib.194a: metaph., π. τῶν φρενῶν Lys.*Fr.*90: abs., οὐχ ὑπὸ γήρως οὐδὲ νόσου π. Plu.*Luc.*43. 5. *change direction*, of the wind, Arist.*Pr.*945$^{a}$36; *deviate from the straight course*, παραλλάξαντι ἐξ Ἀβύδου ὡς ἐπὶ τὴν Προποντίδα Str.13.1.22; οὐδαμῇ οὐδὲν π. Pl.*R.*530b; *go astray, be out of one's wits*, Id.*Ti.*27c, 71e; λόγοι παραλλάσσοντες *delirious*, E.*Hipp.*935; *degenerate, decline*, εἰς μοναρχίαν ἐπαχθῆ Plu.*Rom.*26. 6. *slip aside* or *away*, παραλλάξασα διὰ χερῶν βέβακεν ὄψις A.*Ag.*424 (lyr.). 7. *to be superior to*, c. gen., π. ἅλιος ἄστρων Epigr.ap.D.L.8.78; π. ταῖς ψυχαῖς Sosyl.1 J.; τῇ διαφορᾷ τοῦ καθοπλισμοῦ πρὸς τὴν χρείαν παραλλάττων *superior in*.., Plb.18.25.2; κατά τι Iamb.*Comm.Math.*8. 8. Geom., of figures, *coincide partially* when applied, Euc.1.8, 3.24, Aristarch.Sam.8. 9. Astron., *display parallax*, Ptol.*Alm.*5.11. **-αττόντως**, Adv. *differently*, Phld.*Rh.*1.196 S.

**παραλληγορέω**, *use allegory*, Sch.Il.13.359.

**παραλληλ-επίπεδον**, τό, *body with parallel surfaces, parallelepiped*, Euc.11.25, Plu.2.1080c. **-επίπεδος**, ον, *with parallel surfaces*, πλινθίς Iamb.*in Nic.*p.95 P., al. 2. π. ἀριθμός, number which is the product of three factors, two of which are equal, Nicom.*Ar.*2.16. **-ία**, ἡ, *being side by side, repetition* of a letter, Eust.149.8; of words of identical meaning, *pleonasm*, ταὐτὸν κατὰ παραλληλίαν δηλοῦν Id.961.32. **-ίζω**, *place side by side*, λέξεις ἰσοδυνάμους Id.437.29, cf. 1539.58. ⊛ **-ισμός**, ὁ, *equating* of payments, *PMasp.*58 ii 13 (vi A.D.). II. *placing side by side, repetition* of ideas in a compound (as μυθολογεύειν, λογολεσχεῖν), Eust.437.25.

**παραλληλόγραμμος**, ον, *bounded by parallel lines*, σχῆμα Str.4.1.3: neut. as Subst., τὸ π. *parallelogram*, Euc.2 *Def.*, Plu.2.1080c, etc.; κατὰ -γραμμον Ascl.*Tact.*11.7. Adv. -γράμμως Iamb.*in Nic.*p.27 P.

⊛ **παράλληλος**, ον, *beside one another, side by side*, αἱ π. (sc. γραμμαί) *parallel lines*, Arist.*APr.*65$^{a}$4, *APo.*77$^{b}$22, cf. *Mech.*856$^{b}$28; π. κύκλοι the five *zones*, D.L.7.155, Nonn.*D.*38.258; ὁ π. κύκλος *parall.l* of latitude, Hipparch.2.2.26, al., Cleom.1.2, etc.: without κύκλος, ὁ διὰ τοῦ Βορυσθένους π. Str.1.4.4, al.; οἱ βίοι οἱ π. the *parallel* lives of Plutarch, Plu.*Thes.*1, cf. *Pel.*2, etc.; ἐκ παραλλήλου *parallelwise*, Id.*Comp.Ag.Gracch.*1. 2. ἐν παραλλήλοις κεῖσθαι, of words used *pleonastically*, A.D.*Adv.*140.13; ἐκ παραλλήλου εἰρηκέναι Alex.Aphr.*in Metaph.*3?1.1, cf. Asp.*in EN*65.30, 104.1. Adv. -λως, τίθεσθαι A.D.*Synt.*247.17; but π. χρώμενοι τοῖς ὀνόμασιν using the forms (Ζῆνα, Δία) *indifferently*, Arist.*Mu.*401$^{a}$14. 3. c. dat., *parallel to* or *with*, χάραξ π. τῷ τείχει Plb.8.32.3, etc.; ὁ Ῥῆνος π. ὢν τῇ Πυρήνῃ Str.4.1.1.

**παραλληλότης**, ητος, ἡ, *repetition*, ἐν π. κεῖσθαι (of τε...τε..) A.D.*Adv.*140.14; κατὰ παραλληλότητα Id.*Synt.*318.22.

**παραλογ-εία**, ἡ, *fraudulent exaction, extortion*, in pl., *PAmh.*2.33.13 (ii B.C.), *UPZ*113.10 (ii B.C.). ⊛ **-εύομαι**, *practise extortion*, *PPetr.*2 p.126 (iii B.C.). ⊛ **-ία**, ἡ, in Gramm., *false form*, *EM*807.57, Eust.

154.2. II. μετὰ παραλογίας, = παραλόγως, Sch.Il.23.388. **-ίζομαι,** in keeping accounts, *cheat*, D.27.29, 41.30, Philem.32: c. dupl. acc., *defraud of*, π. τρία ἡμιωβέλια τοὺς ναοποιοὺς Arist.*Rh.*1374b26, cf. Isoc. 12.243; *reckon fraudulently*, τὸν μισθόν LXX *Ge.*31.41; τὰ πορθμεῖα Luc.*DMort.*4.1: generally, *defraud*, τινα LXX *Ge.*29.25, *PMagd.*29.5 (iii B.C.):—Pass., δαπάνας παραλογισθείσας *OGI*665.15 (Egypt, i A.D.). II. *reason falsely, use fallacies*, Arist.*Ph.*186a10, 239b5. b. *draw a false inference*, π. ἡ ψυχή Id.*Po.*1460a25, *Rh.*1408a20; π. ὁ ἀκροατής ib.1401b8. 2. *mislead by fallacious reasoning*, σφᾶς αὐτοὺς Isoc.*Ep.*6.12; σαυτόν Aeschin.3.221, Phld.*Rh.*1.134 S.; ἀπάτῃ τινὶ π. τινάς Aeschin.1.117; μεγάλα τὴν πόλιν π. Id.2.128:—Pass., *to be misled by fallacious reasoning*, π. ἡ διάνοια ὑπό τινων Arist. *Pol.*1307b35, Iamb.*Protr.*2; αἰτίαις Phld.*Lib.*p.49 O.:—Pass. and Med. opposed, παραλογισθῆναι καὶ παραλογίσασθαι Arist.*Top.*108a27. III. *disguise*, τῆς ἐσθῆτος ὄψις παραλογιζομένη τὴν ἐπιδημίαν ἡμῶν Plu.2.597a. ⊛ **-ισμός,** ὁ, *false reasoning, fallacy*, τοὺς π. κατά τινων ποιήσονται Lycurg.31, cf. Gal.11.465, etc.; *false inference*, τοῦ θεάτρου Arist.*Po.*1455a13; οἱ ἔξω τῆς λέξεως π. material fallacies, opp. οἱ παρὰ τὴν λέξιν ἔλεγχοι, Id.*SE*166b21. 2. *weakness of reasoning power*, Aristeas 250. II. *deception, fraud*, Plb. 1.81.8, *PLond.*1.24.26 (ii B.C.), etc. **-ιστής,** οῦ, ὁ, *one who cheats by false reckoning*, Arist.*EE*1232a14; or *by false reasoning*, δεινὸς ὁ τῦφος π. M.Ant.6.13, cf. Procl.*Par.Ptol.*225; *cheat*, Artem.4.57. **-ιστικός,** ή, όν, *fallacious*, Arist.*Rh.*1367b4; *given to fallacious reasoning*, Id.*SE*172b3, Jul.*Or.*7.216a. Adv. -κῶς Poll.9.135; gloss on παραβλήδην, Sch.A.R.3.107. ⊛ **-ος,** ον, (λόγος I, IV. 1 fin.) *beyond calculation, unexpected, unlooked for*, ἄτοπον καὶ π. Arist.*de An.* 411a14; π. τι ἡ τύχη Id.*Ph.*197a18; π. ἀτυχήματα Id.*Rh.*1374b7; εὐδίαι Id.*HA*599b15; αἱ π. τῶν βαρβάρων ἔφοδοι *casual, uncertain*, Plb.2.35.6; *strange*, π. πόθος Palaeph.52; π. καὶ ἀπρεπὴς βούλησις Hdn.1.16.4; παράλογον, τό, an *unexpected event*, τὰ π. τῆς τύχης D.S. 17.66, etc.; εἴ τι σπάνιον καὶ ὡς ἐν παραλόγῳ *abnormal*, Thphr.*CP*1.3.2 (but παράλογα, *over-portions of food* given to guests *which were not to be reckoned upon*, X.*Lac.*5.3). Adv. -γως Hp.*Aph.*2.27, etc.; τοὺς π. δυστυχοῦντας D.27.68, cf. Arist.*EN*1135b16: Sup. -ώτατα J.*BJ*2.19.7. 2. (λόγος III) *beyond reason, unreasonable*, τὰ π. καὶ ἄτοπα Plu.2.626e, etc.; ἐν παραλόγῳ ποιεῖσθαί τι App.*BC*2.146; παράδοξα μέν, οὐ μὴν π. Cleanth.ap.Arr.*Epict.*4.1.173. Adv. -γως, εἰκῇ καὶ π. Plb.1.74.14, etc. 3. Gramm., *contrary to analogy* or *rule, irregular*, A.D.*Pron.*27.26, al. 4. Adv. -γως *fraudulently*, *OGI* 665.33 (Egypt, i A.D.). II. **παράλογος,** ὁ, as Subst., *incalculable element*, τοῦ πολέμου ὁ π. Th.1.78; πολύς, μέγας ὁ π., the *event* is much, greatly *contrary to calculation*, Id.3.16, 7.55; τὸν π. τοσοῦτον ποιῆσαι τοῖς Ἕλλησι τῆς δυνάμεως, i.e. so belied the calculations of the Greeks, ib.28; ἐν τοῖς ἀνθρωπείοις τοῦ βίου παραλόγοις by *miscalculations* such as men make, Id.8.24; τὸ πλείστῳ παραλόγῳ ξυμβαῖνον Id.2.61.

**παράλοιπος,** ον, *remaining besides*, Arist.*APo.*93b13.

**παρα-λοξαίνομαι,** Pass., *to be placed obliquely*, Hp.*Nat.Mul.*40, *Mul.*2.141. **-λοξος,** ον, *oblique*, Sor.*Fract.*7.

⊛ **πάρᾰλος,** ον, (ἅλς) *by* or *near the sea*, ἄντρα S.*Aj.*413 (lyr.); χέρσοι E.*Ion* 1584; ἡ δ' ὠπτημένη σίζουσα πάραλος, of a cuttle-fish, with a pun on ἡ Πάραλος (infr. III), Ar.*Ach.*1158. 2. generally, *concerned with the sea, naval*, ὁ π. στρατός Hdt.7.161. II. ἡ πάραλος γῆ *the coast-land* of Attica (cf. παράλιος II. 2), Th.2.55: hence οἱ Π. *the people of the coast-land*, Hdt.1.59; αὐτόν τε Πάραλον ἐστολισμένον δορί, i.e. τοὺς Π., E.*Supp.*659. III. ἡ Πάραλος ναῦς, Th.8.74, or ἡ Π. alone, D.21.173, or Π. alone, Ar.*Av.*1204, the *Paralos*, one of the Athenian sacred galleys, cf. Arist.*Ath.*61.7, *IG*2².1623.225, and v. Σαλαμινία. 2. οἱ Π. the *crew of the Paralos*, which contained none but free citizens, Th.8.73, 74, Aeschin.3.162, Poll.8.116 (cf. παραλίτης): generally, *seamen*, Ar.*Ra.*1071, cf. Sch. ad loc. IV. ἡ π., name of a plant *which grew near the sea*, π. ἀμμότροφος *AP*4.1.20 (Mel.).

⊛ **παραλοῦμαι,** *bathe together*, Ar.*Frr.*55, 524.

**παρᾰλουργ-ής,** Ion. -οργής *Michel* 832 (Samos, iv B.C.), ές, *edged with purple*, προσκεφάλαια Clearch.25; ἱμάτιον λευκὸν π. *IG*2².1514.27. II. of persons, *wearing a garment with purple border* (i.e. less distinguished than those who wore garments of purple), Hsch. **-ίδιον,** τό, Dim. of sq., *IG*2².1514.54. **-ίς,** ίδος, ἡ, *woman's garment edged with purple*, Poll.7.56, Phot. **-ός,** όν, = παραλουργής I, χιτώνιον Plu.2.583e.

**παραλοφία,** ἡ, *the back of the horse's neck where the mane grows*, Poll.2.135.

**παραλοχίζω,** *lay an ambush*, J.*AJ*14.16.3.

**παράλπιος,** ον, *dwelling near the Alps*, Plu.*Aem.*6.

**παρᾰλυκίζω,** *to be changed and become salt*, Antipho Soph.32.

⊛ **παραλῡπέω,** *grieve* or *trouble besides*, ἄλλο παρελύπει.. οὐδὲν no disease *attacked* them *besides* the plague, Th.2.51, cf. X.*Vect.*4.32, Thphr.*CP*1.7.8; *annoy by a diversion*, Th.4.89; ὅταν αὐτὴν μηδὲν.. παραλυπῇ Pl.*Phd.*65c; π. τοὺς πολεμίους τι Plu.*Per.*35; οἱ παραλυποῦντες the *troublesome*, the *refractory*, X.*An.*2.5.29:—Pass., *to be molested*, ὑπὸ βασιλέων Str.9.1.20, etc.

**παράλυπρος,** ον, *rather poor*, χωρία Str.3.2.3; χώρα Id.17.3.23.

**παρά-λυσις,** εως, ἡ, *secret* or *illicit undoing* or *breaking open*, ἡ πολυπραγμοσύνη π. τῶν ἀπορρήτων Plu.2.519c (v.l. -δυσις). II. *disabling of the nerves, paralysis*, Thphr.*Fr.*11, Dsc.1.6, Ruf.ap.Orib.8.39.2, Gal.8.208; also of the eyes, i.e. *nystagmus*, Cels.6.6.36: generally, π. τῶν σωμάτων, of the effect of strong wine, *Com.Adesp.* 106.13; ἡ λύπη ψυχῆς π. Cleanth.*Stoic.*1.130, cf. Plb.30.32.10. 2. = δελφίνιον II, Ps.-Dsc.3.73; = κώνειον I. 1, Id.4.78. III. *diaeresis* (in Gramm.), κατὰ π. Eust.ad D.P.384. **-λῠτέον,** *one must set free from*, τινος Pl.*Lg.*793e, cf. Sor.1.111 tit. **-λῠτικός,** ή, όν, *paralytic*, *Ev.Matt.*4.24, Dsc.1.16, Ruf.ap.Orib.8.39.8. ⊛ **-λῠτος,** ον, = foreg., Artem.4.67.

**παραλυτρόομαι,** Pass., *to be ransomed*, Παραλυτρούμενος, name of a Comedy by Sotades, Ath.9.368a.

⊛ **παραλύω** [v. λύω]: I. c. acc. rei, *loose and take off, detach*, τὰ πηδάλια τῶν νεῶν Hdt.3.136 (so in Med., παραλυόμενοι τὰ πηδάλια *taking off* the rudders, X.*An.*5.1.11:—Pass., παραλελυμέναι τοὺς ταρσοὺς *with* their oars *taken off*, Plb.8.4.2); τὴν πτέρυγα -λύσασα τοῦ χιτωνίου Ar.*Fr.*325; τὸν θώρακα Plu.*Ant.*76:—Med., π. τὴν ῥαφὴν [τοῦ χιτῶνος] Id.*Cleom.*37; τοὺς στεφάνους Id.2.646a:—Pass., Hdt.3.105. b. *hamstring*, ἅρματα LXX 2*Ki.*8.4. 2. *undo, put an end to*, πόνους E.*Andr.*304 (lyr.); τὴν τοῦ παιδίου ἀμφισβήτησιν *relinquish* it, Is.4.10:—Med., *get rid of*, τὸν κίνδυνον D.H.6.28. 3. *undo secretly*, τὰ σακκία τῶν χρημάτων Plu.2.10b, cf. D.S.13.106. 4. *pay* a penalty, LXX *Ge.*4.15; = Lat. *persolvo*, νόμισμα *PStrassb.*50.8, 14 (vi A.D.). II. c. acc. pers. et gen. rei, *part from*, πολλοὺς ἤδη παρέλυσεν θάνατος δάμαρτος E.*Alc.*932 (lyr., dub. l.); μία γὰρ σφέων παρελύθη ὑπὸ Ἰώνων one city (Smyrna) *was detached from* them, Hdt.1.149; π. τινὰ τῆς στρατιῆς *release from* military service, Id.7.38 (and in Pass., *to be exempt from* it, 5.75), cf. Plb.6.33.10; τοῦ ὅρκου *OGI*266.46 (Pergam., iii B.C.); π. τινὰ δυσφρονᾶν *set free from* cares, Pi.*O.*2.52; π. τινὰ τῆς στρατηγίης *dismiss from* the command, Hdt.6.94, cf. Th.7.16, 8.54; τῆς δυνάμεως τινά Arist.*Pol.*1315a12 (so in Pass., π. τῆς φυλακῆς Plu. *Cleom.*37; τῆς ἀρχῆς Eun.*VS* p.481 B.); also τὴν ἀρχήν τινι π. ib. p.479 B.; τοὺς Ἀθηναίους π. τῆς ἐς αὐτὸν ὀργῆς *set* them *free, release* them *from* .., Th.2.65; φαρμάκῳ π. ἑαυτὸν τοῦ ζῆν Str.8.6.14; παραλελύσθαι τοῦ φόβου Plb.30.4.7: c. acc. only, *set free*, δυστάνου ψυχάν E.*Alc.*117 (lyr.):—Med., *obtain leave of absence from*, τοὺς παιδονόμους *SIG*577.56 (Milet., iii/ii B.C.). III. *loose besides, in addition*, π. καὶ ἑτέραν [κύνα] X.*Cyn.*6.14. IV. *disable, enfeeble*, Pl.*Ax.*367b; π. τροφῆς ἀποχῇ τὸ σῶμα Plu.*Demetr.*38:—mostly in Pass., *to be paralysed*, δεξιῇ χεὶρ παρελύθη Hp.*Epid.*1.26.ιγ'; τὰ παραλελυμένα τοῦ σώματος μόρια Arist.*EN*1102b18: generally, *to be exhausted, flag*, ἡ δύναμις..τῆς πόλεως παρελύθη Lys.13.46; τῇ σωματικῇ δυνάμει παραλυόμενος ὑπὸ τῶν τραυμάτων Plb.16.5.7; παραλελυμένοι καὶ τοῖς σώμασι καὶ ταῖς ψυχαῖς Id.20.10.9; τὴν δύναμιν παρελέλυντο Id.1.58.9; τὰς χεῖρας Teles p.38 H.

**παράλωμα,** ατος, τό, (λῶμα) prob. = παράρρυμα, Hsch. (pl.).

**παραμαίνομαι,** *to be quite mad*, Amips.10.

**παρᾰμαξεύω,** *drive along*, π. θύσθεν τᾶς κελεύθω *IG*5(2).3.23 (Tegea, iv B.C.).

**παραμαρμαίρω,** *gleam beside*, Onos.29.2.

**παρᾰμαρτάνω,** *err, trespass*, εἰς ἥρων τι παρήμαρτον Ar.*Fr.*692a, cf. Plu.2.89e, Hierocl.p.58 A.: c. dat., *damage*, στήλῃ *Ath.Mitt.*30.327 (Temenothyrae).

**παραμαρτῠρία,** ἡ, as law-term, = παραγραφή II. 1, Poll.8.57 (v.l.).

**παραμᾰσ-ήτης,** ου, ὁ, (μασάομαι) *trencher-companion, parasite*, Alex.236, Timocl.9.6. **-ύντης,** ου, ὁ, = foreg., Alex.222.8, Ephipp. 8.6.

**παραμάχαιρον** [μᾰ], τό, *side-dagger*, colloquial word, Eust.413.39.

**παραμβλύνω,** *blunt, deaden*, metaph., Plu.2.788f.

**παραμεθίημι,** *let pass*, τὴν κάθαρσιν Hp.*Mul.*1.67: c. gen. part., π. τοῦ αἵματος ib.25; τῆς αὔξης τῷ ἐμβρύῳ ib.21.

**παρᾰμείβω,** *change* or *alter*, τινὰ ὅλον Alciphr.3.40. II. = Med., *leave on one side, pass by*, c. acc. loci, A.R.2.660, Plu.*Mar.*18, etc.; of a river, *flow past*, Arist.*Mir.*846b30. 2. *outrun, excel*, σοφίᾳ σοφίαν S.*OT*504 (lyr.). 3. c. acc. cogn., παράμειβε κέλευθον *pass on* your way, *Arch.Pap.*1.220.—Rare in Act.

B. Med., *pass by, leave on one side*, τὸν παραμειψάμενος Od.6.310; παρημείβοντο Μάλειαν *h.Ap.*409; ἔθνεα πολλὰ παραμειψάμενοι Hdt.1.94; πόλιας τάσδε Id.7.109, etc.; Κόρας (i.e. their shrine) S.*OC*130 (lyr.); π. τὰς πηγὰς τοῦ Εὐφράτου Plu.*Pomp.*32; of rivers, *run past* a place, Hdt.1.72, 75; *march past*, τῶν βαρβάρων τὴν τάξιν Plu.*Ant.*39; but πύλας παραμείψεται *shall pass through* the gates, Thgn.709. 2. *pass over, omit to mention*, Hdt.2.102. 3. *outstrip*, καὶ θαλασσαίων π. δελφῖνα Pi.*P.*2.50; μή τίς σε λάθῃ.. ὄχοις παραμειψαμένη E.*IA*146 (anap.). 4. of time, *pass, go by*, Hes. *Op.*409. II. causal, *turn aside, divert*, τίνα πρὸς.. ἄκραν ἐμὸν πλόον παραμείβεαι; Pi.*N.*3.27.—Cf. παραμεύομαι.

**παραμείγνυμι** and -ύω, Ion. -μίσγω, also in Thphr.*HP*9.7.2 and later Prose, Phld.*Ir.*p.54 W. (Pass.):—*intermingle, mix with*, τινί τι Ar.*V.*878; ψόγον καὶ νουθεσίαν Plu.2.59b:—Pass., metaph., ἡδονὴν παραμεμεῖχθαι τῇ εὐδαιμονίᾳ Arist.*EN*1177a23. II. c. acc. only, *mix in, add by mixing*, ὕδωρ παραμίσγειν Hdt.1.203, 4.61; μέλι, σμύρνην, Hp.*Morb.*2.47, *Mul.*2.162; στεατίου μικρόν Alex.84:—Pass., ὅ τι αὐτοῖς τούτων ἐν ταῖς ψυχαῖς παραμέμεικται Pl.*R.*415b.

**παράμειξις,** εως, ἡ, *admixture*, ἡδονῆς Phld.*Mus.*p.72 K.

⊛ **παρᾰμελέω,** *disregard, pay no heed to*, τινων Gorg.*Pal.*20, Th.1.25; τοῦ πράγματος Lys.9.1; τῆς μητρὸς X.*Mem.*2.2.14, etc.: abs., παρημελήκεε *he recked little*, Hdt.1.85; παραμελοῦντες *being negligent*, Pl.*R.*555d; *neglect* a duty, τῆς χορηγίας Mitteis *Chr.*96 iii 4 (iv A.D.):—Pass., *to be slighted* or *abandoned*, θεοῖς by the gods, A.*Th.*702; ὑπό τινων Pl.*R.*620c: abs., A.*Eu.*300; ἀνὴρ.. οὐ τῶν παρημελημένων ἐν ἱστορίᾳ no *mean* historian, Plu.2.862b.

⊛ **παραμεμπτέον,** *one must blame*, Gal.14.305.

**παραμένιος**, ον (later form of παραμόνιμος), etym. of Πράμνιος, Ath.1.30e codd., *EM*686.38: παραμένειος Eust.871.24. Adv. -ενίως (codd. -μένως) Sch.Opp.*H*.2.612.

⊕ **παραμένω**, poet. **παρμένω** Pi.*P*.8.40, S.*Ichn*.169 (trim.):—*stay beside* or *near, stand by*, οὐδέ τις αὐτῷ Ἀργείων παρέμεινε Il.11.402, cf. 15.400; παράμεινον τὸν βίον ἡμῖν Ar.*Pax* 1108 (hex.), cf. Pl.*Ap*.39e, al.; of slaves, *remain, stay*, opp. δραπετεύω, ἀποδιδράσκω, Id.*Men*. 97d, X.*Oec*.3.4; in Law, of slaves whose manumission was deferred, *SIG*1208 (Thespiae, ii B.C.), etc.: hence Παρμένων, *Trusty*, as a slave's name, Men.*Sam*.302, etc. II. abs., *stand one's ground, stand fast*, Il.13.151, cf. Hdt.1.82, 6.14, Ar.*Pl*.440, etc.; more fully, μάχαις τλάμονι ψυχᾷ π. Pi.*P*.1.48; παρμένοντας αἰχμᾷ ib.8.40; εὐανθεῖ ἐν ὀργᾷ π. ib.1.89; πρὸς τὰ ὑπόλοιπα τῶν ἔργων Th.3.10; ἀδύνατός εἰμι..παραμένειν *to remain with* the army, Id.7.15; of fortune, *remain steady*, παραμένει γὰρ οὐδὲ ἕν Men.51. 2. *stay* at a place, *stay behind* or *at home*, Hdt.1.64, Antipho 5.13, And.1.2. 3. *survive, remain alive*, Hdt.1.30. 4. of things, *endure, last*, Id.3.57, etc.; ἀεὶ παραμένουσα [ἡ φύσις] E.*El*.942; π. ἡ πολιτεία Lys.25.28; αἱ εὐπραγίαι Isoc.7.13; ἡ ὑγίεια X.*Cyr*.1.6.17, etc.; δίχα τῆς σφοδρότητος π. τὸ μέγεθος Longin.9.13; of money, *stay by one, last for ever*, Alex. 281, Timocl.9.1, Men.128.2; of wine, *last, keep good*, εἰς τριγονίαν π. ἐν ἀπιττώτοις ἄγγεσι Str.11.10.1, cf. *Ostr.Bodl*.i 145 (iii/ii B.C.), Plu. 2.655f.

**παράμερος** [ᾰ], ον, Dor. for παρήμερος, Pi.*O*.1.99.

**παραμεσάζω**, *act as mediator*, Tz.*H*.3.217.

**παράμεσος**, ον, *next the middle*, δάκτυλος Ruf.*Onom*.83, Poll.2. 145, Gal.2.264. 2. *out of the centre of gravity*, π. ἠρτῆσθαι prob. in Apollod.*Poliorc*.158.7. II. **παραμέση** (sc. χορδή), ἡ, the string *next above the* μέση (q.v.), the lowest note in the disjunctive tetrachord, Arist.*Pr*.922ᵇ5, Aristox.*Harm*.p.34 M., etc.:—also **παράμεσος**, Euc.*Sect.Can*.19, Nicom.*Harm*.11.

**παραμετρ-έω**, *measure* one thing *by* another, *compare*, τὰς δυνάμεις Phld.*Rh*.2.255 S., cf. Plu.2.78f (v.l.), Luc.*Pr.Im*.21, Arr.*Epict*.1.2. 10:—Med., *compare oneself*, τινι *with* another thing, Pl.*Tht*.154b; τὸ παραμετρούμενον *that which makes the comparison*, ibid.:—Pass., εἰ τῷ μικρῷ παραμετροῖτο Luc.*Prom*.15; τὰ καθήκοντα ταῖς σχέσεσι π. Epict. *Ench*.30. 2. *measure* by a standard, Chrysipp.*Stoic*.3.188, Ph.1. 147:—Pass., ib.92; *supply a standard of measurement for*, ὁ [τὴν κίνησιν] -μετρῶν χρόνος Plu.2.569c. 3. *adjust expenditure*, τοῖς πράγμασιν Phld.*Oec*.p.71 J.; *measure out*, εἰς τὸ βασιλικόν *PHib*.1.47. 23 (iii B.C.), cf. *PPetr*.3 p.143 (iii B.C.), etc.; ἀπὸ τῆς ἅλω *PRev.Laws* 39.9 (iii B.C.); ἀρσίχῳ *IG*12(7).62.42 (Amorgos, iv B.C.); εἴκοσι μεδίμνους τινί Luc.*Nav*.25:—Med., *cause to be measured out*, σῖτον *SIG* 976.44 (Samos, ii B.C.):—Pass., *PTeb.ined*.703.46. b. *supply according to specified measurements*, *Inscr.Délos* 372 *A* 142 (iii/ii B.C.). 4. *scan, peruse*, ἀρχὴν πίνακος Nonn.*D*.41.369. II. *measure* a distance *past..*, *pass by*, c. acc. loci, A.R.1.595, 1166, 2.937, Nonn.*D*. 14.271; *pass along*, ἀτραπὸν ib.7.314. -ησις, εως, ἡ, *comparison*, Hierocl. *in CA* 16 p.456 M.; *measurement by a standard*, Phld.*Herc*. 1251.13 (pl.). II. *distribution*, σίτου *IG*5(1).1379.21 (Thuria, ii/i B.C.). -ητής, οῦ, ὁ, *one who measures out*, *PLond*.1821. 375. -ητικός, ή, όν, *concerning adjustment*, τὸ π. τῷ φυσικῷ τέλει Phld.*Oec*.p.52 J.

**παρᾰμεύομαι**, Dor. form of παραμείβομαι, μορφᾷ παραμεύσεται ἄλλων *will surpass* the beauty of others, Pi.*N*.11.13: an Act. form παραμεῦσαι· παραλλάξαι, ἐκτραπῆναι, Hsch.

**παραμήκ-ης**, ες, *oblong* or *oval*, ὑποχονδρίου σύντασις π. πρὸς ὀμφαλόν Hp.*Epid*.1.26.β'; τρῆμα, αὐλῶνες, Plb.1.22.6, Agatharch.44; λόφος D.S.15.32; ἀσπίς, πίνακες, Ascl.*Tact*.1.3, Gem.16.4; π. σφαιροειδές *prolate* spheroid, Archim.*Con.Sph.Praef*., al.; γῆ Str.17.3.23; τὸ π. ἔντερον the *rectum*, Aret.*SA*2.10, *SD*1.7; of military formations, opp. πλάγιος, φάλαγξ Ascl.*Tact*.10.21, cf. Arr.*Tact*.26.2: Comp. -κέστερος *Gp*.19.6.1; κύκλου παραμηκεστέρου Paus.5.26.3. Adv., Ion. παραμηκέως, κληῒς π. καταγεῖσα, of a bone fractured *obliquely*, opp. ἀτρεκέως, Hp.*Art*.14. 2. *long*, π. ὅσον ἑξήκοντα σταδίων τὸ μῆκος Str.9.1.22. 3. *lengthened*, of strokes in a letter, Aen.Tact. 31.3. -ύνω, *prolong*, Anon.ap.Ath.11.502d.

**παρα-μήνας**· παραναγνούς, Hsch. -μήξας· παραλλάξας, Id.

**παραμηρ-ιαῖος**, α, ον, = sq., Poll.2.187. -ίδιος, ον, *along the thighs*: τὰ π. *armour for the thighs, cuisses*, X.*An*.1.8.6; for horses, Id.*Cyr*.6.4.1, Arr.*Tact*.4.1. -ιον, τό, *dagger*, Just.*Nov*.85.4 (also Adj. **παραμήριος** μάχαιρα, Hsch. s.v. κλονιστήρ). II. **παραμήρια**, τά, *inside of the thighs*, Dsc.1.99, Ruf.*Onom*.119, Antyll.ap.Orib.10. 31.1, Poll.2.188, Hsch. s.v. κίκκασος.

**παραμηχᾰνάομαι**, *devise wickedly*, Celsus ap.Orig.*Cels*.2.49.

**παραμίγνυμι**, v. παραμείγνυμι.

**παραμικτέον**, *one must mix*, Herod.Med.ap.Aët.5.129, Orib.*Fr*.74.

**παρᾰμιλλ-άομαι**, *outvie, outdo*, *CIG*2271.33 (Delos), J.*BJ*7.8.1; τινί τινα *in* a thing, Plb.12.10.4. -ος, ον, *beyond rivalry*, Astyd. *Eleg*.3. II. *entering into competition*, κατὰ τὴν τῶν ἀποδείξεων ἀκρίβειαν Iamb.*Comm.Math*.23.

**παραμῑμέομαι**, *imitate*, Satyr.*Vit.Eur.Fr*.1, D.H.*Dem*.23.

**παραμιμνήσκομαι**, *mention besides, make incidental mention of*, c. gen. rei, Hdt.7.96, 99, S.*Tr*.1124: abs., ὡς..παρεμνήσθημεν Phld. *Ir*.p.65 W.; cf. παραδέδρομα (-ωμαι cod.)· παρεμνήσθην, Hsch.

**παραμίμνω**, poet. for παραμένω, *abide, tarry*, Od.2.297, 3.115.

**παραμίξ**, Adv. *mixedly*, Nicom.*Harm*.6, Iamb.*VP*26.115.

**παραμιξολῡδιάζω**, *introduce the mixolydian mode*, Plu.2.1144f.

**παραμίσγω**, v. παραμείγνυμι.

**παραμισθόομαι**, *lease from*, τινος *Inscr.Prien*.111.31 (i B.C.).

**πάραμμα**, ατος, τό, *thong* for carrying burdens, in Lat. form *paramma* (fem.), *Edict.Diocl*.10.3 (pl.).

**παραμολύνω**, aor. Pass. -εμολύνθην dub. sens. in Phld.*Rh*.2.27 S.

⊕ **παραμονάριος**, ὁ, *watchman*, *Cod.Just*.1.3.45.3.

⊕ **παρα-μονή**, ἡ, *obligation to continue in service*, of a slave whose manumission is deferred, *SIG*²863 (Delph.), etc.; ἐγγύους παρά τινος λαμβάνειν παραμονῆς *PHal*.1.48 (iii B.C.), cf. *PHib*.1.41.5 (iii B.C.). 2. *endurance, constancy*, Iamb.*Protr*.[2]. 3. *keeping*, οἶνος πρὸς παραμονὴν ἐπιτήδειος Ath.1.30e; γλεῦκος εἰς π. χρήσιμον *Gp*.6.16.3; εἰς πλείονα π. χρωμάτων Dsc.5.159. 4. διὰ τὴν τοῦ βρέφους παραμονήν to make *room* for the foetus, Alex.Aphr.*Pr*.1. 125. -μόνιμος, ον, poet. fem. παρμονίμα Pi.*P*.7.18, cf. Aglaïas 6: (παραμένω):—*constant, steadfast, permanent*, παρμόνιμον χρῆμα Thgn.198, cf. Hp.*Morb*.1.22, etc.; π. εὐδαιμονία Pi.l.c.; ὠφέλεια Pl. *Thg*.130a; ἀλοιφή Gal.6.292; ἐπὴν..παραμόνιμα ᾖ when things are *stable*, Hp.*Mul*.2.162. 2. of slaves, *trusty*, X.*Mem*.2.4.5, prob. for παράμονον ib.2.10.3; θηρίον, metaph. of a man, ib.3.11.11. Adv. -μως Phryn.*PS* p.57 B. ⊕ -μονος, poet. πάρμονος, ον, rarer form of foreg. (q.v.), πένθος Plu.2.114f; εὐτυχία *Cat.Cod.Astr*.8(4).207, cf. Vett.Val.292.30; οἶνος *Gp*.1.12.32; ὄλβος παρμονώτερος Pi.*N*.8. 17.

**παράμουσος**, ον, (Μοῦσα) *out of tune with, discordant with*, c. dat., Ἄρης Βρομίου π. ἑορταῖς E.*Ph*.786 (lyr.); *harsh, horrid*, ἄτας πλαγά A. *Ch*.467 (lyr.).

**παραμπ-έχω** or -ίσχω, *cover with a cloak* or *robe*, τὴν τοῦ σώματος αἰσχύνην Alcid.ap.Arist.*Rh*.1406ᵃ29. 2. *wrap* a thing *round as a cloak* or *disguise*: metaph., παραμπίσχειν (v.l. -έχειν) λόγους *use a cloak of* words, E.*Med*.282:—Med., *allege as a pretext*, c. acc., Hp. *Morb.Sacr*.1.

**παραμπύκ-ια** [ῠ], τά, *headbands*, Eust.1280.57. -ίζω, *bind with a headband*, κόμαν χερί Ar.*Lys*.1316, in Lacon. form **παραμπυκίδδω**:—Pass., *have one's hair so bound*, Eust.1280.58.

**παραμῡθ-έομαι**, *encourage, exhort* one *to do* a thing, c. dat. pers. et inf., τοῖς ἄλλοισιν ἐγὼ παραμυθησαίμην οἴκαδ' ἀποπλείειν Il.9.417, cf. 684, 15.45; later c. dat. pers. only, *PFay*.19.6 (ii A.D.): also c. acc. pers. et inf., πῶς οὖν αὐτοὺς παραμυθησόμεθα προθύμους εἶναι; Pl.*Lg*. 666a; παραμυθοῦ μ' (sc. ποιεῖν) ὅ τι καὶ πείσεις A.*Pr*.1063 (anap.); θαρσεῖν (sc. σε) οὐδὲν παραμυθοῦμαι S.*Ant*.935 (anap.). 2. *speak soothingly to*, c. acc., παρεμυθεῖτο *attempted to reassure* them, Th.3. 75, cf. Pl.*R*.476e, etc.; *encourage* a dog, X.*Cyn*.6.25: metaph., παραμυθεῖται ὁ σκάφος τὴν διψῶσαν ἄμπελον *Gp*.3.5.4; *console, comfort*, τινα Hdt.2.121.δ', Th.2.44, Alcid.*Soph*.10, Pl.*Prt*.346b, al.; ἡ φιλοσοφία τὴν ψυχὴν ἠρέμα παραμυθεῖται Id.*Phd*.83a; π. τινὰ λόγοισι Ar.*V*.115; τινὰ ὀψαρίοις Id.*Fr*.45; τινὰ ἐπὶ τῇ κολάσει Luc. *Tox*.33; ἑαυτὸν τῆς ἥττης D.C.48.46; ταῖς ἐλπίσιν τἀλγεινὰ π. Men. 641: c. neut. Adj., πόλλ' ἂν εἶχέ τις αὐτὸν παραμυθήσασθαι D.21.214; π. τὰς πόλεις ὡς.. *console..by saying* that.., X.*HG*4.8.1. 3. *relieve, assuage, abate*, π. ὁ οἶνος τὴν τοῦ γήρως δυσθυμίαν Thphr.*Fr*. 120; Ἐπίκουρος τἀποθνήσκειν π. Demetr.Lac.*Herc*.1013.13; ἀδουσιν ἡσυχῇ τὸ ἔργον -ούμενοι D.Chr.1.9; π. τὰς ἐν στρατοπέδοις συμφοράς Onos.1.13; π. τὸν φθόνον, τὸ πένθος, τὴν ξυμφοράν, Plu.*Alc*.13, Luc. *Philops*.27, *DMort*.28.3; [θρίδακες] κόρυζαν π. *Gp*.12.13.11; πῦρ ἀνάψαντες τὸ πικρὸν τοῦ κρυμοῦ π. Alciphr.1.1. 4. *soften down, palliate*, τὸ τῆς μοναρχίας ὄνομα Plu.*Cleom*.11; διὰ τῶν τῆς γοργότητος ἰδίων τὸ λίαν ὕπτιον Hermog.*Id*.2.4; *explain away*, τὸ μυθῶδες Plu.2. 248b; *excuse*, τὴν ἀπὸ μικρῶν ἐπίκλησιν Str.13.1.64. 5. *support, justify* a thesis, S.E.*M*.7.66, al., cf. παραμυθητέον 3; *explain*, Simp. *in Ph*.9.32. -ημα, ατος, τό, *consolation*, Suid. and Phot. s.v. παραρρητοῖς. -ητέον, *one must gently talk to*, Pl.*Lg*.899d. 2. *one must soften*, τὸ ἐπαχθές Sopat.ap.Stob.4.5.52. 3. *one must explain, justify*, Corn.*ND*22. -ητής, οῦ, ὁ, *consoler*, Hsch. s.v. παρακλήτορες. -ητικός, ή, όν, *consolatory*, -μυθητικὸν ὁ φίλος καὶ τῇ ὄψει καὶ τῷ λόγῳ Arist.*EN*1171ᵇ2; *able to assuage* (sc. τῶν ἑαυτοῦ παθῶν), Chrysipp.ap.S.E.*P*.1.70; π. λόγος a letter *of consolation*, such as Plu. wrote to Apollonius, 2.101e sq.; π. ὑπόληψις D.Chr.12.40; τὸ -κόν *consolation*, D.H.*Rh*.6.4. Adv. -κῶς Eust.225.41, Sch.A.R.2. 622. -ητός, ή, όν, *consolable*, Sch.Il.9.526. ⊕ -ία, ἡ, *encouragement, exhortation*, Pl.*R*.450d, Phld.*Ir*.p.65 W. (pl.); *reassurance, gentle persuasion*, Pl.*Phd*.70b, *Lg*.720a. 2. *consolation*, Id.*Ax*. 365a, Arr.*Epict*.1.1.18; *diversion, distraction*, Pl.*Sph*.224a. 3. *relief from, abatement of*, φθόνου Plu.*Them*.22; τῶν πόνων καὶ τῶν κινδύνων Id.*Dio*52, etc.; π. ταλαιπωρούντων, of sleep, Secund.*Sent*. 13. 4. *explanation, solution* of a difficulty, π. πρὸς τὴν ἀπορίαν Plu. 2.395f, cf. 929f, Simp. *in Ph*.361.19. 5. *excuse*, ἔχειν τινὰ π. Longin.4.7, cf. Hermog.*Id*.1.11, al. ⊕ -ῐᾰκός, ή, όν, *of* or *for relief*, ἐργασία, i.e. digging in a vineyard, to relieve the effects of drought, *POxy*.1631.13 (iii A.D.). ⊕ -ιον, τό, *address, exhortation*, Pl.*Lg*. 773e, 880a (both pl.); *encouragement*, τοῦ μὴ φοβεῖσθαι Id.*Euthd*. 272b. 2. *assuagement, abatement of*, καμάτων S.*El*.130 (lyr.); πυρσῶν *of* the fires of love, Theoc.23.7; ἐλπὶς κινδύνῳ π. οὖσα Th.5. 103; παραμύθια ποιήσασθαι τῆς ὁδοῦ Pl.*Lg*.632e, cf. 704d; τοῖς γὰρ πλουσίοις πολλὰ π. φασιν εἶναι many *consolations*, Id.*R*.329e, cf. *Phdr*.240d, Phld.*Mort*.19; λύπης παραμύθιον *Epigr.Gr*.298.7 (Teos), cf. *IG*3.768a. 3. παραμύθια πλησμονῆς *stimulants* of a sated appetite, Pl.*Criti*.115b.

**παραμῡκάομαι**, *bellow beside* or *in answer*, of thunder following on earthquake, A.*Pr*.1082 (anap.).

**παρᾰμύσσω**, *scarify*, Gal.13.256.

**παραμφοδ-έω**, *go astray, make a miscalculation*, c. gen., τοῦ χρόνου Vett.Val.360.22. **-ίζω**, = foreg., Id.53.3. **-ισις**, εως, ἡ, *miscalculation*, Id.250.30.

**παράμωρος**, ον, *almost foolish*, Hsch. s. v. ἀκκός.

**παρανα-βαίνω**, *mount a chariot beside* one, Callix.2. **-βλαστάνω**, *shoot* or *grow up beside*, Ph.1.438 : c. dat., ib.667. **-γιγνώσκω**, later -γῑνώσκω, *read beside, compare, collate* one document *with* another, τοὺς λόγους ἡμῶν. . π. τοῖς αὐτῶν Isoc.12.17; π. τοὺς νόμους τῷ ψηφίσματι Aeschin.3.201; so π. τὰς συνθήκας τάς τ' ἐφ' ἡμῶν γενομένας καὶ τὰς νῦν ἀναγεγραμμένας Isoc.4.120; παρὰ μαρτυρίας τὰς ῥήσεις D. 18.267, cf. 24.38; *read as well*, τὰ τῶν ἄλλων Στωϊκῶν βιβλία Gal. 5.244 :—Pass., Pl.*Tht.*172e. II. *read publicly*, Plb.2.12.4, al., Lxx 2*Ma.*8.23, *PGrenf.*2.68.16 (iii A.D.) :—Pass., τοῦ νόμου παραναγνωσθέντος Lxx 3*Ma.*1.12, cf. Ph.2.531.

**παρᾰναγκάζω**, *accomplish* a thing *by force*, v.l. for προσ- in D.H. *Lys.*13. 2. Medic., π. ὀστέα *force* the ends of a bone *together*, Hp.*Art.*34.

**παρανάγνωσις**, εως, ἡ, *reading before* or *to*, Gloss.

**παρανάγω**, *displace*, γνάθον v.l. in Hp.*Mochl.*4; *remove*, τὸ ἐνοχλοῦν (in cataract), Max.Tyr.16.3.

**παρανα-δύομαι**, Med., with aor. 2 and pf. Act., *creep, crawl out*, ἐκ τῶν λίκνων Plu.*Alex.*2. **-θλίβω** [ῑ], *force up*, Sor.1.118.

**παραναιετάω**, *dwell beside* or *near*, c. acc. loci, S.*Tr.*635 (lyr.).

⊕ **παραναίω**, aor. 1 παρένασσα, *cause to dwell, settle*, Call.*Aet.Oxy.* 2080.53. 2. in Med., aor. 1 παρενασσάμην, = παροικίζω, καί μιν . . σφετέρῃ παρενάσσατο χώρῃ D.P.776. II. Med., = foreg., κακὸς παρενάσσατο γείτων Call.*Fr.*143.

**παρανα-κλίνω** [ῑ], *lay beside*, τὰς λαγόνας γυναιξί Lxx *Si.* 47. 19 (v. παρακλίνω I. 3). **-κύπτω**, *emerge, come to light*: hence, *occur*, Heracl.ap.Orib.48.8.2.

**παρᾰνᾰλ-ίσκω** or **-όω**, fut. -ανᾰλώσω, *spend amiss, waste, squander, throw away*, παραναλώσετε πάνθ' ὅσ' ἂν δαπανήσητε D.*Prooem.*21; ἐκ τῶν ἰδίων π. εἰς οὐδὲν δέον Id.13.4, cf. J.*BJ*3.7.13; *ruin*, τὴν πόλιν ib.2.21.7 :—Pass., of persons, *to be sacrificed incidentally*, παραναλώθησαν Plu.*Lys.*28, cf. D.S.14.5; ἀπολώλαμεν, παρανηλώμεθα Lxx *Nu.* 17.12(27): in Com., *to be spent incidentally*, pres. part. Pass. παραναλούμενος Antiph.164.5: pf. παραναλωμένος Arched.2.11. **-ωμα**, ατος, τό, *useless expense, waste*, Plu.*Pyrrh.*30, *Cic.*17; χρόνου Ael. *VH*1.17; *incidental waste*, J.*BJ*4.5.2, 5.1.3; of persons, π. γινόμενοι *perishing incidentally*, Aesop.345, cf. Demad.2; μὴ π. γένηται τελευτήσαντος αὐτοῦ lest his death should *involve* that of . ., Ph.2.519; ἐπ' οὐδενὶ λυσιτελεῖ παρανάλωμα γενησόμενοι ib.600.

**παρανα-παύομαι**, *rest beside*, Jul.*Or.*7.206c. **-πείθω**, *persuade* one *to change one's mind*, *BGU*1141.40 (I B.C.). **-πίπτω**, *fall back on one side*, of dogs copulating, Artem.1.79 (interpol.). **-τείνω**, *extend along*, εἰς τὸν κόλπον *Peripl.M.Rubr.*37. **-τέλλω**, *rise* or *appear beside*, of stars, Ptol.*Tetr.*77, Vett.Val.8.15, Porph.ap.Eus.*PE* 3.4, Serv.ad Virg.*G.*1.218; poet. **παραντέλλω**, of a building, *AP*9. 614 (Leont.). **-τολή**, ἡ, *simultaneous rising*, in pl., Eudem.ap. Theon.Sm.p.200 H., *Cat.Cod.Astr.*8(4).207. **-φύω**, v.l. for παραφύω, Ph.1.345. **-φωνέω**, in Pass., *to be parenthetical*, Sch.Il.*Oxy.* 1086.43.

**παρανδρόομαι**, *remain unmarried*, παρθένοι . . παρανδρούμεναι Hp. *Virg.*1.

**παρανεάτη**, ἡ, = παρανήτη (q. v.).

**παρανέμω**, *pasture beside* or *near*, Ael.*NA*1.20 :—Med., *dwell by* or *near*, Lyd.*Mag.*1.50.

**παρανέομαι**, *go* or *pass by*, A.R.2.357, *Ath.Mitt.*17.272 (Athens, ii A.D.).

**παρανευρίζομαι**, *to be ill strung*, χορδαὶ -νενευρισμέναι Arist.*HA* 581ᵃ20, *Pr.*902ᵇ34.

**παρανεύω**, *incline to one side*, Hippiatr.33; παρανενευκότα τοὺς ὀφθαλμούς Anatolius in *Cat.Cod.Astr.*8(3).188.

**παρανέω**, (νέω A) *swim beside*, τῷ σκάφει Luc.*DMar.*8.2; δελφὶς τῇ γῇ π. Philostr.*VA*1.23: abs., Ael.*NA*9.38.

**παρανηνέω**, Ep. for παρανέω, (νέω C, cf. νηέω, νηνέω) *heap* or *pile up beside*, only impf., σῖτον παρενήνεον ἐν κανέοισιν Od.1.147, cf. 16. 51.

**παρανήτη** (sc. χορδή), ἡ, *string next below the* νήτη, Arist.*Ph.*248ᵇ9, *Metaph.*1018ᵇ28, Plu.2.1137c, etc. :—also **παρανεάτη**, Cratin.134.

**παρανήχομαι**, *swim along* the shore, εἰ δέ κ' ἔτι προτέρω παρανήξομαι Od.5.417; ἐν χρῷ παρενήχοντο τὴν γῆν Plu.2.161f: c. acc. loci, *swim past*, Poet.ap.eund.2.90d: metaph., παρενήξατο τὸ πλεῦν ἥβης *AP*6. 206 (Leon.); *swim beside*, τῇ τριήρει Plu.*Them.*10; παρὰ τὰ πλοῖα Id. *Tim.*19.

⊕ **παρανθέω**, *bloom partially*, of plants which produce flowers in succession, Thphr.*HP*7.11.3 and 4, 8.2.5. II. *flower beside*, Ps.-Callisth.3.13.

⊕ **παρανθινολογέω**, dub. sens. in *BGU*1121.20 (I B.C.).

**παρανίημι**, *relax, slacken* the strings, Plu.2.1145d.

**παρανῑκάω**, *subdue to* or *for evil, pervert*, A.*Ch.*600 (lyr.).

⊕ **παρανίσσομαι**, aor. 1 παρενῑσάμην, = παρανέομαι, *pass beside, near*, or *beyond*, c. acc., *h.Ap.*430, A.R.2.1030.

**παραν-ίστημι**, fut. -αναστήσω, *set up beside*, Ath.4.156c. II. Med. with aor. 2 Act., *stand up beside*, J.*BJ*2.21.1. **-ίσχω**, trans., *raise in answer*, ἀπὸ τοῦ τείχους φρυκτοὺς Th.3.22. II. intr., *stand forth beside*, Plu.*Aem.*32.

**παρανο-έω**, *think amiss*, παρακούουσι καὶ παρανοοῦσι Pl.*Tht.*195a: c. acc., *misconceive, misunderstand*, τὰ λεγόμενα Simp.*in Ph.*1360. 9. II. *to be deranged* or *senseless, lose one's wits*, E.*IA*838, Ar.*Nu.* 1480, Lys.*Fr.*74, Arist.*Ath.*56.6. **-ησις**, εως, ἡ, = παράνοια, Herod. Med. in *Rh.Mus.*58.70. **-ητέον**, *one must deviate from accurate thought*, ἐν τοῖς λόγοις Plot.6.8.13.

**παράνοιᾰ** (παρανοιᾱ Ar.*Fr.*226 (anap.)), ἡ, *derangement, madness*, A.*Th.*756 (lyr.), E.*Or.*824 (lyr.), Hp.*Prog.*23, And.2.10; οἴμοι παρανοίας Ar.*Nu.*1476; παρανοίας τινὰ εἰσαγαγὼν ἑλεῖν, γράφεσθαι, ib.845, Pl.*Lg.*928e, etc.; δίκαι παρανοίας Arist.*Ath.*56.6: pl., παρανοίας ποιεῖ καὶ θανάτους Id.*PA*653ᵇ5.

**παρανοίγνυμι** and **-οίγω**, *open at the side* or *a little, set ajar*, θύραν D.25.28; ἀγγεῖα *Placit.*4.22.1 (Pass.); παρηνεῳγμένοι ὀφθαλμοί *half-closed* eyes, Gal.18(2).300, cf. Dem.Ophth.ap.Aët.7.98: metaph., π. τὸ πρᾶγμα D.H.*Rh.*10.13.

**παρανομ-έω**, impf. παρενόμουν Lys.3.17, D.17.22, Aeschin.3.77: fut. -ήσω Luc.*Tim.*45: aor. παρενόμησα Hdt.7.238, Th.3.67, Luc. *Am.*20, later παρην- Plu.*Demetr.*37: pf. παρανενόμηκα D.59.126, later παρηνόμηκα D.S.16.61: plpf. παρενενομήκεσαν X.*HG*2.1.31 :—Pass., aor. παρενομήθην Th.5.16, etc.: pf. παρανενόμημαι D.44.31, 54.2; part. παρηνομημένος *SIG*167.38 (Mylasa, iv B.C.):—*transgress the law, act unlawfully*, Th.3.65, al.; κοινῇ τι π. ib.82; παρανομοῦντά τε καὶ ἀδικοῦντα Pl.*R.*338e, etc.: c. acc. cogn., παρανομίαν π. Them.*Or.*1.15b. 2. *commit a crime* or *outrage*, τι Antipho 5.15, And.4.21, Aeschin. l. c., Arist.*Pol.*1307ᵇ31; ἐς τὸν νεκρὸν ταῦτα παρενόμησε Hdt.7.238, cf. Lys. 3.17; εἰς θεούς D.59.126; εἰς τὸ μαντεῖον D.S.16.61; also π. τὸ θεῖον καὶ πάτριον ἀξίωμα τῆς εὐσεβείας Plu.2.166b; περὶ σφᾶς Th.8.108; π. τὰ δημόσια *act illegally* in public matters, Id.2.37 :—Pass., κάθοδος παρανομηθεῖσα a return *illegally procured*, Id.5.16. II. Pass., *to be ill-used*, D.35.45, 44.31, *PSI*4.330.8 (iii B.C.); εἰς τὸ σῶμα Plu.*Tim.*13; ἡ φύσις παρανομεῖται, ἡ συνήθεια παρανενόμηται, Id.2.755c, 1070c. **-ημα**, ατος, τό, *unlawful act, transgression*, Th.7.18, Chrysipp.*Stoic.*3.71, Plb.23. 10.2 (pl.), Plu.*Cat.Mi.*47 (pl.), Porph.*Abst.*1.2 (pl.), *POxy.*1119.10 (iii A.D.). **-ησις**, εως, ἡ, *unlawful conduct*, App.*Hisp.*61. **-ητικός**, ή, όν, *inclined to transgress*, Hierocl. *in CA*11 p.440 M. **-ία**, ἡ, *transgression of law, decency*, or *order*, Antipho 5.12, Th.4.98, Pl.*R.* 537e, etc.; ἡ κατὰ τὸ σῶμα π. ἐς τὴν δίαιταν *loose and disorderly habits* of life, Th.6.15, cf. 28; π. εἴς τινας Plb.3.6.13; περὶ τὰς σπονδάς D.H. 8.44; *illegality*, personified, Plb.18.54.10. **-ος**, ον, *lawless, violent*, ὀργά, δάκος, E.*Ba.*997 (lyr.), *Tr.*284 (lyr.); π. δή. . δόξει γεγονέναι ἐκ νομίμου Pl.*R.*539a; εἰς γυναῖκας καὶ εἰς τὴν ἄλλην δίαιταν Antisth.ap. Ath.5.220c; χειρὶ παρανομωτάτῃ Ar.*Fr.*387.10; οὐ. . τίς ἂν δύναιτο παρανομώτερον φράσαι; Anaxil.22.2. II. of things, *unlawful*, διὰ τὴν π. ἐνοίκησιν Th.2.17; τὰ π. τά τ' ἀνόσια Ar.*Th.*684; πέπονθα δεινὰ καὶ π. Id *Pl.*967; ἄδικα καὶ π. Pl.*Ap.*31e; τὸ π. *illegality*, Aeschin.3. 197. Adv. -μως *illegally*, Antipho 5.94, Th.3.65; opp. κατὰ νόμους, Pl. *Plt.*302e: Comp. -ωτέρως And.4.22: Sup. -ώτατα Antipho 5.8. 2. in Law, παράνομα γράφειν, εἰπεῖν, to propose an *illegal* or *unconstitutional measure*, D.21.182, 183; παρανόμων γράψασθαί τινα to indict one *for proposing such a measure*, And.1.17; γράφοντα παράνομα παρανόμων γραφόμενος D.18.13; παρανόμων γραφή Aeschin.3.197, etc.; παρανόμων φεύγειν, ἁλῶναι, Lys.18.14, Antiph.196.14: Sup., παρανομώτατα γεγραφότα Aeschin.3.31.

**παράνοος**, ον, contr. -νους, ουν, *demented*, A.*Ag.*1455 (anap.).

**παρανοσφίζομαι**, Med., *appropriate by stealth*, Eust.754.44.

**πάραντα**, Adv. *sideways*, Il.23.116.

**παραντέλλω**, poet. for παρανατέλλω (q. v.).

**παραντίχειρ**, χειρος, ἡ, *forefinger*, *PLond.*1821.302.

**παρανυκτερεύω**, *pass the night on guard*, Plu.*Pel.*35, *Arat.*8, al.

**παρανυμφ-εύω**, *act as* παράνυμφος, *LW*2823 (Amathus). **-ιος**, ὁ, = sq., v.l. in Poll.3.40; correct acc. to Eust.652.41. ⊕ **-ος**, ὁ, *bridegroom's friend* or *best man*, Poll.3.40; gloss on θυρωρός, Sch. Sapph.*Oxy.*2076.9. II. fem., *bridesmaid*, one of the *dramatis personae* in Ar.*Ach.*, cf. Hsch., *EM*145.31, Moer.p.269 P.

**παρανύσσω**, Att. -ττω, *prick on*, Ps.-Luc.*Philopatr.*22.

**πάραξ**, ακος, ὁ, = βάραξ (q. v.), *Test.Epict.*6.11.

**παράξενος**, ον, *half-foreign, counterfeit*, παράσημα καὶ π. Ar.*Ach.*518 (where it includes a charge of ξενία), cf. Them.*Or.*21.255d. II. *strange, extraordinary*, Anon. *in EN*419.24.

**παραξέω**, *graze* or *rub in passing*, *AP*7.478 (Pass., Leon.), Hld.5. 32; τὸν ὁρίζοντα Procl.*Hyp.*7.46. 2. *make smooth*, *IG*7.3073.140 (Lebad.) :—Med., παραξεσάμενον ib.2².1666 *B*86. II. *keep close to*, ἑαυτόν τισι Eun.*VS*p.495 B.: generally, *imitate*, Eust.1097.24.

**παρα-ξηραίνω**, *cause to dry up*, in Pass., *Hippiatr.*9, 10. **-ξηρος**, ον, *somewhat dry*, Str.17.3.23.

**παράξιος**, ον, *inequitable*, διαθήκη *CPR*18.13 (ii A.D.).

**παρα-ξιφίδιον**, τό, Dim. of sq., Hsch. s. v. κολοίδιον. ⊕ **-ξιφίς**, ίδος, ἡ, *knife worn beside the sword, dirk*, Lxx 2*Ki.*5.8, D.S.5.33, Str. 3.3.6, Plu.*Arat.*25.

**παραξοή**, Dor. παρξοά, ἡ, *planing down, smoothing*, *IG*7.3073.140 (Lebad.), *SIG*247 ii 71 (Delph., iv B.C.).

**παραξόν-ιος**, ον, (ἄξων) *beside the axle*: τὸ π. *linchpin*, Phryn.*PS* p.100 B.: metaph., σχινδαλάμων παραξόνια, expld. by Sch. κινδυνώδη καὶ παράβολα, *audacious, venturesome* quibbles, Ar.*Ra.*819. **-ίτης** [ῑ], ου, ὁ, *linchpin*, Phryn.*PS* p.100 B. II. *nave of a wheel*, Sch. A.*Th.*153.

**παραξῠράω**, Ion. -έω, *shave beside*, Hp.*Morb.*2.26.

**παρά-ξυσμα**, ατος, τό, *superfluous scratch*, metaph., Demetr.*Eloc.* 55. **-ξυστον**, τό, *mason's tool*, gloss on ὑπαγωγεύς, Sch.Ar.*Av.* 1150. **-ξύω**, = παραξέω I. 1, παραξύοντες ἐγγύθεν ἔπαιον prob. in J.*BJ*3.10.9; πέλαγος π. τὴν Συρίαν Anon.*Geog.Comp.*50, cf. Procop.

*Aed.*2.6; π. κανόνα *AP*6.65 (Paul. Sil.): metaph., π. τὸν ἰδιώτην *graze the edge of* vulgarity, Longin.31.2.

**παράορος**, v. παρήορος. **παραός**· ἀετός (Maced.), Hsch.

**παράπᾰγος**, poet. **πάρπᾰγος**, ὁ, *upper bolt of a door*, Hsch.

⊛ **παράπαιγμα**, ατος, τό, *knavery, trickery*, *PPetr.*3 p.156 (iii B.C.).

**παραπαίγνιον**, τό, *stage-trick*, Porph.*Chr.*27.

**παραπαιδᾰγωγ-έω**, *help to train* or *form*, Plu.2.321b. II. *improve, reform gradually*, π. καὶ μεθαρμόττειν Luc.*Nigr.*12. **–ησις**, εως, ἡ, *correction*, αἴσθησις δεῖται τῆς ἐκ τοῦ λόγου π. Ptol.*Harm.*1.1.

**παραπαίζω**, *jest by the way*, πρός τι Sch.Ar.*Pl.*811; εἴς τινα *EM* 463.45. II. παραπαίζων, ὁ, epith. of Dionysus, Ἀρχ.Δελτ.8.171 (Eleusis).

**παρα-παιόντως**, Adv. *in a foolish way*, Hsch. **–παισμα**, ατος, τό, *madness*, Oenom.ap.Eus.*PE*5.25 (pl.):—in form **παραίπαιμα**, Hsch. **–παιστος**, ον, *demented*, Id. **–παίω**, *strike on the side, strike falsely*, χέλυν A.*Fr.*314. II. intr., *strike a false note*: metaph., *to be infatuated, lose one's wits*, Id.*Pr.*1056 (anap.); ληρεῖν καὶ π. Ar.*Pl.*508, cf. *Pax*90 (anap.); μαίνομαι καὶ π. Pl.*Smp.*173e, cf. Plb.12.8.1; παραπεπαικότας Plu.2.963f; *to be in error*, Phld.*Sign.*32; π. τι *commit a folly*, Luc.*Hist.Conscr.*2; π. πρὸς ὑλικὰς δυνάμεις Eun.*VS* p.474B.:—also in pf. part. Pass., φωναὶ –πεπαισμέναι *mad, foolish*, S.*Ichn.*234. b. Medic., *to be delirious*, Gal.10.850, al. 2 *fall away from*, τῆς ἀληθείας Plb.3.21.9; τοῦ δέοντος Id.4.31.2, al. 3. *dash in*, prob. in Philox.2.26.

**παραπάλλομαι**, *bound beside*, τινι E.*IA*228 (lyr.).

⊛ **παράπᾶν**, Adv. for παρὰ πᾶν, *altogether, absolutely*, in correct writers always joined with Art., τὸ π. Hdt.1.61, Th.6.80, etc.; εἰς τὸ π. in *perpetuity*, *Rev.Bibl.*39.532 (Palmyra, ii A.D.). 2. freq. with neg., τὸ π. οὐδέν not *at all*, Hdt.1.32; τὸ π. οὐδὲ γρῦ Ar.*Pl.*17, cf. Isoc.17.35, etc.; μὴ ζητεῖν αὐτὴν..τὸ π. Pl.*Tht.*187a; οὐκ εἰμὶ τὸ π. ἄθεος Id.*Ap.*26c; φωνὴν οὐκ ἔχειν ἰχθύν γε..τὸ π. Pherecr.113: with a neg. Verb, τὸ π. ἀρνούμενοι Antipho 3.3.7. 3. in reckoning, ἐπὶ διηκόσια τὸ παράπαν two hundred *on the average*, Hdt.1.193; οὐδὲ πεντήκοντα δραχμῶν τὸ π. *in all*, D.55.28.

**παρα-πάσσω**, Att. **–ττω**, *sprinkle beside* or *into*, Thphr.*CP*5.6.10 (Pass.); τινί τι Plu.2.954b, cf. Hp.*Ulc.*21, Damocr.ap.Gal.13.944; εἴς τι Dsc.3.23 (Pass.). **–παστον**, τό, *sprinkling powder*, Hp.*Mul.*1.105.

⊛ **παρᾰπᾰτάω**, *deceive, cajole*, οἴνῳ θεάς A.*Eu.*728.

⊛ **παρᾰπᾰφίσκω**, only in aor. 2 παρήπᾰφον, Ep. for παραπατάω, *mislead*, παρά μ' ἤπαφε δαίμων Od.14.488, cf. Theoc.27.12, *APl.*5.361; μολπῇσι π. πέτρας Orph.*A.*704; *cajole*, δῶρα καὶ θεοὺς π. *Trag.Adesp.*434: c. inf., *induce to do* a thing *by craft* or *fraud*, Ἥρη δ' ἐν φιλότητι παρήπαφεν εὐνηθῆναι Il.14.360, cf. A.R.2.952.

⊛ **παραπείθω**, fut. –πείσω *Com.Adesp.*25.17 D. (dub.): Ep. aor. παρ- or παραι-πέπῐθον:—*win by persuasive arts, prevail upon*, Il.24.208; Πηλείωνα..σπουδῇ παρπεπιθόντες 23.37, cf. 606, Od.24.119; freq. with a notion of deceit or guile, *beguile, cajole*, ὅς μ' ἄγε παρπεπιθὼν ᾗσι φρεσί Od.14.290: c. acc. et inf., μή σε ἔπεσσι παραιπεπίθησιν Ὀδυσσεὺς μνηστήρεσσι μάχεσθαι 22.213; παράπεισον..ἐλθεῖν..Ἰσμηνόν E.*Supp.*60 (lyr.):—rare in Prose, μή πῃ πρεσβύτας ἡμᾶς ὄντας..παραπείσῃ *may cajole* us, Pl.*Lg.*892d, cf. Nic.Dam.130.24 J.:—Pass., παραπεπεῖσθαι *to be beguiled* into doing a thing, Arist.*LI*969$^b$17.

**παραπειράομαι**, *make trial of* one, so as to ascertain his will, π. Διός, εἰ.. Pi.*O.*8.3.

**παράπεισις**, εως, ἡ, *over-persuasion, cajolery*, Sch.Il.14.217.

**παρα-πειστέον**, (παραπείθω) *one must win over*, τοὺς δικαστάς S.E.*M.*2.11. **–πειστικός**, ή, όν, *able to persuade* or *cajole*, Poll.4.21.

**παραπελεκάομαι**, Pass., *to be hewn at the side with an axe*, Thphr.*HP*4.16.2, *CP*5.4.7.

⊛ **παρα-πεμπτέος**, α, ον, *that must be dismissed, rejected, inadmissible*, A.D.*Pron.*31.18. II. παραπεμπτέον, *one must reject*, τὴν γραφήν Id.*Adv.*195.8; *one must omit*, Phld.*Hom.*p.60 O., Porph.*Abst.*4.10. 2. *one must inject*, τι τῇ ἕδρᾳ Paul.Aeg.3.45. ⊛ **–πέμπω**, *send past*, ἀλλ' Ἥρη παρέπεμψεν *conveyed* [the Argo] *past* or *through* the Symplegades, Od.12.72: metaph., σαρκὶ καὶ γάλακτι π. τὸν βίον *support* life, Agatharch.30, cf. 99, Hyp.*Fr.*219a; π. τὴν νύκτα *pass* the night, Poll.6.109:—Med., π. τὸν κάματον *while* it *away*, Sch.Ar.*Nu.*1360. 2. *send by* or *along the coast*, Th.8.61 (Pass.). 3. *escort*, of ships of war *convoying* merchant vessels, D.21.167, cf. 8.25 (Pass.); π. τὰ ἱερὰ στρατεύματα *IGRom.*3.1421.7 (Prusias, iii A.D.): generally, *escort*, *Lyr.Alex.Adesp.*1.12, etc.; π. τινὰ πρὸς τὴν οἰκίαν Plu.*Per.*5; π. τὰ ἱερά *IG*2$^2$.1078 (iii A.D.); esp. *escort to the grave*, χορῷ..τὸ σῶμα Posidon.14 J. (so in Med., τὸ σῶμα παραπέμψασθαι ἐπὶ τὴν κηδείαν *IG*12(7).53.19 (Amorgos)):—Pass., ἐτάφη καὶ παρεπέμφθη πανδημεί D.L.3.41; of a bridal procession, *to be escorted* to the bride-chamber, Luc.*DMar.*5.1. b. *attend* a person, of Roman clients, Epict.*Ench.*25.2; *escort, attend* to or from the forum, D.C.43.22, 58.11: metaph., of philosophy, τὸ –πέμψαι δυνάμενον M.Ant.2.17; τὸν ὑπόλοιπον βίον ὑπὸ δόξης χρηστῆς παραπεμφθῆναι Hyp.*Dem.*21. 4. *convoy* supplies, provisions, etc., to an army, π. τισὶ παραπομπήν X.*HG*7.2.18; σῖτον Philipp.ap.D.18.77, cf. 50.58. 5. *send* troops *along* the line or *along* the flanks, in support, ἐπ' οὐρὰν καὶ τὸ ἀπὸ τοῦ στόματος ἱππικόν X.*HG*4.3.4; εὐζώνους εἰς τὰ πλάγια Id.*An.*6.3.15, cf. *Ages.*2.3. 6. *bring also* or *besides*, φέρε, παῖ,..ὕδωρ, π. τὸ χειρόμακτρον Ar.*Fr.*502:—Pass., *to be sent in addition*, *SIG*613.19 (Delph., ii B.C.). 7. *swallow*, Dionys.*Av.*2.6. II. of voice, etc., *pass on, send to*, of an echo, π. στόνον τινί S.*Ph.*1459 (anap.); θόρυβον π. τινί *waft* him applause, Ar.*Eq.*546; μουσικῇ π. ἑαυτόν *give* oneself *up* to.., Plu.*Sol.*29, cf. Phld.*Mus.*p.108 K.; χάριτι π. ἀτύφῳ Plu.*Cat.Mi.*46:—Med., φωνὴν π. D.C.74.14. b. of light, *reflect*, M.Ant.8.57. c. metaph., δόγματα φαντάζεσθαι καὶ π. Id.10.9. III. *dismiss*, Philipp.ap.D.18.166, Plb.30.19.17, D.S.26.1, etc.:—Med., *dismiss one's* pupil, D.L.8.87; *put away one's* wife, Apollod.1.9.28. 2. *give up, omit*, τὸ λουτρόν Sor.1.46, cf. Phld.*Rh.*1.181 S.; *reject*, Sor.1.118, M.Ant.1.8; τὰς δεήσεις J.*AJ*6.3.5:—Med., *reject*, A.D.*Synt.*6.7, al.; *omit*, πλείονα..ἱστορούμενα Philum.*Ven.*36.3. IV. *transmit* an inheritance, Arg.Is.10, Procop.*Arc.*11: metaph., π. ἔχθος εἰς τριγονίαν ib.15; μνήμην εἰς τοὺς ἐπιγόνους Id.*Aed.*1 *Praef.* **–πεμψις**, εως, ἡ, *escorting, conveyance*, of a person, D.S.34/35.39 codd. (παράληψιν cj. Dind.).

**παραπεπλεγμένως**, Adv. pf. part. Pass. *entwined*, Hsch.

**παραπεριπᾰτέω**, *walk beside*, τῷ φορείῳ J.*AJ*18.6.6.

**παραπέρνημι**, Aeol. **–νᾶμι**, *sell at a reduced price*, σῖτον παραπέρναις (pres. part.) λυσιτελέως τοῖς πολίταισι Bechtel *Aeolica* (Halle 1909) p.33 (Eresus); cf. παραπιπράσκω.

**παραπέσσια**, τά, (πεσσός) *buildings abutting on larger buildings*, *Cod.Just.*8.11.14.

**παραπέτᾰλος**, ον, *covered with leaves* of gold or silver, τριήρεις χρυσῷ τὰς πρύμνας π. Anon.ap.Suid.

**παραπετάννῠμαι**, pf. –πέπτᾰμαι (in pres. sense), v. infr.:—Pass., *to be hung before*, pf. part. Pass. –πεπετασμένος Plb.33.5.2; *to be stretched, extend along*, σκαιῇ παραπέπταται ἰσθμός D.P.98, al. II. παραπέπταται Ὄρνις the Bird (i.e. Cygnus) *hovers before* it *with outspread wings*, Arat.312.

**παραπέτασμα**, ατος, τό, *that which is spread before* a thing, *hanging, curtain*, παραπετάσματα ποικίλα Hdt.9.82; π. Μηδικά Ar.*Ra.*938; τὸ π. τὸ Κύπριον Id.*Fr.*611; π. λιτόν *IG*1$^2$.330.6: metaph., *screen, cover*, ταῖς τέχναις ταύταις παραπετάσμασιν ἐχρήσαντο Pl.*Prt.*316e, cf. D.45.19; τὰ χρήματα..π. τοῦ βίου Alex.340 (=Antiph.327); εἶχεν δὲ π. τὴν ἐρημίαν Men.406.4. II. pl., *mantlets*, Agath.3.7.

**παραπέτομαι**, poet. **παρπέταμαι** Call.*Epigr.*33.6: aor. 2 παρεπτόμην or –επτάμην (v. infr.); also παρέπτην, 3 pl. παρέπτησαν Id.*Iamb.Fr.*9.327 P.:—*fly alongside*, κορώνη..ἤδη πετομένων [τῶν νεοττῶν] σιτίζει παραπετομένη Arist.*HA*563$^b$12; τὰς π. μυίας Id.*Pol.*1323$^a$29. 2. *fly past*, of specks before the eyes, Gal.1.363. 3. *escape*, *AP*6.19 (Jul.). 4. *fly to*, ἡμῖν ἑρπετὸν παρέπτατο Semon.13, cf. Philostr.*VA*1.7; *fly to one's succour*, οὐ γὰρ ἂν παρέπτετο Ar.*Th.*1014: metaph., παραπτῆναι, of a λόγος, Philostr.*Her.*19.14.

**παραπεφῠλαγμένως**, Adv., (παραφυλάττω) *cautiously, circumspectly*, Aps.p.314 H., Aët.12.23.

**παράπηγμα**, ατος, τό, *astronomical and meteorological calendar*, inscribed on stone, the days of the months being inserted on movable pegs at the side of the text (see the extant specimen, *Berl.Sitzb.*1904.102), π. ἐνιαύσιον Cic.*Att.*5.14.1, cf. Gem.17.6 (pl.), Ph.1.173 (pl.); Παράπηγμα, name of astron. and meteorol. work by Democritus, D.L.9.48; π. chronological *annals*, D.S.1.5. II. *rule*, π. καθολικόν S.E.*M.*1.223, cf. 269; ἰδιωτικὸν π. M.Ant.9.3.

**παραπήγνῡμι** (also –ύω Plu.2.4c), *fix beside* or *near*, as a spear in the ground, Hdt.4.71:—in Med., of stakes to support vines, χάρακα παραπήξασθαι ταῖς ἀμπέλοις Poll.1.224: hence, metaph. in Act., παραινέσεις π. τοῖς νέοις Plu. l.c.; also, *engraft* a twig, Id.2.640f. 2. of Gramm., *add by way of note*, Eust.190.33, 300.22, etc. II. Pass., with pf. 2 –πέπηγα, *to be fixed beside*, of spears, παρὰ δ' ἔγχεα μακρὰ πέπηγεν Il.3.135; ἔνθεν καὶ ἔνθεν τὰ ξύλα π. Hp.*Fract.*13; of the pegs in a παράπηγμα I, *Berl.Sitzb.*1904.102 (Milet.). 2. *to be affixed to*, [τῷ βωμῷ] παρεπεπήγεσαν δᾷδες Callix.2; *to be engrafted*, Thphr.*CP*5.6.10: metaph., αἱ λῦπαι ταῖς ἡδοναῖς παραπεπήγασι *are annexed to*.., Isoc.1.46; ταῖς βασιλείαις ὁ φθόνος παρεπεπήγει Lib.*Or.*59.151, cf. Hierocl.*in CA*25 p.475 M. 3. *to be petrified*, Luc.*Im.*1. III. Med., *register as on a* παράπηγμα I, τὰ τοῦ κόσμου παθήματα πρὸς τὸν αἰῶνα Pl.*Ax.*370c.

**παραπηδάω**, *overleap, transgress*, τοὺς νόμους Aeschin.3.192. II. *leap upon*, of hounds, X.*Cyn.*6.22: metaph., δημαγωγὸς αὐτοῖς ἐκ παιδαγωγείου παραπεπήδηκεν ὁ Πομπήϊος Plu.*Pomp.*6; ὁ πλοῦτος παραπηδήσας ἐρεῖ.. Crantor ap.S.E.*M.*11.53.

**παραπηκτέον**, *one must add*, τινί τι Eust.827.39.

**παραπηλωτός**, ή, όν, *besmeared with mud*, *Gp.*12.1.6.

**παραπηρόομαι**, Pass., *to be mutilated*, Ph.2.230.

**παραπήχιον**, τό, *radius* or *small bone of the forearm*, opp. προπήχιον (*ulna*), Poll.2.142.

**παράπηχυ**, τό, *a woman's garment*, with a purple border on each side, Macho ap.Ath.13.582d, cf. Poll.4.118, 7.53, Hsch. s.v. καταγωγίς: pl. παραπήχη *PSI*4.341.7 (iii B.C.).

**παρα-πῑέζω**, *press from one side, press down*, ὀφθαλμόν S.E.*M.*7.192, cf. Archig.ap.Orib.8.1.18, Heliod.ap.eund.50.9.3. **–πῑέσις**, εως, ἡ, *pressing aside*, Leonid.ap.Aët.15.7. **–πῑεσμός**, ὁ, = foreg., Heliod.ap.Orib.45.9.2, cf. Orib.46.17.1.

**παραπικρ-αίνω**, *embitter, provoke*, c. acc., Lxx *Ez.*20.21; *rebel against*, τὸ ῥῆμα τοῦ Κυρίου ib.3*Ki.*13.26: abs., ib.*Ez.*24.3, al.; παραπικραίνουσα παρεπικράνθην ib.*La.*1.20, cf. *Ep.Hebr.*3.16. **–ασμός**, ὁ, *provocation*, Lxx *Ps.*94(95).8, *Ep.Hebr.*3.8, 15. **–ος**, ον, *somewhat bitter*, Sch.Ar.*V.*873.

**παραπίμπλημι**, *fill*, Tim.Gaz. in Ar.Byz.*Epit.*93.26.

**παραπίμπραμαι**, Pass., *to be inflamed*, X.*Eq.*1.4, Thphr.*Sud.*15, Gal.11.234.

⊛ **παραπιπράσκω**, *sell at a reduced price*, *BSA*23.73 (Macedonia, ii A.D.):—Pass., *SIG*731.24 (Tomi, i B.C.). II. *sell in addition*, in Pass., τὸ παραπεπραμένον ἀπὸ τῶν πλέθρων ib.990 (Smyrna, iii B.C.).

**παραπίπτω**, *fall beside*, ἐγγὺς τῶν τειχῶν -πεπτωκός Plu.*Lys.*29; *come side to side*, Arist.*GA*718ᵃ1,al. **2.** Math., as Pass. of παραβάλλω, *to be applied*, Archim.*Con.Sph.*2. **II.** *fall in one's way*, κατὰ τύχην παραπεσοῦσα νηῦς Hdt.8.87, cf. Lys.27.15; ἀκοντίσαι ὅπου ἂν παραπίπτῃ [θηρίον] X.*Cyr.*1.2.10; ἀγοράσαι.. χιτωνάριον, μάλιστα μὲν ἐὰν παραπίπτῃ χειριδωτόν *PCair.Zen.*469.5 (iii B.C.); π. κατὰ βοήθειαν *come in time* to aid, Plb.31.5.2, etc.; ὁπότε καιρὸς παραπέσοι as opportunity *offered*, X.*Eq.Mag.*7.4, cf. Th.4.23; οὐ δεῖ τοιοῦτον παραπεπτωκότα καιρὸν ἀφεῖναι D.1.8; εἴ ποθεν ἄελπτος παραπέσοι σωτηρία E.*Or.*1173; ὁ -πίπτων παρὰ τῶν πολλῶν ἔπαινος Epicur.*Sent.Vat.*29; ὁ παραπεσὼν *the first that comes*, ἡ παραπίπτουσα ἀεὶ [ἡδονή] Pl.*R.*561b; ὁ παραπεπτωκὼς λόγος *that happened to arise*, Id.*Lg.*832b, cf. *Phlb.*14c; πᾶν τὸ παραπῖπτον or παραπεσὸν all *that befalls*, Plb.3.51.5, 11.4.5; κατὰ τὸ -πῖπτον *incidentally*, Phld.*Mort.*37. **2.** c. dat., *befall*, θαυμαστὸν κτῆμα παραπεσεῖν τοῖς Ἕλλησι *fell to* their *lot*, Pl.*Lg.*686d; π. τῇ πόλει νομοθέτης *comes to* its *aid*, ib.709c: in bad sense, ἀσθένειά τινι παραπεπτωκυῖα Phld.*Lib.*p.49O.; παραπέπτωκε τῇ πόλει ὥστε ἀνακτᾶσθαι X.*Vect.*5.8. **III.** *fall, rush in*, εἰς τὸ Σαμικόν Plb.4.80.9, etc. **IV.** *go astray, err*, X.*HG*1.6.4; τοῖς ὅλοις πράγμασιν ἀγνοεῖν καὶ π. Plb.18.36.6; π. τῇ διανοίᾳ Vett.Val.73.25. **b.** *to be mislaid* or *lost*, of a document, *Ostr.Bodl.*i 62 (ii B.C.), *POxy.*95.34 (ii A.D.), etc.; σανδάλιον παραπεσόν Luc.*Philops.*27. **2.** *fall aside* or *away from*, c. gen., τῆς ὁδοῦ Plb.3.54.5; τῆς ἀληθείας Id.12.12.2; τοῦ καθήκοντος Id.8.11.8; τῆς ἱστορίας Str.1.1.7: abs., *fall away*, *Ep.Hebr.*6.6. **V.** *fall down before, cringe, flatter*, παραπεπτωκῶς D.45.84. **VI.** Astrol., *to be unfavourably situated*, Vett.Val.5.5, 27.18.

**παραπιστεύω**, = πιστεύω, Hld.6.8 (καταπ- cj. Coraës).

**παραπιτνάω**, = παραπετάννυμι, *Michel*832.20 (Samos, iv B.C.).

⊛ **παρα-πλάγιάζω**, *go obliquely*, v.l. in Lxx1*Ki.*23.26, Hsch.:—Med., π. τῇ πληγῇ *present oneself obliquely* to.., Sch.Od.5.440. **-πλάγιος** [ᾰ], ον, *sidelong, oblique*, Thphr.*HP*4.12.2.

**παραπλάζω**, used by Hom. in aor. Act. παρέπλαγξα and Pass. -επλάγχθην:—*cause to wander from the right way*, of seamen, *drive out of their course*, ἀλλά με.. Βορέης παρέπλαγξε Κυθήρων Od.9.81, cf. 19.187: metaph., *lead astray, perplex*, παρέπλαγξεν δὲ νόημα 20.346; αἱ φρενῶν ταραχαὶ παρέπλαγξαν καὶ σοφόν Pi.*O.*7.31:—Pass., παρεπλάγχθη δέ οἱ ἄλλῃ ἰὸς χαλκοβαρής the arrow *went aside*, Il.15.464; ποῖ παρεπλάγχθην γνώμης ἀγαθῆς; E.*Hipp.*240: abs., *err, be wrong*, Pi.*N.*10.6. **II.** Act. intr., *go astray*, κραδίη παραπλάζουσα μέμηνε Nic.*Th.*757.

**παραπλᾰνάομαι**, Pass., = foreg., Sch.A.*Eu.*104: intr. in Act., Sch.Ar.*Eq.*806.

**παρά-πλασμα**, ατος, τό, *piece of coloured wax stuck on to the margin* of books, to mark doubtful or obscure passages, Hsch. **II.** *monster*, Suid. s.v. τέρας. **-πλασμός**, ὁ, *change of grammatical form*, S.E.*M.*1.176. **II.** *wax used to stop the holes of flutes*, Hsch. **-πλάσσω**, Att. -ττω, *transform*, in fut. Med. -πλάσομαι S.E.*M.*1.208:—Pass., *receive another form*, Hero *Spir.*1 *Prooem.* **II.** Med., *append*, παραπλάσασθαι τῇ τοῦ γεννηθέντος ὥρᾳ τὰ κατ' οὐρανὸν βλεπόμενα S.E.*M.*5.70, cf. Phld.*Rh.*1.6 S. **-πλαστος**, ον, *counterfeit*, Sosith.2.4 ap.Tz.*H.*2.596; *forged*, διαθήκη *BGU*592.10 (ii A.D.).

**παρά-πλεγμα**, ατος, τό, *basket-work for a chariot*, Hsch. s.v. θέργυνον. **-πλεκτέον**, *one must mix with* medicine, Aët.5.131, Paul.Aeg.2.57. **-πλέκω**, *braid* or *weave in*, Hp.*Vict.*1.14: metaph., μύθους Str.1.2.35:—Pass., *to be woven into*, τῇ δραματουργίᾳ τοῦτο παραπέπλεκται Id.1.2.27; τὸ μηδ' ὅλως ἐν τῷ κόσμῳ μηδαμοῦ -πεπλέχθαι κενόν Gal.4.474. **II.** *braid* or *curl along the forehead*, τὰς τρίχας Poll.2.35; π. ἑαυτόν *becurl* himself, Plu.2.785e:—Med., παραπλέκεσθαι Ael.*NA*16.11; παραπεπλεγμένη Ἀθηνᾶ ἢ ἀναπεπλεγμένη Poll. l.c. **III.** *mix with* medicines, Ruf.ap.Orib.8.39.5, Philum.ap. eund.45.29.45, Gal.11.88; so of pigments, τὸ ξανθὸν τῷ κυανῷ π. Procop.Gaz.p.157 B.

**παραπλευρ-ίδια**, τά, *covers for the sides of war-horses*, X.*Cyr.*6.4.1, Arr.*Tact.*4.1. ⊛ **-ιος**, ον, *at* or *in the side* of anything, θύρα Tz.*H.*5.843. **-όω**, *cover on the sides with* a thing, τινι Philostr.*VA*3.35.

**παραπλευστέος**, α, ον, *that must be sailed past*, Str.8.3.27.

**παραπλέω**, Ion. -πλώω Orph.*A.*733, 1271: Ep. aor. 2 παρέπλων (v. infr.):—*sail by* or *past*, abs., οἴη δὴ κείνῃ γε παρέπλω.. Ἀργώ was the only ship that *sailed through* that way, Od.12.69, cf. X.*An.*5.1.11; ἐν χρῷ παραπλέοντες *sailing close in*, Th.2.84, cf. 90; π. παρὰ τὰς πρῴρας τῶν νεῶν Hdt.7.100; π. τὴν Ἔφεσον *sail past* Ephesus, *Act.Ap.*20.16. **2.** *coast by* or *along*, ὃς τῆς Ἀττικῆς ταῦτα μὴ -πέπλωκε Hdt.4.99, cf. Isoc.15.123; ἐς Σικυῶνα Th.1.111; ἐνθένδε μὲν εἰς Σινώπην π., ἐκ Σινώπης δὲ εἰς Ἡράκλειαν X.*An.*5.6.10, cf. D.35.31; ἐκεῖθεν X.*HG*5.4.61; π. ἀπὸ κάλω, v. κάλως. **3.** metaph., π. τὰς συμφορὰς *sail past, escape* them, Amphis 3.4.

**παραπληγίη, παραπληγικός**, Ion. for παραπληξία, παραπληκτικός.

**παρα-πληκτεύομαι**, *to be mad*, Aq.1*Ki.*21.14(15), 15(16). **-πληκτικός**, Ion. -πληγικός, ή, όν, *suffering from hemiplegia*, παραπληκτικοὺς ποιέουσι τοὺς ἀνθρώπους Hp.*Aër.*3; τὰ -πληγικά Id.*Epid.*1.12; π. τρόπον ib.26.ιγ'. Adv. -κῶς Id.*Coac.*60. **2.** = sq., Antioch. Astr. in *Cat.Cod.Astr.*7.112. **-πληκτος**, Dor. -πλακτος, ον, *frenzy-stricken*, χείρ S.*Aj.*230 (lyr.); ὀμφά Melanipp.4.4; *mad*, Lxx *De.*28.34. **II.** = foreg., π. τὰ δεξιὰ ἢ τὰ ἀριστερά Hp.*Aër.*10. ⊛ **-πλήξ**, ῆγος, ὁ, ἡ, *stricken sideways* or *aslant*, ἠϊόνες π. a *retreating* beach, on which the waves *break obliquely*, Od.5.418. **II.** metaph., = παράπληκτος, *mad*, Hdt.5.92.ζ', Ar.*Pl.*242, X.*Oec.*1.13, Demetr.*Eloc.*275. **2.** *paralysed*, Hp.*Acut.*(*Sp.*)7. **3.** pl., *paralyses*, Id.*Morb.*1.3, Aret.*CA*1.4. ⊛ **-πληξία**, Ion. -πληγίη, ἡ, *hemiplegia* (opp. ἀποπληξία), Hp.*Epid.*1.14, 2.3.1 (both pl.), *IG*12(9).1179 (Euboea, ii A.D.). **II.** *derangement, madness*, Lxx*De.*28.28, al., Ph.2.556, Oenom.ap.Eus.*PE*5.22.

**παραπληρ-όω**, *fill up*, δικαστήρια εἰς ἕνα καὶ διακοσίους *IG*2².1629.206 (nisi leg. παρα[κλ]ηρῶσαι). **II.** Gramm., *fill up*, of an expletive particle, Trypho ap.A.D.*Conj.*247.25; σύνδεσμον παραπληροῦντα τὴν φάσιν Dam.*Pr.*300. **III.** Geom., in Pass., παραπληρωθεισῶν τῶν πλευρῶν *being completed also*, Arist.*Mech.*848ᵇ28. **-ωμα**, ατος, τό, *expletive*, ὀνομάτων π. words and phrases of such kind, D.H.*Dem.*39, cf. 19; λέξεων Id.*Isoc.*3. **II.** Geom., *complement* of a parallelogram, Euc.1.43, etc. **III.** = *sagina*, *Gloss.* **-ωματικός**, ή, όν, *expletive*, σύνδεσμοι Demetr.*Eloc.*55, D.T.642.27, A.D.*Conj.*247.22, al. Adv. -κῶς Id.*Synt.*307.18 (s.v.l.), Hellad.ap.Phot.*Bibl.*p.532 B., Eust.72.32. **-ωσις**, εως, ἡ, *filling up*, Anon.*Trop.*10, Eust.467.13.

**παραπλήσιος**, α, ον Hdt.1.202, 4.128, Isoc.7.78, etc.; also ος, ον Th.1.84, Plb.1.37.8:—*coming alongside of*: hence, *coming near, nearly resembling*; of numbers, *nearly equal, about as many*; of size, *about as large*; of age, *about equal*; etc.: **1.** abs., Hdt.4.128, etc.; τοιαῦτα καὶ π. such and *such-like*, Th.1.22; τὰς πράξεις ὁμοίας καὶ π. ἀποβαίνειν Isoc. l.c.; ταὐτόν ἐστι σοφιστὴς καὶ ῥήτωρ, ἢ ἐγγύς τι καὶ παραπλήσιον Pl.*Grg.*520a; ναυσὶ παραπλησίαις τὸν ἀριθμόν Th.7.70; ἱππεῖς π. τὸ πλῆθος X.*HG*4.3.15; ἀγωνίζεσθαι πρὸς π. ἱππέας Id.*Eq.Mag.*8.17. **2.** freq. c. dat., ἐν τῇ ναυμαχίῃ παραπλήσιοι ἀλλήλοισι ἐγίνοντο were *about equal*, of a drawn battle, Hdt.8.16; νῆσοι Λέσβῳ μεγάθεα παραπλήσιαι Id.1.202; ἐσθὴς τῇ Κορινθίῃ παραπλησιωτάτη Id.5.87; π. τούτῳ καὶ ὅμοιον D.19.196; ὅμοι' ἢ π. τούτοις ib.307: with dat. of the person for dat. of that which belongs to the person, ἔπαθε παραπλήσια τούτῳ Hdt.4.78, cf. Plb.1.14.2, etc.: rarely c. gen., Id.1.23.6; ἦχος συριγμοῦ π. Philum.*Ven.*21.1 (in Pl.*Sph.*217b the gen. ὧν is due to the attraction). **3.** folld. by a relat., τρόπῳ παραπλησίῳ, τῷ καὶ Μασσαγέται Hdt.4.172; by καί, Λυδοὶ νόμοισι π. χρέωνται καὶ Ἕλληνες Id.1.94, cf. Th.5.112, 7.71; also π. πάσχουσιν ὥσπερ ἂν εἰ.. Isoc.1.27: neut. παραπλήσια as Adv., π. ὡς εἰ.., *perinde ac si*.., Hdt.4.99: sg., παραπλήσιον καὶ οὐ πολλῷ πλέον *about the same distance* and not much more, Th.7.19; τὸ π. D.S.19.43: more freq. regul. Adv. -ίως, Pl.*Ap.*37a, al.; ἆρά γ' ὁμοίως ἢ π.; D.3.27; ἀγωνισάμενοι π. having fought *with nearly equal advantage*, Hdt.1.77; π. τοῖς εἰρημένοις πράττοντας Isoc.5.51, etc.; π. καὶ.., Lat. *perinde ac*.., Hdt.7.119; π. ἔχει καθάπερ.. Pl.*Ep.*321a: Comp. παραπλησιαίτερον Id.*Plt.*275c.

**παραπλήσσω**, Att. -ττω, *strike at the side*, τὰς νευράς, of a harper, Philostr.*Im.*1.10:—Pass., *to be palsy-stricken*: hence, *to be deranged, mad*, Ar.*Lys.*831, *Ec.*139, etc.; γέλως παραπεπληγμένος E.*HF*935; π. τὸν λογισμόν Plu.*Aem.*34; παραπλήσσεσθαί τι *to be astonished at*.., Agatharch.103.

**παραπλόκᾰμος**, ον, *having curls at the sides*, Hsch.

**παραπλοκή**, ἡ, *weaving in*, τοῦ στήμονος *EM*498.9: metaph., *intertwining*, τῶν ποιημάτων ἐν λόγῳ (i.e. of poetical quotations in Prose) Hermog.*Id.*2.4 (pl.). **II.** *intermingling*, S.E.*M.*1.95; *admixture*, κενοῦ Erasistr.ap.Gal.4.475; ὑγροῦ Dsc.5.79; νάπυος Xenocr.ap.Orib.2.58.146.

⊛ **παραπλομένοισι**· παροῦσι, Hsch.

**παράπλοος**, contr. -πλους, ὁ, *coasting voyage*, τῆς Ἰταλίας καλῶς παράπλου κεῖται Th.1.36; ἐν παράπλῳ κεῖσθαι ib.44, cf. 2.33, etc.; simply, *passage*, *POxy.*525.1 (ii A.D.), Luc.*VH*1.28. **2.** *shore to be coasted along*, π. τραχὺς Πλατανιστὸς καλούμενος Str.14.5.3, cf. 14.3.2; ὁ π. αὐτοῦ (sc. of the Red Sea) ἔχει νήσους μικράς D.S.3.38. **II.** Adj. *fit for coasting*, π. ποιησάμενος τοὺς Σιδητῶν παρῶνας Plb.*Fr.*193.

**παράπλωμα**, ατος, τό, (ἁπλόω) *curtain*, Suid. s.v. παραπέτασμα.

**παραπλώω**, Ion. for παραπλέω.

**παραπνέω**, *blow beside, escape by a sideway*, of the winds confined by Aeolus, Od.10.24; *blow beside* or *next to*, c. acc., ὁ Ἀπηλιώτης ἔχει παραπνέοντας αὐτὸν τὸν Εὖρον καὶ τὸν Καικίαν *Gp.*1.11.2. **2.** *admit the air*, παραπνευσάσης τῆς σικύας Hero *Spir.*1 *Prooem.*:—Pass., ὡς μηδαμόθι -πνεῖσθαι Gal.6.577. **II.** *have a slight smell* or *whiff of* a thing, τινος Dsc.1.19.3.

**παραπνοή**, ἡ, *passage, opening*, τῷ ὕδατι Hp.*Nat.Puer.*25, cf. *Gp.*10.56.6.

**παραποδ-ίζω**, *entangle the feet, fetter, tether*: hence, generally, *hinder, impede*, Plb.2.28.8, 18.31.6:—Pass., *to be entangled, hampered*, Pl.*Lg.*652b, *Ep.*330b, Plb.16.4.10, Gal.9.575; τῶν αἰσθήσεων -πεποδισμένων Metrod.*Herc.*831.5; π. εἴς or πρός τι, S.E.*M.*1.171, 193; τὴν ῥύμην τοῦ δρόμου Hld.10.30. **-ιος**, poet. παρπ-, ον, *at the feet*, i.e. *imminent*, φόνος Pi.*N.*9.38. **-ισμός**, ὁ, *hindering*, τῶν χρειῶν Artem.3.42, cf. Meno *Iatr.*6.9, Gal.19.386; ἕξεως, ψυχῆς π., Hierocl.p.21 A., Iamb.*Protr.*21. **-ιστός**, ή, όν, *impeded, obstructed*, Arr.*Epict.*1.25.3.

**παραπο-δύομαι**, Med., *pull off one's clothes, strip so as to compare oneself with others*, Pl.*Tht.*162b. ⊛ **-θνήσκω**, = παραπόλλυμαι, cj. in D.C.*Fr.*102.11.

**παραποι-έω**, *make falsely*, π. μέτρα καὶ σταθμά *make false* measures and weights, D.S.1.78; οἱ παραποιοῦντες *forgers*, Just.*Nov.*73 *Praef.*; παραποιησάμενος σφραγῖδα *having got a false* seal *made*, Th.1.132 (nisi leg. παρασημηνάμενος, cf. Poll.8.27); π. βίον ἀνθρώπου *falsify* his record, Philostr.*VA*2.30. **2.** *alter slightly*, τὸ ὄνομα, τὴν λέξιν, Paus.5.10.

1, Jul.*Or.*2.70a; τὰ παραπεποιημένα, e.g. τὰ παρὰ γράμμα σκώμματα, Arist.*Rh.*1412ᵃ28. 3. *adopt as one's own by altering, imitate*, Ath. 12.513a: abs., *make a parody*, D.Chr.32.81:—Pass., παρ' ὑπόνοιαν παραποιηθὲν ἐκ.. Sch.Ar.*Pl.*782: abs., *PLond.*3.854.5 (ii A.D.). II. *introduce as an episode* into a poem, κατὰ (= καθ' ἃ) παρεποίησε (prob. for κατὰ γὰρ ἐποίησε) Hdt.2.116, cf. *POxy.*1611.165,175 (prob. l.). ⊕ -ησις, εως, ἡ, *imitation, adulteration*, Gal.14.62, al.; *forgery*, Just.*Nov.*73 *Praef.*; *slight alteration*, ὀνόματος Phoeb.*Fig.*1.3, cf. Eust. 1403.60.

**παραπο-λαύω**, *share the fruits of*, τῆς τιμωρίας Ph.2.15; τῆς ἐνίων κακοβουλίας J.*BJ*2.16.4; τῆς τινων μωρίας Luc.*Alex.*45; παραπολαύειν ἐστὶ τῆς τοῦ εἴδους ὑποστάσεως τὴν ἔκπτωσιν Dam.*Pr.*7.

**παραπόλλυμι**, *destroy, consume* or *spend to no purpose, waste, lose*, τὸ ναῦλον Plu.2.439e, cf. Gal.*UP*12.5; καιρὸν Charito 1.7; ἡλικίαν τὴν ἐκ τῆς Ἰταλίας D.C.74.2:—more freq. in Med. and Pass., with pf. 2 παραπόλωλα, *perish*, παραπολεῖ βοώμενος Ar.*V.*1228; παραπόλωλεν ἡ τέχνη Dionys.Com.2.35; ἠτίμωται καὶ παραπόλωλεν D.21.91; ἀκαρὴς παραπόλωλας Men.835; ὁ βίος μελλησμῷ παραπόλλυται Epicur.*Sent. Vat.*14; λιμῷ παραπολοῦμαι *PCair.Zen.*160.5 (iii B.C.), cf. *PPetr.*3 p.74 (iii B.C.), Sor.1.31; οἷος τεχνίτης παραπόλλυμαι, = *qualis artifex pereo!* D.C.63.29.

**παραπολύ**, Adv. *by much, by far*, Hp.*Art.*7; π. ἔλασσον Dsc.3.80: better divisim παρὰ πολύ.

**παραπομένω**, *remain with*, Lyd.*Mag.*1.12, 2.13.

**παραπομπ-εύω**, = παραπέμπω, νῆα Sch.Opp.*H.*1.186. ⊕ -ή, ἡ, *conveying*, σίτου Decr.ap.D.18.73; ἡ κατὰ θάλασσαν π. Onos.6.14. 2. *escort, convoy*, π. δώσειν Arist.*Oec.*1351ᵇ24; πέμψαι, ἐξαποστέλλειν, Plb.30.9.13, 15.5.7; παραπομπῆς τυχεῖν D.S.20.45, cf. *PSI*5.446.12 (ii A.D.): pl., παραπομπαὶ ὄχλων Ph.1.592; of a funeral *procession*, π. καὶ κηδεία *IG*12(7).239.32 (Amorgos); of athletes, *being escorted* by a body of supporters, Charito 6.2. II. *transport, conveyance*, αἱ τῶν καρπῶν π., whether by importation or exportation, Arist.*Pol.*1327ᵃ8; ἑκάστης ἡμέρας π. ἐγίγνοντο *supplies* were introduced, X.*HG*7.2.23; π. ποιεῖν τῶν ἰχθύων Antiph.190.15; παραπέμψαι τὴν π. X.*HG*7.2.18; συμπαραπέμπειν τὴν εἰς Φλιοῦντα π. Aeschin.2.168. 2. *production*, ἡ ἔξω π. *bringing forth* the statue from the mould, Ph.2.318. ⊕ -ικά, τά, *expenses of transport*, Just.*Nov.*128.9. -ιμος, ον, *attending, escorting*, epith. of Hermes, Sch.E.*Med.*759. ⊕-ός, όν, = foreg., π. νῆες ships *attending as convoy*, Plb.1.52.5, cf. 15.2.6. 2. *purveyor*, *POxy.*1844.1 (vi A.D.). II. (proparox.) = παράνυμφος, Hsch. s.v. πάροχοι.

⊕ **παραπόντιος**, ον, *beside* or *near the sea*, *AP*7.71 (Gaet.).

**παραπορεύομαι**, with fut. Med. and aor. Pass., *go beside* or *alongside*, Arist.*HA*577ᵇ31; παρὰ τὰ ὑποζύγια Plb.6.40.7; of παιδαγωγοί, D.H.7.9: metaph., ἀκρόαμα οὐδὲν παρεπορεύετο *accompanied* the meal, Phylarch.44 J. codd. Ath. II. *go past, pass by*, *PPetr.*2 p.36 (iii B.C.); τὸν χάρακα Plb.3.99.5; παρὰ τὸ χεῖλος Id.3.14.6; ὑπὸ λόφον τινὰ Id.2.27.5; διὰ τῶν σπορίμων *Ev.Marc.*2.23 (v.l. διαπ-), cf. 9.30; of stars, *pass through* the zodiac, *Cat.Cod.Astr.*8(4).210.

**παραπορθμεύω**, *convey* goods *across* a lake, *CIG*4302a (Myra).

⊕ **παραπόρφῠρος**, ον, *edged with purple*, Poll.7.46, 10.42; τὰ π. τῶν ἰσχίων Alciphr.1.39.

**παραποτάμιος**, α, ον, also ος, ον D.S.3.8, *beside* or *near a river, lying* or *dwelling on a river*, πόλις Hdt.2.60; πεδίον E.*Ba.*874 (lyr.); [χώρα] D.S.l.c., Hld.10.1; Παραποτάμιοι, name of a city in Phocis on the Cephisus, Hdt.8.33; π. ζῷον, of the elephant, opp. ποτάμιον ζ., Arist.*HA*630ᵇ26; τὰ π., of plants, Thphr.*HP*3.2.4, 4.5.6.

**παραποφαίνομαι**, fut. inf. -φανεῖσθαι, dub. in Luc.*Nav.*35 (leg. ὕπαρ ἀπο-).

**παράπρᾶσις**, εως, ἡ, *sale below cost price*, παρασχόμενος -πρασιν τῶν ἐν τῇ ἀγορᾷ πωλουμένων *BCH*11.307 (Caria, i A.D.), cf. Ἀρχ.Δελτ.2. 148 (Beroea): pl., παραπράσεις ποιήσαντα ἐν τῷ μακέλλῳ *Inscr.Magn.* 179.20.

**παραπράσσω**, Att. -ττω, Ion. -πρήσσω, *do* a thing *beside* or *beyond* the main purpose, Hdt.5.45; οὔτε πολυπραγμονῶν οὔτε π. D.C. 76.7. II. *help in doing*, μηδενὸς ἄλλου παραπράξαντος S.*Aj.*261 (anap.). III. *act unjustly*, esp. *exact money illegally*, Plu.*Agis* 16:—Pass., Wilcken *Chr.*238.6 (ii A.D.), etc.

**παραπρεσβ-εία**, ἡ, *faithless* or *dishonest embassy*, D.21.5; περὶ τῆς π., title of speeches by D. and Aeschin.; παραπρεσβείας κατακριθέντες Phld.*Rh.*2.224 S. -ευτής, οῦ, ὁ, *dishonest ambassador*, Sch.Ar. *Nu.*691. -εύω, *execute an embassy faithlessly* or *dishonestly*, D.19. 191, *SIG*167.5 (Mylasa, iv B.C.); πρεσβείαν π. Aeschin.2.94:—more freq. in Med. -εύομαι, Pl.*Lg.*941a, Isoc.18.22; εἰς Αἴγυπτον D.24. 127.

**παράπρημα**, ατος, τό, in pl., *swellings on horses' legs*, *PCair.Zen.* 225.3 (iii B.C.); later **παραπρήσματα**, *Hippiatr.*77.

**παράπρῖσις**, εως, ἡ, perh. *swelling, inflammation*, Aët.6.27 (leg. -πρησις).

**παράπρισμα**, ατος, τό, *sawdust, filings*, in pl., ἐλέφαντος, ἐβένου, *Inscr.Délos* 298*A* 181, 320*B*68 (iii B.C.): metaph., παραπρίσματ' ἐπῶν Ar.*Ra.*881.

**παραπρό-ειμι** (εἶμι *ibo*), part. -ιών, *go forward*, *Lyr.Alex.Adesp.* 20.8. -θεσμία, ἡ, *missing the due time*, Sch.Luc.*Tox.*44. -λέγω, *prophesy falsely*, Sm.*Je.*29(36).26. -νοέω, *consider beforehand*, Hsch.

**παραπροσ-δέχομαι**, *admit heedlessly*, Arr.*Epict.*1.20.11. -έχω, *pay attention to*, τισι *PGen.*75.10 (iii/iv A.D.); τῷ ἔργῳ *POxy.*1493.12 (iii/iv A.D.). -ποιέομαι, *dissemble*, *Cod.Just.*1.4.34.15; π. τὸν νόμον *pretend ignorance of* the law, Just.*Nov.*113.3. -ποίησις, εως, ἡ, *dissimulation*, *Cod.Just.*1.4.34.15, *Gloss.*

**παραπροστάτης** [στᾰ], ου, Dor. -ας, ὁ, *assessor* or *secretary of a* προστάτης, *IG*14.952 (Acragas).

**παραπροσωπίς**, ίδος, ἡ, *mask*, Eust.1281.1.

**παραπροχέομαι**, Pass., *throw oneself beside*, παραπροχυθεῖσα δὲ πηγῇ Nonn.*D.*48.599.

**παραπρῠτᾰν-εύω**, *maladminister*, τὰ τῆς δικαιοσύνης ζυγὰ Rh.3. 608 W. -ις, εως, ὁ, perh. *colleague* or *assessor of a* πρύτανις, *CIG* 3168 (Smyrna, pl.).

**παρά-πταισμα**, ατος, τό, f.l. for παράπαισμα in Oenom.ap.Eus. *PE*5.25. -πταίω, *stumble by the way, blunder*, *Placit.*5.20.5 (fort. παραπεπαικότος), Al.*De.*22.1.

**παραπτερῠγίζω**, *fly beside*: metaph., *flatter*, Phot.

⊕ **παράπτομαι**, Med., *apply*, of ointments, Asclep.ap.Gal.12.584, 681, cf. 13.250, Aët.12.34:—Pass., χερσὶ παραπτομένα πλάτα *fitted to* the hands, *plied by* the hands, dub. l. in S.*OC*717 (lyr.); π. σανίδων *fixed along* planks, Apollod.*Poliorc.*173.15. II. Med., *touch in passing* or *slightly*, Men.66.4, Plu.*Cleom.*37; αὐτοῦ δακτύλῳ π. Sor. 1.108. 2. *touch by mistake*, *Hippiatr.*49. 3. *have dealings with*, γυναικὸς ἢ ἀνδρὸς *PMag.Par.*1.2173. 4. *approach*, τῆς εἰς τὸ νοσῶδες παρατροπῆς Apollon.ap.Orib.7.19.5.

**παραπτύω**, *spit out at the side*, Ael.ap.Ar.Byz.*Epit.*53.1; π. ἀφρόν *foam at the corners* of the mouth, Philostr.*VA*4.10; π. τοῦ μέλιτος *drop with* honey, Id.*Im.*1.31: metaph., *write carelessly*, Id.*VS*2.9.3; τοὺς τῶν σοφιστῶν ἐξ ἐπιδρομῆς μετὰ χάριτος παρέπτυσε βίους Eun.*VS* p.454 B. II. *reject scornfully*, Ph.1.488:—Pass., Call.*Hec.*1.3.2.

⊕ **παρά-πτωμα**, ατος, τό, *false step, slip, blunder*, Plb.9.10.6, Phld. *Herc.*1251.14 (pl.), Longin.36.2. 2. *defeat*, D.S.19.100. 3. *transgression, trespass*, Lxx *Ez.*14.13, al., *Ev.Matt.*6.14, *Ep.Gal.*6.1, al. 4. *error in amount of payments*, *PTeb.*5.91 (ii B.C.). -πτωσις, εως, ἡ, *falling beside, lying side by side*, Arist.*GA*718ᵃ28. II. *falling from the right way*, π. τοῦ καθήκοντος Plb.15.23.5: abs., = παράπτωμα 1, Id.16.20.5, Lxx *Je.*22.21, Phld.*Lib.*p.17 O.; grammatical *mistake*, S.E.*M.*1.210. III. ἡ τοῦ τόπου π. the *situation* of a place *off the road*, Plb.4.32.5. IV. κατὰ ⟨τὴν⟩ τοῦ διώγματος π. in the *course* of.., Id.11.17.3; κατὰ τὴν ἐπὶ τοὺς Κελτοὺς π. as they were *pursuing*, Id.3.115.11.

**παραπύημα**, ατος, τό, *suppuration*, Hp.*Mochl.*5 (pl.).

**παραπύθια** [ῠ], τά, Com. word, *sickness which prevented one from being victor at the* Πύθια, *AP*11.129 (Cereal.); cf. παρίσθμια.

**παραπυΐσκω**, impers. in infin., *suppuration begins*, Hp.*Epid.*4. 11.

**παράπυκνος**, ὁ, name of the foot ⏑ – ⏑ ⏑ ⏑, Diom.p.481 K.

**παρα-πύλιον** [ῠ], τό, *side-gate, wicket*, *IG*5(1).538.18 (pl.). -πυλίς, ίδος, ἡ, = foreg., Hld.8.12.

**παράπυξος**, ον, *veneered with boxwood*, κλίνη Cratin.47.

**παραπωλέω**, = παραπιπράσκω, π. ἔλαιον ἀφθόνως ἔλαττον παρὰ πολὺ τῆς ἐνεστώσης τιμῆς *Inscr.Magn.*179.25, cf. *SIG*708.39 (Istropolis, ii B.C.). II. *sell unlawfully*, *PTeb.*38.4, al. (ii B.C.).

**παραπωμάζω**, *cover with a lid*, v.l. for περι-, Arist.*Juv.*470ᵃ9.

**παραρθρ-έω**, *to be partially dislocated*, ἄρθρον παραρθρῆσαν Hp.*Art.* 17 codd., cf. Apollon.Cit.2, Gal.*UP*12.10, 15.7, Heliod.ap.Orib.49. 14.7. II. trans., *dislocate*, v.l. in Pl.*Ax.*367b. -ημα, ατος, τό, *subluxation*, Gal.18(1).666, Heliod.ap.Orib.48.65.3. -ησις, εως, ἡ, *dislocation*, Plu.*Comp.Cim.Luc.*2; *subluxation*, Gal.6.870. -όω, = παραρθρέω II, Pl.*Ax.*367b (codd. Stob.).

**παραριγόω**, v. παραρριγόω.

**παρᾰριθμ-έω**, *reckon in*, τὰς αἶγάς τινι *PSI*6.596.5 (iii B.C.), cf. Ph. 1.613, *PStrassb.*116.13 (i A.D.). 2. *count over, check* items in an inventory, *PMich.Zen.*31.12 (iii B.C.), *IG*11(2).163*Bg*19 (Delos, iii B.C.), *SIG*874*A*5 (Delph., ii A.D.), v.l. in Lxx *To.*9.5. 3. *pay over*, τοὺς λόγους -ούμενοι καὶ -οῦντες *receiving* and *giving in payment*, Plu.2.78f. II. *deceive in counting*: generally, *cheat*, τινα *Stoic.*3.147 (Act. and Pass.). -ησις, εως, ἡ, *false reckoning*, Chrysipp.*Stoic.*2.41.

**παραρίπτω**, v. παραρρίπτω. **πάραρμα**, v. παραίρημα. **πάρᾱρος**, ον, v. παρήορος III. **παράρους**, v. παράρροος.

**παραρπάζω**, *filch away*, *AP*11.153 (Lucill.).

**παραρρᾱθῡμέω**, *to be neglectful of*, τῆς φυλακῆς D.S.14.116.

**παραρραίνω**, *sprinkle in passing*, Posidon.20 J.

**παράρραμμα**, v. παράρρυμα.

**παραρράπτομαι**, Pass., *to be sewn as a fringe along*, Hdt.4.109. 2. of bandages, *to be sewn on*, Gal.18(2).917.

**παραρρέγχω**, *snore beside* or *near*, Lucil.*Fr.*1223 Marx.

⊕ **παραρρέω**, aor. -ερρύην (v. infr.): pf. -ερρύηκα (v. infr.):—*flow beside, by*, or *past*, τὴν Νίνον Hdt.2.150; τὰς Πλαταιὰς Str.9.2.31; παρὰ πόλιν Hdt.6.20, etc.: abs., Hp.*Aër.*6: prov., ὕδωρ παραρρέει, of those who promise to spare no effort, Cratin.60, cf. Lib.*Ep.*109.2. II. *slip off* or *out*, εἴ τί μοι τόξων..παρερρύηκεν S.*Ph.*653; ὅτῳ μὴ παραρρυείη [ἡ χιών] whom it did not *slip off*, X.*An.*4.4.11: metaph., πολλὰ ὑμῖν παρέρρει many points *escaped* you, Pl.*Lg.*781a; φιλοσοφίαν καὶ ῥητορικὴν παρερρυηκυίας *having disappeared from memory*, *Gp.Prooem.*4. 2. of persons, π. τῶν φρενῶν *slip away from* one's senses, Eup.357.6; also, *to be careless, neglect* advice, etc., υἱὲ μὴ παραρρυῇς Lxx *Pr.*3.21; μήποτε παραρρυῶμεν *Ep.Hebr.*2.1. III. *run off*, Arist.*Pr.*866ᵃ9; π. παρὰ (v.l. πρὸς) τὴν ἀρτηρίαν *slip* into the windpipe, Id.*PA*664ᵇ29. 2. *slip in unawares* or *by stealth*, λόγοι παρερρυήκασι πρὸς ἡμᾶς ψευδεῖς D.13.16; παραρρυεὶς ἄνθρωπος εἰς τὸν νεῶν Plu.2.969e; ὅθεν παρερρύηκεν ὁ τοιοῦτος λόγος Theon *Prog.*6; εἴ τι ἐν τῷ τῆς ποιήσεως δρόμῳ παραρρυὲν λάθῃ any irregularity which *slips in*, Luc.*Hes.*5. IV. φωναὶ σαθραὶ καὶ παρερρυηκυῖαι cracked and *unsteady*, Arist.*Aud.*804$^{a}$32.

**παρα-ρρήγνυμι** or -ύω (Plu.*Fab.*19), *break at the side*, esp. *break* a line of battle, Th.4.96; π. τοῦ πύργου μέρος *make a breach in* it, Polyaen.2.27.2:—Pass., *to be broken*, Th.5.73, 6.70, Arr.*An.*2.22.7, 4.26.5. 2. metaph., *break through, violate*, τὸν νόμον Them. *Or.*15.190b, cf. *Or.*16.212d. II. Pass., with pf. 2 παρέρρωγα, *break* or *burst at the side*, παρέρρωγεν ποδὸς φλέψ S.*Ph.*824; χιτωνίου παραρραγέντος Ar.*Ra.*414 (lyr.); τὰ παρερρωγότα τῆς ὀρεινῆς *broken ground, ravines*, Plu.*Alex.*17; τὸ παρερρωγὸς τοῦ στρατεύματος Arr. *An.*2.11.1. 2. φωνὴ παρερρωγυῖα *broken* (by passion), Thphr.*Char.* 6.7; so τραχυνόμενον τῇ φωνῇ καὶ παραρρηγνύμενον Plu.*TG*2. -ρρηξις, εως, ἡ, *breaking* of a line of battle, Arr.*An.*2.11.7.

**παρά-ρρησις**, εως, ἡ, *incorrect expression*, Plu.2.994d (pl.). -ρρητός, ή, όν, of persons, *that may be moved by words*, π. ἐπέεσσιν Il. 9.526. II. of words, *persuasive*, παραρρητοῖσι πιθέσθαι 13.726.

**παρριγόω**, 2 sg. fut. παρᾰριγώσεις, *freeze beside* or *near*, τινι *AP* 5.42 (Rufin.).

**παραρρινάω**, *clip* coin, [τετράδραχμον] παρερρινημένον *IG*11(2).158 *A*5 (Delos, iii B.C.).

**παραρρίπτω**, later -έω Lxx *Ps.*83(84).10, Alciphr.3.51, and in late Poets **παρᾰρίπτω**, *AP*9.174,441 (both Pall.):—*throw, cast*: metaph., *run the risk* of doing a thing, c. part., π. λαμβάνων ὀνείδη S.*OT*1493 codd. 2. c. acc. rei, *hazard*, λεπταῖς ἐπὶ ῥοπῇσιν ἐμπολὰς μακράς Id.*Fr.*555.5; π. σώματα τοῖς κινδύνοις *expose* them.., D.S.13.79. II. *throw down* or *aside*, ὀστέα καθάπερ τοῖς κυσὶ παραρριπτοῦντες Alciphr. l.c., cf. *AP*6.74 (Agath.):—more freq. in Pass., παραρριπτεῖσθαι ἐν τῷ οἴκῳ τοῦ θεοῦ Lxx *Ps.*83(84).10; τῆς θυγατρὸς παρερριμμένης J.*AJ* 19.2.4, cf. Jul.*Or.*7.229c, *AP*9.174,441 (both Pall.). 2. *utter*, in Pass., οὐ μάτην αὐτῷ παρέρριπται τὸ εἰπεῖν Sch.Pi.*P.*1.3. 3. *admit*, τινὰ ἐπὶ ἱερατείαν Lxx 1*Ki.*2.36.

**παραρροή**, ἡ, *effusion*, Poll.4.203.

**παραρροιζέομαι**, Pass., *whizz past*, J.*BJ*5.2.2.

**παράρροος**, ον, in acc. pl. παράρους κεραμίδας, prob. *rainpipes, gutters*, *Inscr.Délos* 439*b*22, 442*A*226 (ii B.C.).

⊕ **παράρρυθμος**, ον, *out of time* (ῥυθμός), corrupt in Ar.*Th.*121 (ubi παράρυθμος); of the pulse, *irregular*, Ruf.*Syn.Puls.*7.4, Gal.8.516, al. II. *in time* or *measure*, Orph.*H.*31.3 (παράρυθμοι).

**παραρρῠ́σκομαι**, *slip into*, τῇ φράσει Eust.1074.4.

⊕ **παράρρῡμα** or **παράρῡμα**, ατος, τό, (ἐρύω A) *anything drawn along* or *over something*: 1. *leathern* or *hair curtain, stretched along* the sides of ships to protect the men, X.*HG*1.6.19, *IG*2$^{2}$.1629.451, 1668. 86, al., Moschio ap.Ath.5.208c (Casaubon for παρατρήματα), Lxx *Ex.* 35.11. 2. π. ποδός *covering* for the foot, S.*Fr.*527. 3. pl., of *fasteners* for bandages, Gal.18(2).748 (nisi leg. παραρραμμάτων).

**παραρρῡπόω**, *mark with the* παράπλασμα, in pf. part. Pass. παρερρυπωμένος, Hsch.

**παράρρῡσις**, εως, ἡ, = παράρρυμα I, A.*Supp.*715 (pl.).

**παραρτ-άω**, *hang alongside, to*, or *upon*, Ael.*NA*1.2; ξιφίδιον ἐκ τῆς ὀροφῆς Plu.2.844e:—Pass., μάχαιρα παρήρτητο Id.*Ant.*4; παρηρτῆσθαι μάχαιραν *to have* it *hung by one's side*, Ael.*NA*5.3; ξίφος παρηρτημένοι γυμνοῦ σώματος Hdn.3.14.8; π. πήραν Luc.*Peregr.*15; τὰ παρηρτημένα *parts appended*, Artemo 12. -έομαι, Ion. Verb (cf. ἀρτέομαι) only Med., I. trans., *fit out for oneself, get ready*, ἐπὶ τέσσερα ἔτεα παραρτέετο στρατιήν *was engaged in preparing*, Hdt.7.20, cf. 142, 8.76, 9.42; so π. τὰς νέας ὡς ἐς πλόον Arr.*Ind.*27.10. II. abs., *prepare, hold oneself in readiness*, παραρτέοντο ὡς ἀλεξησόμενοι Hdt.8. 108, cf. 81; πᾶς τις παρήρτητο ὡς ἐς πόλεμον Id.9.29. -ημα, ατος, τό, *anything hanging at the side, amulet, appendage*, Luc.*Philops.* 8. II. dub. sens. in *SIG*$^{2}$554.25 (Magn. Mae.). -ίδιον, τό, τοῦ αὐλυδρίου dub. sens. in Mitteis *Chr.*96.7 (iv A.D.). ⊕ -ίζομαι, Med., *prepare beside*, Hsch. -ῦμα, ατος, τό, *seasoning, condiment*, Ph.1.441, 679. -ῦσις, εως, ἡ, *preparing*, βελῶν M.Ant.(?) ap.Just.M.101e. II. *seasoning*, Ph.1.389, 604, etc. ⊕ -ύω, of food, *season*, Id.2.477, 483 (Pass.): metaph., ἱστορίαις π. τὴν ποίησιν Eust.100.30. II. Med., *get ready*, Plu.*Luc.*7.

**παράρυμα**, v. παράρρυμα. **παραρυμίς**· τὸ παρὰ τὸν ῥυμόν, Hsch. **παραρυτεῖν**· παρέχειν (fort. παραχεῖν), Id. **παρασαβάζω**, v. παραισαβάζω.

**παρασάγγης**, ου, ὁ, *parasang* (Persian *farsang*), containing thirty stades, Hdt.2.6, 5.53, 6.42, Arr.*An.*1.4.4; τέτταρες π. τῆς ὁδοῦ X.*An.* 1.10.1. II. *messenger*, S.*Frr.*125, 520, E.*Fr.*686, cf. Hsch. s. v. παρασαγγιλόγῳ (leg. παρασάγγῃ· ἀγγέλῳ).

**παρασαίνω**, *decoy*, βροτὸν εἰς ἄρκυας cj. in A.*Pers.*97 (lyr.).

**παρασᾰλεύω**, *shake to the foundations, sap, undermine*, metaph., νόμους παλαιούς Ph.2.69 (dub. l.); τὰ δικαίως τετυπωμένα Just.*Nov.* 135.1 *Ep.*; *upset, disturb* an agreement, *PLond.*1.113$^{5}$1 (vi A.D.):—Pass., *PLips.*34$^{r}$19 (iv A.D.).

**παράσαμον**, τό, Dor. for παράσημον.

**παρασᾰρόω**, *sweep beside* or *at the side*, Hsch.

**παρασάττω**, *stuff in beside*, τι παρά τι Hdt.6.125; λίθους γῇ *IG*7. 4255.27 (Oropus, iv B.C.).

**παράσειον**, τό, *topsail*, Callix.1, Luc.*Nav.*5.

⊕ **παράσειρος**, ον, (σειρά) *tied* or *fastened alongside*, π. ἵππος a horse *harnessed alongside* of the regular pair, = σειραφόρος, Poll.1.141, Them.*Or.*4.50a: metaph., *associate*, E.*Or.*1017 (lyr.). II. generally, *at the side*, X.*Cyn.*5.23, Ael.*NA*15.10; παράσειρα, τά, *parts on each side of the tongue*, Ruf.*Onom.*57, Poll.2.107, cf. περισείρια; δύο [πλευραὶ] π. two *lowest of the true ribs*, ib.182.

**παρά-σεισμα**, ατος, τό, *swinging of the arms* in running, Hp.*Vict.* 2.64. -σείω, *shake at the side*, τὰς χεῖρας *swing* one's arms in running, οἱ θέοντες θᾶττον θέουσι παρασείοντες τὰς χεῖρας Arist.*IA*705$^{a}$17: without χεῖρας, φεύγειν παρασείσας Id.*EN*1123$^{b}$31; ὁ δὲ θᾶττον θεῖ παρασείων ἢ μὴ π. Id.*Pr.*881$^{b}$6, cf. Thphr.*Char.*3.6; τοὺς δὲ ἄλλους παρασεσεικέναι *hurried to the spot*, prob. in *UPZ*119.30 (ii B.C.).

**παρασεσυρμένως**, Adv. pf. part. Pass., *mockingly*, Ph.2.599.

⊕ **παρασεύω**, *drive past*, aor. παρέσσ(ε)υα Hsch.:—Pass., *rush past*, παρεσσύμενοι Q.S.2.214, 8.44.

⊕ **παρασημ-αίνομαι**, Med., *set one's seal beside another's, counterseal*, τὰ σεσημασμένα παρασημηνάσθω Pl.*Lg.*954b. 2. *put one's seal on, seal up*, τὰ οἰκήματα D.42.2 (Pass., τὰ παρασεσημασμένα τῶν οἰκημάτων ib.26); παρασημήνασθαι.. τὰς διαθήκας, of the witnesses, *put their seals on* the will of the deceased, Id.28.5. b. *stamp on*, in Pass., θυμιατήριον ἵνα τὸ ἄλφα -σεσήμανται *IG*2$^{2}$.1425.95 (iv B.C.). 3. *note* or *mark in passing* (cf. παράσημον I), δόξας Arist.*Top.*105$^{b}$16: generally, *take note of*, Id.*Rh.*1397$^{a}$2, Plb.16.22.1. 4. *note* or *conclude from* a thing, τι ἔκ τινος Id.3.90.14. 5. *mark with musical notation*, μέλη, τὰ μεγέθη τῶν διαστημάτων, Aristox.*Harm.*p.39 M.: abs., ib. p.40 M. II. *mark falsely*, ἀργύριον παρασεσημασμένον Poll.3.86; [ὄνομα] π., of an incorrect word, Thom.Mag.p.204 R.; v. παραποιέω I. 1. III. later in Act., *betray by one's expression*, of animals, Phld. *D.*1.11. -αντέον, *one must note*, Eust.1451.63. -αντικός, ή, όν, *marking by symbols*: ἡ -κή (sc. τέχνη) *musical notation*, Aristox. *Harm.*p.39 M. -ασία, ἡ, *indication*, Ptol.*Tetr.*93, *Geog.*2.1. 7. II. *honourable mention*, γυνὴ ἀξία -σημασίας Plb.22.20. 1. III. *qualifying addition* (e.g. ὀξυ- in ὀξύκεδρος), cj. in Thphr. *HP*3.12.3. -εῖον, τό, *counterfeit seal*, σημεῖα παρασημεῖα Pl.Com. 77. -ειόομαι, *make a marginal note*, *POxy.*34.14 (ii A.D.); *annotate in the margin*, Sch.Il.10.398; *note down*, Eust.419.6. 2. *countersign*, ἐπιστολήν *BGU*82.11 (ii A.D.). II. *note in passing*, Dsc.*Ther.*3: generally, *note, observe*, Theon *Prog.*4, S.E.*M.*5.69; *indicate, designate*, Gal.7.467, Sor.2.2. -είωσις, εως, ἡ, *marginal note*, Ptol.*Geog.* 1.24.7, Eust.1512.3; = Lat. *adnotatio, interlocutory judgement*, *IG*2$^{2}$. 1121 (iv A.D.), Just.*Nov.*82.5, 86.2. 2. *passing mention*, Dsc.*Ther.* 26. 3. *indication*, Philum.ap.Aët.5.127. -ειωτέον, *one must note*, Antyll.(? ap.Orib.8.6.16, Dsc.*Ther.Praef.*, Sor.2.53, Aët.9.35. ⊕ -ον, τό, *marginal mark* or *note*, παράσημα ποιεῖσθαι Arist.*SE*177$^{b}$6. II. *distinguishing mark*, in various senses: *ensign* of a ship, παρασήμῳ Διοσκούροις with the Dioscuri as the *sign* or *emblem*, *Act.Ap.*28.11, cf. Plu.2.162a; of a city, ib.399f; of patricians and plebeians, Id. *Cor.*20; τὰ τῆς ἡγεμονίας π. Id.*Ant.*33; τὸ π. ὃ ἐπετίθεντο τῇ κεφαλῇ οἱ τῶν Περσῶν βασιλεῖς Ath.12.514a, cf. *PGnom.*194 (ii A.D.) π. στρατηγικά, = Lat. *insignia praetoria*, Plu.*Sull.*9; *characteristic mark*, τὸ βασιλικὸν τῆς ἐσθῆτος π., i.e. its purple colour, Eun.*VS*p.456 B.; βασιλικὰ π. Id.*Hist.*p.239 D.; τῷ π. τοῦ σχήματος by the *badge* of his costume, App.*BC*1.16; figs are called τὸ π. τῶν Ἀθηνῶν, Alex.117; εἰ τὸ.. λαλεῖν ἦν τοῦ φρονεῖν π. Nicostr.Com.27; τὰ τοῦ πένθους π. '*the trappings and the suits* of woe', Plu.2.118b; τέχνας μὲν παράσαμον ἔχει τάφος *IG*12(1).150 (Rhodes); *indication*, ταῦτα τοῦ μὴ Ῥωμαῖον εἶναι π. Plu.*Caes.*29. b. π. σωματικά *birthmarks*, Ptol.*Tetr.*122, cf. Porph.*Gaur.*5.2. 2. *password*, Plu.2.598b. -ος, ον, (σῆμα) *marked amiss* or *falsely, counterfeit*, esp. of money, D.24.213, Poll.3.86, Plu.2.65b: metaph., of men, Ar.*Ach.*518; δόξα π. E.*Hipp.*1114 (lyr.); π. ῥήτωρ D.18.242; δύναμις π. αἰνῷ power *falsely stamped* with praise, i.e. praised by a wrong standard, A.*Ag.*780 (lyr.). 2. of words and phrases, *false, incorrect*, *AP*11.144 (Cereal.); Ἀττικῶν παράσημος (leg. -σήμων) ἓν (sc. βιβλίον) Gal.*Lib.Propr.*17; τὸ π. *eccentricity* of style, Demetr.*Eloc.*208. 3. *marked by the side, noted*, Plu.2. 1010d; π. τινί *marked, notorious for* a thing, ib.823b, etc.; π. ἐπιτηδεύων τι *remarked as* studying it, Id.*Brut.*2; τὸ π. φεύγουσαι (of women) *conspicuousness*, Gal.12.439. 4. *indicative*, c. gen., τὸ π. ὄνομα τῆς πρὸς ὑμᾶς ἔχθρας Plu.*Cor.*23. II. Adv. -μως *with false accent*, *EM*191.34. 2. *with a distinguishing prefix*, Thphr.*HP*3. 12.3 codd.

**παρασιγάω**, *pass by in silence*, Str.12.3.26; Ion. -σιγέω Hp.*Ep.*19 (in *Hermes* 53.63).

**παράσῑμος**, ον, = ὑπόσιμος, *Cat.Cod.Astr.*7.91.

⊕ **παράσιρον**, τό, dub. sens., τὸ π. τὸ στυππεῖνον *Sammelb.*6801.10 (iii B.C.).

**παρασῑτ-έω**, *board and lodge with*, τινι Pl.*La.*179b. 2. *play the parasite*, ἀφ' οὗ παρασιτῶ from the time I *became a parasite*, Alex.195, cf. Axionic.6.1, Diph.63, Luc.*Par.*4; π. τινί Alex.201.1; τινα Phld. *Herc.*223; ἀλλοτρίων π. ἀγαθῶν Socr.*Ep.*1.4. II. *to be honoured with a seat at the public table*, Plu.*Sol.*24; prop. of the priests named παράσιτοι (v. παράσιτος II. 1), π. ἐν τῷ Δηλίῳ Lex ap.Ath.6.234f. -ησις, εως, ἡ, = *commeatus*, *Gloss.* -ία, ἡ, *profession of a parasite*, Luc. *Par.*37. -ικός, ή, όν, *of a* παράσιτος: ἡ -κή (τέχνη) *the trade of a* παράσιτος, *toad-eating*, ib.4; in full, Ath.6.240b. -ιον, τό, *meeting-place of* παράσιτοι, Crates Gramm.ap.Ath.6.235d, Poll.6. 35. ⊕ -ος, ὁ, *one who eats at the table of another, and repays him with flattery and buffoonery, parasite*, Epich.36, Arar.16, etc.; name of plays by Antiph., Alex., and Diph.; περὶ Παρασίτου, title of work by Luc.: c. gen., κενῆς π. τραπέζης *AP*11.346 (Autom.): metaph., ἰχθὺς ἦν π. (v. ὄψον) Luc.*Lex.*6. II. of *priests who had their meals at the public expense*, Clitodem.11, Polem.Hist.78. 2. *one who dines with a superior officer*, Arist.*Fr.*551.

**παρασῐωπ-άω,** *pass over in silence, omit mention of,* τι Hyp.*Oxy.*1607.69, Plb.2.13.7, Lxx *Ps.*108(109).1, Phld.*Rh.*2.293 S.:—Pass., Plb.6.11.8, Alex.*Fig.*1.16. 2. *keep silence,* περί τινος Plb.24.10.7, D.S.30.9: abs., Lxx *Ge.*34.5, al., Plb.22.4.16, al.; *stand by in silence,* of the chorus, Hsch. s.v. διαύλιον; also παρασιωπῶν· μακροθυμῶν, Id. **-ησις,** εως, ἡ, *passing over in silence,* a rhetor. figure, Quint.*Inst.*9.3.99, Trypho *Trop.*p.199 S., Herm. *in Phdr.*p.188 A. 2. metaph., *intermission,* Sch.Ptol.*Tetr.*161. **-ητέον,** *one must pass over in silence,* Ph.2.152.

**παρασκαίρω,** *bound beside* or *near,* Nonn.*D.*36.172.

**παρασκάπτω,** *dig up,* γῆν νειάν *IG*12(7).62.46 (Amorgos, iv B.C.).

**παρα-σκελής,** ές, *with unequal sides,* opp. ἰσοσκελής, Hero *Mens.*55. **-σκέλια,** τά, *side-tails* of a bandage, Heliod.ap.Orib.48.58.3. II. *accessory supports* of a machine, Id.ib.49.4.20.

**παρασκέπ-ασμα,** ατος, τό, *side-covering,* v.l. in Poll.7.208. **-άστρα,** ἡ, *bandage* for the head, Gal.18(1).785. **-ω,** *cover at the side,* Apollod.*Poliorc.*169.1 (Pass.).

⊛ **παρασκευάζω,** fut. -άσω X.*Cyr.*1.6.18 (but 3 sg. -σκευᾷ Epicur.*Nat.*14.2, 2 pl. -σκευᾶτε *SIG*1106.113 (Cos, iv/iii B.C.)): Ion. 3 pl. plpf. Pass. παρεσκευάδατο Hdt.7.218, etc.: later sts. **-σκεάζω,** as παρεσκεασμένων *IPE*1$^{2}$.32*B*12 (Olbia, iii B.C.):—*get ready, prepare,* δεῖπνον Hdt.9.82, Pherecr.172; στρατείαν Th.4.74; ὀθόνια Ar.*Ach.*1176; πλοῖα Lys.13.26; ἱππέας, ὅπλα, τριήρεις, X.*Ages.*1.24, *Cyr.*2.1.9, *HG*1.4.11; *hold ready,* τῆς θύρας παρεσκευασμένης Lys.1.24: κατασκευάζω is prop. *fit out and prepare what one has,* παρασκευάζω *provide and prepare what one has not*; cf. κατασκευή II. 2. *provide, procure, contrive,* θανάτους τοῖς πέλας Antipho 1.28; τῇ νηῒ οἶνον καὶ ἄλφιτα Th.3.49; πᾶσαν ἡμῖν εὐδαιμονίαν Pl.*Smp.*188d, etc.; ὀργὰς τοῖς ἀκούουσι κατά τινων π. Lys.1.28: in bad sense, *get up,* ἀντίδοσιν ἐπί τινα D.28.17; v. infr. B.I.2. 3. *make* or *render* so and so, with part. or Adj., π. τὰ σώματα ἄριστα ἔχοντας, π. τινὰς ὅτι βελτίστους, X.*Cyr.*1.6.18, 5.2.19; τοὺς θεοὺς ἵλεως αὐτῷ π. Pl.*Lg.*803e; τοὺς κριτὰς τοιούτους π. Arist.*Rh.*1387$^{b}$17, cf. 1380$^{b}$31: c. inf., *accustom,* τὸ στράτευμα παρεσκευακέναι ὡς πόνον μηδένα ἀποκάμνειν *accustom* it not to.., X.*HG*7.5.19, cf. *Eq.*2.3; π. τὸν βίον αὑτῷ μηδὲν δεῖσθαί τινος Pl.*R.*405c; π. τινὰς τὴν τιμὴν ἀποδιδόναι *PFlor.*347.2 (v A.D.); π. ὅπως ὡς βέλτισται ἔσονται αἱ ψυχαί Pl.*Grg.*503a, cf. *Ap.*39d; π. τινῶν τὰς γνώμας, ὡς ἰτέον εἴη X.*Cyr.*2.1.21; δεῖ παρασκευάσαι τὸν ἀκροατὴν ἐν τῷ προοιμίῳ D.H.*Rh.*10.13. 4. *adapt* for a purpose, τὴν τῆς γυναικὸς [φύσιν] ἐπὶ τὰ ἔνδον ἔργα X.*Oec.*7.22; v. B.II. 5. *produce, cause,* τοὺς ὄγκους καὶ τὰ καύματα Diocl.*Fr.*43.

B. Med. and Pass.: I. in proper sense of Med., *get ready* or *prepare for oneself,* ὅπλα ἐς τὰς γεφύρας Hdt.7.25; π. τὰ πολέμια, ναυτικόν, στρατείαν, Th.1.18, 2.80, 4.70 ἑκατὸν νεῶν ἐπίπλουν τῇ Πελοποννήσῳ π. Id.2.56; τὸν γὰρ τοῦ πράττειν χρόνον εἰς τὸ παρασκευάζεσθαι ἀναλίσκομεν in *preparation,* D.4.37; τοῖον παλαιστὴν νῦν π. ἐπ' αὐτὸς αὑτῷ *is preparing* such an adversary *for himself,* A.*Pr.*920. 2. in Oratt., *procure, suborn* persons as witnesses, partisans, etc., so as to obtain a verdict by fraud or force (cf. παρασκευή I.3); π. τοὺς συκοφάντας And.1.105; ῥήτορας παρασκευασάμενοι Is.1.7; ψευδεῖς λόγους ib.17; μάρτυρας ψευδεῖς παρεσκεύασται D.29.28; π. τινὰς τῶν δημοτῶν *bring* them *over to one's side,* Id.44.39: abs., *form a party, intrigue,* Is.10.1, D.27.2:—so in Act., X.*HG*1.7.8, Is.8.3; παρασκευάζειν τινὶ δικαστήριον *pack* a jury to try him, Lys.13.12:—Pass., ὑπὸ σοῦ παρεσκευάσθη *was 'squared'* by you, D.20.145. II. Med. also abs., *prepare oneself, make preparations,* τῷ ναυτικῷ.. παρασκευασαμένῳ Th.2.80; παρασκευασάμενος μεγάλως Hdt.9.15; παρασκευάσασθαι ὥστε ἀμύνασθαι X.*An.*7.3.35: in pres. and impf. it may be regarded either as Pass. or Med., D.18.19, etc.; π. ἐς ναυμαχίην, μάχην, Hdt.9.96, 99; π. πρός τι Th.3.69, etc.; στρατεύεσθαι π. Hdt.1.71, cf. A.*Ag.*353, Ar.*Av.*227: c. fut. inf., X.*Cyr.*7.5.12. 2. freq. folld. by ὡς with fut. part., παρεσκευάσαντο ὡς πολιορκησόμενοι Hdt.5.34; π. ὡς ἐλῶν Id.2.162, cf. 9.122; π. ὡς ναυμαχήσοντες (expressed just above by ὡς ἐπὶ ναυμαχίαν) Th.4.13; ὡς προσβαλοῦντες ib.8; π. ὡς μάχης ἐσομένης X.*HG*4.2.18, cf. *Cyr.*3.2.8: c. fut. part. without ὡς, τέχνῃ παρεσκευάζετο ἐπιθησόμενος Th.5.8, cf. 6.54, 7.17, X.*HG*4.1.41; also π. ὅπως ἐσβαλοῦσιν ἐς τὴν Μακεδονίαν Th.2.99, cf. Pl.*Tht.*183d. 3. in pf. παρεσκεύασμαι, *to be ready, prepared,* κάρτα εὖ παρεσκευασμένοι Hdt.3.150; τράπεζαι.. παρεσκ. Ar.*Ec.*839; λῃστρικώτερον π. *equipped* in pirate fashion, Th.6.104; παρεσκ. ἔρχομαι ἐπὶ τὸν λόγον Pl.*Phd.*91b; εὖ παρεσκ. καὶ τὰς ψυχὰς καὶ τὰ σώματα X.*Oec.*5.13; ἐς τὴν πολιορκίην παρεσκευάδατο v.l. in Hdt.3.150; παρεσκευάδατο ὡς ἀπολεόμενοι Id.7.218; ταῖς ψυχαῖς παρεσκευασμένους ὡς χεῖρας ξυμμείξοντας X.*Cyr.*2.1.11: folld. by ὥστε c. inf., παρεσκευάσμεθ' ὥστε κατθανεῖν E.*HF*1241; παρεσκευάσθαι ὡς ἱκανοὶ εἶναι X.*Cyr.*4.2.13: c. inf. only, δρᾶν παρεσκευασμένος A.*Th.*440, E.*Heracl.*691, cf. A.*Ag.*1422, Ar.*Nu.*607, etc.: so in aor., ὥστε ἂν.. παρασκευασθῶσιν οὕτως ἔχειν Arist.*Rh.*1388$^{a}$26. 4. Med., = *exonerare alvum,* Lxx 1*Ki.*24.4. III. παρεσκευάσθαι τι *to be prepared* or *provided with* a thing, ἀδίκῳ δόξαν δικαιοσύνης παρεσκευασμένῳ Pl.*R.*365b; π. λαμπρὸν ἱμάτιον Thphr.*Char.*21.11. IV. in Pass., of things, *to be got ready, prepared,* ἐπειδὴ παρεσκεύαστο when *preparations had been made,* Th.4.67; τούτῳ ἄριστα παρεσκεύασται ζῆν Pl.*Mx.*248a; in Hdt.9.100, for ὡς παρεσκευάδατο τοῖσι Ἕλλησι, Reiske proposed παρεσκεύαστο.

**παρασκεύ-ᾰσις,** εως, ἡ, = παρασκευή, ναυτικῶν δυνάμεων D.S.21.16. **-ασμα,** ατος, τό, *arrangement,* Aen.Tact.22.19; τὰ πρὸς τὴν ὑγίειαν π. X.*Oec.*11.19. **-αστέος,** α, ον, *to be prepared,* Nicostr.ap.Stob.4.23.62. II. -τέον, *one must prepare* or *provide,* τὸ μὴ κινδυνεῦσαι Pl.*R.*467b; ὅπως μή.. Id.*Grg.*480e; ὅπως εὐπειθεῖς οἱ ἄνδρες ὦσιν X.*Eq.Mag.*1.7; τούτῳ πολλοὺς ἐπαινέτας π. Id.*Mem.*1.7.2. 2. (from Pass.) *one must prepare oneself, be ready,* μηδὲν δεῖσθαί τινος Pl.*Grg.*507d. **-αστής,** οῦ, ὁ, *provider,* ἐπιθυμιῶν ib.518c. ⊛ **-αστικός,** ή, όν, *skilled in providing,* τῶν εἰς τὸν πόλεμον X.*Mem.*3.1.6, cf. Arist.*VV*1250$^{a}$3; π. ἡδονῆς, λύπης, ἀταραξίας, *causing* them, Thphr.*Char.*5.1, 19.1, Phld.*Piet.*65; βεβαίου τόπου Epicur.*Nat.*11.11; νόσου Alcmaeon 4 (v.l.), cf. Porph.*Abst.*1.33; ὄγκου αἱ φαντασίαι παρασκευαστικώταται Longin.15.1; π. πρός τι Andronic.Rhod.p.574 M. 2. abs., *preparatory,* opp. ἀποθεραπευτικός, Gal.6.117, cf. Asclep.Bith.ap.Cael.Aur.*TP*2.13. 3. ἡ π. βίβλος treatise *on preparaions for defence,* Aen.Tact.7.4, al.; τὸ π. the *signal for making ready* (to march), D.C.47.43. **-αστός,** ή, όν, *that can be provided* or *procured,* Pl.*Prt.*319b, 324c. ⊛ **-ή,** ἡ, *preparation,* δείπνου Hdt.9.82; παρασκευὴν σίτου παραγγείλας having ordered corn *to be prepared,* Id.3.25, cf. Pl.*R.*369e; π. νεῶν Ar.*Ach.*190; ἐν τούτῳ παρασκευῆς ἦσαν in this state of *preparation,* Th.2.17; *preparation, practice,* as of a speaker preparing his speech, Isoc.4.13, X.*Mem.*4.2.6; ἡ π. τῆς πραγματείας Plb.3.26.5 (elsewh. προκατασκευή, q.v.); λέγειν ἀπὸ παρασκευῆς, opp. αὐτοσχεδίως, Alex.*Fig.*1.2; also, in a speech, *preparatory section,* D.H.*Is.*15 (pl.); cf. παρασκευάζω A.3 fin. b. with Preps., ἐκ παρασκευῆς *of set purpose, by arrangement,* Antipho 6.19, Lys.31.30; μάχη ἐγένετο ἐκ π. a *pitched* battle, Th.5.56; ἀπὸ παρασκευῆς Id.1.133; ἀπὸ π. οὐδεμιᾶς Antipho 5.22; δι' ὀλίγης παρασκευῆς at short *notice,* offhand, Th.4.8; τὸ ναυτικὸν ἐν π. ἦν Id.2.80; ἦσαν ἐν π. πολέμου were engaged in *preparing* for it (cf. κατασκευή), Id.8.14; ἐν παρασκευῇ εἶναι Arist.*Rh.*1382$^{b}$3; μετὰ παρασκευῆς πλείστης ἠδίκησεν Id.*Rh.Al.*1427$^{a}$4; ἄνευ παρασκευῆς Pl.*Ep.*326a. 2. *providing, procuring,* φίλων καὶ οὐσίας Id.*R.*361b; ὑγιείας σώματι π. Id.*Lg.*962a; *way* or *means of providing,* τίς..τέχνη τῆς π. τοῦ μηδὲν ἀδικεῖσθαι; Id.*Grg.*510a; δύ' εἶναι τὰς π. ἐπὶ τὸ θεραπεύειν ib.513d; in E.*Ba.*457, λευκὴν..χροιὰν εἰς παρασκευὴν ἔχεις, ἐκ π. shd. be read. 3. *intrigue, cabal,* for the purpose of gaining a verdict or carrying a measure, Cratin.185, Antipho 5.79, And.1.1, Lys.12.75, al., D.43.32. II. *that which is prepared, equipage,* πλοῦτοί τε καὶ πᾶσα ἡ τοιαύτη π. Pl.*R.*495a, cf. X.*Cyr.*8.3.14. 2. freq. in military sense (v. supr. I.1), *armament,* And.1.107, Th.6.31, X.*Ages.*1.13, *HG*5.2.23; ἵπποι καὶ ὅπλα καὶ ἡ ἄλλη π. Th.2.100, cf. 5.17; γίγνεσθαι τὰς παρασκευὰς ἐποίησα I got the *armaments* ready for service, D.18.102; αἱ πρὸς πόλεμον π. Arist.*Rh.*1383$^{b}$3. 3. generally, *power, means,* Th.1.1; *natural equipment,* Arr.*Epict.*1.2.30, 2.19.30; φύσις καὶ π. ib.4.8.42, cf. 1.6.37; of the *physical constitution* of a new-born infant, Gal.6.32; of mental faculties, *predisposition,* δύναμις καὶ π. Plot.4.6.3. III. among the Jews, *the day of Preparation,* before the sabbath of the Passover, *Ev.Marc.*15.42, *Ev.Jo.*19.14, 31, etc.; ἡμέρα παρασκευῆς *Ev.Luc.*23.54.

**παρασκην-άω** or **-έω,** (σκηνή) *pitch one's tent beside,* τινι X.*An.*3.1.28, in aor. παρεσκηνήσαμεν. **-ιον,** τό, *side-scene,* τῆς λιθείας τῆς εἰς τὸ π. *IG*11(2).203*A*88 (Delos, iii B.C.): elsewh. in pl., D.21.17, *IG*11(2).199*A*91 (Delos, iii B.C.), al.; ἐν τοῖς π. cj. for ἐν τοῖς προσκηνίοις in Alciphr.2.4. II. in sg., *use of one of the chorus as a fourth actor,* Poll.4.109. ⊛ **-όω,** = παρασκηνάω, X.*Cyr.*4.5.8 (v.l. μεθ' ὧνπερ ἐσκήνου); *to be near,* τινι Plu.2.51e; μῆνες τῷ χειμῶνι -σκηνοῦντες ib.735d. II. φᾶρος π. *throw* a wide garment *like a tent* or *canopy over* one, v.l. in A.*Eu.*634.

**παρασκήπτω,** *glance beside and fall,* εἴς τι Luc.*Tim.*10.

**παρασκῐάζω,** *overshadow, obscure,* τὰς ἰδιότητας τοῦ ὄντος Porph.*Sent.*38.

**παρασκιρτάω,** *leap beside* or *near,* of fish, Ael.*NA*13.2 (v.l. περισκ-); π. παρά τινα *leap upon..,* Plu.*Mar.*38.

**παρασκοπέω,** *give a sidelong glance at,* τινας Pl.*Smp.*221b. II. παρεσκόπεις, f.l. for παρεκόπης, A.*Ag.*1252.

**παρασκυτόω,** dub. sens., κιβώτιον παρεσκυτωμένον *IG*11(2).205*Ab*20 (Delos, iii B.C.).

**παρασκώπτω,** *intervene with jests,* h.*Cer.*203; π. τι εἴς τινας Plu.*Cic.*38, cf. *Demetr.*28.

**παρασμήχω,** *rub gently,* ἁλσὶ λεπτοῖς *Hippiatr.*16.

**παρασοβέω,** *scare away* birds, Arist.*Mir.*841$^{b}$22, as v.l. for κατασοβ-. II. intr., *stalk haughtily past,* Plu.*Cat.Ma.*24.

**παρασοφ-ίζομαι,** *apply art wrongly, refine overmuch,* π. πονηρῶς Chrysipp.*Stoic.*3.199. 2. c. acc., π. τὸν ἰατρόν *wish to be wiser than* the physician, Arist.*Rh.*1375$^{b}$21; π. ταῖς δόξαις τὴν φύσιν Agatharch.49. **-ισμα,** ατος, τό, *additional invention,* Phryn.*PS* p.103 B. (pl.).

**παρα-σπάς,** άδος, ὁ, ἡ, *shoot torn off and planted,* Thphr.*HP*2.1.1, *Cp.*10.3.4 and 5; opp. παραφυάς, Thphr.*HP*2.2.4. **-σπᾰσις,** εως, ἡ, = sq., gloss on παραίρεσις, Sch.Th.1.122; *dragging away* of victims by beasts, Porph.*Abst.*1.10. **-σπασμός,** ὁ, *drawing sideways,* [μήτρας] *Placit.*5.13.1, cf. Aët.16.72. **-σπάω,** fut. -άσω [σπᾰ] S.*OC*1185:—*draw forcibly aside, wrest aside,* Id.*El.*732; τὸ παρασπώμενον, = παρασπάς, Thphr.*HP*2.1.3: metaph., τινὰ πρὸς βίαν π. γνώμης S.*OC* l.c.; ἀδίκους φρένας παρασπᾷς, i.e. ὥστε εἶναι ἀδίκους (cf. ἀδάκρυτος) Id.*Ant.*792 (lyr.); κρίσιν Phld.*Rh.*1.174 S.:—Med., παρασπᾶσθαί τινά τινος *detach* him *from* another's side *to* one's own, X.*HG*4.8.33, cf. D.1.3; π. λόγου *detract* from an argument, Pl.*Sph.*241c; μαντικῆς ἴχνος παρεσπάσατο Iamb.*Myst.*3.27:—Pass., παρεσπασμένος *pulled away,* of a circle viewed obliquely, Euc.*Opt.*36. II. *cull for oneself,* Iamb.*VP*1.1.

**παρασπειράομαι,** Pass., *lie coiled beside,* τῷ βρέφει Apollod.3.14.6.

**παρασπείρω**, *sow among*, Thphr.*CP*3.10.3 (Pass.), *PCair.Zen.* 269.35 (iii B.C., prob. Act.), *BGU*591.14 (i A.D., Pass.): metaph., in Pass., [ψυχὴ] παρεσπαρμένη τοῖς πόροις Pl.*Ax.*366a; *to be diffused over*, τῷ λοιπῷ παρεσπάρθαι σώματι Sch.Epicur.*Ep.*1 p.21 U., cf. *Nat.Herc.* 1420*Fr.*1; *to be interspersed in*, ἡ πιμελὴ παρέσπαρται τῇ σαρκί Gal.1. 345; τοῖς σιτίοις παρέσπαρται [τὸ αἷμα] Id.*Nat.Fac.*2.8; τὸ Ἰουδαίων γένος πολὺ κατὰ πᾶσαν τὴν οἰκουμένην παρέσπαρται τοῖς ἐπιχωρίοις J.*BJ* 7.3.3, cf. Str.17.3.9.

**παρασπ-ίζω**, *bear a shield beside*, i.e. *fight beside, stand by*, ἅρμασιν E.*Ion* 1528; τινι D.H.3.19: abs., E.*Ph.*1435: metaph., [τόξα] παρασπίζοντ' ἐμοῖς βραχίοσι Id.*HF*1099: Arith., of numbers, *place beside* or *on the flanks*, Iamb. *in Nic.*p.40 P. (Act. and Pass.). ❋ **-ιστής**, οῦ, ὁ, *shield-bearer, companion in arms*, E.*El.*886, *Ph.*1165, *Cyc.*6.

**παρασπόνδ-ειος**, ον, *at* or *for a libation*: παρασπόνδεια, τά (sc. μέλη), Ph.2.484. **-έω**, *break a compact* or *treaty*, D.7.36, 18.71, Onos.37.3; εἴς τινα D.H.2.72. II. trans., 1. π. τινάς *break faith with* them, Plb.1.7.8, cf. Plu.*Sull.*3; τοὺς παρεσπονδηκότας τὰς πόλεις *IG*2².687.32:—Pass., *suffer by a breach of faith*, Plb.3.15.7, J. *BJ*1.19.4; ὑπό τινος Id.*Vit.*59. 2. π. πίστεις, δεξιάς, *violate* pledges, etc., D.H.6.30, 7.46. **-ημα**, ατος, τό, *breach of faith*, *IG*7.411 (Orop.), Plb.2.58.4, Plu.*Caes.*22, App.*Gall.*18. **-ησις**, εως, ἡ, *breaking of faith*, Plb.2.7.5; πρός τινα Str.7.1.4; εἴς τινα App.*BC*2. 110. **-ητής**, οῦ, ὁ, = sq. 2, Eust.1400.39. **-ος**, ον, (σπονδή) *contrary to a compact* or *treaty*, ἐπιδρομή Th.4.23; μηδὲν π. ποιεῖν, παθεῖν, X.*HG*2.4.30, *Ages.*3.5; π. τι προστάττειν Isoc.14.45; τοῦ θηριώδους καὶ π. βίου *bound by no compacts*, Athenio 1.4. Adv. -δως App.*BC*5.80. 2. of persons, *breaker of treaties, forsworn*, Lys.12. 74, J.*AJ*10.8.2, Heraclit.*Incred.*15.

❋ **παρασπορά**, ἡ, *sowing*, ἀγρῶν *Inscr.Magn.*116.53 (ii A.D.); *sprinkling on*, S.E.*P.*1.46. 2. *dispersion*, Gal.19.441.

**παράσσον**, Adv., = παραυτίκα, *immediately, at once*, A.R.1.383, 2.961. II. of Place, *side by side*, Id.3.969.

**παραστάδιον** [στᾰ], τό, = παραστάς 1, *IG*2².1668.70, Ἀρχ.Ἐφ.1923. 39 (Oropus, iv B.C.), Hero *Aut.*26.5.

**παραστᾰδόν**, Adv. *standing beside, at one's side*, Il.15.22, Od.10. 173, Thgn.473, A.*Ch.*991; π. ἐγγύς Theoc.25.103.

**παραστάζω**, *drop upon*, Hp.*Mul.*1.78, 84, D.S.2.4:—Pass., Menemach.ap.Orib.7.22.3.

**παρασταθμ-ίδες**, αἱ, *parts of the door next the* στρόφιγξ, Hsch. **-ίζω**, *praepondero*, Gloss. **-ον**, *interpondium*, ib. **-ος**, ον, *deficient in weight*, νόμισμα *Cod.Just.*10.27.2.6.

**παράστᾱμα**, v. παράστημα. **παράστανον**· λόγχη, Hsch.

**παραστάνω** [στᾰ], = παρίσταμαι (v. παρίστημι c. I. 1), *IG*2².1368.76.

❋ **παρα-στάς**, άδος, ἡ, (παρίσταμαι) prop. *anything that stands beside*: pl. παραστάδες, *doorposts*, παραστάδας καὶ πρόθυρα βούλει ποικίλα Cratin. 42, cf. *IG*2².1668.32, Poll.1.76, Hsch.; also, *pilasters* or *returns* which cover the ends of walls in the front of a house or temple, τὰς λευκολίθους π. *CIG*2782.29 (Aphrodisias): also in sg., Vitr.10.10.2: pl., of the *wings* of a stage, Callix.2. 2. *space enclosed between the* παραστάδες, *vestibule* or *entrance* of a temple or house, in pl., E.*Ph.*415, *IT*1159, X.*Hier.*11.2, *IG*2².1672.131, 186, Poll.7.122: also in sg., E.*Andr.* 1121, *IG*1².372.73, *SIG*307.12 (Iasos, iv B.C.), *Supp.Epigr.*4.447.11, 453.46 (Didyma, ii B.C.); of a bath, S.E.*P.*1.110, 2.56. ❋ **-στάσις**, εως, ἡ, I. (παρίστημι) *putting aside, removal*, esp. *relegation, banishment*, π. ἐπὶ τὰ τῆς χώρας ἔσχατα Pl.*Lg.*855c; ἀποδημητικὰς ποιεῖσθαι τὰς π. αὐτῶν, i.e. to ostracize them, Arist.*Pol.*1308ᵇ19; παράστασις· φυγή, καὶ τὸ φυγαδεῦσαι παραστήσασθαι, Hsch. 2. *display, exposure for sale*, Arist.*Pol.*1258ᵇ23. 3. generally, *setting forth, exhibition, manifestation*, εἰς τύπωσιν καὶ π. Phld.*Rh.*2.34 S.; πρὸς παράστασίν τινος *placing before one, representation*, Arr.*Epict.*2.19.1, Corn.*ND*12, Sor.*Vit.Hp.*12, cf. Porph.*Antr.*4, Procl.*in Prm.*p.504 S., Dam.*Pr.*46, 301; κατὰ ἀπόφασιν ὧν οὐκ ἔστιν, οὐ κατὰ παράστασιν ὧν ἔστι προσηγόρευται Porph.*Sent.*19. b. εἰς π. τινός *in proof* of, Gal.1. 149. 4. *placing beside*, D.C.42.48. 5. *production* in court, etc., π. προσώπων *POxy.*1033.17 (iv A.D.). 6. ἡ π. τῶν δημοσίων the *provision* of public sacrificial victims, i.e. the revenues earmarked for that purpose, *SIG*562.68 (Paros, iii B.C.). II. (παρίσταμαι) intr., *being beside*: 1. *position* or *post near* a king, X.*Cyr.*8.4.5. 2. *arrival, visit*, στρατηγοῦ *POxy.*2139 (ii/iii A.D.). 3. *assistance, succour*, *JHS*37.101 (Lydia, ii A.D.); *manifestation* of divinity, *SIG*695.12 (Magn. Mae., ii B.C.); αἱ τῶν εἰδώλων π. *Placit.*5.2.1. 4. *proximity, presence*, Dam.*Pr.*145, 394; ἀνάγκης π. Phld.*Acad.Ind.*p.54 M. 5. *room, space* for standing, οὐχ ἕξει π. Ph.*Bel.*85.3, cf. D.S.20.91: in pl., *free spaces* adjoining a line of wall, *SIG*1182.5, 10 (= 936 note, Ephesus, iii B.C.). 6. *pomp, magnificence*, Lxx 1*Ma.*15.32. 7. *mental excitement, ardour, exaltation*, μεγίστη π. εἶχέ τινας, ὡς δικαίως πράττοντας Plb.5.9.6; μετὰ παραστάσεως ἠσπάζετο Id.10.5.4. b. *desperate courage*, ὁρμὴ καὶ π. Id.3.63.14; μετὰ παραστάσεως ἠγωνίζοντο Id.16.33.2; ἡ ἐν ταῖς βασάνοις π. τῆς ψυχῆς D.S.10.17, cf. J.*BJ*2.20.7. c. *fury, desperation*, τὸ λυποῦν ἤγαγ' ἐς π. Antiph.104, cf. Plb.8.21.4, 9.40.4; ἡ π. τῆς διανοίας Id.3.84.9. d. *propensity, desire*, ψυχῆς πονηρᾶς δυσσεβὴς π. Men.540.8; ἄλογος π. Epicur.*Ep.*1 p.30 U.; π. πρός τινα Id.*Fr.*138; π. ψυχῆς πρὸς ἐλευθερίαν D.S.33.16; *impulse*, Plu.2.589a; ἡ π. τῆς ψυχῆς, as gloss on λῆμα, Ps.-Hdn.Gr. post Moer.p.470 P. III. as law-term, *money deposit, court fee* on entering certain public suits, And.1.120, Is.3.47, Dem.Phal.*Fr.*7 J.; π., μία δραχμή Men.327, cf. *Com.Adesp.*778, Harp. s.v. **-στᾰτέον**, *one must set beside*, τινί τι *Hippiatr.*33, *Gp.*5.22.4. II. *one must set before* the reader, Ph. 2.19. **-στᾰτέω**, *stand by* or *near*, abs., A.*Ag.*877; φόβος ἀνθ' ὕπνου π. ib.14; πέλας τινὶ π. Id.*Th.*669, cf. S.*OT*400, E.*Ph.*160. 2. *stand by*, i.e. *support, succour*, c. dat., S.*El.*917, Ar.*Th.*370 (lyr.), etc.; ἐν γόοις π. [τινι] A.*Ag.*1079 (lyr.). **-στάτης** [στᾰ], ου, ὁ, *one who stands by* or *near, defender*, φρουροὶ καὶ π. πυλῶν E.*Rh.*506. II. *one's comrade on the flank* (opp. προστάτης, front-rank-man, ἐπιστάτης, rear-rank-man), τὸν ἑωυτοῦ π. Hdt.6.117, cf. X.*Cyr.*3.3.59, 8.1. 10; παρήγγειλε τοὺς ἐπιστάτας μεταβαίνειν εἰς παραστάτην Polyaen. 2.10.4. 2. generally, *comrade*, Pi.*N.*3.37, A.*Pers.*957 (lyr.), Hdt. 6.107 (pl.), S.*Ant.*671, etc.; the ephebi were bound by oath μὴ καταλείπειν τὸν π., Poll.8.105, cf. Arist.*EN*1130ᵃ30, Stob.4.1.48; of a horse, π. ἐν μάχαις Babr.76.3: hence, *assistant, supporter*, δίκης E.*Fr.*205; of the gods, π. ἀγαθοὺς καὶ συμμάχους X.*Cyr.*3.3.21; esp. of the Dioscuri, *Trag.Adesp.*14. 3. *right-* or *left-hand-man* in a chorus when drawn up in order, Arist.*Pol.*1277ᵃ12, *Metaph.*1018ᵇ 27. 4. *official of a collegium*, *IG*14.925 (Portus). III. *the ministers of the Eleven* at Athens, *AB*296, Phot., *EM*652.16. IV. Medic., οἱ π. *testicles*, Ph.1.45, Ath.9.395f, etc.: personified, in dual, Pl.Com.174.13; also, of the *epididymis*, Hp.*Oss.*14, cf. Gal.19. 128. 2. of the σπερματικοὶ πόροι, π. ἀδενοειδεῖς, κιρσοειδεῖς, Herophil.ap.Gal.*UP*14.11, cf. Ruf.*Onom.*185, Gal.4.643. 3. in sg., = ὀστέον ὑοειδές, Herophil.ap.Poll.2.202 and Ruf.*Onom.*155. V. in a ship, *pieces of wood* to stay the mast, *IG*2².1606.36, 1607.5, 15, 78, 1611.38; dual παραστάτα ib.1608.34. VI. *outer vertical standard* in plinth of torsion-engine, Ph.*Bel.*55.10, Hero *Bel.*91.10. **-στᾰτικός**, ή, όν, *fit for standing by*. Adv. -κῶς Phot., Suid. II. *bringing to light, displaying*, ἑαυτοῦ τε καὶ τοῦ ἑτέρου Antioch.Ascal. ap.S.E.*M.*7.162; ἀληθοῦς *Stoic.*2.73; *indicative*, c. gen., τὰ καιροῦ π. (sc. ἐπιρρήματα) οἷον σήμερον D.T.641.28, cf. A.D.*Pron.*7.26, al., S.E. *M.*8.202; *making manifest*, ὁλοτελῶν κόσμων π. Dam.*Pr.*224. III. *able to exhort* or *rouse*, c. gen., ἀγωνίας Plb.3.43.8; ὁρμῆς Plu.*Lyc.*21; *creating a disposition* or *propensity*, πρὸς τὰς πράξεις Phld.*Mus.*p.71 K.; π. πρὸς συνουσίαν S.E.*M.*1.307; π. ἀπό τινος εἴς τι Phld.*Oec.*p.52 J. IV. *desperately courageous*, Plb.16.5.7 (Comp.). Adv. -κῶς Id.16.28.8, D.S.18.22: Comp. -ώτερον Id.20.11. 2. *desperate, furious*, διάθεσις Plb.1.67.6, etc.; π. τὰς διανοίας Id.18.46.10. V. *parastatica*, = παραστάς, Vitr.5.1.6, 10.10.2, Plin.*HN*33.52. VI. -κόν, τό, *tomb*, *MAMA*3.10, al. (Seleucia ad Calycadnum). ❋ **-στάτις** [στᾰ], ἴδος, fem. of παραστάτης, S.*Tr.*889; *helper*, Id.*OC*559, X.*Mem.* 2.1.32, etc. II. παραστατίς (sic)· ἀγγεῖον θερμαντικόν, Hsch.

**παρασταυρόω**, *enclose by palisades*, Anon.ap.Suid.

❋ **παρα-στεγάζω**, *roof in*, τὸν πυλῶνα καὶ τὰ ἐχόμενα οἰκήματα *PSI*5. 546.14 (iii B.C.). **-στέγη**, ἡ, *roof*, Sch.Opp.*H.*2.153.

**παραστείχω**, aor. παρέστῐχον, *go past, pass by*, c. acc. loci, *h.Ap.* 217; δόμους π. (prob. for δόμοις) A.*Ch.*568: abs., *pass by*, S.*OT*808 (sed leg. ὄχους), *AP*9.679, *Sammelb.*4312.9 (Ptolemaic), *Ath.Mitt.* 17.272 (ii A.D.). 2. *transgress*, ἤν τι τούτων ὧν λέγω -στείξῃς Herod.5.50. II. *pass into, enter*, δόμους S.*Ant.*1255.

**παραστέλλω**, *draw aside*, of a curtain, Hld.10.28; τὴν γαστέρα Gal.2.523; *contract*, τοὺς μῦς ib.225:—Pass., *to be drawn aside*, Sor. 2.61. 2. *reduce* a swelling, Hp.*Epid.*5.69. 3. *check*, πλάδον Sor.1.49 (Pass.).

**παράστεμα**, v. παράστημα.

**παραστενάχομαι** [ᾰχ], *sigh beside* or *near*, A.R.4.1297.

**παραστήκω**, = παρίσταμαι, Lxx *Nu.*7.2, v.l. in *Jd.*3.19.

**παραστήλη** ἡρώων, *rogus*, Gloss.

❋ **παράστημα**, ατος, τό, Dor. and Arc. **παράστᾱμα** *IG*4²(1).109 ii 147, 155 (Epid., iii B.C.), 5(2).515 *B a* (Megalopolis); later Gr. **παράστεμα** *Ath.Mitt.*9.222 (Mesambria): (παρίσταμαι):—*statue placed beside another*, *IG*4²(1).ll. cc. (pl.), *Ath.Mitt.* l. c. 2. = παραστάς 2, τοῦ προναίου *IG*5(2).l.c. II. = παράστασις II. 7, π. τῆς ψυχῆς *desperate courage, exaltation*, D.S.17.11, D.H.*Dem.*22, J.*BJ*2.18.4, S.E. *M.*5.66; εὐγενῆ παραστήματα λαβόντες D.S.26.14, cf. Longin.9.1, Ph.2.220; θείῳ τινὶ π. κινηθεῖσα divine *inspiration*, D.H.8.39. 2. in pl., *principles, maxims*, M.Ant.3.11. III. of Time, *present moment*, Porph.*Sent.*44.

**παραστίζω**, *prick, mark* the names of defaulters, Hsch., cf. Id. s.v. καταστίζων.

**παραστίλβω**, *gleam*, *Placit.*3.3.2, prob. in Dsc.4.135.

**παραστῐχ-ίδιον**, τό, Dim. of sq., v.l. in D.L.8.78. **-ίς**, ἴδος, ἡ, (στίχος) *anything written at the side*, esp. = ἀκροστιχίς, Id.5.93, Gell. 14.6.4; of a *magical formula*, *PMag.Leid.W.*21.22.

**παραστολεύς**, έως, ὁ, (παραστέλλω) a surgical instrument, *Hermes* 38.283.

**παραστορέννυμι**, *lay flat, lay low*, ἐγώ σε..παραστορῶ (Att. fut.) Ar.*Eq.*481:—Pass., παραστόρνυται Hsch. (with corrupt expl.):—so -στρώννυμι, aor. -έστρωσα J.*BJ*7.9.1.

**παραστοχάζομαι**, *aim at*, τῆς συντομίας S.E.*P.*3.222 codd., cf. Herod.Med.ap.Orib.5.30.25: abs., *estimate*, Sor.1.20.

**παράστρᾰβος**, ον, *with a slight squint*, *PSI*9.1028.8 (i A.D.), Eust. 206.29.

❋ **παραστρᾰτ-εύομαι**, *march with an army*, of camp-followers, Anon.ap.Suid. s.v. λεῖξαι. **-ηγέω**, *issue orders interfering with those of the general*, D.H.10.45, Plu.*Aem.*11, *Alex.*39, Jul. *ad Ath.* 278c. II. Pass., *to be outmanoeuvred*, διὰ τῶν φίλων Arist.*Ath.* 6.2. **-ηγία**, ἡ, metaph., *machinations*, *UPZ*39.25 (ii B.C.). **-οπεδεύω**, *encamp beside* or *opposite to*, τινι Plb.2.6.3; ἀλλήλοις D.H.2.41: abs., Plb.3.17.4, Polyaen.5.2.10, etc.:—Med., c. dat., Chio *Ep.*3.1.

**παρά-στρεμμα**, ατος, τό, *distortion*, of facial paralysis, Hp.*Prorrh.* 2.38 (pl.). **-στρέφω**, *turn aside, alter*, Pl.*Cra.*418a:—Pass., *to* *be displaced to one side*, π. ἢ ἔνθα ἢ ἔνθα ἡ ῥίς Hp.*Art.*35; τὸ στόμα παρεστραμμένος *Com.Adesp.*386; of trees, οὐκ εὐφυές, ἀλλὰ παρεστραμμένον Thphr.*HP*4.2.6, etc.; παρέστραπται δὲ καὶ ὅσσε Nic.*Th.*758. 2. metaph., *turn aside*, esp. for the worse, *pervert*, τὴν μοῖραν ἐς τὸ μὴ χρεών E.*Fr.*491.3; ψυχαὶ παρεστραμμέναι τῆς κατὰ φύσιν ἕξεως Arist. *Pol.*1342ᵃ22. 3. π. τὸν τρίβωνα, as a sign of ἀνελευθερία, dub. in Thphr.*Char.*22.13.

**παραστρόγγῠλος**, ον, *roundish*, Apollod.*Poliorc.*150.8.

**παραστροφ-ή**, ἡ, *distortion*, τοῦ ἰνίου Erasistr.ap.Gal.11.208. II. *selvage* of a robe, Gal.18(1).776, Hsch. s. v. λέγνη. **-ίς**, ίδος, ἡ, = foreg. II, Sor.1.83 (pl.), Hsch. s. v. ἐπίξυλον.

**παραστρώννυμι**, v. παραστορέννυμι.

**παραστρωφάω**, poet. for παραστρέφω, A.R.2.665 (Pass.).

**παραστύφω** [ῡ], *to be rather astringent*, Diph.Siph.ap.Ath.3.73a, Sor.1.95, 2.13.

**παρασυγγρᾰφ-έω**, *break contract with*, τινα D.56.28: abs., ib.34, *PPetr.*3p.161 (iii B. C.); τι *PTeb.*105.34 (ii B. C.), etc.

**παρασυγ-χέω**, *confuse*, τὰς συντάξεις A.D.*Conj.*239.4. **-χωρέω**, *sublet* property *by agreement*, *BGU*86.25 (ii A. D., written παρσ-).

**παρασυζεύγνυμι**, *join alongside*, Sch.E.*Or.*1016 (Pass.).

**παρασῡκοφαντέω**, *cavil at*, τὸ πρόχειρον τοῦ λόγου Ph.1.340: abs., *find fault*, Plu.2.73b.

**παρασυλ-λέγομαι**, *assemble with others*, παρασυλλεγέντες And.1.133. **-λογιστικός**, ή, όν, *fallacious*, *EM*35.28.

**παρασυμ-βάλλομαι**, Pass., *to be compared, to be like*, τοῖς κτήνεσιν Lxx *Ps.*48(49).12,20. **-βᾰμα**, ατος, τό, (συμβαίνω) in the technical language of the Stoics, *secondary accident* or *circumstance*, Chrysipp.*Stoic.*2.59: Gramm., *impersonal verb governing a dative*, A.D.*Pron.*115.12, *Synt.*300.4,6.

**παρασυν-άγχη**, ἡ, *inflammation of the muscles of one side of the throat*, Gal.8.248, Cael.Aur.*CP*3.1. **-ᾰγωγή**, ἡ, Rhet., *production for comparison*, προσώπων καὶ πραγμάτων Alex.*Fig.*1.24. ❋**-αξις**, εως, ἡ, *clandestine religious assembly*, *Cod.Just.*1.5.8.3,5. **-απτικὸς σύνδεσμος**, *connective* particle *which implies a fact*, i. e. *causal* (e.g. ἐπεί as opp. εἰ), D.T.642.25, A.D.*Conj.*220.14, al., Simp.*in Ph.*9.29. **-άπτομαι**, Pass., *to be connected by a causal particle*, Crinis *Stoic.*3.269; [τῶν ἀξιωμάτων] τὰ μὲν συνημμένα, τὰ δὲ παρασυνημμένα τὸ μᾶλλον ἢ ἧττον Ph.1.321, cf. A.D.*Synt.*8.10. **-εργός**, όν, *counter-acting*, opp. συνεργός, δύναμις Vett.Val.78.22. **-εσις**, εως, ἡ, *misunderstanding*, Hp.*Art.*10, cf. 51, Gal.18(1).370. **-ήθως**, Adv. *in a manner contrary to custom*, *PMasp.*6.5 (vi A. D.). **-θετος**, ον, *formed from a compound*, A.D.*Synt.*330.5, *EM*131.42, 155.56, 493.18. Adv. **-τως** *An.Ox.*3.182. ❋**-θημα**, ατος, τό, *sign which accompanies the password*, Aen.Tact.25.1, Plb.9.13.9, Onos.26. **-ίσταμαι**, *to be at one's side*, as an amanuensis, τινι *Sammelb.*5676.5 (iii A. D.).

**παρασῡρίζω**, *play the σῦριγξ beside*, τινι Nonn.*D.*1.521.

**παρά-συρμα**, ατος, τό, *excoriation*, Paul.Aeg.4.14 (pl.). ❋**-σύρω** [ῡ], fut. -σῠρῶ Hsch.:—Pass., pf. παρασέσυρμαι and aor. 2 παρεσύρην [ῠ] (v. infr.):—*sweep away, carry away*, of a rapid stream, [Κρατῖνος] πολλῷ ῥεύσας ποτ' ἐπαίνῳ διὰ τῶν ἀφελῶν πεδίων ἔρρει καὶ τῆς στάσεως παρασύρων ἐφόρει τὰς δρῦς κτλ. *sweeping* the oaks *from* their stations, Ar.*Eq.*527; τοῦ ῥεύματος ἡ ὀξύτης πολλοὺς.. παρέσυρε D.S.17.55: metaph., of orators, τῷ ῥοθίῳ τῆς φορᾶς.. ἅπαντα.. π. Longin.32.4:—Pass., *to be swept away*, τῇ τοῦ κατακλυσμοῦ φορᾷ Ph.1.223: metaph., εἰς ἑτέραν παρασύρεσθαι τέχνην Chor.*Lyd.*17(21), cf. Anon.*in EN*418.21; π. ὑπὸ τῶν ὅπλων *to be swept* into rebellion, Them.*Or.*7.93c; ἐκ λήθης π. Tz.*H.*9.751. 2. π. τῶν νεῶν τοὺς ταρσοὺς *sweep off* the oars of the ships by brushing past them, Plb.16.4.14, cf. D.S.13.16 (Pass.): intr., τὰ ἐς πλάγιον τοῦ ὀστέου παρασύραντα βέλεα *grazing* it obliquely, Hp.*VC*11. 3. *snatch away*, ἴκτινος π. κρέας S.*Fr.*767. 4. π. ἔπος *drag* a word *in*, *use* it *out of time and place*, A.*Pr.*1065 (anap.). 5. generally, *drag, hale*, τινὰ εἰς τὰ κριτήρια Mitteis *Chr.*89.22 (ii A. D.). 6. *drag out*, τὸν λοιπὸν χρόνον Lyd.*Mag.*3.67. 7. *ridicule*, παρώφθη καὶ παρεσύρη Ph.2.566:—Med., παιδιὰς παρασεσυρμένας *mocking*, ib.570. 8. Pass., in Geom., *glide, slide* along the circumference of a curve, Procl.*Hyp.*4.4,34. 9. παρασεσυρμένοι, = ὑπεσκελισμένοι, of wrestlers, Hsch.

**παρασφᾰγίς**, ίδος, ἡ, *the part near the throat*, Poll.2.133.

**παρασφάζω**, *wound in the side*, Anon.ap.Suid. s. v. πνεύσας.

**παρασφᾰλ-ής**, ές, *unsteady, erring*, of men, Nic.*Al.*416. **-ίζω**, *fortify next in order*, in Med., Lxx *Ne.*3.8 (v.l.). **-ισμα**, ατος, τό, *bond, security*, *BGU*246.14 (ii/iii A. D.).

**παρασφάλλω**, aor. παρέσφηλα (v. infr.), *cause to glance off to the side*, of an arrow, παρέσφηλεν γὰρ Ἀπόλλων Il.8.311; π. τινὰ καλῶν *foil* one *of*.., Pi.*N.*11.31; π. τινὰ νόσῳ Opp.*H.*3.200:—Pass., *err, be deceived*, νοῦς παρέσφαλται Critias 6.13; ἀληθείας.. ἐκτὸς παρεσφαλμένοι *having wandered from* it, Pl.*Epin.*976b, cf. Procl.*in Prm.*p.548 S.; ταύτης ὁ Μῶμος ἄχθεται -σφαλείς *Com.Adesp.*262; εἴ τι παρεσφάλη Ph.2.440.

**παρα-σφήνιον**, τό, *side-block for wedging*, *IG*11(2).159*A* 38 (Delos, iii B. C.), *PCair.Zen.*759 (iii B. C.). **-σφηνόω**, *wedge in*, Sor.2.31 (Pass.), Hsch. s. v. ἀραρινοί (Pass.), Aspasia ap.Aët.16.22 (Pass.).

**παρασφίγγω**, *bind up with*, ἡ φύσις π. εἰς αὐτὴν τὸ ὑγιές Alex.Aphr. *Pr.*1.43.

**παρασφρᾱγ-ίζω**, *set a seal upon*:—Med., Teles p.38 H.; π. τὰ ἀποδόχια *PRev.Laws* 54.18, al. (iii B. C.), cf. *PCair.Zen.*454.5 (iii B. C.), *UPZ*5.19 (ii B. C.):—Pass., *to be sealed up*, Teles l. c. II. *counterfeit a seal*, Hsch. s. v. παραποιήσασθαι. **-ισμός**, ὁ, *sealing*, *PRev.Laws* 51.3 (iii B. C.).

**παρα-σφύριος** [ῠ], ον, *beside, near the ankles*, Opp.*H.*3.307. **-σφῠρος**, ον, *with diseased fetlocks*, *Hippiatr.*53,96.

**παρασχάζω**, *lance, prick*, τὰς φλυκταίνας Gal.12.412.

**παρασχεδιάζω**, = παραχαράσσω, Hsch.

**παρασχεδόν**, Adv. *beside, near*, of Place, A.R.2.10,859, Opp.*H.*5.104: c. dat., ib.4.442. 2. of Time, *straightway*, A.R.1.354, Nic. *Th.*800. II. *nearly, almost*, D.H.7.45.

**παρασχεῖν, παρασχέμεν, παρασχεθεῖν**, v. παρέχω.

**παρά-σχεσις**, εως, ἡ, *furnishing, provision*, ἵππων D.C.55.10. **-σχετέον**, *one must impart*, τινί τι Hierocl.p.58 A.

**παρασχημᾰτ-ιαῖον**, *deferendum*, dub. in *Gloss.* **-ίζω**, *change from the true form, transform*, ὀνειδισμὸς ἐστι τῆς ἁμαρτίας παρεσχηματισμένος τὸ σκῶμμα Thphr.ap.Plu.2.631e, cf. D.L.6.9; ὁ βασιλεὺς ..θεὸς ἐν ἀνθρώποις παρεσχημάτισται *has been transformed into*.., Diotog.ap.Stob.4.7.61. 2. in Gramm., *form from another word by a slight change*, Porph.*in Cat.*69.20, Sch.Ar.*Ach.*424, etc.; dub. sens. in Phld.*Rh.*2.97 S.; παρασχηματίσας τῷ πατρὶ *forming a derivative* word (πατρίς) from πατήρ, Hierocl.p.50 A.:—Pass., A.D.*Conj.*237.27; θηλυκῷ καὶ οὐδετέρῳ γένει *Et.Gen.* s. v. πλειότερος. II. *speak incorrectly*, Suid. s. v. σχηματιζόμενος. 2. *make false pretences*, Anon.ap.eund. s. v. παρασχηματίζειν. **-ισμός**, ὁ, *formation by a slight change*, A.D.*Synt.*50.25, al.; *change in the form* of expression, Sch.E.*Hec.*763. II. *malposition* of the foetus, Paul.Aeg.3.76.

**παρα-σχίδες** [ῐ], αἱ, *splinters*, π. ὀστέων, in a fracture, Hp.*Fract.*24: sg., Gal.18(2).536. **-σχίζω**, *rip up lengthwise, slit up*, π. παρὰ τὴν λαπάρην Hdt.2.86; *open* fish, Alex.133.4:—Pass., τὸ παρεσχισμένον σῶμα D.S.1.91; ἱμάτια παρεσχισμένα παρὰ μῆκος Polyaen.6.49. ❋**-σχιστής** or **-σχίστης**, οῦ or ου, ὁ, *one who rips up lengthwise*, e.g. *one who opens* corpses to embalm them, D.S.1.91, Procl.*Par. Ptol.*250. II. ἀνδροφόνοι καὶ π. *mutilators*, Plb.12.6.4. **-σχιστικός**, ή, όν, *pertaining to a παρασχιστής* I, θεραπεία *PTaur.*9.12, cf. 8.14, 20 (ii B. C., dub. l.).

**παρασχοιν-ίζω**, *fence off with lines*, παρεσχοίνισται ἡ ὁδὸς Str.15.1.55. **-ισμα**, ατος, τό, *cord drawn beside* or *along*, Poll.7.160.

**παρασῴζω**, *keep* a criminal *for* delivery to the officer of the law, *PLond.*2.422.1 (iv A. D.).

❋**παρασωρεύω**, *heap beside*, gloss on παρανηνέω, Sch.Od.1.147, 16.51.

**παρατᾱγή**, ἡ, *order for payment*, *CIG*2817.14 (Aphrodisias).

**παραταινᾰρίζω**, *celebrate the Taenaria* like the Laconians, Hermipp. 32.

**παρατάν-υσμα** [τᾰ], ατος, τό, *anything stretched out, covering*, Aq., Sm.*Ex.*27.16. **-ύω**, = παρατείνω, Od.1.138 (tm.), Hp.*Art.*44.

**παράταξις**, εως, ἡ, *placing side by side*, Thphr.*CP*1.6.1. 2. *marshalling, line of battle*, π. ποιεῖσθαι Isoc.10.53; ἐν τῷ μεταξὺ χωρίῳ τῶν π. Plb.15.12.3; ἡ π. τοῦ πολέμου Lxx *Nu.*31.14; ἐν π. ἀποθνήσκειν Phld.*Mort.*29; ὡς ἐν παρατάξει Arr.*Epict.*3.22.69; ἐκ παρατάξεως *in pitched battle*, Th.5.11, D.9.49, Aeschin.3.88; ἐν ταῖς προγεγενημέναις π. in the previous *battles*, Plb.1.40.1; μετὰ τὰν π. τὰν γενομέναν αὐτοῖς ποτὶ Πριανεῖς *Schwyzer* 289.105 (Priene, ii B. C.), cf. *IG*4²(1).28.1 (Epid., ii B. C.). b. *front rank* of the phalanx, Ascl.*Tact.*2.5, Ael. *Tact.*7.1. II. *of marshalling* a political party, τὴν μὲν παρασκευὴν ὁρᾶτε.. καὶ τὴν παράταξιν, ὅση γεγένηται Aeschin.3.1; *conspiracy, intrigue*, ὑπὸ παρατάξεως ἀδίκου D.44.3; *partisanship*, φιλονεικία καὶ π. τῶν θεατῶν Plu.*Cim.*8; *obstinate opposition*, κατὰ ψιλὴν π. ὡς οἱ Χριστιανοί M.Ant.11.3.

**παρατᾰράσσω**, *confuse, confound*, ὑπὸ τῶν φαντασιῶν -ταραχθείς Arr.*Epict.*3.22.25.

**παράτᾰσις**, εως, ἡ, (παρατείνω) *extension* or *continuance of* or *in time*, S.E.*P.*3.107, Ptol.*Tetr.*75; χρονικὴ π. Procl.*Inst.*50; ἐπιθυμία ..μετὰ προκοπῆς τινος καὶ παρατάσεως *Stoic.*3.96; π. τοῦ ἐνεστῶτος *continuance* of the present, A.D.*Synt.*252.4; ἐν παρατάσει γενέσθαι τοῦ τρέχειν *continue* to run, ib.273.17; εἰ ἐν π. χρόνου τὸ εὐδαιμονεῖν Plot.1.5 tit.; παρ' ὃ ἡ κίνησις τὴν π. ἔχει, of time, Id.3.7.8, cf. 3.6.17; τὸ ἀεὶ φαμεν παράτασιν ἔχειν Dam.*Pr.*298. b. π. δοῦναί τισι grant them an *extension* of time for payment, *PTeb.*37.8 (i B. C., pl.). 2. *extension in space, long stretch*, ἡ τῶν ἐντέρων π. Arist.*PA*677ᵇ37, cf. Iamb.*Myst.*1.9. 3. *direction of extension, dimension*, ἐξ π. S.E.*M.*9.367, al. II. Gramm., *time of the tempus imperfectum* (cf. παρατατικός), A.D.*Synt.*70.27, *EM*472.22, Eust.19.28; opp. ἐνεστὼς χρόνος, A.D.*Adv.*124.5.

**παρατάσσω**, Att. -ττω, *place* or *post side by side, draw up in battle-order*, Hdt.9.31, Th.7.3, X.*HG*1.1.33, etc.: also c. inf., τοὺς φρουροὺς παρέταξε φυλάττειν τὸ τεῖχος *drew* them *up with orders* to guard.., ib.4.5.11:—Med., in prop. sense, *draw up one's men in battle-order*, ib.7.5.23 codd.; of ships, π. μετεώρους Th.1.52; *post by one's side*, αὐτὸς αὐτῷ με παρετάξατο Isoc.19.38; αὐτοῖς π. τὰ παιδικὰ εἰς τὸν ἀγῶνα X.*Smp.*8.34:—Med. and Pass., *draw up* or *be drawn up beside*, τῶν ὁπλιτέων οἱ παρατετάχατο παρὰ τὴν ἀκτὴν Hdt.8.95; παραταχθεὶς ἐν μάχῃ πλουσίῳ Pl.*R.*556d; *to be drawn up in battle-order*, ἑκατέρωθεν παρατεταγμένοι Th.4.32, cf. 43, etc.; παραταξάμενοι τοῖς πολεμίοις *against*.., Isoc.12.92; ὡς παρετάξαντο ἀλλήλοις X.*HG*4.3.5; παρατάξασθαι πρὸς τὰς δυνάμεις Isoc.4.96; πρὸς τοὺς πολεμίους Plb.2.1.8; ἐπί τινα App.*BC*5.22: abs., *stand side by side in battle*, οἱ παρατεταγμένοι Th.4.96, cf. Ar.*V.*1123, X.*HG*3.4.23; παραταξάμενοι ἐναυμάχησαν *in order of battle*, Th.1.29, cf. X.*Cyr.*5.3.5; μὰ.. τοὺς ἐν Πλαταιαῖς παραταξαμένους D.18.208. 2. Med. and Pass., *stand prepared*, παρατετάχθαι πρὸς τὸ ἀποκρίνεσθαι Pl.*Prt.*333e; πρὸς τὰ κακὰ Epicur.

Fr.489: c. inf., *refuse obstinately*, π. μὴ ἐπινεύειν Arr.*Epict.*1.5.3, cf. M.Ant.8.48. II. *set side by side, compare*, Isoc.11.7.

**παρατᾰτικός**, ή, όν, *extending, continuing*: χρόνος παρατατικός *the imperfect*, A.D.*Synt.*10.19, al.; π. διάθεσις, προφορά, ib.70.8, 262.16; *incomplete*, opp. συντελεστικός, S.E.*M.*10.91: so in Adv. -κῶς, opp. συντελεστικῶς, Diod.ap.S.E.*M.*10.101.

**παραταυτότης**, ητος, ἡ, *spurious* or *simulated identity*, Dam.*Pr.* 224.

**παρατείνω**, fut. -τενῶ Hsch.: pf. -τέτᾰκα Plu.2.832f:—*stretch out along, beside*, or *near*, χεῖρες παρατεταμέναι Hp.*Fract.*13; βραχίων παρὰ τὰς πλευρὰς παρατεταμένος Id.*Art.*1; *extend, deploy*, τὴν φάλαγγα X. *An.*7.3.48; π. ἔλυτρον Hdt.1.185; παρετέτατο ἡ τάφρος X.*An.*1.7.15: —Pass., *extend along* (v. infr. II. 1); *to be stretched at length, laid low*, Ar.*Nu.*213. 2. *stretch on the rack, torture*, Plu.2.135d: metaph., X. *Cyr.*1.3.11:—Pass., *to be tortured*, λιμῷ Pl.*Smp.*207b; *to be worn out*, c. part., παρετάθη μακρὰν ὁδὸν πορευθεὶς X.*Mem.*3.13.6; παρατέταμαι λιπαρὰ κάπτων *I am nigh dead* with eating dainties, Ar.*Fr.*506.1; γελῶντες.. ὀλίγου παρετάθησαν Pl.*Euthd.*303b; παραταθήσεται ὑπὸ σοῦ.. θαμὰ λέγοντος Id.*Ly.*204c; but πολιορκίᾳ παρατενεῖσθαι ἐς τοὔσχατον *will strain themselves* to the uttermost, *hold out* to the last, Th.3.46. 3. *prolong, protract*, τοὺς λόγους Arist.*Po.*1455b2; μῦθον ib.1451b38; ἐπὶ πλεῖον τὴν διάσκεψιν Luc.*Icar.*29, cf. *DMort.*4.2; τὴν ἀκρόασιν Id.*Im.* 13:—Pass., Id.*Am.*4, etc.; ἐνεστῶτος τοῦ παρατεινομένου A.D.*Synt.* 253.3. b. *delay*, τὴν ἀπόδοσιν *POxy.*237 viii 10 (ii A.D.). 4. *apply* a figure to a straight line, Pl.*Men.*87a: abs., Id.*R.*527a. 5. κοιλίαν π. *relax* the bowels, Philistio ap.Ath.3.115e. 6. *lengthen in pronunciation*, ὄνομα Luc.*Luct.*13; *prolong* a sound, of echo, Id. *Dom.*3. II. intr., *stretch* or *lie beside* or *along*, of a wall, a line of country, etc., Hdt.1.180: c. acc. loci, τὰ πρὸς τὴν ἑσπέρην φέροντα ὁ Καύκασος παρατείνει ib.203, cf. Th.4.8:—Pass., παρατέταται ὄρος Hdt.2.8, cf. 4.38; ἡ δέ γ' Εὔβοια.. ἡδὶ παρατέταται (with a pun on signf. I. 1 in next line), Ar.*Nu.*212; also παρατείνειν παρὰ τὰ μέρη Plb.6.31.5: c. dat., π. τῷ κόλπῳ Str.8.2.2: so metaph., ψυχὴ μικρῷ σώματι -τείνουσα Demetr.Lac.*Herc.*1055.10. 2. *extend*, ἀπὸ τοῦ ἐντέρου κάτω π. Arist.*HA*529a22; *extend over*, πάντας χρόνους καὶ τόπους Aristid.1.11 J. 3. of Time, *extend*, ἐνιαυτοῦ μῆκος π. J.*AJ* 15.7.4; παρατείνοντος τοῦ πότου Parth.8.5; πόλεμος π. εἰς ἔτη μ' App. *Syr.*48; *continue* one's life, *live*, ἕως.., μέχρι.., Plu.2.832f, 839e; ἐπὶ τρεῖς γενεάς Luc.*Macr.*3. 4. as aux. Verb, c. part., ποῖ παρατενεῖς δεδιὼς ταῦτα; how *long will you go on* fearing this? Philostr. *VA*7.22, cf. 5.26.

**παρατειχ-ίζω**, *fortify besides*, τὰς Ἀθήνας Philostr.*Ep.*39. **-ισμα**, ατος, τό, *cross-wall*, Th.7.11, 42, al., *SIG*784.2 (Ephesus, i A.D.).

**παρατεκταίνομαι**, Med., prop. of timber, *work into another form*: then, generally, *transform, alter*, οὐδέ κεν ἄλλως Ζεὺς παρατεκτήναιτο not even he could *make them any way else*, Il.14.54; αἶψά κε.. ἔπος παρατεκτήναιο *could disguise, falsify* it, Od.14.131. II. later in Act., *build besides*, οἰκίαν Plu.*Pomp.*40.

**παρατελευτ-αῖος**, α, ον, *penultimate*, ἡ π. (sc. συλλαβή) Ath.3. 106c. **-άω**, *to be penultimate*, Ps.-Plu.*Vit.Hom.*12, Eust.1557. 39. **-ος**, ον, = παρατελευταῖος, Aristid.Quint.1.29, Ps.-Plu.*Metr.* 2, Simp.*in Ph.*62.1, Sch.Ar.*Pl.*598.

**παρατελωνέομαι**, *cheat the revenue*, D.L.4.46.

**παρατέμνω**, fut. -τεμῶ, Lacon. παρταμῶ Ar.*Lys.*116 cod. R:—*cut off at the side*, π. τινὸς θήμισυ *cut off* half *from*.., Ar. l. c. and 132; τυροῦ τροφάλια Alex.172.12, cf. Posidon.15 J.; *cut a rebate* in an ἀκρογείσιον, π. ἐκ τοῦ ἔνδοθεν πάχος ἱμάντος *IG*2$^2$.463.65: c. gen. partit., *cut off part of*.., Aristid.*Or.*48(24).27:—Pass., [ξύλα] παρατετμημένα planks *with rebates cut in them*, *IG*11(2).287*B*147, 150 (Delos, iii B.C.). 2. *cut amiss, make a wrong cut*, Thphr.*HP* 6.3.2.

**παρατεταγμένως**, Adv. pf. part. Pass. (παρατάσσω) *as in battle-array, steadily*, Pl.*R.*399b; *in a self-possessed manner*, Gal.8.362. II. π. ἄγεσθαι, of a straight line, to be drawn *parallel to the ordinate* of a conic, Apollon.Perg.*Con.*1.27, al.

**παρατετᾰμένως**, Adv. *extendedly, throughout the whole length*, Sch. D Il.17.748.

**παρατετηρημένως**, Adv. *carefully*, Ph.1.221, Heliod.ap.Orib.49. 8.7; *according to rule*, A.D.*Conj.*238.29.

**παρατετραμμένως**, Adv. = παρακλιδόν, Eust.1499.4.

**παρατεχνάομαι**, gloss on παρατεκτήναιο, Sch.Od.14.131.

**παρατεχνολογέω**, *introduce incidentally* into a treatise, Demetr. *Eloc.*178 (Pass.).

**παρατηρ-έω**, *watch closely*, θεία φύσις -τηροῦσα τὰς τῶν ζῴων ἐξόδους Epicur.*Ep.*2 p.54 U., cf. Ceb.9; of a general, π. τόπους Plb.1.29.4; σφᾶς αὐτοὺς π. Id.11.9.9; *observe*, -τετηρηκότες μόνον (opp. scientific explanation) Phld.*Rh.*1.248 S.: folld. by an interrog. clause, π. τινά, ὁπότερα.. X.*Mem.*3.14.4; π. τίς ἔπταρεν Philem.100.1: by a part., π. [ὄρνιθα] ἀποδυόμενον Arist.*HA*620a8; with evil design, *lie in wait for, watch one's opportunity*, abs., Id.*Rh.*1384b7; in argument, Id. *Top.*161a23; ἐνεδρεύειν καὶ π. Plb.18.3.2; π. καιροὺς εἰς κόλασιν Phld. *Ir.*p.43 W.:—Med., παρετηροῦντο αὐτὸν οἱ Φαρισαῖοι *Ev.Luc.*6.7: abs., Vett.Val.205.13:—Pass., ὑπό τινος Dicaearch.1.16; *to be kept under observation*, Men.542.6. 2. *take care*, ὅπως μή.. D.18.161; π. ἵνα .. D.H.*Dem.*53. 3. *observe carefully*, τὸ μέτριον Arist.*Rh.*1405b 33:—Med., *observe religiously*, ἡμέρας καὶ μῆνας *Ep.Gal.*4.10; τὴν τῶν σαββάτων ἡμέραν J.*AJ*14.10.25: generally, ὅσα προστάττουσιν [οἱ νόμοι] ἀκριβῶς π. D.C.53.10. **-ημα**, ατος, τό, *observation*, D.H. *Amm.*2.17 (pl.), *Dem.*13; of auguries, Hsch., Phot. 2. *condition to be observed*, Alex.Aphr.*in Top.*515.9 (pl.). **-ήσιμος**, ον, gloss on ἀποφράδας, Hsch. **-ησις**, εως, ἡ, *observation*, διειλημμένοι εἰς παρατήρησιν kept under *surveillance*, Aen.Tact.10.25; παρατηρήσεις ἄστρων D.S.1.28, cf. 5.31; π. παθέων ἀλλοτρίων *IG*4$^2$(1).687.14 (Epid., ii A.D.); ποιεῖσθαι τὴν π. Plu.2.363b; μετὰ παρατηρήσεως so that *it can be observed*, *Ev.Luc.*17.20: in bad sense, *close observation*, to detect faults, etc., Plb.16.22.8; ἐνέδρα καὶ π. Plu.2.266b; *empirical observation*, opp. λογισμός, Gal.1.127; so κατὰ ἱστορίαν ἢ π. Phld.*Rh.* 1.40 S. 2. *observance* of rules, etc., D.T.629.21. 3. *remark, note*, παρατηρήσεως ἄξια Longin.23.2, cf. Sch.Ar.*Ra.*1258; ψιλὴ π. bare *notice*, A.D.*Pron.*41.8. **-ητέον**, *one must observe*, Vett.Val. 156.20, *Gp.*3.13.10, Iamb.*in Nic.*p.25 P. 2. *one must take care*, ὅπως μή.. Arist.*APr.*66a25. 3. Gramm., *one must note*, ὅτι.. Harp. s. v. περίπολος, Ath.1.18f, Sch.Ar.*Pax*32, al. **-ητής**, οῦ, ὁ, *observer*, φύσεως D.S.1.16; *scrutinizer*, τῶν ξενικῶν βίων Dicaearch. 1.4. **-ητικός**, ή, όν, *good at observing*, Dsc.*Ther.Praef.*, Ptol.*Tetr.* 4 (Comp.). Adv. -κῶς *by observation*, ibid., Procl.*in Cra.*p.74 P.

**παρατίθημι**, Dor. and poet. παρτίθημι (late forms from παρατίθω *PMag.Par.*1.333, *Tab.Defix.Aud.*26.27); 3 sg. παρτιθεῖ, παρατιθεῖ, Od.1.192, Hdt.4.73: impf. -ετίθει Ar.*Ach.*85, *Eq.*1223: aor. Act. παρέθηκα, Med. παρεθέμην: pf. παρατέθεικα: in Att. παράκειμαι generally serves as the Pass.:—*place beside*, πὰρ δὲ τίθει δίφρον Od.21. 177, cf. 182 (tm.), *Berl.Sitzb.*1927.167 (Cyrene), etc.; [εἰκόσι] κόσμον *OGI*90.40 (Rosetta, ii B.C.). b. freq. of meals, *set before, serve up*, σφιν δαῖτ' ἀγαθὴν παραθήσομεν Il.23.810, cf. 9.90 (tm.); ἥ οἱ βρῶσίν τε πόσιν τε παρτιθεῖ Od.1.192; πὰρ δ' ἐτίθει σπλάγχνων μοίρας 20.260; [νῶτα βοὸς] γέρα πάρθεσαν αὐτῷ 4.66; νῦν οἱ πάρθες ξεινήϊα καλά Il.18.408; ξεινιά τ' εὖ παρέθηκεν 11.779, cf. Od.9.517 (tm.); θεὰ παρέθηκε τράπεζαν 5.92: c. gen., τῷ νεκρῷ πάντων παρατιθεῖ Hdt. 4.73, cf. 1.119 (Pass.); παρετίθεσαν ἐπὶ τὴν τράπεζαν κρέα X.*An.*4.5. 31; οἱ παρατιθέντες *the serving-men*, Id.*Cyr.*8.8.20; τὰ παρατιθέμενα *meats set before one* (with or without βρώματα), ib.2.1.30, 5.2.16: in Com., Ar.*Ach.*85, *Eq.*52, 57, Aristomen.12, etc.; of a sacrificial meal, σκέλος τοῦ πράτου βοὸς παρθέντω τῷ θιῷ *IG*4$^2$(1).41.11 (Epid., v/iv B.C.). c. of a mother, *put to the breast*, Sor.1.105. 2. generally, *provide, furnish*, αἳ γὰρ ἐμοὶ.. θεοὶ δύναμιν παραθεῖεν (v. l. περιθεῖεν) oh that they *would place* power *at my disposal!*, Od.3.205; π. ἑκάστων τῶν σοφῶν ἀπογεύσασθαι, i.e. π. ἕκαστα τὰ σοφὰ ὥστε ἀπογεύσασθαι αὐτῶν, Pl.*Tht.*157c; π. αὐτοῖς.. ἀναγιγνώσκειν.. ποιήματα Id.*Prt.* 325e:—Med., *expose for sale*, Arist.*HA*622b34. 3. *place upon*, στεφάνους παρέθηκε καρήατι Hes.*Th.*577 (nisi leg. περίθηκε). 4. *lay before* one, *explain*, X.*Cyr.*1.6.14; π. ἔν τισι ὡς οὐ χρή.. *POxy.* 2110.6 (iv A.D.); *allege, produce*, Is.9.32; ὑποδείγματα Phld.*Mus.* p.79 K.; παραβολὴν π. αὐτοῖς *Ev.Matt.*13.24:—Med., v. infr. B. 5. 5. *put* or *provide side by side*, ὁμοῦ λύπας ἡδοναῖς π. Pl.*Phlb.*47a; παρατεθείσης τῆς ἀπολογίας (sc. τῇ κατηγορίᾳ) Demad.6; *set side by side, compare*, τινά τινι Plu.*Demetr.*12. b. Gramm., *place side by side, juxtapose* (opp. συντίθημι *form a compound*), A.D.*Pron.*42.5, al. (Pass.). 6. *deposit*, = παρακατατίθημι, Charito 8.4 (s. v. l.), v. infr. B. 2.

B. Med., *set before oneself, have set before one*, ἐπὴν δαῖδας παραθεῖτο Od.2.105 codd., cf. 19.150, 24.140; σκύφος παραθέσθαι E.*Cyc.*390; τράπεζαν Περσικήν Th.1.130; σῖτον X.*Cyr.*8.6.12; οἱ τὰ εὐτελέστερα παρατιθέμενοι those *who fare* less sumptuously, Id.*Hier.*1.20; *have* meat *set before* others, ἠῶθεν δέ κεν ὔμμιν ὁδοιπόριον παραθείμην Od.15. 506; *provide for oneself, supply oneself with*, παρετίθεντο τῶν ἀναγκαίων πρὸς τὸν πόλεμον, ὅσα.. Plu.*Per.*26. 2. *deposit what belongs to one* in another's hands, *give in charge*, τοῦ παραθεμένου τὰ χρήματα Hdt.6.86 β'; τὴν οὐσίαν ταῖς νήσοις π. X.*Ath.*2.16; τῶν ἀβακείων ἃ παρεθέμεθα παρ' αὐτῷ *PCair.Zen.*71 (iii B.C.), cf. Plb.3.17.10, *PGrenf.* 1.14.1 (ii B.C.), etc.; *deposit* deeds or documents, *POxy.*237 iv 38 (ii A.D.), etc.; *give a person in charge to*, τινὶ ὀρφανόν Arr.*Epict.*2.8.22; *commend* or *commit* into another's hands, εἰς χεῖράς σου τὸ πνεῦμα *Ev.Luc.*23.46; τινὰς τῷ Κυρίῳ *Act.Ap.*14.23, cf. 20.32, 1 *Ep.Pet.*4. 19; *commend* by a letter of introduction, *PGiss.*88.5 (ii A.D.). b. *store up* in one's mind, ἅ τις ὁρᾷ π. παρ' αὐτῷ Plot.4.4.8. 3. *venture, stake, hazard*, σφὰς γὰρ παρθέμενοι κεφαλὰς Od.2.237; τοί τ' ἀλόωνται ψυχὰς παρθέμενοι 3.74, cf. Tyrt.12.18. 4. *apply* something *of one's own* to a purpose, *employ it*, ὄψιν ἐν τῷ διανοεῖσθαι Pl.*Phd.*65e. 5. *cite in one's own favour, cite as evidence* or *authority*, π. μῦθον, παράδειγμα, Id.*Plt.*275b, 279a; ἀντίγραφον [ἐπιστολῆς] *BGU*1004.12 (iii B.C.); ἀποδείξεις Wilcken *Chr.*77.5 (ii A.D.); ψήφισμα Plu.2.833e, cf. D.Chr.17.10, Ath.11.479c, Porph.*Abst.*1.3, etc.; *mention*, ἔννοιάν τινος A.D.*Synt.*65.9; ἐκδόσεις π. *quote* editions, Id.*Pron.*89.22: abs., *quote instances*, ib.52.7, al.:—rarely in Act., λέξεις π. D.H.*Dem.*37, v. l. in Id.*Comp.*23. 6. *affix, apply a name*, τῷ χωρίῳ ὄνομα Paus. 2.14.4. 7. *explain, allege*, Wilcken *Chr.*20 iii 12 (ii A.D.).

**παρα-τίλλω**, fut. -τῐλῶ Ar.*Eq.*373:—*pluck the hair* from any part of the body but the head, τὰς βλεφαρίδας τινός l. c. (vulg. περιτιλῶ):—Med., *pluck out one's hairs*, Id.*Ach.*31: fut. παρατῐλοῦμαι Men.363.5: —Pass., freq. in pf. part. παρατετιλμένος, η, *clean-plucked*, a practice among voluptuaries and women, Ar.*Lys.*89, *Ra.*516, Pl.Com.174. 14; δέλτα π. Ar.*Lys.*151; ὁ ἀλοὺς μοιχὸς παρατίλλεται Id.*Pl.*168, cf. Luc.*Fug.*33. II. Med., *pull up weeds*, *Gp.*2.38.2. **-τιλμός**, ὁ, *plucking out hair*, Sch.Ar.*Pl.*168 (pl.). **-τίλτρια**, ἡ, *female slave who plucked the hairs* from her mistress's body, Cratin.256, Philostr.*VA*4.27.

**παρατῑμασία**, ἡ, *extra assessment*, *IG*5(1).1433.16 (Messene).

**παρατῑμάω**, f.l. for προτιμάω in Lib.*Decl.*4.11.

**παράτῑμον**, τό, *reduction of price, rebate*, Benndorf-Niemann *Reisen in Lykien* p.156 (pl.), *Ephes.*3 No.71, *PRyl.*225.39 (ii/iii A.D.).

⊛ **παράτιτλον**, τό, *explanatory note* appended to a statute, *Cod.Just.* 1.17.2.21.

**παρατιτρώσκω**, *wound besides*: metaph., *do violence to*, τὴν ἀλήθειαν Men.Prot.p.116 D.; *violate*, νόμον Lyd.*Mag.*1.41.

**παρατμήγω**, = παρατέμνω, aor. 1 παρέτμηξεν· ἐξηφάνισεν, Hsch.

**παρατμίζω**, *fumigate*, *Gp.*11.18.13.

**παρατολμ-άω**, pf. -τετόλμηκα, *to be foolhardy*, Plb.*Fr.*66; τὰ παρατετολμημένα *overbold phrases*, Longin.8.2. **-ος**, ον, *foolhardy*, Plu.*Pomp.*32, al. Adv. -μως Hld.9.21.

**παρατομή**, ἡ, *rebate* cut in a rock, *Inscr.Délos* 507bis 9 (pl., iii B.C.). II. *section* of a settlement, *quarter, district*, *PVat.*11ʳ iii 32, al. (ii A.D.), *Stud.Pal.*20.35.2 (iii A.D.).

**παράτομον** (sc. ξύλον), τό, *plank with a rebate cut in it*, *IG*11(2).287 *B*148, al. (Delos, iii B.C.); cf. παρατέμνω.

**παράτομος**, ον, dub. sens. of rugs, *PCair.Zen.*48 (iii B.C.).

**παράτονος**, ον, *stretched beside*, π. χέρες hands *hanging down by the side*, E.*Alc.*399 (lyr.). II. *ill-sounding*, διάλεκτος Hsch. s.v. βαρβαρισμός. III. *ill-strung*, of a bow, παράτονόν σοι ἐγένετο Ps.-Callisth.1.31.

**παρατόξευσις**, εως, ἡ, *a casting side-glances*, Plu.2.521b. II. *shooting wide of the mark*, Greg.Cypr.*Prov.*4.5.

⊛ **παρᾱτούριον**, τό, Dim. of Lat. *paratura*, = ἀντίπανον (Lat. *antepannus*), Hsch.

**παρατρᾰγεῖν**, v. παρατρώγω.

**παρατρᾰγῐκεύομαι**, *burlesque tragedy*, Sch.Ar.*V.*1473.

⊛ **παρατρᾰγῳδ-έω**, *use mock-tragic style*, Poll.10.92; *ut paratragoedat carnufex!* Plaut.*Pseud.*707. **-ος**, ον, *pseudo-tragic, bombastic*, Plu. 2.7a, Longin.3.1.

**παρατράχηλος** [ᾰ], ον, *with the neck on one side*, of the statues of Alexander by Lysippus, Tz.*H.*8.421:—Verb -έω, ib.11.100.

⊛ **παρατρέπω**, aor. 2 παρέτραπον Hes.*Th.*103:—**Med.** (v. infr.):—**Pass.**, aor. 2 παρετράπην App.*Mith.*1:—*turn aside, off*, or *away*, παρατρέψας ἔχε μώνυχας ἵππους ἐκτὸς ὁδοῦ Il.23.423, cf.398; Ταντάλου λίθον παρά τις ἔτρεψεν ἄμμι θεός *pushed* it *from* our heads, Pi.*I.*8(7).11; ποταμὸν π. *divert* a river *from* its channel, Hdt.7.128, cf. 130; π. ἄλλῃ τὸ ὕδωρ Th.1.109, cf. Pl.*Lg.*736b; [τὸ ὕδωρ] παρατρέψαι τοῦ εἴδους Philostr.*Im.*1.23:—Med. and Pass., -τραπόμενος τοῦ λόγου X.*Oec.*12.17; ἔξω τοῦ βελτίστου D.C.*Fr.*83.1; ἐκ τοῦ νοῦ παρετράπη Paus.4.4.8; παρατρεπόμενος εἰς Τένεδον *turning aside* to.., X.*HG*5.1.6. 2. *turn* one *from* his *opinion, change* his *mind*, ταχέως δὲ παρέτραπε δῶρα θεάων Hes.*Th.*103; τινὰ ἐπέεσσι π. A.R.3.902:—Med., Theoc.22.151:—Pass., π. παρὰ τὸ δίκαιον ὑπὸ δώρων Pl.*Lg.*885d; λοιβῇ τε οἴνου κνίσῃ τε ib.906e. 3. of things, π. λόγον *pervert, falsify* a story, Hdt.3.2; π. τὸν λόγον ἔξω τοῦ ἀληθοῦς D.H.6.75. 4. generally, *alter*: *revoke* a decree, Hdt.7.16.γʹ; π. ἐμμέλειαν Ael.*NA*2.11; π. ὄνομα D.Chr. 12.67, cf. App.*Mith.*1 (Pass.). 5. *remove*, τὸ ἐν κακίᾳ εἰρημένον A.D.*Synt.*37.12. 6. *deceive*, τὴν ὄψιν Ael.*NA*2.14. 7. π. τὰς κράσεις, of air in epidemics, Aët.5.94:—Pass., of wine, *turn sour*, *Gp.* 2.47.5. 8. Pass., π. εἴς τινα *have dealings* with, *PMasp.*295 iii 7 (vi A.D.).—Cf. παρατροπέω, παρατρωπάω.

**παρατρέφω**, aor. 1 παρέθρεψα Hdn. (v. infr.):—Pass., aor. 2 παρετράφην Men.866:—*feed beside* or *with* one, τὸν βουλόμενον Timocl. 9.2; *maintain in addition*, Arist.*Ath.*62.2, *PSI*6.571.15 (iii B.C.); ἵππους, κύνας, Plu.2.830c, cf. Ael.*NA*3.1 (Pass.):—Pass., of slaves, etc., *to be brought up with* the children, Posidon.36 J., Harp. s.v. μόθωνας; οὐχ αὑτῷ παρετράφην ἀλλὰ σοὶ Men. l.c.; of concubines, *live with* the wives, Plu.*Art.*27; of men and animals, *feed at another's expense*, D.19.200, Men.244, Plu.2.13c. 2. *bring up alike*, ἀμφοτέρους ἴσους ἐκ παίδων παραθρέψαι Hdn.3.15.5. 3. Pass., *to be educated*, ἐν φιλοσοφίᾳ Plu.2.37e, 138c.

⊛ **παρατρέχω**, fut. -δρᾰμοῦμαι *Com.Adesp.*555: aor. παρέδρᾰμον (the only tense used by Hom., v. infr.): pf. -δέδρομα (v. infr. 4): plpf. -δεδραμήκεσαν X.*An.*7.1.23: aor. 1 part. παραθρέξας A.R.3.955:—*run by* or *past*, ὁ δ' ἄρ' ὦκα παρέδραμεν Il.10.350, cf. 22.157; ἐς τὰ Πιττάλου Ar.*V.*1432; π. παρ' οἰκίαν X.*An.*7.4.18; οἱ -τρέχοντες the *runners* of a king's bodyguard, Lxx 3*Ki.*14.27, al.; οἱ περὶ τὴν διοίκησιν -τρέχοντες *Arch.Pap.*8.206 (i B.C.). b. *accompany*, c. dat., χάρις π. ταῖς συνουσίαις Eun.*VS* p.499 B. c. παράτρεχε *be off!*, Alex.16. 11. 2. *outrun, overtake*, Ἴφικλον δὲ πόδεσσι παρέδραμον Il.23.636, cf. Ar.*Eq.*1353; χελώνη π. δασύποδα *Com.Adesp.*555; π. τὰ τότε κακά *go beyond, exceed* them, E.*HF*1020; π. τινὰ ἔν τινι, π. τινὰ τοσοῦτον, *excel, surpass* him, Plb.31.25.2 and 29.12; ἔς τι Eun.*Hist.*p.252 D. 3. *run through* or *over*, τὸ λοιπὸν [τοῦ χωρίου] X.*An.*4.7.6; ἑπτά εἰσιν αἱ ἡλικίαι ἃς π. ὁ ἄνθρωπος Sch.Philostr.*Her.*p.391 Boissonade; *run across* (a space of ground expressed or implied), ἐπὶ.., εἰς.., X.*An.*7.1.23, 4.7.11: abs., dub. in ib.4.5.8. 4. *run over*, i.e. *treat cursorily*, Isoc.4.73; παρέργως π. D.H.*Rh.*5.3; τὰ γράμματα τῇ ὄψει π. Plu.2.520e; cf. παραδέδρομα (-ωμαι cod.)· παρεμνήσθην, Hsch. b. *pass over, omit*, Plb.10.43.1, Gal.8.869; ἵνα ταῦτα παραδράμω D.C.79.12; *slight, neglect*, Theoc.20.32. 5. *escape unnoticed*, τινας Plb.6.6.4; παρὰ δὲ φρένας ἔδραμον ἀνδρῶν Opp.*H.*3.96: abs., of Time, Hdn.2.12.4.

**παρατρέω**, *start aside from fear*, παρέτρεσσαν δέ οἱ ἵπποι Il.5.295.

**παρά-τρημα**, v. πάραρρυμα I. ⊛ **-τρητος**, ον, *pierced at the side*, αὐλὸς π., of a flute used for mournful airs, Poll.4.81; π. αὐλίσκος an injecting tube, Ruf.ap.Orib.8.24.62; π. πόροι Antyll.ib.50.3.3.

⊛ **παρα-τρῐβή**, ἡ, *rubbing against one another*, ξύλων Ph.Bybl.2. 2. metaph., *friction*, ἐν ὑποψίαις ἦν πρὸς ἀλλήλους καὶ παρατριβαῖς Plb.2. 36.5; αἱ ἐν ἀλλήλοις π. καὶ φιλοτιμίαι Ath.14.626e. 3. *by-path*, Max.Tyr.39.3. **-τριβος**, *limes, Gloss.* **-τρίβω** [ῑ], *rub beside* or *alongside*, π. χρυσὸν ἀκήρατον ἄλλῳ χρυσῷ (sc. ἐς βάσανον) *rub* pure gold *by the side of* other gold on the lapis Lydius and see the difference of the marks they leave, Hdt.7.10.αʹ:—Pass., *to be rubbed beside* or *upon*, καθάπερ πρὸς τὰς βασάνους Arist.*Col.*793ᵃ33; ἐς βάσανον ἐλθὼν παρατρίβομαι ὥστε μολύβδῳ χρυσός Thgn.417. 2. *rub on* or *against*, τινί τι Ael.*NA*17.44; πρὸς θάμνους Suid. s.v. ὅπου αἱ ἔλαφοι:—Pass., *rub oneself against*, τὰ ὕπτια πρὸς τὰ ὕπτια Arist.*HA*540ᵇ12; dub. in Sor.1.7. 3. *rub slightly, brush*, π. οὔρῳ τοὺς ὀδόντας D.S.5. 33, cf. Diocl.*Fr.*141; τοὺς ὀφθαλμούς S.E.*M.*7.258. II. παρατρίβεσθαι πρός τινα *clash against, fall out with* one, Plb.27.15.6; ἔκ τινων πρός τινας Id.4.47.7: abs., διά τι Id.9.11.2. III. παρατρίψασθαι τὸ μέτωπον *harden* the forehead *as it were by perpetual rubbing*, i.e. *to be utterly hardened, dead to shame*, Str.13.1.45. IV. Pass., *to be exhausted*, ἀναβάσει *POxy.*1668.24 (iii A.D.). **-τριμμα**, ατος, τό, *abrasion caused by friction* in riding or walking, *intertrigo*, Dsc.1. 39, Antyll.ap.Orib.10.24.10, Gal.13.395, al. **-τριπτέον**, *one must rub*, τὰ περὶ τὸ στόμα τρυγὶ οἴνου *Gp.*16.4.4. **-τριψις**, εως, ἡ, *rubbing against one another, friction*, νεφῶν Epicur.*Ep.*2 p.45 U. (pl.), cf. Arist.*Mu.*395ᵇ5, Thphr.*Lap.*45, Ph.*Bel.*78.10, D.S.3.36, *Placit.*3.3. 11 (pl.), M.Ant.6.13; τῇ τοῦ ποδὸς πρὸς τὴν γῆν π. Chrysipp.ap.S.E. *P.*1.70.

**παρα-τροπέω**, = παρατρέπω, τί με ταῦτα παρατροπέων ἀγορεύεις; why tell me this, *trying to lead* me *astray, to mislead* me? Od.4.465, cf. A.R.3.946. **-τροπή**, ἡ, *turning away, means of averting*, θανάτου E.*Ion* 1230 (lyr.); τῶν ἀβουλήτων Plu.2.168e (pl.). 2. *slight alteration*, τοῦ ὀνόματος ib.376a, cf. Suid. s.v. χρεών; f.l. for παρεκτροπή, A.D.*Synt.*167.3; τρόπος ἐστὶ λόγος κατὰ παρατροπὴν τοῦ κυρίου λεγόμενος Trypho *Trop.Praef.* 3. *misleading*, τοῦ φρονοῦντος Plu.2.758e. II. intr., *deviation*, τῆς ὁδοῦ ib.1106b; εἰς τὸ νοσῶδες Apollon.ap.Orib.7.19.5; εἰς τὸ παρὰ φύσιν Gal.18(1).181. 2. of the mind, *aberration, error*, Plu.2.40b, Iamb.*Myst.*3.25 (pl.); *perversion*, Plu.2.1104d. 3. metaph., *side-stream*, Longin.13.3 (pl.); *digression*, Plu.2.855d (pl.), Luc.*Dem.Enc.*6. ⊛ **-τροπος**, ον, *turned aside*: *turned from the right way, lawless*, εὐναί Pi.*P.*2.35. 2. *strange, unusual*, Opp.*H.*1.515, 4.18, cf. Plu.*Lys.*12. II. Act., *averting*, μόρου π. μέλος E.*Andr.*528 (lyr.):—where Sch. expl. **παρατροπικός**.

**παράτροφος**, ον, *reared with* or *in the same house*, Plb.38.15.3 and 5.

⊛ **παρατροχ-άζω**, poet. for παρατρέχω, *run past*, τινα *AP*9.372, 11.163 (Lucill.). 2. *pass by* or *over, leave unnoticed*, *APl.*4.169: metaph., εὐσεβίη οὔ με παρετρόχασεν Puchstein *Epigr.Gr.*p.10. II. *run alongside*, App.*BC*3.70; τινι *by* one, Id.*Syr.*64. **-ια**, τά, part of a chariot *beside the wheel*, Poll.1.147.

**παρατρῠγάω**, *pluck grapes*, Aristaenet.1.3: metaph., of love, ὀμφακίζῃ παρατρυγῶν παιδισκάριον ἄωρον Id.2.7.

**παρατρύζω**, *coo beside* or *near*, Hsch., Phot.

**παρατρύπημα** [ῠ], ατος, τό, *sidehole*, Procl.*in Alc.*p.197 C.

**παρατρώγω**, fut. -τρώξομαι Suet.*Galb.*4: aor. παρέτρᾰγον Hp.*Epid.* 5.86:—*nibble at, take a bite of*, τοῦ ὄφιος Hp. l.c.; τίς ἐλάας παρέτραγεν; Ar.*Ra.*988, cf. *Pax* 415: metaph., τῆς ἀρχῆς παρατρώξῃ August. ap.Suet. l.c.; δικῶν τε καὶ δικαστηρίων Philostr.*VS*2.15.1.

**παρατρωπάω**, poet. for παρατρέπω, [θεοὺς] θυέεσσι.. παρατρωπῶσ' ἄνθρωποι *turn away* the anger of the gods.., Il.9.500.

**παρατρωτής**, οῦ, ὁ, (παρατιτρώσκω) *one who perverts*, τῶν εὖ τεθέντων νόμων Hsch. s.v. παραχαράκτης.

**παράττω**, Att. for παραΐσσω.

**παρατυγχάνω**, pf. -τέτευχα and -τετύχηκα (v. infr.): aor. παρέτῠχον:—*happen to be near, be among*, παρετύγχανε μαρναμένοισιν Il. 11.74; τῷ λόγῳ, τῷ πάθεϊ, *to be present at*.., Hdt.7.236, 9.107; εἰς καιρόν γε παρατετύχηκεν ἡμῖν ἐν τοῖς λόγοις Πρόδικος Pl.*Prt.*340e; τῇ μάχῃ Plb.3.70.7; οἱ -τετυχηκότες τοῖς κινδύνοις Id.12.28ᴬ.5; but ὁ πλείστοις κινδύνοις -τετευχὼς *who had met with*.., Id.12.27.8: with Preps., *visit*, εἰς κώμην *POxy.*76.11 (ii A.D.); ἐπὶ διάγνωσιν *put in an appearance* at.., Mitteis *Chr.*89.18 (ii A.D.). 2. abs., *happen to be present*, Hdt. 1.59, 6.108; of things, *offer, present itself*, Hp.*Art.*38; παρατυχούσης τινὸς σωτηρίας Th.4.19; ἕως ἄν τις παρατύχῃ διαφυγή Id.8.11; λαβόντας ὅ τι ἑκάστῳ παρέτυχεν ὅπλον Pl.*R.*474a. 3. freq. in part. παρατυχών, *whoever chanced to be by*, i.e. *the first comer, any chance person*, οὐκ ἐκ τοῦ παρατυχόντος πυνθανόμενος Th.1.22; σὺν τοῖς π. ἱππόταις X. *Cyr.*1.4.18; also τὸ παρατυγχάνον or παρατυχόν *whatever turns up* or *chances*, ποιεῖν τὸ παρατυγχάνον αὐτῷ to do *whatever circumstances required*, Id.*Eq.Mag.*9.1; πρὸς τὸ παρατυγχάνον as *circumstances* required, Th.1.122; ἐν τῷ παρατυχόντι Id.5.38; ἀποκρίνασθαι ἐκ τοῦ παρατυχόντος answer *offhand*, Plu.2.154a: παρατυχόν, abs., *it being in one's power, since it was in one's power* to do, c. inf., Th.1.76; ἐν καλῷ π. σφίσι ξυμβαλεῖν Id.5.60.

**παρατῠλάριον**, τό, *small cushion*, *Sammelb.*7181 *B*29 (iii A.D.).

⊛ **παράτῠλος**, ὁ, *socket for a* τύλος, *Supp.Epigr.*4.447.48 (Didyma, ii B.C., pl.).

**παρατῠπ-όομαι**, *counterfeit*, σφραγῖδα Poll.8.27. 2. *to be constantly changing one's method*, Sor.1.4. II. in pass. sense, *to be counterfeited*, Harp. s.v. παράσημος ῥήτωρ, Poll.3.86. **-ος**, ον, *counterfeit*, νομίσματα Sch.Ar.*Ach.*516, cf. *POxy.*1411.12 (iii A.D.). **-ωσις**, εως, ἡ, *illusory representation*, Plu.2.404d (pl.), cf. Gal.16.567 (pl.). **-ωτικός**, ή, όν, *misrepresenting as by an illusory copy*, S.E.*M.*8.67, Gal.7.107. Adv. -κῶς ib.104, 8.225.

⊛ **παραύα,** ἡ, Aeol. = *παρειά*, Hdn.Gr.2.563, prob. in Theoc.30.5. II. v. *παρείας* II.

**παραυαίνομαι,** Pass., *dry up*, Thphr.*CP*3.7.11.

**παραυγάζω,** *present the appearance of*, *κριοῖο κάρηνον* D.P.89; *τριήρους σχῆμα* Eust.1405.47. II. Med., *shine*, of the sun, Str.2.1.18:—Pass., *to be illuminated*, *ὑπὸ τοῦ ἡλίου* Id.2.5.42.

**παραυγέω,** *see crookedly*, *μονάδι γλήνᾳ* Cerc.4.20.

**παραυδάω,** *console*, *encourage* (Hom. only in Od.), *μύθοις ἀγανοῖσι παραυδήσας* Od.15.53; *μειλιχίοις ἐπέεσσι παραυδῶν* 16.279, cf. Q.S.5.261; *μὴ ταῦτα παραύδα, χρῶτ' ἀπονίπτεσθαι do* not *coax* me thus, to wash, Od.18.178. II. c. acc. rei, *speak lightly of*, *make light of*, *μὴ δή μοι θάνατόν γε παραύδα* 11.488.

⊛ **παραυλ-έω,** *play the flute beside*, or *play it ill*, Poll.4.67. **-ια,** *τά*, *parts adjoining the αὐλή*, Hsch., Phot. **-ίζω,** *lie near*, *παραυλίζουσα πέτρα..Μακραῖς* E.*Ion* 493 (lyr.):—Med., *π. οἱ δορυφόροι τοῖς βασιλείοις* Ath.5.189e. **-ος** (A), *ον*, (*αὐλή*) *dwelling beside*, *π. οἰκίσαι τινά on the borders*, S.*OC*785; *τίνος βοὴ π. ἐξέβη νάπους; close at hand*, Id.*Aj.*892; *ἔνθ' ἡ πάροικος πηλαμὺς χειμάζεται π. Ἑλλησποντίς* Id.*Fr.*503. II. *μίτρη π.* dub. sens. in *Michel* 832.18 (Samos, iv B.C.). **-ος** (B), *ον*, (*αὐλός*) *discordant*, *out of tune*, *μέλη Com. Adesp.*1254 = *Trag.Adesp.*93. II. = *παρεξηυλημένος*, Eust.1597.26.

**παραύξ-η,** ἡ, *increase*, Ph.1.359. **-ησις,** *εως*, ἡ, *waxing*, *ἡμερῶν καὶ νυκτῶν* Gem.6.29 (pl.); opp. *μείωσις*, Id.18.4; *τῆς σελήνης* Dsc.5.141; *φωτός* Porph.ap.Eus.*PE*3.11, cf. Jul.*Or.*4.147b. 2. *progressive increase of parallel series*, Vett.Val.295.6. 3. *metrical lengthening*, *φωνῶν* S.E.*M.*1.126 (pl.). 4. *singing of high notes*, *ἡ παραυξήσεως φιλοτεχνία* Antyll.ap.Orib.6.10.7. 5. Rhet., *amplification*, *exaggeration*, Quint.*Inst.*9.2.106. **-ητέον,** *one must increase*, *augment*, Herod.Med.ap.Aët.9.37. **-ητικῶς,** Adv. *by increasing*, S.E.*M.*3.42. **-ω,** aor. *παρηύξησα*, aor. Pass. *-ηυξήθην*:—*increase*, *augment*, Str.15.2.8, Ph.1.22, S.E.*M.*6.26, Iamb. *in Nic.* p.70 P. (Pass.); *τὰς ὑπεροχὰς τῶν ἐγκλίσεων* Ptol.*Alm.*2.6. 2. *lengthen* a syllable metrically, D.H.*Comp.*11, cf. 15 (Pass.). II. intr., *wax*, *ἡ ἡμέρα -αύξει* Gem.6.39.

**παραύστηρος,** *ον*, *somewhat austere*, *αὐθέκαστος καὶ π. μισοπονηρία* Dicaearch.1.9.

**πάραυτᾰ** or **παραυτά,** Adv. for *παρ' αὐτά* (sc. *τὰ πράγματα*), *immediately*, *straightway*, A.*Ag.*737 (lyr.), D.23.157; *π. δ' ἡσθεὶς ὕστερον στένει διπλᾶ* E.*Fr.*1079.5 codd. Stob., cf. Plb.23.5.11; *ἡ π. χάρις* Id.38.11.11 (better divisim, *παρ' αὐτά*); *τὸ π. πεφυγμένον κακόν* prob. in Epicur.*Fr.*423. 2. c. gen., *ἥκοντες π. τοῦ θανεῖν* Socr.*Ep.*11 (Aristipp.).

**παραυτεῖ,** Adv. = *αὐτεῖ*, *Riv.Ist.Arch.*3.38 (Crete).

**παραυτίκᾰ,** Adv. = *πάραυτα*, A.*Supp.*767, Hdt.2.89, 6.35, etc.; *ἢ καὶ π. ἢ χρόνῳ* E.*Fr.*273; *τὸ π.* Hdt.1.19, 7.137, Ar.*V.*833, etc.; *ἐκ τοῦ π.* Plu.*Cor.*20; *ἐν τῷ π.* Th.2.11, Pl.*Phdr.*240b, etc. 2. with Substs., *Ἅιδην τὸν π. ἐκφυγεῖν present* death, E.*Alc.*13; *ἡ π. λαμπρότης momentary* splendour, Th.2.64; *ἡ π. ἐλπίς* Id.8.82; *αἱ π. ἡδοναί* X.*Cyr.*1.5.9, 8.1.32; *τὸ π. ἡδύ* Pl.*Phdr.*239a.

**παραυτόθεν,** Adv. = *αὐτόθεν*, Arr.*Fr.*159 J.

**παραυχεν-ίζω,** *bend the neck aside*, *cut the throat*, Hsch. (glossed by *παρακλίνων*), Phot. (glossed by *παρακρούων*). **-ιος,** *η*, *ον*, *hanging from the neck*, *φαρέτρη* *APl.*4.253.

**παραφᾰγεῖν,** aor. 2 inf. of *παρεσθίω*.

⊛ **παραφαίνω,** poet. **παρφ-,** *show beside* or *by uncovering*, *μηδ' αἰδοῖα..παραφαινέμεν* Hes.*Op.*734; *σπάθην* Philem.70; *οὐδὲν παραφῆναι τοῦ σώματος give* no *glimpse of* it, Ar.*Ec.*94; *π. τῶν ὀδόντων ὅσον ἀπόχρη τῷ ᾄδοντι* Philostr.*Im.*1.10; *οἱ μαζοὶ μικρὰ τῆς ὁρμῆς παραφαίνουσιν* ib.2.32. 2. *produce*, *τὸν ὅρκον* the form of oath, Ar.*Lys.*183. 3. *walk beside and light*, *show the way to* a place, Id.*Ra.*1362, Plu.*TG*14. 4. *show*, *demonstrate*, *παρέφηναν εἶναι τῆς σοφίας οὐκ ἀμύητοι* Eun.*VS* p.468 B. II. Pass., *appear*, *disclose itself*, Pl.*Tht.*199c; *ἐν τῷ νῦν λόγῳ παραφανέντι* Id.*Sph.*231b, cf. Arist.*Po.*1449$^a$2; *π. σωτηρία* Hierocl. *in CA* 2 p.422 M.; *παραφανεὶς ὁ θεὸς ἔλεξε Archiv f.Religionswiss.*18.258; *come into view*, of an enemy, Ascl.*Tact.*10.11, 14.

**παραφαίρ-εσις,** *εως*, ἡ, *taking away*, gloss on *παραίρεσις*, Sch.Th.1.122. **-έω,** c. gen., *detract from*, v.l. in Artem.3*Pr.*

⊛ **παράφᾰσις** (A), *εως*, ἡ, (*παράφημι*) only in poet. forms **παραίφᾰσις, πάρφᾰσις,** *address*, *encouragement*, *consolation*, *ἀγαθὴ δὲ παραίφασίς ἐστιν ἑταίρου* Il.11.793; *παραίφασιν εὗρεν ἐρώτων a way of calming* them, *APl.*5.373.3. 2. *allurement*, *persuasion*, in the cestus of Aphrodite, *πάρφασις, ἥ τ' ἔκλεψε νόον πύκα περ φρονεόντων* Il.14.217; *deceitful speaking*, *ἐχθρὰ πάρφασις* Pi.*N.*8.32.

**παράφᾰσις** (B), *εως*, ἡ, (*παραφαίνομαι*) *image in a mirror*, Chalcidius *in Ti.*240 (p.273 Wrobel).

**παρ-ᾰφάσσω,** *feel gently with the finger*, Hp.*Nat.Mul.*6:—Med., Id.*Mul.*1.13:—hence **παρ-αφάσιες,** *αἱ*, *interior of the pudenda muliebria*, ib.2.171, cf. Gal.19.128.

**παρα-φάσσω,** = *ἀλλοφάσσω*, Gal.19.128.

**παράφερνα,** *τά*, *goods which a bride brings over and above her dowry*, *Sammelb.*7260 ii *b* 7 (i A.D.), *POxy.*905.7 (ii A.D.), Just.*Nov.*97.5, etc.: sg. in Hsch. s.v. *εἴλιον*.

⊛ **παραφέρω,** poet. **παρφέρω,** fut. *παροίσω* S.*OC*1675 (lyr.):—**Pass.,** aor. 1 *παροισθέντι· παρενεχθέντι*, Hsch.:—*bring to* one's *side*, esp. of meats, *serve*, *set before* one, Hdt.1.119, X.*Cyr.*1.3.6, etc.; *π. ποτήρια* Ar.*Fr.*466; *πάρφερε τὸν σκύφον* Sophr.15; *τὰς κεφαλὰς π. exhibit* them, Hdt.4.65; *μάστιγάς τε καὶ κέντρα π. ἐς μέσον* Id.3.130:—Pass., *to be set on table*, *served*, Id.1.133; *τοῦ ἀεὶ παραφερομένου ἀπογεύονται* Pl.*R.*354b; *τὰ π.* Luc.*Merc.Cond.*26. 2. *bring forward*, *allege*, *cite*, *νόμον* Antipho 3.4.8, cf. *PFlor.*48.8 (iii A.D.); *π. καινὰ καὶ παλαιὰ ἔργα* Hdt.9.26; *λόγους* E.*IA*981, cf. S.*OC*1675 (lyr.); *π. αὐτὸν ἐν σκώμματος μέρει* Aeschin.1.126, cf. 132; *πίστεις π. τοῦ μή..* D.H.7.27; *μάρτυρα* Eust. ad D.P.306, cf. *PAmh.*2.81.12 (iii A.D.), etc. 3. *hand over*, *ξύνθημα παρφέροντι ποιμέσιν λόχων* E.*Ph.*1140. 4. Pass., *come up*, *hasten along*, Arist.*HA*534$^a$3. II. *carry beside*, [*λαμπάδας*] *ἵπποις* E.*Hel.*724. III. *carry past* or *beyond*, Pl.*R.*515a, etc.; *π. τὴν χεῖρα wave* the hand, of gesture in speaking, D.18.232; *π. τὸν βραχίονα παρὰ τὰς πλευρὰς swing* it in a vertical plane parallel to the sides, opp. lifting the elbow outwards, Hp.*Art.*12:—Pass., *to be carried past* or *beyond*, Th.4.135; *δρόμῳ παρενεχθέντας* Plu.*Mar.*35, cf. *Sull.*29; *πρὸς κοντὸν π.* Id.*Dio* 25; *τοῦ χειμῶνος παραφερομένου while* it *was passing*, Id.*Pel.*10. 2. *turn aside* or *away*, *ἑκάστου π. τὴν ὄψιν* X.*Cyn.*5.27; *π. τοὺς ὑσσούς put* them *aside*, Plu.*Cam.*41; *put away*, *avert*, *ποτήριον ἀπό τινος Ev.Marc.*14.36; but also, *turn towards* an object, *κάτω ὁρᾶν καὶ μηκέτι παρενεγκεῖν τὸν ὀφθαλμόν* Luc.*DMeretr.*10.2; *τὴν αὐτὴν αἴσθησιν παραφέρω πρὸς ἑκάτερον* Dam.*Pr.*414. 3. Pass., *move in a wrong direction*, of paralysed limbs, *τὸ παραφερόμενον* Arist.*EN*1102$^b$22; *π. ἐν ταῖς χερσίν*, of feigned madness, Lxx 1 *Ki.*21.13; *π. τοῖς σκέλεσι*, of a drunken man, D.L.7.183; *τὸ βλέμμα παρενήνεκται is distorted*, Phryn.*PS* p.112 B. 4. *mislead*, *lead astray*, Plu.2.41d:—Pass., *παραφέρεσθαι τῷ τέρποντι πρὸς τὸ βλάπτον* ib.15d; *err*, *go wrong*, Pl.*Phlb.*38d, 60d; *ἴσως μὲν ἀληθοῦς τινος ἐφαπτόμενοι, τάχα δ' ἂν καὶ ἄλλοσε -φερόμενοι* Id.*Phdr.*265b; *παρενεχθείς* (sc. *τῆς γνώμης*) *mad*, Hp.*Prorrh.*1.21. 5. *change*, *γνώμην alter* the text of a decree, App.*BC*3.61; *παρενεχθέντος τοῦ ὀνόματος* ib.2.68; *π. τὸ πεπρωμένον* Id.*Syr.*58. IV. *sweep away*, of a river, Plu.*Tim.*28, cf. D.S.18.35 (Pass.); *τοῦ χρόνου καθάπερ ῥεύματος ἕκαστα π.* Plu.2.432b:—Pass., *to be carried away*, *σέ, Βάκχε, φέρων ὑπὸ σοῦ τᾄμπαλι παρφέρομαι AP*11.26 (Marc. Arg.). V. *let pass*, *τὰς ὥρας παρηνέγκατε τῆς θυσίας* Orac.ap.D.21.53; *let slip*, *τὸ ῥηθέν* Plu.*Arat.*43:—Pass., *slip away*, *escape*, X.*Cyn.*6.24. VI. *overcome*, *excel*, *τινά τινι* Luc.*Charid.*19.

B. intr., *to be beyond* or *over*, *ἡμερῶν ὀλίγων παρενεγκουσῶν*, *ἡμέρας οὐ πολλὰς παρενεγκούσας*, a few days *over*, *more or less*, Th.5.20, 26. 2. *differ*, *vary*, as dialects, Xanth.1; *to be altered*, *παρενεγκόντος τοῦ ὀνόματος* Conon 46.4; *παραφέροντα ἢ κατ' ἄλλον τρόπον διαλλάττοντα* Phld.*Sign.*20; *π. παρά τι differ from..*, D.C.59.5; *πρὸς τὴν ἀλήθειαν* Eun.*Hist.*p.237 D.

**παραφεύγω,** *flee past* or *beyond*, *τῇ δ' οὔ πώ ποτε ναῦται..εὐχετόωνται παρφυγέειν* (Ep. aor. 2) Od.12.99.

**παραφηλόω,** = *φηλόω*, Hsch. (*παραιφη..εύμεθα* cod.).

**παράφημι,** poet. **παραίφημι** and **πάρφημι,** *speak gently to*, *advise*, *μητρὶ δ' ἐγὼ παράφημι* Il.1.577:—Med., *persuade*, *appease*, *μνηστῆρας μαλακοῖς ἐπέεσσι παρφάσθαι* Od.16.287, 19.6; *τιν' ἄλλον παρφάμενος ἐπέεσσιν ἀποτρέψεις πολέμοιο* Il.12.249, cf. Od.2.189; *μαλακοῖσι παραιφάμενοι ἐπέεσσιν* Hes.*Th.*90, cf. Parm.1.15. 2. freq. with collat. notion of deceit, *speak deceitfully* or *insincerely*, *παρφάμεν ὅρκον, λόγον*, Pi.*O.*7.66, *P.*9.43:—Med., *πολλά μιν παρφαμένα beguiling* him, Id.*N.*5.32.

**παρα-φθᾰδόν,** Adv. *overtaking*, c. gen., Opp.*H.*3.298: abs., *in rivalry*, ib.4.97. **-φθάνω** [ᾰν], aor. 2 *παρέφθην*, part. Act. and Med. *παραφθάς, -φθάμενος* (the only tense used by Hom.):—*overtake*, *outstrip*, *τοσσάκι μιν..ἀποστρέψασκε παραφθάς* Il.22.197; *εἰ δ' ἄμμε παραφθαίησι πόδεσσιν* (nisi leg. *-φθήῃσι*) 10.346; *κέρδεσιν, οὔ τι τάχει γε, παραφθάμενος Μενέλαον* 23.515; of a horse, *win a race*, Paus.5.8.8, cf. Hld.4.4.

**παρα-φθέγγομαι,** *add a qualification*, in replying, Pl.*Euthd.*296a. 2. *say casually*, *let drop*, *π. ἐν τῷ λόγῳ πολλάκις, ὡς πλούσιός ἐστιν* Hyp.*Eux.*32; *τοῦτο π., ὡς..* Is.8.23; *π. πρός τινας, ὅτι..* Plb.28.17.13; *εἴ τι παρεφθέγξατο* Philostr.*VA*1.19. 3. *speak amiss*, J.*BJ*2.14.8, cf. Sch.S.*Ph.*1194; *talk nonsense*, Hld.10.33. 4. *interrupt* a speaker, *murmur*, Plu.*Alex.*6, 2.738f. 5. *say secretly*, Hld.5.8; *whisper* a question, *τί πρακτέον* Eun.*VS* p.484 B. 6. *gainsay*, Gal.14.630. 7. *utter beside*, *π. τὴν εὐχὴν τῷ τροπαίῳ* Philostr.*Im.*2.5. **-φθεγκτήρια,** *τά*, *greeting* in the marriage festival, Poll.2.118 (v.l.). **-φθεγμα,** *ατος*, *τό*, *qualification added*, Pl.*Euthd.*296b. II. *incidental remark*, Aristid.*Or.*28(49) tit.

**παρα-φθείρω,** *destroy*, *corrupt*, *spoil*, *τὴν ἀρχαίαν μουσικὴν* Artemo 11; *τὸν λόγον* A.D.*Synt.*82.20; *τὴν ἀγορὰν τῶν ὠνίων SIG*799.22 (Cyzicus, i A.D.). 2. *debase*, *νόμισμα, φιλοσοφίαν*, Philostr.*VA*2.29. 3. *alter*, *corrupt*, *τὴν ἄρχουσαν* (sc. *συλλαβήν*) St.Byz. s.v. *Μέγαρα*, cf. Eust.1532.1. 4. *lose*, *τὸ ε̄* A.D.*Synt.*134.8; *τὴν εὐθεῖαν lose* its nominative force (of *τύ*), ib.15.13. II. Pass., with pf. *παρέφθορα*: aor. 2 *παρεφθάρην*:—*to be destroyed* or *spoilt*, *οἱ παρεφθαρμένοι στάχυες* Ph.2.57; *τῆς γῆς παρεφθορυίας* Philostr.*Her.*10.4; *παρεφθορὸς ὕδωρ* Id.*Im.*2.5; *παρεφθορὼς τὸ λογιστικόν demented*, A.D.*Synt.*292.4; of character, *ὑπό τινος -εφθορέναι* Philostr.*VS*1.16.2. 2. *to be lost*, *αἱ φωναὶ παραφθαρεῖσαι* A.D.*Adv.*164.26 (but *παραφθαρεὶς τὴν φωνὴν having lost* one's voice, Plu.2.848b). 3. *become obsolete*, *τὰ τῆς τοιαύτης χρήσεως παρεφθάρη* A.D.*Synt.*139.25; *περὶ παρεφθορυίας λέξεως*, title of work by Didymus, Ath.9.368b; *fall into desuetude*, *νόμος ἄρτι παρεφθάρη* Lyd.*Mag.*2.15. **-φθορά,** ἡ, *corruption*, *ἐν ταῖς φωναῖς* A.D.*Adv.*164.24; of music, Plu.2.1131f; of language, *κατὰ παραφθοράν* Hermog.*Meth.*3, St.Byz. s.v. *Ἀμαζόνειον*, Eust.1936.23.

**παραφίημι,** *put out at the side*, Thphr.*HP*7.4.12. 2. *release*, *discharge* from service, *BGU*1011 iii 10 (ii B.C.), *PGen.*51.17 (iv A.D.).

**παραφῐλάγᾰθος** [ᾰγ], ὁ, title conferred by religious guild at Panticapaeum, *IPE*2.60, al.

**παραφίμωσις**, v. περιφίμωσις.

**παραφλόγισμα**, ατος, τό, *savoury roasted dish*, in pl., Achae.7.

**παραφλῠᾱρέω**, *keep on chattering*, Gal.18(1).763, Eun.*Hist*.p.265 D.

**παραφομοιόω**, *liken*. in Pass., Dexipp.*in Cat*.65.24.

**παρα-φορά**, Ion. -ρή, Dor. **παρφορά**, ἡ, *going aside*, παραφορὰς ποιεῖσθαι to make itself *by-streams*, of a river, Agatharch.23. 2. *movement to and fro*, Sor.1.73: pl., Id.2.14. 3. *waving* of a sword, Onos.26.1. II. mostly of the mind, *derangement, distraction*, A. *Eu*.330(lyr.); τῆς αἰσθήσιος Aret.*CD*1.5; π. ἐν μέθῃ Id.*SD*1.6; *frenzy*, π. καὶ ἔκστασις Iamb.*Myst*.3.7; π. τῆς διανοίας Plu.2.249b; ποδῶν π. *irregular* gait, Adam.2.21. III. Act., *bringing up, furnishing, purveying*, ζυγάστρων *SIG*247 ii 21 (Delph., iv B.C.), cf. *PLond*.3.974 ii 5 (iv A.D.). **-φορέω**, = παραφέρω, *set before*, τινί τι Ar.*Eq*.1215:—Pass., Hdt.1.133. 2. Med., *accumulate*, Pl.*Lg*.858b.

**παραφορμά**· ἀρχή τις τῶν συνεξιόντων βασιλεῖ, Hsch.

⊛ **παρά-φορος**, ον, (παραφέρω) *borne aside, carried away*, οὕτω π. πρὸς δόξαν Plu.*Them*.3; of a bandage, *liable to slip*, Hp.*Art*.14; of a shot, *deviating* from its course, Ph.*Bel*.80.9, al.; *glancing off* an obstacle, ib.84.16. 2. *reeling, staggering*, στείχειν π. ποδί E.*Hec*.1050; δρόμοι π. Plu.2.501d; παράφορον βαδίζειν, of a drunkard, Luc.*Vit.Auct*. 12; τὸ π. τῶν πινόντων Corn.*ND*30: c. inf., σπείρειν π. ὁ μεθύων *unsteady* for sowing seed, Pl.*Lg*.775d. 3. c. gen., *wandering away from*, παράφορος ξυνέσεως *deranged*, Id.*Sph*.228d: abs., *mad, frenzied*, μῦθοι ἀπίθανοι καὶ π. Plu.*Art*.1; simply, *misled*, prob. in Teles p.9 H. (-φρονοι codd. Stob.): neut. as Adv., of a madman, παράφορον δέρκεσθαι, ἀναβοᾶν, Luc.*Fug*.19, *Am*.13. II. Act., *confusing*, γνώμης Hp.*Prorrh*.1.36. III. **παράφορον**, τό, a kind of *alumina*, Plin.*HN*35.184. **-φορότης**, ητος, ἡ, *lurching movement, awkwardness*, Pl.*Ti*.87e.

**παραφορτίζομαι**, *cram as an additional load into*, ταῦτα τῷ λόγῳ Plu.2.8e, cf. Poll.2.139.

**παράφραγμα**, ατος, τό, *breastwork on the top of a wall or mound*, mostly in pl., Th.4.115; of a ship, *bulwarks*, Id.7.25; *screen* or *curtain*, Pl.*R*.514b; τὰ τοῦ βουλευτηρίου π. App.*BC*2.118. 2. metaph. in sg., *barrier*, π. καὶ ἐμπόδιον Dam.*Pr*.400.

**παραφράζω**, *say the same thing in other words, paraphrase*, ἐνθύμημα μεταφράζειν καὶ π. Ph.2.140; γνώμην Hermog.*Prog*.4, cf. Gal. 15.467; βιβλίον ὅλον Eust.1406.19: abs., τὸ π. Hermog.*Meth*.24, cf. Gal.5.678; ἐξ Ὁμήρου π. Eust.239.23.

**παραφρακτικός**, ή, όν, *producing constipation*, Xenocr.ap.Orib.2. 58.87 (v.l. παρεκ-).

**παράφρᾰσις**, εως, ἡ, *paraphrase*, Hermog.*Prog*.3, Gal.17(2).258, Quint.*Inst*.1.9.2.

**παραφράσσω**, Att. -ττω, *barricade*, πάσας εἰσόδους Hdn.4.1.5, etc.:—Pass., παραπεφράχθαι Plb.10.46.3; ὑπό.. Hdn.3.3.2.

**παρα-φραστής**, οῦ, ὁ, *paraphrast*, Ammon.*in APr*.31.17. **-φραστικός**, ή, όν, *paraphrastic*, κεφάλαιον Aphth.*Prog*.3, 4. Adv. -κῶς Eust.55.32.

**παρ-αφρίζω**, (ἀφρός) *foam at the side*, of the mouth, Nic.*Al*.223.

**παραφρον-έω**, *to be beside oneself, deranged*, Hdt.1.109, 3.34, 35, A. *Th*.806, S.*Ph*.815, Ar.*Nu*.844, Antipho 2.2.9, etc.: poet. **παραιφρ-** Theoc.25.262 (v.l.). 2. *to be delirious*, v.l. in Hp.*Prog*.10. **-ησις**, εως, ἡ, = παραφροσύνη, Lxx *Za*.12.4, Hp.*Ep*.18, Herod.Med. in *Rh. Mus*.58.70. **-ία**, ἡ, = foreg., 2*Ep.Pet*.2.16. **-ιμος**, ον, = παράφρων, S.*OT*691 (lyr.).

**παραφροσύνη**, ἡ, *wandering of mind, derangement*, Pl.*Sph*.228d, Aps.p.333 H. 2. *delirium*, Hp.*Aph*.2.2, 6.53 (pl.), *Prog*.10.

**παραφρουρέω**, *keep guard beside*, παραφρουρεῖ τὴν πέραν τοῦ Δουρίου *guards the frontier* beyond the Douro, Str.3.4.20:—Pass., Hld.8.3.

**παραφρῠγᾰνίζω**, *bank up, revet* a canal *with brushwood*, *PPetr*.3 p.108 (iii B.C.):—hence Subst.⊛ **-ισμός**, ὁ, ib.p.100, *PTeb*.180 (i B.C.), prob. in *PCair.Zen*.296.3, 19 (iii B.C.).

**παραφρύγομαι** [ῡ], Pass., metaph., *go into raptures*, Eun.*VS* p.503 B.

**παραφρυκτωρ-εύομαι**, = sq., τοῖς πολεμίοις Lys.13.67. **-έω**, *make secret signals to the enemy*, Din.*Fr*.9.3.

**παράφρων**, poet. **πάρφρων**, ον, gen. ονος, (φρήν) *wandering from reason, senseless*, μάντις S.*El*.473 (lyr.); *out of one's wits, deranged*, Pl. *Lg*.649d; λύσσας πάρφρονος B.10.103; τί τόδ' αὖ παράφρων ἔρριψας ἔπος; E.*Hipp*.232 (anap.); π. καὶ παραπλὴξ τὴν διάνοιαν Plu.*Pomp*.72. Adv. -νως, γελᾶν Zen.1.43.

**παραφῠ-άδιον**, τό, Dim. of sq., Hsch. s.v. Ἑρμαῖ. **-άς**, άδος, ἡ, (παραφύω) *side-growth*, 1. in plants, *sucker, offshoot*, opp. παρασπάς, Thphr.*HP*2.2.4, cf. 1*Enoch* 26.1: metaph., παραφυάδι ἔοικε τοῦ ὄντος Arist.*EN*1096ᵃ21, cf. Ph.1.330 (pl.). 2. in animals, *branch* of a vein, Hp.*Oss*.18; of certain *appendages* in the ἀστακός, Arist.*HA*526ᵃ29, cf. *PA*672ᵇ27. 3. metaph., of *branches* of a discussion, Stob.2.7.2, *EM*784.28, etc.; also, τὸ πρός τι παραφυάδι ἐοικός Plot.6.2.16. [ῠ in Nic.*Fr*.80, perh. metri gr.] **-ής**, ές, *growing beside*, of extra fingers, Paul.Aeg.6.43: παραφυές, τό, = παραφυάς, Arist.*Rh*.1356ᵃ25.

**παραφυκτός**, v. παρφυκτός.

**παραφῠλᾰκ-έω**, *perform garrison duty*, *IGRom*.3.516 (Cadyanda). ⊛ **-ή**, ἡ, *guard, garrison*, Plb.2.58.1, 4.17.9; πόλεως, etc., *POxy*.1033.7 (iv A.D.), etc. II. *keeping securely, safeguarding*, ἡ τῶν χρημάτων π. D.S.17.71, cf. *Peripl.M.Rubr*.19, *POxy*.2121.75 (iii A.D.); *watchfulness*, ἐν λόγοις καὶ ἔργοις Hierocl.*in CA*10 p.436 M. b. *police-* or *garrison-duty*, *Not.Arch*.4.20 (Cyrene, Aug.). 2. *observation*, καιρῶν Hp.*Ep*.16. **-ισμός**, ὁ, *observation, surveillance*, εἰς π. ἐλθεῖν Ps.-Callisth.3.31 (v.l. προπηλακ-). ⊛ **-ίτης** [ῑ], ου, ὁ, *soldier of a garrison*, *OGI*338.17 (Pergam., ii B.C.), *IGRom*.4.896 (Phrygia), *CIG*4366x (Pisidia). **-τέον**, *one must observe*, Vett.Val.314.34, Heph.Astr.1.23, Eust.1352.15. 2. *one must avoid*, Aët.3.25; *one must beware*, *Cod.Just*.1.3.52.3. II. Adj. -τέος, α, ον, *to be avoided*, Aët.7.24. **-τικός**, ή, όν, *of* or *for observation*, Artem.3.58 (v.l.).

⊛ **παραφύλ-αξ** [ῠ], ᾰκος, ὁ, *watcher, guard*, *BCH*32.499 (Aphrodisias), Suid. s.v. δεξιολάβος. ⊛ **-άσσω**, Att. -ττω, *watch beside, guard closely*, of soldiers in garrison, χώραν, πόλιν, Plb.4.3.7, etc. (Med., Id.5.92.8): metaph., π. τὴν ἐλευθερίαν Id.2.58.2; τισὶ τὸ ἀνεπηρέαστον *protect, maintain* their immunity, *POxy*.1106.4 (vi A.D.): abs., *to be on guard*, Plu.*Galb*.20. 2. *watch, observe narrowly*, τὸ τῆς νεὼς.. ἀεὶ ξυμφέρον Pl.*Plt*.297a; τὸν φαῦλον παραφυλάττειν δεῖ, μή.. Democr.87; π. ἀλλήλους, ἐάν.. X.*Lac*.4.4; καιρὸν π. ἐν ᾧ.. *watch for* a time at which.., Plu.2.775e; ἀπ' ὀφθαλμοῦ π. [τινά] *keep* one *in sight*, of a dog following and watching a person, ib.969f. 3. *watch so as to secure*, π. [τινὰς] ὥστε εἶναι φίλους Pl.*Lg*.628a; π. αὐτόν, μή.. *to be on* one's *guard*, lest.., Plu.2.418d:—Med., *to be on one's guard*, Arist.*Pr*.951ᵃ18; π. τι *stand on one's guard against*, Plb.16. 14.10. II. *to be guarded, be careful*, περί τι Pl.*Plt*.284a; π. ἀλλήλους ὅπως μή.. Id.*Lg*.715a; ὅπως.. Arist.*Rh.Al*.1424ᵃ22:—Med., π. μή.. τάττειν *Gp*.2.26.1. III. *serve as* παραφύλαξ, *Jahresh*.8.172 (Notium), *Ath.Mitt*.8.328 (Tralles).

**παραφυλλίς**, ίδος, ἡ, = *virgultum*, *Gloss*.

**παράφυλλον**, *pagus*, *Gloss*.

**παράφυμα**, ατος, τό, Medic., *growth*, Mich.*in PN*143.11.

**παραφῡσάω**, *blow upon*: metaph., *excite*, Aesop.94.

**παράφῠσις**, εως, ἡ, = παραφυάς 1, Thphr.*HP*7.2.5. 2. παραφύσιες μυῶν, = ψόαι, Hp.*Art*.45. b. *attachment* of veins or tendons, Gal.4. 662, *UP*1.21. 3. *monstrous growth* in animals, Arist.*GA*773ᵃ2 (pl.).

**παραφύτ-ευσις** [ῠ], εως, ἡ, *planting beside*, *Gp*.9.10.10. **-εύω**, *plant beside*, Plu.2.92b, etc.:—Pass., Ph.1.301. **-ος**, ον, *that has grown beside*, Thphr.*CP*3.10.8.

**παραφύω**, with fut. and aor. 1, *produce at the side*, βολβώδη κεφαλὴν Thphr.*HP*7.2.2, cf. 7.7.4. II. Pass., with pf. and aor. 2 Act., *grow beside* or *at the side*, Hdt.2.92, Arist.*PA*658ᵃ26, Thphr.*HP*3.17.3, Plu.*Dem*.31, Plot.5.2.2; ἐκ τῶν παραπεφυκότων δένδρων Ael.*VH*3.1; ἀλλ' ἐγγὺς ἀγαθοῦ παραπέφυκε καὶ κακόν Men.407; παραπέφυκεν ἡ Γνάθαινα πλησίον Anaxil.22.13; τῶν ὀδόντων οἱ παραφυόμενοι τοῖς κατὰ φύσιν Gal.18(2).980, cf. Dsc.*Eup*.1.50; *to be adherent*, Gal.2.258.

**παραφων-έω**, *interrupt and say*, Plu.2.183c. II. gloss on παρατρύζω, Hsch., Phot. **-ή**, ἡ, *pseudo-sound*, as it were *the reflexion* or *image of a sound* in the ear, Epicurei ap.Ael. *in Pl. Ti*. (= Porph. *in Harm*.p.216 W.). **-ησις**, εως, ἡ, dub. in *POxy*.1235.102 (Arg. Men.). **-ία**, ἡ, *harmony*, Bacch.*Harm*.61. **-ος**, ον, *sounding beside*: πάρφωνοι, οἱ, *accompaniment, obbligato*, Longin.28.1. II. *sounds midway between consonances and dissonances*, e.g. the tritone, Gaud.*Harm*.8.

**παραφωτισμός**, ὁ, (φωτίζω) *false light*, as of the sun after setting, Posidon.45 J. (v.l. περιφωτ-).

**παραχάζω**, = παραχωρέω, aor. imper. -χασον, and aor. Med. -χάσσατο (-εχάσετο cod.), Hsch.

**παραχᾰλ-ασμάτιον**, τό, = χαλασμάτιον, Hero *Aut*.23.8. **-άω**, *open a passage for*, τὴν λοχείην κάθαρσιν Hp.*Mul*.1.38. 2. intr., of a ship, *let in water, leak*, Ar.*Eq*.434.

**παραχαλκεύω**, *forge beside*, πυρί Aphth.*Prog*.8 (s.v.l.).

**παραχάρ-αγμα**, ατος, τό, perh. *false coinage*, *Supp.Epigr*.3.565.17 (Tyras, iii A.D.): metaph., π. τῆς φύσεως *Hippiatr*.115. **-ακτής**, οῦ, ὁ, *counterfeiter, coiner*, Vett.Val.74.18, Sch.Ar.*Ach*.516. **-άξιμος**, ον, of coinage, *debased*, Suid. s.v. ὑπόχαλκον. **-άσσω**, Att. -άττω, *re-stamp*, i.e. *re-value* the currency, metaph., Diog.Cyn.ap. D.L.6.20, 71, Str.*Chr*.12.23, Jul.*Or*.7.211b, c, Suid. s.v. γνῶθι σαυτόν; δεῖ κἀμὲ νόμισμα παρακόψαι καὶ π. τὸ βαρβαρικὸν Ἑλληνικῇ πολιτείᾳ Alexander Magn.ap.Plu.2.332c; π. τὰ εἰς τὴν δίαιταν *set up a new standard of* life, Luc.*Demon*.5. II. esp. *debase* the currency, οἱ -οντες τὸ νόμισμα, κἂν μέρος λυμήνωνται, τὸ σύμπαν διεφθαρκέναι δοκοῦσιν D.Chr.31.24:—Pass., Harp. s.v. παράσημος ῥήτωρ. 2. metaph., τὰ καθωσιωμένα παρακόπτειν καὶ π., of sabbath-breakers, Ph.2.298, cf. 562, al., Luc.*Am*.22; π. τὴν πάτριον ὑπόθεσιν Dam.*Pr*. 113. b. ὀνόματα κεκαινοτομημένα καὶ -κεχαραγμένα *re-minted*, i.e. used with new meanings, Aristid.*Rh*.1 p.508 S., cf. Gal.7.834.

⊛ **παραχειμ-άζω**, pf. part. -κεχειμακώς *Act.Ap*.28.11:—*winter at a* place, Hyp.*Fr*.260, D.34.8, 56.30, *Peripl.M.Rubr*.32, etc.; π. ἐν πόλει Plu.*Sert*.3. **-ασία**, ἡ, *wintering in* a place, Plb.3.35.1, *SIG*762.16 (Odessus, i B.C.), D.S.14.38, *Act.Ap*.27.12; ἐνταῦθα τὴν π. ἐποιεῖτο D.S.20.28. ⊛ **-αστικός**, ή, όν, *fit for wintering in*, λιμὴν *Stad*.125, 345.

**παραχειρογρᾰφ-έω**, *violate a written agreement*, *PLond*.2.359.1 (i/ii A.D.), *PFay*.42a ii 14 (ii A.D.), *POxy*.2112.19 (ii A.D.):—hence Subst. **-ία**, ἡ, *PGnom*.218 (ii A.D.).

**παρᾰχελῳ-ίτης** [ῑ], ου, ὁ, *dweller by the Achelous*, Str.9.5.10 (pl.):—fem. **-ῖτις** (sc. χώρα), ιδος, *country along the Achelous*, Id.10.2.19.

**παραχερσία**, ἡ, (χέρσος) *neglected condition* of unirrigated land, *PTeb*.378.13 (iii A.D.).

**παραχέω**, aor. 1 παρέχεα, Pass. παρεχέθην Arist.*Pr*.926ᵇ37 (s.v.l.), παρεχύθην Id.*Fr*.110:—*pour in beside*, παρὰ τὸν οἶνον ὕδωρ (fraudulently) *BCH*50.214 (Thasos, v B.C.): generally, *pour in*, ὕδωρ Hdt. 4.75, cf. Hp.*Int*.32; τινι for one, Plu.2.235a; σπονδάς, τὸ μύρον, Pl. Com.69.4, 6:—Pass., παραχεομένου ὕδατος Dsc.2.77. 2. *pour on*, τοῖς σκέλεσι ἔλαιον Gal.6.328. II. of solids, τὸν χοῦν.. ἀναισίμου, παρὰ τὰ χείλεα τοῦ ποταμοῦ παραχέουσα Hdt.1.185. III. *ply the trade of bath-attendant* (cf. παραχύτης), *PMagd*.33.2 (iii B.C.).

**παράχηλος**, ον, *by the hoof*, στρέμματα Hippiatr.96.

**παραχλιαίνω**, *warm slightly*, Hp.*Nat.Mul.*32; ἐν πυρὶ μαλθακῷ, παρὰ τὸ πῦρ, Id.*Mul.*2.205,158.

**παραχναύω**, *nibble at*, τινος Ael.*NA*1.47.

**παραχορδίζω**, *strike a wrong note*, Ar.*Ec.*295.

**παραχορηγ-έω**, *supply*, τινί τι Ath.4.140e. **-ημα**, ατος, τό, *part of a subordinate chorus*, which retires when no longer wanted, as the children of Trygaeus, Sch.Ar.*Pax*113, cf. Sch.Id.*Ra.* 211. II. *part taken by a fourth actor*, Poll.4.110.

**παραχραίνω**, *mix, defile beside*, Plu.*Fr.*7.26 (Pass.).

**παραχράομαι**, *misuse, abuse*, οἱ μὲν οὐ χρῶνται, οἱ δὲ παραχρῶνται Arist.*Fr.*56; χρῶ μὴ παραχρώμενος Ph.2.61: c. dat., π. τῷ σώματι Plb.6.37.9, etc.; π. ὥσπερ ἀνδραπόδοις D.H.6.93. 2. π. ἐς τοὺς συμμάχους *deal wrongly* or *unworthily* with them, Hdt.5.92.α'. II. *treat with contempt, disregard*, c. acc., Id.1.108, 4.159, 8.20: part. παραχρεώμενοι, abs., of combatants, *fighting without thought of life, setting nothing by their life*, Id.7.223. III. *use for a further* or *subsidiary purpose*, Arist.*PA*688ᵃ23.

B. Act. **παραχράω**, = παραχρηστηριάζω, Str.*Chr.*9.8.

⊕ **παραχρῆμα**, Adv. for παρὰ τὸ χρῆμα (cf. χρέος) *on the spot, forthwith*, Hdt.3.15, 7.150, Lys.25.17, etc.; πάλαι τε καὶ οἱ πλεῖστοι π. Th. 7.75; εἰ καὶ μὴ π., ἀλλ' ὀλίγον ὕστερον Isoc.18.64; ταχέως καὶ π. Cratin.6; *at the moment*, π. τέρψασαι Critias 6.23 (nisi divisim scribendum); τὰ π. *the present*, opp. τὰ μέλλοντα, Th.1.138; ἡ π. ἀνάγκη *present* necessity, Id.2.17; τὸ π. περιχαρές ib.51; τὸ π. περιδεές Id.8. 1; τὸ π. ἡδύ *immediate* pleasure, Pl.*Prt.*356a; αἱ π. ἡδοναί Antipho Soph.58: with the Art., τὸ π. Hdt.6.11, etc.; ἐκ τοῦ π. λέγειν to speak *offhand*, Pl.*Cra.*399d, cf. D.1.1; ἐκ τοῦ π. στρατεύεσθαι X.*HG*6. 4.11; αἱ ἐκ τοῦ π. ἡδοναί Id.*Mem.*2.1.20; λέγειν ἀπὸ τοῦ π. Id.*HG*1.1. 30; ἐν τῷ π. Antipho 5.73, Pl.*R.*455a, etc.; ἐς τὸ π. ἀκούειν Th.1.22; ἀσθενεῖς εἰς τὸ π. γίγνονται Pl.*Lg.*646c.—More freq. in Hdt. and Att. Prose than in later writers (hence expld. by Hsch. παραχρῆμα· παραυτίκα.., εὐθέως), cf. Call.*Fr.*106.3, *SIG*577.12 (Milet., iii/ii B.C.), Plu.*Cam.*42; νόμοι ἐκ τοῦ π. κείμενοι Jul.*ad Them.*262a; ἐκ τοῦ π. εἰπεῖν Plu.2.6e, cf. Longin.18.2; ἐν τῷ π. Aristid.2.407 J.:—hence Cobet treats ἄρτι, εὐθύς, εὐθέως, when joined with παραχρῆμα as glosses, π. ἄρτι X.*HG*1.4.14; εὐθέως π. Antipho 1.20; εὐθὺς π. Is.1. 11, Din.1.94, D.48.40. 2. in later writers, c. gen., π. τῆς εὐεργεσίας D.Chr.11.130; π. τῆς διαβάσεως Eun.*Hist.*p.240 D., cf. *Gp.*10. 75.16.

**παράχρησις**, εως, ἡ, (παραχράομαι) *abuse*, τοῦ σώματος Anon.ap. Suid. s. v. Ὠριγένης.

**παραχρηστηριάζω**, *give a false oracle*, Str.9.2.4.

**παραχρηστικῶς**, Adv. = καταχρηστικῶς, Sch.Ar.*Pl.*313 cod. R.

**παρά-χριστα**, τά, *ointments*, Sever.ap.Aët.7.96. **-χρίω** [ῑ], *daub*, μάλθη τὴν τρόπιν Hippon.50, cf. Suid. s. v. κονιᾶται:—Pass., *to be used for ointment*, Gal.12.183.

**παρά-χροος**, ον, contr. **-χρους**, ουν, *colourless, faded*, Luc.*Hist. Conscr.*51. **-χρωμος**, ον, = foreg., Poll.4.139. **-χρώννυμι**, *corrupt* music *by the* ἁρμονία χρωματική, τῶν μελῶν τὰ.. παρακεχρωσμένα Arist.*Pol.*1342ᵃ24. **-χρωσις**, εως, ἡ, *use of the chromatic scale*, αἱ ἐν τοῖς μέλεσι π. Plu.2.645d. 2. *colouring*, metaph. of character, Simp.*in Cat.*216.5. 3. *faint image*, σκιάς τινας ἡδονῶν καὶ -χρώσεις Id.*in Epict.*p.21 D., cf. *in Ph.*280.16.

**παρά-χῠμα**, ατος, τό, *liquor added*, *EM*172.13. **-χῠσις**, εως, ἡ, *pouring in*, ὕδατος, i.e. fraudulent watering of wine, *BCH*50.214 (Thasos, v B.C.). **-χῠτέον**, *one must pour in*, Aret.*CA*1.1, Antyll. ap.Orib.10.23.14, *Gp.*7.26.1. **-χύτης** [ῠ], ου, ὁ, *one who pours in*, esp. *who brings water for bathing, bath-attendant*, *PCair.Zen.*799.7 (iii B.C.), *PMagd.*33.14 (iii B.C.), Plu.2.538a, Ath.12.518c, *Ostr.Bodl.* ii 81 (iii A.D.); π. δημοσίου βαλανείου *POxy.*1499.2 (iv A.D.). II. prob. *attendant at the religious ceremony* καταχυτήρια, *PCair.Zen.*176. 38 (iii B.C.).

**παρά-χωμα**, ατος, τό, *embankment, dyke*, in pl., Str.5.1.5, 10.2. 19. **-χώννυμι**, *throw up beside*, χῶμα παρέχωσε παρ' ἑκάτερον τοῦ ποταμοῦ τὸ χεῖλος Hdt.1.185; *bank up*, Ἀρχ.Ἐφ.1923.39 (Oropus, iv B.C.).

**παραχωρ-έω**, fut. -ήσομαι D.23.105, later -ήσω Lxx 2*Ma.*8.11:—*go aside*: rarely in lit. sense, *to be displaced*, Hp.*Loc.Hom.*47: mostly, *make way, give place*, abs., Ar.*Ra.*767, *Ec.*633, And.1.26, Pl.*Smp.* 213b, D.17.1, etc.; τινι for one, X.*HG*5.4.28, Arr.*Epict.*4.1.107, etc. b. *give way, yield, submit*, τινι to one, Pl.*Prt.*336b; τινί τινος in respect of.., ib.c: c. acc. cogn., εἴ τις ταῦτα παραχωρήσειε *should concede* this, Arist.*de An.*410ᵇ25: c. acc. et dat., π. τῷ νομοθετοῦντι τοιάδε Pl.*Lg.*959e. 2. π. τινός *retire from*.., ὅμως ἀξιῶ.. μὴ παραχωρεῖν τῆς τάξεως D.3.36; ἐκ τῆς πόλεως v.l. in D.H.6.50. 3. *step aside out of the way for* another, as a mark of respect, ὁδοῦ π. τὸν νεώτερον πρεσβυτέρῳ X.*Mem.*2.3.16: in full, c. dat. pers. et gen. rei vel loci, ὁ ποταμὸς ἡμῖν παρακεχώρηκε τῆς ὁδοῦ Id.*Cyr.*7.5.20; π. σοι τοῦ βήματος Aeschin.3.165; τοῖς ἐχθροῖς τῆς ἡμετέρας π. Isoc.6.13; Φιλίππῳ.. Ἀμφιπόλεως παρακεχωρήκαμεν *we have given up* Amphipolis to him, D.5.25; τῆς ἐλευθερίας π. Φιλίππῳ Id.18.68; π. τινι τῶν αὑτοῦ Id.37.50; οὐ γὰρ ἐπ' εὐνοίᾳ γ' ἐμοὶ παρεχώρεις ἐλπίδων Id. 18.273; τῇ πόλει παραχωρῶ τῆς τιμωρίας *I leave the task* of punishment to the state, Id.21.28; π. τισὶ τῆς πολιτείας, τῆς ἀρχῆς, etc., Aeschin.3.5, Plb.4.5.1, etc. 4. *concede*, π. τινί τι Lxx 2*Ma.*2.28; τὰ ὁμολογημένα Arr.*Epict.*1.7.15; π. τινὶ θέσθαι τι *allow, permit*, Pl. *Plt.*260e; εἰ δὲ ἐπελάθετο, νῦν παρασχέσθω· ἐγὼ παραχωρῶ (sc. αὐτῷ παρασχέσθαι) Id.*Ap.*34a; *deliver, hand over*, σώματα ταλάντου π. Lxx 2*Ma.*8.11:—Pass., *to be permitted* or *conceded*, Corn.*Rh.*p.366 H., Plu. 2.787d. b. in Law, *give up, surrender* a holding, claim, or right, *PTeb.*5.82 (ii B.C.), *PGrenf.*2.33.3 (ii/i B.C.), etc.; δάνειον *PSI*1.64.15 (i B.C.): c. dat., *Arch.Pap.*5.390 (i A.D.):—Pass., *PTeb.*30.28 (ii B.C.); also παρακεχωρημένος τὸν Μενάνδρου κλῆρον *having had* his holding *ceded to me*, ib.31.16 (ii B.C.); ἀλλότρια δάνεια -χωρούμενοι *OGI*669.15 (Egypt, i A.D.). 5. ἐνταῦθα π. *comes to* this, *results in* this, Plu.2. 365c. 6. *flow*, of saliva, Orib.*Syn.*8.9 (v.l. προχ-). **-ημάτων·** ἐκβολῶν, Hsch. **-ησις**, εως, ἡ, *retiring*, Str.10.2.12 (pl.); *recession*, Procl.*Hyp.*5.110. 2. c. gen., *retiring from, giving up, surrender*, *BGU*1127.13 (i B.C.); δανείου ib.1171.12 (i B.C.); of a holding of land, *surrender*, λαβεῖν κατὰ -χώρησιν *PPetr.*3 p.40 (iii B.C.), cf. *PTeb.*30.12 (ii B.C.): generally, *cession, withdrawal from*, τῆς χώρας, τῆς ἀρχῆς, D.S.13.43, Plu.*Cat.Mi.*58; ἡγεμονίας D.H.4.27; π. ἄλλων ἄλλοις *surrender* of one point to one, another to another, Arr.*Epict.* 3.24.10. **-ητέον**, *one must give way*, ἐν ὁδοῖς π. τινί X.*Lac.*9. 5. 2. c. gen. et dat., *one must give way* in a thing to a person, τοῦ ἀκριβοῦς ἄλλοις Str.4.1.1. **-ητικός**, ή, όν, *disposed to yield in respect of*, δόξης καὶ δυνάμεως Plu.2.485c; τὸ -κόν *complaisance*, M.Ant. 1.16. II. in Law, *received or executed in consideration for a surrender*, ἀργύριον *BGU*906.10 (i A.D.); διεγγύημα *PLond.*2.300.14 (ii A.D.); ὁμολογία *Sammelb.*6000.15 (vi A.D.). **-ίζω**, *hand over*, θανάτῳ π. *condemn* to death, *SIG*684.20 (Dyme, ii B.C.). **-ιος**, ον, *situated beside*, gloss on παραβ[ώ]μιος, Sch.S.*OT*184.

**παραψάλλω**, *touch, pluck lightly*, τὰς νευρὰς τῶν τόξων Plu.*Demetr.* 19, cf. 2.133a: c. dat., Philostr.*Im.*2.1: c. gen., χορδῆς Onos.10.3.

**παρά-ψαυσις**, εως, ἡ, *touching lightly*, Plu.2.588f. **-ψαύω**, pf. παρεψαυκέναι S.E.*M.*7.116:—*touch gently* or *lightly*, Hp.*Mul.*2.160; τινος Plu.2.971c, *Eum.*7, etc. 2. metaph., *touch lightly* or *slightly on* a subject, τῆς δόξης S.E. l. c.:—Pass., παρέψαυσταί μοι ἀποφῆναι.. Hp.*Morb.*4.44.

**παραψάω**, *brush sideways*, παρεψησμέναι τρίχες *smoothed down* hair, Poll.4.152. 2. *wipe*, σπόγγῳ τὸ ἄγγος Zos.Alch.p.234 B.

**παραψελλίζω**, *stammer out somewhat of the truth*, Str.2.1.9.

**παραψεύδομαι**, *falsify, cheat*:—Pass., παρεψευσμένος *falsified*, opp. εἰλικρινής, Agatharch.55.

**παραψηλᾰφάω**, *grope about, fumble*, Phld.*Rh.*1.240 S.: c. acc., *fumble with*, Id.*Po.*5.32.

**παράψηξις**, εως, ἡ, *rubbing*, Paul.Aeg.6.87 (pl.).

**παράψησις**, εως, ἡ, = παράτριμμα, *Gloss.*

**παράψηστος**, η, ον, *with smoothed-down hair*, Poll.4.151, 154.

**παραψηφ-ίζομαι**, *deceive, cheat*, Hsch. s. v. παρεκρούσατο. **-ισμός**, ὁ, *deception*, *An.Bachm.*1.329.

**παραψήχω**, *rub at the side*, τὸ ὄμμα Ael.*NA*9.16. II. *smooth down*, τοὺς τοίχους Plu.2.641e.

⊕ **παραψῑδάζω**, dub. sens. et l. in Hippon. in *PSI*9.1089.9.

**παραψ-ίδιον**, τό, written for παροψ-, Dim. of παροψίς, *small dish*, *PLond.*1.124.2 (iv/v A.D.). **-ίς**, = παροψίς, Hsch., *Gloss.*

**παράψιμον**, τό, *charm acting by means of touch*, *PMag.Leid.V.*2.23; ἀγώγιμον π. *PMag.Lond.*121.973.

**παράψογος**, ὁ, *incidental censure*, Rhet. word used by Evenus of Paros, Pl.*Phdr.*267a (pl.).

**παραψοφέω**, gloss on διαψοφέω, Hsch.

**παρα-ψυκτήριον**, τό, = sq., λύπης ἄκεστρον καὶ π. S.*Ichn.*317. **-ψῡχή**, ἡ, *cooling, refreshment, consolation*, ἀντὶ πολλῶν E.*Hec.*280; ἀλγέων π. Id.*Or.*62; π. βίου Is.2.13; π. κινδύνων Aristid.*Or.*44(17). 12; χαλεπῶν Iamb.*Protr.*20; π. τῷ πένθει D.60.32: in pl., παραψυχὰς.. φροντίδων ἀνεύρετο ταύτας Timocl.6.4. **-ψύχω** [ῡ], *cool*, v.l. in *Placit.*5.25.1 (Pass.). 2. metaph., *console, soothe*, ἐπέεσσιν Theoc. 13.54 (Med.), cf. Call.*Cer.*46.

⊕ **παρ-βαίνω**, **-βασία**, **-βάτης**, **-βεβαώς**, **-βολάδην**, poet. for παραβ-.

**παρδᾰκός**, όν, *wet, damp*, χωρίον Ar.*Pax*1148; ἐπίσιον Archil.140 (v.l. παρδοκός); εἵματα Semon.21 (v.l. πορδακός here and in Ar.ap. Str.13.2.6).

**παρδᾰλ-έη** (sc. δορά), ἡ, *leopard-skin*, Il.3.17, 10.29, Hdt.7.69: prov., παρδαλέην ἐνεῖσθαι, of a shifty person, Eust.374.44; Dor. **παρδᾰλέα** Pi.*P.*4.81; Att. contr. **παρδαλῆ** Ar.*Av.*1250, Anaxandr.65, Corn.*ND*27. **-ειος** or **-εος** (which is said to be Ion., *EM*652.35), ον, *of* or *like a pard*, π. στέαρ Dsc.2.76; π. φάρμακον, prob. = παρδαλιαγχές, Arist.*Mir.*831ᵃ5: metaph., of savage men, παρδάλεοι θῆρες Lxx 4*Ma.*9.28. **-ηφόρος**, ον, *leopard-borne*, π. δέρος *leopard's* skin, S.*Fr.*11. **-ια**, τά, *leopards*, Arist.*HA*503ᵇ5. **-ιαγχές**, έος, τό, = ἀκόνιτον I, ib.612ᵃ7, Dsc.4.76, Plin.*HN*20.50, 27.7; Ion. **πορδαλιαγχές** Nic.*Al.*38:—also **παρδαλίαγχος**, Ael.*NA*4.49. II. = ἀπόκυνον, Dsc.4.80. **-ιδεύς**, Ion. πορδ-, έως, ὁ, *young leopard*, Eust.1625.46. **-ιοκτόνος**, ον, *leopard-killing*, Lemma to *AP*7. 578 (Agath.).

⊕ **πάρδᾰλις** or **πόρδᾰλις** (v. infr.), ἡ, gen. εως, Ep. and Ion. ιος Il.17. 20, etc.; dat. ει Ar.*Nu.*347:—*leopard, Felis pardus*, Il.13.103, 17.20, 21.573, Od.4.457, *h.Ven.*71, Semon.(?) in *PLit.Lond.*53ʳ.3, Arist. *HA*500ᵃ28, *Phgn.*809ᵇ36, Opp.*C.*3.63, etc.—Acc. to Apion (ap. Apollon.*Lex.* s. v. πόρδαλις) πόρδαλις was the male, πάρδαλις the female, cf. Hsch.; but πόρδαλις was used of the animal, παρδαλέη of its skin, acc. to *EM*652.38, Phot.; Aristarch. wrote πάρδ- in Hom.; Ar. has πάρδ- *Nu.* l. c., but πόρδ- *Lys.*1015; πάρδ- is found in Pl. *La.*196e, Thphr.*CP*6.5.2, 6.17.9, and always in Arist.; πόρδ- in S. *Ichn.*296. II. a ravenous sea-fish, Ael.*NA*9.49, Opp.*H.*1. 368. III. = πάρδαλος II, Hsch. IV. name of a *plaster*, Aët.12.1.

**πάρδᾰλος**, ὁ, v.l. for πάρδος in Ael.*NA*1.31. II. a gregarious bird, perh. the *plover*, Arist.*HA*617$^{b}$6.

**παρδᾰλ-ώδης**, ες, *leopard-like*, Ath.2.38f. **-ωτός**, ή, όν, *spotted like the pard*, Luc.*Bis Acc.*8.

**παρδαμάλη**, ἡ, = καρδαμάλη, *Com.Adesp.*1107.

**παρδεῖν**, v. πέρδομαι.

**παρδή**, ἡ, = πορδή, Alex.Aphr.*Pr.*1.144 (s.v.l.).

**παρδιαῖος**, α, ον, prob. of colour, *spotted* (like the πάρδος), *Annuario* 4/5.465 (Halic., iv B.C.).

**παρδίας**, f.l. for περαίας, Plu.2.965f.

**πάρδιον**, τό, an unknown animal, Arist.*HA*498$^{b}$33 (v.l. ἱππαρίδιον).

**παρδοκός**, v. πανδοκός.

**πάρδος**, ὁ, later form of πάρδαλις, Ael.*NA*1.31; Lat. *pardus*, the male of the *panthera*, Plin.*HN*8.63.

**πάρδω**, v. πέρδομαι. **παρέασι**, v. πάρειμι (εἰμί *sum*).

**παρε-ᾰτέον**, *one must pass by* or *over*, Tz.*ad Hes.*p.10 G. **-άω**, *let pass, neglect*, Olymp.*in Alc.*p.117 C.; *fail to observe* a testamentary disposition, *IGRom.*4.1168 (Attalea). 2. gloss on παρεῖναι (παρίημι), Sch.E.*Ph.*508. II. Pass., *to be omitted*, Sopat.*in Hermog.* in Rh.5.177 W.

**παρεγγίζω**, *resemble*, τινι Crateuasap.Dsc.2.127.

**παρέγ-γραπτος**, ον, *illegally registered*, π. πολῖται *intrusive* citizens, Aeschin.2.177; of deified heroes, Luc.*JTr.*21: metaph., *assumed*, αἱ τροφοὶ τὴν εὔνοιαν π. ἔχουσιν Plu.2.3c; *interpolated*, συγγραφή Eust. 1379.62. ⊛ **-γρᾰφος**, ον, = foreg., πολίτης Posidon.36 J.; *interpolated*, Ath.5.180f. **-γράφω** [γρᾰ], *write by the side, subjoin*, τὸ αὑτοῦ ὄνομα Pl.*Lg.*753c. 2. in bad sense, *interpolate*, τι ἐν ψηφίσματι Aeschin.3.74, cf. Plu.*CG*17, Gal.15.9 (Pass.), 17(1).606; ἔπος ἐν τῷ καταλόγῳ Str.9.1.10; π. ἑαυτὸν ταῖς διαθήκαις Luc.*Ind.*19; *enrol illegally* among the citizens, εἰς τοὺς φυλέτας Id.*Bis Acc.*27; παρεγγραφεὶς πολίτης Aeschin.2.76.

**παρεγγῠ-άω**, *hand over* to another, *entrust* or *commend* to his care, τοῖσι φίλοισι π. τὸν ξεῖνον Hdt.3.8; τὴν ἀρχήν τινι Plu.*Ant.*11; of life, π. τοῖς ἐπιγιγνομένοις Antipho Soph.50: c. inf., τοῖς φίλοις τηρεῖν παρεγγυηκώς Phld.*Piet.*110; παῖδα τῇ Ἀθηνᾷ τιθηνεῖσθαι π. D.C.59.28:—Pass., π. τι *to be entrusted with*.., Is.*Fr.*31. 2. of things, *recommend*, τοῦτ' ἐγὼ π. Men.487, cf. *POxy.*1101.15 (iv A.D., Pass.), Olymp. Alch.p.94 B. (Med.); μέθοδος ἣν οἱ σοφισταὶ παρεγγυῶσιν Phld.*Rh.*1. 137 S. II. as a military term, *pass on* the watchword or word of command *along* the whole line, παρηγγύων κελευσμὸν ἀλλήλοισι.., "θεῖν", ἀντέρειδε" E.*Supp.*700; σύνθημα παρεγγυήσας "Ζεὺς σωτήρ" X.*Cyr.*7.1.10, cf. 3.3.58, Moer.p.324 P.: abs., σπεύδοντες π. ἐπί τινας eager *to pass the word* to attack them, Plb.7.18.4: without any notion of command, βοώντων τῶν στρατιωτῶν "θάλαττα, θάλαττα", καὶ παρεγγυώντων X.*An.*4.7.24: metaph., c. acc. et inf., σημεῖα δ' ἥξειν τῶνδέ μοι παρηγγύα ἢ σεισμὸν ἢ βροντήν τιν' S.*OC*94. 2. of a general, *give the word of command*, τινί c. inf., X.*Cyr.*3.2.8, 7.5.17: c. inf. only, ib.2.3.21, *An.*4.1.17, etc.:—Med., Id.*Lac.*11.8, Plu.*Oth.* 16. 3. of soldiers, π. ἀλλήλοις μὴ ἀπολείπεσθαι *exhorted* one another not.., Id.*Cam.*37: generally, *exhort*, π. αὐτοῖς παύσασθαι c. part., Luc.*DMort.*1.2, cf. Hierocl.*in CA*2 p.423 M. **-η**, ἡ, *command*, X.*An.*6.5.13. 2. = *allegatio, insinuatio, Gloss.* II. Dor. **παρεγγύα**, *deposit paid by a contractor*, *IG*4$^{2}$(1).109 ii 152 (Epid., iii B.C.). **-ημα**, ατος, τό, *command*, Aristid.Quint.2.6. **-ησις**, εως, ἡ, *passing on the word of command*, X.*Lac.*11.4. II. *instruction, exhortation*, θεία π. Oenom.ap.Eus.*PE*5.28. **-ητέον**, *one must advise, recommend*, Antyll.ap.Orib.6.6.2.

**πάρεγγυς**, Adv. *near at hand, close by*, ἐν τοῖς π. τόποις Arist.*HA* 605$^{b}$25. 2. of Time, *near*, λίαν π. εἶναι, i.e. in age, Id.*Pol.*1335$^{a}$1; π. τινός *following closely on*.., Id.*GA*773$^{b}$9. 3. *nearly alike*, π. γενέσθαι Id.*Metaph.*1040$^{b}$11; τὸ π. τῆς λέξεως Id.*SE*167$^{a}$5; π. ταύτης (sc. τῆς πολιτείας) *nearly resembling* it, Id.*Pol.*1271$^{b}$20, cf. Thphr.*CP* 6.17.9.

**παρεγείρω**, *raise partly*, διὰ τροχιλίας Plu.*Eum.*11.

**παρεγ-κάμπτω**, *bend aside*, Antyll.ap.Orib.6.34.2. **-κάπτω**, *swallow besides*, παρεγκέκαπταί τ' ἀρνί' ἐννέ' ἢ δέκα Eub.15.9; τὸ πνεῦμα prob. cj. in Plu.2.130b. **-κειμαι**, Pass., *to be interpolated*, Gal.18(1). 178, al., Simp.*in Ph.*44.22. **-κελεύομαι**, *exhort*, c. acc. et inf., Plu.2.188e. **-κεράννῡμι**, *mix in besides*, in pf. part. Pass., Poll.3. 86. **-κεφαλίς**, ίδος, ἡ, *cerebellum*, Arist.*HA*494$^{b}$32, Herophil.ap. Gal.*UP*8.11, etc. **-κλίνω** [ῑ], *cause to incline sideways*, Orph.*H.*63. 7; *wave*, μετέωρα τὰ ξίφη.. παρεγκλίνοντες Onos.29.2; *lay beside* or *by*, π. τὰς λαγόνας γυναιξὶ Lxx *Si.*47.19 (as v.l.):—Pass., *incline sideways*, v.l. in Hp.*Art.*54; λοξῷ καὶ παρεγκεκλιμένῳ πορείας σχήματι χρώμενος Plu.*Phoc.*2; κατὰ τὴν θέσιν π. TheoSm.p.128 H. 2. intr. in Act., μικρὸν εἰς τὸ πλάγιον π. Arist.*HA*498$^{a}$16: c. gen., *deviate* from, [πολιτεία] μικρὸν -κλίνουσα τῆς βασιλικῆς Id.*Ath.*41.2: c. acc., μικρὸν π. τὴν ἀκμήν *not far from* their prime, Thphr.*CP*6.17.3: abs., of the sun, *pass the meridian*, Id.*Vent.*16. b. *swerve*, of atoms, Epicur.*Frr.*281 p.351 U., 383 p.355 U. II. *alter slightly*, τὴν λέξιν Ath.15.701d, cf. 10.454b; τῷ τόνῳ Sch.Ar.*Eq.*950. **-κλῐσις**, εως, ἡ, *swerving*, [τῶν ἀτόμων] Epicur.*Fr.*280, Phld.*Sign.*36 (pl.), Plot.3.1.1 (pl.); *divergence*, Vett.Val.342.11. 2. *flexure* of the womb, Sor.2.7, Paul. Aeg.3.64. 3. *alteration*, μικρὰ π. καὶ μετάθεσις σχήματος Plu.*CG*5; τῆς οὐσίας Dam.*Pr.*440. **-κλῐτικός**, ή, όν, *in a slanting direction*, κίνησις Diog.Oen.33. II. Adv. **-κῶς** *symbolically*, Tz.*Proll.Com.* 2.10 p.27 Kaib. **-κόπτω**, *intercept, stop*, τὸ πνεῦμα v.l. in Plu.2. 130b. **-κυκλέω**, *introduce*, τὸ δόγμα τῶν ἰδεῶν Elias *in Porph.*121. 3. **-κύκλημα**, ατος, τό, *something added to a drama, interlude*, Hld.7.7. II. *stage-direction*, in the margin of a play, Sch.Ar.*Nu.* 18, al.

**παρεγχειρ-έω**, *interfere with*, τὴν φύσιν Ph.*Fr.*49 H.; π. ὡς.. *argue falsely* that.., Plu.*Comp.Tim.Aem.*1: c. inf., *attempt illegally*, *Jahresh.*23 *Beibl.*180 (Thrace). 2. *interpret symbolically*, τὴν κόλασιν (sc. τοῦ Ἰξίονος) Asclep.Tragil.3 J.; μηδὲν π. εἰς τὰ κεκριμένα Artem.4.72. 3. *disturb*, μηδενὸς μέρους τῶν ἀρχαίων ἐθῶν παρεγχειρουμένου Epist.Domit. in *SIG*821 C3; *tamper with*, τοῖς ὑπ' ἐμοῦ διατεταγμένοις *POxy.*495.16 (ii A.D.). II. *impugn as false*, τι Sch.Pi. *P.*2.78, etc. III. *put into one's hands, transfer to*, τινί τι S.E.*P.*1. 234. **-ησις**, εως, ἡ, *encroaching on other people's business*, Cic.*Att.*15. 4.3; *interference*, μηδεμιᾷ -ήσει *BMus.Inscr.*481*.402 (Ephesus, ii A.D.).

**παρεγ-χέω**, *pour in beside*, Arist.*EE*1235$^{b}$39:—Pass., Id.*Mete.*359$^{a}$ 2, Gal.18(2).469; κριθαὶ παρεγκεχυμέναι v.l. in Plu.2.82e. **-χρίμπτομαι**, Pass., *approach*, in fut. παρεγχρί(μ)ψεται, Hsch. **-χρώννυμι**, *touch slightly, allude to*, Ath.5.215e. **-χῠμα**, ατος, τό, *anything poured in beside*, name given by Erasistratus to the peculiar substance of the lungs, liver, kidneys, and spleen, as if *formed separately* by the veins that run into them, the word σάρξ being used of the muscular flesh, Gal.14.697, Alex.Aphr.*Pr.*2.72. **-χῠματίζω**, *drop in* liquid, Gal.12.740:—Pass., *have a little liquid dropped into* the eye, Alex. Trall.2. **-χῠσις**, εως, ἡ, *pouring in beside*, of dropsy, Aret.*SD* 2.1, Gal.8.350; esp. of cataract, Ruf.*Fr.*116; *accumulation* of fat, Sor.2.7. **-χωρεῖ**, impers., *it is also allowed*, c. inf., Sch.E.*Med.*900.

⊛ **παρεδρ-εία**, ἡ, *attendance*, π. ποιούμεναι τῆς θεοῦ *SIG*695.28 (Magn. Mae., ii B.C.). II. *close study, application*, Phld.*Oec.*p.71 J. (pl.). **-ευτικός**, ή, όν, *persistent*, Antyll.ap.Orib.10.29.1. **-εύω**, *wait, attend upon*, Ἅιδου νύμφη παρεδρεύοις E.*Alc.*746 (anap.); οἱ παρεδρεύοντες, of those who *attend on* the sick, Phld.*Ir.*p.29 W.; of sluice-*keepers*, *Sammelb.*7174.16 (i A.D.); of a familiar spirit, *PMag. Par.*1.1979 (hex.). 2. *frequent, attend*, θυμέλαις *IG*5(1).734 (Sparta); γυμνασίοις ib.14.1728.6; π. ταῖς ἐκκλησίαις ἐν ὅπλοις ib.2$^{2}$. 1028.35; ἐν τῷ ἱερῷ *SIG*695.27 (Magn. Mae., ii B.C.); παρήδρευσαν ἕως.. Plb.29.27.10. 3. of judges, *act as assessor* (πάρεδρος), παρεδρεύοντος ἄρχοντι D.21.178; δοκιμάζονται [οἱ πάρεδροι] πρὶν παρεδρεύειν Arist.*Ath.*56.1, cf. *CIG*2855.6 (Didyma, ii B.C.); of Aeacus, as *assessor* with Pluto and Persephone, Isoc.9.15. 4. in Tactics, *occupy rear rank*, Ascl.*Tact.*3.6; τὸ παρεδρεῦον ζυγόν ib.7.7. 5. Gramm., ἡ παρεδρεύουσα [συλλαβή] *penultimate*, A.D.*Adv.*135.16, al.; ὁ παρεδρεύων χρόνος the quantity *of the penultimate*, ib.167.10; τῷ ᾱ, τῷ ῡ παρεδρεύεσθαι, *to have* α or υ *in the penultimate*, ib.177.14, Ath. 9.392b. **-ήσσω**, poet. for foreg., Nonn.*D.*9.112. **-ία**, Ion. **-ίη**, ἡ, *attendance*, Memn.60; *service*, ἡ τῶν Γάλλων π. Corn. *ND*6. 2. of things, ἡ τοῦ ἐναντίου π. its *association, constant presence*, Arist.*PA*652$^{a}$32; *persistence*, κακοπαθείης Hp.*Praec.* 8. II. *office of* πάρεδρος, Test.ap.D.59.84. ⊛ **-ιάω**, = παρεδρεύω, παρεδριόων A.R.2.1039. **-ικῶς**, Adv. *after the manner of a familiar spirit*, *PMag.Berol.*1.1. ⊛ **-ος**, ον, (ἕδρα) *sitting beside*, as at table, τὰς γυναῖκας ἐσάγεσθαι π. Hdt.5.18: generally, *sitting beside, near*, τινι E.*Or.*83, *Hec.*616; Διὸς αἰετῶν π. ἱέρεα Pi.*P.* 4.4. II. Subst., *assessor, coadjutor*, folld. by dat. or gen., Διὸς π., of Themis, Id.*O.*8.22, cf. Ar.*Av.*1753, Phylarch.24 J.; ἕτοιμος αὐτῷ (sc. Διί) π., of Rhadamanthys, Pi.*O.*2.76; ἵμερος.. τῶν μεγάλων π. ἐν ἀρχαῖς θεσμῶν S.*Ant.*798 (lyr.); τᾷ Σοφίᾳ παρέδρους Ἔρωτας E. *Med.*843; Ἑρμᾶς Ἀφροδίτᾳ π. *Epigr.Gr.*783 (Cnidus), cf. 817, *IG*2. 1298; καί με καλεῦσι πάρεδρον *Hymn.Is.*139: freq. in Prose, of the *counsellors* of Xerxes, Hdt.7.147, cf. 8.138; of the Ephors at Sparta, Id.6.65; at Athens, of the *assessors* of the Archons, Decr.ap.And. 1.78, Archipp.27, Arist.*Ath.*56.1, *IG*2$^{2}$.1230, D.59.72, etc.; of the *assessors* of other magistrates, as the Ἑλληνοταμίαι, *IG*1$^{2}$.302.3; the στρατηγοί, ib.40; the εὔθυνος, ib.127.19, 2$^{2}$.1629.239; *lieutenant* of a military commander, *Hell.Oxy.*10.1; τοξόται πάρεδροι in a naval battle, dub. in *IG*1$^{2}$.950.137. 2. metaph., Ἐρεχθέα τοῖς ἐν τῇ ἀκροπόλει θεοῖς π. ἀποδείξασα Aristid.1.119 J.; π. ἡδονή *secondary* pleasure, Aristaenet.2.16. III. in Magic, *assistant divinity, familiar spirit*, *PMag.Berol.*1.54, *PMag.Lond.*121.884, *Tab.Defix.Aud.*155 A 20, *PMag.Par.*1.1850: hence, 2. of things, *giving magical aid*, τρίστιχος Ὁμήρου π. ib.2145.

**παρέζομαι**, *sit beside*, Thgn.563; in Hom. we find only forms that prob. belong to an aor. παρεζόμην, viz. παρέζεο καὶ λαβὲ γούνων Il.1. 407; παρέζετο καὶ λάβε γούνων ib.557; μή τι.. παρεζόμενος μινύριζε 5. 889, cf. Od.4.738, 20.334.

**πᾰρειά**, ἡ, Hom. (v. infr.), *IG*2$^{2}$.1421.124, 1455.11, etc.; but **παρεά** ib.1425.246; Aeol. **παραύα** (q.v.); Dor. ***παράα** (implied in εὐπάραος); Old Ion. ***παρηή** (implied in καλλιπάρηος, μιλτοπάρηος, and the adjectival παρή-ϊον):—*cheek*, used by Hom. always in pl. (sg. being supplied by the Ion. παρήϊον), Il.3.35, al.; of an eagle, Od.2. 153: also Trag., in pl., S.*Ant.*783 (lyr.): in sg., A.*Pr.*401 (lyr.), S. *Ant.*1239, E.*Tr.*280 (lyr.): rare in Prose, as Pl.*Plt.*270e, X.*Cyr.*6. 4.3 (pl.). II. *cheekpiece* of a helmet, *h.Hom.*31.11 (s.v.l.), *IG*2$^{2}$. 1421.124, 1455.11, al. 2. = τῆς πρῴρας τὰ ἑκατέρωθεν Poll.1.89. 3. γῆς παρειά *earth-flush*, = ἀνεμώνη ἡ φοινική, cj. in Ps.-Dsc.2.176. (Perh. fr. παρά, οὖς, lit. *beside the ear*.)

**πᾰρείας**, ου, ὁ, mostly Adj., π. ὄφις *reddish-brown snake*, sacred to Asclepius, Cratin.225 (pl.), Ar.*Pl.*690, D.18.260 (pl.); π. alone, Hyp.*Fr.*80, Thphr.*Char.*16.4; ὁ παρείας ἢ παρούας, οὕτω γὰρ Ἀπολλόδωρος ἐθέλει Ael.*NA*8.12:—also **πάρωος**, Philum.*Ven.*32, Hsch. II. **παρώας** ἵππος a *chestnut* horse (μεταξὺ τεφροῦ καὶ πυρροῦ Phot.), αἱ παρῶαι ἵπποι Arist.*HA*630$^{a}$29: fem. **παρόα**, *PPetr.*

3p.159 (cf. p.xviii); **παραύα**, ibid.; **παρούα**, ib.2p.117 (iii B.C.); cf. ὑαλοπάρανος.

**παρειάς**, άδος, ἡ, *bandage for the cheek*, Heliod.ap.Orib.48.20.9, Gal.18(1).787. 2. *cheek*, A.R.4.172 (nisi leg. παρήϊσιν), Heliod. l. c.

**παρεῖδον**, aor. 2, παροράω being used as pres., *observe by the way, remark, notice*, τινί τι something *in* one, οὔτε τινὰ δειλίην μοι παριδών Hdt.1.37, cf. 38; π. ἀνδρὶ τῷδε ἄχαρι οὐδέν ib.108. II. *overlook, disregard*, τοὺς νόμους Antipho1.24, cf. Lycurg.64; παρεῖδε πρὸς τὰ δίκαια Μειδίαν D.21.96. 2. *cast a side glance*, Ar.*Ra*.815.

**παρείθη**, v. παρίημι.

**παρεικάζω**, *liken, compare*, τινί τι Pl.*R*.473c, *Plt*.260e; ὡς μεγάλῳ π. μικρόν Arist.*PA*653ᵃ3, etc.; ταῖς γλαυξὶν ἡμᾶς Phld.*Rh*.1.253 S.:—Pass., τὸ ὀσφραντὸν..παρείκασται οἷον βαφή τις εἶναι *appeared by analogy* to be, Arist.*Sens*.445ᵃ13, cf. Ph.2.111. II. *make like*, νεφέλην τῇ Ἥρᾳ Sch.E.*Ph*.1185.

❋**παρείκω**, aor. 2 παρεικάθον (v. infr.), *give way*, σε..αἰτῶ πιθέσθαι καὶ παρεικαθεῖν S.*OC*1334, cf. *Ant*.1102; *permit, allow*, ὅσον γ' ἂν ἡ δύναμις παρείκῃ Pl.*R*.374e; ὅπως ἂν παρείκωσι θεοὶ νομοθετεῖν Id.*Lg*. 934c; οἷσπερ ἂν ὁ θεὸς παρείκῃ Id.*Tht*.150d; κατὰ τὸ αἰεὶ παρεῖκον by *such* ways *as permitted a passage, as were practicable*, Th.4.36; χωρίοις ἀποτόμοις καὶ χαλεποῖς, οὐ μὴν ἀλλὰ..παρείκουσιν Plu.*Cam*.27. 2. *relax, let fall*, τὴν χεῖρα Clearch.25. II. impers., παρείκει μοι *it is competent, allowable* for me, εἴ μοι παρείκοι S.*Ph*.1048; ὅπῃ παρείκοι wherever *it was practicable*, Th.3.1; καθ' ὅσον παρείκει Pl.*Smp*.187e: c. inf., τόν γε βουλόμενον..οὐκέτι παρείκει..ἀκολάστως ζῆν Id.*Lg*. 734b; ἐὰν ἄρα ἡμῖν πῃ παρεικάθῃ (Böckh for -ασθῇ)..ἀπαλλάττειν Id. *Sph*.254c.

**παρειλέω**, *wind round*, ταινίαν Gal.18(1).788.

**παρειμένως**, Adv. pf. part. Pass. of παρίημι, *remissly, slackly*, Hsch.; π. ἔχειν αὐτῶν (sc. τῶν ἐξόπισθεν) to be *paralysed* in the hind limbs, Ael.*VH*1.7.

**πάρειμι** (εἰμί *sum*), inf. -εῖναι, Ep. 3 pl. παρέασι Il.5.192, Od.13. 247; Ion. subj. παρέω Hdt.4.98; Ep. inf. παρέμμεναι Od.4.640, part. παρεών Il.24.475: Ep. impf. παρέην Od.3.267 (tm.); 2 sg. παρῆσθα v.l. in Od.4.497 (Sch., *Lex.Mess.*); 3 pl. πάρεσαν Il.11.75; Att. impf. παρῆ A.*Ch*.523; in later Greek παρήμην Luc.*VH*2.25: Ep. fut. παρέσσομαι Od.13.393:—*to be by* or *present*, ὑμεῖς θεαί ἐστε πάρεστέ τε ἴστε τε πάντα Il.2.485, etc.: in tmesi, πὰρ δ' ἄρ' ἔην καὶ ἀοιδός Od. 3.267; πάρα used for πάρεστι and πάρεισι, Il.20.98, 23.479, etc.: freq. in part., ποίπνυον παρεόντε 24.475; σημάντορος οὐ π. 15.325, etc.; ἀπεόντα νόῳ παρεόντα Parm.2.1, cf. Heraclit.34. 2. *to be by* or *near* one, c. dat., Od.5.105; μήλοισι 4.640; π. τινὶ παροινοῦντι Antipho4. 1.7; π. παρά τινι S.*Ph*.1056; π. τινὶ *to be* his *guest*, Ar.*Av*.131. 3. *to be present in* or *at*, μάχῃ Od.4.497; ἐν δαίτῃσι Il.10.217; δόμοις π. E.*Hipp*.805; τοῖς πράγμασιν D.1.2, etc.; ἐν λόγῳ Ar.*Ach*.513; ἐν ταῖς συνουσίαις Pl.*Prt*.335b; ἐπὶ τοῖς ἀγῶσι D.24.159. 4. *to be present so as to help, stand by*, τινι Il.18.472, Od.13.393, A.*Pers*.235; πλησίον παρῆσθα κινδύνων ἐμοί E.*Or*.1159, etc.; esp. of one accused, οἱ νῦν παρόντες αὐτῷ καὶ συνδικοῦντες D.34.12, cf. 24.159: Medic., of nurses, assistants, etc., Hp.*Aph*.1.1, Herod.Med.ap.Orib.10.37. 11. 5. παρεῖναι εἰς.. *to have arrived* at, ἐς κοῖτον Hdt.1.9; ἐς τὸν Ἰσθμὸν π. τινί Id.8.60.γ'; ἐς τὴν Λακεδαίμονα Th.6.88; εἰς τὴν ἐξέτασιν X.*An*.7.1.11; Ὀλυμπίαζε Th.3.8: c. acc. loci, πάρεισι..Αἰτναῖον πάγον E.*Cyc*.95, cf. 106, *Ba*.5; π. τινὶ ἐπὶ δεῖπνον Hdt.1.118, cf. Ar.*Av*.131; π. ἐπὶ τὸ στράτευμα X.*An*.7.1.35; π. πρὸς τὴν κρίσιν ib. 6.6.26; πρός τινα Id.*Cyr*.2.4.21; also π. ἐνταυθοῖ Pl.*Ap*.33d; v. πάρειμι (εἶμι) IV. 2. 6. π. ἐκ.. *to have come* from.., ἐκ ταύτης [τῆς πόλιος] π. ἐς τὴν Ἀσίην Hdt.6.24; τοὐκ θεοῦ παρόν S.*OC*1540; Φίλιππος ἐκ Θράκης π. Aeschin.2.101; Θείβαθεν αὐλητὰλ πάρα Ar.*Ach*. 862. II. of things, *to be by*, i.e. *ready* or *at hand*, τά τε δμώεσσι πάρεστι Od.14.80, etc.; πάρα ἔργα βόεσσιν Hes.*Op*.454; οὐ γάρ οἱ πάρα νῆες Od.4.559; εἴ μοι δύναμίς γε παρείη if power *were at* my *command*, 2.62; ὅση δύναμίς γε πάρεστι 23.128; ὅ τι πάρεστι Men.62; τὰ παρεόντα what is *ready*, χαριζομένη παρεόντων Od.1.140; ἡ τοῦ πλέονος ἐπιθυμίη τὸ παρεὸν ἀπόλλυσι Democr.224, cf. 191; ἐκ τῶν παρεουσέων αὐγέων the best light *available*, Hp.*Off*.3; ἐκ τῶν παρεόντων τὸ εὔπορον εὑρίσκειν Id.*Art*.78; εἰ τὰ δεσμὰ μὴ παρείη ibid.; of feelings, conditions, etc., φόβος βαρβάροις παρῆν A.*Pers*.391; θαῦμα παρῆν S.*Ant*.254; ἐν τοῖς τότε παρεοῦσι..κακοῖσι Hdt.8.20, cf. A.*Pr*.26; ὡς παρεσομένου σφι πολέμου Hdt.8.20: in Philos., of qualities or predicates, παρείη γ' ἂν αὐταῖς (sc. θριξίν) λευκότης Pl.*Ly*.217d, cf. Plot.5.6. 4; of Time, ὁ παρὼν νῦν χρόνος S.*El*.1293, cf. Aeschin.1.93, Arist.*Po*. 1457ᵃ18; ἡ νῦν π. ἡμέρα Pl.*Lg*.683c; ἡ ἱερὰ συμβουλὴ π. X.*An*.5.6.4; τὰ παρόντα (Ion. παρεόντα) *the present state of affairs*, Hdt.1.113, etc.; τὰ π. πρήγματα Id.6.100; opp. τὰ γεγονότα, τὰ μέλλοντα, Pl.*Tht*.186b: sg., τὸ παρόν (Ion. παρεόν), πρὸς τὸ π. βουλεύειν, τὸ π. θεραπεύειν, Hdt.1.20, S.*Ph*.149 (lyr.); πρὸς παρεὸν Emp.106: Adverbial phrases, τὸ παρόν *just now*, τὸ π. εἴπομεν Pl.*Lg*.693b; τὰ παρόντα S.*El*.215 (lyr.): in Prose, ἐκ τῶν π. according to *present circumstances*, Th.5.40, etc.; ἐν τῷ π., opp. τὸ ἔπειτα, ib.63, etc.; ἐν τῷ νῦν π. καὶ ἐν τῷ ἔπειτα Pl.*Phd*.67c; ἐν τῷ τότε π. Th.1.95; πρὸς τὸ παρόν Isoc.15.94; ὡς πρὸς τὸ π. S.E.*P*.1.201; πρὸς τὸ π. αὐτίκα Th.3.40; πρὸς τὴν π. ὄψιν Id.2.88; ἐπὶ τοῦ π. for *the present*, *IG*9(2). 517.6 (Epist. Philipp.), Epict.*Ench*.2.2; ἐς and πρὸς τὰ π., Arr.*An*.1. 13.5, 5.22.5. III. impers., πάρεστί μοι *it depends* on me, *is in* my *power* to do, c. inf., τοιαῦθ' ἑλέσθαι σοι πάρεστιν ἐξ ἐμοῦ A.*Eu*.867, cf. S.*Ph*.364, etc.: also impf. παρῆν Hdt.8.20, 9.70: without dat., παρῆν ..κλύειν A.*Pers*.401; πάρεστι χαίρειν Ar.*Pl*.638; δρᾶν πάρεστιν Democr.164, cf. And.2.2, etc. 2. part. παρόν, Ion. παρεόν, *it being possible* or *easy, since it is allowed*, παρεὸν αὐτῷ βασιλέα γενέσθαι Hdt. 1.129, cf. 6.72, S.*Ph*.1098 (lyr.), *Fr*.564.3, Th.4.19. IV. part. masc. παρών is freq. in Trag., at the end of a verse, to give vividness, ἀνδρ' ἐνουθέτει παρών *to his face*, S.*Aj*.1156; τοὺς θανόντας οὐκ ἐᾷς θάπτειν π. you *come here* and forbid.., ib.1131, cf. 338, *El*.300, *Tr*. 422; dub. in Com., Ar.*Fr*.657.

❋**πάρειμι** (εἶμι *ibo*), inf. -ιέναι (Dor. -ίμεν *Berl.Sitzb*.1927.170 (Cyrene)), used as fut. of παρέρχομαι, also in pres. sense, παρῄειν being used as impf.:—*pass by, pass*, παριών Od.4.527, 17.233; οἰκτίρας.. παρίτω *IG*1².976; παρῄε Hdt.4.79; οἱ ἀεὶ παριόντες Pl.*R*.616a, etc.; *go alongside*, Th.4.47; *march along* the coast, of an army, Id.8.16, 22,32, X.*HG*2.1.18 (cj.), 4.5.19. 2. c. acc. loci, *pass by*, Hdt.7.109; τὸν χῶρον Id.1.167; τὴν οἰκίαν And.1.146, Str.14.5.14; π. παρὰ τοὺς πατέρας (prob. for παρῆσαν) Hdt.3.14; παρ' αὐτὴν τὴν Βαβυλῶνα π. X.*Cyr*.5.2.29. II. *pass by, overtake, surpass*, ib.1.4.5. III. *pass on*, esp. in the sense of *entering*, π. ἐς τὰ βασιλήϊα Hdt.3.84, cf. 72,77, Pl.*Phd*.59e; ἔσω π. E.*Hel*.451; πάριτ' ἐς θυμέλας, ἐπὶ δ' ἀσφάκτοις μήλοισι δόμων μὴ πάριτ' ἐς μυχόν Id.*Ion* 228 (anap.); βίᾳ εἰς οἰκίαν παριέναι X.*Cyr*.1.2.2. 2. in discourse, *pass on* from one part of a subject to another, ἐντεῦθεν ἐς.. Ar.*Nu*.1075; ὁ παριὼν τῷ λόγῳ ἔτυχον εἰπών *in passing*, Pl.*Lg*.776d. IV. *come forward*, X.*An*. 7.3.46; πάριτ' ἐς τὸ πρόσθεν Ar.*Ach*.43; τὸ μάχιμον εἰς τὸν μέγιστον τῶν ἀγώνων τολμήσει παριέναι Pl.*Lg*.830c: metaph., ἐς πρώτους νεωστὶ παριών Hdt.7.143. 2. *come forward to speak*, Pl.*Alc*.1.106c; παρῄει οὐδεὶς D.18.170; παριὼν ἐπὶ τὸ βῆμα Aeschin.3.159; παρῆσαν ἐπὶ τὸ βῆμα (cj. Dobree for παρῆσαν) D.1.8; παρῆμεν (cj. Cobet for παρῆμεν) εἰς τὴν ἐκκλησίαν Aeschin.3.71; at Athens, οἱ παριόντες *orators*, And.2.1, D.13.14, etc.; πᾶσι τοῖς παριοῦσι λόγον διδόναι Id.2. 31. V. *pass from man to man*, τὸ σύνθημα παρῄει X.*An*.6.5.25.—Cf. παρέρχομαι.

**παρεῖπον**, aor. 2 with no pres. in use, παράφημι being used, *talk over, win over*, Il.1.555, 6.337, A.*Pr*.131 (lyr.); εἰ..θυμὸν ὀρίναις παρειπών *by thy persuasions*, Il.11.793, cf. 15.404: c. acc. cogn., *give* such and such *advice*, αἴσιμα παρειπών 6.62, 7.121. [In Il. πᾰρειπών, πᾰρειποῦσα, i.e. παρϝειπών, -οῦσα; but μή σε πᾰρέλπῃ 1.555.]

**παρείργω**, *keep off, shut out*, in aor. παρεῖρξα, Hsch.

**παρειρύω**, v. παρερύω.

❋**παρείρω**, (εἴρω A) *thread in, insert*, παρείρας πλεκτάνην A.*Fr*.281.3; οὐδ' ἂν τρίχα, μὴ ὅτι λόγον π. X.*Smp*.6.2; τὴν χεῖρα Plb.18.18.13; νόμους παρείρων is corrupt in S.*Ant*.368 (lyr.).

**παρείς**, aor. 2 part. Act. of παρίημι, and Pass. of πείρω. **παρεῖσα**, v. παρίζω.

**παρεισ-άγω** [ᾰγ], pf. παρεισῆχα Phld.*Piet*.32:—*lead in by one's side, bring forward, introduce*, of persons brought into a public assembly, τοὺς παῖδας τῶν ἐν τῷ πολέμῳ τετελευτηκότων Isoc.8.82; τοὺς αἰχμαλώτους Plb.3.63.2; *propose* a candidate for a succession, Plu.*Galb*. 21. 2. with a notion of secrecy, π. [τοὺς Γαλάτας] εἰς Ἔρυκα *introduce, admit* them into the city, Plb.2.7.8, cf. 1.18.3. 3. *introduce into* a poem or narrative, κινδύνους Arist.*Fr*.142, cf. Phld. l. c., etc.; τὸν Ἀννίβαν ἀμίμητόν τινα π. στρατηγόν *represent* him as.., Plb.3.47.7, cf. 5.2.6, Corn.*ND*9:—Pass., ib.20, al. 4. *introduce* doctrines, customs, etc., τὰς ὑπὲρ τῶν ἐν Ἅιδου διαλήψεις εἰς τὰ πλήθη π. Plb.6.56.12, cf. D.S.1.96; ξένα π. δαιμόνια Plu.2.328d; αἱρέσεις 2*Ep.Pet*.2.1:—Pass., μουσικὴν παρεισῆχθαι τοῖς ἀνθρώποις Ephor. 8J. -ἀγωγή, ἡ, *introduction*, προσώπου Theon *Prog*.10, cf. Plot. 2.9.5. -ακτος, ον, *introduced privily*, *Ep.Gal*.2.4: nickname of Ptolemy XI, Str.17.1.8.

**παρείσανον**· κράσπεδον, ἀκρωτήριον, Hsch.

❋**παρεισ-βαίνω**, *enter*, Orph.*Fr*.32*b*iv3. -**βάλλω**, *throw in beside* or *secretly*, Suid. s.v. παρείραντα. II. intr., gloss on παρεισκρίνει, Phot., Suid.; cf. Hsch. -**βᾰτικός**, ή, όν, = παραβατικός, περίοδος π. πρὸς τὸ θέατρον Sch.Ar.*Ach*.970. -**βῐάζομαι**, *force one's way in*, Iamb.*in Nic*.p.14P. -**γρᾰφή**, ἡ, *illegal registration*, Plu.2. 756d. -**δέχομαι**, *take in beside* or *as well*, S.*Tr*.537; τὸ ὑγρὸν ἅμα τῇ τροφῇ Arist.*PA*662ᵃ9. ❋-**δύνω**, *slip in, penetrate*, τὸ ἔλαιον π. Id.*Pr*.881ᵃ7: metaph., εἰς τὰς γνώμας π. Demad.3: pf. -δέδῡκα, εἰς τὰς ἄλλας διαλέκτους A.D.*Synt*.319.24:—also -**δύω**, τὰ παρεισδύοντα τῶν διαλέκτων Id.*Pron*.4.23. II. Med. **παρεισδύομαι**, ἐς τὸ στόμα Hp.*Epid*.5.86, cf. Sor.1.101, Gal.2.653; ἀλλοφυλίας..κατὰ μικρὸν -δυομένης Epicur.*Ep*.2p.48U.; εἰς τὴν πόλιν Hdn.2.12.1, etc.; [τὸ ὕδωρ] παρεισδυόμενον πνίγει Arist.*Pr*.933ᵃ16; of a leech's bite, *penetrate into*, Aret.*CA*2.6; of customs, Plu.2.216b, *Agis* 3, etc. -**δῠσις**, εως, ἡ, *slipping in*, Chrysipp.*Stoic*.3.199, Gal.8.581; τοῦ ἑτέρου ἄρθρου A.D.*Synt*.81.9; of poison, Philum.*Ven*.4.1; *way to get in, opening*, Thphr.*CP*1.7.2; *loophole* of entrance, *chink*, Epicur.*Sent.Vat*.47, Dam.*Pr*.68; *means of entry*, *PStrassb*.22.30 (i A.D.); but also, *loophole* of escape (in argument), Hero *Spir*.1 *Prooem*. (fort. παρέκ-). II. dub. sens., ἔχουσι π. καὶ φιλαυτότητα καὶ λύπην Vett.Val.345.8. -**ειμι** (εἶμι *ibo*), = παρεισέρχομαι, Men.202, Nicostr.Com.4, Philippid.8, Arist.*Resp*.476ᵃ30. -**έρπω**, aor. -ειρπῠσα, *creep in secretly*, Ph.ap.Eus.*PE*8.14. -**έρχομαι**, with aor. and pf. Act., *come* or *go in beside*: Medic., of fingers or instruments, *to be inserted*, Gal.18(1).323,332: generally, *come in*, ὅπως..τύχῃ παρεισέλθῃ Epicur.*Fr*.281 p.351 U.; παρεισελθόντες ὡς φίλιοι Plb.1.7. 3, al.; νόμος παρεισῆλθεν ἵνα πλεονάσῃ τὸ παράπτωμα *Ep.Rom*.5.20; π. ἄφνω πρὸς τὴν ἑστίαν Plu.*Cor*.23; *to be introduced*, of a side-issue, Gal.8.749: c. inf., π. κατασκοπῆσαι *Ep.Gal*.2.4. II. *occur, suggest itself*, of an idea, τινι Vett.Val.357.9. -**κομίζω**, *bring in*, νύκτωρ κεκαλυμμένας εἰκόνας J.*BJ*2.9.2:—Pass., ib.5.12.1. **-κρίνω** [ῐ], *bring in, introduce beside*, of a digression, Eust.1397.63:—Pass., *to be introduced*, Id.263.5, Hsch. **-κυκλέω**, *smuggle in*, Athenio 1.32; esp. *introduce* a digression, etc., Procl. *in Prm.*p.829 S., *in Ti.*1.31 D. (Pass.), Dam.*Pr.*23. II. παρὰ τοῖς ὕστερον παρεισκυκλεῖν λόγους τὸ ὡς ἐκ περιόδου τινὸς κυκλικῶς παρεισάγειν καὶ στρογγύλλειν τὸ φραζόμενον· ἔτι δὲ καὶ ἄλλως, τὸ πολλάκις περὶ τὸ αὐτὸ στρέφεσθαι καὶ οἷον τροχοειδῶς εἰλεῖσθαι, Eust.683.61. **-οδεύω**, *cause to walk*, τινὰς εἰς τὰ τῶν μακάρων ἴχνια Ps.-Luc.*Philopatr.*12. ⊛ **-οδος**, ἡ, *entrance*, Sor.1.58. **-πέμπω**, *let in*, J.*BJ*5.3.1, Plu.2.760b. **-πίπτω**, *get in by the side, steal in*, Thphr.*CP*5.16.1, Luc.*Jud.Voc.*11, etc.; -πεσόντες ἔλαθον D.H.7.11; esp. in war, εἰς τὰς πολιορκουμένας πόλεις Plb.1.18.3, cf. D.S.20.44, Str.14.1.38, Plu.*Sert.*3. II. *fall in the way of*, Id.*Luc.*17. **-πλοκή**, v. παρεμπλοκή. ⊛ **-πορεύομαι**, *enter*, λεληθότως Lxx 2 *Ma.*8.1. **-πράσσω**, Att. -ττω, *exact beside what is due*, i.e. *illegally*, of tax-gatherers, Poll.9.32. **-ρέω**, *flow* or *stream in*, [ὕδωρ] εἰς τὰς μυωπίας π. Thphr.*Fr.*174.7; *glide* or *slip in*, εἰς τὰ συσσίτια, εἰς τὴν πόλιν, Plu.*Lyc.*17, 27:—Pass., in lit. sense, ἐὰν παρεισρυῇ ὑγρὸν εἰς τὴν ἀρτηρίαν *glide in by the side* or *imperceptibly*, Arist.*PA*664$^b$5, cf. Agathin.ap.Orib.10.7.28. **-φέρω**, *bring in beside*, π. νόμον *propose* an *amending* law, D.20.88, cf. 99 (Pass.); *smuggle in*, *PTeb.*38.12 (ii B.C.): generally, *introduce*, Στωϊκὰς δόξας A.D.*Conj.*213.9; τρόπον Aps.p.243 H.; *apply besides*, σπουδήν 2*Ep.Pet.*1.5; *interpolate*, Sch.D.T.p.29 H.:—Pass., *to be brought in*, χυτρίδες εἰς τὰς μέθας -φέρονται Arist.*Fr.*110. **-φθείρομαι**, *steal in to the hurt* of another, Ph.2.341, J.*BJ*4.2.1, 4.3.3. **-φρέω**, *slip in*, λαθραίως Tz.*H.*8.493. **-χέω**, *pour in beside*, metaph., in Pass., γυναῖκες π. παρά τινα πλαγίᾳ θύρᾳ Eun.*VS* p.477 B.

⊛ **πᾰρέκ** (on the accent, v. infr.), before a vowel **πᾰρέξ** (also before a conson., Od.12.276, *SIG*4.6 (Cyzicus, vi B.C.), Pl.*Epin.*976d, *UPZ* 81 iii 20 (ii B.C.), etc., and always in Hdt., Lxx (*Jd.*8.26, al.), and J. (*AJ*7.1.3, al.)): (παρά, ἐκ): A. as Prep., 1. c. gen. loci, *outside, before*, νῆσος.. π. λιμένος τετάνυσται Od.9.116; παρὲξ ὁδοῦ *out of* the road, Il.10.349. 2. *besides, except*, *SIG* l.c., etc.; οὐδὲν ἔστιν ἄλλο π. τοῦ ἐόντος Parm.8.37; πάρεξ τοῦ ἀργύρου χρυσὸν.. ἀνέθηκε Hdt.1.14, cf. 93, 192; πάρεξ ὀστέου καὶ νεύρου Hp.*Alim.*51; ἑτέραν [ἐπιστήμην] πάρεξ τῶν εἰρημένων εὑρεῖν Pl. l.c., cf. Epicur.*Nat.*14 G.; μηδὲν ἰδιοπραγεῖν πάρεξ τῶν προσταττομένων Plb.8.26.9. 3. οἰωνοῖο π. *contrary to* the omen, A.R.2.344; π. οὗ πατρὸς *against the wish of*.., Id.3.742. II. c. acc., *along the side of, along*, παρὲξ ἅλα φῦκος ἔχευεν Il.9.7; παρὲκ μίτον 23.762; παρὲξ τὴν νῆσον *past, clear of* the island, Od.12.276; παρὲξ περιμήκεα δοῦρα *alongside of*.., ib.443; παρὲξ.. νῆα *past* it, 15.199; παρὲκ μέγα τειχίον 16.165, 343; σῆμα παρὲξ Ἴλοιο Il.24.349; παρὲκ νόον *aside from* sense and reason, 10.391 (v. παρεξάγω II); *foolishly*, 20.133; παρὲξ ὀλίγον θανάτοιο *within* a little of death, A.R.2.1113. 2. παρὲξ Ἀχιλῆα *without the knowledge of* Achilles, Il.24.434. 3. *contrary to*, νόον τινός A.R.1.130; π. Διὸς βουλήν ib.1315; π. ἐμὰ θέσφατα βῆναι Id.2.341. 4. *beside*, πολίσματα π. αὐτὰς Πάτρας ἄλλα Paus.7.18.6. 5. *except*, *Supp. Epigr.*2.710.3 (Pednelissus, i B.C.).

B. as Adv., 1. of Place, *out beside, out and away*, λαβὼν περιμήκεα κοντὸν ὦσα παρέξ Od.9.488; νῆχε παρέξ *out along shore*, 5.439; στῆ δὲ παρέξ *hard by*, Il.11.486; τῆλε παρέξ far *away*, A.R.2.272. 2. metaph., *beside the mark*, παρὲξ ἀγορευέμεν Il.12.213; παρὲξ ἐρέουσα Od.23.16. 3. ἄλλα παρὲξ μεμνώμεθα let us talk *of something else*, 14.168. 4. *excepting*, Μῆδοι.. ἄρξαντες τῆς Ἀσίης ἐπ' ἔτεα τριήκοντα καὶ ἑκατὸν δυῶν δέοντα πάρεξ ἢ ὅσον οἱ Σκύθαι ἦρχον *except* so long as.. (i.e. *including* that period), Hdt.1.130 (but Δωριεῖ π. ἢ Ὀλυμπίασιν Ἰσθμίων μὲν γεγόνασιν ὀκτὼ νῖκαι *besides, exclusive of*.., prob. in Paus.6.7.4): abs., *besides*, ταῦτα π. δὲ μηδέν Plb.2.23.3. (Acc. to Hdn.Gr.2.63, 931, παρέξ is correct in Hom., πάρεξ in Hdt., as in codd., cf. *EM*652.39, Eust.732.40.)

⊛ **παρεκ-βαίνω**, *step aside from, deviate from*, c. gen., δικαίου Hes. *Op.*226; τοῦ εὖ Arist.*EN*1109$^b$19; τῆς ἀρετῆς Id.*Pol.*1325$^b$6; π. τῆς ἀριστοκρατίας ἡ τάξις ib.1273$^a$21; τοῦ καθήκοντος Plb.12.7.1; π. ἐκ τοῦ γένους Arist.*GA*767$^b$6; ἐκ τῆς τάξεως Plb.8.26.8; ἀπὸ τῶν κρειττόνων Procl.*Inst.*124. 2. c. acc., *overstep, transgress*, Διὸς σέβας A.*Ch.*645 (lyr.); τὰ πάτρια Arist.*Pol.*1310$^b$19; ἐπὶ μικρὸν π. τὸ τῆς πολιτείας εἶδος Id.*EN*1160$^b$20; τὴν φύσιν Id.*GA*771$^a$12; δίς ἐστι παρεκβεβηκυῖα τὴν εὐθύτητα Id.*Pol.*1309$^b$23; τὸν κοινὸν νοῦν Phld.*Po.*5.15; ποταμοῦ -βάντος τὸ ῥεῖθρον Thphr.*HP*3.1.5. 3. abs., *deviate*, ὁ μικρὸν παρεκβαίνων Arist.*EN*1126$^a$35; αἱ παρεκβεβηκυῖαι πολιτεῖαι Id.*Pol.*1275$^b$1; opp. ὀρθαὶ [πολιτεῖαι], ib.1282$^b$13; π. ἐς ἃ μὴ θέμις *APl.*4.243 (Antist.); prob. l. in Ph.*Bel.*61.49, 62.51. II. *make a digression*, ὅθεν παρεξέβημεν Arist.*EN*1095$^b$14; περί τινος Id.*PA*658$^b$11; ἀπό τινος Plb.4.9.1, al.; εἰς ταῦτα Id.6.50.1. **-βάλλω**, *throw out at the side*, Sch.E.*Hipp.*237 (Pass.), Hsch. s.v. ἀμβητιῶν. II. *extract and compile* the remarks of others, Eust.3.1. **-βᾰσις**, εως, ἡ, *going aside from*: metaph., *deviation from*, τοῦ δικαίου Arist.*Pol.*1307$^a$7. 2. esp. of the *deviations* of constitutional forms, as τυραννίς is a π. of monarchy, oligarchy of aristocracy, democracy of ἡ πολιτεία, Id.*EN*1160$^a$31, cf. *Pol.*1279$^a$20, 1283$^a$29, al. II. *digression*, Is.6.59 (pl.), Plb.1.15.13, al., Apollon.Cit.3; τὴν π. ποιήσασθαι, ποιεῖσθαι τὰς π., D.H.1.53, D.S.1.37, cf. Phld.*Rh.*1.157 S.; κατὰ παρέκβασιν Plb.3.2.7, 31.30.4, S.E.*P.*3.101. **-βᾰτικός**, ή, όν, *discursive*, λόγος Alex.Aphr.*Febr.*18 (Comp.). Adv. -κῶς *by way of digression*, Eustr. *in EN*7.12, Tz. ad Lyc.653, Phot., Suid. **-βολεύομαι**, *narrate in a digression*, ὡς.. Sch.A.R.4.284. **-βολή**, ἡ, *digression*, Iamb.*Bab.*8. II. *compilation of a set of critical remarks*, as those of Eust. on Homer, Pindar, and Dionysius Periegeta, cf. eund. ad D.P.426; παρεκβολαὶ διαφόρων γραμματικῶν, title of Sch.D.T. in *Cod.BMus.Add.*5118. **-βολικός**, ή, όν, *discursive*, τὸ π. Eust. 4.38. ⊛ **-δέχομαι**, *take in a wrong sense, misconstrue*, M.Ant.5.6, Anon. *in Tht.*19.46. **-δίδωμι**, *give in marriage secretly*: Παρεκδιδομένη, name of a play by Antiphanes. **-δοχή**, ἡ, in pl., *varieties of interpretation*, Ph.Bybl.ap.Eus.*PE*1.10. **-δοχικῶς**, Adv., = συνεκδοχικῶς, Sch.Od.3.486. **-δύομαι**, Pass. with aor. 2 Act., *slip out secretly*, Luc.*JTr.*41. **-δυσις**, v. παρείσδυσις I.

**παρεκεῖ**, Adv. *thereabouts*, Hsch. and Suid. s.v. ἐπέκεινα.

**παρεκέσκετο**, v. παράκειμαι.

**παρέκ-θεσις**, εως, ἡ, *insertion* of part of a metrical system intermediate between εἴσθεσις and ἔκθεσις, Sch.Ar.*Ach.*1007, *Pax* 458. **-θέω**, *run past*, c. acc. loci, A.R.1.592: abs., *penetrate*, ἐλλέβορος -θέων εἴσω Aret.*CD*2.13. **-θλίβω** [ῑ], *jostle aside*, Arist. *Pr.*932$^a$13 (Pass.). **-κᾰθαίρω**, *clear up, explain incidentally*, Epicur.*Nat.*119 G. **-κλίνω** [ῑ], *turn somewhat aside*, ἑαυτόν Archig. ap.Gal.12.656. 2. *alter slightly*, of the form of a word, D.H.5.47. II. *turn aside from, shun*, ἀλλήλας Arist.*HA*578$^b$10. 2. abs., *turn aside, deviate*, Aeschin.1.176; ἡ καρδία μικρὸν εἰς τὰ εὐώνυμα π. Arist.*PA*666$^b$7; ὄνομα μικρὸν παρεκκλῖνον ἀπὸ.. *formed by a slight deviation* from.., as ἦθος from ἔθος, Id.*EN*1103$^a$18 (here and elsewh. with v.l. παρεγκλ-). **-λέγω**, *collect covertly*, π. τὰ κοινά *embezzle* the public moneys, D.19.204, cf. Ph.2.575, D.C.54.21, 76.7. 2. of birds, *collect food here and there*, ὅ τι ἂν τύχῃ παρεκλέγων Ael.*NA*8.25, cf. 17.16. 3. *seek to acquire*, τὸ τῆς δόξης ἀθάνατον Eun.*Hist.*p.251 D. **-λείπω**, *leave out*, Aristid.1.171 J. II. *run short*; c. acc., *fail*, π. αὐτοὺς τὰ βρώματα v.l. in Lxx *Ju.*11.12. **-λύω**, *relieve from*, τοῦ ἐπισπασμοῦ Sor.2.11. 2. Pass., *to be cut off from, unreceptive of*, πρὸς ἅπαντα δι' ὧν ἄμεινον βιώσονται Phld.*Herc.*1251.18. **-μανθάνω**, *learn incidentally* or *gradually*, τὴν μουσικήν Phld.*Mus.*p.105 K. ⊛ **-νέομαι**, *sail past*, c. acc. loci, A.R.2.941. **-νεύω**, *diverge from* the road, Eust.891.11. **-πέμπω**, *convey forth*, Ph.2.224. **-περάω**, *go past*, c. acc. loci, A.*Fr.*31. ⊛ **-πίπτω**, *slope*, εἰς τὰ μεσημβρινὰ μέρη *Placit.*3.12.1. **-πληρόω**, *pack*, μότῳ ξηρῷ Heliod.ap.Orib. 50.49.2. **-προφεύγω**, *flee forth from, elude one's grasp*, ἵνα μή σε παρεκπροφύγῃσιν ἄεθλα Il.23.314. **-πῡρόομαι**, Pass., *take fire by the way*, Arist.*Mete.*341$^b$30. **-πύρωσις** [ῠ], εως, ἡ, *taking fire by the side*, Phlp. *in Mete.*75.7 (pl.). **-ρέω**, aor. 2 inf. παρεκρυῆναι, *run out at the side*, Dsc.*Eup.*1.235. **-ρίπτω**, *throw up*, εἰς τοὺς αἰγιαλούς, of the sea, prob. in Cyran.33. **-στροφή**, ἡ, *turning towards*, π. προσώπων, of lovers, Malch.p.394 D. (pl.). **-τᾰνύω**, = παρεκτείνω, Q.S.3.337 (Pass.), *AP*5.250 (Iren.). **-τᾰσις**, εως, ἡ, *stretching out, extension*, ἀέρος *expanse*, Epicur.*Ep.*2 p.53 U. (pl.); χρονικὴ π. S.E.*M.*6.57, cf. *Theol.Ar.*52 (pl.); χρόνου Sor.2.43; τῶν ἐπισημασιῶν Alex.Philalethes ap.Gal.7.467. 2. *projection* of the false ribs, Ruf. *Oss.*25. II. *lengthening* of a syllable, D.H.*Comp.*15. **-τᾰτέον**, *one must attribute extension to*, τὸ ἀδιάστατον Plot.1.5.7. ⊛ **-τείνω**, *stretch out in line, deploy* an army *into line*, Plb.11.12.4, etc.; of a fleet, π. ἐπὶ μίαν ναῦν Id.1.26.15; ὅτι πλεῖστον π. τὰς ναῦς D.S.13.98: generally, *stretch out beside*, τὸ σῶμά τινι Plu.*Agis* 20; *stretch out*, εἰς λόγους ταῦτα π. Ps.-Luc.*Philopatr.*23:—Pass., τῆς στρατοπεδείας παρὰ τὸν Ἀσωπὸν -τεταμένης Plu.*Arist.*11. II. intr., *extend*, of Place, ἐπὶ τὴν θάλασσαν Lxx *Ez.*47.19; τὸ δεξιὸν κέρας παρὰ τὸν Εὐφράτην -τεῖνον D.S. 14.22; αἱ ἀπὸ Πισιδίας.. ἕως Λυκίας Str.13.4.17; of Time, Thphr.*CP*1.13.9; τριταῖοι -τείνοντες, of semi-tertian fevers, Agathin. ap.Gal.7.367; -τεινόντων τῶν ἀγώνων Phld.*Mus.*p.109 K. 2. of a man, *extend his life, survive*, μέχρι τινός D.H.*Is.*1. 3. in Logic, *to be of wider extent*, Arist.*APo.*99$^a$35. III. in Pass., c. dat., *extend beside* or *be coextensive with*, π. χείλεσι ποταμοῦ D.S.3.10; ὅλα ὅλοις -τείνεται *Stoic.*2.156; -τείνεσθαι τῷ χρόνῳ Diog.Bab.*Stoic.*3.216; ὕλης -τεινομένης τοῖς σώμασιν Jul.*Or.*4.134a. 2. metaph., *measure oneself with*, παρεκτείνεσθαί τινι Democr.238; μὴ -τείνου πένης ὢν πλουσίῳ Lxx *Pr.*23.4. **-τελέω**, *accomplish against one's wish*, Mosch.4.125.

**παρεκτέον**, (παρέχω) *one must furnish, afford*, ἡμῖν γέλωτα X.*Cyr.*2.2.15; τινὶ χάριν Andronic.Rhod.p.577 M.; π. ἑαυτὴν ἐπιτηδείαν Theano *Ep.*5.4, cf. Gal.17(2).355.

**παρεκτίθημι**, *set forth*, τὰ πραχθέντα ὅπως γέγονε Eun.*Hist.*p.223 D.:—Med., *Cat.Cod.Astr.*1.80. II. Med., *expose one's* child, Sch. E.*Andr.*69.

**παρεκτικός**, ή, όν, (παρέχω) *able to cause*, *Stoic.*2.119; ἀλγηδόνος S.E.*M.*7.203, cf. Alex.Aphr. *in Metaph.*58.29; ἐλπίδος Gal.17(2).147; δυάδος *Theol.Ar.*6; τοῦ εὖ Procl.*Inst.*9. II. *liberal*, Ar.Byz. *Epit.*43.7 (Comp.), Vett.Val.47.3, al.

**παρέκτοπος**, ον, *somewhat out of the way*, Gloss.

⊛ **παρεκτός**, Adv. *besides* or *except for* a thing, c. gen., *Ev.Matt.*5.32, *Act.Ap.*26.29. II. abs., χωρὶς τῶν π. besides things *external*, 2*Ep. Cor.*11.28.

**παρεκ-τρέπω**, *turn aside*, ὀχετὸν ὥστε μὴ θανεῖν E.*Supp.*1111:—Pass., *to be turned aside, deviate*, παρεκτετράφθαι Arist.*GA*773$^a$15; π. εἰς.. Plu.2.114d; π. τῆς ὁδοῦ Sch.Ar.*Ach.*81. **-τρέχω**, *run out past*, in aor. part. -δραμόντες Plu.*Flam.*8. II. metaph., παρεκδεδραμηκότα παρὰ τὰς εὐθείας forms *derived from* the nominative, A.D.*Adv.* 171.25; of the *outcome* of astrological influences, Vett.Val.185. 2. **-τρίβομαι** [ῑ], Pass., *suffer friction*, Arist.*Cael.*289$^a$20. **-τροπή**, ἡ, *turning aside, diverting*, of a stream, D.C.*Fr.*77. II. (from Pass.) *swerving aside, deviation, divergence*, τῆς τάξεως Demetr.*Eloc.* 84; κυριωτέρου σχήματος A.D.*Synt.*167.3; παράλλαξις καὶ π. ἡ πρὸς τὸ ὄν Simp. *in Ph.*232.35. 2. *abnormality*, Steph. *in Hp.*1.110 D. **-τροχάζω**, *pass by*, *IG*12(8)p.vii (found in Egypt). II. *run from the path, yield the road*, τινι Tz.*H.*10.84.

**παρέκτωρ**, ορος, ὁ, *provider*, Ramsay *Studies in the Eastern Roman Provinces* p.128 (Phrygia).

**παρεκ-φαίνομαι**, *appear beside* or *gradually*, Gal.19.354. **-φέρω**, *abuse*, τὸ μέγεθος τῆς δωρεᾶς prob. in *IG*2².1099.33 (ii A.D.):—Pass., *to be carried beyond bounds*, Aristipp.ap.Stob.3.17.17; πέρα τοῦ μέτρου Plu.2.102c, cf. Metrod.*Herc.*831.1. II. *to be excreted with*, Aët.5.28. **-φρακτικός**, v. παραφρακτικός. **-χέω**, *pour out by degrees*, ἔκ τινος εἴς τι κατὰ σταγόνα S.E.*M.*7.90:—Pass., Gal.18(2).447; of rivers and lakes, *overflow*, Str.16.2.39, D.S.5.47; also π. εἰς πιμελώδη ὄγκον *become obese*, Sor.1.32. **-χῠμα**, ατος, τό, *effusion*: hence πιμελή ἐστι π. λευκόν Ruf.*Anat.*66. **-χῠσις**, εως, ἡ, *overflowing*, of rivers, Plb.34.10.4, Str.3.5.7, etc. 2. *effusion*, αἵματος Gal.19.124; of humours, Cass.Fel.76; = ὕδερος, Cael.Aur.*TP*3.8.

**παρελᾱσις**, εως, ἡ, *riding past*, Arr.*Tact.*37.4.

❀ **παρελαύνω** or **-ελάω**, aor. παρήλᾰσα Il.23.638, Ep. παρέλασσα ib.382:—*drive by* or *past*, ἐναντίω δύ' ἅρματε π. *drive* them *past* one another, Ar.*Av.*1129; π. τὸν ἵππον X.*Cyr.*5.3.55; τὰς αἶγας παρελᾶντα (Dor. pres. part.) Theoc.5.89, cf. 8.73, Longus 3.15. II. as if intr., 1. *drive by* (sc. δίφρον, ἅρμα, ἵππους, etc.), Il.23.382,427. b. c. acc. pers., *drive past, overtake* another, οἱοισίν μ' ἵπποισι παρήλασαν ib.638; but π. Τρηχῖνα *drive on* to Trachis, Hes.*Sc.*353; also π. ἐφ' ἅρματος, ἐφ' ἵππου, X.*An.*1.2.16, 3.4.46. 2. *row* or *sail past*, παρήλασε νηΐ Od.12.186. b. c. acc. pers., [Σειρῆνας] παρήλασαν ib.197. 3. in Prose, *ride by, run by*, c. acc., freq. in X., *An.*1.2.17, al.; π. τὰς τάξεις ib.3.5.4. 4. less freq., *ride up to, rush towards*, πρὸς αὐτόν, ἐπὶ τοὺς πολεμίους, *Cyr.*4.2.12, *Eq.Mag.*8.18; *ride on one's way*, *Cyr.*3.3.4.

**παρελέγχω**, *rebuke*, Lxx 2 *Ma.*4.33, Gal.2.645.

**παρέλευσις**, εως, ἡ, = παροδεία, Suid., Mich.*in PN*79.22.

**παρελκ-όντως**, Adv. *superfluously*, Dsc.*Ther.Praef.*, Ptol.*Harm.*2.8, Eust.76.7. **-ῠσις**, εως, ἡ, *protraction, delay*, Lxx *Jb.*25.3, Hsch., Phot. (-εσις cod.). **-υσμός**, ὁ, *protraction* of disease, Aët.9.28. II. *prolongation* of sound, Eust.1005.6. **-υ(σ)τής**, οῦ, ὁ, *one who protracts*, *Gloss.*:—fem. **παρελκύστρ(ι)α**, ib.

❀ **παρέλκω**, fut. -ελκύσω Lxx *Si.*29.8 (v.l. -ελκύσῃς): aor. -είλκυσα Ar.*Nu.*553: pf. -είλκυκα *PMagd.*6.10 (iii B.C.): pf. Pass. -είλκυσμαι:—*draw aside*, π. πραγμάτων ὀρθὰν ὁδόν Pi.*O.*7.46; π. τὸ ἀκόντισμα *draw* it *out sideways*, Plu.*Cam.*2; π. ἑαυτόν *withdraw secretly*, Id.*Cleom.*8; π. τινὰ ἀπό.. Chrysipp.ap.D.L.7.182 (v.l.); π. ἡ φαντασία πρός τι S.E.*P.*2.77:—Med., *draw aside to oneself, get hold of by craft*, οὕνεκα τῶν μὲν δῶρα παρέλκετο Od.18.282. 2. *lead alongside*, as a led horse, Hdt.3.102:—Med., ὁ ἐλαύνων τὸν ἕτερον παρέλκεται Harp. s.v. ἅμιπποι:—Pass., παρέλκεσθαι ἐκ γῆς *to be towed* from the bank, Hdt.2.96. 3. κενὰς παρέλκειν (τὰς κώπας, acc. to Sch.) *pull* them through the air, without dipping them, i.e. make a mere show of working, Ar.*Pax* 1306. 4. *drag in*, ὅταν ἀπορήσῃ.., τότε π. αὐτόν (sc. τὸν νοῦν) Arist.*Metaph.*985ᵃ20; τὰ Ἰουδαϊκὰ εἰς τὸν μῦθον π. Plu.2.363d:—Pass., *to be brought in as an accompaniment*, Phld.*Mus.*p.95 K. 5. *lug on the stage*, or *maul* a play, Εὔπολις μὲν τὸν Μαρικᾶν.. παρείλκυσεν Ar.*Nu.*553. II. *spin out* in time, τὰ κατὰ τὸν κίνδυνον π. ὀλίγας ἡμέρας Plb.2.70.3, etc.; μηδὲν παρέλκων without *delay*, *SIG*306.43 (Tegea, iv B.C.): c. acc., *put off, fob off*, τινα *PMagd.*l.c., etc.: abs., μὴ μύνῃσι παρέλκετε *put* not things *off* by excuses, Od.21.111; also π. τὸν χρόνον D.H.2.45, Luc.*Am.*54:—Pass., *to be delayed*, Plb.5.30.5, 22.4.11, D.H.10.19. III. intr., *to be prolonged, continue*, Luc.*Am.*25, Eun.*Hist.*p.260 D.; ἡδονῆς παρέλκοντα μέτρα Luc.*Am.*21. 2. *to be redundant*, περιττὰ καὶ παρέλκοντα Ph.1.227, cf. Phld.*D.*3.14, Arr.*Epict.*1.7.29, S.E.*P.*2.175; περὶ τῶν παρελκόντων λόγων, title of work by Chrysippus, *Stoic.*2.7: so in Gramm., τὰ παρέλκοντα A.D.*Pron.*3.6:—Pass., τὰ ἐκ περιττοῦ παρελκόμενα τοῖς ἐπιτηδεύμασι things *merely appended* to the arts, *extraneous additions* to them, Plb.9.20.6, cf. D.H.4.20, Plu.2.386d, A.D.*Pron.*79.27. IV. intr., *to be derived*, ἀπό.. ib.6.16.

**παρέλλειψις**, εως, ἡ, *loss of one of two similar consonants*, as κάλιον for κάλλιον, Trypho *Pass.*1.26, al. II. π. τῆς φύσεως *defect* of nature, prob. in Anon. *in Prm.* in *Rh.Mus.*47(1892).601.

**παρελπίζω**, *to be disappointed in one's hopes of*, τινας Phld.*Lib.* p.8 O.

❀ **παρεμ-βαίνω**, *fit in*, εἰς ἐπιτομήν Ph.*Bel.*66.39; *go in beside* another, Plu.2.593f; τεθρίππῳ π. *to be mounted beside* another *on..*, D.H.2.34; ἐφ' ἁρματίου Id.5.47, etc. **-βάλλω**, fut. -βᾰλῶ Ar.*V.*481:—*put in beside* or *between, insert, interpose*, τι l.c.; π. λόγους ἑτέρους D.40.61; ὑποψίας π. *insinuate* suspicions, Aeschin.1.167; π. δημηγορίας ib.174; ὅτε νυστάζοιεν οἱ ἀκροαταί, π. τῆς πεντηκονταδράχμου *interpose* [a touch] of his 50 drachmae lecture, of Prodicus the Sophist, Arist.*Rh.*1415ᵇ16, cf. *Top.*157ᵃ1; *interpolate*, π. τι εἰς τὰ Ἡσιόδου Plu.2.730f, cf. Alex.Aphr.*in Top.*309.27 (Pass.). b. in Tactics, *insert* troops in a line of battle, Plb.1.33.7, al.; *insert* men in the ranks, Ascl.*Tact.*10.17, etc. c. *place in* a class or order, Pl.*Lg.*741a. d. *feed* olives into a press, *PFay.*91.6, al. (i A.D.). e. *add* an ingredient in medicine, Sor.1.122, Aët.16.85. f. εἰς ἔκθεσμα πράγματα π. ἑαυτόν *engage* in.., *POxy.*129.4 (vi A.D.). 2. *draw up in battle-order*, Plb.2.27.7, al., Plu.2.618d, etc. II. intr., *fall into line*, ἐς ναυμαχίαν Plb.5.69.7, cf. Plu.*Sull.*17, etc. 2. of an army, *encamp*, Lxx *Ex.*15.27, al., Plb.1.77.6. 3. of guests at table, *take* their *places*, Plu.2.615d. 4. *advance*, Plb.11.23.5; εἰς.. Id.5.14.9, 29.19.8. **-βλαστάνω**, *grow in beside*, Ph.1.573. **-βλέπω**, *look askance*, εἴς τι E.*Hel.*1558, cf. Phld.*Vit.*p.37 J., Sm.*Ca.*1.6, Hsch. s.v. παριλλαίνουσα. **-βλησις**, εως, ἡ, *encamping*, Aq.*Is.*29.1. ❀ **-βολή**, ἡ, *insertion, interpolation*, ἑτέρων πραγμάτων Aeschin.3.205, cf. 1.166 (pl.), Phld.*Rh.*1.261 S. 2. Gramm., *parenthesis*, Alex.*Fig.*25, Tib.*Fig.*48. II. *drawing up in battle-order*, Plb.11.32.6; in Tactics, *insertion of men in the ranks* (dist. fr. παρένταξις and παρεμπλοκή), Ascl.*Tact.*6.1, 10.17. b. *company* of soldiers, etc., Lxx *Ge.*32.2(3); *host*, ib.33.8 (pl.), Ezek.*Exag.*81. 2. *encampment*, Diph.57, Theophil.9, Crito Com.1, Lxx *Ex.*14.19, al., Plb.3.74.5, al., Plu.*Galb.*27: generally, *soldiers' quarters*, Plb.6.29.1; *barracks*, *Act.Ap.*21.34, cf. *Ostr.*901, al. (ii A.D.); name of an ἄμφοδον, *POxy.*2131.8 (iii A.D.). III. = παρεξειρεσία (q.v.), Plb.21.7.4 (sed leg. παραβολαί). IV. in boxing and wrestling, π. βάλλειν *trip* an adversary by a twist of the leg, Luc.*Ocyp.*60, cf. Plu.2.638f (pl.). ❀ **-βολικός**, ή, όν, *as in a camp*, δεῖπνα ib.643d.

**παρεμβολο-ειδής**, ές, *like an interjection*, Hsch. s.v. βόμβαξ. **-θέτης**, ου, ὁ, *one who fixes a camp*, *Gloss.*

**παρεμ-βύω** [ῡ], *stuff in*, Luc.*Hist.Conscr.*22. **-μαίνομαι**, Pass., *to be somewhat mad*, Tim.*Lex.* s.v. κορυβαντιᾶν. **-μᾰνής**, ές, *somewhat mad*, *Gloss.*

**παρέμμεναι**, Ep. inf. of πάρειμι (εἰμί *sum*).

**παρεμ-μίγνυμι**, *mix in besides*, Ael.*NA*2.30, Olymp.*in Alc.*p.7 C. (Pass.), Tz.*H.*2.347:—also **-μίσγω**, Ps.-Dsc.4.137. **-πάσσω**, *sprinkle* or *mix in besides*, Dsc.5.76, Democr.ap.Gal.14.121; τινί τι *Gp.*2.34.1:—Pass., c. dat., ib.3.9. **-πηδάω**, *make an incursion, interfere*, *PPetr.*3p.78 (iii B.C.). **-πίνω**, *drink to excess*, Hsch. **-πίπλημι**, *fill secretly with*, τὸ τεῖχος ὅπλων Plu.*Marc.*18:—Pass., *to be overfull*, τινος Erasistr.ap.Gal.7.538. **-πίπραμαι**, Pass., *to be chafed by rubbing*, Str.15.1.52. ❀ **-πίπτω**, fut. -πεσοῦμαι Arist.*APo.*95ᵇ23:—*creep in, effect an entrance*, ἀρχαὶ π. λοιμῶν Democritei ap. Plu.2.733d, cf. Pl.*Chrm.*173d, Lxx *Wi.*7.25, Alciphr.1.13; *intrude*, εἰς τὴν πολιτείαν Aeschin.2.173; βραχέα σοφῷ τύχη -πίπτει Epicur.*Sent.*16, cf. Plu.*Fab.*19; παρεμπεσοῦσα ἡ σώματος φύσις πρὸς αὐτὴν ἡμᾶς εἵλκυσεν Plot.6.9.9; of enemies, *effect an entrance*, Ph.*Bel.*80.43; of humours, *find their way, are diverted*, Arist.*GA*768ᵇ26. 2. in Logic, of a term, *to be inserted*, Id.*APr.*42ᵇ8, *APo.*l.c. 3. Gramm., τὸ παρεμπίπτον ἄρθρον the *inserted* article, A.D.*Synt.*33.18. 4. Medic., of *intercident* critical days, Gal.9.928. b. of the *intercident* pulse, Ruf.*Syn.Puls.*8.3, Gal.8.525. 5. generally, *intervene*, μὴ δυναμένου παρεμπεσεῖν σημείου S.E.*M.*9.423, cf. Plot.5.3.11, Iamb.*Myst.*1.4: Geom., of a line, *fall in* between curve and tangent, Euc.3.16, Apollon.Perg.*Con.*1.32. 6. *occur, present itself*, Arist.*GA*742ᵇ8; τὰ ἀεὶ -πίπτοντα Epicur.*Ep.*1 p.31 U.; εἰ ἀμφισβήτησις παρεμπέσοι Hermog.*Inv.*4.14. II. *fall under the head of*, τινι Plu.2.570f: abs., *to be included in one form*, A.D.*Synt.*259.5, cf. 21.2. **-πλάσσω**, Att. -ττω, *stop up*, τοὺς πόρους Alex.Trall.2, cf. Antyll.ap.Orib.10.22.1, Dsc.5.81, Aët.7.28:—Pass., *stop up*, τοῖς πόροις Dsc.*Alex.Praef.* **-πλαστικός**, ή, όν, *of* or *for stopping the pores*, δύναμις Id.1.109, cf. Aët.9.42, Alex.Trall.5.5 (Comp.). **-πλέκω**, *insert* men in ranks, Ascl.*Tact.*10.17; *mingle*, τῷ ποτῷ τὴν τροφήν Orib.*Fr.*41:—Med., prob. in Phot. (παρεπλεξάμην cod.): metaph., *interweave*, Eust.2.2, al.:—Pass., *to be blended with, contained in*, Diph.Siph.ap.Ath.2.57c; *to be involved*, Vett.Val.181.35. **-πλοκή**, ἡ, *fitting in, inclusion*, κενοῦ Epicur.*Frr.*92, 274; ἡ κατὰ κένωσιν π. prob. in Hero *Spir.*1 *Prooem.* (παρεισ- codd.); of cogs in a machine, Theo Sm.p.180 H. 2. in Tactics, = παρένταξις 2, Ascl.*Tact.*10.17. 3. Astrol., *complication*, Petos.ap.Vett.Val.281.23. 4. generally, *complication, interposition*, ἡ τοῦ μᾶλλον καὶ ἧττον π. Procl.*in Prm.*p.578 S. 5. *interlude, digression*, ἱστορικὴ π. Eust.103.39. II. in concrete sense, *stuffing, forcemeat*, Agatharch.34.

**παρεμποδ-ίζω**, *to be a hindrance*, τινι Luc.*Am.*15: abs., Gal.4.574, 10.63. **-ισμός**, ὁ, *obstruction*, Erot. s.v. κώφωσις, Gal.14.776, Aspasia ap.Aët.16.72. **-ών**, Adv. *in the way*, Procop.Gaz.*Ep.*127, Alex.Trall.2.

**παρεμ-ποιέω**, *create in* one *besides*, Plu.2.520e. **-πολάω**, *traffic underhand in* a thing, *smuggle* it *in*, π. γάμους dub. in E.*Med.*910; πολίτης παρημπολημένος an *intrusive* citizen, *Com.Adesp.*96. **-πολή**, ἡ, late spelling of παρεμβολή, *BGU*514.14 (iii A.D.).

**παρεμπόρ-ευμα**, ατος, τό, in pl., *merchandise of small value, small gains*, Hsch. s.v. ῥωπικά. II. metaph., *appendix*, = πάρεργον, Luc.*Dem.Enc.*10, 22, M.Ant.3.12, etc. 2. *by-product*, π. τῆς εἰσπνοῆς ἡ τῶν ὀσμῶν γίγνεται διάγνωσις Gal.*UP*8.7. **-εύομαι**, *traffic in besides*: metaph., μικρὰ π. τῆς ἀφροδίτης Alciphr.*Fr.*6.16; τὸ τερπνὸν π. *yield* delight *besides* instruction, Luc.*Hist.Conscr.*9.

❀ **παρέμ-πτωσις**, εως, ἡ, *influx, entrance*, τοῦ ὑγροῦ Arist.*Resp.*476ᵇ8; *occurrence*, S.E.*M.*7.175. 2. *insertion* of words, A.D.*Synt.*16.11, al.; *parenthesis*, D.H.*Amm.*2.2. 3. *implication*, A.D.*Synt.*202.6, 203.22. 4. Medic., *transfusion* of blood into arteries, Erasistr.ap.Gal.7.542, al., Id.ap.Anon.Lond.27.7, Herod.Med. in *Rh.Mus.*49.553, Plu.2.948c. b. *intercidence* of crisis, Gal.9.868. c. *embolism of the retinal artery*, Id.14.777. **-φαίνω**, aor. παρενέφηνα Phld.*Piet.*18:—*display along with*, τὴν αὑτοῦ ὄψιν Pl.*Ti.*50e. 2. generally, *suggest, indicate*, Arist.*Aud.*801ᵇ13, Chrysipp.*Stoic.*2.52, 245, Plb.12.24.2, Phld.l.c., D.H.*Comp.*6, Plu.*Per.*16, 2.107e, A.D.*Adv.*204.22, *Synt.*9.22:—Pass., Ph.1.488, A.D.*Pron.*11.28. b. *emphasize*, Phld.*Rh.*1.85 S.; τὸν νοῦν D.L.6.3. 3. π. ὀσμήν τινος *show* the smell of, i.e. smell like, Dsc.1.47; π. σμύρνης ib.61. II. Pass., *appear in* a thing *incidentally*, Arist.*de An.*429ᵃ

20, Ph.212$^a$8, 224$^a$1; of water, *appear at the same time*, Id.Pr.932$^b$ 23. -φᾰνίζω, Dor. aor. 1 παρενεφάνιξα, = foreg. I. 2, π. τὴν παρουσίαν IG4$^2$(1).122.34 (Epid.). -φάρακτος· ἀσελγής, πέρπερος, Hsch.; = *cerritus*, Gloss. -φᾰσις, εως, ἡ, *signification* of words, περὶ παρεμφάσεως, title of work by Chrysippus, Stoic.2.6, cf. Phalar. Ep.84.4, Apollod.Fr.Hist.102 J., Gal.10.83; ψυχικὴ π. psychical *meaning* (opp. πρᾶγμα), A.D.Adv.131.23. II. *indication*, χρονικὴ π. Id.Synt.334.15. III. *perversion of meaning, misrepresentation*, Phld.Vit.p.38 J. -φᾰτικός, ή, όν, *indicative*, προσώπου, πλήθους, A.D.Pron.63.10, Synt.68.6; τὰ π. *finite* verb-forms, opp. ἀπαρέμφατα, D.H.Comp.5. ⊛-φερής, ές, *somewhat like*, v.l. in Arist.HA 524$^b$10, cf. D.S.1.35,98, etc. Adv. -ρῶς Zos.5.16. ⊛-φέρω, *to be somewhat like*, Asclep.ap.Gal.14.168. II. Pass., *to be brought in besides*, Vett.Val.246.15. 2. *float in as well*, Gal.19.616. -φράσσω, Att. -ττω, *block up beside*, τὰς διόδους Id.6.768; τοὺς πόρους Cass. Pr.60. ⊛-φύομαι, Pass., *grow in beside, hang upon*, Luc.Fug. 10. -φῠσις, εως, ἡ, *point of attachment*, Heliod.ap.Orib.45.9.3.

παρεν-αλλᾰγή, ἡ, *dislocation*, Gal.14.796. -αλλάσσομαι, Pass., *to be interchanged*, Id.Phil.Hist.19. ⊛-δείκνῡμαι, Med., *exhibit*, of actors, Poll.4.98,113. 2. *denote* (of a mask), πολυπραγμοσύνην ib. 145: generally, *display*, Dam.Pr.116:—Act. in Olymp.Alch.p.79 B. ⊛-δημέω, *take up residence in* a place, Sammelb.5223.2. -δίδωμι, *give in*, Plu.2.813d, App.BC1.12. 2. *relax, remit*, of acute disease, Gal.12.494. 3. παρενδοθῇ· παρατεθῇ, Hsch. -δύομαι, Pass. with aor. 2 Act., *slip in*, PCair.Zen.534.50 (iii B.C.), Plu.2.479a. -εῖδον, inf. -ιδεῖν, aor. 2 with no pres. in use (cf. παρεῖδον), *take a side look at*, παρενιδών τι Ar.Lys.156 (s.v.l.). -είρω, *put in by the side*, τὴν χεῖρα Sor.2.60: metaph., ἑαυτὸν εἰς πάντα π. *intrude* oneself into everything, Plu.2.793d; τῷ λόγῳ περιττὰς προτάσεις Alex.Aphr.in Top.521. 34, cf. Eust.7.39. -εκτέον, *one must bring in, apply*, βοηθήματα v.l. in Philum.Ven.36.4 (ap.Aët.13.37).

παρενήνεον, v. παρανηνέω.

παρενήνοθε, = παράκειται, ἡμετέρη..τοίη π. μῆτις A.R.1.664; cf. ἐνήνοθε.

παρενθεῖν, Dor. for παρελθεῖν, v. παρέρπω.

παρέν-θεσις, εως, ἡ, *putting in beside*: *giving besides* or *wrongly*, τῆς τροφῆς Gal.19.193 (pl., s.v.l.); *injection*, Orib.Fr.58. II. *insertion*, of a tent in a wound, Aët.8.27: Gramm., of letters, Eust.30. 43: in Tactics, of men in a rank, Ascl.Tact.6.1; τῶν ἱστοριῶν Eust. 100.33. 2. *parenthesis*, Quint.Inst.9.3.23; κατὰ -θεσιν Hermog. Id.1.12. 3. *application*, τῶν χειλέων Gal.5.708. ⊛-θετος, ον, *interpolated*, στίχος Eust.67.29. II. π. πρόσωπον a 'man of straw', Sammelb.5248.7 (ii B.C.), etc. ⊛-θήκη, ἡ, *something put in beside, addition*, τοιήνδε..παρενθήκην ἐποιήσατο, of works undertaken *in completion of others*, Hdt.1.186; παρενθήκην ἔχρησε ἐς Μιλησίους delivered an oracle *by way of parenthesis*, Id.6.19; τοῦ λόγου π. ποιεέσκετο τήνδε, ὡς.. Id.7.5, cf. 171; ἑτέρας τοῦ πολέμου π. ἐποιεῖτο undertook other *business in the intervals of* the war, Plu.Pomp.41; π. ὄψου, = παροψώνημα, Poll.6.56; of a remedy *interposed* in a difficult situation, Lib.Or.59.95. II. *smaller wares taken as an addition to the cargo*, opp. ἡ ἐμπορία, Plu.2.151e, cf. Poll.1.99, Hsch. -θῡμέομαι, *disregard*, Ph.1.78, M.Ant.5.5, etc.: aor. Pass. in act. sense -θυμηθείς TAM2.245.13 (Lycia); ἵνα μὴ παρενθυμηθῇς Sammelb.7404. 39 (ii A.D.). -θύμησις [ῡ], εως, ἡ, *want of attention, disregard*, Gloss. -θυρσος, ὁ, *false sentiment* or *affectation of style*, Theod. ap.Longin.3.5.

παρενῐαυτοφόρος, ον, *fruiting every other year*, Thphr.CP1.20.3.

παρεννέπω, *tell tales*, A.R.3.367.

παρεν-οχλέω, *cause one much annoyance*, Hp.Ep.13, Arist.Rh.1381$^b$15, Mem.453$^a$16; π. τινὶ περί τινος Plb.1.8.1: simply τινί Lxx Jd.14. 17, al., Phld.Ir.p.86 W., Act.Ap.15.19. 2. c. acc., *annoy*, Plb.16. 37.3, OGI139.16 (Egypt, ii B.C.), Hierocl.in CA8p.431 M.:—Pass., παρηνώχλησθε D.18.50; ὑπό τινος Plb.3.53.6; of disease, ὑπὸ νευρικῆς διαθέσεως OGI331.10 (Pergam., ii B.C.). -όχλημα, ατος, τό, *annoyance*, Ph.2.519, al. -όχλησις, εως, ἡ, *annoyance*, Aët.8. 16. -σᾰλεύω, *swing to and fro*, π. τοῖν ποδοῖν Ar.Pl.291; π. πρὸς αὐλόν Philostr.VA2.13. -σπείρομαι, *to be strewn among*, pf. part. -εσπαρμένος Procl.ap.Simp.in Cael.656.14. -στάζω, *let drop in besides* or *by mistake*, Sor.1.86, Gal.12.794, Aët.4.9. -σταξις, εως, ἡ, *dropping in*, Sor.2.28. -σφηνόομαι, *to be wedged in beside*, '*impacted*', cj. ib.31. -ταξις, εως, ἡ, *insertion*, τῶν μεσοτήτων Plu.2.1022d (pl.). 2. in Tactics, *insertion*, e.g. of light-armed troops among hoplites, Ascl.Tact.6.1. -τάττω, *insert*, μεσότητας Plu.2.1020a, 1022c. -τείνω, *stretch beside*, in Med., ταῖς ἑπτὰ χορδαῖς δύο παρεντεινάμενος ib.84a. II. π. τὴν φωνήν *strain, exert* it, ib.623b, cf. D.H.Dem.54; *aggravate*, τὰς ἐντάσεις Ruf.Sat.Gon.43. III. π. τὸν Ἀναξαγόραν *interlarded* his speech with A.'s doctrines, Plu.Per. 8. -τευξις, εως, ἡ, *meeting by chance*, Gloss. ⊛-τίθημι, *insert*, Dsc.5.120 (Pass.), Sor.1.84 (Pass.), Gal.6.574; καυτήριον PMed. Lond.155.2.22: in Tactics, *insert* men in ranks, Ascl.Tact.10.18 (Pass.). 2. *interpolate*, Gal.18(1).179, Longin.27.1:—Pass., Hermog.Id.2.10. II. π. ἑαυτόν *mix* oneself *up* in an affair, POxy. 907.21 (iii A.D.). -τρώγω, *gnaw besides*, Eub.15.8 (Pass.). -τυγχάνω, = παρατυγχάνω, ὁ παρεντυχὼν *any chance comer*, GDI1702.10, 1716.4, al. (Delph., ii B.C.). -τῠχία, ἡ, *meeting by chance*, Gloss. -ῠφαίνω, aor. -ύφᾰνα, *interweave*, ἡ φύσις τὸ νεῦρον εἰς πολλὰς ἶνας π. Alex.Aphr.Pr.2.52.

πᾰρέξ or πάρεξ, v. παρέκ.

παρεξ-άγω [ᾰγ], *lead past*, c. acc. loci, v.l. in Hdt.4.158. II. *mislead*, παρὲκ Ζηνὸς νόον ἤγαγε h.Ven.36, so perh. in Il.10.391; v. παρέκ A. II. 1. -ᾰγωγή, ἡ, *march past*, of athletes, Artem.5. 13. -αιρέω, *take out*, συλλαβὴν Tz.in An.Ox.3.321. II. Med., *take by choice*, παρεξελόμενοι οἰκήματα εἰς ἀπόθεσιν τῶν σκευῶν SIG1106.107 (Cos, iv/iii B.C.). -αίρω, *thrust up*, βακτηρίας Str.11.14.4:—Pass., *to be lifted up*, παρεξαρθέντες οὐκ ἀνθρωπίνως Scymn.343. -αλλάττω, *change*, παρεξήλλαξέ τι *changed her tone* somewhat, Men.Sam.42: pf. part. Pass. παρεξηλλαγμένος *different, strange*, gloss on ποταίνιος, Sch. S.Ant.849. ⊛-ᾰμείβω, *go* or *sail by*, c. acc., A.R.1.581. -αρκέω, *last out, be extant*, μέχρι.. Tz.H.3.976. -αυλέω, pf. part. Pass. παρεξηυλημένοι *worn out by being played upon*: hence, generally, *worn out, having lost voice and strength*, Ar.Ach.681; π. νοῦς Suid., cf. Hsch., Phot. -ειμι (εἶμι *ibo*), *pass by* or *alongside of*, τὴν λίμνην Hdt.7.58, cf. 109; παρὰ τὴν οἰκίαν Plu.2.754f: abs., Hdt.3.14, 4.92, Th.8.62, E.Ph.1248, Sosith.2.12; *emerge*, of sun from eclipse, Phld. Sign.10: c. acc. cogn., τὴν αὐτὴν ὁδὸν π. Hdt.5.12: freq. of rivers, Paus. 4.31.2, etc. 2. *turn aside*, metaph., -ιόντος τοῦ λόγου Pl.R.503a; *deviate from*, τὴν τάξιν τῆς διδασκαλίας Paul.Aeg.3.45. 3. *avoid*, τοὔνομα Them.Or.21.246b. II. *overstep, transgress*, dub. l. in h.Cer.478; ἁρμονίαν Διὸς θνατῶν παρεξίασι βουλαί A.Pr.551 (lyr.); ψῆφον τυράννων ἢ κράτη παρεξίμεν S.Ant.60. 2. *disregard, neglect*, κακῶς πράττοντά τινα Socr.Ep.6.11. -ειρεσία, ἡ, *outrigger, oar-box*, a closed structure built out from the sides of a ship, through which the oars passed, Th.4.12, 7.34 (pl.), Plu.2.347b, Arr.Peripl.M.Eux.3 (pl.), Fr.160 J., Polyaen.3.11.13. -ελαύνω (sc. ἅρμα, ἵππους, etc.), *drive past, pass* in a race, Il.23.344; *row past*, c. acc., ἐπὴν δὴ τάς γε (sc. Σειρῆνας) παρεξελάσωσιν (or παρὲξ ἐ–) ἑταῖροι Od.12.55; παρά τι Plu.Alc.35; *march by*, Hdt.8.126; ἵππῳ π. *ride past*, Plu.Art.12. II. *ride alongside of*, ἀλλήλοις Id.Phil.10, cf. Pyrrh.16. -έλεγχος, ὁ, *confutation on a side-issue*, Arist.SE176$^a$24, al. II. *super-refutation* (i.e. proving an adversary doubly wrong), Gal.17(1).618. -ελέγχω, *confute on a side-issue*, Arist.Top.112$^a$8 (Pass.), Alex.Aphr.in Top.172.10 (Act.). -ερέομαι, *interrogate*, A.R.3.979. -έρχομαι, Med. with aor. and pf. Act.: aor. -ῆλθον (inf. and part.) is the only tense used by Hom.:—*slip past* another, ῥεῖα παρεξελθοῦσα Od.10.573; π...τυτθὸν *pass by* (us) a little way, Il.10.344; π. τινά *pass by*, Hdt. 1.197, 6.117; παρά τι Plu.Alex.76; *pass out*, διὰ [τῶν πόρων] Steph. in Hp.1.112 D. 2. c. gen., π. τι τῆς ἀληθείας *go aside from* the truth, Pl.Phlb.66b. II. *overstep, transgress*, Διὸς νόον Od.5.104, 138; δίκην S.Ant.921. ⊛-ετάζω, *put* one thing *by* another, *compare* them, τινὰς παρά τινας D.24.132; τί τινι D.C.53.7. 2. *examine*, Procop.Gaz.Ep.78. II. c. inf., *determine, establish* the fact that.., Phalar.Ep.147.1. -εύρημα, ατος, τό, *invention, pretext*, Phryn.PSp.103 B. (pl.). -ευρίσκω, *find out besides*, π. ἄλλον νόμον *find out* a law *which neutralizes* another, Hdt.3.31; νόμιμα -ευρημένα Ph.2.46, cf. Polystr.Herc.346 p.80 V. -ηγέομαι, *misinterpret*, τὸν Ἀριστοτέλην Simp.in Cael.378.29. -ίημι, *allow to pass through*, ἅρματα D.C.40.2, cf. 50.31; of Time, *let pass*, τέσσερας ἡμέρας Hdt.7. 210 (v.l.). II. aor. inf. παρεξέμεν, *divulge*, dub. in h.Cer.478; cf. παρέξειμι II.

παρέξις, εως, ἡ, (παρέχω) *presenting*; esp. *presenting oneself to be operated on*, Hp.Off.3, Mochl.41. 2. *provision*, κεράμου κτλ. SIG 57.32 (Milet., v B.C.).

παρεξ-ισόω, *place beside as equal, rank with*, τινί τι Archestr.Fr.59. 6, cf. Hsch. s.v. παραζηλῶν. -ίστημι, *remove from its place*, π. τὴν διάνοιαν βόμβυξι *distract* it, Plu.2.713a. II. Pass., with aor. 2, pf. and plpf. Act., *undergo a change*, Epich.170.16; παρεξέστη τῇ διανοίᾳ *went mad*, Plb.32.3.6, cf. Fr.192: abs., προφήτης ὁ παρεξεστηκὼς Lxx Ho.9.7; κυλίκιον παρεξεστηκός wine *that has turned, sour* wine, Lyc. Fr.2.3. -οδος, ἡ, *side-way*, Et.Gud. s.v. ἐκσκουβίτωρες. 2. *passage* of injections, Mnesith.ap.Orib.8.38.2. II. surgeon's *travelling companion, case of instruments*, Hp.Decent.8. -ουδενέω, *set at naught*, POxy.1757.8 (ii A.D.).

παρέξω, *outside*, c. gen., v.l. in Lxx Le.8.17.

παρεξωθέω, *push along sideways*, Arist.Mu.395$^b$31 (Pass.).

παρέοικα, *to be somewhat like*, c. dat., Dsc.2.160, Philagr.ap.Orib. 5.20.5, Sch.Ar.Nu.178, etc.

παρεοικότως, Adv. *in a manner somewhat like*, Poll.9.131.

παρέπαινος, ὁ, *by-praise, subordinate* or *incidental praise*, rhetorically used by Evenus of Paros, Pl.Phdr.267a (pl.).

παρεπ-αίρομαι, *to be puffed up*, pf. part. -ηρμένοι ταῖς διανοίαις Vett. Val.9.18, cf. 201.10. -αισθάνομαι, *supplement sensation*, Phld.D. 1.13. -αίσθημα, ατος, τό, *supplement of sensation*, Demetr.Lac. Herc.1013.12. -έχω, aor. inf. -επισχεῖν, *suspend for a time*, PTeb. 29.16 (ii B.C.).

παρεπι-βάλλω, dub. sens. in Demetr.Lac.Herc.1647.26. -βοηθέω, *come in addition to help*, c. dat., v.l. in D.S.2.6. -γρᾰφή, ἡ, *something written in the margin*, Sammelb.6995.26, 7362.1 (both ii A.D.); esp. *stage-direction* (such as αὐλεῖ, Ar.Av.223), Sch.A.Eu. 117, Sch.Ar.Nu.3, al. 2. *incidental statement*, as a rhetorical figure, Tz. ad Lyc.1. -γράφω [γρᾰ], *write by the side of an inscription*, i.e. *correct it*, Str.14.5.14; *write in the margin*, in Pass., PCair.Zen. 147 (iii B.C.), PTeb.30.25, al. (ii B.C.), Sch.Ar.Av.222. -δείκνῡμι, *point out beside* or *at the same time*, Lxx 2Ma.15.10. 2. *display*, κακῶς [τὴν τέχνην] Gal.8.600. II. Med., *display* one's ideas, Phld. Vit.p.39 J.; also in a depreciatory sense, *exhibit out of season, make a display*, Plu.2.43d, Luc.Hist.Conscr.57. -δημέω, Boeot. pres. part. -δᾱμίων Supp.Epigr.3.356 (Haliartus):—*sojourn as a stranger in a place*, Macho ap.Ath.13.579a, Plb.27.6.3, IG7.190 (Megara), 2712.15

(Acraeph.), *PCair.Zen.*368.20 (iii B.C.): *travel*, ἀπὸ..εἰς.. Plb.13.8.3. **-δημία**, Dor. **-δᾱμία**, ἡ, *residence in a foreign city*, Id.4.4.2; παρεπιδαμίαν ποιήσασθαι *SIG*697 *L* 4 (Delph., ii B.C.), cf. *CIG*3052.32 (Teos). II. metaph. of life, π. τίς ἐστιν ὁ βίος Pl.*Ax.*365b, cf. Hipparch.ap.Stob.4.44.81. **-δημος**, ον, *sojourning in a strange place*, esp. as Subst., Lxx *Ge.*23.4, *PPetr.*3 p.14 (iii B.C.), Callix.2, Plb. 32.6.4, etc. **-δῐκος**, *veterator, Gloss.* **-κουρέω**, *to be a help to*, τισι S.E.*M.*5.75. **-κρίνω** [ῑ], *criticize unfairly*, *PLond.*5.1727.13 (vi A.D.). **-μένω**, *continue, survive*, Lyd.*Mag.*1.12. **-μολύνω**, *overlay with foreign matter*, Phld.*D.*3.8. **-νοέω**, *invent besides*, Sch.Ar.*Av.* 454:—Med., v.l. in D.S.12.11. II. Pass., *to be conceived* or *apprehended at the same time*, Plot.6.6.10. **-πάσσω**, *sprinkle beside*, Dsc. 5.81. **-πλέκομαι**, Pass., of stars, *to be in conjunction*, Gal.19. 557. **-σκοπέω**, *examine besides* or *also*, Arist.*MM*1197$^b$32, Plu.2. 129e. **-σπάομαι**, Med., *draw to oneself, claim*, v.l. in Ph.1. 540. **-στέλλω**, *issue instructions*, καθὰ παρεπέσταλται *PTeb.*27.9 (ii B.C.). **-στρέφω**, intr., *turn aside*, μικρὸν πρὸς τὴν ἕω Eratosth. ap.Str.17.1.2, cf. Marcian.1.11. II. Pass., *turn in passing and look at*, Plu.2.521b, D.L.2.23. **-στροφή**, ἡ, *turning round in passing*, Plu.*Sull.*35. **-τείνομαι**, Pass., *become intensified*, of the action of drugs, Archig.ap.Orib.8.2.4. **-τηδεύομαι**, *practise as well*, Philum.ap.Aët.5.78 (Pass.). **-τομή**, ἡ, *incision at the side*, Ph.*Bel.*63.24. **-φαίνομαι**, Pass., *appear beside*, Herod.Med. ap.Orib.10.17.2. II. τὸ -φαινόμενον περιττὸν *incidental*, Phld. *Po.*5.33. ❋**-φέρω**, *employ upon*, τι πρός τι *Peripl.M.Rubr.*57 (sed leg. **παρεπίφορον**, a *suitable* wind). **-χέω**, *add by pouring*, τι εἴς τι Hero *Aut.*2.4, cf. Sor.1.100, Heras ap.Gal.12.430, *Sammelb.*7350 (iii/iv A.D.). **-ψαύω**, *graze*, *Placit.*2.12.1. **παρέπλω**, v. παραπλέω.

**παρέπομαι**, *accompany, attend*, Hp.*Epid.*1.8, etc.; of an escort, X. *Ap.*27; π. τῇ ἐκφορᾷ *IPE*1$^2$.17.24 (Olbia, i B.C.): abs., Pl.*Phd.*89a, etc.: metaph., ἐδωδῇ μὲν καὶ πόσει..παρέπεσθαι τὴν χάριν Id.*Lg.*667b; τοῦτο μάλιστα ἐπὶ πάντων π. *is common* to all, Id.*Tht.*186a; π. τισί *to be imparted* to them, Plb.4.21.1. 2. *to be a constant attribute*, τοῖς ἀνθρώποις τοῦτο π. τὸ σύμπτωμα Phld.*Sign.*23: in Logic, τὸ παρεπόμενον *consequence*, necessary or accidental, Arist.*SE*168$^b$31; τὰ παρεπόμενα *concomitant circumstances*, Longin.10.1. 3. τὰ παρεπόμενα γήδια the lands *appertaining* to a village, *POxy.*1134.15 (v A.D.).

**παρεργ-άτης** [γᾰ], ου, ὁ, (πάρεργον) *workman in addition*, κομψὸς γ' ὁ κῆρυξ καὶ π. λόγων, i.e. argumentative too, E.*Supp.*426:—later **-είτης**, ου, ὁ, *assistant* in a trade, *POxy.*1731.19 (iii A.D.).

**παρεργολᾰβέω**, *convert to one's own use*, Ph.1.541.

❋ **πάρεργος**, ον, (ἔργον) *beside the main subject, subordinate, incidental*, ὁ λόγος π. ὢν Pl.*Ti.*38d; παρέργῳ τῇ ποιήσει καταχρήσασθαι treat it *as a mere accessory*, ib.21c; ὅ τι μὴ π. Id.*Phdr.*274a, etc.; πάντα π. ποιησάμενος *PHib.*1.44.5 (iii B.C.). Adv. -γως *by the way, cursorily*, opp. ἀκριβῶς, Pl.*Lg.*793e; opp. ἐξεταστικῶς, D.17.13; π. ἔχειν πρός τι Din. 3.14; οὐ π. ἔμαθον Hegesipp.Com.1.6, cf. Men.462.6; φέροντα μὴ π. Id.*Sam.*293, cf. Porph.*Abst.*2.61, *PMag.Par.*1.2640; *transiently*, Phld.*Mus.*p.39 K. II. as Subst. **πάρεργον**, τό, *subordinate* or *secondary business*, πόνων E.*Or.*610; πάρεργ' ὁδοῦ *a secondary purpose* of my journey, Id.*El.*509; π. τῆς τύχης *a trifling set-off* to my fortune, Id.*Hel.*925; πάρεργα ἐμῶν κακῶν *baubles in comparison with* my ills, Id.*HF*1340; πάρεργα δόμων, = νόθοι, Id.*El.*63; π. γίγνεσθαι to be slain *among the rest*, Paus.10.27.2; ἐν παρέργῳ *as a by-work, as subordinate* or *secondary*, Th.6.69, etc.; ἐν π. θοῦ με treat in such a way, S.*Ph.*473: ὡς ἐν π. τῆς ἐμῆς δυσπραξίας feeling it *no great addition* to.., E.*IT*514, cf. Pl.*Smp.*222c; ἐν παρέργου μέρει Id.*R.*370c; ἐκ παρέργου πόλεμον ποιεῖσθαι Th.7.27; ἐκ π. μελετᾶται τι Id.1.142; εἴ τις ἐν π. σκέψεται Pl.*Tht.*184a; τἄλλα πάρεργα πρός τι νομίζειν D.51. 17; π. ἐᾶν τι γίγνεσθαι Pl.*Lg.*766a, cf. *Euthd.*273d; πρὸς τὸ κέρδος.. πάντα τἄλλα..π. γίγνεται Alex.98.2; ὅπως μὴ τὰ π. τῶν ἔργων πλείω γίνηται Arist.*EN*1098$^a$32.

**παρερεθίζω**, *irritate*, ταῖς φωναῖς J.*Vit.*45 (Pass.), cf. Sm.*Pr.*24.19, Thd.*Ps.*36(37).1, Aët.16.61, Simp. *in Epict.*p.66 D.

**παρερέττω**, *move as with oars*, τὸ σῶμα Poll.5.71.

**πάρερμα**, v. παραίρημα.

**παρερμηνεύω**, *misinterpret*, τὸν ποιητήν Str.7.3.10, cf. *PGiss.*40 ii 7 (iii A.D.).

**παρερπ-ύζω**, = sq. 1, παρερπύζων Διονύσῳ Nonn.*D.*9.110. **-ω**, *creep secretly up to*, Theoc.15.48: aor. 1 παρείρπυσα *creep in*, Ar.*Ec.* 511; of an orator, *creep forward* (to speak), ib.398. II. Dor. = παριέναι, ἐς τῶ Ῥιττηνίω *Schwyzer*177.8 (Crete, v B.C.); ἐν τὸ ἱερὸν *IG* 5(2).514.3 (Lycosura, ii B.C.): aor. subj. παρένθη, inf. παρενθεῖν, ib.8, Theoc.15.60; μηδὲ παρερπέτω μηθεὶς ἀμύητος εἰς τὸν τόπον *IG*5(1). 1390.36 (Andania, i B.C.); *appear in public*, *Dialex.*2.9. 2. *pass by*, *APl.*1.11 (Hermocr.), *Epigr.Gr.*195 (Crete).

**παρερύω**, Ion. **παρειρύω**, only aor. Act. and Pass., *draw along the side*, φραγμὸν παρείρυσαν Hdt.7.36. II. *draw on one side*, στόμα παρειρύσθη the mouth *was distorted*, Hp.*Epid.*3.1.α'.

❋ **παρέρχομαι** (the other moods of the pres., and the impf. (παρήρχοντο is found in Alciphr.*Fr.*6.15), as also the fut., are borrowed from πάρειμι (εἶμι *ibo*), cf. ἔρχομαι): aor. παρῆλθον, inf. -ελθεῖν, more rarely -ήλυθον Theoc.22.85 (for παρενθεῖν, v. παρέρπω II):—*go by, beside*, or *past, pass by*, of a ship, Od.16.357; ἦος μέγα κῦμα παρῆλθεν 5. 429; of birds, 12.62; of persons, A.*Supp.*1004, etc.; [παρῆλθεν ὁ κίνδυνος] ὥσπερ νέφος *passed away*, D.18.188. 2. of Time, *pass*, Hdt. 2.86; παρεληλύθει τὰ Διονύσια Aeschin.3.69; ὁ παρελθὼν χρόνος time *past*, E.*Fr.*1028 (anap.); ὁ π. ἄροτος the *past* season, S.*Tr.*69; π. ὁδοί wanderings *now gone by*, Id.*OC*1397; οἱ παρεληλυθότες πόνοι Pl. *Phdr.*231b, X.*An.*4.3.2; τῆς παρελθούσης νυκτὸς Pl.*Prt.*310a; ἐν τῷ παρελθόντι χρόνῳ in time *past, of old*, X.*Cyr.*8.8.20, etc.; τὰ παρεληλυθότα *past events*, D.18.191; τὸ παρελθόν, opp. τὸ μέλλον, Arist. *Ph.*218$^a$9; ὁ παρεληλυθώς (sc. χρόνος) Id.*Po.*1457$^a$18, cf. *Cat.*5$^a$8, S.E.*P.*3.106. II. *pass by, outstrip*, esp. in speed, τινα Il.23.345; ποσὶν μή τίς με παρέλθῃ Od.8.230; π. ἐν δόλοισιν *surpass* in wiles, 13.291; οὔ με δόλῳ παρελεύσεαι Thgn.1285; δυνάμει E.*Ba.*906 (lyr.); ἀναιδείᾳ Ar.*Eq.*277; π. τῇ πρώτῃ στρατείᾳ *to be superior, have the advantage*, Aeschin.3.129; τοὺς λόγους τἄργα παρέρχεται D.10.3; τὸ ψυχρὸν τοῦτ' ὄνομα, τὸ "ἄχρι κόρου", παρελήλυθε has *outdone* that hackneyed phrase, 'to satiety', Id.19.187. 2. *outwit, elude*, '*give the go-by to*', μὴ δὴ οὕτως..κλέπτε νόῳ, ἐπεὶ οὐ παρελεύσεαι οὐδέ με πείσεις (unless in signf. v) Il.1.132; οὐκ ἔστι Διὸς κλέψαι νόον οὐδὲ παρελθεῖν Hes.*Th.*613; φυλακὰς..ἐούσας οὐδὲν χαλεπὰς παρελθεῖν Hdt.3.72; π. τὴν πεπρωμένην τύχην E.*Alc.*695; τὴν ἐν τῷ ὅλῳ ψυχὴν Plot.6.7.11; τὰς αἰτίας καὶ τὰς διαβολάς D.18.7. III. *pass on and come to* a place, *arrive at*, ἐς τὰ δίκαια Hes.*Op.*216; εἰς τὴν δυναστείαν D.9.24; εἰς τὴν οὐσίαν Luc.*Gall.*12; ἐπὶ τὰ πράγματα Id.*DMort.*12. 4. 2. *pass in*, ἐς τὴν αὐλὴν Hdt.3.77, 5.92.γ'; ἔσω or εἴσω π. *go into* a house, etc., A.*Ch.*849, S.*El.*1337, etc.; ἔσω θυρῶνος Id.*OT*1241; εἴσω παρὰ τοὺς γηγενεῖς Ar.*Nu.*853: c. acc., π. δόμους E.*Med.*1137, *Hipp.*108; of an army, π. εἰς τὴν πόλιν βίᾳ X.*An.*5.5.11; π. εἴσω Πυλῶν D.18.35. 3. metaph., εἰς παροιμίαν παρῆλθε τὸ πρᾶγμα *passed* into a proverb, Arist.*Fr.*593; εἰς τὴν τραγικὴν..ὀψὲ π. [ἡ ὑπόκρισις] Id.*Rh.*1403$^b$23. IV. *pass without heeding*, τεὸν βωμόν Il. 8.239; *disregard, slight*, θεούς E.*Supp.*231; νόμους D.37.37; *pass over, omit*, οὐδὲν π. Ar.*V.*637, cf. Pl.*Phdr.*278e, etc. 2. *overstep, transgress*, Antipho 5.12, Lys.6.52. V. *pass unnoticed, escape the notice of* (v. supr. II. 2), mostly of things, πολλά με καὶ συνιέντα π. Thgn.419; οὐδέ μ' ὄμματος φρουρὰν παρῆλθε τόνδε μὴ λεύσσειν στόλον S.*Tr.*226; τουτὶ γὰρ αὖ μικροῦ παρῆλθέ μ' εἰπεῖν D.21.110: abs., ὡς μὴ παρέλθωσ' αἱ κόραι S.*OC*902. VI. *come forward* to speak, ἐς τὸν δῆμον π. Th.5.45; εἰς τὴν ἐκκλησίαν Aeschin.3.95: freq. abs., ταῦτα ἔλεγε παρελθὼν ὁ Ἀριστείδης Hdt.8.81; ὀλίγων ἕνεκα καὐτὴ παρῆλθον ῥημάτων Ar.*Th.*443, cf. *Av.*1612; παρελθὼν ἔλεξε τοιάδε, π. εἶπε, Th. 2.59, X.*Ap.*10; ὁ βουλόμενος παρελθὼν ἐλεγξάτω Lys.25.14. VII. pf. παρελήλυθα, = πάρειμι, *adsum*, Th.4.86.

**πάρεσαν**, Ep. 3 pl. impf. of πάρειμι (εἰμί *sum*).

**παρεσθίω**, *eat besides*, Hp.*Dent.*16. II. *gnaw* or *nibble at*, c. gen., ὥσπερ θύρας..τῶν λογίων Ar.*Eq.*1026; μαθημάτων Jul.*Gal.* 229c. 2. metaph., *carp, sneer at*, c. acc., D.L.2.66.

**πάρεσις**, εως, ἡ, *letting go, dismissal*, τινὸς ἐκ Συρακουσῶν Plu. *Comp.Dion.Brut.*2; *release*, D.H.7.37. II. *slackening* of strength, *paralysis*, Hp.*Epid.*4.45; παραπληγίη π. ἀφῆς καὶ κινήσιος Aret.*SD* 1.7, cf. 2.5, Plu.2.652e. 2. metaph., ἡ ἀπὸ τῆς ὕλης π. Dam.*Pr.* 440. III. *remission* of debts, χρημάτων π. Phalar.*Ep.*81.1; of sins, *Ep.Rom.*3.25. IV. *neglect*, App.*Reg.Fr.*13.

**παρέσκεθον**, v. παρέχω. **παρεσκευάδαται**, **-άδατο**, v. παρασκευάζω. **παρεστάμεν**, **-άμεναι**, v. παρίστημι.

❋ **παρέστιος**, ον, (ἑστία) *by* or *at the hearth*, λοιβαί S.*El.*269, cf. *Ant.* 372, E.*Med.*1334; ἡ δ' εἴσω πελάνους καῖεν π. A.R.4.713.

**παρεσχᾰτος**, ον, *last but one*, Ph.2.66: fem. **παρεσχάτη** (sc. συλλαβή), *penultimate*, Apollon.*Lex.* s.v. ἀγρονόμοι.

**παρετάζω**, *put beside and compare*, Hsch. II. *approve*, ὅτινι ἂμ μή..παρετάξωνσι ὀμοθυμαδόν *IG*5(2).6.28 (Tegea, iv B.C.). 2. Med., aor. part. παρhεταξάμενος, c. acc., *after obtaining the consent of*, ib.3.20 (ibid.). (Perh. from πάρ(h)ετος (παρίημι) 'regard as admissible'.)

❋ **παρετέον**, (παρίημι) *one must let pass, neglect*, Pl.*Lg.*796a, Aen. Tact.19, Hierocl.p.48 A. II. *one must leave*, ταῦτα π. τοῖς μετεωροθήραις σκοπεῖν Ph.1.674.

**παρετοιμ-άζω**, *make ready besides*, metrical version of Aesop.62 (Chambry 2 p.300). ❋ **-ᾰσία**, ἡ, *preparation, Gloss.*

**πάρετος**, ον, *relaxed, palsied*, μέλη *AP*5.54 (Diosc.); π. ποιεῖν τινα D.S.3.26, cf. Aret.*SA*1.5.

**παρετῠμολογέω**, *allude to the etymology* of a word, Ath.1.35c, Ach. Tat.*Intr.Arat.*15.

**παρευδῐ-άζομαι**, *live at peace with one's neighbours*, Plb.4.32. 5. **-αστής**, οῦ, ὁ, of a kind of water-fowl *that comes on land in fine weather*, prob. for παρευδιστ-, Clearch.73.

**παρευδοκῐμ-έω**, *surpass in fame*, etc., τινα Plu.*Pomp.*37, etc.; αἱ χελῶναι τοὺς ἵππους π. Lib.*Or.*62.44; ῥώμῃ καὶ ἰσχύϊ D.H.*Vett.Cens.* 3.1; τῇ ἀκολασίᾳ τινά Alciphr.1.39:—Pass., *to be surpassed*, ὑπό τινος Teles p.26 H., Luc.*Herm.*51, Ach.Tat.*Vit.Arat.*6, Philostr.*Ep.* 9. **-ησις**, εως, ἡ, *superiority in favour*, Sch.Od.5.215.

**παρευημερέω**, *flourish, abound*, Ph.1.19, al.:—Pass., *to be surpassed*, ἐν ταῖς χειροτονίαις ὑπὸ τοῦ τυχόντος D.S.20.79.

**παρευθύνω**, *control*, χερσί S.*Aj.*1069.

**παρευθύς**, Adv., = εὐθύς, D.C.63.19, Prisc.p.325 D.

**παρευκηλέω**, *calm, soothe*, E.*HF*99.

**παρευλᾰβέομαι**, *beware at the same time*, μή ποτε.. Sch.S.*Tr.*1.

**παρευμᾰρέω**, aor. 1. -ημάρησα, *think lightly of, hold cheap*, Hsch.

**παρευν-άζομαι**, *lie beside*, δμῳῇσι Od.22.37, cf. Poll.5.41:—later Act., Nonn.*D.*10.200, 25.17. **-άομαι**, = foreg., Orph.*A.*136, Nonn.*D.*2.355. **-αστήρ**, ῆρος, ὁ, *one who sleeps beside*: hence, *chamberlain*, Men.Prot.p.10 D., Agath.3.16 (pl.). **-ετάω**, *sleep with*, τινι dub. in Afric.*Cest.Oxy.*412.23. **-έτις**, ιδος, ἡ, *bedfellow*, Nonn.*D.*8.243. **-ος**, ον, *lying beside* or *with, bedfellow*, Ion Eleg. 2.9: metaph., πῆμα πατρὶ πάρευνον A.*Th.*1009 (lyr.).

**παρεύρ-εσις**, εως, ἡ, *pretext, pretence*, μηδεμιᾷ παρευρέσει Decr.ap.D.

18.37, cf. *PEleph.*1.9 (iv B.C.), *IG*9(1).694.109 (Corcyra), *Test.Epict.* 2.15, *SIG*581.45 (Crete, iii/ii B.C.), etc.; διὰ παρευρέσεως *Sammelb.* 4638.10 (ii B.C.); = Lat. *fraus*, *Supp.Epigr.*3.378 C16 (Delph., ii/i B.C.): prov., Θρᾳκία π. Str.9.2.4, Zen.4.37. **–ημα**, ατος, τό, = foreg., Paus.2.16.3 (pl.), Oenom.ap.Eus.*PE*5.27. **–ημένως**, Adv. pf. part. Pass., *craftily*, οἱ δικαιότατα καὶ π. κρίνοντες f.l. in Zen.2. 60. **–ησις**, εως, ἡ, = παρεύρεσις, *Gloss.* **–ίσκω**, *discover besides, invent*, Hdt.1.26, Str.16.2.25 (Pass.), Hermog.*Inv.*3.1 (Pass.); π. τι ἔς τινας Paus.9.5.3. 2. Pass., ἐς οὓ..σφι ἄδικόν τι παρευρεθῇ *be discovered in* them, Hdt.3.31. II. *fabricate*, in Pass., ἀληθῆ καὶ μὴ παρευρημένα Philostr.*Her.*3.1, cf. 11.

⊛ **παρευτακτ-έω**, *perform one's duty regularly*, of sentries, Plb.3.50. 7; of courtiers, Id.5.56.7. 2. *serve as a* παρεύτακτος, *BCH*55.439 (Delos, ii B.C.). ⊛ **–ος**, ὁ, member of a particular class of ἔφηβοι (cf. εὔτακτος), ibid., Lucil.321,752 Marx, *IG*3.107, Ἐφ.Ἀρχ.1893.74; fem. prob. in Varro ap.Non.p.93 L.

**παρευτρεπίζω**, *put in order, arrange, make ready*, E.*IT*725:—Med., παρευτρεπίσασθαι τὰ κατὰ τὴν Ἰλλυρίδα Plb.5.108.4:—Pass., E.*Cyc.*594.

**παρευωχέομαι**, *feast beside*, App.*BC*1.48.

**παρεφάπτομαι**, *touch on the side*, c. gen., Plu.2.573f. II. *touch upon, allude to*, Phld.*Mus.*p.96 K., al.

**παρεφεδρεύω**, *lie near to guard*: *keep guard*, ἐν Σικελίᾳ Plb.2.24.13, cf. *PAmh.*2.36.8 (ii B.C.), *OGI*182.2 (Egypt, i B.C.), etc.; π. τισί *keep watch upon* them, Plb.3.100.7. 2. *stand immediately behind*, Ael.*Tact.*13.3.

⊛ **παρεφηβεία**, Ion. **–είη**, ἡ, *status of a* *παρέφηβος (perh. = παρεύτακτος), Epigr. in *Abh.Berl.Akad.*1909(2).62 (Samos, ii/i B.C.).

**παρεφθαρμένως**, Adv., (παραφθείρω) *corruptly*, Eupolem.ap.Alex. Polyh.18, Gal.18(1).193.

⊛ **παρέχω**, fut. παρέξω Od.18.317, Th.8.48, παρασχήσω Id.6.86, Isoc. 6.71, 15.248: pf. παρέσχηκα: aor. παρέσχον, Ep. inf. παρασχέμεν Il. 19.147; imper. παράσχες E.*Hec.*842 (παράσχε is f.l.); poet. παρέσχεθον Hes.*Th.*639, inf. παρασχεθεῖν Ar.*Eq.*321; Aeol. παρέσκεθον Alc. *Oxy.*1788 *Fr.*15 ii 11; παρεχέσκετο is f.l. for παρεκέσκετο in Od.14. 521. [In Od.19.113, πᾰρέχῃ.]

A. Act., *hand over*, Il.18.556; *furnish, supply*, φάος πάντεσσι παρέξω Od.18.317; δῶρα Il.19.147; esp. in Od., ἱερήϊα, βρῶσίν τε πόσιν τε, σῖτον, 14.250, 15.490, 18.360: abs., ἐγὼ δ' εὖ πᾶσι παρέξω I *will provide* for all, 8.39; π. νέας Hdt.4.83, 7.21; τεταρτημόριον τοῦ μισθώματος Id.2.180; χρήματα Th.8.48; ἀργύριον, ποίμνια, *IG*1$^2$.39. 69, 45.4; αἱ δὲ Συράκουσαι σῦς..παρέχουσιν Hermipp.63.9; πληρώμαθ' ἡ πόλις παρέχει the state *finds* men to man the ships, D.21.155, cf. Lys.19.43. 2. of natural objects, *yield, produce*, θάλασσα π. ἰχθῦς Od.19.113; [σίδηρον] παρέξει (sc. σόλος) Il.23.835. 3. of incorporeal things, *afford, cause*, φιλότητα, ἀρετήν, γέλω τε καὶ εὐφροσύνην, 3.354, Od.18.133, 20.8; ὀνίαις Alc.88; π. εἰράναν τισί Pi.*P.*9. 23; ὕμνον Id.*N.*6.33; αἶσαν Id.*O.*6.102; Σάρδεσι πένθος A.*Pers.*322; τύχην, φρίκην, S.*OT*53, 1306 (anap.); χάριν, εὔνοιαν, Id.*OC*1498 (lyr.), *Tr.*708; ὄχλον, πρήγματα π., Hdt.1.86, al. (v. πρᾶγμα); πόνον Alc.19, Hdt.1.177; ἔργον Ar.*Nu.*523; π. εὔνοιαν εἴς τινα Antipho 5.76; αἴσθησιν παρέχει τινός *enables* one to observe a thing, Th.2.50; but αἴσθησιν π., abs., it *causes* remark, is perceived, Id.3.22, X.*An.*4.6.13; πενία ἀνάγκῃ τὴν τόλμαν π. Th.3.45; ὑφειμένου δόξαν π., = ὑφειμένῳ ἐοικέναι, Plu.2.131a. II. *present* or *offer* for a purpose, 1. c. inf., [ὄϊες] παρέχουσι..γάλα θῆσθαι Od.4.89; π. τὸ σῶμα τύπτειν Ar.*Nu.*441; τὸ στράτευμα π. τισὶ διαφθεῖραι Th.8.50 (without inf., πτήξας δέμας παρεῖχε A.*Pers.*210): with reflex. Pron., ἐμαυτόν σοι ἐμμελετᾶν π. I *give* myself *up* to you to practise upon, Pl.*Phdr.*228e; π. ἐμαυτὸν ἐρωτᾶν Id. *Ap.*33b, cf. *Prt.*312c; π. ἑαυτοὺς τοῖς ἄρχουσι χρῆσθαι ἤν τι δέωνται X.*Cyr.*1.2.9: rarely with a part., π. ἑαυτὸν δεδησόμενον Luc.*Tox.* 35. 2. *give oneself up, submit oneself*, ἑαυτόν being omitted, π. [ἑωυτοὺς] διαφθαρῆναι Hdt.9.17; πατεῖν παρεῖχε τῷ θέλοντι [ἑαυτόν] S. *Aj.*1146, cf. Ar.*Nu.*422; τοῖς ἰατροῖς παρέχουσι..ἀποτέμνειν καὶ ἀποκάειν X.*Mem.*1.2.54, cf. Pl.*Grg.*456b; τῷ λόγῳ ὥσπερ ἰατρῷ παρέχων ἀποκρίνου ib.475d, cf. *Tht.*191a; ἕτοιμός εἰμί σοι παρέχειν ἀποκρινόμενος Id.*Prt.*348a; esp. of a woman, sens. obsc., Ar.*Lys.*162, 227, Luc. *DMeretr.*5.4, etc. (in full, π. ἑαυτήν Id.*DMar.*13.1, Artem.1.78). 3. with reflex. Pron. and a predicative, *show, exhibit* oneself so and so, π. ἐμαυτὸν ὅσιον καὶ δίκαιον Antipho 2.2.2; σπάνιον σεαυτὸν π. Pl. *Euthphr.*3d; σαυτὸν σοφιστὴν π. Id.*Prt.*312a; ἑαυτὸν π. εὐπειθῆ X.*Cyr.* 2.1.22; μέτριον ἐμαυτὸν π. Aeschin.1.1; τοιοῦτον πολίτην Lys.14.1; π. ἐν τῷ μέσῳ ἐμαυτόν X.*Cyr.*7.5.46; δέμας ἀκέντητον παρέχων Pi.*O.*1. 21. III. *allow, grant*, σιγὴν παρασχὼν κλῦθί μου S.*Tr.*1115: c. inf., ἐπεὶ παρέσχες ἀντιφωνῆσαι *did'st allow* me to.., ib.1114; π. αὐτοὺς δικαστὰς..γίγνεσθαι Th.1.37: abs. in imperat., πάρεχε *make way*, E. *Tr.*308, *Cyc.*203, Ar.*V.*1326, *Av.*1720 (all lyr.); πάρεχ' ἐκποδών Id.*V.* 949. 2. impers., παρέχει τινί c. inf., *it is allowed, in one's power* to do so and so, παρεῖχε ἄν σφι εὐδαιμονέειν Hdt.1.170, cf. 3.73, al., Pi.*I.* 8(7).76; ὑμῖν οὐ παρασχήσει ἀμύνασθαι Th.6.86; σωφρονεῖν παρεῖχέ σοι E.*El.*1080: neut. part. used abs., παρέχον *it being in one's power, since one can*, like ἐξόν, παρόν, παρέχον [ὑμῖν] ἄρχειν Hdt.5.49; also εὖ, καλῶς παρασχόν, Th.1.120, 5.14; κάλλιον π. ib.60. IV. *produce* a person *on demand*, ἐς τὸ κοινόν X.*HG*7.4.38; εἰς τὴν βουλήν, εἰς ἀγοράν (leg. αὔριον), εἰς κρίσιν, Lys.13.23, 23.9, Aeschin.2.117, cf. *PHib.* 1.168 (iii B.C.), etc. V. with a predic. added, *make* so and so, τὴν διέξοδόν οἱ ἀσφαλέα π. Hdt.3.4; π. τινὰς βελτίους And.1.136, cf. Pl.*Phdr.*274e, 277a: with part., π. ξυμμάχους τὰς σπονδὰς δεχομένους Th.5.35, cf. X.*Oec.*21.4; κοινὴν τὴν πόλιν π. *offer* it as a common resort, Isoc.4.52; γῆν ἄσυλον καὶ δόμους ἐχεγγύους π. E.*Med.*388, etc.

B. Med. παρέχομαι, fut. –έξομαι Antipho 5.20, Lys.23.8, etc.; also παρασχήσομαι Antipho 5.24, Lys.9.8: aor. 2 παρεσχόμην Is.3.18, 19: pf. Pass. (in med. sense) παρέσχημαι X.*An.*7.6.11, D.27.49, 36. 35: freq. used much like Act., without any reflex. sense: 1. *supply of oneself* or *from one's own means*, νέας Hdt.6.8, 15, al.; δαπάνην οἰκηΐην Id.8.17; π. ὅπλα *furnish* a suit of armour, *IG*1$^2$.22.11, Th. 8.97; οἱ τὰ τιμήματα παρεχόμενοι the tax-*paying* citizens, Arist.*Ath.* 39.6; μηδεμίαν δύναμιν π. εἰς τὴν στρατιάν *supply* no contingent *of one's own* to.., X.*An.*6.2.10; freq. with ἑαυτόν, εὔνουν καὶ πρόθυμον ἑαυτὸν παρέχεται *SIG*333.11 (Samos, iv/iii B.C.), cf. 620.6 (Tenos, ii B.C.), etc. 2. of natural objects, *furnish, present, exhibit*, [ποταμὸς] κροκοδείλους π. Hdt.4.44; π. λίμνην ὁ Πόντος..οὐ πολλῷ τεῳ ἐλάσσω ἑωυτοῦ ib.86, cf. 46, Pl.*Phd.*81d. 3. of works, ἓν ἔργον πολλὸν μέγιστον π. Hdt.1.93. 4. of incorporeal things, *display on one's own part*, πᾶσαν προθυμίην Id.7.6, cf. X.*An.*7.6.11; πᾶν τὸ πρόθυμον Th.4.85, cf. 61; εὔνοιαν D.18.10; χρείας Decr.ap.D.18. 84. II. in Law, παρέχεσθαί τινας μάρτυρας, π. τεκμήρια, *bring forward* witnesses or proofs, Pl.*Ap.*19d, *Prm.*128b, Antipho 1.11, cf. 5.20, 22, Lys.23.8, etc.; π. ἐκμαρτυρίαν, μαρτυρίαν, Is. ll. cc. III. *produce as one's own*, ἄρχοντα παρέχεσθαί τινα *acknowledge as one's* general, Hdt.7.61, 62, 67; Ἀθηναῖοι ἀρχαιότατον ἔθνος παρεχόμενοι *presenting themselves as*.., ib.161; π. πόλιν μεγίστην, of an ambassador, *represent* a city *in one's own person*, Th.4.64, cf. 85. IV. *offer, promise*, ἀψευδέα μαντήϊα Hdt.2.174; ἔστιν ἃ π. Th.3.36; *put forward*, τὸ εὐπρεπὲς τῆς δίκης Id.1.39. V. *render* so and so *for* or *towards oneself*, θεὸν παρασχέσθαι εὐμενῆ E.*Andr.*55; δυσμενεστέρους π. τοὺς ἀνθρώπους Pl.*Prt.*317b, cf. *R.*432a, *Lg.*809d; v. supr. A. V. VI. Arith., *make up, amount to*, ἐνιαυτοὶ..παρέχονται ἡμέρας.. Hdt.1.32, cf. X.*Cyr.*6.1.28.

**παρέψησις**, εως, ἡ, (ἕψω) = ἕψησις, Palaeph.43.

**παρηβ-άσκω**, = sq. 1. 2, Ph.1.604. **–άω**, pf. παρήβηκα Th.2. 44:—*to be past one's prime, to be elderly*, Hdt.3.53, Th. l. c., J.*BJ*7. 8.7, Luc.*Tim.*2, etc.; π. τὸ σῶμα Longus 3.15: metaph., χρόνος παρήβησεν A.*Ag.*985 (lyr.). 2. metaph., *lose strength*, οἶνος Luc.*Lex.* 13. II. *to be on the point of puberty*, Gal.14.755.

**πάρηβος**, ον, (ἥβη) *past one's prime*, *APl.*4.289. 2. *past boyhood*, Ph.2.59. II. πάρηβον, τό, an Indian wood said to have magnetic properties, *peepul, Ficus religiosa*, Ctes.ap.Apollon.*Mir.*17.

**παρηγεμονικὰ** ζῴδια, *associated with the dominant signs*, *Cat.Cod. Astr.*1.165.

**παρηγέομαι**, *disregard*, *Sammelb.*5232.22 (i A.D.), *PRyl.*119.33 (i A.D.).

**παρηγμένως**, Adv., (παράγω) *redundantly*, of a compound word, part of which loses its significance, Apollon.*Lex.* s. v. τανύηκες.

**παρηγοναῖς**· παραγώγως, ἀπάταις, Hsch.

**παρηγορ-έω**, impf. παρηγόρουν A.*Pr.*646; Ep. παρηγορέεσκε A.R. 4.1740, Musae.39: fut. –ήσω Plu.*Ant.*83: aor. –ησα E.*Hec.*288, Pl. *Ax.*364c:—Med., impf., Hdt. (v. infr.): aor. –ησάμην Luc.*Am.*52:—Pass., pres., Ath.15.687d: fut. –ήσομαι Hp.*Hum.*1, Aret.*CD*2.3: aor. –ήθην Plu.*Caes.*28, etc.: (παρήγορος):—*address, exhort*, τινα A.*Pr.*646, Hdt.9.54, etc.; ὀχλεῖς μάτην με κῦμ' ὅπως παρηγορῶν A.*Pr.*1001, cf. *Eu.*507 (lyr.); π. ὡς.. *advise, give counsel* that.., E.*Hec.*288: c. acc. pers. et inf., S.*Fr.*176:—Med., τὸν Γόργον παρηγορέετο ἀπίστασθαι Hdt.5.104, cf. 7.13; π. τινὰ μὴ κινδυνεύειν v.l. in Id.9.55, cf. 54, Pi. *O.*9.77. II. *console, comfort*, A.*Pers.*530, E.*Ph.*1449; τὰ παρηγοροῦντα *consolations, emollients*, D.60.35; *appease*, Ἔρωτα θυηλαῖς Musae. l. c. 2. c. acc. rei, *assuage, soothe*, τὰ κακὰ δι' ἑτέρων κακῶν Philem.234, Men.549.5; τὴν λύπην, τὰ πάθη, D.H.1.77, Plu.2.156c; τὴν χωλότητα Id.*Publ.*16; τὸν βίον τρυφῇ π. *IG*9(1).883.3 (Corc.); of medicines, *allay* irritation, π. τὸν πνεύμονα Hp.*Acut.*58, cf. Aret. l. c.:—Pass., *Epigr.Gr.*1096.6 (Stratonicea), Ath. l. c.—In correct Att. Prose παραμυθέομαι prevails. **–ημα**, ατος, τό, *exhortation, consolation*, ἄτεγκτος παρηγορήμασιν A.*Fr.*348; π. βίου Ph.2.39; λυπουμένων S.E.*M.*6.18. 2. *remedy*, Plu.2.543a (pl.). **–ητέον**, *one must assuage, remedy*, ib.486e, Orib.*Fr.*1. **–ητικός**, ή, όν, = παρηγορικός, Sch.Il.13.726. **–ία**, Ion. **–ίη**, ἡ, *exhortation, persuasion*, A.R.2.1281 (pl.): metaph., χρίματος..ἀδόλοισι παρηγορίαις A.*Ag.*95 (anap.); ἴση παρηγορία, = ἰσηγορία, Jul.*Or.*1.17b. 2. *surname*, J.*BJ*4.8.3 (sed leg. προσηγ–). II. *consolation*, τοῦ πένθους Plu. *Cim.*4, cf. *Per.*34; υἱοῖο for his loss, *IG*7.2544 (Thebes); ὀδευόντων π., of the moon, Secund.*Sent.*6. 2. *assuagement*, Diocl.*Fr.*142, etc.; τοῦ παροξυσμοῦ Aret.*CD*1.3. **–ικός**, ή, όν, *encouraging, consoling*, λόγοι Poll.3.100. II. *soothing*, βηχός Hp.*Acut.*53, cf. *Aph.* 5.22; κεφαλαλγίας Philonid.ap.Ath.15.676c; π. φάρμακον, καταπλάσματα, Gal.12.268, 10.884, cf. 10.966 (Comp.). Adv. –κῶς *by gentle means*, Hp.*Art.*62: Comp. –ώτερον Gal.1.211. ⊛ **–ος**, Dor. **παρᾱγ–**, ον, (ἀγορεύω) *consoling, soothing*, μῦθοι A.R.1.479: as Subst., *comforter*, S.*El.*229 (lyr.), *Epigr.Gr.*344; Παρήγορος, ἡ, personified, Paus. 1.43.6. 2. c. gen., π. δίψης καὶ λιμοῦ *assuaging* them, M.Ant.(?) ap.Justin.M.*Apol.*1.71.

**παρηδύνω** [ῡ], *sweeten* or *season*, Dorio ap.Ath.7.309f: metaph., of language, D.H.*Dem.*45.

**παρηθ-έω**, *filter through*, Hp.*Dent.*14 and 17 (of the bowels):—Pass., Gal.*UP*6.16. **–ημα**, ατος, τό, *filterings*, Id.19.85.

**πᾰρηϊάς**, άδος, ἡ, = παρειά, Ep. dat. pl. παρηϊάδεσσι *Epic.Alex.Adesp.* 9 iii 6.

**πᾰρήϊον**, τό (Ion. for παρεῖον, which is not in use), used in Il. as the sg. for παρειά (which Hom. uses only in pl.), *cheek*, Il.23.690; of the *jaw* of a wolf, πᾶσιν δὲ π. αἵματι φοινόν 16.159: in pl., of a lion, παρηΐα τ' ἀμφοτέρωθεν αἱματόεντα πέλει Od.22.404; in Ion. Prose, λουσαμένους παρήϊα prob. in *IG*12(5).593.30 (Ceos, v B.C.). II. π. ἔμμεναι ἵππων *cheek-ornament* of a bridle, Il.4.142.

**παρηΐς**, ΐδος, ἡ, later form of παρήϊον, A.*Ch*.24(lyr.), *Trag.Adesp.* 548(lyr.); παρειὰν προσβαλεῖν παρηΐδι E.*Hec*.410; λευκὴν..παρηΐδα Id.*El*.1023: pl., διὰ παρηΐδων A.*Th*.534:—contr. **παρῇς**, ῇδος, E.*IA* 187 (lyr.), *AP*9.745 (Anyt.); pl. παρῇδες E.*IA*681; dat. παρῇσι Phryn.Trag.13 (lyr.).

**παρηκουσμένως**, Adv., (παρακούω) *negligently*, Iamb.*VP*29.157.

**παρήκτης**· πάντα πράττων ἐπὶ κακῷ, Hsch.

⊛ **παρήκω**, *to have come alongside*: hence, *lie beside, stretch along*, παρὰ πᾶσαν [τὴν θάλασσαν] Hdt.2.32, cf. 4.39,42, 9.15; παρὰ τὸ ὀστέον Hp.*Loc.Hom*.6; πρὸς ἡλίου δύσιν μέχρι τοῦ Ὀσκίου ποταμοῦ Th.2.96; εἰς τὸ πλάγιον X.*Cyn*.4.1; π. πρὸς τὸ πλῆθος *extend* to the length, Arist.*Po*.1459b22. II. *pass* in any direction, ἔνδοθεν στέγης μὴ 'ξω παρήκειν S.*Aj*.742. III. of Time, *to be past*, ὁ παρήκων χρόνος *the past*, opp. ὁ μέλλων, Arist.*Ph*.222b1; but also 2. εἰς τὸ παρῆκον τοῦ χρόνου up to the *present* time, Pl.*Alc*.2.148c. 3. ὡς ἂν παρήκῃ as occasion *arises*, Archig.ap.Orib.8.23.1. IV. *remit*, of fever, Aret.*CA*1.1 (v.l. -έκῃ), cf. 2.3: metaph., *come to an end*, παρήκοντος ἤδη τοῦ πολέμου Parth.4.4.

⊛ **παρῆλιξ**, ικος, ὁ, ἡ, *past one's prime*, Plu.*Alex*.32: with neut., παρήλικα παιδικά *AP*12.228(Strat.): Comp. -έστερος Sor.1.15. II. *past the age-limit of service*, *POxy*.1257.2 (iii A.D.), etc.

**παρήλιος**, ὁ, *parhelion, mock sun*, Arist.*Mete*.372a16, Thphr.*Sign*. 22, etc.; also παρήλιον, τό, Arat.881. II. Adj. παρήλιος, ον, *beside the sun*, νέφη Ptol.*Tetr*.100.

**παρηλλαγμένως**, Adv., (παραλλάσσω) *differently, strangely*, Plb.15.13.6, D.S.14.112.

⊛ **πάρημαι**, used as pf. Pass. of παρίζω, *to be seated beside* or *by*, c. dat., only part., νηυσὶ παρήμενος *seated by*.., Il.1.421,488; Δηοῦς ἐσχάραις παρημένη E.*Supp*.290; ἀλλοτρίοισι π. *seated at* another man's table, Od.17.456: generally, *dwell beside*, σύεσσι π. 13.407. 2. abs., *sit by* or *near*, παρήμενοι ἄλλοθεν ἄλλος Il.9.311, cf. Od.19.209; of the vultures of Tityos, ἑκάτερθε παρημένω ἧπαρ ἔκειρον 11.578.

**παρημελημένως**, Adv., (παραμελέω) *negligently*, διατρεφόμενος Plu. 2.340d, f.l. in D.H.7.12.

**παρημερ-εύω**, *pass the day with* one or *in doing* a thing, π. τινὶ ἔργῳ ἢ ἀνθρώπῳ Poll.1.65. **-ος**, Dor. **παράμ-**, ον, *coming day by day, daily*, ἐσλόν Pi.*O*.1.99. II. *every other day*, Poll.1.65 cod. B.

**παρημοσύνη**· θεραπεία, Hsch.

**πάρηξις**, εως, ἡ, *gangway*, A.*Ag*.556.

**παρηονῖτις**, ιδος, fem. Adj. *on the shore*, χερμάς *AP*7.693 (Apollonid.).

**παρηορία**, ἡ, in pl., *side-traces, by which the* παρήορος *was attached beside* the regular pair, ἵπποιο παρηορίας ἀπέταμνε Il.8.87; ἐν δὲ παρηορίῃσι.. Πήδασον ἵει he harnessed Pedasus with *side-traces*, 16.152. II. in pl., *outlying reaches* of a river, Arat.600.

**παρηόριος**, η, ον, later form for sq., τὴν δὲ [νῆα] παρηορίην κόπτεν ῥόος drove it *from side to side*, A.R.4.943; = παρήορος III, π. νόημα *AP*9.603 (Antip.).

**παρήορος**, so in Ep. and Ion., but Dor. and Att. **παράορος** [ρᾰ], ον (as always in Trag.), also Dor. **πάρᾱρος** Theoc.15.8: (παραείρω, cf. συνήορος):—*joined* or *hung beside*: hence παρήορος (sc. ἵππος), *horse which draws by the side of the regular pair* (ξυνωρίς), *outrunner*, = σειραφόρος, Il.16.471,474, D.H.7.73. II. *lying along, outstretched, sprawling*, ἔκειτο π. ἔνθα καὶ ἔνθα Il.7.156; ἀχρεῖον καὶ π. δέμας κεῖται A.*Pr*.365. III. metaph., *reckless, senseless*, οὔ τι π. οὐδ' ἀεσίφρων Il.23.603, cf. Theoc. l.c.; π. ὄμμα τιταίνειν Tryph.371; νόου παρήορος *distraught*, Archil.56.5.

**παρήπαφε**, v. παραπαφίσκω. **παρηρία**· μωρία, Hsch.; cf. παραρρέω, and v. παρήορος III; also **πάρηρος** (πάρερος cod., sed post παρηρία)· ὁ μωρός, Id. **παρῇς**, contr. for παρηΐς.

**παρησυχάζω**, *pass over in silence*, Ph.1.93,504 (Pass.).

**παρηχ-έομαι**, *resemble in sound*, τινι Sch.Ar.*Pl*.586; πρός τι Eust. 139.31; π. ἔκ τινος *to be derived* from a word *by such resemblance*, Id. 87.24. ⊛ **-ημα**, ατος, τό, *succession of similar sounds, alliteration*, Suid. s.v. παραγραμματίζων. ⊛ **-ησις**, εως, ἡ, = foreg., Hermog. *Inv*.4.7. ⊛ **-ητικός**, ή, όν, *alliterative*, interpol. in Suid. s.v. Ναύκων. Adv. -κῶς Eust.1638.17.

⊛ **παρθεν-εία**, ἡ, *virginity*, E.*Heracl*.592, *Tr*.980:—more freq. **παρθενία**, Ep. **-ίη**, Sapph.102, Pi.*I*.8(7).48, A.*Pr*.898 (lyr.), E.*Ph*.1487 (lyr.), Arist.*Pr*.894b35, A.R.2.502, Lxx*Je*.3.4, Parth.26.2, Sor.1.30; ἀπὸ τῆς π. or ἀπὸ π., *Ev.Luc*.2.36, *IG*12(7).395.20 (Amorgos); ἐκ π. Plu.*Brut*.13, *PSI*1.41.5 (iv A.D.); of a man, Ach.Tat.5.20. **-εια**, τά, *songs sung by a chorus of maidens*, Ar.*Av*.919, Sch.Pi.*P*.3.139. II. *festival* of ἡ Παρθένος at Chersonesus, *IPE*1$^2$.352.49 (ii B.C.). ⊛ **-ειος**, poet. also **-ήϊος**, ον, *of* or *belonging to a maiden*, π. γλέφαρα Pi.*N*.8.2; αἰὼν π. *the maiden's* life, A.*Ag*.229 (lyr.); π. λέχος E.*Tr*.676; later in Prose, π. τέκνα *PRyl*.435.2 (ii A.D.); π. ζώματα St.Byz. s.v. Ἐρυσίχη. ⊛ **-ευμα**, ατος, τό, in pl., *pursuits* or *amusements of maidens*, E.*Ph*.1265: sg., *maiden's work*, ἱστῶν π. Id.*Ion* 1425. 2. νόθον π. *child of an unmarried woman*, ib.1472. **-ευσις**, εως, ἡ, = παρθενεία, Luc.*Salt*.44. ⊛ **-εύω**, *bring up as a maid*, π. παῖδας ἐν δόμοις καλῶς E.*Supp*.452, cf. Luc.*DMar*.12.1, etc.:—Pass., *lead a maiden life*, Hdt.3.124, A.*Pr*.648, E.*Ph*.1637; πολιὰ (neut. pl.) παρθενεύεται *grows* grey *in maidenhood*, Id.*Hel*.283. 2. intr. in Act., = Pass., Hld.7.8. **-εών**, ῶνος, ὁ, poet. for παρθενών, *AP*9.790 (Antip.), Musae.263. **-η**, = παρθένος, *Gloss*. **-ην** (acc. sg.), perh. misspelling of -ειον (sc. ζώνην), *UPZ*101.21 (ii B.C.). ⊛ **-ία**, ἡ, = παρθενεία (q.v.). II. old name of Samos, Arist.*Fr*.570. **-ια**, τά, *signs of virginity*, Lxx*De*.22.15; τὰ π. μου my *virginity*, of Jephthah's daughter, ib.*Jd*.11.37. **-ιανός**, ή, όν, *born under the sign of Virgo*, *Cat.Cod.Astr*.7.112, 8(4).191. **-ίας**, ου, ὁ, *son of a concubine*: οἱ Π. the youths born at Sparta during the Messenian War, Arist.*Pol*.1306b29, Str.6.3.2. II. = ἀβυρτακῶδες πέμμα, Hsch. ⊛ **-ική**, ἡ, poet. for παρθένος, Il.18.567, Od.11.39, Hes.*Op*.699, Alcm.26, Alc.*Supp*.11.5, Sapph.*Supp*.20a.15, Pi.*P*.9.99, B.16.11, E.*El*.174 (lyr.); παρθενικὴ νεῆνις Od.7.20; π. κόρη E.*Epigr*.2. ⊛ **-ικός**, ή, όν, *of* or *for a maiden*, σκευή D.S.16.26; ὁ π. χιτών Plu.*Comp.Lyc.Num*.3; ἀνὴρ π. Lxx*Jl*.1.8 (cf. παρθένιος I.2); π. ἀνδριάς statue of a matron *represented as a maiden*, *BMus.Inscr*.1047; παρθενικὰ πράττειν Ael.*VH*12.1. II. παρθενικόν, τό, = ἀρτεμισία, Ps.-Dsc.3.113. **-ιον**, τό, *feverfew*, *Pyrethrum Parthenium*, Hp.*Ulc*.14, Nic.*Th*.863, Dsc.3.138, Plin.*HN*21.176. 2. = ἑλξίνη, Dsc.4.85, etc. 3. = λινόζωστις, Thphr.*HP*7.7.2, Dsc.4.189. II. *girl*, Alciphr.3.33. ⊛ **-ιος**, α, ον, also ος, ον Pi.*P*.12.9, E.*Ph*.224 (lyr.):—*of a maiden, maidenly*, λῦσε δὲ παρθενίην ζώνην Od.11.245; ὄαροι Hes.*Th*.205; ἔρως Anacr.13A; κεφαλή Pi. l.c.; αἷμα A.*Ag*.215 (lyr.); χλιδά E.*Ph*.224 (lyr.): π. θύραι *of the temple of the Virgin Goddess*, *AP*6.202 (Leon.); παρθένιον βλέπειν Anacr.4; π. αὐλός, v. αὐλός I.1. 2. παρθένιος, ὁ, *the son of an unmarried girl*, Il.16.180; παρθενία ὠδίς Pi.*O*.6.31; but π. ἀνήρ the husband *of maidenhood*, *first* husband, Plu.*Pomp*.74. II. metaph., *pure, undefiled*, Π. φρέαρ, name of a well, *h.Cer*.99; π. μύρτα, of *white* myrtle-berries, Ar.*Av*.1099 (lyr.). III. π. γαῖα, = *Samia terra*, Nic.*Al*.149. IV. Π., ὁ (sc. μήν), a month in Elis, Sch.Pi.*O*.3.35. **-ίς**, ίδος, ἡ, pecul. fem. of παρθένιος, name of a flower used in garlands, Poll.6.106; = ἀρτεμισία, Plin.*HN*25.73. **-ισκάριον**, τό, Dim. of παρθένος, *Gloss*.; **-ίσκη**, ἡ, Hdn.Gr.1.317.

**παρθενο-κόμος**, ον, *taking care of maidens*, *An.Ox*.2.398:—also **-κομία**, ἡ, ibid. **-κτονία**, ἡ, *slaughter of a maiden*, Plu.2.314c. **-κτόνος**, ον, *maiden-slaying*, Lyc.22.

**παρθεν-οπίπης** [ῐ], ου, ὁ, (ὀπιπεύω) *one who ogles maidens, seducer*, Il.11.385.

⊛ **παρθένος**, Lacon. **παρσένος** Ar.*Lys*.1263 (lyr.), ἡ, *maiden, girl*, Il.22.127, etc.; αἱ ἄθλιαι π. ἐμαί my unhappy *girls*, S.*OT*1462, cf. Ar.*Eq*.1302; also γυνὴ παρθένος Hes.*Th*.514; π. κόρα, of the Sphinx, dub. in E.*Ph*.1730 (lyr.); θυγάτηρ π. X.*Cyr*.4.6.9; of Persephone, E.*Hel*.1342 (lyr.), cf. S.*Fr*.804; *virgin*, opp. γυνή, Id.*Tr*.148, Theoc.27.65. 2. of unmarried women who are not virgins, Il.2.514, Pi.*P*.3.34, S.*Tr*.1219, Ar.*Nu*.530. 3. Παρθένος, ἡ, *the Virgin Goddess*, as a title of Athena at Athens, Paus.5.11.10, 10.34.8 (hence of an Att. coin bearing her head, E.*Fr*.675); of Artemis, E.*Hipp*.17; of the Tauric Iphigenia, Hdt.4.103; of an unnamed goddess, *SIG*46.3 (Halic., v B.C.), *IG*1$^2$.108.48,54 (Neapolis in Thrace); αἱ ἱεραὶ π., of the Vestal Virgins, D.H.1.69, Plu.2.89e, etc.; αἱ Ἑστιάδες π. Id.*Cic*.19; simply, αἱ π. D.H.2.66. 4. the constellation *Virgo*, Eudox.ap.Hipparch.1.2.5, Arat.97, etc. 5. = κόρη III, *pupil*, X.ap.Longin.4.4, Aret.*SD*1.7. II. as Adj., *maiden, chaste*, παρθένον ψυχὴν ἔχων E.*Hipp*.1006, cf. Porph.*Marc*.33; μίτρη π. *Epigr.Gr*.319: metaph., π. πηγή A.*Pers*.613. III. as masc., παρθένος, ὁ, *unmarried man*, *Apoc*.14.4. IV. π. γῆ *Samian earth* (cf. παρθένιος III), *PMag.Berol*.2.57.

**παρθενό-σφαγος**, ον, π. ῥέεθρα streams *of a slaughtered maiden's blood*, A.*Ag*.209 (lyr.). **-τροφέω**, *bring up from girlhood*, Suid. s.v. διαπαρθενεῦσαι:—Pass., Theano *Ep*.6.1. II. Pass., *keep virgin*, Sor.1.32. **-τροφητέον**, *one must keep virgin*, ib.33 tit. **-χρως**, ωτος, ὁ, ἡ, *of maidenly, delicate colour*, κρόκος *AP*4.1.12 (Mel.).

**παρθεν-ώδης**, ες, *maiden-like*, St.Byz. s.v. Παρθένιος. ⊛ **-ών**, ῶνος, ὁ, *maidens' apartments* in a house, mostly in pl., A.*Pr*.646, E.*Ph*.89, *IT*826, etc. II. in sg., *the western cella of the Parthenon* or *temple of Athena* at Athens, *IG*1$^2$.301.13, al., D.22.76, etc.; also, of the cella of the temple of Artemis at Magnesia on Maeander, *SIG* 695.23 (ii B.C.); of the Great Mother at Cyzicus, *Michel*538.6, and Hermione, *IG*4.743. III. name of a month at Alexandria, Ptol. *Alm*.11.3. **-ωπός**, όν, (ὤψ) *of maiden aspect*, E.*El*.949: metaph., *of feminine softness*, ὀνόματα D.H.*Comp*.23.

**παρθεσίη**, ἡ, (παρατίθημι) *deposit, pledge*, *AP*7.37 (Diosc.).

**Παρθικά**, = φλογοβαφῆ δέρματα, Lyd.*Mag*.2.13.

**Παρθιστί**, Adv. *in the Parthian tongue*, Plu.*Ant*.46.

**Πάρθοι**, οἱ, *the Parthians*, Hdt.3.93, etc.; **Παρθυαῖοι**, Plb.10.31.15, etc.; **Πάρθιοι**, Anacreont.26B, cf. St.Byz.: **Παρθυαία**, ἡ, *Parthia*, Str.11.1.4, etc.; **Παρθυηνή**, Plb.10.28.7, etc.:—Adj. ⊛ **Παρθικός**, ή, όν, Str.11.9.3, Luc.*Hist.Conscr*.16; **Παρθικά**, τά, *history of Parthia*, Str.15.1.3; so **Παρθίς**, ίδος, ἡ, Luc.*Hist.Conscr*.32; and **Παρθονικικά**, τά, ibid. (fort. Παρθυηνικά).

⊛ **πάρθυμα**, ατος, τό, *additional sacrificial victim*, prob. in *GDI*4990.9 (Crete).

**παριαμβ-ίς**, ίδος, ἡ, *air set for the harp*, ὑπαυλεῖν κιθάρᾳ π. Epich. 109 (pl.), Apollod.ap.Hsch. ⊛ **-ος**, ὁ, = πυρρίχιος (⏑ ⏑), Aristid. Quint.1.22, Ter.Maur.1461, etc. II. = παριαμβίς, Phot. III. a kind of *harp*, Poll.4.59. **-ώδης**, ες, *characteristic of the* παριαμβίς, of the foot ⏑ – ⏑ – –, Diom.p.482 K.

**παριαύω**, *sleep beside* or *with*, τῇ παριαύων τερπέσθω Il.9.336, cf. A.R.1.806; in tmesi, Il.9.470, Od.14.21.

**παριδρύω**, *set up beside*, Hsch.:—Med., *AP*9.315 (Nic., παριδρῦεται, s.v.l.), Ph.2.347:—Pass., ib.151, al.

**παριέρη**, ἡ, *ex-priestess*, Ephesian word in Plu.2.795e.

**παρίζω**, Aeol. -ίσδω, *sit beside*, Τηλεμάχῳ δὲ πάριζεν Od.4.311, cf. Alc.52; π. βουλεύουσι τοῖσι γέρουσι Hdt.6.57; ἐν βουλῇ Id.4.165; but, II. causal, *seat beside*, π. Πέρσῃ ἄνδρι ἄνδρα Μακεδόνα Id.5.20: aor. 1, παρὰ δὲ σκοπὸν εἷσεν Il.23.359:—hence Med. in intr. sense, *seat oneself* or *sit beside*, Hdt.7.18, 8.58, cj. in Bion 2.22; cf. παρέζομαι.

⊛ **παρίημι**, fut. παρήσω Hdt.7.161, S.*Ant.*1193: aor. 1 παρῆκα Id.*OC*570: 3 pl. aor. 2 παρεῖσαν Antipho 6.44; part. παρείς S.*El.*732: pf. παρεῖκα (v. infr.); παρῆκα Thphr.*HP*5.3.6:—Pass., aor. 1 παρείθην Il.23.868; inf. παρεθῆναι D.21.105: aor. 2 παρείμην S.*OC*1666: pf. παρεῖμαι E.*Ph.*852:—*let fall at the side, let fall*, πὰρ δ' ἴεισι τὰ πτέρα Sapph.16; τὴν χεῖρα παρεικώς Clearch.25; παρεῖσ' ἐμαυτήν S.*El.*819; π. ἀπ' ὀμμάτων πέπλον E.*HF*1203 (lyr.); τὸ μάργον τῆς γνάθου Id.*Cyc.*310:—Pass., ἡ δὲ παρείθη μήρινθος ποτὶ γαῖαν it *hung down* to earth, Il.23.868. II. *pass by, pass over*, πᾶν ἔθνος καταστρεφόμενος καὶ οὐδὲν παριείς Hdt.1.177; π. κλύδων' ἔφιππον S.*El.*732, cf. D.18.263; π. τι ἄρρητον Pl.*Lg.*754a:—Pass., περὶ μὲν τούτου παρείσθω Plb.2.59.3. 2. *pass unnoticed, disregard*, τι Pi.*P.*1.86, Hdt.1.14, A.*Ag.*291, *Ch.*925, 1032, S.*Ant.*1193, etc.; τὰ παθήματα..παρεῖσ' ἐάσω Id.*OC*363:—Pass., παίδων πόθος παρεῖτο Id.*El* 545; μηδαμῇ παρεθῆναι D.21.105: c. inf., *omit* to do, παρέντα τοῦ μὲν τὸ φρόνιμον ἐγκωμιάζειν, τοῦ δὲ τὸ ἄφρον ψέγειν Pl.*Phdr.*235e, cf. *PCair.Zen.*369.2 (iii B.C.), Iamb.*Comm.Math.*1: with a neg. repeated, μὴ παρῇς τὸ μὴ οὐ φράσαι S.*OT*283: c. part., οὐ παρίει σείων ὁ θεός Paus.3.5.9: abs., αἰ δέ κα παρῇ *Berl.Sitzb.*1927.169 (Cyrene):—Med., *neglect*, E.*HF* 778 (lyr.); τὸν δῆμον D.C.51.5. 3. of Time, *let pass*, τὸν χειμῶνα Hdt.1.77; ἕνδεκα ἡμέρας Id.7.183; νύκτα μέσην Id.8.9; τὸν καιρόν Th.4.27, etc. III. *relax*, τοὺς τερθρίους παρίει Ar.*Eq.*440; οἶνος παρίησι *weakens*, D.L.9.86; *remit*, γόον, πόθον, χόλον, E.*Supp.*111, *Tr.*650, *IA*[1609]; *give up*, μελέτας Th.1.85; τὸν φελλὸν *give up the use of*.., Thphr. l. c.:—Pass., *to be relaxed, weakened*, κόπου δ' ὕπο.. παρεῖται E.*Ba.*635; κόπῳ παρεῖμαι Id.*Ph.*852; παρειμένος νόσῳ Id.*Or.* 881; ὕπνῳ Id.*Cyc.*591; γήρᾳ Pl.*Lg.*931d; σώμασι παρειμέναι E.*Ba.* 683; παρειμένα μέρη τοῦ σώματος Dsc.3.73, cf. Aret.*SD*1.7, etc.; καὶ δὴ παρεῖται σῶμα E.*Supp.*1070; τῷ λίαν παρειμένῳ Id.*Or.*210; τὰ σώματα παρειμένοι D.S.14.105; ὥστε καὶ τοῦ σώματός τι παρεθῆναι D.C.68.33. 2. τοῦ ποδὸς παρίει *slack away* the sheet, Ar.*Eq.*436: so perh. metaph., τοῦ μετρίου παρείς *letting go* one's *hold of* moderation, i.e. giving it up, S.*OC*1212 (lyr.). 3. *remit* punishment, τιμωρίαν Lycurg. 9 (Pass.); *pardon*, τὴν συμφοράν Ar.*Ra.*699:—Pass., ἐποίησεν παρεθῆμεν (Dor. for παρεθῆναι) secured our *release* from the obligation, *IG*4²(1).66.47 (Epid., i B.C.): c. gen., παρεῖσθαι τὰς πόλεις τῶν τόκων *OGI*444.15 (Ilium, i B.C.). IV. *yield, give up*, νίκην τινί Hdt.6.103, cf. A.*Ag.*943; τυραννίδα τινί E.*Ph.*523; αὐτοὺς κυμάτων δρομήμασιν Id.*Tr.*693; π. τινὶ τὴν ἀρχήν Th.6.23, cf. Arist.*Pol.*1285$^{b}$15; οὐδὲ δεῖν δυνάμενον ἄρχειν παριέναι τῷ πλησίον ib.1325$^{a}$37; *leave* a thing to another, σοὶ παρεὶς τάδε S.*Ph.*132; Ζεὺς τὰ μικρὰ..ἄλλοις δαίμοσιν παρεὶς ἐᾷ *Trag.Adesp.*353:—Med., *give up*, συμμαχίαν Arist.*Rh.Al.* 1446$^{b}$28; *resign*, στρατηγίαν D.C.39.23, etc.:—Pass., [γῆ] παρειμένη *left* in private ownership, *PHib.*1.53.5 (iii B.C.). 2. *permit, allow*, c. dat. pers. et inf., ἄλλῳ δὲ παρήσομεν οὐδενὶ ναυαρχέειν Hdt.7.161, cf. S.*El.*1482, Ar.*Eq.*341, Arist.*Pol.*1336$^{b}$29: c. subj., πάρες ὑπερβῶ *suffer* me to.., E.*Fr.*308 (anap.): abs. (the inf. being understood), S.*OC*591, Ar.*Eq.*340, Pl.*Smp.*199c, etc.; μὴ παρῇς σαυτοῦ βροτοῖς ὄνειδος *do* not *allow* them to have cause to reproach thee, S.*Ph.*967; παρῆκεν, ὥστε βραχέα μοι δεῖσθαι φράσαι *has allowed* that there should be but little for me to say, Id.*OC*570. V. *allow to pass, admit*, οὐδεὶς ὅστις οὐ παρήσει [ἡμέας] Hdt.3.72, cf. 4.146; π. ἐς τὴν Ἑλλάδα τοὺς βαρβάρους, τὸν Μαρδόνιον ἐπὶ τὴν Ἑ., Id.8.15, 9.1; Ἄδραστον εἰς γῆν π. E.*Supp.*468; λόγον π. εἰς τὸ φρουρίον Pl.*R.*561b; μὴ παρίωμεν εἰς τὴν ψυχήν *let us* not *admit* [the thought], Id.*Phd* 90e:—Med., βαρβάρους εἰς τὰς ἀκροπόλεις παρεῖνται *have admitted* them into *their very* citadels, D.15.15; of innkeepers, *admit*, τοὺς καταλύτας ἡμιασσαρίου Plb.2.15.6. VI. Med., *obtain the leave of* a magistrate, παρέμενος τοὺς ἄρχοντας Pl.*Lg.*742b, cf. 951a. 2. *beg to be excused* or *let off* something, οὐδέν σου παρίεμαι I ask no *quarter*, Id.*R.*341b; οὐκ ἂν παρείμην οἷσι μὴ δοκῶ φρονεῖν I *ask* no *favour* of them, S.*OC*1666; so παριέμεσθα καί φαμεν κακῶς φρονεῖν I *ask pardon*.., E.*Med.*892; τοῦτο ὑμῶν δέομαι καὶ παρίεμαι Pl.*Ap.*17c.

**παρικτόν**· παρερχόμενον, Hsch.

**παρίκω** [ῐ], *to be past*, of Time, Pi.*P.*6.43: pf. part., τῶν παρικότων *IG*12(5).109.13 (Paros), unless pf. of πάρειμι (εἶμι *ibo*).

**παριλλαίνω**, *look askance at*, Hsch. ⊛ **Πάρινα**, τά, = *marmorea*, *Gloss.* **πάριον**· πιστόν, κάτοχον, Hsch. (leg. πάγιον).

**Πᾰριουργής**, ές, *wrought in Paros*, *IG*11(2).203*B*99 (Delos, iii B.C.).

**παριππ-άζω**, = παριππεύω, Afric.*Cest.*p.57 V.:—Med., Onos.23.1; ταῖς τάξεσιν Id.33.6. -**ᾰσία**, ἡ, *riding past*, Arr.*Tact.*27.3, Ael.*Tact.* 35.3. -**εύω**, *ride along* or *over*, πόντον E.*Hel.*1665; *ride alongside*, Th.7.78, Plb.5.83.7, Luc.*Par.*61; *ride past*, Arr.*Tact.*37.1, 40.5. 2. *ride up to*, ἐπὶ τὰ μέσα Plb.3.116.3. 3. *pass by*, δεινὸν παριππεῦσαι Κυπρίους ἄρτους Eub.77. 4. *surpass*, Philostr.*VS*1.24.9. -**ος**, ον, *riding beside*, Plb.11.18.5. 2. *keeping pace with a horse*, Poll.5.40. II. *additional horse, outrunner*, *Cod.Just.*12.50.4, Lyd.*Mag.*3.7.

**παρίπταμαι**, = παραπέτομαι, Diog.Oen.25, Aesop.140.

**παρῐσάζομαι**, = παρισόομαι, S.E.*M.*1.166, 9.323.

**παρίσθμιον**, τό, (ἰσθμός 'neck') *fauces*, Arist.*HA*493$^{a}$1: pl., Plu. 2.1005a, Gal.6.674. 2. pl., *tonsils*, Hp.*Gland.*7, Ruf.*Onom.* 64. II. in pl., *inflammation of the tonsils*, Hp.*Aph.*3.26, *IG* 4²(1).126.31 (Epid.), Gal.17(2).632; with a pun on *the Isthmian games*, *AP*11.129 (Cereal.).

**παρίσκε[ψις]**, ιος, ἡ, Dor. for περίσκεψις, prob. in *Foed.Delph.Pell.* 1*A* 13 (*Class.Phil.*20.144).

**πάρῐσ-ος**, ον, *almost equal, evenly balanced*, ἀγών, κίνδυνος, Plb.2.10.2, 5.69.8; π. ταῖς δυνάμεσι Id.1.13.12; πέλαγος π. τῷ Ποντικῷ Str.11.7.1; ἴση ἢ π. γε (sc. ἡ εὐθεῖα) Id.2.1.28. II. in Rhet., of the clauses of a sentence, *exactly balanced and even*, π. καὶ ὁμοιοτέλευτον Arist.*Rh.*1410$^{b}$1, cf. Phld.*Rh.*2.258 S.; ἰσόκωλα καὶ πάρισα D.S.12.53; ἀντίθετα καὶ π. καὶ ὁμοιόπτωτα Plu.2.350d; οὔτε π. τὰ κῶλα ἀλλήλοις εἶναι οὔτε παρόμοια *parallel in structure*, D.H.*Comp.*22, cf. 23; ἵνα τὸ τελευταῖον κῶλον π. καὶ ἐφάμιλλον τοῖς πρὸ αὐτοῦ γένηται ib.9; π. σχῆμα Hermog.*Meth.*16. -**ότης**, ητος, ἡ, *approximation* to a limit, Dioph.5.17.

**παρῐσόχρονος**, ον, *almost contemporaneous*, prob. for περισσόχρονος in Thphr.*CP*1.18.3.

**παρῐσόω**, (ἴσος) *make equal*, αἱ συλλαβαὶ αἱ κατὰ τὸ τέλος παρισοῦσαι τὰ κῶλα Hermog.*Id.*1.12: c. acc. et dat., π. τῷ τῆς ἀρχῆς μεγέθει τὸν λόγον Aristid.*Or.*26(14).108; τὰ στέρνα τῇ κεφαλῇ π. Hld.10.30: abs., *use the figure* παρίσωσις, Hermog. l. c. II. Pass. (fut. παρισώσομαι Aristid.*Or.*26(14).2), *make oneself equal to, measure oneself against*, τινι Hdt.4.166, 8.140.α'; ἐπεί χ' Ἑλένᾳ παρισωθῇ Theoc.18. 25. 2. *to be made equal* or *like to*, ἄνδρα ἀρετῇ παρισωμένον καὶ ὡμοιωμένον Pl.*R.*498e; *to be as large as*, Paus.8.25.13; *to be comparable with*, Hermog.*Id.*2.10.

**παριστάνω**, = sq. (q.v.), Plb.3.96.3, 3.113.8, Phld.*Sign.*29, *Ep. Rom.*6.13, etc.:—also **παριστάω**, A.D.*Synt.*272.13 (v.l.), S.E.*P.*2. 42, 108, etc.:—Pass., παριστᾶται Parm.16.2; cf. παραστάνω.

⊛ **παρίστημι**, A. causal in pres., impf., fut., and aor. 1; later pf. παρέστᾰκα in same sense, *PTeb.*5.196 (ii B.C.), Plb.3.94.7, S.E.*M.*7. 273, etc. I. *cause to stand, place beside*, π. τοὺς ἱππεῖς ἐφ' ἑκάτερον τὸ κέρας Plb.3.72.9, cf. 3.113.8; παραστήσας τὰ ὅπλα *having brought* his arms *into view*, D.18.175; π. τινὰ φυλάττειν *set* one *near* a thing to guard it, v.l. in Id.49.35; π. σορὸν σορῷ *Anatolian Studies* p.204 (Termessus). II. *set before the mind, present*, ὑπόθεσιν..οὐχὶ τὴν οὖσαν παριστάντες ὑμῖν D.3.1; τοῦτο π. τοὺς θεοὺς ὑμῖν that they may *put* this *into* your *minds*, Id.18.1; τὸ δεινὸν π. τοῖς ἀκούουσιν Id.21.72; π. ἐλπίδας, ὁτιοῦν τῶν δεινοτάτων, Id.19.333, 21.15; *arouse, inspire*, οὐ γὰρ ἡ πληγὴ παρέστησε τὴν ὀργὴν ἀλλ' ἡ ἀτιμία ib.72; π. φόβον καὶ ἀπορίαν ταῖς πόλεσι Plb.3.94.7; π. ὁ κίνδυνος διαλογισμόν, μὴ.. Aeschin.2.159: so τοῦτο π. ὑμῖν γνῶναι *prompt* you to that decision, D.18.8; π. τινὶ θαρρεῖν *give* one confidence, v.l. in Aeschin.1.174; π. τινί c. inf., *put* it *into his head* to.., Paus.9.14.6; also π. τινὶ ὅτι or ὡς.., X.*Oec.*13.1, Pl.*R.*600c. 2. *dispose* a person, πρὸς μελαγχολίας Phld.*Ir.*p.28 W., cf. *Mus.*p.73 K.; also Ἀθηναίους ἄλλα παρέστησεν ὡς ἥρωα τιμᾶν Θησέα Plu.*Thes.*35:—also in Pass., v. B. v. 1. 3. of a Poet, *represent, describe*, τὸν Νέστορα παρέστησε [ὁ ποιητὴς] πείθοντα Phld.*Hom.* p.65 O., cf. Ath.3.110f, 4.133b; δι' ἐτυμολογίας Corn.*ND*1:—Pass., παριστάσθω ὅτι.. *let it be stated* that.., S.E.*M.*7.310. 4. *furnish, supply, deliver*, *PCair.Zen.*790.10 (iii B.C.), *PTeb.*5.196 (ii B.C.), *Abh. Berl.Akad.*1925(5).31 (Cyrene). 5. *make good, prove, show*, τι πολλοῖς τεκμηρίοις Lys.12.51, cf. *Act.Ap.*24.13; καθάπερ προϊόντες -στήσομεν Phld.*Ir.*p.85 W., cf. *Mus.*p.37 K. 6. c. acc. pers., *present, offer*, ἑαυτοὺς τῷ θεῷ, ἑαυτοὺς δούλους εἰς ὑπακοήν, *Ep.Rom.*6. 13, 16. b. *commend*, βρῶμα ἡμᾶς οὐ παραστήσει τῷ θεῷ 1*Ep.Cor.*8. 8. 7. *render*, [ἡ πίσσα] τὸν οἶνον εὔποτον παρίστησι ταχέως Plu.2. 676c. 8. in later Greek, as in Med. (v. c. I), *produce* in court, etc., *BGU*759.22 (ii A.D.), etc.:—Pass., *Sammelb.*4512.82 (ii B.C.), etc. III. *set side by side, compare*, [πόλεις] μικρὰς μεγάλαις Isoc. 12.40.—The use of these act. tenses occurs in Pl. l. c., but first becomes common in Oratt.

B. Pass., with aor. 2, pf. and plpf. Act., intr.: I. *stand by, beside*, or *near*, θεῶν δέ οἱ ἄγχι παρέστη Il.15.442, cf. 483; ἀμφίπολος δ' ἄρα οἱ κεδνὴ ἑκάτερθε παρέστη Od.1.335, cf. 8.218, 18.183; ἑξείης πάντεσσι παρίστασαι, of a beggar, 17.450; οὐδ' ἄρα οἱ τις ἀνουτητί γε παρέστη Il.22.371; ζωγράφῳ παρεστηκυῖα, of a painter's model, X.*Mem.*3.11.2: freq. in part. παραστάς with a Verb, εἶπε παραστάς Il.12.60; οὖτα π. 20.472; παρασταθείς, v.l. for κατασταθείς, E.*Or.*365. 2. *stand by*, i.e. *help, defend*, τινι Il.10.279, etc.; Τρωσὶ παρεστάμεναι καὶ ἀμύνειν 21.231, cf. 15.255; Ὀδυσῆι πῆ δ' ἀρήγει 23.783, cf. Hes.*Th.*439, Hdt.1.87, etc.; π. τινι χερσί S.*Aj.*1384; βοηθοὶ π. X.*Cyr.*5.3.19; οὐ παρέστη οὐδ' ἐβοήθησεν D.45.64. II. more freq. in past tenses, *to have come*, δεῦρο παρέστης Il.3.405; *to be at hand*, νῆες δ' ἐκ Λήμνοιο παρέσταν 7.467, etc. 2. of events, *to be near, be at hand*, ἀλλά τοι ἤδη ἄγχι παρέστηκεν θάνατος 16.853; κακὴ Διὸς αἶσα παρέστη ἡμῖν Od.9.52, cf. 16.280: in fut. Med., σοί..παραστήσεσθαι ἔμελλεν μοῖρ' ὀλοὴ 24.28; ἐάν τοι καιρὸς ἢ χρεία παραστῇ D. 21.101, cf. 73: freq. in pf., παρέστηχ' ὡς ἔοικ' ἀγὼν μέγας E.*Hec.*229, cf. *Med.*331; in part., τὸ χρῶμα τὸ παρεστηκός Ar.*Eq.*399; ὁ νῦν παρεστηκὼς ἡμῖν λόγος Pl.*Lg.*962d: in Att. form παρεστώς, ῶσα, ός, τῆς παρεστώσης νόσου S.*Ph.*734; τοῦ π. θέρους ib.1340; τὰς παρεστώσας τύχας E.*Or.*[1024]; τὰ παρεστῶτα *present circumstances*, τὰ λῷστα, κράτιστα τῶν π., A.*Ag.*1053, *Pr.*218; πρὸς τὸ παρεστός Ar.*Eq.*564; πρὸς τὸ παριστάμενον X.*Eq.Mag.*9.1. III. *come to the side of* another, *come over to* his *opinion*, παραστῆναι ἐς τῶν Περσέων τὴν γνώμην Hdt.6.99: abs., *come to terms, surrender, submit*, Id.3.13, 5.65, 6.140; οἱ πολέμιοι παραστήσονται Id.3.155; τῷ πολέμῳ παραστῆναι D. 22.15, cf. *EM*653.2. IV. *happen* to one, τῷ δὴ λέγουσι..θῶμα μέγιστον παραστῆναι Hdt.1.23; τὸ φρονεῖν ἀλλοῖα παρίσταται Emp. 108; esp. *come into one's head, occur to* one, τὼς νόος ἀνθρώποισι παριστᾶται Parm.16.2; δόξα μοι παρεστάθη ναοὺς ἱκέσθαι S.*OT*911; δόξα π.

τινὶ ὥστε.. Pl.*Phd.*66b; σοὶ τοῦτο παρέστηκεν, ὡς.. Id.*Phdr.*233c; π. θαῦμα, γνώμη, And.2.2,24 (s.v.l.); ἔκπληξις παρέστη Th.8.96: impers., παρίσταταί μοι *it occurs* to me; τῷ οὐ παραστήσεται..τεθνάναι βούλεσθαι to whom *it will* not *occur* to wish for death, Hdt.7.46: folld. by ὡς, Th. 4.61,95, Lys.12.62, etc.: c. inf., Id.7.17; οὐχὶ παρίσταταί μοι ταὐτὰ γιγνώσκειν D.3.1: c. acc. et inf., Lys.21.12, Pl.*Phd.*58e; part., τὸ παριστάμενον *that which comes into one's head, a thought*, Luc.*Cont.*13; ἐκ τοῦ π. λέγειν speak *offhand*, Plu.*Dem.*9, cf. Gal.14.295. V. *to be disposed*, πρὸς τὰς πράξεις Phld.*Mus.*p.71 K.; εἰρηνικῶς παρεστώτων Id.*Hom.*p.45 O. 2. *collect oneself*, παραστῆναι πρὸς τὸν κίνδυνον D.S. 17.43; τῷ θυμῷ παραστάς ib.99; π. πρὸς τὴν ἀπολογίαν Plu.*Alc.*19; παρεστηκότες ταῖς γνώμαις Arr.*Fr.*161 J. 3. metaph., οἶνος παρίσταται the wine *improves, becomes fit for drinking*, opp. ἐξίσταται, Thphr. *CP*6.14.10, cf. Dsc.5.8. b. of a crop, *to be ripe*, ὅταν ὁ πρώϊμος σπόρος παραστῇ *OGI*56.68 (Egypt, iii B.C.); so prob. ἡ γῆ παρέστηκεν *PLille*8.5 (iii B.C.). VI. παρεστηκέναι φρενῶν *to be beside oneself, lose one's* wits, Plb.18.53.6; π. ταῖς διανοίαις Id.14.5.7, etc.; ἐπὶ τοσοῦτον π. Id.22.8.13; cf. παρεξίστημι II. 2. *to be passionately devoted to*, ἵπποισι παρεστεῶτες Hp.*Ep.*17. VII. abs., παρεστηκός, = παρόν, *since it was in their power, since the opportunity offered*, Th.4.133.

C. Some tenses of Med., pres. and impf. sts., fut. and aor. I almost always (for exceptions, v. supr. B. II. 2, III, IV), are used in causal sense: I. *set by one's side, bring forward, produce*, π. ἱερεῖα X.*An.*6.1.22; esp. in a court of justice, τοὺς παῖδας παραστησάμενοι Lys.20.35; παιδία παραστήσεται (of a culprit) D.21.99; ταῦτα παραστησάμενος ib.187; μάρτυρας παρίστανται Is.4.13, etc.; παραστήσασθαί τινα *produce* him *as witness*, Id.9.9, D.34.28, etc.; π. τινὰ εἰς κρίσιν Pl.*R.*555b. 2. *commend*, τινί τινα J.*AJ*15.7.3. II. *bring to one's side, bring over by force, bring to terms*, ἀέκοντας παραστήσασθαι Hdt.8.80; π. βίᾳ S.*OC*916; π. πολιορκίᾳ Th.1.98; πολιορκοῦντας π. ὁμολογίᾳ ib.29: abs., π. τινά, π. πόλιν, Hdt.3.45, Th.1.124, etc.; τοὺς οἰκοῦντας τὴν Ἀττικὴν π. εἰς φορὰν δασμοῦ Pl.*Lg.*706b. 2. generally, *dispose for one's own views* or *purposes*, τινὰ παραστήσασθαι οὕτως ὥστε..so *to dispose* a person that.., Hdt.4.136; ἑαυτοὺς πρὸς τὴν μάχην Plb.3.109.9; *dispose, induce* a person, πρὸς τὸ κοινωνεῖν Id. 29.3.5: c. acc. et inf., Chio *Ep.*3.

**παριστία**, ἡ, (ἑστία) *side-hearth*, in the vulgar dialect (ἰδιωτικῶς), Eust.132.32.

**παριστίδιος** [ῐδ], ον, *at the loom*, *AP*7.726 (Leon.).

⊕ **παριστορέω**, *inquire by the way*, Cic.*Att.*6.1.25. II. *narrate* or *notice incidentally*, *Placit.*2.24.4, Dam.*Pr.*123.

**παρίστριος**, α, ον, *by* or *on the Danube*, γέφυρα Tz.*H.*3.482.

**παρίσχιος**, ον, *beside the hips*, Hsch. s. v. κλονιστήρ; f.l. for ταρίχιον in D.L.2.139.

**παρισχναίνω**, *make thin* or *lean*, Arist.*HA*546[a]3 (Pass.).

**παρίσχω**, = παρέχω, *hold in readiness*, Ep. inf. παρισχέμεν Il.4.229; *present, offer*, 9.638, Pi.*P.*8.76; *provide*, *IG*7.3073.10 (Lebad.), *SIG* 245 *G*i 46 (Delph., iv B.C.).

**παρῐσ-ώδης**, ες, *after the manner of* πάρισα (πάρισος II), *Vit.Isoc.* p.257 W. **-ωμα**, ατος, τό, = sq., Cratin.Jun.7.4. **-ωσις**, εως, ἡ, Rhet., *even balancing of the clauses* in a sentence, Isoc.12.2 (pl.), cf. Arist.*Rh.*1410[a]23, *Rh.Al.*1435[b]39, Hermog.*Id.*1.11; of clauses equal in number of syllables, ib.12; *assonance*, Syrian.*in Hermog.*1.51 R. (pl.). II. *equalization*, Iamb.*Myst.*1.9. **-ωτικός**, ή, όν, *equalizing*, Eust.789.59.

**παρῐτ-έον**, *one must pass by, omit*, Ph.1.532. II. *one must pass in*, εἰς τὰ βασίλεια Them.*Or.*15.184b. **-ητέα**, (πάρειμι (εἶμι ibo)) *one must come forward*, ἐς τοὺς Λακεδαιμονίους Th.1.72:—also **-ητέον**, Luc.*Merc.Cond.*42, Them.*Or.*26.313a. II. Adj. παριτητέος, α, ον, *to be traversed*, Philostr.*Dial.*2. **-ός**, ή, όν, *accessible*, Call.*Lav. Pall.*90.

**παρκαθήκα**, ἁ, Dor. for παρακαταθήκη, *IG*5(2).159.9 (Tegea).

**παρκαλέω**, v. παρακαλέω.

**παρκάλισις**, εως, ἡ, either *unpacking from a wooden crate* or *transport by rollers*, *IG*4[2](1).103.46,63 (Epid.); cf. διακάλισις, ἐσκάλισις.

**παρ-κατέλεκτο, -κλίνω, -κύπτω, -λαμβάνω**, poet. for παρα-. **παρμέμβλωκε**, v. παραβλώσκω.

**Παρμενίδειος**, α, ον (ος, ον Dam.*Pr.*423), *of Parmenides*, ξένος Plu. 2.1017c: Παρμενίδεια, τά, *his writings*, D.L.2.106.

**παρμένω**, v. παραμένω.

**πάρμη**, ἡ, *light shield, buckler*, Lat. *parma*, Plb.6.22.1, D.H.2.71, etc.

**παρμόνιμος, πάρμονος**, poet. for παρα-.

⊕ **Παρνᾱσός**, Ion. **Παρνησός**, ὁ, *Parnassus*, Od.19.432, *h.Ap.*269, etc.: —also **Παρνασσός**, Th.3.95, Philod.Scarph.23 (prob.), Aristonous 1.41, Hdn.*Gr.*1.209: Adj. **Παρνάσιος** [ᾱ], α, ον (also ος, ον E.*IT* 1244 (lyr.)), *Parnassian*, Pi.*P.*10.8, Limen.22, etc.: also **Παρνήσσιος**, *IG*2[2].1258.24 (iv B.C.); fem. **Παρνᾱσιάς**, άδος, Ion. **Παρνησιάς** E.*Ion* 86 (anap.); also **Παρνασσίς**, ίδος, *Pae.Delph.*4; **Παρνησίς**, A. *Ch.*563.

**Πάρνης**, ηθος, ἡ (ὁ, only in Euphanes 1 = *CAF* ii 297), *Parnes*, Ar. *Nu.*323, etc.: Adj. **Παρνήθιος**, α, ον, Id.*Ach.*348 (Bentl. for Παρνάσιοι), cf. *Ra.*1057.

**πάρνοψ**, οπος, ὁ, a kind of *locust*, = κόρνοψ, Ar.*Ach.*150, *Av.*588, Nicopho 1, Gal.*UP*3.2, Ael.*NA*6.19:—hence **Παρνόπιος** Ἀπόλλων, *averter of locusts*, Paus.1.24.8: also **Παρνοπίων**, ωνος, ὁ, Str.13.1.64; as name of a month among the Aeolians of Asia, ibid. (nisi leg. **Πορν-**, v. Πορνόπιος).

**παρξοά**, ἁ, (παρά, ξέω) *tooling* of stone, *SIG*247 *K*[1] ii 71 (Delph., iv B.C.).

**παρό**, i.e. παρ' ὅ, *wherefore*, Arist.*Col.*798[a]23, *Aud.*802[a]1, *Mir.*834[b] 29, D.S.31.15a, Ph.1.46, al., Sor.1.85: with Comp. sense, πλεονάσαντα παρὸ ἔστι S.E.*M.*7.278.

**παρόα**, v. παρείας.

**παρογκόομαι**, *to be slightly curved*, *Cat.Cod.Astr.*7.238.

**παροδ-εία**, ἡ, *passing by*, Suid. **-έομαι**, = παροιμιάζομαι, Hsch. **-εύσιμος**, η, ον, = παριτός, Sch.Call.*Lav.Pall.*90. **-ευσις**, εως, ἡ, = παροδεία, Procl.*Par.Ptol.*200. **-ευτικός**, ή, όν, *causing to pass*, of the ureters, Steph.*in Hp.*2.432 D. ⊕ **-εύω**, *pass by*, Theoc. 23.47, *AP*9.341 (Glauc.), etc.; of flowing water, Polyaen.3.9.61; of the ureter, Archig. and Philagr.ap.Aët.11.4; διὰ τῶν καιρῶν ὁ χρόνος παροδεύει Porph.ap.Eus.*PE*3.11. 2. c. acc., *pass by* or *through*, D.S.32.27, Plu.2.973d, Herm.ap.Stob.1.49.44, Luc.*Nigr.*36, *IG*14. 881 (Sinuessa): Astron., *pass through* or *across*, Plu.2.670c, Ptol. *Tetr.*109; τὰ αὐτοῦ ὅρια Vett.Val.145.9:—Pass., *to be passed by*, J. *BJ*5.10.2, Plu.2.759f. 3. *pass, spend*, τὸν βίον *BCH*27.261 (Argos). **-ία**, ἡ, *by-road*, as expl. of παροιμία, Hsch. **-ικός**, ή, όν, *of a* πάροδος III. 2, Arg.A.*Pers.*, cj. in D.H.*Dem.*54; = παρόδῳ χρώμενος, Hsch. 2. Astron., π. ἀποκατάστασις restoration *of a transit*, i.e. complete revolution, Procl.*Hyp.*1.30. II. *transient, brief*, ἀποδημία Vett.Val.98.26. Adv. **-κῶς** *in passing*, Id.171.17, Pall. *in Hp.Fract.*1. III. Astrol., *according to chronocratory*, opp. κατὰ γένεσιν, Vett.Val.100.29. Adv. **-κῶς** ib.26. **-ιος**, ον, *by* or *on the road-way*, τοῖχος Hyp.*Fr.*261, *PCair.Zen.*663.4 (iii B.C.); θύρα *PTeb.*45.22 (ii B.C.); θυρίδες π. windows *looking to the street*, Plu.2.521d. II. Subst. παρόδιον, τό, *frontage*, *IG*2[2].2561, 2566. 2. *toll*, καμήλων *PLond.*2.330 (ii A.D.), etc. **-ίτης** [ῑ], ου, ὁ, *passer-by, traveller*, Hp. *Ep.*17, *AP*9.249 (Maec.), *IG*14.494 (Catana):—fem. **-ῖτις**, ιδος, *AP* 7.429 (Alc.), 9.373. ⊕ **-οιπόρος**, ὁ, = παροδίτης, *IG*14.1839.3 (Rome).

**παροδοποιέω**, *make a side-road*, Ath.Mech.16.11.

**πάροδος** (A), ὁ, = παροδίτης, Lxx *Ez.*16.25, *IG*14.1372 (Rome), 12(7).445 (Aegiale), *BCH*46.355 (Lebedus), *CIG*3273 (Smyrna).

⊕ **πάροδος** (B), ἡ, *way by* or *past, passage*, Th.3.21, Arist.*Cael.*294[b] 26; π. καὶ τροπαὶ τῶν ἄστρων ib.296[b]4, cf. Simp.*in Cael.*507.24; π. τοῦ χρόνου *passage, lapse* of time, Porph.*Sent.*44. b. Astrol., *rotation* of chronocratory, Vett.Val.37.9, cf. Ptol.*Tetr.*109. 2. *going by* or *past, passing, entrance*, Th.4.82; ἐν τῇ π. as they *passed by*, Id.1.126, cf. Plb.5.68.8; κατὰ τὴν π. Id.21.46.12; ἐκ π., ἐν π., *by the way, cursorily*, Arist.*Cael.*306[b]27, Phld.*Rh.*1.245 S., D.S.18. 16; π. τινὶ ἐπὶ τὰς ὕστερον πράξεις διδόναι Plu.2.345c; τὴν π. ἵν' ἔχῃς τῶν θυρῶν εὐνουστέραν *entrance* by the door, Dionys.Com.3.17. II. *narrow entrance* or *approach, mountain-pass*, as Thermopylae, etc., Lys.2.30, X.*An.*4.7.4, etc.; λαβεῖν τὰς π. take the *pass*, D.5.20, cf. 9.32, Phld.*Rh.*1.334 S.; opp. δίοδοι, X.*Cyn.*6.6. b. esp. *side-entrance* on the stage, Semus 20, Poll.4.126. c. *gallery* or *passage-way* surmounting fortifications, *IG*2[2].463.49,52, 1672.110. III. *coming forward, appearance*, esp. before the assembly, D.*Ep.*3.29, Jul.*Or.*7.205b, etc. 2. *first entrance* of a chorus in the orchestra, which was made *from the side wings*, Arist.*EN*1123[a]23, Poll.4.108; ὥσπερ δράματος Plu.2.805d. b. *first song* sung by the chorus *after its entrance*, Arist.*Po.*1452[b]22, Plu.2.785a. 3. *use of stage for* an artist's *performance*, ἡ π. εὗρεν δραχμὴν *Michel* 908, 909 (Iasos). 4. *public recitation*, *AP*11.422 (Antioch.). IV. in a ship, *gangway, passage along the deck*, Plu.*Demetr.*43: metaph., π. καὶ ἐπιβάθρα τοῦ συγγράφειν Artem.3 *Praef.*

**παροδύρομαι** [ῡ], *lament beside* or *along with*, D.C.43.19.

**παροδώτης**, ου, ὁ, = παροδίτης, *IG*7.2852 (Haliartus).

**παροίγνυμι** or **παροίγω**, *open at the side* or *a little, half-open*, πύλας E.*IA*857, παροίξας τῆς θύρας *having opened a bit of* the door, *put* it *ajar*, Ar.*Pax*30.

**παροιδ-αίνω**, *swell slightly*, Aret.*SD*2.1. **-έω**, = foreg., Herod.Med.*in Rh.Mus.*58.88, Antyll.ap.Orib.6.27.2, Dsc.*Alex.*27: metaph., τὸ παρῳδηκὸς [τῆς ψυχῆς] Ph.1.276. **-ησις**, εως, ἡ, *swelling*, Orib.*Fr.*128; πελάγους *Placit.*4.1.1. **-ίσκω**, *raise a slight swelling*, Aret.*CA*1.2.

**πάροιθα**, Aeol., = sq., Alc.*Oxy.*1789 *Fr.*1 ii 5 (fort. πάροιθ').

**πάροιθε** [ᾰ], and before a vowel **-θεν** (but sts. elided, as Il.3.162, E.*Hec.*58): (πάρος): I. Prep. c. gen. loci, *before*, and c. gen. pers., *in the presence of*, π. μεγάροιο, αὐτοῖο, Od.4.625, Il.1.360, etc.; separated from its case, π. ἐλθοῦσα, φίλον τέκος, ἵζευ ἐμεῖο 3.162, cf. 14.427, etc.; after its case, Κορωνήας..π. Alc.9. 2. of Time, π. ἐμοῦ *before* me, A.*Pr.*503; κείνου π. S.*Tr.*605. II. Adv., 1. of Place, *before, in front*, οἳ δεύτεροι οἵ τε πάροιθεν Il.23.498, cf. 213, 6.319, etc. 2. of Time, *formerly*, 23.20,180, Od.6.174, Pi.*O.*13.102, A. *Ag.*1372; *before* it got so far, Il.4.185; τὸ πάροιθεν Od.1.322, 2.312, 18.275; οἱ π. men *of old*, Pi.*P.*2.60; τῆς π. ἡμέρας E.*Ph.*853, cf. A. *Pers.*180; πάροιθεν πρὶν..ἐκπέμψαι, = Lat. *priusquam*, S.*El.*1131: also c. inf., = πρίν, π. ἐπὶ νῆα κατελθεῖν Theoc.17.48; cf. παροίτερος, παροίτατος.

**παροικ-εσία**, ἡ, = παροικία, Lxx *Ez.*20.38, *Za.*9.12. **-έω**, *dwell beside*, c. acc., ἀπὸ Κνίδου μέχρι Σινώπης τὴν Ἀσίαν π. *dwell along the coasts of* Asia, Isoc.4.162: c. dat., *live near*, πόλει Th.1.71; ταῖς πυραμίσι *OGI*666.13 (i A.D.); *dwell among*, τισι Th.3.93: abs., Id.6. 82; of places, *lie near*, X.*Vect.*1.5. II. *live in* a place *as* πάροικος, οἱ παροικοῦντες ξένοι D.S.13.47, cf. *SIG*709.9 (Chersonesus, ii B.C.); ὡς ἐπὶ ξένης Ph.1.416; *sojourn in*, Ἱερουσαλὴμ *Ev.Luc.*24.18. III. metaph., τὸν ἀνθρώπινον βίον παρῳκηκότες Phld.*Mort.*38. **-ησις**, εως, ἡ, *dwelling beside* or *near, neighbourhood*, Th.4.92. **II.** = sq., Lxx *Ge.*28.4, al. **2.** *transmigration* of souls, Plot.2.9.6. **-ία,** ἡ, (πάροικος II) *sojourning* in a foreign land, Lxx *Wi.*19.10, *Act.Ap.* 13.17; οἱ ἐν τῇ π., = οἱ ἐκτός, Lxx *Si.Prol.* ⊛ **-ίζω,** *place near*, τινά τινι Sm.*Ez.*12.25:—Med., Call.*Epigr.*26:—Pass., *settle near, dwell among*, τισι Hdt.4.180; ἔθνος Ἰονίῳ κόλπῳ παρῳκισμένον *settled upon*, Luc.*Am.*6. **-ικός,** ή, όν, *of a colonus*, δίκαιον *Cod.Just.*1.2.24 *Intr.*, cf. Just.*Nov.*7 *Praef.* **-ίς,** ίδος, f.l. for περιοικίς, Str.5.3.10.

**παροικοδομ-έω,** *build across* or *past*, Th.2.75; π. ἡμῖν τεῖχος Id.7.11. **II.** *build up*, π. τὰς εἰσόδους *narrow* them *by building*, Arist.*HA*623$^{b}$32; π. [τὸ ὕδωρ] *keep* it *off by a wall*, D.55.17. **-ημα,** ατος, τό, *partition wall*, Arist.*PA*672$^{b}$19. **II.** *building beside* a road, prob. cj. in D.C.68.15 (pl.).

**πάροικος,** ον, *dwelling beside* or *near, neighbouring*, c. gen., Κάδμου πάροικοι..δόμων S.*Ant.*1155; [πόλεις] π. Θρηκίων ἐπαύλων A.*Pers.*869 (lyr.): c. dat., ποταμῷ παροίκους Ἅλυϊ Diog.Trag.1.7, cf. Th.3.113: abs., ἡ π. πηλαμύς S.*Fr.*503; *neighbour*, οὐκ ἀσίνης π. Sapph.80; Ἀττικὸς π., prov. of a restless neighbour, Arist.*Rh.*1395$^{a}$18, Duris 96 J. **2.** π. πόλεμος war *with neighbours*, Hdt.7.235. **II.** *foreign, alien*, Lxx *Ge.*15.13, al.; σπέρμα π. ἐν γῇ ἀλλοτρίᾳ *Act.Ap.* 7.6: as Subst., *sojourner* in another's house, D.L.1.82: generally, *alien, stranger*, Lxx *Le.*22.10: in later Greek, = μέτοικος, *SIG*398.37 (Cos, iii B.C.), *IG*7.2712.64 (Acraeph.), *OGI*338.12, 20, al. (Pergam., ii B.C.), etc.; = *colonus*, *Cod.Just.*1.34.1 (pl.).

**παροιμ-ία,** ἡ, *proverb, maxim, saw*, A.*Ag.*264, S.*Aj.*664, Ar.*Th.* 528, etc.; κατὰ τὴν π. as *the saying* goes, Pl.*Smp.*222b; τὸ κατὰ τὴν π. λεγόμενον Id.*Sph.*261c; καθάπερ ἡ π. Pl.Com.174.3: in pl., of *the Proverbs* of Solomon, Lxx. **2.** *figure, comparison*, *Ev.Jo.*10.6, al. **3.** *digression, incidental remark*, Herod.2.61, Hsch., Phot. **-ιάζω,** τὸν Σαλομῶντα π. *cite the Proverbs of* Solomon, Lxx *4Ma.*18.16:—Med., *make proverbial*, ὁ τὸν θεὸν πρῶτον παροιμιασάμενος Pl.*Lg.*818b:—Pass., *pass into a proverb, become proverbial*, ὁ -ιαζόμενος λόγος Id.*Phlb.*45d; τὸ περὶ τῆς Λιβύης π. Arist.*GA*746$^{b}$7; ὁ π. διὰ πικρότητα κόρχορος Thphr.*HP*7.7.2; τὸ π. *as the proverb goes*, Plu.2.95cf; ὥστε π. πρὸς τοὺς προσποιουμένους *it is proverbial* of pretenders, Str. 10.4.17. **II.** Med., *speak in proverbs*, Pl.*Hp.Ma.*301c, Arist.*EN*1129$^{b}$29; οἱ παροιμιαζόμενοι *people who quote proverbs*, Pl.*Tht.* 162c. **-ιακός,** ή, όν, *proverbial*, Plu.2.636f. Adv. -κῶς Str.11.2.16, *AP*9.379 (Pall.). **II.** παροιμιακόν (sc. μέτρον), τό, *paroemiac*, i.e. an anapaestic dimeter catalectic, freq. at the end of an anapaestic system, Heph.8.6. **-ιαστής,** οῦ, ὁ, *author of proverbs*, of Solomon, Sm.*Ec.*12.10 (dub.). **-ιογράφος** [γρᾰ], ὁ, *collector of proverbs*, Zen.2.45. **-ιον,** *proverbium*, *Gloss.* **-ιώδης,** ες, *proverbial*, Plu.2.302b, 616c, Philostr.*VA*1.8. Adv. -δῶς Asp. *in EN* 160.23, Sch.Ar.*Pl.*287.

**πάροιμος,** ον, *by the road, neighbour*, Hsch.:—also **παροιμώσαντες·** ἐκτραπέντες τῆς ὁδοῦ, Id.

**παροιν-έω,** in the augm. tenses with double augm., impf. ἐπαρῴνουν D.23.114, 54.4, Men.*Pk.*410: aor. ἐπαρῴνησα X.*An.*5.8.4, *PSI*4.352.6 (iii B.C.), Luc.*Symp.*2: pf. πεπαρῴνηκα Henioch.5.18, Aeschin. 2.154 (παρῴνηκα dub. in Phld.*Mort.*38):—Pass., aor. ἐπαρῳνήθην D.22.63: pf. πεπαρῴνημαι *PCair.Zen.*288 (iii B.C.), Luc.*JTr.*14, cf. Moer.p.332 P.: used only in Com. and Prose:—*behave ill at wine, play drunken tricks*, Ar.*Ec.*143, Antipho 4.1.7, Lys.3.19, etc.; οὐ νήφοντα δεῖ παροινεῖν Antiph.40.2; οὐχ οἱ σφόδρα μεθύοντες παροινοῦσιν, ἀλλ' οἱ ἀκροθώρακες Arist.*Pr.*871$^{a}$8, cf. 875$^{a}$29, X.l.c.; εἴς τινα towards one, Ar.*Fr.*249 (prob.), Antipho 4.1.6, D.54.4: so, generally, *insult, maltreat*, *PEleph.*12.2 (iii B.C.), Lxx *Is.*41.12; εἰς ἱκέτας Phld.*Ir.*p.35 W.; εἰς αὐτόν D.23.114; *revile, abuse*, εἰς τοὺς τετελευτηκότας Stob.4.57 tit.:—Pass., π. εἰς τὸ σῶμα Phalar.*Ep.*121.3. **2.** *act like a drunken man*, Plu.*Alc.*38, etc.; παροινήσας *in a drunken fit*, Pl.*Euthphr.* 4c. **II.** trans., *treat with drunken violence*, *PSI* l.c.:—Pass., *to be so treated*, D.19.198; ὑπό τινων Id.54.5. **2.** generally, *maltreat, do violence to*, λῃσταὶ παροινήσαντες ἡμᾶς *PCair.Zen.*659.5 (iii B.C.), cf. D.S. 28.5:—Pass., *to be insulted*, *PCair.Zen.*288, 462.8 (iii B.C.). **-ημα,** ατος, τό, *drunkard's butt*, Plu.2.350c, Longus 4.19. ⊛ **-ία,** ἡ, *drunken behaviour*, Lys.1.45, X.*Smp.*6.1 sq., Amphis 29, D.10.198, Aeschin. 1.61; π. εἰς γυναῖκα ἐλευθέραν Id.2.4. **-ιάζω,** = παροινέω, Hsch. **-ικός,** ή, όν, *addicted to wine, drunken*: Sup. -ώτατος Ar.*V.*1300. ⊛ **-ιος,** ον, f.l. for πάροινος, Id.*Ach.*981. **II.** *befitting a drinking party*, ὄρχησις Ath.14.629e, cf. Luc.*Salt.*34; ἀγών Ph.1.353; π. ᾠδαί, μέλη, *drinking* songs, Sch.Ar.*V.*1217, 1231; τὰ Πραξίλλης παροίνια *drinking songs*, ib.1232; τρυφερὰ καὶ π. γράφειν Plu.*Dem.*4. **-ος,** ον, = παροινικός, Pratin.Lyr.1.8, Lys.4.8, Antiph. 146, etc.; μάχαι π. *Anacreont.*40.12; τὸ σὸν π. Men.*Pk.*444. Adv. -νως Poll.6.21. **II.** = παροίνιος II, ὄρχησις Ath.14.629e.

**παροινοχοέω,** *pour out wine ready for* one, Q.S.4.279.

**πάροιος·** πρᾷος, Hsch.

**παροιστρ-άω,** and **-έω,** = οἰστράω, ὡς δάμαλις παροιστρῶσα παροίστρησεν Ἰσραήλ Lxx *Ho.*4.16, cf. *Ez.*2.6, D.S.34/5.28$^{a}$. **II.** trans., *provoke, incite*, μαινάδων ἐπ' αὐτὸν χοροὺς παρῴστρησεν Pap. in Gercke-Norden *Einleitung*$^{3}$ 1(9)p.42, cf. Hsch.:—Pass., ὑπὸ [δαιμόνων] παροιστρούμενοι Jul.*Ep.*89b. **-ησις,** εως, ἡ, *frenzy, madness*, *PMag.Par.*1.2489, Tz.*H.*10.53. **-ος,** ον, *frenzied, frantic*, ἐπιθυμία, φαντασίαι, Simp. *in Epict.*pp.78, 20 D.

⊛ **πᾰροίτερος,** η, ον, Comp. Adj., (πάροιθε) *before* or *in front*, Il.23.459, 480: c. gen., *in front of*, A.R.4.982. Adv. παροιτέρω *beyond, further than*, Id.3.686. **2.** of Time, *former*: neut. pl. παροίτερα *of old*, Euph. 34. **II.** Sup. **πᾰροίτατος,** η, ον, *first, foremost*, A.R.1.910, 2.29.

**παροίχησις,** εως, ἡ, *departure*, Tz.*H.*8.430.

⊛ **παροίχομαι,** fut. -οιχήσομαι: pf. παρῴχηκα, Ion. παροίχωκα, and in later writers παρῴχημαι, *Act.Ap.*14.16, J.*AJ*8.12.3; also in X.*An.* 2.4.1, but with v.l. παροιχομένων:—*to have passed by*, παρῴχετο γηθόσυνος κῆρ *he passed on, went on his way*, Il.4.272. **2.** of Time, *to be past*, παροίχωκεν (v.l. παρῴχηκεν) δὲ πλέων νύξ 10.252; ἡ παροιχομένη νύξ the *by-gone* night, Hdt.1.209, 9.58; ὁ π. χρόνος Id.2.14; Ὀλύμπια παροιχώκεε Id.8.72; παροιχόμενοι ἀνέρες men *of by-gone times*, Pi.*N.* 6.29 (dub. l.); δεῖμα παροιχόμενον Id.*I.*8(7).12; τὰ παροιχόμενα κακά X.*HG*1.4.17; τὰ παροιχόμενα *the past*, *IG*1$^{2}$.90.15, Hdt.7.120, cf. X.*An.*2.4.1; also, *the aforesaid*, Hp.*Fract.*14; τοὔστρακον παροίχεται the danger of ostracism *has gone by*, Cratin.71. **3.** Gramm., ὁ παρῳχημένος [χρόνος] *past* tense, A.D.*Adv.*123.17, Plu.2.1081c; παρῳχημέναι φωναί forms *of past tenses*, A.D.*Synt.*272.5. **II.** *to be gone, dead*, δείματι with fright, A.*Supp.*738 (lyr.); ὅσον παροίχῃ how *art thou fallen*, E.*Med.*995 (lyr.). **III.** c. gen., *shrink from*, νείκους τοῦδε A.*Supp.*452; later, *neglect*, τῶν πραγμάτων *BGU*288.2 (ii A.D.).

**παροκλάζω,** = ὀκλάζω, Tim. Gaz. in Ar. Byz. *Epit.*147.11, Hsch., Phot., Suid.

**παροκωχή,** ἡ, (παρέχω) *supplying, furnishing*, νεῶν Th.6.85 (ap. Phot., Suid.; παροχή codd.); γνωμῶν J.*AJ*17.9.5 (v.l. παρακωχή).

**παρολῐγωρ-έω,** *neglect, disregard*, X.*HG*7.4.13, Plb.4.46.6, etc.:—Pass., *to be neglected*, Pl.*Epin.*991d, Plb.5.27.6, Phld.*Ir.*p.42 W., Ph. 2.319. **-ητέον,** *one must disregard*, Plb.5.21.7.

**παρολισθ-άνω,** later **-αίνω,** Apollod.*Poliorc.*154.4:—*slip aside*, ἐς τὸ πλάγιον Hp.*Art.*16; *slip in*, εἰς ἔντερα Dsc.*Alex.*11, cf. Plu.2.698c, 701b, Luc.*Laps.*15. **II.** *make a mistake*, Plb.31.31.1.

⊛ **παρολκ-ή,** ἡ, (παρέλκω) *spinning out of time, delay*, J.*AJ*16.11.8, Charito 1.5, 12, etc.; π. χρόνου Porph.*Abst.*1.45; *retardation*, *Theol. Ar.*52; ἡ π. τῆς βραδυτῆτος Alciphr.1.22; παρολκῇ τῆς ἀγγελίας Hld. 6.5; π. εὐχῆς Id.5.34. **II.** Gramm., *redundancy*, ἐν π. εἶναι A.D.*Synt.*327.4, cf. *Adv.*207.4 (pl.); so in Logic, κατὰ παρολκήν *Stoic.* 2.79. **III.** *overdue payment*, *POxy.*997 (iv A.D., pl.). **-ημα,** ατος, τό, *towing* of vessels, *Ostr.*1153 (pl.). ⊛ **-ος,** ὁ, *tow-rope*, *Ostr. Bodl.* ii 72 (ii A.D.), *PLond.*3.1164$^{h}$10 (iii A.D.), Sch.Th.4.25. **II.** Adj., = *lentus*, *Gloss.*

**παρόλου,** = διόλου, Porph.*Gaur.*10.4.

**παρομαρτέω,** *accompany*, Plu.*Ant.*26, Aret.*SA*2.2, Jul.*Caes.*312c, etc.; πρεσβύτῃ χαλεπὰ π. Junc.ap.Stob.4.50.85; ἡ γοητεία προηγεῖται καὶ ἡ ἀναισχυντία π. Luc.*Tim.*55, cf. *Im.*9, Porph.*Abst.*2.49, *CPHerm.* 6.15 (iii A.D.).

**παρομοι-άζω,** *to be like*, τισι *Ev.Matt.*23.27. **-ος,** ον Th.1.80; fem. η Hdt.4.183; α Arist.*HA*616$^{a}$19, v.l. in Isoc.15.192:—*closely resembling*, τινι Hdt.2.73, Th.1.132; τινος Cyran.6. **2.** abs., Hdt. 4.99, Th.1.80; παρόμοιόν ἐστιν, ὅπερ καὶ.. D.1.11; π. ποιεῖν ὡσπερανεί τις.. Plu.2.4d. **3.** of numbers, *nearly equal*, π. τοῖς Ἕλλησι τὸν ἀριθμόν X.*HG*3.4.13. Adv. -ως Arist.*Resp.*478$^{b}$30. **4.** Gramm., *employing assonance*: π., τό, = παρομοίωσις, Rutil.2.12; κῶλα π. D.H.*Comp.*22, Demetr.*Eloc.*25. **-όω,** *compare, describe by a comparison*, τινά τινι Anon.*Geog.Comp.*53, Philum.*Ven.*35.1, Dion.Byz.109:—Pass., *assume the form of*, θεῷ ἢ θεᾷ *PMag.Leid.V.*2.2. **-ωσις,** εως, ἡ, *assimilation*, esp. of sounds in the ends of successive clauses, *assonance*, Arist.*Rh.*1410$^{a}$24, D.H.*Amm.*2.17 (pl.), *Lys.*14 (pl.). **2.** *comparison*, Arist.*Rh.Al.*1430$^{b}$0.

**παρομολογ-έω,** *grant* or *admit besides*: generally, = ὁμολογέω, Plb.3.89.3, 7.3.7:—so in Med., *PPetr.*3 p.129 (iii B.C.). **-ία,** ἡ, *partial admission*, a rhet. figure, Rutil.1.19, Quint.*Inst.*9.3.99. **2.** *agreement*, *OGI*607.7 (Syria, ii A.D.).

**παρόμφημα,** ατος, τό, (ὀμφή) = παρωνυμίασμα, Hsch. (-ώμφ- cod.).

**παρονειδίζω,** = ὀνειδίζω, τινι D.S.38/9.10, cf. Sch.Ar.*Nu.*543.

**παρονομ-άζω,** *call with a slight change of name*, Str.13.1.45:—Pass., *have one's name slightly changed*, Id.6.1.15; Ἀκτικὴν τὴν νῦν Ἀττικὴν παρονομασθεῖσαν Id.9.1.3. **2.** *form a derived name*, τὰ μὲν καινὰ ἔθεσαν, τὰ δὲ παρωνόμασαν Id.11.11.5, cf. Demetr.*Eloc.*97:—Pass., *to be named after*, παρωνομασμένον ἀπό τινος D.S.2.4, cf. Str.11. 2.15; *to be derived*, ἔκ τινος Plu.*Cic.*17; παρά τι A.D.*Adv.*148.11; ἔν τισι Id.*Pron.*3.17; ἀπό τινος Plot.6.1.9; but διὰ τὸ παρωνομάσθαι because of *the employment of* παρονομασία II.2, Hermog.*Id.*2.5. **II.** τῇ Τύχῃ τὴν ἀνδρείαν παρωνόμασεν *added the epithet 'virilis' to 'Fortuna'*, Plu.2.318f. ⊛ **-ᾰσία,** ἡ, *play upon words which sound alike*, but have different senses, *assonance*, Cic. *de Orat.*2.63.256, Rutil.1.3, Alex.*Fig.* 2.20, Hdn.*Fig.*p.95 S. **2.** *use of a word first in its proper, then in a derived sense*, Hermog.*Id.*2.5. **II.** *derivative*, Dionysodor.ap.A.D.*Pron.*3.16 (pl.); *by-name*, dub. in Ath.14.629c (pl.). ⊛ **-ᾰτοποιέω,** *form a derivative name*, Demetr.Lac.*Herc.*1014.56.

**παροξ-ίζω,** *have a somewhat sharp smell*, Dsc.1.19. **-ίς,** ίδος, ἡ, a measure, = $1\frac{1}{2}$ κεράτια, Gal.19.764. **-υντέον,** *one must make paroxytone*, Poll.1.55. **-υντής,** οῦ, ὁ, *stimulator*: hence οἱ τρεφόμενοι ὑπὸ τῶν ἑταίρων ὡς ἂν δὴ ἐρασταί, Hsch. ⊛ **-υντικός,** ή, όν, *fit for inciting* or *urging on*, εἴς τι X.*Cyr.*2.4.29; λόγοι π. πρός τι D.20.105; ἐπί τι Plu.*Pomp.*37. **2.** *exasperating, provoking*, Isoc.1.31: Medic., *aggravating* bad symptoms, Hp.*Prorrh.*1.50. Adv. -κῶς Plu.2.21a. **II.** *easily provoked*, τὸ π. τοῦ ἤθους Arist.*VV*1251$^{a}$8. **III.** π. ἡμέρα day *of the fit* in intermittent fevers, Gal. 7.340. **-ύνω,** pf. inf. παρωξυκέναι Plb.31.1.3, but παρωξυγκέναι J.*AJ*11.6.7:—Pass., pf. παρώξυμμαι Lys.4.8, Men.*Sam.*276:—*urge, spur on, stimulate*, τινα X.*Cyr.*6.2.5, etc.; [τινὰ] πρὸς τὰ καλά Id.*Mem.* 3.3.13; ἐπὶ τὸν πόλεμον Isoc.5.3, cf. Epicur.*Nat.*54 G.; τὰ ζεύγη πρὸς τὸ ἔργον Arist.*HA*577ᵇ31; τινα c. inf., Isoc.12.37; κινδυνεύειν X. *Mem*.3.5.3; opp. ἀποτρέπω, D.21.37. **2.** *provoke, irritate*, πατρὸς μὴ π. φρένας E.*Alc*.674; ξὺν κατηγορίᾳ π. Th.1.84:—Pass., *to be provoked*, τινι at a thing, Id.5.99; διά τινα Id.6.56; ἐπί τινι *OGI*48.15 (Egypt, iii B. C.), Plb.4.7.5; πρός τι X.*HG*6.4.6, D.57.2; πρὸς ἀλλήλους Arist.*Pol*.1302ᵃ39; ὑπό τινος Lys. l. c.; κατὰ τῶν πολιτῶν Plu. *Them*.31: c. dat., Lycurg.87 (s. v. l.), D.S.10.11: c. inf., τίς οὐκ ἂν παροξυνθείη πολεμεῖν; Isoc.5.101:—Pass., of sicknesses, *grow virulent*, π. οἱ πυρετοί Hp.*VM*6. **3.** *make* an application *stronger*, Gal.12.710. **II.** = παροξυτονέω, Ath.11.485a:—Pass., A.D.*Adv*.180.28, al., Gal.18(2).167, Ath.7.323c. **III.** intr., *hasten*, *Peripl.M.Rubr*.20. * **-υς**, υ, *pointed*, of a fractured bone, Hp.*Fract*.31. **II.** metaph., *precipitate*, Antiph.80.8. **-υσμός**, ὁ, *irritation, exasperation*, D.45.14, Lxx *Je*.39(32).37, *Act.Ap*.15.39; π. ἀγάπης *provoking* or *exciting to . .*, *Ep.Hebr*.10.24. **2.** *severe fit of a disease, paroxysm*, Hp.*Aph*.1.11,12, Gal.17(2).387, etc.

**παροξῠτον-έω**, *pronounce paroxytone*, Eust.1600.18 (Pass.):—hence **-ησις**, εως, ἡ, Id.1409.54, al. **-ητέον**, = παροξυντέον, Sch.Il. 21.279. **-ος**, ον, *paroxytone* (*with acute accent on the penultima*), Jo. Alex.τον.παραγγ.6. Adv. **-νως** Agatharch.6, Hermog.*Stat*.2, Ath. 9.409a.

**παροπαιδία**· εἶδός τι πήρας, Hsch.; **παροπαίδιον**· μικρὰ μάχαιρα, Id.

**παροπλ-ίζω**, pf. -ώπλικα D.S.4.10:—*disarm*, Plb.2.7.10, etc.:—Med., 2 sg. Ep. aor. -οπλίσσαιο Numen.ap.Ath.7.306c:—Pass., Plu. *Cat.Mi*.68. **-ισμός**, ὁ, *disarming*, D.S.33.4.

**παροπτ-άω**, *roast slightly, half-roast, toast*, Plb.12.25.2 (Pass.), Agatharch.47; as medical treatment, Herod.Med.ap.Orib.10.10. 2. **-έος**, α, ον, (παροράω, παρόψομαι) *to be overlooked*, Luc.*Tim*.9, Them.*Or*.26.326c. **II.** παροπτέον, *one must overlook*, τὸ γὰρ σύνηθες οὐδαμοῦ π. Men.53, cf. D.26.16. **-ησις**, εως, ἡ, *half-roasting* or *-baking*, Herod.Med.ap.Orib.10.10.4, Sor.2.15, Cael.Aur.*TP*3. 4. **-ος**, ον, *half-roasted*, Apic.6.9.6, Orib.*Fr*.128, *Gloss*.

**παρόρ-ᾰμα**, ατος, τό, *oversight, error*, Phld.*Sign*.29 (pl., *Rh.Mus*. 64.33), Plu.2.515e (pl.), 1123c, Procl.*in Prm*.p.556 S.; opp. ἁμάρτημα ἑκούσιον, Longin.33.4. **-ᾰσις**, εως, ἡ, *false vision*, Ruf.*Fr*.116 (pl.), Gal.7.99. **II.** *overlooking*, συγγνώμη καὶ π. Plu.*Arm*.3, cf. Lxx 2*Ma*.5.17, Luc.*Jud.Voc*.3, etc. **-ᾰτέον**, *one must overlook* or *disregard*, Onos.12.2, *Hippiatr*.14. **-ᾰτικός**, ή, όν, *apt to overlook*, τοῦ συμφέροντος Plu.2.716b. **-άω**, aor. παρεῖδον (q. v.): aor. Pass. παρώφθην D.10.8: pf. Pass. παρῶμμαι Men.207:—*look at by the way, notice, remark*, X.*Cyr*.7.1.5 codd.; τινί τι something in one, Hdt.1.37,108, Ar.*Av*.454. **II.** *look past*, i. e. *overlook* a thing, Arist.*HA*602ᵇ3 (Pass.), Macho ap.Ath.6.244d, etc. **2.** *disregard*, τοὺς νόμους Antipho 1.24, cf. X.*HG*7.4.21, D.18.161, etc.; cf. παρωθέω I. 1:—Pass., τυγχάνει παρεωραμένον Arist.*Metaph*.995ᵃ27, cf. Lxx *Ec*.12.14. **3.** *neglect*, ἐν οὐδενὶ τῶν συμφερόντων παρεωράκασι τὴν σύνοδον *SIG*704*E* 20 (Delph., ii B. C.). **4.** *concede*, *OGI*5.15 (Scepsis, iv B. C.), Phld. *Rh*.2.267 S. **III.** *see amiss, see wrong*, παρακούειν ἢ παρορᾶν Pl. *Tht*.157e, cf. *Hp.Ma*.300c. **IV.** *look sideways*, εἴς τινα or πρός τι, X.*Smp*.8.42, *Cyr*.7.1.4; εἰς τὸ πλάγιον π. μᾶλλον ἢ εἰς τὸ πρόσθεν Arist.*HA*630ᵇ1; ἐπὶ τὸν ἡγούμενον Ascl.*Tact*.12.11, Ael.*Tact*.42.1.

**παροργ-ίζω**, fut. -ιῶ Lxx *De*.32.21:—*provoke to anger*, Arist.*Ath*. 34.1, Lxx 3*Ki*.16.13,33, Ph.1.682, *Ep.Eph*.6.4. **II.** Pass., *to be* or *be made angry*, Thphr.*HP*9.16.6, prob. in Str.7.2.1; τι πρός τινας v. l. in D.26.17. **-ισμα**, ατος, τό, *provocation, cause of anger*, Lxx 3*Ki*.16.33, 20(21).22. **-ισμός**, ὁ, *provocation*: *anger*, ib.15.30, al., *Ep.Eph*.4.26.

**παρορέγω**, *stretch out beside*, Ael.*NA*1.4.

* **παρόρειος**, ον, (ὄρος) *near a mountain* or *mountains*, Str.12.8.13, J.*BJ*1.4.7:—written **παρόριος**, Sch.Il.20.490, 22.190.—The form παρώρειος found in codd. (as in Str. l. c.) is incorrect, whereas παρώρεια (q. v.) is the only correct form of the Subst.

**παρορέω**, *to be adjacent*, ἡ παροροῦσα χώρα τῷ ἱερῷ *SIG*685.78, cf. 40 (Crete, ii B. C.).

**παρόρθιος**, ον, *tolerably straight, not quite straight*, Apollod.*Poliorc*. 146.7, 154.4:—also **πάρορθος**, ον, ib.143.11.

**παρορία**, ἡ, *failure to preserve landmarks*, *SIG*679.76 (Magn. Mae., ii B. C.).

* **παρορίζω**, *limit, define*, Longin.2.2, 10.6. **II.** *outstep one's boundaries, encroach on a neighbour's property*, *AP*11.209 (Ammian.), *AB*293:—Pass., *have the boundaries extended*, *Inscr.Prien*.37.142, al. (ii B. C.); *have one's land encroached upon*, *BGU*615 iii 4 (ii/iii A. D.). **III.** Pass., *to be displaced*, Plu.2.353e.

**παρορίνω** [ῑ], *excite a little*, Alc.99.

* **παρόριος**, v. παρόρειος. **II.** (ὅρος) *on the border* or *edge*, Plu. 2.366b: c. dat., τῇ Αἰθιοπίᾳ *bordering on*, *OGI*168.57 (Syene, ii B. C.). **III.** (ὅρος) παρόρια, τά, *boundaries*, τῆς πόλεως *POxy*.1475. 22 (iii A. D.).

* **παρορ-ισμός**, ὁ, *removal of landmarks*, *SIG*742.43 (Ephesus, i B. C., pl.), *CPHerm*.40.5 (iii A. D.). **-ιστέον**, *one must set a limit*, Longin.38.1. **-ιστής**, οῦ, ὁ, *encroacher*, Lemma to *AP*11.209 (Ammian.).

* **παρορκέω**, *forswear oneself*, Philostr.*VA*5.35, App.*Gall*.19.

**παρορμ-άω**, *urge on, stimulate, incite*, τινα X.*Cyr*.2.4.10; εἰς τἀγαθόν ib.2.2.1; ἐπὶ τὰ καλὰ ἔργα ib.8.1.12; πρός τι Arist.*MM*1206ᵇ9, Phld.*Rh*.2.60 S.; εἰς ἀκολασίαν Id.*Mus*.p.35 K.: c. acc. rei, π. συνουσίαν Dsc.2.140, 3.129; ἀφροδίσια Id.1.16: c. inf., X.*Cyr*.8.1.43, Arist. *EN*1179ᵇ7:—Pass., *to be eager*, ἐπί τι Plb.2.22.6; ἐπ' ἀλλήλους D.C. 40.46; πρὸς τὸ φιλοδοξεῖν *OGI*339.91 (Sestus, ii B. C.):—intr. in Act., παρορμᾶν πρός τι D.L.6.83; παρορμῶντος τοῦ σώματος when the body *has started* (perspiring), Thphr.*Sud*.28. **-έω**, *lie at anchor beside* or *near*, D.S.14.49.50, *PFlor*.155.8 (iii A. D.); τινι Plu.*Ant*.32. **-ημα**, ατος, τό, *incitement, stimulant*, εἴς τι J.*AJ*17.12.1. **-ησις**, εως, ἡ, *urging on, incitement*, εἴς τι X.*Eq.Mag*.1.25, v. l. in *Cyr*.1.6.19, cf. Plb. 6.39.8, Phld.*Mus*.p.98 K., Andronic.Rhod.p.572 M.; ἐπί τι Iamb. *Protr*.5; τινος ib.1 (pl.). **-ητικός**, ή, όν, *stimulative*, Longin.14.3; πρὸς γάμον Plu.*Lyc*.15; π. ὀρέξεων, ἀφροδισίων, Xenocr.ap.Orib.2.58. 146, Dsc.2.110; π. ῥήματα verbs *denoting incitement*, A.D.*Synt*.289. 16. * **-ίζω**, *bring to anchor alongside the shore*, δύο πλοῖα Μουνυχίασιν Lys.13.25. **-ιστέον**, *one must moor beside*, Ph.*Bel*.100. 38.

**πάρορνῑς**, ῑθος, ὁ, ἡ, *having ill omens*, πόροι *ill-omened* voyages, A. *Eu*.770.

**παρόρνυμι**, *urge on*, παρὰ μητέρα μύθοις ὄρνυθι A.R.3.486.

**παρορύσσω**, Att. -ττω, *dig alongside* or *parallel*, τάφρον Th.6. 101. **II.** *dig one against another*, D.L.6.27:—Med., Arr.*Epict*.3. 15.4, Epict.*Ench*.29.2.

**παρορφνῖδωτός**, ή, όν, *with a black border*, χιτών *Schwyzer* 462 *B* 40 (Tanagra, iii B. C.).

**παρορχέομαι**, *represent in dancing out of season*, τὰς Διὸς γονὰς ὀρχούμενος . . καὶ τὴν τοῦ Κρόνου τεκνοφαγίαν π. Luc.*Salt*.80.

* **πάρος**, poet. Particle: **A.** Adv., **I.** of Time, *aforetime, formerly*, π. μεμαυῖα Il.4.73, etc.; κάρη π. χαρίεν 22.403; οὐ γὰρ ἐμὴ ἲς ἔσθ' οἵη π. ἔσκεν 11.669, cf. Od.2.119, etc.; opp. νῦν, 6.325, etc.; π. γε Il.17.270, etc.; π. περ Od.5.82, etc.: with the Art., τὸ π. γε, τὸ π. περ, Il.19.42, 23.480, etc.; once in Hdt., καὶ π. 9.2; never in Att. Prose (rarely later, *PPetr*.2 p.22 (iii B. C.), *POxy*.1121.36 (iii A. D.)), but freq. in Trag., θεοὶ οἱ π. A.*Pr*.406 (lyr.); τά τε π. τά τ' εἰσέπειτα S.*Aj*.34; ἐν τῷ π. χρόνῳ Id.*El*.1445, etc. **2.** with pres., *up to now, hitherto*, οἳ τὸ π. περ ζαχρηεῖς τελέθουσι Il.12.346; οἷος π. εὔχεαι εἶναι 4.264; π. γε μὲν οὔ τι θαμίζεις Od.5.88, cf. 4.810, Il.1.553. **3.** as Conj. like πρίν, *before*, c. aor. inf., πάρος τάδε ἔργα γενέσθαι 6. 348; πάρος ἣν γαῖαν ἱκέσθαι Od.1.21, cf. 8.376, etc.: rarely with pres., πάρος δόρποιο μέδεσθαι Il.18.245. **4.** with neg., as antec. to πρίν γε, π. δ' οὐκ ἔσσεται ἄλλως, πρίν γε . . *not until*, 5.218, cf. Od.2.127. **5.** *before the time, too soon*, τί π. λαβρεύεαι; Il.23.474. **6.** *rather, sooner*, π. τοι δαίμονα δώσω 8.166; π. τινὰ γαῖα καθέξει 16.629, cf. E. *Or*.345 (lyr.). **II.** rarely of Place, *first*, σοὶ βαδιστέον π. S.*El*.1502. **B.** Prep., poet. for πρό, **I.** of Place, *before*, once in Hom., Τυδεΐδαο π. Il.8.254; δωμάτων π. S.*Aj*.73, E.*Hec*.1049, *Ph*.1271; δόμων π. Id.*Or*.112, 1217; τῶν σῶν π. πίτνουσα γονάτων Id.*Andr*. 572. **II.** of Time, θανεῖν πάρος τέκνων ib.1208. **III.** *before, above*, π. τοὐμοῦ πόθου προὔθεντο τὴν τυραννίδα S.*OC*418. **2.** *instead of*, ἀδελφῶν πάρος . . θανεῖν E.*Heracl*.536.—When πάρος is a Prep. it usually follows its case, but not always, S.*OC*418, E.*Andr*.1112, 1208. (Cf. Skt. *purás* 'before'.)

**Πάρος** [ᾰ], ἡ, *Paros*, *h.Ap*.44, *Cer*.491:—Adj. * **Πάριος**, α, ον, Πάριος λίθος *Parian* marble, Pi.*N*.4.81, Hdt.3.57; ἡ Παρία λύγδος D.S.2. 52.

**πᾶρος**, τό, Aeol. for πῆρος.

**παρόσον**, = παρ' ὅσον, *in so far as*, S.E.*M*.7.419, al.; *inasmuch as*, Phld.*Sign*.12.

**παροσφραίνω**, *hold* for one *to smell*, τινί τι *Gp*.13.17.

**παροτρ-υντικός**, ή, όν, *fit for inciting*, εἰς μάχην Eust.1169. 55. **-ύνω**, *urge on*, c. inf., πὰρ θυμὸς ὀτρύνει φάμεν Pi.*O*.3.38, cf. *Act.Ap*.13.50, J.*AJ*7.6.1, Luc.*Tox*.35. **2.** Medic., *displace* the uterus, Hp.*Mul*.2.138.

**παρούα, παρούας**, v. παρείας.

**παρουάτιος** [ᾰτ], ον, (οὖς) *with hanging ears*, κύνες Call.*Dian*.91 (nisi leg. παρουαίους, = παρώους).

* **παρουλίς**, ίδος, ἡ, (οὐλή) *gumboil*, Cels.6.13.1, Gal.6.422, 7.731, Aët.8.26, Paul.Aeg.3.26.

**πάρουλος**, ον, (οὖλος B) *somewhat curled*, Poll.4.135.

**παρουλότρῐχος**, ον, *with slightly curling hair*, *Gp*.18.1.6.

**πάρουρος**, ὁ, (οὖρος B) *one who keeps watch beside*, v. l. in Od.11.489.

**πάρουρος**, ον, (οὐρά) *beside the tail*, Ptol.*Alm*.8.1, al.

* **παρουσ-ία**, ἡ, (πάρειμι) *presence*, of persons, δεσπότου, etc., A.*Pers*. 169, etc.; ἀνδρῶν π., = ἄνδρες οἱ παρόντες, E.*Alc*.606; πόλις μείζων τῆς ἡμετέρας π., = ἡμῶν τῶν παρόντων, Th.6.86; παρουσίαν μὲν οἶσθα . . φίλων, ὡς οὔτις ἡμῖν ἐστιν, i. e. that we have no friends *present* to assist us, S.*El*.948; of things, κακῶν E.*Hec*.227, Ar.*Th*.1049; ἀγαθῶν Pl.*Grg*.497e: abs., παρουσίαν ἔχειν, = παρεῖναι, S.*Aj*.540; τὰ τῆς τύχης . . κοινὰς [ἔχει] τὰς παρουσίας D.*Prooem*.39; αὐτὸ τὸ ἀγαθὸν [αἴτιον] τῇ π. τοῖς ἄλλοις τοῦ ἀγαθὰ εἶναι Arist.*EE*1217ᵇ5, cf. Pl.*Phd*. 100d, etc. **2.** *arrival*, ἡμῶν κοινόπουν π. S.*El*.1104, cf. E.*Alc*.209, Th.1.128; εἰς Ἰταλίαν D.H.1.45; esp. *visit* of a royal or official personage, βασιλέως, etc., *PTeb*.48.14 (ii B. C.), *IPE*1².32 *A* 85 (Olbia, iii B. C.), etc.; of a god, *IG*4²(1).122.34 (Epid.). **3.** *occasion*, v. l. in S. *El*.1251. **4.** π. τισὶ ποιεῖσθαι entertain them on their official *visits*, *OGI*139.9 (Philae, ii B. C.). **5.** in *NT*, *the Advent*, *Ev.Matt*.24.27, al. **6.** Astrol., *situation* of a planet at a point on the zodiac, ἤτοι κατὰ παρουσίαν ἢ κατὰ συμμαρτυρίαν Vett.Val.49.26. **II.** *substance, property*, ὡς . . ἔχομεν παρουσίας Pl.Com.177, cf. Men.471; π. χρημάτων Crates Com.16. **2.** *contribution* in money, Sch.Luc.*Phal*.1.3 (pl.). **-ιάζω**, *to be present*, Anon.*in EN*438.6.

**παροφθαλμιστής**, οῦ, ὁ, = *praestigiator*, *Gloss*.

* **παροχέομαι**, Pass., *sit beside in a chariot*, τινι X.*Cyr*.8.3.14, Luc. *DMar*.15.3, D.C.63.20.

**παροχέτ-ευσις**, εως, ἡ, *diversion, derivation*, Hp.*Hum.*1, Gal.16.149. ⊛ **-ευτέον**, *one must divert*, opp. ἀντισπαστέον, Aët.5.100. **-ευτικός**, ή, όν, *by diversion*, opp. ἀντισπαστικός, Gal.10.641. **-εύω**, *turn from its course, divert*, ὑφαιρουμένους τὸ ὕδωρ καὶ π. Plu.*Them.*31:—Med., εἰς ἑτέρους τὸ τῆς ἀρχῆς π. Id.2.779f: metaph., τοῦτ' αὖ παρωχέτευσας εὖ E.*Ba.*479; π. λόγοις Pl.*Lg.*844a:—Pass., *to be diverted*, Thphr.*CP*5.17.4.

**παροχεύομαι**, *copulate with other males*, Arist.*HA*613ᵃ7.

**παροχ-εύς**, έως, ὁ, *provider, purveyor*, πάσης τέχνης, of Hermes, Cyran.15, cf. Hdn.*Epim.*116; gloss on βραβεύς, Sch.E.*Or.*1650. **-ή**, ἡ, (παρέχω) *supply, furnishing*, νεῶν παροχῇ *with liability to furnish* ships, Th.6.85 (nisi leg. παροκωχῇ (q.v.)); βολίμου, ἐλάτας, etc., *IG*4²(1).103.109,102.25, al. (Epid.); αἱ τῶν ξενίων π., in the case of ambassadors, Plb.21.18.3; θυμάτων π. *IG*5(1).1390.64 (Andania, i B.C.), cf. *OGI*764.44 (Pergam., ii B.C.); χρημάτων παροχαί D.H.6.96: abs., Plb.32.13.2, Hippod.ap.Stob.4.1.94, Wilcken*Chr.*412.2 (ii A.D.). 2. *payment, furnishing*, *PLond.*3.1159.2 (ii A.D.), etc. **-ιον**, τό, *public guest-house*, *IGRom.*3.639 (Lycia, ii A.D.).

**παροχλ-έω**, *trouble besides*, Arist.*Ath.*16.7 (Pap.), Thphr.*CP*3.10.5. **-ίζω**, *move as with a lever, dislodge*, *AP*9.204 (Agath.).

⊛ **πάροχος** (A), ὁ, (ὄχος) *one who sits beside* another *in a chariot*, Hsch., Suid.; esp. of the groomsman in wedding ceremonies, hence of Ἔρως, Ζηνὸς π. γάμων τῆς τε.. Ἥρας Ar.*Av.*1740; π. καὶ νυμφαγωγὸς συμπαρέστη Luc.*Herod.*5.

**πάροχος** (B), ὁ, (παρέχω) *provider*, c. gen., Porph.*Abst.*2.12 (pl.): gloss on πρόξενος, Sch.Ar.*Pl.*182. II. π., οἱ, in the Roman provinces, *those who supplied public officers* with necessaries, Hor.*Sat.*1.5.46, cf. *IG*5(1).209.30 (Sparta, i B.C.): metaph., Cic.*Att.*13.2a.2.

**παροψ-άομαι**, *eat dainties*, Luc.*Merc.Cond.*26. **-ημα**, ατος, τό, *dainty side-dish*, Ath.9.367c; παροψήματα τῶν ἀμπέλων, i.e. other fruits planted among the vines, Philostr.*Her.Prooem.*1:—Dim. **-ημάτιον**, τό, Poll.6.56. **-ίδιον**, τό, Dim. of sq., *PGiss.*77.13 (ii A.D.). **-ίς**, ίδος, ἡ, (ὄψον) = παρόψημα, Pherecr.147, Ar.*Fr.*187, al., X.*Cyr.*1.3.4: metaph., τῶν κακῶν παροψίδες *fresh tastes* of misery, Magn.2. II. *dish on which such meats are served*, Antiph.60, Alex.86, Archestr.*Fr.*6, *Ev.Matt.*23.25, Juv.3.142, Artem.1.74 (παραψ- codd., cf. Hsch.). (The second use is condemned by Phryn.153.) **-ωνέω**, *buy dainties*, Cratin.92, Ar.*Ec.*226. **-ώνημα**, ατος, τό, *addition to the regular fare, dainty*: metaph., εὐνῆς π. τῆς ἐμῆς χλιδῆς *a new relish* to the pleasures of my bed, A.*Ag.*1447.

**παρόω**, v. πηρόω. **πάρπᾰγος**, ὁ, = πάρδαπαγος, Hsch.

**Πάρπαρος**· ἐν ᾧ ἀγὼν ἤγετο καὶ χοροὶ ἵσταντο, Hsch. (name of a mountain in Argolis):—hence **Παρπαρώνια**, τά, festival held there, *IG*5(1).213.44 (Sparta, v B.C.). II. **Παρπάρων**, ωνος, ὁ, name of a place in Aeolis, Apollod.*Fr.Hist.*7 J.:—hence **Παρπαρώνιος**, ὁ, a citizen of it, St.Byz.; also **Παρπαριώτης**, ου, ὁ, *IG*1².195.8.

**παρπεπῐθών**, Ep. redupl. aor. 2 part. of παραπείθω. **παρπόδιος**, ον, poet. for παραπόδιος. **παρπόρφυρος**, = παραπόρφυρος, *IG*7.2421 (Thebes):—also **παρπόρφουρος**, *Schwyzer*462*B*39 (Tanagra, iii B.C.). **παρράλιος** [ᾰλ], η, ον, Ep. for παράλιος, A.R.4.1560, v.l. in D.P.253. **παρρέκτης**, ου, ὁ, = πανοῦργος, Hsch.

⊛ **παρρησί-α**, ἡ, (πᾶς, ῥῆσις) *outspokenness, frankness, freedom of speech*, claimed by the Athenians as their privilege, ἐλεύθεροι παρρησίᾳ θάλλοντες οἰκοῖεν πόλιν κλεινῶν Ἀθηνῶν E.*Hipp.*422, cf. *Ion*672; παρρησίᾳ φράζειν Id.*Ba.*668; ἔχειν π. Id.*Ph.*391; οὔσης παρρησίας Ar.*Th.*541; διδόναι π. τισί Isoc.2.28; ἐλευθερίας ἡ πόλις μεστὴ καὶ π. γίγνεται Pl.*R.*557b; τἀληθῆ μετὰ παρρησίας ἐρῶ D.6.31; τὴν ὑπὲρ τῶν δικαίων π. ἀποδόμενος Din.2.1; δημοκρατίας οὔσης οὐκ ἔστι π. Isoc.8.14; π. καὶ ἰσηγορία καὶ δημοκρατία Plb.2.38.6; περὶ παρρησίας, title of work by Philodemus. 2. in bad sense, *licence of tongue*, ἡ εἰς τοὺς θεοὺς π. Isoc.11.40, cf. Pl.*Phdr.*240e, Cic.*Att.*1.16.8. 3. *freedom of action*, Aristaenet.2.7; π. ζωῆς καὶ θανάτου *power* of life and death, Vett.Val.6.3, al.; *licence, permission*, Just.*Nov.*1.1.1; παρρησίᾳ ἐκτέμνεται τὸ δέρμα *without fear*, Aët.15.8; ἤγαγον ὑμᾶς μετὰ παρρησίας *openly*, Lxx *Le.*26.13. 4. *liberality, lavishness*, κεκόσμηκε τὸν αὐτοῦ βίον τῇ καλλίστῃ π. *OGI*323.10 (Pergam., ii B.C.); ἐπὶ τῇ.. τῶν καμάτων καὶ πάσης ἐπιμελείας παρρησίᾳ *IG*5(1).547 (Sparta, iii A.D.); = *copia, Gloss.* **-άζομαι**, fut. -άσομαι Pl.*Chrm.*156a, etc. (but παρρησιασθήσομαι Lxx *Jb.*22.26): aor. ἐπαρρησιασάμην Isoc.11.1, dub. in Aeschin.1.80: pf. (v. infr.): used only in Prose:—*speak freely, openly*, Pl.*Grg.*487d; τι ib.491e, cf. Aeschin. l.c.; πρὸς ὑμᾶς Pl.*La.*178a, etc.; τινὶ περί τινος Id.*Chrm.*156a, D.18.177; πολλὰ κατά τινος Plb.12.13.8: pf. πεπαρρησίασμαι in act. sense, ἃ γιγνώσκω πάνθ' ἁπλῶς.. πεπ. D.4.51, cf. Plb. l.c.; but τὰ πεπαρρησιασμένα in pass. sense, *free expressions*, Isoc.15.10; -ασμέναι φωναί Phld.*Lib.*p.4 O.:—once in Act., ib.p.58 O. **-αστής**, οῦ, ὁ, *outspoken person*, Arist.*EN* 1124ᵇ29, Phld.*Lib.*p.62 O. (pl.), D.S.14.5, Luc.*Deor.Conc.*3. **-αστικός**, ή, όν, *outspoken*, Arist.*Rh.*1382ᵇ20, Phld.*Ir.*p.74 W. Adv. -κῶς M.Ant.6.30: Comp. -ώτερον J.*BJ*2.21.4. **-ώδης**, ες, *outspoken*: Comp. Adv. -έστερον D.S.15.6.

**παρσᾶς**, ὁ, dub. sens. in *PFlor.*71.76,122 (iv A.D.).

**παρσένος**, Lacon. for παρθένος, Alcm.1, Ar.*Lys.*1263 (lyr.).

**παρσουλακίρ**· τρίβων, Hsch. (Lacon. for *παραθυλακίς).

**παρσταίη, παρστᾶσα**, etc., Ep. for παραστ-. **παρστήετον**, Ep. 2 dual subj. aor. 2 of παρίστημι, Od.18.183. **πάρταξον**· ὕγρανον (Lacon.), Hsch. **παρτέμνω, παρτᾰμεῖν, παρτιθεῖ**, Ep. for παρατ-. **παρτομίς**, ίδος, ἡ, *small book*, Id.

**παρυβρίζομαι**, *insult*, Salač & Škorpil *Několik Archeol. Památek v Vychodniho Bulharska* p.57 (Mesembria).

**παρυγρ-αίνω**, *moisten* or *soften a little*, Herod.Med.ap.Orib.5.27.23, Ath.8.356e. II. Pass., *to be relaxed*, of the bowels, Sor.1.122, Mnesith.ap.Orib.*inc.*19.5. **-ος**, ον, *somewhat wet*, Man.1.87 (leg. πάνυγρος); τὸ π. a kind of *plaster* invented by Heras, Gal.2.703, 13.952; also ἡ π. Orib.*Fr.*90. II. πάρυγρα πράσσοντες plying *waterside* trades, Vett.Val.2.6.

**πάρυδρος**, ον, *living near water*, of the halcyon, Arist.*HA*593ᵇ8; of water-plants, Thphr.*HP*4.12.4.

**παρῡλ-ίζω**, *make dykes with brushwood*, *BGU*14 iii 1,9 (iii A.D.):—hence Subst. **-ισμός**, ὁ, τενάγους ib.13.

**παρυμνέω**, *celebrate unduly*, Aristid.2.157 J.

**παρυπ-αντάω**, *come into the way of, meet*, J.*BJ*1.31.4. ⊛ **-άρχω**, *attend*, π. τινὶ βοηθοί, σύμμαχοι, Sch.E.*Hec.*1041, *Or.*579.

**παρῠπάτη** [πᾰ] (sc. χορδή), ἡ, *string next the* ὑπάτη (q.v.), Arist.*Pr.*917ᵇ30, Plu.2.1134f, etc.

**παρῠπᾰτοειδής**, ές, of a note in music, *sounding like the* παρυπάτη, Aristid.Quint.1.6.

**παρυπνόω**, *sleep by* or *with*, τινι Q.S.10.128.

**παρυπο-γράφομαι** [γρᾰ], *subjoin*, Sch.E.*Or.*126. **-δύνω**, *insinuate, adapt oneself*, ὁμιλίᾳ Metrod.*Fr.*45. **-λαμβάνω**, *assume falsely*, Aristox.*Harm.*p.30 M. **-μιμνήσκω**, *record incidentally*, Plb.5.31.3; τινος Phld.*Vit.*p.24 J. **-μνησις**, εως, ἡ, *reminding by the way*, M.Ant.1.10. **-νοέω**, *suppose incidentally*, Phld.*Lib.*p.49 O.; *conclude as well*, Gal.16.537; *suspect besides*, Dam.*Pr.*118. **-στᾰσις**, εως, ἡ, *coordinate* or *parallel existence*, Porph.*Sent.*44 (pl.), Procl.*in R.*1.38 K., al.; *by-product*, ἐκτροπὴ καὶ π. ἐστι τοῦ κατὰ φύσιν τὸ παρὰ φύσιν Simp.*in Cael.*429.34, cf. *in Ph.*1262.8. **-ψύχω** [ῡ], *cool gently*, Dsc.2.85.

**παρυπτιάω**, of the stomach, *to be turned* (in nausea), Sor.1.36 (Pass.).

**παρῠφ-αίνω**, pf. παρύφαγκα Ph.Byz.*Mir.*2.5:—*weave beside* or *along*, ἐσθὴς παρυφασμένη a garment *with a purple hem* or *border* (παρυφή), D.S.12.21; παρυφασμένα ὅπλα armed men *hemming in* an unarmed crowd, X.*Cyr.*5.4.48; παρύφανται.. τῷ στομάχῳ.. πόρος *is set along its edge*, Arist.*HA*529ᵃ15, cf. *PA*676ᵇ21, *PPetr.*3 p.305 (iii B.C.). II. *excel in weaving*, τινα Philostr.*Im.*2.28. **-ασμα**, ατος, τό, = sq., Gal.18(2).776. **-ή**, ἡ, *border woven along* a robe, *IG*2².1514.29, Clearch.9, Phylarch.45 J., Plu.2.239c, Gal.18(2).791: metaph., π. κακῶν εἰργάσασθε Jul.*Gal.*238b. **-ής**, ές, *with a border*, παρυφές *bordered robe*, Ar.*Fr.*320.7, Poll.7.53, Phot. s.v. παράπηχυ:—also **-ίς**, ίδος, ἡ, Men.479, Poll.7.46.

**παρυφιζάνω**, *to be a concomitant*, of symptoms in disease, Sever.*Clyst.*p.3 D.

**παρυφίστημι**, *place close beside*:—pres. Act. only in form **παρυφιστάνω**, *indicate*, A.D.*Adv.*129.18: pf., *stand close beside*, παρυφέστηκε τῇ χρηστῇ παρασκευῇ εἴδωλον *Proll.Hermog.* in Rh.4.21 W. II. Pass., with aor. 2 -υπέστην, *subsist coordinately with*, τινι *Stoic.*2.48, S.E.*P.*1.205, D.L.9.105, Plot.2.9.14, Porph.*Sent.*43, Ascl.*in Metaph.*371.2: abs., Simp.*in Cat.*110.5. 2. *arise in consequence*, J.*AJ*15.8.4; παρυφιστάμενος φόβος *instinctive* dread, Herod.Med.ap.Orib.8.3.7; τὸ ἐξ ἑκάστης λέξεως παρυφιστάμενον νοητόν A.D.*Synt.*4.5; τὰ ποικίλως παρυφιστανόμενα ἐκ τῶν ῥημάτων ib.297.5. 3. τὸ παρυφιστάμενον *deposit* in urine, Gal.6.251 (pl.), 19.574.

⊛ **πάρφαινε, παρφάμενος, παρφάσθαι, παρφᾰσία, πάρφᾰσις, παρφέρομαι, παρφῠγέειν**, poet. for παραφ-.

**πάρφυκτος**, ον, poet. for *παράφ(ε)υκτος, *to be avoided*, τὸ μόρσιμον οὐ π. Pi.*P.*12.30.

**παρῴα**, ἡ, *hem, border*, Sor.1.83.

**παρῳάς**, v. παρειάς.

**παρῳδ-έω**, *write by way of parody*, D.L.4.52, Luc.*Cont.*14, etc.; π. ἐπί τινι τόδε τὸ ἐλεγεῖον Philostr.*VS*1.5; ἅπερ ἐκ τῶν Ἡσιόδου.. Ἠοίων πεπαρῴδηται Ath.8.364b, cf. Sch.Ar.*Pl.*253, etc. **-ή**, ἡ, = παρῳδία, Phld.*Hom.*p.53 O., Quint.*Inst.*9.2.35. **-ητέον**, *one must parody, burlesque*, τὰ ἔπη Eust.1423.2. **-ία**, ἡ, *burlesque, parody*, Ἡγήμων ὁ Θάσιος ὁ τὰς π. ποιήσας πρῶτος Arist.*Po.*1448ᵃ13, cf. Ath.15.698b. **-ικός**, ή, όν, *burlesque*, μέλη D.H.*Dem.*54 codd. ⊛ **-ός**, όν, (ᾠδή) *singing indirectly, obscurely hinting*, αἰνίγματα E.*IA*1147. II. Subst., *parodist*, such as Matro, Ath.1.5b; and Sopater, Id.4.158d. 2. *reciter of parodies*, *IG*12(9).189.11,19 (Eretria, iv B.C.).

⊛ **παρωθέω**, late aor. παρώθησα Lyd.*Mag.*2.28:—*push sideways*, ἐς χώρην Hp.*Art.*18; *push aside* or *away, reject*, Ἔρωτα S.*Tr.*358; δοῦλον λέχος E.*Andr.*30, cf. *El.*1037:—Pass., *to be set aside, slighted*, X.*HG*2.3.14; παρεῶσθαι καὶ ἐν οὐδενὸς εἶναι μέρει D.2.18, cf. 23.105 (in both places with v.l. παρεωρᾶσθαι). 2. *supersede*, Gal.14.2. 3. *surpass*, Lyd. l.c. II. Med., *push away from oneself, reject*, ξένους E.*Heracl.*237; ἄνδρα Aeschin.1.103, cf. Lxx 2*Ma.*4.11; π. [τὸν Δία] τῆς τιμῆς *put* him *out* of his place of honour, Luc.*Tim.*4; π. τὸ χρεὼν *put* fate *aside*, *Epigr.Gr.*519 (Thessalonica). 2. of Time, *put off*, Pl.*R.*471c. 3. Gramm., *not to admit of*, A.D.*Pron.*24.21, 115.16.

**παρωκεάν-ιος** [ᾱν], ον, *near* or *on the ocean*, Plu.*Caes.*20. **-ῖται**, οἱ, *dwellers near the ocean*, Theopomp.Hist.65, Str.17.3.19 and 24. **-ῖτις** (sc. γῆ), ἡ, *sea-coast*, Plb.34.5.6, Str.2.5.33, etc.:—Adj. **-ῑτικός**, ή, όν, Id.4.2.1, 4.3.1.

**παρωλένιος**, ον, *next the elbow, on the arm*, τὰ ἔνδον π. Poll.2.138; cf. παρωλένια· τῶν χειρῶν τὸ ὄπισθεν, Hsch.: **παρωλενίς**, ίδος, ἡ, dub. sens. in Demioprat.ap.Poll.10.170.

**παρωμᾰλος**, ον, *nearly even* or *equal*, Str.3.5.1.

**παρωμίς**, ίδος, ἡ, *shoulderstrap*, Lxx *Ex.*28.14.

**πᾰρών**, ῶνος, ὁ, a kind of *light ship*, Plb.*Fr.*193, Sch.Ar.*Pax* 142.

**παρωνῠμ-έω**, = παρωνυμιάζω, Eust.84.28 (Pass.), etc. 2. intr., *to be of like signification with*, τινι Ph.1.486, 2.39. 3. *to have a corresponding name*, τινι Iamb.*in Nic.*p.15 P. **-ησις**, εως, ἡ, *denomination*, ib.pp.46, 47 P. **-ία**, ἡ, *by-name, nickname*, Plu. 2.401a, 421e; *punning perversion of words*, ib.853b (pl.). 2. *alternative name*, Dam.*Pr.*61. **-ιάζω**, *call by a derived name*, Arist.*Ph.* 245$^{b}$11:—Pass., = παρωνύμως λέγεσθαι, Id.*EE* 1228$^{a}$35. **-ίασμα**, ατος, τό, *by-name*, Hsch. s.v. παρώμφημα. ⊛ **-ιος**, ον, *deviating from the sense, slightly altered in sense*, Pl.*Lg.*757d. II. as Subst. παρωνύμιον, τό, *name formed from another by a slight change, derivative*, Id.*Sph.*268c, Chrysipp.*Stoic.*3.198, A.D.*Adv.*160.3; in full, ὄνομα π. Id.*Conj.*253.22. 2. *surname*, *Sammelb.*3787.4; = Lat. *cognomen* or *agnomen*, Plu.*Num.*21, *Fab.*1. **-ος**, ον, *formed by a slight change, derivative*, Φοίβης ὄνομ' ἔχει παρώνυμον (sc. Φοῖβος) A.*Eu.*8, cf. Arist.*Cat.*1$^{a}$12. Adv. -μως, λέγεσθαι ἀπό τινος Id.*Top.*109$^{b}$5; ὁ θρασὺς παρὰ τὸ θράσος λέγεται π. Id.*EE* 1228$^{a}$36. II. Subst. παρώνυμον, τό, *by-name*, Pherecyd.25(*a*) J. 2. = παρωνύμιος II. 2, Plu.*Dem.*4; = Lat. *agnomen*, Dosith.p.390 K.

**παρωνῠχ-ία**, ἡ, *whitlow*, Hp.*Epid.*2.6.27, Plu.2.43b, al., Jul.*Gal.* 245d. II. *plant reputed to be a cure for whitlow*, Dsc.4.54, Gal.12. 96, Paul.Aeg.7.3. III. *trifle*, Plb.12.4$^{a}$.1. **-ίς**, ίδος, ἡ, = foreg. I, Hierocl.*Facet.*199, 200, *Gloss.*, v.l. in Paul.Aeg.7.3, interpol. in Suid.

**πάρῳον**, τό, = παρῴα, Gal.18(1).776.

**παρώπανος** (-όπ- cod.)· ἐμβρόντητος, Hsch.

**παρωπία**, ἡ, *corner of the eye* next the temple, Poll.2.71.

**παρώπια**, τά, *blinkers*, Poll.2.53, 10.54, Suid.

**παρωπίς**, ίδος, ἡ, *woman's mask*, Poll.2.53.

**παρωραϊσμός** and **-ωρισμός**, ὁ, *unseasonableness*, vv.ll. in Aq.*Is.* 24.7.

**παρώρεια**, ἡ, (ὄρος) *district on the side of a mountain*, Plb.2.14.6, Onos.21.3, Babr.19.1, etc.: pl., Plb.2.34.15: freq. as pr. n., *IPE* 1$^{2}$. 32 *B* 16 (Olbia, iii B.C.), Str.8.3.18, etc.:—hence **Παρωρεᾶται**, οἱ, Hdt.4.148; Ion. **Παρωρεῆται** Id.8.73.

**παρωρείτης**, ου, ὁ, *mountaineer*, Πάν *APl.*4.235 (Apollonid.).

**παρωρμημένως**, Adv. pf. part. Pass., (παρορμάω) *violently*, Hsch. and Phot. s.v. περιόργως.

**πάρωρος**, ον, (ὥρα) *out of season, untimely*, βλαστήσεις, καρποτοκίαι, Thphr.*CP*5.1.3: neut. πάρωρα as Adv., *AP*12.199 (Strat.). II. *beyond the proper time*, π. πρός τι *too old* for.., Epicur.*Ep.*3 p.59 U.

⊛ **παρωροφίς**, ίδος, ἡ, (ὄροφος) *projecting eaves* or *cornice* of a roof, Hdt.2.155, Poll.1.81.

**παρώτιον**, τό, *part of the* κανθός I, Sch.Nic.*Th.*673.

**παρωτίς**, ίδος, ἡ, (οὖς) *tumour of the parotid gland*, Dsc.2.80, Gal. 16.484, etc. 2. *lobe of the ear*, Lyc.1402. 3. *lock of hair* or *curl by the ear*, Poll.2.28. 4. Archit., = οὖς II. 2, *ornament depending from the end of the* ὑπέρθυρον, λίθοι παρωτίδες *Rev.Phil.*44.250 (Didyma, ii B.C.), cf. Vitr.4.6.4.

**παρῳχημένως**, Adv., (παροίχομαι) *in the past tense*, Sch.E.*Ph.*622.

**πάρωχρος**, ον, *rather pale, sallow*, Plu.2.364b, Poll.4.135, 137.

⊛ **πᾶς**, πᾶσα, πᾶν, Aeol. **παῖς**, παῖσα Sapph.*Supp.*13.8, 21.2, 20a.14, Alc.*Supp.*12.6, 25.8; Cret., Thess., Arc. fem. **πάνσα** *GDI*4976 (Gortyn), *IG*9(2).234.2 (Pharsalus, iii B.C.), 5(2).343.16 (Orchom. Arc., iv B.C.): gen. παντός, πάσης, παντός: gen. pl. masc. and neut. πάντων, fem. πασῶν, Ep. and Ion. πασέων, Ep. also πασάων [σᾱ] Od.6.107: dat. pl. masc. and neut. πᾶσι, Ep. and Delph. πάντεσσι Il.14.246, *IG*2$^{2}$.1126. 22, 44; also Locr. πάντεσιν *Berl.Sitzb.*1927.8 (v B.C.); Delph. πάντεσι *SIG*452.5 (iii B.C.); πάντοις *GDI*2652 (Delph., ii B.C.), *Tab.Defix.Aud.* 75.8: πᾶν as acc. masc. in LXX, π. ἄνδρα, οἰκέτην, οἶκον, 1 *Ki.*11.8, *Ex.* 12.44, *Je.*13.11. [Dor. and Aeol. πάν [ᾰ] Hdn.Gr.2.12, Pi.*O.*2.85, Sapph.*Oxy.*1787 *Fr.*3 ii 5, al., and Att. in compds., as ἅπᾰν, πάμπᾰν, etc. (but in compds. sts. long in Att., *AB*416).]—Coll. Pron., when used of a number, *all*; when of one only, *the whole*; of the several persons in a number, *every*. I. in pl., *all*, πάντες τε θεοὶ πᾶσαί τε θέαιναι Il.8.5, etc.; πάντες ὅσοι.. Od.1.11, etc.; πάντας ᾧ ἂν περιτυγχάνῃ, for ὅσοις ἄν, Pl.*R.*566d: also with the Art., v. infr. B. 2. strengthd. by Advbs., ἅμα πάντες *all* together, Il.24.253, etc.; πάντες ἅμα 1.495 (in Prose commonly ἅπαντες, but not always, v. Hdt.9.23, X.*Cyr.*1. 3.10, etc.): with a collect. noun, ἅμα πᾶς ὁ δῆμος D.H.2.14; πάντες ὁμῶς Il.15.98; ὁμοῦ πάντες S.*El.*715; πάντα μάλα Il.22.115, Od.5. 216, etc.; πάντες ὁμοίως D.20.85, etc. 3. with Sup., πάντες ἄριστοι *all the* noblest, Il.9.3, Od.4.272, etc. 4. *consisting* or *composed wholly of*, i.e. *nothing but, only*, φρουρούμενος ὑπὸ πάντων πολεμίων Pl. *R.*579b; ἐκ πασῶν δυνάμεων συνεστώς *Corp.Herm.*13.2; cf. II. 2. II. sg., *all, the whole*, πᾶς δ' ἄρα χαλκῷ λάμπε Il.11.65, cf. 13.191; πᾶσα ὕλη *all the* wood, Hes.*Op.*511, cf. *Th.*695, etc.; πᾶσα ἀληθείη *all the* truth, Il.24.407, Od.11.507; τὴν φάτνην ἐοῦσαν χαλκέην πᾶσαν *all* of bronze, Hdt.9.70; ἦν ἡ μάχη καρτερὰ καὶ ἐν χερσὶ πᾶσα, ἦν γὰρ τὸ χωρίον πρόσαντες πᾶν, Th.4.43, etc.; πᾶν κράτος *the whole* power, *sovereign* power, S.*Ph.*142 (lyr.); τὸ πᾶν κράτος Hdt.6.35; μετὰ πάσης ἀδείας D.18.305; πᾶσα ἀνάγκη Pl.*Phdr.*240a; πᾶσαι δ' ὠΐγνυντο πύλαι, πᾶσαι γὰρ ἐπῴχατο [πύλαι], the *whole* gate was open (shut), i.e. the gate was *wide* open, *quite* shut, Il.2.809, 12.340, as expld. by Aristarch.; v. infr. B. 2. as in I. 4, with attraction, ὁ πάντ' ἄναλκις οὗτος, ἡ πᾶσα βλάβη who is *nought but* mischief, S.*El.*301, cf. *Ph.*622, 927. III. *every*, οἱ δ' ἄλκιμον ἦτορ ἔχοντες..πᾶς πέτεται Il.16.265, cf. Od.13.313, S.*El.*972, E.*Ba.*1131, 1135; ἄκουε πᾶς, = ἀκούετε πάντες, Ar.*Th.*372; πᾶς χώρει Id.*Pax* 555: with partit. gen., παντὶ βροτῶν (v.l. βροτῷ) Pi.*O.*1.100; πᾶς τοῦτό γ' Ἑλλήνων θροεῖ S.*OC*597; τῶν ἀνθρώπων πᾶς D.Chr.3.70; also πᾶς ἀνήρ S.*Aj.* 1366, Ar.*Ra.*1125, etc.; πᾶσα ἀνθρώπου ψυχή Pl.*Phdr.*249e: with the Art., v. infr. B; πᾶς τις *every single* one, Thgn.621, Hdt.1.50, 3.79, S.*Aj.*28, etc.; πᾶς τις βροτῶν Id.*El.*984, cf. *OC*25, etc.; πᾶς ὅστις.. Id.*Aj.*1413; πᾶν ὅσον.. A.*Pr.*787, etc. 2. less freq., *any one*, τὸ μὲν ἐπιτιμᾶν..φήσαι τις ἂν..παντὸς εἶναι D.1.16; παντὸς ἀνδρὸς [ἐστι] γνῶναι Pl.*Ion* 532e; χαλεπόν τι καὶ οὐχὶ παντός Id.*Alc.*1.129a; παντὸς ἀκούοντος.. when *any one* hears.., *Ev.Matt.*13.19; ἀμήχανον δὲ παντὸς ἀνδρὸς ἐκμαθεῖν ψυχήν *any* man's soul, S.*Ant.*175; πάντων ἀποστερεῖσθαι λυπηρόν to be deprived of *anything*, D.18.5; cf. D. III. 2, VI.

B. with the Art., in the sense of *all, the whole*, when the Subst. is to be strongly specified, πᾶς being put either before the Art. or after the Subst., πᾶσαν τὴν δύναμιν *all his* force, Hdt.1.214; τὰ ἀγαθὰ πάντα X.*An.*3.1.20 (s.v.l.): with abstract Nouns and others which require the Art., πάντα τὰ μέλλοντα A.*Pr.*101; πᾶσαν τὴν ἀλήθειαν Th.6.87; τὰ τῆς πόλεως π. *all* the affairs of state, Lys.19.48, etc.: emphatically, τὰς νέας τὰς πάσας Hdt.7.59. II. πᾶς is put between the Art. and Subst., to denote totality (v. A. II), ὁ πᾶς ἀριθμός A.*Pers.*339; τὴν πᾶσαν ἵππον Hdt.1.80; τὸ πᾶν πλῆθος Th.8.93; οἱ πάντες ἄνθρωποι *absolutely all*.., X.*An.*5.6.7, etc.; so πᾶν the neut. with the Art. itself becomes a Subst., τὸ πᾶν *the whole*, A.*Pr.*275, 456, etc., v. infr. D. IV; τὰ πάντα *the whole*, Id.*Eu.*415; τοῖς πᾶσιν *in all points*, Th.2.64, 5.28; οἱ πάντες *all of them*, Hdt.1.80; but also, *the community*, opp. οἱ ὀλίγοι, Th.4.86; ἡ μὲν [τάξις] πάντα ἕν, ἡ δὲ πάντα ὅλον, ἡ δὲ πάντα πᾶν *all things* as a unity, as a totality, as an *integral sum*, Dam.*Pr.* 206.

C. with Numerals to mark an exact number, ἐννέα πάντες *full* nine, Od.8.258, cf. 24.60; ἐννέα πάντ' ἔτεα Hes.*Th.*803; δέκα πάντα τάλαντα Il.19.247, etc.; but κτήνεα τὰ θύσιμα πάντα τρισχίλια ἔθυσε 3,000 *of all kinds*, Hdt.1.50; τὸν ἀρχιτέκτονα..ἐδωρήσατο πᾶσι δέκα with ten presents *of all kinds*, Id.4.88; Πανσανίῃ πάντα δέκα ἐξαιρέθη Id.9.81; τὰ πάντα μυρία Id.3.74; πάντα θύειν ἑκατόν Pi.*Fr.*170; πάντα χίλια ἔθυεν Porph.*Abst.*2.60. II. with the Art., *in all*, οἱ πάντες... εἷς καὶ ἐνενήκοντα Hdt.9.70, cf. 1.214, Th.1.60, 3.85, etc.; τριήρεις... τὰς πάσας ἐς διακοσίας Id.1.100, cf. 7.1; ἐν εἴκοσι ταῖς πάσαις ἡμέραις Arr.*An.*1.11.5.

D. Special Usages: in dat. pl. masc. πᾶσι, *with* or *in the judgement of all*, Il.2.285, S.*OC*1446; ὁ πᾶσι κλεινός Id.*OT*8; κράτιστον πᾶσιν Οἰδίπου κάρα ib.40. 2. fem. pl., ἔδοξε πάσαις (sc. ταῖς ψήφοις) carried *unanimously*, *IG*12(3).168.14 (Astypalaea, ii/i B.C.), cf. Luc. *Bis Acc.*18, 22. II. neut. pl. πάντα *all kinds of things*, Hom., freq. in phrase δαίδαλα πάντα, Il.5.60, al.; οἰωνοῖσι πᾶσι 1.5. 2. πάντα γιγνόμενος becoming *all things*, i.e. assuming every shape, Od.4. 417. 3. πάντα εἶναί τινι to be *everything* to one, ἦν οἱ..τὰ πάντα ἡ Κυνώ Hdt.1.122; ἦσάν οἱ πάντα (ἅπαντα codd.) αἱ Συρήκουσαι Id.7. 156; Εὔβοια αὐτοῖς πάντα ἦν Th.8.95; πάντ' ἐκεῖνος ἦν αὐτοῖς D.18. 43; π. ἦν Ἀλέξανδρος (sc. ὑμῖν) Id.23.120; π. εἶναι ἔν τισι to be *all in all* among them, Hdt.3.157. 4. πάντα as Adv. for πάντως, *in all points, entirely, wholly*, π. νοήμονες Od.13.209; π. γὰρ οὐ κακός εἰμι 8.214; ὁ πάντ' ἄναλκις S.*El.*301; τῷ πάντ' ἀγαθῷ Id.*Aj.*1415 (anap.); τὸν πάντ' ἄριστον Id.*OC*1458; πάντ' ἐπιστήμης πλέων Id. *Ant.*721 (hence παντάγαθος, παντάριστος, etc. as compd. words); τὰ πολλὰ π. *almost throughout*, Hdt.5.67, cf. 1.203, 2.35; but τὰ π. *in every way, by all means, altogether*, Id.5.97; οἰόμενοι τὰ π. νικᾶν X. *An.*2.1.1; ὁ τὰ π. φιλαίτατος Theoc.7.98; also ἐς τὰ π. Th.4.81; κατὰ π. ibid., Pl.*Ti.*30d. III. neut. sg., τὸ πᾶν *the whole* (v. B. II), περὶ τοῦ π. δρόμον θέειν Hdt.8.74; πολλοῦ γε καὶ τοῦ π. ἐλλείπω A. *Pr.*961; τοῦ π. ἡμαρτηκέναι Pl.*Phdr.*235e; ἄξιοι τοῦ π. Id.*Sph.*216c; τὸ πᾶν as Adv., *completely, altogether*, A.*Supp.*781 (lyr.), S.*El.*1009, Pl.*Lg.*959a, etc. (but, *for all that, nevertheless*, A.D.*Synt.*188.27): with neg., *at all*, οὐκ ἠξίωσαν οὐδὲ προσβλέψαι τὸ πᾶν A.*Pr.*217, etc.; also πᾶν alone, Hdt.1.32, etc. b. in Philos., τὸ πᾶν *the universe*, Emp.13, Pythag.ap.Arist.*Cael.*268$^{a}$11, Pl.*Ti.*28c, 30b, etc.; including τὸ κενόν (opp. τὸ ὅλον), *Placit.*2.1.7; also, Pythag. name for *ten*, Iamb.*in Nic.*p.118 P., *Theol.Ar.*59. c. τῷ παντί *in every point, altogether*, X.*HG*7.5.12, etc. d. τὸ π., = μολυβδόχαλκος, Ps.-Democr. Alch.p.56 B., Maria ap.Zos.Alch.p.192 B. 2. πᾶν *anything*, πᾶν μᾶλλον ἢ στρατιήν οἱ ἐδίδου Hdt.4.162; εἴη δ' ἂν πᾶν *anything* is possible, ib.195; πᾶν ποιῶν by *any* means *whatever*, Pl.*Ap.*39a (also πᾶν ποιεῖν καὶ λέγειν ibid.; πᾶν ποιεῖν ὥστε.. Id.*Phd.*114c), cf. Pi.*I.* 4(3).48; πᾶν ἂν ἔπραξαν Lys.9.16: more freq. in pl., πάντα ποιῶν Id. 12.84, D.21.2; π. ποιεῖν ὅπως.. X.*HG*7.4.21; πάντα τολμῶν S.*OC* 761; cf. A. III. 2. 3. ἐπὶ πᾶν *on the whole, in general*, Pl.*Lg.* 875d; ὡς ἐπὶ πᾶν εἰπεῖν Id.*Euthd.*279e, etc.; τὸ πρὸς ἅπαν ξυνετὸν ἐπὶ πᾶν ἀργόν Th.3.82. 4. παντὸς μᾶλλον more than *anything*, i.e. *above all*, Pl.*Cri.*49b, *Prt.*344b, *Grg.*527b; π. μᾶλλον οὐ Id.*Phdr.*228d: in answers, π. γε μᾶλλον *quite so*, Id.*Phd.*67b. IV. with Preps., εἰς πᾶν προελήλυθε μοχθηρίας D.3.3; ἐς τὸ πᾶν *altogether*, A.*Ag.*682 (lyr.), *Eu.*52, 83; ἐν παντὶ ἀθυμίας εἶναι to be in *utter* despair, Th.7.55: more freq. ἐν παντὶ εἶναι, ἐν παντὶ κακοῦ εἶναι, to be in *great* danger or fear, Pl.*Smp.*194a, *R.*579b; ἐν π. γενέσθαι Id.*Euthd.*301a; ἐμ παντὶ ἐοῦσα *IG*4$^{2}$(1).122.27 (Epid., iv B.C.); ἐν παντὶ εἶναι μή.. to be *in great fear* lest.., X.*HG*5.4.29; ἐς πᾶν κακοῦ ἀπίκατο Hdt.7.118; ἐς πᾶν ἀφικέσθαι X.*HG*6.1.12; εἰς πᾶν ἐλθεῖν D.54.13; ἐπὶ πᾶσιν in *all things*, καιρὸς δ' ἐπὶ π. ἄριστος Hes.*Op.*694; but also, *finally*, Philostr.*VS*2.11. 1, al.; περὶ παντὸς ποιεῖσθαι esteem above *all*, X.*HG*7.1.26, *An.*1.9. 16; πρὸ παντὸς εὔχεσθαι wish above *all*, Pl.*Phdr.*239e; διὰ παντός (sc. χρόνου) *for ever, continually*, S.*Aj.*705 (lyr.), Th.1.38, etc.; also, *altogether*, Pl.*R.*407d; διὰ πάντων Id.*Sph.*254b; ὁ κατὰ πάντων λόγος the *common* formula, *PMag.Par.*1.2186; ἡ κ. π. τελετή ib.1596, *PMag.Lond.*121.872; μέχρι παντὸς *for ever*, Str.8.6.18; εἰς τὸ πᾶν ἀεί A.*Ch.*684; ἐς τὸ πᾶν χρόνου Id.*Eu.*670. V. διὰ πασῶν (sc. χορδῶν), v. διαπασῶν. VI. οὐ πᾶς not *any*, i.e. *none*, Lxx *Ps.*142(143).2, *Ev.Luc.*1.37, *Ep.Gal.*2.16, al.; ἄνευ πάσης ταραχῆς without *any* disturbance, D.S.15.87.

⊛ **πᾶς** (B), Cypr., = παῖς, *Inscr.Cypr.*106, 210 H.

**πᾶς** (C), = πατήρ (Syracus.), *EM*651.7.

**πάσασθαι** [ᾰ], v. πατέομαι, πάσσω: **πάσασθαι** [ᾱ], v. πάομαι.

**πᾱσῐ-άναξ** [ᾰν], ακτος, ὁ, *universal king*, Ζεύς Orac.ap.Phleg.1.6 J.: applied to the ruler of the dead, and hence to the dead, *Tab.Defix.Aud.*43, 44. ⊛ **-γνωστος**, ον, *all-known, famous*, Sch.Lyc. 12. **-δάμεια** [δᾰ], ἡ, *universal queen*, epith. of the moon-goddess, prob. in *PMag.Lond.*121.694. **-δηλος**, ον, *all-manifest*, Hdn. *Epim.*20. ⊛ **-θέα**, ἡ, magical plant, *PMag.Leid.V.*12.13. II. τὰ μεγάλα Πασίθεα, festival at Ephesus, *Ephes.*3 p.103. **-θρύλητος** [ῡ], ον, *world-famous*, Tz.*H.*9.19. ⊛ **-κράτεια** [κρᾰ], ἡ, *universal queen*, a goddess of the underworld, *IG*14.268 (Selinus), *PMag.Par.*1.2774:—also ⊛ **Πασικράτη**, Dor. **-α**, Ἀρχ.Ἐφ.1910.397 (Ambracia). **-μεδέουσα**, ἡ, *ruling over all*, of Hecate, *PMag.Par.*1. 2775. **-μέλων**, ουσα, ον, *a care* or *interest to all, world-famous*, πλοῦς Str.1.2.40; esp. of the ship Argo, Od.12.70.

⊛ **πάσιολος**, ὁ, = Lat. *phaseolus*, *Edict.Diocl.*6.33, 39, prob. for πάσωλος in *Gloss.*

⊛ **Πάσιος** [ᾱ], ὁ, (πᾶσις) = Κτήσιος, epith. of Zeus, Ἀρχ.Ἐφ.1911.152 (Arc.), *SIG*1106.148 (Cos, iv/iii B.C.).

**πᾱσῐπόρνη**, ἡ, *common prostitute*, Hermipp.10 (nisi scrib. divisim).

**πᾶσις**, εως, ἡ, (πάομαι) *acquisition, possession*, Hsch.; cj. in B.9. 42; μοιριδία π. prob. for πρᾶσις in Philic. in *Stud.Ital.*9.44.

**πᾱσῐ-φαής**, ές, *shining on all*, Orph.*H.*8.14, Man.3.346:—fem. **-φάεσσα** [φᾰ], Epigr. in Arist.*Mir.*843b29. **-φάνης**, ές, = foreg., Ἀρετά *shining* Virtue, B.12.176. ⊛ **-φίλητος** [φῐ], ον, *loved by all*, *IG*5(2).254 (Tegea). ⊛ **-φίλος**, ον, = foreg., ib.221 (ibid.), *Sammelb.*6160.10, al. (Tell-el-Yahoudiyeh); ironical in *PCair.Zen.*454.12 (iii B.C.):—fem. **πασιφίλη**, *Sammelb.*7254 (Tell-el-Yahoudiyeh); as pr. n., Archil.19.

**πάσκος**, ὁ, = πηλός, Hsch.

**πάσμα**, ατος, τό, *sprinkling*, ἅλμης πάσμασι σῶμα λιπάνας Axionic. 4.9. 2. Medic., *powder*, Posidon.ap.Aët.6.21, Alex.Trall.12. II. = πεῖσμα, *leaf-stalk*, also, *flock of wool*, Hsch. III. dub. sens. in *Ostr.Bodl.*i 306 (i B.C.).

**πασμάτιον**, τό, Dim. of foreg., in pl., *spangles*, π. ἐπίτηκτα, π. χρυσᾶ, *IG*2².1524.178, 181.

**πάσομαι** [ᾰ], v. πατέομαι:—but **πάσομαι** [ᾱ], v. πάομαι.

**πασπᾰλέτης**, ου, ὁ, = κεγχραλέτης, Gal.19.128.

**πασπάλη** [ᾰ], ἡ, = παιπάλη, *the finest meal*, Hsch., Phot., Suid. s.v. ἀλευρότησις: metaph., ὕπνου οὐδὲ π. not *a morsel* of sleep, Ar.*V.*91.

**πασπᾰληφάγος** [φᾰ], ον, *meal-fed*, γρόμφις Hippon.69.

**πάσπᾰλος**, ὁ, = κέγχρος, Gal.19.128.

**πασπερμεῖον**, τό, = πανσπερμία, *PTeb.*11.9 (ii B.C.):—also **πασπέρμη**, ἡ, ib.9.12 (ii B.C.).

⊛ **πασσᾰγία**, Ion. **-ίη**, ἡ, = πανσαγία, Poet.ap.Suid.

**πασσᾰκίζω**, = πασσαλεύω, and **πασσᾰκίον**, Dim. of πάσσαξ, Hsch.

**πασσᾰλ-εῖον**, Att. πατ**τ**-, τό, Dim. of πάσσαλος, *peg, rivet*, *EM* 323.9: metaph., πάσης κακίας ὡσανεὶ π. ἐστιν ἡ φιλαργυρία Plb.29.8. 10. **-ευτός**, ή, όν, *pinned down*, δεσμοῖσι π. ὤν (as Turneb. for the reading of cod. Med. πασσαλευμένος) A.*Pr.*113. **-εύω**, Att. πατ**τ**-, *peg, pin*, or *fasten to*, λαβών νιν..π. πρὸς πέτραις ib.56; λάφυρα..δόμοις ἐπασσάλευσαν Id.*Ag.*579; ὡς πασσαλεύσῃ κρᾶτα τριγλύφοις E.*Ba.*1214. 2. *drive in like a peg* or *bolt*, σφηνὸς..γνάθον στέρνων διαμπὰξ π. A.*Pr.*65. ⊛ **-ιον**, τό, = sq., Hsch. **-ίσκος**, ὁ, Dim. of πάσσαλος, Plb.*Fr.*163; used to force open the mouth, Hp. *Mul.*2.203; esp. *peg* or *pin in musical instruments*, οἱ π. τῆς κιθάρας Sch.Ar.*V.*572; = κόλλοψ, *EM*525.31. ⊛ **-ιστής**, οῦ, ὁ, *one who plays with pegs*, Hsch. s.v. κυνδαλοπαίστης.

**πασσᾰλοκοπ-έω**, Att. πατ**τ**-, *drive in pegs*, Dosith.p.432 K. **-ία**, ἡ, *making a palisade*, Apollod.*Poliorc.*143.4.

⊛ **πάσσᾰλος**, Att. πάτ**τ**-, ὁ, Ep. gen. πασσαλόφι (v. infr.), (πήγνυμι) *peg* on which to hang clothes, arms, etc., ἀπὸ πασσάλοφι ζυγὸν ᾕρεον Il. 24.268, cf. 5.209; ἀπὸ πασσάλου αἴνυτο τόξον Od.21.53; ἀπὸ φόρμιγγα πασσάλου λάμβαν' Pi.*O.*1.17, cf. B.*Scol.Oxy.*1361.1.1; ἐκ πασσαλόφι κρέμασεν φόρμιγγα Od.8.67; χαλινοὺς..ἐκ πασσάλων δέουσι Hdt.4.72, v. ἐκ I. 6; [χιτῶνα] πασσάλῳ ἀγκρεμάσασα Od.1.440; κύλιξ..κρέμαται περὶ πασσαλόφιν Hermipp.55; ἐπὶ τῶν παττάλων Arist.*PA*681a25; παττάλους ἐνέκρουεν εἰς τὸν τοῖχον Ar.*V.*129; *peg* for making a hole in a vine-stem, Thphr.*HP*2.5.5, *CP*3.12.1; used to force open the mouth or as a gag, Ar.*Eq.*376, *Th.*222; of *stakes* used to mark boundaries, *IG*14.352 i 38 (Halaesa); *pale*, Apollod.*Poliorc.*140.7, al.:—prov. of things very small or worthless, ἔχουσι μηδὲ πάτταλον not *a pin* (i.e. no part of their fee), Ar.*Ec.*284; μηδὲ π. καταλιπεῖν Luc.*Jud.Voc.*9; παττάλου γυμνότερος Aristaenet.2.18; also πάσσαλος πασσάλῳ ἐκκρούεται Eust.126.13, cf. *Com.Adesp.*494; εἶναι ἐν πασσάλοις, i.e. to be hung up, not in use, Lib.*Or.*1.268. II. from the likeness of form, 1. *membrum virile*, Ar.*Ec.*1020, *AP*5.128 (Autom.). 2. = ἵππος ὀρθόκωλος, *Hippiatr.*115.

**πασσᾰλόω**, *furnish with pegs*, Sch.Ar.*Av.*436 (Pass.).

**πασσάμενος, πάσσασθαι**, v. πατέομαι.

**πάσσαξ**, ακος, ὁ, Megar. form of πάσσαλος, Ar.*Ach.*763.

**πασσάριος**· σταυρός, Hsch. **πασσέληνος**, v. πανσ—.

⊛ **πάσσον**, τό, = Lat. *vinum passum, raisin* wine, Plb.6.11a.4.

**πάσσοφος**, v. πάνσοφος. **πασσῠδεί, -δί, -δίῃ, -δίην**, v. πανσ—.

**πασσῠδιάζω**, *assemble*, *IGRom.*4.1302.4 (Cyme, written with one -σ-).

**πασσῠδόν**, Adv. *together*, Nonn.*D.*27.243, 32.230.

**πασσῠρ-εί**, = πασσυδεί, rejected by Poll.9.143:—also **-ως**, Hsch.

**πασσύριον**, Aeol. for πασσυδίην, Hsch.

**πάσσω**, Att. πάττω Ar.*Nu.*912: fut. πάσω [ᾰ] Crates Com.14.10, Ar.*Eq.*99 (κατα-): aor. ἔπᾰσα Lxx *Ex.*9.8 and in compds.:—Med., aor. ἐπᾰσάμην ib.3*Ma.*1.18:—Pass., aor. ἐπάσθην (ἐπ-) Pl.*R.*405e: pf. πέπασμαι Lxx *Es.*1.6, etc.: plpf. ἐπέπαστο A.R.1.729, πέπαστο Longus 1.12: Hom. uses only pres. and impf., and these only in Il.:—*sprinkle*, ἐπὶ..ὀδυνήφατα φάρμακα πάσσων *laying* healing drugs *upon* a wound, Il.5.401, 900, etc.; τὰ Δέλφιδος ὀστία πάσσω Theoc.2.21; esp. *sprinkle* salt, c. gen. partit., πάσσε δ' ἁλὸς θείοιο *sprinkle some* salt, Il. 9.214; π. τῶν ἁλῶν ἐπὶ τὸ πῦρ Luc.*DMeretr.*4.5. 2. *besprinkle*, οὔκουν..σεαυτὸν ἁλσὶ πάσεις; Crates Com. l. c., cf. Thphr.*Char.*9.2; χρυσῷ, ῥόδοις π. τινά, Ar.*Nu.*912, 1330. II. Med., *sprinkle oneself* with ashes, Lxx 3*Ma.*1.18.

**πάσσων**, ον, gen. ονος, Ep. Comp. of παχύς, *thicker, stouter*, μείζονά τ' εἰσιδέειν καὶ πάσσονα Od.6.230, cf. 8.20; of a woman, μακροτέρην καὶ π. 18.195.

⊛ **πασταί**, αἱ, = παστά (v. παστός, ή, όν II), Eup.365.

⊛ **παστάς**, άδος, ἡ, *porch in front of the house*, Hdt.2.148 (pl.), 169. 2. *colonnade*, such as ran round temples, X.*Mem.*3.8.9 (pl.), prob. for παραστάσι in Id.*Hier.*11.2; τὰς δὲ παστάδας κοινὰς εἶμεν πάντεσσι, at Delphi, *IG*2².1126.22, cf. 4²(1).109 ii 122 (Epid.); = Lat. *porticus*, D.H.4.44 (pl.), Plu.*Galb.*25. 3. *part of the house next the porch, hall*, A.R.1.789, *AP*6.172. II. *inner room, bridal chamber*, ἀκτέριστον ἀμφὶ π., of the cave in which Antigone was immured, S.*Ant.* 1207; κεδρωτὰ παστάδων τέραμνα E.*Or.*1371 (lyr.), cf. Theoc.24.46, *AP*9.245 (Antiphan.), Menemach.ap.Orib.10.14.3: παστάδος ὥρη, of marriageable age, *Epigr.Gr.*521 (Thessalonica), cf. Chor. in *Rev.Phil.* 1.241; ἄμοιρος ἔτι παστάδος, of a bachelor, Id.*Proc.*1, cf. 4.

⊛ **πάστας**, α, ὁ, (πάομαι) *owner*, *Leg.Gort.*2.43, al.

**παστάτᾱς**, ὁ, = παραστάτης, *SIG*556 *D* 3 (Delph., iii B.C.).

**παστείλη**, ἡ, *last day of the year*, *EM*655.48 (expld. as from πᾶς, τέλος).

**παστέος**, α, ον, (πάσσω) *to be besprinkled*, τοῖς ἁλσί Ar.*Pax* 1074.

⊛ **παστή**, ἡ, *case, container*, *PLond.*2.191.9 (ii A.D.).

**παστῆον**, τό (for παστεῖον), perh. *case for a curtain*, *SIG*996.22 (Smyrna), cf. *BCH*11.159 (Lagina).

**παστήρια**, τά, *feast on sacrificial meats*, prob. in E.*El.*835 (παστηρίαν codd.), cf. Hsch.

**παστιλλ-άριος**, ὁ, *confectioner*, *MAMA*3.495, al. (Corycus). ⊛ **-ᾶς**, ᾶ, ὁ, = foreg., *POxy.*1891.4, 21 (v A.D.), *PIand.*42.2 (vi A.D.). **-ος**, ὁ, *pastille*, Orib.*Fr.*88, Aët.9.15:—Dim. **-ιον**, τό, *BGU*34 v 19 (ii/iii A.D.). **-όω**, *make into a paste*, Orib.*Fr.*102, Alex.Trall.5.4:—Pass., Aët 8.74. **-ώδης**, ες, *like a pastille*, Sever.*Clyst.*p.40 D. (πάστιλλος, borrowed fr. Lat. *pastillus*, replaces τροχίσκος, cf. Cels. 5.17.2; written παστελ(λ)- in Orib.*Fr.*88, Alex.Trall. l. c.)

**παστός**, ή, όν, (πάσσω) *sprinkled with salt, salted*, Hp.*Int.*41; ἰχθύς, ἐχῖνος, *Edict.Diocl.Aeg.*5.5, 9. 2. παστόν, τό, *powder*, Hp. *Loc.Hom.*13. II. παστά, τά, a kind of *barley-porridge*, Ael.Dion. *Fr.*173; mixed of cheese and meal, acc. to Hsch.

**παστός**, ὁ, = παστάς II, *woman's chamber, bridal chamber*, Lxx *Ps.*18(19).5, *Supp.Epigr.*1.567.5 (Karanis, iii B.C.), Posidipp. in *PLit. Lond.*60.8, Luc.*DMort.*23.3. 2. *bridal bed*, *AP*5.51 (Diosc.), 7.711 (Antip.), *IG*12(8).441.13 (Thasos, ii/i B.C.), Epigr. in *Berl.Sitzb.* 1894.908 (Asia Minor). 3. *embroidered bed-curtain*, *SIG*996.23 (Smyrna), *BMus.Inscr.*1084 (Naucratis, i B.C.), *Hymn.Is.*109, D.Chr. 62.6, Poll.3.37. 4. *bridal hymn*, *Epigr.Gr.*236.5. 5. perh. *shrine*, Herod.4.56. II. παστόν (acc.) is dub. l. in Pherecyd.13(*b*) J.

⊛ **παστο-φόριον** (-εῖον Phot., Cyr.), τό, *chamber assigned to παστοφόροι*, *PPetr.*2 p.1 (iii B.C.), *UPZ*119.25, al. (ii B.C.), *SIG*977*a* (Delos, ii B.C.), Hsch.; used of the *priest's chamber* in the temple at Jerusalem, Lxx *Je.*42(35).4, J.*BJ*4.9.12 (pl.). ⊛ **-φόρισσα**, ἡ, *female παστοφόρος*, *PSI*9.1096.31 (iii A.D.). ⊛ **-φόρος**, ον, *carrying a παστός* (perh. *shrine*): οἱ π. priests appointed for this purpose, *PHib.*1.77 (iii B.C.), *PLille* 11.2, 7 (iii B.C.), D.S.1.29, *IG*14.1366, Porph.*Abst.*4.8, etc. II. *bringing the marriage-bed*, π. Παφίη Epigr. in Stob.1.5.14 (Hermes).

**παστόω**, (παστός, ὁ) *build a bridal chamber*, Aq.*De.*33.12.

**πάστρια**, ἡ, (πάσσω) *embroiderer*, Sch.E.*Hec.*1151 (pl.).

**πάσχα**, τό, indecl., the Hebrew *Passover* (from *pāsaḥ* 'pass over') or *Paschal feast*, Lxx *Ex.*12.48, etc. 2. *paschal supper*, *Ev.Matt.* 26.17, 19, al. 3. *paschal lamb*, θύειν τὸ π. Lxx *Ex.*12.21, al.; τὸ π. ἐτύθη Χριστός 1*Ep.Cor.*5.7.

**πασχαλκεύς**, v. παγχαλκεύς.

**πασχητι-ασμός**, ὁ, *unnatural lust*, Luc.*Gall.*32. **-άω**, *feel lust*, Erot. s. v. γαργαλισμόν, D.C.79.16; esp. of *unnatural lust*, Luc.*Am.* 26, Ath.5.187c, *Cat.Cod.Astr.*2.175.6.

**πασχικός**, ή, όν, *one possessed*, Hsch. s.v. ἐπιληπτικός.

⊛ **πάσχω**, Il.20.297, etc.: impf. ἔπασχον 17.375, etc.: fut. πείσομαι Od.2.134, etc.; Dor. 3 sg. παισεῖται *Abh.Berl.Akad.*1925(5).21 (Cyrene, iii B.C.): aor. ἔπᾰθον Il.9.492, etc.: pf. πέπονθα Od.13.6, etc.: plpf. ἐπεπόνθειν ib.92, etc.; Att. ἐπεπόνθη Pl.*Smp.*198c (all the above tenses in Hom., pres. and aor. only in Hes.).—Rarer forms, 2 pl. pf. πέποσθε (so Aristarch.) Il.3.99, πέποσθε Od.23.53; fem. pf. part. πεπᾰθυῖα 17.555; Dor. pf. πέποσχα Stesich.89, Epich.11, *PCair.Zen.*482.18 (iii B.C.):—*have* something *done to one, suffer*, opp. *do*, ὅσσ' ἔρξαν τ' ἔπαθόν τε Od.8.490; ῥέζοντά τι καὶ παθεῖν ἔοικεν Pi.*N.*4.32; δρᾶν καὶ πάσχειν, v. δράω; πολλὰ μὲν.. πείσεσθαι, πολλὰ δὲ ποιήσειν Hdt.5.89, etc.: hence used as Pass. of ποιέω (cf. Arist.*Cat.*2ᵃ4, *Metaph.*1017ᵃ26, Plot.3.6.8, etc.), π. τι ὑπό τινος *to be treated* so and so by another, *suffer* it at his hands, ἃ πάσχοντες ὑφ' ἑτέρων ὀργίζεσθε, ταῦτα τοὺς ἄλλους μὴ ποιεῖτε Isoc.3.61, cf. Hdt.1.44,124, al.; ἐξ ἐμοῦ μὲν ἔπαθες οἷα φῂς παθεῖν, δρᾷς δ' οὐδὲν ἡμᾶς εὖ E.*Hec.*252; οἷα πρὸς θεῶν πάσχω θεός A.*Pr.*92, cf. Hdt.1.36. **II.** *to have* something *happen* to one, *to be* or *come to be in a state* or *case*, καί τι ἔφη γελοῖον παθεῖν Pl.*Smp.*174e; ὅπερ οἱ τὰς ἐγχέλεις θηρώμενοι πέπονθας Ar.*Eq.*846, cf. *V.*946; δρᾶτε μὴ ταὐτὸ πάθητε τῷ ἵππῳ see that it be not with you as with the horse in the fable, Arist.*Rh.*1393ᵇ20, cf. Pl.*R.*488a; παραπλήσιον π. ὥσπερ ἂν εἰ.. Isoc.1.27; ὁμοιότατον πεπονθέναι ὥσπερ ἂν εἴ τις.. Pl.*Phd.*98c. **2.** of the influence of *passion* or *feeling, to be affected* in a certain way, *be* (or *come to be*) *in a* certain *state of mind*, οἱ Καμαριναῖοι ἐπεπόνθεσαν τοιόνδε Th.6.88, cf. 1.80, D.20.56; ὅ τι μὲν ὑμεῖς πεπόνθατε ὑπὸ τῶν ἐμῶν κατηγόρων οὐκ οἶδα Pl.*Ap.*17a, cf. 21c,22c, *Alc.*1.118b, *Smp.*198c: π. τι πρός τινας Isoc.2.42, Pl.*Grg.*485b, cf. X.*Smp.*4.11,8.15, etc.; τι ἔς τινας Th.6.11: sts. with Adj., ὑϊκὸν πάσχει *he is* swinishly *disposed*, X.*Mem.*1.2.30: abs., ὁ πάσχων *the man of feeling* or *impulse*, ὁ μὴ πάσχων *the unimpassioned man*, Arist.*MM*1203ᵇ21. **3.** of things, πεπόνθασι.. αἱ Ἰώνων ὁρταὶ τοῦτο this *is the case with*.., Hdt.1.148; πάσχει δὲ ταὐτὸ τοῦτο καὶ τὰ κάρδαμα this *is just the way with*.., Ar.*Nu.*234; οἷον τὰ γράμματα πεπονθότ' ἂν εἴη Pl.*Sph.*253a; ὁμοίως π. τῷ Νείλῳ *to be in* the same *case* with.., Hdt.2.20. **4.** Gramm., of words, *to be subject to* certain *changes*, *EM*200.11, 491.2, etc.; τὸ πεπονθός a *modified* form, A.D.*Adv.*137.16. **b.** *to be passive* in meaning, Id.*Synt.*244.6, al. **III.** freq. with Advbs., κακῶς πάσχειν or παθεῖν *to be in evil plight, unlucky*, Od.16.275, Hdt.3.146, etc.; κακῶς π. ὑπό τινος *to be ill used, ill treated by*.., A.*Pr.*1041 (anap.); ἐκ Διὸς π. κακῶς ib.759 (but also κακὸν π. ὑ. τ. Th.8.48): freq. with an Adj., κακά, αἰνά, λυγρὰ π., Il.3.99, 22.431, Hdt.9.37; ἀνάρσια πρός τινος Id.5.89: freq. in Trag., π. δύσοιστα, τάλανα, ἀμήχανα, οἰκτρά, σχέτλια, ἀνάξια, A.*Eu.*789 (lyr.), *Th.*988 (dub.), E.*Hipp.*598, *Hec.*321, *Andr.*1180 (dub.), *IA*852: also in Prose, δεινά, βίαια π., D.51.19, 21.1, etc.; πρέποντα πάσχειν Antipho 3.3.9: in Hom. also with Subst., ἄλγεα, κήδεα, πήματα, ἀεκήλια ἔργα, Il.20.297, Od.17.555, Il.5.886, 18.77: rarely in Att., πράγματ' αἴσχιστ' ἂν ἐπάθομεν D.21.17. **b.** εὖ πάσχειν *to be well off, in good case*, c. gen., τῶν αὑτοῦ (leg. ὧν αὐτοῦ, cf. ὅς Possess.) κτεάνων εὖ πασχέμεν *to have the good of, enjoy* one's own, like ἀπολαύω, γεύομαι, etc., Thgn.1009, cf. Pi.*N.*1.32; εὖ πάσχειν *receive benefits*, opp. εὖ δρᾶν, A.*Eu.*868, Th.2.40, etc.; ἀνθ' ὧν ἔπασχον εὖ.. χάριν δοῦναι S.*OC*1489; τιμᾶσθαι.. ἐν τῇ μνήμῃ τῶν εὖ πεπονθότων Aeschin.3.182; εὖ παθεῖν ὑπό τινων Pl.*Grg.*519d, etc.: also with an Adj., π. ἀγαθά Hdt.2.37; τι ἐσλόν Pi.*P.*9.89, cf. Alc.*Supp.*22.5; τερπνόν τι S.*Aj.*521, cf. Theoc.7.83; χαρτά, ὅσια, E.*Ph.*618, *Hec.*788; γλυκέα, χαρίεντα π., Ar.*Pax*591, *Ec.*794; δίκαια Din.1.10; φιλικὰ ὑπό τινος X.*Cyr.*4.6.6. **2.** without Adv., with reference to *evil*, used for κακῶς or κακὰ π., μάλα πόλλ' ἔπαθον καὶ πόλλ' ἐμόγησα Od.5.223, cf. Il.23.607; εἴ κεν μάλα πολλὰ πάθοι 22.220; ὁτιοῦν π. *suffer* anything whatever, Isoc.12.133, etc.: abs., παθὼν δέ τε νήπιος ἔγνω *by hard experience*, Hes.*Op.*218, cf. S.*OT*403; ὁ παθὼν *the injured party*, Pl.*Lg.*730a, 878c:—Phrases: μή τι πάθῃς or πάθοι, lest *thou*, lest *he suffer* any *ill*, Od.17.596, Il.5.567, cf. 11.470, etc.; μή τι πάθωμεν 13.52: hence εἴ τι πάθοιμι or ἤν τι πάθω, as euphemism, if aught *were to happen* to me, i.e. if I were to *die*, Callin.1.17, Hdt.8.102, Ar.*Ec.*1105, *V.*385, Lys.19.51, Theoc.8.10; ἐὰν οὗτος τι πάθῃ D.4.11; ἐάν τινα ἀνθρώπινα πάσχῃ *IG*3.74.13; so εἴ τι πείσεται.. ἅδε γᾶ E.*Ph.*244 (lyr.); ἤν τι ναῦς πάθῃ Id.*IT*755, cf. Syngr.ap.D.35.13. **b.** in Law, *suffer punishment, pay the penalty*, Lys.20.30; π. ὡς ἱερόσυλος *SIG*1016.7 (Iasos, iv B.C.), cf. 1*Ep.Pet.*4.15; ὡς προδότης καὶ ἐπιβουλεύων τῷ δήμῳ πασχέτω τι Aen.Tact.11.9; τιμᾶν ὅ τι χρὴ παθεῖν.. ἢ ἀποτεῖσαι Pl.*Plt.*299a (-τίνειν codd.), cf. *Ap.*36b, X.*Mem.*2.9.5, *IG*1².65.50, etc. **3.** τί πάθω; what *is to become of me?* ὤμοι ἐγώ, τί π.; Il.11.404, Od.5.465, S.*OC*216 (lyr.), Theoc.3.24; sts. what (else) *am I to do?* Ar.*Nu.*798; so esp. τί γὰρ π.; E.*Hec.*614, *Supp.*257, Ar.*Av.*1432, etc.; ὡμολόγηκα· τί γὰρ π.; I allow it—how *can I help it?* Pl.*Euthd.*302d, cf. Hdt.4.118. **4.** in 2 sg., τί πάσχεις; what's *the matter with you?* Ar.*Nu.*708, *Av.*1044; τί χρῆμα πάσχεις; Id.*Nu.*816: so in aor. part., τί παθών; τί παθόντε λελάσμεθα θούριδος ἀλκῆς; what *possesses us that* we have forgotten..? Il.11.313; but τί παθόντες γαῖαν ἔδυτε; what *befell you that* you died? Od.24.106; also οὐδὲν θαυμαστὸν ἔπαθεν.. πεισθεὶς *no wonder that* he was induced, Antipho 2.4.7. **5.** *to be ill, suffer*, c. acc. of the part affected, π. τοὺς πόδας, τὴν πλευράν, *PSI*4.293.23 (iii A.D.), *PGen.*56.27 (iv A.D.): abs. in part., ὁ πάσχων, almost = ὁ κάμνων, the *patient*, *PMag.Par.*1.3017; μεταβαίνει ἀπὸ τῶν παθῶν ἐπὶ τοὺς πάσχοντας ἀνθρώπους Gal.16.583, cf. 15.501, Sor.*Fasc.*45, al. **IV.** in later Stoic Philos., πάσχειν is *to be acted upon by outward objects, take impressions from* them, opp. ἀποπάσχω, mostly folld. by ὅτι, *to be led to suppose that*.., Arr.*Epict.*1.2.3, 1.18.1, etc.: also c. acc., *have experience of*, ἀρετήν, λόγον, Ph.2.449, 1.121. (*πηθ-σκω, fut. *πένθ-σομαι, cf. πένθος.)

⊕ **πάσωλος**, v. πασίολος.

**πατά**, Scythian word, = κτείνω, Hdt.4.110.

⊕ **πᾰτᾰγ-έω**, Aeol. impf. πατάγεσκον Alc.*Supp.*25.9:—*clatter, clash*, of the sharp loud noise caused by the collision of two bodies, Ar.*Nu.*378 sq.; βαρὺ δ' ἄγριοι χειμῶνες παταγεῦσιν Anacr.6; of Bacchants, Pratin.Lyr.1.3; τὼ δὲ πίθω πατάγεσκ' ὀ πύθμην Alc.l.c.; of the sea, *dash, plash*, Theoc.22.15; *chatter*, as birds, S.*Aj.*168 (anap.); ὁ κότ-τυφος ἐν μὲν τῷ θέρει ᾄδει, τοῦ δὲ χειμῶνος παταγεῖ Arist.*HA*632ᵇ17; *gnash*, as teeth, Philostr.*Im.*1.28: prov., καλὰ δὴ παταγεῖς *well hit!* prob. from the game described under πλαταγών, Ar.*Fr.*116. **II.** trans., τύμπανα π. *beat* drums, Luc.*Syr.D.*50:—Pass., αἷς ἔντεα παταγεῖται *Lyr.Adesp.*121; ἐπαταγεῖτο Luc.*Tim.*3. **-ή**, ἡ, = πάταγος, D.P.574; χειρὸς παταγῇ *clapping*, Longus 1.22 (v.l. χειροπλατάγῃ). **-ημα**, ατος, τό, *rattle*, metaph. of persons, Men.913.

**πᾰτᾰγοδρόμος**, ον, *clattering as it runs*, Orph.*H.*20.3.

**πάτᾰγος** [πᾰ], ὁ, *clatter, crash*, as of trees falling, π. δέ τε ἀγνυμενάων (sc. γίγνεται) Il.16.769; π. δέ τε γίγνετ' ὀδόντων *chattering* of the teeth, 13.283; *plash* of a body falling into water, ἐν δ' ἔπεσον μεγάλῳ π. 21.9, cf. Pi.*P.*1.24; *rattle* or *crash* of thunder, Ar.*Nu.*382, cf. Arist.*Mu.*395ᵃ13; π. ἀνέμων D.H.*Comp.*16; *rumbling* caused by flatulence, Hp.*VM*22; but never of the human voice (exc. in late Greek, βληχᾶσθαι καὶ κρώζειν ἐν ὑποκρίσει τὸν ἔξηχον π. Porph.*Chr.*35): hence βοῇ καὶ πατάγῳ χρεώμενοι means, with a great shouting and *clashing* of arms, Hdt.3.79, cf. 7.211; π. δορός A.*Th.*103 (lyr.); τόξων S.*Tr.*518 (lyr.); ἀσπίδων E.*Heracl.*832, Ar.*Ach.*539; π. χύτρειος Id.*Lys.*329 (lyr.). (Onomatop. word.)

⊕ **Πᾰταίκεια**, τά, festival at Delos, in honour of a donor called Πάταικος, *Inscr.Délos* 366 *A* 58, al. (iii B.C.): sg. Παταίκειον, τό, fund for its maintenance, ib.438.2 (ii B.C.).

**Πᾰταικίων**, ωνος, ὁ, the name of a notorious thief, Aeschin.3.189, Diog.Cyn.ap.Plu.2.21f.

**Πάταικοι**, οἱ, Phoenician deities of dwarfish shape, whose images formed the figure-heads of Phoenician ships, Hdt.3.37; χρυσοῖ'.. ἀπέφθα τοῖς Π. ἐμφερῆ *Com.Adesp.*423.

**πᾰτακτ(ρ)οράφος** [ρᾰ], ὁ, *whip-maker*, prob. in *PGoodsp.Cair.*30 xxix 12 (ii A.D.).

**πᾰτάνεψις** [τᾰ], εως, ἡ, *an eel dressed in a* πατάνη, Epich.211.

**πᾰτάνη** [τᾰ], ἡ, a kind of *flat dish*, Sophr.13, cf. Poll.10.107:—also **πάτᾰνον**, τό, Id.6.90 (v.l.), Hsch.:—Dim. **πᾰτάνιον**, τό, Antiph.70, Eub.38, 47; **Πᾰτανίων** is the name of a cook in Philetaer.14, 15.—For the Sicil. forms **βατάνη, -ιον**, v. sub vocc.

**πατάξ**, v. εὐράξ II. **παταπῶ·** πάλαι ποτέ, Hsch.

⊕ **πᾰτάσσω**, Ep. impf. πάτασσον Il.7.216: fut. -άξω Ar.*Lys.*657, *Ra.*646, Arist.*Mete.*371ᵇ9: aor. ἐπάταξα Thgn.1199:—**Pass.**, aor. ἐπατάχθην Luc.*Anach.*3, 40, Ach.Tat.7.4: fut. παταχθήσομαι Luc.*Fug.*14: pf. πεπάταγμαι (ἐκ-) Od.18.327 (elsewh. Hom. has only pres. and impf.): Att. and Lxx mostly fut. and aor. Act. (τύπτω and πλήσσω being used in other tenses): **I.** intr. in Hom., *beat, knock*, θυμὸς ἐνὶ στήθεσσι πάτασσεν Il.7.216; πάτασσε δὲ θυμὸς ἑκάστου 23.370; ἐν δέ τέ οἱ κραδίη στέρνοισι πατάσσει 13.282, cf. Arr.*Cyn.*15. **II.** with acc. of the thing set in motion, *strike, smite*, [ξίφος] πάταξον εἰς ἄκρον πόδα S.*Ph.*748; πρὸς κίονα νῶτον π. E.*HF*1007: c. acc. cogn., π. πληγὴν Pl.*Grg.*527c, cf. *Lg.*879e: abs., or with acc. of person or thing struck, ὁ πατάξας *the man who struck the blow*, Antipho 4.3.4, Th.8.92; ἐὰν μὲν τὸν ἄρχοντα πατάξῃ τις D.21.33; of a deadly blow, ἐὰν λίθος.. ἢ σίδηρος πατάξῃ Id.23.76; *sting*, of a bee, Ach.Tat.2.7; of lightning, *strike*, Arist.l.c.; π. τινὰ δορί E.*Ph.*1463; πύξ Ar.*Ra.*548, cf. *Eq.*1130 (lyr.): freq. in phrase πατάξαι θύραν, v. θύρα:—Pass., ὁ μηρὸς παταχθήσεται Luc.*Rh.Pr.*19. **b.** *smite, slaughter*, Lxx *Jd.*9.43, al.: simply, *kill*, ib.1*Ki.*17.9, al. **c.** *afflict, visit*, πατάξαι σε Κύριος παραπληξίᾳ ib.*De.*28.28, cf. *IG*12(9).1179.23 (Euboea, ii A.D.). **2.** metaph., ἄτη πατάξαι θυμόν S.*Ant.*1097; πόθος καρδίαν π. Ar.*Ra.*54 (also μοι κραδίην ἐπάταξε ὅττι.. Thgn.l.c.); πατάξω.. μεγάλοις ποτηρίοις Timocl.20; cf. παίω I.6.

**πάταχνον**, τό, = πατάνη, Hsch., Phot.

**πᾰτελίς**, ίδος, ἡ, a species of *limpet*, Sch.Opp.*H.*1.138.

**πάτελλα** [πᾰ], ἡ, *dish*, Poll.6.85:—also **πάτελλον**, τό, *BGU*781 vi 2 (i A.D.):—Dim. **πᾰτέλλιον**, τό, Poll.6.90, 10.107, Zos.Alch.p.142 B.: also ⊕-ίδιον, *Gloss.* (-ίcιον cod.); cf. βάτελλα.

**Πᾰτελλοχάρων** [χᾰ], οντος, ὁ, (πάτελλα, χαίρω) comic name of a parasite, *Dish-friend, 'pique-assiette'*, Alciphr.3.54 tit.

**πᾰτέομαι**, Hdt.2.47, Call.*Fr.*437, Agathocl.*Fr.Hist.*6, etc.: fut. πάσομαι [ᾰ] A.*Th.*1041: aor. ἐπᾰσάμην, Ep. also ἐπασσάμην (v. infr.): plpf. πεπάσμην Il.24.642, elsewh. in Hom. only aor.:—*eat*, c. acc., σπλάγχν' ἐπάσαντο Il.1.464, etc.; πασάμην Δημήτερος ἀκτὴν 21.76; also, of *drink*, νέκταρ ἐπάσαντο Hes.*Th.*642; ταύρου νέον αἷμα πάσηται Nic.*Al.*312: more freq. c. gen. partit., *eat of, partake of*, σίτοιό τ' ἐπασσάμεθ' ἠδὲ ποτῆτος Od.9.87; δείπνου πασσάμενος 1.124; πάσσασθαι ἐδητύος ἠδὲ ποτῆτος 10.384, etc.; so always in Hdt., 1.73, al.: rarely abs., *eat, taste food*, πάρος γε μὲν οὔ τι πεπάσμην Il.24.642.—Ep. and Ion. word, twice in A., τούτου σάρκας.. λύκοι πάσονται Th.1041; τί κακὸν.. ἐδανὸν ἢ ποτὸν πασαμένα..; *Ag.*1408 (lyr.); once in S., ἠθέλησε δ' αἵματος κοινοῦ πάσασθαι *Ant.*202; twice in Ar., in mock heroic lines, *Pax*1092, 1281.—Act. form πατέω only in Orion 162.20. (Cf. Skt. *pitús* 'food', Lat. *pasco*, Goth. *fōdjan* 'feed', etc.)

⊕ **πᾰτερ-εύω**, *hold office of* πατὴρ πόλεως, *Milet.*1(7) No. 206 (vi A.D.). ⊕**-ία**, ἡ, *office of* πατὴρ πόλεως, *Cod.Just.*10.56(55).1. **-ίζω**, Att. fut. -ιῶ, (πατήρ) *say* or *call father*, Ar.*V.*652. ⊕ **-ιον**, τό, Dim. of πατήρ, *little father*, Luc.*Nec.*21.

**πᾰτ-έω**, Delph. βατέω Plu.2.292e; Aeol. μάτημι [ᾰ] Sapph.54: (πάτος):—*tread, walk*, π. ὁδοῖς σκολιαῖς Pi.*P.*2.85; πρὸς βωμὸν A.*Ag.*

1298; ὑψοῦ π. *walk* on high, of a king, Pi.*O*.1.115: π. ἐπάνω ὄφεων *Ev.Luc*.10.19:—Pass., οἱ ἔχεις πατηθέντες Porph.*Abst*.1.14. II. trans., *tread on, tread*, πόας τέρεν ἄνθος μάτεισαι Sapph. l.c.; πορφύρας πατεῖν A.*Ag*.957; δωμάτων πύλας Id.*Ch*.732; χῶρος οὐχ ἁγνὸς πατεῖν holy ground, S.*OC*37; π. τὸν ἁδὺν οἶνον ἀπ' ἀμπέλω *tread* grapes, Hybrias(*Scol*.28.4); ληνούς Lxx*Ne*.13.15, cf. *Apoc*.19.15, Ruf.ap. Orib.5.12.1; also, *thresh* corn, π. τὰ θέρη *PFlor*.150.5(iii A.D.); κριθὴν καλῶς πεπατημένην *POxy*.988 (iii A.D.); π. ἐκ τοῦ χόρτου σπέρματα *PFlor*.388.5 (ii A.D.). 2. *walk in*, i.e. *dwell in, frequent*, Λῆμνον πατῶν S.*Ph*.1060; γαῖαν Theoc.18.20; π. πόντον Opp.*C*.2.218; νῶτα ἁλός *AP*7.532 (Isid.); rarely of vehicles, τὰ μὴ πατέουσιν ἅμαξαι Call. *Aet.Oxy*.2079.25: metaph., εὐνὰς ἀδελφοῦ π. *frequent*, A.*Ag*.1193; ἐμεῖο δέμνιον οὐκ ἐπάτησε Call.*Del*.248; οὐδ' Αἴσωπον πεπάτηκας *hast not thumbed* Aesop, Ar.*Av*.471; τὸν Τεισίαν..πεπάτηκας ἀκριβῶς *you have studied* him carefully, Pl.*Phdr*.273a:—Pass., *to be hackneyed*, τῇ ποιητικῇ πεπατῆσθαι Phld.*Po.Herc*.1676.10; πεπατημένος *well-worn, trite*, ῥήσεις, λόγοι, Ph.2.345,444, cf. Porph.ap.Eus.*PE*10.3; τὸ πεπατημένον A.D.*Pron*.45.6. 3. *tread under foot, trample on*, τινα S.*Aj*. 1146, Pl.*Phdr*.248a, etc.; βουλήν Ar.*Eq*.166; πόλιν *Apoc*.11.2: abs., πατοῦσι καὶ λακτίζουσι καὶ δάκνουσι Gal.16.562: metaph., π. κλέος, τιμὰς τὰς θεῶν, A.*Ag*.1357, S.*Ant*.745; τὰ τοῖν θεοῖν ψηφίσματα Ar.*V*. 377:—and in Pass., τὰ..δίκαια..λάγδην πατεῖται S.*Fr*.683, cf. A.*Ch*. 644 (lyr.), *Eu*.110. ❋ **-ημα**, ατος, τό, *that which is trodden: refuse*, *Gp*.20.46.2: metaph., of persons, Lxx*Ez*.34.19, cf. 4*Ki*.19.26. II. *being trodden on*, Aret.*SD*2.12.

**πατηνόν**· πεπατημένον, κοινόν, Hsch.

❋ **πᾰτήρ**, ὁ, gen. and dat. πατέρος, πατέρι in Ep. and Lyr., Att. πατρός, πατρί (which is also the commoner form in Hom., Hes., and Pi.); acc. always πατέρα; voc. πάτερ: pl. πατέρες, πατέρας, πατέρων (πατρῶν only Od.4.687, 8.245); dat. πατράσι [ᾰ] (cf. Skt. loc. pl. *pitṛṣu*, no dat. pl. occurs in Hom. or Hes.), late Ep. πατέρεσσι Q.S.10.40:—*father*, Il.1.98, etc.; πατρὸς πατήρ *grandfather*, 14.118, Od.19.180, X.*HG*6.3.4, etc.; τοῦδε κεκλῆσθαι πατρός S.*Fr*.86; μητρὸς καλεῖσθαι παῖδα τοῦ π. παρόν ib.564; τὰ πρὸς πατρός *by the father's side*, Hdt.7. 99, cf. *SIG*1015.7 (Halic.), etc.; esp. of God, the *father* of the Israelites, Lxx*De*.32.6, al.; *father* of men, *Ev.Matt*.6.8, al.; *father* of Jesus Christ, ib.7.21, al. II. esp. as epith. of Zeus, πατὴρ Ζεύς, π. Κρονίδης, π. ἀνδρῶν τε θεῶν τε, Il.4.235, 21.508, 1.544, al.; Ζεὺς π. A.*Th*. 512, etc.; Ζεῦ πάτερ καὶ θεοί Ar.*Ach*.225; π. Οὐρανιδᾶν Ζ. Pi.*P*.4. 194; ὁ τῶν ἁπάντων Ζεὺς π. Ὀλύμπιος S.*Tr*.275, etc. III. respectful mode of addressing persons older than oneself, ξεῖνε πάτερ Od.7.28,48, 8.145, cf. *POxy*.1296.15 (iii A.D.), etc.; in addressing an elder brother, *UPZ*65.3 (ii B.C.). IV. metaph., *father, author*, ἀοιδᾶν π...εὐαίνητος Ὀρφεύς Pi.*P*.4.176; Χρόνος ὁ πάντων π. Id.*O*.2.17, cf. Pl.*Ti*.41a; τοῦ λόγου π. Id.*Smp*.177d, cf. *Phdr*.257b, etc.; ὁ π. τῶν φώτων, i.e. God, the *father* of the stars, *Ep.Jac*.1. 17; οἱ π. τῶν ἀτόμων the *authors* of the atomic theory, Gal.1.246; of capital, τοῦ πατρὸς ἐκγόνους τόκους Pl.*R*.555e. V. title of a grade in the mysteries of Mithras, *IG*14.1272, etc. VI. π. πατρίδος, = Lat. *pater patriae*, Plu.*Cic*.23, *BGU*1074.1 (i A.D.), *IG*7.2713. 33 (Acraeph., i A.D.), etc.; similarly, π. τῆς πόλεως ib.5(1).1417.11 (Methone). VII. in pl., 1. *forefathers*, Il.6.209, etc.; ἐξέτι πατρῶν *from our fathers' time*, Od.8.245; ἐκ πατέρων Pi.*P*.8.45. 2. *parents*, D.S.21.17, Alciphr.3.40, *Epigr.Gr*.227 (Teos). 3. *parent-nation*, opp. colonists, Hdt.7.51, 8.22, Plu.*Them*.9. (Cf. Skt. *pitár-*, Lat. *pater*, etc.)

**πάτ-ησις** [ᾰ], εως, ἡ, *treading* of grapes, Corn.*ND*30, *PLond*.2. 163.32 (i A.D.), *Gp*.8.36.2. **-ησμός**, ὁ, *treading on, trampling*, εἱμάτων A.*Ag*.963. II. *threshing* of corn, *PFlor*.388.7 (ii A.D.). **-ητήριον**, τό, *place where grapes are trodden*, *CIG*2694*a* 10 (Mylasa), Androtion or Philippus ἐν τῷ Γεωργικῷ ap.Harp. s.v. σταφυλοβολεῖον. ❋ **-ητής**, οῦ, ὁ, *one who treads* grapes, *POxy*.1340 (i A.D.), Hsch. **-ητός**, ή, όν, *trodden*, ληνός Lxx*Is*.63.2; φοῖνιξ π. a juicy kind of date which bursts on the tree, as if trodden on, Plin.*HN*13.45, *BGU*591 (i A.D.), *PHamb*.5.17 (i A.D.), *Gp*.20.9, Gal. 10.704, Alex.Trall.7.5.

**πατικουρᾶς**, ὁ, dub. sens. in *BGU*594.3 (i A.D.).

**πατνή**· καλή (Parth.), Hsch. **πατνώματα**· στεγάσματα οἴκου, Id. (for φατν-, q.v.).

❋ **πάτος** [ᾰ] (A), ὁ, *trodden* or *beaten way, path*, κιόντες ἐκ πάτου ἐς σκοπιήν Il.20.137; πάτον ἀνθρώπων ἀλεείνων 6.202; οὐ μὲν γὰρ πάτος ἀνθρώπων ἀπερύκει Od.9.119; ὅ τις πάτου ἔκτοθεν ἦεν ἀνθρώπων A.R. 3.1201: metaph., ἔξω πάτου ὀνόματα *out-of-the-way* words, Luc.*Hist. Conscr*.44. 2. *floor*, βαλανείου *PFlor*.384.27 (pl., v A.D.). 3. *treading*, prob. cj. in Thphr.*HP*6.6.10. II. *dirt, dung*, Nic.*Al*. 535, *Th*.933; *scrapings* of oil, etc., Gal.12.116,283. III. πύρινος π. prob. wheat-*field*, *PSI*8.883.8 (ii A.D.): the sense *food*, Sch.Ar. *Pl*.1185, invented to explain ἀπόπατος. (Cf. Skt. *pánthās*, Slav. *pǫtĭ* 'path', Lat. *pons* 'causeway'; v. πόντος.)

❋ **πάτος** [ᾰ] (B), εος, τό, *robe worn by Hera*, Call.*Fr*.495.

❋ **πάτρᾱ**, Ion. and Ep. **πάτρη**, ἡ, (πατήρ) *fatherland, native land*, Il. 12.243, 24.500, Pi.*O*.12.16, A.*Pr*.665, S.*Ph*.222, $IG4^2$(1).244.8 (Epid., epigr., iii B.C.), etc., used in parody of Trag. by Ar.*Ach*.147, *Ra*.1427, *Th*.136, Alex.193, Diph.73.9:—πατρίς (q.v.) was the common prose form, but Hdt. uses πάτρη in 6.126,128, πατρίς in 3.140, 8.61. II. *fatherhood, descent from a common father*, ἀμφοτέροισιν ὁμὸν γένος ἠδ' ἴα π. Il.13.354 (nowh. else in this sense in Hom.); βασιλεὺς Ἰώνων ἀνὰ πάτρην by *hereditary descent*, *IGRom*.4.1730 (Samos, ii A.D.): hence, 2. *body of persons claiming descent from a common ancestor, house, clan*, π. Μειδυλιδᾶν Pi.*P*.8.38, cf. *N*.6.36, 8.46, *IG*5(2).495 (Megalopolis); also, of a *union of families* recognized by the state, ἰέναι αὐτοὺς καὶ ἐπὶ πάτρην ἣν ἂν πείθωσιν ib.12(8).267.10 (Thasos). III. *father's sister, aunt*, *IGRom*.4.621 (Temenothyrae, iii A.D.):—in form **πατρεία**, Keil-Premerstein *Zweiter Bericht* No.138 (nr. Thyatira, ii A.D.); cf. πιάτρα, πινάτρα.

**πατρ-ᾰγᾰθία**, ἡ, *virtue of one's father* or *ancestors*, opp. ἀνδραγαθία, Plu.2.183d, 534c. **-ᾰδελφεός**, ὁ, poet. and Dor. for πατράδελφος, Pi.*I*.8(7).72, *Michel*995*C*44 (Delph., v B.C.). ❋ **-ᾰδέλφεια**, ἡ, *cousin by the father's side*, A.*Supp*.38 (anap.). ❋ **-άδελφος** [ᾰδ], ὁ, *father's brother*, Is.4.23,26, D.44.13, etc.

**πάτρᾱθε**, Adv., Dor. for πάτρηθε.

**Πάτραι**, ῶν, αἱ, *Patrae*, Th.2.83, etc.: **Πατρεύς**, έως, ὁ, one of its citizens, St.Byz.; pl. Πατρέες Hdt.1.145, etc.; gen. Πατρέων Plb.4.6.9.

**πατρ-ᾰλίτωρ** [ῐ], ορος, ὁ, *one who sins against a father*, dub. in Tz.*H*. 6.443. **-ᾰλοίας**, gen. α and ου, ὁ, voc. -αλοῖα: (ἀλοιάω):—*one who slays* or *strikes his father, parricide*, Ar.*Nu*.911, 1327, *Ra*.274, Lys.10. 8, Pl.*Phd*.114a, *Sph*.241d, etc.: as fem., Hld.10.38:—sts. written **πατραλῴας** or **πατρολῴας** (-λώας, -λόας) in codd., as 1*Ep.Ti*.1.9, J.*AJ*16.11.1. **-αρχος**, ὁ, (ἄρχω) *tutelary god*, Lxx*Is*.37.38.

**πατρεία**, v. πάτρα III. **πατρέμβατοι**· ὑψηλοί, Hsch. **πάτρη**, ἡ, Ep. and Ion. for πάτρα.

**πάτρηθε** and **-θεν**, Adv., = ἐκ πάτρης, *from one's native land*, A.R. 2.541, etc. II. *from a family* or *clan*, Dor. **πάτρᾱθε** Pi.*N*.7.70.

❋ **πατρι-ά**, Ion. **-ιή**, ἡ, (πατήρ) *lineage, descent*, esp. *by the father's side*, ἐγενεηλόγησε τὴν π. τὴν Κύρου Hdt.3.75, cf. 2.143, *Ev.Luc*.2. 4. II. = πάτρα II. 2, *clan*, Hdt.1.200, *Michel*195.1 (Elis, v B.C.), 995*A*26 (Delph., v B.C.). 2. *family*, Lxx*Ex*.12.3, al., *Ep.Eph*.3. 15. III. in pl., = *patrum officia*, *Cod.Just*.1.5.14. **-άζω**, *take after one's father*, Poll.3.10. ❋ **-άρχης**, ου, ὁ, (πατριά) *father* or *chief of a race, patriarch*, Lxx1*Ch*.27.22, *Act.Ap*.2.29, 7.8, *Ep.Hebr*.7. 4. II. *title borne by the Bishops* of Rome, Constantinople, Jerusalem, Antioch, and Alexandria, Just.*Nov*.3.2, etc.:—Adj. **-αρχικός**, ή, όν, *of* or *belonging to him*, θρόνος ib.7*Praef*.1, cf. *Cod. Just*.1.5.12.22. **-αστί**, later **-εί**, Adv. *with the father's name*, *PHal*. 1.248 (iii B.C.), *SIG*1023.32 (Cos, iii/ii B.C.), 793.13 (ibid., i A.D.).

**πατρίδιον**, τό, Dim. of πατήρ, *papa, daddy*, Ar.*V*.986, Xenarch.4. 15, Theophil.4.

**πατρίκιος**, ὁ, = Lat. *patricius*, Plb.10.4.2, D.H.2.8, 10, 48, etc. 2. = *patricius calceus*, Plu.2.470c (but κάλτιος πα(τρι)κιᾶτος *Edict.Diocl*. 9.7 (pl.). II. later, as a title, *POxy*.1206.1 (iv A.D.), Procop. *Pers*.1.8, Just.*Nov*.38 tit., etc.:—fem. **πατρικία**, *PKlein.Form*.1091 (vi A.D.), etc.

**πατρικιότης**, ητος, ἡ, *patriciate*, Prisc.p.343 D., Just.*Nov*.38 *Praef*.3.

❋ **πατρῐκός**, ή, όν, (πατήρ) *derived from one's fathers, hereditary*, νόμοι Cratin.116; ἀρίς Call.Com.16; φίλος Ar.*Av*.142; φίλοι *OGI*227.9 (Didyma, iii B.C.); βασιλεῖαι Th.1.13, Arist.*Pol*.$1285^a$19; ἁμαρτεῖν τοῦ π. τύπου Democr.228; αἱ π. ἀρεταί Th.7.69; ξένος And.2.11, Th. 8.6; ἐχθρός Lys.14.40; φύσει τῆς πρὸς ὑμᾶς ἔχθρας αὐτοῖς ὑπαρχούσης πατρικῆς D.21.49; εἰς τὸ π., = *by right of inheritance*, *PTeb*.5.12 (ii B.C.). II. = πάτριος, *of* or *belonging to one's father*, γᾶρυς S.*Ichn*. 65 (lyr.); ὁ π. λόγος Pl.*Sph*.242a; ἡ π. πρόσταξις Arist.*EN*$1180^a$19; οἰκονομία π., opp. δεσποτική and γαμική, Id.*Pol*.$1253^b$10; ἐνευχόμενός σοι τοὺς π. θεούς the gods *of your father(s)*, *PCair.Zen*.421.2 (iii B.C.); ἡ πατρική (sc. οὐσία) *patrimony*, E.*Ion*1304; π. οἰκία *PStrassb*.99.4 (ii B.C.); τὰ π. *AP*11.75 (Lucill.); but τὰ π., also, *father's house*, Lxx*Si*.42.10. 2. *like a father, paternal*, π. γὰρ ἀρχὴ βούλεται ἡ βασιλεία εἶναι Arist.*EN*$1160^b$26; π. καὶ συγγενικὴ αἵρεσις Plb.31.25.1; παρρησία π. Plu.2.802f; π. θεός *OGI*418 (Judaea, i A.D.). Adv., τὰς κολάσεις πατρικῶς ποιεῖσθαι Arist.*Pol*.$1315^a$21; ὁ θεὸς π. κηδόμενος τοῦ ἀνθρωπείου γένους Plu.2.117d. 3. Gramm., ἡ πατρική, = ἡ γενική, the *genitive*, Choerob. *in Theod*.1.111 H.

**πατρίληκτος**, ον, *inherited from a father*, Phot.

❋ **πάτριος**, α, ον, Lyr. and Trag.; also ος, ον E.*Hel*.222, and Att. Com., Prose (exc. And.3.27), and Inscrr. (so elsewh., *SIG*539*A*14 (Delph., iii B.C.), 558.21 (Ithaca, iii B.C.), etc.): (πατήρ):—*of* or *belonging to one's father*, ἄρουρα Pi.*O*.2.14; ὅσσα ib.6.62; γῆ S.*Ant*.806 (lyr.), E.*Med*.651 (lyr.); χθών Id.*Hel*.222; τεύχεα, δώματα, S.*Ph*.398 (lyr.), *OT*1394. II. = πατρικός, *derived from one's fathers, hereditary*, οἱ π. θεοί Hdt.1.172, *Sammelb*.6664.5 (Egypt, ii B.C.), *IG*7.2713. 51 (i A.D.); πάτριος θεά *Milet*.7.64 (ii/iii A.D.); αἱ π. τελεταί Ar.*Ra*.368; ἱερά Th.2.16; νόμοι Id.4.118, Decr.ap.Arist.*Ath*.29.3, X.*HG*2.3.2; θυσίαι Isoc.10.63, $IG2^2$.780, etc.; π. πολιτεία Thrasym.1, Arist.*Ath*.34.3, D.S.14.3, etc.; π. ἀρχαί X.*Cyr*.1.1.4, cf. Arist.*Pol*.$1285^a$24,33; αἱ τιμαὶ αἱ π. Isoc.9.32; π. καὶ ἀρχαῖα νόμιμα Pl.*Lg*.793b; τὸν π. ὅρκον *PPetr*.3 p.163 (iii B.C.); -ωτέρα ἡγεμονία *more ancient*, Isoc.4.37; πάτριόν ἐστιν (sc. αὐτοῖς) it is *an hereditary custom* [among them], Ar.*Ec*.778, cf. Th. 1.123, X.*HG*7.1.3, *SIG*695.16 (Magn. Mae., ii B.C.), etc.; οὐ γὰρ π. τᾷ Σπάρτᾳ Tyrt.15.6; οὐκ ἦν ταῦτα τοῖς τότε Ἀθηναίοις πάτρια D.18.203, cf. Pl.*Hp.Ma*.284b; τάδε π. Ὀλβιοπολίταις καὶ Μιλησίοις, in a treaty, *SIG*286.1 (iv B.C.); τὰ πάτρια *ancestral customs*, κατὰ τὰ π. $IG1^2$.76.4, Ar.*Ach*.1000, Th.2.2, etc.; παρὰ τὰ π. Pl.*Plt*.296c; ποιεῖν πρὸς τὴν πόλιν τὰ π. to serve the state *as our fathers* before us, Isoc.4.31: less freq. in sg., τὸ π. παρείς neglecting *the inherited constitution*, Th.4.86. Adv., πατρίως Ἰουδαίοις *according to the custom of* their *fathers*, J.*BJ* 1.24.2; π. καλούμενον *in their native language*, ib.5.2.1, cf. Lyd.*Mens*. 4.64; v. πατρῷος sub fin. III. Subst. πάτριος, ὁ, *uncle*, *BSA*17. 240 (Pamphyl.).

⊛ **πατρίς**, ίδος, poet. fem. of πάτριος, *of one's fathers*, πατρὶς αἶα, ἄρουρα, *one's fatherland, country*, Od.10.236, 20.193; π. γαῖα 24.322, Hes.*Sc.*1,12, A.*Th.*585; γῆ π. S.*OT*641, Ar.*Th.*859 (paratrag.); π. πόλις the city *of one's sires*, Pi.*O.*10(11).36. **II.** Subst., = πάτρα I, Il.5.213, Od.4.586, 9.34, Hdt.3.140, Th.6.69, etc.; κοινὴ π., i.e. *the nether world*, Plu.2.113c: prov., π. γάρ ἐστι πᾶσ' ἵν' ἂν πράττῃ τις εὖ, *ubi bene, ibi patria*, Ar.*Pl.*1151; simply, *native town* or *village*, *UPZ* 9.5 (ii B.C.), *Ev.Marc.*6.1, etc.: pl., ἐν ταῖς αὑτῶν π. D.18.296, cf. 325, Pl.*Plt.*308a, Hyp.*Epit.*10.

**πατριστί**, Adv. = πατρόθεν, *OGI*46.7 (Halic., iii B.C.), *Bull.Soc. royale des lettres de Lund* 1928/9 iv 3 (Thuria, ii B.C.).

**πατρι-ώτης**, ου, Dor. **-τας**, ὁ, voc. **-ῶτα** Nico 1: (πάτριος):—*fellow-countryman*: prop. of barbarians who had only a common πατρίς, πολῖται being used of Greeks who had a common πόλις, Poll.3.54, Hsch., Phot.: hence μήτε πατριώτας ἀλλήλων εἶναι τοὺς μέλλοντας ῥᾷον δουλεύσειν Pl.*Lg.*777c; τοῖσι Λυκούργου π., Lycurgus being satirized as an Egyptian, Pherecr.11, cf. Alex.326; also ἵπποι π., = ἐγχώριοι, X.*Cyr.*2.2.26: metaph., of Mt. Cithaeron, π. Οἰδίπου S.*OT* 1091 (lyr.); π. θεός, of Dionysus, Plu.2.671c; π. ἐστί μοι.—Ans. ἐλάνθανες ἄρα βάρβαρος ὤν Luc.*Sol.*5; cf. πατριῶτις. **II.** later, = πολίτης, Iamb.*VP*5.21. **III.** *member of a* πατριά II. 1, *IG*4.757 *B* 12 (Troezen), *Michel*995 *B*4 (Delph., v B.C.). **-ωτικός**, ή, όν, *of* or *belonging to a* πατριώτης or πατριά, ἀργύριον *BCH*50.16 (Delph., iv B.C.); τεμένη Arist.*Oec.*1346ᵇ15; ἱερά Dicaearch.Hist.9. **-ῶτις**, ιδος, fem. of πατριώτης, π. γῆ, = πατρίς, E.*Heracl.*755 (lyr.); π. στολή *one's own country's* dress, said by a barbarian, Luc.*Scyth.*3. **II.** Ἄρτεμις π. *IG*5(1).602.11 (Sparta).

**πατρό-βουλος**, ὁ, *hereditary senator*, *IG*12(5).141.7 (Paros), Jul. *Ep.*54, *PLond.*3.971.7 (iv A.D.). **-γένειος**, ὁ, epith. of Poseidon, *ancestral*, Plu.2.730e (s.v.l.). **-γενής**, ές, *begotten of the father*, Orac.ap.Dam.*Pr.*206. ⊛ **-γέρων**, οντος, ὁ, *hereditary member of the* γερουσία, *Ephes.*2.20 iii 4 (ii A.D.). **-δίδακτος** [ῐ], ον, *taught by a father*, Sch. ad Tz.*H.*7.959 in *An.Ox.*3.370. **-δώρητος**, ον, *given by a father*, Luc.*Trag.*268.

**πατρόθεν**, Adv., (πατήρ) *from* or *after a father*, π. ἐκ γενεῆς ὀνομάζων naming him *and giving his father's name*, Il.10.68, cf. Hdt.3.1, Th.7.69, Pl.*Ly.*204e; τὸ μὲν π. ἐκ Διὸς εὔχονται *on the father's side*, Pi.*O.*7.23; εἴπερ.. ἔστ' ἐμὸς τὰ π. S.*Aj.*547, cf. *OC*215 (lyr.); ἐν στήλῃ π. ἀναγραφῆναι to have one's name inscribed on a tablet *with the addition of one's father's name*, Hdt.6.14, cf. 8.90; γράψαι τοὔνομα π. καὶ φυλῆς καὶ δήμου to write one's name adding that *of one's father*, tribe, and township, Pl.*Lg.*753c, cf. *OGI*222.44 (Clazomenae, iii B.C.), *Milet.*3 No.152.93 (ii B.C.), etc.; π. καὶ πατρίδος *PRev.Laws* 7.3 (iii B.C.). **2.** *coming from, sent by one's father*, ἀνάγκα π., imposed by Zeus, Pi.*O.*3.28; π. ἀλάστωρ A.*Ag.*1507 (lyr.); π. εὐκταία φάτις a *father's* curse, Id.*Th.* 841 (lyr.). **3.** *from the time of one's fathers*, π. φίλοι τοῦ δήμου *IG* 2².237.8.

**πατρο-κᾰσιγνήτη**, ἡ, *father's sister*, *IG*4²(1).483 (Epid.), Q.S.10. 58. **-κᾰσίγνητος**, ὁ, *father's brother*, Il.21.469, Od.6.330, 13.342, Hes.*Th.*501.

**Πάτροκλος**, ὁ, *Patroclus*, Hom., who has also obl. cases from Πατροκλῆς (-κλέης), viz. gen. Πατροκλῆος, acc. Πατροκλῆα, voc. Πατρόκλεες: gen. pl. Πατρόκλων Ar.*Ra.*1041: nom. **Πατροκλῆς**, Theoc. 15.140: **Πατρόκλεια**, ἡ, name of the sixteenth book of the Iliad, Ael. *VH*13.14, Eust.1041.19.

**πατρο-κόμος**, ον, *taking care of her father*, Nonn.*D.*26.103. **-κτονέω**, *murder one's father*, A.*Ch.*909, Luc.*Tyr.*1. **-κτονία**, ἡ, *murder of a father, parricide*, Hipparch.ap.Stob.4.44.81, Plu.*Rom.*22, Iamb.*VP*17.78 (pl.). **-κτόνιον**, *parricidium*, *Gloss.* ⊛ **-κτόνος**, ον, *murdering one's father, parricidal*, A.*Th.*752 (lyr.), etc.; π. δίκη trial *for parricide*, S.*Fr.*696; π. μίασμα the foul *slayer of my father*, A. *Ch.*1028. also in later Prose, Ph.2.73, Porph.*Abst.*3.19. **II.** χείρ π. *a father's murdering* hand, E.*IT*1083. **-λάθησις** [λᾰ], εως, ἡ, *neglect of one's father*, *PMasp.*97 *B* 51 (vi A.D.).

**πατρ-ολέτωρ**, ορος, ὁ, *parricide*, *AP*11.348 (Antiphan.). **-ολοός**, ὁ, = foreg., *PMasp.*353.7 (vi A.D.). **-ολῴας**, v. πατραλοίας.

⊛ **πατρο-μήτωρ**, ορος, ὁ, *mother's father*, Luc.*Alex.*58. **2.** fem., *grandmother*, Lyc.502. **-μύστης**, ου, ὁ, *one whose father was a* μύστης, *hereditary* μύστης, *IGRom.*4.1393 (Smyrna).

**πατρονομ-έω**, *hold office of* πατρονόμος, *IG*5(1).18 *B*4 (Sparta). **II.** Pass., *to be under a patriarchal government*, Pl.*Lg.*680e, Plu.*Dio* 10. **-ία**, ἡ, *paternal government*, Luc.*Dem.Enc.*12. **II.** *office of* πατρονόμος, at Sparta, *IG*5(1).311, al.; ἡ θεοῦ Λυκούργου π. ib.541. 17. **-ικός**, ή, όν, *pertaining to fatherly rule*: ἡ -κή (sc. ἀρχή or τροφή) *the rule* or *nurture of a father*, Pl.*Lg.*927e. **-ος**, ὁ, *member of the council* instituted by Cleomenes III at Sparta, *IG*5(1).32, al., Plu.2.795f, Paus.2.9.1, Philostr.*VA*4.32; ἐπὶ π. σεῶ Λυκούργω *IG*5 (1).311.

**πατρο-παράδοσις**, εως, ἡ, *ancestral tradition*, *PMasp.*151.183 (vi A.D.). **-παράδοτος**, ον, *handed down from one's fathers, inherited*, ἡ μικρὰ καὶ π. οὐσία D.H.5.48; ἡ π. ἡγεμονία D.S.17.4; ἀναστροφή 1*Ep.Pet.*1.18; Ζεύς *OGI*331.49 (Pergam., ii B.C.), παρέχεσθαι π. τὴν εὔνοιαν *CIG*2134*b*4 (prob.), cf. *IG*12(5).860.4 (Tenos). **-πάτωρ** [ᾰ], ορος, ὁ, *father's father*, Pi.*P.*9.82, *N.*6.16, A.R.1.170, *IG*12(5).303 (Paros); as title of gods, π. Σάραπις *Sammelb.*5802.4 (i A.D.), cf. 1570. 4 (i B.C.). ⊛ **-ποίητος**, ον, *adopted as a father*, *Supp.Epigr.*6.77 (Galatia, iii A.D., in form -πόητος), *Klio* 24.61 (Galatia, written -φοίητος). **-πολις**, εως, ἡ, coined by Antiph.220 in the line μητρόπολίς ἐστιν οὐχὶ π. πόλις. **-ρραίστης**, ου, ὁ, *parricide*, Suid. **-στερής**, ές, *reft of father, fatherless*, A.*Ch.*253. **-τῠπία**, ἡ, *act of beating one's father*, *Corp.Herm.*9.3 (pl.). **-τύπτης**, ου, ὁ, *one who beats his father*, Is.*Fr.*166, Ph.1.135, S.E.*M.*2.44, Theon *Prog.*13. ⊛ **-τυψία**, ἡ, *beating of one's father*, S.E.*M.*2.46.

**πατρούεος**, α, ον, Thess. for πατρῷος, πατρῷος, *IG*9(2).234.4 (Pharsalus, iii B.C.).

**πατροῦχος παρθένος**, ἡ, *heiress*, Hdt.6.57 codd. (fort. πατρωοῦχος, cf. πατρωιῶχος).

**πατρο-φάγος** [φᾰ], ον, *devouring one's patrimony, spendthrift*, *Gloss.* **-φονεύς**, έως, Ep. ῆος, ὁ, *murderer of one's father*, [Ὀρέστης] ἔκτανε πατροφονῆα Αἴγισθον.., ὅ οἱ πατέρα κλυτὸν ἔκτα Od.1.299, cf. 3. 197. **-φονέω**, *commit parricide*, Phld.*Sto.*339.10. **-φόνος**, ον, *slaying a father*, χείρ A.*Th.*783 (lyr.); μάτηρ E.*Or.*193 (lyr.). **II.** Subst., *parricide*, Pl.*Lg.*869b. **-φόντης**, ου, ὁ, = foreg., S.*OT* 1441: fem., τῆς π. μητρός Id.*Tr.*1125.

**πατρυιός**, ὁ, *stepfather*, *CIG*3445 (Lydia), *Cat.Cod.Astr.*8(4).128, Eust.560.26: also **πατρυός**, *Cat.Cod.Astr.*2.174.

**πατρῴζω**, = πατριάζω, Hdn.1.7.1, Alciphr.3.14, Them.*Or.*5.71b: c. acc. modi, π. τὴν σοφίαν Philostr.*VA*6.16; τὴν δεινότητα Id.*VS*2. 9.3.

**πατρώϊος**, v. πατρῷος.

**πατρωϊστής**, οῦ, Dor. **-τάς**, ὁ, *worshipper of a* θεὸς πατρῷος, *Schwyzer* 137 (Corc.).

⊛ **πατρωϊῶχος**, = πατροῦχος, *Leg.Gort.*7.15, al.

⊛ **πάτρων**, ωνος, ὁ, = Lat. *patronus*, *SIG*656.23 (Abdera, found at Teos, ii B.C.), *IG*7.83 (Megara), D.S.29.27, Plu.*Fab.*13, Arr.*Epict.* 3.9.18, etc.:—fem. **πατρώνα**, dub. in *GDI*2282 (Delph.). **II.** *uncle*, *IGRom.*4.621 (Temenothyrae, iii A.D.).

**πατρων-εία** or **-ία**, ἡ, = Lat. *patronatus*, D.H.2.10, Plu.*Rom.*13, Paul.Al.*L.*3. ⊛ **-εύω**, *to be a patron*, *GDI*2688.7 (Delph., i B.C.):—Pass., D.S.40.5, *PMasp.*151.229 (vi A.D.). **-ης**, ου, ὁ, = πάτρων I, *IGRom.*4.170, 171 (Cyzic.). **-ίκιον**, τό, in pl., *rights of a patron*, *PMasp.*29.5 (vi A.D.). ⊛ **-ικός**, ή, όν, *of* or *for a* πάτρων, *POxy.* 1205.6 (iii A.D.), Just.*Nov.*1.4.1, Suid. ⊛ **-ισσα**, ἡ, *patroness*, *IG* 14.1671, *Stud.Pont.*3.190, *POxy.*478.27 (ii A.D.), etc.

**πατρωνῠμ-έομαι**, Pass., *have the patronymic formed*, Eust.13. 41. **-ία**, ἡ, *name taken from one's father, patronymic*, as Πηλεΐδης, Ἀτρεΐδης, Id.1388.24. **-ικός**, ή, όν, *derived from one's father's name, patronymic*, ὄνομα D.H.3.48, cf. D.T.634.26, S.E.*M.*1.133; τύπος A.D.*Conj.*248.6: -κόν, τό, ib.7. **-ιος**, ον: τὸ π., as Adv., *by the father's side*, A.*Pers.*146 (s.v.l., anap.). ⊛ **-ος**, ον, *named after his father*, *Quarterly of Dept. of Antiquities in Palestine* 1.155 (Gaza, iii A.D.).

⊛ **πατρῷος**, α, ον, also ος, ον A.*Ag.*210 (lyr.), E.*Supp.*1147 (lyr.), etc.; Ep. and Ion. **πατρώϊος**, η, ον, the only form used in Hom., Hes., and Hdt.; the former first in Thgn.888, Pi.*P.*4.290, though both use the longer form, Thgn.521, Pi.*P.*4.220; Thess. **πατρούεος** (q.v.): (πατήρ):—*of* or *from one's father, coming* or *inherited from him*, σκῆπτρον, ἔγχος, Il.2.46, 19.387; τέμενος, δῶμα, οἶκος, 20.391, 21.44, Hes.*Op.*376; ξεῖνος πατρώϊός ἐσσι παλαιός my old *hereditary* friend, Il.6.215; π. ἑταῖροι Od.2.254, 17.69; γαῖα πατρωΐη one's *fatherland*, 13.188, 251; πατρῴα γῆ Thgn.888, Pi.*P.*4.290, S.*El.*67, etc.; π. οὖδας A.*Ag.*1450; ἄστυ S.*OT*1450; δῶμα, ἑστία, κοῖται, E. *Or.*1595, *Hec.*22, S.*El.*194 (lyr.); πατρώϊα one's *father's goods, patrimony*, Od.17.80, 20.336, 22.61; τὰ π. Hdt.9.26, Ar.*Th.*819, Lys. 27.11, v.l. in Arist.*Pol.*1303ᵇ34; τὰ π. χρήματα Ar.*Av.*1658; θρόνος A.*Pr.*230, cf. S.*El.*268, etc.; δοῦλοι π. Hdt.2.1; γέρεα Id.7.104; θυσίαι D.*Ep.*3.30 codd.; ἀρχή X.*An.*1.7.6; π. δόξα *hereditary* glory, Id.*HG*7.5.16 (but πατρῷα καὶ παππῷα δόξα *of our fathers* and grandfathers, D.10.73); π. οἰκία, κλῆρος, And.1.62, Pl.*Chrm.*157e, *Lg.* 923d, etc.; οὐσία Anaxandr.45; ἡ εἰρήνη ἡ π. *IG*4²(1).68.13 (Epid., iv B.C.); ἔχων π. ἡμῶν ὑποθήκην *Sammelb.*7339.6 (i A.D.); π. θεοί tutelary gods *of a family* or *people*, as Apollo at Athens, S.*Ph.*933, cf. Pl.*Euthd.*302d, Arist.*Ath.*55.3, *Sammelb.*6262.5 (iii A.D.); Zeus among the Dorians, A.*Fr.*162.3; πρὸς θεῶν π. καὶ μητρῴων X.*HG* 2.4.21, cf. Th.7.69: sg., *Berl.Sitzb.*1927.169 (Cyrene); Zeus was the θεὸς π. of Heracles, S.*Tr.*288, 753; of Orestes, E.*El.*671; Ζεὺς π. was also the god *who protects parents' rights*, Ar.*Nu.*1468, Pl. *Lg.*881d, etc. **II.** = πάτριος, *of* or *belonging to one's father*, μῆλα Od.12.136; π. πρὸς στάθμαν Pi.*P.*6.45; π. ἄεθλοι *imposed by him*, ib.4. 220; but π. ἆθλος *of him*, S.*Ant.*856 (lyr.); π. γνώμη ib.640; π. φόνοι, πήματα, Id.*OC*990, 1196; π. χέρες A.*Ag.*210 (lyr.), etc.; τὰ πατρῷα *the cause of one's father*, opp. τὰ μητρῷα, Hdt.3.53.—Gramm. distd. πατρῷος, as expressing *patrimonial possession*, from πάτριος as expressing hereditary manners, customs, institutions; v. Ammon. *Diff.* s.v., *AB*297, Suid., etc.—The distn. holds in Att. Prose; but Hom. and Hdt. use πατρώϊος only, and in all these senses; so also Trag. [πάτριος shd. be restored in all passages in Trag. where the 2nd syll. is made short in anap. and lyr., E.*Hec.*82, *Tr.*162, *Ba.* 1368, *El.*1315, *Alc.*249; but γῆς ἀπὸ πατρωΐης ends a pentameter in *IG*1².978.]

**πατρωός**, ὁ, = πατρυιός, *stepfather*, Cerc.4.43, Plu.*Cleom.*11, *Arat.* 41, Artem.3.26, *POxy.*1257.2 (iii A.D.).

⊛ **πάτρως**, ὁ, gen. ωος and ω; dat. πάτρῳ Pi.*P.*6.46, Hdt.6.103, *PCair.Zen.*580 (iii B.C.); acc. πάτρωα Stesich.17, *Leg.Gort.*12.29, J.*AJ* 19.2.1, πάτρων Hdt.4.76, 9.78: pl. πάτρωες Eust.316.15 (but οἱ πάτρω *BCH*11.471 (Lydia)); Cret. acc. pl. πάτρωανς *Leg.Gort.*8.44; dat. pl. πάτρωσι Dessau *ILS* 8897: (πατήρ):—*father's brother, uncle*, ll. cc.

**παττᾰλεύω**, Att. for πασσαλεύω.

**πατταλίας**, ου, ὁ, *two-year-old stag* or *buck*, when the horns are still mere pegs or 'dags', *brocket* or *pricket*, Arist.*HA*611ᵃ34.

**πάτταλος, πάττω**, Att. for πασσ-.

⊛ **πάτωρ** [ᾰ], ορος, ὁ, (*πάομαι) *possessor*, prob. for πατήρ in Critias 15. 4 D., cf. Hsch.

**πατώσας** (-ώμας cod.)· διατριβούσας, Hsch. **παῦ**, v. παύω.

**παῦλα**, ἡ, (παύω) *rest, pause*, S.*OC*88 ; οὐκ ἐν παύλῃ ἐφαίνετο there seemed to be no *end of it*, Th.6.60. 2. c. gen., π. νόσου *cessation* or *end* of disease, S.*Ph.*1329, cf. Hp.*Mul.*2.124 ; κακῶν S.*Tr.*1255, Plu.*Thes.*15 ; μόχθων prob. in B.9.8 ; παροξυσμοῦ Gal.10.604 ; παῦλαν ἔχον κινήσεως παῦλαν ἔχει ζωῆς Pl.*Phdr.*245c ; ἡδονὴν.. παῦλαν λύπης εἶναι Id.*R.*584b ; π. ταῖς γυναιξὶ τοῦ τεκνοῦσθαι Arist.*HA*585ᵃ35 ; ἡ π. τῆς τεκνοποιίας Id.*Pol.*1335ᵃ31 ; παῦλάν τιν' αὐτῶν some *means of stopping* them, X.*An.*5.7.32. (Written παῦλλα Puchstein *Epigr.Gr.*p.7.)

⊛ **παυνί**· μικρόν, οἱ δὲ μέγα ἢ ἀγαθόν, Hsch. **παῦνις**· ἀπόχρεως, Id. **παῦνον**· μέγα, Id. ⊛ **παυράκις**· ὀλιγάκις ἢ οὐδὲν ὅλως, Id. **παυρακίς**, = ἡ πέμπτη (Samothrac.), Id.

**παυράς**, άδος, poet. fem. of παῦρος, Nic. *Th.*210.

**παυρίδιος** [ῐδ], η, ον, = παῦρος, π. ἐπὶ χρόνον Hes.*Op.*133.

⊛ **παυρο-επής**, ές, *of few words*, *AP*7.713 (Antip.). **-λόγος**, v. πραϋλόγος.

⊛ **παῦρος**, ον (not found in fem., cf. παυράς), *little, small*, στήμων Hes.*Op.*538 ; π. ἔπος Pi.*O.*13.98 ; of Time, *short*, Hes.*Op.*326 ; ζωῆς μέρος Emp.2.3 ; π. ὕπνος Pi.*P.*9.25 (s.v.l.) ; *speedy*, τέλος βιότοιο Q.S.7.613 : neut. as Adv., *for a short time*, παῦρον ἀνθήσας Lyc. 1429. 2. mostly of Number, *few*, poet. for ὀλίγος (q.v.) in this sense, Ep., Lyr., and Trag., π. ἄνδρες Thgn.79 ; π. τινές Pi.*O.*10(11).22 ; π. ἀνδρῶν A.*Ag.*832 : rare in Prose, as Thphr.*HP*8.7.4 ; παῦρα, opp. πολλά, Il.9.333, cf. Od.2.241 : with a collect. Subst., π. λαός *small in number*, Il.2.675 : Comp. παυρότερος 4.407, 8.56, al., Thgn. 644 : neut. pl. παῦρα as Adv., *seldom*, Hes.*Th.*780, Ar.*Pax*764. (Cf. Lat. *paucus*, Goth. *fawai* 'few'.)

**παῦς**, ὁ, ἡ, in nom. sg., = παῖς, Kretschmer *Griech.Vaseninschr.* p.188.

**παυσ-άνεμος** [ᾰ], ον, *stilling the wind*, θυσία A.*Ag.*215 (lyr.). ⊛**-ανίας** [ῑ], ου, ὁ, *allayer of sorrow*, S.*Fr.*887 (ubi leg. π. κάκ' Ἀτρειδᾶν *allaying the sorrows* of the A.).

**παυσί-κακος** [ῐ], ον, *ending evils*, Sch.Pi.*O.*2.1. **-κάπη** [ᾰ], ἡ, (κάπτω) *projecting collar worn by slaves* while grinding corn or kneading bread, to prevent them from eating any of the ἄλφιτα, Ar.*Fr.*302, cf. Ael.Dion.*Fr.*276 ; also by animals, Suid. **-λῡπος**, ον, *ending pain*, Ζεύς S.*Fr.*425 (lyr.) ; ἄμπελος E.*Ba.*772 ; ὁ π. οἶκος, i.e. the grave, *IG*14.2136. **-νοσος**, ον, *curing sickness*, ib.3.900. **-νύσταλος**, ον, *stopping drowsiness*, Ael.Dion.*Fr.*277. **-πονος**, ον, *ending toil* or *hardship*, c. gen., E.*IT*451 (lyr.), Ar.*Ra.*1321 (lyr.) ; παυσιπόνῳ λάθας πόματι *Epigr.Gr.*244.10 (Cyzic.).

⊛ **παῦσις**, εως, ἡ, *stopping, ceasing*, Lxx *Je.*31(48).2.

**παυστέον**, (παύω) *one must stop, put an end to*, Pl.*R.*391e, *Grg.* 523d, etc. II. (παύομαι) *one must cease*, Plu.2.6c : c. gen., τῆς ὁρμῆς Dexipp.Hist.26.10 J.

**παυσ-τήρ**, ῆρος, ὁ, *one who stops* or *relieves*, νόσου S.*Ph.*1438, cf. *El.*304, Alex.240.9. **-τήριος**, ον, *fit for ending* or *relieving*, νόσου S.*OT*150. II. **παυστήριον**, τό, *alleviation*, Nic.*Th.*746 ; τοῦ κακοῦ Ar.Byz.Arg.S.*OT*11. 2. *outwork, fence*, Hsch. 3. pl., name of mountains on which Orion died, Id. **-τικός**, ή, όν, = foreg. I, δίψης *EM*543.51. **-τωρ**, ορος, ὁ, = παυστήρ, νόσων Isyll. 56. **-υβρις**, ι, *checking insolence*, cj. in A.*Fr.*360. **-ώδῡνος**, ον, (ὀδύνη) *soothing pain*, Sch.S.*Ph.*44. **-ωλή**, ἡ, *rest*, Il.2.386.

**παύω**, Il.19.67, etc. : Ion. impf. παύεσκον Od.22.315, S.*Ant.*963 (lyr.) : fut. παύσω Il.1.207, etc. ; Ep. inf. παυσέμεν (κατα-) 7.36 : aor. ἔπαυσα 15.15, etc., Ep. παῦσα 17.602 : pf. πέπαυκα D.20.70, Antisth. *Od.*10 :—**Med.** and **Pass.**, Ion. impf. παυέσκετο Il.24.17 : fut. παύσομαι Od.2.198, Hdt.1.56, S.*OC*1040, *Ph.*1424, E.*Med.*93, etc. ; πεπαύσομαι only S.*Ant.*91, *Tr.*587 (though held to be the true Att. form by Moer.p.293 P.) ; παυσθήσομαι (v.l. παυθ-) Th.1.81 ; later παήσομαι (ἀνα-) *Apoc.*14.13 : aor. ἐπαυσάμην Il.14.260 ; ἐπαύθην, Ep. παύθην, Hes.*Th.*533, Th.5.91 (v.l. παυσθῇ), etc. ; ἐπαύσθην Hdt.5.94, etc. ; later ἐπάην Choerob. *in Theod.*2.141 H. : pf. πέπαυμαι Il.18.125, A.*Pr.*615, Hdt.1.84, Ar.*Pax*29, etc. (πεπάσθαι is f.l. in Vett.Val.359.31) : I. causal, *make to end*. 1. c. acc. only, *bring to an end, check*, sts. of persons, ἵνα παύσομεν ἄγριον ἄνδρα Il.21.314, cf. S.*Ant.*963 (lyr.), Ar.*Eq.* 330 ; *stop* or *silence* by death, Od.20.274, S.*OT*397 :— Pass. and Med., *take one's rest*, ἐνὶ κλισίῃ Il.24.17, cf. Hdt.9.52, etc. ; *cease, have done*, Il.8.295, Od.4.103, etc. : of one singing or speaking, 17.359, Hdt.7. 8.δ' : generally, Med. denotes *willing*, Pass. *forced, cessation*. b. mostly of things, *make an end of, stop, abate*, χόλον, μένος, νεῖκος πολέμοιο, ῥόον, ὀδύνας, etc., Il.19.67, 1.282, Od.24.543, 5.451, Il.16. 528, etc. ; μέριμναν Pi.*I.*8(7).13 (s.v.l.) ; λύπας ᾠδαῖς π. E.*Med.*197 (anap.), etc. ; π. τόξον *let* the bow *rest*, Od.21.279 ; π. τοὺς γάμους S. *Ant.*575 ; πόντου σάλον E.*El.*1242 ; π. τὸν νόμον *annul* it, Id.*Or.*571 ; π. τὸν λόγον *close* it, X.*Cyr.*8.6.7 ; τυραννίδα καταλύσαντα πεπαυκέναι D.20.70 ; π. τείχη *raze* them, D.C.69.9 :—Pass., Th.5.91, etc. 2. c. acc. pers. et gen. rei, *hinder, keep back*, or *give one rest, from* a thing, π. Ἕκτορα μάχης, πόνοιο Ἀχιλῆα, Θάμυριν ἀοιδῆς, Πηνελόπειαν κλαυθμοῖο, Il.15.15, 21.137, 2.595, Od.4.801 ; π. τινὰ ἀλκῆς, ἄλης, καμάτοιο, ὀδυνάων, Il.15.250, Od.15.342, 5.492, Il.4.191 : so π. χεῖρας πολέμοιο 21.294 ; ὀρχηθμοῖο πόδας Od.23.298 ; π. τινὰ τῆς βοῆς S.*El.*798 ; τῆς ὕβρεως Ar.*Av.*1259 ; τῆς λυγγός Pl.*Smp.*185d ; τῆς ἁμαρτίας καὶ ἀμαθίας Id.*Lg.*784c ; τῶν ἐπιθυμιῶν X.*Mem.*1.2.5 ; [τῆς νόσου] *IG*4²(1). 121.71 (Epid., iv B.C.) ; π. τινὰ τῆς βασιληΐης *depose* one *from* being king, Hdt.1.123 ; τινὰ τῆς ἀρχῆς, τῆς στρατηγίας, X.*Cyr.*8.6.3, *HG*6. 2.13 ; τῆς ἔξω ξυμμαχίας τινάς Th.3.65 ; also π. τινὰ ἐκ κακῶν S.*El.*987 ; τινὰ ἀπὸ παιδαγωγῶν X.*Lac.*3.1 ; with acc. unexpressed, αἴ κέ ποθι Ζεὺς.. παύσῃ ὀϊζύος Od.4.35 ; φάρμαχ' ἅ κεν παύσῃσι.. ὀδυνάων Il.4. 191 :—Pass. and Med., *rest* or *cease from* a thing, πολέμοιο, μάχης, ἔργων, πόνου, γόοιο, κλαυθμοῦ, ὀδυνάων, κλαγγῆς, etc., 21.432, 467, Od.4.683, 24.384, 9.540, 17.7, 4.812, Il.2.100, etc. ; τῆς μάχης, τοῦ δρόμου, Hdt.1.74, 4.124 ; γόων E.*Med.*1211 ; τῆς ὀργῆς Lys.19.6 ; φιλανθρώπου τρόπου A.*Pr.*11 ; παύεσθαι ἀρχῆς *to be deposed from*, or *reach the term of*, office, Hdt.1.56, cf. 6.66, *IG*1².114.46 ; ἐκ μεγάλων ἀχέων παυσαίμεθ' ἄν Ar.*Ra.*1531 (lyr.) ; ἐκ τρόχων πεπαυμένοι E.*Med.*46, cf. *El.*1108. 3. c. pres. part., *stop* a person *from*.., π. τινὰ ἀριστεύοντα *stop* him *from* doing bravely, Il.11.506 ; τὸν ἄνδρα παῦσον ταῦτα ποιεῦντα Hdt.5.23 ; γελῶντας ἐχθροὺς π. S.*El.*1295 ; παύσω δέ σ' ὄντ' ἄπαιδα E.*Med.*717 :—Pass. and Med., *leave off doing*.., ὄθ' ὕπνος ἕλοι, παύσαιτό τε νηπιαχεύων when *he stopped* playing, Il.22. 502, cf. A.*Pr.*615, *Ag.*1047, Hdt.1.133, etc. ; of things, ἄνεμος μὲν ἐπαύσατο.. θύων Od.12.400 : the part. is freq. to be supplied, αἷμα, φλόξ, ἄνεμος ἐπαύσατο, the blood *stopped* [flowing], the fire [burning], the wind [blowing], Il.11.267, 23.228, Od.12.168, etc. ; so Ῥοδώπιος πέρι πέπαυμαι (sc. λέγων) Hdt.2.135, cf. 7.10. 4. less freq. c. inf., *stop* a person *from*.., ἔμ' ἔπαυσας ἐπὶ Τρώεσσι μάχεσθαι Il.11. 442 ; ῥαψῳδοὺς ἔπαυσε ἀγωνίζεσθαι Hdt.5.67, cf. 7.54 : sts. with μή inserted, θνητούς γ' ἔπαυσα μὴ προδέρκεσθαι μόρον A.*Pr.*250 ; παύσας ὑμᾶς μὴ λίαν ἐξαπατᾶσθαι Ar.*Ach.*634 ; also π. τὸ μὴ προσελθεῖν.. τὴν ὁλκάδα Th.7.53 ; π. τοῦ.. εἶναι Pl.*R.*416c. b. Med. c. inf., Batr.193, *AP*6.21.8, and later Prose, as Plu.2.216d. 5. Med., *yield, give*, of timber, opp. ἵστασθαι, Thphr.*HP*5.6.3. II. intr. in imper. παῦε, *cease, leave off* (παύου is rare, S.*Ichn.*359, Ephipp.5.20, Luc.*Im.*2), παῦε μάχης Hes.*Sc.*449 codd., cf. *h.Cer.*351 ; παῦε γόοιο *Epigr.Gr.*320.5 (Thyatira) : mostly abs., παῦε *stop! have done! be quiet!* παῦε, μὴ λέξῃς πέρα S.*Ph.*1275, cf. Ar.*V.*1208, *Ra.*122, 269, Pl.*Phdr.*228e ; παῦε, παῦε, μὴ βόα Ar.*Av.*1504, cf. *V.*1194 ; also παῦε, παῦε τοῦ λόγου Id.*Ra.*580 ; παῦε, παῦ' ὀρχούμενος Id.*Pax*326 ; παῦ' ἐς κόρακας Id.*Ach.*864, where the other Verbs are pl. ; παῦ, apoc. for παῦε, παῦ, μηδὲν ὄμνυ' Men.*Sam.*96, cf. Ael.Dion.*Fr.*275, etc. : also imper. Med., παῦσαι λέγουσα E.*Hipp.*706 ; παῦσαι φαρμακοπωλῶν Ar.*Fr.*28 ; π. μελῳδοῦσ' *Com.Adesp.*601 ; π. δυσωνῶν Pl.Com.224, cf. Theopomp.Com.62, Philetaer.6, Philem.213.1 ; παύσασθε νοῦν ἔχοντες (leg. λέγοντες) Men.482.1.

**Παφλᾰγ-ών**, όνος, ὁ, *Paphlagonian*, Il.2.851, al. (pl.) ; of Cleon (with play on παφλάζω), Ar.*Eq.*2, 6, *Nu.*581, al. :—Adj. **-ονικός**, ή, όν, X.*An.*5.4.13 : ἡ -κή *the country*, ib.6.1.15.

⊛ **παφλ-άζω**, Aeol. **-άσδω** Alc.*Supp.*25.4 (p.28 Lobel) :—*boil, bluster*, of the sea, κύματα παφλάζοντα Il.13.798 ; αἰθὴρ παφλάζων καταΐσσεται Emp.100.7 ; of *boiling* soup, Ar.*Fr.*498 ; λοπὰς π. βαρβάρῳ λαλήματι Eub.109 :—Med., ἔγχελυς.. παφλάζεται Antiph.217. 4. II. metaph., *splutter, bluster*, of Cleon (cf. foreg.), Ar.*Pax* 314, *Eq.*919 ; κόμποις π. Timocl.15.3. 2. κραδίη πάφλαζεν, of passion, Musae.91. 3. *seethe*, τοῖς λωποδύταις ὁ πόρος π. Cratin. 206. 4. π. τῇ γλώσσῃ *stammer, stutter*, Hp.*Epid.*2.5.2, *Judic.*43. (Redupl., perh. cf. φλέδων.) **-ασμα**, ατος, τό, *boiling* : metaph., in pl., *blusterings*, Ar.*Av.*1243.

**Πάφος** [ᾰ], ἡ, *Paphos*, Od.8.363, *h.Ven.*59 :—Adj. ⊛**Πάφιος** [ᾰ], α, ον, freq. of Aphrodite, νὴ τὴν Π. Ἀφροδίτην Ar.*Lys.*556 : abs. ἡ Παφίη *AP*5.30 (Antip. Thess.), 93 (Rufin.), etc.

**παφών**· κτείνας, Hsch. (v. θείνω II).

**παχάνοψ**, οπος, ὁ, ἡ, dub. sens., γῆ *PTeb.*214 (ii B.C.).

**πάχετος** [ᾰ], ον, = παχύς, *thick, massive*, twice in Od., λάβε δίσκον μείζονα καὶ πάχετον 8.187 ; πάχετος δ' ἦν ἠΰτε κίων 23.191. (Wrongly expld. by Hsch. and *EM*656.53 as sync. from παχύτερον ; for the termination cf. περιμήκετος.) 2. *tight*, of a knot or ligature, Hp. *Mul.*2.110 : neut. as Adv., Id.*Cord.*6. II. in later Ep. as neut. Subst., = πάχος, *thickness*, Nic.*Th.*385 (dub.), 387, 465, Opp.*H.*4.535 codd. (Oxyt. in cod. Hp. ll. cc.)

**παχήμερον**· τὸ Μενδήσιον λεγόμενον, Hsch.

**πάχης** [ᾰ], ητος, ὁ, ἡ, *fleshy, stout*, Tz.*H.*9.305. II. **πάχητες**· πλούσιοι, παχεῖς, Hsch. ; cf. παχύς II.

**πᾰχίων** [ῑ], **πάχιστος**, v. παχύς.

⊛ **πᾰχν-η**, ἡ, (πήγνυμι) *hoar-frost, rime* (defined as frozen rain, Posidon.ap.D.L.7.153), Od.14.476 ; π. ἑῴα A.*Pr.*25 ; τὸ ἐπὶ γῆς συμπαγὲν ἐκ δρόσου γενόμενον π. λέγεται Pl.*Ti.*59e ; opp. κρύσταλλος, Theognet.1.3 : pl., πάχναι καὶ χάλαζαι Pl.*Smp.*188b ; ἀπέκαυσεν ἡ π. τὰς ἀμπέλους Philippid.25.4. 2. metaph., γήρως εὐρῶτα καὶ πάχνην the mould and *frost* of age, descriptive of an old man's grey hair, *Com.Adesp.*650a, cf. 381 ; π. κουροβόρος *clotted blood* of the eaten children, A.*Ag.*1512 (lyr.). **-ήεις**, εσσα, εν, *frosty*, Nonn. *D.*3.4. **-όω**, *congeal, solidify*, Plu.2.396b :—Pass., ib.736a. b. πεπαχνῶσθαι *to be covered with rime*, *Gp.*12.17.1. 2. metaph., *strike chill*, ἐπάχνωσεν φίλον ἦτορ *made* his blood *curdle*, Hes.*Op.*360 :— mostly in Pass., ἦτορ παχνοῦται his heart *is cold and stiff* [with grief], Il.17.112 ; παχνοῦσθαι πένθεσιν, λύπῃ, A.*Ch.*83 (lyr.), E.*Hipp.*803 : in later Prose, ἐπαχνώθη J.*BJ*1.28.3. **-ώδης**, ες, = παχνήεις, *Gp.* 1.12.27 : metaph., *chill, cold*, αὐχμός *Hymn.Is.*146.

**πάχος** [ᾰ], εος, τό, (παχύς) *thickness*, τόσσον ἔην μῆκος τόσσον π. Od.9.324 ; εἰ ἔχοι π. ἔχοι ἂν μόρια Meliss.9 ; τὸ π. τοῦ τείχους Th.1. 93 ; τῆς πλίνθου Id.3.20 : pl., τὰ π. τῶν τριχῶν Arist.*HA*517ᵇ8 ; τὰ π.

αὐτῶν ἐκμυελιεῖ Lxx *Nu.*24.8; σκήνεια ὀρθὰ καὶ πάχη ἔχοντα *PCair.Zen.*353.11 (iii B.C.): abs., πάχος *in thickness*, Hdt.4.81, *IG*1$^2$.372.11; also πάχει μάκει τε Pi.*P.*4.245. **2.** σαρκὸς π. *stoutness*, E.*Cyc.*380; διὰ πάχος τοῦ σώματος Antiph.19; opp. λεπτότης, Pl.*R.*523e, etc. **3.** *consistency, thickness*, of liquids or fluids, Arist.*Sens.*441$^a$29, *GA*739$^a$12; τὸ π. τῆς θαλάσσης, attributed to its saltness, Id.*Mete.*359$^a$7; ὥστε γίνεσθαι τὸ π. ὡς κυκεῶνα Ph.*Bel.*89.21. **4.** in concrete sense, *thick mass*, Dsc.5.18.

**πᾰχύ-αιμος** [ῠ], ον, *thick-blooded*, Hp.*Vict.*2.46. **-βλεφᾰρία**, ἡ, *swelling of the eyelids*, Cyran.35. **-δάκτῠλος**, ον, *thick-fingered*, Polem.*Phgn.*86. **-δενδρος**, ον, *thick with trees*, ἄλση Him.*Or.*23.17. **-δερμέω**, *to be thick-skinned*, *Gloss.* **-δερμία**, Ion. -ίη, ἡ, *thickness of skin*, Hp.*Epid.*5.9. **-δερμος**, ον, *thick-skinned*, Arist.*GA*783$^a$2: Comp., ib.782$^b$5. **2.** metaph., *dull, stupid*, Men.*Epit.*574, Luc.*Tim.*23. **-θριξ**, ὁ, ἡ, gen. τρῐχος, *with thick hair*: Comp. -τριχώτερος Arist.*GA*782$^b$5. **-κάλᾰμος** [κᾰ], ον, *thick-stalked*, Thphr.*CP*3.21.2. **-κάρδιος**, ον, = βαρυκάρδιος, *Gloss.* **-καυλος**, ον, *with a thick stalk* or *stem*, Thphr.*HP*6.2.6 (Comp.). **-κνημος**, ον, *with fat* or *thick legs*, Ar.*Pl.*560, D.L.7.1.

**πᾰχῠλός**, ή, όν, Dim. of παχύς, *thickish*: only Adv. -λῶς *coarsely, roughly*, opp. ἀκριβῶς, Arist.*EN*1094$^b$20.

**πᾰχῠ-μέρεια**, ἡ, *thickness of parts*, S.E.*M.*9.86; opp. λεπτομέρεια, Theo Sm.p.97 H. ⊛ **-μερής**, ές, *consisting of thick* or *coarse parts*, Ti.Locr.100e (Comp.), Arist.*Pr.*873$^a$6; ἀήρ Corn.*ND*5 (Sup.); τὸ παχυμερές *the dense part*, Epicur.*Ep.*2 p.51 U.; τὸ -έστερον, opp. τὸ λεπτομερέστερον, Arist.*Cael.*304$^a$31; τὸ -έστατον *Placit.*1.3.11. **II.** metaph. in Adv., *loosely, broadly, roughly*, εἴρηται παχυμερῶς Str.1.4.7, cf. 8 (Comp.), Ach.Tat.*Intr.Arat.*18; *cursorily*, ἐξετάζειν Just.*Nov.*53.4.1. **-νευρέω**, *have swollen sinews*, Str.14.5.12. **-νοος**, ον, contr. **-νους**, ουν, *thick-witted*, Hsch., Phot. (-νοοι and -νοες).

**πάχυν-σις** [ᾰ], εως, ἡ, *thickening*, Arist.*Mete.*383$^a$11, Thphr.*CP*6.11.7; *hardening* of eggs by boiling, Gal.6.707. **-τικός**, ή, όν, *having the power of thickening*, c. gen., Dsc.5.71; *fattening*, Ath.Med. ap.Orib.*inc.*23.27; τροφαί Sor.1.21. **-ω**, pf. Pass. πεπάχυσμαι Arist.*Mu.*394$^a$28, Philostr.*Gym.*52, but πεπάχυμμαι Gal.6.678, Herm. ap.Stob.1.49.68:—*fatten*, τὰ σώματα Pl.*Grg.*518c; βοῦν Id.*R.*343b; ἵππον X.*Oec.*12.20:—Pass., *grow fat*, Hp.*Aph.*5.44, Ar.*Ach.*791; δαιτὶ παχυνόμενος *AP*7.207 (Mel.); παχυνθῇ ἡ ἀκρίς Lxx *Ec.*12.5. **b.** *thicken, strengthen*, δεσμόν Porph.*Abst.*1.38. **2.** metaph., *cause to wax fat, increase*, κότον π. A.*Supp.*618:—Pass., ὄλβος ἄγαν παχυνθείς Id.*Th.*771 (lyr.). **b.** metaph., *make gross* or *dull*, τὰς ψυχὰς ὑπὸ πλησμονῆς π. Plu.2.995d; βρώσεις τὸν νοῦν π. Philostr.*VA*1.8:—Pass., Lxx *Is.*6.10; πεπαχυσμένος Philostr.*VS*1.21.1; *to be coarsened*, [ψυχὴ] παρὰ τὴν ἰδίαν φύσιν πεπαχυμμένη Herm. l. c.; περιβλήματα.. παχυνόμενα ὑπὸ τῆς γηΐνης φύσεως Procl.*in R.*1.119 K. **II.** Pass., *become thick*, π. πρὸς τὸν ἥλιον, of the skull, Hdt.3.12; of humours, Hp.*VM*19; of excrements, Id.*Prog.*11, cf. Arist.*GA*735$^a$36, al.; distd. from πήγνυσθαι, Id.*Mete.*383$^a$11, $^b$18; of fruit juices, *become concentrated*, Thphr.*CP*6.16.2; of oil, Philostr.*Gym.*52. **2.** *to be dulled*, of the sun's light, D.P.35.

⊛ **πᾰχύ-πους** [ῠ], ὁ, ἡ, gen. ποδος, *thick-footed*, v.l. in Arist.*HA*557$^a$23, cf. Adam.2.48. **-ρῑν**, ῑνος, ὁ, ἡ, better **παχύρριν**, *thick-nosed*, *PPetr.*3 p.13 (-ρρ-, iii B.C.), Adam.2.48. **-ρραβδος**, ον, *with thick shoots*, Dsc.[1.14] (Comp.). **-ρριζος**, ον, *with thick roots*, Thphr.*HP*3.11.4, Dsc.1.14. **-ρρυγχος**, ον, *thick-snouted*, Alex.Aphr.*Pr.*1.141.

⊛ **πᾰχύς**, εῖα (Ion. -έα Hp.*Superf.*21), ύ, *thick, stout*, χειρὶ παχείῃ Il.5.309, etc.; παχέος παρὰ μηροῦ 16.473; παχὺν αὐχένα Od.9.372; π. πούς Hes.*Op.*497; of trees, ib.509; ῥίζα Thphr.*HP*6.3.1; later of persons, περὶ σφυρὸν παχεῖα, μισήτη γυνή *thick*-ankled, Archil.184; *fat*, οἱ παχύτατοι τῶν παίδων Hp.*Aph.*3.25; π. γυνή Id.*Superf.* l. c.; χοῖρος π., ὗς π., Ar.*Ach.*766, Men.21: metaph., of soil, *rich, fertile*, X.*Oec.*17.8 (Comp.); π. τράπεζα a *well-spread* table, Philostr.*VA*3.26. Adv., παχέως διαιτᾶσθαι ibid. **2.** of inorganic things, *thick, massive*, π. λᾶας Il.12.446; σκῆπτρον 18.416; αὐλὸς αἵματος Od.22.18; θρυαλλίδες Ar.*Nu.*59; πέδαι Id.*V.*435; π. δραχμή a *thick* drachma, i.e. the Aeginetan, which weighed more than the Attic, Poll.9.76, or (Hsch.), = δίδραχμον; *thick, coarse*, opp. λεπτός, ἱμάτιον Pl.*Cra.*389b, cf. Poll.7.57,61, etc.; χλαῖναν..παχεῖαν ἐπιβαλῶ Λακωνικήν Theopomp.Com.10; of hair, Arist *HA*502$^a$26; π. τὴν σάρκα, of the pig, Jul.*Or.*5.177c. Adv. *coarsely, roughly*, of stating or arguing, παχέως ὁρίζεσθαι, prob. for ταχέως, Arist.*Pol.*1275$^b$25; παχύτερον or -έρως, Pl.*Plt.*294e, 295a. **3.** of liquids, *thick, curdled, clotted*, αἷμα Il.23.697; ἀπορρέει..παχὺ καὶ μέλαν Hdt.4.23; of *marsh*-water, Hp.*Aër.*7; of urine, Id.*Prog.*12; τὸ παχύτερον τῶν γαλάκτων Arist.*HA*521$^b$28; τὸ παχὺ τῆς δυνάμεως [τῶν οἴνων] Ath.1.33b. **b.** τὰ παχέα καλούμενα νοσήματα, of certain diseases supposed to be due to thickened phlegm, Hp.*Int.*47, al. **4.** in Com., *fat, great*, π. πρᾶγμα, χάρις, Ar.*Lys.*23, *Ec.*1048. **5.** of timbre, *thick*, opp. λεπτός, Arist.*Aud.*803$^b$29, cf. 804$^a$10 (Comp.). Adv., κορώνη παχέα κρώζουσα Arat.953. **6.** of speech, *coarse, heavy*, διάλεκτος παχυτέρα D.H.*Pomp.*2; παχύτερος τὴν λέξιν Id.*Is.*19; παχύτερον ποιεῖν τὸν λόγον Hermog.*Id.*1.6. **b.** *ample*, of periphrasis, Longin.29.1 (Sup.). **7.** of flame, *dull*, Thphr.*HP*5.9.3. **II.** οἱ παχέες *men of substance, the wealthy*, Hdt.5.30,77, 6.91; τοὺς π. καὶ πλουσίους Ar.*Pax*639; ὃς ἂν ᾖ π. Id.*Eq.*1139; ἀνὴρ π. Id.*V.*287; cf. πάχης. **III.** Com. and Prose, *thick-witted, gross, stupid*, ἀμαθὴς καὶ π. Id.*Nu.*842; τὸ τῶν παχυτέρων πλῆθος Phld.*Rh.*1.202 S.; π. καὶ ἠλίθιοι, π. καὶ ἀπαίδευτοι, Luc.*Alex.*9,17; ἐς τὰς τέχνας π. καὶ οὐ λεπτοὶ οὐδὲ ὀξέες Hp.*Aër.*24; π. τὴν μνήμην Philostr.*VS*2.1.10; π. λόγος Gal.8.606. Adv., παχύτερον ἔχειν τῆς ἀκοῆς Hld.5.18. **IV.** prov., πηλοῦ παχύτερος, of a dullard, Eun.*Hist.*p.265 D. **V.** Adv. -έως, v. supr. **VI.** Comp. πάσσων, ον, Od.6.230, 8.20, 24.369; πᾰχίων, ον, Arat.785: Sup. πάχιστος Il.16.314, Call.*Aet.Oxy.*2079.23: regul. forms πᾰχύτερος, πᾰχύτατος (v. supr.). (I.-E. *bhn̥ghú-*, cf. Skt. *bahús*, Lett. *biezs* 'thick'.)

**πᾶχυς**, Aeol. for πῆχυς.

**πᾰχύ-σαρκος** [ῠ], ον, *with stout fibres*, Dsc.1.85. **-σκελής**, ές, *thick-legged*, *Lyr.Adesp.*21, Gal.6.322, Adam.2.31.

**πάχ-υσμα** [ᾰ], ατος, τό, *thickening*, Aët.1.59. **II.** metaph., τὰς μερικὰς ψυχὰς ἀπὸ τῶν π. χωρίζων τῆς ὕλης Procl. *in Cra.*p.101 P. **-υσμός**, ὁ, *a growing fat*, Hp.*Epid.*6.8.11. **II.** *thickening*, νεύρων Damocr.ap.Gal.13.988.

**πᾰχύ-σπερμος**, ον, *having thick semen*, Gal.1.339. **-στομος**, ον, *thick at the brim*, κώθων Henioch.1; *with a large mouth*, of the oyster, Arist.*Fr.*304. **II.** metaph., *speaking with a broad accent*, π. ἢ τραχύστομοι, of the Κᾶρες βαρβαρόφωνοι, Str.14.2.28:—hence **-στομέω**, **-στομία**, ibid.

⊛ **πᾰχύτης**, ητος, ἡ, (παχύς) *thickness*, of stalks, skin, ropes, Hdt.4.74,183, 7.36; of hair, Arist.*GA*782$^a$24; of animals, *fatness*, Id.*HA*611$^a$25: pl., v.l. in Pl.*Plt.*284e. **2.** *thickness* or *sediment* of liquor, Hdt.4.23; *density*, Hp.*Aph.*6.41; *thick consistency*, αἵματος, γάλακτος, Arist.*PA*668$^b$2, 676$^a$11; π. ἀέρος Ascl.*Tact.*12.10. **II.** *thickness of wit, dullness*, D.H.*Dem.*26, S.E.*M.*1.70.

**πᾰχυ-τράχηλος** [τρᾰ], ον, *bull-necked*, Adam.2.21. **-φλοιος**, ον, *with thick rind* or *bark*, Thphr.*HP*1.5.2, Dsc.1.13, Gal.6.270, *Gp.*10.75.2. **-φρων**, ον, gen. ονος, = παχύνοος, Tz.*H.*5.716, Hsch. s.v. Βοῦθος περιφοιτᾷ. **-φωνος**, ον, *of coarse sound*, στοιχεῖον Aristid. Quint.1.21 (Comp.). **-χειλής**, ές, *thick-lipped*, of shell-fish, Arist.*HA*528$^a$29:—also **-χειλος**, ον, Ruf.*Fr.*70; τὰ π. τῶν ἑλκῶν Gal.13.491. **-χῡμος**, ον, *with thick juices*, Id.6.261, Alex.Aphr.*Pr.*1.52, etc.

**πάων** (i.e. Lat. *pavo*), = ταῶς, *Edict Diocl.*4.39,40.

**πᾱώταρ** (παθιώταρ cod.), α, ὁ, Lacon. for παός, πηός, Hsch., who also has π[ρ]αῶται· συγγενεῖς, οἰκεῖοι, Λάκωνες.

⊛ **πε**, reduced form (before initial τ) of πετ(ά), = μετά, *IG*5(2).6.98 (Tegea, iv B.C.), 262.16 (Mantinea, v B.C.).

⊛ **πεδά**, Aeol. for μετά, Sapph.38, Alc.48 A, Pi.*Fr.*26, Theoc.29.38: also Dor., *Leg.Gort.*3.27; πεδ' ἱαρόν *Schwyzer*89.14 (Argos, iii B.C.). (Cogn. with πούς.)

**Πεδᾰγείτνυος**, ὁ, name of a month at Rhodes, etc., = Att. **Μεταγειτνιών**, *GDI*4245.298 (Rhodes):—also **Πεδᾰγείτνιος**, *IG*12(1).1104.1 (ibid.); **Πετᾰγείτνυος**, *SIG*1106.60 (Cos); **Πετᾰγείτνιος**, ib.1009.19 (Chalcedon).

⊛ **πεδάγρετος**, ον, Aeol. for *μετάγρετος (ἀγρέω), in neut. sg., glossed μεταμέλητον, μεταληπτόν, ποικίλον, μεταδίωκτον, Hsch.

**πεδάγω**, = μετάγω, ἐνς τάξιν *Schwyzer*89.16 (Argos, iii B.C.).

**πεδαίρω**, Aeol. or Dor. for μεταίρω (q.v.).

**πεδαίχμιος**, ον, Aeol. or Dor. for μετ-, A.*Ch.*589 (lyr.).

**πέδαλα**· ποικίλα, Hsch. **πεδαλευόμενος**· μεταμελόμενος, μεταδιωκόμενος, Id., cf. Alc.50.4 Pap. Demetr. Lacon.

**πεδάμαρος**, v. μετήορος I fin.

**πεδᾰμείβω**, Aeol. for μεταμείβω, Pi.*O.*12.12.

⊛ **πεδᾰνός**, ή, όν, (πέδον) *low-growing, short*, ἀλκαίη, οὐρή, Nic.*Th.*226, 289. **II.** *light*, ὕπνος Ion Trag.4 (ἠπεδ- Hsch.).

**πεδάϝοικος**, ον, Dor. for μέτοικος, *IG*4.552,615 (Argos).

**πεδαοριστής**, v. πεδαωριστής.

⊛ **πεδάορος** [ᾱ], ον, Aeol. and Dor. for μετήορος, μετέωρος, Alc.100; cf. μετήορος I fin. and πεδήορος.

**πεδάρσιος**, ον, Aeol. or Dor. for μετάρσιος, A.*Pr.*271, 710, 916, *Ch.*846, Ar.*Av.*1197 (paratrag.).

**πεδαρτάω**, Pythag. word for μεθαρμόζω, = νουθετέω, ἐκάλουν δὲ τὸ νουθετεῖν πεδαρτᾶν (Schäfer for παιδ.) Iamb.*VP*31.197; ἐκάλει [Πυθαγόρας] τὸ νουθετεῖν πεδαρτᾶν (to be restored for πελαργᾶν) D.L.8.20, cf. Suid.; τὰς..νουθετήσεις, ἃς δὴ **πεδαρτάσεις** ἐκάλουν Iamb.*VP*22.101, 33.231.

**πέδασος**, dub. sens. in *UPZ*149 i 19 (iii/ii B.C.).

**πεδατρέπω**, v. μετατρέπω.

**πεδαυγάζω**, Aeol. for μεταυγάζω, Pi.*N.*10.61.

**πεδᾰφορά**, = μεταφορά, *removal*, *IG*4$^2$(1).102.276 (Epid., iv B.C.).

**πέδαχνον**, **πεδαχνόομαι**, v. πετ-.

**πεδάω**, Ep. 3 sg. πεδάᾳ Od.4.380: Ep. and Ion. impf. πεδάασκον 23.353: pf. part. Pass. πεπεδημένος Paus.8.49.6: (πέδη):—prop. *bind with fetters*: hence, simply, *bind, make fast*, ἐπέδησε θύρας (unless this be from ἐπιδέω) Od.21.391; π. ἄνδρα δαιδάλῳ πέπλῳ A.*Eu.*635; τὸν μούναρχον πεδήσας Hdt.6.23. **2.** *shackle, trammel*, πέδησε δὲ φαίδιμα γυῖα Il.13.435; δόλῳ ἅρμα πεδῆσαι 23.585, cf. Pi.*P.*6.32, *N.*5.26; ἕρκος Ἀχαιῶν θρασεῖ φόνῳ πεδάσαις Id.*Pae.*6.86; νῆα θοὴν ἐπέδησ' ἐνὶ πόντῳ Od.13.168; of sleep, ὅς μ' ἐπέδησε φίλα βλέφαρ' ἀμφικαλύψας 23.17; ὕπνος λύει πεδήσας S.*Aj.*676; esp. of a deity or fate overruling a mortal's will, μοῖρ' ἐπέδησε c. acc. pers., Il.4.517; ὅς τίς μ' ἀθανάτων πεδάᾳ Od.4.380; πέδησε δὲ καὶ τὸν Ἀθήνη 18.155; ἐμὲ θεοὶ πεδάασκον ἐμῆς ἀπὸ πατρίδος αἴης 23.353: c. inf., Ἕκτορα δ' αὐτοῦ μεῖναι..μοῖρ' ἐπέδησε *constrained* him to remain on the spot, Il.22.5; μιν μοῖρα θεῶν ἐπέδησε δαμῆναι *constrained* him to be slain, Od.3.269; τό γε Μοῖρ' ἐπέδησε οὖλον ἀκίνητόν τ' ἔμεναι Parm.8.37, cf. 10.6: rare in Prose, καθ' ὕπνον τὴν τῆς φρονήσεως πεδηθεὶς δύναμιν Pl.*Ti.*71e, cf. 43d, Plot.3.5.7; εἰ πεδᾶται ὁ ταὐτοῦ κύκλος Dam.*Pr.*400; τῷ ἀξιώματι πεδηθείς D.C.60.29.

**πεδᾱωριστής**, οῦ, ὁ, Aeol. or Dor. for ἵππος φρυαγματίας, μετεωριστής, Hsch. (fort. **πεδαορ-**). **πεδεινός,** v. πεδιεινός. **πεδέπω,** Aeol. = μεθέπω (q. v.). ⊛ **πεδέρχομαι,** v. μετέρχομαι III, IV. 5: aor. imper. πέδελθε, = ἱκέτευσον, Id.; subj. πεδέλθῃ, = ἱκετεύῃ, Id. (prob.). **πέδευρα·** ὕστερα (Lacon.), Id., and **πέδευρον·** ὕστερον, πάλιν, ὀπίσω (Lacon.), Id.

⊛ **πεδέχω,** Aeol. for μετέχω, Alc., Sapph. (v. μετέχω), Pi.*Pae.*4.37: aor. inf. πεδασχεῖν Id.*Fr.*27; also Dor., *Abh.Berl.Akad.*1925(5).21 (Cyrene).

⊛ **πέδη,** ἡ, (πέζα) *fetter*: in pl., *shackles*, ἀμφὶ δὲ ποσσὶ πέδας ἔβαλε χρυσείας, of horses, Il.13.36; of men, τοῖς ἀδίκοις ἀμφιτίθησι πέδας Sol.4.34, cf. Thgn.539, A.*Pr.*6, Men.*Her.*3, Herod.3.95; πεδέων ζεῦγος pair *of fetters*, Hdt.7.35; ἐν πέδαις (v. l. ἐς πέδας) δῆσαί τινα put one in *fetters*, Id.5.77; αἱ πέδαι, ἐν τῇσι ἐδεδέατο ibid.; ἐν πέδαις δῆσαι, φυλάττειν, etc., Pl.*Lg.*882b, Plu.2.181b, etc.: metaph., πέδαις ἀχαλκεύτοισι, of the robe in which Agamemnon was entangled, A.*Ch.*493; πέδας χειροῖν καὶ ποδοῖν ib.982: in sg., of the poisoned robe of Nessus, S.*Tr.*1057; π. Ἑλληνικαί, of the fortresses of Chalcis, Corinth, and Demetrias, Plb.18.11.5, etc. **2.** *anklet, bangle*, Ar.*Fr.*320.11, Philem.81, Luc.*Lex.*9. **3.** of fishing-*nets*, E.*Fr.*670.5. **II.** *mode of breaking in a horse by riding him in a figure-of-eight course* (cf. ἱπποπέδη), X.*Eq.*3.5, 7.13; π. ἑτερομήκης, κυκλοτερής, ib.14.

**πεδήορος,** = πεδάορος, Nic.*Th.*729.

**πεδητής,** οῦ, Dor. **-τάς,** ὁ, *one who fetters*: metaph., *hinderer*, *AP* 9.756 (Aemil.).

**πεδήτης,** ου, ὁ, Pass., *one fettered, prisoner*, Ar.*Fr.*65, Herod.3.69, Lxx *Wi.*17.2, Plu.2.165e, Luc.*Sat.*10, etc.: in pl., title of play by Call. Com. (*Fr.*2 D.). **II.** at Samos, building in which certain fetters were kept, Plu.2.303e.

⊛ **πεδῐᾰκός,** ή, όν, *of* or *on the plain*, τὰ π. Lys.*Fr.*238 S. **II.** π., οἱ, in Attica, *party of the plain*, Arist.*Pol.*1305$^{a}$24, *Ath.*13.4; cf. πεδιάσιος, πεδιεῖς.

**πεδῐάλλω,** = *μετιάλλω, *send for*, aor. inf. πεδιᾶλαι, Hsch.

**πεδιανόμος,** ὁ, title of magistrate at Sparta, *IG*5(1).123.

⊛ **πεδῐάς,** άδος, used as fem. of πεδιεινός, *flat, level*, of Scythia, Hdt.4.23,47, Hp.*Aër.*18; of Egypt, Hdt.2.8; of Thessaly, Pl.*Lg.*625d; ἡ π. (sc. γῆ) Hdt.9.122, Onos.6.8; π. ὁδός, ἁμαξιτός, Pi.*P.*5.91, E.*Rh.*283; ἡ π. χώρα Plb.2.16.7. **II.** *on* or *of the plain*, ὕλη S.*Ant.*420; λόγχη π. the spearmen *of the plain*, Id.*Tr.*1058; π. μάχη battle *in the plain*, Plu.*Sull.*19, prob. in *IG*14.1290.59.

**πεδιασιμαῖος,** *campester*, *Gloss.*

**πεδῐάσιος,** ον, *of the plain*, σμύρνα Dsc.1.64 (v.l. -άσιμος); οἱ π. *dwellers in the plain*, Str.15.1.58; = πεδιεῖς, Phot., Suid. s. v. πάραλοι.

**πεδῐεινός,** ή, όν, *flat, level*, χῶρος Hdt.7.198 (v.l. πεδινός); πεδιναὶ ὑποχωρήσεις Plb.1.34.8; τὰ πεδινά Arist.*Pr.*880$^{b}$28, Aen.Tact.1.2, Onos.18, Plu.*Nic.*26: Comp. πεδιεινότερος Pl.*Lg.*704d; πεδινώτερος X.*An.*5.5.2. **II.** *of the plain, found on the plain*, opp. ὄρειος, λαγώς Id.*Cyn.*5.17 (πεδινός, v.l. πεδεινός); [δένδρα] πεδεινά Thphr.*HP*1.8.1, cf. 3.11.2; πεδινὸν ἄνθος, = ἀργεμώνη, Ps.-Dsc.2.177. (πεδιεινός may have become πεδῑνός (written also πεδεινός) about 150 B.C.; πεδῐνός is dub., since πεδινώτερος may be f. l. in X.*An.* l. c.)

⊛ **πεδῐεῖς,** έων, οἱ, in Attica, *party of the plain* (cf. πεδιακός II), Plu.*Sol.*13, D.L.1.58.

**πεδίζω,** (πέδη) *fetter*, *Gloss.*

**πεδῐήρης,** ες, *abounding in plains*, Θρῄκης ἂμ πεδιήρεις (vulg. ἀμπεδιήρεις)..κελεύθους A.*Pers.*566 (lyr.).

⊛ **πέδῑλον,** Aeol. **πέδιλλον** Choerob. in *An.Ox.*2.239: τό: (πέδη):— mostly in pl., *sandals*, ἀμφὶ πόδεσσιν..ἀράρισκε π., τάμνων δέρμα βόειον Od.14.23; ὑπὸ ποσσὶν ἐδήσατο καλὰ π. ἀμβρόσια χρύσεια, τά μιν φέρον ἠμὲν ἐφ' ὑγρὴν ἠδ' ἐπ' ἀπείρονα γαῖαν, of Hermes, Il.24.340; of Athena, Od.1.96; πτερόεντα π. Hes.*Sc.*220; ποτανά E.*El.*460 (lyr.). **II.** *any covering for the feet, shoes* or *boots*, π. ἐς γόνυ ἀνατείνοντα Hdt.7.67; περὶ τοὺς πόδας τε καὶ τὰς κνήμας π. νεβρῶν ib.75, cf. Pi.*P.*4.95, Plu.*Thes.*3; ἱμάτιον καθαρὸν καὶ καινὰ π. Ar.*Av.*973. **III.** metaph., Δωρίῳ φωνὰν ἐναρμόξαι π., i. e. to write in Doric *rhythm* (cf. πούς), Pi.*O.*3.5; also ἐν τούτῳ π. πόδ' ἔχειν to have one's foot in this *shoe*, i. e. to be in this condition or fortune, ib.6.8.

**πεδινός,** v. πεδιεινός.

**πέδιον,** τό, Dim. of πέδη, *EM*658.23.

**πεδίον,** τό, (πέδον) *plain*, in Hom. mostly sg., Il.5.222, al.: in pl., 12.283, Hes.*Op.*388, etc.; ἐν πεδίῳ on *a fertile plain*, opp. ἐν πέτραις, Men.719. **b.** metaph., of the sea, δελφινοφόρον πεδίον πόντου A.*Fr.*150; πόντου π. Αἰγαῖον Ion Trag.60; π. πλόϊμα Tim.*Pers.*89. **2.** freq. with gen. or adj. of particular plains (mostly in sg.), πεδίον Αἰσώπου A.*Ag.*297; τὸ Τροίας π. S.*Ph.*1435 (but τὰ Τ. π. 1376); τὸ Θήβης π. Id.*OC*1312; Καϋστρίων π. Ar.*Ach.*68; τὸ Κιρραῖον π. Aeschin.3.107; τὰ Θετταλικὰ π. Pl.*Plt.*264c; τὸ Ἄρειον π., = Lat. *Campus* Martius, D.H.7.59. **b.** esp. *the plain of Attica*, *IG*1$^{2}$.842 *C*7, Hdt.1.59, Th.2.55, Is.5.22. **3.** ἱππέας εἰς π. προκαλεῖσθαι, prov. of challenging persons to do that in which they excel, Pl.*Tht.*183d, cf. Men.268. **II.** *part of the foot next the toes, metatarsus*, Gal.*UP*3.5, al., Poll.2.197. **III.** *pudenda muliebria*, Ar.*Lys.*88.

**πεδίονδε,** Adv. *to the plain*, Il.11.492, Od.15.183, *h.Merc.*88, Ar.*Av.*507.

**πεδιονόμος,** ον, *dwelling in the plain*, π. θεοί *rural* deities, A.*Th.*272.

⊛ **πέδιjος,** fem. **πεδίjα,** = πεδιεινός, *Schwyzer* 679.18 (Cyprus).

**πεδῐοῦχος,** ον, *having a plain*, gloss on στερνοῦχος, Sch.S.*OC*691.

⊛ **πεδιοφύλαξ** [ῠ], ἄκος, ὁ, *guard of an estate*, *PFay.*113.4 (100 A.D.), *PLond.*2.189.20 (ii A.D.), etc.

**πεδίσκη,** ἡ, Dim. of πέδη, *small fetter*, *IG*7.2420.27 (Thebes, iii B.C.).

**Πεδιώ,** οῦς, ἡ, *goddess of the Plain*, epith. of Hera, *IG*14.595, 596 (Sicily).

**πεδῐώδης,** ες, *like a plain, level*, Sch.S.*OC*691.

**πεδιών,** Dor., = μετών, *IG*12(3).1259.17 (Cimolus, iv B.C.).

**πεδο-βάμων** [ᾱ], ον, gen. ονος, *earth-walking*, πτανά τε καὶ π. A.*Ch.*591 (lyr.). **-εις,** εσσα, εν, (πέδον) = πεδιεινός, Nic.*Th.*662. **-θεν** (parox.), Adv., (πέδον) *from the ground*, Hes.*Th.*680, E.*Tr.*98 (anap.). **II.** *from the bottom*, Pi.*O.*7.62: metaph., οἵ τοι π. φίλοι εἰσίν which are dear to thee *from the bottom of thy heart*, Od.13.295. **2.** *from the beginning*, Pi.*I.*5(4).38.

⊛ **πέδοι,** Adv. *on the ground, on earth*, A.*Pr.*274; cf. πέδον 4.

**πέδοικος,** Aeol. and Dor. for μέτοικος, Pi.*Fr.*25; π. χελιδών A.*Fr.*53.

**πεδοιχνέω,** = *μετ-, *go in search of, pursue*, παιηόνων ἄνθεα B.15.9.

**πεδοκοίτης,** ου, ὁ, *lying on the ground*, σίκυος *AP*6.102 (Phil.).

⊛ **πέδον,** τό, (πούς) *ground, earth*, first in *h.Cer.*455 (πέδονδε is used in Hom.): freq. in later Poetry, Pi.*O.*10.46, *P.*1.28, etc.; χθονὸς π. A.*Pr.*1; γῆς π. Ar.*Nu.*573 (lyr.); π. κελεύθου στρωννύναι A.*Ag.*909. **2.** of a particular site, esp. of sacred ground (poet. and used only in sg.), Ζηνὸς εὐθαλὲς π., of Nemea, B.8.5; Κρισαῖον π. S.*El.*730; Λοξίου π. A.*Ch.*1036; Παλλάδος κλεινὸν π., i.e. the Acropolis, Ar.*Pl.*772; ἁγνὸν ἐς Θήβης π. Eub.10, cf. 66; πέδον c. gen. loci periphr. for the place itself, Εὐρώπης π. A.*Pr.*734; Λήμνου S.*Ph.*1464 (anap.), etc. **3.** with a Prep., νεύειν ἐς π. Id.*Ant.*441; πρὸς πέδῳ βαλεῖν, κεῖσθαι, A.*Fr.*183, S.*OT*180 (lyr.). **4.** πέδῳ *on the ground, to earth*, *h.Cer.*455; πεσόντος αἵματος π. A.*Ch.*48 (lyr.), cf. *Eu.*263 (lyr.), 479, S.*El.*747; ῥίπτειν πέδῳ E.*IA*39 (anap.), cf. *Or.*1433, 1440 (both lyr.); πέδῳ σκήψασα A.*Pr.*749; πέδοι shd. perh. be read for πέδῳ in Trag., as also for πέδον in the phrases πέδον πατεῖν, πέδον πατεῖσθαι, A.*Ag.*1357, *Ch.*643 (lyr.).

**πέδονδε,** Adv. *to the ground, earthwards*, Il.13.796, *h.Cer.*253, S.*Tr.*786. **2.** *to the bottom*, π. κυλίνδετο λᾶας ἀναιδής Od.11.598.

**πεδορραντήριον,** τό, v. ῥαντήριος.

**πέδορτος** (A), ον, (πέδον, ὄρνυμαι) *rising from the ground*, κτύπος S.*Ichn.*212.

**πέδορτος** (B), ον, = μεθέορτος, expld. by ἡμέρα ἐν ᾗ οὐ γίνεται ἑορτή, Hsch.

**πεδόσε,** Adv., = πέδονδε, E.*Ba.*136, 600 (both lyr.).

**Πεδο-σείων,** οντος, ὁ, *earth-shaker*, coined as etym. of Ποσειδῶν, Corn.*ND*4. ⊛ **-σκᾰφής,** ές, *digging the earth*, Nonn.*D.*12.331. **-στῐβής,** ές, *earth-treading*, opp. πτεροῦς, A.*Supp.*1000; ὄχος, πούς, E.*Med.*1123, *Hel.*1516; ηὕδομεν πεδοστιβεῖς Id.*Rh.*763 (s. v. l.). **2.** *on foot*, opp. ἱππηλάτης, λεώς A.*Pers.*127 (lyr.). **-τρῐβής,** ές, *wearing the ground*, Nonn.*D.*10.361. ⊛ **-τριψ,** ῐβος, ὁ and ἡ, (πέδη, τρίβω) *wearing out fetters*, Com. epith. of good-for-nothing slaves, Luc.*Sat.*8.

**πέδουρος,** ον, = πεδάορος, μετέωρος, Hsch., Phot.

**πέδων,** ωνος, ὁ, *one in fetters*, of a slave, Ar.*Fr.*837.

**πεδωριστός,** v. πέλωρος.

**πεδώρῠχος,** ον, (ὀρύσσω) *digging the soil*, *AP*10.101 (Bianor).

⊛ **πέζᾰ,** ης, ἡ, said to be Dor. and Arc. for πούς, Gal.19.129, cf. Ruf. ap.Orib.25.1.56; τῶν ἄπο πέζαν ἐκτὸς ἔχων Androm.ap.Gal.14.37; but distd. from it as the *instep* by Poll.2.192; πρὸς πέζῃ ποδός Paus.5.11.2, cf. *AP*12.176 (Strat.); οἱ πόδες οἰδίσκονται καὶ αἱ πέζαι μάλιστα Hp.*Mul.*2.169. **2.** περίσφυρος π., = πέδη I. 2, *AP*6.211 (Leon.). **II.** metaph., *bottom, end* of a body, ἐπὶ ῥυμῷ πέζῃ ἔπι πρώτῃ on the pole at the far *end*, Il.24.272. **2.** *edge, border* of a garment, A.R.4.46, *AP*6.287 (Antip.), J.*AJ*3.7.4, Hld.3.3; of the sea, *strand, bank*, Ἐλευσῖνος παρὰ πέζαν Hermesian.7.17; of a country, *coastline*, π. ἠπείροιο A.R.4.1258, cf. D.P.61; εἰς ὁδοῦ π. στενήν Luc.*Trag.*238; of a mountain, D.P.535, App.*Pun.*103. **III.** *round fishing-net*, Opp.*H.*3.83.

**πεζ-ᾰκοντιστής,** οῦ, ὁ, *foot-javelin-man*, Plb.3.65.10, 3.72.2. **-αρχέω,** *command infantry*, Them.*Or.*11.152c. ⊛ **-αρχος,** ὁ, *leader of infantry*, X.*Cyr.*5.3.41. **-έμπορος,** ον, *trafficking by land*, Str.16.3.3. **-έταιροι,** οἱ, *foot-guards* in the Macedon. army (cf. ἑταῖρος), D.2.17, Anaximen.Lampsac.4 J., Plu.*Flam.*17, 2.197c. **-ευτικός,** ή, όν, *able to walk, going on foot*, π. ζῷα, opp. πτηνά, νευστικά, Arist.*GA*715$^{a}$27. **-εύω,** *go* or *travel on foot, walk*, ἐπὶ γαίας πόδα πεζεύων (where πόδα is pleon.) E.*Alc.*869 (anap.); οὔτε ἄπουν οὔτε πεζεῦον Arist.*PA*669$^{b}$7; π. περὶ τὴν τροφήν, of certain birds, Id.*HA*593$^{a}$25, cf. *GA*751$^{b}$13. **2.** *go* or *travel by land*, opp. going by sea, X.*An.*5.5.[4], Plb.16.29.11; π. μετὰ τῶν ἵππων Id.10.48.6; οἱ πεζεύοντες *land-forces*, Arist.*Pol.*1327$^{b}$10; π. διὰ τῆς θαλάσσης, of Xerxes passing by his bridge over the Hellespont, Isoc.4.89; π. τὴν θάλασσαν *pass* it *like dry land*, Philostr.*Im.*1.8; simply, *march, pass through*, ἀνοδίας Ph.2.257:— Pass., ὁ Ἄθως πλείσθω καὶ ὁ Ἑλλήσποντος πεζευέσθω Luc.*Rh.Pr.*18; ἡ ἐκ Βρεντεσίου πεζευομένη ὁδός *by land*, Str.6.3.5; πεζεύεται impers., ταῖς ἁρμαμάξαις Id.4.1.14. **-ῆ,** v. πεζός III. ⊛ **-ίδιον,** τό, Dim. of πέζα II. 2, *ribbon*, to be read for πεζετίον, *EM*749.37, πεζίτιον, Suid. **-ικός,** ή, όν, (πεζός) *on foot*, π. εἰκών (opp. ἔφιππος) *IG*4$^{2}$(1).86.29 (Epid.), 5(2).432.13 (Megalop.), etc. **2.** *of* or *for a foot-soldier*, ὅπλα ἱππικὰ ἢ π. Pl.*Lg.*753b; τὸ π. *the infantry*, X.*Cyr.*5.3.38 codd.; π. καὶ ἱππικαὶ δυνάμεις *CIG*4860 (Ombi); τὰ π. *the evolutions of infantry*, οἱ ἀγαθοὶ τὰ π. X.*Cyr.*1.3.15. **3.** of *a land force*, opp. a fleet, ἥ τε π. καὶ ἡ ναυτικὴ δύναμις Id.*Mem.*3.6.9, cf. Th.6.33, Din.3.10, Aeschin.3.85, Plb.2.2.4, *IPE*1$^{2}$.352.39 (Chersonesus), etc.; πεζός is v.l. and shd. prob. be read in all passages of early writers. 4. *in prose*, π. λόγων συντάξεις Vett.Val.150.23.

πέζις, εως, ἡ, *bullfist, Lycoperdon Bovista*, Thphr.*HP*1.6.5.

⊛ πεζίς, ίδος, ἡ, = πέζα II. 2, *border*, Ar.*Fr.*485, *IG*2$^{2}$.1525.4.

πεζίτης [ῑ], ου, ὁ, = πεζός, Suid.

πεζο-βατέω τὸ πέλαγος, *walk* the sea, *AP*9.551 (Antiphil.). -βόας, α, Dor. for -βόης, ὁ, *one who responds to the battle-cry on foot, foot-soldier*, Pi.*N.*9.34. -γρᾰφέω, *write prose*, D.L.4.15. -γρᾰφία, ἡ, *prose-writing*, Eust.1753.29, Sch.E.*Hec.*581 (pl.) -γράφος [ᾰ], ὁ, *prose-writer*, D.L.4.15, Sch.E.*Hec.*795, al. -θηρικός, ή, όν, *of* or *for the hunting of land-animals* (opp. fishing), τὸ π. εἶδος Pl.*Sph.*220a (but -θηρία, ἡ, ib.223b, is prob. spurious). -λεκτέω, *write prose*, Eust.1424.15. -λέκτης, ου, ὁ, *prose-writer*, Id.569.7. -λογία, ἡ, *prose-writing*, Phld.*Rh.*1.197 S. (pl.), Eust.1888.1. -λογικῶς, Adv. *in prose*, Id.1533.30. -λόγος, ὁ, *prose-writer*, A.D.*Pron.*65.27, Phlp. *in Cat.*24.34, *EM*424.24. -μᾰχέω, *fight by land* or *on foot*, perh. to be restored in Sapph.*Supp.*5.20; of one whose horse is killed, Plb.2.69.2; opp. ναυμαχέω, Hdt.3.45; opp. πολιορκέω, Ar.*V.*685; τισι Th.1.112; π. καὶ ναυμαχοῦντες Isoc.7.75; π. ἀπὸ τῶν νεῶν *fight like soldiers* from shipboard, Th.7.62; ἐπὶ τῶν νεῶν D.S.13.16; of infantry, opp. cavalry, Lyd.*Mag.*1.11. -μάχης [ᾰ], ου, ὁ, = πεζομάχος, ἄνδρες Pi.*P.*2.65. -μᾰχία, Ion. -ίη, ἡ, *battle by land*, opp. ναυμαχία, Hdt.8.15, Th.1.23, etc. 2. *fighting on foot*, opp. ἱππομαχία, Ph.1.191 (pl.), cf. Arr.*An.*1.15.4. -μάχος [ᾰ], ον, *fighting on foot*, Luc.*Macr.*17. II. *fighting as a soldier*, opp. ναυμάχος, Plu.*Alex.*38; π. ἀνὴρ Id.*Ant.*64. -νομικός, ή, όν, *of* or *for the management of quadrupeds* (opp. birds); ἡ π. ἐπιστήμη the business *of managing them*, Pl.*Plt.*265c, cf. 264e; τὸ π. ib.267b. -νόμος, ον, *commanding by land*, A.*Pers.*76 (lyr.). -πορέω, *go on foot*, X.*Eq.Mag.*4.1. II. *go by land, march*, Plb.3.68.14, Luc.*Alex.*53. -πορία, ἡ, *land-journey*, Hdn.*Epim.*105. -πόρος, ον, *going by land*, οὐ ναύταν ποσσὶ δὲ π. *AP*12.53 (Mel.); ναύτην ἠπείρου, π. πελάγους, of Xerxes, ib.9.304 (Parmen.).

⊛ πεζός, ή, όν, (v. πούς): 1. in Poets, esp. Ep., a. *on foot, walking*, πεζοί *fighters on foot*, opp. those in chariots, πεζοί θ' ἱππῆές τε Il.8.59, cf. 5.13, 11.150; πλῆτο δὲ πᾶν πεδίον πεζῶν τε καὶ ἵππων Od.17.436, cf. 9.50. b. *on land, going by land*, opp. sea-faring, esp. in Od.; εἰ δ' ἐθέλεις π., πάρα τοι δίφρος τε καὶ ἵπποι 3.324; οὐ μὲν γάρ τί σε πεζὸν ὀΐομαι ἐνθάδ' ἱκέσθαι 1.173; ἔφθης πεζὸς ἰὼν ἢ ἐγὼ σὺν νηῒ μελαίνῃ 11.58, cf. Pi.*P.*10.29; ἐν νηῒ θοῇ ἢ π. Il.24.438. 2. in Prose, ὁ π. (with or without στρατός), a. sts. *infantry*, opp. cavalry (ἡ ἵππος), Hdt.1.80, 4.128; σὺν δυνάμει καὶ π. καὶ ἱππικῇ X.*Cyr.*2.4.18; but, b. more freq. *land-force, army*, opp. naval force, Hdt.4.97, 6.95, Th.1.47, 2.94, etc.; τὸ π. v.l. in Hdt.7.81; στρατιὰ καὶ ναυτικὴ καὶ π. Th.6.33, cf. 7.16 (and v. πεζικός); ἡ π. στρατιὰ καὶ τὸ ναυτικόν Lys.2.34, cf. A.*Pers.*558 (lyr.), 719, 728 (both troch.); οἱ μὲν ἐφ' ἵππων, οἱ δ' ἐπὶ ναῶν, πεζοί τε βάδην ib.19; τὰ π. κράτιστοι strongest *by land*, Th.4.12; καὶ ναυσὶ καὶ πεζοῖσι Ar.*Ach.*622; π. μάχαισιν Id.*Eq.*567; ἡ π. μάχη battle *by land*, Pl.*Lg.*707c; ἐν τοῖς ναυτικοῖς κινδύνοις, ὥσπερ ἐν τοῖς π. Isoc.4.91. 3. of animals, *land*, opp. birds and fishes, τὰ π. καὶ τὰ πτηνά *beasts* and birds, Pl.*Smp.*207a, cf. *Plt.*264e; π. καὶ ἔνυδρον ib.288a, cf. *Lg.*823b, Arist.*Top.*143$^{b}$1, etc.; ἡ π. θήρα Pl.*Sph.*222b, cf. *Lg.*824a. II. metaph. (cf. αὐτὰρ ἐγὼ Μουσέων πεζὸν ἔπειμι νομόν Call.*Aet.*4.1.9), of language, *prosaic*, λόγοι π. *prose* (cf. III. 3), D.H.*Comp.*6, Paus.4.6.1; διὰ πεζῶν [λ.] Phld.*Mus.*p.87 K.; λόγος *POxy.*724.10 (ii A.D.); ἡ π. διάλεκτος D.H.*Comp.*3; ἡ π. λέξις ib.1; opp. ἡ ἔμμετρος, ib.4; ἡ π. alone, Str.1.2.6; τινὰ καὶ πεζὰ καὶ ἐν ἔπεσι ποιήματα D.C.69.3; π. τις ποιητική, of bombastic prose, Luc.*Hist.Conscr.*8; κομιδῇ πεζὸν καὶ χαμαιπετές ib.16, cf. Plu.2.853c; τὰ ἄγαν π. καὶ κακόμετρα [ὀνόματα] ib.747f; π. ὀνόματα, opp. ποιητικά, Demetr.*Eloc.*167. 2. of verse, *unaccompanied by music*, καὶ πεζὰ καὶ φορμικτά S.*Fr.*16; πεζῷ γόῳ· ἄνευ αὐλοῦ ἢ λύρας, Phot.; cf. III. 2. 3. *common, ordinary*, ἑταῖραι Theopomp.Hist.205; μόσχοι Eup.169; π. αὐλητρίς Pl.Com.155. III. dat. fem. πεζῇ (sc. ὁδῷ) as Adv., 1. *on foot*, opp. σὺν ἵππῳ, X.*Oec.*5.5. b. more commonly, *by land*, Hdt.2.159, Th.2.94, etc.; π. ἕπεσθαι to follow *by land*, Hdt.7.110, 115; στρατιὰν μέλλων π. πορεύσειν Th.4.132; π. πορευθέσθαι X.*An.*5.6.1; οὔτε π. οὔτε κατὰ θάλατταν ib.5.6.10; καὶ π. καὶ ναυμαχοῦντες *by land* and by sea, D.3.24. 2. *without musical accompaniment* (cf. II. 2), παῦσαι μελῳδοῦσ' ἀλλὰ π. μοι φράσον *Com.Adesp.*601, cf. Pl.*Sph.*237a. 3. regul. Adv. πεζῶς *in prose*, Phld.*Rh.*1.165 S., Suid. s. v. ἱστορῆσαι. IV. Comp. πεζότερος *more like a foot-journey*, Plu.2.804d; *more like prose*, στίχοι π. τῇ συνθέσει Sch. Il.2.252, etc.: Sup. πεζότατος, τὸ π. μόριον τῆς ψυχῆς Suid. s. v. ψυχή, cf. Procl. *in Ti.*3.317 D.

πεζότης, ητος, ἡ, *the being furnished with feet*, Simp. *in Cat.*100.16.

πεζο-φᾰνής, ές, (φαίνομαι) *like prose*, Procl. *in Alc.*p.292 C. (Comp.). -φόρος, ον, (πέζα II. 2) *bordered*, ζώματα A.*Fr.*246.

πεῖ, τό, name of the letter π, v. Π:—later πῖ, Sch.D.T.p.489 H., etc.

⊛ πεῖ, Dor. Adv. *where?* Sophr.5:—indef. πει, *anywhere*, *SIG*527.126 (Dreros, iii B.C.).

Πεῖα, τά, games in honour of Antoninus *Pius*, *Delph.*3(1).551.

πειθ-ᾰνάγκη, ἡ, *compulsion under the disguise of persuasion, force majeure, duress*, Plb.21.42.7; π. προσάγειν τισὶ τοῦ συγχωρεῖν Id.*Fr.*194, cf. Cic.*Att.*9.13.4; π. Θετταλική 'Hobson's choice', Zos.1.21, cf. Jul.*Or.*1.32a; euphemism for *torture* or *bastinado*, *PAmh.*2.31.11 (ii B.C.), *PTeb.*5.58 (ii B.C.). -αναλογία, ἡ, *special pleading*, *PLips.*40 iii 7 (iv A.D.). -άνιος [ᾱ], Dor. for πειθήνιος. -ανός, -ανότης, = πιθ-, *CPHerm.*7.20 (iii A.D.), *CPR*232.13 (ii A.D.). -άνωρ [ᾱ], ορος, ὁ, ἡ, *obeying men, obedient*, A.*Ag.*1639.

πειθαρχ-έω, *obey one in authority*, abs., πειθαρχεῖ.., ἄπληκτος ὥσπερ ἵππος Eup.232, cf. Arist.*Pol.*1262$^{b}$3: mostly c. dat., π. πατρί S.*Tr.*1178; τοῖς νόμοισι Ar.*Ec.*762; τοῖς ἐφεστῶσι X.*Mem.*3.5.19, cf. Pl.*R.*538d; ὡς ἂν.. τοῖς πηδαλίοις ἡ ναῦς π. Cratin.139; τοῖς προσταχθεῖσιν Isoc.3.13; τῷ λόγῳ Arist.*Pol.*1295$^{b}$6: c. gen. (cf. πείθω B. I. 3), ἐπιταγμάτων Epist.Darei in *SIG*22.7 (v B.C.); στρατηγοῦ *OGI*12.11 (Priene, iii B.C.), cf. 244.38 (Syria, ii B.C.); τινος *PGiss.*2.16 (ii B.C.):—Med., ἔθνος.. πειθαρχέεσθαι ἑτοῖμον Hdt.5.91. -ησις, εως, ἡ, = sq., Eustr. *in EN*118.10. -ία, ἡ, *obedience to command*, A.*Th.*224, S.*Ant.*676, Isoc.12.115, Pl.*R.*538e. -ικός, ή, όν, *obeying readily*, Arist.*EN*1102$^{b}$31; τοῖς νόμοις Id.*Metaph.*1061$^{a}$25. -ος, ον, (ἀρχή) *obedient*. π. φρήν A.*Pers.*374.

πειθ-ήμων, ον, gen. ονος, *persuaded, obedient*, Nonn.*D.*24.171, 34.92, al.; μῦθος ib.8.165. II. *persuading, convincing*, φωνή Tryph.456. -ήνιος, Dor. -άνιος [ᾱ], ον, (ἡνία) *obedient to the rein*, of a horse, Plu.*Lyc.*30: metaph., Id.2.592c: generally, *obedient*, γυνή M.Ant.1.17, *Hymn.Is.*101, cf. Plu.2.90b; στράτευμα *well-disciplined*, Onos.10.9; ψυχή Hierocl. *in CA*16 p.456 M.; τὸ π. *submissiveness, docility*, Plu.2.442c. Adv. -ίως ib.102e, Ph.1.184; in Surgery, *gently*, Herod.Med.ap.Orib.10.18.15, Sor.1.70$^{b}$, 2.10. II. Act., *that makes obedient*, χαλινοί Plu.2.369c; λόγος Vett.Val.150.28.

πειθοδῐκαιόσῡνος, ον, *pleading the cause of justice* or *obedient to justice*, *PMag.Lond.*46.403.

πειθός, ή, όν, = πιθανός, 1*Ep.Cor.*2.4.

⊛ πείθω, *persuade*, impf. ἔπειθον Il.22.91, etc.; Ep. and Lyr. πεῖθον 16.842, B.8.16: fut. πείσω Il.9.345, etc.; Ep. inf. πεισέμεν 5.252: aor. 1 ἔπεισα Pi.*O.*2.80, A.*Eu.*84, Ar.*Pl.*304, etc. (Hom. has only opt. πείσειε Od.14.123); Aeol. part. πείσαις Pi.*O.*3.16: aor. 2 ἔπιθον Id.*P.*3.65 (poet. πίθον), Corinn.*Supp.*2.58 (poet. dual πιθέταν), A.*Supp.*941, Ar.*Pl.*949, Theoc.22.64, used by Hom. only in Ep. redupl. forms πεπίθωμεν Il.9.112, πεπίθοιμι 23.40, A.R.3.14, πεπιθεῖν Il.9.184, A.R.3.536, πεπιθών Pi.*I.*4(3).72 (v. infr.), πεπιθοῦσα Il.15.26 (ind. not in Il. or Od., πέπιθον A.R.1.964, πέπιθε *h.Ap.*275): pf. πέπεικα Lys.26.7, Is.8.24, Isoc.14.15:—Med. and Pass. πείθομαι, *obey*, Il.1.79, etc.: fut. πείσομαι ib.289, etc.: aor. 2 ἐπῐθόμην, Ep. πιθόμην 5.201, ἐπίθετο Ar.*Nu.*73, ἐπίθοντο Il.3.260, *IG*2$^{2}$.29.14, redupl. πεπίθοντο Orph.*Fr.*135; imper. πιθέο Pi.*P.*1.59, πιθοῦ S.*Ant.*992, pl. πίθεσθε A.*Eu.*794; subj. πίθωμαι Il.18.273, etc.; opt. πιθοίμην 4.93, etc. (redupl. πεπίθοιτο 10.204); inf. πιθέσθαι 7.293, etc. (πεπιθέσθαι *AP*14.75); part. πιθόμενος S.*Ph.*1226: aor. 1 Med. ἐπεισάμην *IG*12(5).720.5 (Andros, ii B.C.), Aristid.1.391 J., Sopat. in Rh.8.150 W.: fut. Pass. πεισθήσομαι S.*Ph.*624, Pl.*Sph.*248e, etc.: aor. 1 ἐπείσθην A.*Eu.*593, S.*OT*526, Ar.*Nu.*866, X.*An.*7.7.29: pf. πέπεισμαι A.*Pers.*697, E.*El.*578, Pl.*Prt.*328e; Thess. pf. inf. πεπείστειν *IG*9(2).517.16 (Larissa, iii B.C.). II. intr. tenses of Act., in pass. sense, pf. 2 πέποιθα Il.4.325, etc. (not freq. in Prose); imper. πέπεισθι A.*Eu.*599 codd.; 2 sg. subj. πεποίθῃς Il.1.524; Ep. 1 pl. πεποίθομεν (for -ωμεν) Od.10.335; opt. πεποιθοίη Ar.*Ach.*940: plpf. ἐπεποίθειν Il.16.171; 3 pl. ἐπεποίθεσαν Hdt.9.88; Ep. πεποίθεα Od.4.434, 8.181; 1 pl. ἐπέπιθμεν Il.2.341, 4.159: Pi. uses aor. 2 part. πιθών = πιθόμενος, *P.*3.28, redupl. πεπιθών *I.*4(3).72. III. as if from fut. πιθέω, Hom. has fut. πιθήσω Od.21.369 (*obey*): aor. part. πιθήσας Il.4.398 (*trust*), cf. Hes.*Op.*359, 671, Pi.*P.*4.109, A.*Ch.*618 (lyr.), Lyc.735; redupl. aor. subj. πεπῑθήσω trans., Il.22.223:—also Aeol. πίθημι, part. πίθεις Alc.*Supp.*9.4.

A. Act., *prevail upon, persuade*, usu. by fair means, τινα Il.9.345, etc.; πεπιθεῖν φρένας Αἰακίδαο ib.184; σοὶ δὲ φρένας ἄφρονι πεῖθε 16.842; τοῦ θυμὸν ἐνὶ στήθεσσιν ἔπειθον 9.587, cf. Od.7.258, 23.337; Ἕκτορι θυμὸν ἔπειθε Il.22.78: c. acc. pers. et inf., *persuade* one *to*.., ib.223, A.*Eu.*724, etc.; π. τινὰς ὥστε δοῦναι, etc., Hdt.6.5, cf. Th.3.31, etc.; ὥστε μὴ.. S.*Ph.*901; later ἵνα.. *Ev.Matt.*27.20, Plu.2.181a; π. τινὰς ὡς χρὴ.., ὡς ἔστι.., Pl.*R.*327c, 364b; π. τινὰ ἐς τὴν ὁμολογίαν Th.5.76; κοὐδείς γέ μ' ἂν πείσειεν.. τὸ μὴ ἐλθεῖν Ar.*Ra.*68; πείθω ἐμαυτόν I *persuade* myself, *am persuaded, believe*, Th.6.33, And.1.70, Pl.*Grg.*453b, etc.; also π. τι ὠφέλιμον ὄν Th.4.17: freq. in part., πείσας *by persuasion, by fair means*, opp. ἐν δόλῳ, S.*Ph.*102, cf. 612; opp. βίᾳ, *Trag.Adesp.*402; πόλιν πείσας *having obtained* the city's *consent*, S.*OC*1298; δᾶμον πείσαις λόγῳ Pi.*O.*3.16; μὴ πείσας unless *by leave*, Pl.*Lg.*844e; οὐ πείσαντες τὸν δῆμον Aeschin.3.41; πείθοντες, opp. βίᾳ, X.*An.*5.5.11; π. γυναῖκα, opp. βιάζεσθαι, Id.*Cyr.*6.1.34; πέπεικε, opp. ἠνάγκακε, Pl.*Hipparch.*232b (but π. ἀνάγκῃ D.C.62.16, cf. πειθανάγκη): with neut. pron., *persuade* one to or of a thing, τοῦτό γε οὐκ ἔπειθε τοὺς Φωκαιέας Hdt.1.163, cf. A.*Pr.*1064 (anap.), Pl.*R.*399b, etc.; ἔπειθον οὐδέν' οὐδὲν A.*Ag.*1212; μὴ πεῖθ' ἃ μὴ δεῖ *do* not *attempt to persuade* me to.., S.*OC*1442; also τοιάνδ' ἔπειθε ῥῆσιν *addressed* them thus, A.*Supp.*615. 2. *prevail on by entreaty*, Il.24.219, Od.14.363; τότε κέν μιν ἱλασσάμενοι πεπίθοιμεν Il.1.100; ὥς κέν μιν ἀρεσσάμενοι πεπίθωμεν 9.112, cf. 181, 386, Hes.*Sc.*450; Ζηνὸς ἦτορ λιταῖς Pi.*O.*2.80, cf. Pl.*R.*366a, *Ap.*37d: c. dupl. acc., τὸν φόρον ὑποτελῶ Ἀθηναίοισιν, ὃν ἂν πείθω Ἀθηναίους *IG*1$^{2}$.39.27. II. in bad sense, *talk over, mislead*, ἐπεὶ οὐ παρελεύσεαι οὐδέ με πείσεις Il.1.132, cf. 6.360; ἔλαθε δόλῳ καὶ ἔπειθεν Ἀχαιοὺς Od.2.106, cf. 14.123; πεπιθοῦσα θυέλλας Il.15.26. 2. π. τινὰ χρήμασι *bribe*, Hdt.8.134, Lys.21.10; π. ἐπὶ μισθῷ or μισθῷ, Hdt.8.4, 9.33, Th.2.96, etc. (Pass., χρήμασι πεισθείς Id.1.137): prov., δῶρα θεοὺς πείθει Hes.*Fr.*272; πείθειν τινὰ alone,

Lys.7.21, X.*An*.1.3.19, *Act.Ap*.12.20. **3.** of food, *tempt*, Xenocr. ap.Orib.2.58.84.

**B.** Pass. and Med., *to be prevailed on, won over, persuaded*, abs., Il.5.201, etc.; imper. freq. in Trag., πείθου *be persuaded*, S.*OC*520, *El*.1015, E.*Fr*.440; but πιθοῦ *comply*, S.*OC*1181, *El*.1207: c. inf.. *to be persuaded* to do, Id.*Ph*.624; πείθεσθέ μοι πρύτανιν ἑλέσθαι Pl.*Prt*.338a; also πείθεσθαί τινι ὥστε.. Th.2.2; ὃ..ὑμεῖς..ἥκιστ' ἂν ὀξέως πείθοισθε (sc. πρᾶξαι) Id.6.34; ἑκὼν καὶ πεπεισμένος of one's own *free will*, *POxy*.iv p 203 (iv A.D.), etc.; τὰ μὲν παρ' ἡμῶν ἴσθι σοι πεπεισμένα we are *won over* to you, Ar.*Th*.1170. **2.** πείθεσθαί τινι *listen to* one, *obey* him, Il.1.79, etc.; τοῖς ἐν τέλει βεβῶσι π. S.*Ant*.67; τοῖς ἄρχουσι, τῷ νόμῳ, X.*Cyr*.1.2.8, *An*.7.3.39; μᾶλλον τῷ θεῷ ἢ ὑμῖν Pl.*Ap*.29d: sts. c. dupl. dat., ἔπεσι, μύθοισι π. τινί, Il.1.150, 23.157: without dat. pers., ἐπείθετο μύθῳ 1.33, cf. Od.17.177; γήραϊ πείθεσθαι *yield, succumb* to old age, Il.23.645; στυγερῇ πειθώμεθα δαιτί *let us comply with* the custom of eating, sad though the meal be, ib.48; νῦν μὲν πειθώμεθα νυκτὶ μελαίνῃ, of leaving off the labours of the day, 8.502; ἀδίκοις ἔργμασι π. Sol.4.11, 13.12. **b.** with Adj. neut., σημάντορι πάντα πιθέσθαι *obey* him *in* all things, Od.17.21; ἅ τιν' οὐ πείσεσθαι ὀΐω wherein I think some *will* not *obey*, Il.1.289, cf. 4.93, 7.48, Hdt.6.100, etc.; πάντ' ἔγωγε πείσομαι S.*Aj*.529; πείσομαι δ' ἃ σοὶ δοκεῖ Id.*Tr*.1180; οὐ..πείθομαι τὸ δρᾶν Id.*Ph*.1252; μύθοις.. πεισθεὶς ἀφανῆ E.*Hipp*.1288 (anap.), cf. Lys.22.3: rarely with Noun in acc., χρήμασι πεισθῆναι [τὴν ἀναχώρησιν] Th.2.21 (s.v.l.). **3.** c. gen., four times in Hdt., πείθεσθαί τινος 1.126, 5.29, 33, 6.12, cf. E.*IA*726, Th.7.73; πείσθητί μευ Herod.1.66; κείνου..πιθοίατο vulg. in Il.10.57. **II.** πείθεσθαί τινι *believe, trust in*, πείθεθ' ἑταίρῳ Od.20.45; οἰωνοῖσι Il.12.238; τεράεσσι θεῶν καὶ Ζηνὸς ἀρωγῇ 4.408; ἐνυπνίῳ Pi.*O*.13.79; λεγομένοισι Hdt.2.146, etc.: c. acc. et inf., *believe that*.., οὐ γάρ πω ἐπείθετο ὃν πατέρ' εἶναι Od.16.192, cf. Hdt.1.8, etc.: c. dat. pers. et inf., π. τινὶ μὴ εἶναι χρήματα, = ὅτι χρήματα οὐκ ἔχει, X.*An*.7.8.3: with ὡς, οὐ πείσονται ὡς σὺ αὐτὸς οὐκ ἠθέλησας Pl.*Cri*.44c, cf. *R*.391b: with neut. Adj. or Pron., τὰ περὶ Αἴγυπτον τοῖσι λέγουσι αὐτὰ π., οὐκ ἐπείθοντο τὰ ἐσαγγελθέντα, Hdt.2.12, 8.81; πείθεσθε τούτῳ ταῦτα Ar.*Th*.592; ταῦτ' ἐγώ σοι οὐ πείθομαι I *do* not *take* this *on your word*, Pl.*Ap*.25e, cf. *Phdr*.235b: abs., ὡς ἐγὼ πείθομαι Phld.*Po*.5.34. **b.** π. τινὰ ὅπως.. *to believe of* him, that.., E.*Hipp*.1251. **III.** pf. 2 πέποιθα *trust, rely on*, c. dat. pers. vel rei, Il.4.325, etc. (not freq. in early Prose, as αὐτῷ πεποιθέναι Pl.*Mx*.248a): c. dat. et inf., οὔ πω χερσὶ πέποιθα ἄνδρ' ἀπαμύνασθαι Od.16.71, cf. Il.13.96, etc.: c. dat., οἷσι..μαρναμένοισι πέποιθε Od.16.98: later c. inf. only, πέποιθα τοῦτ' ἐπισπάσειν κλέος I *trust* to win this fame, S.*Aj*.769; αἰχμὴν..μᾶλλον θεοῦ σέβειν πεποιθώς *daring to*.., A.*Th*.530: once in Hdt., χρήμασι ἐπεποίθεσαν διώσεσθαι 9.88: rarely c. acc. et inf., πέποιθα..τὸν πυρφόρον ἥξειν κεραυνόν A.*Th*.444; εἴ τις πέποιθεν ἑαυτῷ Χριστοῦ εἶναι 2*Ep.Cor*.10.7; π. εἴς τινας ὅτι.. *Ep.Gal*.5.10; ἐπί τινας ὅτι.. 2*Ep.Cor*.2.3; ἐπὶ χρήμασι *Ev.Marc*.10.24: abs., ὄφρα πεποίθῃς that *you may feel confidence*, Il.1.524, Od.13.344; πεποιθώς *in sure confidence*, Lxx *De*.33.28. **IV.** post-Hom. pf. Pass. πέπεισμαι *believe, trust*, c. dat., νεκροῖσι A.*Eu*.599; ὀνείροις E.*Hel*.1190, etc.: c. acc. et inf., συνοίσειν ταῦτα πέπ. D.4.51, cf. Pl.*R*.368a: abs., νῦν δὲ πέπεισμαι Id.*Prt*.328e; πεπεισμένος ἔκ τινων λογίων *persuaded* by.., Plu.*Rom*.14; πεπείσμεθα περὶ ὑμῶν τὰ κρείττονα *Ep.Hebr*.6.9. (Cf. Lat. *fīdo, fīdes*.)

⊛ **Πειθώ**, gen. όος, contr. οῦς, ἡ, Ion. acc. πειθοῦν (v. infr. II. 3):—*Persuasion* as a goddess, Hes.*Op*.73, *Th*.349, Sapph.135, Ibyc.5, Pi.*P*.9.39, *Fr*.123.10, A.*Supp*.1040 (lyr.), Men.*Epit*.338, Hermesian.11, Paus.1.22.3, 2.7.7; Πειθὼ καὶ Ἀναγκαίη Hdt.8.111; Π. καὶ Βία Plu.*Them*.21. **II.** as Appellat., *persuasiveness*, πειθοῦς ἐπαοιδαῖσιν A.*Pr*.173 (anap.), etc.; π. τις ἐπεκάθιζεν ἐπὶ τοῖς χείλεσιν, of Pericles, Eup.94.5; ἀργύριον παρά του πειθοῖ λαβών X.*Mem*.1.7.5; πειθοῦς δημιουργός ἐστιν ἡ ῥητορική Pl.*Grg*.453a; δύο εἴδη πειθοῦς, τὸ μὲν πίστιν παρεχόμενον ἄνευ τοῦ εἰδέναι, τὸ δ' ἐπιστήμην ib.454e; πειθοῖ καὶ βίᾳ *by persuasion* or compulsion, Id.*Lg*.722b; μετὰ πειθοῦς ib.720d. **2.** *persuasion* in the mind, A.*Ag*.385 (lyr.). **3.** *means of persuasion, inducement*, E.*IA*104; πειθώ τινα ζητεῖν Ar.*Nu*.1398; κοίην οὐ προσήγαγον πειθοῦν αὐτῷ; Herod.6.75. **4.** *obedience*, X.*Cyr*.2.3.19, 3.3.8, Hierocl. *in CA*5 p.427 M.; τῶν παρηγγελμένων *POxy*.474.37 (ii A.D.).

**πεικαμμαῖς**· ὀξείαις καὶ λεπταῖς, Hsch. **πεικόν**· πικρόν, πευκεδανόν, Id. **πεῖκος, πείκω**, v. πέκος, πέκω. **πειλός**· πᾶν τὸ πεπιλωμένον (–πηλ– cod.), Id.

**πεῖν**, later form for πιεῖν, v. πίνω.

**πεῖνα**, Ion. **πείνη**, ης, ἡ, *hunger, famine*, πείνη δ' οὔ ποτε δῆμον ἐπέρχεται Od.15.407; πεῖνα (v.l. πείνη) καὶ δίψα Pl.*R*.585a; δίψαν..καὶ πεῖναν ib.437d; δίψα καὶ πεῖνα Arist. *de An*.414$^{b}$11; πείνην τε καὶ δίψος Pl.*Phlb*.34d; πείνη ib.31e, *Ly*.221a: pl., δίψαι καὶ πεῖναι Arist.*Rh*.1389$^{a}$9. **2.** metaph., *hunger* or *longing for* a thing, διὰ μαθημάτων πείνην Pl.*Phlb*.52a. (In nom. and acc. sg. Pl. usu. has πείνη –ην, v. supr.)

**πεῖνα**, v. πίννα; cf. πινώτιον.

**πειν-ᾰλέος**, α, ον, *hungry*, *Com.Adesp*.29 D., *AP*6.218 (Alc.), Opp.*C*.4.94; π. πίνακες *empty* dishes, *AP*11.313 (Lucill.); διψᾶδες καὶ π. Plu.2.129b. **–άω**, forms in αε contr. into η not ᾱ (as in διψάω, cf. Phryn.42), πεινῇς, –ῇ Ar.*Eq*.1270; inf. πεινῆν Id.*Nu*.441, *Pl*.595, Pl.*Grg*.496c; Ep. πεινήμεναι Od.20.137 (only here in Od.): impf. ἐπείνων X.*HG*6.2.15: fut. πεινήσω Hdt.2.13, Ar.*Pl*.539, X.*Mem*.2.1.17; later πεινάσω [ᾱ] Lxx *Si*.24.21, al., *Apoc*.7.16: aor. ἐπείνησα X.*Cyr*.8.3.39, ἐπείνᾱσα Lxx *Ge*.41.55, Luc.*Epigr*.50, Aesop.62, Ps.-Callisth.3.6: pf. πεπείνηκα Pl.*R*.606a: later we find the contr. of αε into ᾱ, ἐπείνας, πεινᾷ, –ᾶν, Lxx *De*.25.18, *Ep.Rom*.12.20, etc.: (πεῖνα):—*to be hungry*, πεινάων, of a lion, Il.3.25; λέοντε..ἄμφω πεινάοντε 16.758; λέοντα..μέγα πεινάοντα 18.162; κακῶς π. *to be starved*, Hdt.2.13, 14; π. βάδην Ar.*Ach*.535; thrice in Trag., πεινῶσα S.*Fr*.199; πεινῶντι E.*Fr*.895, Achae.25; πεινᾶντι δὲ μηδὲ ποτένθῃς Theoc.15.148: metaph., πεινῆν φασι τὴν γῆν Thphr.*HP*8.6.2. **II.** c. gen., *hunger after*, σίτου δ' οὐκέτ' ἔφη πεινήμεναι Od.20.137. **2.** metaph., *hunger, crave after*, χρημάτων X.*Cyr*.8.3.39, etc.; ἐπαίνου Id.*Oec*.13.9; simply, *to be in want of, lack*, πεινῶντες ἀγαθῶν Pl.*R*.521a; μάλα π. συμμάχων X.*Cyr*.7.5.50, etc.: later c. acc., οἱ π. καὶ διψῶντες τὴν δικαιοσύνην *Ev.Matt*.5.6. [ᾱ in uncontr. forms in Hom. With this the Dor. contractions δια-πεινᾶμες (v. διαπεινάω) and πεινᾶντι Theoc. l. c., and the Att. contractions (–η– from –ηε–) agree; but πεινῶντι Dor. 3 pl. pres. ind. in X.*HG*1.1.23 codd. points to –ᾰοντι.] **–έω**, Ion. for foreg., Hsch. **–η**, v. πεῖνα. **–ητικός**, ή, όν, *suffering from hunger*, Arist.*EE*1222$^{a}$36, Plu.2.635e (Comp.):—later **–ᾱτικός**, ib.204d. **–ώδης**, ες, = foreg., Gal.7.576. **–ωλκός**, όν, dub. in *Hymn.Is*.55.

**πεῖρα**, ας (Ion. πείρα, acc. πεῖραν, gen. –ης), Aeol. **πέρρα** Choerob. in *An.Ox*.2.252: ἡ:—*trial, attempt*, π. τοι μαθήσιος ἀρχά Alcm.63; opp. δόξα, Thgn.571; πείρᾳ δ' οὐ προσωμίλησά πω S.*Tr*.591; πικρὰν πεῖραν τολμήσειν Id.*El*.471; πείρᾳ σφαλῆναι Th.1.70; ἢν μὲν ξυμβῇ ἡ π. Id.3.3; πείρᾳ θην πάντα τελεῖται Theoc.15.62; πεῖραν ἔχοντες *being proved*, Pi.*N*.4.76; but πεῖραν ἔχειν τινός to have *experience* of.., X.*Cyr*.4.1.5; π. τινῶν ἔχειν ὅτι.. Id.*An*.3.2.16; π. ἔχει τῆς γνώμης involves *a trial* of your resolution, Th.1.140; πεῖράν τινος λαμβάνειν or λαβεῖν to make *trial* or *proof* of.., E.*Fr*.691, Isoc.12.236, Pl.*Grg*.448a, X.*An*.6.6.33, etc.; also, gain *experience* of.., ἐν ἑαυτῷ ib.5.8.15; π. λ. τινός, ὅπως ἔχει Pl.*Prt*.342a; π. λ. τινός, εἰ ἄρα τι λέγει Id.*Thg*.129d; πεῖράν τινος διδόναι (cf. Lat. *specimen sui edere*) Darei Epist. in *SIG*22.21, Th.1.138, Isoc.3.45; π. τῆς δόξης δοῦναι Th.6.11; π. ἔργῳ δεδωκέναι D.18.107, cf. 195; π. ἀλλήλων λαμβάνοντες καὶ διδόντες Pl.*Plt*.348a; πεῖραν ποιήσασθαι Th.1.53; π. ποιεῖσθαι εἰ.. Id.2.20; ταῖς π. βασανίζειν Arist.*GA*747$^{a}$3; πεῖραν καθεῖναι Ael.*VH*2.13, cf. *NA*1.39; π. δέξασθαι *undertake*, Plu.*Pyrrh*.5. **2.** with Preps., ἀπὸ πείρης by *experiment*, opp. αὐτόματον, Hdt.7.9.γ'; διὰ πείρας ἰέναι Pl.*Ax*.369a; διὰ π. ἔργων ἐλήλυθε Onos.*Praef*.7; ἀποδοκιμασθῆναι διὰ τῆς π. Arist.*Pol*.1341$^{a}$37; ἐς πεῖραν ἤλθομεν φίλων E.*Heracl*.309, etc.; ἰέναι ἐς τὴν π. τοῦ ναυτικοῦ *try* an action by sea, Th.7.21; ἀκοῆς κρείσσων ἐς π. ἔρχεται turns out *on trial* greater than report, Id.2.41; ἐκ τῆς π. δῆλον Arist.*Pr*.938$^{b}$38; Κύρου ἐν πείρᾳ γενέσθαι to have been *acquainted* with Cyrus, X.*An*.1.9.1; ἐν π. τέλος διαφαίνεται Pi.*N*.3.70; ἐπὶ πείρᾳ by way of *test* or *trial*, Ar.*Av*.583; ἐπὶ π. δούς *on trial*, Men.118; π. θανάτου πέρι καὶ ζωᾶς a *contest* for.., Pi.*N*.9.28. **II.** *attempt on* or *against* one, πεῖράν τιν' ἐχθρῶν ἁρπάσαι *a means of attacking*.., S.*Aj*.2; τοιοῦδε φωτὸς π. εὖ φυλακτέον A.*Th*.499; esp. *attempt to seduce* a woman, Plu.*Thes*.26, *Cim*.1: abs., *attempt, enterprise*, A.*Pers*.719 (troch.), Th.3.20; πεῖραν ἀφορμᾶν to go forth upon *an enterprise*, S.*Aj*.290; cf. πειρατής. (Cf. Lat. *experior, peritus*.)

**πειρά**, ἡ, *sharp point*, κοπάνων A.*Ch*.860 (anap.).

⊛ **πειράζω**, (πεῖρα) used by early authors only in pres. and impf., the other tenses being supplied by πειράω, –άομαι: Cret. fut. πειράξω *GDI*5181: aor. 1 imper. πείρᾰσον *AP*11.183 (Lucill.): aor. Pass. ἐπειράσθην Lxx *Wi*.11.9, *Ev.Matt*.4.1: pf. part. πεπειρασμένος *Ep.Hebr*.4.15:—*make proof* or *trial of*, c. gen., Od.16.319, 23.114: abs., 9.281. **2.** c. inf., *attempt* to do, Plb.2.6.9, Lxx *Jd*.6.39, *Act.Ap*.16.7, 24.6; π. τι *attempt* a thing, ἄλλος ἄλλην ἐπ' ἐμὲ πειράζει τέχνην Luc.*Trag*.149, cf. S.E.*M*.1.40; τόδε τόξον *make trial of*, *Anacreont*.31.24: abs., *make an attempt*, Plb.*Fr*.195. **3.** Pass., ἤθη..ἐν χρόνῳ πειράζεται *are tried, proved*, Men.*Mon*.573; *to be experienced*, Phld.*Sign*.32. **II.** c. acc. pers., *try, tempt* a person, *put* him *to the test*, Lxx *Ge*.22.1, al.; ἑαυτοὺς πειράζετε, εἰ.. 2*Ep.Cor*.13.5, al.; τί πειράζετε τὸν Κύριον; Lxx *Ex*.17.2, cf. *Act.Ap*.15.10, 1*Ep.Cor*.10.9, al. **2.** in bad sense, *seek to seduce, tempt*, Ἀθηναίην A.R.3.10: abs., ὁ πειράζων *the Tempter*, 1*Ep.Thess*.3.5, etc.:—Pass., *to be sorely tried*, πειραζομένη βασανίζομαι *PLit.Lond*.52.5; στομακάκκῃ Str.16.4.24; *to be attacked*, ὑποχύσει Alex.Aphr.*Pr*.2.54; ἐπιληψίᾳ Cyran.47; *to be tempted to sin*, *Ev.Matt*.4.1, al.

**Πειραιεύς** or **Πειρᾱεύς** (v. infr.), ὁ, *Piraeus*: gen. Πειραιέως, Att. Πειραιῶς Th.2.93, Isoc.16.46, D.8.7, 24.134, Moer.p.314 P.; dat. Πειραιεῖ X.*HG*2.4.30; acc. Πειραιᾶ ib.5.4.34, Th.2.93, Pl.*R*.327a, D.17.26; Ion. Πειραιέα Hdt.8.85:—Loc. **Πειραιοῖ**, *in Piraeus*, X.*HG*2.4.32, Ael.*VH*2.13; **Πειραιόθεν**, *from P.*, Alciphr.2.4.—The form **Πειραεύς** is freq. in Inscrr., *IG*2.2459*b*2, etc.; Πειρᾰέως *AP*6.349 (Phld.); Πειρᾱεῖ Ar.*Pax*165, but –ᾰεῖ ib.145:—Adj. **Πειραϊκός**, ή, όν, *IG*2$^{2}$.456.33, Plu.*Sull*.14, etc.

**πειραϊκός**, ή, όν, *over the border*, γῆ π. *border*-country, *the March*, f.l. in Th.2.23.

**πειραίνω**, aor. ἐπείρηνα (v. infr.), (πεῖραρ) *fasten by the ends*, σειρὴν ἐξ αὐτοῦ πειρήναντε *having tied* a rope to.., Od.22.175. **II.** poet. for περαίνω (q. v.).

⊛ **πεῖραρ** (also **πεῖρας**, v. infr. I. 5), ᾰτος, τό, Ep., Ion., and Lyr. form of πέρας, *end, limit*, οὐδ' εἴ κε τὰ νείατα πείραθ' ἵκηαι γαίης καὶ πόντοιο Il.8.478, cf. Od.5.463, 11.13. **2.** *completion*, οὐ γάρ πω πάντων ἐπὶ πείρατ' ἀέθλων ἤλθομεν the *end* of our labours, 23.248. **3.** *achievement, execution, mode* or *means of execution*, ᾧ παιδὶ ἑκάστου πείρατ' ἔειπε Il.23.350; πείρατ' ἀέθλων δείκνυεν Pi.*P*.4.220; εἰ δέ τις ἀνδρῶν ἡμετέρης τέχνης πείρατά φησιν ἔχειν says he possesses the *secret*

(=*power of execution*) of my art, Zeuxis in *PLG*2.318, cf. *IG*3.399; *νίκης πείρατ' ἔχονται ἐν ἀθανάτοισι θεοῖσι* the *achievement* of victory is dependent on the gods, Il.7.102; *νίκης ἐν θεοῖσι πείρατα* Archil. 55. 4. *final decision, verdict*, *ἐπὶ ἵστορι πεῖραρ ἑλέσθαι* Il.18.501. 5. *doom*, *ἐκφυγέειν μέγα π. ὀϊζύος* Od.5.289; *ὥς κεν θᾶσσον ὀλέθρου πείραθ' ἵκηαι* Il.6.143; *πεῖρας θανάτου* Pi.*O*.2.31. II. *instrument, tool*, *ἦλθε δὲ χαλκεὺς ὅπλ' ἐν χερσὶν ἔχων χαλκήϊα, πείρατα τέχνης, ἄκμονά τε σφῦράν τ' εὐποίητόν τε πυράγρην* Od.3.433, cf. Sch.D ad loc. 2. esp. *tackle, rope*, *δησάντων σ'..ὀρθὸν ἐν ἱστοπέδῃ, ἐκ δ' αὐτοῦ πείρατ' ἀνήφθω* Od.12.51; *οὐδ' ἔτι δεσμά σ' ἔρυκε, λύοντο δὲ πείρατα πάντα* *h.Ap*.129: metaph., *πτολέμοιο πεῖραρ..τάνυσσαν* Il.13.359: *Τρώεσσιν ὀλέθρου πείρατ' ἐφῆπται* 7.402; *πᾶσιν ὀλέθρου πείρατ' ἐφῆπτο* Od.22.33; *καιρὸν εἰ φθέγξαιο, πολλῶν πείρατα συντανύσαις ἐν βραχεῖ* Pi.*P*.1.81. (*περ-ϝr̥-, περ-ϝn̥-τ-*, cogn. with *πείρω, πόρος*.)

**πείρ-ᾱσις**, εως, ἡ, *attempt*, D.C.47.25; esp. *at seduction*, Th.6.56. **-ασμός**, ὁ, *trial*, Lxx *De*.4.34, al., 1 *Ep.Pet*.4.12; *οἱ ἐπὶ τῶν παθῶν π.* Dsc.1 *Praef*.5; *πειρασμοὶ ἐν τῇ γῇ καὶ θαλάσσῃ* Cyran.40. 2. *worry*, Lxx *Ec*.5.2. II. *temptation*, ib.*Si*.44.20, *Ev.Marc*.14.38, etc. **-αστής**, οῦ, ὁ, *tempter*, Ammon.*Diff*.p.109 V. **-αστικός**, ή, όν, *fitted for trying* or *testing, tentative*, *ἔστι δ' ἡ διαλεκτικὴ π. περὶ ὧν ἡ φιλοσοφία γνωριστική* Arist.*Metaph*.1004$^{b}$25; *ἡ -κή* (sc. *τέχνη, ἐπιστήμη*) as a branch of dialectic, Id.*SE*169$^{b}$25; *π. λόγοι* ib.165$^{a}$39, cf. Gal.17(2).350; *οἱ π. διάλογοι* of Plato, as the Euthyphro, Theaetetus, Meno, Ion, Thrasyll.ap.D.L.3.58 sq. Adv. *-κῶς* Ascl. *in Metaph*.246.9. **-ᾱτέον**, *one must attempt*, c. inf., Pl.*R*.453d, Arist.*EN*1166$^{b}$28, etc.; *π. εἶναι* Isoc.5.58:—also **-τέα**, Pl.*Lg*.770b. ⊛ **-ᾱτεύω**, *to be a pirate*, Str.14.3.2. II. *attack*, of a robber-band, *τινα* Lxx *Ge*.49.19, prob. in *SIG*582.12 (Delos, ii B.C.): —Pass., Sch.E.*Hec*.934. **-ᾱτήριον**, Ion. **πειρητ-**, τό, = *πεῖρα*, *φόνια πειρατήρια* the *trial* for murder, E.*IT*967, cf. Lxx *Jb*.7.1; *test*, Hp.*Mul*.1.78, *Nat.Mul*.96, Hld.10.22; *temptation*, *PLond.ined*.2491.8 (iv A.D.). II. *pirate's nest*, Str.14.5.7, Hld.5.6 (pl.). 2. *gang of brigands* or *pirates*, Lxx *Ge*.49.19, D.H.7.37, Ach.Tat.6.21. **-ᾱτήριος**, Ion. **πειρητ-**, ον, *tentative*: *directed to production*, c. gen., *θεραπεῖαι κυήσιος -ήριοι* Hp.*Steril*.217. **-ᾱτής**, οῦ, ὁ, *brigand*, Plb.4.3.8, Lxx *Jb*.16.10(9); esp. *pirate*, Plb.4.6.1, *Supp. Epigr*.3.378 *B*11 (Delph., ii/i B.C.), Str.14.3.2, Plu.*Luc*.2,13, etc.: later word for *λῃστής*, Ammon.p.109 V. **-ᾱτικός**, ή, όν, *fit for piracy*, Ach.Tat.2.17; *piratical*, *σκάφη* Ph.2.567; *πόλεμος* Plu.*Pomp*.30; *τὸ π. ἅπαν* ib.45; *πλάνη* Vett.Val.288.3; *τὰ π.* *gangs of pirates*, *IG*2².1225.13, Str.14.5.2, Plu.2.779a. Adv. *-κῶς* Ph.1.664 (Comp.) (also, = *πειραστικῶς*, Procl.*in Prm*.p.774 S. (s.v.l.)).

⊛ **πειράω**, Il.8.8, etc.: impf. *ἐπείρων* Th.4.25: fut. *-άσω* [ᾱ] ib.9, 43: aor. *ἐπείρᾱσα* S.*OC*1276, Ar.*Eq*.517, Th.6.54: pf. *πεπείρᾱκα* Luc.*Am*.26:—**Pass.**, aor. *ἐπειράθην* [ᾱ] Th.6.54; cf. *πειράζω*. B. more freq. in Med. **πειράομαι**, Il.2.193, 24.390, etc.: fut. *-άσομαι* [ᾱ] S.*OC*959, etc.; Dor. 2 pl. *πειρασεῖσθε* Ar.*Ach*.743, cf. Hippod.ap. Stob.4.1.94; later *πειρᾱθήσομαι* *Gp*.12.13.12: aor. *ἐπειρᾱσάμην*, Ion. *ἐπειρησάμην*, Od.8.120, Hdt.7.135, Th.2.44, al.; but aor. Pass. *ἐπειρήθην*, Att. *ἐπειράθην* [ᾱ], found in med. sense, Il.19.384, al., Hdt.3.152, al., Th.2.5 (v.l.), 33, 6.92, and in later Prose: pf. *πεπείρᾱμαι*, Ion. *-ημαι*, Od.3.23, Pi.*Fr*.110, Hdt.9.46, S.*Fr*.584, Antipho 5.1, etc.: 3 pl. plpf. *ἐπεπείραντο* D.C.*Fr*.24.3, Ion. *ἐπεπειρέατο* Hdt. 7.125. (From *πεῖρα*.)

A. Act., *attempt, endeavour, try*, c. inf., *μήτε τις..πειράτω διακέρσαι ἐμὸν ἔπος* Il.8.8; *πειρήσω* (*δύναμαι*) *φηλητέων ὄρχαμος εἶναι* *h.Merc*.175; *π. ἐς τὴν Μηδικὴν ἐσβάλλειν* Hdt.6.84, cf. Ar.*V*.1025, al.: folld. by *ὡς*.., Il.4.66, Od.2.316, etc.; by *ὅπως*.., 4.545: c. Adj. neut., *πολλὰ πειρῶντες* Th.6.38; *πάντα* Plu.2.1122b: with inf. understood, Th.7.32. II. c. gen. pers., *make trial of* one, *μή μευ πειράτω*, for the purpose of persuading, Il.9.345, cf. 24.433; of things, *τευχέων* A.R.3.1249: in hostile sense, *make an attempt on*, *μήλων πειρήσοντα* Il.12.301, Od.6.134; *οὐ πειρᾶν τῆς πόλιος, πρὶν..* Hdt.6.82; *π. τοῦ χωρίου* Th.1.61; *Νισαίας* Id.4.70; *ἀλλήλων* Id.7.38; *νυμφείας εὐνᾶς* Pi.*N*.5.30. III. abs., *ναυσὶ π.* *make an attempt* by sea, Th.4.25; *π. ἐπὶ τὴν κώμην* ib.43. IV. c. acc. rei, *experience*, *τύχης ἐπήρειαν* Luc.*Am*.46. 2. c. acc. pers., *make an attempt on* a woman's honour, Ar.*Eq*.517 (ubi v. Sch.), *Pl*.150, 1067, Lys.1.12, X.*Cyr*.5.2.28, etc.:—Pass., *πειραθεὶς ὁ Ἁρμόδιος ὑπὸ Ἱππάρχου* Th.6.54, cf. Pl.*Phdr*.227c; v. infr. B.IV, cf. *πεῖρα* II.

B. more freq. in Med., c. inf., *try to* do, Il.4.5, Hdt.5.71, 6.138, al., Ar.*Pl*.459, X.*Oec*.6.2, Lys.12.64, Isoc.3.41, Pl.*Tht*.186b: c. fut. inf., J.*AJ*17.8.4: the inf. is sts. understood, *πειρήσεται* (sc. *ἀλύξαι*) Od.4.417: folld. by *εἰ*, Il.13.806, Pl.*Phd*.95b; *πειρήσεται αἴ κε θέῃσιν* Il.18.601; by *ἐάν* or *ἄν*, A.*Pr*.327, Pl.*Lg*.638e; by *μή*.., *lest*.., Od.21.394; by *ὅπως*.., X.*An*.3.2.3: c. part., freq. in Hdt., *ἐπειρᾶτο ἐπιών* 1.77; *προσβαίνων* ib.84; *π. βιώμενοι* 4.139; *π. ἀποσχίζων* 6.9, cf. 5.50, 7.139, al.; *π. σκοπῶν* Pl.*Tht*.190e· c. neut. Adj., *τὰ μεγάλα καὶ τὰ μικρὰ π.* X.*Cyr*.1.5.14. II. most freq. (v. A.II) c. gen., 1. c. gen. pers., *make trial of* one, Il.10.444, Od.13.336, etc.; *νῦν σεῦ, ξεῖνε, ὀΐω πειρήσεσθαι, εἰ..* 19.215; *ἕο αὐτοῦ ἐν ἔντεσι..εἰ οἷ ἐφαρμόσσειε* Il.19.384; with gen. not expressed, *ἔπεσιν πειρήσομαι* 2.73; *ἦ πρῶτ' ἐξερέοιτο ἕκαστά τε πειρήσαιτο* *test* him in each particular, Od.4.119 (v.l. *μυθήσαιτο*); *π. θεοῦ* *make trial of, tempt* a god. Hdt.6.86.γ', cf. A.*Ag*.1663 (troch.): in hostile sense, *πρὶν πειρήσαιτ' Ἀχιλῆος* Il.21.580 (with acc. cogn. added *ἀέθλους..ἐπειρήσαντ' Ὀδυσῆος* Od.8.23): freq. in Hdt., esp. *ἀλλήλων πειρᾶσθαι*, as *ἐπειρῶντο κατὰ τὸ ἰσχυρὸν ἀλλήλων* 1.76; *πειρᾶσθέ μου γυναικὸς ὡς ἀφράσμονος* A.*Ag*.1401, etc.; *π. τῆς Πελοποννήσου* *make an attempt* on it, Hdt.8.100; *π. τοῦ τείχους* Th.2.81. 2. c. gen. rei, *make proof* or *trial of*.., *σθένεος* Il.15.359; *ἥβης* 23.432; *χειρῶν καὶ σθένεος π., ἤ..ἤ..* Od.21.282; *try one's chance at* or *in* a work or contest, *ἔργου* 18.369; *ἀέθλου, ἀέθλων*, Il.23.707, Od.8.100, etc.; *παλαιμοσύνης* ib.126; *make proof of, try* a weapon, *τόξου* 21.159,180; *νευρῆς* ib.410 (but [*ὀϊστοί*,] *τῶν τάχ' ἔμελλον πειρήσεσθαι* arrows whose force they were soon *to make trial of*, i.e. *feel*, ib. 418); also, *make proof of, have experience of*, esp. in pf. Pass., first in Hes., *νηῶν* *Op*.660; *οὐ πεπειρημένοι πρότερον* [*οἱ*] *Αἰγύπτιοι Ἑλλήνων* Hdt.4.159, cf. Pl.*Phd*.118; *πειρασάμενος ἀγαθῶν, δουλείας*, Th.2.44, 5.69, cf. Antipho 5.1; *κακῶν* D.18.253; *ὀρφανίας π.*, i.e. to be an orphan, Phalar.*Ep*.49; but *π. τινὸς μετρίου* *find* him moderate *by experience* or *on trial*, Plu.*Aem*.8, cf. *Arat*.43; also, *πεπείρανται ὅτι..* Lys.27.2. 3. abs., *try one's fortune, try the chances of war*, *αἴ κε θεὸς πειρώμενος ἐνθάδ' ἵκηται* Il.5.129; *πειρώμενος ἢ ἐν ἀέθλῳ ἠὲ καὶ ἐν πολέμῳ* *making trial of one's powers*, 16.590; *Ἕκτορι πειρηθῆναι ἀντιβίην, ἤ.. ἤ..* *to try one's fortune* against him, 21.225; *περὶ δ' αὐτῆς πειρηθήτω* (sc. *τῆς ἵππου*) *let* him *try* for her, as a prize, 23.553. III. *make a trial* or *put* a matter *to the test*, *ἐν σοὶ πειρώμεθα* Pl.*Phlb*.21a: c. dat. modi, *ἐγχείῃ πειρήσομαι* Il.5.279; *ἐπειρήσαντο πόδεσσι* *tried their luck* in the foot-race, Od.8.120, cf. 205; *σφαίρῃ* 8.377; also *π. σὺν ἔντεσι, σὺν τεύχεσι π.*, Il.5.220, 11.386: but in pf., *οὐδέ τί πω μύθοισι πεπείρημαι* I *have* not *tried myself, have* not *found my skill*, in words, Od.3.23: abs., *ὁ πειραθεὶς πιστεύσει* X.*Eq.Mag*.1.16; *πεπειραμένος σαφῶς οἶδα* *by experience*, Id.*Hier*.2.6. IV. c. acc. pers., *make an attempt on* (v. A.IV.2), *Διὸς ἄκοιτιν* Pi.*P*.2.34.

**πειρήθηξαι**· *πεῖραν λαμβάνῃ*, Hsch.

**πειρήν**, ῆνος, ὁ, a fish, Numen.ap.Ath.7.306c.

⊛ **πειρητίζω**, Ep. form of *πειράω*, only pres. and impf., *attempt, try, prove*, abs., Il.15.615, Od.24.221: c. inf., *ῥήγνυσθαι μέγα τεῖχος..πειρήτιζον* Il.12.257; *πλήκτρῳ ἐπειρήτιζε* *touched the strings* with it, *h.Merc*.53,419. II. c. gen. pers., *make trial of*, *συβώτεω πειρητίζων εἰ..* Od.14.459; *συβώτεω π., ἤ μιν ἔτ' ἐνδυκέως φιλέοι..ἦ..* 15.304; *μή τί μευ, ἠΰτε παιδός.., πειρήτιζε* Il.7.235. 2. c. gen. rei, *σθένεος καὶ ἀλκῆς* Od.22.237; *τόξου* 21.124,140. III. c. acc., *στίχας ἀνδρῶν π.* *attempt*, i.e. *attack*, the lines, Il.12.47.

⊛ **πείρινς**, ινθος, ἡ, *wicker basket* tied upon the *ἅμαξα*, *body of the cart*, *πείρινθα δὲ δῆσαι ἐπ' αὐτῆς* [*ἁμάξης*] Il.24.190, cf. 267; *τὰ μὲν ἐς πείρινθα τίθει* Od.15.131.—Hom. only uses the acc. *πείρινθα*; gen., A.R.3.873: **πείρινθος** cited as nom. by Hsch., *EM*668.21:—also **πείρινθα**, ibid.

**πείρω**, aor. 1 *ἔπειρα*, Ep. *πεῖρα* Il.7.317, etc.:—**Pass.**, pf. *πέπαρμαι* 1.246, etc.: aor. *ἐπάρην* [ᾰ] (*ἀνα-*) Hdt.4.94:—*pierce, run through*, mostly of cooking, *κρέα τ' ὤπτων, ἄλλα τ' ἔπειρον* they *spitted* meat, Od.3.33, cf. Paus.4.17.1; in full, *μίστυλλόν τ' ἄρ' ἐπισταμένως πεῖράν τ' ὀβελοῖσιν* Il.7.317; *ἀμφ' ὀβελοῖσιν ἔπειραν* *they stuck* the meat round (i.e. on) the spits, 1.465; also *ἔγχεϊ νύξε..διὰ δ' αὐτοῦ πεῖρεν ὀδόντων* *ran* it *through* his teeth, 16.405: c. acc., *τόν γε φίλης διὰ χειρὸς ἔπειρεν αἰχμῇ* 20.479; *ἰχθῦς ὣς πείροντες* Od.10.124, cf. Ach.Tat.3.4 (Pass.); *τῇ τριαίνῃ..ἔπειρε καὶ ἀνεῖλε* Str.13.1.38:—Pass., *σκῆπτρον, δέπας χρυσείοις ἥλοισι πεπαρμένον*, *studded* with golden nails, Il.1.246, 11.633; *ὀδύνῃσι πεπαρμένος* *pierced* with pain, 5.399, Archil.84 (also *π. ἀμφ' ὀδύνῃσι* A.R.4.1067); *περὶ δουρὶ πεπαρμένη* Il.21.577; *ἀμφ' ὀνύχεσσι* Hes.*Op*.205. II. metaph., *ἀνδρῶν τε πτολέμους ἀλεγεινά τε κύματα πείρων* *cleaving a way through*, Il.24.8, Od.8.183; *πεῖρε κέλευθον* *clave* her way [through the sea], 2.434: abs. in the same sense, A.R.2.326,398. (Cf. *περόνη*, OSlav. *na-perją* 'pierce'.)

**πεῖσα**, ης, ἡ, (*πείθω*) poet. for *πειθώ*, *obedience*, *τῷ δὲ μάλ' ἐν πείσῃ κραδίη μένε*, i.e. it remained calm, Od.20.23, cf. Plu.2.453d, Hdn.Gr.1.266.

**πείσει**, v. *τίνω*.

**Πεισῐᾰνάκτειος**, ον, *of Peisianax*: *ἡ Π. στοά*, older name for the *Ποικίλη* at Athens, Plu.*Cim*.4, D.L.7.5.

**πεισί-βροτος**, ον, *persuading mortals*, *π. βάκτρον*, i.e. the sceptre, A.*Ch*.362 (lyr., *πισίμβροτον* cod. Med.). **-θάνᾰτος** [θᾰ], ον, *persuading to die*, epithet of Hegesias, D.L.2.86.

**πεισίμβροτος**, ον, *won by persuading mortals*, *δόξα* B.8.2.

**πεῖσις**, εως, ἡ, (*πάσχω, πείσομαι*) = *πάθος*, Hp.*Loc.Hom*.1, Sor.2.3, Gal.1.141; *ἡ χολέρα π. τοῦ στομάχου* Cass.*Pr*.59, cf. Alex.Aphr.*Pr*.1.138: generally, *affection, susceptibility*, *κινήσεις καὶ π. ψυχῆς* Ph.1.617; *αἰσθητικαί, σωματικαὶ π.*, M.Ant.3.6, 7.55; *πείσεων καὶ παθῶν* S.E.*M*.7.384; *ποίησίν τε καὶ π.* Plot.3.1.4, cf. 3.6.7, al. II. (*πείθω*) *persuasion*, Id.2.9.14 (pl.).

**πεισῐχάλῑνος** [ᾰ], ον, *obeying the rein*, *ἅρματα* Pi.*P*.2.11.

**πεῖσμα** (A), ατος, τό, *ship's cable*, usu. the *stern-cable* by which the ship was made fast to the land, *λιμήν.., ἵν' οὐ χρεὼ πείσματός ἐστιν—οὔτ' εὐνὰς βαλέειν, οὔτε πρυμνήσι' ἀνάψαι* Od.9.136; *πεῖσμα δ' ἔλυσαν ἀπὸ τρητοῖο λίθοιο* 13.77; *πεῖσμα..κίονος ἐξάψας μεγάλης* 22.465: pl., *ἀπὸ πείσματ' ἔκοψα νεός* 10.127, cf. A.*Supp*.765, *Ag*.195 (lyr.); *πίσυνοι λεπτοδόμοις π.*, of Xerxes' bridge of boats, Id.*Pers*.112 (lyr.): metaph., *ἐχόμενοι ὥς τινος ἀσφαλοῦς π.* Pl.*Lg*.893b; *ἔλυσεν οἷον νεὼς πείσματα* Id.*Ti*.85e; *τύχης π. λυσάμενος* *BCH*25.327 (Mysia); of the marriage-*tie*, Ph.1.563: prov., *πᾶν πεῖσμα διέρρηκται* Hld.7.25: metaph., of *reins*, *νέμειν πείσματα Θήβης* Epic. in *BKT*5(1)p.115. 2. generally, *rope*, Od.10.167; *boat-rope, painter*, Theophil.6. 3. *stalk of the fig*, *Gp*.10.56.2 and 4; cf. *πάσμα, πέσμα*. (**πενθ-σμα*, cf. Goth. *bindan* 'bind', etc.)

**πεῖσμα** (B), ατος, τό, (*πείθω*) *persuasion, confidence*, *μετὰ βεβαίου π.* S.E.*P*.1.18, cf. Arr.*Epict*.2.20.26 (pl.), Porph.*Abst*.2.37; *μετὰ πείσματος τεθαρρηκότος* *confidently*, Plu.2.106d.

**πεισμ-ᾰτικός**, ή, όν, *like a cable*: metaph., *pertinacious*, *PMasp.*97 ii 43(vi A.D.), Eust.1927.7. **-άτιον**, τό, Dim. of πεῖσμα (A) 3, *umbilical cord*, Sch.D Il.19.119. **-άτιος** [ᾰ], η, ον, *busied with cables*, epith. of Rhea, Orph.*A.*628. **-ονή**, ἡ, *persuasion*, *Ep.Gal.*5.7, cf. *PMag. Par.*2.274, *PLond.*5.1674.36 (vi A.D.). 2. *confidence*, ἡ ἐξ ἀλλήλων πρὸς ἀλλήλους γινομένη π. A.D.*Synt.*299.17. II. *quality of a cable*, *pertinacity*, Eust.28.24, 741.8, etc.

**πείσομαι**, fut. Med. of πείθω. II. fut. of πάσχω.

**πεῖσος**, τό, v. πίσεα.

**πεισ-τέον**, (πείθω) *one must persuade*, Pl.*R.*421c. II. (Pass.) *one must obey*, S.*OT*1516, E.*Hipp.*1182, Pl.*Ap.*19a. 2. *one must believe*, Id.*R.*365e, Ph.1.135, Agath.2.25. **-τήρ**, ῆρος, ὁ, (πείθομαι) *one who obeys*, Suid. **-τήριος**, α, ον, *persuasive*, *winning*, λόγοι E.*IT* 1053. **-τικός**, ή, όν, *persuasive*, Pl.*Grg.*455a, *Lg.*723a, Arist.*Rh.* 1355ᵇ29, Plb.30.2.3, Phld.*Rh.*2.12S. (in codd. and Pap. freq. written πιστικός, as *Grg.* l.c., Men.472.4, *PMag.Par.*1.2170): ἡ -κή (sc. τέχνη) Pl.*Plt.*304d; τὸ π. ib.c. Adv. -κῶς Ruf.Rh.p.399 H., S.E.*M.* 2.62 (πιστικῶς Phld.*Rh.*2.191S.): Comp. -ωτέρως Thphr.*Metaph.*4.

**πείχισον**· δοκίμασον, Hsch. (fort. πύρωσον, cf. *An.Ox.*2.464).

**πειώλης**, ου, ὁ, Ion. for πεώλης, = κίναιδος, Suid., *EM*668.36.

**πέκος**, Aeol. **πέκκος**, τό, = πόκος, *An.Ox.*3.358; also **πεῖκος**, Hsch. (-κός cod.).

⊕ **πεκούλιον**, τό, = Lat. *peculium*, *BGU*96.14 (iii A.D.), Hsch.

**πέκ-τειον**, τό, name of a plant, Sch.Nic.*Th.*626 (s.v.l.). **-τέω**, (πέκω) *shear*, *clip*, πεκτεῖν.. προβάτων πόκον Ar.*Av.*714:—Pass., *to be shorn*, metaph., of persons, πεκτούμενος Id.*Lys.*685. ⊕ **-τήρ**, ῆρος, ὁ, *shearer*, Suid.; cf. ποκτήρ.

**πέκω**, Ep. 2 pl. pres. imper. **πείκετε** Od.18.316 (metri gr.), but also inf. **πείκειν** (v. infr.): aor. ἔπεξα *AP*6.279 (Euph.):—Med., aor. ἐπεξάμην Il.14.176:—Pass., aor. ἐπέχθην Ar.*Nu.*1356:—*comb*, εἴρια π. *card* it, Od.18.316; ἔπεξε καλὰς Εὔδοξος ἐθείρας *APl.* c.:— Med., χαίτας πεξαμένη *when she had combed her* hair, Il.14.176. 2. *shear*, ὄϊς πείκειν Hes.*Op.*775, cf. Theoc.5.98, Ael.*NA* 1.38:—Med., πόκοις πέξασθαι *have their* wool *shorn*, Theoc.28.13; ἐπέξαθ' ὁ Κριός Simon.13 (cf. Ar.*Nu.*1356):—Pass., Ar.l.c.; πέκεται Eust.531.5. (Cf. Lith. *pěšti* 'pluck'.)

**πελᾰγ-αῖος**, = πελάγιος, epith. of Poseidon, Paus.7.21.7. **-ίζω**, (πέλαγος) *form a sea* or *lake*, of a river that has overflowed, ἐώθεε ὁ ποταμὸς ἀνὰ τὸ πεδίον πᾶν πελαγίζειν Hdt.1.184; λίμνη πελαγίζουσα Str.5.3.12; of places, *to be flooded*, *under water*, ἐπεὰν τὰ πεδία πελαγίσῃ Hdt.2.92, cf. Str.17.1.4. 2. of islands, *lie out in the open sea*, Id.10.2.19. 3. metaph., in Rhet., *to be verbose*, *exuberant*, Phld. *Rh.*1.239, 240S., cj. in D.H.*Is.*14; ἀλαζονεύεσθαι, ψεύδεσθαι μεγάλα, Hsch. 4. *have a chattering of the teeth*, Id. II. trans., = πελαγόω, *flood*, Jul.*Or.*1.27b. III. *cross the open sea*, X.*Oec.*21.3, Hyp.*Fr.*262; πλοίῳ Posidon.28 J.; opp. παρὰ γῆν πλεῖν, Str.1.3.2; *to be on the high sea*, Ach.Tat.2.32:—Med., Charito 8.6. **-ικός**, ή, όν, = sq., θεοί Plu.2.685f. **-ιος**, α, ον, also ος, ον E.*Hel.*1062, 1436:—*of the sea*, κλύδων Id.*Hec.*701; ἀγκάλαι Id.*Hel.* ll. cc.; πλάξ Ar. *Ra.*1438; πελαγίαν ἅλα *the broad* sea, A.*Pers.*427, cf. 467; of animals, *living in the sea*, E.*Hipp.*1276 (lyr.); τῶν δὲ θαλαττίων [ζῴων] τὰ μὲν π. τὰ δὲ αἰγιαλώδη Arist.*HA*488ᵇ7; opp. παράγεια, ib.602ᵃ16; π. ἰχθύες, opp. πρόσγειοι, ib.598ᵃ2; φῦκος π. Thphr.*HP*4.6.4; ἱέραξ π. *PMag.Par.*1.211. 2. *out at sea*, *on the open sea*, S.*Tr.*649 (lyr.); of seamen or ships, π. πλεῖν Th.8.39, cf. 101; π. ἐπιφανῆναι ib.44; π. ἀνάγεσθαι X.*HG*2.1.17; π. ἄνεμοι Str.3.2.5. 3. epith. of Poseidon, *IG*2².410.17; of Aphrodite, Artem.2.37; of Isis, Paus.2.4.6; θεοὶ π. Plu.2.161c. 4. *near the sea*, π. τόποι, opp. μεσόγειοι, Sor.1. 22. 5. γῆ π., a kind of earth, Androm.ap.Gal.13.928. 6. πελάγια· τὰ κρόταλα, ἡ δὲ ῥίνος πελαγία, Hsch. **-ισμός**, ὁ, *being at sea*, Alciphr.2.4 (pl.). **-ῖτις**, ιδος, fem. Adj. *of* or *on the sea*, νᾶες *AP*12.53 (Mel.).

**πελᾰγο-δρομέω**, *run* or *sail on the open sea*, Zen.5.32, Diogenian. 7.20. **-δρόμος**, ον, *sailing on the sea*, Orph.*H.*74.5; *flying over the sea*, ἱέραξ *PMag.Par.*1.2590.

**πέλᾰγ-ος**, εος, τό, gen. pl. πελαγέων Hdt.4.85, S.*Aj.*702 (lyr.), πελαγῶν Th.4.24; Ep. dat. πελάγεσσι (v. infr.):—*the sea*, esp. *high sea*, *open sea*, π. μέγα Il.14.16, Od.3.179, etc.; ἐν πελάγεϊ ἀναπεπταμένῳ Hdt.8.60.α'; διὰ πελάγους out at *sea*, opp. παρὰ γῆν, Th.6.13: freq. coupled with other words denoting *sea*, ἁλὸς ἐν πελάγεσσιν Od.5.335; π. θαλάσσης A.R.2.608; π. πόντιον, πόντου π., Pi.*O.*7. 56, *Fr.*235; ἅλιον π. E.*Hec.*938 (lyr.). 2. of parts of the sea (θάλασσα), freq. with geographical epith., Αἰγαῖον π. A.*Ag.*659, etc., cf. Hdt.4.85 (π. Αἰγαίας ἁλός E.*Tr.*88, Men.*Pk.*379); Ἰκαρίων ὑπὲρ πελαγέων S.*Aj.*702 (lyr.), cf. Luc.*Icar.*3; ἐκ μεγάλων πελαγῶν τοῦ τε Τυρσηνικοῦ καὶ τοῦ Σικελικοῦ Th.4.24. 3. *flooded plain*, γίνεται π. Hdt.2.97, cf. 3.117. II. metaph., of any vast quantity, πλούτου π. Pi.*Fr.*218; κακῶν π. a '*sea* of troubles', A.*Pers.*433; π. ἄτηρᾶς δύης Id.*Pr.*746; ἄτης ἄβυσσον π. Id.*Supp.*470; κακῶν π. εἰσορῶ τοσοῦτον ὥστε μήποτ' ἐκνεῦσαι E.*Hipp.*822 (lyr.); ἀληθινὸν εἰς π. αὐτὸν ἐμβαλεῖς.. πραγμάτων Men.65.6; φεύγειν εἰς τὸ π. τῶν λόγων Pl.*Prt.* 338a; φανήσεται μακρὸν τὸ δεῦρο π. οὐδὲ πλώσιμον S.*OC*663; of great difficulties, μέγ' ἄρα π. ἐλαχέτην τι ib.1746 (lyr.). **-όσδε**, Adv. *to*, *into*, or *towards the sea*, A.R.4.1233.

⊕ **πελᾰγό-στροφος**, ον, *roving through the sea*, ἰχθῦς Opp.*H.*3.174 (v.l. -τροφος, ον, *sea-nourished*).

**πελᾰγόω**, *turn into sea*, *flood*, Ach.Tat.4.12.

⊕ **πελάζω**, Il.5.766, etc.: fut. -άσω E.*El.*1332 (lyr.), etc.; Att. πελῶ A.*Pr.*284 (anap.), S.*Ph.*1150 (lyr., codd.), *OC*1060 (lyr.), *El.*497 (lyr.): aor. ἐπέλᾰσα E.*Hel.*671 (lyr.); Ep. πέλασα Il.12.194; Ep. and Lyr. ἐπέλασσα 21.93, πέλασσα 13.1, Pi.*P.*4.227:—Med., aor. opt. (trans.) πελασαίατο Il.17.341; inf. πελάσασθαι Emp.133:—Pass., aor. ἐπελάσθην, Ep. 3 pl. πέλασθεν Il.12.420, inf. πελασθῆναι S.*OT* 213 (lyr.); Ep. aor. Pass. ἔπλητο Hes.*Th.*193, ἔπληντο Il.4.449, etc., πλῆτο 14.438, πλῆντο ib.468; later ἐπλάθην [ᾱ] A.*Pr.*897 (lyr.), E. *Tr.*203 (lyr.), etc.: pf. Pass. πέπλημαι *AP*5.46 (Rufin.); 3 pl. πεπλήαται Semon.31A (fort. πεπλέαται); part. πεπλημένος Od.12.108; cf. πελάω, πελάθω, πλάθω: (πέλας):

A. intr., *approach*, *draw near*, c. dat., πέλασεν νήεσσι Il.12.112; ὅς τις ἀϊδρείῃ πελάσῃ Od.12.41; ἐὸν.. ἐόντι πελάζει Parm.8.25; τούτοις σὺ μὴ π. A.*Pr.*807, cf. S.*Ph.*301, etc.: rarely in Prose, π. πολεμίοισι Hdt.9.74; θηρίοις X.*Cyr.*1.4.7, cf. 3.2.10, *An.*4.2.3: τῷ φθινοπώρῳ Hp.*Prog.*24: prov., ὅμοιον ὁμοίῳ ἀεὶ πελάζει like *draws to* like, Pl. *Smp.*195b. 2. less freq. c. gen., ἐπὴν [ἡ γυνὴ] τόκου π. Hp.*Mul.*1. 34; πάρα.. πελάσαι φάος.. νεῶν light may *come near* the ships, S. *Aj.*709 (lyr.); εἴργω πελάζειν [σῆς πάτρας] Id.*Ph.*1407 (but σῆς πάτρας shd. be deleted); π. πηγῆς Call.*Ap.*88 (nisi leg. πηγῇσι); π. τῆς πόλεως Th.2.77, Plb.21.6.3; also μὴ πελάσητ' ὄμματος ἐγγύς E.*Med.*101 (anap.). 3. with a Prep., πρὸς τοῖχον π. Hes.*Op.* 732; ἐς τὸν ἀριθμόν Hdt.2.19; [τὸ ὕδωρ] ἐς τὸ θερμὸν π. gets hotter, Id.4.181; ἐς τούσδε τόπους S.*OC*1761 (anap.); εἰς ὄψιν, ἐς σὸν βλέφαρον, E.*IT*1212, *El.*1332 (anap.); ἐπί τινος Orph.*A.*888; πρὸς ἀλλήλας Plu.2.564b. 4. c. acc. loci, δῶμα πελάζει E.*Andr.*1167 (anap.); elsewh. dub., S.*OC*1060 (fort. εἰς νομόν), *Ph.*1150 (but φυγᾷ μ' οὐκέτι.. πελᾶτ' shd. be taken in trans. sense, *will* no more *draw* me *after* you). 5. abs., X.*Cyr.*7.1.48. II. *approach* (in marriage), ματρὶ τεᾷ πελάσαις Pi.*N.*10.81; ἐπὶ παρθενικῆς λέχος *AP*5.301 (Agath.).

B. causal, only in Poets, *bring near* or *to*, freq. in Hom. (Hes. only *Op.*431), both of persons and things, [νέας] Κρήτῃ ἐπέλασσεν Od.3.291, cf. 300; με.. γαίῃ Θεσπρωτῶν πέλασεν μέγα κῦμα 14.315; τοὺς δ' Ἰθάκῃ ἐπέλασσε φέρων ἄνεμος 15.482; π. τινὰ Ἀχιλῆϊ Il.24.154, cf. 2.744, etc.; Ζεύς.. Ἕκτορα νηυσὶ π. *let* him *approach* the ships, 13. 1; νευρὴν μὲν μαζῷ πέλασεν τόξῳ δὲ σίδηρον *brought* the string *up* to his breast, etc., of one drawing a bow, 4.123; ἐπέλασσα θαλάσσῃ στῆθος, in swimming, Od.14.350; πάντας.. πέλασε χθονί *brought* them *to* earth, Il.8.277; οὐδέ τινα πελάσσαι 23.719, etc.; ἱστὸν δ' ἱστοδόκῃ πέλασαν 1.434; βόας ζεύγλᾳ π. Pi.*P.*4.227; δεσμοῖς τινὰ π. A.*Pr.*155 (anap.); βρόχῳ δέρην E.*Alc.*230 (lyr.); μὴ πέλαζε ματρί (sc. τέκνα) Id.*Med.*91; κορώνη νευρειήν Theoc.25.212; ἐπεί ῥ' ἐπέλασσέ γε δαίμων *brought* [him so far], Il.15.418, cf. 21.93; γόμφοισιν πελάσας [γύην] *when he has fixed* [the plough-tree *to* the pole] with nails, Hes.*Op.*431: metaph., ἑ.. κακῇς ὀδύνῃσι π. *bring* him *into* pain, Il.5.766; ἐμὲ.. κράτει πέλασον *endue* me with might, Pi.*O.*1.78; Βορέα σῶμα π. *exposing* it.., Ar.*Av.*1399 (anap.); ἔπος ἐρέω, ἀδάμαντι πελάσσας (sc. αὐτό) *having made* it *firm as* adamant, Orac.ap.Hdt.7. 141. 2. folld. by a Prep., με.. νῆσον ἐς Ὠγυγίην πέλασαν θεοί Od. 7.254; κτήματα δ' ἐν σπήεσσι πελάσσατε 10.404, cf. 424; also δεῦρο π. τινά 5.111; οὐδάσδε πελάζειν τινά 10.440. 3. Med., *bring near to oneself*, οὐκ ἔστιν πελάσασθαι ἐν ὀφθαλμοῖσιν ἐφικτόν Emp. l.c.

C. Pass., like the intr. Act., *come nigh*, *approach*, etc., c. dat., ἀσπίδες.. ἔπληντ' ἀλλήλῃσι Il.4.449; πλῆτο χθονί he *came near* (i.e. *sank to*) earth, 14.438; οὔδεϊ πλῆντο ib.468; σκοπέλῳ πεπλημένος Od. 12.108: abs., ἐπεὶ τὰ πρῶτα πέλασθεν (sc. τείχει) Il.12.420, cf. A.*Th.* 144 (lyr.). 2. rarely c. gen., Χρύσης πελασθεὶς φύλακος S.*Ph.* 1327. 3. folld. by a Prep., πελασθῆναι ἐπὶ τὸν θεόν Id.*OT*213 (lyr.). II. *approach* or *wed*, of a woman, μηδὲ πλαθείην γαμέτᾳ A.*Pr.*897 (lyr.), cf. E.*Andr.*25; v. supr. A. II.

**πελάθω** [ᾰ], collat. form of πελάζω (intr.), only pres., used by Trag. in lyr. and anap., A.*Fr.*132, E.*Rh.*557, *El.*1293, cf. Ar.*Th.*58 (paratrag.).

**πέλαινα**· πόπανα, μειλίγματα, Hsch. **πέλαιτον**· τὸ ἐφικτόν, μέγιστον, Id.

**πέλανορ**, ὁ, v. πελανός sub fin.

⊕ **πελᾰνός** (on the accent, v. Hdn.Gr.1.178, Eust.1601.4; πέλανος freq. in codd.), ὁ, *any thick liquid substance*, of various consistency, πελανῷ *with oil*, A.*Ag.*96 (anap.); ῥοφεῖν ἐρυθρὸν ἐκ μελέων π. the red *blood*, Id.*Eu.*265 (lyr.); π. αἱματοσταγής a reeking *mass* of slaughter, Id. *Pers.*816; π. αἱματηρός, of *clotted* blood, E.*Alc.*851, *Rh.*430; ἀφρώδης π., of *foam* at the mouth, Id.*Or.*220; π. μελίσσης honey, Id.*Fr.*467.5; πιαλέοι π., of *gum* in the eyes, Heliod.ap.Stob.4.36.8. II. *mixture offered to the gods and the dead*, of meal, honey, and oil, *liquid enough to be poured*, χέουσα τόνδε π. ἐν τύμβῳ πατρός A.*Ch.*92; χοὴν π. τε E.*Fr.* 912 (anap.); burnt on the altar, Id.*Ion*707 (lyr.), *Tr.*1063 (pl., lyr.), Ar.*Pl.*661, etc.; θῦσαι πελανόν A.*Pers.*204, E.*Ion* 226 (anap.), cf. Pl.*Lg.* 782c, *IG*1².76.36, 2².140; ἐς τὴν τρώγλην τὸν π. ἔνθες τοῦ δράκοντος Herod.4.91. 2. *meal* made from barley and wheat, of which this mixture was made, π. καλοῦμεν ἡμεῖς οἱ θεοί, ἃ καλεῖτε.. ἄλφιθ' ὑμεῖς οἱ βροτοί Sannyr.1; μύλης πελανοί A.R.1.1077. III. *round cakes* offered to the gods, πέμματα ἐπιχώρια.., ἃ πελανοὺς καλοῦσιν ἔτι καὶ ἐς ἡμᾶς Ἀθηναῖοι Paus.8.2.3: hence (from the shape), 2. as a *measure* of weight, = ὀβολός, Nic.*Al.*488, cf. Suid.; θη'αυρὸν.. τοῖς π. κλακτόν *Schwyzer*89.12 (Argos, iii B.C.), cf. 322.2 (Delph., v/iv B.C.):—Lacon. πέλανορ, = τετράχαλκον, Hsch.

**πελαργ-άω**, f.l. for πεδαρτάω (q.v.). **-ιδεύς**, έως, ὁ, *young stork*, Ar.*Av.*1356, Plu.2.992b. **-ικός**, ή, όν, *of the stork*, Hsch., Suid. II. = Πελασγικός: τὸ Π. the northern slope of the Acropolis at Athens, *IG*1².76.55, Ar.*Av.*832; τὸ Π. τεῖχος Arist.*Ath.*19.

5; written τὸ Πελαργικόν in Hdt.5.64, Th.2.17 (with v.l. Πελασγ-, but cf. Πελαργικόν· ἀντὶ τοῦ Πελασγικόν, Hsch.); also Τυρσηνῶν τείχισμα Π. Call.*Fr.*283. **-ῖτις,** *ιδος, ἡ,* = ἀναγαλλὶς ἡ κυανῆ, Asclep.ap.Gal.13.242, Ps.-Dsc.2.178. 2. a kind of γεράνιον, Id. 3.116. ⊛ **-ός,** *ὁ, stork, Ciconia alba,* Ar.*Av.*1355, Pl.*Alc.*1.135d, Arist.*HA*615$^{b}$23, *Mir.*832$^{a}$15, Suid. s.v. ἀντιπελαργεῖν. II. sts. confounded with Πελασγός (cf. πελαργικός II), Str.5.2.4, 9.1.18, D.H. 1.28; ὁ π. ἀλοίτης Call.*Fr.anon.*72. (A pronunciation πελᾱργός (or Πελᾱργός?) with ᾱ by nature is condemned by Phryn.88.) **-όχρως,** *ωτος, ὁ, ἡ, stork-coloured,* of ships, Lyc.24. **-ώδης,** *ες, like a stork,* π. κατὰ σχῆμα Str.17.2.4.

⊛ **πέλᾰς,** Adv. *near, hard by,* c. gen., which commonly stands before π., Τηλεμάχου π. ἵστατο Od.15.257; Νείλου π. A.*Supp.*308, cf. *Ag.* 1038, 1671; καὶ τάδ' ἀγχόνης π. E.*Heracl.*246, cf. *HF*1109; also before its case, π. τῆς Κασταλίης Hdt.8.39, cf. 138; αὕτη π. σοῦ S.*El.* 1474; separated from its case, Id.*Ant.*580. 2. c. dat., π. ἐμβόλῳ, σκάπτῳ π., Pi.*O.*7.18, *N.*11.4; σοὶ π. A.*Supp.*208, cf. *Fr.*102. 3. abs., χριμφθεὶς πέλας Od.10.516; π. στείχειν, παρεῖναι, παραστατεῖν, E.*Or.*877, S.*Aj.*83, A.*Th.*669. II. οἱ π. (sc. ὄντες) *one's neighbours,* Democr.293, Antipho Soph.58, Hdt.1.97, Critias 15.6 D., Th. 1.69, 4.78, 92, Arist.*EN*1169$^{a}$14, etc.; *one's fellow creatures,* E.*Heracl.* 2, *Hipp.*441; τὰ τῶν πέλας κακά, opp. τὰ οἰκήϊα, Hdt.7.152: sg., ὁ π. *one's neighbour,* Id.3.142, Th.1.32; πᾶς τις αὐτὸν τοῦ π. μᾶλλον φιλεῖ E.*Med.*86; cf. πλησίον. III. Sup. πελαστάτω *nearest,* Hp.*Loc. Hom.*12, 45, *Mul.*1.66: a Sup. Adj. πελάστατος, η, ον, *IG*14.352 ii 65 (Halaesa).

**Πελασγικός,** *ή, όν, Pelasgian,* Ζεῦ ἄνα Δωδωναῖε, Πελασγικέ Il.16.233; τὸ Π. Ἄργος 2.681, cf. Hdt.1.56, Str.5.2.4, 9.5.15; = *Argive,* E.*Ph.* 107:—also **Πελάσγιος,** A.*Supp.*634 (lyr.), E.*IA*1498 (lyr.): fem. **Πελασγίς,** *ίδος,* Hdt.7.42, A.R.4.243; **Πελασγιάς,** *άδος,* Call.*Lav. Pall.*4:—**Πελασγίη,** *ἡ,* = Ἑλλάς, Hdt.2.56; cf. πελαργικός II.

**Πελασγι-ῶται,** *οἱ, inhabitants of Pelasgiotis* in Thessaly, Str.9.5.3; used for *Greeks* in general, E.*Fr.*228.7: **-ῶτις,** *ιδος, ἡ* (with or without γῆ), Str.9.5.3 and 15; -ώτιδες γυναῖκες Hdt.2.171.

**Πελασγός,** *ὁ, Pelasgian,* Il.2.843, 17.288: in pl., 2.840, 10.429, Od. 19.177, Hdt.1.57, etc.; Δωδώνην Πελασγῶν ἕδρανον Hes.*Fr.*212; used generally for *Greeks,* E.*Or.*857; Τυρσηνοὶ Π. S.*Fr.*270 (anap.); cf. πελαργός II.

**πελᾰσείω,** Desiderat. of πελάζω, τῇ πολιορκίᾳ Agath.3.21.

**πέλᾰσις,** *εως, ἡ, approach,* Iamb.*Comm.Math.*8, Procl.*in Prm.* p.513 S.; π. καὶ ἅψις *Stoic.*2.119.

**πελάστατος,** v. πέλας III.

**πελαστής,** *οῦ, ὁ,* = πελάτης (quod fort. legend.), Ammon.*Diff.* p.108 V.

**πελάτ-ης** [ᾰ], *ου,* Dor. **-ας,** *ὁ,* (πελάζω) *one who approaches* or *comes near,* S.*Ph.*1164 (lyr.); *neighbour,* Τμώλου π. A.*Pers.*49 (anap.). II. esp. of one who *approaches* a woman, τὸν πελάταν λέκτρων Διός, of Ixion, S.*Ph.*677 (lyr.). III. *one who approaches to seek protection, dependant, client,* Pl.*Euthphr.*4c, Arist.*Ath.*2.2, Phot.; = Lat. *cliens,* D.H.1.83, Plu.*Rom.*13, etc.:—fem. **πελάτις,** *ιδος,* Id.*Cat.Ma.*24. (Cf. ἱκέτης from ἱκνέομαι.) **-ικός,** *ή, όν, of* or *for a* πελάτης: τὸ π. *the body of clients,* D.H.9.23.

**πελάχνιν·** τρύβλιον ἐκπέταλον, Hsch. (cf. πεδάχνη).

**πελάω,** poet. form for πελάζω, 3 sg. πελάει Arat.74, Opp.*C.*1.515; imper. πέλα *Lyr.Adesp.*22; inf. πελάειν Opp.*H.*5.496, Ep. πελάαν *h.Hom.*7.44; πελῶ is Att. fut. of πελάζω (q.v.).

**Πελδεκεῖτις,** *ιδος, ἡ,* title of Artemis, *BCH*12.269 (Panamara).

**πελέα,** v. πτελέα.

**πελεθοβάψ,** *ὁ, ἡ, one who washes away ordure,* Hdn.Gr.1.246, Hsch.

**πέλεθος,** *ὁ, ordure, dung,* Ar.*Ach.*1170, *Ec.*595 (σπέλεθος codd., cf. Moer.p.310 P.): pl., πελέθοις βοῶν S.*Ichn.*414.

**πελέθρ-ισμα,** *ατος, τό,* = πλέθρισμα, Hsch. **-ον,** *τό,* = πλέθρον, *a measure of land,* Il.21.407, Od.11.577, *IG*$2^{2}$.1126.17 (Delph.), 9(1). 693 (Corc., from Cydonia). II. *stadium, running-ground,* οἰκοδομήσας π. ib.14.10 (Syrac.).

**Πελεθρονιάς,** *άδος, ἡ,* = κενταύρειον τὸ μέγα, Ps.-Dsc.3.6.

**πέλεια,** *ἡ,* (cf. πελλός) *dove* or *pigeon,* esp. *wild rock-pigeon, Columba livia,* Od.15.527, etc.; φύγεν ὥς τε π. Il.21.493; τρήρων (q.v.) πέλεια 23.853, Od.12.62, etc.; πτηνὴ π. S.*Aj.*140, cf. E.*Ion*1197; ὑπόπτεροι π. S.*Ph.*289; cf. sq. I. II. πέλειαι, *αἱ, prophetic priestesses* at Dodona, Paus.7.21.2, 10.12.10; cf. sq. II and πελείους.

⊛ **πελειάς,** *άδος, ἡ,* = foreg. I, mostly in pl., Il.11.634, Hdt.2.55, A. *Supp.*223, E.*Andr.*1140, etc.; τρήρωσι πελειάσιν..ὁμοῖαι Il.5.778; Ep. dat. πεληϊάδεσσι Opp.*C.*1.351: in sg., Hdt. l.c., S.*OC*1081 (lyr.): distd. from περιστερά, Arist.*HA*544$^{b}$2, 597$^{b}$3; but used for περιστερά by Sophr.ap.Ath.9.394d, Hp.*Mul.*2.110, 189. 2. an Indian *fruit-pigeon, Crocopus chlorogaster,* Ael.*NA*16.2. II. = foreg. II, Hdt. 2.55, 57, S.*Tr.*172. III. Πελειάδες, *αἱ,* = Πλειάδες (q.v.).

**πελειοθρέμμων,** *ον,* gen. *ονος,* (τρέφω) *dove-nurturing,* νῆσος A.*Pers.* 309.

⊛ **πελείους·** Κῷοι καὶ οἱ Ἠπειρῶται τοὺς γέροντας καὶ τὰς πρεσβύτιδας, Hsch.; written πελίους and πελίας, and used as etym. of πέλεια II, Str.7 *Frr.*1, 2. 2. πέλειος, = *lividus, Gloss.*

**πελεκάν,** *ᾶνος, ὁ, pelican, Pelecanus onocrotalus,* Anaxandr.41.66 (anap.), Arist.*HA*597$^{b}$29, 614$^{b}$27, Ant.Lib.11.10, Ael.*NA*3.20; cf. πελεκῖνος.

**πελεκανός,** *fulica, Gloss.*

**πελεκᾶς,** *ᾶντος, ὁ, woodpecker,* as if *joiner-bird* (from πελεκάω), Ar. *Av.*884, 1155.

**πελεκ-άω,** (πέλεκυς) *hew* or *shape with an axe,* Od.5.244 (in Ep. form πελέκκησε), Hp.*Art.*12, Ar.*Av.*1157, *IG*$2^{2}$.1666 *A*81, *B*16, Lxx 3*Ki.*6.1 (5.18[32]); λίθοι πεπελεκημένοι Ph.*Bel.*82.5, cf. *Supp.Epigr.* 4.446.17, 18, 21 (Didyma, iii B.C.). II. sens. obsc., Arar. 5. **-ημα,** *ατος, τό,* in pl., *chips,* Aët.8.3, *Gp.*9.11.9. II. in pl., *splinters* of stone or wood, *POxy.*498.23 (ii A.D.). **-ησις,** *εως, ἡ, hewing* of wood, etc., Thphr.*HP*3.9.3; κρηπιδίων *Milet.*7.60, cf. *Supp. Epigr.*2.569.12 (Didyma, ii B.C.). **-ητής,** *οῦ, ὁ, hewer* of wood or stone, *Gloss.,* restd. in *IG*$1^{2}$.349.20. **-ητός,** *ή, όν, hewn,* Thphr. *HP*5.5.6. **-ητρίς,** *ίδος,* fem. of πελεκητής, ἀξίνη π., = Lat. *dolabra, Gloss.* **-ήτωρ,** *ορος, ὁ,* poet. for πελεκητής, Man.4.324. **-ηφόρος,** *ὁ,* = πελεκοφόρος, ἀνήρ Eust. ad D.P.536. **-ίζω,** *cut off with an axe,* esp. *behead,* τινα Plb.1.7.12, 11.30.2 (Pass.), Str.16.2.18, D.S.19.101, *Apoc.*20.4 (Pass.).

**πελεκῖνοειδής,** *ές, in the shape of a dovetail,* σωλήν Hero *Spir.*2.36, *Bel.*75.16, Procl.*Hyp.*4.88.

⊛ **πελεκῖνος,** *ὁ, pelican,* Ar.*Av.*884, Dionys.*Av.*2.6. II. *axeweed, Securigera Coronilla,* Hp.*Mul.*2.181, Thphr.*HP*8.8.3. 2. = ἡδύσαρον, Dsc.3.130, Gal.11.883. 3. = ἱπποφαές, Ps.-Dsc.4.159. III. in masonry and carpentry, *dovetail, IG*7.3073.171 (Lebad.), Ph.*Bel.* 66.36 (pl.), Aristeas 71 (pl.), Hero *Bel.*76.4, *Aut.*10.1.

**πελέκ-ιον,** *τό,* Dim. of πέλεκυς, *IG*$2^{2}$.1424a.392, Sch.D.T.p.195 H., Hsch. s.v. σάγαρις. **-ισμός,** *ὁ, death by the axe,* D.S.32.26 (pl.).

**πελέκκησε,** v. πελεκάω.

**πέλεκκον,** *τό,* or **πέλεκκος,** *ὁ,* (πέλεκυς) *axe-handle,* Il.13.612, cf. Poll.10.146, Hsch.

**πελεκοφόρος,** *ὁ, axe-bearer,* Arr.*Alan.*21.

**πέλεκρα·** ἀξίνη, Hsch.

**πέλεκυ,** = δεκάμνουν (Paph.), Hsch. s.v. ἡμιπέλεκκον.

**πελεκῠνάριον,** *τό,* = πέλεκκον, Theo *in Ptol.*p.311 Manitius (Appendix III to Procl.*Hyp.*).

⊛ **πέλεκῠς,** *εως,* Ion. *εος* (not πελέκυος Hdn.Gr.2.707), *ὁ,* acc. πέλεκυν Od.5.234, etc.: dat. pl. πελέκεσι, Ep. πελέκεσσι Il.13.391:—two-edged *axe* for felling trees, opp. ἡμιπέλεκκον (q.v.), π...χάλκεος, ἀμφοτέρωθεν ἀκαχμένος Od.5.234; ὑλοτόμους πελέκεας Il.23.114; ἐξέταμον πελέκεσσι νεήκεσι 13.391, cf. Pi.*O.*7.36, *P.*4.263, E.*Fr.*472.6 (anap.); π. ξυλοκόπος X.*Cyr.*6.2.36, etc. 2. *battle-axe,* πελέκεσσι καὶ ἀξίνῃσι μάχοντο Il.15.711; οὐ δόρασι μάχεσθαι, ἀλλὰ καὶ πελέκεσι Hdt.7.135; πελέκεως δίστομος γένυς E.*Fr.*530.5; *sacrificial axe,* Il.17.520, Od.3.442; *executioner's axe, Trag.Adesp.*412; Τενέδιος π., prov. of impartial and over-harsh justice, Arist.*Fr.*593; or of summary justice by 'cutting the knot', from the story of Tennes, St.Byz. s.v. Τένεδος (also ὁ Τέννου π. Conon 28); τοὺς π. ἀπέλυσε τῶν ῥάβδων took the *axes* from the fasces of the lictors, Plu.*Publ.*10, cf. Plb.6.53.8. 3. as an image of perseverance, κραδίη π. ὥς..ἀτειρής Il.3.60. 4. "ἀσκός, π." in a child's game, Thphr.*Char.*5.5. 5. nickname in *Com. Adesp.*824; cf. πρίων. 6. *coin* in Cyprus, prob. in *Inscr.Cypr.* 135.26 H.; cf. πέλεκυ. II. a geometrical figure, *like the head of a double axe,* title of *AP*15.22 (Simm.). (Cf. Skt. *paraśús*; loan-word from Bab. *pilaḳḳu,* Sumer. *balag* 'axe'.) [The ῠ of nom. and acc. sg. is in Hom. sts. lengthd., Il.3.60, 17.520: acc. pl. πελέκεας is in Hom. always trisyll., ⏑⏑–.]

**πελεκύστερον·** τὸ στελεόν, Hsch.

**πελεμίζω,** Ep. inf. -έμεν Il.16.766: Ep. aor. πελέμιξα 21.176:—Pass., Hes.*Th.*458: Ep. impf. πελεμίζετο Il.8.443: aor. πελεμίχθην 17.528:—Ep. Verb, *shake, cause to quiver* or *tremble,* βαθέην πελεμιζέμεν ὕλην Il.16.766; τρὶς μέν μιν πελέμιξεν 21.176; οὐρίαχον πελέμιζεν ἔγχεος 13.443; π. [τόξον] *struggle at* the bow, in order to bend it, Od.21.125:—Pass., *to be shaken, tremble, quake,* ὑπὸ ποσσὶ μέγας πελεμίζετ' Ὄλυμπος Il.8.443, cf. Hes.*Th.*842; ὑπὸ βροντῆς πελεμίζεται εὐρεῖα χθών ib.458; ἐπὶ δ' οὐρίαχος πελεμίχθη ἔγχεος it *quivered,* Il.17.528; πελεμίζετο γυῖα θεοῖο Emp.31. 2. *shake* or *drive from his post,* Il.16.108: aor. Pass., χασσάμενος πελεμίχθη 4.535; πελεμιζόμενος ὑπὸ λόγχᾳ Pi.*N.*8.29.

**πελένα·** ζεῦγος βοῶν, Hsch. **πελέσκεο, πέλευ,** v. πέλω. **πελεσσύδραι·** συστρέμματα ὑδάτων, Id. **πελήαρ·** περιστεράς (Lacon.), Id. **πεληϊάδεσσι,** v. πελειάς. **πέληος·** γέρων, Id. (πολητός cod.); cf. πελλᾶς.

**πελιαίνομαι,** Pass., *to be* or *become livid,* Hp.*Coac.*209, 214.

⊛ **πελιγᾶνες·** βουλευταί (Syr.), Hsch.; but **πελιγόνες,** Maced., = οἱ ἐν τιμαῖς, Str.7 *Fr.*2; also Lacon. and Massaliot., = γέροντες, ibid.

**πελίγξαι·** ἐπιδραμεῖν, Hsch.

**πελιδν-αῖος,** *α, ον,* = πελιδνός, Nonn.*D.*4.383. **-ήεις,** *εσσα, εν,* poet. for πελιδνός, Marc.Sid.47. ⊛ **-όομαι,** Pass., = πελιαίνομαι, Hp.*Art.*86, Arist.*Pr.*887$^{b}$13. **-ός,** *ή, όν,* = πελιός, *livid,* Hp.*Aph.* 4.47, Arist.*Pr.*887$^{b}$10, *HA*523$^{a}$9 (Comp.), Nic.*Th.*272, al.; of the mask worn by Tyro in Sophocles' play, Poll.4.141; Att. **πελιτνός** acc. to Ael.Dion.*Fr.*278, Moer.p.325 P., which shd. be read in Th. 2.49, Alex.110.17, *Com.Adesp.*342. **-ότης,** *ητος, ἡ,* = πελίωσις, Aret.*SA*1.5, Gal.18(2).126. **-ωμα,** *ατος, τό, livid spot,* Sch.Theoc. 5.99, Suid. s.v. ὑπώπια. **-ωσις,** *εως, ἡ,* = πελίωσις, Aret.*CA*1.8, Gal.17(1).622.

**πελίκη,** *ἡ* = χοῦς, Poll.10.73; Att. acc. to Crates Gramm.ap.Ath. 11.495a: Aeol. **πελίκα** = λεκάνη, Poll.10.78.

⊛ **πέλιξ,** *ικος, ἡ,* = κύλιξ or προχοΐδιον, Cratin.ap.Poll.10.67.

⊛ **πελῐ-όομαι,** Pass., = πελιαίνομαι, Hellanic.123 J., Hp.*Fract.*11, Arist.*Pr.*887$^{b}$13 (as v.l.), Lxx *La.*5.10, Apollod.1.9.8. **-ός,** *ά, όν,* (cf. πελλός) prop. of parts of the body, *discoloured by extravasated blood,* *black and blue*, *livid*, interpol. in Hp.*Prog.*2, D.47.59, Nic.*Th.*279; π. νοῦσος Hp.*Morb.*2.68: generally, *dark*, *dull*, χρῶμα Thphr.*HP*3.17.5. II. πελιὸς ὁ πολιός Hdn.Gr.1.123. III. πελίους, πελίας, v. πελείους. **-ότης**, ητος, ἡ, *livid colour*, Archig.ap.Orib.8.2.9.

**πελιτνός**, ή, όν, v. πελιδνός.

**πελίχνη**, ἡ, = πέλλα I, Alcm.74B, Seleuc. and Euphron.ap.Ath. 11.495c.

**πελι-ώδης**, ες = πελιός I, Sch.D Il.23.717. **-ωμα**, ατος, τό, = πελίδνωμα, Hp.*Coac.*394, *Acut.*(*Sp.*)2, Arist.*Pr.*$891^{a}1$, Thphr.*HP*9.20.3, Crito ap.Gal.12.448, *BGU*928.13, al. (iii A.D.). **-ωσις**, εως, ἡ, *extravasation of blood*, φλεβῶν Hp.*Fract.*11 (pl.), *Art.*86 (pl.).

⊛ **πέλλα**, Ion. **πέλλη**, ης, ἡ, *wooden bowl*, *milk-pail*, Il.16.642, Theoc. 1.26, Nic.*Al.*311, cf. Ath.11.495. 2. *drinking-cup*, Hippon.39. II. *stone*, Ulp. ad D.19.155, Hsch.

**πελλαϊκόν**, τό, dub. sens. in *Palestine Expl. Fund Quarterly* 1931.66.

**πελλαῖος**, α, ον, = πελλός, Hsch. **πελλαιχρὸν ἢ πελλαιχνόν**· πυρρόν, Id. **Πελλάνιος**, ὁ, epith. of Poseidon at Cyrene, Id.

**πελλαντήρ**, ῆρος, ὁ, (πέλλα) *one who milks into a pail*, Hsch.; ⊛**πελλητήρ**, Clitarch.ap.Ath.11.495e; also, = κύλιξ, Philet.ibid.

**πελλᾶς**, ᾶ, ὁ, (πελλός) *old man*, Hdn.Gr.1.55 (πέλλας Hsch.).

**πελλασταί**, v. πέλλυτρα. **πέλληον**· στέψον, Hsch. **πελλία**· σπέλεθοι, Id.

**πελλίνιον**, τό, dub. sens. in *AJA* 31.351 (vase).

**πέλλιξ**· κράνος, Hsch.

**πελλίς**, ίδος, ἡ, = πέλλα I, Hippon.38, *Trag.Adesp.*595 (codd. Poll.), Phoen.4, 5, Nic.*Al.*77; cf. πελίκη, πελίχνη, πέλυξ. (Cf. Lat. *pelvis.*)

**πελλοπλαύραστον**· ὀξύθυμον, ἢ ἔκλιμον, Hsch.

**πελλοράφος** [ᾰ], ον, (Lat. *pellis*, ῥάπτω) *sewing skins together*, *Gloss.*

**πελλός** (or **πέλλος**, the accent varies in codd.), ή, όν, *dark-coloured*, *dusky*, πελλὴ μηκὰς dub. in S.*Fr.*509; πελλὰ ὄϊς Theoc.5.99, cf. S.*Fr.*114; βοῦς *EM*659.38; πελλὸς ἐρῳδιός Arist.*HA*$609^{b}22$; π. σποδός cj. in Phoen.1.24; = Lat. *pullus*, [ἱμάτιον] *IG*14.644 (*Supp.Epigr.*4.70, Western Locr.); Sicyonian for κιρρός, Zenod.ap.Gal.19.129. (Cf. πελιός, πελιδνός, πολιός: Skt. *palitás* 'grey', Lat. *palleo*, *pullus.*)

**πέλλυρον**· μετέωρον, Hsch. (Fort. πέδαυρον.)

**πέλλυτρα**, τά, *sock* or *bandage* worn by runners on the ankle, A.*Fr.*259, S.*Fr.*1080; **πελλασταί, πελλύτα, πελλύτεμα**, are corrupt in Hsch. (Perh. fr. πεδ-ϝλῦτρα 'foot-wrapper', cf. πούς, ἔλυτρον.)

⊛ **πέλμα**, ατος, τό, *sole of the foot*, Hippon ap.Menon.*Iatr.*11.30, Lxx *Es.*4.17(13.13), *PMag.Par.*1.320, Ael.*NA*14.3, Artem.5.81; of camels, Hdn.4.15.3; but τὰ π. τῶν δακτύλων finger-*tips*, Alex.Aphr. *Pr.*1.46. 2. *sole of the shoe*, Hp.*Mochl.*32, Aen.Tact.31.4, Herod. 7.116, Nic.*Fr.*85.6, Plb.12.6.4; συάγρεα πέλματα *PCair.Zen.*692.18 (iii B.C.). II. *stalk* of apples and pears, *Gp.*10.25.1.

**πελμᾰτ-ίζω**, *scrape the sole of the foot*, Et.Havn.ap.Gaisf. ad *EM* s.v. πέλμα. II. *sole* boots, *PMasp.*5.18 (vi A.D.). **-όομαι**, *become worn in the sole*, prob. in Phot., Suid. s.v. πεπελτωμένα (due to misreading of Lxx *Jo.*9.5).

**πέλομαι**, v. πέλω.

**Πελοπόννησος**, ἡ, for Πέλοπος νῆσος, *the Peloponnesus*, *h.Ap.*250, Hermipp.45, etc.; οἱ **Πελοποννήσιοι**, Hdt.2.171, etc.; ὄνομα Πελοποννήσιον Aen.Tact.27.1: Adj., ὁ ⊛**Πελοποννησιᾰκὸς** πόλεμος Str.13.1.39, D.S.13.24 (also ὁ **Πελοποννήσιος** π. Paus.4.6.1); τὰ Πελοποννησιακά Str.14.2.9: Adv., **Πελοποννᾱσιστὶ** λαλεῖν talk *in the Peloponnesian*, i.e. *Dorian*, *dialect*, Theoc.15.92.

**Πέλοψ**, οπος, ὁ, *Pelops*, Il.2.104, etc.: Adj. **Πελόπιος**, E.*Fr.*515, etc.; **Πελοπήϊος**, A.R.1.758, al.: pecul. fem. **Πελοπηΐς**, ΐδος, Call. *Del.*72, A.R.4.1570, Nic.*Fr.*104.

**πελτ-άζω**, (πέλτη) *serve as a* πελταστής, opp. ὁπλιτεύω, X.*An.*5.8.5, *Vect.*4.52, App.*BC*2.70. **-άριον** [ᾰ], τό, Dim. of πέλτη, Callix. 2, Luc.*Bacch.*1. **-αστής**, οῦ, ὁ, *one who bears a light shield* (πέλτη), *targeteer*, E.*Rh.*311, Th.2.29, Lys.19.21, X.*Cyr.*2.1.5. II. in pl., generally, *light troops*, Id.*HG*4.4.16, *IG*$1^{2}$.97.17, 99.5, etc. **-αστικός**, ή, όν, *skilled in the use of the* πέλτη, Pl.*Tht.*165d; οἱ π. Id.*Prt.*350a: ἡ -κή (sc. τέχνη) *tactics of a targeteer*, Id.*Lg.*813e; τὸ -κόν, = οἱ πελτασταί, X.*An.*7.6.29, etc. Adv. Sup. πελταστικώτατα *in the best manner of* πελτασταί, Id.*Oec.*21.7. ⊛ **-η**, Dor. **πέλτα** *Tab.Heracl.*1.5, 2.4: ἡ:—*small light shield* of leather *without a rim*, orig. Thracian, Hdt.7.75; Θρῃκίας π. ἄναξ E.*Alc.*498, cf. *Ba.*783, Ar.*Lys.*563, *IG*$1^{2}$.282.120, *PCair.Zen.*14(*b*)12 (iii B.C.), etc.; π. Ἀμαζονική Plu.*Pomp.*35. 2. *body of* πελτασταί, E.*Rh.*410. 3. *horse's ornament*, ib.305. II. = παλτόν, *shaft*, *pole*, X.*An.*1.10.12: expld. by δόρυ, ἀκόντιον, Hsch., by λόγχη, Suid.

⊛ **πέλτης**, ου, ὁ, *the Nile-fish* κορακῖνος *salted*, Diph.Siph.ap.Ath.3.121b.

⊛ **πελτ-ίδιον** [ῐδ], τό, = πελτάριον, Sch.Luc.*DMort.*12.2. **-ίον**, τό, Dim. of πέλτη II, Men.*Pk.*202.

⊛ **πέλτον**, τό, *platform for a sarcophagus*, *Supp.Epigr.*6.307, 428, 434 (Lycaonia); cf. πλάτας, πλάτος (B).

**πελτοφόρος** (Boeot. **-φόρας** *IG*7.210 (Aegosthena), 2823 (Hyettos), also **πελταφόρας**, *Supp.Epigr.*3.354 (Thisbe, iii B.C.)), ον, (πέλτη) *bearing a target*, [Arist.]*Pepl.*30; οἱ π., = πελτασταί, X.*Cyr.* 7.1.24, etc.; π. ἱππεῖς *light* horse, Plb.3.43.2.

**πέλυξ**, υκος, ὁ, = πέλλα I, Poll.10.105. II. a kind of *axe*, Lxx *Je.*23.29, Babr.64.9 (with ῡ), Ath.9.392b, *PHamb.*10.40 (ii A.D.); rejected as barbarous by Phot. s.v. πέλεκυς:—Dim. **πελύκιον**, τό, *Peripl.M.Rubr.*6, 17, *PRyl.*$393^{v}15$ (ii/iii A.D.).

**Πελυσιών**, ῶνος, ὁ, name of month at Samos, *SIG*976.56 (ii B.C.).

⊛ **πέλω** and **πέλομαι**, only pres., impf., and aor.:—**Act.**, mostly 3 sg. πέλει, Il.9.134, Sol.13.16, Pi.*P.*4.145 (s.v.l.), A.*Ch.*534; 1 sg. πέλω S.*OT*245; 2 sg. πέλεις Nonn.*D.*44.193: 3 pl. πέλουσι *AP*7.56, Dor. πέλοντι Pi.*O.*6.100: impf. πέλεν Il.8.64, Hes.*Sc.*164, Ar.*Pax* 1276 (hex.), ἔπλεν Il.12.11, ἔπελεν Pempel.ap.Stob.4.25.52; rarely in other persons, ἔπελες, πέλες, Pi.*O.*1.46, Q.S.3.564; Aeol. 1 pl. πέλομες Theoc.29.27 (s.v.l.); imper. πέλε A.R.1.304; subj. πέλω A.*Supp.*340, πέλῃ Theoc.28.22; opt. πέλοι Pi.*P.*1.56, A.*Pers.*526, etc.; inf. πέλειν Id.*Supp.*620, 801, *Ch.*304; Ep. πελέναι (v.l. πελέμεν) Parm. 8.45; part. πέλουσα A.*Pr.*896 (lyr.):—more freq. in Med. in same sense, πέλει Id.*Eu.*149 (lyr.), 199, πέλεται Il.11.392, Alc.26, 49, etc., πελόμεσθα Theoc.13.4, πέλεσθε A.R.2.643, πέλονται Il.10.351, S.*Aj.*159 (anap.), Archyt.ap.Stob.3.1.106 (nisi leg. πέλοντι): impf. 3 pl. πέλοντο Il.9.526: aor. (always augmented) ἔπλεο 1.418, etc.; contr. ἔπλευ 9.54, etc.; ἔπλετο 22.116, Hes.*Th.*836, Sapph.*Supp.*23.26, Emp. 21.2, B.1.31; Ion. Iterat. πελέσκεο Il.22.433, πελέσκετο Hes.*Fr.*14.4, Antim.Col.3P.; imper. πέλευ Il.24.219, πελέσθω A.R.1.1320; subj. πέληται, -ώμεθα, -ωνται, Il.3.287, 6.358, 16.128; opt. πέλοιτο 22.443, A.*Ag.*255 (lyr.); inf. πέλεσθαι A.R.1.160; part. πελόμενος A.*Supp.*123, 810, πλόμενος Euph.58 (as Hom. in the compds. ἐπιπλόμενος, περιπλόμενος).—Poet. and Aeol., Dor., and Ion. Prose, Pittac.ap. D.L.1.81, Archyt. l.c., Aret.*CA*1.4:—*come into existence*, *become*, *be*: **A.** as Subst. Verb, οὐ γάρ τις πρῆξις πέλεται . . γόοιο Il.24.524; ὀδόντων καναχὴ πέλεν 19.365; ἤϋτε περ κλαγγὴ γεράνων πέλει οὐρανόθι πρό 3.3; εὐχωλὴ πέλεν ἀνδρῶν 4.450; ἄθλων, οἷά τε πολλὰ μετ' ἀνθρώποισι πέλονται Od.8.160; τιμὴν . . ἥ τε καὶ ἐσσομένοισι μετ' ἀνθρώποισι πέληται Il.3.287; ὅτε δὴ Πυλίων καὶ Ἐπειῶν ἔπλετο νεῖκος 11.737; τῷ δ' ἤδη δεκάτη . . πέλεν ἠὼς οἰχομένῳ it *was* the tenth day since his departure, Od.19.192; γαλήνη ἔπλετο νηνεμίη 5.392; ἂν κῦδος Ἀχαιῶν ἔπλετο Il.13.677, cf. Od.4.441; σέο δ' ἐκ τάδε πάντα πέλονται Il.13.632; τοῦ δ' ἐξ ἀργύρεος ῥυμὸς πέλεν 5.729; ἐν δὲ γυνὴ . . πέλεν Od.24.211; τὰ δ' ὀλοὰ πελόμεν' οὐ παρέρχεται *when once in being* they pass not away, A.*Th.*768 (lyr.), cf. *Supp.*123, 810 (both lyr.). **B.** as Copula: **1.** *become*, αἶψά τέ οἱ δῶ ἀφνειὸν πέλεται Od.1.393, cf. Il.24.219; λύκων ἧϊα πέλονται 13.103; ἀπὸ κροτάφων πελόμεσθα πάντες γηραλέοι Theoc. 14.68; ἦ τ' ἄλλως ὑπ' ἐμεῖο . . ὀξὺ βέλος πέλεται quite otherwise *does* my spear *become* sharp, i.e. in a very different way does my (emphat.) spear prove its edge, Il.11.392, cf. A.*Ag.*392 (lyr.). **2.** *be*, οὐ μέν πως ἅλιον πέλει ὅρκιον Il.4.158; τριηκόσιοί τε καὶ ἑξήκοντα πέλοντο Od.14.20; ὅσσον τ' ἐν νειῷ οὖρον πέλει ἡμιόνοιιν 8.124, cf. Il.10. 351, 23.431; ῥεῖά τ' ἀριγνώτη πέλεται Od.6.108; ὀξύτατον πέλεται φάος Il.14.345, cf. A.*Ag.*1124 (lyr.), *Eu.*233, S.*Ant.*333 (lyr.), E.*Med.*520, etc.—In Lesbian verse the Copula, which is usu. omitted, is sts. expressed by πέλεται and πέλονται, as Sapph.101. **3.** in aor., *to have become*: hence, *to be*, τίς . . ὅμιλος ὅδ' ἔπλετο; what gathering *is* this? Od.1.225; ἔρξον ὅπως ἐθέλεις καί τοι φίλον ἔπλετο θυμῷ 13.145; ἔνθα μάλιστα ἀμβατός ἐστι πόλις καὶ ἐπίδρομον ἔπλετο τεῖχος Il.6.434: with part., λελασμένος ἔπλευ 23.69; ὀϊζυρὸς περὶ πάντων ἔπλεο 1.418 (so as Subst. Verb, Od.2.364); in similes, Il.2.480, 8.556. (πελ- fr. $q^{u}el$- 'turn', cf. τέλομαι, πόλος, ἀμφι-, ἐπι-, περι-πέλομαι, also ἐπιτέλλω (B), περιτέλλομαι, Skt. *cárati* 'move'; for the sense cf. Germ. *werden*, cogn. with Lat. *verto.*)

**πελώϊος**, gen. sg., dub. sens. in *PAmh.*56.7 (ii B.C.).

**πέλωρ**, τό, *portent*, *prodigy*, *monster*, Ep. Noun, only nom. and acc., in early writers always of living beings, mostly in bad sense, as of the Cyclops, π. ἀθεμίστια εἰδώς Od.9.428; αὐτὴ δ' αὖτε π. κακόν, of Scylla, 12.87; of the serpent Python, *h.Ap.*374; of a dolphin, π. μέγα τε δεινόν τε ib.401; even of Hephaestus, π. αἴητον ἀνέστη χωλεύων Il.18.410; later, of things, εὐρυτενὴς ὠγκοῦτο π. μίτος Nonn.*D.*24.257.—Cf. πέλωρος.

⊛ **πελωρ-ιάς**, άδος, ἡ, = πελωρίς, π. κόγχαι Archestr.*Fr.*56.4, cf. *AP*6.224 (Theodorid.), Nic.*Fr.*83. **-ιος** (also **τελώριος** (q.v.)), ον, fem. (not in Hom.) -ιος Hes.*Th.*179, -ίη A.R.4.1682: = πέλωρος, freq. in Hom., mostly of gods, Ἀΐδης, Ἄρης, Il.5.395, 7.208; or heroes, as Αἴας, Ἕκτωρ, Ἀχιλεύς, 3.229, 11.820, 21.527; Ὠρίων Od.11.572; ἀνὴρ π., of Polyphemus, 9.187, cf. Il.3.166, Pi.*O.*7.15; also of things, ἔγχος, τεύχεα, Il.8.424, 10.439; λᾶας Od.11.594; κύματα 3.290; ἅρπη Hes.*Th.*179; κλέος Pi.*O.*10(11).21: rare in Trag. (only lyr.), γᾶς π. τέρας, of a dragon, E.*IT*1248 (lyr.); τὰ πρὶν π. *the mighty things*, or *mighty ones*, of old, A.*Pr.*151 (lyr.); used by Com. in mock-heroic style, Ar.*Av.*321; in exaggerated language, Arist.*Rh.*$1408^{b}13$: in later Prose, Ath.3.84e. 2. π. (sc. ἱερά), τά, *a harvest-festival*, celebrated in honour of Zeus in Thessaly, Bato Sinop.4; Πελώριος, epith. of Zeus, Q.S.11.273. **-ίς**, ίδος, ἡ, a kind of *mussel*, Xenocr. ap.Orib.2.58.52 and 97, Alciphr.1.2; π. κόγχη Ath.1.4c. **-ον**, τό, = πέλωρ, of the Gorgon, Il.5.741, Od.11.634; of the offspring of the earth, Hes.*Th.*295, cf. 845, 856; of a large stag, Od.10.168; of the enchanted animals of Circe, ib.219; πέλωρα θεῶν *portents* sent by the gods, Il.2.321.—Prop. neut. from sq. **-ος**, η, ον, also ος, ον Od. 15.161 (the only example of the fem. in Hom.):—*monstrous*, *prodigious*, *huge*, with collat. notion of *terrible*, in Hom. much rarer than the form πελώριος, but in Hes. the more common; δράκοντα φέρων ὀνύχεσσι πέλωρον Il.12.202; χῆνα φ. ὀ. π. Od.l.c.; π. ὄφιν, δεινόν τε μέγαν τε Hes.*Th.*299; Γαῖα πελώρη ib.159, 173, Q.S.2.225; θάμβος Maiist.55; ὡς φοβερός, ὡς π. Ezek.*Exag.*125: neut. pl. as Adv., πέλωρα βιβᾷ with *gigantic* tread, *h.Merc.*225, cf. 349: Sup. **πελώριστος** Theoc.*Ep.*18.5 (fort. **πεδωρισταί** = *μεθορισταί (Dor. ὦρος = ὅρος), i.e. μέτοικοι).

**πελωχικόν**, τό, *tax paid by millers*, *PRyl.*167.20 (i A.D.), *POxy.* 2128.10 (ii A.D.), etc.

**πέμμα**, ατος, τό, (πέσσω) *any kind of dressed food*: mostly in pl., *pastry, cakes, sweetmeats*, Stesich.2, Panyas.26, Hdt.1.160, Antiph. 174.2; Ἀττικὰ π. Pl.*R.*404d.

**πεμμάτιον**, τό, Dim. of foreg., *small cake*, Ath.14.645e.

**πεμμᾰτολόγος**, ον, *discoursing of cakes*, Ath.14.648a.

**πεμμᾰτουργός**, ὁ, *pastrycook*, Luc.*Sat.*13.

**πεμπάδ-αρχος** [πᾰ], ὁ, *commander of a body of five*, X.*Cyr.*2.1.23 (v.l. πενταδαρχῶν), *Eq.Mag.*4.9 (v.l. -άρχης): **-άρχης**, ου, ὁ, Hsch. s.v. δωδεκάδαρχοι (pl.). **-ικός**, ή, όν, *five-fold*, Dam.*Pr.*264.

**πεμπ-άζω**, (πέμπε) prop. *count on the five fingers*, i.e. *count by fives*, and then, generally, *count*, A.*Eu.*748, Thphr.*Char.*23.2 (cj.), A.R.2. 975, Plu.2.387e, etc.:—Med., ἐπὴν πάσας πεμπάσσεται (Ep. aor. 1 subj.) when he *has done counting* them all, Od.4.412. II. metaph., *count up, reckon over*, θεοπροπίας θυμῷ π. A.R.4.1748:—Med., πάντα νόῳ πεμπάσσατο ib.350.—In Prose ἀναπεμπάζω is more common. (Aeol. acc. to *EM*660.4.) **-αθλον**, τό, = πένταθλον, dub. in *IG*1$^2$. 472. ⊛ **-άκι**, Adv., = πεντάκις, ib.5(1).222 (Sparta). ⊛ **-άμερος** [ᾰ], ον, = πενθήμερος, Pi.*O.*5.6 (prob.), *Inscr.Cypr.*134 H. **-άς**, άδος, ἡ, *the number five*, Pl.*R.*546c, *Phd.*104a (πεμπτάς codd.), Plu.2. 387e, Plot.6.3.11. II. *group of five*, X.*Cyr.*2.1.22 and 24, *HG*7.2. 6, Dam.*Pr.*203; cf. πεντάς. III. *fifth part*, *SIG*57.35,39 (Milet., v B.C.). **-αστής**, οῦ, Dor. -ας, ὁ, *one who counts*: as a Verbal c. acc., μύρια π. *reviewing by* tens of thousands, A.*Pers.*980 (lyr.).

⊛ **πέμπε**, Aeol., = πέντε, Ps.-Hdt.*Vit.Hom.*37; gen. πέμπων Alc.33.7: **πεμπεκαιδέκοτος**, Aeol. for πεντεκαιδέκατος, *IG*12(2).82.5 (Mytil.).

**πεμπεβόηος**, ον, *made of five ox-hides*, σάμβαλα Sapph.98 (πενταβόεια codd. Heph.).

**πέμπελος**, ον, *aged*, Lyc.682, 826, Gal.6.380, Choerob.*in Theod.* 1.357 H. (alternatively expld. as = στωμύλος, λάλος by Hsch.).

**πέμποτος**, Arc., = πεμπτός, *IG*5(2).33.13 (Tegea, iii B.C.).

⊛ **πεμπτ-αΐζω**, part. -αΐζοντες *on the fifth day*, Thd.*Ex.*13.18. **-αῖος**, α, ον, *on the fifth day*, mostly agreeing with the Subject, π. ἱκόμεσθα *on the fifth day* we came, Od.14.257, cf. Hp.*Aph.*4.36; π. γεγενημένος born *five days before*, Pi.*O.*6.53; πεμπταῖα λογίζομαι..γενέσθαι D.19.59; προκεῖσθαι π. to have been *five days* laid out as dead, Ar. *Av.*474; [νεκροὶ] ἤδη ἦσαν π. X.*An.*6.4.9; ἔκρινεν [ὁ πυρετὸς] πεμπταίοισι came to a crisis *with those who had had it five days*, Hp.*Epid.* 1.20; π. ἀπὸ τῆς νίκης, ἐκ γενετῆς, Plu.*Fab.*17, Luc.*Halc.*5. II. *every fifth day*, π. πυρετοί *quintan* fevers, Hp.*Epid.*1.24, cf. Alex. Aphr.*Pr.*2.10; ποτισμοί *POxy.*729.24 (ii A.D.). **-άκις**, Adv. *five times*, D.C.53.16. **-άς**, v. πεμπάς.

**πεμπτέος**, α, ον, *to be sent*, Luc.*Phal.*1.11. II. **πεμπτέον**, *one must send*, X.*Cyr.*8.1.11.

**πεμπτημόριον**, τό, *fifth part*, Hp.*Nat.Mul.*50, Pl.*Lg.*956c.

**πεμπτήρ**, ῆρος, ὁ, = πομπεύς, ἁλίων ἐρετμῶν S.*Fr.*142 ii 10 (lyr.).

⊛ **πέμπτος**, η, ον, (πέντε) *fifth*: *with four others*, πέμπτος μετὰ τοῖσιν Od.9.335; π. αὐτός Th.1.61, 3.19; π. σπιθαμή, i.e. four cubits and a span, Hdt.2.106; ἐς π. μῆνα by *the fifth* month, Id.1.77; τὸ πέμπτον μέρος *a fifth*, Pl.*Ap.*36b, etc.; τὸ π., as Adv., *for the fifth time*, ὕπατοι, ὑπατεύων, D.S.19.77, Plu.*Fab.*19. II. ἡ πέμπτη (sc. ἡμέρα) *the fifth day*, Hes.*Op.*802, 803, Ar.*Nu.*1131. b. ἡ π. (sc. ὥρα) *the fifth hour*, Arr.*Epict.*1.1.29. 2. ἡ π. (sc. ὁδός), in the Roman camp, = *via quintana*, Plb.6.30.6. 3. ἡ π. tax *of one-fifth*, *PLond.*3.1107.5, al. (iii A.D.). III. τὸ π. σῶμα the *fifth* or celestial element, Philol.12, *Placit.*1.3.22; called π. στοιχεῖον ib.2.6.2; π. οὐσία ib.2.25.7, Phlp. *in Ph.* 9.29.

**πεμπτός**, ή, όν, *sent*, ἀπὸ τῶν τετρακοσίων π. πρέσβεις f.l. in Th.8.86.

**πέμπω**, Ep. inf. -έμεναι, -έμεν, Od.13.48, 10.18: Ion. impf. πέμπεσκε Hdt.7.106: fut. πέμψω Od.5.167, etc.; Dor. πεμψῶ Theoc.5. 141; Ep. inf. πεμψέμεναι Od.10.484: aor. ἔπεμψα, Ep. πέμψα Il.1.442, 21.43, etc.: pf. πέπομφα Th.7.12, X.*Cyr.*6.2.10, D.4.48: plpf. ἐπεπόμφει, Ion. -εε, X.*Cyr.*6.2.9, Hdt.1.85:—Med. (not in early Prose, exc. in compds. ἀπο-, μετα-, προ-πέμπομαι), fut. πέμψομαι only f.l. in E. *Or.*111: aor. ἐπεμψάμην Id.*Hec.*977:—Pass., fut. πεμφθήσομαι Str.1. 1.4, Plu.*Demetr.*27: aor. ἐπέμφθην Pi.*N.*3.59, S.*El.*1163, etc.: 3sg. pf. πέπεμπται A.*Th.*473, (προ-) Th.7.77; part. πεπεμμένος D.23.159, Luc. *Alex.*32, D.C.50.13: plpf. ἐπέπεμπτο Id.36.18, (προὔπ-) Th.8.79 (cj.):—*send*, freq. of persons, as messengers, spies, etc., Il.3.116, A.*Th.*37, Hdt.7.15, etc.; of troops, A.*Pers.*34 (anap.), *Th.*470: c. dupl. acc., ὁδὸν π. τινά *send* one *on* a journey, S.*Aj.*739, cf. *El.*1163 (Pass.); also of things, πέμψω δέ τοι οὖρον ὄπισθεν Od.5.167, etc.; π. γράμματα, ἐπιστολήν, Pl.*Ep.*310d, 323b; in letters, in the epistolary aorist, Th.1.129, X.*An.*1.9.25, Lxx 2*Es.*4.14; π. κακόν τινι *send* one evil, Il.15.109; π. παραβᾶσιν Ἐρινύν A.*Ag.*59 (anap.); ποινάς, ζημίαν, Id.*Eu.*203 (dub.), E.*Fr.*506; ψόφον π. ἔσω Id.*IT*1308; ὕπνον, ὀνείρατα, S.*Ph.*19, *El.*460; freq. of omens, π. οἰωνόν, τέρατα, Il.24.310, X.*Mem.* 1.4.15, cf. *Smp.*4.48; μαντείας S.*OT*149; also ἱκεσίους π. λιτάς Id. *Ph.*495; π. ἀρωγάς, ἀλκάν, A.*Eu.*598, S.*OT*189 (lyr.):—Constr.: 1. c. acc. of place to which, π. τινὰ Θήβας, ἀγρούς, Id.*OC*1770 (anap.), *OT*761: also c. dat., Ἀΐδᾳ E.*IT*159 (anap.): but usu. with Preps., ἐς Τροίην, φίλην ἐς πατρίδα γαῖαν, etc., Il.6.207, Od.5.37, etc.; π. εἰς Ἀΐδαο Il.21.48; δόμον Ἄϊδος εἴσω Od.9.524; π. εἰς διδασκάλων *send* to school, Pl.*Prt.*325d (so πέμπειν alone, Ar.*Fr.*216); π. ἐπ' εὐρέα νῶτα θαλάσσης *over*.., Od.4.560, etc.; π. ἐπὶ Θρῃκῶν ἵππους to them, Il.10. 464; but πέμπειν ἐπί τι *send for* a purpose, ἐπ' ὕδωρ Hdt.5.12; ἐπὶ κατασκοπήν X.*Cyr.*6.2.9 (π. εἰς κ. S.*Ph.*45); π. ἀρωγὴν ἐπὶ νίκην A.*Ch.*477 codd. (anap.); π. ἐπί τινι *send to* him, Il.2.6; *against*.., A.*Ag.*61 (anap.), etc.; *for* a purpose, ἐπὶ πολέμῳ X.*HG*4.8.17; περί τινος about something, Th.1.91, X.*Cyr.*6.2.10; ὑπέρ τινος Epist. Philipp. ap.D.12.12; παρά or πρός τινα *to* some one, Th.2.81, X.*An.*5.2.6; ὥς τινα Th.8.50. 2. folld. by Advbs., οἴκαδε, οἰκόνδε, Od.19. 281, 24.418; ὅνδε δόμονδε Il.16.445; θύραζε Od.9.461; πόλεμόνδε Il. 18.452, etc.; ἕταρον γὰρ..πέμπ' Ἄϊδόσδε *was conducting* or *convoying* Patroclus to Hades, 23.137. 3. folld. by inf. of purpose, τὴν.. ἅρμασι π. νέεσθαι Od.4.8; ἕπεσθαι Il.16.575; ἰέναι Od.14.396; ἱκανέμεν 4.29; ἄγειν 24.419; φέρειν Il.16.454; φέρεσθαι ib.681; μήτηρ με πέμπει πατρὶ τυμβεῦσαι χοάς S.*El.*406; *send word*, πέμπεις..σῇ δάμαρτι, παῖδα σὴν δεῦρ' ἀποστέλλειν E.*IA*360; πέμπουσιν οἱ ἔφοροι.. στρατεύεσθαι *sent him orders* to march, X.*HG*3.1.7: also c. part., κήρυκας π. ἀγγέλλοντας *IG*1$^2$.76.22: the place from which is expressed by ἀπό or ἐκ, Il.16.447, Od.11.635, etc. 4. abs., ἐπέμψαμεν πρὸς ὑμᾶς περὶ ἀποστάσεως Th.3.13; πέμπει κελεύων Th.1.91, 2.81; ἐκέλευε..πέμπων X.*An.*2.3.1; ἔπεμπε πρὸς Κῦρον δεόμενος Id.*Cyr.*1.5.4; ἔπεμπον ἐρωτῶντες Id.*An.*6.6.4, etc. 5. *send forward, nominate* a person for a post, ὀνόματα Wilcken *Chr.*28.20 (ii A.D.):—Pass., ib.392.7 (ii A.D.). II. *send forth* or *away, dismiss, send home*, τὸν ξεῖνον Od.7.227, al.: less freq. in Il., as 24.780; χρὴ ξεῖνον παρεόντα φιλεῖν, ἐθέλοντα δὲ πέμπειν 'welcome the coming, *speed* the parting guest', Od.15.74; ὑπέδεκτο καὶ πέμπε 23.315; of the father who sends off his daughter to go to her husband, c. dat., 4.5; π. τινὰ ἄποικον S.*OT*1518, etc. 2. of missiles, *discharge, shoot*, πέτρας Hes.*Th.*716: metaph., ὄμματος..τόξευμα A.*Supp.*1005: abs., οἱ πολλάκις πέμποντες ἔστιν ὅτε τυγχάνουσι τοῦ σκοποῦ Eun.*VS* p.495 B. 3. of words, *send forth, utter*, A.*Th.*443, S.*Ph.*846 (lyr.), 1445 (anap.). III. *conduct, escort*, Il.1.390, Od.14.336, S.*Tr.*571, etc.; freq. of Hermes and other gods, Od.11.626, A.*Eu.*12, *Supp.*219; ὁ πέμπων abs., of Hermes, S.*Ph.*133 (cf. πομπός, πομπαῖος, etc.); of a ship, *convey, carry*, Od.8.556, cf. A.*Supp.*136 (lyr.); κραιπνοφόροι δέ μ' ἔπεμψαν αὖραι Id.*Pr.*132 (lyr.), cf. Pi.*P.*4.203 (Pass.). 2. πομπὴν π. *conduct*, or *take part in*, a procession, Hdt.5.56, Ar.*Ec.*757, Th.6. 56, Lys.13.80, D.4.26, etc.; π. χορούς *move in* dancing *procession*, E.*El.*434 (lyr.); Παναθήναια π. Men.494, Philostr.*VA*4.22:—Pass., φαλλὸς Διονύσῳ πεμπόμενος *carried in procession* in his honour, Hdt.2. 40, cf. Plu.*Aem.*32, *Demetr.*12; τῆς πομπῆς ὅπως ἂν ὡς κάλλιστα πεμφθῇ *IG*1$^2$.84.27; χορὸς ὁ εἰς Δῆλον πεμπόμενος X.*Mem.*3.3.12. IV. *send* as a present, εἵματα, σῖτον, Od.16.83, 4.623; π. δῶρα, σκῦλα, ξένια, Hdt.7.106 (Act. and Pass.), S.*Ph.*1429, X.*Cyr.*3.1.42. V. *send up, produce*, ὅσα πέμπει βιόδωρος αἶα S.*Ph.*1162 (lyr.).

B. Med., πέμπεσθαί τινα *send for* one, S.*OC*602, ubi v. Sch.; τί χρῆμ' ἐπέμψω τὸν ἐμὸν ἐκ δόμων πόδα; E.*Hec.*977. II. *send in one's own service* or *cause to be sent*, S.*OT*556, Luc.*Tox.*14.

**πεμπώβολον**, τό, (πέμπε, ὀβελός) *five-pronged fork*, Il.1.463, Od.3. 460, cf. Ps.-Hdt.*Vit.Hom.*37.

**πεμφηρίς**, ίδος, ἡ, a kind of *fish*, Numen.ap.Ath.7.309f.

**πεμφῑγώδης**, ες, (πέμφιξ) *accompanied by vesicular eruption*, Hp. *Epid.*6.1.14, cf. Gal. ad loc. (17(1).878), Id.19.399; **πεμφιδ-**, Hsch.

⊛ **πέμφιξ**, ῑγος, ἡ, *breath, blast*, ἀπῇξε πέμφιξ Ἰονίου πέλας πόρου prob. in S.*Fr.*337; κεραυνία π. βροντῆς Id.*Fr.*538; δυσχείμερος π. A.*Fr.* 195.4. 2. *ray*, τηλέσκοπον πέμφιγα χρυσέαν ἰδών S.*Fr.*338; ὃς οὔτε π. ἡλίου προσδέρκεται οὔτε κτλ. A.*Fr.*170. 3. *drop*, Id.*Fr.*205; μηδ' αἵματος πέμφιγα πρὸς πέδῳ βάλῃς Id.*Fr.*183. 4. *cloud*, πέμφιγι ..ἀγγέλῳ πυρός *cloud*, harbinger of lightning, S.*Fr.*539; *driving rain* or *rain-cloud*, Ibyc.17; πελιδναὶ φλύκταιναι πέμφιξιν ἐειδόμεναι ὑετοῖο, ..ἀμυδρήεσσαι ἐς ὠπήν livid pustules like rain *clouds* (in colour)..dim to the sight, Nic.*Th.*273 (but = *bubbles* acc. to Sch.); dub. sens. in Call.*Fr.*483 (prob. = *Oxy.*2080.43). 5. *ghost*, Lyc.1106, and so prob. in Euph.134. 6. *pustule* or *part surrounding a pustule*, ἐφίσταται π. οἷον ἐλαίου χλωρῆς ὥσπερ ἀράχνιον Euryphon ap.Gal.17 (1).886.

**πεμφίς**, ίδος or ῖδος, ἡ, = foreg. 5, Lyc.686 (v.l. πεμφίγων).

**πεμφρηδών**, όνος, ἡ, a kind of *wasp* that builds in hollow oaks, Nic.*Al.*183 (cf. Sch.), *Th.*812; cf. τενθρηδών, ἀνθρηδών.

**πέμψις**, εως, ἡ, (πέμπω) *sending, mission*, Hdt.8.54; ἡ π. τῶν νεῶν Th.7.17; ἐπιστολῶν πέμψεις Aen.Tact.31.1, cf. Arist.*Po.*1452$^b$6; ἡ π. τῶν νικητηρίων, of a triumphal *procession*, D.C.44.41 (μέμψιν codd.).

**πενεστ-εία**, ἡ, = οἱ πενέσται, *the class of serfs*, Arist.*Pol.*1264$^a$35 (pl.), 1269$^a$37. **-ερος, -ατος**, Comp. and Sup. of πένης. **-ης**, ου, ὁ, (πένομαι, cf. D.H.2.9) *labourer*, mostly in pl., of the Thessalian *serfs*, Theopomp.Com.75, X.*HG*2.3.36, 6.1.11, D.23.199, Arist.*Fr.* 586, Theoc.16.35 (cf. Sch. ad loc.), Philocrat.ap.Ath.6.264a, Archemach.1. II. generally, *slave, bondsman*, τινος E.*Heracl.*639; π. ἀμὸς ἀρχαίων δόμων Id.*Fr.*830; *labourer, poor man*, Ar.*V.*1273 (lyr.), Timo 39, *AP*6.300 (Leon.). **-ικός**, ή, όν, *in the state of a πενέστης*, τὸ Θετταλῶν π. ἔθνος the caste *of serfs*, Pl.*Lg.*776d.

**πενέω**, *to be poor*, Hsch.: aor. part. Pass. πενηθείς Lxx *Pr.*24.32 (30.9).

**πένης**, ητος, ὁ, (πένομαι) *one who works for his living, day-labourer, poor* man, opp. πλούσιος, Democr.283; opp. δυνάμενος, Archyt.3; πτωχοῦ μὲν γὰρ βίος..ζῆν ἐστιν μηδὲν ἔχοντα· τοῦ δὲ πένητος ζῆν φειδόμενον καὶ τοῖς ἔργοις προσέχοντα Ar.*Pl.*553; οἱ π. αὐτῶν Hdt.1.133, 2.47; πλούσιος ἐκ πένητος Lys.1.4; πένητες ἄνθρωποι Hdt.8.51; οἱ ἀνὴρ π. S.*Ph.*584; π. ἵππος X.*Oec.*11.5. II. as Adj., π. δόμοι E. *El.*1139: c. neut., ἐν πένητι σώματι ib.372: c. gen., χρημάτων πένητες *poor in* money, ib.38; π. φίλων Pl.*Ep.*332c; π. ἀπολογίας Luc.*Apol.* 11: Comp. πενέστερος X.*Ath.*1.13: Sup. πενέστατος D.21.123.

**πένησσα**, ἡ, fem. of foreg., Hsch.

**πενητεύω**, *to be poor*, Ps.-Phoc.28, Crates *Ep.*18, Phld.*Rh.*2.172S., Nic.Dam.44.3J., etc.; π. τινός Emp.57.3.

**πενητῠλίδας**, α, ὁ, *starveling*, Cerc.4.4.

⊛ **πενθ-ᾰλέος**, α, ον, *sad, mourning*, ἐστόρεσαν παλάμαις π. *AP*7.604 (Paul. Sil.); π. τοκῆας *Supp.Epigr.*6.140.6 (Cotiaeum); μορφᾶς εἰκὼν π. *IG*3.1416. 2. *mourned*, θάνατος *Supp.Epigr.*6.140.22 (Cotiaeum). ⊛ **-άς**, άδος, ἡ, fem. of foreg., ὄρνιθες Mosch.3.49, cf. Nonn.*D.*14.271. ⊛ **-εια**, ἡ, poet. form of πένθος, A.*Ag.*430 (lyr.). **-εινός**, ή, όν, *mourning*, Aq., Thd.*Is.*61.2.

⊛ **πενθερ-ά**, Ion. -ρή, ἡ, fem. of πενθερός, *mother-in-law*, D.45.70, Call.*Dian.*149, *Ev.Marc.*1.30, Plu.*TG*8, etc. **-ῐδεύς**, έως, ὁ, *brother-in-law*, *CIG*4079 (Ancyra), Keil-Premerstein *Erster Bericht* No.137 (Daldis), 149 (Gordos), *Zweiter Bericht* No.145 (ibid.), *BCH*8.382,386 (Lydia):—later ⊛ **-ίδης**, ου, ὁ, *PLond.* 5.1676.8, 37 (vi A.D.). **-ικός**, ή, όν, = sq., Man.5.297, *MAMA*3.512 (Corycus). ⊛ **-ιος**, α, ον, *of* or *for a* πενθερός, Arat.252. II. πενθέριον· τὴν προῖκα Θάσιοι, Hsch., cf. *BCH*50.227 (Thasos, ii A.D.).

**πενθεροκτόνος**, ον, gloss on πενθεροφθόρος, Tz. ad Lyc.161.

⊛ **πενθερός**, ὁ, *father-in-law*, Il.6.170, Od.8.582, Lex Draconis ap.D.43.57 (pl.), Hdt.3.52, *PCair.Zen.*369.2 (iii B.C.); λαβὼν Ἄδραστον π. S.*OC*1302: in pl., *parents-in-law*, E.*Hipp.*636. II. generally, *connexion by marriage*, e.g. *brother-in-law*, Id.*El.*1286; also, = γαμβρός, *son-in-law*, S.*Fr.*305 (pl.). (Cf. Skt. *bándhus* 'kinsman', Lith. *beñdras* 'comrade', Goth. *bindan* 'bind'.)

**πενθεροφθόρος**, ον, *slaying one's father-in-law*, Lyc.161.

**πενθετηρ-ικός**, ή, όν, = πεντετηρικός: neut. **-κόν**, τό, = πεντετηρίς II, *SIG*577.70 (Milet., iii/ii B.C.), *PGrad.*6.7 (iii B.C.). ⊛ **-ος**, ον, *in the fifth year* (inclusively), τροπαί Philod.Scarph.131.

**πενθ-έω**, Ep. 3 dual πενθείετον Il.23.283; Ep. inf. πενθήμεναι Od.18.174, 19.120: fut. -ήσω A.*Fr.*207: aor. ἐπένθησα Id.*Ch.*173, Aeschin.3.211: pf. πεπένθηκα Luc.*Demon.*25, (συμ-) D.60.33: (πένθος):—*bewail, lament*, esp. for persons, νέκυν πενθῆσαι Il.19.225, cf. *Trag. Adesp.*331; πενθέειν τινα ὡς τεθνεῶτα Hdt.4.95; π. γόοις A.*Pers.*545 (anap.); π. τινὰς δημοσίᾳ Lys.2.66; π. τινὰ τριχί A.*Ch.*173; ἐπί τινι π. καὶ κείρασθαι Aeschin.3.211: abs., *mourn, go into mourning*, Pl.*Phdr.*258b, etc.: c. acc. cogn., πενθεῖ νέον οἶκτον A.*Supp.*64:—Pass., *to be mourned for*, Isoc.10.27; πένθος ἀμφί τινι πενθεῖται Arr.*Tact.*33.4. 2. of things, π. κακά S.*OT*1320, Lys.2.2; πήματα S.*OC*739; τύχας E.*Med.*268. **-ημα**, ατος, τό, *lamentation, mourning*, A.*Ch.*432 (pl., lyr.), Theoc.26.26 (with play on Πενθεύς); διπλοῦν πένθιμον δαιμόνων (leg. πένθημ' ὁμαιμόνων) ἔχειν E.*Supp.*1035. **-ήμεναι**, v. πενθέω.

⊛ **πενθ-ημερία**, ἡ, *five days' labour*, *PLond.* 2.321(*c*)5 (ii A.D., abbrev.), *PTeb.*662 (ii A.D.). **-ήμερος**, ον, *of five days*, ἀγών Sch. Pi.*O.*5.13; κατὰ πενθήμερον for alternate *periods of five days*, X.*HG* 7.1.14; *once in every five days*, Arist.*Ath.*30.4; also καθ' ἑκάστην πενθήμερον *SIG*364.9 (Ephesus, iii B.C.).

⊛ **πενθημῐ-αρτάβη** [τᾰ], ἡ, *two and a half* ἀρτάβαι, *PCair.Zen.*376.4 (iii B.C.). **-γῠον**, τό, *two and a half* γύαι, *Tab.Heracl.*2.20. **-μερής**, ές, *consisting of five halves*, i.e. *of two and a half*: in Prosody, τομὴ π. the caesura *after two feet and a half*, as in Hexam. and Iamb. Trim., Aristid.Quint.1.25, etc.; τὸ π. (with or without μέτρον) *the first two feet and a half* of a verse, Quint.*Inst.*9.4.78, Heph.7.3, al., Sch.Ar.*Av.*627. **-πόδιος**, α, ον, *consisting of five half-feet*, i.e. of $2\frac{1}{2}$ *feet*, X.*Oec.*19.3,5, *IG*2².1682.11, *Milet.*7.56. **-σπίθαμος** [σπῐ], ον, $2\frac{1}{2}$ *spans long*, Ph.*Bel.*59.11. **-τᾰλαντιαῖος**, α, ον, *weighing* $2\frac{1}{2}$ *talents*, ib.51.43.

**πενθ-ήμων**, ον, gen. ονος, *mournful*, A.*Ag.*420 (lyr.). ⊛ **-ήρης**, ες, *lamenting, mourning*, E.*Ph.*323 codd., *Tr.*141 (both lyr.). **-ηρός**, ά, όν, *of* or *for mourning*, ἱμάτιον Anaxil.37: in later Prose, Sm.*Je.*9.19(18). **-ησις**, εως, ἡ, *mourning*, Sch.rec.A.*Ag.*429. **-ητέον**, *one must lament*, τὸν θάνατον Ap.Ty.*Ep.*58. **-ητήρ**, ῆρος, ὁ, ἡ, *mourner*, A.*Pers.*946 (lyr.), *Th.*1067 (anap.):—fem. **-ήτριᾰ**, *she who mourns for*, κακῶν E.*Hipp.*805. **-ητήριος**, α, ον, *of* or *in sign of mourning*, πλόκαμος A.*Ch.*7; βόθροι π. trenches *in which mourners lay*, Ion Trag.51. **-ητικῶς**, v. sq. fin. ⊛ **-ῐκός**, ή, όν, *of* or *for mourning, mournful*, ὀδυρμοί Plu.2.102b; θέα Porph.*Abst.*2.50; ἐσθής Chor.p.6 B.; ἐν πενθικοῖς (sc. ἐσθήμασι) Lxx *Ex.*33.4. Adv. -κῶς, ἔχειν τινός to be *in mourning* for a person, X.*Cyr.*5.2.7; πάνυ π. ἐσκευασμένη Luc.*Cal.*5, cf. Plu.2.113d (v.l. -ητικῶς). ⊛ **-ῐμος**, ον, also η, ον D.S.11.57:— = foreg., δακρύων π. αἰδώς A.*Supp.*579 (lyr.); κουρά E.*Alc.*512, *Or.*458; π. πρέπεις ὁρᾶν prob. in Id.*Supp.*1056; ἐσθής D.S. l.c.; τὰ π. *mourning garments*, Plu.2.114e, cf. D.S.13.101. II. *sorry, wretched*, γῆρας E.*Alc.*622; π. ὕπνον ἰαύειν, of death, *Epigr.Gr.*204.7 (Cnidus).

**πενθοποιέω**, *cause lamentation*, Al.*Le.*26.22.

**πένθος**, εος, τό, *grief, sorrow*, Il.11.658, etc.; τινος *for* one, Od.18.324, etc.; π. ἄλαστον ἔχουσα Il.24.105; π. λαγχάνειν S.*Fr.*659; Τρῶας λάβε π. Il.16.548, etc.; μέγα π. Ἀχαιΐδα γαῖαν ἱκάνει 1.254, etc.; πένθεϊ δ' ἀτλήτῳ βεβολήατο πάντες 9.3; θυμὸς ἐτείρετο π. λυγρῷ 22.242, etc. 2. esp. of grief for the dead, *mourning*, τοκεῦσι γόον καὶ π. ἔθηκας 17.37; παιδὸς γάρ οἱ ἄλαστον ἐνὶ φρεσὶ π. ἔκειτο Od.24.423; Σάρδεσι π. παρασχών A.*Pers.*322; δμωαῖς προθήσειν π. οἰκεῖον στένειν S.*Ant.*1249; π. ποιήσασθαι make *a public mourning*, Hdt.2.1; so π. προεθήκαντο Id.6.21; π. τίθεται Id.2.46; π. τινὸς κοινοῦσθαι E.*Alc.*426; ἐν πένθει [εἶναι] S.*El.*290, 847 (lyr.); πολὺ π. ἦν κατὰ τὸ στράτευμα X.*HG*4.5.10; π. λιπεῖν *IG*3.1311; π. λύεσθαι, ἀποθέσθαι, Plu.*Fab.*18, *Alex.*75: in pl., Pi.*I.*8(7).6, *Fr.*154, A.*Ch.*333 (lyr.), Pl.*R.*395e, Arist.*Rh.*1370b25, etc. II. *unhappy event, misfortune*, π. τινός one's *ill-fortune*, Hdt.3.14; ἔτλαν π. οὐ φατόν Pi.*I.*7(6).37. III. of a person, *a misery*, S.*Aj.*615 (lyr.); π. ἔδωκε φέρειν, i.e. the body, *Epigr.Gr.*228.6 (Ephesus). (Cf. πείσομαι from *πένθ-σομαι, fut. of πάσχω, pf. πέπονθα, Lith. *kenčiù* 'suffer', *pa-kantà* 'patience'; πενθ- is reduced to πηθ- (παθ-) in αἰνο-παθής, etc.)

**πενία**, Ion. -ίη, ἡ, (πένομαι) *poverty, need*, πενίῃ εἴκων Od.14.157; οὐλομένην π. Hes.*Op.*717; στάσις πενίας δότειρα Pi.*Fr.*109.5; τῇ Ἑλλάδι π. σύντροφός ἐστι, ..[ἀρετῇ] δὲ διαχρεωμένη τὴν πενίην ἀπαμύνεται Hdt.7.102; τῆς πτωχείας πενίαν φαμὲν εἶναι ἀδελφήν Ar.*Pl.*549; π. δὲ σοφίαν ἔλαχε διὰ τὸ συγγενές (v.l. δυστυχές) E.*Fr.*641; ἐν πενίᾳ εἶναι, γίγνεσθαι, Pl.*Ap.*23c, *R.*613a; εἰς π. πολλὴν καὶ ἀπορίαν καταστῆναι And.1.144: pl. πενίαι Isoc.8.128, Pl.*Prt.*353d, *R.*618a, etc. 2. *lack, need*, τινος Plot.2.4.16. II. Πενία personified, *Poverty*, Alc.92, Pl.*Smp.*203b.

**πενιχρ-ᾰλέος**, α, ον, collat. form of πενιχρός, *AP*6.190 (Gaet.). **-ός**, ά, όν, *poor, needy*, Od.3.348, Alc.49, Thgn.165, 181, Sol.4.23, Pi.*N.*7.19.—Poet. word, found in Com., as Ar.*Pl.*976, Philetaer.4, Diod. Com.2.8, in Pl.*R.*578a, and in later Prose, as *PPetr.*3 p.73 (iii B.C.), Socr.ap.Stob.3.13.64, Lxx *Ex.*22.25, etc.; π. δίαιτα Phld.*Oec.*p.48 J.: Comp. πενιχρότερος Ph.2.284, Sup. -ότατος Plb.6.21.7. Adv. -χρῶς Arist.*Pol.*1252b3. [ῐ by nature, Pi. and Ar. ll. cc., also Man.2.416, elsewh. ῑ by position.] **-ότης**, ητος, ἡ, = πενία, S.E.*M.*2.103, Hsch. s.v. εὐτέλεια.

⊛ **πένομαι**, used only in pres. and impf., (cf. πενέω): I. intr., *toil, work*, ἀμφίπολοι.. ἐνὶ μεγάροισι πένοντο Od.10.348; περὶ δεῖπνον ἐνὶ μεγάροισι π. *were busy* preparing a meal, 4.624; ἀμφ' αὐτὸν ἑταῖροι ἐσσυμένως ἐπένοντο Il.24.124. 2. after Hom., (*to have to work for one's living*, hence) *to be poor* or *needy*, Sol.15, E.*Hec.*1220, Th.2.40, etc.; πλουσία ἢ πενομένη πόλις Pl.*R.*577e; πλουτοῦντες ἢ π. Id.*Plt.*293a; π. καὶ κάμνειν Id.*Grg.*477d. 3. c. gen., *to be poor in, have need of*, τῶν σοφῶν (i.e. τῆς σοφίας) A.*Eu.*431; ὡς διαλλαγὰς ἔχοιμεν ἀλλήλοισιν ὧν πένοιτο γῆ E.*Supp.*210; πάντων Porph.*Marc.*27; πενόμενον τὴν ψυχὴν τῶν ἐπιβαλλόντων αὐτῇ καλῶν Hierocl. *in CA*14 p.451 M.: c. acc., χρήματα Them.*Or.*(i.e. Constant. *pro Them.*)22b. II. trans., *work at, get ready*, δόμον κάτα δαῖτα πένοντο Od.2.322, cf. 3.428, etc.; ἔργα Hes.*Op.*773; ὁππότε κεν δὴ ταῦτα πενώμεθα when we *are a-doing* this, Od.13.394; τί σε χρὴ ταῦτα πένεσθαι; 24.407, cf. Il.19.200.—On the precise meaning of πένομαι, πενία, cf. Ar.*Pl.*551 sqq. (Cf. πένης, πόνος, πονηρός.)

**πενόν**· μεμελανωμένον, Hsch. (leg. πελιόν).

**πενόομαι**, = πένομαι, aor. part. πενωθείς, *poor, needy*, v.l. for πενόμενος in Men.*Mon.*43.

**πεντά-βρᾰχυς** (sc. πούς), ὁ, *foot consisting of five short syllables*, Choerob. *in Heph.*p.247 C. **-γαμβρος**, ον, *with five sons in-law*, νυμφεῖα Lyc.146. **-γραμμον**, τό, *pentagram* ☆ formed by Pythagoreans, Luc.*Laps.*5; cf. πένταλφα. **-γωνικός**, ή, όν, *pentagonal*, σχῆμα Nicom.*Ar.*2.10; ἀριθμός Iamb. *in Nic.*p.60 P. Adv. -κῶς Theo Sm. p.39 H., Iamb. *in Nic.*p.60 P. **-γωνισμός**, ὁ, κατὰ πενταγωνισμόν *pentagonwise*, Nicom.*Ar.*2.13. **-γωνος**, ον, *pentagonal*, Arist.*Fr.*310; ἀριθμός, βάσις, Nicom.*Ar.*2.10,13: πεντάγωνον, τό, *pentagon*, Plu.2.1003d, Gal.5.67. **-δακτῠλιαῖος**, α, ον, = sq. 2, Orib.49.23.20. II. *five-pointed, five-rayed*, ἀστέρες *PMag.Par.*1.580. ⊛ **-δάκτῠλος**, ον, *with five fingers* or *toes*, Arist.*HA*498a34, *PA*688a4. 2. *five fingers broad*, Hp.*Art.*7. 3. = foreg. II, κοχλίαι Xenocr.ap.Orib.2.58.85. II. as Subst., = πεντάφυλλον, Dsc.4.42.

**πεντάδαρχος**, ὁ, f.l. for πεμπάδαρχος in Poll.1.128.

**πεντάδιον** [ᾰ], τό, *group of five*, *BGU*812.2 (ii/iii A.D.).

**πεντά-δραχμος**, ον, *of the weight* or *price of five drachmae*, Hdt.6.89; π. συναλλάγματα *to the amount of five drachmae*, Arist.*Pol.*1300b33: π., τό, *piece of five drachmae*, Poll.9.60; cf. πεντέδραχμος. **-δωρος**, ον, (δῶρον II. 2) *five palms long*, Vitr.2.3.3.

**πεντάεθλος**, ον, poet. and Ion. for πένταθλος, -ον (q.v.).

**πεντάειδος**, ον, (εἶδος IV) *composed of five ingredients*, of a remedy, Aët.15.30.

**πεντάετ-ηρής**, ές, = πενταετής, χρόνος Sch.Ar.*Pax*876. **-ηρία**, ἡ, *period of five years*, Gloss. ⊛ **-ηρικός**, ή, όν, *falling every four* (= *five inclusive*) *years, quinquennial*, ἀγών Plu.2.748f, *IG*5(1).662 (pl., Sparta); ἄρχων ib.14.617 (Rhegium), cf. 741 (Naples). **-ηρίς**, ίδος, ἡ, = πεντετηρίς I, Lycurg.102, Arist.*Pol.*1308b1, *Tab.Heracl.*1.105, etc.; = Lat. *lustrum*, Plb.6.13.3; = *quinquennalia*, D.C.54.19. II. as Adj. *coming every fourth year*, π. ἑορτά Pi.*O.*10(11).57, *N.*11.27; alone in same sense, Id.*O.*3.21, *PMich.Zen.*46.8 (iii B.C.), etc. ⊛ **-ηρος**, ον, poet. for sq., *five years old*, βοῦς Il.2.403, 7.315; ὗς Od.14.419, cf. *PMasp.*5.11 (vi A.D.). II. = πενταετηρικός, τῶν Πτωΐων τῶν π. *BCH*44.251 (i B.C.). **-ής**, ές, Att. πεντᾰέτης, ες (v. διέτης), = foreg. I, ἀπὸ πενταέτεος ἀρξάμενοι Hdt.1.136; πενταετεῖ.. ἥθει ψυχῆς Pl.*Lg.*794e:—fem. πεντᾰετίς, Plu.2.844a. II. *lasting five years*, σπονδαί Th.1.112 codd.; χρόνος *IG*12(5).860.29 (Tenos): neut. as Adv., πεντάετες *for five years*, Od.3.115. **-ία**, ἡ, = πενταετηρίς I, D.H.8.75, Plu.*Per.*13, *IG*7.2227 (Thisbe), 2712.62 (Acraeph.), *PFlor.*61.45 (i A.D.). II. *the age of five*, Ph.2.276. **-ίζομαι**, *to be five years old*, *IG*14.1971.

**πεντά-ζωνος**, ον, *with five girdles* or *zones*, [χθών] Alex.Eph.ap. Theon.Sm.p.140 H.; γῆ, οὐρανός, Str.2.2.1, 2.5.3. **-θετος**, ον, *composed of five ingredients*, ἀντεμβροχή Orib.*Fr.*90: πεντάθετον, τό, Aët.15.37.

**πενταθλ-εύω**, *practise the* πένταθλον, Xenoph.2.2:—also ⊛ **-έω**, ib. 16, Paus.6.14.13, Artem.1.57. **-ητικός**, ή, όν, *in the* π., νίκη Sch. Pi.*N.*7.9. **-ία**, ἡ, = πένταθλον, Arr.*Epict.*3.1.5. **-ιον**, Lyr.

**πενταέθλιον**, τό, = sq., Pi.*P.*8.66, *I.*1.26. **-ον**, Lyr. and Ion. **πεντάεθλον**, τό, *contest of the five exercises* (viz. ἅλμα, ποδωκείην, δίσκον, ἄκοντα, πάλην, Simon.153), Pi.*O.*13.30, *N.*7.8, B.8.104, etc.; πεντάεθλον ἐπασκέειν or ἀσκέειν Hdt.6.92, 9.33; πένταθλ' ἃ νομίζεται is corrupt in S.*El.*691; cf. πέμπαθλον. **-ος**, Lyr. and Ion. **πεντάεθλος**, ὁ, *one who practises the* πένταθλον *or conquers therein*, B.8.27, Arist.*Rh.*1361ᵇ10, Plu.2.737f; π. ἀνήρ Hdt.9.75, *IG*4²(1).99.19 (Epid.). II. metaph., of *one who tries everything*, Pl.*Amat.*138e; ἐν φιλοσοφίᾳ π. *versed in every department* of philosophy, D.L.9.37; in depreciation, 'jack of all trades', X.*HG*4.7.5.

**πένταιχμος**, ον, *five-pointed*, ποδῶν ἀκμαί *AP*6.57 (Paul. Sil.).

**πεντᾰκάτιοι** [κᾰ], = πεντακόσιοι, *GDI*1154 (Elis), 5100.16 (Crete), *Foed.Delph.Pell.*2 *A* 21, *IG*4.498 (Mycenae), 7.3193 (Orchom.Boeot.).

**πεντᾰκαττίς**, ίδος, ἁ, Dor. for πεντηκοστύς, dub. rest. in *CIG*1834 (Issa).

⊕**πεντᾰ-κέλευθος**, ον, *with five ways*, Orac.ap.Paus.8.9.4. **-κέφᾰλος**, ον, *with five heads*, φοῖνιξ Thphr.*HP*2.6.9.

⊕**πεντάκῐς** [ᾰ], Adv. *five times*, Pi.*N.*6.19, A.*Pers.*323, Ar.*Pax*242, Isoc.5.5:—later **πεντάκῑ**, Opp.*C.*3.56, *AP*13.15, Iamb. *in Nic.*p.80 P., al.

**πεντᾰκισ-μύριοι** [ῡ], αι, α, *fifty thousand*, Hdt.7.103, Luc.*Pisc.* 20. **-χίλιοι** [χῑ], αι, α, *five thousand*, Hdt.1.104, Pl.*Lg.*738a: in sg., π. ἀσπίς *five thousand* men-at-arms, Luc.*DMeretr.*9.4; π. ἵππος Lxx 1*Ma.*4.28:—Dor. form **πεντακιχήλιοι** *Abh.Berl.Akad.*1925(5). 25 (Cyrene, iii B.C.).

**πεντά-κλᾰδος**, ον, *five-branched*, π. ἡ χείρ *EM*127.41. **-κλῑνικός**, ή, όν, = sq., σκηνὴ π. *PCair.Zen.*54.34 (iii B.C.). **-κλῑνος**, ον, of a room, *with five couches*, Chares 2 J., Callix.1; σκηνὴ π. *PSI*5. 533.3 (iii B.C.): as Subst., Arist.*Mir.*842ᵇ21, *PCair.Zen.*445.13 (iii B.C.). **-κοινον**, τό, = πεντέφυλλον, Ps.-Dsc.4.42, *Gloss.* **-κόλουρος**, ον, *five times truncated*, Nicom.*Ar.*2.14.

**πεντᾰκοσι-άρχης**, ου, ὁ, *commander of* 512 *men*, Ascl.*Tact.*2.10, Arr.*An.*7.25.6, Ael.*Tact.*9.5:—also **-αρχος**, ὁ, *PPetr.*3 p.4 (iii B.C.), *Sammelb.*7245.2 (iii B.C.), Plu.*Alex.*76. **-αρχία**, ἡ, *command of* 512 *men*, Ascl.*Tact.*2.10: pl., Arr.*Tact.*10.9.

**πεντακοσιόδραχμος**, ον, *consisting of* 500 δραχμαί, ἔρανος *SIG* 1215.6 (Myconos).

**πεντᾰκόσιοι**, Ep. **πεντηκόσιοι**, αι, α, *five hundred*, Od.3.7, Hdt.1. 7, etc.: in sg., πεντακοσία ἵππος *five hundred* horse, Longus 3.1. II. at Athens, οἱ π. *the senate of* 500, τὴν βουλὴν τοὺς π. *IG*2².1629.243, Lycurg.37, Aeschin.3.2; ἡ βουλὴ τῶν π. D.47.18.

**πεντᾰκοσιομέδιμνος**, ὁ, *possessing land which produced* 500 *medimni yearly*, of the first class in the Solonian constitution, Th.3.16, Lys.*Fr.*207 S., Arist.*Pol.*1274ᵃ19 (but attributed to Draco, Id.*Ath.*4. 3), Plu.*Sol.*18.

**πεντᾰκοσι-οστός**, ή, όν, *five-hundredth*, Lys.26.11: -οστή, ἡ, *tax of one-fifth per cent.*, Ar.*Ec.*1007. **-οστύς**, ύος, ἡ, *company of* 500, cj. for πεντηκοντύς in Sch.Od.3.7, cf. *EM*728.55.

**πεντα-κῡμία**, ἡ, *fifth wave*, supposed to be larger than the four preceding, Luc.*Merc.Cond.*2; cf. τρικυμία. **-κωπος**, ον, *five-oared*, *Gloss.* **-λεκτρος**, ον, *five times married*, Lyc.143. **-λῐθα**, **-λῐθίζω**, dub. l. for πεντελ- in Poll.9.126. **-λῑτρος**, ον, *weighing five* λίτραι or *pounds*, Id.4.173.

⊕**πεντ-αλκία**, ἡ, a measure, *GDI*4984 (Gortyn). **-αλφα**, τό, = πεντάγραμμον, Sch.Luc.*Laps.*5. **-ᾱμᾰρῑτεύω**, (ἀμάρα, Dor. for ἡμέρα) *hold office for five days*, *Schwyzer* 323 *D* 16 (Delph.).

**πεντᾰ-μερής**, ές, *consisting of five parts*, χώρα Str.3.4.19, cf. Diom. p.498 K. Adv. -ρῶς, φύλλα π. ἐπεσχισμένα Dsc.3.48.

**πεντ-άμεροι** [ᾱ], οἱ, *officials appointed for five days*, *AJA*19.446 (Halae, iii B.C.).

⊕**πεντά-μετρος** [ᾰ], ον, *consisting of five measures* or *feet*, ἔπη Poll.4. 52: π. (sc. στίχος), ὁ, *pentameter*, Hermesian.7.36: also neut. πεντάμετρον ἐλεγειακόν D.H.*Comp.*25, cf. Heph.6.2, etc. ⊕**-μηνιαῖος**, α, ον, = sq., *Epigr.Gr.*344.17 (Bithynia), *Hippiatr.*20:—also **-μήνιος**, *BGU*859.8 (ii A.D.). ⊕**-μηνος**, ον, *five months old*, Arist.*HA*568ᵃ 12; π. τέκνον, παιδία, *five months' child(ren)*, ib.585ᵃ19, Men.*Epit.* 576. 2. *consisting of five months*, περίοδοι Plu.2.933e; ὁ π. (sc. χρόνος) Hp.*Epid.*3.1.ιαʹ. ⊕**-μναῖος**, ον, = sq., σάρξ *IG*12(2). 498.16 (Methymna, iii B.C.):—also **-μναος**, *SIG*945.9 (Assos, iv B.C.). **-μνους**, ουν, *weighing five minae*, τυροῦ πεντάμνουν Harmod.1, cf. *IG*2².1013.33. **-μοδιαῖος**, α, ον, *holding five modii*, σκάφη *Edict.Diocl.*15.48. **-μοιρία**, ἡ, *arc of five degrees*, Paul. Al.*S.*3. **-μοιριαῖος**, α, ον, *of five degrees*, διαστήματα Procl.*Hyp.* 6.9. **-μοιρον**, v. πεντάμυρον. **-μορφος**, ον, *having five shapes*, of evil, Simp. *in Epict.*pp.71, 72 D. **-μῠρον**, τό, a kind of *ointment*, Orib.*Fr.*70, Alex.Trall.7.8:—written **-μοιρον**, perh. rightly, Aët. 12.61 (v.l. -μυρον). **-νᾱΐα**, ἡ, *squadron of five vessels*, *Hell.Oxy.* 2.4, Polyaen.3.4.2. **-νούμμιον**, τό, *a piece of five sesterces*, Zonar. ⊕**-ξεστιαῖον**, τό, *measure containing five sextarii*, *PSI*8. 881.5 (vi A.D.).

**πενταξός**, ή, όν, *five-fold*, π. στιγμαί *five sets of* points, Arist.*Metaph.* 1076ᵇ32.

**πεντά-οζος** [ᾰ], ον, *having five knots*, Thphr.*HP*1.8.3. **-ούγκιον**, τό, = *quincunx*, *Gloss.* **-πᾰλαιστιαῖος**, α, ον, = sq., Orib.49.23. 1. **-πάλαιστος** [πᾰ], ον, *five handbreadths wide, long*, etc., X.*Cyn.* 9.14, 10.3; cf. πεντεπάλαστος. **-πεδος**, ον, *five feet long*, θριγκοί *IG*7.3073.75 (Lebad.). **-πέτᾰλον**, τό, = sq., *Cat.Cod.Astr.*8 (3).162. **-πετές**, έος, τό, = πεντέφυλλον, Thphr.*HP*9.13.5, Dsc. 4.42. **-πέτηλον**, τό, = foreg., Nic.*Th.*839, Androm.ap.Gal. 14.40. **-πήχης**, ες, = sq., Str.17.3.11 codd. **-πηχυς**, υ, gen. εος, *five cubits long* or *broad*, Hdt.9.83, Thphr.*HP*9.4.2, *PPetr.*3 p.113 (iii B.C., gen. -ους), Lxx 1*Ch.*11.23, *OGI*332.7 (Elaea, ii B.C.); cf. πεντέπηχυς.

**πενταπλᾰσι-άζομαι**, Pass., *to be multiplied by five*, interpol. in Nicom.*Ar.*1.21. **-επίπεμπτος**, ον, *five and* $\frac{1}{5}$ *times as large*: **-επιτέταρτος**, ον, *five and* $\frac{1}{4}$ *times*: **-επίτρῐτος**, ον, *five and* $\frac{1}{3}$ *times*: **-εφήμῐσυς**, υ, *five and* $\frac{1}{2}$ *times*; all in Nicom.*Ar.*1.22. **-ος**, α, ον, Ion. **-πλήσιος**, η, ον, *five-fold*, Hdt.6.13, Arist.*Pol.*1265ᵇ22; π. τινός *five times as large as*.., ib.1266ᵇ6; *five times as much*, Orib.*Fr.*99. Adv. -ως Lxx *Ge.*43.34. **-ότης**, ητος, ἡ, *a being the fifth multiple*, Nicom.*Ar.*2.5. **-ων**, ον, gen. ονος, = πενταπλάσιος, c. gen., J.*AJ* 12.2.8, Ael.*NA*16.12, Heliod. *in EN*98.25; πενταπλασίονα ἀποτεῖσαι to make *five-fold* restitution, Plu.2.846c.

**πεντά-πλεθρος**, ον, *five* πλέθρα *long*, Hecat.Abd.ap.J.*Ap.*1. 22, Max.Tyr.8.6. **-πλευρον**, τό, *figure with five sides*, Papp.396. 13, al. **-πλήσιος**, v. πενταπλάσιος. ⊕**-πλοκος**, ον, *five times twisted*, Hp.ap.Paul.Aeg.6.78 (πεντάπλουν Hp.*Fist.*4). **-πλόος**, α, ον, contr. **-πλοῦς**, ῆ, οῦν, *five-fold*, *PRev.Laws* 11.6, al. (iii B.C.), Lxx 3*Ki.*6.31; ἡ πενταπλόα (sc. κύλιξ) a cup *of five ingredients*, Philoch.43, Aristodem.ap.Ath.11.495f. 2. = πεντάπλοκος, Hp. *Fist.*4. **-πολις**, εως, Ion. ιος, ἡ, *league of five cities*, Hdt.1.144, Lxx *Wi.*10.6, Str.6.2.4, *POsl.*1.300: metaph., of the five senses, Ph. 2.22. **-πορος**, ον, *with five passages*, D.P.301. **-πους**, v. πεντέπους. **-πρωτεία**, ἡ, *board of the first five men*, Lat. *quinqueprimi*, *Cod.Just.*12.28.2.1. **-πτωτος**, ον, *with five cases*, Priscian. *Inst.*5.76. **-πῠλος**, ον, *with five gates*: τὰ Π., a quarter of Syracuse, Plu.*Dio* 29.

⊕**πεντ-άρουρος** [ᾰ], ὁ, *holder of five* ἄρουραι, *PPetr.*3 p.243 (iii B.C.).

**πεντά-ρραβδος** or **-ραβδος**, ον, *consisting of five staves* or *lines*, Telest.4 (dub. l.). II. [στρατηγὸς] π., = Lat. *praetor quinquefascalis*, *IGRom.*1.971 (Gortyn). **-ρρᾱγος**, ον, *with five berries*, *AP*6.300 (Leon.) ap.Suid. (-ρρωγος cod. Pal.).

**πενταρτᾰβ-ία**, ἡ, *contribution of five* ἀρτάβαι, *POxy.* 1445.3 (ii A.D.). **-ιαῖος**, ον, *of five* ἀ., ib.1760.8 (ii A.D.).

**πενταρχία**, ἡ, *magistracy of the Five*, at Carthage, Arist.*Pol.*1273ᵃ13.

⊕**πεντάς**, άδος, ἡ, = πεμπάς, *group of five*, Ascl.*Tact.*7.6, Str.15.1.51 (pl.); *the number five*, Arist.*Metaph.*1082ᵃ2, Ph.1.14, Plu.2.264a, Iamb.*Comm.Math.*18.

**πεντά-σημος** [ᾰ], ον, in Prosody, = πεντάχρονος, Quint.*Inst.*9.4.51, Aristid.Quint.1.14. **-σκαλμος**, ον, *with five sets of tholes* (σκαλμοί), Ephipp.5.17. **-σπῐθᾰμος** [ῐ], ον, *five spans long, broad*, or *high*, X.*Cyn.*2.4, 7, Str.15.1.57; ἀνδριαντίδιον *BCH*54.97 (Delos, ii B.C.). **-στᾰδιαῖος**, α, ον, = sq., Luc.*VH*1.40. **-στάδιος** [στᾰ], ον, *of five stades*, πορθμός, σκιά, Str.7.6.1, 15.1.21: -στάδιον, τό, *distance of five stades*, Id.7.6.2. **-στάτηρος** [στᾰ], ον, *five* στατῆρες *in weight*, Sosicr.1 codd. Poll. **-στῐχος**, ον, *of five lines* or *verses*, *AP*9.173 (Pall.). **-στοιχος**, ον, *five-rowed*, κριθή Thphr. *HP*8.4.2. **-στομος**, ον, *with five mouths* or *openings*, of the Nile, Hdt.2.10; of the Ister, Id.4.47; of the Rhone, Str.4.1.8. **-συλλᾰβία**, ἡ, *having five syllables*, Eust.ad D.P.916. **-συλλάβως** [ᾰ], Adv. *in five syllables*, Id.ib.431. **-σύριγγος**, v.l. for πεντεσ- in Poll.8. 72. **-σχημος**, ον, *of five different forms*, Ps.-Plu.*Metr.*3. **-σχοινος**, ον, *five* σχοῖνοι *long*: -σχοινον, = στάδιον, Hsch. **-τάλαντος**, ον, v. πεντετ-. **-τευχος**, ὁ, *the Pentateuch*, Isid.*Etym.*6.2.1, 2, *Gloss.* **-τομον**, τό, = πεντέφυλλον, Dsc.4.42. **-φάρμᾰκος**, ον, *consisting of five drugs* or *ingredients*: *pentapharmacum*, *Hist. Aug.Hel.*5. **-φυής**, ές, *of five-fold nature*: *five*, ὄνυχες *AP*7.383 (Phil.). **-φύλᾰκος** [ῠ], ον, *divided into five watches*, νύξ Stesich. 55 (πεντε- codd.). **-φῠλία**, ἡ, *five-fold order of priests* in Egypt, *OGI*111.20 (ii B.C., prob. rest.), *BGU*149.6 (ii/iii A.D.), etc. **-φυλλος**, ον, *five-petalled*, Thphr.*HP*6.6.4: **-φυλλον**, τό, *cinquefoil*, *Potentilla reptans*, Hp.*Morb.*2.42, Thphr.*HP*9.13.5, Gal.12.96; also *Potentilla argentea*, Hp.*Ulc.*20:—written **πεντέφυλλον** Dsc.4.42, but πεντάφ- Id.1 *Prooem.*

**πένταχᾰ**, Adv. *five-fold*, *in five divisions*, Il.12.87; but **πένταχα**· ἡ χείρ, Hsch.

**πενταχῇ**, Adv., = πένταχα, Arist.*HA*526ᵇ8, Str.16.4.25, Ph.1.79, Plu.2.429e.

**πεντᾰ-χίλιοι** [χῑ], αι, α, *five thousand*, Tz.*H.*7.96. **-χοίνῐκος**, ον, *containing five* χοίνικες, Poll.4.168. **-χοος**, ον, contr. **-χους**, -ουν, *holding five* χόες, κεράμια *PMagd.*26 (iii B.C.). **-χορδος**, ον, *five-stringed*, [μάγαδις] Ath.14.637a: -χορδον, τό, *a five-stringed instrument*, Poll.4.60; π. συστήματα scales *of five notes*, Theo Sm.p.49 H.

**πένταχος**· τὴν τάλαρον (Boeot.), Hsch.

**πεντᾰχοῦ**, Adv. *in five places*, Hdt.3.117.

**πεντάχρονος**, ον, *consisting of five time-units*, ῥυθμός D.H.*Comp.* 25; πούς Heph.3.2.

**πεντᾰχῶς**, Adv. *in five ways*, Theo Sm.p.23 H., S.E.*M.*1.122, Eust. 32.40.

⊕**πέντε**, Aeol. πέμπε (q.v.), οἱ, αἱ, τά, indecl. (declined in Aeol.), *five*, Il.10.317, etc.; τὰ πέντε κρατήσας having won the πένταθλον, Simon.155.11. (I.-E. *penqᵘe*, cf. Skt. *páñca*, Lith. *penkì*, etc. 'five'.)

**πεντέ-βαθμος**, ον, *of five steps*, κλῖμαξ J.*BJ*5.5.2. **-βάλᾰνος** [βᾰ], ον, *with five wards*, κλειδίον *IG*2².1533.27 (iv B.C.). **-γραμμος**, ον, *consisting of five lines*, πεσσὰ π. draughts *played on a board with five lines*, S.*Fr.*429; cf. πεντάγραμμον. **-δάκτῠλος**, ον, *measuring five finger-breadths*, ἐμπόλια π. πανταχῇ *IG*2².1675.8. ⊕**-δραχμία**, ἡ, *sum of five* δραχμαί, X.*HG*1.6.12, Din.1.56; *coin worth five* δραχμαί, cj. in Polyaen.3.10.14. **-δραχμος**, ον, *at the price of five* δραχμαί, μεδίμνους πυρῶν π. *IG*2$^2$.360.9; σῖτος π. *at the price of five* δραχμαί *per* μέδιμνος, ib.30.

**πεντεκαίδεκα**, οἱ, αἱ, τά, indecl., *fifteen*, Simon.125, Th.3.94, Pl.*R.* 540a, etc.; οἱ π. ἄνδρες, *quindecimviri sacris faciundis*, D.C.53.1, cf. 42.51; ἱερεῖς οἱ π. καλούμενοι Id.44.15.

**πεντεκαιδεκά-γωνον** [ᾰ], τό, *figure with fifteen angles*, Hero *Deff.* 138.11, Theo Sm.p.151 H., Procl.*Hyp.*3.28. **-ετηρίς**, ίδος, ἡ, *term of fifteen years*, Sch.Th.1.18: as Adj., π. περιφορά *fifteen-year* cycle, Men.Prot.p.49 D. **-ετής**, ές, Att. -έτης, ες, *fifteen years old*, Arist. *HA*546$^a$14, dub. in Plu.2.113d. 2. *of* or *for fifteen years*, ἀνοχαί D.H.4.85.

**πεντεκαιδεκάκις** [ᾰ], Adv. *fifteen times*, Sch.Ptol.*Geog.*1.24.2, Theo Sm.p.203 H.

**πεντεκαιδεκα-μναῖος**, α, ον, *weighing fifteen minae*, Ph.*Bel.*51. 37. **-ναΐα**, ἡ, *squadron of fifteen ships*, D.14.18.

**πεντεκαιδέκανδρος**, ὁ, ἱερεὺς π. ἐπὶ τῶν ἱεροποιῶν, = Lat. *XVvir sacris faciundis*, *IGRom.*3.172.14 (Ancyra); but π. τῶν ἐκδικαζόντων τὰ πράγματα wrongly used for *decemvir stlitibus iudicandis*, ib.5.

**πεντεκαιδεκά-πηχυς** [ᾰ], υ, *fifteen cubits long* or *broad*, Arist.*Mir.* 838$^a$21; ξύλα *Inscr.Délos* 370.34 (iii B.C.); δᾷδες D.S.17.115:—also **-πηχυαῖος**, α, ον, Tz.*H.*1.813. **-πλάσιος** [πλᾰ], ον, = sq. (which is v.l.), *Placit.*2.30.1. **-πλᾰσίων**, ον, gen. ονος, *fifteen-fold*, Ath.2.57f.

**πεντεκαι-δεκᾰταῖος**, α, ον, *on the fifteenth day*, Str.15.2.10, 16.4.23; π. τύπος πυρετοῦ Gal.7.500. **-δεκᾰτάλαντος** [τᾰ], ον, *worth fifteen talents*, οἶκοι D.28.11. **-δεκᾰτημόριον**, τό, *fifteenth part*, Hp.*Oct.* 13. ⊛**-δέκᾰτος**, η, ον, *fifteenth*, Arist.*Pr.*941$^b$14, D.S.12.81, *Ev. Luc.*3.1; π. τόκοι *Supp.Epigr.*4.664.17 (Ilium, i B.C.). **-δεκά-χορδος** [ᾰ], ον, *with fifteen strings*, Adrast.ap.Theon.Sm.p.64 H., Ptol.*Harm.*3.1 tit., Porph. *in Harm.*p.168 D. **-δεκήρης**, ες, *with fifteen banks of oars*, Plu.*Demetr.*20. **-δεχήμερος**, ον, *of fifteen days*, ἀνοχαί Plb.18.34.5. **-εικοσάσημος**, ον, *of twenty-five time-units*, Aristid.Quint.1.14. **-είκοσι**, οἱ, αἱ, τά, *twenty-five*, better divisim πέντε καὶ εἴκοσι. ⊛**-εικοσιέτης**, ες, *twenty-five years old*, D.C.52.20. **-εικοστός**, ή, όν, *twenty-fifth*, Pl.*Tht.* 175b. **-πεντηκονταετής**, ές, Att. -έτης, ες, *fifty-five years old*, Id.*R.* 460e. **-τεσσᾰρᾰκονθήμερος**, ον, *in forty-five days*, ὑγιέες γίνονται π. Hp.*Nat.Hom.*12. **-τεσσᾰράκοντα** [ρᾰ], *forty-five*, Iamb. *in Nic.* p.16 P. **-τριᾱκοντάμετρος**, ον, *of thirty-five metres*, Sch.Ar.*Pax* 974. **-τριᾱκοντούτης**, ες, (ἔτος) *thirty-five years old*, Pl.*Lg.*774a.

**πεντέ-κλῑνον**, τό, Att. for πεντάκλινον, Moer.p.321 P. **-κοσμος**, ον, *of five worlds*, Dam.*Pr.*124 bis. **-κτενος**, ον, (κτείς 8b) *with five purple threads woven zig-zag round the border*, Antiph.297, Men.92, cf. Poll.7.52:—also **-κτενής**, ές, Hsch. **-λῐθα**, τά, *the five stones*: πεντελίθοις παίζειν, a game played by women, in which *five pebbles, potsherds, dice*, etc., were tossed from the back of the hand and caught in the palm, *jackstones*, Ar.*Fr.*366. **-λῐθίζω**, *play* πεντελίθοις (cf. foreg.), Hermipp.34. **-λοιπος**, ον, *remaining out of five, last of five*, Cic.*Att.*14.21.4, 15.2.4. ⊛**-μηνον**, τό, Att. for πεντάμηνον, Moer.p.321 P. **-μῡριομέδιμνος**, ον, *of fifty thousand medimni burden*, Tz.*H.*2.108. **-μῡχος**, ον, *of five sanctuaries*, Dam.*Pr.*124 bis.

**πεντενῑαύσιος**, ον, *lasting five years*, σιγή Tz.*H.*8.280.

**πεντε-πάλαστος**, ον, = πενταπάλαιστος, *IG*1$^2$.372.27,164, 2$^2$.1682. 12, 12(8).266 (Thasos). **-πηχυς**, υ, Att. for πεντάπηχυς, Ael. Dion.*Fr.*153.

**πεντεπικαιδέκᾰτος**, η, ον, poet. for πεντεκαιδέκατος, *AP*9.482.18 (Agath.).

⊛**πεντέ-πους**, πουν, gen. ποδος, *of five feet, five feet long*, *IG*1$^2$.372.128, al., 2$^2$.1668.44, Pl.*Tht.*147d:—later **πεντάπους**, *Milet.*7.57 (Didyma, iii/ii B.C.); ἄγαλμα Arr.*Peripl.M.Eux.*3; πεντάπους τὸ ὄρυγμα, = *car-recta*, *Gloss.* **-σύριγγος** [ῡ], ον, *with five holes*, ξύλον π. *pillory*, Ar.*Eq.*1049, cf. Poll.8.72: metaph., of palsy, π. νόσος Polyeuct.ap. Arist.*Rh.*1411$^a$22. **-τάλαντος** [ᾰ], ον, *worth* or *consisting of five talents*, οὐσία D.27.62, etc.; π. δίκη an action *for the recovery of five talents*, Ar.*Nu.*759, 774. II. *weighing five talents*, βάρος Simp. *in Ph.*1104.10 (v.l. πενταт-).

⊛ **πεντ-ετηρικός**, ή, όν, *happening every five years, quinquennial*, Str. 7.7.6, D.C.51.1; cf. πενθετηρικός. **-ετηρίς**, ίδος, ἡ, *term of five years*, διὰ πεντετηρίδος *every fifth year* (inclusively), Hdt.3.97, 4.94. II. *festival celebrated every fifth year* (inclusively), Id.6.111, Th.3.104, *IG* 1$^2$.84.6,32, 2$^2$.1172.27. **-έτης**, ες, *of five years*, σπονδαί Ar.*Ach.* 188. 2. *five years old*, ἐλέφας Arist.*HA*546$^b$8, cf. *IG*3.1307, etc.

**πεντε-τρῐάζομαι**, Pass., *to be conquered five times*, *AP*11.84 (Lucill.). **-φυλλον**, v. πεντάφυλλον. **-χαλκον**, τό, *piece of five* χαλκοῖ, Aristopho 2. **-χους**, ουν, *holding five* χόες, ὑδρία Ar.*Fr.* 136. **-χρονον**, τό, *space of five years*, Sch.Ar.*Pl.*584.

**πεντηκονθήμερος**, ον, *of fifty days*, προθεσμία D.H.2.57.

**πεντήκοντα**, οἱ, αἱ, τά, indecl., *fifty*, Il.2.509, etc.: Boeot. **πεντεί-κοντα** Corinn.*Supp.*2.67: gen. pl. πεντηκόντων *Schwyzer*688 *D*7 (Chios, v B.C.).

**πεντηκοντά-δραχμος**, ον, *worth fifty drachmae*, Pl.*Cra.*384b. 2. *weighing fifty drachmae*, *IG*7.3498.26 (Orop.). II. πεντηκοντά-δραχμον, τό, *gold coin nominally worth fifty silver drachmae*, *PCair. Zen.*22 (iii B.C.); at Cyrene, Poll.9.60. **-έξ**, *fifty-six*, Lxx 1*Es.* 5.10, al. **-ετηρίς**, ίδος, ἡ, *period of fifty years*, Sch.Th.1.18. **-ετής**, ές, Att. -έτης, ες, *fifty years old*, Pl.*Alc.*1.127e, D.H.4.29, etc. II. *of* or *lasting fifty years*, χρόνος D.S.4.58, etc.: fem., πεντηκονταέτιδες σπονδαί Th.5.32 codd. (leg. -ούτ-). **-ετία**, ἡ, *the age of fifty years*, D.H.4.32, Ph.1.551. II. *period of fifty years*, ib.532, Sch.Th.1.97. **-καιτριέτης**, ες, *of fifty-three years*, χρόνος Plb.3. 4.2. ⊛ **-κάρηνος** [κᾰ], ον, *fifty-headed*, Hes.*Th.*312 (-κέφαλον (sic) codd.). ⊛ **-κέφᾰλος**, ον, = foreg., Simon.203, f. l. in Pi.*Fr.*93 (ἑκατοντακάρανον cj. Herm.); cited from Hes. (v. foreg.) by Sch.S. *Tr.*1098. **-κολλος**, ον, *made of fifty sheets*, χάρται *PCair.Zen.*54. 46 (iii B.C.). **-λῑτρος**, ον, *of fifty* λίτραι, νόμισμα D.S.11.26. **-μηναῖος**, α, ον, *happening every fifty months*, Tz.*H.*1.581. **-μναῖος**, ον, *weighing fifty minae*, Ph.*Bel.*51.40. ⊛ **-παις**, παιδος, ὁ, ἡ, *consisting of fifty children*, γέννα A.*Pr.*853. II. *having fifty children*, Δαναός Id.*Supp.*321 (πεντηκοστόπαις codd.). **-πηχυς**, υ, gen. εος, *fifty cubits high*, Callix.2, J.*BJ*5.5.8. **-πλεθρος**, ον, *fifty plethra large*, Eust.776.60: poet. **-πέλεθρος**, Nonn.*D.*25.504.

**πεντηκονταρχ-έω**, *to be* πεντηκόνταρχος, D.50.25. **-ία**, ἡ, *his office*, Pl.*Lg.*707a. II. *company of sixty-four light-armed men*, Ascl.*Tact.*6.3, Arr.*Tact.*14.3, Ael.*Tact.*16.1: pl., Onos.34.2. **-ος**, ὁ, at Athens, *commander of fifty men*, serving under the τριήραρχος, X.*Ath.*1.2, D.50.18,19,24 (wrongly expld. by Harp. as *commander of a* πεντηκόντερος). 2. generally, *leader of a company of fifty*, Lxx *Ex.*18.21, 4*Ki.*1.9.

**πεντηκοντάς**, άδος, ἡ, *body of fifty*, S.*Fr.*432.5 (pl.). II. *the number fifty*, Ph.2.481.

**πεντηκοντα-στάτηρον** [στᾰ], τό, *matter of fifty staters*, *Leg.Gort.* 2.38. **-τᾰλαντία**, ἡ, *fifty talents*, D.ap.Poll.9.52. **-τέσσᾰρες**, α, *fifty-four*, Lxx 2*Es.*2.7. **-τρεῖς**, -τρία, *fifty-three*, ib.*Ge.*5. 31. **-χοος**, ον, contr. -χους, ουν, (χέω) *yielding fifty-fold*, Thphr. *HP*8.7.4.

**πεντηκόντ-ερος** (sc. ναῦς), ἡ, *ship with fifty oars*, Pi.*P.*4.245, *IG*1$^2$. 23, Hdt.1.152, al., Th.1.14; **-ορος** is v.l. in Pi. l.c., Hdt.6.138, Th. l.c., and is found in E.*IT*1124 (lyr.), *Marm.Par.*15. **-ήρ**, ῆρος, ὁ, *commander of fifty men*, name of an officer in the Spartan army, Th.5.66, X.*An.*3.4.21:—written **πεντηκοστήρ** in Id.*Lac.*11.4, 13.4, *HG*3.5.22, 4.5.7. **-ήρης**, ες, f.l. for πεντήρης, Polyaen.4.11. 3. **-ηρικὰ πλοῖα**, = πεντηκόντεροι, Plb.24.6.1.

**πεντηκοντόγῠος**, ον, (γύης) *of fifty acres of corn land*, Il.9.579, Pherecyd.30 J.

**πεντηκοντομέσοδμος**, ον, *with fifty stories*, Hsch. (-ολμον cod.).

**πεντηκοντόργυιος**, ον, *fifty fathoms deep* or *high*, Hdt.2.149.

**πεντηκόντορος**, v. πεντηκόντερος.

**πεντηκοντόστολον**· ὅπου οἱ δραπέται ἀνάγονται, Hsch.

**πεντηκοντούτης**, ες, contr. fr. *πεντηκοντοέτης (= πεντηκονταέτης), *fifty years old*, Pl.*R.*540a, *Lg.*670b. II. *of* or *lasting fifty years*, σπονδαί Foed.ap.Th.5.27.

**πεντηκοντοφύλαξ** [ῠ], ἄκος, ὁ, *watcher over fifty*, *EM*729.16.

⊛ **πεντηκόσιοι**, αι, α, Ep. for πεντᾰκόσιοι, *five hundred*, Od.3.7.

**πεντηκοστ-αῖος**, α, ον, *on the fiftieth day*, Gal.7.478. **-αρχος**, ὁ, *chairman of the company which farmed the* πεντηκοστή, *AB*297, Phot. (-οντ- cod.). **-εύομαι**, Pass., *to be charged with a tax of two per cent.* on any articles, D.35.29; also of the articles, *to have the tax paid upon* them, οὐδ' ὁτιοῦν εὑρίσκομεν..πεπεντηκοστευμένον ib. 30. **-ή**, v. πεντηκοστός II. **-ήρ**, v. πεντηκοντήρ.

**πεντηκοστό-εκτος**, ον, *fifty-sixth*: π., τό, *fifty-sixth part*, σχοινίου Hero *Geom.*90.5. **-λογέω**, *collect the* πεντηκοστή, Philonid.5 ap.Poll. 9.27. **-λόγιον**, τό, *office of* πεντηκοστολόγοι, *IG*11(2).154 *A* 38 (Delos, iii B.C.), Anon.ap.Suid. ⊛ **-λόγος**, ὁ, *collector of the* πεντηκοστή, at Athens, D.21.133, 34.7, Eub.122; at Delos, *SIG*975.10 (iii B.C.); at Cyparissia, ib.952.9 (iv/iii B.C.). **-παις**, f.l. for πεντηκονταπ- (q.v.). **-πρωτος**, ον, *fifty-first*, Hero *Geom.*15.10, al.

**πεντηκοστ-ός**, ή, όν, *fiftieth*, Pl.*Tht.*175b. II. Subst. **πεντηκοστή**, ἡ, 1. (sc. μερίς), *fiftieth part*: hence, *tax of two per cent.* on exports and imports, at Athens, And.1.133, D.59.27: pl., Id.24.120; ἐς Ἀθάνας πεντηκοστὰ τῶν λίθων *IG*4$^2$(1).103.46 (Epid.); at Delos, ib.2$^2$.1635.38 (iv B.C.), 11(2).161 *A* 26 (iii B.C.); at Halicarnassus, *OGI* 46.12 (iii B.C.); τῶν πρηθέντων τελείτω π. *SIG*229.5 (Erythrae, iv B.C.); = Lat. *quinquagesima*, D.C.55.31 (s. v.l.): metaph., ταύτην εὗρηκε Μειδίας καινὴν ἱππικήν τινα πεντηκοστήν invented a new sort of *composition of two per cent.* in lieu of his cavalry service, i. e. paid this instead of it, D.21.166. 2. (sc. ἡμέρα), *fiftieth day* (after the Passover), *Pentecost*, Lxx 2*Ma.*12.32; ἡ ἡμέρα τῆς Π. *Act.Ap.*2.1. ⊛ **-ύς**, ύος, ἡ, *body of fifty*, as a division of the Spartan army, Th.5.68; κατὰ πεντηκοστῦς (acc. pl.) X.*An.*3.4.22. **-ώνης**, ου, ὁ, *farmer of the* πεντηκοστή, prob. in *AB*297 (pl.), cf. *Ostr.*43 (i A.D.), *Theb.Ostr.*130 (ii A.D.).

**πεντήρης** (sc. ναῦς), ἡ, *quinquereme*, Plb.8.4.2, al. (but f.l. for πεντετηρίς Hdt.6.87); in full, ναῦς π. D.S.2.5, 14.41: **πεντηρικὰ πλοῖα**, σκάφη, Plb.1.59.8, 3.41.2, cf. D.S.14.41.

**πεντό-δρῡον**, τό, = στρύχνον μανικόν, Dsc.4.73.

**πέντ-οζος**, ον, *with five branches*: as Subst., of the human *hand*, Hes.*Op.*742, Hsch. s. v. ἐμῇ πεντόζῳ (prob.). **-όργυιος**, ον, *of five fathoms*, *AP*11.87 (Lucill.); cf. πεντώρυγος. **-ορκία**, ἡ, *oath by five gods*, *IG*9(1).333.16 (Locr., v B.C.). ⊛ **-ὄροβος**, ὁ, = γλυκυσίδη, Dsc.3.140, Plin.*HN*25.29, 27.84. 2. an architectural ornament in this form, *IG*11(2).161 *B* 19 (Delos, iii B.C.): **πεντώροβος**, *BCH*32.11 (ibid., iv B.C.), *IG*2$^2$.1451.29, 1452.7. ⊛**-ώβολος**, ον, (ὀβολός) *of* or *worth five obols*, π. ἡλιάσασθαι to sit in the Heliaea *at five obols a day*, Ar.*Eq.*798; τόκος π. *IG*11(2).146 *B* 17 (Delos, iv/iii B.C.); δραχμᾶν δύο πεντωβόλου ib.4$^2$(1).109 ii 123 (Epid.); κυλίκιον τοῦ πεντωβόλου a cup *of five-obol wine*, Lyc.*Fr.*2.2. ⊛ **-ώγκιον**, τό, = πενταούγκιον, prob. in Epich.9. **-φδουμένη μονάς**, = 10,000, Iamb.

*in Nic.*p.89 P. (Fort. πεντοδ-.) -ώνῠμος, ον, *called by five names*, Tz.*Proll.Com.*p.29 K. -ώνῠχος, ον, *with five nails*, Philostr.*VA* 2.13. -ώροφος, ον, (ὄροφος) *with five stories*, D.H.*Rh.*1.3, D.S. 1.45, etc. ⊛-ώρῡγος, ον, = πεντόργυιος, X.*Cyn.*2.5.

***πένω**, v. πένομαι.

**πέξις**, εως, ἡ, (πέκω) *shearing* or *combing*, Hsch.

⊛ **πεξὸν** ἱμάτιον, *prosa pexa tunica*, *Gloss.*

**πεοίδης**, ες, *with a swollen* πέος, *Com.Adesp.*1111.

⊛ **πέος**, εος, τό, *membrum virile*, Ar.*Ach.*158, etc. (Cf. Skt. *pásas* 'membrum virile'.)

**πεπάγουσα**· ἁπαλή, Hsch. **πεπᾰθυῖα**, v. πάσχω.

**πεπαιδευμένως**, Adv. *in a well-bred manner*, Isoc.11.30, Ael.*VH* 12.1.

⊛ **πεπαίνω**, aor. ἐπέπᾱνα (v. infr. 2):—Pass., fut. πεπανθήσομαι: aor. ἐπεπάνθην (v. infr.): pf. inf. πεπάνθαι Arist.*Pr.*925ᵃ13: (πέπων):—*ripen*, Hdt.1.193; ὀρχάτους ὀπωρινούς E.*Fr.*896; π. τὴν ὀπώραν, of the vine, *bring* its fruit *to maturity* or *perfection*, X.*Oec.*19.19, cf. Arist.*Mir.*846ᵇ1; [ἡ συκῆ] π. τέτταρας καρπούς Thphr.*HP*4.2.3; but [συκῆ] π. τὴν σάρκα τοῦ ὄρνιθος, by being boiled with it, Plu.2.697b: abs., διασκοπῶν ἥδομαι τὰς.. ἀμπέλους, εἰ πεπαίνουσιν ἤδη, i.e. if the grapes are ripening, Ar.*Pax* 1163 (lyr.):—Pass., *become ripe*, Hdt.4.199, Ion Trag.57, *Trag.Adesp.*396, *Gp.*4.6.1, etc. 2. metaph., *soften*, *assuage*, πεπᾶναι ὀργήν Ar.*V.*646; χρόνος ὁ πάντα πεπαίνειν εἰωθώς Plu.2.102a; ὀργὴ πεπανθήσεται X.*Cyr.*4.5.21; τὸ πεπανθὲν ἔρωτος τραῦμα *AP*12.80 (Mel.); of a person, ἢν πεπανθῇς E.*Heracl.* 159. 3. in Pass., of tumours, *soften and suppurate*, Hp.*Epid.*6.2.16; of illness generally, *come to a head*, *mature*, Id.*Aph.*2.40, *Prog.*12; μέχρι ἂν τῆς νούσου ἡ ἀκμὴ πεπανθῇ Id.*Acut.*38; also οὖρα πεπαινόμενα Id.*Epid.*1.3. 4. χρὼς ἐπὶ χρωτὶ πεπαίνετο *grew warm*, Theoc.2.140.

**πεπαίτερος** and **-τατος**, v. πέπων. **πεπᾰλαγμένος, πεπάλακτο**, v. παλάσσω. **πεπᾰλών**, v. πάλλω, ἀμπεπαλών. **πέπᾱμαι**, v. *πάομαι. **πέπανα**· πλακούντια, Hsch. (leg. πόπανα).

**πέπ-ᾰνος**, ον, rarer collat. form of πέπων, Artem.1.73, 2.25, Porph. *Gaur.*13.4; = *maturus*, *mitis*, *passus*, *Gloss.*; πεπανός· ὁ πολὺν χρόνον ἔχων παρὰ τὸ ὀπτηθῆναι, Hsch.: Comp. -ώτερος Paus.9.19.8: metaph., *more experienced*, Lyd.*Mag.*3.10 (Comp.). [Oxyt. in Artem.2.25, Hsch.] ⊛ -ανσις, εως, ἡ, *ripening*, of fruits, Arist.*Mete.*380ᵃ11, Thphr.*HP*5.1.2, 3.4.1 (pl.), Corn.*ND*30. 2. Medic., *maturation*, of tumours and the like, Arist.*Mete.*380ᵃ21. -αντικός, ή, όν, *able to ripen* or *soften*, c. gen., πτυάλου Hp.*Acut.*66; π. δύναμις Dsc.5.125; π. μέλος (of music) *soothing* strain, prob. cj. in Iamb.*VP*25.113.

**πεπᾰρεῖν**, aor. 2 inf., only in Pi.*P.*2.57 (v.l. πεπορεῖν, also cited by Hsch., who expl. πεπαρεῖν by ἐνδεῖξαι, σημῆναι, *display*, *manifest*; and cites **πεπᾰρεύσιμος**· εὔφραστος, σαφής).

**πεπαρμένος**, v. πείρω. **πεπάσμην**, v. πατέομαι.

**πεπασμός**, ὁ, = πέπανσις: in Medic., *concoction of sputum* or *urine*, Hp.*Epid.*1.2, 3.10 (pl.); πεπασμοὶ σπέρματος Aret.*CD*1.4. 2. *suppuration*, Hp.*Epid.*3.4.

**πέπειρᾰ**, ἡ, rare fem. of πέπων (formed on analogy of πίειρα, fem. of πίων), used of women, *mellow*, *ripe*, ἐν ταῖς πεπείραις (v.l. -οις) Ar.*Ec.*896; *over-ripe*, *passée*, π. γίνομαι Anacr.87; πέπειρα· γραῖα, Hsch. 2. of things, *soft*, *pulpy*, τὴν σάρκα πέπειραν ποιεῖ Hp.*VC* 11 (v.l. -ον): metaph., ὀργὴ π. S.*Tr.*728.

**πέπειρος**, ον, *ripe*, of fruit, Thphr.*CP*3.6.9 (Comp.), Lxx *Ge.*40.10, *AP*12.185 (Strat.); of girls, opp. νέαι, v.l. in Ar.*Ec.*896; παρθένοι Plu.*Comp.Lyc.Num.*4, cf. *Lyc.*15; φιλέουσι πέπειρος *AP*12.9 (Strat.). 2. metaph., of persons, *mild*, πεπειροτέρους γεγονότας D.H.9.49. 3. π. νοῦσος a disease *come to its crisis*, Hp.*Acut.*39; also πεπειρότερον πτύελον *more concocted*, Id.*Epid.*2.3.4.

**πεπεισμένως**, Adv. *confidently*, π. διεγγυώμενος D.L.9.71, cf. 4.56; *from conviction*, Ptol.*Alm.*2.6, Iamb.*VP*30.175: f.l. in Str.15.1.24 (ἀπεφεισμένως cj. Mein.).

**πεπερασμενάκις** [ᾰ], *a definite number of times*, Arist.*APo.*82ᵇ32.

**πεπερᾶτος**, ον, *peppered*, *Gp.*8.39 tit.: πεπερᾶτον, τό, *wine flavoured with pepper*, *SIG*1171.10 (Crete).

**πεπερημένος**, v. πέρνημι.

⊛ **πέπερῐ**, τό, *pepper*, *Piper nigrum*, Antiph.277, Arist.*Po.*1458ᵃ15, Dsc.2.159, etc.: gen. πεπέρεως Plu.*Sull.*13, Ath.9.381b; πεπέριος Thphr.*HP*9.20.2: pl., τὰ τρία πεπέρια Orib.*Fr.*67: other forms imply nom. **πέπερις**, ὁ, gen. τοῦ πεπέριδος Eub.128; dat. πεπέριδι Ael.*NA*9.48; acc. πέπεριν Nic.*Al.*332, *Th.*876; gen. pl. πεπερίδων Ath.9.376d: also fem., αἱ πεπέριδες *pepper-trees*, Philostr.*VA*3.4. 2. π. πρόμηκες, μακρόν, *long pepper*, *Piper officinarum*, Thphr.*HP*9.20.1, Dsc. 2.159. (Gen. sg. πιπέρεως *Stud.Pal.*20.27.3 (ii/iii A.D.).)

**πεπερίζω**, *taste like pepper*, τῇ γεύσει Dsc.2.160.

**πεπερό-γᾰρον**, τό, *peppered* γάρον, Alex.Trall.1.15 (written πιπερό-). -ζωμος, ὁ, *peppered broth*, Cyran.109.

**πεπῐασμένως** or **-εσμένως**, Adv., (πιέζω, -άζω) *closely*, Hsch. s.v. βύζην.

**πεπῐθεῖν, -θοῦσα, -θοιμεν, -θοιεν, -θήσω, -θμεν**, v. πείθω.

**πεπῑνωμένως**, v. πινόομαι.

**πεπιστευμένως**, Adv., (πιστεύω) *truly*, Aristox.ap.Stob.4.25.45, Phld.*Rh.*1.352 S.: -ωμένως, Aq.*Is.*25.1, *Nu.*5.22, al.

⊛ **πεπλᾰνημένως**, Adv., (πλανάομαι) *mistakenly*, *in error*, περί τινος π. ἔχειν Isoc.9.43; π. λέγεσθαι Str.2.4.3. II. *irregularly*, of fits of disease, Hp.*Epid.*1.3.

**πεπλασμένως**, Adv., (πλάσσω) *artificially*, *by pretence*, opp. ἀληθῶς, Pl.*R.*485d; opp. ἀληθινῶς, Bato 7.5; opp. πεφυκότως, Arist.*Rh.*1404ᵇ 19; π. λαρυγγίζοντες Phld.*Rh.*1.200 S.

**πεπλᾰτυσμένως**, Adv., (πλατύνω) *widely*, Tz. ad Lyc.1414.

**πέπληγον, πεπληγέμεν, πεπλήγετο, πεπληγώς**, v. πλήσσω.

**πεπληθυσμένως**, Adv., (πληθύω) *by way of multiplication*, *as a plurality*, Porph.*Sent.*33.2, Procl.*in Cra.*p.51 P.; opp. διῃρημένως, Id. *in Alc.*p.52 C.

**πεπλημένος**, v. πελάζω.

**πεπληρωμένως**, Adv., (πληρόω) gloss on νουθετικῶς, Sch.Ar.*V.* 1285; = Lat. *plene*, Dosith.p.409 K., *Gloss.*

**πεπλίς**, ίδος, ἡ, *wild purslane*, *Euphorbia Peplis*, Dsc.4.168:—also in Dim. form **πέπλιον**, τό, Hp.*Acut.*23, Gal.12.97.

⊛ **πεπλο-γρᾰφία**, ἡ, *description of the peplos*, or the subjects worked on it, title of work by Varro, being a sort of 'Book of Worthies', Cic.*Att.*16.11.3. -δόχος, ον, *receiving the* πέπλος, χηλοί Eust.1776.42. ⊛ -θήκη, ἡ, *wardrobe*, *IG*2².1462.12. -ποιία, ἡ, *making of the peplos*, metaph., Dam.*Pr.*339.

**πέπλος**, ὁ, in late Poets also with heterocl. pl. πέπλα, *AP*9.616, *Epigr.Gr.*418 (Cyrene):—*any woven cloth* used for a covering, *sheet*, *carpet*, *curtain*, *veil*, to cover a chariot, funeral-urn, seat, Il.5.194, 24.796, Od.7.96; laid over the face of the dead, E.*Tr.*627, cf. *Hec.* 432, *Ion* 1421. II. *upper garment* or *mantle* in one piece, worn by women, π. ἑανός, ποικίλος Il.5.734, cf. Batr.182, Od.18.292, X.*Cyr.*5.1.6. 2. at Athens, the embroidered *robe* carried in procession at the Panathenaea, *IG*1².80.11; τὸν π... ἕλκουσ', ὀνεύοντες.. εἰς ἄκρον ὥσπερ ἱστίον τὸν ἱστόν Stratt.30; ὁ π. μεστὸς τῶν τοιούτων ποικιλμάτων Pl.*Euthphr.*6c, cf. E.*Hec.*468, Arist.*Ath.*49.3, 60.1. b. metaph. of a mythological work by Aristotle, Porph.ap.Eust.285.25: pl., Tz. ad Lyc.488. 3. less freq. of *a man's robe*, esp. of long Persian dresses, A.*Pers.*468, 1030 (lyr.), 1060 (lyr.), X.*Cyr.*3.1.13; *a man's cloak* or *robe*, S.*Tr.*602, al., E.*Cyc.*301, Theoc.7.17. III. *peritoneum*, dub. in Orph.*A.*312. IV. *wartweed*, *Euphorbia Peplus*, Hp.*Superf.*32, Dsc.4.167.

**πέπλῡφος**, ὁ, *weaver of* πέπλοι, *PTeb.*5.250 (ii B.C.).

**πέπλωμα**, ατος, τό, in Trag., *robe*, *garment*, A.*Th.*1044, S.*Tr.*613, E.*Supp.*97, *Trag.Adesp.*42 (= Ar.*Ach.*426).

**πέπνῡμαι**, Ep. pf. Pass. with pres. sense, *to be conscious*, *in full possession of one's faculties*, τῷ καὶ τεθνηῶτι νόον πόρε Περσεφόνεια οἴῳ πεπνῦσθαι· τοὶ δὲ σκιαὶ ἀΐσσουσιν Od.10.495; π. ἐν νεκύεσσι Call.*Lav. Pall.*129. 2. more freq. *to be wise*, πέπνυσαι.. νόῳ Il.24.377; οὔ σ' ἔτυμόν γε φάμεν πεπνῦσθαι Ἀχαιοί 23.440; imper. πέπνῠσο Thgn.29: plpf. with impf. sense, τά περ ἄλλα μάλιστα ἀνθρώπων πέπνῠσο Od.23.210: most freq. in part. πεπνυμένος, of persons, Il.3.203, Od.3.52; also of things, π. μῦθος, π. μήδεα, I.361, Il.7.278; στόμα Hsch.; πεπνυμένα ἀγορεύειν, βάζειν, etc., Od.19.352, Il.9.58, etc.; once in Hes., πεπνυμένα εἰδώς *Op.*731; in later Prose, πεπνυμένη ῥῆσις Anaxarch. 1; τὰ θεῖα πεπνυμένος Plu.*Num.*4; αἱ (v.l. οἱ) π. the *experts*, Aret.*SD*2.11.—In aor. opt. Pass., πνυθεὶς ἀκόνιτον *understand* it, Nic.*Al.* 13. 3. *breathe*, ζῶντες καὶ πεπν. ἄνδρες Plb.6.47.9; εἰκόνες Id.6.53.10. (From root πενῠ- which becomes πινῠ- in πινυτός (cf. Σικυών from Σεκυών, Λιβύη from Λεβύα), ἀπινύσσω; πνῠ- also in pr. n. Πνυταγόρας, πνυτός: not cogn. with πνέω, with which however it soon began to be confused, cf. ἄμπνυντο, ἀναπνέω I. 1.)

**πεποιημένως**, Adv. *as a made up* or *onomatopoeic word*, Sch.Il.15.607.

**πεποίθ-ησις**, εως, ἡ, *trust*, *confidence*, *boldness*, Lxx 4 *Ki.*18.19, Phld.*Lib.*p.22 O., Ph.2.444, *Ep.Eph.*3.12, Philum.*Ven.*2.4; π. ἐπὶ τῇ δυνάμει J.*AJ*1.3.1; ἡ ἀπὸ τοῦ θεοῦ π. ib.10.1.4: in pl., Babr.43.19. -ία, ἡ, = foreg., Hsch. -ότως, Adv. = πεπεισμένως, Lxx *Za.*14.11, D.Chr.12.26.

**πεποικιλμένως**, Adv. *in a manner diversified*, πολλαῖς ἰδιότησι Phld.*Po.*5.29.

**πεπονημένως**, Adv. pf. part. Pass., *elaborately*, Ael.*NA* in epilogo. 2. *with toil*, μόλις καὶ π. Agath.4.17.

**πέπονθα**, pf. of πάσχω.

**πεπονθ-έω**, *to be affected*, in aor. ἐπεπονθήθησα, Dam.*Pr.*60. -ησις, εως, ἡ, *passivity*, *modification*, Simp.*in Cat.*130.1, Dam.*Pr.*58, al.; opp. μέθεξις, ib.176.

**πεπονώδης**, ες, *somewhat puffy*, of the face in fever, Gal.7.466.

**πεπορεῖν**, v. πεπαρεῖν.

**πεπορθημένως**, Adv. *so as to be destroyed*, *AB*393, Suid. s.v. ἀναστάτως.

**πεπόσθαι**, v. πίνω. **πέποσθε, πέποσχα**, v. πάσχω.

**πεπρᾱδίλη** [ῐ], ἡ, (πέρδομαι) *crepitus ventris*, in pl. πετραδεῖλαι (sic), Hsch. (**πραδίλη** Theognost.*Can.*111). II. a kind of *fish*, Hsch. (pl.).

**πεπρίλος**, ὁ, a kind of *fish*, Hsch.

⊛ **πεπρωΐων** or **πεπρῴων**, dub. sens. (perh. gen. pl.) in *Rev.Phil.*2 (1928).192 (Erythrae, v B.C.).

**πέπρωται, πέπρωτο, πεπρωμένος**, v. *πόρω. **πέπτᾰμαι, πεπτᾰμένος**, v. πετάννυμι. **πεπτεῶτα**, v. πίπτω.

**πεπτήριος**, α, ον, = πεπτικός, κοιλίη, σπλάγχνον, Aret.*SD*2.7.

**πεπτηώς**, v. πτήσσω.

**πεπτ-ικός**, ή, όν, (πέσσω) *able to digest*, π. εἶναι τῆς τροφῆς Arist.*GA* 766ᵃ32; ἔχειν τὴν κοιλίαν.. πεπτικωτάτην ib.749ᵇ24; δύναμις π. *digestive* power, Dsc.1.14. II. *promoting digestion*, Arist.*PA*677ᵇ 32, *Long.*466ᵇ32, Thphr.*Lass.*16, Str.15.2.10, Xenocr.ap.Orib.2.58.98; πόα Dsc.3.31; φάρμακον Gal.11.779. III. *promoting concoction*, hence of the male seed, σπέρμα π. Zeno *Stoic.*1.36. -ός, ή, όν, *cooked*, E.*Fr.*467.4; ἄλφιτα καὶ π. σῖτα *PCair.Zen.*698.1 (iii B.C.); ἑφθὰ καὶ ὀπτὰ καὶ π. Plu.2.126d. -ρια, ἡ, *cook*, Hsch. s.v. σιτοποιός.

**πέπτω**, v. πέσσω. **πέπυσμαι**, v. πυνθάνομαι. **πεπωγμένον**· κεκλασμένον, Hsch.

**πέπων**, ον, gen. ονος: Comp. and Sup. πεπαίτερος, -τατος:—prop. of fruit, *cooked by the sun, ripe*, B.*Fr*.34, Hdt.4.23, S.*Fr*.181; ἄπιος Alex.33.5 (Sup.); opp. ὠμός, Ar.*Eq*.260, X.*Oec*.19.19; of wine, *mellow*, Ar.*Fr*.579, etc.; πέπονα ποιεῖν τινα, by beating him, *Com. Adesp*.125. b. of abscesses, *ripe, ready to suppurate*, Hermipp. 30. 2. σίκυος π. a kind of *gourd* or *melon, not eaten till quite ripe* (whereas the σίκυος was eaten unripe), Hp.*Morb*.3.17, *Vict*.2.55, Pl. Com.64.4, Anaxil.36, Arist.*Pr*.926b4, Diocl.*Fr*.120; πέπων alone distd. from σίκυος, τοὺς σικύους καὶ τοὺς πέπονας LXX *Nu*.11.5, cf. Speus.ap.Ath.2.68e, Phan.Hist.34, Dsc.2.135, etc.: prov., μαλθακώτερος πέπονος σικύου Theopomp.Com.72; ἀνὴρ ἐκεῖνος ἦν πεπαίτερος μόρων A.*Fr*.264; π. ἀπίοιο Theoc.7.120. II. metaph., as always in Hom. (more freq. in Il. than in Od.), and in Hes., in addressing a person, mostly as a term of endearment or familiarity, *kind, gentle*, πέπον Καπανηϊάδη Il.5.109; Κύκνε πέπον Hes.*Sc*.350; ὦ πέπον *good* brother!, *gentle* sir!, Il.6.55, 9.252, Hes.*Th*.544, 560, etc.; κριὲ πέπον my *pet* ram (says Polyphemus), Od.9.447: Comp., of a ἑταίρα, Xenarch.4.9: in bad sense, ὦ πέπονες *ye weaklings!* Il.2. 235. 2. *mild, less acrid*, ῥεύματα Hp.*VM*19 (Comp.): hence metaph., *mild, gentle*, πεπαιτέρα γὰρ μοῖρα τῆς τυραννίδος A.*Ag*.1365; μόχθος πέπων *softened* pain, S.*OC*437, etc.: c. dat., ἐχθροῖσι π. *gentle* to thy foes, A.*Eu*.66. (Cf. πέπειρος, πέσσω.)

**περ** (A), enclit. Particle, adding force to the word to which it is added, prob. a shortd. form of περί (q.v.) in the sense of *very much, however much*.—Chiefly Ep. and Lyr.; also in Trag. with relats. and parts.: 1. in Hom. freq. with Adj. and part. ὤν, ἐπεί μ' ἔτεκές γε μινυνθάδιόν π. ἐόντα *all* shortlived as I am, Il.1.352; φίλην π. ἐοῦσαν ib.587; Ἰθάκης κραναῆς π. ἐούσης 3.201: mostly concessive like καίπερ (q.v.), ἀγαθός π. ἐών *however* brave thou art, 1.131, al.; κρατερός π. ἐών 15.164; κυνεός π. ἐών 9.373; δουρικτητήν π. ἐοῦσαν ib.343; μέγαν π. ἐόντα 5.625: so in Trag., ἄελπτά π. ὄντα A.*Supp*.55 (lyr.); γενναῖός π. ὤν S.*Ph*.1068: with a Subst., ἀλόχῳ π. ἐούσῃ Il.1.546; γυνή π. οὖσα A.*Th*.1043: with Adj. and Subst., λιγύς π. ἐὼν ἀγορητής Il.2. 246: with καί preceding, καὶ κρατερός π. ἐών 15.195, etc.: with the part. ὤν omitted, φράδμων π. ἀνήρ *however* shrewd, 16.638; κρατερός π. 21.63; χερείονά π. 17.539; καὶ θεός π. A.*Ag*.1203, cf. 1084: with parts., ἱεμένων π. *however* eager, Il.17.292; καὶ ἀχνύμενός π. ἑταίρου grieved *though* he was for.., 8.125. 2. intens., ἐλεεινότερός π. more pitiable *by far*, 24.504; μίνυνθά π. for a *very* little, 1.416, 13.573; ὀλίγον π. 11.391; πρῶτόν π. first *of all*, 14. 295; ὑστάτιόν π. 8.353; ὀψέ π. Pi.*N*.3.80: to strengthen a negation, οὐδὲ.. π. not *even*, not *at all*, οὐδ' ὑμῖν ποταμός π. ἐΰρροος ἀρκέσει Il.21.130, cf. 8.201, 11.841, 21.410, Od.1.59, 3.236; μή ποτε καὶ σὺ γυναικί π. ἤπιος εἶναι 11.441; ἦν μή π. Hdt.6.57. 3. to give emphasis, ἀλλὰ καὶ αὐτοί π. πονεώμεθα Il.10.70; ἡμεῖς δ' αὐτοί π. φραζώμεθα 17.712; σθένος ἀνέρος ἀμφότεροί π. σχῶμεν 21.308: esp. *at any rate*, τιμήν π. μοι ὄφελλεν ἐγγυαλίξαι honour (*whatever else*) he owed me, 1.353, cf. 2.236, 17.121, 239; τόδε π. μοι ἐπικρήηνον ἐέλδωρ 8. 242: in imper. clauses with the pers. Pron., ἀλλὰ σύ π. μιν τῖσον *at all events*, 1.508: in the apodosis of a conditional sentence, εἰ δέ τοι Ἀτρεΐδης μὲν ἀπήχθετο.., σὺ δ' ἄλλους π... ἐλέαιρε 9.301, cf. 11.796, 12.349. II. after Conjs. and relat. words, with which it commonly coalesces: 1. after hypothetical Conjs., v. εἴπερ. 2. after temporal Conjs., ὅτε π. *just* when, Il.4.259, 5.802, etc.; ἦμος.. π. 11. 86; ὅταν π. S.*OC*301, etc.; πρίν π. before *even*, Il.15.588. 3. after causal Conjs., v. ἐπείπερ, ἐπειδήπερ; δι' ὅ τι π. *just* because, Hdt.4. 186. 4. after relats., v. ὅσπερ, οἷός περ, ὅσοσπερ, ἔνθαπερ, ὅθιπερ, οὗπερ, ᾗπερ, ὥσπερ. 5. after the comp. particle, v. ἤπερ, ἠέπερ. 6. after καί, v. καίπερ.

**περ** (B), Aeol. for περί.

⊕ **πέρᾱ** (A), Adv. *beyond, further*, μέχρι τοῦ μέσου καθιέναι, π. δ' οὔ Pl. *Phd*.112e; μέχρι τούτου.., π. δὲ μή Id.*R*.423b: with Art., τὸ π. λέγειν Id.*Phdr*.241d. 2. c. gen., π. ὅρου ἐλαύνειν *further than*, Lex ap.D. 23.44; τούτου μὴ π. προβαίνειν Arist.*Pol*.1319b14, cf. Pl.*Ti*.29d. II. of Time, *longer*, οὐκέτι π. ἐπολιόρκησαν X.*An*.6.1.28: with Art., τὸ π. καθεύδειν τοῦ πρέποντος Aeschin.Socr.52. 2. c. gen., π. μεσούσης τῆς ἡμέρας X.*An*.6.5.7; τῶν πεντήκοντα π. γεγονότας *above* fifty years old, Pl.*Lg*.670a (v.l. πέραν). III. freq. metaph., *beyond measure, extravagantly*, π. λέξαι, φράσαι, S.*El*.633, *Ph*.332, cf. E.*Hipp*. 1033; Ζεύς.. με λυπήσει πέρα Ar.*Av*.1246; π. ματεύειν S.*OC*211 (lyr.); μέλεα καὶ π. παθεῖν E.*El*.1187 (lyr.); οἵ τοι π. στέρξαντες οἶδε καὶ π. μισοῦσιν *Trag.Adesp*.78; τὸ π. Arr.*Fr*.123 J.; but π. is f.l. in S.*OC*1745 (lyr.). 2. c. gen., *more than, beyond, exceeding*, π. δίκης, καιροῦ π., A.*Pr*.30, 507; τοῦ εἰκότος π. S.*OT*74; π. τῶν νῦν εἰρημένων Id.*OC*257; π. τῶν νόμων Id.*El*.1506; π. τοῦ προσήκοντος Antipho 5.1; π. ὧν προσεδεχόμεθα Th.2.64; π. τοῦ δέοντος, π. τοῦ μετρίου, Pl.*Grg*.487d, *Ti*.65d; π. τοῦ μεγίστου φόβου Id.*Phlb*.12c; θαυμάτων π. *more than* marvels, E.*Hec*.714; δεινὸν καὶ π. δεινοῦ D.45.73; π. μεδίμνου *more than* a medimnus, Is.10.10; ἐλπίδος π. Plu.*Sull*.11. b. abs., *more, further*, οὐδὲν ἐρρήθη π. E.*IT*91; ἄπιστα καὶ π. κλύων things incredible, and *more than that*, Ar.*Av*. 417; πᾶν τολμήσασα καὶ π. S.*Fr*.189. 3. as Comp., folld. by ἤ, Id. *OC*651, *Ph*.1277. IV. *above, higher than*, τῶν ἐμῶν ἐχθρῶν μ' ἔνερθεν ὄντ' ἀνέστησας π. ib.666; π. ἀνθρώπου, π. τέχνης, Philostr. *Her*.18.1, 19.4.—In all senses πέρα may stand either before or after the gen., but commonly before.—Comp. περαίτερος, α, ον, Adv. περαίτερον and -τέρω (qq.v.); cf. sq.

⊕ **πέρα** (B), ἡ, = περαία, ἐκ πέρας Ναυπακτίας A.*Supp*.262; Χαλκίδος πέραν ἔχων Id.*Ag*.190 (lyr.):—hence **πέρανδε**, *to a foreign city*, *SIG* 56.13 (Argos, v B.C.).

**περαᾶν, περάασκε**, v. πέρνημι.

**περᾱγείς**, Boeot., = *περιαγής, *very reverend*, Corinn.*Supp*.2.86.

**περάγην**, = διέρρωγα, dub. in Rhinth.21.

**πέρᾱθεν**, Adv., (πέρα) *from beyond, from the far side*, E.*Heracl*.82 (lyr.), X.*HG*3.2.2: Ion. **πέρηθε** Hdt.6.33; **πέρηθεν** τοῦ Εὐφρήτεω Luc.*Syr.D*.13.

**περαίας**, ου, ὁ, a kind of *mullet* (κεστρεύς) *found beyond*, i.e. *at a distance from*, the bank, opp. πρόσγειος, Arist.*HA*591a23.

**περαίη**, ἡ, v. περαῖος.

⊕ **περαίνω**, Pi.*P*.10.28, Philol.1, etc.; poet. πειραίνω Arat.24: also impf. ἐπείραινε Pi.*I*.8(7).25: fut. περᾰνῶ Ar.*Pl*.563, Pl.*Lg*.672e; Ion. -ανέω, 3 sg. -εῖ, Hp.*Nat.Puer*.15, Meliss.5: aor. ἐπέρᾱνα S.*Aj*.22, Pl. *Tht*.207c; Ion. aor. part. πειρήνας *h.Merc*.48:—**Med.**, pres., Th.7.43: fut. περᾰνοῦμαι (δια-) Pl.*Phlb*.53c: aor. ἐπερανάμην (δι-) E.*Hel*.26, Pl.*Lg*.900b:—**Pass.**, fut. περανθήσομαι Gal.*UP*4.12 (περασθήσομαι is corrupt in Crito ap.Stob.3.3.63): aor. ἐπεράνθην X.*HG*3.2.19, Pl. *Grg*.501c, etc.: pf. 3 sg. πεπέρανται Id.*R*.502e, Arist.*Cael*.273a4; poet. πεπείρανται Od.12.37, S.*Tr*.581; imper. πεπεράνθω Pl.*Lg*.736b; inf. -άνθαι Id.*Grg*.472b, Arist.*Sens*.445b23, -άσθαι Id.*Xen*.977b3 (s.v.l.); part. πεπερασμένος Zeno Eleat.3, Pl.*Prm*.145a, Arist.*APo*. 82b32, al.: (πέρας):—*bring to an end, finish, accomplish*, Hom. only in Pass. (v. infr.); π. ἄταν A.*Ch*.830 (lyr.); πρᾶγος π. *rem transigere*, S. *Aj*.22; πρᾶγμα καὶ χρησμοὺς θεοῦ E.*Ion*1569; ἐλπίδα, δόκησιν, Id. *Andr*.1062, *Or*.636; π. τινὰ πρὸς ἔσχατον πλόον *bring* him *to the end of* his voyage, Pi.*P*.10.28; π. δίκας τινί Id.*I*.8(7).25; without δίκην, *finish the business*, D.38.24; π. τὰ δέοντα X.*Cyr*.4.5.38; τὸ προσταχθὲν ib.5.3.50; ἐπέραινεν ἐφ' οἷς ἐμισθώθη D.18.149; π. ὁδόν Ar.*Ra*. 403; πολλήν (sc. θάλασσαν) Arat.289:—Pass., *to be brought to an end, finished*, πάντα πεπείρανται Od.12.37, cf. S.*Tr*.581; περαίνεται δὴ τοὔργον A.*Pr*.57, etc.; *to be fulfilled, accomplished*, χρησμός, τὰ λόγια περαίνεται, E.*Ph*.1703, Ar.*V*.799; ἡ συμμαχία ἐπεραίνετο X.*HG* 7.4.3; ἔργῳ π. Id.*An*.3.2.32. 2. *limit*, Iamb.*Comm.Math*.3:—elsewh. Pass., *to be limited* or *finite*, τὸ ὅλον πεπεράνθαι Arist.*Ph*.207a 16; πεπέρανται [ὁ οὐρανός] Id.*Cael*.273a4; esp. in part. πεπερασμένος, opp. ἄπειρος, π. μέγεθος, χρόνος, Id.*Ph*.266b22, *Cael*.272a15. 3. in speaking, π. μῦθον, λόγον, *proceed with* a discourse, A.*Th*.1056, E.*Med*. 701; εἰπὲ καὶ π. πάντα A.*Pers*.699; π. ὅ τι λέγεις Ar.*Pl*.648: abs., περὶ σωφροσύνης ἤδη.. περανῶ ib.563, cf. *Ra*.1283; πέραιν' ὥσπερ ἦρξω Pl.*Prt*.353b; πέραινε· σωθεὶς δὲ.. Men.65.5. 4. *recite from beginning to end*, ἰαμβεῖον Ar.*Ra*.1170, cf. D.19.245; τραγῳδίαν Antiph.1. 6, cf. 85.4; νόμον Pl.*Ti*.29d; *recount, relate*, E.*Ion*362, *IT*781. 5. abs., *effect one's purpose*, esp. with a neg., οὐδὲν π. *come to* no *issue, make* no *progress*, περαίνει δ' οὐδὲν ἡ προθυμία Id.*Ph*.589, cf. Th.6.86, Lys.8.8; ἰατρευόμενοι.. οὐδὲν περαίνουσι Pl.*R*.426a; ἵνα τι περαίνωμεν ib.346a; περαίνειν ἤδη ὥρα X.*An*.3.2.32. 6. *draw a conclusion, infer*, διὰ τοῦ ἀδυνάτου π. by a reductio ad impossibile, Arist.*APr*. 41a23; ὁ περαίνων [λόγος], a kind of syllogism, D.L.7.44; περὶ τῶν π. λ., title of work by Chrysippus:—freq. in Pass., τὸ ἐν πλείοσι σχήμασι.. περαινόμενον *the conclusion which is drawn*, Arist.*APr*. 42b30, etc.; περαίνεται c. acc. et inf., *it is inferred* that.., Muson.*Fr*.1 p.2 H., cf. Phld.*Rh*.1.137 S. II. sens. obsc., Artem.1.80, D.L.2. 127:—Pass., *Com.Adesp*.14, *AP*11.339, D.L.l.c. III. intr., *reach, penetrate*, δι' ὤτων A.*Ch*.57 (lyr.); εἰς τὸν ἐγκέφαλον Arist.*HA*492a21; πρὸς [τὴν καρδίαν] Id.*PA*666a13; εἰς τὸ ἔξω Id.*GA*716b28: abs., *penetrate*, Id.*HA*497a10. 2. *come to an end*, τὸ πεπερασμένον ἀεὶ πρός τι περαίνει the finite always *comes to* some *limit*, Id.*Ph*.203b 21, cf. *Xen*.977b6; *end in*.., εἴς τι E.*Fr*.340, cf. Pl.*Men*.76a, Plu. *Arat*.52, etc.; ἡ ὁδὸς π. ἐπὶ τὸ στρατόπεδον Id.*Cat.Ma*.13. IV. *pierce*, *h.Merc*.48.

**περαι-όθεν**, Adv. = πέραθεν, A.R.4.71, Arat.606. **-ος** (properisp.), α, ον, (πέραν) *on the further side* or *bank*, ἤπειρος, γαῖα, A.R. 2.392, 4.848; τὰ π. Call.*Fr*.1.15 P. 2. Comp., περαιότερόν τι anything *further*, *PFay*.124.8 (ii A.D.). II. Subst., ἡ περαία (sc. γῆ, χώρα) *the country on the other side of the river*, etc., Str.4.1.12; τῆς χώρας τῆς π. *SIG*588.29 (Milet., ii B.C.): freq. with gen. whether partitive or objective, ἡ π. τῆς Βοιωτίης χώρης *the part* of Boeotia *over against* [Chalcis], Hdt.8.44; ἡ π. τῆς Ἀσίας *the coast* of Asia *over against* [Rhodes], D.S.20.97 (but ἡ τῶν Ῥοδίων π. Str.14.2.1, 14.5.11: hence pr. n. ἡ Περαία, Plb.18.2.3, 18.6.3; also of *the country beyond* Jordan, J.*BJ*3.3.3, St.Byz.); πᾶσα περαίη Θρηϊκίης all *the opposite coast* of Thrace, A.R.1.1112; ἡ Τενεδίων π. *the coast* [of the Troad] *opposite to* Tenedos, Str.13.1.32. ⊕ **-όω**, *carry over* or *across*, στρατιὰν πλείω ἐπεραίωσε Th.4.121, cf. Plu.*Crass*.10, al.; π. τοὺς στρατιώτας εἰς τὴν Λιβύην Plb.1.66.1; ἐπὶ Καρχηδόνα τὸν στόλον Plu.2.196c: metaph., ἡ ψυχὴ διὰ φιλοσοφίας ἐπεραιώθη Arist.*Mu*.391a12: c. dupl. acc., τοὺς λοιποὺς π. τὸ ῥεῖθρον Plb.3.113.6:—Pass. (with fut. Med. in Th.1.10), *pass over, cross*, μὴ φθέωσι περαιωθέντες ἐκεῖνοι Od.24.437; πῶς περαιωθήσομαι; Ar.*Ra*.138 (nowh. else in Poets); περαιοῦσθαι ναυσὶν ἐπ' ἀλλήλους Th.1.5; περαιωθεὶς Id.4.120; ἐς νῆσον π. Id.5.109; εἰς τὴν Ἀσίαν X.*An*.7.2.12: c. acc. loci, ἐπεραιώθη τὸν Ἀράξεα Hdt.1.209; περαιωθεὶς (sc. τὸν Ἑλλήσποντον) Id.5.14; τὸ πέλαγος Th.1.10; τὸν Ἰόνιον Id.6.34. 2. intr. in Act., ἔμελλον τὸν Ἑλλήσποντον περαιώσειν Id.2.67. 3. in Pass., *pass through*, of cauteries, Hp.*Art*.11, cf. *Oss*.7, Aret.*SD*1.7. II. = περαίνω, *complete* a transaction, etc., *Leg.Gort*.7.11, *GDI*4998 vii 15, dub. in Epicur.*Nat*.2.6:—Pass., ἔνθα αἱ συνουσίαι περαιοῦνται Ruf.*Anat*.64; ὁ -ούμενος χρόνος Vett.Val.276.

34 :—περαιωθέντων is f.l. for περανθέντων in X.*HG*2.4.39 ; περαιοῦται (*is bounded*) shd. perh. be περατοῦται in Philol.[21].

**✻περαίτερος**, α, ον, Comp. of πέρα (A), *beyond*, ὁδοὶ περαίτεραι roads *leading farther*, Pi.*O*.9.105. II. Adv. **περαιτέρω**, *further*, μανθάνειν π. E.*Ph*.1681 ; ἓν οἶδα κοὐ π. Id.*IT*247 ; δεινὰ καὶ π. Ar.*Th*.705 ; βουλυτὸς ἢ π. Id.*Av*.1500 ; οὐδὲν ὅ τι οὐ ξυνέβη καὶ ἔτι π. Th.3.81 ; π. τι λέγειν Antipho 5.65 ; φιλοσοφεῖν Thphr.*Char*.23.4. 2. c. gen., τῶνδε καὶ π. A.*Pr*.249 ; π. τοῦ μετρίου X.*Mem*.3.13.5 ; π. τοῦ δέοντος Pl. *Grg*.484c ; π. τόλμης Plu.*Galb*.8 : abs., π. (sc. τοῦ δέοντος) πεπραγμένα *beyond what is fit, too far*, S.*Tr*.663 : neut. περαίτερον as Adv., π. ἄλλων *beyond, better than* others, Pi.*O*.8.63.

**Περαΐτης** [ῑ], ου, ὁ, *native of Peraea* (cf. περαῖος II), J.*BJ*2.20.4, Sch. Ar.*Av*.823.

**✻περαίωσις**, εως, ἡ, *crossing over*, Str.12.5.1, al., Plu.*Tim*.16.

**✻πέρᾱμα**, ατος, τό, *ferry*, Just.*Nov*.59.5, *Gloss*.

**πέρᾱν**, Ion. and Ep. **πέρην**, Adv. *on the other side, across*, in early Poets always c. gen., esp. of water, νήσων αἳ ναίουσι π. ἁλὸς Il.2.626 ; πέρνασχ' ὅν τιν' ἕλεσκε π. ἁλός 24.752 (never in Od.) ; π. κλυτοῦ Ὠκεανοῖο Hes.*Th*.215 ; π. Χάεος ζοφεροῖο ib.814 ; π. πόντοιο Pi.*N*.5.21 ; τὰ π. τοῦ Ἴστρου Hdt.5.9 ; πόντου π. τραφεῖσαν A.*Ag*.1200 ; πολιοῦ π. πόντου S.*Ant*.334 (lyr.) ; π. τοῦ Ἑλλησπόντου, τοῦ ποταμοῦ, Th.2.67, X. *An*.4.3.3 ; π. Ἕβρον is corrupt in E.*HF*386 (leg. Ἕβρου). 2. abs., *on the other side*, esp. of water, προσορμίζεσθαι.. π. ἐν τῇ Ῥηναίῃ Hdt. 6.97 ; π. εἶναι X.*An*.2.4.20, 3.5.12, etc. ; π. γενέσθαι ib.6.5.22. 3. with Verbs of motion, folld. by εἰς, *over* or *across to*.., π. ἐς τὴν Ἀχαιίην διέπεμψαν Hdt.8.36 ; π. εἰς τὴν Ἀσίαν διαβῆναι X.*An*.7.2.2 ; διαπλεύσαντες π. τῆς Ἀκαρνανίας ἐς Οἰνιάδας Th.1.111 ; also without εἰς, ἐκ Θάσου διαβαλόντες π. having crossed *over* (sc. ἐς τὴν ἤπειρον), Hdt.6.44. 4. freq. c. Art., διαβιβάζεσθαι εἰς τὸ π. τοῦ ποταμοῦ X.*An*. 3.5.2 ; διέβη εἰς τὸ π. Id.*HG*1.3.17 ; ἐν τῷ π. Id.*An*.4.3.11 ; τὰ π. things *done on the opposite side*, ib.4.3.24 ; τὰ π. πράγματα, opp. τὰ ἐπὶ τάδε, Plb.3.97.5 ; οἱ π. those *on the other side*, Plu.*Mar*.23 ; ἡ ὄχθη ἡ π. Arr.*An*.5.10.2. II. *over against, opposite*, c. gen., π. ἱερῆς Εὐβοίης Il.2.535 : freq. in Paus., 2.22.2, 5.15.8, al. III. less freq. = πέρα (A), *beyond*, c. gen., π. Νείλοιο παγᾶν Pi.*I*.6(5).23 ; π. γε πόντου καὶ τόπων Ἀτλαντικῶν E.*Hipp*.1053, cf. *Alc*.585 (lyr.), *Supp*.676. IV. *right through*, καῦσις [ἔστω] μὴ πέρην Hp.*Mochl*.37 ; ἐς τὸ π. Id.*Art*. 11.—π. c. gen. usu. precedes its case, but follows it in A. l. c., Paus. 5.15.8. (Cf. πέρα (B).)

**πέρανδε**, v. πέρα (B).

**περαν-τέον**, *one must bring to an end*, Gal.4.460. **-της**, ου, ὁ, = *paedicator*, Sch.Theoc.13 (Pap.). **-τικός**, ή, όν, *conclusive*, Ar. *Eq*.1378 ; π. λόγος, a kind of syllogism, *Stoic*.2.77, cf. Gal.18(1). 219. II. περαντικά, τά, dub. sens. in *POxy*.2032.61 (vi A. D.).

**περάπτων**, Aeol. for περιάπτων, Pi.*P*.3.52.

**✻πέρᾰς**, Ep. **πεῖραρ** (q. v.), ἄτος, τό, *end, limit, boundary*, I. in local sense, ἐκ περάτων γᾶς Alc.33.1, cf. Th.1.69 ; π... αὐλ(ε)ιος θύρα ἐλευθέρᾳ γυναικὶ νενόμιστ' οἰκίας Men.546 ; τὸ π. *tip*, τοῦ αἰδοίου Arist. *GA*773ᵃ21 ; [τῆς ῥινός] Gal.18(2).28 ; τισὶ τὰ π. ἀλγέει *the extremities*, Aret.*SD*1.7. II. generally, *limit*, either opp. ἀρχή, Arist.*Ph*.264ᵇ 27, or including it, τελευτή γε καὶ ἀρχὴ π. ἑκάστου Pl.*Prm*.137d, cf. Arist.*GA*777ᵇ29, *Metaph*.1022ᵃ4 ; οὐκ ἔχων π. κακῶν E.*Andr*.1216, cf. *Or*.511, A.*Pers*.632, Lys.12.88, etc. ; π. ἅπασιν ἀνθρώποις ἐστὶ τοῦ βίου θάνατος D.18.97, cf. Arist.*EN*1115ᵃ26 ; εἰ π. μηδὲν ἔσται σφίσι τοῦ ἀπαλλαγῆναι τοῦ κινδύνου Th.7.42 ; π. ἔχειν, = περαίνεσθαι, *come to an end*, Isoc.4.5, Lycurg.60, etc. ; π. λαμβάνειν Plb.5.31.2 ; ἐπιθεῖναι τῇ γενέσει π. Arist.*GA*776ᵃ4 ; ἐν π. εἶναι Thphr.*CP*5.18.2. 2. *perfection* of a thing, τὸ π. τῆς μαγειρικῆς.. εὑρηκέναι Hegesipp.Com. 1.4, cf. 10, Posidipp.26.17. b. Philos., τὸ τῶν ἀγαθῶν π., τὰ π. τῆς ἡδονῆς, Epicur.*Ep*.3 p.65 U., *Sent*.20 ; ἐν τῷ κατὰ φύσιν π. κατακέκλειται τἀγαθόν Metrod.*Herc*.831.8. 3. *end, object*, εὐχῆς, ἐλπίδος, Luc.*Harm*.2 sq. 4. Philos., *that which limits* or *has limits*, opp. τὸ ἄπειρον, Pythag.ap.Arist.*Metaph*.986ᵃ23, Pl.*Phlb*.30a, etc. ; τὰ ἐλάχιστα καὶ ἀμιγῆ π. [τῆς ἀτόμου] Epicur.*Ep*.1 p.17 U. : Com., of a person, τὸν καλούμενον Π. Philosteph.Com.1.3. III. *final decision*, [οἱ] τὸ π. ἔχοντες τῶν ἐν τῇ πόλει ἁπάντων δικαίων the supreme court, from which there is no appeal, Din.3.16. IV. πέρας as Adv., *at length, at last*, Aeschin.1.61, Plb.2.55.6, etc. ; πέρας δ' οὖν D.56.10 ; τὸ π. Lys.9.17, Alex.261.13 ; but also, τὸ π. 'to cut a long story short', Men.*Epit*.70, 316, 470. [In Aeol. the first syll. is short in Alc.33, long in 84.]

**περ-άσιμος** [ᾰ], ον, (περάω A) *that may be crossed, passable*, ἀὴρ αἰετῷ π. E.*Fr*.1047 ; ποταμοί Arr.*An*.5.9.4, cf. Scymn.818, Str.7.4.1 ; ᾗ μάλιστα π. ἦν [τὸ ῥεῦμα] Plu.*Luc*.27 ; θαλάσσας.. π. μόχθον the labour *of crossing* the sea, *Hymn.Is*.35. **-ᾱσις**, εως, ἡ, *crossing*, βίου π. *a completing* of life, S.*OC*103. 2. Pythag. name for *nine*, *Theol.Ar*.57. **-ασμός**, ὁ, (περαίνω) *finishing*, Lxx *Ec*.4.8, 16, 12.12.

**περᾰτ-εύω**, = περαίνω, Hsch. **-η**, ἡ, fem. of πέρατος (wh. is not found) (sc. χώρα), *farthest quarter, extremity* of the heavens, whether East, A.R.1.1281, or (more freq.) West, Od.23.243, Call.*Del*. 169. 2. of the *southern hemisphere*, Arat.499. **-θεν**, Adv. = πέραθεν, A.R.4.54, Man.3.417, Orph.*L*.606.

**περᾰτ-ής**, οῦ, ὁ, (περάω A) = πορθμεύς, Suid. s. h. v., Procl.*Par.Ptol*. 250. II. *wanderer, emigrant*, Lxx *Ge*.14.13 : expl. of Ἑβραῖος, Ph.1.439. **✻-ικός**, ή, όν, *coming from abroad, foreign*, λίβανος *Peripl.M.Rubr*.8, 10, 11.

**περᾰτοειδής**, ές, *of limited* or *finite nature*, opp. ἄπειρος, Pl.*Phlb*. 25d, Procl.*Inst*.90 : Comp. -έστερος Dam.*Pr*.50.

**περᾱτός**, Ion. **περητός**, ή, όν, (περάω A) = περάσιμος, Γαδείρων τὸ πρὸς ζόφον οὐ π. Pi.*N*.4.69 ; ποταμὸς νηυσὶ π. *navigable*, Hdt.1.189, al. (better νηυσιπέρητος) ; τάφρος οὐ π. Plu.*Pyrrh*.28. 2. = περατικός, *PCair.Zen*.536.7 (iii B. C.).

**περᾰτ-όω**, (πέρας) *limit, bound*, Str.2.3.1, al. ; νύκτα καὶ ἡμέραν ἀνατολαῖς καὶ δύσεσιν Ph.1.347 ; π. τὴν ὕλην ἄπειρον οὖσαν Plu.2.719d ; αὐτὴ [μέθοδος] περατοῖ τοῦτο [τὸ ἄπειρον] S.E.*M*.1.81 :—Med., ἡ σελήνη τὸν ἑαυτῆς κύκλον περατοῦται Ph.2.240 :—Pass., Arist. *de An*.407ᵃ28, *Mu*.391ᵇ15, Plu.2.389f ; *to be terminated, finished off*, Aret.*SD*1.7 (dub. cj.), Gal.18(2).766. b. Gramm. in Pass., *terminate*, εἰς ῡς A.D.*Pron*. 95.6, al. ; of verses, εἰς μέρος λόγου Heph.1.4 ; ἕως ὀκτωκαιδεκασήμου Aristid.Quint.1.14. II. *bring to an end*, λόγον *Corp.Herm*.18. 11 ; *accomplish*, τὴν διάβασιν τριήρει J.*AJ*19.1.1 (s. v. l.). **-ωσις**, εως, ἡ, *ending*, φλεβῶν Aret.*SA*2.8 (pl.). 2. *consummation*, Plot. 4.4.20. **-ωτικός**, ή, όν, *limitative*, Simp.*in Ph*.456.16, Dam.*Pr*.232 ; δυνάμεις Procl.*in Prm*.p.567 S. **-ωτός**, ή, όν, *subject to limitation*, Dam.*Pr*.315.

**περάω** (A), late Ep. part. περόων *IG*12(8).441.3 (Thasos), *Epigr.Gr*. 1068.8 (Syria) ; Ep. inf. περάαν Od.5.174 : Ion. impf. περάασκε ib.480 : fut. περάσω [ᾱ], Ion. and Ep. περήσω Il.5.646 ; inf. περησέμεναι 12. 200 : aor. ἐπέρᾱσα, Ion. and Ep. ἐπέρησα, πέρησα Od.24.118 (ἐπέρασσα f.l. in 5.409, late opt. περάσειας [ᾰ] D.P.608) ; Aeol. ἐπέραισα Alc. *Supp*.7.8 : pf. πεπέρᾱκα A.*Pers*.65 (lyr.), Eup.192 :—*drive right through*, λευκοὺς δ' ἐπέρησεν ὀδόντας Il.5.291. 2. more freq. *pass right across* or *through* a space, *traverse*, freq. of water, θάλασσαν, πόντον, Od.6.272, 24.118 ; λαῖτμα θαλάσσης 5.174 ; ὕδωρ Hes.*Op*. 738 ; Ἀχέροντα Alc. l. c. ; ἅλα Pi.*N*.3.21 ; Τάναϊν Hdt.4.115 ; πόντου φλοῖσβον, [ποταμόν], A.*Pr*.792, 718 ; πέλαγος Αἰγαῖον S.*Aj*.461 ; also *pass* a barrier or boundary, πύλας Ἀΐδαο περήσει Il.5.646, cf. Thgn. 427 ; [τάφρος] ἀργαλέη περάαν hard *to pass*, Il.12.63, cf. 53, al. ; τὰς φυλακὰς π. *pass* the guards, secretly or by force, Hdt.3.72 ; π. Τεύθραντος ἄστυ Μυσῶν A.*Supp*.549 (lyr.) ; γῆς ὁρίσματα E.*Rh*.437 : metaph., κίνδυνον π. *pass through* a danger, A.*Ch*.270 ; π. πλοῦς *accomplish* them, X.*Oec*.21.3 (s. v. l.) ; π. ὅρκον, prob. *go beyond, transgress* the oath, A.*Eu*.489 (sed leg. πορόντας). 3. less freq. of Time, *pass through, complete*, τέλος δωδεκάμηνον περᾶσαι an office of twelve months' duration, Pi.*N*.11.10 ; τοῦ βίου τέρμα S.*OT*1530 ; τὴν τελευταίαν ἡμέραν E.*Andr*.102 ; οἱ τὴν ἡλικίαν πεπερακότες X.*Lac*. 4.7. II. intr., *penetrate, pierce*, of a pointed weapon, Il.21.594 ; of violent rain, οὔτ' ὄμβρος περάασκε διαμπερές Od.5.480, cf. 19.442 ; διὰ κροτάφοιο through the temples, Il.4.502 ; ὀστέον εἴσω into the bone, ib.460 ; *extend, reach* to a place, οὐδαμοῖ π. X.*Cyn*.8.5. 2. *pass*, δι' Ὠκεανοῖο Od.10.508 ; διὰ (or διὲκ) προθύροιο *h.Merc*.271, 158 ; ὡς ὁπότ' ὠκὺ νόημα διὰ στέρνοιο περήσῃ ib.43 ; ἐπὶ πόντον, ἐφ' ὑγρήν, Il.2.613, Od.4.709 ; διὰ πόρον *across* the strait, A.*Pers*.501 ; διὰ Κυανέας ἀκτὰς *through* the Symplegades, E.*Andr*.864 (lyr.) ; διὰ ῥοάς Id.*Rh*.919 ; ἐπ' οἶδμα Id.*IT*417 (lyr.) ; ὑπ' οἴδμασιν S.*Ant*.337 (lyr.) ; μή σε λάθῃ.. ταύτῃ περῶν Ar.*Av*.1195. 3. *pass to* or *from* a place, εἰς Ἀΐδαο Thgn.906 ; ποτὶ Φᾶσιν Pi.*I*.2.41 ; εἰς χώραν A.*Pers*. 65 (lyr.) ; ἐξ ἐνέρων Id.*Pr*.572 (lyr.) ; ἐκ δόμων, ἔξω δωμάτων, S.*Ant*. 386, *OT*531 ; γῆς ἔξω E.*Med*.272 ; δόμων ἔσω Id.*Or*.1572 ; ποῖ περῶ ; Id. *Ph*.981 : c. acc. loci, π. Δελφοὺς ib.980 ; μέλαθρα, δόμους, ib.299 (lyr.), *Hipp*.782. 4. rarely of Time, διὰ γήρως π. X.*Mem*.2.1.31 ; εὐδαίμων π. *live* happy, Orac.ap.X.*Cyr*.7.2.20. 5. *pass all bounds*, S.*OC*155 (lyr.) : c. gen., θυμοῦ π. in wrath, Id.*OT*674. 6. with instrument of motion in acc., π. πόδα E.*Hec*.53.

***περάω** (B), v. πέρνημι. **περβέβαται**, v. περιβαίνω III.

**περγάμιον**· δήμιον, Hsch.

**Πέργᾰμος**, ἡ, *Pergamus*, the citadel of Troy, Il.5.446, etc. ; τὸ Πριάμου **Πέργᾰμον** Hdt.7.43 : pl., τὰ Πέργαμα S.*Ph*.347, 1334, E.*Tr*. 556 (lyr.), etc. ; Πέργαμα Τρωίας Stesich.32 ; τἀπὶ Τροίᾳ Π. S.*Ph*.353, 611 :—also **Περγᾰμία**, ἡ, Pi.*I*.6(5).31. 2. generally, *citadel, acropolis*, A.*Pr*.956, E.*Ph*.1098, 1176. II. *Pergamum* in Mysia, X. *HG*3.1.6, etc. :—also **Πέργᾰμον**, τό, Plb.4.48.11 : Adj. **✻Περγαμηνός**, ή, όν : Π., ἡ, *district of P.*, Str.12.8.2 ; also, *parchment*, introduced there, Suid. (pl.) : so in neut. pl., Ῥωμαῖοι τὰ μέμβρανα Περγαμηνὰ καλοῦσιν Lyd.*Mens*.1.28.

**Περγασή**, ἡ, a deme of the φυλὴ Ἐρεχθηΐς : **Περγασῆθεν** *from P.*, Is.*Fr*.73 ; **Περγασῆσι** *at P.*, Ar.*Eq*.321 ; **Περγασήνδε** *to P.*, St.Byz.

**✻πέργουλος**, ὁ, a small bird (Argive (?)), Hsch. **πέργουν**· πρέσβεις, Id. **πέρδησις**, f.l. for πράδησις (q. v.).

**περδῐκ-ειος** [ῐ], α, ον, *of a partridge*, κρέα Poll.6.33, cf. Suid. **-ιάς**, άδος, ἡ, = περδίκιον II, Gal.12.885. **-ιδεύς**, έως, ὁ, *young partridge*, Eust.753.56. **-ικός**, ή, όν, *of* or *for a partridge*, οἰκίσκος Ar.*Fr*. 406. **-ιον**, τό, Dim. of πέρδιξ, Eub.123, Ephipp.15.8. II. a plant, *Polygonum maritimum*, Thphr.*HP*1.6.11 ; = ἑλξίνη, Dsc.4. 85 (also ἡ περδίκιος βοτάνη Hsch. s. v. ἑλξίνη). **-ίτης** [ῑτ] (sc. λίθος), ὁ, a kind of stone, Alex.Trall.12.

**περδῑκο-θήρας**, ου, ὁ, *partridge-catcher*, name of a species of *hawk*, Ael.*NA*12.4. **-τροφεῖον**, τό, *partridge-coop*, Hyp.*Fr*.45. **-τρόφος**, ον, *keeping partridges*, Str.14.2.5.

**✻πέρδιξ**, Cret. **πήριξ** Hsch., ῑκος S.*Fr*.323, Nicopho 18, ῐκος Archil. 106, Epich.84, ὁ and ἡ :—*partridge*, Ar.*Av*.767 ; οἱ ὄρτυγες καὶ οἱ π. X.*Mem*.2.1.4 ; σκοπέλων μεταναάστρια π. *AP*7.204 (Agath.) : prov., πέρδιξ ὄρουσον 'look sharp', Ar.*Fr*.523.

**✻πέρδομαι**, *break wind*, Ar.*Ach*.30, etc. : aor. ἔπαρδον only in compds., v. ἀπο-, κατα-πέρδομαι : pf. πέπορδα in pres. sense, Id.*Pax* 335 : plpf. 3 sg. ἐπεπόρδει as impf., Id.*V*.1305. (Cf. Skt. *pardate*, etc. 'break wind'.)

**πέρηθεν, πέρην,** Ion. and Ep. for πέρᾱθεν, πέραν.

**περητήριον,** τό, (περάω A) *borer*, Hp.ap.Gal.19.129.

**περητός,** ή, όν, Ion. for περᾱτός.

**περήτρια·** ἡ περιαγγέλλουσα τὴν ὥραν, Suid.

® **πέρθω,** Il.18.342: fut. πέρσω 21.584: aor. 1 ἔπερσα Od.1.2, al.; Ep. inf. περσέμεν Q.S.12.20: aor. 2 ἔπρᾰθον Pi.*Pae*.6.91; poet. πράθον Id.*N*.7.35; also Ep. (cf. δια-, ἐκ-πέρθω), but in Hom. aor. 1 is more common: Ion. impf. πέρθεσκον A.R.1.800:—**Pass.**, pres. and impf., Il.2.374, 12.15: fut. Med. πέρσομαι in pass. sense, 24.729: aor. inf. Pass. πέρθαι 16.708:—poet. Verb, *waste, ravage, sack*, in Hom. only of towns, Il.18.342, Od.1.2, al.: freq. in later poets, Orac.ap.Hdt.7.220 (Pass.), Corinn.16, Pi.*N*.7.35, etc.:—Pass., πόλιν περθομέναν ἀτίμως A.*Th*.325 (lyr.). **2.** of persons, *destroy, slay*, στρατόν Pi.*O*.10(11).32; ἀνθρώπους S.*Aj*.1198 (lyr.); δείματα θηρῶν E.*HF*700 (lyr.); and even of one man, ἔπραθέ [νιν] φασγάνου ἀκμᾷ Pi.*P*.9.81, cf. *N*.3.37; μήτε μ' ἂν νόσον μήτ' ἄλλο πέρσαι μηδέν S.*OT*1456: metaph., of love, E.*Hipp*.542 (lyr.); of fire, πυρὶ περθόμενοι δέμας Pi.*P*.3.50. **3.** of things, γενείου πέρθε τρίχα A.*Pers*.1056; φύλλον ἐλαίης..χερὶ πέρσας S.*OC*703 (lyr.). **II.** *get by plunder, take* at the sack of a town, τὰ μὲν πολίων ἐξ ἐπράθομεν Il.1.125; δμωαὶ..ἃς ἔπερσ' ἐμὸς πατήρ E.*El*.316.

® **περί,** Thess., Delph. **περ** *IG*9(2).517.17 (iii B.C.), al., *Schwyzer* 323 *A* 4 (v/iv B.C.), also Aeol., v. infr. A. v; Elean **παρ** ib.413.4: Prep. with gen., dat., and acc.:—*round about, all round* (prop. different from ἀμφί, *on both sides*). (Cogn. with Skt. *pári* 'round about'.)

A. WITH GENITIVE, **I.** of Place, sts. in Poets, *round about, around*, τετάνυστο π. σπείους ἡμερίς Od.5.68; τείχη π. Δαρδανίας E.*Tr*.818 (lyr., s.v.l.); εἴλυμα π. χροός A.R.2.1129: rarely, like ἀμφί, *on both sides*, v. περιβαίνω I fin. **2.** *about, near*, π. σοῦ πάντα γένοιτο ῥόδα *IG*14.2508 (Nemausus). **II.** to denote the object *about* or *for* which one does something: **1.** with Verbs of fighting or contending, π. τινός *for* an object—from the notion of the thing's lying in the middle to be fought *about*, π. τῶνδε *for* these prizes, Il.23.659; π. πτόλιος..μαχήσεται 18.265; π. Πατρόκλοιο θανόντος ib.195, cf. 17.120; π. σεῖο 3.137; π. νηὸς ἔχον πόνον 15.416; ἀμύνεσθαι π. πάτρης, π. νηῶν, π. τέκνων, 12.243, 142, 170, etc.; δόλους καὶ μῆτιν ὕφαινον, ὥς τε π. ψυχῆς since it was *for* my life, Od.9.423; π. ψυχῆς θέον Ἕκτορος Il.22.161; π. ψυχέων ἐμάχοντο Od.22.245; in Prose, τρέχειν π. ἑωυτοῦ, π. τῆς ψυχῆς, Hdt.7.57, 9.37; ἀγῶνας δραμέονται π. σφέων αὐτῶν Id.8.102; νεναυμάχηκε τὴν π. τῶν κρεῶν Ar.*Ra*.191; ⟨τὸν⟩ π. τοῦ παντὸς δρόμον θέοντες Hdt.8.74; κινδυνεύειν π. τινός ibid., etc.; οὐ π. τῶν ἴσων ὁ κίνδυνός ἐστι X.*HG*7.1.7; and without a Verb, π. γῆς ὅρων διαφοραί Th.1.122; π. πάντων ἀγαθῶν ὁ ἀγών X.*Cyr*.3.3.44, cf. S.*Aj*.936 (lyr.), etc.; μάχη π. τινός Pl.*Tht*.179d; ἐπειγόμενοι π. νίκης Il.23.437, cf. 639, Hdt.8.26; πεῖραν θανάτου π. καὶ ζωᾶς ἀναβάλλεσθαι Pi.*N*.9.29; π. θανάτου φεύγειν Antipho 5.95; but ἐρίσσαι π. μύθων contend *about* speaking, i.e. who can speak best, Il.15.284; καὶ ἀθανάτοισιν ἐρίζεσκον π. τόξων Od.8.225, cf. 24.515. **2.** with words which denote care or anxiety, *about, on account of*, π. Τρώων..μερμηρίζειν Il.20.17; ἄχος π. τινός Od.21.249; φόνου π. βουλεύειν 16.234; φροντίζειν π. τινός Hdt.8.36, etc.; κήδεσθαι π. τ. S.*Ph*.621; δεδιέναι π. τ. Pl.*Prt*.320a, etc.; ἀπολογεῖσθαι π. τ. X.*Cyr*.2.2.13; κρίνειν, διαγιγνώσκειν π. τ., Pi.*N*.5.40, Antipho 5.96; π. τ. ψηφίζεσθαι, διαψηφίζεσθαι, ψῆφον φέρειν, *IG*1$^2$.57.42, X.*HG*2.3.50, Lycurg.11; βουλεύεσθαι π. τῆς κοινῆς σωτηρίας Isoc.5.69; π. Μεθωναίων *IG*1$^2$.57.49; διανοεῖσθαι, σκοπεῖν π. τινός, Pl.*Phdr*.270d, *Phd*.65e; μαντεύεσθαι π. τ. Hdt.8.36, cf. S.*Tr*.77; π. πότου γοῦν ἐστί σοι; so with you it is a question *of* drink? Ar.*Eq*.87, cf. Plu.2.43b. **3.** with Verbs of hearing, knowing, speaking, etc., *about, concerning*, π. νόστου ἄκουσα Od.19.270; οἶδα γὰρ εὖ π. κείνου 17.563; π. πομπῆς μνησόμεθα 7.191; π. πατρὸς ἐρέσθαι 1.135, 3.77; π. τινὸς ἐρέειν, λέγειν, λόγον ποιήσασθαι, etc., Hdt.1.5, S.*OT*707, X.*Cyr*.1.6.13, etc.; λέγειν καὶ ἀκούειν π. ἑκάστου Th.4.22, etc.; λόγος π. τινός Pl.*Prt*.347b, etc.; ἡ π. τινὸς φήμη Aeschin.1.48; π. τινὸς ἀγγεῖλαι, κηρῦξαι, S.*El*.1111, *Ant*.193; π. τινὸς διελθεῖν, διεξελθεῖν, διηγεῖσθαι, Isoc.9.2, Pl.*Plt*.274b, *Euthphr*.6c, etc.; παίζειν π. τινός X.*Mem*.1.3.8; ἐμπειροτέρως ἔχειν π. τινός Aeschin.1.82; νόμον γράψαι π. τινός X.*HG*2.3.52, etc.; νόμῳ χρῆσθαι π. τινός S.*Ant*.214. **4.** of impulse or motive rather than object, ἐμαρνάσθην ἔριδος πέρι fought *for very* enmity, Il.7.301, cf. 16.476, 20.253. **5.** *about, in regard to*, μεμνημένος π. τινός Th.6.53; οὕτως ἔσχε π. τοῦ πρήγματος τούτου Hdt.1.117; τὰ π. τῶν Πλαταιῶν γεγενημένα Th.2.6; τὸ π. τούτου γεγονός Plb.1.54.5: in Prose freq. without a Verb, ἡ π. τῶν Μαντινικῶν πρᾶξις Th.6.88; τὰ π. τινός *the circumstances* of.., ib.32, 8.14, 26, etc. (cf. infr. C. I. 5); οὕτω δὴ καὶ π. τῶν ἀρετῶν (sc. ἔχει) Pl.*Men*.72c, cf. *R*.534b, 551c, etc.; π. τοῦ καταλειφθῆναι τὸν σῖτον *as for* reserving the corn, *PMich.Zen*.28.5 (iii B.C.): without the Art., ἀριθμοῦ πέρι *as to* number, Hdt.7.102; χρηστηρίων δὲ πέρι.. Id.2.54. **III.** *before, above, beyond*, of superiority, chiefly in Ep., π. πάντων ἔμμεναι ἄλλων Il.1.287; π. δ' ἄλλων φασὶ γενέσθαι 4.375; τετιμῆσθαι π. πάντων 9.38; ὃν π. πάσης τῖεν ὁμηλικίης 5.325; ὃν..π. πάντων φίλατο παίδων 20.304; π. πάντων ἴδριες ἀνδρῶν Od.7.108; κρατερὸς π. πάντων Il.21.566, cf. 1.417, Od.11.216: in this sense freq. divided from its gen., π. φρένας ἔμμεναι ἄλλων in understanding to be *beyond* them, Il.17.171, cf. 1.258, Od.1.66; π. μὲν εἶδος, π. δ' ἔργα τέτυκτο τῶν ἄλλων Δαναῶν Il.17.279; π. μὲν κρατέεις, π. δ' αἴσυλα ῥέζεις ἀνδρῶν 21.214; π. δ' ἔγχει Ἀχαιῶν φέρτατός ἐσσι 7.289, cf. Pi.*O*.6.50, Theoc.25.119.—In this sense π. is sts. adverbial, and the gen. is absent, v. infr. E. II. **IV.** in Hdt. and Att. Prose, to denote value, ἡμῖν π. πολλοῦ ἐστι it is *of* much *consequence, worth* much, to us, Hdt.1.120, cf. Antipho 6.3; π. πολλοῦ ποιεῖσθαί τινας to reckon them *for*, i.e. *worth*, much, Hdt.1.73, X.*Mem*.2.3.10, etc.; π. πλείονος, π. πλείστου ποιεῖσθαι, Id.*An*.7.7.44, *Cyr*.7.5.60; π. πλείστου ἡγεῖσθαι Th.2.89; π. παντὸς ποιεῖσθαι X.*Cyr*.1.4.1; π. ἐλάττονος ἡγούμενοι, π. οὐδενὸς ἡγήσασθαι, Lys.2.71, 31.31. **V.** Aeol. περί and περ = ὑπέρ, στροῦθοι περὶ γᾶς..δίννεντες πτέρα Sapph.1.10; περ κεφάλας prob. in Alc.93, cf. 18; περρ ἀπαλῶ στύματός σε πεδέρχομαι Theoc.29.25; also Hellenistic, ὁ διέγραψε Πωῖτος περί μου paid *on* my *behalf*, *PCair.Zen*.790.23 (iii B.C.), cf. *UPZ*57.12 (ii B.C.).

B. WITH DATIVE (in Att. Prose mostly in signf. II, esp. in Th.), **I.** of Place, *round about, around*, of close-fitting dresses, armour, etc., ἔνδυνε π. στήθεσσι χιτῶνα Il.10.21; χιτῶνα π. χροΐ δῦνεν Od.15.60; δύσετο τεύχεα καλὰ π. χροΐ Il.13.241; ἕσσαντο π. χροΐ χαλκόν Od.24.467; κνημῖδας..π. κνήμῃσιν ἔθηκε Il.11.17; βεβλήκει τελαμῶνα π. στήθεσσι 12.401: in Prose, π. τῇσι κεφαλῇσι εἶχον τιάρας Hdt.7.61; θώρακα π. τοῖς στέρνοις ἔχειν X.*Cyr*.1.2.13; οἱ στρεπτοὶ οἱ π. τῇ δέρῃ καὶ τὰ ψέλια π. ταῖς χερσί ib.1.3.2; π. τῇ χειρὶ δακτύλιον ὄντα Pl.*R*.359e, etc.; χαλκὸς ἔλαμπε π. στήθεσσι Il.13.245; χιτῶνα π. στήθεσσι δαΐξαι 2.416; πήληξ..κονάβησε π. κροτάφοισι 15.648; in other relations, π. δ' ἔγχεϊ χεῖρα καμεῖται will grow weary *by grasping* the spear, 2.389; δράκων ἑλισσόμενος π. χειῇ 22.95; κνίση ἑλισσομένη π. καπνῷ 1.317; π. σταχύεσσιν ἐέρση 23.598; μάρναντο π. Σκαιῇσι πύλῃσιν 18.453: rarely in Trag., π. βρέτει πλεχθείς A.*Eu*.259 (lyr.); κεῖται νεκρὸς π. νεκρῷ S.*Ant*.1240. **2.** in Poets, also, *around* a weapon, i.e. *spitted upon* it, *transfixed by* it, π. δουρὶ πεπαρμένη Il.21.577; ἐρεικόμενος π. δουρί 13.441; κυλινδόμενος π. χαλκῷ 8.86; π. δουρὶ ἤσπαιρε 13.570; πεπτῶτα π. ξίφει S.*Aj*.828; αἷμα ἐρωήσει π. δουρί Il.1.303. **3.** of a warrior *standing over* a dead comrade so as to defend him, ἀμφὶ δ' ἄρ' αὐτῷ βαῖν', ὥς τις π. πόρτακι μήτηρ 17.4; ἑστήκει, ὥς τίς τε λέων π. οἷσι τέκεσσι ib.133; Αἴας π. Πατρόκλῳ..βεβήκει ib.137, cf. 355; π. σκύμνοισι βεβηκώς Ar.*Eq*.1039. **II.** of an object *for* or *about* which one struggles (cf. supr. A. II. 1), π. οἷσι μαχειόμενος κτεάτεσσι Od.17.471; μαχήσασθαι π. δαιτί 2.245; π. παιδὶ μάχης πόνος Il.16.568; ἄνδρα π. ᾗ πατρίδι μαρνάμενον Tyrt.10.2; π. τοῖς φιλτάτοις κυβεύειν Pl.*Prt*.314a; π. τῇ Σικελίᾳ ἔσται ὁ ἀγών Th.6.34 codd.; κινδυνεύειν π. αὐτῷ Antipho 5.6. **2.** with Verbs denoting care, anxiety, or the opposite (cf. supr. A. II. 2), π. γὰρ δίε ποιμένι λαῶν, μή τι πάθοι Il.5.566; ἔδεισεν δὲ π. ξανθῷ Μενελάῳ 10.240, cf. 11.557; δεδιότες π. τῷ χωρίῳ Th.1.60, cf. 74, 119, Ar.*Eq*.27; θαρρεῖν π. τῇ ἑαυτοῦ ψυχῇ Pl.*Phd*.114d, cf. *Tht*.148c; π. πλέγματι γαθεῖ Theoc.1.54. **3.** generally, of the cause or occasion, *on account of, by reason of*, ἀτύζεσθαι π. καπνῷ, v.l. for ὑπὸ καπνοῦ in Il.8.183; μὴ π. Μαρδονίῳ πταίσῃ ἡ Ἑλλάς Hdt.9.101; π. σφίσιν αὐτοῖς πταῖσαι Th.6.33; π. αὐτῷ σφαλῆναι Id.1.69: in Poets, π. δείματι *for* fear, Pi.*P*.5.58; π. τιμᾷ *in* honour or praise, ib.2.59; π. τάρβει, π. φόβῳ, A.*Pers*.696 (lyr.), *Ch*.35 (lyr.); π. χάρματι *h.Cer*.429:—but π. θυμῷ is f.l. in Hdt.3.50.

C. WITH ACCUSATIVE, **I.** of Place, prop. of the object *round about* which motion takes place, π. βόθρον ἐφοίτων came flocking *round* the pit, Od.11.42; π. νεκρὸν ἤλασαν ἵππους Il.23.13; π. τέρματα ἵπποι τρωχῶσι 22.162; ἄστυ πέρι..διώκειν ib.173, 230; ἐρύσας π. σῆμα 24.16, cf. 51, etc.; π. φρένας ἤλυθ' ἰωή 10.139; π. φρένας ἤλυθε οἶνος Od.9.362: also of extension *round*, ἑστάμεναι π. τοῖχον, π. βωμόν, Il.18.374, Od.13.187, etc.; λέξασθαι π. ἄστυ Il.8.519; μάρνασθαι π. ἄ. 6.256, etc.; φυλάσσοντας π. μῆλα 12.303; οἳ π. Πηνειὸν ..ναίεσκον, π. Δωδώνην..οἰκί' ἔθεντο, 2.757, 750; σειρὴν κεν π. ῥίον Οὐλύμποιο δησαίμην 8.25, cf. Od.18.67: in Prose, ἰκριῶσαι π. τὼ ἀγάλματε *IG*1$^2$.371.22; φυλακὰς δεῖ π. τὸ στρατόπεδον εἶναι X.*An*.5.1.9; π. τὴν κρήνην εὕδειν *somewhere near* it, Pl.*Phdr*.259a, cf. X.*Cyr*.1.2.9; εἶναι π. τὸν λαγώ Id.*Cyn*.4.4; π. λίθον πεσών *upon* it, Ar.*Ach*.1180; π. αὑτὰ καταρρεῖν collapse *upon* themselves, D.2.10; ταραχθεῖσαι [αἱ νῆες] π. ἀλλήλας Th.7.23; πλεῦνες π. ἕνα many *to* one, Hdt.7.103; π. τὸν ἄρξαντα..τὸ ἀδίκημά ἐστι is *imputable to* him who.., Antipho 4.4.2: freq. with a Subst. only, ἡ π. Λέσβον ναυμαχία the sea-fight *off* Lesbos, X.*HG*2.3.32; οἱ π. τὴν Ἔφεσον Pl.*Tht*.179e; στρατηγοὶ π. Πελοπόννησον *IG*1$^2$.324.18: strengthd., π. τ' ἀμφί τε τάφρον Il.17.760; π. τ' ἀμφί τε κύματα Hes.*Th*.848; cf. ἀμφί C. I. 2. **2.** of persons who are *about* one, ἔχειν τινὰ π. αὐτόν X.*HG*5.3.22; esp. οἱ π. τινά a person's attendants, connexions, associates, or colleagues, οἱ π. τὸν Πείσανδρον πρέσβεις Th.8.63; οἱ π. Ἡράκλειτον his school, Pl.*Cra*.440c, cf. X.*An*.1.5.8, etc.; οἱ π. Ἀρχίαν πολέμαρχοι Archias *and his colleagues*, Id.*HG*5.4.2, cf. *An*.2.4.2, etc.; οἱ π. τινά so-and-so *and his family*, *PGrenf*.1.21.16 (ii B.C.), etc.; later οἱ π. τινά, periphr. for the person himself, οἱ π. Φαβρίκιον Fabricius, Plu.*Pyrrh*.20, cf. *Tim*.13, *IGRom*.3.883.14 (Tarsus, ii/iii A.D.); cf. ἀμφί C. I. 3. **3.** of the object *about* which one is occupied or concerned, π. δόρπα πονεῖσθαι, π. δεῖπνον πένεσθαι, Il.24.444, Od.4.624 (but π. τεύχε' ἕπουσι, tmesis for περιέπουσι, Il.15.555); later mostly εἶναι π. τι, Th.7.31, X.*HG*2.2.4; γενέσθαι Isoc.3.12; π. γυναῖκας γενέσθαι Vett.Val.17.20; ὄντων ἡμῶν π. ταύτην τὴν πραγματείαν D.48.6; διατρῖψαι π. τὴν θήραν X.*Cyr*.1.2.11, etc.: less freq. ἔχειν π. τινάς Id.*HG*7.4.28, Gal.15.442; in periphr. phrases, οἱ π. τὴν ποίησιν καὶ τοὺς λόγους ὄντες poets and orators, Isoc.12.35; οἱ π. τὴν φιλοσοφίαν ὄντες Id.9.8; οἱ π. τὴν μουσικήν ib.4; οἱ π. τὰς τελετάς ministers of the mysteries, Pl.*Phd*.69c; ὁ π. τὸν ἵππον the groom, X.*Eq*.6.3; cf. ἀμφί C. I. 6. **4.** *round* or *about* a place, and so *in*, π. νῆσον ἀλώμενοι Od.4.368, cf. 90; ἐμέμηκον π. σηκούς 9.439; ἂν π. ψυχὰν γάθησεν *in* his heart, Pi.*P*.4.122; χρονίζειν π. Αἴγυπτον Hdt.3.61, cf. 7.131; εὕροι ἄν τις [βασιλείας] π. τοὺς βαρβάρους Pl.*R*.544d, etc.; οἱ π. Φωκίδα τόποι Plb.5.24.12, etc. 5. *about, in the case of*, τὰ π. τὴν Αἴγυπτον γεγονότα, τὰ π. Μίλητον γενόμενα, Hdt.3.13, 6.26; εὐσεβεῖν π. θεούς Pl.*Smp.*193a; ἀσεβεῖν π. ξένους X.*Cyr.*5.2.10; ἁμαρτάνειν π. τινάς Id.*An.*3.2.20; ἀνήρ ἐστιν ἀγαθὸς π. τὸν δῆμον τὸν Ἀθηναίων *IG*1$^{2}$.59.10; ἄνδρ' ἀγαθὸν ὄντα Μαραθῶνι π. τὴν πόλιν Ar.*Ach.*696; τοιαύτην γνώμην ἔχειν π. τὸν πατέρα Lys.10.21; οὐδεμία συμφορὴ.. ἔσται.. π. οἶκον τὸν σόν Hdt.8.102; ποιέειν or πράττειν τι π. τινά, Id.1.158, Pl.*Grg.*507a; τὰ π. Πρηξάσπεα πρηχθέντα Hdt.3.76; καινοτομεῖν π. τὰ θεῖα Pl.*Euthphr.*3b; π. θεοὺς μὴ σωφρονεῖν X.*Mem.*1.1.20; σπουδάζειν π. τινά promote his cause, Isoc.1.10: without a Verb, αἱ π. τοὺς παῖδας συμφοραί X.*Cyr.*7.2.20; ἡ π. αὐτὸν ἐπιμέλεια Isoc.9.2; ἡ π. ἡμᾶς ἡνιόχησις Pl.*Phdr.*246b: generally, of all relations, *about, concerning, in respect of*, π. μὲν τοὺς ἰχθύας οὕτως ἔχει Hdt.2.93, cf. 8.86; πονηρὸν π. τὸ σῶμα Pl.*Prt.*313d; ἀκόλαστος π. ταῦτα Aeschin.1.42; γελοῖος π. τὰς διατριβάς ib.126; ξυνηνέχθη θόρυβος π. τὸν Ἀστύοχον Th.8.84; *as to* (cf. A. II. 5), π. τὸ παρὸν πάθος Pl.*Tht.*179c, cf. *Phd.*65a: freq. in place of an Adj., ὄργανα ὅσα π. γεωργίαν, i.e. γεωργικά, Id.*R.*370d; οἱ νόμοι οἱ π. τοὺς γάμους Id.*Cri.*50d; αἱ π. τὰ μαθήματα ἡδοναί Id.*Phlb.*51e; also in place of a gen., οἱ π. Λυσίαν λόγοι the speeches *of* L., Id.*Phdr.*279a; ἡ π. Φίλιππον τυραννίς the despotism *of* P., X.*HG*5.4.2; ἀκρασίας τῆς π. τὸν θυμόν Arist.*EN*1149$^{b}$19: in Prose, to denote circumstances *connected with* any person or thing, τὰ π. Κῦρον, τὰ π. Ἑλένην, τὰ π. Βάττον, Hdt.1.95, 2.113, 4.154; τὰ π. τὸν Ἄθων the *works at* Mount Athos, Id.7.37; τὰ π. τὰς ναῦς naval *affairs*, Th.1.13; τὰ π. τὴν ναυμαχίαν (v.l. for τῆς ναυμαχίας) the *events of*.., Id.8.63; τὰ π. τὸν πόλεμον Pl.*R.*468a; τὰ π. τὸ σῶμα Id.*Phdr.*246d; τὰ π. τοὺς θεούς X.*Cyr.*8.1.23, etc.; cf. ἀμφί C. I. 4. II. of Time, π. λύχνων ἁφάς *about* the time of lamp-lighting, Hdt.7.215; π. μέσας νύκτας *about* midnight, X.*An.*1.7.1; π. πλήθουσαν ἀγοράν ib.2.1.7; π. ἡλίου δυσμάς ib.6.5.32; π. τούτους τοὺς χρόνους Th.3.89, etc. 2. of round numbers, π. ἑβδομήκοντα *about* seventy, Id.1.54; π. ἑπτακοσίους X.*HG*2.4.5, etc.

D. Position: π. may follow its Subst., when it suffers anastrophe, ἄστυ πέρι Il.22.173; ἔριδος πέρι 16.476: most freq. with gen., τοῦδε πράγματος πέρι A.*Eu.*630; τῶνδε βουλεύειν πέρι Id.*Th.*248, etc. (S only once uses it *before* its gen., *Aj.*150 (anap.)): in Prose, σφέων αὐτῶν πέρι Hdt.8.36; σοφίας πέρι Pl.*Phlb.*49a; δικαίων τε πέρι καὶ ἀδίκων Id.*Grg.*455a, etc.; γραμμάτων εἴπομεν ὡς οὐχ ἱκανῶς ἔχεις πέρι Id.*Lg.*809e, cf. *Ap.*19c.

E. περί abs., as Adv., *around, about*, also, *near, by*, freq. in Hom., γέλασσε δὲ πᾶσα π. χθών Il.19.362, al.: strengthd., περί τ' ἀμφί τε κάλλος ἄητο *round about*, *h.Cer.*276, cf. Call.*Hec.*1.1.13. II. *before* or *above others* (cf. A. III), *exceedingly*, only Ep., in which case it commonly suffers anastrophe, Τυδεΐδη, πέρι μέν σε τίον Δαναοί Il.8.161, cf. 9.53; σε χρὴ πέρι μὲν φάσθαι ἔπος ἠδ' ἐπακοῦσαι ib.100; τοι πέρι δῶκε θεὸς πολεμήϊα ἔργα 13.727; ἅ οἱ πέρι δῶκεν Ἀθήνη Od.2.116, cf. 7.110; πέρι γάρ μιν ὀϊζυρὸν τέκε μήτηρ 3.95; πέρι κέρδεα οἶδεν 2.88; τὸν πέρι Μοῦσ' ἐφίλησεν 8.63. 2. π. does not suffer anastrophe in the Ep. phrase π. κῆρι *right heartily*, π. κῆρι φίλησε Il.13.430, etc. (κῆρι φιλεῖν alone, 9.117); ἀπέχθωνται π. κῆρι 4.53; π. κῆρι τιέσκετο ib.46, cf. Od.5.36, 7.69; π. κῆρι.. ἐχολώθη Il.13.206; also π. φρεσὶν ἄσπετος ἀλκή 16.157; π. φρεσὶν αἴσιμα ᾔδη Od.14.433; ἀλύσσοντες π. θυμῷ Il.22.70, cf. Od.14.146; π. σθένεϊ Il.17.22. 3. for περὶ πρό, v. περιπρό. 4. περὶ κάτω bottom *upwards*, δῖνος π. κάτω τετραμμένος Stratt.34, cf. Phot.; τὴν κόγχην στρέψας π. τὰ κάτω Ael.*NA*9.34.

F. In Compos. all its chief senses recur, esp. I. extension in all directions as from a centre, *all round*, as in περιβάλλω, περιβλέπω, περιέχω. II. completion of an orbit and return to the same point, *about*, as in περιάγω, περιβαίνω, περίειμι (εἶμι *ibo*), περιέρχομαι, περιστρέφω. III. a going over or beyond, *above, before*, as in περιβαίνω III, περιβάλλω V, περιγίγνομαι, περιεργάζομαι, περιτοξεύω. IV. generally, a strengthening of the simple notion, *beyond measure, very, exceedingly*, as in περικαλλής, περίκηλος, περιδείδω, like Lat. *per-*. V. the notion of *double*-ness which belongs to ἀμφί is found in only one poetic compd., περιδέξιος (q.v.).

G. Prosody: περί never suffers elision in Il. or Od. (περ' ἰγνύσι *h.Merc.*152); once in Hes., περίαχε Th.678 (cf. Q.S.3.601, 11.382), v. ἰάχω fin.; περ' ἰγνύησι Theoc.25.242; περ' Ἠδάλιον *Inscr.Cypr.*135.27 H.; also in Pi., περάπτων *P.*3.52; περόδοις *N.*11.40; περιδαῖος *Fr.*154; περ' αὐτᾶς *P.*4.265; ταύτας περ' ἀτλάτου πάθας *O.*6.38: not in Trag. (περεβάλοντο, περεσκήνωσεν are ff.ll. in A.*Ag.*1147, *Eu.*634); in Com. and codd. of Prose writers only in part. of περίειμι (εἶμι *ibo*) (q.v.):—π. stands before a word beginning with a vowel in Com., περὶ Ἀθηνῶν, περὶ ἐμοῦ, Ar.*Eq.*1005 sq.:—Aeol. περρ metri gr., v. A. 5.

**περιᾰγᾰπ-άζομαι**, *love very much*, Hsch. s.v. ἀμφαγαπαζόμενος. -άω, = foreg., Eun.*VS* p.469 B., Sch.Opp.*H.*5.90.

**περιαγγέλλω**, *announce by messages sent round*, τὴν ἐκεχειρίαν Th.4.122; τούτων περιαγγελλομένων Hdt.7.1; π. τὸ γεγονός Id.6.58. 2. abs., *send* or *carry a message round*, Id.7.119; v.l. for παρήγγελκεν in D.21.4. II. c. inf., *send round orders for* people to do something, περιήγγελλον κατὰ τὴν Πελοπόννησον.. στρατιὰν παρασκευάζεσθαι ταῖς πόλεσι Th.2.10; τῷ δὲ ναυτικῷ περιήγγειλαν.. ὡς τάχιστα πλεῖν ib.80; περιήγγελλον.. κατὰ τὴν Πελοπόννησον βοηθεῖν ὅτι τάχιστα Id.4.8, cf. 1.116, X.*HG*6.4.2; π. οὐχ ὑποκαίειν Ephipp.5.18 (s.v.l.): with inf. omitted, ναῦς περιήγγελλον κατὰ πόλεις, = Lat. *imperabant naves*, v.l. in Th.2.85; σίδηρον π. κατὰ τοὺς ξυμμάχους Id.7.18.

**περιᾰγείρομαι**, *collect for oneself as pay* or *salary*, Pl.*R.*621d.

**περι-ᾱγή**, ἡ, (περιάγνυμι) *curvature*, Arat.688. -ᾱγής, ές, *broken in pieces*, αἰγανέαι *AP*6.163 (Mel.). II. = περιηγής (q.v.), *round*, τρύπανον ib.204 (Leon.); σχῆμα π. ὡς κύρτου Plu.2.494b; ὅλμος Androm.ap.Gal.14.38; of the *rounded* front of the vertebrae, Ruf.*Oss.*24. 2. *bent*, opp. εὐθές, Ph *Bel.*52.32, 62.8; π. ἠρέμα χωρίον gently *curving*, Dion.Byz.28, cf. Porph. *in Harm.*p.21 D.

**περιᾱγῑνέω**, = περιάγω, Arat.23 (tm.).

⊛ **περιαγκων-ίζω**, *tie the hands behind the back*, Lxx 4*Ma.*6.3: pf. part. Pass. περιηγκωνισμένος Eust.643.44 (cf. περιακονίζω). -ισμα, ατος, τό, *tying of the hands behind the back*, Phot.

⊛ **περιαγν-ίζω**, *purify all round*, τὰ ἱερὰ ὕδατι D.H.7.72, cf. Plu.2.074c; δᾳδίοις τινά Luc.*Nec.*7, etc. -ίστρια, ἡ, *woman who purifies*, Hsch. s.v. ἐγκιλικίστρια.

**περιάγνῡμι** and -ύω (Chio *Ep.*13.2): pf. part. (in pass. sense) περιεᾱγώς *Inscr.Délos* 396 *B* 86 (ii B.C.):—*bend and break all round*, τὸν βραχίονα Chio l.c.; κρημνοῖς τὰς ναῦς π. *wreck* the ships *upon* them, App.*BC*2.150:—Pass., ὅσσους.. μέλαν περιάγνυται ὕδωρ A.R.2.791. 2. once in Hom., of sound, ὄψ περιάγνυται the voice *is broken all round*, i.e. *spreads all round*, Il.16.78; περὶ δέ σφισιν ἄγνυτο ἠχώ echo *broke forth around* them, Hes.*Sc.*279. 3. κόλπου περιαγνυμένου, Lat. *recurvus*, Agath.5.22.

**περιᾰγόρ-αιος**, ὁ, *haunter of the market-place*, Hsch., Phot., Suid. -ευτής, οῦ, ὁ, = foreg., Hsch.

**περιάγχω**, *strangle, throttle*, Suid.

⊛ **περιάγω** [ᾰ], fut. -άξω Men.532.13, etc.:—*lead* or *draw round*, Hdt.1.30, al.; τὰ φορτία ἐν βάρισι περὶ τὸ Δέλτα Id.2.179; π. τινὰς ἐν ἁμάξῃσι κειμένους Id.4.73: c. acc. loci, περιάγουσι τὴν λίμνην κύκλῳ (sc. τὴν παρθένον) ib.180 (s.v.l.), cf. Men. l.c.; *carry about* for sale, Pl.*Prt.*313d:—Med., *lead round with one*, ἐλέφαντα Epin.2.4. b. *cause to revolve*, ψυχὴ π. πάντα Pl.*Lg.*898d, cf. Plot.5.1.2:—Pass., *rotate*, οἷον τροχοῦ περιαγομένου Pl.*Ti.*79b. 2. *lead about with one, have always by one*, X.*Cyr.*2.2.28, cf. 1.3.3:—more freq. in Med., ἀκολούθους πολλοὺς περιάγεσθαι Id.*Mem.*1.7.2, cf. Theopomp.Hist.89(*a*), Posidon.7 J., etc. b. metaph., *lead round and round, perplex*, τὼ θεώ με περιάγουσιν, ὥστε.. And.1.113 (s.v.l.), cf. Luc.*Nigr.*8:—Pass., περιαγόμενος τῷ λόγῳ Pl.*La.*187e. 3. *turn round, turn about*, τὴν κεφαλήν, τὸν τράχηλον, τὸν αὐχένα, Ar.*Pax* 682, *Av.*176, Pl.*R.*515c, cf. Hp.*Art.*18; τινὰ πρὸς τἀριστερά E.*Cyc.*686 (s.v.l.); μύλην Poll.7.180; π. τὴν σκυταλίδα *twist it round* in order to tighten a noose, Hdt.4.60; τὼ χεῖρε περιαγαγὼν εἰς τοὔπισθεν καὶ δήσας *twisting back* the hands *behind the back*, Lys.1.25; simply π. τὼ χεῖρε D.H.6.82:—Pass., περιαχθεὶς τὼ χεῖρε Philostr.*Her.*10.7; so prob. περιαχθείς alone, π. κρεμήσεται *PCair.Zen.*202.9 (iii B.C.). 4. *pass round*, τὸ περιαγόμενον ποτήριον Ath.10.420a, etc., cf. Hld.3.11. 5. *protract*, ἐς ὥραν τινά Luc.*Merc. Cond.*31. 6. *bring round* to.., [τὴν πολιτείαν] πάλιν εἰς τὴν ἑτέραν πολιτείαν Arist.*Pol.*1265$^{a}$4; εἰς αὐτὸν τὴν ἀρχήν Hdn.4.3.1:—Pass., π. εἰς ὁμόνοιαν Id.3.15.7; εἰς τόδε, εἰς ἀνάγκην, Luc.*Nigr.*5, J.*AJ*5.2.8. 7. Rhet., *round* a period, etc., περίοδος, σύνθεσις περιηγμένη, Demetr.*Eloc.*19, 30. II. intr., *come round*, πάλιν κύκλῳ π. εἰς τὴν ἀρχήν Arist.*Mete.*356$^{a}$8; περιφερομένης καὶ περιαγούσης Epicur.*Nat.*11.2. 2. c. acc. loci, *go round*, π. τὴν ἐσχατιάν D.42.5; π. τὰς πόλεις *Ev.Matt.*9.35, cf. 4.23, etc.

⊛ **περιάγωγ-εύς**, έως, ὁ, *windlass*, Luc.*Nav.*5. -ή, Dor. -γά, ἡ, *turning round*, ὄνου Hp.*Fract.*31; περιαγωγαὶ τῆς ἐπιδέσιος Id.*Art.*62; χειρῶν Gal.6.92, cf. Pl.*R.*518d; *whirling* of a sling, Plb.27.11.6. b. metaph., *distraction*, Plu.2.588d. 2. *carrying round*, τοῦ ὕδατος εἰς τὸ βαλανεῖον *IG*4$^{2}$(1).109 iii 44 (Epid., iii B.C.); τῶν ἐπιτηδείων Plu.*Nic.*7. II. *rotation, revolution*, στρέφεσθαι διττὰς καὶ ἐναντίας π. Pl.*Plt.*270a; τοῦ οὐρανοῦ Arist.*Mu.*399$^{a}$2; of the moon, Plu.2.923c; π. περὶ τὸν ἄξονα Hierocl. *in CA* 24 p.474 M.; τῆς ὀρχηστικῆς περιαγωγαί Luc.*Salt.*71; ἡ τῆς ψυχῆς π. Plot.2.1.3. 2. in Tactics, *wheeling*, J.*BJ*3.5.7, Ael.*Tact.*18.4 (both pl.). 3. *circuit*, καμπὴ καὶ π. Plu.2.819a, cf. 407c. 4. *circumference*, ὀστέων, λοβῶν, Aret.*SD*1.8, 13. 5. *enclosure*, π. φυτώδης, of a grass-*plot*, Erot. s.v. ἐκχλοιούμενα. 6. Rhet., *rounding* of a period, Demetr.*Eloc.*19; ἐκ περιαγωγῆς συντεθεῖσθαι Anon.*Fig.*p.114 S. -ίς, ίδος, ἡ, = περιαγωγεύς, Heliod.ap.Orib.49.4.1, Sor.1.68. -ός, όν, *causing to turn round*, π. καὶ ἀναγωγὸς ὠφέλεια ταῖς ψυχαῖς Syr. *in Metaph.*14.36. II. Subst. -ᾰγωγός, ὁ, *circular canal*, *Sammelb.*7379.25 (ii A.D.).

**περιαδεῖς**· περίρρυτοι, περίπνοοι, Hsch.

**περιᾴδω**, *go about singing*, ἰαμβεῖα Luc.*Salt.*27. II. Pass., *to be buzzed about*, κωνώπων χορῷ Plu.2.663d. 2. *to be harped upon, repeated*, τὰ ὑπὸ τῶν πολλῶν -όμενα Agath.2.30.

**περιαθρ-έω**, *inspect all round, consider narrowly*, τὴν φύσιν Pl.*Ax.*370d; ἅπαντα Ph.2.533; ἑαυτόν Philostr.*Her.*15; π. μή τις εἴη.. J.*BJ*1.33.7: abs., Ph.2.445. 2. *look round upon*, τὸ πλῆθος Hld.10.35. -ησις, εως, ἡ, *looking at on all sides*, Ph.1.142, al. -ητέον, gloss on περιοπτέον, Sch.Th.8.48.

**περιαθροίζομαι**, *gather about*, Hsch. s.v. ἀμφαγέροντο.

**περιαίνῡμαι**, = περιλαμβάνω, περιαίνυνται ὀστέα τύμβος *BCH*24.380 (Bithyn.), cf. Hsch.

**περιαίρ-εμα**, ατος, τό, *anything taken off*, Sch.Ar.*Eq.*767. -εσις, εως, ἡ, *stripping off*, φλοιοῦ Thphr.*CP*5.17.1, cf. Epicur.*Ep.*1 p.15 U.; *removal, extirpation*, Antyll.ap.Orib.44.8.26, Gal.1.173; *excision*, Id.10.887. II. *taking away* a person's goods, etc., φιλονικία ἐπιθυμία περιαιρέσεως *Stoic.*3.96. -ετέος, α, ον, *to be done away with*, ἡ συγγνώμη π. Arist.*Rh.Al.*1427$^{a}$19. II. neut. -έον, *one must remove*, τὴν πόσθην Antyll.ap.Orib.50.2.10; φύλλα *Gp.*5.29.4; τὴν τροφήν Aët.7.26; *one must do away with*, ἀναλώματα Arist.*Oec.*1345$^{b}$

26; τὴν συγγνώμην Id.*Rh.Al.*1427ᵃ7; τραγῳδίαν D.S.19.8. **-ετός**, ή, όν, *that may be taken off, removable*, ἅπαν [τὸ χρυσίον] Th.2.13; κόσμος Paus.1.25.7; προσωπεῖον Luc.*Pr.Im.*3, cf. Plu.2.818b. **-έω**, aor. περιεῖλον Hdt.3.159, etc.:—*take away something that surrounds, strip off, remove*, c. acc. rei, τεῖχος Hdt. l. c., cf. 6.46, Th.1.108, 4.51, 133; π. τὸν κέραμον *taking off* the earthen jar into which the gold had been run, Hdt.3.96; π. τὸν χιτῶνα Arist.*HA*557ᵇ20; δέρματα σωμάτων π. *strip* skins *off from*.., Pl.*Plt.*288e; αὐτοῦ τὰ κοινὰ πάντα περιελόντες Id.*Sph.*264e; π. τινὰ αὐτοῦ τῆς ἐξουσίας Hdn.3.11.3; simply, *take away from*, τῶν πολεμικῶν τὸ μελετᾶν X.*Cyr.*2.1.21, etc.:—Med., *take off from oneself*, π. τὴν κυνέην, τὴν σφρηγῖδα, *take off one's* helmet, *one's* signet-ring, Hdt.2.151, 3.41; τὰς ταινίας Pl.*Smp.*213a; βυβλίον περιαιρεόμενος *taking* [*the cover*] *off one's* letter, i. e. *opening* it, Hdt.3.128; π. τὴν ἐξουσίαν τῆς ἀπολογίας αὐτοῦ Lycurg.35: but Med. is freq. used like Act., *strip off, take away*, τὸ περιελέσθαι αὐτῶν τὰ ὅπλα X.*Cyr.*8.1.47; εἴ τις περιέλοιτο τῆς ποιήσεως τὸ μέλος Pl.*Grg.*502c (v.l. for περιέλοι); τὴν Ἀττικὴν ὑμῶν περιῄρηνται D.19.220; ἁπάντων τὴν ἐλευθερίαν περιείλετο Id.18.65; περιείλοντό μου ὑποζύγια δύο *PCair. Zen.*659.7 (iii B.C.):—Pass., *to be taken off*, τοὐπίβλημ' ἐπεὶ περιῃρέθη Nicostr.Com.15; τοῦ ἄλλου περιῃρημένου *when* the rest *has been taken away*, Th.3.11; περιῃρημένων τοσούτων κακῶν Pl.*Phdr.*231b; τείχη περιῃρημένα D.19.65. 2. *make void, cancel* a vow, Lxx *Nu.*30.13. 3. *strike off, cancel* an item in an account, *PCair.Zen.*147 (iii B.C.):—Pass., *Sammelb.*5136.8 (iii A.D.). II. Pass., c. acc. rei, *to be stripped of* a thing, *have* a thing *taken off* or *away from* one, περιῃρημένοι χρήματα καὶ συμμάχους D.3.31; περιαιρεθεὶς τὰ ὄντα Id.21.138; τοὺς στεφάνους περιῄρηνται Id.26.5: with acc. understood, περιαιρεθήσεσθαι ἤμελλον Epicur.*Nat.*15.34.

**περιαίρω**, *raise up*, ἐπὶ τὸν ἀγκῶνα π. ἑαυτόν J.*AJ*17.7.1.

**περιαιωρέομαι**, *hang about*, λευκαὶ κορυφᾷ περιαιωρεῦνται Cerc. 7.12.

**περιᾰκολουθέω**, *follow about*, Heraclid.*Pol.*44. 2. *encircle*, Polem.*Phgn.*9, al.

**περιᾰκονίζω**, dub. l. in Zos.Alch.p.118B. (fort. περιηγκωνισμένον).

**περιᾰκοντίζω**, *dart at from all sides*, Plu.*Galb.*26.

**περιακτέον**, *one must turn round*, Pl.*R.*518c.

**περίακτος**, ον, (περιάγω) *turning on a centre* or *pivot*, δίφροι π. Artemo Hist.12; π. τροχοί *water-wheels*, Ph.*Bel.*91.44; π. ἄντλημα *water-wheel*, Plu.2.974e; μηχανήματα π. machines *for draining* land, Ph.*Bel.*97.23; μηχαναὶ ἀπὸ σκηνῆς π. machines *for changing the scene* on the stage, Plu.2.348e; also περίακτοι, αἱ, as Subst., Poll.4.126, Vitr.5.6.8. 2. π. ὁδός a *winding* road, Anon.Hist.(*FGrH*151) p.819J. II. metaph., τὸ π. 'the old saw', Plu.*Comp.Lys.Sull.*3; τὸ π. ἐκ τῆς Ἀκαδημείας Id.2.922f.

**περιαλγ-έω**, *to be greatly pained at* a thing, τῇ συμφορᾷ Antipho Soph.54; τῷ πάθει Th.4.14; τῇ ἀτιμίᾳ Pl.*Hipparch.*229d; ἐπὶ τούτοις Ael.*VH*2.4, cf. Ph.2.178; κατά τι Id.*Fr.*57 H.: c. acc., Id.2.436. **-ημα**, ατος, τό, *severe pain*, Aët.16.119(109). **-ής**, ές, (ἄλγος) *feeling extreme pain*, mental or physical, opp. περιχαρής, Pl. *R.*462b, Plu.*Fab.*6. II. *very painful*, φόνος Nic.*Th.*497. Adv. -γῶς D.C.78.24: Comp. -έστερον, κτείνειν Aret.*SD*1.13.

**περι-άλειμμα** [ᾰλ], ατος, τό, *pigment*, J.*AJ*15.9.3(pl.). **-ᾰλειπτέον**, *one must anoint all over*, κηρωτῇ Sor.1.56. **-ᾰλείφω**, fut. -ψω *SIG*1097.7 (iv B.C.):—*smear all over*, ἑλκύδρια Ar.*Eq.*907; πάντα π. τὸν νεὼν ἀργύρῳ *overlay* it with silver, Pl.*Criti.*116d; *whitewash*, τῶν τοίχων τοὺς δεομένους *SIG* l. c., cf. *IG*2².1672.140: metaph., ὑμένες ὅσοι π. τὸν πνεύμονα Gal.5.535:—Pass., περιαλήλιπται μίτυϊ, of the mouth of the hive, Arist.*HA*624ᵃ14.

**περιᾰληθής**, ές, *very true*, Phld.*Po.*2.11.

**περιᾰλιφή**, ή, *whitewashing*, *IG*2².1672.61.

**περιαλλόκαυλος**, ον, *twining around other plants*, of creepers, Thphr.*HP*7.8.1, *CP*2.18.2.

**περιάλλομαι**, *leap around*, Sch.Nic.*Al.*13.

**περίαλλος**, ον, *before all others*: Adv. περίαλλα *before all*, *h.Pan.*46, Pi.*P.*11.5, Ar.*Th.*1070 (= E.*Fr.*115, lyr.), A.R.2.217, 3.529, dub. in S.*OT*1219 (lyr.). II. as Adj., *superlative*, γλωττισμοί *AP*5.131 (Phld.).

⊛ **περίαλλος**, ὁ, = ἰσχίον, Hdn.Gr.1.158, Hsch., prob. in Alciphr. 1.39.

**περιᾰλουργός**, όν, *with purple all round*, π. τοῖς κακοῖς *double-dyed* in villainy, Ar.*Ach.*856.

**περιᾰμάομαι**, Med., *gather from all sides*, γῆν περιαμησάμενος *Gp.*1.14.8, cf. Hsch., Phot.

**περιᾰμαρτ-ίζω**, *make a sin-offering*, Aq., Sm., Thd.*Ex.*29.36. **-ισμός**, ὁ, *sin-offering*, Sm.*Za.*13.1.

**περίαμμα**, ατος, τό, (περιάπτω) *anything worn about the body, amulet*, Plb.33.17.2, D.S.5.64, Dsc.5.141, *AP*11.257 (Lucill.).

**περι-άμπαξ**, Adv. *round again*, *SIG*685.60 (Crete, ii B.C.). **-αμπέτιξ**, = foreg., ib.67, al.

**περιαμπέχω** (also **περιαμπίσχω** Ph.1.369, Philostr.*Im.*2.26 (cf. II)), -ήμπεσχον Ar.*Eq.*893:—*put round about*, π. τινά τι *put a* thing *round* or *over* one, Ar. l. c.:—Med., *put around oneself, put on*, metaph., ὀνόματα καὶ ῥήματα Pl.*Smp.*221e. II. *cover all over*, τὰ ὀστᾶ μετὰ τῶν σαρκῶν Id.*Phd.*98d; later περιαμπίσχω τί τινι Ph. l. c.: metaph., τὰ πράγματα γυμνὰ ἐξέκειτο καὶ οὐ περιήμπισχεν αὐτὰ ἡ λέξις Philostr.*VS*2.22.

**περιᾰμύνω** [ῡ], *defend* or *guard all round*, Plu.*Alc.*7.

**περιᾰμύσσω**, Att. -ττω, *prick* or *wound on all sides*, τὸν νοῦν Pl. *Ax.*365c: gloss on περιξύσας, Gal.19.130.

**περιαμφιέννῡμι**, *clothe on all sides*, Pl.*Ti.*76a.

**περιαμφίς**, ίδος, ή, *turning round and round*, Eup.436 (pl.).

**περιάμφοδος**, ον, *having a way all round it*, of a detached house or block of houses, Hsch. s. v. διάλαυρος.

**περιᾰναγκ-άζω**, *force round*, Hp.*Art.*62, Gal.18(1).336:—hence Subst. **-ᾰσις**, εως, ή, Apollon.Cit.3.

**περιαναιρέω**, prob. f.l. for περιαιρέω, Ocell.4.13.

**περιανθ-έω**, *bloom*: hence, *glow all round*, of heat, Plu.2.648a. **-ής**, ές, *with flowers all round*, Nic.*Fr.*130.

**περιανίστημι**, *rouse up*, τινα dub. in Ph.2.552:—Pass., with aor. 2, pf., and plpf. Act., *arise from sleep, start up*, Id.1.672, al., Apollod.2.1.4.

**περιανοίγω**, *open all round*, Ph.2.597 (Pass.).

**περιαντλ-έω**, *pour all over*, Dsc.2.114 (Pass.), Archig.ap.Aët.3.194: metaph., σοφοὺς λόγους τινί Plu.2.502c:—Pass., *to be completely drowned*, ὑπὸ θαλάσσης Sch.Opp.*H.*1.155: metaph., ἐν τῷ τῶν παθῶν κατακλυσμῷ Lxx 4*Ma.*15.32; ὑπὸ τοῦ πλήθους τῆς τῶν ἰατρῶν διαφωνίας Gal.10.469. **-ητέον**, *one must pour all over*, Philum.ap.Aët.9.23.

**περιαοιδός**· ἡ ἐγκύκλιος ᾠδή, Hsch., Phot., Suid.

**περιαπλόω**, *unfold and spread around*, f. l. in *Placit.*5.26.4 (Pass.).

**περιαποστέλλω**, *send round* begging letters, *PCair.Zen.*599 (iii B.C.).

**περι-απτέον**, *one must hang round*, Cyran.79. **-απτος**, ον, *hung round, appended*, ἄκος π., i. e. an amulet, Cratin.22 D.; σέμνωμα π. Eust.95.42. II. as Subst. περίαπτον, τό, = περίαμμα, *amulet*, Pl. *R.*426b, Thphr.*HP*9.19.2, etc.; *adventitious charm*, Arist.*EN*1099ᵃ16: pl., *ornaments*, Ph.1.608. **-άπτω**, fut. -ψω Lys.21.24, etc.:—*tie, fasten, hang about* or *upon*, γυίοις περάπτων φάρμακα Pi.*P.*3.52, cf. Call.*Hec.*1.1.1; τὰ ἐρινεὰ πρὸς τὰς συκᾶς Arist.*HA*557ᵇ29:—Med., *put round oneself, wear*, [χρυσὸν ἢ ἄργυρον] Pl.*R.*417a, cf. Plu.*Per.*12, etc. 2. metaph., π. ὄλβον τινί X.*Cyr.*1.5.9; ἀγαθὸν [τῇ πόλει] Id. *Mem.*2.6.13; π. αὐτοῖς τὰ διὰ μέσης θεωρούμενα φυσιολογίας Phld.*Rh.*1.208 S.: mostly in bad sense, π. πήματα, τῆς πενίας πρᾶγμ' αἰσχρόν τινι, *attach to* one, Simon.97 (tm.), Ar.*Pl.*590; π. ὀνείδη τινί Lys. l. c., cf. Pl.*Euthd.*272c; αἰσχύνην τῇ πόλει Id.*Ap.*35a; π. ἀνελευθερίαν (sc. αὐτοῖς) X.*Cyr.*8.4.32; ἀντὶ καλῆς [δόξης] αἰσχρὰν π. τῇ πόλει D.20.10 (hence π. alone, *defame*, Vett.Val.285.32); τουτονὶ π. βίον (sc. ἡμῖν) *imposed* this life upon us, Athenio 1.7; also σχῆμα π. τῷ πυρί Arist. *Cael.*304ᵃ9; τινὰς αἰτίαις π. J.*AJ*12.5.5; π. τινὰ ψόγῳ Lxx 3*Ma.*3.7. II. *light a fire all round*, Phalar.*Ep.*122.2 codd.; π. πῦρ *Ev. Luc.*22.55.

**περιᾰράσσω**, *break all in pieces*, Nic.*Th.*842 (tm.), Poll.1.111, 114.

**περιάργῠρ-ος**, ον, *set in silver*, κίονες Chares 4 J., cf. Lxx *Ep.Je.*8; ὅπλα App.*BC*1.106. **-όω**, *case, plate with silver*, Theopomp.Hist. 40(*a*):—Pass., *IG*11(2).161 *B*77 (Delos, iii B.C.), Lxx *Ex.*27.11, Diog.ap.Theon.*Prog.*5, *PRyl.*110.14 (iii A.D.).

**περιαρμόζω**, *fasten, fit on*, Pl.*Ax.*366a; τοῖς θυρεοῖς κύκλῳ π. λεπίδα χαλκῆν Plu.*Cam.*40; τάφον τινί Philostr.*Her.*1.2:—Pass., of persons, πώγωνας περιηρμοσμέναι *having* them *fastened on*, Ar.*Ec.*274; of things, *to be fastened on*, περί τι Arist.*HA*500ᵃ9; τῷ πέρατι Antyll.ap.Orib.10.19.4; τοῖς σφυροῖς Jul.*Or.*2.57c. II. intr., *fit closely round*, Arist.*Mech.*854ᵃ22.

**περιάρ-οσις** [ᾰ], εως, ή, *ploughing round*, χωρίων D.H.1.88. **-όω**, fut. -αρόσω Id.5.25:—*plough round*, l. c., Plu.2.820e, etc.

**περίαρσις**, εως, ή, dub. sens. in *Stud.Pal.*22.95.2 (iii A.D.).

**περιαρτάω**, *hang round* on, ἐρινά [ταῖς συκαῖς] Poll.1.242; χρυσὸν τοῖς δακτύλοις Max.Tyr.36.2:—Pass., of persons, πήραν περιηρτημένος *having* it *hung round one*, S.E.*M.*2.105; τὸ σύμβολον τῆς εὐγενείας -ηρτημένος τῷ ὑποδήματι Philostr.*VS*2.1.8; of things, *to be hung round*, τῷ τραχήλῳ Plu.*Per.*38, cf. Poll.5.101.

**περιασθμαίνω**, *breathe round*, τινα Ach.Tat.4.4. II. *breathe hard*, Hld.8.9.

**περίᾳσις**, εως, ή, *circumsonance, resonance*, Plu.2.41d (pl.).

**περιασπάζομαι**, *embrace*, Socr.*Ep.*17.3, *PMag.Leid.V.*7ᵃ.16.

**περιαστράπτω**, *flash around*, φῶς π. τινά *Act.Ap.*9.3, cf. Jul.*Or.*4.131a; περί τινα *Act.Ap.*22.6: abs., ἄγγελοι περιαστράπτοντες τοῖς ὅπλοις Lxx 4*Ma.*4.10. 2. *dazzle*, ὁ ἀνὴρ περιαστράπτεται ὑπὸ κάλλους *is dazzled* with beauty, Junc.ap.Stob.4.50.95, cf. Gal.19.22c.

**περιασχολέω**, *keep busy about a thing*, v.l. in Luc.*Bis Acc.*11.

**περιατμισμός**, ὁ, *steaming*, Sor.2.39 (pl.).

**περιαυγ-άζω**, *beam round about, illuminate*, Ph.1.264, Hld.8.9. **-ασμα**, ατος, τό, *encircling gleam*, ibid. **-ασμός**, ὁ, *halo, splendour*, Dam.*Pr.*81. **-εια**, ή, *illumination*, Aristeas 77, Str.1.85. **-έομαι**, Pass., *to be surrounded with light*, Str.16.4.6 (v.l. ὑπερ-), Longin.17.2. **-ή**, ή, = περιαύγεια, Plu.2.936b (pl.). **-ής**, ές, *beaming round about*, τὸ π. τῶν ἀκτίνων Ph.1.570: Sup., -έστατον φέγγος ἀρετῆς ib.443; ἔποψις Metop.ap.Stob.3.1.115. **-ος**, ον, *shining round*, c. gen., Arist.*Mu.*395ᵇ1.

**περιαυθᾰδίζομαι**, *to be exceeding wilful*, Hsch.

**περι-αύλισμα**, ατος, τό, *enclosure*, Agath.4.14 (pl.), 19. ⊛ **-αυλον**, τό, *courtyard, enclosure*, Keil-Premerstein *Zweiter Bericht* No.87 (ii A.D.), *Supp.Epigr.*2.481 (Scythia, iii A.D.).

**περιαυτίζομαι**, Med., (αὐτός) *to be busy about oneself, brag*, Hsch., Phot., Suid. 2. *speak much on one subject*, Hsch., Phot., Suid.

**περιαυτο-λογέω**, *speak about oneself, brag*, Phld.*Hom.*p.60 O., S.E. *P.*1.62, Iamb.*Myst.*2.10, Eust.100.37. **-λογία**, ή, *speaking about oneself, bragging*, Plu.2.41b, al., Alex.*Rh.*p.4 S. **-λογικός**, ή, όν, *boastful*, στομφασμός Eust.897.2. Adv. -κῶς Id.1866.28.

**περιαυχένιος**, ον, (αὐχήν) *put round the neck*, στρεπτός Hdt.3.20;

κόσμος Ph.2.62, Alciphr.3.3; δεσμοί Agath.4.1. II. Subst. περιαυχένιον, τό, *necklace, collar*, App.*Mith*.85, Aristaenet.1.19, Hld.7.27.

**περίᾰχε**, Ep. for περιίαχε, Hes.*Th*.678, Q.S.3.601, 11.382; v. περί G.

**περιᾰχῠρίζω**, *free from husks*, Dieuch.ap.Orib.4.7.21.

**περιβάδην** [ᾰ], Adv. *astride*, of a rider, Plu.*Art*.14; opp. κατὰ πλευράν, Ach.Tat.1.1. II. *with crossed legs*, Sch.Poll.3.90.

**περιβαίνω**, fut. -βήσομαι: aor. περιέβην, Ep. περίβην (v. infr.):—*go round*, esp. of one defending a fallen comrade, *bestride* him, ἀλλὰ θέων περίβη καί οἱ σάκος ἀμφεκάλυψε Il.8.331, 13.420, cf. Plu.*Nic*.13; π. τὰ πίπτοντα σώματα D.S.17.25: c. gen., περιβῆναι ἀδελφειοῦ κταμένοιο Il.5.21; περὶ τρόπιος βεβαῶτα Od.5.130: and c. dat., Πατρόκλῳ περιβάς Il.17.80, cf. 313; ὡς δὲ κύων.. περὶ σκυλάκεσσι βεβῶσα Od.20.14, cf. Ar.*Eq*.1039. 2. *bestride*, as a rider does a horse, ἵππον Plu.*Pyrrh*.11, 2.213e; ἐς ἵππον Malch.p.394 D.; οἱ περιβεβηκότες *those mounted on* the elephants, D.S.17.88; of the male camel, Arist.*HA* 540ᵃ14; περὶ τὴν ψωλὴν π. Ar.*Lys*.979 (anap.). II. of sound, *come round* one's ears, τινι S.*Ant*.1209. III. Aeol., *pass by* or *beyond*, in Pass., περβέβαται χρόνος Alc.*Oxy*.1788 *Fr*.15 ii 17 (p.38 Lobel).

⊛ **περιβάλλω**, fut. -βᾰλῶ: aor. περιέβᾰλον (v. infr.):—*throw round, about*, or *over, put on* or *over*, c. acc. rei, φίλας περὶ χεῖρε βαλόντε Od.11.211; περὶ πτερὰ πυκνὰ βαλόντες Il.11.454; περὶ δ' ἄντυγα βάλλε φαεινήν 18.479; π. χέρας Ar.*Th*.914, E.*Or*.1044: freq. c. dat., χέρας π. τινί Id.*Ph*.1459, etc.; περὶ δ' ὠλένας δέρᾳ.. βάλοιμι ib.165 (lyr.); π. τινὶ δεσμά, βρόχους, A.*Pr*.52, E.*Ba*.619; Τροίᾳ ζευκτήριον A.*Ag*.529; κρατὶ π. σκότον E.*HF*1159; π. τινὰ χαλκεύματι *put* him *round* the sword, i.e. stab him, A.*Ch*.576; also περὶ τὰ στέρνα θώρηκας π. Hdt.1.215, cf. 5.85; αἱμασιὴν π. κατὰ τὸν κύκλον Id.7.60; περὶ ἕρμα π. ναῦν *wreck* it *on*.., Th.7.25:—Med., *throw round* or *over oneself, put on*, c. acc. rei, περιβαλλόμενοι τεύχεα *putting on their* arms, Od.22.148; περὶ δὲ ζώνην βάλετ' ἰξυῖ 5.231; ξίφος περὶ στιβαροῖς βάλετ' ὤμοις 14.528; εἷμα, φᾶρος περιβάλλεσθαι, Hdt.1.152, 9.109; φάρεα καὶ πλοκάμους E.*IT*1150 (lyr.); κόσμον σώμασιν Id.*HF*334; κύκλον ὅσον περιβάλλεται αἰθήρ Hermesian.7.87; freq. of defences, τεῖχος καὶ σωτηρίην περιβαλέσθαι τοῖς τε χρήμασι καὶ τοῖς σώμασιν Democr.280; also ὅταν περιβάλωνται χειρισμοὺς παραλλάττοντας Phld.*Rh*.1.8 S.; π. ἕρκος ἔρυμα τῶν νεῶν Hdt.9.96; τείχεα Id.1.141, cf. 6.46, Th.1.8; ταῖς πόλεσιν ἐρύματα περιβάλλονται X.*Mem*.2.1.14; Πελοποννήσῳ π. ἓν τεῖχος Arist.*Pol*.1276ᵃ27; λιμένι τεῖχος, χάρακα τῇ παρεμβολῇ, Plb.4.65.11, 5.20.5; also περὶ τὴν Πελοπόννησον τεῖχος π. Lys.2.45: c. dupl. acc., τεῖχος περιβαλέσθαι πόλιν *build* a wall *round* it, Hdt.1.163: in pf. Pass., *have* a thing *put round one*, Pl.*Smp*.216d; τὸ τεῖχος περιβεβλημένος *having* his wall *around* him, *encompassed by* it, Id.*Tht*.174e, cf. Arist.*Pol*.1331ᵃ8. 2. metaph., *put round* or *upon* a person, i.e. *invest* him *with* it, π. τινὶ ἀγαθόν (i.e. βασιληΐην), τυραννίδα, Hdt.1.129, E.*Ion*829; π. σωτηρίαν [τισί] Id.*HF*304; ὕδασι δουλείαν Id.*Ph*.189 (lyr.); οἶκτον Id.*IA*934; τινὶ π. ἀνανδρίαν, i.e. make him faint-hearted, Id.*Or*.1031; π. τὴν αἰτίαν τῷ ἰατρῷ *impute* blame to.., Pall.*in Hp*.12.283 C.:—Pass., c. acc., *to be involved in*, μεγίστην ζημίαν τὸ ταμεῖον περιβληθήσεται *SIG*888.87 (Scaptopara, iii A.D.). II. reversely c. dat. rei, *surround, encompass with*.., περιβαλεῖν πλῆθος τῶν ἰχθύων (sc. τῷ ἀμφιβλήστρῳ) Hdt.1.141; βρόχῳ π. τὸν αὐχένα Id.4.60 (tm.); [Βόσπορον] πέδαις π. A.*Pers*.748; π. τινὰ ὑφάσματι E.*Or*.25; δοραῖσι σῶμα Id.*Cyc*.330; π. τινὰ χερσί embrace, Id.*Or*.372:—Med., *surround* or *enclose for one's advantage* or *defence*, τὴν νῆσον π. τείχει Pl.*Criti*.116a; χωρίον X.*Cyr*.6.3.30; π. θύννους *net* them, Arist.*HA* 537ᵃ20, cf. 533ᵇ25. 2. metaph., π. τινὰ κακῷ, συμφοραῖς, *involve* one in evil or calamity, E.*Or*.906, Antipho 3.2.12; ἀνηκέστοις πόλιν συμφοραῖς And.1.142, cf. Lys.4.20; ὀνείδει D.22.35; π. τινὰ φυγῇ, i.e. banish him, Plu.2.775c; τινὰ κλοπῆς καταδίκῃ Id.*Arist*.4:—Pass., [συμφοραῖς] Phld.*Piet*.35ᵇ. III. c. acc. only, *encompass, surround*, περιβάλλει με σκότος, νέφος, E.*Ph*.1453, *HF*1140; π. ἀλλήλους *embrace* each other, X.*An*.4.7.25, cf. Men.*Pk*.36, 111; also, *clothe*, τινα *Ev.Matt*.25.36; τὸ περιβεβλημένον *the space enclosed, enclosure*, Hdt.2.91; cf. περίβολος II. 2:—Med., ἤλαυνον περιβαλόμενοι [τὰ ὑποζύγια] *surrounding* them, Id.9.39, cf. X.*Cyr*.1.4.17. 2. *fetch a compass round, double*, ἵπποι περὶ τέρμα βαλοῦσαι Il.23.462; esp. of ships, *round* a cape, π. τὸν Ἄθων Hdt.6.44; Σούνιον Th.8.95: abs., of a hare, *double*, X.*Cyn*.5.29, 6.18. 3. *amplify, expand*, λόγον Hermog.*Id*.1.4, cf. 11: abs., ib.3, al. IV. Med., *bring into one's power, compass*, ἰδίῃ π. ἑωυτῷ κέρδεα Hdt.3.71; πολλὰ [χρήματα] Id.8.8, cf. 7.190; σωφροσύνης δόξαν π. X.*Mem*.4.2.6; τὰ λοιπὰ τῶν πραγμάτων περιβαλλόμενος D.18.231; πλῆθος λείας Plb.1.29.7, cf. 3.69.7: pf. Pass., *to have come into possession of*.., πόλιν Hdt.6.24; δυναστείας Isoc.4.184, cf. 2.25. 2. *appropriate mentally, comprehend*, περιβάλλεσθαι τῇ διανοίᾳ τὰς πράξεις Id.5.118; πολλὰ περιβεβλῆσθαι πράγματα *to have aimed at learning* many things, Men.683; logically, ξύμπαντα τὰ οἰκεῖα.. γένους τινὸς οὐσίᾳ π. *embrace*, Pl.*Plt*.285b. 3. *use circumlocution*, κομψῶς κύκλῳ π. Id.*Smp*.222c, cf. *Phdr*.272d. V. *throw beyond, beat in throwing*: hence generally, *excel, surpass*, μνηστῆρας δώροισι Od.15.17; π. ἀρετῇ *to be superior* in.., Il.23.276. VI. π. τὸ λουτρόν *take* a bath, Cass.*Pr*.5; π. πρὸς λουτρόν ibid.

**περιβᾱρίδες**, αἱ, (βᾶρις) a sort of *women's shoes*, Ar.*Lys*.45, Theopomp.Com.52, Cephisod.4:—also **περίβᾱρα**, τά, Poll.7.94, Hsch., Phot.

**περίβᾰρυς**, υ, gen. εος, *exceeding grievous*, A.*Eu*.161 (lyr.).

**περίβᾰσις**, εως, ἡ, (περιβαίνω) *going round, circuit* *GDI*5075.72 (Crete); οὐρανοῦ ταχύτητα τὴν περὶ ταῦτα π. *Corp.Herm*.5.5 codd.; ἐσχίσθω ὁ ἱμὰς τὴν ἀμφὶ τὸ οὖς περίβασιν let the bandage be slit *so as to go round* the ear, Hp.*Art*.33, cf. Gal.18(1).754.

**περιβασώ**, οῦς, ἡ, (περιβαίνω) obsc. name of Aphrodite in Argos, Hsch., prob. in Clem.Al.*Protr*.2.39.2.

**περιβεβλημένως**, Adv. pf. part. Pass., metaph. in Rhet. *diffusely*, Hermog.*Id*.1.10, 11; cf. περιβολή III. 3.

**περιβῐάζομαι**, *use great force*, Aesop.103: c. acc., *do violence to*, τὴν φύσιν Gal.17(2).177.

**περιβῐβάζω**, *put astride, mount* a rider on a horse, Plu.*Crass*.31.

**περιβιβρώσκω**, *gnaw all round*, pf. -βέβρωκα Diph.34; π. πλεκτάνας Plu.2.1059e:—Pass., of leaves, Dsc.2.133; περιβεβρωμένους τυρούς D.S.2.4; *to be corroded* by ulcers, Dsc.1.71, 2.74, Gal.12.875.

**περιβῐόω**, *survive*, aor. inf. -βιῶναι Plu.*Cor*.11: fut. inf. -βιώσεσθαι Id.*Ant*.53; τὴν παροῦσαν ἡμέραν -βεβιωκότες Lxx 3*Ma*.5.18. II. trans., in fut., *keep alive*, v.l. in ib.*Ex*.22.18(17) cod. A.

**περιβλαστάνω**, *grow round about*, Plu.2.829b.

**περι-βλεπτικός**, ή, όν, *circumspect*, *Cat.Cod.Astr*.2.166. ⊛ **-βλεπτος**, ον, *looked at from all sides, admired of all observers*, βίος E.*Andr*.89; ταῶς Antiph.175.5; ἵππος X.*Eq*.10.1 (Comp.); π. τὴν φύσιν τινὸς ποιεῖν Isoc.10.17; mostly of persons, π. βροτοῖς E.*HF*508, cf. Epicur.*Sent*.7, Lxx *Pr*.31.23, etc.; πάντων.. -ότατοι X.*HG*7.1.30; διὰ ταῦτα π. εἶναι ἐν Ἕλλησι καὶ ἐν βαρβάροις Id.*Smp*.8.38, etc.; π. παρά τισι Carneisc.*Herc*.1027.12, D.S.13.92; π. ἐπ' ἀρετῇ Isoc.8.141, cf. 16.48; ὑπὸ πάντων ἐπὶ κακίᾳ Id.6.95; π. τὸ σῶμα Anon.ap.Suid. s.v. Ἀρσάκης (Sup.), Philostr.*VA*1.7; freq. as a title of honour, *POxy*.1038.11 (vi A.D.), etc. Adv. -τως, ἀγωνίσασθαι D.S.18.30. **-βλεπτότης**, ητος, ἡ, *celebrity*, as a title, *BGU*547.3 (Byz.), *Gloss*. **-βλέπω**, *look round about, gaze around*, περιβλέψας ἔφη Ar.*Ec*.403; πρὸς τοὺς παρόντας Pl.*Erx*.395c; μηδαμοῖ X.*Lac*.3.4; πάντῃ Luc.*Sacr*.9, etc.:—Med., *look about one*, Plu.*Cat.Mi*.37, Arr.*Epict*.3.14.3; περιεβλέποντο ζητοῦντες.. D.S.16.32. II. trans., *look round at*, πάσας X.*Cyr*.5.1.4:—Med., ἀλλότρια ἡγεμονικὰ π. M.Ant.7.55, cf. *Ev.Marc*.3.5. 2. *seek after, covet for oneself*, ἀρχήν App.*BC*3.7. 3. *look about for*, τινα Luc.*Vit.Auct*.12; τόπον εὐφυῆ Plb.5.20.5:—Med., Id.9.17.6, Lxx *To*.11.5. 4. *admire, respect*, τοὔνδικον π. S.*OC*996 (unless in signf. II. 3):—Pass., περιβλέπεσθαι τίμιον E.*Ph*.551, cf. Philostr.*Her*.15. 5. Med., *look up, consult*, βίβλους Zos.Alch.p.138 B. **-βλεψις**, εως, ἡ, *looking* or *gazing about*, Hp.*Epid*.7.11 (pl.); ὀμμάτων -βλέψεις Arist.*Phgn*.808ᵃ16. 2. *close examination*, Plu.*Alex*.23. II. *admiration*, Epicur.*Sent.Vat*.81: pl., Phld.*Oec*.p.66 J.

**περί-βλημα**, ατος, τό, *garment*, Arist.*Pr*.870ᵃ27, Lxx *Nu*.31.20, Democr.Eph.1; as name of a particular garment, *PCair.Zen*.92.2 (iii B.C.); = Lat. *palla*, *Gloss*.; τὰ ἐν Διονύσου π. actors' *robes*, Max.Tyr.7.10; π. σαρκῶν Ph.1.281; of a membrane, Gal.*UP*7.3. II. = περίβολος II. 2, Ph.2.148; *enceinte, fortification*, Pl.*Plt*.288b. **-βλησις**, εως, ἡ, *putting round, enwrapping*, Sor.*Fasc*.18. **-βλητέον**, *one must put round*, τινί τι Muson.*Fr*.14 p.73 H., Antyll.ap.Orib.7.9.2, Sor.2.10. 2. *one must surround*, τι θριγκῷ *Gp*.10.1.1. **-βλητικός**, ή, όν, *fit for amplifying*, σχῆμα Hermog.*Id*.1.9, Eust.1968.23. Adv. -κῶς Id.1949.17.

**περίβληχρος**, ον, *very weak*: neut. as Adv., *even to faintness*, π. βαρύθοντες A.R.4.621.

**περιβλύζω** and **περιβλύω**, *boil* or *bubble all round*, κύματα περιβλύει σπιλάδεσσι A.R.4.788; περὶ δ' ἔβλυσεν αἷμα βοείῃ Q.S.10.150; γῆ.. νάμασι περιβλύζουσα *gushing* with streams, Arist.*Mu*.397ᵃ25. 2. c. acc., *cause to gush around*, λίμνην αὐτῷ περιβλύσαι νέκταρος Philostr.*VA*3.25.

**περιβο-άω**, *defame*, Poll.8.154, Phalar.*Ep*.135.1, 142.3. **-ησία**, ἡ, *scandal*, Ptol.*Tetr*.170, Vett.Val.40.30 (pl.), al., Artem.2.30 (pl.). **-ησις**, εως, ἡ, = foreg., in pl., Vett.Val.230.34, Artem.1.51. **-ητος**, ον, Dor. **-ᾱτος**, poet. **περίβωτος** (q.v.), *noised abroad, much talked of, famous*, π. τινὰ ποιεῖν D.34.29, cf. *Com.Adesp*.120; π. ξένοι Men.*Pk*.281; π. λαβρώνιος Hipparch.Com.3; π. στιχίδια Plu.*Per*.30; π. καθ' ὅλην τὴν οἰκουμένην ἱερόν Lxx 2*Ma*.2.22; ὁ στόλος.. π. ἐγένετο Th.6.31, cf. D.40.11; μέγα καὶ π. ἔργον Men.402.3. 2. in bad sense, *notorious, scandalous*, ἵνα μὴ π. εἴην Lys.3.30; π. ἐργαστήριον Antiph.25; ταύτης τῆς.. αἰσχρᾶς καὶ περιβοήτου συστάσεως D.18.297, cf. Din.2.15. Adv. -τως *notoriously*, Aeschin.1.113, D.17.5. 3. [Ἄρης] περιβόατος ἀντιάζων meeting me *amid shouts and cries*, S.*OT*192 (lyr.); περιβοήτους ἀπεργάζεται makes them *utter frantic cries*, Pl.*Phlb*.45e.

**περιβοθρόομαι**, Pass., *have a trench dug round*, Thphr.*CP*5.13.1.

⊛ **περιβολ-άδιον**, τό, Dim. of sq., *wrapper*, *POxy*.921.2 (iii A.D.). **-αιον**, τό, (περιβάλλω) *that which is thrown round, covering*, θανάτου περιβόλαια corpse-*clothes*, E.*HF*549; σαρκὸς π. ἡβῶντα youthful *incasements* of flesh, i.e. youth, manhood, ib.1269, cf. *PStrassb*.91.9 (i B.C.); freq. in Lxx, *De*.22.12, al. (metaph., π. χαλκοῦν ἡ ἰσχύς σου *Je*.15.12); woman's *headgear*, 1*Ep.Cor*.11.15; *covering* for the feet, Plu.*Arat*.43; *chariot-cover*, Id.*Alex*.67; *bedcover*, Gal.18(1).103; *padding*, περιβόλαια σπληνῶν ib.(2).381; *dressing-gown, warm wrap*, Herod.Med.ap.Orib.10.18.13, Archig.ap.Gal.13.264. II. = περίβολος II. 2, *CIG*4590 (Palestine). **-ή**, ἡ, *covering, garment*, Pl.*Plt*.280b; *dress*, Phld.*Vit*.p.36 J., Arr.*Epict*.3.1.1, Luc.*Herm*.19; π. ἱματίων Lxx *Si*.11.4; *turn* of a bandage, Hp.*Fract*.14 (pl.): in various senses acc. to context, χειρῶν περιβολαί *embraces*, E.*IT*903 (περιβολαί alone, X.*Cyn*.7.3, Plu.*Rom*.8); περιβολαὶ χθονός, i.e. the *grave*, E.*Tr*.389; ἐς σκοτεινὰς π. μεθῶ ξίφος *scabbard*, Id.*Ph*.276; ἄτοιχοι π. σκηνωμάτων tents, Id.*Ion* 1133; π. σφραγισμάτων the sealed *coverings*, Id.*Hipp*.

864; π. τοῖς σώμασι, of clothes and houses, Diog.Oen.10; σαρκῶν π. *putting on* of flesh, Aret.*SD*2.6: abs., of *walls round* a town, ἑπτάπυργοι π. E.*Ph*.1078; αἱ ἔκτοσθεν π. Luc.*Anach*.20; ἐνιαυσία π. χλαμύδος annual *investiture*, Phld.*Vit*.p.27 J. 2. *circumnavigation*, περιβολαὶ τῆς Πελοποννήσου Luc.*Ner*.1. II. *space enclosed, compass*, οἰκίης μεγάλης π. a house of large *compass*, Hdt.4.79; *precinct*, Jul.*Or*.7.239c. b. *extent, degree*, π. νοσήματος Hp.*Epid*.1.9. 2. *circumference, circuit*, χωρίου.. γωνιώδη π. ἔχοντος Th.8.104; μείζω τὴν π. ποιεῖσθαι X.*Cyr*.6.3.30; κύκλον τινὰ καὶ π. ἔχουσα ὁδὸς Plu.*Luc*.21. III. metaph., 1. *compassing, endeavouring after*, τῆς ἀρχῆς π. X.*HG*7.1.40, cf. Afric.*Cest*.p.18 V. 2. ἡ π. παντὸς τοῦ λόγου the *compass* of the whole matter, *scope*, Isoc.5.16, cf. 12.244, J.*AJ Prooem*.2; ἡ καθόλου π. τῶν πραγμάτων Plb.16.20.9. 3. Rhet., *expansion, amplification*, Hermog.*Inv*.1.5, al.; ἡ π. τῶν λόγων Philostr. *VS*1.6; σοφιστικὴ π. ib.1.19.1; *prolixity*, Porph.*Plot*.21, Longin.ap. eund.20.

**περιβολῐβόω**, *case in lead*, *IG*12(1).694 (Rhodes).

**περιβόλιον**, τό, = sq. II. 2, of a temple, *UPZ*119.15 (ii B.C.), prob. in *Arch.Pap*.2.433 (i A.D.).

* **περίβολος**, ον, (περιβάλλω) *compassing, encircling*, στέφεα E.*IA* 1477 (lyr.); κάνναι Pherecr.63. II. as Subst. περίβολος, ὁ, = περιβολή, ἐχίδνης περίβολοι *spires* or *coils* of a serpent, E.*Ion*993: in pl., π. λάϊνοι, of a tomb, Id.*Tr*.1141: sg., *enclosing wall*, Hdt.1.181; of a town *wall*, Th.1.89; ἐν οἰκείῳ π. in *a cage* of his own, Pl.*Tht*.197c; of the body as *the case* of the soul, Id.*Cra*.400c; περίβολοι οἰκήσεων Id.*R*.548a; *wall* of the heart, Hp.*Cord*.4. 2. *area enclosed, enclosure*, π. νεωρίων E.*Hel*.1530; ὁ τῆς πόλεως π. Pl.*Lg*.759a; ἀμπελώνων *PGrenf*.2.28.13 (ii B.C.); of a temple, *precinct*, π. ἱεροῦ LXX *Si*.50.2, cf. 2*Ma*.6.4, 4*Ma*.4.11, J.*AJ*15.11.5, Porph.*Abst*.2.54; ὁ τῶν Ὠρῶν π. *BMus.Inscr*.1044 (Attaleia): metaph., πρόθυρα καὶ περιβόλους καὶ αὐλὰς τῇ ἀρχῇ περιέθηκεν Plu.*Sol*.32. III. neut., περίβολα πυρὶ φλεγόμενα fire-balls, Tim.*Pers*.27.

**περιβομβέω**, *buzz, hum round*, Luc.*Lex*.16, *Im*.13, Alciphr.2.4; ποιητοῦ λόγος π. ἀκοάς Max.Tyr.23.4:—Pass., π. δεινοῖς, τῷ θορύβῳ καὶ τῇ βοῇ πάντοθεν, Agath.1.17, 3.18.

**περιβόρειος**, ον, *northern*, Tz.*H*.8.757.

**περιβόσκομαι**, of beasts, fishes, etc., *feed on all round*, Nic.*Al*. 391, *Th*.611, Luc.*Asin*.17; of tribes, π. ἔθνεα γαῖαν D.P.383: metaph., οὐδέ ποτε χθιζὸν περιβόσκεται ἄνθρακα τέφρη Call.*Ap*.84.

**περίβουνος**, ον, *surrounded by hills*, χώρα Plu.*Phil*.14.

**περιβρᾰχῑόνιος**, ον, *round* or *on the arm*, φόρημα Plu.*Dem*.30: Subst. περιβραχιόνιον, τό, *armlet*, X.*Cyr*.6.4.2, D.H.10.37.

* **περιβρέμω**, *roar* or *bellow round about*, περὶ στυφελὴ β. ἀκτὴ A.R.2. 323, cf. Orph.*A*.689:—Med., c. dat., D.P.132, Opp.*C*.2.67.

**περιβρίθω** [ῐ], intr., *to be exceeding heavy, droop*, Nic.*Al*.180, *Th*. 851; *bear a heavy crop*, Arat.1049; πετάλοισι *with* leaves, Nic.*Al*. 143.

**περιβρομέω**, = περιβρέμω, Ep. impf. περιβρομέεσκον ἀκουαί A.R.4. 17: c. acc., *buzz about*, λείρια περιβρομέουσι μέλισσαι Id.1.879.

**περιβροντάομαι**, *resound with thunder*, ὁ κόσμος ἐν κύκλῳ περιεβροντᾶτο *Erotic.Fragm.Papyr*.p.20 Lavagnini.

**περιβρυής**, ές, *very luxuriant*, Nic.*Th*.531, 841.

**περιβρύχιος** [ῠ], ον, *engulfing*, οἴδματα S.*Ant*.336 (lyr.).

**περί-βρωσις**, εως, ἡ, *ulceration*, Dsc.5.5 (pl.). **-βρωτος**, ον, *ulcerated*, Aret.*SD*2.9.

**περιβυρσόομαι**, Pass., *to be covered with hides all round*, Ath.Mech. 25.1.

**περιβύω**, *stop up round about*, in Pass., ὡς ἅπασαν τὴν στεφάνην περιβεβύσθαι Agath.5.7, cf. Hsch. II. *stuff in all round*, τί τινι Luc.*Gall*.11.

**περιβώμ-ιος**, ον, *round the altar*, Suid. s.v. ἔλεγος: Subst., τὰ π. *images placed about the altar*, LXX 2*Ch*.34.3:—but περιβωμόῳ (sic), *space round a* βωμός, *Rev.Hist.Rel*.97.275; περιβώμιοι, οἱ, functionaries attached to Asiatic cults, *IG*12(3).1126 (Melos): hence *Peribomius*, name of an Archigallus, Juv.2.16, cf. Sch. ad loc. **-ίς**, ίδος, ἡ, pecul. fem., = foreg., τιμή *Milet*.7.64 (Didyma, ii/iii A.D.). **-ισμός**, ὁ, *altar-precinct*, ibid.

* **περίβωτος**, ον, poet. for περιβόητος, *IG*3.716, 7.94 (Megara), 14. 1942.3 (Rome), Afric.*Cest*.30.

**περιγᾰνόω**, *polish all round*, Cass.*Pr*.62.

**περιγεγονότως**, Adv., (περιγίγνομαι) *successfully*, Phlp.*in Cat*.135. 6, prob. in Choerob.*in Theod*.1.305 H. 2. = ἐκ περιουσίας, i.e. *superfluously*, Simp.*in Ph*.1023.16.

**περιγεγραμμένως**, Adv., (περιγράφω I. 2) *definitely, explicitly*, Sch. Ar.*Pax*418.

**περιγέγωνα**, *shout round about*, τὸ περιγεγωνός *sonorousness*, restd. for -γεγονός by Casaubon in D.L.5.65.

**περίγειος**, ον, *surrounding the earth*, φῶς, opp. αἰθέριος, *Stoic*.1. 28; τὰ π. Cleanth.ib.111; π. χῶρος Ph.1.196; κόσμος Alex.Aphr. *Pr*.2.47. 2. *of the earth*, opp. ἀέριος etc., θεοί *Cat.Cod.Astr*.8(4). 252. II. Astron., *near the earth*, σελήνη Vett.Val.55.23, etc.: Comp., Ptol.*Alm*.9.1: Sup., ib.3.3; τὸ π. (sc. σημεῖον) *perigee*, ibid.; π. ἐναντίωσις Phlp.*in Cat*.80.9.

**περιγειότης**, ητος, ἡ, *proximity to the earth*, Ptol.*Tetr*.17.

**περιγελάω**, *deride*, τινα A.D.*Synt*.284.21. 2. *smile all around* (expl. of γέλασσε δὲ πᾶσα περὶ χθών), ib.311.27, cf. Phot. s.v. περιεκόκκασα.

**περιγενητικός**, ή, όν, *superior to, victorious over*, εἱμαρμένη π. ἁπάντων Plu.2.1055e.

* **περιγηθής**, ές, *very joyful*, A.R.3.814, 4.888.

**περιγηράσκω**, *grow old in succession*, J.*BJ*3.10.8.

* **περιγίγνομαι**, Ion. and later -γίνομαι [γῐ], fut. -γενήσομαι Th.4. 27, etc.: aor. -εγενόμην Hdt.1.122, etc.: pf. -γέγονα ib.82, etc.; -γεγένημαι Th.1.69, etc.:—*to be superior to* others, *prevail over, overcome*: Constr. in full, c. gen. pers. et dat. rei, μήτι δ' ἡνίοχος περιγίγνεται ἡνιόχοιο Il.23.318; ὅσσον περιγιγνόμεθ' ἄλλων πύξ τε παλαισμοσύνῃ τε Od.8.102, cf. 252; πολυτροπίῃ τινὸς π. Hdt.2.121.ε', cf. Th.1. 55, Pl.*Ap*.22c; τάχει τοσοῦτον π. τινός X.*Cyr*.3.1.19; τῶν χρημάτων τῶν ἐν Δελφοῖς π. ταῖς ἐκ τῶν ἰδίων δαπάναις Isoc.5.54: c. acc. rei, ὅσα .. περιγένοιντο ἐμοῦ D.18.236; τὰ Ὀλύμπια π. Plu.2.242b: c. gen. pers. only, Hdt.1.207, Ar.*V*.604; π. καὶ πλεονεκτεῖν τῶν ἐχθρῶν Pl. *R*.362b, etc.: c. acc. pers. (in an anacoluthon), κατὰ τὸ ἰσχυρὸν Ἕλληνας ὁμοφρονέοντας χαλεπὰ εἶναι π. Hdt.9.2: abs., *to be superior, prevail*, Id.1.214, Th.4.27, etc.; π. τῇ συμβολῇ, τῷ πλῷ, Hdt.6.109, Th.8.104; π. πρός τινας, πρὸς τὰ ἀντιτεταγμένα, Id.1.69, 5.111. 2. of things, ἤν τι περιγίγνηται αὐτοῖς τοῦ πολέμου if they *gain any advantage* in the war, Id.6.8; π. ὑμῖν πλῆθος νεῶν you *have a superiority in* number of ships, Id.2.87; π. ἡμῖν μὴ προκάμνειν we *have the advantage* in not.., ib.39. II. *live over, survive, escape*, Hdt.1.82, 122, Th.4. 27, etc.; οἱ περιγενόμενοι the *survivors*, Hdt.5.64, etc.: c. gen. rei, περιεγένετο τούτου τοῦ πάθεος *he survived, escaped from* this disaster, ib.46; τῆς δίκης π. Pl.*Lg*.905a; ἐκ τῶν μεγίστων π. Th.2.49. 2. of things, *remain over and above*, opp. ἐπιλείπειν, Ar.*Pl*.554, cf. Lys. 30.20; περιγενόμενον ἐκ τοῦ προτέρου ἐνιαυτοῦ *IG*1².352.10; τάλαντα ἃ περιεγένοντο τῶν φόρων *which remained from* the tribute, the *surplus*, X.*HG*2.3.8; τὸ περιγιγνόμενον τῶν πόρων ἀργύριον Isoc.8.82, cf. Pl. *Lg*.742b, *PRev.Laws*19.8 (iii B.C.), etc.; τὰ περιγινόμενα the *revenues*, Arr.*An*.7.17.4. 3. of things, *to be left over*: hence, *to be a result* or *consequence*, ἐκ τῶν μεγίστων κινδύνων καὶ πόλει καὶ ἰδιώτῃ μέγισται τιμαὶ π. Th.1.144; ἀμαχητὶ π. τινί τι Id.4.73; ἡ ἠθικὴ ἐξ ἔθους π. Arist. *EN*1103ᵃ17; τί αὐτῷ περιγέγονεν ἐκ τῆς φιλοσοφίας; D.L.2.68; περιεγένετο ὥστε καλῶς ἔχειν X.*An*.5.8.26; τούτου μόνου περιγίγνεσθαι μέλλοντος, παθεῖν τι κακὸν D.3.12; ἐκ τούτων περιγίγνεταί τι *the upshot* of the matter *is*.., Id.8.53; τοῖς μὲν.. πεισθεῖσιν ἡ σωτηρία περιεγένετο to those who complied safety *was the result*, Id.18.80; περίεστι δέ μοι τοιαῦτα οἷα τοῖς κακόν τι νοοῦσιν ὑμῖν περιγένοιτο that is what I have got by the business, and I hope that your enemies *may get* the like, Id.*Ep*.3.36; ἀηδὴς δόξα τῇ πόλει παρὰ τοῖς πολλοῖς π. Id.*Prooem*. 23; ἡ ἐκ τῆς πραγματικῆς ἱστορίας περιγινομένη ἐμπειρία Plb.1.35.9.

**περιγλᾰγής**, ές, (γλάγος) *full of milk*, Il.16.642.

**περιγληνάομαι**, (γλήνη) *turn round the eyeballs, glare around*, περιγληνώμενος ὄσσοις, of a lion, Theoc.25.241. **-ής**, ές, *having eyes all round*, τροχαλόν, i.e. the Milky Way, Arat.476.

**περίγλισχρος**, ον, *very sticky*, Hp.*Aph*.4.53, *Epid*.4.46.

**περίγλῠκυς**, εια, υ, *very sweet*: Sup. -κιστος Ael.*NA*15.7.

**περι-γλυπτέον**, *one must cut away*, Philum.*Ven*.2.6. **-γλῠφή**, ἡ, *peeling*, Antyll.ap.Orib.50.3.6, Paul.Aeg.6.54. **-γλῠφον**, τό, *carved figure*, LXX 3*Ki*.6.29. **-γλύφω** [ῠ], *peel*, ᾠά Aristid.*Or*.47 (23).45 (Pass.). 2. *trim*, of papyrus, Heliod.ap.Orib.50.9.11 (Pass.). 3. *hollow out*, ῥοιάν Orib.*Fr*.54. 4. *excise*, Antyll.ap. Orib.44.23.44. **-γλυψις**, εως, ἡ, *excision*, Philum.*Ven*.22.4.

**περίγλωσσος**, ον, *ready of tongue, eloquent*, Pi.*P*.1.42.

**περιγλωττίς**, ίδος, ἡ, *covering of the tongue*, Ath.1.6c.

**περιγλώχῐν**, ῖνος, ὁ, ἡ, v.l. for πυρι-, Opp.*C*.2.166.

**περιγνάμπτω**, *double* a headland, Μάλειαν Od.9.80; ἄκρην A.R.2. 364. 2. intr., *curve*, ὀρθαὶ ἑκάτερθε π. κεραῖαι Arat.790. 3. *bend*, στάχυν Nonn.*D*.41.225: metaph., φρένα π. κεστῷ ib.8.174.

**περιγογγύζω**, *murmur round about*, ἅσσ' ἂν π. πολῖται Phoc.6.

**περιγομφάομαι**, Pass., *to be pierced by nails*, f.l. for περιοφθεὶς in Lib.*Or*.56.20. **-γομφος**, ον, *fitted with dowels*, φάτναι, προσαρμογαί, *Inscr.Délos*504 *A*6,9 (ii B.C.).

**περιγονᾰτίς**, ίδος, ἡ, in pl., *knee-caps*, Jul.*Or*.2.57c.

**περίγρα**, ἡ, *pair of compasses*, Eust.1960.18, Suid.

**περί-γραμμα**, ατος, τό, *that which is written around* or *upon*, Aristaenet.1.10. II. *enclosed space, ring*, Luc.*Anach*.38. **-γραπτέον**, *one must trace around*, κύκλῳ περὶ ἐμαυτὸν σκιαγραφίαν ἀρετῆς π. Pl.*R*. 365c. II. *one must cancel*, Ath.5.180b. III. *one must set a limit to*, λόγον A.D.*Synt*.18.20. **-γραπτος**, ον, *circumscribed*, ἐκ περιγράπτου Th.7.49. **-γρᾰφεύς**, *circumscriptor, Gloss.*; διαθηκῶν π. *will-forger*, ib. * **-γρᾰφή**, ἡ, *outline*, π. τις ἔξωθεν περιγεγραμμένη Pl. *Lg*.768c, cf. *Plt*.277c; διαρθρῶσαι τὰ καλῶς ἔχοντα τῇ π. Arist.*EN*1098ᵃ 23; ταῖς π. διορίζεται πρότερον, ὕστερον δὲ λαμβάνει τὰ χρώματα Id.*GA* 743ᵇ20; κύματος Gal.9.311; ἴδοι τις ἂν καὶ ἐπ' ἐσθῆτος καὶ ἐν τῇσιν ἄλλῃσι π. *general appearance*, Hp.*Decent*.2; ἡ τοῦ προσώπου π. Luc.*Im*. 6; κατὰ περιγραφὴν *in outline*, Iamb.*Myst*.1.9, cf. Thphr.*Fr*.69. 2. *circumference, circuit*, [ἡ Βαβυλὼν] ἔχει π. μᾶλλον ἔθνους ἢ πόλεως Arist. *Pol*.1276ᵃ28, cf. Plb.4.39.1, 9.26ᴬ.3. b. *surface*, Gal.6.504. c. *section*, Id.19.644. 3. *that which is marked by an outline, impression*, π. ποδοῖν A.*Ch*.207. 4. Geom., *circumscribed figure*, Archim.*Sph. Cyl*.1.6. II. *limit*, τῆς ἀπολαύσεως D.S.3.16; *termination*, τῶν κακῶν cj. in J.*AJ*16.11.6, cf. *BJ*1.19.4. 2. *individuality*, μία ψυχὴ κἂν φύσεσι διείργηται μυρίαις καὶ ἰδίαις π. M.Ant.12.30; κατὰ περιγραφὴν in their *individual content*, S.E.*M*.8.161. 3. Rhet., *compass of expression*, ἡ π. τῆς ἐννοίας Hermog.*Id*.1.3; αἱ π. τῶν διανοιῶν Luc. *Dem.Enc*.32; κῶλόν ἐστι νοήματός τινος π. Corn.*Rh*.p.395 H. III. Gramm., *breaking off, conclusion*, prob. in A.D.*Conj*.251.24, 253.15, *Synt*.267.5. IV. αἱ π. *descriptive passages*, Hermog.*Inv*.2.7. V. in Law, *circumvention, fraud*, π. τοῦ ταμείου *on* the treasury, prob. for ἐπιγρ- in *PTeb.*288.8(iii A.D.), cf. *Arch.Pap.*1.301 (iv A.D.), etc.; διατυπώσεως *Cod.Just.*1.2.24.1, cf. Just.*Nov.*7 *Praef.* **-γρᾰφικός**, ή, όν, *indicating a conclusion*, σύνδεσμοι prob. in A.D.*Conj.*253.18. **-γράφιον** [ᾰ], τό, and **-γρᾰφος**, ὁ, = Lat. *praeductal*, *Gloss.* ⊛ **-γράφω** [ᾰ], *draw a line round*, περιγράφει τῇ μαχαίρῃ ἐς τὸ ἔδαφος τὸν ἥλιον Hdt.8.137; π. κύκλον *draw* a circle *round*, Id.7.60; π. ὅσον ἐναριστᾶν κύκλον Eup.250; ἡ ταῦτα τὰ πεδία περιγράφουσα γραμμή Plb.2.14.8: abs., *describe a circle*, Ar.*Pax*879. b. Geom., *circumscribe*, περὶ κύκλον τρίγωνον Euc.4.3,5, cf. Archim.*Sph.Cyl.*1.3, al.; τὸ περιγεγραμμένον σχῆμα τῷ τομεῖ ib.40. 2. *define*, *determine*, *limit*, π. τοῦ ἔτους χρόνον X.*Mem.*1.4.12; π. ὅτι.. ἐγγύτατα τοῦ πράγματος Arist.*Rh.*1396[b]8; τὴν πολλὴν βρῶσιν Heraclid.Tar.ap.Ath.2.64e:— Med., Arist.*Metaph.*1064[a]2: Pass., περιεγέγραπτο, ὡς ἔοικε, ..μέχρι ὅσου ἡ νίκη ἐδέδοτο αὐτοῖς X.*HG*7.5.13; *to be bounded*, D.S.3.41; *to be circumscribed*, Ti.Locr.97e, Plot.6.4.7, Dam.*Pr.*113, etc.: Rhet., αἱ ἔννοιαι.. ἐφ' ἑαυτῶν περιγραφόμεναι *being* self-*contained*, Hermog.*Id.*1.3. 3. *terminate*, *conclude*, τὴν βίβλον D.S.2.60, 3.74, etc.; τὰς ὑποθήκας Plu.2.14a; ἀγχόνῃ τὸ ζῆν Ath.9.388c:—Pass., *Placit.*3.8.2. 4. *bring to an end*, *cure* a disease, Archig.ap.Gal.8.90, Sor.2.16 (Pass.), Gal.13.860. II. *draw in outline*, *trace* or *sketch*, *delineate*, τοὺς θεούς Phld.*Piet.*81:—Med., σκιὰν περιγράψασθαι *draw oneself* an outline, Poll.7.129:—Pass., περιγεγράφθω ταύτῃ Arist.*EN*1098[a]20; τὰ δυνατὰ -γραφῆναι Phld.*Ir.*p.62 W.; περιγεγραμμένους μῦς *well-marked* muscles, Antyll.ap.Orib.7.7.8. III. *enclose* as it were *within brackets*, *cancel*, *annul* (cf. διαγράφω), Demonic.1.3, Plu.2.334c, *PSI*1.64.15 (Pass., i A.D.); τὸ φιλεῖν *AP*5.67 (Lucill. or Polemo Rex); τὸ πρὸς δόξαν ἢ τρυφὴν ἅπαν π. Epict.*Ench.*33; π. τινὰ ἐκ πολιτείας *exclude from* civic privileges, Aeschin.3.209; τινὰ τοῦ ζῆν Vett.Val.150.10:—Pass., Hld.10.20. 2. *reject as spurious*, Ath.5.180e; *remove* from a text, A.D.*Synt.*6.3, al. IV. in Law, *defraud*, in Pass., *PAmh.*2.77.7 (ii A.D.), etc.; also, *circumvent*, διάταξιν Just.*Nov.*55 *Praef.*

**περιγῡρ-εύω**, (γῦρος) *make a trench round*, βωμόν *PMag.Par.*1.33, 37. **-ίς**, ίδος, ἡ, *circumference*, Hsch. (pl.).

**περιγώνιον**, τό, carpenter's *set-square*, Aq.*Is.*44.13 (pl.).

**περιδαίδᾰλος**, ον, *all-variegated*, Opp.*C.*4.388.

**περῐδαῖος** [ᾱ] νομός, dub. sens. in Pi.*Pae.*4.51.

⊛ **περιδαίω**, in Pass., *to be exceedingly heated*, Opp.*H.*5.411: metaph., περιδαίομαι Ἐνδυμίωνι I *burn with love for* him, A.R.4.58.

**περίδακρυς**, υ, *tearful*, gloss on ἀμφιδάκρυτος, Sch.E.*Ph.*330.

**περιδάμναμαι**, *subdue utterly*, Q.S.1.165, 3.21, al.

**περιδᾰπᾰνάομαι**, *to be wasted away all round*, Philum.ap.Aët.5.127.

**περιδαρδάπτω**, *devour greedily*, Hsch. (Act. and Pass.).

**περιδέεια**, ἡ, *exceeding fear*, Suid.

**περιδεής**, ές, (δέος) *very timid* or *fearful*, π. γενέσθαι Hdt.5.44, cf. And.4.40, Th.3.28, Isoc.2.23, Alciphr.2.4, etc.; τινι *at* a thing, Hdt.7.15; τινος Pl.*Ep.*348b; π. μή.. Th.3.80. Adv. -εῶς *in great fear*, Id.6.83, etc.; πρός τινα π. σχεῖν Isoc.9.58.

**περιδείδῐα**, pf. in pres. sense, Il.10.93, al.; imper. περιδείδιθι Hsch.: aor. 1 περίδεισα, Hom. (only in Il.) always in forms with ῑ, for περίδϝεισαν, περιδϝείσασα, etc. (v. infr.):—*to be in great fear* or *dread about*. c. gen., αἰνῶς γὰρ Δαναῶν π. Il.1.c., cf. 17.240: c. dat., *to be in great fear for*, Ἀθήνῃ πᾶσι περιδείσασα θεοῖσι 15.123; Αἴαντι περιδείσαντες 23.822; τῷ ῥα περίδεισαν 11.508; ἐμῇ κεφαλῇ περιδείδια, μή τι πάθῃσιν 17.242; περιδείσασ' Ἀχιλῆϊ, μή.. 21.328: c. inf., *fear greatly* to do, A.R.2.1203: c. acc., γαλέην περιδείδια Batr.51.

**περιδεικνύω**, *demonstrate*, ἐπιλογιστικῶς ὅτι.. Phld.*Lib.*p.14 O.

**περίδειλος**, ον, *very cowardly*, Apostol.15.32.

**περίδεινον**· πειρατήν, and **περίδεινος**· περιπαθής, Hsch.; cf. περίδινος.

**περιδειπν-έω**, *cause* one *to eat a funeral feast*, Lxx 2*Ki.*3.35 (v.l. παραδειπνίσαι):—Pass., Artem.4.81. **-ον**, τό, *funeral feast*, D.18.288, Aen.Tact.10.5, Men.367, Hegesipp.Com.1.11, *PTeb.*118.1 (ii B.C.), Phld.*Acad.Ind.*p.35 M., etc.; τὸ π. τοῦ βίου λαμπρὸν ποιῶ Anaxipp.1.42; Ἀρκεσιλάου π., title of work by Timo, D.L.9.115.

**περι-δειρίδιον**, τό, (δειρή) *necklet*, *IG*11(2).161 *B*42 (Delos, iii B.C.). **-δειρον**, τό, *circumference of the neck*, Poll.2.135.

⊛ **περιδέξιος**, ον, *with two right hands*, i.e. *ambidextrous*, Il.21.163, *AP*12.247 (Strat.). 2. *very dexterous* or *expert*, λόγοι Ar.*Nu.*949 (lyr.). Adv. -ίως Philostr.*VS*1.19.1. 3. *convenient*, Opp.*C.*1.114,455. 4. δένδρον π., name of a fabulous Indian tree, Cyran. 95. II. *going round the right arm*:—Subst. **περιδέξιον**, τό, *armlet for the right arm*, *PPetr.*2 *Intr.*p.22 (iii B.C.), Lxx *Ex.*35.22, *Is.*3.20.

**περι-δέραιος**, ον, (δέρη) *passed round the neck*, ὁ π. κόσμος Plu.*Galb.*17; οἱ π. τῶν στεφάνων Id.2.647f. II. Subst. περιδέραιον, τό, *necklace*, Ar.*Fr.*320.5, *Com.Adesp.*146, Arist.*Po.*1454[b]24, Plu.*Sert.*14, Luc.*Pisc.*12, etc. 2. *collar* of a pillory, Id.*Lex.*10. **-δερίς**, ίδος, ἡ, *necklace*, Poll.2.235, 5.55.

⊛ **περιδέρκομαι**, poet. for περιβλέπω, Nonn.*D.*22.58, *AP*5.288 (Agath.).

**περιδέρω**, *dissect off all round*, τὸ δέρμα Gal.2.691:—Pass., *to be flayed*, Antyll.ap.Orib.50.2.4.

**περίδεσ-ις**, εως, ἡ, *tying round*, Muson.*Fr.*19 p.107 H. **-μεύω**, *tie round*, Sch.Ar.*Ec.*118, 319 (Pass.):—also **-μέω**, *Gp.*17.19.3, Sch.Opp.*H.*2.34:—Pass., Zos.Alch.p.233 B. **-μιος**, ον, *tied round*, π. ἅμματι χειρῶν παρθενικήν Nonn.*D.*48.142. **-μος**, ὁ, *band*, *belt*, *girdle*, Gal.18(2).762, Aristaenet.1.25.

**περίδετος**, ον, *bound*, θώραξ ταινίαις π. App.*Mith.*77.

**περιδευκές**· περισσῶς πεποικιλμένον, Hsch.

**περιδέω**, *bind*, *tie round* or *on*, τινί τι Hdt.1.193, Ar.*Ec.*127:—Med., *bind round oneself*, περισφύριον περιδέεται Hdt.4.176; τὴν φὰν π. περὶ τὴν ὀσφύν Hermipp.53; λόφον, πώγωνα, στεφάνους π., Ar.*Ra.*1038, *Ec.*100, 122; of pugilists, ἐπισφαίροις π. τὰς χεῖρας Plu.2.825e; ἀντὶ ἱμάντων σφαίρας ἂν περιεδούμεθα Pl.*Lg.*830b. 2. *bind round*, *bandage* with, ἱμᾶσι πόδα Hp.*Fract.*13; ἀραχνίοις Arist.*HA*623[a]14.

**περίδηλος**, ον, *very clear*, *manifest*, Hsch.

**περίδημα**, ατος, τό, *anything bound round*, *band*, D.Chr.31.116.

**περιδηρ-ῐάω**, *fight about*, Ep. part. περιδηριόωντα Q.S.6.287:—Med., περιδηριόωνται Id.4.165. **-ῑτος**, ον, *fought about*, Κύπριδος ἐργασίη *AP*5.218 (Paul. Sil.).

**περιδιαιρέω**, *part off*, *remove all round*, Heliod.ap.Orib.44.8.24, Gal.2.296.

**περιδιαρθρόομαι**, *to be articulated on all sides*, Gal.18(2).433.

**περιδιατείνω**, *distend*, τὸ κῶλον Herod.Med. in *Rh.Mus.*58.111.

**περιδίδωμι**, only in Med., *stake*, *wager*, c. gen. pretii, τρίποδος περιδώμεθον ἠὲ λέβητος *let us make a wager of* a tripod, i.e. *let us wager* a tripod (to be paid by the loser), Il.23.485; ἐμέθεν περιδώσομαι αὐτῆς I *will wager* myself, i.e. my life, Od.23.78; π. πότερον.. *lay a wager* whether.., Ar.*Ach.*1115; περὶ τῆς κεφαλῆς περιδόσθαι Id.*Eq.*791: with dat. pers. added, περίδου μοι περὶ θυματιδᾶν ἁλῶν *have a wager* with me for a little thyme-salt, Id.*Ach.*772; περίδου νυν ἐμοί, εἰ μή.. Id.*Nu.*644, cf. Diph.130.

**περιδιείρω**, *pass through and embrace*, Philostr.*Im.*2.6.

**περιδῑν-εύω**, *hover around*, prob. for sq. in S.*Fr.*334 (anap.); *revolve round*, ἄξονας οὓς περιεδίνευον τροχοί D.S.18.27. ⊛ **-έω**, *whirl*, *wheel round*, κύκλῳ αὐτόν Aeschin.3.167; τὴν κεφαλήν D.Chr.1.56; ὁ ἥλιος π. περὶ αὐτὸν τὸν πόλον Men.Rh.p.442 S.; τυφὼν π. τὴν ναῦν Luc.*VH*1.9; *set in motion all round*, Alciphr.1.39:—Med., περιδινήσασθε ἀνελίγματα χαίτης *AP*7.485 (Diosc.); also, *take a stroll*, περιδινησόμεθα ἐν Λυκείῳ Luc.*Lex.*2:—Pass., *to be whirled round*, Ph.1.145, Ti.Locr.97c, Iamb.*Myst.*5.20; *spin round* like a top, X.*Smp.*7.3, Luc.*Syr.D.*36, etc.—Cf. περιδονέω. **-ής**, ές, *circular*, κύρτος *AP*6.23. **-ησις**, εως, ἡ, *whirling round*, *rotation*, *revolution*, ἀέρος Plu.*Flam.*10, cf. Plot.2.2.1, *Theol.Ar.*60; τροχοῦ Arr.*Tact.*38.3, Philostr.Jun.*Im.*10; τρυπάνου Heliod.ap.Orib.46.11.12. **-ήτειρα**, ἡ, fem., *causing to revolve*, of Aphrodite, *PMag.Par.*1.2918. **-ητής**, οῦ, ὁ, *one who causes to revolve*, Hsch. (pl.). **-ητος**, ον, *revolving*, ἄξων *PMag.Par.*1.680. ⊛ **-ος**, ὁ, ἡ, *rover*, *pirate*, Pl.*Lg.*777c (-δεινον Hsch.).

**περιδιπλόω**, *wrap round*, *pack up*, Lxx *Ju.*10.5.

**περιδίω** [ῐ], = περιδείδια, *to be in great fear for*, c. dat., used by Hom. only in 3 sg. impf. and always in tmesi, περὶ γὰρ δίε νηυσὶν Ἀχαιῶν Il.9.433, 11.557: folld. by relat. clause, περὶ γὰρ δίε ποιμένι λαῶν, μή τι πάθοι 5.566: without dat., περὶ γὰρ δίε, μή μιν Ἀχαιοὶ.. ἕλωρ δηΐοισι λίποιεν 17.666, cf. Od.22.96.

**περιδῐώκω**, *pursue on all sides*, Str.6.1.8, S.E.*M.*1.227 (Pass.), Aq.*Jb.*13.25.

**περιδνοφέω**, *wrap round with darkness*, Arat.876 (Pass.).

**περιδομ-έω**, *build round*, J.*AJ*15.11.5 (Pass.). **-ημα**, ατος, τό, *surrounding edifice*, *EM*255.40.

**περιδονέω**, v.l. for -δινέω, D.H.1.19 (Pass.); of a wounded elephant, Agath.3.27 (Pass.).

**περιδορά**, ἡ, *removal of skin all round*, Aët.15.8, Paul.Aeg.6.39.

**περίδοσις**, εως, ἡ, (περιδίδομαι) *bargain*, *wager*, Hsch.

**περιδρᾰμητέον**, gloss on περιθρεκτέον, Hsch.

**περί-δραξις**, εως, ἡ, *grasping with the hands*, τινος Plu.2.392b, cf. 979d. **-δράσσομαι**, Att. -ττομαι, *grasp*, τινος Ph.2.136, Hierocl.p.37 A., Plu.*Cam.*26, *Lys.*17: c. acc., -δεδράχθαι θαυμάσιον ἀγαθόν Phld.*Mort.*18; ἡ φύσις τοῦ παντὸς π. τὰ ἐν αὐτῇ Iamb.ap.Simp. in *Cat.*375.9: abs., Ph.2.353; ὥσπερ ἔνιοι -δράττονται *arrogantly claim*, Phld.*Rh.*1.214 S.

**περιδρομ-άς**, άδος, pecul. fem. of περίδρομος, μίτρη *AP*5.12 (Phld.). **-εύς**, έως, ὁ, = Lat. *ambitiosus*, *Gloss.* ⊛ **-ή**, ἡ, *running round*, *encircling*, Plu.*Aem.*20 (pl.); πλάναι καὶ -δρομαί Id.2.493d, etc.; π. ποιεῖσθαι wheel about, X.*Cyn.*10.11. 2. *revolution*, περιδρομαὶ ἐτῶν E.*Hel.*776. 3. a military manœuvre, = Lat. *decursio*, στρατιωτῶν D.C.76.15; π. ἐνόπλιοι Id.77.16. II. κατὰ περιδρομήν *cursorily*, J.*AJ*20.12.1; ἐκ π. Ptol.*Tetr.*55. III. *getting round*, *cajolery*, Memn.8.1, *PLond.*2.415.12 (iv A.D.); π. θεραπείας, = Lat. *ambitus*, D.C.78.22. **-ικός**, ή, όν, *sidereal*, κύκλος, opp. συνοδικός, of the moon, Vett.Val.298.28. **-ίς**, ίδος, ἡ, *circular track* on the top of the walls of Babylon, prob. in Ph.Byz.*Mir.*5.2 (pl.). **-ος**, ον, *running round*, *encircling*, δοιαὶ δὲ π. ἄντυγές εἰσι Il.5.728; πλῆμναι π. ἀμφοτέρωθεν ib.726; of the rim of a shield, E.*El.*458 (lyr.), A.*Th.*495; of a net, Opp.*H.*3.99; κύκλον π. αἰὲν ἑλίσσων Orph.*Fr.*236: c. dat., [ἅλς] νήσοισι περίδρομος D.P.60: dub. sens. in *IG*2².463.54. 2. *wandering*, *roaming*, ἱκέτις φυγὰς π. A.*Supp.*350 (lyr.); κύνες Ar.*Ra.*472; γυνὴ π. *gadabout* woman, Thgn.581. II. Pass., *that can be run round*: hence, *standing apart*, *detached*, κολώνη.. π. ἔνθα καὶ ἔνθα Il.2.812; αὐλὴ π. Od.14.7; αὐλῶν Carc.1; *circular*, D.P.5, 718. 2. *surrounded*, κοίλη.. ὄρεσι π., of Laconia, E.*Fr.*1083; π. οὔρεσι γαῖα A.R.3.1085. **-ος**, ὁ, Subst., *that which surrounds*, *edge*, *rim*, of a shield, E.*Tr.*1197; τοῦ τείχους ὁ π. *circuit* of the wall, Pl.*Criti.*116b; τῆς τομῆς, in amputation, Archig.ap.Orib.47.13.7; *string that runs round the top of a net*, X.*Cyn.*2.6, 10.7, etc.; *gallery running round a building*, Ar.*Fr.*133, X.*Cyr.*6.1.53, Hld.4.8; *line round the head* which defines the scalp, Poll.2.40; ὁ π. τῶν τριχῶν Arist.*Phgn.*808[a]26; ὠκεανὸς πάσης φύσεως π. Secund.*Sent.*2; ἐν π. in a circle, Plu.2.731d. II. orbit, ἡλίου Placit.2.1.4; lap of a race, αἱ περίοδοι τῶν π. D.C.49.43. III. pl., circuit-judges at Mytilene, IG 12(2).6.12 (iv B.C.).

**περιδρύπτω**, tear all round, peel the bark off a tree, AP9.706 (Antip.):—Pass., ἀγκῶνας περιδρύφθη (Ep. aor. Pass.) had the skin all torn from off his arms, Il.23.395, cf. Q.S.4.540; π. χεῖρας καὶ πρόσωπα Ph.1.311; δορὰς Id.2.527; περιδρύπτεσθαι τραύμασιν Ach. Tat.1.12.

**περιδύω**, strip off, ἐπεὶ περίδυσε χιτῶνας Il.11.100; τῶν αὐλητρίδων τὰ ἱμάτια περιέδυεν Ath.13.607f. 2. c. acc. pers., strip, εἰ μὴ ἔφθησαν περιδύσαντες αὐτόν Antipho 2.2.5; π. τὰ νεκρὰ App.BC5.68, etc.: metaph., deprive of authority, J.AJ13.15.3. 3. c. acc. pers. et rei, strip one of a thing, αὐτὰ [ποιήματα] περιδύσας τὸ μέτρον Epich.[254] (dub.); τὰ λοιπὰ π. τινάς App.BC5.67; ἑαυτὸν τὴν ἐσθῆτα J.AJ6.11.5. b. c. acc. et gen., π. τὸν ναὸν τῶν ἀναθημάτων ib.9.12.3.

**περιεγείρω**, arouse, J.AJ5.9.3:—Med., part. -εγρόμενος ib.17.13.3:—Pass., ib.2.9.4.

**περιεγκεντρίζω**, fut. -ίσω, surround with beams laid in cuttings in rafters, IG2².463.62.

**περιεζόμενον**· περιεχόμενον, Hsch.

**περιειλ-άς**, άδος, ἡ, encircling, ζῶναι Eratosth.Fr.16.3 (v.l. περιηγέες). -έω, v. περιείλω. -ημα, ατος, τό, that which is wrapped round, Poll.7.91, Sch.Ar.Nu.10.

**περιειλημμένως**, Adv., (περιλαμβάνω) = περιεκτικῶς, Hsch.

**περιείλ-ησις**, εως, ἡ, wrapping round, Herod.Med.ap.Orib.10.18.15, Sor.1.77,84(pl.). 2. revolution, [ἄστρων] Poll.4.156. -ίσσω, v. περιελίσσω.

**περι-είλω**, -ειλέω, or -ίλλω, wrap round, περὶ τοὺς πόδας σάκια περιειλεῖν (v.l. περιδεῖν, Cobet περιίλλειν) X.An.4.5.36; τῷ αὐτοῦ τραχήλῳ τι περιειλήσας Luc.Alex.15. 2. wrap up, swathe, τὸ βρέτας περιειλῆσαι πάντοθεν Ath.15.672d:—Med., swathe oneself, ῥακίοις περιειλάμενος (Phot., Suid., -ειλλόμενος or -ειλόμενος codd.) Ar.Ra.1066:—Pass., to be wrapped up, Ath.15.672e; to be coiled, of a snake's tail, Gal.14.265, cf. OGI56.63 (Egypt, iii B.C.); to be concentrated, τοῦ πυρώδους περιειληθέντος εἰς τὸ αὐτό Ach.Tat.Intr.Arat.3. II. build a vaulting, Arch.Anz.19.8 (Milet.).

⊛ **περίειμι** (εἰμί sum) to be around, χωρίον ᾧ κύκλῳ τειχίον περιῆν Th.7.81; but more freq. II. to be superior to another, surpass, excel, c. gen. pers., τόσσον ἐγὼ περί τ' εἰμὶ θεῶν περί τ' εἴμ' ἀνθρώπων Il.8.27, cf. Emp.113, Hdt.3.146, X.Mem.3.7.7: c. acc. rei, περὶ φρένας ἔμμεναι ἄλλων Il.13.631; περίεσσι γυναικῶν εἶδός τε μέγεθός τε Od.18.248, cf. 19.326, etc.; οἳ περὶ μὲν βουλὴν Δαναῶν περὶ δ' ἐστὲ μάχεσθαι Il.1.258, cf. Od.1.66: later c. dat. rei, σοφίᾳ τῶν Ἑλλήνων π. Pl.Prt.342b, cf. Smp.222e; τῇ ἐπιμελείᾳ π. τῶν φίλων X.An.1.9.24: without gen. pers., to be superior, ναυσὶ πολὺ π. Th.6.22; πολλὸν π. πλήθεϊ Hdt.9.31, cf. X.An.1.8.13: abs., ἐλπὶς τοῦ περιέσεσθαι hope of success, Th.1.144, cf. Men.Sam.134; ἐκ περιόντος ἀγωνιεῖσθαι at an advantage, Th.8.46. III. to be spared, τινι Hdt.3.119: abs., survive, Id.1.11,120, al., Hp.Prog.20; τῇ σεωυτοῦ μοίρῃ περίεις by your own destiny, Hdt.1.121; τὴν Ἑλλάδα π. ἐλευθέρην shall remain free, Id.7.139, cf. D.21.222, etc.; of things, to be extant, still in existence, Hdt.1.92, etc. 2. to be over and above, remain, freq. in part., τὸ περιὸν τοῦ στρατοῦ Th.2.79; esp. of property, money, etc., ἡ περιοῦσα παρασκευή Id.1.89; π. τινὶ εἰς τὸν ἐνιαυτόν Pl.R.416e; οἰόμενοι περιεῖναι χρήματά τῳ imagining that any one has a balance in his hands, D.18.227; τὰ περιόντα τοῦ κλήρου the surplus, balance, Pl.Lg.923d, cf. Lys.21.16, Is.5.41; τὰ περιόντα χρήματα τῆς διοικήσεως the money remaining after paying the expenses, D.59.4, cf. IG1².91.31, PRev.Laws 16.16 (iii B.C.), etc.; ἃ δὲ νῦν περιόντ' αὐτὸν ὑβρίζειν ἐπαίρει but the superfluous wealth which now incites him.., D.21.211. b. metaph., ἐκ τοῦ περιεῦντος γενέσθαι to be a luxury, Democr.144; ἐκ τοῦ π. in one's leisure, D.Ep.3.36; as a work of supererogation, Phld.Mus.p.108K.; τοῖς ἐκ τοῦ π. εἰς εὐπρέπειαν ἠσκημένοις Luc.Am.33; τοσοῦτον ὑμῖν περίεστι τοῦ πρὸς ἐμὲ μίσους you have such an excess of hatred against me, Ps.-Philipp.ap.D.12.7; τοσοῦτον αὐτῷ περιῆν (sc. τῆς ὕβρεως) D.21.17, cf. Philostr.VA3.46, Ael.NA5.34, Aristid.Or.22(19).6, al.; τοσοῦτον περίεστιν (sc. τῆς ὕβρεως), ὥστε τοὺς ἠδικημένους πρὸς συκοφαντοῦσιν D.55.29. 3. to be left over and above, to be the net result, ὑμῖν περίεστιν ἐκ τούτων the net result to you of all this is.., Id.13.20; ἐνίοις..τὸ μηδὲν ἀναλῶσαι..περίεστιν to some the net result is that they spend nothing, Id.21.155; ὥστε μηδὲν ἄλλ' ἢ τὰς αἰσχύνας αὐτῷ περιεῖναι Aeschin.1.154; ψηφίσμαθ' ὑμῖν περιέσται, βελτίω δ' οὐδ' ὁτιοῦν τὰ πράγματ' ἔσται you will have plenty of decrees, but.., D.Prooem.21.3: c. inf., περίεστι τοίνυν ὑμῖν ἀλλήλοις ἐρίζειν Id.2.29; cf. περιγίγνομαι.

**περίειμι** (εἶμι ibo). [In Com. the ι in περί is sts. elided in the part., περιών, περιόντες, Pherecr.186, Phryn.Com.3.4, Pl.Com.193, Antiph.279, and the part. is so written in Pap. of Arist.Ath.53.1, Hyp.Dem.Fr.4, Lyc.2, also in all or some codd. of Th.1.30, al., X.HG 3.2.25, D.4.10,48, al.]: go round, fetch a compass, Hdt.2.138, etc.; π. κατὰ νώτου τισί get round and take them in rear, Th.4.36; π. κατὰ τὰς κώμας go round to every village, Pl.Min.320c; π. κατ' ἀγρούς Lys.31.18. b. go about, Hp.Fract.15, Gland.12; βούλεσθε περιιόντες πυνθάνεσθαι D.4.10, cf. 48, 6.14, 18.158, etc.; κατὰ τὴν ἀγορὰν π. Phryn.Com.l.c. 2. c. acc. loci, go round, compass, π. τὸν νηὸν κύκλῳ Hdt.1.159; π. φυλακὰς go round the guards, visit them, Id.5.33; τὸν βωμόν Ar.Pax957; ἐν κύκλῳ περιῄει πάντα Id.Pl.709; ὁ ἥλιος κύκλῳ π. τὴν σελήνην Pl.Cra.409b, cf. La.183b; τὴν Ἑλλάδα περιῄει X.An.7.1.33; αἱ μὴ περιιεῖεν [τὰν ἱερὰν γᾶν] IG2².1126.18 (Amphict. Delph.); of sounds, αὐλῶν σε περίεισιν πνοή Ar.Ra.154. II. come round to one, esp. in one's turn or by inheritance, ἡ ἀρχή, βασιληΐη περίεισι ἔς τινα, Hdt.1.120, 2.120. 2. of revolving periods, χρόνου περιιόντος as time came round, ib.121.α', 4.155; ὁ κύκλος τῶν ὡρέων ἐς τὠυτὸ περιιὼν Id.2.4; περι(ι)όντι τῷ θέρει, τῷ ἐνιαυτῷ, Th.1.30, X.HG 3.2.25.

**περιείργω**, Att. for περιέργω (q.v.).

**περιείρω**, insert or fix round, περὶ γόμφους π. τὰ ξύλα Hdt.2.96.

**περιεκλεπτύνω**, reduce to extreme smallness or fineness, in Pass., Zos.Alch.p.223B.

**περιεκτικός**, ή, όν, (περιέχω) containing, c. gen., π. ἑτέρου Zeno Stoic.1.33; θυλάκια π. σπερματίων Dsc.2.148, cf. Cleom.1.8, S.E.M.10.24, Gal.4.722, 5.147, Ruf.Anat.30; ὁ κόσμος ὁ νοητὸς ὅ τε αἰὼν περιεκτικὰ ἄμφω καὶ τῶν αὐτῶν Plot.3.7.2, cf. Procl.Inst.177, Theol.Ar.60, etc. 2. all-embracing, τὸ -ώτατον πάντων Arr.Epict.1.9.4; comprehensive, Ptol.Geog.1.1.1 (Comp.), Dam.Pr.85 (Comp.); διάλυσις PLond.3.1008.4 (vi A.D.). Adv. -κῶς comprehensively, gloss on περιειλημμένως, Hsch.: Comp. -ώτερον Anon.in Cat.25.28, Hsch. 3. profit-making, opp. ἐκχύτης, Luc.Vit.Auct.24, Cat.Cod.Astr.8(4).173. II. Gramm., 1. π. ὄνομα a noun denoting a place in which a number are collected, as παρθενών, D.T.636.14, Ph.1.541, Hdn.Gr.1.35, al. 2. π. ῥῆμα a verb of both active and passive signification, as βιάζομαι, Sch.A.R.1.1.

**περιεκχέομαι**, flow out all round, Gal.18(2).446.

⊛ **περιέλᾰσις**, εως, ἡ, driving about, Hp.Aër.20 (pl.); hurling about, cj. in Plu.2.916d (pl.). II. place for driving round, roadway, Hdt.1.179.

**περιελαύνω**, fut. -ελῶ Ar.Eq.290, etc.:—drive round, τὰς κύλικας π. push the cups round, X.Smp.2.27, Poll.6.30; drive, round up cattle, etc. as booty, λείαν πολλήν Parth.20.1, App.Hann.12; [πρόβατα] Palaeph.18; βοῦς Porph.Abst.2.30:—also in Med., Plb.4.29.6, etc. 2. drive about, harass, οἵοις πιθηκισμοῖς με περιελαύνεις Ar.Eq.887; περιελῶ σ' ἀλαζονείαις (Elmsl. for -είας) ib.290:—Pass., περιελαυνόμενος τῇ στάσι Hdt.1.60; μή με περιελαθέντα περιιδεῖν ὑπὸ τούτων D.42.32. 3. draw or build round, περὶ δ' ἕρκος ἔλασσε Il.18.564; περὶ δ' ἕρκος ἐλήλαται ἀμφοτέρωθεν Od.7.113; ἐληλαμέναι πέρι πύργον A.Pers.872 (lyr.); π. αὔλακα βαθεῖαν Plu.Rom.11. II. seemingly intr. (sc. ἅρμα, ἵππον, etc.), drive or ride round, Hdt.1.106, Th.7.44, X.Cyr.1.4.24, Eq.Mag.3.2; εἰς τὸ ὄπισθεν Id.Cyr.7.1.36: c. acc. loci, ὅσα ἂν ἵππῳ ἐν ἡμέρῃ μιῇ περιελάσῃ as much ground as.., Hdt.4.7, cf. X.Cyr.4.2.32. 2. metaph., have recourse, οὐδὲ ἐς ὁτιοῦν περιελᾷ ψεῦδος Philostr.VA7.14.

**περιέλευσις**, εως, ἡ, coming or going round, dub. in Plu.2.916d (pl.), cf. περιέλασις: gloss on περίοδος, Phot., Suid.

**περι-ελιγμός**, ὁ, winding of a river, καμπὰς καὶ π. ποιεῖσθαι Agath.2.21. -έλιξις, εως, ἡ, circumvolution, Porph.Gaur.10.3, cj. in Plu.Thes.21; winding round of bandages, Gal.18(2).809. -ελίσσω, Att. -ττω, Ion. -ειλίσσω, roll or wind round, τι περί τι Hdt.8.128, X.Cyn.6.17, IG4²(1).122.103 (Epid.); τί τινι Hp.Art.80, Aen.Tact.18.12:—Med., ἱμάντας περιειλίττονται wind caestus straps round their arms, Pl.Prt.342c:—Pass., to be wound round, περιελιχθέντα περὶ τὴν γῆν ὥσπερ οἱ ὄφεις Id.Phd.112d, cf. 113b,c; οἱ ὄφεις περιελίττονται ἀλλήλοις Arist.HA540b2; δράκων..περὶ τὸν ἄξονα περιηλιγμένος IG4²(1).122.71 (Epid.); τριβόλους στιππύῳ περιειλιγμένους Ph.Bel.95.8. 2. intr., wind about, of a guide, μηδὲν ὑγιὲς στρέφειν καὶ π. Plu.Crass.29:—Pass., rotate, ἅρματος ὡς πέρι χνοίη ἑλίσσεται Emp.46 (dub.); of troops, wheel, Arr.Tact.21.3: so intr. in Act., ib.39.3. II. envelop by winding round, of a spider, περιδεῖ καὶ π. τοῖς ἀραχνίοις Arist.HA623a14; [ὁ ἐλέφας τῷ μυκτῆρι] τὰ δένδρα π. Id.PA659a1:—Med. c. dat., ἐπιτίθεται καὶ περιελίττεται (v.l. -ελίττει) καὶ τοῖς μείζοσι ζῴοις Id.HA623a34. 2. construct around, διαδρομὰς ἰχθυοτρόφους τοῖς οἰκητηρίοις π. Plu.Luc.39.

**περιελκ-υσμός**, ὁ, distraction, τῆς ψυχῆς Plot.4.4.25 (pl.). -ω, Att. aor. περιείλκυσα, later -εῖλξα Philostr.Her.19.8:—drag round, drag about, X.An.7.6.10; π. τινὰ ὡς ἀνδράποδον Arist.EN1145b24; π. [τὸν Ἕκτορα] τῷ τείχει Philostr. l.c.:—Pass., Hp.Fract.13, Art.3, Pl.Prt.352c, Arist.EN1147b16. 2. metaph., π. τοὔνομα drag one's good name in the mire, Jul.Or.7.214d. 3. divert, distract, κύκλῳ π. τινά Pl.Chrm.174b; π. διάνοιαν ἐπί τι Gal.6.851:—Pass., ἀπό τινος εἴς τι Longin.15.11.

**περιεμφανίζω**, demonstrate, Hero Aut.24.1 (s.v.l.).

**περιέννυμι**, Ep. Verb used in aor. Act. and Med., put round, περὶ δ' ἄμβροτα εἵματα ἕσσον Il.16.670,680; περὶ μὲν τὰ ἃ τεύχεα ἕσσε 18.451:—Med., [χλαῖναν] περιέσσασθαι to put on one's cloak, Hes.Op.539.

**περιεξ-αιρέω**, expunge, Gal.16.837. -ανθέω, break out all round, μέλασιν ἐξανθήμασιν Id.5.115. -άπτομαι, to be kindled round, Id.7.674.

**περιεπτισμένως**, Adv., (περιπτίσσω) in a winnowed, clean style, metaph., of speech, Poll.6.150 (ante 146).

**περιέπω**, impf. περιεῖπον Hdt.7.181, X.Mem.2.9.5: fut. περιέψω Id.Cyr.4.4.12, Luc.Tim.12: aor. περιέσπον Hdt.1.73, al.; inf. περισπεῖν ib.115: fut. Med. περιέψομαι Id.2.115: aor. Pass. περιεφθῆναι Id.5.1 (not in correct Att. Prose):—treat, handle, whether well or ill, usu. with an Adv. or some modal word to determine the sense: 1. in good sense, π. εὖ τινα treat him well, Hdt.1.73, etc.; κροκόδειλον..π. ὡς κάλλιστα Id.2.69; π. τινὰ ταῖς μεγίσταις τιμαῖς X.Smp.8.38; π. τινὰ ὡς εὐεργέτην καὶ φίλον, οὐχ ὡς δοῦλον Id.Cyr.4.4.12: without any modal word, treat with respect or honour, Id.Mem.2.9.5, D.H.

8.45, Plu.*Num.*3, Anon.*Incred.*17; τὰ ἀγάλματα τῶν θεῶν Porph. *Marc.*17; ἐπήνεις καὶ περιεῖπες αὐτόν Arr.*Epict.*3.23.14. 2. in bad sense, τρηχέως κάρτα π. *handle* very *roughly*, Hdt.1.114; ἀεικείῃ περισπεῖν τινα ib.115; τρηχέως κάρτα π. ἀεικείῃ ib.73; π. [κροκοδείλους] ἅτε πολεμίους Id.2.69; π. ὡς ἀνδράποδα Id.7.181; εἰ δὲ μή, ἅτε πολεμίους περιέψεσθαι (either Act., *we will treat* you as enemies, or Pass., *you shall be treated* as ..) Id.2.115, cf. 7.149:—Pass., περιεφθῆναι ὑπό τινων τρηχέως Id.5.1,81, al.; ὑπὸ τοῦ νοσήματος κακῶς περιέπεσθαι Hp.*Prorrh.*2.23; οὐ πάνυ τι καλῶς π. X.*HG*3.1.16. 3. abs., in part., *with vigilance*, Plb.4.10.5.—The synon. ἀμφιέπω is poet.

**περιεργ-άζομαι**, fut. -εργάσομαι, (περίεργος) *take more pains than enough about* a thing, *waste one's labour on* it, c. part., περιεργάζοντο δοκέοντες πρῶτοι ἀνθρώπων γεγονέναι Hdt.2.15; Σωκράτης π. ζητῶν τά τε ὑπὸ γῆς καὶ οὐράνια Pl.*Ap.*19b; περιείργασμαι μὲν ἐγὼ περὶ τούτων εἰπὼν περιείργασται δ' ἡ πόλις ἡ πεισθεῖσ' ἐμοί D.18.72: c. dat. modi, τῷ θυλάκῳ περιεργάσθαι *that they had overdone it* with their 'sack' (i.e. need not have used the word), Hdt.3.46; π. τοῖς σημείοις *overact one's part*, Arist.*Po.*1462$^a$6; π. τῷ οἰκιδίῳ *go to a needless expense* with his house, Ael.*VH*4.11; οὐδὲ περιείργασται ἐν αὐτοῖς nor has he *lavished useless pains* upon.., Luc.*Herod.*6 (but pf. in pass. sense, πλέον οὐδὲν περιείργασται τῷ Θέωνι Ael.*VH*2.44). 2. c. acc., π. τι καινόν *to be busy about* 'some new thing', Ar.*Ec.*220; αἱ μέλιτται π. τὸ παιδίον Philostr.*Im.*2.12; *meddle, interfere with*, τὰ ἀλλότρια Chilo ap.Stob. 3.1.172; τῶν κατὰ τὴν Ἰταλίαν οὐδέν Plb.18.51.2: abs., *to be a busy-body*, D.26.15, 32.28, Men.*Epit.*358, Lib.*Ep.*1068.3. 3. *bargain, haggle*, περὶ τῆς τιμῆς *PCair.Zen.*393.5 (iii B.C.). 4. in good sense, *elaborate*, Men.Rh.p.394 S., al. 5. *investigate thoroughly*, τὰ λεληθότα Jul.*Or.*7.217c, cf. Eun.*Hist.*p.250 D.; *seek diligently*, π. πόθεν ἡ εἴσοδος Zos.Alch.p.111 B. 6. ταῦτα π. *have* this *effect*, of substances, Gal.18(1).484. -ᾰσία, ἡ, = περιεργία I. 1, Longin.3.4: pl., Aristid. *Rh.*2 p.535 S. -αστέον, *one must take pains*, π. ἵνα.. Antipho 2.4.3; οὐδὲν π. Plu.2.1004c. -έω, *to be meddlesome*, Sch.S.*Aj.* 586. ⊛ -ία, ἡ, *futility, needless questioning*, Pl.*Sis.*387d; *curiosity*, Plu.2.516a. 2. *over-elaboration*, Men.Rh.p.342 S.; πεμμάτων περιεργίαι *curiosities* of cakes, Luc.*Nigr.*33. 3. *useless learning*, Hp.*Decent.*1. II. *intermeddling with other folk's affairs, officiousness*, Thphr.*Char.*13, Luc.*VH*1.5, Lib.*Or.*2.53; ὑπὸ περιεργίας Luc. *DDeor.*7.4. III. *jugglery*, Simp.*in Cael.*536.1.

**περιεργοπένητες**, οἱ, *poor scholars*, name of a book written by Diogenianus for their use, Hsch.*Ep. ad Eulog.*

⊛ **περίεργος**, ον, *taking needless trouble*, Lys.12.35; γραμματικῶν π. γένη *AP*11.322 (Antiphan.). Adv. -γως Hp.*Decent.*7. 2. *officious, meddlesome*, Isoc.5.98, X.*Mem.*1.3.1, Men.*Sam.*85; π. εἰμι I am *a busy-body*, Id.*Epit.*45; περίεργα βλέπειν look *curiously* at, c. acc., *AP* 12.175 (Strat.), cf. Hdn.5.3.8 (Comp.). 3. *of an inquiring mind*, Arist.*Resp.*480$^b$27; *inquisitive, curious*, Hdn.4.12.3 (Sup.); π. παιδία Gal.6.635; τὸ π. Luc.*Alex.*4. Adv. -γως, ἔχειν Astramps.*Orac.*p.1 H.: Comp. -ότερον, ἔχειν πρός τινα Jul.*Or.*4.130d. II. Pass., *overwrought, elaborate*, ὀδμή (perfume) Hp.*Praec.*10; φορήματα Ar.*Fr.* 321; ζωγράφημα Plu.2.64a; τὸ τῆς κόμης π. Luc.*Nigr.*13; esp. of language or style, ὀνόματα, λόγοι, Aeschin.3.229, D.H.*Lys.*14; τὸ π. Θουκυδίδου Id.*Vett.Cens.*3.2: Comp. -οτέρα λέξις Id.*Is.*3. Adv. -γως Antyll.ap.Orib.9.14.7: Comp. -ότερον, ἠσκημένος τὴν κόμην Arr.*Epict.*3.1.1; ἐξορχεῖσθαι Hdn.5.5.3. 2. *superfluous*, π. καὶ μακρὰ λέγειν Pl.*Plt.*286c; ὅπως εἴ τις π. ἀφαιρεθῇ (sc. δαπάνη) Arist. *Rh.*1359$^b$27; π. ἐστί τι And.3.33, cf. Is.1.31; π. [ἐστι] τὸ λέγειν Arist.*Pol.*1315$^a$40, cf. *Rh.*1369$^a$8; *futile, useless*, πόλεμος Isoc.15.117. Adv. -γως Timocl.13.4, etc. 3. *curious, superstitious*, ἱερουργίαι Plu.*Alex.*2; τὰ π. *curious arts, magic*, *Act.Ap.*19.19.

**περιέργω**, Att. -είργω, *enclose, encompass*, Hdt.2.148, Th.1.106, 5.11; ἐν περιειργμένοις παραδείσοις X.*HG*4.1.15; ἐν σκώλοισι τὸ πρόσωπον περιειργμένος Ar.*Lys.*810 (lyr.).

**περιερεία**· καθαρσία, Hsch.; cf. **περίεσι**· καθαρά, Phot. (leg. περίστια· καθάρσια).

**περιερέσσω**, Att. -ττω, *row round*, Hsch.

**περίερκτος**, ον, *enclosed*, κάνναισι Pherecr.63.

⊛ **περιέρπω**, *walk about*, *IG*4$^2$(1).121.7,34 (Epid.). 2. *creep round*, Gal.2.549. II. *wind round*, Ael.*NA*6.21: c. acc., Id.*VH*3.42, 13.1.

**περιέρρω**, *wander about*, Ar.*Eq.*533, Pherecr.90, *Com.Adesp.*1112.

⊛ **περιέρχομαι**, impf. περιηρχόμην Ar.*Th.*504 cod.:—*go round, go about*, Th.4.36, etc.; πάντοθεν Hdt.7.225; κατὰ τὴν ἀγοράν Ar.*Lys.* 558; κατὰ πᾶσαν χώραν D.23.139; ἐν κύκλῳ Pl.*Plt.*283b; *go about* like a beggar, πρὸς τοὺς φίλους X.*Cyr.*8.2.16; like a stranger seeing sights, Id.*Oec.*10.10: c. part., *go about* doing a thing, Ar.*Th.*504 cod., Pl.*Ap.*30a, Critias 37 D., D.13.19: c. acc. cogn., π. στάδια χίλια Ar.*Av.*6; π. ἀπέραντον ὁδόν Pl.*Tht.*147c; δύ' ἢ τρεῖς δρόμους Id.*Euthd.* 273a; [πρεσβείας καὶ κατηγορίας] D.9.72; ποικίλως τὸν βίον π. Vett. Val.40.28: c. acc. loci, π. [τὸν βωμόν] Ar.*Pax*958; βωμοὺς ἅπαντας ἐν κύκλῳ Id.*Fr.*679; τὴν πόλιν And.1.99; τὴν ἀγορὰν κύκλῳ D.19. 225; τὴν χώραν π. *survey* it, Id.18.150. 2. c. acc. pers., in Hom. (only in tmesi), *encompass*, of sounds, τὸν.. περὶ φρένας ἤλυθ' ἰωὴ Il. 10.139, cf. Od.17.261; τὸν.. περὶ κτύπος ἦλθε ποδοῖιν 19.444; of the effect of wine, Κύκλωπα περὶ φρένας ἤλυθεν οἶνος 9.362. 3. *overreach, cheat*, σοφίῃ π. τινά Hdt.3.4, cf. Ar.*Eq.*1142 (lyr.), Plu.*Nic.*10. 4. later, in lit. sense, *surround*, κύκλῳ π. τοὺς πολεμίους Id.*Publ.*22, cf. *Ages.*38. II. *go round and return* to a point, *come round*, αὖτις ἐς τυραννίδας περιῆλθον Hdt.1.96; περιῆλθεν ἐς ὀκτὼ ὁμιλητὰς ἐκ τεττάρων καὶ τριάκοντα *came down* to.., Philostr.*VA*4.37; of things, events, etc., ἡ ἡγεμονίη περιῆλθε.. ἐς τὸ γένος, ἡ βασιληΐη περιῆλθε ἔς τινα, Hdt. 1.7,187, al.; περιελήλυθε ὁ πόλεμος καὶ ἀπῖκται ἐς ὑμέας Id.7.158; ἐς φθίσιν περιῆλθε ἡ νοῦσος the disease *ended* in.., ib.88; π. εἰς ἅπαντας ὁ λόγος Plu.2.151a, cf. Pl.*Lg.*866b; ἐπειδὰν οἱ προκείμενοι λόγοι περιέλθωσι X.*Smp.*4.20: c. acc., Πανιώνιον ἡ τίσις περιῆλθε vengeance *came at last upon* him, Hdt.8.106; ταῦτα ἰσχυρῶς περιελήλυθε τοὺς πολλούς has taken strong *hold upon* them, Luc.*Luct.*10; τὸ πάθος.. τοὺς πολλοὺς.. π. Id.*Hist.Conscr.*2. 2. of Time, *come round*, περιῆλθεν ὁ ἐνιαυτός X.*Cyr.*8.6.19. 3. of the heavenly bodies, *rotate, revolve*, ὁ οὐρανὸς π. Arist.*Cael.*272$^b$14; ὁπόταν ὁ ἥλιος τὸν ἑαυτοῦ περιέλθῃ κύκλον Pl.*Ti.*39c.

**περιεσθίω**, *eat all round, nibble at*, Luc.*Merc.Cond.*26: metaph., Id.*Lex.*23: aor., τοῦ ἰοῦ περιφαγόντος τὸ ἀσθενὲς τοῦ σιδήρου D.S. 5.33.

**περιεσκεμμένως**, Adv., (περισκέπτομαι) *circumspectly*, Pl.*Ax.*365b, Ph.1.672, J.*BJ*1.24.1.

**περιέσκληκα**, pf. of περισκέλλω, in intr. sense, *to be dried up*, Sch. S.*Ant.*475.

**περιεσταλμένως**, Adv., (περιστέλλω) *covertly*, Arr.*Epict.*3.7.13, D.L.7.16; τὰ αἰσχρὰ π. ἀπαγγέλλειν *gloss* them *over*, Theon *Prog.*2: gloss on εὐσταλέως, Erot.

**περιεστικός**, ή, όν, (περίειμι (εἰμί *sum*)) *indicating recovery*, opp. θανατώδης, Hp.*Epid.*1.25, cf. *Prog.*9, al. (with v.l. περιεστηκώς). Adv. -κῶς ib.24; π. ἔχειν Paul.Aeg.6.74.

**περιεστραμμένως**, Adv., (περιστρέφω) gloss on ἑλίγδην, Sch.rec. A.*Pr.*882.

⊛ **περιέσχᾰτα**, τά, *extremities, edges*, Hdt.1.86, 5.101.

**περιευντίζομαι**, = περιαυτ-, Hsch.

**περίεφθος**, ον, (ἕψω) *thoroughly well cooked*, Luc.*VH*2.21.

**περιεχής**, ές, *surrounding, embracing*, κῦμα κυρτὸν καὶ π. Philostr. *Im.*2.8 (v.l. -ηχές). 2. *stooping*, π. μᾶλλον ἢ ὀρθοί, of athletes, Id. *Gym.*40.

⊛ **περιέχω**, also -ίσχω, Th.5.71; Aeol. περρέχω Sapph.*Supp.*25.9, Theoc.30.3: fut. περιέξω (and περισχήσω Th.5.7): aor. περιέσχον, inf. περισχεῖν: aor. Med. περιεσχόμην, inf. περισχέσθαι:—*encompass, embrace, surround*, κυκλόθεν ὁδὸς π. [τὸ χωρίον] Lys.7.28; ἡ περιέχουσα [πέλαγος] γῆ Pl.*Ti.*25a, cf. Arist.*Mete.*354$^a$6; γραμμαὶ περιέχουσαι τὸ χωρίον Pl.*Men.*85a, cf. Arist.*Mech.*851$^a$14; ἡ περιέχουσα [ἶρις] Id.*Mete.* 375$^a$31; τόπον κύκλῳ πέτραις περιεχόμενον *IG*4$^2$(1).122.21 (Epid.); τὸ περιέχον the *envelope* of a seed, Thphr.*HP*1.11.1. b. esp. of that which *encompasses* the earth or the universe, τὸν κόσμον πνεῦμα καὶ ἀὴρ π. Anaxim.2; ὁ περὶ χθόν' ἔχων αἰθήρ E.*Fr.*919 (s.v.l.), cf. Thphr.*CP*3.17.4; τὸ περιέχον πάντα ὁπόσα νοητὰ ζῷα Pl.*Ti.*31a, cf. 33b; τὸ περιέχον the *environment*, Epicur.*Nat.*79 G., al., Plot.2.3.14; τὸ περιέχον ἡμᾶς ἅπαντας καὶ γῆν καὶ θάλατταν, ὃ καλοῦμεν οὐρανόν Str. 16.2.35; ὁ περιέχων ἀήρ (ἠήρ) Hp.*Lex*3, Arist.*Mete.*379$^a$28, D.H.3.47, Plu.2.333f, etc.; ὁ περιέχων alone, Id.*Cor.*38; but usu. τὸ περιέχον, Anaxag.2, Arist.*Juv.*468$^a$3, Ptol.*Phas.*p.10 H., S.E.*M.*8.286; τὸ ἄπειρον καὶ τὸ π. Arist.*GC*332$^a$25, cf. *Ph.*253$^a$13, 259$^b$11; φαμὲν τὸ μὲν π. τοῦ εἴδους εἶναι, τὸ δὲ περιεχόμενον τῆς ὕλης Id.*Cael.*312$^a$12, cf. *Ph.* 211$^b$12. c. τὸ π. the *atmosphere*, Plb.1.37.9, D.S.4.38, etc.; δυσκρασίαι τοῦ π. Plu.*Alex.*58. 2. *embrace*, τινὰ ταῖς χερσίν Id.*Ant.* 79, cf. *Alex.*51, Philostr.*VS*2.5.3; πατρὸς περὶ χεῖρας ἔχοντος Simon. 115.1. 3. *surround* so as to guard, Plu.*Caes.*16, etc.:—but, Pass., *to be shut in, beleaguered*, Hdt.8.10; ὑπὸ τῶν πολεμίων κύκλῳ ib.79; πανταχόθεν ib.80, cf. X.*Cyr.*7.1.24: metaph., *to be hard pressed*, Men. *Epit.*289; περισχομένη κακότητι A.R.3.95. 4. *embrace, comprise, comprehend*, Pl.*Men.*87d, etc.; πλείω γένη Arist.*Pol.*1285$^a$2; περιέχεται ὑπὸ τοῦ ὅλου τὰ πάντα Pl.*Prm.*145c; *contain*, βίβλος π. τὰς πράξεις D.S.2.1; λόγος π. ἐγκώμιον Men.660; of a letter, J.*AJ*12.4. 11: impers., περιέχει ἐν γραφῇ, folld. by a quotation, 1*Ep.Pet.*2.6; καθὼς ἡ ὠνὴ π. as *is contained in* the deed of sale, *Supp.Epigr.*3.421.33 (Locr., ii A.D.). b. in Logic, τὸ περιέχον *universal*, opp. τὰ περιεχόμενα, the *individuals* or *particulars*, Arist.*Metaph.*1023$^b$27, cf. *APr.* 43$^b$23; ὀνόματα περιέχοντα *generic* terms, Id.*Rh.*1407$^a$31; καλοῦσι δ' αὐτοὺς πλάτακας ἀπὸ τοῦ περιέχοντος from the *generic name*, Ath.7. 309a. 5. Math., ὁ ὑπὸ δύο ἀριθμῶν περιεχόμενος [ἀριθμός] the *product* of two numbers, Euc.7 *Def.*19; but π. ἑαυτόν, of a number of which a higher power terminates in the same digit, *Theol.Ar.*33. 6. τὸν ἔλεγχον π. *to be involved in, open to* criticism, Phld.*Rh.*1.49 S. II. *surpass, excel*, πάντα περρέχοισ' ἄστρα, of the moon, Sapph. *Supp.*25.9; *overcome, gain the victory* or *advantage*, Th.5.7, 8.105. 2. *outflank* the enemy, Id.5.71; περιέσχον τῷ κέρᾳ οἱ Πελοποννήσιοι Id. 3.108, cf. 5.73. III. Med., *hold one's hands round* or *over* another: hence, *protect, defend*, c. gen. pers., περίσχεο (Ion. imper. aor. 2 Med.) παιδὸς ἑῆος Il.1.393: c. acc., οὕνεκά μιν περισχόμεθα Od.9.199. 2. *hold fast by, cling to*, c. gen., γούνων περισχομένη A.R.4.82 (but c. acc., περίσχετο γούνατα χερσίν Id.3.706); περιίσχετο κούρης Mosch.2.11: hence, *cleave to, be fond of* a person or thing, γευσάμενοι τῶν ἡμετέρων ἀγαθῶν περιέξονται Hdt.1.71, cf. 3.53, 5.40, 7.39, 160, etc.; τὠυτοῦ περιεχόμεθα *we are compassing, aiming at* the same end, Id.3.72, cf. Plu.*Them.*9; κρίσιν.. ἧς μᾶλλον περιέχομαι on which I *place* more *reliance*, Alciphr.2.4. 3. rarely c. inf., περιείχετο.. μένοντας μὴ ἐκλιπεῖν τὴν τάξιν *clung to his resolution* that they should stay and not leave their post, Hdt.9.57. IV. Aeol. περρέχω, = ὑπερέχω, ὁπόσον τῷ ποδὶ περρέχει τᾶς γᾶς, τοῦτο χάρις, i.e. every inch of his stature is grace, Theoc.30.3.

**περιζᾰμενῶς**, Adv. *very powerfully* or *violently*, κεχολῶσθαι h.*Merc.* 495.

**περιζᾰφελῶς,** Adv. *furiously*, βοῶσα Epic. in *Arch.Pap.*7 p.4.

**περιζεύγνυμι,** *yoke*, χαλινῷ νῶτα λεόντων Nonn.*D.*15.184.

**περιζέω,** *boil round*, Plu.2.567c, Luc.*Tox.*20, Gal.7.707; ὑπὸ πρῴρης περιέζεεν ὕδωρ Orph.*A.*1253: poet. **-ζείω** *AP*9.632, Q.S.13.150. b. metaph., π. τῷ θυμῷ Eun.*VS* p.463 B.

⊛ **περίζυξ,** ὔγος, ὁ, ἡ, neut. pl. περίζυγα, Boeot. **περίδδυγα** *Schwyzer* 462 *B* 54 (Tanagra, iii B.C.):—*over and above a pair*, ἣν μή τις ἔχῃ περίζυγα (sc. ἱμάντα) a *spare* strap, X.*Cyr.*6.2.32; ἐνωτίδια π. *odd* ear-rings, *Schwyzer* l.c.; περιζύγ[ων], of harness, prob. in *GDI*5633.4 (Teos): nom. περίζυξ dub. sens. in Eup.385, Ar.*Fr.*838, *IG*2$^{2}$.1469.75. II. = ὁμόζυγος, σύζυγος, Hsch.

⊛ **περί-ζωμα,** ατος, τό, *girdle worn round the loins*, *PRev.Laws* 94.7 (iii B.C.), Plu.*Rom.*21 (in form **-ζωσμα**), Poll.7.65, etc.; worn by athletes, Paus.1.44.1; by priests, Plu.*Aem.*33; by smiths, Arr.*Epict.*4.8.16; ἔχειν π. wear *the apron*, of a cook, Hegesipp.Com.1.7: hence οἱ λόγοι σου περιζώματος ὄζουσιν Plu.2.182d; ἀσκεῖν ἐκ περιζώματος practise an art *with the apron on*, i.e. *merely with the outward appendage of an art, superficially*, D.H.*Din.*1; of soldiers, *underclothing*, ἐν περιζώμασιν, opp. ἐν θώραξι, Plb.6.25.3. **-ζωμᾰτίας,** ου, ὁ, *affecting the waist*, of shingles, etc., Orib.*Fr.*102. **-ζωμάτιον,** τό, Dim. of περίζωμα, Timae.134, D.H.10.17. ⊛ **-ζώννυμι,** *gird upon* a person, π. τὸ ξίφος [τινί] J.*AJ*6.9.4, cf. App.*Hann.*20, Nonn.*D.*40.460 (prob. l.); *gird*, τὸ παιδίον prob. in Ruf.ap.Orib.*inc.*20.1 —more freq. in Med. with pf. Pass., *gird oneself with*, ᾤαν λουτρίδα Theopomp.Com.37; ἐσθῆτα, τήβεννον, Plu.*Rom.*16, *Cor.*9; γυμνὸς ὢν τοῦτον τὸν ἄνδρα περιεζώσατο *put* him *on* as a defence, παρ' ὑπόνοιαν for ἐπίτροπον ἐποιήσατο, Ar.*Pax* 687; περιεζῶσθαι τὴν φορβειάν *to have* their halter *girded round them*, Arist.*Pol.*$1324^{b}16$: c. dat., -ζώσασθαι τοῖς ἐντέροις τινός Phld.*Ir.*p.26 W.: abs., Κλέων.. περιζωσάμενος ἐδημηγόρησε Arist.*Ath.*28.3; π. κοσμίως ἄνωθεν καὶ κάτωθεν Sor.1.70$^{a}$; of a cook, περιεζωσμένος *with his apron on*, Alex.174.11, cf. Anaxandr.41.12 (anap.); αἱ νῆτται περιεζωσμέναι ἐπλινθοφόρουν Ar.*Av.*1148; of athletes, Paus.1.44.1; of a dancer, Plb.30.22.10. **-ζωσις,** εως, ἡ, *praecinctus*, *Gloss.* **-ζωσμα,** v. περίζωμα. **-ζώστρα,** ἡ, *apron*, Anaxandr.69. II. *ribbon twined round* a garland, dub. in Theoc.2.122.

**περιηγ-έομαι,** Dor. **περιᾱγ-,** fut. -ήσομαι Men.*Her.Fr.*9:—*lead round*, π. τὸ ὄρος τοῖσι Πέρσῃσι *show* them *the way round* the mountain, Hdt.7.214: abs., *IG*9(1).689 (Corc.), *Delph.*3(1).362 i 16. 2. abs., *explain, describe*, Luc.*Cont.*1, *DMort.*20.1. 3. Pass., *to be made to revolve*, Philol.[21]. II. *draw in outline, describe in general terms*, συμπληροῦν τὸ περιηγηθέν (used in pass. sense), Pl.*Lg.*770b.—Act. only περιήγει· ἐζωγράφει, Hsch. **-ημα,** ατος, τό, *topographical description*, Sch.D.P.1. **-ημᾰτικός,** ή, όν, *descriptive*, Theon *Prog.*11, Aphth.*Prog.*12. **-ής,** ές, *lying in a circle*, of the Cyclades lying round Delos, Call.*Del.*198; κωμῆται π. *round about, neighbouring*, Id.*Fr.*66b. 2. of the arms, *tied behind one*, *APl.*4.195 (Satyr.). 3. *circular*, κρίκοι Hp.*Anat.*1; λίμνη Call.*Ap.*59; ἀκτή, ἁψῖδες, A.R.1.559, 3.138; τόξον D.P.157; ζῶναι v.l. in Eratosth.*Fr.*16.3. 4. *surrounding*, μονίη π. γαίων *circumambient* solitude, Emp.27. 5. *revolving*, Ἑλίκη Q.S.2.105. ⊛ **-ησις,** εως, ἡ, *leading round and explaining*, as is done by guides and cicerones, Luc.*Cont.*22. II. *geographical description*, ἡ π. τῆς χώρας Str.9.2.6; οἱ τὰς π. καὶ τοὺς περίπλους ποιησάμενοι Ath.7.278d; π. γῆς γράφειν Aristid.*Or.*26(14).102, cf. Porph.*Antr.*2 (pl.); τῆς οἰκουμένης π., title of poem by Dionysius of Alexandria; π. Συρακουσῶν, title of work by Crito, Suid. III. *outline*, αἰετῷ περιήγησιν ὁμοιότατος καὶ τὸ μέγαθος *in shape* and size, Hdt.2.73. **-ητής,** οῦ, ὁ, *one who guides strangers, cicerone*, π. καὶ ἀρχιατρός *IG*4.723 (Hermione), cf. 3.1335, Plu.2.675e, Luc.*VH*2.31; at Delphi, Plu.2.395a (pl.), etc.; ὁ π. τῆς εἰκόνος *the man who explains* it, Luc.*Cal.*5. II. *author of geographical descriptions*, as Dionysius ὁ περιηγητής; also of Polemo, Ath.5.210a, cf. Plu.*Them.*32. **-ητικός,** ή, όν, *of* or *befitting a* περιηγητής, *traditional*, ἡ κοινὴ καὶ π. δόξα Id.2.386b; *descriptive*, βιβλία π. *guide*-books, ib.724d; τὸ τῆς Παρθίας π. the *handbook* of Parthia by Isidorus of Charax, Ath.3.93e. **-ητός,** όν, *with a border round it*, χιτών Antiph.153; χιτωνίσκος *IG*2$^{2}$.1514.52.

**περιῄδη,** Att. plpf. of περίοιδα.

**περιήθημα,** ατος, τό, *that which drains off, drainings, filtrate*, Dsc.1.73, Gal.17(1).983. 2. pl., *means of purging*, τὰ τοῦ παντὸς ὄγκου π. Longin.43.5.

**περιήκασε·** περιώρυξε, περιέγραψεν, Hsch. (fort. περιήλασε).

⊛ **περιήκω,** *to have come round to one*, εἰς τὸν φονέα ἡ ἀρχὴ π. X.*Cyr.*4.6.6, cf. Arr.*An.*4.13.4: metaph., [κεφαλαὶ] εἰς κρανία π. *are turned* into.., Philostr.*Im.*2.19: c. acc., τὰ σὲ περιήκοντα *that which has fallen to* thy *lot*, Hdt.7.16.α'; τοῦτον τὸν ἄνδρα φαμὲν περιήκειν τὰ πρῶτα we say that the greatest luck *came round to, befel*, this man, Id.6.86.α'; ἔμελλε.. δίκη περιήξειν καὶ Φιλοποίμενα Paus.8.51.5. 2. of Time, *to have come round*, καιρῷ περιήκοντι Plu.*Ages.*35; ἔτει δεκάτῳ περιήκοντι Aristid.*Or.*50(26).1, cf. Parth.30.2. 3. *surround*, πέτραν [τὸν ὄχθον] περιήκουσαν Philostr.*VA*3.13; κύκλῳ περὶ τὸ σπήλαιον π. ἄμπελος D.Chr.2.41.

**περιήλῠσις,** εως, ἡ, = περιέλευσις, *coming* or *going round*, ἡ Περσικὴ π. καὶ κύκλωσις Plu.*Cat.Ma.*13. 2. *revolution, cycle*, Hdt.2.123.

**περιημεκτέω,** *to be aggrieved, chafe*, τῇ συμφορῇ, τῇ δουλοσύνῃ, τῇ ἀπάτῃ, etc., Hdt.1.44, 164, 4.154, al.: c. gen. pers., *to be aggrieved at* or *with* him, Id.8.109: abs., Id.1.114. (ἠμεκτέω only in Hsch.)

**περιήνεικα,** Ion. aor. 1 of περιφέρω, Hdt.1.84.

**περιηχ-έω,** *ring all round*, περιήχησεν δ' ἄρα χαλκός Il.7.267, cf. Iamb.*Myst.*2.8: c. acc. loci, θόρυβος π. τὴν οἰκίαν Plu.2.720c:—Pass., τηγάνοισι περιηχούμενοι *Com.Adesp.*140: νῆσος περιηχουμένη τῷ κύματι Luc.*VH*1.6. II. Pass., *to be noised abroad, to be celebrated*, Ph.Bybl.ap.Eus.*PE*1.10: c. inf., περιηχήθησάν τινα κατέχειν δημόσια *Cod.Just.*10.11.8 *Intr.* 2. *get wind of* a fact, *POxy.*1119.7 (iii A.D.), *PFlor.*36.24 (iv A.D.). **-ή,** ἡ, *noise all around*, Choerob.Rh.p.249 S. **-ημα,** ατος, τό, *circumsonance, resonance*, Iamb.*VP*25.114 (pl.). ⊛ **-ησις,** εως, ἡ, *resounding, echoing*, Ph.2.159, Plu.*Sull.*19. ⊛ **-ητικός,** ή, όν, *resonant*, Porph. *in Harm.*p.64 D. (Comp.).

**περι-θάλλω,** pf. περιτέθηλα, f.l. for παρα-, Philostr.*Im.*2.6. **-θαλπής,** ές, *very hot*, ὄχημα ἠελίου *AP*7.742 (Apollonid.). **-θαλπτέον,** *one must warm all round*, Paul.Aeg.3.28. **-θάλπω,** *warm all round, cherish*, Gal.14.304:—Pass., Aen.Gaz.*Thphr.*p.70 B.

**περιθαμβής,** ές, *marvelling greatly*, A.R.2.1158. 2. *much alarmed*, Id.4.1528; τὸ π. Plu.*Cat.Mi.*59.

**περιθαρσ-ής,** ές, *very confident*, A.R.1.152, 195. **-ύνω,** *encourage greatly*, Sch.A.R.2.611 (fort. παρα-).

**περιθεάομαι,** *look round*, Lyd.*Mag.*3.39.

⊛ **περιθει-όω,** *fumigate thoroughly*, Hsch., Phot.: περιθεωσάτωσαν prob. in Men.530.22. **-ωμα,** ατος, τό, in pl., *fumigations*, gloss on ἀπομάγματα, Hsch. **-ωσις,** εως, ἡ, *thorough fumigation, purification*, Pl.*Cra.*405b (pl.).

**περίθεμα,** ατος, τό, *anything put round*: 1. *headband*, τὰ τοῦ στεφάνου π. Sch.Ar.*Pl.*22. 2. *necklace*, Hsch. s.v. κάθορμα, Suid. s.v. καθόρμια. 3. *enclosure, covering*, Lxx *Nu.*16.38(17.3).—Cf. περίθημα.

**περιθεόω,** v. περιθειόω.

**περίθερμος,** ον, *very hot*, Thphr.*Sens.*58, Plu.2.642c, Dsc.*Ther.*4, etc.: metaph., of the mind, Sch.Ar.*Nu.*144.

**περι-θέσιμος,** ον, *to be put round* or *on*, κόσμος J.*AJ*15.8.2. **-θεσις,** εως, ἡ, *putting round, putting on*, ἐκ περιθέσεως in the act of *application*, Heraclas ap.Orib.48.12.1; π. χρυσίων 1*Ep.Pet.*3.3; βρόχου Philum.*Ven.*7.8; στραγγάλης S.E.*P.*3.15: pl., π. πλοκαμίδων J.*AJ*19.1.5; κωνωπίων Sor.1.85. **-θετέον,** *one must put round*, Philum.ap.Aët.8.48, Jul.*Or.*2.90d, *Gp.*5.9.7. ⊛ **-θετος,** ον, also **περιθετός,** ή, όν, (περιτίθημι) *put round* or *to be put round*, π. πρόσωπον a *mask*, Aristomen.5; κεφαλὴ περίθετος a mask *with a wig attached*, Ar.*Th.*258, cf. Sch.; περιθεταὶ τρίχες *false* hair, *wig*, Plb.3.78.2; περίθετος κόμη Ael.*VH*1.26, *EM*790.19; προκόμια π. Ath.12.523a; περιθέτη alone, Amphis 2, Men.359.

**περιθέω,** *run round*, περὶ δὲ χρύσεος θέε πόρκης Il.6.320, cf. Od.24.208; τάφρος, τεῖχος περιθέει, Hdt.1.178, 181; π. περὶ τὴν νῆσον Pl.*Criti.*115e: c. acc. loci, τὸ ἄγκος αἱμασιῆς τις π. κύκλος Hdt.6.74: π. κύκλῳ τὸν φραγμόν X.*Cyn.*11.4, cf. Luc.*Nigr.*22; π. τὴν Ἰταλίαν Plu.*Ant.*16; τὸν βωμόν Porph.*Abst.*2.54: c. acc. pers., περιθέοντες ἑκάστους from one to another, App.*BC*1.59: metaph., π. τοῖς ὄμμασι τὴν γραφήν Aristaenet.1.10; τὸ φάρμακον τὴν ψυχὴν π. Luc.*Nigr.*37; τὰ στοιχεῖά τινος π. Dam.*Pr.*28 bis: c. dat., τοῖς βωμοῖς Hdn.5.5.9. II. *run* or *gad about*, Ar.*Eq.*65, Pl.*R.*475d: metaph., Plot.2.2.2, 5.1.4, al. III. *rotate, revolve*, ἀσπίδος αἰεὶ περιθεούσης, i.e. as he was always *swaying* his shield *round and round*, Hdt.9.74, cf. Poll.4.156.

**περιθεωρέω,** *go round and observe*, Luc.*Herm.*44; *survey, consider thoroughly*, Diog.Oen.24.

**περι-θήκη,** ἡ, *galericulum*, *Gloss.* **-θημα,** = περίθεμα 2, Nicostr. ap.Stob.4.23.62.

**περί-θλᾰσις,** εως, ἡ, *crushing, contusion*, Plu.2.609e, Herod.Med. ap.Orib.10.37.6, Sor.1.80, Gal.18(1).468. **-θλάω,** *bruise* or *crush all round*, Plu.2.341a (Pass.), Sor.1.118 (Pass.), Gal.18(1).640.

**περιθλίβω** [ῑ], *press all round*, Nonn.*D.*10.370; τὴν ὄψιν, τὸν τῆς ὄψεως κῶνον, Plu.*Fr.*13.2. 2. *squeeze out*, αἷμα Nonn.*D.*17.361.

**περιθνῄσκω,** of flesh, *mortify round* a wound, Hp.*Fract.*33 (v.l. ἀμφιθνήσκουσιν).

**περί-θραυσις,** εως, ἡ, gloss on ἀγμούς, *EM*11.47 (pl.); cf. παράθραυσις. ⊛ **-θραύω,** *break small, grind down*, Arist.*Pr.*$935^{b}2$:—mostly Pass., ib.$^{a}$38, Hp.*Morb.*4.55, J.*BJ*6.1.3, Plu.2.626b, Gal.*UP* 2.17. 2. metaph., *crush*, Ph.1.564, al.

**περιθρεκτέον,** *one must run round*, Pl.*Tht.*160e.

**περιθρηνέομαι,** Pass., *resound with wailing*, Plu.*Ant.*56.

**περιθριγκόω,** *edge* or *fence all round*, τοῖς ὀστέοις τοὺς ἀμπελῶνας Plu.*Mar.*21.

**περίθριξ,** τρῐχος, ὁ, *the first growth of hair* before it is cut, Call.*Fr.anon.*56.

**περιθρομβόομαι,** Pass., *to be clotted up*, of blood, Heliod.ap.Orib.50.52.3, Gal.10.345.

**περιθρόνιος,** α, ον, *round about the throne*, Orph.*H.*7.4 (s.v.l.).

**περιθρῡλέω,** *devulgo*, *Gloss.*

**περιθρύλητος** [ῡ] and **περίθρῡλος,** ον, *famous*, Tz.*H.*8.371, 7.929. Adv. -ήτως *Cat.Cod.Astr.*8(4).205.

**περιθρύπτω** and **-θρύβω** (D.S.3.51), *rub* or *pound in pieces*, l.c. (Pass.); τὰ περιθρύπτοντα τὴν ψυχήν Ph.1.501; περιθρυφθείς Id.2.527.

**περιθῡμῐάω,** *surround with burning incense*, ἡ κεφαλὴ τοῦ ἰχθύος -ωμένη μετὰ σμύρνης Cyran.33.

**περίθῡμος,** ον, *very wrathful*, A.*Th.*724 (lyr.), *Cat.Cod.Astr.*8(4).181; τὸ π. Ph.1.684. Adv. -μως A.*Ch.*40 (lyr.); π. ἔχειν or ἴσχειν to be *very angry*, Hdt.2.162, Pl.*Ti.*88a: neut. as Adv., Plu.*Mar.*19.

**περιθῠρ-έω,** *to be about the door*, Ael.*NA*1.11, 14, Phot. ⊛ **-ον,** τό, *door-way*, i.e. door-posts and lintel, *Ephes.*4(1) No.28.

**περιῐάλλω,** *put around*, περὶ χερσὶ δὲ δεσμὸν ἴηλα Il.15.19.

⊛ **περιῐάπτω,** *wound all round*, περὶ θυμὸς ἰάφθη Theoc.2.82.

**περιῐάχω** [ᾰ], *ring around, re-echo*, περὶ δ' ἴαχε πέτρη Od.9.395: Ep. impf. περίαχε [ῑ], for περιίαχε, Hes.*Th.*678.

**περιίδμεναι**, Ep. inf. of pf. περίοιδα, Il.13.728.

**περιιδνόομαι**, *become bent* or *curved*, Hp.*Mul.*1.36.

**περιιδρόω**, *sweat all over* or *excessively*, S.E.*M.*11.159, Aët.8.7.

**περιιδρύομαι**, *to be set up around*, [στῆλαι] π. ⌊νεῷ⌋ Philostr.*Im.* 1.12.

**περιίδρωσις**, εως, ἡ, *sweating all over*, Dsc.*Ther.*9, Sor.1.28, Orib. *Fr.*53.

**περιιζομαι**, *sit round about*, κύκλῳ περιιζόμενοι Hdt.1.202, 6.78: c. acc. objecti, π. τινά Id.5.4, cf. 41.

**περιικνέομαι**, *reach on all sides*, περὶ φρένας ἵκετο θαῦμα Arat.473, cf. Sch.Arat.862.

**περιίκω** [ῐκ], Dor. for περιήκω 2, ἐπεί κα ἑκαστάκις ὁ χρόνος περιίκῃ *Inscr.Magn.*44.18 (Corc.).

**περιιππάζομαι**, Med., = sq., Polyaen.4.3.29, Zos.1.53, *PMag. Leid.V.*7.10.

**περιιππεύω**, *ride round*, Plb.5.73.12, Arr.*Tact.*4.6 (cj.), Polyaen. 4.8.4.

**περιίπταμαι**, later form for περιπέτομαι, Arist.*HA* 542$^b$24, D.C. 58.5, Alex.Trall.*Febr.*4.

**περιῖσος**, ον, *more than equal*, coined as etym. of περισσός, *Theol. Ar.*13.

**περιιστάνω**, later form of sq., Vett.Val.285.33:—also※-άω, Chamael.ap.Ath.1.21e.

※**περιΐστημι**, A. in the trans. tenses (with pf. περιέστᾰκα Pl. *Ax.*370d), *place round*, π. τοὺς ἑαυτοῦ Th.8.108, etc.; π. στήλην τινί Hdt.3.24; π. κύτος τῷ ζῴῳ Pl.*Ti.*78c; στράτευμα περὶ πόλιν X.*Cyr.*7. 5.1: metaph., π. τινὶ ἔτι πλείω κακά D.21.123; κινδύνους τοῖς Καρχηδονίοις Plb.12.15.7; π. ἀγῶνάς τισι Plu.*Comp.Ag.Gracch.*5. 2. *bring round*, ὁ δῆμος εἰς ἑαυτὸν περιέστησε τὴν πολιτείαν Arist.*Pol.* 1304$^a$33; εἰς τοὐναντίον π. τινὰ τῷ λόγῳ Pl.*Ax.*l.c.; εἰς τοσοῦτον π. τινά, ὥστε.. Heraclid.Pont.ap.Ath.12.537c; esp. into a worse state, εἰς τοῦθ' ἡ τύχη τὰ πράγματα αὐτῶν περιέστησεν ὥστε.. Isoc.6.47, cf. Aeschin.3.82; π. εἰς μοναρχίαν τὴν πολιτείαν Plb.3.8.2; οἴκους εἰς πενίαν π. Hdn.7.3.5; *convert*, εἰς τὸ περιφερὲς [τὸν ἀέρα] Epicur.*Ep.*2 p.51 U.; *transfer*, π. τὰς ἑαυτοῦ συμφορὰς εἴς τινα D.40.20; π. τὴν αἰτίαν εἴς τινα D.H.3.3. II. in aor. 1 Med., *place round oneself*, ξυστοφόρων κύκλον X.*Cyr.*7.5.41; φρουρὰν περὶ τὸ σῶμα App.*BC*3.4.

B. Pass. and Med., with aor. 2 (aor. 1, v. infr. 2), pf., and plpf. Act.:—*stand round about*, περίστησαν γὰρ ἑταῖροι Il.4.532; κῦμα περιστάθη a wave *rose around* (Ep. aor. Pass.), Od.11.243; περιστῆναι περί τι Pl.*Ti.*84e; τοῦ περιεστῶτος ἔξωθεν πνεύματος ib.76b; οἱ περιεστῶτες the *bystanders*, Antipho 6.14; ὄχλου πολλοῦ περιστάντος *IG*4$^2$(1).123.25 (Epid.). 2. c. acc. objecti, *encircle, surround*, χορὸν περιίσταθ' ὅμιλος Il.18.603; βοῦν δὲ περιστήσαντο (fort. περίστησάν τε) 2.410, cf. Od.12.356; μή πώς με περιστήωσ' ἕνα πολλοί (Ep. 3 pl. subj. aor. 2 for -στῶσι) that their numbers *surround* me not, Il. 17.95, cf. Od.20.50; so περιστάντες [τὸ θηρίον] κύκλῳ Hdt.1.43, cf. 9.5, A.*Fr.*379, Pl.*R.*432b; π. τὸν λόφον τῷ στρατεύματι X.*Cyr.*3.1.5: metaph., τὸ περιεστὸς ἡμᾶς δεινόν Th.4.10, cf. 7.70; τοσούτου πολέμου τὴν Ἀσίαν περιστάντος Isoc.4.162; χωρὶς τῆς περιστάσης ἂν ἡμᾶς αἰσχύνης D.3.8; διὰ τὸν φόβον τὸν περιστάντα αὐτοὺς Aeschin.3.137; φόβος π. τινά Th.3.54, cf. D.18.195. 3. c. dat., περιισταμένους τῇ κλίνῃ Pl.*Lg.*947b: mostly metaph., *come round to* one, ἡμῖν.. ἀδοξία τὸ πλέον ἢ ἔπαινος περιέστη Th.1.76; τῇ [Ἑλλάδι] δουλεία περιέστηκε Lys.2.60; τοῦ πολέμου περιεστηκότος Θηβαίοις D.16.28; ἡλίκα τῇ πόλει περιέστηκε πράγματα Id.19.340; ἀνάγκη π. τινί, c. inf., ib.212: abs., of *circumstances*, mostly bad, τὰ περιεστηκότα πράγματα Lys. 2.32, cf. Epicur.*Sent.*38; οἱ περιεστῶτες καιροί Plb.3.86.7. II. *come round, revolve*, κύκλῳ Arist.*Ph.*217$^a$19; of winds, ἐκ τῶν ἀπαρκτίων εἰς θρασκίας Id.*Mete.*365$^a$6; of Time, περιισταμένης τῆς ὥρας Thphr.*CP*2.11.2, cf. Hp.*Nat.Hom.*7. 2. *come round to, devolve upon*, περιειστήκει ὑποψία ἐς τὸν Ἀλκιβιάδην Th.6.61; νομίσαντες τὸ παρανόμημα ἐς τοὺς Ἀθηναίους τὸ αὐτὸ περιεστάναι Id.7.18; εἰς ὀλίγους ἡμᾶς περιέστη [ἡ στατίων] *IG*14.830.8 (Puteoli, ii A.D.). 3. of events, *come round, turn out*, esp. *for the worse*, ἐξ ἀρρωστίης π. τινὶ ἐς ὕδερον Hp.*Coac.*471 (but also of persons, ἐς ὕδρωπα περιίσταντο *became* dropsical, Id.*Epid.*3.13); ἐς τοῦτο περιέστη ἡ τύχη fortune *was* so completely *reversed*, Th.4.12; τοὐναντίον περιέστη αὐτῷ *it turned out* quite contrary for him, Id.6.24, cf. Lys.12.64, Pl.*Men.*70c; ὁ τοῦ δικαίου λόγος εἰς τοὐναντίον περιειστήκει Id.*R.*343a; φιλεῖ ἐς τύχας τὰ πολλὰ περιίστασθαι *come to be dependent* on chances, Th.1.78; εἰ τὰ μὲν πράγματ' εἰς ὅπερ νυνὶ περιέστη D.18.201, cf. 3.9; τὸ πρᾶγμ' εἰς ὑπέρδεινόν μοι περιέστη Id.21.111, cf. 37.10; ἐνταῦθα τὰ πράγματα π. ὥστε.. Isoc.8.59, cf. 5.55; περιέστηκεν εἰς τοῦτο ὥστε.. Lycurg.3: c. inf., περιειστήκει τοῖς βοηθείας δεήσεσθαι δοκοῦσιν αὐτοὺς βοηθεῖν ἑτέροις D.18.218, cf. Pl.*Mx.*244d: c. part., περιέστηκεν ἡ πρότερον σωφροσύνη νῦν ἀβουλία φαινομένη Th.1.32. III. later, *go round so as to avoid, shun*, τὰς ἁμαρτίας Phld.*Rh.*1.384 S.; τὴν ὁμιλίαν J.*AJ* 1.1.4; κύνας Luc.*Herm.*86 (though he censures this usage, *Sol.*5), cf. Gal.*UP*10.14, Porph.*Abst.*4.7, etc.; τὸν κίνδυνον Iamb.*VP*33.239; τὸ μοναρχικόν ib.31.189; τὴν ἀφροσύνην S.E.*M.*11.93; κενοφωνίας 2*Ep.Ti.*2.16; τὸ εἰκῇ καὶ μάτην M.Ant.3.4; τοὺς ἡγουμένους Artem.4. 59; π. μή.. *to be afraid* lest.., J.*AJ*4.6.12; *sneak round*, Phld.*Rh.*1. 99 S.; *circumvent*, τοὺς λογιστάς Mitteis *Chr.*88 iv 11 (ii A.D.):—so in Pass., περιεσταμένης τῆς λογοθεσίας *BGU*1019.8 (ii A.D.).

**περιισχναίνομαι**, Pass., *become exceedingly attenuated*, Hp.*Epid.* 6.8.18.

**περιίσχω**, v. περιέχω.

**περιιτέον**, (περίειμι (εἶμι)) *one must make a circuit*, Pl.*Phdr.*274a; τὴν μακροτέραν π. τινί he *must take* the longer *round*, Id.*R.*504c.

**περιιχνεύω**, *follow all round*, τοῖς ὀφθαλμοῖς καὶ τοῖς μυκτῆρσί τι Ph.2.479 (fort. περιλιχνεύω).

**περικαγχᾰλάω**, *exult exceedingly*, Opp.*H.*4.326.

**περικάδομαι**, Dor. for -κήδομαι.

※**περικᾰής**, ές, *exceedingly fiery, burning hot*, π. πρὸς χεῖρα Hp.*Coac.* 154; πρὸς τὴν ἁφήν ib.223, cf. *Aph.*5.62, etc.; χωρίον J.*BJ*4.8.3; π. θερμότης Thphr.*Ign.*44. Adv. -καῶς, ἔχειν τινός to be *hot with love* for.., Plu.*Ages.*11, Eun.*Hist.*p.274 D., cf. Id.*VS* p.501 B.

**περικᾰθαίρω**, *cleanse on all sides* or *completely*, τὰ δίκτυα Arist.*HA* 598$^b$14, cf. Gal.12.877; τὰς ῥίζας Thphr.*HP*4.13.5. 2. metaph., *purify completely*, π. ἐπαοιδαῖς Arist.*Fr.*496, cf. Thphr.*Char.*16.14; τὴν στήλην Pl.*Criti.*120a; τὸν υἱὸν ἐν πυρί Lxx *De.*18.10; πόλιν μὴ σκίλλῃ [ἀλλὰ] τῷ λόγῳ D.Chr.48.17.

**περικαθάπτω**, *fasten* or *put on*, τῷ ἀγκίστρῳ ἰχθῦς Plu.*Ant.*29:—Med., *fasten on oneself, put on*, νεβρίδας Id.2.364e. 2. = περικαταστρέφω, ἀγγεῖον Str.16.4.6; ἄμβικα Dsc.5.95; τρύβλιον τῷ ἀλγοῦντι μέρει Id.*Eup.*2.45; *enclose*, πυξίδα πυξίδι Ps.-Callisth.3.31. 3. intr. c. dat., *grasp, enclose*, ἀκτῖνες οἷον χειρῶν ἐπαφαῖς π. τοῖς ἐκτὸς σώμασι *Placit.*4.13.9, Gal.*Phil.Hist.*94.

**περικᾰθᾰρ-ίζω**, *purge entirely*, τὴν καρδίαν Lxx *De.*30.6. II. *purge away*, τὴν ἀκαθαρσίαν ib.*Le.*19.23. ※-μα, ατος, τό, *expiation*, ib.*Pr.*21.18. II. = κάθαρμα I. 2, περικαθάρματα τοῦ κόσμου 1 *Ep.Cor.* 4.13, cf. Arr.*Epict.*3.22.78. -σις, εως, ἡ, *clearing round*, τῶν ῥιζῶν Thphr.*CP*5.9.11 (pl.). -τήρια, τά, *purificatory offerings*, Hsch. s.v. θεώματα. -τής, οῦ, ὁ, *purifier*, *PMag.Osl.*1.158, Hsch. s.v. ἀπομάκτης.

**περικαθεζόμενος, περικαθεσθείς**, v. περικαθίζω III.

**περικάθ-ημαι**, Ion. -κάτημαι, Ion. 3 pl. impf. περιεκατέατο or περικατέατο Hdt.8.111 (also περιεκαθέατο 6.23 codd.):—*to be seated all round*, τραπέζῃ at table, Id.3.32 codd.: mostly c. acc., *invest, besiege* a town, τὴν Νίνον Id.1.103, al., cf. Lxx *Jd.*9.31; also περιεκάθητο ἐπὶ Γαβαθών ib.3*Ki.*15.27; of ships, *blockade*, Hdt.9.75: c. acc. pers., *sit down by* one as a companion, Id.3.14. -ίεμαι, Pass., *have hung round* one, περιβραχιόνια καὶ περιαυχένια περικαθειμένη Ph.2.266. -ίζω, *cause to sit around* or *over*, Hp.*Mul.*1.51. 2. π. στρατὸν τῇ πόλει *invest* a city, J.*AJ*8.14.1, cf. 13.5.5. II. intr., *sit round*, τῇ πυρᾷ Max.Tyr.27.6, cf. Ach.Tat.3.5, Orib.*Eup.*4.113.4: but usu. *besiege*, φρούριον Wilcken *Chr.*11 *B* 10 (ii B.C.); τὸ τεῖχος v.l. in D.S.20.103; π. κύκλῳ τὴν πόλιν App.*Hisp.*53; περὶ or ἐπὶ τὴν πόλιν, Lxx 1*Ma.*11. 61, 4*Ki.*6.24: abs., J.*AJ*12.8.1, al. III. Med., *invest*, περικαθεζόμενοι (aor. part.) τὸ τεῖχος D.59.102; τὴν πόλιν περικαθισάμενος Memn.45.1: intr. in pass. form, περικαθεσθέντες *having sat down round about*, Luc.*VH*1.23, S.E.*P.*3.232: pres. inf. περικαθέζεσθαι, = *obsidere*, *Gloss.* -ισις, εως, ἡ, *siege*, ib. -ίσταμαι, *take up position around, invest*, χωρίον Iamb.*Bab.*3.

**περικαίνυμαι**, *overcome*: of fire, *consume*, Nic.*Th.*38.

※**περικαίω**, Att. -κάω, *scorch*, Thphr.*CP*2.3.8, Str.17.1.27, etc.:—Pass., *to be scorched*, Hdt.4.69, Thphr.*Ign.*74. II. metaph., *inflame, excite*, τῆς φιλοτεκνίας περιέκαιεν ἐκείνη φύσις Lxx 4*Ma.*16. 3:—Pass., And.2.2.

**περικᾰκ-έω**, *to be in extreme ill-luck*, Plb.1.58.5; τοῖς ὅλοις Id.3. 84.6. -ησις, εως, ἡ, *extreme ill-luck*, Id.1.85.2, al. -ος, ον, *very bad*, Ptol.*Tetr.*68.

**περικᾰλᾰμῖτις**, ιδος, ἡ, = φλοιὸς καλάμου, Gal.12.422.

**περικᾰλίνδησις**, εως, ἡ, *rolling about*, Plu.2.919a (pl.).

**περικαλλής**, ές, (κάλλος) *very beautiful*, in Hom. mostly of things, φόρμιγξ, κίθαρις, Il.1.603, Od.1.153; ἀγροί, αὐλή, βωμός, δίφρος, δόμος, δῶρα, ἔργα, εὐνή, θρόνος, etc., 14.263, 1.425, Il.8.249, 4.486, 3.421, Od.8.420, 2.117, 10.347, 22.438, al.; of women only Il.5.389, 16.85, Od.11.281; of men first in *h.Merc.*322, 397, 504; of a man's eyes, Od.13.401, 433; of a statue, Orac.ap.Hdt.5.60; Κύπρον, περικαλλέα νῆσον Thgn.1277, cf. Hdt.7.5; ἄνθη -έστατα Hellanic.55 J.: also in later Prose, Arist.*Fr.*11, *Mu.*397$^a$4 (Sup.), Ph.2.269, J.*BJ*6.1.1, D.C. 37.17 (Sup.), etc.: but rare in Att., Hermipp.Hist.6 (Comp.); π. Θεσμοφόρω Ar.*Th.*282: irreg. Sup. περικάλλιστος v.l. in Alciphr.3. 59. Adv. -καλλῶς *Cat.Cod.Astr.*2.171, Longin.*Rh.*p.186 H., Eust. 836.41.

**Περικαλλιμᾰχοι**, οἱ, *followers of Callimachus*, Com. word in *AP* 11.347 (Phil., s.v.l.).

**περι-κάλυμμα** [κᾰ], ατος, τό, *covering, garment*, Pl.*Plt.*279d: metaph., *pretext*, Ph.1.608 (pl.). -καλυπτέα, *one must muffle* or *wrap oneself up*, Ar.*Nu.*727. -κᾰλύπτω, *cover all round*, πολέμοιο νέφος περὶ πάντα καλύπτει Il.17.243, cf. 10.201; π. δένδρεον πίλῳ Hdt. 4.23; τινὰ ἱματίοισι or ἐν ἱματίῳ, Hp.*Aph.*5.59, X.*Cyr.*7.3.14: metaph., π. σωτηρίᾳ τοὺς νόμους Pl.*Lg.*793b; τὸ θνητὸν περικάλυπτε τῷ θεῷ (sc. Διονύσῳ), i.e. get drunk, Diph.20; τὰ πάθη Plu.2.100f; π. καὶ ἀρνεῖσθαι ib.1013e:—Med. and Pass., *cover oneself all round*, ib. 51d, etc. II. *put round as a covering*, αὐτῷ.. περὶ κῶμα κάλυψα *put* sleep *as a cloak around* him, Il.14.359; τὸ σῶμα [ψυχῇ] Pl.*Ti.*34b; π. τὰ Χερουβεὶν ἐπὶ τὴν κιβωτόν Lxx 3*Ki.*8.7: metaph., π. τοῖσι πράγμασι σκότον *throw a veil of* darkness *over* the deeds, E.*Ion* 1522. -κᾰλυφή, ἡ, *wrapping, covering*, Pl.*Lg.*942d.

**περικάμνω**, *make great efforts*, ἐπεὶ Καῖσάρ εἰμι καὶ περικέκμηκα τὸ κλῖνον ἀναλήμψεσθαι *PFay.*20 ii 14 (iii/iv A.D.).

**περικαμπ-ή**, ἡ, *bending round*, ἐξ ὀλίγου χωρίου τὴν π. ἔχειν a sharp *curve*, Hp.*Art.*46. -ής, ές, *bent round*, Aq.*Is.*40.4, *Ho.*6.8; διὰ π. τόπων by *zigzag* paths, Vett.Val.263.13. **-της,** *tergiversator*, Gloss. **-τω,** *bend round*, Hp.*Art*.18; π. τὸν τοῖχον *make a return in* the wall, *IG*2².1668.24; π. τὴν χεῖρα τοῖς βλεφάροις Ps.-Luc. *Philopatr*.19. II. intr., *turn round* a corner or bend, Pl.*Euthd*. 291b: c. acc. loci, π. [ὁ ἦχος] τοὺς ὄζους Arist.*Aud*.802ᵃ35; π. τὸν Ἄθω Ael.*VH*1.15: abs., *bend* or *sweep round*, ἐπὶ τοὺς λιμένας App. *Pun*.95. 2. *go round so as to shun* or *escape from*, τὴν τῶν κυάμων χώραν Hermipp.Hist.23; ὁμιλίας, prob. for παρέκαμπτε in D.S.5.59; τὴν πόλιν Plu.2.246b; κακοπαθίαν οὐδεμίαν *IG*12(5).129.23 (Paros); διήγησιν Apollon.Cit.1; ὀσμάς Archig.ap.Gal.12.790, cf. *PMed*. in *Arch.Pap*.4.270 (iii A.D.); φιλίας Porph.*VP*59.

**περίκαμψις,** *tergiversatio*, Gloss.

**περικαπνίζω,** = περιθυμιάω, *PMag.Leid.W*.1.33.

**περικάρδιος,** ον, (καρδία) *about* or *around the heart*, αἷμα Emp.105.3; χιτών Ruf.*Onom*.163, Gal.*UP*6.16 (ὁ π. alone, ibid.); σκέπασμα ib.18.

**περικαρπϊάκανθος** [ᾰκ], ον, *having thorns* or *prickles upon the* περικάρπιον, Thphr.*HP*6.1.3, 6.5.3.

**περικάρπιον,** τό, *case of fruit* or *seed, pod, husk*, or *shell*, Arist.*de An*.412ᵇ2, *Mete*.380ᵃ11, *GA*770ᵃ15, *Pr*.925ᵇ30, Thphr.*HP*1.2.1, al., Phan.Hist.34, Dsc.2.110. II. *bracelet*, Poll.5.99, Malch.p.423 D.

**περικαρφισμός,** ὁ, (κάρφος) *covering oneself with chaff*, a practice of hens, Plu.2.700d.

**περικαταβάλλω,** only in Ep. aor. περικάββαλον (also -καμβ-), *throw down around* or *upon*, κάρη κόλποις A.R.3.707; π. τινὰ γαίῃ *lay* him *prostrate* on.., Nonn.*D*.37.582; δέρας περικάμβαλε μήλου *wrap* a sheepskin *round* it, Orac. in Damocr.ap.Alex.Trall.1.15: metaph., π. πένθος τινί, π. τινὰ ἄτῃ, Q.S.1.819, 5.469.

**περικατ-αγμᾰτική** ἀγωγή, treatment *for fractures*, Gal.18(2).589 (s.v.l.). **-άγνῡμι,** *break all round*, Thphr.*HP*3.7.4 (Pass.), Ph.1.657 (Pass.); π. ξύλον τύπτοντα *break* it *about* his back, Ar.*Lys*.357; π. τινὶ φιάλην Alciphr.3.45; ἀμίδας ἀλλήλοις Ath.1.17c: intr. in pf. part. -κατεαγώς, D.H.8.67.

**περικατα-κλάω,** *break all round about*, Apollon.*Lex*. s.v. περιάγνυται. **-λαμβάνω,** *embrace, enclose, hem in on all sides*, Arist.*Pr*. 946ᵇ38 (Pass.). 2. *overtake*, περικαταλαμβάνει γὰρ ὁ νέος [καρπὸς] ἀεὶ τὸν ἔνον Thphr.*HP*4.2.5, cf. 3.4.5, 3.16.1, D.S.4.54, 20.74, al.; θάλασσα π. τοὺς Αἰγυπτίους J.*AJ*2.16.3:—Pass., Archyt.1, J.*AJ*20.4.1; π. τῇ ὥρᾳ *to be overtaken by*.., Thphr.*CP*2.8.1; π. ὑπὸ τοῦ ῥεύματος, ὑπὸ τῆς φλογός, Arist.*Mu*.400ᵇ1, Plb.14.4.10; περικαταλαμβανόμενος τοῖς καιροῖς *compelled* by circumstances, Id.16.2.8. II. intr., περικαταλαβούσης τῆς ὥρας the season *having come round* or *returned*, Thphr.*Od*.39. **-λᾰμψις,** ιος, ἡ, Doricized form of *περικατάληψις, = -ληψις, of planets, Ti.Locr.97b (pl.). **-λείπω,** *leave behind in*, κέντρον πληγῇ Nic.*Th*.809; f.l. in Plb.4.63.10 (Pass.). **-ληπτος,** ον, *overtaken and surrounded*, Philippid.24, D.S.2.50, etc.; by death, Phld.*Mort*.39. 2. *detected*, Lxx 2*Ma*.14.41, D.S.4.76, Theodor.ap.Stob.4.20.71. **-ληψις,** εως, ἡ, *overtaking*, ὑπ' ἀλλήλων Thphr.*HP*7.10.3; cf. περικατάλαμψις. **-μάσσω,** *detergo*, Gloss. **-πίπτω,** only Ep. aor. περικάππεσον, *fall down upon*, ἀφλάστῳ A.R.3.543; τεθνειῶτι Q.S.5.502, cf. 9.168; esp. *fall upon so as to be pierced*, θοῷ π. δουρί A.R.2.831, cf. Tryph.576. **-ρρέω,** *fall in and go to ruin*, Lys.30.22. **-ρρήγνῡμι,** *tear off round about, strip off*, ἐσθῆτα D.H.9.39, Nic.Dam.62 J.:—Med., περικατερρήξατο τὸν ἄνωθεν πέπλον she *tore off and rent her* outer garment, X.*Cyr*.5.1.6.

**περικατάσσομαι,** Pass., late form of περικατάγνυμαι, Sch.Il.11.631; cf. περικατεάσσω.

**περικατα-στρέφω,** *turn round over*, ἀγγεῖον ἀτμῷ Dsc.2.61:—Pass., *to be overturned*, Str.16.2.13. **-σφάζω,** aor. -έσφαξα, *slaughter over*, τινὰς περὶ σῶμα Plb.1.86.6. **-τίθεμαι,** Med., *put round* one, ἰοδόκην περικάτθετο μίτρῃ A.R.3.156. **-χέω,** *pour down over*, Posidon.70 J.

**περικατ-εάσσω,** *frango, infringo*, Gloss.; cf. περικατάσσομαι. **-έχω,** *shut in all round*, τὴν πόλιν, τὸν ναόν, J.*BJ*3.7.3, 6.4.5:—Pass., aor. 1 part. περικατασχεθείς v.l. in Ph.1.657.

**περικάτω** [ᾰ], Adv. *upside down*, Stratt.34 (nisi divisim leg.); π. ὁ λόγος τρέπεται Epicur.*Nat*.87 G., cf. *Nat.Herc*.1420.4; *headlong*, π. τρέπεσθαι Plu.2.943d.

**περικατωτροπή,** ἡ, *complete overthrow, refutation*, Phld.*Sign*.30.

**περί-καυσις,** εως, ἡ, *burning all round*, π. καὶ ἐκπύρωσις *Placit*.3.16.6. 2. *spray, douche*, f.l. for περίκλυσις in Thphr.*Sud*.16. **-καυστέον,** *one must cauterize all round*, τὸν ὀφθαλμόν *Hippiatr*.12. **-καυστος,** ον, *consumed*, σποδός D.H.14.2 (fort. πυρικαύστῳ).

**περικάω,** Att. for περικαίω.

⊛ **περίκειμαι,** inf. -κεῖσθαι: fut. -κείσομαι:—used as Pass. of περιτίθημι, *lie round about*, c. dat., εὗρε δὲ Πατρόκλῳ περικείμενον ὃν φίλον υἱόν *lying with his arms round* him, Il.19.4; [γωρυτὸς τόξῳ] περίκειτο *there was* a case *round* the bow, Od.21.54; πασσάλοις (acc. pl.) κρύπτοισιν περικείμεναι.. κνάμιδες Alc.15; οἷς στέφανος περίκειται Pi.*O*.8.76; τὸ σχῆμα καὶ τὸ ὄνομα τῆς βασιλείας τινὶ π. Hdn.6.1.1; π. τινὶ τῶν πράξεων κηλίς Plu.*Dio*56: c. acc., σφέας εὐδίη καὶ γαληναίη περικέαται Luc. *Astr*.3: with a Prep., περὶ [τὰς φλέβας] τὸ σῶμα π. τὸ τῶν σαρκῶν Arist. *GA*764ᵇ30: abs., τὰ περικείμενα χρυσία plates of gold *laid on* (an ivory statue), Th.2.13; [ὁ κημὸς] περικείμενος *put round* the horse's mouth, X.*Eq*.5.3. 2. metaph., οὐδέ τί μοι περίκειται *there is* no *advantage* for me, I have nought *laid by*, Il.9.321. b. οἱ περικείμενοί τινι his *supporters*, *POxy*.1408.24 (iii A.D.). II. c. acc. rei, *have round one, wear*, mostly in part., [τελαμῶνας] περὶ τοῖσι αὐχέσι περικείμενοι Hdt.1.171, cf. *OGI*56.67 (Canopus, iii B.C.); τιάρας π. Str.15.3.15; στεφάνους Plu.*Arat*.17; πτέρυγα Luc.*Icar*.14; προσωπεῖον Id.*Nigr*.11, Aesop.360; στρατιωτικὴν δύναμιν π. *invested with*.., Plu.*Pomp*.51; ὕβριν π. *clad in* arrogance, Theoc.23.14 (s.v.l.): rarely in other moods, περίκεισο ἄνθεα *have* garlands *put round thee*, *AP*11.38 (Polem.); περιέκειτο ξίφος, σχῆμα βασιλικόν, Hdn.3.5.7, 5.4.7; τὴν ἅλυσιν ταύτην περίκειμαι *Act.Ap*.28.20; περίκειται ἀσθένειαν *Ep.Hebr*.5.2.

**περικειμένως,** Adv. *completely*, τοῦτο π. διεκρούσατο Ἀσκληπιάδης Cass.*Pr*.1.

**περικείρω,** aor. inf. -κεῖραι Philostr.*Ep*.61: pf. -κέκαρκα Luc.*Symp*.32:—*shear* or *clip all round*, τὴν κόμην κακῶς π. Hdt.3.154; π. τινά *clip* him *close*, Philostr. l.c.:—Med., τρίχας περικείρεσθαι *clip one's* hair, Hdt.4.71:—Pass., π. κατὰ πρόσωπον Lxx *Je*.32.9(25.23); τοὺς πλοκάμους περικειρόμενος Luc.*Tim*.4; Περικειρομένη, title of play by Menander. II. metaph., *shear* of its walls, τὴν ἀκρόπολιν Ael.*VH*7.8.

**περικεκᾰλυμμένως,** Adv. *covertly*, Apollon.*Lex*. s.v. ἐντυπάς, Ascl. *in Metaph*.30.9.

**περικεκλεισμένως,** Adv. *self-containedly*, Gal.*Phil.Hist*.33.

**περικέλλιον,** τό, dub. sens. in *BGU*459.11 (ii A.D.).

**περικεντέω,** *pierce on all sides*, δόρασι App.*BC*4.22.

**περικεράννυμι,** *temper* acrid humours, Alex.Trall.7.3:—Pass., f.l. in Plu.2.924b; cf. περικρεμάννυμι.

**περικεράω,** (κέρας) *outflank*, π. τοὺς ὑπεναντίους Plb.11.1.5; ὑπὲρ τὰ θηρία Id.5.84.8.

**περικερδής,** ές, *very grasping*, Sch.D Il.1.149 codd. (περὶ τὰ κέρδη Barnes).

⊛ **περικεφάλ-αιος** [ᾰ], α, ον, *round the head*: hence, II. Subst. περικεφαλαία, ἡ, *covering for the head, helmet, cap*, Call.Com.1 D., Aen. Tact.24.6, *PPetr*.3 p.328 (iii B.C.), etc.; π. σιδηρᾶ περιηργυρωμένη *IG*11(2).161 *B*77 (Delos, iii B.C.), cf. 2².1478.16, 12(5).647.30 (Ceos), Plb.3.71.4, J.*AJ*6.9.4. Antyll.ap.Orib.6.36.3. b. *wig*, Hsch. 2. *disorder of the oak*, Thphr.*HP*3.8.7. 3. in a ship, = ὁ στόλος ὑπὲρ τὴν σπεῖραν, Poll.1.86, cf. Thphr.*HP*3.13.4. 4. name of a *bandage*, Sor.*Fasc*.24. **-ον,** τό, *top* of an upright in an engine, Ath.Mech.23.3, al.

⊛ **περικήδομαι,** *to be very anxious* or *concerned about*, c. gen., Ὀδυσσῆος Od.3.219; ἀνδρῶν δικαίων περικαδόμενοι Pi.*N*.10.54; π. τινὶ βιότου *take care of* his substance for him, Od.14.527.

**περίκηλος,** ον, (κηλόν) *very dry, well-seasoned*, of timber, αὖα πάλαι, περίκηλα Od.5.240, 18.309.

**περίκηπος,** ὁ, *garden near* a town or *round* a house, *PCair.Zen*.193.8 (iii B.C.), *PSI*5.547.22 (iii B.C.), D.S.34/5.2.13, D.L.9.36; opp. παράδεισος, Longus 4.19, 28, 29. 2. *border of a garden-plot*, Sch. Ar.*V*.478, Phot. and Suid. s.v. οὐδ' ἐν σελίνοις.

**περικίδναμαι,** Pass., *spread round about*, μοι ἔρως π. *AP*5.291 (Agath.); λέκτροις π. ib.9.765 (Paul.Sil.); π. ἠὼς εἴς τινα ib.651 (Id.).

**περικινδῡνευτικός,** ή, όν, *risky*, Gal.9.764.

**περικῑνέω,** *move round*, gloss on περιδ[ε]ινεῖσθαι, Hsch. (Pass.), cf. Dosith.p.434 K.

**περικῑ-όνιος,** ὁ, a name of Dionysus at Thebes, Orph.*H*.47.1, Mnaseas 18. **-ων,** ον, gen. ονος, *surrounded with pillars*, θάλαμοι E.*Fr*.369.5 (lyr.); περικίονας ναούς (Elmsl. for ναοῦ or ναῶν) Id.*IT*405 (lyr.).

**περικλᾰδής,** ές, *with branches all round*, ὕλη A.R.4.216.

**περικλάζω,** *make a noise round*, αἰετὸν.. π. κολοιοί Tryph.249.

⊛ **περικλαίω,** *stand weeping round*, Opp.*H*.5.674; π. τὸ σῶμα Plu. *Brut*.44.

**περί-κλᾰσις,** εως, ἡ, *twisting round*, τῆς πόας Plu.2.325b (pl.); σώματος ib.45d. 2. *breaking round* or *on* something, π. τοῦ αἰθέρος Id.*Lys*.12; κάταγμα γιγνόμενον κατὰ περίκλασιν Gal.18(2).436. II. *wheeling round* of an army, Plb.10.23.6, 11.23.2; π. λαμβάνειν Plu.*Flam*.8. 2. generally, *change of direction*, of winds, Thphr.*Vent*.28. 3. *modification*, τοῦ κόσμου *Stoic*.2.300 (pl.). 4. Gramm., κατὰ περίκλασιν with the *circumflex accent*, D.T.630.2. III. of ground, *brokenness, ruggedness*, Plb.3.104.4 (pl.). ⊛ **-κλάω,** *twist round, bend*, [τὴν φλόγα] Thphr.*Ign*.53; τοὺς ἀγκῶνας Lxx 4*Ma*.10.6: but usu. *break off*, [τὰς δρῦς] Ael.*VH*9.18; τῷ κράνει π. τὸ ξίφος *break* it *round* the helmet, Plu.*Sull*.14:—Pass., περικεκλασμέναι ῥάβδοι Thphr.*HP*4.6.10; περικλασθήσονται κλῶνες Lxx *Wi*.4.5; κολοσσὸς -κλασθεὶς ἀπὸ τῶν γονάτων Str.14.2.5; περικλώμενα τοῖς αὐτῶν βρίθεσι *bent and broken* by.., Plu.*Sull*.12; περικεκλασμένον σχῆμα *bent and bowed down*, Id.2.878c; of persons, τοῖς σώμασι -κλώμενοι Arist.*Phgn*.813ᵃ16, cf. Theoc.21.48; but also, *arched*, θώραξ Gal.18(1).420; περικλώμενος κλύδων J.*AJ*15.9.6. 2. in Optics, *refract*, Cleom.2.1 (Pass.). II. *wheel* an army *round* to the right or left, ἐπὶ δόρυ or ἐπ' ἀσπίδα Plb.11.12.4, cf. 11.23.2; also π. τὸν Τίβεριν ἐπὶ τὸ Κίρκαιον *divert* it, Plu.*Caes*.58. 2. Pass., of missiles, *ricochet*, Ph.*Bel*.79.19. III. τόποι περικεκλασμένοι *rough, broken* ground, Plb.12.20.6; so λόφοι περικεκλ. Id.18.22.9; οἰκίαι περικεκλ. houses *on such ground*, Id.9.26ᴬ.7; περικεκλασμένας λόφοις ἐρημίας Onos.6.7.

⊛ **περικλεής,** ές, = περικλειτός, *AP*7.119, A.R.1.1069: irreg. Sup. -κληέστατος Epic. in *BKT*5(1).85 (iv A.D.).

⊛ **Περίκλειος,** α, ον, *of Pericles*, Πειθώ Luc.*Am*.29; τύπος Aristid. *Or*.28(49).77.

**περί-κλεισις,** εως, ἡ, *enclosing all round*, Theol.Ar.60. **-κλεισμα,** ατος, τό, *enclosed place*, Sch.Lyc.615. **-κλειστικός,** ή, όν, *able to enclose*, ὁ κύκλος π. παντὸς πολυγώνου σχήματος Iamb. *in Nic*.p.61 P.

❀ **περικλειτός**, ή, όν, (κλείω (B), κλέος) *far-famed*, Theoc.17.34, *AP*9.434.3 (Theoc.), Q.S.3.305.

**περίκλειτρον**, v. περίκλιτρον.

**περικλείω**, Ion. -κληΐω, old Att. -κλῄω, (κλείω (A), κλείς) *shut in all round, enclose*, ἐκ τοῦ περικληΐοντος ὄρεος Hdt.3.117, cf. 7.129,198; ὅπως αἱ νῆες περικλῄσειαν Th.2.90: abs., περικλειούσης θαλάττης Ph.2.544:—Med., περικλῄσασθαι τὰς ναῦς τῶν ἐναντίων *get* them *surrounded*, Th.7.52:—Pass., ὑπὸ πλήθους περικλῃόμενοι Id.2.100. II. metaph., in Pass., *to be confined, reduced*, εἰς τοὺς ἐσχάτους κινδύνους D.S.16.35; εἰς ἀνενεργησίαν S.E.*M.*11.162, cf. *POxy.*1666.12 (iii A.D.):—later in Act., *limit*, εἰς τρία τὴν πραγματείαν Steph. *in Hp.*1.179; ἐπεὶ δέ με ὁ χρόνος περιέκλειε τὸ τέλος ἐπάγων Vett.Val.354.1.

**περικλῄζω**, *celebrate far and wide*, Hsch. (περικλυζόμενος cod.).

❀ **περικλῄϊστος**, ον, *far-famed*, Coluth.273, 292.

**περίκλησις, περικλητεύομαι**, ff.ll. for παρακλ- (q.v.).

**περικλινής**, ές, *sloping on all sides*, of the roof of the Odeion, Plu.*Per.*13; λόφοι π. Id.*Pel.*32; σκοπαί, νάπαι, Id.*Marc.*29, *Mar.*20.

**περί-κλῐνον**, τό, *couch all round a table*, f.l. for πολύκλινα, Ph.2.478. II. *couch-cover, Gloss.* ❀ **-κλίνω** [ῑ], *decline*, of the sun, Posidon.28 J.:—Pass., *lean upon*, περικλινθεῖσα τιθήνῃ παρθένος Nonn.*D.*35.14. II. Pass., *to be deflected, distorted*, Phld.*Rh.*1.157 S. III. dub. sens. in *IG*5(2).437.5 (Megalop., ii B.C.). **-κλῐσις**, εως, ἡ, *sloping sideways, Placit.*2.29.3 (pl.). **-κλῐτέον**, *one must decline, avoid*, Archig.ap.Orib.47.13.6. **-κλιτρον**, τό, *torale, Gloss.*:—also written **-κλειτρον**, ib.

**περικλονέω**, *stir up all round*, κυδοιμόν Q.S.2.649:—Pass., *to be massed together*, of clouds, Id.3.707.

**περικλύδην** [ῠ], Adv., λούεσθαι π. take a *shower* bath, Hp.*Vict.*1.35.

**περικλύζω**, *wash all round*, τὸ παιδίον ὕδατι Arist.*Mir.*837$^b$21:—Pass., *to be washed all round* by the sea, of an island, Th.6.3; of a boat, Plu.*Mar.*36; μὴ περικλύζοιο θαλάσσῃ, i.e. venture not on the sea, Arat.287: metaph., *to be overwhelmed*, κακοῖς Lib.*Decl.*30.61; τῷ πλήθει τῶν σκοπῶν Gal.15.584.

❀ **περικλύμενον** [ῠ], τό, *honeysuckle, Lonicera etrusca*, Dsc.4.14; *periclymenos*, v.l. in Plin.*HN*27.120.

**περί-κλῠσις**, εως, ἡ, = περικλυσμός, Ael.*NA*16.15; *spray, douche*, cj. in Thphr.*Sud.*16. **-κλυσμα**, ατος, τό, *wash, lotion*, gloss on περινήματα, Gal.19.130. **-κλυσμός**, ὁ, *ablution, Gloss.* (pl.). **-κλυστος**, η, ον, also ος, ον A.*Pers.*880 (lyr.):—*washed all round by the sea*, of islands, Δῆλος *h.Ap.*181, cf. A.*Pers.*596 (lyr.), E.*HF*1080 (lyr.), Ephipp.5.3 (anap.); πέτρα Str.16.2.13; ἀπόψεις '*belvederes*', Plu.*Comp.Cim.Luc.*1; π. ὑπὸ τοῦ Αἰγαίου Str.2.5.24; ἐκ τοῦ ποταμοῦ D.H.5.13.

**περικλῠτός**, ή, όν, (κλύω) *famous, renowned*, of Hephaestus, Il.1.607, Od.8.287, Hes.*Th.*571; of heroes, Il.11.104, 18.326; of a minstrel, Od.1.325, 8.83, etc.; of places, ἄστυ π. 4.9, 16.170; of things, π. δῶρα, ἔργα, *excellent, noble*, Il.7.299, 6.324, cf. Orph.*Fr.*238, al.

**περικλώζομαι**, Pass., *to be hooted off on all sides*, Eust.1504.31.

**περικνήμ-ια**, τά, *flesh of the leg*, Hp.*Epid.*2.4 (dub.). **-ίς**, ῖδος, ἡ, *covering for the leg, gaiter*, D.H.4.16, Plu.*Phil.*9, Thd.*Da.*3.21, *PLond.*1.191.13 (ii A.D.).

**περικνίδιον** [κνῐ], τό, θυμέων περικνίδια *stalks* or *leaves* of thyme, *AP*9.226 (Zon., dub.).

**περικνίζω**, *scratch all round*, v.l. in Poll.9.113: metaph., *keep nibbling at* a thing, D.H.9.32, Plu.2.10e: aor. Med. περικνίξασθε, of bees, *AP*9.226 (Zon.).

**περικνύω** [ῡ], *scratch* or *rub all round*, Phot.

**περικοιμάομαι**, *pass the night round*, τῇ σκηνῇ τινος App.*BC*5.79.

**περικοκκάζω**, *cry cuckoo all round*, Ar.*Eq.*697 ap.Phot. (περιεκόκκυσα vulg.).

**περικολάπτω**, *trim all round*, v.l. for περικόπτω in *Hippiatr.*8.

**περικολλάω**, *glue all round*, τὸ κυμάτιον *IG*1$^2$.374.132,136; τοῖς βλεφάροις *Gp.*12.33 (Pass.), cf. Aët.7.106.

❀ **περικολούω**, *cut short, clip all round*, περὶ πτορθεῖα κολούσας Nic.*Al.*267. II. metaph., *humble*, Plu.2.139b.

**περικολπίζω**, *sail round a bay*, *Peripl.M.Rubr.*57: c. acc., τὴν ἤπειρον ib.34.

**περικομ-ιδή**, ἡ, *carrying round*, *Gp.*1.14.9. **-ίζω**, *carry round*, ἐς τὸν Στρυμόνα π. τριήρεις Th.7.9:—Pass., *go round*, Id.3.81.

**περί-κομμα**, ατος, τό, *that which is cut off all round, trimmings, mincemeat*, Metag.6.7 (pl.), Alex.175, etc.; περικόμματα ἐκ σοῦ σκευάσω Ar.*Eq.*372, cf. Men.*Sam.*78. II. = περικοπή II, π. τοῦ καλοῦ Plu.2.765c. **-κομμάτιον**, τό, Dim. of foreg. I, Ar.*Eq.*770, Alex.132, Athenio 1.31.

❀ **περίκομος**, ον, *covered all over with leaves*, Thphr.*HP*3.8.4, al.

**περικομπέω**, *sound round about*, Lxx *Wi.*17.4. II. *declare loudly*, J.*BJ*1.25.2.

**περίκομψος**, ον, *very subtle*, ὑπόνοιαι Ar.*Pax* 994.

**περι-κονδῠλο-πωρο-φίλα** [φῐ], ἡ, *loving chalk-stones on the knuckles*, epith. of the gout, Luc.*Trag.*202.

**περικονιάω**, *whitewash all round*, πύλην *IG*11(2).144*A* 118 (Delos, iv B.C.).

**περι-κοπή**, ἡ, *cutting all round, mutilation*, e.g. of the Hermae at Athens, Th.6.28, And.1.15, Plu.*Alc.*18, etc.; *lopping* of a tree, Thphr.*CP*5.4.7; *docking* of hair, Plu.2.42b; *trepanning*, Id.*Cat.Ma.*9. 2. metaph., *cutting down, diminution*, τῆς πολυτελείας ib.18, cf. 2.84a. 3. *mason's work*, *PTeb.*406.19 (iii A.D.). II. *outline, general form* of a person or thing, Plb.6.53.6; λιτὸς κατὰ τὴν π. in *externals*, Id.10.22.5; π. καὶ χορηγία Id.31.26.7, cf. *Fr.*199, al.; π. κόσμου καὶ θεραπαινίδων D.S.31.27, cf. 32$^a$. III. Rhet., *section*, ἡ π. ἐκ δύο κώλων καὶ τριῶν Longin.*Rh.*p.193 H., cf. Hdn.*Fig.*p.89 S. 2. in Metric, *passage, section*, κατὰ π. ἀνομοιομερῆ Heph.*Poëm.*4.5, cf. Sch.Heph.p.170 C., Sch.Ar.*Pl.*619. **-κοπίς**, ίδος, ἡ, *lectio, Gloss.* (dub., *-capis* cod.). **-κοπτέον**, *one must cut away all round*, Antyll.ap.Orib.45.2.5: metaph., π. ἐπιφυομένας κῆρας τῷ φιλίας φυτῷ Ph.1.345, cf. Porph.*VP*22. II. Adj. -κοπτέος, α, ον, τὰ πολλὰ π. τῶν ἀκροαμάτων Plu.2.711e. **-κόπτης**, ου, ὁ, *mason*, *POxy.*1146.15 (iv A.D.). II. *thief, robber*, Hsch., Phot. **-κοπτικός**, f.l. for παρα-, Gal.10.930. **-κόπτω**, pf. -κέκοφα Lys.14.42:—*cut all round, mutilate*, τοὺς Ἑρμᾶς περιέκοπτεν D.21.147, cf. And.1.34, Lys.6.51; οἱ Ἑρμαῖ περιεκόπησαν τὰ πρόσωπα Th.6.27; π. τὰ ἀκρωτήρια τῆς Νίκης D.24.121; τὰ παράσημα [τῆς νεώς] Plu.*Them.*15; π. τὰ βιβλία *cut* them *round the edges*, Luc.*Ind.*16; *trim off*, τὰς ἀκάνθας τὰς κύκλῳ (of fish) Alex.133.3; *prune*, δένδρεα *Tab.Heracl.*1.173:—Pass., *to be pruned* or *cut away*, Thphr.*HP*4.16.1,5; of fish, *to be trimmed*, Arist.*Mir.*835$^a$19; of a statue, *to be rough-hewn*, Plu.2.74d. 2. *lay waste* (from the practice of *cutting down* the fruit-trees), τὰ ἐν Ἑλλησπόντῳ D.8.9: hence, *plunder* a person, Id.9.22:—Pass., *PCair.Zen.*44.24, 145.4 (iii B.C.), D.H.10.51, Str.11.13.2, etc.; πόλεις περικεκομμέναι χρημάτων Plu.*Ant.*68: abs., π. καὶ λῃστεύειν D.S.4.19: hence, simply, *intercept, cut off*, ἀγορὰς D.H.10.43, cf. Plu.*Luc.*2 (Pass.); τὰ σιτηγά Id.*Mar.*42; τινῶν τὴν ἀπὸ τῆς γῆς εὐπορίαν Id.*Sert.*21; *restrain, check*, πολυπραγμοσύνην Id.*Per.*21:—Pass., *to be hindered*, ἐν ταῖς πράξεσι *Cat.Cod.Astr.*2.166. 3. *cut off, destroy, kill*, D.H.10.51, J.*BJ*4.5.2. 4. *take no account of, eliminate*, Gal.9.781, *Sect.Intr.*6. 5. π. λογάριον *close* an account, *PFay.*134.5 (iv A.D.).

**περικορδᾰκίζω**, *dance the* κόρδαξ *around*, gloss on περιεκόκκασα, Sch.Ar.*Eq.*694.

**περικόρημα**, ατος, τό, *sweepings*, *EM*529.46, Phot.

**περικοσμ-έω**, *deck all round*, ῥάβδοις καὶ πελέκεσι App.*BC*4.94, interpol. in J.*Ap.*2.35: in tmesi, Phoronis 4:—Pass., Lxx *Ps.*143 (144).12. **-ιος**, ον, *mundane*, τὰ π. γένη Prisc.Lyd.32.16, cf. Iamb.*Myst.*2.1, Procl. *in Prm.*p.527 S., Dam.*Pr.*127, Syrian. *in Metaph.*26.10. Adv. -ίως Iamb.*Myst.*2.4. II. *embracing the* κόσμος, νοῦς Procl.*Theol.Plat.*5.7. **-ος**, ον, = foreg., Dam.*Pr.*98 (s.v.l.).

**περίκουρος**, ον, (περικείρω) *shorn all round*, of the female slave's mask in Comedy, Poll.4.151. II. *surrounded and taken prisoner*, Hsch.

**περικόχλιον**, τό, (κοχλίας) *female screw*, Heliod.ap.Orib.49.4.66.

**περικράζω**, *croak* or *scream all round*, Dionys.*Av.*1.9 (v. παρακρώζω).

**περικράνιος** [ᾱ], ον, *round the skull*, πῖλος π. *skull*-cap, of the *apex* of the Roman *flamines*, Plu.*Num.*7 (pl.); ἡ π. χιτών or ὑμήν the membrane *under the skin of the skull*, Ruf.*Onom.*129, Antyll.ap.Orib.44.8.1, Gal.*UP*8.9. II.❀ **περικράνιον**, τό, = *cervicale, Gloss.*

**περίκρᾱνον**, τό, *cap*, π. θήρεια Str.11.4.5, cf. Poll.2.42.

❀ **περικρᾰτ-έω**, *have full command of*: *hold fast*, βέλος χειρί Hp.*VC* 11: c. gen., εὐγενείας Herm.ap.Stob.1.49.44. 2. *lord it over*, Ἑλλάδος Σφίγγα περικρατοῦσαν *Carm.Pop.*46.24, cf. Iamb.ap.Simp. *in Cat.*375.17; *prevail over*, ἐχθρῶν Ph.2.383; *control*, π. τῶν παθῶν ὁ λογισμός Lxx 4*Ma.*1.9; ἄνθρωποι π. πάντων J.*AJ*11.3.4; προσώπου, of an actor, Simp. *in Epict.*p.125 D.; *master* with the mind, θεωρημάτων Ph.1.105, cf. *PGnom.Praef.* (ii A.D.), *Theol.Ar.*59: abs., v.l. in Plu.2.526f:—Pass., *to be mastered, cured*, of a disease, Archig.ap.Aët.9.40. **-ής**, ές, *grasping, tenacious*, γαμφηλαί Simm.1.11; *having full command over*, π. γενέσθαι τῆς σκάφης *Act.Ap.*27.16, cf. Thd.*Su.*39 (v.l.); cf. περικρεμής. **-ησις**, εως, ἡ, *predominance*, Iamb.ap.Simp. *in Cat.*374.27. II. *prevailing signification*, κατὰ -κράτησιν *EM*584.4. III. *retention*, οὔρων Sch.Nic.*Al.*337.

**περικρεμ-άννῡμι**, *hang round*, τινί τι *AP*11.66 (Antiphil.), Nonn.*D.*26.254:—Pass., *hang round, cling to*, cj. in Plu.2.924b (v. περικεράννυμι): c. dat., μητρί *AP*9.78 (Leon.). **-ής**, ές, *hanging*, cj. for περικρατές in Opp.*H.*4.541. II. c. dat., *hung round with*, ἀγάλμασι Luc.*Trag.*142. **-νάω**, = -κρεμάννυμι, Apollod.*Poliorc.*142.2 (Pass.).

**περίκρημνος**, ον, *steep all round*, J.*BJ*5.5.8, Plu.*Sull.*16; λόφος App.*BC*4.105, cf. *Pun.*95.

**περι-κροτέω**, *cause to rattle round*, χερσὶ π. νῶτα βοείης Nonn.*D.*14.351. **-κροτος**, ον, *rattling round*, κύμβαλα ib.9.117, cf. 10.223.

❀ **περικρούω**, *strike off all round*, περικρουσθεῖσα πέτρας τε καὶ ὄστρεα *having* stones and shells *knocked off, stripped* of them, Pl.*R.*611e; ὅταν περικρουσθῶσιν οἱ ἀγκῶνες when the headlands *are broken away*, by the river overflowing, Str.12.8.19. 2. *strike all round, ring* a metal or earthen vessel, to see if it is cracked, εἴ πῄ τι σαθρὸν ἔχει (ἠχεῖ Wytt.), πᾶν περικρούωμεν Pl.*Phlb.*55c: metaph., Iamb.*Myst.*8.5: hence περικεκρουμένος *unsound, cracked*, *Com.Adesp.*888. 3. *twist round*, of a wrestler, Plu.2.234d. 4. Pass., *to be buffeted on every side*, ib.831a. 5. π. πέδας *fasten* fetters *on* one, ib.499a.

**περικρύπτω**, late impf. -έκρυβον *Ev.Luc.*1.24:—*conceal entirely*, Luc.*DMort.*10.8, Eun.*Hist.*p.248 D., etc.:—Med., *conceal oneself from*, τινα D.L.6.61.

**περικρώζω**, *caw all round*, τινα, of crows, D.C.58.5.

**περι-κτάομαι**, *acquire*, J.*AJ*13.16.6: aor. περιεκτήθην Vett.Val.41.10, al. **-κτησις**, εως, ἡ, *acquisition*, οὐσίας A.D.*Synt.*278.8, cf. S.E.*M.*7.166, 11.146, App.*Prooem.*11, Vett.Val.41.21, etc. **-κτητικός**, ή, όν, Astrol., *promoting acquisition*, of planets, Id.38.30, 70.28. **-κτητος**, ον, *acquisitive, rich*, Heph.Astr.1.1.

**περικτίονες** [κτῐ], όνων, οἱ, Ep. dat. περικτιόνεσσι, (κτίζω, cf. ἀμφικτύονες) *dwellers around, neighbours*, Il.18.212, 19.104,109; π. ἄνθρωποι, π. ἐπίκουροι, Od.2.65, Hes.*Fr.*103, Il.17.220, cf. Orac.ap.Hdt. 7.148, Simon.10, Pi.*N.*11.19, *I.*8(7).69.—The sg. is not in use.—Rare in Prose, π. νησιῶται Th.3.104, cf. Ath.13.591b.

**περικτίται** [τῐ], ῶν, οἱ, = foreg., Od.11.288.

**περικτῠπέω**, *sound around*, ἄξονες π. διαύλῳ *Hymn.Is.*33, cf. Eun. *Hist.*p.246 D. (Pass.).

**περικῠβιστάω**, *tumble headlong*, Philostr.*Gym.*50.

**περικῡδής**, ές, *very famous*, Nic.*Th.*345, Q.S.9.65.

**περικυκλ-άς**, άδος, ἡ, *revolving*, Ὧραι Orph.*H.*43.5. **-εύω**, *encircle, encompass*, Sch.Ar.*Ra.*195. **-έω**, *move in a circle, move around*, ἅρμα Ael.*NA*13.9:—Pass., *fluctuate*, Alex.Trall.10. II. intr., *revolve*, c. acc. cogn., τὴν αὐτὴν δίνην π. Epicur.*Ep.*2 p.53 U. **-ησις**, εως, ἡ, *revolution*, cj. in D.L.1.9 (pl.); τοῦ χρόνου Lyd.*Mens.*4.51. **-ιον**, τό, *periphery*, *Corp.Herm.*3.2b codd. **-ος**, ον, *all round, spherical*, Tryph.34; Στέφανος Nonn.*D.*25.145: περικύκλῳ, = πέριξ, *round about*, Lxx *De.*6.14, *Ps.*88(89).7, Hero *Aut.*4.2, Plu.2.755a, A.D.*Synt.*336.24: in earlier writers divisim, as Pl.*Phd.* 112e. **-όω**, *encircle, encompass*, Arist.*HA*533$^{b}$11, Lxx *Ge.*19.4, *PLond.*2.681.9 (iv A.D.), etc.:—more freq. in Med., *surround* an enemy, Hdt.8.78, X.*An.*6.3.11, etc.; in tmesi, Ar.*Av.*346. II. intr., *go round*, Luc.*Ocyp.*63. **-ωσις**, εως, ἡ, *encircling, encompassing*, Th.3.78.

⊛ **περικῠλ-ινδέω**, later **-κυλίω** [ῑ], fut. -κυλίσω Vett.Val.115.21: aor. 1 -εκύλῑσα:—*roll round*, [ὀνίδα] περικυλίσας τοῖν ποδοῖν Ar.*Pax* 7; περικυλίοντες εἰς τὴν γῆν τὰ σώματα D.H.9.21, cf. D.S.18.34:—Pass., of an infant, Sor.1.85; of the shoulder in reducing dislocation, Gal.18(1).327: abs., *roll about*, Pl.*Lg.*893e: metaph., *to be involved in*, βιαίοις πράγμασι Vett.Val.42.9, cf. *Cat.Cod.Astr.*2.206; εἰς ἕτερα πάθη Gal.19.572. **-ῖσις**, εως, ἡ, *rolling round, revolution*, Gal.18(1).326.

**περικῡμαίνω**, *heave* or *surge around*, c. acc., Orph.*H.*83.3.

**περικύμων** [ῡ], ον, gen. ονος, *surrounded by the waves*, of islands, E.*Tr.*800 (lyr.); Λέσβος Archestr.*Fr.*59.4, cf. *Fr.*4.5.

**περικυρτ-όομαι**, Pass., *to be quite convex*, Parth.ap.Ath.11.783b. **-ος**, ον, *convex*, S.E.*M.*7.307, Gal.18(1).787; τὸ π. [τῆς γαστρός] Ruf. *Anat.*40.

**περικῡτόω**, (κύτος) *cover with leather*, Suid. s.v. κύτος.

**περικῡφ-όομαι**, Pass., *to be bent all round*, Apollon.*Lex.* s.v. κύπελλον. **-ος**, ον, *bent all round*, π. ἔκπωμα, = ἀμφικύπελλον, *EM* 549.14, Orion 81.18.

**περικωδωνίσαι**· περιβομβῆσαι, prob. in Hsch.

**περικωκύω** [ῡ], *wail around*, Opp.*H.*4.259, Q.S.3.742:—Pass., Hsch.

**περικωμάζω**, *carouse round*, παλαίστρας Ar.*V.*1025.

**περικωνέω**, *smear all over with pitch*, π. τὰ ἐμβάδια *black* shoes, Ar. *V.*600.

**περιλᾰβεύς**, έως, ὁ, a surgical instrument, *Hermes* 38.283.

**περιλᾰκίζω**, *rend all round*, Lxx 4*Ma.*10.8 (Pass.).

**περιλᾰλ-έω**, *chatter exceedingly, gossip*, Ar.*Ec.*230, M.Ant.1.7; τὰς τραγῳδίας..τὰς περιλαλούσας (sc. of Euripides) Ar.*Fr.*376. 2. *describe*, Philostr.*Im.*2.9. 3. *talk round* a subject, Gal.8.675, 18(2). 901. **-ημα**, ατος, τό, *prating, gossip*, gloss on στωμύλματα, Hsch., *EM* 729.32 (pl.). **-ησις**, εως, ἡ, *gossip*, Gal.8.943, 17(1).547. **-ητος**, ον, *much talked of, famous*, of things and persons, Agath.2.15, 4.26, Hsch. s.v. περιλεσχήνευτος. **-ος**, ον, *very talkative*, Suid. s.v. κομψόν.

**περιλαμβάνω**, fut. -λήψομαι: aor. περιέλᾰβον:—*embrace*, τινα X. *An.*7.4.10, *Smp.*9.4, Lxx *Ge.*29.13, etc.; *grasp*, ταῖς χερσὶν πέτρας Pl.*Sph.*246a: hence πολλὸν τοῦ ἀσφαλέος π. Hp.*VM*9. 2. *encompass* or *surround* an enemy, Hdt.8.7,16, Plb.2.29.5, etc.; μετεώρους τὰς ναῦς π. *intercept* them at sea, Th.8.42; χάρακι π. κύκλῳ τὴν πόλιν Plb.1.48.10; ἐπεὰν δὲ αὐτὸν περιλάβῃς when *you get hold of* him, *catch* him, Hdt.5.23; πανοικίῃ τινὰ π. Id.8.106; π. τὸν θῆρα Pl.*Sph.*235b; π. τόπον ὑπὸ [διφθέραις] *cover* it *over*, Phylarch.41 J.; also of water, πλείω π. τόπον Plb.4.39.8:—Pass., *to be caught, trapped*, οἴμοι, περιείλημμαι μόνος Ar.*Pl.*934; τῷ καιρῷ περιληφθέντες *constrained by..*, Plb.6. 58.6, etc. 3. *compass, get possession of*, ἅπαντα τὰ ἐκείνου Is.8.37; πάντα π. ταῖς ἐλπίσιν Plb.8.1.3; *acquire* an art, Phld.*Rh.*2.21 S. 4. Geom., *enclose* a rectangle, Pl.*Tht.*148a; of a sphere, *contain* the regular solids, Id.*Ti.*33b. II. *encase* or *cover all round*, τοῦ τείχους χαλκῷ τὸν περίδρομον Id.*Criti.*116b; νεύροις..κύκλῳ κατὰ κορυφὴν περιειλημμένη Id.*Ti.*77e; χρυσαῖς λεπίσι περιληφθῆναι Plb.10.27.10; χαλκοῖς ἥλοις Moschio ap.Ath.5.207b:—Pass., of substances taken in a medium, Ph.*Bel.*89.17. III. *comprehend, include*, ἐν κεφαλαίοις τὴν δύναμιν ὅλου τοῦ πράγματος Isoc.2.9; τῷ λόγῳ Id.8.141; τῷ λόγῳ τὸ ὄν Pl.*Sph.*249d; πολλὰ εἴδη ἑνὶ ὀνόματι ib.226e, cf. *Plt.*288c (Pass.); δύο γὰρ ὄντα αὐτὰ καὶ..τρίτον ἄλλο εἶδος ἓν ὄνομα περιλαβόν *since* one name *includes* the two, and a third class besides, Id.*Lg.*837a; μιᾷ ἰδέᾳ καθ' ἓν ἕκαστον π. Id.*Phdr.*273e; π. πάντα D.61.30; π. τῇ διανοίᾳ τὸ μέλλον Plu.*Luc.*9; τὴν ἱστορίαν γραφῇ Id.*Cic.*41; π. τὴν..διάλεκτον *compass* it (Coraës παραλαβεῖν), Id.*Ant.*27; βραχεῖ λόγῳ π. Luc. *Peregr.*42; π. ταῖς συνθήκαις τινά Plb.5.67.12; ὅσα μὴ σφόδρα περιείληφε ἓν ὁ νόμος τι προσαγορεύσας Lycurg.9:—Pass., θήρα πάμπολύ τι πρᾶγμά ἐστι περιειλημμένον ὀνόματι νῦν σχέδον ἑνί Pl.*Lg.*823b; περιληφθῆναι τοῖς νόμοις Arist.*Pol.*1287$^{b}$19; τοσούτων περιειλημμένων κακῶν Phld.*Sto.*339.13 (-ειλλημε- Pap.).

**περι-λαμπής**, ές, *very brilliant*, αὐγαί Ph.1.485 (Sup.), cf. Max.Tyr. 39.4 (Comp.): metaph., Plu.*Fab.*19: neut. as Adv., στίλβων ὀξὺ καὶ π. Id.*Crass.*24, etc. **-λάμπω**, *shine around* or *brightly*, Id.*Cam.* 17; πρὸς τὴν σελήνην Id.*Arat.*21, etc.:—Med., περιλαμπομένας φύσεις ὑπερβάλλειν λαμπρότητι D.S.3.12; τῷ χρυσῷ Luc.*Ind.*9. II. c. acc., *light up*, πολεμίῳ πυρὶ τὴν Ἑλλάδα π. Demad.39; *illuminate*, τὰ κεκρυμμένα τῶν ἀδικημάτων ταῖς ἀκτῖσι Ph.1.634; *shine around*, Plu.*Cic.* 35; φῶς π. τινά *Act.Ap.*26.13, cf. *Ev.Luc.*2.9:—Pass., *to be illumined*, φωτί, ὑπὸ τῆς φλογός, Plu.*Per.*39, *Dio* 46; ὑπὸ τῶν ἀστέρων Luc.*Dom.* 8. **-λαμψις**, εως, ἡ, *shining round, radiation*, Plu.2.931a, Plot.5. 1.6, 5.3.15.

**περιλάπτω**, *suck* or *lick all round*, Pherecr.23 (περιλέψαντες Herm.).

**περιλεγνής**, ές, (λέγνη) *with a variegated border*, Hsch.

**περιλέγω**, *express by circumlocution*, Hermipp.92, Poll.2.125.

**περίλειμμα**, ατος, τό, *remainder, residue*. Pl.*Mx.*236b (pl.).

**περιλείπομαι**, Med. and Pass., *remain over, survive*, ὅσσοι δ' ἂν πολέμοιο περὶ στυγεροῖο λίπωνται Il.19.230; τὸν περιλειφθέντα Hdt.1.82; ὑπὸ τῶν κόρεων εἴ μού τι περιλειφθήσεται Ar.*Nu.*725; τοὺς περιλελειμμένους φίλων E.*Hel.*426, cf. Pl.*Ti.*23c (Pass.), Arist.*Oec.*1350$^{a}$29, etc.

**περιλείχω**, *lick all round*, τὰ βλέφαρα Ar.*Pl.*736; Σοφοκλέους..τὸ στόμα Id.*Fr.*581; of a parasite, πολλῶν..λοπάδων τοὺς ἄμβωνας -λείξας *having licked* them *clean*, Eup.52; τὸ τρύβλιον Luc.*Gall.*14. II. *lick off*, τι Arist.*HA*605$^{a}$4; τῶν ὀβολῶν τὸν ῥύπον Luc.*Icar.*30.

**περίλεξις**, εως, ἡ, *circumlocution*, Ar.*Nu.*318.

**περιλεπίζω**, = sq., Ph.*Bel.*88.47, Dieuch.ap.Orib.4.7.15, Paul. Aeg.1.81, Sch.Ar.*Lys.*736.

**περιλέπω**, *strip off all round*, περὶ γάρ ῥά ἑ χαλκὸς ἔλεψεν φύλλα Il. 1.236; περιλέποντες τὸν φλοιόν Hdt.8.115; *peel*, Thphr.*HP*6.4.10 (Pass.); v. περιλάπτω.

**περιλεσχήνευτος**, ον, *talked of in every club* (λέσχη), *matter of common talk*, Hdt.2.135.

**περιλευκ-αίνω**, *whiten all round*, πέτρας Ach.Tat.1.1. **-ιος** (sc. λίθος), ὁ, name of a stone, Herm.Trism. in *Rev.Phil.*32.274. ⊛ **-ος**, ον, *edged with white*, Callix.2. 2. **περίλευκον** (sc. ἱμάτιον), τό, *garment edged with white*, Antiph.297.

**περί-ληµµα**, ατος, τό, *embrace*, Lxx *Ec.*3.5 (v.l.), *EM* 175.7. **-ληπτικός**, ή, όν, *that may be taken hold of*, of loose skin, Arist.*GA* 719$^{b}$6. II. *comprehending*, i.e. *understanding*, π. τρόπος Epicur. *Nat.*28.2. Adv. -κῶς *with comprehension*, ib.7, prob. in Id.*Ep.*1 p.6 U. 2. *comprehending, including* (as the greater the less), τινος Plu. 2.428d, cf. 1003d, etc.; πάντων A.D.*Synt.*40.13 (v.l.), cf. 285.4; τὸ καθολικὸν π. τῶν ἐπὶ μέρους S.E.*M.*11.9, cf. 7.143: Comp. -ώτερος Procl.*Inst.*143: Sup. -ώτατος Id. *in Prm.*p.858 S.; *collective*, ὄνομα D.T. 637.13, Hdn.*Fig.*p.87 S., *EM* 264.45; σχῆμα, in Rhet., Ulp. ad D.23. 63. **-ληπτός**, ή, όν, *embraced* or *to be embraced, comprehensible*, οὔτε νόῳ περιληπτά Emp.2.8; νοήσει, δόξῃ π., Pl.*Ti.*28a,c; τὰ π. *things mentally comprehended*, Epicur.*Ep.*1 p.6 U.; πᾶν μῆκος π. any *conceivable* distance, ib.p.10 U.; π. διανοίᾳ Phld.*D.*3.15, S.E.*M.*9.409; π. ἀριθμῷ Plu.*Cam.*43. Adv. -τῶς, f.l. for -τικῶς, Epicur.*Ep.*1 p.6 U. 2. c. dat., *involved in*, παραισθήσει..περιληπτὴν αἴσθησιν Phld. *Piet.*116.

**περιλῆσαι** (-ιειλῆσαι cod.)· περι⟨σ⟩τρέψαι, Hsch.

**περίληψις**, εως, ἡ, *grasping with the hand*, Poll.9.98; *embracing*, Lxx *Ec.*3.5. II. *comprehension*, ἐν τῇ π. τῆς ἀρχῆς τῆς ψυχικῆς *in the fact of their comprehending* the vital principle, Arist.*GA*762$^{a}$25, cf. Epicur.*Ep.*1 p.16 U. (pl.); ἐπιστημονικὴ π. Procl. *in Alc.*p.276 C.; εἰς καθολικὴν καὶ ἔντεχνον π. πεσεῖν admit of general and technical *comprehension*, D.H.*Comp.*12. III. *inclusion*, κατὰ περίληψιν S.E.*M.*10.99, 286, cf. Procl. *in Euc.*p.395 F. 2. concrete, *that which includes* or *comprehends*, [θεὸς] πάντων π. καὶ μέτρον Plot.6.8.18; ἡ ἡνωμένη π. ἣν σπέρμα πάντων ἐκάλεσε Dam.*Pr.*98.

**περιλιμνάζω**, *surround with water, insulate*, τὴν πόλιν Th.2. 102. II. intr., *become a lake*, Ael.*NA*16.15.

**περιλιμπάνω**, later form of περιλείπω, Simp. *in Epict.*p.119 D. (Pass.), Sch.Ar.*Pl.*554, etc.

**περιλίπᾰρος** [λῐ], ον, *very moist and shiny*, βλέμμα Paul.Aeg.3.71.

**περιλῐπής**, ές, *left remaining, surviving*, c. gen., π. τῆς φθορᾶς Pl. *Lg.*702a: abs., Plb.1.73.2; π. σχεῖν Str.8.7.5.

**περιλιχμ-άζω**, *lick*, Opp.*H.*1.786, 2.650. **-άομαι**, = foreg., γλώσσῃ γένειον Theoc.25.226, cf. Arat.1115, Phylarch.27 J., Luc. *Merc.Cond.*34, *DDeor.*12.2: in pass. sense, Pl.*Ax.*372a. 2. *lick up*, τὸν ἑαυτῶν φόνον Plu.*Pyrrh.*31; τοῦ ψωμοῦ τι Luc.*Prom.*10. **-ησις**, εως, ἡ, *licking all round*, Sch.Arat.1114.

**περιλιχνεύω**, *desire greedily*, Ph.1.446; cf. περιιχνεύω.

**περιλογισμός**, v.l. for ἐπιλογισμός in D.H.*Amm.*2.3.

⊛ **περίλοιπος**, ον, = περιλιπής, Ar.*Fr.*160, Th.1.74, al., Arist.*Oec.*1350$^{b}$ 13, Lxx *Am.*5.15.

**περιλοπίζω**, = περιλεπίζω, Thphr.*HP*3.15.2.

**περιλούω**, *wash all over*, Plu.*Lyc.*16, *Pomp.*80.

**περιλῠγίζω**, *bend*, [ῥάβδους] πρὸς τὸ ἐναντίον Olymp. *in Alc.*p.54 C.:—Pass., Hsch.

**περιλῡπ-ία**, ἡ, *extreme grief*, D.L.7.97. **-ος**, ον, *very sad, deeply grieved*, Hp.*Acut.*42; opp. περιχαρής, Isoc.1.42, Arist.*EN* 1124$^{a}$16; στυγνὸς καὶ π. Demad.17, cf. Lxx *Ge.*4.6, al.

**περίλῠσις**, εως, ἡ, dub. sens., ὅταν ἡ πόλις συνάγῃ στοὰν ἢ περίλυσιν *Abh.Berl.Akad.*1925(5).32 (Cyrene, ii/i B.C.). 2. *cancellation*, δανείων *Sammelb.*5761.4 (i A.D.), cf. *PGiss.*33.11 (iii A.D.), etc.; τοῦ πρὸς ἀλλήλους γάμου *Stud.Pal.*22.51.3 (ii A.D.); = *repudium*, *Gloss.* 3. pl., title of a work by Musaeus, Sch.Ar.*Ra.*1065 codd.

⊛ **περιλύω**, *loosen round about*, Aq.1*Ki.*5.9 (Pass.), *Is.*52.2 (Med.), cf. Dosith.p.434 K. II. *cancel*, μισθοκαρπίαν *PLips.*10 ii 31 (iii A.D.), cf. *POxy.*323 (i A.D., Pass.), etc.

**περιλωπίζω**, *strip*, gloss on (or perh. glossed by) περιδῦσαι, Poll.7.44 ( = Hyp.*Fr.*263).

**περιμάδᾰρος** [μᾰ], ον, *bald round about*, π. ἕλκεα *where the skin peels* or *scales off all round*, Hp.*Aph.*6.4 ( = *Epid.*6.8.2).

**περιμάθησις** [ᾰ], εως, ἡ, dub. l. in Diog.*Ep.*44 (pl.).

**περιμαιμάω**, *seek round*, ἰχθυάᾳ σκόπελον περιμαιμώωσα (Ep. part.) Od.12.95. 2. *seek eagerly*, ἀπὸ μαζῶν.. χείλεσσι γλάγος π. Q.S. 14.16.

**περιμαίνομαι**, *rage round about, rush furiously about*, ἄλσος Hes. *Sc.*99. II. *to be madly in love with*, τινα Ael.*Ep.*7: c. dat. rei, *to be mad for*, χρυσῷ Naumach.ap.Stob.4.23.7 (dub. l.).

**περιμάκης**, Dor. for περιμήκης.

**περιμάκτρια**, ἡ, (περιμάσσω) *one that purifies by magic*, γραῦς π. *a witch*, Plu.2.166a.

**περιμᾰνής**, ές, *furious, mad*, Plu.2.43d,52d, al. Adv. -νῶς ib. 1100a.

**περιμανώς**, name of a *song*, Eub.46.

**περιμαρμαίρω**, *sparkle all round*, Q.S.5.114.

**περιμάρμᾰρος**, ον, *sparkling*, π. ἄνθεσιν ἄχνας φλοῖσβος *Hymn.Is.* 165.

**περιμάρνᾰμαι**, poet. for περιμάχομαι, Epigr.ap.Paus.5.19.4.

**περιμάσσω**, Att. -ττω, *wipe all round*, τὠφθαλμὼ τούτῳ (sc. τῷ σύκῳ) π. Pherecr.132; τοὺς ὀδόντας ὀθονίοις Plu.2.976b; σπόγγῳ τι Aët.8.3, cf. Gal.12.840; τὸ πρόσωπον Sor.2.28:—Med., περιμάξασθαι τὸν κόλπον Id.1.61, cf. Philum.ap.Orib.45.29.44. 2. *wipe off*, τὴν ἀκαθαρσίαν Dsc.5.94. 3. *purify by magic*, Men.530.21, Ph.2.316, Plu.2.168d (Pass.).

**περιμαστεύω**, *go round and visit*, πολλὰ ἔθνη Ps.-Callisth.1.3 (v.l.).

**περιμάχ-ητος** [ᾰ], ον, *fought about, fought for*, τοῖσι φυλαῖς Ar.*Av.* 1404; τοῖς πολλοῖς [ὕδωρ] Th.7.84; [πενία] ἥκιστα περιμάχητον not *a thing one would fight for*, X.*Smp.*3.9, cf. Pl.*R.*521a, *Lg.*678e; δυναστεία ὑπὸ πάντων ἐρωμένη καὶ π. γεγενημένη Isoc.8.65, cf. 7.24, 10.17; τὰ π. ἀγαθά *such as are matters of contention, highly prized*, Arist.*EN* 1169a21, cf. *Pol.*1271b8, *Rh.*1363a8, Epicur.*Sent.Vat.*45: Sup. -ότατος Isoc.9.40, Plu.*Lyc.*26: in Ar.*Th.*319, πόλις π., prob. with collat. sense of *fought around, surrounded by battle*. -ομαι, *fight around* one, X.*Cyr.*7.1.41.

**περιμελαίνομαι**, Pass., *to be black all round*, π. λαμπρὰ σκιεροῖς *to have* bright parts *shaded off* into dark, Plu.2.368c.

**περιμέλας**, αινα, αν, *very black*, ὄνος *BGU*806.4 (i A.D., cf. Index p.5).

**περιμεμφής**, ές, *blaming greatly*, v.l. for πολυμεμφής, Arat. 109.

**περιμενεαίνω**, *wish for ardently*, in tmesi, A.R.1.670,771.

**περιμενετέον**, *one must await*, D.H.*Rh.*9.5; τοὺς καιρούς Herod. Med.ap.Orib.7.8.1.

**περιμένω**, *wait for, await*, c. acc. pers., Hdt.4.89, Ar.*Pl.*643, etc.; π. Τισσαφέρνην ἡμέρας πλείους ἢ εἴκοσι X.*An.*2.4.1, etc.: c. acc. rei, π. ἐξ ἀγορᾶς ἰχθύδια Ar.*Fr.*387.8; τοῦ καιροῦ μὴ περιμένοντός τι as the time could not *wait for*.., Plu.*Caes.*17. 2. *require, expect*, σχολάζουσαν φιληκοΐαν Id.2.172e. 3. *endure, put up with*, μακρὰ λέγοντας ἡμᾶς αὐτοὺς περιεμείναμεν Pl.*Lg.*890e. 4. of events, *await, be in store for*, τίς με πότμος ἔτι π.; S.*Ant.*1296 (lyr.); μὴ θύσαντας δεινὰ π. Pl.*R.*365a; ἃ τελευτήσαντα ἑκάτερον π. ib.614a. II. c. inf., οὐ περιμενοῦσιν ἄλλους σφᾶς διολέσαι *will* not *wait for* others to destroy them, ib.375c; ἕκαστος [τῶν λόγων] π. ἀποτελεσθῆναι *awaits* its accomplishment, Id.*Tht.*173c; μηδ' ἐφ' ἑαυτὸν [τὰ τοιαῦτα] ἐλθεῖν π. D.21.220; π. τὰ λοιπὰ μαθεῖν D.H.1.13. III. abs., *wait, stand still*, Hdt.7.58, Ar.*Ec.*517, etc.; π. αὐτοῦ Id.*Ach.*815; ὀλίγον χρόνον Pl.*Ap.*38c; π. ἕως ⟨ἂν⟩ τὸν ὄχλον διωσώμεθα X.*Cyr.*7.5.39; ἕως ἀνοιχθείη τὸ δεσμωτήριον Pl.*Phd.*59d, cf. 116a; μέχρι τούτου, ἕως ἂν.. D.9.10; ἄχρι ἂν.. X.*An.*2.3.2; μέχρις ἂν.. Epict.*Ench.*15.

**περίμεσος**, ον, *in the middle*: τὸ π. *the middle part*, *AB*354.

**περίμεστος**, ον, *full all round, quite full of*, τινος X.*Smp.*2.11, Plu. *Caes.*5.

**περι-μετρέω**, *measure all round*, Luc.*Icar.*6, *Nav.*12. ⊛ -μετρον, τό, *circumference*, Hdt.1.185, 2.15,41, Arist.*Mir.*840b34, Luc.*VH*2. 40; τὸ π. τῆς περιόδου Hdt.2.149; τὸ π. τῆς γῆς Ach.Tat.*Intr.Arat.* 29. -μετρος, ον, (μέτρον) *very large*, Hom., only in Od., as epith. of Penelope's web, ἱστὸν.. ὕφαινε λεπτὸν καὶ π. 2.95, cf. 19.140; later, of bulk, π. δέμας, κήτεα, Opp.*H.*3.190, 5.47. 2. *well-fitting*, of a garment, Aristaenet.1.1. II. -μετρος (sc. γραμμή), ἡ, = περίμετρον, Arist.*Mir.*838b21, Thphr.*HP*4.12.4, *PLille* 1.4 (iii B.C.), Plb.1. 56.4, Phld.*Sign.*1, Str.2.5.4.

**περιμετωπίδιος**, ον, *on the forehead*, ἱδρώς Hp.*Mul.*2.171 (cod. θ).

**περιμηκάομαι**, *bleat round*, cj. for -μυκάομαι, Orph.*L.*209.

**περιμήκ-ετος**, ον, poet. for sq.. *very tall* or *high*, ἐλάτη Il.14.287; Τηΰγετος Od.6.103: c. gen., π. ἄλλων Arat.250. -ης, ες, Dor. **περιμάκης** [ᾱ], ες, *AP*6.125 (Mnasalc.): (μῆκος):—*very tall* or *long*, κοντός Od.9.487; ῥάβδος 10.293; ἱστοί 13.107; δοῦρα 12.443; ὀϊστοί Hes.*Sc.*133; *very high*, πέτρη Il.13.63; ὄρος Od.13.183; *very large, huge*, οἴκημα Hdt.2.100; ἀνδρόσφιγγες ib.175; λίθους μεγάθεϊ περιμήκεας ib.108; ἄγκυραι Id.7.36: Comp. -μηκέστερος Ael.*Tact.*2.7: but Sup. -μήκιστος Plu.2.1077b.

**περιμήρια**, τά, *covering for the thighs*, *Gloss.*:—also **περιμηρίδες**, αἱ, ib.:—but **περιμηρίδιον**, τό, is f.l. for παρα–, Arr.*Tact.*4.1.

**περιμηρύομαι**, Dor. -μᾱρύομαι, Med., *wind round*, περὶ ταῦτα τοὺς τόνους Ph.*Bel.*65.39, cf. 46:—Pass., *to be surrounded by a cord*, of a temple, prob. in *Abh.Berl.Akad.*1928(6).33 (Cos, iii B.C.).

**περίμητρος**, ον, (μήτρα) *with tough sap-wood*, ξύλον π. Thphr.*HP*3. 9.6.

**περιμηχᾰνάομαι**, *prepare very craftily, contrive cunningly*, ἄλλο τι .. περιμηχανόωνται Od.7.200; δούλιον ἦμαρ ἐμοὶ περιμηχανόωντο 14. 340.

**περιμῐνύθω** [ῡ], *decrease on all sides*, περὶ δὲ ῥινοὶ μ. Od.12.46.

**περιμολυβδοχοέω**, *run lead round*, *IG*7.3073.73 (Lebad.).

**περιμοτ-όω**, *dress a wound with lint*, Heliod.ap.Orib.44.10.18, 47. 15.8:—Subst. -ωσις, εως, ἡ, *dressing with lint*, Id.ap.Orib.46.19.4.

**περιμοχθέω**, *sorrow greatly over*, τινι Opp.*H.*4.258.

**περιμῠδάω**, *remove by softening*, Sor.1.73.

**περιμῡκ-άομαι**, *roar round*, τινα Plu.*Crass.*26; cf. περιμηκάομαι. -ής, ές, *loud-bellowing*, cj. in Orph.*A.*313.

**περιμύρομαι** [ῡ], *lament around*, Mosch.3.89, Q.S.12.489.

**περιναιετ-άω**, *dwell round about* or *in the neighbourhood*, Od.2.66, 8.551, 23.136, Hes.*Th.*370, Pi.*N.*8.9, etc. 2. of cities, *to be* or *lie near*, Od.4.177. -ης, ου, ὁ, *one of those who dwell round, neighbour*, Il.24.488, A.R.4.470.

**περίναιον**, **περίναιος**, v. περίνεος.

**περιναΐος** [ᾱ], ον, *round the temple*, στοαί *IPE*2.352 (Phanagoria).

**περιναίω**, *dwell round*, A.*Supp.*1021 (lyr.).

**περιναύτιος**, ον, *sea-sick, squeamish*, D.S.2.58.

**περινάω**, *float* or *flow around*, ἄμυλοι π. ἡμῖν Metag.6.11.

⊛ **περινέμομαι**, Pass., *spread round*, of fire, Plu.*Dio* 46.

**περινενοημένως**, Adv. *in a carefully thought-out fashion*, opp. ἁπλῶς καὶ ἀνειμένως, Hermog.*Id.*2.5, cf. 9.

**περίνεος**, ὁ, *space between the anus and scrotum*, Hp.*Art.*71, 77, *Aph.*4.80, Arist.*HA*493b9; *male genital organs*, Id.*GA*716a33 (v.l. -ναίους), 766a5: Gal.19.130 has **περινῷ**· περινέῳ, Hsch. **περίνα**· περίναιον, τὸ αἰδοῖον, and **περίνος**· τὸ αἰδοῖον.

**περί-νευσις**, εως, ἡ, *oscillation, swing*, Apollod.*Poliorc.*178. 6. -νεύω, *bend forward and look round timidly*, App.*BC*4.46. II. *incline first to one side then to the other, sway*, Arist.*Phgn.*808a15; of a chariot, = ἀμφαξονέω, Phryn.*PS* p.40 B. 2. of lands, *slope, incline*, ἐπὶ τὸν Νότον Str.8.4.1; παρὰ τὴν ἑσπέραν Id.4.1.6; πρὸς τὴν Ἰταλίαν Id.7.1.5; καθὰ ἡ φύσις π. *IG*5(1).1431.35 (Messene, i A.D.). 3. *project*, Apollod.*Poliorc.*166.11, al. 4. περινενευκὼς σφυγμός perh. *compressible* pulse, Archig.ap.Gal.8.479, 9.86.

**περινέφελος**, ον, *clouded, overcast*, ἀήρ Ar.*Av.*1194.

**περίνεφρος**, ον, *fat about the kidneys*, Arist.*HA*520a31, *PA*672b2.

**περινέω** (A), *swim round*, Hp.ap.Gal.19.130; π. κύκλῳ τινός Arist. *HA*621a18.

**περινέω** (B), Hdt.6.80: aor. part. περινήσας Id.4.164, also uncontr. inf. -νηῆσαι v.l. in Id.2.107, cf. Q.S.3.678 (Med.):—*pile, heap round*, ὕλην (sc. περὶ τὸν πύργον) Hdt.4.164; πολὺ πῦρ Anon.ap.Suid., cf. Plu.2.583a. 2. π. τὴν οἰκίην ὕλῃ *pile* it *round* with wood, Hdt.2. 107; ὕλῃ τὸ ἄλσος Id.6.80.

**περίνεως**, ὁ, gen. νεω, nom. pl. νεῳ, (ναῦς, Att. gen. νεώς) *supernumerary* or *to spare in a ship*, κῶπαι περίνεῳ *IG*2².1607.9,19, al.; π. ὁ δεύτερος ἱστὸς καὶ.. τὰ διττὰ τῆς νεὼς σκεύη, Hsch., cf. Phot.; of persons, *supercargo, passenger*, opp. πρόσκωπος, Th.1.10; opp. ναύτης, Ael.*NA*2.15, Anon.ap.Suid.; opp. αὐτερέτης, Procop.*Vand.*1.11, cf. Philostr.*VA*6.12, Phot.; but, *marines*, opp. τριηρῖται, D.C.49.1: in sg., *petty officer*, gen. -νέου Artem.1.35.

**περίνημα**, ατος, τό, *lotion*, Gal.19.130.

⊛ **περίνησος**, ον, *edged with purple* (or *with a fringe*): περίνησον (sc. ἱμάτιον), τό, *robe with a purple border* (or *with a fringe*), Antiph.297, Men.92, cf. Hsch.

**περινήχομαι**, *swim* or *float about*, D.H.1.15; ἐν κύκλῳ Plu.2. 977a; π. τινί *swim round*.., Q.S.14.548.

**περινίζω**, *wash off all round*, περὶ δ' αἷμα νένιπται Il.24.419, cf. Hp. *Fist.*9:—Med., Id.*Mul.*2.158; π. τὸ σῶμα D.S.4.51.

**περινίσομαι** [νῐ], *go round about*, κυλίκων περινισομενάων as the cups *go round*, Phoc.11; *revolve*, Orph.*Fr.*247.11; *come round*, of time, ἁνίκα Καρνείου περινίσεται ὥρα E.*Alc.*449 (lyr.).

**περινο-έω**, *contrive cunningly*, Ar.*Ra.*958; μεγάλα ταῖς ἐλπίσι π. *form* great *projects*, Plu.*Phoc.*14; τὴν αὐτοκράτορα ἀρχὴν π. *meditate* empire, Philostr.*VA*5.27; περινοησάτω ὅπως.. prob. in Diocl.Com. 14:—Pass., περινενοημέναι ἔννοιαι Hermog.*Id.*2.9, cf. 5. II. *consider on all sides, consider well, study carefully*, Epicur.*Nat.*11.6; πάντα τὸν κίνδυνον Plu.*Brut.*13, cf. Hierocl.*in CA*23 p.469 M.; *understand* a thing, M.Ant.1.7, S.E.*M.*2.9. -ημᾰτικός, ἡ, όν, = -νοητικός, Herm.ap.Stob.2.8.31, *Cat.Cod.Astr.*2.172. -ησις, εως, ἡ, *shrewdness, subtlety*, Plu.2.509e. 2. *sustained thought*, Plot.6.9. 11. -ητικός, ἡ, όν, *thoughtful*, Poll.2.229. 2. *discursive in thought*, λόγος Herm.ap.Stob.1.49.4. 3. *subtle*, Procl.*Par.Ptol.* 231.

**περίνοια**, ἡ, *thoughtfulness, quick comprehension*, τινος Pl.*Ax.*370c: abs., Philostr.*VS*2.4.2, Luc.*Zeux.*2; ἐν περινοίᾳ γεγονέναι to have *comprehended*, Gal.18(1).331. 2. *deliberation*, ἐν περινοίᾳ τοῦ μεταστήσοντος αὐτὸν ἦν J.*AJ*18.6.2. II. *over-wiseness*, Th.3.43; *subtlety*, λογικὴ π. Simp.*in Ph.*1205.28. III. *disdain, contempt*, Aristid.1.141 J. (v.l.), Lib.*Or.*12.48, Phot., Suid. IV. *sharp practice, fraud*, π. καὶ ἀπάτη Just.*Nov.*7.12, cf. *Cod.Just.*1.3.41.5.

**περινομή**, ἡ, (νέμω) *distribution in regular order*, ἐκ περινομῆς *in turn*, D.H.10.57 (leg. περιτροπῆς). II. *procession round* a place, Men.894 (pl.).

**περίνοος**, ον, contr. -νους, ουν, (νοέω) *very intelligent*: Sup. περινούστατος S.E.*M.*7.326.

**περινοστ-έω**, *go round, visit, inspect*, περὶ τὰς κλίνας Ar.*Th.*796; παλαίστρας Id.*Pax*762; τὰ τεκτόνων ἔργα Plu.2.155c: metaph., π. τινὰ ἀπάτῃ *circumvent*, Aesop.204b. 2. abs., *go about, stalk about*, π. ὥσπερ ἥρως Pl.*R.*558a; of vagrants, Ar.*Pl.*121, 494, D.19.255; π. σχολὴν ἄγοντα Alex.28, cf. Alciphr.1.10 (cj.), Jul.*Ep.*89. **-ησις**, εως, ἡ, *a going about, wandering*, Agath.2.6.

**περινοτ-ίζω**, *moisten all round*, Sor.1.22 (Pass.); τὸ πρόσωπον Alex. Trall.1.15. **-ισις**, εως, ἡ, *wetting all round*, Archig.ap.Aët.3.194.

**περινυκτίδες**, gloss on ὀλοφλυκτίδες, Erot.

**πέριξ**, strengthd. for περί, mostly Ion. Prose and Trag. (in latter usu. Adv.): I. Prep., *round about, all round*, c. gen., Hdt.1.179, 2.91, X.*An.*7.8.12, Epicur.*Ep.*2 p.51 U., etc. 2. rarely c. dat., E.*Ph.*710. 3. commonly c. acc., Hdt.1.196, 3.158, 4.36, al.: mostly before its case, but also after, ib.52, 79, as also in A.*Pers.*368, dub. in E.*HF*243. II. Adv. *round about*, π. ὑπορύσσοντες τὸ τεῖχος Hdt.5.115; π. λαβεῖν ἄνθρωπον *to surround him*, ib.87; κύκλῳ π. A.*Pers.*418, dub. in S.*Ant.*1301, E.*Andr.*266; [Ὠκεανὸς] π. γᾶν ἀμπέχει Limen.10: metaph., πᾶν π. φρονοῦντες *circuitously*, E.*Andr.* 448: rare in Att. Prose, π. πολιορκεῖν Th.6.90; ὁ π. τόπος, οἱ π., Pl.*Ti.*62e, X.*Cyr.*1.5.2, cf. Epicur.*Ep.*2 p.47 U.; ὁ π. χρόνος, i.e. all times save the present, Arist.*Int.*16$^b$18; τὸ π. ὕδωρ Thphr.*Sens.*26; later αἱ π. πόλεις *Act.Ap.*5.16; αἱ π. κῶμαι *SIG*880.44 (Pizus, iii A.D.).

**περιξαίνομαι**, *suffer laceration upon*, ταῖς ἀπορρῶξιν J.*BJ*3.9.3.

**περιξεστός**, ή, όν, *polished round about*, πέτρη Od.12.79.

**περιξέω**, *polish all round*, Theoc.22.50, *Supp.Epigr.*4.446.13 (Didyma, iii B.C.), Gal.*UP*16.11:—Pass., Lib.*Or.*18.219. 2. *scrape all round*, Hp.*Mul.*2.144.

**περιξηραίνομαι**, *become dry all round*, Arist.*GA*758$^b$25, *Pr.*870$^a$24.

**περίξηρος**, ον, *dry round about*, ἀήρ Thphr.*Ign.*41; χώρα *Gp.*2.13; σύγκρισις Philum.ap.Orib.45.29.36; τὸ π. *the crust*, Arist.*GA*737$^a$36.

**περιξῠράω**, Ion. -έω, *shave all round*, τοὺς κροτάφους v.l. in Hdt.3. 8:—Pass., περιεξυρημένος τὸν πώγωνα Luc.*Merc.Cond.*33.

**περί-ξῦσις**, εως, ἡ, *stringor*, *Gloss.* **-ξυσμα**, ατος, τό, in pl., *shavings, scrapings*, Sch.Pl.*Chrm.*161e. **-ξυστήρ**, ῆρος, ὁ, *surgical instrument for scraping* or *smoothing bones*, Heliod.(?)ap.Orib.46.11. 29. **-ξύστης**, ου, ὁ, = foreg., *Hermes* 38.283. **-ξύω**, *scrape all round*, Hp.ap.Gal.19.130; *scrape off* or *away*, φλοιόν Lxx *Wi.*13. 11, cf. Gal.2.653; *nibble at*, ἄκροισι.. στομάτεσσι δαῖτα Opp.*H.*3. 525:—Med., *scrape oneself*, Diocl.*Fr.*141, Alex.Aphr.*in Top.*455. 25:—Pass., Hp.*Mul.*2.192; περιξυομένη γῆ *drilled out* by a borer, Apollod.*Poliorc.*149.3.

**περίογκος**, ον, *of great size, bulky*, Arist.*Phgn.*810$^b$15, Heliod.ap. Orib.44.8.23.

* **περιοδ-εία** or **-ία**, ἡ, *going round, circuit*, Str.8.6.3, 9.3.1. 2. *patrolling, rounds*, Aen.Tact.1.1 (pl.), al. II. *going through* a subject, *diligent study*, Epicur.*Ep.*1 p.4 U.: pl., ib.p.32 U.; π. φυσική Phld. *Rh.*2.53 S. 2. medical *practice, routine*, ἐν π. Gal.17(1).518; κατὰ τὴν π. ἐν Ῥώμῃ Id.14.295. **-εύσιμος**, ον, *with circuitous ways*, *Gloss.* **-ευσις**, εως, ἡ, = περιοδεία, Suid. **-ευτής**, οῦ, ὁ, *traveller*, Eust.1382.59. II. *medical practitioner*, Gal.12.844, Steph. *in Hp.*2.457 D. III. *visitor* of an ecclesiastical foundation, *Cod. Just.*1.3.38.2, 1.3.41.19. **-ευτικός**, ή, όν, *of a* περιοδευτής: -κά, τά, *inspector's report*, *PLips.*105.16 (i/ii A.D.). 2. of medical treatment, *systematic*, Dsc.*Ther.Praef.* (dub.). 3. *making a systematic study of*, μαθημάτων Ptol.*Tetr.*57. 4. = περιοδικός II, χρόνοι *Placit.*2.4.13. **-εύω**, *go all round*, τὴν γῆν Lxx *Za.*1.10; τὸν νομόν *PCair.Zen.*541.2 (iii B.C.); τὸ Παλάτιον Plu.*Cam.*32, cf. *Phoc.* 21; ἐν πάσῃ τῇ γῇ Lxx 2*Ki.*24.8; *make a revolution*, of the moon, Gal.19.554. 2. in military sense, *patrol*, Aen.Tact.22.10; π. τὴν πρώτην φυλακήν Id.26.2; of dyke-watchers, *PPetr.*2 p.17 (iii B.C.); of an inspector, *go round* vineyards, *PCair.Zen.*300.7 (iii B.C.); *march round*, App.*BC*1.58, al. II. metaph., *go systematically through*, βίον τινός Plu.2.87b; τὸν περὶ τῶν οὐρανίων λόγον *Placit.*3 *Prooem.*, cf. Ptol.*Tetr.*1 (Pass.); *study diligently*, Epicur.*Ep.*2 p.35 U., Demetr. Lac.*Herc.*1013.18, 1055.23 (Pass.), Epict.*Ench.*29.3; περιοδευομένη φαντασία Academici ap.Gal.5.802. III. *circumvent, cheat*, J.*AJ* 17.4.2. IV. *practise*, of a midwife, Sor.1.3; οἱ περιοδεύοντες *practitioners*, Alex.Trall.8.2:—Pass., *to be treated*, ibid., Id.11.4. V. Rhet., *write in periods*, Demetr.*Eloc.*229; διαπορητικῶς π. Hermog. *Inv.*4.3:—Pass., ἡ περιωδευμένη προφορὰ καὶ γραφή Phld.*Rh.*1.158 S.; but τὸ περιωδευμένον *path traversed in a circle*, expl. of περίοδος, Demetr. *Eloc.*11. **-ία**, v. περιοδεία. **-ίζω**, *to be periodical*, esp. in pres. part., π. ἐπιτάσεις καὶ ἀνέσεις Str.7.2.1; of fevers, *intermittent*, Ph.2.576, Gal.10.627. **-ικός**, ή, όν, *acquired in one's travels*, ἱστορία Ptol.*Geog.*1.2.2. II. *periodical*, ἀριθμὸς π. σελήνης Plu.2. 1018d; ὧραι Vett.Val.243.13; *recurrent, intermittent*, νόσοι Chrysipp. *Stoic.*3.116; ῥίγη, πυρετοί, Dsc.1.51, 3.81; περιστάσεις Ptol.*Tetr.*54 (Comp.); πυρετοῦ λῆψις Tim.*Lex.* s.v. καταβολή, cf. Harp., Suid., etc. Adv. -κῶς Chrysipp.*Stoic.*3.117, Herod.Med.ap.Orib.10.37.18, Procl. *Inst.*199, Aët.12.21. III. Rhet., *periodic*, κῶλα, συμμετρία, Demetr. *Eloc.*13, 16; σχῆμα Anon.*Fig.*p.112 S. Adv. -κῶς, συγκεῖσθαι Demetr. *Eloc.*33; λέγειν, ἑρμηνεύειν, Hermog.*Inv.*4.3, 8. IV. π. μέτρον, i.e. a hexameter in which dactyls and spondees alternate, Ps.-Plu. *Metr.*2. **-ιον**, τό, Dim. of περίοδος V, Arr.*Epict.*2.1.31.

**περιοδοιπορέω**, *walk about*, Hp.*Prorrh.*2.3.

* **περιοδονίκης** [νῑ], ου, ὁ, *one who gains victories in all the great games* (cf. περίοδος IV. 2), *IG*3.809, 5(1).669, al., Ph.2.438, *POxy.*1643.2 (iii A.D.), D.C.63.8, al.

* **περίοδος**, ὁ, *one who goes the rounds, patrol*, Aen.Tact.22.3, al., *Rev.Arch.*1911(2).424 (Mesembria, i B.C.).

* **περίοδος** (Dor. **πέροδος**, q.v.), ἡ, *going round, marching round, flank march*, τῶν Περσέων ἡ π. Hdt.7.219, 229; π. καὶ κύκλωσις Th.4. 35. 2. *slow walk*, Gal.17(2).99. 3. *passage* of fluids, Aret. *SD*1.10, cf. Arist.*Pr.*870$^a$10. II. *way round*, Hdt.7.223; λίμνης Id.1.185; *circumference, circuit, compass*, σήματος, τείχεος, ib.93, 163: abs., τὴν π. *in circumference*, Id.7.109. III. γῆς π. *chart* or *map* of the earth, Id.4.36, 5.49, Ar.*Nu.*206, Arist.*Mete.*362$^b$12, Agathem.1.1; αἱ τῆς γῆς π. *books of descriptive geography*, Arist. *Pol.*1262$^a$19, *Rh.*1360$^a$34, *Mete.*350$^a$16. IV. *going round in a circle, coming round to the starting-point, circuit*, ἡ τοῦ τρίποδος π. Plu. *Sol.*4. 2. esp. of Time, *cycle* or *period of time*, πάσαις ἐτέων π. Pi. *N.*11.40; freq. in Pl., ἐν πολλαῖς χρόνου καὶ μακραῖς π. *Phd.*107e; π. χιλιετής *Phdr.*249a: abs., *R.*546b, Epicur.*Ep.*1 p.27 U. (pl.), etc.; κατὰ φύσιν π. Arist.*GA*777$^b$18; of the *Great Year* of the Stoics, Chrysipp.*Stoic.*2.189 (pl.); ἐκ περιόδου *periodically, in rotation*, Heraclid.*Pol.*58, Plb.2.43.1, etc.; ἐν περιόδῳ Plu.*Eum.*8; esp. *the period embracing the four great public games*, κατὰ τὰν π. ἑκάσταν *IG*9(1). 694.31 (Corc.); ἐνίκησε τὴν π. Ath.10.415a; νικώμενος τὴν π. Arr. *Epict.*3.25.5, cf. Poll.4.89; v. περιοδονίκης. 3. of events, *periodic recurrence, cycle*, Isoc.15.174, Thphr.*CP*1.13.1. b. *cycle, roster* of public officials, τῇ πρὸ ταύτης π. τῶν μελλόντων λειτουργεῖν *POxy.* 1119.6 (iii A.D.), cf. 1552.3 (iii A.D.). 4. Medic., *a regular prescribed course of life*, ἐν τῇ καθεστηκυίᾳ π. ζῆν to live in the regular *course*, Pl.*R.*407e; αἱ ἰατρικαὶ π. the *periodical visits* of a regular physician, the doctor's *rounds*, Luc.*Gall.*23, cf. *Nigr.*22: hence, medical *practice*, Heraclas ap.Orib.48.18.2. b. *the period of menstruation*, Arist.*GA*738$^a$17. c. *fit* of intermittent fever, or the like, Hp. *Aph.*4.59 (pl.), D.9.19; ὁ ἐκ περιόδου πυρετός an *intermittent* fever, Luc.*Philops.*9. 5. *course at dinner*, X.*Cyr.*2.2.2; π. λόγων *table-talk*, Id.*Smp.*4.64. 6. *orbit of a heavenly body*, Id.*Mem.* 4.7.5; ἀστέρος κυκλικὴ π. Vett.Val.94.20; also θεριναὶ π., = τροπαί, Hp.*Aër.*19; *revolution* of a heavenly body, Epicur.*Ep.*1 p.28 U. V. *survey* in thought, ἡ ἅμα νοήματι π. τῶν κυριωτάτων ib.p.32 U. VI. Rhet., *period*, Thrasymach.ap.Suid. s.v. Θρασύμαχος, etc.; defined as λέξις ἔχουσα ἀρχὴν καὶ τελευτὴν αὐτὴ καθ' αὑτὴν καὶ μέγεθος εὐσύνοπτον, Arist.*Rh.*1409$^a$35, etc.; also in Music and Metric, Heph.*Poëm.*3.5, Aristid.Quint.1.14. VII. *vessel used in iron-founding*, Arist.*Fr.*261. VIII. *entrance to a temple-enclosure*, *IG*11(2).158*A* 65 (Delos, iii B.C.). IX. = Lat. *regio*, π. Καρίας Maiuri *Nuova Silloge* 562 (Cos).

**περιοδῠνάομαι**, v. περιωδ-.

**περιοδώδης**, ες, *recurrent*, Anon.Rhythm.*Oxy.*9 iii 20.

**περίοιδα**, **περιῄδη**, pf. and plpf. (in pres. and impf. sense), *know well*, c. inf., περίοιδε νοῆσαι Il.10.247: c. dat., ἴχνεσι γὰρ περιῄδη for he *was very skilled in* the tracks, Od.17.317: c. acc. rei et gen. pers., *know better than* others, περίοιδε δίκας ἠδὲ φρόνιν ἄλλων 3.244 (nisi leg. περὶ (Adv.) οἶδε); βουλῇ περιίδμεναι ἄλλων *to be better skilled in* counsel than others, Il.13.728.

**περιοιδέω**, *swell round about*, Hp.*Vict.*3.82, Herod.Med.ap.Orib.6. 20.24.

**περιοικ-έω**, (περίοικος) *dwell round* persons or places, c. acc., Hdt.1.57, al., X.*An.*5.6.16: abs., Hdt.5.23, Lys.7.28:—Pass., *to be inhabited all round*, κύκλῳ Arist.*Mete.*354$^a$4, Scyl.107, Scymn. 766. **-ία**, ἡ, = *territorium*, *Gloss.* 2. v. περιοικίς II. 2 fin. **-ίζω**, *place around*, [τῷ ἐγκεφάλῳ] τὰς αἰσθήσεις Gal.*UP*8.2 (s.v.l.):—Pass., Id.5.230. **-ιον**, τό, *space round a dwelling*, Is. *Fr.*102, Aristid.*Or.*51(27).55. **-ίς**, ίδος, ἡ, pecul. fem. of περίοικος, *dwelling* or *lying round about, neighbouring*, [πόλιες] Hdt.1.76, 9.115, cf. X.*HG*3.2.23; νῆσοι Th.1.9; κῶμαι Plb.5.8.4, Plu.*Cat.Ma.* 1. II. as Subst. (sc. γῆ, χώρα), *country round* a town, as of Sparta, Th.3.16; of Elis, Id.2.25. 2. *town of* περίοικοι, *dependent town*, Arist.*Pol.*1320$^b$6, *Po.*1448$^a$36, Str.10.2.2, 6.1.6 (v.l. περιοικίας).

**περιοικοδομ-έω**, *build round*, αἱμασιάν D.55.11; θριγκούς Poll.7. 120:—Med., π. τεῖχος Id.1.160. II. *enclose by building round*, τὸ χωρίον D.55.3; ὑμᾶς ib.29; αὐλήν *UPZ*10.16 (ii B.C.):—Pass., *to be built up, walled in*, ἐν τῷ ἱερῷ Th.3.81; περιῳκοδομημένα [θηρία] X. *Cyr.*1.4.11; τὸ περιοικοδομημένον *space built round, enclosure*, Hdt.7. 60. **-ημα**, ατος, τό, *wall built round*, *IG*11(2).161*A* 56 (Delos, iii B.C.): but in pl., *surrounding buildings*, *SIG*685.75 (Crete, ii B.C.). **-ησις**, εως, Dor. ιος, ἡ, = sq., *IG*4.823.43 (Troezen). **-ία**, ἡ, *building round*, ib.11(2).161 *A* 42 (Delos, iii B.C.), *Inscr.Délos* 290.188 (iii B.C.).

**περιοικονομέω**, *administer, manage*, τὰ περί τινων *POxy.*94.13 (i A.D.).

* **περίοικος**, ον, *dwelling round*, οἱ π. Λίβυες Hdt.4.159; οἱ π. *neighbours*, Id.1.166, 175, Ephipp.5.6; ἡ π. (sc. χώρα) Lxx *Ge.*19.25; τὸ π. τοῦ Ἰορδάνου ib.3*Ki.*7.33(46); τὰ π. the *neighbouring countries*, App.*Mith.* 112, Hdn.6.2.1. II. in Laconia, οἱ π. the *inhabitants of the towns dependent on Sparta*, Hdt.6.58, 9.11, Th.1.101, etc.; also in Crete, Arist.*Pol.*1271$^b$30; at Argos, ib.1303$^a$8: hence generally, *dependent, subject*, περιοίκους τε καὶ οἰκέτας ἔχοντες Pl.*R.*547c; ἐξὸν.. ἅπαντας τοὺς βαρβάρους περιοίκους τῆς Ἑλλάδος καταστῆσαι Isoc.4.131. III. geographically, περίοικοι, οἱ, *those who live on the same parallel of latitude as ourselves but* 180° *East or West of us*, opp. ἄντοικοι (v. Addenda), ἀντίποδες (qq. v.). Gem.16.1, Cleom.1.2.

**περιοιστ-έος**, α, ον, *to be carried about*, κλείς Men.343. **-ικός**, ή, όν, *of* or *for carrying about*, Phot. **-ος**, ον, *mobile*, of war-engines, *IG*2$^2$.468.

**περιοιχνέω**, *run round* or *about*, Agathocl.2.

**περιοκέλλω**, prop. of a ship, *run aground*: metaph., εἰς ἐπιτηδεύσεις χειρίστας π. *fall into* the worst habits, D.S.12.12.

**περιοκωχή**, ἡ, = περιοχή, Hsch.

⊛ **περιολισθ-άνω**, *slip about*, Hp.*Art*.47; *slip away all round*, Id.*VM* 22, cf. D.H.14.10; ναῦς π. *slips off* the engine, Plu.*Marc*.15; τὰ βέλη π. ἀπὸ [τῶν βυρσῶν] *glance off* them, J.*BJ*3.7.10: metaph., ἡδονὴ π. εἰς τὸ σῶμα (v.l. for δι-) Plu.2.1089d: later **-ολισθαίνω**, metaph., *wander, stray from the point*, Plot.2.2.1. **-ησις**, εως, ἡ, *slipping away*, in pl., Plu.*Cam*.26, Id.2.930e; ῥαμμάτων Antyll.ap.Orib.45.24.9.

**περιολκή**, ἡ, (περιέλκω) *drawing away, evacuation*, Archig.ap.Orib. 8.1.1. 2. *revulsion*, Philum.ib.45.29.17. II. in war, *diversion*, J.*AJ*15.6.6 (pl.). III. *distraction* of mind, Simp.*in Epict*.p.128D.

**περιόλλῡμι**, *destroy utterly*, ἣν περὶ Ζεὺς ὀλέσει *Epigr.Gr*.336 (Alexandria Troas).

**περιομμᾰτοποιός**, όν, *providing with eyes*, τῆς ψυχῆς Iamb.*VP*6.31.

**περιομφᾰκώδης**, ες, *looking quite unripe*, dub. in Hp.*Epid*.4.30 (πέρι, ὁ φακώδης Littré).

**περιονῠχίζω**, fut. -ιῶ, *pare* a person's *nails*, γυναῖκα Lxx *De*.21.12.

**περιοπάζω**, *enclose, surround*, σάρκα (of a nut) περὶ σκύλος αὖον ὀπάζει Nic.*Al*.270; θνητοὺς.. κακὸν περὶ γῆρας ὀπάζει Id.*Th*.356.

**περιοπτέος**, α, ον, (περιοράω) *to be overlooked* or *suffered*, c. part., οὔ σφι π. Ἑλλὰς ἀπολλυμένη Hdt.7.168; ἡμῖν τοῦτό ἐστι οὐ π., γένος τὸ Εὐρυσθένεος γενέσθαι ἐξίτηλον Id.5.39. 2. *to be watched* or *guarded against*, Th.8.48. II. περιοπτέον *one must overlook* or *suffer*, X.*Lac*.9.5, Agath.3.10.

**περίοπτος**, ον, *to be seen all round, in a commanding position*, ὄρος Str.8.6.21; τόπος Plu.*Arat*.53, etc.; of a person, π. ἐπιστὰς τοῖς σώμασι J.*BJ*2.18.4; ἐκ περιόπτου D.H.*Comp*.23. b. Subst. περίοπτα, τά, *belvederes*, Plu.*Luc*.39. 2. *conspicuous*, Isoc.ap.Poll.2.58, etc.; βίος D.S.14.1; κάλλεα *AP*5.26 (Rufin.), etc.; ἔργα Plu.*Caes*.16. Adv. -τως *gloriously*, Id.*Sull*.21, etc.

**περιορ-ᾱτέον**, *one must overlook, suffer*, D.S.20.2. **-άω**, impf. περιεώρων, Ion. περιώρων Hdt.3.118: pf. περιεόρᾱκα D.18.64 (περιωρακυῖα cod. S), etc.: fut. περιόψομαι Ar.*Nu*.124, etc.: aor. 2 περιεῖδον (v. infr.):—*look round upon*, Arist.*Mete*.345ᵇ8:—Pass., ib.ᵃ28. 2. abs., *take a look round*, Thphr.*Char*.25.3. II. *look over, overlook*, i.e. *look on without regarding, allow, suffer*: 1. mostly c. part., ἣν τούτους περιίδῃς διαρπάσαντας Hdt.1.89; μὴ περιιδεῖν τὴν ἡγεμονίην αὖτις ἐς Μήδους περιελθοῦσαν Id.3.65, cf. 2.110, 4.118, Ar.*Ach*.167, *Ra*.509, Antipho 3.1.2, Th.1.24; ταῦτα περιιδεῖν γιγνόμενα D.18.63, cf. 21.115 (but with Art., εἰ ὑμᾶς τοὺς ἐναντιουμένους περιίδοιμεν if we should *leave* you who are opposing us *alone*, Th.4.87): with gen. abs., σφετεριζομένων Θηβαίων τὴν Εὔβοιαν οὐ περιείδετε D.18.99: rarely without part., οὐ περιόψεταί μ' ἄνιππον [ὄντα] Ar.*Nu*.124; μηδέν' ἐν συμφορᾷ (sc. ὄντα) τῶν πολιτῶν π. D.19.230: simply c. acc. pers., *disregard* a suppliant, Men.*Per*.6, *PMagd*.6.11 (iii B.C.), etc. 2. c. inf., περιιδόντες τοὺς Πέρσας ἐσελθεῖν Hdt.1.191; τοὺς προπόλους.. οὐ περιορᾶν παριέναι Id.2.63, cf. 1.24, Th.1.35, etc.; ἀποθανεῖν Porph.*Abst*.3.14: with inf. omitted, οὐκ ἄν με περιεῖδες [ποιέειν] Hdt.3.155; ὁ πυλουρὸς καὶ ὁ ἀγγεληφόρος οὐ περιώρων [αὐτὸν ἐσιέναι] ib.118, cf. Th.1.39, etc.; περιιδεῖν τινα ἐπὶ πράγματι Hyp.*Eux*.38; ἐάν τ' οὖν δοῦλον ἐάν τ' οὖν καὶ ἐλεύθερον περιορᾷ Pl.*Lg*.934d; π. τὴν ὕβριν τινός X.*HG*2.1.9: rarely c. gen., π. τῶν ἄλλων Plu.2.764d codd.; τοῦ πλείονος βίου Polem.*Cyn*.20. III. *watch closely, observe*, περιορώμενοι ὑπὸ τῶν Λακεδαιμονίων Th.5.31. 2. *wait for*, τὸ μέλλον περιιδεῖν Id.4.71; π. εἴ τινες βοηθήσουσιν Isoc.9.30. IV. *keep watch for* or *on behalf of*, θεοῦ J.*AJ*4.2.2. V. Med., *watch the turn of events*, Th.6.93, 103, 7.33; π. ὁποτέρων ἡ νίκη ἔσται Id.4.73. 2. c. gen., *look round after, watch over*, τῆς Μένδης περιορώμενος ib.124. 3. *consider anxiously*, τοὺς πολεμικοὺς κινδύνους Id.2.43.

**περιοργ-ής**, ές, *very angry* or *wrathful*, Th.4.130, J.*AJ*18.8.1, D.C.39.19. Adv. -γῶς A.*Ag*.216 (lyr., dub., fort. -όργῳ from Adj. περίοργος). **-ίζομαι**, *to be very angry*, Plb.4.4.7.

**περιοργυιόομαι**, Med. with pf. Pass., *clasp in the arms*, περιωργυιωμένοι περιλαβεῖν Ctes.*Fr*.57.6.

**περίορθρος**, ον, *towards morning*: τὸ π. *dawn*, Th.2.3, Hdn.6.9.3, 7.4.5 (v.l. περιόρθριον).

**περιόρ-ια**, τά, festival in Cyprus, Hsch. ⊛ **-ίζω**, *mark by boundaries*: *set a limit*, μέχρις οὗ δεῖ ἔχειν.. Plu.2.226d; ἄνευ τοῦ περιορίζοντος without *any boundary*, ib.719e:—Pass., ἡγεμονία τῷ Ὠκεανῷ περιορισθεῖσα Id.*Caes*.58; τούτῳ διαστήματι περιωρίσθω Luc.*Salt*.37. 2. *draw up the description of the boundaries of* a property, π. τὴν χώραν *OGI*225.30 (Didyma, iii B.C.):—Pass., ἀπὸ τῶν περιωρισμένων τόπων *SIG*1231.9 (Nicomedia, iii/iv A.D.). II. *banish*, Lat. *deportare*, ἐν νήσῳ -ορισθείς D.C.76.5, cf. Just.*Nov*.42.3*Intr*. (Pass.). 2. *dislocate*, Apollon.Cit.1 (Pass.). **-ισμα**, ατος, τό, *anything surrounded by boundaries, enclosed place*, Sch.Pi.*O*.13.62, Phot. s.v. οὐρούς. **-ισμός**, ὁ, *marking out by boundaries*, D.H.8.75, Plu.*Num*.16; *description of the boundaries* of a property, *OGI*225.31 (Didyma, iii B.C.), *SIG*685.57 (Crete, ii B.C., pl.); π. τῆς οἰκουμένης *description* of.., Scymn.74. 2. *boundary*, Hero *Geom*.4.12. 3. in Metric, *division* of a strophe, κατὰ περιορισμοὺς ἀνίσους Heph.*Poëm*.6. 4. gloss on δρύφακτοι, *EM*228.33. II. as Law-term, = Lat. *deportatio*, Phot., Suid. **-ιστικός**, ή, όν, c. gen., *serving to determine* or *define*, Ascl.*in Metaph*.78.25. 2. *able to enclose* or *limit*, τοῦ ἀσωμάτου οὐδέν ἐστι π. *Corp.Herm*.11.18. **-ιστος**, ον, *bounded, determined*, Hsch.

**περιορμ-έω**, *anchor round, blockade*, Th.4.23, 26, Poll.1.122, D.C.59.17. **-ίζω**, *bring round* [a ship] *to anchor*, D.51.4.7, *PCair.Zen*.343.3 (iii B.C.), Plu.*Ant*.35:—Med., *come to anchor*, Th.3.6.

**περίορος** γῆ, land *marked out by boundary-stones*, Eust.1535.40.

**περιορύσσω**, Att. -ττω, *dig round*, π. λίμνην *dig* a lake *round*.., Hdt.2.99; π. πρὸς τὰς ῥίζας Arist.*Pr*.923ᵇ10; μέχρι τῶν ῥιζῶν Thphr.*CP*5.6.3; τὴν ῥίζαν J.*BJ*7.6.3:—Pass., τάφρου κύκλῳ περιορυχθείσης Pl.*Criti*.118c; ῥίζης -ορυχθείσης Dsc.1.126. 2. *dig up around*, τὰ πλησίον Plu.*Rom*.20. 3. *dig out around*, τοὺς λίθους Id.*Ant*.45.

**περιορχέομαι**, *dance around*, Thphr.*HP*9.8.8, Luc.*Salt*.8: c. acc., Call.*Dian*.240 (tm.).

**περίοσμος**, ον, *strong-smelling, fragrant*, Sch.Ar.*Pl*.808.

**περιόστεος**, ον, *round the bones*, χιτών, ὑμήν, Ruf.*Onom*.129, Gal.2.591 (περιόστιος and -εως are ff. ll., 13.415, 4.550).

**περιοσφραίνομαι**, *sniff all round*, Aesop.311.

**περιουργός**, ὁ, in pl., *meddlers*, contemptuously of the θεουργοί II, Aug.*Civ.D*.10.16.

⊛ **περιουσί-α**, ἡ, (περίειμι (εἰμί *sum*)) *that which is over and above, surplus, abundance*, ἐρίων Ar.*Nu*.50; νεῶν Th.3.13; χρημάτων Id.1.2, 2.13; οὔτε σοφίας ἐνδείᾳ οὔτ' αἰσχύνης π. Pl.*Grg*.487e; τοσαύτῃ π. χρῆσασθαι πονηρίας D.19.55; ἄν.. μοι π. ᾖ τοῦ ὕδατος, i.e. time enough for speaking, Id.59.20. 2. *residuum*, Hp.*Cord*.11. II. abs., *net gain, profit*, ἀπὸ παντὸς π. ποιεῖσθαι Pl.*R*.554a; οὐ γὰρ εἰς π. ἐπράττετ' αὐτοῖς τὰ τῆς πόλεως so as to bring them *advantage*, D.3.26; τῆς ἰδίας τρυφῆς εἵνεκα καὶ π. Id.21.159, cf. Plb.4.21.1; στρατεία οὐ φέρει περιουσίαν Men.382: pl., opp. τὰ ἀναγκαῖα, Isoc.11.15: with Preps., ἀπὸ περιουσίας *with plenty of other resources*, Th.5.103; πρὸς περιουσίαν, opp. πρὸς τὰς ἀναγκαίας χρείας, Plb.4.38.4: most freq. ἐκ π. out of *the abundance* (of their store), Pl.*Tht*.154e, etc.; ἐκ π. χρῆσθαι D.S.20.59; ἐκ π. ζῆν to live *on one's own resources*, Ath.4.168a; ἐκ π. κατηγορεῖν τινος *at an advantage*, D.18.3; also ξενοτροφεῖν ἐκ τῆς π. J.*BJ*1.2.5; τὰ ἐκ π. *superfluities*, opp. τὰ ἀναγκαῖα, Arist.*Top*.118ᵃ6. 2. *superiority* of numbers or force, Th.5.71; τοσαύτην ἔχειν π., ὥστε.. D.S.4.12; π. τῆς δυνάμεως Iamb.*Myst*.5.23. III. *survival*, τίς οὖν ἡ ταύτης π.; what is its *chance of being saved?* D.19.79. **-άζω**, *have more than enough*, of persons, Phalar.*Ep*.81.2, Heraclit.*Ep*.8.3: c. dat., *abound in* a thing, δυναστείᾳ D.H.6.75, cf. Crantor ap.S.E.*M*.11.58; τρυφῇ D.S.8.18; *to be abundantly supplied*, ὑπό τινος Alciphr.2.1:—Med., Corn.*ND*15, S.E.*M*.1.31, Eust.33.12. 2. *expend one's means*, εἴς τινα Phalar.*Ep*.69.2. 3. of an orator, *speak at unnecessary length*, Corn.*Rh*.p.396 H. II. of things, *abound*, τὰ ἐν τῇ πόλει -άζοντα Hippod.ap.Stob.4.1.94; ὅκα ἐν οἴκῳ καὶ πόλει περιουσιάζῃ whenever *there is a surplus*, Callicrat.ib.4.28.16. III. Act., *enrich*, τοὺς ἱππέας App.*BC*5.9, cf. 75. **-ασμός**, ὁ, = πλῆθος, Hsch. II. *private possession*, εἰς π. Lxx *Ps*.134(135).4, cf. *Ec*.2.8. **-αστικός**, ή, όν, *full in treatment*, of a treatise, Apollon.Perg.*Con*.1 *Praef*. (Comp.). 2. Astrol., of influences, *bringing wealth*, Ptol.*Tetr*.158. 3. *superfluous*, Ammon.*in APr*.37.9. **-ος**, ον, *having more than enough, wealthy*, Hsch.; dub. sens. in *PGen*.11.17 (iv A.D.). II. *especial, peculiar*, λαός Lxx *Ex*.19.5, al., *Ep.Tit*.2.14.

**περιοφθάλμιος**, ον, *round the eye*, Gal.19.436.

**περιοχ-έομαι**, Pass., *to be traversed in all directions*, ἡ γῆ.. περιοχουμένη ζῴοις Arist.*Mu*.397ᵃ25. ⊛ **-ή**, ἡ, (περιέχω) *a containing, enclosing*, Plu.2.1078b, Herm.ap.Stob.1.49.69. 2. *compass, circumference*, σφαίρας *Placit*.3 *Prooem*., cf. J.*BJ*5.4.3, Cleom.1.11, 2.3, Diog.Oen.24; opp. μῆκος, *BGU*492.10 (ii A.D.); ἡ ἐκτὸς π., of the body, Arist.*Col*.797ᵇ22, cf. *Pr*.870ᵃ10, D.S.1.91; κατὰ τὰς τῶν ἐθνῶν π. according to their *extent*, Id.17.58; *mass, body*, Plu.*Lys*.12; π. τις οὐρανοῦ Epicur.*Ep*.2p.37U.; ἀκατάληπτος π., of the world, Secund.*Sent*.1. 3. generally, *compass, extent*, ἡ π. τῆς ὅλης περιβολῆς καὶ πράξεως Plb.11.19.2; *aggregate*, Dam.*Pr*.88, 95bis. b. *content* of a definition, etc., Corn.*Rh*.p.382H., Alex.Aphr.*in APr*.278.11, etc. c. *summary*, Herm.ap.Stob.1.41.1; σύντομος π. Procl.*in Ti*.1.73; *periochae*, title of summaries of books of Livy. 4. *inclusion*, S.E.*P*.3.101; κατὰ περιοχήν τινος *including*.., Ph.2.488. II. *portion circumscribed* or *marked off, section* of a book, Cic.*Att*.13.25.3, *Act.Ap*.8.32. III. *pod, husk, shell*, Thphr.*CP*1.19.2. 2. *fence, fortification*, Lxx 1*Ki*.22.4, al.; πόλις περιοχῆς ib.*Ps*.30(31).21, al. IV. *straitness*, = θλῖψις, συνοχή, Phot.; esp. *siege*, Lxx *Je*.19.9; ἦλθεν πόλις ἐν περιοχῇ ib.4*Ki*.24.10; ὕδωρ περιοχῆς ib.*Na*.3.14. V. = περιπέτεια, Phot.

**περί-οχος**, Aeol. πέρροχος, ον, *superior*, Sapph.92: Boeot. πέροχος, *pre-eminent*, restd. in Corinn.2.68. **-οψία**, ἡ, *arrogance*, Nic.Dam.130.29J. (ὑπεροψία cj. Dind.).

**περιπάθ-εια** [πᾰ], gloss on τερθρεία, Tim.*Lex*., *EM*752.47. **-έω**, *to be in a state of violent emotion* or *indignation*, Conon 38.3, Plu.2.168d, etc.; π. εἰ.. Ph.2.176, etc. **-ής**, ές, *deeply moved*, τῇ συμφορᾷ Plb.1.81.1; ἔρωτι Plu.*Art*.27; χαρᾷ καὶ δέει J.*AJ*15.2.7; π. τοῖς ὄψοις *eager* for.., Phan.Hist.13; π. ταῖς ψυχαῖς *in* spirit, Plb.4.54.3: abs., Plu.*Cim*.8. 2. *passionate*, ῥήτορες Longin.8.3; σὺν οἰμωγῇ π. Luc.*Hist.Conscr*.26: Comp., ἑταίρα τῶν ἐν τοῖς μίμοις -εστέρα Ael.*Fr*.123: Sup., ὅρκος -έστατος Sch.Par.A.R.2.257. Adv. -θῶς Lxx 4*Ma*.8.2, Luc.*Tim*.46; ἐπιδραμεῖν Ael.*NA*9.8: Comp. -έστερον, λέγειν Plu.2.456a. 3. *pathetic, heartrending*, D.C.40.41; λόγος Id.76.9 (Sup.). **-ησις**, εως, ἡ, *intensity of emotion*, Ph.2.26: pl., *expressions of emotion* in Rhetoric, Id.1.158.

**περιπαιφάσσω**, *look wildly round*, Q.S.13.72.

**περιπαίω**, *strike on all sides*, *EM*288.54.

⊛ **περιπάλαξις** [πᾰ], εως, ἡ, *collision, combination* of atoms, Democr. ap.Simp. *in Cael.*609.25 (v.l.), prob. in Arist.*Cael.*303$^{a}$8, Thphr.*Sens.* 66.

⊛ **περιπᾰλάσσομαι**, *to be hurled about*, of atoms, cj. for περιπαλαίσεσθαι in Democr.168 and for περιπλάττεσθαι in Thphr.*Sens.*66: περιπαλαχθῆναι· περιπλακῆναι, Hsch.

**περιπάλλομαι**, Pass., *tremble all round*, Q.S.10.371, 14.44; περιπάλλετο δ' ἐν φρεσὶ θάμβος *Hymn.Is.*156.

**περίπαμπαν**, Adv., strengthd. for πάμπαν, Opp.*C.*2.348 (better divisim).

**περιπαμφᾰνάω**, only Ep. 3 pl. -όωσιν, *beam all around*, D.P.530.

**περιπαπταίνω**, *look timidly round*, ἔνθα καὶ ἔνθα Mosch.4.108 (tm.): c. acc., πέλαγος π. Arat.297.

**περι-πάσσω**, Att. **-ττω**, *strew, sprinkle all round*, ὀρίγανον Sotad. Com.1.28; τευθίδας ἡδύσμασι Alex.84.4; ἄλευρον π. αὐτῷ πρὸς τὴν πῆξιν Thphr.*HP*9.1.7, cf. Arist.*Mir.*845$^{a}$32:—Pass., *to be sprinkled*, ὑπ' ὀριγάνου Id.*HA*534$^{b}$22; τινι with a thing, Gal.6.533. **-παστος**, ον, *sprinkled over*, Hp.*Int.*51, Archestr.*Fr.*18.3.

**περιπᾰτ-έω**, *walk up and down*, as in a cloister, opp. βαδίζειν (take a walk), ἐν ταῖς στοαῖς Dicaearch.ap.Plu.2.796d; *walk about*, Ar.*Eq.* 744, *V.*237; περιπατῶν ἀνδριάς Alex.204; ἐν τῷ καταστέγῳ δρόμῳ Pl. *Euthd.*273a; π. ἄνω κάτω Ar.*Lys.*709; π. περιπάτους X.*Mem.*3.13.5, cf. Men.*Pk.*156; περιπατεῖται ἡ ὁδός the road *is for walking on*, A.D. *Synt.*279.19: c. acc., *traverse*, ὅλην τὴν Αἴγυπτον *POxy.*471.124 (ii A.D.). 2. *walk about while teaching, discourse*, Pl.*Ep.*348c, D.L.7. 109; π. ἐς τοὺς ἀκροωμένους *dispute, argue* with them, Philostr.*VA* 1.17, cf. 7.22. 3. metaph., *walk*, i.e. *live*, Phld.*Lib.*p.12 O.; κατὰ τὴν παράδοσιν *Ev.Marc.*7.5; ἀτάκτως 2*Ep.Thess.*3.6. **-ήματα**, gloss on διαβήματα, Hsch. **-ησις**, εως, ἡ, *walking about*, A.D. *Synt.*19.10, Sor.1.112 tit., S.E.*M.*1.74, D.L.7.98. **-ητής**, οῦ, ὁ, *one who walks about*, *Gloss.* **-ητικός**, ή, όν, *of walking*, δύναμις Alex. Aphr.*de An.*110.31. II. *given to walking about*, esp. *while teaching* or *disputing*: of Aristotle and his followers (cf. περίπατος II. 3), *Supp.Epigr.*1.368.5 (Samos, iii/ii B.C.), Demetr.Lac.*Herc.*1055.19, Phld.*Acad.Ind.*p.112 M., Cic.*Acad.Post.*1.4.17, Ceb.13 (-πατικοί is f.l.), Plu.2.1115a, Luc.*Herm.*14, *CIG*4814*c* Add. (Egypt); τὰ π. *their doctrines*, Posidon.36 J., Cic.*Att.*13.19.4; ἡ π. φιλοσοφία S.E.*M.*11. 179. **-ος**, ὁ, *walking about, walk*, ποιεῖσθαι τοὺς π. Pl.*Phdr.* 227a; εἰς π. ἰέναι ib.228b; ἐξανίστασθαι εἰς π. X.*Smp.*9.1; ἐν π. εἶναι Id.*An.*2.4.15: metaph., *exercise*, γλώσσης π. ἐστιν ἀδολεσχία Astyd. 7; ψυχῆς π. φροντὶς ἀνθρώποισιν Hp.*Epid.*6.5.5. II. *place for walking*, esp. *covered walk*, X.*Mem.*1.1.10, Plu.*Luc.*39, *IG*2$^{2}$.2639; Ἀριστοτέλους..ὑποσκίους περιπάτους Plu.*Alex.*7; cf. infr. 2, 3. 2. *discourse during a walk, discussion, argument*, Ar.*Ra.*942, Bato 2. 3; π. περί τινος Ar.*Ra.*953; ἑωθινὸς π., δειλινὸς π., Aristotle's names for his morning and evening *lectures*, Gell.20.5.5. 3. *school* of philosophy, first used of the Academy, ἀναπεπταμένου τοῦ Πλάτωνος π. Epicur.*Fr.*171; ἔτη ὀκτὼ κατασχὼν τὸν π. (sc. Σπεύσιππος) Phld. *Acad.Ind.*p.38 M.; οἱ ἀπὸ τοῦ Π., name given to Xenocrates and Aristotle, because their teacher Plato was accustomed to walk about while teaching, Ammon. *in Cat.*3.8; οἱ ἐκ τοῦ π. *the school of Aristotle*, Luc.*Pisc.*43; οἱ ἐκ τῶν π. Str.13.1.54; οἱ ἀπὸ τοῦ π. φιλόσοφοι Plu.2. 1131f; τοῦ Π. προστάς Antig.Car.ap.Ath.12.547d: generally, any *school* of philosophy, ἕτερος π. Phld.*Acad.Ind.*p.39 M.; αὐτὸς ἴδιον π. κατασκευάσας ib.p.79 M., cf. p.53 M. (pl.); οἱ τὸν αὐτὸν Ἀριστοτέλει ἐμβαίνοντες π. Diog.Oen.4. III. Astrol., *progression* along the Zodiac in order to determine κλῆροι, Vett.Val.205.10, *Cat.Cod.Astr.* 8(1).245, al.

**περιπαύομαι**, Pass., *become quite quiet*, Ach.Tat.2.5.

**περιπαχνόομαι**, Pass., *to be congealed all round*, Orph.*L.*526.

**περι-πεζία**· ταπείνωσις, Hsch.; cf. sq. II. 1. **-πέζιος**, ον, *round the foot*: **-πέζια**, τά, *ornaments for the feet, anklets*, Poll.5.99; so **-πεζίδες**, αἱ, ibid.; **-πεζα**, τά, Id.7.62. II. metaph., 1. *lowly, 'earthy'*, δυνάμεις Herm. *in Phdr.*p.102 A., p.128 A., Procl. *in Cra.* p.69 P., etc.; μέρος ψυχῆς Simp. *in Epict.*p.126 D. Adv. -ζίως, εἰπεῖν *in common language*, Eust.899.56. 2. *accessible, intelligible*, Zonar.

⊛ **περιπείρω**, *put on a spit*, π. τι περὶ λόγχην Plu.*Galb.*27: metaph., *pierce*, ἑαυτοὺς π. ὀδύναις 1*Ep.Ti.*6.10:—Pass., *to be spitted* or *pierced*, ξίφεσι καὶ λόγχαις D.S.16.80; χάρακι Id.19.84; σκόλοπι Ael.*NA*7.48; ὀβελοῖς Luc.*Gall.*2: metaph., *to become entangled*, δυσαναπορεύτοις βαράθροις περιπαρέντες Ph.1.672; δίκτυα, οἷς ἀνάγκη περιπείρεσθαι Id. 2.411, cf. Vett.Val.250.11. II. *run into*, τοὺς ὀδόντας τῇ δειρῇ Lib. *Descr.*12.2 (Pass.):—Pass., ἄγκιστρα περιπαρέντα τοῖς ἰχθύσι Ael.*NA* 15.10.

**περιπέλομαι**, Hom. only in Ep. aor. 2 part. περιπλόμενος (the true pres. being περιτέλλομαι, q.v.): I. *move round, be round about*, only in part., 1. of Place, c. acc., ἄστυ περιπλομένων δηΐων the enemy *who have surrounded* the town, Il.18.220, cf. A.R.3.1150; of things, μίτρα μαστοῖς σφιγκτὰ περιπλομένα *AP*6.272 (Pers.). 2. of Time, περιπλομένου δ' ἐνιαυτοῦ when the year *has gone round*, Od.11.248, cf. Hes.*Op.*386; περιπλομένων ἐνιαυτῶν Od.1.16, Hes.*Th.* 184; πέντε π. ἐνιαυτούς for five *revolved*, i.e. complete, years, Il.23. 833. II. *surpass, conquer*, οὐδὲ δίκῃ περιέπλεο νῆϊν ἐόντα A.R.3.130.

**περί-πεμπτος**, ον, *sent round about*, περίπεμπτα θυοσκεῖς A.*Ag.*87 (anap.). **-πέμπω**, *send round* from one place to another, [νέας] π. ἔξωθεν Σκιάθου Hdt.8.7; δύο τέλη τῶν ἱππέων Th.4.86; αἱ νῆες..αἱ ἐς τὸν λιμένα περιπεμφθεῖσαι Id.5.3. 2. *send round* to a number of places, οἱ περιπεμφθέντες Hdt.1.48. **-πεμψις**, εως, ἡ, *sending round*, dub. in D.C.56.14.

**περιπεπλεγμένως**, Adv., gloss on περιπλέγδην, Sch.Opp.*H.*2.376; on σπειρηδόν, Suid.

**περιπέπληκα**· περιπεπόληκα, περιπέπληγμαι, Hsch.

**περί-πεπτος** (-πεμπτος cod.), ον, *cooked up*, Hsch.; cf. sq. **-πέσσω**, Att. **-ττω**, *bake a crust round*: only metaph., *disguise*, ὀνόματι π. τὴν μοχθηρίαν Ar.*Pl.*159; π. αὑτὰς προσθέτοις *deck* themselves *out* with false hair, Id.*Fr.*321; πεπλασμένως τὸ πρᾶγμα π. Bato 7.6; π. ἀβλαβῶς *cover* Marius without hurting him, Plu.*Mar.*37 (-πεσεῖν codd.):—Pass., [ἄνδρες] χλανίσι περιπεπεμμένοι *Com.Adesp.*338; λόγοισιν εὖ πως εἰς τὸ πιθανὸν περιπεπεμμένα *dressed up*, Pl.*Lg.*886e; λῦπαι ἡδοναῖς περιπεπεμμέναι X.*Oec.*1.20; also ῥηματίοις περιπεφθείς *cajoled* by words, Ar.*V.*668.

**περιπετᾰλόω**, *cover with metal plates*, *Gloss.*

**περι-πετάννῡμι**, also **-ύω**, X.*Oec.*19.18: pf. Pass. -πέπτᾰμαι:— *spread* or *stretch around*, χέρα [τινί] E.*Hel.*628 (lyr.); κατάδεσμον π. ἥβης *spread* bathing-drawers *over*.., Theopomp.Com.37 (s.v.l.); [ὀθόνιον] τῷ ἀγγείῳ Dsc.5.75; π. φοινικίδας *spread* them *out*, Aeschin.3.76; ἄμπελος..π. τὰ οἴναρα X. l.c.:—Pass., φορεῖον χρυσοῦν περιπεπετασμένον πορφύραν *covered with*.., D.S.31.8; ἀμφὶ δέπας περιπέπταται ὑγρὸς ἄκανθος *is spread over* it, Theoc.1.55, cf. A.R.1.1036 (tm.). **-πεταστός**, ή, όν, *spread round* or *over*, π. φίλημα *lewd* kiss, Ar.*Ach.*1201.

**περιπέτ-εια**, ἡ, (περιπετής) *turning right about, reversal* of the normal order, Arist.*HA*590$^{b}$13; esp. *sudden change* of condition or fortune, Id.*Rh.*1371$^{b}$10; π. τύχης D.S.8.10; mostly from good to bad, Plb.1.13.11, etc.: less freq. from bad to good, Id.21.26.16, D.S. 4.43: generally, *any strange occurrence, unexpected event*, Plb.9.12.6, 38.9.2, D.S.3.57, etc.; ἐκ π. Arist.*Po.*1454$^{b}$29, cf. Plb.32.8.4, Sch. BT Il.2.156. 2. esp. *sudden reversal of circumstances* on which the plot in a Tragedy hinges, such as Oedipus' discovery of his parentage, ἔστι δὲ π. ἡ εἰς τὸ ἐναντίον τῶν πραττομένων μεταβολή Arist.*Po.*1452$^{a}$ 22, cf. 1450$^{a}$34 (pl.). b. the *plot* itself, = ὑπόθεσις, S.E.*M.*3.3. 3. ἡ π. τοῦ λόγου the *varied course* of the argument, Olymp. *in Mete.*98.12, 274.28: but in pl., of cheap sensational effects, Phld.*Po.*5.33. **-ής**, ές, (περιπίπτω) *falling round*, ἀμφὶ μέσσῃ π. προσκείμενος lying *with his arms clasped round* her waist, S.*Ant.*1223. 2. *surrounded by, wrapped in*, πέπλοισι A.*Ag.*233 (lyr.). 3. ἔγχος π. the sword *round which* (i.e. *on which*) *he has fallen*, S.*Aj.*907. II. *falling in with, falling into* evil, καταστῆσαί τινα δεινῷ μηδενὶ π. D.*Ep.*5.1; π. γίγνεσθαι, = περιπίπτειν, *fall among*, τοῖς σταυροῖς καὶ τοῖς ὀρύγμασι Plu. *Pomp.*62; πολέμοις Id.*Cic.*42; π. εἶναι τῇ χολῇ τινος Luc.*Pseudol.*1; πόλις αὐτὴ ἑαυτῇ π. γενομένη Plu.*Phoc.*33; ἀλλήλοις Anon.ap.Suid.; π. ποιεῖν αὐτοῖς τοὺς πολεμίους cause them to *fall foul of* each other, Plu.*Marc.*26; π. τοῖς ἑαυτῶν λόγοις Hermog.*Stat.*1 (cf. περιπίπτω II. 3); π. τῇ αἰτίᾳ γενέσθαι become *liable* to the charge, Plu.*CG*10. III. *changing* or *turning suddenly*, of a man's fortunes, esp. from good to bad, περιπετέα ἐποιήσαντο σφίσι..τὰ πρήγματα a *sudden reverse*, Hdt. 8.20; π. τύχαι E.*Andr.*982; cf. foreg. **-ικός**, ή, όν, *concerned with vicissitudes of fortune*, διηγήσεις Corn.*Rh.*p.363 H.

**περιπέτομαι**, *fly around*, Ar.*Av.*165: c. acc., ib.1721; περιεπέτετο τὰ οἰκία Ant.Lib.16.3; π. τὰ πελάγη Luc.*Halc.*1; τὴν ἑκάστου γνώμην π. Id.*Hist.Conscr.*1: the form **περιπέταμαι** occurs in codd. of Arist. *HA*609$^{a}$14; cf. περιίπταμαι.

**περιπετρ-ίζομαι**, Pass., *to be dashed upon a rock*, Hsch. **-ος**, ον, *surrounded by rocks*, Id.

**περιπέττω**, Att. for περιπέσσω (q.v.).

**περιπευκής**, ές, (πεύκη) *very sharp, keen*, or *painful*, βέλος Il.11.845.

**περιπεφρασμένως**, Adv. *very thoughtfully*, gloss on περιφραδέως, Hsch.

**περιπεφῠλαγμένως**, Adv. *very cautiously*, gloss on ἀνακῶς, Erot. (περιφυλ- codd.).

**περι-πηγής**, ές, *congealed around*, λιβάνοιο χύσις π. θάμνοις Nic.*Al.* 107. **-πῆγις**· πόρνος, μάχλος, Hsch. (fort. -πυγίς). **-πηγμα**, ατος, τό, *frame*, Ph.*Bel.*78.15, Hero *Bel.*82.12.

**περιπήγνῡμι** and **-ύω** (Plu.2.433b): also **περιπήττω** (v. infr.):— *fix round, fence round*, c. acc. loci, περὶ δὲ πάξαις Ἄλτιν Pi.*O.*10(11). 45; π. τῷ σώματι χιτῶνα Plu.2.966d:—Pass. with pf. περιπέπηγα, αἷς π. ἡ σαρκώδης οὐσία Gal.18(2).597; περιπησσέσθωσαν σανίδες Apollod. *Poliorc.*173.13; περιπαγῆναί τινι τὸν αὐχένα *to have one's neck fixed* in it, Ar.*Fr.*301. 2. *make to congeal round*, τὴν τέφραν τῷ βωμῷ Plu.2.433b:—Pass. with pf. intr. -πέπηγα, τὰ ὑποδήματα π. *are frozen on the feet*, X.*An.*4.5.14; περιπήττεται τὸ ὕδωρ τινί Str.12.5.4; τὸ δάκρυον [τῆς ἀμπέλου] π. τοῖς στελέχεσι Dsc.5.1; of a *coated* tongue, Gal.17(2).277: metaph., τἀγαθῷ -πεπηγός Dam.*Pr.*70.

**περιπηδάω**, *leap round* or *upon*, Luc.*Anach.*31.

**περιπηλ-όω**, *encase in clay*, Gal.12.727, *PHolm.*8.34, Olymp.Alch. p.76 B. **-ωσις**, εως, ἡ, *encasing in clay*, Zos.Alch.p.135 B.

**περίπηξις**, εως, ἡ, *congealing all round*, τῶν ἁλῶν Str.12.5.4.

**περιπηχύνω**, aor. part. -πηχύναντες, *take into one's arms*, Call.*Fr.* 344.

**περιπῑαίνω**, *make very fertile*, D.P.1071.

**περιπῐ-έζω**, *squeeze*, Heliod.ap.Orib.50.9.5 (Pass.). **-έσματα**, v.l. for περιπτίσματα.

**περίπικρος**, ον, *very harsh* or *bitter*, Phld.*Ir.*p.6 W., Ptol.*Tetr.*160, Procl.*Par.Ptol.*225.

**περιπῑλέω**, *cover thick all round*, οἶκον χρυσίῳ Lxx 3*Ki.*6.20(21).

**περιπίμελος** [πῑ], ον, *very fat*, Xenocr.ap.Orib.2.58.11, Poll.2.233.

**περιπίμπλαμαι**, Pass., *to be filled full of*. λευκότητος περιεπλήσθη Pl.*Tht.*156e: abs., περιεπλήσθη ἡ οἰκία X.*HG*3.2.28.

**περιπίμπρημι**, *set on fire round about*: impf. περιεπίμπρα X.*Cyn.* 10.17 codd.; -επίμπρασαν Th.3.98:—Pass., aor. περιεπρήσθησαν D.C. 51.24.

**περιπιπράσκω**, fut. Pass. περιπραθήσεται, expld. by ἀπωνηθήσεται, *AB*432 (dub. l.).

⊛ **περιπίπτω**, fut. -πεσοῦμαι Ar.*V.*523, etc.: Ep. pf. part. fem. περιπεπτηυῖαι Eratosth.16.9:—*fall around*, i.e. *so as to embrace*, τινι X.*An.*1.8.28; ἐπί τινι Plu.*Crass.*17; εἰς τὸ στῆθος Id.*Sert.*26. 2. *fall around*, i.e. *upon*, a weapon, τῷ ξίφει Ar.*V.*523; τῷ βέλει Antipho 3.3.6. 3. [ζῶναι] πόλοις περιπεπτηυῖαι *encircling* the poles, Eratosth. l. c. 4. *fall over*, ἑκατέρωσε Plu.*Pyrrh.*24; πλαγία περιπεσοῦσα Id.*Ant.*67. II. c. dat., *fall in with*, Hdt.6.105; ἀλλήλοις X.*An.*7.3.38, etc.; freq. of ships meeting at sea, Hdt.6.41, 8.94, Th. 8.33, 103; π. μουσικῇ τε καὶ ταῖς μέθαις *having encountered* them in our discussion, Pl.*Lg.*682e; ἡ ὄψις κάμνουσα ἐν τοῖς μικροῖς τοῖς μεγάλοις ἀσμένως π. Plot.6.9.3: abs., *supervene*, Petos.ap.Vett.Val.278.8. 2. *fall foul of* other ships, τῇσι σφετέρῃσι νηυσί Hdt.8.89; περὶ ἀλλήλας of one another, ib.16; also π. περὶ τὴν Σηπιάδα *to be wrecked* on.., Id.7. 188. 3. metaph., *fall in with, fall into*, mostly of evil, c. dat., π. ἀδίκοισι γνώμῃσι *fall in with, encounter* unjust judgements, Id.1.96; π. τοιαύτῃσι τύχῃσι, δουλοσύνῃ, Id.6.16, 106; νούσοις, νοσήμασι, Hp. *VM*3, X.*Cyr.*6.2.27; λουτροῖσιν ἀλόχου E.*Or.*367; αἰσχρᾷ τύχῃ Id. *Hec.*498; ἀκουσίοις κακοῖς Antipho 3.3.7; τοιούτῳ πάθει Th.2.54; τοιαύτῃ συμφορᾷ περιπέπτωκεν ὑπὸ τούτου D.21.96, cf. And.1.51; ἀβροχίαις *OGI*56.15 (Canopus, iii B.C.); π. συκοφάνταις Lys.7.1; αἰσχύνῃ X.*HG*7.3.9; ταῖς μεγίσταις ζημίαις Isoc.7.27, cf. 12.146; αἰτίᾳ Plu. *Ant.*67; also σοὶ αὐτῷ περιπίπτειν *to be caught in* your own *snare*, Hdt.1.108, cf. 8.16, Luc.*DMort.*26.2; τοῖς ἐμαυτοῦ λόγοις περιπίπτω Aeschin.2.144: with a Prep., ἐν σφίσι κατὰ τὰς ἰδίας διαφορὰς π. Th.2. 65: abs., *come to grief*, Plb.8.36.4, Vett.Val.16.2. 4. of events, *befall* one, ἤν μοί τι περιπίπτῃ κακόν Ar.*Th.*271: abs., δεῖ τι περιπεσεῖν Philostr.*VA*1.33. III. *change suddenly*, εἴς τι Plb.3.4.5.

**περιπίσματα**, v.l. for περιπτίσματα.

**περιπίτνω**, poet. for περιπίπτω, c. acc., καρδίαν π. κρύος *comes over* or *upon* the heart, A.*Th.*834 (lyr.).

**περιπλᾰν-άομαι**, *wander about*, [Κρήτην] Hdt.4.151: metaph., *float round about* one, as the lion's skin round Heracles, Pi.*I.*6(5).47. 2. abs., *wander*, Luc.*Herm.*59, D.C.47.21, etc.: metaph., ταῦτα π. *to be in* this state of *uncertainty*, X.*Cyr.*1.3.5; περιπλανᾶσθαι τὸν αὐλ..κὸν.. ἠρημένον βίον Phld.*Ind.Sto.*13; περιπεπλ..ν..μένα μέτρα *erratic, irregular*, D.H.*Dem.*50. -ής, ές, *wandering about*, Plu.2.1001e. -ησις, εως, ἡ, *wandering about*, ib.520f (pl.). -ία, poet. -ίη, ἡ, = foreg., *Jahresh.*4 *Beibl.*20 (Tithorea). -ιος, ον, poet. for περιπλανής, βίος *AP*7.736 (Leon.).

**περί-πλᾰσις**, εως, ἡ, *plastering round*, Gal.6.690. -πλάσσω, Att. -ττω, *plaster* one thing *over* another, *form as a mould* or *cast round*, περίπλασον αὐτοῖς εἰκόνα Pl.*R.*588d; οἱ πλάττοντες ἐκ πηλοῦ ζῴων ὑφιστᾶσι τῶν στερεῶν τι σωμάτων, εἶθ' οὕτω περιπλάττουσιν Arist. *PA*654$^b$31; τοῦ αἵματος τὸ πηγνύμενον μύρμηκες τοῦ ποδὸς περὶ τὸν μέγαν δάκτυλον περιέπλαττον Plu.*Cim.*18; ἡ μύξα περιπλάττεται περὶ .. Arist.*HA*621$^b$8; [ὁ κηρὸς] -πλάσσεται τοῖς ὀδοῦσι *PMed.Lond.*155. 2.8; [κόκκον] ἐν ἄρτῳ περιπλάττοντες *kneading it up* in.., Thphr.*HP* 9.20.2: metaph., *smooth over, disguise*, τι χρηστοῖς λόγοις Men.652; but οἱ [τῷ ζῆν] κενῶς -πλαττόμενοι those who *cleave to* life, Epicur. *Sent.Vat.*47 (= Metrod.*Fr.*49). 2. *plaster over with* a thing, περιπλάττεται πηλῷ Arist.*Pr.*924$^b$37; περιπεπλασμέναι ψιμυθίοις Eub.98. 1. -πλαστεύω, *surround with a bank of clay*, in Pass., *Sammelb.* 4481.8 (v A.D.).

**περιπλᾰτᾰγέω**, *rattle all round*, Q.S.7.500.

**περιπλέγ-δην**, Adv. *closely entwined*, Eratosth.27; π. ἔχειν τινά *in close embrace*, *AP*5.258 (Paul. Sil.), cf. 254.16 (Id.), Opp.*H.*2.376; cf. ivy, Luc.*Am.*12, etc. -μα, ατος, τό, gloss on πρόσπτυγμα, Sch.E. *Or.*1049. -νυμαι, late for περιπλέκομαι, Eust.1456.14.

**περίπλειος**, v. περίπλεως.

**περιπλέκ-εια**, ἡ, *intricacy*, μαθημάτων Iamb.*Protr.*21.κα'. -ής, ές, = περίπλεκτος, Nonn.*D.*12.199. -τέον, *one must mix*, μέλιτι ταῖς τροφαῖς Aët.4.20. -τικός, ή, όν, *embracing*, τινος Gal.19.131. -τος, ον, *intertwining, crossing*, of the feet of dancers, Theoc.18.8 (nisi leg. περίπλικτος). ⊛ -ω, aor. 2 part. Pass. περιπλακείς Tim.*Pers.*157:—*twine* or *fold round*, π. τινὶ τὰ σκέλη περὶ τὴν γαστέρα Luc.*Anach.* 31; *embrace*, ταῖς χερσὶν τοὺς πόδας τινός D.H.8.54; τινα Call.*Epigr.* 45:—Med., *hug one another*, Luc.*Anach.*1:—used by Hom. only in Pass., *fold oneself round, embrace*, c. dat., [ἱστῷ] περιπλεχθείς Od. 14.313; γρηῒ περιπλέχθη 23.33; περιπλάκηθι τῷ λοιπῷ πατρί E.*Fr.* 930; ἀμφὶ γόνασι π. Tim. l. c.; περιπλέκονται ἀλλήλοις οἱ ὄφεις Arist. *GA*718$^a$27, cf. *HA*550$^a$12; δεσμὰ π. τινί Luc.*DDeor.*17.1: abs., [δίκτυον] εὖ μάλα περιπλεκόμενον *close folding*, X.*Mem.*3.11.10; τὰ στοιχεῖα.. περιπλεκόμενα γεννᾶν Arist.*GC*325$^a$34 (also c. acc. cogn., περιπλέκεσθαι περιπλοκήν, of atoms, Id.*Fr.*208); περιπλακεῖσα συκῇ Thphr. *CP*5.5.3: metaph., *embrace* an idea, Iamb.*VP*35.258 (s.v.l.). 2. *twine round* with something, τὰ νέα φυτά Thphr.*CP*5.15.6. 3. *mix* drugs, Philum.ap.Aët.5.78 (Act. and Pass.). II. *complicate, entangle*, τὸν λόγον Luc.*Herm.*81, cf. Gal.5.339; περιπεπλεγμένον *intricate, involved*, Pl.*Plt.*265c; περιπεπλ. φιλία, of a flatterer, Plu.2. 62d. 2. *wrap up in words*, i.e. in *circumlocutory* and *indirect* phrases, αἰσχυνόμενος δὲ π. τὴν συμφορὰν *Com.Adesp.*576; οὐκ οἶδ' ὅπως δυνήσομαι π. Aeschin.1.52; ἐμπλέκοντες καὶ περιπλέκοντες καὶ οὐδὲν βουλόμενοι λέγειν ἐφεξῆς D.Chr.11.24; σαφῶς, μηδὲν περιπλέκων Gal.8.948, cf. Arr.*Epict.*2.19.27, Hermog.*Meth.*8, D.C.63.20.

**περίπλεξις**, εως, ἡ, = περιπλοκή, συμπλοκῇ καὶ π. πάντα γεννᾶσθαι Arist.*Cael.*303$^a$8 (v.l. ἐπαλλάξει; περιπαλάξει cj. Diels).

**περίπλεος**, ον, v. περίπλεως.

**περιπλευμον-ία** or **περιπνευμονία** (both forms freq. in codd.), Ion. -ίη, ἡ, (πλεύμων) *inflammation of the lungs*, Hp.*VM*17 (pl.), *Aph.* 3.23 (pl.), al., Pl.*La.*192e, Hipparch.ap.Stob.4.44.81 (= *Com.Adesp.* 344, pl.), Aret.*SA*2.1, Luc.*Merc.Cond.*31, Gal.19.419. -ιᾰκός, ή, όν, = περιπλευμονικός, Cels.4.14.1. -ιάω, *have* περιπλευμονία, Poll.4.187 (in form περιπν-). -ικός, ή, όν, *affected with* περιπλευμονία, Hp.*Prog.*3, al., Dsc.3.25; π. πάθη Plu.2.699e. Adv. -κῶς Hp. *Coac.*67.

**περιπλευρ-ίζω**, fut. -ιῶ, *embrace*, Phryn.*PS*p.99 B. -ῑτικός, ή, όν, *affecting the* πλευρά, νοσήματα Hp.*Coac.*502 (v.l. for πλευριτικά). -ος, ον, *covering the sides*, κύτος E.*El.*472 (lyr.).

**περιπλέω**, Ion. -πλώω, *sail* or *swim round*, abs., Hdt.6.44, Ephipp. 5.16 (anap.), etc.; *float*, of an island, Hecat.305 J.: c. acc., Λιβύην, Πελοπόννησον, τὴν ἄκρην, τὴν Εὔβοιαν, Hdt.4.42, 179, 5.108, 8.14; π. αὐτοὺς κύκλῳ Th.2.84; ἀνὴρ πολλὰ περιπεπλευκώς Ar.*Ra.*535; π. ἐκ τοῦ Κωρύκου Th.8.34; ἀπ' Ἰωνίας εἰς Κιλικίαν X.*An.*1.2.21, cf. Th.8. 92; εἰς Πύλας D.18.32; π. ἐκεῖσε X.*HG*1.1.11. II. metaph., *to be unstable, slip about*, Hp.*Fract.*4. 2. *recur*, ἐς περίοδον π., of a headache, Aret.*SD*1.2. III. Pass., *to be wrapped up*, Heliod.ap. Orib.44.23.20.

**περίπλεως**, ων, pl. περίπλεῳ, neut. -πλεα: also **περίπλεος**, ον, Arist.*Phgn.*810$^a$32, A.R.1.858; poet. **περίπλειος** Arat.1118:— c. gen., *quite full of* a thing, Th.4.13, Arist.*HA*585$^a$24, etc.; μυκηθμοῖο π. βόες Arat. l. c.; ψυχὴ π. σώματος soul *burdened with* body, Plu.*Rom.*28: c. dat., *filled with* a thing, A.R. l. c., Dsc.3.4, *AP*6.28 (Jul. Aegypt.). II. abs., *supernumerary, spare*, ἔχειν ξύλα περίπλεα καὶ ἅρμασι καὶ ἁμάξαις X.*Cyr.*6.2.33. 2. *full, large*, νεφροί Arist.*PA*672$^a$27; κνῆμαι Id.*Phgn.* l. c.

**περιπληθ-ής**, ές, *very full of people*, νῆσος Od.15.405; of a speech, *full of matter*, Plu.*Cat.Mi.*5. 2. *very full* or *large*, σάρξ Id.*Mar.*34, cf. Luc.*Anach.*25: Comp. -έστερος Id.*VH*2.40. II. *very full of* a thing, c. gen., καρπῶν Ph.2.494 (Sup.); σπέρματος Dsc.3.23: c. dat., Opp.*H.*1.796, al. ⊛ -ω, *to be quite full*, c. gen., πόλις νεκρῶν περιπλήθουσα, γαῖα ν. περιπεπληθυῖα, Tryph.595, Q.S.11.160: also c. dat., βουκολίοισι Theoc.25.13; σαρκί Opp.*H.*5.591:—Med., abs., ib.678.

**περι-πλίγδην**· περιβάδην, Hsch. -πλικτος, ον, *crossing*, ποσσὶ π., of dancers, Theoc.18.8 (v.l. -πλέκτοις). -πλίξ, *embracing* with the legs, Hsch. -πλίσσομαι, *put the legs round* or *across*, τὰ θυγάτρια περὶ τὴν λεκάνην.. περιπεπλιγμένα Stratt.63, cf. Eust.1564. 49, Hsch.

**περιπλοκ-άδην** [ᾰ], Adv. = περιπλέγδην, *AP*5.251 (Paul. Sil.). -άς, άδος, ἡ, = *capreolus, cincinnus*, *Gloss.* (pl.). ⊛ -ή, ἡ, *twining round, interlacing*, Arist.*HA*540$^b$4; περιπλοκαὶ γυναικῶν Plb.2.56.7, cf. Luc.*Alex.*39, etc.; περιπλοκῆς δεῖται [ὁ κιττός] Plu.2.649c. b. in the philos. of Epicurus, *interlacing* of atoms, *Ep.*1 p.8U., 2 p.41U. (pl.), al.; περιπλοκὴν περιπλέκεσθαι Arist.*Fr.*208. II. metaph., of one wrestling in argument, Ph.1.199. 2. *entanglement, complication*, *POxy.*533.10 (ii/iii A.D.). 3. *intricacy*, περιπλοκὰς λόγων *circumlocutions*, E.*Ph.*494, cf. Hermog.*Meth.*8; περιπλοκὰς λίαν ἐρωτᾷς Antiph.74.1; τί οὖν.. π. λέγεις; Strato Com.1. 35; χωρὶς -πλοκῆς λέγειν τἀληθῆ M.Ant.12.1. -ος, ον, *entwined*, δεσμῷ *AP*9.362; σειρῇσι Tryph.300; *coiled*, of a snake, Nonn.*D.*22. 54: c. dat., *twined about*, ὅρμος π. αὐχένι ib.6.195.

**περιπλόμενος**, v. περιπέλομαι.

**περίπλοος**, ον, contr. -πλους, ουν, *sailing round*, ἡγητὴρ π. *AP*9. 559 (Crin.). II. Pass., *that may be sailed round*, π. ἐστὶν ἡ γῆ Th. 2.97; κολωνός Philostr.*Im.*2.17. III. τὸν Ἰσθμὸν περίπλουν ἐργαζόμενος making it a *passage by water*, Id.*VA*4.24. IV. *enfolding*, σὺν λοβοῖς πολλάκις κοίλῃ περιπλόοις *enfolding* the vena cava, Hp.*Ep.* 23.

⊛ **περίπλοος**, ὁ, contr. -πλους, gen. πλου, nom. pl. -πλοι:—*circumnavigation*, c. gen., τὸν π. τοῦ Ἄθω Hdt.6.95; περὶ Πελοποννήσου Th. 2.80, cf. 8.4; τὸν π. τὸν εἰς Κέρκυραν Aeschin.3.243; esp. round the enemy's fleet, X.*HG*1.6.31: metaph., of a *journey by land*, Call.*Fr.* 278; of the *journey* of the soul in transmigration, Diog.Oen.35. II. *account of a coasting voyage* (opp. περίοδος of a land-journey), γράφειν τὸν π. τῆς ἔξω θαλάσσης Luc.*Hist.Conscr.*31: *Periplus* is the title of several geograph. works, still extant, by Scylax, Agatharchides, Arrian, etc.

**περιπλούσιος**, ον, *very rich*, Sch.Opp.*H.*3.221.

**περί-πλῠμα**, ατος, τό, *soluble portion*, ἡ κονία π. τῆς τέφρας Gal.12. 35. -πλύνω [ῡ], *wash clean, scour*, D.54.9, Plu.2.69c; ὅπὸν Diocl.*Fr.*141, etc.:—Pass., *have* a thing *washed off* one, Arist.*HA* 591$^a$28; also of the thing, ὅταν ἡ ἅλμη περιπλυθῇ Thphr.*CP*4.14. 4. ⊛ -πλῠσις, εως, ἡ, *thin discharge* from the bowels, Hp.*Coac.*600; π. κοιλίης Id.*Prorrh.*1.2, Aret.*SA*1.5.

**περιπλώω**, Ion. and poet. for περιπλέω.

**περιπνευμονία**, **-πνευμονιάω**, **-πνευμονικός**, v. περιπλευμ-.

**περιπνέω**, *breathe round*, c. acc., Μακάρων νᾶσον αὖραι περιπνέοισι Pi.*O.*2.72, cf. Luc.*VH*2.5: abs., D.S.3.19:—Pass., ἡ γῆ περιπνεομένη αὔραις Arist.*Mu.*397$^a$34; οἴκησις περιπνεομένα (Dor.) Myia *Ep.*4. II. *exhale a scent of*, οἰκία περιπνεῖ Ἑρμοῦ καὶ Μουσῶν Eun.*VS*p.483 B.

**περι-πνῑγή**, ἡ, *asphyxiation*, Vett.Val. in *Cat.Cod.Astr.*8(1).168

(pl.). -πνῑγής, ές, *suffocated, choked*, Nic.*Th*.432, J.*AJ*7.13.3; ὑπὸ τοῦ θυμοῦ Agatharch.76; τῇ τῆς ἀναπνοῆς φθορᾷ D.S.38.4:—also -πνῑγος, ον, Sch.Nic.*Th*.432. -πνίγω [ῑ], *suffocate*, *Gp*.6.1.2 (Pass.).
❀ **περι-πνοή**, ἡ, *blowing round about*, ἀνέμων D.S.3.19 (pl.), cf. Serv. ad Verg.*A*.5.772 (pl., in form -πνοία). 2. *ventilation*, Gal.7.393 (pl.). -πνοος, ον, contr. -πνους, ουν, *blown round about, airy*, ἐν περίπνῳ [εἶναι] Thphr.*HP*5.1.11.

**περιπόδιος**, α, ον, (πούς) *going round the feet*, σύρμα Ptol.*Alm*.8.1, cf. *AB*354. II. Subst. **περιπόδιον**, τό, *part about the feet*, Ptol. *Alm*.7.5; **περιποδίη** (Ion.), ἡ, *foot-bandage*, Hp.ap.Gal.19.130.

**περιπόθητος**, ον, *much-beloved*, J.*AJ*16.11.8, Luc.*Tim*.12, *DMort*. 9.2, Chor.*Proc*.8: Comp., App.*BC*3.4; π. ταλαιπώρημα Secund. *Sent*.9.

❀ **περιποι-έω**, *cause to remain over and above, keep safe, preserve*, Hdt. 3.36, al., Th.2.25, al., Lys.13.63, etc.; ἐκ κακῶν καὶ πολέμου ὑμᾶς αὐτοὺς π. Id.6.47. 2. of money, food, etc., *save up, lay by*, X.*Oec*.11. 10; ἀπ' ὀλίγων ib.2.10; τῶν προσόδων *part* of the revenues, Is.6.38, cf. *POxy*.2148.17 (i A.D.). 3. *obtain a net product* or *residue*, Thphr.*Lap*.58. 4. generally, *procure, secure, achieve, lay up*, αἰσχύνην τῇ πόλει Isoc.15.301; π. τῇ πόλει τὰ εἰς τιμὴν ἀνήκοντα *Milet*.3 No.146.84 (iii B.C.); πολλὰ καὶ μεγάλα τῶν συμφερόντων τῇ πατρίδι *IGRom*.4.1757 (Sardes, i B.C.); δυναστείας ἑαυτοῖς Aeschin.3.3 (Med.), cf. D.15.11; τὰ πράγματα ἐς ἑαυτοὺς π. *get* things into their own hands, Th.8.48, cf. Is.7.6. II. Med., *keep* or *save for oneself*, [τὸ παιδίον] Hdt.1.110 (sed leg. -ποιήσῃς); τὸ ζῆν Arist.*Pol*.1315ᵃ26; ἐλπίδας ἑαυτῷ D.19.240; *compass, acquire, gain possession of*, δύναμιν, ἰσχύν, Th.1.9, 15; ἑαυτῷ ὄνομα καὶ δύναμιν π. X.*An*.5.6.17, cf. Lxx 1*Ma*.6.44; παρὰ τοῦ πλήθους δόξαν D.12.19; αὐτοῖς δυναστείαν Arist. *Pol*.1306ᵃ24; πρόβατα *PMich.Zen*.87.7 (iii B.C.); [ἐκκλησίαν] διὰ τοῦ αἵματος *Act.Ap*.20.28; *save*, τοσαῦτα ὥστε καὶ πλουτεῖν X.*Mem*.2. 7.3; χρυσίον Lxx 1*Ch*.29.3; *make gain*, ἀπό τινος X.*Mem*.4.2.38:— Pass., χρήματα περιποιηθησόμενα *Cod.Just*.1.4.26 *Intr*. 2. in sense of Act. I. 1, freq. in Lxx, as *Ge*.12.12, al. -ημα, ατος, τό, *acquisition*, Vett.Val.90.7. -ησις, εως, ἡ, *keeping safe, preservation*, Pl.*Def*.415c, Lxx 2*Ch*.14.13(12), *Ma*.3.17, *Ep.Hebr*.10. 39. 2. concrete, *those who are saved*, *Ep.Eph*.1.14. II. *gaining possession of, acquisition*, 1*Ep.Thess*.5.9, 2*Ep.Thess*.2.14, *PTeb*. 317.26 (ii A.D.), Vett.Val.85.16, Just.*Edict*.13.15; *procuring*, A.D. *Synt*.294.9. 2. λαὸς εἰς περιποίησιν, = λ. περιούσιος, 1*Ep.Pet*.2. 9. -ητικός, ή, όν, *able to procure, productive*, c. gen., πνευμάτων Mnesith.Ath.ap.Ath.8.357f; ζημίας καὶ ὠφελείας Ph.1.463; εὐχροίας Dsc.2.104; πειθοῦς S.E.*M*.2.9, etc.; expld. by διοικητής, Hsch. Adv. -κῶς Sch.Ar.*Pl*.717. 2. *grasping*, αὐτῷ τοῦ πλείονος Arr. *Epict*.4.7.11. 3. *indicating the procuring of*, ἐνεργειῶν A.D.*Synt*. 297.27. 4. Astrol., *wealth-bringing*, τόπος Nech.ap.Vett.Val.291. 15. -ητός, ή, όν, *abundantly produced*, Hsch. s.v. περιούσιον.

**περιποικίλλομαι**, Pass., *to be variegated*, Apollon.*Lex*. s.v. κεστός.

**περιποίκῐλος**, ον, *variegated, spotted*, οὐρά X.*Cyn*.5.23, cf. *IG*2². 1514.8.

**περιποιπνύω**, *busy oneself with*, Q.S.4.210:—Med., Opp.*H*.2.615 (divisim edd.).

**περιπολ-άζω**, f.l. for ἐπι-, Plu.2.587b. -αῐος, ον, *open all round, flat*, of eyes, Arist.*Phgn*.810ᵃ1 (Comp., nisi leg. ἐπι-, cf. foreg.). -άρχης (Hsch. s.v. κωδωνοφορῶν) or -αρχος (*IG*2².204. 20, 1193, 2.1219, 1219*b*), ου, ὁ, (περίπολος) *commander of military patrol*, Th.8.92, *IG* and Hsch. ll. cc. -εύω, later form for sq., [Ἥλιον] περιπολεύοντα τὸν κόσμον Phylarch.25 J. (v.l.); ἄλγη περιπολεύοντα Sch.Nic.*Al*.339. ❀ -έω, *go round* or *about, wander about*, S.*OT*1254; καθ' Ἑλλάδα E.*IT*84, 1455; μετά τινος Pl.*Phdr*.252c; ἡ στρατιὰ ἡ μετὰ βασιλέως περιπολοῦσα Isoc.4.145; of the sun or stars, Pl.*Ti*.41a, Arist.*Fr*.10, Epicur.*Ep*.2 p.52 U.: aor. Pass. in med. sense, D.L.8. 4. II. c. acc. loci, *traverse*, οὐρανόν Pl.*Phdr*.246b; τόνδε τὸν τόπον Id.*Tht*.176a; π. στρατόν *prowl about* it, E.*Rh*.773; ἔρως ὁ τὰς πόλεις π. Philostr.*Ep*.5, etc. 2. at Athens, οἱ ταχθέντες..περιπολεῖν τὴν χώραν *to patrol* the country, X.*Vect*.4.52; οἱ ἔφηβοι..π. τὴν χώραν Arist.*Ath*.42.4, cf. *IG*1².99.22 (prob.). -ημα, ατος, τό, Astron., = sq., π. κοσμικόν Vett.Val.259.20. -ησις, εως, ἡ, *revolution*, of the stars, Ph.1.10 (pl.); τῶν οὐρανίων TheoSm.p.120 H., cf. Iamb. *VP*15.65; τὴν π. ποιεῖσθαι, of the sun, Porph.ap.Eus.*PE*3.12; π. τῆς ψυχῆς, of metempsychosis, Max.Tyr.38.3, D.L.8.4. -ίζω, *wander about*, Str.14.5.15; *move in society*, *PMed*. in *Arch.Pap*.4.270 (iii A.D.). -ιον, τό, *station for* περίπολοι, *guard-house, fort*, *SIG*38.17 (Teos, v B.C.), Th.3.99, 6.45, 7.48, etc. II. *suburb* or *township*, Lxx 1*Ch*.6.71(56), *IG*12(1).1033 (Carpathos), etc.; τὸ π. τῆς θεοῦ *the quarter round* her *temple*, *CIG*2715.16 (Lagina). -ιος, ον, *lying round* a place, c. gen., κατοικίαι π. τῆς Νικοπόλεως Str.7.7.6, cf. 14.2. 22, 17.3.21. -ις, εως, ὁ, ἡ, *street-walker, vagrant*, Phryn.Com. 33. -ισμα, ατος, τό, = περιπόλημα, Vett.Val.331.20. -ιστικός, ή, όν, *disposed for wandering*: hence σύνοδος π. a company *of travelling artistes*, *IG*2².1350, 14.747 (Naples), *IGRom*.4.1361 (Thyatira), etc.

❀ **περιπολλόν**, Ep. Adv. of πολύς, *very much*, A.R.2.437.

❀ **περίπολος**, ον, (περιπέλομαι) *going the rounds, patrolling*: hence, as Subst., 1. *watchman, patrol*, Epich.35.10, Plu.*Num*.16, Luc. *VH*2.6, etc.; π. τῶν βασιλείων Lib.*Or*.59.144. 2. pl., at Athens, *patrol*, in which ἔφηβοι (and also non-Athenians, cf. Lys.13.71 with Th.8.92) served, Ar.*Av*.1177, Th.4.67, 8.92; τοὺς π. ἀπιέν' εἰς τὰ φρούρια Eup.341: sg. in Aeschin.2.167. 3. generally, *attendant, follower*, as fem., S.*Ant*.1150 (lyr.). 4. π. πάσης τῆς ὑφ' ἥλιον '*globe-trotter*', Him.*Or*.14.25, cf. Lib.*Ep*.168. 5. περίπολος (sc. ναῦς), ἡ, *guardship*, Arr.*An*.2.20.2.

**περιπομπεύω**, *carry round in procession*, Sch.Ar.*Pl*.1198 (Pass.).

**περιπομπή**, ἡ, *sending round about*, Sch.A.*Eu*.11.

**περιπονέω**, *toil about*, Vett.Val.361.21 (Pass.).

**περιπόνηρος**, ον, *very rascally*, as a pun on περιφόρητος, Ἀρτέμων Ar.*Ach*.850.

**περιπορ-εία**, ἡ, in pl., gloss on ἀμφιπολῇσιν, *EM*91.8. -εύομαι, *travel, go about*, Pl.*Lg*.716a, Ceb.7; κατ' οὐρανόν Iamb.*Protr*.13; *walk about*, *IG*4²(1).123.125 (Epid.). II. c. acc. loci, *go round*, τὰ ἱερά Arist.*Oec*.1353ᵇ20; τὰς πόλεις, τοὺς ναούς, etc., Plb.3.7.3, 9.6.3, etc.; τὴν πόλιν κύκλῳ Id.4.54.4; τὰς οἰκίας τῶν συγκλητικῶν D.S.40.1, cf. Corn.*ND*17.

**περιπορπ-άομαι**, *fasten with a clasp round oneself*, App.*Hisp*. 42. -ημα, ατος, τό, *that which is so fastened*, Cyr.

**περι-πόρφῠρος**, ον, *edged with purple*, ἱμάτια Crates Com.31, Heraclid.*Pol*.69; χιτωνίσκοι Plb.3.114.4, etc. 2. π. ἐσθῆτες garments *with a purple border*, of the Roman *toga praetexta* or *laticlavia*, Id.6. 53.7; π. τήβεννα, τήβεννος, D.H.2.70, Plu.*Rom*.26; and περιπόρφυρος alone, ib.25, 2.283a; π. (sc. παῖδες), *pueri praetextati*, Id.*Publ*. 18. 3. π. ἀγών part of name of an athletic contest at Sidon, *IG*3. 129 (iii A.D.), *CPHerm*.54.13 (iii A.D.). -πορφῠρόσημος παῖς, ὁ, = Lat. *puer praetextatus*, *AP*12.185 (Strat.). -πορφύρω [ῠ], strengthd. for πορφύρω, Man.5.24.

**περιποτάομαι**, poet. for περιπέτομαι, *hover about*, τὰ δ' αἰεὶ ζῶντα (sc. τὰ μαντεῖα) περιποτᾶται S.*OT*482 (lyr.): c. acc., Hld.2.22.

**περίποτος**, ον, (πίνω) of a cup, *to be drunk from on both sides* (to explain δέπας ἀμφικύπελλον), Ath.11.783b.

**περίπου**, or divisim περί που, *about*, ἔτη γεγονὼς περίπου ἑκκαίδεκα Hdn.5.7.4, cf. 7.5.2, Paul.Aeg.4.1, etc.

**περίπους**, ποδος, ὁ, ἡ, *fitting close*, as a shoe to the foot, Hsch., Phot. (better divisim, περὶ ποδός and περὶ πόδα).

**περιπρακτορία**, ἡ, *district for purposes of taxation*, *PMasp*.9 ii 20 (vi A.D.).

**περίπρησις**, εως, ἡ, *burning all round*, ὅλου τοῦ σώματος Philum. *Ven*.24.3.

**περιπρό**, Adv. *very, especially*, Il.11.180, Call.*Jov*.86.

**περιπρο-βάλλω**, *throw round before*, τινί τι Opp.*H*.4.657. -θέω, *run forward and round*, ib.2.440, 4.89. -χέομαι, *to be poured all round*, used by Hom. in aor. part., ἔρος..θυμὸν ἐνὶ στήθεσσι περιπροχυθεὶς ἐδάμασσε love *rushing in a flood over* my heart overcame it, Il. 14.316.

**περιπρωκτιάω**, = σαυλοπρωκτιάω, *Com.Adesp*.1114.

**περιπταίω**, *stumble upon*, c. dat., Polyaen.1.3.2; *fall into*, ἐνέδρᾳ Id.4.2.18: mostly metaph. of calamity, Plu.*Pyrrh*.10 (v.l.); ἑτέροις ἀφ' ἑτέρων J.*AJ*17.5.5; ὀλέθρῳ Tryph.312: abs., Ph.2.62. 2. *fall in with*, ὀνείδεσι f.l. for περιπεπτωκότων in Arist.*Fr*.487.

**περιπτέρνια**, τά, metallic *joints* connecting the arms of an air-catapult with the air-chambers, Ph.*Bel*.78.19.

**περιπτερνίς**, ίδος, ἡ, *bandage for the heel*, Sor.*Fasc*.60, Orib.48. 67 tit.

**περίπτερος**, ον, *flying round about*: περίπτερα πυρός *sparks* of fire, Lxx *Ca*.8.6. II. Archit., of a temple, *with a single row of columns all round it*, προστάς, οἶκος, Callix.1, cf. Lxx *Am*.3.15, Vitr.3.2.1. 2. *surrounded by a gallery*, Ath.Mech.11.8.

**περι-πτίσματα**, τά, *skins* of grapes, Sch.Ar.*Nu*.45, *Eq*.803 (with vv.ll.). -πτίσσω, *strip off the husk* or *skin*, Thphr.*HP*9.16.9, Dieuch.ap.Orib.4.7.21:—Pass., Thphr.*HP*4.4.10, Sor.1.122: metaph., περιεπτισμένοι *free from the chaff, clean-winnowed*, Ar.*Ach*.507; π. τὸ εἶδος *clean-built, taper* of form, Philostr.*Her*.3.4.

**περί-πτυγμα**, ατος, τό, *anything folded round, covering*, E.*Ion* 1391. -πτυκτος, η, ον, *folding*, π. ἐξαιρῖτις *folding* ladder, Ath. Mech.36.7. -πτυξις, εως, ἡ, *folding oneself round, embracing*, τοῦ νεκροῦ Plu.*Cat.Mi*.11 (pl.); περιπτύξεις καὶ ἁφαί Plot.4.7.8. ❀ -πτύσσω, *enfold, enshroud*, τινὰ τύμβῳ S.*Ant*.886; πέπλοι περιπτύσσοντες δέμας E.*Hec*.735; π. γόνυ, δέμας, *clasp, embrace* it, Id.*IA*992, *Med*.1206 (v.l. χέρας); ὥς σε περιπτύξω Bion 1.44; π. ταῖς χερσί Plb.13.7.8, etc.; ὁλοῇσι π. γενύεσσι, of a dragon, A.R.4.155:—Pass., Aristaenet. 1.1. 2. as military term, *outflank*, X.*An*.1.10.9:—Pass., Id.*Cyr*. 7.1.26. 3. Med., *embrace*, Jul.*Ep*.193. II. *fold round*, π. χέρας *fold* the arms *round* another, E.*Alc*.350, *Andr*.417:—Med. and Pass., *fold oneself round, coil round*, Pl.*Smp*.196a; ἡ γαστὴρ -πτύσσεται τῇ τροφῇ Gal.6.303: c. acc., τήνδε τὴν μερίδα τῆς βασιλείας δύο..ἔθνη περιπτύσσεται Lib.*Or*.59.89. 2. *apply*, τι τόπῳ Philum.*Ven*.7.6.

**περιπτῠχ-ή**, ἡ, *that which enfolds*, used in pl. in poet. periphrasis, τειχέων περιπτυχαί *enfolding* walls, E.*Ph*.1357; δόμων Ar.*Av*.1241 (parody of E.); Ἀχαιῶν ναύλοχοι π. their naval *cloak* or *fence*, E.*Hec*. 1015; πέπλων π. *Trag.Adesp*.91. II. *enfolding, embracing*, περιπτυχαῖσι δὴ χέρας προσαρμόσασα E.*Supp*.815 (lyr.); ἐν ἡλίου περιπτυχαῖς in *all that* the sun *embraces*, i.e. all the world, Id.*Ion* 1516. -ής, ές, *folded round*, φᾶρος S.*Aj*.915. 2. φασγάνῳ π. *fallen around* (i.e. *upon*) his sword, ib.899.

**περιπτύω**, *spit upon*, περιπτυόμενον ἀμελεῖται Aristaenet.1.21, cf. Porph.*Chr*.63.

❀ **περί-πτωμα**, ατος, τό, *accidental happening*: hence, 1. *calamity*, Pl.*Prt*.345b. 2. *lucky chance*, Lxx *Ru*.2.3. -πτωσις, εως, Ion. ιος, ἡ, *encountering, falling into* the earth's shadow, Cleom.2.6. II. = foreg., S.E.*P*.1.144 (pl.), Hld.6.14, etc.; ἀπὸ περιπτώσεως S.E.*M*.1. 25. III. *experience*, ξυγκαταινέω..τὸν λογισμόν, ἥνπερ ἐκ περιπτώσιος ποιέηται τὴν ἀρχήν Hp.*Praec.*1; οὔτε πεῖρα οὔτε π. Plu.2.918c tit.; ἄλογος τριβὴ καὶ π. ib.440a; κατὰ περίπτωσιν ἐγνωσμένον *Stoic.*2.29, al., cf. Phld.*Rh.*2.164S., Diog.Oen.10(pl.).

**περιπτώσσω**, *fear greatly*, τι Musae.206 (dub.): abs., *APl.*4.110.

**περιπτωτικός**, ή, όν, *falling into that which one seeks to avoid*, Epicurei ap.Plu.2.420d, Arr.*Epict.*3.6.6, etc.; τῷ κακῷ M.Ant.10.7. Adv. -κῶς Arr.*Epict.*4.10.6. II. *accidental*, π. εἶδος ἐμπειρίας Gal.*Sect.Intr.*2. Adv. -κῶς S.E.*M.*1.25.

**περιπύημα** [ῠ], ατος, τό, (πυέω) *suppuration round about*, Hp.*Epid.*4.52.

**περιπῠκάζω**, *encompass thickly*, κόμῃ *with* foliage, Ach.Tat.1.15:—Med., *have thick round*, τὰς τρίχας περὶ τὸ σῶμα Ctes.*Fr.*57.11.

**περίπῠρον**, τό, *vessel for containing fire*, *IG*11(2).203*B*45,219*B*53 (Delos, iii B.C.), *SIG*996.13 (Smyrna, i A.D.).

**περίπυστος**, ον, *widely known, celebrated*, A.R.4.213, Parth.25.3, App.*BC*2.88, Coluth.75, *AP*7.42, etc.

**περιπωμ-άζω**, *cover with a lid all over*, Hp.*Loc.Hom.*47, Ph.2.324:—Pass., *to be closely covered*, Arist.*Juv.*470a9. 2. Pass., *to be shut up in*, ἐὰν περιπωμασθῇ ὀλίγος ἀήρ Id.*HA*592a22. -ᾰτίζω, = foreg. 1, Id.*Pr.*930b2 (Pass.), Thphr.*Ign.*43.

**περιρρᾰγής**, ές, *torn* or *broken round about*, *AP*7.542 (Stat. Flacc.).

**περιρραίνω**, *besprinkle*, Thphr.*Lap.*13; esp. in sacred rites, μιᾶς ἐκ χέρνιβος βωμοὺς π. Ar.*Lys.*1130:—Med., *purify oneself*, ὕδατι περίρραν' (i.e. περίρραναι) Men.530.23, cf. Plu.*Lyc.*2; ἀπὸ συνουσίας περιρανα-μένους *IG*12(1).789.15 (Rhodes, ii A.D.), cf. *SIG*982.8 (Pergam., ii B.C. in form -ρασάμενοι); π. ἀπὸ ἱεροῦ Thphr.*Char.*16.2; ἐπὶ θαλάττης ib.13; ἀπὸ [κρήνης] Aristobul.6 J.; οὐλοχύταις Nonn.*D.*5.7 (Pass.), etc. II. generally, *moisten*, ὕδασι..ἀρούρας ib.14.48. 2. *pour*, οἶνον..Ὑμεναίῳ ib.29.156. 3. metaph., -έρρανται στιγμαῖς Philum.*Ven.*20.1.

⊛ **περίρραμμα**, ατος, τό, *something stitched on*, Hsch. s.v. ἄκανθος.

**περίρραν-σις**, εως, ἡ, *lustral besprinkling*, Pl.*Cra.*405b. -τήριον, τό, *utensil for besprinkling*, esp. *whisk for sprinkling* water at sacrifices, or *vessel for lustral water*, Hdt.1.51, Porph.*Abst.*2.27 (pl.):—written **περιραντήριον** in Inscrr., *IG*2².1641.38, 11(2).287*A* 93 (Delos, iii B.C.), *SIG*253 ii 10 (Delph., iv B.C.). II. περιρραντήρια ἀγορᾶς *the parts* of the market-place *sprinkled with lustral water*, Lex ap.Aeschin.1.21, cf. 3.176, Luc.*Sacr.*12, 13. III. = foreg., Ph.1.156, al., Luc.*Pseudol.*23. -τής, οῦ, ὁ, *sprinkler*, temple-official at Sardes, *BMus.Inscr.*1031 (= *Sardis* 7(1).117, i B.C.). -τίζω, = περιρραίνω, Lxx *Nu.*19.13, al.; v.l. for -νοτίζω in Alex.Trall.1.15. -τισμός, ὁ, *sprinkling with water*, Sm.*Za.*13.1.

**περιρρᾰπίζω**, *lash round about*, τῇ οὐρᾷ π. τὸ ἐδώδιμον, of fish, Plu.2.977b.

**περι-ρράπτρια**, ἡ, *she who sews* or *stitches*: title of priestess at Piraeus, *IG*2².2361.12. -ρράπτω, *stitch all round*, D.S.20.91 (Pass.), Poll.7.84 (Pass.). -ρράσσω, *dash to pieces*, κέρατα Hierocl.p.15A. (written περιράσσει).

**περιρρέζω**, *purify by sacrifice*, Hsch.

**περιρρέμβομαι**, *wander, roam about*, μὴ περιρέμβου ζητοῦσα θεόν Zos. Alch.p.244 B., cf. *Gloss.*; περιρεμβαῦσαι (sic)· περιφθαρῆναι, Hsch.

**περι-ρρεπής**, ές, *falling over on one side*, opp. ἰσόρροπος, Hp.*Art.*50; αἱ πλάγιαι [κλίσεις] περιρρεπεῖς γίγνονται τῇ κύστει *cause* the organs *to press* on the bladder, Ruf.*Ren.Ves.*11. -ρρέπω, *incline to one side*, Hp.*Fract.*4, Gal.18(2).828. -ρρεψις, εως, ἡ, *slipping to one side*, Hp.*Off.*12.

⊛ **περιρρέω**, fut. -ρεύσομαι Arist.*Cael.*287b10: aor. 1 inf. -ρρεῦσαι Lycurg.96 (s.v.l.): aor. 2 -ερρύην (v. infr.): pf. -ερρύηκα Pl.*Criti.* 111b: I. c. acc., *flow round*, τὸν δ' αἷμα περίρρεε Od.9.388; νῆσον π. ὁ Νεῖλος Hdt.2.29, cf. 127; νήσους, ἃς περιρρεῖν τὸν ἀέρα Pl.*Phd.* 111a; κύκλῳ..τὸν τόπον περιρρεῦσαι τὸ πῦρ Lycurg. l.c. codd.; of persons, ἅπαντες π. ἡμᾶς κύκλῳ Pl.*Chrm.*155d:—Pass., *to be surrounded by water*, X.*An.*1.5.4, Arist.*Mu.*393a11, al. II. abs., *flow round*, Στρυμόνος ἐπ' ἀμφότερα περιρρέοντος Th.4.102, cf. X.*HG*4.1.16 (v.l.), Arist.*Cael.* l.c. 2. *fall away*, περιερρυηκυίας τῆς γῆς Pl.*Criti.* l.c.; *waste away*, πῆχυς ὅλος περιερρύη Hp.*Epid.*3.4, cf. Lxx 4*Ma.*9.20; *fall off*, of flowers, Thphr.*HP*4.8.9. 3. *slip from off* a thing, ἡ ἀσπὶς περιερρύη ἐς τὴν θάλασσαν *slipped off his arm* into the sea, Th.4.12; [αἱ πέδαι] αὐτῷ αὐτόμαται π. X.*An.*4.3.8; [αἱ πέδαι] π. Plu.2.304b; οἱ στέφανοι π. Luc.*VH*2.11: c. gen., ἵππου π. *slip off* it, Plu.*Art.*15, cf. Id. 2.970d; τροχοὶ π. τῶν ἁρμάτων Parth.6.4. 4. *overflow on all sides*, σοὶ περιρρείτω βίος let thy means of living *abound*, S.*El.*362; of excessive wealth, Diog.Oen.60; οὐδενὸς περιρρέοντος *being in excess*, Plu.*Per.*16:—Pass., *to be all running* or *dripping*, ἱδρῶτι *with* sweat, Id.*Aem.*25; δάκρυσι Suid. s.v. ἄναυδος: freq. metaph., *abound*, περιρρεομένη ἀφθονίᾳ ἀγαθῶν Ph.2.455; of persons, c. dat., περιρρεόμενος ταῖς ἐκτὸς οὐσίαις Id.1.592, cf. 2.445; περιρρέονται μαθηταῖς *have a crowd* of pupils *about them*, Lib.*Or.*64.90.

**περιρρήγνῡμι** and -ύω (Plu.*Publ.*6), *break off all round*, τὸν γήλοφον κύκλῳ Pl.*Criti.*113d: freq. of clothes, *rend and tear off*, τὸν χιτωνίσκον D.19.197; τὴν χλαμύδα Plb.15.33.4: also c. acc. pers., *strip*, Parth. 15.3:—Med., περιερρήξατο τοὺς πέπλους *tore off her own* garments, Plu.*Ant.*77, cf. Ph.2.44: abs., J.*AJ*9.7.3, Arr.*An.*7.24.3, D.Chr.35. 9; [γυναῖκες] περιερρηγμέναι Id.46.12:—Pass., with aor. 2 -ερράγην, intr. pf. περιέρρωγα, περιρρηγνυμένων φαρέων A.*Th.*328 (lyr.); of the case or membrane that encloses pupa or shellfish, περιρρήγνυται τὸ κέλυφος Arist.*HA*551a23, cf. 552a6; περιερρωγέναι τὸ ὄστρακον ib. 601a13 (so in Act., ἡ σχάδων..τὸν ὑμένα περιρρήξας (sic) ἐκπέταται ib. 554a30.—Med., τὰ ζῷα τὰ ἐκ τῶν σκωλήκων περιρρηγνύμενα ib.552a9); πέτρα περιρραγεῖσα ib.578b22; of dead flesh, *break away*, Hp.*Fract.* 26. II. *cause* a stream *to break* or *divide round* a piece of land, [Βούσιρις] τὸν Νεῖλον περὶ τὴν χώραν περιέρρηξε Isoc.11.31:—Pass., τοῦ Δέλτα κατὰ τὸ ὀξὺ περιρρήγνυται ὁ Νεῖλος Hdt.2.16, cf. Ael.*NA*7. 24; βρονταὶ περιερρήγνυντο *kept breaking round* a place, Plu.*Crass.* 19. III. *break* a thing *round* or *on* another, *wreck*, τὸ σκαφίδιον πρὸς πέτραν Luc.*Merc.Cond.*2, cf. Poll.1.114; ἀλλήλοισι π. ἀέλλας Q.S.8.61. IV. ὄρος περιερρωγὸς *broken all round*, i.e. *precipitous*, Nic.Dam.1 J.

**περι-ρρήδην**, Adv. of sq. II, *sloping*, A.R.4.1581. -ρρηδής, ές, *sprawling*, περιρρηδὴς δὲ τραπέζῃ κάππεσε he fell *sprawling over* the table, Od.22.84; περιρρηδὴς κεράεσσι *pitching forward over* them, A.R.1.431, cf. Orus in *EM*664.39. II. *falling away*, or *sloping on each side*, Hp.*Art.*16; of the body in bed, Id.*Mul.*2.158, Gal.18(1). 420. (*EM* l.c. explains the word by περιρραγής, περιρρυής. Prob. cogn. with ῥαδινός, cf. βραδανίζω.)

**περί-ρρηξις**, εως, ἡ, *breaking away all round*, as of mortified flesh, Hp.*Art.*69 (pl.). 2. *open wound*, *Hippiatr.*100,104. II. *circular fracture*, Gal.ap.Orib.46.21.5. -ρρήσσω, collat. form of περιρρήγνυμι, Gal.11.138, f.l. in Q.S.8.332:—also -ρρήττω, D.S.17.35, Ph.2.230, Dsc.2.107.

**περιρρητῑνόομαι**, *to be treated with resin*, dub. in Gal.12.659.

**περιρρίπτω**, *cast around* or *over*, μυίῃσι..χεῖρα prob. in Q.S.8. 332:—Pass., aor. 2 inf. περιρριφῆναι Sch.A.R.2.1210; *to be thrown about*, νεκρά, ὀστᾶ, Agath.2.1,23.

⊛ **περιρρογχάζω**, *mock, ridicule*, Sch.Ar.*Eq.*694.

**περι-ρροή**, ἡ, *flowing round*, ὡς ἂν ἑκάστοις [τοῖς ποταμοῖς] τύχῃ..ἡ π. γιγνομένη according as each flows round, Pl.*Phd.*111e. II. *fluid*, ξὺν π. αἱμάλωψ Aret.*CD*1.13. -ρροια, ἡ, = foreg., Plu.2. 1128c. II. *fluid discharge* in dysentery, Hp.*Epid.*1.5 (pl.); cf. περίρροος II.2.

**περιρρομβέω**, *cause to spin round like a top*, Plu.*Ant.*67, Tz. ad Lyc. 310.

**περίρροος**, ον, contr. **περίρρους**, ουν, = περίρρυτος, Hdt.1.174. 2. *flowing round*, γῆς π. ὠκεανός Aristid.*Or.*43(1).24. II. Subst., = περιρροή I, J.*AJ*18.9.1. 2. = περίρροια II, Hp.*Epid.*1.26.δ', 3.17.ιε', *Coac.*629.

**περιρροπή**, ἡ, *inclining to one side*, Gal.18(2).430.

**περιρρυής**, ές, *falling down all round*, gloss on περιρρηδής, Pius ap. Orum in *EM*664.39.

**περίρρῡπος**, ον, *all dirty*, cj. in Crates Theb.4.

**περιρρύπτω**, *scour all round*, Gal.11.129, Orib.*Eup.*2.1 s.v. γάλα.

**περί-ρρῠσις**, εως, ἡ, = περιρροή I, Agatharch.50. II. *violent discharge*, Gal.19.456. -ρρῠτος, ον, also α, ον Alcm.21, A.*Eu.*77:—*surrounded with water*, π. Κρήτη *sea-girt* Crete, Od.19.173, cf. Hes. *Th.*193, 290; Λιβύη, Εὐρώπη, Hdt.4.42,45; πόλεις A. l.c., cf. S.*Ph.*1, Th.4.64, Plu.2.941c, Aristid.*Or.*44(17).8; Ὠκεανὸς τῷ πᾶσα π. ἐνδέδεται χθών Neoptol.2. 2. Act., *flowing round*, c. gen., περιρρύτων ὑπὲρ ἀκαρπίστων πεδίων Σικελίας over the barren plains *that flow round* Sicily, i.e. the sea, E.*Ph.*209 (lyr.), sed leg. -ρρύτῳ.

**περιρρώξ**, ῶγος, ὁ, ἡ, *broken off all round, abrupt*, πέτρα ἀπότομος καὶ π. Plb.9.27.4, cf. D.H.9.15 (= Plb.*Fr.*200).

**πέρις**, Boeot. for πέριξ (if not an engraver's error), *IG*7.2712.33.

**περισαίνω**, Ep. περισσ-, *wag the tail round, fawn upon*, Τηλέμαχον δὲ περίσσαινον κύνες Od.16.4; οὐρῇσιν μακρῇσι περισσαίνοντες 10.215; of σαργοί, Opp.*H.*4.361: metaph., π. γλώσσῃσιν Orph.*L.*430, cf. Them.*Or.*7.92d, 21.258d; τινὰ ὡς δεσπότην Simp. *in Epict.*p.52 D.

**περισαλπ-ίζω**, *sound trumpets around*:—Pass., οὐ περισεσάλπισται or -πικται *has never had the trumpets sounding round* him, Eudamid.ap.Plu.2.192b (= Stob.4.13.65). -ισμός, ὁ, *blowing the trumpet round*, Jul.*Or.*5.168d.

**περίσαξις**, εως, ἡ, *heaping round*, Arist.*Pr.*924b9, Thphr.*CP*5. 6.6.

**περισαρκ-ίζω**, *make an incision all round*, Heliod.ap.Orib.46.22. 12, Philum.*Ven.*3.5, Paul.Aeg.5.3. -ισμός, ὁ, *incision all round*, Philum.*Ven.*7.5. -ιστέον, *one must make such an incision*, ib.16.6, Paul.Aeg.5.19. -ος, ον, *surrounded with flesh, fleshy*, Arist.*Phgn.* 809b7 (Comp.), Adam.2.2 (Comp.): Com. metaph., φωνάριον π. Clearch.Com.2 (cj. for -σαργ-). -όω, *surround* or *cover with flesh*, Gal.10.324,336. -ωσις, εως, ἡ, *covering with flesh*, ibid., Orib.46.9.2.

**περισάρωμα** [σᾰ], ατος, τό, *sweepings*, *AB*296, *EM*529.46.

**περισάττω**, *heap up all around*, τὴν γῆν περὶ τὰς ῥίζας Arist.*Pr.*924b 4, cf. a28 (Pass.); π. [τὰς ῥίζας] Thphr.*CP*5.6.5; π. τὰ χείλη *block up*, Plb.21.28.14:—Pass., cj. in Antyll.ap.Orib.6.10.12.

**περισβέννῡμι**, *quench all round*, τῇ βαφῇ τοῦ σιδήρου περισβεννύμενον τὸ αἷμα Plu.2.997a: metaph., περισβέννυσθαι αὐτῶν τὰς ὁρμάς J.*BJ* 3.7.18.

**περισείομαι**, Pass., *to be shaken all round*, περισσείοντο ἔθειραι the hair *floated round*, Il.19.382, 22.315.

**περισείρια**· τὰ πλάγια τῆς γλώττης, Hsch.; cf. παράσειρος II.

**περισέμνος**, ον, *very august*, ἀρχή Ar.*V.*604, cf. Eup.333.

**περίσεπτος**, η, ον, *much-revered, much-honoured*, A.*Eu.*1038 (lyr.), Agathocl.2.

**περίσημος**, Dor. -σᾱμος, ον, (σῆμα) *very famous, notable*, E.*HF* 1018 (Sup., lyr.), Call.*Fr.*1.54 P., Mosch.1.6, Ph.2.330 (Sup.); περι-στερεῶν *POxy.*1278.12 (iii A.D.).

**περισήπομαι**, Pass., *decay all round*, ὅταν περισαπῇ τὰ λευκὰ καὶ τὰ κύκλῳ Thphr.*HP*3.9.3; ἐπὴν περισαπῇ Hp.*Morb.*2.36.

**περισθεν-έω**, *to be exceeding strong*, part. περισθενέων Od.22.

368. -ής, ές, (σθένος) *exceeding strong*, Pi.*N*.3.16; θάνατος Id.*Fr.* 131.2.

**περισῐᾰλόομαι**, Pass., *to be broidered round the edge*, χρυσίῳ Lxx *Ex*.36.13(39.6).

**περισιγᾶν**· ἀφέλκειν τοῦ προκειμένου, Hsch. (leg. περισπᾶν).

**περισῐδηρ-όομαι**, Pass., *to be cased with iron*, Bito 49.5, *Stud.Pal.* 20.67$^r$.6 (ii/iii A. D.). -**ος**, ον, *cased with iron*, D.S.3.33.

**περισκαίρω**, *jump about*, τινι Opp.*C*.1.143.

**περισκάλλω**, *hack round about*, Gal.6.619: aor. 1 imper. περίσκᾰλον *Gp*.5.42.1 (leg. -σκαψον).

**περισκάπτω**, *dig round*, Thphr.*HP*4.14.7, *CP*5.9.3 (Pass.), Ph. 2.294, etc.; δένδρεα *Tab.Heracl*.1.173; π. ἀμπέλους *Gp*.3.3.6, etc.; γύρους Alciphr.3.13.70. II. *turn up all round*, περισκαφείσης τῆς γῆς D.H.2.31. III. *cut* the thread of a screw, Heliod.(?)ap.Orib. 49.4.66 (Pass.).

**περισκᾰρίζω**, gloss on περισκαίρω, Hsch.

**περίσκαψις**, εως, ἡ, *digging all round*, *Gp*.9.9.2, *PGiss*.56.13 (vi A. D.).

**περισκελ-ᾰσία**, ἡ, *harshness in action*, of hellebore, Orib.*Fr*.80 (nisi leg. περισκέλεια, cf. περισκελής (A) II. 2). -**εια**, ἡ, *hardness, harshness*, τῶν ἀναγκαίων Porph.*Marc*.2. 2. *difficulty*, Arist.*Fr.* 29. (Written **περισκελία**, Antyll.(?) ap.Orib.8.6.6, al., Paul.Aeg.6. 112.) -**ής** (A), ές, (σκέλλω) *very hard*, σίδηρον ὀπτὸν ἐκ πυρὸς περισκελῆ S.*Ant*.475. II. metaph., *obstinate, stubborn*, φρένες Id.*Aj.* 649; ἦθος M.Ant.4.28; χαρακτήρ *AP*9.578 (Leo Phil.): Comp. -έστερος Simp. *in Epict*.p.62 D. Adv. Comp. -έστερον, φέρειν to bear *more unflinchingly*, Men.6.3. 2. of medicines, *harsh, irritating*, Hp.*Ulc*.1; ἐλλέβοροι σκληροὶ καὶ π. Thphr.*HP*9.10.4. 3. *excessive, violent*, καύματα Philoch.171; ἀὴρ π. ἐφ' ἑκάτερα *excessive* in heat or cold, Thphr.*CP*5.14.9, cf. 2.3.3. 4. *hard, difficult*, τὸ π. τῆς τοιαύτης γεωγραφίας Str.14.1.9, cf. S.E.*M*.1.39; λοξῶν καὶ π. ὄντων τῶν χρησμῶν Corn.*ND*32; πρᾶγμα φύσει π. Theon *Prog*.4. -**ής** (B), ές, (σκέλος) *round the leg*: hence περισκελῆ, τά, *drawers*, Lxx *Ex*.28.38(42), Ph.2.157: sg., περισκελὲς λινοῦν Lxx *Le*.16.4; cf. περισκέλια. II. *with the legs apart*, ἄγαλμα π., such as Daedalus first made, Sch.Pl. *Euthphr*.11b. -**ία**, ἡ, v. περισκέλεια. ⊛ -**ια**, τά, *drawers*, Anon. ap.Suid., v.l. in Lxx *Ex*.28.38(42). -**ίζω**, *supplanto*, *Gloss.* -**ίς**, ίδος, ἡ, *leg-band*, i.e. *anklet, bangle*, Men.1054, Nicostr.Com.33, *Inscr. Délos* 442 *B* 199 (ii B. C.), *Peripl.M.Rubr*.6, Plu.2.142c, Alciphr.*Fr*.4; περισκελίδες χρυσαῖ Longus 1.5. II. *ornament round the stem* of a cup, *IG*2$^2$.1407.38, 1408.17 (quoted by Ath.11.476e).

**περισκέλλω**, pf. part. περιεσκληκώς *dried up*: *wiry, lean*, [στέρνα] Philostr.*Gym*.35.

**περίσκεμμα**, ατος, τό, *inquiry, examination*, *PLond ined*.2082 (ii/i B. C.).

**περισκεπ-άζω**, *cover, screen all round*, βύσσῳ τι *AP*5.103 (Marc. Arg.), cf. *Gp*.2.4.2:—Pass., Thphr.*HP*4.5.3, Dsc.2.76. -**ής**, ές, (σκέπας) *covered all round*, ὄρος θάμνοισι π. Call.*Jov*.11; οἶκοι Moschio Trag.7.27: metaph., λόγος π. ἑτέρῳ κόσμῳ, of a myth, Max.Tyr.10.5 (s. v. l.). II. *covering* or *screening all round*, πύργοι Call.*Del*.23; [ὥρα] τῷ ἀέρι περισκεπής (fort. -σκελής) Thphr.*HP*7.1.4. -**τέον**, *one must consider*, ἕκαστα Ph.2.195. ⊛ -**τος**, ον, *to be seen on all sides, far-seen*, περισκέπτῳ ἐνὶ χώρῳ Od.1.426, 10.211, Pl.*Epigr*.26.3; [ἀστέρες] Arat.213. 2. *worth seeing*, Call.*Epigr*.6.8; *admired*, Χαρίτεσσι *AP*12.91 (Polystr.). ⊛ -**ω**, = περισκεπάζω, Plb.2.30.3, Mosch.2.61, Ascl.*Tact*.1.3, *AP*6.250 (Antiphil.).

**περί-σκεψις**, εως, ἡ, Delph. **παρίσκεψις** (q. v.), *consideration*, τοῦ πράγματος Eudor.ap.Stob.2.7.2; μετά, ἄνευ περισκέψεως, Str.4.4.2, Chrysipp.(?) *Stoic*.3.115. -**σκέψομαι**, fut. of περισκοπέω.

**περισκήνια**, τά, bronze *balustrade* in a theatre, *EM*743.30; but, = ὀρχήστρα, ib.33.

**περισκήπτω**, *prop* or *press all round*, Hsch.

**περισκῐ-άζομαι**, Pass., *to be overshadowed*, Plu.2.1129d; of the moon, *to be obscured*, Id.*Nic*.21. -**ασμός**, ὁ, *obscuration*, Id.2.372e (pl.). -**ος**, ον, (σκιά) *throwing a shadow all round*, of the inhabitants of the polar circles, Posidon.76 J., Cleom.1.7.

**περισκιρτάω**, *leap round* or *about*, c. acc., τὸ ἅρμα Ael.*NA*14.28, cf. *AP*12.181 (Strat.), Luc.*Bacch*.2, etc.

**περίσκληρ-ος**, ον, *very hard*, Hp.*Aff*.59, *Epid*.6.1.10: metaph., *very rough, strong*, πνεῦμα Antiph.202.17; of persons, *very tough*, Heliod. (?)ap.Orib.44.14.4. ⊛ -**ύνω**, *make hard all round*, Hp.*Aph*.5.20, *Liqu*.6.

**περίσκον**, v. περισσός A. v.

⊛ **περισκοπ-έω**, fut. -σκέψομαι: pf. -έσκεμμαι in act. sense, S.E.*M.* 2.53; in pass. sense, v. infr. II. 3:—*look round*, S.*El*.897, Pl.*Tht*.155e, *Ax*.364a, Luc.*Prom*.1, etc.:—Med., Ar.*Ec*.487. II. *examine, observe carefully*, τὸ αὐτίκα Th.1.36; τὸν αἰγιαλόν Plu.*Pomp*.80; νύκτα -σκέψασθαι Arat.199; τὰ πάντα Luc.*VH*1.32. 2. *consider well*, εὖ περισκέψασθαι τὰ μέλλει ἀσφαλέστατα εἶναι Hdt.1.120; π. ὁπότεροι κρατήσουσι *watch and see*.., Th.6.49; π. εἴτε.. εἴτε Pl.*Prt*.313a; τἀφανῆ π. *speculate on* hidden things, S.*Fr*.737; τὴν φύσιν περιεσκεμμένος cj. in Pl.*Ax*.365b. 3. περιεσκεμμένος, in pass. sense, *circumspect, guarded*, γνώμη, ἔπαινος, D.Chr.34.27, Luc.*Hist.Conscr.* 59. -**ησις**, εως, ἡ, = περίσκεψις, J.*AJ*17.9.1: pl. in concrete sense, θαλάσσης ἀπέραντοι π. Sch.Opp.*H*.1.364.

**περισκορπίζω**, *scatter on all sides*, Olymp. *in Mete*.108.19, 26.

**περισκουτλόω** (Lat. *scutula*), *cover* or *surround with marble slabs*, *Jahresh*.3.206 (Termessus, ii A. D.).

**περισκῠθ-ίζω**, *scalp in Scythian fashion*, Lxx 2 *Ma*.7.4, Phalar.*Ep.* 147.3 (Pass.). II. as a surgical operation, Gal.18(1).790 (Pass.): —hence -**ισμός**, ὁ, Id.14.784; ὁ κατὰ θέξιν π. *PMed*. in *Arch.Pap*.4. 270 (iii A. D.); cf. περισκυφίζω. III. sens. obsc., *AP*12.95.6 (Mel.). -**ιστής**, οῦ, ὁ, *one who scalps*, Str.11.14.14.

**περισκῠλᾰκισμός**, ὁ, *a purifying rite in which a puppy was sacrificed and carried or applied all round*, Plu.*Rom*.21 (pl.), Id.2.280b.

**περισκῡτόω**, *cover with leather*, *Chron.Lind.B*.23 (Pass.).

**περισκῠφίζω**, (σκύφος) *make an incision round the scalp*:—hence -**ισμός**, ὁ, Aët.7.56 (pl.), 93, Paul.Aeg.6.7 (v.l. ὑπο-).

**περισμᾰρᾰγέω**, *rattle all round*, Anon.ap.Luc.*Hist.Conscr*.22, D.P. 844.

**περισμ-άω**, *wipe all round*, Hdn.Gr.1.468, f.l. in Dsc.3.45 (Pass.). -**ημα**, ατος, τό, in pl., *filings*, *IG*7.3498.21 (Oropus). -**ήχω**, *wipe over*, τόπους Sor.[2.88], f.l. in Dsc.3.45 (Pass.).

⊛ **περισμύχω** [ῡ], *consume by a slow fire*, Orph.*L*.602; of love, *AP* 5.291.11 (Agath.).

**περισοβέω**, *chase about*, π. ποτήριον *push round* the wine-cup, Men.224, cf. Hippoloch.ap.Ath.4.130c:—Pass., κύλικος, φιλοτησίας περισοβουμένης, Alciphr.1.22, 3.55, cf. Luc.*Symp*.15. II. *run bustling round*, κύκλῳ τὰς πόλεις Ar.*Av*.1425.

**περισ[σ]ομένη**· πορθουμένη, Hsch. (leg. περθ-).

**περισοφίζομαι**, *overreach, cheat*, τινα Ar.*Av*.1646.

**περισπᾰθίζω**, (σπάθη) *stir about*, Orib.*Fr*.88.

⊛ **περισπαίρω**, *quiver round*, δουρί Q.S.1.624; *struggle convulsively*, Lyc.68, Nic.*Th*.773, etc.

**περί-σπᾰσις**, εως, ἡ, = sq. II, *PGen*.56.15 (iv A. D.). II. = sq. III, Ephor.108 J., Eust.630.28. ⊛ -**σπασμός**, ὁ, *wheeling round*, Plb. 10.23.3, 12.18.3. II. *distracting circumstances, distraction*, Metrod. *Herc*.831.7, Plb.3.87.9 (pl.), Phld.*Mus*.p.98 K., Plu.2.831f (pl.); ἐν περισπασμοῖς εἶναι Plb.4.32.5, etc.; οἱ τῆς πόλεως π. καὶ φόβοι D.S.12. 38; περισπασμοὶ καὶ πιθανότητες Chrysipp.*Stoic*.3.77: rarely in sg., θυμοῦ π. Lxx *Ec*.2.23, cf. Arr.*Epict*.3.22.71. III. *circumflex accent*, D.H.*Comp*.11, A.D.*Pron*.34.24. -**σπαστέον**, *one must make circumflex*, Ath.14.644b, Sch.E.*Ph*.697, etc. -**σπαστικός**, ή, όν, *distracting*, δύναμις S.E.*M*.6.21, cf. Orib.*Eup*.4.14. ⊛ -**σπάω**, fut. -σπάσω D.S.20.3, A.D.*Pron*.87.15:—*draw off from around, strip off*, Isoc.*Ep*.9.10; τὸ χλαμύδιον αὐτοῦ π. D.S.19.9, etc.:—Med., *strip oneself of*, τὴν τιάραν X.*Cyr*.3.1.13 (so also in Act., π. τὴν πορφύραν Plu. *Aem*.23). 2. *strip bare*, περισπάσας ξίφος (Pierson χερὶ σπάσας) E. *IT*296. II. *wheel about*, of a general, Plb.1.76.5; intr. of the troops, Id.3.116.5; esp. *wheel twice* through a right angle, Ascl. *Tact*.12.6, al.; of a horse's bit, οὐ πάνυ π. not *pulling* it violently *round*, Luc.*Merc.Cond*.21. III. *draw off* or *away, divert*, εἰς τοὐναντίον [τὴν πολιτείαν] Arist.*Pol*.1307$^a$24; τροφὴν εἰς τὸ περικάρπιον Thphr.*CP*1.16.2; π. τοὺς Ῥωμαίους Plb.9.22.5; τὸν πόλεμον Id.1.26. 1; π. τὴν δύναμιν αὐτοῦ *draw* it *away*, Plu.*Cic*.45; ἀπὸ τῆς πατρίδος π. τοὺς βαρβάρους D.S.20.3; τὸν ἐντὸς.. θόρυβον ἐπὶ τοὺς ἔξω πολέμους D.H.6.23; π. περὶ τὰς ἔξω στρατείας τὸν δῆμον Id.9.43:—Pass., π. ὑπό τινων *PStrassb*.112.13 (ii B. C.); πάντῃ τὰς ὄψεις περισπώμενος Luc. *DDeor*.30.11; ἕως τοῦ ἔξω τόπου π. *to be drawn away and expanded*, opp. συστέλλεσθαι, Arist.*Pr*.863$^a$5. b. *detach*, Συρίαν τινός App. *Syr*.1, cf. *Hann*.56; τινὰς αὐτοῦ τῶν ἀκροατῶν Phld.*Acad.Ind*.p.79 M. 2. *disturb, vex*, Men.*Epit*.504, Lxx *Ec*.5.19:—Pass., ὑπὸ τῶν τελωνῶν *PSI*3.384.5 (ii B. C.). 3. *divert, distract*, Plu.2.96b, 160c; π. [τὴν διάνοιαν] ἀπό τινος Metrod.*Herc*.831.4, cf. Phld.*Rh*.2.53 S., al., Onos.42.6:—Pass., *to be distracted* or *engaged*, π. ταῖς διανοίαις Plb. 15.3.4; ὑπὸ βιωτικῆς χρείας D.S.2.29, cf. Phld.*Po.Herc*.994.24, al.; μηδ' ὑφ' ἑνὸς περισπωμένη ἡ πόλις *IG*2$^2$.1304.7; περί τινος Lxx *Si*.41. 2; περὶ πολλὴν διακονίαν *Ev.Luc*.10.40: abs., Plb.4.10.3. 4. *steal*, ἀργυροῦν ἢ χρυσοῦν ἀνάθημα Philostr.*Gym*.45:—Pass., ἅπαντα περιέσπασμαι I *have been robbed of* all, Men.*Epit*.143. 5. Pass., c. inf., *to be compelled* to do a thing, περιησπάσθην (sic) ἀνενεγκεῖν *PUniv.Giss*.19.4 (i A. D.). IV. Gramm., *pronounce* a vowel or word *with the circumflex*, A.D.*Pron*.33.24, al., Plu.*Thes*.26, etc.; esp. on the last syllable, Ath.2.52f, etc.; π. τὸν τόνον A.D.*Pron*.87.15; τῷ τόνῳ Gal.16.495; περισπώμεναι [λέξεις] D.H.*Comp*.11; π. [προσῳδία] D.T.630.2, Ph.1.29; περισπώμενος [φθόγγος] ib.46.

**περισπεῖν**, v. περιέπω.

**περισπειράω**, *wind round*, τὴν ἐσθῆτα τῇ κεφαλῇ Plu.*Cam*.25:—Med., τὰ μέσα.. ὁπλίταις περιεσπειραμένος *having concentrated his troops around*.., Id.*Ages*.31:—Pass., *form round*, ἀνδρῶν κύκλῳ περιεσπειραμένων Id.*Cic*.22; of serpents, etc., *twine, coil round*, δράκοντα περιεσπειραμένον τὸ δέρος D.S.4.48: c. dat., τισι Luc.*Hist. Conscr*.29; τῷ ποδί Id.*Dips*.6: metaph., *insinuate oneself into*, τὰς αὐλάς Eun.*Hist*.p.257 D.

**περισπείρω**, *spread all round*, Apollod.*Poliorc*.145.13 (Pass.), Ach. Tat.*Intr.Arat*.1:—Pass., -σπείρεται φλόξ Gal.7.314.

**περισπένδω**, v. περισπεύδω.

**περισπέρχ-εια**, ἡ, (σπέρχω) *expedition, quickness*, Eust.832.12; = ἡ ἄγαν σπουδή, Sch.Opp.*H*.2.334. -**έω**, v. περισπέρχω. -**ής**, ές, *very hasty*, π. πάθος a *rash, overhasty* death (such as the self-slaughter of Ajax), S.*Aj*.982; π. βοή *Trag.Adesp*.254; πικρὸς καὶ π. Plu.2.59d. 2. π. ὀδύνῃσι *goaded* by pains, Opp.*C*.4.218, *H*.5. 145. -**ω**, intr., *to be in great agitation*, ib.2.334, 3.449, 4.330. II. Pass., *to be agitated, angered*, Λοκρῶν περισπερχθέντων τῇ γνώμῃ (Valck. for -σπερχεόντων) Hdt.7.207.

**περισπεύδω**, *pursue on all sides*, τινα dub. in J.*AJ*17.1.1 (v.l. -σπένδ-). 2. *go in search of* a thing, αἶγες π. ἀκάνθαις Arat.1122.

**περισπιλόω**, *subject to heat*, Cyran.77 (s. v. l.).

**περίσπλαγχνος**, ον, *great-hearted*, Theoc.16.56.

⊛ **περισπογγ-ίζω**, *sponge all round*, Hp.*Morb*.2.13, Thphr.*Char*.25.5, Gal.13.357. **-ισμός**, ὁ, *sponging all over*, τοῦ προσώπου Sor. [2.28].

⊛**περισπόρια**, τά, *suburbs*, Lxx *Jo*.21.2, 1 *Ch*.6.55(40), al.

⊛**περισπουδ-άζω**, *to be very eager*, Sm.*Ps*.67(68).17. **-αστος**, ον, *much sought after, much desired*, Theopomp.Hist.114; ἔνδοξον καὶ π. D.H.*Rh*.7.3, cf. Muson.*Fr*.18 *B* p.104 H. (Comp.), Luc.*Tim*.38, Men. Rh.p.366 S., etc.; τινι *by* one, M.Ant.5.36, Gal.6.519, Hdn.6.8.4, Iamb.*Comm.Math*.26, etc. 2. *diligent, eager*, *PMasp*.20 ii 11 (vi A.D.). Adv. -τως *with due care*, Phylarch.30 J., Ath.4.164b. **-ος**, ον, *very eager*, Poll.6.29, etc.; τινος *for*.., Simp. *in Epict*.p.51 D.

**περισπωμένως**, Adv. pres. part. Pass., (περισπάω) *pronounced with a circumflex*, esp. on the last syllable, Gal.19.120, Ath.9.400a, Sch. Ar.*Pl*.109, etc.

**περισσάδελφος** [ᾰ], ον, *having an extraordinary number of brothers*, Vett.Val.18.33.

**περισσαίνω**, (περισσός) *feel repletion* or *oppression*, Ruf.(?)ap. Orib.*inc*.6.25, Orib.*Syn*.5.1, Paul.Aeg.1.1. II. v. περισαίνω.

**περισσ-άκις**, Att. περιττ-, Adv. of περισσός, of numbers, *taken an odd number of times, multiplied by an odd number*, Pl.*Prm*. 144a, Plu.2.744a, etc. **-ακῶς**, Adv. = foreg., Iamb. *in Nic*.p.13 P. (s. v. l.). **-άρτιος**, ον, *odd and even*: Arith. of numbers *which become uneven when divided by some power of two*, such as 24 (for $24 \div 2^3 = 3$), Nicom.*Ar*.1.10, Poll.4.162. **-εία**, ἡ, *surplus, abundance*, 2 *Ep.Cor*.8.2; χρημάτων *IG*5(1).550. II. *advantage*, Lxx *Ec*. 1.3, al. **-ευμα**, Att. -ττευμα, ατος, τό, *superfluity*, Orib.22.7.1; *that which remains over*, κλασμάτων *Ev.Marc*.8.8; *abundance*, opp. ὑστέρημα, 2 *Ep.Cor*.8.14; ἐκ τοῦ περισσεύματος τῆς καρδίας τὸ στόμα λαλεῖ *Ev.Matt*.12.34. II. = περίσσωμα, *excrement*, Sor.1.108, f.l. in Plu.2.962f. **-ευσις**, εως, ἡ, = περισσεία, *Gloss*. **-εύω**, Att. -ττεύω, impf. ἐπερίσσευον (περιέσσευον is condemned by Phryn.20), (περισσός) *to be over and above* the number, μύριοί εἰσιν ἀριθμόν.., εἷς δὲ π. Hes.*Fr*.160; περιττεύσουσιν ἡμῶν οἱ πολέμιοι the enemy *will go beyond* us, *outflank* us, X.*An*.4.8.11. II. *to be more than enough, remain over*, τἀρκοῦντα καὶ περιττεύοντα Id.*Smp*.4.35; τὸ π. [ἀργύριον] Id.*Vect*.4.7; ἂν ᾖ τι.. περιττεῦον Pl.*Lg*.855b; εἴ τι π. ἀπὸ τῶν τόκων *SIG*672.19 (Delph., ii B.C.); ἡ περιττεύουσα τροφή Arist.*HA* 619ᵃ20; τὸ π. τῶν κλασμάτων *Ev.Matt*.14.20; τοσοῦτον τῷ Περικλεῖ ἐπερίσσευσε, κτλ. such *abundance* of reason *had* Pericles for his belief, Th.2.65; τοσόνδ' ἐπερίσσευσεν αὐτοῖς εὐνοίας J.*AJ*19.1.18; τὸ ἀνδρεῖον ἐπερίττευεν αὐτῇ D.H.3.11. 2. in bad sense, *to be superfluous*, τὰ περισσεύοντα τῶν λόγων S.*El*.1288; ἵν' ἐμοὶ περιττεύῃ, i.e. that I may be over-rich, Diog.Oen.64. III. of persons, *abound in*, χορηγίᾳ, opp. ἐλλείπω, Plb.18.35.5, etc.; αἱ ἐκκλησίαι ἐπερίσσευον τῷ ἀριθμῷ *Act.Ap*.16.5:—Med., c. gen., περισσεύονται ἄρτων *have more than enough of*.., *Ev.Luc*.15.17. 2. *to be superior*, π. παρά τινα *to be better than*.., Lxx *Ec*.3.19; ὑπέρ τινα ib.1 *Ma*.3.30 (v.l.); *be better, have the advantage*, 1 *Ep.Cor*.14.12; π. μᾶλλον *abound* more and more, sc. in Christian graces, 1 *Ep.Thess*.4.1, 11:—Med., περισσευόμεθα, opp. ὑστερούμεθα, 1 *Ep.Cor*.8.8. IV. causal, *make to abound*, πᾶσαν χάριν π. 2 *Ep.Cor*.9.8; τινὰς τῇ ἀγάπῃ 1 *Ep.Thess*.3.12:—Pass., *to be made to abound*, *Ev.Matt*.13.12, 25.29. 2. of Time, π. τὰς ὥρας *make* them *longer*, Ath.2.42b.

**περισσο-γονία**, ἡ, *production of odd numbers*, Iamb. *in Nic*.pp.21, 34 P. ⊛ **-δάκτυλος**, ον, *with more than the usual number of fingers* or *toes*, *Gp*.14.7.9. **-ειδής**, ές, *partaking of the nature of odd numbers*, of the δυάς, Theo Sm.p.24 H., *Theol.Ar*.19, Iamb. *in Nic*.p.31 P. **-επέω**, *speak superfluously*, Hsch., Suid. **-καλλής**, ές, *exceeding beautiful*, Cratin.238. **-κομος**, ον, *exceeding hairy*, Opp.*C*.3.317. **-λογέω**, Att. περιττο-, *speak superfluously*, Simp. *in Ph*.770.14; gloss on περισσοεπέω, Hsch., Suid. **-λογία**, ἡ, *over-talking, wordiness*, Isoc. 12.88; π. καὶ ἀκρίβεια Id.15.264. II. *elaborate writing*, D.H. *Pomp*.2. III *exaggeration*, J.*AJ*14.7.2. **-λόγος**, ον, *talking too much, wordy*, Sch.Ar.*Eq*.89. **-λοφος**, ον, *with an over-big crest*, Opp.*C*.3.369. **-μελής**, ές, *with superfluous limbs*, Heph.Astr. 1.1, Man.4.464, Vett.Val.18.33, al. **-μῦθος**, ον, = περισσολόγος, *superfluous*, E.*Fr*.52. Adv. in form -μυθεί (s. v. l.), Phld.*Rh*.1.101 S. **-νοος**, ον, *eminent for understanding*, Opp.*H*.3.12, Nonn.*D*. 5.222. **-πᾰθέω**, (παθεῖν) *suffer exceedingly*, Cass.*Pr*.15. **-ποιός**, όν, *making odd*, of numbers, Syrian. *in Metaph*.131.36. **-πους**, ὁ, ἡ, gen. ποδος, *with a foot too many*, Nonn.*D*.7.43 (of old age).

⊛ **περισσός**, Att. περιττός, ή, όν, (from περί, as ἔπισσαι from ἐπί, μέτασσαι from μετά) *beyond the regular number* or *size, prodigious*, δῶρα Hes.*Th*.399 (never in Hom.); ὦμος *Trag.Adesp*.458.3; στάθμα, dub. sens., v. ἕλκω B. 3. 2. *out of the common, extraordinary, strange*, εἴ τι περισσὸν εἰδείη if he has any *signal* knowledge, Thgn.769; εἴ τι φρονεῖς καί τι περισσὸν ἔχεις Philisc.(*PLG*2.327); π. λόγος S.*OT* 841; ἄγρα E.*Ba*.1197 (lyr.); πάθος Id.*Supp*.791 (lyr.); βίος οὐδὲν ἔχων π. ἀλλὰ πάντα σμικρά Antipho Soph.51; οὐ γὰρ π. οὐδὲν οὐδ' ἔξω λόγου πέπονθας E.*Hipp*.437; περισσότερα παθήματα Antipho 3.4.5; τὰ π. τῶν ἔργων καὶ τερατώδη Isoc.12.77; ἴδια καὶ π. Id.15.145; π. καὶ θαυμαστά Arist.*EN*1141ᵇ6; πρᾶξις π. Id.*Pol*.1312ᵃ27; οὐθὲν δὴ λέγοντες π. φαίνονταί τι λέγειν Id.*Metaph*.1053ᵇ3; τί π. ποιεῖτε; *Ev.Matt*.5.47; περιττοτάτη φύσις Arist.*HA*531ᵃ9; συνανθρωπίζον.. πάντων περισσότατον, of the dog, Ath.13.611c, cf. Clearch.24; in Literature, *striking*, τὸ περιττόν, as a quality of οἱ τοῦ Σωκράτους λόγοι, Arist.*Pol*.1265ᵃ 11; τὰ σοφὰ καὶ τὰ π. *refinements*, Epicur.*Fr*.409; opp. κοινὸς καὶ δημώδης, Longin.40.2 (but also, *elaborate*, π. καὶ πεποιημένος Id.3.4; in bad sense, *far-fetched*, D.H.*Pomp*.2, *Dem*.56). 3. of persons, *extraordinary, remarkable*, esp. for great learning, π. ὢν ἀνήρ E.*Hipp*. 948; τοὺς.. π. καί τι πράσσοντας πλέον Id.*Fr*.788; δυστυχεῖς εἶναι τοὺς π. Arist.*Metaph*.983ᵃ2; π. γένος τῶν μελιττῶν Id.*GA*760ᵃ4: freq. with the manner added, π. κατὰ φιλοσοφίαν Id.*Pr*.953ᵃ10; περὶ τὸν ἄλλον βίον περιττότερος *somewhat extravagant* or *eccentric*, Id.*Pol*.1267ᵇ24; τῇ φύσει π. Id.*HA*622ᵇ6; κάλλει Plu.*Demetr*.2; ἐν ἅπασι Id.*Dem*. 3; τὴν ὥραν Alciphr.1.12: c. inf., D.H.*Comp*.18. 4. c. gen., περισσὸς ἄλλων πρός τι *beyond* others in.., S.*El*.155; θύσει τοῦδε περισσότερα *greater things than* this, *AP*6.321 (Leon.Alex.); περιττότερος προφήτου *one greater than*.., *Ev.Matt*.11.9. II. *more than sufficient, superfluous*, αἱ π. δαπάναι X.*Mem*.3.6.6; περιττὸν ἔχειν to have *a surplus*, Id.*An*.7.6.31; οἱ μὲν.. περιττὰ ἔχουσιν, οἱ δὲ οὐδὲ τὰ ἀναγκαῖα.. Id. *Oec*.20.1: c. gen., τῶν ἀρκούντων περιττά *more than* sufficient, Id.*Cyr*. 8.2.21; τὰ π. τῶν ἱκανῶν Id.*Hier*.1.19: freq. in military sense, οἱ π. ἱππεῖς the *reserve* horse, Id.*Eq.Mag*.8.14; οἱ π. τῆς φυλακῆς ib.7.7; π. σκηναί *spare* tents, Id.*Cyr*.4.6.12 (but τοῖς περιττοῖς χρῆσθαι *their superior numbers*, Id.*An*.4.8.11, cf. *Cyr*.6.3.20); τὸ π. the *surplus, residue*, Inscr.ap.eund.*An*.5.3.13 (but τὸ π. τοῦ Ἰουδαίου the *advantage* of the Jew, *Ep.Rom*.3.1); Ἀρπυιῶν τὰ π. their *leavings*, *AP*11.239 (Lucill.); τὸ π. τῆς ἡμέρας the *remainder* of the day, X.Eph.1.3; π. γράμματα *supplementary* provisions in a will, *BGU*326 ii 9 (ii A.D.). 2. in bad sense, *superfluous, useless*, οὐδέ τι τοῦ παντὸς κενεὸν πέλει οὐδὲ π. Emp.13; μόχθος π. A.*Pr*.385, cf. S.*Ant*.780; π. κἀνόνητα σώματα Id.*Aj*.758; βάρος π. γῆς ἀναστρωφώμενοι Id.*Fr*.945; ἄχθος Id.*El*.1241 (lyr.); τὰ γὰρ π. πανταχοῦ λυπήρ' ἔπη Id.*Fr*.82; αὐδῶ σε μὴ περισσὰ κηρύσσειν A.*Th*.1048; π. πάντες οὑν μέσῳ λόγοι E.*Med*.819; π. φωνῶν Id.*Supp*.459. 3. *excessive, extravagant*, μηχανᾶσθαι περισσά *commit extravagances*, Hdt.2.32; περισσὰ δρᾶν, πράσσειν, to be *over-busy*, S.*Tr*.617, *Ant*.68; π. φρονεῖν to be *over-wise*, E.*Fr*.924 (anap.); ἡ π. αὕτη ἐπιμέλεια τοῦ σώματος Pl.*R*.407b; μῆκος πολὺ λόγων π. Id.*Lg*. 645c; *redundant, overdone*, οἱ καρτεροὶ καὶ π. λόγοι Id.*Ax*.365c, etc.; of dress, ἐσθὴς π. Plu.2.615d; περισσοτέρα λύπη 2 *Ep.Cor*.2.7; τοῦ τὰ δέοντ' ἔχειν περιττὰ μισῶ I hate *extravagance* in comparison with moderation, Alex.254, etc. 4. of persons, *over-wise, over-curious*, περισσὸς καὶ φρονῶν μέγα E.*Hipp*.445, cf. *Ba*.429 (lyr.); ὁ πολυπράγμων καὶ π. Plb.9.1.4; τὴν περὶ τὸ σῶμα θεραπείαν ἀκριβὴς καὶ π. Plu.*Cic*.8; so, of speakers, π. ἐν τοῖς λόγοις Δημοσθένης Aeschin.1.119. 5. as a term of praise, *subtle, acute*, ἀκριβὴς καὶ π. διάνοια Arist.*Top*. 141ᵇ13. III. Arith., ἀριθμὸς π. an *odd, uneven* number, opp. ἄρτιος, Epich.170.7, Philol.5, Pl.*Prt*.356e, etc.; π. ἡμέραι Hp.*Aph*. 4.61; τὸ π. καὶ τὸ ἄρτιον the nature of *odd* and even, Pl.*Grg*.451c, etc.; π. χῶραι the *odd* places in a verse, Heph.5.1; ἀρτιάκις π. ἀριθμός a number divisible by an odd number an even number of times, as 2, 6, 10, Euc.7 *Def*.9. IV. περισσότεροι *more in number, extra*, Carnead.ap.S.E.*M*.9.140. V. περιττόν, τό, = στρύχνος μανικός, θρύον II, Thphr.*HP*9.11.6; περισσόν Dsc.4.73; περίσκον Orib.12.8. 56.

B. Adv. περισσῶς *extraordinarily, exceedingly*, θεοσεβέες π. ἐόντες Hdt.2.37; ἐπαινέσεται π. E.*Ba*.1197 (lyr.); π. παῖδας ἐκδιδάσκεσθαι to have them educated *overmuch*, Id.*Med*.295; περιττοτέρως τῶν ἄλλων *far above* all others, Isoc.3.44; περισσότερον τοῦ ἑνὸς Luc. *Pr.Im*.14; also περισσά Pi.*N*.7.43, E.*Hec*.579, etc. 2. *remarkably*, περισσότερον τῶν ἄλλων θάψαι τινά *more sumptuously*, Hdt.2. 129; οἴκησις π. ἐσκευασμένη Plb.1.29.7; περιττότατα ἔχειν to be *most remarkable*, Arist.*HA*589ᵃ31; κοσμουμένη π. καὶ σεμνῶς Plu.2.145e; περισσότατα ἀνθρώπων θρησκεύειν *in the most singular way*, D.C.37.17; ἡδέως καὶ π. *in an uncommon manner*, D.H.*Comp*.3; εἰπεῖν στρογγύλως καὶ π. Id.*Is*.20; ἰδίως καὶ π. Plu.*Thes*.19; τὰ καινῶς ἱστορούμενα καὶ π. Id.2.30d. 3. *abundantly*, ἐχέτω π. τῆς κρόκης Alciphr.3. 41. 4. with a neg., οὐδὲν περισσὸν τούτων nothing *more than* or *beyond* these, Antipho 3.4.6; οὐδὲν τῶν ἄλλων περιττότερον πραγματεύεσθαι Pl.*Ap*.20c; οὐδὲν π. ἢ εἰ.. no *otherwise* than if.., Id.*Smp*. 219c; περισσόν alone, *furthermore*, Lxx *Ec*.12.12, al. 5. τὰ περισσά *in vain*, *AP*12.182 (Strat.). II. ἐκ περιττοῦ *superfluously, uselessly*, Pl.*Prt*.338c, *Sph*.265e; but ὑπερέχειν ἐκ π. to be *far* superior, Id.*Lg*.734d, cf. 802d; ἡ κάμινος ἐκαύθη ἐκ π. Thd.*Da*.3.22; ἐκ π. χρησάμενος τῇ παρρησίᾳ Luc.*Pro Merc.Cond*.13; cf. ὑπερεκπερισσοῦ.

**περισσό-σαρκος**, ον, *over-fleshy*, Suid. s. v. Πρίαπος. **-συλλαβέω**, *to have one syllable more than*, τινος or τινι, *EM*35.41, 131.57: abs., A.D.*Pron*.28.11, etc. **-σύλλαβος**, ον, *with a syllable more*, γενική Id.*Adv*.166.26, St.Byz. s. v. Φλεγύα. Adv. -βως Id. s. v. Ἄβαι, Sch. E.*Or*.18, etc. **-τᾰγής**, ές, (τάσσω) *put in a series of uneven numbers*, opp. ἀρτιοταγής, Nicom.*Ar*.1.22. **-τεχνία**, ἡ, *over-exactness in art*, Demetr.*Eloc*.247. **-της**, Att. περιττ-, ητος, ἡ, (περισσός) *extravagance, excess*, in pl., Isoc.10.7; π. μιαιφονιῶν D.C.77.16; *pomp*, ἡ ἐν τοῖς βίοις π. καὶ πολυτέλεια Plb.9.10.5. 2. in style, *redundancy*, Hermog.*Meth*.5. 3. ἐκ περισσότητος [κατηγορεῖν], *ex abundanti*, Aps.*Rh*.p.223 H. II. *eminence, excellence*, D.S.1.94; ἡ κατὰ τὴν τέχνην π. Id.18.26. III. of numbers, *unevenness*, opp. ἀρτιότης, Arist.*Metaph*.1004ᵇ11. **-τρύφητος** [ῠ], ον, *over-luxurious*, ὀϊζύς Timo 3.3 (nisi leg. πᾶσ' ἀπερισσοτρύφητος). **-φρονέω**, gloss on περιφρονέω, Hsch. (περισωφρονέω cod.). **-φρων**, ὁ, ἡ, gen. φρονος, = περισσόνοος, *over-wise*, A.*Pr*.330. 2. in good sense, *extremely clever*, Vett.Val.17.22. **-χορηγία**, ἡ, *extra largess* of corn, *Cod.Theod*.14.26.2. **-χρονος**, ον, corrupt in Thphr.*CP*1.18.3 (leg. παρισόχρονα).

**περίσσ-ωμα**, Att. περίττ-, ατος, τό, *that which is over and above*, esp. *that which remains after the digestion of food*, either as *a secretion* or *an excretion*, defined as τὸ τῆς τροφῆς ὑπόλειμμα, Arist.*GA*724ᵇ26, cf. Epicur.*Fr.*293, Meno *Iatr.*4.35, Diocl.*Fr.*141, Plu.2.130a, etc.; ταῦτα δὲ [τὰ π.] ἐστὶ κόπρος, φλέγμα, χολή Arist.*HA*511$^b$9; also of hair and nails, Jul.*Or.*6.189b. 2. metaph., *refuse, dregs*, ὥσπερ π. τῆς πόλεως Plu.*Cor.*12. -ωματικός, Att. περιττ-, ή, όν, *of the nature of* περιττώματα, *excretive, excrementitious*, ἀπόκρισις Arist.*PA* 681$^b$36; ὑγρότης Plu.2.130b; π. [μόριον] *for excretion*, Arist.*HA*531$^a$29, etc. 2. of persons, *abounding in* περιττώματα, ib.584$^a$6, *Pr.* 873$^a$18; σώματα Id.*GA*766$^b$35 (Comp.); βρέφη Alex.Aphr.*Pr.*1.2; π. καὶ παχὺς τὴν σάρκα, of a pig, Jul.*Or.*5.177c. -ωνῠμέω, of numbers, *to be odd*, Iamb.*in Nic.*p.22 P.:—Adj. -ώνῠμος, *odd*, ib. p.84 P. -ωσις, Att. περίττ-, εως, ἡ, *superfluity*, Hp.*Epid.*6.5.10. 2. = περίσσωμα, Arist.*HA*489$^a$7, *GA*717$^b$6, al., Thphr.*Sud.* 20.

* **περιστᾰδόν**, Adv. *standing round about*, Il.13.551, Hdt.7.225, E. *Andr.*1136, Theoc.2.68, Call.*Hec.*1.1.14, etc. 2. *from all sides*, ἐβάλλοντο π. Th.7.81.

**περιστάζω**, *sprinkle all round*, Alex.Trall.9.1:—Pass., *AP*7.36 (Eryc.).

**περιστάθη**, v. περίστημι.

**περιστάθμια**, τά, dub. sens. in *IG*1$^2$.310.190.

**περιστᾰλάδην**, and -αδόν, v. περιστολάδην.

**περισταλτικός**, ή, όν, (περιστέλλω) *clasping and compressing*, δύναμις π. the *peristaltic* action of the bowels, by which their contents are propelled, Gal.*Nat.Fac.*3.4; also of the bladder, Id.8.404; ἡ π. ἐνέργεια Id.*Nat.Fac.*3.8; ἡ π. κίνησις Id.*UP*4.9. Adv. -κῶς Id.*Nat.Fac.* 3.4.

**περι-στάσιμος** [ᾰ], ον, *filled with people standing round, crowded with hearers*, στοά Lyr.ap.Timae.80 (Cerc.(?)10). * -στάσις, εως, ἡ, *standing round*, τίς ἥδε κραυγὴ καὶ δόμων π.; *crowds standing round* the house, Telecl.35; π. ποιεῖσθαι, of crowds, Thphr.*Char.*8. 12(pl.); ὄχλοιο π. Timo 34.1: hence, in concrete sense, *crowd standing round*, Plb.1.32.3, 18.53.11. 2. *surrounding*, ἡ τοῦ ψυχροῦ π. Arist.*Pr.*869$^a$21: in concrete sense, *environment*, π. ἀέρος ψυχροῦ Epicur.*Ep.*2p.50 U., cf. p.48 U.; *surrounding space*, Plb.6.31.1, 6.41.2; esp. *free space round* a building, *OGI*483.123, al. (Pergam., ii A.D.), *IG*14.352i 8,70 (Halaesa). b. *portico surrounding* a hall or temple, ib.4$^2$(1).102.6 (Epid., iv B.C.), Callix.1; ἡ ἔξω π. τοῦ σηκοῦ *IG*7.3073.90 (Lebad.). c. *district surrounding* a village, *neighbourhood*, *PTeb.*14.19 (ii B.C.), al. II. *circumstances, situation, state of affairs*, Plb.1.35.10, 4.67.4, etc.; αἱ π. [τῶν πόλεων] Id.10.21.3; τὸ παράδοξον τῆς π. Posidon.36 J.; π. *nostra, the position of my affairs*, Cic.*Att.*4.8b.2; *the actuality*, μείζων τῆς π. ἡ φαντασίη Aret.*SD*2.9; τὰ κατὰ περίστασιν καθήκοντα duties dependent on *circumstances*, *Stoic.*3.135, al., cf. Cic.*Att.*16.11.4, Phld.*Rh.*1.219 S. (pl.): sg. of a particular *circumstance*, Ael.*Tact.*35.1, A.D.*Synt.*145.4, etc.; κατά τινα π. γραμμάτων Gal.11.242. b. esp. *difficult position, crisis* (both senses distd. in Arr.*Epict.*2.6.17, M.Ant.9.13); δὸς π. καὶ λάβε τὸν ἄνδρα *Stoic.*3.49; κατὰ τὰς π. in *critical times*, Plb.1.82.7, cf. 4.33.12, etc.; διὰ τὰς τῶν καιρῶν π. *SIG*731.2 (Tomi, i B.C.); εἰς πᾶν ἐλθεῖν περιστάσεως Plb.4.45.10, cf. 1.84.9, etc.; χαλεπὴ π. Lxx 2*Ma.*4.16, cf. Dsc.*Alex.Praef.*; μετὰ τὴν κατασχοῦσαν τὴν πόλιν π. *SIG*708.7 (Istropolis, ii B.C.), cf. *IG*2$^2$.1338.27, Orph.*Fr.*285.63; ἐν π. ἰσχυρᾷ τῶν ἔξωθεν Porph.*Abst.*1.55. 2. Rhet., *circumstances* of the case treated by a speaker, Quint. *Inst.*3.5.18, 5.10.104, Corn.*Rh.*p.362 H.; classified by Hermog.*Inv.* 3.5. 3. *outward pomp and circumstance*, ἡ τοῦ βίου π. Plb.3.98.2, cf. 31.26.3; τρυφὴ καὶ π. Antig.Car.ap.Ath.12.547f; ὑπάρχων ἐν μεγάλῃ π. Phld.*Acad.Ind.*p.101 M. 4. in Meteorology, of climatic *conditions*, ἡ κατὰ τὸν ἀέρα π. Plb.3.84.2; λοιμικαὶ π. pestilential *conditions*, Id.6.5.5, cf. *SIG*731.7 (Tomi, i B.C.); καυματώδης π. D.S.4.22. b. Astron., *position* of the heavenly bodies, ἐκλειπτικὴ π. Sch.Arat. 862. III. *veering round*, of winds, Arist.*Mete.*364$^b$14, *Pr.*942$^b$27. 2. *cycle*, ἡ τοῦ μεγάλου ἐνιαυτοῦ π. Eudem.ap.Theon.Sm. p.198 H. 3. *direction* of motion, αἱ ἓξ π., i.e. up, down, forwards, backwards, right, left, Nicom.*Ar.*2.6,16. 4. *materials* for use, *PFlor.*369.2 (ii A.D.). -στᾰτέον, *one must avoid*, τι Philonid.ap. Ath.15.675e. -στατήρια· σπλάγχνα, Hsch. -στᾰτικός, ή, όν, *of* or *in critical circumstances*, τὰ π. πράγματα, = περιστάσεις, *critical circumstances*, Plu.2.169c, cf. Heliod.*in EN*103.17; π. ἐνοχλήσεις Alex.Aphr.*in Top.*255.26. 2. *dependent on circumstances*, καθήκοντα *Stoic.*3.135; ἐνέργειαι Plot.1.4.13; *precarious*, διαγωγὴ τοῦ βίου Max.Tyr.36.4. Adv. -κῶς *according to circumstances*, ἐνεργεῖν Plot.1.2.7. 3. *circumstantial, accidental, extraneous*, κακά Hierocl. *in CA*11 p.439 M. 4. Rhet., *concerned with the circumstances* of a case, προοίμια Corn.*Rh.*p.354 H.; μόρια Men.Rh.p.366 S.; τὰ ὑποκείμενα τῷ διαλόγῳ π. Procl.*in Prm.*p.482 S. 5. *full of business*, βίος Gal.6.403 (cj.), 15.177. -στᾰτος, ον, *surrounded and admired by the crowd*, Eup.176, Iamb.*VP*7.35; π. ὑπὸ πάντων Isoc.6.95, cf. 15.269. 2. περιστατόν· τὸ ἀνάστατον, Hsch. II. Act., *standing round and wondering, agape*, π. τὴν κώμην ποιεῖ Theopomp. Com.41.

**περισταυρ-όω**, *fence about with, palisade*, τινὰς δένδρεσιν Th.2.75:—Pass., αἱ οἰκίαι κύκλῳ περιεσταύρωντο X.*An.*7.4.14:—Med., περισταυρωσάμενοι *having entrenched themselves*, Id.*HG*3.2.2. -ωμα, ατος, τό, *entrenchment*, D.H.5.42, 8.67 (pl.).

* **περιστᾰχυώδης**, ες, *with an ear* or *spike* (as of corn) *growing round* or *on it*, μίσχοι Thphr.*HP*4.12.2.

**περιστεγᾰνός**, όν, *covered all round, well covered*, Hsch.

**περιστεγνόω**, *solder* a pipe *all round*, Hero *Spir.*2.23 (Pass.).

**περιστέγω**, *retain* heat, etc. *by covering*, Hp.*Acut.*21, Thphr.*Ign.* 19; *contain* a fluid, Gal.15.709:—Pass., Arist.*Pr.*900$^a$1, Thphr.*CP* 1.19.2.

**περιστείνω**, Ep. for περιστένω (A).

**περιστείχω**, *go round about*, c. acc., τρὶς δὲ περίστειξας κοῖλον λόχον Od.4.277, cf. *AP*5.138 (Mel.): abs., περιστείχοντος ἀλείσου Call.*Aet.* 1.1.13, dub. in Alc.Com.35.

* **περιστέλλω**, fut. -στελῶ S.*Aj.*1170:—*dress, clothe, wrap up*, θνατὰ π. μέλη Pi.*N.*11.15; σαρκῶν π. χιτῶνι Emp.126; τινα Thphr.*Char.* 2.10; τοὺς πόδας Arist.*Pr.*868$^b$38; κεφαλὴν τοῖς κόλποις Plb.21.38.5; χλαμυδίῳ π. ἑαυτόν Plu.*Pyrrh.*11; ἔπηξα δ' αὐτὸν εὖ περιστείλας I planted the sword *wrapping* it well *with earth*, i.e. planted it *firmly*, S.*Aj.*821:—Med., *wrap oneself up*, Hp.*Epid.*3.17.ιε':—Pass., *to be wrapped up*, περιεσταλμένον ἀναπαύεσθαι Arist.*Pr.*866$^a$25. b. Rhet., *employ compression*, δεῖ π. καὶ μὴ περιουσιάζειν Corn.*Rh.*p.396 H. c. *cut down, retrench*:—hence in Pass., *to be dispensed with*, περιέσταλται ἡμῖν πᾶν τὸ τῆς δέσεως τῶν περιτρήτων Ph.*Bel.*62.28. 2. *lay out* a corpse, Od.24.293, Hdt.2.90, 6.30, S.*Ant.*903, E.*Or.*1066, Men.325.12, etc. (also τάφον π. S.*Aj.*1170); simply, *bury*, Pl.*Hp.Ma.*291e, *AP* 7.613 (Diog. Episc.), etc. II. Medic., in Pass., *to be contracted round*, κοιλίης περιστελλομένης ἀμφὶ τὸ ἔμβρυον Hp.*Mul.*1.34; [ἡ γαστὴρ] περισταλεῖσα τοῖς ἐνυπάρχουσι Gal.*UP*4.7; τοῖς σιτίοις Id.7.67, cf. 8. 440. III. metaph., *wrap up, cloak, cover*, τἄδικ' εὖ π. E.*Med.*582; τὰ ἁμαρτήματα, τὴν ἀμαθίαν, etc., Plb.30.4.14, Plu.2.47d, etc.; αἰσχρορρημοσύνην Phld.*Rh.*1.175 S. b. ἐμαυτὸν περιστέλλων *putting on a grave countenance*, Aen.Gaz.*Ep.*12. c. c. dupl. acc., *conceal* something *from*, τινά τι Phld.*Lib.*p.20 O. 2. *protect, defend*, ἀλλήλους Hdt.9.60; πόλισμα Id.1.98; π. τοὺς νόμους *maintain* the laws, Id.2.147, cf. 3.31; τὸ τοιοῦτο (sc. monarchy) ib.82; τὸ μὴ ἄναρχον A. *Eu.*697; εὖ π. αὐτὰ δαίμονες S.*Ph.*447; τὰ πάτρια D.24.139; [τὸν Ἐπίκουρον] Phld.*Mort.*27:—Pass., περισταλεὶς ὑπὸ τῆς τῶν Ἀχαιῶν πρᾳότητος Plb.2.60.4. 3. *attend to, cherish*, ἀοιδάν Pi.*I.*1.33; ἔργα Theoc.17.97; ταῦτα κοσμεῖν καὶ περιστέλλειν D.36.47. 4. Med., τὰ σὰ περιστέλλου κακά *attend to your own* ills, E.*HF*1129. 5. Med., *withdraw from society*, Archig.ap.Aët.13.120.

**περιστεμματόω**, = περιστέφω, *IG*5(1).1390.35 (Andania, i B.C.).

**περιστενάζω**, *lament round*:—Pass., οἰκουμένη -στεναζομένη *filled with lamentation*, Plu.*Ant.*56.

**περιστενᾰχέω**, *resound all around*, γαῖα περιστενάχησε Hes.*Sc.*344 (v.l. -στονάχιζε).

**περιστενᾰχίζομαι**, Med., = foreg., *resound all round* or *re-echo with..*, μέγα δῶμα περιστεναχίζετο ποσσὶν ἀνδρῶν παιζόντων Od.23.146, cf. 10.454 (tm.); κνισῆεν δέ τε δῶμα περιστεναχίζεται ib.10:—later in Act., Q.S.12.415.

**περιστενάχω** [ᾰ], = περιστενάζω, Q.S.9.49:—Med., Id.3.591.

**περιστενοχωρέομαι**, Pass., *to be confined within a narrow compass*, Apollon.*Lex.* s.v. στείνοντο.

**περιστένω** (A), Ep. -στείνω, (στενός) *make narrow, compress, contract*, περιστένεται δέ τε γαστήρ, of wolves, Il.16.163; νεκύεσσι περιστείνοντο ῥέεθρα Q.S.3.23, cf. 14.607, Opp.*H.*4.458.

**περιστένω** (B), *moan about* or *over*: generally, *sound round about*, κορυφὴν π. οὔρεος ἠχώ *h.Pan.*21: abs., Dionys.Iamb.ap.Clem.Al. *Strom.*5.8.47:—Med., περιστένεται δέ οἱ ὕδωρ Opp.*H.*5.209.

**περίστεπτος**, ον, *crowned, wreathed*, ταινίαις Emp.112.6.

**περιστερ-ά**, ἡ, *common pigeon* or *dove*, Hdt.1.138, S.*Fr.*866, Democr.164, etc.; specifically, *Columba livia domestica*, and so distd. from φάψ, φάττα, οἰνάς, τρυγών, Arist.*HA*562$^b$5, 593$^a$16; ἐλάττων μὲν ἡ πελειάς, τιθασὸν δὲ γίνεται μᾶλλον ἡ π. ib.544$^b$3: περιστερός, ὁ, *cock-pigeon*, Pherecr.33 (of a carrier-*pigeon*), Alex.214; censured by Luc.*Sol.*7. -εών, ῶνος, ὁ, *dovecole*, Pl.*Tht.*197c,d, 198b, *POxy.*1127.8 (ii A.D.), etc. II. = περιστέριον II, Ps.-Dsc.4.59, prob. (for ἀριστερεών) in Plu.2.614b; π. ὕπτιος *holy vervain*, *Verbena supina*, Ps.-Dsc.4.60. -ῐδεύς, έως, ὁ, *young pigeon*, *PCair.Zen.* 354.5 (iii B.C.), etc. (misspelt περιστρ- *PGrenf.*2.14(*b*)4 (iii B.C.)), Sch.Ar.*Ach.*866, Eust.753.56. -ίδιον, τό, Dim. of περιστερά, *PGoodsp.Cair.*30v20, al. (ii A.D.), *PLips.*97 xxvi9 (iv A.D.), f.l. in Lxx *Le.*1.14, interpol. in Ath.14.654a. * -ιον, τό, = foreg., Pherecr. 135, Phryn.Com.51, *BGU*1095.16 (i A.D.), etc. II. *vervain*, *Verbena officinalis*, Dsc.4.59. -ίς, ίδος, ἡ, = foreg. I, *BGU*594.9 (i A.D.), Aq.*Ge.*15.9, v.l. in Gal.6.708. II. a woman's ornament, *Com.Adesp.*1115.

**περιστερν-ίδιον**, v. περιστέρνιον. -ίζω, *put round the breast*, Aristaenet.1.25 (Med.). -ιον, glossed by περιστερνίδιον (prob. a *breast-band*), Phot.

**περιστερο-ειδής**, ές, *of the pigeon kind*, Arist.*HA* 562$^b$3, 593$^a$24. -εις, εσσα, εν, *of the verbena*, πέτηλα Nic.*Th.*860. -ποιός, *columbarius*, *Gloss.* -πώλης, ου, ὁ, *pigeon-dealer*, *BGU*1258.10 (ii B.C.).

**περιστερός**, ὁ, v. περιστερά.

**περιστεροτροφ-εῖον**, τό, *place where doves are reared*, Varro *RR* 3.7. -ος (parox.), ὁ, *pigeon-keeper*, *PCair.Zen.*498.2 (iii B.C.).

**περιστερ-ώδης**, ες, = περιστεροειδής, Arist.*GA*749$^b$18, 750$^a$15. -ών, ῶνος, ὁ, = περιστερεών I, *PPetr.*3 p.195 (iii B.C.), *PGrenf.*1.21.11 (ii B.C.), etc.

**περιστεφ-ᾰνίς**, ίδος, ἡ, *coronary vein* of the hoof, *Hippiatr.*117. -ᾰνόω, = περιστέφω, *encircle*, ἐμὲ ποῖος οὐκ ὄχλος π. Ar.*Pl.*787, cf. *IG Rom.*4.1725 (Samos, tm.); φλὲψ -στεφανοῦσα τὴν καρδίαν *coronary* vein, Gal.*UP*6.14:—Pass., πῖλοι πτεροῖσι περιεστεφανωμένοι Hdt.7.92; ὄρεσι περιεστεφάνωται πᾶσα Θεσσαλίη ib.130. II. *put round in a circle*, τὸν ὄχλον D.H.3.30; τὸν χάρακα Id.8.66:—Pass., νῆσοι κύκλῳ περιεστεφάνωνται τὴν οἰκουμένην Arist.*Mu.*393$^b$17, cf. Ph.2.

324. **-ής**, ές, *wreathed, crowned*, ἀνθέων π. *with a crown* of flowers, S.*El*.895. II. Act., *twining, encircling*, κισσός E.*Ph*.651 (lyr.). **-ω**, *enwreathe, surround*, νεφέεσσι περιστέφει οὐρανὸν εὐρὺν Ζεύς Od.5.303; τὴν νησῖδα τοῖς ὅπλοις Plu.*Arist*.9; κύκλῳ τὰ τείχη Id.2.245e; Παρνησὸν π. ἐννέα κύκλοις, of the serpent Pytho, Call.*Del*.93:—Pass., Orph.*Fr*.186: metaph., ὁ παῖς ἀρετῇ περιστέφεται Aphth.*Prog*.3.

**περιστήθιον**, τό, *breastband*, Lxx *Ex*.28.4, Ph.1.653, 2.226.

**περιστηλόομαι**, *to be set up as* στῆλαι *round about*, οἱ περιεστηλωμένοι ὅροι *Jahrb.Ergänzungsheft* 10.64 (Nysa, i B.C.).

**περιστηρίζω**, *adhere firmly all round*, Hp.*Morb*.4.51.

❀ **περίστια**, τά, *sacrifice of a pig* at the lustration of the popular assembly at Athens, or *the lustration* itself, Ister 32, Sch.Ar.*Ec*.128:—hence **περιστίαρχος**, ὁ, *one who offers the* περίστια, Ar. l.c., Ister l.c.

❀ **περιστιγής**, ές, *spotted all over, variegated*, ἕρφος Nic.*Th*.376 (v.l. **-στιβής**, *trodden all round, compact*).

**περιστίζω**, *prick* or *dot all round*, περιέστιξε [τοῖσι μαζοῖσι] τὸ τεῖχος she *stuck* the wall *all round* with the breasts, Hdt.4.202; περιστίξαντες (v.l. περιστήσαντες, πέριξ στήσαντες Dobree) κατὰ τὰ ἀγγήϊα τοὺς τυφλούς *having set* them *at equal distances round*.., ib.2 (expld. by Hsch. ἀπὸ τοῦ στίχειν). II. Gramm., *mark with dots*, τὸ λ Gal. 16.800; τὸ ι καὶ τὸ υ *EM*169.37, cf. 462.39 (Pass.): pf. part. Pass. περιεστιγμένος, η, ον, *marked with dots*, διπλῆ Sch.Il.p.xliii Dind., etc.; ὀβελός, etc., D.L.3.66.

**περίστικτος**, ον, *dappled*, φολίδεσσι Nic.*Th*.464: metaph., λωβητοῖσι π. μελέεσσι *branded with*.., Tryph.227.

**περιστίλβω**, *glitter all round*, D.S.3.45, Plu.2.693d; π. τι Eun.*VS* p.459 B.

**περιστῐχ-άω**, *stand round in rows*, Nic.*Th*.442, Nonn.*D*.26.223. **-ες** (parox.), οἱ, αἱ, *placed round in a row*, v.l. for περὶ στίχες, ib.2.170. **-ίζω**, = περιστοιχίζω, A.*Ag*.1383.

**περιστλεγγίζω**, *scrape all round with a* στλεγγίς, Hsch.

**περιστόϊον**, v. περίστῳον.

❀ **περιστοιχ-έω**, = sq., *comprehend within limits*, Men.Rh.p.348 S. (Pass.); f.l. for sq. in D.C.60.30 (Pass.). ❀ **-ίζω**, *surround as with toils* or *nets*, of a besieging army, interpol. in Plb.8.5.2, etc.; dub. in Sm.*Ps*.47(48).13, Quint.*Ho*.8.13: metaph., J.*AJ*17.2.4:—Med. (fut. -ιοῦμαι D.C.50.31), κύκλῳ πανταχῇ μέλλοντας ἡμᾶς καὶ καθημένους περιστοιχίζεται D.4.9, cf. D.C.39.3:—Pass., ὑπό τινων Id.49.30, al., Aristaenet.1.9; ψυχὴ π. ὑπὸ πονηρῶν πνευμάτων Ph.*Fr*.104 H.; κλύδωνι φροντισμάτων Hld.7.4, cf. Pall.*in Hp*.2.112 D. **-ος**, ον, *set round in rows*, D.53.15.

**περιστολ-άδην**, Adv. *surrounding*, Nic.*Al*.475 codd.; prob. -σταλάδην, *by drops*, cf. Sch.ad loc., and **περισταλαδόν**· περισταζόμενον, περιρρεόμενον τῷ χόλῳ, Hsch. ❀ **-ή**, ἡ, *wrapping up*, περιστολῇ καὶ κατακλίσει συνθάλπειν Plu.2.652e. b. *laying out*, of a corpse, D.H.3.21, *BGU*896.7 (ii A.D.). 2. Medic., *peristaltic action* of internal organs, Gal.8.440; γαστέρος Id.7.219; φλεβῶν Id.*Nat.Fac*.2.1. 3. *adornments*, Lxx *Ex*.33.6: metaph., π. δόξης ib.*Si*.45.7. II. metaph., *restraint, decorum*, ὅσα παίζεται μετὰ περιστολῆς Aristeas 284. 2. ἐν π. *secretly*, *Psalm.Solom*.13.7. **-ίζομαι**, Med., *wrap oneself up*, Suid. s.v. ἐπαναβάλεσθε:—Pass., Dsc.*Eup*.2.115.

**περιστόμ-ιος**, ον, *round a mouth* or *aperture*, Opp.*H*.3.603. II. Subst. **περιστόμιον**, τό, *mouth of a vessel*, πίθου Plb.21.28.12. 2. *mouth-band*, φορβειᾷ καὶ περιστομίοις Plu.2.456b. 3. *region of the epiglottis*, Hsch. 4. *collar* of a garment, Lxx *Jb*.30.18. 5. *edge* of a ravine, ib.*Ez*.39.11. **-ίς**, ίδος, ἡ, wooden *gauge* or *spanner* for testing thickness of τόνοι, Ph.*Bel*.54.46, Hero *Bel*.108.8. 2. iron *clamp*, Apollod.*Poliorc*.155.11. 3. π. φρέατος, *puteal*, *Gloss*. **-ος**, ον, *presenting a front all round*, τετράπλευρον Ascl.*Tact*.11.6.

**περιστονᾰχέω**, *bemoan*, υἷα περιστονάχησε πεσόντα Q.S.3.397. II. *groan all around*, γαῖα περιστονάχησε cj. in Hes.*Sc*.344; cf. περιστεναχίζω.

**περιστορέννῡμι**, aor. inf. Med. περιστορέσασθαι, Pass. περιστρωθῆναι, *spread all round* or *over*, Orph.*A*.1335 (tm.), Nonn.*D*.18.81, etc.; cf. περιστρώννυμι.

**περιστρᾰτοπεδεύω**, *encamp about, invest, besiege*, Lycurg.128, Plb.1.30.5, 2.2.7, D.H.6.29, Plu.*Fab*.22:—used by X. in Med., abs., *HG*3.1.7, *Cyr*.3.1.6, al.:—Pass., *HG*4.7.1.

**περί-στρεμμα**, ατος, τό, = διάστρεμμα, Gal.18(2).888. **-στρέφω**, *whirl round*, of one preparing to throw, ἔρριψεν.. χειρὶ περιστρέψας Il.19.131; τόν ῥα περιστρέψας ἧκε Od.8.189; *turn round*, π. τὸν τράχηλον εἰς τοὐπίσω Arist.*HA*504$^a$16; θέαμα πρὸς αὐγὴν Gal.*UP*17.1; π. ἵππον *wheel* it *round*, Plu.*Marc*.6; ὁ ἥλιος κύκλον ἄγει καὶ π. περὶ τὴν σελήνην Id.2.931a:—Pass., *to be turned* or *turn round, spin round*, Pl.*Cra*.411b; περιστρεφόμενος.. θαμὰ ἐπεσκοπεῖτο *turning round*, Id.*Ly*.207a; of the heavens, *complete a rotation*, Arist.*Cael*.273$^a$2: metaph., π. εἰς τἀληθῆ *turn* towards them, Pl.*R*.519b; κινδυνεύει εἰς τοὺς πολιτικοὺς περιεστράφθαι τὸ ῥῆμα *to be fixed on*.., Id.*Plt*.303c; οὐ -στραφήσεται κλῆρος *shall* not *be removed* from tribe to tribe, Lxx *Nu*.36.9. 2. π. τὼ χεῖρε *tie* his hands *behind* him, Lys.1.27:—Pass., *to be twisted*, of an intestine, Gal.8.388. 3. *attract* a person's *attention*, π. τὸν θεατὴν Lib.*Or*.11.236; *convert* a person, *Cat.Cod.Astr*.2.180.

**περιστροβέω**, *cause to revolve*, κύλινδρον Herm.ap.Stob.1.49.44.

**περιστρόγγῠλος**, ον, *perfectly round*, Ath.Mech.38.11.

**περιστροφ-άδην** [ᾰ], Adv. = περιφοράδην, π. ὁδοιπορέειν ὡς βόες Hp.*Mochl*.20. 2. *spinning round*, Opp.*H*.5.146. **-έω**, v. περιστρωφάω. **-ή**, ἡ, *turning* or *spinning round*, ὀστράκου Pl.*R*.521c; ἄστρων περιστροφαί *courses* of the stars, S.*Fr*.432.8; κόσμου Euc.*Phaen*.p.8 M.; τοῦ ἡλίου Hld.1.18, etc.; ἐν περιστροφῇ λαοῦ *amidst* them, Lxx *Si*.50.5: pl., *contortions*, Gal.15.126; *whorls* in hair-growth, δύο π. ἕξει ἐν τῇ κεφαλῇ Heph.Astr.1.1. **-ίδιον**, τό, name of a garment, π. ἀνδρεῖον dub. in *BCH*29.432 (Delos). ❀ **-ίς**, ίδος, ἡ, *wooden implement that is turned round, strickle*, Poll.4.170, 10.113. 2. *handle for turning a fuller's press*, ib.135. **-ος**, ον, *turning round*: *turning in a socket*, κοτύλαι Aret.*SD*2.12. II. Subst., *twisted rope*, f.l. for περιδρόμους in X.*Cyn*.2.6. III. περίστροφος· ὁ τῆς ὑποσφραγῖδος τόπος, Hsch.

❀ **περίστρωμα**, ατος, τό, *covering of a bed*, *PCair.Zen*.60.9 (iii B.C.), D.S.13.84, Lycon ap.D.L.5.73; *counterpane*, opp. στρώματα, Ath.2.48c (pl.). 2. in pl., *carpets and hangings* of rooms, Philist.28, Callix.2, Simyl.1.

**περιστρώννῡμι**, aor. -έστρωσα, = περιστορέννυμι, [δίφρους] ἱματίοις Duris 49 J., cf. Aq., Thd.*Pr*.7.16.

**περιστρωφάω**, *ply hither and thither*, μενοινήν Nonn.*D*.41.264. II. intr., *turn hither and thither*, prob. (for -στροφέοντες) in Q.S.6.504. III. Med., περιστρωφώμενος πάντα τὰ χρηστήρια *going round* to all the oracles, Hdt.8.135; περιστρωφῶντο δ' ὀπωπαί Q.S.12.404.

**περιστύλ-ιον** [ῠ], τό, Dim. of περίστυλον, *IG*11(2).199 *A*108 (Delos, iii B.C.). ❀ **-ος**, ον, *surrounded with a colonnade*, αὐλή Hdt.2.148, 153, Muson.*Fr*.19 p.108 H., Aphth.*Prog*.12; δόμοι E.*Andr*.1099; σῦριγξ Callix.2; ναὸς στοαῖς..περίστυλος Paus.6.25.1. II. Subst. **περίστῡλον**, τό, *peristyle, colonnade round a temple* or *round the court of a house*, Lxx *Ez*.42.3 (pl.), D.S.18.26, *IG*5(2).268.50 (Mantinea, i B.C.), J.*BJ*1.21.11 (pl.); also, *area surrounded by a colonnade*, Lxx 3*Ma*.5.23, al.:—so **περίστῡλος**, ὁ, D.S.1.48: gender indeterminate in *IG*4$^2$(1).109 ii 132, al. (Epid., pl.), Callix.2, Plb.10.27.10 (pl.), 15.25$^A$.3, D.S.1.47, Plu.*Arat*.26, 2.586b.

**περιστῠφελίζομαι**, Med., *beat, dash all round*, κρᾶθ' ἑκατὸν πέτρῃσι Opp.*H*.3.23.

**περιστύφω** [ῡ], *dry up by astringents*, τὸ δάκρυον Plu.2.659d.

❀ **περίστῳον**, τό, later Gr. for περίστυλον, *BCH*54.97 (Delos, ii B.C.), D.S.5.40, Hierocl.p.54 A., J.*BJ*5.4.4, 5.5.8, D.C.44.16, 54.23.—In codd. freq. spelt περίστοον (περιστόϊον *IG*11(2).165.21, 49 (Delos, iii B.C.)), but cf. *EM*665.1.

**περισυγ-καταλαμβάνομαι**, Pass., *to be included*, τοὺς ἑτέρους ἤχους π. ὑπὸ τῶν ἑτέρων Arist.*Aud*.803$^b$41. **-χωρέω**, = συγχωρέω, dub. in Mitteis *Chr*.31 i 24 (ii B.C.).

**περισῡλάω**, *strip off all round*, τὸ ἱμάτιον Ph.1.637. II. *strip, plunder*, ἄγαλμα Ael.*VH*1.20; *strip of* one's property, Id.*Fr*.48; ἀποκτείνει αὐτοὺς καὶ π. ὅσα ἐπηγάγοντο ib.167:—Pass., περισυλᾶσθαι πᾶσαν τὴν οὐσίαν Pl.*Grg*.486c, cf. Luc.*Philops*.20, *JConf*.8.

**περισυμπλέκω**, in Pass., *to be wound round*, of a screw, dub. in Bito 47.4 (v.l. συμπεπλεγμένος).

**περισυν-άγω**, gloss on ἀθροίζω, Sch.E.*Hec*.1139:—Pass., gloss on ἀμφαγέρονται, Sch.Opp.*H*.3.231; περισυνηγμένων *collected from all round*, gloss on παντοδαπῶν, Sch.Them.*Or*.16.201a. **-ίσταμαι**, *arise about*, Dam.*Pr*.34.

❀ **περίσυνος**, ον, *adjacent*, ὅρια *PFlor*.383.77, 104 (iii A.D.), cf. *PMasp*.128.15 (vi A.D.).

**περισῡρίττω**, *hiss on all sides*, Eust.1816.46:—Pass., ibid., Id.1504.31.

**περί-συρμα**, ατος, τό, (περισύρω I.2) *mockery*, Eust.1816.45. **-συρμός**, ὁ, *drawing* or *whirling round*, Thphr.*Ign*.53. ❀ **-σύρω** [ῡ], *drag about*, ἄνω καὶ κάτω Luc.*Merc.Cond*.30 (Pass.); περισυρέντα τὴν πόλιν *dragged round* the city, J.*BJ*2.12.7. 2. metaph., *satirize, ridicule*, Eust.1816.46 (Act. and Pass.). II. *tear off, pick off*, τὸ χλωρὸν Lxx *Ge*.30.37. 2. *tear away, take by violence from*, τὴν λείαν τινῶν -συρεῖν (fut. inf.) Plb.3.93.1, cf. 4.19.4:—Med., *carry off*, λείαν περιεσύραντο Hyp.*Fr*.264, cf. App.*Hisp*.65: metaph., *destroy*, Ph.1.178:—περισύρεται is f.l. for παρασύρεται in D.P.864.

**περισφᾰλ-άω** or **-έω**, = περισφάλλομαι, *stagger*, Nic.*Al*.542 (part. -σφαλόωντες cod. Π, -σφαλέοντες cett.). ❀ **-εια**, ἡ, *slippery nature*, χωρίων prob. in Herod.8.19. **-ής**, ές, *very slippery*, τόποι Plu.*Alex*.16: metaph., τύχη Id.2.317e.

❀ **περι-σφάλλω**, *cause to slip about*, Apollon.Cit.1:—Pass., *slip about*, Hp.*Art*.6. **-σφαλσις**, εως, Ion. ιος, ἡ, *causing to slip round*, ἐμβολὴ ἐκ π. in reduction of a dislocation, Id.*Mochl*.15, cf. *Art*.25.

**περισφᾰρᾰγέω**, *to be ready to burst*, γάλακτι Nic.*Th*.553.

**περισφᾰτος**, ον, = ἐπιθρήνητος, ἐπονείδιστος, Hsch. Adv. **-τως**, ἔχειν *Trag.Adesp*.333.

**περισφηκόω**, *tie tight all round*, as one does a jar, Dsc.5.18:—Pass., *to be tight bound*, Hp.*Ep*.15, 16.

**περι-σφίγγω**, *bind tightly all round*, βοὸς οὐρᾷ τὸν αὐχένα π. D.S.3.33; κύκλος οὐρανοῦ π. πάντα Ph.1.227; χεῖρα σπατάλῃ *AP*6.74 (Agath.); δεσμῷ.. Ἄρηα περισφίγξας Ἀφροδίτῃ Nonn.*D*.5.585; *apply closely*, of a cupping-instrument, Aret.*CA*1.10:—Pass., Hp.*Oss*.13, J.*AJ*3.7.4; τῷ πυθμένι -σφίγγεται σωλήν Str.16.2.13: abs., *contract, shrink*, Hp.*VC*15; π. τοῖς ἱδρῶσι τοὺς λινοῦς Sor.1.83. 2. metaph., *tighten up, make more stringent*, νόμον Just.*Nov*.46 *Praef*. **-σφιγξις**, εως, ἡ, *tying tight all round, constriction*, Herm.ap.Stob.1.49.69; βρόχων Sor.2.40 (pl.), cf. Pall.*in Hp*.12.284 C.

**περισφρᾱγισμός**, ὁ, *birthmark*, Heph.Astr.1.1 (pl.).

❀ **περισφριγάω**, gloss on περιφλίω, Sch.Nic.*Al*.62.

**περι-σφύριος** [ῠ], ον, *round the ankle*, δράκων *AP*6.207.7 (Arch.). II. Subst. **περισφύριον**, τό, *anklet*, Hdt.4.176, *AP*6.172, S.E.*P*.3.201. **-σφυρίς**, ίδος, ἡ, *ankle-bandage*, Orib.48.67 tit. **-σφῡ-**

ρος, ον, = περισφύριος, πέζα *AP*6.211 (Leon.); τὰ περίσφυρα σκέλη Luc.*Am*.41, shd. prob. be written τὰ περὶ σφυρά (σκέλη being a gloss). II. as Subst. **περίσφῡρον**, τό, = περισφύριον, Gal.19.144.

**περισχαδόν**, applied to an actor taking the part of Perseus as a beggar; also ψίαθον ἐν ᾧ περιειλοῦσι τὰς ἰσχάδας, Hsch. **περισχελές**· δυσχερές, Id. **περισχέμεν, περίσχεο**, v. περιέχω.

**περίσχεσις**, εως, ἡ, *surrounding* or *taking in flank*, D.C.50.31; ἡ π. τῶν βαρβάρων the *surrounding host* of barbarians, Id.60.30, cf. 40.39. II. Astrol., planetary *blockade*, Heph.Astr.1.15.

**περίσχετος**, ον, *surrounded, encompassed*, Opp.*H*.4.146.

**περι-σχῐδής**, ές, *slit all round*, κεφάλιον Dsc.4.119. II. Subst. περισχιδεῖς, αἱ, a kind of *shoe*, Ephipp.Olynth.ap.Ath.12.537e; used by slaves, Phot., cf. Hsch. (neut. sg. -σχιδές Phot.). **-σχίζω**, *slit and tear off*, ἐσθῆτα Plu.*Cic*.36, Luc.*DMeretr*.8.1; κιτῶνα *BGU*22.16 (ii A. D.); *slit open*, Arist.*HA*550ᵃ30:—Pass., π. τῷ μετώπῳ κόμη Poll.2.25. II. Pass., of a river, περισχίζεσθαι τὸν χῶρον *to split round* a piece of land, i.e. *divide into two branches and surround* it, Hdt.9.51; π. περὶ τὸ χωρίον Plb.3.42.7, etc.: abs., of a stream of men, *part and go different ways*, περιεσχίζοντο ἔνθεν καὶ ἔνθεν Pl.*Prt*.315b; of light, αὐγὴ πολλαχοῦ π. Plu.2.407e, cf. Thphr.*Ign*.52; of sound, Sch.Poll.2.116. III. *strip of all his clothes*, τινα Arr.*Epict*.1.25.20. **-σχῐσις**, εως, ἡ, = sq., Olymp.*in Mete*.18.28. **-σχισμός**, ὁ, *division, fission*, σπέρματος *Placit*.5.10.1.

**περισχοιν-ίζω**, *part off by a rope*, τῆς ἀγορᾶς μέρος Poll.8.20; τὸ δικαστήριον ib.141; χωρία τῆς ἀγορᾶς D.H.7.59:—Med., of the Areopagitic Council, *part itself off by a rope*, D.25.23:—Pass., Poll. 8.123. **-ισμα**, ατος, τό, *space marked off by a rope*, Plu.2.847a, App.*Pun*.78, Alciphr.2.3; [τοῦ δικαστηρίου] Poll.8.124. ⊕ **-ισμός**, ὁ, *roping off*, τοῦ περιστύλου *BCH*23.566 (Delph.).

⊕ **περισῴζω**, *save alive* (= σῴζειν τινὰ ὥστε περιεῖναι), *save from death* or *ruin*, X.*HG*2.3.25, etc.; π. τὴν πόλιν ib.6.5.47:—Med., ἑταίραν χρηστὴν σεαυτῷ περιεσώσω Alciphr.1.30:—Pass., *escape with one's life*, of a prisoner, X.*HG*2.3.32, cf. 4.8.21, Phld.*Rh*.1.28 S.; αἰσχρῶς App.*Sam*.4.7; ἐκ μάχης D.C.46.50; of things, *survive*, οἷον λείψανα περισεσῶσθαι Arist.*Metaph*.1074ᵇ13.

**περισωρεύω**, *heap up all round*, ἀγγείῳ χιόνα Arist.*Fr*.216, cf. Aesop.12. II. Pass., *to be heaped up with*, λαφύροις Plu.*Tim*.29; π. ὑπὸ τῶν θυρεῶν *to be buried under* the shields, of Tarpeia, D.H.2.40.

**περιταινία**, f.l. for περιτένεια.

**περιτάμνω**, Ion. and Ep. for περιτέμνω.

**περίτᾰνος**, ὁ, Arc. for εὐνοῦχος, Ptol.Heph.ap.Phot.*Bibl*.p.147 B.

**περιταρχύομαι**, *honour with funeral rites*, νεκρούς Q.S.7.157.

**περίτᾰσις**, εως, ἡ, *extension all round*, Plu.2.1003d. II. *distension*, κοιλίης, τοῦ δέρματος, Hp.*Prorrh*.1.99, *Epid*.4.55; μαστῶν Dsc. 3.34. 2. *tight fit*, Thphr.*CP*4.12.11. 3. *contraction*, νεύρων Androm.ap.Gal.13.1036. (Dub. sens. in Vett.Val.14.2.)

**περιταφρεύω**, *surround with a trench*, τὴν πόλιν, τὸ στρατόπεδον, Plb.1.48.10, Plu.2.191c; λόφον App.*Pun*.72; τὴν ἐπαρχίαν Phleg. 36.18 J.:—Pass., στρατοπεδεύεσθαι ἐν περιτεταφρευμένῳ X.*Cyr*.3.3.28; περιταφρευόμενος ἠνέσχετο Plu.*Mar*.33.

**περιτείνω**, *stretch all round* or *over*, π. τούτοισι (sc. τοῖσι νομεῦσι) διφθέρας Hdt.1.194; ὠμοβοέην π. Id.4.65; περὶ ταῦτα (sc. τὰ ξύλα) πίλους..π. ib.73; ἐπὶ τράπεζαν ὕδατος κύαθον Arist.*Mete*.355ᵇ28:—Pass., δέρμα περιτεταμένον *tight-stretched*, Hp.*Prog*.2, cf. Arist.*HA* 548ᵇ32, al.; νοτίδος περὶ ἀέρα περιταθείσης *being spread round*.., Pl. *Ti*.66b, cf. Arist.*Mete*.354ᵇ24; ἀσπὶς δέρματι περιτεταμένη *covered* with a skin, Id.*Fr*.498; περιτετάσθαι τῷ κελύφει *fit* the pod *tight*, Thphr. *CP*4.12.11; ἡ κοιλία περιτείνεται *is distended*, Arist.*HA*591ᵇ2; οἱ ὄνυχες περιτεταμένοι εἰσὶν *become aduncate*, Hp.*Loc.Hom*.14.

**περιτείρω**, *vex exceedingly*, Orph.*A*.878 (tm.).

**περιτειχ-ίζω**, *wall all round*, πλίνθοις ὥσπερ Βαβυλῶνα Ar.*Av*.552:—Pass., τόπος -τετειχισμένος *BGU*993 iii 1 (ii B. C.), etc. 2. *surround with a wall*, so as to beleaguer, πόλιν κύκλῳ Th.2.78, cf. 4.69; Μυτιλήνην ἐν κύκλῳ ἁπλῷ τείχει Id.3.18; τείχει διπλῷ D.59.102:—Pass., Th.3.68. II. *build round*, in Med., ξύλινον τεῖχος πολίταις Themist.*Ep*.8:—Pass., ὁ περιτετειχισμένος κύκλος X.*HG*5.3.22. III. metaph., *fortify*, θεωρίαν ἐρείσμασι Vett.Val.334.10. **-ισις**, εως, ἡ, *walling round* so as to blockade, *circumvallation*, Th.2.77, 4.131; but also for defence, π. τοῦ ἄστεος Themist.*Ep*.4.3. **-ισμα**, ατος, τό, *wall of circumvallation, blockading wall*, Th.3.25, 5.2, X.*HG*1.3.5. 2. *surrounding wall* of a precinct, *SIG*818.5 (Ephesus, i A. D.). **-ισμός**, ὁ, = περιτείχισις, Th.4.131, 6.88. **-ος**, τό, *surrounding wall*, Lxx 4*Ki*.25.1, al.

**περιτελέθω**, *grow around*, περὶ γλῶχες τελέθουσι Hes.*Sc*.398.

**περιτελέω**, *complete in a circle*, περὶ δ' ἤματα μακρὰ τελέσθη Od.10.470, cf. 19.153 (= Hes.*Th*.59).

**περιτέλλομαι**, Pass., *go* or *come round*, mostly of Time, ἂψ περιτελλομένου ἔτεος as the year *came round*, Od.11.295, cf. *h.Cer*.445; περιτελλομένων ἐνιαυτῶν as years *go round*, Il.2.551, cf. 8.404; π. ὥραις S.*OT*156 (lyr.), cf. Ar.*Av*.696 (anap.); cf. περιπέλομαι. 2. of the sun and stars, *rise above the horizon*, Alc.39, Arat.215, 232. II. Act. in later Poets in signf. I. 1, Orph.*Fr*.247.25; in signf. I. 2, Arat.828.

**περιτέμνω**, Ep. and Ion. -τάμνω, *cut* or *clip round about*, οἴνας περιταμνέμεν *prune* them, Hes.*Op*.570; [τὴν κεφαλὴν] π. κύκλῳ περὶ τὰ ὦτα Hdt.4.64; of a goldsmith, *CPR*22.6 (ii A. D.):—Med., βραχίονας περιτάμνονται *make incisions all over their* arms, Hdt.4.71:—Pass., *to be cut up*, of fish, Arist.*Mir*.835ᵃ19. 2. of circumcision, τῶν ἐπιγινομένων οὐ περιτάμνουσι τὰ αἰδοῖα Hdt.2.104, cf. D.C.79.11; π. τοὺς παῖδας D.S.1.28, cf. Lxx *Jo*.5.2, al., *PCair.Zen*.76.13 (iii B. C.), etc.:—Med., περιτάμνονται τὰ αἰδοῖα Hdt.2.36, 104, cf. D.S.3.32; περιετέμοντο τὴν σάρκα Lxx *Ge*.34.24: abs., *practise circumcision*, Hdt.2.104:—Pass., Lxx *Ge*.17.10, al. 3. *cut off* the extremities, τὰ ὦτα καὶ τὴν ῥῖνα Hdt.2.162; τοὺς μαστούς D.C.62.7; τὰ περιττά Luc. *Anach*.20:—Pass., περιτάμνεσθαι γῆν *to be curtailed of* certain land, Hdt.4.159; πᾶσαν..περιτεμνόμενον σοφίαν E.*Fr*.473 (anap.). II. *cut off and hem in all round*:—Med., βοῦς περιταμνόμενον *cutting off* cattle *for oneself*, '*lifting*' cattle, Od.11.402, 24.112:—Pass., *to be cut off*, ἅρματα π. ὑπὸ τῶν ἱππέων X.*Cyr*.5.4.8.

**περιτέν-εια**, ἡ, *tension* of the skin, Antyll.ap.Orib.10.27.11, Aret. *SD*1.8 (περιταινία is f.l.), Cass.*Pr*.43. II. Archit., *prepared surface, finished section*, *IG*2².1670.17 (iv B. C.), 7.3073.69 (Lebad., ii B. C.). **-ής**, ές, *stretched all round, distended*, Hp.*Art*.46, Paul.Aeg. 5.8; glossed περιτεταμένος by Erot., Greg.Cor.p.556 S.

**περιτεραμνίζω**, *cover all over*, χρυσῷ τὰ χείλη Polem.Hist.63.

**περιτέρμων**, ον, gen. ονος, *bounding all round*, κύκλος Orph.*H*.83.3. II. Pass., *bounded all round*, Ῥώμη ὠκεανῷ π. *AP*9.297 (Antip.).

**περιτεύοντες**· συλῶντες, Hsch. (fort. πειρατεύοντες).

**περιτεχν-άομαι**, *contrive with great cunning*, Anon.ap.Suid. **-ησις**, εως, ἡ, *extraordinary art* or *cunning*, τῶν ἐπιχειρήσεων Th.3.82; σοφία καὶ π. D.C.46.19.

**περί-τηγμα**, ατος, τό, *that which is cast off in smelting, dross, scum*: metaph., ἰσοτιμίας π. ἡ εὐγένεια Chrysipp.*Stoic*.3.85. **-τήκω**, *melt, melt away*, τὸν σίδηρον Hp.*Vict*.1.13; *wash away*, γῆν Pl.*Criti*.112a; τῶν σωμάτων τὰ νοσερά Herod.Med.ap.Orib.10.40.1:—Pass., with pf. -τέτηκα, *melt entirely, melt away*, ἡ χιὼν π. Plu.2.648c; περιτετηγμένον ὀστέων πῆγμα Lxx 4*Ma*.9.21; *become emaciated*, Hp.*Prorrh*.2.6, Aret.*SD*2.13; *to be washed away*, Arist.*Mir*.833ᵇ7. II. τι κασσιτέρῳ π. *cover with a coat* of tin, Pl.*Criti*.116b. **-τηξις**, εως, Ion. ιος, ἡ, *discharge of humour*, as in dropsy, Hp.*Coac*.471.

**περιτῐάρα** [ᾰρ], ας, ἡ, *round cap*, Tz.*H*.8.310:—Dim. **-άριον**, τό, Sch.Tz. in *An.Ox*.3.358.

**περιτίθημι**, *place* or *put round, put on*, περὶ δὲ ξύλα θῆκαν Od. 18.308; δέραισι περθέτω (Aeol.)..ὑποθυμίδας Alc.36; π. κυνέην τινί Hdt.2.162; στεφάνους τινί Id.6.69; πιλίδια περὶ τὴν κεφαλὴν Pl.*R*. 406d; χρυσόν ib.420e; φωνήεσί τε καὶ ἀφώνοις π. γράμματα *attach* letters to.., Id.*Cra*.393e, cf. 414c; π. σφαῖραν Arist.*Cael*.285ᵇ3; σκληρὸν περὶ τὸ σαρκῶδες περιέθηκεν ἡ φύσις Id.*PA*685ᵃ8; δέρματα ἐπὶ τοὺς βραχίονας Lxx *Ge*.27.16; περίβολον τῷ τεμένει *IG*12(9).906.7 (Chalcis, iii A. D.):—Med., *put round oneself, put on*, περὶ δὲ τρυφάλειαν..κρατὶ θέτο Il.19.381; περὶ δὲ ξίφος ὀξὺ θέτ' ὤμῳ Od.2.3, 4.308; περθέμενον χλάμυν (Aeol. for περι-) prob. in Sapph.64; π. στέφανον E.*Med*.984 (lyr.), cf. Ar.*Th*.380, al.; στρεπτόν X.*Cyr*.2.4.6; σκευήν Pl.*Cri*.53d; δακτύλιον Id.*R*.360b; βασιλείαν *OGI*90.44 (Rosetta, ii B. C.); διάδημα αὐτὸς περιεθήκατο App.*Mith*.67. II. metaph., *bestow, confer upon*, π. τινὶ βασιληΐην, κράτος, ἐλευθερίην, Hdt.1.129, 3.81, 142, Simon.100; πόλει τὸ κάλλιστον ὄνομα, τινὶ δόξαν, Th.4.87, Isoc.5.149, etc.; π. τινὶ ὄνειδος, ἀτιμίαν, *put* reproach, dishonour *upon* him, Antipho 5.18, Th.6.89; πίστιν τισί Aeschin.2.103; συμφοράν Antipho 2.3.1; Μηδικὴν ἀρχὴν τοῖς Ἕλλησι *put* the Median yoke *round* their necks, Th.8.43; ὁ πυκτικὸς..οὐ πᾶσι τὴν αὐτὴν μάχην π. *does* not *prescribe*.., Arist.*EN*1180ᵇ11; τῇ Ἀθηνᾷ τὴν τέχνην *ascribe*, Id.*Pol*.1341ᵇ8; [ταῖς πράξεσι] μέγεθος π. καὶ κάλλος Id.*Rh*.1368ᵃ29:—Med., *assume*, ἰσχὺν ἑαυτῷ Democr.252; σχῆμα ἀλλότριον Arr.*Epict*. 2.19.28. 2. reversely, π. τινὰ ὕβρει *envelop* him with.., D.L.6.33.

**περιτίλλω**, *pluck all round, strip*, θρίδακα *strip the outside leaves off* a lettuce, Hdt.3.32; θρίδαξ περιτετιλμένη ibid.: metaph., περιτετιλμένος τὰ πτερὰ *having one's* feathers *all plucked off*, Luc.*Gall*.23. II. *pluck out*, v. παρατίλλω.

**περιτῑμήεις**, εσσα, εν, *much-honoured*, *h.Ap*.65.

⊕ **περιτῑνάσσω**, gloss on δνοπαλίζω, *EM*281.22.

⊕ **Περίτιος**, ὁ, *fourth month* of the Macedonian year, Men.Eph.ap.J. *AJ*8.5.3, *PCair.Zen*.1.3, al. (iii B. C.): **Περίτια**, τά, festival held in this month, Hsch. (περιπέτεια cod.).

**περιτῑταίνω**, *stretch round about*, περὶ μέσσῳ χεῖρε τιτήνας Il.13.534.

**περιτίτραμαι**, Pass., *to be trephined by a circle of perforations*, Heliod.(?) ap.Orib.46.11.34, Leonid.ap.Aët.15.12.

**περιτίω**, *honour very highly*, περὶ μέν σε τίον Il.8.161:—Pass., A.R. 3.74. [ῐ Il., ῑ A.R.]

**περίτμημα**, ατος, τό, *piece cut off, trimming, clipping*, σκυτῶν π. cj. in *IG*1².363.26 (pl.), cf. Hsch. s. v. κόλλεα; πινάκων ἀργυρῶν π. *IG*2². 1436.61 (pl.), cf. M.Ant.8.50: metaph., τῶν λόγων Pl.*Hp.Ma*.304a.

**περιτομ-εύς**, έως, ὁ, *shoemaker's knife*, Poll.7.83, 10.141. **-ή**, ἡ, *circumcision*, Lxx *Ge*.17.13, Agatharch.61, Str.16.2.37 (pl.), Ph.1.450, al., Dsc.2.82: metaph., π. καρδίας *Ep.Rom*.2.29. II. *section* of a machine, ἡ κάτω π. Apollod.*Poliorc*.173.4. III. *circular incision*, Heliod.ap.Orib.45.6.9, 45.7.3, Aët.15.8. **-ίς**, ίδος, ἡ, part of a ship, Hsch. **-ος**, ον, *cut off all round, abrupt, steep*, ὄρος Plb.1.56.4; λόφος D.H.5.19; περίτομα *steep places*, *Inscr.Prien*.363.28 (iv B. C.).

**περι-τόναιος**, ον, *stretched* or *strained over*, esp. of *the membrane which contains the lower viscera*, τοῦ π. χιτῶνος ἢ ὑμένος ἢ σκεπάσματος Gal.*UP*4.9:—freq. as Subst.⊕ **περιτόναιον**, τό, Hp.*Epid*.7.20, Gal. l.c., 18(1).164, etc.; **περιτόναιος**, ὁ, Cels.4.1.13. II. περιτόναιον, τό, = ἐντερονεία, Poll.1.92, cf. περίτονος II; but 2. περιτόναια, τά, *projecting beams at the stern* of a ship, ib.89. **-τονία**, ἡ, f.l. for περιτένεια, Orib.10.27.11. —τόνιον, τό, v.l. for ἐπιτόνιον, Heliod. ap.Orib.49.4.65. II. = περιτόναιον (which is v.l.), *Hippiatr.* 73. —τονος, ον, *covered with* something *stretched over*, βύρσῃ D.H. 4.58. II. Subst. περίτονον, τό, = περιτόναιον II. 1, Eust.1533.41.

**περιτοξεύω**, *overshoot, outshoot*, τινα Ar.*Ach.*712 (nisi leg. ὑπερ-). II. *shoot to death with arrows*, App.*Num.*3 (i p.324 M.):— Pass., -τοξευθεὶς ὑπὸ τῶν βαρβάρων Aristid.1.125 J.

**περιτορνεύω**, *turn as in a lathe*, περὶ . . τὸν ἐγκέφαλον . . σφαῖραν περιετόρνευσεν ὀστεΐνην *he framed* a globe round it, Pl.*Ti.*73e; θνητὸν σῶμα [τῇ ψυχῇ] π. ib.69c: metaph. in Pass., *to be well-turned*, of style, D.H.*Dem.*21.

**περίτρᾱνος**, ον, *very distinct*, Antig.*Mir.*45; περίτρανα λαλεῖν Plu. 2.4a; of an orator, *very lucid*, Phld.*Rh.*1.336 S. Adv. -νως, λαλεῖν, λέγειν, M.Ant.8.30, *EM*729.31.

**περιτρᾰχηλ-ίδιον**, τό, Dim. of sq. II, *IG*2².1407.9, 1428.31, *PMagd.* 42.5 (iii B.C.). —ιος, ον, *round the neck*, Hsch. s.v. κλοιός; κόσμος *EM*477.31, al. II. Subst. περιτρᾰχήλιον, τό, *neckpiece, gorget*, *IG*2².1492.54, Str.3.4.17 (pl.), Plu.*Alex.*32, Arr.*Epict.*2.14.12, *POxy.* 1273.7 (iii A.D.). —ος, ον, = foreg. I, ἄλυσις *PSI*10.1116.6 (ii A.D.); ἀλγηδών Hsch. s.v. βραγχία.

**περιτρέμω**, *tremble for*, τοῖς ἱματιδίοις Arr.*Epict.*3.26.36; v. περιτρέπω I. 3.

**περιτρεπτικῶς**, gloss on περιτροπάδην, Sch.Par.A.R.2.143.

**περιτρέπω**, *turn and bring round, divert*, τὴν ἀναθυμίασιν εἴσω -τρέπεσθαι *is diverted* inwards, Arist.*Mete.*367ᵃ32; μὴ βούλεσθε εἰς ὑμᾶς τὴν αἰτίαν -τρέψαι Lys.6.13; γυναικάς φασι τοῖς ἀνδράσι περιτρέπειν τὰ σφέτερ' αὐτῶν ἁμαρτήματα Aristid.2.420 J.; εἰς τοὐναντίον τὸν λόγον Eus.Mynd.2; ἐπὶ θάτερα Aristid.1.112 J.; τὸ σφάλμα εἰς ἄλλο μακρῷ αἰσιώτερον περιετράπη Luc.*Laps.*15; ὁ λόγος εἰς ὄνειδος -τέτραπται Plu.2.1036f; π. τινὰ εἰς μανίαν, εἰς χαράν, *Act.Ap.*26.24, J.*AJ*9.4.4; εἰς ἄλγημα Sor.1.26 (Pass.): c. inf., τοὐναντίον π. τι μηνύειν *bring* a thing *round* to signify the opposite, Pl.*Cra.*418b. 2. *turn upside down, upset*, χειμὼν π. τὴν ναῦν Luc.*Cont.*7; περιτραπεὶς Ὀδυσσεύς *capsized*, Plu.2.831d; τῇ ῥύμῃ τοῦ ἵππου τινὰ π. Id.*Marc.*7: metaph., [ὕψος] περιέτρεψεν ἢ χρόνος τις ἢ φθόνος *Trag.Adesp.*547.4; π. θρόνους δικαστῶν Lxx *Wi.*5.23; π. εἰς κακοτροφίαν *pervert*, Ath.Med.ap.Orib. *inc.*21.1; μή τις . . βασκανία π. τὸν λόγον Pl.*Phd.*95b; *refute*, π. σεαυτόν Id.*Ax.*370a, cf. Aps.p.278 H.:—Pass., τὸ παράδειγμα περιτέτραπται Luc.*JTr.*49; of a person, *collapse in argument*, Phld.*Sign.*29; *refute oneself*, D.L.3.35; περιτρέπεται ὁ λόγος Dam.*Pr.*7. 3. *turn away from*, δοῦλ' ἔργα καὶ δύην π. Semon.7.58 (nisi leg. περιτρέμει). 4. Pass., *to be folded over*, of skin, Gal.*UP*3.12. 5. περιτρέπεται· ἰλιγγιᾷ, Hsch. II. intr. in aor. 2, *turn* or *go round*, περὶ δ' ἔτραπον ὧραι Od.10.469.

❋ **περιτρέφω**, pf. -τέτροφα A.R.2.738:—*cause, make to congeal around*, πάχνην l.c.: metaph., ἄλγος π. κραδίην Nic.*Th.*299:—Pass., περιτρέφεται κυκόωντι [the milk] *forms curds* as you mix it, Il.5.903; σακέεσσι περιτρέφετο κρύσταλλος the ice *froze hard upon* the shields, Od.14.477; τὸ περιτεθραμμένον σοι σαρκίδιον M.Ant.12.1, cf. Gal.2.504.

❋ **περιτρέχω**, fut. -θρέξομαι Ar.*Ra.*193, -δρᾰμοῦμαι Id.*V.*138: aor. περιέδρᾰμον Id.*Eq.*56; but inf. -θρέξαι Id.*Th.*657: pf. -δεδράμηκα Pl. *Clit.*410a, -δέδρομα (v. infr. II. 1b):—*run round and round*, τὸ δῶμα π., said by a drunken man, Thgn.505; π. τὰ κυνίδια X.*Oec.*13.8; π. δεῦρο Ar.*V.*138; π. εἰς ταὐτόν *come round, return* to the same point, Pl.*Tht.*200c, cf. *Clit.* l.c. 2. *run about everywhere*, οἱ δὲ πυππάζουσι περιτρέχοντες Cratin.52; κύκλῳ π. καὶ βοᾶν Alex.174.1; π. ὅπῃ τύχοιμι Pl.*Smp.*173a, cf. Lys.30.21: generally, *to be in motion, circulate*, Plot.6.3.24; ἡ περιτρέχουσα ὑγρότης flexibility *of movement*, of a surgeon operating, Plu.2.67e. 3. metaph., *to be current, in vogue*, ταῦτα περιτρέχοντα πᾶσι προσφέρεσθαι Pl.*Tht.*202a; ἡ περιτρέχουσα ἑταιρεία *common* society, Id.*Ep.*333e; ὀνόματα περιτρέχοντα *current*, D.H.*Din.*2; τέχνη περιτρέχουσα, of Rhetoric, *comprehensive* art, *ars circumcurrens*, Quint.*Inst.*2.21.7. II. c. acc., *run round*, τὴν λίμνην κύκλῳ Ar.*Ra.*193; *run round searching*, τὴν Πύκνα πᾶσαν Id.*Th.*657; *run up to from all sides*, τὸν δὲ βληθέντα περιέδραμε ὅμιλος Hdt.8.128. b. of things, esp. in pf. -δέδρομα, *encompass, surround*, περιδέδρομεν ἄψεα νοῦσος A.R.3.676; φήμη κακὴ -δέδρομεν αὐτούς Man.2.298; ὠκεανὸς π. γαῖαν D.P.41, cf. Theoc.*Ep.*4.5. 2. metaph., *circumvent, take in*, Ar.*Eq.*56.

**περιτρέω**, *flee round about*, λαοὶ δὲ περίτρεσαν the people *fled on all sides*, Il.11.676.

**περί-τρημα**, ατος, τό, f.l. for περίτρητα, Ph.*Bel.*72.9. —τρησις, εως, ἡ, *trephining by a circle of perforations*, Heliod.(?) ap.Orib.46.11. 35. —τρητος, ον, *perforated*: Subst. περίτρητον, τό, *perforated horizontal beam* in a torsion-engine, Ph.*Bel.*55.5, al.: pl., Hero *Bel.* 93.9.

**περιτρηχής**, ές, Ion. for *-τρᾱχής, *very rough*, Numen.ap.Ath.7. 315b.

**περι-τρῐβής**, ές, *worn all round by use*, δόνακες *AP*6.63 (Damoch.): metaph., *worn with work*, χεῖρες A.R.1.1175. —τρίβω [ῑ], *rub* or *wear away all round*, -τρίψας ὁ χρόνος [τὸ ἄγαλμα] Philostr.*Her.*2.1, cf. *Im.*1.23 (Pass.); πτερὰ περιτετριμμένα *battered*, Arist.*HA*627ᵃ13; κόγχος ἅλμῃ . . περιτρῐβείς (aor. 2 Pass.) Lyc.790: metaph., περιτετριμμένοι 'old hands', Arr.*Epict.*2.6.5. II. *smear*, τί τινι Nonn. *D.*6.190, 41.110.

**περιτρίζω**, pf. περιτέτρῑγα, *creak all round*, Q.S.12.431, prob. in 14. 265.

❋ **περί-τριμμα**, ατος, τό, *anything worn smooth by rubbing*: metaph., π. δικῶν, of a pettifogger, Ar.*Nu.*447; π. ἀγορᾶς D.18.127; π. πραγμάτων *Com.Adesp.*889. II. Medic., *preparation for rubbing in*, Crito ap.Gal.12.447. —τριπτος, ον, *smooth-worn*, κέλευθος Orac.ap. Sch.E.*Ph.*638. —τριψις, εως, ἡ, *rubbing round*, Sch.Nic.*Al.*256.

**περι-τρομέω**, *tremble*, Q.S.13.184, al.: c. acc., *tremble at*, θῆρα, δμοκλήν, Id.3.182, 364: c. gen., *tremble by reason of*, ὑετοῖο, ὠδίνων, Arat.861, Opp.*H.*4.194: c. dat., *tremble for*, ib.1.293, 4.202:—Med., σάρκες περιτρομέοντο μέλεσσιν all the flesh *crept on* his limbs, Od.18. 77: abs., Q.S.1.477. —τρομος, ον, *trembling, terrified*, Opp.*H.* 2.309. Adv. -μως, ἔχειν πρός τι Phalar.*Ep.*109.

**περιτροπ-άδην** [ᾰ], Adv. *by rounding up*, A.R.2.143. —έω, Ion. and Ep. form of περιτρέπω: I. intr., περιτροπέων ἐνιαυτός a *revolving* year, Il.2.295. II. trans., *turn from all sides to a centre, round up, drive in*, πολλὰ [μῆλα] περιτροπέοντες ἐλαύνομεν Od. 9.465; περιτροπέων φῦλ' ἀνθρώπων *shepherding* them *about*, *h.Merc.* 542. ❋ -ή, ἡ, *turning round, revolution*, ἐτέων περιτροπάς Semon.1. 8, cf. Pl.*Tht.*209e; ὅταν περιτροπαὶ ἑκάστοις . . περιφορὰς συνάπτωσι Id. *R.*546a; π. ἔτους Wilcken *Chr.*27.32 (ii A.D.): prov., ὑπέρου π., v. ὕπερος I. 2. *turning about, changing*, ἐν περιτροπῇ *by turns, one after another*, Hdt.2.168, 3.69; ἐκ περιτροπῆς D.H.5.2, Aristid.*Or.*43(1). 24, *BGU*149.9 (ii/iii A.D.), D.C.53.1; ἐκ τῆς π. Id.54.19. 3. *overturning*, ὠθισμοὶ καὶ π. ἀλλήλων Plu.2.639f. b. Rhet., ἡ π. τοῦ λόγου *turning* an opponent's arguments against himself, S.E.*P.*2. 128, al., cf. Dam.*Pr.*13. ❋ -ος (proparox.), ον, *turned round, whirled round*, κίνησις π. *rotatory* motion, prob. l. in Plu.*Lys.*12: Subst. περιτρόπου· ἴλιγγος, Hsch.

**περιτροχ-άζω**, = περιτρέχω, Apollod.1.9.26; *walk round*, *Hippiatr.* 33. —ᾰλος, ον, = περίτροχος: neut. pl. as Adv., περιτρόχαλα κείρεσθαι to have one's hair clipped *round about*, Hdt.3.8, Plu.2.261f; κουρὰ π. Phot. s.v. σκάφιον. —ασμός, ὁ, f.l. for -ισμός in Antyll.ap. Orib.6.22.10. —άω, = περιτρέχω, *AP*7.338: c. acc., πολέες σε περιτροχόωσιν ἀοιδαί Call.*Del.*28:—Med., Arat.815. —ιον, τό, *wheel revolving round* an axle, ὁ ἄξων ἐν τῷ περιτροχίῳ *the wheel and axle*, Papp.1060.9, cf. Tz.*H.*11.607. —ισμός, ὁ, *running round*, Antyll. ap.Orib.6.22.7. —ος, ον, *circular*, of a star in a horse's forehead, π. ἠΰτε μήνη Il.23.455; of the sun or moon, A.R.3.1229, Tryph.518; of a hat, Call.*Fr.*124; of a *round* lake, π. ὕδασι λίμνη D.P.987. II. neut. pl. as Adv., = περιτρόχαλα, περίτροχα κείρεσθαι Agath.1.3.

**περιτρύζω**, *grunt round about*, Q.S.14.36.

**περιτρῡπ-άω**, *perforate with a circle of holes*, Aët.9.38, Paul.Aeg. 6.3. —ησις, εως, ἡ, *perforation with a circle of holes*, ib.90.

**περιτρύχω** [ῡ], *afflict exceedingly*, Sch.E.*Ph.*873.

**περιτρώγω**, fut. -τρώξομαι Luc.*Gall.*28: aor. περιέτρᾰγον Ar.*Ach.* 258:—*gnaw round about, bite off*, v.l. in Arist.*HA*605ᵃ4, cf. Luc. *Tim.*8, etc.; τοὺς δακτύλους Pherecr.13; π. τὰ χρυσία τινός *nibble off, purloin* her jewels, Ar.*Ach.*258; τῆς ἀρχῆς τοὺς ἀργελόφους Id.*V.*672: metaph., *carp at*, τινα ib.596.

**περιτρωχάω**, Ep. collat. form of περιτρέχω, Q.S.7.459.

**περιττός, -άκις, -εύω, -ωμα**, etc., v. περισσ-.

**περιτυγχάνω**, fut. -τεύξομαι: aor. -έτῠχον: pf. -τετύχηκα Isoc.11. 2: 1. mostly of persons, *happen to be about, at*, or *near*: hence, *light upon, fall in with*, c. dat. pers., Th.1.20, Lys.13.23, etc.; ἀγνώμονι κριτῇ π. X.*Mem.*2.8.5: abs., Th.1.135, Pl.*Smp.*221a: c. dat. rei, π. τῷ πράγματι And.1.37; πλοίῳ Th.4.120; φαρμακίοις Pl.*Phdr.* 268c; τῇ ἀρετῇ Id.*Prt.*320a; ἀτυχήμασι Plb.1.37.6; π. ἰητρικῇ *stumble upon* medical success, without science, Hp.*de Arte* 5. 2. reversely of events, *befall*, μή ξυμφορά τις αὐτοῖς περιτύχῃ Th.4.55.

**περιτῠλίσσω**, *wrap round*, Sor.1.82, 84, Hsch. s.v. ἐσπαργάνωσεν, Phot.

**περί-τῠλος**, ον, *callous*, Sor.2.16. II. *surrounded with bead-moulding*, *Inscr.Délos* 504.14. ❋ -τῠλόω, *make callous*, Crito ap.Gal. 13.798:—Pass., *become callous all round*, Cass.*Pr.*13. —τύλωσις [ῠ], εως, ἡ, *callosity*, Sor.2.7, 9.

**περιτύμβιος**, ον, *at the grave*, δάκρυα *AP*7.560 (Paul. Sil.).

**περιτυμπᾰνίζομαι**, Pass., *to be maddened by drums*, Plu.2.144d, 167c.

**περιτῡπόω**, *embrace, enfold*, as the atmosphere does our bodies, S.E.*P.*3.75, *M.*10.95: Peripatetic term, Id.*P.*3.131.

**περιυβρίζω**, *insult wantonly*, τινα Hdt.5.91, J.*AJ*7.6.1, Jul.*Or.*5. 159a, etc.; τοιαῦτα π. αὐτοὺς ἐν μέρει Ar.*V.*1319, cf. *Th.*535; τὰ θεῖα π. Plu.*Cam.*18:—Pass., *to be so treated*, πρός or ὑπό τινος, Hdt.2.152, 4.159; ὧδε or ταῦτα π., Id.1.114, 3.137; οἷα π. Ar.*Eq.*727; ψυχὴ ὑπὸ λαιμαργίας π. Ph.1.488.

**περιῠλακτέω**, *howl around*, Jul.*Or.*2.88b: metaph., ἡ ὀργὴ π. τὴν καρδίαν Ach.Tat.2.29.

**περιύομαι** [ῡ], Pass., *to be rained round*, Str.14.2.20.

**περιυπν-ίζω**, *expergiscor*, *Gloss.* —ος, ον, *awakened*, Aristodem. 8.1 J.

**περιῠφαίνω**, *weave round*, Poll.7.62 (Pass.), *An.Ox.*3.9 (Pass.).

**περιφᾰγεῖν**, v. περιεσθίω.

**περιφᾰής**, ές, *gleaming all round*, βλεφάρων περιφαέα [ᾱ metri gr.] κύκλα Opp.*H.*2.6.

**περιφαίνομαι**, Pass., *to be visible all round*, ὄρεος . . ἕκαθεν περιφαινομένοιο Il.13.179; ἐν σκοπιῇ, περιφαινομένῳ ἐνὶ χώρῳ, βωμὸν ποιήσω *h.Ven.*100; ἐν περιφαινομένῳ (without Subst.) Od.5.476: generally, *to be visible*, ὅσσῃ π. ὀκλάξ Arat.517. 2. *shine around*, Plu.2. 932b. II. later, in Act., *display all round*, ἶριν D.S.17.10. III. intr. in Act., Parth.17.4.

**περιφάλλια**· πομπὴ Διονύσῳ τελουμένη τῶν φαλλῶν, Hsch.

**περιφάν-εια** [φᾰ], ἡ, *conspicuousness*, πολλὴ π. τῆς χώρης ἐστί it is thoroughly *known*, Hdt.4.24; τοσαύτη π. τοῦ πράγματός ἐστι D.45.2, cf. Is.7.28; διὰ τὴν π. τῶν ἀδικημάτων D.29.1; ἐκ π. ὁρᾶσθαι *on every side*, D.H.*Comp*.22, 23; *celebrity, distinction*, Jul.*Or*.3.108d. II. = ἐπιφάνεια II, *superficial appearance*, Plu.2.674a. -ής, ές, *seen all round*, of a city, Th.4.102; π. ζῷα figures *standing free and unattached*, opp. those in relief, Callix.2, cf. 1. 2. *conspicuous, notorious*, S.*Aj*.66, etc.; π. τὰ πράγματα Ar.*Lys*.756; π. ἀδίκημα Lys.9.22; τὰ δημόσιά που καὶ π. Pl.*Phlb*.31e; μεγάλη καὶ π. ἀναισχυντία D.27.38; τεκμήριον Lys.22.11 (Sup.); πενία Antiph.167; περιφανές [ἐστι], ὡς.. X.*HG*7.2.17: Comp. -φανέστερος, Sup. -έστατος, ib.7.3.8, Ar.*Eq*.206, etc. Adv. -νῶς *conspicuously, notably, evidently*, S.*Aj*.81, Ar.*Eq*.1186, *Pl*.948, Th.6.60, Lys.16.8, Pl.*Men*.91d, *Ep*.346a: Comp. -έστερον D.27.7: Sup. -έστατα Is.8.17 codd. -τάζομαι, *frame an imaginative notion of* a thing, Simp.*in Epict*.p.112 D., *in Cael*.313.8. ⊛ -τος, ον, = περιφανής: metaph., π. θανεῖται *too plainly* he will die, S.*Aj*.229 (lyr.). II. *famous, renowned*, πᾶσιν ib.599 (lyr.).

**περίφᾰσις**, εως, ἡ, = περιφάνεια, αἱ τῶν τόπων π. *wide views over* the country, Plb.10.42.8.

**περιφέγγ-εια**, ἡ, *radiance*, *Placit*.3.5.11. -ής, ές, *radiant*, φῶς θεοῦ Ph.1.631 (Sup.). II. *shedding light around*, φλόξ Id.2.505; σῶμα, of Zeus, Orph.*Fr*.168.22; μήνη Man.6.57; ἀκτίς *Cat.Cod.Astr*.1.109. ⊛ -ω, *illuminate round about*, in Med., Sm.*Ez*.1.27.

**περιφείδομαι**, *spare and save alive*, ἀμῶν Isyll.26; πατρός A.R.1.620, cf. Plu.*Luc*.3; ζωῆς *AP*7.534 (Alex. Aet. or Autom.). 2. *to be careful*, τοῦ μὴ..[ἀφελεῖν] Archig.ap.Orib.46.25.2.

⊛ **περιφέρ-εια**, Ion. -είη, ἡ, *circumference*, κύκλου Heraclit.103; (*rounded*) *surface*, σφαίρας Ti.Locr.100e; of helmets, Plu.*Cam*.40 (pl.); τὰ ὦτα ἐπὶ τῆς αὐτῆς π. τοῖς ὄμμασι Arist.*HA*494$^b$14; more generally, *curve*, Id.*EN*1102$^a$31; *curvature* of the edge of a leaf, Thphr.*HP*3.10.5; *roundness*, Hp.*Art*.61; *spherical* or *curved shape*, Epicur.*Ep*.2 pp.49,51 U. 2. *arc of a circle*, Arist.*Ph*.264$^b$25, Euc.3.28; marked on concave sun-dial (πόλος), *Sammelb*.358.1 (iii B.C.). II. *wandering, error*, ἐν καρδίᾳ Lxx*Ec*.9.3. ⊛ -ής, ές, *revolving*, ὧν δὲ π. (sc. ὁ ἐνιαυτὸς) τελευτὴν οὐδεμίαν οὐδ' ἀρχὴν ἔχει Hermipp.4; π. ὀφθαλμοί *rolling* eyes, Luc.*JTr*.30. 2. *rounded* or *curved*, a. of surfaces and lines, ἄκρον Hp.*Art*.7; π. κύρτωμα Id.*Epid*.1.26.α'; κύλικες Pherecr.143.5; ἀσπίδες Ael.*Tact*.2.7; τὰ στρογγύλα τε καὶ π. Hp.*VC*11; opp. εὐθύς, Pl.*Prm*.137e, 138a, Arist.*Ph*.248$^a$12, al.; τὸ π. *circularity*, Id.*APo*.73$^a$39; but, *circumference*, Pl.*R*.436e, Dsc.3.6, 48. Adv. -ρῶς *in a rounded shape*, Procl.*Hyp*.3.6. b. of bodies, *spherical, globular*, Democr.164, Pl.*Phd*.108e, *Smp*.190b; π. τὸ σχῆμα τῆς γῆς Arist.*Cael*.298$^a$7; π. σχηματισμός Epicur.*Ep*.2 p.50 U.; [σώματα] Phld.*Mort*.8 (Sup.); π. στέγαι *domed*, Demetr.*Eloc*.13. c. metaph., of style, *rounded*, D.H.*Comp*.22; τὰ στρογγύλα καὶ τὰ π. προοίμια Id.*Rh*.10.13. 3. Adv. -ρῶς *in a circle*, Hero *Deff*.5. II. *surrounded by*, δῶμα περιφερὲς θριγκοῖς τόδε E.*Hel*.430. 2. Adv. -ρῶς *disposed in a circle*, Dsc.4.169. III. *wavering*, π. στίβον χθονός thy *wavering* steps, E.*Ion*743. IV. cf. Περφερέες.

**περιφερόγραμμος**, ον, *bounded by a curved line*, opp. εὐθύγραμμος, Arist.*Cael*.286$^b$14, Str.5.1.2, Simp.*in Cael*.413.4.

**περιφέρω**, *carry round*, τὸν ὀϊστὸν περιέφερε κατὰ πᾶσαν γῆν Hdt.4.36; *carry about* with one, ib.64; παῖδ' ἀγκάλαισι π. E.*Or*.464, cf. Men.*Sam*.29; τὴν γαλῆν Ar.*Ec*.128; ὀκλαδίαν prob. in Id.*Eq*.1385:—Pass., c. acc. loci, περιενειχθέντος τοῦ λέοντος τὸ τεῖχος *being carried round* the wall, Hdt.1.84: abs., Σωκράτη.. περιφερόμενον *swinging about* (in a basket), Pl.*Ap*.19c; πίνειν.. σκύφον περιφερόμενον Arist.*Pol*.1324$^b$18. 2. *move round*, π. τὸν πόδα *bring* the foot *round* in mounting a horse, X.*Eq*.7.2; *hand round* at table, Id.*Cyr*.2.2.2, al. (Act. and Pass.); τὸ βλέμμα π. εἰς τοὺς παρόντας Plu.*Agis* 18; π. κλήρους Id.2.737d (Pass.). 3. *turn round*, τὴν κεφαλήν Id.*Marc*.20:—Med., τὰ σκέλη π. Pl.*Smp*.190a. b. in Tactics, *wheel*, τοῦ συντάγματος περιενεχθέντος Ascl.*Tact*.10.4, cf. Ael.*Tact*.25.5. c. intr., *turn round*, ὡς ὁ στεφὼν περιφέρει κύκλῳ *GDI*5597.8 (Ephesus, iii B.C.). 4. *carry round, publish, make known*, π. τι πανταχόσε Plu.2.80f:—Pass., τοῦ Πιττακοῦ.. περιεφέρετο τοῦτο τὸ ῥῆμα *was passed from mouth to mouth*, Pl.*Prt*.343b, cf. *R*.402a,c, *Demod*.383c; ὁ περιφερόμενος στίχος Plb.5.9.4, etc.; of a person, περιενεχθῆναι εὐνοίᾳ καὶ θαυμασθῆναι παρὰ τοῖς Ἀθηναίοις Phld.*Acad.Ind*.p.75 M. 5. *carry to and fro*, Plu.*Caes*.37, cf. infr. III. 2. 6. *bring round in the end, determine, reduce, subject*, περιήνεγκεν εἰς ἑαυτὸν τὰς Ἀθήνας Id.*Per*.15, cf. *Galb*.8; τὴν Ἰταλίαν π. ἐς λιμόν App.*BC*5.143; εἰς συμφορὰς π. Id.*Pun*.86; εἰς ἀπάθειαν Plu.2.165b, cf. 546c:—Pass., ἐς Ῥωμαίους πάντα περιηνέχθη App.*Mith*.68; τὸ σπέρμα ἐς θῆλυ περιηνέχθη Hp.*Genit*.6. 7. *carry round* or *back* (in memory), οὔτε μέμνημαι τὸ πρῆγμα οὔτε με περιφέρει οὐδὲν εἰδέναι τούτων nor *does* any of these things *carry* me *back* to the knowledge of it, Hdt.6.86.β'; π. τίς με καὶ μνήμη Pl.*La*.180e; τοῦ πράγματος ἤδη -φέροντος αὐτὸν τῇ ὑπονοίᾳ Plu.2.522c. 8. *turn round, make dizzy, turn mad*, ἡ συκοφαντία π. σοφόν Lxx*Ec*.7.8(7):—Pass., *to be turned giddy*, -φερόμενος τῷ μεγέθει τῶν τολμωμένων Plu.*Caes*.32; ψυχὴ δυνάμει -φερομένη Id.*Dio*11; κακοῦ μεγέθει -φερόμενος J.*AJ*17.5.2. 9. *transfer, refer, shift*, τὴν ἀπορίαν ἐς τοὺς δικαστάς App.*BC*1.54. II. intr., *survive, endure, hold out*, Th.7.28, Thphr.*HP*9.12.1, J.*AJ*17.6.1: also c. acc., *survive, outlast*, ἡμέραν App.*BC*2.149; τὰς εἰδοὺς ib.153. 2. *come round, recover*, ἐκ τῆς νόσου Hsch., Suid. III. Pass., *go round, rotate*, ἐν τῷ αὐτῷ κύκλῳ Pl.*Prm*.138c; πάντα -φερόμενα ὁρᾶν Ath.4.156c; ἐνιαυτοῦ -φερομένου Hdt.4.72; ἐν ἴσῳ χρόνῳ π. Arist.*Cael*.290$^a$5; κύκλος τῶν ἀνθρωπηΐων πρηγμάτων -φερόμενος Hdt.1.207; of argument, εἰς ταὐτὸ π. ἀεί Pl.*Grg*.517c, cf. *Lg*.659d; εἰς τὰ πρότερα Id.*R*.456b. 2. *wander about*, X.*Cyn*.3.5; λόγος.. ἀνοήτως π. ἐν συμποσίῳ Plu.2.716f; *to be unstable*, ἡ περιφερομένη εἱμαρμένη Id.*Aem*.27, cf. *Galb*.6; περιφερόμενοι τύπτουσι *at random*, Arist.*Metaph*.985$^a$14.

**περιφεύγω**, *flee from, escape*, πόλεμον περὶ τόνδε φυγόντε Il.12.322; ψάμμος ἀριθμὸν περιπέφευγεν the sand *escapes* thy numbering, Pi.*O*.2.98; π. τὴν φθοράν Pl.*Lg*.677b; ῥαθυμίας Men.*Mon*.467; ἔφοδον, πῦρ π., Plu.2.171e. 2. abs., *escape from illness, come out of it alive*, D.54.1, 28; π. ἐκ [κυναγχέων] v.l. in Hp.*Prog*.23, cf. Arist.*HA*604$^a$10. 3. *avoid especially*, ὅπως μὴ.. ἔσται Hp.*Fract*.48.

**περιφημ-ίζω**, *announce, publish*, σύμβολα τῷ πλήθει Lyd.*Mag*.1.46. II. *celebrate all round*, εἰς πᾶσαν τὴν γῆν *EM*517.17. -ιστος, ον, *famous*, Ps.-Callisth.3.18. -ος, ον, (φήμη) *very famous*, Archil.63, Orph.*A*.24, Poll.5.158. II. in bad sense, *notorious*, Paul.Al.*N*.3.

**περιφθέγγομαι**, *speak with all kinds of people*, Gal.4.448.

⊛ **περιφθείρομαι**, Pass., *to be utterly destroyed*, Ph.2.627. II. *wander about in destitution*, Isoc.*Ep*.9.10, Lycurg.40. III. = τὰς φθεῖρας συλλέγω, Com.ap.Hsch.

**περιφθῐνύθω** [ῠ], *go to ruin*, Orph.*L*.521.

**περιφίλητος** [ῑ], ον, *greatly beloved by*, ἅπασιν App.*BC*4.85.

**περιφῑμ-όω**, *close all round*, ἀγγεῖον Afric.*Cest*.p.45 V., Ps.-Democr.Alch.p.48 B., cf. Zos.Alch.p.141 B. -ωσις, εως, ἡ, *disorder of the penis in which the prepuce cannot be drawn forward*, Antyll.ap.Orib.50.5.2, Paul.Aeg.6.55: παραφ- is f.l. in Gal.19.445.

⊛ **περι-φλεγής**, ές, *very burning*, δίψος Plu.2.699e (Sup.; fort. πυρι-). Adv. -γῶς, διψῆσαι Id.*Cat.Ma*.1. -φλέγω, *burn, blaze all round*, Id.2.648c. II. trans., *burn up, wither*, θέρος π. τὰ γεννώμενα Ph.2.391; ἆσθμα π. χαίτην D.Chr.36.47: with acc. understood, πρὶν ἢ τὸν ἥλιον -φλέγειν Poll.10.51; *overheat*, Plu.2.651b, Sor.1.72:—Pass., of victims in the bull of Phalaris, Plb.12.25.2; *to be singed*, Philum.*Ven*.7.12: metaph., Plu.2.498b; cf. περιφλεύω.

**περι-φλέκτως**, Adv. *with burning passion*, ἐρᾶν Eun.*VS*p.455 B. -φλεξις, εως, ἡ, τοῦ ἡλίου *excessive* sun-*burn*, Aët.7.106 (pl.). -φλευσμός, ὁ, *scorching*, Aq.*De*.28.22. -φλεύω or -φλύω [ῡ], *scorch, singe*, or *char all round*, τοὺς ζῶντας περιφλύει, of lightning, Ar.*Nu*.396:—Pass., τειχέων περιπεφλευσμένων πυρί Hdt.5.77; γαλῆ -φλευσθεῖσα (v.l. -φλεχθεῖσα) Dsc.2.25; cf. περιφλοίζω.

⊛ **περιφλίω** [ῐ], *to be almost bursting with*, ἀλοιφῇ Nic.*Al*.62 (v.l. -φλῐδόωντος from -φλῐδάω).

⊛ **περιφλίωμα** [ῐ], ατος, τό, *portico*, *CRAcad.Inscr*.1906.168 (Aphrodisias, ii A.D.).

**περιφλογ-ίζω**, *blaze around*, *PMag.Par*.1.3073. -ισμός, ὁ, *scorching*, Sm., Thd.*De*.28.22.

**περι-φλοίζω**, *strip off the bark*, περιφλοῖσαι (nisi leg. -φλεῦσαι) Thphr.*HP*9.5.3; [ξύλα] περιφλοισθέντα Id.*Ign*.72, cf. Dsc.1.20:—Med., Id.4.148 (s.v.l.). -φλοιος, ον, *with bark all round*, X.*Cyn*.9.12. -φλοισμός, ὁ, *stripping off the bark*, Thphr.*CP*5.15.1.

**περιφλύω**, v. περιφλεύω.

**περιφοβέω**, *terrify, scare*, Phot. and Suid. s. v. στροβεῖ:—Pass., *fear greatly*, X.*Cyn*.9.17 (s.v.l.).

**περίφοβος**, ον, *in great fear*, τάρβος A.*Supp*.736 (lyr.), cf. Th.6.36, X.*An*.3.1.12, Lycurg.40, Hyp.*Ath*.13; τινος of a thing, Pl.*Phdr*.239b; περὶ σφῶν αὐτῶν Plb.5.74.3; πρὸς τὸν θάνατον μαλακὸς καὶ π. Arist.*EE*1229$^b$7. Adv. -βως Epicur.*Fr*.532, D.H.11.22, Plu.*Arat*.26.

**περιφοιτ-άω**, *wander about*, prov., Βοῦθος -φοιτᾷ Cratin.245, cf. Arist.*Fr*.616; πανταχοῦ Aristid.*Or*.26(14).18, cf. Ph.1.305. 2. c. acc., ψυχὴ π. τὰ μόρια τὰ ἑωυτῆς Hp.*Vict*.1.6; π. τὰ ἄστη Philostr.*VS Praef*. -ησις, εως, ἡ, *wandering about*, Plu.*Lys*.20, Id.2.592d. -ος, ον, *revolving*, ἔργα σελήνης Parm.10.4; of persons, *wandering about*, Call.*Epigr*.30.3, 39.2, Nonn.*D*.3.297, al.; ψυχὴ π. καὶ πεπλανωμένη Ph.1.484; but f.l. for περίφημον, Id.2.248.

⊛ **περιφορ-ά**, ἡ, *carrying round*, of dishes at table: hence, *meats carried round, course* at dinner, X.*Cyr*.2.2.4, Heraclid.Tarent.ap.Ath.3.120c (pl.), cf. 7.275b. II. (from Pass.) *going round, circular* or *rotatory motion, revolution*, of a wheel, E.*Ba*.1067; of the heavens and heavenly bodies, Ar.*Nu*.172, X.*Mem*.4.7.5, Pl.*Phdr*.247c, *Lg*.898c, Arist.*Mete*.341$^a$2, *Cael*.291$^a$35, Epicur.*Nat*.11.10, al.; αἱ τῶν ὡρῶν π. J.*AJ*1.1.1, cf. Pl.*R*.546a, *Plt*.271a, 274e. 2. *revolving vault* of heaven, Id.*R*.616c, *Tht*.153d; ἡ ὕπερθε π. *the heavens*, Critias 25.31 D. 3. metaph., in pl., *twists, circumvolutions*, Eub.73. 4. ἐν ταῖς περιφοραῖς *in social intercourse*, Plu.*Per*.5. 5. *error*, v.l. for παραφορά in Lxx*Ec*.2.12, 7.26(25). III. *story* or *tier* of a funeral pile, D.S.17.115. IV. *turntable* (?), *PTeb*.12.17 (ii B.C.). -άδην [ᾰ], Adv. *trailing round*, of the peculiar movement of the hind feet of oxen walking, Hp.*Art*.52, cf. Gal.18(1).586. -άριος, *circumlator*, *Gloss*. -έω, = περιφέρω, Hdt.2.48. -ημα, ατος, τό, *anything handed round, dish*, *Gloss*. -ητικός, ή, όν, *current*, λόγος S.E.*M*.10.87. -ητός, όν, *portable*, οἰκήματα Hdt.4.190; δεῖπνον Str.3.3.7, cf. A.D.*Synt*.310.14. II. *notorious, infamous*, Anacr.21.2: with a pun in Diph.36, Plu.*Per*.27.

⊛ **περιφόρῑνος**, ον, (φορίνη) *covered with skin*, χοιρίδια Diph.90; cf. περίφουρνος.

**περίφορος**, ον, *carried about* by passing impulse, M.Ant.1.15. II. Subst. περίφορος, ἡ, f.l. for περιφορά or περίοδος in Luc.*Astr*.5.

⊛ **περίφουρνος**, ον, perh. misspelling of περιφόρινος, ὑποδήματα λευκὰ π. *Edict.Diocl*.9.20.

**περιφρᾰγ-ή**, ἡ, = sq., *Gp.*11.5.4. ® **-μα**, ατος, τό, *fence round a* place, Agath.2.4 (pl.): metaph., Ti.Locr.100b. II. *place fenced round, enclosure, IG*11(2).287 A 117 (Delos, iii B.C.), *PMich.Zen.*84. 12 (iii B.C., pl.), Str.15.1.55 (pl.), *BCH*11.395 (Aegae); = περίβολος, *precinct*, τοῦ Διονύσου *IG*12(5).481.28 (Siphnos, iii B.C.). III. *covered part of a chariot*, Poll.1.142. **-νῡμι**, = περιφράσσω, Them. *Or.*32.357c.

® **περιφρᾰδής**, ές, (φράζομαι) *very thoughtful, very skilful, h.Merc.* 464, S.*Ant.*348 (lyr.). Adv. -δέως Hom., always in phrase ὤπτησάν τε π., Il.1.466, al.

**περιφράζομαι**, Med. with aor. 1 Pass. περιεφράσθην, *think* or *consider about*, περιφραζώμεθα πάντες νόστον Od.1.76, cf. Nic.*Th.*715; περιφρασθεὶς ἀλεξητήρια ib.7. II. Act., *express periphrastically*, τὴν νόησιν D.H.*Amm.*2.4: abs., *use periphrasis*, Phld.*Po.*5.28:—Pass., D.H.*Th.*29; τὸ μὴ σύνηθες.., ἀλλὰ λοξὸν καὶ περιπεφρασμένον Plu.2.407a.

**περι-φράκτης**, ου, ὁ, = οἰκοδόμος φραγμῶν, Aq.*Is.*58.12. **-φρακτος**, ον, *fenced round*: Subst. -φρακτον, τό, *enclosure, IG*3.1866, Plu. *Thes.*12, Luc.*Bacch.*6. **-φραξις**, εως, ἡ, *fencing round*, Agath.2.20 (pl.), dub. in *SIG*1231.17 (Nicomedia, iii/iv A.D.).

**περίφρᾰσις**, εως, ἡ, *circumlocution, periphrasis*, D.H.*Pomp.*2.5, *Th.*29, Plu.2.406f (pl.).

**περιφράσσω**, Att. -ττω, *fence, fortify all round*, ἐμαυτόν Pl.*R.* 365b; κύκλον δένδρεσι Str.4.5.2; of armour, Hld.9.15; *enclose*, πέρόνῃ π. λίθον Procop.*Aed.*3.1:—Med., *separate off* for oneself, μέρος [τῆς στοᾶς] αὐλαίᾳ Hyp.*Fr.*139:—Pass., πίλοις περιπεφραγμένα Hp. *Aër.*18; πόλις περιπεφρ. Sm.*Ps.*30(31).22; *to be obstructed*, f.l. for παραφρ- in Gal.*UP*8.6. 2. *make a dam*, φρυγάνοις καὶ λίθοις Arist. *HA*603a9.

**περιφραστικός**, ή, όν, *periphrastic*, Eust.557.37 (Comp.). Adv. -κῶς Erot. s.v. μανδραγόρου ῥίζαν, Zos.Alch.p.182 B., Sch.Theoc.1. 1, etc.

**περιφρίσσω**, *shudder at*, νέκυν Q.S.3.184. 2. c. dat., *tremble for*, παιδί Nonn.*D.*6.8. II. *bristle with*, κορύμβοις ib.11.502.

**περιφρον-έω**, *compass in thought, speculate about*, τὸν ἥλιον Ar.*Nu.* 225; τὰ πράγματα ib.741. II. *contemn, despise*, τινας Th.1.25; τὰ δαιμόνια D.H.1.71, etc.: c. gen., τοῦ ζῆν Pl.*Ax.*372b; τοῦ πιθανοῦ Plu.*Thes.*1, cf. Ael.*Tact. Praef.*3, etc.: metaph., of diseases or difficult patients, *defy* remedies, Alex.Trall.1.15, Archig.ap.Aët.6.8:—Pass., J.*AJ*4.5.2. III. intr., *to be very thoughtful*, οὐ περιφρονοῦσα ἡλικίᾳ Pl.*Ax.*365b (s.v.l.). **-ησις**, εως, ἡ, *contempt*, τῶν θεῶν Plu. *Cam.*6, *Per.*5; τῶν νόμων J.*AJ*5.5.2. **-ητικός**, ή, όν, *contemptuous*, c. gen., Eun.*Hist.*p.233 D.

® **περιφροσύνη**, ἡ, *cunning*, Them.*Or.*21.259b, Coluth.197 (pl.).

**περιφρουρ-εύω**, = sq., Opp.*H.*4.233. **-έω**, *guard on all sides, blockade closely, OGI*199.17 (Adule), D.C.40.36:—Pass., τὸ τεῖχος, ᾧ περιεφρουροῦντο οἱ Πλαταιῆς Th.3.21: metaph., πλήθει βίβλων -πεφρούρημαι Vett.Val.271.8; but, *to be protected*, Paul.Aeg.6.105.

**περιφρῠγής**, ές, *parching, wasting*, μαρασμός Philipp.ap.Gal.7. 686. II. *parched*, Alex.Trall.*Febr.*4. III. Adv. -γῶς, καυσούμενοι Sever.*Clyst.*p.25 D.

**περιφρύγω** [ῡ] (also **-φρύσσω**, Att. -ττω, Olymp.*in Mete.*157.10, al., Pall.*in Hp.*2.100 D. (Pass.), Pass. -φρύσσομαι Steph.*in Hp.*1. 175 D.), *scorch, parch*, Thd.*Ca.*1.6, Olymp.*in Mete.*292.33:—Pass., aor. 2 inf. -φρῠγῆναι Alex.Trall.*Febr.*4.

® **περίφρων**, ονος, ὁ, ἡ, voc. περίφρον Od.16.435, etc., but = nom., 19. 357, 21.381: (φρήν):—*very thoughtful, very careful*, freq. in Od. of Penelope, 16.435, al.; of other women, 11.345, 19.357, once in Il., 5. 412, Theoc.3.45; also of Hephaestus, first in Hes.*Sc.*297, 313; τέκνα Id.*Th.*894; *artful, crafty*, θήρη Opp.*H.*3.205. II. *haughty, overweening*, A.*Supp.*757 (lyr.); περίφρονα δ' ἔλακες Id.*Ag.*1426 (lyr.). 2. c. gen., *despising*, τῶν παθῶν Lxx 4*Ma.*8.28.

**περιφῠγή**, ἡ, *place of refuge*, Plu.*Demetr.*46 (pl.).

**περιφυής**, ές, (περιφύω) *growing round about*, π. τῇ γῇ *growing close to the ground*, v.l. for προσφυής in Dsc.4.103.

**περιφῠλάσσω**, Att. -ττω, *guard all round*, Ph.*Bel.*83.29 (Pass., s.v.l.), J.*BJ*5.10.1 codd., Sch.E.*Hec.*1209.

**περιφύρω** [ῡ], *throw into confusion*, in Pass., -πεφυρμένος βίος Ph. 2.656.

**περιφύσητος** [ῡ], ον, *blown upon from all sides*, Ar.*Lys.*323 (lyr.).

**περίφῠσις**, εως, ἡ, *growing round* or *over, overgrowth*, τῆς σαρκός Arist.*IA*710a32, cf. Gal.*UP*16.5; χόνδρου Ruf.*Oss.*38: abs., Thphr. *HP*5.2.2.

**περιφῠτεύω**, *plant round about*, περὶ δὲ πτελέας ἐφύτευσαν Il.6.419; πέριξ δένδρων ἄλσος π. Pl.*Lg.*947e: metaph., π. τὰ πάθη τινί Lxx 4*Ma.* 2.21.

**περίφῠτος**, ον, *planted all over*, ὄρος π. ἐλάαις App.*Hisp.*64.

**περιφύω**, fut. -φύσω [ῡ]: aor. 1 περιέφῡσα:—*make to grow round* or *upon, stick* or *fix upon*, κύτος περὶ τὸ σῶμα Pl.*Ti.*78d; τοῖς κερασφόροις.. ἡ φύσις ὀστᾶ π. τὸ κέρας Philostr.*VA*2.13. II. Pass., with fut. Med. -φύσομαι [ῡ]: pf. and aor. 2 Act. περιπέφῡκα, περιέφῡν: aor. 2 inf. περιφῦναι, part. περιφύς [ῠ]:—*grow round about*, περὶ δ' αἴγειροι πεφύασιν Od.9.141; περὶ τὰ ὀστᾶ αἱ σάρκες περιπεφύκασι Arist. *PA*654b27, cf. *GA*754a2; π. καὶ ἐμφυόμενα Thphr.*CP*5.5.4; πέτρα κύκλῳ.. περιπέφυκε *there is* rock *all round*, Plu.*Cam.*25. 2. of persons, *cling to*, c. dat., περιφῦσ' Ὀδυσῆϊ Od.19.416: abs., Τηλέμαχον.. κύσεν περιφύς 16.21; κύσσαι καὶ περιφῦναι ἐὸν πατέρα (where the acc. depends on κύσσαι) 24.236, cf. 320; of shoes, περιέφυσαν Περσικαί τινι Ar.*Nu.*151; of ivy, κισσὸς καλάμῳ περιφύεται Eub.104 (lyr.); [τῇ ψυχῇ] γεηρὰ.. πολλὰ καὶ ἄγρια περιπέφυκε Pl.*R.*612a, cf. *Lg.* 898e; of a report, φήμη π. τινί Isoc.5.78. 3. *sprout*, of ears of corn, prob. f.l. (for θερισθῇ) in Thphr.*HP*8.11.4.

**περιφων-έω**, *sound round, re-echo*, Plu.*Mar.*20. **-ησις**, εως, ἡ, *sounding round about*, prob. in Id.2.587c.

**περίφωρος**, ον, (φώρ) *detected*, Plu.2.49c.

**περιφωτ-ίζω**, *shine round about, illuminate*, Cleom.2.1; πᾶσαν τὴν ψυχήν Plot.6.9.4:—Pass., Plu.2.953a, Dam.*Pr.*83. **-ισμός**, ὁ, *shining round about*, Hld.9.22; but v.l. for παραφ- in Str.3.1.5.

**περιχαίνω**, v. περιχάσκω.

**περιχαίρω**, *rejoice exceedingly*, Eun.*VS*p.461 B.

**περιχᾰλάω**, *relax all round*, περικεχαλασμένων τῶν σαρκῶν Lxx 4*Ma.*7.13.

**περιχᾰλῑνόω**, *put a bridle on*, ἵππους App.*Syr.*26.

**περιχαλκ-ίζω**, = περιχαλκόω, in Pass., *BGU*283.16 (i A.D.). ® **-ος**, ον, *covered with brass* or *copper*, Theodor.Hierap.ap.Ath.10. 413b. ® **-όω**, *cover with brass* or *copper*, Lxx *Ex.*27.6.

**περιχαμπτά**, corrupt word in A.*Supp.*878 (lyr.).

**περιχανδής**, ές, *capacious*, χύτρος Nic.*Fr.*72.3.

**περιχᾰρᾰκ-όω**, *surround with a stockade*, τὸ τεῖχος Aeschin.3. 236; *fortify*, Plb.4.56.8; π. [πόλιν] ἐκ θαλάσσης ἐς θάλασσαν Ph.*Bel.* 96.39; *blockade, besiege*, App.*Hisp.*90:—Pass., *to be besieged*, Polyaen. 2.2.5 (-εύομαι ibid., s.v.l.): metaph., πατρίδα συμβουλίαις -κεχαρακωμένην Din.1.64. **-τέον**, *one must incise around*, Archig.ap. Orib.44.26.8. **-τήρ**, ῆρος, ὁ, *instrument for detaching* the gums before drawing teeth, Cael.Aur.*TP*2.4, Aët.8.36, Pall.*in Hp.*2.174 D. **-τικός**, ή, όν, *causing tissues to form a line of demarcation round*, ἐσχαρῶν Dsc.1.105; π. δύναμις Id.2.100. **-ωμα**, ατος, τό, *entrenchment*, Hsch. s.v. θρι[γκ]ός, *EM*455.55.

**περι-χάραξις** [χᾰ], εως, ἡ, *demarcation by incision*, Orib.44.11.1; *incision* made for purposes of grafting, *Gp.*10.77.2. **-χᾰράσσω**, Att. -ττω, *entrench all round*, χωρίον τάφρῳ Str.15.1.42: in Medicine, *demarcate*, Dsc.1.72, 2.112; also, *detach from gums all round*, ὀδόντας Gal.14.431:—Pass., φύλλον περικεχαραγμένον *serrated*, cj. Scalig. in Thphr.*HP*3.12.5, cf. 3.14.1.

**περιχάρ-εια** [ᾰ], ἡ, *excessive joy*, Pl.*Phlb.*65d, Ph.1.460; opp. περιωδυνία, Pl.*Lg.*732c: in pl., Plu.2.83d, Gal.10.841, Plot.1.4.12:—incorrectly written -ία, D.C.44.8, Alciphr.3.38, Adam.2.38, etc. **-ής**, ές, (χαίρω) *exceeding glad*, Hdt.1.119, 3.35, 157, S.*Aj.*693 (lyr.), Diph. 43.19; τινι *at* a thing, Hdt.1.31, Ar.*V.*1477, *Pax* 309; ἐπί τινι Pl.*R.* 462b (opp. περιαλγής), Plb.1.41.1, D.S.11.57; διά τι Plb.4.86.5; τὸ π., = περιχάρεια, Th.2.51, 7.73.

**περιχάσκω**, aor. 2 περιέχᾰνον and pf. περικέχηνα (as if from περιχαίνω, which is post-classical):—*open the mouth wide, gape*, Hp. *Morb.*2.26, Phld.*Rh.*1.194 S. b. *open* a girdle, Heliod.ap.Orib. 48.58.5 (s.v.l.). II. *close the jaws over, take into the mouth*, Arist. *HA*604b18, D.S.10.18, Dsc.*Eup.*2.138, Luc.*Merc.Cond.*3, Ael.*NA*4. 33, *Hippiatr.*119; π. τὸν ἀέρα *snap at* the air, of a lion, Ach.Tat. 2.22.

**περιχειλόω**, *edge round*, σιδήρῳ *with* iron, X.*Eq.*4.4.

® **περί-χειρον**, τό, *armlet, bracelet*, Plb.2.29.8:—Dim. ® **-χειρίδιον**, τό, Hsch. s.v. ἀβάκχευτον; also **-χείριον**, τό, Poll.1.185.

**περιχειρίδες**, αἱ, *sleeves*, Lyd.*Mag.*1.17.

**περιχέω**, Ep. **περιχεύω**, aor. περίχευα (v. infr.), *pour, spread*, or *scatter round* or *over*, ἣν [ἠέρα] οἱ περίχευεν Ἀθήνη Od.7.140, cf. 13. 189 (tm.), Il.5.776 (tm.); of solids, ἅλις χέραδος περιχεύας 21.319; χρυσὸν κέρασιν περιχεύας *having spread* gold leaf *round* its horns, 10. 294: metaph., τῷ περίχευε χάριν κεφαλῇ τε καὶ ὤμοις Od.23.162; σκότος τοῖς δικασταῖς 'throw dust in the eyes of..', Plu.*Cic.*25:—Med., ὡς δ' ὅτε τις χρυσὸν περιχεύεται ἀργύρῳ Od.6.232, 23.159:—Pass., *to be poured around*, περὶ δ' ἀμβρόσιος κέχυθ' ὕπνος Il.2.19; ἣν σκότος περιχυθῇ Hp.*VC*11; τῶν ὀστέων περικεχυμένων *scattered all round*, v.l. in Hdt.3.12: metaph., -χυθεῖσα θεωρία, εὐδαιμονία, Vett.Val.241.5, 246.18. 2. of persons, π. στρατὸν τείχει Hld.9.1:—freq. in Pass., περιχυθέντες *crowding round*, Hdt.9.120; τῷ ναυκλήρῳ περικεχύσθαι Pl.*R.*488c, cf. *Plt.*268c, X.*HG*2.2.21. 3. π. τινί (sc. ὕδωρ) *pour water over* one, D.L.2.36:—Med., *pour* or *have poured over oneself*, πρὶν ἐνβῆναι ἐν τῷ βαλανείῳ εἰς τὸ θερμὸν ὕδωρ οἶνον περιχέασθαι *IG*4²(1).126.13 (Epid.); μικρὸν περιχέασθαι *take* a moderate *bath*, Mnesith.ap.Ath.11.484b; ψυχρῷ π. Anon.Lond.38.39; στολὴν.. π. Eun.*VS*p.477 B. II. Pass., *embrace*, τινι Luc.*Luct.*13, cf. *Alex.*45, Parth.28.2 (cj.); πανταχόθεν αὐτῷ -χυθεῖσα Hld.1.2. III. *drench*, τι ὕδατι Dsc.4.150.4.

**περίχθων**, ὁ, ἡ, gen. ονος, *round about the earth, AP*9.778 (Phil.), dub. in Orph.*Fr.*285.57.

**περιχῑλόω**, *eat one's fill*, Hsch.

**περιχλαιν-ίζομαι**, Med., *wrap oneself in a cloak*, Hsch. (-χλαν- cod.), Phot.:—Act., and also Subst. **-ισμός**, ὁ, Hdn.*Epim.*149.

**περίχολος**, ον, *full of bile*, διαχωρήματα Hp.*Prorrh.*1.53, *Coac.* 590.

**περιχονδριάω**, *to be swollen*, cj. in *Com.Adesp.*1116.

**περιχόραι**· περιχορεῖαι, Hsch.

**περιχορ-εύω**, *dance round*, [ἐκεῖσε καὶ τὸ δεῦρο] E.*Ph.*316 (lyr.); τινα Luc.*DMar.*15.3; τὸν βωμόν Id.*Salt.*24: metaph., ἡ φιλία π. τὴν οἰκουμένην Epicur.*Sent.Vat.*52. **-ίζω**, = foreg., Hsch.

**περί-χρισις**, εως, ἡ, *anointing*, ὀφθαλμικαὶ π. Dsc.1.99. **-χρισμα**, ατος, τό, *ointment, salve*, Alex.Trall.7.8: metaph., τὰ π. τῶν παιδευόντων, of music used as 'jam to coat the pill', Phld.*Mus.* p.96 K. **-χριστέον**, *one must anoint, Gp.*17.5.1. **-χριστος**, ὁ, *ointment*, Archig.ap.Orib.44.26.11 (pl.); συναγχικῶν περίχριστος Dsc. 1.77; δίχα τῆς τῶν ἔξωθεν περιχρίστων ἐπιθέσεως Plu.2.102a. -χρίω [ῑ], *smear* or *cover over*, κλινόποδας σκορόδοις Str.17.3.11; τοὺς ὀδόντας Archig.ap.Gal.12.873; τι ὑάλῳ Luc.*Luct.*21; τὸ πρόσωπον Poll.5. 102:—Pass., Dsc.1.77. II. *pour as unguent over*, ἔλαιον J.*AJ*7. 14.5, cf. Nonn.*D.*14.175. III. metaph. (cf. περίχρισμα), prob. in Phld.*Mus.*p.97 K. (Pass.).

**περίχροος**, ον, contr. **-χρους**, χρουν, *highly-coloured*, Gal.16.627.

**περίχρῡσ-ος**, ον, *set in gold*, *IG*1$^2$.280.78; σφραγὶς π. ib.2$^2$.1388.91, 1459.18, Chares 4 J., Luc.*Nec.*12; cf. κατάχρυσος, ἐπίχρυσος. **-όω**, *gild all over*, Agatharch.*Fr.Hist.*2 J., v.l. for κατα- in Hdt.4.65:—but in Pass., σφραγὶς περικεχρυσωμένη, = περίχρυσος, *with a gold mount* or *setting*, *IG*2$^2$.1388.88, cf. *POxy.*1449.22 (iii A.D.).

**περί-χῠδᾰ**, Adv. *by sprinkling*, Hp.*Aff.*52. **-χῠμα**, ατος, τό, *that which is poured round* or *over*, *wash*, Dsc.1.87; of whey, Gal.17 (1).983. II. *that which is diffused around the earth*, *atmosphere*, τὸ ἱερὸν π. Herm.ap.Stob.1.49.44. III. *ablution*, Marin.*Procl.* 26. **-χῠσις**, εως, ἡ, *pouring over*, ἐλαίου Orib.46.20.11; *washing out*, Dsc.5.103; *douche*, Gal.12.461. II. *diffusion*, Herm.ap. Stob.1.49.69; π. ὑγροῦ, ἀκτίνων, Porph.*Gaur.*3.3, 11.2: in concrete sense, τοῦ θείου ἐν πυρὸς αἰθερίου π. διάγοντος Id.ap.Eus.*PE*3.7. **-χῠτέον**, *one must pour over*, Herod.Med.ap.Aët.4.47. **-χῠτήριον**, τό, *perfusorium*, *Gloss.* ⊕ **-χύτης** [ῠ], ου, ὁ, *attendant at baths*, π. λουτροῦ *POxy.*148 (vi A.D.), cf. Ptol.*Tetr.*179, *Cod.Just.*3.43.1.4.

**περιχύτρισμα**, ατος, τό, *space round an olive-tree marked by potsherds*, *IG*2$^2$.2492.44.

**περί-χωμα**, ατος, τό, *embankment*, *dyke enclosing an area*, *PPetr.*3 p.339 (iii B.C.), *Ostr.Bodl.*i 245 (iii B.C.), *PTeb.*61(*b*).167 (ii B.C.). II. *area enclosed by dykes*, *PCair.Zen.*182.7, 362.24 (iii B.C.), *PTeb.*13.12, 84.3 (ii B.C.). ⊕ **-χωμᾰτίζω**, *surround with a dyke*, *PLond.*3.1170*B* 298 (iii A.D.):—hence **-ισμός**, ὁ, *PRyl.*172.22 (iii A.D.), etc.

**περιχωνεύομαι**, *to be fused in an amalgam with*, χρυσῷ Dsc.*Eup.* 2.168.

**περιχώννῡμι**, *heap earth round*, τὰς ἀμπέλους D.S.17.82, cf. Dsc.5. 148 (Pass.):—Pass., *to be covered with* mud, etc., D.S.3.40: metaph., περιχωσθῆναι τοῖς τοξεύμασιν Philostr.*VA*4.23. II. *embank*, γῆν *PSI*6.577.8 (iii B.C.), cf. *PLille* 1$^v$ 20 (iii B.C.).

**περιχώομαι**, Med., *to be exceeding angry*, ὅς μοι παλλακίδος περιχώσατο (al. παλλακίδος πέρι χ., v. Sch.) Il.9.449; Ἡρακλῆος περιχώσατο 14.266.

**περιχωρ-έω**, *go round*, σὺ περιχώρει λαβὼν τὴν χέρνιβα Ar.*Av.*958; π. τὴν Ἑλλάδα Thales ap.D.L.1.44. II. *rotate*, Anaxag.9, 12. 2. *to be transferred to*, *come to in succession*, ἡ βασιληΐη π. ἐς Δαρεῖον Hdt. 1.210; ἡ ὀργὴ π. ἐς τό τινων μίασμα D.C.40.49. **-ησις**, εως, ἡ, *rotation*, Anaxag.12, 13. ⊕ **-ιος**, ον, = περίχωρος: τὰ π. Str.1.2.15 (s.v.l.). **-ιστος**, ον, *separate*, *isolated*, Elias *in Porph.*19.23. ⊕ **-ος**, ον, *round about a place*: οἱ π. *the people about*, D.19.266, Plu.*Cat.Ma.* 25, *Eum.*15, etc.; ἡ π. (sc. γῆ) *the country round about*, Lxx *Ge.*13. 10, al., *Ev.Matt.*14.35; τὰ π. Palaeph.20.

**περίχωσις**, εως, ἡ, *covering over with earth*, *PSI*6.577.13 (iii B.C.). 2. *dyke*, *embankment*, *PLille* 1$^v$ 20 (iii B.C., pl.).

**περιψαύω**, *touch*, *attack* a part, of pains, Nic.*Al.*122.

⊕ **περιψ-άω**, *wipe all round*, *wipe clean*, τῷ φθαλμιδίῳ περιψῆν Ar.*Eq.* 909; τὰ βλέφαρα περιέψησεν Id.*Pl.*730; σφόγγοι περιψῆσαι τὰ ἀναθήματα *IG*11(2).287 *A* 84 (Delos, iii B.C.); π. σπόγγῳ τὸ ἄγγος Zos. Alch.p.224 B. ⊕ **-ημα**, ατος, τό, *anything wiped off*, *offscouring*, of a vile person (or *scapegoat*), 1*Ep.Cor.*4.13, Phot.; π. σου your *humble servant*, *CIL*8.12924 (Carthage), *LW*2493 (Syria), *Classical Studies in honor of J.C.Rolfe* 318 (Ostia); *peripsuma su* (sic), Dessau *ILS* 5725 (Brixia). **-ησις**, εως, ἡ, *wiping clean*, μύλωνος Suid. s.v. ψαιστά.

⊕ **περίψηφος**, ὁ, *calculator*, Sch.Ar.*Pl.*237, Hsch. s.v. ῥυπαρός, Suid. s.v. λογισταί.

**περιψήχω**, sine interpr., *Gloss.*

**περιψῐθῠρίζω**, *whisper around*, Suid. s.v. περιηχήθην (Pass.).

**περιψῑλ-όομαι**, Pass., *to be made bare all round*, περιψιλωθῆναι τὰς σάρκας *to have one's* flesh *all stripped off*, Hdt.9.83. **-ωσις**, εως, ἡ, sine interpr., *Gloss.*

**περιψοφ-έω**, *sound loudly around*, in Pass., τοῖς κυμβάλοις J.*AJ*11. 3.9; πατάγῳ Plu.2.266d. **-ησις**, εως, ἡ, *sounding all round*, *loud noise*, ib.549c (pl.).

**περι-ψυγμός**, ὁ, *cold*, *chill*, Pl.*Ax.*366d; *excessive cold*, as a cause of injury, *Cat.Cod.Astr.*8(4).188 (pl.). **-ψυκτος**, ον, *very cold*, *chill*, of places, Plu.*Aem.*14, Id.2.649c; f.l. (for περὶ ψῦχος) in Eratosth.16.12. II. *fanned all round*: hence, *fondled*, *beloved*, Alciphr.3.59; π. κάλλος Eun.*VS* p.455 B.; cf. περιψύκτης (sic)· περιπόθητος, Hsch. **-ψυξις**, εως, ἡ, *shivering*, Hp.*Prorrh.*1.134 (pl.), Ph.1.39, Herod.Med.ap.Orib.10.37.1, etc. II. *chilling*, *cooling*, Arist.*Fr.*231, Thphr.*Ign.*52, Chrysipp.*Stoic.*2.222, Plu.2.73c, etc. **-ψῡχρος**, ον, *cold all round* or *very cold*, ἄκρεα Hp.*Epid.*1.18 (v.l. ὑποψ-), Thphr.*Sens.*58. **-ψύχω** [ῡ], *chill all round*, τὴν σάρκα Arist.*Pr.*966$^b$11:—Pass., *to be chilled all over*, Hp.*Epid.*1.26.γ′; *grow cool*, Thphr.*Ign.*52, Plu.2.690d:—also intr. in Act., Hp.*Coac.*176, *Epid.*3.17.α′, Thphr. l.c. II. metaph., *refresh*, *revive*, *cherish*, τινα Lxx *Si.*30.7 (v.l.), D.H.7.46 (cj. Reiske), Alciphr.1.39.

**περιώγανα**· ἐπίσσωτρα, Hsch. II. = κνημίαι II. 1, Id.

**περιωδευμένως**, Adv. pf. part. Pass. of περιοδεύω, *fully*, *in detail*, Phld.*Rh.*1.248 S., Plu.2.537d.

**περιῳδ-έω**, *subdue by spells*, Ps.-Luc.*Philopatr.*9. **-ή**, ἡ, = καμπή III. 1, Sch.Ar.*Nu.*332. **-ικά**, τά, *metrical systems in which the strophic correspondence is of the form abbb..c*, Heph.*Poëm.*4, cf. Sch.

**περιωδῡν-άω**, *suffer great pain*, Dsc.3.23, Gal.12.603:—Med., v.l. in Hp.*Aph.*7.52. **-έω**, = foreg., π. κεφαλήν ib.6.10, *Morb.*3.1, *Epid.* 5.12, Herod.Med.ap.Orib.10.10.4. **-ής**, ές, = περιώδυνος, Id.ib.10. 5.6. **-ία**, ἡ, *excessive pain*, Pl.*R.*583d; opp. περιχάρεια, Id.*Lg.* 732c; of headache, Hp.*Aff.*2: in pl., αἱ ἀπὸ τῶν φρενῶν π. Id.*Acut.* (*Sp.*)34; ἥπατος π. ib.4; οἱ θάνατοι καὶ π. Arist.*Po.*1452$^b$12. **-ος**, ον, (ὀδύνη) *exceeding painful*, of death, A.*Ag.*1448 (lyr.); τύχη Pl.*Lg.* 873c. II. *suffering great pain*, Hp.*Acut.*(*Sp.*)34, D.54.12, Parth. 5.5. Adv. -νως Hsch. s.v. περισφάτως.

**περιωθέω**, *push*, *shove about*, περιωθῶν καὶ ἐλαύνων τοὺς ἀνθρώπους D.21.173. 2. *push* or *force round*, π. εἴσω τὴν ἀναπνοήν Pl.*Ti.*79c, cf. e, Arist.*Resp.*472$^b$18:—Pass., *to be pushed away*, περιεώσμεθα ἐκ πάντων Th.3.57; π. ἔν τινι *lose one's place* in a person's favour, ib. 67; ἀσθενὲς ὂν π. ὑπὸ τοῦ βιαιοτέρου D.H.7.25; εἰς τὴν φάραγγα -ωσθεὶς App.*BC*1.45: abs., *to be rejected*, *defeated*, Arist.*Pol.*1304$^a$8 (v.l. περιωρισθείς), cf. 1306$^a$32. 3. λόγων ἀρετῇ -ωθούμενος *moved by..*, J.*AJ*17.3.1.

**περίωμα**, written for πελίωμα, *POxy.*52.16 (iv A.D.).

**περιωμιάζω**, *surround with an espalier* (ὠμία), περίβολος περιωμιασμένος *PVat.*11$^r$ v 5 (ii A.D.).

**περιώνῠμος**, ον, *far-famed*, Orph.*A.*149, *IG*3.914; γένους λαμπρότητι App.*BC*2.2, etc.

**περιωπ-έω**, *gaze around upon*, τὰ ἀνθρώπου Philostr.*Dial.*2:—Med., -ήσασθαι πάντα Sch.D Il.14.8. **-ή**, ἡ, (ὤψ) *place commanding a wide view*, Il.14.8, 23.451, Od.10.146, Pl.*Plt.*272e; παράκτιος π. *AP* 6.167 (Agath.); ἐκ περιωπῆς from *a place of vantage*, by *a bird's-eye view*, Luc.*Symp.*11, *Im.*1; ἐκ π. τοῦ Πηλίου from *the summit* of P., Philostr.*Her.*19.1. II. *circumspection*, πολλὴν π. τινὸς ποιεῖσθαι to show much *caution* in a thing, Th.4.87. III. *contemplation*, ἐπιστήμης, τοῦ θείου, Procl *in Alc.*pp.19, 21 C.: pl., ταῖς τοῦ νοῦ π. Dam.*Pr.*54. ⊕ **-ος**, ον, *visible all round*, Hsch. s.v. ἀμφίσωπον: in Orph.*A.*14 περιωπέα..Ἔρωτα is prob. f.l. for πυριωπέα.

**περιωρεσία**, ἡ, *surrounding hills*, *IG*14.352 ii 38 (Halaesa).

**περιώσιος**, ον, *immense*, *countless*, χρήματα Sol.24.7; μήδεα *Lyr. Adesp.* in *TGF* p.xx; φῦλα A.R.2.394; ἔργον *AP*9.197 (Marin.); ὀργιοφάντης ib.688; θεάτρου κύκλος *Epigr.Gr.*1050 (Ephesus). 2. = περισσός, *unusual*, *rare*, περιώσια εἰδώς, of Pythagoras, Emp.129.1; ἄγρη Opp.*C.*4.354. II. Hom. only neut. as Adv. περιώσιον, *beyond measure*, Il.4.359, Od.16.203: pl., περιώσια *h.Pan.*41. 2. c. gen., περιώσιον ἄλλων *far beyond* the rest, *h.Cer.*362, Pi.*I.*5(4).3, A.R.1.466.—Regul. Adv. -ίως only in Hsch.; cf. περώσιος.

**περίωσις**, εως, ἡ, *driving round* of the breath, Arist.*Resp.*472$^b$6, Gal.5.708.

**περιωτειλόομαι**, *to be cicatrized all round*, Hp.*Art.*63.

**περιωτίς**, ίδος, ἡ, = ἀμφωτίς, Method.ap.*EM*93.14.

**πέρκα**, ἡ, = πέρκη, *Gloss.*

**περκ-άζω**, (πέρκος = περκνός) *become dark*, *turn dark*, of grapes beginning to ripen, ὀπώρα ἄκραισι περκάζουσα οἰνάνθαις Chaerem. 12.2; ὅταν ἄρτι π. σταφυλή Thphr.*HP*9.11.7, cf. *Hymn.Is.*168, Lxx *Am.*9.13; ὅταν ἄρχωνται π. οἱ βότρυες Thphr.*CP*3.16.3, etc.; of olives, *Gp.*9.19.2; of flowers, Porph.*VP*44. 2. metaph., of young men, whose beard begins to *darken* their faces, Call.*Lav.Pall.* 76. II. Act., *make dark-coloured*, Dsc.5.2. **-αίνω**, = foreg., σέλας οἰνωπὸν ἐξέλαμπε περκαίνων γένυν E.*Cret.*15; = διαποικίλλεσθαι, Hsch.

**πέρκανα**· ἱστοῦ περιπλέγματα, Hsch.; cf. πευκάνα.

**περκάς**, άδος, poet. fem. of πέρκος, κίχλη Eratosth.12.2.

**πέρκ-η**, ἡ, a river-fish, *perch*, Epich.47, 48, Philyll.13.3, Antiph. 194.2, Arist.*HA*505$^a$17, 599$^b$8, Numen.ap.Ath.7.313c. (Perh. cogn. with περκνός.) **-ίδιον**, τό, Dim. of foreg., Anaxandr.27 (anap.):—also -ίον, τό, *PCair.Zen.*66.14 (iii B.C.). **-ίς**, ίδος, ἡ, = πέρκη, Dsc. 2.33.

**περκνόπτερος**, ον, *dusky-winged*, name of a kind of *vulture*, Arist. *HA*618$^b$32.

**περκνός**, ή, όν, *dusky*, *dark in colour*, of grapes when beginning to ripen, or of olives, Poll.1.61, 5.67; περκνὴν (prob. for πρέκνην)..ἐλάην *AP*6.102 (Phil.); also π. ἔχις Arist.*Mir.*846$^b$18, Nic.*Th.*129; π. ἰχθύες Marc.Sid.7; *livid*, Hp.*VC*19. II. Subst., name of a kind of *eagle*, αἰετὸν.., μόρφνον θηρητῆρ', ὃν καὶ περκνὸν καλέουσι Il.24.316 (Aristarch. πέρκνον), cf. Arist.*Mir.*835$^a$2, Lyc.260; = πλάγγος acc. to Arist.*HA*618$^b$23. (Cf. πρακνόν, Skt. *pṛ́śnis* 'spotted', OIr. *erc*, Welsh *erch* 'speckled', 'dusky'.)

**πέρκος**, ὁ, a kind of *hawk*, Arist.*HA*620$^a$20.

**πέρκωμα**, ατος, τό, *dusky spot on the face*, Hsch. (pl.).

**πέρνα** (late Ep. πτέρνα Batr.37 (s.v.l.)), ης, ἡ, *ham*, Str.3.4.11, Poll.2.193 (πτέρνα codd.), *PSI*6.683.33 (ii A.D.), Ath.14.657e, *Edict. Diocl.Aeg.*4.8:—also πέρνη, Hdn.Gr.2.939 (fort. Πέρνη). (Borrowed from Lat. *perna*.)

**πέρναξ**· θρίδαξ, Hsch.

**περνάω**, *sell*, aor. imper. πέρνησον Hsch.; cf. sq.

⊕ **πέρνημι**, 3 pl. περνᾶσι Thgn.1215, Hippon.46 (2 sg. περνᾷς dub. in 52); part. περνάς Il.22.45, Hippon.52 (v.l.), E.*Cyc.*271: Ep. Iterat. 3 sg. πέρνασκε Il.24.752: Ep. fut. inf. περάαν 21.454 (but pres. περάω is wrongly inferred from forms like ἐπέρασσα): aor. ἐπέρασσα ib.40, Od.15.387; part. περάσαντες *h.Cer.*132; aor. opt. 3 sg. περάσειε [ᾰ] Od.14.297; aor. subj. 2 pl. περάσητε 15.453, cf. ἀποπέρνημι; also aor. ἔπρησα *Schwyzer* 714 (Samos, vi B.C.): pf. πέπρᾱκα Alex.146.1,

Is.7.31, etc. (v. infr.): plpf. ἐπεπράκειν [ᾰ] D.18.23:—**Pass.**, pres. 3 sg. πέρνᾰται Ar.*Eq.*176, Hsch.: impf. 3 pl. ἐπέρναντο Pi.*I.*2.7; part. περνάμενος [ᾰ] Il.18.292: pf. part. once πεπερημένος 21.58; elsewh. the pf. is Att. πέπρᾱμαι, A.*Ch.*132, S.*Ph.*978, etc., inf. πεπρᾶσθαι Ar. *Ach.*734, *Pax* 1011, And.1.73, etc.; Ion. πέπρημαι Hdt.2.56, imper. πεπρήσθω *SIG*45.35 (Halic., v B.C.), inf. πεπρῆσθαι ib.38: plpf. ἐπέπρᾱτο Ar.*Ach.*522: aor. Trag. and Att. ἐπράθην [ᾰ] Sol.36.7, A.*Ch.* 915, And.1.133, etc.; Ion. ἐπρήθην Hdt.1.156, *SIG*229.5 (Erythrae, iv B.C.), etc.: Att. fut. πεπράσομαι [ᾰ] Ar.*V.*179, X.*An.*7.1.36, later πρᾱθήσομαι Sopat.6, Lxx *Le.*25.23, etc., cf. Moer.p.294 P.: Aeol. pres. inf. **πόρναμεν** Hsch. (fort. πορνάμεναι): pres. part. Pass. πορνάμεναι Id.—In Att. the usual pres. in act. sense is πωλέω, fut. ἀποδώσομαι, aor. ἀπεδόμην: from πέπρᾱμαι, ἐπράθην, etc. is formed the later pres. Pass. **πιπράσκομαι**, first found in Lys.18.20, interpol. in Pl.*Phd.* 69b, *Sph.*224a, and from this the pres. Act. **πιπράσκω** first found in Luc.*Asin.*32: impf. ἐπίπρασκον Plu.2.178c, *Per.*16; Ion. **πιπρήσκω** Call.*Iamb.*1.93, v.l. in Hp.*Ep.*17:—*export for sale*, in Ep. usu. of *exporting* captives to foreign parts *for sale* as slaves, πολλοὺς ζωοὺς ἕλον ἠδὲ πέρασσα Il.21.102, cf. Od.14.297; π. τινὰ Λῆμνον *sell* one *to* Lemnos, Il.21.40; ἐς Λῆμνον ib.58 (Pass.), 78; σέ γε.. νησοῖν λάβον ἠδ' ἐπέρασσαν τοῦδ' ἀνδρὸς πρὸς δῶμαθ' Od.15.387; κατ' ἀλλοθρόους ἀνθρώπους ib.453; δήσειν καὶ περάαν νήσων ἔπι τηλεδαπάων Il.21.454; κτείνων καὶ περνὰς v. ἕ. τ. 22.45; πέρνασχ' ὅν τιν' ἕλεσκε πέρην ἁλὸς.. ἐς Σάμον 24.752; οὐδ' ἡμᾶς περνᾶσι Thgn. l.c., cf. Hippon.46; later also of other merchandise, ὡς χαραδριὸν περνάς Id.52 (v.l. μῶν..περνᾷς;); τοῖς ξένοις τὰ χρήματα περνάντα σ' εἶδον E.*Cyc.* l.c.:—Pass., κτήματα περνάμεν' ἵκει Il.18.292, cf. Pi.*I.*2.7; πάντα..πέρναται Ar.*Eq.*176. 2. simply, *sell* (as always in the Att. forms), τὰ κτήματα πέντε ταλάντων πεπρακότας Is. l.c.:—Pass., *to be sold*, esp. for exportation, Sol. l.c., Hdt.1.156, A.*Ch.*915, E.*Ion* 310; ἐς Λιβύην, ἐς Θεσπρωτούς, Hdt.2. 54,56; ἐπ' ἐξαγωγῇ *SIG*45.38 (Halic., v B.C.); ὠνούμενά τε καὶ πιπρασκόμενα interpol. in Pl.*Phd.*69b; τὸ ὠνηθὲν ἢ πραθὲν Id.*Lg.*850a; πραθείσης ὀλίγου [τῆς πεντηκοστῆς] the tax of 2 per cent. *having been sold* or *let* for a small sum, And.1.133. II. *sell* for a bribe, of political leaders, τοὺς πεπρακότας αὐτοὺς ἐκείνῳ D.10.63, cf. 17.13; τὰ ὅλα πεπρακέναι Id.18.28; τἄλλα πλὴν ἑαυτοὺς οἰομένους πωλεῖν πάντους ἑαυτοὺς πεπρακόσιν αἰσθέσθαι ib.46; τὴν πατρῴαν γῆν πεπρακέναι Din.1.71; πεπρακότες τὴν τοῦ βίου παρρησίαν Alex.146.1: metaph. in Pass., πέπραμαι *I am bought and sold!*, i.e. *betrayed, ruined*, πέπραμαι κἀπόλωλα S.*Ph.*978; εὐμορφίᾳ πραθεῖσα E.*Tr.*936. (Cogn. with περάω (A), πέραν, OIr. *renaid* 'he sells'.)

**πέροδος**, ἡ, Dor. for περίοδος, Pi.*N.*11.40, *IG*2².1126.16 (Delph., iv B.C.).

**περομνύναι**· ἐλέγχεσθαι, Hsch.

**περόν-ᾱμα**, Dor. for περόνημα. **-άω**, *pierce, transfix*, δουρὶ μέσον περόνησε Il.7.145, 13.397; π. μέσον τὸν βραχίονα D.H.6.11; ἔδειξε..τὰς χεῖρας ὡς ἦσαν πεπερονημέναι Cels.ap.Orig.*Cels.*2.55. 2. Med., *buckle on one's* mantle, *one's* robe, χλαῖναν περονήσατο, ἑανὸν περονᾶτο, Il.10.133, 14.180; λῶπος περονᾶσθαι Theoc.14.66, cf. A.R. 1.722. ⊛ **-η**, ἡ, (πείρω) *pin* or *tongue of a buckle* or *brooch, buckle* or *brooch* itself, Il.5.425, Od.19.226,256, E.*Ph.*805 (lyr.); ἐν δ' ἄρ' ἔσαν [πέπλῳ] περόναι δυοκαίδεκα πᾶσαι χρύσειαι Od.18.293, cf. *IG*1². 369.11, 2².1388.20; used for wounding, Hdt.5.87, S.*OT*1269. 2. *pin* for twisting ropes round, on board ship, A.R.1.567. 3. *pivot* of door-post, περόνησιν ἀρηρότε Parm.1.20; of a machine, Heliod.ap.Orib.49.24.1, al. 4. *linchpin*, Parth.6.4. 5. *rivet, bolt*, π. χαλκαῖ *Inscr.Délos* 504.12 (iii B.C.); π. κεφαλωτή Ph.*Bel.*76. 3. b. *rivet* in the Roman *pilum*, Plu.*Mar.*25. II. *small bone of the arm, radius*, Hp.*Loc.Hom.*6 (dub.), *Oss.*3: more freq. *of the leg, fibula*, Gal.*UP*3.9, al., v.l. in Hp.*Art.*62. 2. *ligament* below the knee of a horse, X.*Eq.*1.5. 3. = ἐπίφυσις 2, Hp.*Loc.Hom.*6. 4. pl., *splint-bones*, Poll.2.191. III. a kind of *fish*, Marc.Sid.15 (pl.). **-ημα**, Dor. **-ᾱμα**, ατος, τό, *garment pinned* or *buckled on*, Theoc.15.79. **-ητήρ**, ῆρος, ὁ, *buckle, brooch*, *IG*2².47.12 (iv B.C.). **-ητρίς**, Dor. **-ᾱτρίς**, ίδος, ἡ, *robe fastened on the shoulder with a buckle* or *brooch*, Theoc.15.21: as Adj., ἀμπεχόναι περονητρίδες cj. for -ήτιδες in *AP*7.413 (Antip.). **-ίδιον**, τό, Dim. of περόνη I.1, *POxy.*496.3 (ii A.D.), Sch.E.*Hec.*1170. **-ιον**, τό, Dim. of περόνη, *small peg* or *pin*, Ph.*Bel.*62.14, Hero *Aut.*28.1, *Spir.* 1.42. II. *shackle* or *ring* into which a bolt fits, Ph.*Bel.*76.4. **-ίς**, ίδος, ἡ, = περόνη, S.*Tr.*925, *IG*11(2).219*A*35 (Delos, iii B.C.), *CPR* 12.4 (i A.D.).

**περόσχια**· τὰ ῥάκη, Hsch.

**περπερ-εύομαι**, *boast, brag*, 1*Ep.Cor.*13.4, M.Ant.5.5. **-ος**, ον, *vainglorious, braggart*, Plb.32.2.5, 39.1.2, Arr.*Epict.*3.2.14, S.E.*M.*1. 54; gloss on παρεμφάρακτος, Hsch.

**πέρρα**, ἡ, Egypt. word in Lyc.1428, = ἥλιος. II. v. πεῖρα.

**πέρρᾰμος**, ὁ, = βασιλεύς, Hsch.; Aeol. for Πρίαμος, Alc.*Supp.*8.2, *EM*665.39, etc.

**περράτων**, v. πεῖραρ. **περρέχω**, v. περιέχω. **περρησιππίαν**· τὴν ἀνατρέχουσαν ἵππον, Hsch. **πέρροχος**, v. περίοχος.

⊛ **περσέα**, ἡ, *persea*, an Egyptian tree, *Mimusops Schimperi*, Hp.*Mul.* 1.90, Thphr.*HP*3.3.5, 4.2.5, *OGI*97.9 (Taposiris, iii/ii B.C.), D.S.1. 34 (-αία codd.), Str.17.2.2, Dsc.1.129 (v.l. -αία), Plu.2.378c, etc.:—later **περσία**, *POxy.*53.7 (iv A.D.); ornament in form of its leaf, *BGU* 1028.9 (ii A.D.): also **περσεία**, poet. **-είη**, Nic.*Al.*99, Paus.5.14.3.

**πέρσειον** (which also = στρύχνον μανικόν, Dsc.4.73) or **πέρσιον**, τό, *fruit of* περσέα, Thphr.*HP*2.2.10, Posidon.3 J.: pl. πέρσεια Clearch. 65:—Dim. **περσίδιον**, *POxy.*1188.21 (i A.D.), Dioscorus in *PLit. Lond.*100 *B*:—Adj. ⊛ **περσεῖνος**, *PCair.Zen.*176.168 (iii B.C.), *CPHerm.* 7 iii 13 (iii A.D.).

**περσέπολις**, poet. also **περσέπτολις**, εως, ὁ, ἡ, (πέρθω) *destroyer of cities*; epith. of Pallas, Lamprocl.1; ὁ π. στρατός A.*Pers.*65 (lyr.; parodied by Eup.192, cf. Phryn.Com.72); π. Τρώων Poet.ap.Hld.3. 2, cf. Call.*Lav.Pall.*43.

**Περσέπολις**, εως, ἡ, *Persepolis*, the ancient capital of Persia, and burial place of her kings, Str.15.3.6, Arr.*An.*7.1.1. (Shd. perh. be written Πέρσαι πόλις (cf. Πέρσης I. 1 b); **Περσαίπολις** is v.l. in Str. and written in codd. of Ael.*NA*1.59.)

**Περσετικά**, τά, f.l. for Περσικά, as title of work by Dieuches, Ath. Mech.5.12.

**Περσεύς**, gen. έως, Ion. έος (Hdt., Pi.), Ep. ῆος, ὁ, *Perseus*, Il.14. 320, Hes.*Th.*280, etc.:—Adj. **Περσεῖος**, α, ον, E.*Hel.*1464 (lyr.); Ep. **Περσήϊος** Theoc.24.73:—Patron. **Περσείδης**, ου, ὁ, Th.1.9, etc.; Ep. **-ηϊάδης** Il.19.116,123. II. a *fish*, Ael.*NA*3.28; in Hsch. **πέρσος**. III. the constellation *Perseus*, Eudox.ap.Hipparch.1.2.15, Arat.249,484. 2. a name for the Sun, *Stoic.*2.197 (fr. περισσῶς, σεύειν). IV. = περσέα, Nic.*Th.*764.

⊛ **Περσεφόνη**, ἡ, Ep. **Περσεφόνεια** Il. and Od., the common form first in *h.Cer.*56, Hes.*Th.*913; **Φερσεφόνη**, Simon.124 B, Pi.*O.*14.21, *BMus.Inscr.*942 (iii B.C.), etc.; **Φερσεφονείη**, *CIG*4588; **Περσέφασσα**, A.*Ch.*490, etc.; **Φερσέφασσα**, S.*Ant.*894, E.*Hel.*175 (lyr.); **Φερσέφαττα**, Ar.*Th.*287, *Ra.*671; **Φερρέφαττα**, Pl.*Cra.*404c, *IG*2².1437. 58, Epicr.9:—*Persephone*, Il.9.569, Hes. l.c., etc.:—hence **Φερρεφάττιον** or **-εῖον**, τό, D.54.8, *AB*314; cf. Κόρα.

**περσεφόνιον**, τό, = ῥάμνος, Ps.-Dsc.1.90; but **φερσεφόνιον**, τό, = περιστερεὼν II, Id.4.60.

**Περσηΐς**, ίδος, ἡ, *sprung from Perseus*, of Alcmena, E.*HF*801 (lyr.). II. name of Hecate, A.R.3.467.

⊛ **Πέρσ-ης**, ου, ὁ, heterocl. acc. Πέρσεα v.l. in Hdt.8.108,109; voc. Πέρσᾰ (but Πέρση when it is the pr. n. of a person, Hdn.Gr.2.690):—*Persian*, Hdt.1.4, etc. (The Greeks derived the name of the people from Perseus, Id.7.61.) b. Πέρσαι, οἱ, the city of *Persepolis*, Beros. 16 (leg. ⟨καὶ⟩ Π.), Arr.*An.*3.18.10; cf. Περσέπολις. II. freq. as pr. n., *Perses*, Hes.*Op.*10,27, Hdt.7.61, etc.; name of a Titan, Hes. *Th.*409. III. the name of *a throw on the dice*, Hsch. **-ίζω**, *speak Persian*, X.*An.*4.5.34, Porph.*Abst.*3.5, etc. 2. *imitate the Persians*, τῇ τε σκευῇ καὶ τῇ φωνῇ Arr.*An.*7.6.3, cf. Str.11.11.8. 3. *take the side of the Persians*, Id.14.2.17. b. *take the side of Perseus*, D.S.30.5a.

**περσιθέα**, epith. of Aphrodite, Hsch.

**περσικία**, ἡ, *peach-tree*, Cyran.25.

**περσίκιον**, τό, *sceptre*, Lyd.*Mag.*2.9.

⊛ **Περσικός**, ή, όν, *Persian*, ἡ Περσική (sc. χώρα) *Persia*, Hdt.4.39, etc. Adv. **-κῶς** Ael.*VH*12.1. 2. Περσικαί, αἱ, *slippers*, Ar.*Nu.* 151; τὼ Περσικά (dual) Id.*Lys.*229. 3. ψιλὴ Π. *Persian carpet*, Callix.2. 4. Περσικός, ὁ, or Περσικόν, τό, *peach*, v. μηλέα, μῆλον (B):—also **περσική**, ἡ, *peach-tree*, Gal.12.76 (but = ἐλένιον, Dsc.1.28); Π. καρύα, ἡ, *the Persian nut, walnut*, *IG*2².1013.18, Thphr.*HP*3.6. 2. 5. Π. ὄρνις *the common cock*, Ar.*Av.*485,707; ὁ Π. alone, Cratin. 259. 6. Περσικόν, τό, *a Persian dance*, Ar.*Th.*1175; τὸ Π. ὠρχεῖτο X.*An.*6.1.10. 7. τὰ Π. *the Persian war*, Pl.*Lg.*642d, etc. (earlier called τὰ Μηδικά); but ὁ Π. πόλεμος the war *with Perseus*, Plb.3.3. 8. 8. *oriental, gorgeous*, στολαί Men.24, cf. Hipparch.Com.1.5.

**περσικών**, ῶνος, ὁ, *peach-orchard*, *IG*2².2776.91,113.

**πέρσιον**, τό, v. πέρσειον.

⊛ **πέρσις**, εως, ἡ, (πέρθω) *sacking, sack*, π. Ἰλίου, name of a tragedy, Arist.*Po.*1456ᵃ16, 1459ᵇ6; of a poem by Lesches, Paus.10.25.5; by Stesichorus, Id.10.26.1.

**Περσ-ίς**, ίδος, pecul. fem. of Περσικός, *Persian*, A.*Pers.*59 (anap.), Th.1.138; χώρη Hdt.3.97, al. II. as Subst., 1. (sc. γῆ), *Persis, Persia*, Str.15.3.1, etc. 2. (sc. γυνή) *Persian woman*, X.*Cyr.*8.5. 21, etc. 3. (sc. χλαῖνα) *Persian cloak*, Ar.*V.*1137. **-ιστί** [ῐ], Adv., (Περσίζω) *in the Persian tongue*, Hdt.9.110, X.*An.*4.5.10. II. *in the Persian fashion*, Aristid.*Or.*34(50).56.

**Περσο-γενής**, ές, *of Persian origin*, Σελεύκεια Cyran.4. **-διώκτης**, ου, ὁ, *chaser of the Persians*, *APl.*4.233 (Theaet.). **-κτόνος**, ον, *Persian-slaying*, Θεμιστοκλῆς Plu.2.349c.

**Περσ-ολέτης**, ου, ὁ, *destroyer of Persians*, Ps.-Callisth.3.22.

**Περσονομέομαι**, Pass., *to be governed by the Persian laws* or *by Persians*, A.*Pers.*585 (anap.):—from **-νόμος**, ον, *ruling Persians*, ib.919 (anap.).

**πέρσος**, v. Περσεύς II.

⊛ **πέρσυ**, = πέρυσι, *Supp.Epigr.*4.707.7 (Cyzicus):—hence **περσύας** (sc. οἶνος), ὁ, for περυσίας (περισύας codd.), *last year's wine*, Hp.ap. Gal.19.130; and **περσυνός**, = περυσινός, *Dura*⁴ 97 (iii A.D.), *PSI*1.50. 12 (iv/v A.D.); περισυνός codd. Gal. l.c.

⊛ **πέρῠσι**, before a vowel **-σιν**, Aeol. **πέρρυσι** Theoc.29.26, Dor. **πέρυτι** A.D.*Synt.*50.19: Adv.:—*a year ago, last year*, Simon.75, Cratin.76, Ar.*V.*1038, Lys.17.5, Pl.*Prt.*327d, Men.731, Theoc.15. 98; ἡ π. κωμῳδία Ar.*Ach.*378; ἡμεῖς ἐσμεν οἱ αὐτοὶ νῦν τε καὶ π. X. *HG*3.2.7; ἀπὸ π. 2*Ep.Cor.*8.10. (Cf. Skt. *parút*, Arm. *heru*, MHG. *vert* 'last year'.)

**περῠσινός**, ή, όν, *of last year, last year's*: 1. of men and animals, οἱ π. ἄρχοντες Pl.*Lg.*855c; π. φόρος *IG*1².216.11,45; π. δήμαρχος ib. 2².1183.26; π. ἔφηβος Poll.2.9; οἱ π. ἡγεμόνες, of queen wasps, Arist. *HA*628ᵃ26; τὰ π. κυήματα ib.556ᵃ7. 2. of things, τρύβλιον π. Ar.*Ra.*986; ὁ π. [καρπός] Thphr.*HP*3.12.4; π. σπέρματα Mnesith.

ap.Orib.2.67.1; ὁ π. οἶνος dub. in Ael.*NA*7.47; ἡ π. ἔγληψις Wilcken *Chr*.167.18 (ii B.C.).

**Περφεραῖος**, ὁ, = Ὑπερβόρειος, epith. of Hermes, prob. in Call.*Fr*. 117.

**Περφερέες**, οἱ, name of the five officers who escorted the Hyperborean maidens to Delos, Hdt.4.33 (vv.ll. Περιφερέες, Περφέρες, cf. Πέρφερες· θεωροί, Hsch.).

⊛ **Περφερέτας**, ου, ὁ, title of Zeus in Thessaly, *Liv.Ann*.3.155; cf. Ὑπερβερεταῖος.

**περώσιος**, dialectic form of περιώσιος, Hsch.

**πεσδο-**, Aeol. for πεζο-.

**πέσημα**, ατος, τό, *fall*, A.*Supp*.937, S.*Aj*.1033, E.*Ba*.588 (lyr.), al.; μόσχος ἀδάματον πέσημα δίκε, = μόσχος ἀδάματος ἔπεσε, Id.*Ph*.640 (lyr.); τὸ οὐρανοῦ π., i.e. the Palladium, Id.*IT*1384; πεσήματα νεκρῶν dead *corpses*, Id.*Andr*.652; Κόδρου τοῦτο π. *place where* K. *fell*, *IG*3.943: rare in Prose, *breach* in a wall, Aen.Tact.32.12.

**πέσκος**, τό, = πέκος, *skin*, *rind*, Nic.*Th*.549; *hide*, Hsch., Phot. (Acc. to A.D.*Synt*.8.21 by transpos. from σκέπω.)

**πέσμα**, = πεῖσμα 3, Hsch.

**πέσος**, εος, τό, = πτῶμα II, πέσεα E.*Ph*.1298 (lyr.).

**πεσσάριον**, τό, *pessary*, Damocr.ap.Gal.13.1050.

**πεσσ-εία**, Att. **πεττ-**, ἡ, *game resembling draughts* or *backgammon*, Socr.ap.Stob.4.56.39, S.*Fr*.1081, Pl.*R*.487c, *Phdr*.274d, al. II. in Music, *repetition of same note*, Cleonid.*Harm*.14. **-ευτήριον**, τό, Egyptian *astronomical table*, *POxy*.470.11 (iii A.D.), Eust.1397.12. **-ευτής**, Att. **πεττ-**, οῦ, ὁ, (πεσσεύω) *draught-player*, Pl.*Plt*.292e; applied to Divine Providence, Id.*Lg*.903d. **-ευτικός**, Att. **πεττ-**, ή, όν, *skilled in draught-playing*: ὁ π., = πεσσευτής, Id.*R*.333b, 374c; π. παιδιά Eust.1397.14; πεττευτική (sc. τέχνη), = πεσσεία, Pl.*Grg*.450d; τὸ -κόν Id.*Chrm*.174b; τὰ -κά Id.*Alc*.1.110e. ⊛ **-εύω**, Att. **πεττ-**, *play at draughts*, Heraclit.52, Pl.*Alc*.1.110e, *R*.487b, X.*Mem*.3.9.9, etc.: prov., τύχη ἄνω καὶ κάτω τὰ ἀνθρώπεια πεττεύει fortune *gambles* with human affairs, Ph.2.85. **-ικός**, Att. **πεττ-**, ή, όν, *of* or *for draught-playing*, Apion ap.Eust.1397.3; πεττική (sc. τέχνη) v.l. in Poll.7.210. **-ιον**, τό, Dim. of πεσσός: in pl., παίξαντα πέττια πρὸς τὴν σελήνην Plu.2.355d (s. v.l.).

**πέσ⟨σ⟩ον**· ὅρος· χωρίον Κύπριοι, πεδίον Αἰολεῖς· τινὲς ὁμαλές, Hsch.

**πεσσο-νομέω**, *set the* πεσσοί *in order for playing*: *play at* πεσσοί, Crates Com.7. 2. metaph., *dispose*, *adjust*, A.*Supp*.13 (anap.). ⊛ **-ποιέομαι**, *make and apply a* πεσσός II. 1 *to oneself*, Poet. *de herb*.103.

⊛ **πεσσός**, Att. **πεττ-**, ὁ, heterocl. pl. πεσσά S.*Fr*.429, Euph.61:— *oval-shaped stone for playing draughts* or *backgammon*, usu. in pl. (λευκοῖο σημήϊα π. *AP*9.482.21 (Agath.)), πεσσοῖσι.. θυμὸν ἔτερπον Od.1.107, cf. Hdt.1.94; τοὶ μὲν ἵπποις.., τοὶ δὲ πεσσοῖς.. τέρπονται Pi.*Fr*.129.4; πεττῶν θέσις Pl.*R*.333b; ἐφηῦρε πεσσοὺς κύβους τε (sc. Palamedes) S.*Fr*.479.4; πόλεις πεσσῶν ὁμοίως διαφοραῖς ἐκτισμέναι as if moved from place to place like draughts, E.*Fr*.360.9; ἓν μὲν τόδ' ἡμῖν, ὥσπερ ἐν πεσσοῖς, δίδως κρεῖσσον you have given me *a piece* (as at chess), Id.*Supp*.409; κατὰ τὸν ἐν πεττοῖς νόμον Ar.*Ec*.987; πεττῶν δίκην τὰς κοινὰς ἐννοίας μετατιθείς Plu.2.1068c; ἐν πεττοῖς καὶ κύβοις διημερεύειν ib.272f; ἄζυξ ὢν ὥσπερ ἐν πεττοῖς Arist.*Pol*.1253$^{a}$7. 2. *the board on which the game was played*, πεσσὰ πεντέγραμμα, since the pieces were placed on five lines, S.*Fr*.429. 3. οἱ π. *the place* in which the game was played, or *the game itself*, E.*Med*.68; ἔνθα Διὸς.. θᾶκοι π. τε καλοῦνται Cratin.7. II. *medicated plug of wool* or *lint* to be introduced into the vagina, anus, etc., *pessary*, Thphr.*HP*9.20.4, Dsc.1.106, 2.61, Cels.5.21, etc. 2. *any oval body*, π. ἐκ μολύβδου App.*Mith*.31. 3. *ticket* or *tally* showing attendance at an ἐκκλησία, *JHS*8.118 (Iasus). 4. *bolt* of a door, *PMag.Lond*.121.616, *POxy*.2146.10 (iii A.D.). III. in Archit., *cubic mass of building*, *terrace*, Str.16.1.5, *POxy*.1272.6 (ii A.D.), Procop.*Aed*.1.1.37. IV. *dark edge of the pupil* (in the eye), Poll.2.71, Hsch.

**πέσσυμπτον**· σκυτεῖον, Hsch., and **πεσσύπτη**· σκυτεύ⟨τ⟩ρια, Id.; cf. πίσυγγος, πεττύκια.

**πέσσω**, Il.4.513 (no other tense in Hom. exc. in the compd. καταπέσσω), Att. **πέττω**, later **πέπτω** Arist.*Ph*.259$^{b}$12, (ἐκ-) Plu.2.683d, corrupted in Ath.3.83f cod. A: fut. πέψω Ar.*Fr*.202 (cj. for πέμψω): aor. ἔπεψα Pherecr.183, Pl.*R*.372b, (κατα-) Il.1.81:—Med. (v. infr.), aor. ἐπεψάμην Hegem.ap.Ath.15.698f:—Pass., fut. πεφθήσομαι Arist.*Pr*.927$^{b}$31, Gal.1.634: aor. ἐπέφθην Herm. *in Phdr*.p.93 A., v.l. in Hp.*Acut*.(*Sp*.)67, Arist.*Pr*.864$^{a}$32: pf. Pass. πέπεμμαι Hp.*Dent*.26, Ar.*Pax* 869:—*soften*, *ripen*, or *change* by means of heat: I. of the West wind, *ripen* fruit, Od.7.119: generally, *bring to maturity*, Arist.*GA* 780$^{b}$10; also ὅταν [ὁ ἥλιος] ὑγρὸν ὄντα τὸν ἀέρα πέττῃ καὶ διακρίνῃ Id.*Pr*.944$^{a}$13. II. by the action of fire, *cook*, *dress*, esp. *bake*, σιτία Hdt.8.137; ἄρτους Ar.*Ra*.505; τὰ μὲν πέψαντες τὰ δὲ μάξαντες Pl.*R*.372b:—Pass., σιτία σφί ἐστι ἱρὰ πεσσόμενα Hdt.2.37; ὁ πλακοῦς πέπεπται Ar.*Pax* 869; ἄρτον εὖ πεπεμμένον Id.*Pl*.1136:—Med., πέσσεσθαι πέμματα *bake oneself* cakes, Hdt.1.160. 2. *distribute largess of cooked food*, *IGRom*.4.1638 (Philadelphia); cf. πέψις. III. by the action of the stomach, *digest*, κοιλίαι πέσσουσι Hp.*VM*11, cf. Arist.*GA*718$^{b}$21, *PA*677$^{b}$31, al.; opp. κατεργάζεσθαι (chew), Plu.*Eum*.11:—Pass., τὸ σηπτὸν περίττωμα τοῦ πεφθέντος ἐστίν Arist.*GA* 762$^{a}$15, cf. *Mete*.381$^{b}$12; of milk, etc., *to be concocted*, Id.*GA*776$^{a}$26, 777$^{a}$7. b. οἶνος π. τὰ σῖτα *promotes the digestion of* food, Ath.1.26a. 2. metaph., of diseases, πέσσεται νοῦσος *is 'concocted'*, *comes to a crisis*, Hp.*Acut*.42. 3. metaph., also, mostly in bad sense, χόλον πέσσειν *nurse*, *brood over* one's wrath, ἀλλ' ἐπὶ νηυσὶ χόλον θυμαλγέα πέσσει Il.4.513, cf. 9.565 (but, *digest*, i.e. allow to cool down, in Arist.*EN*1126$^{a}$24); κήδεα π. Il.24.617,639; αἰεί Philet.1; βέλος πέσσειν *have* a dart in one *to brood over*, Il.8.513; γέρα πεσσέμεν *gorge himself on* them, 2.237 (later, simply, *enjoy*, θρεπτήρια A.R.1.283); also ἀκίνδυνον αἰῶνα πέσσειν *lead a sodden* life of ease, Pi.*P*.4.186. (I.-E. *peqʷ*-, cf. Skt. *pácati* 'cook', Lat. *coquo*, Slav. *pekǫ* 'I bake'.)

**πέσυρες**, ρα, Aeol. for τέσσαρες, *Epigr.Gr*.988 (Balbilla).

**πετά**· πτῶσις, στάχυα, Hsch. **Πεταγείτνυος**, v. Πεδαγείτνυος. **πετάζω**, = πετάννυμι, Id. **πεταιτά**· μετέωρα, ἀμπελουργία. ὡς αἱ ἀναδενδράδες, Id. **πέτακνον**, = πέταχνον, Id.

**πετάλ-ειον** [ᾰ], τό, poet. for πέταλον, Nic.*Th*.628, 638. **-η**, ἡ, = πέταλον, *AP*9.226 (pl., Zon.). ⊛ **-ία**, ἡ, *flat dish* or *crate*(?), *PCair.Zen*.99.3 (iii B.C.). II. *crown of leaves*, *Ostr*. in *Arch.Pap*.6.220. **-ίζω**, *put forth leaves* or *strip off leaves*, Hsch. **-ιον**, τό, Dim. of πέταλον, *small splint*, Paul.Aeg.6.8. **-ίς**, ίδος, ἡ, *full-grown*, of swine, Achae.8; cf. πέτηλος. **-ισμός**, ὁ, *petalism*, method of banishing citizens practised at Syracuse, like the ὀστρακισμός at Athens, exc. that the name was written on *olive-leaves* instead of potsherds, D.S.11.87. **-ῖτις**, ιδος, ἡ, = φυλλῖτις, Nic.*Th*.864.

**πετᾰλοειδής**, ές, *leaf-shaped*, Phlp. *in Cat*.86.26.

⊛ **πέτᾰλον**, τό, poet. dat. pl. πέταλσι as well as πετάλοις, Poet. in *An.Ox*.1.121, cj. in Simon.10; also **πέτηλον**, first in Hes.*Sc*.289, *Fr*.96.87: (πετάννυμι):—*leaf*, mostly pl., Il.2.312, Od.19.520, Hes.*Op*.486, 680, Alcm.39, Alc.39, E.*Hel*.244 (lyr.), etc.; εὐδαιμονίας πέταλον, of the Olympian *wreath* of wild olive, B.5.186; ἁβρά τε λειμώνων π. flowers, *AP*7.23 (Antip. Sid.): rare in Prose, X.*An*.5.4.12, *Cyn*.9.15; used in divination, Phld.*D*.1.25: sg. in Ael.*VH*5.16; poet., νεικέων πέταλα contentious *votes* (cf. πεταλισμός), Pi.*I*.8(7).46; Ὠκεανοῦ πέταλα, of springs, Id.*Fr*.326. II. *leaf of metal*, χρυσίων πέταλα *IG*1$^{2}$.374.283; πέταλα χρυσᾶ ib.2$^{2}$.1394.5; π. χρυσίῳ ἐπίτηκτα *Inscr.Délos* 442*B*138 (ii B.C.), cf. Dsc.5.79, Luc.*Philops*.19; used for gilding the horns of victims, *IG*2$^{2}$.1635.36: sg., π. χρυσοῦν Lxx *Ex*.28.32(36); π. πύρινα, of the stars, *Placit*.2.14.4. 2. *slice*, ῥαφανῖδες κατατμηθεῖσαι εἰς πέταλα Orib.*Fr*.81.

**πετᾰλοποιός**, όν, *making leaves of metal*, *goldbeater*, *Gloss*.

⊛ **πετᾰλ-ουργός**, όν, = foreg., *Gloss*. **-όω**, *cover with leaves* or *plates* (of metal), χρυσίῳ Lxx 3*Ki*.6.21 cod. A; cf. πέταχνον:—Pass., *PLeid.X*.89. **-ώδης**, ες, *full of flakes*, ὑποστάσιες ἐν τοῖσιν οὔροισιν Hp.*Prog*.12, cf. Gal.8.411. **-ωσις**, εως, ἡ, *covering with gold-leaf*, *EM*69.44. II. *putting forth of leaves*, Aristeas 68. **-ωτόν**· ἀκμαιότατον, εὐειδέστατον, Hsch.

**πέτᾰμαι**, = πέτομαι (q.v.).

**πεταμνῠφάντειρα**, ἡ, *weaver of hangings* (from *πέταμνον, cf. τέραμνον, etc.), *AJA*19.446 (Halae, iii B.C.).

**πετάννῡμι** and **-ύω** (ἀνα-); later **πετάω** (ἀνα-) Luc.*Cal*.21; poet. **πίτνημι** (q.v.): fut. πετάσω (ἐκ-) E.*IT*1135 (lyr.); Att. πετῶ (ἀνα-) Men.26,458: aor. ἐπέτᾰσα (κατ-) Ar.*Pl*.731, etc.; Ep. πέτασα, πέτασσα, Hom. (v. infr.): pf. πεπέτακα (δια-) D.S.17.115:—Med., Ep. aor. πετάσαντο Nonn.*D*.2.704:—Pass., aor. ἐπετάσθην, Ep. πετ-, Od.21.50, (ἐκ-) E.*Cyc*.497 (lyr.): pf. πέπταμαι Hom. (v. infr.), πεπέτασμαι (ἐκ-) Orac.ap.Hdt.1.62, (παρα-) Plb.33.5.2, (ἀνα-) Pl.*Phd*.111c, Luc.*Gall*.29: plpf. ἐπέπτατο, Ep. πέπτ- Il.17.371: forms prop. belonging to πέτομαι are ἀνα-πτάς Zenod. in Il.1.351; ἀνα-πτάμεναι (for -πεπτάμεναι) πύλαι Parm.1.18; conversely πετασθέντα in signf. *fly*, Sotion p.186 W.—The simple Verb is rare exc. in aor. Act. and Pass., and pf. Pass.; cf. ἀνα-, δια-, κατα-, περι-πετάννυμι:—*spread out*, οὔρῳ πέτασ' ἱστία Od.5.269; [εἵματα] πέτασαν παρὰ θῖνα 6.94; χεῖρε πετάσσας, of one swimming, 5.374; ἄμφω χεῖρε φίλοις ἑτάροισι πετάσσας Il.4.523, 13.549: abs., πετάσας *opening his doors*, Theoc.16.6: metaph., θυμὸν πετάσαι '*flutter*', *elate* one's heart, Od.18.160:—Pass., mostly pf., *to be spread on all sides*, ἀμφὶ δὲ πέπλοι πέπτανται Il.5.195; αἴθρη πέπταται ἀνέφελος Od.6.45; πέπτατο δ' αὐγὴ Ἠελίου Il.17.371; part., *spread wide*, *opened wide*, of folding doors, πεπταμέναι πύλαι 21.531; also πετασθεῖσαι τεῦξαν φάος ib.538; θύρετρα.. πετάσθησαν Od.21.50; later κῶας πεπταμένον A.R.2.405; πεπτ. πέλαγος the *open* sea, Arat.288; ὄστρεον χείλεσι πεπτ. *AP*9.86 (Antiphil.); πεπταμέναι περὶ τέκνα μέγα κλαίουσι γυναῖκες Opp.*C*.3.106; also ὡς ἄνεμος ἐπετάσθη *was scattered abroad*, *dispersed*, of death, *Riv.Fil*.57.380 (Crete). (Cf. Lat. *pateo*, OE. *fæþm* 'fathom'.)

**πετάομαι**, false form for ποτάομαι, f.l. in Arist.*Metaph*.1009$^{b}$38, Str.16.4.11, *AP*14.63 (Mesom.):—also in Act., ὅ τι πετᾷ *Cat.Cod.Astr*.8(1).249.

**πετάσ-ιον** [ᾰ], τό, Dim. of πέτασος, Posidon.2 J.; π. κανωπικά Sch.Orib.2.745. **-ῖτις**, ιδος, ἡ, *butter-bur*, *Petasites officinalis*, Dsc.4.107 (v.l. -ίτης, as in Gal.12.98).

**πέτ-ασμα**, ατος, τό, (πετάννυμι) *anything spread out*, of the feelers of the polypus, Arist.*HA*541$^{b}$6: pl., *carpets*, πέδον.. στρωννύναι πετάσμασιν A.*Ag*.909. **-ασμός**, ὁ, *spreading out*, Al.*Nu*.23.22.

⊛ **πέτᾰσ-ος**, ὁ, also ἡ Eratosth.ap.Ath.11.499e; πετάσῳ Θετταλικῇ is prob. cj. for πίλῳ Θετταλικῇ in Thphr.*HP*4.8.7 (cf. 9): (πετάννυμι):—*broad-brimmed felt hat*, worn by ἔφηβοι and hence used as their badge, Poll.10.164, Suid.; γυμνάσιον καθίδρυσε καὶ τοὺς κρατίστους τῶν ἐφήβων ὑπὸ πέτασον ἦγεν, i.e. made them practise gymnastics, Lxx 2*Ma*.4.12; also in representations of Hermes, Ephipp. ap.Ath.12.537f. II. from its shape, *broad umbellated leaf*, as of the lotus, Thphr.*HP*4.8.9; φύλλον μέγα ὡς π. Dsc.2.106. III. from its shape, also, *awning*, ὁ π. τοῦ θεάτρου *OGI*510.4 (Ephesus, ii A.D.), *CIG*3422.17 (Philadelphia); also, of the *circular tomb* of

Porsenna, Plin.*HN*36.92; *baldacchino*, *PMag.Leid.W*.3.11. **-ώδης**, ες, *hat-shaped*, σπερμάτων φύσις Phan.Hist.27; φύλλον Dsc.4.107. ⊛ **-ών**, ῶνος, ὁ, *ham*, Ath.14.657e.

**πεταυρισμός**, **-ιστής**, **-ον**, later forms for πετευρ- found in Phot., Suid., also as vv.ll. and in Latin derivatives; cf. **παίταυρα** and **πέταυρα**, expld. by σίγνα (Lat. *signa*), Hsch.

**πέταχνον**, τό, (πετάννυμι) *broad flat cup*, Alex.59, prob. in *Ostr. Bodl.* i 318 (ii/i B.C.); cf. πέτακνον:—hence **πεταχνόομαι**, *drink from* πέταχνα, *drink deep*, Ar.*Fr.*288 (ap.Phot., cf. Hsch. s. v. πεταλοῦνται; πεταχνεῦται codd. Ath.).

**πετάω**, v. πετάομαι. **πετεηνός**, v. sq.

⊛ **πετεινός**, ή, όν, also **πετηνός** (v. fin.), and **πτηνός** (v. sub voc.), Ep. and poet. **πετεηνός** (also **πετεεινός** *AP*9.337 (Leon.), 363.22 (Mel.)):—*able to fly*, *full-fledged*, of young birds, τάρος πετεηνὰ γενέσθαι Od.16.218; of birds generally, *able to fly*, *winged*, πετηνῶν.. ὑπ' οἰωνῶν A.*Th.*1025; πετηνοῖς γυψί E.*Rh.*515; also π. ἵππος Men.*Pk.* 342: abs., πετεηνά *winged fowl*, αἰετὸς.. τελειότατος πετεηνῶν Il.8.247, al.; πετεινόν *a bird*, Thgn.1097; τὰ πετεινά (with v.l. πετηνά) Hdt.1.140, 2.123, 3.106, Lycurg.132.—Thom.Mag.p.272 R. rejects the form πετεινός: Πετηνή is the name of an Att. ship in *IG*2².1611.138.

**πετελκές**· καμπύλον, Hsch.

**πετευρ-ίζομαι**, *jump from a springboard*, *vault*, *perform acrobatic feats*, Phld.*Rh.*1.74 S.: pf. πεπεταύρισται *Gloss.* **-ιον**, τό, Dim. of πέτευρον IV, *small notice-board*, *Jahresh.*13 *Beibl.*23 (Erythrae, iv B.C.). **-ισμός**, ὁ, *vaulting*, *tumbling*: only metaph. (in later form), ὁ τῆς τύχης πεταυρισμός Plu.2.498c. **-ιστέω**, = πετευρίζομαι, prob. in Gal.*Protr.*9. **-ιστήρ**, ῆρος, ὁ, *tumbler*, *acrobat*, Man.4.278. ⊛ **-ιστής**, οῦ, ὁ, = foreg., in Lat. form *petaurista*, Varro ap.Non.p.79 L.: metaph., of fleas and the like, Plin.*HN*11.115.

⊛ **πέτευρον**, τό, *roosting-perch* for fowls, Ar.*Fr.*839, Theoc.13.13, Nic.*Th.*197 (pl.), Hsch. 2. generally, *pole*, *spar*, *plank*, Lyc. 884. II. *springboard*, used by tumblers and acrobats, Man.6.444, Epic. in *Arch.Pap.*7 p.5; Lat. *petaurus*, Juv.14.265, etc., but abl. *peteuro* (v.l. *petauro*), Lucil.*Fr.*1298 Marx. 2. *platform*, *stage*, Plb.8.4.8. III. *springe*, *trap*, ἐπὶ πέτευρον ᾄδου συναντᾷ Lxx *Pr.*9.18. IV. *public notice-board*, *IG*7.235.42 (Oropus, iv B.C.); π. τῷ λόγῳ (for publication of accounts) ib.11(2).145.44 (Delos, iv B.C.).

**πετήλη**, ἡ, small kind of *palm*, Hsch.

**πετηλίας**· καρκίνος, ὁ, a kind of *crab*, Ael.*NA*7.30.

**πετηλίς**, ίδος, ἡ, *locust*, Hsch. **πέτηλον**, τό, v. πέτᾰλον.

**πέτηλος**, η, ον, *outspread*, *stretched*, ἐπὶ σκελέεσσι πέτηλον (acc. to others *flying*) Arat.271. II. *full-grown*, μόσχοι Ath.9.376b (expld. ἀπὸ τῶν κεράτων ὅταν αὐτὰ ἐκπέταλα ἔχωσι), cf. Hsch. s. v. βοῦς π. (-ηνός cod.).

**πετηλώδης**, ες, *like a leaf*, *worn thin*, ὀβολός Eust.136.12.

**πετήν**, ῆνος, ὁ, ἡ, poet. form of πετηνός, *EM*407.1.

⊛ **πετηνίς**· κόρις, Hsch. **πετηνός**, ή, όν, v. πετεινός. **πετοῖσαι**, = πεσοῦσαι, v. πίπτω.

⊛ **πέτομαι**, 2 sg. πέτεαι Anacr.9: impf. ἐπετόμην, Ep. πετ- Il.5.366, etc.: fut. πετήσομαι Ar.*Pax*77, cf. 1126 (ἀπο-); shortd. πτήσομαι (ἐκ-) Id.*V.*208, and always in early Prose, (ἀνα-) Pl.*Lg.*905a, al., Aeschin.3.209, (ἐπι-) Hdt.7.15 (mostly in compds., but πτήσεσθαι in later Prose, Lib.*Or.*2.27): aor. ἐπτόμην, inf. πτέσθαι S.*OT*17; elsewh. in compds., (ἐπι-) Il.4.126, (ἀν-) Antipho *Fr.*58, etc.; freq. also ἐπτάμην, Il.13.592, E.*Hel.*18, (παρ-) Semon.13, (ἐσ-) Hdt.9.100; Ep. 3 sg. πτάτο Il.23.880, inf. πτάσθαι (δια-) E.*Med.*1, part. πτάμενος Il.5.282, 22.362, etc. (in codd. of Pl. forms of ἐπτόμην in compds. predominate over those from ἐπτάμην; δι-έπτατο is found in codd. of Ar. *V.*1086, ἐκ-πτόμενος folld. by κατ-έπτατο Id.*Av.*788 sq.; ἀν-επτάμαν is prob. in S.*Aj.*693 (lyr.), προσ-έπτατο ib.382); subj. πτῆται for πτᾶται, Il.15.170: also aor. of act. form ἔπτην, ἔπτης, *IG*14.2550, Luc. *Trag.*218, ἔπτη Batr.208, Nonn.*D.*2.223, al., *Anacreont.*22.3; opt. πταίης *AP*5.151 (Mel.); part. πτᾶσα *h.Cer.*398, Hdn.Gr.1.532; elsewh. only in compds., (δι-) *IG*3.1386, (ἐξ-) Hes.*Op.*98, (ἀν-) S.*Ant.* 1307, E.*Med.*440, (προσ-) A.*Pr.*115, (ὑπερ-) S.*Ant.*113 (Trag. only in lyr.): pf. πέπτηκα only as a coinage in Choerob. *in Theod.*2.79, elsewh. πεπότημαι (v. ποτάομαι): aor. Pass. ἐπετάσθην Arist.*HA*624ᵇ 6 (εἰσ-), Lxx *Ps.*17(18).10, *Ho.*9.11 (ἐξ-), Sotion p.186 W., D.S.4.77 (ἐξ-): fut. Pass. πετασθήσομαι Lxx *Hb.*1.8.—The only pres. in Hom. and Att. Prose is πέτομαι; **πέταμαι** is used by Sapph.*Supp.*10.8, Simon. 30, Pi.*P.*8.90, *N.*6.48, E.*Ion* 90 (anap.), *AP*11.208 (Lucill.), and in later Prose, as Arist.*IA*709ᵇ10, *HA*609ᵃ14 (περι-), cf. Moer.p.311 P.; noted as archaic by Luc.*Pseudol.*29: aor. imper. πέτασσαι *Anacreont.* 14.2; **ἵπταμαι** (q. v.) is first found in late writers, Mosch.3.43, Babr. 65.4, etc. (mostly in compds., cf. ἐξίπταμαι; ἀφίπτατο in E.*IA*1608 is spurious), and is censured by Luc.*Lex.*25, *Sol.*7:—*fly*, of birds, Il. 12.207, 13.62, Od.2.147, etc.; of bees, gnats, etc., Il.2.89, Hdt.2.95; of a departing spirit, ψυχὴ ἐκ ῥεθέων πταμένη Ἄϊδόσδε βεβήκει Il.22. 362; ἐκ μελέων θυμὸς πτάτο 23.880: metaph., of young children, οὐδέπω μακρὰν πτέσθαι σθένοντες S.*OT*17; also of arrows, javelins, etc., Il.20.99, etc.; ὀλοοίτροχος.. ἀναθρῴσκων π. 13.140 (but ἐκ χειρῶν ἔπτατ' ἐρετμά, τεύχεα *fell suddenly*.., Od.12.203, 24.534); of any quick motion, *dart*, *rush*, of men, Il.13.755, 22.143, etc.; of horses, μάστιξεν δ' ἐλάαν, τὼ δ' οὐκ ἀέκοντε πετέσθην 5.366, cf. 768, etc.; of chariots, Hes.*Sc.*308; of dancers, E.*Cyc.*71 (lyr.); πέτου *fly!* i.e. *make haste!* Ar.*Lys.*321; ἔχρην πετομένας ἥκειν πάλαι ib.55; πολλοὶ ἥξουσι πετόμενοι Pl.*R.*567d, cf. 467d; πέτονται.. ἐπὶ ταῦτ' ἄκλητοι, of parasites, Antiph.229. II. metaph. and proverbial usages:—*to be on the wing*, *flutter*, of uncertain hopes, ἐξ ἐλπίδος π. Pi.*P.*8.90; π. ἐλπίσιν S.*OT*487 (lyr.); of fickle natures, πέτει τε καὶ φρονῶν οὐδὲν φρονεῖς E.*Ba.*332; ἐφ' ἕτερον π. Ar.*Ec.*899; ὄρνις πετόμενος a bird *ever on the wing*, Id.*Av.*169; πετόμενόν τινα διώκεις 'you are chasing a butterfly', Pl.*Euthphr.*4a, cf. Arist.*Metaph.*1009ᵇ38; of fame, *fly abroad*, πέταται τηλόθεν ὄνυμ' αὐτῶν Pi.*N.*6.48. 2. c. dat., πτάμενος νοήματι *flying* in mind, Id.*Fr.*122.4. (Cf. πίπτω, Skt. *pátati* 'fly', 'fall', Lat. *prae-pes*, etc.)

**πετόντεσσι**, Aeol. dat. pl. aor. 2 part. of πίπτω, Pi.*P.*5.50.

**πέτρα**, Ion. and Ep. **πέτρη**, ἡ, *rock*; freq. of *cliffs*, *ledges*, etc. by the sea, λισσὴ αἰπεῖά τε εἰς ἅλα πέτρη Od.3.293, cf. 4.501, etc.; χῶρος λεῖος πετράων free from *rocks*, of a beach, 5.443; π. ἠλίβατος.. ἁλὸς ἐγγὺς ἐοῦσα Il.15.618, etc.; χοιρὰς π. Pi.*P.*10.52; also, *rocky peak* or *ridge*, αἰγίλιψ π. Il.9.15, etc.; ἠλίβατος 16.35, etc.; λιττὰς π. Corinn.*Supp.*1. 30, cf. A.*Supp.*796 (lyr.); π. Λευκάς, Ὠλενίη, etc., Od.24.11, Il.11.757, etc.; π. σύνδρομοι, Συμπληγάδες, Pi.*P.*4.209, E.*Med.*1264 (lyr.); πρὸς πέτραις ὑψηλοκρήμνοις, of Caucasus, A.*Pr.*4, cf. 31, 56, al.; π. Δελφίς, π. δίλοφος, of Parnassus, S.*OT*464 (lyr.), *Ant.*1126 (lyr.); π. Κωρυκίς A.*Eu.*22; π. Κεκροπία, of the Acropolis, E.*Ion*936. 2. π. γλαφυρή a hollow *rock*, i.e. a cave, Il.2.88, cf. 4.107; σπέος κοιλῇ ὑπὸ π. Hes. *Th.*301; δίστομος π. *cave in the rock* with a double entrance, S.*Ph.*16, cf. 937; κατηρεφεῖς αὐτῇ τῇ π. Pl.*Criti.*116b; π. ἀντρώδης X.*An.*4.3. 11; τόπος κύκλῳ πέτραις περιεχόμενος *IG*4²(1).122.21 (Epid.); ἕως τῆς π. down to *virgin rock*, *PCair.Zen.*172.14 (iii B.C.), *OGI*672 (Egypt, i A.D.), cf. *Ev.Matt.*16.18. 3. *mass of rock* or *boulder*, Od.9.243, 484, Hes.*Th.*675; πέτρας κυλινδομένα φλόξ Pi.*P.*1.23; ἐκυλίνδουν πέτρας X.*An.*4.2.20, cf. Plb.3.53.4. 4. *stone* as material, π. λαρτία, Τηΐα, *SIG*581.97 (Crete, iii/ii B.C.), 996.13 (Smyrna, i A.D.): distd. from πέτρος (q. v.), which is v.l. in X. l. c.; πέτρᾳ shd. be read in S.*Ph.*272; the distn. is minimized by Gal.12.194. II. prov., οὐκ ἀπὸ δρυὸς οὐδ' ἀπὸ πέτρης, etc. (v. δρῦς); as a symbol of firmness, ὁ δ' ἐστάθη ἠΰτε π. ἔμπεδον Od.17.463; of hard-heartedness, ἐκ πέτρας εἰργασμένος A.*Pr.*244; ἁλίαν π. ἢ κῦμα λιταῖς ὣς ἱκετεύων E.*Andr.* 537 (anap.); cf. πέτρος I. 2. (Written πε-τε-ρα in a text with musical accompaniment, *Pae.Delph.*5.)

**πετραία**, ἡ, = κάππαρις, Dsc.2.173.

**πετραῖον**, τό (= ἀσπάραγος ἄγριος, acc. to Ps.-Dsc.2.125), *a rock plant*, Thphr.*HP*9.15.7 (nisi leg. κατὰ), Nic.*Fr.*71.2 (πετρίου codd. Ath.).

**πετραῖος**, α, ον, *of a rock*, σκιή Hes.*Op.*589; *living on* or *among the rocks*, Σκύλλη Od.12.231; ὄρνις A.*Fr.*304.3; Νύμφαι π. *rock*-Nymphs, E.*El.*805; ἠχώ *Com.Adesp.*669; τὰ π. τῶν ἰχθυδίων *rock*-fish, Theopomp.Com.62.3, cf. Sotad.Com.1.22; πετραῖα, as a class of marine animals, opp. πελάγια, αἰγιαλώδη, Arist.*HA*488ᵇ7, cf. 598ᵃ11; *growing on* or *among rocks*, συκῆ Archil.19. 2. *rocky*, ἀγκάλη A.*Pr.* 1019; τάφος π. S.*El.*151 (lyr.); π. δειράς, λέπας, χθών, ἄντρα, etc., Id.*Aj.* 697 (lyr.), E.*HF*120 (lyr.), *Cyc.*382 (s. v.l.), *IA*1082 (lyr.), etc.; χωρία Arist.*HA*570ᵇ26. II. Πετραῖος, epith. of Poseidon in Thessaly, as he *who clave the rocks* of Tempe, and drained Thessaly, Pi.*P.*4.138.

⊛ **πετρᾰκισχείλιη**, Boeot. for τετρακισχίλιαι, *IG*7.3172.172 (Orchom. Boeot.).

**πετράμβᾰτοι** (for πετρανάβατοι)· ὑψηλοί, Hsch. (πατρέμβ- cod.).

**πετράμεινος** [ᾰ], ον, Boeot. for τετράμηνος, *IG*7.3172.115 (Orchom. Boeot.).

**πετρανός**, perh. written for οὐετρανός (Lat. *veteranus*), Judeich *Altertümer von Hierapolis* No.202.

⊛ **πετράς**, άδος, ἁ, Boeot. for τετράς, *fourth day* of the month, *IG*7. 506.1 (Tanagra, iii B.C.).

**πέτρᾰτος**, α, ον, Boeot. for τέταρτος, *IG*7.3172.142 (Orchom. Boeot.).

**πετρεντῑνάκτης**, ου, ὁ, *shaker of rocks*, of Poseidon, *PMag.Par.*1. 183.

**πετρεφράμη**· θρασεῖα, θερμή, Hsch.

**πετρη-γενής**, ές, *rock-born*, Marc.Sid.38. **-δόν**, Adv. *like stones*, of hail, Luc.*Tim.*3. **-εις**, εσσα, εν, *rocky*, in Hom. always epith. of places, Αὐλίς, Πυθών, Καλυδών, Il.2.496, 519, 640; νῆσος Od.4.844; γλάφυ πετρῆεν Hes.*Op.*533. II. *haunting rocks*, ἰουλίς *AP*7.504. 5 (Leon.); ἠχώ *APl.*4.154 (Luc. or Arch.).

**πετρ-ηρεφής**, ές, (ἐρέφω) *o'er-arched with rock*, *rock-vaulted*, ἄντρα A.*Pr.*302, E.*Cyc.*82. **-ήρης**, ες, *rocky*, στέγαι S.*Ph.*1262. **-ίδιον**, τό, Dim. of πέτρα, Arist.*HA*547ᵇ21, *Fr.*338, Thphr.*Fr.*160, *AP*9.570 (Phld.), Porph.*Abst.*2.17.

⊛ **πέτρῐνος**, η, ον, *rocky*, ὄρος Hdt.2.8; κοίτη S.*Ph.*160 (anap.); ὄχθος, δειράδες, etc., E.*IT*290, 1089 (lyr.), etc.; στάλα *IG*5(1).1111.37 (Geronthrae); ποτήριον Anon.Vat.56; λίθοι (opp. λευκοί, 'marble') *Supp.Epigr.*4.446 (Didyma, iii B.C.); π. ῥόος, τοῖχος π., *Schwyzer*89.9, 18 (Argos, iii B.C.): metaph., of a person, Anaxipp.3.3 (s. v.l.). II. *changed into rock*, of Niobe, Tz.*H.*4.715. III. π. ἀκοντισμός, a Celtic manœuvre, Arr.*Tact.*37.4.

**πέτριον**, v. πετραῖον.

**πετρίς**, ίδος, ἡ, = πετραῖον, *SIG*1171.16 (Lebena).

**πετρο-βᾰτέω**, *climb rocks*, D.S.2.6, Arr.*An.*4.19.1, App.*BC*4. 79. **-βάτης** [ᾰ], ου, ὁ, *one who climbs rocks*, ib.56; of Pan, Poet. ap.Stob.1.1.31a. **-βᾰτικός**, ή, όν, *given to rock-climbing*, ζῷον Eust.733.36. **-βλητος**, ον, *pelted with stones*, Phot. II. *affected by the stone*, νεφροί Id.

**πετροβολ-έω**, *pelt with stones*, in Pass., Sch.rec.A.*Th.*560. **-ία**, ἡ, *stoning*, X.*An.*6.6.15. **-ικός**, ή, όν, *of* or *for throwing stones*, ὄργανα Plb.5.99.7. **-ισμός**, ὁ, *pelting with stones*, Sch.rec.A.*Th.* 342 (pl.). **-ος** (parox.), ον, *throwing stones*, X.*HG*2.4.12. II.

Subst. πετροβόλος, ὁ, *engine for throwing stones*, Plb.5.4.6, Lxx *Jb*.41.19, Ath.Mech.34.2, etc.; distd. from καταπέλτης, Plb.8.7.2 (but καταπέλτας ὀξυβελεῖς τε καὶ πετροβόλους D.S.18.51, cf. *IG*2².468.1): neut. πετροβόλα (sc. ὄργανα), opp. δορυβόλα, J.*AJ*9.10.3. 2. *sling*, v.l. in Lxx 1*Ki*.14.14. III. λίθοι πετρόβολοι *hurled as from a sling*, of hailstones, ib.*Ex*.13.11,13.

**πετρο-γενής**, ές, = πετρηγενής, epith. of Mithras, Lyd.*Mens*.4.30. **-ετηρίς**, ίδος, ἡ, Thess., = τετραετηρίς, *Rev.Phil*.35.123 (Larissa, i B.C.). **-κατοίκητος**, ον, *having its abode in the rocks*, ἀχώ Limen.15. **-κοιτος**, ον, *with bed of rock*, εὐνά Simm.26.18. **-κόραξ**, ἄκος, ὁ, *raven of the rocks*, nickname in *IG*14.1517. **-κόσσυφος**, *saxamerulus*, *Gloss*. **-κῠλιστής**, οῦ, ὁ, *rolling rocks* or *stones*, κερκοπίθηκοι Str.15.1.56: Σίσυφος π., name of a play by Aeschylus, Anon.*in EN*145.25. **-λάπᾰθον**, τό, *rock-sorrel*, dub. l. in Dsc.*Eup*.2.49. **-ποιία**, ἡ, *stone-fabric*, Callix.1. **-ποιός**, όν, *producing stones*, δύναμις Porph.ap.Eus.*PE*3.11. ⊛ **-ρρῐφής**, ές, *hurled from a rock*, π. θανεῖν E.*Ion* 1222. **-ρῠτος**, ον, *flowing from a rock*, Orph.*H*.51.9.

⊛ **πέτρος**, ὁ (in later Poets ἡ, *AP*7.274 (Honest.), 479 (Theodorid.)), *stone* (distd. from πέτρα, q.v.); in Hom., used by warriors, λάζετο πέτρον μάρμαρον ὀκριόεντα Il.16.734; βαλὼν μυλοειδέϊ πέτρῳ 7.270, cf. 20.288, E.*Andr*.1128 (never in Od.); ἔδικε πέτρῳ Pi.*O*.10(11).72; ἄγαλμ' Ἀΐδα ξεστὸν π. ἔμβαλον στέρνῳ Id.*N*.10.67; νιφάδι γογγύλων πέτρων A.*Fr*.199.7; ἐκ χερῶν πέτροισιν ἠράσσοντο Id.*Pers*.460; λευσθῆναι πέτροις S.*OC*435; πέτρους ἐπεκυλίνδουν X.*HG*3.5.20, etc.; ἐν πέτροισι πέτρον ἐκτρίβων, to produce fire, S.*Ph*.296; of a *boulder* forming a landmark, Id.*OC*1595; τόνδ' ἀνέθηκα π. ἀειράμενος *IG*4²(1).125 (Epid., iii B.C.). 2. prov., πάντα κινῆσαι πέτρον 'leave no stone unturned', E.*Heracl*.1002, cf. Pl.*Lg*.843a; of imperturbability, καὶ γὰρ ἂν πέτρου φύσιν σύ γ' ὀργάνειας S.*OT*334, cf. E.*Med*.28. II. a kind of *reed*, *Peripl.M.Rubr*.65.—The usual Prose word is λίθος.

**πετρο-σελῑνίτης** [νῑ] οἶνος, ὁ, *parsley-wine*, Dsc.5.65, *Gp*.8.12. **-σέλῑνον**, τό, *parsley*, *Petroselinum sativum*, Dsc.3.66, Gal.12.99, Alex.Aphr.*Pr*.1.110, *POxy*.2144.3 (iii A.D.), *Edict.Diocl*.32.56. **-τόμος**, ον, *cutting stones*, ἀκίδες *APl*.4.221 (Theaet.). ⊛ **-φῠής**, ές, *clinging to rock*, πολύπους Ps.-Phoc.49. II. Subst. πετροφυές, τό, = ἀείζων τὸ λεπτόφυλλον, Ps.-Dsc.4.90, cf. 89.

⊛ **πετρ-όω**, *turn into stone, petrify*, mostly in Pass., Lyc.901, *APl*.4.132 (Theodorid.), Orph.*L*.527: aor. Med. πετρώσατο Nonn.*D*.25.81. 2. Pass., *to be frozen*, ib.47.591. II. Pass., *to be stoned*, E.*Or*.564; πετρουμένους θανεῖν ib.946, cf. *Ph*.1177, *Ion* 1112. 2. *to be filled with stones*, Nonn.*D*.43.131. **-ώδης**, ες, *like rock* or *stone, rocky, stony*, π. κατῶρυξ, of a grave, S.*Ant*.774, cf. Porph.*Antr*.9; of ground, Hp.*Aër*.1; γεηρὰ καὶ πετρώδη καὶ ἄγρια Pl.*R*.612a; ἐν τοῖς τραχέσι καὶ πετρώδεσι Arist.*HA*549ᵇ14; τὸ π. *BMus.Inscr*.3.407.8 (Priene): ἄνθρωποι π. καὶ δενδρώδεις Heraclit.*Incred*.23; π. κεφαλή Philum.*Ven*.15.4. **-ώεις**, εσσα, εν, *haunting rocks*, ἴουλοι Marc.Sid.15. **-ωμα**, ατος, τό, *mass of stone*, ἱερὸν π. καλούμενον, λίθοι δύο πρὸς ἀλλήλους ἡρμοσμένοι Paus.8.15.1. II. θανεῖν.. λευσίμῳ πετρώματι to die *by stoning*, E.*Or*.50,442. ⊛ **-ών**, ῶνος, ὁ, *rocky* or *stony place*, *Inscr.Prien*.37.166 (ii B.C.). **-ώνιον**, τό, = βήχιον, Dsc.3.112. **-ώροφος**, ον, (ὄροφος) = πετρηρεφής, Tz.Lyc.*Arg*.

⊛ **πεττᾰράκοντα** [ρᾰ], Boeot. for τετταράκοντα, *IG*7.3171.51 (Orchom. Boeot.).

⊛ **πέτταρες, πέτταρα**, Boeot. for τέττ-, *IG*7.2418.10 (Thebes, iv B.C.), 3171.38 (Orchom. Boeot.), *Schwyzer* 462 *B* 54 (Tanagra, iii B.C.).

**πεττεία, -ευτής, -εύω, -ός**, Att. for πεσσεία, etc. **πεττύκια**, τά, *clippings of leather*, Moer.p.305 P. (Cf. πεσσύγγιον.) **πέττω**, Att. for πέσσω. **πευδρία·** ἀρτοθήκη, Hsch. **πευθείς** (i.e. πεφθείς)· ἑψηθείς, Id. **πεύθη**, ἡ, (πεύθομαι) = πεῦσις, Id.

**πευθήν**, ῆνος, ὁ, *inquirer, spy*, Luc.*Phal*.1.10, *Alex*.23,37, Lib.*Or*.4.25, al., Them.*Or*.34 p.461 Dind.; simply, *questioner*, ib.21.253c; περίεργοι καὶ π. *inquisitive persons*, Arr.*Epict*.2.23.10.

**πεύθομαι**, older form of πυνθάνομαι, Od.3.87, al. (Hom. uses the later form (q.v.) only twice), Hes.*Th*.463, Mimn.14.2, Pi.*P*.4.38,109, A.*Ch*.679, S.*OT*604, E.*IA*1138, Herod.6.38: impf. ἐπευθόμην Il.17.408, E.*Rh*.767:—Act. ⊛πεύθω, *give notice, lay an information*, *Leg. Gort*.8.55, *SIG*525.9 (Gortyn, iii B.C.). (Cf. Skt. *bódhati* 'wake up', 'notice', Lith. *budėti* 'to be awake'.)

**πευθώ**, οῦς, ἡ, *tidings*, A.*Th*.370.

**πευῖδας·** λαμπάδας, Hsch. **πευκάεις**, v. πευκήεις.

**πευκᾰλέομαι**, = ξηραίνομαι, and **πευκᾰλέος**, α, ον, = ξηρός, Aristeas Epic.ap.Hsch.

**πευκάλῐμος** [ᾰ], η, ον, Ep. word used by Hom. only in phrase φρεσὶ πευκαλίμῃσι Il.8.366, 14.165, 15.81, 20.35; μετὰ φρεσὶ π. Hes.*Fr*.170; πραπίδεσσιν ἀρηρότα πευκαλίμῃσιν Orac.ap.D.L.1.30; πευκαλίμοις μήδεσι *IG*4.787 (Troezen); πευκαλίμας ἀχέων φρένας Q.S.10.388. (πευκαλίμῃσι expld. by πυκναῖς, συνεταῖς, also by πικραῖς, ὀξείαις, Hsch.)

**πευκάνα·** πευκονία, ἱστοῦ παράπλεγμα, τροχίαι, Hsch.; cf. πέρκανα, πεύκλα.

**πευκέδᾰνον**, τό, *sulphur-wort*, *Peucedanum officinale*, Thphr.*HP* 9.14.1, Nic.*Th*.76: also **πευκέδανος**, ἡ, v.l. in Dsc.3.78, cf. Sch. Nic.*Th*.76. II. = σίκυς ἄγριος, Ps.-Dsc.4.150.

**πευκεδᾰνός**, ή, όν, = πευκήεις II, πτολέμοιο μέγα στόμα πευκεδανοῖο Il.10.8; βέλεμνα, ἀσπίς, Orph.*L*.500,609; θάλασσα Opp.*H*.2.33.

⊛ **πεύκ-η**, ἡ, *pine*, esp. *Pinus Laricio*, *Corsican pine*, Il.11.494, 23.328, E.*Med*.4, Ar.*Eq*.1310, Dsc.1.69, etc.: distd. fr. πίτυς (q.v.), Thphr.*HP*3.9.5; of other species, π. ἥμερος *stone pine*, *Pinus Pinea*, ib.3.9.4; π. παραλία *Aleppo pine*, *P. halepensis*, ib.3.9.1; πεύκης τρόπον, prov. of utter destruction, Zen.5.76; cf. πίτυς. II. *anything made from the wood of the* πεύκη, *torch of pine-wood*, A.*Ag*.288 (dub.), S.*OT*214 (lyr.), E.*Ion*716 (lyr.), etc.; κάμακες πεύκης οἱ πυρίφλεκτοι A.*Fr*.171. 2. *wooden writing-tablet*, E.*IA*39 (anap.), *Hipp*.1254. (Cf. OPruss. *peuse*, Lith. *pušis*, OHG. *fiuhta* 'pine'; perh. orig. 'needle-tree', cf. ἐχεπευκής, περιπευκής.) **-ήεις**, Dor. **-άεις**, εσσα, εν, *pine-covered*, οὔρεα D.P.678; νῆσος Orph.*A*.1189. 2. *of pine* or *pine-wood*, π. σκάφος E.*Andr*.863 (lyr.); πευκάενθ' Ἥφαιστον the fire *of pine-torches*, S.*Ant*.123 (lyr.). II. metaph., *sharp, piercing*, πευκήεντ' ὀλολυγμόν A.*Ch*.386 (lyr., codd.; Dind. metri gr. πῡκάεντ', cf. πυκᾶες· ἰσχυρόν, Theognost.*Can*.23, but πεύκαες· τὸ πικρόν, Hdn.Gr.1.394); πευκάεν σέλας ἀστραπῆς A.*Fr*.25 A; π. κέντρα Opp.*H*.2.457. **-ία**, ἡ, *bitter taste of pitch*, Tz.*H*.9.835. **-ῐνος**, η, ον, *of, from*, or *made of pine* or *pine wood*, κορμοί E.*Hec*.575; λαμπάς S.*Tr*.1198; π. δάκρυ tear *of the pine*, i.e. the resinous drops that ooze from it, E.*Med*.1200; ῥητίνη Dsc.1.71; πεύκινα, τά, *pine-logs*, Plb.5.89.1, cf. *IG*1².342.70.

**πεύκλα·** ἁματροχιαί, Hsch. **πευκονία**, v. πευκάνα.

**πευκών**, ῶνος, ὁ, *pine-forest*, Hdn.Gr.1.29, al.

**πεῦσις**, εως, ἡ, (πεύθομαι) *inquiry, question*, Ph.1.202, al., Ruf.*Interrog*.2, Plu.2.614d (pl.), Philostr.Jun.*Im*.10, etc.: as a rhet. figure, D.H.*Dem*.54, Longin.18.1. 2. *information*, αἱ ἀπὸ σοῦ π. Phalar.*Ep*.125.

**πεύσομαι**, fut. of πυνθάνομαι.

**πευσ-τέον**, (πυνθάνομαι) *one must inquire*, Pl.*Sph*.244b. **-τήριος**, α, ον, *of* or *for inquiry*, ὅπως πευστηρίαν θοινασόμεσθα (sc. θυσίαν) a sacrificial feast *for learning the will of the gods*, cj. for παστηρίαν in E.*El*.835. **-τής**, οῦ, ὁ, *asker, inquirer*, gloss on πευθήν, Sch.Luc.*Phal*.1.10. **-τικός**, ή, όν, *interrogative*, ἐπίρρημα A.D.*Adv*.193.26, al.; [ὄνομα] D.T.637.7; τὸ π. Ph.1.97. Adv. **-κῶς** A.D.*Adv*.209.26; ἔχειν Sch.A.R.4.1405. **-τός·** ὑπήκοος, Hsch.

**πέφανται**, 3 sg. pf. Pass. of φαίνω and 3 pl. pf. Pass. of θείνω II.

**πεφάσθαι**, pf. inf. Pass. of θείνω II: **πεφάσθω**, 3 sg. pf. imper. Pass. of φημί: **πεφασμένος**, pf. part. Pass. both of φαίνω (cf. also φημί) and of θείνω II: **πεφασμένως**, Adv. pf. part. Pass. of φαίνω, *manifestly, expressly*, Lexap.Lys.10.19.

**πεφειράκοντες**, v. θηράω.

⊛ **πεφεισμένως**, Adv., (φείδομαι) *sparingly, cautiously*, D.S.31.31, Vett.Val.187.6, *Hippiatr*.96, Ael.*NA*7.45, etc.: c. gen., π. ἔχουσα τοῦ στόματος ib.6.24.

**πέφη·** ἐφάνη ἢ πεφύκασι, Hsch. **πεφήσομαι**, fut. Pass. of φαίνω and θείνω II. **πεφῐδέσθαι, πεφῐδοίμην, πεφῐδήσομαι**, v. φείδομαι. ⊛ **πεφλάζει·** βράζει, Id. **πεφλοιδώς·** τὸν φλοιὸν ἀποβαλών, and **πεφλοιδέναι·** φλυκταινοῦσθαι, Id.

**Πεφναῖος**, α, ον, *of Pephnos* in Laconia, κύων, i.e. Helen, Lyc.87.

**πέφνε, πεφνέμεν, πεφνών**, etc., v. θείνω: hence a late pres. πέφνουσι, Opp.*H*.5.390.

**πεφοβημένως**, Adv., (φοβέομαι) *timorously*, X.*HG*7.5.25.

**πεφραγμένως**, Adv., (φράσσω) *guardedly*, συγκατατίθεσθαι πρὸς τοὺς ἐναντίους Chrysipp.*Stoic*.2.42; *with a good defence*, δέχεσθαι τὴν ἐκδρομήν J.*BJ*7.6.4.

**πέφρᾰδε, πεφρᾰδέειν, πεφρᾰδέμεν**, v. φράζω.

**πεφρασμένως**, Adv., (φράζω) *thoughtfully*, *EM*399.33.

**πέφρῐκα**, v. φρίσσω.

**πεφρονημένως**, Adv., (φρονέω) *thoughtfully*, π. ἔχει, i.e. has been thought out, Diotog.ap.Stob.4.1.96.

**πεφροντισμένως**, Adv., (φροντίζω) *carefully*, Str.15.1.2, D.S.12.40, Ph.2.214, J.*AJ*15.2.7, Antyll.ap.Orib.44.8.7, Themist.*Ep*.8, etc.; π. ἔχειν Ael.*NA*3.33.

**πεφύασι**, v. φύω.

**πεφύγγων**, Aeol. for πεφευγώς, Alc.147.

**πεφυζότες**, Ep. pf. part. for πεφευγότες, cf. φύζα.

**πεφῡκότως**, Adv. of φύω (πέφῡκα), *naturally*, opp. πεπλασμένως, Arist.*Rh*.1404ᵇ19.

**πεφύκω**, Ep. pres. formed from pf. πέφῡκα, = φύω: hence impf. ἐπέφῡκον, Hes.*Op*.149, *Th*.152.

**πεφυλαγμένως**, Adv., (φυλάσσω) *with due caution*, X.*An*.2.4.24, *Eq.Mag*.6.2, Aen.Tact.15.7, D.7.29, Plu.*Oth*.7, al., Luc.*Philops*.6; πρός τι π. ἔχειν Isoc.8.97.

**πεφυρμένως**, Adv., (φύρω) *confusedly*, M.Ant.2.11, cj. in Diotog. ap.Stob.4.1.133.

**πεφυυῖα, πεφυῶτες**, v. φύω.

**πέχαρι·** ἔλαφος, Amerias ap.Hsch.

**πέψις**, εως, Ion. ιος, ἡ, (πέσσω) *softening, ripening*, or *changing* by means of heat (Arist.*Mete*.379ᵇ18, *GA*775ᵃ17, *Pr*.907ᵃ18): I. of fruit, πέπανσίς ἐστι π. τις Id.*Mete*.380ᵃ11, cf. Thphr.*HP*1.12.2, 5.1.3 (pl.). II. *cooking* of food, including both ἕψησις and ὄπτησις (cooking by water or by dry heat), Arist.*Mete*.380ᵇ13, 381ᵃ23; κλίβανος καιόμενος εἰς π. Lxx *Ho*.7.4. b. *largess of cooked food*, *IGRom*.4.1637 (Philadelphia). 2. of wine, *fermentation*, Plu.2.656a. III. Medic., *digestion* of food, ὁμοία ἑψήσει Arist.*Mete*.381ᵇ7, cf. *PA*650ᵃ4, al.; τὰ τῆς π. ὄργανα Gal.*Nat.Fac*.1.10; π. καὶ ἀνάδοσις Porph.*Abst*.1.45: pl., Agatharch.77. 2. *ripening*, '*concoction*' of acrid humours, Hp.*VM* 18, cf. Plu.2.102a. b. *concoction*, as a function of the animal organs, ἡ τοῦ σπέρματος π. Arist.*GA*719ᵇ2; ἡ διάκρισις π. ἐστί ib.775ᵃ17; of milk, ib.776ᵇ35.

**πεώδης**, ες, *with a large* πέος, Luc.*Lex*.12; cf. πεοίδης.

**πη**, Dor. Adv. *somewhere, anywhere*, ἄλλη πη *Berl.Sitzb*.1927.

167 (Cyrene). II. indirect interrog. πῇ, *where*, ἴσατι πῇ ἐστι *Supp.Epigr.*4.70 (Locr. Epizeph.); cf. sq. B. II. 2. (Panhellenic η and no iota, cf. πήποκα.)

⊛ **πη**, Ion. (but not in Hom.) **κη**, Dor. **πᾳ**: enclit. Particle: I. of Manner, *in some way, somehow*, with a neg. *in any way, at all*, οὐδέ πῃ ἔστι Il.6.267, cf. Od.12.433, 13.207; οὐδέ τί πῃ δύναμαι Il.21.219; οὔτι πῃ Hes.*Op.*105; οὕτω πῃ *in some* such *way*, Il.24.373; ταῦτά κῃ Hdt.5.40; τῇδέ πῃ Pl.*Phd.*73b, etc.; ταύτῃ πῃ Id.*R.*432e, etc.; ἦ ἔχεις πῃ ἄλλῃ κάλλιον λέγειν; Id.*Cra.*427e; ἄλλῃ γέ πῃ λέγειν ἢ ᾗ.. Id.*Smp.*189c; εἴ πῃ if *any way*, Id.*Prt.*355a; μή πῃ..that *in no way*, Id.*Sph.*242c, etc.; ἦ πᾳ..; can it *possibly*..? Theoc.4.3; so ἆρά γέ πᾳ..; Id.7.149,151; μάλιστά κῃ *somewhere* about, *approximately*, Hdt.2.75, 4.86, etc.: to limit a Sup., ἀπορώτατά πῃ Pl.*Ti.*51b, etc.; opp. ἁπλῶς, Arist.*APr.*49ᵃ8. II. of Space, *by some way, to some place*, Il.6.378,383; οὔτε πῃ ἄλλῃ Od.2.127, cf. 3.251: c. gen., ἦ πῄ με..πολίων..ἄξεις; wilt thou carry me *to some* city? Il.3.400. 2. *somewhere, anywhere*, οὐδέ πῃ ἀσπὶς ἔην Od.22.25 (ap. Eust.); εἴ πῃ πιέζοιντο Th.1.49; πεσόντος πῃ τοῦ τείχους X.*HG*5.2.5, etc.; οὐδέ πῃ ἄλλῃ Od.22.140; ἀέρι πᾳ Theoc.17.120. 3. πῇ μέν.., πῇ δέ.. *on one side*.., *on the other*.., Plu.*Caes.*25; *partly*.., *partly*.., v.l. in X.*An.*3.1.12; πῇ μέν.., ἔστι δ' ὅτε Plu.*Alc.*6.

B. **πῇ**, Ion. (but not in Hom.) **κῇ**, Dor. **πᾷ**: interrog. Particle: I. of Manner, *in what way? how?* Od.12.287, Pl.*Phd.*76b, *Prt.*353c, etc.; πῇ δή; *how, pray?* Pl.*R.*376b, etc.; πῇ δὴ οὖν ποτε; *how in the world?* Id.*Lg.*694c; πῇ μάλιστα; *how exactly?* Id.*R.*537e; πῶς οὖν καὶ πῇ; Id.*Lg.*686b: in indirect questions, ἐκαραδόκεον τὸν πόλεμον κῇ ἀποβήσεται Hdt.8.67, cf. D.29.1; εἰδέναι πῇ διαφέρει X.*Hier.*1.2, cf. *Cyr.*1.6.14, etc.; πῇ καὶ τί πρακτέον ἑκάστοις Plb.11.2.6. 2. *to what end? wherefore?* Od.2.364, etc.; πῇ δή; 17.219, Il.10.385, etc. II. of Space, *which way? whither?* πῇ ἔβη Ἀνδρομάχη; 6.377, etc.; πῇ ἔβαν εὐχωλαί; 8.229; πᾷ τις τράποιτ' ἄν; A.*Ch.*409 (lyr.); πῇ δή; Il.5.472, 24.201; πῇ γάρ; Od.15.509; δεῦρο ἕπου. Answ. πῇ; Pl.*Plt.*258e. 2. less freq. like ποῦ; *where?* Il.13.307; πᾷ πᾷ κεῖται; S.*Aj.*912 (lyr.), cf. E.*Hec.*1056 (lyr.): in indirect questions, X.*HG*2.4.31: c. gen., ἐπειρώτα.., κῇ γῆς οἰκημένοι.. cj. in Hdt.5.73. (Freq. written πη, πῆ in codd.)

**πηγ-άζω**, (πηγή) *spring, gush forth*, πηγάζει τὸ διαυγὲς ἐν ὄμμασι *APl.*4.310 (Damoch.); πηγάζοντες μαστοί, φλέβες πηγάζουσαι, Ph.1.31, 2.324. 2. c. acc. cogn., *gush forth with*, νᾶμα μέλισσα πηγάζει *AP*9.404 (Antiphil.); π. ῥεῖθρα Heraclit.*All.*9; [Ζεὺς] π. ζωὴν νοερὰν Procl. *in Cra.*p.52 P. **-αῖος**, α, ον, also ος, ον E.*Alc.*99 (lyr.):—*from a spring*, ὕδατα Hp.*Aër.*8; π. ῥέος *spring*-water, A.*Ag.*901; χέρνιψ E. l. c.; π. ἄχθος a weight *of water*, Id.*El.*108; π. κόραι *water* Nymphs, Id.*Rh.*929; π. ὕδωρ, ὕδατα, Pl.*Lg.*845e, *Criti.*113e; opp. συλλογιμαῖα, Arist.*Mete.*353ᵇ25: metaph., *belonging to the primal source*, Dam.*Pr.*96. Adv. -αίως Procl. *in Prm.*p.566 S. II. πηγαῖον, τό, = ἀρδάνιον, Hsch.

**πηγάν-ειος** [ᾰ], α, ον, = πηγάνινος, Gal.12.511. **-έλαιον**, τό, *oil of rue*, Herod.Med. in *Rh.Mus.*58.75, Alex.Trall.1.16. **-ηρά**, ἡ, *rue-plaster*, Antyll.ap.Paul.Aeg.7.17, Alex.Trall.5.4:—also **-ηρόν**, τό, Aët.15.40. **-ίζω**, *to be like rue*, Dsc.1.14, Gal.14.258. **-ινος**, η, ον, *of rue*, ἔλαιον Id.11.489. **-ιον**, τό, = πήγανον, Thphr.*HP*1.10.4 (pl.), Nic.*Th.*531, *Al.*49. **-ίτης** [ῑ] οἶνος, ὁ, wine *flavoured with rue*, *Gp.*8.13; fem., -ῖτις χολή *rue*-juice, Sopat.18. **-όεις**, εσσα, εν, *of rue*, ὄραμνοι Nic.*Al.*154.

⊛ **πήγᾰνον**, τό, *rue, Ruta graveolens*, Diocl.*Fr.*138, Theopomp.Hist.177(*a*), Alex.127.8, Thphr.*HP*1.3.4, al., Nic.*Al.*413; π. ὀρεινόν, ἄγριον, *mountain rue, Ruta halepensis*, Dsc.3.45 (but π. ἄγριον, = μῶλυ, ib.46): prov., οὐδ' ἐν σελίνῳ οὐδ' ἐν πηγάνῳ, i.e. scarcely at the *edge* or *beginning* of a thing, because these herbs were planted for borders in gardens, Ar.*V.*480; cf. περίκηπος.

**πηγᾰνόσπερμον**, τό, *rue-seed*, *Gp.*8.30.

**πηγᾰνώδης**, ες, *like rue*, Thphr.*HP*6.5.3, 9.9.6.

**πηγάς**, άδος, ἡ, (πήγνυμι III): 1. = πάχνη, *hoar-frost, rime*, Hes.*Op.*505 (pl.). 2. (sc. γῆ) *earth hardened after rain*, Hsch.

**Πήγᾰσος**, Dor. **Πάγᾰσος** [ᾱγ], ὁ, *Pegasus*, Hes.*Th.*281, 325, E.*Fr.*306, Apollod.2.3.2, Str.8.6.21, Paus.2.4.1, etc.: pl. Πήγασοι, as a sample of prodigies, Pl.*Phdr.*229d, cf. Cic.*Pro Quinct.*25.80, Plin.*HN*8.72, 10.136:—Adj. **Πηγάσειος** [ᾰ], α, ον, *of Pegasus*, Ar.*Pax*76: fem. **Πᾱγᾰσὶς** κράνα, *Hippocrene*, Mosch.3.77, cf. *AP*11.24 (Antip.).

**πηγεσίμαλλος** [ῐ], ον, *thick-fleeced*, ἀρνειός Il.3.197; cf. πηγός.

**πηγετός**, ὁ, = παγετός, D.P.667.

⊛ **πηγή**, Dor. **πᾱγά**, ἡ, *running water*, used by Hom. always in pl., *streams*, πηγαὶ ποταμῶν Il.20.9, cf. Hdt.1.189, A.*Pr.*89, 434 (lyr.), *Pers.*311, E.*HF*1297, *Rh.*827 (lyr.); κρουνὼ δ' ἵκανον καλλιρρόω, ἔνθα δὲ πηγαὶ δοιαὶ ἀναΐσσουσι Il.22.147: sg., καλλιρρόου ἔψαυσα π. A.*Pers.*202, cf. 613. 2. metaph., of tears, πηγαὶ κλαυμάτων, δακρύων, *streams*.., Id.*Ag.*888, S.*Ant.*803, *Tr.*852 (lyr.): abs., παρειὰν νοτίοις ἔτεγξα παγαῖς A.*Pr.*402 (lyr.), cf. E.*Alc.*1068, etc.; also πηγαὶ γάλακτος, βοτρύων, S.*El.*895, E.*Cyc.*496 (lyr.); πόντου πηγαῖς with sea-*water*, Id.*IT*1039; πηγαὶ τροφῆς τῷ γεννωμένῳ, of mother's milk, Pl.*Mx.*237e; π. μαστῶν *Inscr.Cos* 218.8. II. *fount, source*, τοῦ Νείλου Hdt.2.28, 4.53 (pl.), *OGI*168.9 (Syene, ii B. C.), Str.17.1.52 (pl.); πηγαὶ ἡλίου *the fount* of light, i.e. the South, A.*Pr.*809; πηγαὶ νυκτός the North, S.*Fr.*956; παγὰ ἐπέων Pi.*P.*4.299; πυρὸς παγαί ib.1.22, cf. A.*Pr.*110, Pl.*Ti.*79d; πηγὴ ἀργύρου, of the silver-mines at Laureion, A.*Pers.*238; τῆς ἀκουούσης π. δι' ὤτων, i.e. the sense of hearing, S.*OT*1387; ἀπὸ μιᾶς ἀρχῆς καὶ π. Arist.*PA*668ᵃ15, cf. Plu.2.856e. 2. metaph., *source, origin*, mostly in sg., κακῶν π. A.*Pers.*743; αἱ τέχναι, ἃς πηγάς φασι τῶν καλῶν εἶναι X.*Cyr.*7.2.13; π. καὶ ἀρχὴ κινήσεως Pl.*Phdr.*245c; π. ἡδονῶν, τοῦ φρονεῖν, νοσημάτων, etc., Id.*Phlb.*62d, *Lg.*808d, *Ti.*85b, etc.; ἀρχαὶ καὶ π. τῶν στάσεων Arist.*Pol.*1301ᵇ5, cf. Pl.*Lg.*690d; π. τῆς κακοπραγμοσύνης Plb.18.40.3; βέβηκα π. εἰς ἐμάς I have returned to *the source* of my existence, *Epigr.Gr.*463 (Crommyon), cf. Dam.*Pr.*95, al. 3. *inner canthus* of eye, supposed source of tears, Poll.2.71, Hsch. (both pl.).

**πηγίδιον**, τό, Dim. of πηγή, Suid.

**πηγῐμαῖος**, α, ον, (πηγή) *from a spring*, Hdn.*Epim.*68, *Gloss.*

**πηγίον**, τό, Dim. of πηγή, *spring*, *PRyl.*233.1 (ii A. D.).

⊛ **πῆγμα**, ατος, τό, (πήγνυμι) *anything fastened* or *joined together, framework*, of a ship, κέλητος π. *AP*5.203 (Mel.); τὸ π. τῆς σχεδίας Ph.Byz.*Mir.*4.5; of a roof, *Annuario* 6/7.450; θύρα κέλλας, στοὰ σὺν πήγμασι, *POxy.*2146.9, 12 (iii A. D.); τὸ τῶν ὀστέων π. Lxx 4*Ma.*9.21; τὸ πιοειδὲς π. Heliod.ap.Orib.49.33.5. 2. *stage* or *scaffold* used in theatres, Str.6.2.6, J.*AJ*14.15.5, *BJ*7.5.5, Juv.4.122, Suet.*Claud.*34, etc. 3. *bookcase*, Cic.*Att.*4.8.2. 4. metaph., π. γενναίως παγέν (Aurat. for πῆμα) *bond* in honour bound, A.*Ag.*1198; but also τὸ τῆς ὅλης π. σοφίας *fabric*, Ph.1.536. II. *anything congealed*, τὸ π. τῆς χιόνος frozen snow, Plb.3.55.5; τὸ π. τῆς τροφῆς, i.e. fat, Ruf.*Onom.*215; *solid mass*, ἔστη π., of the waters of Jordan, Lxx *Jo.*3.16. III. *that which makes to curdle*, as rennet does milk, Arist.*HA*516ᵃ4.

**πηγμάτιον**, τό, Dim. of foreg., *small attachment*, Procl.*Hyp.*3.15.

⊛ **πήγνῡμι**, 3 pl. πηγνύουσι Hdt.4.72 (v.l.), Thphr.*HP*6.6.9, but πηγνῦσι Hdt.1. c. codd. plur., Hp.*Vict.*2.60; opt. πήγνυτο Pl.*Phd.*118a codd.; inf. πηγνύειν X.*Cyn.*6.7, Dsc.4.95: impf. πήγνυον Orph.*L.*567 (περι-), Nonn.*D.*5.50: late form of pres. πήσσω (q.v.): fut. πήξω Il.22.283; Dor. πάξω Pi.*O.*6.3: aor. ἔπηξα, Ep. πῆξα Od.12.15, etc.; Aeol. part. πάξαις Pi.*O.*10(11).45: pf. πέπηχα, only plpf. ἐμ-πεπήχεσαν D.C.40.40:—**Med.** in trans. sense, πήγνῠμαι Hes.*Op.*809: fut. πήξομαι Gal.10.388: aor. ἐπηξάμην Hes.*Op.*455, Hdt.6.12, etc.:—**Pass.** πήγνῠμαι: fut. πᾰγήσομαι Ar.*V.*437, Th.4.92; πήξομαι (as Pass.) Hp.*Aër.*8: aor. 1 ἐπήχθην, Ep. 3 pl. πῆχθεν Il.8.298, Dor. subj. παχθῇ Theoc.23.31, part. πηχθείς E.*Cyc.*302: more freq. aor. 2 ἐπάγην [ᾰ], Ep. πάγην, Ep. 3 pl. πάγεν Il.11.572; part. παγείς A.*Eu.*190, E.*IA*395: pf. πέπηγμαι (κατα-, συμ-) D.H.5.46, Arr.*An.*2.21.1: plpf. ἐπέπηκτο Jul.*Or.*3.123b; but in the best authors, πέπηγα is used as the pf. Pass., Il.3.135, etc.; Aeol. πέπᾱγα Alc.34; opt. πεπαγοίην Eup.435: plpf. ἐπεπήγειν Il.13.442, Th.3.23: I. *stick* or *fix in*, ἐν δὲ μετώπῳ πῆξε [τὴν αἰχμήν] Il.4.460, etc.; ἔνθα οἱ ἔγχος ἔπηξε 13.570; ἐν γαίῃ π. ἐρετμόν Od.23.276 (or γαίῃ 11.129); π. ἐπὶ τύμβῳ ἐρετμόν 11.77 (or τύμβῳ 12.15); [γύην] ἐν ἐλύματι π. Hes.*Op.*430; ἔπαξε διὰ φρενῶν ξίφος Pi.*N.*7.26; *fix in the earth, plant*, σκῆπτρον S.*El.*420, cf. *Aj.*821; σκηνήν, σκηνὰς π., *pitch* a tent, And.4.30, Pl.*Lg.*817c (in Med., σκηνὰς πηξάμενοι *pitching themselves* tents, Hdt.6.12); σταύρωμα π. Th.6.66; τὰς σχαλίδας π. ὑπτίας X.*Cyn.*6.7; *plant* seeds or cuttings, Thphr.*HP*6.6.9, 7.4.10: intr. pf. and Pass., δόρυ δ' ἐν κραδίῃ ἐπεπήγει the spear *stuck fast* in his heart, Il.13.442; [δοῦρα] ἐν χροΐ πήγνυτο 15.315; [ὀϊστοὶ] ἐν χροΐ πῆχθεν 8.298; δοῦρα ἐν σάκεϊ πάγεν 11.572; [ξίφος] πέπηγεν ἐν γῇ S.*Aj.*819; σκηνὴ ἔσκε πεπηγυῖα ἑτοίμη Hdt.7.119; κυρβασίας ὀρθὰς πεπηγυίας ib.64, cf. 70:—Med., ἐν ἀλλήλοις χείλεα πηξάμενοι, of kissing, *AP*5.254 (Paul. Sil.). 2. *stick* or *fix on*, κεφαλὴν ἀνὰ σκολόπεσσι Il.18.177; σκόλοψι δέμας E.*IT*1430; κρᾶτα πήξασ' ἐπ' ἄκρον θύρσον Id.*Ba.*1141:—Pass., ἀμφὶ βουπόροισι πηχθέντας μέλη ὀβελοῖσι *having their* limbs *fixed* on spits, Id.*Cyc.*302; ὑπὸ ῥάχιν παγέντες *impaled*, A.*Eu.*190. 3. *fix upon* an object, κατὰ χθονὸς ὄμματα π. Il.3.217: intr. pf., πρὸς ἀστρονομίαν ὄμματα πέπηγεν Pl.*R.*530d, cf. Jul. l. c. (Pass.); πεπηγυῖα τὰς τῶν ὀμμάτων βολὰς ἐς τὰ τῆς ψυχῆς ἀπόρρητα Philostr.Jun.*Im.*11: c. inf., ἡ σοφία ἀρέσκειν πέπηγε *is bent upon* pleasing, Pl.*R.*605a: abs., τὸ πεπηγὸς ὄμμα *immovable* eye, *fixed* gaze, Hp.*Prorrh.*1.46, cf. Gal.16.610. II. *fasten* [different parts] *together, fit together, build*, νῆας πῆξαι Il.2.664; ἴκρια π. Od.5.163:—Med., πήξασθαι ἅμαξαν *build oneself* a wagon, Hes.*Op.*455; νέας πηξάμενοι Hdt.5.83:—Pass., *to be joined* or *put together*, ψυχὴ καὶ σῶμα παγέν Pl.*Phdr.*246c. III. *make solid* or *stiff*, esp. of liquids, *freeze*, θεὸς..πήγνυσι πᾶν ῥέεθρον A.*Pers.*496; τοὺς ποταμοὺς ἔπηξε (sc. ὁ θεός) Ar.*Ach.*139; βορρᾶς πηγνὺς τοὺς ἀνθρώπους X.*An.*4.5.3; *curdle*, γάλα Dsc.4.95:—Med., τυροὺς πήγνυσθαι *to make oneself* cheese (by curdling the milk), Luc.*VH*1.24:—Pass. and intr. pf., *become solid, stiffen*, γοῦνα πήγνυται Il.22.453; ἄρθρα πέπηγέ μου E.*HF*1395 (but also, *become firm* or *set*, of limbs, Ael.*NA*2.11; πεπηγυῖα ὑγιεινὴ κατάστασις Gal.*Thras.*7); of liquids, *freeze*, ἡ θάλασσα πήγνυται Hdt.4.28; ἅλες πήγνυνται salt *crystallizes*, ib.53, cf. 6.119; φόνος πέπηγεν A.*Ch.*67 (lyr.); πεπάγαισιν ὐδάτων ῥόαι Alc.34, cf. X.*An.*7.4.3; κρύσταλλος ἐπεπήγει οὐ βέβαιος *was* not *frozen* so as to bear, Th.3.23; ἀνίκα [χιὼν] παχθῇ Theoc.23.31; ὄστρακον [ᾠοῦ] π. Arist.*GA*752ᵃ35; γάλα π. Id.*PA*676ᵃ14; ὀφθαλμῶν οἱ μὲν ὑγιεῖς, οἱ δὲ πεπηγότες *blind*, of buds, Thphr.*CP*5.12.10: metaph., *to be petrified, struck dumb*, Antiph.166.7. IV. metaph., *fix*, ὅρους τοῖς βαρβάροις Lycurg.73, cf. Aristopho 9.7: Astrol., *fix, determine* a nativity, Sch.Ptol.*Tetr.*103:—Med., ὄφρα ἐν φρασὶ πάξαιθ', ὅπως.. that *he might keep it fixed in his* heart, Pi.*N.*3.62; *establish*, χορούς Him.*Or.*16.6:—Pass. and intr. pf., *to be irrevocably fixed, established*, εἰς ὅρος ἡμῖν παγήσεται Th.4.92; πῆγμα (Aurat. for πῆμα) γενναίως παγέν A.*Ag.*1198; κακῶς παγέντας ὅρκους E.*IA*395; ὀρθὰς παγείσας φρένας Carc.6.2; μὴ γὰρ ὡς θεῷ νομίζετ' ἐκεῖνῳ τὰ παρόντα πεπηγέναι πράγματα ἀθάνατα D.4.8; τὰ καλῶς πεπηγότα τῇ φύσει Id.25.90. (Cf. Lat. *pango*.)

**πήγνῡσις**, εως, ἡ, = πῆξις, Ps.-Thales ap.Gal.16.37.

**πηγό-μαλλος**, = πηγεσίμαλλος, coined by Eust.404.1. **-ρρῦτος**, ον, *flowing from a spring*, ἰκμάδες Orph.*H*.83.5.

⊛ **πηγός**, ή, όν, Dor. **πᾱγός**, (πήγνυμι II) *well put together, solid, strong*, ἵππους πηγοὺς ἀθλοφόρους Il.9.124, cf. Alcm.23.48 ; κύματι πηγῷ Od. 5.388, 23.235, *AP*9.143 (Antip.). 2. Subst. πηγός (sc. ἅλς), ὁ, *salt* (cf. πηκτός III), mock-Epic use in Strato Com.1.36. II. *white*, πλόκος Lyc.336 ; ὀστέα *Sammelb*.4314.5 (Alexandria, iii B.C.) ; κύνας ἥμισυ πηγούς Call.*Dian*.90. 2. Hsch. has πηγόν· οἱ μὲν λευκόν, οἱ δὲ μέλαν ; and Eust.403.43 explains κῦμα π. as κ. μέλαν, cf. 740.50, 1539.42.

**πηγῠλίς**, ίδος, ἡ, (πήγνυμι III) *frozen, icy-cold*, νὺξ δ' ἄρ' ἐπῆλθε κακὴ Βορέαο πεσόντος π. Od.14.476 ; αὐτμή A.R.2.737. II. as Subst., *hoar-frost, rime*, *AP*9.384.24, Alciphr.1.23 : pl., *frosts*, Orph.*Fr*.270.4.

**πηδάλι-ον** [ᾰ], τό, (πηδόν) *steering-paddle, rudder*, Hom., only in Od. ; π. μετὰ χερσὶ.. νηὸς ἔχοντα 3.281 ; π. ποιήσατο, ὄφρ' ἰθύνοι 5. 255 ; πηδαλίῳ ἰθύνετο τεχνηέντως ἥμενος ib.270 ; π. δὲ ἐκ χειρῶν προέηκε ib.315 ; π. δὲ ἓν ποιεῦνται (sc. Αἰγύπτιοι) καὶ τοῦτο διὰ τῆς τρόπιος διαβύνεται Hdt.2.96 ; Greek ships had a pair, hence in pl., of a single ship, Id.4.110, Cratin.139, Ar.*Eq*.542, Diph.43.11 ; πηδάλια ζεύγλαισι (cross-bars) παρακαθίετο E.*Hel*.1536 ; ἀνέντες τὰς ζευκτηρίας τῶν π. *Act.Ap*.27.40 ; πηδάλια εἶχε τέτταρα τριακονταπήχη, of the τεσσαρακοντήρης of Ptolemy IV, Callix.1 : metaph. in Com., [γυνὴ] ..οὐδὲ μικρὸν πείθεται ἑνὶ πηδαλίῳ Theophil.6 : prov., π. κρεμάσαι to retire from a seafaring life, Ar.*Av*.711. 2. metaph., ἱππικὰ π., of reins, A.*Th*.206 (lyr.) ; νώμα δικαίῳ π. στρατόν Pi.*P*.1.86 ; τὰ π. τῆς διανοίας Pl.*Clit*.408b. II. in pl., of *the oars* by which the nautilus is said to steer himself, Arist.*HA*622ᵇ13 ; of *the long hind legs* of the locust and grasshopper, ib.532ᵃ29, 535ᵇ12, cf. *IA*710ᵃ3. III. = πολύγονον ἄρρεν, Ps.-Dsc.4.4. **-όομαι**, *to be furnished with a rudder*, Simp.*in Cat*.187.14. **-ουργική** (sc. τέχνη), ἡ, art *of rudder-making*, Asp.*in EN*5.1. **-ουχέω**, *steer*, Ph.1.131 : metaph., π. τὴν τῆς εὐσεβείας ναῦν Lxx 4*Ma*.7.1 ; π. τὸ κοινὸν τοῦ κόσμου σκάφος, of God, Ph.1.516 ; *govern*, τὰ σύμπαντα Boeth.*Stoic*.3.266, Ph. 1.370. ⊛ **-οῦχος**, ὁ, (ἔχω) *steersman* : metaph., *ruler*, ib. 145. **-ώδης**, ες, *rudder-shaped*, Arist.*PA*683ᵃ36. **-ωτός**, ή, όν, *furnished with a rudder*, Id.*Cat*.7ᵃ12.

**πηδ-άω**, E.*Ion*717 (lyr.), etc. ; Dor. 3 sg. παδῇ Sophr.20 ; Lacon. imper. πάδη Ar.*Lys*.1317 (lyr.) ; Ion. part. πηδεῦντα, πηδεῦσαι, Herod. 3.96, 4.61 : fut. -ήσομαι Thphr.*Char*.21.6, (ἐπι-) Pl.*Ly*.216a, (προσ-) Alex.124.16 ; later -ήσω *APl*.4.54*, 142 : aor. ἐπήδησα Il.14.455, etc. : pf. πεπήδηκα Aesop.203, (ἀπο-) Hp.*Art*.47, (ἐκ-) X.*HG*7.4.37, (ὑπερ-) D.23.73 :—**Pass.**, plpf. ἐπεπήδητο (in act. sense) Hp.*Nat.Puer*.13 :— *leap, spring*, ὑψόσε ποσσὶν ἐπήδα Il.21.269, cf. 302 ; ἐς σκάφη π. S.*Aj*. 1279 ; πρὸς πυγήν Hp.*Nat.Puer*.l.c. ; opp. βαδίζω, X.*Cyn*.5.31 ; of fish in the frying-pan, Eub.75.6, 109, al. : c. acc. cogn., π. δυστυχῆ πηδήματα E.*Or*.263 ; π. μείζονα (sc. πηδήματα) S.*OT*1300 (anap.) ; λαιψηρὰ π. E.*Ion*717 (lyr.) : c. acc. loci, πεδία π. *bound over* them, S.*Aj*.30 ; π. πλάκα E.*Ba*.307. 2. *stamp with the feet*, οἱ φίλοι πηδάτωσαν Luc.*Rh. Pr*.21. II. metaph. of things, οὐκ ὀΐω.. ἅλιον πηδῆσαι ἄκοντα Il.14. 455 ; πάλος..'πήδησεν εὐχάλκου κράνους A.*Th*.459 ; τροχοὶ π. E.*Ph*. 1194 : freq. of the heart or pulse, *leap, throb*, ἁ καρδία παδῇ Sophr. l.c., cf. Pl.*Smp*.215e : folld. by interrog. clause, οἶμαι τὰς καρδίας πηδᾶν ὅ τι λέξει Ar.*Nu*.1392 ; κατὰ δ' ἐγκέφαλον πηδᾷ σφάκελος E.*Hipp*. 1352 ; πηδῶσα οἷον τὰ σφύζοντα Pl.*Phdr*.251d ; αἱ σάρκες οἷα θερμὰ θερμὰ πηδεῦσαι Herod.4.61 ; of the mind, πηδῶν ὁ θυμὸς ἔνδοθεν μαντεύεται *Trag.Adesp*.176, cf. 390 ; of sudden change, τί πηδᾷς ἄλλοτ' εἰς ἄλλους τρόπους E.*Tr*.67 ; εἰς τἀπίσημα δ' ὁ φθόνος πηδᾶν φιλεῖ Id. *Fr*.294 ; π. πρός τινος εὐπραγίαν Philostr.*VS*2.25.4. **-ηθμός**, ὁ, *pulsation*, φλεβῶν Hp.*Epid*.7.39. **-ημα**, ατος, τό, *leap, bound*, A. *Pers*.95, 305, S.*Aj*.833, E.*Andr*.1139, etc., cf. πηδάω I ; *leaping up* in admiration, of an audience, Plu.2.41c (pl.). II. *beating* or *throbbing* of the heart, τὸ μέλλον καρδία πήδημ' ἔχει E.*Ba*.1288 ; ἴσχεσθαι καρδίαν πηδήματος Plu.2.83b. **-ησις**, εως, ἡ, *leaping*, πηδήσεις σατυρικαί Id.*Ant*.75 ; πηδήσεις ἐπὶ τοὺς ἵππους Arr.*Tact*.43.3 ; of wood burning, Thphr.*Ign*.69. II. *beating* or *throbbing* of the heart, Pl.*Ti*.70c, *Lg*.791a, Arist.*PA*669ᵃ20, Phld.*Ir*.p.27 W. **-ητής**, οῦ, ὁ, *leaper, dancer*, Ptol.*Tetr*.64. **-ητικός**, ή, όν, *good at leaping, springing*, of the locust, grasshopper, flea, Arist.*HA*532ᵃ27, *PA*683ᵃ 33 : Sup. -ώτατος, σατύρων Luc.*Bis Acc*.10.

**πήδῐνος**, η, ον, *made of* πηδός, read by Gramm. for φήγινος in Il.5. 838, Hsch., *EM*669.40, Eust.613.9.

**πηδόν**, τό, *blade of an oar* : hence generally, *oar*, ἀναρρίπτειν ἅλα πηδῷ Od.7.328, cf. 13.78 ; πηδοῖσιν ἐρέσσετε A.R.4.200 ; γῆ δὲ ναυσθλωθήσεται ῥήσσοντι πηδοῖς χέρσον Lyc.1416. II. in pl. πηδά, = πηδάλια, Arat.155. (Written πῆδον, also πῆδος, Hsch.)

⊛ **πηδός**, ὁ, tree whose timber was used for axles, etc., Thphr.*HP* 5.7.6 ; perh. = πάδος (q.v.) ; cf. πήδινος. (Variously accented in codd.)

**πηδύειν, πηδυλίς**, written for πιδ-, Hsch.

**πήθω**, = πάσχω, etym. of πηρός, Phlp.*in Cat*.180.24, *EM*671.1. (Inferred from παθεῖν.)

⊛ **πηΐσκος**, ὁ, Dim. of παῖς, *child, son*, *Supp.Epigr*.2.509.5 (Crete, v B.C.).

**πήκασμα**, ατος, τό, f.l., perh. for πύκασμα, in pl., *trappings* for horses, *Hippiatr*.14.

**πηκτή**, Dor. **πακτά**, ἡ, v. πηκτός.

**πήκτης**, dub. sens. in *Arch.Pap*.5.387 (ii A.D.).

**πηκτικός**, ή, όν, *freezing*, Thphr.*CP*6.1.3 : Comp., ib.5.14.3. 2. *coagulating, curdling*, γάλακτος Dsc.1.128.

⊛ **πηκτίς**, Dor. **πᾱκτίς**, ίδος, Aeol. **πᾶκτις**, ιδος, ἡ, *stringed instrument* used by the Lydians, Sapph.122, Alc.*Supp*.5.5, Pi.*Fr*.125, Hdt. 1.17, S.*Frr*.241 (pl.), 412, Telest.5.4 (pl.), Sopat.11 ; played with finger (not πλῆκτρον), Aristox.*Fr.Hist*.66 : pl., Ar.*Th*.1217, Pl.*R*.399c, Arist.*Pol*.1341ᵃ40, Anaxil.15 ; said to have been introduced (from Lydia) by Sappho, Menaechm.5 ; later, = λύρα, Luc.*DMar*.1.4. 2. *shepherd's pipe, Pan's pipes*, *APl*.4.244 (Agath.) ; ἐπὶ χείλεσι σύρων π. *AP*9.586 (Cometas), cf. Procop.Gaz.p.137 B. 3. *cage* or *net for catching birds*, in pl., Dionys.*Av*.3.1, Sch.Ar.*Av*.528. II. *carving-knife*, Suid.

⊛ **πηκτός**, ή, όν, Dor. **πᾱκτός**, ά, όν, (πήγνυμι I) *stuck in, fixed*, ἔγχος ἐν χθονὶ S.*Aj*.907 ; π. θάνατος, of the death of Ajax, *Trag.Adesp*. 255. 2. *planted*, opp. raised from seed, [σκόροδον] Thphr.*HP*7.4. 11 : πηκτή, ἡ, a variety of σύμφυτον (q.v.), Dsc.4.10. II. (πήγνυμι II) *well put together, compacted, built*, of wood-work, ἄροτρον Il.10.353, Od.13.32 ; opp. αὐτόγυος, Hes.*Op*.433 ; π. ἕδος a chair *of several pieces*, *h.Cer*.196 ; π. κλίμακες E.*Ph*.489 ; π. λύραι S.*Fr*.238 (anap.). 2. πηκτή, ἡ, *net* or *cage* set to catch birds, Ar.*Av*.528, Arist.*HA*614ᵃ12 ; cf. πηκτίς I. 3. 3. πηκτὰ δωμάτων *barriers* of the house, *door*, E.*Fr*. 1003 (πακτὰ codd. Poll.), parodied in Ar.*Ach*.479. III. (πήγνυμι III) *congealed, curdled*, γάλα E.*Cyc*.190 ; πακτά, ἡ, *cream-cheese*, Theoc.11.20, cf. *AP*6.55 (Barb.), *POxy*.1923.19 (pl., v/vi A.D.) ; ἅλς π. salt *obtained from brine*, Nic.*Al*.518 ; κηρός Theoc.1.128 ; *frozen*, ὕδατα Pl.*Ti*.59c ; ὕδωρ τὸ μὲν ῥέον τὸ δὲ πακτόν Ti.Locr.99c. 2. *capable of solidification*, Arist.*Mete*.385ᵃ12.

**Πηλᾰγόνες**, οἱ, v. πηλόγονος. **πῆλαι**, v. πάλλω.

**πηλαῖος**, α, ον, (πηλός) *made of clay*, πλίνθος Man.4.292. II. *living in mud*, of fish, Paus.4.34.2.

**πηλᾰκ-ίζω**, etym. of προπηλακίζω, *EM*669.49, cf. πήλαξ ; also found in *PSI*5.495.9 (iii B.C.). **-ισμός**, ὁ, etym. of προπηλακισμός, Suid.

**πηλᾰμῠδ-εία**, ἡ, *tunny-fishery*, Str.12.3.19. **-εῖον**, τό, *fishing-ground for tunnies*, Id.12.3.11.

⊛ **πηλᾰμύς**, ύδος, ἡ, *young tunny* (of the first year, acc. to Arist.*HA* 571ᵃ11), S.*Fr*.503, Phryn.Com.35, Hices.ap.Ath.3.116e, Sostrat.ap. eund.7.303b, Opp.*H*.1.113, 4.504 ; *vas pelamydum*, Juv.7.120.

**πήλαξ**, ακος, = πηλός, etym. of πηλακίζω, *EM*669.49.

**πηλάριον**, τό, name of an *eye-salve*, Aët.7.9 (pl.), Alex.Trall.2.

**πῆλε**, v. πάλλω.

**Πηλεύς**, ὁ, gen. έως, Ep. ῆος or έος, acc. έα (monosyll.) S.*Fr*.487, E.*Andr*.22 :—*Peleus*, Il.18.18, etc. ; Πηλέως μάχαιρα, prov. of unexpected aid, Sch.Ar.*Nu*.1059 :—Adj. **Πήλειος**, α, ον *AP*9.476b ; Ep. **Πηλήϊος**, η, ον Il.18.60 ; Patron **Πηλεΐδης**, ου, Ep. εω and αο, ὁ, *son of Peleus*, 15.64, 614 ; Ep. also **Πηληϊάδης**, 1.1 ; Dor. **Πηλεΐδας** Pi. *P*.6.23 :—also **Πηλεΐων**, ωνος, ὁ, Il.16.195, etc. (also as name of a frog, with play on πηλός, Batr.206) ; **Πηλεΐωνάδε** *to Peleus' son*, Il. 24.338. (Popularly derived from πηλός (which however has ᾱ in Dor.) : hence prov. μὴ δεῖν τὸν Οἰνέα Πηλέα ποιεῖν don't make wine into lees, Ath.9.383c, cf. Demetr.*Eloc*.171.)

**πηλεφάνης**, v. τηλεφανής.

⊛ **πήληξ**, ηκος, ἡ, *helmet*, ἀμφὶ δέ οἱ κροτάφοισι φαεινὴ σείετο πήληξ Il. 13.805 ; ἤμυσε κάρη πήληκι βαρυνθέν 8.308 ; ἱππόκομος π. 16.797 ; old Ep. word, used by Ar.*Ra*.1017, Arist.*Top*.173ᵇ20. 2. serpent's *crest*, E.*Hyps.Fr*.16(18).4. (Commonly derived from πάλλω, πῆλαι, from the nodding of the plume, Apollon.*Lex*., etc.)

**Πηλιάς**, άδος, ἡ, *of* or *from Mount Pelion*, μελίη Il.16.143, etc.

**πηλιδνός**, = πελιδνός, Hsch.

**πηλίκ-ος** [ῐ], η, ον, interrog. correl. to τηλίκος, ἡλίκος, *how great* or *large?* πηλίκη τις ἔσται ἡ γραμμή; Pl.*Men*.82d, cf. 83e ; πηλίκον τινὰ οἴεσθε μέγεθος; Eub.82 ; after τηλικοῦτος, D.19.284 ; πόσα καὶ πηλίκα *of what* number and *magnitude*, Plb.1.2.8 : with Art., ὁ πηλίκος; *quantulus?* Babr.69.4 ; τὸ π. *magnitude*, opp. τὸ ποσόν (quantity), Nicom. *Ar*.1.2 ; ὁ χρόνος.. ἐστὶ μῖγμα πηλίκου καὶ ποσοῦ Dam.*Pr*.371. Adv. -κως Hdn.Gr.2.925. II. *of what age*, π. ἦσθ' ὅθ' ὁ Μῆδος ἀφίκετο; Xenoph.22.5. 2. indef., *of a certain age*, Arist.*EN*1134ᵇ11 : Comp. -ώτερος, f.l. for ἀπηλικέστερος, Aret.*SA*2.11. **-ότης**, ητος, ἡ, *magnitude, size*, A.D.*Pron*.26.13, Gal.1.333, Sch.Ar.*Pl*.377 : opp. ποσότης (quantity), Nicom.*Ar*.1.7.

**πήλῐνος**, η, ον, also ος, ον D.Chr.31.152 : (πηλός) :—*of clay*, ἀνδριὰς π. Arist.*Metaph*.1035ᵃ32 ; οἱ π. *clay figures*, D.4.26 ; τοῖχοι π. Plu. *Dem*.11 ; π. εἰκόνες D.Chr.l.c. ; π. βωμός *Com.Adesp*.341 ; π. ὀξὺ pointed nest *of clay*, built by the mason-bee, Arist.*HA*555ᵃ14 ; π. ἔργα *PPetr*.3 p.143 (iii B.C.).

**Πήλιον**, Dor. **Πάλιον** [ᾰ], τό, *Pelion*, a mountain in Thessaly, Il.2. 757, etc. :—Adj. **Πηλιάς** (q.v.) ; **Πηλιῶτις**, ιδος, *on* or *at the foot of Pelion*, E.*Med*.484 ; **Πηλιωτικός**, ή, όν, S.*Fr*.154 ; **Πηλιακός**, ή, όν, *APl*.4.110.

**πηλο-βάτης** [ᾰ], ου, ὁ, *mud-walker*, name of a frog, v.l. in Batr. 241. ⊛ **-γονος**, ον, *born from clay*, = γηγενής, used of the giants in Call.*Jov*.3 (but Πηλαγόνες, *Pelagonians*, Hdn.Gr.1.24). **-δευστέω**, *make mortar*, *IG*2².1672.29. **-δομέω**, *build of clay*, θάλαμον *AP* 10.4 (Marc. Arg.), cf. 5 (Thyill.). **-δομος**, ον, *clay-built*, τοῖχοι ib. 9.662 (Agath.). **-εργία**, ἡ, v. πηλουργία. **-εψητής**, *coctiliarius, figulus*, *Gloss*.

**πήλοθεν**, v. τηλόθεν. **πήλοι**, v. τηλοῦ.

⊛ **πηλο-πᾰτέω**, *trample in the mire*, *PMasp*.87.9 (vi A.D., Pass.). 2. *walk on clay* or *mud*, Sch.Ar.*Pax*1148. **-πᾰτίδες**, αἱ, *mud-treaders*, ἀρβύλαι π. a kind of boots with thick soles, Hp.*Art*.62 (v.l. πηλοβατίδες ap.Gal.18(1).680). **-πλάθος** [ᾰ], ὁ, *potter*, Luc.*Prom. Es*1. **-πλαστος**, ον, *moulded of clay*, π. σπέρμα, of a man, A.*Fr*.

369. -πλάτων [ᾰ], ωνος, ὁ, *Mud-Plato*, nickname of the sophist Alexander, Philostr.*VS*2.5.1. -ποιέω, *make muddy*, χθόνα Lyc.473, cf. *EM*629.34. -ποιητικός and -ποικός, ff.ll. for πιλοπ-. -ποιία, ἡ, *potter's trade*, *PPetr.*2p.32 (iii B.C.), *CPHerm.* p.80. ⊛ -ποιός, ὁ, = πηλοπλάθος, *BGU*362 viii 8 (iii A.D.), Alex. Aphr.*Pr.*1.49.

⊛ **πηλός** (Dor. **πᾱλός** Sophr.32, Cerc.3.3, *IG*5(1).1447.16 (Messene, iii/ii B.C.)), ὁ, Syrac. ἡ Phryn.38:—*clay, earth*, used by masons and potters, Hdt.2.36,136, Ar.*Av.*1143, Th.2.76, Pl.*Tht.*147a, Plb.15.35.2; πηλὸν ὀργάζειν Eup.248, S.*Fr.*482, cf. 510,787, Ar.*Av.*839; π. ἠχυρωμένος *clay* mixed with chaff for use as mortar, *IG*2$^2$.463.42, cf. 5(1) l. c., Lxx *Ge.*11.3; εὐώδει πηλῷ, of *earth* on which wine has been poured, Tryph.349; Βρομιώδεα π. φύρησαν..Χάριτες, of a drinking-cup, *AP*11.27 (Maced.): metaph., *clay* from which man was made: hence ὁ π. ὁ Προμηθεῖος, of man, Call.*Fr.*87, cf. 133, Ar.*Av.*686; ἐκ ποίου πηλοῦ πεφύρητ' εἰδότα Herod.2.29. 2. *mud, mire*, Hdt.2.5, 4.28, Ar.*V.*248, Th.2.4, Pl.*R.*363d, etc.: prov., ἔξω κομίζειν πηλοῦ πόδα A.*Ch.*697; κάσις πηλοῦ ξύνουρος, i.e. dust, Id.*Ag.*495: metaph., ἀνέρες ὧν τὸ κέαρ παλῷ σέσακται Cerc. l. c. II. Poet., *thick* or *muddy wine, lees*, S.*Fr.*783; of wine spilt on the floor, Plu.2.463a, Charito 1.3; cf. Πηλεύς fin. III. metaph., *dolt, blockhead*, *Com.Adesp.*890.

**πηλο-στρόφιον**, τό, *machine for kneading mortar*, *Stud.Pal.*20.67.20 (ii/iii A.D.). -τροφος, ον, *reared in mud* or *soft soil*, Opp.*C.*1.288.

**πηλουργ-ία**, in Ion. form **πηλοεργίη**, ἡ, *working in clay*, Aret.*SD*1.6. -ός, όν, *working in clay*, of bees, *Lyr.Alex.Adesp.*7.16: Subst. π., ὁ, Lxx *Wi.*15.7, Luc.*Prom.Es*2, *PKlein.Form.*63 (vi A.D.).

**Πηλούσιον**, τό, *Pelusium* in Egypt, Hdt.2.15, etc.: **Πηλουσιώτης**, ου, ὁ, *inhabitant of P.*, Luc.*JTr.*42; Adj., τὸ **Πηλούσιον** στόμα the Eastern mouth of the Nile, Hdt.2.17,154; τὸ **Πηλουσιακὸν** στ. Str.17.1.18; also Ταριχῆια Πηλουσιακά Hdt.2.15: Subst. Πηλούσιον, τό, an Egyptian festival, expld. with ref. to πηλός, Lyd.*Mens.*4.57.

**πηλο-φορέω**, *carry clay* or *mortar*, Ar.*Av.*1142, *Ec.*310 (lyr.), *BGU* 699.5 (ii A.D.). -φόρος, ον, *carrying clay* or *mortar*, ib.1290.3 (ii B.C.), Poll.7.130, Suid. -χῠτος, ον, *moulded of clay*, θάλαμοι, of swallows' nests, *AP*10.16 (Theaet.).

⊛ **πηλόω**, *coat* or *daub with clay*, *PMag.Berol.*2.151, Gal.14.291:—Med., *smear oneself with clay*, ἁφῇ (cf. ἁφή II. 5) πηλώσασθαι *IG*4$^2$(1).126.11 (Epid., ii A.D.), cf. Plu.2.980e:—Pass., *to be covered with mud*, J.*AJ*1.3.5, Plu.2.831a; ὅλον τὸ σῶμα πεπηλωμένος Lyd.*Mens.*4.57; *to be smeared with clay*, Apollod.*Poliorc.*147.4; of athletes, Luc.*Anach.*6.

**πήλυι**, v. τηλοῦ.

⊛ **πῆλυξ**, = ῥαγάς, *rent, cleft*, Hsch., Phot.

**πηλ-ώδης**, ες, *clayey, muddy*, ἀταρπιτός Parm.20; of places, Th.6.101, Arist.*HA* 549$^b$15, etc.; of the river Acheron, Pl.*Phd.* 113b. -ώεις, εσσα, εν, poet. for foreg., Opp.*H.*4.520, Nonn.*D.*2.59. ⊛ -ωμα, ατος, τό, *mud*, Charis.p.33 K. -ωσις, εως, ἡ, *smearing with mud*, Plu.2.166a (pl.).

**πῆμα**, ατος, τό (same form in Dor.), poet. word, *misery, calamity*, π. κακόν Od.5.179; π. κακοῖο 3.152; δύης π. 14.338; π. τῆς ἄτης S.*Aj.* 363; π. θεὸς Δαναοῖσι κυλίνδει Il.17.688; τοῖσι..πῆμα κυλίνδεται Od.2.163, cf. Il.11.347; ἡμῖν πήματα πολλὰ θέσαν 15.721; τοι πῆμα τόδ' ἤγαγον Οὐρανίωνες 24.547; ἓν παρ' ἐσλὸν π. σύνδυο δαίονται βροτοῖς ἀθάνατοι Pi.*P.*3.81; πημάτων ἔξω πόδα ἔχει A.*Pr.*265; πήματα ἐπὶ πήμασι πίπτοντ' S.*Ant.*594 (lyr.); πῆμ' ἐπὶ πήματι κεῖται, i.e. iron upon iron, the sword forged upon the anvil, Orac.ap.Hdt.1.67, cf. 68; σοφιστὴς πημάτων deviser of *pains* (i.e. the *labours* of Heracles), E.*Heracl.*993. II. of persons, *bane, calamity*, ὅς μιν ἔτικτε..π. γενέσθαι Τρωσί Il.22.421, cf. 3.50,160,6.282, S.*OT*379; π. κακὸς γείτων Hes.*Op.*346. (Cf. Skt. *pīyati*, Goth. *fijan* 'hate'.)

**πημ-αίνω**, Il.15.42: fut. -ᾰνῶ S.*Aj.*1314, *OC*837; Ion. -ανέω Il.24.781: aor. ἐπήμηνα 3.299, S.*Tr.*715, Pl.*R.*364c; Dor. part. πημάνας [ᾱ] *IG*1$^2$.1085.8:—Med., fut. πημᾰνοῦμαι Ar.*Ach.*842 (s. v. l.), also πημανούμενος in pass. sense, S.*Aj.*1155: Ep. aor. πημήναντο Q.S.13.379:—Pass., aor. ἐπημάνθην (v. infr.):—*plunge into ruin, undo*, and in milder sense, *grieve, distress*, π. Τρῶάς τε καὶ Ἕκτορα Il.15.42; [Ὅρκος] ἀνθρώπους π. Hes.*Th.*232, cf. Thgn.689; π. τὴν γῆν *damage* it, Hdt.9.13; ἄτρακτος θεὸν π. S.*Tr.*715; π. τινὰ φαρμάκοις Pl.*Lg.*932e; ὑγρότης π. τὰ ὄμματα Arist.*Pr.*957$^b$24: abs., *do harm*, Il.24.781, Democr.258; ὑπὲρ ὅρκια πημήνειαν *might work harm* in transgression of oaths, Il.3.299:—Med., ὅρκια πημήναντο *violated their* oaths, Q.S. l. c.:—Pass., *suffer hurt* or *harm*, οὐδέ τις οὖν μοι νηῶν πημάνθη Od.14.255, cf. 8.563, A.*Pr.*336, etc.; ἴσθι πημανούμενος S.*Aj.*1155.—Poet. word, used also *IG*1$^2$.18.7 and by Hdt. l. c., Pl.*R.* l. c., *Lg.*862a, 932e, 933e (Pass.), and in later Prose, as Corn.*ND*32 (Pass.), Porph.*Abst.*2.12, Agath.5.23. -αντέος, α, ον, *deserving to be injured*, Thgn.689. -ονή, ἡ, = πῆμα, freq. in Trag., A.*Pr.*239 (pl.), 278, 308 (pl.), S.*Tr.*1189 (pl.), E.*Fr.*682; also ὅπλα μὴ ἐπιφέρειν ἐπὶ πημονῇ with *hostile* intent, Foed.ap.Th.5.18.

**πῆμος**, interrog. Adv. *when?* Hdn.Gr.2.925, Hsch.; cf. ἦμος, τῆμος.

**πημοσύνη**, ἡ, = πημονή, A.*Pr.*1058 (pl., anap.), E.*Fr.*910.3 (anap.), Orph.*Fr.*285.10.

**πήμων**, ον, gen. ονος, *baneful*, Orph. Εὐχή 31.

**πῆν**· πῆ καὶ πῆν ἐπὶ τοῦ κατάπασσε καὶ καταπάσσειν, Hsch. (Prob. Dor. contr. forms of *πάω = πάσσω, cf. ἐπιπάσσω.)

**πήνα**, = ἀπήνη, Hsch.

**πηνάομαι**, = πηνίζομαι, Hsch. s. v. πηνώμενον (-όμενον cod.), Phot.

**Πηνελόπεια**, ἡ, *Penelope*, Od.24.194, etc.; **Πηνελόπη**, first in Hdt. 2.145, Ar.*Th.*547; Dor. **Πᾱνελόπα** *AP*6.289 (Leon.).

**πηνέλοψ**, Aeol. and Dor. **πᾱν-**, οπος, ὁ, a parti-coloured *duck*, Alc. 84, Ibyc.8, Ar.*Av.*298, 1302, Ion Trag.68, Arist.*HA*593$^b$23.

**πήνη**, ἡ, *thread on the bobbin* in the shuttle, *woof*, and in pl., *web*, E.*Hec.*471 (lyr.), *Ion* 197 (lyr.). II. *bobbin, spool*, *AP*6.160 (Antip. Sid.).

**πηνήκ-η**, ἡ, *false hair, wig*, Luc.*DMeretr.*5.3, 11.4, 12.5: distd. from ἔντριχον and προκόμιον, Phot., cf. Poll.2.30, 10.170. -ίζω, *cheat, gull*, Cratin.319, Hsch. (-ικ- cod., ante πήνην), Suid.; cf. διαπηνηκίζω. -ισμα, ατος, τό, *fraud*, Hsch. (pl.).

**πηνίζομαι**, Dor. **πᾱνίσδομαι**, (πήνη) *wind thread off a reel for the woof*, Philyll.33, prob. in *BGU*1141.34 (i B.C.): generally, *wind off a reel*, ἐκ ταλάρω π. ἔργα Theoc.18.32:—later in Act., Orib.*Fr.*137.

⊛ **πηνίκα**, interrog. Adv. correl. to τηνίκα and ἡνίκα, *at what precise point of time? at what hour?* Luc.*Sol.*5; π. μάλιστα; about *what o'clock* is it? Pl.*Cri.*43a, cf. Aeschin.1.9, Plu.*Cat.Mi.*13; πηνίκ' ἄττα; *at about what hour?* Ar.*Av.*1514; in full, πηνίκ' ἐστὶν ἄρα τῆς ἡμέρας; ib.1498; π. τῆς νυκτός; Anon.ap.Suid. 2. in indirect questions, ἐρωτᾷ π. δεῖπνόν ἐστι Men.367. II. generally, for πότε; *when?* D.18.313, Philostr.*VA*4.25, Luc.*Tim.*4, etc. 2. in an indirect question, φυλάττει πηνίκ' ἔσεσθε μεστοί D.18.308.

⊛ **πην-ίον**, Dor. **πᾱνίον**, τό, Dim. (in form) of πῆνος or πήνη, *bobbin, spool* (ἄτρακτος, εἰς ὃν εἰλεῖται ἡ κρόκη Hsch.), π. ἐξέλκουσα παρὲκ μίτον Il.23.762: pl., τὰ τροχαῖα πανία *AP*6.288 (Leon.), cf. Thphr.*HP*6.4.5, *AP*6.285 (Nicarch.(?)); prob. in *POxy.*1740.6 (iii/iv A.D.). 2. *quill*, *IG*2$^2$.1522.22. II. a kind of *pupa*, perh. of *currant-moth*, *Abraxas grossulariata*, Ar.*Fr.*377, Arist.*HA*551$^b$6. III. *ornament put on cakes*, Poll.6.79, Hsch. ⊛ -ισμα, ατος, τό, *woof on the spool*, *AP*6.283; ἱστότονα π. (A.ap.) Ar.*Ra.*1315, cf. *Sammelb.*5873.6 (Cyrene). -ῖτις, ιδος, ἡ, *the weaver*, i.e. Athena, Ael.*NA*6.57; Dor. dat. **Πᾱνίτιδι** cj. Mein. for -άτιδι in *AP*6.289 (Leon.).

**πηνοειδής**, ές, *thread-like*, Paus.Gr.*Fr.*228.

**πῆνος**, ὁ, *web*, Hsch.

**πηξῐθάλαττα** [θᾰ], ἡ, *she that freezes the sea*, *Com.Adesp.*1118.

⊛ **πῆξις**, εως, Ion. ιος, ἡ, (πήγνυμι) *fixing, putting together*, esp. of woodwork, θυρωμάτων Pl.*Plt.*28cd (pl.). 2. Astrol., *fixing*, τοῦ ἀναφορικοῦ Vett.Val.24.18, cf. *Cat.Cod.Astr.*2.196. II. *solidity*, πῆξιν λαβεῖν D.S.1.7 (but metaph., acquire *fixity*, Chrysipp.*Stoic.*3.138, cf. Dam.*Pr.*56). 2. *coagulation*, Pl.*Phlb.*32a; *freezing*, Hp.*Aër.*8; [ὕδατος] π. Epicur.*Ep.*2 p.49 U., cf. p.45 U.; caused by cold, as τῆξις, διάχυσις, ζέσις by heat, Arist.*Mete.*382$^b$31, *GC*330$^b$27 (but also π. θερμότητος Ocell.2.9); *formation of gum* in plants, Thphr.*HP*9.1.5; *curdling*, γάλακτος D.S.4.81.

**πηός**, ὁ, Dor. **πᾱός** (also in Nic.*Th.*3), *kinsman by marriage*, Il.3.163, Od.8.581, 10.441, 23.120, Hes.*Op.*345, Call.*Fr.*6.8 P.: generally, *kinsman*, *Sammelb.*7423.14 (Egypt), prob. in *Supp.Epigr.*2.461.1 (Histria). (Wrongly derived from πέπαμαι by Eust.134.43.)

**πηοσύνη**, ἡ, *relationship by marriage*, A.R.1.48.

**πηόω**, only in form παόω (q. v.).

**πήποκα**, Adv., Dor. = πώποτε, *IG*5(1).213.5 (Sparta, v B.C.), Theoc. 8.34, *Com.Adesp.* in *Gött.Nachr.*1922 p.28, Epigr.ap.Poll.4.102.

**πήρα**, Ion. **πήρη** (**πάρη** [ᾰ] Heraclid.ap.Eust.29.3), ἡ, *leathern pouch* for victuals, etc., *wallet*, Od.13.437, al., Ar.*Pl.*298, *Fr.*273, *Ostr.Bodl.* iii 264 (i A.D.), etc.

**πήραξον**· ἀφόδευσον, Hsch. **πηρία⟨ν⟩**· Ἀ⟨σ⟩πένδιοι τὴν χώραν τοῦ ἀγροῦ, Id.

**πηρίδιον** [ῐδ], τό, Dim. of πήρα, Ar.*Nu.*923 (anap.), *Fr.*486; π. γνωρισμάτων Men.*Epit.*114, cf. Ant.Diog.6, Hld.10.9, Porph.*Abst.* 2.15.

⊛ **πηρίν** or **πηρίς** (both forms in Choerob. in *An.Ox.*2.248), ῖνος, ἡ, *scrotum*, Nic.*Th.*586, Antig.ap.Erot. (not found in text of Hp.); ἐλάφου πηρίς Hsch.

**πηρίνα**, ἡ, = περίνεον, Gal.19.130 (not in text of Hp.); also cited from Hp.*Haem.* and *Fist.*, = ἕδρα, ibid.

**πῆριξ**, = πέρδιξ (Cret.), Hsch.

**Πηριφόνα**, = Περσεφόνη, prob. in *IG*14.631 (Locri).

**πηρό-δετος**, ον, *binding a wallet*, ἱμὰς *AP*9.150 (Antip.). -**μελής**, ές, *disabled in the limbs, maimed*, Epigr.ap.D.L.5.40.

⊛ **πηρός** (Dor. **πᾱρός** implied in ἔμπαρος, παρόω, qq. v.), ά, όν, *disabled in a limb, maimed*, αἱ δὲ χολωσάμεναι πηρὸν θέσαν [the Muses] made him *helpless* or *blind* (cf. Aesop.57), Il.2.599; πηρὸς ὁ μὲν γυίοις, ὁ δ' ἄρ' ὄμμασι *AP*9.11 (Phil. or Isid.); πηραὶ τὰ σκέλεα Hp.*Mul.*2.131. 2. of the mind, Semon.7.22; ἀμβλεῖς καὶ π. Ph.1.624; π. τῷ νῷ Sch.Ar.*Pl.*48; πηροὶ οἱ λογισμοί Luc.*Am.*46.

⊛ **πῆρος**, Aeol. **πᾶρος**, εος, τό, *loss of strength, dotage*, Alc.98.

**πηρ-όω**, Dor. **πᾱρόω** (v. infr.), (πηρός) *maim, mutilate*, esp. in the limbs, Ar.*Ra.*623; ἐὰν παῖδας ὄντας πηρώσῃ τις *castrate*, Arist.*HA*631$^b$31; αἴ κα σῦς καρταῖπος παρώσει *GDI*4998 i 14 (Gortyn): more freq. in Pass., πηροῦται τὸ σκέλος τουτοισὶ Hp.*Art.*60, cf. *GDI* l. c. i 8; τὸ σκέλος πεπηρωμένος D.18.67; πεπήρωται τοὺς ὀφθαλμοὺς Arist.*HA*620$^a$1, cf. Ephor.1 J.; so of moles, lobsters, *to be defective* in point of eyes, claws, Arist.*HA*491$^b$34, *PA*684$^a$35; ὥσπερ πεπηρωμένον τετράπουν, of the seal, Id.*HA*498$^a$32; τὸ πηρωθὲν ἐν τῇ ὑστέρᾳ Id.*GA*749$^a$2, etc. 2. metaph., *incapacitate*, τέχνην..πηρῶσαι Pl.*Phdr.*257a; π. τὴν ἱστορίαν Str.17.3.3:—Pass., πεπηρωμένος πρὸς ἀρετὴν *incapacitated* for practising virtue, Arist.*EN*1099$^b$19; πρὸς τὴν γνῶσιν Anaxarch.ap.S.E.*M.* 7.55, cf. 298; πρὸς καρπογονίαν Thphr.*CP*1.5.5. -ώδης, ες, *maimed*, Hsch. s. v. γυιός. -ωμα, ατος, τό, *mutilated* or *imperfect animal*, opp. τέλειον, Arist.*de An.*415a27, 432b22, *Metaph.*1034b4. **II.** = πήρωσις, Id.*GA*746b32, Gal.*UP*14.6. **-ώνῠμος**, ον, (πήρα, ὄνομα) *named after a wallet*, gloss on οὐλαδώνυμος, Tz. ad Lyc.183. ⊛ **-ωσις**, εως, ἡ, *maiming, disabling* in the limbs or senses, γῆρας ὁλόκληρός ἐστι π. Democr.296, cf. Arist.*EN*1131a9: freq. in pl., Hp.*Art.*61, Pl.*Lg.* 874e, 925e, Arist.*EN*1148b17; νόσοι καὶ πηρώσεις ib.1145a31; πηρώσις τῶν ὀφθαλμῶν Plu.2.633c, Luc.*DMar.*2.4 (abs., *blindness*, Dsc.2. 180, Plu.2.791d, Luc.*Dom.*29); ἀκοῆς Plu.2.167c: generally, π. τινὸς αἰσθήσιος Aret.*SD*1.4; π. ψυχῆς Man.4.518; of plants, Thphr.*HP*2. 4.3, 4.14.8 (pl.).

**πῆς**, Boeot. = παῖς, Corinn.*Supp.*2.51,76 (but Boeot. Inscrr. have nom. παις (prob. = πάϊς), v. παῖς).

**πήσασθαι**· μέμψασθαι, Hsch.

**πῆσις**, late form for πεῖσις (from πάσχω), Olymp.*in Cat.*99.22.

**πήσσω**, Att. **πήττω**, later form for πήγνυμι, Lxx *Si.*14.24, Ph.1. 420, Dsc.4.188, Arr.*Epict.*1.19.4, S.E.*M.*9.247, (κατα-) Str.4.3.5, D.H.3.22: impf. ἔπησσον Satyr.1:—Pass. πήττομαι Antig.*Mir.*174, Str.13.4.14, 7.3.18 (συμ-).

**πηχίζω**, *measure by the cubit*, Sm., Al.*Ez.*43.13, *Supp.Epigr.*6.636 (Termessus Major).

**πήχιον**, τό, = βήχιον I, Dsc.3.112.

**πηχ-ίσκος**, ὁ, Dim. of πῆχυς, Anon.ap.Suid. **-ισμα**, ατος, τό, *cubit-measure*, Sm.*Ez.*43.13. **-ισμός**, ὁ, *measuring by the cubit*, *Ostr.Bodl.*190 (ii B.C.), *PTeb.*164.14 (ii B.C., pl.), Sm., Al. l.c., Judeich *Altertümer von Hierapolis* No.262.

⊛ **πηχῠαῖος**, α, ον, *a cubit long*, *IG*1².88.8, Hdt.2.48,78, Hp.*Fract.*8, Pl.*Phd.*96e, Plb.6.23.12, etc.; τὸ π. Plot.6.3.21.

**πηχυαλὲς ἱμάτιον**, τό, Ion. word, = παρυφές, Poll.7.53.

**πήχυιος**, α, ον, = πηχυαῖος, βόθρος A.R.3.1207; π. χρόνος '*but a span*', Mimn.2.3; ἐρετμὰ πήχυιον προὔχοντα projecting *for the space of a cubit*, A.R.1.379 (wrongly expld. as = τροπωτήρ by *EM*671.8).

⊛ **πηχύνω**, *take in one's arms, embrace*, A.R.4.972, Nonn.*D.*25.177; τινὰ ἀγοστῷ ib.3.340: more freq. in Med., χείρεσσι *AP*12.121 (Rhian.), Opp.*H.*4.286, Nonn.*D.*9.30; ἀγοστῷ ib.14.152.

⊛ **πῆχυς** (Aeol. **πᾶχυς** Alc.33), ὁ, gen. πήχεος Hp.*Fract.*2, al., Hdt. 1.178, Pl.*Alc.*1.126d, Arist.*Mir.*813a10, Lxx *Ex.*25.9, al., Plb.10.44.2, Ph.*Bel.*73.42, πήχεως Arist.*HA*606a14 (v.l. -εος), *PCair.Zen.*484.10 (iii B.C.), πήχως (condemned by Phryn.222) corrected to πήχεος *PCair.Zen.*665.1 (iii B.C.): gen. pl. πήχεων *IG*1².314.39, 2².1673.15, *PCair.Zen.*353.10 (iii B.C.); later contr. πηχῶν X.*An.*4.7.16 codd., Arist.*Pol.*1302b37, *PCair.Zen.*54.4 (iii B.C.), *PStrassb.*85.20 (ii B.C.), Phld.*Sign.*2, Phryn.222, Moer.p.327 P.:—*forearm*, from wrist to elbow, Hp.*Fract.*2, 3, al., Poll.2.140; opp. βραχίων, Pl.*Ti.*75a, X. *Eq.*12.5: in Poets, generally, *arm*, ἀμφὶ δ' ἑὸν φίλον υἱὸν ἐχεύατο πήχεε λευκώ Il.5.314, cf. Od.17.38, 23.240; λευκὸν ἀντείνασα π. B.*Fr.*13.4, cf. E.*Or.*1466 (lyr.); λαιὸν ἔπαιρε π. Id.*Heracl.*728. **2.** Anat., *ulna*, Ruf.*Onom.*80, Gal.*UP*2.2, Sor.*Fract.*20. **II.** *centrepiece, which joined the two horns of the bow*, τὸν ῥ' [ὀϊστὸν] ἐπὶ πήχει ἑλὼν ἕλκεν νευρήν Od.21.419; ὁ δὲ τόξου πῆχυν ἀνέλκε Il.11.375, 13. 583. **III.** in pl., *horns of the lyre*, opp. ζυγόν (the bridge), Hdt.4. 192; πήχεις ἐναρμόσας καὶ ζυγώσας Luc.*DDeor.*7.4. **2.** also, = ζυγόν, *crosspiece* or *bridge* in which the horns were fitted, Artemo Hist.12. **IV.** in the balance, *beam*, *IG*2².1013.32, *Theol.Ar.* 29. **V.** as a measure of length, *distance from the point of the elbow to that of the middle finger*, = 6 παλασταί = 24 δάκτυλοι, Poll.2.158; π. μέτριος Hdt.1.178; π. ἰδιωτικός, κοινός, Sch.Luc.*Cat.*16; but π. βασιλήϊος, = 27 δάκτυλοι, Hdt.1.178, 7.117; ὁ Αἰγύπτιος π. τυγχάνει ἴσος ἐὼν τῷ Σαμίῳ Id.2.168, cf. Luc. l.c.; for later measurements, Hero *Deff.*131, *Geom.*4.2, al. **2.** *cubit-rule*, as we say 'foot-rule', Ar. *Ra.*799, Gal.1.47; π. ἀκαμπής *AP*6.204 (Leon.); as epith. of Nemesis, *APl.*4.223, 224. **3.** metaph. of any small amount (cf. πήχυιος), *Ev.Matt.*6.27; κατὰ πῆχυν *little* by *little*, Marin.*Procl.*26. **VI.** πήχεις, οἱ, the *cubits* (of inundation), represented in pictures as children one cubit high playing round the Nile, Luc.*Rh.Pr.*6, Philostr. *Im.*1.5. (Cf. Skt. *bāhú-*, Avest. *bāzu-* (masc.) 'arm', ONorse *bógr* 'shoulder'.)

**πῖ**, v. πεῖ.

**πιάζω**, Dor. and late Att. for πιέζω (q.v.).

⊛ **πιαίνω**, fut. πιᾰνῶ A.*Th.*587: aor. ἐπίᾱνα Id.*Ag.*276, Hp.*Mul.*1.47; poet. πίᾱνα Pi.*N.*9.23; later ἐπίηνα D.L.1.83:—Pass., fut. πιανθήσομαι Lxx *Ps.*64(65).12: aor. ἐπιάνθην Anan.5.9, Theoc.17.126, (κατ-) Ael.*NA*2.13; but aor. inf. συμ-πιασθῆναι Hp.*Epid.*7.68 (s.v.l.): pf. πεπίασμαι (κατα-) Pl.*Lg.*807b, cf. Ael.*NA*13.25: (πίων): *fatten*, τὸ σῶμα Hp. l.c.; ἡ γῆ π. τὰ βοτά E.*Cyc.*333; [τὰς ὗς] Arist.*HA*603b 27; π. χθόνα *enrich* the soil, of a dead man, A.*Th.*587; σώμασι πίαναν καπνόν, of bodies being burnt, Pi. l.c.:—Pass., *to be* or *become fat*, Semon.7.6, Pl.*Lg.*807a, Arist.*HA*520b7, etc.; π. ὁ στάχυς Theoc. 10.47. **II.** metaph., **1.** *increase, enlarge*, πλοῦτον Pi.*P.*4.150 (where ῐ); μυχοὺς πόλεως Xenoph.2.22. **2.** *make wanton*, ἀλλ' ἦ σ' ἐπίανέν τις ἄπτερος φάτις; A.*Ag.*276; π. τὰ πάθη Porph.*Abst.*1.34:—Pass., *wax fat and wanton*, πρᾶσσε, πιαίνου A.*Ag.*1669 (anap.); ἔχθεσιν πιαίνεσθαι *batten on* quarrels, Pi.*P.*2.56; φθόνῳ π. B.3.68. **3.** *cherish, cheer*, ἵππον.. π. ὁ τοῦ δεσπότου ὀφθαλμός Anon.ap.Arist.*Oec.* 1345a3; π. ἑὴν φρένα Opp.*H.*5.372; μέλος ib.620; μάστακα π. χείλεος εὐαφίη *AP*5.293.16 (Agath.).—Rare in Prose.

**πῑᾰλέος**, α, ον, Ion., poet., and late Prose for πίων, Hp.*Mul.*1.17, *AP*6.190 (Gaet.), 299 (Phan.), Artem.1.46, Opp.*C.*1.86, etc.; *rich*, πόσις Nic.*Al.*360, cf. Nonn.*D.*3.146, al.

**πίαλος**, v.l. for σίαλος in Hp.*Mul.*2.133; but, = παράλευκος, Hsch.

**πῑαν-τήριος**, α, ον, *fattening*: τὰ π. *fattening food*, Hp.*Loc.Hom.* 28. **-τικός**, ή, όν, = foreg., Apollon.*Lex.* s.v. πίονα ἔργα.

**πῖαρ**, τό, only nom. and acc. (exc. dat. πίαρι Suid.): (πίων):—*fat*, Ep. and Ion. word, βοῶν ἐκ πῖαρ ἑλέσθαι Il.11.550; of men, Hp.*Nat. Puer.*21. **b.** *any fatty substance*, π. ἐλαίης A.R.4.1133; π. μελιηδές prob. *cream*, *AP*9.224 (Crin.), cf. Sol.36.21 (πῦαρ Pap. Arist.*Ath.*); *thick juice* from trees, Hp.*Nat.Puer.*26; of the fig, Id.*Mul.*2.205, *Ulc.* 15; *richness* of soil, ἐπεὶ μάλα π. ὑπ' οὖδας Od.9.135, cf. *h.Ap.*60; ἐσθλῆς ἀρούρης π. ἔγκληρον χθονός Lyc.1060, cf. *AP*9.555 (Crin.). **2.** metaph., *cream, choicest part* of a thing, *h.Ven.*30.

**πῑᾰρός**, ά, όν, *fat, rich*, τὸ πιαρόν Hp.*Nat.Puer.*21 (p.514 L., sed leg. τὸ πῖαρ, cf. p.512):—πιαρά and πιερά are prob. ff.ll. for πίειρα in ib.22, Arist.*Pr.*892b33, and πίεραι, πιεραῖς ff.ll. for πίειραι, πιείραις in Hp.*Aër.*21, Ath.Med.ap.Orib.1.2.4.

**πίασμα** [ῐ] (A), ατος, τό, (πιαίνω) *that which makes fat*, of a river, π. Βοιωτῶν χθονὶ *bringing fatness and riches* to.., A.*Pers.*806.

**πίασμα** [ῐ] (B), ατος, τό, Dor. and later Gr. for πίεσμα (q.v.).

**πιασμός**, ὁ, (πιαίνω) *fatness, fat*, Ael.*NA*13.25.

**πιαστήριος**, ον, = πιεστήριος (q.v.).

**πιάτοις**· τὸ ἄσημον ἀργύριον, Hsch.

⊛ **πιάτρα**, ἡ, a term of relationship, = πάτρα, *TAM*2.385 (Xanthus), 611 (Tlos); cf. πινάτρα.

⊛ **πιβρᾶτος**, = Lat. *privatus*, *Edict.Diocl.*7.76.

**πίγγαλος**, ὁ, a kind of *lizard*, = χαλκίς, Hsch. **πίγγαν**· νεοσσίον, Amerias ap. Hsch.

⊛ **πιγκέρνης**, = Lat. *pincerna, cupbearer*, *PLond.*5.1656.3 (iv A.D.).

**πῑδάκ-ῖτις**, ιδος, ἡ, (πῖδαξ) *growing at* or *about a spring*, βοτάναι Hp.*Ep.*16. **-όεις**, εσσα, εν, *full of springs*, Hegesin.ap.Paus.9. 29.1; *gushing*, λιβάς E.*Andr.*116 (eleg.). **-ώδης**, ες, *full of springs*, τόποι Plu.*Aem.*14; π. σάρξ, of a woman's breasts, Id.2.496a.

**πῖδαξ**, ᾰκος, ἡ, *spring, fountain*, μάχεσθον π. ἀμφ' ὀλίγης Il.16.825, cf. Theoc.7.142, Call.*Ap.*112, etc.; [γῆ] ἔνυδρος πίδαξι Hdt.4.198; οὐρειᾶν πιδάκων.. ῥοαῖς E.*Andr.*285 (lyr.); π. ῥωγός *AP*6.238 (Apollonid.), cf. 158 (Tull. Sab.), 334 (Leon.), etc.

**πῑδ-άω**, = πιδύω, Arist.*Mete.*349b34, Hsch., Choerob. in *An.Ox.*2. 249; prob. cj. in Hp.*Epid.*5.16, Theoc.8.42. **-ήεις**, εσσα, εν, *rich in springs*, Ἴδη Il.11.183. ⊛ **-ῠλίς**, ίδος, ἡ, = πιδακόεσσα, Hsch. (πηδ- cod.). ⊛ **-ύω**, *gush forth*, *AP*9.322 (Leon.), 10.13 (Satyr.); ὀλίγον καὶ πονηρὸν ἐπίδυε [τὸ ποτόν] Plu.*Aem.*14, cf. Antig.*Mir.*144:—Med., Nic.*Th.*302. [ῡ exc. in Nic. l.c.]

⊛ **πιέζω**, impf. ἐπίεζον, Ep. πίεζον Od.12.174, etc.: fut. πιέσω Diph.18.3; Ep. πιέσσω Nonn.*D.*4.146: aor. ἐπίεσα Hp.*Fract.*6, Hdt.9.63, Th.2.52, etc. (but subj. πιέξῃς Hp.*Fract.*5, inf. πιέξαι *IG*4²(1).123.116 (Epid., iv B.C.), part. πιέξας (v.l. πιάξας) Nic.*Al.*224): pf. πεπίεκα Demetr.Lac. *Herc.*1012.44:—Pass., fut. πιεσθήσομαι Gal.11.317 (δια-), Heliod.ap. Orib.10.18.15: aor. ἐπιέσθην Od.8.336, Sol.13.37, Hdt.4.11, etc.; ἐπιέχθην Hp.*Fract.*5, etc.: pf. πεπίεσμαι Arist.*Mu.*392b33, Procl.*Hyp.*5. 49, cj. in Alciphr.3.55, etc.; πεπίεγμαι Hp.*Fract.*5.—From **πιεζέω** we have πιεζέουσι v.l. in Id.*Fract.*31: impf. πιέζευν v.l. in Od.12.174,196; part. πιεζεῦντα Hp.*Off.*25, *Fract.*9, πιεζεῦσαν Herod.8.47:—Pass., part. πιεζεύμενος Hdt.3.146, 6.108, 8.142 (always with v.l. -όμενος), Hp.*Nat.Puer.*21, πιεζούμενος Plb.3.74.2; imper. πιεζείσθω *IG*4.364.7 (Corinth, iv A.D.): impf. ἐπιεζοῦντο Plb.11.33.3; so in later Gr., as Plu. *Thes.*6, *Alc.*2, etc.; Dor., Aeol., and later Gr. **πιάζω** Alcm.44, Alc.148: aor. 1 ἐπίασα Lxx *Ca.*2.15, *Ev.Jo.*8.20; ἐπίαξα Theoc.4.35, (ἀμφ-) *Ep.*6: Pass., fut. πιασθήσομαι Lxx *Si.*23.21: aor. ἐπιάσθην *Apoc.*19.20: pf. πεπίασμαι *POxy.*812 (i B.C.), Dsc.1.15, *Hippiatr.*34:—*press tight, squeeze*, χειρὶ ἑλὼν ἐπίεζε βραχίονα Il.16.510, cf. Hes.*Op.*497; ἀστεμφέως ἐχέμεν μᾶλλόν τε π. Od.4.419; μ' ἐν δεσμοῖσι δέον μᾶλλόν τε πίεζον 12.196, cf. 164; π. τὰ χείλεα *compress* them, Hp.*VM*22; ῥύγχος εἰς ὄξος π. Axionic.8.5; π. τοὺς ὑπευθύνους *squeezing* them (like figs), to try if they are ripe, Ar.*Eq.*259; σφόδρα π. αὐτοῦ τὸν πόδα Pl. *Phd.*117e; π. [τὴν δεξιὰν] ἐμπαθῶς Plb.31.24.9: abs., X.*Mem.*3.10. 13, Arist.*Rh.*1361b17:—Pass., *to be pressed tight*, ἐν δεσμοῖς Od.8.336, cf. Hp.*Fract.*25, al.; of wrestlers, Plu.*Alc.*2; πιέζεται ὅσα πόρους ἔχει κενούς *are compressible*, Arist.*Mete.*386b1. **II.** *press* or *weigh down*, of a heavy weight, Σικελία αὐτοῦ π. στέρνα Pi.*P.*1.19, cf. Ar.*Pax* 1032:—and in Pass., ὁ δ' ὦμος.. πιέζεται Id.*Ra.*30, cf. X.*Cyr.*7.5.11: metaph., *oppress, distress*, π. τινὰ ἡ δαπάνη Hdt.5.35; λιμὸς A.*Ch.* 250; καὶ πρὸς π. χρημάτων ἀχηνία (Abresch for προσπιέζει) ib.301; συμφορὰ δ' ἑτέρους ἑτέρα π. E.*Alc.*894 (lyr.); αὐχμὸς π. τὰς ἀμπέλους Ar. *Nu.*1120; π. ἡ ἀνάγκη ib.437, cf. Th.2.52:—freq. in Pass., ὑπὸ νούσοισι Sol.13.37; ὑπὸ λιμοῦ Th.1.126; πολέμῳ Hdt.4.11, 6.34; τῇ νούσῳ Pherecyd.ap.D.L.1.122, cf. Th.7.47; ταῖς εἰσφοραῖς Lys.28.3; ταῖς συμφοραῖς X.*Cyr.*7.2.20; σπάνει σίτου Id.*HG*5.4.56, etc.: abs., Hdt.7.121, etc.; of a river, *to be exhausted* from the heat of the sun, Id.2.25. **2.** *press hard*, of a victorious army, τοὺς ἐναντίους Id.9.63:—Pass., τὴν πιεζομένην μάλιστα τῶν μοιρέων ib.60; εἴ πῃ πιέζοιντο Th.1.49, cf. X.*HG*2.4.34; ὑπό τινων ib.7.1.43. **3.** *bear hardly upon*, τινα Pl.*Cra.*409a; τῷ λόγῳ Plu.*Alc.*6; ὑπὸ τῶν ἐλέγχων πιέζεσθαι Phld.*D.*3.8; of a point in the argument, *hold fast to*, Pl.*Lg.*965d; *press* it, Plb.3.21.3, Demetr.Lac. l.c., etc.; *lay stress on*, Plu.2.31e: c. dat., *insist upon*, τοῖσι περιπάτοισι Hp.*Insomn.*88. **b.** *determine precisely*, ἀποστήματα Procl.*Hyp.*5.19, cf. 49 (Pass.); π. δεῖ πῶς ἓν ἐκεῖνο καὶ ἕτερον Porph.*Sent.*36. **4.** *repress, stifle*, ἐν θυμῷ χόλον Pi.*O.*6.37; τὸν τῦφον Plu.*Alc.*4. **5.** *outweigh*, τἀγαθῷ τὸ δυστυχές E.*Hipp.*637, cf. *Supp.*249 (s.v.l.). **III.** later, *lay hold of*, ταῦρον.. πιάξας τᾶς ὁπλᾶς *by* the hoof, Theoc.4.35; αὐτὸν τῆς χειρὸς *Act.Ap.*3.7, cf. *Ev.Jo.*7.30, etc.

**πίειρα** [ῐ], ἡ, fem. of πίων, *fat, rich*, mostly of land, ἄρουρα π. Il.18.541, Od.2.328, etc.; χθών Sol.ap.Arist.*Ath.*12.3, cf. Pl.*Criti.*111b, Thphr.*HP*8.6.2; Σικελία Pi.*N.*1.15; δαὶς π. *rich, plenteous* meal, Il.19.180; of wood, *resinous, juicy*, S.*Tr.*766. cf. Hp. *Nat.Puer.*26; of doves, *plump*, Arist.*HA*600ᵃ23. (Cf. Skt. *pīvarī*, fem. of *pīvā*, v. πίων.)

**πίεξις** [ῐ], ιος, ἡ, = πίεσις, Hp.*Fract.*6, *Art.*63, Aret.*CD*1.3 (pl.).

⊛ **Πιερία**, ἡ, Ion. -ίη, *Pieria*, in the S.W. of Macedonia, Il.14.226, Od.5.50, Hes.*Th.*53. Adv. **Πιερίηθεν**, *from Pieria*, Id.*Op.*1, *h.Merc.*85. ⊛**Πιερίδες**, αἱ, *Pierides*, name of the Muses, as haunting Pieria, Hes.*Sc.*206, Pi.*O.*10(11).96, *P.*1.14, etc.: Adj. ⊛**Πιερικός**, ή, όν, Hdt. 4.195, etc.

**πιερός**, v. πιαρός.

**πιέσ-ῐμος**, ον, (πιέζω) *pressing. Gloss.* **-ις**, εως, ἡ, *squeezing, compression*, Arist.*PA*687ᵇ11 (pl.), *Mete.*387ᵃ16; *pinching*, ποδῶν Aret.*CA*1.2; *pressure, close contact*, Gal.18(2).398. **-μα**, ατος, Dor. and later Gr. **πίασμα**, τό, *anything pressed*: 1. *pulpy mass left after pressing, pomace*, μυροβαλάνου Gal.10.911, *Gp.*20.28: pl., of *cakes* of olive-pulp, *PSI*9.1030.11 (ii A.D., in form πιάσματα). 2. *juice pressed out*, Dsc.1.78. II. = πίεσις, δακτύλου πιέσματι Eub.75.11 (πιάσματι codd. Ath.), cf. *AP*12.41 (Mel.). **-μός**, ὁ, = πίεσις, Hp.*Nat.Puer.*21 (v.l. for ἐκπ-), Eust.1181.63: metaph., in pl., *constraint, pressure* of circumstances, Epicur.*Nat.*28.3. **-τέος**, α, ον, *to be pressed*, Hp.*Fract.*25. II. πιεστέον *one must squeeze, press*, τὴν κεφαλήν Orib.*Fr.*48. ⊛**-τήρ**, ῆρος, ὁ, *squeezer*: *press*, *IG*2².1672.304 (pl.), Dsc.4.64 (v.l. πιαστ-), Gal.13.1044, Aët.12.55. ⊛ **-τήριος**, later **πιαστήριος**, ον, *pressing, squeezing*, πιαστήρια ὄργανα Heliod.ap.Orib.49.4.68. II. πιεστήριον, τό, *press*, Dsc.4.75; Dor. πιαστήριον *Gloss.* **-τός**, ή, όν, *compressible*, Arist.*Mete.*385ᵃ15, Thphr.*Lass.*8. **-τρον**, τό, = πιεστήριον, Hp.*Mul.*1.70, Gal.19.104,130.

**πιήεις**, εσσα, εν, poet. for πίων, *AP*6.300 (Leon.).

**πῐθάκνη**, ἡ, Att. **φιδάκνη** Moer.p.392 P., Phot., Lacon. **πισάκνα** Hsch.: (πίθος):—*cask* or *jar*, Ar.*Pl.*546, Ion Trag.10, *BCH*50.214 (Thasos, v B.C.); used for storing figs, etc., D.30.28, Pl.Com.114, Thphr.*Sign.*49, *OGI*483.149 (Pergam., ii A.D.); οἰκεῖν ἐν ταῖς φιδάκναις *live in casks*, as the poorer Athenians were forced to do during the Peloponn. war, Ar.*Eq.*792; π. ἰατρική a medicine-*jar*, Gal.19.115, cf. *UP*4.3:—also **πῐθακνίς**, ίδος, ἡ, Att. **φιδακνίς**, Poll.10.74,131; Dim. ⊛ **πῐθάκνιον**, τό, Eub.132, Hyp.*Fr.*265, Luc.*Hist.Conscr.*4, etc. (Dim. of πίθος, as πολίχνη of πόλις, Sch.Ar.*Eq.* l.c.)

**πίθᾱκος**, Dor. for πίθηκος; also in *Sammelb.*2629 (Naucratis).

**πῐθᾰνεύομαι**, = sq., Artem.2.32.

**πῐθᾰνο-λογέω**, *use probable arguments*, Arist.*EN*1094ᵇ26, D.S.1.39:—Med., Dam.*Pr.*405, Sch.E.*Or.*424:—Pass., Epicur.*Ep.*2 p.36 U., Orib.49.22.22. **-λόγημα**, ατος, τό, *probable argument*, Sch.E.*Hec.*258. **-λογία**, ἡ, *use of probable arguments*, opp. demonstration (ἀπόδειξις), Pl.*Tht.*162e, cf. *Ep.Col.*2.4, Gal.17(1).619. **-λογική**, ἡ, *art of using probable* or *specious arguments*, Arr.*Epict.*1.8.7. **-λόγος**, ον, *speaking persuasively*, Sch.Ar.*Ra.*91. **-ποιέω**, *sharpen the wits of one*, Hsch. s.v. κομψεύεται.

**πῐθᾰν-ός**, ή, όν, (πείθω) of persons, *persuasive, plausible*, esp. of popular speakers, πιθανώτατος τοῖς πολλοῖς Th.6.35; τῷ δήμῳ παρὰ πολὺ..-ώτατος, of Cleon, Id.3.36, cf. 4.21; ἐν ὄχλῳ π. Pl.*Grg.*458e; -ώτατος πάντων ἀνθρώπων D.37.48; -ώτεροι οἱ ἀπαίδευτοι τῶν πεπαιδευμένων ἐν τοῖς ὄχλοις Arist.*Rh.*1395ᵇ27; -ώτατοι οἱ ἐν τοῖς πάθεσιν Id.*Po.*1455ᵃ30; π. καὶ πανοῦργος Plu.2.26a; π. συνταγματάρχης Luc. *Bacch.*2: c. inf., -ώτατοι λέγειν Pl.*Grg.*479c; π. περιβαλεῖν τινα κακῷ *apt* at.., E.*Or.*906; πιθανώτατος στρατηγῆσαί τε καὶ προσαγαγέσθαι App.*Hisp.*15, etc.: with a Prep., π. ἐς στρατηγίαν, ἐς ἐνέδρας, Id. *Mith.*51, *Pun.*108, etc. 2. of arguments, *plausible*, Ar.*Th.*464 (lyr.); λέγων πιθανώτατ' Id.*Eq.*629; λόγος, φωναὶ π., Pl.*Phd.*88d, *R.*568c; λόγοι θαυμασίως ὡς π. D.35.16; τὸ περὶ λόγους π., = πιθανότης, Pl.*Tht.*178e: freq. in Arist.*Rh.*, as 1356ᵇ26, 1403ᵇ20; μόνον ἐφρόντισαν τοῦ π. τοῦ πρὸς αὑτούς Id.*Metaph.*1000ᵃ10. 3. of manners, *winning, plausible*, τὸ -ώτατον ἦθος X.*Mem.*3.10.3; τὸ π. ἰσχὺν τῆς ἀληθείας ἔχει μείζω Men.622 codd. Stob.; οὐ π. ἔσχεν ὄχλῳ τὸ ἦθος Plu.*Phoc.*3. 4. of reports, etc., *plausible, specious, credible*, λόγος πιθανώτατος Hdt.1.214, cf. 2.123; π. τινί Pl.*Lg.*677a: c. inf., πιστεύεσθαι πιθανά ib.782d; πιθανὸν [ἐστι] c. inf., it is *probable* that.., Arist. *Top.*151ᵃ29. 5. of works of art, *producing illusion, true to nature*, X.*Mem.*3.10.7 (Comp.). II. Pass., *easy to persuade, credulous*, A. *Ag.*485 (lyr.), Pl.*Grg.*493a. 2. *obedient, docile*, X.*Cyr.*2.2.10, *Oec.*13.9 (Comp.). III. Adv. -νῶς *persuasively, plausibly*, Ar.*Th.*268, Pl.*Phdr.*269c, al.: Comp. -ώτερον Id.*Phd.*63b, *Grg.*456c, Arist.*EN*1096ᵇ5. **-ότης**, ητος, ἡ, *persuasiveness, plausibility*, of persons, Plb. 22.20.2, Plu.2.1040b (pl.). 2. of arguments, Pl.*Lg.*839d, *Cra.*402a; π. τινὰ ἔχει ὁ λόγος Arist.*EN*1097ᵃ4, cf. Phld.*Rh.*1.209 S.; πιθανότητας ἐλάμβανε κατὰ τῶν ἀνθρώπων provided himself with *plausible charges* against.., Plb.27.15.9, cf. 12.26ᶜ.2, Ph.1.94 (pl.). **-ουργία**, ἡ, *faculty of persuasion*, Them.*Or.*26.330a. **-ουργικός**, ή, όν, *having the faculty of persuasion*, Numen.ap.Eus.*PE*14.5; τέχνη *art of persuasion*, Pl.*Sph.*222c sq. **-ουργός**, όν, *making probable*, τῶν ἀπιθάνων Sch.Hermog. in Rh.7.218 W. **-όω**, *make probable*, Arist.*Rh.*1408ᵃ19.

**πῐθάριον**, τό, Dim. of πίθος, Hsch. s.v. φιδάκνη, *EM*671.46.

**πῐθείας**, v. πιθίας.

**πιθέσκετο**, *πῐθέω, v. πείθω.

⊛ **πῐθεών**, ῶνος, ὁ, later form of πιθών (q.v.), D.S.13.83, *AP*9.403 (Maec.), *Gp.*6.12.3.

**πῐθήκ-ειος**, α, ον, *of an ape, ape-like*, Gal.2.386, *UP*3.8, Suid. ⊛ **-η**, ἡ, = ψύλλα, Ael.*NA*6.26. **-ῐδεύς**, έως, ὁ, *young ape*, ib.7.47. ⊛ **-ίζω**, *play the ape*, of flatterers, Lib.*Ep.*424.1, 1397.5:—Med., Sch.rec.D.18.242 (viii p.325 Dindorf): barbarous form ἐπιτήκιζι or ἐπιτήκιζε cj. for ἐπιθηκίζει in Ar.*Th.*1133. ⊛ **-ιον**, τό, Dim. of πίθηκος, Lat. *pithecium* Plaut.*Mil.*989. II. weight hung between two ships coupled for carrying engines of war, Ath.Mech.32.11. III. = ἀντίρρινον, Ps.-Apul.*Herb.*86. **-ισμός**, ὁ, *playing the ape, playing monkey-tricks*, Ar.*Eq.*887, M.Ant.9.27.

**πῐθηκο-ειδής**, ές, *ape-like*, Arist.*HA*498ᵇ15, Gal.2.545. **-μορφος**, ον, *ape-shaped*, Lyc.1000, Sor.1.39.

⊛ **πίθηκος** [ῐ], Dor. **πίθᾱκος**, ὁ, *ape, monkey*, Archil.89.3,91, S.*Ichn.*122, Ar.*Ach.*120, Arist.*HA*502ᵃ17: as fem., πίθηκος μήτηρ Babr.56; πίθηκον ἐνδυομένην putting on *an ape's form*, Pl.*R.*620c; cf. πιθήκη. 2. nickname for a trickster, *jackanapes*, Ar.*Ach.*907, *Av.*440, *Ra.*708, etc.; αὐτοτραγικὸς π., of Aeschines, D.18.242. 3. prov., ἀντὶ λέοντος π. γίγνεσθαι Pl.*R.*590b; ὑπὸ τῇ λεοντῇ πίθηκον περιστέλλειν Luc.*Philops.*5; π. ἐν πορφύρᾳ 'borrowed plumes', Diogenian.7.94; ἐν πιθήκοις ὄντα δεῖ εἶναι π. 'in Rome we do as the Romans do', Apollod.Com.1.3; ὄνος ἐν πιθήκοις 'parmi les aveugles le borgne est roi', Men.402.8. 4. *dwarf*, Suid. II. a ζῷον σελαχῶδες, Ael.*NA*12.27.

**Πῐθηκοῦσσαι** (as if from πιθηκόεις) (sc. νῆσοι), ῶν, αἱ, *Ape-islands*, off the coast of Campania, Arist.*Mir.*833ᵃ14, Str.1.3.10, etc.; one of them being specially named Πιθηκοῦσσα, Id.1.3.19; **Πιθήκινοι** νῆσοι, v. l. in Harp.

**πῐθηκο-φᾰγέω**, *eat ape's flesh*, Hdt.4.194. **-φόρος**, ον, *branded with the mark of an ape*, Luc.*Pisc.*47.

**πῐθηκώδης**, ες, = πιθηκοειδής, Arist.*Phgn.*812ᵃ9, Ael.*NA*12.27.

**πίθηξ** [ῐ], ηκος, ὁ, *dwarf*, Procop.*Goth.*4.24. II. = πίθηκος, Aesop.43b, Zonar.; = μιμώ, Suid.

**πιθήσας**, v. πείθω. **πῖθι**, v. πίνω.

**πῐθίας**, ου, ὁ, *jar-shaped comet*, Seneca *QN*1.14, Phlp. *in Mete.*92.34:—written **πιθείας**, Procl.*Par.Ptol.*131.

**πίθιον** [ῐ], τό, = βήχιον I, Dsc.3.112.

**πῐθίσκος**, ὁ, Dim. of πίθος, in pl., = Lat. *Doliola*, prob. l. in Plu. *Cam.*20.

**πῐθῖτις**, ιδος, ἡ, *corn poppy, Papaver Rhoeas*, Dsc.4.64.

**πῐθοειδής**, ές, *cask-shaped*, σχῆμα Hero *Stereom.*2.22.

**πῐθοίγια**, τά, (οἴγνυμι) *festival at the opening of casks* of new wine, held at the Anthesteria, Plu.2.655e, 735e:—later **πιθοιγία**, ἡ, Eust. 1363.26. ⊛**πῐθοιγὶς** ἠώς, the morning of this festival, Call.*Aet.*1.1.1; **Πιθοιγιών**, ῶνος, ὁ, month in which the festival took place, prob. in *IG*12(8).645 (Peparethus, -κιών lapis).

**πῐθοκοίτη**, ἡ, gloss on πιθάκνη, Sch.Ar.*Eq.*789.

⊛ **πίθος** [ῐ], ὁ, *large wine-jar*, Il.24.527, Od.2.340, 23.305, Hes.*Op.*98, 368, *IG*1².328.2, etc.: usu. of earthenware, π. κεράμινοι Hdt.3.96, cf. Ar.*Pax*703, Pl.*La.*187b, *Grg.*493a; π. ἀργύρεοι, sent by Croesus to Delphi, Hdt.1.51; but π. ξύλινοι *casks*, Str.5.1.12, cf. Hdn.8.4.5. 2. prov., εἰς τὸν τετρημένον π. ἀντλεῖν, of the task of the Danaids, i.e. of labour in vain, X.*Oec.*7.40, cf. Philetaer.18.5, Luc.*Herm.*61, *DMort.*11.4; applied to insatiable appetites, Pl.*Grg.*493b; to largesses made by demagogues, Arist.*Pol.*1320ᵃ32, cf. *Oec.*1344ᵇ25; ἐκ πίθω ἀντλεῖς you have wine by the *caskful*, i.e. your purse is deep, Theoc. 10.13; ἐν πίθῳ ἡ κεραμεία γιγνομένη 'trying to run before you can walk', Pl.*La.*187b, cf. *Grg.*514e, Ar.*Fr.*469; ζωὴ πίθου a Cynic's life, like that of Diogenes, Zen.4.14; π. φρενῶν *a cask full of* wit, Men.*Mon.*240 (= *IG*14.699), expld. with ref. to Diogenes by Eust. 1363.40. II. = πιθίας, Arist.*Mu.*395ᵇ12, Ptol.*Tetr.*90. (Cf. Lat. *fidelia*.)

**πιθόω**, Boeot. for πείθω, *IG*7.3172.58 (Orchom. Boeot., iii B.C.).

**πῐθώδης**, ες, *like a jar* or *cask*, βόθυνος Arist.*HA*558ᵃ8.

**πίθων** [ῐ], ωνος, ὁ, *little ape*, Babr.56.4: καλὸς π. παρὰ παισίν Pi.*P.*2.72, cf. Sostrat.ap.Eust.1665.53.

**πῐθών**, ῶνος, ὁ, (πίθος) *cellar*, Pherecr.138, Eup.111, *IG*11(2).287*A* 168 (Delos, iii B.C.), 12(5).872.52 (Tenos, iii B.C.(?)); cf. πιθεών.

**πῐθών**, aor. 2 part. of πείθω, Pi.*P.*3.28.

**πικᾶσι**· πικραῖς, Hsch.

**πικέριον**, τό, = βούτυρον, Hp.*Mul.*1.63, Arist.*Fr.*636, Aret.*CA*1.1, Gal.19.131: Phrygian acc. to Erot.

**πίκρα**, ἡ, an *antidote*, '*higry-pigry*' (i.e. ἱερὰ π.), Alex.Trall.7.6, *Febr.*6.

**πικρ-άζω**, = sq., S.E.*P.*1.211:—Pass., *taste bitter*, ib.2.51, etc. II. metaph., π. τὸν λόγον τῇ κακίᾳ Epict.*Gnom.*22. **-αίνω**, *make sharp* or *keen*, esp. to the taste, π. τὴν κοιλίαν *make it bitter*, *Apoc.*10.9:—Pass., τὸ στόμα πικραίνεται Hp.*Acut.*30: opp. γλυκαίνεσθαι, Arist. *Ph.*244ᵇ20. 2. metaph., *embitter, irritate*, τὴν ψυχήν Lxx *Jb.*27.2; τὴν ἀκοήν *affect* it *harshly*, opp. γλυκαίνω, D.H.*Comp.*12, 15; *make harsh*, νόμους cj. in A.*Eu.*693:—Pass., *to be exasperated, embittered*, Pl.*Lg.*731d, Theoc.5.120; ὁ ζωγράφος πονεῖ τι καὶ π. *vexes himself*, Antiph.144.3; π. ἐπί τισι Lxx *Ex.*16.20; ἔν τισι ib.*Ru.*1.20; also ἐπικράνθη μοι it *grieved* me, ib.13. 3. of style, *make harsh* or *rugged*, διάλεκτον D.H.*Dem.*55, cf. 34. **-αντικός**, ή, όν, *disposed to bitterness*. Adv. -κῶς, διατίθεσθαι S.E.*M.*7.367. **-άς**, άδος, ἡ, = ἀνδρόσακες, Ps.-Dsc.3.133. **-ασμός**, ὁ, *bitterness*: *bitter feeling*, ψυχῆς Lxx *Ez.*27.31: pl., Ph.1.441:—written **πικραμμός**, Aq.*Jb.*3.5. ⊛ **-ία**, ἡ, *bitterness*: 1. of taste, Thphr.*CP*6.10.7, *Od.*32,

Lxx *Je.*15.17, *Placit.*3.16.2, Dsc.1.61, etc. 2. of temper, τὴν ἀπὸ τῆς ψυχῆς π. D.21.204, cf. 25.84, *Ep.*3.33, Arist.*VV*1251$^{a}$4, Phld.*Ir.* p.56 W.; ἡ ἐπὶ τοῖς γεγονόσι π. Plb.15.4.11; πρὸς τὸν δῆμον Plu.*Cor.* 15; ἡ ἐν τοῖς λόγοις π. D.S.16.88; λόγος π. ἔχων μεμιγμένην χάριτι Plu.*Lyc.*19. 3. of circumstances, ἡ τοῦ καιροῦ π. *BGU*417.5 (ii/iii A.D.). ⊛ **-ίδιον**, τό, = σέρις ἥμερος, *endive, Cichorium Endivia*, Ps.-Dsc.2.132, *Gp.*12.1. **-ίδιος**, α, ον, *somewhat bitter*, σῦκα Ath.3.78a. **-ίζω**, *to be* or *taste bitter*, Str.11.2.17, Archig.ap.Orib.8.1.37; π. ἐν τῇ γεύσει Dsc.1.20.

**πικρίς**, ίδος, ἡ, *ox-tongue, Helminthia sepioides*, Arist.*HA*612$^{a}$30, Thphr.*HP*7.11.4. 2. = κιχόριον, Dsc.2.132. II. *sour soil*, *Sammelb.*6797.12 (iii B.C.), prob. in *PCair.Zen.*517.17, 728.3,8 (iii B.C.).

**πικρό-γᾰμος**, ον, *attaining a bitter kind of marriage* (cf. πικρός III), Od.1.266, al., Hld.5.30, 7.28. **-γλωσσος**, ον, *of sharp* or *bitter tongue*, ἀραί A.*Th.*787 (lyr.). **-καρπος**, ον, *bearing bitter fruit*, ἀνδροκτασία ib.693 (lyr.). **-λογία**, ἡ, *bitterness of language*, Arist.*VV*1251$^{a}$9. **-λόγος**, ον, *speaking bitter things*, γλῶσσα prob. in *Epigr.Gr.*288*c*4 (Cyprus). ⊛ **-λωτος**, ον, *of the bitter lotus*, σπέρμα Gal.14.159. **-ποιός**, όν, *causing bitterness*, Eust.820.49; ἔχις Sch. Opp.*H.*1.559.

⊛ **πικρός**, ά, όν, poet. also ός, όν Od.4.406:—prop. *pointed, sharp, keen*, ὀϊστός Il.4.118, al.; βέλεμνα 22.206; γλωχίς S.*Tr.*681: metaph., γλώσσης πικροῖς κέντροισι E.*HF*1288. II. generally, *sharp* to the sense: 1. of taste, *pungent*, ῥίζα Il.11.846; ἅλμη Od.5.323; δάκρυον (v.l. for πυκνόν) 4.153; of salt water, opp. γλυκύς, Hdt.4.52, cf. 7.35; ἁλμυρὸς καὶ π. Pl.*Lg.*705a; τριγλία π. *PCair.Zen.*82.8 (iii B.C.); ἀπ' ὄμφακος πικρᾶς A.*Ag.*970; ὑγρότης π., opp. ὀξεῖα, Meno *Iatr.*5.13; also of smell, *pungent*, Od.4.406; πικρὸν ὀδωδώς Alciphr.3.59. (This sense prevails in the derived and compd. words.) 2. of feeling, *sharp, keen*, ὠδῖνες Il.11.271, S.*Tr.*41. 3. of sound, *piercing, shrill*, οἰμωγά Id.*Ph.*189 (lyr.); φθόγγος Id.*OC*1610; γόοι, ὄδυρμα, E.*Ph.*883, *Tr.*1227 (lyr.); πικροτάτη ὄψ Ar.*Pax* 805 (lyr.). III. metaph., 1. of things, *bitter*, esp. of what yields pain instead of expected pleasure, freq. in threats, μὴ τάχα πικρὴν Αἴγυπτον καὶ Κύπρον ἵκηαι (v.l. ἴδηαι) Od.17.448, cf. Ar.*Av.*1045, *Th.*883 (lyr.), E.*Med.*399, *IA*955, *Ba.*357, *Cyc.*589; π. Σίγειον κατηγόμην S.*Ph.*355; τὸ πὰρ δίκαν γλυκὺ πικροτάτα μένει τελευτά Pi.*I.*7(6).48, cf. A.*Ag.*745 (lyr.); τιμωρία, ἀγῶνες, Id.*Pers.*473, S.*Aj.*1239; δύαι, χεῖμα, A.*Pr.*180 (lyr.), *Ag.*198 (lyr.); πικρότερ' ἀχέων Id.*Supp.*875 (lyr.); λόγοι E.*Hel.*481; πικροτάτου χρυσοῦ φύλαξ Id.*Hec.*772; τὸ δὴ λεγόμενον γλυκὺ πικρῷ μεμειγμένον Pl.*Phlb.*46c; ἔχει τι τὸ π. τῆς γεωργίας γλυκύ Men.795: c. inf., μὴ λίαν πικρὸν εἰπεῖν ᾖ D.1.26. 2. so of persons, prob. in Sapph.*Supp.*4.1 (Comp.); γλυκὺν ὧδε φίλοις ἐχθροῖσι δὲ π. Sol.13.5, cf. Thgn.301, A.*Ch.*234, *Eu.*152 (lyr.), etc.; ἔς τινας Hdt.1.123: abs., A.*Pr.*739, *Th.*940 (lyr.); π. θεοῖς *hateful* to them, S.*Ph.*254; π. πολίταις E.*Med.*224, cf. *Supp.*1222; ἐμοὶ π. τέθνηκεν ἢ κείνοις γλυκύς his death is *matter of sorrow* to me, S.*Aj.*966; δαίμων π., of *untimely* death (Lat. *acerbus*), *IG*3.1338. 3. *embittered, angry*, πικρὰ ὄρνις S.*Ant.*423. 4. *relentless*, οὐδὲν πικρότερον τῆς ἀνάγκης Antipho 2.2.4; *spiteful, mean, vindictive*, βάσκανον καὶ πικρὸν καὶ κακόηθες οὐδέν ἐστι πολίτευμα ἐμόν D.18.108; π. καὶ συκοφάντης Id.25.45, cf. Arist.*Rh.*1368$^{b}$21, *EN*1126$^{a}$19: in Com. of old men, σκυθρός, π., φειδωλός Men.10, cf. 825, 843, *Georg.Fr.*3. Adv. -ρῶς *pedantically*, D.H.*Lys.*6; *with rigid accuracy*, Apollon. Cit.3, Plu.2.659f. IV. Adv. -ρῶς *harshly, bitterly, vindictively*, A.*Pr.*197, S.*OC*990; π. ἐξετάσαι D.2.27, 18.265; π. ἔχειν τισί, πρός τινας, Id.10.54, *Ep.*3.10; π. φέρειν τι E.*Ion*610, cf. *Andr.*190; ἔκλαυσε π. *Ev.Matt.*26.75: Comp. -ότερον Men.*Mon.*659, etc.: Sup. -ότατα Plb.1.72.3. [ῑ in Hom. and Ep.; ῐ freq. in Trag., as A.*Pers.*473, *Ag.*970, S.*Aj.*500, E.*Hec.*772, and in Theoc.8.74: ι therefore is not long by nature as in μικρός.]

⊛ **πικρότης**, ητος, ἡ, *pungency*, of taste, *bitterness*, Hp.*Acut.*23, *VM* 19, Pl.*Tht.*159e, *Ti.*83b: in pl., ib.82e. II. metaph., *bitterness, harshness, cruelty*, τὴν [Ἀστυάγεος] π. Hdt.1.130; γλώσσῃ π. ἔνεστί τις E.*El.*1014: pl., αἱ τῶν συκοφαντῶν π. Isoc.15.300.

**πικρόχολος**, ον, *full of bitter bile, bilious*, opp. μελάγχολος; οἱ π. τὰ ἄνω Hp.*Acut.*34, cf. 61, Aret.*SA*1.5; π. χυμός Gal.6.247: metaph., *splenetic*, *AP*7.69 (Jul.).

**πικρόω**, *make bitter*:—Pass., *become so*, Alex.Aphr.*Pr.*2.70.

**πικτίς**, v. πυκτίς.

**πίλα**, ἡ, = Lat. *pila, mortar*, *POxy.*1890.12 (vi A.D.).

**πιλάριον**, τό, an *eye-salve*, Aët.7.103, Paul.Aeg.7.16, Alex.Trall.2. 2. a lead *plaster*, Orib.*Fr.*90. 3. *cap*, Leonid.ap.Aët.6.1.

**πίλεος**, ὁ, (πῖλος) = Lat. *pileus*, cj. in Plb.30.18.3; cf. πιλίον.

**πῖλ-έω**, (πῖλος) = πιλόω (which is rejected by *EM*672.12), *compress wool, make it into felt*, πιληθεὶς πέτασος a *felt* hat, *AP*6.282 (Theod.). II. generally, *compress, close up*, πιλοῦντες ἑαυτούς Ar.*Lys.*577; πιλήσαντες τοὺς λόχους D.H.9.58; *make firm* or *solid*, π. καὶ πυκνοῦν τὴν σάρκα, τὸ σῶμα, Gal.11.758, 394; τρίψει..π. τὸ δέρμα Id.6.417:—Pass., *to be close pressed*, διὰ τὸ πολὺ εἰς ὀλίγον πιληθῆναι τόπον Arist.*Mete.*366$^{b}$13; χθὼν .. οὔπω πιληθεῖσα *made solid*, A.R.4.678; ὕδατι πιληθεῖσα μᾶζα *kneaded*, *APl.*4.333 (Antiphil.); *to be condensed*, [σελήνην] νέφος εἶναι πεπιλημένον Xenoph.ap.*Placit.*2.25.4; of air, Hero *Spir.*1 *Praef.*; of a man, παγκρατιαστὴς ὑπὸ τῆς πυκνότητος σαρκῶν πεπιλημένος Ph.2.449, cf. Porph.*Chr.*35; ἰσχνός, τὴν σάρκα πεπιλ. J.*BJ*6.1.6; τοῖς χείλεσι πιλουμένοις *compressed*, Sch.D.T.p.43 H. 2. π. πουλύπουν *pound* a polypus so as to make it tender, πουλύπου πιλουμένου Ar.*Fr.*191; π. πλεκτάνας Eub.150.7, cf. Arist.*HA*622$^{a}$16 (Pass.), Zen.3.24. 3. metaph. in Pass., *to be oppressed, overwhelmed*, κακοῖς Hegesias ap.D.H.*Comp.*18; τῷ θανάτῳ πεπιλημένος Agath.5.3. **-ημα**, ατος, τό, *compressed wool* or *hair, felt*, Dsc.1.58, Gal.12.504; π. τῆς πολυτελεστάτης πορφύρας Duris 14 J., cf. Posidon.9(*a*) J. 2. *anything made thereof, hat* (cf. πῖλος), Call.*Fr.*124, 125. II. *compression*, νιφετοῦ βρῖθος ἐκ π. λαβόντος Arist.*Mu.*394$^{b}$2, cf. Anaximand.ap.*Placit.*2.13.7; π. φλογός, of the angel's sword, Ph.1.143; π. αἰθέριον, αἰθέρος, of the sun and moon, ib.284, 624.

**πῑλήσει**, for φιλήσεις, barbarism in Ar.*Th.*1190.

**πίλ-ησις** [ῑ], εως, ἡ, *compression of wool, felt*, Pl.*Lg.*849c. II. generally, *compression, solidification*, esp. of *contraction* by cold, Id.*Ti.*76c, cf. Xenoph.ap.*Placit.*3.4.4, Pl.*Ti.*58b, Thphr.*CP*5.8.3 (v.l. πιλώσει); *compression* of air, Ph.*Bel.*77.22; opp. ἐξάπλωσις, Ph.1.385: pl., πιλήσεις ἀέρος Epicur.*Ep.*2 p.44 U., cf. Gal.*Nat.Fac.*1.3. III. *overloading* of animals, Anon.ap.Suid. (pl.). **-ητικός**, ή, όν, *of* or *for felt-making*: ἡ -κή (sc. τέχνη) *felter's art*, Pl.*Plt.*280c. II. of cold, *contractive*, Arist.*Pr.*909$^{b}$18; π. δύναμις Gal.11.711; τὸ π. cj. for τὸ πλατικόν in Hp.*Cord.*8. **-ητός**, ή, όν, *made of felt*, κτήματα Pl.*Ti.*74b, Gal.*UP*6.4; στολαί Agatharch.20; φοινικίδες D.S.17.115; θώρακες Anon.ap.Suid. s. v. πίλοις. II. generally, *compressible*, Arist.*Mete.*385$^{a}$17, 387$^{a}$15. **-ίδιον**, τό, Dim. of πῖλος, Ar.*Ach.*439, Antiph.33.4, Pl.*R.*406d, D.19.255. **-ῐνος**, η, ον, *made of felt*, ὑποδήματα *IG*5(1).1390.23 (Andania, i B.C.), cf. Poll.7.171. ⊛ **-ίον**, τό, Dim. of πῖλος II, Arist.*Fr.*235, *PCair.Zen.*659.23 (iii B.C.), *PTeb.*230 (ii B.C.), Plb.35.6.4, Plu.*Flam.*13. 2. name of a *bandage*, Sor.*Fasc.*2.

**πῑλῑπής**, ές, *wanting the letter* π, Theoc.*Syrinx*4 (fort. **πειλιπής**, cf. πεῖ).

**πῑλίσκος**, ὁ, Dim. of πῖλος, Dsc.3.4.

**πιλλᾶτος**, ὁ (fort. πιλλεᾶτος), = Lat. *pilleatus, freedman*, Arr.*Epict.*4.7.37 (pl.).

**πιλνάω**, = πελάζω, *bring near*, once in Hes., Βορέας..δρῦς..πιλνᾷ χθονί *brings* them to earth, *Op.*510; also intr., δόμοισι πιλνᾷς thou *drawest nigh to* the house, *h.Cer.*115 (nisi leg. πίλνασαι):—elsewh. Pass. **πίλνᾰμαι** (with no act. form πίλνημι), *draw near to, approach*, c. dat., ἅρματα χθονὶ πίλνατο the chariots *went close to* the ground, Il.23.368; ἐπ' οὔδει πίλναται 19.93, cf. A.R.4.952, Simm.7: abs. with two subjects, Γαῖα καὶ Οὐρανὸς πίλνατο earth and sky *threatened to encounter* (in the storm), Hes.*Th.*703:—πίτναντο must be read for πίλναντο with Aristarch. and some codd. in Il.22.402; conversely πίλναντο for πίτναντο in Euph.63.2.

**πῖλο-ειδής**, ές, *like a cap*, Cleanth.*Stoic.*1.113 (πηλ- codd.), Heliod.ap.Orib.48.50.1 (πηλ-). Adv. -δῶς Sor.1.14 (rest. from Orib.). **-ποιία**, ἡ, *felting*, Poll.7.171. **-ποιικός**, ή, όν, *good for felting*, πηλοποιικὸν (sic) ὕδωρ Gal.13.938 (**-ποιητικός** ib.361); ἡ -κή *the felter's art*, Poll.7.171. ⊛ **-ποιός**, ὁ, *felt-maker, hatter*, Id.1.149, 7.171.

**πιλός**· κοχλιός, Hsch.

**πῖλος**, ὁ, *wool* or *hair wrought into felt*, used as a lining for helmets, Il.10.265; for shoes, Hes.*Op.*542, cf. Pl.*Smp.*220b, Luc.*Rh.Pr.*15; but τὴν τῶν οἰκείων πίλων γένεσιν, playfully, of the human hair, Pl.*Lg.*942e. II. *anything made of felt*, esp. close-fitting *cap*, Hes.*Op.*546, Arist.*GA*785$^{a}$27, *AP*6.90 (Phil.), etc.; πίλους τιάρας φορέοντες wearing turbans *for caps*, Hdt.3.12; ἀντὶ τῶν π. μιτρηφόροι ἦσαν Id.7.62, cf. 61, 92; πῖλοι τοῖς δημοσίοις *IG*2$^{2}$.1672.70; π. λευκός ib.5(1).1390.13 (Andania, i B.C.); of various fashions, π. Ἀρκαδικός Polyaen.4.14; Λακωνικός Poll.1.149; Μακεδονικός, = καυσία, Id.10.162; π. χαλκοῦς a brazen *cap*, i.e. helmet, Ar.*Lys.*562; of the *apex* worn by Roman *flamines*, D.H.2.64 (pl.). 2. *felt shoe*, λευκοὺς ὑπὸ ποσσὶν ἔχων π. Cratin.100. 3. *felt cloth*, used for carpets, mats, tents, etc., Hdt.4.23, 73, 75, Hp.*Aër.*18 (pl.), cf. X.*Cyr.*5.5.7, Aen.Tact.33.3 (pl.), etc.; for horse-cloths, Plu.*Art.*11. 4. *felt cuirass, jerkin*, Th.4.34. III. *amadou, Polyporus igniarius*, Thphr.*HP*3.7.4. b. *embryo of Nelumbium*, ib.4.8.7. 2. *ball*, σφαιρίζουσα πίλῳ Suid. Hist.(*FHG* ii p.464) *Fr.*2. IV. = Lat. *pilus*, as in *primus pilus*, Suid. (Cf. Lat. *pilleus.*)

**πῖλοφορ-έω**, *wear a* πῖλος or *apex*, like the Roman *flamines*, App.*BC*1.65. **-ικός**, ή, όν, *accustomed to wear a* πῖλος, Luc.*Scyth.*1. **-ος**, ον, *wearing a cap*, Ἀρμένιοι *AP*9.430 (Crin.); of the Dacian nobles, D.C.68.9.

**πῖλ-όω**, = πιλέω, of the effect of cold, *contract*, opp. μανόω, ὁ χειμὼν πιλώσας τὰς ῥίζας Thphr.*CP*3.23.5:—Pass., ib.1.12.3; νέφη ἐκ τῶν ἀτμῶν πιλοῦσθαι Democr.ap.*Placit.*4.1.4. **-ώδης**, ες, *like felt*: *close-pressed*, Ptol.*Judic.*p.25 B. (Comp.). **-ωσις**, εως, ἡ, v. πίλησις. **-ωτάριος**, ὁ, = πιλοποιός, Aët.12.49. **-ωτός**, ή, όν, (πιλόω) = πιλητός, *of felt*, σκηναὶ π., of the Scythians, Str.7.3.17; τιάρας περικείμενοι πιλωτάς Id.15.3.15. II. *compressed*, = Lat. *densus*, Serv.Dan. ad Verg.*A.*12.121.

**πῖμελ-ή**, ἡ, (πίων, πῖαρ) *soft fat, lard*, Hdt.2.40, 47, Hp.*Aër.*19, S.*Ant.*1011, Democr.ap.Ael.*NA*12.18, Alex.83: distd. from στέαρ as being χυτὸν καὶ ἄπηκτον, Arist.*HA*520$^{a}$8, cf. *PA*651$^{a}$20; ἡ ἐπιπολάζουσα [γάλακτι] π., of *cream*, Philostr.*Im.*1.31. **-ής**, ές, *fat*, Aq.*Jd.*3.17, Luc.*Tim.*15, Babr.100.1, etc.: Comp. -έστερος Luc.*Symp.*43.

⊛ **πῖμελοσαρκοφάγος** [φᾰ], ὁ, *sepulchre of fat*, Cerc.7.5.

**πῖμελώδης**, ες, *like fat, fatty*, Arist.*PA*652$^{a}$7, al.; τὸ π. Hp.*Art.*41.

* **πῑμεντάριος**, ὁ, *spicer, apothecary*, Olymp.*in Grg.*p.362 J., al., cj. for ποιμενταρίων (v.l. ποιμενικῶν) in Aët.15.29. (Late Lat. *pi(g)mentarius*.)

**πιμπλάνομαι**, Ep. pass. form, = πίμπλαμαι, Il.9.679.

**πιμπλάω**, = πίμπλημι: imper. πίμπλα Xenarch. 3 codd.; pres. part. πιμπλῶν, -ῶσαι, Lxx *Si.*24.25, Hp.*Epid.*6.8.7, ἐμ-πιπλῶντα v.l. in Id. *Morb.*2.12: impf. ἐπίμπλων *Lyr.Adesp.*90:—Pass. πιμπλῶνται Hp. *Morb.*1.32.

**Πίμπλεια** (**Πίμπλα** Str.10.3.17), ἡ, a place in Pieria, sacred to the Muses and Orpheus, Call.*Del.*7, Str.7 *Fr.*18. 9.2.25:—Adj. **Πιμπληϊάς**, κούρη v.l. in Orph.*Fr.*342; ***Πιμπληΐδες** Μοῦσαι *AP*5.205 (Leon.); σκοπιὴ Πιμπληΐς, Π. ἄκρη, A.R.1.25, Epic. in *EM*588.4.

* **πίμπλημι**, in pres. and impf. formed like ἵστημι; Aeol. 3 pl. πίμπλεισι Alc.*Supp.*25.3; Ep. 3 sg. subj. πιμπλῇσι Hes.*Op.*301; imper. πίμπλη cj. in Xenarch.3, ἐμ-πίμπλη Ar.*Av.*1310; part. πιμπλάς Pl.*R.* 586b; but nom. pl. fem. πιμπλεῖσαι Hes.*Th.*880: impf. 3 pl. ἐπίμπλασαν X.*An.*1.5.10: other tenses from πλήθω (which in pres. and impf. is intr.): fut. πλήσω E.*Hipp.*692, (ἀνα-) Od.5.302: aor. ἔπλησα E.*Med.* 905, etc.; Ep. πλῆσα Il.13.60, al.: pf. πέπληκα (ἐμ-) Pl.*Ap.*23e, *Ly.* 204d:—Med., fut. πλήσομαι (ἐμ-) Arat.1121, App.*Syr.*7: aor. ἐπλησάμην Il.9.224, etc.:—Pass., fut. πλησθήσομαι *Ev.Luc.*1.15, Charito 5.5, Him.*Or.*23.14, (ἐμ-) E.*Hipp.*664, Isoc.6.69; also πεπλήσομαι Porph. *Abst.*1.16: aor. ἐπλήσθην Il.20.156, etc.; Ep. 3 pl. πλῆσθεν 17.211, Od.4.705: pf. πέπλησμαι Babr.60, (ἐμ-) Pl.*R.*518b, 3 pl. πεπλήαται Semon.31 A, πέπληνται Hp.*Flat.*8; also shortd. form πλῆνται Parm. 1.13: aor. 2 ἐπλήμην, Ep. 3 sg. and pl. πλῆτο, πλῆντο, Il.17.499, Od.8. 57, Parm.12.1; ἐν-έπλητο Ar.*V.*911, 1304; imper. ἔμ-πλησο ib.603; opt. ἐμ-πλήμην, -ῆτο, Id.*Ach.*236, *Lys.*235; part. ἐμ-πλήμενος Id.*V.* 424, 984, etc.—In the compd. ἐμπίμπλημι (q.v.; more freq. in Prose) the second μ is sts. dropped, as ἐμπίπλημι; but returns with the augm., as in ἐνεπίμπλασαν; cf. πίμπρημι:—*fill*, c. gen. rei, *fill full of..*, τράπεζαν ἀμβροσίης Od.5.93; πήρην σίτου καὶ κρειῶν 17.411; π. τινὰ μένεος, θάρσευς φρένας, Il.13.60, 17.573; καλάμης τὸ πλοῖον Hdt.1.194; π. κρητῆρα κακῶν A.*Ag.*1398; πίμπλημ' ὄμμα δακρύων S.*El.*906; δακρύων ἔπλησεν ἐμέ *filled* me *full* of tears, E.*Or.*368: c. dat. rei, *fill with* .., ἰαχῇ τε φόβῳ τε πάσας πλῆσαν ὁδούς Il.16.374; δακρύοις Ἑλλάδ' ἅπασαν ἔπλησεν E.*Or.*1363 (lyr.); simply, *fill*, ἰχθύες.. πιμπλᾶσι μυχούς Il.21.23, cf. 14.35, Hes.*Op.*411, Pl.*Grg.*494a; π. μέλος A.*Fr.*57.4: abs., πίμπλη σὺ μὲν ἐμοί (sc. τὴν κύλικα) Xenarch.3. 2. *fill full, satisfy, glut*, E.*Cyc.*146, etc. 3. *fill, discharge* an office, A.*Ch.*361 (dub.). II. Med., *fill for oneself*, or *what is one's own*, πλησάμενος οἴνοιο δέπας *having filled himself* a cup of wine, Il.9.224, cf. Od.14.112, etc.; π. νῆας *load* ships, ib.87; π.. θυμὸν ἐδητύος ἠδὲ ποτῆτος *fill up, satiate* one's desire with.., 17.603; παρθένῳ δυσώνυμα λέκτρ' ἐπλήσω S.*OC*528 (lyr.); πεδία πίμπλασθ' ἁρμάτων *fill* the plain *full of your* chariots, v.l. in E.*Ph.*522. III. Pass., *to be filled, be full of*, τῶν.. ἐπλήσθη πεδίον Il.20.156; πλῆτο ῥόος.. ἵππων τε καὶ ἀνδρῶν 21.16; ὄσσε δακρυόφι πλῆσθεν Od.4.705, etc.; μένεος.. φρένες.. πίμπλαντο Il.1.104; πλῆσθεν.. μελέ' ἐντὸς ἀλκῆς 17.211; ἀλκῆς πλῆτο φρένας.. ib.499; αὐτῆς.. ἐπλήσθη στέγος E.*Heracl.*646: rarely c. dat., λέκτρα δ' ἀνδρῶν πόθῳ πίμπλαται δακρύμασι A.*Pers.*134 (lyr.); δάκρυσι τὸ στράτευμα πλησθέν Th.7.75. 2. *to be filled, satisfied, have enough of* a thing, αἱμάτων γέννυσιν πλησθῆναι S.*Ant.*121; π. τῆς νόσου ξυνουσίᾳ *to be wearied of it by* being with it, Id.*Ph.*520; ἡδονῶν Pl.*R.*442a, etc. 3. of females, *become pregnant*, Arist. *HA*576ᵇ29, 578ᵇ32. (Cf. Skt. *piparti* 'fill', *pūrṇá-*, Lat. *plenus*, Goth. *fulls*, etc. 'full'.)

* **πίμπρημι**, pres. and impf. non-thematic; imper. πίμπρη E.*Ion* 527, 974; part. nom. pl. πιμπράντες Th.6.94; inf. πιμπράναι A.*Pers.* 810, E.*Tr.*81, (ἐμ-) Plb.11.5.6, etc.: impf. ἐν-επίμπρην Th.6.94; 3 pl. ἐνεπίμπρασαν X.*HG*6.5.32:—other tenses formed from πρήθω (q.v.): fut. πρήσω A.*Th.*434, (ἐμ-) Il.9.242, etc.: aor. ἔπρησα 2.415, E.*Andr.*390, etc.; 3 sg. shortd. ἔπρεσε Hes.*Th.*856: pf. πέπρηκα (ὑπο-, ἐμ-, κατα-) Hp.*Ep.*17, Alciphr.1.32, D.C.59.16:—Med., Nic.*Al.*345: aor. ἐπρησάμην (ἐν-) Q.S.5.485:—Pass., fut. πρησθήσομαι Lxx *Nu.*5.27; πεπρήσομαι (v.l. πρήσομαι (ἐμ-)) Hdt.6.9: aor. ἐπρήσθην Hp.*Nat.Mul.*10, Amphis 30.10 (dub.), (ἐν-) Hdt.8.55, Pl.*Grg.*469e: pf. (ἐμ-)πέπρησμαι Hdt.8.144, Paus.2.5.5; but πέπρημαι is the Att. form acc. to Phot. s.v. σέσωται, and ἐμ-πέπρημαι is found in Ar.*V.*36 cod. Rav.; imper. πέπρησο Pherecr.80.—Collat. pres. **ἐμ-πιπράω** (v. ἐμπίμπρημι).—In the compd. ἐμπίμπρημι (q.v.; more freq. in Prose) the second μ is sts. dropped, as ἐμπίπρημι; but returns with the augm., as ἐνεπίμπρασαν; cf. πίμπλημι:—*burn, burn up*, γῆν.. πυρὶ πρῆσαι κατάκρας S.*Ant.*201, cf. E.*Tr.*81; πρῆσαι δὲ πυρὸς.. θύρετρα Il.2.415, cf. 9.242 (v.l.); without πυρί or πυρός, Hes.*Th.*856; πρήσω πόλιν A.*Th.*434, cf. *Pers.*810; δῶμα E.*Andr.*390, etc.:—Pass., πίμπραμαι *to be burnt*, Ar.*Lys.*341; πέπρησο *burn with fever*, Pherecr. 80, cf. *SIG*1180.10 (Cnidus); of wounds, *to be inflamed*, Nic.*Th.*306 (but intr. in Act. πίμπρησι δὲ χείλη Id.*Al.*438): metaph., ἐπί τινι πίμπρασθαι Luc.*Jud.Voc.*8; ἐπὶ Ῥωμαίοις App.*Ital.Fr.*3. II. = πρήθω 1.1, *blow up, distend*, in Pass., Hp.*Nat.Mul.*10, *Flat.*8, Nic.*Al.* 477, *Act.Ap.*28.6 (v.l.); ἐπέπρητο ὅλα *IG*4²(1).122.123 (Epid.):—Act., Arist.*HA*522ᵇ28, Dsc.4.32. (Cf. Russ. *prĕt'* 'sweat', 'stew'.)

**πῖνα**, ἡ, = πίνη (q.v.).

**πῐνᾰκ-ηδόν**, Adv., (πίναξ) *like planks*, ῥήματα π. ἀποσπῶν Ar.*Ra.* 824, cf. Sch. ad loc. **-ιαῖος**, α, ον, *of the size* or *thickness of a* πίναξ, *Hippiatr.*104. **-ιδᾶς**, ᾶ, ὁ, *seller of* πινακίδες, Hdn.Gr.2.657 (πινακᾶς Lentz). **-ίδιον** [κῐ], τό, = πινάκιον, Hp.*Epid.*6.8.7, Arist.*Mir.* 834ᵇ12, Sm.*Ez.*9.2, Gal.7.855; *writing-tablet*, Plu.*Eum.*1. **-ικός**, ή, όν, *of* or *by means of tables*, τῶν ἀστέρων θεωρία Vett.Val.173.26, cf. Ptol.*Tetr.*120, Paul.Al.*L.*1. Adv. -κῶς *in tabular form*, Ptol.*Tetr.* 53. **-ιον**, τό, Dim. of πίναξ, *small tablet* on which the δικασταί wrote their verdict, π. τιμητικόν Ar.*V.*167, cf. Arist.*Pol.*1268ᵃ2; εἰς π. γράφειν Pl.*Lg.*753c; also used in drawing lots for offices, D.39.12; π. πύξινον, given to dicasts as *badge* of office, Arist.*Ath.*63.4. 2. *notice-board* on which laws, decrees, etc. were written, Ar.*Av.*450, Plu.*Per.*30, etc.; ἐν πινακίῳ λελευκωμένῳ *IG*2².1237.62, cf. 1².66.31; also for notices of charges against officials, Arist.*Ath.*48.4, cf. D.8. 28, *PHal.*1.225 (iii B.C.); ἀναγράψαντες ἐμ π. τὸ μέτρον τοῦ καρποῦ *IG*1².76.27. 3. *tablets, memorandum book*, τά τε π. καὶ τὰ γραμματεῖα ib.91.11; π. ὀνειροκριτικόν Plu.*Arist.*27. 4. *votive tablet*, *IG*2².1388.57. II. *tablet for painting upon*, τὰ τῶν ζωγράφων π. Thphr. *HP*3.9.7, cf. *Inscr.Délos* 290.100 (p.191, iii B.C.), Luc.*Im.*17. b. *small* or *bad picture*, Isoc.15.2. 2. *small plate* or *dish*, Arr.*Epict.* 1.19.4, 2.22.31; π. ἀργυροῦν *BGU*387 ii 10, etc. 3. *astronomical table*, π. ἀστρολογικόν ib.1674.8 (ii A.D.). **-ίς**, ίδος, ἡ, = foreg. 1.3, Philyll.11, Macho ap.Ath.13.582c; in the Kingdom of Bosporus, ἐπὶ τῆς π., as title, prob. in *IPE*2.29.29 (Panticapaeum, iii A.D.), cf. *BMus.Inscr.*183 (πινακεῖδος): pl., π. Ἑλληνικαί *codicils* in Greek, *PGnom.*36 (ii A.D.). 2. in pl., *tablets*, Plu.*TG*6, Id.2.47e, Arr.*Epict.* 1.10.5. II. a kind of *dance*, Poll.4.103, Ath.14.629f. **-ίσκιον**, τό, Dim. of sq., Antiph.55.8. **-ίσκος**, ὁ, Dim. of πίναξ 2, Ar.*Pl.* 813, *Fr.*532, Pherecr.108.14, Pl.Com.119, Lync.1.6.

**πῐνᾰκογρᾰφ-έω**, *inscribe on a* πίναξ, in Pass., Eust.633.25 (Pass.), etc. **-ία**, ἡ, *drawing of maps*, Str.2.1.11. **-ικός**, ή, όν, *in the manner of a map*, Eust.1167.39. **-ος**, ὁ, *map-maker*, Id. ad D.P. 4. II. *maker of lists* or *catalogues*, St.Byz. s.v. Ἄβδηρα.

**πῐνᾰκο-ειδής**, ές, *like a tablet*, Diogenian.5.72. * **-θήκη**, ἡ, *picture-gallery*, Str.14.1.14. **-ποιός** (**-ποίς** Pap.), ὁ, *tablet-maker*, *PTeb.*278.16 (i A.D.). **-πώλης**, ου, ὁ, *one who sells small birds plucked and ranged upon a board*, Ar.*Av.*14, cf. Sch.

**πῐνάκωσις** [ᾰ], εως, ἡ, *timber-work*, Plu.2.658e.

* **πίναξ** [ῐ], ᾰκος, ὁ, *board, plank*, πινακάς τε νεῶν Od.12.67; εὐγόμφοισιν.. πινάκεσσιν Opp.*H.*1.194, cf. πινακηδόν; πίνακος κουρά sawdust, Hsch.: hence of things made of flat wood, metal, etc., 1. *drawing-* or *writing-tablet*, = δέλτος, γράψας ἐν π. πτυκτῷ Il.6.169; πίναξιν.. ἐγγεγραμμένα A.*Supp.*946; πινάκων ξεστῶν δέλτοι Ar.*Th.*778; ἐν χρυσῷ π. γράψαντες Pl.*Criti.*120c, cf. *R.*501a; of a *votive tablet* hung on the image of a god, A.*Supp.*463, cf. Arist.*Pol.*1341ᵃ36, *IG*4²(1). 121.24 (Epid., iv B.C., pl.), Herod.4.19, Str.8.6.15 (pl.), etc.; Πίνακες *tables* or *catalogues* of authors, name of a work by Callimachus, D.L. 8.86, cf. Ath.6.244a, 13.585b, Suid. s.v. Καλλίμαχος; *lists* of philosophers, Plu.*Sull.*26; αἵ τ' ἀναγραφαὶ τῶν π. αἵ τε βυβλιοθῆκαι Phld. *Sto.*339.13. 2. *trencher, platter*, κρειῶν πίνακας παρέθηκεν Od.1. 141, cf. 16.49; ἐπ' ἀργυροῦ π. Philippid.9.4; π. χαλκοῦς Ath.4.128d; *salver*, πίνακα.. μέγαν, ἔχοντα μικροὺς πέντε πινακίσκους Lync.1.5, cf. 17, 19; πίνακες ὑέλινοι Aët.7.106. 3. *board* for painting on, *picture*, Simon.178, Anaxandr.33.2; π. οἱ γραφόμενοι Thphr.*HP*5.7.4, cf. *IG* 11(2).161 *A* 75 (Delos, iii B.C.). 4. generally, *plate with anything drawn* or *engraved on it*, χάλκεος π., of a map, Hdt.5.49, cf. Plu. *Thes.*1; π. γεωγραφικός, first made by Anaximander, Str.1.1.11. 5. *board* or *tablet* on which astronomical tables were drawn, ἡ περὶ πίνακα μέθοδος the art of casting nativities, Plu.*Rom.*12; ἀγυρτικοὶ π. Id.*Comp.Arist.Cat.*3, cf. πινάκιον II. 3. b. prov., ἐκ πίνακος καὶ πυλαίας, of a trivial fiction, Id.2.386b. 6. *public notice-board* or *register*, π. ἐκκλησιαστικός D.44.35, etc.; but δαμόσιος π. public *archive*, *SIG*671 *A* 15 (Delph., ii B.C.). 7. *strop*, to sharpen knives on, Thphr.*HP*5.5.1. 8. *toy-theatre* for marionettes, Hero *Aut.* 23.1, al. (Cf. OSlav. *pĭnĭ* 'tree-stump'.)

**πῐνάριον**, τό, a sort of *vitriol*, Dsc.[5.98]. II. *piece of mother-of-pearl* (cf. πίνη), *PHolm.*3.12, *PSI*3.183.5 (v A.D.).

**πῐνᾰρ-όομαι**, Pass., *to be dirty*, Suid. s.v. πεπελτωμένα. * **-ός**, ά, όν, (πίνος) *dirty, squalid*, Cratin.372, E.*El.*184 (lyr.); πιναρὸν.. ἀλουτίᾳ κάρα Eup.251; of *unwashed* wool, Aret.*CA*1.1; cf. πινηρός. **-ότης**, ητος, ἡ, *filthiness*, Eust.1561.25.

**πινάτρα**, ἡ, perh. = πιάτρα, *JHS*25.174 (Isaura), *Papers of Amer. Sch. at Athens* 3 No.207 (Pisidia), unless a pr. n.

**πινάω**, *to be dirty*, Ar.*Lys.*279.

**Πινδάρειος** [ᾰ], α, ον, *of Pindar*, ἔπος Ar.*Av.*939 (lyr.):—also **Πινδᾰρικός**, ή, όν, Plu.2.602f; σχῆμα Π. Eust.1110.52. Adv. -κῶς Id. 21.14.

**Πινδόθεν**, Adv. *from Mount Pindus*, Pi.*P.*1.66.

**πίνη** [ῑ] (Antiph.194.15) and **πῖνα**, ἡ, *pinna*, a long-shaped bivalve, with a silky beard or byssus, of which several species inhabit the Mediterranean, freq. mentioned as a delicacy in Com. Poets, e.g. Cratin.8, Philyll.13, cf. Arist.*HA*528ᵃ24, 547ᵇ15, Isid.Char.20, Opp. *H.*2.187, Artem.2.14. II. *pearl*, acc. pl. πίνας *UPZ*121.9 (ii B.C.); πεῖνας *POxy.*1273.10 (iii A.D.), cf. ἀληθινόπινος, πινώτιον, πινάριον.—Written with one ν, *UPZ* l.c., *POxy.* l.c., and sts. in codd., cf. Cic. *Fin.*3.63, *ND*2.123, Plin.*HN*9.115, 142; πῖνα Hdn.Gr.2.570, Hsch., Choerob. in *An.Ox.*2.250; the spelling πινν- in this word and its derivatives is freq. in codd., but is not found in Inscrr. or Papyri.

**πῑνηρός**, ή, όν, Ion. for πιναρός, ἔρια πινηρά Hp.ap.Erot.

**πῑνίκιος**, ον, *of the* πινικόν, π. κόγχος, = πινικόν, *Peripl.M.Rubr.*35: **πῑνικόν**, τό, *pearl produced by the* πίνη, ib.36, 59.

**πίνινος** λίθος *mother-of-pearl*, Lxx *Es.*1.6 (v.l. πίννινος).

**πῑνόεις**, εσσα, εν, = πιναρός, Hp.*Mul.*2.187, A.R.2.301, *AP*7.146 (Antip. Sid.).

* **πῖνον**, τό, *liquor made from barley, beer*, Arist.*Fr.*106, cj.

in *Atti della reale Accad. di Archeologia di Napoli* 11.41 (Gortyn, iv B.C.).

**πῑνόομαι**, Pass., *to be dirty*, χιτὼν πεπινωμένος Philet.17; of Alexander's complexion as painted by Apelles, Plu.*Alex.*4: metaph. (cf. πῖνος 2), *literae* πεπινωμέναι or πεπινωμένως *scriptae, in archaic style*, Cic.*Att.*14.7.2, 15.16; ἡ αὐστηρὰ καὶ πεπ. σύνθεσις D.H.*Dem.*45.

* **πῖνος**, ὁ, *dirt, filth*, in clothes or hair, S.*OC*1259, E.*El.*305; of the natural *grease* in wool, Paul.Aeg.7.17.88: metaph., σὺν πίνῳ χερῶν, i.e. by *foul* means, A.*Ag.*776(lyr.). 2. *patina* on bronze statues, Plu.2.395b: hence, metaph. of style, ὁ τῆς ἀρχαιότητος π. D.H.*Dem.* 5, cf. 39, *Comp.*11, al. 3. Alch., *wash* on metals, Olymp.Alch.p.75 B. [πίνος Hdn.Gr.2.945, and ῑ in Poets, S.l.c., A.R.2.200, etc.: πῖνος is incorrect in Phryn.*PS*p.37 B. cod., *EM*672.39.]

**πῑνο-τήρης**, ου, ὁ, (τηρέω) *pinna-guard, a small crab* that lives in the pinna's shell, said to give warning of approaching danger, Arist. *HA*547ᵇ28, Chrysipp.*Stoic.*2.207, Plu.2.980b; cf. πινοφύλαξ. 2. metaph., of a diminutive person, '*baby-crab*', Ar.*V.*1510; ὁ π. τοὐδὲ μάντεως χορός (prob. for χοροῦ), posted to give warning, S.*Fr.* 113. **-τρόφος**, ον, *nourishing the pinna*, Tz.ad Lyc.418. **-φύλαξ** [ῠ], ἄκος, ὁ, = πινοτήρης, Arist.*HA*547ᵇ16, Isid.Char.20, Xenocr.ap. Orib.2.58.98, Artem.2.14.

**πινσός**, ὁ, = πεσσός III, *cubical block of masonry*, Sch.Pi.*O.*2.146.

**πίνῡμι** [πῑ], = sq., Hsch. s.v. πινυμένην: **πίνῠσις** [πῑ], εως, ἡ, *prudence*, Id.

**πῑνύσκω** and **πῑνύσσω**, Ep. aor. ἐπίνυσσα: aor. Pass. ἐπινύσθην:—*make prudent, admonish, correct*, ἤδη γάρ με καὶ ἄλλο τεὴ ἐπίνυσσεν ἐφετμὴ Il.14.249; ἀφραδέοντα πινυσσέμεν Naumach.ap.Stob.4.23.7; ἐκεῖνον.. πινύσκετ' εὐλόγοισι νουθετήμασι A.*Pers.*830; κερδαλέῳ μύθῳ σε πινύσκει Call.*Dian.*152; ὁπόταν πινύσκῃ Ζεὺς ἄματα *makes* the days *calm*, Simon.12; simply, *teach*, ταλασήϊα ἔργα Orph.*Fr.*178:—Pass., ὑπὸ τᾶς ματρὸς πινυσθεὶς Pythag.ap.Iamb.*VP*28.146. (Cf. πέπνυμαι.)

**πῑνῠτ-ή**, ἡ, *understanding, wisdom*, Il.7.289, Od.20.71, Hp.*Ep.* 18. **-ής**, ῆτος, Dor. ᾶτος, ἡ, = foreg., *AP*7.490(Anyt.). **-ός**, ή, όν, *prudent, discreet*, Od.1.229, 4.211, 11.445, etc.; πινυτὸς θυμόν Pi.*I.*8(7). 28; πάντα ἄρτια καὶ π. Sol.4.40, cf. Luc.*Bacch.*8: Comp. -ώτερος Q.S.5.166. Adv. -τῶς, λέγειν Epicr.11.6 (anap.).—Poet. word, cf. Plu.2.797e.

**πῑνῠτό-της**, ητος, ἡ, = πινυτή, Eust.681.43. **-φρων**, ονος, ὁ, ἡ, *of wise* or *understanding mind*, of Odysseus, Q.S.14.630, *AP*3.8 (Inscr. Cyzic.); εὐμαθίη ib.7.22(Simm.); σιγή *APl.*4.325(Jul.); *ingenious*, εὐχωλή (of an acrostic) Puchstein *Epigr. Gr.*p.10; νοῦς Jul. *Caes.*319a; restd. in *Epic.Alex.Adesp.*7.19.

* **πίνω** [ῐ], Ep. inf. πινέμεναι and -έμεν, Il.4.346, Od.7.220: Ion. impf. πίνεσκον Il.16.226: fut. πίομαι 13.493, Thgn.962, A.*Ch.*578, S. *OC*622, Ar.*Eq.*1289, 1401, *Fr.*311; later πιοῦμαι Arist.*Rh.*1370ᵇ18, Ael.*VH*12.49, etc.; also as f.l. in earlier authors, πιεῖσθαι Hp.*Int.*12, πιεῖσθε X.*Smp.*4.7, but rejected by Phryn.23, Ath.10.446d; 2 sg. πίεσαι Lxx *De.*28.39, *Ev.Luc.*17.8: aor. ἔπῐον, Ep. πίον Il.22.2, etc.; 2 sg. subj. πίησθα 6.260; imper. πίε Od.9.347, Men.151, *Carm.Pop.* 33, (ἐκ-) E.*Cyc.*563, Orph.*Fr.*32 biii; also πῖθι Cratin.141, Ion Trag. 27, Ar.*V.*1489, Amips.18, Antiph.163.1, etc., (ἔκ-) E.*Cyc.*570; πίει, πίεις, Kretschmer *Griech.Vaseninschr.*p.195; inf. πιεῖν Od.8.70, Hdt. 4.172, etc.; later contr. πεῖν *AP*11.140(Lucill.), *Mim.Oxy.*413.66, *PMag.Lond.*121.738, *PFlor.*101.8(i A.D.), etc.; Ep. πιέμεν Od.15. 378, πιέειν Il.4.263, πιέναι f.l. for ὑπιέναι in Hp.*Epid.*5.18; part. πιών, πιοῦσα, Il.24.102, etc., πιέουσα Hp.*Epid.*7.11:—Med., subj. πινώμεθα Hermipp.25; imper. πίνεο Nic.*Th.*912: πίομαι [ῑ] as pres. Med., Ibyc.17(s.v.l.), Pi.*O.*6.86, and so ἐκπίομαι [ῑ] Ar.*Ach.*199, ἐμπίομαι [ῑ] Thgn.1129(Pass. in *AP*5.43(Rufin.)):—Pass., Od.20.312, Hp.*Aër.* 9, etc.: Ep. impf. πίνετο Od.9.45.—Other tenses are from πω- or πο-, pf. πέπωκα A.*Th.*821, etc.:—Pass., fut. ποθήσομαι (κατα-) Ar.*V.*1502, (ἐκ-) Plu.2.240e: aor. ἐπόθην (ἐξ-) A.*Ch.*66, (κατ-) Pl.*Criti.*111d: pf. inf. πεπόσθαι Thgn.477: Aeol. pres. πώνω Alc.20, 52, *Supp.*20.3: aor. imper. πῶθι, πῶ, *EM*698.52. [ῐ always in πίνω, πίνομαι; ῐ always in aor. ἔπιον, hence πίε must be read for πῖνε in *AP*11.19(Strat.), and ἔπινον for ἔπιον in *Anacreont.*5.5: Hom. has ἐθέλουσι δὲ πιέμεν ἄμφω Il.16.825, cf. Od.18.3; but καὶ φαγέμεν πιέμεν τε 15.378; in imper. πῖθι, ῑ always.—In fut. πίομαι Hom. and Trag. use ῑ, Il.13.493, A.*Ch.* 578, S.*OC*622, cf. Thgn.962, Ar.*Eq.*1289, 1401, *Fr.*311; but ῐ in Ion Lyr.2.10 (nisi leg. πιέτω), (ἐκ-) Pl.Com.9, Amips.22; also in later Poetry, *AP*11.8, 25.5(Apollonid.); for pres. Med. πίομαι, v. supr.]:—*drink*, freq. from Hom. downwds., c. acc., π. οἶνον, ὀρόν, αἷμα, etc., Od.15.391, 17.225, S.*OC*622, etc.; π. ὕδωρ Αἰσήποιο *drink* its water, i.e. live on its banks, Il.2.825, cf. Pi.*O.*6.86 (Med.): c. gen. partit., *drink of* a thing, π. οἴνοιο Od.22.11; εἰς οἶνον.., ἔνθεν ἔπινον *whereof*.., 4.220; αἵματος ὄφρα πίω 11.96, cf. 15.373; also πίνειν κρητῆρας οἴνοιο *to drink* bowls of wine, Il.8.232; κύπελλα οἴνου 4.346; π. ἀπὸ κρήνης *drink* of a spring, Thgn.959 (but κρήνης 962); π. ἀπ' αὐτοῦ (sc. δέπαος) αἴθοπα οἶνον *from* it, Il.16.226; δέπα ἔνθεν ἔπινον Od.19.62; ἐκ κεράμων μέθυ πίνετο Il.9.469; ἐκ τῆς χειρὸς διδοῖ πιεῖν Hdt.4.172; ἐκ ταὐτοῦ.. ποτηρίου Ar.*Eq.*1289; ἐξ ἀργύρου ἢ χρυσοῦ Pl. *R.*417a; ἀπὸ τοῦ ποταμοῦ X.*Cyr.*4.5.4; σκύφος ᾧ περ ἔπινεν *with* which.., Od.14.112; π. κερατίνοις ποτηρίοις v.l. in X.*An.*6.1.4; τὰ φάρμακα π. παρὰ τοῦ ἰατροῦ draughts sent by him, Pl.*Grg.*467c. 2. abs., *drink*, ἐσθιέμεν καὶ πινέμεν Od.2.305; ὁ πίνε καὶ ἧσθε 5.94, 6.249, cf. Il.24.476, etc.; μῆλα πιόμεν' ἐκ βοτάνης *going to drink* after pasture, 13.493; πρὸς βίαν πώνην Alc.20; πῖνε, πῖν' ἐπὶ συμφοραῖς Simon.14; π. πρὸς ἡδονήν Pl.*Smp.*176e; εἰς μέθην Id.*Lg.*775b; διδόναι πιεῖν Cratin.124; πιεῖν αἰτεῖν X.*Cyr.*8.3.41; τινὶ πιεῖν ἐγχέας ib.1.3.9; πιεῖν τις ἡμῖν ἐγχεάτω Philem.9: in pf. πέπωκα, *to be drunk*, E.*Cyc.* 536; πίνοντά τε καὶ πεπωκότα *drinking* and *having finished drinking*, Pl.*Phd.*117c. II. *celebrate by a carouse*, νίκην Philostr.*Gym.* 54. III. metaph., *drink up*, as the earth does rain, τὸ ὕδωρ, ὄμβρον, Hdt.3.117, 4.198; πιοῦσα κόνις μέλαν αἷμα A.*Eu.*979(lyr.), cf. *Th.*736 (lyr.), 821, S.*OT*1401; of plants, X.*Smp.*2.25; of a lamp, π. τοὔλαιον Luc.*Cat.*27; λύχνος.. πολλὰ πιὼν μέλη *AP*5.196(Mel., dub. l.). (I.-E. *pōy-* and *pī-*, cf. Skt. *pāy-áyati* 'cause to drink', *pītí-* 'a drink', Lat. *pōtus*, etc.)

**πῑνώδ-ης**, ες, (πῖνος) *greasy*, of wool, Hp.*Mul.*2.185 (Sup.); *dirty, foul*, of hair, E.*Or.*225, cf. Lyc.675. **-ία**, ἡ, *dirt, filth*, Hsch.

**πῑνώτιον**, τό, *pearl ear-ring*, *POxy.*1449.25 (iii A.D.).

**πιοειδής**, ές, *shaped like the letter* πῖ, μέρη [τοῦ διαπήγματος] Sor.1.68; φλιά Orib.49.4.30, 49.33.4. Adv. -δῶς Ruf.*Anat.*45, cj. in Sor.1.14.

**πίομαι**, v. πίνω.

**πῖον** (sc. γάλα), τό, *fat, rich milk*, Nic.*Al.*77.

**πῖος**, α, ον, poet. form of πίων, ἄρνες Epich.136; μῆλα Orph.*A.*506: hence πιότερος, πιότατος, v. πίων.

**πιότης**, ητος, ἡ, *fattiness*, τῆς σαρκός Hp.*Aër.*21, cf. Arist.*HA*520ᵃ 23, *PA*651ᵇ9, Thphr.*HP*9.1.3. II. metaph., *wealth, prosperity*, Ph.1.299, Eust.1146.10.

**πιόφυλλος**, ον, *with oily leaves*, of the olive, etc., Alex.Aphr. *in Top.* 118.31.

**πιπαλίς**, ίδος, ἡ, a kind of *lizard*, Hsch.; also, = χαλκίς, Id.

**πιπεράδιον**, τό, *pepper*, *POxy.*1299.10 (iv A.D.).

**πιπεράς**, dub. in *POxy.*921.26 (iii A.D.), *PCornell* 33 (iii A.D.); perh. *pepper-pot*.

**πίπερι**, = πέπερι (q.v.).

**πιπεροτριβεύς**, *piperoterarium*, *Gloss.*

**πῑπίσκω**, Hp.*Mul.*1.63, Luc.*Lex.*20: fut. πίσω [ῑ] Pi.*I.*6(5).74, Eup.115: aor. ἔπῑσα Hp.*Mul.*1.59, al., prob. in Arist.*EN*1111ᵃ14 (for παίσας), (ἐν-) Pi.*Fr.*111 (πιπίσαι is f.l. in Hp.*Fract.*36):—Med., aor. ἐπῑσάμην (ἐν-) Nic.*Th.*573, 877, etc.:—Pass., aor. ἐπίσθην (ἐν-) ib.624:—causal of πίνω, *give to drink*, Hp.*Acut.*2, Aret.*CA*1.1, etc.: c. dupl. acc., πίσω σφε Δίρκας ὕδωρ I *will make* them *drink* the water of Dirce, Pi.*I.* l.c.; π. τινά τινος Luc. l.c.: c. dat. et acc., ταύτῃσι γάλα Hp.*Mul.*1.63.

**πίπον**· ἄκρον, Hsch.

**πίπος**, ὁ, v.l. for πιπώ in Arist.*HA*609ᵃ30, 617ᵃ28. II. ὁ, *a young piping bird*, cj. for ἵππους in Ath.9.368f.

**πιππίζω**, *pipe, cheep*, or *chirp like young birds*, Ar.*Av.*306.

**πίπρα**, ἡ, v.l. for πιπώ in Arist.*HA*609ᵃ7.

**πιπράσκω**, v. πέρνημι.

**πιττᾰκάριος**, ὁ, prob. *seller of pistachio-nuts* (cf. πιστάκη), *MAMA* 3.495 (Corycus).

* **πίπτω**, Aeol. πίσσω, acc. to Gramm. in Hilgard *Exc. ex libris Herodiani* p.28 (cf. Hdn.Gr.2.377 note); poet. subj. πίπτησι Pl.Com. 153.5: Ep. impf. πῖπτον Il.8.67, etc. (for the quantity of ι cf. Hdn. Gr.2.10); Ion. πίπτεσκον (συμ-) Emp.59.2: fut. πεσοῦμαι A.*Ch.*971 (lyr.), etc.; Ion. 3 pl. πεσέονται Il.11.824, 3 sg. πεσέεται Hdt.7.163, 168: aor. ἔπεσον, inf. πεσεῖν, Il.13.178, etc.; 2 sg. opt. πεσοίης Polem.*Call.* 10.14; Aeol. and Dor. ἔπετον Alc.60, Pi.*O.*7.69, *P.*5.50, (κάπετον) *O.*8.38, (ἔμ-) *P.*8.81, cf. Isyll.8, *IG*14.642 (Thurii); in later writers ἔπεσα, Orph.*A.*521, Lxx *Le.*9.24, al., f.l. in E.*Tr.*291 (προσ-): pf. πέπτωκα A.*Eu.*147, Ar.*Ra.*970, etc.; Ep. part. πεπτεώς, ῶτος (the εω forming one syll. by synizesis), Il.21.503, etc.; also πεπτηώς, υῖα, Od.14.354, Simon.183.7, Hp.*Mul.*1.69, A.R.4.1298, *AP*7.427 (Antip. Sid.), cf. πτήσσω; Trag. part. πεπτώς S.*Aj.*828, *Ant.*697. (Redupl. from πετ-, which appears in Aeol. and Dor. aor. ἔ-πετ-ον (v. supr.), and the poet. form πίτ-νω; cogn. with πέτομαι, q.v.)

A. Radical sense, *fall down*, and (when intentional) *cast oneself down*, πρηνέα πεσεῖν, ὕπτιος πέσεν, Il.6.307, 15.435, etc.; νιφάδες.. π. θαμειαί 12.278; ὀπίσω πέσεν Od.12.410; etc.:—Constr., with Preps., in Hom. almost always ἐν.., ἐν κονίῃσι π. *fall* in the dust, i.e. to rise no more, Il.11.425, cf. 13.205; ἐν αἵματι καὶ κονίῃσι πεπτεῶτας Od.22.384; π. ἐν ἀγκοίνῃσί τινος *fall into* his arms, Hes.*Fr.*142.5; ἐν χθονὶ πεπτηώς Simon. l.c. (cf. πτήσσω); π. ἐν δεμνίοις E.*Or.*35, cf. A.*Pers.*125 (lyr.) (v. infr. B. I): rare in Prose, π. ἐν ποταμῷ X.*Ages.*1.32: c. dat. only, πεδίῳ πέσε Il.5.82; δεμνίοις π. E.*Or.*88 (s.v.l.); π. ἐπὶ χθονί Od.24.535; οὐδέ οἱ ὕπνος πῖπτεν ἐπὶ βλεφάροις Hes.*Fr.*188.4; ἐπὶ γᾷ S.*Ant.*134 (lyr.); πρὸς πέδῳ E.*Ba.* 605; πρὸς ἀγκάλαις Id.*Ion* 962; ἀμφὶ σώμασίν τινων A.*Ag.*326: with a Prep. of motion first in Hes., Πληϊάδες π. ἐς πόντον *Op.*620; [ποταμὸς] εἰς ἅλα *Th.*791; εἰς ἄντλον E.*Hec.*1025 (lyr.); ἐπὶ γᾶν π. αἷμα A.*Ag.* 1019 (lyr.); ἐπὶ στόμα X.*Cyn.*10.13; πρὸς οὖδας E.*Hec.*405. 2. in Hom. with Advs. of motion as well as of rest, χαμάδις π. Il.7.16, 15.714, etc.; χαμαὶ π. 4.482, cf. 14.418, etc.; π. ἔραζε 12.156, cf. Od.22. 280. 3. with Preps. denoting the point from which one falls, ἀπ' ὤμων χαμαὶ πέσε Il.16.803; ἀπ' οὐρανοῦ A.*Fr.*44.3; ἀπό τινος ὄνου Pl. *Lg.*701d; ἐκ χειρῶν π. ἡνία Il.5.583; π. ἐκ νηός Od.12.417; πεσὼν ἐκ νηὸς ἀποφθίμην ἐνὶ πόντῳ 10.51. 4. Geom., of perpendiculars or parts of applied figures, π. ἐπί τι *fall* upon, Euc.3.11, Archim.*Fluit.* 2.8, al., Apollon.Perg.*Con.*1.2; but π. ἐπί τι, ποτί τι, *intersect, meet*, Archim.*Con.Sph.*16, *Spir.*15; π. διά τινος *pass* through, Id.*Con.Sph.* 17; π. κατά τινος Id.*Sph.Cyl.*1 *Def.*2; ἐπί τι κατά τινα Apollon.Perg. *Con.*1.2.

B. Special usages: I. πίπτειν ἔν τισι *fall violently upon, attack*, ἐνὶ νήεσσι πέσωμεν Il.13.742 (but ἐν νήεσσι πεσόντες *tumbling* into the ships, 2.175); ἐν βουσὶ π. S.*Aj.*375 (lyr.); Ἔρως, ὃς ἐν κτήμασι π. Id.*Ant.*782 (lyr.); ἐπ' ἀλλήλοισι, of combatants, Hes.*Sc.*379, cf. 375; πρὸς μῆλα καὶ ποίμνας S.*Aj.*1061; πρὸς πύλαις A.*Th.*462. 2. *throw oneself down, fall down*, πρὸς βρέτη θεῶν ib.185; ἀμφὶ σὸν γόνυ E.*Hec.*787; ἐς γόνατα on one's knees, of a wrestler, Simon.156; ἐς τὸν ὦμον Ar.*Eq.*571. II. *fall* in battle, πῖπτε δὲ λαός Il.8.67, etc.; οἱ πεπτωκότες *the fallen*, X.*Cyr.*1.4.24; νέκυες πίπτοντες Il.10.200; νεκροὶ περὶ νεκροῖς πεπτωκότες E.*Ph.*881: πεσήματα.. πέπτωκε δοριπετῆ νεκρῶν Id.*Andr.*653; π. ὑπὸ Ἀθηναίων Hdt.9.67; ὡς.. θάμνοι πρόρριζοι πίπτουσι.., ὣς ἄρ' ὑπ' Ἀτρεΐδῃ πῖπτε κάρηνα Τρώων Il.11.157, cf. 500, etc.; τὸ Περσῶν ἄνθος οἴχεται πεσόν A.*Pers.*252. 2. *fall, be ruined*, δόμον δοκοῦντα κάρτα νῦν πεπτωκέναι Id.*Ch.*263, cf. Pl.*Phlb.*22e; πεσεῖν.. πτώματ' οὐκ ἀνασχετά A.*Pr.*919, cf. Pl.*La.*181b; στάντες τ' ἐς ὀρθὸν καὶ πεσόντες ὕστερον S.*OT*50; ἀβουλίᾳ, ἐξ ἀβουλίας π., Id.*El.*429, 398; ἀπὸ σμικροῦ κακοῦ Id.*Aj.*1078; of an army, μεγάλα πεσόντα πρήγματα ὑπὸ ἡσσόνων Hdt.7.18, cf. Th.2.89; ὁ Ξέρξεω στρατὸς αὐτὸς ὑπ' ἑωυτοῦ ἔπιπτε Hdt.8.16; of a city, π. δορί E.*Hec.* 5. 3. *fall, sink*, ἄνεμος πέσε the wind *fell*, Od.19.202 (but in Hes. *Op.*547, Βορέαο πεσόντος is used for ἐμπεσόντος, *falling on, blowing on* one): metaph., πέπτωκεν κομπάσματα A.*Th.*794, cf. S.*Ant.*474: c. dat., ταῖς ἐλπίσι πεσεῖν *fail* in one's hopes, Plb.1.87.1. 4. *fall short, fail*, Pl.*Phd.*100e; of a playwright, *fail*, Ar.*Eq.*540. III. πίπτειν ἔκ τινος *fall out of, lose* a thing, unintentionally, σοι ἐκ θυμοῦ πεσέειν *fall out of, lose* thy favour, Il.23.595; ἐξ ἐλπίδων π. E.*Fr.*420. 5; τοὔμπαλιν π. φρενῶν Id.*Hipp.*390; also of set purpose, ἐξ ἀρκύων π. *escape* from.., A.*Eu.*147; ἔξω τῶν κακῶν Ar.*Ra.*970. 2. reversely, πολλὴν ἐς κακότητα π. Thgn.42; εἰς ἄτην Sol.13.68; εἰς δουλοσύνην Id.9.4; ἐς δάκρυα Hdt.6.21; ἐς νόσον A.*Pr.*478; εἰς ἔρον, ἔριν, ὀργήν, φόβον, ἀνάγκας, E.*IT*1172, *Fr.*578.8, *Or.*696, *Ph.*69, Th.3. 82; also ἐν γυιοπέδαις π. Pi.*P.*2.41; ἐν μέσοις ἀρκυστάτοις S.*El.*1476; ἐν φόβῳ E.*Or.*1418 (lyr.); ἐν σολοικισμῷ Luc.*Sol.*3; πρὸς τόλμαν S.*Ichn.* 11: c. dat. only, π. δυσπραξίαις Id.*Aj.*759; αἰσχύνῃ Id.*Tr.*597, etc.; οὐκ ἔχω ποῖ γνώμης πέσω I know not which way *to turn*, ib.705. 3. εἰς ὕπνον π. *fall* asleep, Id.*Ph.*826; but ἐν ὕπνῳ Pi.*I.*4(3).23; simply ὕπνῳ, A.*Eu.*68. 4. π. εἰς (ἰατρικὴν) χρῆσιν *to be applied* to (medicinal) use, Dsc.5.19,151, al. 5. π. ὑπ' αἴσθησιν *to be accessible* to perception, Iamb.*Comm.Math.*8, *in Nic* p.7 P. IV. πίπτειν μετὰ ποσσὶ γυναικός *to fall* between her feet, i.e. to be born, Il.19.110. V. of the dice, τὰ δεσποτῶν εὖ πεσόντα θήσομαι I shall count my master's lucky *throws* my own, A.*Ag.*32: ἀεὶ γὰρ εὖ πίπτουσιν οἱ Διὸς κύβοι S.*Fr.*895; ὥσπερ οἱ κύβοι· οὐ ταὔτ' ἀεὶ πίπτουσιν Alex.34; ὥσπερ ἐν πτώσει κύβων πρὸς τὰ πεπτωκότα τίθεσθαι τὰ πράγματα according to *the throws*, Pl.*R.*604c; ὄνασθαι πρὸς τὰ νῦν π. E.*Hipp.*718; πρὸς τὸ πῖπτον as matters *fall out*, Id.*El.*639; of tossing up with oyster-shells, κἂν μὲν πίπτῃσι τὰ λεύκ' ἐπάνω Pl.Com.153.5; of lots, ὁ κλῆρος π. τινί or παρά τινα, Pl.*R.*619e, 617e; ἐπί τινα *Act.Ap.*1.26: Astrol., π. καλῶς ὁ οἰκοδεσπότης Vett.Val.7.15. 2. generally, *fall, turn out*, εὖ πίπτειν *to be lucky*, E.*Or.*603; παρὰ γνώμαν π. Pi.*O.*12.10; of a battle, καραδοκήσοντα τὴν μάχην τῇ πεσέεται to wait and see how *it would fall*, Hdt.7.163, cf. 8.130; λόγων κορυφαὶ ἐν ἀλαθείᾳ π. *turn out* true, Pi.*O.*7.69; συμφοραὶ παντοῖαι πίπτουσαι παντοίως Pl.*Lg.*709a. 3. *fall to* one, i.e. to his lot, esp. of revenues, *accrue*, τῷ δήμῳ πρόσοδος ἔπιπτε Plb.30.31.7; φησιν.. ἐξακισχίλια τάλαντα τοῖς Λακεδαιμονίοις πεσεῖν Id.2.62.1; τὴν πεπτωκότα (sic) μοι οἰκίαν *BGU*251.12 (ii A.D.); τὰ πίπτοντα διάφορα ἐκ τῶν μυστηρίων *IG*5(1).1390.45 (Andania, i B.C.); τὸ πεσὸν ἀπὸ τῆς τιμῆς ἀργύριον D.H.20.17; *to be paid*, τῶν εἰς Καίσαρα πίπτειν ὀφειλόντων ἐξεταστής Str.17.1.12; τὰ πεπτωκότα εἰς τὸ.. ἱερόν *PEleph.*10.2 (iii B.C.); π. ἐπὶ τράπεζαν *PCair.Zen.*236.7 (iii B.C.), *PLond.*3.1200.1 (ii B.C.); μὴ πιπτόντων τῶν τόκων *BMus.Inscr.*1032. 40 (Teos); πέπτωκεν ἁλικῆς διά τινος.. *Ostr.Bodl.*13 (iii B.C.) (but τὰ ἀπὸ τῶν προσόδων πίπτοντα *deficiencies*, *IPE*1².32*B*75 (Olbia)). VI. *fall*, of a date or period of Time, π. κατὰ τὴν ρκθ' Ὀλυμπιάδα Plb.1.5.1; οἱ χρόνοι οἱ πίπτοντες ὑπὸ τὴν ἡμετέραν ἱστορίαν Id.4.2.2. VII. *fall under, belong to* a class, εἰς γένη ταῦτα Arist.*Metaph.*1005ᵃ2, al.; ἐπὶ τὴν αὐτὴν ἐπιστήμην ib.982ᵇ8; ὑπὸ τὴν αὐτὴν μέθοδον Id.*Top.*102ᵃ37, cf. 151ᵃ15; ὑπὸ τέχνην οὐδεμίαν Id.*EN*1104ᵃ8; ἔξω τῶν διηρημένων γενῶν Id.*PA*681ᵇ1; τὸ μακάριον ἐνταῦθα πεπτωκέναι Epicur.*Ep.*1 p.28 U.; ὅσα πέπτωκεν ὑπὸ τὴν.. ἱστορίαν Plb.2.14.7.

**πιπώ**, οῦς, ἡ, *woodpecker*, *Picus major* and *minor*, Arist.*HA*593ᵃ4, al. (cf. πίπρα, πῖπος), Lyc.476, Nic.*Fr.*54, prob. in Antim.Col.4 P.

**πίρωμις**, ὁ, Egypt. word, = καλὸς κἀγαθός, Hdt.2.143 (*pi romi* 'the man').

**πίσα** [ῐ], ἡ, (πιπίσκω) = πίστρα, Sch.Pi.*I.*6(5).108.

⊛ **Πῖσα** or **Πίση**, Dor. **Πίσα**, ης, ἡ, a fountain at Olympia (Str.8.3. 31), which gave a name to Olympia itself, Stesich.90, Pi.*O.*1.18, Hdt. 2.7, etc.: Adv. **Πίσηθεν** *AP*7.290 (Antip. Thess.); **Πισαῖοι**, οἱ, *the people of Pisa*, D.S.15.82: Adj. ⊛**Πισαῖος**, α, ον, Nic.*Fr.*74.5, *AP*6.350 (Crin.), etc.:—also **Πισάτης**, ου, ὁ, Pi.*O.*9.68; fem. **Πισᾶτις**, ιδος, ἐλαία ib.4.13; ἡ Πισᾶτις (sc. γῆ) Str.8.3.1; also ἡ Πισαία Paus.5.1.6, etc. II. *Pisa* in Etruria, Plb.2.16.2, etc.: elsewh. in pl. Πίσαι, αἱ, Id.2.27.1, etc. [Πῖσα in Pi., in other Poets Πῑσα.]

**πισάκιον**· περιστόμιον, Hsch.

⊛ **πισγίς**, ίδος, ἡ, dub. sens. in *IG*11(2).287*B*50,54 (Delos, iii B.C.).

**πισεύς**, έως, ὁ, *dweller in meadows*, Theoc.25.201.

**πίσῐνος** [πῐ], η, ον, (πίσος) *made of peas*, ἔτνος *pea*-soup, Ar.*Eq.* 1171, Antiph.183.7, Dieuch.ap.Orib.4.8.14, Ael.*Ep.*4.

**πίσιρα**· πίτυρα (Achaean), and **πισιρῖται**· πιτύρινοι ἄρτοι, Hsch.

**πισμός**, ὁ, (πιπίσκω) = ποτισμός, Hsch. **πίσορ**, Lacon. for πίθος, Id.

**πίσος** [ῐ], ὁ, *pease*, *Pisum sativum*, Ar.*Fr.*22, Eup.301, Thphr. *HP*8.1.4, Phan.Hist.31, *PTeb.*9.11 (ii B.C.), etc.:—also **πίσον** [ῐ], τό, Alex.327. [On the accent v. Hdn.Gr.1.205; πισός freq. in codd.]

**πῖσος**, εος, τό, old Ep. Noun, only in pl., *meadows*, πίσεα ποιήεντα Il.20.9, cf. Call.*Fr.anon.*57, A.R.1.1266.

**πίσσᾰ**, Att. **πίττᾰ**, ἡ, *pitch*, Il.4.277, Hdt.4.195, Call.*Hec.*1.4.4, etc.: gen. pl. written πισᾶν *IG*4²(1).102.278 (Epid., iv B.C.); but sg. πίσσας ib.238,240: distd. as π. ὠμή and ἑψηθεῖσα, Thphr.*HP*3.9.2, cf. Plb.5.89.6, Hp.*Mul.*1.37; π. ὑγρά raw *pitch*, Dsc.1.72.1, *PLond.* 3.1171.11; opp. ξηρά, Dsc.1.72.5, *PLond.*3.929.66, *SIG*1171.14 (Lebena), cf. παλίμπισσα; ὀρὸς πίσσης, = πίσσανθος, Hp.*Ulc.*12: prov., μελάντερον ἠΰτε πίσσα Il. l. c.; ἄρτι μῦς πίττης γεύεται, i.e. he has got the first taste of misery, D.50.26, cf. Theoc.14.51; πέπονθα.. ὅσσα κῆμ πίσσῃ μῦς Herod.2.62. II. *resin*, used for treating wine-jars, *PCair.Zen.*481 (iii B.C.). (Cf. Lat. *pix*.)

**πισσ-ᾰλῐφής**, ές, *tarred, pitched*, Eust.1561.9. **-αλοιφέω**, *smear with pitch*, Aen.Tact.11.3. **-ανθος**, εος, τό, *the oily fluid that rises to the surface when the raw pitch is left to stand*, Gal.11.520. **-άριον**, τό, *a little pitch*, Archig.ap.Gal.12.978. **-άσφαλτος**, Att. πιττ-, ἡ, *compound of asphalt and pitch*, Dsc.1.73, Plin.*HN*24.41, etc. **-έλαιον**, τό, = πίσσανθος, Dsc.1.72; also, *mixture of oil and pitch*, *Hippiatr.*20, al. **-ήεις**, εσσα, εν, *of pitch, pitchy*, Nic.*Th.*717, Man.4.346. **-ήρης**, ες, = foreg., κηκίς A.*Ch.*268. 2. = πισσοκώνητος, Orac.ap.Ath.12.524b. **-ηρός**, ά (Ion. ή), όν, = πισσήεις, ἡ π. (sc. κηρωτή) *pitch ointment*, Hp.*Fract.*24, cf. Gal.18(2). 365. **-ησις**, Dor. **-ᾱσις**, εως, ἡ, = πίσσωσις, *IG*4²(1).102.238,245 (Epid., iv B.C.). **-ίζω**, *taste of pitch*, οἶνος πισσίζων Sch.Ar.*Ach.*189; f.l. for ἰΐζω in Dsc.5.75. **-ῐνος**, Att. πίττινος, η, ον, *of* or *from pitch, pitched*, κάδος π. Ar.*Fr.*269, *IG*2².1648.27 (pl.); *like pitch*, δρόσος Luc. *VH*2.29. **-ιος**, α, ον, v. ἐργατήσιος. **-ίτης** [ῑ], ου, ὁ, *flavoured with pitch*, οἶνος Str.4.6.2, Dsc.5.38, Plu.2.676c.

**πισσο-ειδής**, ές, *like pitch, pitchy-looking*, κηκίς Thphr.*HP*3. 5.2. **-κάμῑνος** [ᾰ], ὁ, *furnace for extracting pitch*, *PMasp.*110.38 (vi A.D.). **-καπνος**, ὁ, *soot obtained by burning pitch, lampblack*, *Hippiatr.*34. **-καυτέω**, *extract pitch by burning*, π. τὴν τέρμινθον Thphr.*HP*9.2.2 (Pass.). **-κηρος**, ὁ, a kind of *propolis*, with which bees line their hives, Arist.*HA*624ᵃ17, Plin.*HN*11.16. **-κοπέω**, Att. πιττο-, (κόπτω) *smear with pitch*, τὰς ὀροφάς *IG*2².1672.179:—more freq. in Pass., πιττοκοπηθέντα [ξύλα] Thphr.*HP*5.4.5, cf. *PLond.* 5.1654.4 (iv A.D.). II. *have the hair removed by pitch-plasters*, πιττοκοπούμενος ἢ ξυρούμενος Alex.264.1; κίναιδοι πεπιττοκοπημένοι *Com.Adesp.*339; ὁ -κοπούμενος, title of play by Philemon:—hence Subst. **-κοπία**, Ion. **-ίη**, ἡ, Aret.*CD*1.2, *POxy.*1911.187 (vi A.D.): Adj. **-κοπικός**, ή, όν, and **-κόπος**, ον, Poll.7.165. **-κώνητος**, ον, (κωνάω II) *daubed with pitch*: π. πῦρ fire *blazing with pitch*, A.*Fr.*118; π. μόρος the death *of one who is pitched and burnt alive*, Hsch. s. v. κωνῆσαι. **-κωνία**, ἡ, *tarring* of sheep, ibid. **-κωνίας Ἄρης**, = πισσοκώνητος μόρος, Cratin.364. **-τρόφος**, ον, *yielding pitch*, φυτά Plu.2.648d.

**πισσουργ-εῖα**, τά, *pitch-works*, Str.5.1.12. **-έομαι**, Pass., *to be made into pitch*, D.H.20.15. **-ία**, ἡ, *making of pitch*, Poll.7. 101. **-ός**, ὁ, *maker of pitch*, ibid.

**πισσόχριστος**, ον, *smeared with pitch*, νῆες Hsch. s. v. μέλαιναι νῆες.

⊛ **πισσ-όω**, Att. πιττ-, (πίσσα) *pitch over*, *pitch*, τὰς ὀροφάς *IG*2².1659. 25; τὰς ναῦς Sch.Ar.*Pl.*1093:—Pass., Chrysipp.*Stoic.*2.110, Dsc.5. 12,31; of bronze statues, in order to take casts of them, Luc.*JTr.* 33; in order to clean them, Id.*Lex.*11. II. Med., *remove the hair by means of a pitch-plaster*, οἱ βάρβαροι πιττοῦνται τὰ σώματα Theopomp. Hist.195, cf. Luc.*Rh.Pr.*23; πιττούμενος τὰ σκέλη Id.*Demon.*50, cf. *Merc.Cond.*33. **-υγγος**, ὁ, = πίσυγγος (q. v.), *PMasp.*141 vᵛ9 (vi A.D.). **-ώδης**, Att. πιττ-, ες, *like pitch*, χρῶμα Arist.*HA*587ᵃ 32; *thick as pitch*, Thphr.*HP*3.1.6; ὑγρότης ib.1.12.2: Sup., ib.9.2. 2. **-ωσις**, Att. πίττ-, εως, ἡ, *a pitching over*, *PCair.Zen.*271.9 (iii B.C.), Gal.6.443, Archig.ap.Aët.3.180. **-ωτέον**, *one must pitch*, *Gp.*6.3.8. **-ωτής**, οῦ, ὁ, *one who pitches*, Luc.*Fug.*33, Gal.10.501. **-ωτός**, Att. πιττ-, ή, όν, *pitched*, Id.11.106, 18(2). 894.

**πιστ-άκη** [ᾰ], ἡ, *pistachio-tree*, *Pistacia vera*, Alciphr.1.22. ⊛ **-άκιον** [ᾰ], τό, *pistachio-nut*, Nic.*Th.*891, Dsc.1.124, *Gp.*10.3.3: written **βιστάκιον**, Posidon.3 J.; **φιττάκια**, v.l. in Nic. l. c. (ap.Ath.14.649e); also **ψιττάκια** ib.c, and in *Gp.*10.12.1).

**πίστ-ευμα**, ατος, τό, = πίστωμα, A.*Ag.*878 (pl.). **-ευσις**, εως, ἡ, *confiding, entrusting*, ἐντολῶν J.*AJ*17.3.3 (pl.). **-ευτέον**, *one must trust*, Pl.*Ti.*20b, 40e, Arist.*GA*760ᵇ31, Str.15.1.34. II. *one must believe*, Plb.12.11.3, Str.1.3.1; τῷ θρυλουμένῳ Longin.44.2; εἰ τοῦτο π. κατ' ἐκεῖνον Aristid.*Or.*20(21).9: in pl. **-ευτέα**, οὐκέτι π. τῶν νῦν οὐδενί Luc.*Tim.*48. **-ευτικός**, ή, όν, *disposed to trust, confiding*, Arist.*Rh.*1372ᵇ29; τὸ -κόν M.Ant.1.14. Adv. **-κῶς**, ἔχειν τινί *rely upon*.., Pl.*Hp.Mi.*364a, cf. Iamb.*VP*28.138. II. *creating belief*, πειθὼ π. Pl.*Grg.*455a, cf. Aristid.2.47 J. **-ευτός**, ή, όν, *trustworthy*, Iamb.*Comm.Math.*8. **-εύω**, fut. -εύσω: plpf. πεπιστεύκειν *Act. Ap.*14.23: (πίστις):—*trust, put faith in, rely on* a person, thing, or statement, τινι Hdt.1.24; τῷ λόγῳ Id.2.118, cf. S.*El.*886, etc.; π. θεῶν θεσφάτοισι A.*Pers.*800; τῇ τύχῃ Th.5.112; σφίσιν αὐτοῖς Id.3.5; ταῖς ἀληθείαις D.44.3; [σημείοις] Antipho 5.81; π. τινὶ περί τινος Arist. *EN*1157ᵃ21; ὑπὲρ τῶν ὅλων Plb.2.43.2: with neut. Adj. or Pron., λόγοις ἐμοῖσι πίστευσον τάδε *believe* my words herein, E.*Hel.*710; τοῦτ'.. Αἰγυπτίοις πιστεῦσαι δεῖ Arist.*Mete.*343ᵇ10; μὴ πάντα πειρῶ πᾶσι πιστεύειν Men.*Mon.*335: later with Preps., π. ἐν τῷ Θεῷ, ἐν τῷ εὐαγγελίῳ, Lxx*Ps.*77(78).22, *Ev.Marc.*1.15; π. εἰς τὸν Θεόν *Ev.Jo.*14.1, al.; εἰς τὸ ὄνομά τινος ib.1.12; π. ἐπὶ τὸν Κύριον *Act.Ap.*9.42: abs., *believe*, περὶ μὲν τούτου.. οὔτε ἀπιστέω οὔτε ὦν π. τι λίην Hdt.4.96; χαλεπὰ παντὶ ἑξῆς τεκμηρίῳ πιστεῦσαι although it is hard *to believe* every single bit of evidence about them, Th.1.20: c. acc. cogn., π. δόξαν *entertain a confident* opinion, Id.5.105:—Pass., *to be trusted* or *believed*, ἄνδρες ἄξιοι πιστεύεσθαι Pl.*La.*181b, cf. *Ep.*309a, X.*Cyr.*4.2.8; πιστευθῆναι ὑπό τινος *enjoy* his *confidence*, ib.6.1.39, cf. *An.*7.6.33; π. παρά τινι D.23.4, 58.44; πρός τινας Id.20.25; ὡς πιστευθησόμενος as if *he would be believed*, Id.27.54, cf. 36.43; π. ὡς δημοτικὸς ὤν Arist.*Pol.* 1305ᵃ28; πιστεύονται [οἱ λόγοι] Id.*EN*1172ᵇ6; ἐπιστεύοντο ἃ ἔλεγον they *were believed* in what they said, D.32.4; πρόγνωσιν ἐπεπίστευντο *were believed to possess* foreknowledge, J.*AJ*17.2.4. 2. *comply*, ὡς οὐχ ὑπείξων οὐδὲ πιστεύσων λέγεις; S.*OT*625, cf. 646; opp. ἀπιστέω, Id.*Tr.*1228. 3. c. inf., *believe that*, *feel confident that* a thing is, will be, has been, E.*HF*146; ἀληθῆ εἶναι Pl.*Grg.*524a, cf. *R.* 450d; ὃς ἂν γνώμῃ πιστεύῃ τῶν ἐναντίων προὔχειν Th.2.62; προέσθαι τὴν προῖκ' οὐκ ἐπίστευσεν D.30.7; π. ὡς.., ὅτι.., X.*Hier.*1.37, Arist. *Ph.*254ᵃ3, al.: the inf. is sts. omitted, τὰ μὲν οὐ πιστεύουσιν οἱ νέοι (sc. εἶναι or γεγονέναι) Id.*EN*1142ᵃ19, cf. *APr.*68ᵇ13, *GA*716ᵃ7:— Pass., παρὰ Διὸς.. οἱ νόμοι πεπιστευμένοι ἦσαν γεγονέναι Pl.*Lg.*636d; πιστευθεὶς ἀληθεύσειν *believed sure to*.., X.*An.*7.7.25; ὁ ἥλιος.. πεπίστευται εἶναι μείζων τῆς οἰκουμένης Arist. *de An.*428ᵇ4; πρῶτοι νόμοις ἐγγράπτοις χρήσασθαι πεπιστευμένοι Str.6.1.8: without inf., πιστευθείσης εἱμαρμένης αἴρεται πᾶσα νουθεσία Diog.Oen.33, cf. 23. 4. c. dat. et inf., τοῖσι ἐπίστευε σιγᾶν to whom *he trusted* that they would keep silence, Hdt.8.110, cf. X.*Cyr.*3.3.55, Lys.19.54. 5. *have faith*, *Act.Ap.*2.44, 19.18, etc. II. π. τινί τι *entrust* something to another, τινὶ ἡγεμονίαν, χρήματα, X.*Mem.*4.4.17, *Smp.*8.36; τὰν ὠνὰν τῷ θεῷ *GDI*1684, al. (Delph.); γυναικὶ μὴ πίστευε τὸν.. βίον Men.*Mon.*86; also περὶ τῶν ἐμῶν τούτῳ ἀξιῶ πιστεύειν ὑμᾶς Lys.30. 7:—Med., *have entrusted to one*, ἀρχήν *Berichte der russ. Akad. für Gesch. der materiellen Kultur* 4.82 (Olbia, ii/iii A.D.):—Pass., πιστεύεσθαί τι *to be entrusted with* a thing, *have* it *committed* to one, παρά or ὑπό τινος, Plb.3.69.1, Phylarch.24 J., cf. Vett.Val.65.3: c. inf., πιστευθέντας τοῖς ἐχθροῖς διαφθείρειν Arist.*Pol.*1287ᵃ39 (nisi leg. πεισθέντας): c. gen., πιστευθεὶς τῆς Κύπρου Plb.18.55.6, cf. 6.56.13, D.S.12.15, etc.

**πιστήρ**, ῆρος, ὁ, (πιπίσκω) = ποτίστρα, Hsch. s. v. πισμός.

**πιστήριον**, τό, = ποτιστήριον, Hsch., Phot.

**πιστῐ-επαγγελτής**, *fidei promissor*, *Gloss.* (pl., prob.). **-κελευστής**, οῦ, ὁ, = Lat. *fidejussor*, *PLips.*4.6, 5 ii 2 (iii A.D.).

⊛ **πιστικός** (A), ή, όν, (πίνω) *liquid*, νάρδος *Ev.Marc.*14.3, *Ev.Jo.*12.3.

⊛ **πιστικός** (B), ή, όν, (πίστις) *faithful*, Vett.Val.10.14, *Cat.Cod. Astr.*8(4).169; γυνὴ π. καὶ οἰκουρός Artem.2.32. Adv. -κῶς, ἔχειν πρὸς ἀλλήλους Plu.*Pel.*8: Sup. -ώτατα Hld.3.9. 2. late spelling of πειστικός (q. v.).

⊛ **πίστιον**, τό, *certified copy*, ἐπιγραφῆς *TAM*2.338 (pl., Xanthus).

**Πίστιος** Ζεύς, ὁ, = Lat. *Juppiter Fidius*, D.H.4.58, al.

⊛ **πίστις**, ἡ, gen. εως, Ion. ιος Parm.8.12, Emp.114; dat. πίστει, Ion. πίστι Hdt.3.74, 9.106: Ion. nom. and acc. pl. πίστις v.l. in Id.3.8; dat. πίστισι Id.4.172: (πείθομαι):—*trust* in others, *faith*, first in Hes., πίστιες καὶ ἀπιστίαι ὤλεσαν ἄνδρας *Op.*372; πίστει χρήματ' ὄλεσσα, ἀπιστίῃ δ' ἐσάωσα Thgn.831; π. ἴσχειν τινί S.*OC*950; τῷ θεῷ πίστιν φέροις Id.*OT*1445, etc.: generally, *persuasion* of a thing, *confidence*, *assurance*, Pi.*N.*8.44 (πιστόν Sch.), etc.; ἡ βεβαιοτάτη π., ἀταραξία καὶ π. βέβαιος, Epicur.*Ep.*1 p.19, 2 p.36 U.; σωφροσύνης π. ἔχειν περί τινος to be *persuaded* of his probity, D.18.215; π. περὶ θεῶν ἔχειν Plu.2. 1101c. 2. in subjective sense, *good faith*, *trustworthiness*, *honesty*, Thgn.1137, A.*Pers.*443, Hdt.8.105; θνῄσκει δὲ π., βλαστάνει δ' ἀπιστία S.*OC*611. b. of things, *credence*, *credit*, τὰν π. σμικρὰν παρ' ἔμοιγ' ἔχει E.*El.*737 (lyr.); πίστιν τὰ τοιαῦτα ἔχει τινά Arist.*EN*1179ᵃ17; π. λαβεῖν Plb.1.35.4. c. καλῇ π., = Lat. *bona fide*, *PGnom.*180 (ii A.D.), etc.; αἱ κατὰ πίστιν γεινόμεναι κληρονομίαι, = Lat. *hereditates fideicommissariae*, ib.56. 3. in a commercial sense, *credit*, π. τοσούτων χρημάτων ἐστί τινι παρά τισι he has *credit* for so much money with them, D.36.57, cf. 44; εἰς πίστιν διδόναι [τί τινι] Id.32.16; εἰ ἔξω ἐλπίδα πίστεως Astramps.*Orac.*68 p.6 H. b. *position of trust* or *trusteeship*, ἐν πίστει κληρονόμος ἀπολειφθείς left *in trust*, as guardian, Plu.*Cic.*41, cf. 2c supr.; ἐν πίστει ὢν τῷ βασιλεῖ *IG*2².646.11. 4. Theol., *faith*, opp. sight and knowledge, 1*Ep.Cor.*13.13, etc. II. *that which gives confidence*: hence, 1. *assurance*, *pledge of good faith*, *guarantee*, οὐκ ἀνδρὸς ὅρκοι π. ἀλλ' ὅρκων ἀνήρ A.*Fr.*394, cf. S.*El.*887, E.*Hipp.* 1055; ὅρκοις καὶ πίστεσιν ἀναγκάζειν Antipho 6.25: distd. from ὅρκοι and δεξιαί, Arist.*Rh.*1375ᵃ10, cf. E.*Med.*22; ἔμβαλλε χειρὸς πίστιν S. *Ph.*813; δός μοι χερὸς σῆς π. Id.*OC*1632; ὅρκους παρασχών, πίστιν οὐ σμικράν, θεῶν E.*Hipp.*1037, cf. *Med.*414 (lyr.); πίστιν καὶ ὅρκια ποιέεσθαι make a treaty by exchange of *assurances* and oaths, Hdt.9.92, cf. And.1.107; οἷσιν.. οὔτε π. οὔθ' ὅρκος μένει Ar.*Ach.*308; ποιέεσθαι τὰς πίστῑς (Ion. for πίστεις) Hdt.3.8; πίστεις ποιήσασθαι πρός τινας Th.4.51; ἀλλήλοις X.*HG*1.3.12; πίστιν δοῦναι to give *assurances*, Hdt.9.91, cf. Th.4.86, 5.45; ὅρκους καὶ πίστιν ἀλλήλοις δότε Ar.*Lys.* 1185; ἔδοσαν πίστιν καὶ ἔλαβον interchanged *them*, X.*Cyr.*7.1.44; πίστεις ἀλλήλοιν δεδωκέναι τε καὶ δεδέχθαι Pl.*Phdr.*256d; π. παρά τινος λαβεῖν Lys.12.9; π. πρός τινας δοῦναι c. inf., Id.19.32; πίστι τε λαβεῖν (or καταλαβεῖν) καὶ ὁρκίοισί τινα bind by *assurances* and oaths, Hdt.3.74, 9.106; θεῶν πίστεις ὀμόσαι Th.5.30; πίστιν ἐπιθεῖναι or προσθεῖναι, D.29.26, 49.42, 54.42: c. gen. objecti, φόβων π. *an assurance against*.., E.*Supp.*627 (lyr.). 2. *means of persuasion*, *argument*, *proof*, φρὴν παρ' ἡμέων (sc. τῶν αἰσθήσεων) λαβοῦσα τὰς πίστεις Democr.125; τοὺς δεομένους πίστεως αἰσθήσει κεκραμένης Plot. 4.7.15; esp. of proofs used by orators, Antipho 5.84, 6.28, Pl.*Phd.* 70b, Isoc.3.8, etc.: in Arist., opp. a demonstrative proof (ἀπόδειξις), π. ἔντεχνοι, ἄτεχνοι, *Rh.*1355ᵇ35, 1375ᵃ22: also, generally, π. ἐκ τῆς ἐπαγωγῆς *APo.*90ᵇ14, al.; π. ἡ διὰ συλλογισμοῦ *Top.*103ᵇ7; ἡ τῶν λόγων π. (cf. λόγος IV. 1) *Pol.*1326ᵃ29; ὁ ἀναιρῶν ταύτην τὴν π. οὐ πολὺ πιστότερα ἐρεῖ *EN*1173ᵃ1. III. *that which is entrusted*, *a trust*, πίστιν ἐγχειρίζειν τινί Plb.5.41.2, cf. 16.22.2, *IG*7.21.12 (Megara, ii B.C.), 5(1).26.6 (Amyclae, ii/i B.C.), *BMus.Inscr.* 422.7 (Priene, ii B.C.); σῇ π. *given in trust* to thee, *IG*14.2012*A* 23 (Sulp.Max.). IV. political *protection* or *suzerainty*, Lat. *fides*, Αἰτωλοὶ.. δόντες αὑτοὺς εἰς τὴν Ῥωμαίων π... τῷ τῆς π. ὀνόματι πλανηθέντες Plb.20.9.10, cf. 3. 30.1; πάντες εἰς τὴν [τῆς συγκλήτου] π. ἐνδεδεμένοι Id.6.17.8. 2. in Egypt, *safe-conduct*, *safeguard*, *UPZ*119.32 (pl., ii B.C.); δοῦναί μοι ἔγγραπτον π. ib.124.30 (ii B.C.). V. Pythag. name for *ten*, *Theol.Ar.*59, 60. VI. personified, = Lat. *Fides*, Plu.*Num.*16, App. *BC*1.16, D.C.45.17; π. δημοσία, = *Fides publica*, D.H.2.75.

**πιστο-ΐασπις**, ιδος, ἡ, *true jewel*, metaph. of Isis, *POxy.*1380.138 (ii A.D.). **-λογευτής**, οῦ, ὁ, *confidential agent for collection* of dues, *PCair.Zen.*199.7 (iii B.C.).

**πιστόν**, τό, v. πιστός (B) III.

⊛ **πιστοποιέω**, *accredit*, *confirm*, Lxx 4*Ma.*7.9:—Med., ib.18.17.

⊛ **πιστός** (A), ή, όν, (πιπίσκω) = ποτός, *liquid*; πιστὰ *liquid medicines*, *draughts*, A.*Pr.*480.

⊛ **πιστός** (B), ή, όν, (πείθω): A. Pass., *to be trusted* or *believed*: I. of persons, *faithful*, *trusty*, ἑταῖρος Il.15.331, etc.; φύλακες Hes.*Th.* 735; μάρτυρες Pi.*P.*1.88; Ζηνὶ π. ἄγγελος A.*Pr.*969, etc.: Comp. -ότερος Th.5.108, Isoc.10.38: Sup. πιστότατος Ar.*Pl.*27: c. dat., -ότατος δέ οἱ ἔσκε Il.16.147; ὁ π. ἡμῖν κἀγαθὸς καλούμενος S.*Tr.*541, cf. E.*IA*153 (anap.), etc.: c. gen., τοῦ Φαλάνθου πιστόν τινα a *trusted friend* of P., Ergias ap.Ath.8.360f; π. πρὸς τὰ συμβόλαια Arist.*Pol.* 1283ᵃ33; οἱ πιστοί, in Persia, *trusty councillors*, X.*An.*1.5.15, cf. Hdt. 1.108 (Sup.); τάδε Περσῶν πιστὰ καλεῖται A.*Pers.*2 (anap.); so πιστὰ πιστῶν, = πιστότατοι, ib.681, cf. 528, 979. 2. *trustworthy*, *worthy of credit*, Antipho 3.3.5 (Comp.), 5.3, Th.3.43. Adv., -τῶς καὶ ἀδόλως *IG*1².90.14, 17. 3. *genuine*, π. Ἀταλάντης γόνος S.*OC*1322; Θηρικλέους π. τέκνον, of a cup, Theopomp.Com.32.1; *unmistakable*, νόσοι πονηραὶ καὶ π. Lxx *De.*28.59. II. of things, *trustworthy*, *sure*, ὅρκια π. Il.3.269, cf. Pi.*O.*11(10).6, etc.; τέκμαρ τῶνδε, τεκμήρια, μαντεῖα, A. *Ag.*272, 352, *Th.*66; τοῖσι Ἕλλησι ὡς πιστὰ δὴ τὰ λεγόμενα ἦν Hdt.8.83; ἔσται πιστὰ καὶ ἄδολα καὶ ἁπλᾶ ἅπαντα τὰ ἀπ' Ἀθηναίων Ῥηγίνοις *IG*1². 51.11; οὐκέτι πιστὰ γυναιξίν no longer *can one trust* women, Od.11. 456; βροτῶν δὲ π. οὐδέν S.*Fr.*667.3; οὐκ ἔχοντες τὴν ἐλπίδα.. πιστὴν ἔτι no longer having such hope *as could be relied on*, Th.5.14; ὑπόληψις ἡ πιστοτάτη, of knowledge, Arist.*Top.*131ᵃ23. 2. *deserving belief*, *credible*, π. καὶ οἰκότα Hdt.6.82, cf. 8.80; π. ὑπόθεσις Pl.*Phd.* 107b; τοῦτο π. ἐκ τῆς ἐπαγωγῆς Arist.*Cael.*276ᵃ14; πιθανὸν καὶ π. Id. *Rh.*1356ᵇ28; [λόγος] ἀποδεικτικὸς καὶ π. ib.1377ᵇ23. III. πιστόν, τό, as Subst., *pledge*, *security*, *warrant*, τὸ π. τῆς ἀληθείας S.*Tr.*398, etc.; τὸ π. τῆς ἐπιστήμης Th.6.72 (but τὸ π. τῆς καθ' ὑμᾶς πολιτείας its *honesty*, Id.1.68); τὸ π. ἔχοντες.. κἂν περιγενέσθαι feeling *confidence* that.., Id.1.141: freq. in pl., τὰ πιστὰ ποιέεσθαι, = πίστιν ποιεῖσθαι, Hdt.3.8; πιστὰ θεῶν, of oaths, X.*Cyr.*4.2.7; ἐδώκαμεν καὶ ἐλάβομεν πιστά we gave and received *pledges*, c. fut. inf., Id.*An.*3.2.5, cf. 4.8.7, etc.; πιστὰ ἠξίου γενέσθαι Id.*Cyr.*7.4.3; τὰ πίστ' ἐδειξάτην A.*Ag.*651; στέργειν τὰ π. τῶνδε Id.*Eu.*673; τὰ π. ἐμαυτῷ τοῦ θράσους παρέξομαι E.*Ph.* 268.

B. Act., *believing*, *relying on*, τινι Thgn.283, A.*Pr.*917, *Pers.*55 (anap.), S.*OC*1031; *trustful*, τῆς ἐλευθερίας τὸ π. Th.2.40, cf. Pl.*Lg.* 824; τινὶ τὸ π. νέμειν App.*BC*3.39. 2. *obedient*, *loyal*, τὴν τῶν Ἀθηναίων χώραν οἰκείαν καὶ π. ποιήσασθαι X.*HG*2.4.30. 3. *faithful*, *believing*, *Act.Ap.*16.1, *IG*3.3435.

C. Adv. πιστῶς *with good faith*, μὴ π. καταμαρτυρηθείς Antipho 2.4.7; *loyally*, D.3.26: Comp. -οτέρως Aen.Tact.22.17. 2. *persuasively*, in Comp., πιστότερον ἢ ἀληθέστερον Antipho 3.3.4; *credibly*, *demonstrably*, Pl.*Epin.*983e; *unmistakably*, κριθῆναι Gal.9. 857. 3. *with disposition to believe*, D.34.49: Comp., πιστότερον πρὸς ἐκείνους ἢ πρὸς ὑμᾶς αὐτοὺς διακείμενοι Lys.18.15.

**πιστόσυνος**, etym. of πίσυνος, *EM*673.30.

**πιστότης**, ητος, ἡ, *good faith*, *honesty*, Hdt.7.52, Pl.*Lg.*630c, etc. 2. πιστότητος ὑμῶν ἕνεκα in order to produce *conviction* in you, And.1.25.

**πιστό-φρων**, ονος, ὁ, ἡ, *true-minded*, Man.4.580. **-φύλαξ** [ῠ], ἄκος, ὁ, ἡ, *guardian of truth*, Orph.*H.*8.17.

⊛ **πιστόω**, *make trustworthy*, πιστοῦν τινα ὅρκοις *bind* him by oaths, Th.4.88. II. Pass., *to be made trustworthy*, *give a pledge* or *warrant*, πιστωθείς *h.Merc.*536; ἐπεὶ δ' ἐπιστώθησαν E.*IA*66; μοι.. ὅρκῳ πιστωθῆναι ἀπήμονά μ' οἴκαδ' ἀπάξειν *bind yourselves* to me by oath.., Od.15.436. 2. *feel trust* or *confidence*, *to be persuaded*, ὄφρα.. πιστωθῆτον ἐνὶ θυμῷ 21.218; πιστωθεὶς ὅτι.. *feeling confidence* that.., S.*OC*1039. III. Med., *give mutual pledges of fidelity*, *exchange troth*, χεῖράς τ' ἀλλήλων λαβέτην καὶ πιστώσαντο Il.6.233; ἐπιστώσαντ' ἐπέεσσιν 21.286; π. περὶ τῶν ὅλων πρὸς ἀλλήλους Plb.18.39.6. 2. πιστοῦσθαί τινα ὑφ' ὅρκου *secure* his *good faith* by oaths, S.*OC*650, cf. Plb.8.15.2. 3. *confirm*, *prove*, τῷ παρόντι τοὐπιόν E.*Fr.*1073.6, cf. Phlp. *in GA* 206.25; *guarantee*, τι Plb.1.43.5, Luc.*Philops.*5, Nonn.*D.*13.407; τι διότι.. Phld.*Rh.*1.122 S.; ἀπὸ τούτων ἕκαστα Polystr.*Herc.*346 p.84 V.; [τι] ταῖς Αἰσχύλου ἐλεγείαις Plu.2.628e; μάρτυρι τῷ Νέρωνι, ὅτι.. Id.*Galb.*5; ἔργοις τὰς ὑποσχέσεις Luc.*Hipp.* 1; πείρῃ τὸ πρῆγμα Aret.*CA*1.7; φιλοσοφίαν σώφρονι βίῳ Hdn.1.2.4;

ἐκ τῆς ἀποβάσεως τὴν φήμην Id.1.14.6, cf. Lib.*Or.*11.77; τίς ἂν τάδε πιστώσαιτο, . . ὅτι . . ; Opp.*C.*3.355: abs., Arist.*Fr.*133, Lxx 3*Ki.*1.36.

**πίστρα**, ἡ, (πιπίσκω) *drinking-trough* for cattle, E.*Cyc.*47 (lyr.), Str.8.3.31, cf. *EM*673.27:—also **πίστρον**, τό, E.*Cyc.*29 (pl.).

**πίστ-ωμα**, ατος, τό, *assurance, warrant, pledge*, mostly in pl., Emp. 5.2, A.*Ch.*977, *Eu.*214; π. περί τινος Arist.*Rh.*1376ᵃ17: in sg., φιλίας π. συγγενέσι Clearch.Com.1; τὸ βεβαιότατον π. ἔχοντες Epicur.*Sent.* 40. 2. *confirmation* of an argument, in pl., Phld.*Rh.*1.285 S., *Sign.*19. II. of persons, γηραλέα πιστώματα, = πιστοὶ γέροντες, A. *Pers.*171 (troch.). **-ωσις**, εως, ἡ, *assurance, confirmation*, μαρτύρων π. λόγων Pl.*Lg.*943c (pl.), cf. Hermog.*Meth.*10; ὅρκου π. D.C.38. 12. **-ωτέος**, α, ον, *to be affirmed as true*, λόγος Luc.*Hist.Conscr.* 60, cf. Plot.5.3.16. **-ωτής**, οῦ, ὁ, *confirmer*, Hsch. s.v. ἐμπαστῆρας. **-ωτικός**, ή, όν, *confirmatory*, Hermog.*Id.*2.9.

**πίσυγγος** [ῐ], ὁ, = πίσσυγγος (q.v.), *shoemaker*, Sapph.98 (v.l. πίσσυγοι), Alex.Aet.5.7, Herod.7.39 (prob.), *Com.Adesp.*330:—hence **πισύγγιον**, τό, *his shop*, ibid., Hdn.Gr.2.567. (Perh. cf. πεττύκια, πέσσυμπτον.)

**πίσῠνος** [ῐ], ον (not η, ον Eust.918.50), (πείθω) *trusting on, relying on*, always c. dat., π. Διί Il.9.238; τόξοισιν π. 5.205; ἠνορέῃ π. καὶ κάρτεϊ χειρῶν 11.9, cf. Hes.*Th.* 506 (Hom. and Hes. use only masc.); θεῷ, θεοῖσι, Pi.*P.*4.232, A.*Th.*212 (lyr.); ἰσχύϊ, ἐλπίδι, B.5.21, 12.221; ἀλκᾷ A.*Supp.*352 (lyr.); τοῖς περιδεξίοισι λόγοισι Ar.*Nu.*949; ὑμῖν Id. *V.*385; χρησμῷ, χρηστηρίῳ, Hdt.1.66,73, cf. 2.141: in Att. Prose only Th., τῇ δυνάμει τὸ πλέον π. ἢ τῇ γνώμῃ 2.89, cf. 5.14, 6.2: in later Prose, Plot.4.8.1, Jul.*Or.*2.57a. II. *obedient*, τινι Orph.*A.*265,707.

**πίσυρες**, v. τέσσαρες. **πίσω**, fut. of πιπίσκω.

**Πῐτάνη** [ᾰ], Dor. **-να**, ἡ, one of the κῶμαι of Sparta, Pi.*O.*6.28, Hdt.3.55, etc.: τοῦ Πιτανητέων λόχου, a battalion of the Spartan army, Id.9.53 codd. (leg. Πιτανήτεω); τὸν Πιτανήτην λ. ibid., Th.1. 20. II. a place in Aeolis, Alc.114.

**πιτεύω**, *irrigate*, *Schwyzer*485.7 (Thespiae, iii B.C.); cf. ἀπίτευτος.

**πίτνημι**, poet. form of πετάννυμι, *spread out*, ἠέρα πίτνα (Ep. impf.) Il.21.7; πιτνὰς εἰς ἐμὲ χεῖρας *stretching out* his arms to me, Od.11. 392; πίτναν τ' ἐς αἰθέρα χεῖρας (impf.) Pi.*N.*5.11; πίτνατε λεπταλέας στολίδας *AP*10.6 (Satyr.): metaph., *excite, flutter*, τὸ λεῖον φαλακρὸν ἡδονῇ πιτνάς S.*Ichn.*359:—Pass., ἀμφὶ δὲ χαῖται . . πίτναντο Il.22.402; θυμέλαι ἐπίτναντο χρυσήλατοι E.*El.*713 (lyr.); πίτνατο . . μαστὸς θαλάμων *AP*7.711 (Antip.):—also **πίτνω**, only ἔπιτνον ἀλωήν Hes.*Sc.* 291.

**πίτνω**, poet. form of πίπτω, Pi.*O.*2.23, *P.*8.93; Νίκας ἐν ἀγκώνεσσι πίτνων Id.*N.*5.42, cf. *I.*2.26, A.*Ch.*1056, *Ag.*1128 (lyr.), E.*Hec.*23, al.: impf. ἔπιτνον, poet. πίτνον, B.16.6, S.*OC*1732 (lyr.), etc.: πιτνῶ is given as pres. by Gramm., as Hdn.Gr.2.290, and πιτνεῖς is found in codd. of E.*Heracl.*77; but cf. Sch.Il.16.827; forms with -ου- from -εο- are not found (προσπιτνοῦμεν, v.l. in S.*OC*1754, is unmetrical).

**πίττα**, ἡ, Att. for πίσσα.

**Πιττάκειος** [ᾰ], α, ον, *of Pittacus*: τὸ Π. *the saying of P.*, Simon. 5.8.

**πιττᾰκιάρχης**, ου, ὁ, *president of a* πιττάκιον II, *BGU*634.2 (ii A.D.), etc.

**πιττᾰκ-ίδιον**, τό, Dim. of πιττάκιον, *PMag.Leid.V.*3.5. **-ίζω**, *attach a label to* a thing, [κωθώνιον] *PMag.Par.*1.2952.

**πιττάκιον** [ᾰ], τό, *tablet for writing on, label, ticket* (cf. Eust.633.19 sq.), Dinol.7; *written message*, γράψας βραχὺ π. Plb.31.13.9, cf. D.L. 6.89, *IG*14.830.18 (Puteoli), *POxy.*136.36 (vi A.D.), etc.; *ticket, pass*, *OGI*674.21 (Egypt, i A.D.); *receipt*, *PStrassb.*44.3 (ii A.D.); *votive tablet*, *CIG*3442 (Philadelphia); *promissory note*, *BGU*1155.15 (i B.C.), etc.; *account-book*, *POxy.*297.4 (pl., i A.D.), *PGoodsp.Cair.* 30iv5 (ii A.D.), etc. II. *list* of members of an association, hence of the association itself, *PTeb.*112 *Intr.* (ii B.C.), etc.; cf. πιττακιάρχης. III. Lat. *pittacium, strip of leather*, Cels.3.10.

**πίτταξις**, εως, ἡ, *fruit of the* κράνεια, Sch.Od.10.242, Eust.1657. 19.

**πιττεύω**, indistinct pronunciation of πιστεύω, ἡ ψελλὴ "οὐ πιττεύω" *App.Prov.*3.17.

**πίττῐνος, πιττόω, πίττωσις, πιττωτός**, Att. for πίσσινος, etc.

**πιτύα** [ῠ], ἡ, v. πυτία.

**πιτυδάνη**· ἀσκὸς μικρός, Hsch.

**πιτύδιον**, τό, Dim. of πίτυς, Theognost.*Can.*125; Lat. *pitydia*, Plin.*HN*15.36.

**πιτύ-ῐνος** [ῠ], η, ον, *of* or *from the pine*, ῥητίνη π. *pine*-resin, Hp. *Mul.*2.203, Thphr.*HP*9.2.2; so πιτυίνη alone, Orib.*Fr.*89, Paul.Aeg. 7.17; π. στέφανος Plu.2.677b; π. φύσημα Gal.13.475. **-ΐς**, ίδος, ἡ, *pine-seed*, Herod.Med. in *Rh.Mus.*58.97, Dsc.1.69, cf. Gal.12.102 (of the stone pine only). II. *pine-resin*, Id.19.131.

**πιτῠκάμπτης**, v. πιτυοκάμπτης.

**πῐτῠλ-εύω**, (πίτυλος) *ply the sweeping oar*, Ar.*V.*678. 2. = sq. 1, *Com.Adesp.*3 D. **-ίζω**, *practise regular swinging of the arms*, as with dumb-bells, Gal.6.133,144. 2. *dart about*, ἰχθύων γένεσιν ἐν κολύμβοις -ίζουσαν Anon.ap.Suid. **-ος**, ὁ, *sweep* of oars, νεὼς π. εὐήρης, periphr. for *a ship and its oars*, E.*IT*1050, cf. 1346, *Tr.* 1123: pl., Hp.ap.Gal.19.131; ναῦς ὅταν ἐκ πιτύλων ῥοθιάζῃ Ar.*Fr.*84: metaph., ἑνὶ π. with one *sweep*, all together, A.*Pers.*976 (lyr.). 2. *shower, torrent*, δακρύων E.*Hipp.*1464 (anap.); of blows, Theoc.22. 127, cf. Poll.2.147; ἄρασσε κρᾶτα πιτύλους διδοῦσα χειρὸς E.*Tr.*1236 (lyr.). 3. *onslaught*, π. Ἀργείου δορὸς Id.*Heracl.*834, cf. *Fr.*495. 11; δὶς δὲ δυοῖν πιτύλοιν τείχη . . κατέλυσεν αἰχμά Id.*Tr.*817 (lyr.); with allusion to signf. 1, ἐρέσσετ' ἀμφὶ κρατὶ πόμπιμον χεροῖν π. A.*Th.* 856 (lyr.). b. *attack, fit*, μανίας E.*IT*307; ἆρ' ἐς τὸν αὐτὸν π. ἥκομεν φόβου; are we victims of the same *attack* of fear, i.e. are we seeing the same phantasms? Id.*HF*816; μαινομένῳ π. πλαγχθεὶς ib.1189 (lyr.); π. σκύφου the mad *fit* of the wine-cup, Id.*Alc.*798: as Adj., *mad*, Phld.*Rh.*1.251 S. (s. v.l.).

**πιτύνη, πίτυνος**, v. πυτίνη, πύτινος.

**πῐτῠό-εις**, εσσα, εν, *abounding in pine-trees*:—only as pr. n. **Πιτυοῦς**, οῦντος, ὁ, a town on the NE. coast of the Euxine, Str.11.2.14; **Πιτυοῦσσαι**, αἱ, two islands off the coast of Spain, *Ebusus* (*Iviza*) and *Ophiussa* (*Formentera*), Id.3.5.1. II. **πῐτῠοῦσσα**, ἡ, *quacksalver's spurge, Euphorbia Pityusa*, Dsc.4.165, Plin.*HN*24.31, Ruf.ap.Orib. 7.26.37. **-κάμπη**, ἡ, *a stinging* or *urticating caterpillar of the pine-woods*, prob. the *processional caterpillar*, Dsc.1.45, Zopyr.ap.Orib.14. 58.2, Gal.11.756:—also written **-κάμπτης**, Hsch. s.v. ἀεροκέλαδοι (pl.). II. *small pine-cone*, Sch.Il.2.868. **-κάμπτης**, ου, ὁ, *pine-bender*, epith. of Sinis, who killed travellers by tying them between two pine-trees bent down so as nearly to meet, and then let go again, Str.9.1.4, Apollod.3.16.2, Plu.*Thes.*8:—also written **πῐτῠκάμπτης**, prob. for παλικάμπῃ in *AP*11.107 (Lucill.). **-τρόφος**, ον, *growing pines*, Φρυγίη *APl.*1.8 (Alc.).

**πῐτῡρ-ίας** (with or without ἄρτος), ὁ, bread *made with bran*, Poll. 6.72, Gal.6.481, etc. **-ίᾱσις**, εως, ἡ, = πίτυρον 2, Dsc.5.106 (pl.), Gal.12.459, Paul.Aeg.3.3. **-ίζω**, *become coated with bran*, *PLeid.* *X.*8,25. **-ίς** (sc. ἐλαία), ίδος, ἡ, *small* kind of *olive*, of the colour of bran, which was gathered before it was ripe, and then preserved, acc. πίτυριν Call.*Fr.*50, cf. Philem.Gloss.ap.Ath.2.56c. [ῡ prop., but ῠ in Call.l.c.] **-ισμα**, ατος, τό, *dandruff*, τῆς κεφαλῆς Hdn. Gr.1.49 cod. C. **-ίτης** [ρῑ] ἄρτος, = πιτυρίας, Philem.Gloss.ap. Ath.3.114e, Gal.8.184.

**πῐτῡροειδής**, ές, *bran-like, scurfy*, Orib.*Fr.*79, Paul.Aeg.3.3.

**πίτῡρον** [ῐ], τό, *husks of corn, bran*, in sg., Thphr.*HP*8.4.4, Dsc.2. 85.2, Gal.6.481: mostly in pl., Hp.*Acut.*21, al., *PCair.Zen.*355.87 (iii B.C.), etc.: used in magical ceremonies, D.18.259, Theoc.2. 33. 2. *bran-like eruption* on the skin, esp. the head, *scurf, dandruff*, Dsc.1.30. 3. *bran-like sediment in urine*, Hp.*Nat.Hom.*14.

**πῐτῡρ-όομαι**, Pass., *to be affected with* πιτυρίασις, Hp.*Prorrh.*2. 30. **-ώδης**, ες, *bran-like*, Thphr.*CP*1.5.4, Gal.6.483; ὑποστάσιες π., of sediment in urine, Hp.*Prog.*12. 2. *scurfy*, Id.*Aph.*4.77, *Coac.*570.

**πίτυς** [ῐ], υος, ἡ, Ep. dat. pl. πίτυσσιν, *pine*, esp. *Pinus Laricio, Corsican pine*, π. βλωθρή, τήν τ' οὔρεσι τέκτονες ἄνδρες ἐξέταμον Il.13. 390; μακρῇσίν τε πίτυσσιν ἰδὲ δρυσὶν Od.9.186; also, *Aleppo pine, P. halepensis*, Thphr.*HP*3.9.5, Nic.*Al.*301, Paus.2.1.3, *Gp.*2.8.2 (called π. ἀγρία Thphr.*HP*1.9.3, 3.3.1, Paus.5.6.4); *stone pine, P. pinea*, Theoc.5.49, Dsc.1.69,72 (π. ἥμερος Paus.6.9.1); *small-seeded pine*, *P. brutia*, π. φθειροποιός Thphr.*HP*2.2.6, cf. Plin.*HN*16.49; the *Isthmian pine* was one species, Callix.2, Plu.2.675e: prov., πίτυος τρόπον ἐκτρίβειν like *a pine*, i.e. *utterly*, because the pine when cut down never grows again, Hdt.6.37 (but this is attributed to the πεύκη, and not to the πίτυς, by Thphr.*HP*3.9.5).

**πῐτύ-στεπτος**, ον, poet. for *πιτυόστ-, *pine-crowned*, Πάν *AP*6.253 (Crin.). **-ώδης**, ες, *abounding in pines*, ἄλσος, ὄρος, Str.8.6.22, 13.1.15; χωρία Plu.2.676a; π. νῆσοι the islands Πιτυοῦσσαι (cf. πιτυόεις), Alcm.147 B. II. *of pine-wood*, δούρατα Nonn.*D.*2.102.

**πιφαλλίς**, = πίφιγξ, Hsch.

**πιφάσκω**, freq. v.l. for sq. in Hom., Il.10.478, al.

**πιφαύσκω**, redupl. form of φαυ- (φαϝ-) (v. *φάω), only pres. and impf., Act. and Med.; Ep. inf. πιφαυσκέμεν Od.11.442:—Ep. and Lyr. Verb (used also by A. in Act., v. infr.), *make manifest, tell of*, ἵπποι οὓς νῶϊν πίφαυσκε Δόλων Il.10.478; ἕκαστα λέγων ἑτάροισι πίφαυσκον Od. 12.165; θέσφατα π., ὅσα μήδεται . . Ζεύς *h.Merc.*540; μειλίγματα βροτοῖς πιφαύσκων εἶπε A.*Ch.*279; *proclaim*, γᾷ ἐπισκήπτων πιφαύσκω B. 5.42: metaph., λαμπτῆρ ἡμερήσιον φάος πιφαύσκων *showing forth*, A. *Ag.*23; τιάρας φάλαρον π. *exhibiting*, Id.*Pers.*662 (lyr.): abs., βοίζησεν δ' ἄρα πιφαύσκων Διομήδεϊ *making signal*, Il.10.502. 2. *declare, utter*, μηδ' οἱ μῦθον . . πιφαυσκέμεν Od.11.442; ἔπος πάντεσσι π. 22.131; πείρατα μύθων Emp.17.15. 3. c. acc. et inf., *tell* one to do, A.*Eu.* 620. II. Med., *make manifest, show*, ἀνθρώποισι π. τὰ ἃ κῆλα Il. 12.280, cf. 21.333; *make known, disclose*, ἀλλά τοι ἄλλον φῶτα π. Od. 15.518; οἷα Ζεὺς κακὰ ἔργα π. Il.15.97, cf. 16.12, Od.2.32,162, Hes. *Th.*655; ἄσχετα ἔργα πιφαύσκετο δημοτέροισιν A.R.3.606. III. later Pass., *have told one, learn about*, c. acc., Nic.*Th.*411,637,725. [In Ep. πῐ- metri gr. in the first half of a hexam., Il.10.478,502, 18. 500, *h.Merc.*540; in the latter half πῑ- (so always in Med.).]

**πίφιγξ**, an unknown bird, Arist.*HA*610ᵃ11 (v.l. πίφηξ), Ant.Lib. 20.8; **πίφιξ**, *EM*673.56; expld. as = κορυδαλλός by Hsch.

**πίων** [ῑ], ὁ, ἡ, neut. πῖον, gen. πίονος (irreg. fem. πίειρα, q.v.), *fat*, in Hom. of beasts, πίονος αἰγός Il.9.207; ὗν . . μάλα πίονα Od.14.419; π. μῆλα Il.12.319, etc.; μῆλα πίονα δημῷ Od.9.464; βοῦν πίονα δημῷ Il.23.750, cf. 2.403; πίονα μηρία καῖε βοὸς 11.773; νῶτα βοὸς π. Od.4. 65; π. δημός rich fat, Il.22.501; ἔγκατα πίονι (fort. πίονα) δημῷ Hes. *Th.*538; of oil, Hdt.2.94; λύχνου π. ἔαρ Call.*Fr.*201; ὀπώρας ποτὸς S.*Tr.*703; πλακοῦς Ar.*Eq.*1190; νεφροί Arist.*PA*672ᵃ35; πίονα μαζὸν αἰγός Call.*Jov.*48; π. καὶ μαλακῷ . . διανήματι Pl.*Plt.*309b. 2. of men, Ar.*Ra.*1092 (anap.), *Pl.*560 (anap.), Pl.*R.*422b. II. metaph., of soil, *rich*, ἀγρός, δῆμος, etc., Il.23.832, 16.437, etc.; πίονα ἔργα rich crops, 12.283; τέμενος Pi.*P.*4.56. 2. of persons and places, *wealthy, abounding*, οἶκος, νηός, Od.9.35, Il.2.549; ἄδυτον 5.512; πίονας πλούτου πνοάς A.*Ag.*820; πίονι μέτρῳ in *plenteous* measure,

Theoc.7.33, etc.; *abundant*, κλαυθμὸς π. LXX *Ge*.46.29; ἐν καταφορᾷ πίονι in a state of *deep* lethargy, Herod.Med. in *Rh.Mus*.58.79 (sed πλείονι ib.72); τὸ πῖον, v. λιπαρός I. 2. 3. *fattening*, *fertilizing*, Ζέφυρος B.*Fr*.34 (Sup.). III. Comp. πιότερος, as if from πῖος (q. v.), *h.Ap*.48, Arist.*HA*596$^a$18, Thphr.*CP*2.4.5: Sup., πιότατον πεδίον Il. 9.577, cf. Hes.*Op*.585, Hp.*Carn*.4, Arist.*HA*600$^a$31. Adv., πιοτέρως διαιτᾶν Hp.*Aph*.1.10. (Cf. Skt. *pívan*-, fem. *pívarī* 'fat', 'rich'.)

**πλαγά**, v. πληγή.

**πλαγγόνιον**, τό, a kind of *ointment*, Polem.Hist.64, Sosib.23, Poll. 6.104. (Named from the inventor, Πλαγγών.)

**πλάγγος**, ὁ, a kind of *eagle*, Arist.*HA*618$^b$23.

**πλαγγών**, όνος, ὁ, *wax-puppet*, *doll*, Call.*Cer*.92.

⊛ **πλᾰγι-άζω**, (πλάγιος) *turn sideways*, τὸν ἵππον Poll.1.204; in wrestling, *throw sideways*, Id.3.155; of ships, π. πρὸς ἀντίους τοὺς ἐτησίας *sail athwart* the trade-winds, Luc.*Nav*.9; dub. sens. in App. *BC*5.88. 2. *hold aslant*, κάτοπτρον Ach.Tat.*Intr.Arat*.21. 3. Pass., πλαγιαζέσθω τὰ τρήματα let the holes *be made obliquely*, Apollod. *Poliorc*.151.6; κύλινδρος ἀπὸ τῆς ὀρθότητος -ασθεὶς Hierocl. in *CA* 24 p.474 M. 4. *lead astray*, LXX *Ez*.14.5; *pervert*, ἐπ' ἀδίκοις δίκαιον ib.*Is*.29.21: abs., *use tortuous methods*, π. καὶ τεχνιτεύειν Ph.2.432; π. ἢ φωνὴν ἢ πρᾶξιν in word or deed, Plu.*Dem*.13. II. *strike with the flat of the sword*, D.C.40.53 (Pass.). III. Gramm., *inflect*, *decline*, Sch.rec.S.*El*.365. 2. Pass., πεπλαγίασται ὁ λόγος, of Tragic irony, Sch.S.*OT*137, 1183. **-ασμός**, ὁ, *obliquity*, of the sun's course, Epicur.*Nat*.11.5. 2. in Obstetrics, *oblique presentation* of the foetus, Sor.2.60. 3. metaph., *deceit*, Sch.Ar.*Ra*.987 (pl.). II. Gramm., *use of oblique cases*, opp. ὀρθότης, Hermog. *Id*.1.3; *inflexion*, Sch.rec.S.*El*.365. ⊛ **-αυλίζω**, *play upon the cross-flute*, Eust.1157.40. ⊛ **-αυλος**, ὁ, *cross-flute*, opp. flûte-à-bec, Theoc. 20.29, Bion *Fr*.7, etc.; cf. πλάγιος.

**πλᾰγιο-βάτης** [βᾰ], ου, ὁ, *walking obliquely*, dub. cj. for πλαγιοβαθεῖς, Vett.Val.110.14. **-καρπος**, ον, *having fruit at the sides*, Thphr. *HP*1.14.2, 3.18.12. **-καυλος**, ον, *having stalks at the sides*, ib.8.3.2.

**πλᾰγι-όμμᾰτος**, ον, *with oblique eyes*, *squinting*, Eust.768.7.

⊛ **πλάγιος** [ᾰ], α, ον, also ος, ον Thphr.*CP*3.6.3, etc.: (v. πλάζω (A) fin.):—*placed sideways*, *athwart*, τριήρεις Th.7.59, etc.; π. φορά oblique motion, Pl.*Ti*.39a; opp. ἀντία (direct), ib.43e; πλάγιον θεῖναί τι, opp. ὀρθόν, X.*Oec*.19.9; τάφρους ὀρύσσειν τὰς μὲν πλαγίους τὰς δὲ ὀρθίας Thphr. l. c.; μαστοὶ π. *pointing sideways*, Arist.*PA*688$^a$35: Geom., π. διάμετρος *transverse* diameter, Apollon.Perg.*Con*.1 *Def*.1.5; π. πλευρά ib.1.14; τὰ π., of the regions round the celestial poles, as being *transverse to* the diurnal rotation, Arist.*Cael*.285$^b$12; *horizontal*, μεσηγὺ δύο στύλων στρωτῆρα π. εὖ προσδῆσαι Hp.*Art*.7; πλάγι' ἐστὶ τἄλλα, τοῦτο δ' ὀρθὸν θηρίον Philem.3; of window bars, opp. ὀρτία, *PCair.Zen*.663.8 (iii B.C.); so ξύλον κρεμάσαι π. Paul.Aeg.6.99; π. Σελήνη, opp. ὀρθή, *Cat.Cod.Astr*.8(3).174; πλαγία φάλαγξ an army in march *with extended front*, *transverse* to the direction of march, Ascl.*Tact*.10.1, 11.1; also of ships, π. παραβάλλουσαι ἀλλήλαις Plb.1. 22.9; παρεδίδου π. [τὰς τριήρεις] τοῖς Ἕλλησι Plu.*Them*.14; π. ὥσπερ πνεύματι παραδιδοὺς ἑαυτόν Id.2.28d. 2. πλάγια, τά, *sides*, *flanks*, τῆς Σκυθικῆς Hdt.4.49; τὸ π., of the body, Arist.*PA*657$^b$21, *IA* 713$^b$31. b. esp. in military sense, τοῖς π. ἐπιέναι attack *the flanks*, Th.4.32; εἰς τὰ π. παραγαγεῖν, παραπέμψαι, to make an army file off *right and left*, X.*An*.3.4.14, 6.3.15; π. λαβεῖν τοὺς πολεμίους to take the enemy *in flank*, Id.*Cyr*.7.1.26, etc.; π. παραπορεύεσθαι Plb.6. 40.7. 3. of ground, *sloping*, *Gp*.2.46.2. 4. freq. with Preps. in adv. sense, εἰς τὸ π. *sideways*, [βὶς] ἐς τὸ π. κατάγνυται Hp.*Art*. 38; δρέπανα εἰς π. ἀποτεταμένα X.*An*.1.8.10; ἐς τὰ π. παραπλέοντες Th.7.40; opp. εἰς τὸ ἀντίον, X.*Eq*.12.12; εἰς πλάγια, opp. καταντικρύ, Pl.*Tht*.194b; ἐκ πλαγίου, opp. καταντικρύ, Id.*R*.598a; ἐκ πλαγίου *in flank*, esp. in military sense, Th.4.33, 7.6, X.*HG*6.5.26; ἐκ τῶν π. Arist.*Mete*.377$^b$29; ἐκ π. Id.*Pr*.912$^b$28; ἐκ πλαγίων τῆς σκηνῆς LXX *Nu*.3.29; ἐκ πλαγίας Arist.*Mete*.372$^a$11; ἐν τῷ π. ib.378$^a$3; ἐπὶ τὸ π. Id.*IA*712$^b$17; πρόσθεν ἢ κατὰ ⟨τὰ⟩ πλάγια in front or *in flank*, X. *Cyr*.5.2.1: regul. Adv. -ίως rare, Aen.Tact.32.2 (cj.), Arist.*Mech*.850$^b$ 37, Luc.*Symp*.47: neut. πλάγιον as Adv., *Inscr.Prien*.363.13 (iv B.C.), al. II. metaph., *crooked*, *treacherous*, φρένες Pi.*I*.3.5; σὺν πλαγίῳ κόρῳ στείχοντα Id.*N*.1.64; πλάγια φρονεῖν E.*IA*332; πλάγιοι ταῖς ψυχαῖς Plb.4.8.11; π. ἐν τῷ πολέμῳ *wavering*, Id.30.1.6, etc.; προβλήματα π. *involving arrière-pensée*, Hermog.*Inv*.4.13. Adv. -ίως, χρώμενοι ταῖς διαβολαῖς Plu.2.856c; but simply, *indirectly*, *by implication*, Ph.2.173; *with an innuendo*, Plu.2.205b. III. Gramm., πτῶσις πλαγία *oblique* case, *Stoic*.2.60: freq. in pl., D.H.*Comp*.6, A.D.*Pron*. 23.1, al., S.E.*M*.1.177. 2. π. λέξις *dependent* construction, Demetr. *Eloc*.198; τὸ π., opp. τὸ εὐθύ, ib.104. IV. πλάγιον, τό, technical term of uncertain meaning in connexion with enrolment of ἔφηβοι, *Chron.d'Égypte* 7 (1932).301, *Sammelb*.7239.25 (ii A.D.), *BGU*1084. 31 (ii A.D.).

**πλᾰγιό-σκελος**, ον, expl. of Lat. *Varus*, *Blaesus*, Lyd.*Mag*.1.23. **-της**, ητος, ἡ, *use of oblique cases*, Demetr.*Eloc*.198 (pl.). **-τομία**, ἡ, *oblique incision*, Leonid.ap.Aët.15.5. **-φορέομαι**, *lie athwart*, Sor.1. 57. **-φύλαξ** [ῠ], ᾰκος, ὁ, ἡ, *guarding the flanks* of an army on the march, ἶλαι π. D S.19.82 (v.l. -φύλακοι); esp. of the *corner* man in the ῥόμβος (q.v.) of cavalry, Ascl.*Tact*.7.2,6, Arr.*Tact*.16.5; cf. πλαγυφύλαξ. **-χαίτης**, ου, ὁ, *with hair across*, Hsch. s. v. δοχμόκορσοι.

**πλᾰγι-όω**, = πλαγιάζω I.1, τὸν ἵππον π. τῷ χαλινῷ X.*Eq*.7.16. **-ωσις**, εως, ἡ, = πλαγιασμός, Hsch. s. v. λόξωσις.

**πλαγκ-τήρ**, ῆρος, ὁ, (πλάζω A) either (Act.) *he that leads astray*, *the beguiler*, or (Pass.) *the roamer*, epith. of Dionysus, *AP*9.524.17: fem. πλάγκτειρα, ἀτραπιτός, of the Zodiac, *Hymn.Is*.29. **-τός**, ή, όν, also ός, όν A.*Ag*.593: (πλάζω A):—poet. Adj. *wandering*, *roaming*, of ships, Id.*Pers*.277 (lyr.); πλαγκτὰ δ' ὡσεί τις νεφέλα E.*Supp*.961 (lyr.); π. ὕδωρ, of the Euripus, *AP*9.73 (Antiphil.); ἰός ib.6.75 (Paul. Sil.); πλαγκτὰν ὁδόν a devious route, *Hymn.Is*.149. b. π. ἄστρα, = πλάνητες, Alex.Eph.ap.Theon.Sm.p.140 H. 2. metaph., *wandering in mind*, *erring*, *distraught*, Od.21.363, A.*Ag*.593. II. Πλαγκταὶ πέτραι rocks near Scylla and Charybdis, Od.12.59sqq., 23.327; later identified with the Συμπληγάδες or Κυάνεαι of the Bosporus, Hdt.4.85, Arr.*Peripl.M.Eux*.25, Eratosth.ap.Sch.E.*Med*.2, etc.; but also with the volcanic islands of Lipari, A.R.4.924, cf. Apollod.1.9. 25. **-τοσύνη**, ἡ, poet. for πλάνη, *roaming*, Od.15.343, Nonn.*D*.2. 692. ⊛ **-τύς**, ύος, ἡ, *wandering*, Call.*Aet*.1.2.7.

**πλάγος** [ᾰ], εος, τό, *side*, Dor. word, *Tab.Heracl*.1.66.

**πλαγυφύλαξ** [φῠ], ᾰκος, ὁ, in pl., written either for πλαγιοφύλακες (q. v.), or for πλακοφύλακες (*guardians of* temple-*inscriptions*), *UPZ* 89.6 (ii B.C.).

**πλᾰδᾰρ-όομαι**, Pass., *become soft and flabby*, Aq.*Is*.19.3. **-ός**, ά, όν, *moist*, *damp*, ἱδρῶτι πλαδαρὴ κόμη *AP*9.653 (Agath.); καρήατα A.R.3.1398; πλαδαραὶ σάρκες *flabby*, *flaccid*, Hp.*Int*.40, etc.; οὖλα Dsc.5.5; διαχωρήματα -ώτερα *loose*, *watery*, Hp.*Acut*.52; ὕλη Sch. Iamb.*Comm.Math*.4; *weak*, δόρυ Plb.*Fr*.69 (nisi leg. κλαδ-); of taste, *insipid*, opp. στρυφνός, Hp.*VM*14,15, cf. Aristid.Quint.2.15 (Comp.). **-ότης**, ητος, ἡ, *flaccidity*, Epicur.*Nat*.140 G., Herm.ap. Stob.1.49.69, Gal.14.770. **-ωμα**, ατος, τό, = πλάδος, Suid. s. v. πλαδαρόν (pl.). **-ωσις**, εως, ἡ, *becoming 'splashy'*, of the stomach, Cass.Fel.42.

⊛ **πλᾰδάω**, (πλάδη) *to be flaccid*, of the flesh, Hp.*Aër*.10; πῆξις πλαδῶσα, as of milk without rennet, Arist.*HA*516$^a$3; οὖλα πλαδῶντα Dsc. 1.110; φλύκταιναι π. Nic.*Th*.241; of corn, Ph.1.179. 2. π. τὸν στόμαχον *have a 'splashy'* stomach, Dsc.*Eup*.2.9, cf. Gal.13.145. 3. metaph. of the mind, *to be* or *become flaccid*, Ph.1.441,459, 2.411:—Hsch. cites pf. part. πεπλαδηκώς· σεσηπώς, ὑγρανθείς, and impf. ἐπλάδα in causal sense = κατέδευεν.

**πλαδδιάω**, *talk nonsense*, Lacon. word in Ar.*Lys*., inf. πλαδδιῆν 171, imper. πλάδδιη 990. (Perh. onomatop.)

**πλάδ-η** [ᾰ], ἡ, = πλάδος, Emp.75, Suid.s.v. πλαδαρόν (pl.). **-ησις**, εως, ἡ, = πλαδάρωσις, τοῦ στομάχου Sor.1.50. **-όεις**, εσσα, εν, = πλαδαρός, Sch.Nic.*Th*.241. **-ος**, ὁ, *abundance of fluids*, like *water-brash*, Hp.*Epid*.1.5, *Acut*.37, *Gland*.3, Aret.*SD*2.6. **-ώδης**, ες, = πλαδαρός, Lycus ap.Orib.8.26.7: Comp., Hp.*Mul*.1.11. **-ωσις**, εως, ἡ, = πλαδάρωσις, τῆς ἑλκώσεως Aët.9.42, cf. Phot. and Suid. s. v. πλαδαρόν.

**πλάζω** (A), Ep. impf. πλάζον Od.2.396: aor. ἔπλαγξα (παρ-) 9.81: Ep. πλάγξα 24.307:—Pass. and Med., 3.106, etc.; Ep. impf. πλαζόμην 5.389: fut. πλάγξομαι 15.312: aor. ἐπλάγχθην (ἀπ-) Il.22.291; Ep. πλάγχθην Od.1.2; inf. πλάγξασθαι dub. in A.R.3.261: pres. Med. also πλάττονται Parm.6.5 codd.:—poet. Verb (rare in Prose, v. infr.), *turn aside* or *away from*, πλάζει δ' ἀπὸ πατρίδος αἴης Od.1.75; ἀλλά με δαίμων πλάγξ' ἀπὸ Σικανίης δεῦρ' ἐλθέμεν 24.307; [πρὼν..ποταμοῖσι] ῥόον πεδίονδε τίθησι πλάζων Il.17.751:—Pass., πλάγχθη δ' ἀπὸ χαλκόφι χαλκός bronze *glanced off* from bronze, 11.351; πάλιν πλαγχθέντας ὀΐω ἂψ ἀπονοστήσειν *balked*, *baffled*, 1.59, cf. Od.13.5; τίς πλάγχθη πολὺ μόχθος ἔξω; what woe *is warded off* afar? S.*OC*1231 (lyr.); κεῖθεν δὲ πλαγχθέντες ἱκάνομεν ἐνθάδε Od.13.278; Σκύρου μὲν ἅμαρτε, πλαγχθέντες δ' εἰς Ἐφύραν ἵκοντο Pi.*N*.7.37 (s. v. l.); [Ἀλέξανδρος] ἐπλάζετο ἄγων [Ἑλένην] Hdt.2.117, cf. 116; ἀκταῖσιν ὁρμεῖ, δαρὸν ἐκ Τροίας χρόνον ἄλαισι πλαγχθείς E.*Or*.56; of an exile, Ἀργεϊ νάσθη πλαγχθείς Il.14.120; γένεσις καὶ ὄλεθρος τῆλε μάλ' ἐπλάχθησαν *have been banished* afar, Parm.8.28: metaph., ὁ νέος..ὑπὸ τῆς τύχης..πλάζεται, ὁ δὲ γέρων καθάπερ ἐν λιμένι τῷ γήρᾳ καθώρμικεν Epicur.*Sent.Vat*. 17; so perh. ἔνθα δύω νύκτας δύο τ' ἤματα κύματι πηγῷ πλάζετο Od.5.389 (v. infr. II). 2. *baffle*, *thwart*, *balk*, esp. mentally, οἵ με μέγα πλάζουσι καὶ οὐκ εἰῶσ' ἐθέλοντα Ἰλίου ἐκπέρσαι..πτολίεθρον Il.2.132; πλάζε δὲ πίνοντας *balked* or *bewildered* them as they drank, Od.2.396; πίνοντες ἐπλάζοντο, i. e. became drunk, Pi.*Fr*.166; μαινομένῳ πιτύλῳ πλαγχθείς E.*HF*1189 (lyr.); ὁκόσα ἰνδαλμοῖσι διαλλάττοντα ἀνὰ τὸν ἠέρα πλάζει ἡμέας Hp.*Ep*.18; *embarrass*, *trip up*, πλάζει τὸν παῖδα τὰ σάνδαλα *AP* 7.365 (Zon.); ἐπλάζοντο πρὸς οὐδένα σκοπὸν *wavered* aimlessly, Plu. *Mar*.36. 3. Pass., *go astray*, πλαγχθέντα ἧς ἀπὸ νηός Od.6.278: c. gen., ἁμαξιτοῦ E.*Rh*.283; μανδρῶν πλαζομένων χοίρων τρεῖων *Supp. Epigr*.4.647.6 (Maeonia, ii A.D.). b. *lose*, *be deprived of*, ὀμμάτων ἐπλάγχθη A.*Th*.784 (lyr., ἀπ' ὀμμ. codd.). 4. Pass., *wander*, *rove*, πλάζομαι ὧδ' Il.10.91; ὃς μάλα πολλὰ πλάγχθη Od.1.2; πῇ..πλάζομαι; 13.204, cf. 3.95, 16.64; ἐπὶ πόντον πλαζόμενοι κατὰ ληΐδ' 3.106; πλάζεσθαι μετ' ἐκεῖνον 16.151; ἀλλά πῃ ἄλλῃ πλάζετ' ἐπ' ἀνθρώπους 3.252; κατὰ δὲ πτόλιν αὐτὸς ἀνάγκῃ πλάγξομαι 15.312; οἱ πλαζόμενοι the *planets*, Ti.Locr.97a: never in Com. or correct Att. Prose. II. μέγα κῦμα πλάζ' ὤμους καθύπερθε *struck* his shoulders, Il.21.269: here and in Od.5.389 (v. supr. I. 1 fin.) Aristarch. (ap.*An.Ox*.1.149) took πλάζω [ᾱ by nature] as a dialectal form of πλήσσω, perh. rightly; cf. ἐπιπλάζω, προσπλάζω. (In signf. I related to πλάγιος as ἅζομαι to ἅγιος; for πλαγξ-, πλαγχθ- codd. sts. have πλαξ-, πλαχθ-, as v.l., Il.1.59, Od.1.2, 9.81 (παρ-), Parm.8.28; in signf. II perh. a different word.)

**πλάζω** (B), = πλάσσω (Tarent.), *An.Ox*.1.62.

⊛ **πλᾰθᾰ**, ἡ, (πλάσσω) *modelled figure*, Plu.2.191d; cf. κοροπλάθος.

⊛ **πλᾰθᾰν-ίτης**, Dor. -ίτας [ῑ], ου, ὁ, *baked in a mould*, ἄμυλος prob. in Philox.3.17. ⊛ **-ον**, τό, *dish* or *mould* in which bread, cakes, etc. were baked, Theoc.15.115, Nic.*Fr*.70.2, Poll.7.22, etc.: hence the baking-woman in Ar.*Ra.* is called Πλαθάνη; cf. πλαθά, κοροπλάθος.

**πλᾶθος**, v. πλῆθος.

⊛ **πλάθω** [ᾰ], poet. form of πελάζω, used by Trag. in lyr., *approach, draw near*, τινι S.*Ph.*728, cf. *El.*220: c. acc., E.*Rh.*14: abs., Id.*Alc.* 119:—Med., στάλαις πλάθεται Ἡρακλέους Inscr. ap. Plu.*Arat.*14.

**πλαῖσι**· κλῆσι, Hsch.

**πλαίσῐ-ον**, τό, = πλινθίον, πλινθεῖον (qq.v.), *oblong case* or *frame* used in moulding bricks and in measuring, Ar.*Ra.*800 (pl.), Pl.Com. 147; χιτωνίσκος ἐμ π. in an *oblong box*, *IG*2².1514.13, al., cf. *BCH*28. 165 (Delos); κεκρυφάλους τρεῖς ἐμ π. *IG*2².1522.18; *oblong scaffold* or *platform*, Plu.*Alex.*67: pl., of the *frames* enclosing Solon's ἄξονες, Id.*Sol.*25; of *frames* in roof-panelling, *IG*1².372 *E*2, al., *Inscr.Délos* 504 *A* 13, 15 (iii B.C.). II. *hollow rectangle*, ἐν π. τετάχθαι Th.7.78, cf. 6.67, X.*An.*1.8.9; = ἐν ἑτερομήκει σχήματι, Ael.*Tact.*37.8, Arr. *Tact.*29.7; ἰσόπλευρον π. X.*An.*3.4.19, Arr.*An.*4.5.6; [Σμύρνα] ἀνέχει ἐν π. Aristid.*Or.*23(42).20; of the shape of the Acropolis of Alexandria, Aphth.*Prog.*12. III. εἰς τὰ π. prob. f.l. for εἰς τὰ πλάγια in D.C.40.2. **-όω**, *enclose in a frame*, *BCH*28.165 (Delos, Pass.).

**πλαισός**, ή, όν, = βλαισός, Phot.

**πλᾰκ-άς**, άδος, ἡ, *floor* of a wine-cellar, *POxy.*729.28 (ii A.D.). **-ερός**, ά, όν, (πλάξ) = πλατύς, *broad*, Theoc.7.18. **-ιανόν**, τό, an eye-salve, Aët.7.118. **-ινος**, η, ον, *made of marble slabs*, *CIG*2846 (Aphrodisias); π. τρίπους a *marble* tripod, *AP*6.98 (Zon.). **-ίον**, τό, Dim. of πλάξ, *IG*4.823.61 (Troezen, iv B.C.), *POxy.*921 *Intr.* (iii A.D.); *small slab* of marble ready for powdering, Aët.12.64. **-ίς**, ίδος, ἡ, *bench, seat, couch* of flowers, used at the Panathenaea, Hsch. ⊛ **-ίτης** [ῑ], Dor. **-ίτας**, ἄρτος, ὁ, *flat* cake, Sophr.29. II. fem. **πλακῖτις**, ιδος, ἡ, = πλακώδης, a form of καδμεία, Gal.12.220. 2. a kind of alum, ib.237. **-όεις**, εσσα, εν, *flat*, πεδίον D.P.*Fr.*12.6, cf. Orph.*A.*951.

**Πλάκος**, ἡ, v. ὑποπλάκιος.

**πλᾰκουντ-άριον**, τό, Dim. of πλακοῦς, Str.17.1.38, Arr.*Epict.*3.12. 11. ⊛ **-άριος**, ὁ, *maker of cakes, pastry-cook*, *IG*3.3445 (Piraeus), *MAMA*3.697 (Corycus). **-ᾶς**, ᾶ, ὁ, = foreg., *POxy.*1495.7 (iv A.D.). **-ήριος**, ον, *for making cakes*, τήγανον Maria ap. Zos.Alch. p.236 B. **-ηρός**, ά, όν, = sq., Chrysipp.Tyan. ap. Ath.14. 647d. **-ικός**, ή, όν, *like a cake*, ὄγκος Phan.Hist.29. **-ινος**, η, ον, = foreg., ἔλατρα *SIG*57.36 (Milet., v B.C.). **-ιον**, τό, Dim. of πλακοῦς, Arr.*Epict.*2.16.25, Aët.9.30, Sch.Porph.*Abst.*2.16:— written **-όντιον**, *PLond.*3.964.20 (iii A.D.). **-ίσκος**, ὁ, Dim. of πλακοῦς, *EM*533.21.

**πλᾰκουντο-ποιικός**, ή, όν, *relating to cake-baking*, συγγράμματα Ath.14.643e. **-ποιός**, όν, *cake-baking*, Σῖμος Sopat.4. II. Subst., *pastrycook*, *Sammelb.*984.6 (i A.D.), *PKlein.Form.*967 (vi A.D.).

**πλᾰκουντώδης**, ες, *like a cake*, Thphr.*HP*4.10.4, Ath.14.646c.

⊛ **πλᾰκοῦς**, οῦντος, ὁ, voc. πλακοῦ Theodos.*Can.*p.3 H.:—contr. from πλακόεις, *flat cake* (perh. *shaped like the mallow-seed*, Phan.Hist.29), freq. in Com., πλακοῦντος κύκλος Ar.*Ach.*1125, cf. Alex.22 (pl., hex.); π. ἄρτος Ath.14.645d: also resolved πλακόεις, *AP*6.155 (Theodorid.). II. *the seed of the mallow*, which seeds children call *cheeses*, Phan.Hist.29, Gal.10.113.

⊛ **πλᾰκόω**, *face with marble slabs*, *BCH*21.48 (Syria):—Pass., *Gloss.*

**πλακτήρ**, ῆρος, ὁ, cock's *spur*, Hsch.

**πλακτός**, ή, όν, = πλαγκτός I. 2, Parm.6.6.

**πλάκτωρ**, ορος, ὁ, Dor. for *πλήκτωρ, *striker*, *AP*6.294 (Phan.).

**πλᾰκ-ώδης**, ες, *laminated*, τραχὺς καὶ π. Arist.*HA*507ᵇ8, cf. *Fr.* 338, etc.; π. σάρξ *flaky*, of a fish, Xenocr. ap. Orib.2.58.41: Comp. **-ωδέστερος** *having more lamellae, more laminar*, Arist.*HA*525ᵇ14, *PA* 684ᵃ20; π. ὑπόνομοι, of gold-mines, Agatharch.29, 96; *with a crust*, of soil, Thphr.*HP*9.4.8. **-ωσις**, εως, ἡ, *facing with marble slabs, revetting*, τοῦ λογείου *TAM*2.408 (Patara, ii A.D.), cf. *CPHerm.*94.2 (iii A.D.). **-ωτή**, ἡ, a form of καδμεία (cf. πλακίτης II), Dsc.5.74.

**πλάν**, Dor. for πλήν. **πλανάτας**, Dor. for πλανήτης.

⊛ **πλᾰν-άω**, fut. -ήσω Lxx 4*Ki.*4.28, etc.:—**Pass.** and **Med.**, fut. -ήσομαι Pl.*Hp.Mi.*376c, Luc.*Peregr.*16, -ηθήσομαι D.H.*Dem.*9, Luc. *VH*2.27: aor. ἐπλανήθην E.*Hel.*598, Th.5.4, etc.: pf. πεπλάνημαι A.*Pr.* 565 (anap.), Hdt.7.16.β', Pl.*Plt.*264c, etc.: (πλάνη):—Prose verb, = πλάζω (used once in Hom., also by Trag., Pi. (v. infr.), and Sapph. *Supp.*10.15), *cause to wander*, A.*Pr.*572 (lyr.), Hdt.4.128. 2. *lead from the subject*, in talking, D.19.335. 3. *lead astray, mislead, deceive*, ἡ γνώμη πλανᾷ S.*OC*316, cf. Pl.*Prt.*356d, *Lg.*655c, Theognet. 2.2, Men.*Pk.*79; τὸν ὄχλον *Ev.Jo.*7.12; τὸ ἀόριστον πλανᾷ Arist.*Rh.* 1415ᵃ14; τὰ μὴ πλανῶντα Id.*Mete.*347ᵇ35; πλανῶν τὴν ἔξοδον, of the Labyrinth, Apollod.3.1.4. II. Pass., *wander, stray*, ἵπποι πλανόωνται ἀνὰ δρόμον Il.23.321; ὅποι γῆς..πεπλάνημαι A.*Pr.*565 (anap.); π. εἰς πόλεις Lys.12.97; κατὰ τὴν χώραν Isoc.6.76; περὶ τὰ πεδία Pl.*Plt.* 264c: abs., S.*OC*347, etc.; of the *planets*, Pl.*Lg.*822a, Arist.*Mete.* 346ᵃ2, etc.: metaph., νοῦς ἐν αὐτῷ ὁ ἀληθινὸς πέφυκε πλανᾶσθαι Plot.6. 7.13; of reports, *travel abroad*, πολλὰ..ἐμπόρων ἔπη φιλεῖ π. S.*OC* 304. b. c. acc. loci, πλανηθεὶς τήνδε βάρβαρον χθόνα *having wandered over* it, E.*Hel.*598; πᾶσαν γῆν Plu.*Luc.*34: c. acc. cogn., πολλοὺς ἑλιγμοὺς πλανώμενοι *wandering about* as in a labyrinth, X.*Cyr.*1.3.4. 2. *wander* in speaking, π. ἐν τῷ λόγῳ Hdt.2.115; *digress*, π. ἀπὸ τοῦ λόγου Pl.*Plt.*263a. 3. c. gen., πλανηθεὶς καιροῦ *having missed* the right moment, Pi.*N.*8.4. 4. *do a thing irregularly* or *with variation*, Hdt.6.52; ἐνύπνια τὰ ἐς ἀνθρώπους πεπλανημένα the *varying* dreams *that visit* them, Id.7.16.β'; πλανωμένη πρὸς ἄλλοτ' ἄλλον πημονὴ προσιζάνει A.*Pr.*277; πεπλανημένον τρόπον *irregularly*, Hp.*Prog.*24; *to be unsettled*, τὰ τῆς ἐλευθερίας ἔτι πλανώμενα καταστήματα *IG*4²(1).81.13 (Epid., i A.D.). 5. *to be in doubt* or *at a loss*, π. τὸ θέλει τὸ ἔπος εἶπαι Hdt.6.37: more freq. abs., A.*Pr.*473, etc.; π. καὶ ἀπορῶ Pl.*Hp. Ma.*304c; ἡ ψυχὴ π. καὶ ταράττεται Id.*Phd.*79c; π. τῇ διανοίᾳ, ταῖς διανοίαις, Isoc.15.52, *Ep.*6.10; πεπλανημένην ἔχειν τὴν διάνοιαν Id.15.265; πλανωμένων θεραπεία παθῶν Diog.Oen.27. 6. in forensic Rhet., χρώματα πεπλανημένα, μετάθεσις πεπ., of *alternative* pleas, Hermog. *Stat.*3. 7. *to be misled*, ὑπὸ φωνῆς κοινότητος Phld.*Sign.*7; ταῖς ὁμωνυμίαις ib.36. **-η**, ἡ, *wandering, roaming*, Hdt.1.30, 2.103, 116: freq. in A.*Pr.*, in sg., 622, 784, al.: in pl., τηλέπλανοι, πολύπλανοι πλάναι, 576 (lyr.), 585 (lyr.), cf. Ar.*V.*873 (lyr.). 2. *discursive treatment*, ἡ διὰ παντὸς διέξοδος καὶ π. Pl.*Prm.*136e; ἡ π. τοῦ λόγου Id.*Lg.*683a. II. metaph., *going astray*, βίοτος ἀνθρώπων π. E.*Fr.* 659.8; π. καὶ ἄνοια Pl.*Phd.*81a; πλάνης ἔμπλεῳ Id.*R.*505c; ἡ περὶ τὰ χρώματα π. τῆς ὄψεως the *illusion*, ib.602c; πολλὴν ἔχει..πλάνην *irregularity*, Arist.*EN*1094ᵇ16; πολλὰς ἀπορίας ἔχει καὶ π. Id.*de An.* 402ᵃ21; ἡ κατὰ τὰς αἰσθήσεις π. Epicur.*Nat.*28 *Fr.*7; π. καὶ παραλογισμός Phld.*Rh.*1.30 S., cf. Diog.Oen.33. 2. *deceit, imposture*, Lxx *Pr.*14.8, *Ev.Matt.*27.64. **-ημα**, ατος, τό, *wandering*, A.*Pr.* 828; π. ψυχῆς S.*OT*727. ⊛ **-ης**, ητος, ὁ, *wanderer, vagabond*, ib.1029, E.*IT*417, Isoc.19.6: c. gen., πόντου πλάνητες *roamers* of the sea, *Trag.Adesp.*100. 2. πλάνητες ἀστέρες *planets*, X.*Mem.* 4.7.5, Arist.*Mete.*342ᵇ28; and, simply, οἱ π. Id.*APo.*78ᵃ30, *Fr.*196, Plu.2.604a, etc.; τοὺς ἀστέρας τοὺς ἐνδεδεμένους, τοὺς δὲ π. Arist. *Cael.*290ᵃ19. 3. πλάνητες [πυρετοί] fevers *that come in irregular fits*, Hp.*Epid.*1.6, *Aph.*3.22; cf. πλανήτης II.2. II. as Adj., ἄπορος καὶ π. βίος Plu.*Brut.*33; π. ὅμιλος Polem.*Call.*18.56: as fem., πλάνητα πτῆσιν Luc.*Musc.Enc.*9. **-ησίεδρος** [ῐ], ον, (ἕδρα) *having a wandering seat*, i.e. *moving about freely*, of the knee-pan, Arist.*HA*494ᵃ5. **-ησις**, εως, ἡ, *making to wander*: *dispersing, scattering*, τῶν νεῶν Th.8.42. 2. metaph., *misleading*, S.E.*M.*7.394 (dub. l.). **-ητέον**, *one must wander*, X.*Lac.*9.5. **-ητεύω**, *wander about*, *AB*375. **-ήτης**, ου, Dor. **πλανάτας**, ὁ, = πλάνης I.1, S.*OC*3, 124 (lyr.), E.*Ba.*148 (lyr.), etc.; τοὺς π. ἐπὶ τὰς πόλεις ἐμπόρους [καλοῦμεν] Pl.*R.*371d; πλανῆται ἐπὶ πάντας τόπους, of hares, X.*Cyn.*5.17. II. as Adj., π. ἄθλιος βίος E.*Heracl.*878, cf. Porph.*Marc.*22. 2. Medic., = πλάνης I.3, Gal.11.18. ⊛ **-ητικός**, ή, όν, *migratory*, ἔθνος Str.8.3.17. 2. *unstable, irregular*, τὰ ὑγρὰ π. ἐστι Arist.*Pr.*940ᵇ4; π. κίνησις Cleom. 2.7. 3. *of a planet*, Vett.Val.332.16. **-ῆτις**, ιδος, ἡ, fem. of πλανήτης, Lyc.998, Phld.*Acad.Ind.*p.77 M., Poll.5.63, Ant.Lib.24. 1. **-ητός**, ή, όν, *wandering*, π. κατὰ πόλεις Pl.*Ti.*19e; ἄστρα π. Id.*Lg.*821b, cf. *Ti.*38c (vv.ll. πλανῆται, πλάνητες), Arist.*Mu.*392ᵃ 13. II. metaph., *shifting*, Pl.*R.*479d; *irregular*, πάθη Plu.2.550e.

**πλάνιος** [ᾰ], ον, poet. for πλάνος, *AP*7.715 (Leon.).

**πλανίς**· τὸ τῆς νύμφης χρυσοῦν διάδημα, Hsch.

**πλᾰνοδαίμων**, ονος, ὁ, *deceitful demon*, *PMag.Lond.*121.636.

**πλανόδιος**, α, ον, *going by by-paths, wandering*, *h.Merc.*75 [πλᾱ-, metri gr.]; cf. πληνοδία.

**πλάνος** [ᾰ], ον, 1. Act., *leading astray, deceiving*, π. κατέσειον ἐδωδάν the bait, Theoc.21.43, cf. *AP*7.702 (Apollonid.); π. δῶρα, ἄγρα, Mosch.1.29, *Fr.*1.10; πνεύματα 1*Ep.Ti.*4.1. 2. Pass., *wandering, roaming, fickle*, ποικίλον πρᾶγμ' ἐστὶ καὶ πλάνον τύχη Men.*Kith.Fr.*8; π. φέγγη *planets*, Man.4.3. II. Subst. πλάνος, ὁ, = πλάνη, *wandering, roaming*, S.*OC*1114, E.*Alc.*482, etc.: in pl., Ar.*V.*873 (lyr.), etc. b. κερκίδος πλάνοι, of the act of weaving, E.*Ion* 1491 (lyr.). 2. metaph., φροντίδος πλάνοι *wanderings* of thought, S.*OT*67; π. φρενῶν *wandering* of mind, madness, E.*Hipp.*283; π. τε καρδίᾳ προσίσταται Id.*Fr.*1038; πλάνοις *in uncertain fits*, of a disease, S.*Ph.*758; = πλάνη II.1, Pl.*Phd.*79d. 3. *digression*, Id.*Ep.*344d. 4. *error*, Ceb.25, Diog.Oen.26; *grammatical mistake*, A.D.*Pron.*84.11. III. of persons, πλάνος, ὁ, *vagabond, impostor*, Nicostr.Com.24, Dionys.Com. 4, D.S.34/5.2.14, *Ev.Matt.*27.63.

**πλᾰνοστῐβής**, ές, *trodden by wanderers*, χθών A.*Eu.*76.

**πλᾰνύττω**, = πλανάομαι, *wander about*, Ar.*Av.*3.

**πλᾰνώδης**, ες, *wandering*, esp. 1. = πλάνης I.3, πυρετοί Hp. *Coac.*582. 2. *liable to slip*, of ligatures, Id.*Off.*9 (Sup.); ἄρθρον Id.*Fract.*45 (Comp.); of the womb, Aret.*SA*2.11. 3. metaph., *rambling*, γνώμη π. Id.*SA*2.11 (Comp.). Adv. **-δῶς** Phld.*Lib.*p.32 O.

**πλάξ**, πλᾰκός, ἡ, *anything flat and broad*, esp. *flat land, plain*, πᾶσαν ἠπείρου πλάκα A.*Pers.*718; Φλεγραίαν π. Id.*Eu.*295; νυχίαν π., of Psyttaleia (fort. μυχίαν), Id.*Pers.*953 (lyr.); πλακὸς ὑλίας *Berl.Sitzb.*1927.7 (Locr., v B.C.); νεκύων πλάκα S.*OC*1564 (lyr.); νεκρῶν πλάκες ib.1577 (lyr.); also of sea and sky, πόντου πλάξ the ocean-*plain*, Pi.*P.*1.24; ἄλοκα Νηρεΐας πλακὸς τέμνοντες Arion 1.15; ποντίᾳ, πελαγίᾳ π., E.*Fr.*578.4, Ar.*Ra.*1438; κατ' Αἰγαίην πόντου πλάκα *BMus.Inscr.*1012 (Chalcedon, i B.C./i A.D.); αἰθερία πλάξ E. *El.*1349 (anap.); *flat top of a hill, table-land*, Σουνίου, Οἴτης π., S.*Aj.* 1220, *Ph.*1430; Παρνασοῦ πλάκες E.*Ion* 1267; ἀπ' ἄκρας πυργώδους πλακός from the *flat top* of the towering hill, S.*Tr.*273; τὰς π. τοῦ ὄρους Ant.Lib.4.1. 2. *flat stone, tablet*, ἐργώνας τᾶν πλακῶν τᾶς τομᾶς εἰς τὸν ὀχετὸν *IG*4²(1).109 iii 154 (Epid., iii B.C.); π. ἐπιγεγραμμέναι *OGI*672.12 (Egypt, i A.D.), cf. Luc.*Somn.*3, etc.; of the *Tables* of the Jewish Law, αἱ π. τοῦ μαρτυρίου, τῆς διαθήκης, Lxx *Ex.* 31.18, *Ep.Hebr.*9.4; λίθων πλαξὶ λείαις Luc.*Am.*12; οὐκ ἐν πλαξὶν λιθίναις ἀλλ' ἐν π. καρδίας 2*Ep.Cor.*3.3; *tombstone*, *AP*7.324, cf. *IG* 12(5).329 (pl., Paros): pl., *slabs* of marble, Chor.p.89 B., cf. eund. in *Rev.Phil.*1877.79; ὥσπερ μαρμάρου π., of ice, Jul.*Mis.*341b. b. πλάκες χρυσίου gold *plates*, Str.4.2.1; σαπφείροιο D.P.1105; ἡ ἐντὸς π. τῶν κογχυλίων the inner *surface*.., Thphr.*Sens.*73. c. ἡ π. τοῦ βαλανίου τούτου prob. part of the furnace, *PMag.Osl.*1.340. **d.** pl., *flakes* of ἀρσενικὸν τὸ πλακῶδες, Dsc.5.104. **3.** in pl., *flaps, tail-fins* of crustacea, Arist.*HA*526$^{b}$9, *GA*758$^{a}$14. **b.** *folds* within certain parts of the ruminant stomach, Id.*HA*507$^{b}$11, *PA*675$^{a}$28. **4.** κοπτῆς πλάκες, = πλακοῦντες, *AP*12.212 (Strat.). (Cf. Lett. *plakt* 'become flat'.)

**πλάξιππος,** v. πλήξιππος. **πλαριᾶν·** μίγνυσθαι, Hsch.

⊛ **πλάσις** [ᾰ], εως, ἡ, (πλάσσω) *moulding, conformation,* τοῦ ἐμβρύου Arist.*GA*776$^{a}$33; of an infant, by massage, Sor.1.85; of a statue, *Rev.Ét.Anc.*33.215 (Theangela, iii B.C.); ὀπτῆς πλίνθου *PSI*6.712.5 (iii A.D.): generally, opp. ὕλη, Plot.3.3.4. **2.** *training* of the voice, Plu.*Cic.*4. **3.** *fiction, invention,* Arist.*Metaph.*1086$^{a}$4, Demetr.*Eloc.*158; πλάσει τῶν ἀδυνάτων Str.1.2.35.

**πλάσμα,** ατος, τό, *anything formed* or *moulded, image, figure,* πλάσματα πηλοῦ Ar.*Av.*686; κήρινον.. οὐκ οἶδ' ὅ τι π. as it were a *piece of* wax-*work,* Pl.*Tht.*197d, cf. 200c, *Sph.*239e; of figures made by bakers, Men.113: pl., *cakes* of incense, *POxy.*2144.29 (iii A.D.). **b.** the *body,* as fashioned by the Creator, *PMag.Par.*1.212. **II.** *counterfeit, forgery,* π. ὅλον ἐστὶν ἡ διαθήκη D.45.29. **b.** *figment, fiction,* πλάσματα τῶν προτέρων Xenoph.1.22, cf. Arist.*Cael.*289$^{a}$6, Str.1.2.36, J.*BJ*1.1.2, Plu.*Thes.*28, etc.; of a *story* which is *fictitious but possible,* opp. ἱστορία II and μῦθος II.3, S.E.*M.*1.263, Aus.*Prof.*21.26, cf. Ph.1.528. **c.** *pretence,* Phld.*Vit.*p.38 J., Plu.*Mar.*43. **2.** *delusion,* Phld.*Lib.*p.56 O. **III.** *formed style* in writing or speaking, π. καὶ τὴν ἄλλην κατασκευὴν δημηγόρου Id.*Rh.*1.199 S.; opp. τρόπος, σχῆμα, ib.164 S.; π. ἱστορικόν, opp. ὑπαγωγικόν, D.H.*Pomp.*4; ἡνίκ' ἂν ᾖ ποιητικὸν τοῦ λόγου τὸ π. Longin.15.8. **2.** in music, *affected execution,* with trills, falsetto, etc., μετὰ πλάσματος αὐλεῖν, opp. ἀπλάστως, Thphr.*HP*4.11.5; of studied *intonation* in orators or actors, π. φωνῆς ἀθόρυβον Plu.*Per.*5, cf. 2.405d; *lectio plasmate effeminata,* Quint.*Inst.*1.8.2; ἀναγνώσεις μετὰ πλάσματος Sor.1.49.

**πλασμᾰτ-ίας,** ου, ὁ, *fabricated, fictitious,* ἄτοπος καὶ π. ὁ λόγος Arist.*GA*734$^{a}$33, cf. 769$^{a}$36, *Metaph.*1076$^{a}$39. **II.** *one addicted to invention,* Plu.*Cam.*22. **-ικός,** ή, όν, *imitative, dramatic,* εἶδος διηγήματος Hermog.*Prog.*2. **II.** *fictitious,* S.E.*P.*1.103.

**πλασμᾰτογράφος** [γρᾰ], ὁ, *writer of speeches for possible* (not real) *occasions,* Anon.*in Rh.*122.5, Eust.61.12:—hence **-γρᾰφέω,** Id.751.19 (Pass.).

⊛ **πλασμᾰτώδης,** ες, *fictitious,* Arist.*GA*764$^{b}$10, *Resp.*472$^{b}$12, Porph.*Gaur.*2.2; λέγω δὲ πλασματῶδες τὸ πρὸς ὑπόθεσιν βεβιασμένον Arist.*Metaph.*1082$^{b}$3; τὸ δραματικὸν καὶ π. Plu.*Rom.*8.

⊛ **πλάσσω,** Att. **-ττω** S.*Aj.*148 (anap.), Pl.*R.*420c, etc.: fut. πλάσω (ἀνα-) Hp.*Mochl.*2: aor. ἔπλᾰσα Hdt.2.70 (κατ-), Ar.*V.*926, etc.; poet. ἔπλασσα Theoc.24.109; Ep. πλάσσα Hes.*Op.*70: pf. πέπλᾰκα Phld.*Mus.*p.85 K., D.S.15.11, D.H.*Th.*41: 3 sg. plpf. ἐπεπλάκει Erot.*Praef.*:—Med., fut. πλάσομαι Alciphr.1.37: aor. ἐπλασάμην Th.6.58, Pl.*Lg.*800b, etc.:—Pass., fut. πλασθήσομαι Phld.*Mus.*p.82 K., (δια-) Gal.4.619: aor. ἐπλάσθην E.*Fr.*1130, Lys.12.48, Pl.*Ti.*26e: pf. πέπλασμαι A.*Pr.*1030, etc.:—*form, mould,* prop. of the artist who works in soft substances, such as earth, clay, wax, ἐκ γαίης π. Hes.*Op.*70, cf. Hdt.2.47, 73; of Prometheus, ὃν λέγουσ' ἡμᾶς πλάσαι καὶ τἄλλα ... ζῷα Philem.89.1, cf. Men.535.5; π. καθάπερ ἐκ κηροῦ Pl.*Lg.*746a; σχήματα ἐκ χρυσοῦ Id.*Ti.*50a; ἐκ πηλοῦ ζῷον Arist.*PA*654$^{b}$29; ἀγγεῖον π. κήρινον Id.*Mete.*359$^{a}$1; οὐκ ἔστιν ἀνδριαντοποιὸς ὅστις ἂν πλάσαι κάλλος τοιοῦτον Philem.72.2; τοὺς πηλίνους D.4.26; opp. γράφειν, as sculpture to painting, Pl.*R.*510e (so in Pass., *Lg.*668e, Isoc.9.75); τὴν ὑδρίαν πλάσαι *mould* the water-jar, Ar.*V.*926; σώματα π. θνητά Pl.*Ti.*42d; π. κηρία, of bees, Arist.*HA*623$^{b}$32; ἔπλαττεν ἔνδον οἰκίας *made clay* houses, Ar.*Nu.*879; *knead* bread, Gal.6.313:—Med., σχῆμα πλασάμενος *having formed oneself* a figure, Pl.*Plt.*297e:—Pass., *to be moulded, made,* τὸ δὲ ἐν τῇσι μήτρῃσι πλάσσεται Hdt.3.108; οἶκος τεκτόνων πλασθεὶς ὕπο E.*Fr.*1130; ἂν ἴδωσι.. κήρινα μιμήματα πεπλασμένα Pl.*Lg.*933b. **2.** *plaster,* τὸν.. ναὸν χρίσαντες καὶ πλάσαντες *BCH*15.209 (Panamara). **II.** generally, *mould, form* by education, training, etc., π. τὰς ψυχὰς τοῖς μύθοις, τὰ σώματα ταῖς χερσίν, Pl.*R.*377c; σῶμα ἐπιμελῶς Id.*Ti.*88c; ἑαυτόν Id.*R.*500d; παιδεύειν τε καὶ π. Id.*Lg.*671c:—Pass., τοὔνομ' ἀνὰ χρόνον πεπλασμένον E.*Ion*830; of the voice, *to be trained,* Arist.*HA*536$^{b}$19. **III.** *form an image* of a thing *in the mind, imagine,* πλάττομεν οὔτε ἰδόντες οὔτε.. νοήσαντες ἀθάνατόν τι ζῷον Pl.*Phdr.*246c, cf. *R.*420c, 466a; τῷ λόγῳ τοὺς νόμους Id.*Lg.*712b; τἀρχαῖα Phld.*Mus.*p.85 K.:—Pass., ib.p.82 K. **IV.** *put in a certain form,* τὸ στόμα π. (so as to pronounce more elegantly) Pl.*Cra.*414d; [κόμιον] Arr.*Epict.*2.24.24; τὴν ὑπόκρισιν Plu.*Dem.*7:—Med., ἀδήλως τῇ ὄψει πλυσάμενος πρὸς τὴν ξυμφοράν *having formed himself* in face, i.e. composed his countenance, Th.6.58, cf. D.45.68. **V.** metaph., *fabricate, forge,* λόγους ψιθύρους πλάσσων S.*Aj.*148 (anap.); ψευδεῖς π. αἰτίας Isoc.12.25; προφάσεις D.25.28; τί λόγους πλάττεις; Id.18.121, cf. Pl.*Ap.*17c; μὴ πλάσῃς κακόν Men.*Mon.*145; π. ἐπιστολήν Plb.5.42.7: abs., δόξω πλάσας λέγειν I shall be thought to speak *from invention,* i.e. not the truth, Hdt.8.80, cf. X.*Mem.*2.6.37:—Med., πλάσασθαι τὸν τρόπον τὸν αὑτοῦ Lys.19.60; ψεύδη X.*An.*2.6.26; τῆς φιλανθρωπίας ἦν... ἐπλάττετο D.18.231; προφάσεις π. Id.19.215; τοιαῦτα πλάττεσθαι τολμᾶτε Id.28.9; καιρὸν πλάττεσθαι Id.21.187: abs., πλαττομένους πρὸς ἑαυτούς (αὑτούς Bonitz) Arist.*Rh.*1381$^{b}$28: c. inf., Νέρων εἶναι πλασάμενος *pretending* to be N., D.C.64.9; π. νοσεῖν Gal.19.1:—Pass., οὐ πεπλασμένος ὁ κόμπος not *fictitious,* A.*Pr.*1030; πεπλάσθαι φάσκοντες saying *it was a forgery,* Is.7.2; μὴ πλασθέντα μῦθον ἀλλ' ἀληθινὸν λόγον Pl.*Ti.*26e; π. ὑπὸ ποιητῶν And.4.23; ἐξ ὧν ἡ δίκη αὕτη πέπλασται D.52.12. (πλαθ-yω, cf. κορο-πλάθος, πηλο-πλάθος.)

**πλασταρεύοντες·** πλάσσοντες, Hsch.

**πλάσ-τειρα,** fem. of πλάστης, Orph.*H.*10.20; φύσις *APl.*4.310 (Damoch.). **-τέον,** *one must mould, Gp.*6.2.4 (sed leg. παστέον); *one must form* (in mathematical calculations), Iamb.*in Nic.*p.44 P. **-τευτής,** οῦ, ὁ, *one who makes* πλασταί, *PFlor.*226.11 (iii A.D.). **-τή,** ἡ, *mud-wall* or *-enclosure, BGU*1503 (iii B.C.), *PSI*2.171.19 (ii B.C.), *POxy.*729.30 (ii A.D.), etc. ⊛ **-της,** ου, ὁ, *moulder, modeller,* in clay or wax, Pl.*R.*588d, *Lg.*671c, Plu.*Per.*12; *sculptor, IG*11(4).1105 (Delos, iii B.C.), Luc.*Im.*9, Gal.*Med.Phil.*2; *brickmaker, Meyer Ostr.*61.6 (iii B.C.); perh. = τριχοπλάστης, Plu.*Dio*9. **II.** *creator,* Ph.1.434.

**πλαστίγγιον,** τό, Dim. of sq., *balance,* Διός Cerc.4.37. **II.** = πλάστιγξ III, *Hippiatr.*74 (pl.).

⊛ **πλάστιγξ,** Ion. **πλήστιγξ** (v. infr. III), ιγγος, ἡ, *scale of a balance,* Ar.*Pax*1248; παρίστασθον παρὰ τὼ πλάστιγγε Id.*Ra.*1378; τιθέναι εἰς πλάστιγγας, ἐν πλάστιγγι ζυγοῦ κεῖσθαι, Pl.*Ti.*63b, *R.*550e: metaph., ἀνώμαλοι πλάστιγγες ἀστάτου τύχης *Trag.Adesp.*179; ὅταν δαίμων ἀνδρὸς εὐτυχοῦς τὸ πρὶν πλάστιγγ' ἐρείσῃ τοῦ βίου παλίρροπον S.*Fr.*576.5 (prob. for μάστιγ'); τὸ τεᾷ π. δοθὲν μακαριστότατον τελέθει *Lyr.Adesp.*139; ὥσπερ ἐπὶ πλάστιγγος ἀντιρρέπων Ph.2.170; εἰς τὴν αὐτὴν τιθεὶς π. τὴν μέθην τῇ μανίᾳ Ath.1.11a. **2.** *disk* poised on the top of the ῥάβδος κοτταβική, καθ' ὅσον ἂν τὸν κότταβον ἀφεὶς ἐπὶ τὴν π. ποιήσῃ πεσεῖν Antiph.55.6, cf. Hermipp.47.8 (anap.); π. ἡ χαλκοῦ θυγάτηρ Critias *Fr.*1 D., cf. Poll.6.110. **3.** *valve of an oyster-shell,* Opp.*H.*2.179. **II.** *collar for horses,* E.*Rh.*303. **III.** pl., *surgical splints, Hippiatr.*24, 74; in form **πλήστιγγες,** Hp.ap.Gal.19.131. **IV.** *scourge,* A.*Ch.*290 (s.v.l.), cf. *EM*674.20, Hsch.

**πλαστῐκ-άριος,** ὁ, *potter* (?), *PSI*8.955 (vi A.D.). **-ός,** ή, όν, *fit for moulding, plastic,* γῆ.. τῶν σωμάτων -ωτάτη Pl.*Ti.*55e; αἱ π. τῶν τεχνῶν the arts *of moulding* clay, wax, etc., *plastic* arts, Id.*Lg.*679a; ἡ -κή Arist.*PA*645$^{a}$13, Phld.*Mus.*p.91 K., Ph.1.34, Luc.*Prom.*2, etc. **II.** of persons, *gifted in sculpture,* Longin.*Rh.*p.203 H.

**πλάστις,** ιδος, fem. of πλάστης, Ael.*NA*5.42.

**πλαστο-γρᾰφέω,** *counterfeit writing,* Artem.4.27, etc. **-γρᾰφία,** ἡ, *forgery,* J.*Vit.*11, *BGU*388 ii 39 (ii A.D.), Vett.Val.40.29 (pl.), Just.*Nov.*80.7. **-γράφος** [γρᾰ], ὁ, *forger,* Artem.1.51, Ptol.*Tetr.*161, Man.2.305, *Cod.Just.*4.20.13 *Intr.* **-κόμης,** ου, ὁ, *one who wears false hair,* Man.4.304. **-λάλος** [λᾰ], ὁ, *fandi fictor, Gloss.* **-λογέω,** *tell fictions, lie,* Suid. (ἐπλ-). **-λόγος,** ὁ, *falsidicus, Gloss.* **-ποιός,** ὁ, *maker of* πλασταί, *POxy.*2155.9 (iv A.D.).

⊛ **πλαστός,** ή, όν, *formed, moulded,* esp. in clay or wax, γυνή Hes.*Th.*513; τὸ π. ὃ δὴ σκεῦος ὠνομάκαμεν Pl.*Sph.*219a; π. ἐκ γαίης Antiph.52.3; π. εἰκών *statue,* opp. painting, Plu.*Ages.*2. **2.** *that can easily be moulded, plastic,* Arist.*Mete.*386$^{a}$27; *in a thick paste,* Thphr.*HP*9.4.10. **II.** metaph., *fabricated, forged, counterfeit,* ἐκ λόγου πλαστοῦ Hdt.1.68; π. βακχεῖαι *sham* inspirations, E.*Ba.*218; π. τὴν φιλίαν παρέχεσθαι X.*Ages.*1.38; πλαστὸς πατρί a *supposititious* son, S.*OT*780, cf. Sosith.2.4; π. ἐπιχείρημα *hypothetical* case, Hermog.*Inv.*3.11, cf. 15. Adv. **-τῶς,** opp. ὄντως, Pl.*Sph.*216c; opp. ἀληθῶς, Id.*Lg.*642d; opp. φύσει, ib.777d; π. ὀδυρόμενοι *feignedly,* Phld.*Rh.*1.381 S. **III.** v. πλατός.

**πλαστουργ-έω,** *mould, form, fashion,* Hsch. **-ία,** ἡ, *work of plastic art,* of statues, Tz.*H.*7.932; ποικίλη π., of cakes, ib.13.325.

**πλάστρια,** ἡ, fem. of πλάστης, of the μονάς, *Theol.Ar.*5; of φύσις, Herm.ap.Stob.1.49.69.

**πλάστρον,** τό, *ear-ring, IG*2$^{2}$.1527.17 (Brauronion, iv B.C.): more freq. in pl., Ar.*Fr.*320.10, *IG*1$^{2}$.313.63, al., 2$^{2}$.1544.11, 12(8).51.17 (Imbros, ii B.C.), Poll.5.97. **II.** pl., *images of gods,* Hsch.

**πλᾰτᾰγ-έω,** *clap the hands,* Theoc.8.88; of broad flat bodies coming together, *clap,* v.l. in Id.3.29, *AP*9.86 (Antiphil.):—Med., ἐπλαταγεῦντο θύραι ib.7.182 (Mel.). **II.** *beat,* so as to make a loud noise, στήθεα Bion 1.4; στέρνα *BMus.Inscr.*1084.6 (Naucratis); τύμπανον *AP*6.218.6 (Alc.). **-ή,** ἡ, *rattle,* Hellanic.104(*a*) J., Pherecyd.72 J.; ἡ Ἀρχύτου π. Arist.*Pol.*1340$^{b}$26; π. χαλκείη, πυξινέη, A.R.2.1055, *AP*6.309 (Leon.). **-ημα,** ατος, τό, *crack,* of the τηλέφιλον (q.v.), Theoc.3.29, *AP*5.295 (Agath.). **-ών,** ῶνος, ἡ, = πλαταγή, Sch.Theoc.11.57. **-ωνίζω,** = πλαταγέω: πλαταγωνίσας· ἀποληκυθίσας, ψοφήσας, Hsch. **-ώνιον,** τό, *broad petal of the poppy* or *anemone,* so called because lovers took omens from it, laying it on the left hand, and striking it with the right, and it was a good omen if it burst *with a loud crack,* Theoc.11.57, cf. Nic.*Fr.*74.43, Poll.9.127; τῷ μηκῶνος π. J.*AJ*3.7.6 (vulg. πλαταγῶνι); cf. τηλέφιλον.

**Πλάταια** [Πλᾰ], ἡ, Il.2.504, Hdt.8.50, Th.2.4:—more freq. pl. **Πλᾰταιαί,** ῶν, αἱ, *Plataea* or *Plataeae* in Boeotia, Hdt.9.25, 30, etc. Adv. **Πλᾰταιᾶσι,** before a vowel **-σιν,** *at Plataeae,* Th.1.130, D.59.97; **Πλᾰταιάζε** *to P.,* **Πλᾰταιόθεν** *from P.,* St.Byz.: **Πλᾰταιεῖς,** έων, οἱ, Ion. **-έες,** *Plataeans,* Hdt.6.108, etc.; Att. nom. **Πλᾰταιῆς,** acc. **-ᾶς,** Th.2.4, Ar.*Ra.*694; οἱ Π., at Athens, were *enfranchised slaves who had the same civic rights as the citizens of Plataea,* Hellanic.171 J.: Adj. **Πλᾰταιικός,** ή, όν, *of P.,* Hdt.9.25; τὰ -κά *the events at P.,* Id.8.126, 9.38; fem. ἡ **Πλᾰταιὶς** γῆ, χώρα, Id.9.25, Th.3.58, al.: abs., ἡ Π. Hdt.9.36; also **Πλαταιᾶτις,** St.Byz.

**πλαταΐσαι·** τὸ ὠμοθετῆσαι, Hsch. (πλαταῖς· τὸ δμο- cod.).

**πλατάκιον,** v. πλάταξ.

**πλᾰτᾰμώδης,** ες, *of flat shape, broad and even,* Arist.*HA*548$^{a}$26; τὰ π. *Placit.*3.15.9, cf. Str.8.3.23.

⊛ **πλᾰτᾰμών,** ῶνος, ὁ, (πλατύς) *any broad flat body* or *space,* esp. *flat* *stone, h.Merc.*128, A.R.1.365; *flat reef* of rocks at the water's edge, Arat.993, Gal.19.131: pl., *ledges of rock*, Str.5.2.6, 12.2.8. **2.** *flat beach*, in pl., *AP*7.404 (Zon.), v. l. in Dsc.4.73. **3.** *shallow reservoir, fish-pond*, Arist.*HA*592$^a$4, cf. *AB*1313. **4.** *flat land*, liable to be overflowed, Plb.10.48.7, D.P.626. **5.** pl., *level sea*, Opp.*H.*1.121, 5.650.

**πλᾰτάνιον** [τᾰ], τό, a kind of *apple*, Diph.Siph.ap.Ath.3.81a.

**πλᾰτᾰνιστ-ής**, οῦ, Dor. **-ιστάς**, ᾶ, ὁ, = πλατανών, Paus.3.11.2, 3.14.8. **II.** an unknown *fish* of the Ganges, Plin.*HN*9.46. **-ῖνος**, η, ον: π. μῆλα inferior kind of apple on which pigs were fed in Asia Minor, Gal.6.597. **-ος**, ἡ, earlier name for πλάτανος, Il.2.307, 310, Hdt.5.119, 7.27,31, Theoc.18.44, al. **-οῦς**, οῦντος, ὁ, contr. for πλατανιστόεις, *grove of plane-trees*, Thgn.882.

**πλᾰτᾰν-ος** [πλᾰ], ἡ, later form of πλατάνιστος, *Platanus orientalis, plane*, Ar.*Eq.*528, *Nu.*1008, Pl.*Phdr.*229a, Thphr.*HP*4.5.6, Nic.*Th.*584, Dsc.1.79. (From πλατύς, because of its *broad crown*.) **-ών**, ῶνος, ὁ, = πλατανιστοῦς, Dsc.4.73 (v. l. πλαταμῶσι), Hdn.Gr.1.34, al., Plin.*Ep.*1.3.

**πλᾰταξ** [ᾰ], ακος, ὁ, Alexandr. name of *the fish* κορακῖνος, Ath.7.309a:—Dim. **πλᾰτάκιον** [τᾰ], τό, *POxy.*920.3, al. (ii/iii A. D.).

⊛ **πλάτας** [πλᾰ], α, also **πλάτης**, ου, ὁ, *platform* on which tombs were placed, *TAM*2.438 (Patara), *CIG*2825, al. (Aphrodisias); cf. πλάτος (B), πέλτον.

**πλᾰτάσσω**, (πλατύς) *slap* or *clap two flat bodies together*, Suid. s. v. πλαταγώνιον. **πλατεῖα**, ἡ, v. πλατύς II.

**πλᾰτει-άζω**, Dor. **-άσδω**, *slap with the flat hand* (πλατείᾳ), Pherecr. 224. **II.** *pronounce broadly*, like the Dorians, Theoc.15.88. **III.** πλατεάζειν (sic)· ἀλαζονεύεσθαι, φενακίζειν, Hsch. **IV.** πλατειάδδοντες· οἱ γυμναζόμενοι τοῖς ἐφήβοις, Id. **-ασμός**, ὁ, *broad Doric accent*, pl. in form πλατεασμοί, Quint.*Inst.*1.5.32.

**πλᾰτεῖον**, τό, (πλατύς) *tablet*, Plb.6.34.8, 10.45.8.

⊛ **πλάτη** [ᾰ], Dor. **πλάτα**, ἡ, (πλατύς) *flat* or *broad object*: **1.** *blade of an oar*: and generally, *oar*, A.*Ag.*695 (lyr.), S.*Aj.*358 (lyr.), E.*Hec.*39, al.; ναυτίλῳ π. *by ship, by sea*, S.*Ph.*220; οὐρίῳ π. with a fair *voyage*, ib.355; βάρβαρος π. E.*Hel.*192 (lyr.); πλάτη φυγεῖν Id.*IT*242; οἷον πλάταις, of the tails of some crustacea, Arist.*PA*684$^a$3; ὥσπερ πτερύγια ἢ πλάτας, of the feet of others, ib.13; of the *membranes* or *lobes* attached to the toes of certain birds, ib.694$^b$5. **2.** χερσαία π. *winnowing fan*, or (as others expl.) shepherd's *crook*, Lyc.96. **3.** in pl., *shoulder-blades*, Hp.*Loc.Hom.*6, Poll.2.133, Hsch.: sg., *SIG* 1024.7 (Myconos, iii/ii B. C.). **b.** *broad ribs*, Poll.2.181. **4.** *sheet of papyrus*, *AP*13.21 (Theodorid.). **II.** *paling*, *POxy.*707.32 (ii A. D.), 1674.10 (iii A. D.).

**πλατηρ**· τὸ πλατείᾳ τῇ χειρὶ πατάξαι, Hsch. **πλάτης**, v. πλάτας.

**πλᾱτιάζω, -ιασμός, πλᾱτίον**, Dor. for πλησιάζω, -ιασμός, πλησίον.

**πλάτιγξ**, ἡ, = πλάτη I. 1, Hsch.

⊛ **πλᾰτικός**, ή, όν, (πλάτος) *of* or *in latitude*, θέσεις, ἀπόστασις, Procl.*Hyp.*5.6,8. **II.** metaph., *broad, general*, π. θεωρία, opp. μοιρική, Vett.Val.112.25; π. καὶ καθολικὴ θ. Id.289.15, cf. 243.3. **2.** of meanings of words, *broad, wide*, or *involving breadth*, ὁ κοινὸς καὶ π. τόπος *in the broad sense*, Simp.*in Ph.*637.24; τὸ νῦν, οὐ τὸ π. ἀλλὰ τὸ ἄτομον Id.*in Cael.*579.16; π. ἐστιν ὁ ἐνεστὼς· οἱονεὶ γὰρ πλάτος ὑπεμφαίνει ὡς πρὸς τὸν.. ἀκαριαῖον λεγόμενον χρόνον Choerob.*in Theod.*2.12 H. Adv. **-κῶς** *broadly speaking*, Ach.Tat.*Intr.Arat.*18, Vett.Val.274.34, Simp.*in Cat.*426.23, Phlp.*in Cat.*46.19. **3.** π. ἐξήγησις *detailed* exegesis, Ammon. in *Porph.*60.6; **-κωτέραν** τὴν ἴασιν εὑρήσεις ἐν.. Paul.Aeg.2.25. Adv. Comp. **-ώτερον**, ἐξηγούμενος, opp. κεφαλαιωδῶς, Id.6.53, cf. Eust. ad D.P.*Proll.*p.71 B. (πλατυκ- is read in Eust. l. c., and as v. l. in inferior codd. of Phlp., Ammon. ll. cc., Simp. *in Cael.* l. c., Paul.Aeg. ll. cc.; cf. Lat. *platicus*.)

**πλᾶτις**, ιδος, ἡ, poet. for πελάτις, *wife*, Ar.*Ach.*132, Lyc.821.

**πλᾰτίστᾰκος**, ὁ, *the fish* μύλλος, Dorio ap.Ath.3.118c; also, = σαπέρδης, Parmeno ap. eund.7.308f: with play on Πλάτων, Timo 30. **II.** *pudenda muliebria*, Hsch., Phot.

**πλατιωχέτας**, v. πλατυχαίτας.

**πλᾰτόομαι**, Pass., *to be made flat* like an oar-blade, Ar.*Ach.*552.

**πλᾰτοποιία**, ἡ, prob. *manufacture of* πλάται, *PLond.ined.*2142 (pl., iv A. D.; written -ειῶν).

**πλατορόα**, name of a festival at Lindos, Hsch.

⊛ **πλάτος** (A) [ᾰ], εος, τό, (πλατύς) *breadth, width*, σώματος Simon.188, etc.: abs., τὸ π. or π., *in breadth*, Hdt.1.193,4.195, X.*Oec.*19.3; ἴση μῆκός τε π. τε Emp.17.20. **b.** Math., *breadth*, i. e. *the second dimension*, ἐν μήκει καὶ π. καὶ βάθει Pl.*Sph.*235d, cf. Arist.*Ph.*209$^a$5; κατὰ π., opp. κατὰ μῆκος, κατὰ βάθος, Id.*Cael.*299$^b$26, *Mete.*341$^b$34. **2.** *plane surface*, Pl.*Plt.*284e, *Lg.*819e; μεγέθους τὸ ἐπὶ δύο [συνεχὲς] π. Arist.*Metaph.*1020$^a$12. **3.** *latitude*, whether terrestrial or celestial, Str.1.4.2, Cleom.1.4, 2.4, Ptol.*Alm.*2.12, Vett.Val.30.12. **4.** metaph., *plane*, ἐν τῷ ψυχικῷ π. Procl.*Inst.*201. **5.** *plane* of flat fish, Arist.*HA*489$^b$33; *flat* of the tail, ib.549$^b$1; *flat part* of the body of the fishing-frog, Id.*PA*695$^b$15. **6.** *extension, breadth* of a subject, Gal.1.316; οὐκ ὀλίγον τὸ π. Id.11.738. **7.** = πλάτας, Judeich *Altertümer von Hierapolis* No.322, al. **II.** metaph., *range* of variation, *latitude*, π. ἔχειν Plot.6.3.20; ἡ ὑγίεια π. ἔχει Gal.6.12, cf. 11.737. **III.** with Preps., ἐν πλάτει in a *loose* sense, *broadly*, Posidon. ap.Stob.1.8.42, Str.2.1.39, D.H.*Comp.*21, *EM*673.24; opp. κατ' ἀκρίβειαν, S.E.*M.*10.108; ὡς ἐν π. Sor.1.24 (but περὶ ὧν ἐν τῷ π. λέγομεν which we will discuss *in detail*, D.L.7.76); also ἐπὶ πλάτει Ἑλληνίζειν talk *loose* Greek, Phld.*Po.*2.9; κατὰ πλάτος λέγεσθαι to be said *loosely*, Chrysipp.*Stoic.*2.164, cf. Sor.1.6,21. **IV.** = πλατύτης 3, Demetr. *Eloc.*177. **V.** π. καρδίας, of Solomon, *width* of knowledge, Lxx 3 *Ki.*2.35a. **VI.** ἀργυρίου πλάτη, = δραχμαί, *IG*9(1).189.15 (Tithora, ii A. D.).

⊛ **πλάτος** (B) [ᾰ], ὁ, = πλάτας, *IGRom.*4.866 (Laodicea ad Lycum).

**πλᾱτός**, ἡ, όν, (πελάζω) *approachable*, οὐ πλατοῖσι φυσιάμασι A.*Eu.*53 (Elmsl. for πλαστοῖσι, cf. πλατά· προσπέλαστα, Phot.).

**πλάττω**, Att. for πλάσσω. **II.** **πλάττομαι**, v. πλάζω (A).

**πλᾰτῠ-ᾰλουργής**, ές, *with broad purple border*, ἱμάτιον *IG*2$^2$.1514.17. **-ᾰμφοδος**, ον, *with broad streets*, gloss on εὐρυάγυια, Sch.D Il.2.12, *AB*332, etc. **-αύχην**, ενος, ὁ, ἡ, *broad-necked*, Man.5.185. **-γάστωρ**, ορος, ὁ, ἡ, *flat-bellied*, Arist.*HA*553$^b$10, 624$^b$25. **-γένειος**, ον, gloss on ἠϋγένειος, Sch.Opp.*H.*2.565.

**πλᾰτῠγίζω**, (πλατύς) of a goose, *beat the water with its wings, splash about*, Eub.115; ὥσπερ πελεκᾶς πλατυγίζων prob. in Ar.*Fr.*22 D.: metaph., *make a splash, swagger*, Id.*Eq.*830.

**πλᾰτῠ-γλωσσος** [ῠ], Att. **-ττος**, ον, *broad-tongued, flat-tongued*, Arist.*HA*504$^b$3: Comp., Id.*PA*660$^a$30. **-γνᾰθος**, ον, *with broad jaws*, Lyd.*Mag.*3.61. **-ίσχιος**, ον, *with broad hips*, Gal.4.629, 5.464. **-καρπος**, ον, *with flat fruit*, v. l. in Dsc.3.144. **-καυλος**, ον, *flat-stalked*, Thphr.*HP*7.4.5. **-κερκος**, ον, *flat-tailed*, οἶες Arist.*HA*596$^b$4. **-κερως**, ωτος, ὁ, ἡ, *flat-horned*, ἔλαφος Dsc.*Eup.*1.21, cf. Plin.*HN*11.123, Poll.5.76: as Subst. (without ἔλαφος), Dsc.2.75. **-κέφᾰλος**, ον, *flat-headed*, Apollod.*Poliorc.*146.7, al., Olymp. Hist.p.459 D. **II.** a venomous *beast* or *reptile*, Philum.*Ven.*32.2. **-κορία**, Ion. **-ίη**, ἡ, (κόρη III) *a disease* of the eye *from dilatation of the pupil, mydriasis*, Aret.*SD*1.7, Aët.7.54. **-κορίᾰσις**, εως, ἡ, = foreg., Gal.14.768.

**πλᾰτῠκός**, v. πλατικός.

**πλᾰτῠ-κύμῑνον** [κῠ], τό, *broad cummin*, Dsc.*Eup.*2.118 (interpol.), Alex.Trall.8.2. **-λέσχης**, ου, ὁ, *diffuse babbler*, *AP*11.382.5 (Agath.). **-λόγος**, ον, *babbling*, *Gloss.* **-λογχος**, ον, *broad-pointed*, ἀκόντια Ar.*Fr.*476, cf. Alex.131, *IG*2$^2$.1487.98. **II.** Subst. π., τό, *partisan*, Str.17.3.7, prob. in Hsch. s. v. μαδάρεις. **-μέτωπος**, ον, *with broad forehead*, βόες Ael.*NA*12.19, cf. Heph.Astr.2.2. **-μήλη**, ἡ, *broad probe*, Antyll.ap.Orib.44.22.2, Heliod.ap.eund. 44.11.2.

**πλάτυμμα** [πλᾰ], ατος, τό, = πλάτυσμα, *plate*, π. χρυσοῦν, ἀργυροῦν, *BGU*162.3,7 (ii/iii A. D.); μολυβοῦν *PMag.Par.*1.329, cf. *PMag.Lond.*121.438. **II.** *flat cake*, *AB*294, 317.

**πλᾰτυν-τέον**, *one must extend*, X.*Eq.Mag.*4.3. **-ω**, (πλατύς) *widen*, τὰ φυλακτήρια *Ev.Matt.*23.5; τὴν εἰσβολὴν J.*BJ*5.8.1; π. τὸ στῖφος *widen* it out, ib.5.2.1; τοὺς ἐφεξῆς στίχους Arr.*Tact.*17.2: metaph., τὴν ψυχὴν εὐγενεστέραν τῆς φύσεως πλατύνας *IG*5(2).268.12 (Mantinea, i B. C.):—Med., τὴν γῆν πλατύνεσθαι *widen one's* territory, X.*Cyr.*5.5.34:—Pass., *grow broad, widen out*, Arist.*Mir.*841$^a$2, *Mu.*393$^a$23, etc.; of the pupils, *to be dilated*, Plu.2.376f: metaph., ἡ καρδία πεπλάτυνται *is opened, relieved from care*, 2*Ep.Cor.*6.11; ἐπλάτυνας τὴν καρδίαν μου Lxx*Ps.*118(119).32. **2.** ἐπλατύνθη.. τὸ στόμα μου *was opened wide*, ib.1*Ki.*2.1: hence, metaph., μὴ πλατυνθῇ ἡ καρδία *be puffed up*, ib.*De.*11.16:—Med., *talk big of oneself*, τί πλατύνεαι, ἠλίθιος ὥς; Timo 34.4. **3.** *pronounce broadly*, τὴν φωνὴν Hermog.*Id.*1.6, Harp. s. v. λαρυγγίζειν. **4.** *amplify*, τὸν λόγον Phld.*Ind.Sto.*24; τὴν ἑρμηνείαν Hermog.*Prog.*3:—Pass., διήγησις πλατύνεται τρόποις Id.*Inv.*2.7: abs., *use amplification*, D.H.*Din.*6.

**πλᾰτῠ-νωτος**, ον, *broad-backed*, Batr.296. **-ουρος**, ον, (οὐρά) *broad-tailed*, Opp.*H.*1.99. **-όφθαλμος**, ον, *widening the eyes*, v. l. in Hp.*Art.*67, cf. Erot.: τὸ π., = στίβι, Dsc.5.84. **-πεδος**, ον, *with broad fields*, Sch.Hes.*Th.*117. **-πήγιον**, τό, *broad-bottomed boat, punt*, *POxy.*1652.2 (iii A. D.), prob. in *PThead.*59.3. **-πῖλος**, ον, *with broad felt*, κυνῆ Sch.S.*OC*313. **-πλευρον**, τό, *plantago*, *Gloss.* (*patipleoron* cod.). **-πόρφῠρος**, ον, *with broad purple border*, ἱμάτιον Archipp.39. **-πους**, ὁ, ἡ, πουν, τό, gen. ποδος, *flat-footed*, D.L.1.81. **-πρόσωπος**, ον, *flat-faced*, *PGrenf.*1.27(2).8 (ii B. C.), *Peripl.M.Rubr.*65, Arist.*Mir.*832$^b$2, Ael.*NA*15.26. **-πῡγος**, ον, (πυγή) *broad-bottomed*, of boats, Str.4.4.1.

**πλατυρ**· δοῦλος ἢ δῆμος, Hsch.

**πλᾰτῠ-ρημοσύνη**, ἡ, (ῥῆμα) *breadth in speaking*, i. e. *prolixity*, Timo 35. **-ρρῖνος**, ον, = sq., Heph.Astr.2.2. **-ρρίς**, ῖνος, ὁ, ἡ, *broad-nosed*, Str.2.2.3. **-ρροος**, contr. **-ρους**, ουν, *broad-flowing*, Νεῖλος A.*Pr.*852. **-ρρυγχος**, ον, *broad-snouted* or *-beaked*, Timocl.14.7, Arist.*PA*662$^b$12. **-ρρῡμος**, ον, (ῥύμη) *with broad streets*, gloss on εὐρυάγυια, Eust.166.21.

⊛ **πλᾰτύς**, εῖα, ύ, Ion. fem. πλατέα Hdt.2.156: acc. pl. fem. πλατέας *PMag.Par.*1.1086:—*wide, broad*, τελαμών Il.5.796; πτύον 13.588; αἰπόλια πλατέ' αἰγῶν *broad* herds, i. e. *large* or *spread over a wide space*, 2.474, Od.14.101, Hes.*Th.*445; π. πρόσοδοι Pi.*N.*6.45; ὁδοί X.*Cyr.*1.6.43, *IG*2$^2$.380.20; τὴν ὁδὸν τὴν π. *Broad Street*, *SIG*57.27 (Milet., v B. C.); similarly, π. ὁδὸς τῶν θεῶν *PStrassb.*85.22 (ii B. C.) (cf. infr. II); κιβώτιον π. *IG*1$^2$.330.20; τάφρος ὡς πλατυτάτη καὶ βαθυτάτη X.*Cyr.*7.5.9. **2.** *flat, level*, χῶρος π. καὶ πολλός Hdt.4.39; πλατυτάτης.. γῆς οὔσης Θετταλίας X.*HG*6.1.9; πότερον ἡ γῆ π. ἐστιν ἢ στρογγύλη Pl.*Phd.*97d; κάρυα τὰ π., i. e. chestnuts, Hp.*Vict.*2.55, Diocl.*Fr.*126, X.*An.*5.4.29; σελάχη, ἰχθύες, Arist.*HA*489$^b$31, *PA*695$^b$7; ποτήρια πλατέα, τοίχους οὐκ ἔχοντ' Pherecr.143.2. **3.** of a man, *broad-shouldered*, οὐ γὰρ οἱ πλατεῖς, οὐδ' εὐρύνωτοι S.*Aj.*1250, cf. *UPZ*121.19 (ii B. C.). **4.** of seasons, *far advanced*, ἔαρ Procl. ad Hes.*Op.*483. **5.** metaph., π. ὅρκος a *broad strong* oath, Emp.30.3, cf. 115.2; καταγέλως π. *flat* (i. e. downright) mockery, Ar.*Ach.*1126; π. φλήναφος Amelius ap.Porph.*Plot.*17, 18; but πλατὺ γελάσαι, καταγελᾶν, laugh *loud and* *rudely*, Philostr.*VA*7.39, *VS*1.20.2; καταχρεμψαμένη πλατύ Ar.*Pax* 815, cf. Luc.*Cat.*12. **6.** *broad*, of pronunciation, π. λέξις Hermog. *Id.*1.6; φωνή Poll.2.116; πλατέα λαλοῦσι πάντα οἱ Δωριεῖς Demetr. *Eloc.*177. **7.** *diffuse*, λέξις D.H.*Dem.*19. Adv. -έως ibid.: Comp. -ύτερον *in fuller detail*, διαλεξόμεθα S.E.*P.*2.219, cf. Sor.2.5, Hdn.2.15.6; -υτέρως Tz.ad Lyc.177: Sup. -υτάτως Id.*H.*12.890. **b.** Adv. -έως *loosely*, opp. ἀκριβῶς, Phld.*Rh.*1.248 S. **8.** *widespread, frequent*, χρῆσις Choerob.*in Theod.*1.332: Comp., ib.267. **9.** π. δρόμος, = Lat. *cursus clabularis*, Lyd.*Mag.*3.61. **II.** Subst. πλατεῖα (sc. ὁδός, cf. S.E.*P.*1.188, and v. supr. I. 1), ἡ, *street*, Philem.58, Herod.6.53, *OGI*491.9 (Pergam.), Lxx *Ge.*19.2, D.S.17.52, Str.17.1.10, *Ev.Matt.*12.19; οἱ ἐν τῇ Σκυτικῇ π. τεχνεῖται *IGRom.*4.790, cf. 791, al. (Apamea); hence Σεβαστὴ π. name of a guild, ib.3.711 (Sura); ἡ ἱερωτάτη π. *CIG*3960b6 (Apamea). **b.** (sc. χείρ) *flat of the hand*, ταῖσι πλατείαις τυπτόμενος Ar.*Ra.*1096; πλατείᾳ τῇ χειρί Philum.*Ven.*5.3. **c.** a kind of *dish* or *cup*, *IG*11(2).110.22, al. (Delos, iii B.C.). **d.** *broad stripe* or *border*, Demetr.*Eloc.*108. **III.** *salt, brackish*, πλατυτέροισι ἐχρέωντο τοῖσι πόμασι Hdt.2.108; πλατέα or πλατύτερα ὕδατα, Arist.*Mete.*358$^{b}$4, 358$^{a}$28 (but πλατὺς Ἑλλήσποντος Il.7.86, 17.432, is not *the salt*, but *the broad*, Hellespont, cf. A.*Pers.*875 (lyr.), wrongly expld. by Ath.2.41b). (Cf. Skt. *pṛthú-* 'broad', *práthati* 'spread out', etc. But in signf. III cogn. with Skt. *paṭu-* 'sharp', 'pungent', *tripaṭu* 'the three saline substances'.)

**πλᾰτύ-σαρκος** [ῠ], ον, *broad-fleshed*, στῆθος Polem.*Phgn.*42. **-σημος**, ον, (σῆμα) *with broad border*, π. χιτών, = Lat. *tunica laticlavia*, D.S.36.7, Str.3.5.1; ἡ π. ἐσθής Hdn.3.11.2; συνθέσεις *PHamb.*10.15 (ii A.D.): abs., ἡ π. Arr.*Epict.*1.24.12; cf. στενόσημος. **II.** of those entitled to wear it, χιλίαρχος π., = *tribunus laticlavius*, *IG*4.588.4 (Argos, ii A.D.), *IGRom.*3.554 (Tlos), 889 (Adana).

**πλάτυσ-μα**, ατος, τό, *flat object*, e.g. *tile*, Herod.3.46; *slab*, κηροῦ Dsc.*Eup.*1.171; metal *plate*, Hero *Dioptr.*5; χαλκοῦν Gal.12.831; *plaster*, Heliod.ap.Orib.46.29.3, Orib.*Syn.*2.59; *flat cake*, Gal.4.526; π. μυώδες, a muscle discovered by Galen, 18(2).930; τὰ π. τῶν κωπῶν *blades*, Eust.1625.17. **-μάτιον**, τό, Dim. of foreg., Hero *Spir.*1.21, Asclep.ap.Gal.13.675, Orib.*Fr.*99. **-μός**, ὁ, *widening, enlarging, dilatation, distension*, Dsc.5.6; ἐξήνεγκέ με εἰς πλατυσμόν *into broad space*, into *open ground*, Lxx 2*Ki.*22.20, al.; ἐν πλατυσμῷ ib.*Si.*47.12. **II.** metaph., *boasting, bragging*, πουλυμαθημοσύνης Timo 20. **2.** *amplitude*, τῆς ποιήσεως Eust.1382.21.

**πλᾰτύ-στερνος**, ον, *broad-breasted*, κύνες *Gp.*19.2.1: Sup., Ruf.*Onom.*74. **-στομέω**, *speak broadly*, Sch.Theoc.15.88. **-στομος**, ον, *wide-mouthed*, λέβης, χύτρα, ἀγγεῖον, Dsc.1.30, Damocr.ap.Gal.13.40, *Gp.*9.24.1; of a cupping instrument, Sor.1.50. **-σχιστος**, ον, *with broad clefts*, of a leaf, Thphr.*HP*9.10.1. **-σωμος**, ον, *with a broad body*, Tz.*H.*6.420.

**πλᾰτύτης** [ῠ], ητος, ἡ, *breadth, width*, of the liver, Hp.*VM*22; of animals, X.*Cyr.*1.4.11. **2.** *amplitude*, ἑρμηνείας D.L.3.4. **3.** *breadth* of pronunciation, Demetr.*Eloc.*177.

**πλᾰτύ-φυλλος** [τῠ], ον, *broad-leaved*, Arist.*APo.*98$^{b}$4, Thphr.*HP*3.8.2, etc.: Comp. -ότερος Id.*CP*5.7.2. **-χαίτας**, corrupt in Plu.2.292d, who says it is Boeot. for *neighbour*: Schneid., comparing ὁμωχέτας, restored **πλᾱτ-ωχέτας** (better **πλᾱτι-ωχέτας**, from πλατίον, Dor. for πλησίον). **-χωρος**, ον, *with broad space, roomy*, σηκοί *Gp.*18.2.1. **-ψῡχος**, ον, *of proud* (or *insatiate*) *soul*, Sm.*Pr.*28.25. **-ώνῠχος**, ον, (ὄνυξ) *with flat nails*, of man, Pl.*Def.*415a, S.E.*P.*2.211; of the swan and goose, Ael.*NA*11.37.

**Πλάτων** [ᾰ], ωνος, ὁ, *Plato* (prop. a nickname, *broad-shouldered*):— hence Adj. ⊛**Πλᾰτώνειος**, α, ον, *of Plato*, Sch.D.T.p.224 H., Suid.; **Πλατώνεια**, τά, *festival in honour of P.*, Porph.ap.Eus.*PE*10.3:— also ⊛**Πλᾰτωνικός**, ή, όν, *AP*11.354.9 (Agath.); Π. φιλόσοφος *Sammelb.*6012 (iii A.D.); ἀποδείξεις Dam.*Pr.*311: Comp. -ώτερος ib.263: Sup. -ώτατος Luc.*VH*2.19. Adv. -κῶς *after the manner of Plato*, τὰς γυναῖκας Π. ἔχοντες κοινάς Str.7.3.7.

**πλάτων**, bronze *ladle* for separating whey from curds, Hsch.

**πλάτωνις**, ιδος, ὁ, *deer with broad antlers*, Cyran.59.

**πλάτωσις** [ᾰ], εως, ἡ, = ἐμπνευμάτωσις, dub. in *Gloss.*

**πλέγ-δην**, Adv. *entwined*, *APl.*4.196 (Alc. Mess.), Opp.*H.*2.317. ⊛ **-μα**, ατος, τό, *anything twined* or *twisted*, π. ἕλικος the *twisting tendril* of the vine, Simon.183.2; γυίων π. *AP*5.245 (Paul. Sil.), cf. 285 (Id.). **2.** *plaited work, wicker-work*, Pl.*Lg.*734e, etc.; τὸ τοῦ κύρτου π. Id.*Ti.*79d: hence, = κύρτος, X.*Cyr.*1.6.28: in pl., *wreaths, chaplets*, E.*Ion* 1393; also, *plaited hair*, 1*Ep.Ti.*2.9. **3.** π. δικτυοειδές *the rete mirabile Galeni*, Herophil.ap.Gal.5.155, Gal.*UP*9.4, al. **II.** metaph., *complex, combination of words*, Pl.*Sph.*262d: generally, *complex*, Ph.1.372,651, Plot.3.3.4. **-μᾰτεύομαι**, Pass., *to be entwined*, Hsch. **-μάτιον**, τό, Dim. of πλέγμα I. 2, Arist.*PA*685$^{b}$5, M.Ant.2.2. **-νύμενος**, pres. part. Pass. (as if from πλέγνυμι = πλέκω), Opp.*C.*2.212, *H.*1.311.

**πλέες, πλέᾰς**, v. πλείων sub fin.

**πλεθρ-ιαῖος**, α, ον, *of the size of a* πλέθρον, φοίνικες X.*Cyr.*7.5.11; ποταμὸς τὸ εὖρος π. Id.*An.*1.5.4; γέφυρα π. τὸ πλάτος οὖσα Pl.*Criti.*116a; δράκων μῆκος π. Str.16.2.17. ⊛ **-ίζω**, *run the* πλέθρον: metaph., '*draw the long bow*', Thphr.*Char.*23.2 (dub. l.). **-ιον**, τό, *wrestling-ground* at Olympia, Luc.*Peregr.*31, Paus.6.23.2. ⊛ **-ισμα**, ατος, τό, *race of a* πλέθρον *in length*, Hsch., Phot. ⊛ **-ον**, τό, *measure of length of* 100 *feet*, Hdt.2.124, E.*Ion* 1137, X.*An.*1.2.5, *SIG*250 F 15 (Delph., iv B.C.), etc. **II.** as a square measure, 10,000 square feet, Hdt.7.199 (s. v. l.), *IG*1$^{2}$.376,385, Pl.*Tht.*174e, *Alc.*1.123c, D.20.115, *SIG*306.13 (Tegea, iv B.C.). **2.** = Lat. *jugerum*, Plu.*Cam.*39, Ael.*VH*3.1; cf. πέλεθρον. **III.** in pl., = δίυγροι καὶ βοτανώδεις τόποι, Hsch. (Written **βλέθρα** in *Rev.Ét.Gr.*10.29 (Thespiae, iii/ii B.C.).)

**Πλειάδες**, Ep. and Ion. **Πληϊάδες** (Aeol. **Πληΐαδες** Sapph.52), αἱ, *Pleiads*, Il.18.486, Od.5.272, Hes.*Op.*383, 572. **II.** later in sg., of the whole constellation, esp. in notes of time, ὑπὸ Πληϊάδα *at the setting of the P.*, Hp.*Epid.*1.1; πρὸ Πλειάδος ἐπιτολῆς Arist.*HA*553$^{b}$31; ἀπὸ Πλειάδος ἀνατολῆς ib.599$^{b}$10; μετὰ Πλειάδα ib.598$^{b}$7; ἀπὸ Πλειάδος δύσεως ib.599$^{a}$28; περὶ Πλειάδος δύσιν ib.542$^{b}$22; πρὸς δύσιν Πλειάδος χειμερινήν ib.566$^{a}$21; Σείριος ἐγγὺς τῆς ἑπταπόρου Π. ᾄσσων E.*IA*8 (anap.), cf. *Ion* 1152: in sg., also a name given to the seven best Alexandrian tragic poets, Heph.9.4, Choerob.*in Heph.*p.236 C., Suid. s. v. Ἀλέξανδρος Αἰτωλός, al. (Πλειάδες is perh. derived from πλέω, *sail*, because they rose at the beginning of the *sailing-season* (if so Πληϊάδες is metri gr. for Πλε(ϝ)ϊάδες).—Poets (Hes.*Frr.*177, 178, 179, Pi.*N.*2.11, A.*Fr.*312), using the lengthened form Πελειάδες (Alcm.23.60, gen. sg. Πελειάδος E.*Or.*1005 (lyr.)), represented them as *doves* flying before the hunter Orion.)

**πλεῖν**, Att. for πλέον, v. πλείων sub fin.

**πλειον-άζω**, *have more than one meaning* or *application*, Alex.Aphr.*in Top.*428.13. **2.** *to be in excess*, *IG*5(1).1390.39 (Andania, i B.C.). (Cf. πλεονάζω.) **-άκις**, v. πλεονάκις. **-αχῶς**, v. πλεοναχῶς.

**πλειόνει**· σπείρει, Hsch.

**πλειονομοιρέω**, *to be further on in the zodiac, have more degrees*, Paul.Al.*H.*1.

**πλειονότης**, ητος, ἡ, *length of string* in the monochord, Nicom.*Harm.*10 (pl., opp. βραχύτητες).

**πλειονο-ψηφία**, ἡ, *dominant astrological influence*, Serapio in *Cat.Cod.Astr.*5(3).87 (πλειοψ-), Paul.Al.*R.*1. **-ψηφοφορία**, ἡ, = foreg., Jul.Laod. in *Cat.Cod.Astr.*4.104.

**πλειοποιός**, όν, *creating plurality*, Dam.*Pr.*55.

**πλεῖος, πλειότερος**, v. πλέως.

**πλειότης**, ητος, ἡ, *plurality*, *Theol.Ar.*12 (v. l.). **πλειοψηφία**, v. πλειονοψηφία.

**πλειστάκις** [ᾰ], Adv., (πλεῖστος) *mostly, very often*, Hp.*Art.*51, Arist.*EN*1153$^{b}$34, Lxx *Ec.*7.23(22), etc.; ὅτι π. X.*Oec.*16.14; ὡς π. Hp.*Art.*67, Antipho 5.86, Pl.*R.*459d, etc.—A form **πλειστάκι** *PRyl.*130.12 (i A.D.), *EM*169.31, Eust.122.7.

**πλείσταρχος**, ον, *holding widest sway*, Ἑλλάνων γέρας B.3.12.

**πλειστᾰχόθεν**, Adv. *from most* or *many places*, Ar.*Fr.*840.

**πλειστήρ-ης**, ες, *manifold*, ἅπας π. χρόνος all *the whole length of* time, A.*Eu.*763. ⊛ **-ιάζω**, *raise the price* of a thing, *make dear*, Lys.*Fr.*7, Pl.Com.18, Them.*Or.*21.261b:—hence Subst. **-ιασμός**, ὁ, Hsch. **-ίζομαι**, (πλειστήρης) *name as chief*, A.*Ch.*1029.

**πλειστοβολ-έω**, *throw highest at dice*, Phot., Suid. **-ίνδα** (sc. παιδιά), ἡ, *dice-playing*, Poll.7.206, 9.95,110, Hsch. **-ος**, ον (parox.), *throwing high*, of dicers, *AP*7.422 (Leon.).

**πλειστο-γονέω**, *produce many at a birth*, Ptol.*Tetr.*126:—hence Adj. **-γόνος**, ον, ib.110. **-δῠνᾰμέω**, *to be dominant, prevail*, Heraclid.Erythr.ap.Gal.8.743; τὸ -δυναμοῦν *the greater part, majority*, Sor.1.11,126, Gal.18(2).324. **-λόγως**, Adv. *in various ways*, *Gloss.* **-λόχεια**, ἡ, *small birthwort*, *Aristolochia Plistolochia*, Plin.*HN*25.96,101. **2.** = ἀλθαία, ib.20.222. **-μβροτος**, ον, *crowded with people*, ἑορτά Pi.*O.*6.69. ⊛ **-νίκης** [ῑ], ου, ὁ, *victor in many contests*, *SIG*1073.3 (Olympia, ii A.D.). *BSA*26.167 (Sparta, ii A.D., πλιστ-), etc.

⊛ **πλεῖστος**, η, ον, Sup. of πολύς, *most, greatest, largest*, in number, size, extent, etc., π. ὅμιλος, λαός, Il.15.616, 16.377, etc.; π. κακόν Od.4.697; πλεῖστοι ἐπιχθονίων ἀνθρώπων Hes.*Fr.*33.1; π. εὐκλείας γέρας S.*Ph.*478; φιλοσοφία παλαιοτάτη τε καὶ πλείστη *most in vogue*, Pl.*Prt.*342a; π. τῶν Ἑλληνικῶν φῦλον τὸ Ἀρκαδικόν X.*HG*7.1.23, etc.; τῇ γνώμῃ πλεῖστός εἰμι, ἡ π. γνώμη, Hdt.7.220 (s. v. l.), 5.126; πλεῖστον σχήσειν, as Sup. of πλέον ἔχειν (v. πλείων), Th.7.36. **2.** with Art., οἱ π. *the greatest number*, Id.4.90, etc.; τὸ π. τοῦ βίου *the greatest part* of.., Pl.*Lg.*718a, etc. (also same gender as the foll. Noun, ὁ π. τοῦ βίου, ἡ π. τῆς στρατιᾶς, Th.1.5, 7.3); τῇ ὄψει τοῦ θαρσεῖν τὸ π. εἰληφότες Id.4.34; τῷ πλούτῳ διδοὺς τὸ π. E.*Supp.*408. **II.** Special usages: with relat., ὅσας ἂν πλείστας δύνωνται καταστρέφεσθαι subdue *the greatest* number that they *possibly* could, Hdt.6.44; ὡς ἂν δύνωνται πλεῖστα *IG*1$^{2}$.98.4, cf. 109.10, 113.37; ὁπόσσω κα πλείστω ἄξιος ᾖ *Berl.Sitzb.*1927.160 (Cyrene); ὅς κα πλεῖστον διδῷ ἀποδόμενοι *Leg.Gort.*5.48; ὡς π. χρόνον Pl.*Grg.*481b; ὅτι π. Th.6.64, etc.: coupled with εἷς (q. v.), εἷς ἀνὴρ π. πόνον ἐχθροῖς παρασχών A.*Pers.*327: in comp. sense, πλείστου ἄξια ἢ ὥς τις οἴεται Hp.*Art.*57 (but πλεῖστα ἢ is corrupt in Hdt.2.35). **III.** Adv. usages: πλεῖστον *most*, Il.19.287, Hes.*Th.*231, etc.; ὡς π. X.*An.*2.2.12: sts. added to a Sup., π. ἐχθίστη S.*Ph.*631; π. ἀνθρώπων..κάκιστος Id.*OC*743; τὴν π. ἡδίστην θεῶν E.*Alc.*790: πλεῖστα as Adv., Pi.*P.*9.97, S.*OC*720, etc.; πολλάκις μὲν.., π. δὲ.. Pl.*Hp.Ma.*281b; π. χαίρειν, freq. in letters, *POxy.*742 (i B.C.), etc. **b.** *furthest*, π. ἀφεστηκέναι Pl.*R.*587a, Arist.*Mu.*391$^{a}$13. **2.** with Art., τὸ π. *at most*, ἡμερῶν τεσσάρων τὸ π. Ar.*V.*260, etc.; τὰ π. *for the most part*, Pl.*Criti.*118c, etc.; opp. ἐνίοτε, Arist.*HA*563$^{a}$31.—The form πλείστως is cited by Gal.17(1).855 from Hp.*Epid.*6.1.10 (πλεῖστα codd.). **IV.** with Preps.: **1.** διὰ πλείστου *furthest off*, in point of space or time, Th.4.115, 6.11. **2.** ἐς πλεῖστον *most*, S.*OC*739. **3.** ἐπὶ πλεῖστον *over the greatest distance, to the greatest extent*, in point of space, time, or extent, ἐπὶ π. χλιδῆς ἀπίκετο Hdt.6.127; ἐπὶ π. τοῦ γενησομένου Th.1.138; ἐκ τοῦ ἐπὶ π. Id.1.2; ἐπὶ π. ἀνθρώπων ib.1; ὡς ἐπὶ π. or ὡς ἐπὶ τὸ π., *for the most part*, Id.4.14, Pl.*Lg.*720d. **4.** κατὰ τὸ π. *for the most part*,

Plb.11.4.7, etc. 5. περὶ πλείστου ποιεῖσθαι, v. περί A. IV. 6. ἐν τοῖς πλεῖσται, v. ὁ, ἡ, τό, A. VIII. 6.

**πλειστο-τόκος**, ον, *bringing forth most offspring*, Man.4.102 cod. **-φόρος**, ον, *bearing most*, Thphr.*HP*3.7.6.

**πλείω**, v. πλέω.

⊛ **πλείων, πλέων**, ὁ, ἡ, neut. πλεῖον, πλέον, πλεῖν, Comp. of πολύς (on the forms v. sub fin.), *more*, of number, size, extent, etc., οἱ δὲ μάχονται παυρότεροι πλεόνεσσι Il.13.739; πλείων μὲν πλεόνων μελέτη Hes. *Op.*380; ἐς πλείονας οἰκεῖν govern for the interest of *the majority*, Th. 2.37; πλέον' ἔλπομαι λόγον Ὀδυσσέος ἢ πάθαν *greater* than.., Pi.*N.*7. 21; τὸν πλείω λόγον all *further* speech, S.*Tr.*731; ὁ ὄχλος πλείων καὶ πλείων ἐπέρρει X.*Cyr.*7.5.39; πλείω τὸν πλοῦν..ποιησάμενοι having made the voyage *longer*, Th.8.39; ὁ π. βίος a *longer* life, Pl.*Ti.*75c; μακροτέρα καὶ π. ὁδός Id.*R.*435d, etc.; of Time, *longer*, π. χρόνος Hdt. 9.111, S.*Ant.*74; πλέων νὺξ τῶν δύο μοιράων Il.10.252. 2. with Art., οἱ πλέονες *the greater number, the mass* or *crowd*, 5.673, Od.2. 277; οἱ πλεῦνες Hdt.1.106, etc.: c. gen., τὰς πλεῦνας τῶν γυναικῶν ib.1; *the people*, opp. the chief men, Id.7.149, Th.8.73,89, etc.; euphem. of the dead, ἀνεστηκυῖα παρὰ τῶν πλειόνων Ar.*Ec.*1073; εὖτ' ἂν ἵκηαι ἐς πλεόνων *AP*11.42 (Crin.); ἐς πλεόνων μετοικεσίην ib. 7.731 (Leon.); τὸ πλεῖον πολέμοιο *the greater part* of.., Il.1.165; ὅστις τοῦ πλέονος μέρους χρῄζει, opp. τοῦ μετρίου, S.*OC*1211 (lyr.); τοῦ πλέονος ἐλπίδι ὀρέγονται Th.4.17, cf. 92. II. pecul. usages of neut.: 1. as a Noun, *more*, πλεῦν ἔτι τούτου Hdt.2.19, etc.; εἴ τι ἐνορῶ πλέον Id.1.89; τὸ δὲ π. nay, what is *more*, E.*Supp.*158 (Musgr. for τί δὲ..); to a *greater* extent, Th.1.90, 7.57, etc.; πλέον or τὸ πλέον τινός *a higher degree* of a thing, τίς πλέον τᾶς εὐδαιμονίας φέρει; S.*OT*1189 (lyr.); τὸ π. τοῦ χρόνου Th.1.118, etc.; also τὸ π. ὃ ἀναφέρει the *excess* which he reports, *PCair.Zen.*661 (iii B.C.); ᾧ πλεῖον the *excess*, prob. in *PPetr.*2 p.42 (iii B.C.), cf. *PCair.Zen.*742.26 (iii B.C.); πλέον ἔχειν to have *the advantage*, have *the best* of it, like πλεονεκτέω, c. gen., Hdt.9.70, Pl.*R.*343d, 349b, etc.; τὸ π. πάντων ἔχειν X.*Cyr.*1.3.18: more fully, μοίρης πλεῖον ἔχειν Thgn.606; π. τινὸς φέρεσθαι Hdt.8.29; π. φέρεσθαι τῶν ἄλλων And.4.4, etc.; π. ποιεῖν *do some good, be successful*, βουλοίμην ἂν πλέον τί με ποιῆσαι ἀπολογούμενον Pl.*Ap.*19a; οὐδὲν π. ποιήσειν, –ῆσαι, And.1.149, 4.7, cf. Pl.*Phd.* 115c, etc.; παραινοῦσ' οὐδὲν ἐς π. ποιῶ S.*OT*918; οὐδὲν π. ὀψοφαγῶν ποιήσεις Ath.8.344b; οὐδὲν εἴργασμαι π. E.*Hipp.*284; οὐδὲν π. πρᾶξαι Id.*IA*1373, And.4.20, etc.; οὐδὲν ἐπίσταμαι π. have no *superior* knowledge, Pl.*Tht.*161b; τί πλέον; what *more*, i.e. what *good* or *use* is it? Antipho 5.95, etc.; τί π. πλουτεῖν..πάντων ἀπορούντας; Ar.*Pl.*531; τί σοι π. λυπουμένῃ γένοιτ' ἄν; E.*Hel.*322; τί π. ἔστ' εἰς τέκνα πονεῖν; *Supp.Epigr.*1.567.1 (Karanis, iii B.C.), cf. *AP*7.261.1 (Diotim.); also οὐδὲν ἦν π. τοῖς πεπονθόσιν Lys.19.4 (=And.1.7), cf. D.35.31; ὧν οὐδέν μοι π. γέγονε Isoc.15.28; οὐδέν γέ σοι π. ἔσται Pl.*R.*341a; τί τὸ π.; *Epigr.Gr.*306a.3; ἐπὶ πλέον as Adv., *more, further*, Hdt.2.171, 5.51, Th.6.54, Pl.*Phdr.*261b, etc.: c. gen., *beyond*, ἐπὶ π. τῶν ἄλλων ἰσχύσας Th.1.9 (but, ἐπὶ τὸ π. ἵκεο μοίσας *to surpassing height in*.., Theoc.1.20); also ὅταν τις ἐς π. πέσῃ τοῦ θέλοντος S.*OC*1219 codd. (lyr.); περὶ πλείονος ποιεῖσθαι, v. περί A. IV. 2. as Adv., *more, rather*, π. ἔφερέ οἱ ἡ γνώμη κατεργάσεσθαι τὴν Ἑλλάδα he inclined *rather* to the belief.., Hdt.8.100; οὐ τοῦτο δειμαίνεις π.; A.*Pr.*41; σέ..τῶνδ' ἐς πλέον σέβω S.*OT*700; ἢ π. ἢ ἔλαττον D.18.125; π. ἔλαττον *more* or less, *BGU*402.9 (vi A.D.), *IG*14.177 (Syracuse); also τὸ π., Ion. τὸ πλεῦν, *for the most part*, Th.1.81, etc.; αὐτῆς τὸ π. μέτοχος εἰμι have *the larger* share, Hdt.3.52; τὸ π.,=μᾶλλον, οὐ χάριτι τὸ π. ἢ φόβῳ Th.1.9, cf. 2.37; ἐστὶν ὁ πόλεμος οὐχ ὅπλων τὸ π., ἀλλὰ δαπάνης not so *much*.., *as*.., Id.1.83. b. with Numerals, τοξότας π. ἢ εἴκοσι μυριάδας X.*Cyr.*2.1.6; οἶκος πλέον ἢ τεττάρων ταλάντων Is.10.23; ἐν πλέον ἢ διακοσίοις ἔτεσι v.l. in D.24. 141 (fort. πλεῖν, v. infr.); π. ἢ ἐν διπλασίῳ χρόνῳ X.*Oec.*21.3:—in this sense a short form πλεῖν is used by Att. writers (cf. Moer.p.294P., but the rule is not universal, cf. *IG*2².657.25 (iii B.C.). etc.), πλεῖν ἢ τριάκονθ' ἡμέρας Ar.*Ach.*858; πλεῖν ἢ χιλίας (sc. δραχμάς) Id.*Eq.* 444; στάδια πλεῖν ἢ χίλια Id.*Av.*6, cf. *Nu.*1041, 1065, al.; πλεῖν ἤ γε διπλοῦν Id.*Lys.*589; πλεῖν ἢ 'νιαυτῷ πρεσβύτερος Id.*Ra.*18, cf. 91; πλεῖν (πλεῖον codd.) ἢ πέντε τάλαντα D.21.173; πλεῖν ἢ δυοῖν ποδοῖν Eub.119.10; ἤ is freq. omitted, πλεῖν ἑξακοσίας Ar.*Av.*1251; ἔτη γεγονὼς πλείω ἑβδομήκοντα v.l. in Pl.*Ap.*17d; but δέκα πλείοσιν ἔτεσι for ten years *more*, Id.*Lg.*932c; τρεῖς μῆνας καὶ πλείω X.*HG*2.2.16; λίθους..ὅσον μναιαίους καὶ πλεῖον καὶ μεῖον Id.*Eq.Mag.*1.16: with number in gen., κώμας..οὐ πλεῖον εἴκοσι σταδίων ἀπεχούσας Id.*An.*3.2.34, cf. 7.3.12. c. Com., πλεῖν ἢ μαίνομαι *more than to* madness, Ar. *Ra.*103, 751. d. pl. πλείω used like πλέον, Th.1.3, Pl.*R.*417b, D. 23.213, etc.; τὰ π. Th.1.81; πλέω A.*Ag.*868 codd. e. regul. Adv. πλειόνως Aen.Tact.7.4, J.*AJ*17.1.1.

B. Forms: Ep. use πλείων or πλέων as metre requires, also nom. and acc. pl. πλέες, πλεᾶς, Il.2.129, 11.395, Call.*Act.Oxy.*2080.85 (so, with ι from ε, Cret. πλίες, πλίας, *Leg.Gort.*7.18,24, *GDI*5125*B*8, also πλίαδ (δὲ) *Leg.Gort.*7.29, πλίανς ib.5.54; πλέας also Aeol., *IG*12(2). 1.9 (Mytil., iv B.C.)); dat. pl. πλεόνεσσι Il.13.739 (πλεόνεσιν is f.l. in Hdt.7.224); Cret. also acc. sg. neut. πλῖον *Leg.Gort.*1.37, al., gen. πλίονος ib.2.39, al., neut. pl. πλίονα ib.4.51, πλία ib.10.17; Aeol. πλήων Hdn.Gr.2.431, also late Dor., *IPE*1².79.18 (Byzant., i A.D.); Att. Inscrr. have -ει- always before -ου- and -ω-, *IG*1².76.7, 2².657. 25, 2498.22, etc., but -ε- and -ει- before -ο-, ib.1².94.33, 40.3,4, 2². 2670.4 (but always πλέον).

⊛ **πλειών**, ῶνος, ὁ, *full time* or *period, year*, Hes.*Op.*617, Call.*Jov.*89, Lyc.201, *AP*6.93 (Antip.), *IG*9(1).880.16 (Corc.).

**πλέκος**, εος, τό, (πλέκω) *wicker-work*, Ar.*Ach.*454, *Pax* 528.

**πλεκόω**, v. σπλεκόω.

**πλεκτᾰν-άομαι**, Pass., = πλεκτανόομαι, πεπλεκτανημένᾳι δράκουσι, of the Erinyes, A.*Ch.*1049. **-η**, ἡ, (πλέκω) *anything twined* or *wreathed, coil, wreath*, ὄφεων πλεκτάναισι περίδρομον κύτος Id.*Th.*495; flame-*wreath*, Id.*Fr.*281.3; π. καπνοῦ *wreath* of smoke, Ar.*Av.* 1717. II. pl., *arms* of the poulp or octopus, *tentacles*, Alex.187.2, Eub.150.7, Diph.34, Arist.*HA*524ᵇ1, *PA*685ᵇ4, Thphr.*HP*8.8.4, 9. 13.6; of the ναυτίλος II, Arist.*HA*622ᵇ10; also of the *antennae* of the καρίς, Dsc.4.77. III. pl., *meshes* of a spider's web, Luc.*Musc.Enc.* 5: metaph., αἱ τῶν λόγων π. Id.*Vit.Auct.*22. IV. Medic., *mastoid growth* in the uterus, Diocl.*Fr.*27, Eudem. and Praxag.ap.Gal.2. 890. 2. *Fallopian tubes*, Ruf.*Onom.*194. 3. *plexus* of veins, Hp.*Oss.*14. **-ιον**, τό, Dim. of foreg. II, Eub.110. **-όομαι**, Pass., *to be intertwined, interlaced*, Hp.*Oss.*18.

**πλεκτᾰνόστολος**, ον, *with cordage rigged*, αἴθυιαι (metaph. of ships), Lyc.230.

**πλεκτᾰνώδης**, ες, *like a* πλεκτάνη II, πόδες Eust.1715.26.

⊛ **πλεκ-τή**, ἡ, prop. fem. of πλεκτός: 1. *coil, wreath*, ἐν πλεκταῖσι ..ἐχίδνης A.*Ch.*248. 2. *twisted rope, cord, string*, E.*Tr.*958, 1010, Pl.Com.21. 3. *fishing-basket* or *weel*, Pl.*Lg.*824b, *POxy.*520.7 (ii A.D.). 4. = πλεκτάνη II, Pl.Com.173.16. 5. pl., *mats*, Orph. *A.*403. **-τικός**, ή, όν, *of, occupied with plaiting*, αἱ π. τῶν τεχνῶν Pl.*Lg.*679a, cf. *Plt.*283b, 288d. II. *entangling* or *interlacing*, Epicur.*Ep.*1 p.8 U. Adv. **-κῶς** Poll.7.172, Sch.Opp.*H.*2.376. **-τός**, ή, όν, *plaited, twisted*, τάλαροι Od.9.247; σειρή 22.175; ἀναδέσμη Il. 22.469; ἅρματα Hes.*Sc.*63; ὑποθυμίδες Sapph.*Supp.*23.16; στέφανοι Xenoph.1.2, cf. E.*Hipp.*73; π. στέγαι *wicker* mansions, of the Scythian vans, A.*Pr.*709; ἀρτάναι, αἰῶραι, S.*Ant.*54, *OT*1264; κύτος E. *Ion* 37; κανίσκιον Ar.*Fr.*160; βρόχων πλεκταὶ ἀνάγκαι Xenarch.1.9 (paratrag.); σκεύη π. *any plaited* or *twisted* instruments, *cordage*, X. *Oec.*8.12. 2. *wreathed*, ἄνθη A.*Pers.*618. 3. as Subst. πλεκτή, ἡ, v. sub voce. b. πλεκτόν, τό, *basket*, *SIG*1016.4 (Iasos, iv B.C.). **-τρα**, τά, *wicker-work*, *Michel* 832.47 (Samos, iv B.C.). II. π., ἡ, prob. f.l. for ἐμπλέκτρια in Hsch. s.v. κομμώ(τ)ρια. ⊛ **-ω**, Pi.*O.* 6.86, etc.: fut. πλέξω *AP*5.146 (Mel.): aor. ἔπλεξα Il.14.176, etc.: pf. πέπλοχα (Att. acc. to Hdn.Gr.2.356), (δια-) Hp.*Oss.*16, (ἐμ-) ibid., but ἐμ-πέπλεχε ib.17:—Med., fut. πλέξομαι Perict.ap.Stob.4.28.19: aor. ἐπλεξάμην Od.10.168, Ar.*Lys.*790:—Pass., fut. πλεχθήσομαι (ἐμ-) A.*Pr.*1079 (anap.); πλᾰκήσομαι (ἐπι-) Gal.6.873: aor. ἐπλέχθην A.*Eu.*259 (lyr.), Pl.*Plt.*283a, (περι-) Od.23.33; but also aor. 2 ἐπλάκην [ᾰ], part. πλᾰκείς (ἐμ-) E.*Hipp.*1236, (συμ-) S.*Fr.*618; also part. κατα-πλεκείς Hsch., v.l. in Plb.3.73.1, περι-πλεκείς Tim.*Pers.*157, συμπλεκείς Hdt.8.84 (v.l. -πλακ-): pf. πέπλεγμαι Id.7.72, etc.:—*plait, twine*, πλοκάμους ἔπλεξε φαεινούς Il.14.176; στέφανον Pi.*I.*8(7).73, cf. Ar.*Th.*458; ἐκ τῆς βίβλου ἱστία Thphr.*HP*4.8.4; ἀνθερίκεσσι ἀκριδοθήραν Theoc.1.52:—Med., πεῖσμα..πλεξάμενος *having twisted me* a rope, Od.10.168, cf. Hdt.2.28; π. ἄρκυς Ar.*Lys.*790 (lyr.):—Pass., κράνεα πεπλεγμένα *of basket-work*, Hdt.7.72; χρέωνται σειρῇσι πεπλεγμένῃσι ἐξ ἱμάντων ib.85; βρόχος πεπλ. σπάρτου X.*Cyn.*9.13. 2. *make by art*, βωμόν Call.*Ap.*61. II. metaph., *devise, contrive*, mostly of tortuous means, π. δόλον ἀμφί τινι A.*Ch.*220: prov., δεινοὶ πλέκειν τοι μηχανὰς Αἰγύπτιοι Id.*Fr.*373; so π. πλοκάς E.*Ion*826; ἐκ τέχνης τέχνην ib.1280; παντοίας παλάμας Ar.*V.*644 (lyr.):—Pass., μηχανὴ πεπλεγμένη E.*Andr.*995. 2. of Poets, π. ὕμνον, ῥήματα, Pi.*O.*6.86, *N.*4.94; ᾠδάς Critias *Fr.*1 D.; π. λόγους E.*Rh.*834, Pl.*Hp.Mi.*369b; *form the plot* of a tragedy, opp. λύειν, Arist.*Po.*1456ᵃ9:—hence in Pass., μῦθοι πεπλεγμένοι *complex*, opp. ἁπλοῖ, ib.1452ᵃ12, cf. ᵇ32, 1459ᵇ9; συλλογισμὸς πεπλ. Arr.*Epict.*1.29.34; πέπλεκται [ἡ τῶν συμπάντων τῶν ὄντων νομοθεσία] ἐκ..λόγων τε καὶ αἰτίων κτλ. Plot.4.3. 15. 3. χρόνον τοῦ ζῆν π., = διαπλέκω II, Euphro 5. 4. *compound*, ἐκ λευκοῦ καὶ μέλανος *AP*12.165 (Mel.):—Pass., of words or syllables, *to be compounded*, Pl.*Tht.*202b, Ael.*NA*5.30. 5. Pass., *twine oneself round*, περὶ βρέτει πλεχθεὶς θεᾶς A.*Eu.*259 (lyr.). 6. Pass., *to be involved, entangled*, Vett.Val.169.32. (Cf. Lat. *plecto, im-plico*, OHG. *flehtan.*)

**πλέκωμα**, ατος, τό, = δράγμα, Sch.Theoc.7.157.

⊛ **πλέννα**· μύξαι, Hsch.; cf. βλέννα. **πλεννεραί**, = μυξώδεις, Hp. ap.Gal.19.131.

**πλεξείδιον**, τό, Dim. of πλέξις, Suid. s.v. ἔρσις.

**πλεξείω**, Desiderat. of πλέκω, Hdn.*Epim.*249.

**πλέξις**, εως, ἡ, *plaiting, weaving*, Pl.*Plt.*308d, *Gp.*10.6 tit.

**πλεο-έλασσον**, Adv. *more or less*, *PMonac.*4.10 (vi A.D.). **-μελής**, ές, *with more than the normal number of limbs*, coined word in Iamb. *in Nic.*p.32 P. **-μισθία**, ἡ, *rise of wages*, *POxy.*1414.13 (iii A.D.).

**πλέον**, = πλήν, c. nom., *JHS*50.267 (Asia Minor).

**πλεον-αζόντως**, Adv. *in the majority of instances, usually*, Phld.*Rh.* 2.74 S., *Lib.*p.43 O., Heliod.ap.Orib.46.10.1, Sor.*Fract.*19; *superfluously*, Eust.934.16. ⊛ **-άζω** (rarely πλειονάζω, q.v.), fut. -άσω: pf. πεπλεόνακα D.S.1.90:—Pass., pf. -ασμαι Hp.*Fract.*7, etc.: aor. -άσθην Id.*Art.*47: (πλέον):—*to be more*, esp. *to be more than enough, superfluous*, opp. ἐλλείπειν, ὑπολείπειν, Arist.*EN*1106ᵃ31, *Col.*799ᵃ 18; τὸ πλεονάζον the *excess*, *PRev.Laws* 57.13 (iii B.C.), Lxx *Ex.*26. 12; π. παρά c. acc., *to be in excess of*.., ib.*Nu.*3.46; ἐπλεόνασεν ἡ ἁμαρτία *Ep.Rom.*5.20; of animals, *have more than the due number* of limbs. opp. κολοβὰ γίνεσθαι, Arist.*GA*770ᵇ32; of visits, *to be frequent*, Plb.4.3.12; of the sea, *encroach*, Arist.*Mete.*351ᵇ6, cf. Plu.2. 366b; πάθος defined as ὁρμὴ πλεονάζουσα, Zeno *Stoic.*1.50; εἰκασία ἐστὶ μεταφορὰ πλεονάζουσα simile is *expanded* metaphor, Demetr.*Eloc.* 80; τὸ σ̄ πλεονάσαν *used to excess*, D.H.*Comp.*14: Gramm., *to be redundant*, Demetr.Lac.*Herc.*1012.21, etc.; Ἀρίσταρχος οὐκ ἔλεγε πλεονάζειν τὸ ἄρθρον A.D.*Synt.*6.2; also of letters, τὸ ε̄ πλεονάζει (in ἑ-ώρων) Id.*Pron.*58.25; but π. τῷ ῑ to have an *added* ῑ (as in ἐμεῖο), ib. 38.20; cf. III.6. **2.** c. gen., *exceed*, opp. λείπω, Ptol.*Geog.*1.20. 7: abs., τὸ -άζον ἔργον the *extra* work, *PLille* 1$^v$.16 (iii B.C.); τοὺς -άζοντας τῶν ρκε′ (sc. ἐρίφους) the *odd* 25 out of 125, *PCair.Zen.*422.7 (iii B.C.). **II.** of persons, *go beyond bounds, take* or *claim too much*, Isoc.2.33, 12.85, D.9.24, 39.14: c. dat., *presume upon* .., εὐτυχίᾳ Th.1.120; but π. κυνηγεσίαις *go beyond bounds in*.., Str.11.5. 1; of a writer, τοῖς ὀνόμασι π. Id.3.3.7: abs., *to be lengthy, tedious*, Id. 9.1.16, D.S.1.90, Lxx 2*Ma.*2.32; περί τινος Parmenisc.ap.Ath.4. 156d. **2.** π. τινός *have an excess of, abound in* a thing, opp. ἐνδεὴς εἶναι, Arist.*Pol.*1257$^a$33, cf. Epicur.*Sent.*4; but π. τοῦ καιροῦ *exceed all bounds*.., of a writer, D.H.*Comp.*22. **III.** c. acc., *state at a higher figure*, Str.6.3.10:—Pass., *to be magnified, exaggerated*, [νομίσειεν ἂν] ἔστιν ἃ πλεονάζεσθαι Th.2.35, cf. Str.2.4.3; πεπλεόνασται *has been overdone*, opp. ἐνδεὲς πεποίηται, Hp.*Fract.*7, cf. *Art.*47. **2.** *make to increase*, τινὰς τῇ ἀγάπῃ 1*Ep.Thess.*3.12. **3.** *eat in too great quantity*, τι Diph.Siph.ap.Ath.8.356d, Dsc.4.75,82 (all Pass.). **4.** *raise the price of*, τι Aristid.1.170 J. **5.** Pass., *to be deceived*, prob. f.l. for πλεονεκτεῖσθαι, Stob.2.7.11$^m$. **6.** Gramm., *use in addition* or *redundantly*, εἰώθασιν οἱ Ἀττικοὶ τὰ ἄρθρα πλεονάζειν Sch.Ar.*Pl.*5; Αἰολεῖς πλεονάζουσιν ἕτερον σύμφωνον *EM*84.18:—Pass., τὸ ῡ πλεοναζόμενον ψιλοῦται ib.440.12. **7.** *to be in excess of unity, partake of plurality*, Procl.*Inst.*2. ⊛ **-άκις** [ᾰ], Adv., (πλέων) *more frequently, oftener*, Hp.*Acut.*29, Lys.14.30, Pl.*Phd.*112d, etc.; *several times, frequently*, Arist.*Pol.*1299$^a$9, *IG*2$^2$.682.25, 1304.5, *PCair.Zen.*31.11 (iii B.C.); *too often*, Hp.*Aph.*5.16. **II.** *taken more times together, multiplied by a larger number*, opp. ἐλαττονάκις, Pl.*Tht.*148a:—also **πλεονάκι,** *PMagd.*25.4 (iii B.C.); **πλειονάκις,** *PCair.Zen.*29.2 (iii B.C.), *IG*12(5).533 (Ceos, iii B.C.), 9(1).694.45 (Corc., ii B.C.); **πλειονάκι,** *Sammelb.*4638.18 (ii B.C.). **-ᾰσις,** εως, ἡ, *superabundance, excess*, Cass.*Pr.*66. **-ασμα,** ατος, τό, *superfluity*, Lxx *Nu.*31.32; opp. ἔνδεια, A.D.*Synt.*133.14, cf. Gal.16.417; opp. τὸ ὁλόκληρον, A.D.*Pron.*59. 7; *surplus* of production, *PTeb.*78.7 (ii B.C.), 81.27 (pl., ii B.C.); π. γῆς *Ostr.Bodl.* i 97 (ii B.C.), cf. *PTeb.*344 (ii A.D.). **-ασμᾰτίζω,** *bring a surplus into account*, *PGiss.*48.20 (Pass., iii A.D.). ⊛ **-ασμός,** ὁ, *superabundance, excess*, ὑγρότητος, τῶν μερῶν, Arist.*GA*780$^a$20, 770$^b$28, cf. Chrysipp.*Stoic.*3.114,130, Porph.*Antr.*11; πλεονασμοὶ λαλιᾶς Plu.2.650e. **b.** *surplus*, *PRyl.*213.82 (pl., ii A.D.), *Sammelb.*4296.7 (iv A.D.), etc. **2.** *usury*, Lxx *Le.*25.37, Critodem. in *Cat.Cod.Astr.*8(1).260, etc. **3.** Rhet. and Gramm., *use of redundant words*, D.H.*Dem.*58, A.D.*Synt.*267.14, al. **b.** *lengthening* of clauses, opp. μείωσις, D.H.*Comp.*7. **4.** *repetition*, Timae.71 (pl.). **-αστέον,** *one must use in abundance*, Gal.11.143. **-αστός,** ή, όν, *numerous*, ὑπὲρ τοὺς πατέρας Lxx *De.*30.5; dub. l. in ib.1*Ma.*4.35. **-ᾰχῆ,** Adv. *from many points of view*, Pl.*R.*477a. **-ᾰχόθεν,** Adv. *from several sources*, λαβεῖν τὴν πίστιν Arist.*Cael.*270$^b$33. **-ᾰχός,** ή, όν, *manifold*, γενέσεως αἰτία Epicur.*Ep.*2 p.36 U.; κατὰ π. τρόπον ibid.; τοῦ π. τρόπου ib.p.41 U.; τὸ π. τὸ τῆς ῥητορικῆς *diversity*, Phld.*Rh.*1.50 S.:—elsewh. only Adv. **-ᾰχῶς** *in various ways* or *senses*, λέγεσθαι Arist. *APo.*89$^a$28, *EN*1125$^b$14, 1129$^a$25, Epicur.*Ep.*1 p.29 U., al.; π. ἐτυμολογεῖν Str.10.3.8: also **πλειοναχῶς,** Iamb.*Comm.Math.*p.93 F.

**πλεονεκτ-έω,** fut. -ήσω Th.4.62, etc. (πλέον ἐκτήσεται shd. be read in Pl.*La.*192e):—Prose Verb. *have* or *claim more than one's due*, mostly in bad sense, *to be greedy, grasping*, Hdt.8.112, X.*Mem.*2.6. 21, Pl.*Grg.*483c, etc. **2.** also, *gain* or *have some advantage*, without any bad sense, δυνάμει τινὶ π. Th.4.62, cf. 86; opp. ἐλαττοῦσθαι, Arist.*Rh.*1360$^a$3; πολὺ ἐπλεονέκτει ὁ Πελοπίδας παρὰ τῷ Πέρσῃ X. *HG*7.1.34: abs., Arist.*Rh.*1402$^b$25, D.S.12.46; π. ἀπὸ τῶν μὴ καθηκόντων Plb.6.56.2: freq. with neut. Pron., π. ταῦτα, etc., Th.4.61, etc. **3.** c. gen. rei, *have* or *claim a larger share of* than others, τῶν ὠφελίμων Id.6.39; τοῦ ἡλίου, τοῦ ψύχους, τῶν πόνων, X.*Cyr.*1.6. 25, cf. *Oec.*7.26; δόξης, χάριτος, Arist.*EN*1136$^b$22, 1137$^a$1. **II.** c. gen. pers., *have* or *gain the advantage over*, τῶν ἐχθρῶν Pl.*R.*362b, cf. Hyp.*Lyc.*8, etc.; παρά τινος X.*Cyr.*1.6.32 (v.l.); παρ' ἀλλήλων Arist.*Pol.*1292$^b$19; τινι *in* a thing, X.*Cyr.*4.3.21, etc.; κατά τι Pl. *Euthphr.*15a; περί τι Id.*La.*183a; also π. τῶν νόμων *gain at the expense of* the laws, Id.*Lg.*691a; τῆς ὑμετέρας π. εὐηθείας *take advantage of* your simpleness, D.*Prooem.*24. **2.** later c. acc. pers., *get* or *have the advantage over*, D.H.9.7, Plu.*Marc.*29, Luc.*Am.*27: usu. in bad sense, *overreach, defraud*, πλεονεκτεῖν μηδένα Men.*Mon.*259, cf. 1*Ep. Thess.*4.6, 2*Ep.Cor.*7.2, D.Chr.17.8, D.C.52.37: in early writers only Pass. in this sense, ὑπό τινων X.*Mem.*3.5.2; πλεονεκτεῖσθαι χιλίαις δραχμαῖς *to be defrauded in* or *of* 1,000 drachmae, D.41.25. In Th.1.77 πλεονεκτεῖσθαι is impers., *to be an act of* πλεονεξία. **3.** Pass., *to be surpassed, excelled*, τινι Apollod.*Poliorc.*173.5. **-ημα,** ατος, τό, *advantage, gain*, Pl.*Lg.*709c, D.5.23 (pl.), 18.60, etc.: pl., *gains, successes*, Gorg.*Pal.*30; ἐν τοῖς πολέμοις X.*Eq.Mag.*5.11; τὰ τοῦ στρατηγοῦντος π. Chor.p.35 B.; *advantages*, *SIG*888.133 (Scaptopara, iii A.D.); *excellences, virtues*, Zos.4.54: so in sg., *superiority, superior quality*, τῆς αἰτίας Diog.Oen.39; τῆς φωνῆς Eun.*Hist.*p.246 D.; π. σωματικά Jul.*Or.*6.194c, cf. Chor.p.209 B.: metaph., τὸ κατ' εὐθεῖαν ἐκ τῶν ἐναντίων π. Dam.*Pr.*350. **II.** *act of overreaching, undue gain*, D.21.60, 50.38, *Ep.*5.3, Arist.*Pol.*1311$^a$5; = *vitium*, *Gloss.* **-ης,** ου, ὁ, = ὁ πλέον ἔχων, *one who has* or *claims more than his due, greedy, grasping*, Th.1.40, etc.: as Adj. λόγος π. a *greedy, arrogant* speech, Hdt.7.158: Sup. πλεονεκτίστατος X.*Mem.*1.2.12. **2.** ἐν παντὶ πλεονέκτην τῶν πολεμίων *making gain* from their losses, Id.*Cyr.*1.6. 27. **3.** metaph. in Math., of τὸ ὑπερτελές, Iamb.*in Nic.*p.32 P. **-ητέον,** *one must take more than one's share*, Pl.*Grg.* 490c. **-ικός,** ή, όν, *greedy, grasping*, of persons, Isoc.12.243; ἡ πονηρία -εκτικόν D.25.24: Comp. and Sup. -ώτερος, -ώτατος, Arist. *Pol.*1333$^b$10, *Rh.*1418$^b$37. Adv. -κῶς Pl.*Phd.*91b, *OGI*665.16 (Egypt, i A.D.); π. ἔχειν πρός τινα D.22.56; also, *at an advantage*, μάχεσθαι Aen.Tact.16.18.

**πλεονεξία,** Ion. -ίη, ἡ, *greediness, assumption, arrogance*, τῶν Σπαρτιητέων ἡ π. Hdt.7.149, cf. And.4.13, Th.3.82, Isoc.12.240, Pl. *R.*359c, X.*HG*3.5.15; π. συγγενική *wrong* done to one's kin, Iamb. *VP*24.108. **2.** *assumption*, αἱ ἐν τῷ πυνθάνεσθαι π. Arist.*SE*175$^a$ 19. **II.** *advantage*, Isoc.4.183, 15.275, D.23.128: pl., αἱ ἐν τῷ πολέμῳ π. Isoc.3.22, etc.; αἱ π. αἱ ἴδιαι, αἱ δημόσιαι, X.*Cyn.*13.10; ἐπὶ πλεονεξίᾳ with a view to *one's own advantage*, Th.3.84, X.*Mem.*1. 6.12; μετὰ πλεονεξίας τινὸς ἀγωνίζεσθαι πρὸς [τὰ θηρία] Id.*Cyr.*1.6. 28; πλεονεξίαι ψυχῆς *excellences*, Plot.4.6.3. **2.** *a larger share of* a thing, τῶν πολιτικῶν δικαίων Arist.*Pol.*1282$^b$29. **3.** *gain derived* from a thing, τὴν ἐπὶ τῶν ἰδίων δικῶν πλεονεξίαν D.21.28; αἱ π. τῶν πλουσίων *undue gains*, Arist.*Pol.*1297$^a$11, cf. Pl.*R.*586b; π. ἔκ τινος Plb.6.56.3. **III.** *excess*, opp. ἔνδεια, Pl.*Ti.*82a.

**πλεονο-δάκτῠλος,** ον, *having more than the normal number of fingers*, Gal.19.454. **-συλλᾰβέω,** *to be of more syllables*, Eust. 1769.56: c. gen., τὰ τρίτα τῶν δευτέρων οὐ -συλλαβεῖ A.D.*Pron.* 78.7. **-σύλλᾰβος,** ον, *having more syllables*, Charis.p.539 K.

**πλεονότης,** v. πλειονότης. **πλεονοτρόφος,** f. l. for ὠλενοστρόφος, *Gloss.* **πλεόνως,** v. πλείων. **πλέος,** v. πλέως.

**πλεοτῑμία,** ἡ, *rise in price*, *POxy.*1414.13 (iii A.D.).

**πλεσώνης,** ου, ὁ, title of Egyptian *priest*, *Rev.Épigr.*1.146 (Abydos). (π– represents the definite article.)

**πλέτο,** v. πέλομαι.

**πλευμάω** or **-όω,** *have disease of the lungs*, ὅταν πλευμᾷ Hp.*Morb.* 2.48 (v.l. πλευμοῖ, and so written in Gal.19.131).

**πλευμον-ία,** ἡ, *disease of the lungs*, *Com.Adesp.*759:—also **πνευμονία,** Mnesith.ap.Plu.2.918d, cj. in *Hippiatr.*6. **-ίς,** ίδος, ἡ, = foreg., Hp.*Int.*3 (v.l. πν–). **-ώδης,** ες, *like the lungs*, σπόγγος Arist.*HA*549$^a$7 (v.l. πν–).

**πλευμορρωγής,** ές, *with a rent in the lungs*, Hp.*Int.*2.

**πλεῦμ-ος,** ὁ, = πλευμονία, Gal.19.131. **-ώδης,** ες, *of, like a disease of the lungs*, ibid., f.l. in Hp.*Epid.*4.1 (Erot.*Fr.*15).

⊛ **πλεύμων** or **πνεύμων,** ονος, ὁ (on the form and deriv., v. sub fin.), *the lungs*, πάγη δ' ἐν πλεύμονι χαλκός Il.4.528, 20.486 (v.l.); ὁ τῶν πνευμάτων τῷ σώματι ταμίας ὁ π. Pl.*Ti.*84d, cf. 70c, Arist.*Resp.*476$^a$9, Lxx 3*Ki.*22.34: mostly in pl., Archil.9.5, Alc.39.1, A.*Th.*61, S.*Tr.*567, etc.; διὰ πνευμόνων θερμὸν ἄησιν ὕπνον A.*Fr.*178 A; πνεῦμ' ἀνεὶς ἐκ πλευμόνων E.*Or.*277; regarded as the most vital part, σπαραγμὸς.. πλευμόνων ἀνθήψατο S.*Tr.*778, cf. Ar.*Lys.*367, *Ra.*474; πλευμόνων πολὺς πόνος ib.829; as the seat of love, [Κύπρις] Διὸς τυραννεῖ πλευμόνων S.*Fr.*941.15. **II.** *sea-lungs, jelly-fish*, Pl.*Phlb.*21c, Arist. *PA*681$^a$18, Thphr.*Sign.*40, Pytheas ap. Plb.34.3.4; term of abuse applied by Epicurus to Nausiphanes, Epicur.*Frr.*114, 236. (Gramm. differ as to the forms. Eust.(483.10, 1436.62) and Phot. both recognize πλεύμων as the Homeric and ancient form; this was also the true Att. form, Moer. p.309 P., Sch.Ar.*Pax* 1069, Eust.483.10; it is found in the best codd. of A.*Th.*61, S.*Tr.*567, as well as in codd. of Alc. (l.c. ap.Ath.10.430b), Hp. (*Art.*41, *Prog.*23, al., cf. i p.cxx K.), Ar., Pl., and Arist., also in Pap., Phld.*Ir.* pp.27, 28 W., and Inscr., *IG*4$^2$(1).122.56 (Epid., iv B.C.), and is doubtless the original form, which was altered in accordance with a supposed deriv. from πνεῦμα suggested by Arist.*Resp.*476$^a$9, cf. *EM*677.31. Cf. Lith. *plaũčiai* 'lungs', cogn. with πλέω, as 'that which floats', cf. Engl. *lights*, also *lungs*, cogn. with ἐλαφρός.)

**πλεῦν, πλεῦνος, πλεῦνες,** Ion. forms; v. πλείων.

**πλεύνως,** Adv. Ion. for πλεόνως, (πλέων) *too much*, Hdt.5.18 (v.l.).

⊛ **πλευρ-ά,** ᾶς, ἡ, = πλευρόν, *rib*, rare in sg., βοὸς π. Hdt.4.64; παρὰ τὴν π. ἑκάστην Arist.*HA*513$^b$29: pl., *ribs*, Id.*PA*654$^b$35. **2.** pl., generally, *side* of a man or animal, ἄλλοτ' ἐπὶ πλευρὰς κατακείμενος, ἄλλοτε δ' αὖτε ὕπτιος Il.24.10; of *both sides*, ἀνὰ πλευράς τε καὶ ὤμους 23.716; οὐρῇ δὲ πλευράς τε καὶ ἰσχία ἀμφοτέρωθεν μαστίεται 20.170, cf. Hes.*Sc.*430, A.*Pr.*71, *Eu.*843 (lyr.): sg., also, of *one side*, S.*OC*1260, *Aj.*834, etc.; a *side* of beef, etc., *PCair.Zen.*381.5 (iii B.C., written πλερά): the pl. form is v.l. in E.*Hec.*826. **II.** *side*, of things and places, νηὸς πλευραί Thgn.513; χωρίου Pl.*Sis.*388e; [Πακτωλοῦ] D.P. 833; of an army, αἱ π. τοῦ πλαισίου X.*An.*3.4.22, cf. 28, Plu.*Mar.* 25, etc.; παρὰ π. τινὶ εἶναι Plb.5.26.6; παρὰ π., opp. κατὰ κεφαλήν, *IG*2$^2$.463.72. **III.** Math., *side* of a triangle or other figure, Antipho Soph.13, Pl.*Ti.*53d, 54c, etc.: esp. **b.** *side* of a rectangle, ib.36c: hence, *one factor* of any product, Id.*Tht.*148a, Arist. *Metaph.*1051$^a$26, Euc.7*Def.*17, etc. **c.** *side* of a square or cube, and *root* of a square or cubic number, Id.8.11,12, *Theol.Ar.*11; κυβικὴ π. cube *root*, Ph.*Bel.*52.4. **d.** *generator* of a cone or cylinder, Archim.*Sph.Cyl.*1.8,12. **-άξ,** coined as etym. of εὐράξ, *EM*395. 17. **-ιαῖος,** α, ον, *of the side*, θύρετρα *BCH*20.324 (Lebad.); κρέα cj. in Poll.6.52. **-ιάς** (sc. γραμμή), άδος, ἡ, = πλευρά III, *Tab.Heracl.*1. 54, al. **-ικός,** ή, όν, *of* or *for the ribs*: τὰ π. τῶν βοῶν *the sides*, Sch. Ar.*Eq.*361. **II.** π. ἀριθμός number of units *in the side* of a square, opp. διαμετρικός: μονάς *Theol.Ar.*3, Iamb.*in Nic.*p.11 P. **-ίον,** τό, Dim. of πλευρά, Hp.*Superf.*7 (pl.), *SIG*247 ii 71 (Delph., iv B.C., pl.). -ισμός, ὁ, dub. sens. in *BGU*1270.14 (ii B.C.), *POxy*.373 (i A.D.), *PSI*8.897.69 (i A.D.). II. = πλευρά III c, v.l. for πλευρικός in *Theol.Ar*.28. -ίτης [ῑ], ου, ὁ, *connected with ribs*, of vertebrae, Poll.2.178. -ῖτικός, ή, όν, *suffering from pleurisy*, Hp. *Aph*.1.12, *IG*14.966.7 (Rome, ii A.D.), Paul.Aeg.3.33. 2. *good for pleurisy*, δυνάμεις Gal.11.711. 3. *causing pleurisy*, Ruf.ap.Orib.5.3.14; π. πυρετός Gal.17(1).890. -ῖτις (sc. νόσος), ιδος, ἡ, *pleurisy*, Hp.*Aph*.3.23 (pl.), Ar.*Ec*.417, *AP*11.382.17 (Agath.), etc. II. = σκόρδιον, Ps.-Dsc.3.111.

**πλευρο-ειδῶς**, Adv. *after the manner of ribs*, π. ἀπὸ τῆς μέσης εὐθείας κατατείνειν Thphr.*HP*3.10.3, cf. 3.17.3. -θεν (parox.), Adv. *from the side*, S.*Tr*.938. -κοπέω, *smite the ribs*, Id.*Aj*.236 (anap.).

**πλευρόν**, τό, = πλευρά, *rib*, in pl., Arist.*HA*496$^b$12, al. (usu. πλευραί). II. twice in Hom., in pl., *side*, πλευρὰ..οὔτησε ξυστῷ Il. 4.468, cf. 11.437, Hdt.9.22,72, A.*Fr*.210, S.*Tr*.833 (lyr.), E.*Or*.223, etc.; π. δελφάκεια Pherecr.108.16: also in sg., Diog.Apoll.6, Pherecr. 45.5, S.*OC*1112; π. ὕειον Hermipp.45; καπριδίου Ar.*Fr*.506. III. of places, π. νεῶν *side* of the entrenchment where the ships lay, S.*Aj*. 874; τὸ δεξιὸν π. the right *flank* (of an army), X.*Cyr*.6.3.34, etc.

**πλευρο-πριστήρ**, ῆρος, ὁ, *rib-saw*, *Hermes*38.283. -τυπής, ές, *with striking of the sides*, κέλαδος, of a cock crowing, *AP*12.137 (Mel.).

**πλευρ-ωμα**, ατος, τό, only pl., *sides*, of a man, ὁμόσπλαγχνα π. A. *Th*.890 (lyr.); also λέβητος π. Id.*Ch*.686. II. *cross-rail*, Ath. Mech.17.13. ⊛-ωνία, ἡ, dub. sens. in Them.*in PN*11.24, Mich.*in PN*25.20 (perh. Πλευρωνία).

**πλεῦσις**, εως, ἡ, *sailing*, Hsch. s.v. νεῦσις, Sch.Theoc.13.51.

**πλευσ-τέον** or -έα, (πλέω) *one must sail*, πλευστέα Ar.*Lys*.411; πλευστέον..αὐτοῖς ἐμβᾶσι D.4.16, cf. Them.*Or*.27.337c. -τικός, ή, όν, *fit* or *favourable for sailing*, οὖρος Theoc.13.52. Adv. -κῶς, ἔχειν Arist.*Mete*.359$^a$10. II. *given to seafaring*, Vett.Val.18.17.

**πλεφίλερ·** ἡ πεφρυγμένη σησαμίς, and **πλεφίς·** σησαμίς, Hsch.

⊛ **πλέω**, Ep. **πλείω** Od.15.34, 16.368: Ep. impf. ἀπ-έπλειον 8.501: also Ep. and Ion. **πλώω** (v. infr.): Att. contr. imper. πλεῖ E.*Tr*.102 (anap.): fut. πλεύσομαι Od.12.25, Il.11.22 (ἀνα-), Hdt.2.29, Th.6.104, etc.; later πλευσοῦμαι *SIG*402.27 (Chios, iii B.C.), found in codd. of Th.1. 143, 8.1, (ἐπεσ-) Id.4.13, (συνεκ-) Lys.13.25, (ἀπο-) Pl.*Hp.Ma*.370d, 371b, (συμ-) Isoc.17.19, etc.; Dor. πλευσοῦμαι Theoc.14.55; but 3 pl. πλεύσονται *GDI*5120*B*11,13 (Crete, iii B.C.); πλεύσω Philem. 116 (s.v.l.), Plb.2.12.3, *AP*11.162 (Nicarch.), 245 (Lucill.), *OGI*572. 30 (Lycia, ii/iii A.D.), etc.: aor. 1 ἔπλευσα A.*Ag*.691 (lyr.), etc.: pf. πέπλευκα S.*Ph*.404, etc.:—Pass., fut. πλευσθήσομαι (περι-) Arr.*An*.5. 26.2: aor. ἐπλεύσθην ib.6.28.6, Babr.71.3: pf. πέπλευσμαι X.*Cyr*.6. 1.16, D.56.12: Hom. uses only pres., impf., and fut. πλεύσομαι (v. supr.).—Of the Ion. πλώω, Hom. uses opt. πλώοιεν Od.5.240, part. ἐπι-πλώων ib.284, πλώων *h.Hom*.22.7: impf. πλῶον Il.21.302; also shortd. aor. ἔπλων, ως, ω, part. πλώς, in the compds. ἀπ-έπλω, ἐπ-έπλως, part. ἐπιπλώς, παρέπλω; and Hes. has ἐπ-έπλων; the pres., impf., and fut. forms occur as vv.ll. in Hdt., inf. πλώειν 4. 156, part. πλωούσας 8.10,22,42: impf. ἔπλωον ib.41; Iterat. πλώεσκον Q.S.14.656: fut. πλώσομαι (ἀπο-) Hdt.8.5 (πλώσω Lyc.1044); but the aor. 1 forms are read in Hdt., ἔπλωσα 4.148; inf. πλῶσαι 1.24; part. πλώσας 4.156, 8.49 (also once in Hom. in compd. ἐπι-πλώσας Il. 3.47): pf. παρα-πέπλωκα Hdt.4.99; πέπλωκα occurs E.*Hel*.532, Ar. *Th*.878 (paratrag.).—Only εε and εει are contracted in Att. (πλέει is f.l. in Th.4.28, and πλέετε v.l. in X.*An*.7.6.37). [Hom. uses πλέων as monosyll., πλέων ἐπὶ οἴνοπα πόντον Od.1.183]:—*sail, go by sea*, Λακεδαίμονος ἐξ ἐρατεινῆς Il.3.444; Ἰλιόθεν 14.251; ἐπὶ Κέρκυραν Th. 1.53; εὐθὺ Λέσβου X.*HG*1.2.11; π. ἐπὶ [σῖτον] to fetch it, Id.*Oec*.20.27; ἐπί τι *IG*1$^2$.105.9; μετὰ [νάκος] Pi.*P*.4.69; εἰς Ἐρέτριαν ἐπ' ἄνδρας Pl. *Mx*.240b; more fully, ἐνὶ πόντῳ νηῒ θοῇ πλείοντες Od.16.368; νηΐ.. πλέων ἐπὶ οἴνοπα πόντον Il.7.88; πλέεν..ποντοπορεύων Od.5.278; ἐν τῇ νηΐ Pl.*R*.341d; ἐν τῇ θαλάττῃ ib.346b; ἐπλέομεν βορέῃ ἀνέμῳ Od.14.253; αὔρᾳ A.*Ag*.691 (lyr.): c. acc. cogn., πλεῖθ' ὑγρὰ κέλευθα *sail* the watery ways, Od.3.71; πλεῖν τὴν θάλατταν And.1.137, Lys.6.19, Isoc.8.20, Antiph.100:—Pass., τὸ πεπλευσμένον [πέλαγος] X.*Cyr*.6.1.16, cf. Babr.71.3; πλεῖται ἡ θάλασσα Muson.*Fr*.18 B p.104 H.; also π. στόλον τόνδε S.*Ph*.1038; τοῦ πλοῦ τοῦ πεπλευσμένου D. 56.12: metaph., πλεῖν ὑφειμένῃ δοκεῖ, cf. ὑφίημι III: prov., ὁ μὴ πεπλευκὼς οὐδὲν ἑόρακεν κακόν Posidipp.22; ἐπὶ γῆς μὴ πλεῖν when on land do not *be at sea*, i.e. avoid the hazards of tax-farming, etc., Pythag.ap.Clem.Al.*Strom*.5.5.28. II. of ships, Il.9.360; νέας ἅμεινον πλεούσας Hdt.8.10, etc.; ὑπὸ τριήρους..εὖ πλεούσης ἐπεδιώκοντο Th.7.23; ἡ ναῦς ἄριστά μοι ἔπλει Lys.21.6; ἔφευγε ταῖς ναυσὶν εὖ πλεούσαις X.*HG*1.6.16; τριήρης ταχὺ π. Id.*Oec*.8.8. 2. of other things, *swim, float*, τεύχεα καλὰ..πλῶον καὶ νέκυες Il.21.302; δένδρεα .., τά οἱ πλώοιεν ἐλαφρῶς Od.5.240; [νῆσος] πλέουσα Hdt.2.156. 3. *to be conveyed by sea*, [σκῦλα] πλέοντα Th.3.114. 4. metaph., ταύτης ἔπι πλέοντες ὀρθῆς while [the ship of] our country bearing us is on an even keel, S.*Ant*.190; οὐδ' ὅπως ὀρθὴ πλεύσεται (sc. ἡ πόλις) προείδετο D.19.250; πάντα ἡμῖν κατ' ὀρθὸν πλεῖ Pl.*Lg*.813d; θεοῦ θέλοντος κἂν ἐπὶ ῥιπὸς πλέοις E.*Fr*.397; also κέρδους ἕκατι κἂν ἐπὶ ῥιπὸς πλέοι Ar.*Pax*699. (With πλε(ϝ)-, πλευ- cf. Skt. *plávate* 'float', 'swim', Lat. *pluit*; with πλω- cf. Goth. *flōdus* 'river', 'flood', OE. *flōwan* 'flow'.)

**πλέων**, neut. πλέον, pl. πλέω; v. πλείων.

⊛ **πλέως**, πλέᾱ, πλέων, pl. πλέῳ, πλέᾳ, πλέᾱ; Ion. **πλέος**, -έη, -έον; Ep. **πλεῖος**, η, ον (Hom. uses πλέον only in Od.20.355); contr. fem. πλῆ Hdn.Gr.2.912: (πίμ-πλη-μι):—*full, filled*, c. gen., πλεῖαί τοι οἴνου κλισίαι Il.9.71; νηῦς πλείη βιότοιο Od.15.446; εἰδώλων δὲ πλέον πρόθυρον, πλείη δὲ καὶ αὐλή 20.355, cf. 4.319, 17.605; πλείη γαῖα κακῶν Hes.*Op*.101; τάφρος πλέη ὕδατος Hdt.1.178; στρατιῆς ἅπαντα πλέα Id.8.4; λήματος πλέος Id.5.111; θράσους πλέως, φόβου πλέα, etc., A. *Pr*.42, E.*Med*.263, etc.; ἀναιδείας πλέων S.*El*.607; ἔπη μωρίας πολλῆς πλέα Id.*Aj*.745; λήθης, ταραχῆς π., Pl.*R*.486c, 391c; φροντίδων πάντα π. Antipho Soph.49. 2. ῥάκη νοσηλείας πλέα *infected with*.., S.*Ph*. 39; ἀτιμίας πλέως Cratin.9; ἀχθόμενος ὅτι πλέα σοι ἀπ' αὐτῶν [τῶν βρωμάτων] ἐγένετο [ἡ χείρ] X.*Cyr*.1.3.5. II. abs., *full*, πλείοις δεπάεσσι Il.8.162, etc.; κνέφαλλον πλέων *IG*1$^2$.330.22. 2. of Time, *full, complete*, δέκα πλείους ἐνιαυτούς ten *full* years, Hes.*Th*. 636; ἤματος ἐκ πλείου, πλέῳ ἤματι, the *longest* day, Id.*Op*.778, 792: Comp. πλειότερος Od.11.359, Arat.1080, Call.*Fr*.51 P., Poet.ap.*Et. Gen*. 3. πλείην· ἔγκυον, Hsch.

**πλεώτερος**, = πλειότερος, *PLond*.5.1722.27 (vi A.D.).

**πληγ-αίνηται**, prob. f.l. for πλείων γένηται, Gal.18(2).514. -ἄνον, τό, *stick, rod*, Hsch. -άς, άδος, ἡ, = δρέπανον, Id. II. Πληγάδες, αἱ, = Συμπληγάδες, A.R.2.596,645.

**πληγεῖον·** παλαιόν, Hsch.

**πληγενής**, ὁ, ἡ, (πέλας, γί-γν-ομαι) *half-brother, half-sister*, Hsch.

**πληγ-ή**, Dor. **πλᾱγά**, ἡ, (πλήσσω) *blow, stroke*, πεπληγὼν πληγῇσιν Il.2.264, etc.; πᾶν ἑρπετὸν πληγῇ νέμεται Heraclit.11, cf. Pl.*Criti*. 109b, Erasistr.ap.Ps.-Dsc.*Ther*.18; ἡ π. τοῦ τραύματος Pl.*Lg*.877b: freq. joined with Verbs of cogn. signf., πέπληγμαι καιρίαν πληγὴν A.*Ag*.1343; τύπτει τὰς ἴσας πληγὰς ἐμοί Ar.*Ra*.636; τύπτεσθαι τῇ δημοσίᾳ μάστιγι ν' πληγάς Lex ap.Aeschin.1.139; πολλὰς πληγὰς μαστιγούσθω Pl.*Lg*.914b (but in such phrases πληγήν or πληγάς is freq. omitted, τρίτην ἐπενδίδωμι A.*Ag*.1386; τυπτόμενος πολλάς Ar. *Nu*.972, cf. D.19.197; ὀλίγας παῖσαι X.*An*.5.8.12; μαστιγωθεὶς ὁπόσας ἂν δόξῃ τοῖς δικασταῖς Pl.*Lg*.854d, cf. 879e, 2*Ep.Cor*.11.24): the person struck is said πληγὰς λαβεῖν, Ar.*Ra*.673; ὑπὸ τῶν ῥαβδούχων Th.5.50, etc.; πληγῶν δεῖσθαι Ar.*Nu*.493; πληγὴν ἔχω Anaxandr.72; ὑπὸ τὴν π. τοῦ ἀκοντίου ὑπελθεῖν Antipho 3.4.4; καιρίῃ (sc. πληγῇ) τετύφθαι Hdt.3.64; πληγὰς ὑπομένειν Aristopho 4.6; εἰληφέναι καὶ δεδωκέναι πληγάς D.54.14; π. ἐμβαλεῖν, ἐντείνειν τινί, X.*An*.1.5.11, 2.4.11, etc.; πατάξαι Pl.*Grg*.527d; ἐντρίβειν τινί Luc.*Ind*.25, cf. *Somn*.14; προστρίβεσθαι Ar.*Eq*.5; τὰς ἐξ ἀνθρώπων πληγὰς μαστιγοῦν τινα Aeschin.1.59; πληγὴν ἐπὶ πληγῇ φέρειν Plb.2.33.6; π. παρὰ πληγήν Ar.*Ra*.643; πληγαῖς ζημιοῦν, κολάζειν, Th.8.74, Pl.*Lg*.762c, etc.; δίκη ὕβρεως ἢ πληγῶν *PHal*.1.115 (iii B.C.); πληγῆς ἄρχειν strike the first *blow*, Antipho 4.2.2; τὰς π. στέγειν, of the shell of a tortoise, Ar.*V*.1295. 2. *stroke by lightning*, Hes.*Th*.857 (pl.); πλαγαὶ σιδάρου *strokes* of axe or sword, Pi.*P*.4.246, *O*.10(11).37; κλυδωνίου..πληγαῖς A.*Th*.796; στέρνων πλαγαί *beating* of breasts, S.*El*. 90 (anap.); π. τῶν ὀδόντων *strokes* from boars' tusks, X.*Cyn*.10.5; *spearing* of fish, Pl.*Lg*.824 (pl.); of pig-*sticking*, οἱ κάπροι οἱ πρὸς τὴν π... ὠθούμενοι Id.*Euthd*.294d: in sg., *fight with clubs*, Hdt.2. 63. 3. *stroke* or *impression* on the ears or eyes, Pl.*Ti*.67b, Plu. 2.490c, etc.; αἱ νοήσεις τύποι ἔσονται· εἰ δὲ τοῦτο, καὶ ἐπακτοὶ καὶ πληγαί Plot.5.5.1. 4. *impact* of bodies, atoms, etc., Archyt.1, Epicur.*Fr*.308, *Placit*.1.4.2, Plot.3.6.19. 5. *beat* of the pulse, Gal.9.464. 6. metaph., *blow, stroke of calamity*, esp. in war, ἐν μιᾷ π. κατέφθαρται..ὄλβος A.*Pers*.251, cf. *Hell.Oxy*.16.2; ἐν πληγαῖς ὄντες ibid.; πληγὴν ὑπήνεγκεν ἡ πόλις Arist.*Pol*.1270$^a$33; πληγῇ περιπεπτωκέναι Plb.14.9.6; πληγαὶ βιότου A.*Eu*.933 (anap.); π. Διός a heaven-sent *plague*, Id.*Ag*.367 (lyr.), S.*Aj*.137 (anap.); μὴ 'κ θεοῦ π. τις ἥκει ib.279; δμαθέντες πλαγαῖσι ποντίαισιν A.*Pers*. 908 (lyr.); of the ten *plagues* of Egypt, J.*BJ*5.9.4. -ίζω, dub. sens., fut. πληγιεῖται ξοΐδι (τοὺς λίθους?) *IG*12(2).10.14 (Mytil.). -μα, ατος, τό, = πληγή, πλήγματα μετώπων, γενειάδων, κρατός, etc., S.*Tr*. 522 (lyr.), E.*IT*1366, *Tr*.794 (anap.), etc.; π. γενῆδος *stroke* of mattock, S.*Ant*.250; τέθνηκε νεοτόμοισι π. ib.1283; of a wasp's *sting*, Arist.*HA*627$^b$27. -μός, ὁ, *apoplectic stroke*, Alex.Trall.12. II. *bite*, ἑρπετοῦ Heraclid.Tar.ap.Gal.14.181; ῥωγὸς Sch.Nic.*Th*.655. -νῦμι, v. ἐκπλήγνυμι.

**πληγοειδής**, ές, *like an impact*, ἐπίρροιαι Cass.*Pr*.25:—also **πληγώδης**, ες, = πληκτικός II, Antyll.ap.Orib.9.13.4.

**πλῆθα**, ἁ, *assembly*, or perh. *majority in the assembly*, *IG*9(1).334. 40 (Locr., v B.C.); Boeot. **πλεῖθα** *Supp.Epigr*.3.342.19 (Thisbe, iii B.C.).

**πληθικῶς**, Adv. *in the majority of instances*, *OGI*669.49 (Egypt, i A.D.).

**πληθο-ειδής**, ές, *having the form of plurality*, Dam.*Pr*.45, al. Adv. -δῶς Olymp.*in Phlb*.p.284 S. II. *numerous*, Simp.*in Ph*.528. 24. -ποιέω, *multiply, increase*, Iamb.*Protr*.21.λη'. -ποιός, όν, *creating plurality*, Procl.*in Prm*.p.592 S., Dam.*Pr*.33.

**πλῆθος**, εος, τό, Dor. and Arc. **πλῆθος** *Schwyzer*84.8, al. (Argive, found in Crete, v B.C.), *IG*5(2).6.20 (Tegea, iv B.C.), etc.; Boeot. **πλεῖθος** ib.7.3171.46 (Orchom. Boeot.); pseudo-Dor. and pseudo-Aeol. **πλᾶθος** *GDI*5176.21 (Crete), *IGRom*.4.1302.18 (Cyme, i B.C./ i A.D.), Hippod.ap.Stob.4.1.93: (πλήθω, v. πίμπλημι):—*great number, multitude*, esp. of people, Il.17.330, Hdt.7.49, etc.; στρατοῦ π., periphr. for στρατὸς πολύς, Id.9.73; ὡς πλήθει for the *mass* of men, Pl.*R*.389d. 2. τὸ π. the *greater number*, the *mass, main body*, τὸ π. τοῦ στρατοῦ Hdt.1.82, cf. 5.92; τὸ π. τῆς ψυχῆς the *largest part* of.., Pl.*Lg*.689a: as Noun of Multitude with pl. Verb, Ἀθηναίων τὸ π. οἴονται Th.1.20; τὸ π. ἐψηφίσαντο πολεμεῖν *the majority*, ib.125, cf. X.*Cyr*.2.4. 20; τῷ π. by *a majority*, *Berl.Sitzb*.1927.8 (Locr., v B.C.): hence, *people, population*, σμικρὸν τὸ π. τῆσδε γῆς E.*Ph*.715. b. *the commons*, Th.

1.9, etc.; ἡ τοῦ π. ἀρχή, δημοκρατία τοὔνομα κληθεῖσα Pl.*Plt.*291d; ἐς τὸ π. φέρειν τὸ κράτος Hdt.3.81: freq. of the popular *assembly*, τὸ ὑμέτερον π., τὸ π. τὸ ὑμέτερον, Lys.12.42, Pl.*Ap.*31c; Ἐρυθραίων τῷ π., Ἀθηναίων τοῦ π., *IG*1$^{2}$.10.21,22; = Lat. *plebs*, Plb.6.15.11, D.S.12.25, D.H.4.71; also, *association, corporation*, or *guild*, τὸ π. τὸ Ἁλιαδᾶν *IG* 12(1).155.6,156.5 (Rhodes); τὸ τῶν Πανιαστῶν π. *IGRom.*4.1680 (Pergam.); τὸ π. τῶν ἱερέων *OGI*56.24 (Canopus, iii B.C.); π. τῶν ἁλιέων *PSI*5.498.2 (iii B.C.); τὸ π. τῶν μαχαιροφόρων *OGI*737 (Memphis, ii B.C.); opp. αἱ ἀρχαί, οἱ ὀλίγοι, Th.5.84; but also, *populace, mob*, opp. δῆμος (commons), X.*Ath.*2.18, App.*BC*1.10: also in pl., πείθειν τὰ π. the *masses*, Pl.*Grg.*452e, cf. *Sph.*268b; ὃ πᾶσι..σωτήριον, μάλιστα δὲ τοῖς π. πρὸς τοὺς τυράννους D.6.24; φιλόσοφον..π. ἀδύνατον εἶναι Pl.*R.*494a. II. *quantity* or *number*, πόσον π. ἦν νεῶν Ἑλληνίδων; A.*Pers.*334; τῆς σῆς δυνάμεως τί φῂς π. εἶναι; X.*Cyr.*2.1.6; ὅμιλος πλήθει φοβερώτατος Th.2.98; ἰσχύϊ καὶ πλήθει προέχων Id.3.74; τῷ π. αὐτῶν καταπλαγέντες Id.4.10; πλήθεϊ πολλοί Hdt.3.11, cf. 6.44; σὺν πλήθει χερῶν S.*OT*123; πλήθει παρόντες *in force*, Th.8.22: abs. in acc., κόσοι πλῆθος Hdt.1.153; πόσοι τὸ π.; Diph.17.1; ἐρέται..π. ἀνάριθμοι A.*Pers.*40 (anap.); π. ὡς δισχίλιοι X.*An.*4.2.2; ἄπειρα τὸ π. Id. *Mem.*1.1.14; ἄπειρα καὶ π. καὶ σμικρότητα Anaxag.1; π. τι πάμπολυ φθειρῶν *IG*4$^{2}$(1).122.45, cf. 32 (Epid., iv B.C.). III. *magnitude, size*, or *extent*, [ὄρος] πλήθεϊ μέγιστον καὶ μεγάθεϊ ὑψηλότατον Hdt.1.203; πεδίον πλῆθος ἄπειρον ib.204; ἡ ἐρῆμος..ἐοῦσα πλῆθος ἑπτὰ ἡμερέων ὁδοῦ Id.4.123; π. χώρας καὶ ἀνθρώπων X.*An.*1.5.9. 2. in Att., of *quantity* or *amount*, διὰ π. τῆς ζημίας Th.3.70; χρημάτων π. Id.1.9; διὰ πλῆθος οὐσίας Pl.*R.*591e, cf. Arist.*Pol.*1279$^{a}$19; ταῦτα οὐδέν ἐστι πλήθει οὐδὲ μεγέθει πρὸς ἐκεῖνα Pl.*R.*614a; μετὰ πλήθους ἱδρῶτος *multa sudans*, Id.*Ti.*84e; τὸ π. τοῦ ῥεύματος Plb.1.75.5; τὸ παρακείμενον π. the *amount* entered against each, *Ostr.Bodl.*i 252 (ii B.C.); of money, τὸ ἴσον π. *TAM*2.526 (Pinara): in pl., *quantities*, ἐμβρύων Cratin.326; θαυμαστὸν ὅσ' ἐστ' ἀγαθῶν π. Mnesim.4.51 (anap.); οἰκοδομημάτων πλήθεσι ἢ μεγέθεσι D.C.52.30, cf. 10. 3. *more than enough*, π. φέρειν Lxx *Ex.*36.5. 4. *plurality*, opp. ἕν, Dam.*Pr.*45. IV. of Time, *length*, χρόνου Th.1.1, Pl.*Tht.*158d, Isoc.12.180; π. ἐτῶν Ar.*Nu.*855; πλήθει πολλῶν μηνῶν S.*Ph.*722 (lyr.). V. with Preps., or Advbs., ἐς π. *in great numbers*, Th.1.14; κατὰ πλῆθος a *large number* at a time, *IG*1$^{2}$.6.112; ὡς ἐπὶ τὸ π. *usually, mostly*, Pl.*Phdr.*275b; ὡς ἐπὶ τὸ π. εἰπεῖν Arist.*GA*786$^{a}$35; κατὰ π. D.H.6.67.

**πληθο-χορεία**· ἡ ἐπὶ πολὺ ἐκτεινομένη χορεία, Phot. **-χορος**, ον, *much-dancing*, or, *gathering a large troupe of dancers*, Id. **-χωρος**, ον, *containing much*, Id.

**πλήθριον**, τό, Dim. of πλῆτρον, Alcm.148.

⊛ **πληθ-υντικός**, ή, όν, *plural*, περὶ τῶν ἑνικῶν καὶ π. ἐκφορῶν, title of work by Chrysippus: ὁ π. (with or without ἀριθμός) D.T.635.30, D.H. *Amm.*1.9, A.D.*Pron.*11.2, al.; τὰ π. Longin.23.3; αἱ π. χρήσεις, opp. αἱ ἑνικαί, Ath.7.299a. Adv. -κῶς *in the plural*, Str.9.1.20. **-ύνω**, fut. -ῠνῶ 2*Ep.Cor.*9.10: aor. ἐπλήθυνα Dam.*Pr.*99:—causal of πληθύω, *increase, multiply*, Lxx *Ge.*17.2, al., Ph.1.496, 2*Ep Cor.* l. c., *Ep. Hebr.*6.14:—Pass., ταῖς γυναιξὶ τὸ γάλα πληθύνεται *abounds*, Arist. *HA*587$^{b}$20. 2. *make multiple, 'plurify'*, κατὰ ἀναλογίαν [τὸ ἡνωμένον] ἐπληθύναμεν τῶν κατωτέρω πεπληθυσμένων τὸν πρῶτον πληθυσμόν Dam. l. c.; θεοὶ -όμενοι μὲν ἐν τῷ κόσμῳ, περὶ αὐτὸν δὲ ἑνοειδῶς ὄντες Jul.*Or.*4.143b, cf. *Or.*7.222a. 3. intr., v. πληθύω II. 4. *use the plural*, Sch.Il.*Oxy.*1087.34. II. Pass., *to be in the majority, prevail*, δήμου..χεὶρ ὅπῃ πληθύνεται (cod. Med. πληθύεται) A.*Supp.* 604: c. inf., ταύτην ἐπαινεῖν..πληθύνομαι I *follow the majority*, Id.*Ag.* 1370: pf. πεπλήθυνται Lxx *Ge.*18.20. 2. Gramm., [τὸ ἀπαρέμφατον] οὐ πληθύνεται the infinitive *has* no *plural*, A.D.*Synt.*31.25. ⊛**-ύς**, ύος, ἡ, Ep. dat. πληθυῖ Il.22.458, Od.11.514, 16.105:—Ion. for πλῆθος, *throng, crowd*, of people, Hom. ll. cc.; = δῆμος, *Leg. Gort.*6.52; *majority*, πληθὺν δὲ νικῆν *IG*9(1).333.18 (Locr., v B.C.): as Noun of multitude with pl. Verb, ὣς φάσαν ἡ π. Il.2.278: in later Prose, Pl.*Ax.* 366b, Lxx 3*Ma.*4.17; τῆς στρατιᾶς τὴν π. συχνὴν Plu.*Pomp.*39, cf. Luc. *Cont.*15, etc.; = Lat. *plebs*, D.H.7.16, etc. [ῡ in nom. and acc. sg., in other cases ῠ.] **-υσμός**, ὁ, *a making multiple, pluralization*, Procl. *in Prm.*p.577 S., *in Ti.*1.184 D., al., Simp. *in Ph.*88.22, Anon. *in Cat.*9.9, Dam.*Pr.*53, Eust.213.23. ⊛ **-ύω**, aor. subj. πληθύσῃ Pl.*Ti.*83e:—intr. form of πληθύνω, *to be* or *become full*, c. gen., νεκρῶν π. πέδον E.*HF*1172; ἡ πόλις π. ἀνδρῶν Arist.*Pol.*1270$^{a}$39; ἡ τοῦ γάλακτος πληθύουσα τροφή ib.1336$^{a}$7: c. dat., πληθύοι αὐτῷ οἶκος παίδων γοναῖς *IG*12(9).1179.38 (Euboea, ii A.D.): abs., ἀγορῆς πληθυούσης, v. ἀγορά IV; ὁ δῆμος ὁ Ἀθηναίων πληθύων *IG*1$^{2}$.114.26, al., cf. *Schwyzer* 412 (Elis); of rivers, *swell, rise*, Hdt.2.19,20, etc.:—Med., ἐπεὰν πληθύεσθαι ἄρχηται ὁ Νεῖλος (v.l. πλήθεσθαι) ib. 93. 2. *increase in number, multiply*, A.*Ch.*1057, Pl.*Lg.*678b; *increase in time*, ὁ πληθύων χρόνος S.*OC*930:—Med., φῦλον ἐν τῷ ἑνὶ -όμενον *possessing multiplicity* in unity, Iamb.*Myst.*1.6. 3. *abound*, Pl.*R.*405a; τινι *in* a thing, S.*Tr.*54. 4. *increase, grow*, of the σπέρμα, Arist.*Pol.*1335$^{a}$27. 5. *spread, prevail*, ὡς ἐπλήθυον λόγοι A.*Ag.*869; ὁ πληθύων λόγος the *current* story, S.*OC*377. II. πληθύνω is generally trans., -ύω intr.; but πληθύω is trans. in S.*Fr.*718, κύναρος ἄκανθα πάντα πληθύει γύην, and πληθύομαι is Pass. (in signf. *make multiple, 'plurify'*) in Procl.*Inst.*125, Dam.*Pr.*139: πληθύνω is intr. in later writers, Arist.*Mete.*351$^{b}$7, *GA*738$^{a}$37 (in both places with v.l.), Lxx *Ex.*1.20, al., v.l. in Nic.Dam.19 J., *Act.Ap.*6.1, Hdn. 3.8.8; and πληθύομαι is Med. in Hdt.2.93 (s.v.l., v. supr.), and in codd. of A.*Supp.*604; cf. συμπληθύω. [ἐπλήθῠον A.*Pers.*421; πληθῠεται dub. in Id.*Supp.*604: quantity of υ elsewh. indeterminate.] **-ω**, poet. pf. (in pres. sense) πέπληθα Pherecr.29, Herod.7.84, Theoc.22.38, etc.: plpf. ἐπεπλήθει A.R.3.271:—intr. form of πίμπλημι, mostly in pres. part., *to be full*, πλήθει..νεκύων ἐρατεινὰ ῥέεθρα Il.21.218; ναῦς..ἀνδρῶν πληθούσας Simon.142.7; θάλασσα..ναυαγίων πλήθουσα καὶ φόνου A.*Pers.*420, cf. 272; χεῖρας κρεῶν πλήθοντες *having* them *full of..*, Id.*Ag.*1220; τὸ στεγύλλιον πέπληθε καλῶν ἔργων Herod. l. c.: later c. dat., κρήνην..ὕδατι πεπληθυῖαν Theoc. l. c.; δόνακι πλήθοντα λιπὼν ῥόον Call.*Fr.*166, cf. *AP*6.63 (Damoch.); πεπληθότα λύθρῳ Maiist.25; but Ἄναυρος ὄμβρῳ χειμερίῳ πλήθων *swollen with* winter's rain, ὄμβρῳ being dat. of cause, Hes.*Sc.*478: abs., of rivers, ποταμῷ πλήθοντι ἐοικώς Il.5.87; ὡς δ' ὁπότε πλήθων ποταμὸς πεδίονδε κάτεισι 11.492; of the *full* moon, σελήνη πλήθουσα 18.484, cf. Sapph.3: in Att. Prose only in the phrases ἀγορᾶς πληθούσης, ἐν ἀγορᾷ πληθούσῃ, etc., v. ἀγορά IV: πληθούσης ἀγορᾶς rarely = in a *full* assembly, *SIG*257.14 (Delph., iv B.C.). II. trans. only in later Poets, *AP*14.7, Opp.*C.*1.126, Q.S.6.345:—Pass., A.R.3.1392, 4.564, *AP*5.232 (Maced.), Q.S.14.607; πάσαις ἀρεταῖς πληθόμενον κραδίην *BCH*50.444 (Thespiae, iv A.D.).

**πληθώρ-α**, Ion. -η, ἡ, *fullness*, π. ἀγορῆς, = ἀγορὰ πλήθουσα, Hdt. 2.173, 7.223. II. *fullness, satiety*, Hp.*Acut.*37; εὐπρηξίης Hdt.7.49: pl., Iamb.*Protr.*21.κβ'. III. Medic., *repletion of blood* or *humours, fullness of habit, plethora*, Gal.10.891, Alex.Aphr.*Pr.*2.10. **-έομαι**, Pass., = πλήθω, *to be full*, Suid. **-ιάω**, *to be plethoric*, Gal.18(1).728. **-ικός**, ή, όν, *plethoric*, διάθεσις, νόσημα, Id.7.578, 18(1).79. Adv. -κῶς, διακεῖσθαι Id.6.130.

**Πληϊάς**, -ϊάδες, Ep. for Πλειάς, -άδες.

**πληκ-τέον**, *one must strike*, Hsch. s. v. παιητέον. **-τήρ**, ῆρος, ὁ, = πλῆκτρον, Hdn.Gr.2.922. **-της**, ου, ὁ, *striker, brawler*, Hp.*Ep.*19 (pl., v.l. πρῆκται), Arist.*EE*1221$^{b}$14, 1*Ep.Ti.*3.3; *violent, fierce*, ἄνδρες π. καὶ μάχιμοι Plu.*Dio* 30, cf. *Phil.*9; of wine, π. καὶ ὀξύς Id.2.132d; of the sun, ib.920c, cf. 653f: Sup. πληκτίστατος Eust.1441.26, *EM*31.16. **-τίζομαι**, *bandy blows with* one, ἀργαλέον δὲ πληκτίζεσθ' ἀλόχοισι Διός Il.21.499. II. *beat one's breast* for grief, *AP*7.574 (Agath.). III. *toy amorously*, μετὰ τῆς σῆς πυγῆς Ar.*Ec.*964; πρός τινα, πρὸς ἀλλήλους, Herod.5.29, Str.11.8.5, cf. D.C.46.18: abs., Id. 51.12. IV. Act. is only f.l. in Plu.2.735d. **-τικός**, ή, όν, *of, for*, or *by striking*, π. θήρα fishing *by means of spearing*, Pl.*Sph.*220d; ἡ πληκτική, τὸ πληκτικὸν [μέρος], ib.220e, 221b; π. δύναμις Epicur.*Fr.* 308. 2. *ready to strike, given to striking*, π. [ὁ σκορπίος] Arist.*Fr.* 331; γυνὴ ἀνδρὸς..πληκτικώτερον Id.*HA*608$^{b}$10. II. metaph., *striking the senses, overpowering*, οἶνος, τροφή, Ath.1.27a, Philum.*Ven.*9; π. τῇ ὀσμῇ Dsc.1.15, cf. S.E.*P.*1.125 (Comp.); of whitewashed rooms, Antyll.ap.Orib.9.13.5; τὸ π. *overpowering effect*, Plu.2.693b, cf. 367c, 735d (cj.). b. *striking the mind, impressive, startling*, S.E.*P.*3.71 (Comp.), 240, etc. Adv. -κῶς Alex.Aphr.*in Sens.*104.16, Ulp.ad D.20.56: Sup. -ώτατα Ph.2.462 (nisi leg. τλητ-). **-τισμός**, ὁ, *amorous toying*, *AP*12.209 (Strat., pl.). **-τός**, ή, όν, *beaten*, χαλκώματα dub. in Man.5.164. **-τρον**, Dor. **πλᾶκτρον**, τό, *anything to strike with*: 1. *instrument for striking the lyre, plectrum*, χρυσέου ὑπὸ π. *h.Ap.*185, cf. *h.Merc.*53, Pi.*N.*5.24, E.*HF*351 (lyr.); κεράτινα π. Pl. *Lg.*795a; π...ξύλινον *IG*2$^{2}$.1388.80; κρούειν τῷ π. Pl.*Ly.*209b; π. ἐς λύρην ῥάψαι Herod.6.51; πλήκτρῳ..πληγῶν γιγνομένων Pl.*R.*531b. 2. *spear-point*, δορὸς διχόστομον π. S.*Fr.*152 (lyr.); διόβολον π., of lightning, E.*Alc.*129 (lyr.); a bee's *sting*, Jul.*Or.*2.90a. 3. *cock's spur*, Ar.*Av.*759, 1365, Arist.*HA*504$^{b}$7, *PA*694$^{a}$13; also, *spur* of crayfish, ὥσπερ π. Id.*HA*526$^{a}$5; *an analogous bone of the ankle*, ib.516$^{b}$2; *part of the thigh-joint*, Poll.2.185, Hsch. 4. = πηδάλιον, Hdt.1.194, S.*Fr.*143. 5. *goad*, E.*Rh.*766. 6. = γλῶσσα, Poll. 2.104.

**πληκτρο-ποιός**, ὁ, *maker of* πλῆκτρα, Poll.7.154:—hence **-ποιία**, ἡ, *manufacture of* πλῆκτρα, ibid.: Adj. **-ποιικός**, ή, όν, ibid. Adv. -κῶς ibid. **-φόρος**, ον, *with spurs*, of birds, Arist.*HA*504$^{b}$9.

***πλήκτωρ**, v. πλάκτωρ. **πλῆμα**, ατος, τό, = πλῆσμα, Hsch., Phot. **πλημαθῆναι**· πλησθῆναι, Hsch. **πλημαινόν**· παλαιόν, Id.

**πλήμη**, ἡ, *flood-tide*, Plb.20.5.11, 34.9.5, D.H.1.79, D.S.17.106 (pl.), Str.3.2.5 (pl.), *Peripl.M.Rubr.*44; cf. πλήσμη.

**πλημμέλ-εια**, ἡ, prop. *mistake in music, false note*, but in usage, metaph., *fault, error*, esp. in taste or judgement, Pl.*Ap.*22d; διὰ π. καὶ ἀμουσίαν Id.*Lg.*691a; *faultiness* in metre, etc., Plu.2.396d; ἀσέβεια ἡ περὶ θεοὺς π. Arist.*VV*1251$^{a}$31 (hence in Lxx, *trespass, sin*, *Le.*6.5, al.; εἰς πλημμέλειαν for a *sin*-offering, ib.5.18): freq. in pl., αἱ π. αἱ ἐν τοῖς πράγμασιν Isoc.8.56, etc. **-έω**, prop. *make a false note in music*, but in usage, metaph., *offend, err*, τί πλημμελήσας; E.*Ph.*1655, cf. Pl.*Phd.*117e, al.; τοὺς ἑκουσίως καὶ δι' ὕβριν πλημμελοῦντας D.21.42; περί τι Antipho 3.3.6; παρὰ τοὺς νόμους Din.1.62; εἰς δίκην Pl.*Lg.*943e, cf. *Rev.Phil.*1929.142 (Iasos), *POxy.*1119.18 (iii A.D.); εἴς τινα τῷ λόγῳ Aeschin.1.167, cf. Phld.*Ir.*p.83 W.: c. part., μὴ οὖν τι πλημμελήσομεν καλοῦντες..; Pl.*R.*480a, cf. *Sph.* 244b: rarely c. acc., *offend against*, τὸν πάλαι προτετελευτηκότα D.S. 10.14:—Pass., τὰ εἰς ἀλλήλους πεπλημμελημένα Isoc.5.37; τὰ πλημμεληθέντα τῷ δήμῳ περὶ τοὺς στρατηγούς Plu.*Arist.*26; *to be wronged* or *sinned against*, Pl.*Phdr.*275e; ὑπό τινων Decr.ap.D.18.155; κατ' οὐδὲν ὑφ' ἡμῶν πεπλημμελημένοι Philipp.ib.166; ἐάν τι πλημμεληθῇ if anything *goes wrong*, Arist.*PA*664$^{b}$29. ⊛ **-ημα**, ατος, τό, *fault, trespass*, εἰς τοὺς θεούς Aeschin.3.106 (pl.), cf. Lxx *Je.*2.5, Phld.*Rh.* 1.188 S. (pl.), Gal.*Anim.Pass.*2.3 (pl.), etc. **-ής**, ές, (πλήν, μέλος) prop. *out of tune*, opp. ἐμμελής, but in usage, metaph., *faulty, erring*, ὁ ἀκράτως..π. καὶ κακός Pl.*Lg.*731d. 2. *wrongful, outrageous*, ἤν τι π. σε δρᾷ E.*Hel.*1085; μή τι π. πάθῃς; Id.*Med.*306; ἐάν *τι πάθωμεν π.* Pl.*R.*451b; *λίαν πλημμελὲς ἂν εἴη* Arist.*EN*1099$^{b}$24, cf. Democr.181, Pl.*Cri.*43b, *Sph.*243a: Sup., *ἀμαθίαι -έσταται* Id.*Lg.*689b. Adv. *-λῶς* ib.793c; *κινούμενον π. καὶ ἀτάκτως wrongly*, Id.*Ti.*30a. **-ησις,** *εως, ἡ, trespassing, sinning*, Lxx 2*Es.*10.19.

**πλήμνη,** *ἡ, nave of a wheel*, Il.5.726, 23.339, Hes.*Sc.*309, Hp.*Fract.*13; *ἄξονος ἐν πλήμνῃσι* A.R.1.757. (Perh. from *πλήθω, the filled up* or *solid part* of the wheel.)

**πλημνόδετον,** *τό, hoop to secure* the spokes *in the nave*, Poll.1.145.

**πλῆμνος·** *ἀφρός*, Hsch. **πλήμνῳ·** *παλαιῷ*, Id.

**πλημοχόη,** *ἡ, (πλήμη, χέω) earthen vessel for water*, E.*Fr.*592 (anap., = Critias *Fr.*17 D.), Pamphil.ap.Ath.11.496a, Poll.10.74; used on the last day of the Eleusinian mysteries, which were hence called *αἱ πλημοχόαι*, Ath. l. c., Hsch.

⊛ **πλήμῡρ-α,** *ἡ, = πλημυρίς, flood-tide, flood*, Thphr.*Sign.*29, Lxx *Jb.*40.18(23), *Placit.*3.17.1, D.H.1.71, *AP*9.291 (Crin.), *Ev.Luc.*6.48, Plu.*Rom.*3, etc.; *inundation* of the Nile, *POxy.*1409.17 (iii A.D.): metaph., *λόγου* Ph.1.175, cf. 690 (pl.); *κακῶν* S.E.*M.*11.157. **2.** Medic., *accumulation, excessive flow*, Lycus ap.Orib.8.25.39, Aret.*SA*2.9, *SD*2.2. **-έω,** *rise like the flood-tide, to be full* or *in flood, be redundant*, Hp.*Morb.Sacr.*10,11, *APl.*4.134 (Mel.), Plu.*Caes.*22, etc.: Medic., *suffer congestion*, Aret.*SD*2.3, *CD*2.1. **-ία,** Ion. **-ίη,** *ἡ, = πλήμυρα*, prob. f.l. in Aret.*CA*2.8 and in Sch.Pi.*O.*5.20. **-ίς,** *ἴδος, ἡ, rise of the sea, as at flood-tide, πλημῡρὶς ἐκ πόντοιο* of *the wave* caused by the rock thrown by the Cyclops, Od.9.486; *flood-tide*, opp. *ἄμπωτις* (ebb), *π. τῆς θαλάσσης μεγάλη* Hdt.8.129; *π. πόντου* B.*Fr.*30; *ἡ ἔξω π.* Arist.*Mete.*366$^{a}$20, cf. Str.3.3.7 (pl.), S.E.*M.*9.79 (pl.). **2.** generally, *flood, deluge*, Arist.*Mu.*397$^{a}$28 (pl.); of tears, *σταγόνες..δυσχίμου πλημῡρίδος* A.*Ch.*186; *ὀφθαλμοτέγκτῳ δεύεται πλημῡρίδι* E.*Alc.*184. **3.** *redundance, congestion* of the fluids of the body, Hp.*Acut.*62. [ῠ Hom. l.c., and prob. in B. l.c.; ῡ Trag., but ῡ̆ in later Ep., cf. A.R.4.1269, 1241: in *πλήμυρα, πλημυρέω, πλημύρω*, ῡ always.] (The spelling *πλημμ-* in this word and its cognates commonly found in codd. arises from the false etymology from *πλήν, μύρομαι*; the correct spelling is found in B.5.107, *POxy.*1409.17, *OGI*666.8 (v. *πλημύρω*), etc., and good Mss. of Hp.*Acut.*62, *AP*5.203 (Mel.), cf. Archil.97.) **-όντως,** Adv. *abundantly*, Dosith.p.409 K. **-ω,** *= πλημυρέω, overflow*, Call.*Del.*263, *AP*5.203 (Mel.), Orph.*A.*1053: hence, *to be filled with food*, Panyas.12.18; of the Nile, *PLond.*3.924.10 (ii A.D.); *γαῖα..αἵματι πλημύρεσκεν* Q.S.11.161: metaph., *π. σθένει* B.5.107, cf. Ph.ap.Eus.*PE*8.14; *πλημύρουσα πᾶσιν ἀγαθοῖς ἡ Αἴγυπτος* *OGI*666.8 (Gizah, i A.D.). **2.** *swell*, Archil.97; *μαζοὶ π.* A.R.4.706. **3.** *ἧπαρ πλημῦρον congested* liver, Aret.*CD*1.3. **II.** causal, *make to flow, μαστούς* Ph.1.8; *νύμφαι καλὰ νάματα πλημύρουσιν* Orph.*A.*494:—Pass., *overflow*, ib.715:—in Hsch. for *πλημυρόν, πλημῦρον* (as part.) shd. be read.

**πλήν,** Dor. and Aeol. **πλάν** *SIG*56.3 (Argos, v B.C.), 421.7 (Thermum, iii B.C.), *IG*9(1).333.4 (Locr., v B.C.), *Berl.Sitzb.*1927.158 (Cyrene), *Schwyzer*633.16,19 (Eresus, ii/i B.C.): **A.** Prep. with gen., *except, save, πάντων Φαιήκων πλήν γ' αὐτοῦ Λαοδάμαντος* Od.8.207; *τίς ἔτλη.. π. Ἡρακλῆος;* Hes.*Sc.*74, cf. A.*Pr.*914, *IG*1$^{2}$.6.108, etc.: with *γε*, S.*El.*909, etc.; *ὑπεγγύους π. θανάτου* liable to any punishment *short of* death, Hdt.5.71; *ἐπιτρέψαι περὶ σφῶν αὐτῶν π. θανάτου save in respect of* death, Th.4.54; *σκυλεύειν τοὺς τελευτήσαντας π. ὅπλων* of anything *save* their arms, Pl.*R.*469c; *διαρπάσαι..ἐπέτρεψε πλὴν ἀνδραπόδων* to carry off all plunder *save* slaves, X.*An.*2.4.27. **2.** later, *besides, in addition to*, Lxx *De.*18.8, 29.1.

**B.** Conj.: **I.** with single words and phrases, esp. when a neg. precedes, *οὐκ ἆρ' Ἀχαιοῖς ἄνδρες εἰσὶ π. ὅδε;* S.*Aj.*1238; *οὐκ οἶδα π. ἕν* Id.*OC*1161, E.*El.*752; *οὐ κάτοιδα π. ἐπὶ σμικρὸν φράσαι* S.*El.*414, cf. Amphis 13: after a question implying a neg., *τί σοι πέπρακται π. τεύχειν κακά;* A.*Eu.*125, cf. S.*Ant.*646: after *πᾶς*, etc., *τὸ δ' ἄρσεν αἰνῶ πάντα π. γάμου τυχεῖν* A.*Eu.*737; *παντὶ δῆλον π. ἐμοί* Pl.*R.*529a, cf. S.*Ph.*299, Isoc.12.19, etc.; *νικᾶν..πανταχοῦ..ἔφυν π. εἰς σέ* S.*Ph.*1053 (*πᾶς* is sts. omitted, *θνῄσκουσι* [*πάντες*] *π. εἷς τις* Id.*OT*118; *ἀλλ' ἔστι* [*πᾶσι*] *πλὴν σοί* ib.370): freq. with *ἄλλος* (much like *ἤ*), *τί οὖν μ' ἄνωγας ἄλλο π. ψευδῆ λέγειν;* Id.*Ph.*100, cf. *Aj.*125, *Ant.*236, Ar.*Pl.*106, X.*An.*1.2.1, Pl.*Prt.*334b, etc.: after a Comp., *ταῦτ' ἐστὶ κρείσσω π. ὑπ' Ἀργείοις πεσεῖν* E.*Heracl.*231, cf. Pl.*Min.*318e, etc.; *πάντα μᾶλλον π. αὐτὸς ἅψασθαι* D.21.179: after a Sup., *τὸ μέγιστον εἴρηται π. αἱ τάξεις τοῦ φόρου* X.*Ath.*3.5. **II.** freq. joined with other Particles: **1.** *π. εἰ, π. ἐάν, ὅταν*, **a.** folld. by a Verb, *π. εἴ τις κωμῳδοποιὸς τυγχάνει ὤν* Pl.*Ap.*18d, cf. *Tht.*177d, D.3.18, 10.39, etc.; *π. ὅταν* A.*Pr.*260, S.*El.*293, etc.; *π. εἰ ἄρα μή* Str.7.3.8; *π. ἐὰν μὴ ἐξέλθῃ* Arist.*HA*554$^{b}$2. **b.** with Verb omitted, *οὐδεὶς οἶδεν.., π. εἴ τις ἄρ' ὄρνις* Ar.*Av.*601, cf. X.*HG*4.2.21, etc.; *π. εἰ μή*, after a neg., *οὐδὲν προσδεησόμεθα, π. εἰ μὴ πάρεργόν τι* Pl.*Plt.*286d (v.l.); *οὐδὲν ἂν πάθοι.., π. εἰ μή που κατὰ συμβεβηκός* Arist.*GC*323$^{b}$26; *οὐ δεῖ..τοῦτο..κινεῖσθαι, π. εἰ μὴ κατὰ σ.* Id.*de An.*406$^{b}$8, cf. *APr.*43$^{a}$30, Thphr.*CP*1.10.6, D.H.4.74.—The pleon. phrase *π. εἰ μή* is censured by Luc.*Sol.*7. **2.** *πλὴν ἤ* (where *ἤ* adds nothing to the sense; *πλὴν εἰ* is a common v.l.), *οὐκ ἄλλῳ π. ἢ Προδίκῳ* Ar.*Nu.*361, cf. 734; *οὐδὲν κάκιον.., πλὴν ἄρ' ἢ γυναῖκες* Id.*Th.*532, cf. Hdt.2.111, Pl.*Ap.*42a (v.l. *π. εἰ*); also *οὐ τὸν ἄνθρωπον ὑγιάζει π. ἀλλ' ἢ..* Arist.*Metaph.*981$^{a}$18 (v.l.). **3.** *π. οὐ only* not, *πάντες προσδέχονται, π. οὐχ οἱ τύραννοι* X.*Hier.*1.18 (v.l. ap.Ath.4.144d), cf. *Lac.*15.6, D.18.45, 56.23, *Berl.Sitzb.* l.c. **4.** *π. ὅτι except* that.., *save* that.., *καίτοι τί διαφέρουσιν ἡμῶν ἐκεῖνοι, π. ὅτι ψηφίσματ' οὐ γράφουσιν;* Ar.*Nu.*1429; *π. ἢ ὅτι* Hdt.4.189; *πλήν γε ὅτι, πλήν γε δὴ ὅτι*, Pl.*Tht.*183a, *Phd.*57b; after *ὁμοίως, τὰ αὐτά*, Plu.*Pel.*4, Artem.1.56. **5.** *π. ὅσον except* or *save* so far as.., *παρήκουσι παρὰ πᾶσαν* [*τὴν Λιβύην*].., *π. ὅσον Ἕλληνες..ἔχουσι* Hdt.2.32, cf. D.H.1.23; *π. ὅσα* Pl.*R.*456a; *π. καθόσον* D.C.72.19; *π. καθόσον εἰ* Th.6.88 codd. **b.** without a Verb, *πάντων ἐρήμους, π. ὅσον τὸ σὸν μέρος save* so far as thou art concerned, S.*OT*1509; *τοὺς πολλοὺς ἀπέκτειναν π. ὅσον ἐκ τριῶν νεῶν οὓς ἐζώγρησαν except* only.., Th.7.23, cf. Pl.*Lg.*670a, 856d; *ἀληθευτικός, π. ὅσα μὴ δι' εἰρωνείαν* Arist.*EN*1124$^{b}$30. **III.** introducing a clause, mostly preceded by *οὐδείς, πᾶς, ἄλλος, save that, νῦν δ' οὐδεμία πάρεστιν.., π. ἥ γ' ἐμὴ κωμῆτις ἥδ' ἐξέρχεται* Ar.*Lys.*5, cf. S.*Tr.*41, X.*An.*1.8.20, etc.; *οὐκ ἀντεξῄεσαν π. ἕως ἀκροβολισμοῦ* Plb.1.18.2: without any such word preceding, *only, albeit, ἀπέπεμπε κήρυκας ἐς τὴν Ἑλλάδα, π. οὔτε ἐς Ἀθήνας οὔτε ἐς Λακεδαίμονα ἀπέπεμπε* Hdt.7.32, cf. S.*OC*1643, Th.8.70, Pl.*Prt.*328e, etc. **2.** to break off and pass to another subject, *only, however, π. γνώριζε ἄτοπος ὤν* *PCair.Zen.*454.10 (iii B.C.), cf. Plb.1.69.14, 2.17.1, 1*Ep.Cor.*11.11, Diog.Oen.8, Plu.*Per.*34, etc.: in late Prose, *π. ἀλλά* Id.*Pyrrh.*5, Luc.*Prom.*20, *DMort.*13.3, 20.4, etc.; *π. ἀλλά γε* Id.*Rh.Pr.*24. **3.** simply for *δέ, but, πολλὴν στρατιὰν ἀθροίσας, π. ἄπειρον μάχης* Hdn.3.4.1; *δυστυχῶν μέν, π. ἀλλ' Ἑλλήνων* Hld.6.7. (Cogn. with *πλησίος, πελάζω*, cf. *ἔμπλην*.)

**πληναρία,** *ἡ, completeness*, *PLond.*5.1674.41 (vi A.D.).

**πληνοδίᾳ·** *παρανόμῳ, τετιμημένῃ, τῇ πεπλανημένῃ τῆς ὀρθῆς ὁδοῦ*, Hsch. **πλῆντο,** 3 pl. Ep. aor. Pass. both of *πίμπλημι* and of *πελάζω*. **πληνώδους·** *ἀσθενοῦς*, Id.

**πλήξ,** *ῆγος, ἡ*, name of a bandage, Sor.*Fasc.*22,24. **2.** coined word (sine expl.) in Hellad.ap.Phot.p.532 B.

**πλήξιππος,** Dor. **πλάξ-,** *ον, striking* or *driving horses*, epith. of heroes, Il.2.104, 4.327, 5.705, Call.*Hec.*1.4.7; *Βοιωτοί* Hes.*Sc.*24; *Θήβα* Pi.*O.*6.85; *ἱμάσθλη* Nonn.*D.*20.227.

**πλῆξις,** *εως, ἡ*, Dor. **πλᾶξις,** *stroke, percussion*, Ti.Locr.101a, *Placit.*4.19.5, 4.20.1, Ph.1.162.

⊛ **πλήρης,** *ες*, gen. *εος*, contr. *ους*: Comp. *-έστερος* Pl.*Smp.*175d: Sup. *-έστατος* S.*Ph.*1087 (lyr.), etc.: (*πίμ-πλη-μι*): **I.** c. gen., *full of, ἄστυ π. οἰκιέων* Hdt.1.180; *φορμοὶ ψάμμου π.* Id.8.71; *ὀμίχλα..π. δακρύων* A.*Pr.*145 (lyr.); *πλῆρες ἄτης στέγος* S.*Aj.*307; *ποταμὸς π. ἰχθύων* X.*An.*1.4.9; *π. μέλιτος τὸ καλὸν στόμα* Theoc.1.146; *ταῦτα πάσης ἀλογίας π.* Plb.1.15.6; of persons, *κενῶν δοξασμάτων π.* E.*El.*384; *αἰδοῦς π. ψυχή* Pl.*Plt.*310d. **2.** *infected by, π. ὑπ' οἰωνῶν τε καὶ κυνῶν βορᾶς polluted* by birds and dogs with meat (torn from the body of Polynices), S.*Ant.*1017; *νόσου* ib.1052. **3.** *satisfied, satiated*, c. gen., *π. ἔχοντι θυμὸν ὧν χρῄζεις* Id.*OC*778: c. part., *θηεύμενοι ἔωσι π.* they should have gazed their *fill*, Hdt.7.146. **II.** less freq. c. dat., *filled with, Ἕλλησι βαρβάροις θ' ὁμοῦ π. πόλεις* E.*Ba.*19. **III.** abs., *full*, of a swollen stream, Hdt.2.92; of the moon, Sapph.53, Hdt.6.106; *π. γαστήρ* S.*Fr.*848; *ὄγκος γαστρός* *Trag.Adesp.*186; *κρατῆρες, δέπας*, etc., E.*Ba.*221, *Hec.*527, etc.; *κεχόρτασμαι..οὐ κακῶς, ἀλλ' εἰμὶ π.* Eub.30, cf. 53; *full of people, ἐπειδὰν π. ᾖ τὸ θέατρον* Isoc.8.82; *π. τὸ βαλανεῖον ποιεῖν* Ar.*Nu.*1054; *εἰ π. τύχοι ὁ δῆμος ὤν* Id.*Ec.*95, cf. X.*Ath.*2.17; *ἡ βουλὴ ἐπειδὴ ἦν π.* And.1.112; *ἐπειδὰν πάντα π. ᾖ τὰ δικαστήρια* Arist.*Ath.*66.1, cf. *IG*1$^{2}$.41.5; *ἐπειδὴ π. αὐτοῖς ἦσαν αἱ νῆες fully manned*, Th.1.29, cf. X.*HG*2.1.28, D.50.32; of persons, *satisfied, gorged*, opp. *κενός*, X.*Oec.*11.18, etc.; *τὸ π.*, opp. *τὸ κενόν*, Leucipp. and Democr.ap.Arist.*Metaph.*985$^{b}$5. **2.** *full, complete, ἐπειρώτων..εἰ λελάβηκε πλήρεα..τὰ ἀκροθίνια* Hdt.8.122; *ὡς ἂν τὴν χάριν πλήρη λάβω* E.*Hel.*1411, cf. *PGiss.*40 ii 6 (iii A.D.); *-εστάτη οἰκειότης fullest* intimacy, Epicur.*Sent.*40; *φέρων π. τὸν μισθόν* X.*An.*7.5.5; *-εστάτῳ δικαίῳ*, = Lat. *optimo jure*, *PFlor.*66.3 (iv A.D.); of numbers or periods of Time, *τέσσερα ἔτεα π.* four *full* years, Hdt.7.20. **3.** *solid, whole*, of a voting-pebble (*ψῆφος*), opp. *τετρυπημένος, τρυπητός*, Aeschin.1.79, Arist.*Ath.*68.2, 69.1; *π. ὁπλαί* Poll.1.191; *αὔλημα* Id.4.73; *ἄγαλμα..ἐποίησε πλῆρες* Paus.9.12.4. **4.** of sound, *full, πληρέστερον μέλος* Iamb.*VP*14.65. **5.** of wine, *full-bodied, with a persistent flavour*, Archig.ap.Gal.8.945; of the pulse, Id.ib.678; of wool, Id.ib.672. **6.** *ἐκ πλήρους fully, ποιεῖν τὰ δίκαια* *IG*2$^{2}$.1343.21; *in full, τὰ ἐκφόρια κομίσασθαι* *PTeb.*105.47 (ii B.C.), etc. **IV.** *πλήρης* is used indecl. in later Greek, esp. of payments *in full*, Wilcken *Chr.*499.9 (ii/iii A.D.), etc.; freq. v.l. in Lxx, *Ge.*27.27, *Nu.*7.20, *Jb.*21.24, al. **V.** Adv. *πλήρως in full*, *Sammelb.*4652.2 (iv A.D.): Sup. *-έστατα* Iamb.*Protr.*21.κγ'.

**πληροσέληνος,** *ον, full*, of the moon, *Μήνη* Man.2.490; *σελήνη* Sch.Ar.*Nu.*750; *ἡμέρα* Suid. s.v. *πλησιφαής*; *τὸ π. full moon*, Lyd.*Mens.*3.10.

**πληροσία,** *ἡ, = προηρόσια*, *IG*2$^{2}$.1177.9 (pl.), 1183.33.

**πληρότης,** *ητος, ἡ, fullness*, Plu.2.721c, Gal.8.671, Orib.6.3.1.

**πληρούντως,** Adv. *completely, exactly*, Nicom.*Ar.*1.18.

**πληροφορ-έω,** *bring full measure: satisfy fully*, *PAmh.*2.66.42 (ii A.D.), *PMag.Lond.*121.910; esp. *assure, τινὰ ὅρκοις* Ctes.*Fr.*29.39, cf. *Cod.Just.*1.1.7.23. **2.** *fulfil, τὴν διακονίαν* 2*Ep.Ti.*4.5; *τὸ πατρῷον συνάλλαγμα* *Arch.Pap.*5.383 (i/ii A.D.):—Pass., *to be fulfilled*, *Ev.Luc.*1.1, Vett.Val.43.18. **3.** *pay in full*, *POxy.*1473.8 (Pass., iii A.D.), etc. **II.** Pass., of persons, *have full satisfaction, to be fully assured, ὅτι..* *Ep.Rom.*4.21: abs., ib.14.5. **2.** *π. τοῦ ποιῆσαι to be fully bent on* doing, Lxx *Ec.*8.11. **-ημα,** *ατος, τό, full satisfaction*, *Gloss.* **-ησις,** *εως, ἡ, maturity, σπερμάτων* Ptol.*Tetr.*4 (pl.). **-ία,** *ἡ, fullness of assurance, certainty*, 1*Ep.Thess.*1.5, *Ep.Col.*2.2, *Ep.Hebr.*6.11. **II.** *assurance given*, *Cod.Just.*1.1.5.4.

⊛ **πληρ-όω,** 3 pl. impf. *ἐπληροῦσαν* cited by Choerob.*in Theod.*2.64 H. from E.*Hec.*574: fut. *-ώσω*: pf. *πεπλήρωκα*, Aeol. part. *πεπληρώ-*

κων *IG*12(2).243.9(Mytil.):—Med., fut. πληρώσομαι (ἐπι-) Th.7.14 (v. infr.): aor. ἐπληρωσάμην Pl.*Grg*.493e, X.*HG*5.4.56, etc.:—Pass., fut. -ωθήσομαι Pl.*Smp*.175e, Aeschin.2.37; fut. Med. in pass. sense, X.*Eq.Mag*.3.6, D.17.28, Gal.2.560:—*make full*: I. c. gen. rei, *fill full of*, λάρνακας λίθων Hdt.3.123, etc.; κρατῆρα, πίστρα (sc. οἴνου), E.*Ion* 1192, *Cyc*.29:—Pass., *to be filled full*, τινος *of* a thing, Hp.*VM* 20, Pl.*R*.550d, etc.; σάλπιγξ βροτείου πνεύματος -ουμένη A.*Eu*.568; ἀπό τινος Porph.*Sent*.32. 2. *fill full* of food, *gorge, satiate*, βορᾶς ψυχὴν ἐπλήρουν E.*Ion* 1170: metaph., π. θυμόν *glut* one's rage, S.*Ph*. 324, E.*Hipp*.1328; τὰς ἐπιθυμίας Pl.*Grg*.494c:—Pass., *to be filled full of, satisfied*, δαιτὸς -ωθείς E.*Fr*.213.3; Αἴγυπτος ἁγνοῦ νάματος -ουμένη A.*Fr*.300.6; φόβου, ἐλπίδος, etc., Pl.*Lg*.865e, *R*.494c, etc.; also οὐ πληρωθήσεται οὖς ἀπὸ ἀκροάματος Lxx *Ec*.1.8. 3. π. τὴν χεῖρά τινος *consecrate*, ib.*Ex*.32.29, al., *Jd*.17.5,12. II. rarely c. dat., *fill with*, πεύκαισιν..χέρας πληροῦντες E.*HF* 373 (lyr.):—Pass., πνεύμασιν -ούμενοι *filled with* breath, A.*Th*.464; πεπληρωμένους πάσῃ ἀδικίᾳ *Ep.Rom*.1.29, cf. 2*Ep.Cor*.7.4. III. without any modal case, π. νέας *man* ships, Hdt.1.171, cf. Th.1.29 (Act. and Pass.) (in full πεντηκόντερον π. ἀνδρῶν Hdt.3.41); π. ναυτικόν Th.6.52; πληροῦτε θωρακεῖα *man* the breastworks, A.*Th*.32:—Med., τριήρη πληρωσάμενος Is.11. 48, cf. X.*HG*5.4.56, etc.; in full, ἐπληρωσάμην τὴν ναῦν ἐρετῶν ἀγαθῶν D.50.15. 2. *impregnate*, [τὰ θήλεα] Arist.*HA* $574^{a}$20, *Metaph*.$988^{a}$6:—Pass., of the female, ibid., *HA* $541^{a}$13. 3. *make full* or *complete*, τοὺς δέκα μῆνας Hdt.6.63; π. τοὺς χρόνους, τὸν ἐνιαυτόν, Pl.*Lg*. 866a, *Ti*.39d; τὸν τῆς καταδίκης χρόνον *Sammelb*.4639.5 (iii A.D.), cf. *POxy*.491.6 (ii A.D.), etc.:—Med., τὰ πάντα ἐν πᾶσι π. *Ep.Eph*.1.23:—Pass., of the moon, *to be full*, S.*Fr*.871.6; ἵνα..ἧ τοι ἀπαρτιλογίη ὑπ' ἐμέο πεπληρωμένη Hdt.7.29; πεπλήρωται ὁ καιρός *Ev.Marc*.1.15, etc.: Math., πεπληρώσθω *let* the figure *be completed*, Arist.*Mech*.$854^{b}$29. 4. π. δικαστήρια *fill* them, D.24.92:—Pass., δικαστήριον πεπληρωμένον ἐκ τούτων Id.21.209, cf. Is.6.37; πληρουμένου..βουλευτηρίου A.*Eu*. 570. 5. *render, pay in full*, τροφεῖα πληρώσει χθονί Id.*Th*.477; π. τὴν χρείαν *supply* it, *make* it *good*, Th.1.70; πεπλήρωκα τὸν τόκον μέχρι τοῦ Ἐπείφ *POxy*.114.3 (ii/iii A.D.), cf. *BGU* 1055.23 (Pass., i B.C.): c. dupl. acc., ἵνα πληρώσῃς αὐτοὺς τὴν τιμήν *PLond*.2.243.11 (iv A.D.), cf. 251.30 (Pass., iv A.D.), etc.: abs., *IG*14.956. 6. *fulfil*, τὸ χρεών (destiny) Plu.*Cic*.17; τὴν ἐπαγγελίαν, τὰς ὑποσχέσεις, Arr. *Epict*.2.9.3, Hdn.2.7.6; π. πᾶσαν ἀρχὴν καὶ λειτουργίαν *IG*12(5).946.1 (Tenos), cf. 12(2) l.c. (Mytil.), *PFlor*.382.40 (iii A.D.), Lyd.*Mag*.3.30, al.; *execute, perform*, τὰ προσταχθέντα *POxy*.2107.5 (iii A.D.):—Pass., λαμπαδηφόρων νόμοι..διαδοχαῖς πληρούμενοι *fully observed*, A.*Ag*.313; *to be fulfilled*, of prophecy, *Ev.Matt*.1.22, *Ev.Jo*.13.18. 7. ἐς ἄγγος..βακχίου μέτρημα πληρώσαντες *having poured* wine into the vessel *till it was full*, E.*IT* 954:—Pass., *assemble, muster*, πληρουμένης τῆς ἐκκλησίας Ar.*Ec*.89; ἀρχαί τ' ἐπληροῦντ' εἰς..βουλευτήρια E.*Andr*.1097 codd.; πολλοὶ δ' ἐπληρώθημεν Id.*IT* 306. 8. *fill up* a document, Lyd.*Mag*.3.11:—Pass., ib.68. IV. intr., ἡ [ὁδὸς] πληροῖ ἐς τὸν ἀριθμὸν τοῦτον the length of road *comes in full* to this number, Hdt.2.7 (s.v.l.). **-ωμα**, ατος, τό, *that which fills, complement*, κρατήρων πληρώματα, i.e. wine, E.*Ion* 1051 (lyr.); so κενὸν τόδ' ἄγγος, ἢ στέγει π. τι; ib.1412; χθονὸς π., i.e. men, Id.*Or*.1642; λίθους τοὺς εἰς τὰ π. τῷ πύργῳ προσάξεται *IG*2².244.109, cf. 90, al. (iv B.C.); τὸ π. τῆς γαστρός Hp.*Aër*.7, *Mul*.2.169, cf. Epicur.*Sent.Vat*. 59; of excrement, Orib.8.35.7. 2. δαιτὸς π. *satiety* of the feast, E.*Med*.203 (anap.); π. τυρῶν *their fill* of cheese, Id.*Cyc*.209. 3. of ships, *full number*, Hdt.8.43,45; but, of single ships, *complement, crew*, in pl., Th.7.4,12, X.*HG*5.1.11, D.21.155, etc.: in sg., Th.7. 14; opp. ὑπηρεσία (q.v.), Lys.21.10; παραλαβὼν τῶν πολιτᾶν ἐπιλέκτους ἐμ π. τρισί *IPE*1².352.40 (Cherson., ii B.C.); π. ἐπίλεκτον Plb. 1.47.6: generally, π. παρέχεσθαι πόλεως make up *the full number* of citizens, Arist.*Pol*.$1267^{b}$16, $1284^{a}$5, cf. $1291^{a}$17, Pl.*R*.371e; τῶν φίλων π. ἀθροίσας E.*Ion* 664; *gang* of workmen, *PPetr*.3 p.130 (iii B.C.). 4. of number, *sum*, ὀγδώκοντα ἔτεα ζόης π. μακρότατον προκεῖσθαι 80 years are fixed as life's longest *sum*, Hdt.3.22; τούτων π. τάλαντ' ἐγγὺς δισχίλια γίγνεται Ar.*V*.660; *sum, total*, τὸ π. τῶν ἀγαθῶν Metrod.*Herc*.831.14, cf. Polystr.*Herc*.346 p.81 V., Diog.Oen. 2. 5. *piece inserted to fill up*, *Ev.Matt*.9.16, Ruf.*Onom*.216. 6. *fullness, full and perfect nature*, *Ep.Rom*.11.12; τὸ π. τοῦ θεοῦ, τοῦ Χριστοῦ, *Ep.Eph*.3.19, 4.13, cf. *Ep.Col*.1.19; τῆς θεότητος ib. 2.9; later τὰ π. τῶν θεῶν Iamb.*Myst*.1.8; *the aggregate of properties which constitute the complete nature of a thing, full specification, substance*, Dam.*Pr*.28 bis; φθαρτὰ π. ib.34; τὰ μέσα π. ib.35 bis; τὰ ἑκάστου πληρώματα τῆς οὐσίας ib.14, cf. 56,58; πᾶς νοῦς, π. ὢν εἰδῶν Procl.*Inst*.177. 7. *reserves* of troops, στρατιῶν Lyd.*Mag*.3.44 (pl.). 8. *mass, complex*, ὁ κόσμος π. ἐστι κακίας, ζωῆς, *Corp.Herm*. 6.4, 12.15; γενομένη π. ἀρετῶν ἥδε ἡ ψυχή Ph.2.418. 9. *duties of an office*, Lyd.*Mag*.3.6, al.; *completion of a term of office* (cf. II), ib. 47. 10. *freight, cargo*, νεώς Ph.2.18, cf. 465: metaph., π. εὐτυχίας ib.547. II. *filling up, completing*, S.*Tr*.1213; Ζηνὸς ἔχεις κυλίκων π. hast *the task of filling*.., E.*Tr*.824 (lyr.). 2. *fulfilment*, νόμου *Ep.Rom*.13.10. **-ωσις**, εως, ἡ, *filling up, filling*, πληρώσεσι καὶ κενώσεσι Pl.*Phlb*.42c; esp. with people, κληρώσεις δικαστηρίων καὶ π. Id.*Lg*.956e; π. τῆς νεώς *manning* the ship, *CIG*2501 (Cos, i B.C.). 2. *sensual satisfaction, gratification*, esp. of eating and drinking, τὸ πίνειν π. τῆς ἐνδείας Pl.*Grg*.496e; ἐκπορίζεσθαι ταῖς ἡδοναῖς π. ib.492a; πληρώσεών τινων καὶ ἡδονῶν Id.*R*.439d: as expl. of the origin of pleasure, Id.*Phlb*.31e sq., 35a sq.; of other passions, θυμοῦ π. Plu.*Lys*.19; of the higher aspirations, Plot.5.8.4. 3. *completion of a number*, μῆνας ἑπτὰ τοὺς ἐπιλοίπους..ἐς τὰ ὀκτὼ ἔτεα τῆς πληρώσιος which remained *to complete* the eight years, Hdt.3.67; εἰς π. ἐκρηγμάτων (ἐκχρημ- Pap.) κδ' making a *total* of 24 sluices, Wilcken *Chr*.11 *A* 14 (ii B.C.). 4. *filling up* a document, Lyd. *Mag*.3.68. II. Pass., *becoming full*, τῆς σελήνης Arist.*HA* $582^{b}$2, Epicur.*Ep*.2 p.40 U.; of women, *impregnation*, Arist. l.c.; αἱ τῶν σιτίων π. *a being filled with* food, opp. αἱ ἔνδειαι, Id.*Phgn*.$810^{b}$22: abs., *repletion*, Hp.*VM* 9, 21, Arist.*Rh*.$1380^{b}$4. **-ωτέον**, *one must fill*, *Gp*.6.2.4. ⊛ **-ωτής**, οῦ, ὁ, *one who completes*, π. ἐράνου *joint-lender* in an ἔρανος, D.21.101, cf. 184, 25.21, Hyp.*Ath*.7 (pl.): in sg., *treasurer of an* ἔρανος, π. καὶ συνερανισταί *IG*2².2721; = ἐράνου συναγωγός, Hsch. II. *one who fills up documents*, Lyd.*Mag*.3.11,68. 2. in Egypt, holder of a local office of unknown nature, *PFay*.23 *Intr*. (ii A.D.); γραμματεὺς πληρωτῶν *PHamb*.59 (ii A.D.). **-ωτικός**, ή, όν, *filling up*, ἑλκῶν Dsc.2.77; δύναμις π. κοιλωμάτων Id.1.68; v.l. for συμπλ. in S.E.*M*.3.26, Ptol.*Tetr*.88. II. Medic., = πληθωρικός, Alex.Trall.1.14; *causing plethora*, ib.15. III. *acknowledging payment in full*, ἀποχή *PFlor*.346.6 (v A.D.), *PStrassb*.15.5 (v/vi A.D.).

⊛ **πλησι-άζω**, Dor. **πλᾱτιάζω** Archyt.ap.Stob.1.41.2: pf. πεπλησίακα Isoc.3.36, Pl.*Tht*.144a: (πλησίος):—*bring near*, [ἵππον] ὄψεσι, ψόφοις, X.*Eq*.2.5; ναῦν λιμένι Sch.Ar.*Ra*.271:—Pass., *come near, approach*, τινι E.*El*.634. II. intr., abs., *to be near*, S.*OT* 91: c. dat., *draw near to, approach*, τῷ πάθει, τοῖς πολεμίοις, X.*Cyr*.7.3.16, *An*.4.6.6, al. (rarely c. gen., τῶν ἄκρων Id.*Cyr*.3.2.8: abs., τὸ πλησιάζον ὀστοῦν Gal.18 (1).304); ἀλλήλοις Pl.*Phd*.97a; π. τόποις Amphis 4; π. τῷ γενειάσκειν Pl.*Smp*.181d; ἀρχαῖς π. *enter on* a career of public office, Thphr.*Char*. 26.3; so π. πρὸς τὴν πολιτείαν, = *accedere ad rem publicam*, Luc.*Anach*. 21. 2. c. dat. pers., *consort, associate with*, τῷδε τἀνδρί S.*OT* 1136, cf. Pl.*La*.197d, *Tht*.143d, 144a, al., Isoc.2.4; οἱ πλησιάζοντες a man's *followers* or *disciples*, Id.15.175, cf. 1.30; οἱ ἐμοὶ πεπλησιακότες Lib.*Ep*.750.1; π. τινὶ ἐπὶ σοφίᾳ, διὰ φιλοσοφίαν, Luc.*Herm*.80, Plu.*Dem*.2; also π. παιδεύσει Pl.*R*.496a. 3. c. dat. pers., *have sexual intercourse with*.., D.40.8, Hyp.*Lyc*.3, Plu.2.769a: metaph., Pl.*R*.490b; οὐδενὶ σώματι πεπλησιακώς Isoc.3.36; of animals, whether of the male, Arist.*HA* $546^{a}$26, $578^{b}$12; or the female, ib. $584^{b}$23, *GA* $727^{b}$25; or both sexes, Id.*HA* $539^{b}$21, al. III. Gramm., *indicate proximity*, A.D.*Pron*.21.11. **-αίτερος, -αίτατος**, v. πλησίος fin. **-ᾰλος**, ον, *near the sea*, Posidon.29 J. **-ᾰσις**, εως, ἡ, = πλησιασμός, Plu.2.1112e. **-ασμα**, ατος, τό, *impregnation*, f.l. for πλῆσμα, Arist.*HA* $577^{a}$30. **-ασμός**, ὁ, Dor. **πλᾱτιασμός** Dius ap.Stob.4.21.16:—*approach*, φοβεροῦ Arist.*Rh*.$1382^{a}$32, cf. A.D. *Adv*.161.21. 2. *sexual intercourse*, Arist.*HA* $536^{a}$15, Poll.5. 93. ⊛ **-αστής**, οῦ, ὁ, *neighbour*, Sch.rec.A.*Pers*.49. **-αστός**, ή, όν, *approachable*, τοῖς ξένοις Sch.rec.A.*Pr*.716. **-γνᾰθος**, ον, *filling the cheeks*, ἄρτος Sopat.9. **-έστερος**, v. πλησίος fin. ⊛ **-μοχθος**, ον, *full of distress*, v.l. for τλησίμοχθος (q.v.).

**πλησίνη**, ἡ, dub. sens. in *PFay*.348 (ii/iii A.D.).

**πλησιοθάλαττος** [θᾰ], ον, *near the sea*, Sch.Opp.*H*.1.309.

**πλησί-οικος** [ῐ], ον, *dwelling near*, D.C.*Fr*.53. ⊛ **-ος**, α, ον, Boeot. **πλᾱτίος** *Rev.Ét.Gr*.10.29 (Thespiae): (πέλας, πελάζω):—*near, close to*, c. gen., πλησίοι ἀλλήλων v.l. in Il.6.249; πλησίαι ἀλλήλων Od.5. 71. 2. c. dat., πλησίοι ἀλλήλοισι Il.23.732, cf. Od.2.149, S.*Ant*. 761. 3. abs., *near, neighbouring*, πλησίαι αἵ γ' ἥσθην Il.4.21; dub.l. in A.*Eu*.195; οἱ π. γύαι S.*OC* 58; τῶν πλησίων ἱερῶν *OGI* 736.5 (Egypt): Subst., *neighbour*, ἰδὼν ἐς π. ἄλλον Il.2.271, etc.; οἱ π. Hdt. 7.152, Ar.*Lys*.471, etc. II. Adv. πλησίον, Aeol. **πλάσιον** [ᾱ] Sapph.2.3, *Supp*.6.1; Dor. **πλᾱτίον**: = πέλας, *near, hard by*, c. gen., τὰ μὲν κατέθεντ' ἐπὶ γαίῃ π. ἀλλήλων Il.3.115, cf. Od.14.14; Σωφροσύνας πλατίον οἰκεῖ Epich.101, cf. *IG*4²(1).123.15 (Epid., iv B.C.); κεῖται στενωποῦ π. A.*Pr*.366; στῆθι π. πατρός S.*Tr*.1076; στρατοπεδεύεσθαι π. τινῶν Hdt.4.111; δρῶ δέ σ' ἤδη τοῦδε π. κακοῦ E.*Hipp*.1439; π. παρῆσθα κινδύνων ἐμοί Id.*Or*.1159: c. dat., σταθεῖσα τῷ τεκόντι π. Id.*IA* 1551; τοῖς πολεμίοις π. προσέρχομαι Plu.2.234d. 2. with the Art., ὁ πλησίον (sc. ὤν) *one's neighbour*, Thgn.221, 611, E.*Hec*.996 (pl.), Antipho Soph.58, Arist.*Pol*.$1267^{a}$25, etc.; ὁ π. καὶ ὁ γείτων Pl. *Tht*.174b; τοὺς μάλιστα π. ἑαυτῶν Id.*Ap*.25d; Dor., ὁ πλατίον Theoc. 5.28, 10.3: with Substs., ταῖς π. κλίναις Pl.*Prt*.315d; ὁ π. παράδεισος, αἱ π. κῶμαι, etc., X.*An*.2.4.16, 3.4.9, etc. III. Sup. -αίτατος ib.1. 10.5, 7.3.29. Comp. Adv. -αιτέρω Hdt.4.112; -αίτερον X.*Mem*.2.1. 23: Sup. -αίτατα Id.*Vect*.4.46: later Comp. -έστερος Simp. *in Cael*. 441.14. Adv. -έστερον Lxx 4*Ma*.12.3, Them.*Or*.1.12a.—The Adj. is poet. and Ion.; in Att. Prose only the Adv. is found.

**πλησιότης**, ητος, ἡ, *neighbourhood*, A.D.*Adv*.161.23, Phlp. *in Mete*.60.9, *EM* 651.32.

⊛ **πλησιόχωρος**, ον, *adjacent, bordering upon*, τισι Hdt.3.97: more freq. abs., οἱ π. ib.89, 4.13, al., Pl.*Lg*.737c; οἱ π. βάρβαροι Th.2.68: sg., τὸν σαυτοῦ π. Ar.*V*.393.

**πλησισέληνος**, ον, *becoming full*, of the moon, Theo Sm.p.103 H.; opp. πανσέληνος, Paul.Al.*G*.3.

**πλησίστιος**, ον, (πίμπλημι, ἱστία) *filling* or *swelling the sails*, οὖρος Od.11.7, 12.149, Them.*Or*.15.195a; πνοαί E.*IT* 430 (lyr.). II. Pass., *with full sails*, π. φέρεσθαι Ph.1.611, 2.571: metaph., Plu.*Cat. Ma*.3.

**πλησῐ-φάεις** [ᾰ], εσσα, εν, = sq., Doroth.ap.Heph.Astr.3.16. **-φᾰής**, ές, *with full light*, of the moon, Ph.1.24, al., Man.1.208, Nonn. *D*.41.258, Epic. in Pap. ap. Kroll *Analecta Graeca* (Greifswald 1901) p.4, Eust.729.20:—also **-φως**, ωτος, ὁ, ἡ, *Theol.Ar*.26. **-φωτέω**, *to be waxing*, of the moon, Anub.ap.Heph.Astr.2.5. **-φωτος**, ον, = πλησίφως, Plot.2.3.5.

⊛ **πλῆσ-μα**, ατος, τό, (πίμπλημι) *impregnation*, π. λαμβάνειν Arist.

*HA* 577ᵃ30. -μη, ἡ, = πλημυρίς, ἐν πλήσμησι διιπετέος ποταμοῖο when it is *full*, Hes.*Fr.*217. ✱ -μιος, α, ον, Hices.ap.Ath.7.298b, but ος, ον Xenocr.ap.Orib.2.58.49:—*filling, satisfying*, ἐδέσματα Plu. *Tim.*6, cf. Philistion ap.Ath.3.115d, Ph.*Bel.*89.9, Hices.l.c., Xenocr. l.c., Dsc.5.8; of wine, Ath.1.32f; τὸ π. *satiety, surfeit*, Epicur.*Fr.* 465, Plu.*Ant.*24; ἔχει τι π. τὸ πρᾶγμα Agathin.ap.Orib.10.7.22: neut. as Adv., πλήσμιον διαιτᾶσθαι Ruf.*Sat.Gon.*33.

πλησμον-ή, ἡ, *a being filled, satiety*, opp. ἔνδεια, κένωσις, Pl.*R.*571e, *Smp.*186c; esp. with food, *repletion, surfeit*, Hp.*Aph.*2.4; οὔτε π. οὔτε μέθη X.*Cyr.*4.2.40, cf. Phld.*Mus.*p.62 K.; ἐς πλησμονὰς E.*Tr.* 1211; ἐν πλησμονῇ τοι Κύπρις, ἐν πεινῶντι δ' οὔ Id.*Fr.*895; ἐσθίειν εἰς π. Lxx *Ex.*16.3: c. gen., τῶν μὲν γὰρ ἄλλων ἐστὶ πάντων π. Ar.*Pl.*189, cf. Isoc.1.20; π. ὑγροῦ Hp.*Aph.*7.62; τιμῆς τε καὶ νίκης Pl.*R.*586d, etc.; also π. περί τι Id.*Lg.*837c; π. ἀπό τινος Luc.*Nigr.*33. II. *abundance*, Lxx *Pr.*3.10, *Gp.*1.10.8 (pl.). -ικός, ή, όν, *fond of gorging*, ταῖς τροφαῖς Pythag.*Ep.*4.2 (Theano). -ώδης, ες, *filling, cloying*, Hp.*Acut.*56. Adv. -δῶς Gal.19.5.

✱ πλήσσω, Nic.*Al.*456, present used by Hom. and Att. writers only in compd. ἐκπλ- (cf. πλήγνυμι); Att. πλήττω Arist.*Ph.*224ᵃ33: fut. πλήξω A.*Fr.*275, and late Prose, Philostr.*VA*5.39, (ἐπι-) Il.23.580, (ἐκ-) Pl.*R.*436e, (κατα-) X.*Lac.*8.3: aor. ἔπληξα, Ep. πλῆξα, Il.2.266, Hes.*Th.*855, Hdt.3.64, and later Greek, J.*AJ*4.8.33, Plu.2.233f, *BGU*759.14 (ii A.D.), etc.; Dor. πλᾶξα Pi.*N.*1.49; never in Att. (E.*IA*1579 is spurious) exc. in compds. ἐκ-, κατα- (qq.v.); in the simple Verb the fut. and aor. of πατάσσω or παίω are used instead, as also in Lxx: pf. πέπληγα, subj. πεπλήγῃ Ar.*Av.*1350, inf. πεπληγέναι X.*An.*6.1.5 (dub., but read by Ath.1.15e), part. πεπληγώς Il.5.763, al. (also in pass. sense in late writers, Lxx 2*Ch.*29.9, Plu.*Luc.*31, Luc.*Trag.*115, Q.S.5.91, etc.); later perf. πέπληχα Men.*Epit.*485, *Sam.*86, J.*AJ*4.8.33: Ep. redupl. aor. 2 ἐπέπληγον Il.5.504, πέπληγον 23.363, Od.8.264; inf. πεπληγέμεν Il.16.728, 23.660; but part. πεπλήγοντες in pres. sense, Call.*Jov.*53, Nonn.*D.*28.327:—Med., fut. πλήξομαι (κατα-) Plb.4.80.2, D.H.6.10, etc.: aor. ἐπληξάμην, Ep. πληξάμην, *h.Cer.*245, Hdt.3.14, and in late Prose, J.*AJ*16.10.7, (κατα-) Plb.2.52.1, etc.; part. πληξάμενος Il.16.125: Ep. aor. 2 πεπλήγετο 12.162, Od.13.198, πεπλήγοντο Il.18.51:—Pass., pres. πλήσσομαι Ptol.*Harm.*1.1: fut. πληγήσομαι X.*Cyr.*2.3.10, D.18.263 (but in compos. ἐκ-πλᾰγήσομαι); also πεπλήξομαι E.*Hipp.*894, Ar.*Eq.*271, Pl.*Tht.*180a: aor. ἐπλήχθην Ph.1.39, Dsc.1.93, *Placit.*4.14.3, but mostly ἐπλήγην, Hdt.5.120, S.*OC*605, etc. (the former nowhere in Trag., exc. ἐκ-πληχθεὶς E.*Tr.*183 (lyr.)); part. πληγείς Il.8.12, A.*Th.*608, *Frr.*139, 180, Antipho 4.4.3, etc.; Dor. πλᾱγείς (v. infr. I. 1a ad fin.); Aeol. πλάγεις [ᾰ] Alc.*Supp.*26.3; (ἐπλάγην [ᾰ] only in compds. ἐξ-, κατ-, of persons *struck with terror* or *amazement*): pf. πέπληγμαι Hdt.1.41, etc.—in Att. and Trag., also Lxx, the simple Verb is scarcely found exc. in fut. 2 and 3, aor. 2, and pf. Pass., but fut. Act. is used once by A., pf. 2 πέπληγα by Ar. and X. (v. supr.); Hdt. uses the Act. (aor.) only in 3.64,78.—The pres. πλήσσω, πλήσσομαι are unknown to Att. writers (also to Lxx, exc. 4*Ma.*14.19), who use the pres. Act. and Pass. of παίω, τύπτω instead (v. sub his vv.); whereas the aor. 2 Pass. ἐπλήγην is used instead of ἐπαίσθην, ἐπατάχθην, or ἐτύφθην (ἐτύπην): hence παίσαντές τε καὶ πληγέντες S.*Ant.*172; πότερον πρότερος ἐπλήγην ἢ ἐπάταξα Lys.4.15; πατάξας καταβάλλω, opp. πληγεὶς κατέπεσεν, Id.1.25,27; ὁ πληγεὶς ἀεὶ τῆς πληγῆς ἔχεται, κἂν ἑτέρωσε πατάξῃ τις, ἐκεῖσ' εἰσὶν αἱ χεῖρες D.4.40; ὅταν ὁ μὲν πληγῇ, ὁ δὲ πατάξῃ Arist.*EN*1132ᵃ8; πατάξαι ἢ πληγῆναι Id.*Rh.*1377ᵃ21; so in D.21.33,38 the Act. πατάξαι corresponds with the Pass. πληγῆναι in ib.36,39:—*strike, smite*, freq. in Hom., esp. of a direct blow, opp. βάλλειν (οὔτε πληγέντα.., οὔτε βληθέντα Hdt.6.117), πλῆξεν..κόρυθος φάλον Il.3.362; σκήπτρῳ δὲ μετάφρενον ἠδὲ καὶ ὤμω πλῆξεν 2.266, cf. 16.791; πλήξας ξίφει αὐχένα ib.332; μή τις..ἐμὲ χειρὶ βαρείῃ πλήξῃ Od.18.57, etc.; ἱστὸς.. πλῆξε κυβερνήτεω κεφαλήν 12.412: c. acc. dupl. pers. et rei, *strike* one *on*.., τὸν δ' ἄορι πλῆξ' αὐχένα Il.11.240, etc.; τὸν..ξιφεῖ..κληῗδα παρ' ὦμον πλῆξ' 5.147; τὸν..κατ' ἄκνηστιν μέσα νῶτα πλῆξα Od.10.162; πὺξ πεπληγέμεν, of boxers, Il.23.660; πλῆξ' αὐτοσχεδίην 12.192; πεπληγὼς ἀγορῆθεν ἀεικέσσι πληγῇσιν *having driven* him *with blows*, 2.264; κῦμα..μιν..πλῆξεν *struck* him, Od.5.431; ὧσε ποδὶ πλήξας 22.20; ἵππω πλήξαντε [ποσὶ τὸν νεκρόν] Il.5.588; πέπληγον χορὸν ποσὶν Od.8.264; ἵππους ἐς πόλεμον πεπληγέμεν *whip* on the horses to the fray, Il.16.728; of Zeus, *strike* with lightning, Hes. *Th.*855:—Med., μηρὼ πληξάμενος *having smitten his* thighs, Il.16.125; καὶ ὣ πεπλήγετο μηρὼ 12.162 (but στῆθος πλήξας Od.20.17); πλήξασθαι τὴν κεφαλήν, as a token of grief, Hdt.3.14:—Pass., *to be struck, smitten*, πληγέντε κεραυνῷ *stricken* by lightning, Il.8.455, etc.; of a ship, Διὸς πληγεῖσα κ. Od.12.416; of a tree, Hes.*Sc.*422, cf. *Th.*861; ἡ κριθὴ ἐπλήγη (by hail?) *PPetr.*2 p.69 (iii B.C.): freq. in Trag., πληγεὶς θεοῦ μάστιγι A.*Th.*608; Διὸς πληγέντα..πυρὶ E.*Supp.*934; πληγείς τινος *stricken* by a man, Id.*Or.*497 (s.v.l.); ἔβραχε θύρετρα πληγέντα κληῗδι *touched* by the key, Od.21.50; ὥσπερ τὰ χαλκία πληγέντα..ἠχεῖ Pl.*Prt.*329a; ὑπὸ δόρατος πλαγεὶς δι' ἀμφοτέρων τῶν ὀφθαλμῶν *IG*4²(1).122.64 (Epid., iv B.C.): c. acc. cogn., πέπληγμαι καιρίαν πληγήν A.*Ag.*1343. b. *sting*, πληγεῖσα ὑπὸ σκορπίου *Sammelb.*1267.6 (i A.D.). 2. with acc. of the thing set in motion, κονίσαλον ἐς οὐρανὸν ἐπέπληγον πόδες ἵππων *struck* the dust up to heaven, Il.5.504; Ζεὺς ἐπ' Ἴδᾳ πλᾶξε κεραυνόν (for Ἴδαν πλᾶξε κεραυνῷ) Pi.*N.*10.71:—Pass., πλήσσονται λινέαις ὄρτυγες ἐν νεφέλαις *are dashed* against the nets, Call.*Aet.*3.1.37. 3. *strike* or *stamp* as one does a coin, Κύπριος χαρακτὴρ..ἐν γυναικείοις τύποις.. πέπληκται A.*Supp.*283. 4. of musical sounds, οὑτωσὶ πληγέντα οὕτως ἐφθέγξατο τὰ φωνήεντα Plot.3.3.5. II. metaph. in Pass., *receive a blow, to be heavily defeated*, Hdt.5.120, 8.130, Th.4.108, 8.38; *to be stricken* by misfortune, συμφορῇ πεπληγμένον Hdt.1.41, cf. A.*Ch.* 31 (lyr.); στρατὸν τοσοῦτον πέπληγμαι *I am smitten* in so great a host, Id.*Pers.*1015 (lyr.); διανταίαν δόμοισι καὶ σώμασιν πεπλαγμένους Id.*Th.*896 (lyr.); φθινάσιν πληγεῖσα νόσοις S.*Ant.*819 (anap.). 2. *to be smitten* emotionally, ἱμέρῳ πεπληγμένοι A.*Ag.*544; also πληγέντες δώροισι *touched* by bribes, Hdt.8.5; ἐξ ἔρωτος Hermesian. 7.42; τὴν καρδίαν πληγεὶς ὑπὸ λόγων Pl.*Smp.*218a, etc. 3. Act. of wines, when smelt or drunk, *overpower*, τὴν κεφαλήν Gal.18(2). 568, 15.672; *shock*, κατασεισμὸς πλήσσει [τινὰ] βιαίως Sor.1.72:—Pass., πληττομένη ἡ μήτρα Id.2.59. (Cf. πλάζω, Lat. *plango*, Goth. *faiflōkun* (redupl.) 'they beat their breasts'.)

πληστεύομαι, *to be full, gorged*, opp. ἀπληστεύομαι, Eust.1382.64.

πλήστιγξ, Ion. for πλάστιγξ. πλήτης· πλησιαστής, Hsch. πλητήσαντα· δηλοῦντα, Id. πλητίνες· δέλτοι, Id. πλῆτο, 3 sg. aor. Pass. both of πίμπλημι and of πελάζω. πλήτομον· παλαιόν (Acarn.), Id. πλῆτρον, τό, = πηδάλιον, *An.Ox.*1.343; cf. πλῆθριον. πλήων, v. πλείων B.

✱ πλίγμα, ατος, τό, (πλίσσομαι) *crossing the legs in walking* or *wrestling*, Hsch.: pl., = πηδήματα, Sch.Ar.*Ach.*217. II. = πλιχάς, Hp. ap.Sch.Od.6.318, *EM*395.12.

πλίκιον, τό, a kind of *cake*, Chrysipp.Tyan.ap.Ath.14.647c.

πλινθ-άριον, τό, = πλινθίον I, Al.*Ex.*5.16, Aët.4.26, *Stud.Pal.*20. 244.34 (vi/vii A.D.). -εία, ἡ, *brickmaking*, Lxx *Ex.*1.14, al., J.*AJ* 2.13.4. II. *drawing up of an army in square*, Suid. s.v. πλινθωτόν. ✱ -εῖον, τό, *brickworks*, Ar.*Fr.*283, Lys.*Fr.*161 S., Lxx 2*Ki.*12. 31. II. *oblong case*, φιάλαι..ἐμ πλινθείοις, φιάλη..ἐμ πλινθείῳ, *IG*11(2).161*B*12,63,66 (Delos, iii B.C.), *Inscr.Délos* 396*B*55, 461*Bb*14 (ii B.C.); φιάλαι ἐκ πλινθείων ἐξῃρημέναι ib.399*B*15, 442*B*15 (ii B.C.); φιάλας ἐμ πλινθείῳ τρεῖς *IG*11(2).199*B*71 (Delos, iii B.C.); στέφανος χρυσοῦς ἐπιγραφὴν ἔχων ἐπὶ τοῦ π. ib.208.13, 287*B*9 (iii B.C.). III. *block of houses*, *PRein.*49.11 (iii A.D.), etc.; *rectangular plan* of land, *PLille* 1.8 (iii B.C.). 2. *frame* of a panel, *IG*11(2).165.22,32 (Delos, iii B.C., pl.); window-*frame* or *-casing*, *PCair.Zen.*663.10 (iii B.C., pl.); πλινθεῖα..τοῖς πύργοις τοῖς Ἐλευσῖνι *IG*2².1672.203. -ευμα, ατος, τό, *brickwork*, *Trag.Adesp.*269: pl., Ezek.*Exag.*9. -ευσις, εως, ἡ, *making of bricks*, prob. in *IG*4²(1).102.172 (Epid., iv B.C.). ✱ -ευτής, οῦ, ὁ, *brickmaker*, Poll.7.163, *POxy.*158.1 (vi/vii A.D.), etc. -εύω, *make into bricks*, τὴν γῆν Hdt.1.179; π. πλίνθους *make* bricks, Lxx *Ge.*11.3: abs., *make bricks*, Ar.*Nu.*1126, *Ra.*800, *PCair.Zen.*633.21,25 (iii B.C.), *PLond.*1.131.302 (i A.D.), Luc.*Sacr.*4:—Med., Th.2.78. II. *build of brick*, τείχη Id.4.67. III. Pass. is variously expld. by Gramm. as *to be changed into bricks, built up with bricks, tortured* or *enslaved*, *EM*367.43, etc.; *to be duped*, Hsch., Suid. IV. πλινθευομένη, ἡ, *tax on brickmaking*, *POxy.*502.44 (ii A.D.). -ηγέω, *cast bricks*, *PCair.Zen.*176.311 (iii B.C.). -ηδόν, Adv. *brick-fashion*, i.e. in courses with the joints alternating, Hdt.2.96. II. of a kind of writing in which the letters were arranged *in a rectangle*, Eust. 1305.33, Sch.D.T.p.191 H., etc. -ήϊον, τό, poet. for πλινθεῖον, βορειότατον ζώνης π., of part of the zodiac, Doroth.ap.Heph.Astr. 3.7. -ιακός, ή, όν, *of* or *for bricks*: ὁ π., = πλινθευτής, D.L.4. 36. -ίδιον, τό, Dim. of πλινθίς II, Iamb. *in Nic.*p.39 P. ✱ -ικός, ή, όν, *of bricks*, *CPR*206.6 (ii A.D.). -ινος, η, ον, *made* or *built of brick*, οἰκίαι, τεῖχος, Hdt.5.101, X.*An.*3.4.11, cf. Arist.*Metaph.*1033ᵃ 19; στήλη J.*AJ*1.2.3; ἔργα *PSI*5.496.3 (iii B.C.). II. *of clay*, κυλίκιον Thphr.*HP*5.9.8; ζῷα Dicaearch.1.3 (dub.). -ίον, τό, Dim. of πλίνθος, *small brick*, Th.6.88, X.*Cyr.*7.1.24; of gold, *IG*2².1377. 13. II. = πλαίσιον: 1. *square* of troops, *Hell.Oxy.*7.2, Plu. *Crass.*23, Arr.*Tact.*11.5, 29.8; τάξας τὴν στρατιὰν ἐν πλινθίῳ J.*AJ*13. 4.4. 2. *sundial*, Vitr.9.8.1. 3. a *bandage*, = ἡμιρρόμβιον, Gal. 18(1).798, cf. Heraclas ap.Orib.48.13.1. b. *machine* invented by Nileus for reducing dislocations, Heliod.ap.Orib.49.7. 4. *rectangular box*, Bito 60.2. III. *checker-board*, Poll.9.98. 2. *table of numbers divided into squares*, Vett.Val.321.1: hence, = διάγραμμα, of a musical scale, Ph.1.27. 3. pl., = Lat. *regiones caeli*, *fields* into which the Augurs divided the *templum* of the heavens, Plu.*Cam.*32, *Rom.* 22. 4. *squares* or *checks* of tartan, D.S.5.30. 5. *front frame* of a torsion-engine, Ph.*Bel.*60.6, Hero *Bel.*81.10; also, *case* or *chamber* in which mechanism is fitted, Id.*Aut.*5.3. 6. generally, *rectangle*, Str. 2.5.36, *PMag.Lond.*46.349,361. ✱ -ίς, ίδος, ἡ, Dim. of πλίνθος, *stone cut in the shape of a brick*, *IG*2².1668.26. 2. *square* or *check*, Callix. 1. b. = πλινθίον III. 1, for a kind of cross-word puzzle, Puchstein *Epigr.Gr.*p.7, *PMag.Par.*1.1305. 3. *sundial*, Plu.2.410e. 4. *paper-weight*(?), *AP*6.295.6 (Phan.). 5. *block of land* 6,000 ft. square, = Lat. *laterculus*, Hygin. in *Corp.Agrimens.Rom.* i p.85 Thulin. 6. *block of wood* inserted to strengthen the χοινικίδες, Ph.*Bel.*57.35. 7. *block of fish-pemmican*, Agatharch.34. II. *number squared and multiplied by a smaller number*, Theo Sm.p.41 H., Nicom.*Ar.*2.6,17, Anon. *in Tht.*43.22. III. = πλινθίον II. 1, *Corp.Herm.*16. 13. -ιτις, ιδος, ἡ, a kind of στυπτηρία, Gal.12.237.

πλινθο-βάψ, ὁ, ἡ, *brickmaker*, Hdn.Gr.1.246. -βολέω, *build of brick*, *IG*2².1672.26. -βολία, ἡ, *bricklaying*, ib.4²(1).115. 17,21 (Epid., iv/iii B.C.). -βόλος, ὁ, *bricklayer*, *Edict.Diocl.*7. 16. ✱ -ειδής, ές, *brick-like*, Phot. s.v. παλάσια. -ομαι, Med., *build as with bricks*, χρυσῷ..ἐπλινθώσασθε μέλαθρον *AP*9.423 (Bianor). -ποιέω, *make bricks*, Eust. ad D.P.511. -ποιία, ἡ, *brickmaking*, *PFay.*36.9 (ii A.D.), Sch.Pi.*O.*5.20. **-ποιός**, ὁ, *brickmaker*, *Gloss.* **-πωλική**, ἡ, *right of selling bricks*, *PFay.*36.10 (ii A.D.).

**πλίνθος**, ἡ, rarely **πλίνθον**, τό (v. infr. II. 1), *brick*, whether sun- or fire-baked, πλίνθοι ὀπταί Hdt.1.180,186, Ar.*Av.*552, X.*An.*2.4.12, cf. Alc.153, *PAmh.*2.99(*a*)9 (ii A.D.), etc.; π. κεραμεαῖ, γήϊναι, X.*An.* 3.4.7, 7.8.14 (opp. ὠμὴ π. Paus.8.8.7); πλίνθους ἑλκύσαι, εἰρύσαι, make *bricks*, Hdt.1.179, 2.136; ὀπτᾶν bake *them*, Id.1.179; δόμοι πλίνθου (in collect. sense) layers of *brick*, ibid., cf. Th.3.20 (pl.); πλίνθους ἐπιτιθέναι, of torture by *pressing*, Ar.*Ra.*621: prov., π. πλύνειν, of useless trouble, *Com.Adesp.*891, Zen.6.48; ὕδατι νίζειν θολερὰν διαειδέϊ π. Theoc.16.62. II. *any brick-shaped body*, 1. *stone squared for building*, *IG*1[2].372.10, al.: pl. πλίνθα *squared blocks* of marble, *Sardis*7(1) No.93.3. 2. *ingot* of gold or silver, Plb.10.27.12, Luc. *Cont.*12; of lead, Dsc.5.88: metal *plate* let into a threshold, *SIG* 247 I 22 (Delph., iv B.C.), *IG*4[2](1).102.73 (Epid., iv B.C.). 3. *plinth of a column*, *Milet.*7.59, *Supp.Epigr.*4.447.17 (Didyma, ii B.C.), Vitr.4.7.3.

**πλινθουλκ-έω**, *make bricks*, *PSI*4.410.13 (iii B.C.), Poll.7.163. **-ία**, ἡ, *brickmaking* (written -ολκία), *PPetr.*2 p.50 (cf. 3 p.139, iii B.C.). **-ιον**, τό, *brickworks*, *SIG*633.82 (Milet., ii B.C.). **-ός**, ὁ, *brickmaker*, *PCair.Zen.*176.22 (pl., iii B.C.), Poll.7.163, etc.

⊛ **πλινθουργ-εῖον**, τό, *brickworks*. *EM*677.27. **-έω**, *make bricks*, Ar.*Pl.*514, Ph.1.418. **-ία**, ἡ, v.l. for πλινθεία I, Lxx *Ex.*5.8. ⊛ **-ιον**, τό, *brickworks*, *PTeb.*402.2 (ii A.D.), etc. **-ός**, ὁ, *brickmaker*, Pl. *Tht.*147a, Gal.4.618, etc.

**πλινθοφορ-έω**, *carry bricks*, Ar.*Av.*1149, *IG*2[2].1672.28, Polyaen.8. 24.3, *BGU*699.6 (ii A.D.). ⊛ **-ος** (parox.), ον, *carrying bricks*, Ar. *Av.*1134: as Subst., *PSI*6.672.5 (iii B.C.), etc. 2. πλινθοφόρος, ἡ, name of a coin (cf. κιστοφόρος II), *Inscr.Délos* 461 *Bb* 49 (ii B.C.).

**πλινθ-υφής**, ές, (ὑφαίνω) *brick-built*, A.*Pr.*450. **-ωτός**, ή, όν, *brick-shaped*, *oblong*, Paul.Aeg.6.66: Subst. -ωτόν, τό, = πλινθεία II, Suid.

**πλίξ**, ἡ, Dor. word for βῆμα, *step*, Sch.Od.6.318, Sch.Ar.*Ach.* 217. II. *pelvis*, Sch.Ar. l.c.

**πλίσσομαι**, aor. 1 ἐπλιξάμην (ἀπ-) Ar.*Ach.*218: pf. πέπλιγμαι (δια-) Archil.58:—*cross the legs*, as in *trotting*, εὖ μὲν τρώχων, εὖ δὲ πλίσσοντο πόδεσσιν well they galloped, well they *trotted*, Od.6.318:—Act., ἵνα πλίσσωσιν ὁμαρτῇ cj. in Call.*Dian.*243; cf. πλίξαντα· διαναβάντα καὶ ἀναστάντα καὶ διαβάντα, Hsch. (πλήξ- cod.).

**πλῐχάς**, άδος, ἡ, *inside of the thighs*, *fork*, *perineum*, Hp.*Fract.*20, *Art.*54, Ruf.*Onom.*108 (pl.), Aret.*CA*2.9, etc.; **πλιγάς**, Gal.18(2). 522; **πλίχος**, εος, τό, Sch.Od.6.318.

**πλῐχώδης**, ες, = ἐξεπτυγμένος, read in Hp.*VC*19 by Bacchius and Lysimachus ap.Erot. s.v. βλιχῶδες.

**πλοητόκος**, ον, *producing navigation*, Ζέφυρος dub. l. in *AP*10.6 (Satyr.).

**πλοιᾰρ-ίδιον**, τό, = sq., *POxy.*602 (ii A.D.), Ps.-Callisth.1.3, dub. in *PGiss.*11.6 (ii A.D.). **-ιον**, τό, Dim. of πλοῖον, *skiff*, *boat*, Ar.*Ra.*139, X.*HG*4.5.17, *Ev.Jo.*6.22, *Peripl.M.Rubr.*15, *BGU*812.5, etc. II. a kind of *woman's shoe*, Poll.7.93.

⊛ **πλοιαφέσια**, τά, *launching of the ship* of Isis, a festival, *Ath.Mitt.* 37.180 (Byzantium, i B.C./i A.D.), Lyd.*Mens.*4.45.

**πλοΐζω**, v. πλωΐζω. **πλοϊκός**, ή, όν, = πλώϊμος, Suid. **πλόϊμος**, v. πλώϊμος.

**πλοῖον**, τό, (πλέω) prop. *floating vessel*: hence, generally, *ship*, A. *Th.*602, *Ag.*625, Hdt.1.168, *IG*1[2].128.5, etc.: more nearly defined, π. λεπτά small *craft*, Hdt.7.36, Th.2.83; π. ἁλιευτικόν a fishing-*boat*, X.*An.*7.1.20; ἱππαγωγὰ π. *transports* for horses, Hdt.6.48; π. μακρά *ships* of war, Id.5.30, Th.1.14; π. στρογγύλα or φορτηγικά *ships* of burden, merchantmen, X.*HG*5.1.21; μεγάλα π. D.S.13.78; ἱερὸν π. τοῦ Ὀσείριος *OGI*56.51 (Canopus, iii B.C.): when distd. from ναῦς, without Adj., mostly *merchant-ship* or *transport*, as opp. ship of war, τοῖς π. καὶ ταῖς ναυσί Th.4.116, cf. 6.44; πλεῖν μὴ μακρᾷ νηΐ, ἄλλῳ δὲ κωπήρει πλοίῳ Foed.ap.eund.4.118; πλοῖά τε καὶ τριήρεις Pl. *Hp.Ma.*295d; πλοῖα alone, = τριήρεις, X.*HG*1.2.1, Docum.ap.D.18. 106.

**πλόκαμα**· τὰ περιόστεα νεῦρα, Hsch.

⊛ **πλοκᾰμ-ίς**, ῖδος, ἡ, poet. for sq., *lock* or *braid of hair*, Euph.140, Bion 1.20, Nonn.*D.*4.133, 5.385: collectively in sg., *braided hair*, τοῦ τὰν πλοκαμῖδα φορεῦντος Theoc.13.7. II. = πλεκτάνη II, in pl., Opp.*H.*2.125, *C.*3.179. ⊛ **-ος**, ὁ, *lock* or *braid of hair*, A.*Ch.*6,187, Hdt.4.34: in pl., *locks*, *curling hair*, prop. of women, Il.14.176; of a man, κομᾶν πλόκαμοι Pi.*P.*4.82; π. Τυφῶ, dithyrambic phrase in Ar. *Nu.*336; τί πλόκαμοι ῥέξωμεν, ὅτ' οὔρεα τοῖα σιδήρῳ εἴκουσιν; Call. in *PSI*9.1092.47: in sg. also, collectively, = κόμη, A.*Fr.*313, etc.; τριχὸς π. Id.*Th.*564 (lyr.); χαίτας π. E.*Ph.*309 (lyr.). 2. Βερενίκης π., a constellation, Hsch., cf. Call. l.c.; ἡ τοῦ π. συστροφή Ptol. *Tetr.*26. II. = πλεκτάνη II, Ael.*VH*1.1. 2. π. θαυμαστός, = πλέγμα δικτυοειδές, v.l. in Gal.*UP*9.4. 3. in pl., of wicker *baskets*, Id.*Nat.Fac.*1.15. **-ώδεα**· τὸν οὖλον βόστρυχον, Hsch.

**πλόκ-ᾰνον**, τό, *plaited work*, *basket-work*, Pl.*Ti.*78c, Thphr.*HP*4. 10.4, D.S.3.37. 2. *wicker fan for winnowing*, Pl.*Ti.*52e, Poll. 1.225. 3. *plaited rope*, X.*Cyn.*9.12, Poll.5.33. 4. *sieve*, *strainer*, Gal.2.500, 6.179:—πλόχανον is v.l. in both passages of Pl. and is cited by Suid.: πλόκαμον is f.l. in Pl.*Ti.*78c, X. l.c., Gal. ll. cc. **-άς**, άδος, ἡ, = πλόκαμος, Pherecr.225. **-ερός**, *plaited*, ζωστήρ v.l. for πλακερός in Theoc.7.18. **-εύς**, έως, ὁ, *plaiter*, *braider*, Epich.171, Hp.*Vict.*1.19; π. ἱματίων *Cat.Cod.Astr.*8(4). 137. ⊛ **-ή**, ἡ, *twining*, *twisting*, Epich.171; οὐ δέχεται π. do not admit *of being made into a web*, Arist.*GA*783a12; ἡ τοῦ δικτύου π. ib.734a20; σχοινίων πλοκαί Dsc.3.148; βρόχου Heraclas ap.Orib.48. 1.1, al. II. *anything twisted* or *woven*, *web*, E.*IT*817 (pl.), Pl. *Lg.*849c; *mesh*, θώραξ τὴν π. λεπτότατος *PGiss.*47.7 (ii A.D.). 2. *histological structure*, Gal.*UP*1.9. III. metaph., *complication* of a dramatic plot, opp. λύσις, Arist.*Po.*1456a9; π. δραματική Plu.2. 973e, etc. b. *interweaving*, [ἐπιτιμήσεως καὶ παραμυθίας] Hermog. *Meth.*36. c. αἱ τῶν σχηματισμῶν π., of rhet. figures, D.H.*Th.*29, cf. Alex.*Fig.*2.22 tit., Phoeb.*Fig.*p.55 S.; π. καὶ ποιότητες Phld.*Rh.* 1.165 S.; *contortions* of speech, Thphr.*Char.*1.7. d. *construction* of a syllogism, π. τοῦ συλλογισμοῦ Phld.*Rh.*2.89 S., cf. Ammon. *in APr.*67.30, Eustr. *in EN*336.4. 2. *web of deceit*, πλοκὰς πλέκειν E. *Ion* 826, cf. *IA*936, *PMonac.*6.53 (vi A.D.). IV. *harmony*, in Music, Mart.Cap.9.958. **-ίζομαι**, Pass., *have one's hair braided*, γυνὴ ἀφελὲς πεπλοκισμένη Hp.*Ep.*15; κόμην ἀφελῶς πεπλ. Aristaenet.1. 19:—Act., *plait* is prob. in *PMag.Par.*1.1336. **-ῖμος**, ον, *for plaiting*, κάλαμος Thphr.*HP*4.11.1. ⊛ **-ιον**, τό, Dim. of πλόκος I, π. Γοργάδος Phot. II. *necklace* or *chain*, *IG*2[2].1524.100, Plu.2. 141d, Eun.*VS* p.455 B.: title of play by Menander, Gell.2.23.6. ⊛ **-ιος**, α, ον, *twined*, v.l. for κλόπιος, Od.13.295; πλοκίη, epith. of φύσις, Orph.*H.*10.11 (prob.). **-ος**, ὁ, *lock of hair*, *braid*, *curl*, A.*Ch.*197, S.*Aj.*1179, A.R.4.30, etc.; χαίτης π. E.*El.*527; τοὺς ἀκηράτους π. κόμης Id.*Ion* 1266, etc. II. *wreath* or *chaplet*, πλόκοι σελίνων the parsley-*wreath* at the Isthmian games, Pi.*O.*13.33; μυρσίνης πλόκοι E.*El.*778; π. ἀνθέων Id.*Med.*841 (lyr.); π. χρυσήλατος ib.786. 2. *plaited bowstring*, Lyc.915.

**πλόμενος**, Ep. sync. pres. part. of πέλομαι, formed after the Homeric περιπλόμενος, Euph.58.

**πλόμος**, ὁ, = φλόμος, Arist.*HA*602b31:—hence **πλομίζω**, *poison with mullein*, ἰχθῦς ib.603a1.

⊛ **πλόος**, ὁ, Att. contr. **πλοῦς**; pl. πλοῖ S.*Ph.*304, X.*An.*5.7.7; gen. πλῶν *OGI*132.9 (Egypt, ii B.C.); dat. πλοῖς Antipho 5.83; acc. πλοῦς Arist.*Mete.*362b24; later, a gen. sg. πλοός, as if of third declens. (cf. χοῦς A), *Peripl.M.Rubr.*62, *OGI*572.21 (Myra, ii/iii A.D.), X. Eph.1.14; dat. πλοΐ D.S.21.2: pl. πλόες Phot.; acc. πλόας *IGRom.* 4.841 (Hierapolis: (πλέω):—*sailing*, *voyage*, Od.3.169, Hdt. (who always has the disyll. form) 2.29, etc.; ἔσσεται Ἀγεάνακτι καλὸς π. ἐς Μιτυλάναν Theoc.7.52; ναῶν π. Pi.*O.*7.32; πλόον ὁρμαίνειν Od. l.c.; πλοῦν στεῖλαι, ποιεῖσθαι, S.*Aj.*1045, *Ph.*552; ἔξω πλόου out of *one's course*, Pi.*P.*11.39; ἐπ' ἡμέρας τέσσερας πλόος Hdt.2.29; μῆκός ἐστι πλόος ἡμέραι τέσσερες its length is four days' *sail*, ib.158; ἐκ τῶν πλόων when *the voyage* is done, Id.1.185: metaph., διὰ τοῦ πλοῦ..τῆς ζωῆς Pl.*Lg.*803b. 2. *time* or *tide for sailing*, ὡραῖος π., εἰαρινὸς π., Hes.*Op.*630,678; καιρὸς καὶ π. S.*Ph.*1450 (anap.); π. ἡμῖν ἐγίγνετο, i.e. the wind was fair, Antipho 5.24, cf. Th.1.137; π. ἐστί τινι E.*Hec.*899, *IA*92; παραπεσόντος π. τισί Plb.4.57.6; πλῷ χρήσασθαι to have a *fair wind*, Th.3.3; πλόον δοκάζων Sophr.52: pl., καλλίστοις ἐχρήσαντο πλοῖς Antipho 5.83. 3. prov., δεύτερος π. 'the next best way', of those who try another scheme if the first fails (from those who use oars when the wind fails, ὁ δ. π. ἐστι δήπου λεγόμενος, ἂν ἀποτύχῃ τις οὐρίου (cj.), κώπαισι πλεῖν Men.241), Pl.*Phd.* 99d, *Phlb.*19c, *Plt.*300c; δεύτερος δὲ π..., πειρᾶσθαι.. the *next best thing* is to try.., Arist.*Pol.*1284b19; κατὰ τὸν δ. πλοῦν Id.*EN*1109a 35; δ. ἂν εἴη π. τὸ.. Plb.8.36.6: prov., οὐ παντὸς ἀνδρὸς ἐπὶ τράπεζάν ἐσθ' ὁ π. Nicol.Com.1.26, cf. Κόρινθος; ἡμέτερος ὁ π. 'our innings', *Com.Adesp.*274. 4. later, = ὁδός, βαιὸν π. αἰὲν ὀκέλλει, of the *crawling* of a serpent, Nic.*Th.*295, cf. Sch. ad loc. b. *highway*, ὑλήεντα διὰ πλόον ἐρχομένοισι Antim.62; ἔχοντα παρὰ πλόον οἰκίον Call.*Hec.*1.4.13.

**πλός**, Arc. Adv. = πλέον, π. ἀμέραυ καὶ νυκτός *IG*5(2).3.16 (Tegea, iv B.C.).

**πλουᾶται**· πλουθήσεται, Hsch.

**πλουδοκέω**, *wait for a fair wind*, Cic.*Att.*10.8.9.

**πλουθῠγίεια**, ἡ, (πλοῦτος) *health and wealth*, Ar.*V.*677, *Eq.*1091; parox. πλουθυγιεία (guaranteed by metre) Id.*Av.*731 (anap.).

**πλουμ-άκιον**, τό (Lat. *pluma*), *embroidery*, *Stud.Pal.*20.172.2 (vi A.D.). ⊛ **-αρικός**, ή, όν, *embroidered*, *Sammelb.*7033.45 (v A.D.). ⊛ **-άριος**, ὁ, *embroiderer*, *MAMA*3.285, al. (Corycus), *PMasp.*163.12 (vi A.D.), Rhetor. in *Cat.Cod.Astr.*8(4).213. **-άρισις**, εως, ἡ, *embroidery*, *Edict.Diocl.*19.6,25. **-ᾶτος**, η, ον, *embroidered*, στιχάριον *POxy.*1741.16 (iv A.D.). **-ίον**, τό, *embroidery*, *Stud.Pal.*20.245.6 (vi A.D.).

**πλοῦς**, Att. contr. for πλόος.

**πλουσιακός**, ή, όν, *peculiar to a rich man*, κακόν Alex.264.5; δρᾶμα Plu.2.528b; ἡ π. διαγωγή M.Ant.1.3.

**πλουσιάω**, = πλουτέω, [πυρετὸς] πλουσιῶν πρὸς ὕλην Alex.Aphr. *Pr.*2.10.

**πλουσιόδωρος**, ον, *giving rich gifts*, Hsch.

**πλουσιομᾰχέω**, *contend with the wealthy*, Phld.*Rh.*2.97 S.

**πλούσιον**· θαλασσιοειδές, οἱ δὲ τὸ ὕδωρ, Hsch.

**πλουσιόρους**, ουν, *of a wealthy stream*, ὕδωρ *CRAcad.Inscr.*1931. 241 (Susa, i A.D.).

**πλούσιος**, Lacon. **πλούτιος** *EM*156.20: α, ον: (πλοῦτος):—*wealthy*, *opulent*, opp. πένης, πενιχρός, Hes.*Op.*22, *h.Merc.*171, Thgn. 621, etc.; πτωχὸς ἀντὶ πλουσίου S.*OT*455; ἐμοὶ πένης..πλουσίου μᾶλλον ξένος E.*El.*395; μέγα π. Hdt.1.32; πλουσίῳ χαίρειν γένει in his *rich and lordly* race, S.*OT*1070: prov., οὐδ' εἰ Μίδου -ώτεροι εἶεν Pl.*R.* 408b. 2. c. gen. rei, *rich in* a thing, ὁ δαίμων δ' ἐς ἐμὲ πλούσιος κακῶν E.*Or.*394; π. οὐ χρυσίου, ἀλλ' οὗ δεῖ τὸν εὐδαίμονα πλουτεῖν Pl.*R.*521a; -ώτερος εἰς τὸ γῆρας..φρονήσεως Id.*Plt.*261e. 3. c. dat., π. τοῖς ἀχρήστοις καὶ περιττοῖς Plu.*Cat.Ma.*18; εἴκοσι μύξαις π...λύχνος Call.*Epigr.*56; π. ἐν ἐλέει *Ep.Eph.*2.4. II. of things, σοὶ δὲ π. τράπεζα κείσθω *richly furnished*, S.*El.*361; *ample, abundant*, κτερίσματα E.*Tr.*1249; ὕδωρ Id.*Fr.*316.3: Sup., θησαυρὸς ἀνάκειται ὁμοῖα τοῖσι πλουσιωτάτοισι Hdt.3.57. Adv. -ίως, ἱρὸν π. κατεσκευασμένον ἀναθήμασι Id.2.44; π. ταφήσεται E.*Alc.*56; κοίτας..π. σεσαγμένας Eup.76, cf. Ph.2.403, etc.; νέον π. ἐπικηρυκευόμενον Aristaenet.2.1.

**πλουσιο-ϋφής** [ῠ], ές, *richly woven*, Tz. ad Lyc.863. **-χειρ**, χειρος, ὁ, ἡ, *open-handed*, Hsch. s.v. ὀμπνιόχειρ. **-ψῡχος**, ον, *generous*, Heph.Astr.1.1.

**πλουτᾰγᾰθής**, v. πλουτογᾰθής.

**πλούταξ**, ἄκος, ὁ, *rich fool*, Eup.159.9, adopted by Men.462.10.

**Πλουτάρχειος**, α, ον, *of* or *by Plutarch*, βίοι Men.Rh.p.392S.

**πλούταρχος**, ον, *fount, source of riches*, of God, Ph.1.669.

⊛ **Πλουτεύς**, ὁ, collat. form of Πλούτων, gen. Πλουτέως Luc.*Trag.*13, *IG* 3.1341, 1355, Πλουτῆος *AP*7.587 (Jul. Aegypt.); dat. Πλουτεῖ Mosch. 3.126, Πλουτῆϊ ib.22, 118, *AP*14.55.7; acc. Πλουτέα ib.9.137 (Hadr.).

⊛ **πλουτ-έω**, (πλοῦτος) *to be rich, wealthy*, opp. πένομαι, τάχα σε ζηλώσει ἀεργὸς πλουτεῦντα Hes.*Op.*313; πενιχρὸς αἶψα μάλ' ἐπλούτησε *becomes rich*, Thgn.663, cf. Pl.*R.*421d, Men.*Kol.*42; π. μέγα, μάλιστα, μεγάλως, Hdt.1.32, 3.57, 6.125; πλούτει κατ' οἶκον μέγα S.*Ant.*1168; ὄναρ πεπλουτηκέναι 'build castles in the air', Pl.*Ly.*218c, cf. *Tht.*208b; μὴ σπεύδετε πλουτεῖν μᾶλλον ἢ χρηστοὶ δοκεῖν εἶναι Isoc.3.50; ταχέως πλουτῆσαι Lys.18.18; π. ἀπὸ τῶν κοινῶν *to be rich* from the public purse, Ar.*Pl.*569; π. ἀφ' ἑαυτῶν Porph.*Sent.*40; π. ἐκ τῶν ἀλλοτρίων Lys.32.25; ὑφ' ὑμῶν πεπλουτηκότας D.21.189 (ἀφ' Cobet). 2. c. gen. rei, *to be rich in* a thing, πόνου A.*Fr.*241; φίλων X.*An.*7.7.42; νομίσματος Arist.*Pol.*1257b13; πλουτίον (i.e. -τεῖον, metri gr. for -τέον) τέκνων..δωμάτιον *IG*12(8).442.8 (Thasos). 3. c. dat. rei, π. ἐμπύροισιν E.*Hel.*756; σιδήρῳ, χαλκῷ, X.*Ath.*2.11. 4. c. acc. cogn., π. πλοῦτον Luc.*Tim.*48; π. φίλους, φιλίαν, Them.*Or.*1.17c, 22.267a. **-ηρός**, ά, όν, *enriching*, ἔργον X.*Oec.*2.10. **-ητέον**, *one must become rich*, Luc.*Tim.*39. **-ίζω**, Att. fut. -ιῶ Timocl.4.8:—*make wealthy, enrich*, τινα A.*Ag.*586, X.*Cyr.*8.2.22; ἀρετῇ τινας Id.*Mem.*4.2.9; τὴν πατρίδα *IGRom.*3.199 (Ancyra): iron., π. τινὰ ἄτης (ἄτην codd.) A.*Ag.*1268:—Pass., Ἅιδης στεναγμοῖς καὶ γόοις π. S.*OT*30; τούτοις π. ὑπὸ σοῦ X.*Cyr.*5.5.27; ἀπὸ βοσκημάτων, ἐκ τῆς πόλεως, *gain one's wealth* from.., Id.*Mem.*2.1.28, *Vect.*4.14. **-ίνδην**, Adv. *according to wealth*, π. αἱρεῖσθαι τοὺς ἄρχοντας Arist.*Pol.*1273a24, cf. *Ath.*3.1, Plb.6.20.9, Plu.2.154c. **-ισμός**, ὁ, *enriching*, Eust. 740.42, etc. **-ιστήριος**, α, ον, *enriching*, ἔργα Ph.1.669. **-ιστής**, οῦ, ὁ, *one who enriches*, *IGRom.*3.204 (Ancyra), *CIG*4018 (ibid.).

**πλουτο-γᾰθής**, ές, Dor. for *-γηθής, (γηθέω) *delighting by* or *in riches, wealthy*, μυχὸς A.*Ch.*801 (lyr., πλουταγαθῆ cod. M.). **-δοτέω**, *enrich*, τινά τινι Orph.*H.*18.5. **-δοτήρ**, ῆρος, ὁ, = sq., epith. of Apollo, *AP* 9.525.17:—fem. ⊛ **-δότειρα**, θεά, of Demeter, Orph.*H.*40.3, cf. *Fr.*302, Luc.*DMeretr.*7.1. ⊛ **-δότης**, ου, ὁ, *giver of riches*, Hes.*Op.*126; θεὸς Ph. 1.232; ἥρωνι π. *Arch.Anz.*45.147 (Chios); epith. of Dionysus, Poet. ap.Sch.Ar.*Ra.*482; of Zeus, Orph.*H.*73.4; of Zeus-Helios-Sarapis, *Not.Scav.*1912.323; of Pluto, Luc.*Tim.*21:—in form **-δώτης**, ου, ὁ, epith. of Mên, *BCH*23.389. **-κρᾰτέομαι**, Pass., *to be in a state governed by the wealthy*, Men.Rh.p.360S. **-κρᾰτία**, ἡ, *oligarchy of wealth*, X.*Mem.*4.6.12, Men.Rh.p.359S. **-ποιός**, όν, *wealth-creating*, τέχνη, ἀδικία, χρῆμα, Plu.*Num.*16, 2.165a, Poll.3.110, cf. Vett.Val.16.20.

⊛ **πλοῦτος**, ὁ, *wealth, riches*, ἄφενος καὶ πλοῦτον ἀφύξειν Il.1.171; ὄλβῳ τε πλούτῳ τε 16.596; π. ἀρεταῖς δεδαιδαλμένος Pi.*O.*2.53; opp. πενία, Pl.*R.*421d; ἀνατετροφέναι πλοῦτον And.1.131: pl., τῶν γὰρ π. οὐδ' ἀριστος *treasures*, E.*Fr.*137 (anap.); πλούτοις καὶ πενίαις Pl.*R.*618b; γένη καὶ πλοῦτοι Id.*Grg.*523c, cf. *Prt.*354b, etc.: c. gen. rei, π. ἀργύρου, χρυσοῦ, *treasure* of silver or gold, Hdt.2.121.α'; *Anacreont.*34.1; οὔτε ἀργυροῦς π. οὔτε χρυσοῦς Pl.*Lg.*801b; ἀφανὴς π., opp. γῆ, Ar.*Ec.*602. 2. metaph., πραπίδων π. Emp.129.2: π. τῆς σοφίας Pl.*Euthphr.*12a; γᾶς π. ἄβυσσος, of the whole earth, A.*Th.*948 (lyr.); πλοῦτον εἵματος κακὸν Id.*Ag.*1383; ὁ ἐν τῇ ἐμῇ ψυχῇ π. X.*Smp.*4.43, cf. 34, etc. II. masc. pr. n. *Plutus*, god of riches, Hes.*Th.*969; represented as blind, Timocr.8; ὁ δὲ Π. ἡμᾶς..τυφλοὺς ποιεῖ Antiph.259:—Hsch. s.v. εὔπλουτον says that π. originally meant wealth in corn. (Prob. from πλέω in an early sense '*flow', '*abound', as φόρτος from φέρω.)

**πλοῦτος**, εος, τό, = πλοῦτος, ὁ, 2*Ep.Cor.*8.2, v.l. in *Ep.Rom.*9.23, *Ep.Col.*1.27, 2.2.

**πλουτο-τρᾰφής**, ές, *bred in riches*, Eust.835.37. **-φόρος**, ον, *wealth-bringing*, Archestr.*Fr.*45.5, Ael.*NA*12.43; αἶξ *Com.Adesp.* 8; of God, Ph.1.544. **-χθων**, ονος, ὁ, ἡ, *rich in treasures of the earth*, in allusion to the silver mines of Laureion, A.*Eu.*947 (lyr.).

**Πλούτων**, ωνος, ὁ, *Pluto*, god of the nether world, first in Trag., as A.*Pr.*806, S.*Ant.*1200, E.*Alc.*360, *HF*808 (lyr.): acc. to Plato (from πλοῦτος) the *wealth-giver*, a name of Hades, ὅτι ἐκ τῆς γῆς ἀνίεται [ὁ πλοῦτος], *Cra.*403a, cf. πλουτοδότης; identified with *Plutus*, and considered as the god of riches, cf. S.*Fr.*273, Ar.*Pl.*727:—hence **Πλουτώνιος**, α, ον, *of* or *belonging to Pluto*; **Πλουτώνιον**, τό, any place *where there are mephitic vapours*, looked upon as entrances to the nether world, Str.5.4.5, 13.4.14; but **Πλουτώνειον**, *temple of Pluto*, *IG*4.203.20 (Corinth):—**Πλουτωνίς**, ίδος, ἡ, *Persephone*, Orac.ap. Phleg.*Fr.*36.10J.; also **Πλουτώνη**, ἡ, Orph.*Fr.*200.

**πλόχᾰνον**, v. πλόκανον.

**πλοχμός**, ὁ, like πλόκαμος, mostly in pl., *locks, braids of hair*, Il.17. 52, A.R.2.677, *AP*6.237 (Antist.), Q.S.5.39. II. *tentacles* of the polypus, *AP*9.10 (Antip. Thess.).

**πλοώδης**, ες, *swimming, floating*: metaph., *loose, slack*, κλητ̀ς Hp. *Art.*14.

**πλῠμα** [ῠ], ατος, τό, (πλύνω) *water in which something has been washed*, π. ἰχθύων Pl.Com.82, cf. Arist.*HA*534a27, Nic.*Al.*258; κρεῶν Gal.18(1).730; π. ἀλεύρου *infusion* of meal, Hp.*Epid.*7.80, *Acut.*(*Sp.*) 63; πλύματα τοῖς παιδαρίοις *PCair.Zen.*398.10 (iii B.C.); *washings, scum*, a by-product of cinnabar, Thphr.*Lap.*58 (in form πλύσματι); from oilworks, *Sammelb.*4425 vii 10 (ii A.D.). II. metaph., *low prostitute*, Poll.7.39.—The form πλύσμα is found in some codd. and preferred by Phot.; but πλύμα is guaranteed by metre in Nic. l.c., also by *PCair.Zen.* l.c.

**πλῠν-εύς**, έως, ὁ, = πλύντης, πλύτης, *IG*2.1327, Poll.7.38. **-ιον**, τό, Dim. of sq. I, *IG*14.217.35 (Acrae, pl.). **-ός**, ὁ, *trough, tank*, or *pit, in which dirty clothes were washed* by treading, pl., Il.22.153, Od.6.40, 86; pl., *washing-places*, Ephor.1J.; later *washing-tubs, fuller's tubs*, Luc.*Fug.*12, D.C.46.4, cf. Phot. II. parox. πλύνος, ὁ, *washing*, Suid.; νιτρικῆς πλύνου *Ostr.Bodl.* i 126 (ii B.C.), cf. *PHib.* 1.114 (iii B.C.): metaph., πλύνον ποιεῖν τινα, = πλύνω II, Ar.*Pl.*1061; π. πλύνεσθαι, = ὑβρίζεσθαι, Phryn.*PS* p.101 B. **-τήριος**, ον, *of* or *for washing*: Πλυντήρια (sc. ἱερά), τά, a festival at Athens (on the 25th Thargelion), *in which the clothes of Athena's statue were washed*, *IG*1².842, X.*HG*1.4.12, Lycurg.*Fr.*44, Plu.*Alc.*34, Phot. s.v. καλλυντήρια. **-τηριών**, ῶνος, ὁ, name of month at Thasos and elsewhere, *BCH* 50.214 (Thasos, v B.C.), *SIG*987.10 (Chios, iv B.C.), *IG*12(5).1010 (Ios). **-της**, ου, ὁ, *clothes-cleaner*, Poll.7.37, rejected by *EM*785.35; cf. πλύτης. **-τικός**, ή, όν, = πλυντήριος, Arist.*Sens.*443a1, Poll.7.39; ἡ π. (sc. τέχνη) *clothes-cleaning*, Pl.*Plt.*282a. **-τρια**, ἡ, fem. of *πλυντήρ, *washerwoman*, *IG*1².473, Poll.7.37; **Πλύντριαι**, name of a Satyric drama by Sophocles and of a comedy by Philyllius. **-τρίς**, ίδος, ἡ, = foreg., Ar.*Fr.*841. II. πλυντρίς (sc. γῆ), ἡ, a kind of *fuller's earth*, Menestor ap.Thphr.*CP*2.4.3, Nicoch.4. **-τρον**, τό, = πλύμα, Arist.*Pr.*880a27. II. πλύντρα, τά, *payment for cleaning* clothes, *Sammelb.*7451.150 (iii B.C.), *PCair.Zen.*176.252 (iii B.C.), Poll.7.38.

⊛ **πλύνω** [ῡ], Ep. impf. πλύνεσκον Il.22.155: fut. πλῠνῶ Ar.*Th.*248, D.39.11; Ion. and Ep. πλῠνέω Od.6.31, 59: aor. ἔπλῡνα, Ep. πλῦνα Od.6.93, (ἐκ-, περι-) Ar.*Pl.*1062, D.54.9:—Med., fut. πλῠνοῦμαι Lxx *Nu.*31.24 (ἐκ-πλυνεῖται in pass. sense, Ar.*Pl.*1064): aor. part. πλυνάμενος Lxx *Le.*13.6, (ἐκ-) Hdt.4.73:—**Pass.**, fut. πλῠθήσομαι (πλυνθ- Hsch.) *Com.Adesp.*715: aor. ἐπλύθην [ῠ], 3 sg. subj. πλυθῇ Thphr.*HP*3.15.4; part. πλυθέν Dsc.2.76.18, πλυθείσης Porph.*VP*34: pf. πέπλῠμαι Hp.*Acut.*(*Sp.*)65, Theoc.1.150, (κατα-) Aeschin.3.178; part. πεπλυμένος *PCair.Zen.*92 (iii B.C.):—*wash, clean*, prop. of linen, clothes, etc. (opp. λούομαι *bathe*, νίζω *wash the hands* or *feet*), εἵματα πλύνεσκον Il.22.155; ἴομεν πλυνέουσαι Od.6.31; πλῦνάν τε (sc. εἵματα) κάθηράν τε ῥύπα πάντα ib.93; π. κῴδια Ar.*Pl.*166; τὸ ἑαυτοῦ ἱμάτιον Pl.*Chrm.*161e; τὰς κοιλίας Ar.*Eq.*160; ἄμμον Thphr.*Lap.*58; ἐάν τις ἢ λόηται ἢ πλύνει τι ἐν ταῖς κρήναις *IG*12(5).569.5 (Ceos, iii B.C.); στολὴν Lxx *Ge.*49.11:—Pass., σησάμου πεπλυμένου *PCair.Zen.*562.19 (iii B.C.); σκίλλης πλυθείσης Porph. l.c. b. metaph., πέπλυται τὸ πρᾶγμα the thing *is washed to pieces*, i.e. *worn out*, Sosip.1.3: hence τὸ πεπατημένον καὶ πεπλυμένον *threadbare, hackneyed*, Longin.*Rh.* p.190H. II. as a slang term, πλύνειν τινά '*give* him *a dressing*', *abuse*, κἀκυκλοβόρει κἄπλυνε Ar.*Ach.*381; ἀλλήλους πλυνοῦμεν D.39.11; πλύνοντες αὐτοὺς τἀπόρρητα Id.58.40; τὸν πατέρα καὶ σὲ τούς τε σοὺς ἐγὼ πλυνῶ Men.608; τοὺς κρείσσονας D.C.46.4: c. dat. modi, τὸν τάριχον τουτονὶ πλύνων ἅπασιν ὅσα σύνοιδ' αὐτῷ κακά Ar.*Fr.*200: c. dupl. acc., πλυνεῖ σε τὰ κακὰ τῶν κακῶν ὑμᾶς Diocl.Com.2. (πλῠ-ν-yω cogn. with πλε(F)-ω, also with Lith. *pláuti* 'bathe', OSlav. *pluti* 'flow', 'sail'.)

**πλύσῐμον** [ῠ], τό, *washing-place*, *Gloss.*: pl., either, *clothes for washing*, or, *payments for washing*, *PCair.Zen.*457.7 (iii B.C.).

**πλύσις** [ῠ], εως, ἡ, *washing*, Pl.*R.*429e, Str.10.1.6, Dsc.5.153, etc.

**πλύσμα**, v. πλύμα. **πλυσμός**, ὁ, = πλυτήρ, Hsch.

**πλῠ-τέον**, *one must wash*, Alex.186.6, Dsc.2.76.5. **-τήρ**, ῆρος, ὁ, gloss on πλυσμός, prob. = πλυνός I, Hsch. 2. = sq., *Gloss.* **-της**, ου, ὁ, = πλύντης, Choerob. *in Theod.*1.187, al., *EM*435.49. **-τικός**, ή, όν, = πλυντικός, Alex.Aphr. *in Sens.*89.12. **-τός**, ή, όν, *washed*, ἄλητον Hp.*Art.*36; π. ἄρτος a *light* form of bread, Gal.6.494, etc.

**πλω-άς**, άδος, ἡ, (πλώω) = πλώουσα, *sailing* or *floating about*, ὄρνιθες A.R.2.1053 (*EM*731.40, but πλωΐδας codd.):—also **πλωϊάδες** νεφέλαι Thphr.ap.Plu.2.292c; αἱ **πλωάδες** νῆσοι (πλοάδες codd.) *floating* islands in Lake Copais, Thphr.*HP*4.10.2, 4.12.4. ⊛ **-ΐζω**, *sail on the sea*, πλωΐζεσκ' ἐν νηυσὶ Hes.*Op.*634 (Pl.*R.*388a implies πλωΐζεσκ' ἀλύων in Il.24.12); οἱ Ἕλληνες μᾶλλον ἔπλωζον *began to use ships* or *practise navigation*, Th.1.13:—Med., *Sammelb.*7332 (iii B.C.), Str.17.1.6, Luc.*Hist.Conscr.*62: aor. inf. Pass. πλωϊσθῆναι, πρὸς πόλιν Just. *Edict.*13.6:—written **πλοΐζομαι** in *Sammelb.*7169.20 (ii B.C.), Plb.4.47.1, 5.88.7, D.S.3.34, Arr.*Peripl.M.Eux.*23.—On the form, v. sq. **-ΐμος** or **πλόϊμος**, ον, (πλώω) *fit for sailing*: 1. of a ship, *seaworthy*, Th.1.29, 50, 2.13, D.56.23, etc.; also, *fit for shipbuilding*, τὴν ξύλων τὰ -ώτατα Plu.2.676a. 2. of navigation, ἤδη πλωϊμωτέρων ὄντων as *navigation* advanced, as circumstances became *favourable for navigation*, Th.1.7, cf. 8; but πλωΐμων γενομένων when the weather was *fit for sailing*, D.H.1.63; τὴν θάλατταν ἐκ Διονυσίων π. εἶναι Thphr.*Char.*3.3; τῆς ὥρας ἐστὶ τὰ π. Hld.

5.21. 3. of a river, *navigable*, ῥαπτοῖς πλοίοις Str.7.4.1. 4. of goods, *sea-borne*, Just.*Nov.*163.2.—Most codd. of Th. and D. give πλόϊμος (also found in Thphr. l. c.), though in Th. they give πλωΐζω. **-ΐσις**, εως, ἡ, *carriage by sea*, Just.*Edict.*13.14.1 (pl.).

⊛ **πλώς**, ὁ, gen. πλωτός, (πλώω) *swimmer*, name of a fish, = κεστρεύς, Epich.44, Xenocr.ap.Orib.2.58.29.

**πλώσιμος**, ον, *navigable*, πέλαγος S.*OC*663.

**πλώσσειν**· φθείρεσθαι, Hsch.

**πλωτ-άρχης**, ου, ὁ, *shipmaster*, σκαφέων Man.1.324. **-εύομαι**, Pass., *to be navigated*, of the sea, Plb.16.29.11. ⊛ **-ήρ**, ῆρος, ὁ, (πλώω) *sailor, seaman*, Archyt.ap.Stob.3.1.112, Ar.*Ec.*1087, Pl.*R.*489a; including rowers, navigators, and passengers, Arist.*Pol.*1276$^{b}$20, 1279$^{a}$4, Plot.4.3.21; epith. of the Dioscuri, *IG*4$^{2}$(1).511 (Epid., ii A. D.). 2. *swimmer*, Nonn.*D.*1.65,al., Musae.2; of fishes, Opp.*H.*2.196. II. as Adj., *floating*, λόφος Nonn.*D.*23.107. **-ικός**, ή, όν, *seafaring*, Pl.*Ax.*368b, Phld.*Rh.*1.342 S., Plu.2.27b, etc.; π. ἄνθρωποι *shipowners*, Id.*Cat.Mi.*61. **-ίς**, ίδος, ἡ, perh. *life-belt* or *float*, Demetr. in *Cat.Cod.Astr.*8(3).98 (pl.). **-ός**, ή, όν, also ός, όν *AP*5.203 (Mel.):—epith. of the island of Aeolus, Od.10.3, i. e. (as expld. by Aristarch.ap.Eust.) *floating*; νῆσος π. *floating* island, Hdt.2.156; [τὴν γῆν] εἰπεῖν Θαλῆν..πλωτὴν εἶναι..ὥσπερ ξύλον Arist.*Cael.*294$^{a}$30; π. ἀπήναισι χαλκεμβόλοις *floating* wains, i.e. ships, *Trag. Adesp.*142 (= *Lyr.Adesp.*117); of fish, *swimming*, ἰχθύων π. γένος S.*Fr.*941.9; π. θῆρες Arion 1; πλωτοί *AP*6.14 (Antip. Sid.), 23,296 (Leon.); πλωταὶ ἄγραι *fishing*, ib.180 (Arch.); π. ἐγχέλεις, so called because they *float on the surface*, Ath.1.4c; *muraenae*, Colum.8.17.8 (prob.); but π. ζῷα *water*-animals generally, Hp.*Flat.*3; opp. πεζά, πτηνά, Arist.*HA*488$^{a}$1, cf. *Pol.*1258$^{b}$19; τὰ π., of *migratory fishes*, opp. τὰ μόνιμα, Id.*HA*621$^{b}$3, cf. 607$^{b}$26; also of *water-birds*, ib.504$^{a}$7, *PA*694$^{a}$7; οἱ π. τῶν ὀρνίθων ib.$^{b}$2. II. *navigable*, ἐς θάλασσαν οὐκέτι πλωτὴν ὑπὸ βραχέων Hdt.2.102; ποταμοί Arist.*Mir.*836$^{b}$32, Plb.10.48.1; *to be passed over in ships*, opp. πορευτός, Id.1.42.2, etc.; π. οἶμος Lyc.889; μήτε γῆν καρπὸν φέρειν μήτε θάλασσαν πλωτὴν εἶναι, formula in curses, *IG*3.1417,al., cf. *BMus.Inscr.*918 (Halic., ii/iii A. D.). 2. of seasons, *fit for navigation*, Plb.1.37.10: Subst. πλωτός (sc. καιρός), ὁ, *the season for sailing*, π. καὶ ἀροτοῦ Heraclit.*All.*7 (s. v. l.).

**πλώω**, Ion. for πλέω. **πνείω**, Ep. for πνέω.

⊛ **πνεῦμα**, ατος, τό, (πνέω) *blast, wind*, first in Anaximen.2, ὅλον τὸν κόσμον π. καὶ ἀὴρ περιέχει: freq. in Trag., etc., ἀνέμων πνεύματα πάντων A.*Pr.*1086 (anap.), cf. 1047 (anap.); θαλάσσας..πνεύματι λάβρῳ Id.*Pers.*110 (lyr.); πνευμάτων ἐπομβρίᾳ Id.*Fr.*300.3; τέως δὲ κούφοις πνεύμασιν βόσκου S.*Aj.*558; πνεύμασιν θαλασσίοις ἐξωσθέντες E.*Cyc.*278 (but πνοή is commoner in Poets; Hom. uses πνοιή); πνεύματα ἀνέμων Hdt.7.16.ά; τὸ π. κατήει Th.2.84; κατὰ πρύμναν ἵσταται τὸ π. ib.97; τὸ π. λεῖον καὶ καθεστηκὸς λαβεῖν Ar.*Ra.*1003; τὸ π. ἔλαττον γίγνεται Id.*Eq.*441; εἰ φορὸν π. εἴη X.*HG*6.2.27; κατὰ πνεῦμα στῆναι τοῦ ἄρρενος to *leeward* of him, Arist.*HA*560$^{b}$14; but κατὰ π. προσιόντες down *wind*, ib.535$^{a}$19; πνεύματος ἀνείλησις, ἐκπύρωσις, Epicur.*Ep.*2 pp.44,45 U.; as an element, *air*, *Corp.Herm.*1.9,16; τὸ π. τὸ περὶ τὴν ψυχήν Plot.2.2.2, cf. Porph.*Sent.*29. 2. metaph., θαλερωτέρῳ π. with more genial *breeze* or *influence*, A.*Th.*708 (lyr.); λύσσης π. μάργῳ Id.*Pr.*884 (anap.); αἰδοίῳ π. χώρας with *air* or *spirit* of respect on the part of the country, Id.*Supp.*29 (anap.); π. ταὐτὸν οὔποτ᾽..ἐν ἀνδράσιν φίλοις βέβηκεν *the wind* is constantly changing even among friends, S.*OC*612; π. συμφορᾶς E.*IT*1317; ὅταν θεοῦ σοι π. μεταβαλὸν τύχῃ Id.*HF*216. II. *breathed air, breath*, σάλπιγξ βροτείου πνεύματος πληρουμένη A.*Eu.*568; αὐλῶν, λωτοῦ π., E.*Ba.*128 (lyr.), *Ph.*787 (lyr., pl.); π. ἀπέρρηξεν βίου *the breath* of life, A.*Pers.*507; π. ἀπώλεσεν Id.*Th.*984 (lyr.); π. ἄθροισον collect *breath*, E.*Ph.*851; π. ἀφεῖναι, ἀνεῖναι, μεθεῖναι, to give up *the ghost*, Id.*Hec.*571, *Or.*277, *Tr.*785 (anap.); π. δειμαίνων λιπεῖν Id.*Supp.*554; π...δυσῶδες ἠφίει Th.2.49; πνεύματος διαρροαί the wind-pipe, E.*Hec.*567; τὰς τοῦ π. διεξόδους ἀποφράττον Pl.*Ti.*91c (v. πνεύμων); πνεύματος ῥώμη Plu.2.804b: prov., ἄνθρωπός ἐστι π. καὶ σκιὰ μόνον S.*Fr.*13. 2. *breathing, respiration*, freq. in Hp., π. πυκνόν, ἀραιόν, ἐκτεῖνον, κατεπεῖγον, *Epid.*2.3.7; π. πυκνότερον *Acut.*16; π. προσκόπτον checked, difficult *breathing*, *Aph.*4.68; π. ἄσημον indistinct, feeble *breathing*, *Epid.*6.7.8; π. βηχῶδες *Coac.*622; π. μετέωρον shallow *breathing*, *Epid.*2.3.1; τὸ π. ἔχειν ἄνω to be out of *breath*, Men.23, cf. Sosicr.1; τὸ π. ἀνήνεγκαν recovered their *breath*, Hp.*Prorrh.*2.12 (so without τὸ π. *Aph.*2.43); but ἀναφέρουσιν.. κλαίοντά τε καὶ ἐς τὰς ῥῖνας ἀνέλκοντα τὸ π. they *sob*.., Id.*Hebd.*51. b. pl., of the air imagined as filling the veins, πνευμάτων ἀπολήψιες ἀνὰ φλέβας Id.*Acut.*(*Sp.*)7, al. 3. *flatulence*, in pl., Eub.107.9, Arist.*Pr.*948$^{b}$25, Dsc.2.112, D.L.6.94. 4. *breath of life*, π. ζωῆς Lxx *Ge.*6.17, 7.15, cf. Plu.*Per.*13, etc.; π. ἔχειν retain *life*, Plb.31.10.4; *living being*, ἐγὼ Νίνος πάλαι ποτ᾽ ἐγενόμην π. Phoen.1.16; οὐ π. πάντα βρότεια σοί (sc. Πλούτωνι) νέμεται; *IG*14.769 (Naples). 5. *that which is breathed forth* or *exhaled, odour*, ὦ θεῖον ὀδμῆς π. E.*Hipp.*1391; π. βαρὺ ἀφιεῖσα, of a tree, Plu.2.647b. 6. Gramm., *breathing with which a vowel is pronounced*, ib.1009e (pl.), A.D.*Adv.*147.18; π. δασύ, ψιλόν, Id.*Pron.*78.6, *Adv.*148.9. III. *divine inspiration*, ἄγρια..πνεύματα θεοφορίης *AP*6.220.4 (Diosc.); εἰ μή τι θεῖον..ἐνῆν π. τῇ ψυχῇ Pl.*Ax.*370c; τὸ ἱερὸν καὶ δαιμόνιον ἐν μούσαις π. Plu.2.605a; καθαρὸν δίκαιον..π. θεοῦ σωτῆρος *BMus.Inscr.*1062 (Cyrene, ii A. D.). IV. the *spirit* of God, π. θεοῦ Lxx *Ge.*1.2, etc.: freq. in *NT*, τὸ π. τὸ ἅγιον *Ev.Marc.*3.29, al. 2. *spirit* of man, εἴτ᾽ ἐστὶ τοῦτο π. θεῖον εἴτε νοῦς Men.482.3: in *NT*, opp. ψυχή, 1*Ep.Thess.*5.23, cf. *Ep.Rom.*8.2; τῷ π., opp. τῷ σώματι, 1*Ep.Cor.*5.3; also, opp. γράμμα, *Ep.Rom.*2.29. V. *spiritual* or *immaterial being, angel*, *Ep.Hebr.*1.14, *Apoc.*1.4; τὰ ἄχραντα π., τὰ κακὰ π., Iamb.*Myst.*3.31; π. πονηρόν, ψευδές, Lxx *Jd.*9.23, 3*Ki.*22.21, cf. *Act.Ap.*19.12,15, *Apoc.*16.14, Porph.ap.Eus.*PE*4.23, etc.; ἀλάλου καὶ κακοῦ π. οὖσα πλήρης (sc. ἡ Πυθία) Plu.2.438b. VI. Rhet., *sentence declaimed in one breath*, Hermog.*Inv.*3.10, 4.4, al.

⊛ **πνευμᾰτ-έμφορος**, ον, = πνευματόφορος, στόμα *EM*677.28. **-ίας**, ου, ὁ, = πνευματώδης 1.3, Hp.*Acut.*17. **-ιάω**, = πνευστιάω, Sch.E.*Med.*1119. **-ίζω**, *fan by blowing*, in Pass., Antig.*Mir.*136. II. *write* or *pronounce with the breathing*, Eust.524.5, al. **-ικός**, ή, όν, *of wind* or *air*, κινήσεις Arist.*Pr.*916$^{b}$4; βίᾳ π. Id.*HA*586$^{a}$17; φύσεις Epicur.*Ep.*2 p.39 U.; ἀέρος ψυχρότης Thphr.*CP*4.12.5; π. [ὄργανον] a machine *moved by wind*, Vitr.10.1.1; μηχάνημα Gal.*Anim.Pass.*2.3. 2. *of the nature of wind* or *air*, τὰ π. Arist.*Mete.*380$^{a}$23; π. ξηρότης, i. e. a dry vapour, Plu.*Alex.*35. b. *of subtle substance*, τὸ π. Str.1.3.5; οὐσία, opp. ὑγρά, Ph.1.15, cf. Cleom.1.8, Gal.7.596. 3. *inflated, distended with air*, ὑστέραι Arist.*HA*584$^{b}$22. 4. Act. (= πνευματώδης 1.3), *causing flatulence*, οἶνος Id.*Pr.*955$^{a}$35; βρώματα Nicom.Com.1.31, cf. Diph.Siph.ap.Ath.3.73a (Sup.), Plu.2.286e, Sor.1.52. Adv. **-κῶς** *by flatulence*, Archig.ap.Gal.12.537. 5. *breathing, exhaling*, εὐοσμία Thphr.*CP*6.16.3. II. *of the breath* or *breathing*, τὸ π. μόριον, ὁ π. τόπος, Arist.*GA*781$^{a}$31, *Pr.*962$^{a}$11. III. *of spirit, spiritual*, interpol. in Plu.2.129c; opp. σαρκικός, ψυχικός, *Ep.Rom.*15.27, 1*Ep.Cor.*2.13, etc. Adv. **-κῶς** ib.14. IV. οἱ Π. a school of physicians *who referred all questions of health to pneumatic agencies*, Gal.8.749, 15.111. V. *conveying* πνεῦμα, κοιλία, of the left ventricle of the heart (opp. αἱματική), Erasistr.ap.eund.*UP*6.12, cf. *Placit.*4.5.7. VI. Rhet., Adv. **-κῶς** *in one breath* (cf. πνεῦμα VI), ἀποτελεῖσθαι Hermog.*Inv.*4.1. **-ιον**, τό, Dim. of πνεῦμα, *a little breath* or *life*, Plb.15.31.5, M.Ant.2.2, etc.; opp. σωμάτιον, Arr.*Epict.*2.1.17. 2. *flatulence*, Damox.2.26 (pl.). 3. *respiration*, Agathin.ap.Orib.10.7.22. 4. *a light breeze*, Antig.*Mir.*51. **-ιος**, η, ον, *portending wind*, σελήνη Arat.785. **-ισμός**, ὁ, *use of the breathing*, Eust.524.26, al.

**πνευμᾰτο-δώτης**, ου, ὁ, *giver of spirit*, *PMag.Par.*1.1371. **-κήλη**, ἡ, *aneurysmal varicocele*, Paul.Aeg.6.64.

**πνευμᾰτ-όμφᾰλος**, ὁ, *sufferer from umbilical hernia*, supposed to be *caused by wind*, Gal.14.786:—also **πνευμ-όμφαλον**, τό, *umbilical hernia*, Id.19.445.

**πνευμᾰτο-ποιέω**, *turn into air, vaporize*, Arist.*Pr.*937$^{a}$5. II. *cause flatulence*, Orib.*Syn.*9.43.8. **-ποιός**, όν, *producing flatulence*, Apollon.*Mir.*46. II. *producing breath* or *spirit*, ψυχή Eust.1090.29. **-ρροος**, ον, contr. **-ρους**, ουν, (ῥέω) *streaming with currents of air*, Pl.*Cra.*410b. **-φορέομαι**, Pass., *to be borne as by the wind*, Lxx *Je.*2.24. ⊛ **-φόρος**, ον, *bearing the spirit, inspired*, ib.*Ho.*9.7; προφῆται ib.*Ze.*3.4. **-φως**, φωτος, ὁ, epith. of a δαίμων, *shining spirit*, *PMag.Par.*1.593.

**πνευμᾰτ-όω**, *turn into vapour*, Arist.*Pr.*965$^{b}$39, 962$^{a}$8:—Pass., *become wind, evaporate*, Id.*Cael.*305$^{b}$14, *GA*737$^{a}$11, al., Thphr.*Vent.*40. 2. Pass., *to be filled with wind*, Epicur.*Ep.*2 pp.44,47 U. b. *effervesce*, Gal.16.569,661; *ferment*, Id.7.549. 3. abs., *cause flatulence*, Dsc.1.106. II. *blow up, inflate*, Anaxipp.1.47:—Pass., ἀσκὸς πεπνευματωμένος Hierocl.p.13 A.; esp. *to be flatulent*, Gal.7.215, *UP*4.9. III. Pass., *to be filled with the breath of life*, *PMag.Leid.W.*12.32. ⊛ **-ώδης**, ες, *like wind* or *air*, opp. ὑδατώδης, Arist.*Mete.*380$^{b}$16, 366$^{b}$7, al., Epicur.*Ep.*1 p.14 U.; opp. ἀτμιδώδης, Arist.*Mete.*341$^{b}$9 (Comp.); π. ζῴδιον in the zodiac, opp. πυρῶδες, γεῶδες, ὑδατῶδες, Palch. in *Cat.Cod.Astr.*8(1).262; γράμματα π. *pronounced with a strong breathing*, as φ, ψ, σ, ζ, Pl.*Cra.*427a; *aerated*, οἶνος Arist.*Pr.*953$^{b}$27. 2. *windy, exposed to the wind*, τόποι Thphr.*CP*1.8.3, Plu.2.648d; ἐνιαυτοὶ π. *windy* years, Arist.*Mete.*344$^{b}$27; ὧραι -έσταται ib.366$^{b}$4. 3. *flatulent*, Hp.*Aph.*5.72, al.; πάθη Arist.*Insomn.*461$^{a}$24, etc. (*asthmatic*, only Hp.*Acut.*(*Sp.*)55). b. Act., *causing flatulence*, [κύαμοι] D.L.8.24; ὄσπρια Plu.2.286e. II. *of the nature of breath, whispered*, φωνεῖν πνευματῶδες, of the elephant, Arist.*HA*536$^{b}$21; φωνὴ π. Id.*Phgn.*807$^{b}$35. **-ωσις**, εως, ἡ, *evaporation*, τοῦ ὑγροῦ Id.*Resp.*480$^{a}$15. II. *inflation*, στομάχου Dsc.1.8, cf. Gal.7.67; f.l. for ἐμπν-, *Placit.*5.8.2. **-ωτικός**, ή, όν, *apt to cause flatulence*, Dsc.2.110, Sor.2.32, Orib.*Fr.*76.

**πνευμόμφαλον**, v. πνευματόμφαλος.

**πνευμον-ία**, v. πλευμονία. **-ίας**, ου, ὁ, *of the lungs*, λοβοί Poll.2.215. **-ικός**, ή, όν, *of the lungs*, τόπος Arist.*Pr.*962$^{b}$37. II. *affected with lung-disease*, Ptol.*Tetr.*152. **-ιον**, τό, Dim. of πνεύμων, Hegesand.29. **-ίς**, v. πλευμονίς. **-ώδης**, ες, v. πλευμονώδης.

**πνευμόρρωξ**, ωγος, ὁ, *rupture of the lungs*, Hippiatr.6. II. *one who suffers therefrom*, ibid.

**πνεύμων**, v. πλεύμων.

**πνεῦσις**, εως, ἡ, (πνέω) *blowing*, Gal.17(1).36 (pl.); *breathing*, gloss on ἀοιδή, Sch.Opp.*H.*1.79.

⊛ **πνευστ-ιάω**, *breathe hard, pant*, Hp.*Int.*44, Sor.1.108; expld. by πυκνὸν ἀναπνεῖν, Arist.*Rh.*1357$^{b}$21; Ep. part. πνευστιόων *AP*11.382.4 (Agath.). **-ικός**, ή, όν, *of* or *for breathing*, ὄργανον Gal.4.506. 2. *flatulent*, v.l. in Diph.Siph.ap.Ath.2.69e (Comp.).

⊛ **πνέω**, poet. πνείω as always in Hom. exc. Od.5.469: fut. πνεύσομαι (ἐκ-) E.*HF*886 (lyr.), (ἐμ-) Id.*Andr.*555, (παρα-) Hp.*Mul.*2.133; also πνευσοῦμαι Ar.*Ra.*1221, Arist.*Mete.*367$^{a}$13, Thphr.*Sign.*34, Palaeph.17; πνεύσω Thphr.*Sign.*32, Lxx *Ps.*147.7(18), *Si.*43.20, *Gp.*1.12.34, *AP*9.112 (Antip. Thess.), (ἀνα-) Q.S.13.516 (συμ-πνευσόντων is f.l. in D.18.169): aor. 1 ἔπνευσα Hes.*Op.*506, Hdt.2.20, etc., (ἐν-) Il.17.456, (ἀν-) S.*Aj.*274: pf. πέπνευκα (ἐπι-) Pl.*Phdr.*262d, (ἐκ-) Arist.*Pr.*904$^{a}$1:—Pass., fut. πνευσθήσομαι (δια-) Aret.*CA*1.1: aor.

ἐπνεύσθην (δι-) Thphr.*HP*5.5.6, etc.—Hom. and early Prose writers use the simple Verb only in pres. and impf., to which Trag. add fut. and aor. 1 Act.—For the form ἄμπνυε, v. ἀναπνέω; for ἀμπνύνθη, -πνυτο, v. ἄμπνυτο; and for pf. Pass. πέπνῡμαι, part. πεπνῡμένος, v. πέπνυμαι.—Like other disyll. Verbs in -έω, this Verb contracts only εε, εει; but ἐκπνέων is disyll. in A.*Ag.*1493, 1517 (both lyr.):—*blow*, of wind and air, οὐδέ ποτ' οὖροι πνείοντες φαίνονθ' Od.4.361; αὔρη δ' ἐκ ποταμοῦ ψυχρὴ πνέει 5.469; ἐτησίαι.. οὐκ ἔπνευσαν Hdt.2.20, etc.; τῷ πνέοντι (sc. ἀνέμῳ or πνεύματι) Luc. *Cont.*3; ἡ πνέουσα (sc. αὔρα) *Act.Ap.*27.40; also of a flute-player, μέγα πνέων Poll.4.72; and of the flutes themselves, αὐλοὺς ἡδὺ πνέοντας *AP*6.254 (Myrin.); πνεῖται flutes *are sounding*, Mnesim.4.57 (anap.). II. *breathe, send forth an odour*, ἀμβροσίη.. ἡδὺ πνείουσα Od.4.446; π. εὐῶδες, δυσῶδες, Poll.2.75, etc.: abs., Dsc.3.80. 2. c. acc., *breathe out, send forth*, Ζεφύρου πνείοντος ἐέρσην Call.*Ap.* 82. 3. c. gen., *breathe* or *smell of* a thing, οὐ μύρου πνέον S.*Fr.* 565; τράγου π. *AP*11.240 (Lucill.); μόγοιο Q.S.6.164; λύθρου καὶ αἵματος Id.5.120 (ἐπιπν- codd.): rarely c. dat., μύροισι π. *smell with*.., *AP*5.199: freq. metaph., *breathe, be redolent of*, Χαρίτων πνείοντα μέλη Simon.184.3; ὄμματα.. πόθον πνείοντα *AP*5.258 (Paul. Sil.); φόνου π. cj. in Tryph.505; αὐθαδείας πολὺς ἔπνει D.H.7.51. III. of perceptible breathing, [ἵππω] πνείοντε κατ' ὤμων Il.13.385; π. ὕπνῳ A.*Ch.*621 (lyr.). IV. generally, *draw breath, breathe*: hence, *live*, Il.17.447; οἱ πνέοντες, = οἱ ζῶντες, S.*Tr.*1160; ὄλβος ἀεὶ πνεῖ Simm.25.12; ἥμισύ μευ ψυχῆς ἔτι τὸ πνέον Call.*Epigr.*42. V. metaph., c. acc. cogn., *breathe forth*, μένεα πνείοντες *breathing* spirit, epith. of warriors, Il.2.536, 3.8, 11.508, etc.; so πῦρ π. Hes.*Th.*319, Pi. *Fr.*146; φόνον δόμοι πνέουσιν A.*Ag.*1309; κότον πνέων Id.*Ch.*34 (lyr.), cf. 951 (lyr.); φρενὸς πνέων τροπαίαν Id.*Ag.*219 (lyr.); Ἄρη πνεόντων ib.376 (lyr.); πνέων χάριν τινί ib.1206; πῦρ πνειόντων.. ἄστρων S.*Ant.* 1146 (lyr.); πῦρ π. καὶ φόνον E.*IT*288; ὠδῖνας Id.*HF*862: paratrag. in Com., πνέοντας δόρυ καὶ λόγχας Ar.*Ra.*1016; τρέχει τις Ἀλφειὸν πνέων, of a swift runner, Id.*Av.*1121, etc.; and in a rhetorical passage, οἱ πῦρ πνέοντες, οἱ νενικηκότες Λακεδαιμονίους X.*HG*7.5.12. 2. with neut. Adjs. or Prons., πνέοντες μεγάλα giving themselves airs, E.*Andr.*189; τόσονδ' ἔπνευσας ib.327; κενὰ πνεύσαις Pi.*O.*10(11). 93; χαμηλὰ πνέων Id.*P.*11.30: abs., ὑπὲρ σακέων πνείοντες *breathing* over their shields, i.e. unable to repress their rage for war, Hes.*Sc.* 24; θρασείᾳ πνέων καρδίᾳ Pi.*P.*10.44: with nom., Ἄρης.. μέγας πνέων E.*Rh.*323; πολὺς ἔπνει καὶ λαμπρός D.25.57; οὗτος.. κaικίας ἢ συκοφαντίας πνεῖ Ar.*Eq.*437; ᾧ σὺ μὴ πνεύσῃς ἐνδέξιος on whom *thou breathest* not favourably, Call.*Epigr.*10.3.

**πνῑγᾰλίων**, ωνος, ὁ, (πνίγω) *nightmare*, from *the sense of throttling* which attends it, Themiso ap.Paul.Aeg.3.15.

**πνιγετός**, ὁ, = πνῖγος, Ptol.*Phas.*p.63 H., Hsch. s.v. ἀγχόνη.

**πνῑγεύς**, έως, ὁ, (πνίγω) *damper, extinguisher, cover* of a stove, Ar. *Nu.*96, *Av.*1001, Arist.*Juv.*470ᵃ9, *PA*654ᵃ7; as a votive offering, *IG* 2².1425.411. II. *hydraulic instrument in which air is pent up*: *regulator*, Hero *Spir.*1.42, al.; *air-chamber* in a water-organ, Ph.*Bel.* 77.44. III. *muzzle* for horses, Ar.*Fr.*60, *Com.Adesp.*664.

**πνῑγ-ηρός**, ά, όν, (πνίγω) *choking, stifling*, whether by throttling or heat, Ar.*Ra.*122 (with play on both senses); π. καλύβαι Th.2.52; [γῆ] ἐν κοίλῳ καὶ π. Hp.*Aër.*1; χωρία ib.24; σκηνώματα Plu.*Per.*34; νύκτες Arist.*Pr.*939ᵇ9 (Comp.); ὥρα D.H.8.89. ❀ **-ίζω**, = πνίγω, *AP*12. 222 (Strat.). **-ῖτις** (sc. γῆ), ιδος, ἡ, a sort of *clay*, Dsc.5.157, Plin. *HN*35.194. **-μα**, ατος, τό, *choking*, βὴξ.. μετὰ π. πολλοῦ Hp.*Epid.* 7.26; εἰς π. τὸν δῆμον ἔχειν to have it fast by the throat, Cephisodot. ap.Arist.*Rh.*1411ᵃ7. **-μονή**, ἡ, = sq., Herm. *in Phdr.*p.163 A. (pl.), Sch.E.*Ph.*327, Hdn.*Epim.*111. **-μός**, ὁ, *choking, suffocation*, Hp. *Coac.*61, Arist.*HA*514ᵃ6, *PA*664ᵇ31 (pl.), Anaxandr.33.8; of weeds, παρέχει π. αὐτῷ [τῷ σίτῳ] X.*Oec.*17.12; *crushing*, of a crowd, Plb. 4.58.9. 2. *stifling heat*, Men.Rh.p.351 S. (pl.). 3. *stewing*, Thphr.*Ign.*24. **-μώδης**, ες, *choking*, βὴξ Hp.*Epid.*7.26; φωνή Id.*Coac.*261. Adv. -δῶς Steph. *in Hp.*1 pp.207, 212 D.

**πνῑγόεις**, εσσα, εν, = πνιγηρός, *AP*7.536 (Alc.), Nic.*Th.*425, v.l. ib.24.

**πνῖγος**, εος, τό, *choking, stifling*, of the effects of heat, and so *stifling heat*, Hp.*VM*16, *Aër.*10, Ar.*Av.*726, 1091, Th.7.87, etc.; ἐν ἡλίῳ τε καὶ πνίγει, διὰ καύματός τε καὶ πνίγους, Pl.*R.*422c, 621a; πνίγους ὄντος τὰ νῦν Id.*Lg.*625b: in pl., Hp.*Epid.*3.2; ἔν γε χειμῶσιν καὶ πνίγεσιν Pl.*Phlb.*26a. II. in the Parabasis of the Att. Comedy, = μακρόν, because spoken at one breath, Sch.Ar.*Ach.*659.

❀ **πνίγ-ω** [ῑ], Sophr.68, al., Antipho 4.1.6, Herod.4.31, etc.: impf. ἔπνῑγον Ar.*Nu.*1376: fut. πνίξω (ἀπο-) Pl.Com.198, Antiph.171; Dor. 2 pl. fut. πνιξεῖσθε Epich.155: aor. ἔπνιξα, imper. πνῖξον, Cratin.27, Hdt.2.92, Batr.158:—Pass., fut. πνῑγήσομαι Gal.*Nat.Fac.*1.17, (ἀπο-) Ar.*Nu.*1504, Hp.*Morb.*3.16; also ἀπο-πεπνίξομαι Eun.*VS*p.463 B.: aor. ἐπνίχθην (ἀπ-) Aret.*SA*1.7; but ἐπνίγην [ῐ] Batr.148, Aret.*SD* 1.11, (ἀπ-) Pherecr.159, Pl.*Grg.*512a, D.32.6, etc.: pf. πέπνιγμαι, v. infr. II.—The simple verb is less freq. than the compd. ἀποπνίγω:—*choke, throttle, strangle*, Sophr. l.c., etc.; of a doctor, πνίγων.. πικρότατα πόματα διδούς Pl.*Grg.*522a; ἂν ὕλη πνίγῃ [τὸν σῖτον] X.*Oec.*17.14: prov., ὅταν τὸ ὕδωρ πνίγῃ, τί δεῖ ἐπιπίνειν; Arist.*EN*1146ᵃ35:—Pass., *to be choked, stifled*, ἐπνιγόμην τὰ σπλάγχνα Ar.*Nu.*1036; αἱ ὑστερικῶς πνιγόμεναι Antyll.ap.Orib.10.19.1. 2. impers. πνίγει, of great heat, *it is stifling*, Arist.*Pr.*941ᵇ4, 944ᵃ7. 3. metaph., *vex, torment*, ἕνα χαλκοῦν ἀποβαλὼν αὐτὸν π. Phld.*Ir.*p.37 W.; ὃ δὲ μάλιστά με πνίγει v.l. in Luc.*Prom.*17; *oppress* by exactions, 'squeeze', Jul. *Mis.*368c. II. *cook in a close-covered vessel, bake, stew*, Hdt.2.92; δικίδιον.. ἐν λοπάδι πεπνιγμένον Ar.*V.*511; πεπνιγμένος Metag.6. 9. III. *drown* (cf. πνῖξις II), in Pass., X.*An.*5.7.25: metaph., of plants, τὰ φυτὰ.. τοῖς πολλοῖς [ὕδασι] πνίγεται Plu.2.9b. **-ώδης**, ες, *choking*, τὸ π. Diph.Siph.ap.Ath.2.61e; of places, *stifling*, Plu. *Alex.*77. 2. Pass., *choked, stopped*, φάρυγξ Hp.*Prorrh.*1.86; φωνή ib.87, v.l. in *Coac.*261.

**πνικ-τήρ**, ῆρος, ὁ, *choking*, κόρυμβος Nonn.*D.*21.62; πόνος, of wrestling, ib.37.607. **-τικός**, ή, όν, v.l. for sq. I. 2 in Hero *Spir.* 1.3. **-τός**, ή, όν, *strangled*, *Act.Ap.*15.20, al. 2. *air-tight*, Hero *Spir.*1.3, 16, al. Adv. -τῶς ib.2.21. II. *baked* or *stewed* (cf. πνίγω II), Pherecr.175, Stratt.29, Antiph.1.4, etc.

**πνίξ**, ῖγός, ἡ, *choking, suffocation*, Hp.*Aph.*4.34, etc.; of women, αἱ ὑστερικαὶ πνίγες Dsc.3.45, 140, cf. Aret.*SA*2.11 tit.

**πνῖξις**, εως, ἡ, *stifling, smothering*, Arist.*Resp.*475ᵃ28, Thphr.*Ign.* 76. II. *drowning*, *PMag.Par.*2.3,41.

**Πνιστία**, ἡ, name of a goddess at Mytilene, *IG*12(2).484.11.

❀ **πνοή**, ῆς, ἡ, Ep. πνοιή, always in Hom.; Dor. **πνοά** (v. infr.); Lyr. **πνοιά** Pi.*O.*3.31, B.5.28: (πνέω):—*blowing, blast*, πνοιαὶ παντοίων ἀνέμων Il.17.55, cf. Od.4.839, Hes.*Th.*253, 268; πνοιῇ Βορέαο Il.5.697: abs., *blast, breeze*, 11.622, 13.590, etc.; ὀλίγη π. a light *breeze*, Arr.*Tact.*34. 4; π. βιαία a stiff *breeze*, ib.35.4; οἷον π. εἰς ἄλλο Plot.6.3.23; esp. to denote excessive swiftness, ἅμα πνοιῇς ἀνέμοιο along with, i.e. swift as, *blasts* of wind, Il.24.342, etc.; ἅμα πνοιῇ Ζεφύροιο 19.415; ἐπέτοντο μετὰ πνοιῇς ἀνέμοιο Od.2.148; πέτετο πνοιῇς ἀνέμοιο Il.12.207; ἅμα πνοιῇσι πετέσθην 16.149; imitated by Ar.*Av.*1396 (lyr.), ἅμ' ἀνέμων πνοαῖσι βαίην; freq. in Trag., ταχύπτεροι πνοαί A.*Pr.*88; πνοαὶ δ' ἀπὸ Στρυμόνος μολοῦσαι Id.*Ag.*192 (lyr.), cf. 654, Ar.*Nu.*161, Arist.*Mu.*392ᵇ11, etc.; *blast* of bellows, Th.4.100. II. *breathing hard, panting*, of horses, Il.23.380, S.*El.*719 (pl.). 2. generally, *breath*, ἔμπνους μέν εἰμι.. καὶ πνοὰς.. πνέω E.*HF*1092; μητρὸς οἴχονται πνοαί Id.*Or.*421: metaph., πνοιὴ Ἡφαίστοιο *the breath* of Hephaestus, i.e. *flame*, Il.21. 355; πυρὸς πνοᾷ E.*Tr.*815 (lyr.); πρὶν καταιγίσαι πνοὰς Ἄρεως A.*Th.* 63, cf. 115 (lyr.); θεοῦ πνοαῖσιν ἐμμανεῖς E.*Ba.*1094; πνοαὶ Ἀφροδίτης Id.*IA*69; θυμοῦ πνοαί Id.*Ph.*454. III. *vapour, exhalation*, σποδὸς προπέμπει πλούτου πνοάς, of a burning city, A.*Ag.*820; τηγάνου π. Eub. 75.8, cf. Antiph.217.7; λιβάνου πνοαί Anaxandr.41.37 (anap.). IV. *breath* of a wind-instrument, Αἰοληῖσιν ἐν πνοαῖσιν αὐλῶν Pi.*N.*3.79; αὐλῶν π. Ar.*Ra.*313; σύριγγος πνοά E.*Or.*145 (lyr.).—Poet. (Pl.*Cra.* 419d is no exception), once in Th. and freq. in later Prose (v. supr.) for πνεῦμα.

**πνοήπους**, ποδος, ὁ, ἡ, *wind-footed*, Hsch. **πνοιή**, Ep. for πνοή. **πνόος**, ὁ, = πνοή, Id. **πνυκίτης**, f.l. for πυκνίτης.

**πνύξ**, gen. πυκνός (v. infr.), ἡ, *the Pnyx*, at Athens, where the ἐκκλησίαι were held, Ar.*Eq.*165, 751, al.; ἐν πυκνὶ τῇ ἐκκλησίᾳ Docum. ap.D.18.55.—The Att. forms are gen. πυκνός, *IG*1².882, Ar.*Eq.*165, Pl.*Criti.*112a; dat. πυκνί Ar.*Ec.*243, Aeschin.1.81; acc. πύκνα Th.8. 97 (πνύκα cod. Vat.), Ar.*Th.*658, Pl. l.c.; later πνυκί Plu.*Them.*19, Luc.*Anach.*17, *JTr.*11. (Perh. cogn. with πυκνός; cf. πυκναία.)

**πνῦτός**, = πινυτός, Hsch. **πό**, v. ποτί.

❀ **πόα**, ἡ, Ion. and Ep. ποίη, Dor. ποία Pi. (v. infr.), also in E.*Cyc.* 333 (trim.), Ar.*Eq.*606 (troch.); Boeot. πύας, αο, ὁ, *Schwyzer*485.1, al. (Thespiae, iii B.C.):—*grass*, νέμεαι τέρεν' ἄνθεα ποίης Od 9.449; κεκορηότε ποίης, of oxen, 18.372; ἐν ποίῃ ib.368; χθὼν.. φύεν νεοθηλέα π. Il.14.347; ἀμφὶ δὲ ποίῃ.. ἀέξετο Hes.*Th.*194, cf. Hdt.4.53, E. l.c., etc.; π. Μηδική, v. Μηδικός. 2. generally, *herb*, π. τὸ ἀπὸ ῥίζης φυλλοφόρον προϊὸν ἀστέλεχες Thphr.*HP*1.3.1; collect., *herbaceous plants*, τῆς π. τὸ ἡλιοτρόπιον ib.7.3.1; esp. of medicinal *herbs*, καλοῦσι πόαν ἔνια τῶν φαρμακωδῶν οἱ ῥιζοτόμοι ib.9.8.1; of φυλλώδεις δυνάμεις, ibid.; ποίαν τρίψας *IG*4²(1).122.121 (Epid., iv B.C.); freq. in Hsch., s.v. ἀβρότονον, al. b. *lye*, Lxx *Je.*2.22, *Mal.*3.2. 3. *plant* in general, π. ἡ βοτάνη *EM*677.49, al.; π. Παρνασίς, i.e. the bay or laurel, Pi.*P.*8.20; στεφάνοισί νιν ποίας ἔρεπτον ib.4.240: hence, metaph., κεῖραι μελιαδέα ποίαν ib.9.37. 4. *the grass*, i.e. *a grassy place*, πόᾳ καθίζεσθαι *grass* to sit on, Pl.*Phdr.*229b, cf. X.*HG*4.1.30, Plu.*Ages.*36; *meadow*, *Schwyzer* l.c. (pl.). II. in later Poets, of Time, *hay-harvest*, i.e. *summer*, ἐπ' ἐννέα.. ποίας for nine *summers*, Call.*Fr.*182; χείματά τε ποίας τε δύω Rhian.54; ἢ τρεῖς ἢ πίσυρας ποίας *AP*7.731 (Leon.), cf. 627 (Diod.), 6.252 (Antiphil.): in this signf. ποιά (oxyt.) acc. to Sch.E.*Tr.*20, *EM*677.49. (Cf. Lith. *pieva* 'meadow'.)

**πο-άζω**, *weed*, cj. in Philem.116.4. II. of ground, *produce grass*, Str.5.3.8, 12.2.7; of the sea, *appear grassy* with seaweed, Id. 16.4.7. **-αλίς**· εἶδος πικρίδος, Hsch. **-άριον**, τό, Dim. of πόα, Thphr.*HP*3.3.6; in form ποιάριον, ib.1.7.3, 9.10.2. **-ασμός**, ὁ, *weeding*, Id.*CP*3.20.6. **-άστρια**, ἡ, *weeder* or *grass-cutter*, Archipp. 44; Ποάστριαι, title of comedies by Magnes and Phrynichus, cf. *IG* 2².2363.31 (dub.). **-άστριον**, τό, *sickle for cutting grass*, Poll.7. 184. **πόθ**, v. ποτί.

**ποδαβρός**, όν, *tender-footed*, Orac.ap.Hdt.1.55.

**ποδαγκώνιδας**, prob. f.l. for ποταγωγίδας, Hsch.

**ποδᾱγός**, v. ποδηγός.

**ποδάγρ-α**, ἡ, *trap for the feet*, X.*Cyr.*1.6.28, Call.*Fr.anon.*379, *AP* 6.296 (Leon.), Opp.*C.*1.156. II. *foot disease* of dogs, oxen, horses, Arist.*HA*604ᵃ5, 14, 23; *gout*, of human beings, *IG*4²(1).122. 133 (Epid., iv B.C.), Dsc.1.104, Arr.*Epict.*3.22.40, Philostr.*VA*4.30: pl., Str.15.1.43. **-άω**, *have gout in the feet*, Ar.*Pl.*559, Pl.*Alc.*2. 139e; of a foot disease in oxen, Arist.*HA*575ᵇ8; in dogs, Ael.*NA* 4.40. **-ιάω**, = foreg., Hp.*Aph.*6.28–30, Gal.14.240, Porph.*Abst.* 3.7. ❀ **-ικός**, ή, όν, *gouty*, of persons, Plb.36.14.2, D.S.32.20, Dsc. 1.15, 3.133, Herod.Med.ap.Orib.10.8.9, Plu.*Cat.Ma.*9. 2. *of* or *from gout, gouty*, πάθη Id.2.1087e, cf. Ph.1.525; νόσος D.L.5.68; τὰ π. Hp.*Aph.*5.25, Thphr.*HP*9.9.1. 3. *for gout*, δυνάμεις, φάρμακον, Dsc.5.128, Gal.11.432. **-ός, όν,** = foreg., *AP*5.38 (Nicarch.), Luc. *Sat.*7, Man.4.501.

**ποδάκνη,** ἡ, = ὁ ἐν τῷ τόξῳ δεσμός, Poll.7.157.

**ποδαλγ-έω,** = ποδαγράω, Sch.Ar.*Pl.*559. II. causal, *produce gout*, Ruf.ap.Orib.5.3.35. **-ής, ές,** *gouty*, Poll.2.196, *AP*7.112 (D.L.). **-ία, ἡ,** *gout in the feet*, Ruf ap.Orib.5.3.35, Poll.2.196, Lyd. *Mens.*4.8. **-ιάω,** = ποδαλγέω, Sch.Pi.*P.*3.111. **-ικός, ή, όν,** = ποδαγρικός, νόσος Lyd.*Mens.*4.89. **-ός, όν,** = foreg., Lycus ap.Orib.9.43.1.

**ποδάνεμος,** ον, v. ποδήνεμος.

**ποδᾰ-νιπτήρ,** ῆρος, ὁ, (νίζω) *vessel for washing the feet in, footpan*, Stesich.30 (v. infr.), Hdt.2.172, Amips.2, Diocl.Com.1, *IG*1$^2$.313.137, 2$^2$.1425.393, 11(2).161*B*127 (Delos, iii B.C.), *CIG*3071.8 (Teos, ii B.C.), Plu.2.151d, etc.: **ποδονιπτήρ** is a later form, Ath.4.168f, Stesich. l.c. (codd. Ath.10.451d). **-νιπτηρίδιον, τό,** Dim. of foreg., *IG*2$^2$.1471.50. **-νιπτρον, τό,** *water for washing the feet in*, mostly pl., Od.19.504; π. ποδῶν ib.343: sg., π. ἐκχεῖν Ar.*Fr.*306; dub. in *Com.Adesp.*35 (cod. Et.Gen.):—later **ποδόνιπτρον,** Ph.2.472, J.*AJ* 8.2.5, Iamb.*Protr.*21.ια'.

⊛ **ποδᾰπός,** ή, όν, *from what country?*: hence, generally, *whence? where born?* Hdt.7.218 (as v.l.), A.*Ch.*575, S.*OC*1160, E.*Cyc.*276, etc.; τίς καὶ π.; Pl.*Ap.*20b; π. τὸ γένος; Ar.*Pax*186, cf. *Av.*108; of wine, π. ὁ Βρόμιος; Θάσιος Alex.230. 2. generally, *of what sort?* π. τὸ δῶρον; S.*Fr.*453: freq. in later Gr., *Ev.Matt.*8.27, *Ev.Luc.*1.29, Hermog.*Inv.*1.1, etc.; in a play on both senses, π. τὸ γένος; πλούσιος Alex.90; π. (sc. κύων); οἷος..μὴ δάκνειν D.25.40. Adv. **-πῶς** Hdn. Gr.2.925; ποταπῶς *Gloss.* (Phryn.39 considers signf. 2 un-Attic, but S. l.c. is cited by Sch.D.T.p.239H.: the spelling **ποταπός** (wh. is f.l. in Alex.230 (codd. Ath.)) is found in later Gr., ll.cc. supr., cf. Phld.*Vit.*p.25J., D.H.7.57, Ph.1.157 (v.l.), Philostr.*VA*3.16, Luc. *Par.*22, Jul.*Or.*4.138c. ποδ- = Lat. *quod*; for the termination cf. ἀλλοδαπός (and v. A.D.*Synt.*20.15). Derived fr. ποίου δαπέδου by Phryn. l.c., Phot.)

⊛ **πόδ-αργος,** ον, *swift-footed*, or acc. to others *white-footed* (cf. Aret. *SD*2.13; **ποδάργης·** λευκόπους, Hsch.), Lyc.166: **Πόδαργος,** ὁ, *Swiftfoot* or *Whitefoot*, a horse of Hector, also of Menelaus, Il.8.185, 23.295; fem. Ποδάργη, name of a Harpy, 16.150. **-αρίζω,** v. πυδαρίζω. ⊛ **-άριον, τό,** Dim. of πούς, Pl.Com.248, Alex.110.15. **-αρκής, ές,** (ἀρκέω I.3) *succouring with the feet, running to the rescue* (cf. βοηθόος): hence, *swift-footed*, epith. of a good runner, freq. in Il., as epith. of Achilles, 1.121, al. (never in Od.); π. ἄγγελος Διός, of Hermes, B. 18.30. II. π. ἀμέρα a day *of swift feet*, i.e. on which swift runners contended, Pi.*O.*13.38; ποδαρκέων δρόμων τέμενος the sacred field of *swift* courses, i.e. the Pythian race-course, Id.*P.*5.33 (s.v.l.). III. *assisting the feet*, name of a remedy for gout, Gal.13.1021. **-αυρος,** ον, (αὔρα) = ποδήνεμος, Hsch. **-άων,** v. ποδεών II.1.

**ποδ-δᾰτέομαι,** Dor. for προσδατέομαι, *assign*, in aor. ποτεδασσάμεθα *Tab.Heracl.*2.54. **-δέχομαι** or **-δέκομαι,** in aor. part., Dor. for προσδέχομαι, *IG*5(1).653*a*9 (Sparta, ii A.D.).

**ποδ-εῖον,** τό, (πούς) *sock* or *legging, puttee* (expld. by εἴλημα τῶν ποδῶν Theognost.*Can.*128): in pl., Critias *Fr.*65D., Crates Com.34, *IG*2$^2$.1425.402, Thphr.*HP*7.13.8, etc.—On the accent, v. Theognost. l.c., Hsch.: written πόδειον in Phot., codd. Thphr. l.c.; ποδέων ζεύγη *PCair.Zen.*778.5 (iii B.C.). **-εκμᾰγεῖον** or **-εκμάγιον, τό,** *cloth for wiping the feet, Gloss.* **-ένδῠτος,** ον, (ἐνδύω) *drawn over the feet*, π. κατασκήνωμα, = πέπλος ποδιστήρ, A.*Ch.*984(998). **-εών,** ῶνος, ὁ, (πούς) in pl., *ragged ends* in the skins of animals, *where the feet and tail have been*, ἄκρων δέρμα λέοντος ἀφημμένον ἐκ ποδεώνων a lion's skin hung round one's neck by *the paws*, Theoc.22.52. II. sg., *neck* or *mouth of a wineskin*, which was formed by one of these ends, the others being sewn up, Hdt.2.121.δ'; *neck* of a skin bag, Hp.*Aff.* 21, prob. in *Art.*77 (pl.); ἀσκοῦ τὸν προὔχοντα ποδάονα (Dor. form), of the *membrum virile*, Orac.ap.Apollod.3.15.6. 2. *neck of the bladder*, Poll.2.196, Phot. 3. generally, of *any narrow end*, π. στεινός a narrow *strip of land*, Hdt.8.31. 4. *lower end* or *corner of a sail, sheet*, which in old times was a strip of hide (cf. πούς II.2), *Chrest.Oxy.*1241 v 1 (ii A.D.), Luc.*VH*2.45. 5. in pl., of a kind of *shoe*, Lyd.*Mag.*1.12 (πεδ- codd.); so perh. *AP*6.95 (Antiphil.).

⊛ **ποδηγ-ετέω,** *guide*, τἀγαθά Democr.173, cf. Lyc.12, Opp.*C.*4.360: abs., Ph.1.16, al.:—Pass., λογίοις, ὑπ' ἔρωτος π., Id.2.442,421. **-έτης,** ου, ὁ, *leader, guide*, Lyc.385, D.C.40.25 (pl.). **-έω,** *lead, guide*, Pl. *Lg.*899a, *Ep.*340c, Lyc.965, Phleg.*Fr.*36.2J.: abs., Ph.1.440, Muson. *Fr.*8p.37H.:—Pass., Clearch.9, D.C.63.9. **-ία, ἡ,** *leading, guiding*, Lyc.846. **-ός, όν,** Dor. and Trag. **ποδᾱγός,** (ἄγω) *guiding the foot, guiding*, τὰ π. Πόθων ὠκύπτερα *AP*5.178 (Mel.): but in Trag., etc., Subst., *guide*, E.*Ph.*1715, Ph.1.109; *attendant*, S.*Ant.*1196: irreg. Comp. ποδηγέστερος Phot., Suid.

**ποδ-ηνεκής,** ές, *reaching down to the foot*, δέρμα λέοντος Il.10.24, cf. A.R.1.324, 4.180; ἀσπίς Il.15.646; κιθὼν π. λίνεος Hdt.1.195. **-ήνεμος** (Dor. **-άνεμος** B.6.13), ον, *wind-swift*, epith. of Iris, π. ὠκέα Ἶρις Il. 2.786, al. (never in Od.); ὦ π. τέκος, of a runner, B. l.c.: Com., καρκίνοι ποδάνεμοι [ᾱ] Crates Com.29 (-ήνεμοι cj. Mein.), cf. Hsch. **-ήρης,** ες, *reaching to the feet*, πέπλοι, χιτὼν π., a robe *that falls over the feet*, E.*Ba.*833, X.*Cyr.*6.4.2, Paus.5.19.6, etc. (later ποδήρης alone (sc. χιτών) of the High Priest's robe, Lxx *Ex.*25.6, Aristeas 96); π. ἀσπίς large shield *which covered the body down to the feet*, X.*An.*1.8.9, *Cyr.*6. 2.10: Com., πώγων π. καθεῖται Plu.2.52c. 2. ναῦς π. a ship *with feet*, i.e. *oars*, Hsch., Eust.1515.29; στῦλος π. a *firmly based* pillar, A.*Ag.*898. 3. τὰ π. *parts about the feet, feet*, ib.1594. (-ήρης perh. from -ᾱρης, cf. Arc. pr. n. Ποδάρης.) **-ία, ἡ,** = πούς II.2, *Gloss.*, cf. Serv.ad Verg.*A.*5.830. **-ιάζειν·** τὸ ἐπὶ τὸ αὐτὸ ἀναστρέφειν καὶ ὑποστρέφειν, Hsch. ⊛ **-ιαῖος** (spelt -ιεῖος Anon.*in Tht.*27.6), α, ον, (πούς) *a foot long, broad*, or *high*, Hp.*Art.*73, *IG*1$^2$.372.119, X.*Oec.*19.4, etc.; φαίνεται μὲν ὁ ἥλιος π. Arist.*de An.*428$^b$3. 2. Math., ἡ π. [γραμμή] side *of one foot long*, taken as the unit of length, Pl.*Tht.*147d, cf. Arist.*Sens.*446$^a$6, *Metaph.*1052$^b$33. II. ποδιαῖον ποιησάμενοι ἐφιᾶσι *loosen* the sail *by the* πούς, Id.*Mech.*851$^b$8. **-ίζω,** *bind* or *tie the feet*:—Pass., *to have the feet tied, to be hobbled*, of horses, ἐπὶ ταῖς φάτναις X.*Cyr.*3.3.27; ἀνὴρ κῶλον ποδισθείς S.*Fr.*63. II. *furnish with feet*, τὰ πεποδισμένα ζῷα *Theol.Ar.*55. III. in Prosody, *measure by feet, scan*, τροχαϊκῶς ποδίζεσθαι Eust.11.37. IV. *dance* (cf. ποδισμός II), cj. in Cratin.219.

**πόδικε·** πρόσριψον, Hsch. (cf. δικεῖν).

**ποδικός,** ή, όν, *of a metrical foot* or *feet*, γένη, λόγος, Aristid.Quint. 1.15,19; π. χρόνοι, opp. ἁπλοῖ, πολλαπλοῖ, ib.14.

**ποδίκρα·** ὄρχησις πρὸς πόδα γινομένη (Lacon.), Hsch.

**ποδίκροτος,** ον, *clanking on the feet*, ἅμμα *APl.*1.15*.

**πόδ-ιον,** τό, Dim. of πούς, Epich.57, Hp.*Epid.*7.52; *foot* of a vase, *BGU*781 i 15 (i A.D.). **-ίς,** ίδος, ἡ, a kind of *shoe*, in pl., Poll.10. 168. **-ίσκος,** ὁ, Dim. of πούς, Herod.7.94, *Anacreont.*28.4. **-ισμός,** ὁ, *measuring by feet*, = Lat. *pedatura*, Veg.2.7: in land-surveying, Frontin. in *Corp.Agrimens.Rom.* i p.16 Thulin. 2. in Metric, *scansion*, π. μετρικός Eust.456.39: hence, metaph., of the pulse, Ruf. *Syn.Puls.*4.4. II. a kind of *dance*, Poll.4.99. ⊛ **-ιστήρ,** ῆρος, ὁ, πέπλος π. a *foot-entangling* robe, A.*Ch.*986(1000). II. a kind of *tripod*, J.*AJ*8.3.7. **-ιστί,** Adv. from ποδίζω, sine expl., *An.Ox.* 2.313. **-ίστρα,** ἡ, *foot-trap*, *AP*6.107 (Phil.); of a spider's web, ib.9.372.

**ποδογλῠφεῖον,** *gulvia* (sic), *Gloss.*

**ποδοῖιν,** Ep. gen. and dat. dual for ποδοῖν.

**ποδο-κάκκη,** ἡ, *stocks* (commonly called ξύλον), Lex ap.Lys.10.16, Lex ap.D.24.105, Pl.Com.249, Theon *Prog.*13, Sch.Ar.*Eq.*366. (Cf. Skt. *kañcatē* 'bind', Lith. *kinkýti* 'harness', κιγκλίς; the spelling -κάκη is due to the false expl. *foot-plague*, ap.Harp.: from ποδοκατοχή acc. to Did.ap.eund.) **-κέφᾰλον,** τό, in pl., prob. = κεφαλόποδες, *POxy.*1513.13 (iv A.D.). ⊛ **-κοίλιον,** τό, written -κύλιον, dub. sens. in *Sammelb.*2253.16. **-κοιλον,** τό, = *aqualegellae* (i.e. *aquale, gello*), *Gloss.* **-κρουστία,** ἡ, *stamping with the feet*, Str.10.3.15 (pl.). **-κτῠπέω,** *strike the earth with the feet*, of dancers, Phot. s.v. ῥαβάττειν. **-κτύπη** [ῠ], ἡ, *dancing-girl*, Luc. *Lex.*8. **-μακτρον,** τό, *towel for wiping the feet, Gloss.* **-μερής,** ές: στίχοι ποδομερεῖς, = *versus partipedes* (*qui in singulis pedibus singulas orationis partes adsignant*), Diom.p.498K. **-νιπτήρ, -νιπτρον,** v. ποδαν-. **-πέδη,** ἡ, *fetter*, Tz.*H.*1.891. **-ρρᾰγής,** ές, (ῥήγνυμι) *bursting forth at a stamp of the foot*, ὕδατα π., of Pirene and Hippocrene, *AP*9.225 (Honest.). **-ρρωρος,** η, ον, (ῥωρός) *swift-footed*, Call.*Dian.*215 (v.l. -ρρώην).

**ποδὸς ῥυτίς·** τὸ τῶν ποδῶν ἕλκεσθαι, Hsch. (Fort. ποδορρυτί.)

**ποδοστράβη** [ᾰ], ἡ, *snare, gin*, X.*Cyn.*9.11 sq. II. *instrument for straining* or *twisting the feet*, in surgical operations, Poll.4.182, Hsch.; or in torture, Hyp.*Ath.*18 (restd. from Harp. s.v. ποδοστράβη), Luc. *Lex.*10, Sch.Ar.*Eq.*366.

**ποδοστρόφια,** = *repotia, Gloss.*

**ποδότης,** ητος, ἡ, (πούς) *footedness*, Arist.*PA*642$^b$28, *Metaph.*1038$^a$15.

**ποδο-τρόχᾰλος,** ὁ, *one who turns a wheel with his foot, potter*, Hsch. **-φύλαξ** [ῠ], ἄκος, ὁ, = ποδοκάκκη, Lyd.*Mag.*1.46 (pl.).

**ποδοχέω,** *guide* a ship *by means of the sheet* (πούς II 2), Antipho Soph.96, *AB*297.5 (written ποδοκέω):—hence **ποδουχέω,** *govern*, is restd. by Dind. in A.*Pers.*656 (lyr.).

**ποδο-ψέλιον,** τό, *anklet*, Ps.-Acro ad Hor.*Ep.*1.17.56:—written **-ψέλλιον,** *POsl.*46 (iii A.D.); **-ψελον,** *Sammelb.*7250.10 (iii/iv A.D.). ⊛ **-ψηστρον,** τό, (ψάω) *footwiper, footcloth*, A.*Ag.*926. **-ψοφία,** ἡ, *noise of feet*, Aesop.237, Sch.A.R.4.86. **-ψόφιον,** τό, *rattle*, *Gloss.* ⊛ **-ψόφος,** ον, *making a noise with the foot* or *feet*, ib.

**ποδ-όω,** *tighten* a sail *with the sheet*, Eust.1534.26. II. Pass., *to be furnished with feet*, Nicostr.ap.Simp.*in Cat.*369.10. **-ώκεια,** ἡ, *swiftness of foot*, Il.2.792 (pl.), E.*IT*33, Plu.*Rom.*25:—written ποδωκία in A.*Eu.*37, X.*Cyn.*5.27 (v.l. -εία), Hld.8.16; ποδωκίην [ῐ] *Anacreont.*24.3. **-ώκης,** ες, (ὠκύς) *swiftfooted*, Hom. (esp. in Il.), mostly epith. of Achilles, 2.860, al.; of Dolon, 10.316; of the mares of Eumelus, 2.764, cf. Hes.*Sc.*191: in Prose, ἄνθρωπος Th.3.98, cf. Plu. *Fab.*7; δρομεύς Alcid.*Soph.*7; ἡμεροσκόποι Aen.Tact.6.5; [ἐφ' ἵππων] ὅτι -εστάτων Pl.*R.*467e, cf. Palaeph.1 (Comp.); κύων Id.4; λαγώς X.*Mem.*3.11.8. 2. generally, *swift, quick*, ὄμμα A.*Th.*623 (nisi leg. οἶμα); ποδώκει χαλκεύματι Id.*Ch.*576; τό τοι κακὸν ποδῶκες ἔρχεται Id. *Fr.*22; θεῶν π. βλάβαι S.*Ant.*1104: metaph., *hasty, impetuous, rash*, οὐ χρὴ π. τὸν τρόπον λίαν φορεῖν *Trag.Adesp.*519: Sup. ποδωκέστατος Pl. l.c.; Ep. ποδωκηέστατος A.R.1.180. ⊛ **-ωμα,** ατος, τό, (πούς) *floor, base*, Apollod.*Poliorc.*192.7, *OGI*510.5 (Ephesus, ii A.D.); of a granary, *BGU*321.13 (iii A.D.), etc. 2. *storage-charge* for grain, *PRyl.*71 *Intr.* (i B.C.), *PTeb.*339.17 (iii A.D.), etc. **-ώνῠχος,** ον, *reaching to the toes* (cf. ποδήρης), Poll.10.191, Hsch. **-ωτός,** ή, όν, *tightened by the sheet*, of a sail, Lyc.1015.

**ποεσι-τρόφος,** ον, (πόα) *abounding in herbs*, Opp.*C.*3.189. **-χροος,** ον, *grass-coloured*, ib.2.409.

**πόεστι,** Arc. for πρόσεστι, *SIG*306.12 (Tegea, iv B.C.).

⊛ **ποέχομαι,** Cypr. for προσέχομαι, *Schwyzer*679.19,21 (Idalium).

**ποέω**, v. ποιέω sub init.

**ποηλογέω**, *gather herbs*, J.*BJ*5.13.7.

**Ποήσιος**, ὁ (sc. μήν), month at Gonni (Perrhaebia), Ἀρχ.Ἐφ.1912.63.

**ποη-φᾰγέω**, *eat grass* or *herbs*, J.*BJ*2.8.8, al.:—written **ποιηφαγέω**, Hdt.3.25,100, Max.Tyr.20.4; **ποοφαγέω**, Arist.*HA*593$^{a}$15. **-φᾰγία**, ἡ, *grass-eating*, Hsch. ⊛ **-φάγος** [ᾰ], ον, *eating grass* or *herbs*, ζῷα π., opp. καρποφάγα, ῥιζοφάγα, Hp *Vict.*2.49, Arist. *HA*595$^{a}$14, al.; **ποιηφάγος** Id.*Fr.*344, Max.Tyr.29.4; **ποοφάγος**, Arist.*PA*693$^{a}$15.

**ποθᾶκον**, Dor. for προσῆκον, v. προσήκω.

**ποθεινοποιός**, όν, *exciting a tender longing*, Sch.E.*Ph.*1737.

⊛ **ποθεινός**, ή, όν, also ός, όν E.*Hel.*623:—shortd. **ποθινός** (q.v.): (ποθέω):—*full of longing*, ἔρος Sapph.*Supp.*4.11; but usu. 2. *longed for, desired, desirable*, τίς ἀδονᾶς ἄτερ βίος π.; Simon.71; οὐκ..δήμῳ φίλος οὐδὲ π. Callin.1.16; χρυσὸς π. κτῆμα τοῖς βροτοῖς E.*Fr.*1132.31; esp. of those absent or lost, παῖς πατρὶ π. Pi.*O.*10(11).87, cf. *I.*5(4).7, etc.; ποθεινὰ Ἑλλάς *desire of* seeing Greece, Id.*P.*4.218; π. ἦλθες E.*IT*515; π. ἂν μόλοις Id.*Hel.*540; π. δάκρυα tears *of regret*, Id.*Ph.*1737 (lyr.): also in Com. and Prose, ἀγαθὸς ποιητὴς καὶ π. τοῖς φίλοις Ar.*Ra.*84; ὦ ποθεινὴ τοῖς..γεωργοῖς ἡμέρα Id.*Pax*556 (paratrag., cf. E.*Hel.*623); τὴν τῶν ἐναντίων τιμωρίαν -οτέραν αὐτῶν λαβόντες Th.2.42; -ότερος θάνατος βίου Lys.2.73; τὸ -ότατον τῆς ψυχῆς ἦθος X.*Mem.*3.10.3; ποθεινοὶ ἀλλήλοις Pl.*Ly.*215b, etc. Adv. Comp. -οτέρως, σφῶν αὐτῶν ἔχειν *long more ardently* for each other, X.*Lac.*1.5. II. *longed for, desired, missed*, E.*Cyc.*620 (lyr.); ποθεινὴ δακρύοισι συμφορά *desired by* tears, i.e. *desiring, calling for* tears, Id.*Med.*1221 (s.v.l.). III. Subst., perh. name of a colour (cf. πόθος III) or kind of paint, χρίσει ποθεινῷ *PCair.Zen.*445.11 (iii B.C.).

**πόθεν**, Ion. **κόθεν**: I. interrog. Adv. *whence?* 1. of Place, εἰρώτα.., τίς εἴη καὶ π. ἔλθοι Od.15.423; ποδαπὸς ὁ ξένος; π.; A.*Ch.*657; ποῖ δὴ καὶ π.; Pl.*Phdr.*227a: c. gen., τίς π. εἰς ἀνδρῶν; Il.21.150, Od.1.170, al.; κ. τῆς Φρυγίης ἥκων; Hdt.1.35; π. γῆς ἦλθες; E.*Ion*258, etc. 2. of origin, π. γένος εὔχεται εἶναι *from what stock* he avows that he is by descent, Od.17.373; τὴν..τέχνην πῶς καὶ π. ἄν τις δύναιτο πορίσασθαι; Pl.*Phdr.*269d; π. ἄλλοθεν..; D.3.28: c. gen., π. ποτὲ..θνητῶν ἔφυσαν; E.*Supp.*841. 3. in speaking, π. ἄρξωμαι; A.*Ch.*855 (anap.); π. ἂν λάβοιμι ῥῆμα; Ar.*Pax* 521, etc. 4. of the cause, *whence? wherefore?* π. χοὰς ἔπεμψεν; ἐκ τίνος λόγου; A.*Ch.*515; to express surprise or negation, π. γὰρ ἔσται βιοτά; i.e. οὐδαμόθεν, S.*Ph.*1159 (lyr.); π. υἱὸς αὐτοῦ ἐστιν; *Ev.Marc.*12.37; πόθεν; *how can it be? impossible! nonsense!* E.*Ph.*1620, Ar.*V.*1145, *Ra.*1455; σὺ δ' ὁμέστιος θεοῖς; π.; Id.*Fr.*655; ἀλλ' οὐκ ἔστι ταῦτα· πόθεν; πολλοῦ γε καὶ δεῖ D.18.47, cf. 24.157, etc.; π. γάρ; E.*Alc.*781. 5. with Verbs of finding, taking, purchasing, etc., π. ἂν πριαίμην ῥῖνα; Ar.*Pax*21; π. ἄν τις τοῦτο τὸ χρῖμα λάβοι; X.*Smp.*2.4; π. πρᾷον..ἦθος εὑρήσομεν; Pl.*R.*375c, cf. *Euthd.*273e, al.; so κάθησθε κλάοντες περὶ τῆς αὔριον π. φάγητε Arr.*Epict.*1.9.19. II. **ποθέν**, enclit. Adv. *from some place or other*, εἴ π. Il.9.380; εἰ καί π. ἄλλοθεν ἔλθοι Od.7.52, cf. 5.490; φανεὶς..π. A.*Pers.*354; ἦλθέ π. σωτήρ Id.*Ch.*1073 (anap.); ἐκ δρυός π. ἢ ἐκ πέτρας Pl.*R.*544d; ἐκ βιβλίου π. ἀκούσας from *some* book *or other*, Id.*Phdr.*268c, cf. 244d; after ἐνθένδε, ἐντεῦθεν, ib.229b, 270a, etc.

**ποθέρπω**, v. προσέρπω. **ποθέσπερος**, v. προσέσπερος.

**ποθ-έω**, Od.1.343, etc.; Aeol. **ποθήω** Sapph.23; Ep. inf. ποθήμεναι Od.12.110: Ep. impf. πόθεον Il.2.726, etc.; also ποθέεσκον 1.492, Call. in *PSI*9.1092.51: fut. ποθήσω X.*Mem.*3.11.3, *Oec.*8.10, (ἐπι-) Hdt.5.93; also ποθέσομαι Lys.8.18, Pl.*Phd.*98a: aor. ἐπόθεσα, Ep. πόθεσα, inf. ποθέσαι, Il.15.219, Od.2.375, 4.748, (προ-) Gal.*Thras.* 29; ἐπόθησα Pl.*Men.*84c, X.*HG*5.3.20, etc.; both forms in codd. of Hdt., ἐπόθησε 3.36, ἐπόθεσαν 9.22; ἐπόθεσα also in codd. of Isoc.4.122, 19.7: pf. πεπόθηκα *AP*11.417, S.E.*M.*11.139, etc.:—Med., S.*Tr.*103 (lyr.):—Pass., pf. πεπόθημαι Orph.*H.*81.3, etc.: (cf. πόθος fin.):—*long for, yearn after* (what is absent), *miss* or *regret* (what is lost), φθινύθεσκε..αὖθι μένων, ποθέεσκε δ' ἀϋτήν τε πτόλεμόν τε Il.1.492; πόθεόν γε μὲν ἀρχόν 2.703; τοίην γὰρ κεφαλὴν ποθέω Od.1.343; π. στρατιᾶς ὀφθαλμὸν ἐμᾶς Pi.*O.*6.16, cf. Hdt.3.36, 9.22, etc.; ἄνδρας πόλις ἥδε ποθεῖ *IG*1$^{2}$.945.10; ποθεῖν ποθοῦντα τήνδε γῆν στρατὸν λέγεις A.*Ag.*545; τὸν δ' ἐμὸν δῆμον ποθῶν Ar.*Ach.*33; ποθεῖς τὸν οὐ παρόντα Id.*Pl.*1127; αἱ κνῆμαι..σου..τὰς πέδας π. ib.276; ἡ χώρα αὐτὴ τὸ μὴ ὂν ποθήσει the place itself *will miss* what is absent, X.*Oec.*8.10; π. τὰς ἐν τῇ νεότητι ἡδονάς Pl.*R.*329a, cf. *Ti.*19a, And.1.70:—Pass., S.*Tr.*632, etc.; ὦ ποθουμένη (sc. Εἰρήνη) Ar.*Pax*586; ποθεῖ καὶ ποθεῖται Pl.*Phdr.*255d. 2. of things, *crave, require*, τί γὰρ π. τράπεζα; E.*Fr.*467; π. ἡ ἀπόκρισις ἐρώτησιν τοιάνδε Pl.*Smp.*204d, cf. *Prt.*352a. II. c. inf., *to be anxious* to do, E.*Hec.*1020, Antipho 5.64, X.*An.*6.4.8; τὸ νοσοῦν ποθεῖ σε ξυμπαραστάτην λαβεῖν my sickness *needs* to take thee.., S.*Ph.*675; ἆρα ἔτι ποθοῦμεν μὴ ἱκανῶς δεδεῖχθαι; *do we* still *feel* that it has not been satisfactorily proved? Pl.*Lg.*896a:—Pass., ποθεῖται..λεχθῆναι *requires* to be stated, Arist.*EN*1097$^{b}$23. III. abs., *love with fond regret*, οἱ δὲ ποθεῦντες ἐν ἤματι γηράσκουσι Theoc.12.2, cf. Luc.*Im.*22, etc. 2. τὸ ποθοῦν *longing, desire* (wrongly expld. by Sch. as = τὸ ποθούμενον), S.*Tr.*196. 3. Med. only in ib.103 (lyr.), ποθουμένᾳ φρήν the *longing* soul, cf. Eust.806.56. **-ή**, ἡ, = πόθος, c. gen., *longing, desire for..*, ἐμεῖο ποθὴν ἀπεόντος ἔχουσιν Il.6.362, cf. 14.368, etc.; σῇ ποθῇ *from longing after* thee, 19.321: in late Prose, π. ψυχροῦ ἠέρος Aret.*SA*1.7. 2. c. gen. rei, *want* of.., ξενίων Od.15.514,546. **-ημα**, ατος, τό, = πόθος, Hsch.

**ποθήνυτο**· προσήσθη, Hsch.

**ποθ-ήσιμος**, ον, *mourned by*, πάσαισι γυναιξί prob. in *IPE*1$^{2}$.527 (Cherson., i A.D.). **-ησις**, εως, ἡ, = ποθή, Sch.D Il.1.240. **-ητικός**, ή, όν, *disposed to long for*, τὸ ὀρεκτικὸν καὶ π. τινός Metop.ap.Stob.3.1.115. ⊛ **-ητός**, ή, όν, *longed for, regretted*, *IG*7.3434 (Chaeronea). **-ητύς**, ύος, ἡ, poet. for πόθησις, Opp.*C.*2.609. **-ήτωρ**, ορος, ὁ, *one who longs*, Man.4.120.

**πόθι**, interrog. Adv., poet. for ποῦ; *where?* Od.1.170: Trag. in lyr., S.*Tr.*98, E.*Ph.*1718: c. gen., π. Νύσας; Id.*Ba.*556; π. φρενός; Pi.*O.*10(11).2. 2. later for ποῖ; *whither?* A.R.1.242, *AP*7.566 (Maced.). B. **ποθί**, enclit. Adv., poet. for που, *anywhere, somewhere*, Il.10.8, etc.; εἴ π. S.*Aj.*886 (lyr.). 2. of Time, αἴ κέ π. Ζεὺς δῷσι if *ever*.., Il.1.128, Od.1.379, cf. Il.6.526. 3. to give an expression of indefiniteness, *haply, probably*, 10.273, Od.1.348, etc.

**ποθίερος**, ον, Dor. for προσ-, *dedicated*, τοῦ θεοῦ to him, *SIG*672.13 (Delph., ii B.C.); τὰ π. καὶ δαμόσια ib.671 *A* 4 (ibid., ii B.C.); μνᾶς π. τριάκοντα Ἀρχ.Δελτ.2.264 (Phocis).

**ποθίζω**, = προσίζω, *stick tightly*, of a plaster, Aret.*CA*2.3.

**πόθικες**, οἱ, (ποτί, ἱκ-νέ-ομαι) *relatives, kinsmen*, τοὶ 's ἄσιστα π. *IG* 5(2).159.17 (Tegea, v B.C.).

⊛ **ποθίκω** [ῑ], Dor. and Boeot. for προσήκω, *belong*, c. dat., *IG*9(1). 189.10 (Tithora, ii A.D.), 7.3083 (Lebad., iii B.C.), etc.

**ποθῑνός**, ή, όν, poet. for ποθεινός, *AP*7.403 (Marc.Arg.), 467 (Antip.).

**ποθόβλητος**, ον, *love-stricken*, Nonn.*D.*4.225, *AP*6.71 (Paul.Sil.), 9.620 (Id.). II. Act., *causing desire*, Nonn.*D.*15.235, al.

**πόθοδος**, v. πρόσοδος.

**ποθόδωμα**, ατος, τό, *proposal* of a decree, *Schwyzer*404.5 (Epirus, ii B.C.). II. pl., = πρόσοδοι, *revenues*, *IG*7.3172.161 (Orchom. Boeot., iii B.C.).

**ποθολκίς**, ίδος, ἡ, Dor. for προσολκίς, *leading-rein*, Hsch.

**ποθόρημι**, v. προσοράω.

⊛ **πόθος**, ὁ, *longing, yearning, regret* (for something absent or lost, cf. Pl.*Cra.*420a), mostly c. gen. obj., ἡνιόχοιο π. Il.17.439; ἀλλά μ' Ὀδυσσῆος πόθος αἴνυται Od.14.144; γλυκὺν π. Ἀργοῦς Pi.*P.*4.184; ἀνδρῶν πόθῳ A.*Pers.*133 (lyr.), cf. *Ag.*414 (lyr.); τοῦ βίου δ' οὐδεὶς π. S.*El.*822; ἔλαβε [αὐτοὺς] π...τῆς πόλιος Hdt.1.165; ἀποθανόντος αὐτοῦ π. ἔχειν πάντας Id.3.67, cf. S.*Ph.*646, Ar.*Ra.*66: with a possess. Pron., σὸς π. *yearning after* thee, Od.11.202, cf. Ar.*Pax*585; τῷμῷ π. S.*OT*969, cf. *OC*419: less freq. abs., τίς ὁ π. αὐτοὺς ἵκετ'; Id.*Ph.*601; σὺν πόθῳ γὰρ ἡ χάρις *desire* to give, Id.*OC*1106: pl., πότερα πόθοισι; was it *by reason of longing?* ib.333; τὰς ἐν τοῖς θρήνοις καὶ π. ἡδονάς Pl.*Phlb.*48a. II. *love, desire*, Hes.*Sc.*41 (who never uses ποθή), A.*Pr.*654, S.*Tr.*107 (lyr.), 368, Men.*Sam.*279, Theoc.2.143, etc.; πόθου κέντρα Pl.*Phdr.*253e; τὸν π. τὸν ἐξ ἐμοῦ S.*Tr.*631: generally, *desire*, πόθῳ θανεῖν (i.e. τοῦ θανεῖν) E.*Andr.*824; π. γυναικός Ar.*Ra.*55. 2. personified, A.*Supp.*1039 (lyr.), where Π. and Πειθώ are children of Κύπρις; Ἔρως καὶ Ἵμερος καὶ Π. Paus.1.43.6; Κύπρι Πόθων μῆτερ *AP*10.21 (Phld.). III. name of two plants, *larkspur, Delphinium Ajacis*, and *asphodel, Asphodelus ramosus* (used at funerals), Thphr.*HP*6.8.3. (ποθέω, ποθή, πόθος are cogn. with θέσσασθαι, q.v.)

⊛ **ποῖ**, interrog. Adv. *whither?* v.l. in Thgn.586 (leg. πῇ), freq. in Trag., Com., and Att. Prose; π. με χρὴ μολεῖν; S.*El.*812; π. τις φύγῃ; Ar.*Pl.*438; π. τις ἂν τράποιτο; π. τις τρέψεται; ib.374, *Th.*603; ellipt., π. Κλυταιμνήστρα; *whither has she gone?* A.*Ch.*882, cf. 405 codd. (lyr.). 2. c. gen., π. χθονός; π. γᾶς; *to what spot* of earth? Id.*Supp.*777 (lyr.), S.*Tr.*984 (anap.), etc.; π. φροντίδος; π. φρενῶν; π. γνώμης; Id.*OC*170 (anap.), 310, *Tr.*705; cf. κῆχος. II. *to what end?* πῶς τε καὶ π. τελευτᾷ; A.*Pers.*735, cf. *Ch.*732; ἃ δ' ὑπέσχεο π. καταθήσεις; S.*OC*227 (anap.). III. *how long?* ποῖ χρὴν ἀναμεῖναι; Ar.*Lys.*526. B. **ποι**, enclit. Adv. *somewhither*, S.*OC*26, Ar.*Pl.* 447, Pl.*R.*420a, etc. 2. Aeol. = που (q.v.). C. **ποί**, Dor. = πρός, v. ποτί. D. **ποῖ** shortd. for ποῖον, Ar.*Lys.*193, 383 (cf. ποίαν monosyll. in *V.*1369 and v. ποῖος I. 2).

**ποία**, v. πόα. **ποιάεις**, v. ποιήεις.

**ποιανθής**, ές, *luxuriant in grass*, νῆσος Orph.*A.*1050.

**ποιάριον**, v. ποάριον. **ποιγράφω**, v. προσγράφω. **ποιδέω**, v. προσδέω (A). ⊛ **ποιδέομαι**, v. προσδέομαι.

⊛ **ποιέω**, Dor. ποιϝέω *IG*4.800 (Troezen), etc.: Ep. impf. ποίεον Il. 20.147; contr. ποίει 18.482; Ion. ποιέεσκον Hdt.1.36, 4.78: fut. ποιήσω: aor. ἐποίησα, Ep. ποίησα Il.18.490: pf. πεποίηκα:—Med., Ion. impf. ποιεέσκετο Hdt.7.119: fut. ποιήσομαι Il.9.397: in pass. sense, Hp.*Decent.*11, Arist.*Metaph.*1021$^{a}$23: aor. ἐποιησάμην, Ep. ποι- Od.5.251, al.: pf. πεποίημαι in med. sense, And.4.22, Decr.ap.D. 18.29:—Pass., fut. ποιηθήσομαι (μετα-) D.23.62, v. supr.; πεποιήσομαι Hp.*Mul.*1.11, 37: aor. ἐποιήθην Hdt.2.159, etc. (used as Med. only in compd. προσ-): pf. πεποίημαι Il.6.56, etc.:—Att. ποῶ (*EM* 679.24), etc., is guaranteed by metre in Trag. and Com., as ποῶ S. *OT*918, ποεῖν Id.*Tr.*385, ποεῖς Ar.*Ach.*410, etc., and found in cod. Laur. of S., cod. Rav. of Ar., also *IG*1$^{2}$.39.6 (ποήσω), 82.9 (ποεῖ), 154.7 (ἐποησάτην), etc.; but ποι- is always written before -οι, -ου, -ω in Inscrr.: πο- also in Aeol. πόημι πόης πόει *PBouriant*8.71,75, Sapph. *Supp.*1.9, al., and Arc. ποέντω, = ποιούντων, *IG*5(2).6.9 (Tegea, iv B.C.); cf. ποιητής.

Used in two general senses, *make* and *do*.

A. *make, produce*, first of something material, as manufactures, works of art, etc. (opp. πράττειν, Pl.*Chrm.*163b), in Hom. freq. of building, π. δῶμα, τύμβον, Il.1.608, 7.435; εἴδωλον Od.4.796; π. πύλας ἐν [πύργοις] Il.7.339; of smith's work, π. σάκος ib.222; ἐν [σάκεϊ] ποίει δαίδαλα πολλά 18.482, cf. 490,573: freq. in Inscrr. on works of art, Πολυμήδης ἐποίϝηἑ (=ἐποίησε) Ἀργεῖος *SIG*5 (vi B.C., cf. *Class.Phil.*20.139); Θεόπροπος ἐποίει Αἰγινάτας *SIG*18 (vi/v B.C.), etc.; ἐποίησε Τερψικλῆς ib.3*b*(Milet., vi B.C.), etc.; τίς.. τὴν λίθον ταύτην τέκτων ἐποίει; Herod.4.22; εἵματα ἀπὸ ξύλων πεποιημένα *made* from trees, i.e. of cotton, Hdt.7.65; ναὸν ἀπὸ τοῦ ἱεροῦ ἀργυρίου X.*An.*5.3.9; πλοῖα ἐκ τῆς ἀκάνθης ποιεύμενα Hdt.2.96; καρβάτιναι πεποιημέναι ἐκ βοῶν X.*An.*4.5.14: c. gen. materiae, πωρίνου λίθου π. τὸν νηόν Hdt.5.62; ἔρυμα λίθων λογάδην πεποιημένον Th.4.31; φοίνικος αἱ θύραι πεποιημέναι X.*Cyr.*7.5.22: rarely ποιεῖσθαί τινι *to be made with*.., Longus 1.4; also τῶν τὰ κέρεα.. οἱ πήχεες ποιεῦνται the horns of which *are made* into the sides of the lyre, Hdt.4.192; also δέρμα εἰς περικεφαλαίας πεποίηται Sch.Patm.D. in *BCH*1.144:—Med., *make for oneself*, as of bees, οἰκία ποιήσωνται *build them* houses, Il.12.168, cf. 5.735, Od.5.251,259, Hes.*Op.*503; [ῥεῖθρον] π., of a river, Thphr. *HP*3.1.5; also, *have* a thing *made*, *get* it *made*, ὀβελούς Hdt.2.135; στεφάνους οὓς ἐποιησάμην τῷ χορῷ D.21.16, cf. X.*An.*5.3.5; τὸν Ἀπόλλω, i.e. a statue of A., Pl.*Ep.*361a; αὑτοῦ εἰκόνας Plu.*Them.*5, cf. *Inscr.Prien.*25.9 (iii B.C.?). 2. *create, bring into existence*, γένος ἀνθρώπων χρύσεον Hes.*Op.*110, cf. *Th.*161, 579, etc.; ὁ ποιῶν *the creator*, Pl.*Ti.*76c; ἕτερον Φίλιππον ποιήσετε D.4.11:—Med., *beget*, υἱόν And.1.124; ἔκ τινος Id.4.22; παῖδας ποιεῖσθαι, = παιδοποιεῖσθαι, X.*Cyr.*5.3.19, D.57.43; *conceive*, παιδίον π. ἔκ τινος Pl.*Smp.*203b:—Act. in this sense only in later Gr., Plu.2.312a; of the woman, παιδίον ποιῆσαι ib.145d. 3. generally, *produce*, ὕδωρ π., of Zeus, Ar.*V.*261: impers., ἐὰν πλείω ποιῇ ὕδατα, = ἐὰν ὕῃ, Thphr.*CP*1.19.3; π. γάλα, of certain kinds of food, Arist.*HA*522$^{b}$32; ἄρρεν π., of an egg, Ael.*VH*1.15; μέλι ἄριστον π., of Hymettus, Str.9.1.23; π. καρπόν, of trees, *Ev.Matt.*3.10 (metaph. in religious sense, ib.8); of men, κριθὰς π. *grow* barley, Ar.*Pax* 1322; π. σίτου μεδίμνους D.42.20; π. πενίαν, πλοῦτον, of the stars, Plot.2.3.1. b. Math., *make, produce*, τομήν, σχῆμα, ὀρθὰς γωνίας, Archim. *Sph.Cyl.*1.16,38, *Con.Sph.*12; ὁ Α τὸν Γ πολλαπλασιάσας τὸν Η πεποίηκεν Euc.7.19:—Pass., πεποιήσθω ὡς.. *let it be contrived* that.., Archim. *Sph.Cyl.*2.6. c. *postulate, imply*, ἡ προσθήκη ἀφαίρεσιν καὶ ἔλλειψιν ποιεῖ Plot.3.9.3. d. π. τὸ πρόβλημα *effect a solution of* the problem, Apollon.Perg.*Con.*2.49,51; π. τὸ ἐπίταγμα *fulfil, satisfy* the required condition, Archim.*Sph.Cyl.*1.2,3. 4. after Hom., of Poets, *compose, write*, π. διθύραμβον, ἔπεα, Hdt.1.23, 4.14; π. θεογονίην Ἕλλησι Id.2.53; π. Φαίδραν, Σατύρους, Ar.*Th.*153,157; π. κωμῳδίαν, τραγῳδίαν, etc., Pl.*Smp.*223d; παλινῳδίαν Isoc.10.64, Pl.*Phdr.*243b, etc.; ποιήματα Id.*Phd.*60d: abs., *write poetry, write as a poet*, ὀρθῶς π. Hdt.3.38; ἐν τοῖσι ἔπεσι π. Id.4.16, cf. Pl.*Ion*534b: folld. by a quotation, ἐπόησάς ποτε.. Ar.*Th.*193; εἴς τινα Pl.*Phd.*61b; περὶ θεῶν Id.*R.*383a, etc. b. *represent in poetry*, Ὅμηρον Ἀχιλλέα πεποιηκέναι ἀμείνω Ὀδυσσέως Pl.*Hp.Mi.*369c, cf. 364c, *Smp.*174b; ποιήσας τὸν Ἀχιλλέα λέγοντα *having represented* Achilles saying, Plu.2.105b, cf. 25d, Pl. *Grg* 525d,e, Arist.*Po.*1453$^{b}$29. c. *describe in verse*, θεὸν ἐν ἔπεσιν Pl.*R.*379a; ἐποίησα μύθους τοὺς Αἰσώπου *put* them *into verse*, Id.*Phd.* 61b; μῦθον Lycurg.100. d. *invent*, καινοὺς θεούς Pl.*Euthphr.*3b; ὑπὸ ποιητέω τινὸς ποιηθὲν [τοὔνομα] Hdt.3.115; πεποιημένα ὀνόματα Arist.*Rh.*1404$^{b}$29, cf. *Po.*1457$^{b}$2; opp. αὐτοφυῆ, κύρια, D.H.*Is.*7, *Pomp.*2. II. *bring about, cause*, τελευτήν Od.1.250; γαλήνην 5.452; φόβον Il.12.432; σιωπὴν παρὰ πάντων X.*HG*6.3.10; τέρψιν τοῖς θεωμένοις Id.*Mem.*3.10.8; αἰσχύνην τῇ πόλει Isoc.7.54, etc.; also of things, ἄνεμοι αὐτοὶ μὲν οὐχ ὁρῶνται· ἃ δὲ ποιοῦσι φανερά X.*Mem.*4.3.14; ταὐτὸν ἐποίει αὐτοῖς νικᾶν τε μαχομένοις καὶ μηδὲ μάχεσθαι Th.7.6, cf. 2.89. b. c. acc. et inf., *cause* or *bring about* that.., σε θεοὶ ποίησαν ἱκέσθαι [ἐς] οἶκον Od.23.258; π. τινὰ κλύειν S.*Ph.*926; π. τινὰ βλέψαι Ar.*Pl.*459, cf. 746; π. τινὰ τριηραρχεῖν Id.*Eq.*912, cf. *Av.*59; π. τινὰ αἰσχύνεσθαι, κλάειν, ἀπορεῖν, etc., X.*Cyr.*4.5.48, 2.2.13, Pl.*Tht.*149a, etc.: with ὥστε inserted, X.*Cyr.*3.2.29, Ar.*Eq.*351, etc.: folld. by a relat. clause, π. ὅκως ἔσται ἡ Κύπρος ἐλευθέρη Hdt.5.109, cf. 1.209; ὡς ἂν.. εἰδείην ἐποίουν X.*Cyr.*6.3.18:—also Med., ἐποιήσατο ὡς ἐν ἀσφαλεῖ εἶεν ib.6.1.23. 2. *procure*, π. ἄδειάν τε καὶ κάθοδόν τινι Th.8.76; ὁ νόμος π. τὴν κληρονομίαν τισί Is.11.1; λόγος ἀργύριον τῷ λέγοντι π. *gets* him money, D.10.76:—Med., *procure for oneself, gain*, κλέος αὐτῇ ποιεῖτ' Od.2.126; ἄδειαν Th.6.60; τιμωρίαν ἀπό τινων Id.1.25; τὸν βίον ἀπὸ γεωργίας X.*Oec.*6.11, cf. Th.1.5. 3. of sacrifices, festivals, etc., *celebrate*, π. ἱρά Hdt.9.19, cf. 2.49 (Act. and Pass.); π. τὴν θυσίαν τῷ Ποσειδῶνι X.*HG*4.5.1; π. Ἴσθμια ib.4.5.2; τῇ θεῷ ἑορτὴν δημοτελῆ π. Th.2.15; παννυχίδα π. Pl.*R.*328a; π. σάββατα *observe* the Sabbath, Lxx *Ex.*31.16; π. ταφάς, of a public funeral, Pl. *Mx.*234b; π. ἐπαρήν *SIG*38.30 (Teos, v B.C.); also of political assemblies, π. ἐκκλησίαν Ar.*Eq.*746, Th.1.139; π. μυστήρια Id.6.28 (Pass.); ξύλλογον σφῶν αὐτῶν Id.1.67:—Med., ἀγορὴν ποιήσατο Il.8.2; ἣν θυσίην τις ποιῆται Hdt.6.57 (v.l.); δημοσίᾳ ταφὰς ἐποιήσαντο Th.2.34; π. ἀγῶνα Id.4.91; π. ἐκκλησίαν τοῖς Θρᾳξὶ περὶ μισθοῦ Ar.*Ach.*169. 4. of war and peace, πόλεμον π. *cause* or *give rise to* a war, πόλεμον ἡμῖν ἀντ' εἰρήνης πρὸς Λακεδαιμονίους π. Is.11.48; but π. ποιησόμενοι *about to make* war (on one's own part), X.*An.*5.5.24; εἰρήνην π. *bring about* a peace (for others), Ar.*Pax* 1199; σπονδὰς π. X.*An.*4.3.14; ξυμμαχίαν ποιῆσαι Th.2.29; but εἰρήνην ποιεῖσθαι *make* peace (for oneself), And.3.11; σπονδὰς ποιήσασθαι Th.1.28, etc.:—Pass., ἐπεποίητο συμμαχίη Hdt.1.77, etc. 5. freq. in Med. with Nouns periphr. for the Verb derived from the Noun, μύθον ποιήσασθαι ἐπισχεσίην *submit* a plea, Od.21.71; ποιέεσθαι ὁδοιπορίην, for ὁδοιπορέειν, Hdt.2.29; π. ὁδόν Id.7.42,110,112, etc.; π. πλόον, for πλέειν, Id.6.95, cf. Antipho 5.21; π. κομιδήν, for κομίζεσθαι, Hdt.6.95; θῶμα π. τὴν ἐργασίην, for θωμάζειν, Id.1.68; ὀργὴν π., for ὀργίζεσθαι, Id.3.25; λήθην π. τι, for λανθάνεσθαί τινος, Id.1.127; βουλὴν π., for βουλεύεσθαι, Id. 6.101; συμβολὴν π., for συμβάλλεσθαι, Id.9.45; τὰς μάχας π., for μάχεσθαι, S.*El.*302, etc.; καταφυγὴν π., for καταφεύγειν, Antipho 1.4; ἀγῶνα π., for ἀγωνίζεσθαι, Th.2.89; π. λόγον [τινός] *make* account of.., Hdt.7.156; but τοὺς λόγους π. *hold* a conference, Th.1.128; also simply for λέγειν, Lys.25.2, cf. Pl.*R.*527a, etc.; also π. δι' ἀγγέλου, π. διὰ χρηστηρίων, *communicate* by a messenger, an oracle, Hdt.6.4, 8.134. III. with Adj. as predic., *make, render* so and so, ποιῆσαί τινα ἄφρονα *make* one senseless, Od.23.12; [δῶρα] ὄλβια ποιεῖν *make* them blest, i.e. prosper them, 13.42, cf. Il.12.30; τοὺς Μήδους ἀσθενεῖς π. X.*Cyr.*1.5.2, etc.; χρήσιμον ἐξ ἀχρήστου π. Pl.*R.* 411b: with a Subst., ποιῆσαι ἀθύρματα *make* into playthings, Il. 15.363; ποιεῖν τινα βασιλῆα Od.1.387; ταμίην ἀνέμων 10.21; γέροντα 16.456; ἄκοιτίν τινι Il.24.537; γαμβρὸν ἐόν Hes.*Th.*818; [μύρμηκας] ἄνδρας π. [καὶ] γυναῖκας Id.*Fr.*76.5; πολιήτας π. τινάς Hdt.7.156; Ἀθηναῖον π. τινά Th.2.29, etc.; π. τινὰ παράδειγμα Isoc.4.39: hence, *appoint, instal*, τὸν Μωϋσῆν καὶ τὸν Ἀαρών Lxx 1*Ki.*12.6; δώδεκα *Ev. Marc.*3.14:—Med., ποιεῖσθαί τινα ἑταῖρον *make* him *one's* friend, Hes. *Op.*707, cf. 714; π. τινὰ ἄλοχον or ἄκοιτιν *take* her *to oneself* as wife, Il.3.409, 9.397, cf. Od.5.120, etc.; π. τινὰ παῖδα *make* him *one's* son, i.e. *adopt* him as son, Il.9.495, etc.; θετὸν παῖδα π. *adopt* a son, Hdt. 6.57: without υἱόν, *adopt*, ἐπειδὴ οὐκ ἦσαν αὐτῷ παῖδες ἄρρενες, π. Λεωκράτη D.41.3, cf. 39.6,33, 44.25, Pl.*Lg.*923c, etc.; π. τινὰ θυγατέρα Hdt.4.180: generally, ἅπαντας ἢ σῦς ἠὲ λύκους π. Od.10.433; π. τινὰ πολίτην Isoc.9.54; μαθητήν Pl.*Cra.*428b; τὰ κρέα π. εὔτυκα Hdt. 1.119; τὰ ἔπεα ἀπόρρητα π. *making* them a secret, Id.9.45, etc.; also ἑωυτοῦ ποιέεται τό..ἔργον *makes* it *his own*, Id.1.129; μηδ' ἃ μὴ 'θιγες ποιοῦ σεαυτῆς S.*Ant.*547. IV. *put* in a certain place or condition, etc., ἐμοὶ Ζεὺς.. ἐνὶ φρεσὶν ὧδε νόημα ποίησ' Od.14.274; σφῶϊν ὧδε θεῶν τις ἐνὶ φρεσὶ ποιήσειεν Il.13.55; αἱ γὰρ τοῦτο θεοὶ ποιήσειαν ἐπὶ νόον νησιώτῃσι Hdt.1.27, cf. 71; ἐν αἰσχύνῃ π. τὴν πόλιν D.18.136; τὰς ναῦς ἐπὶ τοῦ ξηροῦ π. Th.1.109; ἔξω κεφαλὴν π. Hdt.5.33; ἔξω βελῶν τὴν τάξιν π. X.*Cyr.*4.1.3; ἐμαυτὸν ὡς πορρωτάτω π. τῶν ὑποψιῶν Isoc.3.37; of troops, *form* them, ὡς ἂν κράτιστα.. X.*An.*5.2.11, cf. 3.4.21; in politics, ἐς ὀλίγους τὰς ἀρχὰς π. Th.8.53; and in war, π. Θετταλίαν ὑπὸ Φιλίππῳ *bring* it under his power, D.18.48; μήτε τοὺς νόμους μήθ' ὑμᾶς αὐτοὺς ἐπὶ τοῖς λέγουσι π. Id.58.61:—Med., ποιέεσθαι ὑπ' ἑωυτῷ Hdt.1.201, cf. 5.103, etc.; ὑπὸ χεῖρα X.*Ages.*1.22; π τινὰς ἐς φυλακήν, τὰ τῶν ξυμμάχων ἐς ἀσφάλειαν, Th.3.3, 8.1; τινὰς ἐς τὸ συμμαχικόν Hdt.9.106; τὰ λεπτὰ πλοῖα ἐντὸς π. *put* the small vessels in the middle, Th.2.83, cf. 6.67; π. τινὰ ἐκποδών (v. ἐκποδών); ὄπισθεν π. τὸν ποταμόν X.*An.* 1.10.9. 2. Math., *multiply*, π. τὰ ιβ' ἐπὶ τὰ ε', τὰ ζ' ἐφ' ἑαυτὰ π., Hero *Metr.*1.8, 2.14. V. Med., *deem, consider, reckon* a thing as.., συμφορὴν ποιέεσθαί τι *take* it for a misfortune, Hdt.1.83, 6.61; δεινὸν π. τι *esteem* it a grievous thing, *take* it ill, Id.1.127, etc. (rarely in Act., δεινὰ π. 2.121.ε', Th.5.42); μέγα π. c. inf., *deem* it a great matter that.., Hdt.8.3, cf. 3.42, etc.; μεγάλα π. ὅτι.. Id.1.119; ἕρμαιον π. τι *count* it clear gain, Pl.*Grg.*489c; οὐκέτι ἀνασχετὸν π. τι Th.1.118: freq. with Preps., δι' οὐδενὸς π. *deem* of no account, S.*OC*584; ἐν ἐλαφρῷ, ἐν ὁμοίῳ π., Hdt.1.118, 7.138; ἐν σμικρῷ μέρει S.*Ph.*498; ἐν ὀλιγωρίᾳ Th.4.5; ἐν ὀργῇ D.1.16; ἐν νόμῳ π. *consider* as lawful, Hdt. 1.131; ἐν ἀδείῃ π. *consider* as safe, Id.9.42; παρ' ὀλίγον π. τι X. *An.*6.6.11; περὶ πολλοῦ π., Lat. *magni facere*, Lys.1.1, etc.; περὶ πλείονος, περὶ πλείστου π., Id.14.40, Pl.*Ap.*21e, etc.; περὶ ὀλίγου, περὶ ἐλάττονος, Isoc.17.58, 18.63; περὶ παντὸς Id.2.15 (rarely πολλοῦ π. τι Pl.*Prt.*328d); πρὸ πολλοῦ π. c. inf., Isoc.5.138. VI. *put the case, assume* that.., ποιήσας ἀν' ὀγδώκοντα ἄνδρας ἐνεῖναι Hdt.7.184, cf. 186, X.*An.*5.7.9: without inf., ἐν ἑκάστῃ ψυχῇ ποιήσωμεν περιστερεῶνά τινα (sc. εἶναι) Pl.*Tht.*197d:—Pass., πεποιήσθω δή *be it assumed* then, ib.e; οἱ φιλοσοφώτατοι ποιούμενοι *those who are reputed*.., Id. *R.*498a, cf. 538c, 573b:—but for τὸν φιλόσοφον ποιώμεθα νομίζειν ib.581d read τί οἰώμεθα..; VII. of Time, οὐ π. χρόνον *make* no long time, i.e. not to delay, D.19.163 codd.; μακρότερον ποιεῖς *you are taking* too long, *PCair.Zen.*48.4 (iii B.C.); μέσας π. νύκτας *let* midnight *come*, Pl.*Phlb.*50d, cf. *AP*11.85 (Lucill.); ἔξω μέσων νυκτῶν π. τὴν ὥραν *put off* the time of business to past midnight, D.54.26; τὴν νύκτα ἐφ' ὅπλοις ποιεῖσθαι *spend* it under arms, Th.7.28 (s.v.l.); ποιήσουσιν ἐν πλοίῳ ἔτη πολλὰ Lxx *Pr.*13.23, cf. *To.*10.7; δύο ἡμέρας ποιεῖ ἐν τῷ Ἀνουβιείῳ *UPZ*70.21 (ii B.C.), cf. *PSI*4.362.15 (iii B.C.); τὰς ἡμέρας ἐν τοῖς ὕδασι π. D.S.1.35; *tarry, stay*, μῆνας τρεῖς *Act.Ap.* 20.3, cf. *AP*11.330 (Nicarch.). VIII. in later Greek, *sacrifice*, μοσχάριον Lxx *Ex.*29.36; καρπώσεις ὑπέρ τινος ib.*Jb.*42.8: without acc., π. Ἀστάρτῃ *sacrifice* to Ashtoreth, ib.3*Ki.*11.33. IX. *make ready, prepare*, as food, μοσχάριον ib.*Ge.*18.7 sq.; π. τὸν μύστακα *trim* it, ib.2*Ki.*19.24(25). X. ποιεῖν βασιλέα *play* the king, ib.3*Ki.*20 (21).7.

B. *do*, much like πράσσω, οὐδὲν ἂν ὧν νυνὶ πεποίηκεν ἔπραξεν D. 4.5; περὶ ὧν πράττει καὶ μέλλει ποιεῖν Id.8.2, cf. 18.62; ἄριστα πεποίηται Il.6.56; πλείονα χρηστὰ περὶ τὴν πόλιν Ar.*Eq.*811; τὰ δίκαια τοῖς εὐεργέταις D.20.12; ἅμα ἔπος τε καὶ ἔργον ἐποίεε Hdt.3.134 fin.; ποιέειν Σπαρτιητικά *act* like a Spartan, Id.5.40; οὗτος τί ποιεῖς; A. *Supp.*911, etc.; τὸ προσταχθὲν π. S.*Ph.*1010; π. τὴν μουσικὴν *practise* it, Pl.*Phd.*60e, etc.; πᾶν or πάντα π., v. πᾶς D. III. 2, etc.: Math., ὅπερ ἔδει ποιῆσαι, = *Q.E.F.*, Euc.1.1, etc. 2. c. dupl. acc., *do* something to another, κακὰ or ἀγαθὰ ποιεῖν τινα, first in Hdt.3.75, al.; ἀγαθόν, κακὸν π. τινά, Isoc.16.50, etc.; μεγάλα τὴν πόλιν ἀγαθὰ Din.1.17; also εὖ ποιεῖν τὸν εὖ ποιοῦντα X.*Mem.*2.3.8; τὴν ἐκείνου (sc. χώραν) κακῶς π. D.1.18; in Lxx with Prep., π. κακὸν μετά τινων *Ge.* 26.29; ταῦτα τοῦτον ἐποίησα Hdt.1.115; κοὐκ οἶδ' ὅ τι χρῆμά με ποιεῖς Ar.*V.*697, cf. *Nu.*259; also of things, ἀργύριον τωὐτὸ τοῦτο ἐποίεε he *did* this same thing with silver, Hdt.4.166: less freq. c. dat. pers., τῷ τεθνεῶτι μηδὲν τῶν νομιζομένων π. Is.4.19; ἵππῳ τἀναντία X.*Eq*.9.12 codd., cf. Ar.*Nu*.388, D.29.37: c. dat. rei, τί ποιήσωμεν κιβωτῷ; Lxx 1*Ki*.5.8:—in Med., φίλα ποιέεσθαί τισι Hdt.2.152, 5.37. 3. with an Adv., ὧδε ποίησον *do* thus, Id.1.112; πῶς ποιήσεις; how *will you act?* S.*OC*652; πῶς δεῖ ποιεῖν περὶ θυσίας X.*Mem*.1.3.1; ποίει ὅπως βούλει Id.*Cyr*.1.4.9; μὴ ἄλλως π. Pl.*R*.328d; πρὸς τοὺς πολεμίους πῶς ποιήσουσιν; ib.469b; ὀρθῶς π. ib.403e; εὖ, κακῶς π. τινά, v. supr. 2: freq. c. part., εὖ ἐποίησας ἀπικόμενος Hdt.5.24, cf. Pl.*Phd*.60c; καλῶς ποιεῖς προνοῶν X.*Cyr*.7.4.13; οἷον ποιεῖς ἡγούμενος Pl.*Chrm*.166c; καλῶς ποιῶν almost Adverbial, καλῶς γ', ἔφη, ποιῶν σύ Id.*Smp*.174e; καλῶς ποιοῦντες..πράττετε D.20.110, cf. 1.28; εὖ ποιοῦν *fortunately*, Id.23.143. 4. in Prose (rarely in Poetry, A.*Pr*.935), used in the second clause, to avoid repeating the Verb of the first, ἐρώτησον αὐτούς· μᾶλλον δ' ἐγὼ τοῦθ' ὑπὲρ σοῦ ποιήσω I will *do* this for you, D.18.52, cf. 292, Hdt.5.97, Is.7.35. II. abs., *to be doing, act*, ποιέειν ἢ παθεῖν πρόκειται ἀγών Hdt.7.11; ποιεῖν, as a category, opp. πάσχειν, Arist.*Cat*.$2^{a}3$, cf. *GC*$322^{b}11$, *Ph*.$225^{b}13$. b. of medicine, *operate, be efficacious*, Pl.*Phd*.117b; λουτρὰ κάλλιστα ποιοῦντα πρὸς νόσους Str.5.3.6; πρὸς στραγγουρίαν, πρὸς τοὺς δαιμονιζομένους, Thphr.*HP*7.14.1, Ps.-Plu.*Fluv*.16.2: freq. in Dsc., πρὸς ἐπιληπτικούς 1.6, al.; εἰς τὰ αὐτά 2.133: c. dat., στομαχικοῖς Gal.13.183: abs., ἄκρως π. ib.265; also of charms, *PMag.Osl*.1.361. 2. Th. has a peculiar usage, ἡ εὔνοια παρὰ πολὺ ἐποίει μᾶλλον ἐς τοὺς Λακεδαιμονίους good-will *made* greatly for, on the side of, the L., 2.8: impers., ἐπὶ πολὺ ἐποίει τῆς δόξης τοῖς μὲν ἠπειρώταις εἶναι, τοῖς δέ.. it was the general character of the one to be landsmen, of the others.., 4.12: the former passage is imitated by Arr.*An*.2.2.3, App.*BC*1.82, D.C.57.6.

C. Med., = προσποιέομαι, *pretend*, c. inf., Zos.2.14.1, Procop.*Arc*.10. (ποιϝέω perh. from *ποι-ϝό-ς (in κλινοποιός, νεωποιός, τραπεζοποιός, etc.) 'builder', 'maker', cf. Skt. *cinóti, cáyati* 'arrange in order', 'build'.)

**ποίη**, ἡ, v. πόα.

**ποιη-βόρος**, ον, (βορά) *grass-eating*, Oenom.ap.Eus.*PE*5.23. **-εις**, εσσα, εν, *grassy*, Ἁλίαρτος, Δουλίχιον, ἄγκεα, Il.2.503, Od.16.396, 4.337: Dor. **ποιάεις** S.*OC*158 (lyr.); Pi. has ποιάεντα (trisyll.) στεφανώματα *N*.5.54.

⊛ **ποί-ημα**, ατος, τό, (ποιέω) *anything made* or *done*: hence, I. *work*, π. χρύσεα, χάλκεα καὶ σιδήρεα, Hdt.4.5, 7.84, cf. 2.135; Γλαύκου τοῦ Χίου π. Id.1.25; of the works of Daedalus, Pl.*Men*.97e; π. ἐραστοῦ a lover's *invention*, Id.*R*.474e; *product*, of land formed by silting-up of rivers, Arr.*An*.5.6.4 (pl.). 2. *poem*, Cratin.186, Pl.*Phd*.60d, *Ly*.221d; τὰ μετὰ μέτρου π. Isoc.2.7, 15.45; π. εἰς τὰς Μούσας *IG*7.1773.17 (Thespiae, ii A.D.): pl., of single *verses*, = ἔπη, D.H.1.41, *Comp*.3. b. *poetical*, esp. *metrical, form*, περὶ ποιήματος, title of work by Hephaestio. 3. *fiction*, Arr.*An*.5.6.5 (pl.). 4. *onomatopoeic word*, Hsch. s.v. μάματα. II. *deed, act*, opp. πάθημα, Pl.*R*.437b (pl.), *Sph*.248b; π. πονηρά Lxx 2*Es*.9.13. (Written ποιϝήματα (in signf. I. 1) in *Mnemos*.57.208 (Argos, vi B.C.).) **-ημᾰτικός**, ή, όν, *poetical*, Plu.2.744f. **-ημάτιον**, τό, Dim. of ποίημα, Id.*Cic*.2, Longin.33.5. **-ημᾰτογράφος** [γρᾰ], ὁ, *writer of poems*, Sch.Il.22.51. **-ηματοκόπος**, gloss on μιξίαμβος, Hsch.

**ποιηρός**, ά, όν, = ποιήεις, E.*Ba*.1048, *Cyc*.45, 61 (both lyr.).

**ποι-ησείω**, Desiderat. of ποιέω, *desire to do*, Hdn.*Epim*.249. **-ησις**, εως, ἡ, *fabrication, creation, production*, opp. πρᾶξις (*action*, v. Arist.*EN*$1140^{a}2$, *Pol*.$1254^{a}5$), [μύρου] Hdt.3.22; νεῶν Th.3.2, etc.; ἡ τῶν ζῴων π. Pl.*Smp*.197a; ἡ τῶν μελῶν π. Id.*Grg*.449d; μίμησις π. τίς ἐστιν, εἰδώλων μέντοι Id.*Sph*.265b, etc.; αἱ ὑπὸ πάσαις ταῖς τέχναις ἐργασίαι ποιήσεις εἰσί Id.*Smp*.205b. 2. of Poetry, ἡ τῶν διθυράμβων π., τῆς τραγῳδίας, τῶν ἐπῶν, Pherecr.145.10, Pl.*Grg*.502a,b, *R*.394c: abs., *art of poetry*, οἱ ἐν π. γενόμενοι Hdt.2.82, cf. Ar.*Ra*.868, etc.; οὕτως..ἀταλαιπώρως ἡ π. διέκειτο Id.*Fr*.254; οἱ ἄκροι τῆς π. ἑκατέρας, i.e. tragedy and comedy, Pl.*Tht*.152e; ᾠδαὶ καὶ ἡ ἄλλη π. Id.*Phdr*.245a; π. ψιλὴ ἢ ἐν ᾠδῇ ib.278c. b. *poetic composition, poem*, ἐς ποίησιν ἐσενείκασθαι Hdt.2.23, cf. Th.1.10, etc.; περὶ ὧν Ὅμηρος τὴν π. πεποίηκεν Pl.*Ion*531d: pl., Id.*Lg*.829e. II. = εἰσποίησις, *adoption*, in pl., Is.7.1, D.44.7, al.; κατὰ ποίησιν ibid., *Michel*836.5 (Didyma, ii B.C.); ποιήσει υἱοί D.H.4.7; τῇ παρ' ὑμῶν π. πολίτης D.20.30. 2. in collect. sense, *those adopted*, τῆς π. ἣν ἐκεῖνος ἐποιήσατο Id.44.61. III. *method of procedure*, in Magic, *PMag.Par*.1.1248. **-ησῐφάρμᾰκον**, gloss on πελεθρόνιον, Hsch. **-ητέος**, α, ον, *to be made* or *done*, Hdt.1.191, 7.15, Hp.*Art*.27, Pl.*R*.361c; εὐλάβειά τινος π. Antipho3.3.11; τὸ π., = τί δεῖ ποιεῖν, Th.4.99. II. ποιητέον, *one must make* or *do*, And.3.16, Onos.22.2, etc.:—from Med., *one must deem*, περὶ πολλοῦ π. τὸ ἑαυτὸν γιγνώσκειν X.*Mem*.4.2.30. **-ητής**, οῦ, ὁ, *maker*, μηχανημάτων Id.*Cyr*.1.6.38; κλίνης Pl.*R*.597d; τὸν π. καὶ πατέρα τοῦδε τοῦ παντός Id.*Ti*.28c; ζῴων, of the painter, Id.*Sph*.234a; *inventor*, θεῶν Id.*Euthphr*.3b; νόμων *lawgiver*, Id.*Def*.415b. 2. *workman*, *PSI*4.388.8, al. (iii B.C., pl.). II. *composer of a poem, author*, π. κωμῳδίας Pl.*Lg*.935e; π. καινῶν δραμάτων, τραγῳδιῶν κτλ. *SIG*1079.2, al. (Magn. Mae., ii/i B.C.): abs., *poet*, Hdt.2.53, Ar.*Ra*.96, 1030, Pl.*Ion*534b, etc.; Homer was called ὁ π., Pl.*Grg*.485d, Arist.*Rh*.$1365^{a}11$, $1380^{b}28$, Teles p.34 H., Plb.12.21.3, Str.1.1.10, A.D.*Synt*.26.19, etc.; so also Hesiod, Pl.*Lg*.901a; and others, Id.*Thg*.125e, D.Chr.78.44. b. *composer* of music, Pl.*Lg*.812d. 2. *author* of a speech, opp. deliverer of it, π. λόγων Id.*Euthd*.305b, cf. *Phdr*.234e, 278e, Alcid.*Soph*.34, Isoc.15.192. (Written ποητής *IG*$2^{2}$.2319.65, *SIG*711*L*35 (Delph., ii B.C.), etc.) ⊛ **-ητῐκεύομαι**, Pass., *to be a poetic invention*, Anon.*Incred*.3. II. Med., *speak poetically*, Eust.79.12, Sch.Arat.696, al. ⊛ **-ητικός**, ή, όν, *capable of making, creative, productive*, opp. πρακτικός (*active*, Arist.*EN*$1140^{a}4$), τινος Id.*Top*.$137^{a}4$, Pl.*Def*.411d; ἡδονῶν Epicur.*Sent*.8: abs., αἱ π. ἐπιστῆμαι, = αἱ τέχναι, the *Productive* Arts, Arist.*MM*$1216^{b}17$, cf. *Pol*.$1254^{a}2$, D.L.3.84; πᾶσαι αἱ τέχναι καὶ αἱ π. ἐπιστῆμαι Arist.*Metaph*.$1046^{b}3$; ἡ -κή *creativity*, Pl.*Sph*.265b; τὰ π. *efficient causes*, Plot.6.3.18,28. Adv. -κῶς (sc. τῆς ὑγιείας) *so as to produce..*, Arist.*Top*.$106^{b}36$, cf. Procl. *in Alc*.p.52 C. 2. of persons, *inventive, ingenious*, Alex.234.5. II. *poetical*, λέξις Isoc.15.47, cf. Phld.*Po*.2.40 (both Comp.); of persons, Pl.*R*.393d; Ὅμηρον -ώτατον εἶναι ib.607a; π. καὶ μουσικοί Id.*Lg*.802b, cf. 700d, etc.; οἱ π. *poets*, ib.656c; ἡ π. τύρβη Epicur.*Fr*.228; but ἡ -κή (sc. τέχνη) *the art of poetry*, Pl.*Grg*.502c, Arist.*Po*.$1447^{a}8$, etc.; π. ἄδεια, ἐξουσία, *poetic* licence, A.D.*Pron*.38.3, al., Jul.*Or*.1.10b. Adv. -κῶς Pl.*R*.332b; *by poetic licence*, Str.9.2.14. 2. *celebrated by poets*, Ἶρις Olymp. *in Mete*.210.7; *quoted from the poets*, μαρτυρίη Hp.*Praec*.12. III. ποιητική, ἡ, = κισσὸς χρυσόκαρπος, *poet's ivy, Hedera Helix* var. *poetica*, Ps.-Dsc.2.179.

**ποιητο-γράφος** [ᾰ], ὁ, = ποιητής, *IGRom*.4.176 (Parium). **-δῐδάσκᾰλος**, ὁ, *poet's master*, *EM*428.19.

**ποι-ητός**, ή, όν, *made*, freq. in Hom., esp. of houses and arms, always in the sense of εὖ ποιητός, *well made*, δόμοις ἔνι ποιητοῖσι Il.5.198, Od.13.306; ποιητὰς.. πύλας Il.12.470; also πύκα ποιητός 18.608, Od.1.333, 436, al.: generally, *made*, εἰ δ' ἦν π. τε καὶ ἔνθετον ἀνδρὶ νόημα Thgn.435; π. φρέατα, opp. natural springs, Plu.*Sol*.23; *cultivated*, opp. ἄγριος, Aret.*CD*1.4; ἕλκεα *self-inflicted*, Tryph.229. II. *made into a son, adopted*, παῖς π., opp. ἀληθινός, γεννητός, Pl.*Lg*.878e, 923e; οἱ π. τῶν πατέρων *adopted* fathers, Lycurg.48; π. πολῖται *factitious* citizens, not so born, Arist.*Pol*.$1275^{a}6$, cf. D.45.78. III. *made by oneself*, i.e. *invented, feigned*, λόγος Pi.*N*.5.29; ποιητῷ τρόπῳ E.*Hel*.1547; of works of art, *imitated*, Nonn.*D*.34.287. **-ήτρια**, ἡ, fem. of ποιητής, Hld.2.8; *poetess*, ἐπέων π. *Supp.Epigr*.2.263 (Delph., iii B.C.), cf. *SIG*532.4 (Lamia, iii B.C.), Str.17.1.33, Plu.2.30cf, Luc.*Musc.Enc*.11, Ath.13.600f, etc.; *par excellence*, of Sappho, Gal.4.771.

**ποιη-τρόφος**, ον, = ποεσιτρόφος, Opp.*C*.1.460. **-φᾰγέω, -φάγος**, v. ποηφαγέω, -φάγος.

**ποικεφάλαιον**, v. προσκεφάλαιον.

**ποικῐλ-άνιος** [ᾱ], ον, Dor. for *-ήνιος, *with broidered reins*, Pi.*P*.2.8. **-είμων**, ον, gen. ονος, (εἷμα) *arrayed in spangled garb*, νὺξ π., in reference to the stars, A.*Pr*.24. **-ερυθρόμελας**, αινα, αν, *marked with red and black*, Arist.*Fr*.296. **-εύομαι**, *to be versatile* or *artful*, Vett.Val.4.9. **-εύς**, έως, ὁ, = ποικιλτής, Alex.328. **-ία**, ἡ, *marking with various colours, embroidering*, Pl.*R*.373a, 401a, cf. *IG*$1^{2}$.338.24,48; *tapestry, weaving*, *PTeb*.703.93. 2. in pl., *pieces of embroidery*, γραφαὶ καὶ π. X.*Mem*.3.8.10. II. *being marked with various colours, striped, spotted*, Arist.*HA*$518^{b}16$, $564^{a}26$. 2. *varied aspect, diversity*, γινομένης π. ἐπὶ τῶν νοσημάτων Hp.*Epid*.1.8; of the stars, ἡ περὶ τὸν οὐρανὸν π. Pl.*R*.529d; π. χρωμάτων Id.*Phd*.110d; Σικελικὴν π. ὄψου Id.*R*.404d; ἔστι περὶ τὴν ἐργασίαν [τῶν μελιττῶν]..πολλὴ π. Arist.*HA*$623^{b}26$, cf. $539^{a}3$; πραγμάτων Plb.9.22.10; τῆς πολιτείας Id.6.3.3. 3. in literary style, music, etc., *variety, intricacy, ornamentation*, αἱ περὶ τὴν λέξιν π. Isoc.5.27, cf. D.H.*Comp*.11, al.; ἡ π. τῆς λύρας Pl.*Lg*.812d; opp. μονῳδία, Plu.2.7b. 4. *versatility, subtlety*, mostly in bad sense, π. πραπίδων E.*Fr*.27 (lyr.); ταῦτ' ἐδεῖτο λόγου τινὸς ἢ ποικιλίας D.29.1: in Surgery, οὔτε τομὴ οὔτε καῦσις οὔτε ἄλλη π. Hp.*Art*.62. 5. *complexity* of a subject, Sor.1.2. ⊛ **-ίας**, ου, ὁ, a kind of *fish*, Philosteph.Hist.20. **-ιον**, *mendiculeia* (sic), *Gloss*. **-ίς**, ίδος, ἡ, an unknown bird which eats the lark's eggs, Arist.*HA*$609^{a}6$.

⊛ **ποικ-ίλλω**, fut. ποικῐλῶ Choerob. in *An.Ox*.2.250: aor. 1 inf. ποικῖλαι (δια-) Isoc.9.9; part. ποικίλας S.*Tr*.412, *Inscr.Délos* 442 *A* 206 (ii B.C.): pf. πεποίκιλκα D.H.*Pomp*.4:—Pass., pf. πεποίκιλμαι, v. infr.: (ποικίλος):—*work in various colours, work in embroidery*, πώλους ἐν ἀνθοκρόκοισι πήναις E.*Hec*.470 (lyr.), cf. *IT*224 (lyr.); ἐν αὐτῷ [τῷ φάρει] π. γῆν Pherecyd.Syr.2; of any elaborate work, ἐν δὲ χορὸν ποίκιλλε *with cunning workmanship he wrought* a χορός, Il.18.590; ἀναθήματα π. Emp.23.1; ἐν πετάλοις στεφανώματα π. Man.2.325: metaph., ποικίλλεται γαῖα πολυστέφανος *Lyr.Adesp*.104A. 2. *embroider* garments, etc., *Inscr.Délos* l.c.; μίτρα καναχηδὰ πεποικιλμένα Pi.*N*.8.15: metaph., *diversify, vary*, ἀνθρώπων βίον E.*Cyc*.339, cf. Pl.*Lg*.927e, Plu.*Mar*.23; π. ἱππικαῖς τάξεσι τὰς πορείας *vary* the order of march with troops of horse, X.*Eq.Mag*.4.3; π. ταῖς συλλαβαῖς Pl.*Cra*.394a; τρόπους D.H.*Comp*.12, al.; σχημάτων μεταβολαῖς π. τοὺς λόγους Id.*Is*.3; ἁρμονίαν Nicom.*Harm*.11; π. εἴδη δυσκολίας..παντοδαπά *produces various* kinds, Pl.*Ti*.87a:—Pass., [πολιτεία] ὥσπερ ἱμάτιον ποικίλον πᾶσιν ἄνθεσι πεποικιλμένον, οὕτω..πᾶσιν ἤθεσιν πεποικιλμένη Pl.*R*.557c; οὐκ ἐπαύξεται ἡ ἡδονή, ἀλλὰ μόνον ποικίλλεται Epicur.*Sent*.18; τὸ φῶς τὸ ἐκεῖ τὸ ποικιλθὲν ἐν λόγοις τοῖς ἄστροις Plot.2.1.7. II. of style, *embellish, adorn*, βαιὰ π. *tell with art and elegance*, Pi.*P*.9.77; of imaginative constructions, πολλά Hp.*Morb.Sacr*.1; κάλλιστα τοῖς ὀνόμασι π. Pl.*Mx*.235a; οὐδὲν ξυνίημ' ὧν σὺ π. S.*Tr*.1121, cf. 412:—Pass., Σπάρτη πεποίκιλται τρόπους E.*Supp*.187. III. intr., *vary, change*, Hp.*Prorrh*.1.92, *Coac*.182; πολλὰ ποικίλλει χρόνος *makes* many *changes*, Men.593.2. 2. metaph., *speak equivocally, mince matters*, μηδὲν π. πρός τινα Pl.*Smp*.218c, cf. *Lg*.863e. **-ιλμα**, ατος, τό, *broidered stuff, brocade*, A.*Ch*.1013; ὑφάσμασι καὶ π. Arist.*Mete*.$375^{a}23$. 2. *embroidery*, ὃς [πέπλος] κάλλιστος ἔην ποικίλμασιν Il.6.294; ποικίλμασι κεκόσμηται [ἡ οἰκία] *with various ornaments*, X.

*Oec*.9.2; ὁ πέπλος μεστὸς τῶν..π. Pl.*Euthphr*.6c; τὰ π. καὶ τὰ ζωγραφήματα καὶ τὰ πλάσματα Id.*Hp.Ma*.298a; of the stars in heaven, Id. *R*.529c; οὐρανοῦ δέμας Χρόνου καλὸν π. Critias *Fr*.25.34 D. II. generally, *variety, diversity*, Pl.*Lg*.747a, *Ti*.67a; τῶν ῥυθμῶν..παντοδαπὰ π. προσαρμόττοντας τοῖσι φθόγγοις τῆς λύρας Id.*Lg*.812e; τὰ ἐν διαίτῃ π. Epicur.*Sent.Vat*.69; τὸ παντοδαπὸν π. τῶν φαινομένων Phld.*Sign*.33. **-ιλμός**, ὁ, *elaboration, refinement*, Epicur.*Fr*. 417 (pl.); *variegation*, Plu.2.382c.

**ποικιλό-βοτρυς**, υος, ὁ, ἡ, *with varied clusters*, Nonn.*D*.5.279. **-βουλος**, ον, *of changeful counsel, wily*, Προμηθεύς Hes.*Th*.521; Ὀδυσσεύς *APl*.4.300.5; Ἑρμείης Orph.*H*.28.3. **-γενής**, ές, = αἰολόφυλος, Sch.Opp.*H*.1.617. **-γηρυς**, Dor. **-γᾱρυς**, υος, ὁ, ἡ, *of varied voice, many-toned*, φόρμιγξ Pi.*O*.3.8. **-γραμμος**, ον, *striped*, Arist.*Fr*.296. **-γρᾰφέω**, *go into elaborate detail*, Hero *Dioptr*.20. **-γράφος** [ᾰ], ον, *writing on various subjects*, D.L.5. 85. **-δακρυς**, υος, ὁ, ἡ, *shedding many tears*, Nonn.*D*.10.45. **-δειρος**, ον, *with variegated neck*, πανέλοπες Alc.84; ἔχις Epigr.ap.Poll.5.48 (Anyte). II. = ποικιλόγηρυς, ἀηδών Hes.*Op*.203. **-δέρμων**, ον, gen. ονος, *piebald*, πῶλοι E.*IA* 226 (lyr.). **-δίνης** [δῑ], ου, ὁ, *whirling in various eddies*, Opp.*H*.1.676. **-διφρος**, ον, *with chariot* or perh. *throne*) *richly dight*, Θετταλὲ π. Orac.ap.Poll.7.112. **-θριξ**, ὁ, ἡ, gen. τριχος, *spotted, dappled*, νεβρός E.*Alc*.584 (lyr.); of birds, v.l. in *Lyr. Adesp*.94. ❋ **-θρονος**, ον, *on richly-worked throne*, Ἀφροδίτα Sapph.1 (v.l. ποικιλόφρον'). **-θροος**, ον, *of varied note*, οἰωνοί *Lyr.Adesp*.94; cf. ποικιλόθριξ. **-καυλος**, ον, *with variegated stalk*, Thphr.*HP*7.4. 6. **-μήτης**, ου, ὁ, voc. μῆτα, *full of various wiles*, epith. of Odysseus, Il.11.482, Od.3.163, 13.293; of Zeus, *h.Ap*.322; of Hermes, *h.Merc*.155. **-μητις**, ιδος, ὁ, ἡ, = foreg., ἆται S.*Fr*.592.5 (lyr.). **-μήχᾰνος**, ον, *full of various devices*, Ἔρως Epigr.ap. Clidem.24. **-μορφος**, ον, *variegated*, ἱμάτια Ar.*Pl*.530; *of many shapes*, [θεά], of Fortune, *Lyr.Alex.Adesp*.34.1. **-μουσος**, ον, *yielding rich music*, χέλυς Tim.*Pers*.234. **-μῦθος**, ον, *of various discourse*, χείλη *AP*5.55 (Diosc.); epith. of Cronus, Orph.*H*.13.5; of Hermes, ib.28.8. **-νους**, ουν, *cunning*, ὀρχίλος cj. in Euph.4. ❋ **-νωτος**, ον, *with back of various hues*, ὄφις Pi.*P*.4.249; δράκων E.*IT*1245 (lyr.); δόρξ Id.*HF*376 (lyr.). **-πτερος**, ον, *with wings of changeful hue*, Ἔρως Id.*Hipp*.1270 (lyr.): metaph., π. μέλος Pratin.Lyr.1.5.

❋ **ποικίλος** [ῐ], η, ον, *many-coloured, spotted, pied, dappled*, παρδαλέη Il.10.30; ὄφις Hes.*Th*.300 codd. (αἰόλον Sch.); δράκων Pi.*P*.8.46; ἴυγξ ib.4.214; νεβρίδες E.*Ba*.249; ὄρνιθες Plot.4.4.29; also of cattle, *PCair.Preis*.37.9 (iii B.C.), etc.: -ώτερον ταὧ Alex.110.14, cf. Ath.9. 397c; opp. ὁμόχρους, Arist.*HA*543ᵃ25; κιθῶνες Hdt.7.61; λίθος Αἰθιοπικὸς π., of the red granite of Syene, Id.2.127, cf. *IG*4²(1). 106 i 96,113 (Epid., iv B.C.); σφαῖρα Pl.*Phd*.110b; in X.*An*.5.4.32, *tattooed*. II. *wrought in various colours*, of woven or embroidered stuffs, in Hom. as epith. of πέπλος, Il.5.735, al.; ἱμάς 14.215; φᾶρος S.*Fr*.586; ἐν ποικίλοις..κάλλεσιν βαίνειν, of a rich carpet, A.*Ag*.923; ποικίλα, τά, ib.926,936, Theoc.15.78; π., τό, *a broidered robe*, Cratin. 38; ἐπίβλημα π. *IG*1².387.28; of Cyprian, Carthaginian, and Sicilian stuffs, Ar.*Fr*.611, Hermipp.63.23, Philem.76.4. Adv. -λως, ὑφασμένον Antiph.99 (dub.); στρωμναὶ π. διηνθισμέναι Lxx *Es*.1.6. 2. of metal work, τεύχεα π. χαλκῷ *cunningly wrought* in bronze, Hes.*Sc*.[423]; θώρηξ Il.16.134; τεύχεα, ἔντεα, σάκος, δίφρος, κλισμός, etc., 4.432, 10.75, 149,501, Od.1.132, etc.; but δεσμὸς π. *intricate*, 8.448. 3. ἡ στοὰ ἡ π. the *Painted* Hall at Athens, Aeschin.3.186; ἡ π. στοά D.45.17, 59. 94, cf. Paus.1.15.1; also Ποικίλη alone, Id.5.11.6, Luc.*DMeretr*.10.2; or ἡ Π., Id.*Pisc*.13, 16, etc.; also π. στοά, at Olympia, Paus.5.21.17; λέσχη π., at Sparta, Id.3.15.8; θρᾶνος π. *PCair.Zen*.445.5 (iii B.C.). 4. of drugs, *complicated*, Aret.*CD*1.4. III. metaph., *changeful, diversified, manifold*, εὐμορφία A.*Pr*.405; π. κακῶν ταμιεῖον Democr.149; -ώτερος αὐτοῦ Πρωτέως Luc.*Sacr*.5; ποικίλα ἀντὶ ἁπλοῦ Pl.*Tht*.146d; -ώτερα ποιεῖν τὰ νοσήματα Id.*R*.426a; παντοδαπὰς ἡδονὰς καὶ π. καὶ παντοίως ἐχούσας ib.559d; οὕτω δὲ π. τί ἐστι τὸ ἀγαθὸν καὶ παντοδαπόν Id.*Prt*.334b; πηδήσεις ὡς ἔνι -ωτάτας ποιεῖσθαι Arr. *Tact*.43.3; π. μῆνες the *changing* months, Pi.*I*.4(3).18 (nisi leg. ποικίλα [χθών]); π. εὐεργεσία *IG*5(2).268.22 (Mantinea, i B.C.). Adv. -λως *in various ways*, Hp.*Art*.33, Gal.13.91: Comp. -ωτέρως, θρεπτέον Herod.Med. in *Rh.Mus*.58.85; but -ώτερον Sor.*Vit.Hp*.4. 2. of Art, π. ὕμνος a song *of changeful strain* or *full of diverse art*, Pi.*O*.6. 87; ποικίλον κιθαρίζων Id.*N*.4.14; δεδαιδαλμένοι ψεύδεσι ποικίλοις μῦθοι Id.*O*.1.29; of style, λέξις ποιητικωτέρα καὶ π. Isoc.15.47 (Comp.); σχηματισμοί D.H.*Is*.3. 3. *intricate, complex*, εἰλιγμοὶ -ώτατοι, of a labyrinth, Hdt.2.148; of an oracle, Id.7.111 (Comp.); ὁ θεὸς ἔφυ τι π. E.*Hel*.711; π. νόμος, opp. νοῆσαι ῥᾴδιος, Pl.*Smp*.182b; π. μηχάνημα, λόγοι, S.*OC*762, Ar.*Th*.438; opp. ἁπλούστερος, Arist. *Rh*.1416ᵇ25; οὐδὲν π. οὐδὲ σοφόν D.9.37. Adv. -λως, αὐδώμενος speaking *in double sense*, S.*Ph*.130; π. ᾐνιγμένος Ar.*Eq*.196. b. of abstruse knowledge, *intricate, subtle*, εἰδέναι τι π. E.*Med*.300; οὐδὲν π. nothing *abstruse* or *difficult*, Pl.*Men*.75e, *Grg*.491d, etc. c. of persons and things, *subtle, artful, wily*, of Prometheus, Hes.*Th*. 511, A.*Pr*.310; of Odysseus, E.*IA*526; π. γὰρ ἀνήρ Ar.*Eq*.758; φύσει π. Plb.8.18.4; ἀλώπηξ κερδαλέα καὶ π. Pl.*R*.365c; π. λαλήματα, of the Sirens, E.*Andr*.937; π. τόξον B.9.43; βουλεύματα Pi. *N*.5.28. Adv. *subtly, artfully*, E.*Ba*.888 (lyr.); σοφῶς..καὶ π. Alex. 110.20; π. χρώμενοι τοῖς πράγμασιν Plb.4.30.7. 4. *changeable, unstable*, ὁ εὐδαίμων οὐ π. καὶ εὐμετάβολος Arist.*EN*1101ᵃ8; π. ἐλπίδες *doubtful* hopes, Plb.14.1.5; π. περιστάσεις *OGI*194.5 (Egypt, i B.C.). Adv. -λως, ἔχειν to be *different*, X.*Mem*.2.6.21; δέος π. περιαμύττον τὸν νοῦν Pl.*Ax*.365c: Comp. -ωτέρως dub. in Epicur.*Nat*.5 G. (Cf. Skt. *pimśáti* 'dress (meat)', 'adorn', *péśas* 'shape', 'colour', 'embroidery', Lith. *piẽšti* 'draw', 'write', Slav. *pĭsati* 'write'.)

**ποικιλο-σάμβᾰλος**, ον, *with broidered sandals*, Anacr.14.3. **-στερνος**, ον, metaph., = ποικιλόβουλος, Hsch. **-στικτος**, ον, *mottled, dappled*, Arist.*Fr*.299. **-στολος**, ον, of a ship, *with variegated prow*, S.*Ph*.343. **-τερπής**, ές, *delighting by variety*, *AP*9.517 (Antip. Thess.). **-τευκτος**, ον, *intricate*, κύβων θέσις ib.482.7 (Agath.). **-τέχνης**, ου, ὁ, *skilled in various arts*, Tryph. 536. **-τραυλος**, ον, *lisping in various notes*, μέλη Theoc.*Ep*. 4.10. **-φόρμιγξ**, ιγγος, ὁ, ἡ, *accompanied by the various notes of the lyre*, ἀοιδά Pi.*O*.4.2. ❋ **-φρων**, ονος, ὁ, ἡ, = ποικιλομήτης, ἀλώπα Alc.*Supp*.22.7; of Odysseus, E.*Hec*.131 (anap.); cf. ποικιλόθρονος. **-φῦλος**, ον, = αἰολόφυλος, Sch.Opp.*H*.1.617. **-φωνος**, ον, *with varied tones*, στίχα λαιμῶν Nonn.*D*.2.510; ἀηδών Tz. ad Hes. *Op*.201; κιθάρα Sch.Pi.*O*.3.11: metaph., = ποικιλόμυθος, Clearch. 26. **-χειρος**, ον, *with changeful hands*, [θεά], of Fortune, prob. in *Lyr.Alex.Adesp*.34.1. **-χροος**, ον, = sq., Lyd.*Ost*.10ᵇ, Aët.15. 13. **-χρωμος**, ον, = sq., *Gloss*. **-χρως**, acc. -χροα, *of various colour*, Arist.*Fr*.295.

**ποικῐλ-όω**, *embroider*, A.*Fr*.304. **-σις**, εως, ἡ, = ποικιλία, Pl. *Lg*.747a (pl.). **-τέον**, *one must work in embroidery*, Id.*R*. 378c. **-τής**, οῦ, ὁ, *broiderer, pattern-weaver*, Aeschin.1.97, Arist. *Mete*.375ᵃ27, Lxx *Ex*.28.6, *BGU*34 ii 24 (ii/iii A.D.), Chor. in *Hermes* 17.226, etc.:—fem. **-τρια**, Str.17.1.36. **-τικός**, ή, όν, *skilful in embroidery*, Poll.7.34: ἡ -κή (with or without τέχνη) *embroidery*, ibid., D.H.*Comp*.2, Ph.1.652, Vett.Val.3.21; π. ἐπιστήμη Lxx *Jb*.38.36; ποικιλτικά, v.l. for ποικιλτά, ib.*Ex*.37.21 (38.23). **-τός**, ή, όν, *variegated, broidered*, Theopomp.Hist.283, Lxx *Ex*.37.21 (38.23), *POxy*. 1277.8 (iii A.D.): metaph., ἀθύρματα *Trag.Adesp*. in *Gött.Nachr*.1922. 27. **-ῳδός**, όν, *of perplexed and juggling song*, of the Sphinx S.*OT*130.

**ποιμαίνω**, Ep. impf. ποιμαίνεσκεν Od.9.188: (ποιμήν):—*herd, tend*, μῆλα Od. l. c.; ἄρνας Hes.*Th*.23; ποίμνας E.*Cyc*.26, A.R.2.1004; πρόβατα v.l. in Pl.*R*.345c; ποιμαίνειν ἐπ' ὄεσσι *to be shepherd* over sheep, Il.6.25, 11.106: abs., *act as shepherd, tend flocks*, Lys.20.11, Pl.*Tht*.174d, Theoc.11.65; ἐν τοῖς ἄλσεσιν μὴ π. *SIG*986.3 (Chios, v/iv B.C.):—Pass., *to be herded, roam the pastures*, of flocks, Il.11.245, E.*Alc*.579 (lyr.): metaph., ἀτρεκέων ποιμαίνεται ἔθνος ὀνείρων Mosch. 2.5 (unless Med., with ὕπνος (l. 3) as subject). 2. πᾶς πεποίμανται τόπος every country *has been traversed* (as by a shepherd or flocks of sheep), A.*Eu*.249. II. metaph., *tend, cherish*, ζῶας ἄωτον Pi.*I*.5(4).12; ἱκέτην A.*Eu*.91; τὸ σῶμα Pl.*Ly*.209a; θεσμόν *AP* 12.99. 2. *guide, govern*, στρατόν E.*Fr*.744; μάλα καὶ κατόπιν ἡμᾶς ἐποίμαινον αὖραι Luc.*Am*.6. 3. *soothe, beguile*, ἔρωτα π. Theoc.11. 80; ὀνομάτων κομψεύμασι τοὺς ἀμαθεῖς π. Luc.*Am*.54: hence, generally, *deceive*, E.*Hipp*.153 (lyr., cod. M and Sch. for πημαίνει). 4. εἴδωλα ἃ ποιμαίνουσιν images which they *send flocking*, i.e. represent as flocking, Plu.2.420b.

❋ **ποιμανδρία**, ἡ, *milk-pail*, Lyc.326.

**ποιμᾱνόριον**, τό, (ποιμάνωρ) *herd*: metaph., *army*, A.*Pers*.74 (lyr.).

**ποιμαν-τήρ**, ῆρος, ὁ, = ποιμήν: metaph., νεῶν π., of pilots, S.*Fr*. 432.10 (pl.). **-τικός**, ή, όν, *pastoral*: ἡ -κή (with or without τέχνη) *the shepherd's art*, Gal.5.750, Hsch.

**ποιμάνωρ** [ᾱ], ορος, ὁ, = ποιμήν II, A.*Pers*.241 (troch.). (From ποιμαίνω and ἀνήρ.)

**ποιμασία**, ἡ, *feeding, tending*, Ph.1.594,596.

**ποιμεν-ικός**, ή, όν, (ποιμήν) *of* or *for a shepherd*, θῶκος Theoc.1.23; πίλημα Call.*Fr*.125; ἀγγεῖον Nic.ap.Ath.11.475d, etc.: ἡ -κή (sc. τέχνη) Pl.*R*.345d. **-ιον**, τό, poet. for ποίμνιον, Opp.*C*.3.264, 4. 269. **-ιος**, α, ον, rare synonym of ποιμενικός, κάματοι, δόναξ, *AP* 6.73 (Maced.), *APl*.4.226 (Alc.). **-ισσα**, ἡ, *shepherdess*, *BGU* 1289.11 (iii B.C.). **-τάριος**, v. πιμεντάριος.

❋ **ποιμήν**, ένος, ὁ, voc. ποιμήν (not -μέν) Hdn.Gr.2.717:—*herdsman*, whether of sheep or oxen, Od.10.82–5, al.; opp. lord or owner (ἄναξ), 4.87. 2. after Hom. always *shepherd*, βουκόλοι καὶ π. E.*Ba*. 714, cf. Cratin.281, Pl.*Tht*.174d, *R*.343a, *Lg*.735b, etc.; π. προβάτων Lxx *Ge*.4.2. II. metaph., *shepherd* of the people, regularly of Agamemnon, Ἀγαμέμνονα π. λαῶν Il.2.243, al.: generally, *captain, chief*, ib.85, al., S.*Aj*.360 codd. (lyr.); ναῶν ποιμένες A.*Supp*.767; λόχων E.*Ph*.1140; ὄχων Id.*Supp*.674; ποιμένες δώρων Κυπρίας, of the Loves, Pi.*N*.8.6: abs., *master, lord*, πλοῦτος ὁ λαχὼν ποιμένα Id.*O*.10(11). 88; for A.*Ag*.657, v. στρόβος. 2. in Lxx and *NT*, *pastor, teacher*, *Je*. 2.8, *Ep.Eph*.4.11, etc. (Cf. Lith. *piemuõ*, gen. sg. *piemeñs* 'shepherd'.)

❋ **ποίμν-η**, ἡ, *flock*, Od.9.122; prop. *of sheep*, βουκολίας ἀγέλας τε καὶ αἰπόλια πλατέ' αἰγῶν ποίμνας τ' εἰροπόκων ὀΐων Hes.*Th*.446; τά τε αἰπόλια καὶ τὰς π. καὶ τὰ βουκόλια Hdt.1.126, cf. A.*Pr*.653, Pl.*R*.415e, etc.: generally, ποῖμναι κάπρων λεόντων τε Pi.*Fr*.238; of a single animal, χρυσεόμαλλος π., of the ram with golden fleece, E.*El*.725 (lyr.), cf. Antiph.52.4. 2. metaph. of persons, A.*Supp*.642 (lyr., of the Furies), *Eu*.197; ποίμνη δίπους, of mankind, Pl.*Plt*.267c. **-ηθεν**, Adv. *of* or *from a flock*, A.R.2.491. **-ήϊος**, η, ον, Ep. Adj. *of a flock* or *herd*, σταθμός, σηκός, Il.2.470, Hes.*Op*.787. **-ικός**, ή, όν, = foreg., *PRein*.51.16 (iii A.D.). ❋ **-ιον**, τό, = ποίμνη, esp. *of sheep*, Hdt.2.2, 3.65 (v.l.), S.*OT*761, 1028, Pl.*R*.416a, etc.; of goats, *IG*1². 45.3 (dub.): pl., *head of cattle*, π. ποικίλια Lxx 1 *Ki*.25.2. II. metaph. of disciples, *Ev.Luc*.12.32, al.; π. Θεοῦ 1 *Ep.Pet*.5.2. **-ιος**, α, ον, *frequented by flocks*, ἄλση E.*Fr*.740.5 (lyr.).

**ποιμνιοτρόφος**, ὁ, = ποιμήν, Aq.4 *Ki*.3.4, *Am*.1.1.

**ποιμνίτης** [ῑ], ου, ὁ, = ποιμενικός, ὑμέναιοι *shepherds'* marriage songs, E.*Alc*.577 (lyr.); π. κύνες *shepherds'* dogs, Poll.7.185.

**ποινά**, = ποιά (Lacon.), Hsch. (Perh. for ποιϝά.)

⊛ **ποιν-αῖος**, α, ον, (ποινή) *punishing, avenging*, ἀήρ Keil-Premerstein *Erster Bericht* p.9 (Troketta); σελίς *AP*5.253.6 (Paul. Sil.); βέλος Aristaenet.1.10; ὄργανα Lyd.*Mag* 3.16. **-άομαι**, Med., *avenge oneself on* one, ὑμᾶς..ποινᾱσόμεσθα E.*IT*1433. **-άτωρ** [ᾱ], ορος, ὁ, ἡ, *avenger, punisher*, A.*Ag*.1281, E.*El*.23, 268. **-ή**, ἡ, *blood-money, were-gild, fine* paid by the slayer to the kinsmen of the slain, c. gen. pers., ἵνα μή τι κασιγνήτοιό γε π. δηρὸν ἄτιτος ἔῃ Il.14.483; π. δ' οὔ τις παιδὸς ἐγίγνετο τεθνηῶτος 13.659, cf. 9.633; ἐνείκεον εἵνεκα ποινῆς ἀνδρὸς ἀποφθιμένου 18.498. 2. generally, *price paid, satisfaction, requital, penalty*, Κύκλωψ ἀπετείσατο π. ἰφθίμων ἑτάρων Od.23.312; δυώδεκα λέξατο κούρους, π. Πατρόκλοιο Il.21.28; πολέων δ' ἀπετίνυτο ποινὴν 16.398; υἷος π. Γανυμήδεος 5.266; τοῖς ἔνι π., ἔστ' ἐπὶ καὶ τῷ π., Hes.*Op*.749, 755; τῶν ποινὴν *in return for* these things, Il.17.207; so also ποινὴν τῆς Αἰσώπου ψυχῆς ἀνελέσθαι accept *satisfaction for* A.'s life, Hdt.2.134; ποινὴν τείσειν Ξέρξῃ τῶν κηρύκων τῶν ἀπολομένων give Xerxes *satisfaction for* the death of the heralds, Id.7.134, cf. A.*Eu*.543 (lyr.), S.*El*.564 (pl.), Antipho 2.4.11; ποινῆς εἵνεκα by way of *penalty*, *Epigr.Gr*.356.3 (Hadriani): freq. in pl., A.*Pr*.270, *Eu*.464, etc.; ποινὰς τεῖσαι to pay *penalties*, Pi.*O*.2.58; τίνειν A.*Pr*.112, X.*Cyr*.6.1.11; δοῦναι E.*IT*446 (lyr.); π. λαμβάνειν exact *them*, Id.*Tr*.360; τᾶς ὕβριος *IG*4²(1).122.98 (Epid.).—Rare in Prose, δίκη being the usual word. 3. in good sense, *recompense, reward for* a thing, τεθρίππων, καμάτων, Pi.*P*.1.59, *N*.1.70; εὐχὰς ἀγαθὰς ἀγαθῶν ποινὰς A.*Supp*.626 (anap.); ποινὴν εὐσεβίης *IG*14.1437. 4. *redemption, release*, π. τίς ἔσται πρὸς θεῶν; Pi.*P*.4.63. II. personified, *the goddess of vengeance*, μᾶτερ, ἅ μ' ἔτικτες..ἀλαοῖσι καὶ δεδορκόσι ποινάν A.*Eu*.323 (lyr.), cf. E.*IT*200 (lyr.): pl., Aeschin.1.190, Plb.23.10.2, etc. III. Astrol., name of a κλῆρος, S.E.*M*.5.15; also of the sixth τόπος, Paul.Al.*M*.1. (I.-E. *q*ᵘ*oi-nā*, cf. Avest. *kaēnā*- 'punishment', 'vengeance', Lith. *kaina*, Slav. *cěna* 'price', cogn. with τίνω, τεῖ-σαι.)

**ποινηλ-ᾰσία**, ἡ, *pursuit by the furies, madness*, Lyd.*Ost*.28. **-ατέω**, *pursue like an avenging fury*, S.E.*M*.11.117:—Pass., *to be so pursued*, Id.*P*.1.27, 3.237, Heph.Astr.3.8 (in *Cat.Cod.Astr*.8(1).151), Eun. *Hist*.p.248 D., Herm. *in Phdr*.p.111 A. **-ᾰτος**, ον, (ἐλαύνω) *pursued by the furies*, Anon.ap.Suid. II. *inflicted by them*, μανία Simp. *in Epict*.p.117 D.

**ποίν-ημα**, ατος, τό, (ποινάω) *penalty*, Hsch. (ποινώματα cod.). **-ητήρ**, ῆρος, ὁ, *avenger*, Opp.*H*.2.421. **-ῆτις**, ιδος, ἡ, *avenging*, *AP*7.745.5 (Antip. Sid.). **-ήτωρ**, ορος, ὁ, = ποινάτωρ, Nonn.*D*.8.281, 48.402. II. Adj. *avenging*, ib.21.145, al. **-ίζομαι**, Arc. aor. 1 inf. ποινίξασθαι, *exact a penalty*, *IG*5(2).261.14 (Mantinea, vi B.C.). **-ῐμος**, ον, *avenging, punishing*, Δίκη, Ἐρινύς, S.*Tr*.808, *Aj*.843; π. πάθεα Id.*El*.210 (lyr.). 2. in good sense, *bringing return* or *recompense*, χάρις cj. in Pi.*P*.2.17. **-ιον**, τό, Dim. (in form only) of ποινή, *fine*, *BCH*50.17 (Delph., iv B.C.). **-ίς**, ίδος, ἡ, perh. = ποτνιάς (cf. E.*Ba*.664), ποινίδες Βάκχαι Theognost.*Can*.23; cf. -ποινα in δέσποινα, if from -ποτνyα.

**ποινο-ποιός**, όν, *taking vengeance*, αἱ π. *the avenging goddesses*, Ps.-Luc.*Philopatr*.23. **-στροβέομαι**, Pass., *to be routed*, of an army, *BCH*55.85 (Panamara).

**ποινουργός**, ὁ, *executioner*, Lyd.*Mag*.3.60.

⊛ **ποιο-λογέω**, *put up corn in sheaves*, Theoc.3.32. **-λογία**, ἡ, *hay-harvest*, *PLille* 5.3, al. (iii B.C., spelt πωο-). **-λόγος**, ον, (λέγω) *picking up grass* or *herbs*, ταῶς Arist.*Fr*.351. **-νόμος**, ον, (νέμω) *feeding on grass* or *herbs*, βοτά A.*Ag*.1169 (lyr.). II. proparox. **ποιόνομος**, ον, (νομή) *with rich grassy fields*, τόποι Id.*Supp*.50 (lyr.).

**ποῖος**, α, ον, Ion. **κοῖος**, η, ον, *of what kind?* in Hom. commonly expressing surprise and anger, π. τὸν μῦθον ἔειπες *what manner of* speech hast thou spoken! Il.1.552, al.; ποῖόν σε ἔπος φύγεν ἕρκος ὀδόντων 4.350, al.; simply, ποῖον ἔειπες 13.824, Od.2.85, al.; ποῖον ἔρεξας Il.23.570; ποῖοί κ' εἶτ' Ὀδυσῆϊ ἀμυνέμεν *what sort* would ye be to..! Od.21.195; in simple questions, ποίῃ..νηΐ σε ναῦται ἤγαγον; 16.222; κοίῃ χειρί; Hdt.4.155, cf. A.*Th*.304 (lyr.), etc.; ποῖος οὐ interrog., equiv. to *every* affirm., Hdt.7.21, S.*OT*420, etc. 2. freq. in Com. and Prose dialogue, used in repeating a word used by the former speaker, to express scornful surprise, Πρωτέως τάδ' ἐστὶ μέλαθρα. Answ. ποίου Πρωτέως; Ar.*Th*.874, cf. *Ach*.62, 157, 761, *Nu*.367, Pl.*Tht*.180b, *Grg*.490e, *Chrm*.174b: twice in Trag., S.*Tr*.427, E.*Hel*.567: with Art., τὰν ποίαν σύριγγα; Theoc.5.5: abbrev. ποῖ (q.v.). 3. with the Art., when the question implies a Noun which is defined by the Art. or the context, τὸ π. εὑρὼν..φάρμακον; A.*Pr*.251; τὰ π. τρύχη; μῶν ἐν οἷς..; Ar.*Ach*.418; λέγεις δὲ τὴν π. κατάστασιν ὀλιγαρχίαν; Answ. τὴν ἀπὸ τιμημάτων πολιτείαν Pl.*R*.550c: freq. with the demonstr., ὁ ποῖος οὗτος Λάμαχος; Answ. ὁ δεινός, ὁ ταλαύρινος.. Ar.*Ach*.963, cf. *Nu*.1270, Timocl.12.4 (corr. Elmsley): sts. the answer is given more generally, S.*OT*120, 291, *OC*1415, *Ph*.1229: in Prose, τὸ π.; Pl.*Sph*.220e, etc.; τὸ π. δή; Id.*Tht*.147d, *Phdr*.279a; τὰ π. ταῦτα; Id.*Cra*.395d, etc.; τῆς π. μερίδος γενέσθαι τὴν πόλιν ἐβούλετ' ἄν; D.18.64: so also without the Art., κοῖα ταῦτα λέγεις; Hdt.7.48; π. Ἐρινὺν τήνδε..; *what sort of* Fury is this that..? A.*Ag*.1119; π. ἐρεῖς τόδ' ἔπος; *what sort of* is this that thou wilt speak? S.*Ph*.1204 (lyr.), cf. 441, etc. 4. ποῖός τις; making the question less definite, κοῖόν μέ τινα νομίζουσι Πέρσαι εἶναι; Hdt.3.34, cf. S.*OC*1163, X.*HG*4.1.6, etc.: with Art., τὰ ποῖ' ἄττα; Id.*Cyr*.3.3.8, cf. Pl.*Sph*.240c. II. like ὁποῖος, in indirect questions, διδάξω..ποῖα χρὴ λέγειν A.*Supp*.519, cf. *Pr*.196, S.*Ph*.153 (lyr.), etc.; ποῖα ἄττα δεῖ ἡμᾶς λέγειν Pl.*R*.398c; οὐκ οἶδα ὁποίᾳ τόλμῃ ἢ ποίοις λόγοις χρώμενος ἐρῶ ib.414d; εἴρετο..κοῖός τις δοκέοι ἀνὴρ εἶναι Hdt.3.34; doubled, ποίαν χρὴ [γυναῖκα] ποίῳ ἀνδρὶ συνοῦσαν τίκτειν Pl.*Tht*.149d. III. = ποδαπός; ποῖος οὑτοσὶ (ὁ) Τιμόθεος;—Μιλήσιός τις.. Pherecr.145.20, cf. Call.*Epigr*.36. 2. *whose?* ἐν π. δυνάμει ἢ ἐν π. ὀνόματι; *Act.Ap*.4.7, cf. *Ev.Matt*.21.23. IV. simply, *what, which?* esp. of place or time, ποίης ἐξ εὔχεται εἶναι γαίης; Od.1.406, cf. Pi.*P*.4.97; ἐν π. πόλει; Eup.23 D., cf. Alex.267.6; ἐκ ποίας πόλεως σὺ εἶ; LXX 2*Ki*.15.2, cf. 3*Ki*.13.12, al., *Act.Ap*.23.34; ποίᾳ ἄλλῃ (sc. ὁδῷ); by *what* other way? Ar.*Av*.1219 (hence κοίῃ metaph., *how?* Hdt.1.30); ποίου χρόνου; since *what* time? A.*Ag*.278, cf. E.*IA*815 (nisi leg. πόσον); ἀπὸ π. χρόνου; Ar.*Av*.920, *UPZ*65.7 (ii B.C.); ἀπὸ ποίου ἔτους *PAmh*.2.68.7 (i A.D.); ποίᾳ ἡμέρᾳ; *Ev.Matt*.24.42, cf. Hyp.*Epit*.31, Arist.*Cat*.5ᵃ20, 22, *SIG*826 *E* ii 28 (Delph., ii B.C.), *IG*5(1).1390.113 (Andania, i B.C.), *PUniv.Giss*.20.18 (ii A.D.); φυλᾶς ἑλομένοις ἑκάστου (= -ῳ) ποίας κε βέλλειτει (= ἥστινος ἂν βούληται, sc. εἶναι) *IG*9(2).517.20 (Larissa, iii B.C.); ποίας φυλῆς ἐστι LXX *To*.5.8; π., = *quis*, *Gloss*. V. = πότερος, *An.Ox*.1.284. VI. Adv. ποίως Hdn.Gr.2.925, Bacch.*Harm*.93. [The first syll. is sts. short in Trag. and Com., A.*Supp*.911, Ar.*V*.1369.]

**ποιός**, ά, όν, indef. Adj. *of a certain nature, kind*, or *quality*, Pl.*Lg*.770d, Arist.*Cat*.10ᵃ27, etc.; esp. joined with τις, Pl.*Sph*.262e, al., Arist.*Cat*.8ᵇ25; ποιά ἄττα Pl.*R*.438b, al.; τὸ ποιόν, = ποιότης, Arist. *Metaph*.1083ᵃ11, al.; μοναχῶς μὲν ἡ ποιότης λέγεται κατ' αὐτοὺς τοὺς Στωϊκούς, τριχῶς δὲ ὁ ποιός *Stoic*.2.129, cf. 131, 168, al.: pl., τὰ τοιαῦτα π. Iamb.*Comm.Math*.14; τὸ π. μέλος *such-and-such*, *PMag.Par*.1.327.

**ποιότης**, ητος, ἡ, *quality*, Pl.*Tht*.182a (where he apologizes for the use of the word as ἀλλόκοτον ὄνομα), Arist.*Cat*.8ᵇ26, *EN*1173ᵃ15 (pl.), Gal.*Nat.Fac*.1.2, *POxy*.2113.16 (iv A.D.), etc.; of size, Babr.28.10, Aesop.84.

**ποιο-φάγος** [ᾰ], ον, = ποηφάγος, Opp.*C*.2.613.

**ποιόω**, (ποιός) *make of a certain quality*, τὸ ποιοῦν αὐτῶν Thphr.*CP* 2.1.5:—Pass., *to be endowed with quality*, *Stoic*.2.220, S.E.*M*.1.108; σῶμα τοιόνδε οἷον ποιωθὲν ψυχῆς εἰδώλῳ Plot.1.1.11, cf. 4.3.26; τὸ πεποιωμένον τῷ οἴνῳ γάλα Sor.1.95.

**ποιπνός**, ὁ, *servant*, Hsch.

**ποιπνύω**, impf. ἐποίπνυον, Ep. ποίπνυον Il.24.475: aor. part. ποιπνύσας 8.219. [ῠ of pres. long before a long syll., short before a short syll., v. infr.: ῡ in fut. and aor. always.]:—Ep. Verb (perh. formed by redupl. from πνῡ-, cf. πέπνυμαι), *bustle about*, of attendants, ὡς ἴδον Ἥφαιστον διὰ δώματα ποιπνύοντα Il.1.600; αἱ μὲν ὕπαιθα ἄνακτος ἐποίπνυον 18.421; ποίπνυον παρεόντε 24.475; ὣς ἔφαθ'· οἱ δ' ἄρα πάντες ἐποίπνυον Od.3.430; ποιπνύοντα μάχην ἀνὰ κυδιάνειραν Il.14.155; δῶμα κορήσατε ποιπνύσασαι *make haste and* sweep the house, Od.20.149; ἐπὶ φρεσὶ θῆκ' Ἀγαμέμνονι πότνια Ἥρη αὐτῷ ποιπνύσαντι..ὀτρῦναι Il.8.219; once in Pi., ἐμὰν ποιπνύων χάριν *labouring* for the sake of me, *P*.10.64. 2. later c. acc., ἰδέα ποιπνύουσα Emp.73; εὖ μάλα π...ἔργα Pythag.ap.Porph.*VP*40 codd.; μαντοσύνην Orac.ap.Phleg.37 J. II. Med. in sense of Act., περί τι Opp.*H*.2.615.

**ποίστᾰσις**, ιος, ἁ, (ποι- = προσ-) prob. in *IG*4²(1).102.41 (Epid., iv B.C.).

**ποιτάσσω**, v. προστάσσω. **ποιτίθημι**, v. προστίθημι.

**Ποιτρόπιος**, ὁ, a Delphic month, *SIG*631.1 (ii B.C.), etc.

**ποιφ-ύγδην**, Adv. *blowing, puffing, hissing*, Nic.*Th*.371. ⊛ **-υγμα**, ατος, τό, *blowing, snorting*, ἐν ματαίοις κἀγρίοις ποιφύγμασι A.*Th*.281, cf. Epic. in *Arch.Pap*.7.6. ⊛ **-ύσσω** (redupl. form from φῦ, cf. φῦσα), *blow, snort*, Nic.*Th*.180 (ποιφύξειν v.l. ap.Sch.): Ζεφύρου μέγα ποιφύξαντος Euph.135; παιδικὰ ποιφυξεῖς, title of mime by Sophr.ap. Ath.7.324f. II. trans., *blow up*, Lyc.198; *puff out*, *AP*7.215 (Anyt.).

**ποι-ώδης** (A), ες, v. ποώδης. **-ώδης** (B), ες, (ποιός) *qualitative*, Simp. *in Cat*.179.4. **-ωσις**, εως, ἡ, *qualification*, ib.99.12. **-ωτίζομαι**, Pass., *to be endowed with quality*, Antyll.ap.Orib.10.2.1. **-ωτικός**, ή, όν, *tending to qualify*, c. gen., Simp. *in Cat*.78.23; also v.l. for sq. (q.v.). **-ωτός**, ή, όν, *endowed with quality*, Antyll.ap.Orib.10.2.1 (v.l. -ωτικός).

**ποκ**, v. ποτί. **πόκα, ποκά** [ᾰ], Dor. for πότε, ποτέ (qq.v.).

**ποκ-άζω**, (πόκος) = ποκίζω, Sch.Ar.*Av*.714, Suid. s.v. πέκτειν. **-άριον**, τό, Dim. of πόκος, Sch.Theoc.15.18, *Hippiatr*.26: pl., *Sammelb*.7247.21 (iii/iv A.D.). **-άς**, άδος, ἡ, *wool, hair*, Ar.*Th*.567 (pl.), dub. in *PThead*.8.9 (iv A.D.).

**πόκες**, αἱ, and **πόκη**, ἡ, v. πόκος II.

**ποκίζω**, (πόκος) = πέκω, *shear wool*:—Med., *shear for oneself*, τρίχας ἐποκίξατο (Dor. aor.) Theoc.5.26.

⊛ **Πόκιος**, ὁ, name of a month in Locris, *GDI*2019, al.

**ποκ-ισμός**, ὁ, *sheep-shearing*, *PSI*3.233.24 (ii A.D.). **-ιστί**, Adv. *by the fleece*, πωλεῖν ib.5.459.11 (i A.D.).

⊛ **ποκκί** or **πὸκ κί**, = πρὸς τί, but in meaning = ὅτι, *that*, *IG*9(2).517.12 (Larissa, iii B.C.).

**ποκο-ειδής**, ές, *like undressed wool*: *rough, crude*, ἔννοιαι Longin.15.5. **-ομαι**, Pass., *to be covered* or *clothed with down*, μῆλον λεπτῇ πεποκωμένον ἄχνῃ *AP*6.102 (Phil.).

⊛ **πόκος**, ὁ, (πέκω) *wool* in its raw state, *fleece*, Il.12.451, Ar.*Lys*.574, *GDI* iv p.886 (Erythrae, iv B.C.), *PCair.Zen*.287, 774 (iii B.C.), LXX *Jd*.6.37; οἶν μελάγχιμον πόκῳ E.*El*.513; πεκτεῖν..προβάτων π. ἠρινὸν Ar.*Av*.714; πέντε πόκως ἔλαβ' ἐχθές Theoc.15.20; *lock* or *tuft of wool*, S.*Tr*.675; ἐρίων π. Cratin.372; νεφέλαι πόκοις ἐρίων ὁμοῖαι

Thphr.*Sign.*13. II. prov., εἰς ὄνου πόκας to an ass-*shearing*, i.e. to no-place, Ar.*Ra.*186; ὄνου πόκους or πόκας ζητεῖς you ask for 'pigeons'-milk', Zen.5.38, etc.:—the nom. of this phrase is given as πόκες by Sch.Ar. l.c., as πόκαι by Suid., Phot.; Ὄκνου πλοκάς (cf. ὄκνος II) was prob. read by Aristarch. in Cratin.348, and shd. perh. be read in Ar. l.c.; οὐδεὶς πόκον εἰς γναφεῖον φέρει Arcesil.ap.Gal.8.624.

**ποκτήρ**, = πεκτήρ, *PUniv.Giss.*23.2 (iii A.D.).

**πόκτος**, ὁ, Aeol., = πόκος, *Lyr.Adesp.*73, Hdn.Gr.1.217 codd. Arc.

**ποκύφος** [ῠ], ὁ, = ἐριοϋφάντης, *PTeb.*5.170 (ii B.C.).

**πολείδιον** or -ίδιον, τό, Dim. of πόλις, Str.8.3.15, 9.2.32, 10.1.5, *EM*147.22.

**πολεμᾱδόκος**, Aeol. and Dor. for πολεμηδόκος.

**πολέμ-αιγις**, ιδος, ἡ, *with warlike aegis*, Ἀθάνα B.16.7. **-αίνετος**, ον, *famed in war*, *Lyr.Oxy.*426.4.

**πολεμάρχ-ειος**, ον, *of* or *belonging to the polemarch*, στοά Polem.Hist.58; τὸ π. *his residence*, X.*HG*5.4.6, Plb.4.79.5; **-άρχιον**, *IG*12(9).279 (Eretria, i B.C.). **-έω**, *to be polemarch*, Ἀθηναίων Hdt.6.109, cf. Cratin.458 (= *Com.Adesp.*51), X.*HG*5.2.25; Boeot. **πολεμαρχίω** *IG*7.4127 (Acraeph.), etc. **-ης**, ου, ὁ, = πολέμαρχος, *Inscr.Magn.*98.57 (ii B.C.), al. **-ία**, ἡ, *office of polemarch*, Polem.*Cyn.*18, Vett.Val.213.1, al. **-ικός**, ή, όν, *concerning the* πολεμάρχης, νόμος *Inscr.Magn.*14.7 (iii B.C.). **-ος**, ὁ, *chieftain, war-lord*, Κνωσίων, Ἀχαιῶν, B.16.39, A.*Ch.*1072 (anap.), cf. *Th.*828 (anap.). II. the title of high officers in several Greek states: 1. at Athens, *the third archon*, Hdt.6.109, Ar.*V.*1042, *IG*1$^2$.16.10, 49.7, al.; ὠφληκέναι παρὰ τῷ π. in his court, Lys.23.3; at Sparta, a *military commander*, Hdt.7.173, Th.5.66, X.*HG*4.4.7, 4.5.7, etc.; at Thebes, officers of chief rank after the Boeotarchs, supreme in affairs of war, ib.5.4.2 sqq., *Michel* 232 (ii B.C., found in Crete), etc.; at Orchomenos, *IG*7.3175.5, etc.; at Mantinea, Th.5.47; in Arcadia, Plb.4.18.2; π. ἐπιμήνιος *SIG*402.1 (Chios, iii B.C.). 2. simply, *chief, leader*, συνεφήβων *IG*2$^2$.2055.

**πολεμέω**, Ion. Iterat. πολεμέεσκε Acus.22 J.: fut. -ήσω X.*An.*2.6.5: pf. πεπολέμηκα Arist.*Rh.*1396$^a$11, Ephipp.9:—Med., aor. ἐπολεμησάμην (κατ-) Plb.11.31.6:—Pass., πολεμηθήσομαι Id.2.41.14, etc.; πολεμήσομαι in pass. sense, Th.1.68, 8.43, D.23.110: aor. ἐπολεμήθην Th.5.26: pf. πεπολέμημαι (κατα-) Id.6.16: (πόλεμος):—*to be at war* or *make war*, Id.1.140, etc.; ἀφ' ἡσυχίας πολεμῆσαι ib.124; opp. εἰρήνην ἄγειν, Id.5.76; τινι *with* one, Hdt.6.37, *IG*2$^2$.236.19, etc.; πολεμοῦσαι πρὸς ἀλλήλας πόλεις X.*Vect.*5.8, cf. Pl.*Lg.*686b, *SIG*182.12 (Argos, iv B.C.), etc.; μετά τινος or σύν τινι in conjunction with.., X.*HG*7.1.27, *An.*2.6.5; περὶ τῆς ἀρχῆς π. Hdt.6.98. 2. *fight, do battle*, ἀπὸ τῶν ἵππων Pl.*Prt.*350a; ἀπὸ [καμήλων] X.*Cyr.*7.1.49; but ἀφ' ὅτου πολεμήσωμεν what *our means of war are*, And.3.16. 3. generally, *quarrel, wrangle with* one, X.*Cyr.*1.3.11; π. χρείᾳ S.*OC*191 (anap.), cf. E.*Ion* 1386; τισὶν ὑπέρ τινος D.18.31: metaph. of disease, Gal.1.103. II. later c. acc., *make war upon*, τὴν πόλιν Din.1.36 codd.; τὰς Ἀθήνας D.S.4.61, cf. 13.84, 14.37, Lxx 1*Ma.*5.30, etc.; τὰς Συρακούσας Plb.1.15.10, etc.: metaph., τὰς σταφυλάς Alciphr.3.22:—Pass., also in early writers, *have war made upon* one, *to be treated as enemies*, Th.1.37, X.*HG*7.4.20; ὑπό τινων Isoc.5.49; καὶ αὐτοὶ.. ἐκ πολλοῦ πολεμούμενοι D.18.43; αὐτὸς μὲν πολεμεῖν ὑμῖν, ὑφ' ὑμῶν δὲ μὴ πολεμεῖσθαι Id.9.9; -ηθείσης τῆς χώρας *OGI*748.8 (Cyzicus, iii B.C.). 2. c. acc. cogn., πόλεμον π. Pl.*R.*551d, Arist. l.c., etc.:—Pass., [πολέμους] τοὺς ἐπὶ Θησέως πολεμηθέντας X.*Mem.*3.5.10; κατὰ θάλατταν ὁ π. ἐπολεμεῖτο Id.*HG*5.1.1, cf. Pl.*R.*600a; ὅσα ἐπολεμήθη whatever *hostilities took place*, X.*An.*4.1.1; τὰ περὶ Πύλον κατὰ κράτος ἐπολεμεῖτο Th.4.23, cf. 3.6.—The form used by Poets is πολεμίζω.

**πολεμηδόκος**, Aeol. and Dor. **πολεμᾱδόκος**, ον, *war-sustaining*, epith. of Pallas, Alc.9 (prob.), Lamprocl.1, Phryn.Com.72, *IGRom.*4.360.14 (Pergam.); ; also π. ὅπλα Pi.*P.*10.13.

**πολεμ-ήϊος**, α, ον, Ep., Ion., and Lyr. Adj. *warlike*, freq. in Hom. (esp. in Il.), πολεμήϊα ἔργα Il.2.338, al.; π. τεύχεα 7.193, Hes.*Sc.*238; πολεμήϊα, = πολέμια, v.l. in Hdt.5.111; π. ἀοιδά *war*-note, of the trumpet, B.17.4. **-ησείω**, Desiderat. of πολεμέω, Th.1.33, D.C.46.30. **-ητέον**, *one must go to war*, Ar.*Lys.*496, Arist.*Rh.*1396$^a$8; ἑκάστοις Pl.*Plt.*304e: pl. -ητέα, Th.1.79, D.C.36.46. **-ητήριον**, τό, *head-quarters of a general*, Plb.4.71.2. **-ητής**, οῦ, ὁ, = πολεμιστής, *IG*5(1).1188 (pl., Gythium, iii A.D.). **-ητόκος**, ον, *bringing forth war*, Nonn.*D.*4.425, etc.; of Athena, Orph.*H.*32.10. **-ήτωρ**, ορος, ὁ, ἡ, *warlike*, Antioch. in *Cat.Cod.Astr.*1.111, v.l. in Opp.*C.*3.205. **-ιεῖον**, τό, written πολημιεῖον corr. to πολεμιεῖον), dub. sens. in *PPetr.*2 p.40 (iii B.C.). **-ίζω**, Il.1.168, al.; Ep. inf. πολεμιζέμεναι 9.337:—also **πτολεμίζω** (metri gr.), 8.428, al.: fut. πολεμίξω or πτολεμίξω, 24.667, 2.328:—poet. form of πολεμέω, *wage war, fight*, τινι *with* one, Il.9.337, al.; π. Διὸς ἄντα, Ἀχιλῆος ἐναντίβιον, 8.428, 20.85; μετ' Ἀχαιοῖσιν *jointly with*.., 9.352; ἄπρηκτον πόλεμον π. 2.121; τόξῳ π. Pi.*O.*9.32 (nisi leg. πελεμ-); τῇ γλώττῃ Ar.*Nu.*419:—Med., Pi.*N.*8.29 (nisi leg. πελεμ-). II. trans., *war* or *fight with*, ῥηΐτεροι πολεμίζειν Il.18.258:—Pass., Opp.C.3.209. **-ικός**, ή, όν, *of* or *for war*, οἱ π. κίνδυνοι Th.2.43; ἀγῶνες π., opp. εἰρηνικοί, Pl.*Lg.*729d; βίος ib.829a; πλοῖα, ὅπλα, ib.706b, 944e; χαλκῆν ἀσπίδα -ωτάτην εἶναι *most fit for service*, X.*Lac.*11.3; χρεία *OGI*54.13 (Egypt, iii B.C.); τέχνη καὶ ἐπιστήμη π. Pl.*R.*522c, cf. *Lg.*639b; ἡ -κή (sc. τέχνη) *the art of war*, Id.*Sph.*222c, etc.; τὰ -κά *warlike exercises*, τὰ π. ἄλκιμος (v.l. πολέμια) Hdt.3.4; τὰ π. ἀσκεῖν X.*HG*3.4.18, *Cyr.*1.5.9; αἱ τῶν π. μελέται Th.2.39, cf. 89 (v.l.). 2. τὸ -κόν *signal for battle* (παιὼν π. in Pl.*Ep.*348b), ἐπειδὰν ὁ σαλπικτὴς σημήνῃ τὸ π. X.*An.*4.3.29, cf. Aen.Tact.4.3; ἀνέκραγε πολεμικόν gave a *war*-shout, X.*An.*7.3.33; also of *an air on the flute*, Trypho ap.Ath.14.618c. b. *fighting part* of the people, opp. civilians, Arist.*Pol.*1291$^a$26, 1329$^a$2. II. of persons, *skilled in war, warlike*, Th.1.84, Pl.*R.*522e, *Lg.*643c, etc.: distd. from φιλοπόλεμος, X.*An.*2.6.1; also ἵπποι π. Id.*Cyr.*7.5.62; τὸ π. *warlike spirit*, Phld.*Mus.*p.27 K. III. *like an enemy, hostile*, X.*Vect.*4.44; *stirring up hostility*, opp. φιλικός, πολεμικὸν ἔρις καὶ ὀργή Id.*Mem.*2.6.21: metaph., ἀντίθεσις π. καὶ ἀσύμβατος Plu.2.946e. Adv. -κῶς, ἔχειν, opp. εἰρηνικῶς, Isoc.5.46; π. διακεῖσθαι Id.6.39: Sup. -ώτατα, ἔχειν πρός τινα X.*An.*6.1.1. **-ιος**, α, ον, also ος, ον E.*Supp.*1192, Ar.*Av.*344 (lyr.):—*of* or *belonging to war*, κάματοι Pi.*P.*2.19; ὅπλα *Expl.Arch. de Délos* 11.140; τὰ π. *war and its business*, Hdt.5.78, Th.4.80 (s.v.l.), etc.; παρασκευάζεσθαι τὰ π. Id.1.18. II. more freq. *of* or *like an enemy, hostile*, ἄνδρες Pi.*P.*1.80; χείρ Id.*N.*4.55; χθών A.*Th.*588; δόρυ ib.216, etc.; ἄνδρα π. ἐχθρόν τε S.*Ph.*1302; π. δυσμενῇ τε ib.1323; π. τινί *hostile* to one, Hdt.1.4, E.*Hec.*1138; π. πῦρ νεύροις Hp.*Art.*11. b. freq. as Subst., *enemy*, Hdt.1.87, Pi.*P.*1.15, etc.; οἱ π. *the enemy*, Th.1.84, 2.43, etc. c. τὸ φύσει π. natural *hostility*, Id.4.60; τὸ π. τῶν Ἀθηναίων *towards* them, Id.5.11. 2. generally, *opposed, adverse*, δύο.. ἐόντα -ώτατα Hdt.7.47; δύο.. ἔτι πολεμιώτερα (sc. γῆ καὶ θάλασσα) ib.49; τὸ ἔλαιον ταῖς θριξὶ -ώτατον ταῖς τῶν ἄλλων ζῴων *most hurtful*, Pl.*Prt.*334b; πολεμία ἡ ὀσμὴ τοῖς ὄφεσιν Arist.*HA*612$^a$29. III. *of* or *from the enemy*, φόβος A.*Th.*270; φρυκτοί Th.2.94; φίλια καὶ π. ναυάγια Lys.2.38; τριήρεις *IG*2$^2$.29.15; πολέμια, τά, *enemy's wares, contraband*, Ar.*Ach.*912; ἡ π. (sc. γῆ, χώρα) *the enemy's country*, X.*Cyr.*3.3.16, etc., cf. S.*Aj.*819. IV. Adv. -ίως *in hostile manner*, φιλίως, οὐ π. Th.3.65, cf. 66, etc.; π. ἔχειν τινί X.*Cyn.*7.11: Sup. -ιώτατα, διακείμενος *SIG*741.19 (Epist. Mithrid., i B.C.).—πολέμιος is older than πολεμικός, being always used by Pi. and Trag., and mostly by Hdt. and Th.; in X. and later writers, πολέμιος is mostly used in the sense of *hostile*, πολεμικός in that of *warlike, skilled in war*. **-ιστήριος**, α, ον, also ος, ον Plu.*Cat.Ma.*26:—*of* or *for a warrior*, ἵπποι Hdt.1.192 (v.l. πολεμιστέων), X.*Ages.*9.6, cf. D.42.24; βοή, θώραξ π., Ar.*Ach.*572, 1132; π. ἅρματα *war*-chariots, Hdt.5.113, X.*Cyr.*6.1.29; ἐλέφαντες Arist.*HA*610$^a$19; ὅπλα *Schwyzer* 633.13 (Eresus, ii/i B.C.), cf. *Supp.Epigr.*4.267 (Panamara); ζεύγη D.S.1.54; παρασκευή Plu. l.c.; ἐλᾶν τὰ π. drive the *war-chariots* (in a race), Ar.*Nu.*28, cf. *IG*2$^2$.2311.58, and πολεμιστής fin.; ἅρμα π. ib.2316.56. II. τὰ π., = τὰ πολεμικά, Pl.*Criti.*119b, X.*Cyr.*8.8.26. III. **-ήριος**, ὁ, = sq., Nic.Dam.4 J. ⊛ **-ιστής**, οῦ, ὁ, Ep. πτολ- Il.22.132:—*warrior*, ib.5.602, al., Pi.*N.*4.27, etc.: freq. in later Prose, Lxx *De.*2.14, Str.11.2.4, J.*BJ*6.2.5, Gal.14.283. II. π. ἵππος *war*-horse, *charger*, D.S.2.41 (pl.), Str.15.1.29, Plu.*Fab.*20; ἵπποι π. are prob. racehorses *trapped as chargers*, Theoc.15.51, cf. *IG*2$^2$.2316.29, *SIG*697*H*3 (Delph., ii B.C.), Phot. s.v. **-ιστρίς**, ίδος, fem. of foreg., Tz.*H.*1.876; **-ίστρια**, Heraclit.*Ep.*7.6.

**πολεμο-γράφος** [ᾰ], ον, *describing wars*, αὐδά, of an historian, *IG*4$^2$(1).687 (Epid., ii A.D.). **-κέλᾱδος**, ον, *exulting in the din of war*, Βρόμιος *Lyr.Adesp.*108. **-κλονος**, ον, *raising the din of war*, ἔργον Ἄρηος Batr.4; Παλλάς ib.275, Orph.*H.*32.2. **-κραντος**, ον, (κραίνω) *finishing war*, τέλος A.*Th.*162 (lyr.). **-λᾱμᾰχᾱϊκός**, ή, όν, comic word in Ar.*Ach.*1080, a compd. of πόλεμος, Λάμαχος, Ἀχαϊκός.

**πόλεμόνδε**, Ep. πτόλ-, Adv. *into the fight*, Il.2.872, al. II. *to the war*, Od.11.448.

**πολεμο-ποιέω**, *stir up war*, X.*HG*5.2.30, D.S.13.53. II. c. acc., *make war on*, τὰ ξυγγενείης Hp.*Ep.*17. **-ποιός**, όν, *making war, bellicose*, π. ὁ τύραννος Arist.*Pol.*1313$^b$28, cf. Plu.2.321f, Jul.*ad Ath.*281b, etc.; π. ἵπποι Them.*Or.*24.307b; διαβολή ib.22.277c.

⊛ **πόλεμος**, and Ep. **πτόλεμος**, ὁ, *war*, Il.1.61, etc. (the usual meaning in post-Homeric Greek); also, *battle, fight*, ib.226, etc.; even of *single combat*, 7.174; πόλεμοί τε μάχαι τε 1.177, 5.891; φυλόπιδος.. καὶ πολέμοιο 18.242; αὐτὴν τε πτόλεμόν τε 1.492, cf. 14.37, 96; π. καὶ δηϊοτῆτος 5.348, etc.: periphr., νεῖκος, φύλοπις, ἔρις πολέμοιο, 13.271, 635, 17.253; π. ἄγριος, αἱματόεις, ἀργαλέος, ἀλίαστος, δακρυόεις, δήϊος, δυσηλεγής, δυσηχής, κακός, λευγαλέος, ὀϊζυρός, ὀκρυόεις, ὀλοός, ὁμοίιος, πευκεδανός, πολυάϊξ, πολύδακρυς, στυγερός, φθισήνωρ, ib.737, 19.313, Od.24.531, Il.2.797, 5.737, 7.119, 20.154, 2.686, 1.284, 13.97, 3.112, 9.64 (leg. κρυόεντος), 3.133, 9.440, 10.8, 1.165, 3.165, 4.240, 9.604; π. Ἀχαιῶν, ἀνδρῶν, i.e. brought by them, 3.165, 24.8 (pl.), etc.; ὁ τῶν βαρβάρων π. Th.1.24; Ἑλλήνων π. X.*HG*3.2.22; ὁ παρὼν π. Κορινθίων Th.1.32; ὁ μέλλων καὶ ὅσον οὐ παρὼν π. ib.36; ὁ πρὸς Δαρεῖον π. Hdt.6.2; ἀσχημοσύνῃ καὶ Ἔρωτι πρὸς ἀλλήλους ἀεὶ π. Pl.*Smp.*196a; Δωριακὸς π. Orac.ap.Th.2.54; ὁ Ἰωνικὸς π. Id.8.11; ὁ Φωκικὸς π. Aeschin.3.148; π. Δεκελεικός Isoc.8.37, 14.31; π. ξενικός Arist.*Pol.*1272$^b$20; δουλικοὶ π. Ath.6.272f; ἱερὸς π. Ar.*Av.*556, etc.; πόλεμον ἄρασθαι levy war, A.*Supp.*342, cf. Ar.*Ach.*913, etc.: c. dat., ἢ τοῖσιν ἢ τοῖς π. αἱρεσθαι μέγαν A.*Supp.*439; π. ἄρασθαι πρός τινας X.*Cyr.*1.6.45; π. θέσθαι τινί E.*Or.*13; π. ἀναιρέεσθαι Hdt.5.36, cf. D.1.7, etc.; π. κινεῖν, ἐγεῖραι, Th.6.34, Hdn.3.5.3; π. τοῖς ἔργοις ἐξενήνοχε D.11.20, cf. Plu.2.829e; ἐς π. καθίστασθαί τισι E.*HF*1168; π. ἐπαγαγεῖν Aeschin.3.140; ἀγαγεῖν ἐπί τινας D.5.19; π. ποιεῖν make *war*, Id.8.7; π. ποιεῖσθαι carry *it* on, X.*An.*5.5.24; π. καταλύεσθαι put an end to *it*, And.3.17, Th.6.36; ὁ π. ἀναπέπαυται X.*Cyr.*7.5.47: prov., οὐ πόλεμον ἐπαγγέλλεις, i.e. that is good news, Pl.*Lg.*702d, *Phdr.*242b: in pl., Democr.250, etc.; διὰ τὴν τῶν χρημάτων κτῆσιν πάντες οἱ π. ἡμῖν γίγνονται Pl.*Phd.*66c, cf. *R.*460a, al. II. personified, *War, Battle*, Ἀλαλὰ Πολέμου θύγατερ Pi.*Fr.*78, cf. Ar.*Pax* 205; Π. πάντων μὲν πατήρ ἐστι, πάντων δὲ βασιλεύς Heraclit.53; ὁ π. τῆς γενέσεως Dam.*Pr.*423. 2. metaph. of womankind, πολυτελὴς π. Secund.*Sent.*8.

**πολεμο-τροφέω,** *maintain war*, Lxx 2*Ma.*10.14. **-φθόρος,** ον, *wasting by war*, ἄται A.*Pers.*653 (lyr.). **-φόνευτος,** ον, *slain in war*, Sch.Opp.*H.*3.562. **-φρων,** gloss on δαΐφρων, Sch.Od.1.48.

**πολεμ-όω,** *make hostile, make an enemy of*, τινα v.l. in Lxx 4*Ma.*4.21:—Med., πῶς οὐ πολεμώσεσθε αὐτούς; surely *you will make* them *your enemies*, Th.5.98:—Pass., *to be made an enemy of*, μετὰ μεγίστων καιρῶν οἰκειοῦταί τε καὶ πολεμοῦται Id.1.36; ἐπολεμώθη δὲ ὅτι.. ib.57:—in other passages (πολεμουμένων Id.3.82, πολεμοῦνται 4.20) it is doubtful whether the word should be referred to πολεμόω or -έω. **-ώδης,** ες, *pertaining to war*, παροιμία Olymp.*in Grg.*p.114 J.

**πολεμώνιον,** τό, name of a plant, *Hypericum olympicum*, Dsc.4.8. 2. ἡ πολεμώνιος βοτάνη *horsemint*, *Mentha longifolia*, *Hippiatr.*32; called πολεμώνιον, τό, ibid.; πολεμωνία βοτάνη ib.86.

**πολεύω,** = sq. I. intr., *turn* or *go about*, κατὰ ἄστυ π. *go about* the city, i.e. live therein, Od.22.223; ὁ πολεύων, in Astrol., *the planet presiding over a day*, Serapio in *Cat.Cod.Astr.*1.99, *PMag.Leid.W.*5.47, Paul.Al.*I.*3; ὕψη τοὺς πολεύοντας ἀναβαίνοντας εἰς οὐρανὸν θεούς, ἄλλους δὲ καταβαίνοντας *PMag.Par.*1.545, cf. Iamb.*Myst.*3.30. II. trans., *turn up* the soil with the plough, γᾶν.. ἱππείῳ γένει π. S.*Ant.*341 (lyr.).—Poet. and late Prose.

**πολέω,** (πέλω) mostly Poet., I. intr., *go about, range over, haunt*, νῆσον Αἴαντος πολεῖ A.*Pers.*307; τί σὺ τῇδε πολεῖς; E.*Alc.*29 (anap.); τίς δδ' ἄρ' ἀμφὶ μέλαθρον πολεῖ; Id.*Or.*1270 (lyr.):—Med., ὄψεις ἔννυχοι πολούμεναι ἐς παρθενῶνας A.*Pr.*645 (dub., leg. πωλεύμεναι), cf. Ar.*Av.*181: abs., πεφασμένως πολοῦνται Lex Sol.ap.Lys.10.19. 2. *revolve*, Pl.*Cra.*405d. II. trans., *turn up* the earth with the plough, *plough*, ἔαρι πολεῖν Hes.*Op.*462; π. ἀρούρας Nic.*Al.*245.

**πόλεων,** gen. pl. of πόλις:—but πολέων, Ion. gen. pl. of πολύς.

**πόληες, πόληος, πόληι,** v. πόλις.

**πολῆον,** τό, prob. misspelling of πωλίον, *colt*, *PFay.*101.6,13 (i B.C.).

**πόλησις,** εως, ἡ, (πολέω) *movement*, coined by Pl.*Cra.*405c.

**πολῐ-ά,** ἡ, *greyness of hair*, Men.*Mon.*705; as a disease, Arist.*GA* 784$^b$13, *Pr.*894$^b$9, *Fr.*235; σεμνὴ π. Lxx 4*Ma.*7.15, cf. Plu.2.41b, Chor. p.15 B., al.; πολιή σε κατεύνασε *AP*5.219 (Agath.): concrete, πολλῆς μὲν νεότητος, πολλῆς δὲ πολιᾶς εἰσιούσης Chor.in Lib.4.516 R. **-άζω,** = sq., of the hair, Sch.Call.*Ap.*14. **-αίνομαι,** (πολιός) Pass., *grow white*, of the foaming sea, A.*Pers.*109 (lyr.).

**πολῑᾱ-νομέω,** *hold office of* πολιανόμος, Pl.*Ep.*363c; at Rome, *to be aedile*, D.C.43.48. **-νόμος,** ὁ, (πόλις, νέμω) *a civic magistrate*, *Tab.Heracl.*1.95 (pl.), *Documenti Ant. dell' Africa Italiana* 2.127 (Cyrenaica, pl.). 2. = Lat. *aedilis*, D.C.43.28,48. **-οχος,** ον, Dor. for πολιήοχος, v. πολιοῦχος.

**πολιαρχ-έω,** *to be praefectus urbi*, D.C.53.33, Malch.p.410 D., Lyd.*Mag.*3.38. **-ης,** ου, ὁ, = πολίαρχος 1, of Zeus, *IPE*1$^2$.183.10 (Olbia, ii A.D.). **-ία,** ἡ, *praefectura urbis*, Them.*Or.*17.214b, 18.224b. **-ος,** ὁ, *ruler of a city, prince*, π. πάτρα Pi.*N.*7.85, cf. E.*Rh.*381 (anap.). II. = Lat. *praefectus urbi*, D.C.40.46, al., Lyd.*Mag.*1.49 (pl.): as Adj., π. ἐξουσία ib.2.19; Thess. **πτολίαρχος** *IG*9(2).1233 (Phalanna, iii B.C., pl.).

**Πολιάς,** άδος, ἡ, (πόλις) *guardian of the city*, epith. of Athena, esp. in her oldest temple on the Acropolis of Athens, Hdt.5.82, S.*Ph.*134, Ar.*Av.*828, *IG*1$^2$.304.6, etc. (Πολιτίδα is f.l. for Πολιάδα in Din. 1.64); simply ἡ Πολιάς, Luc.*Pisc.*21, etc.; in other Greek cities, *Mnemos.*57.208 (Argos, vi B.C., dat. πολιιάδι), *IG*12(7).386.43 (Amorgos), 12(8).640.37 (Peparethus), etc.; at Troezen, Paus.2.30.6; at Erythrae, Id.7.5.9:—so **Πολιᾶτις,** ιδος, at Tegea, Id.8.47.5.

**πολιάς,** άδος, ἡ, pecul. fem. of πολιός, *grey-haired*, γυνὴ τὴν κεφαλὴν π. Luc.*Lex.*12.

**πολιάτ-ας** [ᾱτ], α, ὁ, Aeol. and Dor. for πολιήτης, opp. ξένος, Alc.*Supp.*14.6, Id.*Oxy.*1233 *Fr.*22.3, Pi.*I.*1.51, *Leg.Gort.*10.35, Isyll. 21. **-εύω,** *to be a citizen*, *Leg.Gort.*9.33.

**πολιᾶχος,** v. πολιοῦχος.

**πολίδιον,** v. πολείδιον. **πολίεθρον,** v. πτολίεθρον.

**Πολιεύς,** έως, ὁ, *guardian of the city*, of Zeus, Arist.*Mu.*401$^a$19, Corn.*ND*9, Paus.1.24.4, etc.; gen. Πολιῶς *IG*2$^2$.1388.48; Πολιέως *Schwyzer* 722.14 (Theb. ad Mycalen, iii B.C.); Coan dat. sg. Πολιῆ *SIG*1025.42 (iv/iii B.C.): nom. sg. written Πολιηύς *IG*12(3).363 (Thera, before v B.C.).

**πολίζω,** Ep. aor. ἐπόλισσα A.R.1.178, πόλισσα Il.7.453: (πόλις):—*build a city*: generally, *build*, [τεῖχος] πολίσσαμεν Il. l. c.; ἣν ἐπόλισσεν (sc. τὴν πάτρην) *Epigr.Gr.*982 (Philae):—Pass., Ἴλιος πεπόλιστο Il. 20.217; Δωδώνη πεπόλισται Hes.*Fr.*134.5, cf. Hdt.4.108, 5.52, al.; ἐφ' ἁμαξῶν πεπολισμένοι Philostr.*VA*6.25:—Med., *build for oneself*, A.R.1.1346; τὴν Ῥώμην σὺν τοῖς ἄλλοις ἐπολίσαντο D.H.1.30. II. *build a city* or *cities on* or *in* a place, χωρίον πολίζειν X.*An.*6.6.4; τὴν χώραν Str.8.5.4; τὸν τόπον Plu.*Rom.*9:—Pass., εἴη ἡ Παιονίη ἐπὶ τῷ Στρυμόνι ποταμῷ πεπολισμένη Hdt.5.13.—Ep., Ion., X., and later Prose.

**πολῐ-ήοχος,** ον, Ep. for πολιοῦχος. **-ήτης,** εω, ὁ, Ep. and Ion. for πολίτης, *citizen*, Il.2.806 (elsewh. Hom. uses the form πολίτης), Simon.137, twice in Trag., A.*Pers.*556, E.*El.*119 (both lyr.); constantly in Hdt. (only in 1.96 codd. have πολιτέων):—*fellow-citizen, countryman*, ib.37,120, al., cf. πολιάτας:—fem. **πολιῆτις,** ιδος, A.R. 1.867: as Adj., ψάμαθοι πολιήτιδος ἀκτᾶς sands on my *country's* shore, E.*Hipp.*1126 (lyr.).

**πόλινδε,** Adv. *into* or *to the city*, Il.5.224, al.

**πολιο-ειδής,** ές, *greyish*, ἄνθη Sch.Nic.*Al.*126. **-θριξ,** τρῐχος, ὁ, ἡ, *greyhaired*, ἱέρειαι Str.7.2.3.

**πολιοκρότᾰφος,** ον, *with grey hair on the temples*, i.e. *just beginning to be grey*, γέροντες Il.8.518, cf. Hes.*Op.*181, Alex.260; π. γῆρας B.*Fr.*21.2.

**πόλιον,** τό, *hulwort*, *Teucrium Polium*, said to cause caprification, Thphr.*HP*2.8.3, cf. 1.10.4, 7.10.5, Nic.*Th.*64, Orph.*A.*919, Dsc.3.110, Gal.6.731. 2. π. θαμνωδέστερον, *Teucrium creticum*, Dsc. l. c. 3. = ἕρπυλλος, Ps.-Dsc.3.38. (Cf. πολιόφυλλον.)

**πολιοπλόκᾰμος,** ον, *greyhaired*, Q.S.14.14.

**πολῐορκ-έω,** fut. -ήσω X.*Cyr.*7.5.12: aor. -ησα Ar.*Lys.*281, Th.1.61, etc.:—Pass., fut. -ηθήσομαι X.*HG*4.8.5; in med. form -ήσομαι, Hdt. 5.34, 8.49, Th.3.109, X.*HG*7.5.18, *Cyr.*6.1.15: aor. ἐπολιορκήθην Isoc. 6.57: pf. πεπολιόρκημαι (ἐκ-) Th.7.75: (πόλις, ἕρκος):—*besiege*, Hdt. 1.17,154, Ar.*V.*685, *Lys.*281, etc.; οἱ πολιορκοῦντες *the besiegers*, opp. οἱ κατακεκλειμένοι, Isoc.6.40:—Pass., *to be besieged, in a state of siege*, Hdt.1.81, al.; ὑπό τινος ib.26; also of a fleet, *to be blockaded*, Isoc.4.142; of Scamander, *to be blocked, dammed back*, ὑπὸ Ἀχιλλέως Pl.*Prt.*340a. 2. metaph., π. τῆς ψυχῆς τὸ φρόνημα Porph.*Chr.*28:—Pass., *to be besieged, pestered*, ὑπὸ τῶν συκοφαντῶν -ούμενοι πολιορκίαν Pl.*Alc.*2.142a, cf. *R.*453a, X.*Mem.*2.1.13, *UPZ*6.33 (ii B.C.); of a banker, π. περὶ ἀργυρίου *PCair.Zen.*62(a)4 (iii B.C.): in Medicine, *to be blocked*, Dsc.5.6.13. **-ητέος,** α, ον, *to be besieged*, X.*Cyr.*7.5.7. **-ητήριος,** α, ον, = πολιορκητικός, μηχαναί Onos.42.3. **-ητής,** οῦ, ὁ, *taker of cities*, surname of Demetrius son of Antigonus, Phld.*Hom.*p.55 O., D.S.20.92, Plu.*Demetr.*42, *Arist.*6 (pl.), etc. **-ητικός,** ή, όν, *of* or *for besieging*, αἱ π. ἐπίνοιαι Plb.1.58.4. II. τὰ π. ἔργα *siege-works*, D.S.20.103; ὄργανα Posidon.36 J., Str.16.1.24. 2. π., τά, title of treatise by Apollodorus of Damascus. **-ία,** Ion. **-ίη,** ἡ, *siege of a city*, Hdt.1.81,190, 5.34, And.1.73, Th.2.78, etc. 2. metaph., *besieging, pestering*, v.l. in Plu.*Sull.*25.

**πολιός,** ά, όν, also ός, όν, ἁλὸς πολιοῖο Il.20.229, Od.5.410, etc.; χήραν πολιόν E.*Andr.*348:—*grey, grizzled, grisly*, λύκοιο Il.10.334; κορῶναι Ar.*Av.*967; σίδηρος Il.9.366, *h.Merc.*41, cf. E.*Heracl.*758 (lyr.); of the surging sea, πολιῆς ἐπὶ θινὶ θαλάσσης Il.4.248; πολιὴν ἅλα ναιέμεν 15.190; π. θάλασσα Alc.51; π. πέλαγος Ar.*Av.*350 (lyr.); γάλα Q.S.10.135; λύκοι *IG*4$^2$(1).131.12 (Epid.); but, 2. most freq. of human hair, *grey* from age, κάρη, κεφαλή, Il.22.74, Od.24.317, etc.; π. στῆθος Alc.*Supp.*20.2; γῆρας π. Pi.*I.*6(5).15, E.*Ba.*258; πολιοί *greyhaired men*, Od.24.499; π. ματέρες S.*OT*182 (lyr.), cf. E.*Supp.*35, Ar.*Ach.*600, 610, 692, Pl.*Prm.*127b (rare in Att. Prose), Call.*Fr.*473; Γραῖαι, ἐκ γενετῆς πολιαί Hes.*Th.*271: Comp. -ώτεροι Arist.*Fr.*235: abs., πολιαί (sc. τρίχες) Pi.*O.*4.28, Arist.*GA*722$^a$7, *Pr.*898$^a$31; πολιῶν ἔσχηκας τὸν πώγωνα μεστόν Thphr.*Char.*2.3; ἅμα ταῖς π. κατιούσαις as the *grey hairs* come down (i.e. from the temples to the beard), Ar.*Eq.*520, cf. 908; ἕως τὸ δὴ λεγόμενον πολιὰς σχῇ *PMich.Zen.*77 (iii B.C.), cf. Lxx *Is.*47.2, al., Phld.*Vit.*p.32 J. 3. τίς σε πολιᾶς ἐξανῆκε γαστρός; what *old woman's* womb bare thee? as a sarcasm, Pi.*P.*4.98; π. δάκρυον ἐκβάλλων *an old man's* tear, E.*HF*1209 (lyr.). b. metaph., *hoary, venerable*, ὃς πολιῷ νόμῳ αἶσαν ὀρθοῖ A.*Supp.*673 (lyr.); κληδὼν ἐν πολιαῖσι μένει φήμαις E.*El.*701 (lyr.); μάθημα χρόνῳ π. Pl.*Ti.*22b; πλοῦτος.. χρόνῳ π. Jul.*Or.*2.82b. II. *bright, clear, serene*, ἔαρ Hes.*Op.*477, 492; αἰθήρ E.*Or.*1376 (lyr.); ἠήρ A.R.3.275, Q.S.2.554.

**πολιότης,** ητος, ἡ, *greyness*, of hair, Arist.*GA*780$^b$6, 784$^a$30, al.

**πολιότρῐχος,** ον, = πολιόθριξ, Opp.*C.*3.293.

**πολιοῦχος** (A), ον, Ep. **πολιήοχος,** Dor. **-άοχος** (v. infr.), Lacon. **πολιᾶχος** *IG*5(1).213.3 (Sparta, v B.C.); cf. πολισσοῦχος: (ἔχω A):—*protecting a city*, ὦ π. κράτος E.*Rh.*821 (lyr., codd., sed v. infr.); π. ἀρετά Isyll.16; but mostly as epith. of the guardian deity of a city, Ἀθηναίη π. in Chios, Hdt.1.160 (also in Attica, *BCH*50.529 (Marathon, ii A.D.)); Παλλὰς π., at Athens, Ar.*Eq.*581 (lyr.); Ἀθάνα π. Id. *Nu.*602 (lyr.), cf. *Av.*827; Παλλὰς πολιάοχος Pi.*O.*5.10; π. θεοί A. *Th.*312 (lyr.); δαίμονες ib.822 (lyr.); Ζεὺς π. Pl.*Lg.*921c; Ἀρτέμιδος πολιηόχου A.R.1.312; π. Ἀλεξανδρείας, title of Diocletian, *OGI*718.2 (Alexandria, iv A.D.): **πολίοχος** (elsewh. known as pr. n. Πολίοχος) shd. be read in E.*Rh.*166, 821.

**πολιοῦχος** (B), ον, (πολιός) *greyhaired*, *PLond.*1821.325.

**πολιοφῠλᾰκέω,** of an army, *keep within the city*, opp. taking the field, Plb.18.39.4.

**πολιόφυλλον,** τό, name of a herb, *Hippiatr.*31 (v.l. πολιουφύλλα), 32; cf. πολίου φύλλον *Gp.*16.9.2.

**πολίοχος,** v. πολιοῦχος.

**πολιόχρως,** ωτος, ὁ, ἡ, *white-coloured*, κύκνος E.*Ba.*1365 (sed leg. κηφῆνα πολιόχρων); μεμβράδες Ar.*Fr.*137.

**πολιόω,** *turn grey*, Dsc.1.30, *Eup.*1.94:—mostly in Pass., *to be* or *become grey*, ὁ ἄνθρωπος πολιοῦται μόνος Arist.*GA*780$^b$4, cf. Gal.12.441; πρῶτον πολιοῦνται οἱ κρόταφοι Arist.*HA*518$^a$16, cf. Plu.*Fr.inc.*149; of things, J.*AJ*10.11.7.

**πολίπορθος,** f.l. for πτολίπ- (q. v.).

**πολιρραίστης,** ου, ὁ, (ῥαίω) = πτολίπορθος, Lyc.210.

**πόλις,** Ep. also **πτόλις** (found sts. in Trag. etc., v. πτόλις), ἡ: Ep. forms, acc. sg. πόληα Hes.*Sc.*105, Call.*Aet.Oxy.*2080.62; gen. πόλιος or πτόλιος, Il.2.811, 4.514, al., πόληος 16.395, al. (also Thgn.757), πόλεος Il.21.567; dat. πόλει 5.686, al., πτόλεϊ 17.152, πόληϊ 3.50 (also Tyrt.12.15): pl., nom. πόλιες Od.15.412, πόληες Il.4.45; gen. πολίων 1.125, al.; dat. πολίεσσι Od.21.252; acc. πόλεις Il.2.648, al., πόληας Od.17.486, Call.*Fr.*9.70 P. (scanned ⏑⏑– *IG*1$^2$.826), πόλιας (disyll.) Od.8.560, 574, (trisyll.) Il.4.308 (s. v. l., πόλεας Aristarch.): Ion. forms, gen. πόλεως *IG*12(8).356 (Thasos), *GDI*5653 *a*13 (Chios), etc., also Xenoph.2.9, 22, v.l. in Thgn.1043; written πόλειως *GDI*5532.19

(Zeleia); πόλεος ib.5339.41 (Orop.), *IG*12(7).103 (Amorgos), Thgn. 776, etc., πόλιος Hdt.1.26, al., Herod.2.8, al., πόληος Thgn. (v. supr.), cj. in Hippon.47, cf. *An.Ox.*1.361; dat. mostly πόλει, but πόλῑ Hdt. 2.60, al., πόληῑ (or –ῃ) *SIG*169.3 (Iasos, iv B.C.): pl., usu. πόλεις, πόλεων, πόλεσι, but in Hdt. πόλῑες 1.142, al., πολίων ib.6, al., πόλισι ib. 151, al.; acc. πόλῑς 2.177, al., πόλιας 1.142, 2.102, al.: Dor. gen. sg. πόλιος *SIG*615.3 (Delph., ii B.C.); dat. sg. πόλι *IG*4.839 (Calaurea, iv B.C.); dat. pl. πολίεσι Pi.*P.*7.8; πολίεσσι Foed.Lac.ap.Th.5.77 (v.l. πολίεσι), 79, *IG*4$^{2}$(1).74.4 (Epid., iii B.C.); Cret. πόλιθι *GDI*5019.3: Aeol. gen. πόλιος *IG*12(2).526*a*8 (πόληος is an Epicism in Alc. *Supp.*17.6); gen. pl. πολίων *IG*11(4).1064*b*20; dat. pl. πολίεσσι ib. 12(2).1.6: Trag., gen. πόλεως disyll. (as also in Com., exc. Ar.*Eq.* 763), thrice πόλεος A.*Ag.*1167 (lyr.), S.*Ant.*162, E.*Or.*897:—Att. Inscrr. earlier than 350 B.C. sts. have dat. sg. πόλῃ, *IG*1$^{2}$.108.35, 2$^{2}$. 17.10, 42.5, 53.7; Att. dual πόλη Isoc.8.116, πόλη or πόλει Aeschin. Socr.8 (where Choerob. cites both forms, *in Theod.*1.314, 136 H.); gen. τοῖν πολέοιν Isoc.4.73: Elean nom. sg. πόλερ *Schwyzer*425.16; gen. πόλιορ ib.20 (iii/ii B.C.):—*city*, Hom. ll. cc., Hes.*Sc.*270, etc.; π. ἄκρη, ἀκροτάτη, = ἀκρόπολις, *the citadel*, Il.6.88, 20.52; which at Athens also was in early times called simply π., while the rest of the city was called ἄστυ, καλεῖται.. ἡ ἀκρόπολις μέχρι τοῦδε ἔτι ὑπ' Ἀθηναίων π. Th.2.15; ἐν πόλει in treaties, Id.5.23,47, cf. *IG*1$^{2}$.372.1, Ar. *Lys.*245, 758; ἐς πόλιν *IG*1$^{2}$.91.4; πρὸς πόλιν Ar.*Lys.*288 (lyr.); ἐκ πόλεως Id.*Eq.*1093; but ἐν τῇ πόλει X.*An.*7.1.27, dub. in Antipho 6.39; so Ἰνάχου π. *the citadel* of Argos, E.*Fr.*228.6; of the Cadmea at Thebes, Plu.*Pel.*18, cf. Str.8.6.8; of Alexandria, Eust.239.13; π. ἡ ἁγία, of Jerusalem, Lxx *Ne.*11.1: with the name of the city added in gen., Ἰλίου π., Ἄργους π., *the city of..*, A.*Ag.*29, Ar.*Eq.*813; also in appos., ἡ Μένδη π. Th.4.130; ἡ π. οἱ Ταρσοί X.*An.*1.2.26. 2. *one's city* or *country*, πόθι τοι π. ἠδὲ τοκῆες; Od.1.170, etc., cf. πόλιν· τὴν χώραν, Hsch. 3. ὁ ἐπὶ τῆς πόλεως *city* governor, *OGI*113.3, 134.2, al. (Cyprus, ii B.C.), Plb.5.39.3: without Art., ἐπὶ πόλιος *IG*7.2809.2 (Hyettus, iii B.C.), etc.; ἐπὶ πόλεως ib.299.1 (Oropus, iii B.C.); στρατηγὸς πόλεως *OGI*743 (Ptol.); στρατηγὸς τῆς π. *BGU*729.1 (ii A.D.); στρατηγὸς κατὰ πόλιν, = Lat. *praetor urbanus*, *IG*14.951.2 (Rome, i B.C.). II. *country*, as dependent on and called after its city, ἀνθρώπων οἳ τήνδε π. καὶ γαῖαν ἔχουσιν Od.6.177, cf. Hes.*Sc.*380, S.*OC* 1533, etc.; esp. of *islands* peopled by men, Λῆμνον π. Θόαντος Il.14.230; π. Αἴαντος, = Σαλαμίς, Pi.*I.*5(4).48, etc.; περιρρύτας π. A.*Eu.*77, cf. E. *Ion*294, Ar.*Pax*251 (v. Sch.); also διώχληκε π. πολλάς.., Σικελίαν, Ἰταλίαν, Πελοπόννησον, Θετταλίαν κτλ. Lys.6.6, cf. Str.8.3.31. III. *community* or *body of citizens* (opp. ἄστυ, their dwellings, Il.17.144, but in δῆμός τε π. τε Od.11.14, π. denotes the *town*), ὧν π. ἀνάριθμος ὄλλυται S.*OT*179 (lyr.): hence, 2. *state* or *community*, ξύμπασα π. κακοῦ ἀνδρὸς ἀπηύρα Hes.*Op.*240, cf. Pi.*P.*2.88, S.*OT*22, E.*Ph.*947, etc.; π. ἄνδρα διδάσκει Simon.67; esp. *free state, republic*, S.*Ant.*738 (cf. 734), X.*Cyr.*8.2.28, Arist.*Pol.*1276a23; τὰ τῆς π. *state affairs, government*, Pl.*Prt.*319a; π. ἡ γενῶν καὶ κωμῶν κοινωνία ζωῆς τελείας καὶ αὐτάρκους Arist.*Pol.*1280b40; τὴν π. φεύγειν shun one's *public duties*, D.45.66; *assembly of citizens*, *Berl.Sitzb.*1927.8 (Locr., v B.C.). 3. *rights of citizenship*, Ar.*Ra.*718, D.21.106. IV. πόλιν παίζειν, a game resembling backgammon, Cratin.56, perh. alluded to in Pl.*R.*422e. (Cf. Skt. *pūr*, Lith. *pilìs* 'fortress'.)

⊛ **πόλ-ισμα**, ατος, τό, *buildings of a city, town*, sts. = πόλις, sts. difft. from it; of Ecbatana, Hdt.1.98; π. Πελασγικά ib.57, cf. 6.6; of Thebes, A.*Th.*63, al.; of Troy, S.*Ph.*1424; of Athens, Id.*OC*1496 (lyr.), cf. Ar.*Av.*553, 1565; ὦ π. Κεκροπίας χθονός Men.*Sam.*110: pl., Call.*Aet. Oxy.*2080.90: in Prose, Th.1.10, 4.54; of the Acropolis, Dicaearch. Hist.72; = *municipium*, *Gloss.* **-ισμάτιον**, τό, Dim. of foreg., Ephor. 27 J., Plb.1.24.12, Str.6.3.9, J.*AJ*15.9.6, Plu.*Them.*26. **-ισμός**, ὁ, *building of a city*, D.H.1.57, 59; π. τῆς Ῥώμης Lyd.*Mag.*1.2.

**πολισσονόμος**, ον, (πόλις, νέμω) *managing* or *ruling a city*, ἀρχαί A.*Ch.*864 (anap.); π. βιοτά a life *of social order*, Id.*Pers.*853 (lyr.).

**πολισσόος**, ον, (σῴζω) *guarding a city* or *cities*, *h.Mart.*2.

**πολισσοῦχος**, ον, poet. for πολιοῦχος, θεοί A.*Th.*69, 185, 271, *Ag.* 338; also of patrons or eponymous heroes, Ἰδομενεύς *GDI*5074 (Crete); Κραταιμένης Call.*Aet.Oxy.*2080.79. II. *dwelling in the city*, λεώς, βροτοί, A.*Eu.*775, 883.

**πολιστής**, οῦ, ὁ, (πολίζω) *founder of a city*, rejected by Poll.9.6.

⊛ **πολῑταρχ-έω**, *hold office of* πολιτάρχης, Demitsas Μακεδ.364, al. (Thessalonica), *Sammelb.*5765.7 (Egypt, iii/iv A.D.). ⊛ **-ης**, ου, ὁ, *civic magistrate*, at Thessalonica, *Act.Ap.*17.6; at Lete, *SIG*700.2 (ii B.C.); in Egypt, *POxy.*745.4 (i B.C./i A.D.):—also **-ος**, ὁ, Aen.Tact. 26.12. **-ία**, ἡ, *office of* πολιτάρχης, *BSA*23.73 (Lete, ii A.D.).

⊛ **πολῑτ-εία**, Ion. -ηΐη, ἡ, *condition and rights of a citizen, citizenship*, Hdt.9.34, Th.6.104, etc.; π. δοῦναί τινι X.*HG*1.2.10: pl., *grants of citizenship*, Arist.*Ath.*54.3. 2. *the daily life of a citizen*, And.2.10, D. 19.184; ἐν εἰρήνῃ καὶ π. Id.20.122; *life, living*, ἡ ἐν Βοιωτίᾳ π. Plb.18. 43.6; so perh. *Ep.Eph.*3.12. 3. concrete, *body of citizens*, Arist.*Pol.* 1292a34. 4. = Lat. *civitas* in geographical sense, *SIG*888.118 (Scaptopara, iii A.D.), Mitteis *Chr.*78.6 (iv A.D.), etc. II. *government, administration*, Ar.*Eq.*219, X.*Mem.*3.9.15, etc.; ἄγειν τὴν π. Th.1.127; θρασύτατα καὶ ἀσελγέστατα τῇ π. κεχρῆσθαι Hyp.*Eux.*29; *course of policy*, τῇ π. καὶ τοῖς ψηφίσμασι D.18.87, cf. 9.3 (pl.), 18.263; ἡ Κλεοφῶντος π. Aeschin.3.150; ἡ πρὸς Ῥωμαίους ὁμιλία καὶ π. Str.16.2.46: pl., *acts of policy*, J.*Vit.*65. 2. *tenure of public office*, πᾶσαν π. ἐπιφανῶς ἐκτελέσαι *IG*4.716.6 (Hermione); ἐν τοῖς τῆς π. χρόνοις *IPE*1$^{2}$.32 *B*76 (Olbia, iii B.C.). III. *civil polity, constitution of a state*, Antipho 3. 2.1, Th.2.37, etc.; τὴν ἐλευθερίαν.., μᾶλλον δὲ καὶ τὰς π. D.18.65; *form of government*, Pl.*R.*562a, etc.; ὁμολογοῦνται τρεῖς εἶναι π., τυραννὶς καὶ ὀλιγαρχία καὶ δημοκρατία Aeschin.1.4, cf. Arist.*Pol.*1293a 37, etc.; αἱ τέτταρες π. Pl.*R.*544b; ἥτις ἂν π. συμφέρῃ Lys.25.8; π. ἐστὶ τάξις ταῖς πόλεσιν ἡ περὶ τὰς ἀρχάς Arist.*Pol.*1289a15, cf. 1274b26 (pl.), 1289b27 (pl.); ὅπου μὴ νόμοι ἄρχουσιν οὐκ ἔστι π. ib.1292a32; τὴν ἀρίστην πολιτεύεσθαι π. ib.1288b31, cf. X.*Ath.*1.1, etc. 2. esp. *republican government, free common-wealth*, Arist.*EN*1160a34, *Pol.* 1293b22; ὅταν δὲ τὸ πλῆθος πρὸς τὸ κοινὸν πολιτεύηται συμφέρον, καλεῖται π. ib.1279a39; ἄπιστον ταῖς π. ἡ τυραννίς D.1.5; οὐ γὰρ ἀσφαλεῖς ταῖς π. αἱ πρὸς τοὺς τυράννους.. ὁμιλίαι Id.6.21; τοὺς τὰς π. μεθιστάντας εἰς ὀλιγαρχίαν Id.15.20; ταῖς μὲν π. πολεμοῦσι τὰς δὲ μοναρχίας συγκαθιστᾶσι Isoc.4.125; ἔστι δήμου ἡ π. βίος Plu.2.826c. ⊛ **-ευμα**, ατος, τό, *business of government, act of administration*, D.18.108, 136: more freq. in pl., *measures of government* or *institutions*, Pl.*Lg.*945d, Isoc.7.78; τῶν τοιούτων π. οὐδὲν πολιτεύομαι D.8.71; ἔν τε τοῖς κατὰ τὴν πόλιν π. καὶ ἐν τοῖς Ἑλληνικοῖς both in my home and foreign *policy*, Id.18.109; κάλλιστον π. ἐποιήσατο *IG*4$^{2}$(1).81.9 (Epid., i A.D.); π. *Catonis* Cic.*Att.*6.1.13, cf. 9.7.3. II. the concrete of πολιτεία III, *the government*, π. ἐστὶν ἡ πολιτεία Arist.*Pol.*1278b11, cf. 1279a26, 1283b 31, etc.; οἱ ἐν π. the *citizens*, ib.1303b26, cf. 1305b34; τὸ τῆς δημοκρατίας π. Aeschin.2.172; τὸ πάτριον π. Plb.5.9.9, cf. 4.25.7 (pl.); π. ἀκέραια, σωφρονικά, Id.1.13.12, D.H.1.41; τὰ π. *free republics*, D.S.18.69; *form of government*, πολίτευμα (sic) εἶναι ἐν Χίῳ δῆμον *SIG*283.3 (Edict of Alexander, Chios, iv B.C.), cf. Decr.Att.ap.Plu.2.851f. III. *citizen rights, citizenship*, ἀξίους τοῦ παρ' ὑμῖν π. *IG*9(2).517.6 (Larissa, Epist. Philipp. V), etc.: metaph., ἡμῶν τὸ π. ἐν οὐρανοῖς ὑπάρχει *Ep.Phil.*3. 20. IV. concrete, *body of citizens*, τὸ π. τὸ Μιλησίων *SIG*633.59 (Milet., ii B.C.), cf. *OGI*229.60 (Smyrna, iii B.C.), etc.; *sovereign body*, Arist.*Pol.*1302b16, 1332b31; π. ἔστω οἱ μύριοι *Abh.Berl.Akad.*1925 (5).6 (Cyrene); πᾶν τὸ π. ib.7. 2. *corporate body of citizens* resident in a foreign city, Καυνίων τὸ π. (at Sidon) *OGI*592; τὸ π. τῶν ἐν Βερενίκῃ Ἰουδαίων *CIG*5361.21; τὸ π. τῶν Κρητῶν (in Egypt) *PTeb.*32. 17 (ii B.C.). b. generally, *corporate body, association*, τὸ π. τῶν γυναικῶν *BCH*15.182, 205 (Panamara); τὸ π. τινός *founded by* a person, *Sammelb.*5793 (i A.D.). **-ευτέον**, *one must take part in politics*, Cic.*Att.*2.6.2, 10.1.4, Plu.2.790e, Arr.*Epict.*3.7.19. ⊛ **-ευτής**, οῦ, ὁ, *statesman*, Artem.1.79, Sch.Ar.*Eq.*161.

⊛ **πολῑτεύω**, fut. -σω Th.1.19, X.*HG*2.3.2:—*to be a citizen* or *freeman, live in a free state*, Th.2.46, 3.34, 4.114, X.*An.*3.2.26; οἶκοι π. *SIG*306.21 (Tegea, iv B.C.); π. παρά τισι X.*HG*1.5.19; πεπολιτευκὼρ πὰρ ἀμέ, = μετοικῶν, *Schwyzer*425.5 (Elis, iii/ii B.C.); κατὰ νόμους π., opp. monarchy, Plb.4.76.2: more freq. in Med., v. infr. 2. *have a certain form of government, administer the state*, κατ' ὀλιγαρχίαν π. Th.1.19, 3.62; π. ὥσπερ εἰώθεσαν Id.4.130; κατὰ τὰ ἴδια κέρδη π. Id. 2.65; πρὸς τὸ ἴδιον κέρδος X.*HG*1.4.13; ἐλευθέρως τὰ πρὸς τὸ κοινὸν π. Th.2.37:—Pass., of the state, *to be governed*, τὰς εὖ -ευομένας πόλεις Isoc.6.35, cf. Pl.*R.*427a, etc.; ἄνευ ὁμονοίας οὔτ' ἂν πόλις εὖ -ευθείη X. *Mem.*4.4.16; τὰ πεπολιτευμένα αὐτοῖς *the measures of* their *administration*, D.1.28; τὰ κοινῇ πεπ. Id.18.8, cf. Isoc.16.45, etc. b. Pass., in Law, *to be customary*, τὸ μέχρι νῦν -ευόμενον Just.*Nov.*73.8.2, cf. 52 *Praef.*; ἡ -ευομένη τῆς ἀρτάβης (sc. τιμή) *customary* price, *PGiss.* 105.7 (v A.D.). 3. Pass., *to be made a citizen*, τοὺς ἐπὶ Γέλωνος πολιτευθέντας D.S.11.72.

B. most freq. in Med., fut. πολιτεύσομαι Ar.*Eq.*1365, X.*Ath.* 3.9: aor. ἐπολιτευσάμην And.2.10, D.18.207; also Pass. ἐπολιτεύθην Th.6.92, Lys.26.5, (ἐν-) Isoc.5.5, etc.: pf. πεπολίτευμαι Lys.25. 10, D.13.35, etc.:—like the Act., *live as a free citizen*, chiefly in Prose (once in E. (v. infr.), twice in Ar. (v. infr.)); π. μεθ' ὑμῶν And. l.c.; ἐν δημοκρατίᾳ X.*Cyr.*1.1.1, etc.; ἐν ἐλευθερίᾳ καὶ νόμοις ἐξ ἴσου D.10.4; opp. μετοικέω, Lys.12.20; ἐν εἰρήνῃ X.*HG*2.4.22; ἀδίκως π. τοὺς ἄλλους π. Lys.14.42; εἰ πένης.. λαὸς πολιτεύοιτο πλουσίων ἄτερ E.*Fr.*21. II. *take part in the government*, Critias 45 D., Th.2.15 (as v.l.), Nausiph.2, Hyp.*Eux.*27, D.18.18; *meddle with politics*, Pl.*R.*561d; opp. ἰδιωτεύειν, Aeschin.1.195; *hold public office, show public spirit*, *IG*4.858 (Methana, cf. *Glotta* 14.78), *SIG*850.14 (Epist. Antonini Pii), etc. 2. c. acc., *administer, govern*, ἅπαντα Ar.*Lys.*573; τὰ καθ' αὐτοὺς πολιτεύεσθαι D.10.74; ἃ καὶ πεποίηκα καὶ πεπολίτευμαι Id.18.4; οὐ τὰ βέλτιστα π. ib.207; π. πόλεμον ἐκ πολέμου *make* perpetual war *the principle of government*, Aeschin.2. 177: abs., *conduct the government*, Ar.*Eq.*1365; κατὰ συμμορίας D. 2.29; διὰ τοὺς ἀδίκως -ομένους ἐν τῇ ὀλιγαρχίᾳ δημοκρατία γίγνεται Lys.25.27; τοῖς ὑπὲρ αὐτοῦ πεπολιτευμένοις D.2.4; οἱ πολιτευόμενοι the *ministers*, Id.3.30, 24.157. III. *have a certain form of government*, τοὺς ἄριστα τῶν ἄλλων πολιτευομένους Isoc.3.24; ἡμῶν ἐγγὺς π. Pl.*R.*568b; κατὰ τὰ πάτρια π. Decr.ap.And.1.83; οἱ τὴν ἄνισον πολιτείαν πολιτευόμενοι, i.e. those living in an oligarchy or a tyranny, Aeschin.1.5. IV. *serve as curialis*, Mitteis *Chr.*97 i 18 (iv A.D.), *PLips.*62 i 2 (iv A.D.), *POxy.*2106.19 (iv A.D.), etc. V. in Law, *execute according to custom*, διαθήκας Just.*Nov.*66.1 *Intr.* VI. *deal with*, in private affairs, ἀλλήλοις *PHib.*1.63.11 (iii B.C.); πρὸς [τοὺς θεοὺς] ὁσίως καὶ δικαίως *UPZ*144.14, cf. 110.78 (ii B.C.), Lxx 2 *Ma.*11. 25, Aristeas 31, *Act.Ap.*23.1; π. πᾶσαν πολιτείαν κατὰ τὸν Ἰουδαϊσμόν *BCH*56.293 (Stobi, i/ii A.D.); *behave*, *Ep.Phil.*1.27. b. metaph., *arrange, bring about*, συνοδίαν, γάμον, Charito 1.1, 2.2.

**πολῑτ-ηΐη**, ἡ, Ion. for πολιτεία. ⊛ **-ης**, ου, ὁ, Ion. **πολιήτης** (q.v.), *citizen, freeman*, Il.15.558, 22.429, Od.7.131, Pi.O.5.16, etc.; π. ἀγαθός Th.3.42, Pl.*Grg.*517c; κακός E.*Ba.*271; πόλεως, πόλεων π., Antipho 5.78, And.1.5; ὦ γᾶς πατρίας πολῖται S.*Ant.*806 (lyr.); π. ὁρίζεται τῷ μετέχειν κρίσεως καὶ ἀρχῆς Arist.*Pol.*1275a22. 2.

*fellow-citizen* (cf. πολιήτης), Sapph.*Supp*.1.14, etc.; Κάδμου π. A.*Th*. 1; Ἀθηναίων π. And.1.139; ὑμῶν Lys.20.12; σός Pl.*Prt*.339e: and by a Com. metaph., οἴνου π. ὢν κρατίστου Amphis 36. II. Adj. *belonging to, connected with one's city* or *country*, θεοὶ πολῖται, = πολιοῦχοι, A.*Th*.253; π. δῆμος, = ὁ τῆς πόλεως, Ar.*Ec*.574. **-ῐκοπραιτώριος**, α, ον, *in accordance with jus civile and praetorian law*, *PMasp*. 151.44 (vi A.D.). ⊛ **-ῐκός**, ή, όν, *of, for,* or *relating to citizens*, σύλλογος Pl.*Grg*.452e; οἶκοι Isoc.2.21; αἱ π. λειτουργίαι, opp. αἱ τῶν μετοίκων, D.20.18; π. κοινωνία, βίος, Arist.*Pol*.1252$^a$7, 1254$^b$30; π. νόμος *IG*9(1).32.22 (Stiris, ii B.C.), *PHal*.1.79, cf. *PPetr*.3 p.49 (iii B.C.), Mitteis *Chr*.31 vii 9 (ii B.C.); π. χώρα, Lat. *ager publicus*, Plb.6.45.3; παῖδες π. *IG*14.748 (Naples); χορὸς π. ib.7.1776 (Helice); at Rome, π. στρατηγία office of praetor *urbanus* (i. e. *qui inter cives ius dicit*), Plu.*Brut*. 7. Adv. -κῶς, κινεῖν bring a *civil* action, *Cod.Just*.4.20.13.1. b. *in a town*, π. τόπος a *city* site, *POxy*.2109.8 (iii A.D.). c. πολιτικός, ὁ, *official*, *PTeb*.208 (i B.C.), *Sammelb*.286 (pl.), *POxy*.34 iii 10 (pl., ii A.D.), etc. 2. *befitting a citizen, civic, civil*, ἰσονομία Th.3.82; σχῆμα π. τοῦ λόγου Id.8.89; ἀγῶνες X.*Mem*.2.6.26; π. ἀρετή Id.*Lac*. 10.7; ἡ -ωτάτη ἔρις ib.4.5; τὰ πολιτικά *civil affairs*, opp. τὰ πολεμικά, Id.*Eq*.2.1, cf. *Hier*.9.5; πολιτικωτέρα ἐγένετο ἡ ὀλιγαρχία *more constitutional*, Arist.*Pol*.1305$^b$10; π. ἀρχή, opp. δεσποτική, ib.1254$^b$4; *observant of social order*, Plb.34.14.2. Adv. -κῶς, ἔχειν act *like a citizen, in a constitutional manner*, Isoc.4.79; οὐδὲ κοινῶς οὐδὲ π. ἐβίωσαν ib. 151; οὐκ ἴσως οὐδὲ π. D.10.74; οὕτω..ἀρχαίως εἶχον, μᾶλλον δὲ π. the Greek states were so much *like members of one state*, Id.9.48; π. ἄρχειν, opp. βασιλικῶς, Arist.*Pol*.1259$^b$1; opp. δεσποτικῶς, ib.1324$^a$37; of animals, πολιτικώτερον χρῶνται τοῖς ἀπογόνοις *more socially*, Id.*HA* 589$^a$2: hence, b. *civil, courteous*, Plb.23.5.7. Adv. *civilly, courteously*, πράως καὶ π. μεμψιμοιρεῖν Id.18.48.7. 3. *consisting of citizens* or *of one's fellow-citizens*, τὸ πολιτικόν the *community*, Hdt.7.103, cf. Th.8.93; τὸ π. στράτευμα, opp. τὸ τῶν συμμάχων, X.*HG*4.4.19: without στράτευμα, ib.5.3.25, etc.; αἱ π. δυνάμεις Aeschin.3.98; opp. οἱ σύμμαχοι, D.18.237, cf. 9.48; π. δικαστήριον a court *composed of* locally appointed *citizens*, opp. ξενικὸν δ. (one composed of foreigners invited from abroad), *SIG*306.28 (Tegea, iv B.C.), 976.9 (Samos, ii B.C.); οἱ π. ἱππεῖς καὶ πεζοί Plb.1.9.4, cf. D.S.19.106; τὰ π. σώματα prob. cj. for τὰ πολεμικὰ σ. in Plb.4.52.7, cf. *SIG*588.64 (Milet., ii B.C.); σῶμα π. *IG*12(7).386.25 (Aegiale, iii B.C.); οἱ π., = οἱ πολῖται, ib.2$^2$.2316.54. 4. *living in a community*, ἄνθρωπος φύσει π. ζῷον Arist.*Pol*.1253$^a$3; πολιτικὰ δ' ἐστίν, ὧν ἕν τι καὶ κοινὸν γίγνεται πάντων τὸ ἔργον Id.*HA*488$^a$7; also, *fit for, characteristic of, free government*, Id.*Pol*.1287$^b$38, 1294$^b$1; πλῆθος ib.1288$^a$12. 5. *secular*, opp. ecclesiastical, πρόσοδοι *SIG*459.6 (Beroea, iii B.C.), cf. 526.35 (Itanus, iii B.C.), *OGI*267.29 (Pergam., iii B.C.); οἱ π. the *laity*, Lyd. *Mens*.3.10. II. *of* or *befitting a statesman, statesmanlike*, δεινότητες Nausiph.2; ψυχαὶ -ώτεραι, opp. οἰκονομικώτεραι, X.*Cyr*.2.2.14, cf. Pl.*Alc*.1.133e; ὁ πολιτικός *the statesman*, Arist.*Pol*.1252$^a$7, 1274$^b$36, 1276$^a$34; also, title of a dialogue by Plato. III. *belonging to the state* or *its administration, political*, οἰκείων καὶ π. ἐπιμέλεια Th. 2.40; τέχνη π. Democr.157, Pl.*Prt*.319a, *Grg*.521d; ἡ π. ἐπιστήμη, ἡ π., the science *of politics*, opp. οἰκονομική, βασιλική, Id.*Plt*.259c, 303e (in Arist. *politics* includes ethics, *EN*1094$^b$11, *Rh*.1356$^a$27, and is divided into πολιτική (proper) καὶ οἰκονομία καὶ φρόνησις, *EE*1218$^b$13, cf. *EN*1141$^b$23 sq.); π. πράγματα Isoc.4.113; πράξεις Pl.*Hp.Ma*. 281c; φρόνησις Arist.*EN*1141$^b$26; λόγος, title of work by Antipho Soph., Hermog.*Id*.2.11, etc.; τὰ π. *public matters*, γνῶναι Th.2.40, cf. 6.15,89; πράττειν τὰ π. Pl.*Grg*.521d, cf. *Ap*.31d, etc.; but τὰ π. βλάπτειν prejudice the *weal of the state*, Id.*R*.407d. 2. *civil, municipal*, opp. natural or general, οὐ γὰρ ἐκ π. αἰτίας D.21.218. IV. generally, *having relation to public life, political, public*, opp. κατ' ἰδίας, Th.8.89; π. τιμαί X.*Mem*.2.6.24; λόγοι *civil* oratory, Isoc.15. 46, D.H.*Comp*.1, al.; τίς π. καὶ κοινὴ βοήθεια; D.18.311. Adv. Comp. -ώτερον, *litterae π. scriptae* Cic.*Att*.5.12.2. V. *suited to a citizen's common life, ordinary*, κάνναθρον X.*Ag*.8.7; *belonging to common usage*, τῶν ὀνομάτων τὰ π. Isoc.9.10; *drawn from ordinary life*, παραδείγματα Gal.5.221; τὰς π...χρείας [τοῦ σκέλους] *ordinary*, opp. wrestling and dancing, Id.2.299; ὁ π., opp. ὁ ποιητής, Phryn.45. Adv. -κῶς, λέγειν, opp. ῥητορικῶς, Arist.*Po*.1450$^b$7; ὁρίζεσθαι Id.*Pol*. 1275$^b$25; ἑρμηνεύειν Gal.18(1).415. VI. πολιτική, ἡ, *concubine, mistress*, *PGrenf*.2.73 (iii A.D.), *POxy*.903.37 (iv A.D.). **-ις**, ιδος (acc. -ῖτιν *SIG*1012.24 (Cos, ii/i B.C., prob.), Porph.*Hist.Phil*.12), fem. of πολίτης, S.*El*.1227, E.*El*.1335 (anap.), Pl.*Lg*.814c, Arist. *Pol*.1275$^b$32, *IG*12(7).386.21 (Aegiale, iii B.C.), etc. **-ισμός**, ὁ, *administration of public affairs*, D.L.4.39.

**πολῑτο-γρᾰφέω**, *enrol as a citizen*, τινας D.S.11.49, Philisc.Com.5: abs., *act as registrar*, *OGI*547.4 (Ancyra, iii A.D.):—Pass., *to be admitted to citizenship*, οἱ πολιτογραφηθέντες ib.229.54 (Smyrna, iii B.C.), cf. Plb. 32.7.3, Phld.*Acad.Ind*.p.35 M., D.S.11.72,86; πεπολιτογράφημαι *IG*9(2).517.41 (Larissa, iii B.C.). ⊛ **-γρᾰφία**, ἡ, *enrolment as a citizen*, ib.2$^2$. 954.17, 981.13, 9(2).517.31 (Larissa, iii B.C., pl.), D.S.11.86. **-γράφος** [ᾰ], ὁ, *registrar*, *OGI*528.5 (Prusias). **-κάπηλος** [ᾰ], ὁ, *jobber in public offices*, Malch.ap.Suid. s. v. Ζήνων. **-κοπέω**, = δημοκοπέω, Antipho Soph.113. II. = λοιδορεῖν, κωμῳδεῖν, Pl.Com.105, Diph. 131. **-κοπία**, ἡ, = δημοκοπία, Sannyr.7. **-κόπος**, ον, = δημοκόπος, Phryn.*PS* p.99 B. **-φθόρος**, ον, *hurtful to the citizens*, Pl.*Lg*. 854c. **-φῠλᾰκέω**, *supervise the citizens*, σώματα..πολιτοφυλακήσοντα Aen.Tact.1.3. **-φῠλᾰκία**, ἡ, *supervision of the citizens*, Id.22.7. **-φύλαξ** [ῠ], ᾰκος, ὁ, *warden of the citizens*, title of a magistrate, Arist.*Pol*.1268$^a$22; at Larissa, ib.1305$^b$29.

**πολίχνη**, ἡ, Dim. of πόλις, *fort, small town*, Th.7.4, Call.*Del*.41, Plu. *Tim*.11, etc.; in earlier writers only as pr. n., Πολίχνη, Att. Πολίχνα, a city in Chios, Hdt.6.26; in Ionia, Th.8.14, etc.; in the Megarid, v.l. in Il.2.557:—hence ⊛ **Πολιχνῖται**, οἱ, inhabitants of a city in Crete, Hdt.7.170.

**πολίχνιον**, τό, Dim. of foreg., Pl.*R*.370d, Isoc.5.145, etc.

**πολι-ώδης**, ες, *greyish, whitish*, Alex.Aphr.*Pr*.1.8, dub. l. in Luc. *Alex*.60. **-ωμα**, ατος, τό, *greyness*, Eust.565.9. **-ωσις**, εως, ἡ, *becoming grey*, Arist.*Col*.798$^a$13, Plu.2.364b, Gal.1.634.

**πολλᾰγόρᾰσος**, ον, = ὁ πολλὰ ὠνούμενος, Pherecr.126.

**πολλαδελφία**, v. πολυαδελφία.

⊛ **πολλάκις** [ᾰ], Ep. and Lyr. **πολλάκι**, sts. in Trag. (only lyr.) metri gr., A.*Th*.227, *Supp*.131, S.*Ph*.1456 (anap.); never in Prose: (πολύς): Adv. I. of Time, *many times, often*, Il.1.396, etc.; π. καὶ οὐκὶ ἅπαξ Hdt.7.46; π. τοῦ μηνός X.*Cyr*.1.2.9; π. ἀγωνοθέτης *Ephes*. 3 p.152 No.70. II. of Degree and Number, π. μυρίοι *many* tens of thousands, Pl.*Lg*.810d, *Tht*.175a; of Quantity, [τὴν] οὐσίαν π. τοσαύτην ἐποίησε Id.*R*.330b; of Size, μεῖζον π. Plu.2.94a. 2. τὸ π. *mostly, for the most part*, Pi.*O*.1.32; *very much, altogether*, χρὼς ὅμοιος ἐγίνετο πολλάκι θάψῳ Theoc.2.88; χαίρετε π. Μοῖσαι Id.1.144. III. in Att., after conditional particles, *perhaps*, σεισμὸς εἰ γένοιτο π. Ar. *Ec*.791; ἐάν τι πολλὰ π. πάθω ib.1105: with ἄρα, ἐὰν ἄρα π. νυμφόληπτος γένωμαι Pl.*Phdr*.238d, cf. *Phd*.60e, D.32.3; also μὴ π. lest *perchance*, Hp.*VC*14, Th.2.13, Pl.*Prt*.361c, al.

**πολλαπλᾰσι-άζω**, *multiply*, ἀριθμοὶ πολλαπλασιάσαντες ἀλλήλους Euc.7.30, cf. Archim.*Aren*.3.6; ὁ Α τὸν Β -πλασιάσας τὸν Δ πεποίηκεν Euc.7.16; also ἀριθμοὺς δι' ἀλλήλων π. Papp.22.4, Hero *Metr*.2 *Praef*.; τι ἐπί τι ib.1.5, 2.3: generally, Porph.*Gaur*.7.2:—Pass., Archim. *Sph.Cyl*.1.2, etc.: c. dat., *to be multiplied by*.., Arist.*Ph*.237$^b$33, Archim.*Aren*.3.7; ἐπί τι Euc.9.36; κατά τι Papp.100.20. II. metaph., *multiply, increase*, εὐεργετήματα, ἐμπειρίαν, Plb.30.4.13, D.S. 1.1. **-ᾰσις**, εως, ἡ, = sq., Procl.*in Prm*.p.551 S.: cf. -ωσις. **-ασμός**, ὁ, *multiplication*, Plu.2.388c, Gal.7.509, Procl.*in Euc*.p.151 F. **-επιμερής**, ές, *containing a number a number of times with more than one aliquot part over* (e.g. $\frac{11}{3} = 3\frac{2}{3}$), and **-επιμόριος**, ον, *containing a number a number of times with one aliquot part over* (e.g. $\frac{10}{3} = 3\frac{1}{3}$), Nicom. *Ar*.1.23. **-ος**, α, ον (ος, ον Alcid.*Soph*.28), Ion. **-πλήσιος**, η, ον, (πολύς) *many* (or *a number of*) *times as many* or *as large*, Hdt.3.135, 8.140.α'; π. πρὸς πολλοστημόριον Arist.*Metaph*.1020$^b$27; π. ἤπερ.., ἢ.., *many times as many as*.., *many times more* or *larger than*.., Hdt.4.50, al., Pl.*R*.530c: c. gen., Hdt.7.48, Antipho 3.2.10, Th. 4.94, etc.; π. τινὸς τῷ αὐτῷ ἀριθμῷ the same *multiple* of.., Archim. *Spir*.19 *Cor*.; also π. τινὸς κατὰ τοὺς ἑξῆς ἀριθμούς ib.*Praef*. Adv. -ίως Hp.*Acut*.62, Epicur.*Nat*.111 G., Archim.*Aren*.1.2, D.C.44.39, etc.; π. ταχύ Anaxag.9: neut. pl. as Adv., X.*Cyr*.1.5.9. II. π. ἀναλογία, prob. *geometrical progression*, Arist.*APo*.78$^a$1. III. πολλαπλάσιον, τό, a *multiple*: in pl., ἰσάκις π. equi*multiples*, Euc.5 *Def*.5; ὡσαύτως π. the same *multiples*, Id.5.15. IV. Adv. -ίως *by multiplication*, Dam.*Pr*.148. **-ότης**, ητος, ἡ, *the being a multiple*, *Theol.Ar*.52, Iamb.*in Nic*.p.38 P., al. **-όω**, *multiply*, Pl.*R*.525e:—Pass., Hp.*Acut*.61, Arist.*Top*.163$^b$26. **-ων**, ον, gen. ονος, = πολλαπλάσιος, *Num.Chron*.1905.114 (Abonuteichos, ii B.C.), Plb.35.4.4, Plu.2.215b: c. gen., Phld.*Sign*.9. Adv. -όνως Poll.4.164. **-ωσις**, εως, ἡ, *multiplication*, Pl.*R*.587e, Arist.*Pol*.1308$^b$5, *Metaph*.1092$^b$33 (pl., -άσεσιν Alex.Aphr. ad loc.).

**πολλαπλήσιος**, η, ον, Ion. for πολλαπλάσιος.

**πολλαπλόος**, η, ον, contr. **-πλοῦς**, ῆ, οῦν, *manifold, many times as long*, βίος διπλοῦς καὶ π. Pl.*Ti*.75b; ὄνομα πολλαπλοῦν *multi-compound*, opp. ἁπλοῦν, διπλοῦν, Arist.*Po*.1457$^a$35; π. ἡ ἐνέργεια Iamb.*Comm. Math*.8. II. metaph., ἀνὴρ διπλοῦς, π., i.e. *not simple and straightforward*, Pl.*R*.397e.

**πολλασταῖος**, v. πολλοσταῖος.

**πολλατεκνία**, ἡ, = πολυτεκνία, *PLond.ined*.2181.

**πολλᾰχ-ῇ**, Adv. *in many places*, δεδήλωται Democr.10; opp. οὐδαμῇ, X.*An*.7.3.12. II. *in divers manners*, A.*Supp*.468; πολλὰ π. S.*OC*1626; τῇ τε ἄλλῃ π. καὶ δὴ καὶ.. Hdt.6.21, cf. Th.8.87; π. καὶ ἄλλῃ Pl.*Tht*.179c, etc.; πολλάκις καὶ π. Id.*R*.538d; *for many reasons*, Hdt.1.42. **-όθεν**, Adv. *from many places* or *sides*, Th.6.32, Lys.6. 20, Pl.*Lg*.842c, etc.; π. ὁμολογεῖται Id.*Smp*.178c. II. *from many considerations, for many reasons*, π. ξυνέβη..ἀναχωρῆσαι Th.4. 6. **-όθῐ**, Adv. *in many places*, Plu.*Pomp*.24, Luc.*Herm*.30. **-όσε**, Adv. *towards many sides, into many parts* or *quarters*, Th.2.47: c. gen., π. τῆς Ἀρκαδίας X.*HG*4.4.16. **-οῦ**, Adv. *in many places*, τοὔνομα γένοιτ' ἂν πολλαχοῦ, τὸ σῶμα δ' οὔ E.*Hel*.588, cf. Pl.*Smp*.209e; ἐμοῦ πολλάκις ἀκηκόατε πολλαχοῦ λέγοντος Id.*Ap*.31c; π. ἐν τοῖς λόγοις Id.*Prt*.329c; Ὅμηρος π. λέγει Id.*Cra*.408a; π. ἄλλοθι X.*Cyr*.7.1. 30. 2. c. gen., π. τῆς γῆς v.l. in Pl.*Phd*.111a. II. = πολλαχῇ, *on many grounds*, interpol. in Hdt.6.122, v.l. in Isoc.4.183. **-ῶς**, Adv. *in many ways*, Diog.Apoll.2, Isoc.4.8, D.22.25, etc.; π. λέγεσθαι *in many senses*, Arist.*Top*.158$^b$10, *Pol*.1276$^a$23.

**πολλοᾰγάπητος** [γᾰ], ον, *much-beloved*, τέκνα *MAMA*1.235 (Laodicea Combusta).

**πολλόγειος**· ἡ ψιθία σταφυλή, Hsch.

**πολλο-δεκάκις** [ᾰ], Adv. *many tens of times*, Ar.*Pax*243. **-ποιός**, όν, *creating plurality*, Dam.*Pr*.34, al.

**πολλός**, πολλόν, Ion. masc. and neut. for πολύς, πολύ.

**πολλοστ-αῖος**, α, ον (formed like εἰκοσταῖος, etc.), *for many days past*, Eub.133 cod.:—written **πολλασταῖος**, *PSI*5.528.12 (iii B.C.).

**πολλοστ-ημόριος**, ον, (μόριον) *a number of times smaller*, opp. πολλαπλάσιος, Arist.*Top.*147ᵃ26, *Metaph.*1020ᵇ28; πολλαπλάσιον ἢ π. τοῦ πρότερον Id.*Pol.*1308ᵇ2; τὸ π. *fraction*, Id.*Top.*125ᵃ9; οὐδὲ π. ὧν σε δεῖ παθεῖν Luc.*DDeor.*1.1, cf. Phld.*Mus.*p.110 K. ⊕ **-ός**, ή, όν (formed from πολύς on the analogy of εἰκοστός, τριακοστός, etc.), *far on in the ordinal series first, second, third*, etc., π. ὧν Συρακοσίων καὶ τῷ γένει καὶ τῇ δόξῃ, i.e. far from the most eminent of the Syracusans, Isoc.5.65; κίνησις..δευτέρα τε καὶ ὁπόσων ἀριθμῶν βούλοιτο ἄν τις ἀριθμεῖν αὐτὴν πολλοστὴν τοσούτων, i.e. infinitely less important, Pl.*Lg.*896b; πότερον..τὰ σκληρότατα..ἢ..τὰ πολλοστὰ σκληρότητι; things *far down in descending order* of hardness, Id.*Phlb.*44e; αἱ π. ἡδοναί, opp. αἱ ἀκρόταται καὶ σφοδρόταται, ibid. Adv., δευτέρως καὶ -στῶς λέγοιντ' ἄν *much less properly*, opp. κυρίως, Arist.*EN*1176ᵃ29; [ὑγείας] πρώτως μὲν θεοί, δευτέρως δὲ ἢ καὶ π. ἄνθρωποι μεταλαμβάνουσιν Herm. *in Phdr.*p.90 A.; but τὸ π. εἰπεῖν *using many* alternative *names* for the same thing, D.H.*Rh.*11.9. 2. with ἀπό, *remote*, τρίται καὶ π. ἀπὸ [τῆς Νυκτός] Herm. *in Phdr.*p.144 A.; ἀπὸ τῆς δημιουργίας Iamb. *Myst.*3.28; ἀπὸ τῆς οἰκείας ἀρχῆς Procl.*Inst.*110; ἀπὸ τῶν θεῶν, ἀπὸ τῆς ἀρχικῆς μονάδος, ib.119, 181. 3. π. μέρος or μόριον, a fraction *with one for numerator and with a large denominator*, i.e. a *small* fraction, π. τι μέρος And.2.8, cf. X.*Mem.*4.6.7; π. μόριον Th.6.86: freq. with a neg., οὐδὲ [τὸ] π. μέρος Lys.14.46, cf. Is.1.34; μηδὲ πολλοστὸν ἐξευρίσκειν τινῶν Phld.*Rh.*1.210 S. 4. of Time, π. ἔτει *in the last of many* years, i.e. after many years, Cratin.Jun.9; π. χρόνῳ *after a very long* time, Ar.*Pax*559, D.24.196, 57.18, Men.329. II. in later Gr., = πολύς, πολλοστὸς ἔργοις one that has done *a great deal*, Lxx 2*Ki.*23.20, cf. *Pr.*5.19.

**πολλότης**, ητος, ἡ, *plurality*, Dam.*Pr.*55.

**πολλύνομαι**, Pass., *to be multiplied*, Phot.

**πολο-γρᾰφία**, Ion. -ίη, ἡ, *description of the heavens*, title of a treatise by Democritus, Hp.*Ep.*18, D.L.9.48. **-κράτωρ** [ᾰ], ορος, ὁ, *ruling the pole*, π. τοῦ οὐρανοῦ *PMag.Par.*1.676 (pl.).

**πόλος**, ὁ, (πέλω, πέλομαι, πολέω) *pivot* on which anything turns, *axis*: 1. *axis of the celestial sphere*, γῆν ἰλλομένην τὴν περὶ τὸν διὰ παντὸς πόλον τεταμένον Pl.*Ti.*40c. 2. *pole* of this axis, ὁ ἄνω, ὁ κάτω π., Arist.*Cael.*285ᵇ9, cf. *Mete.*362ᵃ33; π. φανερός, ἀφανής, Id.*Cael.* 285ᵇ21; π. ἀρκτικός, ἀνταρκτικός, Id.*Mu.*392ᵃ2; π. βόρειος, νότιος, Hipparch.1.4.1, 1.8.14, cf. Gem.16.11, Cleom.1.4, Ptol.*Alm.*2.6; π. τοῦ ὁρίζοντος *the zenith*, Euc.*Phaen.*p.18 M.; λόξωσις τοῦ π. inclination of the *pole* (of the zodiac), Ocell.2.23. b. *pole-star*, Eratosth. *Cat.*2. 3. *celestial sphere, vault of heaven, sky*, A.*Pr.*429 (lyr.), E.*Fr.* 839.11 (anap.); ἄστρων π. Id.*Or.*1685 (anap.), cf. eund.*Eleg.*2; τὸ τοῦ π. τοῦ παντὸς ἡμισφαίριον Alex.261.7; ὀρνίθων π. Ar.*Av.*179; ψυχὴ δ' αἰθέριον κατέχει π. *Epigr.Gr.*225 (Ephesus); ἀπ' ἀντολίης πόλον ἥλατο χρύσεα κύκλα ἠελίου *AP*14.139 (Metrod.). b. ὑπὸ τὸν αὐτὸν π. in the same *latitude*, Gal.17(1).16. 4. *orbit of a star*, Pl.*Epin.*986c. 5. *crown of the head*, Hsch.; *the whole head*, Poll.2.99. II. *centre* of the circular threshing-floor, X.*Oec.*18.8. III. *pole passing through the axle-tree* of a carriage, as a shock-absorber, D.S.18.27. IV. *concave sun-dial* (called πόλος from being shaped like the vault of heaven), on which the shadow was cast by the γνώμων, Hdt.2.109, Ar.*Fr.*163: fem. in Luc.*Lex.*4. 2. διακόσμησις τοῦ π. organization of the *calendar*, *OGI*56.46 (Canopus, iii B.C.). V. *head-dress*, worn by goddesses, e.g. Aphrodite, Paus.2.10.5; Tyche, Id.4.30. 6. VI. Archit., *dowel*, *IG*2².1675.4, al. VII. *crescent-shaped projection* on a machine for reducing dislocations, Philistion ap. Orib.49.4.37. VIII. *windlass, capstan*, *BGU*544.24 (pl., ii A.D.).

**πολτ-άριον** [ᾰ], τό, Dim. of πόλτος, *little porridge, poor bad porridge*, Dsc.2.92, Philum.ap.Orib.45.29.3. **-άριος** [ᾱ], ὁ, = Lat. *pultarius*, Gal.13.280, *Gloss.*:—Dim. **βουλτᾱρίδιον**, τό, *PHolm.*2.40.

**πολτοποιέω**, *make into porridge*, Orib.*Fr.*75:—Pass., *to be made into porridge*, Dsc.2.106.

**πόλτος**, ὁ, *porridge*, Alcm.75, Plu.2.201c, etc.; π. ἕψειν Epich. 23; sts. oxyt., as Archig.ap.Orib.8.1.7, 8.46.11, Gal.12.45.

**πολτοχάρυβδις**, v. ποντο-.

**πολτώδης**, ες, *porridge-like*, Erot. s. v. πολφοί.

**πολῠ-ᾰγάπητος** [γᾰ], ον, *much-beloved*, Hsch. s. v. πολύθεστος, Sch.Opp.*H.*4.138. **-ἄγκιστρος**, ον, *with many hooks*, Opp.*H.*3. 78. II. πολυάγκιστρον, τό, *night-line*, Arist.*HA*532ᵇ25, 621ᵃ 16. **-αγρής**, ές, = πολύαγρος, Opp.*C.*1.88. **-αγρία**, ἡ, *catching much game*, Poll.5.13. **-αγρος**, ον, *catching much game*, *AP*6.184 (Zos., Comp.). **-ᾰδελφία**, ἡ, *possession of many brothers*, Sch.Ptol. *Tetr.*102:—also **πολλᾰδελφία**, *Cat.Cod.Astr.*6.70. **-άδελφος** [ᾰ], ον, *with many brothers*, Vett.Val.16.29, Poll.6.171, Paul.Al.*L.* 3, Sch.S.*Ant.*1. **-άης**, ές, (ἄημι) *blowing hard*, αὖραι Q.S.1. 253. **-άθλιος**, ον, *much-toiling*, *Supp.Epigr.*1.459 (Miscamus; πολι- lapis, fort. n. pr.). **-αθλος**, ον, *of many labours*, epith. of Heracles, Luc.*DDeor.*10.1. **-αιγος**, ον, *having many goats*, *AP* 9.744 (Leon.). ⊕ **-άϊκος**, ον, = πολυᾶιξ, Sch.E.*Med.*10. **-αίμᾰτος**, ον, *full of blood*, Emp.150, Ath.7.301f. **-αιμέω**, *to have much blood*, Arist.*PA*648ᵃ30, *GA*765ᵇ18. **-αιμία**, ἡ, *fullness of blood*, Id.*PA*669ᵇ4, Gal.10.611. **-αιμος**, ον, *full of blood, of a full habit*, Hp.*Flat.*14, Arist.*HA*515ᵃ20, 520ᵇ27 (Comp.); πλεύμων Id.*PA*669ᵃ 27. **-αίμων**, ον, gen. ονος, *bloody*, A.*Supp.*840 (lyr.). **-αίνετος**, ον, = sq., E.*Heracl.*761 (lyr.), *BCH*29.412 (Callatis):—also **-αίνητος**, *IG*4²(1).616.5 (Epid., iv B.C.); to be restored in *BCH*21.599 (Delph., iv B.C.). **-αινος**, ον, (αἰνέω) *much-praised*, Homeric epith. of Odysseus, Il.9.673, 10.544, 11.430, Od.12.184; but expld. alternatively by Hsch. as = πολύμυθος (cf. αἰνέω I, αἶνος I). **-ᾶιξ** [ᾰ], ικος, (ἀΐσσω) *much-rushing, impetuous, furious*, πόλεμος Il.1.165, Od. 11.314; κάματος π. weariness *caused by impetuosity in fight*, Il.5. 811. **-άκανθος** [ἄκ], ἡ, *welted thistle, Carduus acanthoides*, Thphr. *HP*6.4.3. **-αλγής**, ές, *very painful*, Antioch.Astr. in *Cat.Cod.Astr.* 1.112, Orph.*H.*67.2. **-άλγητος**, ον, *feeling much pain*, Sch.S.*Aj.* 946. II. = ἀνάλγητος, Sch.E.*Hipp.*1386. **-αλδής**, ές, (ἀλδαίνω) *much-nourishing*, Q.S.2.658. **-αλθής**, ές, (ἄλθος) *curing many diseases*, Dsc.3.146. **-αλφής**, ές, (ἀλφάνω) *fetching a high price*, Nonn.*D.*37.715. **-άλφῐτος**, ον, *yielding much meal*, κριθαί Thphr.*HP*8.4.2. **-αμμος**, ον, *abounding in sand, sandy*, Hsch. s. v. ἠμαθόεντος. **-άμπελος**, ον, *with many vines*, B.7(*Fr.*), Sch. DIl.2.507, etc. **-αναγνωσία**, ἡ, *much reading, much learning*, Ath.14.654a. **-ανάλωτος** [ᾰλ], ον, *prodigal*, Vett.Val.48.25. II. *causing much expense, very expensive*, gloss on πολυτελές, *EM*750. 47. **-αναφορία**, ἡ, Astrol., *slowness in rising*, Sch.Ptol. *Tetr.*118. **-ανάφορος**, ον, Astrol., *slow in rising*, ζῴδια Vett.Val. 227.12, Sch.Ptol.*Tetr.*118.

**πολῠανδρ-εῖον**, τό, *common burial-place*, *IG*2².1035.33, al., Favorin. in *PVat.*11.8.20; Λακώνων *SIG*826 *E*iii 32 (Delph., ii B.C.); cf. πολυάνδριος II. 2. **-έω**, *to be full of men, to be populous*, ὄχλοις π. αἱ πόλεις Th.6.17, cf. Str.8.7.1, *Sammelb.*7462.7 (i A.D.):—Med., πολυανδρέομαι D.S.8.1, Ocell.4.4, Ael.*NA*5.13. **-ία**, ἡ, *populousness*, τοῦ Ἰταλικοῦ γένους App.*BC*1.7, cf. Them.*Or.*6.74c. **-ιος**, ον, *of or connected with many men*, τὸ π. κακὸν μεταδιώκειν, i.e. *prostitution*, Ph.1.568 (sed leg. -ανδρον); π. τάφος, = πολυανδρεῖον, Eun.*Hist.*p.264 D.; π. δαίμονες spirits *which haunt a* πολυανδρεῖον, *Tab.Defix.Aud.*22. 30. II. Subst. **-ιον**, τό, *place where many people assemble*, Plu. 2.823e (pl.). 2. = πολυανδρεῖον, Ph.*Bel.*86.14, D.H.1.14, Str.9.4. 16, J.*BJ*5.1.3, Plu.*Flam.*7, Ael.*VH*12.21. ⊕ **-ος**, ον, of places, *full of men, populous*, A.*Pers.*73 (lyr.), 899 (lyr.); κῶμαι *BGU*903.10 (ii A.D.): Sup., χωρίον Palaeph.38. 2. of persons, *many, numerous*, Πέρσαι A.*Pers.*533 (anap.), cf. *Ag.*693 (lyr.); ἥβα νέων π. Tim.*Pers.* 194; δύναμις π. Onos.21.5; π. συμβολή *much* experience *of men*, Vett.Val.172.25. II. γυνὴ π. wife *of many husbands*, Ptol.*Tetr.* 72; πολύανδρον, τό, *prostitution*, Ph.1.563; cf. πολυάνδριος I.

**πολῠάνθ-εμον**, τό, = βατράχιον I, Plin.*HN*27.112, *Gloss.* **-εμος**, ον, (ἄνθεμον) *rich in flowers*, ἄρουραι Sapph.*Supp.*25.11; μίτραι Anacr. 65.3; Ὧραι Pi.*O.*13.17: in later Prose, χώρα Plu.2.294f. ⊕ **-ής**, ές, (ἀνθέω) *blooming*, ὕλη Od.14.353; ἔαρ *h.Hom.*19.17; πτερύγων χροιή Mosch.2.59, cf. Opp.*C.*1.320, al.: in later Prose, θύμβρα *Gp.*15.4.4; *parti-coloured*, στρωμναί D.S.31.8, cf. 5.30: poet. fem. πολυάνθεα, γλήχων Nic.*Th.*877. **-ος**, ον, = foreg., dub. l. in Orph.*H.*51.7 (leg. -ανθεῖς).

**πολῠάνθραξ**, ᾰκος, ὁ, ἡ, *rich in coal*, Sch.Ar.*Ach.*34.

**πολῠάνθρωπ-έω**, *to be populous*, J.*AJ*1.4.1 (v.l.), St.Byz. s. v. Ἀρτύμνησος. **-ία**, ἡ, *large population, multitude of people*, X.*HG*5.2.16, *Vect.*4.49, Arist.*Pol.*1326ᵇ20, D.S.1.73, etc. **-ος**, ον, *populous*, πόλις Hp.*Art.*72, Th.6.3, Arist.*Pol.*1326ᵃ25; δύναμις Th.1.24: Comp. and Sup., Arist.*Pol.*1321ᵇ25, Th.2.54. II. *much-frequented, crowded*, πανήγυρις Luc.*Peregr.*1 (Sup.). III. *numerous*, ἔθνη Plb.3.37.11, al.

**πολῠ-ανώδῠνος**, ον, *with much anodyne power*, = κώνειον, Ps.-Dsc. 4.78. **-άνωρ** [ᾱ], ορος, ὁ, ἡ, *with many men, much-frequented*, θρόνος E.*IT*1281 (lyr.); πόλις Ar.*Av.*1313 (lyr.); εὐνομία *IG*4²(1). 129.12 (Epid.). II. γυνὴ π. wife *of many husbands*, A.*Ag.*62 (anap.). **-απεχθής**, ές, *much-hated*, Vett.Val.248.2. **-απόδημος**, ον, *much-travelled*, Id.98.7, al. **-άρᾱτος** [ᾰρ], Ep. **-άρητος** [ᾰ], ον, (ἀράομαι) *much-wished-for, much-desired*, ἥ τίς οἱ εὐξαμένῃ π. θεὸς ἦλθεν Od.6.280, cf. 19.404, *h.Cer.*220: in Att. Prose, τὴν πολυάρατον σοφίαν Pl.*Tht.*165e. II. *cursed*, κολακεία, γόητες, Dam.*Isid.*18, 92. **-άργῠρος**, ον, *rich in silver*, of persons or places, πολυαργυρώτατοι, of the Lydians, Hdt.5.49, cf. Ph.2.30; πλάκες τῆς γῆς D.S.5.36; οἶκοι Plu.*Comp.Lys.Sull.*3 (Sup.). **-αρής**, v. l. for ταχυήρης ap.Sch.Opp.*H.*4.569. **-αρθρος**, ον, *with many articulations*, πόδες Gal.*UP*3.6. **-άριθμος** [ᾰ], ον, *numerous, manifold*, Callicrat.ap.Stob.4.28.16; δύναμις D.S.14.25. **-αρκής**, ές, (ἀρκέω) *much-helpful, supplying many wants*, mostly in Sup. -έστατος, [ποταμός] Hdt.4.53; γῆ D.H.1.36; πόλις Plu.*Alex.*26; λογισμός Ael.*NA Prooem.*; τὸ πολυαρκὲς τῆς ταριχείας *durability*, Luc.*Nec.*15. Adv. -κῶς Hsch. 2. = ἀσφόδελος, *Gloss.* (dub.). **-αρκῠς**, ῠος, ὁ, ἡ, *with many nets*, ἄγρη Opp.*C.*4. 10. **-άρμᾰτος**, ον, *with many chariots*, S.*Ant.*149 (lyr.). **-αρμόνιος**, ον, *capable of being played upon in many modes*, ὄργανα Pl.*R.* 399d. **-αρνι**, v. πολύρρην. **-άρουρος** [ᾰ], ον, *with many fields*, Hsch. s. v. πολυλήιος. **-άρτῡτος**, ον, *highly spiced*, Sor.1. 94. **-αρχία**, ἡ, *command or government shared by many*, τὸ πλῆθος τῶν στρατηγῶν καὶ ἡ π. Th.6.72, cf. X.*An.*6.1.18, J.*AJ*4.8.41, Plu. *Cam.*18, etc. **-άρχιος**, ον, *invented by* the physician *Polyarchus*, μάλαγμα π. Sor.2.32, Gal.13.184. **-αρχος**, ον, *ruling over many*, Corn.*ND*35. **-ασπις**, ιδος, *many-shielded*, i.e. *of a large host*, [ὕβρις] *Inscr.Cos*350. **-άστερος**, ον, = πολύαστρος, Man.4.26: gen. πολυάστερος (as if from -άστηρ) Orac.ap.Eus.*PE*3.15. **-αστράγᾰλος** [ᾰγ], ον, *strung with many knucklebones*, μάστιξ π., = ἀστραγαλωτή, *AP*6.234 (Eryc.). **-αστρος**, ον, *with many stars, starry*, Διὸς ἕδος E.*Ion*870 (anap.). **-άσχολος**, ον, *very busy*, μαθηματική Ps.-Luc.*Philopatr.*25, cf. *Cat.Cod.Astr.*8(3).93. **-αῦλαξ**, ᾰκος, ὁ, ἡ, τό, *with many furrows*, πεδίον π. *AP*6.238 (Apollonid.). **-αυξής**, ές, *full-grown, strong, large*, μόσχος, μαράθου ῥίζα, Nic.*Th.*73, 596 (v. l. πολυαξής, cf. εὐαυξής fin.). **-αύχενος**, ον, (αὐχήν) *with many necks*, ὕδρα *APl.*4.92; αἷμα νέων μακάρων Nonn.*D.*2.352. **-αύχην**, ενος, ὁ, ἡ, *full-necked*, κύνες *Gp.*19.2.2. **-αυχής**, v. l. for -αυξής ap.Sch. Nic.*Th.*73. **-άφορμος**, ον, *with abundant materials*, γραφαί

Eust.5.4. **-άχητος** [ᾱ], ον, Dor. for πολυήχητος. **-αχθής**, ές, very grievous, Τρώων πεδίον Q.S.3.421; λιμός Id.10.38, cf. Sch.Nic.*Al.* 322. **-άχῠρος** [ᾰ], ον, with much chaff, Thphr.*CP*4.11.4. **-βάδιστος** [ᾰ], ον, = πολύβατος, Sch.Opp.*H.*3.502. **-βᾰθής**, ές, very deep, ib.1.633, 5.61. **-βᾰτος**, ον, much-trodden, ἄστεος ὀμφαλός, of the ἀγορά, Pi.*Fr.*75.3. **-βᾰφής**, ές, much-dipped, of drowned men, A.*Pers.*275 (lyr.), but v. ἁλιβαφής. **-βέλεμνος**, ον, with many darts, *Trag.Adesp.*597. **-βενθής**, ές, very deep, ἅλς Od.4.406; λιμήν Il.1.432, Od.10.125, 16.324; λίμνη A.R.4.599. **-βήμᾰτος**, ον, taking many steps, Hsch. s.v. πολυσκάρθμοιο. **-βιβλος**, ον, in many books, ἱστορία Ath.6.249a; πραγματεία Gal.1.409, cf. *IGRom.* 4.1655 (Notium: -βυβλον lapis). **-βῐος**, ον, (βίος II) well-to-do, *Cat.Cod.Astr.*2.209. II. (βία) powerful, Eust.916.21. **-βλᾰβής**, ές, very hurtful, *EM*1.22, Sch.A.R.2.232, Sch.Il.14.271. II. Pass., easily hurt, τὸ τῆς σαρκὸς π. Plu.2.1090b. **-βλαστής**, ές, shooting vigorously, Thphr.*CP*3.7.4, v.l. for παλιμβλαστής ib.3.19. 2. **-βλαστία**, ἡ, vigorous shooting, ib.3.7.5. **-βλέπων**, οντος, blind (by euphemism), *PLond.*1821.269. **-βλέφᾰρος**, ον, with many eyes, Nonn.*D.*20.65. **-βλής**, ῆτος, ὁ, ἡ, having struck many, Apollon.*Lex.* s.v. ἀβλῆτα. **-βόειος**, ον, covered with many oxhides: Ep. fem. πουλυβόεια Q.S.3.239 (s.v.l.). **-βοησία**, ἡ, f.l. for περιβοησία, Artem.2.30. **-βόητος**, ον, much-talked-of, gloss on παλαίφατος, Sch.A.*Supp.*532; much-sounding, gloss on πολυάχητος, Sch. E.*Alc.*918. **-βόλος**, ον, throwing many missiles, καταπάλτης Ph. *Bel.*73.34. **-βόρος**, ον, much-devouring, voracious, Pl.*Criti.*115a (Sup.); opp. πολυπότης, Hp.*Aër.*4; ζῷα Gal.*UP*4.18. **-βοσκος**, ον, (βόσκω) much-nourishing, γαῖα Pi.*O.*7.63. **-βότᾰνος**, ον, abounding in herbs, Eust.1624.10. **-βότειρα**, ἡ, fem. Adj., (βόσκω) much- or all-nourishing, in Ep. form πουλυβότειρα, epith. of χθών, Il.3.89, al.; of Ἀχαΐς, 11.770. **-βοτος**, ον, (βόσκω) much-nourishing, αἰὼν βροτῶν A.*Th.*774 (lyr.). II. having much pasture, Κελαιναί Tim.*Pers.*153; γῆ D.H.1.37. **-βοτρυς**, υος, ὁ, ἡ, abounding in grapes, of places, Hes.*Fr.*122, Simon.53, Theoc.25.11; ἄμπελος E.*Ba.* 651. **-βουλος**, ον, much-counselling, exceeding wise, Ἀθήνη Il.5.260, Od.16.282; of Isis, *Hymn.Is.*26; γνώμα Pi.*I.*4(3).72. 2. shifty, *Cat.Cod.Astr.*8(1).259. **-βους**, ὁ, ἡ, = sq., gloss on Περίβοια, Eust.562.40. ⊛ **-βούτης**, ου, ὁ, (βοῦς) rich in oxen, ἄνδρες .. πολύρρηνες, πολυβοῦται Il.9.154, Hes.*Fr.*134.3:—also in form πουλυβώτης, Carm.Naupact.2 (*EGF*p.199 K.). **-βρομος**, ον, (βρέμω) loud-roaring, Sch.Il.13.41. **-βροχος** (A), ον, (βρέχω) freshly infused several times, Dsc.1.128.6, al. **-βροχος** (B), ον, (βρόχος) with many nooses, E.*HF*1035 (lyr.). **-βρώμᾰτος**, ον, composed of many meats, Sch.Opp.*H.*2.221. **-βρωτος**, ον, devoured, mangled, μέλεα, of Actaeon, Nonn.*D.*5.502. **-βυβλος**, v. πολύβιβλος. **-βῠθος**, ον, = πολυβενθής, Ph.1.6. **-βυρσος**, ον, of many hides or skins, gloss on πολύρρινος, Sch.A.R.3.1231. **-βῶλαξ**, ἄκος, ὁ, ἡ, = sq., Cypr.7.11. **-βωλος**, ον, with large clods, fruitful, E.*Fr.*229 (anap.). **-βωμος**, ον, with many altars, Call.*Del.*266, 316. **-βωτος**, ον, prob. from βόσκω, many-feeding, fertile, as ironical epith. of the barren island of Seriphos, Cratin. 211. **-γᾱθής**, ές, Dor. for πολυγηθής. **-γᾰλακτέω**, have much milk, Plu.2.640f; ζῷα -γαλακτοῦντα Sor.1.97. **-γάλακτος** [γᾰ], ον, with much milk, Arist.*PA*688$^b$3: poet. Sup. πουλυγαλακτοτάτη *AP*9.224 (Crin.). **-γᾰλον**, τό, (γάλα) milk-wort, Polygala venulosa, Dsc. 4.139, Plin.*HN*27.121. 2. = πέπλιον, Ps.-Dsc.4.168. **-γᾰλος**, ον, = πολυγάλακτος, Aët.2.17. **-γᾰμία**, ἡ, polygamy, Ph.1.568; frequent marriage, Vett.Val.119.22. **-γᾰμος**, ον, often-married, or, living in polygamy, Poll.3.48, Ptol.*Tetr.*183. **-γελως**, ὁ, ἡ, gen. pl. -γέλων, f.l. for πολυτελῶν (corr. Cobet) in Plu.2.552a. **-γενής**, ές, (γένος) of many families, Poll.9.21; π. τὸν Δία προσηγόρευσεν *PMich.* in *Class.Phil.*22.9. **-γέωργος**, ον, farming much land, Vett.Val.69.26. **-γηθής**, Dor. -γᾱθής, ές, (γηθέω) much-cheering, delightful, gladsome, ὧραι Il.21.450; Διώνυσος Hes.*Th.*941, *Op.*614, cf. Pi.*Fr.*29.5; Διὸς εὐναί Id.*P.*2.28; ὀρχηθμός *AP*9.189, etc.: also voc. -γηθὲ (as if from -γηθος) Orph.*H.*10.10. **-γήρᾱος**, ον, very old, Asius 1: -γήρως, = vivax, *Gloss.*: nom. pl. -γήρως (sic) Pl. *Ax.*367b. **-γηρία**, ἡ, attainment of great age, Melamp.παλμ.p.24 D. **-γηρος**, ον, = -γήραος, Vett.Val.62.5. ⊛ **-γιος**, epith. of Hermes at Troezen, Paus.2.31.13. **-γλᾰγής**, ές, (γλάγος) = πολυγάλακτος, ἐνιαυτός Arat.1100; μαζοί Nonn.*D.*9.176. **-γλευκος**, ον, abounding in sweet juice, βότρυς *AP*6.238 (Apollonid.). **-γληνος**, ον, many-eyed, Nonn.*D.*3.272, *AP*5.261 (Paul. Sil.). II. with many meshes, σαγήνη Opp.*C.*1.157. **-γλῠφής**, ές, (γλύφω) much-carved, Nonn.*D.*3.136, etc. **-γλωσσος**, Att. **-ττος**, ον, many-tongued, δρῦς π. the vocal (oracular) oak of Dodona, S.*Tr.*1168; π. βοή an oft-repeated or loud-voiced cry, Id.*El.*641, 798. II. speaking many tongues or languages, Lyc.1377, Luc.*JTr.*13, Gal.8.585; ἐπίκουροι Tryph.24. **-γλωχῑν**, ῖνος, ὁ, ἡ, many-barbed, σίδηρος D.P.476; ἀκόντιον App.*BC*5.82: metaph., ἐλάφοιο κεραίη Nic.*Th.* 36. **-γναμπτος**, ον, much-bent, much-twisting, μυχοί Pi.*O.*3.27; λαβύρινθοι *AP*9.191; προχοαί Q.S.1.286; curly, σέλινον Theoc. 7.68. **-γνωμοσύνη**, ἡ, depth of knowledge, Poll.4.22. **-γνώμων**, ον, gen. ονος, very sagacious, Pl.*Phdr.*275a, D.C.76.16 (v.l. -γνωμος); sententious, Philostr.*VS*1.16.4. Adv. -μόνως Poll.4.23. **-γνώριστος**, ον, easy to be recognized, Eust.1421.48. **-γνωστος**, ον, = sq., Vett.Val.15.9, Paul.Al.*L.*3, Tz.*H.*13.507. **-γνωτος**, ον, well-known, Pi.*N.*10.37 (s.v.l.). **-γόητος**, Ep. πουλυ-, ον, much lamented, *BMus.Inscr.*829 b 7 (Cnidos). **-γομφος**, ον, with many nails, well-riveted, νῆες Hes.*Op.*660, cf. Ibyc.*Oxy.*1790.1.18, A.*Pers.* 71 (lyr.). **-γόμφωτος**, ον, = foreg., Eust.174.12. **-γόνᾰτος**, ον, having many joints, Dsc.1.14, al. II. Subst. -γόνατον, τό, seal-wort, Polygonatum multiflorum, Id.4.6. 2. = λευκάκανθα 2, Id.3.19, Plin.*HN*22.40. 3. = πολύγονον ἄρρεν, Ps.-Dsc.4.4. 4. = πολύκνημον, Dsc.3.94. **-γονέομαι**, Pass., multiply, spread, νόσος Luc.*Nigr.*38. **-γονία**, ἡ, fecundity, Pl.*Prt.*321b, Arist.*HA*580$^b$27, 624$^a$1, Ph.2.211. **-γονοειδές**, τό, = κληματίς, Dsc.4.7; but = δαφνοειδές, Gal.12.31. ⊛ **-γονον**, τό, π. ἄρρεν knot-grass, Polygonum aviculare, Dsc.4.4; in Ep. form πουλύ-, Nic.*Al.*264. 2. π. θῆλυ mare's tail, Hippuris vulgaris, Dsc.4.5. **-γονος**, ον, producing much offspring, prolific, Hdt.3.108; γένος Hp.*Aër.*19, cf. A.*Supp.* 692 (lyr.); π. διχῶς, οἱ μὲν τῷ πολλάκις, οἱ δὲ τῷ πολλά Arist.*HA*558$^b$26: Sup., Ph.1.519: metaph. c. gen., π. ἀρετῆς Id.2.399: abs., Lysis ap.Iamb.*VP*17.77: Comp., Thphr.*CP*4.1.5. II. of the Nile, much-producing, fertilizing, Id.*Fr.*159 (Sup.), D.S.1.10:—Ep. **πουλύγονος** Opp.*C.*3.519. **-γουνος**, ον, = πολυγόνατος, many-jointed, ὄνωνις Nic.*Th.*872. **-γράμμᾰτος**, ον, marked with many letters, = στιγματίας, Ar.*Fr.*64, cf. Duris 66 J. 2. of words, composed of many letters, Phld.*Po.Herc.*994.32, al. II. of great knowledge, very learned, Plu.2.1121f: Comp., Philostr.*VS*2.27.4. ⊛ **-γραμμος**, ον, (γραμμή) marked with many stripes, Arist.*Fr.*298. **-γραος**, ον, (γράω) eating much, Hp.ap.Gal.19.132. **-γρᾰφέω**, write much or at length, Ath.Mech.4.9, Apollon.Cit.3. **-γρᾰφία**, ἡ, writing much, D.L.10.26, dub. in Phld.*Rh.*1.143 S. **-γράφος** [ᾰ], ον, writing much, Id.*Ind.Sto.* 32, Ath. Mech.6.2: Sup. -ώτατος Cic. *Att.*13.18, D.L.10.26. **-γύμναστος**, ον, of much experience, κακόν, of a woman, Luc.*Tox.*14. **-γύναιος** [γῠ], ὁ, (γυνή) having many wives, Ptol.*Tetr.*72, Ath.13.556f. **-γύνης** [γῠ], ου, ὁ, = foreg., Poll.6.171: nom. pl. πολυγύναικες Str.17.3.19. ⊛ **-γώνιος**, ον, = πολύγωνος, Thphr.*Sens.*66, *CP*6.1.6, Poll.4.161. **-γωνοειδής**, ές, like a polygon, Arist.*Pr.*911$^b$19. **-γωνος**, ον, polygonal, Id.*Sens.* 442$^b$20, Plu.2.1121c: Subst. -γωνον, τό, polygon, Antipho Soph.13, Gal.*Anim.Pass.*2.3. **-δάηρ** [ᾰ], ερος, ὁ, ἡ, having many brothers-in-law, Hdn.Gr.1.48. **-δαίδᾰλος**, ον, highly, richly wrought, chiefly of metal work, θώρηξ, ἀσπίς, ὅρμος, Il.3.358, 11.32, Od.18.295, etc.; χρυσός 13.11; κλισμός Il.24.597; θάλαμος Od.6.15: of weaving, π. ἱστὸν ὑφαίνειν Hes.*Op.*64; κεράων π. ἔρνος Opp.*C.*2.194. II. Act., working with great art or skill, very skilful, Il.23.743, *APl.*4.80 (Agath.). **-δαίμων**, ον, f.l. for πολυδέγμων in Orph.*H.*18.11. **-δαισία**, ἡ, eating much, Suid. s.v. Ἀπίκιος; cf. πολυποσία. **-δάκρῠος**, ον, = sq., μάχης πολυδακρύου Il.17.192, cf. Alc.*Supp.*1 A 7 (cj.); Ἄρης Tyrt. 11.7; ἆμαρ prob. in B.3.30; Ἅιδας E.*HF*427 (lyr.); ψυχή A.R.2.916; π. εἰς Ἀχέροντα *CR*29.196 (Oloösson); Ἴλιον Q.S.7.263. **-δακρύς**, ῠος, ὁ, ἡ, (δάκρυ) of or with many tears: hence, I. much-wept, lamented, Ἄρης, πόλεμος, ὑσμίνη, Il.3.132, 165, 17.544; μῆτις B. 15.24; Ἴτυς Ar.*Av.*212 (anap.); tearful, ἰαχά, γόος, A.*Pers.*940 (lyr.), *Ch.*419 (lyr.); π. ἀδονά E.*El.*126 (lyr.). II. of persons, much-weeping, Id.*Ph.*366, *Supp.Epigr.*4.719 (Bithynia). ⊛ **-δάκρῡτος**, ον, much-wept or lamented, παῖς Il.24.620. 2. lamentable, tearful, γόος Od. 19.213, Ar.*Th.*1040 (lyr.); πένθη A.*Ch.*333 (lyr.). II. Act., much-weeping, E.*Hec.*651 (lyr.), cj. in *Tr.*1105 (lyr.). [πολυδάκρῡτος is f.l. in Il.17.192, E.*HF*427 (lyr.); cf. πολυδάκρυος.] **-δάκτῠλος**, ον, many-toed, Arist.*HA*499$^b$8, *PA*659$^a$23, al. **-δαμνος**, ον, (δάμνημι) taming much, Hsch., cf. Sch.Od.4.228. **-δάπᾰνος** [δᾰ], ον, causing great expense or outlay, ἱρά Hdt.2.137 (Comp.), cf. Porph.*Abst.*2.15; τράπεζα X.*Lac.*5.3. II. of a person, expensive, extravagant, Id.*Ap.*19, Vett. Val.90.15. Adv. -νως D.S.1.52, Plot.1.4.7; at great expense, *IGRom.* 4.1241, 1242, 1273, *JHS*37.108 (Thyatira). **-δαφνος**, ον, with many laurels, Ἑλικών Sch.Hes.*Th.*30. **-δέγμων**, ον, gen. ονος, (δέχομαι) containing or receiving much, Lyc.700. II. πολυδέγμων, ὁ, like πολυδέκτης, a name of Hades, *h.Cer.*17, 31, prob. in Orph.*H.*18.11, cf. *Fr.*49 iv 64, v 69. **-δεής**, ές, (δέομαι) wanting much, Max.Tyr. 21.4. **-δειράς** (A), άδος, ὁ, ἡ, (δειράς) with many ridges, Οὐλύμποιο Il.1.499, 5.754. **-δειράς** (B), άδος, ὁ, ἡ, (δειρή) many-necked, ὕδρη Q.S.6.212. **-δειρος**, ον, = foreg. (B), Nonn.*D.*25.199. **-δέκτης**, ου, ὁ, the All-receiver, i.e. Hades, *h.Cer.*9. **-δένδρεος**, ον, Ep. for sq., κῆπος, ἀγρός, Od.4.737, 23.139; γῆ Sol.13.47. ⊛ **-δενδρος**, ον, abounding in trees, of a country, Str.17.3.4: heterocl. dat. pl. πολυδένδρεσσιν Ὀλύμπου θαλάμαις E.*Ba.*560 (lyr.). **-δερκής**, ές, much-seeing, far-seeing, Ἠώς Hes.*Th.*451; φάος ib.755; cf. πολυδευκής. **-δερμος**, ον, = πολύρρινος, *EM*395.56 (v.l. -δέρματον). II. with several layers, of the abdominal wall, Gal.8.952. **-δεσμος**, ον, fastened with many bonds, strong-bound, ἐπὶ σχεδίης πολυδέσμου Od.5.33, v.l. ib.338.

**Πολῠδεύκης**, εος, ὁ, Pollux, Il.3.237, Od.11.300: hence Adj. **Πολυδεύκειος**, Ep. fem. Πολυδευκείη, χείρ Call.*Fr.*496. II. Adj. πολυδευκής, ές, v.l. for πολυηχής in Od.19.521 ap.Ael.*NA*5.38 (τὴν ποικίλως μεμιμημένην) and Hsch. (πολλοῖς ἐοικυῖαν, cf. δευκές). 2. = ποικίλος, μορφή prob. for -δερκής in Nic.*Th.*209. 3. (δεῦκος) very sweet, ἐλίχρυσος ib.625 (cf. Sch. ad loc.).

**Πολῠδεύκιον**, τό, Com. Dim. of Πολυδεύκης, Luc.*DMort.*1.3.

**πολύ-δημος**, ον, populous, Poll.9.21. **-δημώδης**, ες, = foreg., D.L.7.14. **-δήνης**, ες, (δήνεα) = πολύβουλος, Hsch. **-δηρις**, ὁ, ἡ, = sq., ἔλεγχος Parm.1.36. **-δήρῑτος**, ον, much-contested, Opp. *H.*5.328. **-διαίρετος**, ον, with many divisions, Eust.425.27. **-διάκρῐτος**, ον, divisible into minute parts, Dam.*Pr.*56. **-διάφθορος**, ον, much-destroyed, Sch.Il.4.171. **-διάχῠτος**, ον, widely diffused, πάθος Hsch. s.v. γάγγραινα. ⊛ **-δῐκέω**, to be litigious, Pl.*Lg.* 938b. ⊛ **-δῐκος**, ον, litigious, Str.15.1.53, Vett.Val.15.17. **-δῑνής**, ές, much-whirling, Opp.*H.*4.585; μίτου πολυδινέα λάτριν *AP*6.39

(Arch.). -δίνητος [ῑ], ον, *much-whirled*, φύλλον D.P.407. -διοίκητος, ον, *widely distributed, all-pervading*, πνεῦμα Secund. *Sent.* 3. -δίψιος, ον, (δίψα) *very thirsty*, of ill-watered countries, Ἄργος Il.4.171, Q.S.3.570. (Expld. as = πολυπόθητος by Str.8.6.7, Ath.10. 433e; Str. also suggests πολυΐψιος (fr. ἴπτω), *much-destroyed*.) -διψος, ον, *making very thirsty*, Xenocr.ap.Orib.2.58.91. -δονος, ον, *much-driven*, πλάνη A.*Pr.*788. -δόξαστος, ον, *much-famed*, Sch.rec.Pi.*O.*6.120. -δοξία, ἡ, *diversity of opinions*, Dam.*Isid.* 37. -δοξος, ον, *having various opinions*, Stob.2.7.4ᵃ. II. *famous*, *BCH*21.599 (Delph., iv B.C.), Timo 44; διδαχαί *IG*14. 2124. -δουλεία, ἡ, *abundance of slaves*, Poll.3.80. -δούλευτος, ον, gloss on ἀτμένιος, Sch.Nic.*Al.*178. -δουλος, ον, *having many slaves*, Poll.3.80, 6.171. -δράστεια, ἡ, (δράω) *she that effects much*, Corn.*ND*13.

⊕πολύδριον, τό, Dim. of πόλις, Sch.D.T.p.227 H. (as v.l.), Hsch. s.v. πολίχνια, *Gloss.*

πολυ-δρομή, ἡ, *long race*, *IG*12(9).95 (Eretria). -δρομος, ον, *much-wandering* or *rapid*, φυγά A.*Supp.*737 (lyr.). -δροσος, ον, *very dewy*, ἰκμὰς Βάκχου *AP*5.133 (Posidipp.). -δρῡμος, ον, *with many woods*, Rhian.20. ⊕-δύνᾰμος [δῠ], ον, *with many powers* or *faculties*, Porph.ap.Stob.1.49.25ᵃ, Herm. *in Phdr.*p.139 A., Procl. *in Cra.*p.75 P. 2. *powerful*, Eust.916.21. -δωρία, ἡ, *open-handedness*, X.*Cyr.*8.2.7, Poll.3.118. ⊕-δωρος, ον, *richly dowered*, ἄλοχος Il.6.394, Od.24.294, etc. II. *open-handed*, Aret.*SD*1.5. -εδνος, ον, *with rich dowry*, Hsch. s.v. πολύδωρος. -εδρος, ον, *with many seats*, Plu. *Per.*13. -εθνής, ές, *many-peopled*: *numerous*, Oenom.ap Eus.*PE* 5.29, Orph.*H.*78.11, *A.*430. ⊕-είδεια, v.l. for πολυειδία. -ειδήμων, ον, gen. ονος, *knowing much*, S.E.*M.*1.63. ⊕-ειδής, ές, *of many kinds* or *forms*, πολυειδῆ φθέγγεσθαι utter cries *of divers kinds*, Th.7.71; opp. μονοειδής, Pl.*R.*612a; opp. ἁπλοῦς, Id.*Phdr.*238a codd.; τὸ δεινὸν.. καὶ π. θρέμμα Id.*R.*590a, cf. *Phd.*80b; λόγος Hippias 6; of music, Phld.*Mus.*p.64 K. (Sup.); τὸ π., = πολυειδία, τῶν χρωμάτων Arist.*Col.* 792ᵇ33: Comp. -έστερος D.H.*Comp.*19: Sup. -έστατος Ti.Locr.101b. Adv. -δῶς D.H.*Comp.*26, Gal.10.113, Iamb.*Myst.*1.1, al. II. π. τροχίσκος, ὁ, name of a *lozenge*, Aët.12.64 bis (nisi leg. Πολυείδου). -ειδία, ἡ, *diversity of kind*, Pl.*R.*580d, Thphr.*HP*3.2.5. -ειδος, ὁ, name of various plants, e.g. κρόμυον, κάππαρις, etc., Ps.-Dsc.2.151, 173, al. 2. Adj. -ειδος, ον, = πολυειδής 1, Zos Alch.p.113 B. -είλητος, ον, *much convoluted*, ἔντερα Ruf.*Anat.*44. -είμων, ον, gen. ονος, *of many garments*, Mesom.*Sol.*25 (prob.). -έλαιος, ον, *owning many oliveyards*, X.*Vect.*5.3. -έλεος, ον, *very merciful*, Lxx *Ex.*34.6, *Nu.*14.18, al. -έλικτος, ον, *much convoluted*, ἔντερον Gal.2.572; τὸ π., of a nerve, Id.*UP*9.13. II. π. ἀδονά the pleasure *of the mazy dance*, E.*Ph.*314 (lyr.); Ep. πουλυ-, π. χορείη Nonn.*D.*21.185. -ελκής, ές, (ἕλκος) *with many sores*, Aret. *SD*1.14. -ενος, ον, (ἔνος A) = πολυετής, Suid. -έξοδος, ον, *with many outgoings*, *lavish*, Procl.*Par.Ptol.*96. -επαίνετος, ον, *much-praised*: Sup. -ώτατος X.*Ages.*6.8. -επής, ές, *much-speaking*, *wordy*, τέχναι A.*Ag.*1134 (lyr.). -έραστος, ον, *much-loved*, X.*Ages.* 6.8 (Sup.), D.S.37.2. -εργής, ές, = sq. 1, *AP*7.400 (Serapio). II. = sq. II, Antioch.Astr. in *Cat.Cod.Astr.*1.111. ⊕-εργος, ον, *hard-working*, ἀροτρεύς Nic.*Th.*4, cf. *Cat.Cod.Astr.*2.179; perh. f.l. for ἀμπελοεργοί, Theoc.25.27. II. Pass., *highly-wrought*, *elaborate*, Ph.1. 665. -ερώμενος, ον, *with many lovers*, Diom.p.326 K. -ερως, ωτος, ὁ, *much-loving*, Hdn.*Epim.*206. -εσθλος, ον, *very excellent*, *Rev. Phil.*46.122 (Kadyn Khan). -έταιρος, ον, *with many fellows* or *comrades*, Poll.3.62. -ετέω, *grant long life*, *PLond.ined.*2181. -ετής, ές, *after many years*, π. σεσωσμένος E.*Or.*473; π. μολεῖν Id.*Hel.*651 (lyr.). II. *lasting many years*, βίος *OGI*383.22 (Nemrud Dagh, i B.C.); ζωή, πόλεμοι, Ph.2.364, 1.677; δουλεία Luc.*Merc.Cond.*17; χρόνος Sor.1.33; *full of years*, γῆρας Lxx *Wi.*4.16; *old*, ἐλέφας Hld.10.25; οἶνος Dsc.2.76; *keeping for many years*, of a remedy, Aët.9.24. -ετία, ἡ, *length of years*, Ph.1.393, al., Gal.6.357, D.L.1.72, D.C.66. 18. -ευκτος, ον, *much-prayed-for*, *much-desired*, ἰὴ παιδός Orac.ap. Hdt.1.85; ὄλβος A.*Eu.*537 (lyr.); πλοῦτος X.*Cyr.*1.6.45; παιδίον Him. *Or.*23.20. II. Act., *with many prayers*, ἱκεσίη Nonn.*D.*40. 66. -εύχετος, ον, = foreg. 1, *h.Cer.*165. -εφθος, ον, = sq., interpol. in Dsc.2.124. -έψητος, ον, *much* or *well boiled*, Sch.Nic. *Al.*130 (*Stud.Ital.*12.340). -ζηλος, ον, *full of emulation*, βίος S. *OT*381. II. *much admired*, βασιλεύς B.10.63; πόσις S.*Tr.* 185. -ζήλωτος, ον, *much admired* or *revered*, B.7.10, al.; Ἄρτεμις E. *Hipp.*168 (lyr.), cf. *IG*4.491.3 (Cleonae, misspelt -σήλωτον), *Hymn.Is.* 16 (-ζάλ-). -ζήμιος, ον, *very hurtful*, *Gloss.* -ζῦγος, ον, (ζυγόν III) *many-benched*, νηῦς Il.2.293, Maiist.9; φορτίς Opp.*H.*5.312. -ζωέω, *to be full of life*, of Isis, *IGRom.*1.1310 (Philae). -ζωνος (sc. λίθος), ὁ, gem *with many layers*, Plin.*HN*37.189. -ζωος, ον, = *long-lived*, π. κακόν, of a *very aged* man, *Com.Adesp.*892; κορῶναι Opp.*C.*3. 117. -ζῳος, ον, *consisting of many animals*, ἀγέλα Ph.1.20, 2.30; ἄστρα, of the Zodiac, Man 4.516. II. π., τό, *multiplex animal*, Plot.2.3.7. -ζωστος, ον, *tight-girded*, Hsch. s.v. ἀζείρου, *EM*23. 1. ⊕-ηγερέες, read for τηλεκλητοί by Aristarch. in Il.11.564. -ηγόρος, ον, *much-speaking*, Φρόντις Philisc.ap.Plu.2.836c, cf. Orph.*A.* 489. -ηδής, ές, *very pleasant*, Hdn.Gr.2.689. -ήθης, ες, *taking many characters*, *versatile*, Eust.1381.41. -ηκοΐα, ἡ, *much learning*, Olymp.*Vit.Pl.*p.1 W., Eust.1459.43. -ήκοος, ον, (ἀκούω) *having heard much*, *much-learned*, π. ἐν ταῖς ἀναγνώσεσιν καὶ πολυμαθεῖς Pl. *Lg.*810e; π. ἄνευ διδαχῆς Id.*Phdr.*275a. -ηλάκᾰτος [λᾰ], ον, (ἠλακάτη II. 1) *very reedy*, ποταμοί A.*Fr.*8. -ήλῐος, ον, *much-sunned*, *very sunny*, Sch.E.*Andr.*534. -ημερεύω, *attain length of days*, Lxx *De.*11.21 (v.l.). -ήμερος, ον, *lasting many days*, δυσεντερίη Hp.*Art.*69, cf. Gal.10.587; ὁδός Plu.*Luc.*21; οὐ π. θνήσκουσι they die *in a few days*, Aret.*SA*1.9. II. *full of days*, *aged*, Lxx *De.*25. 15, al. -ήρᾰτος, ον, (ἐράω) *much-loved*, *very lovely*, γάμος Od.15. 126; εὐνή Hes.*Th.*404; εἶδος ib.908; ὕδωρ Id.*Op.*739; ἥβη *h.Ven.* 225; of places, Θήβη Od.11.275; Ἀθᾶναι B.18.9; Λιβύη Orac.ap. Hdt.4.159; γᾶ Κέκροπος Ar.*Nu.*301 (lyr.). 2. of persons, Hes.*Fr.* 192.1; Λαΐς Plu.2.767f; φέγγος π. Αἰνεαδάων, of Caracalla, Opp.*C.*1. 2. -ήρης, ες, *with many oars*, ἐπακτρίδες Agath.5.22. -ηρος, ον, (ἔρα) *rich in land*, Hsch. -ήσῠχος, ον, *very quiet*, Sch.rec.A.*Pr.* 139. -ηχής, ές, (ἦχος) *many-toned*, of the nightingale's voice, Od. 19.521; χοροῦ π. φωνή *AP*9.504; *much-* or *loud-sounding*, αἰγιαλός Il.4.422; ἄνεμος, πέτραι, A.R.4.609, 963. -ήχητος, Dor. πολυάχ-, ον, *loud-sounding*, E.*Alc.*918 (anap.). -ηχία, ἡ, *variety of sound*, Demetr.*Eloc.*73. -ηχος, ον, = πολυηχής, γῆρυς, θάλασσα, Ph.1. 373, Sch.S.*Aj.*695: metaph., χωρίον ψυχῆς Ph.1.372; βίος ταραχώδης καὶ π. *noisy*, Epict.*Gnom.*1. Adv. -χως Ael.*NA*12.28. -θάητος [ᾱ], ον, poet. for πολυθέατος, τέμενος Epigr.ap.Paus.6.3.14. -θάλμιος, ον, *much-nourishing*, Orph.*H.*68.1. -θαλπής, ές, *very hot*, ἀτμός Nonn.*D.*14.424. -θαμβής, ές, *much frighted* or *astonied*, ib.418, al. -θαρσής, ές, *much-confident*, μένος Il.17.156, Od.13.387; *valorous*, πόλεμος A.R.2.912. ⊕-θαύμαστος, ον, *much-admired*, Suid. s.v. Ἱπποκράτης. -θεάμων [ᾰ], ον, gen. ονος, *having seen much*, c. gen., Pl.*Phdr.*251a. -θέᾰτος, ον, *much-seen*, *conspicuous*, Hsch. s.v. πολύοπτος. -θεΐα, ἡ, *polytheism*, Ph.1.609, Procop.*Arc.*19, *Aed.*6. 2. -θελγής, ές, *bewitching*, dub. in *Hymn.Is.*104. -θεος, ον, *of* or *belonging to many gods*, ἕδρα A.*Supp.*424 (lyr.); ἐκκλησία Luc.*JTr.*14 (Sup.). II. *believing in many gods*, Procop.*Arc.*11; δόξα π. *polytheism*, Ph.1.41, al. III. *consisting of many gods*, θίασος, στῖφος, ib.609, 426. -θερής, ές, gloss on βουθερής, Sch.S.*Tr.*188. -θερμος, ον, *very hot*, τοῦ σώματος κρᾶσις Plu.*Alex.*4, cf. Heliod.ap.Orib. 49.8.11, Gal.17(2).201, Theo Sm.p.187 H. -θεστος, ον, *much-desired*, τοκεῦσι Call.*Cer.*48. -θηρία, ἡ, *great plenty of game*, Poll. 5.13. -θηρος, ον, *with much game*, *full of wild beasts*, νάπος E.*Ph.* 801 (lyr., Sup.). II. *mighty huntress*, epith. of Δίκτυννα, Id.*Hipp.* 145 (lyr.). III. *taking many fish*, Hld.5.18. ⊕-θλῐβής, ές, *much-pressed*, Nonn.*D.*2.494. -θουρος, ον, *very salacious*, Opp. *C.*3.516. -θραυστος, ον, *much-broken*, *EM*1.52. -θρέμμᾰτος, ον, *rich in cattle*, J.*AJ*6.13.6. -θρέμμων, ον, gen. ονος, *feeding many*, epith. of the Nile, A.*Pers.*33 (anap.); Νύμφαι Orph.*H.*51. 13. -θρεπτος, ον, *much-nourished*, ἄνθη π. *the many* flowers *that grow*, ib.43.6. -θρήνητος, ον, *lamentable*, γενεή *AP*7.334.15, cf. *IG*12(8).445.6 (Thasos); gloss on ἀδινός, Sch.S.*Tr.*848. -θρηνος, ον, *much-wailing*, αἰών A.*Ag.*714 (lyr.); ὕμνος ib.711 (lyr.); π. Ἀλκυών Luc.*Halc.*1; π. ὑάκινθος Nic.*Th.*902. II. *much-lamented*, παιδίον Him.*Or.*23.20 (Sup.). ⊕-θρῖδαξ, ἄκος, *abounding in lettuces*, Diom.p.326 K. ⊕-θριξ, τρῐχος, ὁ, ἡ, *with much hair*, of persons, *AP*6.276 (Antip.); οὐρά *Gp.*17.2.1. II. Subst., = ἀδίαντον, Plin.*HN*25.132. ⊕-θρόνιος, ον, (θρόνον) = πολυφάρμακος, Androm. ap.Gal.14.32: πολύθρονος is f.l. in Nic.*Th.*875. ⊕-θροος, ον, contr. -θρους, ουν, *clamorous*, μάται A.*Supp.*820 (lyr.); φήμη Tryph.236; κυκλίων στίχος *App.Anth.*3.186. -θρῡλής, ές, = sq., Ptol.*Tetr.* 170 (s.v.l.). -θρύλητος [ῡ], ον (freq. written -θρύλλητος in codd.), *much-spoken-of*: hence, *well-known*, *notorious*, [Thales] 3, Pl.*R.*566b, *Phd.*100b, Plb.9.31.4, Plot.1.4.5. Adv. -τως Vett.Val. 285.31, Poll.6.207. -θῠρος, ον, (θύρα) *with many doors* or *windows*, αὐλαί Plu.2.99e: generally, *with many holes*, τριβώνιον Luc.*DMort.* 1.2. II. *with many plates* or *leaves*, δέλτου.. πολυθύρου διαπτυχαί E. *IT*727. -θύσᾰνος [θῠ], ον, *with many tassels*, epith. of Artemis, Poet. ap.Hsch. (also expld. by -θῠσίαστος, *honoured with many sacrifices*, and -θώϋστος (θωΰσσω), *rushing violently*). -θῠτος, ον, *abounding in sacrifices*, ἔρανος, πομπαί, Pi.*P.*5.77, *N.*7.47; σφαγαί S.*Tr.*756; ἄλσος Ἀρτέμιδος E.*IA*185 (lyr.); τιμά Id.*Heracl.*777 (lyr.). -ἴᾰχος [ῐ], ον, *crying much*, Apollon.*Lex.* s.v. ἄβρομοι. -ΐδμων, ον, gen. ονος, = πολυΐστωρ, μάγοι, θεοπροπίη, Orph.*L.*697, 715. -ϊδρεία, ἡ, *much knowledge* or *wisdom*, in pl., ἡ πάντ' ἐφύλασσε νόου πολυϊδρείῃσι Od.2.346, cf. 23.77 (v.l.); πολυϊδρίῃσιν Thgn.703 codd.: later in sg., Call.*Aet.*3.1.8. -ϊδρίδας, α, ὁ, = sq., S.*Inach.* in *PTeb.* 692 ii 1. -ϊδρις, Ion. gen. ιος, Att. εως, ὁ, ἡ, *of much knowledge*, *wisdom*, Od.15.459, 23.82, Hes.*Th.*616, Alc.*Supp.*7.7, Ar.*Eq.*1068 (hex.); σίττη Arist.*HA* 616ᵇ24, etc.; dat. πολυΐδριδι Sapph. 166. -ῖνος [ῑ], ον (ἴς A) *with many fibres*, Thphr.*HP*3.10.3, al. -ιππία, ἡ, *abundance of horses*, *Gloss.* -ιππος, ον, *rich in horses*, Il.13.171, D.P.308, Tryph.171. -ϊστορία, ἡ, *great learning*, *erudition*, prob. in Phld.*Rh.*1.143 S. -ΐστωρ, ορος, ὁ, ἡ, *very learned*, D.H. *Din.*1, Str.3.2.12, Gal.17(1).605; esp. as epith. of Alexander Polyhistor, J.*AJ*1.15.1, etc.; βίβλος *AP*9.280 (Apollonid.):—also -ΐστορος, ον, Sch.Lyc.5. -ϊχθυς, υος, ὁ, ἡ, *abounding in fish*, ποταμός Str.3.3.1:—also -ιχθύος, ον, *h.Ap.*417. -ΐψιος, ον, v. πολυδίψιος. -καγκής, ές, (κάγκω, καίω) *parching*, δίψα Il.11. 642. 2. *very dry*, χέρη *AP*9.678. -κᾰδία, ἡ, *chain of buckets*, Hero *Dioptr.*6. -κᾰής, ές, (καίω) *much burning*, dat. -καέϊ (metri gr.) *AP*7.648 (Leon.). -κάθεδρος, ὁ, = πολύζυγος, Sch.D Il.2. 74, Eust.174.10. -καισᾰρίη, ἡ, (Καῖσαρ) *a plurality of Caesars*, formed after πολυκοιρανίη, Arius ap.Plu.*Ant.*81. -κάλᾰμος [κᾰ], ον, *of* or *with many stalks*, βρόμος Thphr.*HP*8.9.2, cf. *CP*4.11.3; σῦριγξ D.S.3.58. -κάμᾰτος [κᾰ], ον, = πολύκμητος, Phot., Suid. -κάμμορος, ον, *very miserable*, *AP*9.151 (Antip.). -καμπής, ές, *with many curves*, Thphr.*Sens.*65, *CP*6.10.3, *AP*6.297 (Phan.), etc.; τὸ π. (sc. τοῦ κισσοῦ) Plu.2.649b; of a zigzag route, ib.615c: metaph. of music, *with many flourishes*, π. μέλη Phrynis ap.Poll.4.66. **-καμπτος**, ον, = foreg., μελέων π. v.l. for πολυπλάγκτων in Parm.16.1. **-κᾰνής**, ές, (καίνω) *much-slaughtering*, θυσίαι π. βοτῶν *with slaughter of many* beasts, A.*Ag.*1169 (lyr.). **-καπνος**, ον, *smoky*, στέγος E.*El.*1140.

**πολῠκάρηνος** [ᾰ], Ep. **πουλ-**, ον, *many-headed*, *APl.*4.91, Nonn.*D.*40.233.

**πολῠκαρπ-έω**, *bear much fruit*, Arist.*GA*750$^{a}$22, Thphr.*CP*2.11.3. **-ία**, ἡ, *abundance of fruit*, *IG*1$^{2}$.76.45, X.*Mem.*3.14.3, Thphr.*CP*4.8.1, *Sammelb.*6944.14 (Edict. Hadriani), Sm.*Ps.*64(65).10. **-ος**, ον, *fruitful*, ἀλωή Od.7.122, 24.221; χθών Pi.*P.*9.7 (Sup.); τὸν π. οἰνάνθας βότρυν E.*Ph.*230 (lyr.); δένδρον Pl.*Ti.*86c (Comp.), cf. Hp.*Insomn.*90, etc.; στέφανος μύρτων Ar.*Ra.*328, cf. *IG*3.726; *rich in fruit*, Φρύγες πολυκαρπότατοι Hdt.5.49; θεοί *CIG*2175. II. πολύκαρπον, τό, = κραταιόγονον, Hp.*Mul.*1.65, acc. to Gal.19.132; = πολύγονον ἄρρεν, Dsc.4.4.

**πολῠ-κατασκεύαστος**, ον, *elaborately wrought*, Sch.D Il.3.358. **-κατέργαστος**, ον, = foreg., ib.4.135. II. gloss on ἀτμένιος, Sch.Nic.*Al.*178. **-καυλος**, ον, *many-stalked*, Thphr.*HP*4.6.8, 7.2.8. **-κέλᾰδος**, ον, *much-sounding*, Luc.*Trag.*118. **-κενος**, ον, *containing much void, porous*, Arist.*Pr.*940$^{a}$4; τόπος Epicur.*Ep.*2 p.37 U.; φύσεις Id.*Nat.*2.9, cf. Dsc.5.108, Plu.2.721c, Gal.9.181. **-κέντητος**, ον, gloss on πολύκεστος, Hsch., Suid., cf. *EM*506.49, Eust.425.24. **-κέρδεια**, ἡ, *great craft*, πολυκερδείῃσιν Od.23.77, 24.167; **-κερδία** is v.l. in Adam.*Phgn.*2.37. **-κερδής**, ές, *very crafty* or *wily*, νόος Od.13.255; *shrewd in business, money-making*, Man.1.132, Polem.*Phgn.*8; *gainful*, τέχναι Opp.*H.*2.15. **-κερως**, ωτος, ὁ, ἡ, *many-horned*, π. φόνος the slaughter *of many horned cattle*, S.*Aj.*55. **-κεστος**, ον, *with much needle-work, well-stitched*, ἱμάς Il.3.371. (For -κεντ-τος.) ✻ **-κέφᾰλος**, ον, *many-headed*, θηρίον Pl.*R.*588c; σοφιστής Id.*Sph.*240c, cf. Arist.*GA*769$^{b}$27; of plants, interpol. in Dsc.2.152; π. στρέβλα (with allusion to Pl.*R.* l.c.) Lxx 4*Ma.*7.14; νόμος π., a celebrated air on the flute, so called from its expressing *the hissing of the serpents round the Gorgon's head*, Plu.2.1133d. **-κήδεια**, ἡ, *much care* or *grief*, Sch.A.R.3.298 (pl.). **-κηδής**, ές, *full of care, grievous*, νόστος Od.9.37, 23.351; μάχη Plu.*Nob.*2 (Sup.); νοῦσος Q.S.8.31; of persons, κασιγνήτη A.R.4.734, cf. Q.S.10.310. **-κήριος**, ον, (κήρ) *very deadly*, ἄτη Nic.*Th.*798; χρημοσύνη *IG*14.1424. **-κήτης**, ες, *full of monsters*, Νεῖλος Theoc.17.98. **-κίνδῡνος**, ον, *very dangerous*, Isoc.10.17 as cited by Demetr.*Eloc.*23. II. *conversant with danger*, Teucer in *Cat.Cod.Astr.*7.198. **-κῑνησία**, Ion. -ίη, ἡ, *manifold motion*, Aret.*SA*2.2. **-κίνητος** [ῑ], ον, *full of movement*, ὄψις Plu.2.681a, cf. Gal.*UP* 16.6; *restless*, Id.8.131; ἔκστασις Iamb.*Myst.*3.2; τὸ ἄρχειν π. καὶ πολυμέριμνον Arist.*Mu.*400$^{b}$9. **-κίων** [ῑ], ον, gen. ονος, *with many pillars*, νηός *Rh.Mus.*59.623 (Lindos). **-κλαγγος**, ον, *clamorous*, ὄρνις Ael.*NA*2.51 (Sup.). **-κλᾰδής**, ές, *with many branches*, Thphr.*HP*1.5.1. **-κλᾰδος**, ον, = foreg., ib.1.3.1, Dsc.1.97, Gal.14.66. ✻ **-κλαυστος** or **-κλαυτος**, ον, also η, ον cj. in A.*Ag.*1526 (anap.):—*much lamented*, Hom.*Epigr.*2.5, A. l.c., E.*Ion* 869 (anap.), etc.; π. φίλοισι A.*Pers.*674 (lyr.). II. Act., *much-lamenting*, γυναῖκες Emp.62; ῥέεθρα Mosch.3.73; π. ὑάκινθος *IG*14.607; π. ποταμός *swollen with tears*, Arat.360; *causing much lamentation*, πόλεμος Q.S.10.141. **-κλεής**, ές, *far-famed*, Man.4.43 (nisi leg. πολὺ κλέος): Comp. -έστερος Them.*Or.*4.53b. **-κλείδωτος**, ον, gloss on πολυκλήϊς, Eust.174.11. **-κλειστος**, ον, (κλείω A) *closely shut*, θάλαμοι Ps.-Phoc.215. **-κλειτος**, η, ον, (κλείω B) *far-famed*, Pi.*O.*6.71, *Fr.*194. **-κλεπτος**, ον, *very thievish*, Tz.*H.*13.361. **-κλήεις**, εσσα, εν, *celebrated*, *APl.*4.331 (Agath.). **-κλήϊς** [ῑ], ῖδος, ἡ, (κλείς IV) *with many benches* of rowers, in Hom. always in dat., as epith. of ships, νηῒ πολυκλήϊδι Il.7.88, Od.20.382; νηυσὶ πολυκλήϊσι Il.2.74, cf. 175, al.; νῆα πολυκλήϊδα Hes.*Op.*817. **-κλήϊστος**, ον, *with many fastenings*, ζυγόν Nonn.*D.*28.77. **-κλημᾰτέω**, *have many branches*, Ph.1.301. **-κληρος**, ον, *with a large portion* of land, *exceeding rich*, Od.14.211, Theoc.16.83. **-κλητος**, ον, *called from many a land*, of the allies of the Trojans, Il.4.438, 10.420. **-κλῐνής**, ές, *lying with many*, Man.3.332. **-κλῑνος**, ον, *with many couches* or *seats*, οἶκος Hld.5.18. **-κλυστος**, ον, *much-dashing, stormy*, πολυκλύστῳ ἐνὶ πόντῳ Od.4.354, 6.204, Hes.*Th.*189, cf. Pancrat.*Oxy.*1085.13. II. Pass., *washed by many a wave*, πολυκλύστῳ ἐνὶ Κύπρῳ Hes.*Th.*199; φάραγγες Ὄσσης A.R.1.597. **-κλωνος**, ον, *with many branches*, Thphr.*HP*6.2.6 (Comp.), Dsc.3.33; ἀρτεμισία π., = ἀμβροσία 4, Ps.-Dsc.3.113: neut. π., τό, name of a plant, *Gp.*12.1.2. **-κμητος**, ον, (κάμνω) *wrought with much toil*, Hom. epith. of iron (as distd. from copper), Il.6.48, al.: generally, *elaborate*, π. θάλαμος Od.4.718; ἑανοί A.R.4.1189. II. later, *laborious*, τέχνη *AP*9.656.6; πόλεμος Q.S.7.424. 2. of persons, *toiling hard*, ἁλιῆες Id.9.173. **-κνημος**, ον, (κνημός I) *with many mountain-spurs, mountainous*, Il.2.497. II. (κνημός II) τὸ π. *field basil, Zizyphora capitata*, Hp.*Mul.*1.65, Nic.*Th.*559, *Al.*57, Dsc.3.94. **-κνῖσος**, ον, (κνῖσα) *steaming*, ἑκατόμβη A.R.3.880, cf. Tryph.446. **-κοίλιος**, ον, *with many stomachs*, Arist.*PA*676$^{a}$6, 677$^{b}$17. **-κοίμητος**, ον, *sleeping much*, Sch.A.*Pr.*139. **-κοινέω**, *to be* πολύκοινος II, *Cat.Cod.Astr.*8(4).169. **-κοινία**, ἡ, *sexual promiscuity*, Heph.Astr.1.1. ✻ **-κοινος**, ον, *common to many* or *to all*, τὰν π. ἀγγελίαν, i.e. death, Pi.*P.*2.41; π. Ἅιδας S.*Aj.*1192 (lyr.); πυρετός Hp.*Flat.*6 (prob.); εὐδαιμονία, ἀγαθόν, Arist.*EN*1099$^{b}$18, *MM*1204$^{b}$1; εὐτυχία Them.*Or.*1.6d. II. *promiscuous in sexual relations*, Ptol.*Tetr.*172, *Cat.Cod.Astr.*8(4).176. **-κοιρᾰνία**, Ep. -ίη, ἡ, *rule of many*, Il.2.204, cf. Arist.*Pol.*1292$^{a}$13. II. *rule over many*, Rhian.1.10. **-κοίρᾰνος**, ον, *wide-ruling*, A.*Fr.*238 (lyr.). **-κοιτέω**, *lie with many women* or *men*, Vett.Val.118.5. **-κοιτος**, ον, *lying with many women* or *men*, Id.75.9, al. **-κολπος**, ον, *with many sinus*, μήτρα Gal.2.890; of a fistula, Heliod.ap.Orib.44.23.68. **-κόλυμβος**, ον, *oft-diving*, μέλη, of the frogs, Ar.*Ra.*245 (lyr.). **-κομος**, ον, *with much down*, στάχυες Dsc.1.7, cf. 4.164.9. **-κομπος**, ον, *loud-sounding*, αὐλός v.l. in Poll.4.67. **-κομψος**, ον, *very elegant*, *EM*729.29, Suid. s.v. στωμύλος. ✻ **-κοπος**, f.l. for πολυπρόσωπος in Ath.1.20e (cf. Plu.2.711f). ✻ **-κοσμος**, ον, *much-adorned*, Hsch. s.v. πολυδαίδαλον. ✻ **-κρᾱνος**, ον, *many-headed*, E.*Ba.*1017 (lyr.).

**Πολυκράτειος** [ᾰ], α, ον, *of Polycrates*, ἔργα Arist.*Pol.*1313$^{b}$24.

**πολυ-κρᾰτέω**, *have much power*, Eun.*VS* p.493 B. **-κρᾰτής**, ές, *very mighty*, Μοῖρα B.8.15; ἀραὶ φθιμένων (leg. τεθυμένων) A.*Ch.*406 (lyr.). **-κρᾱτος**, ον, *much-mixed*, *AB*371. **-κρεκτος**, ον, *much-sounding*, κιθάρη Orph.*H.*34.16. **-κρεως**, ων, *with many meats*, εὐωχία Ph.ap.Eus.*PE*8.14. **-κρημνος**, ον, *with many steeps* or *mountains*, χθών B.1.11, cf. Call.*Fr.*477. **-κρῑθέω**, *have plenty of barley*, Eust.658.43. **-κρῑθος**, ον, *abounding in barley*, γᾶ B.10.70, cf. Euph.51.14, Suid. s.v. κρίμνον. **-κριμνος**, ον, = foreg., *EM*681.37. **-κρῐτος**, ον, *widely separate*, Orph.*H.*11.18. **-κρόκᾰλος**, ον, *full of pebbles*, Call.*Fr.anon.*110. **-κροσσος**, ον, *with many battlements*, Tz.*H.*10.228. **-κρότᾰλος**, ον, *much-rattling*, χείρ Nonn.*D.*5.255. **-κρότητος**, ον, *much struck* or *beaten*, Hsch. s.v. ἀκρότητα. ✻ **-κροτος**, ον, also η, ον (v. infr.), *ringing loud* or *clearly*, *h.Pan.*37; χελωνίς Posidon.10 J. II. *sly, cunning, wily*, v.l. in Od.1.1, cf. Hes.*Fr.*94.22, Anacr.90.2 (fem. πολυκρότη). **-κρουνος**, ον, *with many springs*, στόματα fountains *many-gushing*, *AP*9.669.4 (Marian.); *with many mouths*, φιάλαι Aristid.*Or.*17(15).22. **-κρωζος**, ον, (κρώζω) *much-croaking*, v.l. in Opp.*C.*3.117. **-κτέᾰνος**, ον, = πολυκτήμων, Pi.*O.*10(11).36, Call.*Ap.*35, Opp.*C.*1.239; Ῥωμαῖοι *IG*14.809. **-κτήμᾰτος**, ον, = foreg., Ptol.*Tetr.*69. **-κτημοσύνη**, ἡ, *great wealth*, Poll.3.110, *Cat.Cod.Astr.*2.163, 204. **-κτήμων**, ον, gen. ονος, *with many possessions, exceeding rich*, Il.5.613, S.*Ant.*842 (lyr.): in later Prose, Eus.Mynd.59, Alex.Aphr.*in Top.*147.14: c. gen., π. βίου E.*Ion* 581. **-κτηνος**, ον, *rich in cattle*, Alex.Polyh.ap.Eus.*PE*9.25. **-κτησία**, ἡ, = πολυκτημοσύνη, Ath.6.233d. **-κτητος**, ον, *of large possessions, wealthy*, δόμοι E.*Andr.*769 (lyr.), v.l. in Sch.S.*El.*508. **-κτῐτος**, ον, (κτίζω) *building much*, Orph.*H.*10.2. ✻ **-κτόνος**, ον, (κτείνω) *murderous*, A.*Ag.*461, 734 (both lyr.); δι' ἐμὲ τὰν πολυκτόνον E.*Hel.*198 (lyr.). **-κύδιστος** [κῡ], ον, *most glorious*, θεσμοσύνα *AP*7.593 (Agath.); πολυκυδίστη Σοφίη ib.9.657 (Marian.). **-κυθνος**, ον, = πολύσπερμος, Hsch. s.v. κυθνόν. **-κυκλος**, ον, *with many circles*, Id. s.v. πολυέλικτον. **-κῠκος**, ον, (κυκάω) *much troubled*, of the sea, Porph. ad Il.2.145. **-κῠλίνδητος**, ον, *much* or *often rolled*, Eust.1471.7, Hsch. **-κύμᾰτος** [κῡ], ον, *swelling with many waves*, Id. s.v. ἀκύμονος (πολυκαμ- cod.), *EM*545.15. **-κύμων** [κῡ], ον, gen. ονος, (κῦμα) = foreg., πόντος Sol.13.19, Emp.38.3. II. (κύω) *bringing forth much*, gloss on ἐρικύμων, Sch.A.*Ag.*119. **-κώθων**, ωνος, ὁ, ἡ, *wine-bibber*, Polem.Hist.79. **-κώκῡτος**, ον, *full of wailing*, Ἀΐδαο δόμοι Thgn.244. **-κωλος**, ον, *of many clauses*, περίοδοι Demetr.*Eloc.*252. **-κωμος**, ον, *much-revelling*, *AP*9.524.17, *Anacreont.*40.14. **-κωπος**, ον, *many-oared*, ὄχημα ναός S.*Tr.*656 (lyr.); σκάφος E.*IT*981; [πλοῖον] *PGrenf.*2.80.11 (V A.D.). **-κώτῐλος**, ον, *much-warbling*, ἀηδόνες Simon.73. ✻ **-λάλητος** [ᾰ], ον, gloss on ἀθυρόστομος, Sch.S.*Ph.*188. II. *often repeated*, of a common epithet, Eust.861.33. **-λᾰλία**, ἡ, *talkativeness*, Gal.16.198. **-λᾰλος**, ον, *talkative*, Cleobul.ap.Stob.3.1.172; οὐ π. ἀλλὰ πολύνους Plot.6.2.21, cf. Sm.*Jb.*11.2, Sch.Ar.*Nu.*1363, Sch.S.*Ant.*324. **-λεκτος**, ον, *requiring full discussion*, ζήτησις Zos.Alch.p.107 B. **-λέξις**, ι, *containing many words*, Sch.D.T.p.25 H. **-λευκτον**· πολυπλάνητον, πανταχοῦ περιφερές, Hsch. **-λήϊος**, ον, (λήϊον) *with many cornfields*, Il.5.613, Hes.*Fr.*134.1; Εὔβοια prob. in B.9.34; *fruitful*, ἄροσις Arat.1058. **-λήμμᾰτος**, ον, *with many premisses*, συλλογισμοί Gal.*Inst.Log.*6.5. **-λίμενος** [ῐ], ον, (λιμήν) *with many ports*, Artem.ap.Eust.287.34. **-λῐμενότης**, ητος, ἡ, *richness in harbours*, Men.Rh.p.352 S. **-λῑμος**, ὁ, *ravenous hunger*, coined as etym. of βούλιμος, prob. in Plu.2.694a. **-λῐτάνευτος** [ᾰ], ον, gloss on πολύλλιστος, Sch.Od.5.445, etc. **-λλῐθος**, ον, *very stony*, *AP*6.3 (Dionys.). **-λλιστος**, ον, also η, ον Orph.*H.*32.14, al.: (λίσσομαι):—*sought with many prayers*, πολύλλιστον δέ σ' ἱκάνω Od.5.445; νηοὶ π. temples *much frequented by suppliants*, *h.Ap.*347, cf. *h.Cer.*28; βωμός B.10.41: later in act. sense, πολύλλιστος δέ σ' ἱκάνω Procl.*H.*7.51 (s.v.l.):—also **-λιστος**, Simon.45, cf. *IG*3.171 iii 12 (restd.). **-λλῐτος**, ον, = foreg., Call.*Ap.*80, *Del.*316, Orph.*H.*12.4. **-λογέω**, *talk much*, Gal.18(1).792, Vett.Val.175.31, al., Poll.10.51, Alex.Aphr.*in Top.*433.19. **-λογία**, ἡ, *loquacity, much to say*, Pl.*Lg.*641e, X.*Cyr.*1.4.3, Arist.*Pol.*1295$^{a}$2, Lxx *Pr.*10.19, etc. **-λογίζω**, = φλυαρέω, Sch.Ar.*Pl.*575. **-λογος**, ον, *loquacious*, Democr.44, Pl.*Lg.*641e, X.*Cyr.*1.4.3 (Comp.). Adv. -γως Poll.4.24. **-λοπος**, ον, *with many layers of bark* or *wood*, Thphr.*HP*1.5.2, 5.1.6. **-λῡπος**, ον, gloss on πολύπονος, Sch.E.*Hec.*721. **-λυχνον**, τό, *lamp with many burners*, *IG*14.915. **-μάθεια** [ᾰ], ἡ, = πολυμαθία (q.v.), Arist.*Fr.*62, Str.1.1.1, Ph.1.652, Luc.*Salt.*37: as pr. n. of a Muse at Sicyon, Plu.2.746e. **-μᾰθέω**, *learn* or *know much*, Pl.*Amat.*137b. **-μᾰθημοσύνη**, Ep. **πουλ-**, ἡ, = πολυμαθία, Timo 20. **-μᾰθής**, ές, *having learnt* or *knowing much*,

Ar.*V.*1175, Democr.64, Pl.*Lg.*811a: Comp. *-έστερος* Aristeas 137: Sup. *-έστατος* Phld.*Vit.*p.35J.; Ἀριστοτέλης Ath.9.398e, cf. Dam. *Isid.*168, Lyd.*Mag.*1.5. **-μᾰθία**, Ion. **πολῠμᾰθίη**, ἡ, *much learning*, π. νόον ἔχειν οὐ διδάσκει Heraclit.40; opp. πολυνοΐη, Democr.65, cf. Anaxarch.1, Pl.*Lg.*811a, 819a; as a subject of competition, *Michel* 913.8 (Teos, ii B.C.). II. cf. Πολύμνια. **-μᾰκᾰρ**, ᾰρος, ὁ, ἡ, *most blissful*, Eust.1542.19. **-μαλλος**, ον, *with abundant fleece*, Sch.Theoc.1.10 (Didot). **-μᾱλος**, ον, v. πολύμηλος. **-μᾰνής**, Ep. **πουλ-**, ές, *troubled by manifold madness*, *AP* 12.87. **-μάντευτος**, ον, *on which many oracles are given*, ἑβδόμη Plu.2.292f. **-μάσχᾰλος**, ον, (μασχάλη II) *with many side-branches*, [ἡμερίς], μίλος, Thphr.*HP*3.8.4, 3.10.2, cf. 3.12.3. **-μάχητος** [μᾰ], ον, *much-fought-for*, Luc.*Cyn.*8. **-μᾰχος**, ον, *much-fighting*, Sch.Opp.*H.*5.328. **-μέδιμνος**, Ep. **πουλ-**, ον, *with many medimni*, epith. of Demeter, Call.*Cer.*2. **-μεθής**, Ep. **πουλ-**, ές, *drinking much wine*, *AP*11.45 (Honest.). **-μέλαθρος**, Ep. **πουλ-**, ον, *with many halls* or *temples*, Call.*Dian.*225. **-μελής**, ές, (μέλος) *with many members*, Pl.*Phdr.*238a. II. *many-toned*, in form πολυμμελές, Alcm.1. Adv. -λῶς Poll.4.57. **-μελπής**, ές, *much-singing*, ib.67. ⊛ **-μεμφής**, ές, *much-blaming*, Nonn.*D.*4.35, al. **-μέρεια**, ἡ, *a consisting of many parts*, Ph.1.506, *Placit.*5.26.4, Porph.*Sent.* 34. **-μερής**, ές, (μέρος) *consisting of many parts, manifold*, opp. εἷς, Ti.Locr.98d (Sup.), cf. Arist.*de An.*411$^{b}$11, *PA*683$^{b}$5 (Comp.); πρᾶξις Id.*Po.*1459$^{b}$1; -έστατον τὸ δωδεκάεδρον Plu.2.427b. Adv. -ρῶς Porph.*Sent.*34. 2. *of divers kinds*, τῆς ὕβρεως οὔσης π. Arist.*Pol.* 1311$^{a}$33. Adv. -ρῶς *in many ways*, *Ep.Hebr.*1.1, Plu.2.537d, Ptol. *Tetr.*127. **-μέριμνος**, ον, *full of care*, τὸ ἄρχειν πολυκίνητον καὶ π. Arist.*Mu.*400$^{b}$10, cf. Vett.Val.2.2, al. **-μέριστος**, gloss on πολυσχιδής, Sch.Opp.*H.*4.409. **-μέρμερος**, ον, = πολυμέριμνος, Hsch. **-μεσος**, ον, *having several means*, of contraries, Olymp. *in Cat.*137.31, Elias *in Cat.*243.31. **-μετάβλητος**, ον, *often transforming oneself*, Eust.1502.62. **-μετάβολος**, ον, *very changeable*, ὕλη Lyd.*Mens.*2.7, cf. Vett.Val.9.2, Procl.*in Alc.*p.301, Tim.*Lex.* s.v. παλίμβολος. **-μετρία**, ἡ, *use of a variety of metres*, Eust.353. 42. ⊛ **-μετρος**, ον, *of many measures*: hence, *copious, abundant*, π. στάχυς E.*Fr.*516 (ap.Ar.*Ra.*1240). II. *written in many metres*, δρᾶμα Ath.13.608e. **-μηκάς**, άδος, ὁ, ἡ, *much-bleating*, αἶγες Bacis ap.Hdt.8.20. **-μήκετος**, ον, poet. for sq., Q.S.2.452. **-μήκης**, ες, (μῆκος) *very long*, αὐλός v.l. in Poll.4.67. **-μηλος**, ον (fem. -μήλη Suid.), (μῆλον A) *with many sheep* or *goats, rich in flocks*, of persons, Il.2.705, 14.490 (never in Od.), Hes.*Op.*308; of places, Il.2.605, Pi.*P.*9.6 (where codd. have πολύμηλος correctly; πολύμᾱλος in *O.*1.12, if correct, means *rich in tree-fruit*). **-μῆναι**· πολύβουλε, Hsch. **-μηνις**, ιος, ὁ, ἡ, *abounding in wrath*, *AP*9.168 (Pall.). **-μήτης**, ου, ὁ, = sq., Hsch.; poet. -μῆτα Opp.*H.*5.6. **-μητις**, ιος, ὁ, ἡ, *of many counsels*, of Odysseus, Il.1.311, Od.21.274, Ar.*V.*351; of Hephaestus, Il.21.355; πολυμήτιδι τέχνῃ Orph.*A.*126. **-μήτωρ**, ορος, ἡ, *mother of many*, Opp.*H.*1.88. **-μηχᾰνία**, Ion. -ίη, ἡ, *resourcefulness, inventiveness*, Od.23.321, Plu.2.233e: pl., Man.6.483. **-μήχᾰνος**, ον, *resourceful, inventive*, epith. of Odysseus, Il.2.173, etc., cf. S.*Ph.* 1135 (lyr.); of Apollo, *h.Merc.*319; π. μήτηρ, of Nature, Orph.*H.*10.1; π. βουλή Opp.*H.*2.54: in later Prose, π. περὶ τοὺς λόγους Aristid. *Or.*41(4).2. **-μῑγής**, metri gr. **πουλυμ-** Pl. (v. infr.), and **πολυμμ-** Maiist. (v. infr.), ές, *much-mixed*, Philol.10, Herm.ap.Stob.1.49.3; ξεῖνοι Maiist.53; *composed of many ingredients*, γονή Arist.*GA*769$^{a}$34, cf. Gal.14.284. II. *confused*, βληχὴ τοκάδων Pl.*Epigr.*24. **-μῑγία**, ἡ, *mixture of many components*, Plu.2.661e, S.E.*M.*9.6; *multifarious composition*, Diog.Oen.8. II. *confusion*, Ph.1.426. **-μίγμᾰτος**, ον, = πολυμιγής, Androm.ap.Gal.14.131, Gal.14.283, al., Paul.Aeg.3.48. **-μικτος**, ον, = πολυμιγής, Orph.*H.*10.11. **-μιξία**, ἡ, = πολυμιγία, αἱ π. τῶν σπερμάτων Epicur.*Fr.*250 (= Metrod.*Fr.*1). **-μῑσής**, ές, *much-hating*, Luc.*Pisc.*20. **-μισθος**, ον, *receiving much pay* or *hire*, v.l. in *AP*5.1. **-μῐτᾱρική** (sc. τέχνη), ἡ, *art of weaving* πολύμιτα, Hsch., Suid. s.v. ποικιλτική. **-μῐτάριος** [ᾱ], ὁ, *damask-weaver*, *Cat.Cod.Astr.*8(4).217. ⊛ **-μῐτος**, ον, *consisting of many threads*, Cratin.436; τὰ π. *damask stuffs, in which several threads were taken for the woof* in order to weave in patterns, Plin.*HN*8.196; πέπλοι π. *damask* robes, A.*Supp.*432 (lyr.); προσκεφάλαια *Sammelb.* 7033.37 (V A.D.). **-μνήμων**, ον, gen. ονος, *remembering many things*, Plu.2.292a, Gal.17(1).605.

**Πολυμνήστεια** (sc. μέλη), τά, *songs of Polymnestus* of Colophon, Ar.*Eq.*1287, Cratin.305, Plu.2.1132d (-μνάστια).

**πολυ-μνήστευτος**, ον, *much-wooed*, Plu.2.766d, *CG*4. ⊛ **-μνήστη**, ἡ, (μνάομαι) = foreg., Od.4.770, 14.64, 23.149:—later in form **-μνηστος**, κούρη Nonn.*D.*42.497; πολυμνάστοιο.. Τίσιδος *AP*6.274 (Pers.). ⊛ **-μνηστος**, ον (η, ον Emp.4.3), (μιμνήσκομαι) *much-remembering, mindful*, Μοῦσα l.c.; θεοῖσι..π. χάριν τίνειν A.*Ag.*821. II. Pass., *much-remembered*, πολύμναστον..αἷμα ib.1459 (lyr.); σπέρμα Orph.*H.*50.2. **-μνήστωρ**, ορος, ὁ, ἡ, = πολυμνήμων, A.*Supp.*535 (lyr.).

⊛ **Πολύμνια**, ἡ, contr. for Πολυύμνια, *Polymnia* or *Polyhymnia, she of the many hymns*, one of the Muses, Hes.*Th.*78; later, the Muse of Lyric poetry, Sch.A.R.3.1; of learning (cf. Πολυμάθεια), Plu.2.746d; **Πολυμνίς**, ίδος, Kretschmer *Griech.Vaseninschr.*p.186.

⊛ **πολύ-μνιος** [ῐ], ον, (μνίον) *full of moss*, v.l. (ap.Sch.) in Nic.*Th.* 950. **-μορφής**, ές, = πολύμορφος, πληθύς Aus.*Ep.*10.25. **-μορφία**, ἡ, *manifoldness*, Longin.39.3, Him.*Or.*21.10. ⊛ **-μορφος**, ον, *multiform, manifold*, Hp.*Aër.*12; π. τοῖς σχήμασιν Arist.*PA*646$^{b}$32: Comp., ib.656$^{a}$4: Sup., Id.*HA*606$^{b}$18; π. λόγων ἰδέα Him.*Or.*34.4. Adv. -φως D.S.2.52. II. of persons, *versatile*, Ph.2.47; π. βίος Id.1.565. III. *of irregular shape*: hence πολύμορφον, τό, the *sphenoid bone*, Gal.14.721. **-μουσος**, ον, *rich in the Muses' gifts*, Plu.2.744a; *many-sided in art*, Luc.*Salt.*7. ⊛ **-μοχθος**, ον, *much-labouring, suffering many things*, S.*OC*165 (lyr.), 1231 (lyr., dub.), E.*Hec.*95 (anap.), *HF*1197 (lyr., Comp.), *IA*1330 (lyr.). II. Pass., *won by much toil, toilsome*, ἀρετά Arist.*Fr.*675.1; κῦδος *IG*3.1374; *wrought with much toil*, ἐλέφας Theoc.28.8. **-μύελος**, ον, *with much marrow*, ὀστέα Hp.*Fract.*35. ⊛ **-μῦθος**, ον, poet. **πουλύ-** Call.*Iamb.*1.170 (πολυ- Pap.):—*wordy*, Il.3.214, Od.2.200. II. Pass., *much talked of, famous in story*, ἀρεταί Pi.*P.* 9.76. III. *full of story*, Καλλιόπη *AP*9.523, cf. Call.*Epigr.*18; *with a number of legends*, [σύστημα] Arist.*Po.*1456$^{a}$12, cf. Str.14.2.7. **-μυξος**, ον, *with many wicks*, of a lamp, Mart.14.41 tit. **-μῠχος**, ον, *with many recesses*, gloss on ἑπτάμυχον, Sch.Call.*Del.*65. **-νᾱος**, ον, *with many temples*, Theoc.15.109; Ion. -νηος *EM*32.9. **-ναστος**, v. πολύνοστος. **-ναύτης**, ου, Dor. **-τας**, ὁ, *with many sailors* or *ships*, A.*Pers.*83 (lyr.). ⊛ **-νεικής**, ές, *much-wrangling*, Id.*Th.*830 (anap.): freq. as pr. n. Πολυνείκης, ὁ, on which the Trag. are fond of playing, ib.578, 658, al. **-νευρον**, τό, = ἀρνόγλωσσον, Ps.-Dsc.2.126. **-νέφελος**, ον, *overcast with clouds*, *EM*7.10; Dor. **πολυνεφέλας**, α, epith. of Οὐρανός, Pi.*N.*3.10. **-νηνεμίη**, ἡ, *great calm*, f.l. for παλι-, *AP*10.102 (Bass.). **-νίκης** [ῑ], ου, ὁ, *a frequent conqueror*, Luc.*Lex.*11. **-νῐφής**, ές, *deep with snow*, δρία E.*Hel.* 1326 (lyr.):—also **-νῐφος**, ον, *EM*7.9. **-νοια**, Ion. **-νοΐη**, ἡ, *thoughtfulness*, opp. πολυλογία, Pl.*Lg.*641e, cf. Aristid.*Or.*50(26).26, D.C.52.41, Dam.*Isid.*37; opp. πολυμαθίη, Democr.65. **-νομος**, ον, *grazing much*, -νομώτατον ὁ βοῦς Thphr.*HP*9.15.4. II. *with much pasture*, χώρα Tz.*H.*7.58 (Sup.). **-νοος**, ον, contr. **-νους**, ουν, *thoughtful*, opp. πολύλαλος, Plot.6.2.21, cf. Porph.*Plot.*14; *profound*, τὸ π. τῆς Πυθαγορικῆς βαθύτητος Hierocl.*in CA*26 p.480 M., cf. Iamb.*in Nic.*p.5 P. Adv. -νως Poll.2.230. **-νοσος**, ον, *liable to many sicknesses*, Str.15.1.43, *Cat.Cod.Astr.*2.208. **-νοστος**, ον, *making much return*; of food, *very nutritious*, σιτία Hp.*Vict.*2.56 (v.l. -ναστα *very compact*): Comp., of seed, *producing fuller grain*, Thphr.*HP*8.8.2.

⊛ **πόλυντρα**· ἄλφιτα (i.e. Lat. *polenta*), Hsch.

**πολύ-νυμφος**, ον, *with many brides*, Poll.3.48. **-ξενος**, Ion. **-ξεινος**, ον, poet. also α, ον Pi.*Fr.*122.1, *N.*3.2:—of persons, *entertaining many guests, very hospitable*, opp. ἄξεινος, Hes.*Op.*715; δαίς ib.722; πολυξενώτατον Ζῆνα τῶν κεκμηκότων A.*Supp.*157 (lyr.), cf. *Fr.*228, Call.*Fr.*478. II. *visited by many guests*, βωμός, νᾶσος, Pi.*O.*1.93 (Sup.), *N.*3.2; νεάνιδες Id.*Fr.*122.1; οἶκος E.*Alc.*569 (lyr.); cf. sq. **-ξεστος**, ον, (ξέω) *much-polished*, πύλαι (of Hades) f.l. in S.*OC*1570 (lyr., leg. πολυξένοις). **-ξηρος**, ον, *very dry*, Hsch. s.v. πολυκαγκέος, *EM*681.39. ⊛ **-ξῠλος**, ον, *very woody*, Sch.Il.11.155, Poll.6.171. **-όδευτος**, ον, *much travelled over*, Sch.Opp.*H.*3.502. **-οδία**, ἡ, *long journey*, Lxx *Is.*57.10. **-οδμος**, ον, (ὀδμή) *strong-smelling*, Thphr.*Od.*27, 44, 55, Orph.*H.*43.4; cf. πολύοσμος. **-όδους**, Ep. **πουλυ-**, ὁ, ἡ, *with many teeth*, Nic.*Th.*53, Nonn.*D.*24.253, al. **-οζία**, ἡ, *having many branches*, Thphr.*HP*5.2.2. **-οζος**, ον, *with many branches*, φλέβες Diog.Apoll.6; of trees, Thphr.*HP* 3.13.3, 7.2.8: Comp., κλάδοι ib.1.8.5. **-οινέω**, *to be rich in wine*, *h.Merc.*91. **-οινία**, ἡ, *abundance of wine*, *Gp.*4.1.14, etc. II. *excess in wine*, Pl.*Lg.*666b, Ph.1.351, Plu.2.239a. **-οινος**, ον, *rich in wine*, of a place, Th.1.138 (Sup.), Lib.*Ep.*19.8; of men, X.*Vect.* 5.3. **-οκνος**, ον, *delaying much, very tardy*, *JRS*17.52 (Phrygia, iv A.D.), Sch.S.*Tr.*841. **-όλβιος**, ον, = sq., Orph.*H.*3.12. **-ολβος**, ον, *very wealthy*, of persons and countries, D.P.934, *AP*6.114 (Simm.), Coluth.280, *BSA*27.245 (Sparta, iv A.D.); *sumptuous, expensive*, ἐδωδή *AP*9.642 (Agath.). II. Act., *rich in blessings*, Ἀφροδίτα Sapph.59, cf. Afric.*Cest.*28; of the Sun, *Epigr.Gr.*361 (Phrygia). **-ομβρία**, ἡ, *much rain*, *Cat.Cod.Astr.*4.155, *Gp.*1.10.5, 1.8.3 (pl.). **-ομβρος**, ον, *very rainy*, *Cat.Cod.Astr.*4.87; gloss on ἀνομβρήεις, Sch.Nic.*Al.* 288. ⊛ **-όμμᾰτος**, ον, *many-eyed*, of Argus, Luc.*DDeor.*3.1. ⊛ **-όμφᾰλος**, ον, *with many bosses* or *shields*, πεδίον π., of the Roman *testudo*, Opp.*C.*1.218. **-όνειρος**, ον, *producing many dreams*, ἡ τῶν μελαγχολικῶν [κρᾶσις] π. Plu.2.437f. **-οπος**, ον, (ὀπός) *full of juice, succulent*, Thphr.*HP*4.2.2, 9.8.2. **-οπτος**, ον, *much-seen*, Hsch. **-όργιος**, ον, *celebrated with many orgies*, Orph.*H.*6.4. **-ορκία**, ἡ, *habit* or *custom of swearing*, Ph.2.196, 271. **-ορκος**, ον, *swearing much*, Lxx *Si.*23.11. **-όρμητος**, ον, *very impetuous*, Suid. s.v. πολυάϊξ. **-όρνῑθος**, ον, *abounding in birds*, αἶα E.*IT*435 (lyr.). **-ορνῑς**, ῑθος, ὁ, ἡ, = foreg., Sch.Ar.*Av.*65. **-όροφος**, ον, v. πολυώροφος. **-οσμία**, ἡ, *strength of smell*, Thphr.*CP*6.16.6. **-οσμος**, ον, Att. for πολύοδμος, ibid., Dsc.4.36, 95. **-όστεος**, ον, *with many bones*: π., τό, = πεδίον II, Poll.2.197; τὸ π. τοῦ σκέλους, i.e. the foot, Arist.*HA*494$^{a}$10. II. of fruits, *with many seeds*, *Cat.Cod.Astr.*8(4).251. **-ούσιος**, ον, (οὐσία) *substantial*, Gal.19.673. 2. *wealthy*, *Gloss.* ⊛ **-όφθαλμος**, ον, *many-eyed*, D.S.1.11, Poll.4.141. 2. *with many eyes* or *buds*, ἄμπελοι *Gp.*5.8.1. II. Subst., a plant, = βούφθαλμον, Hp.*Art.* 67, Diocl.*Fr.*154. **-όχευτος**, ον, *very salacious*, *EM*425.40 (spelt -όχητ-), Suid. s.v. ἠλέκτωρ. **-οχλέω**, *to be numerous*, -οχλοῦσαι δυνάμεις D.H.6.64, cf. 5.6:—Pass., *to be much-peopled*, of a city, Str.8.6.20, D.S.14.95, Timae. in *Cat.Cod.Astr.*1.99, prob. in Ceb. 15. **-οχλία**, ἡ, *crowd of people*, Plb.10.14.15, Lxx *Jb.*39.7; τῶν νέων *Inscr.Perg.*252.22. **-οχλος**, ον, *much-peopled, populous*, χώρα Plb.3.49.5. II. *very prolific*, δήμου εἴδη Arist.*Pol.*1291$^{b}$23; for E.*Rh.*166 v. πολιοῦχος. **-οψία**, ἡ, *abundance* or *variety of meats* or *fish*, X.*Mem.*3.14.3, Plu.2.662a. **-οψος**, ον, *abounding in fish*, λίμνη Str.12.3.38. 2. *luxurious*, δεῖπνον Luc.*Gall.*

11. ⊛-πάθεια [πᾰ], ἡ, *suffering of many calamities*, π. βίου J.*AJ*15.6.4. II. *receiving of diverse impressions* or *sensations*, formed after ἀπάθεια, Plu.2.167e,734a. -πᾰθής, ές, (παθεῖν) *subject to many passions* or *impressions*, π. κακῶν ταμιεῖον Democr. 149; ψυχή Plu.2.97b; *full of diverse reactions*, νόσημα ib.171e; poet. πουλ-, *much perturbed*, τύραννοι *AP*9.98 (Stat. Flacc.). -παίγμων, ον, gen. ονος, *very sportive*, v.l. in Od.23.134, so cited by Sch.Ar.*Th*.954. -παιδία, ἡ, *abundance of children, fecundity*, Isoc.9.72, App.*BC*1.7, Hierocl.*in CA*24p.472M., Chor.*Proc*. 6. ⊛-παίπᾰλος, ον, *exceeding crafty*, Φοίνικες Od.15.419, cf. Opp. *H*.3.41. II. = πεποικιλμένος, αἰθήρ Call.*Fr.anon*.225. -παις, παιδος, ὁ, ἡ, *with many children*, Str.17.3.19, Lxx 4*Ma*.16.10; of swans, Ael.*VH*1.14: metaph., of Tyre, mother of many colonies, *AP*7.428.14 (Mel.). ⊛-παλτος, ον, *much-brandished*, of a weapon, Call.*Sos*.4.1. -πάμφᾰος, ον, *bright-shining*, Φαέθων *AP*9. 591. -πάμων [ᾱ], ον, gen. ονος, (πᾶμα, πέπαμαι) *exceeding wealthy*, Il.4.433. -παρθένευτος, ον, *having been long a maid*, Sch.E. *Ph*.1732. -πάρθενος, ον, *having many maidens*, Orph.*H*.52. 12. -παστος, ον, *much-besprinkled*, Hsch. s.v. κερχνωτά. ⊛-πᾰταξ, ᾰγος, ὁ, ἡ, (πάταγος) *full of tumult*, found in acc., πολυπάταγα θυμέλαν Pratin.Lyr.1.2; dat. -πάταγι Choerob.*in Theod*.1. 377 H., prob. in *EM*280.1. -πάτητος [ᾰ], ον, *much trodden*, Sch.Call.*Jov*.26: metaph., *common-place, threadbare*, ῥαψῳδία Plu. 2.514c. -πατρις, ιδος, ὁ, ἡ, *having more than one country*, Eust.4.20. -πείρητος, ον, *much-tried*, κέλευθος *CR*11.136 (Asia Minor). -πειρία, ἡ, *great experience*, Th.1.71, Pl.*Lg*.811a, Lxx *Wi*.8.8, D.S.5.1, Plu.*Sol*.2. ⊛-πειρος, ον, *much-experienced*, Parm. 1.34, Ar.*Lys*.1109, Lxx *Si*.21.22, D.S.1.1 (Sup.), Sor.1.4; ἰατρῶν ὦ πολυπειρότατε *Epigr.Gr*.202 (Halic., from Cos). Adv. -ρως Sch.Theoc. 15.48. ⊛-πείρων, ον, gen. ονος, (πεῖρας) *with many boundaries, manifold*, λαός *h.Cer*.296. 2. *with wide boundaries*, opp. ἀπείρων, Orph.*A*.33. -πέλαστος, ον, gloss on δασπλῆτι, Sch.Theoc.2. 14. -πέλεθρος, Ep. πουλ-, ον, = πολύπλεθρος, Q.S.3.396. -πενθής, ές, *much-mourning*, ἀλκυών Il.9.563, cf. Od.14.386; θυμός 23. 15; of events, *very lamentable*, π. μόρος A.*Pers*.547 (anap.): Sup. -έστατος Plu.2.114f. -περίσπαστος, ον, *much-distraught*, Vett. Val.4.29. -πευθής, ές, *much-inquiring*, ἑβδόμη a day *on which many persons consult the oracle*, Plu.2.292f. -πήδητος, ον, gloss on πολύσκαρθμος, Hsch. ⊛-πήμων, ον, gen. ονος, *causing manifold woe, baneful*, *h.Cer*.230, *h.Merc*.37; π. νόσοι diseases *manifold*, Pi.*P*.3.46; λώβη, ἄτη, A.R.4.1044, Opp.*C*.2.287: hence pr. n. **Πολυπημονίδης**, ου, ὁ, *son of Polypemon*, with a play on πολυπήμων, Od.24.305. II. Pass., *much-suffering*, Man.1.85, 4.49. ⊛-πηνος, ον, *thick-woven, close-woven*, φάρεα E.*El*.191 (lyr.). -πηχυς, υ, gen. υος, *many cubits long*, ξύλον Plot.6.4.7. II. *many-armed*, Nonn.*D*.1. 204. -πῖδαξ, ᾰκος, ὁ, ἡ, *with many springs, many-fountained*, Ἴδην πολυπίδακα Il.8.47, 14.283, etc.; πολυπίδακος Ἴδης ib.157, 20.59, 218 (v.l. πολυπιδάκου, rejected by Aristarch., but found in *h.Ven*.54, Cypr.5.5, Pl.*Lg*.681e, Hsch.); σκοπιαί A.R.3.883.

**πολῠπῐκός**, ή, όν, *of* or *for a polypus*, σπαθίον π. knife *for removing polypi*, Heliod.ap.Orib.46.6.3, Sor.2.63, Paul.Aeg.6.25.

**πολύ-πικρος**, ον, *very keen* or *bitter*: neut. pl. as Adv., Od.16.255: regul. Adv. -κρως Eust.1801.35. -πῑνής, ές, (πῖνος) *very squalid*, κάρα E.*Rh*.716 (lyr.). -πιστος, ον, *very faithful*, Hsch. -πλαγκτος, ον, (πλάζω) *much-wandering, wide-roving*, λῃστῆρσι π. Od.17. 425, cf. 511; of Io, A.*Supp*.572 (lyr.); π. ἔτεα S.*Aj*.1186 (lyr.); οὐκ ἂν εἰδείης ἕτερον..πολυπλαγκτότερον E.*HF*1197 (lyr.). 2. *ever-moving*, ἰκτῖνοι (prob. l.) Thgn.1257; μέλεα Parm.16.1. 3. *much-erring*, πραπίδες *IG*14.1424 (Rome). II. *driving far from one's course*, ἄνεμος Il.11.308 (unless in signf. I.1).—In S.*Ant*.615 (lyr.) π. ἐλπίς may be either *wandering, uncertain* hope, or, *misleading, deceitful*; cf. πολυπλανής II. -πλαγκτοσύνη, ἡ, *wandering far* or *long*, Man.4.222. -πλᾰνής, ές, (πλανάομαι) *roaming far* or *long*, ἐν ἁλὶ πολυπλανής (sc. Menelaus) E.*Hel*.203 (lyr.); εἶδος κτημάτων π., opp. ἀπλανές, Pl.*Plt*.288a; π. κισσός the *straying* ivy, *AP*6.154 (Leon. or Gaet.); π. πορεία *devious*, Plu.*Crass*.29; π. ἐν γράμμασι Id. 2.422d. Adv. -νῶς *wandering in all directions*, Hp.*Oss*.12. II. *much-erring* (or Act., *leading much astray*), Ἐλπὶς καὶ Τύχη *AP*9.134; ἔπεα Musae.175. [-πλᾶνης metri gr. in Opp.*C*.4.358.] ⊛-πλάνητος [ᾰ], ον, = foreg., γένος, of the Dorians, Hdt.1.56; αἰὼν π. αἰεί E.*Hipp*.1110 (lyr.); π. πόνος the pains *of wandering*, Id.*Hel*.1319 (lyr.). II. of blows, *falling in every direction*, A.*Ch*.425 (lyr.). -πλᾶνος, ον, = πολυπλανής, πλάναι Id.*Pr*.585 (lyr.); κόραι E.*Ph*.661 (lyr.), cf. *AP*6.69 (Maced.): in late Prose, Paul.Al. *M*.3.

**πολυπλᾰσι-άζω**, later form for πολλαπλ-, *multiply*, Lxx *De*.8.1 (Pass.), Gal.10.352, Hdn.8.2.4 (Pass.), Jul.*Or*.4.139a (Pass.), Them. *Or*.21.261a; τι ἐπί τι Phlp.*in Mete*.15.10; τὸ βάθος Ael.*Tact*.8. 2. -ασμα, ατος, τό, *product of multiplication*, Vett.Val.349. 2. -ασμός, ὁ, *multiplication*, v.l. in Plu.2.388c,1020c, cf. Aenesidem.ap.S.E.*M*.10.217; in tactical sense, *deepening*, Arr.*Tact*.9.4 (pl.). -αστέον, *one must multiply*, τί τινι Iamb.*in Nic*.p.34P. -ος, α, ον, = πολλαπλ-, *AP*6.152 (Agis), Lxx 2*Ma*.9.16, Alex.Aphr.*de An*. 123.33, Them.*Or*.6.74c. -ων, ον, gen. ονος, = πολλαπλ-, Isoc. 15.177 codd., *SIG*711 *L* 11 (Delph., ii B.C.), Them.*Or*.15.186b.

**πολύ-πλεθρος**, ον, *many* πλέθρα *in size, far-stretching*, γύαι E.*Alc*. 687; of persons, *rich in land*, Luc.*Icar*.18 (Sup.). -πλεκής, ές, = sq., δεσμοί Nonn.*D*.42.452. -πλεκτος, ον, = πολύπλοκος I, ib.5.247; σειραί ib.26.106. -πλευρος, ον, *many-sided*, Plu.2.966e, Plot.6. 3.14. 2. -πλευρον, τό, = ἀρνόγλωσσον, Dsc.2.126 (v.l. πολύνευρον).

⊛ **πολυπλήθ-εια**, Ion. -είη, ἡ, *great quantity* or *number*, ὕδατος Hp. *Aër*.15, cf. Aen.Tact.3.1; [τῶν φαττῶν] Arist.*HA*562b29, cf. Ocell.4. 5, Aen.Gaz.*Thphr*.p.47 B., *SIG*880.40 (Pizus, iii A.D.), etc.:—written -πληθία, S.*Fr*.667.1 (lyr.), Hyp.*Fr*.266, D.ap.Poll.4.163, Lxx 2*Ma*.8.16, Str.16.2.23. -έω, *multiply*, Lxx *Ex*.5.5; π. ποσί *abound* in feet, ib.*Le*.11.42. -ής, ές, *very numerous*, Sch.Ar.*Pax* 519. 2. *plethoric*, ἦν π. ὁ νοσέων ἢ Aret.*CA*1.1. -ία, ἡ, v. πολυπλήθεια. -ύνω, fut. -υνῶ Lxx *Ex*.32.13:—*multiply*, l.c.

**πολυ-πλόκᾰμος**, ον, *with many feelers*, of the poulp, Marc.Sid. 36. -πλοκία, ἡ, *cunning, craft*, Thgn.67 (pl.). ⊛-πλοκος, ον, (πλέκω) *tangled*, σπεῖραι E.*Med*.481; καμπαί, of the labyrinth, *Trag.Adesp*.34; of the brain, *with many convolutions*, Erasistr.ap. Gal.5.603, cf. Gal.*UP*8.13. 2. metaph., *tangled, complex*, θηρίον Τυφῶνος -ώτερον Pl.*Phdr*.230a; -ωτάτη ἡ ἐν ὅπλοις τάξις X.*Lac*.11.5; μέτρα μολπᾶς Simm.26.20; πεσσῶν μορφαί E.*IA*197 (lyr.). Adv. -κως D.H.*Th*.54: neut. as Adv., φωνὴ πολύπλοκον ἠχοῦσα cj. in Thphr.*Sign*.40. b. of the poulp, *crafty*, Thgn.215; of persons and thoughts, *subtle, acute, tortuous*, οὔπω..ἤκουσα -ωτέρας γυναικός Ar.*Th*.435 (lyr.); π. νόημα ib.463 (lyr.); -πλοκοι μεθόδων παραλογισμοί Lxx *Es*.8(16).13; ὑπόδοξοι καὶ π. Phld.*D*.1.16; π. ἔννοιαι Luc. *DMort*.10.8, cf. Eun.*Hist*.p.218 D. (Comp.). c. *complex*, φύσις, opp. ἁπλῆ, Herm.*in Phdr*.p.186 A. -πλοος, ον, contr. -πλους, ουν, *of* or *for many voyages*, λιμένες Men.Rh.p.352 S. -πνοος, ον, contr. -πνους, ουν, *blowing hard*, Hsch. s.v. ζαής. II. *fragrant*, Opp.*C*. 1.461.

**πολῠπόδ-ειος**, ον, *of a poulp*, κρέα Poll.6.33,47; πολυπόδειον (sc. κρέας), τό, Theopomp.Com.6 (πουλ-), Philyll.13, Mnesim.4.43 (anap.), etc. -ης, ου, ὁ, poet. πουλ-, = πολύπους, ἰχθῦς *AP*9.227 (Bianor), cf. Man.6.748. -ία, ἡ, *having many feet*, Arist.*PA*682b1. -ίνη [ῑ], ἡ, = ὀσμύλη, Arist. and Speus.ap.Ath.7.318e. -ιον, τό, Dim. of πολύπους, f.l. in Philox.2.13, cf. Arist.*HA*550a4, 622a23. II. *polypody, Polypodium vulgare*, Thphr.*HP*9.13.6, Dsc.4.186, etc. -ίτης [ῑ] οἶνος, ὁ, wine *flavoured with polypody*, Aët.3.61. -ώδης, ες, *of the poulp kind*, Arist.*PA*685a24.

**πολῠ-πόθεινος**, ον, *much longed-for*, i.e. *regretted*, *Supp.Epigr*.6. 382 (Lycaonia, Sup.). ⊛-πόθητος, ον, *much longed-for*, as expl. of πολυδίψιος, Str.8.6.7, Ath.10.433e; τῆς δίψης οὐδὲν -ότερον ibid. ⊛-ποίκῐλος, ον, *much-variegated*, φάρεα E.*IT*1149 (lyr.); στέφανος Eub.105 (anap.); διαχωρήματα Steph.*in Hp*.1.157 D. 2. *manifold*, σοφία τοῦ θεοῦ *Ep.Eph*.3.10; φαντασία τῶν οἰνωμένων Anon. *Incred*.17; τελετή Orph.*H*.6.11. -ποίκιλτος, ον, gloss on πολύκεστος, Eust.425.24. -ποινος, ον, *punishing severely*, Δίκη Parm.1.14, Orph.*Fr*.158. -πολις, εως, Ion. ιος, ὁ, ἡ, poet. πολύπτ-, *with many cities*, Call.*Dian*.225; ἡ π. Ἀλεξάνδρεια *a congeries of cities*, Ph.2.541.

**πολῠπόν-ηρος**, ον, *very bad*, Melamp.*Naev*.p.506 F. -ία, ἡ, *much labour* or *toil*, Pl.*Amat*.133e. -ος, ον, of men, *much-labouring, much-suffering*, as a general epith. of mankind, π. ἄνδρες Pi.*N*.1.33; βροτοί A.*Supp*.382 (lyr.), E.*Or*.175 (lyr.), etc.; -ωτάτη βροτῶν Id.*Hec*. 722, cf. Ar.*Th*.1023 codd.; *laborious*, Puchstein *Epigr.Gr*.p.7. 2. of things, *painful, toilsome*, δόρυ A.*Pers*.320; [τόξα] S.*Ph*.777; αἰκία Id. *El*.515 (lyr.); ἀνάγκαι E.*Or*.1011 (lyr.); νοῦσος Hp.*Aff*.23; κρυπτεία π. πρὸς τὰς καρτερήσεις Pl.*Lg*.633b; δι' ἐμὸν ὄνομα π. (i.e. Helen's) E.*Hel*.199 (lyr.). Adv. -νως Plu.*Alex*.63, Phalar.*Ep*.34.

**πολῠποξύστης**, ου, ὁ, *instrument for removing polypi*, Paul.Aeg. 6.25.

**πολῠ-πόρευτος**, ον, *much-travelled*, Hsch. s.v. πολύστιπτος, Phot. s.v. πολυστείνοις. -πορος, ον, *furnishing abundant harvests*, πεδία Ar.*Av*.952 (dub.). II. *with many passages*, Plu.2.650c.

**πολῠποσία**, Ion. -ίη, ἡ, (πόσις) *hard-drinking*, Hp.*Aph*.7.7, Plb. 5.15.2, Ph.1.682, Demoph.*Sim*.49.

**πολῠ⟨πο⟩σφάκτης**, ου, ὁ, = πολυποξύστης, *Hermes* 38.284.

**πολῠ-πότᾰμος**, ον, *with many* or *large rivers*, E.*HF*410 (lyr.). -ποτέω, *drink hard, drink much wine*, Hp.*Prorrh*.2.2. -πότης, ου, ὁ, (πίνω) *hard drinker*, Hp.*Aër*.4, Ath.10.442f, Cass.*Pr*.48; poet. πουλ- *AP*9.524.17:—fem. -πότῐς, ιδος, Ael.*VH*2.41. -ποτμος, ον, *of many fates* or *fortunes*, Εὐμενίδες Orph.*H*.70.9. -πότνια, ἡ, strengthd. for πότνια, *h.Cer*.211, A.R.1.1125, Orph.*H*.40.16.

**πολῠποτόμος**, ον, *for excising* πολύποδες, Philum.ap.Aët.16.23.

**πολύποτος**, ον, *much-drinking*, Hp.*Vict*.2.49 (πουλυ-), Arist.*HA* 601b4.

⊛ **πολύπους** (A), ὁ, ἡ, neut. πουν; acc. masc. πολύποδα Arist.*Pol*. 1281b6: neut. pl. πολύποδα Pl.*Epin*.981d:—*many-footed*, Pl.*Ti*.92a, Dsc.2.35; Ἐρινύς S.*El*.488 (lyr.); οὕτω τι πολύπουν ἐστὶν ἡ λύπη κακόν Posidipp.19 (dub.). 2. Pass., *trodden by many feet*, χῶρος Orac.ap. Polyaen.6.53.

⊛ **πολύπους** (B) (first in Arist.), later Gr. for πουλύ-, ποδος, ὁ:—Declension: nom. πουλύπους S.*Fr*.307, Ar.*Fr*.318, Eup.110, etc.; gen. πουλύποδος Od.5.432, Pl.Com.173.16, Eub.101; acc. πουλύπουν Ion Trag.36, Ar.*Fr*.190, Hegem.1, Alex.170, etc.: pl., nom. πουλύποδες *h.Ap*.77, Hp.*Vict*.2.48, Diocl.*Fr*.132; acc. -ποδας Pherecr.13, Pl.Com.93; gen. πουλυπόδων Anaxandr.41.29 (anap.); later, acc. sg. πολύποδα Luc.*Vit.Auct*.10, πολύπουν Id.*DMar*.4.2: pl. πολύποδες, etc., Arist.*HA*541b1, al.; acc. πολύπους ib.534a25, Dsc.1.74 (in signf. III):—in Poets freq. declined as if from πούλυπος, gen. πουλύπου Thgn. 215, Ar.*Fr*.191: pl., gen. πουλύπων Amips.6; acc. πουλύπους Ar.*Fr*. 189: Dor. pl. nom. πώλυποι Epich.61; acc. πωλύπους Id.124: also nom. sg. πώλυπος Hp.*Aff*.5 (v.l.); πῶλυψ Diph.Siph.ap.Ath.8.356e, (in signf. III) Poll.4.204 : acc. pl. πώλυπας Dsc.2.166 ; also acc. pl. **πόλυπας** and acc. and gen. sg. πόλυπα, πόλυπος, Paul.Aeg.6.25 :— the common *poulp* or *octopus*, Od. l.c., Thgn. l.c., Arist.*HA*$524^{a}3$, etc. II. of insects, Id.*PA*$682^{a}36$, al. ; esp. of the myriapods, Id. *HA*$531^{b}29$, al. III. *polypus* or *morbid excrescence in the nose*, Hp. *Aff.*5, Thphr.*HP*9.13.6, Gal.7.106, Poll.l.c. IV. π. βοτάνη, = πολυπόδιον, *Gp.*15.1.14.

**πολυπραγμ-ᾰτέω,** = πολυπραγμονέω, Arist.*Pol.*$1299^{b}1$. **-ᾰτος,** ον, = πολυπράγμων, Palaeph.*Praef.*, Procl.*Par.Ptol.*228. ⊛ **-ονέω,** Ion. **πολυπρηγμ-,** pf. πεπολυπραγμόνηκα Phld.*Sign.*33 :—*to be busy about many things*, μὴ πολυπραγμόνει *take* no *trouble* about it, Pherecr. 154 ; π. τὰς αἰτίας ἐρευνῶντας Pl.*Lg.*821a ; περί τι ib.952d ; περί τινα Phld.*Ind.Sto.*22 ; ὑπὲρ σοῦ Pl.*Tht.*184e. 2. mostly in bad sense, *to be a meddlesome, inquisitive busybody*, Ar.*Pl.*913, etc. ; τὰ αὑτοῦ πράττειν καὶ μὴ π. Pl.*R.*433a : c. acc., τὰ ὀθνεῖα Democr.80 ; *interfere*, εἴς τι *IG*5(1).1208.24 (Gythium). b. esp. *meddle in state affairs, intrigue*, Hdt.3.15, X.*An.*5.1.15. 3. c. acc., *to be curious after, inquire closely into*, ἀλλότρια κακά Men.*Mon.*583, cf. Plb.3.38.2 ; οἱ τὰ φαινόμενα πεπολυπραγμονηκότες Id.9.15.7 ; τὰ μετέωρα π. Diog.Oen.3, etc. :—Pass., Plb.12.27.4. ⊛ **-όνησις,** εως, ἡ, = πολυπραγμοσύνη, dub. l. in Plot.6.3.23. **-ονητέον,** *one must search after knowledge*, ἔκ τινος Plb.9.19.5 ; περί τινος Ph.2.312. **-οσύνη,** ἡ, *curiosity, officiousness, meddlesomeness*, Ar.*Ach.*833, Lys.1.16, etc. ; joined with ἀλλοτριοπραγμοσύνη, Pl.*R.*444b ; opp. ἀπραγμοσύνη, Th.6.87. 2. later, *search after knowledge*, Plb.5.75.6.—Cf. Plu. περὶ πολυπραγμοσύνης (2.515b). **-ων,** ον, gen. ονος, (πρᾶγμα) *busy about many things*, mostly in bad sense, *meddlesome, officious, a busybody*, Eup. 222, Ar.*Av.*471, Lys.24.24, Isoc.15.98,230,237 : freq. as epith. of the *restless* Athenians, as in the plays so entitled by Timocles, Diphilus, and Heniochus ; applied to Socrates, Arr.*Epict.*3.1.21. Adv. -νως Mitteis *Chr.*31 viii 30 (ii B.C.). 2. later and rarely in good sense, *curious after knowledge*, π. καὶ περιττός Plb.9.1.4 ; Ἡρόδοτος ὁ π. D.S.1.37, cf. Antig.*Mir.*24.

**πολύ-πρακτος,** ον, = πολυπράγμων, Vett.Val. in *Cat.Cod.Astr.*8(1).163. **-πράκτωρ,** ορος, ὁ, poet. **-πρήκτωρ,** = πολυπράγμων, Man.4.160. **-πρεμνος,** ον, *with many trunks*, ὕλη A.R.4.161 ; Ἴδη prob. in Coluth.195. **-πρεπής,** ές, *magnificent*, πλοῦτος Philostr.*VS* 2.23.2. **-πρηγμονέω,** Ion. for πολυπραγμονέω. **-πρήων,** ωνος, ὁ, ἡ, *with many hillocks*, Κολωνός Hermesian.7.57. **-πρόβᾰτος,** ον, *rich in sheep* or *cattle*, Φρύγες Hdt.5.49 (Sup.), cf. X.*Vect.*5.3. **-προικος,** ον, (προίξ) *richly-dowered*, Eust.1383.16. **-πρόσωπος,** ον, *many-faced, multiform*, οὐρανός the *ever-changing* sky, Lyc.Sophist. ap.Arist.*Rh.*$1405^{b}35$ ; πράγματα Vett.Val. in *Cat.Cod.Astr.*8(1).166 ; *with many masks* or *characters*, δρᾶμα Luc.*Nigr.*20 ; [ὄρχησις] Plu.2.711f ; τὸ π. τῶν ὀρχημάτων Luc.*Asin.*49. 2. *of many persons*, γενεά J.*BJ*1.28.4. Adv. -πως, συναγωνιζόμενοι, of conspirators, Id. *AJ*16.3.3. **-πρώτιστος,** written for πολὺ π. in some texts of Il. 2.702, Eust.326.12. **-πτερος,** ον, *many-winged*, Arist.*HA*$486^{b}11$, *PA*$682^{b}13$. **-πτόητος,** poet. **-πτοίητος,** ον, *timorous*, Plu.2.44c, etc. ; ὄμμα *AP*5.289 (Paul. Sil.) ; *much-agitated*, θάλασσα ib.7.624 (Diod.), cf. Nonn.*D.*27.189, al. **-πτυκτος,** ον, *manifold, intricate*, ῥυθμοί *IG*3.82. **-πτῠχία,** *frequentia*, *Gloss.* **-πτῠχος,** ον, (πτύξ, πτυχή) *of* or *with many folds* ; esp. of mountains, *with many valleys*, πολυπτύχου Οὐλύμποιο Il.8.411, cf. 20.5, Hes.*Th.*113 ; Ἴδης ἐν κνημοῖσι πολυπτύχου Il.21.449, cf. 22.171, etc. ; χθών, of the mountainous tract of Phocis, E.*IT*677 ; of a compress, *many times folded*, σπλήν Hp.*Fract.*8, etc. II. *folded many times, with many leaves*, δέλτοι Luc.*Am.*44 ; γραμματεῖον Poll.4.18. **-πτώξ,** ῶκος, ὁ, ἡ, *abounding in hares*, Call.*Fr.*528. **-πτωτος,** ον, (πτῶσις) *with* or *in many cases*, σχῆμα, a rhetorical figure, *employment of the same word in various cases*, Hermog.*Id.*1.12, Eust.349.39 ; σχηματισμός Id.105.26 ; τὸ π. alone, Quint.*Inst.*9.3.37, Longin.23.1 (pl.). **-πῠλος,** ον, *with many gates*, D.S.1.45. **-πυργος,** ον, *with many towers*, *h.Ap.*242. **-πύρηνος** [πῡ], ον, *with many stones*, Thphr.*CP*4.4.12. **-πῡρος,** ον, (πυρός) *rich in corn*, epith. of fruitful lands, Il. 11.756, 15.372, Od.14.335, al., A.*Supp.*555 (lyr.), *AP*6.258 (Adaeus), Dsc.1.127 ; ἄγυια *Hymn.Is.*2. **-πῠρος,** ον, (πῦρ) *full of fire*, Sch. rec. A.*Pr.*880. **-πυστος,** ον, *much-heard-of, far-famed*, Nic.*Al.* 303. **-ρημονέω, -ρήμων,** v. πολυρρ-. **-ριζος,** ον, = πολύρριζος, ἀσφόδελος *Epigr.Gr.*1135 (Naples, vase). **-ρραβδος,** ον, *with many stripes*, Arist.*Fr.*294. **-ρρᾰγής,** ές, epith. of a river, either *with many branches*, or *violent*, Nic.*Th.*59. **-ρράθᾰγος** [ᾰθ], ον, *far-sounding*, Opp.*C.*3.21, *H.*5.652. **-ρρᾰθάμιγξ** [ᾰμ], ιγγος, ὁ, ἡ, *with many drops*, Nonn.*D.*7.174. **-ρραίστης,** ου, ὁ, *slayer of many*, Opp.*H.*1.463, v.l. for πολιρραίστης in Lyc.210. **-ρραπτος,** ον, *much-sewn, well-stitched*, φαρέτρη Theoc.25.265. **-ρρᾰφής,** ές, = foreg., *EM*148.37. **-ρρᾰφος,** ον, = foreg., πόρπαξ S.*Aj.* 575. **-ρρημονέω,** *speak much*, Eust.805.41, etc. **-ρρήμων,** ον, gen. ονος, (ῥῆμα) *much-speaking, wordy*, M.Ant.3.5 ; πνεῦμα τοῦ στόματος Lxx *Jb.*8.2 ; σοφία Max.Tyr.31.1. **-ρρην,** ηνος, (ἀρήν) *rich in lambs*, *Carm.Naupact.*2 (*EGF* p.199 K.) : dat. sg. -ρρηνι Hsch. (-ρρήνη cod.) : nom. pl. -ρρηνες, ἄνδρες Il.9.154,296, Hes.*Fr.*134.3, cf. Theoc. 25.117 : the older dat. of πολύρρην (= *πολύ-ϝρην) is πολύαρνι (from *πολύ-ϝr̥νι) Il.2.106 (-ϝρην is to -ϝr̥ν-ι as πατήρ to πατρ-ί). ⊛ **-ρρηνος,** ον, = foreg., of a person, Od.11.257 ; of a country, A.*Eleg.*3 ; σταθμός Q.S.2.331. ⊛ **-ρρητος,** ον, = πολύφραστος, Hsch. ; also, = πολύπονος, Id. **-ρριζία,** ἡ, *possession of many roots*, Thphr.*CP*3.10.6. **-ρριζος,** ον, *with many roots*, Id.*HP*9.10.2, Epigr.ap.Poll.5.48 (Anyt.) ; *full of roots*, γῆ *Gp.*3.10.8. 2. *bearing many* ῥίζαι, i.e. *fertile in herbs*. Str.5.3.6, 15.1.22. 3. metaph., *firmly rooted*, πολιτεία Plu.2.787f. 4. *fibrous*, of tissue in malignant disease, Hp. *Mul.*2.156. II. πολύρριζον, τό, = ἐλλέβορος μέλας, Dsc.4.162. 2. = πτερίς, ib.184. 3. = ἐπιμήδιον, Ps.-Dsc.4.19. **-ρρῑνος,** ον, *with many hides*, σάκος A.R.3.1231. **-ρροδος,** ον, *abounding in roses*, λειμῶνες Ar.*Ra.*449 (lyr.). **-ρρόθιος,** ον, *much-dashing, loud-roaring*, θάλασσα Q.S.7.395 ; *buffeted by many waves*, ἄνθρωποι Arat.412. **-ρροθος,** ον, = foreg., φροίμια π. the cries *of many voices*, A.*Th.*7. **-ρροίβδητος,** ον, *much-whirring*, ἄτρακτος *AP*6.160 (Antip. Sid.). **-ρροιζος,** ον, *with a loud rushing noise*, Q.S. 1.156 ; f.l. for πολυστίοιο, Nic.*Th.*792. **-ρρομβος,** ον, *with many turns*, of a bandage, Sor.*Fasc.*23,57. **-ρροος,** ον, contr. **-ρους,** ουν, = πολύρυτος, Poll.6.148, Eust.96.28. **-ρρῡμος,** ον, *with many chariot-poles*, ἅρματα Arr.*Tact.*2.5. **-ρρῠτος,** f.l. for παλίρρυτος, S. *El.*1420. **-ρῠτος,** ον, *with many currents*, πόρος A.*Supp.*843 (lyr.).

⊛ **πολύς,** Att. πολλή, πολύ ; gen. πολλοῦ, ῆς, οῦ ; dat. πολλῷ, ῇ, ῷ ; acc. πολύν, πολλήν, πολύ :—Ion. **πολλός** Anacr.43.3, πολλή, πολλόν Xenoph.9, Democr.219, Hp.*VM*1, Herod.3.19 ; also in Trag., S.*Ant.*86, *Tr.*1196 ; acc. πολλόν, πολλήν, πολλόν : Hdt. uses the Ion. forms, but codd. have πολύν 2.121.δ′, 3.57, v.l. in 6.125, πολύ 2.106, 3.38, 6.72, 7.46,160 (πολύ also in Heraclit.114, Democr. 244) :—both sets of forms are found in Ep., also gen. sg. πολέος Il.4. 244, etc. : nom. pl. πολέες 2.417, al., once contr. πολεῖς 11.708 ; gen. πολέων (trisyll.) 5.691, (disyll.) 16.655 ; dat. πολέσι 10.262, al. ; πολέσσι 13.452, al. ; πολέεσσι 9.73, Od.5.54, Hes.*Op.*119, etc. ; acc. πολέας (trisyll.) Il.3.126, etc., (disyll.) 1.559, 2.4, Hes.*Op.*580 (freq. with v.l. πολεῖς Il.15.66, etc.) ; in later Ep. πολέες is used as fem., Call.*Del.*28, also πολέας Id.*Dian.*42, A.R.3.21 ; neut. πολέα Q.S.1.74 (v. infr.) :—Ep. also have **πουλύς** (once in Hes., *Th.*190, also Thgn. 509, sts. fem. in Hom., πουλὺν ἐφ' ὑγρήν Il.10.27, ἠέρα πουλύν 5.776), neut. πουλύ Od.19.387 ; these forms are found in codd. of Hp. and Aret. (who uses πολύ, πουλύ and πολλόν in neut.), but not in Hdt. :— Lyr. and Trag. (lyr.) sts. use Ep. forms, dat. sg. πολεῖ A.*Supp.*745 ; nom. pl. πολέες B.10.17 ; neut. πολέα A.*Ag.*723 ; πολέων E.*Hel.*1332 (fem., B.5.100) ; dat. pl. πολέσι E.*IT*1263. [ῠ always.] I. of Number, *many*, Il.2.417, etc. ; ἐκ πολλῶν, opp. ἐξ ὀλίγων, Hes.*Th.*447 ; τριηκόντων ἐτέων πόλλ' ἀπολείπων wanting *many* of thirty years, Id.*Op.*696 ; παρῆσάν τινες, καὶ πολλοί γε Pl.*Phd.*58d ; οὐ πολλοί τινες A.*Pers.*510 : with Nouns of multitude, πουλὺς ὅμιλος Od.8.109 ; πλῆθος πολλόν Hdt.1.141 ; ἔθνος πολλόν Id.4.22 ; later πουλὺ . . ἐπ' ἔτος *many* a year, *AP*6.235 (Thall.) ; π. ἦν ὁ καταπλέων Plb.15.26.10 ; of anything often repeated, περὶ σέο λόγος ἀπῖκται π. Hdt.1.30 ; πολλὸν ἦν τοῦτο τὸ ἔπος Id.2.2, cf. 3.137, etc. ; πολὺ . . τὸ σὸν ὄνομα διήκει πάντας S.*OC*305 ; τούτῳ πολλῷ χρήσεται τῷ λόγῳ *often*, D.21.29 ; τοῦτο ἐπιεικῶς πολὺ νῦν ἐστι is fairly *frequent*, Luc.*Hist.Conscr.*15. 2. of Size, Degree, Intensity, *much, mighty*, ὄμβρος, νιφετός, Il.10.6 ; π. ὕπνος Od.15.394 ; πῦρ . . π. 10.359 ; π. ὑμέναιος a *loud* song, Il.18.493 ; π. ὀρυμαγδός, ῥοῖζος, etc., 2.810, Od.9.315, etc. ; π. ἀνάγκη *strong* necessity, E.*Ph.*1674 ; π. γέλως, βοή, *much* or *great*, S.*Aj.*303, 1149 ; μωρία ib. 745 ; ὄλβος, αἰδώς, A.*Pers.*251, *Ag.*948 ; ἀσφάλεια Th.2.11 ; ἀλογία, εὐήθεια, Pl.*Phd.*67e, *Phdr.*275c, etc. b. rarely of a single person, *great, mighty*, μέγας καὶ πολλὸς ἐγένεο Hdt.7.14, cf. E.*Hipp.*1 ; ὁ π. σοφιστής, στρατηγός, Chor.p.23 B., Id. in *Rev.Phil.*1.68 ; ὁ πάντα π. Id.p.27 B. ; ὁ πολύς alone, of Hippocrates, Gal.19.530 ; of Trajan, Lyd.*Mag.*2.28 ; ῥώμην σώματος πολύς D.H.2.42. c. joined with a Verb, Κύπρις γὰρ οὐ φορητός, ἢν πολλὴ ῥυῇ if she flow *with full stream*, metaph. from a river, E.*Hipp.*443 ; θρασυνομένῳ καὶ πολλῷ ῥέοντι D. 18.136 ; from the wind, ὡς π. ἔπνει καὶ λαμπρός was blowing *strong* and fresh, Id.25.57, cf. Ar.*Eq.*760, *AP*11.49 (Even.) : generally, *with might* or *force*, ὅταν ὁ θεὸς . . ἔλθῃ πολύς E.*Ba.*300 ; ἦν π. παρῇ Id.*Or.*1200 ; π. καὶ τολμηρὸς ἄνθρωπος D.40.53 : with part. and εἰμί, πολλὸς ἦν λισσόμενος was *all* entreaties, Hdt.9.91 ; ἦν πολλὸς ὑπὸ παντὸς ἀνδρὸς αἰνεόμενος Id.1.98 ; Ἐτεοκλέης ἂν εἷς π. . . ὑμνοῖθ' A.*Th.*6 ; π. ἐνέκειτο λέγων Hdt.7.158 ; π. τοῖς συμβεβηκόσιν ἔγκειται D.18.199 ; also π. ἦν ἐν τοῖσι λόγοισι Hdt.8.59 ; πρὸς ταῖς παρασκευαῖς Plb.5.49.7 ; ἐπὶ τῇ τιμωρίᾳ D.S.14.107 : without a Prep., π. ἦν τοῖς ἐπαίνοις καὶ ἐπαχθής Aeschin.2.41 ; π. μὲν γὰρ ὁ Φίλιππος ἔσται will be *often mentioned*, Id.1.166. 3. of Value or Worth, πολέος δέ οἱ ἄξιος ἔσται Il.23.562, cf. Od.8.405 ; πολλοῦ ἄξιος X.*An.*4.1.28, etc. ; πολλῶν ἄξιος Ar.*Pax*918 ; περὶ πολλοῦ ποιεῖσθαί τι, Lat. *magni facere*, cf. περί A. IV ; ἐπὶ πολλῷ at *a high price*, D.8.53 ; ἐπὶ π. ἐρραθυμηκότες Id.1.15 ; πολύ ἐστί τι it is *worth much, of great consequence*, X.*Oec.*18.7. 4. of Space, *large, wide*, π. χώρη, πεδίον, Il.23.520, 4.244, etc. ; πόντος, πέλαγος, Hes.*Op.*635, S.*Ph.*635 ; χῶρος πλατὺς καὶ π. Hdt.4.39 ; λίμνη μεγάλη τε καὶ π. ib.109 ; π. ἡ Σικελία Th. 7.13 ; π. ἡ Ἑλλάς Pl.*Phd.*78a, etc. ; πολλὸς ἔκειτο he lay *outstretched wide*, Il.7.156, cf. 11.307 ; π. κέλευθος a *far* way, A.*Pers.*748 (troch.) : without ὁδός, πολλὴ μὲν εἰς Ἡράκλειαν . . , πολλὴ δὲ εἰς Χρυσόπολιν . . X.*An.*6.3.16 : διὰ πολλοῦ, ἐκ πολλοῦ, v. infr. IV. 5. of Time, *long*, χρόνος S.*Aj.*1402 (anap.), etc. ; πολὺν χρόνον Il.2.343, etc. ; οὐ π. χρ. S.*Ph.*348, etc. ; so πολλοῦ χρόνου Ar.*Pl.*98 ; χρόνῳ πολλῷ S.*Tr.*228 ; διὰ πολλοῦ (sc. χρόνου) Luc.*Nec.*15 ; ἐκ πολλοῦ Th.1.58, D. 21.41 ; πρὸ πολλοῦ *long* before, D.S.14.43 ; οὐ μετὰ πολύ Luc.*Tox.*54 ; ἔτι πολλῆς νυκτός while still *quite* night, Th.8.101 ; πολλῆς ὥρας *late* in the day, Plb.5.8.3 ; ἤδη ὥρα πολλή *Ev.Marc.*6.35 ; ἔτι ἔστιν ἡμέρα πολλή Lxx *Ge.*29.7. II. Special usages : 1. c. partit. gen., e.g. πολλοὶ Τρώων, for πολλοὶ Τρῶες, Il.18.271, etc. ; neut., πολλὸν σαρκός, for πολλὴ σάρξ, Od.19.450 : in Prose, the Adj. generally takes the gender of the gen., τὸν πολλὸν τοῦ χρόνου Hdt.1.24 ; τῆς γῆς οὐ πολλήν Th.6.7; τῆς ἀθάρης πολλήν Ar.*Pl*.694; πολλὴν τῆς χώρας X.*Cyr*.3.2.2; ὁ π. τοῦ λόγου D.44.6; v. infr. 3. **2.** joined with another Adj., πολλὰ δυστερπῆ κακά A.*Ch*.277, cf. 585 (lyr.), etc.: more freq. joined to another Adj. by καί, πολέες τε καὶ ἐσθλοί *many* men and good, Il.6.452, etc.; πολέες τε καὶ ἄλκιμοι 21.586; πολλὰ καὶ ἐσθλά Od.2.312; παλαιά τε πολλά τε ib.188; ἄκοσμά τε π. τε Il.2.213; πολλαί γε..καὶ ἄλλαι Hes.*Th*.363; π. τε καὶ κακά Hdt.4.167, etc.; π. κἀγαθά Ar.*Th*.351 (but π. ἀγαθά *IG*1$^{2}$.76.45); π. καὶ ἀνόσια Pl.*R*.416e; π. καὶ μακάρια Id.*Plt*.269d; π. καὶ πονηρά X.*Mem*.2.9.6; πολλά τε καὶ δεινά Id.*An*.5.5.8; μεγάλα καὶ π. D.36.22; π. καὶ καλοὺς (s.v.l.) κινδύνους, π. καὶ καλὰ παραδείγματα, Din.1.109. **3.** with the Art. (in Hom. without the Art., Il.2.483, 5.334, 22.28), of persons or things well known, Ἑλένα μία τὰς πολλάς, τὰς πάνυ π. ψυχὰς ὀλέσασ' those *many* lives, A.*Ag*.1456 (lyr.), cf. S.*OT*845, Th.3.87, Pl.*Phd*.88a, *Ti*.54a, *Act.Ap*.26.24: with abstract Nouns, τᾶς πολλᾶς ὑγιείας A.*Ag*.1001 (lyr., dub.); τὸ πολλόν *numbers*, Hdt.1.136. **b.** οἱ π. the *many*, i.e. the *greater number*, Ἀθηναῖοι..ἀπῆλθον οἱ πολλοί Th.1.126, cf. 3.32, etc. (so in sg., ὁ πολλὸς λόγος the *prevailing* report, Hdt.1.75); τοῖς π. κριταῖς S.*Aj*.1243: with gen., τοῖς π. βροτῶν ib.682; οἱ π. τῶν ἀνθρώπων X.*Cyr*.8.2.24; οἱ πολλοὶ ἅπαντες *far the most*, Hp.*Aër*.20 (v.l. μάλιστα for ἅπαντες); for τὰ πολλὰ πάντα, v. infr. III. 1a: hence οἱ πολλοί the *people*, the *commonalty*, opp. οἱ μείζω κεκτημένοι, Th.1.6; opp. οἱ κομψότεροι, Pl.*R*.505b; οἱ π., = Lat. *plebs*, D.S.20.36; τῶν πολλῶν εἷς one *of* the *multitude*, D.21.96; also ὁ π. λεώς Luc.*JTr*.53, cf. *Rh.Pr*.17; ὁ π. ὅμιλος Id.*Luct*.2, Hdn.1.1.1, etc.; ὁ π. δῆμος Luc.*Apol*.15; ὁ π. ὄχλος Ph.2.4; ὁ π. alone, = *vulgus*, v.l. in D.S.2.29; the *ordinary man*, Epicur.*Fr*.478, Phld.*Rh*.2.154S.; νίμμα ὁ π. λέγει, ἡμεῖς ἀπόνιπτρον λέγομεν Phryn.170, cf. 369; ὁ ἐμπαθὴς καὶ π. ἄνθρωπος 'l'homme *moyen sensuel*', Herm.*in Phdr*.p.146A.; ὁ π. ἄνθρωπος (with pl. Verb) the *average* man, opp. τὸ ἐξαίρετον, Eun.*Hist*.p.216D. **c.** τὸ πολύ, c. gen., τῆς στρατιῆς τὸ πολλόν Hdt.8.100; τὸ π. τοῦ χρόνου Hp.*Aër*.20; τῶν λογάδων τὸ π. Th.5.73; τῶν ὅπλων τὸ π. Pl.*Plt*.288b; also ὁ στρατὸς ὁ πολλός Hdt.1.102; ἡ δύναμις ἡ π. Th.1.24; ὁ π. βίοτος *the best part* of life, S.*El*.185 (lyr.). **d.** τὰ πολλά *the most*, Od.22.273, and perh. 2.58, 17.537 (elsewh. in Hom. πολλά, as Subst., means *much riches*, *great possessions*, Il.11.684, Od.19.195); τὰ π. τοῦ πολέμου Th.2.13; πρὸς τὸ τῶν π. μέγεθος in regard to the size of *the average*, Arist.*Rh*.1363$^{b}$11. **4.** pl. πολλά *very much*, *too much*, πολλὰ πράσσειν, = πολυπραγμονεῖν, E.*Supp*.576, Ar.*Ra*.228; π. ἔπαθεν Pi.*O*.13.63, etc.; π. ἔρξαι τινά to do one *much harm*, A.*Th*.923 (lyr.). **5.** πολλάς with Verbs of beating (πληγάς being omitted), v. πληγή I. **6.** πολύς repeated, ἦ πολλὰ πολλοῖς εἰμι διάφορος βροτῶν E.*Med*.579, cf. A.*Supp*.451; τὰ μὲν οὖν πολλὰ πολλοῦ χρόνου διηγήσασθαι Pl.*R*.615a, etc.; πολλοῦ πολύς, v. infr. III. 1b: with Advbs. πολλάκις, πολλαχῇ, etc. (qq.v., cf. III. 1e). **III.** Adverbial usages: **a.** neut. πολύ (Ion. πολλόν), πολλά, *much*, πόλλ' ἀεκαζομένη Il.6.458, etc.; strengthd., μάλα πολλά 8.22, al.; πάνυ πολύ Pl.*Alc*.1.119c; πολύ τι Id.*R*.484d; esp. of repetition, *often*, Il.2.798, Od.13.29, Hes.*Op*.322; so of *earnest* commands and entreaties, πολλὰ κελεύων, πόλλ' ἐπέτελλον, πολλὰ λισσομένη, πολλὰ μάλ' εὐχομένω, Il.5.528, 11.782, 5.358, 9.183: with the Art., τὸ πολύ *for the most part*, Pl.*Prt*.315a, etc. (but with numerals, *at most*, Vett.Val.9.5); ὡς τὸ π. X.*Mem*.1.1.10, etc.; τὰ πολλά Th.1.13, 2.11, 87, etc.; ὡς τὰ π. Id.5.65, etc.; τὰ π. πάντα Hdt.1.203, 2.35, 5.67. **b.** of Degree, *far*, *very much*, ἀπέφυγε πολλὸν τοὺς διώκοντας Id.6.82: also abs. gen. πολλοῦ *very*, θρασὺς εἶ πολλοῦ Ar.*Nu*.915, cf. Eup.74; πολλοῦ δύνασθαι Alciphr.1.9 (s.v.l.); πολλοῦ πολύς, πολλὴ πολλοῦ, *much too much*, Ar.*Eq*.822, *Ra*.1046. **c.** of Space, *a great way*, *far*, οὐ πολλόν Hdt.1.104; πολὺ οὐκ ἐξήεσαν Th.1.15, etc. **d.** of Time, *long*, ὡς πολλὸν τοῦτο ἐγίνετο Hdt.4.126, cf. 6.129. **e.** of Probability, ἐὰν πολλὰ πολλῶν τέκῃς, perh. = ἐὰν πολλάκις τέκῃς, *POxy*.744.9 (i B.C./i A.D.); ἐάν τι πολλὰ πολλάκις πάθω Ar.*Ec*.1105. **2.** πολύ is freq. joined with Adjs. and Advbs., **a.** with a Comp. to increase its comp. force, πολὺ μεῖζον, πολλὸν παυρότεροι, Il.1.167, Od.14.17; πολὺ μᾶλλον *much* more, Il.9.700; πολύ τι μᾶλλον f.l. in D.H.*Comp*.4 (p.22 U.-R.): with words, esp. Preps., between πολύ and its Adj., π. ἐν πλέονι, π. ἐπὶ δεινοτέρῳ, Th.1.35, Pl.*R*.589e; πολὺ ἔτι ἐκ λαμπροτέρων Id.*Phd*.110c; π. σὺν φρονήματι μείζονι X.*An*.3.1.22, cf. 3.2.30, *Smp*.1.4 (but the Prep. freq. comes first, ἐκ π. ἐλάττονος And.1.109, etc.); so πολλῷ is freq. used with the Comp., *by far*, A.*Pr*.337, Hdt.1.134, etc.; π. μᾶλλον S.*OT*1159, Pl.*Phd*.80e; οὐ πολλῷ τεῳ ἀσθενέστερον not *a great deal* weaker, Hdt.1.181, cf. 2.48, 67, etc.: πολύ with all words implying comparison, πολὺ πρίν *much* sooner, Il.9.250; π. πρό 4.373: with the comp. Verb φθάνω, ἦ κε πολὺ φθαίη 13.815; so πολὺ προβέβηκας ἁπάντων, πολὺ προμάχεσθαι ἁπάντων, 6.125, 11.217; προὔλαβε πολλῷ Th.7.80: with βούλομαι, = *prefer*, ἡμῖν πολὺ βούλεται ἢ Δαναοῖσι νίκην Il.17.331, cf. Od.17.404; πολύ γε in answers, after a Comp. or Sup., ἀργὸς..γενήσεται μᾶλλον; Answ. πολύ γε Pl.*R*.421d, cf. 387e, etc. **b.** with a Sup., πολὺ πρώτιστος, πολλὸν ἄριστος, *far* the first, etc., Il.2.702, 1.91, etc.; προθυμία π. τολμηροτάτη Th.1.74, etc.; πολλόν τι μάλιστα Hdt.1.56; π. δή, π. δὴ γυναῖκ' ἀρίσταν E.*Alc*.442 (lyr.), cf. Ar.*Av*.539, Archestr.*Fr*.34.9; also πολλῷ πλεῖστοι Hdt.5.92.έ, 8.42; π. μεγίστους Id.4.82. **c.** with a Positive, to add force to the Adj., ὦ πολλὰ μὲν τάλαινα, πολλὰ δ' αὖ σοφή A.*Ag*.1295; also ἐς πόλλ' ἀθλία πέφυκ' ἐγώ E.*Ph*.619 (troch.); πολὺ ἀφόρητος Luc.*DMeretr*.9.3; cf. πλεῖστος. **IV.** with Preps., **1.** διὰ πολλοῦ at *a great interval* of Space or Time, v. διά A. I. 5, II. 2. **2.** εἰς πολύ for *a long time*, Plot.2.1.3. **3.** ἐκ πολλοῦ from *a great distance*, Th.4.32, etc.; for *a long time*, v. ἐκ II. 1. **4.** ἐπὶ πολύ, **a.** over *a great space*, *far*, οὐκ ἐπὶ πολλόν Hdt.2.32; ἐπὶ π. τῆς θαλάσσης, τῆς χώρας, Th.1.50, 4.3, etc.; to *a great extent*, Id.1.6, 18, 3.83; cf. ποιέω B. II. 2. **b.** for *a long time*, *long*, Id.5.16; τῆς ἡμέρας ἐπὶ π. Id.7.38, cf. 39. **c.** ὡς ἐπὶ π. *very generally*, Id.1.12 (v.l.), Archyt.ap.Stob.3.1.195; ὡς ἐπὶ τὸ π. *for the most part*, Th.2.13, Pl.*Plt*.294e, etc.; μὴ καθ' ἓν ἕκαστον, ἀλλ' ὡς ἐπὶ τὸ π. Isoc.4.154; τό γ' ὡς ἐπὶ τὸ π. Id.8.35. **5.** παρὰ πολύ by *far*, v. παρά C. III. 5. **6.** περὶ πολλοῦ, v. supr. I. 3. **7.** πρὸ πολλοῦ *far* before, τῆς πόλεως D.H.9.35; also of Time, οὐ πρὸ π. not *long* before, Id.5.62. **8.** σὺν πολλῷ *in no small degree*, *only too much* or *too well*, Hld.2.8, 9.20, 10.9 (cf. *CR*41.53). **V.** for Comp. πλείων, πλέων, Sup. πλεῖστος, v. sub vocc. (Cf. Skt. *purú-*, Goth. *filu* 'much'.)

**πολύ-σαθρος** [ῠ], ον, *very rotten*, *unsound*, Ps.-Luc.*Philopatr*.21. **-σαρκία**, ἡ, *fleshiness*, *plumpness*, X.*Mem*.2.1.22, Plu.2.641a, Gal.1.607. **-σαρκος**, ον, *very fleshy*, Arist.*HA*583$^{a}$7, *PA*656$^{a}$19, Dsc.5.124, Gal.10.607, etc. **II.** metaph., *very stupid*, Them.*Or*.23.288c. **-σέβαστος**, ον, Ep. **πουλυ-**, = Lat. *augustissimus*, *AP*9.419 (Crin.). **-σεμνος**, ον, *exceeding venerable*, Ὄσιρις *Epigr.Gr*.1029 (Cios), Orph.*H*.22.9. **-σεπτος**, ον, *much-revered*, ib.26.6, Porph.*Chr*.78. **-σήμαντος**, ον, *with many significations*, Heliod.*in EN*86.8; προσηγορία Lyd.*Mag*.2.2; περὶ π. λέξεων, title of work by Orus, Reitzenstein *Gesch.d.Gr.Etym*.p.336. **-σημάντωρ**, ορος, ὁ, *giving commands to many*, *ruling over many*, Ἀϊδωνεύς *h.Cer*.84, 376, cf. 31. **-σημος**, ον, = πολυσήμαντος, Democr.26, Nicostr.ap.Simp.*in Cat*.368.15, etc. **-σθενής**, ές, *of great might*, νηῶν ὅπλον *Epic.Alex.Adesp*.9 ii 11, cf. Luc.*Trag*.192, Q.S.2.205, al. **σῑνής**, ές, (σίνομαι) *very hurtful*, *baneful*, κύων A.*Ch*.446 (lyr.). **-σῖνος**, ον, *with many defects* or *blemishes*, Vett.Val.111.12. **-σῑτέω**, *eat heavily*, Pall.*in Hp*.2.95D. **-σῑτία**, ἡ, *abundance of corn* or *food*, X.*HG*5.2.16. **II.** *much eating*, Luc.*Par*.16. **-σῖτος**, ον, *rich in corn*, of persons, X.*Vect*.5.3; of a country, Thphr.*HP*8.6.6, Str.15.3.11. **II.** *high-fed*, *full of meat*, Theoc.21.40. ❋ **-σκαλμος**, ον, *many-oared*, *AP*7.295. **-σκαρθμος**, ον, (σκαίρω) *much-springing*, *bounding*, Il.2.814; or (as expld. by Str.12.8.6), *driving swift horses*, but π. ὄνος Nic.*Th*.350; νῆες Q.S.5.657. ❋ **-σκάριστος**, ον, gloss on foreg., Apollon.*Lex*. s.v. εὔσκαρθμοι. **-σκεπής**, ές, *sheltering entirely*, πέτρα Ael.*NA*14.26. **-σκεπτος**, ον, *far-seen*, Βοώτης Arat.136. **-σκηπτρος**, ον, *wide-ruling*, *AP*4.3$^{b}$.17 (Agath.). **-σκῐος**, ον, *very shady*, Hp.*Aff*.60, A.R.4.166, Jo.Gaz.*Ecphr*.2.289, interpol. in Dsc.1.126. **-σκόπελος**, ον, *very rocky*, Marc.Sid.5. **-σκοπος**, ον, *far-seeing*, Pi.*Fr*.107.1. **-σκῠλαξ** (or **-σκύλᾰκος**), ὁ, ἡ, *with many dogs*, in gen. pl. -άκων κεφαλάων of *many dogs'* heads, Nonn.*D*.18.246. **-σκώμμων**, ονος, ὁ, ἡ, *fond of mocking*, Poll.6.171. **-σμάρᾰγος** [σμᾰ], ον, *loud-roaring*, θάλασσα Opp.*C*.2.138, cf. Hsch., Suid. **-σμηνος**, ον, *in many swarms*, μέλισσαι Choeril.2. **-σοφος**, ον, *very wise*, Philostr.*VS*2.19 (nisi leg. πολὺ σ.), Vett.Val.15.24. **-σπᾰθής**, ές, (σπάθη) *close-woven*, πέπλοι *AP*6.39 (Arch.). **-σπαστος**, ον, (σπάω) *drawn by many cords*: πολύσπαστον, τό, *compound pulley*, Hero *Bel*.84.11, Ath.Mech.33.3, Plu.*Marc*.14, Gal.18(1).747. **-σπείρητος**, ον, (σπεῖρα) *with many coils*, ἑρπηστήρ Nonn.*D*.40.482. **-σπειρος**, ον, = foreg., Hsch. **-σπερής**, ές, (σπείρω) *wide-spread*, *spread over the earth*, ἄνθρωποι Il.2.804, Od.11.365; Ὠκεανῖναι Hes.*Th*.365; φήμη Theodect.16; συνόδοντες Opp.*H*.3.577; Boeot. pl. πολουσπερίες Corinn.*Supp*.2.63. **II.** *fruitful*, καμασῆνες Emp.74. **-σπέρμᾰτος**, ον, = πολύσπερμος, Thphr.*HP*7.3.4. **-σπερμία**, ἡ, *abundance of semen*, Horap.2.115. **-σπερμος**, ον, *abounding in seed*, Arist.*GA*725$^{b}$29, Thphr.*HP*6.7.4; πολύσπερμος, ἡ, a plant, *Hippiatr*.2, *Gp*.17.5.5. **II.** *abounding in seminal fluid*, Gal.1.339. **2.** *prolific*, *Cat.Cod.Astr*.1.166, Vett.Val.10.26. **-σπερχής**, ές, *very diligent*, *zealous*, Eust.1385.23. **-σπῐλάς**, άδος, ἡ, *with many rocks*, Dem.Bith.4.2. **-σπλαγχνος**, ον, *of great mercy*, *Ep.Jac*.5.11. ❋ **-σπορος**, ον, *with many crops*, *fruitful*, E.*Tr*.748, Opp.*C*.3.23, Orph.*H*.6.10; φύσις ib.10.19; *rendering prolific*, Ptol.*Tetr*.34, Vett.Val.6.6. Adv. -ρως *widely scattered*, S.E.*M*.5.58. **II.** = πολύσπερμος II, Ptol.*Tetr*.72, *Cat.Cod.Astr*.7.212. **-σπούδαστος**, ον, = πολυσπερχής, Eust.442.8, 1385.23. **-στᾰγῶς**, Adv. *dropping fast*, Sch.A.R.3.805. **-στάδιος** [ᾰ], ον, *many stades long*, Eudem.ap.Simp.*in Ph*.974.5. **-στακτί**, Adv. = πολυσταγῶς, Sch.S.*OC*1646. **-στᾰσίαστος**, ον, *much harassed by factions*, App.*BC*2.151. **-στᾰτος**, ον, (ἵστημι) *standing thick*, πύργοι Ph.Byz.*Mir*.5.2 cod. (πολύστεγοι Hercher). **-στάφῠλος** [ᾰ], ον, *rich in grapes*, of places, Il.2.507, S.*Ant*.1133 (lyr.); also Διόνυσε *h.Hom*.26.11; ἄμπελος Hecat.15J. **-στᾰχυς**, υ, gen. υος, *rich in ears of corn*, Δάματερ Theoc.10.42; ὕψος τοῦ φυτοῦ τετράπηχυ, π. καὶ πολύκαρπον Str.15.1.18. **-στεγος**, ον, *with many ceilings* or *stories*, Id.16.2.23; πύργοι cj. in Ph.Byz.*Mir*.5.2. **-στεινος**, ον, = πολυπόρευτος, Phot. (leg. -στειβ-, i.e. -στῐβ-). **-στειος**, v. πολύστιος. **-στελέχης**, ες, *with many stems*, Thphr.*HP*1.3.1. **-στέλεχος**, ον, = foreg., παλίουρος *AP*9.312 (Zon.). **-στένακτος**, ον, *causing many groans*, ποδάγρα Luc.*Trag*.2; *full of groaning*, βίος *AP*7.155. ❋ **-στέφᾰνος**, ον, *with many wreaths* or *crowns*, Emp.123.2, Cratin.317, *Supp.Epigr*.6.246 (Phrygia, iii A.D.). **II.** Subst., = *Feronia*, *Gloss*. ❋ **-στεφής**, ές, *decked with many wreaths*, A.*Eu*.39; *earning many crowns*, μόχθοι *APl*.5.338: c. gen., *wreathed with*, δάφνης S.*OT*83. **II.** *twisted in many a wreath*, κότινος Nic.*Th*.378; of a serpent (expld. by Sch. as πολλοὺς στεφάνους ἔχοντες καὶ γραμμάς), μύαγροι ib.490 (s.v.l.; fort. -στρεφέας). **III.** *containing many circles*, οὐρανός Herm.ap.Stob.1.

49.44. **-στημος**, ον, (στῆμα) *thick-woven*, Hsch. s. v. στημνίον. **-στῐβία**, Ep. -ίη, ἡ, *constant treading*, ἀτραπιτοῖο Opp.*C*.4.433. **-στικτος**, ον, (στίζω) *much-spotted*, Orph.*Fr*.238; χελῶναι Marc.Sid.16; δορά Anon.*Incred*.17. **-στῖος**, ον, (στία) *with many small stones, pebbly*, Call.*Jov*.26; ποταμοί, ἅλμη, Nic.*Th*.950, *Al*.466. **-στιπτος**, ον, *much-trodden*, Hsch. (πολύστικτος cod.). **-στῐχία**, poet. -ίη, ἡ, *length in lines*, ἐπιγράμματος *AP*9.342 (Parmen.). **-στῐχος**, ον, = sq., στῦλοι Str.17.1.28. II. *of many lines* or *verses*, Ammon.*in Int*.134.22, Paul.Aeg.*Praef*. III. *prolix*, Ammon.*in Porph*.38.18. **-στοιχος**, ον, *in many rows*, ὀδόντες Arist.*HA*505ᵃ29; κριθαί Thphr.*HP*8.4.2 (Comp.); π. γνάθοι jaws *set with many rows of teeth*, Lyc.414. **-στομέω**, *speak much*, A.*Supp*.502. **-στομος**, ον, *many-mouthed*, φλέψ Hp.*Oss*.13; of a fistula, Heliod.ap.Orib.44.23.67; Νεῖλος v.l. for sq. in Nic.*Th*.175. II. *uttered by many mouths*, φήμη Nonn.*D*.26.275. **-στονος**, ον, *much-sighing, mournful*, of persons, Od.19.118, A.*Th*.845 (lyr.). 2. *noisy*, Νεῖλος f.l. for foreg. in Nic.*Th*.175; οἶδμα.. πολυστόνου Ἀμφιτρίτης Q.S.14.644. 3. of things, *causing many sighs, mournful, grievous*, κήδεα, Ἔρις, ἰός, Il.1.445, 11.73, 15.451; ξιφέων πολύστονον ἔργον Archil.3.3; τάφος Pi.*Pae*.6.99; π. φάτις A.*Eu*.380 (lyr.); Τροία S.*Ph*.1346; ἀρά, δαίμων, Ἐρινύς, E.*Or*.996 (lyr.), *Hel*.212 (lyr.), *Supp*.835 (lyr.); ἰός A.R.3.279, etc. **-στρεπτος**, ον, *much-twisted*, δεσμοί v.l. for πολυπλέκτοισι in Nic.*Al*.224, cf. Orph.*A*.1096, etc.; τὸ ἄστατον καὶ π. τῆς θαλάσσης Lyd.*Mens*.4.159. **-στρεφής**, ές, *winding*, ποταμός *Inscr.Magn*.17.33. 2. *much-twisted*, [θῶμιγξ] Opp.*H*.5.132. **-στροιβος**, ον, *much-tossed, tempestuous*, θάλασσα, Νεῖλος, Nic.*Al*.6, *Th*.310. **-στρόφᾰλιγξ**, ιγγος, ὁ, ἡ, *much-whirling*, ἄελλαι Musae.294; ῥιπή Nonn.*D*.23.263. **-στροφάς**, άδος, ἡ, = foreg., ib.6.147. **-στροφία**, poet. -ίη, ἡ, *complication, variety* of melody, *AP*7.198 (Leon.). ❀ **-στροφος**, ον, *much-twisted*, λίνα ib.6.107 (Phil.); ἀκτίς Mesom.*Sol*.12. 2. *versatile*, γνῶμα Pi.*Fr*.214; π. τὴν γνώμην Poll.6.131. 3. *making many turns*, of a dancer, Nonn.*D*.30.108; ἡνιοχεύς (of a steersman) ib.40.464. **-στῦλος**, ον, *with many columns*, σκηνή, οἶκος, Str.15.1.21, 17.1.28; of the Odeum, Plu.*Per*.13. **-σύγκρᾱτος**, ον, *mixed up of many things*, Hsch. s. v. ἀμφιμιγές. **-σύγκρῐτος**, ον, *compounded of many things*, Id. s. v. παγχυρισμός. **-σύλλᾰβος**, ον, *polysyllabic*, D.H.*Comp*.11, Luc.*Nec*.9. **-σύνδεσμος**, ον, *using many conjunctions* or *connecting particles*, Θουκυδίδης Sch.Th.2.41. **-σύνδετος**, ον, = foreg., *versus* π. Serv.Dan.ad Verg.*A*.11.634; τὸ π. Diom p.447 K., cf. Donat.ad Ter.*Ad*.301. **-σύνθετος**, ον, *much-compounded*, Plot.5.9.3; of medicines, *with many ingredients*, Alex.Trall.5.5; of words, *with many elements*, Sch.Ar.*Ra*.844, etc. II. τὸ π. *the union of clauses by many particles*, Rutil.1.14. **-σφᾰγής**, ές, *murderous*, σίδηρος Ps.-Callisth.1.46. **-σφαιρία**, ἡ, *multiplication of spheres*, Theo Sm.p.201 H. **-σφακτος**, corrupt in Plu.*Lib*.9 (fort. -σφυκτον, *much-pulsating*). **-σφάρᾰγος** [σφᾰ], ον, = πολυσμάραγος, Opp.*C*.4.445, Nonn.*D*.2.36. **-σφελμος**, ον, (σφέλμα) *with thick rind*, Hsch. **-σφόνδῠλος**, ον, *many-jointed*, Luc.*Dips*.3. **-σφράγιστος** [ᾰ], Ion. **-σφρήγιστος**, ον, *with many seals, well-secured*, Nonn.*D*.4.14. **-σφυκτος**, v. πολύσφακτος. **-σχεράς**, άδος, ἡ, *shingly*, Euph.25. **-σχημάτιστος** [ᾰ], ον, *multiform*, Poll.5.170; τὸ π. *variety of rhetorical forms*, D.H.*Vett.Cens*.3.1. 2. of verses, *composed of various metres*, στίχοι Sch.Ar.*Eq*.322, etc.; [μέτρον] Heph.10.4. **-σχήμᾰτος**, ον, = foreg., λόγος Philostr.*VS*2.1.14, cf. Porph.*in Ptol.(Tetr.)*185. **-σχημος**, ον, = πολυσχήμων, χείρ Aristaenet.1.26 (nisi leg. πολυσήμῳ). **-σχημοσύνη**, ἡ, *use of a variety of forms*, Eust.1463.27. **-σχήμων**, ον, gen. ονος, *of many shapes, varied in form*, *Placit*.1.14.4, Poll.6.171, Artem.1.2: Sup. -σχημονέστατος Str.2.5.18. Adv. -μόνως Poll.4.98. **-σχῐδής**, ές, (σχίζω) *split into many parts*, ἁπλῷ τρόπῳ καὶ μὴ πολυσχιδέϊ by a single and not *a splintered fracture*, Hp.*Fract*.24; λώβῃσι πολυσχιδέεσσι λυθέντα, of a wreck, Opp.*H*.4.409. 2. *much-cloven*, opp. ἀσχιδής, of certain figs, Arist.*Pr*.930ᵇ33; of a deer's antlers, *branching*, Id.*HA*517ᵃ24, cf. *PA*663ᵃ10; of the lungs, Id.*HA*495ᵇ1; of leaves, Thphr.*HP*3.12.5; καυλοί Dsc.2.185; of a mountain range, Str.11.12.1; ἀτραποί Plu.2.969b; of the Nile, Opp.*C*.2.85, cf. Lib.*Or*.61.18. 3. of the hand, *cloven into fingers*, Arist.*PA*687ᵇ7; of the foot, *into toes*, ib.690ᵇ6: hence τὰ π. *animals that have toes*, not hoofs, Id.*HA*497ᵇ20, 499ᵇ7, 502ᵇ34; esp. of birds, ib.504ᵃ6. 4. generally, *much divided*, γνῶμαι S.E.*M*.7.349; ἔμφασις Iamb.*VP*29.161; ψεῦδος Id.*Protr*.21κ'; *complex*, Ammon.*in Cat*.66.9. Adv. -δῶς Ph.1.31. **-σχῐδία**, Ion. -ίη, ἡ, *a splitting into many parts*: *manifold division*, νούσων Hp.*Acut*.3; *diversity*, δογμάτων Id.*Praec*.13. **-σχιστος**, ον, *split into many parts, branching*, κέλευθοι S.*OC*1592. **-σχοινος**, ον, *of many cords*, of a net, Marc.Sid.92. **-σώμᾰτος**, ον, *with many bodies*, γίγαντες D.S.1.26, cf. Plu.2.427b, Poll.2.235; *composed of many corpuscules*, πῦρ *Placit*.3.3.4 (Comp.), cf. Gal.19.482 (Comp.). **-σωρος**, ον, *rich in heaps of corn*, of Demeter, *AP*6.258 (Adaeus). **-τάλαντος** [τᾰ], ον, *worth many talents*, γάμος, μισθός, Luc.*DMeretr*.7.4, *Pro Merc.Cond*.12; of a book, πραγματεία π. Ath.9.398e. 2. *possessing many talents*, οἶκος Luc.*Tox*.14, cf. Poll.9.54. 3. *weighing many talents*, λίθος Alciphr.3.10; τράπεζα τὴν ὁλκὴν π. J.*BJ*7.5.5, cf. Luc.*JTr*.7. **-τάρακτος** [τᾰ], ον, *much-disturbed*, Ach.Tat.1.13. **-τάρᾰχος** [τᾰ], ον, *tumultuous*, Sch.D Il.1.34, Hsch. s. v. πολυφλοίσβοιο, Erot. s. v. κιγκλισμός. **-ταρβής**, ές, *much-frightened*, Nonn.*D*.43.360, *AP*9.816. **-τειρής** (A), ές, (τείρω) *wearying much*, Q.S.4.120, 5.314. **-τειρής** (B), ές, (τείρεα) *rich in stars*, Ἀργώ Arat.604. **-τεκνέω**, *have many children*, Arist.*Pol*.1272ᵃ24, Ephor.216 J. **-τεκνία**, ἡ, *abundance of children*, Arist.*Rh*.1360ᵇ20, Hierocl.p.55 A. **-τεκνος**, ον, *bearing many children, prolific*, Τηθύς A.*Pr*.137 (anap.), cf. Arist.*HA*616ᵇ10. 2. *consisting in many children*, γενέθλη Nonn.*D*.25.561. II. epith. of rivers, *giving increase*, A.*Supp*.1027 (lyr.). ❀ **-τέλεια**, Ion. -είη, ἡ, *great expense, extravagance*, opp. εὐτέλεια, Hdt.2.87, Th.6.12; τρυφὴ καὶ π. X.*Mem*.1.6.10; π. τῶν βίων Plb.13.1.1, cf. 9.10.5, etc. 2. *costliness*, ἐσθῆτος X.*Lac*.7.3, etc. **-τελεύομαι**, *feast luxuriously*, Epicur.*Fr*.182. **-τελέω**, *to be extravagant*, Phot. ❀ **-τελής**, ές, (τέλος) *very expensive, costly*, opp. εὐτελής, οἰκίη Hdt.4.79; τράπεζα Democr.210; παρακομιδή Th.7.28; ζῶναι Pl.*Hp.Mi*.368c; παρασκευαί X.*Hier*.1.20 (Comp.); π. νεκρός *honoured with a costly funeral*, Men.*Per.Fr*.2; λίθοι, λιθεία, *precious* stones, *OGI*90.34 (Rosetta, ii B.C.), 132 (Egypt, ii B.C.): generally, *valuable*, -εστάτην τὴν τοῦ δρᾶν.. δύναμιν ἐδημιούργησεν Pl.*R*.507c; -έστατον ζῷον, v.l. for πολυφρονέστατον, Euryph.ap.Stob.4.39.27. II. of persons, *lavish, extravagant*, coupled with ἄσωτος, Men.615; γυνὴ π. ἐστ' ὀχληρόν Id.325.7; ἑταίρα π. Id.824; π. τῷ βίῳ Antiph.80.5. Adv. -λῶς Eup.335, Lys.7.31, X.*Mem*.3.11.4: Sup., τὰ -λέστατα *in the costliest manner*, Hdt.2.87. **-τενής**, poet. πουλ-, ές, *far-stretching*, D.P.99, 340. **-τερπής**, ές, *much-delighting*, ὕμνοι *AP*9.504; Ἔρως Orph.*Fr*.168.9, 169. II. *much-delighted*, ἀκουαί Nonn.*D*.10.236. **-τέχνης**, ου, ὁ, *skilled in divers arts*, Ἥφαιστος Sol.13.49. **-τεχνής**, ές, *wrought with much art*, Orph.*A*.585. **-τεχνία**, ἡ, *skill in many arts*, Pl.*Alc*.2.147a, Aristeas 51, v.l. in D.S.1.64: in pl., Perict.ap.Stob.4.28.19. **-τεχνος**, ον, *skilled in many arts*, πόλις Aristeas 114; Σιδόνιοι Str.16.2.24; π. ὑποθέσεις ἔργων Plu.*Per*.12. Adv. -νως, ἔχειν Aristeas 73. II. *the work of many craftsmen*, δημιούργημα D.Chr.78.24.

**πολῠτῑμ-ητίζω**, *esteem highly*, Numen.ap.Eus.*PE*14.5, Hsch.:—Pass., *to be addressed as* "πολυτίμητε", *Com.Adesp*.1120. **-ητος**, Dor. -τίμᾱτος, ον, also η, ον Ar.*Pax*978: (τιμάω): *highly honoured*, freq. used in addressing a divinity, Ἀφροδίτη [Parm.]20; ὦ Ζεῦ πολυτίμητ' Pherecr.73, Ar.*Fr*.319; ὦ πολυτίμηθ' Ἡράκλεις Id.*Ach*.807; ὦ π. θεοί Id.*V*.1001; θεώ Id.*Th*.594; ὦ π. Νεφέλαι Id.*Nu*.269; ὦ π. Αἰσχύλε Id.*Ra*.851; and (ironically) ὦ π. Εὐθύδημε Pl.*Euthd*.296d; so τὸ π. ἰατρεῖον, of Aristotle, Timae.ap.Plb.12.8.4. II. *at a high price, very costly*, Epich.71, Ar.*Fr*.387.9, Alex.Trall.1.15; with play on signf. I, [σῖτος] π. ᾧπερ τοὶ θεοί Ar.*Ach*.759. **-ία**, ἡ, *high price*, Iamb.*VP*3.14. ❀ **-ος**, ον, (τιμή) *much-revered*, θεοί Men.109.1. II. *highly priced*, μουσοεργός Hp.*Nat.Puer*.13; *very costly*, *AP*5.35.5 (Rufin.), Babr.57.9. Adv. -μως Plb.14.2.3 (nisi leg. -τελῶς). **-ώρητος**, ον, *much-punished*, Suid., Tz.ad Lyc.1047.

**πολύ-τῖτος** [ῡ], ον, (τίω) *worthy of high honour*, Orac.ap.Hdt.5.92.β'. **-τλας**, ὁ, (τλῆναι) *much-enduring*, epith. of Odysseus, Hom. and S. only in nom., Il.8.97, al.; ironically, S.*Aj*.956 (lyr.); gen. πολύτλα Eust.700.32; acc. πολύτλαν Antisth.*Od*.14 codd., Man.5.268. (Perh. Aeol. for *πολυτλής, ῆτος.) **-τλήμων**, ονος, ὁ, ἡ, *much-enduring*, θυμός Il.7.152; of Odysseus, Od.18.319; βροτοί Ar.*Pax*236. **-τλητος**, ον, *having borne much, miserable*, γέροντες Od.11.38, cf. Orph.*Fr*.354, Q.S.1.135, al.; also ὠδίνεσσι πολυτλήτοισι Id.11.25; γῆρας Id.2.341. **-τμητος**, ον, (τέμνω) *much-cut, lacerated*, παρειά *AP*11.66 (Antiphil.), cf. Opp.*C*.2.252. II. Act., *cutting much* or *deeply*, of sharp pain, Id.*H*.5.288. **-τοιοῦτος**, αύτη, οῦτον, *having many of so and so*, e.g. πολυγλώχιν is a πολυτοιοῦτον of γλωχίς and τριγλώχις, Eust.89.19. **-τοκέω**, *to be prolific*, Arist.*HA*558ᵇ20, *GA*750ᵃ27, Thphr.*CP*1.22.1. **-τοκία**, ἡ, *fecundity*, Arist.*GA*750ᵃ28, 771ᵃ16. **-τόκος**, ον, *bearing more than one child*, Hp.*Nat.Puer*.30. 2. *bringing forth many children* or *young ones, prolific*, Arist.*PA*688ᵃ34, *GA*749ᵇ31 (Comp.), Porph.*Abst*.4.14. **-τολμος**, ον, *very bold*, Plu.2.731c, Sch.E.*Hipp*.642, *Cat.Cod.Astr*.8(4).195. **-τόρος**, ον, (τορέω) *much-piercing*, *Com.Adesp*.716. **-τραφής**, ές, *much-nourishing, productive*, χώρα D.S.2.52. **-τράχηλος** [ᾰ], ον, *with large* or *stubborn neck*, Heraclit.*All*.17 codd. (misquoting Pl.*Phdr*.253d). **-τρεπτος**, ον, *much-turning, changeable*, Plu.2.423a. **-τρεφής**, ές, = πολυτραφής, ὕδωρ Nonn.*D*.40.362 (s. v.l.). **-τρήρων**, ωνος, ὁ, ἡ, *abounding in doves*, Il.2.502, 582. **-τρητος**, poet. -πουλύ-, ον, *much-pierced, full of holes, porous*, σπόγγοι Od.1.111, 22.439; φῷδες Cratin.213; φύλλα Dsc.2.182; of the flute, λωτοί, δόνακες, *AP*9.266 (Antip.), 505.5; ἠθμός ib.6.101 (Phil.); of honeycombs, ib.9.363.15 (Mel.); σίμβλοι Luc.*Epigr*.12; of the lungs, Aret.*SD*1.10; τὸ π. τῆς χώρας Str.12.8.16. **-τρίπους** [ῐ], ὁ, ἡ, gen. ποδος, *abounding in tripods*, *AP*7.709 (Alexander). **-τριπτος**, ον, *rubbed very fine*, Nic.*Th*.104. II. *much-trodden, frequented*, Opp.*H*.3.502. **-τρίχιον** μάλαγμα, perh. f.l. for Πολυάρχιον, Herod. Med. in *Rh.Mus*.58.96. ❀ **-τρῐχος**, ον, (θρίξ) *very hairy, bushy*, πώγων Philonid.10. II. **-τρῐχον**, τό, = ἀδίαντον, Dsc.4.134, *Sammelb*.7350.8 (iii/iv A.D.), Phot. s. h. v., *AB*343. **-τροπία**, Ion. -ίη, ἡ, *versatility, craft*, Hdt.2.121.ε'. II. *multifariousness, variety*, Hp.*Acut*.3 (pl.), D.H.*Amm*.2.3, Corn.*ND*25, M.Ant.12.24. ❀ **-τροπος**, ον, (τρέπω) *much-turned*, i.e. *much-travelled, much-wandering*, epith. of Odysseus, Od.1.1, 10.330. II. *turning many ways*: metaph., *shifty, versatile, wily*, of Hermes, *h.Merc*.13, 439; τοῖς ἀσθενέσι καὶ π. θηρίοις Pl.*Plt*.291b; and in this sense Plato took the word as applied to Odysseus, *Hp.Mi*.364e (Sup.), al.; τὸ π. τῆς γνώμης their *versatility* of mind, Th.3.83; τὸ π., of Alcibiades, Plu.*Alc*.24. 2. *fickle*, ὅμιλος Ps.-Phoc.95. 3. of diseases, *changeful, complicated*, Plu.*Num*.22; also πόλεμος τοῖς πάθεσι ποικίλος καὶ ταῖς τύχαις πολυτροπώτατος Id.*Mar*.33; στρατεία Eun.*Hist*. p.223 D. III. *various, manifold*, ξυμφοραί Th.2.44; ἐπιθυμίαι, ἐθισμοὶ τῶν λέξεων, Epicur.*Fr*.471, *Nat*.28.1 (p.7V.); κακά Ph.2.567; ἔθνη Plu.*Marc*.12; τύχαι Id.*Alc*.2; ὄργια *Lyr.Alex.Adesp*.36.3; τὸ π. Phld.*Sign*.26. Adv. -πως *in many manners*, Meno *Iatr*.20.31, Ph.2.512, *Ep.Hebr*.1.1, Iamb.*Comm.Math*.12: Comp., -ωτέρως καὶ ποικιλωτέρως Epicur.*Nat*.5 G. **-τροφία**, ἡ, *excess of nourishment*, Thphr.*CP*6.16.4, Aret.*CA*1.2. ⊛ **-τροφος**, ον, *well-fed, plump*, Thphr.*CP*4.3.5, Plu.*Lyc*.17, Ptol.*Tetr*.163. II. parox. πολυτρόφος, ον, Act., *supplying food*, Δάματερ π. Call.*Cer*.2; [γαῖα] *Mém. Miss.Arch.Perse* 20.90 (Susa, Hymn to Apollo). 2. *nutritious*, τυρός Dsc.2.71, cf. Anon.Lond.31.9 (Comp.), Xenocr.ap.Orib.2.58.19, Gal.6.261. **-τρόχᾰλος**, ον, *in constant motion*, κέντρα (of the celestial sphere) *IGRom*.4.607 (Phrygia). **-τρῡτος**, ον, *much-wearied*, Sch.S.*Aj*.788. **-τρωτος**, ον, *with many wounds*, Polem.*Call*. 50. **-τῡρος**, ον, *with much cheese*, Pherecr.130.7. **-υγρος**, ον, *containing much fluid*, Dsc.5.99. **-υδρία**, ἡ, *plenty of water*, Thphr.*CP*2.14.2. **-υδρος**, ον, *abounding in water*, τόποι Pl.*Lg*. 761b. **-ῡλία**, ἡ, *plethora*, Sor.1.38. **-ῡλος**, ον, *abounding in forests*, *Gloss*. 2. *abounding in materials*, Poll.6.171; π. σῶμα *plethoric*, Antyll.ap.Orib.9.13.2, cf. Heliod.ib.46.20.7. 3. *consisting of many kinds of matter*, opp. μονόϋλος, Zos.Alch.p.112 B.; *requiring abundance of materials*, of a remedy, Afric.*Cest*.p.30V. II. Rhet., τὸ π. τῆς ῥητορικῆς Sch.Hermog. in Rh.4.63W. **-ύμνητος**, ον, *much-famed in song*, Pi.*N*.2.5, M.Ant.7.6, Chor. in *Jahrb*.9. 187. ⊛ **-υμνος**, ον, *abounding in songs, much sung of, famous*, θεὸς π., of Dionysus, E.*Ion* 1074 (lyr.), cf. *h.Hom*.26.7; πόρνη Anacr.159; Ἀθῆναι Ar.*Eq*.1328; θησαυρὸς Μουσᾶν Tim.*Pers*.244. **-υπνία**, ἡ, *sleeping much*, Cass.*Pr*.24. **-υπνος**, ον, *bestowing sound sleep*, Orph. *H*.3.4. **-φᾰγέω**, *eat to excess*, Eust.1386.51, al. **-φᾰγία**, ἡ, *excess in eating*, Arist.*GA*768ᵇ29, Ph.1.686, Plu.2.624a, Iamb.*Protr*. 2. **-φάγος** [ᾰ], Ion. πουλ-, ον, *eating to excess*, Hp.*Vict*.2.49, Arist.*Fr*. 520. **-φᾱμος**, ον, Dor. for πολύφημος (q.v.). **-φᾰνής**, poet. πουλ-, ές, *very conspicuous*, Jo.Gaz.*Ecphr*.2.322, Eust.254.6. **-φᾱνος**, ον, *with many torches*, ἑορτά Alcm.34.2. **-φάνταστος**, ον, *with many apparitions*, εἴδωλα Plu.2.167a. **-φαντος**, ον, *conspicuous*, δόξα B.12.61. **-φάρμᾰκος**, ον, *knowing many drugs* or *charms*, ἰητροί Il.16.28; Κίρκη Od.10.276; Παιών Sol.13.57; of Medea, A.R. 3.27. 2. *given to the use of drugs*, Gal.10.169. 3. of countries, *abounding in healing* or *poisonous herbs*, Τυρρηνία Thphr.*HP*9.15. 1. 4. *compounded of many drugs*, δυνάμεις Plu.2.408b, Gal.13. 365. **-φᾰσία**, ἡ, (φημί) *wordiness*, Hsch. (pl.). **-φάσμᾰτος**, ον, *of many appearances, multiform*, Φοίβη Orac.ap.Lyd.*Mens*.3. 10. **-φᾰτος**, ον, (φημί) *much spoken of, famous*, ἀγῶνες Pi.*P*.11.47; π. ὕμνος *excellent, noble* strain, Id.*O*.1.8, cf. *N*.7.81. **-φαυλος**, ον, *very bad*, Eust.1311.62. **-φεγγής**, ές, *bright-shining*, Doroth. in *Cat.Cod.Astr*.2.81, Man.2.347, Orph.*Fr*.274; σελήνη *IGRom*.4.607 (Phrygia). **-φεγγος**, ον, = foreg., *Cat.Cod.Astr*.1.173. **-φειδής**, ές, *very sparing*, Eust.1967.20. **-φερβής**, ές, = πολύφορβος, Nonn. *D*.5.218. **-φερνος**, ον, (φερνή) = πολύεδνος, Hsch. s.v. πολύδωρος. **-φημία**, ἡ, *far-spread fame*, Poll.5.158. **-φημος**, Dor. -φᾱμος, ον, *abounding in songs and legends*, ἀοιδός Od.22. 376. 2. = πολύφατος, θρῆνος πολύφαμος Pi.*I*.8(7).64. II. *many-voiced, wordy*, ἀγορὴν πολύφημον ἱκέσθην Od.2.150; ἐς πολύφημον ἐξενεῖκαι to bring it forth to *the many-voiced*, i.e. *the agora* (*the 'parliament'*), Orac.ap.Hdt.5.79. III. *much spoken of, famous*, ὁδός Parm. 1.2; ὁ π. καὶ πολυώνυμος σοφός Ph.1.371. ⊛ **-φήτωρ**, ορος, ὁ, ἡ, = foreg. II, as gloss on ἀφήτωρ, Sch.Il.9.404. **-φθεγγής**, ές, *complicated*, μῦθος Cyran.5. **-φθερής**, ές, *subject to many forms of destruction*, ἄνθρωποι Emp.113. ⊛ **-φθογγος**, ον, *of many notes*, ψαλτήρια Plu.2. 827a, cf. 973c, Ael.*NA*5.51. **-φθονερός**, όν, *very envious*, as Epicurus called the Dialectic school of Megara, *Fr*.237sq. (ap.D.L.10.8; Plu.2.1086e writes πολυφθόρος). **-φθοος**, ον, epith. of a day at Delphi, *on which the oracle was much consulted*, Plu.2.292f. **-φθόρος**, ον, *destroying many, fraught with death* or *ruin*, ἁμέραι, ὄμβρος, Pi.*N*.8. 31, *I*.5(4).49; of persons, π. ἐν δαΐ A.*Th*.925 (lyr.). 2. v. πολυφθονερός. II. proparox. πολύφθορος, ον, Pass., *utterly destroyed* or *ruined*, Οἰχαλία, δῶμα, S.*Tr*.477, *El*.10. 2. (φθείρω II. 4) *involving* or *enduring many wanderings*, π. τύχαι, πλάνη, A.*Pr*.633, 820; of merchants, S.*Fr*.555.5. **-φίλητος** [ῐ], ον, *much-loved*, gloss on τριφίλατος, Sch.Theoc.15.86. **-φῐλία**, ἡ, *abundance of friends*, Arist.*Rh*. 1360ᵇ20, *Pol*.1284ᵃ20, al.; ὑπερτείνειν ταῖς..πολυφιλίαις ib.1293ᵃ31, cf. Lib.*Or*.25.59. **-φῐλος**, ον, *having many friends, dear to many*, Pi.*P*.5.4, Lys.8.7, Arist.*EN*1170ᵇ23, *Rh*.1372ᵃ13, Him.*Or*.8. 6. **-φιλτρος**, ον, *suffering from many love-charms, love-sick*, Theoc.23.1. **-φλέγμᾰτος**, ον, *having much phlegm*, Ptol.*Tetr*. 151, Antyll.ap.Orib.6.8.3. **-φλογος**, ον, (φλόξ) *fiercely blazing*, Hsch. s.v. ζαφλεγές, *EM*408.16. **-φλοιος**, ον, *with much* or *thick bark*, Hsch. s.v. πολυσφέλμου. **-φλοισβος**, ον, *loud-roaring*, θάλασσα Il.1.34, Hes.*Op*.648, Archil.9.3, Diph.126.4, etc.; σπουδή *confused* dissertation, Olymp.Alch.p.92 B. **-φοβος**, ον, *very timid*, Sch.S.*Tr*.841. **-φοιτος**, ον, *much-roaming*, Musae.181. **-φόνος**, ον, *murderous*, E.*HF*420 (lyr.), *Rh*.62,465. **-φορβος**, ον, also η, ον Il.9.568, Hes.*Th*.912: (φορβή):—*feeding many, bountiful*, γαῖα Il. 14.200, 301; Δημήτηρ Hes. l.c.

**πολῠφορ-έω**, *to be prolific, bear* or *yield much*, Thphr.*CP*5.5.4. II. Pass., *to be found in a variety of forms*, μυρία τῶν ῥημάτων -φοροῦνται ταῖς κλίσεσι Eust.1502.58. **-ητος**, ον, *bearing much*, Phot. and Suid. s.v. πολύχουν. II. *carried about, well-known*, *An.Ox*.3. 187. **-ία**, ἡ, *productiveness*, X.*Oec*.19.19, Poll.1.240. **-ος**, ον (parox.), *bearing much, productive, prolific*, π. καὶ παμφόρος Pl.*Lg*. 705b, cf. Str.6.3.9: Comp. -ώτεροι, φοινικῶνες J.*BJ*4.8.2. 2. metaph., χρόνος π. πονηρίας ib.7.8.1: Sup., τὸ κακὸν -ώτατον Ph. 1.361. II. *that will bear much water*, opp. ὀλιγοφόρος, of strong wine, Gal.15.669, *Gp*.7.23: metaph., πολυφόρῳ δαίμονι συγκεκρᾶσθαι to have a fortune *that wants tempering*, Ar.*Pl*.853.

**πολύφορτος** [ῠ], ον, *heavily laden*, Man.3.241; σύγχυσις Lyd.*Mag*. 3.1. 2. *rich*, Ps.-Hdt.*Vit.Hom*.1.

**πολυφρᾰδ-έω**, *to be very eloquent* or *wise*, only in part. πολυφραδέων, = sq., Hes.*Fr*.197. **-ής**, ές, (φράζω) *very eloquent* or *wise*, ἐννεσίῃσι πολυφραδέεσσι δολωθείς Id.*Th*.494, cf. Semon.7.93 (Sup.). II. *much talked of, famous*, ἔργον *IG*14.2012 *A*26 (Sulp. Max.). **-ία**, poet. -ίη, ἡ, ὕμνων *eloquence* of song, Hermesian. 7.50. **-μοσύνη**, Dor. -α, ἡ, = foreg., Archyt.ap.Stob.1.48. 6. **-μων**, ον, gen. ονος, = πολυφραδής, A.R.1.1311, Opp.*H*.4.28, *AP*9.816, Tryph.455.

**πολύ-φραστος**, ον, = πολυφραδής, *very wise*, ἵπποι Parm.1.4; so π. δόλοι *shrewd*, Opp.*C*.4.6; μενοινὴ π. Nonn.*D*.4.275. **-φροντις**, ιδος, ὁ, ἡ, *full of thought*, βουλαί *Anacreont*.48.6; ὁ νοῦς Lxx *Wi*.9. 15. **-φρόντιστος**, ον, *thoughtful*, Θάλης *AP*7.84; *very anxious*, Sch. S.*Tr*.109, Suid. s.v. πολυκηδέος. Adv. -τως *IG*2².1042 *b*21. ⊛ **-φροσύνη**, ἡ, *fullness of understanding, great shrewdness*, Hdt.2.121.ζ', Democr.40; pl., Thgn.712. **-φρων**, ον, gen. ονος, (φρήν) *ingenious, inventive*, Il.18.108, al.; epith. of Odysseus, Od.14.424; of Hephaestus, Il.21.367, Od.8.297; ἄλοχος Q.S.1.727: Sup. -έστατος Euryph.ap.Stob.4.39.27. 2. *embodying much thought*, ἀτρέκεια Orac.ap.Dam.*Pr*.161. **-φυής**, ές, (φυή) *divided into many, manifold*, Arist.*HA*493ᵃ1. ⊛ **-φυλλος**, ον, *with many leaves, thick-leaved*, of the yew, Eup.14.3, cf. Thphr.*HP*1.10.8, etc. **-φῡλος**, ον, *consisting of many tribes*, θνητοί Orph.*H*.62.3; epith. of Egypt, Timo 12. **-φῠτος**, ον, *rich in plants*, Cass.*Pr*.58.

**πολῠφων-έω**, *sound* or *speak much*, gloss on τρύζειν, Eust.751. 11. ⊛ **-ία**, ἡ, *variety of tones*, αὐλῶν Plu.2.1141c, cf. 674f; ὀρνέων D.S.2.56; *variety of speech*, J.*AJ*1.4.3. **-ος**, ον, *having many tones*, ὄρνιθες Arist.*PA*660ᵃ34; κίττα Plu.2.973c, etc.: neut. pl. as Adv., πολύφωνα κρῶξαι Arat.1002. 2. *having many voices*, Βοιωτία ἕνεκα χρηστηρίων π. οὖσα Plu.2.411e; *loquacious, talkative*, π. ὁ οἶνος ib.715a, cf. Luc.*Hist.Conscr*.4. 3. *manifold in expression*, of Homer, D.H.*Comp*.16 (Sup.), Str.3.2.12; τὸ π., of Plato, Stob.2.7.3ᶠ; of Hyperides, -ότερος [τοῦ Δημοσθένους] Longin. 34.1.

**πολῠ-φωτιστής**, οῦ, ὁ, *illuminator of many things*, *PMag.Berol*.2.121 (s.v.l.). **-χαίτης**, ου, ὁ, *with much hair*, Hdn.*Epim*.166. **-χαλκος**, ον, *abounding in copper* or *bronze*, πολύχρυσος π., of Troy, Il.18.289; of Sidon, Od.15.425; of Dolon, Il.10.315. II. *wrought of bronze, brazen*, οὐρανός 5.504, Od.3.2; ἄξονες Parm.1.18. **-χανδής**, ές, *wide-yawning, capacious*, Orph.*Fr*.56; ψυχῆς π. κόλπον *Stud. Ital*. (N.S.) 2.398 (Crete); κρωσσός Theoc.13.46; ὅλμος Nic.*Th*.951; λαιμός Nonn.*D*.11.162; νηδύς Q.S.1.527; σίμβλος Tryph.535: in late Prose, κοτύλη -εστέρα Them.*Or*.23.299c. **-χάρακτος** [χᾰ], ον, *variously formed*, Secund.*Sent*.3. **-χᾰρής**, ές, (χαίρω) *feeling* or *causing much joy*, *An.Ox*.3.138, Hsch. s.v. πολυγηθές; *graceful*, ὁμοίωσις Phld.*Lib*.p.26 O. **-χᾰρίδας**: ὦ πολυχαρίδα, or πολυχαρείδα (cj. Mein., to suit the metre), Lacon. term of endearment, *dearest! sweetest!* Ar.*Lys*.1098, 1242. **-χᾰρίεις**, εσσα, εν, *very gracious*, in Sup., *Cat.Cod.Astr*.8(4).154, 174. **-χαρμος**, ον, (χάρμη) *very warlike*, *AP*5.201 (Asclep. or Posidipp.). **-χείμερος**, ον, (χειμών) *very wintry*, Opp.*C*.1.429. **-χείμων**, ὁ, ἡ, gen. ονος, *very stormy*, θάλασσα App.*BC*5.108. ⊛ **-χειρ**, χειρος, ὁ, ἡ, *with many hands, many-handed*, Ἐρινύς S.*El*.488 (lyr.), Arist. *Pol*.1281ᵇ6. II. *with a large band of soldiers*, A.*Pers*.83 (lyr.); π. δύναμις Heraclit.*All*.25. **-χειρία**, ἡ, *multitude of hands*, i.e. *workmen* or *assistants*, Th.2.77, X.*Cyr*.3.3.26, Arist.*Mu*.398ᵇ12, Man.ap.J.*Ap*.1.26. II. *possession of many hands*, Βριάρεω π. Polem.*Cyn*.43. **-χεσος**, ον, (χέζω): π. νόσημα *diarrhoea*, *Com. Adesp*.19. **-χεύμων**, ον, gen. ονος, *strong-flowing*, πηγή Lib.*Ep*. Basil.19.1. **-χηλος**, ον, *with divided hoof*, opp. μονώνυχος, Ph.2. 353. **-χίτων** [ῑ], ωνος, ὁ, ἡ, *having many coats*, πυρός, σπέρματα, Thphr.*CP*3.21.2, 5.18.2, etc.; of the eyes, Hp.*Ep*.23. **-χλωρος**, Ion. πουλυ-, ον, *dark yellow*, τὸ π. Id.*Epid*.2.1.10.

**πολύ-χνοος**, ον, contr. -χνους, ουν, *very downy*, φύλλα κονύζης Nic.*Th*.875. **-χοέω**, *yield much, be productive*, Arist.*GA*749ᵇ 9. **-χοΐα**, ἡ, *diversity, variety*, Thphr.*HP*1.14.5:—also **πολυχοια**, ἡ, *abundant crop*, Max.486. **-χοος** or **-χόος**, ον, contr. **-χους**, ουν, (χέω) *pouring forth much, yielding much*, of animals, *prolific*, Arist.*HA*629ᵃ35, cf. Vett.Val.10.28; of fruit and grain, Thphr.*HP*8. 4.3; πολυχούστερα τὰ χεδροπά Id.*CP*4.8.1; τὸ καταβληθὲν πολύχουν ἀποδίδωσιν J.*BJ*4.8.3: metaph. of a writer or orator, *copious*, τῶν καθ' αὑτὸν πολυχούστατος Phld.*Acad.Ind*.p.102 M., cf. *Rh*.1.157 S. 2. *capable of great diffusion*, Hp.*Vict*.2.56. 3. *in large quantity*, κόπρος Heraclit.*All*.33. II. *manifold, various*, Arist.*Rh*.1418ᵇ9: Comp. -χούστερος Id.*PA*656ᵃ5; πολύχουν τὸ φυτὸν καὶ ποικίλον Thphr.*HP* 1.1.10; τὸ πολύχουν *variety*, Ptol.*Geog*.1.15.1; τὸ π. τῆς φύσεως the *prodigal variety* of Nature, Plot.6.2.3; ποικίλον καὶ π. χρῆμα ἡ ψυχή Them.*Or*.2.35a; π. καὶ πολύτροπος Iamb.*Protr*.21.λη'; π. ἐν πᾶσιν ἰητρός *IG*14.1813. 2. *frequent*, π. κακία, σπάνιον δ' ἡ ἀρετή Ph.2. 4, cf. Iamb. *in Nic*.p.33 P. **-χορδία**, ἡ, *the use of many strings in* the lyre, Pl.*R.*399c, Phan.Hist.17, etc.: pl., Plu.2.661d. ⊛ **-χορδος,** ον, *many-stringed,* βάρβιτον Theoc.16.45; *many-toned,* of the flute, Simon.46, cf. Pl.*R.*399d (Sup.); π. ᾠδαί E.*Med.*196 (anap.); πολυχορδοτάτα γῆρυς the sound *of many strings,* Id.*Rh.*548 (lyr.): metaph., δημοκρατία Plu.2.827b. **-χορτος,** ον, *with much grass,* gloss on βαθυλείμων, Eust.743.30.

**πολυχρημ-ᾰτέω,** *abound in money,* prob. in Str.9.2.40. **-ᾰτία,** ἡ, *greatness of wealth,* opp. εὐτέλεια, X.*Smp.*4.42, cf. Poll.3.110. **-ᾰτίας,** ου, ὁ, *man of great wealth,* v.l. in D.L.6.28. **-ᾰτος,** ον, *very wealthy,* Str.16.4.22, al., Eus.Mynd.17; *characteristic of wealth,* Phint.ap.Stob. 4.23.61ᵃ. **-οσύνη,** ἡ, = πολυχρηματία, Poll.3.110. **-ων,** ον, gen. ονος, = πολυχρήματος, Plb.18.35.9 (Sup.), Man.4.21.

⊛ **πολυ-χρήσῐμος,** ον, *very useful,* f.l. in Gal.6.480 (Sup.). **-χρηστία,** ἡ, *great usefulness,* Thphr.*HP*9.20.5. **-χρηστος,** ον, *useful for many purposes, very useful,* Arist.*GA*789ᵇ9, *Pol.*1337ᵇ26, Dsc. 1.1, Gal.6.534,480 (Sup.); τὸ π. Corn.*ND*9: Comp., Muson.*Fr.* 20p.112 H., Alex.Aphr. *in Top.*277.4. Adv. -τως v.l. in Paul.Aeg.7. 16. **-χροια,** ἡ, *variety of colour,* Arist.*Pr.*963ᵇ37, Ael.*NA* in epilogo. ⊛ **-χρονία,** ἡ, *length of time,* τοῦ τόκου Arist.*Pr.*896ᵃ 27. ⊛ **-χρονίζω,** fut. -ῐῶ, *prolong,* ἡμέρας Lxx *De.*4.26: abs., *live long,* Ptol.*Tetr.*132. **-χρόνιος,** ον, *of olden time, ancient, h.Merc.* 125. 2. *of long standing,* τὴν πολυχρονίων (leg. -χρόνιον) Μαρμαριτῶν θρασύτητα *Sammelb.*6026 (Cyrenaica, iii A.D.). II. *lasting for long,* νουσήματα Hp.*Aph.*4.23, cf. 7.6; μουναρχίη Hdt.1.55; π. ἔχειν τὴν ζωήν Arist.*Long.*464ᵇ25; ἀρχαί Id.*Pol.*1299ᵃ7 (Comp.); opp. αἰώνιος, Epicur.*Sent.*28; βιότω τέρμα *long-protracted,* Call.*Lav. Pall.*128; πολιορκίαι Onos.38.6; πλέγμα *AP*5.254.14 (Paul. Sil.): Comp., Hp.*Fract.*10, Pl.*Ti.*75b: Sup., τὰ -ώτατα τῶν ἀνθρωπίνων X.*Mem* 1.4.16. Adv. -ίως dub. l. in Hp.*Ep.*17. 2. *long-lived,* Arist.*HA*629ᵇ32, al.: Comp. -ώτερος Pl.*Phd.*87c, Arist.*HA*613ᵃ25, Thphr.*CP*5.18.4: Sup. -ώτατος, αἷμα Call.*Del.*282, cf. Dam.*Pr.* 23. **-χρονιότης,** ητος, ἡ, *long duration,* Phld.*Herc.*1251.4, Ptol. *Tetr.*10, etc.; *longevity,* Phld.*Sign.*17, Sch.Ar.*Av.*604; *keeping quality,* Thphr.*Od.*19. **-χρονος,** ον, later form for πολυχρόνιος, Jo.Gaz.*Ecphr.*2.211. **-χροος,** ον, contr. **-χρους,** ουν, (χρόα) *many-coloured, variegated,* φάρμακα Emp.23.3, cf. Arist.*Pr.*963ᵇ37, Opp.*C.*1.348; ἄνθρωπος π. τὰ ὄμματα Arist.*HA*492ᵃ5: poet. **πουλ-** Opp.*C.*4.389. **-χρῡσος,** ον, *rich in gold,* of persons, cities, etc., Μυκήνη Il.11.46, cf. S.*El.*9; Ὄλυμπος B.10.4; δῶμα, of Delphi, Pi.*P.* 4.53; of Dolon, Il.10.315; Γύγης Archil.25.1, cf. A.*Pers.*3 (anap.), etc.: rarely in Prose, π. ἀνήρ X.*Cyr.*3.2.25, cf. Ph.2.30, al., Jul.*Or.*2. 93d; φρούριον Plu.*Pomp.*36 (Sup.); of Croesus, Pittac.ap.D.L.1.81 (Sup.). II. as epith. of Aphrodite, = χρύσεος, Hes.*Op.*521, *Fr.* 143.3, *h.Ven.*1. **-χρώμᾰτος,** ον, = πολύχροος, Pl.ap.Poll.4.48, Str. 15.1.22, Ph.1.383. **-χρωμος,** ον, = foreg., Man.5.248, Hdn.*Epim.* 153, Zos.Alch.p.107 B. **-χρως,** ων, = πολ χροος, Arist.*GA*779ᵇ 9. **-χῡλος,** ον, *with much juice,* Ath.Med.ap.Orib.1.2.14, Xenocr. ib.2.58.50. 2. = πολύχοος I. 2, Dsc.1.26, 5.96 (v.l. -χυτος). **-χῡμος,** ον, = foreg. I, Xenocr.ap.Orib.2.58.117 (Comp.). **-χῠτος,** ον, (χέω) *capable of great diffusion,* Orib.*Syn.*2.56.77; *widely diffused,* ἀρετή Plu. *Cat.Mi.*25; σχῆμα Id.2.423a, etc. **-χώρητος,** ον, *capacious, spacious,* κόσμος *PMag.Par.*1.2828, cf. Sch.Theoc.13.46; *of large area,* Sophon. *in de An.*9.17 (Sup.): Comp., *of larger area* or *of greater cubic content,* Simp.*in Cael.*414.15, *in Ph.*291.18: Sup., Damian.*Opt.*3. **-χωρία,** ἡ, *comprehensiveness,* ὀ ομάτων Ptol.*Judic.*p.8 B. ⊛ **-χωρος,** ον, *spacious, extensive,* Ἀΐδης Luc.*Luct.*2: Sup., Gal.*UP*8.11. II. π. ἀριθμοί *large,* 'round' numbers, Vett.Val.274.27. III. *divided into many squares* or *compartments,* Puchstein *Epigr.Gr.*p.9. **-χωστος,** ον, *high-heaped,* τάφος A.*Ch.*351 (lyr.). **-ψάμᾰθος** [ψᾰ], ον, *very sandy,* Id.*Supp.*870 (leg. πολύψαμμον, lyr.), Opp.*C.*1.374. **-ψαμμος,** ον, = foreg., ψάμαθος dub. l. in *AP*7.214 (Arch., fort. **πολυξάντους**). **-ψεκτος,** ον, (ψέγω) *much-blamed,* Eust.1962.18. **-ψευδόκαυχος,** ον, *boasting much falsely, Et.Gud.*270.28. **-ψηφία,** ἡ, *number* or *diversity of votes,* Th.3.10, Ph.2.567. **-ψήφῐς,** ῐδος, ὁ, ἡ, *with many pebbles, pebbly,* of river-beds or the sea-shore, πολυψήφιδα παρ' Ἕρμον Orac.ap.Hdt.1.55; ῥηγμὶν θαλάσσης Naumach.ap.Stob. 4.31ᶜ.76: Ep. **πουλυ-,** Κυρήνη Opp.*C.*1.292. **-ψηφος,** ον, = foreg., Sch.Call.*Jov.*26, Sch.Nic.*Th* 950. II. *with many votes,* Luc.*Harm.* 3 (Sup.). **-ψογος,** ον, *very scandalous,* Ptol.*Tetr.*172, *Cat.Cod.Astr.* 8(4).195. **-ωδῠνία,** ἡ, *great anguish,* E.*Ep.*4.2, Suid. ⊛ **-ώδῠνος,** ον, (ὀδύνη) *very painful,* ἰός Theoc.25.238; λαμπὰς [ἔρωτος] *APl.*4. 201.3 (Marian.); ἄλγος *IG*7.583.5 (Tanagra, v A.D.). II. Pass., *suffering great pain* or *distress, APl.*4.111 (Glauc.); Νίκη *AP*11.386 (Pall.).

**πολῠωνῠμ-έω,** *have many names,* Eust.8.26. **-ία,** poet. **-ίη,** ἡ, *multitude of names,* Democr.26, Call.*Dian.*7. **-ος,** ον, poet. **πουλυ-** *Mém. Miss. Arch. Perse* 20.91 (Susa, Hymn to Apollo): (ὄνομα):— *having many names,* Pl.*Phdr.*238a, Arist.*HA*489ᵃ2. 2. of divinities, *worshipped under many names, h.Cer.*18, B.*Epigr.*1.1, S.*Ant.*1115 (lyr.), Ar.*Th.*320 (lyr.), Theoc.15.109; εἷς ὢν ὁ θεὸς π. ἐστιν Arist. *Mu.*401ᵃ12; π. δύναμις Secund.*Sent.*3. 3. Gramm., π., τό, = συνώνυμον, Speus.ap.Porph.ap.Simp. *in Cat.*36.27, Porph. *in Cat.* 69.1 (pl.), Sch.D.T.p.390 H. II. *of great name,* i.e. *famous, h.Ap.*82, Hes.*Th.*785, Pi.*P.*1.17. III. π., τό, = ἑλξίνη, Dsc.4. 85.

**πολῠ-ώνῠχος,** ον, *with many claws,* of birds, Arist.*HA*504ᵃ5; τὰ π. (sc. ζῷα) *dividing the hoof,* Id.*Pr.*895ᵃ38. **-ωπής,** ές, (ὀπή) *with many holes* or *meshes,* λίνον *AP*6.27 (Theaet.); ὀθόνης κόλπος Nic. *Al.*323; πολυωπέες ὄμπναι, i.e. honeycombs, ib.450:—late poet. fem. **πολυωπέτις,** ιδος, Max.584. II. (ὤψ) *many-eyed,* ποιμένα τοῦ Ἄργου -έστερον Eun.*Hist.*p.266 D. **-ωπός,** όν, = foreg. I, δίκτυον Od.22.386; λίνου π. ὄλεθρος Opp.*H.*3.579, cf. Tryph.223.

**πολῠωρ-έω,** (ὥρα) *treat with much care,* c. gen., *Supp.Epigr.*2.257. 12 (Delph., iii B.C.), *PCair.Zen.*38.23 (iii B.C.), D.L.6.9: Dor. aor. ἐπολυώρη'ε *IG*4.497.8 (Mycenae, ii B.C.): later c. acc., πεπολυωρηκότες τὴν Ὀλυμπιάδα *having observed* her *carefully,* D.S.18.65; ὑπέρ τινων *PCair.Zen.*462.10 (iii B.C.): abs., Test.ap.Aeschin.1.5, Corn.*ND*1; *esteem highly,* Carneisc.*Herc.*1027.16:—Pass., Aen.Tact.22.17: ὑπό τινος Arist.*Rh.*1378ᵇ34; πεπολυωρῆσθαι *to have been cared for, PCair. Zen.*50 (iii B.C.). **-ητικός,** ή, όν, *attentive, careful,* θεός Plu.2. 276a. **-ία,** ἡ, *care, attention, consideration,* opp. ὀλιγωρία, Chrysipp. *Stoic.*3.187, *Delph.*3(2).88 (iii B.C.), *PCair.Zen.*527 (iii B.C.), etc.

**πολύ-ωρος,** ον, (ὥρα) *many years old,* οἶνος Dius ap.Stob.4.21. 17. **-ώροφος,** ον, (ὀροφή) *of many roofs* or *stories,* Eust.640.1:—written **πολυόροφος** in Str.16.2.13. **-ωτος,** ον, (οὖς) *many-eared,* Ps.-Luc.*Philopatr.*3. **-ωφελής,** ές, (ὄφελος) *very useful,* Arist.*EN* 1095ᵃ11, D.H.1.36, etc.: Comp., *SIG*1164 (Dodona, iv/iii B.C.): Sup., λογισμός Ael.*NA Praef.* Adv. -λῶς, τῇ πόλει Ar.*Th.*304: Sup. -έστατα X.*Eq.Mag.*1.1. **-ώψ,** ῶπος, ὁ, ἡ, = πολυωπός, κίστη *AP*6. 65 (Paul. Sil.), cf. 9.765 (Id.).

**πολφός** (on the accent v. Hdn.Gr.1.225), ὁ, mostly in pl., a sort of *farinaceous food,* eaten with porridge, Ar.*Fr.*681, Metag.16; dub. in *BMus.Inscr.*968A17 (Cos).

**πολφοφάκη** [ᾰ], ἡ, *dish of macaroni and pulse,* Poll.6.61.

**πόλφυκα·** τὸν κόγχον, Hsch.

⊛ **πόλχος,** ὁ, coin-inscription of doubtful meaning, *BMus.Cat.Coins Crete* p.23 (Cnossos, ii/i B.C.).

**πόμα,** τό, v. πῶμα. II. = φοῖνιξ, cj. in Dsc.1.109.

**πομάτιον,** τό, Dim. of foreg. I, Gloss. in *POxy.*1802.36.

**πομμοῦσαν·** ὁμιλεῖν, Hsch.

**πομπ-ᾰγωγέω,** = πομπὴν ἄγω, Hsch. (πομφ- cod.). **-ᾰγωγία,** ἡ, *conduct of a procession, POxy.*2127.6 (ii A.D.). **-αῖος,** α, ον, *escorting, conducting,* π. οὖρος a *fair* wind, Pi.*P.*1.34; so of a ship, εἰς ὅρμους. ἐλάτα π. E.*IA*1322 (lyr.). II. epith. of Hermes, *who escorted the souls of the dead* to the nether world, A.*Eu.*91, S.*Aj.*832, E.*Med.*759 (anap.), D.L.8.31. **-εία,** ἡ, *leading in procession, solemn procession,* Plb.30.25.2. II. *abuse, ribaldry,* such as was allowed to those who took part in the processions at the festivals of Dionysus and Demeter, D.18.11, Men.*Per.Fr.*4 (pl.): metaph., ἡ τοῦ δαίμονος καθ' ἡμῶν π. the *mock* that fate makes of us, Hld.5.6, cf. Philostr.*VS*2.27. ⊛ **-εῖον,** τό, (πομπή) *vessel employed in solemn processions,* mostly pl., And.4. 29, D.22.48, 69; πομπείων ἐπιστάται *IG*1².379.7, cf. Philoch.124; at Rome, *the apparatus of a triumph,* D.C.43.42; πομπεία σκευή is dub. (leg. πομπεῖα [σκεύη]) in D.S.12.40: sg., of a wax *bust* of Cleopatra *carried in triumph,* D.C.51.21; πομπείου τυχεῖν to have one's *image carried in procession,* Aristid.2.38 J. II. at Athens, *storehouse where such vessels were kept,* D.34.39, D.L.2.43, 6.22. **-εύς,** gen. έως, Ion. ῆος, ὁ, Att. pl. πομπῆς Pl.Com.85: (πομπός):—*one who attends* or *escorts, conductor, guide,* Od.3.325, 376; of favourable winds, οὖροι νηῶν πομπῆες 4.362. 2. *one who takes part in a procession,* Th.6.58, *IG*2². 334.14. **-ευσις,** εως, ἡ, = πομπεία I, Pl.*Lg.*949c (pl.). **-ευτήριος,** α, ον, *of* or *for a procession,* D.H.*Dem.*32. ⊛ **-ευτής,** οῦ, ὁ, = πομπεύς 2, Id.7.72: as Adj., π. ἵππος πάντα διδάσκεται Iamb.post Polem.p.50 Hinck. 2. *organizer* or *marshal of a procession,* Luc. *Nec.*16. **-ευτικός,** ή, όν, *processional,* of the foot παλιμβάκχειος, Sch.Heph.pp.216, 302 C. ⊛ **-εύω,** poet. Iterat. πομπεύεσκε Theoc.2. 68: (πομπή):—*conduct, escort,* as a guide, Od.13.422, Erinn.1; ἐν δέπαϊ Ἠελίου Antim.*Eleg.*5; Ἑρμοῦ τέχνην π. play the part of Hermes, S.*Tr.*620. 2. *carry* sinning Vestal Virgins *in procession,* D.H.8. 89. II. *lead a procession,* π. πομπήν Test.ap.D.21.22, Plb.6.39.9, etc.; κατὰ κάλλος π. *Michel*731.27 (Ilium, ii B.C.), cf. *OGI*309.9 (Teos, ii B.C., prob.):—Pass., *to be led in triumph* (at Rome), Str.7.1.4, Plu. *Aem.*34, *Flam.*14, etc. b. metaph., *parade ostentatiously,* [ἀρχήν] Arr.*Epict.*3.24.118; opp. ὑποσταλμένως ἀλληγορῆσαι, Heraclit.*All* 29: —Pass., Phld.*Rh.*1.223 S. 2. abs., *take part in a procession, IG* 1².40.25, D.21.180, Arist.*IA*712ᵃ34, Isyll.17, 21, Theoc. l.c., *IG*12 (8).150.26 (Samothrace, iii B.C.), D.S.16.92; π. μετὰ τῶν ἱππέων Thphr.*Char.*21.8; of sinning Vestal Virgins carried on a bier, D.H. 2.67; of prisoners led in triumph, Str.7.1.4, 15.3.15; but of the victorious general, Procop.*Vand.*2.9: metaph., *make a fine show,* τοῖς προσώποις Cic.*Att.*13.32.3; *swagger, strut,* Luc.*DMeretr.*12.2. III. *abuse with ribald jests* (cf. πομπεία II), opp. κατηγορεῖν, D.18.124: abs., Phld.*Lib.*p.42 O.; εἴς τινα Philostr.*Her.*2.10. **-ή,** ἡ, (πέμπω) *conduct, escort,* θεῶν ὑπ' ἀμύμονι πομπῇ Il.6.171; οὔτε θεῶν πομπῇ οὔτε θνητῶν ἀνθρώπων Od.5.32; π. δόμεναι 9.518; πομπᾷ Διὸς ξενίου A.*Ag.*748 (lyr.); θείῃ π. χρεώμενος Hdt.1.62, cf. 3.77; οὐρία π., of a fair wind, E.*IA* 352 (troch.); also ἀνταίαν πνεῦσαι π. ib.1324 (lyr.): in pl., Ἀπολλωνίαις πομπαῖς Pi.*P.*5.91; Ζεφύροιο πομπαί Id.*N.*7.29; βασιλέως ὑπὸ πομπαῖς A.*Pers.*58 (anap.), etc. b. concrete, *an escort,* ὑπ' εὔφρονι πομπᾷ Id.*Eu.*1034 (lyr.). 2. *sending away, sending home,* ἔπειτα δὲ καὶ περὶ πομπῆς μνησόμεθα Od.7.191, cf. 8.545, etc.; ὄφρα τάχιστα πομπῆς καὶ νόστοιο τύχῃς 6.290; τεῦχε δὲ πομπὴν 10.18, cf. Pi.*P.*4.164; πομπᾶς ἁγεμών E.*Rh.*229 (lyr.). 3. *mission,* θεοῦ τινος πομπῇ *sent by . .,* of a dream, Hdt.7.16.β', cf. Pl.*R.*383a; κατὰ σημείων πομπάς ib.382e: simply, *sending,* ξύλων Th.4.108. II. *solemn procession,* Διονύσῳ πομπὴν ἐποιοῦντο Heraclit.15; ὑπὸ πομπῆς *in procession,* Hdt.2.45; σὺν πομπῇ Id.7.197; πομπὴν πέμπειν Id.5.56, Ar.*Av.*849, Th.6.56; τὰς π. πεμπειν, πομπεῦσαι, D.4.26, *IG*2².1028.14; τῆς π., ὅπως ἂν ὡς κάλλιστα πεμφθῇ ib.1$^2$.84.26; τινι in honour of a god, Ar.*Ach.*248; μήλων κνισάεσσα πομπά the flesh of sheep for sacrifice carried in *procession*, Pi.*O.*7.80. **b.** at Rome, *triumphal procession*, Plb.6.39.9, etc.: generally, τείνειν π. lead a long *procession*, of a military expedition, A.*Th.*613. **2.** metaph., *pomp, parade*, π. καὶ ῥημάτων ἀγλαϊσμός Pl.*Ax.*369d. **3.** personified, on a vase, *AJA* 30.424. **-ηγορῶσι·** προπέμπουσι, Hsch. ⊛ **-ικός,** ή, όν, *of* or *for a solemn procession*, π. ἵππος a horse *of state*, X.*Eq.*11.1, cf. Poll.1.211; ἀσπίδια, ζεῦγος, *IG* 2$^2$.1424a.395, 2311.65; στέμμα D.S.18.26; ἅρμα D.C.56.34; μέλος Plu.*Aem.*33, etc. **2.** metaph., *stately, magnificent*, ὄψις Id.*Mar.*22; of literary style, *impressive*, Phld.*Rh.*2.96S., D.H.*Is.*19, Longin.8.3. Adv. -κῶς Id.32.5, etc. **-ίλος** [ῐ], ὁ, a fish *which follows ships, Gasterosteus ductor* L., Erinn.1, A.R.*Fr.*9, et alii ap. Ath.7.282e, al. ⊛ **-ῐμος,** ον, also α, ον E.*Hipp.*578 (lyr.), *Ph.*1711 (lyr.): (πομπή):—*conducting, escorting, guiding*, A.*Th.*371, 855; π. κῶπαι S.*Tr.*560; πνοαί E.*Hec.*1290, *Hel.*1073; π. ὁ δαίμων Id.*Ph.*984; π. ἔχειν τινά ib.1711 (lyr.): c. gen., φίλων π. χώρα a land *that lends escort* to friends, Id.*Med.*848 (lyr.); νόστου πόμπιμον τέλος the *home-sending* end of one's return, i.e. one's safe return home, Pi.*N.*3.25. **II.** Pass., *sent, conveyed*, τινι to one, S.*Tr.*872, cf. E.*Hipp.*578 (lyr.). **-ιος,** α, ον, *conveyed by transmission*, Plot.6.5.10. **-ός,** ὁ, (πέμπω) *conductor, escort, guide*, Il.13.416, 24.153, 182, Od.4.162, Hdt.1.121, 122; epith. of Hermes (cf. πομπαῖος), A.*Pers.*626 (anap.), S.*OC* 1548; πομποί *attendants, guards*, ib.723: fem. πομπός, ἡ, *conductress*, Od.4.826. **2.** c. gen. rei, τῆσδε προστροπῆς π. *conveyor, carrier of* these suppliant offerings, A.*Ch.*86; π. ἴσθι τῶν ἐσθλῶν ἄνω (for πέμπε τὰ ἐσθλά) ib.147. **3.** *messenger, envoy*, S.*OT* 289, *OC* 70, *Tr.*617. **II.** as Adj., π. ἀρχαί *conducting* chiefs, A.*Ag.*124 (lyr.); π. [ἄνεμος] Ael.*NA* 3.13; πῦρ π. *signal, beacon* fire, A.*Ag.*299.

**πομποστολέω,** (στέλλω) *conduct a procession*, *IG* 2.1325, 1358. **2.** c. acc., *lead* or *carry in procession*, πομποστολεῖται τὰ ἱερά Str.14.2.23; π. τὸ σκάφος Luc.*Am.*11. **b.** metaph., *make a pompous display of*, τὰ μηδεμιᾶς ἄξια σπουδῆς Ph.2.70.

**πομφολῠγ-ηρόν,** τό, *a plaster containing* πομφόλυξ IV, Paul.Aeg.7.17. **-ίζω,** *bubble up* like boiling water, Dsc.1.68.4, 5.74, Simp.*in Ph.*460.22 (τονθ- shd. be read in Pherecr.108.4).

**πομφολῠγοπάφλασμα,** ατος, τό, *noise made by bubbles rising*, Ar.*Ra.*249 (pl.).

**πομφολῠγ-όω,** *cause to bubble* or *boil*, τὴν θάλατταν Arist.*Pr.*931$^b$34:—Pass., *form bubbles*, Herod.Med. in *Rh.Mus.*58.76, Dsc.5.126. **-ώδης,** ες, *like bubbles*, Archig.ap.Gal.8.509, 931. **-ωτός,** ή, όν, *provided with* πομφόλυγες II, περόναι rivets *with bosses*, Ph.*Bel.*66.44.

**πομφολύζω** or -ύσσω, *bubble* or *boil up*, πομφόλυξαν δάκρυα tears *gushed forth*, Pi.*P.*4.121.

⊛ **πομφόλυξ,** ῠγος, ἡ (ὁ, ἡ, acc. to Gal.13.639): (πομφός):—*bubble*, Hp.*Aph.*7.34, Pl.*Ti.*66b, 83d, Thphr.*Metaph.*15, etc.; πομφόλυγες are the constituent parts of ἀφρός, Arist.*GA* 735$^b$12. **II.** *boss of a shield*, = ὀμφαλός, Hsch.; as architectural ornament, *IG* 1$^2$.373.254 (pl.). **III.** *ornament for the head* worn by women, Ar.*Fr.*320.13, *IG* 2$^2$.1524.50. **IV.** *zinc oxide*, Dsc.5.75, Paul.Aeg.7.17.

**πομφός,** ὁ, *blister* on the skin, Hp.*Mul.*2.118, *Morb.*2.70. (Cf. πομφόλυξ, πομφολύζω; perh. akin to πέμφιξ.)

⊛ **πον-έω, πονέομαι,** **A.** in early Greek only Med. πονέομαι, inf. -έεσθαι Il.10.116: impf. ἐπονεῖτο, Ep. πονεῖτο 9.12: fut. πονήσομαι 23.159, Hp.*Mul.*1.4, later πονέσομαι Luc.*Asin.*9: aor. ἐπονησάμην, Ep. πονήσατο Il.9.348, (δια-) Pl.*Lg.*966c, X.*Eq.*5.10; ἐπονήθην f.l. in E.*Hel.*1509 (lyr.), (δια-) Isoc.15.267: pf. πεπόνημαι, Ion.3pl. -έαται Hdt.2.63, Ep. -ήαται Arat.82, Att. -ηνται Pl.*Phlb.*58e: plpf. πεπόνητο Il.15.447, Ep.3pl. -ήατο A.R.2.263: **I.** abs., *work hard*, ὡς ἐπονεῖτο Il.2.409; ὄφελεν πονέεσθαι λισσόμενος he ought *to suffer toil* in praying, 10.117; ὅπλα.., τοῖς ἐπονεῖτο with which *he did his work*, of Hephaestus, 18.413, cf. Od.16.13; περὶ δόρπα..πονέοντο *were busied* about their supper, Il.24.444, cf. Hdt.2.63, Pl.*Phlb.*58e; so πεπόνητο καθ' ἵππους *was busy* with the horses, of a charioteer, Il.15.447; πονέοντο κατὰ κρατερὴν ὑσμίνην *were toiling* in the fight, 5.84, etc.; hence πονεῖσθαι alone = μάχεσθαι, 4.374, 13.288; π. τινός *to be busy* with.., Arat.82, cf. 758. **2.** *suffer* from illness, *be sick*, Th.2.51. **II.** c. acc., *work hard at, make* or *do with pains* or *care*, τύμβον Il.23.245; ταῦτ' ἐπονεῖτο ἰδυίῃσι πραπίδεσσι 18.380; ὅπλα..πονησάμενοι κατὰ νῆα Od.11.9; πονησάμενος τὰ ἃ ἔργα 9.250, cf. Il.9.348, Hes.*Op.*432 (sc. ἄροτρα); πονεύμενος ἕρκος ἀλωῆς Mosch.4.100; πεπονήατο δαῖτα γέροντι A.R.2.263.

**B.** after Hom., the act. form πονέω prevails: fut. πονήσω A.*Pr.*344, Pl.*R.*410b, Hp.*Mul.*1.2, 5; later πονέσω Arist.*Mech.*856$^b$9, *Lyr.Alex.Adesp.*37.3, Lxx *Is.*19.10, al., and in codd. of Hp.*Aph.*4.32: aor. ἐπόνησα, Dor. -ᾱσα, E.*Hipp.*1369 (anap.), Pl.*R.*462d, Hp.*Acut.*46, Theoc.15.80; poet. πόνησα Pi.*N.*7.36; later ἐπόνεσα Lxx 1*Ki.*23.21, al., Ph.*Bel.*58.1, al., Polyaen.3.10.6, etc., and in codd. of Hp.*Coac.*489, *Morb.*1.4, 14: pf. πεπόνηκα Ar.*Pax* 820, X.*Cyr.*4.5.22, Hp.*Vict.*2.66; later πεπόνεκα *PMich.Zen.*104.3 (iii B.C.): plpf. ἐπεπονήκει Th.7.38:—Pass., aor. ἐπονήθην (ἐξ-) Id.6.31; Dor. subj. πονᾱθῇ Pi.*O.*6.11: pf. πεπόνημαι S.*Tr.*985 (anap.), Pl.*Phdr.*232a (v. infr. I.3): **I.** intr., *toil, labour*, περὶ λήϊον Hdt.2.14; ἐς ἄκαιρα πονεῖν Thgn.919; πόνει μετ' εὐκλείας Anon.ap.Stob.3.1.173 = *JHS* 27.63 (Cyzicus, iv/iii B.C.); ἄλλως, μάτην π., *labour* in vain, S.*OT* 1151, E.*HF* 501: c. acc., τὰ μηδὲν ὠφελοῦντα μὴ πόνει μάτην do not *labour at*.., A.*Pr.*44; ἀνήνυτα π. Pl.*R.*531a: rarely of things, τίς..αἶνος ἐπ' ἀνδρὶ θείῳ..πονήσει; A.*Ag.*1550 (lyr., dub., leg. αἶνον). **2.** c. acc. cogn., π. πόνον *go through, suffer* toil, Id.*Pers.*682, E.*Hec.*779, cf. S.*Ph.*1419, E.*Hipp.*1369 (anap.), Pl.*R.*410b, etc.; περὶ τῶν παθημάτων ὧν νοσέουσί τε καὶ πονέουσι Hp.*VM* 2, etc.; ἅμιλλαν ποδοῖν E.*IA* 212 (lyr.); π. πολλά Id.*Supp.*577: with modal words, π. τινί *suffer in* or *by* a thing, Pi.*N.*7.36; δίψῃ A.*Pers.*484; ὑπὸ χειμῶνος Antipho 2.2.1; τῇ κυήσει Arist.*HA* 570$^b$3; εἰρεσίᾳ Polyaen. l.c.: c. acc. partis, πεπόνηκα..τὼ σκέλει my legs *ache*, Ar.*Pax* 820; π. τὰς κεφαλάς, τοὺς ὀφθαλμούς, τὰ γόνατα, *have a pain* in.., Arist.*HA* 557$^a$10, *Pr.*959$^b$21, 882$^b$25: with modal dat. added, π. πλευρὰν πικρᾷ γλωχῖνι S.*Tr.*681: abs., *labour under sickness, suffer*, Hp.*VM* 8; *suffer damage*, ἅπαν ἂν συμπαθὲς ἦν ἑνὸς μορίου πονήσαντος Arist.*PA* 690$^b$4; also, *suffer pain*, ἀεὶ π. τὸ ζῷον Anaxag.ap.eund.*EN* 1154$^b$7; of an army, *to be hard-pressed, suffer*, Th.5.73, X.*Cyr.*1.4.21, etc.; of ships, Th.7.38; of implements, arms, etc., *to be worn out, spoilt*, or *damaged*, D.18.194, Plb.3.49.11, *Inscr.Délos* 442*B*204, al. (ii B.C.): τὰ σπαρτία ἧττον πονέσει Arist.*Mech.* l.c.; ῥίζαι πεπονηκυῖαι Thphr.*HP* 3.7.1; of buildings, *to be dilapidated*, *PEnteux.*6.3 (iii B.C.), etc. **3.** Pass., impers., οὐκ ἄλλως αὐτοῖς πεπόνηται, = πεπονήκασι, Pl.*Phdr.*232a. **II.** trans., **1.** c. acc. pers., *afflict, distress*, Pi.*P.*4.151, cj. in *Anacreont.*33.14:—Pass., *to be afflicted* or *worn out, suffer greatly*, πεπονημένος ὀδύναις S.*Tr.*985 (anap.); πόλεως πονουμένης τῷ πολέμῳ Th.4.59; τόν τε θνῄσκοντα καὶ τὸν πονούμενον Id.2.51. **b.** Pass., *to be trained* or *educated*, δοκεῖ ὁ κατ' ἀλήθειαν πολιτικὸς πεπονῆσθαι περὶ [τὴν ἀρετήν] Arist.*EN* 1102$^a$8; πεπονημένην ἔχειν τὴν ἕξιν Id.*Pol.*1335$^b$8, cf. Theoc.13.14; πεπονημένον ὑπό μου though he *owes his training* to me, *PCair.Zen.*378.16 (iii B.C.). **2.** c. acc. rei, *gain by toil* or *labour*, [χρήματα] X.*An.*7.6.41:—Pass., *to be won* or *achieved by toil*, καλὸν εἴ τι πονᾱθῇ Pi.*O.*6.11, cf. *P.*9.93. **b.** Pass., of meats, *to be dressed, cooked*, Ptol.Euerg.9J., Phld.*Mort.*24; ἄρτος πεπονημένος *specially prepared*, Sor.1.94.—The rule of Choerob.*in Theod.*2.137H., *EM* 130.3, that when πονέω means *toil*, the fut. and aor. are πονήσω, ἐπόνησα, when *suffer pain*, πονέσω, ἐπόνεσα, is not borne out by the examples (v. supr.).—The fut. Med. κατα-πονήσομαι is used as trans. by D.S.11.15; so aor. Pass. πονήθη in *IG* 9(1).867.6 (Corc., vii/vi B.C.); and the intr. and trans. senses are united in *Anacreont.*33.14 (cj.), 15.

**πόνημα,** ατος, τό, *that which is wrought, work*, μελισσᾶν E.*IT* 165 (anap.); *a work, book*, *AP* 4.3.42 (pl., Agath.), 9.166 (Pall.).

**πονήρ-ευμα,** ατος, τό, in pl., *villainies*, D.19.257, D.H.6.84: sg., Jul.*Or.*3.115a. **II.** Medic., in sg., *bad state* or *condition*, Gal.19.138. **-εύομαι,** *to be in a bad state*, Hp.*Coac.*194; πονηρευόμενα ἕλκη *malignant* ulcers, Dsc.1.106, cf. Ruf.ap.Orib.45.30.31. **II.** *act wickedly, play the knave*, Heraclit.125$^a$, Arist.*Rh.*1411$^a$17, Men.*Epit.*133; οἱ πεπονηρευμένοι D.19.32, cf. Phld.*Rh.*1.43S., Plu.*Cat.Ma.*9, etc.: c. dat., *towards* or *against*.., Thd.*Su.*61: with Preps., ἐν τοῖς προφήταις Lxx 1*Ch.*16.22; κατ' ἐμοῦ Thd.*Su.*43: also c. acc., τινα Lxx *Ec.*7.22(23); *intend maliciously*, c. inf., ib.*De.*19.19; τοῦ ἀποκτεῖναί τινα ib.*Ge.*37.18, al. ⊛ **-ία,** ἡ, *bad state* or *condition*, ὀφθαλμῶν Pl.*Hp.Mi.*374d; ἡ τοῦ σώματος π. Id.*R.*609c; π. ψυχῆς ibid. **II.** in moral sense, *wickedness, vice, knavery*, ἡ μωρία..ἀδελφὴ τῆς π. ἔφυ S.*Fr.*925, cf. Ar.*Th.*868, Lys.22.16; εἰς τὴν π. πάλιν τρέπεται turns again to *vice*, X.*Cyr.*7.5.75: in pl., *knavish tricks, rogueries*, D.21.19, Arist.*Rh.*1389$^a$18. **2.** *baseness, cowardice*, E.*Cyc.*645, Lys.14.9. **3.** with a political connotation, *mob-rule*, Th.8.47.

**πονηρο-δῐδάσκᾰλος,** ον, *teaching wickedness*, Str.7.3.8. **-κάρδιος,** ον, *bad-hearted*, *Gloss.* **-κρᾰτέομαι,** Pass., *to be governed by the* πονηροί III, Arist.*Pol.*1294$^a$2, D.H.8.31. **-κρᾰτία,** ἡ, *government by the* πονηροί III, ib.5. **-λογία,** ἡ, *bad reasoning*, Arist.*Top.*164$^b$13. **-πολις,** εως, ἡ, *Roguetown*, a nickname given to some place by Philip, Theopomp.Hist.107, Plu.2.520b.

**πονηρός,** ά, όν, in physical sense, *oppressed by toils*, πονηρότατος καὶ ἄριστος, of Heracles, Hes.*Frr.*138, 139. **2.** of things, *toilsome, painful, grievous*, ἔργα Hom.*Epigr.*14.20; νούσων πονηρότερον Thgn.274; φορτίον Ar.*Pl.*352. **II.** *in bad case, in sorry plight, useless, good-for-nothing*, σύμμαχοι ib.220, cf. *Nu.*102; στράτευμα X.*An.*3.4.34; ἰατρός Antipho 4.2.4 (v.l. for μοχθηρός); κύων, ἱππάριον, Pl.*Euthd.*298d, X.*Cyr.*1.4.19; δίαιτα, τροφή, σιτία, *injurious*, Pl.*R.*425e, *Lg.*735b, *Grg.*464d, etc.; π. ἕξις σώματος Id.*Ti.*86e; π. σῶμα, opp. χρηστόν, Id.*Prt.*313a, cf. *R.*341e; π. σκώμματα *sorry* jests, Ar.*Nu.*542; π. βούλευμα Id.*Lys.*517 (Comp.); π. πράγματα a *bad* state of things, Th.8.97, cf. 24; π. ἀρχὴ τῆς παιδείας a *bad* beginning, Aeschin.1.11; π. τὴν ναυτιλίαν ναυτίλλεσθαι Pl.*R.*551c; π. πολιτεία Arist.*Pol.*1294$^b$38. Adv., -ρῶς ἔχειν to be *in bad case*, Th.7.83, etc.; ἃ πονηρῶς ἔχει τῶν πραγμάτων Lys.14.35; π. διακεῖσθαι, διατεθῆναι, Isoc.19.12, D.59.55. **III.** in moral sense, *worthless, knavish*, φήμη, βίος, ζόη, A.*Ch.*1045, *Frr.*90, 401, etc.; οὐδεὶς ἑκὼν π. Epich.78; π. ἦθος Democr.192; πονηρὸς..κἀκ πονηρῶν *rogue* and son *of rogues*, Ar.*Eq.*336–7; ὦ πόνῳ πονηρέ, in a comic jingle, Id.*V.*466, cf. *Lys.*350; π. πόρρω τέχνης past master in *knavery*, Id.*V.*192; π. τοῖς φίλοις X.*Cyr.*8.4.33; πρὸς ἀλλήλους Id.*An.*7.1.39; π. λόγων ἀκρίβεια Antipho 3.3.3; πονηρότεροι σύμβουλοι Id.5.71; π. [ῥῆμα] *malicious*, *Ev.Matt.*5.11; τὰ π. *wickednesses*, X.*Cyr.*2.2.25; πονηρὰ δρᾶσαι E.*Hec.*1190; τὸ π. Lxx *De.*17.2; δόλῳ πονηρῷ, Lat. *dolo malo*, *SIG* 693.6 (Methymna, ii B.C.); ὁ π. the *evil one*, *Ev.Matt.*13.19; π. δαίμων *PLips.*34.8 (iv A.D.), etc. **2.** *base, cowardly*, S.*Ph.*437, etc.; π. χρώματα, i.e. the coward's hue, X.*Cyr.*5.2.34 (interpol.). **3.** with a political connotation, *of the baser sort*, E.*Supp.*424; οἱ λεγόμενοι π. Pl.*R.*519a; opp. καλοὶ κἀγαθοί, Isoc.15.100, 316, cf. Ar.*Eq.*186.—On the variation of accent, πονηρός and πόνηρος, v. μοχθηρός fin.

**πονηρόφθαλμος**, ον, *with evil* (i.e. *envious*) *eye*, Al.*Pr*.23.6.

**πονηρό-φῐλος**, ον, *fond of bad men*, π. ἡ τυραννίς Arist.*Pol*.1314$^a$ 1. **-ψῡχος**, ον, *of evil soul*, *Gloss*.

**πόν-ησις**, εως, ἡ, *toil, exertion*, D.L.6.70: pl., f. l. in Critias *Fr*.25.30. **-ητέον**, *one must toil*, Hp.*Insomn*.90, Isoc.15.285, Pl.*R*.504d, Men.*Mon*.735; μὴ πάντα ⟨χρόνον⟩ π. ἀνθρώποις Chor.*Brum*.8. **-ητικός**, ή, όν, *laborious*, ὁ τῶν γυναικῶν βίος Arist.*GA*775$^a$33; ὅσα π. τῶν ἀρρένων Id.*Long*.466$^b$12; *painstaking*, Gal.7.437. **-ικός**, ή, όν, *toilsome, hard-working*, D.L.7.170: Sup. -ώτατος ib.180. Adv. -κῶς, πιστῶς καὶ π. ὑπηρετῶν *IPE*1$^2$.39.15 (Olbia, ii A.D.): -ώτερον J.*AJ*11.8.3. II. *toilsome, oppressive*, Thd.*Pr*.15.1.

**πόννα**· τὸ γράφος ἢ μάγος, Hsch. **πόννος**· μάγος, Id.

**πονόεις**, εσσα, εν, *toilsome*, Man.4.373.

**πονοπαίκτωρ**, ορος, ὁ, *one that sports with danger*, Man.4.276.

❀ **πόνος**, ὁ, (πένομαι) *work*, esp. *hard work, toil*, in Hom. mostly of *the toil of war*, μάχης π. the *toil* of battle, Il.16.568; πόνος alone, = μάχη, 6.77, Od.12.117, al.; πόνον ἔχειν, = μάχεσθαι, Il.6.525, cf. 13.2, al.; ἀνδράσι δυσμενέεσσι π. καὶ δῆριν ἔθεντο 17.158; π. ἀνδρῶν Thgn.987; πόνοι Ἐνυαλίου Pi.*I*.6(5).54; ἐν τούτῳ τῷ π. ὁ πολέμαρχος διαφθείρεται in this *struggle* (at Marathon), Hdt.6.114; ἐν τοῖσι Τρωϊκοῖσι π. Id.9.27. 2. generally, *toil, labour*, ἐπεὶ παύσαντο πόνου Il.1.467, al.; π. ὀρνίθεσσι τιθείη cause *toil* to them, Hes.*Op*.470; π. λαβόντας incurring *toil*, Hdt.7.24; π. παρέχειν μανθάνοντι Pl.*R*.526c; μάταιος π. *labour* in vain, Id.*Ti*.40d; οἱ κατὰ τὰ σώματα π. Id.*Plt*.294e; π. συνεχής Democr.241; πολλῷ π. A.*Pers*.509; μετὰ πολλοῦ π. Pl.*Sph*.230a; σὺν π. X.*Cyn*.9.6; οὐ μακρῷ π. A.*Pr*.75; ἄνευ π. X.*Mem*.2.6.22; ἔχει πόνον πολύν involves much *trouble*, Ar.*Pax* 1216 (also εἰνάλιον π. ἐχοίσας σκευᾶς when the tackle *labours* in the sea, Pi.*P*.2.79): pl., π. ἑκούσιοι Democr.240. 3. of special kinds of labour, *bodily exertion, exercise*, στρατιωτικοὶ π. X.*Cyr*.3.3.9; of *exertions* in the games, Hes.*Sc*.305, Pi.*N*.4.1, *I*.4(3).47, etc.; γυμνάσια.., νεανιᾶν (prob.) πόνον *the scene of* youthful *labours*, E.*Hel*.211 (lyr.); εἰναλίοισι πόνοισι Theoc.21.39. 4. *work, task, business*, ἐπεὶ π. ἄλλος ἔπειγεν Od.11.54; *enterprise, undertaking*, S.*Ph*.864 (lyr.), etc. 5. *implements for labour, stock-in-trade*, οὗτος τοῖς ἁλιεῦσιν ὁ πᾶς πόνος Theoc.21.14; καὶ πόνος ἐντὶ θάλασσα the sea is their *workshop*, Mosch.*Fr*.1.10. II. *stress, trouble, distress, suffering*, Il.19.227; Τρώεσσι πόνον καὶ κήδε' ἔθηκεν 21.525; ἦ μὴν καὶ π. ἐστίν.. 2.291; ἐν τούτῳ τῷ π., of a storm, Hdt.7.190; ὁ Μηδικὸς [π.] the *trouble* from the Medes, Id.4.1; παῦροι ἐν πόνῳ πιστοί Pi.*N*.10.78: freq. in Trag., πόνος πόνῳ πόνον φέρει S.*Aj*.866 (lyr.); πόνον ἔχειν Id.*OC*232 (lyr.), etc.: in pl., *sufferings*, A.*Pr*.66, 328, etc.; πόνους πονεῖν (cf. πονέω B.I.2); διά τινα πόνους ἔχειν Ar.*Ec*.975 (lyr.); also of *disease*, κατέβαινεν ἐς τὰ στήθη ὁ π. Th.2.49; πλευρᾶς πόνοι καὶ θώρακος καὶ ἥπατος Dsc.1.2; ἰσχίων π. καὶ πλευρᾶς ib.73. 2. *pain*, esp. physical, δύο π. ἅμα γενομένων, μὴ κατὰ τὸν αὐτὸν τόπον, ὁ σφοδρότερος ἀμαυροῖ τὸν ἕτερον Hp.*Aph*.2.46, cf. Erot. s.v. πόνοι, Gal.17(2).699; π. ἐν κεφαλῇ Hp.*Acut*.(*Sp*.)40; ἐς τὰ ἄρθρα πόνοι Id.*Aph*.4.44.45, cf. Sor.1.27, al.; π. ἐς ἀμφοτέρας κνήμας Hp.*Epid*.1.26.γ', cf. δ', al., Lxx *Ge*.34.25; distd. from λύπη (pain in general), Alex.Aphr.*Quaest*.125.33; but sts. = λύπη, Epicur.*Ep*.3 p.65 U., *Sent.Vat*.4, *Fr*.442, Phld.*Mus*.p.72 K. III. *anything produced by work, a work*, μελισσᾶν τρητὸς π., of honey, Pi.*P*.6.54; ὑψηλὸς τεκτόνων π. A.*Fr*.357, cf. E.*Or*.1570; ὁ ἐμὸς ὠδίνων π., of a child, Id.*Ph*.30; so, πόνον ὀρταλίχων ὀλέσαντες, i.e. the nestlings, A.*Ag*.54 (anap.); τοὺς ἡμετέρους π. the *fruits of* our *labour*, X.*An*.7.6.9. IV. Πόνος personified as son of Eris, Hes.*Th*.226.

**πονοψῡχία**, ἡ, *distress of soul*, *Gloss*.

**Ποντάρχ-έω**, *hold office of* Ποντάρχης, *IGRom*.3.97 (Amisus), *OGI* 529.7 (Sebastopolis, ii A.D.). **-ης**, ου, ὁ, *president of the provincial council of Pontus*, *IGRom*.3.69, al., *OGI*531.10 (iii A.D.). II. epith. of Achilles at Olbia, *IPE*1$^2$.134, al. **-ία**, ἡ, *office of* Ποντάρχης, *IGRom*.3.1427 (Bithynia).

❀ **ποντ-ιάς**, άδος, ἡ, poet. fem. of πόντιος, ἅλμα Pi.*N*.4.36; γέφυρα π., i.e. the Isthmus, Id.*I*.4(3).20; π. αὔρα E.*Hec*.444 (lyr.); χελώνη Crates Com.29. ❀ **-ίζω**, *plunge* or *sink in the sea*, σκάφος A.*Ag*.1013 (lyr.):—Pass., ὁ ποντισθεὶς Μυρτίλος S.*El*.508 (lyr.).

**Ποντικός**, ή, όν, *from Pontus, Pontic*, Π. (sc. δένδρεον), τό, perh. *Prunus Padus*, Hdt.4.23; τάριχος Π. Cratin.40, cf. Gal.6.563; Π. μῦς a kind of *weasel*, Arist.*HA*600$^b$13, 632$^b$9; Π. ῥίζα, = γλυκύρριζα, Dsc.3.5; Π. κάρυον *hazel-nut*, Gal.6.355, cf. *PCair.Zen*.702.22 (iii B.C.); ῥέον Π. *rhubarb*, Julianus Alex.ap.Alex.Trall.12. II. Ποντικός (sc. μήν), ὁ, name of month at Gortyn, *GDI*5031 (*Riv.Fil*. 58.475).

**ποντίλιον**, *pons*, *Gloss*.

**ποντίλος**, ὁ, = ναυτίλος II, Arist.*HA*525$^a$21.

❀ **πόντ-ιος**, α, ον, also ος, ον E.*Alc*.595 (lyr.): (πόντος):—*of the sea*, epith. of Poseidon, *h.Hom*.22.3, S.*OC*1072 (lyr.), etc.; πόντιε E.*Andr*.1010 (lyr.); π. Θέτις, Νηρηΐδες, Pi.*N*.3.35, *P*.11.2; π. δάκη *sea monsters*, A.*Pr*.582 (lyr.); π. βόσκημα Id.*Fr*.275; π. ὕδωρ, πέλαγος, Pi.*O*.2.64, 7.56; κύματα, θύελλα, A.*Pr*.89, S.*OC*1659, etc.; ᾅδην π. πεφευγότες, i.e. death by drowning, A.*Ag*.667. b. π. ῥάκη, of sponges or fragments of such, *Trag.Adesp*.258. 2. *by the sea*, of places, Ἰσθμός, ἀκτή, Χρύση, Pi.*O*.8.48, A.*Pers*.449, S.*Ph*.269. 3. *in the sea*, of islands, Pi.*N*.8.18; esp. of those *far out to sea*, opp. πρόσγειοι, Arist.*Mete*.368$^b$33, cf. Thphr.*HP*4.6.2, 8.6.6; of ships, βάριδες A.*Pers*.553 (lyr.); ὅπλισμα E.*IA*253 (lyr.). 4. of persons, ἱκέτας δέχεσθαι ποντίους *from the sea*, Id.*Cyc*.300; ἀφιέναι πόντιον *into the sea*, Id.*Hec*.797. 5. *brought by sea* or *from beyond sea*, of iron, A.*Th*.940 (lyr.). **-ισμα**, ατος, τό, *that which is cast into the sea*, esp. as an offering, E.*Hel*.1548 (pl.). **-ιστής**, οῦ, ὁ, *one who casts into the sea*, Paus.8.52.2.

**ποντῐφεξ**, φῖκος, ὁ, *pontifex*, *SIG*857 (Eleusis, ii A.D.).

**ποντο-βαφής**, ές, (βάπτω) *dipped in the sea*, Jo.Gaz.*Ecphr*.2.88. **-βροχος**, ον, (βρέχω) *drowned in the sea*, Lxx 3*Ma*.6.4, Phot. **-γενής**, ές, (γενέσθαι) *seaborn*, Orph.*H*.55.2, 81.1:—fem. -γένεια, poet. -είη, ἡ, formed like ἀφρογένεια, Opp.*C*.1.33.

**ποντόθεν**, Adv. *from* or *out of the sea*, Il.14.395.

**ποντο-θήρης**, ου, ὁ, *one who fishes in the sea*, *AP*6.193 (Phal.?). **-κράτωρ** [ᾰ], ορος, ὁ, *lord of the sea*, Orph.*H*.17b.7. **-κύκη** [ῠ], ἡ, *woman who disturbs the sea*, i.e. *shrew*, prob. in *Com.Adesp*.893 (πρωτοκύκη cod. Phryn., παντοκύνη, παντογύνη codd. Arc.). **-μέδων**, οντος, ὁ, *lord of the sea*, of Poseidon, Pi.*O*.6.103, A.*Th*.131 (lyr.), E.*Hipp*.743 (lyr.), Ar.*V*.1532, *IG*1$^2$.706; σεισίχθονα π. Hes.(?) in *PMich*.11.17; of Priapus, *AP*10.16 (Theaet.):—heterocl. gen., ποντομέδοιο Ποσειδάωνος Orac.ap.St.Byz. s.v. Τρινακρία. **-ναύτης**, ου, ὁ, *seafarer*, S.*Fr*.555.

**πόντονδε**, Adv. *into the sea*, Od.9.495, 10.48, A.*Supp*.33 (anap.).

**ποντο-πᾰγής**, ές, (παγῆναι) *fixed, founded on the sea*, Nonn.*D*.41.15. **-πλάνητος** [ᾰ], ον, *roaming over the sea*, Orph.*H*.38.5. **-πλάνος** [ᾰ], ον, (πλάνη) = foreg., δελφῖνες, νῆες, ib.24.8, 75.6.

**ποντοπορ-εύω**, *pass over the sea*, Ep.inf. -έμεναι Od.5.277: elsewh. in part., πλέεν.. ποντοπορεύων ib.278, cf. 7.267: later in Med., Orac.ap. Plu.*Thes*.24. **-έω**, = foreg., νηῦς ποντοπορούσα *sea-sailing*, Od.11.11, cf. Lxx *Pr*.24.54(30.19), Q.S.7.397; *sail the open sea*, opp. a coasting voyage, Plu.*Dio*25; κύματα.. ποντοπόρει βιότου *AP*10.74 (Paul. Sil.). **-ος**, ον, *seafaring*, of ships, Il.1.439, 2.771, Od.12.69, S.*Ph*.721 (lyr.), *Aj*.250 (lyr.); ναῦται Hom.*Epigr*.8.1, cf. Opp.*C*.1.120; π. βοῦς Mosch.2.49.

**Ποντοποσειδῶν**, ῶνος, ὁ, *Sea-Poseidon*, Com. compd. in Ar.*Pl*.1050.

❀ **πόντος**, ὁ: Ep. gen. ἐκ ποντόφιν Od.24.83:—*sea*, esp. *open sea*, common from Hom. downwds., exc. in Prose, where it is chiefly used of special seas (v. infr. II); in the general sense, ὁπότε πνεύμα ἐκ πόντου εἴη Th.4.26, cf. Pl.*R*.611e, *Ti*.25a, Lxx *Ex*.15.5; π. ἀπείριτος, ἀπείρων, εὐρύς, μεγακήτης, Od.10.195, Il.1.350, 6.291, Od.3.158; π. ἠεροειδής, ἰοειδής, μέλας, οἶνοψ, 2.263, 11.107, Il.24.79, 23.316; π. ἀτρύγετος, ἰχθυόεις, 15.27, 19.378; opp. γαῖα, 8.479, etc.; κέλευθοι, πλάξ, πεδίον πόντου, Pi.*P*.4.195, 1.24, A.*Fr*.150 (anap.); π. ἁλὸς πολιῆς the *wide waters* of the grey brine, Il.21.59, Thgn.10, 106; πόντου γέφυρα, πύλαι, of the Isthmus, Pi.*N*.6.39, 10.27. 2. metaph., π. ἀγαθῶν Sophr.159; π. χρυσίου Phoen.1.2; ἐκπεσεῖν εἰς τὸν ἀνομοιότητος π. Pl.*Plt*.273d (ap.Dam.*Pr*.5). II. of special seas, π. Ἰκάριος, Θρηΐκιος, Il.2.145, 23.230; ὁ Αἰγαῖος π. Hdt.2.97, etc.; ὁ π. οὗτος Id.4.177 (v.l); Ἰόνιος, Σαρωνικός, Σικελός, E.*Tr*.225 (lyr.), *Hipp*.1200, *Cyc*.703: esp. π. Εὔξεινος, Id.*IT*125 (lyr., nisi leg. Ἄξεινος); ὁ Εὔξεινος π. Hdt.1.6, Th.2.96, 97 (called Ἄξεινος, E.*IT*218 (lyr.)); generally called simply ὁ Πόντος or Πόντος, A.*Pers*.878 (lyr.), Hdt.7.147, Ar.*V*.700, Arist.*Mete*.354$^a$14, al.; but Hdt. has also ὁ πόντος for *the sea*, 4.99, 177. 2. the country *Pontus* on the S. shore of the Black Sea, App.*Mith*.8, etc.: Adj. Ποντικός (q.v.). III. personified as son of Gaia, Hes.*Th*.132, 233 sq. (Cogn. with πάτος, q.v.)

**ποντο-τίνακτος** [ῐ], ον, *shaken by the sea*, Hom.*Epigr*.4.6 (Pierson for ποτνιάνακτον). ❀ **-φᾰρυξ**, ῠγος, ὁ, ἡ, = sq., *Com.Adesp*.1121. **-χάρυβδις** [ᾰ], εως, ἡ, *seagulf, whirlpool*, Com. epith. for a glutton, Hippon.85.1 (codd. Ath.). Cf. παντοχάρυβδις.

**ποντ-όω**, *throw into the sea*, τινας Nic.Dam.10 J. II. Pass., *become a sea*, Q.S.14.604. **-ωσις**, εως, ἡ, *throwing into the sea*, Tz.*H*.7.215.

**ποο-φᾰγέω, -φάγος**, v. ποηφαγέω, -φάγος.

**ποπᾰν-εῖον**, *panificium*, *Gloss*. **-ευμα**, ατος, τό, = sq., *AP*6.231 (Phil.), cj. in Theoc.26.7. ❀ **-ον**, τό, (πέσσω) *round cake*, used at sacrifices, π. θύειν Ar.*Th*.285, al., cf. Pl.*R*.455c, Arist.*Fr*.489, *IG*2.1651, Men.12.9, *PCair.Zen*.569.86 (iii B.C.), Dieuch.ap.Orib.4.7.32, Porph.*Abst*.2.16; cj. in Thphr.*Char*.16.10.

**ποπᾰνο-ποιέω**, *make cakes*, Procl.*in R*.1.245 K. **-ποιός**, όν, *making cakes*, ibid.

**ποπᾰνώδης**, ες, *like a* πόπανον, Hsch. s.v. φυσακτήρ.

**πόπαξ**, Interj. = πόποι: ἰού, ἰού, πόπαξ A.*Eu*.143.

**πόπαρ**· πατήρ, καὶ πατρὸς πατήρ, Hsch.

**ποπάς**, άδος, ἡ, = πόπανον, *AP*6.232 (Crin.).

**πόποι**, exclam. of surprise, anger, or pain, ὦ π. freq. in Hom., always at the beginning of a verse and sentence; ὦ π., οἷον ἔειπε.. Od.17.248; ὦ π., οἷον δή νυ.. 1.32; ὦ π., ὡς.. 10.38, al.; ὦ π., ἦ μάλα.. Il.16.745, al.; ὦ π. οὐδέ νύ σοί περ 8.201, cf. Od.17.454; ὦ π... καὶ δὴ Il.21.420; in later Ep. and Eleg., A.R.3.558, al., *AP*5.253 (Paul. Sil.); Trag. only in lyr., exc. A.*Pers*.731 (troch., c. gen.), as ib.852, *Eu*.145, S.*OT*168: with other exclam., ἰὼ π. A.*Pr*.575, *Ag*.1100; ὀτοτοτοτοῖ πόποι δᾶ ib.1072, 1076.—Later writers expld. πόποι as a Dryopian word = δαίμονες, Plu.2.22c, or, = ἀγάλματα ὑπόγαια τῶν θεῶν, *EM*823.32, and πόποι = θεοί Lyc.943; dat. πόποις Euph.136.

**πόποπο**, onomatop. word to express the cry of the hoopoe, Ar.*Av*.227.

❀ **ποππ-ύζω**, Dor. -ύσδω, onomatop. word, *smack the lips* or *cluck*: hence, I. *call to* horses, etc., Ar.*Pl*.732, cf. D.S.1.83:—Med., *call to* a horse, S.*Fr*.878: Com., *call to* a man, πόρρωθεν ἀπιδὼν ἐπόππυσεν Timocl.21.7; παιδίον ὑποκορίζεσθαι ποππύζων Thphr.*Char*.20.5;

Ποππύζουσα, title of play by Alexis; κἂν ἀστράψῃ ποππύζουσιν.. οἱ πάνυ σεμνοί Ar.*V*.626 (cf. ποππυσμός). II. *applaud*, Phld.*Acad. Ind.*p.14 M.:—Pass., εἰ ποππυσθείη καὶ κροτηθείη Pl.*Ax*.368d. III. *smack*, of loud kisses, *AP*5.244 (Maced.), 284 (Agath.). IV. in bad sense, *play badly* on the flute, *let the breath be heard* in playing, Theoc.5.7. -ὑλιάζω, Dor. -άσδω, = foreg. I, ib.89. -υσμα, ατος, τό, *smacking of lips, clucking*, Dexipp.*in Cat*.11.27: Lat. *poppysma*, Juv.6.584. -υσμός, ὁ, = foreg., X.*Eq*.9.10, Plu.2.713b (pl.), Poll.1.210, v.l. in D.H.*Comp*.14; σιγμοῖς καὶ π. Nicom.*Harm*.6, cf. *PMag.Leid.W*.1.37; of applause, Plu.2.545c: Lat. *poppysmus*, of the sound made on seeing lightning, Plin.*HN*28.25 (pl.); ὁ ἱερακοπρόσωπος κορκόδειλος.. τὸν θεὸν ἀσπάζεται τῷ π. *PMag.Leid.W*.2.1.

**πόρ**· πούς (Lacon.), Hsch. **πορδᾱκός**, v. παρδακός.

**πορδάλεος** [ᾰ], α, ον, = παρδάλεος, Opp.*C*.3.467. II. (πορδή) *flatulent*, Luc.*Lex*.10.

**πορδᾰλ-ιαγχές, -ιδεύς, -ις**, v. παρδ-.

**πορδ-ή**, ἡ, (πέρδομαι) *crepitus ventris*, Ar.*Nu*.394. -ῶ, *pedo*, Gloss. -ων, ωνος, ὁ, (πορδή) *stinker*, nickname of Cynics, Arr.*Epict*.3.22.80.

❀ **πορ-εία**, ἡ, (πορεύω) *mode of walking* or *running, gait*, Democr.126, Pl.*Smp*.190b, *Ti*.45a; τὰ ὀργανικὰ μέρη τῆς π. Arist.*de An*.432ᵇ26; περὶ πορείας ζῴων, title of work by Aristotle. II. *journey*, A.*Pr*.823, al.; ἡ ἐκεῖσε π. Pl.*Phd*.107d; ἡ κατὰ τὰ ἄγκη π. Id.*Cra*.420e; αἱ κατὰ γῆν π. Isoc.1.19; ἡ εἰς Ἅιδου, εἰς Πέρσας π., Pl.*Phd*.115a, X.*Cyr*.8.5.1: metaph., π. ἕως εἰς ἄπειρον *processus ad infinitum*, Phld.*Mort*.19. 2. in military sense, *march*, Th.2.18; κατὰ θάλατταν τὴν π. ποιεῖσθαι X.*An*.5.6.11; π. ἀνύτειν Id.*Cyr*.8.6.18; ἰέναι ib.5.2.31 (nisi leg. εἶναι); ἐκ π. μάχεσθαι Plu.2.198b; *order of march*, Ascl.*Tact*.11 tit., Arr.*Tact*.28.1, al. 3. generally, *course* taken by a person, etc., Antipho 3.2.4; ἡ [τοῦ κόσμου] π. Pl.*Plt*.274a; of the sun, *Hymn.Is*.32 (pl.), Eudox.*Ars* 2.15; χρόνου π. Procl.*Inst*.50. 4. *travelling expenses*, *IG*2².1.34, *PRev.Laws* 50.11 (iii B.C., pl.), *PGrenf*.1.43.8 (ii B.C.). 5. *visitation, inspection*, οἰκοπέδων *BGU*83.1 (ii/iii A.D.), etc. ❀ -εῖον, τό, *means of conveyance, carriage*, *GDI*5043 (Crete), Pl.*Lg*.678c, v.l. in Id.*Ti*.44e; π. ὑπότροχα *trolleys* for conveying ships by land, Plb.8.34.11, cf. *SIG* 581.23 (Hierapytna, ii B.C.); τὸ σκῆπτρον Ἑρμοῦ πρoκαθηγέτου ἐστὶ π., τούτῳ γὰρ κατάγει ψυχάς *BSA*16.107 (Attalia):—Dor. and Aeol. πορήϊον *GDI*5040.29 (Crete), *Milet*.3 No.152.13 (Methymna, ii B.C.). II. *load*, *PPetr*.2 p.128 (iii B.C.), etc.; written πορῆον, *PTeb*.195 (i B.C.), etc.

**πορενβῆκις** and **πορεμβῆκις, -βαῖκις, πουερενπβῆκις**, etc. (variously spelt and declined), ὁ, *keeper of the falcons*, *Sammelb*.6028.10, al. (i B.C.). (Egypt. *pwr bik* 'the great one of the falcon'.)

**πορ-ευμα**, ατος, τό, *place in which one walks*, βροτῶν πορεύματα their *haunts*, A.*Eu*.239. 2. *means of going, carriage*, ναΐον π. a fleet, E.*IA*300 (lyr.). -εύς, έως, ὁ, = πορθμεύς, Hsch. -εύσιμος, ον, also η, ον Them.*Or*.6.83c:—*that may be crossed, passable*, ἡ τοῦ ποταμοῦ ὁδὸς π. ἀνθρώποις ἐγίγνετο X.*Cyr*.7.5.16; εἰ π. εἴη τὸ ἔδαφος τοῦ ποταμοῦ ib.18; π. ἦν τὸ.. πέλαγος Pl.*Ti*.24e; [θύραι] ἀνθρώποις π. Porph.*Antr*.3; παρεχέτωσαν.. π. τὰς ὁδοὺς *OGI*483.30 (Pergam.): in neut., [ὁδόν], ἥνπερ ἦν πορεύσιμον by which it was *possible to pass*, E.*El*.1046. II. Act., *able to go* or *travel*, Pl.*Epin*.981d. 2. *able to carry*, π. ὄχημα τοῖς κομιζομένοις, of the sea, Plu.2.86e. -ευσις, εως, ἡ, = πορεία, γένεσις π. εἰς τὸ εἶναι Pl.*Def*.411a, cf. Lxx *Ge*.33.14. -ευτέος, α, ον, *to be traversed*, ὁδὸς S.*Ph*.993; ὄρη X.*An*.2.5.18. II. neut. πορευτέον, *one must go*, S.*Aj*.690, E.*Heracl*.730, Pl.*R*.452c. -ευτικός, ή, όν, *going on foot, walking*, τὰ π. ζῷα, opp. πτηνά, ἑρπυστικά, νευστικά, Arist.*HA*487ᵇ16, al.; π. κίνησις Id.*de An*.432ᵇ14. II. *of* or *for a march*, τὰ π. διαστήματα Plb.12.19.7; π. ἀγωγή Id.12.20.6. 2. *for conveyance*, ὁ π. Ἀλεξανδρεῖνος στόλος, of the corn-fleet, *IG*14.918 (ii A.D.); ὁ στόλος.. ὁ ἐκ πλοίων πορευτικῶν *Arch. Pap*.2.447 (Alexandria, ii A.D.). -ευτός, ή, όν (also ός, όν A.*Ag*.287), *gone over, passed, passable*, ὁδὸν ζυγίοις π. *Milet*.3 No.149 (ii B.C.), cf. Plb.1.42.2, etc.; καιρὸς π. the season *for travelling*, Id.1.37.10; τὸ πέλαγος π. θέσθαι Lxx 2 *Ma*.5.21. II. Act., *going, travelling*, ἰσχὺς πορευτοῦ λαμπάδος A.l.c. ❀ -εύω, fut. -σω E.*Hec*.447 (lyr.), etc.: aor. ἐπόρευσα, poet. πόρευσα Pi.*P*.11.21:—Pass. and Med., fut. πορεύσομαι S.*OT*676, Pl.*Smp*.190d; πορευθήσομαι *IG*2².141.2, Lxx 3 *Ki*.14.2: aor. ἐπορευσάμην (only compds. ἐν-, προ-, Pl.*Ep*.313d, Plb.2.27.2); ἐπορεύθην Pi.*Fr*.75.8, Hdt.8.107, Th.1.26, E.*Hec*.1099 (lyr.), etc.: pf. πεπόρευμαι Pl.*Plt*.266d, D.53.6: (πόρος): I. Act., *make to go, carry, convey*, by land or water, τινα Arion 1.13, Pi.*O*.1.77, *P*.11.21, etc.; ἐπ' εὐστόλου νεὼς πορεύσαιμ' ἂν ἐς δόμους S.*Ph*.517 (lyr.); ὡς τάχιστά μοι μολὼν ἄνακτα.. τις πορευσάτω Id.*OC*1476; ἐμὲ πόντιον σκάφος πορεύσει Ἄργος E.*Tr*.1086 (lyr.); ποντιὰς αὔρα,.. ποῖ με πορεύσεις; Id.*Hec*.447 (lyr.); βασά νιν δεῦρο πόρευσον Id.*Med*.181 (lyr.); στρατιὰν πεζῇ π. ὡς Βρασίδαν Th.4.132, etc.: c. dupl. acc., *carry* or *ferry over*, [Νέσσος] ποταμὸν.. βροτοὺς μισθοῦ 'πόρευε S.*Tr*.560; γυναῖκ' ἀρίσταν λίμναν.. πορεύσας ἐλάτᾳ E.*Alc*.443 (lyr.). 2. of things, *bring, carry*, ἐπιστολὰς πατρί S.*OC*1602; *furnish, bestow*, χρυσὸν E.*Ph*.985; *set in motion*, κίνησις.. βραδυτῆτάς τε καὶ τάχη.. π. Pl.*Lg*.893d. 3. abs., *conduct a search*, S.*Ichn*.324 (lyr., s.v.l.). II. Pass. and Med., *to be driven* or *carried*, μέγας βοῦς ὑπὸ σμικρᾶς μάστιγος εἰς ὁδὸν π. Id.*Aj*.1254; πρὸς βίαν π. Id.*OC* 845. 2. *go, walk, march*, Hdt.8.22, Thphr.*Char*.2.1, etc.; ἐφ' ἑνὸς σκέλους Pl.*Smp*.190d; σύνδρομά τινι Id.*Plt*.266d; ταχέως X.*An*.2.2.12; τοῖν ποδοῖν Id.*Cyr*.4.3.13; *go by land*, opp. going by sea, Id.*An*.5.3.1; also *cross, pass over*, διαφυλάσσειν τὰς σχεδίας, πορευθῆναι βασιλέϊ for the king's *crossing*, Hdt.8.107; π. δι' Εὐρίπου Th.7.29: freq. with Preps., π. ἐκ δόμων, ἔξω δωμάτων, S.*Tr*.392, E.*Hipp*.1156; εἰς ἀγρόν Pl.*R*.563d; εἰς ἐκκλησίαν Thphr.*Char*.4.1; ἐξ.. ἐς.. Hdt.4.35; ἐπὶ τὸν Ἀχέροντα Pl.*Phd*.113d: c. acc. loci, *enter*, π. στέγας S.*Tr*.329, cf. E.*Hel*.51; π. διὰ Θεσσαλίης *march* through T., Hdt.7.196; π. παρὰ βασιλέος *come* from his presence, Id.6.95; παρὰ βασιλέως πρὸς τὸν σατράπην X.*An*.4.5.10; π. πρὸς τὸν ἴδιον ἄνδρα *go in* to her husband, Theano ap.D.L.8.43: freq. c. acc. cogn., μακροτέραν (sc. ὁδόν) π. X.*An*.2.2.11, etc.; π. φυγάν E.*Ion* 1239 (lyr.); τὴν εἱμαρμένην πορείαν Pl.*Mx*.236d: c. acc. loci, γῆν πολλὴν π. *go over, traverse*, Arr.*An*.6.23.1; π. τὰ δύσβατα X.*Cyr*.2.4.27; τοσαῦτα ὄρη Id.*An*.2.5.18: Geom., π. διὰ τοῦ κέντρου *pass* through the centre, Archim.*Con.Sph*.16; π. γραμμάν *traverse, move along* a line, Id.*Spir*.14.—Special phrases: ἐς ἄρκυν π. *fall* into.., E.*El*.965; ἐπ' ἔργον π., ἐπὶ τὰ δευτερεῖα π., Id.*Or*.1068, Pl.*Phlb*.23b; π. εἰς τὰ κτήματα *enter into possession of*.., D.44.32; ἣν αἱ καθάρσιες πορεύωνται if the menses *come*, Hp.*Aph*.5.60. 3. *walk*, i.e. *live*, εἴ τις ὑπέροπτα.. π. S.*OT*884 (lyr.); freq. in Lxx, as π. τοῖς νομίμοις *Le*.18.3. 4. metaph., ἡ πονηρία διὰ τῶν ἡδονῶν π. X.*Cyr*.2.2.24; of discourse, ἐκτὸς τῶν λόγων π. Pl.*Lg*.812a; διὰ τῶν ὁμολογουμένων X.*Mem*.4.6.15; καθ' ὁμοιότητα π. *proceed* by analogy, Phld.*Sign*.31. 5. *proceed* at law, *PEleph*.3.5, 4.6 (iii B.C.). 6. *go on one's way*, i.e. *die*, Jul.*Ep*.14.

**πορήϊον**, τό, v. πορεῖον.

**πορθ-έω**, collat. form of πέρθω (more used in Prose), *destroy, ravage, plunder*, πόλεας καὶ τείχεα Il.4.308; ἀνδρῶν ἀγρούς Od.14.264; τοὺς χώρους Hdt.3.58; πόλιν A.*Th*.583, etc.; Φοινίκην Isoc.9.62; τὴν Σελλασίαν ἔκαον καὶ ἐπόρθουν X.*HG*6.5.27; τὴν Ἤπειρον Th.8.57; τὴν χώραν λεηλατῆσαι καὶ τὴν πόλιν πορθῆσαι D.S.12.34; π. ἐκ τῶν ἱερῶν τὰ ἀγάλματα Ath.12.523b:—Pass., πᾶν τὸ ἄστυ ἐπορθέετο Hdt.1.84; ὅλης τῆς Ἑλλάδος πεπορθημένης Isoc.10.49; τἀργύρια πορθεῖται *is carried off*, Eup.155. 2. in pres. and impf., sts. *endeavour to destroy, besiege* a town, Hdt.1.162, Decr.ap.D.18.164, D.S.12.34, 15.4. 3. of persons, *destroy, ruin*, θεοὺς τοὺς ἐγγενεῖς A.*Th*.583; φίλους E.*Fr*.605: abs., *do havoc*, Id.*Andr*.633: esp. in Pass., αὐτοὶ ὑφ' αὑτῶν.. πορθούμεθα A.*Th*.194; κατ' ἄκρας.. ὡς πορθουμένα Id.*Ch*.691; of women, κόραι βίᾳ πρὸς ἀνδρῶν πορθούμεναι E.*Ph*.565; σκόροδα πορθούμενος *robbed* of them, Com. phrase in Ar.*Ach*.164. -εών, ῶνος, ὁ, *ravager*, Hdn.Gr.1.19. -ημα, ατος, τό, = sq., Plu.*Sull*.16 (pl.). -ησις, εως, ἡ, *sack* of a town, D.18.70, Plu.*Sull*.33, etc. -ητήριος, ον, *ravaging*, Tz.*H*.11.595. -ητής, οῦ, ὁ, *destroyer, ravager*, E.*Tr*.213 (lyr.), Lyc.524, Str.17.1.6. -ητικός, ή, όν, *ravaging*, Hsch. s.v. ἀγρεμόνες; π. μηχανή, gloss on *sambuca*, Gloss. -ήτωρ, ορος, ὁ, = πορθητής, A.*Ag*.907, *Ch*.974.

**πορθμ-εία**, ἡ, *ferrying across* a river, *SIG*1262.10 (Smyrna), Apollod.2.7.6. II. *conveyance by water*, Str.5.3.7. ❀ -εῖον, Ion. -ήϊον, τό, *place for crossing, passage, ferry*, πορθμήϊα Κιμμέρια (where it is pr. n.) Hdt.4.12,45. II. *passage-boat, ferry-boat*, Id.7.25, X.*HG*5.1.23, Antiph.86.4, Luc.*DMort*.10.1; πορθμείων ὅρμου ὅρος *IG*1².890. III. *ferryman's fee*, Call.*Fr*.110, Luc.*DMort*.22.1 (pl.); τὸ εἰς Ῥήνειαν π. *Inscr.Délos* 442 *A* 153 (ii B.C.). IV. *landing-place*, Wilcken *Chr*.392.10 (ii A.D.), etc. [This word and its cognates are sts. written προθ- in Pap., e.g. *POxy*.1421.6 (iii A.D.).] -ευμα, ατος, τό, *passage, ferry*, ὠκύπορον π. ἀχέων, of the river Acheron, A.*Ag*.1558 (anap.). -εύς, έως, Ion. ῆος, ὁ, *ferryman*, Od.20.187, Aeschin.3.158, *SIG*633.104 (Milet., ii B.C.), *BGU*1188.11 (i B.C.), etc.; π. νεκύων, of Charon, E.*Alc*.253 (lyr.), cf. Call.*Fr*.440. 2. generally, *boatman, seaman*, esp. as one of the crew of a passenger-ship, Hdt.1.24, Ar.*Ec*.1086, Theoc.1.57. 3. metaph., *conveyer, 'purveyor'*, τῶν καθ' ἡμέραν λεγομένων Lib.*Or*.18.15. -ευτής, οῦ, ὁ, = foreg., Eust.1888.10. -ευτικός, ή, όν, *engaged in ferrying*, Arist.*Pol*.1291ᵇ21. ❀ -εύω, *carry* or *ferry over* a strait, river, etc., στρατόν E.*Rh*.429; τινὰς εἰς Σαλαμῖνα Aeschin.3.158: then, generally, *carry over, carry*, ἐφετμὰς τάσδε πόρθμευσον πάλιν A.*Ch*.685; δεῦρο π. βρέφος E.*Ion* 1599; γραφὰς πρὸς Ἄργος Id.*IT*735; also, π. τινὰ ἐκ γῆς S.*Tr*.802, cf. E.*IT*1358; π. πόδα, ἴχνος, *advance*, ib.936, 266: metaph., εἰς δάκρυα π. ὑπομνήσει κακῶν Id.*Or*.1032; τινὰ εἰς αἱματηρὸν γάμον δόλῳ Id.*IT*371; ποῖ διωγμὸν πορθμεύεις; how far *dost thou carry* it? ib.1435; Ἀχέρων ἄχεα π. βροτοῖσιν Licymn.2; πορθμεύει γὰρ ἔμοιγε κύλιξ παρὰ σοῦ τὸ φίλημα *AP*5.260 (Agath.):—Pass., *to be carried* or *ferried over from place to place*, Hdt.2.97; ἐπ' ὄχοις π. E.*Tr*.569 (anap.): c. acc. loci, *pass over* or *through*, λευκὴν αἰθέρα πορθμευόμενος Id.*Andr*.1229 (anap.). II. Act. intr., *pass over*, ποταμοὺς Pl.*Ax*.371c; Ἀχέροντος ὕδωρ *AP*7.68 (Arch.); κύματα *Epigr.Gr*.522.1 (Thessalonica); τίς ἀστὴρ ὅδε π.; E.*IA*6 (anap.). -ήϊον, Ion. for πορθμεῖον. -ικός, ή, όν, *of* or *for conveyance* or *transit* by water, Arist.*Pol*.1291ᵇ24 codd.; τέλη Str.12.8.19; ὠνή *OGI*572.8 (Myra, ii/iii A.D.); τὰ π. *Sammelb*.4372 (Ptol.). -ιον, freq. f.l. for πορθμεῖον, e.g. Luc.*Luct*.10. -ιος, ὁ, epith. of Poseidon at Carpathos, *IG*12(1).1032.34, 1036.12 (ii B.C.). -ίς, ίδος, ἡ, = sq., D.P.80, 344. II. = πορθμεῖον II, *ship, boat*, E.*Hipp*.753 (lyr.), *Hel*.1061, *IT*355, etc.; μόνος μόνῳ γέμιζε πορθμίδος σκάφος load this *boat* for yourself alone, Id.*Cyc*.362; π. ναῦς Paus.8.25.13. b. τὸ τέλος τῆς π. *ferry*-toll, *SIG*633.100 (Milet., ii B.C.), cf. *Inscr.Délos* 442 *A* 175 (ii B.C.): pl., *PPetr*.3 p.85 (iii B.C.), *Ostr.Bodl*.i 54 (ii B.C.). 2. metaph. of a table *that brings in another course*, Philox.3.2 (pl.). ❀ -ός, ὁ, (πείρω, πόρος) *ferry* or *place crossed by a ferry, strait, narrow sea*, π. Ἰθάκης τε Σάμοιό τε Od.4.671; of the straits of Salamis, Hdt.8.76,91; πορθμὸν ἀμείψας Ἕλλας, i.e. the Hellespont, A.*Pers*.68 (lyr.), cf. 722, 799; π. Σαρωνικός Id.*Ag*.307; ὁ ἐς Ἀΐδα πορθμός the Styx, E.*Hec*.1106 (lyr.); ὁ π. ὁ περὶ τὴν Σκύλλαν, i.e. the *straits* of Messina, Pl.*Ep*.345e, cf. Arist.*Mir*.834ᵇ3, *Vent*.973ᵇ1: hence prov., π. Σικελίας a 'slough of despond', Lib.*Ep.*221.1. b. generally, *the sea*, Pi.*I.*4(3).57. 2. *any narrow passage, tube*, as of the κλεψύδρα I, Emp.100.10,17. II. *crossing by a ferry, passage*, S.*Tr.*571, E.*Hel.*532 (both pl.); χωρεῖ ὁ π. Macho ap.Ath.8.341c; π. χθονὸς *a passage to* it, E.*Cyc.*108; οὐ πᾶσι π. αὐτὸς Ἀργείοισιν ἦν; Id.*Hel.*127; τηρήσαντες τὸν π. watching for the *opportunity to cross*, Th.6.2.

**πορθμοφῠλᾰκία**, ἡ, *custody of a ferry*, *PRyl.*185.6, al. (ii A.D.).

**πόρθος**· πτόρθος κτλ., Hsch. **πορθυγγίς**· σπατίλη, τρύβλιον, Id.

**πορθώτης** (variously declined), ὁ, *priest of Thoth*, hence *superintendent of the ibises*, *Sammelb.*6028.7, al. (i B.C.). (Egypt. *pwr Tḥwt* 'the great one of Thoth'.)

**πορ-ίζω**, Att. fut. ποριῶ Ar.*Eq.*1079,1101, Th.6.29, etc., late πορίσω Artem.2.68: aor. ἐπόρισα Pl.*Lg.*966e: pf. πεπόρικα Id.*Phlb.*30d:—Med., fut. Att. ποριοῦμαι D.35.41: aor. ἐπορισάμην Ar.*Ra.*880, etc.:—**Pass.**, fut. πορισθήσομαι Th.6.37,94: aor. ἐπορίσθην ib.37, etc., Dor. -ίχθην Lysis ap.Iamb.*VP*17.75: pf. πεπόρισμαι Isoc.15.278, D.44.3 (in med. sense, Lys.29.7, Aeschin.3.209, Philem.123): plpf. ἐπεπόριστο Th 6.29: (πόρος):—rarely, like πορεύω, *carry, bring*, σὲ θεὸς ἐπόρισεν ἁμέτερα πρὸς μέλαθρα (prob. for ἐπῶρσεν, ἔπορσεν) S.*El.*1267 (lyr.). II. *bring about, furnish, provide*, κακά τινι Hom.*Epigr.*14.10; νίκην, χρήματα, etc., Ar.*Eq.*593, *Ec.*236, Democr.78, *IG*2$^2$.834.14, etc.; ἀρχὴν πολέμου Ar.*Fr.*81; τροφὴν τοῖς στρατιώταις Isoc.12.82; τοῖς μαθηταῖς δόξαν, οὐκ ἀλήθειαν Pl.*Phdr.*275a: abs., θεῶν ποριζόντων καλῶς E.*Med.*879: freq. with a notion of *contriving* or *inventing*, μηχανὰν κακῶν, πόρους, Id.*Alc.*222 (lyr.), Ar.*Eq.*759, etc.; τοῖσι φιλτάτοις τέχνας E.*IA*745; π. τριβάς Ar.*Ach.*386; διαβολὴν Th.6.29; σωτηρίαν τῷ γένει Pl.*Prt.*321b; τῇ ζητήσει ἀπόκρισιν Id.*Phlb.*30d, etc.:—Med., *furnish oneself with, procure*, ῥήματα Ar.*Ra.*880; δαπάνην, χρήματα, ὅπλα, Th.1.83,142,4.9; τὰς ἡδονάς, τἀγαθά, τἀπιτήδεια, etc., Pl.*Grg.*501b, *La.*199e, *Ax.*368b, etc.; μηχανήν Id.*Smp.*191b; τὰ δεῖπνα Alex.257.2; καινὰ ῥήματα Philem. l.c.; φῶς ποθέν Pl.*R.*427d; ἐκ τῶν ἀλλοτρίων π. τὸν βίον Isoc.12.116; also π. μάρτυρας Lys.29.7; πρόφασιν Id.8.3; λόγους περὶ ἀδίκων πραγμάτων D.35.41; αἰτίας χρηστὰς ἐπὶ πράγμασι φαύλοις Plu.2.868d: sts. also πορίζεσθαί τι ἑαυτοῖς X.*HG*5.1.17, Pl.*Smp.*208e; σημεῖα πεπορίσθαι *to have acquired* the signs, i.e. *know* them, Hp.*Medic.*14; also, *have provided for one, receive*, Men.Prot.p.16 D.:—Pass., *to be provided*, τὰ τῆς παρασκευῆς ἐπεπόριστο Th.6.29; ῥᾳδίως αἱ ἐπαγωγαί..ἐπορίζοντο inducements *were* easily *provided*, Id.3.82; δύναμις ἐκ θεῶν π. Pl.*R.*364b; πίστεις ὑπὸ τοῦ λόγου πεπορισμέναι Isoc.15.278, cf. Arist.*Rh.*1356$^a$1; τὸ γηροβοσκοὺς κεκτῆσθαι τοῖς ἀνθρώποις πορίζεται X.*Oec.*7.19; πράξεις πρὸς τὰ ψύχη καὶ τὰς ἀλέας πεπορισμέναι behaviour *adapted to*.., Arist.*HA*596$^b$22, cf. *PA*665$^b$3. 2. Act. in med. sense, *find* money, *raise* a loan, *PCair.Zen.*477.16 (iii B.C.); *obtain*, προστάγματα εἰς τὸ τιμωρηθῆναι αὐτούς *PMich.Zen.*57.9 (iii B.C.); *earn*, τὸ ζῆν ἀπὸ τῆς γερδιακῆς *PLond.*3.846.11 (ii A.D.):—Pass., ἀπ' ἄλλων συντόμως σοι ποριοσθὲν ἀποδοθήσεται (sc. τὸ ἀργύριον) *PMich.Zen.*56.8 (iii B.C.). III. Math., *find* something, opp. proving it (as in a theorem) and constructing it (as in a problem), Papp.650.22, al.; cf. πόρισμα II. **-ῐμος**, ον, also η, ον Hp.*Acut.*50:—*able to provide, resourceful, inventive*, Gorg.*Pal.*25; πόριμον αὐτῷ, τῇ πόλει δ' ἀμήχανον Ar.*Ra.*1429; πόριμος τόλμα Id.*Pax* 1031; φρονήσεως ἐπιθυμητὴς καὶ π. [ὁ ἔρως] Pl.*Smp.*203d; ῥήτωρ Poll.4.34: c. acc., ἄπορα πόριμος *making possible* the impossible, A.*Pr.*904 (lyr.). 2. of things, *affording means of safety, saving*, ἔργον Ar.*Th.*777; ἐπιβολή Anon.ap.Suid. (Sup.); [τὸ] π. the *profitable*, Gal.5.751. 3. Medic., *finding* or *making a passage*, ἡ ἀπὸ τοῦ γλυκέος οἴνου φῦσα π. Hipp. l.c.; *passing rapidly through* the system, τροφή Gal.6.570. II. Pass., *compassable, practicable*, ἄπορα γίγνεται τὰ π. J.*AJ*Prooem.3; ἔρωτι πάντα π. Luc.*Dem.Enc.*14. 2. *well-provided*, ποριμώτεροι ἐς πάντα Th.8.76; ἐποίησε τὸν ἀνθρώπινον βίον π. ἐξ ἀπόρου Gorg.*Pal.*30. **-ῐμότης**, ητος, ἡ, *inventiveness*, Eust. ad D.P.69.

**πό[ρι]ον**, τό, = πορεῖον (dub.), *Inscr.Magn.*57.32.

**πόρις**, ιος, ἡ, = πόρτις (q.v.), ἄγραυλοι πόριες Od.10.410, cf. E.*Ba.*737, Arat.1120; of a girl, E.*Supp.*629 (lyr.), Lyc.184, etc. (Cf. Lat. *pario*, Lith. *perìù* 'hatch'.)

**πόρ-ισμα**, ατος, τό, Geom., *deduction from a previous demonstration, corollary*, as it were a *windfall* or *bonus* (cf. πορίζω II.2), Euc.3.1, etc.: metaph., Procl. *in Alc.*p.139 C., Hierocl. *in CA*23 p.469 M., Dam.*Pr.*251. II. (πορίζω III) *a kind of proposition intermediate between a theorem and a problem*, defined by Papp.648.18 sqq., Procl. *in Euc.*p.301 F. **-ισμός**, ὁ, *providing, procuring*, τῶν ἐπιτηδείων Plb.3.112.2; *earning a living*, Chrysipp.*Stoic.*3.172; ἐφήμερος π. Phld.*Oec.*p.44 J.; συγγνώμης J.*BJ*2.21.3: abs., Man.4.448 (pl.); *money-getting*, Plu.2.524d, 92b (pl.), 136c (pl.), etc.; *means of gain*, Chaerem.ap.Porph.*Abst.*4.8; δυσὶ π., γεωργίᾳ καὶ φειδοῖ Plu.*Cat.Ma.*25; π. μέγας ἡ εὐσέβεια 1*Ep.Ti.*6.6; *means of livelihood*, Muson.*Fr.*11 p.59 H. **-ιστέον**, *one must provide*, Epicur.*Fr.*481, Chrysipp.*Stoic.*3.172, Iamb. *in Nic.*p.58 P. ❀**-ιστής**, οῦ, ὁ, *one who supplies* or *provides*, π. τῶν κακῶν τῷ δήμῳ Th.8.48; φύλαξ καὶ π. ἀλλοτρίων χρημάτων Eus.Mynd.24; δόξης Phld.*Rh.*2.53 S. (Comp.). b. abs., *money-maker*, J.*AJ*19.2.5. 2. pl., at Athens, *a financial board appointed to raise extraordinary supplies*, Ar.*Ra.*1505, Antipho 6.49, etc.: hence metaph., τῶν χρημάτων αὐτοὶ ταμίαι καὶ π. D.4.33. 3. the name used by robbers of themselves, οἱ λῃσταὶ αὑτοὺς ποριστὰς καλοῦσι νῦν Arist.*Rh.*1405$^a$26. **-ιστικός**, ή, όν, *able to supply* or *procure*, τῶν ἐπιτηδείων τοῖς στρατιώταις X.*Mem.*3.1.6; ἀρετή ἐστι δύναμις π. ἀγαθῶν Arist.*Rh.*1366$^a$37, cf. Pl.*Grg.*517d; π. βίβλος treatise *on supply*, Aen.Tact.14.2; π. ἕξις τῶν πρὸς τὸ ζῆν καθηκόντων *Stoic.*3.67; π. καὶ φυλακτικός Phld.*Oec.*p.67 J.

**πόρκας**· ἐλάφους, Hsch.

**πορκεύς**, έως, ὁ, *one who fishes with the net called* πόρκος, Lyc.237, 596, 1217, Pancrat.ap.Ath.7.321f.

**πόρκης**, ου, ὁ, *ring* or *hoop*, passed round the joint of the spearhead and shaft, περὶ δὲ χρύσεος θέε πόρκης Il.6.320, cf. Il.Parv.5.

❀ **πόρκος**, ὁ, a kind of *fish-trap, weel*, Pl.*Sph.*220c, Antiph.120, Diph.78, Plu.2.730c. II. transliteration of Lat. *porcus*, Id.*Publ.*11.

**πορκώδης**, ες, (πόρκης) *like a ring*, Eust.795.39.

**πορν-εία**, Ion. -είη, ἡ, *prostitution*, Hp.*Epid.*7.122, etc.; of a man, D.19.200; *fornication, unchastity*, *Ev.Matt.*19.9: pl., 1*Ep.Cor.*7.2. II. metaph., *idolatry*, Lxx *Ho.*4.11, al. **-εῖον**, τό, *brothel*, Ar.*V.*1283, *Ra.*113, Antipho 1.14, etc. **-ευμα**, ατος, τό, = πορνεία, *PGrenf.*1.53.20 (iv A.D., pl.). **-ευσις**, εως, ἡ, = foreg., Secund.*Sent.*14. **-εύτρια**, ἡ, = πόρνη, Ar.*Fr.*121. **-εύω**, *prostitute*, mostly in Pass., of a woman, *prostitute herself, be* or *become a prostitute*, Hdt.1.93, Eup.67, Lys.*Fr.*59; of a man, Aeschin.1.52,119, D.19.233. II. intr. in Act., = Pass., Lxx *De.*23.17(18), Luc.*Alex.*5, Phalar.*Ep.*121, Harp. s.v. πωλῶσι; *fornicate*, 1*Ep.Cor.*6.18. 2. metaph., *practise idolatry*, Lxx 1*Ch.*5.25, al. ❀**-η**, ἡ, *harlot, prostitute*, Archil.142, Ar.*Ach.*527, etc. (Prob. from πέρνημι, because Greek prostitutes were commonly *bought slaves*.) **-ίδιον**, τό, Dim. of foreg., Ar. (v. infr.), etc. [πορνῐδῐον, Ar.*Nu.*997, Men.*Pk.*150, *Com.Adesp.*120, but -ῑδῐον (Dim. of *πορνίον), Ar.*Ra.*1301.] **-ικός**, ή, όν, *of* or *for harlots*, εἶδος Lxx *Pr.*7.10, cf. *AP*12.7 (Strat.); of planetary influences, Vett.Val.17.31; π. τέλος the tax *paid by brothel-keepers*, Aeschin.1.119; οἱ π. *libertines*, *Cat.Cod.Astr.*2.166.

**πορνοβοσκ-εῖον**, τό, *brothel*, Sch.Ar.*V.*1344. ❀ **-έω**, *keep a brothel*, Ar.*Pax* 849, Hyp.*Ath.*3, Herod.2.77, Vett.Val.61.23. II. *waste one's substance on harlots*, Palaeph.6. **-ία**, ἡ, *trade of a brothel-keeper*, Aeschin.3.214, *Stoic.*3.36. **-ός**, ὁ, *brothel-keeper*, Myrtil.4, Aeschin.3.246, D.59.30, Arist.*EN*1121$^b$33: title of plays by Eubulus, Anaxilas, and Posidippus, and mime by Herodas.

**πορνο-γενής**, *spurius*, *Gloss.* **-γέννητος**, ον, *born of a harlot*, Hsch. s.v. νοθογέννητα. **-γράφος** [ᾰ], ον, *writing of harlots*, Ath.13.567b. **-δῐάκονος** [ᾱ], ὁ, = *bacario*, *Gloss.* **-δῐδάσκᾰλος**, ὁ, ἡ, *teacher of fornication*, Aristaenet.1.14. **-δύτης**· *ganeo*, *Gloss.* **-κοπέω**, *to be a whoremonger*, Poll.6.188. **-κοπία**, ἡ, *whoremongering*, Sch.Ar.*Av.*286. **-κόπος**, ὁ, *one who has commerce with prostitutes, fornicator*, Men.1057, Lxx *Pr.*23.21. **-μᾰνής**, ές, *mad after prostitutes*, Sch.Ar.*Ra.*432.

❀ **Πορνόπιος**, ὁ (sc. μήν), name of month at Cyme, *BCH*37.166, 51.375; cf. Παρνόπιος.

❀**πόρνος**, ὁ, *catamite*, Ar.*Pl.*155, X.*Mem.*1.6.13, D.22.73, Alex.242, etc. 2. *sodomite*, D.*Ep.*4.11, Phalar.*Ep.*4. 3. in Lxx and *NT*, *fornicator*, Lxx *Si.*23.16, 1*Ep.Cor.*5.9, al. II. *idolater*, Suid.

**πορνοσύνη**, ἡ, = πορνεία, Man.4.314.

**πορνο-τελώνης**, ου, ὁ, at Athens, *farmer of the* πορνικὸν τέλος, Philonid.5: nickname for *tax-gatherers*, Poll.9.29. **-τριψ**, ῐβος, ὁ, (τρίβω) = πορνοκόπος, Phryn.389, Thom.Mag.p.291 R. **-τρόφος**, ὁ, = πορνοβοσκός, Ph.1.550. **-φίλης** [ῐ], Dor. **-ας**, α, ὁ, *loving harlots*, *AP*11.416.

**πορο-ποιέω**, *open the pores*, Dsc.5.6; σῶμα πεποροποιημένον *provided with pores*, S.E.*M.*8.309. **-ποιία**, ἡ, *state of the pores*, term in 'Methodic' medicine, Gal.10.268, Cass.*Pr.*79.

❀ **πόρος**, ὁ, (πείρω, περάω) *means of passing a river, ford, ferry*, Θρύον Ἀλφειοῖο π. Thryum *the ford* of the Alphēus, Il.2.592, *h.Ap.*423, cf. *h.Merc.*398; πόρον ἷξον Ξάνθου Il.14.433; Ἀξίου π. A.*Pers.*493; ἀπικνέεται ἐς τὸν π. τῆς διαβάσιος to the place of the passage, Hdt.8.115; π. διαβὰς Ἅλυος A.*Pers.*864 (lyr.); τοῦ κατ' Ὠρωπὸν π. μηδὲν πραττέσθω *IG*1$^2$.40.22. 2. *narrow part of the sea, strait*, διαβὰς πόρον Ὠκεανοῖο Hes.*Th.*292; παρ' Ὠκεανοῦ..ἄσβεστον π. A.*Pr.*532 (lyr.); π. Ἕλλης (Dor. Ἕλλας), = Ἑλλήσποντος, Pi.*Fr.*189, A.*Pers.*875 (lyr.), Ar.*V.*308 (lyr.); Ἰόνιος π. the Ionian Sea which is the *passage-way* from Greece to Italy, Pi.*N.*4.53; πέλαγος Αἰγαίου πόρου E.*Hel.*130; Εὔξεινος, ἄξενος π. (cf. πόντος II), Id.*Andr.*1262, *IT*253; διάραντες τὸν π., i.e. the sea between Sicily and Africa, Plb.1.37.1; ἐν πόρῳ in the *passage-way* (of ships), in the *fair-way*, Hdt.7.183, Th.1.120, 6.48; ἐν π. τῆς ναυμαχίης Hdt.8.76; ἕως τοῦ π. τοῦ κατὰ τὸν ὅρμον τὸν Ἀφροδιτοπολίτην *PHib.*1.38.5 (iii B.C.). 3. periphr., πόροι ἁλός the *paths* of the sea, i.e. the sea, Od.12.259; Αἰγαίου πόντοιο πλατὺς π. D.P.131; ἐνάλιοι π. A.*Pers.*453; π. ἀλίρροθοι ib.367, S.*Aj.*412 (lyr.); freq. of rivers, π. Ἀλφεοῦ, Σκαμάνδρου, i.e. the Alphēus, Scamander, etc., Pi.*O.*1.92, A.*Ch.*366 (lyr.), etc.; ῥυτοὶ π. Id.*Eu.*452, cf. 293; Πλούτωνος π. the river Pluto, Id.*Pr.*806: metaph., βίου π. *the stream* of life, Pi.*I.*8(7).15; π. ὕμνων Emp.35.1. 4. *artificial passage over a river, bridge*, Hdt.4.136,140, 7.10.γ'; *aqueduct*, *IG*7.93 (Megara, v A.D., restd.), *Epigr.Gr.*1073.4 (Samos). 5. generally, *pathway, way*, A.*Ag.*910, S.*Ph.*705 (lyr.), etc.; *track* of a wild beast, X.*Cyr.*1.6.40; αἰθέρα θ' ἁγνὸν πόρον οἰωνῶν their *pathway*, A.*Pr.*284 (anap.); ἐν τῷ π. εἶναι to be in the *way*, *Sammelb.*7356.11 (ii A.D.): metaph., πραπίδων πόροι A.*Supp.*94 (lyr.). 6. *passage through* a porous substance, *opening*, Epicur.*Ep.*1 pp.10, 18 U.; esp. *passage through* the skin, οἱ πόροι the *pores* or *passages* by which the ἀπορροαί passed, acc. to Empedocles, πόρους λέγετε εἰς οὓς καὶ δι' ὧν αἱ ἀπορροαὶ πορεύονται Pl.*Men.*76c, cf. Epicur.*Fr.*250, Metrod.*Fr.*7, Ti.Locr.100e; νοητοὶ π. S.E.*P.*2.140; opp. ὄγκοι, Gal.10.268; so of sponges, Arist.*HA*548$^b$31; of plants, Id.*Pr.*905$^b$8, Thphr.*CP*1.2.4, *HP*1.10.5. b. of other *ducts* or *openings* of the body, π. πρῶτος, of the womb, Hp.ap.Poll.2.222; πόροι σπερματικοί, θορικοὶ π., Arist.*GA*716$^b$17, 720$^b$13; π.

ὑστερικοί *the ovaries*, Id.*HA*570ᵃ5, al.; τροφῆς π., of the oesophagus, Id.*PA*650ᵃ15, al.; of the rectum, Id.*GA*719ᵇ29; of the urinal duct, ib.773ᵃ21; of the arteries and veins, Id.*HA*510ᵃ14, etc. **c.** *passages* leading from the organs of sensation to the brain, ψυχὴ παρεσπαρμένη τοῖς π. Pl.*Ax*.366a; οἱ π. τοῦ ὄμματος Arist.*Sens*.438ᵇ14, cf. *HA*495ᵃ11, *PA* 656ᵇ17; ὤτων, μυκτήρων, Id.*GA*775ᵃ2, cf. 744ᵃ2; of the optic nerves, Heroph.ap.Gal.7.89. **II. c.** gen. rei, *way* or *means of achieving, accomplishing, discovering*, etc., οὐκ ἐδύνατο π. οὐδένα τούτου ἀνευρεῖν Hdt.2.2; οὐδεὶς π. ἐφαίνετο τῆς ἁλώσιος Id.3.156; τῶν ἀδοκήτων π. ηὗρε θεός E.*Med*.1418 (anap.); π. ὁδοῦ a *means of performing* the journey, Ar.*Pax* 124; π. ζητήματος Pl.*Tht*.191a; but also π. κακῶν a *means of escaping* evils, a *way out* of them, E.*Alc*.213 (lyr.): c. inf., πόρος νοῆσαι Emp.4.12; π. εὐθαρσεῖν And.2.16; π. τις μηχανή τε.. ἀντιτείσασθαι E.*Med*.260: with Preps., π. ἀμφί τινος A.*Supp*.806 codd. (lyr.); περί τινος dub. in Ar.*Ec*.653; πόροι πρὸς τὸ πολεμεῖν X.*An*.2.5.20. **2.** abs., *providing, means of providing*, opp. ἀπορία, Pl.*Men*.78d sq.; *contrivance, device*, οἵας τέχνας τε καὶ π. ἐμησάμην A.*Pr*. 477; δεινὸς γὰρ εὑρεῖν κἀξ ἀμηχάνων πόρον ib.59, cf. Ar.*Eq*.759; μέγας π. A.*Pr*.111; τίνα π. εὕρω πόθεν; E.*IA*356 (troch.). **3.** π. χρημάτων a *way of raising* money, financial *provision*, X.*Ath*.3.2, *HG*1.6.12, D.1.19, *IG*7.4263.2 (Oropus, iii B.C.), etc.; ὁ π. τῶν χρ. D.4.29, *IG*12(5).1001.1 (Ios, iv B.C.); without χρημάτων, *SIG*284.23 (Erythrae, iv B.C.), etc.; μηχανᾶσθαι προσόδου π. X.*Cyr*.1.6.10, cf. *PTeb*.75.6 (ii B.C.): in pl., '*ways and means*', *resources, revenue*, πόροι χρημάτων D.18.309: abs., πόρους πορίζειν Hyp.*Eux*.37, cf. X.*Cyr*.1.6.9 (sg.), Arist.*Rh*.1359ᵇ23; πόροι ἢ περὶ προσόδων, title of work by X.: sg., *source of revenue, endowment*, *OGI*544.24 (Ancyra, ii A.D.), 509.12,14 (Aphrodisias, ii A.D.), etc. **b.** *assessable income* or *property, taxable estate*, freq. in Pap., as *BGU*1189.11 (i A.D.), etc.; *liability*, *PHamb*.23.29 (vi A.D.), etc. **III.** *journey, voyage*, μακρᾶς κελεύθου π. A.*Th*. 546; παρόρνιθας π. τιθέντες Id.*Eu*.770, cf. E.*IT*116, etc.; ἐν τῷ π. πλοῖον ἀνατρέψαι on its *passage*, Aeschin.3.158. **IV.** Π. personified as father of Ἔρως, Pl.*Smp*.203b.

**πορόω**, *furnish with pores*, Dam.*Pr*.454 (Pass.).

**πορπ-ακίζομαι**, Med., (πόρπαξ) *grasp* a shield *by the handle, bear a shield*, Ar.*Lys*.106. **-ᾱμα**, ατος, τό, *garment fastened with a πόρπη*, always in pl., E.*El*.820, *HF*959, *Rh*.442. **II.** = πόρπη, *IG* 2².1126.31 (Decr. Amphict.).—E. ll. cc. preferred the Dor. form πόρπαμα: πόρπημα v.l. in Suid. ⊛ **-αξ**, ᾰκος, ὁ, (πόρπη) *handle* of a shield, B.*Fr*.3.6, S.*Aj*.576, E.*Ph*.1127, etc.; prob. *ring* or *loop*, inside the shield, which could be taken out at pleasure, ἔχουσι πόρπακας [αἱ ἀσπίδες], i.e. they are ready for use, Ar.*Eq*.858, cf. 849, and Sch. ad loc. **II.** *part of the headgear of a horse*, E.*Rh*.385 (anap.). **III.** surgical *fibula*, *Hippiatr*.24 (pl.). **-ᾱφόρος**, ον, *wearing a brooch*, S.*Inach*. in *PTeb*.692 ii 16. ⊛ **-άω**, aor. imper. πόρπᾱσον A.*Pr*.61:—*fasten with a brooch, pin down*, l.c. (πορπάζω is f.l. in Plu.*Num*.20). ⊛ **-η**, ἡ, (πείρω) = περόνη, *brooch, clasp* for fastening dresses, esp. on the shoulders; used for piercing the eyes, E.*Ph*.62, *Hec*.1170: mostly pl., of the fastenings for women's dresses, Il.18.401, *h.Ven*.163, E.*El*.318, etc.; worn as emblem of rank by συγγενεῖς τῶν βασιλέων, Lxx 1 *Ma*.10.89; by a Roman officer, = *fibula*, *IGRom*.1.1299 (Egypt); of a *hair-clasp*, Luc.*Dom*. 7. **-ηδόν**, Adv. *like a buckle*, Suid. **-ημα**, v. πόρπαμα. ⊛ **-ίον**, τό, Dim. of πόρπη, Roussel *Cultes Égyptiens* 219 (Delos, ii B.C.). **-όω**, = πορπάω, in Pass., Phot., Suid. **-ωμα**, ατος, τό, = πόρπαμα, Id. (v.l. πόρπημα).

**πόρρω, -ωθεν, -ωτέρω**, v. πρόσω, πρόσωθεν, etc. **πορσαίνω**, v. πορσύνω. **πόρσῐον, πόρσιστα**, v. πρόσω.

⊛ **πορσύνω** [ῠ], fut. -ῠνῶ A.*Supp*.522, Ep. -ῠνέω (v. infr.): aor. ἐπόρσῡνα S.*OT*1476, Ep. πόρσῡνα Od.7.347; imper. πόρσυνον S.*Ichn*.304: also **πορσαίνω**, Ep. Iterat. πορσαίνεσκον A.R.4.897: Ep. fut. -ᾰνέω (v. infr.):—in Hom always of the wife *preparing* her husband's bed, hence a euphem. expression for *lie with* the husband, *share* his bed, Ἀλκίνοος δ' ἄρα λέκτο μυχῷ δόμου.., πὰρ δὲ γυνὴ δέσποινα λέχος πόρσυνε καὶ εὐνήν Od. l.c., cf. 3.403; κεῖσε δ' ἐγὼν οὐκ εἶμι (says Helen) κείνου πορσυνέουσα λέχος Il.3.411; later Ep. λέχος.. πορσυνέεις A.R.3.1129; λέκτρον.. πορσαίνουσα Id.4.1107, 1119. **II.** generally, *prepare, provide*, τρίτον [κρατῆρα] σωτῆρι πορσαίνοντας Pi.*I*.6(5).8; δαῖτα ib. 4(3).61; βίου τροφεῖα S.*OC*341; τὸ κατ' ἆμαρ Id.*Fr*.593.5; παισὶν οἷα χρὴ καθ' ἡμέραν E.*Med*.1020; Νύμφαις π. ἔροτιν Id.*El*.625; γαμβροῖς χάριν Id.*Supp*.132; τὰ ἐπιτήδεια X.*Cyr*.4.2.47:—Med., *provide for oneself*, δεῖπνον A.*Pers*.375. **2.** of evils, ἐχθροῖς ἐχθρὰ Id.*Ag*. 1374; τόνδε.. μοῖρ' ἐπόρσυνεν μόρον Id.*Ch*.911, cf. E.*Andr*.1063; μεγάλα κακὰ ib.352; ὅταν ὁ δαίμων ἀνδρὶ πορσύνῃ κακὰ *Trag.Adesp*. 455; δίκην Maiist.57; π. τοῖς πολεμίοις κακὰ X.*Cyr*.1.6.17:—Pass., τίνος πρὸς ἀνδρὸς τοῦτ' ἄχος πορσύνεται; A *Ag*.1251; ἐπορσύνθη κακά Id.*Pers*.267. **3.** *execute, order, arrange*, κατὰ δώματα πορσαίνουσι *manage* (all things) in the house, *h.Cer*.156; τὰ τοῦ θεοῦ π. Hdt.9.7; ταῦτα A.*Supp*.522; τάδε S.*OT*1476; τἄλλα πάντα Id.*Aj*.1398; πρᾶγμα π. μέγα Id.*El*.670; προκείμενον πόνον E.*Alc*.1150; μοῖρα ἑτέραν ἐπόρσυν' ὁδὸν B.16.89:—Pass., τὸ τοῦ ποταμοῦ οὕτως ἐπορσύνετο X.*Cyr*.7.5.17; ἅμα δὲ ταῦτα ἐπορσύνετο ἀπὸ σημείου Aen.Tact.29.9; θεᾶς π. μῆτις *was accomplished*, A.R.1.802, cf. 2. 1050. **III.** *treat with care, tend*, ἐκέλευσεν ἥρωϊ πορσαίνειν δόμεν.. βρέφος Pi.*O*.6.33; οὕτως ὅπως ἂν μὴ 'γκαλῇ πορσύνετε [αὐτόν] E.*Rh*. 878; πορσαίνειν δαίμονα *honour, adore* him, A.R.2.719, cf. 4.897: of things, τεὸν οἶκον ταῦτα πορσύνοντ' Pi.*P*.4.151; τῶν δ' Ὁμήρου καὶ τόδε.. ῥῆμα πόρσυν' *regard, esteem* it, ib.278.—Both forms are found in Pi. and A.R., only πορσύνω in Prose and prob. always to be read in Trag. (never found in Com.): πορσανέουσα was read by Aristarch. in Il.3.411, but πορσυνέουσα most codd., as in Od. ll. cc.: πορσύνων, -ουσα are expld. by ἐρεθίζων, -ουσα in Hsch. (leg. ὀροθυν-).

**πόρσω, πορσώτατα**, v. πρόσω.

**πορτάζει**· δαμαλίζεται, Hsch. **πορτάκινον**· μοσχίον, Id.; cf. πόρταξ. **πόρτακος**· ὦμος, Id.

⊛ **πόρταξ**, ᾰκος, ἡ, = πόρτις, *calf*, Il.17.4.

⊛ **πορτᾶς**, ᾶ, ὁ, (πόρτις) *dealer in calves*, *POxy*.1519.7 (iii A.D.).

**πορτί**, v. προτί.

⊛ **πόρτῐς**, ῐος, ἡ, poet. word (in later Prose, acc. pl. πόρτιας Ant.Lib. 23.3), *calf, young heifer* (younger than δαμάλη, Sch.Theoc.1.75), Il.5. 162, *h.Cer*.174, S.*Tr*.530 (lyr.), etc.; δαμάλαι καὶ πόρτιες Theoc.1.75; ἀεργηλὴν ἔτι π. A.R.4.1186; *young cow*, Theoc.1.121, Mosch.3.82: rarely masc., A.*Supp*.41 (lyr.), 314. **2.** metaph., *young maiden*, Lyc.102; cf. πόρις. (Cf. Skt. *pṛthukas* 'young of an animal', Arm. *orth* 'calf'.)

**πορτιτρόφος**, ον, *nourishing calves*, ἤπειρος *h.Ap*.21; [πεδίον] B. 10.30.

**πορτιφόροι**· οἱ αἴροντες τὰ κόρροια ἐπὶ τῶν ὤμων, Hsch. **πορύναν**· μαγίδα; and **πορύνωμεν** μᾶζαν· τῇ χειρὶ προσπιέζωμεν, Id. **πορφίτῳ**· περόνῃ, Id.

⊛ **πορφύρ-α** [ῠ], Ion. -ρη, ἡ, *purple-fish*, *Murex trunculus* and *Purpura haemastoma*, S.*Fr*.504, Archipp.23, Arist.*HA*528ᵃ10, al., Speus.ap.Ath.3.86c; τρέφουσα.. πορφύρας ἰσάργυρον κηκῖδα A.*Ag*. 959. **II.** *purple dye obtained from it*, Sapph.44, Hdt.3.22, Isoc. 12.39, Pl.*Lg*.847c; ἡ π. ἡ θαλαττία Phylarch.45 J., etc.; π. βαθυτάτη Ael.*NA*4.36; used as an application, βρέξαντες ἐν [τῷ νάρδῳ] τὴν π. ἐπιτιθέναι Orib.*Eup*.3.2. **III.** = πορφυρίς I, Plu.*Aem*.23, etc.: in pl., *cloths of purple*, πορφύρας πατῶν A.*Ag*.957: collectively in sg., κωμῳδοῖς.. πορφύραν εἰσφέρων, ὥσπερ οἱ Μεγαρεῖς Arist.*EN*1123ᵃ 23. **IV.** *purple stripe* or other *adornment* of a garment, τῆς σκιᾶς τὴν π. πρῶτον ἐνυφαίνουσ', εἶτα μετὰ τὴν π. τοῦτ' ἔστιν οὔτε λευκὸν οὔτε π. ἀλλ' ὥσπερ αὐγὴ τῆς κρόκης κεκραμένη Men.561; ποτικεφάλαια.. μὴ ἔχοντα μήτε σκιὰν μήτε πορφύραν *IG*5(1).1390.24 (Andania, i B.C.), cf. *BGU*1141.41 (i B.C.), Luc.*Par*.58, Gal.18(2). 791; π. πλατεῖα, = Lat. *latus clavus*, Plb.10.26.1, Demetr.*Eloc*.108 (pl.); π. alone, *IGRom*.3.1422 (Prusias). **V.** metaph., σελήνη οὐρανοῦ π. Secund.*Sent*.6. (Perh. formed from πορφύρεος II, cf. μαρμαίρω, μαρμάρεος, μάρμαρος.) **-άνθεμος**, ον, = sq., Ps.-Plu. *Fluv*.7.4. **-ανθής**, ές, *with purple blossom*, Thphr.*HP*6.6.3 ap. Ath.15.681b (πορφυρᾶ codd. Thphr.), Dsc.3.137. **II.** τὸ π., = ἡμεροκαλλές, Ps.-Dsc.3.122; = ὑάκινθος, Id.4.62. **-εῖον**, τό, *dye-house for purple*, Str.16.2.23 (f.l. πορφυρίοις). **-ειος**, ον, = sq., ἐσθής Suid. ⊛ **-εος**, η, ον, Att. -ῠροῦς, ᾶ, οῦν, Aeol. -ῠριος Sapph.64, Alc.*Supp*.11.2 (πόρφυρον ἄνθος is corrupt in Sapph.94, and πορφυρ[α] as neut. pl. (-◡-) is found in Sapph.*Supp*.20a.9); -ύριος also in *IG*5(1).1390.179 (Andania, i B.C.): **I.** in Hom., **1.** of the sea (cf. πορφύρω), *heaving, surging*, [χαράδραι] ἐς.. ἅλα πορφυρέην μεγάλα στενάχουσι ῥέουσαι Il.16.391; ἀμφὶ δὲ κῦμα στείρῃ πορφύρεον μεγάλ' ἴαχε νηὸς ἰούσης 1.482, Od.2.428; π. κῦμα.. ποταμοῖο ἵσταντ' ἀειρόμενον Il.21.326, cf. Od.11.243; θάλασσα Alc. l.c. **2.** of blood, *gushing*, αἵματι δὲ χθὼν δεύετο π. Il.17.361; so, π. θάνατος *onrushing* death, of death in battle, 5.83, al. (but, π. θάνατος· ὁ μέλας καὶ βαθὺς καὶ ταραχώδης, Hsch.). **3.** of the rainbow, Il.17. 547; to which a supernatural π. νεφέλη is compared, ib.551; perh. *lurid*. **II.** *purple*, of stuff, cloths, etc., π. φᾶρος Il.8.221; χλαῖνα Od.4.115; πέπλοι Il.24.796; δίπλαξ 3.126, Od.19.242; ῥήγεα Il.24. 645; τάπητες 9.200, Od.20.151; σφαῖρα 8.373; χλάμυς Sapph.64; σπάργανα, πτερά, Pi.*P*.4.114, 183; χλανίς, χιτών, Simon.37.11, B.17. 52, cf. A.*Pers*.317, Hdt.1.50, E.*Or*.1457 codd. (lyr.), etc. **2.** of human complexion, *bright-red, rosy, flushing*, π. Ἀφροδίτη Anacr.2.3; στόμα Simon.72; παρῇδες Phryn.Trag.13; χείλη *IG*3.1376. **3.** *purple-clad, in purple*, Luc.*Tim*.20. **4.** neut. pl. πορφυρᾶ *purple colour* or *purple spots*, Ael.*NA*17.33. **5.** πορφυροῦν (sc. ἄνθος), τό, *Woodfordia floribunda* (an Indian shrub), Ctes.*Fr*.57.21. **6.** Adv. -ῶς, στύφειν mordant *for purple*, *PHolm*.24.37. **-εύς**, έως, ὁ, *fisher for purple fish*, Hdt.4.151, Arist.*Pr*.966ᵇ25, Ph.1.35, prob. in E. *Fr*.670. **-ευτής**, οῦ, ὁ, = foreg., Poll.1.96. **-ευτικός**, ή, όν, *of* or *for a purple-fisher* or *purple-dyer*, στέγαι E.*IT*263; ἡ -κή (sc. τέχνη) *his art*, Poll.7.139. **-εύω**, *catch purple fish*, Philostr.*VA* 1.24:—Med., Hices.ap.Ath.3.87b. **II.** *dye purple*, in Pass., Acus. 37 J. **-έω**, = πορφύρω, ἁλὶ πορφυρεούσῃ v.l. in Arat.158; ἀμέθυστον.. πορφυρέουσαν (v.l. πορφύρουσαν) D.P.1122; χρυσῷ πορφυρέοντι Opp.*C*.2.597 (vv.ll. πορφύρεον, πορφυρόεντι; πορφύροντι cj. Schneider); λειμῶνες ἀνήροτα πορφυρέουσι v.l. for -φύρουσι ib.1.462. **-ίζω**, *to be purplish*, Dsc.3.36, Apollod.Ath.ap.Ath.7.281f; of the sea, Arist. *Mir*.843ᵃ26:—Med., Apollon.*Lex*. s.v. πορφύρη. **-ική**, ἡ, *monopoly of purple-dyeing industry*, ἡ κατὰ Λυκίαν π. *PTeb*.8.31 (iii B.C.). **-ιον**, τό, Dim. of πορφύρα, Arist.*HA*546ᵇ32; *purple-dyed stuff*, *PLond*.3. 899.3 (ii A.D.), etc. **-ιος**, α, ον, Aeol. for πορφύρεος (q.v.). **-ίς**, ίδος, ἡ, *purple garment* or *covering*, X.*Cyr*.2.4.6; distd. from φοινικίς, ib.8.3.3, cf. Poll.7.55; π. θαλαττία Plb.38.7.2; π. ἐξίτηλοι, opp. ἀληθιναί, X.*Oec*.10.3, cf. Chrysipp.*Stoic*.3.196, Luc.*Hist.Conscr*.10, *Nigr*. 13, etc. **II.** *a purple-coloured bird*, τανύπτερος ὡς ὅκα π. Ibyc.4, cf. Ar.*Av*.304, Call.*Fr*.100ᶜ2. **III.** = ἄγχουσα, Ps.-Dsc.4.23. **2.** = ὠκιμοειδές, ib.28. **-ίτης** [ῑ], ου, ὁ, *like purple*, π. λίθος *porphyry*, Plin.*HN*36.57, cj. in D.C.76.15: as Subst., *porphyry-quarry*, *Ostr*.951 (ii A.D.); κίονες π. columns *of porphyry*, *IGRom*.4.1431.42 (Smyrna): in fem., ἡ λιθοτομία ἡ -ῖτις the *porphyry* quarry, Aristid.*Or*.36(48).

67. -ιτικός, ή, όν, *of porphyry*, κίων *PLond.*2.328.20 (ii A. D.); πλάκες *CPHerm.*86.7 (iii A. D., dub.). -ίων, ωνος, ὁ, *purple coot* or *water-hen*, *Fulica porphyrion*, Ar.*Av.*707, al., Arist.*HA*509ᵃ11, 595ᵃ 12, Lxx *Le.*11.18, Polem.Hist.59; distd. from the πορφυρίς, Call.*Fr.* 100ᶜ.2. II. a kind of *polypus*, Artem.2.14. 2. a kind of *fish*, Hsch.

πορφῠρό-βαπτος, ον, *purple-dyed*, Pl.Com.208. -βᾰφεῖον, τό, *dye-house for purple*, Str.17.3.18. -βᾰφής, ές, = πορφυρόβαπτος, *AB*379, Poll.7.63, v. l. in Artem.2.3. -βᾰφία, ἡ, *purple-dyeing*, Vett.Val.3.21. ❀-βάφος [ᾰ], ὁ, *dyer of purple*, *Inscr. Délos* 400.7 (ii B. C.), *IGRom.*4.816 (Hierapolis, πορφυραβ–), Ath.13. 604b. -δίνης [ῑ], Dor. -ας, α, ὁ, *with purple eddies*, B.8.39. -ειδής, ές, *purply*, λίμνα A.*Supp.*529 (lyr.); ἅλς E.*Tr.*124 (lyr.), cf. Arist. *Col.*792ᵃ17. Adv. -δῶς Dsc.1.73. -εις, εσσα, εν, *purple*, καρπός, χρυσός, Nic.*Al.*623 (v.l. πορφυρέοντα), v.l. for πορφυρέοντι in Opp.*C.* 2.597. -εργής, ές, *wrought of purple*, *EM*63.46. -ζωνος, ον, *with purple girdle*, θεά B.10.49, cf. Hsch. s. v. ἰόζωνος. -καυλος, ον, *with purple stalk*, Thphr.*HP*7.4.6. -κλέπτης, ου, ὁ, *stealer of purple*, D.L.6.57. -μῐγής, ές, *mixed with purple*, ἐσθής Poll.7.48, cf. 10.42. -νωτος, ον, *purple-backed*, φᾶρος Nonn.*D.*44.56. -πεζα, ἡ, *purple-edged*, Tryph.66. ❀-πώλης, ου, ὁ, *dealer in purple*, *IG Rom.*4.1071 (Cos), Judeich *Altertümer von Hierapolis* No.156: fem. -πωλις, ιδος, *IGRom.* l. c. (prob.), *Act.Ap.*16.14, *PFlor.*71.641 (iv A. D.):—hence -πωλική (sc. τέχνη), ἡ, *their trade*, *AB*379, Harp. s. v. ἁλουργοπωλική. -στρωτος, ον, *spread with purple cloth*, A.*Ag.* 910. -σχήμων, ον, gen. ονος, (σχῆμα) *purple-clad*, Polyaen.4.3.24.

πορφῠροῦς, ᾶ, οῦν, Att. contr. for πορφύρεος.

❀ πορφῠρο-φορία, ἡ, *wearing of purple garments*, Jul.Laod. in *Cat. Cod.Astr.*5(1).189 (pl.). -χροος, contr. -χρους, ουν, *purple-coloured*, *PHolm.*22.18.

❀ πορφύρω [ῡ], poet. Verb, only pres. and impf., of the sea, ὡς ὅτε πορφύρῃ πέλαγος μέγα κύματι κωφῷ as when the huge sea *heaves, surges, swirls* with dumb swell (i. e. with waves that do not break), Il.14.16, cf. Arat.158, Artem.2.23; ὑπὸ στείρῃσι θάλασσα πορφύρει Arat.296; διάνδιχα νηὸς ἰούσης δίνῃ πορφύροντα διήνυσαν Ἑλλήσποντον A.R.1.935; of flame, [φλόγα] φονίῳ σβέσεν αἵματι πορφύρουσαν Id.4. 668:—later in Med., κἂν ἡ γαλήνη πορφύροιτο even in a *gently heaving* calm, Him.*Or.*31.2; εὔδια μὲν πόντος πορφύρεται *AP*10.14 (Agath.). 2. metaph., πολλὰ δέ οἱ κραδίη πόρφυρε much *was* his heart *troubled*, Il.21.551, cf. Od.4.427,572, 10.309; though others take it trans., his heart *brooded, pondered on* many things, as in Q.S.2.85, al., Epic. ap. Suid.: abs., *ponder*, A.R.3.456; π. οἷον.. ib. 1161. II. after Hom., *grow red*, of a river, καὶ τὺ δὲ Κρᾶθι οἴνῳ πορφύροις may'st thou *flush* with wine, Theoc.5.125 (= βλύζοις Sch., i. e. signf. I.1; prob. both senses are meant); τόσον ἄνθος χιονέαις πόρφυρε παρῇσι Bion 2.19; αἰδοῖ π. παρήϊον Q.S.14.47; πορφύρων βότρυς *AP*9.249 (Maec.); δαίδαλα πορφύρων, of the tiger's skin, Opp. *C.*3.347; of ringlets, ὑακίνθοις.. ὅμοια πορφύροντες Luc.*Am.*26, cf. Him.*Or.*1.19; γῆ π. ἄνθεσι ib.13.7. 2. trans., *dye red*, χεῖρας φόνῳ Nonn.*D.*44.106:—Pass., [οἴνῳ] πορφύρετο πέτρη ib.45.308, etc. (πορ-φύρ-yω, redupl., cogn. with Lat. *fervere*, *fermentum*, OE. *beorm* 'barm, froth on fermenting malt liquors, yeast'; for the sequence of meanings cf. English *flush* (1) 'flow suddenly in great volume', (2) of blood, 'rush to the cheeks', (3) of the cheeks, etc., 'become red'; cf. πορφύρεος.)

πορφῠρ-ώδης, ες, = πορφυροειδής, *EM*486.46, v. l. in Artem.2. 36. -ώματα, τά, *flesh of the swine sacrificed to Demeter and Persephone*, Hsch.

❀ *πόρω, assumed as pres. to aor. Act. ἔπορον and pf. Pass. πέπρωμαι: no example occurs of fut. πορῶ, Aeol. πόρσω, cited by *EM*683.54: I. aor. ἔπορον, Hom. mostly without augm.; part. πορών Il.21.80, Od. 19.460, A.*Pr.*946; inf. πορεῖν S.*OT*1255:—*furnish, offer, give*, of things, π. ἀμφιφορῆα, δέπας, δόρυ, δῶρα, ξεινήϊα, ἕδνα, εἵματα, ἵππον, κρέας, μελίην, οἶνον, ὅπλα, τεύχεα, τόξον, φάρμακα, χλαῖναν, Il.23. 92, 24.234, 23.893, Od.4.130, Il.6.218, 16.178, Od.5.321, Il.23. 540, Od.8.477, Il.16.143, Od.9.360, Il.19.21, 7.146, 15.441, 4.219, Od.14.460; of conditions or qualities, π. μαντοσύνην Il.1.72; νόον Od.10.494; πένθος, κακά, θάνατον, etc., 19.512, 9.460, 18.202, etc.; τιμήν Hes.*Th.*904; εὖχος π. *fulfil* a wish, Od.22.7; ἀνδρὶ παράκοιτιν π. Il.24.60; θυγατέρας π. υἱάσι Od.10.7; πόρεν δέ οἱ υἱόν *he gave* her a son, i. e. begat one upon her, Il.16.185; οἱ ἔπορεν χρυσόν Pi.*O.*13.77; ἀγλαΐαν, αἶσαν, κῦδος, etc., Id.*I.*2.18, *N.*6.47, *P.*4.66, etc.; π. τινὶ γέρα, δωρεάν, τιμάς, etc., A.*Pr.*108, 616, 946, etc.; ἔπορε χρήματα Eup.12.2 D. (s. v. l.); λύσιν εὐαγῆ S.*OT*921; Κύκνον θανάτῳ πόρεν Pi. *O.*2.82; ὅρκον π. *offer to take* an oath, A.*Eu.*489: c. inf., πόρε καὶ σὺ κούρῃσιν ἕπεσθαι τιμήν [so as] to attend on them, Il.9.513, cf. 6. 228; νιν.. πόρε Κενταύρῳ διδάξαι Pi.*P.*3.45: abs., σοὶ θεοὶ πόροιεν, ὡς (= οἷα) ἐγὼ θέλω S.*OC*1124. 2. = πορεύω, *bring*, εἴ τις.. δεῦρο Θησέα πόροι ib.1458. II. pf. πέπρωμαι, only 3 sg. πέπρωται (Hes. also in plpf. πέπρωτο):—*it has* or *had been* (*is* or *was*) *fated*, c. acc. pers. et inf., ἄμφω γὰρ πέπρωται.. γαῖαν ἐρεῦσαι Il.18.329, cf. Pi.*O.*8. 33, E.*Alc.*21: c. dat. pers. et inf., οἱ πέπρωτο.. δαμῆναι Hes.*Th.*464, cf. 475; τί γὰρ πέπρωται Ζηνὶ πλὴν ἀεὶ κρατεῖν A.*Pr.*519, cf. 815, Antiph.227.10; πεπρωμένον ἐστί, = πέπρωται, ὁπποτέρῳ θανάτοιο τέλος πεπρωμένον ἐστί Il.3.309; ὅτῳ θανεῖν μέν ἐστιν οὐ πεπρ. A.*Pr.*753; ἐκ θεῶν πεπρ. ἐστὶ πολέμους γίγνεσθαι X.*HG*6.3.6. 2. part. as Adj., of persons, *destined to* a thing, δμῇ πεπρωμένον αἴσῃ Il.15.209, cf. 16.441, E.*Tr.*340 (lyr.). b. abs., *destined*, π. βασιλεύς Pi.*P.*4.61; τὸν πεπρ. μόρον A.*Fr.*362.4; βίος π. one's *natural* life, Pi.*P.*6.27; τὸ μόρσιμον π. Id.*N.*4.61; ἀρετὰ π. ib.43; π. αἶσα, ξυμφορά, etc., A.*Pr.*103, S.*Ant.* 1337, etc.; ὅταν ἔλθῃ τὸ π. τέλος X.*Mem.*2.1.33; ἡ π. (with and without μοῖρα) *appointed lot, Fate, Destiny*, Hdt.1.91, E.*Hec.*43, etc.; twice in Isoc., 1.43, 10.61 (also, οὐ ταῦτα ταύτῃ μοῖρά πω τελεσφόρος κρᾶναι πέπρωται, i. e. ἡ πεπρωμένη μοῖρα οὐ ταῦτα ταύτῃ κρανεῖ, A.*Pr.* 512); also, τὸ π. Pi.*Fr.*232, A.*Ag.*68 (anap.), 684 (lyr.), E.*Rh.*634; τὰ π. Id.*Ion* 1388, etc.—Poet. word, pf. part. Pass. being used rarely in Prose (v. supr.). (Cf. Lat. *pars, portio.*)

πός (A), Dor. = ποὺς, Choerob. in *Theod.*1.192, 243 H., *EM*635.22.

πός (B), Arc., Cypr. = πρός (q. v.).

ποσάγω, = προσάγω, *JRS*15.159 (Cotiaeum).

ποσάκις [ᾰ], Adv. *how many times? how often?* Pl.*Ep.*353d; poet. ποσσάκι Call.*Dian.*119. II. Indef., *so many times*, οἱ π. ποσοὶ [ἀριθμοί], i. e. *square* numbers, and οἱ π. π. ποσοὶ *cubes*, Arist.*Metaph.* 1020ᵇ5.

ποσα-πλάσιος [πλᾰ], α, ον, *how many times multiplied? how many fold?* Pl.*Men.*83b. 2. c. gen., *what multiple of..?* ib.84e. -πλοῦς, ῆ, οῦν, = foreg., Gal.13.872. Adv. -πλῶς; *how many times?* Lxx *Ps.*62(63).1. -πους, ποδος, ὁ, ἡ, *of how many feet?* Pl.*Men.* 85b. -χορδος, ον, *with how many strings?* Bacch.*Harm.* 63. -χῶς, Adv. *in how many ways*, Arist.*Pol.*1289ᵃ11, Gal.14. 791, 19.47; esp. *in how many senses?* π. λέγεται; Arist.*Top.*105ᵃ23; περὶ τοῦ π. λέγεται ἕκαστον Id.*Metaph.*1028ᵃ5, cf. *Rh.*1398ᵃ28.

πόσε, Adv. *whither?* πόσε φεύγετε; Il.16.422, Od.6.199; πόσ' ἴμεν; 10.431:—Ep. for later ποῖ.

ποσεία, ἡ, (πόσος) *enumeration*, *POxy.*918 *Intr.* (ii A. D.).

Ποσειδαῖα, τά, *games in honour of Poseidon*, *IG*5(1).1387 (Thuria, iii B. C.); also Ποσείδεα ib.7.47 (Megara); Lacon. Ποʽοίδαια ib.5(1). 213.12,18 (Sparta, v B. C.).

Ποσειδάνιασταί, οἱ, guild of *worshippers of Poseidon* at Rhodes, *Annuario* 8/9.322; Ποσειδωνιασταί, at Delos, *SIG*726.1 (i B. C.).

Ποσειδάνιος, v. Ποσειδώνιος. Ποσειδεών, v. Ποσιδηϊών.

Ποσείδιος, Ποσείδιον, v. Ποσιδήϊος, -ήϊον.

❀ Ποσειδῶν (perispom. in Att., Hdn.Gr.2.914), ὁ; gen. ῶνος, also ῶ Aristias 1; acc. Ποσειδῶ Ar.*Lys.*1165, *IG*2².111.67; voc. Πόσειδον S. *Fr.*371.1 (lyr.), Ar.*Ra.*664: contr. (first in Hes.*Th.*732 (s. v. l.)) from Ep. form (also used by Pi.*P.*4.204, al., and S.*Tr.*502 (lyr.)) Ποσειδάων [ᾰ], άωνος, acc. άωνα, voc. Ποσείδαον Il.14.357, Od.3.55, al.:—Ion. Ποσειδέων, έωνος, Hdt.1.148, al.:—Aeol. Ποσείδαν Alc.26; Lyr. Ποσειδάν Pi.*O.*1.26, al., B.16.79; also in Crete, *SIG*56.15 (v B. C.); at Epidaurus, *IG*4²(1).150 (v B. C.); at Lindus, ib. 12(1).809, etc.; and in Arc., *SIG*306.57 (Tegea, iv B. C.):—Dor. Ποτειδάν (oxyt., Hdn.Gr. 2.916) *IG*4.210, 219, al. (Corinth), *SIG*1000.17 (Cos, i B. C.), etc., prob. in Pi.*O.*13.5,40, Epich.54,115, X.*HG*3.3.2; also Ποτειδάϝων *IG*4.211, al. (Corinth), Ποτειδάων *GDI*5085 (Crete, iii B. C.): also Ποτῖδᾶς or Ποτειδᾶς (codd. vary), gen. ᾶ Eup.140, acc. ᾶν Epich.81, dub. in Ar.*Ach.*798 (Megarian), voc. ᾶ Sophr.131:—Boeot. Ποτειδάων (leg. Ποτῖδάων) Corinn.1, cf. Corinn.*Supp.* 2.26 (*BKT*5(2)p.31); gen. [Ποτ]ιδάωνος ib.76; but dat. Ποτειδάονι *IG*7.2465 (Thebes):—Arc. Ποσοιδάν ib.5(2).95 (Tegea):—Lacon. Ποʽοιδάν ib.5(1).1228, al.:—Aeol. (?) Ποτοίδαν *Schwyzer* 642 (Pergam., v B. C.):—*Poseidon.*

❀ Ποσειδώνιος, α, ον, *sacred to Poseidon*, v.l. in E.*Ph.*188 (lyr.):—also Ποσειδαώνιος, *AP*6.4 (Leon.); Dor. Ποσειδάνιος [ᾰ] Pi.*O.*5. 21, 10(11).26, B.*Fr.*6, S.*OC*1494 (lyr.), E. l. c. (lyr.). II. Ποσειδώνιον (sc. ἱερόν), τό, *temple of Poseidon*, Th.4.129, Paus.10.38.8; Ποσειδώνειον, Arist.*Vent.*973ᵃ16; Dor. Ποσειδάνειον *AB*430, Suid. s. v. Ἀπολλώνιον; Delph. Ποτειδάνιον *SIG*247 III 12 (iv B. C.). III. Ποσειδώνια, τά, *his festival*, Str.10.5.11, Ath.13.590f; Dor. Ποσειδάνια *GDI*4271.10 (Rhodes), *SIG*1028.24 (Cos, ii B. C.).

Ποσειδωνοπετής, ές, *coming from Poseidon*, formed like διοπετής, Oenom.ap.Eus.*PE*5.36.

ποσέτης, ες, *how many years old?*, *Riv.Fil.*53.217 (Gortyn).

ποσθ-ᾰλίσκος, ὁ, = πόσθων II, Ar.*Th.*291. -η, ἡ, *membrum virile*, Id.*Nu.*1014. II. *foreskin*, Dsc.4.153, Ruf.*Onom.*102, Orib.*Fr.*84. -ία, ἡ, *foreskin*, Ph.2.211. II. *stye on the eyelid*, Gal.12.741, Aët.7.84. -ιον, τό, Dim. of πόσθη, Hp.*Ulc.*12, Ar. *Th.*254,515. ❀ -ων, ωνος, ὁ, (πόσθη) prop. *one with a large πόσθη*, Luc.*Lex.*12. II. Com. word for a *little boy*, Ar.*Pax* 1300.

ποσίδεσμος, ὁ, *foot-shackler, fetterer*, word coined by Pl.*Cra.*402e.

❀ Ποσιδήϊος, η, ον, Ion. for Ποσιδεῖος (v. infr.), Π. ἄλσος the grove *sacred to Poseidon*, Il.2.506, *h.Ap.*230; written Ποσείδιον ἄλσος in Str.8.3.20; but the Att. form is Ποσῖδεῖος, S.*Fr.*506 (anap.). 2. Dor. Ποσῖδαῖος [ᾱ], ὁ (sc. μήν), a month at Epidaurus, *IG*4²(1).103.35; Hellenistic Ποσῖδεῖος *CIG*6850 (incert. loc.). II. Ποσιδήϊον, τό, Ion. for Ποσῖδεῖον (which is found in *Inscr.Délos* 372 *A* 158 (iii/ii B. C.)), *temple of Poseidon*, Od.6.266; written Ποσείδιον in Paus.2. 34.9. III. Ποσῖδεῖα, τά, *festival of Poseidon*, *IG*11(2).203 *A* 57, 287 *A* 89 (Delos, iii B. C.), *Inscr.Délos* 372 *A* 114 (iii/ii B. C.); written Ποσίδεα, *IG*1².190.8.

❀ Ποσιδηϊών, ῶνος, ὁ, sixth month in the Athenian and some Ionic calendars, Anacr.6, *IG*1².377.17; later Ποσιδεών, in Att. inscrr., ib. 2².204.11 (iv B. C.), al., and at Delos, Tenos, Paros, ib.11(2).203 *A* 32, 56 (iii B. C.), 12(5).872.43 (iii B. C.), *SIG*562.49 (iii B. C.) written Ποσειδεών in one inscr., ib.1017.10 (Sinope, iii B. C.), and in codd. of Arist.*HA*543ᵃ11, 570ᵃ32, etc.:—Aeol. (?) Ποσίδάων, *Hemerolog. Flor.*

πόσιμος, ον, *drinkable*, *PSI*8.948.2, al. (iv A. D.).

ποσίνδα, Adv., (πόσος) *how many times?* π. παίζειν, = ἀρτιάζειν, *play morra*, X.*Eq.Mag.*5.10.

❀ πόσις, ὁ, poet. πόσσις *AP*6.323 (Leon.); gen. πόσιος (no gen. is found in Att., πόσεως only in Hdn.Gr.2.700); dat. πόσει, Ep. πόσεϊ Il.5.71; voc. πόσι E.Alc.323, Ar.Th.913; also πόσις E.Hel.1399: pl. πόσεις Id.IA176 (lyr.); acc. πόσιας Il.6.240:—*husband, spouse*, Il.3.329, Alcm.29, *Inscr.Cypr.*93 H., Pi.P.9.99, etc.; τὸν ὁμοδέμνιον π. A.Ag.1108 (lyr.); esp. *lawful husband*, μὴ π. μὲν Ἡρακλῆς ἐμὸς καλῆται, τῆς νεωτέρας δ' ἀνήρ S.Tr.550 (but cf. Il.24.725 and 763): rare in Prose, Arist.Pol.1335b41; π. καὶ ἄλοχος ib.1253b6; κρυπτὸς π., of a paramour, E.Or.561. (I.-E. *potis* 'lord, master', cf. πότνια, δεσπότης, Skt. *pátis* 'lord, master, husband', *pátnī* 'lady, wife', Lat. *potis* (*sum*), etc.)

**πόσῐς**, ιος, Att. εως, ἡ; dat. πόσει, Ion. πόσι Hdt.5.19: (πίνω):—*drinking, drink, beverage*, πόσιος καὶ ἐδητύος ἐξ ἔρον ἕντο Il.1.469, al.; βρῶσίς τε π. τε Od.10.176, cf. Hes.Sc.395: pl., βρώσεσιν ἢ πόσεσιν Democr.235; *carousal*, Alc.101, Critias 6.9 D.; συγγίνεσθαι ἐς πόσιν to meet for a *carousal*, Hdt.1.172, cf. *Bull.Soc.Arch.Alex.*7.66; πρὸς πόσιν τετράφθαι Th.7.73; λιπαρέειν τῇ πόσι Hdt.5.19; παρὰ τὴν π. *over their cups*, Id.2.121.δ'; ἐκ δὲ θοίνας π. ἐγένετο, ἐκ δὲ πόσιος μῶκος Epich.148; πόσιος ἐν βάθει Theoc.14.29: pl., Pl.Lg.641a. 2. *draught*, αἷμα πίεται τρίτην πόσιν A.Ch.578; ἐκπίνειν ὑστάτην π. Antipho 1.20; πόσις φαρμάκου Id.6.22.

**Ποσοιδαία**, ἡ, name of a tribe at Mantinea, *IG*5(2).271.14 (iv B.C.).

**Ποσοιδάν**, v. Ποσειδῶν.

**ποσοποιός**, όν, *making a certain quantity*, prob. l. in Arist.*Metaph.*1083a13.

❋ **πόσος**, Ion. κόσος, η, ον, interrog. Adj. *of what quantity?* 1. of Number, *how many?* κόσοι τινές εἰσι οἱ Λακεδαιμόνιοι Hdt.7.234; π. καὶ ποῖα.. ; X.Mem.4.4.7; π. χρήματα; Id.Cyr.3.1.35; π. ἄττα δὴ ὑποδήματα Arist.EN1133a21: with sg. Nouns, *how great? how much?* π. πλῆθος νεῶν; A.Pers.334; π. τις ἀριθμός; Pl.Tht.198c; π. χρυσίον; X.An.7.8.1. 2. of Distance, *how far?* πόσον ἄπεστιν ἐνθένδε τὸ στράτευμα; Id.Cyr.6.3.10; π. τις ὁδὸς εἴη ib.4.6.10; μέχρι πόσου; Anon.ap.Gell.1.3.9, cf. E.Fr.953.32. 3. of Time, *how long?* π. τινὰ χρόνον; S.OT558, etc.; π. χρόνου; = πότε; Ar.Ach.83. 4. of Value, *how much?* πόσον δίδως; Id.Pax 1262; πόσου; *at what price?* Id.Ach.812, 898, Pl.Ap.20b, etc.; ἐπὶ πόσῳ; ib.41a, X.Cyr.3.1.43; ἐκ πόσου is f.l. for ὁπόσου in D.50.30. 5. of Degree, *how great?* πόθος; πόσος τις; Ar.Ra.55; πόσης γέμει σωφροσύνης; Pl.Smp.216d: neut. Adv. πόσον; πόσα; *to what amount?* Ar.Ec.399, X.Mem.2.2.8. II. **ποσός**, ή, όν, indef. Adj. *of a certain quantity* or *magnitude*, Gorg.Fr.3 D., Pl.Sph.245d, etc.; ποσὰ τῶν περιφερῶν *a certain number of..*, Epicur.Ep.2 p.50U.; ἐπὶ ποσόν *for a certain time*, Plb.2.34.15, etc.; οὐδ' ἐπὶ π. Id.1.1.2; κατὰ ποσόν *to a certain extent*, Vett.Val.81.22. 2. ποσόν, τό, = ποσότης, Pl.Phlb.24c,d, Arist.Cat.4b20, Metaph.1020a7, etc.; κατὰ ποσόν in point of *quantity*, Id.EN1158b31. III. Adv. ποσῶς Corn.ND34, Ruf.Oss.18, Sor.Fract.2, Vett.Val.238.24, S.E.P.1.120, 227. (I.-E. *qᵘ̯oty-os*, cf. Lat. *quot*, Skt. *káti* 'how many?')

**ποσότης**, ητος, ἡ, *quantity*, freq. in pl., Arist.Metaph.1028a19, Longin.2.2, S.E.P.1.129: sg., Plb.16.12.10, Vitr.1.2.2, Ph.1.9, al., Longin.12.1, *CIG*2712 (Mylasa), etc. II. *amount, sum of money*, *IG*14.956 A 11 (Rome, iv A.D.), *BGU*412.12 (iv A.D.). III. *quantity* of syllables, v.l. in *An.Ox.*3.282; *number*, στοιχείων Longin.Proll.Heph.p.87 C.

**ποσόω**, *reckon the quantity of, count*, τὰς ψήφους Thphr.Char.23.6:—Pass., τῶν ποσω[θεισέων δραχμέων] prob. in *SIG*279.41 (Zeleia, iv B.C.); *make up a quantity, amount to*, Hero *Geom.*5.4. II. *quantify*, ποσῶν τοῦτο τὸ δέκα Plot.6.6.16:—Pass., *to be quantified* or *quantitatively determined*, Dam.Pr.54, Elias *in Porph.*154.35, Ascl. *in Metaph.*104.36, Phlp. *in de An.*543.31.

**ποσσαέτης**, ες, = ποσέτης, used as fem. (nisi leg. -ις), *Bull.Soc.Arch.Alex.*7.244 (i B.C./i A.D.).

**ποσσῆμαρ**, Adv. *for how many days?* Il.24.657.

**ποσσί-κλῦτος**, ον, *famed for swiftness of foot*, Dionys.ap.St.Byz. s.v. Κάσπειρος. ❋ **-κροτος**, ον, *struck with the foot* in dancing, Orac.ap.Hdt.1.66. II. Act., *striking with the feet*, Orph.H.31.2.

**ποσταῖος**, α, ον, (πόστος) *on which day in the ordinal series?* π. ἂν ..ἐκεῖσε ἀφικοίμην; i.e. in how many days! X.Cyr.5.3.28; π. πάρει; Diog.Cyn.ap.D.L.6.39, cf. Gal.9.861.

**ποστημόριον** and **ποστήμορον**, τό, *fraction*, Gloss.

**πόστιον**, τό, for πόσθιον, barbarism in Ar.Th.1188.

**πόστος**, η, ον, *which in the ordinal series?* π. δὴ ἔτος ἐστὶν ὅτε ξείνισσας ἐκεῖνον; *how many* years is it since..? Od.24.288; πόστην (sc. γραμμήν, i.e. on the sun-dial) ἥλιος τέτραπται; Ar.Fr.163; π. ῥύμη; *which* side-street? *which* turning? Philippid.22; κατὰ π. σφόνδυλον; Gal.8.238; ἐνθυμήθητι π. ἀφ' Ἡρακλέους ἐγένετο Arr.Epict.2.18.22; κατανόησον πόστῳ αὐτῶν μέρει πάντες μαχεσάμενοι νενικήκαμεν with *what* fraction, i.e. *with how small* a part, X.Cyr.4.1.16, cf. Jul.Mis.340b; Ξενοφῶν π. μέρος τοῦ λόχου ἢ ἐνωμοτία ἐστὶν οὐ διασαφεῖ Arr.Tact.6.3. II. **ποστός**, ή, όν, *holding a certain place in the ordinal series*, τῇ ποστῇ (sc. ἡμέρᾳ) on *such-and-such* a day of the month, PMag.Leid.W.3.35, cf. S.E.M.5.37. (Prob. from *ποσσοστος, formed from πόσ(σ)οι on analogy of πολλοστός from πολλοί.)

**ποσφέρω**, fut. 3 sg. ποσοίσει, = προσ-, *JRS*15.155 (Cotiaeum).

**ποσώδης**, ες, *quantitative*, Simp. *in Cat.*178.10.

**πότ**, apocop. for ποτί (q.v.). **ποτα**, Aeol. for ποτε, as ὅτα for ὅτε. ❋ **πόταγε**, Dor. for πρόσαγε. **ποτάγορος**, Dor. for προσήγορος. **ποτάγχυμεν**· προσορμίζομεν, Hsch. **ποταγωγίς**, v. προσαγωγεύς. **ποταείδω**, Dor. for προσαείδω, v. προσᾴδω.

**ποταινί**, Adv. *recently* (glossed προσφάτως), Zonar.

**ποταίνιος**, α, ον, also ος, ον S.Fr.149.5:—*fresh, new*, στέφανος Pi.O.10(11).60; αἷμα A.Ch.1055, cf. Eu.282; ἄλφιτα Hp.Acut.37, Nat.Mul.15; ἡ τῶν π. προσθήκη Aret.CA2.3. 2. metaph., *new, unexpected, unheard of*, μῆτις B.16.51; πῆμα A.Pr.102; πάταγος Id.Th.239 (lyr., dub.); τάφος S.Ant.849 (lyr.); ἡδοναί Id.Fr. l.c. (Expld. as = πρόσφατος by Eust.1106.23 and Phot. (who calls it Doric, i.e. from ποτί, αἶνος), but it is found in Hp. (v. supr.), cf. Bacch.ap.Erot.)

**ποταινός**, ή, όν, f.l. (ποτ' αἰναί) for ποταναί in Epich.61.

**ποτᾰμέλγω**, Dor. for προσαμέλγω (q.v.).

**ποτᾰμ-εύς**, έως, ὁ, name of *the East wind* at Tripolis, Arist.Vent.973a13. **-ηγός**, όν, (ἄγω) *towed upon a river, going by river*, σκάφαι D.H.2.53,55, 3.56. **-ηδόν**, Adv. *like a river*, Luc.Sat.7, Aret.SD2.13. **-ήϊος**, η, ον, Ion. and poet. for ποτάμιος, Nonn.D.11.309, al. **-ηΐς**, ΐδος, poet. fem. of ποτάμιος, Νύμφαι A.R.3.1219, Nic.Al.128. **-ηνή**, ή, *River-goddess*, Μήτηρ *Supp.Epigr.*6.556 (Yalovadj). **-ηπόρος**, ον, *crossing rivers*, Opp.C.2.178; *going to the river*, ib.4.84. **-ιαῖος**, α, ον, = ποτάμιος (which is v.l. in Arist.), Arist.Mete.353b28, Ruf.Fr.66. **-ιον**, τό, Dim. of ποταμός, Metag.6.5, Str.6.3.9, 8.3.12. **-ιος**, α, ον, also ος, ον E.El.309, but cf. 56:—*of* or *from a river*, ὄχθαι A.Th.392; ποτά S.Fr.659.5; δρόσος, ὕδατα, χεύματα, ῥεῖθρα, E.Hipp.127 (lyr.), Alc.159, Hel.1304 (lyr.), El.152 (lyr.), 794; κύκνος Id.Rh.618; οἱ ἵπποι οἱ π. Hdt.2.71, cf. Arist.HA502a9; ὁ π. χοῖρος Id.Fr.300; τὰ π. (sc. ζῷα), opp. τὰ θαλάττια, etc., Id.HA487a27; of plants, Thphr.HP4.10.1; ναῦς Jul.Or.1.22a; ναῦται PGiss.40 ii 18 (iii A.D.). 2. of cities, *on a river*, Pi.P.6.6; ποταμία (sc. χώρα) Str.11.3.2, al. 3. epith. of Artemis, from the connexion of her worship with that of rivers, Pi.P.2.7; π. θεοί Artem.2.34. 4. Ποτάμιος (sc. μήν), ὁ, month at Chalcedon, *GDI* 3053. **-ίσκος**, ὁ, Dim. of ποταμός, Str.14.1.8. **-ίτης** [ῑ], ου, ὁ, *water-finder*, Lat. *aquilex*, Gloss. II. *worker employed by the Nile conservancy*, *BGU*14 ii 19 (iii A.D.), *PSI*1.83.11 (iii A.D.): dat. pl. spelt -ίτοις PMasp.p.53 (vi A.D.).

**ποτᾰμο-γείτων**, ονος, ὁ, *pondweed, Potamogeton natans*, Dsc.4.100, Luc.Trag.152, Ael.NA6.46. 2. = ἄρκιον, Ps.-Dsc.4.106. II. epith. of a crocodile, PMag.Leid.W.25.21. **-διάρτης**, ου, ὁ, (διαίρω) *river-ferryman*, Artem.4.66. **-καρίδες**, *cammariunculi*, Gloss. **-κλυστος**, ον, *washed by a river*, Str.3.4.12, 4.1.12.

**ποτᾰμόνδε**, Adv. *to* or *towards a river*, Il.21.13, Od.10.159, al.

**ποτᾰμόρρῠτος**, ον, (ῥέω) *watered by rivers*, Phryn.PSp.103 B. II. *washed down by rivers*, κασσίτερος Scymn.165.

❋ **ποτᾰμός**, ὁ, *river, stream*, Ὠκεανοῖο ἐξ οὗ περ πάντες π. Il.21.196; π. ἁλιμυρήεις, ἀργυροδίνης, βαθυδίνης, βαθύρροος, δεινός, διιπετής, δινήεις, ἐΰρροος, ἐρίδουπος, εὐρὺ ῥέων, θεῖος, ἱερός, ἴφθιμος, καλλίροος, κελάδων, λάβρος, πλήθων, χειμάρροος, ὠκύροος, Od.5.460, Il.21.8, 212, 8, 25, 17.263, Od.11.242, Il.21.130, Od.10.515 (pl.), Il.21.304, Od.11.238, 10.351 (pl.), Il.17.749 (pl.), Od.5.441, Il.18.576, 21.270, 5.87, 87, 598; νυκτὸς π., of the *rivers* of hell, Pi.Fr.130.9: prov., ἄνω ποταμῶν, of extraordinary events, A.Fr.335, etc. (in full, ἄνω π. ἱερῶν χωροῦσι παγαί E.Med.410 (lyr.)); π. οὐκ ἔστιν ἐμβῆναι δὶς τῷ αὐτῷ Heraclit.91; π. θαλάσσῃ ἐρίζεις, of unequal combats, Suid., etc. 2. metaph., *rivers of fire* or *lava*, Pi.P.1.22, A.Pr.370: Com., ζωμοῦ π. κρέα θερμὰ κυλίνδων Telecl.1.8, cf. Pherecr.108.3; also π. πραγμάτων Porph.Marc.5. 3. *artificial stream, canal*, Str.16.1.10, Arr.An.7.21.1; οἱ ὀρυχθέντες π. OGI54.23 (Adule, iii B.C.). II. personified, *river-god*, Il.20.7, 73, etc. III. name of the constellation Eridanus, Eudox.ap.Hipparch.1.2.20, Arat.358, etc.

❋ **ποτᾰμο-φόρητος**, ον, *carried away by a river*, Apoc.12.15, PMag.Par.1.876, Cyran.39; γῆ π. PStrassb.5.10 (iii A.D.). **-φῠλᾰκία**, ἡ, *office of river-guard*, *CIL*2.1970 (in Lat. form), prob. in PAmh.2.32.13 (ii B.C.). ❋ **-φῠλᾰκίδες** νῆες, *guardships on river*, Ostr.293 (i A.D.), PFlor.91.4 (ii A.D.). **-χοος**, ον, contr. -χους, ουν, = sq., ἡ π. (sc. γῆ) Hero *Geom.*23.68. **-χωστος**, ον, *deposited by a river*, Ephor.65(e) J., Str.13.3.4.

**ποτᾰμώδης**, ες, *like a river*, δάκρυον Eun.Hist.p.206 D.

**ποτᾰνής**, ές, Dor. for προσηνής, Cleobul.ap.D.L.1.93 (Sup.).

**ποτᾰνός**, ά, όν, *winged, flying*, ἐν ποτανοῖς among *fowls*, Pi.N.3.80; π. οἰωνοί E.Hel.1478 (lyr.); πέδιλα Id.El.460 (lyr.); π. εἴ σέ τις θεῶν κτίσαι Id.Supp.620 (lyr.), cf. 1142 (lyr.): prov. of vain pursuits, διώκει παῖς ποτανὸν ὄρνιν A.Ag.394 (lyr.): metaph., ποτανὸς ἐν Μοίσαισι, i.e. *soaring* in the arts of the Muses, Pi.P.5.114; ποτανᾷ μαχανᾷ by *soaring* art, i.e. by poesy, Id.N.7.22; ἐμᾷ ποτανὸς ἀμφὶ μαχανᾷ Id.P.8.34; ποταναί (v.l. ποτ' αἰναί) τευθίδες Epich.61.—Dor. for **ποτηνός**, which occurs only in Poet.ap.Pl.Phdr.252b.

❋ **ποτάομαι**, poet. Frequentat. of πέτομαι, Ep. also **ποτέομαι** (imper. ποτεῦ Call.Fr.1.50P.) (v. infr.), also Alc.43; Aeol. 2 sg. πότῃ Sapph.41 (dub.); Dor. 3 sg. ποτῆται Alcm.26.3; Aeol. part. ποτήμενος Theoc.29.30: fut. ποτήσομαι Mosch.2.145 (s.v.l.): aor. ἐποτήθην, Dor. -άθην [ᾱ] S.Fr.476 (ἀμ-, lyr.): pf. πεπότημαι, Dor. -ᾱμαι in lyr. passages of Trag., A.Pers.668, Eu.378, E.Hipp.564:—*fly hither and thither*, ὀρνίθων ἔθνεα..ἔνθα καὶ ἔνθα ποτῶνται Il.2.462; νυκτερίδες..τρίζουσαι ποτέονται Od.24.7; κεραυνοί..ποτέοντο Hes.Th.691; ποτώμεναι ἄλλοτε ἄλλῃ h.Merc.558; in Trag. also simply = πέτομαι, *fly*, A.Ag.576, etc.; τὰ ποτήμενα συλλαβῆν Theoc. l.c.; of sounds, [βοά] π. A.Th.84 (lyr.); ἐκ στομάτων π. εὐχά Id.Supp.657 (lyr.): pf. (with pres. sense), *to be upon the wing*, ψυχὴ δ'..ἀποπταμένη πεπότηται Od.11.222; [μέλισσαι] αἱ μέν τ' ἔνθα..πεποτήαται, αἱ δέ τε ἔνθα Il.2.90; Ἔρις πεπότητο Hes.Sc.148. 2. metaph., δεῖμα προστατήριον καρδίας..ποτᾶται *hovers*, A.Ag.977 (lyr.), cf. Ch.390 (lyr.); τοῖον ἐπὶ κνέφας ἀνδρὶ..π. Id.Eu.378 (lyr.), cf. Pers.668 (lyr.); *to be fluttered*, ἐπὶ τραγῳδίᾳ ἀνεπτερῶσθαι καὶ πεποτῆσθαι τὰς φρένας Ar.*Av.*1445, cf. *Nu.* 319.

**ποταπός,** v. ποδαπός.

**ποταποφωνέω,** Dor. for προσ-, *declare in addition, Chron.Lind.* D.45.

**ποταρός·** γνώριμος, Hsch.

**ποταρχέω,** = συμποσιαρχέω, *Lyr.Alex.Adesp.*21.9.

**ποτὰς** ἡ ἀναβάλλουσα, *bibulus* (sic), *Gloss.*

**ποταυδάω,** Dor. for προσαυδάω. **ποταυλέω,** Dor. for προσαυλέω.

**ποτᾶφος,** ῴα, ῷον, Dor. for προσηῷος, Theoc.4.33.

⊛ **πότε,** Ion. **κότε,** Dor. **πόκα** Theoc.4.7, al.:—interrog. Particle used in direct and indirect questions, *when? at what time?* Il.19.227, Od.4.642; πότ' εἰ μὴ νῦν..; A.*Th.*101 (lyr.), cf. *Ch.*394 (lyr.); πότ' ἆρα; = πότε with ἆρα I. 4 or II, E.*Ion* 563; πότε δή; A.*Ch.*720 (lyr.); ἐς πότε λήξει; S.*Aj.*1185 (lyr.); ἐκ πότε..ἤρξασθε *SIG*832.9 (Astypalaea, ii A.D.). II. indef. **ποτε** (Att., also Arc. in οὔποτε *IG*5(2).343.48,66 (Orchom., iv B.C.), οὔτε ποτέ *Tab.Defix.* in *Philol.* 59.201, and Cypr. in μήποτε *Inscr.Cypr.*144 H.), Ion. **κοτε,** Dor. **ποκα,** Aeol. **ποτα** Sapph.1.5, enclit. Particle: 1. *at some time* or *other, at some time,* τάχ' ἄν ποτε θυμὸν ὀλέσσῃ Il.1.205, cf. Od. 2.76, etc.; π. καὶ ἄλλοτε *at certain* other *times,* X.*An.*6.4.12, Arist. *Po.*1451ᵃ9, Luc.*Herm.*24. 2. in hypoth. clauses, questions, etc., *at any time, ever,* S.*Aj.*755,1133; εἴ κοτε Call.*Aet.Oxy.*2080.69; cf. εἴ ποτε: also with relatives (cf. δήποτε), Ζεὺς ὅστις ποτ' ἐστίν A.*Ag.* 160 (lyr.), etc.; ὅποι ποτέ, ὅπου π., etc., S.*Ph.*780, *Aj.*194 (lyr.), etc.; after πω, πη, v. πώποτε, πήποκα: very freq. with negatives, οὔτε ποτ' ..Il.1.226; οὐδέ ποτ' Hes.*Th.*759; οὐδέν ποτ' ἄλλο A.*Ch.*16; οὐδεὶς ἐρεῖ ποθ' S.*Aj.*481; οὐκ ἂν δή ποτε Il.19.271, etc.; τοῦτο μὴ δόξῃς ποτέ S.*Ant.*762, cf. 648, 750, etc.; cf. οὔποτε, μήποτε, οὐδέποτε, μηδέποτε, οὐπώποτε, μηπώποτε. 3. in correl. clauses it stands first, with accent, ποτὲ μὲν.., ποτὲ δὲ.. *at one time.., at another..,* Pl. *Tht.*170c (s.v.l.), Plb.4.38.6, etc.; ποτὲ μὲν.., αὖθις δὲ.. Pl.*R.*560a; ποτὲ.., τοτὲ δ' οὔ Id.*Tht.*192d; ποτ' εἶχε.., εἶτά γε νῦν D.36.50; ποτὲ μὲν..νῦν δέ Luc.*DMort.*11.1; ποτὲ δὲ.., without any preceding Part., Thphr.*Char.*9.7 (dub.). III. of some unknown point of time, 1. in ref. to the past, *once,* ὅν ποτ' Ἀθήνη θρέψε Il.2.547, etc.; οὕς ποτ' ἀπ' Αἰνείαν ἑλόμην, of the day before, 8.108 (v. Sch.), cf. 14.45; ἤδη π. 1.260, S.*Aj.*1142, Ar.*Nu.*346, *Ra* 931; ποτ' ἤδη A.*Eu.*50; πρόσθε πού ποτ' S.*OC*1549; χρόνῳ ποτ' Id.*Ant.*303; esp. in telling a story, *once upon a time,* οὕτω ποτ' ἦν μῦς καὶ γαλῆ Ar.*V.*1182, cf. Pl. *Phdr.*237b: with historic pres., S.*OT*715, E.*El.*416, *Ba.*2: with a Subst., εἰς τὴν π. φιλίαν And.3.22; τυράννου..πάλαι π. S.*OT*1043, cf. *Ph.*677 (lyr.), *Tr.*555. b. *at length,* μόγις δή κοτε εἶπε Hdt.1.116; μόγις οὖν π. Pl.*Prt.*314e, etc.; ὀψὲ γοῦν π. Hierocl. in *CA*27 p.484M. 2. in ref. to the future, *at some time,* καὶ π. τοι..παρέσσεται..δῶρα Il.1.213, cf. 240, S.*OC*386, *Ant.*912, etc.: also to denote earnest expectation, *at length,* εὔχεται π. οἶκον ἰδεῖν Pi.*P.*4.293; ἔμελλον ἄρα παύσειν π. Ar.*Ra.*268; esp. with imper., μέθες π. *dimitte tandem aliquando,* S.*Ph.*816; τείσασθ', ἀλλὰ τῷ χρόνῳ π. ib.1041, etc.; ὀψέ π. Jul.*Or.*1.31d. 3. with intensive force, in questions, τίς ποτε; who *in the world?* τίνες ποτ' ἐστέ; A.*Eu.*408, cf. S.*Ph.*220, etc.; τί ποτ' ἐστὶ τοῦτο τὸ πάθος what it can *possibly* be, Pl.*Tht.* 187d; οὐκ ἐξερεῖς ποτε; S.*OT*335, cf. 754, *Aj.*1290, etc.; to strengthen ἀεί, ἀεί ποτε *from all time, always in the past,* ἀεί ποτε ζῇ ταῦτα Id.*Ant.*456, cf. *Aj.*320, Th.6.82, al., D.C.42.5; ἀεὶ δή π. Th.1.13, 8.73.

**Ποτείδαια,** ἡ, *Potidea, IG*1².201.14, etc.:—**Ποτειδεᾶται,** οἱ, *citizens of Potidea,* ib. 205.50:—Adj. **Ποτειδεᾱτικός,** ή, όν, *concerning the Potideans,* Th.1.118.

**Ποτειδάν,** v. Ποσειδῶν. **Ποτειδάνιον,** τό, v. Ποσειδώνιος II.

**ποτεῖδον, ποτιδών,** Dor. for προσεῖδον, προσιδών. **ποτεκλεπτόμαν·** προσεπορευόμην, Hsch. **ποτεκχετήρια·** τορνευτήρια, Id.

**ποτένθης,** Dor. for προσέλθῃς, Theoc.15.148.

**ποτεξορκίζω,** v. προσεξορκίζω.

**ποτέομαι,** Ep. for ποτάομαι.

**ποτέος,** α, ον, (πίνω) *to be drunk,* οὐ π. οἶνος Pl.*Lg.*674b. II. ποτέον, *one must drink,* Id.*Cri.*47b, *Smp.*213e.

**ποτερίσδω,** Dor. for προσερίζω.

⊛ **πότερος,** α, ον; Ion. **κότερος,** η, ον: *whether of the two?* both in direct and indirect questions; once in Hom., οὐκ ἂν γνοίης ποτέροισι μετείη Il.5.85; κότερα τούτων αἱρετώτερά ἐστι..; Hdt.3.52, cf. 1.126; πότερα τύχης καὶ πότερα γνώμης ἔργα κρίνεις; X.*Mem.*1.4.4; σκόπει πρὸς ποτέρους διαλέγῃ Pl.*R.*528a, etc.: sts. the two objects referred to follow in apposition, ἐρωτώσης τῆς μητρός, π. καλλίων.. δοκεῖ εἶναι, ὁ πατὴρ ἢ οὗτος X.*Cyr.*1.3.2, cf. *Mem.*1.6.9; πότερος.., ὁ ἰατρὸς ἢ ὁ ὀψοποιός; Pl.*Grg.*464d, cf. 498a, etc.; modified by τις, Id. *Lg.*715a, etc.; repeated in the same sentence, πότερος ποτέρου φίλος γίγνεται; Id.*Ly.*212a. II. neut. πότερον and πότερα (interchangeable, πότερον δέδρακεν ἢ οὔ, καὶ πότερ' ἄκων ἢ ἑκών; D.23.79, cf. X. *Mem.*3.6.16), as Adv. at the beginning of an interrog. sentence containing two alternative propositions, the second being connected by ἤ.., *whether..or,* a. in direct questions, Pi.*P.*11.22, *Fr.*213, B.17.33, Hdt.1.88, etc.; τίνες κατῆρξαν, πότερον Ἕλληνες ἢ παῖς ἐμός; A. *Pers.*351, etc.; πότερα δικαστὴν ἢ δικηφόρον λέγεις; Id.*Ch.*120, cf. *Supp.*336. b. in indirect questions, ἐπείρεσθαι κότερα τὴν ἑωυτοῦ ἢ τὴν Κύρου λέγοι ἀρχήν Hdt.1.91, cf. 3.32, etc.: the Verb is sts. repeated, π. οὐδενὶ δύναται ἀρέσαι, ἢ ἔστιν οἷς καὶ πάνυ ἀρέσκει; X.*Mem.* 2.3.6: sts. π. precedes the common Verb, π. βούλοιτο μένειν ἢ ἀπιέναι; Id.*Cyr.*1.3.15, cf. *Oec.*18.1. 2. sts. a third clause (with ἤ) is inaccurately added, κότερα παρὰ δήμου ἢ ὀλιγαρχίης ἢ μουνάρχου; Hdt. 3.82, cf. A.*Supp.*247, S.*OT*112; and a fourth, Id.*El.*539. 3. the second alternative is sts. left to be supplied, πότερα δὴ κερτομῶν λέγεις τάδε (sc. ἢ μή..); Id.*Ph.*1235, cf. *OC*333, A.*Pers.*239, *Th.*94 (lyr.), *Ag.*274, Pl.*Sph.*228a, *R.*501d, etc. 4. πότερον is sts. omitted in the first clause, ἐπισκέψασθαι.., ὀρθὴ ἢ ψευδής Id.*Tht.*161d, cf. *Lg.* 670b. 5. in affirmative sentences, π...ἤ, *either..or,* Corn.*ND*14, al.; so π...ἤ..ἤ ib.27. III. indef., *one or other, either of the two,* τί οὐ λέγει π. ὑμῶν; Pl.*La.*181d; τούτων ποτέροις ἐπακολουθῆσαι Id. *Chrm.*171b, cf. *R.*499c, *Phlb.*20e, *Tht.*145b, etc.; ἄτεροι πότεροι, = ὁποτεροιοῦν, *SIG*421.31 (Thermon, iii B.C.): for ὁπότερος, ἐξέστω αὐτῷ πότερον ἂν βούληται, ἤ..ἤ.. *Abh.Berl.Akad.*1925(5).7 (Cyrene, iii B.C.): in this sense Phot. would make it oxyt. ποτερός, ά, όν. IV. Adv. ποτέρως, v. sub voc. (I.-E. *qᵘo-tero-s,* cf. Skt. *katarás,* Goth. *hwaþar* 'which of two?')

**ποτέρχομαι,** Dor. for προσέρχομαι.

**ποτέρ-ωθεν,** Adv., (πότερος) *from which of two quarters,* Arist. *Mete.*361ᵃ25. **-ωθι,** Adv. *on whether of the two sides? on which side* (of two)? π. οὖν εὐαπατητότεροί ἐσμεν; Pl.*Phdr.*263b; π. τὴν ἀπάτην ταύτην θήσομεν; Answ. πρὸς τὴν δικαιοσύνην X.*Mem.*4.2.17. **-ως,** Adv. of πότερος, *in which of two ways?* π. ἂν μᾶλλον ἄνθρωποι σωφρονοῖεν, ἀργοῦντες ἢ.. ἐπιμελόμενοι; ib.2.7.8, cf. 1.6.15, etc.; ποτέρως ἐστὶν αὐτῆς (sc. τῆς τραγῳδίας) τὸ ἐπιχείρημα.., χαρίζεσθαι.., ἢ καὶ διαμάχεσθαι; π. σοι δοκεῖ..; Pl.*Grg.*502b, cf. *Cra.* 435e; π. οὖν οἴει μᾶλλον ἂν φοβεῖσθαι.., εἰ ὁρῷεν.., ἢ εἰ καταδοξάσειαν ..; X.*An.*7.7.30. 2. in indirect questions, διορίσαι, π. λέγεις Pl. *R.*341b; διερευνήσασθαι..π. ἔχει ib.368c, cf. *Plt.*272d. **-ωσε,** Adv. *to which of two sides?* π. οὖν θῶμεν τοῦτο; Answ. πρὸς τὴν ἀδικίαν X. *Mem.*4.2.14; π. νόον τράποι Orph.*Fr.*135.

**ποτευχά,** ἁ, Dor. for προσευχή, *IG*4²(1).106 i 27 (Epid., iv B.C.).

**ποτεχεῖ,** Dor. Adv. = ἑξῆς, τὸ π. ϝέτος *Tab.Heracl.*1.121.

**ποτέχω,** Dor. for προσέχω, Ar.*Ach.*733, etc.; also Ep.aor. part. ποτισχομένη A.R.3.150.

⊛ **ποτή** (A), ἡ, *flight,* ποτῇ ἀνεδύσατο λίμνης Od.5.337; ποτῆσι v.l. in *h.Merc.*544; ποτὴν ἴσον dub.l. in Alex.Aet.5.5.

**ποτή** (B), ἡ, *sample of wine,* ἐκ ληνοῦ *POxy.*1673.12, al. (ii A.D.), cf. *BGU*1143.18 (i B.C.).

**πότημα** (A), ατος, τό, *flight,* A.*Eu.*250 (πωτήμασι codd.).

**πότημα** (B), ατος, τό, (πίνω) *draught, potion,* Hp.*Aff.*18 (pl.), Erasistr.ap.Gal.11.200, Dsc.2.159 (pl.), Orib.*Fr.*50 (pl.). II. *pill,* Paul.Aeg.3.20.

**ποτημᾰτοποιός,** όν, *preparing drink,* Parmenio ap.Ath.13.608a.

**ποτῆμεν,** Dor., = προσεῖναι, Melissa *Ep.*11.1.

**ποτηνός,** ή, όν, v. ποτανός.

⊛ **ποτήρ,** ῆρος, ὁ, *drinking-cup,* E.*Alc.*756, *Cyc.*151.

⊛ **ποτηρίδιον,** τό, Dim. of ποτήριον, Men.24 (pl.), *IG*11(2).161 *C* 87 (Delos, iii B.C.), *PCair.Zen.*38.7, al. (iii B.C.).

**ποτηριοκλέπτης,** ου, ὁ, *cup-stealer,* title of poem by Euphorio.

⊛ **ποτήριον,** τό, *drinking-cup, wine-cup,* Alc.52, Sapph.*Supp.*20a.10, Hdt.2.37, 3.148, Ar.*Eq.*120, 237, etc.; οὔποτ' ἐκ ταὐτοῦ μεθ' ἡμῶν πίεται π. ib.1289; π. ἀργυρᾶ *IG*1².232, al.; κεραμεᾶ Ath.11.464a, etc. 2. *the Cup* in the Eucharist, 1*Ep.Cor.*11.25 sq. 3. *jar,* Gal.13.385. 4. *receptacle* for offerings in temples, *PTeb.*6.27 (pl., ii B.C.). II. *absorbent preparation,* Gal.13.258, Alex.Trall.10 (pl.). III. v. ποτίρριον.

**ποτηριοφόρος,** ον, *bearing a drinking-cup,* Autocr.Hist.ap.Ath.11.460d.

**ποτηρο-θήκη,** ἡ, *table for setting out cups, sideboard, buffet, Gloss.* **-πλύτης** [ῠ], ου, ὁ, = foreg., *PLond.*5.1657 (iv/v A.D.), *Ostr.*1218; gloss on κυλικεῖον, Sch.Luc.*Lex.*7 (-πλύτης perh. adapted from Lat. *pluteus,* cf. Engl. cup*board*).

⊛ **ποτής,** ῆτος, ἡ, (πότος, πίνω) *drink,* opp. ἐδητύς, σῖτος, βρώμη, Il.11.780, 19.306, Od.10.379, etc.; Dor. gen. ποτᾶτος Philox.2.38.

⊛ **πότης,** ου, ὁ, *drinker, tippler, toper,* usu. in fem. πότις (masc. only metaph., v. infr.), πότις γυνή Phryn.Com.71; Λαΐς ἀργὸς καὶ πότις Epicr.3: metaph., πότης λύχνος a *tippling* lamp, i.e. that consumes much oil, Ar.*Nu.*57; στίλβη πότις Pl.Com.190: Com.Sup., ποτίσταται γυναῖκες Ar.*Th.*735, cf. Ael.*VH*12.26.

**ποτητός,** ή, όν, (ποτάομαι) *flying, winged:* ποτητά, τά, *fowls, birds,* Od.12.62: sg., A.R.4.1240.

**ποτητύν·** τὸ πίνειν, Hsch.

⊛ **ποτί** [ῐ], Dor. for πρός, also used in Ep. (as Il.1.426, al., Call.*Del.*210, al.), and rarely in Hp., esp. in phrase π. καί *and also,* i.e. *especially, Art.* 8, 41, 46, 57, 69, without καί only in *Fract.*3 (but not in Hdt.), whether in or out of compos.; sts. in Trag. (lyr., exc. A.*Eu.*79) as A.*Th.*295, 346, *Ag.*725, *Eu.* l.c., S.*Fr.*245, E.*Hipp.*140 (and in compds., as ποτινίσσομαι, ποτιμάστιος, ποτιπίπτω, ποτιτρόπαιος). The elision of ι before a vowel is found once in Pi., viz. *O.*7.90 (elsewh. Pi. uses πρός before a vowel); but found in later Dor., as Epich.170.7, *IG*4²(1).121.20 (Epid., iv B.C.), Theoc.7.26, esp. in compds., v. ποθ-ίερος, πόθ-οδος, ποθ-ολκίς, πότ-αγε, ποτ-αγωγίς, ποτ-αείδω, ποτ-αμέλγω, ποτ-αυλέω, etc.; freq. apocop. before the Art., πὸτ τῶ, for πρὸς τοῦ, Theoc.4.50, 5.74; πὸτ τῷ *SIG*247 iii 11 (Delph., iv B.C.); πὸτ τόν *IG*5(1).1.18, al. (Sparta); πὸτ τάν, for πρὸς τήν, Pi.*Fr.*122.5 (s.v.l.), Ar.*Ach.*732, etc.; πὸτ τό ib.751, *Lys.*117, etc.; πὸτ τώς Foed.Lacon.ap.Th.5.77; πὸτ τάς Ar.*Lys.*1264 (lyr.); πὸτ τά ib.1253 (lyr.); πὸτ τούτοισι Epich.60: less freq. in Verbs, ποτθέμειν Id.170.10; ποτθέντες *Tab.Heracl.*2.30; also ποτ-, as in ποτόν *Schwyzer* 412 (Elis), ποτούς *IG*9(1).334.32 (Locr.); **πὸδ** Δάφνῃ ib.7.518.5 (Tanagra, iii B.C.); **πὸκ** κατόπτας *Schwyzer* 485.10

(Thespiae, iii B.C.); ποί in Argolic, esp. before dentals, *IG*4²(1).102.63, al. (Epid., iv B.C.), sts. in other Dor. dialects, as Delphic, ib. 2².1126.26, etc. Cf. προτί. (Cf. Avest. *paiti* 'to': the form ποί has prob. lost τ by dissimilation from a following dental.)

**ποτι-βαίνω, -βλέπω, -γλέπω**, Dor. for προσβ- (q.v.). **Ποτιδᾶς, Ποτιδάων**, v. Ποσειδῶν. **ποτιδέγμενος, ποτιδέχνυσο**, v. προσδέχομαι. **ποτιδεῖν**, Dor. for προσιδεῖν.

**ποτιδέρκομαι**, Ep. and Dor. for προσδ-, Il.16.10, Od.17.518, Theoc.1.36.

**ποτιδεύομαι**, Dor. for προσδέομαι, Theoc.5.63.

**ποτιδίδωμι**, Dor. for προσδ-.

**ποτιδόρπιος**, ον, Ep. form of προσδ- (which is not found), *of or serving for supper*, ὄβριμον ἄχθος ὕλης.., ἵνα οἱ ποτιδόρπιον εἴη that it might *serve to dress his supper*, Od.9.234, cf. 249; ὕδωρ A.R.1.1209; τὰ π., = τὰ προσσίτια, Hsch.

⊛ **ποτίζω**, Att. fut. ιῶ *Gp*.17.12.3: (πότος) :—*give to drink*, ἄκρητον ποτίσας Hp.*Aph*.7.46; ἐπότισεν.. ὁ ἰατρὸς τὸ φάρμακον Arist.*Ph*.199ᵃ34, cf. Ruf.*Fr*.118; οἶνον [ὑποζυγίοις] Aen.Tact.27.14:—Pass., Dsc.1.11, al. 2. c. dupl. acc., τοὺς ἵππους νέκταρ ἐπότισε *gave* them nectar *to drink*, Pl.*Phdr*.247e; μικρὸν ὕδωρ π. τινά Lxx *Ge*.24.17; ποτήριον π. τινά *Ev.Marc*.9.41, cf. 1*Ep.Cor*.12.13 (Pass.). 3. *water*, [τὰ φυόμενα] X.*Smp*.2.25, cf. Lxx *Ge*.2.6; *irrigate*, φυτὰ *PCair.Zen*.72.4 (iii B.C.); π. τὴν γῆν ἀπὸ χερός ib.155.3 (iii B.C.); also *water* cattle, ταύρως καὶ πόρτιας Theoc.1.121:—Pass., of land, *to be watered, to be irrigated*, *CPR*1.9 (i A.D.), Luc.*Abd*.27, etc. 4. π. οἴνῳ *OGI*200.16 (Axum, iv A.D.); οἴνου Porph.*Abst*.2.54 (ap.Eus.*PE*4.16; οἴνῳ codd. Porph.). 5. *moisten*, μετά τινος Zos.Alch.p.167B.; τινι Moses ap.eund.p.183B.

**ποτίθες**, Dor. for πρόσθες, Theoc.14.45.

**ποτικαρτερέω**, v. προσκαρτερέω.

**ποτικατάβλημα**, ατος, τό, Dor. for προσ-, *additional payment*, Herzog *Koische Forschungen* 10 p.41.

**ποτικλῄζω**, Dor. for προσκλῄζω, Lamprocl.1.

**ποτικλίνω**, = προσκλίνω, pf. Pass. -κέκλιται Od.6.308.

**ποτίκολλος**, ον, Dor. for πρόσκ-, Pi.*Fr*.241.

⊛ **ποτικός**, ή, όν, (πότος, πίνω) *fond of drinking*, Plu.*Demetr*.1, etc.; *boon-companion*, Alc.Com.9. 2. *able to drink*, Gal.(?) ap.Orib.*Syn*.8.12. Adv. -κῶς, ἔχειν Plu.*Demetr*.36.

⊛ **ποτίκρᾱνον**, Dor. form of πρόσκρ- (which is not found), = προσκεφάλαιον, *cushion*, Sophr.10, *Com.Adesp*.1372, Theoc.15.3.

**ποτιλέγω, ποτιμάσσω**, Dor. for προσλέγω, προσμάσσω (qq.v.).

**ποτιμάστιος**, ον, an Ep. form, not found in the common form προσμ-, *at the breast*, π. ἔσχεθε κοῦρον Epic.ap.Sch.S.*OC*378 (attributed to Sophocles in cod., cf. *Coll.Alex*.p.247).

**πότῐμος**, ον, (πότος, πίνω) mostly of water, *drinkable, fresh*, Heraclit.61, Hdt.8.22, Hp.*Medic*.2, X.*HG*3.2.19; κρήνη Plb.34.9.5: generally, τὰ π. Thphr.*Od*.65. 2. metaph., *fresh, sweet, pleasant*, καρποὶ γλυκεῖς καὶ π. Id.*CP*4.4.12; π. λόγος, opp. ἁλμυρὰ ἀκοή, Pl.*Phdr*.243d; of the writings of Isoc., Phld.*Rh*.1.200S., cf. *Lib*.p.46O.(Comp.); π. δόγματα, ἔννοιαι, Ph.2.275, 1.72; τὰ χρηστὰ καὶ π., opp. τὰ δυσχερῆ καὶ μοχθηρά, Plu.2.469c. b. of persons, *pleasant, sociable*, Theoc.29.31 (Comp.); so also ποτιμώτερον συμπόσιον Hld.3.10. Adv., σοφῶς καὶ π. Philostr.*VS*1.8.4. 3. *porous*, λίθος Pl.*Lg*.947d. 4. *watered, irrigated*, Apollon.*Lex*. s.v. πείσεα. 5. = δευτερίας, Dsc.5.6.15.

**ποτιμυθέομαι**, v. προσμυθέομαι.

**ποτινεύμενος**, = προσνεόμενος, Orph.*Fr*.94(s.v.l.).

**ποτινίσσομαι**, = προσνίσσομαι, A.*Pr*.530 (lyr.).

**ποτιπελάζω**, Dor. for προσπελάζω, *Chron.Lind*.D.4.

**ποτιπίαμμα** [ῐ], ατος, τό, (ποτί, πιαίνω) *fat* remaining *on* the altar, *Berl.Sitzb*.1927.159 (Cyrene).

**ποτιπίπτω**, = προσπ-, A.*Th*.94 (lyr.).

**ποτιπλάσσω**, poet. for προσπ-, Call.*Epigr*.52 (Pass.).

**ποτιπορεύομαι**, v. προσπορεύομαι.

**ποτιπταίω**, poet. for προσπτ-, Q.S.7.81.

**ποτιπτήσσω**, = προσπτ- (which is not found), *crouch* or *cower towards*, ἀκταὶ λιμένος ποτιπεπτηυῖαι (Ep. pf. part.) *verging towards* it, so as to shut it in, Od.13.98.

**ποτιπτύσσω**, = προσπτύσσω, Od.2.77 (Med.).

**ποτιρραίνω**, *sprinkle on*, αἷμα ποτὶ τὸν βωμόν *Abh.Berl.Akad*.1928(6).12 (Cos, iv B.C.).

**ποτίρριον**, τό, *goat's thorn, Astragalus Poterium*, Dsc.3.15 (v.l. ποτήριον).

**πότις**, v. πότης.

**ποτίσδω**, Dor. for ποτίζω, Theoc.1.121.

**πότ-ισμα**, ατος, τό, *draught*, Asclep.ap.Gal.14.137. ⊛ **-ισμός**, ὁ, = foreg., Call.*Fr.anon*.121, *BGU*912.20 (i A.D.), Aq.*Pr*.3.8. 2. *irrigation*, *PCair.Zen*.268.36 (iii B.C.), *PAmh*.2.91.11 (pl., ii A.D.), etc.

**ποτισπαστήρ**, ῆρος, ὁ, Dor. for προσ-, *thong which draws* the bolt of a door, *IG*4²(1).110.22,24 (Epid., iv/iii B.C.).

**ποτιστάζω**, Dor. for προσστάζω, Pi.*O*.6.76, *P*.4.137.

**ποτίστᾰσις**, ιος, ἡ, Dor. for πρόσ-, (προσίστημι) *admission*, αἱ ἐκ ποτιστάσιος δίκαι suits brought by persons *admitted* to plead, *SIG* 629.21 (Delph., ii B.C.).

**ποτίστατος**, v. πότης.

**ποτ-ιστέον**, *one must water*, *Gp*.17.20.3. II. *one must give a draught to*, Herod.Med.ap.Aët.5.130, Orib.*Fr*.58, Aët.7.24, etc. **-ιστήριον**, τό, *drinking-trough for cattle*, Lxx *Ge*.24.20, 30.38. 2. = *popina*, *Gloss*. **-ιστής**, οῦ, ὁ, *one who gives to drink*, Aq.*Ge*.40.5. **-ίστρα**, ἡ, *watering-place, drinking-trough*, Call.*Dian*.50, D.S.3.17, Str.8.3.31, Al.*Ex*.2.16, *PFlor*.50.107 (iii A.D.). 2. *conduit* or *channel*, *CPR*121.1 (pl., iii A.D.), *PTeb*.374.14 (ii A.D.), etc. **-ιστρέα**, ἡ, = foreg., κρεμαστὴ π. ib.527 (ii A.D.). ⊛ **-ιστρίς**, ίδος, ἡ, = ποτίστρα 1, Tz.*H*.4.890 (pl.).

**ποτί-ταξις**, ιος, ἡ, = πρόσ-, *command, injunction*, τᾶς Ἀθάνας *Chron. Lind*.D.17. **-τάσσω**, v. προστάσσω. **-τέμνω**, v. προστέμνω.

**ποτιτέρπω**, Ep. for προστ-, Il.15.401.

**ποτιτρόπαιος**, ον, Dor. for προστρ-, A.*Eu*.176 (lyr.).

**ποτιφαίνω**, = προσφαίνω, *shine in opposition*, Antioch.Astr. in *Cat. Cod.Astr*.1.111 (prob. cj.).

**ποτιφόριμος**, ον, Dor. for προσφ-, = πρόσφορος, Epich.102.

**ποτίφορος**, Dor. for πρόσφ-, Pi.*N*.3.31, Ti.Locr.104a.

**ποτιφωνήεις**, εσσα, εν, Ep. for προσφ-, Od.9.456.

⊛ **ποτιψαύω**, Dor. for προσψ-, Pi.*Fr*.121.3.

**ποτιψᾱφίζομαι**, Med., Dor. for προσψη-, *vote in addition*, ἀγῶνα *Mélanges Glotz* 290 (Delph., ii B.C.).

⊛ **πότμος**, ὁ, (πίπτω) poet. word, *that which befalls one, lot, destiny*: 1. in Hom. always of *evil destiny*, esp. of *death*; of the killer, πότμον ἐφῆκε, ἐφήσω, Il.4.396, Od.19.550; or of the killed, πότμον ἐπισπεῖν Il.6.412, Od.2.250, al.; θάνατον καὶ π. ἐπισπεῖν Il.2.359, 20.337, al.; also θανέειν καὶ πότμον ἐπισπεῖν 7.52, Od.4.562, al.; ὀλόμην καὶ πότμον ἐπέσπον 11.197; αἴ κε θάνῃς καὶ πότμον ἀναπλήσῃς βιότοιο Il.4.170, cf. 11.263; also πότμον ἐφάψαι, = π. ἐφεῖναι, Pi.*O*.9.60, cf. B.5.158, etc.; πότμον ἀμπιπλάντες ὁμοῖον, of the Dioscuri who lived on alternate days, Pi.*N*.10.57. 2. after Hom. without a sense of evil, π. συγγενής one's natural *gifts*, ib.5.40; εὐτυχεῖ π. A.*Pers*.709; καλλίπαις π. Id.*Ag*.762 (lyr.), cf. 1005 (lyr.); π. ξυνήθης πατρός my father's customary *fortune*, S.*Tr*.88; π. ἄποτμος E.*Hipp*.1143 (lyr.); τίνα ποτ' Ἠλέκτρα πότμον εἴληχε βιότου; Id.*IT*913; θανεῖν ζηλωτὸν ἐν Ἑλλάδι π. Arist.*Fr.Lyr*.6.4. II. personified, *Destiny*, ὁ μέγας Π. Pi.*P*.3.86. [The first syll. long in Hom., but sts. short in later poets, *IG*9(1).871 (Corc., iii B.C.), Orph.*A*.1291; commonly short in Trag., but long in S.*Tr*.88, *Fr*.871.1.]

⊛ **πότνᾰ**, mostly Voc., = sq., π. θεά Od.5.215, 13.391, 20.61; π. θεάων *h.Cer*.118 (nom.); Ὁσία π. θεῶν E.*Ba*.370 (lyr.); π. Σελάνα Theoc.2.69, al.; addressed to a mistress, *AP*5.253 (Paul. Sil.), 285 (Id.).

⊛ **πότνια**, ἡ, poet. title of honour, used chiefly in addressing females, whether goddesses or women: 1. as Subst., = δέσποινα (cf. Apion ap.Apollon.*Lex*.), *mistress, queen* (v. sub fin.), πότνιαν ἁγνὴν *h.Cer*.203: mostly c. gen., πότνια θηρῶν (nom.) *queen* of wild beasts, of Artemis, Il.21.470; πότνια βελέων Pi.*P*.4.213; τὰν ἐρώτων πότνιαν, of Aphrodite, E.*Fr*.781.16 (lyr.); π. λαῶν, τοξοφόρων, Arat.112, Call.*Fr.anon*.338: without a gen., π. Αὔως Sapph.153; πότνι' Ἐρινύς A.*Th*.887 (lyr.), *Eu*.951 (anap.); πότνιαν ἐξαπαφῶν ἐμάν E.*Ion* 704 (lyr.); [Ἱστίην] πότνιαν *h.Ven*.24; ναὶ τὰν πότνιαν Theoc.15.14: in voc., ὦ πότνι' Ἥρα A.*Th*.152 (lyr.); ὦ πότνια (sc. Ἀθηναία) Ar.*Eq*.1170, al.; ὦ πότνι' E.*IT*533, Ar.*Pax*445; addressed to a mistress, *AP*5.269 (Paul. Sil.). 2. in pl. of the Eumenides, ὦ πότνιαι δεινῶπες S.*OC*84; τὸ τῶν ποτνιέων ἱρόν Hdt.9.97; of Demeter and Kore, S.*OC*1050 (lyr.), Ar.*Th*.1149 (lyr.); θεσμοφόρους ἁγνὰς π. *Inscr.Prien*.196.3. 3. as Adj., *revered, august*, in Hom. of Hebe, Enyo, Calypso, Circe, Il.4.2, 5.592, Od.1.14, 8.448; most freq. of Hera, Il.1.551, al., cf. Sapph.*Supp*.6.2; in Hes. of Hera, Tethys, and Peitho, *Th*.11, 368, *Op*.73; Τριτογένεια Id.*Th*.926; Νίκη Bacis ap.Hdt.8.77, cf. B.11.5; π. μήτηρ Il.1.357, al., Od.6.30, al.; esp. in invocation, π. γῆ Hom.*Epigr*.7.1; ὦ π. χθών A.*Ch*.722 (anap.), E.*Hec*.70 (anap.); μᾶτερ π., addressed to Earth, S.*Ph*.395 (lyr.) (also of a bird, Mosch.4.24); π. νύξ E.*Or*.174 (lyr.); ὦ π. λήθη τῶν κακῶν ib.213; Ἔνοσι π. Id.*Ba*.585 (lyr.); ὦ μεγάλα Θέμι καὶ π. Ἄρτεμι Id.*Med*.160 (anap.); ὦ π. αἰδώς Id.*IA*821; ὦ π. μοῖρα καὶ τύχη ib.1136: the phrase π. συκῆ is used by Arist.*Rh*.1408ᵃ16 as a parody of Cleophon's style.—Mostly used in voc. [The first syll. is short in A.*Th*.152, *Ch*.722, E.*Med*.160, *Ion* 873, al., Theoc. l.c., but elsewh. long, cf. πότμος: the final syll. always short in nom., voc., and acc. sg.]

**ποτνιάζομαι**, = ποτνιάομαι, Hsch.

**Ποτνιαί**, αἱ, an ancient Boeot. town called after αἱ Πότνιαι (= Demeter and Kore), Paus.9.8.1; conjectured to be the Ὑποθῆβαι of Homer, Str.9.2.32: hence Adj. **Ποτνιεύς**, έως, ὁ, *Potnian*, Γλαῦκος Π. title of play by A.

**ποτνιάνακτος**, f.l. for ποντοτίνακτος (q.v.).

**ποτνιάομαι**, *cry* ὦ πότνια: hence generally, *cry aloud in horror* or *indignation*, Att. acc. to Moer., but found only in later Prose; of women, Plu.*Caes*.63, *Ant*.35, 2.507c, Ach.Tat.6.15, etc.; of a man, J.*AJ*9.8.6, al., Plu.2.408a, Luc.*Merc.Cond*.17, *Gall*.20; ἐπὶ τοῖς δρωμένοις Eun.*VS*p.501B.; even of elephants, Ael.*NA*5.49. 2. c. acc., *implore loudly*, Ph.1.391: c. inf., Id.2.227: abs., ib.65, al.

**Ποτνιάς**, άδος, fem. Adj. *of Potniae, Potnian*, κέλευθοι Ποτνιάδες A.*Fr*.173; ἡ Ποτνιὰς κρήνη a spring near the town, Ael.*NA*15.25, Paus.9.8.1; Ποτνιάδες ἵπποι the mares that tore Glaucus in pieces, Str.9.2.24; hence, generally, Π. πῶλοι *Boeotian* mares, E.*Ph*.1124 (but expld. by Sch. as = μανικαί). II. = πότνια, Βάκχαι ποτνιάδες (expld. by Hsch. as = μαινάδες καὶ λυσσάδες) E.*Ba*.664, cf. ποινίς; π. θεαί, of the Eumenides (expld. by Sch. as = μανικαί, but v. πότνια 2), Id.*Or*.318 (lyr.); cf. ποτνιάομαι.

**ποτνι-ασις**, εως, ἡ, *loud lamentation*, Poll.6.201. **-ασμός**, ὁ, = foreg., of women, Str.7.3.4 (pl.). **-αστής**, οῦ, ὁ, *lamenter*, Phld.*Herc*.1457.12.

**ποτόδδω**, Lacon. for προσόζω, Ar.*Lys*.206.

**ποτοκέλλω**, Dor. for προσοκέλλω, Dius ap.Stob.4.21.17 (nisi leg. ποτοπτίλλουσιν).

**ποτόμφει·** προσόζει, Hsch.; cf. ὀμφά.

**ποτοπτάζω**, Dor. Verb, = προσοράω, *AP*6.353 (Noss.): also **ποτοπτίλλω**, prob. in Dius ap.Stob.4.21.17.

**πότορθρος**, Dor. for πρόσορθρος (q.v.).

**ποτός**, ή, όν, (πίνω) *drunk, for drinking*, τί κακὸν ἐδανὸν ἢ ποτὸν πασαμένα.. ; A.*Ag.*1408 (lyr.); φάρμακον E.*Hipp.*516; ὕδωρ Th.6.100. II. Subst., **ποτόν**, τό, *that which one drinks, drink*, esp. of wine, κρητῆρας ἐπεστέψαντο ποτοῖο Il.1.470, etc.; θεῖον ποτὸν ἐντὸς ἔχοντες Od.2.341; κρόμυον ποτῷ ὄψον Il.11.630; of wine, A.*Pers.*615, S.*Tr.*703; τῷ ποτῷ χρησαμένους Hdt.2.121.δ'; σῖτα καὶ ποτά meat and *drink*, Id.5.34, X.*An.*2.3.27; βρωτοῖσι καὶ ποτοῖσι E.*Supp.*1110; σιτία καὶ π. Pl.*Prt.*334a, etc. 2. *drinking water*, ἰὼ Σκαμάνδρου πάτριον π. *water* of Sc. *drunk* by my sires, A.*Ag.*1157 (lyr.); Σπερχειὸς ἄρδει πεδίον εὐμενεῖ π. Id.*Pers.*487; π. κρηναῖον S.*Ph.*21, cf. 1461 (anap.); ποτάμια π. Id.*Fr.*659.5.

⊛ **πότος**, ὁ, (πίνω) *drinking-bout, carousal*, πῶς τις αὐτὸν..ἂν ἀπὸ τοῦ πότου παύσειεν..; Cratin.187; προὐχώρει ὁ π. X.*An.*7.3.26; ἧς π. ἁδύς Theoc.14.17; παρὰ πότον over the *wine*, X.*An.*2.3.15, *Smp.*8.41; ἀλλήλοις..συνεῖναι ἐν τῷ πότῳ Pl.*Prt.*347c; τρέπεσθαι πρὸς τὸν π. Id.*Smp.*176a: pl., Ar.*Nu.*1073; αἱ ἐν τοῖς πότοις συνουσίαι Isoc.1.32, cf. Aeschin.2.47; περὶ πότους τὰς διατριβὰς ποιεῖσθαι Lys.16.11, cf. Pl.*R.*329a, Isoc.15.286.

**ποτόσδω**, Dor. for προσόζω, Theoc.1.28.

**πότωπον**, Dor. for πρόσωπον, Eust.684.17.

**ποῦ**, Ion. **κοῦ**, interrog. Adv. *where?* Hom., etc.; freq. c. dat. pers., ποῦ δέ οἱ ἔντεα κεῖται..; Il.10.407; π. τοι τόξον; 5.171; π. τοι Δηΐφοβος..,π. δέ τοι Ὀθρυονεύς; 13.770,772; ἀλλ' ἡμὶν Αἴας ποῦ 'στιν; S.*Aj.*733; π. μοί ποτε ναίει; Id.*OC*137 (lyr.); rarely with Verbs of motion in early authors, v. που sub fin.:—c. gen. loci, π. χθονός; *where* in the world? A.*Pers.*231; π. γῆς; S.*Aj.*984, *OT*108, etc.; π. τῆς χώρας; X.*Eq.Mag.*7.14; τὴν σοφίαν..π. χοροῦ τάξομεν; *in what part of* the chorus? Pl.*Euthd.*279c. 2. so in a sense not strictly local, π. ποτ' εἶ φρενῶν; S.*El.*390; π. γνώμης ποτ' εἶ; Id.*Ant.*42; π. ποτ' εἰμὶ πράγματος; Id.*Tr.*375; π. σοι τύχης ἕστηκεν; *at what point* of fortune stands he? Id.*Aj.*102. II. of manner, *how?* E.*IA*406, *Or.*802; to express an inference very strongly, κοῦ γε δὴ..οὐκ ἂν χωσθείη κόλπος..; *how* then would it not..? i.e. it certainly would.., Hdt.2.11, cf. Th.8.27 codd.; in Trag., in indignant questions, *how? by what right?* π. σὺ στρατηγεῖς τοῦδε; S.*Aj.*1100; ποῦ σὺ μάντις εἶ σαφής; Id.*OT*390, cf. *Ph.*451, E.*Heracl.*369 (lyr.), 510; π. γάρ ἐστι δίκαιον; D.37.41, cf. 23.58.

**που**, Ion. **κου**, Aeol. **ποι** Sapph.*Supp.*25.17, Pi.*P.*5.101, *BCH*37.157 (Cyme, iii B.C.), prob. in Alc.9:—enclit. Adv. *anywhere, somewhere*, Il.16.514, etc.; freq. with other Advs. of Place, οὐχ ἑκάς π. *somewhere* not far off, S.*Ph.*41; πέλας π. ib.163 (anap.); μηδαμοῦ.. π. ib.256 (dub. l.); π. πέραν τοῦ ποταμοῦ X.*An.*4.3.3; ἄλλοθί π. D.4.41; τῇδέ π. Plb.3.108.3, etc.: c. gen., ἀλλά π. αὐτοῦ ἀγρῶν in *some part* there of the fields, Od.4.639; ἐμβαλεῖν π. (fort. ποι) τῆς χώρας *some part* of the country, X.*Cyr.*6.1.42; εἴ π. τῆς χώρας ταὐτὸ τοῦτο πάθος συνέβη D.18.195. II. without reference to Place, *in some degree*, καί πού τι Th.2.87: freq. to qualify an expression, *perhaps, I suppose*, Hom., etc.; added to introductory Particles, οὕτω π... Il.2.116; Ζεὺς μέν π. τό γε οἶδε 3.308; ὡς ὅτε π. 11.292; ἦν π., εἰ μή π., X.*Hier.*3.2, Pl.*R.*372a: strengthd., τάχ' ἄν π. S.*OT*1116; ἴσως π. E.*El.*518: attached to single words to limit their significance, πάντως κ. Hdt.3.73; τί π. δράσεις; what *in the world?* A.*Pr.*743; οὐδείς π. Pl.*Phlb.*64d; with numerals, ἔτεα τρία καὶ δέκα κ. μάλιστα *about* thirteen years, Hdt.1.119, cf. 209,7.22, etc.: οὔ τί που denies with indignation or wonder, *surely it cannot be*.., οὔ τί π. οὗτος Ἀπόλλων Pi.*P.*4.87, cf. S.*Ph.*1233, Ar.*Nu.*1260, *Pax* 1211, *Ra.*522, Pl.*R.*362d, etc.; οὐ δήπου adds a shade of suspicion, οὐ δήπου Στράτων; Ar.*Ach.*122, cf. *Av.*269, Pl.*Smp.*194b: for δήπου, ἦπου, v. sub vocc.—In late writers (Lxx *Jo.*2.5, al., *Ev.Jo.*7.35, al., Arr.*Epict.*1.27.9, 4.1.93, etc.) ποῦ, που take the place of ποῖ, ποι, with Verbs of motion, as in Engl. *where* for *whither?* This idiom (condemned by Phryn.30, ποῦ ἄπει.. ἁμάρτημα) is found occasionally in early authors, ποῦ τοι ἀπειλαὶ οἴχονται; Il.13.219; ἐξελθὼν που Antipho 2.4.8; ἰόντα που X.*Cyr.*1.2.16; but in pure Att. only as f.l. for ποῖ, ποι.

**ποῦαν·** οἱ κύαμοι ἑφθοί, Hsch. (leg. πύανοι· κ. ἑ., cf. πύανος).

**πουερενπβῆκις**, v. πορενβῆκις. **πουκότατος**, v. πυκνός.

⊛ **πουλβῖνον**, τό, = Lat. *pulvinus, cushion, bolster, Sammelb.*1.10 (iii A.D.), dub. l. in Arr.*Epict.*3.23.35: also Dim. **πουλβινάριον**, prob. in *Gloss.*

**πούλιμος**, ὁ, Aeol. (prob. Boeot.) for βούλιμος, Plu.2.694a. (πουperh. not cogn. with βου- but late Boeot. spelling of πῡ- (cf. pr. n. Πυλιμιάδας *IG*7.602 (Tanagra)), cogn. with Skt. *ku*-(I.-E. $q^u\breve{u}$- 'what') in *ku-purusas* '*what* a man!', i.e. 'a *bad* man', etc.)

**πουλῠβότειρα**, ἡ, metri gr. for πολυβότειρα, Hom. and Hes.; so all other compds. with πολύ may be lengthd. in hexameter verse to πουλυ-, metri gr., v. πολυ-:—Hom. however uses the licence only in this word, in the gen. sg. of πουλύπους, and in the pr. n. Πουλυδάμας.

**πουλυγόητος**, v. πολυγόητος.

**πουλῠπόδειος**, poet. for πολυπόδιος, Theopomp.Com.6, Philyll.13, Ephipp.12.7.

**πουλύπους**, ὁ, v. πολύπους. **πουλύς**, πουλύ, Ion. for πολύς, πολύ, Ep., but not in Ion. Prose. **πουμμά** (ποῦμμα cod.)· ἡ τῆς χειρὸς πυγμή, Hsch. **πουνιάζειν·** παιδικοῖς χρῆσθαι, πούνιον γὰρ ὁ δακτύλιος, Id.

**ποῦπος**, ὁ, *hoopoe*, Cyran.20.

**πουράγγιον**, τό, name of a plant, Ruf.*Fr.*80.

**πούρδαιν·** μαγειρεῖον (Lacon.), Hsch. (cf. πυροδάνσιον). **πουρέακος** (Lacon.), *ring* for leading pigs, Ar.Byz.ap.Hsch.

**πουρεινίς**, ίδος, ἡ, Boeot., = πυρηνίς, *knob*, *Schwyzer* 462 *B* 30 (Tanagra, iii B.C.).

**πούριον**, τό, a kind of cake, Chrysipp.Tyan.ap.Ath.14.647d.

**ποῦρος**, ὁ, = πῶρος, *SIG*245 *G* 22, al. (Delph., iv B.C.).

**πουροφόρος**, ὁ, = πῡρο-, *IG*5(1).997, 1018 (Lacon.).

⊛ **πούς**, ὁ, ποδός, ποδί, πόδα (not ποῦν, Thom.Mag. p.257 R.): dat. pl. ποσί, Ep. and Lyr. ποσσί (also Cratin.100 (lyr.)), πόδεσσι, once πόδεσι S.*Fr.*240 (lyr.): gen. and dat. dual ποδοῖν, Ep. ποδοῖιν Il.18.537:—Dor. nom. πός (cf. ἀρτίπος, πούλυπος, etc.) *Lyr.Adesp.*72, but πούς *Tab. Heracl.*2.34 (perh. Hellenistic); **πῶς·** πός, ὑπὸ Δωριέων, Hsch. (fort. **πός·** πούς, ὑ.Δ.); Lacon. **πόρ**, Id. (on the accent v. Hdn.Gr.2.921, A.D. *Adv.*134.24):—*foot*, both of men and beasts, Il.7.212, 8.339 (both pl.), etc.; in pl., also, a bird's *talons*, Od.15.526; *arms* or *feelers* of a polypus, Hes.*Op.*524: properly *the foot from the ankle* downwards, Il.17.386; ταρσὸς ποδός 11.377, 388; ξύλινος π., of an artificial *foot*, Hdt.9.37: but also of *the leg with the foot*, as χείρ for the arm and hand, Il.23.772, Od.4.149, Luc.*Alex.*59. 2. *foot* as that with which one runs, πόδας ὠκὺς Ἀχιλλεύς Il.1.215, al.; or walks, τῷ δ' ὑπὸ ποσσὶ μέγας πελεμίζετ' Ὄλυμπος 8.443; freq. with reference to swiftness, περιγιγνόμεθ' ἄλλων πύξ τε..ἠδὲ πόδεσσιν Od.8.103; ποσὶν ἐρίζειν to race *on foot*, Il.13.325, cf. 23.792; πόδεσσι πάντας ἐνίκα 20.410, cf. Od.13.261; ἀέθλια ποσσὶν ἄροντο Il.9.124, etc.; ποδῶν τιμά, αἴγλα, ἀρετά, ὁρμά, Pi.*O.*12.15, 13.36, *P.*10.23, B.9.20; ἅμιλλαν ἐπόνει ποδοῖν E.*IA*213 (lyr.): the dat. ποσί (ποσσί, πόδεσσι) is added to many Verbs denoting motion, π. βήσετο, παρέδραμον, Il.8.389, 23.636; π. θέειν, πηδᾶν, σκαίρειν, πλίσσεσθαι, ib.622, 21.269, 18.572, Od.6.318; ὀρχεῖσθαι Hes.*Th.*3; ἔρχεσθαι Od.6.39; πάρος ποσὶν οὖδας ἱκέσθαι 8.376; νέρθε δὲ ποσσὶν ᾔιε μακρὰ βιβάς Il.7.212; also emphatically with Verbs denoting *to trample* or *tread upon*, πόσσι κατάστείβοισι Sapph.94; ἐπεμβῆναι ποδί S.*El.*456; πόδα βαίνειν, v. βαίνω A.II.4; πόδα τιθέναι to journey, Ar.*Th.*1100: metaph., νόστιμον ναῦς ἐκίνησεν πόδα started on its homeward way, E.*Hec.*940 (lyr.); νεῶν λῦσαι ποθοῦσιν οἴκαδ'.. πόδα ib.1020; χειρῶν ἐκβαλλον ὀρείους πόδας ναός, i.e. oars, Tim.*Pers.*102; φωνὴ τῶν π. τοῦ ὑετοῦ sound of the *pattering* of rain, Lxx 3*Ki.*18.41. 3. as a point of measurement, ἐς πόδας ἐκ κεφαλῆς from head to *foot*, Il.18.353; ἐκ κεφαλῆς ἐς πόδας ἄκρους 16.640; and reversely, ἐκ ποδῶν δ' ἄνω..εἰς ἄκρον κάρα A.*Fr.*169; ἐκ τῶν ποδῶν ἐς τὴν κεφαλήν σοι Ar.*Pl.*650; also ἐκ τριχὸς ἄχρι ποδῶν *AP*5.193 (Posidipp. or Asclep.); ἐς κορυφὰν ἐκ ποδός ib.7.388 (Bianor). 4. πρόσθε ποδός or ποδῶν, προπάροιθε ποδῶν, *just before* one, Il.23.877, 21.601, 13.205; τὸ πρὸ ποδός..χρῆμα Pi.*I.*8(7).13; αὐτὰ τὰ πρὸ τῶν ποδῶν ὁρᾶν X.*Lac.*3.4, cf. *An.*4.6.12, Pl.*R.*432d. b. παρά or πὰρ ποδός *off-hand, at once*, ἀνελέσθαι πὰρ ποδός Thgn.282; γνόντα τὸ πὰρ ποδός Pi.*P.*3.60, cf. 10.62; πὰρ ποδί *close at hand*, Id.*O.*1.74; but παραὶ ποσὶ κάππεσε θυμός sank to their *feet*, Il.15.280; παρὰ πόδα *in a moment*, S.*Ph.*838 (lyr.), Pl.*Sph.*242a; *close behind*, Νέμεσις δέ γε πὰρ πόδας (leg. πόδα) βαίνει Prov.ap.Suid.; also παρὰ πόδας *immediately afterwards* Plb.1.35.3, 5.26.13, Gal.5.272; παρὰ π. οἱ ἔλεγχοι Luc.*Hist. Conscr.*13, cf. Aristid.2.115 J.; τὰ ἔμπροσθεν αὐτοῦ καὶ παρὰ πόδας *at his very feet*, Pl.*Tht.*174a; περὶ τῶν παρὰ πόδας καὶ τῶν ἐν ὀφθαλμοῖς ib.c; τὸ πλησίον καὶ παρὰ π. Luc.*Cal.*1. c. ἐν ποσί *in one's way, close at hand*, τὸν ἐν π. γινόμενον Hdt.3.79, cf. Pi.*P.*8.32; τὰν ποσὶν κακά S.*Ant.*1327, cf. E.*Andr.*397; τοὐν ποσὶν κακόν Id.*Alc.*739; τὴν ἐν ποσὶ [κώμην] αἱρεῖν Th.3.97; τὰ ἐν ποσὶν ἀγνοεῖν *everyday matters*, Pl.*Tht.*175b, cf. Arist.*Pol.*1263ᵃ18, etc. d. τὸ πρὸς ποσί, = τὸ ἐν ποσί, S.*OT*130. e. all these phrases are opp. ἐκ ποδῶν *out of the way, far off*, written ἐκποδών Hdt.6.35, etc.; also, βίαια πάντ' ἐκ ποδὸς ἐρύσαις Pi.*N.*7.67. 5. to denote close pursuit, ἐκ ποδὸς ἕπεσθαι follow *in the track*, i.e. *close behind*, Plb.3.68.1, cf. D.S.20.57, D.H.2.33, etc.; ἐκ ποδῶν διώξαντες Plu.*Pel.*11. b. in earlier writers κατὰ πόδας *on the heels* of a person, Hdt.5.98, Th.3.98, 8.17, X.*HG*2.1.20, Lxx *Ge.*49.19 (also κατὰ πόδα ὑπολαβεῖν *on the moment*, Pl.*Sph.*243d); ἡ κατὰ πόδας ἡμέρα the *very next* day, Plb.1.12.1 (but κατὰ πόδας αἱρεῖν catch it *running*, X.*Cyr.*1.6.40, cf. *Mem.*2.6.9): c. gen. pers., κατὰ πόδας τινὸς ἐλαύνειν, ἰέναι, march, come close *at his heels, on his track*, Hdt.9.89, Th.5.64; τῇ κατὰ π. ἡμέρᾳ τῆς ἐκκλησίας on the day *immediately after* it, Plb.3.45.5; κατὰ π. τῆς μάχης Aristid.1.157 J., etc. 6. various phrases: a. ἀνὰ πόδα *backwards*, Hsch. b. ἐπὶ πόδα *backwards facing the enemy*, ἐπὶ π. ἀναχωρεῖν, ἀνάγειν, ἀναχάζεσθαι, to retire *without turning to fly, leisurely*, X.*An.*5.2.32, *Cyr.*3.3.69, 7.1.34, etc.; also ἐπὶ πόδας Luc.*Pisc.*12; but γίνεται ἡ ἔξοδος οἷον ἐπὶ πόδας the offspring is as it were born *feet-foremost*, Arist.*GA*752ᵇ14. c. περὶ πόδα, properly of a shoe, *round the foot*, i.e. *fitting exactly*, ὡς ἔστι μοι τὸ χρῆμα τοῦτο περὶ πόδα Pl.Com.197, cf. 129: c. dat., ὁρᾷς ὡς ἐμμελὴς ἡ ἀρχὴ καὶ περὶ πόδα τῇ ἱστορίᾳ Luc.*Hist.Conscr.*14, cf. *Ind.*10, *Pseudol.*23. d. ὡς ποδῶν ἔχει as he is off *for feet*, i.e. as quick as he can, ὡς ποδῶν εἶχον [τάχιστα] ἐβοήθεον Hdt.6.116; ἐδίωκον ὡς ποδῶν ἕκαστος εἶχον Id.9.59; φευκτέον ὡς ἔχει ποδῶν ἕκαστος Pl.*Grg.*507d; so, σοῦσθε..ὅπως ποδῶν ⟨ἔχετε⟩ A.*Supp.*837 (lyr.). e. ἔξω τινὸς πόδα ἔχειν keep one's *foot* out of a thing, i.e. be clear of it, ἔξω κομίζων πηλοῦ πόδα Id.*Ch.*697; πημάτων ἔξω πόδα ἔχει Id.*Pr.*265; ἐκτὸς κλαυμάτων S.*Ph.*1260; ἔξω πραγμάτων E.*Heracl.*109: without a gen., ἐκτὸς ἔχειν πόδα

Pi.*P.*4.289 : opp. εἰς ἄντλον ἐμβήσῃ πόδα E.*Heracl.*168 ; ἐν τούτῳ πεδίλῳ . . πόδ' ἔχων Pi.*O.*6.8. **f.** ἀμφοῖν ποδοῖν, etc., to denote energetic action, Ar.*Av.*35, cf. Il.13.78 ; συνέχευε ποσὶν καὶ χερσὶν 15.364 ; χερσίν τε ποσίν τε καὶ σθένει 20.360 ; τιμωρήσειν χειρὶ καὶ ποδὶ καὶ πάσῃ δυνάμει Aeschin.2.115, cf.3.109 ; τερπωλῆς ἐπέβημεν ὅλῳ ποδί with all the *foot*, i.e. *entirely*, A.R.4.1166, cf. D.Chr.13.19 (prob.); καταφεύγειν ἐπὶ τὴν πόλιν ὥσπερ ἐκ δυοῖν ποδοῖν Aristid.1.117J. ; opp. οὐκ ἂν προβαίην τὸν πόδα τὸν ἕτερον Ar.*Ec.*161 ; οὐκ ἂν ἔφασκεν ἐξελθεῖν οὐδὲ τὸν ἕτερον πόδα Din.1.82. **g.** τὴν ὑπὸ πόδα [κατάστασιν] *just below them*, Plb.2.68.9 ; ὑπὸ πόδας τίθεσθαι trample under *foot*, scorn, Plu.2.1097c ; οἱ ὑπὸ πόδα those *next below them* (in rank), Onos.25.2 ; ὑπὸ πόδα χωρεῖν *recede, decline*, of strength, Ath. Med. ap.Orib.*inc.*21.16. **h.** for ὀρθῷ ποδί, v. ὀρθός II.1. **k.** ἁλιεῖς ἀπὸ ποδός prob. fishermen who fish *from the land*, not from boats, *BGU*221.5 (ii/iii A.D.); ποτίσαι ἀπὸ ποδός perh. irrigate *by the feet* (of oxen turning the irrigation-wheel), *PRyl.*157.21 (ii A.D.); τόπον . . ἀπὸ ποδὸς ἐξηρτισμένον dub. sens. in *POsl.*55.11 (ii/iii A.D.). **l.** ἀγγεῖον . . τρήματα ἐκ τῶν ὑπὸ ποδὸς ἔχον *round the bottom*, Dsc.2.72. **7.** πούς τινος, as periphr. for a person *as coming*, etc., σὺν πατρὸς μολὼν ποδί, i.e. σὺν πατρί, E.*Hipp.*661 ; παρθένου δέχου πόδα Id.*Or.*1217, cf. *Hec.*977, *HF*336 ; χρόνου πόδα Id.*Ba.*889 (lyr.), Ar.*Ra.*100 ; also ἐξ ἑνὸς ποδός, i.e. μόνος ὤν, S.*Ph.*91 ; οἱ δ' ἀφ' ἡσύχου π., i.e. οἱ ἡσύχως ζῶντες, E.*Med.*217. **II.** metaph., of things, *foot, lowest part*, esp. *foot of a hill*, Il.2.824, 20.59 (pl.), Pi.*P.*11.36, etc. ; of a table, couch, etc., Ar.*Fr.*530, X.*Cyr.*8.8.16, etc. ; cf. πέζα ; of the side strokes at the foot of the letter Ω, Callias ap.Ath.10.454a ; = ποδεών II.1, ἀσκοῦ . . λῦσαι π. E.*Med.*679. **2.** in a ship, πόδες are *the two lower corners of the sail*, or *the ropes fastened thereto*, by which the sails are tightened or slackened, *sheets* (cf. ποδεών II.4), Od.5.260 ; χαλᾶν πόδα ease off *the sheet*, as is done when a squall is coming, E.*Or.*707 ; τοῦ ποδὸς παρίει let go hold *of it*, Ar.*Eq.*436 ; ἐκδοῦναι ὀλίγον τοῦ ποδός Luc.*Cont.*3 ; ἐκπετάσουσι πόδα ναός (with reference to the sail), E.*IT*1135 (lyr.) : opp. τεῖναι πόδα haul *it* tight, S.*Ant.*715 ; ναῦς ἐνταθεῖσα ποδί a ship with her *sheet* close hauled, E.*Or.*706 ; κὰδ δ' . . λαῖφος ἐρυσσάμενοι τανύοντο ἐς πόδας ἀμφοτέρους A.R.2.932 ; ἱστία . . ἐτάνυσσαν ὑπ' ἀμφοτέροισι πόδεσσι Q.S.9.438. **b.** perh. of the *rudder* or *steering-paddle*, αἰεὶ γὰρ πόδα νηὸς ἐνώμων Od.10.32 (cf. Sch. ad loc.); πὰρ ποδὶ ναός Pi.*N.*6.55. **III.** *a foot*, as a measure of length, = 4 palms (παλασταί) or 6 fingers, Hdt.2.149, Pl.*Men.*82c, etc. **IV.** *foot* in Prosody, Ar.*Ra.*1323 (lyr.), Pl.*R.*400a, Aristox.*Harm.* p.34 M., Heph.3.1, etc. ; so of a metrical *phrase* or *passage*, ἔκμετρα καὶ ὑπὲρ τὸν π. Luc.*Pr.Im.*18 ; of a long passage declaimed in one breath, κήρυκες ὅταν τὸν καλούμενον πόδα μέλλωσιν ἐρεῖν Gal.4.459, cf. Luc.*Demon.*65, Poll.4.91. **V.** *boundary stone*, Is.*Fr.*27. (Cf. Lat. *pes*, Goth. *fotus*, etc. 'foot'; related to πέδον as noted by Arist. *IA*706$^{a}$33.)

**πούστακος,** ὁ, sine expl., Ar.Byz. ap.Hsch. s.v. πουρέακος.

⊛ **ποῦ⟨τ⟩ριν·** σαπρόν, Hsch. **ποῶ,** v. ποιέω sub init.

**ποώδης** and **ποιώδης,** ες, *herbaceous*, Thphr.*HP*1.1.10, Gal.6.644 ; *grassy*, Hdt.4.47, Arr.*Ind.*32.4 ; ὄζειν ποωδέστερον Arist.*Pr.*906$^{b}$36. **II.** *grass-green*, Id.*Col.*794$^{b}$20 ; φύλλα, καυλός, Thphr.*HP*4.10.3, 6.6.9 ; χρῶμα ib.4.6.2, al. : Comp. ποιωδέστερος ib.1.10.2, Aret.*SD*2.13.

⊛ **πρᾶγμα,** ατος, τό, Ion. **πρῆχμα** *Schwyzer* 688 *B* 16, *C* 5 (Chios, v B.C.), *GDI*5598.4 (Ephesus) ; also **πρῆγμα** Hdt.5.33, al., but Hdt. perh. wrote **πρῆχμα,** which is v. l. in 1.133 ap.Ath.4.144a (cod. A), and in 3.49,57 (*POxy.*1619.326,379) ; cf. πρήχματος οὐχ ὁσίου imitated from Hdt. in *Epigr.Gr.*1092 (Erechtheum) : (πράσσω) :—*deed, act*, the concrete of πρᾶξις, but freq. approaching to the abstract sense, Thgn.116, al. ; opp. λόγοι, D.2.12, etc. ; πραγμάτων ὀρθὰν ὁδόν Pi.*O.*7.46 ; γυναίου π. ἐποίει did the *act* of a woman, D.25.57, cf. 18.24, etc. **II.** *occurrence, matter, affair*, πᾶσαν τελευτὰν πράγματος Pi.*O.*13.75, cf. *P.*4.278 ; τί τοῦδε σοὶ μέτεστι π. λέγε A.*Eu.*575, cf. 584 ; π. τοιόνδε συνηνείχθη γενέσθαι Hdt.5.33, cf. 9.92, Th.2.64 ; ἐς μέσον σφι προετίθεε τὸ π. Hdt.1.206 ; τί δ' εἰδὼς τοῦδε π. πέρι ; S.*Aj.*747 codd. ; τὸ π. εἰς ὑπέρδεινόν μοι περιέστη D.21.111 ; δρᾶτε τὸ π., οἷ προελήλυθε κτλ., Id.4.9, cf. 8.7. **2.** *thing, concrete reality*, ἆρ' ἔστιν αὔλησίς τι π. ; Epich.171.1 ; opp. ὄνομα, Pl.*Cra.*391b, 436a, And.4.27 ; δύο π. . . τοιάδε, οἷον Κρατύλος καὶ Κρατύλου εἰκών Pl.*Cra.*432b ; ὡς ἀργαλέον π. ἐστίν c. inf., Ar.*Pl.*1 ; οὐδὲ π. οὐθέν ἐστι παρὰ τὰ μεγέθη . . τὰ αἰσθητὰ κεχωρισμένον Arist.*de An.*432$^{a}$3, cf. *Mete.*379$^{a}$32, *Ph.*226$^{b}$30, 227$^{b}$28 ; διαμάχονται περὶ τοῦ λευκὸν ἢ μὴ λευκὸν εἶναι τὸ π. Plu.2.1109d, cf. 1112d ; ἐξ ἀζωΐας καὶ ζωῆς συγκείμενον π. Porph.*Sent.*21 : pl., τῶν π. ἀΐδιος ἔσσα Philol.6, cf. Democr.164, Arist.*Xen.*974$^{a}$25, *Pol.*1252$^{a}$24 ; τὰ μετέωρα π. Ar.*Nu.*228, cf. 250, 741 ; opp. ὀνόματα, Pl.*Cra.*390e, D.9.15. **b.** contemptuously, *thing, creature*, κακῷ πράγματι wretched *creature*, viz. the sophist, Pl.*Prt.*312c ; τούτῳ τῷ π., viz. the demos, Id.*Grg.*520b ; ὁ δῆμος ἀσταθμητότατον π. D.19.136 ; ἄμαχον π., of a woman, X.*Cyr.*6.1.36. **3.** like πρᾶξις I.2, ὄφελος I, in Hdt., πρῆγμά ἐστι or ἐστί μοι, c. inf., it is *advantageous* for me, εὕρισκε π. οἱ εἶναι ἐλαύνειν 1.79, cf. 4.11 : with a neg., εὕρισκέ οἱ οὐ π. εἶναι στρατεύεσθαι Id.7.12 : also c. acc. et inf., οὐδὲν ἂν εἴη π. γνώμας ἐμὲ σοὶ ἀποφαίνεσθαι there will be no *advantage* or *need*, Id.1.207 ; π. ἂν ἦν μοῦνον the only *thing needful*, Id.7.130. **4.** *thing of consequence* or *importance*, π. ποιήσασθαι [τι] ib.150 ; π. οὐδὲν ἐποιήσαντο Id.6.63 ; οὐδὲν π., ὦ Σώκρατες no *matter*, S., Pl.*Grg.*447b, cf. E.*Med.*451 ; ὡς . . οὐδὲν ὂν π., εἰ καὶ ἀποθάνοι Pl.*Euthphr.*4d ; δῆλον ἦν ὅτι π. τι εἴη that there was *something the matter*, X.*An.*4.1.17. **b.** π. ἐστί μοι it *concerns* me, σφίσι τε καὶ Ἀθηναίοισι εἶναι οὐδὲν π. they had *nothing to do* with the A., Hdt.5.84, cf. D.18.283 ; ᾧ μὴ π. μὴ εἰσίναι no admittance except on *business*, *Sammelb.*6152.22 (i B.C.) : c. gen. rei, οἷς μηδὲν ἦν π. τοῦ πολέμου who were not *concerned* in the war, Plu.*Pomp.*65 ; τὸ σὸν τί ἐστι π. ; what is your *pursuit* or *business*, what are you about? Pl.*Ap.*20c, cf. *Alc.*1.104d. **c.** μέγα π. a man *of consequence*, D.35.15 ; τὸ μέγα π. ἐν τῇ πόλει Men.*Sam.*175 ; ἦν μέγιστον π. Δημοκήδης παρὰ βασιλέϊ he was made much of by the king, Hdt.3.132 ; π. μέγα φρέατος a *fine large* tank, Alex.179. **5.** used of a battle, *action, affair*, ὡς οἱ σωθέντες ἐκ τοῦ π. ἀπέφυγον X.*HG*7.1.17. **6.** τὸ π. the love-*affair* of Harmodius and Aristogeiton. Aeschin.1.132. **7.** *fact*, opp. λόγος, ὄνομα, Arist.*Top.*146$^{a}$3, *SE*175$^{a}$8 ; πρὸς τὸ π. καὶ τὴν ἀλήθειαν Id.*Ph.*263$^{a}$17 : pl., οὐκ ἐχρῆν τῶν π. τὴν γλῶσσαν ἰσχύειν πλέον E.*Hec.*1188. **8.** *matter in hand, question*, Hp.*Acut.*39 ; πρὸς τὸ π. Pl.*Men.*87a, Arist.*APr.*70$^{a}$32, D.54.26 ; διαιρεῖν κατὰ τὸ π. Arist.*Pol.*1299$^{b}$18 ; ἔξω τοῦ π., v. ἔξω I.2b. **III.** in pl., πράγματα, **1.** *circumstances, affairs*, τὰ ἀνθρωπήϊα π. Hdt.1.207 ; ἐν εἰρήνῃ καὶ ἀγαθοῖς π. Th.3.82, cf. 1.89 ; τοῖς π. τέθνηκα τοῖς δ' ἔργοισιν οὔ by *circumstances*, not by acts, E.*Hel.*286 ; ἐν τοιούτοις π. X.*Mem.*2.7.2, *An.*2.1.16, etc. ; δεινὸς πράγμασι χρῆσθαι D.1.3, cf. X.*HG*3.5.1 ; τύχη τὰ θνητῶν πράγματ', οὐκ εὐβουλία Chaerem.2 ; ἀποτυγχάνειν τῶν π. fail *to prosper*, X.*Mem.*4.2.28 ; the *condition* of a patient, τὰ τῶν νοσεύντων π. Hp.*Prog.*1 (also in sg., ἐξαπίνης ὅλῳ τῷ π. μεταβάλλειν Id.*Acut.*35 ; so also poet., ποῦ ποτ' εἰμὶ πράγματος ; S.*Tr.*375, cf. *Aj.*314). **2.** *state-affairs*, τὰ πολιτικὰ π. Pl.*Ap.*31d ; ἔστ' ἐν ἡμῖν τῆς πόλεως τὰ π. the *fortunes* of the state, Ar.*Lys.*32 ; a *state* or *empire*, τὰ Περσικὰ π. the Persian *power*, Hdt.3.137 ; τὰ Περσέων π. Id.7.50, etc. ; διαπεπόρθηται τὰ Περσῶν π. A.*Pers.*714 ; ἐν ταῖς ναυσὶ τῶν Ἑλλήνων τὰ π. ἐγένετο Th.1.74 ; μὴ ὥσπερ θεῷ νομίζετ' ἐκείνῳ τὰ παρόντα πεπηγέναι π. ἀθάνατα D.4.8, cf. 44, etc. ; παρασπάσασθαί τι τῶν ὅλων π. Id.1.3 ; of *government*, καταλαμβάνειν τὰ π. Hdt.6.39, cf. Th.3.30 (Pass.) ; ἔχειν τὰ π. ib.62,72, cf. Hdt.6.83 ; κατέχειν τὰ π. Th.4.2 ; ἐς μέσον Πέρσῃσι καταθεῖναι τὰ π. Hdt.3.80 ; οἱ ἐν τοῖς π. those who are in *power* or *office*, Th.3.28, D.9.56, Arist.*Pol.*1307$^{b}$10 ; οἱ ἐπὶ τοῖς π. ὄντες D.9.2 ; οἱ ἐπὶ τῶν π. Id.18.247, cf. Plb.3.69.4, Lxx 1*Ma.*3.32 ; ἐν τυραννίδι καὶ πλούτῳ καὶ πράγμασι Plu.2.150c ; τριῶν ἀνδρῶν δημοσίων π. ἀποκαταστάσεως, = Lat. *triumvir reipublicae constituendae*, *Sammelb.*4224.2 (i B.C.) ; κοινωνοὶ τῶν π. X.*HG*2.3.17 ; νεώτερα π. *innovations*, Lys.13.6, Isoc.7.59, etc., cf. Hdt.5.19 ; but εὐνούστατος τοῖς π. a friend *to things as they are*, Lys.12.65. **3.** *fortunes, cause, circumstances*, Hdt.7.236, 237 ; κοινὰ π. E.*IT*1062 ; τέρας γὰρ ὁ βίος καὶ τὰ π. ἐστί μου Id.*Hel.*260 ; ἔρρει τἀμὰ π. X.*Smp.*1.15, cf. E.*Alc.*280 : τὰ π. alone, one's *all*, one's *fortunes*, ἐν ᾧπέρ ἐστι πάντα μοι τὰ π. Ar.*Ach.*474 ; = κτήματα, Hp.(*Lex* 5?) ap.Erot. : in sg., φαῦλον γὰρ ἂν εἴη τὸ ἐμὸν π. Pl.*Hp.Ma.*286e, cf. *Cri.*53d, *Ap.*42a. **4.** *business*, esp. *law-business*, πρός τινα Antipho 6.12, Th.1.128 ; οὔτε ἐμαυτοῦ οὔτε ἀλλότρια π. πράξας Lys.12.3 ; δικῶν γὰρ οὐ δέομ' οὐδὲ πραγμάτων Ar.*V.*1426 ; πράγματα κἀντιγραφάς Id.*Nu.*471 : metaph. in sg., πονηρὸν τὸ π. ἔχειν to have a bad *case*, Arist.*Rh.*1415$^{b}$22. **5.** in bad sense, *trouble, annoyance*, ἁπάντων αἰτίους τῶν π. Ar.*Ach.*310 ; πρήγματα ἔχειν, c. part., to have *trouble* about a thing, Hdt.7.147, cf. Pl.*Tht.*174b, etc. ; π. ἔχειν ἐν τῷ δείπνῳ X.*Cyr.*1.3.4, etc. ; π. λαμβάνειν Id.*Lac.*2.9 ; π. παρέχειν τινί to cause one *trouble*, Hdt.1.155, Ar.*Pl.*20, al. : c. inf., cause one the *trouble* of doing, Pl.*Phd.*115a, X.*Cyr.*4.5.46, Ar.*V.*313 ; πραγμάτων . . ἀπαλλαγείς Id.*Ach.*269 (lyr.), cf. Pl.*Ap.*41d, *R.*406e ; ἄνευ πραγμάτων, σὺν πράγμασι, D.1.20, X.*An.*6.3.6 : less freq. in sg., μηδὲν πρῆγμα παρέχειν Hdt.7.239.

**πραγμᾰτ-ᾶς,** ᾶ, ὁ, = πραγματευτής, *agent* or *official* of a religious guild, *IPE*2.61, al. (Panticapaeum). ⊛ **-εία,** Ion. **πρηγμᾰτίη,** poet. **πραγμᾰτίη** Man.1.38 : ἡ :—*prosecution of business, diligent study*, Isoc.1.44, 5.7, Pl.*Cra.*408a, al. ; πόνων πολλῶν καὶ πραγματείας εἶναι D.8.48 ; πλείονος εἶναι πρηγματίης Hp.*VM*7 ; ἡ μάταιος π. [λογισμῶν] this idle *attention to* argumentations, X.*Mem.*4.7.8 ; μετὰ πολλῆς π. with a great deal of *trouble*, *PCair.Zen.*19.4 (iii B.C.). **II.** *occupation, business*, ἡ π. αὐτῆς (sc. τῆς ῥητορικῆς) ἅπασα . . εἰς τοῦτο τελευτᾷ Pl.*Grg.*453a ; ἡ τοῦ διαλέγεσθαι π. the *business* of dialectic, Id.*Tht.*161e ; τοῦ πολιτικοῦ . . πᾶσα ἡ π. περὶ πόλιν [ἐστί] Arist.*Pol.*1274$^{b}$37, cf. *EN*1105$^{a}$11 ; ἡ δημηγορικὴ π. the *business* of oratory, Id.*Rh.*1354$^{b}$24 ; ἀπὸ τῆς ἀναισχύντου π. ἀποστῆναι Aeschin.3.242 ; πραγματεῖαι *official duties*, opp. ἀρχαί, ib.13, cf. *PTeb.*5.143, al. (ii B.C.) ; esp. *law-business, lawsuit*, Isoc.2.18, al. ; ἡ περὶ τὰ δικαστήρια π. Id.15.31 : pl., *affairs* in general, κάτω βλέπειν εἰς ἀνθρώπων πραγματείας Pl.*R.*500c ; μεθισταμένων πραγματειῶν Antipho 2.4.9 (nisi leg. πραγμάτων) ; *troubles*, D.61.37, Epicur.*Ep.*1 p.28 U. ; πρὸς ἔθνη τὴν π. ἔχειν to have *dealings* with . . , Str.9.2.2. **b.** pl., *works*, of the buildings of Solomon, Lxx 3*Ki.*9.1. **III.** *treatment* of a subject, εἰδέων Archyt.4 ; ἡ τοῦ ἐπιπέδου π., as a definition of plane geometry, Pl.*R.*528d ; ἡ Πλάτωνος π. Plato's *system*, Arist.*Metaph.*987$^{a}$30, cf. 986$^{a}$8, Epicur.*Ep.*1 p.3 U., Phld.*D.*1.17 ; *manner of dealing with*, ἡ περὶ τοὺς μάρτυρας π. Arist.*Rh.*1376$^{b}$4. **2.** *philosophical argument* or *treatise*, Id.*Top.*100$^{a}$18, 101$^{a}$26 ; τοῦ εἰδέναι χάριν ἡ π. Id.*Ph.*194$^{b}$18 ; ἡ παροῦσα π. οὐ θεωρίας ἕνεκα Id.*EN*1103$^{b}$26 ; *the subject of such a treatise*, τρεῖς αἱ π. Id.*Ph.*198$^{a}$30, cf. *SE*183$^{b}$4 ; ἡ περὶ τῶν ἀγαθῶν ἐκδοθεῖσα π. Str.1.2.2, etc. **3.** *systematic* or *scientific historical treatise*, Plb.1.1.4, 1.3.1, D.S.1.1, D.H.1.74, Luc.*Hist.Conscr.*13 ; Τρωϊκὴ π. *the legends* of the Trojan war, Arg.S.*Aj.* ; π. συνέταξεν ἐν δράματι τῶν Δαρδάνου πράξεων τὰς μνημοσύνας *BMus. Inscr.*3.444.18 (Iasus). **4.** *magical operation, spell*, ἡ Σολομῶνος π. *PMag.Par.*1.853, cf. 776. **-ειώδης,** ες, *laborious, like work* rather than play, παιδιά Pl.*Prm.*137b. **2.** *serious, important, based on reality*, ἀπορία Simp.*in Ph.*1299.4, cf. Ammon.*in Int.*86.5, Simp.*in Cat.*

1.22. b. *concerned with facts* or *realities, material*, opp. λογικός (formal), Procl. *in Prm.* p.820 S., Dam. *Pr.* 201 (Comp.). Adv. -κῶς Simp. *in Cat.* 194.4 (Comp.), Ascl. *in Metaph.* 123.33, Diotog. ap. Stob. 4.7.62 (-δέως), Eust. 1762.5: Comp. -εστέρως Olymp. *in Grg.* p.355 J. **-ευμα**, ατος, τό, *business, concern*, τὸ π. τὸ τῶν ῥητόρων Phld. *Rh.* 1.82 S., cf. 79 S. ⊕ **-εύομαι**, Ion. **πρηγμ-**, aor. ἐπραγματευσάμην, Ion. ἐπρηγμ-, Hp. *Epid.* 6.8.32, X. *Oec.* 10.9, etc.; also ἐπραγματεύθην, Ion. ἐπρηγμ-, Hdt. 2.87, Isoc. 12.249: pf. πεπραγμάτευμαι Id. 11.1, Pl. *Phd.* 99d, 100b, al.; also in pass. sense, v. infr.:—*busy oneself, take trouble*, ἀπέδωκαν τὸν νεκρὸν οὐδὲν ἔτι πρηγματευθέντες Hdt. l.c., cf. Pl. *Cra.* 437c; π. περὶ σωφροσύνης Id. *R.* 430d, cf. *Cra.* 425c; περὶ τὰ ὄντα Id. *Tht.* 187a, cf. X. *Mem.* 4.2.7, Arist. *EN* 1102ᵃ22, etc.; πολλὰ ἐπί τινι π. *work at* a thing, *labour to bring* it *about*, X. *Mem.* 1.3.15; πρός τι Pl. *Erx.* 398a; πραγματεύονται ὅπως ἄρξουσι *exert themselves* to.., X. *Lac.* 14.5: abs., Thphr. *HP* 4.4.1; μηδὲν πραγματεύου do not *worry*, Id. *Char.* 18.9: c. inf., *exert oneself* to.., Plu. *Them.* 19. 2. *to be engaged in business, spend one's time in business*, ὅλην τὴν νύκτα all night long, X. *Cyr.* 2.4.26; π. καὶ κακοπαθεῖν τὸν βίον ἅπαντα Arist. *EN* 1176ᵇ29, cf. 1122ᵃ9; simply, *conduct a business*, *PCair.Zen.* 199.11 (iii B.C.); *transact business*, of clerks, ib. 647.11 (iii B.C.); π. ἀπὸ ἐμπορίας καὶ δανεισμῶν *make money* by trade and loans, Plu. *Cat.Mi.* 59, cf. *Sull.* 17, etc.; οἱ πραγματευόμενοι, = Lat. *negotiatores*, *OGI* 532.6 (Galatia), cf. *SIG* 797.10 (Assus, i A.D.): c. acc., π. τὸ συνηγορικὸν καὶ (τὸ) ἐπιδέκατον, of a tax-farmer, *Ostr.* 1537 (ii B.C.), *PLeid.F* in *Ostr.* i p.302; τὴν ὑϊκὴν π. *PSI* 4.384.2 (iii B.C.); generally, of officials, *to be employed in public affairs*, *PGnom.* 174 (ii A.D.), etc. II. c. acc. rei, *take in hand, treat laboriously, be engaged in*, Pl. *Prt.* 361d, *Hp.Ma.* 304c, D. 18.26, etc.; *undertake*, τὸν δεύτερον πλοῦν Pl. *Phd.* 99d. 2. of authors, *elaborate* a work, Ar. *Nu.* 526; of a science, *work out*, ἃ θέλει Archyt. 4; *treat of*, περὶ φύσεως πάντα Arist. *Metaph.* 989ᵇ33, cf. Epicur. *Nat.* 15.34; περί τινος Arist. *Ph.* 193ᵇ31; περί τι Id. *Metaph.* 1025ᵇ17, Phld. *Mus.* p.96 K., al.; τοιαύτην οὐκ ἐπραγματεύθησαν ἀκριβολογίαν περὶ τὰς φλέβας *did* not *use* such precision *in treating* of.., Arist. *HA* 513ᵃ9. 3. of historians, *treat systematically*, τὰς πράξεις Plb. 1.4.3: abs., οἱ πραγματευόμενοι *systematic historians*, Id. 5.33.5, etc. 4. simply, *write, treat*, ποιητὴς ὧν πεπραγμάτευται περὶ τὸ ἱερόν *IG* 11(4).544.5 (Delos, iii B.C.); τὰ πεπραγματευμένα ὑπ' αὐτῶ his *works, compositions*, *SIG* 721.8 (Crete, ii/i B.C.), cf. 702.5 (Delph., ii B.C.). III. Pass., mostly pf. πεπραγμάτευμαι, *to be laboured at, elaborated*, Pl. *Ap.* 22b, *Prm.* 129e; δόρυ ὡσαύτως -ευμένον X *Eq.* 8.10; αἱ εἰς τὸν παῖδα -ευμέναι μεταφοραί Aeschin. 1.167; also pres., Arist. *EE* 1215ᵃ30. **-ευτέος**, α, ον, *to be laboured at*, τοῦτο τῷ νομοθέτῃ π., ὅπως.. Id. *Pol.* 1333ᵃ14; τῷ νομοθέτῃ π. περί τι ib. 1337ᵃ11. II. **-τέον**, *one must treat*, περί τινος Id. *Top.* 105ᵇ31, cf. 106ᵃ2, Ruf. *Ren.Ves.* 13.11. 2. *one must arrange, distribute*, Paul.Al. *C.* 4. ⊕ **-ευτής**, οῦ, ὁ, *business representative*, = Lat. *actor*, Plu. 2.525a, *PColumb.* in *JEA* 18.16 (ii A.D.), *PMasp.* 158.17 (v A.D.), etc.; π. Πτολεμαίου his *agent* or *attorney*, *CIG* 4299 (Antiphellus), cf. 3104 (Teos), *IG* 14.2057, *OGI* 525.3 (Halic.), *PTeb.* 357.5 (ii A.D.), etc. ⊕ **-ευτικός**, ή, όν, *occupied in business*, Procl. *Par. Ptol.* 95, Sch.Ar. *Pl.* 521, f.l. in Porph. *Abst.* 1.3. II. *levied on traders*, χρυσάργυρον *PLips.* 64.30 (iv A.D.). **-ίας**, ου, ὁ, *tiresome*, λόγος *Com.Adesp.* 894. ⊕ **-ικός**, ή, όν, *fit for action* or *business, businesslike, statesmanlike*, later Greek for πρακτικός, βασιλεύς, ἄνδρες, Plb. 7.11.2, 7.12.2, al.; *pragmatici homines*, men *of the world*, men *of affairs*, Cic. *Att.* 2.20.1; *wise and prudent men*, Vett.Val. 17.22; πραγματική, = ἐπιστήμη τῶν ἀνθρωπίνων πραγμάτων, Andronic. Rhod. p.574 M. Adv. -κῶς Cic. *QF* 2.14.2. 2. Subst. πραγματικός, ὁ, *agent, attorney*, π. τῆς πόλεως, τοῦ νομοῦ, *Inscr.Magn.* 189 (ii A.D.), *PAmh.* 2.107.15 (ii A.D.), cf. *SIG* 888.101 (Scaptopara, iii A.D.). b. Lat. *pragmaticus, legal adviser*, Cic. *de Or.* 1.45.59, Quint. *Inst.* 12.3.4, Juv. 7.123. c. *civil official*, opp. military officer, *PTeb.* 58.18 (ii B.C.), *OGI* 139.7 (Egypt, ii B.C.), 669.21, al. (ibid. i A.D.); *civilian*, opp. στρατιωτικός, Plb. 14.1.13; ἱερόδουλοι καὶ π. τοῦ ἱεροῦ Lxx 1 *Es.* 8.22. 3. π. τύπος, νόμος, = Lat. *pragmatica sanctio*, Just. *Nov.* 7.2.1, *Cod.Just.* 1.3.38.6. II. of things, 1. of history, *political* (including *military*), Plb. 1.2.8, 9.2.4, al., Plu. *Galb.* 2, etc.; π. ἀποφάσεις *political* utterances, Plb. 32.2.7. 2. of speech or action, *able, prudent, statesmanlike*, ἔργον, λόγοι, Id. 3.116.7, 36.5.1; τρόπος Id. 23.5.5; ὥστε μὴ ὑποπτεῦσαί τι περὶ αὐτοῦ πραγματικόν anything *machiavellian*, Id. 30.27.2, cf. 30.19.11. Adv. -κῶς Id. 2.13.1, al.; *by statecraft*, Id. 31.10.6. III. *relating to subject-matter*, opp. style, ὁ π. τόπος, opp. ὁ λεκτικός, D.H. *Comp.* 1: Sup., -ωτάτη εὕρεσις Hermog. *Inv.* 1.1. 2. *relating to fact*, θεωρήματα, ζήτησις, Epicur. *Nat.* 28 *Fr.* 4 (p.5 V.), Demetr.Lac. *Herc.* 1014.62; πίστις Syrian. *in Hermog.* i p.57 R. (v.l.): -κή, ἡ, *deliberation on matter of fact* or *on action*, ib. ii p.161 R.; π. ἔγγραφος, ἄγραφος, ib. p.162 R. b. *material* (opp. formal, verbal), διαφωνία Simp. *in Cael.* 640.28. Adv. -κῶς, ζητεῖν Phld. *Rh.* 2.238 S., cf. Plu. 2.960b; διαφέρεσθαι ib. 1113c; τὸ π. ἀπορούμενον difficulty *arising from facts* (opp. verbal), Simp. *in Ph.* 1289.35: Sup., ἐν τοῖς Στωικοῖς -ώτατα φιλοσοφῆσαι Porph. *Abst.* 4.8: opp. ψυχικῶς, στοιχειακῶς, Anon. in Westermann *Mythogr.* p.328. IV. πραγματικόν, τό, in Magic, *effective spell*, *PMag.Par.* 1.2432. V. *troublesome, formidable*, of a citadel, Plb. 4.70.10; λίαν δυσάλωτος καὶ π. πόλις Beros. ap. J. *Ap.* 1.20; of an attack, Plb. 5.5.4; ἀήττητα καὶ π. πλήθη Id. 1.35.5. **-ιον**, τό, Dim. of πρᾶγμα, *trifling matter, petty lawsuit* or *business*, Ar. *Nu.* 197, 1004, Arr. *Epict.* 1.27.16, *POxy.* 746.6 (i A.D.), etc.

**πραγμᾰτο-δίφης** [ῐ], ου, ὁ, *one who hunts after lawsuits, pettifogger*, Ar. *Av.* 1424. **-ειδής**, ές, *laborious, troublesome*, Hp. *Mul.* 1.70 (Comp.). **-κοπέω**, *meddle in business, to be meddlesome, seditious*, Plb. 29.23.10, 38.13.8, Phld. *Rh.* 2.53 S. **-κόπος**, ὁ, *meddler, busybody*, ib. 1.226 S. ⊕ **-λογέω**, *narrate facts*, Arist. *Rh.Al.* 1438ᵇ20, Ph. 1.554, 655. II. *quarrel, argue*, D.L. 9.52. **-μᾰθής**, ές, *skilled in business*, Anon. ap. Suid. **-ποιία**, ἡ, *statecraft*, Plb. 36.9.11. **-ρράφος** [ᾰ], ὁ, *author of troubles*, Gloss.

**πραγμᾰτώδης**, ες, = πραγματοειδής, *laborious*, αἱ ἀλύσεις πρὸς τὰ τοιαῦτα -ώδες Aen.Tact. 39.7: Sup., Id. 31.16; *tedious*, συγγράμματα Isoc. 10.2 (Comp.); οὐδέν ἐστι -ωδέστερον D. 19.270; πραγματῶδες τὸ τοῦτο παρατηρεῖν Phld. *Rh.* 2.44 S.

**πραγορίτης**, ου, ὁ, a kind of *wine*, Hsch.

**πρᾶγος**, εος, τό, poet. for πρᾶγμα, Pi. *N.* 3.6, *Fr.* 108, A. *Th.* 861 (anap.), *Pers.* 248 (troch.), S. *Ichn.* 74, Ar. *Av.* 112, *Lys.* 706 (paratrag.). 2. = πράγματα, *state-affairs*, A. *Th.* 2.

**πράδησις** [ᾰ], ιος, ἡ, *breaking wind*, Hp. *Prog.* 11, *Coac.* 485 (v.l. πέρδησις).

**πραδίλη**, ἡ, = πεπραδίλη (q.v.).

**πρᾰθέειν**, v. πέρθω; **πρᾰθείς**, v. πέρνημι.

**πραθενεύεσθαι**· θρασύνεσθαι, ἐπαγγέλλεσθαι λόγοις, Hsch.

⊕ **πραιδεύω**, = Lat. *praedor*, Petr.Patr. in Boissevain *Dio Cassius* iii p.746, Hsch. s.v. δηώσαντες: written **πραιτεύω**, *PLond.* 5.1674.91 (vi A.D.), etc.

⊕ **πραίκων**, ωνος, ὁ, = Lat. *praeco*, *Stud.Pal.* 20 p.77 (iv A.D.), Hsch.

**πραῖνοι**· πρηνίζει, καταστρέφει, Hsch. (leg. πρανοῖ, cf. πρανόω).

⊕ **πραιπόσιτος**, ὁ, = Lat. *praepositus*, a military title, *PCair.Preis.* 33.2 (iv A.D.), etc.: hence **πραιποσιτεύομαι**, *PAmh.* 2.140.1 (iv A.D.); **πραιποσιτούρα**, ἡ, *PLips.* 111.16 (iv A.D.).

**πραισίδια**, τά, = Lat. *praesidia, garrison*, *PMich.* in *Class.Phil.* 28.250 (ii A.D.).

**πραισιμνάω**, = προαισιμνάω (which shd. perh. be read), *Rev.Arch.* 22 (1925).62 (Callatis).

**πραιτωριανοί**, οἱ, *soldiers of the praetorian guard*, D.C. 53.25, Lyd. *Mag.* 2.6, etc.

**πραιτωρίδιον**, τό, Dim. of sq., *small house*, Arr. *Epict.* 3.22.47.

⊕ **πραιτώριον**, τό, = Lat. *Praetorium*, *official residence of a governor*, *Ev.Matt.* 27.27; later, of private *residences*, Just. *Nov.* 159 *Praef.* II. *praetorian guard*: ἔπαρχος πραιτωρίου, τοῦ π., = *praefectus praetorio*, *OGI* 707 (Tyre, ii A.D.), *IG* 14.911, etc. 2. *imperial household*, *Ep. Phil.* 1.13.

**πράκες**, = πρόκες, Hsch. **πράκνον**· μέλανα, Id.; cf. περκνός.

**πρακ-τεῖον**, τό, *post, official position*, τὰ πρακτῖα τῶν δουκικῶν μηκέτι πιπράσκεσθαι *Princeton Exp.Inscr.* A3 No. 562 (Bosra, v A.D.). **-τέος**, α, ον, (πράσσω) *to be done*, Pl. *Prt.* 356c, etc. II. πρακτέον, *one must do*, S. *OT* 1439, Pl. *Prt.* 356b, etc. 2. *one must exact*, χρήματα X. *Hier.* 8.9. **-τευτής**, οῦ, ὁ, = πράκτωρ II, *PKlein.Form.* 1270 (vi A.D.). **-τήρ**, Ion. **πρηκτήρ**, ῆρος, ὁ, *doer*, πρηκτῆρά τε ἔργων Il. 9.443: in pl., *traders*, ναυτάων, οἵ τε πρηκτῆρες ἔασιν Od. 8.162; παίδων π. *dealers in*.., Man. 6.447. II. = πράκτωρ II. 1, *BCH* 50.16 (Delph., iv B.C.), *IG* 2².45.8 (prob.), 9(1).32.38 (Stiris, ii B.C.), Them. *Or.* 8.114a, *POxy.* 1829.7 (vi A.D.), etc. **-τήριος**, ον, *efficacious, effectual*, τύχη A. *Supp.* 523. **-της**, ου, ὁ, = πρακτήρ I, Suid. s.v. ῥέκτῃ ἀνδρί: Ion. **πρήκτης** *treacherous person*, Hp. *Ep.* 19 (*Hermes* 53.67, cf. 76). **-τικεύομαι**, *to be practical*, Eustr. *in EN* 284.38. ⊕ **-τικός**, ή, όν, *fit for* or *concerned with action, practical*, λεκτικοὶ καὶ π. καὶ μηχανικοί X. *Mem.* 4.3.1; φιλότεχνοι καὶ π. Pl. *R.* 476a; ζωὴ π., βίος π., Arist. *EN* 1098ᵃ3, *Pol.* 1325ᵇ16, etc.; αἱ π. ἀρχαί the principles *of action*, Id. *EN* 1144ᵃ35; ἡ π. διάνοια, opp. ἡ θεωρητική, ib. 1139ᵃ27, cf. *Metaph.* 1025ᵇ25, *de An.* 433ᵃ18; ἡ -κή (with or without ἐπιστήμη) *practical science*, opp. theoretical, Pl. *Plt.* 258e, 259d; τὸ λαμβεῖον π. *representative of action*, Arist. *Po.* 1460ᵃ1; μέλη π. Id. *Pol.* 1341ᵇ34; π. χρόνοι times *appropriate for action*, Vett.Val. 96.28. 2. *active, effective*, τὸ -ώτατον τῆς δυνάμεως the *most effective* part, Plb. 1.30.9, cf. 10.25.2; παρὰ θεῶν -ώτερος *more effectual in carrying one's point* with.., X. *Cyr.* 1.6.3; περὶ τὴν πολιτείαν -ώτατος Plb. 7.10.5: so of things, *drastic, effective*, ῥίζα Dsc. 3.54; also νεῦρα π. *motor* nerves, Gal. 1.321: πρακτικόν, τό, *spell, magical rite*, *PMag. Par.* 1.2359. 3. c. gen., *able to effect*, τῶν καλῶν, τῶν δικαίων, Arist. *EN* 1099ᵇ31, 1129ᵃ8, etc. 4. *active, vigorous, strong*, οἴνου τι πρακτικώτερον Ar. *Eq.* 91; ἰταμότης ὀξεῖα καὶ π. Pl. *Plt.* 311a; [ἡ ὀργὴ] -ώτερον τοῦ μίσους Arist. *Pol.* 1312ᵇ27. II. Adv. -κῶς, διακεῖσθαι πρός τι Plb. 6.25.4; ὠφελεῖν Archig. ap. Aët. 9.28: Comp. -ώτερον Plb. 5.18.7. ⊕ **-τῖμος**, ον, *liable to a money-penalty*, *SIG* 671 *A* 12 (Delph., ii B.C.). **-τορεία** (freq. also -ία, *Sammelb.* 5982.4 (ii A.D.), etc.), ἡ, *office of* πράκτωρ, *collectorship*, Stob. 2.7.26, *PTeb.* 27.106 (ii B.C.), *POxy.* 2119.9 (iii A.D.), etc.; π. ξενικῶν *PLips.* 120.1 (i A.D.), cf. 116.6 (ii A.D.). II. proparox. **πρακτόρεια**, ἡ, pecul. fem. of πράκτωρ, A.D. *Conj.* 233.8. **-τόρειον**, τό, *office of the* πράκτωρ (-opes) II. 1, which includes a *debtors' prison*, *OGI* 515.32 (Mylasa, iii A.D.), 669.15 (Egypt, i A.D.). 2. *tax-collector's office*, *Ostr.* 517 (ii A.D.). **-τόρειος**, α, ον, *subject to collection*, εἴδη *PTeb.* 72.463 (ii B.C.). ⊕ **-τορεύω**, *act as collector*, *PLond.* 2.306.9 (ii A.D.). ⊕ **-τορικός**, ή, όν, *kept by* or *with the* πράκτωρ, διαλογισμός *UPZ* 114(1).13 (ii B.C.). **-τός**, Ion. **πρηκτός**, ή, όν, (πράσσω): τὰ π. *things to be done*, i.e. *matters of moral action*, Arist. *EN* 1094ᵃ19, 1097ᵃ22; τὰ π. ἀγαθά ib. 1095ᵃ16, cf. Andronic. Rhod. p.574 M. 2. *traversed*, νηυσὶ πρηκτὰ κέλευθα A.R. *Fr.* 5.3. II. πρακτὸς ὑπό τινος *liable to be called on to pay money* by one, *Test.Epict.* 7.2, 21, cf. *IG* 12(7).237.60 (Minoa, i B.C.); π. ἔστωμ Πραξικλεῖ ἡμιόλιον τὸ ἀργύριον ib. 67.46 (Arcesine, iv/iii B.C.); π. ἔστω τοῦ ἡμιολίου τοῖς ταμίαις ib. 62.50 (ibid., iv B.C.). **-τύς**, ύος, ἡ, Ion. for πρᾶξις, *EM* 316.34. ⊕ **-τωρ**, ορος, ὁ, = πρακτήρ, *one who does* or *executes, accomplisher*, Ζεὺς ὅτου π.

φανῇ S.*Tr.*251; π. τῶν ἀκουσίων Antipho 3.2.6; with fem. Subst., Κύπρις..τῶνδ' ἐφάνη π. S.*Tr.*861 (lyr.). II. *official who executes a judgement for debt*, esp. *public debt, bailiff*, *IG*1².75.49, al., Antipho 6.49, Decr.ap.And.1.77, D.25.28, *IG*12(8).51.9 (Imbros, ii B.C.), *OGI* 483.7 (Pergam.), *Ev.Luc.*12.58; βασιλικὸς π. *PSI*4.335.2 (iii B.C.); τῶν ξενικῶν *PTeb.*5.222 (ii B.C.). 2. *collector* of taxes, π. βαλανήου *Ostr.* in Wilcken *Grundzüge* p.213 (i A.D.), *Ostr.*399 (i A.D.); π. ἀργυρικῶν *PIand.*29.1 (ii A.D.), *BGU*434.3 (ii A.D.), etc.; π. σιτικῶν *PLond.*2.367*a* 1, al. (ii A.D.). 3. in Poets, *one who exacts punishment, avenger*, A.*Supp.*647 (lyr.); π. αἵματος Id.*Eu.*319 (anap.); φόνου S.*El.*953: as Adj., with a fem. Subst., *avenging*, σὺν δορὶ καὶ χερὶ πράκτορι A.*Ag.*111 (lyr.).

**πράληξ**· ὁ λίαν ἀγροῖκος, Hsch.

**Πράμνειος** οἶνος, ὁ, *Pramnian* wine, Il.11.639, Od.10.235; also **Πράμνιος**, Hp.*Mul.*1.52, Ar.*Eq.*107, *Fr.*317. Phryn.Com.65; Π. οἶνος Λέσβιος Ephipp.28 (but from Icarus acc. to Eparchides ap.Ath.1.30b, from Smyrna acc.to Plin.*HN*14.54); *raisin-wine*, Dsc.5.6.

**πράμνη**, ἡ, = δίκελλα, Hsch. 2. = ἄμπελος, Id.

**πράμνημα**, ατος, τό, *shoot of the Pramnian vine*, Poll.7.150.

**πράμος** [ᾰ], ὁ, = πρόμος, dub. in Ar.*Th.*50.

**πρᾶν** [ᾱ], Dor. = πρῴην, *aforetime*, Theoc.3.28, 5.132, etc.; πρᾶν ποκα 2.115, 5.81.

**πρᾱν-ής**, ές, Ion. **πρηνής** (also in Arist.*Mete.*350ª11, *Spir.*484ᵇ29, *Fr.*106, J.*AJ*18.3.1, 19.8.2, Plu.2.680a, *Tim.*11, Gal.*UP*2.2, 7.22, *PMag.Par.*1.194, etc.), gen. έος, Att.contr. οῦς:—of posture, *with the face downwards, lying on the front, falling forwards*, opp. ὕπτιος, πρηνεῖς τε καὶ ὕπτιοι ἔκπεσον ἵππων Il.11.179; ἐκ δίφροιο.. ἐξεκυλίσθη πρηνὴς ἐν κονίῃσιν ἐπὶ στόμα 6.43, cf. 2.418, 4.544, Hes.*Sc.*365; πρηνὴς ἐπὶ γαίῃ κεῖτο ταθείς Il.21.118; mostly with Verbs of falling, πρηνὴς κάππεσε, ἤριπε, ἐλιάσθη, 16.413, 5.58, 15.543; πρηνέα..τανύσσας [Ἕκτορα] 23.25; κατὰ πρηνὲς βαλέειν Πριάμοιο μέλαθρον *headlong down*, 2.414; π. γενόμενος *Act.Ap.*1.18 (fort. = πρησθεὶς *becoming distended*); ἐπὶ τὸ πρηνὲς ῥέπειν incline towards *pronation*, Hp.*Fract.* 1; ἐς τὸ π. Id.*Mochl.*8; of the arm and hand, *with the palm downwards*, v.l. in *Fract.*2; opp. ὕπτιος, Arist.*Spir.* l.c., Plu.*Tim.*11; of ἀστράγαλοι, ὀρθοὶ πίπτοντες ἢ πρηνεῖς Id.2.680a, cf. Poll.7.204; of seeds, *hollow side downwards*, Thphr.*HP*2.6.1; of a ship, *bottom upwards*, implied in Plu.*Tim.* l.c. II. of parts of animals or man, that part which is uppermost and visible when the animal or man is in the πρανής position (the normal one for a quadruped), the *back* part, τὰ τετράποδα .. ἐν τοῖς ὑπτίοις οὐκ ἔχει τὰς τρίχας, ἀλλ' ἐν τοῖς πρανέσι μᾶλλον· οἱ δ' ἄνθρωποι τοὐναντίον ἐν τοῖς ὑπτίοις μᾶλλον ἢ ἐν τοῖς πρανέσιν Arist.*PA*658ª17, cf. *HA*498ᵇ20, 519ª21, 540ª2, *GA*717ᵇ30. 2. of leaves and of the hand, the *back* or '*wrong*' side, τὰς ἶνας καὶ τὰς φλέβας ἐν τοῖς π. ἔχουσιν ὥσπερ ἡ χείρ Thphr. *HP*1.10.2 (misunderstood as the opposite by Plin.*HN*16.88), cf. 3.14.2. III. of the sides of hills, πρὸς ἄναντες καὶ κατὰ πρανοῦς καὶ πλάγια ἐλαύνειν *down hill*, X.*Eq.*3.7, cf. *An.*1.5.8, 4.8.28, Plu.*Sull.*18; κατὰ τὰ π. X.*Eq.*8.6; τὸ π., opp. τὸ ὄρθιον, ibid., cf. *Cyr.*2.2.24. 2. *convex*, Arist.*Mete.*350ª11. -ίζω, Ion. πρηνίζω, aor. ἐπρήνιξα, πρήνιξα, = καταστρέφω, πόλιν Euph.18, Nonn.*D.*4.340, al.:—Pass., *capsize*, ἅμα νηὶ πρηνιχθεὶς *AP*7.532 (Isid.); πρανιχθῆναι· τὸ ἐπὶ στόμα πεσεῖν, Phot., cf. Hsch.: plpf. ἐπρήνικτο Nonn.*D.*30.86. -όν· τὸ κατωφερές, πρανές, Hsch. -όω, = πρανίζω, aor. ἐπράνωσε Id.; cf. πραϊνοι.

**πρανώ**· ἀκρίδος εἶδος, Hsch.

**πραξείδιον**, τό, Dim. of πρᾶξις, *EM*230.10.

**Πραξῐδίκη** [δῐ], ἡ, *she who exacts penalties*, a goddess, represented with a bare head, to whom the heads of victims were offered, Orph. *A.*31, Paus.3.22.2, etc.: pl., *Tab.Defix.*109.2 (iii B.C.). II. = Περσεφόνη, Orph.*H.*29.5.

**πραξιεργίας**, ου, ὁ, expl. of Lat. *pontifex*, Lyd.*Mens.*4.15.

**πραξικοπέω**, *take by surprise* or *treachery*, πόλιν Plb.3.69.1. 2. *overreach, outwit*, τινας Id.2.46.2, *OGI*315.7 (Pessinus, ii B.C.), cf. *Supp.Epigr.*4.671 (Alexandria Troas, ii B.C.).

**Πραξίλλειον** μέτρον, metre *used by Praxilla*, Heph.7.8.

※ **πράξῐμος**, ον, of money, *recoverable*, Plb.21.43.17; π. τῆς ἡγεμονικῆς τάξεως *BGU*306.3 (vi A.D.). II. τὰ π. *practical aims*, γένοιτο αὐτῷ..τὰ π. ἄπρακτα *Supp.Epigr.*6.802 (Cyprus, ii/iii A.D.).

※ **πρᾶξις**, εως, Ep. and Ion. **πρῆξις**, ιος, ἡ: (πράσσω):—*doing, transaction, business*, [πλεῖν] κατὰ πρῆξιν *on a trading voyage*, Od.3.72; ἐπὶ πρῆξιν ἔπλεον *h.Ap.*397; π. δ' ἥδ' ἰδίη, οὐ δήμιος a private, not a public *affair*, Od.3.82; π. μηδὲ φίλοισιν ὅμως ἀνακοινέο πᾶσιν Thgn. 73; ἡ περί τινος π. the *transaction* respecting.., Th.6.88. 2. *result* or *issue of a business*, esp. *good result, success*, οὐ γάρ τις πρῆξις πέλεται..γόοιο no *good* comes of weeping, Il.24.524; οὔ τις π. ἐγίγνετο μυρομένοισιν Od.10.202; λυμαίνεσθαί τινι τὴν π. to spoil one's *market*, X.*An.*1.3.16; π. φίλαν δίδοι grant a happy *issue*, Pi.*O.*1.85; π. οὐρίαν θέλων A.*Ch.*814 (lyr.); ταχεῖά γ' ἦλθε χρησμῶν π. their *issue*, Id.*Pers.* 739; ἄνευ τούτων οὐκ ἂν εἴη π. X.*Cyn.*2.2; δὸς πόρον καὶ π. τῷ τόπῳ τούτῳ *PMag.Par.*1.2366. II. *doing*, τῶν ἀγαθῶν (of persons) πρήξιες Thgn.1026; ἡ τῶν ἀγαθῶν π. Pl.*Chrm.*163e; ἡ π. τῶν ἔργων Antipho 3.4.9; *achievement*, Th.3.114; π. πολεμική, ποιητική, πολιτική, Pl.*R.*399a, *Sph.*266d, *Men.*99b; *action*, opp. πάθος, Id.*Lg.*876d; opp. ἕξις, Id.*R.*434a; *moral action*, opp. ποίησις, τέχνη, Arist.*EN* 1140ª2, 1097ª16; opp. ποιότης, Id.*Po.*1450ª18, cf. *EN*1178ª35 (pl.); ἤθη καὶ πάθη καὶ π. Id.*Po.*1447ª28; opp. οἱ πολιτικοὶ λόγοι, D.61.44; ἔργῳ καὶ πράξεσιν, οὐχὶ λόγοις Id.6.3; ἐν ταῖς πράξεσι ὄντα τε καὶ πραττόμενα exhibited *in actual life*, Pl.*Phdr.*271d; *action* in drama, opp. λόγος, Arist.*Po.*1454ª18; μία π. ὅλη καὶ τελεία ib. 1459ª19, cf. 1451ᵇ33 (pl.). 2. *action, exercise*, χειρῶν, σκελῶν, στόματος, φωνῆς, διανοίας, Pl.*La.*192a. 3. euphem. for *sexual intercourse*, Pi. *Fr.*127, Aeschin.1.158, etc.; in full, ἡ π. ἡ γεννητική Arist.*HA*539ᵇ 20. 4. magical *operation, spell*, *PMag.Par.*1.1227, al., *PMag. Lond.*125.40. III. *action, act*, S.*OT*895 (lyr., pl.), *OC*560, etc.; μιᾶς μόνον μνησθήσομαι π. Isoc.12.127. b. *military action, battle*, Plb.3.19.11, etc. IV. *doing, faring* well or ill, *fortune, state, condition*, ἀπέκλαιε.. τὴν ἑωυτοῦ π. Hdt.3.65, cf. A.*Pr.*695 (lyr.), S.*Aj.*790, 792; εὐτυχὴς π. Id.*Tr.*294; κακαὶ π. Id.*Ant.*1305. V. *practical ability*, π. καὶ σύνεσις Plb.2.47.5; ἡ ἐν τοῖς πολεμικοῖς π. Id.4.77.1. 2. *practice*, i.e. *trickery, treachery*, ἐπὶ τὴν πόλιν Id. 2.9.2; κατὰ τῆς πόλεως, ἐπὶ τοὺς Αἰτωλούς, Id.4.71.6, 5.96.4. VI. *exaction of money, recovery of debts, arrears*, etc., *IG*1².57.13, al.; συμβολαίων πράξεις And.1.88; τοῦ μισθοῦ Pl.*Prt.*328b; τελῶν Id. *R.*425d (pl.); παρὰ Ἀρτέμωνος.. ἔστω ἡ π. τοῖς δανείσασι let the lenders have *an action of recovery* against Artemon, Syngr.ap.D.35. 12, cf. *SIG*364.61, 67 (Ephesus, iii B.C.), *Test.Epict.*5.31; ἡ π. ἔστω καθάπερ ἐκ δίκης *PEleph.*1.12 (iv B.C.), etc.; αἱ π. τῶν καταδικασθέντων Arist.*Pol.*1321ᵇ42. 2. *exaction of vengeance, retribution*, βαρβάρων χάριν γάμων πρᾶξιν ὡς Ἑλλὰς λάβοι E.*IA*272 (lyr.). VII. *public office*, ἡ διοικηθεῖσα π. Epist.Macrin.ap.Hdn.5.1.2. VIII. *discourse, lecture* of a rhetorician or philosopher, Jul.*Or.*2.59c, Marin.*Procl.*22.

※ **πραόνως**, Adv. *temperately*, Ar.*Ra.*856, Ael.*NA*5.39. (Formed from *πραό-νους.)

**πραο-παθέω**, etc., v. πραϋ-.

※ **πρᾶος**, ον, also **πραΰς**, Ion. **πρηΰς**, εῖα, ύ:—**πρᾶος** supplies sg. in Att., Trag., and Com., exc. that the fem. is always πραεῖα (πρᾶος as fem. only in Plu.2.168d); but sg. **πραΰς**, Ion. **πρηΰς**, is used in Ep. and Lyr. (also in X. and usu. in Lxx, Plb., etc.):—pl., nom. πρηέες Hp.*Epid.*1.10, πρηεῖς *AP*5.208 (Posidipp. or Asclep.), πρᾶοι Pl.*R.* 562d, etc.; fem. πρηεῖαι *AP*6.244 (Crin.); neut. πραέα X.*Oec.*15.4, *Eq.*9.10, etc., πρᾶα Arist.*HA*488ᵇ22, f.l. in Ph.2.351; gen. πραέων X.*An.*1.4.9; dat. πραέσι Pl.*Lg.*888a, 930a, fem. πραίαις written for πραείαις *IG*7.3101 (Lebad., iii A.D.); acc. πραεῖς Plb.18.37.7, πράους Isoc.3.55: Comp. πραότερος Lys.20.21, πραΰτερος Epich.153, Pl.*Ti.* 85a, etc., Ion. πρηΰτ- Hdt.2.181: Sup. πραότατος Pl.*Phd.*116c, etc., πραΰτατος *Syria* 5.337 (Sidon); Ep. and Ion. πρηΰτατος A.R.2.937, *AP*6.349 (Phld.); πράϋστος *MAMA*1.237 (Phrygia). (The ι subscr. is freq. written in codd., but Πρᾶος is written in *IG*2².1928.20 (pr. n., iv B.C.), *IGRom.*4.504 (Pergam.), cf. Phot., *Et.Gud.*478.31; πρᾳύτερος is found once in codd., Pl.*Ti.* l. c. (proved wrong by πραῢς *Com. Adesp.* in *Gött Nachr.*1922.31, πραέα (neut. pl.) in *PCair.Zen.*33.12 (iii B.C.), πραέως *UPZ*144.6 (ii B.C.), and by the absence of iota in Ion. πρηΰς)):—*mild, soft, gentle* (not in Il. or Od.): 1. of things, πρηῢ σέλας *h.Hom.*8.10; πραῢς ὄαρος Pi.*P.*4.136; *mild*, πυρετοί Hp.l.c.; ἰητρείη πρηεῖα Id.*Art.*69; of sound, *soft, gentle*, τὴν φωνὴν πραοτέραν ποιοῦνται X.*Smp.*1.10; ἀνέμων πρηΰτατε Ζέφυρε *AP*6.349 (Phld.); ὠδῖνες ib.244 (Crin.); κέντρον ib.229 (Id.). 2. of persons, *mild, gentle, meek*, πραῢς ἀστοῖς Pi.*P.*3.71; πᾶσιν ἵλεώς τε καὶ πρᾶος Pl.*R.* 566e; πρὸς τοὺς οἰκείους π. ib.375c; π. τὸ ἦθος Id.*Phdr.*243c; π. ἐν τοῖς λόγοις Id.*Euthd.*303d; esp. after having been angry, Hdt.2.181 (Comp.); ὁ θὴρ ὅδ' ἡμῖν π., of Dionysus, E.*Ba.*436; of a horse, *gentle*, ἀλλήλοις πραότεροι X.*Cyr.*2.1.29; of other animals, *tame*, ἰχθύων μεγάλων καὶ πραέων Id.*An.*1.4.9, cf. Arist.*HA*488ᵇ22; ζῷα..πραέα πρὸς τοὺς ἀνθρώπους X.*Oec.*15.4: prov., πραΰτερος μολόχας Epich.153; also, τόπος ἡμερώτερος καὶ πραότερος Isoc.9.67. 3. of actions, feelings, etc., *mild*, τιμωρίαι πραότεραι Pl.*Lg.*867b; πραότεραι ἡδοναί ib.815e; λόγοι, ἤθη, φύσις, ib.888a, 930a, *R.*375c; ὅσσοισι πρηέσιν δέρκευ *BMus.Inscr.*921*b*8 (Branchidae, i/ii A.D.); τὰ πραέα *caresses*, X.*Eq.* 9.10; πραότερα πάσχειν Pl *Cri.*49b. II. *making mild, taming*, φάρμακον πραῢ τείνων ἀμφὶ γένυι, of a bridle, Pi.*O.*13.85; προκινεῖν αὐτὸν [τὸν ἵππον] ὡς πραοτάτοις σημείοις X.*Eq.*9.3. III. Adv. **πράως**, *mildly, gently*, πράως πείθειν τινά, φέρειν τι, Pl.*R.*589c, *Cri.*43b; πράως ἔχειν πρός τι Id.*Ly.*211e; πράως λέγειν τὸ πάθος to speak *lightly* of it, X.*An.*1.5.14; πράως διακεῖσθαι, opp. ὀργίζεσθαι, D.21.183; πράως, μὴ πικρῶς Id.18.265; in physical sense, *gently*, Orib.*Fr.*134: Comp., πραότερον προδιδάσκειν, κολάζειν, Pl *Grg.*489d, *Phd.*94d; πραοτέρως (v.l. -ύτερως) ἔχειν τινί J.*AJ*17.6.4: Sup., φέρειν..ὡς πραότατα Pl.*R.*387e: later form **πραέως** (πράως [Ἀττικοί], οὐ πραέως Phot.), *UPZ*144.6 (ii B.C.), D.S.1.36, Dsc.1.13, dub. in *Com.Adesp.*336.5 (cf. πρατίας), etc.: Ion. **πρηέως** cj. in Democr.46 (πράως and πραέως codd.). (Cogn. with Skt. *prīṇā́ti* 'love, give pleasure to', Goth. *frijon* 'love', *frijonds* 'friend'.)

**πρᾱότης**, ητος, ἡ, *mildness, gentleness*, Th.4.108, Lys.6.34, Isoc.3.55, Pl.*R.*558a, etc.; opp. ἀγριότης, Id.*Smp.*197d; opp. ὀργιλότης, Arist.*EN*1125ᵇ26; opp. ὀργή, Id.*Rh.*1380ª6: pl., Isoc.5.116: later **πραΰτης**, Lxx *Ps.*44(45).4, *Ep.Gal.*5.23 (v.l.), *CIG*2788 (Aphrodisias).

**πρᾰπῐ́δες**, αἱ, dat. πραπίσιν Pi.*O.*2.94, Ep. πραπίδεσσι (v. infr.):—poet., 1. = φρένες, *midriff, diaphragm*, βάλε..ἧπαρ ὑπὸ πραπίδων Il. 11.579, cf. 13.412, 17.349: then, since this was deemed the seat of mental powers and affections, 2. *understanding, mind*, ἰδυίῃσι πραπίδεσσι 1.608, 18.380, etc.; περὶ μὲν πραπίδες, περὶ δ' ἐστὶ νόημα Hes. *Th.*656; as the seat of desire, *heart*, ἀπὸ πραπίδων ἦλθ' ἵμερος Il.24. 514; ἔσχεν ἄκοιτιν ἀρηρυῖαν πραπίδεσσιν wins a wife after his own *heart*, Hes.*Th.*608; πάσῃσιν ὀρέξαιτο πραπίδεσσιν Emp.129.4; πραπίδων πλοῦτος ib.2, cf. Pi.*O.*11(10).10, *P.*4.281; Trag. in lyr., εὖ πραπίδων λαχόντα A.*Ag.*380, cf. 802, E.*Andr.*480: rarely in sg. πραπίς, ἴδος, Pi.*P.*2.61, *Fr.*109, E.*Ba.*427 (lyr.), 999 (lyr.); *ἔργον ἐμῆς π.* *IG* 14.1500.

**Πρᾱράτιος** (sc. *μήν*), ὁ, name of month at Epidaurus, *IG*4$^{2}$(1).105.10, 108.141, al.; once written **Πραράτριος,** ib.106.107: cf. Πρηροσία, προηρόσια.

**πρᾰσεά,** ἡ, = *πρασιά*, *BGU*530.27 (i A.D.).

**πρᾰσεῖος,** *α, ον,* f.l. for *πράσινος*, Poll.10.42.

**πρᾰσι-ά,** Ion. -ιή, ἡ, *bed in a garden, garden-plot,* Od.7.127, 24.247, Thphr.*HP*4.4.3, Nic.*Al.*532, Lxx *Si.*24.31, Dsc.4.17, Gal.*UP*9.6; *ἀνθῶν πρασιαί* Longus 4.2: metaph., *πρασιαὶ πρασιαί in companies* or *groups*, *Ev.Marc.*6.40. (Prob. from *πράσον*, and so prop. *bed of leeks.*) II. a surgical instrument, *Hermes* 38.283. **-άζω,** *divide into beds*, Aq., Quint.*Ps.*41(42).2 (Pass.). **-ανός,** *όν*, = *πράσινος* 3, M.Ant.1.5.

**πρᾰσίζω,** (*πράσον*) *to be greenish*, Dsc.3.80.2, 4.150.5, Ruf.ap.Orib.8.24.64, Gal.6.742.

**πράσῐμος** [ᾱ], *ον*, (*πρᾶσις*) *for sale*, Pl.*Lg.*848a, X.*Cyr.*4.5.42, *PSI* 4.413.4 (iii B.C.).

**πρασίμοχθος,** ὁ, ἡ, corrupt in E.*Fr.*998 (fort. *περισσόμοχθοι*).

**πρᾰσῐνίζω,** = *πρασίζω*, interpol. in Dsc.3.54, cf. Sch.rec.A.*Pers.*617, David *Proll.*163.27.

**πρᾰσῐνοειδής,** *ές*, *leek-green*, Olymp. *in Mete.*211.10.

⊛ **πράσῐν-ος** [ᾰ], *ον*, (*πράσον*) *leek-green, light green*, Arist.*Mete.*372$^{a}$8, al. 2. *λίθος π.*, = *πρασῖτις*, Lxx *Ge.*2.12. 3. *οἱ π. the green faction* in the Circus, Mart.11.33.1, *POxy.*145.2 (vi A.D.); *τὸ π.* (sc. *μέρος*) J.*AJ*19.4.4; cf. *πράσιος*. **-ώδης,** *ες*, = *πρασινοειδής*, Sch.Theoc.4.28.

⊛ **πράσιον** [ᾰ], *τό*, *horehound, Marrubium vulgare*, Hp.*Steril.*224, Thphr.*HP*6.2.5, Dsc.3.105; also *Marrubium peregrinum*, Thphr. l.c., Nic.*Th.*550. 2. = *τραγορίγανος λεπτόφυλλος*, Dsc.3.30. 3. = *βαλλωτή*, Ps.-Dsc.3.103. II. a seaweed, Arist.*HA*591$^{a}$16.

**πράσιος** [ᾰ], *ον*, = *πράσινος*, Pl.*Ti.*68c; *στολή* D.C.79.14; *οἱ π.*, = *πράσινοι* 3, Id.73.4; *vomitus*, Cael.Aur.*CP*3.20; (sc. *lapis*) = *πρασῖτις*, Plin.*HN*37.113.

**πρᾰσιόω,** = *πρασιάζω*, Aq.*Jl.*1.20 (Pass.).

**πρᾶσις,** *εως*, Ion. **πρῆσις,** *ιος*, *Schwyzer* 688 *C* 6 (Chios, v B.C.), Hdt. (v. infr.), ἡ: (*πέρνημι*):—*sale*, *ὠνῇ τε καὶ πρήσι χρέωνται* Hdt.1.153, cf. S.*Fr.*909, Pl.*Sph.*223d; *ἐπὶ πρήσι* for *sale*, Hdt.4.17; *κατὰ πρᾶσιν* Hermipp.63.15; *πρᾶσιν ἐποιήσατο τοῦ ἀγῶνος* Aeschin.1.115; *εὑρεῖν π.* Ar.*Fr.*567; *π. αἰτεῖν* Eup.225: pl., Arist.*Pol.*1291$^{a}$5. II. of legal documents, *contract for farming of taxes, sale*, etc., *PRev.Laws* 55.16 (iii B.C.), *POxy.*95.13 (ii A.D.), etc.

**πρᾰσίτης** [ῑ] *οἶνος*, ὁ, wine *flavoured with horehound*, v.l. in Dsc.5.48. II. **πρᾰσῖτις,** *ιδος*, ἡ, a precious stone, prob. *emerald* (from *πράσον, leek-green*), Thphr.*Lap.*37.

**πρᾰσο-ειδής,** *ές*, *leek-green*, Hp.*Prog.*11, Arist.*Col.*795$^{a}$4. **-εις,** *εσσα, εν*, (*πράσον* II) *overgrown with seaweed*, Opp.*H.*1.107. **-κεφᾰλον,** *τό*, = *porrum capitatum*, *Gloss.* ⊛ **-κουρίς,** *ἴδος*, ἡ, (*κείρω*) *a creature* (prob. *milliped*) *which destroys leeks*, Stratt.66.1, Arist.*HA*551$^{b}$20, Thphr.*HP*7.5.4. **-κουρον,** *τό*, (*κείρω*) *leek-slicer*, *AP*11.203, *BGU* 1522 (iii B.C.): Adj., *δρέπανα πρασόκουρα* *PCair.Zen.*782(a).51 (iii B.C.).

**πράσον** [ᾰ], *τό*, *leek, Allium Porrum*, Batr.54 (v.l.), Chionid.7, Ar.*Ra.*621, Thphr.*HP*7.1.2, etc.; *π. κεφαλωτόν* Dsc.2.149; *πράσα τὰ κειρόμενα* sliced *leeks*, Artem.1.67: prov., *φύλλῳ πράσου τὸ τῶν ἐρώντων συνδέδεται βαλλάντιον* *Com.Adesp.*197. II. *leek-like seaweed, Posidonia oceanica, Ligurian grass-wrack*, Thphr.*HP*4.6.2, Plin.*HN* 13.135; also, *riband-weed, Laminaria saccharina*, Thphr.*HP*4.6.4. (Cf. Lat. *porrum*, from I.-E. *pr̥som.*)

**πρᾰσοργη,** ἡ, = *πρασόκουρον*, Hsch.

**πρᾰσό-σπερμον,** *τό*, *leek-seed*, Paul.Aeg.7.11. **-φᾰγέω,** *eat leeks*, Lyd.*Mens.*4.135. **-χρους,** *ουν*, (*χρόα*) *leek-coloured*, Dem.Ophth. ap.Aët.7.33, Tz.*H.*8.971.

**Πρασσαῖος,** ὁ, mock-Ep. for **πρασαῖος* (= *πράσινος*), *Leek-green*, name of a frog, Batr.252:—so **Πρασσο-φάγος** [φᾰ], ὁ, *Leek-eater*, v.l. ib.232.

⊛ **πράσσω,** Ep. and Ion. **πρήσσω,** Att. **πράττω** (first in *IG*1$^{2}$.7.11, al., Ar. and X.), Cret. **πράδδω** *Leg.Gort.*1.35: fut. *πράξω*, Ion. *πρήξω*: aor. *ἔπραξα*, Ion. *ἔπρηξα*: pf. *πέπραχα*, Ion. *πέπρηχα*, (trans.) Hdt.5.106, X.*HG*5.2.32, *Cyr.*3.1.15, Din.3.21, Men.610, *IG*9(2).517.36 (Larissa, iii B.C.), *PHib.*1.80.11 (iii B.C.), (intr.) Pl.Com.187 codd., Arist.*Rh.Al.*1440$^{a}$36: plpf. *ἐπεπράχει(ν)* (trans.) X. l.c., (intr.) App.*BC*5.83: pf. 2 *πέπρᾱγα*, Ion. *πέπρηγα*, (intr.) Pi.*P.*2.73, Hdt.2.172, Ar.*Pl.*629, *Ra.*302, X.*HG*1.4.2, (trans.) Arist.*EN*1168$^{b}$35, al., *SIG* 364.70 (Ephesus, iii B.C.): plpf. *ἐπεπράγεσαν* (intr.) Th.2.4, 7.24:—pf. *πέπραγα* Att., *πέπραχα* Hellenistic, acc. to Moer.p.293 P., Phryn.*PS* p.103 B., but see above:—**Med.**, fut. *πράξομαι* Antipho *Fr.*67, X.*HG*6.2.36 (also in pass. sense, Pi.*P.*4.243 (prob.), Pl.*R.*452a): aor. *ἐπραξάμην* S.*OT*287, Th.4.65, etc.:—**Pass.**, fut. (v. supr.), also *πραχθήσομαι* Aeschin.3.98, Arist.*Rh.*1359$^{a}$11, etc.; fut. 3 *πεπράξομαι* S.*OC* 861, Ar.*Av.*847, Eup.9.3 D.: aor. *ἐπράχθην* S.*Tr.*679, Th.4.54, etc.: pf. *πέπραγμαι* A.*Pr.*75, etc. (sts. in med. sense, v. infr. VI). [ᾱ by nature, as is shown by the Ion. form *πρήσσω*, and by the accent in *πρᾶγμα, πρᾶξις*, etc.]

I. in Ep. only, *pass through, pass over*, *δὶς τόσσον ἅλα πρήσσοντες ἀπῆμεν* Od.9.491; *ῥίμφα πρήσσοντε κέλευθον* Il.14.282, 23.501; *ῥίμφα πρήσσουσι κέλευθον* Od.13.83; *ὁδὸν πρήσσουσιν ὁδῖται* *h.Merc.*203: c. gen., *ἵνα πρήσσωμεν ὁδοῖο* Il.24.264, Od.15.219; *ὄφρα πρ. ὁδοῖο* ib.47; *ἵνα πρήσσῃσιν ὁδοῖο* 3.476: Gramm. note that this sense is found only in pres., *An.Ox.*1.355, *EM*688.1. II. *experience certain fortunes, fare* well or ill, *ὁ στόλος οὕτως ἔπρηξε* Hdt.3.26, cf. 4.77, Th.7.24; so *ὡς ἔπρηξε* Hdt.7.18; *κατὰ νόον π.* Id.4.97, cf. Ar.*Eq.*549; *πράξασαν ὡς ἔπραξεν* A.*Ag.*1288; *εὖ πέπραγεν, ὅτι..* Pi.*P.*2.73, cf. Hdt.1.24, 42, etc.; *φλαύρως π. τῷ στόλῳ* Id.6.94; *π. καλῶς* A.*Pr.*979; *χαλεπώτατα π.* Th.8.95; *ταπεινῶς π.* Isoc.5.64; *ὅστις καλῶς πράττει, οὐχὶ καὶ εὖ πράττει;* Pl.*Alc.*1.116b; *π. εὐτυχῶς* S.*Ant.*701; *κάλλιστα* E.*Heracl.*794; *μακαρίως, εὐδαιμόνως*, Ar.*Pl.*629, 802: freq. with neut. Pron. or Adj., *εὖ π. τι* S.*OT*1006, cf. *OC*391; *μηδὲν εὖ π.* X.*Mem.*1.6.8; *χρηστόν τι π.* Ar.*Pl.*341; *καλά* Th.6.16; *χείρω* Id.7.71; *μεγάλα* E.*IA* 346; *πάντ' ἀγαθά* Ar.*Ra.*302, cf. *Eq.*683 (lyr.); *εὐδαίμονα* E.*El.*1359 (anap.); *πολλὰ καὶ ἀγαθά* X.*An.*6.4.8; *οἷον ἤθελεν* S.*OC*1704 (lyr.); *πράξας ἅπερ ηὔχου* E.*Or.*355 (anap.), cf. X.*Mem.*3.9.14. III. *achieve, effect, accomplish*, *οὔ τι* Il.1.562, 11.552, Od.2.191, etc.; *οὐδέ τι ἔργον ἐνθάδ' ἔτι πρήξει* 19.324, cf. 16.88; *χρῆμα μὲν οὐ πρήξεις, σὺ δ' ἐτώσια πόλλ' ἀγορεύσεις* Hes.*Op.*402; *κλέος ἔπραξεν won* it, Pi.*I.*5(4).8; *ἔπραξε δεσμόν achieved* bondage, i.e. brought it on himself, Id.*P.*2.40; *τινὰ Νηρεΐδων π. ἄκοιτιν* Id.*N.*5.36; *ὕμνον π. grant power of* song, ib.9.3; *λεόντεσσι π. φόνον do* slaughter upon them, ib.3.46; *τὴν Κυπρίων ἀπόστασιν π.* Hdt.5.113; *π. εἰρήνην, φιλίαν, bring* it *about*, D.3.7, 18.162; *π. τι παρά τινος get* something from.., *ὧν δέονται πάντων πεπραγότες εἶεν παρὰ βασιλέως* X.*HG*1.4.2; *ἐλπὶς πράξειν τι παρὰ τῶν θεῶν ἀγαθόν* Isoc.2.20; also, *attempt, plot*, *δήμου κατάλυσιν* And.3.6: c. dat. pers., *δαίμοσιν π. φίλα* A.*Pr.*660; *Λοξίᾳ χάριν* E.*Ion*37, cf. 896 (lyr.), *El.*1133, etc.; *σὺ τοῦτο πράξεις ὥστε..;* A.*Eu.*896:—Pass., *πέπρακται τοὔργον* Id.*Pr.*75; *φεῦ φεῦ πέπρακται* E.*Hipp.*680; *τὰ πεπραγμένα* Pi.*O.*2.15, etc.; *ἡ ἐπὶ τοῖς πεπρ. ἀδοξία* D.1.11; *τὰ πεπρ. λῦσαι* Id.24.76; *τὰ πραχθέντα* A.*Pr.*683, etc.; *τὰ ἔργα τῶν πραχθέντων* the facts *of what took place*, Th.1.22; *οὐ γὰρ ἂν τό γε πραχθὲν ἀγένητον θείη* Pl.*Prt.*324b. 2. abs., *effect an object, be successful*, *δὸς Τηλέμαχον πρήξαντα νέεσθαι* Od.3.60; *ἐπρήξας καὶ ἔπειτα* Il.18.357. 3. of sexual intercourse, *ἐπράχθη τὰ μέγιστα* Theoc.2.143. 4. *to be busy with*, *σὺ μὲν τὰ σαυτῆς πρᾶσσ' mind* your own *business*, S.*El.*678; *πράττων ἕκαστος τὸ αὑτοῦ* Pl.*Phdr.*247a, cf. *Plt.*307e; *τὰ αὑτοῦ π. καὶ μὴ πολυπραγμονεῖν* Id.*R.*433a, cf. 400e, etc. (whereas *πολλὰ π.* = *πολυπραγμονεῖν*, Hdt.5.33, E.*HF*266, Ar.*Ra.*228, etc.); *φιλοσόφου τὰ αὑτοῦ πράξαντος καὶ οὐ πολυπραγμονήσαντος* Pl.*Grg.*526c, cf. *Ap.*33a, etc.; *οὐδ' εὖ..οἰκοῦνται αἱ πόλεις, ὅταν τὰ αὑτῶν ἕκαστοι πράττωσι* (ironical) Id.*Alc.*1.127b; *μὴ τὰ αὑτῶν π.* not to *act* their *part*, Id.*R.*452c; *π. τὰ δέοντα* X.*Mem.*3.8.1. 5. *manage* affairs, *do* business, *act*, *εἰπεῖν τε καὶ πρᾶξαι* ib.2.9.4, cf. 2.8.6; *πράττειν τὰ πολιτικὰ πράγματα, τὰ τῆς πόλεως*, *manage* state-affairs, take part in government, Pl.*Ap.*31d, Lys.16.20; *τὰ Ἀθηναίων* Pl.*Smp.*216a; *οἱ τὰ κοινὰ π. καὶ πολιτευόμενοι* Arist.*Pol.*1324$^{b}$1: abs., without any addition, *ἱκανωτάτω λέγειν τε καὶ πράττειν*, of able statesmen, X.*Mem.*1.2.15, cf. 4.2.1, 4; *πολιτεύεσθαι καὶ π.* D.18.45, cf. 59, Pl.*Prt.*317a. 6. generally, *transact, negotiate, manage*, *οἱ πράξαντες πρὸς αὐτὸν τὴν λῆψιν τῆς πόλεως* Th.4.114; *Θηβαίοις τὰ πράγματα π. manage* matters for their interest, D.19.77:—so in Pass., *τῷ Ἱπποκράτει τὰ..πράγματα ἀπό τινων ἀνδρῶν..ἐπράσσετο* matters *were negotiated* with him by.., Th.4.76: but freq. abs., *treat, negotiate, manage, act*, *οἱ πράσσοντες αὐτῷ* ib.110, cf. 5.76; *π. πρός τινα* Id.2.5, 4.73, etc.; *ἐς* (v.l. *πρὸς*) *τοὺς βαρβάρους, ἐς τοὺς Εἵλωτας*, Id.1.131, 132:—Pass., *ἐπράττετο οὐ πρὸς τοὺς ἄλλους* Aeschin.3.64; also *π. τι ὑπὲρ τῶν κοινῶν* D.26.2; *π. ὑπὲρ τῆς πόλεως τὰ πάτρια* Id.59.73; *π. περὶ εἰρήνης* X.*HG*6.3.3; *π. τῇ δύναιτο ἄριστα* Hdt.5.30; *π. ὡς ἄριστα καὶ πιστότατα* Th.1.129; *οἱ πράσσοντες the traitors*, Id.4.89, 113:—folld. by dependent clauses, *πρᾶσσε καὶ τὰ ἐμὰ καὶ τὰ σὰ ὅπῃ κάλλιστα ἕξει* Id.1.129; *ἐς τὴν Πελοπόννησον ἔπρασσεν, ὅπῃ ὠφελία τις γενήσεται* ib.65; *π. ὅπως πόλεμος γένηται* ib.57; *π. ὅπως τιμωρήσονται* ib.56, cf. 3.4, 70, etc.: c. acc. et inf., *μὴ δεῦρο πλεῖν τὴν ναῦν ἔπραττεν* D.32.22. b. esp. of secret practices and intrigues, *εἴ τι μὴ ξὺν ἀργύρῳ ἐπράσσετ' ἐνθένδ'* unless some bribery *was being practised*, S.*OT*125; *καί τι αὐτῷ καὶ ἐπράσσετο ἐς τὰς πόλεις προδοσίας πέρι* Th.4.121, cf. 5.83; *μετάστασις ἐπράττετο* Lys.30.10; *τούτοις ἔπρασσον τὴν πόλιν* Plb.4.17.12; *νῦν δ' αὔτ' Ἀτρεῖδαι φωτὶ παντουργῷ φρένας ἔπραξαν have jobbed them* (the arms) *away* to a villain, S.*Aj.*446. IV. *practise*, *πόνῳ π. θεοδμάτους ἀρετάς* Pi.*I.*6(5).11; *δίκαια ἢ ἄδικα* Pl.*Ap.*28b, etc.; *ταῦτ' ἔπραξάν τε καὶ ἔλεξαν* X.*Cyr.*5.1.1; *ἃ καὶ λέγειν ὀκνοῦμεν οἱ πεπραχότες* Men.619: then abs., *act*, *π. ἔργῳ μὲν σθένος βουλαῖσι δὲ φρήν* Pi.*N.*1.26; *ὡς πράττοντες* as *doing*, Pl.*R.*527a; *μεθ' ἡμῶν ἔπραττεν*, i.e. he took our side, Is.5.14. 2. *study*, *δράματα* Suid. s.v. Ἀριστοφάνης; *συλλογισμούς* Arr.*Epict.*2.17.27; *ἐν τοῖς πραττομένοις* in the poems *which are now studied, made the subject of commentaries*, Sch.Nic.*Th.*11. V. c. dupl. acc. pers. et rei, *πράττειν τινά τι do* something *to* one, E.*Hel.*1394, Isoc.12.93; *ἀγαθόν τι π. τὴν πόλιν* Ar.*Ec.*108. VI. *exact payment from* one, *αὐτοὺς ἑκατὸν τάλαντα ἔπρηξαν* Hdt.3.58; *πράσσει με τόκον* he *makes* me *pay* interest, Batr.185; *π. τινὰ χρέος* Pi.*O.*3.7, cf. *P.*9.104; *ὅσοι πράξεις πεπράγασιν* *SIG*364.70 (Ephesus, iii B.C.); *τοὐφειλόμενον π. Δίκη* A.*Ch.*311 (anap.); *ἀντίποινα* Id.*Pers.*476: freq. of tax-gatherers or other collectors of public debt, *IG*1$^{2}$.116.16, al., Pl.*Lg.*774d; *π. τὰς εἰσφοράς* D.22.77, etc.; *φόρον ἔπρησσον παρ' ἑκάστων obtained* or *demanded* from.., Hdt.1.106: c. acc. pers., *press for payment*, *μὴ π. τοὺς ὀφειλέτας* Plb.38.11.10; *π. τινά τι ὑπέρ τινος demand* from one *as the price* for a thing, Luc.*Vit.Auct.*18: metaph., *φόνον π. exact punishment* or *vengeance for* a murder: hence, *avenge, punish*, A.*Eu.*624; *τὰ περὶ τὸν φόνον ἀγριωτέρως π.* Pl.*Lg.*867d:—Pass., *ὑπὸ βασιλέως πεπραγμένος φόρους called on to pay up* the tribute, Th.8.5; *πραχθεὶς* ὑπὸ τῶνδε Lys.9.21 codd., cf. Pl.*Lg*.921c:—Med., *exact for oneself*, πράξασθαί τινα μισθόν Pi.*O*.10(11).30; ἀργύριον, χρήματα, Hdt.2.126, Th.4.65, cf. Ar.*Ra*.561, etc.; τὴν διπλασίαν π. τὸν ὑποφεύγοντα Pl.*Lg*.762b, cf. Plb.5.54.11; π. τοὺς ἐξάγοντας τριακοστήν D.20.32; πράσσεσθαι χρέος Antipho *Fr*.67; φόρους πράσσεσθαι ἀπό, ἐκ τῶν πόλεων, Th.8.5, 37; παρ' αὐτῶν ἃ ὤφειλον Lys.17.3, cf. And.2.11: metaph. of exacting punishment, etc., μεγάλ' ἀντ' ὀλίγων ἐπράξαο Call.*Lav.Pall*.91:—Pass. pf. and plpf. in med. sense, εἰ μὲν ἐπεπράγμην τοῦτον τὴν δίκην if I *had exacted* from him the full amount, D.29.2. VII. c. acc. pers., πράττειν τινά *deal with, finish off*, euphem., ἔπρασσε δ' ᾇπέρ νιν, ὧδε θάπτει A.*Ch*.440 (lyr.); πεπραγμένοι is f.l. ib.132.

**πρᾰσώδης**, ες, (πράσον) = πρασοειδής, *leek-green*, Thphr.*HP*9.10.1, Gal.19.488; of part of the Indian Ocean, Anon.*Geog.Comp*.32, Marcian.*Peripl*.1.40.

**πρατά**· ἡ νουμηνία, Hsch. **πρατάνιον**· μαλλόν, Id. **πρατασία**, ἡ, *prayer offered at commencement of ploughing*, Id.; cf. προηρόσια.

**πρᾱτέος**, α, ον, *to be sold, for sale*, Pl.*Lg*.849c; γράψον μοι πόσου σοι π. [ὁ ἵππος] *PCair.Zen*.393 (iii B.C.). II. πρατέον *one must sell*, ib.382 (iii B.C.).

**πρᾱτεύς**, έως, ὁ, Dor. for πρωτεύς, *first principle*, Pythag.ap.Syrian. *in Metaph*.10.4 (πρακτέα codd., cf. Πρωτεύς in 175.4).

⊛ **πρατήνιον**, τό, Att. for ὕπερον, Hsch. II. = πρητήν, Id.

⊛ **πρᾱτ-ήρ**, ῆρος, ὁ, *seller*, Pl.*Lg*.915d, Is.10.24 (prob.), D.37.5,16, *IG*12(5).872.15, al. (Tenos, iii B.C.), etc. II. π. λίθος the stone *on which slaves were sold*, Poll.3.78. **-ήριον**, Ion. **πρητ-**, τό, *place for selling, market*, Hdt.7.23, Aen.Tact.10.14, *PTeb*.701(*a*).7 (ii B.C.), Plu.2.972d, D.C.59.14 (un-Attic acc. to Moer.p.314P.). **-ης**, ου, ὁ, = πρατήρ, Is.*Fr*.167, Hyp.*Fr*.163, *POxy*.1454.2,10 (ii A.D.), etc. **-ίας**, ου, ὁ, = πρατήρ, *Com.Adesp*.336.5 (dub., cf. πρᾶος). **-ικός**, ή, όν, *of* or *for selling*, only as Subst., -κή, ἡ, *tax on sales*, *IG*5(1).18*B*12 (Sparta): -κόν, τό, *commission on sales*, *POxy*.1454.6 (ii A.D.): pl., *Sammelb*.4425 v 13 (ii A.D.).

**πρᾱτιστεύω**, Dor. for πρωτ-, *GDI*3059 (Byzantium).

**πράτιστος**, v. πρᾶτος.

**πρᾱτο-μηνία**, ἁ, Dor. for πρωτο-, = νουμηνία, *IG*4$^2$(1).103.35 (Epid., iv B.C.), 4.498.1 (Mycenae, ii B.C.). **-παις**, παιδος, ὁ, Dor. for πρωτό-, at Sparta, in pl., *boys in their first year*, prob. in ib.5(1).213.36 (v B.C., cf. *Class.Phil*.20.139). ⊛**-πάμπαις**, παιδος, ὁ, *chief of the* πάμπαιδες (v. Addenda), *IG*5(1).256, 279.

**πρᾱτορεύω**, *act as* πράτωρ, *IG*12(5).872.84 (Tenos, iii B.C.).

⊛ **πρᾱτός**, ή, όν, *for sale*, πρατόν νιν ἐξέπεμψεν S.*Tr*.276, cf. *Test.Epict*.7.11, *POxy*.1117.24 (ii A.D.), *PGnom*.190, 193 (ii A.D.).

⊛ **πρᾶτος**, α, ον, Dor. for πρῶτος, Epich.88, al., *IG*4$^2$(1).40.11 (Epid., v/iv B.C.), etc.: Sup. πράτιστος Theoc.1.77, *IG*12(3).436, 540 (Thera), *Berl.Sitzb*.1927.161 (Cyrene).

**πράττω**, v. πράσσω.

**πράτωρ**, ορος, ὁ, = πρατήρ, *IG*12(5).872.33 (Tenos, iii B.C.), *Milet*.3.308 No.140, *PCair.Zen*.497.3 (iii B.C.).

**πρᾱΰ-γελως**, Ion. **πρηΰ-** [ῠ], ὁ, ἡ, *softly-smiling*, Licymn.4, *AP*9.229 (Marc.Arg.); Ζέφυρος ib.10.4 (Id.). **-θῡμος**, ον, *of gentle mind*, LXX *Pr*.14.30. **-λόγος**, ὁ, ἡ, *gentle in speech*, Erinn.2 in *PSI*9.1090.32 (παυρο- codd.Stob.). ⊛**-μενής**, ές, *of gentle spirit*, Hsch., in Adv. -νῶς; in form **πρηϋ-**, *IG*14.2012*A*40 (Sulp.Max.); more freq. in the contr. form πρευμενής (q.v.). **-μητις**, ιος, ὁ, ἡ, *of gentle counsel, gracious*, Pi.*O*.6.42. ⊛ **-νοος**, Ion. **πρηΰ-**, ον, *of gentle mind*, Orph.*H*.69.13; κραδίη *AP*7.592, etc.; with v.l. πρηΰνομος, ib.9.769 (Agath.).

**πρά-ϋνσις** [ᾱ], εως, Ion. **πρήϋνσις**, ἡ, *softening, appeasing*, Arist.*Rh*.1380$^a$8: Medic., *relief*, Aret.*CA*2.11 (pl.). **-ϋντής**, οῦ, ὁ, *one who appeases*, *EM*436.6. **-ϋντικός**, ή, όν, *fit for appeasing*, Arist.*Rh*.1380$^a$31: esp. Medic., *relieving*, ἰσχιάδος Dsc.2.80, cf. Sor.2.38.

**πρᾱΰνω**, Ion. **πρηΰνω** [ῡ], fut. ὑνῶ: aor. ἐπράῢνα:—**Med.**, Ep. aor. πρηΰνατο Nonn.*D*.29.276:—**Pass.**, fut. πραϋνθήσομαι Ph.1.135, Gal.13.478: aor. ἐπραΰνθην Pl.*R*.440d: pf. πεπράϋσμαι (v. infr.): (πραΰς):—*make soft, mild*, or *gentle, soothe, calm*, πνοιὰς..πρηΰνει Hes.*Th*.254; π. τινά *h.Merc*.417; π. ἕλκος *soothe* a raging sore, S.*Ph*.650; π. τινὰ λόγοις A.*Pers*.837; π. τινὰς πρὸς ἀλλήλους Isoc.4.47; π. ὑπερήφανα ἔργα Sol.4.38; ὀργήν E.*Fr*.822; τὸν θυμόν, τὸ θυμοειδές, Pl.*Lg*.731d, *R*.572a, cf. X.*Eq*.9.5:—Pass., *become milder, abate*, πρηϋνομένου τοῦ χειμῶνος Hdt.2.25; of persons, *grow milder, be appeased*, ib.121.δ', Pl.*R*.440d, Arist.*Rh*.1380$^a$5. 2. *tame* wild animals, οὐρῆας, κύνα, Hes.*Op*.797, X.*Mem*.2.3.9; [ἐλέφαντα] π. καὶ ἡμερῶσαι Ael.*NA*10.10:—Pass., πεπραϋσμένος πέρδιξ ib.4.16; opp. ἐγείρεσθαι, of horses, X.*Eq*.9.10; θῆρες ἀνὰ δρυμὰ πρηΰνονται Euph.177 (= Call.*Fr.anon*.74).

**πρᾱϋπάθ-εια** [πᾰ], ἡ, *gentleness of temper*, Ph.2.31, Hsch.; written **-παθία**, 1 *Ep.Ti*.6.11 (v.l.). **-έω**, *to be gentle in temper*, Ph.1.547. **-ής**, ές, *mild-tempered*, Id.2.351, prob. ib.595 (v.l. πραο-).

**πρᾱΰς**, v. πρᾶος.

**πρᾱϋσμός**, ὁ, *gentle treatment*, Sor.2.29.

**πρᾱϋ-τένων**, Ion. **πρηϋ-**, οντος, ὁ, *with tamed neck*, ταῦροι *AP*9.299 (Phil.). **-της**, ητος, ἡ, v. πραότης. **-τοκος**, ον, *with easy parturition*, Ph.1.577. **-τροπος**, ον, *gentle of mood*, τὸ π. τοῦ λόγου Plu.2.493d (s.v.l.).

**πράως**, v. πρᾶος III.

**πρείγ-α**, ἁ, *assembly of elders*, *Berl.Sitzb*.1927.8 (Locr., v B.C.). **-εία**, ἁ, Cret., = πρεσβεία, *SIG*712.18 (ii B.C.). **-ευτάς**, ᾶ, ὁ, Cret., = πρεσβευτής, ib.26, *CIG*3058.4 (found at Teos), etc. **-εύω**, Cret., = πρεσβεύω, *GDI*5149, etc. **-ήϊα**, τά, Cret., = πρεσβεῖα, ib.5040.29. **-ηΐα**, ἡ, = πρεσβεία, ib.5075.22. ⊛**-υς**, ὁ, Cret., = πρέσβυς, *old man*, ib.4992*a* iii 2; also in Comp., acc. sg. πρείγονα *older*, *Leg.Gort*.12.34, cf. *Supp.Epigr*.1.414.9 (Crete, v/iv B.C., dub. sens.), and Sup. πρείγιστος *oldest*, *Leg.Gort*.7.23, al.—Cogn. forms are **πρεγγευτάς**, **πρεσγευτάς**, **πρεισγευτάς**, = πρεσβευτής, *Supp.Epigr*.4.599.13, 17 (Teos, ii B.C.), *GDI*5148.12, 5167.11; **πρήγιστος**, = πρέσβιστος, *president*, ib.5034.5; βουλῆς ib.2562.23 (Hierapytna); also **πρίγιστος**, *Sammelb*.1042 (vi B.C.); **πρεσγέα**, ἁ, Argive for πρεσβεία, *SIG* 56.38 (Argos, v B.C.). (For the etym. v. πρέσβυς fin.)

**πρεμν-ιάζω**, = sq., Hsch. **-ίζω**, *stub up, root up*, Test.ap.D.43.70 (Pass.), Poll.7.146, Phot. **-ιον**, τό, Dim. of πρέμνον, Hsch. **-οθεν** or **-όθεν**, Adv. *from the stump*, i.e. *utterly*, cj. for πρυμνόθεν, A.*Th*.71, 1061 (anap.); *from the bottom*, cj. in Call.*Del*.35. **-ον**, τό, *bottom of the trunk of a tree, stump*: generally, *stem, trunk*, *h.Merc*.238, Ar.*Lys*.267, Lys.7.19, X.*Oec*.19.13, etc. 2. *enlarged bark* of the stem of the olive, Thphr.*HP*1.8.6. II. *base* or *bottom* of a pillar, πρέμνα χθόνια Pi.*Fr*.88.4; of a *trunk* artery, Gal.5.189, 659: metaph., πρέμνον πράγματος πελωρίου Ar.*Av*.321; Ἀρετῆς π. the *trunk* of the tree Virtue, Q.S.14.197; of a woman, τὴν ἀρετῆς πινυτὴν.. πρέμνον dub. in *Epigr.Gr*.416 (Alexandria). **-ος**, ὁ, = foreg. 1, *Theol.Ar*.31. **-ώδης**, ες, *like a trunk*, τὸ π. the *trunk-like stock*, i.e. *rhizome*, Thphr.*HP*4.10.5, etc.

⊛ **πρεπ-όντως**, Adv. part. of πρέπω, *fitly, meetly*, A.*Ag*.687 (lyr.); *gracefully*, Pi.*O*.3.9, Th.4.126. 2. c. dat., *in a manner befitting, suitably to*, σαυτῷ τε καὶ τῇ πατρίδι π. Pl.*Lg*.699d, cf. 835b: c. gen., *in a manner worthy of*, π. τῶν πραξάντων Id.*Mx*.239c. ⊛ **-τός**, ή, όν, *distinguished, renowned*, A.*Eu*.914, Ar.*Lys*.1298 (lyr.). ⊛ **-ω**, impf. ἔπρεπον, which were the tenses chiefly in use: fut. πρέψω A.*Eu*.995 (anap.), Pl.*Plt*.269c, 288c: aor. ἔπρεψα Id.*Chrm*.158c:—prop. of impressions on the senses, 1. on the eye, *to be clearly seen, to be conspicuous* among a number, ὁ δ' ἔπρεπε καὶ διὰ πάντων Il.12.104; μετὰ δὲ π. ἀγρομένοισιν Od.8.172, Hes.*Th*.92; *to be distinguished in* or *by* a thing, φάρεσιν μελαγχίμοις A.*Ch*.12, cf. *Th*.124 (lyr.), E.*Alc*.512, 1050; π. παρηΐς φοινίοις ἀμυγμοῖς A.*Ch*.24 (lyr.); *shine forth, show itself*, πειρῶντι χρυσὸς ἐν βασάνῳ π. Pi.*P*.10.67; πανσέληνος ἐν σάκει π. A.*Th*.390, cf. *Pers*.239 (troch.), *Ag*.389 (lyr.); πρέπουσά θ' ὡς ἐν γραφαῖς ib.242 (lyr.); ἐπί τοι πρέπει ὄμμασιν αἰδώς *h.Cer*.214; Ζεὺς πρέπων δι' αἰθέρος E.*Hel*.216 (lyr.): sts. c. part., *to be clearly seen* as doing or being, ὁ φρυκτὸς ἀγγέλλων πρέπει A.*Ag*.30; σπλάγχνα..πρέπουσ' ἔχοντες ib.1222, cf. *Eu*.995 (anap.). 2. on the ear, βοὰ π. the cry *sounds loud and clear*, Pi.*N*.3.67, cf. A.*Ag*.321. 3. on the smell, *to be strong* or *rank*, ὅμοιος ἀτμὸς ὥσπερ ἐκ τάφου π. ib.1311. II. *to be conspicuously like, resemble*, π. τινὶ εἶδος *to be like* one in form, Pi.*P*.2.38; πρέποντα..ταύρῳ δέμας A.*Supp*.301; εἴ τι σῇ δοκεῖ πρέπειν γυναικί E.*Alc*.1121; πρέπεις..θυγατέρων μορφὴν μιᾷ Id.*Ba*.917: c. inf., τοῦδε γὰρ δράμημα φωτὸς Περσικὸν πρέπει μαθεῖν his running *is like* Persian to behold, A.*Pers*.247, cf. *Supp*.719; more freq. with ὡς or ὥστε, πρέπει ὡς τύραννος εἰσορᾶν S.*El*.664; ὡς πένθιμος πρέπεις δρᾶν E.*Supp*.1056; πρέπει γ' ὥστε θὴρ ἄγραυλος φόβῃ Id.*Ba*.1188 (lyr.). III. *to be conspicuously fitting, beseem*, c. dat. pers., θνατὰ θνατοῖσι πρέπει Pi.*I*.5(4).16; τοῖς ὀλβίοις γε καὶ τὸ νικᾶσθαι πρέπει A.*Ag*.941, cf. Pl.*Chrm*.158c, etc.; with Preps., ποῦ τάδ' ἐν χρηστοῖς πρέπει; E.*Heracl*.510; οἷα δὴ εἰς πλῆθος πρέπει X.*Cyr*.2.1.24: c. part., ὅ τι γιγνόμενον ἂν πρέποι Pl.*Epin*.976c, cf. *Plt*.269c, 288c; πρέποι γὰρ ἂν (sc. λεχθεῖσα) Id.*Sph*.219c. 2. freq. in part., ὕμνοι πρέποντες γάμοις Id.*R*.460a, etc.; esp. in part. neut., πρέπον τε εἶναι καὶ ἁρμόττειν Id.*Grg*.503e; ἤν τι ἄλλο π. δοκῇ εἶναι Th.6.25; τὸ π. τῇ γραφῇ Plb.2.40.3: rarely c. gen., π. ἦν δαίμονος τοὐμοῦ τόδε S.*Aj*.534, cf. Plu.*Caes*.14, Thom.Mag.p.306R.; τὸ π. that which is *seemly, propriety*, Pl.*Hp.Ma*.294a; πρὸς τὸ μέτριον καὶ τὸ π. Id.*Plt*.284e, etc.: pl., πρέποντα πάσχειν Antipho 3.3.9; πρέποντα τῇ συγγενείᾳ ποιοῦντες Isoc.10.23. 3. rarely with personal subject, πρέπων ἔφυς πρὸ τῶνδε φωνεῖν art *the fit person* to.., S.*OT*9; Πομπήϊος..πάνυ τοῖς ἔπεσι πρέπων *suiting* them, Plu.*Pomp*.72, cf. *Publ*.17. 4. mostly impers., πρέπει *it is fitting*, both of outward circumstances and moral fitness, c. dat. pers. et inf., Hdt.9.79, etc.; οὐ πρέπει νῷν..δάσασθαι Pi.*P*.4.147; πρέπει ἐσλοῖσιν ὑμνεῖσθαι Id.*Fr*.121, cf. A.*Ag*.483 (lyr.), E.*Hipp*.115, etc.: with inf. unexpressed, πρέπει γοῦν σοι [ἀποκρίνεσθαι] X.*HG*4.1.37. b. c. acc. pers. et inf., πρέπει τὸν Αἰνησιδάμου ἐγκωμίων τε μελέων λυρᾶν τε τυγχανέμεν Pi.*O*.2.46, cf. A.*Supp*.203, S.*Tr*.728, Th.1.86, etc. c. c. inf. only, πρέπει γαρυέμεν Pi.*N*.7.82, cf. *P*.5.43, A.*Th*.656, *Ag*.636, etc. d. with inf. understood, an acc. may be subject, ἀπήλλαξαν οὕτω ὡς κείνους ἔπρεπε Hdt.8.68.α', cf. A.*Supp*.195, Pl.*Prt*.312b; or object, τείσασθαι οὕτως, ὡς κείνους [τείσασθαι] πρέπει Hdt.4.139; so with dat. of indirect object, Id.8.114. IV. trans., *liken*, τινί τι A.*Ag*.1328 (ap.Phot.). **-ώδης**, ες, *fit, proper*, Ar.*Pl*.793: c. dat., ib.797: Comp., τὸ κάλλιον -δέστερον Pl.*Alc*.1.135b, cf. Phld.*Mus*.p.82K.: esp. in Sup., -δέστατα γυναικί X.*Mem*.2.7.10, cf. Isoc.15.277, D.H.*Pomp*.4, Luc.*Hipp*.5, etc.

**πρέπων**, οντος, ὁ, a sea-fish, Opp.*H*.1.146, Ael.*NA*9.38.

**πρέσβ-ᾰ** (only nom.), ἡ, Ep. fem. of πρέσβυς, *august, honoured* (never *aged*); in Il. mostly of Hera, Ἥρη πρέσβα θεά 5.721, 8.383, al.; πρέσβα Διὸς θυγάτηρ Ἄτη 19.91; later, π. Δίκη Q.S.13.378; in Od., of a mortal, πρέσβα Κλυμένοιο θυγατρῶν 3.452. **-εᾰ**, ἡ, fem. of πρέσβυς, π. μήτηρ *BMus.Inscr*.1036.6 (Caria, ii/i B.C.). **-ειᾰ**, ἡ, = foreg., St.Byz. s.v. Ἀγάμμεια. **-εία**, ἡ, *age, seniority, right of the elder*, κατὰ πρεσβείαν A.*Pers*.4 (anap.), Arist.*Pol*.1259$^b$12: hence, 2. *rank, dignity*, πρεσβείᾳ καὶ δυνάμει ὑπερέχειν Pl.*R*.509b. II. *embassy*, Ar.*Lys*.570, Pl.*R*.422d, al. 2. *body of ambassadors*, Ar.*Ach*.647, *Eq*.795, Th.1.72, 4.118, X.*Cyr*.2.4.1, Aeschin.

1.23 (pl.), etc.; καλέσαι ἐπὶ ξένια τὴν π. *IG*1².19.14, al.; καλέσαι τὴν π. ἐπὶ δεῖπνον ib.2².1.54. III. *intercession*, Phalar.*Ep*.33. ⊛ -εῖον, Ion. and Ep. -ήϊον, τό, *gift of honour*, πρώτῳ τοι μετ' ἐμὲ πρεσβήϊον ἐν χερὶ θήσω Il.8.289; λαχὼν πρεσβήϊα τέχνης *AP*9.656.6. 2. *privilege of age*, Plu.2.787d, cf. D.39.29: hence, generally, *privilege*: pl., *prerogatives*, πρεσβεῖα διδόναι τινί, c. inf., give him *as a privilege*, to.., Pl.*Grg*.524a; πρεσβείων ἐπιλαμβάνειν Arist.*EE*1242ᵃ6: c. gen., γῆς πρεσβεῖα *chief share* or *sovereignty* of the land, S.*Fr*.24.3. 3. *right of the eldest, his share of the inheritance*, πρεσβεῖα λαβεῖν D.36.35, cf. J.*AJ*2.1.1; ἀπολιπεῖν π. τὴν ἀρχήν Plu.*Art*.26; κατὰ τὰ π., = κατὰ πρεσβείαν, Lxx *Ge*.43.33, cf. Nic.Dam.58 J. II. *old age* itself, Lxx *Ps*.70(71).18. -ειόομαι, Med., *hold in honour*, [πατρῷ' ἀγάλματα] Lyc.1265. ⊛ -ειρα, ἡ, fem. of πρέσβυς, θεῶν π. *h.Ven*.32; π. Ἐρινύων E.*IT*963; opp. νεᾶνις, Ar.*Lys*.86; Com. of a large eel, π. Κωπᾴδων κορᾶν Id.*Ach*.883. -ευμα, ατος, τό, *ambassador*, in pl., πρεσβεύματ' οὐ Δήμητρος ἐς μυστήρια E.*Supp*.173, cf. *Rh*.936; collectively, *the embassy*, Plu.*Tim*.9; but, *embassies, missions*, Id.2.541e. -εύς, έως, ὁ, *ambassador*, acc. sg. πρέσβεια (i.e. -ηα or -εα) Hoffmann *Griech.Dialekte* ii No.160.31 (Lampsacus); dat. pl. πρεσβεῦσι Lyc.1056, v.l. in Anon. *in EN*200.14; nom. dual πρεσβῆ Ar.*Fr*.639: Sch. Ar. denies that πρέσβεως Ar.*Ach*.93 is gen. of this word: Boeot. pl. πριστεῖες *IG*7.2418.6,18 (Thebes, iv B.C.), 1720.6 (Thespiae, ii B.C.) (πρεσβῆες in Hes.*Sc*.245 belongs in form to this word, in meaning to πρέσβυς I.1). -ευσις, εως, ἡ, *dispatch on an embassy*, ἡ π. ἐγένετο Th.1.73, D.C.42.46; poet. acc. to D.H.*Amm*.2.3. ⊛ -εύτειρα, ἡ, prop. fem. of πρεσβευτής, only metaph., ὀσμὴ π., of the scent of hounds, Opp.*C*.1.464. -ευτεύω, = πρεσβεύω, *Sammelb*.4309.9 (iii B.C.). ⊛ -ευτής, οῦ, ὁ, *ambassador*, *IG*1².22.27, Th.5.4, Pl.*Lg*.941a, *POxy*.933.31 (ii A.D.), etc.: pl. πρεσβευταί is at first less freq., later more freq., than πρέσβεις, πρεσβευτὰς πάντας ὑμᾶς ἡμεῖς οἱ πρέσβεις ποιοῦμεν And.3.41, cf. Th.8.77 (interpol.), *IG*2².858.6 (iii B.C.), 1224.26 (ii B.C.), Alciphr.2.2. II. *agent* or *commissioner*, ὑπέρ τινος D.45.64. 2. = Lat. *legatus*, *staff officer*, etc., Plb.35.4.5, Plu.*Mar*.7, etc.; π. καὶ ἀντιστράτηγος, = *legatus pro praetore*, *IG*14.1121, etc. ⊛ -ευτικός, ή, όν, *of* or *for an ambassador* or *embassy*, ἀγῶνες, ἐξουσία, Plb.9.32.4, D.H.11.25; πομπεία οὐ π. Philostr.*VS*2.27.3. Adv. -κῶς Poll.4.26. ⊛ -εύω, pf. πεπρέσβευκα Ar.*Ach*.610, D.19.310:—**Med.**, aor. ἐπρεσβευσάμην Th.1.92, etc.:—**Pass.**, pf. πεπρέσβευμαι (v. infr.): I. prop. of age, 1. intr., *to be the elder* or *eldest*, S.*OC*1422; οἱ ἀεὶ πρεσβεύοντες Pl.*Lg*.951e: c. gen. pers., *to be older than, be the eldest of* a number, τῶν προτέρων ἐπρέσβευε Hdt.7.2; π. τῶν ἄλλων κατὰ τὴν ἡλικίαν Timae.114; π. ἀπ' αὐτοῦ *to be* his *eldest* son, Th.6.55; of wine, πολλαῖς π. ἐτέων.. ὥραις Archestr.*Fr*.60.2; π. τοῖς χρόνοις τὰ ἡρωικά Ath.1.19a: hence, b. *take the first place, be best*, S.*Ant*.720; οἷσι πρεσβεύει γένος, of the male sex, E.*Heracl*.45. c. c. gen., *rank before, take precedence of* others, π. τῶν πολλῶν πόλεων Pl.*Lg*.752e: hence, *rule over*, Ὀλύμπου π. S.*Aj*.1389; Ἴναχε.. μέγα πρεσβεύων Ἄργους γύαις Id.*Fr*.270 (anap.); also, *have at one's command* or *disposal*, c. gen., καὶ εἰ (καὶ σὺ Kaibel) τῶν λόγων αὐτοῦ πρεσβεύεις Ath.8.352d. 2. trans., *place as oldest* or *first, put first in rank*, πρῶτον.. πρεσβεύω θεῶν Γαῖαν A.*Eu*.1: hence, *pay special honour* or *worship to*, πρῶτον τόνδε πρεσβεύσω τάφον Id.*Ch*.488, cf. S.*Tr*.1065, Pl.*Smp*.186b; joined with τιμῶ Id.*Cri*.46c; τὰ δίκαια πρὸ παντὸς ἰδίου συμφέροντος Plu.*Luc*.3, cf. Arr.*An*.6.30.3:—Pass., *hold the first place*, Παλλὰς.. ἐν λόγοις π. A.*Eu*.21; ὁ δ' ὕστατός γε τοῦ χρόνου π. *is first* in point of time, Id.*Ag*.1300: c. gen., κακῶν πρεσβεύεται τὸ Λήμνιον *is most notable* of mischiefs, Id.*Ch*.631 (lyr.); τὸ πρεσβύτερον τοῦ νεωτέρου ἐστὶ πρεσβευόμενον is *more honoured than*.., Pl.*Lg*.879b. b. later, *cultivate* arts, etc., διαλεκτικόν, τὸ.. τοὺς λόγους πρεσβεῦον D.L.1.18; π. παρὰ Ῥοδίοις ἃ μήπω ἐγίγνωσκον Philostr.*VS*1 *Praef*.; πόλις ὄρχησιν μάλιστα πρεσβεύουσα Luc.*Salt*.76. II. *to be an ambassador* or *serve as one*, *IG*1².135.5; ἀπὸ Κορίνθου Hdt.5.93; εἰς Θετταλίαν And.4.41; παρά or πρός τινα, Pl.*Chrm*.158a, X.*Cyr*.5.1.3; τινος *for* one, E.*Heracl*.479: abs., Ar.*Ach*.610, etc.: c. acc. cogn., ἃς ἐπρέσβευσεν [εἰς Θήβας] πρεσβείας Din.1.16. b. at Rome, *act as legatus*, Plu.*Sull*.4. 2. c. acc. objecti, π. εἰρήνην *negotiate* peace, And.3.23, Isoc.4.177, D.19.134, etc.; π. ὑπὲρ τουτωνὶ τὰ βέλτιστα ib.189; π. πολλὰ καὶ δεινά ibid.:—Pass., τὰ αὐτῷ πεπρεσβευμένα his *negotiations*, ib.20; πολλὰ καὶ δεινὰ πεπρεσβεῦσθαι ib.240. 3. Med., *send ambassadors*, ἐς χωρία, ἐς τὴν Θουρίαν, Th.2.7, 6.104; πρεσβεύεσθαι παρά τινας Id.4.41, etc.; πρός τινας Id.1.126; ἐς Λακεδαίμονα περὶ καθόδου Id.3.85. b. *go as ambassador*, Id.5.39. III. c. acc. rei, *represent, urge, maintain*, Luc.*Pisc*.23; [δόγματα] Gal.6.753; τὴν ὄψιν κατὰ εἰσδοχὴν π. Olymp. *in Mete*.5.6: c. inf., κατὰ ἐκπομπὴν εἶναι τὴν ὄψιν ib.10. -η, ἡ, = πρέσβεα, St.Byz. s.v. Ἀγάμμεια, dub. in A.*Supp*.727. -ήϊον, v. πρεσβεῖον. -ηΐς, ΐδος, ἡ, = πρέσβα, π. τιμή *highest* or *most ancient* honour, *h.Hom*.29.3. ⊛ -ις (A), εως, ὁ, *ambassador*, πρέσβις οὐ τύπτεται οὐδὲ ὑβρίζεται Prov.ap.Sch.Il.4.394; alleged as the word of which πρέσβεως (Ar.*Ach*.93) is gen., Choerob. *in Theod*.1.233, Sch.Ar.l.c., Suid. ⊛ -ις (B), εως, ἡ, poet. for πρεσβεία, *age*, κατὰ πρέσβιν according to *age*, *h.Merc*.431, Pl.*Lg*.855d, etc. II. *aged woman*, v.l. for πρεσβῦτις in Aesop.107ᵇ (pp.182, 183 Chambry). 2. *ambassadress*, Ael.ap.Eust.738.62. -ιστος, η, ον, poet. Sup. of πρέσβυς, *eldest*, *most august, most reverend*, *h.Hom*.30.2, A.*Th*.390, S.*Frr*.582, 605; πρεσβίστα κόσμου μᾶτερ *Lyr.Alex.Adesp*.35.2; ἁ π. φιλοσοφία Ti.Locr.104b; πόλις *Sardis*7(1).13: irreg. form **πρεσβίστατος**, η, ον, Nic.*Th*.344. -ος, εος, τό, poet. word, *object of reverence*, Πέρσαις to them, A.*Pers*.623 (anap.); π. Ἀργείων *august assembly* of.., Id.*Ag*.855, 1393.

**πρεσβῠ-γένεθλος**, ον, = πρεσβυγενής, Orph.*H*.4.2. -γένεια, Ion. -είη, ἡ, *seniority of birth*, Hdt.6.51, Plu.2.636e. -γενής, ές, *first-born*, Il.11.249, E.*Tr*.593 (lyr.): generally, *ancient, primeval*, Κρόνος Cratin.240. II. οἱ π., Lacon. for οἱ γέροντες, Plu.*Lyc*.6, 2.789e. -γονία, ἡ, = πρεσβυγένεια, Hsch. s.v. κατὰ προΐθην.

⊛ **πρέσβῠς**, Pi.*P*.4.282, A.*Ag*.530, εως or εος (v. infr. II), ὁ, voc. πρέσβυ E.*Or*.476, Ar.*Th*.146:—*old man* (poet. for prose πρεσβύτης), in this sense only used in nom., acc., and voc., ὁ π. Πόλυβος S.*OT*941; Φοῖνιξ ὁ π. Id.*Ph*.562; δριμὺς π. Ar.*Av*.255 (lyr.); πατέρα πρέσβυν S.*Ph*.665; πρέσβυ Id.*OT*1013, 1121; ὦ πρέσβυ E.l.c., Ar.l.c.; ὁ π. *the elder*, A.*Ag*.184 (lyr.), 205 (lyr.), 530; cf. πρέσβα, πρέσβειρα, πρεσβηΐς, πρέσβις: pl. πρέσβεις, *elders*, three times in Trag., always voc. (v. infr. III), A.*Pers*.840, S.*OT*1111, E.*HF*247; for πρεσβῆ, πρεσβῆες, πριστεῖες, v. πρεσβεύς: Comp. and Sup. are the only forms found in Hom., Comp. πρεσβύτερος, α, ον (late πρεσβυτερωτέρα *PLond*.2.177.15 (i A.D.)), *elder*, Il.11.787, 15.204, Hdt.2.2, etc.; πλεῖν ἢ 'νιαυτῷ by more than a year, Ar.*Ra*.18; πρεσβυτέρα ἀριθμοῦ *older* than the fit number, Pi.*Fr*.127; βουλαὶ πρεσβύτεραι thy counsels *wise beyond thy years*, Id.*P*.2.65; γνώμη π. τῆς ἡλικίας D.H.5.30; οἱ σοφοὶ καὶ π. Arist.*EE*1215ᵃ23; of animals, Id.*HA*546ᵃ7; ἵππος π. ἤδη ὤν *rather old*, *PCair.Zen*.225.8 (iii B.C.); also δένδρα π. Thphr.*CP*1.13.8; ἐπὶ τὸ π. ἱέναι *become older*, Pl.*Lg*.631e; ἵνα μὴ π. ὢν ῥέμβωμαι *in my old age*, *PCair.Zen*.447.9 (iii B.C.): Sup. πρεσβύτατος, η, ον, *eldest*, Il.4.59, 11.740, Hes.*Th*.234, etc.; π. γενεῇ Il.6.24; as a term of respect, ἐγὼ παλαιότατός εἰμι σὺ δὲ π. Plu.*Nic*.15; of animals, Arist.*HA*546ᵃ4, al.: for the poet. forms πρέσβιστος, πρεσβίστατος, v. πρέσβιστος, and cf. πρεῖγυς. 2. Comp. and Sup., of things, *more* or *most important, taking precedence*, esp. πρεσβύτερόν τι (or οὐδὲν) ἔχειν deem *higher, more important*, τὰ τοῦ θεοῦ πρεσβύτερα ἐποιεῦντο ἢ τὰ τῶν ἀνδρῶν Hdt.5.63; οὐδὲν πρεσβύτερον νομίζω τᾶς σωφροσύνας E.*Fr*.959 (lyr.); ἐμοὶ οὐδέν ἐστι πρεσβύτερον τοῦ.. Pl.*Smp*.218d; πρεσβύτατον κρῖναί τι Th.4.61; merely of magnitude, πρεσβύτερον κακοῦ κακόν one evil *greater than* another, S.*OT*1365 (lyr.); χρεὼν πάντων πρεσβύτατα Pl.*Lg*.717b. Adv., -τέρως γυμναστικὴν μουσικῆς τετιμηκέναι Id.*R*.548c, cf. Jul.*Or*.4.132c. II. = πρεσβευτής, *ambassador*, in nom. sg. only cj. in A.*Supp*.727 (v. πρέσβη) and in Prov.ap.Sch.Il.4.394 (v. πρέσβις (A)); gen. πρέσβεως Ar.*Ach*.93 (at end of line); πρέσβεος Choerob. *in Theod*.1.233: dual πρέσβει (written πρεσβε) *IG*12(1).977.45, 57 (Carpathos, iv B.C.): pl. πρέσβεις, Dor. uncontr. πρέσβεες ib.14.952.11 (Acragas, iii B.C.) (at first more freq. than πρεσβευταί (q.v.)), Ar.*Ach*.61, *IG*1².52.1, 2².1.20, al., D.19.183; acc. πρέσβεις *IG*1².46.24, Foed.ap.Th.4.118, X.*HG*4.8.13; gen. πρέσβεων, dat. πρέσβεσι, Ar.*Ach*.76, 62, *IG*2².1.7. III. at Sparta a political title, *president*, τῶν ἐφόρων ib.5(1).51.6, 552.11; νομοφυλάκων ib.555b19; βιδέων ib.556.6; συναρχίας ib.504.16; τῆς φυλῆς ib.564.3; [σφαιρέων] ib.675.5; gen. sg. πρέσβεως ib.504.16, al. 2. Comp. πρεσβύτερος, *elder, alderman*, τῆς κώμης *BGU* 195.30 (ii A.D., pl.), cf. *POxy*.2121.4 (iii A.D.), etc.; ἐκρίθημεν ἐπί τε Νουμηνίου καὶ ἐπὶ τῶν π. *PCair.Zen*.520.4 (iii B.C.), cf. *UPZ*124.22, 36 (ii B.C.): τοῖς ἱερεῦσι καὶ (*both*) τοῖς π. καὶ τοῖς ἄλλοις πᾶσι *OGI*194.3 (Egypt, i B.C.); οἱ π. τῶν ὀλυροκόπων ib.729 (Alexandria, iii B.C.); π. τῶν γεωργῶν *PTeb*.13.5 (ii B.C.); π. γέρδιοι *IGRom*.1.1122 (Theadelphia, ii A.D.); τέκτονες π. ib.1155 (Ptolemaïs Hermiu, i A.D.): *elder of the Jewish Sanhedrin*, *Ev.Matt*.16.21, etc.; later, *elder of the Christian Church, presbyter*, *Act.Ap*.11.30, 20.17, 1*Ep.Ti*.5.19, *POxy*.1162.1 (iv A.D.), etc.; of the Apostles, 2*Ep.Jo*.1.1, 3*Ep.Jo*.1.1. IV. *wren*, Arist.*HA*609ᵃ17, 615ᵃ19, Hsch.; cf. σπέργυς. (-βυ-, Cret. -γυ- (in πρεῖγυς), cogn. with Skt. -*gu* in *vanar-gú-* 'one who lives or moves in the forest', Lith. *žmogùs* 'man' (lit. 'one who moves on the ground'); πρεσ- cogn. with Lat. *prae, pris-tinus*; the oldest sense of π. is 'going in front, taking precedence'.)

**πρεσβῠτέριον** or -εῖον, τό, *council of elders, presbytery*, *Ev.Luc*.22.66, *Act.Ap*.22.5, 1*Ep.Ti*.4.14. II. *honour* or *privilege of an elder*, Thd.*Su*.50.

**πρεσβύτης** [ῠ], ητος, Dor. -ας, ατος, ἡ, *age, seniority*, *Test.Epict*.4.28, 6.29: opp. νεότας, prob. rest. in *IG*5(1).1427.5 (Messene).

**πρεσβ-ύτης** [ῡ], ου, ὁ, prose form of πρέσβυς I, Hp.*Aër*.10 (pl.), Th.3.67 (pl.), Arist.*EN*1157ᵇ14 (pl.), etc.; the sixth of the seven ages, Hp.*Hebd*.5; also in Trag. and Com., E.*Ph*.847, Ar.*Eq*.525, *Nu*.358; πατέρα π. Κρόνον A.*Eu*.641; ἀνὴρ π. Ar.*Ach*.707, Antipho 4.1.6; ὁ ἐκ παιδὸς μέχρι πρεσβύτου χρόνος Pl.*R*.608c, etc.; of animals, [λέοντες] ὅταν γένωνται πρεσβῦται Arist.*HA*629ᵇ28:—fem. **πρεσβῦτις**, ιδος, A.*Eu*.731, 1027, E.*Hec*.842, Pl.*Hp.Ma*.286a, Theopomp.Com.78; πρεσβύτιδες γυναῖκες Aeschin.3.157; π. ἄνθρωπος Lys.1.15. -ῠτικός, ή, όν, *like an old man, elderly*, ὄχλος Ar.*Pl*.787; κακὰ π. the evils *of age*, ib.270, cf. Ael.*VH*2.34 (vulg. πρεσβυτιδίου); ἕλκη Dsc.*Eup*.1.172; ᾄδουσαι μέλος π. Ar.*Ec*.278; παιδιά Pl.*Lg*.685a; οἱ στρυφνοὶ καὶ π. Arist.*EN*1158ᵃ2; ἀρχαῖον λίαν καὶ π. Plu.*Fab*.25: Comp., εἴ τι περιεργότερον καὶ πρεσβυτικώτερον εἰρήκαμεν Isoc.*Ep*.4.13. Adv. -κῶς Plu.*Thes*.14. II. πρεσβυτικόν, τό, *hall of the elders, senate-house*, *Milet*.7.60 (Didyma), *Sardis*7(1).8.72. -ῦτις, ιδος, fem. of πρεσβύτης (q.v.).

**πρεσβῡτοδόκος**, ον, *receiving the aged*, A.*Supp*.667 (lyr., dub.).

⊛ **Πρέσβων**, ωνος, ὁ, pl. Πρέσβωνες the *Elders*, name of a family or χιλιαστύς, *Abh.Berl.Akad*.1909(2).17 (Chios).

**πρεσγέα**, v. πρεῖγυς.

**πρευμέν-εια**, ἡ, *gentleness of temper, graciousness*, E.*Or*.1323. -ής, ές, contr. fr. πρηϋμενής (v. πραϋμενής), *soft of temper, gentle, gracious*, τινι to one, A.*Ag*.840, E.*Hec*.538: abs., ἴδοιτο.. πρευμενοῦς ἀπ' ὄμματος A.*Supp*.210 (207); Ἀχαιῶν πρευμενεστέρων τύχοις E.*Tr*.739.

Adv., πρευμενῶς αἰτεῖσθαι, παραινέσαι, A.*Pers.*220, 224; δέχεσθαι Id. *Eu.*236. 2. of events, *favourable*, κατελθὼν.. πρευμενεῖ τύχῃ Id.*Ag.*1647; τελευτὰς.. πρευμενεῖς κτίσειεν Id.*Supp.*140 (lyr.); πρευμενοῦς.. νόστου τυχόντας E.*Hec.*540 (s.v.l.). II. *propitiating*, χοαί A.*Pers.*609.

**πρεών**, v. πρών.

⊛ **πρηγιστεύω**, *hold office of* **πρήγιστος** (v. πρεῖγυς), *GDI*3742.4 (Cos).

**πρῆγμα, πρηγματεύομαι**, Ion. for πραγμ-. II. οἷον πρῆγμα (sic codd.) πνίγεται (sic cod. θ, v.l. πνέεται) Hp.*Aff.*5, perh. f.l. for οἷον πρῆμά τι γίνεται a sort of *swelling* (cf. παράπρημα) arises.

**πρηγορεύω**, = προαγορεύω, Hsch.

**πρηγορεών**, ῶνος, ὁ, *crop* of birds, Ar.*Eq.*374 (metaph. of Cleon), *Av.*1113 (πρηγορῶνα, -ῶνας cj. Bentley); from πρό, ἀγείρω, because birds *collect* their food there *before* it passes into the second stomach, Hsch., Poll.2.204, *EM*688.33, Suid., Apollonius ap.Zonar.: written **προηγορεών**, *EM* l.c., cf. Suid.

**πρηδών**, όνος, ἡ, (πρήθω) *swelling*, Nic.*Th.*365 (pl.); αἱ τῆς φλεγμονῆς π., of intestinal *distension*, Aret.*CA*1.1.

**πρηθῆναι**, v. πέρνημι.

**πρῆθμα**· πολύποδος κεφαλή· ἔνιοι πλεκτάνη, Hsch.

⊛ **πρήθω**, impf. ἔπρηθον (ἐν-): aor. ἔπρησα (v. infr.):—Pass., pf. πέπρησμαι: aor. ἐπρήσθην (v. infr.): A.R. seems to use πρήσοντα, πρήσοντος as pres. part., 4.819, 1537: (for the signf. *burn*, v. πίμπρημι; cf. also ἐμπρήθω, πρηστήρ):—Ep. Verb (rarely if ever in Com., v. infr.), *blow out, swell out by blowing*, ἔπρησεν δ' ἄνεμος μέσον ἱστίον Od.2.427; ἐν δ' ἄνεμος πρῆσεν μέσον ἱστίον Il.1.481; νότου πρήσαντος ἅλα *AP*13.27 (Phal.); πρῆσαι γαστέρα Lxx *Nu.*5.22:—Pass., ἐπρήσθη dub. in Amphis 30.10; κοιλία πεπρησμένη Lxx *Nu.*5.21; πέπρησται ἱστία Ael.*NA*2.17; λαίφεα πρησθέντα Q.S.14.416. 2. *spout*, τὸ δ' [αἷμα] ἀνὰ στόμα καὶ κατὰ ῥῖνας πρῆσε he *spouted* blood from his mouth and nostrils, Il.16.350. 3. *blow into a flame*, π. πυρὸς μένος, of Hephaestus, A.R.4.819. II. intr., *blow*, ib.1537.

**πρῄον**· πρότερον, Hsch. **πρηκτήρ, πρήκτης, πρηκτός**, v. πρακτήρ, πράκτης, πρακτός. **πρῆμα**, v. πρῆγμα II.

**πρημάδη**, ἡ, name of a kind of *olive*, Nic.*Al.*87.

**πρημαίνω**, (πρήθω) *blow hard*, πρημαινούσας τε θυέλλας Ar.*Nu.*336: later c. acc., πρήμηνον ὀξίην φωνὴν σεωυτοῦ Herod.7.98.

**πρημνάς**, άδος, ἡ, a kind of *tunny-fish*, Pl.Com.44, Nicoch.11 (πρημάδας codd. Ath.), Opp.*H.*1.183; **πριμάδες** and **πριμαδίαι** in codd. of Arist.*HA*599$^b$17 (where the meaning is apptly. *young tunny*).

**πρημονάω**, perh. *fume, seethe* or *swell* with indignation, Herod.6.8.

**πρην-ής, -ίζω**, v. πρανής, -ίζω.

**πρῆξαι, πρῆξις**, Ion. for πρᾶξαι, πρᾶξις.

**πρηξών**, όνος, ὁ, = ἀγοραῖος (Sicel), Theognost.*Can.*38.

⊛ **πρηροσία**, ἡ, a sacrifice at Athens (i.e. προηρόσια), Hsch.

**πρῆσις** (A), v. πρᾶσις.

**πρῆσις** (B), ιος, ἡ, (πρήθω) *blowing up, distension*, τράχηλος οἰδέει πνεύματος πρήσι Aret.*SD*1.11; ἔντασις καὶ π. (in εἰλεός) Id.*CA*2.5; ὑπὸ τῆς π. (in dropsy) Id.*SD*2.1; *filling out, development*, τραχήλου (by gymnastics) Id.*CD*1.3 (pl.). 2. *inflammation*, ὀφθαλμῶν ibid. (pl.); τῶν παρισθμίων, τοῦ ὑπεζωκότος, τοῦ πνεύμονος, τῶν νεύρων, Id. *CA*1.7,10, 2.1,11 (pl.).

**πρῆσ-μα**, ατος, τό, = ἐμφύσημα, Gal.19.132. 2. *swelling*, *Hippiatr.*77. **-μονή**, ἡ, = foreg., ibid.

**πρήσσω**, v. πράσσω.

⊛ **πρηστήρ**, ῆρος, ὁ, (πρήθω) *hurricane* or *waterspout attended with lightning* (*Placit.*3.3.1, Arist.*Mete.*371$^a$16, Chrysipp.*Stoic.*2.203, Epicur.*Ep.*2 p.47 U., Lucr.6.424,445), πρηστήρων ἀνέμων Hes.*Th.*846; θαλάσσης τὸ μὲν ἥμισυ γῆ, τὸ δ' ἥμισυ π. Heraclit.31; βρονταί τε καὶ πρηστῆρες ἐπεσπίπτουσι Hdt.7.42; τυφῷ καὶ πρηστῆρι Ar.*Lys.*974; ὁ.. νεὼς τῆς Ἀθηνᾶς ἐνεπρήσθη π. ἐμπεσόντος X.*HG*1.3.1; π. χθόνιος *tornado*, Arist.*Mu.*395$^a$10; πρηστῆρες καὶ κεραυνοί Thphr.*Ign.*1. 2. ὀμμάτων ἄπο αἱμοσταγῆ πρηστῆρε ῥεύσονται κάτω two *jets* of blood, E.*Fr.*384. II. *pair of bellows*, πρηστῆρος αὐλός *Placit.*2.20.1, 2.25.1: pl., A.R.4.777. III. pl., *veins of the neck when swollen by anger*, Poll.2.134, Hsch. IV. a kind of *serpent*, whose bite is poisonous, Dsc.4.37, Philum.*Ven.*19, Ael.*NA*6.51.

**πρηστηριάζω**, *burn up as with lightning*, Hdn.*Epim.*111.

**πρηστηροδόχος**, ον, *receiving thunderbolts*, κόλποι Orac.Chald.ap. Procl.*in Cra.*p.58 P.

**πρηστικός**, ή, όν, = ἐμφυσητικός, Hp.ap.Gal.19.132 (Sup.).

**πρῆστις**, ἡ, v. πρίστις.

**πρητήν**, ῆνος, ὁ, *yearling lamb*, Ar.Byz.ap.Eust.1625.35, Hsch.

**πρητήριον**, v. πρατήριον. **πρηϋ-γελως**, κτλ., v. πραϋ-. **πρῆχμα**, v. πρᾶγμα. **πρηών**, v. πρών.

⊛***πρίαμαι** (assumed as Pres.), 1 aor. ἐπριάμην freq. in Att., supplying aor. of ὠνέομαι, *buy*; 2 sg. ἐπρίω Ar.*V.*1440; 3 sg. ἐπρίατο *IG*1$^2$.94.22, Ep. πρίατο Od.1.430; imper. πρίασο Ar.*Ach.*870; πρίω ib.34, 35, Eup.1, etc.; Dor. πρίᾶ Epich.137; subj. πρίωμαι Ar.*Ach.*812, 2 sg. πρίῃ Id.*Nu.*614, 3 sg. πρίηται D.18.247, Thphr.*Fr.*97.3; opt. πριαίμην S.*Ant.*1171, *Leg.Gort.*6.13, etc.; inf. πρίασθαι *IG*1$^2$.10.5, E.*Med.*233, Ar.*V.*253, etc. (πριάσασθαι v.l. in Lxx *Ge.*42.10); part. πριάμενος Hdt.1.196, *IG*1$^2$.94.22, *Leg.Gort.*6.20, etc.:—*buy*, Od.l.c., etc.; ὁ πριάμενος, opp. ὁ ἀποδόμενος, *Leg.Gort.*6.20: c. dat. pretii, τίς σε πρίατο κτεάτεσσιν ἑοῖσιν Od.14.115, cf. 452; τὸ κάλλος ἀνονήτοις γάμοις E.*Hel.*885, cf. *Med.*233. etc.: c. gen., π. θανάτοιο *purchase by* his death, Pi.*P.*6.39; π. καπίθην ἀλεύρων τεττάρων σίγλων X.*An.*1.5.6; π. πολλοῦ Id.*Cyr.*3.2.19 (also πρὸ πάντων χρημάτων Id.*Mem.*2.5.3); πρίασθαι οὐδενὸς λόγου *to buy at* no price, S.*Aj.*477: with dat. pers. added, πόσου πρίωμαί σοι τὰ χοιρίδια; Ar.*Ach.*812, cf. *Ra.*1229, S.*Ant.*1171; π. τι παρὰ τῶν ἐκτημένων Hdt.9.94; π. τὴν χώραν παρά τινων τριάκοντα ταλάντων X.*HG*3.2.30: c. inf., π. παρά τινων μὴ δοῦναι δίκην And.3.38; τῆς ψυχῆς π. ὥστε μή.. X.*Cyr.*3.1.36, cf. 8.4.23: π. alone, π. τίμιον [τοὔλαιον] *buy* it dear, Ar.*V.*253; τὴν εἰρήνην π. Aeschin. 2.178; ὀπώραν D.53.21; π. τὸ ποιῆσαι *buy* the power of doing, X.*Cyr.*5.3.10. 2. of slaves, π. Σκύθας τοξότας And.3.5, cf. Posidipp. 23; ἐπιστάτην ταλάντου X.*Mem.*2.5.2; τέκτονα πέντε μνῶν Pl.*Amat.*135c. 3. π. τοὺς δικαστὰς *buy*, i.e. *bribe* them, D.7.7. 4. *rent, farm* a tax, etc., τέλος X.*Vect.*4.20; μέταλλον Din.ap.D.H.*Din.*13; ὠνὴν ἐκ τοῦ δημοσίου And.1.92, etc.: abs., οἱ πριάμενοι [τὸ θέατρον] the *contractors* for the management of the theatre, *IG*2$^2$.1176.15,31. (Cf. Skt. *krīṇā́ti*, OIr. *crenid*, Welsh *prynu* 'buy', Old Lith. *krienas* 'bride-price'.)

**πρῐᾰμόομαι**, Med., *to have one's head shaven*, because Priam was represented on the stage with a bald head, *Com.Adesp.*1123.

**Πρίαμος** [ῐ], ὁ, *Priam*, Il.1.19, etc.; Aeol. **Πέρρᾰμος** (wh. = βασιλεύς, acc. to Hsch.) Alc.*Supp.*8.2; also **Πέρᾰμος**, Sapph.*Supp.*20a.16:—Patron. **Πριᾰμίδης** [Πρῑ- metri gr.], ὁ, Ep. gen. -ίδαο, -ίδεω, Il.3.356, 20.77: Adj. **Πριαμικός**, ή, όν, *of* or *like Priam*, τύχαι Arist. *EN*1101$^a$8; poet. fem. **Πριαμίς**, ίδος, E.*Hel.*1158 (lyr.), *Or.*1482 (lyr.): Dim. **Πριαμιλλύδριον** and **Πριαμύλλιον**, τό, Sch.D.T.pp.375, 376 H.

**Πρῐάπ-ειος** [ᾱ], α, ον, Ion. **Πριήπ-**, *of Priapus*, *AP*6.254 (Myrin.); Π. μέτρον Heph.10.4; τὰ Π. (sc. μέλη) D.H.*Comp.*4, Str.8.6.24. **-ήϊον**, τό, = σατύριον, Ps.-Dsc.3.126. 2. = ἴον πορφυροῦν, ib.4.121. ⊛ **-ίζω**, Ion. **Πριηπ-**, *to be lewd*, πάντα Πριηπίζω, κἂν ᾖ Κρόνος *APl.*4.237 (Tymn.); *to be ithyphallic*, τραγέλαφος πριαπίζων prob. in *IG*2$^2$.1388.62. **-ίσκος**, ὁ, Dim. of Πρίαπος, *dilator* or *suppository* for the anus, Heliod.ap.Orib.44.23.72, 44.14.7. 2. *perineal peg*, in the Hippocratic bench, Ruf. (or Heliod.) ap.Orib.49.26.6. 3. *plug* for the nose, Heraclid.Tar.ap.Gal.12.692. II. = σατύριον, Ps.-Dsc.3.126,128 (called *priapisce*, *Gloss.*). **-ισκωτός**, ή, όν, *shaped like the membrum virile*, μοτός Gal.14.795. **-ισμός**, ὁ, *priapism*, Id.8.448, 13.318, Alex.Trall.11.8. **-ισταί**, οἱ, *worshippers of Priapus*, *Ausonia*4.242 (Crete, i B.C.). ⊛ **-ος**, Ion. **Πρίηπος** (also written **Πρίεπος**, Arr.*Fr.*23 J., cf. Πριέπιος), ὁ, *Priapus*, D.S.4.6, Luc.*DDeor.*23.1, Paus.9.31.2: pl. Πρίηποι, like Σάτυροι, Mosch.3.27. **-ώδης**, ες, *like Priapus*, *lewd*, Sch.Ar.*Lys.*981.

**πρῑβᾰτάριος**, ὁ, *keeper of a private bath*, Lat. *balneator privatarius* (*Edict. Diocl.*7.76), *MAMA*3.259, al. (Corycus); written **πριβαρίου** (gen.) ib.557 (ibid.).

**πρίγιστος**, v. πρεῖγυς.

⊛ **πρίγκῖπες**, οἱ, = Lat. *principes*, Plb.6.21.7, etc.

⊛ **Πριέπιος** (sc. μήν), ὁ, a month in Bithynia, prob. in *Hemerolog. Flor.* ⊛ **Πρίεπος**, v. Πρίαπος.

**πρίζω**, = πρίω, *saw*, Pl.*Thg.*124b (s.v.l.), D.S.4.76, Heliod.ap. Orib.47.14.3: impf. ἔπριζον Lxx *Am.*1.3. II. *file*, ῥίνῃ πρίζειν Gal.12.848.

**πριμάς**, άδος, ἡ, v. πρημνάς.

⊛ **πρίν**, Adv. and Conj., *before, until*. [πρῖν 19 times in Hom., Il.2.344, al.; πρῐν in Il.6.81, 13.172, al.; once written πρείν, *Leg.Gort.*7.40, but πρίν *IG*1$^2$.60.11, 94.9, 114.46, etc.; Trag. and Com. always πρῐν (πρίν γ' must be read in Ar.*Ach.*176).]

A. Adv. of Time, *before*, either in the sense of *sooner* or in that of *formerly, erst* (implying duration up to a certain time): I. of future time, with fut. Indic., πρίν μιν καὶ γῆρας ἔπεισιν Il.1.29, cf. 18.283, Od.2.198, etc.: with Subj. = fut., πρὶν καὶ κακὸν ἄλλο πάθησθα Il.24.551: with Opt. and κεν, πρίν κεν ἀνιηθεὶς σὴν πατρίδα γοῖαν ἵκοιο Od.3.117, cf. 11.330, 14.155, Ar.*Pax*1076, 1112: with Opt., Il.24.800: with Imper., 9.250: with Inf. (expressing a wish), 2.413, (expressing an oath) Od.4.254. II. of past time, 1. *formerly, once*, πρὶν μέν μοι ὑπέσχετο.., νῦν δὲ.. Il.2.112, v.l. in 9.19, cf. 23.827; πρὶν μὲν πόσιν ἐσθλὸν ἀπώλεσα Od.4.724, cf. 3.408. 2. *formerly* (up to a certain point), *before*, in this sense freq. with Art., τὸ πρίν γ' ἐκέκαστο Il.5.54; τὸ πρίν γε.., νῦν δὲ.. 13.105; νῦν δὲ.. τὸ πρίν γε 16.208, cf. A.*Pr.*443, Hdt.1.129: without Art., τὰς ἐπιστήμας ἅς ποτε καὶ π. εἴχομεν Pl.*Phd.*75e: with ellipsis of part. γενόμενος, τὰ π. πελώρια (sc. γενόμενα) the giants *of old*, A.*Pr.*151 (lyr.); τοῦ π. Αἰγέως Aegeus *gone before*, S.*OC*69; ἐν τῷ π. χρόνῳ Id.*Ph.*1224; ἐν τοῖς π. λόγοις Th.2.62: with part. expressed, τὸ π. γενόμενον τέρας Hdt.8.37; τοὺς πρὶν φυλαττομένους Pl.*R.*547c, etc. 3. *hitherto*, π. μέν.. B.12.114; *until that time*, and so *meanwhile*, Id.15.13. 4. sts. folld. by gen., π. ὥρας Pi.*P.*4.43; π. ἀνηκέστου πάθους J.*BJ*1.6.1; π. γενέσεως Thd.*Su.*42; π. τῆς συνόδου S.E.*M.*9.371; π. φάους Arr.*An.*3.18.6; π. τοῦ βλέψαι, π. τοῦ ἀποθανεῖν, S.E.*P.*7.162, v.l. in Lxx *To.*14.15; also πρὶν οὐ c. inf., *SIG*953.16 (Calymna, ii B.C.); c. indic., Test.ap.D.46.21.

B. Conj. *before, ere*: freq. following an antecedent clause with adverbial π. (chiefly in Ep.), or its equivalents πρότερον, πρόσθεν, πάρος (poet.), esp. with negat., οὐδὲ π.., π.. Il.1.98, 7.481, Od.19.475; μὴ π.., π.. Il.2.355, E.*HF*605; π.., π.. Il.2.348, 8.453, Od.19.586; οὐ πρότερον.., π.. Ar.*Ec.*620, And.4.17, D.9.61; μὴ πρότερον.. π.. S.*Ph.*199 (anap.), Pl.*Phd.*62c, Aeschin.1.10; πρότερον.., π.. And.4.1, X.*Cyr.*5.2.9; οὐ πρόσθεν.., π.. Od.17.9, X.*Cyr.*1.4.23; μὴ πρόσθεν.., π.. Id.*An.*1.1.10; πρόσθε.., π. τυχεῖν Pi.*P.*2.92; οὐ πάρος.., π.. Od.2.128, Il.5.219; preceded by φθάνω, 16.322, Antipho 1.29, Th.4.79,104, 6.97, 8.12, X.*An.*4.1.21,

Cyr.2.4.25; sts. folld. by ἤ, οὐ..πρίν γ' ἀποπαύσεσθαι πρίν γ' ἢ ἕτερόν γε πεσόντα αἵματος ἆσαι Ἄρηα Il.5.288, cf. 22.266, Hdt.1.136, 165, al.; dub. and perh. always corrupt in Att. and X., Th.5.61, Lys.6.11, Isoc.4.19 (v.l.), Lycurg.128, Aeschin.2.132 (v.l.), X.*Cyr.*1.4.23, *An.* 4.5.1, but freq. in later Greek, Lxx *Ge.*29.26, etc. I. c. inf., the prevailing constr. in Hom., after positive and negative clauses alike: in Att. mostly after positive clauses, and always used with them when the action does not or is not to take place: the tense is, 1. regularly aor., a. after a positive clause, ναῖε δὲ Πήδαιον, πρὶν ἐλθεῖν υἷας Ἀχαιῶν Il.13.172, cf. 8.453, 16.322, Od.1.210; Ζεὺς ὀλέσειε βίην, πρὶν ἥβης μέτρον ἱκέσθαι 4.668, cf. Il.6.465, 24.245, Pi.*P.*2.92, 3.9, *N.*8.19, Hdt.6.119, A.*Pers.*712, *Ag.*1539 (anap.), S.*Ant.*120 (lyr.), *Tr.*396, E.*Alc.*281, Ar.*Eq.*258, al., Antipho 5.67, Th.1.125, X.*An.*4.1.7, Pl.*Prt.*350b, al.; after negat. questions which expect a posit. answer, E.*Andr.*1069, *Ion* 524, *Rh.*684, Ar.*Ra.*481, etc. b. after a negat. clause, οὐδ' ὅ γε πρὶν Δαναοῖσιν ἀεικέα λοιγὸν ἀπώσει, πρίν γ' ἀπὸ πατρὶ φίλῳ δόμεναι ἑλικώπιδα κούρην Il.1.98, cf. 19.423, Od.2.128, 4.747: after Hom. a negat. antecedent is commonly folld. by πρίν with finite Verb (v. infr. II); but Inf. is found where π. precedes, π. ἰδεῖν δ', οὐδεὶς μάντις S.*Aj.*1419 (anap.); π. μὲν γὰρ κριθῆναι, οὐ ῥᾴδιον ἦν εἰδέναι τὰς αἰτίας And.4.8; π. νικῆσαι.., οὐκ ἦν.. Lys.19.28; π. δὲ ταῦτα πρᾶξαι, μὴ σκοπεῖτε D.3.12, cf. Lycurg.135; also, οὔτε..π. ἱδρῶσαι δεῖπνον ᾐρεῖτο X.*Cyr.*8.1.38; also after Verbs of fearing (the positive being the thing dreaded), ὅταν..δεδίωσι μὴ πρότερόν τι πάθῃς, π. τέλος ἐπιθεῖναι τοῖς πραττομένοις Isoc.5.70, cf. E.*Fr.*453.6, S.*Tr.* 632; in unfulfilled conditions and wishes, οὔθ' ὁ Πλούτωνος κύων οὔθ' οὑπὶ κώπῃ ψυχοπομπὸς ἂν Χάρων ἔσχον π. εἰς φῶς σὸν καταστῆσαι βίον E.*Alc.*362, cf. *Rh.*61; otherwise not common, ὤφθην οὐδεπώποτε π. ταύτην τὴν συμφορὰν γενέσθαι Lys.19.55; οὐδὲ παύσεται χόλου.., π. κατασκῆψαί τινα E.*Med.*94, cf. *HF*605; καί μοι μὴ θορυβήσῃ μηδεὶς π. ἀκοῦσαι D.5.15, cf. X.*Oec.*4.24: after neg. opt. with ἄν, οὕτω γένοιτ' ἂν οὐδ' ἂν ἔκβασις στρατοῦ καλή, π. ὅρμῳ ναῦν θρασυνθῆναι A.*Supp.*772, cf. Pl.*Lg.*769e: after a past tense (in orat. obliq.), ὤμοσαν μὴ π. ἐς Φώκαιαν ἥξειν, π. ἢ τὸν μύδρον τοῦτον ἀναφανῆναι Hdt.1.165, cf. 4.9, Th. 7.50, X.*HG*6.5.23, Pl.*Phd.*61a. 2. also pres., to convey a special sense of continuance, effort, or the like, 'before undertaking to', 'before proceeding to', π. ἐξοπλίζειν Ἄρη A.*Supp.*702 (lyr.), cf. *Ag.* 1067; π. νυν τὰ πλείον' ἱστορεῖν.., ἔξελθε S.*OC*36, cf. *El.*20; π. κλαίειν τινὰ E.*Andr.*577, cf. *Or.*1095; π. λέγειν Ar.*Th.*380, cf. *Ach.*383, Hdt. 8.3, And.4.1, Th.3.24, Pl.*Lg.*666a, X.*Cyr.*2.4.25, *Mem.*1.2.40, etc. 3. also perf., after a fut., π. τόδ' ἐξηντληκέναι E.*Med.*79; after pres. or impf., Id.*El.*1069, cf. Hdt.3.25; π..., τί μέλλετ'..; E.*Ph.*1145; π. καὶ τεθύσθαι Ar.*Av.*1034, cf. *V.*1156, *Pax* 375, *Lys.*322 (lyr.), *Ra.*1185, X. *An.*4.1.21, Pl.*Tht.*164c, *Prt.*320a, etc.; with ἥκειν in pf. sense, Hdt.6. 116; οὐ βουλόμενος διαγωνίσασθαι π. οἱ τοὺς βοηθοὺς ἥκειν Th.5.10. II. with a finite Verb: 1. with Ind., chiefly aor.: not in Hom. (first in *h. Ap.*357), who uses Ind. only with πρίν γ' ὅτε, πρίν γ' ὅτε δή, after both posit. and neg. clauses, ἠλώμην..., πρίν γ' ὅτε.. ἤγαγες Od.13.322; πρίν γ' ὅτε δή με..κάλεσσεν 23.43, cf. Il.12.437; οὐδέ κεν ἡμέας ἄλλο διέκρινεν.., πρίν γ' ὅτε δὴ θανάτοιο..νέφος ἀμφεκάλυψεν Od.4.180: rarely with impf., οὐδ' ὣς τοῦ θυμὸν..ἔπειθον, πρίν γ' ὅτε δὴ θάλαμος πύκ' ἐβάλλετο (*began to be hit*) Il.9.588: freq. after Hom., with aor., a. after neg. clauses: of a fact in the past, οὐκ ἦν ἀλέξημ' οὐδὲν.., πρίν γ' ἐγώ σφισιν ἔδειξα A.*Pr.*481; οὐ πρότερον ἀπανέστη..Μαρδόνιος, πρὶν ἤ σφεας ὑποχειρίους ἐποιήσατο Hdt.6.45; ἀλλ' οὐδ' ὣς..ἠξίωσαν νεώτερόν τι ποιεῖν ἐς αὐτόν.., πρίν γε δὴ αὐτοῖς..μηνυτὴς γίγνεται (histor. pres. = aor.) Th.1.132, cf. 3.101, 5.61, Hdt.6.79, Ar.*Av* 700, X.*Cyr.*1.4.23, 4. 5.13 (histor. pres.), *HG*5.4.58, etc.; once in Pl., *Phdr.*266a; as part of an unfulfilled condition, οὐκ ἂν κατέσχε δῆμον οὐδ' ἐπαύσατο π. ἀνταράξας πῖαρ ἐξεῖλεν γάλα Sol.ap.Arist.*Ath.*12.5; οὐκ ἂν ἐσκεψάμεθα πρότερον.., πρὶν ἐζητήσαμεν Pl.*Men.*86d, cf. *Tht.*165e; χρῆν τοίνυν Λεπτίνην μὴ πρότερον τιθέναι τὸν ἑαυτοῦ νόμον, πρὶν τοῦτον ἔλυσε γραψάμενος D.20.96; after verbs implying a neg., ἀμφιγνοεῖν X.*An.*2.5.33, θαυμάζειν Th.1.51, λανθάνειν Id.3.29; also with impf., οὔπω ᾔδει..π. ἐν τῷ κακῷ ἦν Antipho 1.19, cf. And.4.17, D.9.61. b. after posit. clauses (both combined, A.*Pr.*481, Th.1.118), with the sense *until*, ἡγόμην δ' ἀνὴρ ἀστῶν μέγιστος.., πρίν μοι τύχη τοιάδ' ἐπέστη S.*OT* 776; σπουδαὶ δὲ λόγων ἦσαν ἴσαι πως, πρὶν..πείθει (histor. pres.) E. *Hec.*131 (anap.); πρίν γ' ὁρᾷ Id.*Med.*1173; freq. folld. by δή, π. δή τις ἐφθέγξατο Id.*Andr.*1147; τὰ περὶ τοὺς ἀγῶνας κατελύθη (neg. idea) ὑπὸ ξυμφορῶν, πρὶν δὴ οἱ Ἀθηναῖοι τότε τὸν ἀγῶνα ἐποίησαν Th.3.104, cf. 7.39 (histor. pres.), 71. 2. with Subj. only after negs. or equiv. of neg., = ἕως or ἣν μή (in Isoc 4.173 ἣν μή and πρὶν ἄν are used almost as synonyms); οὐ καταδυσόμεθ', ἀχνύμενοί περ.., πρὶν μόρσιμον ἦμαρ ἐπέλθῃ Od.10.175; μή πω καταδύσεο.., πρίν γ' ἐμὲ..ἴδηαι Il.18.135, cf. 190, 24.781; ἀλλ' ὄμοσον μὴ μητρὶ φίλῃ τάδε μυθήσασθαι, πρίν γ' ὅτ' ἂν ἑνδεκάτη τε δυωδεκάτη τε γένηται Od.2.374, cf. 4.477: in Prose usu. πρὶν ἄν (πρίν κα *Berl.Sitzb.*1927.161 (Cyrene)), rarely π. alone, as also πρὶν ἤ: a. generally with aor., to express an action preceding the action of the anteced. clause, the Verb in which is fut. (or some equiv. of the fut.) or imper., οὐ γαμέεται παρθένος οὐδεμία, πρὶν ἂν τῶν πολεμίων ἄνδρα ἀποκτείνῃ Hdt.4.117, cf. 1.82 (v.l.), 3.109 (v.l.); νῦν δ' οὐδέν ἐστι τέρμα μοι προκείμενον μόχθων (the sense here is fut.), πρὶν ἂν Ζεὺς ἐκπέσῃ τυραννίδος A.*Pr.*756, cf. 166 (lyr.), 177 (anap.); οὐ γάρ ποτ' ἕξει τῆσδε τῆς χώρας, πρὶν ἂν..στήσῃς ἄγων S.*OC*909; cf. 48, 1041, *OT*1529, etc.; οὐκ ἂν ἐκμάθοις.., πρὶν ἂν θάνῃ τις Id.*Tr.*2; οὐκ ἄπειμι πρὸς δόμους πάλιν, πρὶν ἄν σε..ἔξω βάλω E.*Med.*276, cf. 680, *Alc.*1145, *IA*324, *IT*19.1302; μὴ προκαταγίγνωσκε.., π. ἄν γ' ἀκούσῃς ἀμφοτέρων Ar.*V.*920, cf. *Ach.*176, 230, X.*Hier.*6.13, *Cyr.*1.2.8, *An.*1. 1.10, 5.7.12, Pl.*Phdr.*228c, *La.*187e (ἄν added in later codd.), etc.; μηδέν' ὀλβίζειν π. ἂν τέρμα τοῦ βίου περάσῃ S.*OT*1529 (troch.); οὐχὶ μὴ παύσησθε, π. ἄν..ὑμᾶς τις ἐκτραχηλίσῃ Ar.*Lys.*704: π. without ἄν, μὴ στέναζε, π. μάθῃς S.*Ph.*917, cf. *Ant.*619 (lyr.), *Aj.*742, 965, *Tr.*608, 946; οὐκ ἔστιν ὅστις αὐτὸν ἐξαιρήσεται.., π. γυναῖκ' ἐμοὶ μεθῇ E.*Alc.* 849, cf. *Or.*1218, 1357 (lyr.); π. χαρίσωνται Ar.*Ec.*629 (s.v.l.); οὐ γὰρ δή σφεας ἀπίει τῆς ἀποικίης, πρὶν δὴ ἀπίκωνται Hdt.4.157; π. διαγνῶσι Th.6.29; π...βεβαιωσώμεθα ib.10 (dub.l.); πρὶν ἀνάγκην τινὰ θεὸς ἐπιπέμψῃ Pl.*Phd.*62c codd.; π. ἐξετάσωσιν Hyp.*Eux.*4: πρὶν ἤ (never with ἄν), π. ἢ ἀνορθώσωσι Hdt.1.19, cf. 136, Pl.*Ti.*57b, etc.: with neg. implied, ὁ δὲ ἀδικέει ἀναπειθόμενος π. ἢ ἀτρεκέως ἐκμάθῃ Hdt.7. 10.η'; αἰσχρὸν ἡγοῦμαι πρότερον παύσασθαι, π. ἂν..ψηφίσησθε Lys. 22.4; ὅστις οὖν οἴεται τοὺς ἄλλους πράξειν τι.., π. ἄν..διαλλάξῃ, λίαν ἁπλῶς ἔχει Isoc.4.16 (where ὅστις οὖν οἴεται = οὐ δεῖ οἴεσθαι, as is shown by ἀλλὰ δεῖ in the next sentence, cf. D.38.24). b. less freq. (never in Hom.) with pres. subj.: μήπω π. ἂν τῶν ἡμετέρων ἄτῃς (the Verb has no aor.) μύθων S.*Ph.*1409 (anap.); ὁ νομοθέτης τὰ διδασκαλεῖα ἀνοίγειν ἀπαγορεύει μὴ πρότερον π. ἂν ὁ ἥλιος ἀνίσχῃ Aeschin.1.10, cf. Antipho 1.29, X.*Cyr.*2.2.8, Pl.*Phdr.*271c. 3. πρίν with Opt.: a. representing subj. after histor. tenses, οὐκ ἔθελεν φεύγειν π. πειρήσαιτ' Ἀχιλῆος Il.21.580; πρίν γ' ὅτε, as with subj., 9.488; ἔδοξέ μοι μὴ σιγᾶ π. φράσαιμί σοι τὸν πλοῦν ποεῖσθαι S. *Ph.*551, cf. Th.3.22, X.*Cyr.*1.4.14, *HG*6.5.19 (cf. 2.4.18), *An.*1.2.2, Pl.*Ap.*36c, etc. b. by assimilation, ὄλοιο μήπω π. μάθοιμι S.*Ph.* 961, cf. *Tr.*657 (lyr.); οὐδὲ γὰρ εἰδείης (potential opt.)..π. πειρηθείης Thgn.126; after opt. with ἄν, οὐκ ἂν πρότερον ὁρμήσειε π. βεβαιώσαιτο Pl.*Lg.*799d, cf. S.*OT*505 (lyr.). 4. π. ἄν c. opt. is doubtful, and (if not corrupt) due to the change required by orat. obl., ἀπαγορευόντων τῶν φίλων τῶν ἐμῶν μὴ ἀποκτείνειν τὸν ἄνδρα, πρὶν ἂν ἐγὼ ἔλθοιμι Antipho 5.34 (s.v.l.), cf. X.*HG*2.3.48, 2.4.18. 5. without a Verb, πρὶν ὥρη (sc. γένηται) Od.15.394.

**πρίνη**, ἡ, = πρῖνος, Eup.360.

**πρῑν-ίδιον** [ῐδ], τό, Dim. of πρῖνος, Ar.*Av.*615 (anap.), Ael.*VH*5. 17. **-ῐνος**, η, ον, *made from the* πρῖνος, γύης Hes.*Op.*429; ἄνθρακες Ar.*Ach.*668; αἱ πρίνιναι (sc. βάλανοι) Dsc.1.106.2; π. ὕλη Orib.49.3.1; μύκητες π. fungi *that grow under the ilex*, Antiph.227.11, cf. *An.Ox.*3. 231. 2. metaph., *oaken*, i.e. *tough, sturdy*, γέροντες Ar.*Ach.*180; τὸ λίαν στρυφνὸν καὶ π. ἦθος Id.*V.*877; ἀθληταί Luc.*Hist.Conscr.*8, cf. *AP*7.37 (Diosc.) (rejected by Hom. in favour of φήγινος for reasons of euphony, acc. to Phld.*Po.*2.9).

**πρῑνο-βάλᾰνος** [βᾰ], ὁ, f.l. for πρίνου βαλάνους (cf. Orib.*Fr.*143), Paul.Aeg.3.62. **-κοκκα**, τά, *galls of the kermes-oak*, *Gloss.*

**πρινοκόπος**· κοπῶν, Hsch.

**πρῖνος**, ἡ, Arat.1047, Dsc.1.106.2 (also ὁ, Amphis 38; both ὁ and ἡ in Thphr., cf. *HP*3.16.1, 3.6.4):—*holm-oak*, *Quercus Ilex*, Hes.*Op.* 436, Ar.*Ra.*859, Theoc.5.95, Call.*Iamb.*1.261. 2. *kermes-oak*, *Quercus coccifera*, Eup.14, Amphis l.c.; ἡ π. τὸν φοινικοῦν κόκκον [φέρει] Thphr.*HP*3.7.3, cf. *Sign.*45; πρίνοιο..ἄκανθαι Arat.1122. (Heterocl. gen. πρινός is f.l. in Simon.54.)

**πρῑν-ώδης**, ες, *tough as oak*, θυμός Ar.*V.*383. ✱ **-ών**, ῶνος, ὁ, *ilex-grove*, *IG*$1^2$.328.1 (dub.), *Gloss.*

**πρῑόν-ιον**, τό, Dim. of πρίων, Ph.*Bel.*67.30. **-ῖτις**, ιδος, ἡ, = κέστρον I. 1, Aret.*CA* 2.8, Alex.Trall.11.1; = ἡμιονῖτις II, Orib.*Fr.* 63. **-ώδης**, ες, *like a saw, serrated*, Thphr.*HP*1.10.5; κῶλα *AP* 7.196 (Mel.); σχήματα Clytus 1; in form **πριονοειδής**, Gal.2.737. Adv. -δῶς Dsc.1.108, al. [ῑ in *AP* l.c.] **-ωτός**, ή, όν, (as if from πριονόω) *made like a saw, jagged, serrated*, στόμια Ar.*Fr.*58; [τοῦ κρανίου] τὸ π. μέρος ῥαφὴ [καλεῖται] Arist.*HA*516$^a$15; π. δράκοντες *with serrated crests*, Philostr.*VA*3.7; π. τῇ λοφιᾷ Philostr.Jun.*Im.* 4; ἡ π. τειχοποιΐα, of a warlike engine, Ph.*Bel.*83.8.

**πρῑόω**, = πρίω, only in 3 sg. subj. πριῷ, *Tab.Heracl.*1.129; pf. part. Pass. πεπριωμένος Hp.*VC*20; cf. πρίωμα, ἀπρίωτος, διαπρίωσις, διαπριωτός.

**πρισγεῖες**, v. πρεσβεύς.

**πρῖσ-ις**, εως, ἡ, (πρίω) *sawing*, Arist.*PA*645$^b$17, Thphr.*HP*5.5.4, Heliod.ap.Orib.47.14.3. 2. in cranial surgery, *trephining*, Hp.*VC*9, 21. II. π. ὀδόντων *grinding* of the teeth, from anger, Plu.2.458d (pl.); or as an effect of disease, Hp.*Prorrh.*1.48. ✱ **-μα**, ατος, τό, *anything sawn, sawdust*, Thphr.*HP*5.6.3, *AP*11.207 (Lucill.), *Gp.*4. 15.9; π. λωτοῦ Dsc.*Eup.*2.50; μαρμάρου Aët.12.64; *rotten wood*, Dsc. 1.66. 2. *wound resulting from trephining with a saw*, ἰῆσθαι ὡς π. Hp.*Morb.*2.15. II. Geom., *prism*, Euc.11*Def.*13. **-μάτιον**, τό, Dim. of foreg. II, Procl.*Hyp.*4.88. **-μᾰτοκαύστης**, ου, ὁ, *slow-burning fire of sawdust*, Ps.-Democr.Alch.p.52 B.:— **-μᾰτόκαυστος**, ον, *forming such a fire*, ἄνθρακες Zos.Alch.p.143 B. ✱ **-μός**, ὁ, *gripping tightly*, Hsch. (pl.). **-τήρ**, ῆρος, ὁ, (πρίω) *saw*, Aret.*CD* 1.2. 2. *sawyer*, πριστῆρες δαιτὸς ὀδόντες *App.Anth.*3.101. **-τηροειδής**, ές, *like a saw*, Lxx*Is.*41.15. **-της**, ου, ὁ, *sawyer*, *IG*$1^2$. 373.256, 374.82, *PCair.Zen.*754.3 (iii B.C.), Poll.7.114. b. metaph., *hairsplitter*, Sch.Ar.*V.*1348. 2. *saw* or *file*, Poll.7.113, Hsch. **-τικός**, ή, όν, *of* or *for sawing*, ξύλον Hero *Geom.*4.10; τέχνη Eustr. in *EN*296.8.

**πριστιν(άριος?)**, ὁ, dub. sens., perh. = Lat. *pistrinarius, miller*, *MAMA*3.667 (Corycus).

**πρίστις**, εως, ἡ, prob. *saw-fish*, *Pristis antiquorum*, Epich.59 (v. infr.), *AP*7.506.10 (Leon.), Polycharm.1, Opp.*H.*1.370, Ael. *NA*9.49; coupled with βοῦς (v. βοῦς III) but distd. from δελφίς, φάλαινα and other animals which have a blow-hole instead of gills in Arist.*HA*566$^b$3. (πρῆστις is read in Epich. l.c., Opp. l.c. (v.l.

πρίστις), Ael. l.c., Suid., but πρίστις in Arist., Polycharm., *AP* ll. cc. and *pristis* is the Lat. form, Plin.*HN*9.4,41; the spelling πρῆστις was perh. due to the idea that it was a 'spouter'; there was further a supposed connexion between πρίω and πρήθω; πρίεται· φυσοῦται, Hsch., cf. *EM*687.39; v. πρίω II. 2 fin.) **II.** *ship of war*, prob. from its shape, Plb.18.1.1, 16.2.9 (pl.). **III.** a kind of *cup*, also from the shape, π., τραγέλαφος κτλ. Diph.80. **IV.** ornamental part of a surgical machine, Orib.49.4.42. **V.** a stone-mason's implement, *IG*1².313.130; gen. pl. πριστίω[ν] dub. sens. in ib.4²(1).118.15 (Epid., iii B.C.).

**πριστός**, ή, όν, *sawn*, ἐλέφας Od.18.196, 19.564; π. λόγχης ῥινήματα E.*Fr.*724; λίθος, of marble, J.*AJ*8.5.2; of a comb, π. ψήκτρης κνῆσμα *AP*6.233 (Maec.).

**πρίω**, imper. of ἐπριάμην, v. *πρίαμαι.

**πρίω** (later πρίζω, πριόω, qq. v.), imper. πρῖε S.*Fr.*897, Ar.*Ra.*927: impf. ἔπριον (ἐξ-) Th.7.25: aor. ἔπρῖσα Hp.*VC*14, Th.4.100: pf. πέπρῖκα (ἐμ-) D.S.17.92:—**Med.**, Babr.28.8, Luc.*DMeretr.*12.2:—**Pass.**, fut. πρισθήσομαι Aen.Tact.19: aor. ἐπρίσθην Hp.*Epid.*5.16, 27: pf. πέπρισμαι Id.*VC*15, Dsc.4.65, (δια-) Pl.*Smp.*193a, (ἐκ-) Ar.*Pax* 1135 (dub.):—*saw*, π. δίχα *saw* asunder, Th.4.100; π. τὸν ἐλέφαντα Luc.*Hist.Conscr.*51: abs., prob. in Ar.*V.*694:—Pass., κέρατα ὅταν πρισθῇ Plu.2.953b; χειρὸς..πριομένης *cut, abraded*, Opp.*H.*3.315. **2.** in surgery, *trephine*, Hp.*VC*12, al., *Epid.* ll. cc. **3.** pf. part. Pass. πεπρισμένος *serrated*, Dsc.4.65. **II.** π. ὀδόντας *grind* or *gnash* the teeth, in disease, Hp.*Prog.*3; esp. with rage, μὴ πρῖε τοὺς ὀδ. Ar.*Ra.*927; τὰς σιαγόνας πρίων Babr.96.3:—Med., Luc.*DMeretr.*12.2. **2.** generally, *bite*, ὀδόντι πρῖε τὸ στόμα S. *Fr.*897; [ἀμίαι] πρίουσι Opp.*H.*2.575: metaph., θυμὸν ὀδὰξ πρίοντες Id.*C.*4.139; ἐπὶ οἱ πρῖεν χόλον *gnashed* fury against him, A.R.4.1671:—Pass., *to be irritated, provoked*, τινι *by* or *at* a thing, πριομένα κάλλει Γανυμήδεος *AP*9.77 (Antip. Thess.); ἔνδοθεν δὲ πρίεται Men.902; but μὴ πρίου is prob. f.l. for μὴ πρήθου (cj. Bgk.) in Babr. 28.8. **3.** *cut off* syllables, Anon.Rhythm.*Oxy.*220 viii 3. **III.** *seize as with the teeth, grip, bind fast*, ζωστῆρι πρισθεὶς ἱππικῶν ἐξ ἀντύγων S.*Aj.*1030, cf. ἐκ I. 6. [ῑ: ĭ only in later Poets, ἀπέπρĭσε *AP*11.14 (Ammian.).]

**πρίωμα**, ατος, τό, = πρίσμα, Hsch.

❋ **πρίων** (A), ὁ, gen. πρίονος S.*Tr.*699:—*saw*, *IG*1².313.129, S.*Tr.*699, *Fr.*797, Cratin.437 (pl.), Lxx *Am.*1.3, Plu.2.654f; π. ὀδοντωτός, opp. π. μαχαιρωτός (toothless *saw* for cutting stone), Gal. 18(2).331; ὀδόντων π. *saw* of teeth, i.e. *jagged row*, *AP*7.401 (Crin.): abs., *serrated ridge of hills*, Spanish *sierra*, Lxx *Ju.*3.9; ὁ καλούμενος Π. Plb.7.15.6, cf. 1.85.7; λόφοι πάντοθεν ὀξεῖς οἷα πρίονες App.*Ill.*25, cf. Str.14.1.4. **2.** *Saw*, nickname of a timber-merchant, *Com.Adesp.*823. **3.** *cylindrical saw, trephine*, Hp.*VC*21. (Oxyt. acc. to Phot., thus differing from part. πρίων, but parox. acc. to Hdn.Gr.1.20.) [ῑ Trag. and Com., also Opp.*H.*5.199; ĭ in later Poets, dat. pl. πρĭόνεσσι Nic.*Th.*52, cf. *AP*6.204 (Leon.).]

❋ **πρίων** (B), ὁ, Com. Noun, from πρίω, imper. of ἐπριάμην, with a pun upon πρίων (A), χὼ π. ἀπῆν *that rasping word, buy..*, Ar.*Ach.* 36; hence πρίων· ἀγοράζων, Hsch.

**πρίωσις** [ῑ], ιος, ἁ, *sawing*, *IG*4²(1).109 ii 153 (Epid., iii B.C.).

❋ **πρό**, *before, forth*:

**A.** PREP. WITH GENIT.: **I.** of Place, *before, in front of*, ἠγερέθοντο π. ἄστεος Od.24.468, cf. Il.15.351, etc.; π. πτόλιος δεδαϊγμένον 19.292; κείνους κιχησόμεθα π. πυλάων 10.126, cf. 6.80, etc.; φύλοπις αἰνὴ ἕστηκε π. νεῶν 18.172; πυρὰ φαίνετο Ἰλιόθι π. 8.561, cf. 10.12, Od.8.581, etc.; κλαγγὴ γεράνων πέλει οὐρανόθι π. Il.3.3; π. τειχέων Pi.*O.*13.56; ἔμπροσθε π. (v.l.) τῆς ἀκροπόλιος, ὄπισθε δὲ τῶν πυλέων Hdt.8.53, cf. 9.52; π. δόμων, π. δωμάτων, *in front of*, i.e. *outside* the house, Pi.*P.*2.18, 5.96, etc.; π. θυρῶν S.*El.*109 (anap.), etc.; τὴν π. τοῦ Ἡραίου νῆσον *before* or *off* the Heraeum, Th.3.75, cf. 7.22; π. ποδός, v. πούς I. 4a; π. χειρῶν *at* hand, S.*Ant.*1279, E.*Rh.*274, dub. in *Tr.*1207; π. τῶν ὀφθαλμῶν προφαίνεσθαι Aeschin. 2.148. **2.** with Vbs. of motion, π. δ' ἄρ' αὐτῶν κύνες ἤϊσαν Od. 19.435, cf. Il.23.115; π. Ἀχαιῶν ἄγγελος ἥκει 10.286, cf. 13.693; π. ἔθεν κλονέοντα φάλαγγας 5.96. **3.** *before, in front of*, for the purpose of shielding or guarding, π. Τρώων ἑσταότ' Il.24.215: hence, *in defence of*, μάχεσθαι..π. τε παίδων καὶ π. γυναικῶν 8.57, cf. 4.156, 373, Hdt.8.74, etc.; ὀλέσθαι π. πόληος, Lat. *pro patria mori*, Il.22. 110; π. τῆς Σπάρτης ἀποθνήσκειν Hdt.7.134, cf. 172, 9.72, E.*Alc.*18, 645, etc.; π. τοῦ θανόντος..ἔθεσθ' ἐπιστροφήν S.*OT*134; διακινδυνεῦσαι π. βασιλέως X.*Cyr.*8.8.4; βουλεύεσθαι, πράττειν π. τινός, ib.1.6.42, 4.5.44, cf. *Mem.*2.4.7; π. τοξευμάτων *as a defence against* arrows, Id. *An.*7.8.18: hence also, *for, on behalf of, instead of*, ἀγρυπνῆσαι π. τινῶν ib.7.6.36, cf. *Leg.Gort.*1.43; of an advocate, π. τῶνδε φωνεῖν S.*OT*10, cf. *OC*811; ὅτι δέ κ' αὐτὸς π. ϝιαυτοῦ [ἀμάρτη] whatever offence he commits *of* his own *volition*, Kohler-Ziebarth *Stadtrecht von Gortyn* p.34. **4.** π. ὁδοῦ ἐγένοντο *further on* the road, i.e. *forwards, onward*, Il.4.382, cf. Ael.*NA*3.16, 7.29 (v. φροῦδος): also to denote *distance*, π. πολλοῦ τῆς πόλεως D.H.9.35; π. τριάκοντα σταδίων *at a distance of* 30 stades, Str.8.6.24. **5.** π. ἠοῦς, π. ἑσπέρης τοῦ βωμοῦ, east*wards*, west*wards of..*, *IG*7.235.45 (Orop., iv B.C.). **II.** of Time, *before*, π. γάμοιο Od.15.524; ἦῶθι π. 5.469; π. ὁ τοῦ ἐνόησεν one *before* the other, Il.10.224; more freq. in later writers, π. τῶν Τρωικῶν Th.1.3, cf. 1.1; π. τοῦ θανεῖν S.*Ant.*883; π. τοῦ θανάτου Pl.*Phd.*57a; π. τοῦ λοιμοῦ Id.*Smp.*201d; π. δείπνου X.*Cyr.*5.5.39; π. ἡμέρας ib.4.5.14; π. τοῦ χρῆσθαι *before* one uses it, Id.*Mem.*2.6.6; π. μοίρας τῆς ἐμῆς *before* my doom, A.*Ag.*1266; π. τῆς εἱμαρμένης Antipho 1.21; π. τοῦ καθήκοντος χρόνου Aeschin.3.126, cf. 124; π. πολλοῦ long *before*, Hdt.7.130, etc.; π. μικροῦ, π. ὀλίγου, Plu.*Pomp.*73, App.*BC*2.116; ὀλίγον π. τούτων Th.2.8; τὸ π. τοῦ (v.l. τούτου) ib.15; π. τοῦ (sts. written προτοῦ) A.*Ag.*1204, Hdt.1.122, 5.83, Ar.*Th.*418, Pl.*Smp.*173a; ὁ π. τοῦ χρόνος A.*Eu.*462, Th.2.58, etc.; π. τοῦ ἤ, = πρὶν ἤ, *IG*7.2225.22 (Thisbe); οἱ π. ἡμῶν γενόμενοι Isoc.13.19; οἱ π. ἐμοῦ Th.1.97. **2.** in later writers freq. with Numerals, π. τριάκοντα ἡμερῶν thirty days *before*, Ael.*NA*5.52; π. μιᾶς ἡμέρας Plu.*Caes.*63; π. ἐνιαυτοῦ Id.2.147e; π. δυεῖν ἡμερῶν ἢ ἐτελεύτα Id.*Sull.*37: freq. c. dupl. gen., π. δύο ἐτῶν τοῦ σεισμοῦ, π. δύο ὡρῶν τῆς ἐπιβολῆς, Lxx *Am.*1.1, Dsc.1.64; π. ἓξ ἡμερῶν τοῦ πάσχα, π. μιᾶς ἡμέρας τῶν γενεθλίων, *Ev.Jo.*12.1, Plu. 2.717d; π. πολλοῦ τῆς ἑορτῆς Luc.*Sat.*14. **b.** in rendering Roman dates, τῇ π. μιᾶς Νωνῶν Ὀκτωβρίων, = *pridie Non. Oct.*, Plu.2.203a, etc. **III.** in other relations: **1.** of Preference, *before, rather than*, κέρδος αἰνῆσαι π. δίκας to praise sleight *before* right, Pi.*P.*4.140, cf. Pl.*R.*361e; πᾶν δὴ βουλόμενοι σφίσι εἶναι π. τῆς παρεούσης λύπης anything *before, rather than*, their actual trouble, Hdt.7.152 (so, *in order to avoid*, π. τοῦ δεινοτάτου D.54.19); πᾶν π. τοῦ δουλεῦσαι ἐπεξελθεῖν Th.5.100, cf. 4.59; ἑλέσθαι, αἱρεῖσθαι, or κρῖναί τι π. τινός to choose one *before* another, Id.5.36, Pl.*R.*366b, *Phlb.*57e; π. πολλοῦ ποιήσασθαι to esteem *above* much, i.e. very highly, Isoc.5.138; π. πολλῶν χρημάτων τιμήσασθαί τι Th.1.33, cf. 6.10; π. ἄλλων *more than* others, Pl.*Mx.*249e (v.l.), cf. A.*Th.*1002; δυσδαίμων..π. πασᾶν γυναικῶν ib.927 (codd., lyr.); π. πάντων θεῶν τῇ Ἑστίᾳ πρώτῃ προθύειν Pl *Cra.* 401d: after a Comp. it is redundant, ἡ τυραννὶς π. ἐλευθερίης ἀσπαστότερον Hdt.1.62, cf. 6.12, Pl.*Ap.*28d, *Cri.*54b, *Phd.*99a; for ἤ after ἄλλος, οὐδεὶς ἄλλος π. σεῦ Hdt.3.85, cf. 7.3. **2.** of Cause or Motive, *for, from*, π. φόβοιο *for* fear, Il.17.667; ἀθλεύων π. ἄνακτος toiling *before the face of*, i.e. *in* his *service*, 24.734; π. τῶνδε there*fore*, S.*El.*495 (lyr.).

**B.** POSITION: words may be put between π. and its case, Il.23. 115; but it does not follow its case, exc. after Ep. forms in -θι, Ἰλιόθι πρό, οὐρανόθι πρό, ἠῶθι πρό (v. supr.).

**C.** πρό, abs. as ADV.: **I.** of Place, *before*, opp. ἐπί (*after*), Il. 13.799, 800; *before, in front*, 15.360; *forth, forward*, ἐκ δ' ἄγαγε π. φόωσδε 19.118; χωρεῖν π. δόμων to come *forth* from, S.*Tr.*960 (lyr.); ἄγειν τινὰ π. δόμων E.*Hec.*59 (anap.); γῆν π. γῆς ἐλαύνομαι I am driven *on* from one land to another, A.*Pr.*682; διώκειν γῆν π. γῆς Ar.*Ach.*235. **II.** of Time, *before*, πρό οἱ εἴπομεν Od.1.37; *earlier*, τά τ' ἐσσόμενα π. τ' ἐόντα Hes.*Th.*32, 38. **III.** when joined with other Preps., ἀποπρό, διαπρό, ἐπιπρό, περιπρό, προπρό, it strengthens the first Prep., or adds to it the notion of *forward, forth*.

**D.** πρό IN COMPOS. **I.** with Substs., to denote **1.** *position before* or *in front*, πρόδομος, προάστιον, πρόθυρον, προπύλαια, etc. **2.** *priority of rank*, πρόεδρος, προεδρία, etc.: also *priority of order*, προάγων, πρόλογος, προοίμιον, προπάτωρ, etc. **3.** standing *in* another's *place*, πρόμαντις, πρόξενος. **II.** with Adjs., to denote **1.** *proximity*, πρόχειρος; and *readiness*, πρόθυμος, πρόφρων. **2.** *away* (cf. III. 3 infr.), προθέλυμνος, πρόρριζος. **3.** *prematureness*, πρόμοιρος, πρώορος. **4.** *intensity*, πρόπας, πρόπαρ, προπάροιθε; so also πρόκακος, πρόπαλαι. **III.** with Verbs, **1.** of Place, *before, forwards*, προβαίνω, προβάλλω, προτίθημι, etc.: also, *before, in defence*, προκινδυνεύω, προμάχομαι, etc. **2.** *forth*, προέλκω, προφέρω. **b.** *publicly*, προγράφω, προειπεῖν, πρόκειμαι. **3.** *away*, προδίδωμι, προϊάλλω, προϊάπτω, προΐημι, προλείπω, προρέω, προτέμνω, προτρέπομαι, προφεύγω, προχέω. **4.** *in preference*, προαιροῦμαι, προτιμάω, etc. **5.** *before, beforehand*, προαισθάνομαι, προγίγνομαι, προκαταλαμβάνω, etc.; of *fore*sight, προνοέω, προοράω.

**E.** Etymology: cf. Lat. *prŏ-*, Slav. *pro-*, Skt. *pra-*, etc., in compounds.

**προαγγ-ελία**, ἡ, *previous announcement*, Ruf.Rh.p.401 H. **-έλλω**, *declare, announce beforehand*, X.*Cyr.*5.3.12; πόλεμον Plb.3.20.8; μάχην ἔσεσθαι X.*Cyr.*3.3.34:—Pass., Th.7.65; τὸν προαγγελέντα *Berl. Sitzb.*1927.170 (Cyrene). **-ελμα**, ατος, τό, *forewarning*, J.*BJ*1.3.5 (v.l.). ❋ **-ελος**, ον, *announcing beforehand*, c. gen., Musae. 164; πολέμοιο π. ἔργον Coluth.60. **II.** Subst., *harbinger*, Plu.2. 127d. **-ελσις**, εως, ἡ, *forewarning, early intimation*, τινος Th.1.137.

**προαγεύων**· προξενῶν, Hsch., cf. eund. s.v. προαγορεύσας (leg. προαγ⟨ωγ⟩εύων).

**προαγκτηριάζω**, *tie with a ligature beforehand*, Gal.12.521, Aspasia ap.Aët.16.102(112).

**προάγν-ευσις**, εως, ἡ, *purification before* [the mysteries], Sch.Ar. *Pl.*846. **-εύω**, pf. -ήγνευκα, *purify beforehand*, τὸ πλῆθος J.*BJ*4.3.12, cf. Arr.*Epict.*3.21.14.

**προαγνοέω**, *to be ignorant of before*, *PTeb.*23.12 (Pass., ii B.C.), f.l. in Gal.2.231.

**προάγνῡμι**, *break before* or *in advance*, πρὸ δὲ κύματ' ἔαξεν Od.5.385.

**προᾰγορ-άζω**, *buy beforehand, forestall*, Cod.Just.12.37.19.2. **-ανομέω**, *to be* ἀγορανόμος, i.e. *aedile, before*, D.C.53.33. ❋ **-αστής**, οῦ, ὁ, *forestaller, regrater*, *Gloss.* **-ευμα**, ατος, τό, *prophecy*, Chio *Ep.*4.1 (pl.); π. Σιβύλλειον App.*BC*2.110. **-ευσις**, εως, ἡ, *foretelling*, Arist.*Po.*1454ᵇ5; *prophecy, prediction*, Diogenian.Epicur.4.18 (pl.), J.*Ap.*1.29, *BJ*2.8.12 (pl.), Plu.*Sull.*7 (pl.); *prognosis*, Hp.*Aph.*2.19 (pl., v.l.). **II.** *proclamation*, App.*BC*1.26; *warning, prohibition*, J.*AJ*18.8.2, 18.9.2, Poll.8.66. **-ευτέον**, *one must say first*, Arist.*SE*176ᵇ27. **-ευτής**, οῦ, ὁ, *foreteller*, gloss on πρηγορεύων, Hsch. **-ευτικός**, ή, όν, *prophetic*, φωνή Poll.1.15; τῶν μελλόντων Chrysipp.ap.Diogenian.Epicur.4.40; κινδύνων Artem.1.66: ἡ -κή (sc. τέχνη) *the art of divination*, Poll.1.19. **-εύω**, aor. -ηγόρευσα Hdt.1.74, 125: pf. -ηγόρευκα D.11.20

(v.l. -ευσε; but in Att. fut. is προερῶ, aor. προεῖπον, pf. προείρηκα):—**Pass.**, fut. (in med. form) X.*Eq.Mag.*2.7: pf. -ηγόρευμαι Id.*Mem.*1.2.[35]:—*tell beforehand*, τι Th.1.68: c. inf., *declare beforehand that*.., Hdt.1.74,91; π. ὅτι.. Th.2.13, X.*Cyr.*3.1.3; ὡς.. ib.7.5.34; *advise beforehand*, πολλοῖς π. τὰ μὲν ποιεῖν τὰ δὲ μὴ ποιεῖν Id.*Mem.*1.1.4, cf. Pl.*Lg.*907d. **2.** *foretell, prophesy*, τὸ μέλλον X.*Smp.*4.5. **II.** *declare* or *proclaim publicly*, τι Hdt.7.10.δ',8.83; τινί τι Id.1.153; ἰσονομίην ὑμῖν π. Id.3.142; πόλεμον (with or without τινι) Th.1.131, D.11.20, etc.: c. inf., Pl.*Cri.*51d: esp. of a herald or public officer, Hdt.3.61,62; also, *have* a thing *proclaimed by herald*, ὑπὸ κήρυκος π. Id.9.98 (though ἀναγορεύειν was properly the word for heralds, προαγορεύειν for magistrates, X.*An.*2.2.20). **2.** *order publicly*, ταῦτα Hdt.1.22: c. inf., ib.21; π. ὑμῖν παρεῖναι ib.125, cf. 6.37; π. τοῖς πολίταις μὴ κινεῖν.. *forbid* them to.., Pl.*R.*426b, etc.; ὁ ἱερεὺς π. καὶ ἀπαγορεύει.. μὴ κόπτειν *IG*2$^2$.1362.2: without a dat., τοὺς Ἕλληνας π. αὐτονόμους ἀφιέναι Th.1.140, cf. X.*HG*7.4.38:—Pass., γυμνάζεσθαι προαγορεύεται..ἅπασι Id.*Lac.*12.5, etc.; τὰ προηγορευμένα Id.*Mem.*1.2.[35]. **b.** *give public notice* to persons accused of murder that they are excommunicated, π. εἴργεσθαι τῶν νομίμων Antipho 6.34, Arist.*Ath.*57.2, cf. Antipho 5.10, Isoc.4.157, D.47.69: abs., Antipho 6.48; τὴν πρόρρησιν π. Pl.*Lg.*871c. **c.** *serve notice on* persons to appear for trial, π. εἰς τρίτην ἀγορὰν παρεῖναι Plu.*Cor.*18. **III.** *forestall* an anticipated argument, Arist.*SE*174$^b$30.

**προᾱγορέω**, Dor. for προηγορέω, *IG*14.952 (Agrigentum).

**προαγρέω**, Aeol. for προαιρέω, pf. part. Med. προαγρήμμενος *having decided*, *IGRom.*4.1302.6 (Cyme, i B.C./i A.D.).

**προαγρυπνέω**, *keep watch for*, ὑμῶν Arr.*An.*7.9.9.

**προάγω** [ᾰ], fut. -άξω: pf. Act. προῆχα D.19.18, 25.8, Paus.3.11.10:—**Med.**, v. infr.: pf. Pass. in med. sense, v. infr. I.7:—*lead forward* or *onward*, μιν ἐς τὰ οἰκία Hdt.3.148, etc.; *escort on their way*, Id.8.132; τοὺς πεζοὺς οὐ πολλὴν ὁδόν X.*Cyr.*3.3.23:—Pass., *to be led on*, προαγομένης τῆς πόλεως ἐπὶ συμφοράς And.2.9. **2.** *carry on*, αἱμασιάν D.55.27; *produce*, Plot.3.7.6:—Pass., [τάξις] εἰς ὀξὺ προηγμένη *brought* to a point, Arr.*Tact.*16.8. **b.** *bring on* in age, etc., προῆγεν αὐτὸν ὁ χρόνος εἰς ὥραν X.*Cyr.*1.4.4:—Pass., ἐπὶ πλείω προῆκται τῆς κατ' ἰητρικὴν ἐπιμελείας *belong to* more *advanced* medical study, Hp.*Medic.*13. **c.** *increase, raise* a dose, ἐπὶ ἓξ κοτύλας Ruf.*Fr.*68 (v.l. προσ-). **3.** *bring forward*, νεκρὸν εἰς τὸ φανερόν, τι εἰς τὸ πρόσθεν, Pl.*Lg.*960a, *Plt.*262c; τὴν φύσιν εἰς φῶς πᾶσιν Id.*Ep.*341d; βουλὴν ἀπόρρητον εἰς φῶς ἡλίου Plu.2.552d; οἱ προαγαγόντες εἰς φῶς, = οἱ γονεῖς, Poll.3.8, cf. Hld.7.23; *call up* an apparition, Thessal. in *Cat.Cod.Astr.*8(3).137. **b.** *bring before* a tribunal, *SIG*826*G*22 (ii B.C., Pass.); π. δάνειον *POxy.*1562.14 (iii A.D.). **4.** *lead on, induce, persuade*, δόλῳ τινὰς π. Hdt.9.90; ὡς ἡ χρεία προάγει Th.3.59: with inf. added, κινδυνεύειν τινὰ π. ib.45; ἐγὼ προήγαγον ὑμᾶς ἄξια τῶν προγόνων φρονεῖν D.18.206: with Preps., π. θυμὸν ἐς ἀμπλακίην Thgn.386 (nisi leg. παράγει); τινὰς ἐς λόγους Pl.*Ti.*22a; εἰς μῖσος X.*HG*3.5.2; τὰς συγγενείας εἰς ἔχθραν, εἰς ἄνοιαν τὴν πόλιν, Isoc.4.174, 8.121; εἰς ὀργὴν ἢ φθόνον ἢ ἔλεον Arist.*Rh.*1354$^a$25; εἰς γέλωτα ib.1415$^a$37; τινὰ ἐπ' ἀρετήν, opp. προτρέψασθαι, X.*Mem.*1.4.1; πάντας ἐκ..πολέμων ἐπὶ τὴν ὁμόνοιαν Isoc.5.141; πρὸς..κακίας ὑπερβολήν D.20.36; ἐμαυτὸν εἰς ἀπέχθειαν Id.23.1:—Med., ἐς γέλωτα προαγαγέσθαι τινά *move* one to laughter, Hdt.2.121.δ'; τὴν ὑγρότητα αὐτῶν τοῦ ἤθους εἰς ἔλεον Lycurg.33; προαξόμεθ'..εἰς ἀνάγκην D.5.14: c. inf., τοῦτο πολεμίους προάγεται ἁμαρτάνειν X.*Eq.Mag.*5.15, cf. Aeschin.3.117, Arist.*Pol.*1270$^b$2:—freq. in Pass., προαχθέντας εἰς φιλοποσίαν X.*Mem.*1.2.22; εἰς τοῦτ' ὀργῆς προήχθησαν ὥστε.. Isoc.20.8: c. inf., οὐ γὰρ ἔγωγε προαχθείην ἂν εἰπεῖν D.21.79, cf. 18.269, Arist.*Ph.*194$^a$31; προάγεται λαλεῖν Men.164; πολλὰ προηγμένον πρᾶξαι D.5.23, etc. **5.** *carry forward, advance*, π. τὴν πόλιν *lead* it *on to power*, Th.6.18, D.19.18; π. αὐτὴν (sc. τὴν ἀρχὴν) ἐς τόδε Th.1.75, cf. Arist.*Pol.*1274$^a$10; λόγοισι προάγει.., ἔργοισι δ' οὐδὲ κινεῖ Cratin.300; οὕτω μέχρι πόρρω προήγαγον [τὴν ἔχθραν] *carried* it so far, D.18.163; π. [τὰ πράγματα] ἐπὶ τὸ βέλτιον Id.*Prooem.*38, etc.; τὴν πραγματείαν π. εἰς τὸ πρόσθεν *promote* the study, Aristox.*Fr.Hist.*81; [τὰ μαθήματα] Arist.*Metaph.*985$^b$24; τὰς τέχνας Id.*SE*183$^b$29, cf. *Po.*1449$^a$13; π. καὶ διαρθρῶσαι τὰ καλῶς ἔχοντα τῇ περιγραφῇ *carry on* and complete.., Id.*EN*1098$^a$22, cf. *Pol.*1282$^b$35:—Med., ἐς τοῦτο [τὰ Περσέων πρήγματα] προηγάγοντο Hdt.7.50:—Pass., *increase, become rife*, D.19.266. **b.** of persons, *promote* or *prefer* to honour, δᾶμος εἰς ἀριστοκρατίαν ἄνδρας αἱ προάγοι καλῶς Isyll.3, cf. Plb.12.13.6, etc.; τινὰς εἰς δόξαν, ἐφ' ἡγεμονίας, Plu.*Them.*7, *Galb.*20, etc.; ἐπὶ μέγα προαχθῆναι Luc.*Alex.*55. **c.** *prefer* in the way of choice, esp. in Pass., αἱ προηγμέναι φυλαί J.*AJ*4.8.44: προηγμένος *distinguished, outstanding*, ὥρα Philostr.Jun.*Im.Praef.* **6.** in Stoic Philos., of things neither good nor bad but *promoted* or *advanced* above the zero point of indifference, προηγμένον..ὃ ἀδιάφορον ⟨ὂν⟩ ἐκλεγόμεθα Zeno *Stoic.*1.48, cf. Aristo ib.83, Chrysipp.ib.3.28, etc.; cf. ἀποπροάγω. **7.** in pf. Pass. with med. sense, οὕτω προῆκται τοὺς παῖδας ὥστε.. *has had* them *brought up* in such a way that.., D.54.23: also in pass. sense, ἐπιεικῶς τοῖς ἔθεσι προηγμένοι Arist.*EN*1180$^a$8. **8.** *pronounce* a discourse, κατὰ θεωρίαν π. πάντα Philostr.*VS*2.9.3; αἱ κατὰ σχῆμα προηγμέναι τῶν ὑποθέσεων ib.2.4.2. **II.** intr., *lead the way, go before*, πρόαγε δή Pl.*Phdr.*227c; σοῦ προάγοντος ἐγὼ ἐφεσπόμην Id.*Phd.*90b, cf. X.*An.*6.5.6, etc.: with acc. added, προῆγε πολὺ πάντας dub. in J.*BJ*6.1.6 (leg. πάντων): of a commander, *lead an advance, push forward*, Plb.2.65.1, 3.35.1, etc. **2.** metaph., ὁ προάγων λόγος the *preceding* discourse, Pl.*Lg.*719a; αἱ π. γραφαί J.*AJ*19.6.2; ὁ π. μήν *PSI*5.450.59 (ii A.D.). **3.** *go on, advance*, ἐπὶ πολὺ προάγει τῇ τε βίᾳ καὶ τῇ ὠμότητι Decr.ap.D.18.181; ἐκ τῶν ἀσαφεστέρων ἐπὶ τὰ σαφέστερα Arist.*Ph.*184$^a$19; πόρρω π. ὕβρεως Clearch.6 (τὸ ἔργον προῆγε(ν) is v.l. for προσῆγε in Hdt.9.92); πᾶς ὁ προάγων καὶ μὴ μένων ἐν τῇ διδαχῇ 2*Ep.Jo.*9: of Time, τῆς ἡμέρας ἤδη προαγούσης Plb.18.8.1; *reach, attain to*, εἰς τὰς ὀκτὼ μυριάδας Phld.*Ind.Sto.*32. **4.** *excel*, τινος Dsc.1.71 (v.l. προέχει); ἀρχαιότητι J.*Ap.*2.15.

**προᾰγωγ-εία**, ἡ, *pandering, procuring*, Pl.*Tht.*150a (-ία codd.), X.*Smp.*4.61, Aeschin.1.14, Arist.*EN*1131$^a$7. **-εύς**, έως, ὁ, = προαγωγός, dub. in D.C.46.6. **-εύω**, *prostitute* or *procure*, ἐλεύθερον παῖδα ἢ γυναῖκα Lex ap.Aeschin.1.14, cf. Ps.-Phoc.177, Plu.*Sol.*23:—Pass., Theopomp.Hist.240. **2.** metaph., αὐτὸς ἑαυτὸν π. ὀφθαλμοῖς Ar.*Nu.*980; π. τινὰ Προδίκῳ X.*Smp.*4.62. ⊛ **-ή**, ἡ, *leading on, promotion*, Posidon.36 J., *Arch.Pap.*6.18; *rank, eminence*, Plb.6.8.4 (pl.), 15.34.5; ἡ χιλιάρχων τάξις καὶ π. D.S.18.48; προαγωγῆς τυχεῖν ἐν τῇ αὐλῇ Arr.*Epict.*4.13.14, cf. Plu.2.466c (pl.), *Cat.Cod.Astr.*2.198 (pl.); ἐν π. τινὰ ποιεῖσθαι *promote* him, J.*AJ*15.1.1: metaph., ὁ θεωρητικὸς βίος π. ἀγῶνος τελειοτέρου Ph.1.551, cf. 2.42. **II.** *progress, prosperity*, *OGI*223.9 (Erythrae, iii B.C.). **III.** *preference*, *Stoic.*3.35. **-ία**, f.l. for προαγωγεία in codd. **-ικός**, ή, όν, *skilful in pandering*, Ptol.*Tetr.*163. **-ός**, όν, *leading on*, εἰς πειθώ Sch.S.*OT*14; πρὸς τὸ ἄμετρον Longin.32.7; π. τοῦ δήμου Poll.4.34. **2.** *producing, dispensing*, ὁ πάντων π., of God, Agath.3.19. **II.** Subst. *pander, pimp*, Ar.*V.*1028, *Ra.*1079, Aeschin.1.184, etc.: fem., *procuress*, ibid., Ar.*Th.*341. **2.** metaph., in good sense, X.*Smp.*4.64.

⊛ **προᾰγών**, ῶνος, ὁ, *a ceremonial parade of actors*, etc., *preceding dramatic contests* at Athens, Aeschin.3.67 (cf. Sch.ad loc.), *IG*2$^2$.780.16 (pl.), *Vit.Eur.*; title of play by Ar., cf. *Fr.*461, al. **2.** *preliminary contest*, προαγῶνας προαγωνιστέον Pl.*Lg.*796d, cf. *IG*12(9).189.23 (Eretria, iv B.C.), Philostr.*Gym.*11: metaph., προαγῶνας ἀεὶ κατασκευάζων αὑτῷ τῆσδε τῆς γραφῆς D.22.59. (προάγων acc. to Hdn.Gr.1.24, 2.729.)

**προᾰγων-ίζομαι**, *fight before*, ἐξ ὧν προηγώνισθε from *the contests you have before had*, Th.4.126; π. περί τινος D.S.19.26; οὐ προηγωνισμένη δύναμις not *having been engaged before*, Hdn.3.7.6:—Pass., οἱ προηγωνισμένοι ἀγῶνες Plu.*Arist.*12; τὰ μὲν οὖν τῶν λόγων προηγώνιστο αὐτοῖς Luc.*Eun.*4. **II.** *fight in front of*, ἡγεμόνες τῶν ὑποτεταγμένων προαγωνιζόμενοι D.S.17.34; χώρα προαγωνιζομένη τῆς φάλαγγος ὅλης D.H.4.16: abs., Ph.2.379; *fight for* or *in defence of* another, ib.177, Plu.*Flam.*11, etc.; *plead in behalf of*, c. acc. cogn., π. Ἀθηναίων οὐ μικρὸν ἀγώνισμα Philostr.*VS*1.18.4. **-ισμα**, ατος, τό, *previous contest*, π. ναυμαχίας App.*Syr.*22, cf. Dexipp.Hist.*Fr.*26 J. (pl.). **-ιστέον**, *one must engage beforehand in*, προαγῶνας Pl.*Lg.*796d. **-ιστής**, οῦ, ὁ, *one who fights for* another, *champion*, Str.16.4.25, Ph.2.312,542, Luc.*Salt.*14, Jul.*Or.*2.87a; π. τῆς δημοκρατίας Poll.4.34.

**προαδῐκέω**, *to be the first in wrong-doing*, Arist.*Rh.Al.*1425$^b$6, Ph.2.128:—Pass., *to be wronged before* or *first*, Decr.ap.D.18.181, Aeschin.3.133, etc.

**προαδῠνᾰτέω**, *to be already very weak*, v.l. for προεξαδυνατέω in Hp.*Prorrh.*1.8 (ap.Gal.16.531).

**προᾴδω**, *sing before, prelude*, Aeschin.2.163: c. acc., τὴν πόλιν προᾷσαι Him.*Or.*5.4:—Pass., στροφὴ προᾳσθεῖσα Poll.4.112.

**προαθετέω**, *reject as spurious first*, Sch.Od.2.322:—Pass., ib.1.185.

**προαθλέω**, = προαγωνίζομαι, Sch.Pi.*O.*8.71.

**προαθρέω**, *foresee*, Eust.86.41.

**προαθροίζω**, *gather* or *collect before*, χρήματα D.C.60.27:—Pass., Gal.4.590, Poll.2.204.

**προαθύροντες** (leg. **προσ-**)· προσπαίζοντες, Hsch.

**προαιδέομαι**, *owe* one *special respect, be under obligations* to one, ἤγειρον δωτίνας ἐκ τῶν πολίων, αἵτινές σφι προαιδέατό κού τι (Ion. 3 pl. plpf.) Hdt.1.61; τίς ἐστι.., τῷ ἐγὼ προαιδεῦμαι; Id.3.140.

**πρόαιθρον**, τό, *vestibule of a courtyard*, *PFlor.*56.14 (iii A.D.).

**προ-αικίζομαι**, Med., *maltreat beforehand*, J.*BJ*2.14.9. **-αινίσσομαι**, *hint* or *indicate before*, 1 aor. -ηνίξατο Heraclit.*All.*66.

**προαίρ-εσις**, εως, ἡ, *choosing* one thing *before* another, Pl.*Prm.*143c; *purpose, resolution*, π. καὶ πρᾶξις Id.*Def.*413a, cf. Arist.*EN*1094$^a$2; opp. ἀνάγκη, Isoc.1.10; ἐκ π. καὶ βουλήσεως D.44.57, cf. Arist.*PA*657$^b$1; ἡ κατὰ π. κίνησις Id.*Metaph.*1015$^a$33; τὰ κατὰ π. ἀδικήματα wrongs done *from malice prepense*, Lycurg.148; ζῆν κατὰ π., as a test of freedom, Arist.*Pol.*1280$^a$34; παρὰ τὴν π. contrary to *one's purpose*, Id.*Metaph.*1015$^a$27; as characteristic of moral action, ἡ π. βουλευτικὴ ὄρεξις τῶν ἐφ' ἡμῖν Id.*EN*1113$^a$10, cf. 1139$^a$23; *inclination*, χρῶ ὡς βούλει τῇ σεαυτοῦ π. Epicur.*Sent.Vat.*51; *motive*, κατὰ προαίρεσιν δακρύειν Hp.*Aph.*4.52. **2.** *purpose, plan*, or *scope* of action, τῇ π. τοῦ βίου D.23.141, 48.56; οὐδενὸς εὐδοκιμεῖ πράγματος ἡ π. Id.*Prooem.*50; ἐπὶ τῇ τοῦ πλεονεκτεῖν π. ζῆν Id.23.127; ἀναίδεια καὶ π. πονηρίας *deliberate* wickedness, Id.*Ep.*3.18; τῶν καλῶν ἔργων Zaleuc.ap.Stob.4.2.19: abs., *course of life, principle* of action, ἐν π. χρηστῇ καὶ βίῳ σώφρονι ζῆν D.*Ep.* l.c.; διὰ τὰς τέτταρας δραχμὰς ἀποβάλω τὴν π.; Strato Com.1.33: pl., *principles*, Isoc.1.9; αἱ κοιναὶ π. D.18.210, etc. **3.** in political language, *deliberate course of action, policy*, ἡ π. ἡ ἐμὴ καὶ ἡ πολιτεία ib.93; ἡ π. τῆς πολιτείας ib.192, cf. 19.27, Plb.3.8.5, 18.37.1, *OGI*763.50 (Milet., ii B.C.); *mode* of government, such as an oligarchy, D.13.8; ἡ π. τῆς πόλεως, opp. ἡ τύχη, Id.18.306; ἡ π. τῶν κοινῶν ib.292: pl., τὰς κοινὰς π. your public *principles, policy*, ib.210, cf. 206; ταῖς τοῦ δήμου π. Id.*Ep.*3.2. **4.** *department* of public life, πολλῶν προαιρέσεων οὐσῶν τῆς πολιτείας, τὴν περὶ τὰς Ἑλληνικὰς πράξεις εἰλόμην Id.18.59. **5.** *political party*, οἱ τῆς ἐκείνου π. Id.10.4. **b.** *sect* or *school* of music, philosophy, etc., Plu.2.1137b, Gal.18(2).658; αἱ ἐν φιλοσοφίᾳ π. Luc.*Demon*.4, etc. **6.** *conduct*, διὰ ταύτης τῆς π. Plb.18.3.3; ἀνεπίληπτος π. Id.14.2.14, cf. 30.8.1, 39.3.11. **7.** *character, reputation*, ἠστόχει τῆς σφετέρας π. had no regard for his own *reputation*, Id.7.14.3; ἀείμνηστον καὶ καλὴν ἔχει τὴν π. Id.9.9.10; καταξίως..τῆς τῶν ἀλειφομένων π. *Arch.Pap*.3.134 (Thera, iii/ii B.C.). **8.** *devotion, affection, goodwill*, τᾷ π. ἂν ἔχων τυγχάνει ἐς τὰν ἁμὰν πόλιν *SIG*721.30 (Crete, ii/i B.C.), cf. 593.4 (Perrhaebia, ii B.C.); ἀποδεξάμενον μετ' εὐνοίας τὴν τοῦ δήμου π. the *homage* of the people, ib.700.43 (Macedonia, ii B.C.); ἐπαινέσαι ἐπὶ τᾷ περὶ..τὰν τέχναν π. her *devotion* to her art, ib.738.11 (Delph., i B.C.), cf. 737.12 (i B.C.); = σπουδή, *zeal*, τὴν π. ἣν ὁ δῆμος..διατελεῖ ποιούμενος τῶν..ἐνδόξων ib.590.33 (Cos, ii B.C.). **9.** *expressed opinion, advice*, τὴν π. ἀποδεξάμενοι τοῦ λέγοντος Plb.29.3.9, cf. 2.42.4, 7.13.4, 7.14.1. **-ετέον**, *one must choose, prefer*, Pl.*R*.535a; θάνατον ἀντί τινος X.*Mem*.2.7.10. ※**-έτης**, ου, ὁ, *steward, keeper*, βιβλιοθήκης *BGU*362 viii 13 (iii A.D.), cf. *PLips*.123.19 (ii A.D.). **-ετικός**, ή, όν, *inclined to prefer, deliberately choosing*, τοῦ πλεονεκτεῖν Arist.*Pol*.1266$^{b}$37, cf. *EN*1137$^{b}$35; τῶν τοιούτων λόγων Id.*Metaph*.1025$^{a}$3. **2.** abs., *purposive, concerned with purpose*, ἔστιν ἄρα ἡ ἀρετὴ ἕξις π. Id.*EN*1106$^{b}$36; τῆς ψυχῆς τὸ πρακτικὸν καὶ π. *power of purposing, will*, Plu.*Cor*.32, etc.; π. ἐνέργειαι Ph.1.279; τὰ π., opp. τὰ ἀπροαίρετα, Arr.*Epict*.2.10.8; π. κίνησις Gal.5.520; π. νεῦρα *motor* nerves, Diagoras Cypr.ap.Erot. s.v. περόνας, Gal.2.739. Adv. **-κῶς** *of set purpose*, φιλόδωρος Ph.1.342, cf. Phld.*Rh*.2.52 S. **-ετός**, ή, όν, *deliberately chosen, purposed*, Arist.*EN*1113$^{a}$10, *Metaph*.1025$^{b}$24. Adv. **-τῶς** *Placit*.1.29.3, Gal.19.452. **II.** *appointed as representative*, in pl., ὑπὸ τᾶς πόλιος *SIG*241.133 (Delph., iv B.C.). ※**-έω**, fut. -ήσω Babr.108.26: aor. προεῖλον:—*bring forth, produce from one's stores*, προαιρούσαις λαθεῖν (prob. l.) ἄλφιτον, ἔλαιον κτλ. Ar.*Th*.419; ἰσχάδας Pherecr.68; τὸν σῖτον..ἐντεῦθεν προαιροῦντας πωλεῖν Th.8.90; ἐκ τοῦ ταμιείου Thphr.*Char*.4.6, cf. Men.*Sam*.15, Luc.*Rh.Pr*.17, Babr. l.c. **II.** mostly **Med.**, late impf. ἐπροῃρούμην Ph.1.72 codd.: fut. -αιρήσομαι: aor. -ειλόμην: pf. Pass. (in med. sense) -ῄρημαι (v. infr.):—*take away first for oneself*, [ἀστραγάλους] ἐκ φορμίσκων Pl.*Ly*.206e; *remove*, Ῥωμαίων τὰς ἀφορμὰς Plb.16.29.1. **b.** *elect previously*, τινὰς ἐκ τοῦ πλήθους Arist.*Pol*.1298$^{b}$27 (s. v. l.); προελομένου τοῦ δήμου θεωροὺς *Inscr.Prien*.108.152 (ii B.C.). **2.** *prefer*, τοῦ παρόντος κινδύνου τὸν μέλλοντα Hdn.6.8.6: but mostly folld. by a Prep., πρὸ τοῦ κεκινημένου τὸν σώφρονα προαιρεῖσθαι φίλον Pl.*Phdr*.245b; ἀντὶ ἀρετῆς..οὐδ' ἂν τὰ Σύρων..πάντα προέλοιντο X.*Cyr*.5.2.12; κριτικὴν τινα [ἐπιστήμην] ἐκ τῶν ἄλλων προειλόμεθα Pl.*Plt*.292b. **3.** c. acc. only, *choose deliberately, prefer*, οὔτε Λακεδαίμονα προῃροῦ οὔτε Κρήτην Pl.*Cri*.52e, cf. *Prt*.327a, *La*.200e, Luc.*DMort*.15.1, etc.; βιοῖ..οὐδεὶς ὃν προαιρεῖται βίον Men.*Mon*.65; ἃ λυσιτελεῖ προελέσθαι D.*Ep*.3.31; οὐ προσήκοντας..προῃρῆσθαι λόγους Id.18.129; τῷ προαιρεῖσθαι τἀγαθὰ ἢ τὰ κακὰ ποιοί τινές ἐσμεν Arist.*EN*1112$^{a}$2, cf. *Rh*.1382$^{a}$35; τοῦτον τὸν ἀγῶνα προελόμενος *having undertaken*, Lycurg.5; πολλὰ καὶ καλὰ καὶ μεγάλ' ἡ πόλις προείλετο δι' ἐμοῦ D.18.285; ταύτην π. τὴν σκέψιν Arist.*Pol*.1324$^{a}$21; opp. φεύγειν τι, Id.*EN*1172$^{a}$25, *Po*.1450$^{b}$9: abs., ὁ ἀκρατὴς ἐπιθυμῶν μὲν πράττει, προαιρούμενος δὲ οὔ not *by preference*, not *deliberately*, Id.*EN*1111$^{b}$14, cf. 1135$^{b}$9, *Rh*.1368$^{b}$11. **4.** c. inf., *choose deliberately* to do, Lys.30.31, Pl.*Demod*.381b, Arist.*Pol*.1315$^{a}$26, *IG* 2$^{2}$.448.53; π. τὸ κατεπεῖγον μᾶλλον πράττειν ἤ.. X.*Mem*.2.1.2. **b.** *purpose* or *propose* to do, εὖ δρᾶν προῃρημένος Democr.96; ὑπὲρ ἐμοῦ προῄρησαι λέγειν Pl.*Phlb*.28b; εἰ προαιρησόμεθα..τούτου μεμνῆσθαι D.18.176; π. λαβεῖν Arist.*Pol*.1290$^{b}$25: with inf. omitted, πλὴν ὧν ἐγὼ προειλόμην (sc. πρᾶξαι) D.18.190, cf. Arist.*EN*1136$^{b}$15, *Pol*.1301$^{a}$19.

**προαίρω**, (αἴρω) *advance before*, Plu.2.211d (sed leg. προάγειν).

※ **προαισθ-άνομαι**, aor. -ησθόμην Th.3.38: pf. -ῄσθημαι ib.112:—*perceive or observe beforehand*, Id.3.38, 5.58, X.*An*.1.1.7, etc.; π. τοῦ στρατοῦ *become aware of*..*beforehand*, Th.3.102. **-ησις**, εως, ἡ, *presentiment*, Plu.2.127d (pl.).

**προαισυμνάω** or **-αισιμνάω**, *to be chairman of a board of* αἰσυμνᾶται (αἰσιμ-), *IPE*1$^{2}$.352.57 (Chersonesus, ii B.C.), *SIG*1011.10 (Chalcedon, iii/ii B.C.):—Pass., *of acts done by such a chairman*, ib.12.

**προαιτέω**, *demand in advance*, ἐνέχυρον D.C.55.5.

**προαιτία**, ἡ, *prior cause*, Dam.*Pr*.122, cf. 118; also **προαίτιον**, τό, ib.31 bis: Adj. **-αίτιος**, ον, θεοί Ammon.*in Int*.134.4.

**προαιτιάομαι**, *accuse beforehand*, τινὰ εἶναι *Ep.Rom*.3.9.

**προαιώνιος**, ον, (αἰών) *before time*, Procl.*Inst*.107.

**προακμάζω**, *ripen before the time, be premature*, Hsch.s.v. πρόδρομα; *arrive at puberty too early*, Ruf.ap.Orib.*inc*.2.8. **II.** *to be at the age just before one's prime*, Hp.*Coac*.625.

**προᾰκολουθέω**, *precede*, Ascl.*in Metaph*.371.26: perh. f.l. for παρακολουθέω, Olymp.*in Mete*.21.16.

**προᾰκονάω**, *sharpen before* or *in front*, Hsch. s.v. προκαταθήγεσθαι (Pass.).

**προᾰκοντίζομαι**, Pass., *to be darted like a javelin before*, Luc.*Tim*.3.

**προᾰκούω**, *hear beforehand*, τι Hdt.2.5, 5.86, etc.; τῶν ἐνυπνίων Plb.10.5.5; περί τινος D.22.35; προακηκόεε ὅτι.. Hdt.8.79; προακηκοότες ὡς εἶχε how matters stood, Id.6.16; of a horse, τοῖς ὠσὶ προακούοντα σημαίνειν X.*Cyr*.4.3.21.

**προακροβολίζομαι**, *skirmish with missiles before the battle*, Poll.1.163.

**προακτ-έον**, *one must carry* to a height, ἀδικίαν Plu.*Fr.inc*.145a. ※**-ικός**, ή, όν, (προάγω, intr.) *progressive*, Hsch. **-ός**, ή, όν, perh. f.l. for προαιρετός, Them.*Or*.11.147d.

**προαλγέω**, *feel pain beforehand*, ὀσφύν in the loins, Hp.*Prorrh*.1.21, Arist.*HA*586$^{b}$31; ὀφθαλμόν Hp.*Coac*.184; of mental *anguish*, Ph.2.326.

**προᾰλείφω**, *coat, cover beforehand*, Aen.Tact.34.1; *anoint beforehand*, Ruf.(?) ap.Orib.8.40.3:—Med., προαλείψασθαι τὸ πρόσωπον Dsc.3.45, cf. Diph.Siph.ap.Ath.3.90a. **2.** Med., *smear on to oneself beforehand*, τοῦτο Hermes Trism. in *Cat.Cod.Astr*.8(3).156.

**προᾰλής**, ές, *sloping*, χῶρος Il.21.262; π. ὕδωρ the *rushing* water, A.R.3.73 (πρόαλες Cypr.Arc.Lac., acc. to Parmenio ap.Sch.Gen.Il. l.c.; expld. by Ptol.Ascal. ἀφ' οὗ ἁλὲς καὶ ἄθρουν καταφέρεσθαι δύναται τὸ ὕδωρ, ibid.). **II.** metaph., = προπετής, πρόχειρος (Hsch.), *heedless*, ἀκουσταί Lysis ap.Iamb.*VP*17.77; *wilful*, Lxx *Si*.30.8; *rash*, A.D.*Pron*.21.23, *Adv*.165.11. Adv. Comp., πλησιάζειν τῇ γῇ προαλέστερον, of dolphins, *rather rashly*, Str.12.3.19: προαλῶς is censured by Phryn.221.

※ **προᾰλίζω**, = προαθροίζω, J.*BJ*3.7.25, Phot.

**προᾰλίσκομαι**, Pass., *to be taken* or *captured beforehand*, J.*BJ*5.9.3; ὑπὸ δόξης καὶ ἀπάτης Plu.2.17d, etc. **II.** *to be convicted beforehand*, D.22.7.

※ **προᾰλιώτης**, ου, Dor. **-τας**, α, ὁ, *president of* ἁλία (A), *SIG*295.14 (Delph., iv B.C.) (nisi leg. π[ρὸ Ἰτ]αλιωτᾶν, cf. *Rev.Arch*.21(1919).77).

**προαλλάσσομαι**, gloss on προαμείψασθαι, Hsch.

**προάλλομαι**, *spring forward*, Q.S.4.510: aor. 1 part. -αλάμενος Anon.ap.Suid.

**προᾰμαρτάνω**, *fail* or *sin before*, 2*Ep.Cor*.12.21, 13.2: pf. part. Pass., τὰ προημαρτημένα *OGI*751.10 (Amblada, ii B.C.), J.*BJ*1.24.4, Hdn.3.14.4.

**προᾰμβολή**, v. προαναβολή.

**προᾰμείβομαι**, Med., *pass to another place*, Hsch. **II.** c. acc. rei, *receive in advance*, Pl.*Lg*.921e.

**προᾰμέλγω**, *milk beforehand*, Paul.Aeg.1.4.

**προᾰμ-εύω**, Dor. for προαμείβω, Hsch.; also **-ευτής**· ἐργάτης προηγούμενος, Id.

**προᾰμύνομαι** [ῡ], Med., *take retaliatory measures beforehand*, Th.3.12. **2.** c. acc., *take such measures against*, τὸν ἐχθρὸν οὐχ ὧν δρᾷ μόνον, ἀλλὰ καὶ τῆς διανοίας προαμύνεσθαι χρή not for his acts only, but for his intention also, Id.6.38.

**πρόαν**, v. πρώην.

**προανα-βαίνω**, *ascend before, preoccupy*, τὸν λόφον Th.3.112; ἐπὶ τὴν ναῦν Polyaen.6.8; f.l. for προσ- in Gal.6.434. **-βάλλομαι**, Med., *say* or *sing by way of prelude*, Ar.*Pax*1267, Isoc.12.39. **-βλέπω**, *look up before*, Hsch. s.v. προαναθρούσης. **-βοάω**, *declaim in advance*, Demetr.*Eloc*.15. **-βολή**, ἡ, *ante-prelude*, = τὰ πρὸ τοῦ προοιμίου, Sch.Pi.*N*.10.61 (pl.); poet. **προαμβολή**, Phot. s.v. προαύλια. **-γαργᾰρίζομαι**, *gargle beforehand*, Gal.14.305. **-γιγνώσκω**, *read aloud*, D.C.38.2; esp. of a teacher *reading aloud* to pupils, Plu.2.790e. **II.** *read previously* or *beforehand*, J.*Vit*.44, Plu.2.36e, Gal.15.745.

**προᾰναγκάζω**, *compel beforehand*, Harp. s.v. ἐκ προαγωγῆς (Pass.), Them.*Or*.6.74b.

**προανα-γράφω** [γρᾰ], *register* or *record beforehand*, App.*BC*5.145: —Med., ib.1.6:—Pass., *POxy*.504.17 (ii A.D.); *to be written beforehand*, J.*AJ*1.3.4. **-γυμνάζω**, *exercise before*, φωνήν, στόμα, Phryn.*PS*p.105 B.

※ **προανάγω** [ᾰγ], *lead up before*, τινὰ ἐπὶ τοῦ τείχους J.*BJ*1.2.4:—Pass., *put to sea before*, Th.8.11, Polyaen.4.2.22, etc.

**προανα-δίδωμι**, *hand in beforehand*, *PRyl*.90.22, al. (Pass., iii A.D.). **-ζέω**, *boil up first*, Gal.12.915. **-ζωγρᾰφέω**, *delineate first*, Simp.*in Ph*.390.14. **-θερμαίνω**, *heat up beforehand*, Herod.Med. in *Rh.Mus*.58.109. **-θλίβω** [ῑ], *push back first*, τὸ ἔντερον Orib.*Fr*.85.

**προαναθρέω**, *look up before*, Hsch.

**προαναθρῴσκω**, *leap up before*, Hsch.

**προαναίρεσις**, εως, ἡ, *previous murder*, ἀδελφοῦ Polyaen.5.11. **-αιρέω**, *take away before*, ἣν μή με προανέλῃ τὸ γῆρας Isoc.12.34; τοὺς χρόνους π. τῆς πόλεως D.19.183; ἃ ἐροῦσι π. *refute by anticipation*, Arist.*Rh*.1418$^{b}$11; *kill, destroy first*, ἀδελφὸν φαρμάκοις J.*AJ*15.4.1, cf. Plu.*Caes*.28, Luc.*JTr*.25, App.*Mith*.48, Ach.Tat.3.4; τῆς αἰσθήσεως προανελὼν τὸ αἰσθανόμενον, i.e. πρὸ τῆς αἰσθήσεως, Plu.2.517a:—Pass., Id.2.820f, Hld.9.24. **II.** Med., *catch first*, [τὴν σφαῖραν] Poll.9.104. **III.** Pass., *to be chosen as a representative*, *IG*12(7).22.5 (Amorgos, iii B.C.).

**προᾰναισῑμόω**, *use up, spend before*, ἐν τῷ προαναισιμωμένῳ χρόνῳ πρότερον ἢ ἐμὲ γενέσθαι in times *past before* I was born, Hdt.2.11.

**προαναισχυντέω**, *to be shameless on behalf of*, ὑπὲρ τῶν ἀδικούντων Hyp.*Dem.Fr*.3.

**προανα-κᾰθαίρω**, *clear away first*, τὰς ἐμποδίους δόξας τῆς τοιαύτης θεωρίας Procl.*in Alc*.p.251 C.: so in Med., ταῦτα..ἀναγκαῖον ἦν -καθήρασθαι Anon. in *Tht*.2.10. **-κειμαι**, Pass., *to be dedicated before*, Gauthier et Sottas *Décret trilingue en l'honneur de Ptolémée IV* p.66 (iii B.C.), *OGI*129 (Egypt, ii B.C.), J.*AJ*12.2.9. **-κεφᾰλαίωσις**, εως, ἡ, *anticipatory summary*, Sch.Il.15.56, Eust.1672.35, Sch.Ptol.*Tetr*.86. **-κήρυξις**, εως, ἡ, *proclamation in advance*, Hsch. s.v. ἀνάρρησις. **-κηρύσσω**, *announce beforehand*, τὸν σκοπὸν τοῦ ὑπολοίπου συγγράμματος Olymp.*in Mete*.14.4. **-κῑνέω**, *stir up before*, ἀγῶνας Plu.*Cat.Ma*.26 (Pass.); τὰ αἰσθητὰ π. *examine* them *before*, Id.2.948c. **II.** οὐδὲν..-ήσας without any *prelude* (cf. ἀνακίνησις 1), Arist.*Rh*.1416$^{a}$2. **-κῑνητέον**, *one must exercise* *before*, ἑαυτούς Agathin.ap.Orib.10.7.14. **-κλαίομαι**, Med., *bewail before*, τὴν συμφοράν D.H.10.49. **-κλίνω** [ῑ], *push back first*, πυλίδα Procop.*Goth*.2.13. **-κοινόομαι**, Med., *unite before*, τὸ ῥεῦμα, of rivers, Paus.8.35.1. ⊛ **-κόπτω**, *cut away first*, τὰς ἐμποδίους ὕλας J.*BJ*3.6.2. **-κουφίζω**, *float up beforehand*, τὸ ἔμβρυον Sor. 1.57. **-κρίνω** [ῑ], *examine beforehand*, of measures to be submitted to the vote of the people, opp. κρίνω, Arist.*Pol*.1298ᵃ31; *conduct a preliminary investigation* of lawsuits, opp. αὐτοτελεῖς κρίνειν, Id.*Ath*. 3.5. II. *inquire beforehand of*, τινα Phld.*Vit*.p.29 J. **-κρουσις**, εως, ἡ, = προαναβολή, Sch.Od.7.208, Sch.Pi.*P*.1.4. ⊛ **-κρούομαι**, Med., *push back before, forestall*, ἀπορίαν Steph.*in Hp*.1.231 D.:—Pass., of diseases, τομαῖς ἢ καύσεσιν Ph.2.205. 2. = ἀναχαιτίζω, Hsch. II. προανακρούσασθαί τι, in Music, *play as a prelude*, Plu.2.161c; *introduce by way of prelude*, π. καὶ προαναφωνῆσαι τὰ τοῦ Ἐμπεδοκλέους ib. 996b; of masters, *play by way of example*, ib.790e:—Pass., τί.. ταυτὶ προανακέκρουσται; Philostr.Jun.*Im.Praef*. **-λαμβάνω**, *lift up first*, τὸ σῶμα cj. in Sor.2.38; *take up before*, εἰς τὴν ἕξιν Ath.2.45e (Pass.), cf. *BGU*421.14 (Pass., ii A. D.). 2. *take up* a narrative *at an earlier point*, βραχὺ τοῖς χρόνοις π. τὴν ἱστορίαν D.S.17.5. 3. *prepare, mix with*, τινι Philum.ap.Aët.16.38:—Pass., cj. in Sor.1. 122. II. *anticipate, forestall*, J.*AJ*16.4.4. **-λέγω**, *mention before*, Mitteis*Chr*.31 v 25, ix 1 (ii B. C., Pass.). II. *collect, gather before*, *Sammelb*.4425 iii 10 (ii A. D.):—also in Med., *Gp*.10.22.1.

**προαν-ἄλείφω**, *anoint first*, Dsc.*Eup*.2.20 (Pass.).

**προανᾱλίσκω**, fut. -ώσω Th.1.141: aor. -ανάλωσα, also **-ανήλωσα** *IG*2².834.3:—*use up* or *spend before*, χρήματα Th. l.c.; μνᾶν ἀργυρίου D.41.11; π., ἵνα διπλάσια κομίσωνται Lys.19.57; π. ἑαυτούς D.C.59. 18; π. τῆς γνώσεως ἑαυτούς, i.e. πρὸ τῆς γνώσεως, Plu.2.517a:—Pass., *throw away one's life first*, Th.7.81; of water, *to be used up before*, Hp.*Vict*.2.42, Arist.*Mete*.349ᵇ11.

**προαναλογ-ία**, ἡ, *previous analogy*, Dam.*Pr*.118. **-ίζω**, *advance a consideration previously*, Phld.*Po.Herc*.994.38 (Pass.).

**προανάλωμα** [νᾱ], ατος, τό, *previous expense*, Artem.1.70 (pl.); also **προανήλωμα**, *PCair.Zen*.333.76 (iii B. C.).

**προανα-μᾰλάσσω**, *soften, relax beforehand*, Hp.*Art*.79 (v.l. προσανα-). **-μέλπω**, *sing before* or *first*, Lxx *Wi*.18.9. **-μιμνήσκω**, *call to mind first*, Gal.12.2, 15.465. **-ξέω**, *scrape first*, Crito ap. Gal.13.794. **-ξηραίνω**, *dry up before*, Gal.12.318, al.:—Pass., pf. part. -εξηραμμένος Id.6.266. ⊛ **-παύω**, *prescribe a previous rest*, Id.12. 683. II. Med., *die before*, *Rev.Bibl*.41.96 (Otranto). **-πειράομαι**, *carry out trial* naval *manœuvres*, cj. for προσ- in Poll.1.123. **-πέμπω**, *throw back* the accent, Sch.Ar.*Pax* 62. **-πηδάω**, *leap up before*, of flames, Cass.*Pr*.1. **-πίπτω**, *fall down beforehand*, Ph.1.154; π. τὴν γνώμην ib.282. **-πλάσσω**, *transform before*, ἐπὶ τὸ βέλτιον Hipparch.ap.Stob.4.44.81; *imagine beforehand*, Posidon.*Stoic*.3. 131. ⊛ **-πλέω**, *set sail first*, *IG*2².1028.27. **-πληρόω**, *fulfil before*, Lxx *Wi*.19.4 (v.l. προσ-). **-πνέω**, *exhale before*, ἀέρα Plu.2. 949c: abs., *take breath beforehand*, Sch.Pi.*N*.8.32. **-πνοή**, ἡ, *previous respiration*, Gal.5.159.

**προαναρπάζω**, *carry off* or *arrest beforehand*, D.21.125; of an enemy, π. τῆς παρασκευῆς τινα, i.e. πρὸ τῆς παρασκευῆς, Plu.*Pomp*.76.

**προαναρρήγνῡμι**, *cause to burst open before*, πηγὰς ὑδάτων Eust. 1524.42.

**προαναρτάω**, *keep in suspense*, τὸν λόγον Aristid.*Rh*.1 p.467 S.

**προανα-σείω**, *brandish before* or *in front*, τὰ ὅπλα D.S.5.29: metaph., γῆρας π. φροντίδας Them.*Or*.8.101c:—Pass., δίκαι π. τῷ Νασικᾷ Plu.*TG*21. II. *agitate beforehand*, τὸν δῆμον Id.*CG*4. ⊛ **-σκευάζομαι**, *pack up and carry off beforehand*, J.*BJ*1.15.6: plpf. Pass. in med. sense, τὰ λαμπρότατα.. προανεσκεύαστο ib.1.13.9. **-σκοπέομαι**, *look at beforehand*, Id.*AJ*17.6.3, prob. in 17.5.6. **-στέλλω**, *check beforehand*, τὸ θρασυνόμενον αὐτῶν Plu.*Per*.15; τὸν κόρον Aristaenet. 2.1; τὸ παρὰ φύσιν Procl.*in Cra*.p.99 P.; νέφη, of the wind, Sch.Arat. 416. 2. in Surgery, *draw back* or *open out first*, in Pass., Sor.*Fract*. 2. **-στολή**, ἡ, *previous opening out*, Paul.Aeg.6.103. **-στομόω**, *open up first*, Dsc.*Eup*.1.197. **-τάσσω**, *prefer*, Lxx *Ps*.136 (137) 6. ⊛ **-τείνω**, *hold up in front*, θυρεὸν ὑπὲρ τῆς κεφαλῆς J.*BJ*6.1.6, cf. Paul.Aeg.6. 33. **-τέλλω**, *rise before*, of stars, Hipparch.1.5.16, Gem.12.7, Ti. Locr.97a, etc. II. *sprout afresh*, Lxx *Ez*.17.9. **-τέμνω**, *open up, clear first*, τὴν εἰς σωτηρίαν ὁδόν Ph.2.662 (= *Fr*.100 H.). II. *dissect first*, Gal.2.300 (Pass.), 504. ⊛ **-τίθημι**, *dedicate before*, προανετέθη *TAM* 2.408.18 (Patara, ii A. D.). **-τολή**, ἡ, *earlier rising* (of the sun), Gem. 16.16 (pl.); of a star, ἑσπερία π. μὴ φαινομένη *rising* above the Eastern horizon just *before* sunset, Ptol.*Alm*.8.4. **-τρέχω**, *run up in front*, prob. for προσ- in Sor.2.64 and Paul.Aeg.6.74. **-τρίβω** [ῑ], *use friction, rub first*, Gal.12.420, Herod.Med.ap.Orib.10.18.15, Ps.-Dsc. 2.115. **-τῠπόω**, *design beforehand, prefigure*, Men.Prot.p.68 D. **-φαίνω**, *display beforehand*, ἔχθος Paus.4.10.7:—Pass., Dam. *Pr*.280. **-φέρω**, *bring up* or *mention before*, v.l. in Sch.E.*Ph*. 777:—Pass., *BGU*255.7 (vi A. D.). II. Pass., *rush up before*, τινος Arist.*Pr*.897ᵃ28. 2. *rise before*, of a star, c. gen., S.E.*M*.5. 15: abs., Ptol.*Tetr*.128, Vett.Val.264.23. **-φθέγγομαι**, *say by way of preface*, Ph.1.680. **-φορά**, ἡ, name of 12th τόπος, Paul. Al.*O*.1, *Cat.Cod.Astr*.8(1).156. **-φῠράω**, *saturate before*, σπόγγον αἵματι -φυραθῆναι Ruf.ap.Orib.8.24.53. **-φῡσάω**, *play a prelude on the flute*, v. προσαναφυσάω.

**προαναφων-έω**, *pronounce before*, S.E.*M*.1.130 (Pass.). 2. *proclaim before, predict*, Sch.Il.5.662; *announce beforehand*, ὅτι μέλλει λέγειν Ps.-Plu.*Vit.Hom*.163. 3. *state first*, Dam.*Pr*.228. II. *say by way of preface*, D.H.*Rh*.2.6, Plu.*Pel*.2; *utter as prelude*, τὰ τοῦ Ἐμπεδοκλέους Id.2.996b. **-ημα**, ατος, τό, *previous exclamation*, Sch.Ar.*Pax* 1. ⊛ **-ησις**, εως, ἡ, *previous proclamation*, μετὰ κήρυκος π. Posidon.36 J. 2. *statement by anticipation*, Ps.-Plu.*Vit.Hom*. 65, Trypho *Trop*.2.12, Hdn.*Fig*.p.103 S. II. *preface, proëm*, Hld. 8.17. **-ητικός**, ή, όν, *signifying beforehand*, σχῆμα π. τῶν ἐφεξῆς Eust.1941.63. Adv. -κῶς Id.1902.30.

**προανα-χᾰλάω**, *relax, loosen before*, Antyll.ap.Orib.10.31.3, prob. for προσ- in Sor.2.61 (Pass.). **-χωρέω**, *go away before*, D.C.49.7: c. gen., Dam.*Isid*.64. II. *proceed beyond*, Sor.1.7, prob. for προσ- in Id.2.64. **-χώρησις**, εως, ἡ, *previous departure*, Th.4.128. **-ψηφίζω**, *determine beforehand*, J.*AJ*18.8.2 (Pass.).

**προάνγρεσις**, Thessal., = προαίρεσις, *IG*9(2).461.28.

**προαν-εγείρω**, *arouse, awaken beforehand*, ἑαυτὸν πρός τι Procl.*in Prm*.p.606 S., cf. Syrian.*in Metaph*.149.12. **-είργω**, *put away beforehand*, τοὺς ἀναξίους ἱεροῦ συλλόγου Ph.2.261. **-έλκω**, *draw up before*, *Placit*.5.6.1 (Pass.). **-έρχομαι**, *go up before*, Arist.*Mete*. 356ᵇ26. **-εσις**, εως, ἡ, *previous relaxation*, Gal.14.736. **-ευρύνω**, *dilate beforehand*, v.l. for προσ- (q.v.). **-έχω**, *hold up before*, βωμὸς π. γωνίας *has projecting* angles, J.*BJ*5.5.6. II. intr., *rise up above* or *jut out beyond*, Th.7.34: c. gen., J.*BJ*5.4.4, etc. **-ήλωμα**, v. προανάλωμα.

**προανθ-έω**, *flower before its season*, Thphr.*CP*1.10.2, Ph.1.602, Plu. 2.377c. 2. *flower before leaves appear*, Thphr.*HP*7.13.7. **-ησις**, εως, ἡ, *previous* or *first bloom*, Sch.Ar.*Pax* 198, Hsch. s. v. κύτταρος.

**προαν-ίημι**, *relax first*, Sor.1.65 (Act. and Pass.). 2. *dissolve first*, γάλακτι Asclep.ap.Gal.13.529 (Pass.). **-ίστημι**, *set up before*, δρυφάκτους τῶν τεκτόνων J.*BJ*3.7.10: aor. 1 Med., ib.5.3.2:—Pass. with aor. 2 Act., *start up first*, Stratt.62; *rise from table first*, Ach. Tat.5.18; *rise before daybreak*, Poll.1.71. **-ίσχω**, = προανέχω II, c. gen., J.*BJ*3.3.5: abs., *arise before*, Plu.2.427e. **-οίγω**, *open before*, Meges ap.Orib.44.24.9: metaph., τὴν ψυχὴν λόγοις Plu.2.36d.

**προανταναιρέομαι**, Pass., *to be removed, withdrawn previously*, *PTeb*.61(*b*).219, 72.147 (ii B. C.).

**προᾰνύτω** [ῠ], aor. -ήνυσα Sch.Ar.*Eq*.1053:—*get forward in, achieve*, ὧν χρῄζομεν X.*Cyr*.4.5.22. 2. *accomplish before*, in Pass., τὸ προανυσθὲν ὑπόμνημα S.E.*M*.8.1, cf. Gal.15.101, Iamb.*Myst*.3.18.

**προανωθέω**, *push up first*, Sor.2.60.

⊛ **προαπ-αγγέλλω**, *announce before*, Aen.Tact.10.5, Lxx *Ez*.33.9, D.C.38.13. **-άγγελμα**, ατος, τό, *previous report*, J.*BJ*1.3.5 (v.l. προάγγ-). **-αγορεύω**, fut. προαπερῶ Ael.*NA*14.11: aor. προαπεῖπον Isoc.4.171, D.C.60.15: pf. προαπείρηκα Isoc.*Ep*.1.1:—*give in* or *fail before*, Id.15.59; π. ὑπὸ τραυμάτων Luc.*Anach*.37; of inscriptions, *disappear first*, Lib.*Or*.12.11. II. *renounce beforehand*, τὴν συμβίωσιν J.*AJ*15.7.10; τὴν ἀρχήν D.C. l.c.:—Med., προαπειπάμενοι τὴν φιλίαν Paus.4.5.8. **-άγχομαι**, Med., *strangle oneself before*, D.C.77.20. **-άγω** [ᾰγ], *remove first*, τέλη ἐς Ἤπειρον ἐκ Βρεντεσίου App.*BC*2.38. **-αίρω**, *depart before*, D.C.36. 48. **-ᾰλείφω**, *strike out first*, Id.43.21. **-αλλάσσω**, Att. **-ττω**, *remove beforehand*, τινὰ ἐκ τῆς δημαρχίας Id.44.10; παῖδας φαρμάκῳ Id.37.13; [ὁ σφυγμὸς] π. τὴν σφοδρότητα *loses* its energy, Marcellin.*Puls*.257:—Pass., *depart* or *die beforehand*, D.C.43.11: also intr. in Act., π. εἰς τὴν οἰκείαν D.S.18.15; προαπαλλάξας *having predeceased*, Phld.*Acad.Ind*.p.83 M. **-ᾰμέλγω**, *milk first*, Orib.*inc*. 12.7 (-απομ- codd.). **-αντάω**, *go forth to meet*, Th.1.69, 4.92, 6.42, Ph.1.286, al., J.*AJ*13.4.1, al., Luc.*VH*1.38. II. *go to meet before* .., τῆς ἑῴας ἀπάσης Them.*Or*.14.183b. 2. *take steps in advance* or *in good time*, *BGU*372 ii 9 (ii A. D.). III. *to be interposed, intervene*, τὰ προαπαντῶντα σώματα Gal.*UP*8.3 (pl.). **-άντημα**, ατος, τό, *representative appearance*, Olymp.*in Phd*.p.237 N. (pl.). **-άντησις**, εως, ἡ, *meeting before*, a Rhet. figure, Zonae.*Fig*.p.170 S., Anon.*Fig*.p.187 S. II. *interposition*, Gal.*UP*8.3. **-αντλέω**, *bathe before*, ὠμοπλάτας ὕδατι θερμῷ *Hippiatr*.26, cf. Paul.Aeg.3.6. **-αυδάω**, = προαπαγορεύω I, Hp. *Prorrh*.1.8 (ap.Erot.); μέσφι ἂν -απαυδήσῃ ἀτροφίῃ ἢ νοῦσος Aret.*CD*2. 13; εἰ μὴ -απηύδηκε [ἡ δύναμις] Id.*CA*2.3; π. τῆς ἐπιθυμίας ὁ ζῆλος Plu 2.783e. **-αφρίζω**, *despumate*, μέλι Gal.6.266 (Pass.), al. ⊛ **-ειλέω**, *threaten beforehand*, *PCair.Zen*.230.3 (iii B. C., corrected), J.*BJ*4.6.1, Onos.14.3, App.*BC*2.108. **-ειμι**, (εἶμι *ibo*) *go away first*, Luc. *DMort*.5.1, *JTr*.52. **-εῖπον**, v. προαπαγορεύω. **-ελαύνω**, *drive away before*, τὰς μελίττας *Gp*.15.5.5. **-έρχομαι**, *go away before*, πρὶν τὸν Βρασίδαν ἰδεῖν Th.4.125, cf. D.19.323: c. gen., οἴκαδε π. τοῦ χρόνου *depart before* the time, Pl.*Lg*.943d. 2. *die before*, Lib. *Or*.55.10, Him.*Or*.23.8; τῆς ἐπιδημίας Eun.*VS* p.494 B. II. *die for*, τῆς πατρίδος Lib.*Eth*.22.5. **-ερῶ**, v. προαπαγορεύω. **-εχθάνομαι**, *become hostile before*, D.14.4. **-έχω**, *receive beforehand*, *POxy*.1287.7 (ii/iii A. D.), etc. **-ηγέομαι**, Ion. for προαφ-. **-ήχημα**, ατος, τό, *preliminary sound*, Dam.*Pr*.438.

**προαπίδων**· φρενῶν, διανοιῶν, Hsch. (leg. πραπίδων).

**προαπιστέομαι**, *to be disbelieved beforehand*, f.l. in Sch.E.*Andr*.297.

**προάπλωσις**, εως, ἡ, gloss on πρόθεσις, Hsch.

⊛ **προαπο-βάλλω**, *throw away, lose before*, τὸ φρόνημα Paus.4.7. 11. **-βάπτω**, *dip first*, τὸν δάκτυλον ὄξει Orib.*Fr*.102. **-βρέχω**, *soak, steep before*, in Pass., Gal.6.611, Herod.Med.ap.Orib.10.10.3: 2 aor. part. -βραχεῖσα *Gp*.14.9.5. **-γεύομαι**, *taste before*, τροφῆς J.*BJ*7.5.4. **-γιγνώσκω**, *despair beforehand*, τινος of a thing, Gal.8. 772: c. acc., Id.18(2).39. **-γλῠκαίνω**, *sweeten beforehand*, ὀρόβους Ruf.*Ren.Ves*.2.21, cf. Gal.6.546 (Pass.). **-γράφομαι** [γρᾰ], *describe before*, χώρας Ptol.*Geog*.2.1.6; *register beforehand*, *POxy*.249.7 (i A. D.). **-δείκνῡμι**, *prove* or *demonstrate before*, in Pass., Isoc.3. 13, Phld.*Sign*.8, 32, J.*Ap*.2.2, Plu.2.720f, Ptol.*Tetr*.50, etc.:—Med.,

App.*BC*5.41. II. Pass., *to be appointed before*, of magistrates, D.C.52.42, 59.9, al. ※ -**δίδωμι**, *pay in advance*, *PTeb*.296.13 (ii A.D.). 2. *give an account of first*, S.E.*M*.7.46 :—Pass., A.D. *Adv*.195.17. II. π. τὴν βάσιν *finish* the rhythmical conclusion of a sentence *before* the speaker reaches it, Longin.41.2. III. of the bowels, *act first*, Aët.7.39. ※ -**δότης**, ου, ὁ, *one who renders payment first*, i.e. *surety*, *SIG*²845 (Delph.), *JHS*13.343 (Aetol.). -**ζέω**, *boil down beforehand*, Gal.15.872 :—Pass., Id.6.623, Philagr.ap.Orib. 5.17.7 : also -**ζέννυσθαι** Alex.Trall.8.1. -**θερᾰπεύω**, *treat first*, Herod.Med. in *Rh.Mus*.58.87 :—Pass., Sor.1.40. -**θεωρέω**, *consider previously*, Phld.*Sign*.38. -**θησαυρίζω**, *store up beforehand*, Phlp. in *GA*10.30. ※ -**θνήσκω**, *die before* or *first*, Hdt.2.1, App. *Mith*.117 ; π. τῆς γηραιοῦ τελευτῆς *die before* old age, Antipho 4.1.2 ; of a coward, π. ὑπὸ τοῦ φόβου, i.e. before his time, X.*Cyr*.3.1.25 ; π. τῷ δέει Ph.2.68 ; π. πρὶν ἐντὸς βέλους γενέσθαι Luc.*Anach*.25. II. *die on behalf* or *in defence of*, ὑπὲρ τῆς βασιλείας Pl.*Smp*.208d ; τῶν τέκνων Arist.*EE*1235ᵃ34 ; κύνες π. τῶν δεσποτῶν Ph.2.200. -**θρηνέω**, *bewail beforehand*, τινὸς τὸ τέλος Plu.*Pomp*.78.

**προαποικίζομαι**, *emigrate beforehand*, App.*BC*2.119.

**προαπο-καθίσταμαι**, Pass., *cease and be cured before*, Hp.*Coac*. 204. -**κάμνω**, *grow tired before the end, give up the task*, μὴ -κάμῃς Pl.*Euthphr*.11e : c. gen., π. τῆς τελευταίας ἐλπίδος Plu.*Mar*. 36. -**κειμαι**, Pass., *to be stored up before*, *Sammelb*.4425 iv 8 (ii A.D.), prob. in Aristid.*Or*.50(26).49. -**κινδῡνεύω**, *risk an engagement first*, D.C.50.19. -**κλείω**, *shut beforehand*, τὰς πύλας App. *BC*4.77 ; *shut out, exclude beforehand*, τραγῳδίαν τῆς ἐξόδου Them.*Or*. 7.92c. -**κληρόομαι**, Pass., *to be allotted beforehand*, Luc.*Bis Acc*. 14. -**κλύζω**, *wash* or *cleanse beforehand*, Gal.12.179 (Pass.), 264 (Act., prob.), Paul.Aeg.3.42 (Pass.). -**κόπτω**, *cut off before*, J.*BJ*4.4.4: —Pass., Paul.Aeg.4.1. -**κρίνομαι** [ῑ], *answer first*, App.*BC*4.69 :—Pass., Aristeas 236. II. Pass., *to be excreted first*, Sor.1.58. -**κτείνω**, *kill beforehand*, J.*AJ*20.2.2, Luc.*Cat*.8, D.C.54.9, etc. ; ἡ ἕκτη π. *proves fatal earlier*, Gal.9.820. -**κτίννῡμι**, = foreg., Philostr.*VA*7. 26, D.C.59.18. -**λαμβάνω**, *receive before*, *Sammelb*.5677.9 (iii A.D., Pass.). -**λαύω**, *enjoy beforehand*, Plu.*Aem*.30. -**λείπω**, *leave beforehand*, οὐ π. τὴν κοινωνίαν, πλὴν ἐὰν χῆρος ἢ χήρα γένηται, of doves, Arist.*HA*612ᵇ33 ; of water, *quit* certain places *first*, Id. *Mete*.352ᵇ11 ; π. τὴν τάξιν *depart from* the natural order *first*, Id.*Rh. Al*.1438ᵃ31. II. intr., *fail before* or *first*, Hp.*Mul*.1.59 : c. gen., *fail before*, i. e. *in comparison with*, τοῦ σώματος . . ἡ ψυχὴ π. Antipho 5. 93 ; προαπολείπει τῆς προθυμίας ἡ δύναμις Plu.2.789d :—Med., ib. 1078f. 2. *desist first*, Paus.2.1.5. -**λεπίζω**, *shell* or *peel beforehand*, Dsc.2.107 (Pass.). -**λήγω**, *cease first*, M.Ant.3.1.

※ **προαπόλλῡμι**, aor. -ώλεσα, *destroy first*, [τὴν πόλιν] αἱ στάσεις -ώλεσαν App.*BC*4.14, cf. Plu.*Phoc*.2. II. more freq. in Pass., with pf. -όλωλα, *to be first destroyed, perish before* or *first*, Antipho 5. 67, Th.5.61, 6.77 ; μὴ ἡ ψυχὴ προαπολλύηται (from -απολλύω) Pl. *Phd*.91d ; προαπόλωλεν τὸ ἐφ' ὃ ἂν ἐκπλέωμεν D.4.37 : c. gen., ὀλίγῳ τῶν ἄλλων προαπολεῖσθαι Lys.2.24.

**προαπο-λύω**, *dismiss, send away before*, App.*BC*4.101. -**μισθόω**, *let out for hire before*, Nic.Dam.130.26a J. -**νίπτω**, *wash first*, Gal.12.834.

**προαπονῠχίζω**, *cut a finger-nail first*, Sor.1.82 (Pass.).

**προαπο-ξηραίνω**, *dry beforehand*, Hp.*Morb*.1.18 (Pass.). -**ξῠρέω**, *shave before*, Orib.9.53.1. -**ξύω**, *scrape off beforehand*, Gal.2.351 :— Pass., ib.686, Dsc.*Eup*.1.166. -**παύω**, *put a stop to first*, τὴν φλεγμονήν Orib.9.52.1 :—Med., *stop before*, c. gen., Id.*inc*.4.53. -**πέμπω**, *send away, dismiss before*, D.C.60.34 :—Med., X.*Cyr*.4.2.29 :—Pass., Th.3.25. -**πίπτω**, *fall off early*, Thphr.*HP*3.7.3. -**πληρόω**, *block up beforehand*, τὰς εἰσβολὰς καὶ τὰς διόδους Aen.Tact.2.2. -**πλύνω** [ῡ], *wash before*, Aët.4.25, Alex.Trall.2.1, *Hippiatr*.26. -**πνέω**, *blow early*, Plu.*Sert*.17. -**πνίγομαι** [ῑ], *to be choked, drowned first*, Aesop.144. -**πτωτος**, ον, *having fallen off before its time*, Thphr. *HP*3.3.8.

**προαπορέω**, *start preliminary doubts and difficulties*, Arist.*Metaph*. 995ᵇ2, *APo*.99ᵇ19 :—Pass., τὸ προηπορημένον, opp. προευπορημένον, Id.*Ph*.208ᵃ35 : aor. in med. sense, προαπορηθῆναι περί τινος Pl.*Ti*.49b.

**προαπο-ρρίπτω**, *throw away before*, τὰ ὅπλα D.C.56.14. -**ρρύπτω**, *wash clean first*, Philagr.ap.Orib.5.21.3 :—Pass., Antyll.ib.10.24. 8. -**σβέννῡμαι**, Pass., fut. -σβήσομαι M.Ant.12.15 :—*to be extinguished* or *go out first*, Id.3.1 ; *die first*, D.C.55.10ᴬ.9. -**σημαίνω**, *signify before*, J.*AJ*18.3.4. -**σμήχω**, *smear beforehand*, οὔρῳ -σμῆξαι *Gp*.18.15.4 ; τρίχας -σμηχθείσας Κιμωλίᾳ γῇ Dsc.1. 106, cf. Gal.12.423. 2. *wash off first*, Menemach.ap.Orib.10.14. 3. -**σπάω**, *tear away before*, τινὸς τὴν γυναῖκα D.C.54.31. -**σπογγίζω**, *sponge first*, Sor.2.41. -**σταυρόω**, *fortify with palisades before*, Sch.Th.6.99. -**στέλλω**, *send away, dispatch beforehand* or *in advance*, Th.4.77, J.*BJ*1.17.2, Plu.*Arat*.6 :—Pass., *to be sent in advance*, Th.3.112 : aor. part. -σταλέντες *PEleph*.28.6 (iii B.C.), Plb.3.45.1 : plpf. -έσταλτο App.*BC*4.20 : also c. gen., προαποσταλῆναι τῆς ἀποστάσεως, = ἀποσταλῆναι πρὸ τῆς ἀ., Th.3.5. -**στερέω**, *rob before*, χάριτος αὐτόν Aristid.1.466 J. -**στρέφομαι**, *turn round first*, εἰ μὴ τὰ σημεῖα -εστράφη App.*BC*2.63. -**στύφω** [ῡ], *apply an astringent first*, Aët.7.42. -**σφάζω**, *slay before*, Paus. 10.1.7, Luc.*Hist.Conscr*.26 ; ἑαυτόν D.C.65.10. -**σχάζω**, *scarify first*, Gal.11.85. -**τάσσομαι**, *bid farewell before*, τῷ βίῳ π. ξίφεσι Ph.2.326. -**τέλεσμα**, ατος, τό, *previous influence of a star*, Procl. *Par.Ptol*.114 :—hence -**τελεσματικός**, ή, όν, *of* or *concerned therewith*, ib.10,109. -**τέμνω**, *cut off first*, τὰς γλώσσας D.C.59.10. -**τήκω**, *melt, dissolve first*, Gal.14.268. -**τίθημι**, *put aside from before*, τοῦ λοιποῦ σώματος Plu. in *Hes*.76 :—Med., π. ἔπαινον *throw out* some praise (sc. *before* beginning to blame), Id.2.856d. II. Med., *excrete previously*, Gal.6.89, etc. -**τίκτω**, *lay eggs before*, [ᾠὰ] εἰς . . Arist.*HA* 555ᵇ7. -**τρέπομαι**, *turn aside before, leave off*, c. part., προαπετράποντο διώκοντες X.*An*.6.5.31 ; *turn aside to attack*, πρός τινα D.C.47. 36. -**τυγχάνω**, *to be unsuccessful before*, Sch.Il.9.223. -**φαίνω**, *declare* or *explain before*, τὴν μουσικὴν δύναμιν Plu.2.1146c ; Καίσαρα π. τύραννον App.*BC*2.127 :—Med., π. τὴν γνώμην *declare one's* opinion *before*, Pl.*Prt*.340b, cf. App.*Mac*.9.1 : abs., Pl.*Hp.Ma*.288d ; *express an opinion off-hand*, εἰς πρᾶγμα Plu.*Mar*.29 :—Pass., τὰ -φανθέντα *PLips*.38.11 (iv A.D.). -**φέρω**, 1 aor. -ήνεγκα, *carry off first* (by death), Lib.*Or*.1.146. -**φημι**, *deny before*, Arist.*SE*177ᵃ 19. -**φθέγγομαι**, *declare before*, J.*AJ*17.6.5. -**φοιτάω**, *depart* (from life) *prematurely*, Plu.2.120a. -**χράομαι**, *use fully before*, Sch.E. *Hipp*.58. 2. *kill before*, ἑαυτόν D.C.57.15, *Fr*.36.8. -**χωρέω**, *depart before*, Th.4.90 ; ἐς, ἐκ . ., D.C.47.27, *Fr*.72.2.

**προάπτω**, *light, kindle before*, Hld.1.12.

**προαργέω**, *live idly before*, J.*BJ*3.5.1 (v.l.).

**προαρθρεμβολέω**, *reduce a dislocation previously*, Gal.18(1).772 (Pass.).

**προαριθμέω**, *enumerate previously*, Lyd.*Mag*.3.43 (Med.).

**προᾰριστ-άω**, *breakfast beforehand*, Hp.*Acut*.30, Polyaen.3.9.53, D.L.2.139.

**προᾰριστεύω**, *be best before*, Sch.E.*Hec*.306.

**προᾰριστίδιος**, ον, *before breakfast* or *luncheon*, πλοῦς (about 20 miles) Scyl.64,113.

**προαρκτούρια**, τά, = προηρόσια, Clitodem.23.

**προαρμόζω**, *fit on before*, Hsch. s. v. προαρτᾷ.

**προάρον**, τό, (ἀρύω A) *large wooden bowl in which wine was mixed*, Pamphil.ap.Ath.11.495a.

**προαρ-οτριάω**, *plough before*, Sch.Ar.*Pax* 1158 (Pass.). -**όω**, = foreg., Ael.*Fr*.339.

**προαρπάζω**, *snatch away before*, ὥσπερ ἰκτῖνος τὰ ὄψα Luc.*Tim*.54 : metaph., τὴν δόξαν J.*AJ*13.5.8 ; τὴν ἡγεμονίαν τινί ib.20.8.2, cf. Luc. *Tox*.6, etc. ; π. ἀλλήλων τὰ λεγόμενα *snap at* a conclusion, *anticipate hastily*, Pl.*Grg*.454c ; τὸ ζητούμενον π. ὡς ὁμολογούμενον S.E.*M*.1.157.

**προαρτᾷ**· προαρμόζει, προτείνει, Hsch.

**προαρτύω**, *season beforehand*, Gal.17(2).181.

**προαρχιερᾰτεύω**, *hold the office of* ἀρχιερεύς *previously*, *Supp.Epigr*. 4.318 (Panamara).

**προάρχω**, *begin first*, ἀδικεῖν J.*AJ*18.9.6 ; ἀδικίας Phalar.*Ep*.147 : —Med., π. μάχης Arist.*Fr*.344. II. *hold office before*, οἱ προάρξαντες αὐτῶν D.C.57.14 ; ἄλλην ἀρχήν Id.76.5 ; ὁ ταμίας ὁ προάρχων *IG*7.303.38 (Orop.). 2. *to be previous governor*, τῆς Μακεδονίας D.C.47.21. 3. *to be chief* or *eponymous archon of*, π. ἐν [Δελ]φοῖς τὴν ἐν[ναετηρίδα] *Inscr.Magn*.17.14.

※ **προασθενέω**, gloss on προκάμνω, Sch.Th.2.49.

**προασῑτέω**, *go without food before*, Antyll.ap.Orib.7.16.2, Gal.14. 663, Orib.*Fr*.80.

**προασκέω**, *train* or *exercise before*, τοὺς ἐπιγιγνομένους Isoc.4.75 : c. gen., τὴν ἕξιν προήσκησαν ἡμῶν, i. e. πρὸ ἡμῶν, Arist.*Metaph*.993ᵇ14, cf. J.*BJ*4.2.1.

**πρόᾳσμα**, ατος, τό, *prelude*, Sch.Theoc.1.64.

**προασπ-ίζω**, *hold a shield before*, τειχῶν Aristid.*Or*.26(14).84 ; τοῦ πατρός, τῆς Ῥωμαίων ἀρχῆς, Philostr.*Her*.3.4, Hdn.6.2.5 ; ὅπλα π. λόγων Them.*Or*.16.200b ; κύνες π. τῶν δεσποτῶν Ph.2.200 : c. acc., *cover with a shield*, D.H.6.93 :—Pass., *to be covered with shields*, τοῖς ὁπλίταις by them, Hld.9.14. II. *put forward as a shield*, τινὰ εἰς θώρακα Id.3.3. -**ιστήρ**, ῆρος, ὁ, *one who holds a shield before, champion*, τινος Nonn.*D*.20.50. -**ιστής**, οῦ, ὁ, = foreg., D.H.3.14 (dub.l.), Ph.1.638.

**προ-άστειον**, v. προάστιον. -**άστειος**, ον, *suburban*, γυμνάσιον D.L.3.7 (nisi leg. -άστιον). -**αστήϊον**, f. l. for sq. in Hdt.3. 142. -**αστεύς**, έως, ὁ, = προαστίτης, St.Byz. s. v. ἄστυ. ※ -**άστιον**, τό, *suburb*, Pi.*Fr*.129.2, S.*El*.1432, E.*Alc*.836, Hdt.1.78, 3.142, 8.129, Th.2.34, *IG*2².1191.19 (iv B.C.), *SIG*1215.27 (Myconus, iii/ii B.C.), *AP*11.38 (Polem. Rex) ; opp. ὁ τῆς πόλεως περίβολος, Pl.*Lg*.759a, cf. Th.5.2, Plb.4.78.11, etc. : pl., Hdt.2.41, X.*HG*3.2.27, Lxx *Nu*.35.2, 7, Luc.*Herm*.24, *OGI*483.160 (Pergam.), 669.48 (Egypt, i A.D.), *PGrenf*.2.70.3 (iii A.D.), etc. 2. *house* or *estate in the suburbs*, Philostr.*VA*1.7, *VS*2.1.11. -**άστιος**, α, ον, *suburban*, γῆ S.*Fr*.721. (The spelling -αστειο- is found in some late Papyri, *Sammelb*.4651.3 (iii A.D.), etc., and is freq. in codd., but is proved wrong by the metre in Pi., S., E., *AP* ll.cc., cf. St.Byz. s.v. ἄστυ, also by *IG*, *SIG* ll.cc.) -**αστίς**, Boeot. -ϝαστίς, ίδος, ἡ, *resident in a suburb*, Schwyzer 462 *A* 7 (Tanagra, iii B.C.). ※ -**αστίτης** [ῑ], ου, ὁ, *dweller in the suburbs*, St.Byz. s.v. ἄστυ.

**προασφᾰλίζομαι**, Med., *secure before*, ἑαυτόν Eust.52.30 :—Pass., *to be so secured*, κεφαλὴν -ησφαλίσθαι τέγξεσι Aret.*CA*2.3 ; προησφαλίσθαι πρὸς τὸ ἄδηλον, τὸ πτῶμα, J.*BJ*1.3.3, 6.1.4 ; ἐλπίδα *in hope*, Id.*AJ*17.5.5.

**προατονέω**, *to be previously relaxed*, Sor.1.65.

**προατῠχέομαι**, *to be unfortunate before*, τὰ προητυχημένα D.S.31.9.

**προαυαίνω**, *dry first*, Hp.*Mul*.2.137 (Pass., cj. for προσ-).

**προαυδάω**, *declare before* or *first*, inf. contr. προυδᾶν, πόλεμόν τινι Ar.*Av*.556.

※ **προαυλ-έω**, *play a prelude on the flute*, Arist.*Rh*.1414ᵇ23. -**ημα**, ατος, τό, *prelude on the flute*, Hsch. (prob. s. v. προαυλία), Phot. -**ία**, ἡ, = προαύλιον II, *EM*689.34. **-ίζομαι**, *encamp before a place*, c. gen., App.*Hisp.*25. **-ιον**, τό, (αὐλός) *prelude on the flute*, Pl.*Cra.*417e, Arist.*Rh.*1414ᵇ20: metaph., π. τοῦ λόγου Them.*Or.*33.367a. II. (αὐλή) *place before a court, vestibule*, Poll.1.77, Suid. 2. *space before a cattle-pen*, Poll.9.16.

**προαυξ-ής**, ές, *well-grown*, παιδία Hp.*Art.*62. II. *pertaining to elderly persons*, νόσοι Id.ap.Gal.19.132. **-ησις**, ιος, ἡ, *growing out*, Hp.*Epid.*2.1.8. **-ω**, *cause to grow out*, ibid.

**προαφαιρέω**, *take away before*, Thphr.*HP*7.3.4; τοῦ πιτυρίτου τὸ καθαρώτατον Gal.11.120, cf. 12.465; π. τοῦ χρόνου *anticipate* the appointed time, App.*BC*2.26:—Med., π. τὸ θάρσος τοῖς λόγοις D.S.5.29, cf. App.*Mith.*90.

**προαφᾰνίζομαι**, *disappear before*, D.S.1.29, Hld.10.36, Orib.*Fr.*75.

**προαφ-αναίνω**, *dry up before*, προαφαυανθέντα Ph.2.370. **-έλκω**, *draw off first*, Aët.6.28 (Pass.). **-έψω**, *boil down before*, Gal.6.290,667:—Pass., Thphr.*HP*7.12.2, Dsc.1.107, Antyll.ap.Orib.9.24.8. **-ηγέομαι**, Ion. προαπηγ-, *relate before*, τὴν συμφορὴν Hdt.3.138, cf. *PMasp.*89.24 (vi A.D.). ⊛ **-ίημι**, *release first*, π. τοῦ αἵματος *let* some blood *before*, Hp.*Vid.Ac.*3; *dismiss first*, τὰ στρατόπεδα D.C.37.50. **-ικνέομαι**, *arrive first*, Th.4.2,8.100, J.*AJ*2.7.4. **-ίσταμαι**, Pass., with pf. and aor. 2 Act., *secede, revolt before*, Th.3.12, etc. 2. *leave off* or *desist before*, Pl.*Smp.*175d, etc.; μὴ π., πρὶν ἄν.. Id.*Phd.*85c; ἅπαντα.. ἐξευρίσκεται, ἂν μὴ προαποστῇς Alex.30.2. II. *depart from before*, τῶν ὅπλων -αποστῆναι, of soldiers laying down arms, D.C.49.41.

**προαφρίζω**, = προαπαφρίζω (which shd. perh. be read), *despumate*, μέλι Gal.6.450:—Pass., Dsc.*Eup.*2.33.

**προβάδην** [ᾰ], Adv., (προβαίνω) *as one walks*, Hes.*Op* 729; π. ἔξαγε lead them out *onward*, Ar.*Ra.*352 (lyr.): metaph., *advancing gradually*, of intervals in musical scales, Iamb.*VP*26.121.

**προβᾰδίζω**, *go before*, σκιὰ π. σώματος Plu.2.707b, cf. *Hippiatr.*1.

**προβᾰθύς**, ύ, *very deep*, A.R.4.283 (v.l. προβαθής).

**προβαίνω**, fut. -βήσομαι: pf. -βέβηκα: aor. 2 προὔβην, imper. πρόβᾱ, Ar.*Ach.*262, E.*Alc.*872 (lyr.), pl. πρόβᾰτε S.*OC*841 (lyr.), E.*HF*1047 (lyr.): Hom. has only pf. and pres. part. προβιβάς (as if from βίβημι), Il.13.18, but προβιβῶντα (-τι) (as if from βιβάω) ib.807, al. codd. (v. infr.); imper. προβιβάσθων Hsch.; part. προβάοντε, read by Aristarch. for προβοῶντε, Il.12.277; προβῶντες Cratin.126:—*step forward, advance*, κραιπνά, κοῦφα ποσὶ προβιβάς, Il.13.18,158, Od.17.27; τὸν δ' ὦκα προβιβάντα (-βιβῶντα codd.) πόδες φέρον 15.555; ὑπασπίδια προβιβάντι (-βιβῶντι codd.) Il.13.807, cf. 16.609; π. εὐθέσι τοῖς σκέλεσι Arist.*HA*604ᵇ5: c. acc. cogn., οἵαν ὁδὸν ἁ δειλαιοτάτα π. E.*Alc.*263 (lyr.); μέγα π. *take a* big *stride forward*, Hp.*Art.*60. b. of hair, *grow*, Lib.*Or.*64.50. 2. as a mark of Time, ἄστρα προβέβηκε they *are far gone* in heaven, i.e. it is past midnight, Il.10.252; ἡ νὺξ π. the night *is wearing fast*, X.*An.*3.1.13: hence of Time itself, τοῦ χρόνου προβαίνοντος as time *went on*, Hdt.3.53,140; ὁ μὲν χρόνος δὴ διὰ χρόνου προὔβαινέ μοι S.*Ph.*285; also τὰ μὲν προβέβηκεν the *past*, Thgn.583; προβαίνοντος τοῦ ἔργου, τοῦ πολέμου, Hdt.7.23, Plb.2.47.3; τοῦ κώθωνος εὖ μάλα προβεβηκότος Hegesand.21; ἐκ τοῦ προβεβηκότος, *e re nata, on the spur of the moment*, Plb.7.12.2: of Age, προβήσεται ἡ ἡλικία X.*Ap.*6; of persons, οἱ προβεβηκότες τῇ ἡλικίᾳ *advanced* in age, Lys.24.16, cf. D.S.12.18; π. τῶν ἡμερῶν, ταῖς ἡμέραις, Lxx*Jo.*13.1, 23.1: abs., οἱ π. Bato 7.9, Luc.*Nigr.*24; ἐπεὶ προέβη τοῖς ἔτεσιν Macho ap.Ath.13.580c; προβεβηκότες ἐν ταῖς ἡμέραις αὐτῶν *Ev.Luc.*1.7, cf. 18; ἡλικίας εἰς τὸ πρόσθε π. Pl.*Ep.*325c; π. εἰς πεντήκοντα ἔτη D.C.68.4 (nisi leg. προεβεβιώκει). 3. metaph. of narrative, argument, action, events, μὴ πέρα προβῇς λόγου Cratin.66; προβήσομαι ἐς τὸ πρόσω τοῦ λόγου Hdt.1.5; προβάς φησιν.. *further on*, Demetr.Lac.*Herc.*1012.12, cf. Phld.*Rh.*1.87 S.; π. ἐκ τῶν κνημέων ἐς τοὺς μηροὺς *went on*.., Hdt.6.75; προέβαινε τὸ ἔθνος ἄρχον καὶ ἐπιτροπεῦον the nation *was organized in a series* of overlordships and mandates, Id.1.134; προὔβης τῶνδε καὶ περαιτέρω A.*Pr.*249; π. ἐπ' ἔσχατον θράσους S.*Ant.*853 (lyr.); οἷ προβαίνει τὸ πρᾶγμα τοῦ βουλεύματος Ar.*Ach.*836; ποῖ προβήσεται λόγος; E.*Hipp.*342; πέρας δὴ ποῖ κακῶν προβήσεται; Id.*Or.*511, cf. 749; τὸ τῆς τύχης ἀφανὲς οἷ προβήσεται Id.*Alc.*785; μὴ προβαίη μεῖζον ἢ τὸ νῦν κακόν Id.*Med.*907; τὸ ἔθος ἐπὶ πολὺ προβαίνει Aeschin.1.179: impers., εἰς τοῦτο προβέβηκε ὥστε.. it *has gone* so *far* that.., Pl.*Lg.*839c; π. πόρρω μοχθηρίας *to be* far *gone* in knavery, X.*Ap.*30; π. εἰς τοῦτο ἔχθρας ὥστε.. D.12.16; εἰς ἀταξίαν Aeschin.3.38; μέχρι τίνος Plb.2.1.3; ἐπὶ τὸ χεῖρον π. τὰ πράγματα Id.5.30.6: in good sense, *make progress*, τοσοῦτον προβεβήκαμεν ὥστε.. Pl.*Tht.*187a; of an enterprise, *prosper, succeed*, *BGU*1209.10 (i B.C.). II. *go before*, i.e. *be superior to*, another, πολὺ προβέβηκας ἁπάντων σῷ θάρσει Il.6.125; κράτεϊ 16.54, cf. 23.890; δυνάμει τε καὶ αἰδοῖ Τρηχῖνος προβέβηκε by might and awe *he is over*, i.e. *rules*, Trachis, Hes.*Sc.*355, cf. Call.*Epigr.*1.5. III. c. acc. rei, *overstep*, τέρμα προβάς Pi *N.*7.71. IV. with acc. of the instrum. of motion, πόδα π. Thgn.283; οὐκ ἂν προβαίην τὸν πόδα τὸν ἕτερον Ar.*Ec.*161, cf. Luc.*Hist.Conscr.*29; προβὰς δὲ κῶλον E.*Ph.*1412; ἀρβύλαν προβάς Id.*Or.*1470 (lyr.); προβεβήκασι τὰ ἀριστερά *have* their *left legs foremost* (v.l. προβεβλήκασι, v. προβάλλω A.II.1), Arist.*IA*706ᵃ7; προβὰς τὸν πόδα τὸν ἀριστερὸν καὶ τὸν δεξιὸν ὑποβάς Poll.5.23. V. Causal, in fut. Act., *move forward, advance*, τίς τρόπος ἄνδρα προβάσει [ᾱ]; Pi.*O.*8.63.

**προβακχήϊος**, ὁ, Ion. for -ειος, of Dionysus, *leader of the Bacchanals*, E.*Ba.*412 (lyr., codd., sed leg. πρόβακχ' εὔιε).

**προβᾰλάνειον** [λᾰ], τό, *ante-room before the bath*, Archig.ap.Gal.13.168: pl., *CIG*3080 (Teos).

**προβαλλός**, ὁ, = πρόβλημα II, *shield*, Hdn.Gr.1.158; cf. **πρόβαλλος** Phot., **προβάλους** Hsch.

⊛ **προβάλλω**, fut. -βαλῶ: pf. -βέβληκα: Ep. aor. 2 προβάλεσκον Od.5.331: Hom. has only aor. Act. and Med. without augm.:—*throw* or *lay before, throw to*, Νότος Βορέῃ προβάλεσκε [σχεδίην] φέρεσθαι l.c.; τοὺς μαζοὺς κυσὶ προέβαλε Hdt.9.112; τρωγάλια τοῖς θεωμένοις Ar.*Pl.*798; πυροὺς ὀλίγους π. Id.*Av* 626; π. τινὰ ταῖς Νύμφαις Pl.*Phdr.*241e; ἀνδρὶ δέμας, of a woman, E.*Cret.*6: without dat., π. ἀκήδευτα τὰ σώματα Plu.*Per.*28. II. *put forward*, π. πρόβλημα Pl.*Sph.*261a; ἄμφω τὰ δεξιὰ προβεβληκώς, of a horse, Arist.*Po.*1460ᵇ19 (also Med., τὰ ἀριστερὰ προβάλλονται Id.*IA*706ᵃ6); χλαμύδα ἀλώπεκι Paus.4.18.6; π. αὑτὸν ἐς τὸ μέσον Luc.*Cat.*25: metaph., ἀγαθὴν ἐλπίδα π. σαυτῷ Men.572:—Pass., v. infr. B.III.1. b. in obstetrics, *present*, Act. and Pass., Hp.*Mul.*1.69, Sor.2.60, al. 2. ἔριδα προβαλόντες *putting forth* strife, i.e. striving, Il.11.529. 3. *put forward* as an argument or plea, ἐπεί μοι τὴν θέμιν προὔβαλες S.*Tr.*810; Κύπριν E.*Hec.*825; τοὔνομα τὸ τῆς εἰρήνης D.9.8:—Pass., τὸν ὑφ' ἁπάντων προβαλλόμενον λόγον Th.6.92; ἐς ἐνθυμίαν αἰεὶ προβαλλόμενος Id.5.16. 4. Med., *put forward, propose for an office*, λῃτουργεῖν π. γυμνασίαρχον And.1.132:—Pass., v. infr. B.I.4. 5. *propound* a question, task, problem, riddle (cf. πρόβλημα IV), Ar.*Nu.*757, Pl.*R.*536d; αἴνιγμα, γρῖφον, Id.*Chrm.*162b, Antiph.74.5; χαλεπὴν π. αἵρεσιν Pl.*Sph.*245b; εὐσκεπτον σκέψιν π. Id.*Phlb.*65d; ἀπορίαν Arist.*Pol.*1283ᵇ35: later folld. by interrog. clause, πρόβαλε σαυτῷ τί ἂν ἐποίησεν ἐν τούτῳ Σωκράτης Epict.*Ench.*33.12; θεοῦ προβαλόντος πότερον.. Aristid.1.41 J.:—Pass., προβάλλεται τάδε θεωρῆσαι, περὶ τοῦ κώνου προβεβλημένα ἐστὶ τάδε, Archim.*Con.Sph.Praef.*, *Spir.Praef.* 6. *put forth beyond*, κάρα.. ὀχημάτων S.*El.*740; τῶν ὀδόντων τὴν γλῶσσαν Aret.*SA*1.7; φλέγμα καὶ ἀφρῶδες ἐκ τοῦ στόματος Philum.*Ven.*1.2. III. *expose, give up*, π. σφέας αὐτοὺς ὑπὸ τοῦ κακοῦ give themselves *up for lost*, Hdt.7.141; ἐμαυτὸν εἰς ἀρὰς δεινὰς S.*OT*745; ψυχὴν π. ἐν κύβοισι δαίμονος *hazard, venture*, E.*Rh.*183. IV. *send forth, emit*, τράγου ὀσμὴν v.l. (for προσ-) in Dsc.4.50; τὴν φωνὴν ὀξεῖαν π. D.S.3.8; ἦχον τραχὺν Id.5.30, etc.; *produce*, καρπὸν J.*AJ*4.8.19; ἄνθος Aët.12.1:—Pass., c. gen., *to be emitted from*, αἱ τῶν θεῶν δυνάμεις προβεβλημέναι τῶν πρώτων Procl.*inPrm.*p.552 S. V. intr., *stick out*, of the tongue, Arist.*PA*660ᵃ24. 2. *fall forward*, εἰς τὸ μέτωπον Sch.Ar.*Av.*487.

B. Med. with pf. Pass. (used also in pass. sense, v. infr.):—*throw* or *toss before one*, οὐλοχύτας προβάλοντο Il.1.458, al.: hence, *throw away, expose*, S.*Ph.*1017. 2. *set before* or *in front*, θεμείλιά τε προβάλοντο Il.23.255. 3. *set before oneself, propose to oneself*, ἔργον Hes.*Op.*779. 4. *put forward, propose for election*, Hdt.1.98, Pl.*Lg.*755c sq., X.*An.*6.1.25, *IG*2².1343.29, etc.; προβαλλόμενος ἑαυτὸν D.21.15:—Pass., Hdt. l.c., Pl. l.c., etc.; προβληθεὶς πυλάγορος οὗτος D.18.149, cf. 285. 5. c. dat. et inf., *challenge* a person to.., π. μοι [ὀμόσαι] Mitteis*Chr.*32 i 14, cf. ii 13 (ii B.C.):—Pass., of the oath, *to be proposed as a challenge*, ib. ii 25, *Sammelb.*5231.9 (i A.D.). II. *throw beyond, beat in throwing*: hence, *surpass, excel*, c. gen. pers. et dat. rei, ἐγὼ δέ κε σεῖο νοήματί γε προβαλοίμην Il.19.218. III. *hold before oneself* so as to protect, λαιᾷ ἴτυν Tyrt.15.3; Πηλεΐδα κατ' ὄμμα πέλταν E.*Rh.*370 (lyr.); τὼ χεῖρε Ar.*Ra.*201; π. τὰ ὅπλα *level* arms, opp. μεταβάλλεσθαι (cf. προβολή I), τὴν φάλαγγα ἐκέλευσε προβαλέσθαι τὰ ὅπλα καὶ ἐπιχωρῆσαι X.*An.*1.2.17, cf. 6.5.16, *Mem.*3.8.4: in pf. Pass., σάρισαν προβεβλημένος *having* his pike *advanced*, with levelled pike, D.S.17.100; τοὺς θυρεοὺς πρὸ τῶν νώτων..-βεβλημένοι Arr.*Tact.*36.1; εἰκοσάπηχύν τινα προβεβλ. κοντόν Luc.*DMort.*27.4; also προβεβλημένοι τοὺς θωρακοφόρους *having* them *to cover* one *in front*, X.*Cyr.*6.3.24; π. τάφρον, ποταμόν, of a general, Plb.1.18.3, 2.5.5; π. τῆς.. στρατοπεδείας τεῖχος Id.1.48.10, etc.; πόλις -βεβλημένη ποταμὸν Str.11.2.17; π. τὰ θηρία πρὸ τῶν κεράτων, λογχοφόρους τῆς δυνάμεως, Plb.3.72.9, 3.113.6: abs., *stand in front*, πρὸ ἀμφοῖν προβεβλημένος *standing so as to cover* both, X.*An.*4.2.21, cf. *Cyr.*2.3.10: c. gen., τούτου προβέβληται Πολύευκτος D.21.139; προβάλλεσθαι ἢ ἐναντίον βλέπειν οὔτ' οἶδεν οὔτ' ἐθέλει Id.4.40; προαίρεσις τῆς πολιτείας προβεβλημένη *a guarded* policy, Id.19.27; πρὸς ἅπαντας -βεβλημένος *on one's guard* against, Plu.*Dio* 9:—Pass., ἱππῆς προβέβληνται πρὸ τοῦ δεξιοῦ κέρως Arr.*Tact.*36.2; κράνη πρὸ τῆς κεφαλῆς π. ib.34.3. 2. metaph., *put forward*, τὴν ἀγαθὴν προβαλλόμενος ἐλπίδα D.18.97; ταύτην τὴν συμμαχίαν ib.195; τὴν Εὔβοιαν προβαλέσθαι πρὸ τῆς Ἀττικῆς ib.301, cf. 300, Isoc.5.122; τι πρὸ τῆς αἰσχύνης Aeschin.3.11. b. *bring forward, cite on one's own part, in defence*, τὸν Ὅμηρον π. Pl.*La.*201b; π. μάρτυρας Is.7.3, etc.; ὁ προβαλόμενος *one who has brought evidence*, Lex ap.D.46.10; *cite as an example*, ἔθνος οὐδὲν ἔχομεν προβαλέσθαι σοφίης πέρι Hdt.4.46; *use as an excuse* or *pretext*, Th.2.87, etc.; τὸ εὐπρεπὲς ἄσπονδον προβέβληνται Id.1.37; π. σκῆψιν, πρόφασιν, Plb.5.56.7, 15.20.3. IV. in Att. law, *accuse* a person by προβολή (v. προβολή V), *present him as guilty* of the offence, προὐβαλόμην ἀδικεῖν τοῦτον περὶ τὴν ἑορτήν D.21.1 (cf. Harp. s.v. προβαλλομένους); π. τινά τι ib.28; τινα alone, ib.175; ὁ προβαλλόμενος the *prosecutor* in a προβολή, ib.179:—Pass., *to be accused* or *presented*, προὐβλήθησαν X.*HG*1.7.35: generally, *attack, censure*, τὸ ἔθος D.H.4.24, cf. Ph.2.137; τοὺς ψευδομένους J.*BJ*2.8.7 (s.v.l.), cf. Plu.*CG*14; opp. ἐπαινεῖν, Id.2.18d.

**προβάπτω**, *dip first*, εἰς γάλα τι Sor.2.32:—Pass., *PHolm.*4.2.

**προβᾰρύνω**, *load beforehand*, τὴν γαστέρα Philostr.*Gym.*46.

**προβᾰσᾰνίζω**, *examine* or *test before*, Hero *Aut.*2.5 (Pass.). 2. *torture before*, Luc.*Tyr.*17:—Pass., Lxx 4 *Ma.*10.16, J.*AJ*17.5.5; τοῦ θανάτου Id.*BJ*5.11.1.

⊛ **προβᾰσῐλεύω**, *rule* or *govern before*, D.S.1.51.

⊛ **πρόβᾰσις**, εως, ἡ, *property in cattle, abundance of cattle*, κειμήλιά τε πρόβασίν τε Od.2.75; cf. προβατεία. II. *advance*, τὰς π. ποιεῖσθαι Str.7.1.5; *progression* of musical sounds, Iamb.*VP*26.120; π. τῶν χρόνων Sor.1.110: pl., ἡ. τοῦ νοῦ Ph.1.595. 2. bodily *growth*, Sor.1.114, Gal.19.373. 3. ἐκ προβάσεως, = ἐκ προσαγωγῆς, Maria ap.Zos.Alch.p.158 B.

**προβασκ-αίνω**, *envy before* or *because of*, τινί τινος, prob. for προσ– in Lib.*Decl.*29.2. ⊛ **-ανία**, ἡ, = βασκανία, *BGU*954.9 (vi A.D.). ⊛ **-άνιον**, τό, *safeguard against witchcraft, amulet* or *scarecrow* hung up before workshops or in fields. Lxx *Ep.Je.*70, Plu.2.681f, Hsch. s.v. κεράμβηλον; = *muttonius*, *Gloss.* (also προβασκαντον, = *muttonium*, ib.); less correct than βασκάνιον, Phryn.68.

**προβαστάζω**, *carry away beforehand*, *POxy.*935.21 (iii A.D.).

**προβᾰτ-άγριον**, τό, *wild sheep*, *Gloss.* **-αία**, ἡ, = ὠκιμοειδές, Ps.-Dsc.4.28. **-εία**, ἡ, *keeping of sheep*, *SIG*1165.4 (Dodona), J.*AJ*1.2.2, *AB*294: pl., Plu.*Sol.*23, *Publ.*11. II. *property in cattle, flock of sheep*, Str.12.3.13, Ael.*NA*4.32 (pl.), etc. **-ειος**, α, ον, *of a sheep*, [γάλα] Arist.*HA*522ᵃ22; στέαρ J.*AJ*3.11.2; κρέας S.E.*P.*3.223, cf. Str.11.8.6. II. **προβάτειον**, τό, = ἀρνόγλωσσον, Ps.-Dsc.2.126; but **προβάτειος**, = θύμβρα, Id.3.37. **-ερον**, v. πρόβατον I. 2. ⊛ **-εύς**, έως, ὁ, = προβατευτής, title of play by Antiphanes, Poll.7.184. **-εύσιμος**, ον, *suited for pasturage*, πόα Ph. 2.91,131. **-ευτής**, οῦ, ὁ, *grazier*, Poll.7.184. **-ευτικός**, ή, όν, *of* or *for cattle*, κύων *sheep*-dog, Philostr.*VA*6.42, Longus 3.7: ἡ π. τέχνη the art *of breeding* or *keeping sheep*, X.*Oec.*5.3, cf. Poll.7.184. **-εύω**, *keep cattle*, *SIG*1165 (Dodona), App.*BC*1.7; *tend sheep*, *AP*7.636 (Crin.):—Pass., *to be grazed by cattle*, D.H.1.37. II. *keep at grass, graze*, ἑκατὸν πλείω τὰ μείζονα App.*BC*1.8. **-εών**, ῶνος, ὁ, *sheep-pen*, Hdn.*Epim.*113; cf. προβατών. **-ημα**, ατος, τό, = πρόβατον, Hsch. **-ικός**, ή, όν, *of sheep* or *goats*, π. χορός a chorus *of goats*, as in the Αἶγες of Eupolis, Eust.1063.44; ἡ π. πύλη the *sheep*-gate, Lxx *Ne.*3.1; without πύλη, *Ev.Jo.*5.2 (nisi leg. π. κολυμβήθρα); χόρτος π. *PGoodsp.Cair.*30 xxxiv 6 (ii A.D.). ⊛ **-ιον**, τό, Dim. of πρόβατον, *little sheep*, Ar.*V.*955, *Pl.*293, Pl.*Phdr.*259a, Strato Com. 1.22, Sotad.9.3, Plu.*Fab.*1, Philostr.*VA*3.43; π. ἀγαπητόν Men.319.3; προβατίου βίος Ar.*Pl.*922; προβατίου γνώμη Procop.*Arc.*13; of a *kid*, Ar.*Av.*856.

⊛ **προβᾰτο-βοσκός**, ὁ, *shepherd*, Hsch. s.v. ἀρηνοβοσκός, *Gloss.* **-γνώμων**, ον, gen. ονος, *good judge of cattle*: metaph., *good judge of character*, A.*Ag.*795 (anap.). ⊛ **-δόρας**, ου, ὁ, *sheep-flayer*, name of the month Ληναιών, Procl.ad Hes.*Op.*502. **-θύτης** [ῠ], ου, ὁ, *slaughterer of sheep*, *PKlein.Form.*326 (vi A.D.). **-κάπηλος** [κᾰ], ὁ, *sheep-dealer, retailer of sheep*, Plu.*Per.*24, *Com.Adesp.*62. **-κόμος**, ὁ, *one who tends sheep*, Anon. in Rh.3.607 W. **-κτηνοτρόφος**, ον, *keeping sheep and cattle*, *OGI*655.5 (Egypt, i B.C.), *PHamb.*34.6 (ii A.D.), etc.

⊛ **πρόβᾰτον**, τό, freq. in pl. πρόβατα (but also in sg., Cratin.43, Pl. *Euthd.*302a, etc.); heterocl. dat. πρόβασι Hdn.Gr.1.414, Hsch.:—used (among the Ionians and Dorians) of all four-footed *cattle*, Hdt. 2.41, etc.; πάντων τῶν π. βόες μάλιστα ἀτονέουσι Hp.*Art.*8; τὰ ἄλλα π. καὶ ἵππους μάλιστα Hdt.4.61, cf. Pi.*Fr.*316, *IG*12(1).677.31 (Rhodes, iv/iii B.C.); of Europa's bull, Simon.28: in Hom. generally of *cattle, flocks* and *herds*, Il.14.124, 23.550, *h.Merc.*571, cf. *IG*12(7).62.35 (Amorgos, iv B.C.); τὰ π. καὶ καρταίποδα *Leg.Gort.*4.35; opp. ἄνθρωποι, Hes.*Op.*558, Hdt.1.203; τὰ λεπτὰ τῶν π. small *cattle*, i.e. sheep and goats, ib.133, 8.137; τὸ μὲν μέζον π. . ., τὸ δὲ μεῖον *IG*5 (2).3.14 (Tegea, iv B.C.); so later, π. ἀπὸ τῶν ἀρνῶν καὶ τῶν ἐρίφων λήψεσθε Lxx *Ex.*12.5: but in Att. Prose and Com. (never in Trag.) almost invariably of *sheep*, Ar.*Av.*714, Th.2.14, *IG*2².1672.289, etc.; ὥσπερ π. βῆ βῆ λέγων βαδίζει Cratin.43; so in later Boeot., *IG*7.3171. 39,44 (Orchom. Boeot.): generally, *animals for slaughter*, whether for sacrifices, Hdt.6.56; or for food, Id.1.207; cf. Antipho 5.29. 2. prov. of stupid, lazy people, ἀριθμός, πρόβατ' ἄλλως Ar.*Nu.*1203, cf. *V.*32: Com. Comp., προβάτου προβάτερον *more sheepish* than a *sheep*, dub. cj. in Sophr.122; χρυσοῦν π., = Lat. *pecus aurea*, as nickname, D.C.59.8: in other provs., τοὺς γενομένους κύνας τῶν π. κατακόπτειν φασὶ δεῖν D.25.40; λέων ἐν προβάτοις Plu.*Cleom.*33, cf. Plb.5.35. 13. II. name of a sea-fish, Opp.*H.*1.146, 3.139, Ael.*NA*9.38. (Orig. of small cattle, sheep and goats, which in primitive mixed herds *walk in front* (προβαίνει) of the larger animals.)

**προβᾰτο-πώλης**, ου, ὁ, *sheep-dealer*, Ar.*Eq.*132, 138. **-στάσιον** [στᾰ], τό, *sheep-pen*, *Gloss.* **-τροφία**, Ion. -ίη, ἡ, *keeping of sheep*, prob. in *Supp.Epigr.*2.579.8 (Teos, iv B.C.). **-τρόφος**, ον, *breeding sheep*, Sch.Pi.*P.*12.1. **-χίτων** [ῐ], ωνος, ὁ, ἡ, *with coat of sheep's skin*, Hsch. s.v. οἰοχίτων.

⊛ **προβᾰτ-ώδης**, ες, *like a sheep, simple*, Simp.*in Epict.*p.34 D., Hsch. s.v. βαίκυλος, Sch.Ar.*Eq.*264. **-ών**, ῶνος, ὁ, = προβατεών, *IG*11(2). 287 *A* 149, al. (iii B.C.), *PCair.Zen.*68.2 (iii B.C.), *Inscr.Délos* 403.51 (ii B.C.), Hdn.Gr.1.36.

**προ-βᾰφή**, ἡ, *previous dipping*, *PHolm.*8.20. **-βάφιον** [ᾰ], τό, *substance used in first stage of alloying*, Zos.Alch. p.193 B., Maria ap. eund. p.212 B.

**προβεβαιόω**, *confirm before*, S.E.*M.*8.181 (Pass.).

**προβέβουλα**, isolated poet. pf. 2 (προβούλομαι does not occur), *prefer* one to another, τινά τινος Il.1.113, Q.S.13.347; θάνατον δουλοσύνας Ion Lyr.16: c. inf., *AP*9.445 (Jul. Aegypt.): abs., *make plans*, Coluth.199.

**προβεβουλευμένως**, Adv. *premeditatedly*, Poll.6.140.

**πρόβημα**, ατος, τό, *a step forward*, Ar.*Pl.*759.

**προβῐάζομαι**, *force* a measure *through*, Aeschin.3.72.

⊛ **προβῐβ-άζω**, fut. -άσω D.C.58.23, Att. προβιβῶ Ar.*Av.*1570:—causal of προβαίνω, *cause to step forward, lead on*, τινα S.*OC*180 (lyr.); ποῖ προβιβᾷς ἡμᾶς ποτε; to what point, how far *do you mean to carry* us? Ar. l. c.; τινὰ εἰς ἀρετήν, εἰς ἐγκράτειαν, Pl.*Prt.*328a, X.*Mem.*1.5. 1; ἕως Μακεδονίας τὴν ἀρχὴν *extend* it.., D.H.1.3; *push on*, οὐδὲν ἠδύνατο π. τῶν ἔργων Plb.5.100.1:—Pass., *to be developed, improved*, of machines, Hero *Bel.*74.4. 2. *push forward, advance*, τὸ ὑπερκείμενον τοῦ κρημνοῦ (by building a wall) D.S.4.78; *exalt*, τὴν πατρίδα Plb.9.10.4; τινὰ ἐς τὰς ἀρχὰς *promote* him, D.C. l. c.; δύναμιν Phld. *Rh.*1.40 S. 3. *teach*, τινάς τι Lxx *De* 6.7, cf. Plu.*Cat.Mi.*36 (dub.); *put forward* as a representative, *Act.Ap.*19.33 (v. l.):—Pass., *to be instructed* or *egged on*, ὑπὸ τῆς μητρός *Ev.Matt.*14.8. II. intr., = προβαίνω, Plb.10.44.1, Aristid.2.231 J. III. of a male, *mount before*, ἄλλην Arist.*HA*546ᵃ10. **-άς**, v. προβαίνω. **-ᾰσις**, εως, ἡ, *leading forward, advancing*, Nicom.*Harm.*12. **-ασμός**, ὁ, *advancing*, Artem.2.12.

**προβιβρώσκω**, *eat first*, ἣν -βεβρώκῃ ὤνθρωπος Aret.*SA*2.2:—Pass., προβρωθέντα φύλλα Dsc.3.45, cf. 1.125.

**προβῐβῶν**, v. προβαίνω.

**προβῐ-οτή**, ἡ, *previous* (i.e. *antenatal*) *existence*, Plu.*Fr.*7.9, Porph.*Gaur.*11.4, Id. ap. Stob.2.8.42, Hierocl.*Prov.* p.172 B., al., Herm. *in Phdr.* p.109 A. **-όω**, *live before*, mostly pf. part. Pass., τὰ προβεβιωμένα *one's previous life*, Plb.11.2.9, J.*AJ*4.8.15, Plu.2. 561a, Hdn.2.1.8, Plot.3.4.5, cf. Plu.2.10b; also pf. Act. in intr. sense, τὸν προβεβιωκότα χρόνον *IG*12(5).655.10 (Syros). **-ωτος**, ον, *having had a prior existence*, οὐ π. [ἡ ψυχὴ] τοῦ σώματος ἔσται Sophon. *in de An.*135.1.

**προβλαστ-άνω**, *shoot* or *sprout before*, Thphr.*CP*5.1.12, Ph.1. 602; π. πρότερον τῶν λοιπῶν Thphr.*CP*1.13.12; *shoot before the season*, Plu.2.377c. **-ημα**, ατος, τό, *previous shoot*, Thphr.*CP*5. 2.2.

**πρόβλαστος**, ὁ, epith. of Dionysus, Lyc.577 (ἐπεί, ὅταν βλαστάνωσιν αἱ ἄμπελοι.., θύουσιν αὐτῷ, Sch.). II. f.l. for πρωΐβλαστος, q.v.

**προβλεπτικός**, ή, όν, *able to foresee*, τῶν μελλόντων Eust.83.33.

**προβλέπω**, *foresee*, ὅτι ἥξει ἡ ἡμέρα Lxx *Ps.*36(37).13; *provide against*, D.H.11.20; λογισμῷ μηδὲν π. Heraclit.*Incred.*11; τῇ ψυχῇ προβλέπειν Him.*Or.*31.1; *provide*, θανάτου μνημόσυνον *IG*12(8).561 (Thasos):—Med., θεοῦ περὶ ἡμῶν τι προβλεψαμένου *Ep.Hebr.*11.40.

**πρόβλημα**, ατος, τό, (προβάλλω) *anything thrown forward* or *projecting*, πόντου π. ἁλίκλυστον sea-washed *promontory*, S.*Aj.*1219 (lyr.). 2. *hindrance, obstacle*, Hp.*Nat.Mul.*67, *Mul.*1.20, Ael. *NA*2.13. II. *anything put before one as a defence, bulwark, barrier*, προβλήματα ἀντ' ἀσπίδων ἐποιεῦντο γεράνων δοράς Hdt.7.70, cf. 4.175; τῶν..π. τὰ μὲν πρὸς τὸν πόλεμον ὁπλίσματα, τὰ δὲ φράγματα Pl.*Plt.* 279d sq., cf. *Sph.*261a; σώματος π., of a shield, A.*Th.*540; νεῶν προβλήματα, of a wall, E.*Rh.*213; χαλκᾶ προβλήματα the brazen *armour* of horses, X.*Cyr.*6.1.51. 2. c. gen. objecti, *defence against* a thing, αἰχμῆς καὶ πέτρων A.*Th.*676; χείματος προβλήματα E.*Supp.* 208; π. χειμώνων Pl.*Ti.*74b; π. κακῶν Ar.*V.*615; κρύους π. ποιοῦνται τὴν ἐσθῆτα Plu.2.691d; but, 3. μηδὲν φόβου π. μηδ' αἰδοῦς ἔχειν to have neither fear nor reverence *as a defence*, S.*Aj.*1076; τὸν ποταμὸν π. λαβεῖν, ποιήσασθαι, Plb.2.66.1, 3.14.5. III. *anything put forward as an excuse*, π. τοῦ τρόπου D.45.69; λαβὼν π. σαυτοῦ παῖδα making *a screen* of him, S.*Ph.*1008. IV. *task, business*, E.*El.*985, Gal.11. 250. 2. *problem* in Geometry, etc., Pl.*R.*530b, *Tht.*180c sq., Plu. *Marc.*14, 19, etc.; φυσικὰ π. Epicur.*Ep.*2 p.36 U.; οἱ κατὰ πρόβλημα λόγοι (opp. τὰ ἐν τῷ βίῳ) theoretical, Phld.*Lib.* p.59 O. 3. in the Logic of Arist., *question as to whether a statement is so or not*, Arist. *Top.*101ᵇ28, cf. 104ᵇ1: τὰ π. title of work by Arist., cf. *Mete.*363ᵃ24, *PA*676ᵃ18, *GA*747ᵇ5, cf. προβληματικός; also of the extant work wrongly ascribed to Arist. 4. practical or theoretical *problem*, εἰς π. παμμέγεθες ἐνέπεσε Plb.28.13.9; εὕροντο λύσιν τοῦ π. Id.30.19. 5; ἐν προβλήμασιν ἢ κρίνομεν ἢ βουλευόμεθα Hermog.*Inv.*1.1. 5. *riddle*, π. προβάλλειν Lxx *Jd.*14.12.

**προβλημ-ᾰτικός**, ή, όν, *of* or *for a problem*: τὰ π. title of work by Arist. (cf. πρόβλημα IV. 3), *Somn.Vig.*456ᵃ29. **-άτιον**, τό, Dim. of πρόβλημα, Arr.*Epict.*2.20.33, *Gloss.* **-ᾰτοπλόκος**, ον, *framing problems* or *riddles*, Tz.*H.*2.518. **-ᾰτουργικός**, ή, όν, *of* or *for the construction of fortifications*, Poll.7.207; -κή (sc. τέχνη), ἡ, ibid.; ἡ π. δύναμις the faculty *of constructing them*, Pl.*Plt.*280d. **-ᾰτώδης**, ες, *problematical*, Plu.*Cat.Mi.*25.

**προ-βλής**, ῆτος, ὁ, ἡ, *thrown forward, jutting out*, προβλῆτι σκοπέλῳ Il.2.396; πέτρῃ ἔπι προβλῆτι 16.407; στήλας τε προβλῆτας 12.259; ἀκταὶ προβλῆτες ἔσαν Od.5.405, cf. 10.89, 13.97, Archil.49 Diehl; προβλῆτες, without subst., *forelands, headlands*, S.*Ph.*936; τόν γε (sc. ποταμόν) εἴργουσιν π. Q.S.10.175: sg., Opp.*H.*5.252; π. ἔπαλξις, ἐρίπνα, *AP*5.293.3 (Agath.), 7.147 (Arch.); π. γενειάς Nonn.*D.*15.8; προσώπου π. γένυς ib.28.75; γναθμοῖς π. ὀδόντες ib.26.301: in later Prose, προβλῆτες λιμένων πύργοι Lxx 4 *Ma.*13.6; λιμένες προβλῆσι λίθοις εἰς τὸ πέλαγος ἐξανεστηκότες Aristid.*Or.*25(43).3; ὀφρύες π. Aret. *SD*2.13. **-βλητέον**, f.l. for προσ–, Sor.2.87. **-βλητικός**, ή, όν, *productive*, τινος Simp.*in Ph.*1138.32, *Gloss.* **-βλῆτις**, ιδος, fem. of προβλής, Sch.Opp.*H.*3.460. **-βλητος**, ον, *thrown forth* or *away*, κυσὶν π. *cast* to the dogs, S.*Aj.*830. II. *spread, beaten out* into plates, ἀργύριον prob. l. in Lxx *Je.*10.5(9). **-βλήτωρ**, ορος, ὁ, *producer*, *Gloss.*

* προβλώσκω, aor. inf. προμολεῖν, *go* or *come forth, go out of the house*, δμῳὰς δ' οὐκ εἴας προβλωσκέμεν Od.19.25; ὁ δὲ προμολών 4.22, cf. 24.388, Il.21.37; μή τι θύραζε προβλώσκειν Od.21.239, cf. Opp.*H*. 2.252: c. gen., προβλώσκειν μεγάρων Orph.*Fr*.270.6.

**προβοάω,** *shout before, cry aloud*, τώ γε προβοῶντε μάχην ὤτρυνον (v. προβαίνω init.) Il.12.277, cf. S.*Ph*.218 (lyr.).

**προβοηθέω,** *hasten to aid before*, προβοηθῆσαι ἐς τὴν Βοιωτίην Hdt.8.144 (v.l. προσβωθῆσαι).

**προβόλ-αιος,** ον, *held out before one, levelled, in rest*, δούρατι προβολαίῳ Theoc.24.125; προβόλαιος alone, = πρόβολος II, εἴσω τὸν π. ἔχων Orac.ap.Hdt.7.148. **-άριος,** ὁ, dub. sens. in *BGU*14v18 (iii A.D.). **-εύς,** έως, ὁ, *producer, originator*, Procl.*in Cra*.p.2 P., *Gloss*. **-ή,** ἡ, (προβάλλω) *putting forward*, esp. of a weapon for defence, τὰ δόρατα εἰς προβολὴν καθιέναι to bring the spears to *the rest*, couch them, X.*An*.6.5.25 (nisi leg. προσβολήν); [τὰ δόρατα] ἀποτείναι ἐς π. Arr.*An*.1.6.2; κοντοὺς ὀρθοὺς ὡς ἐς π. φέροντες Id.*Tact*.43.2; ἵστανται ἐς π. ib.36.3; ἐν προβολᾷ θεμένα ξίφος bringing it to *the guard*, *AP*7.433 (Tymn.); ὁπλίτας ἑστῶτας ἐν π. standing *with spear in rest*, Plu.*Caes*.44, cf. Plb.2.65.11; ὑπελθεῖν τὴν π. τοῦ πολεμίου get under his *guard*, D.H.3.19; of a pugilist, δοχμὸς ἀπὸ π. κλινθείς Theoc.22.120; παγκρατίου προβολὰν διδάξαι *IG*4²(1).122.53 (Epid., iv B.C.), cf. 7.2470.3 (Thebes, iv/iii B.C.); *Carneades* προβολὴν *pugilis ..similem facit* ἐποχῇ Cic.*Att*.13.21.3; ἀνέχοντες ἐν π. τὰς χεῖρας, of long-distance runners, Philostr.*Gym*.32; ἡ π. τῶν χειρῶν, of boxers, ib.34; αἱ π. τοῦ σώματος X.*Cyn*.10.22; ἡ τῆς φάλαγγος π. the phalanx *with its pikes couched*, Plb.18.30.1; αἱ τῶν θυρεῶν π. Id.1.22.10, cf. Arr.*Tact*.37.5; of the legs, *putting foremost*, Arist.*IA*706a6. 2. *putting forth*, βλαστοῦ *Gp*.5.25.1. 3. *putting forward* of a plea or case, Hermog.*Stat*.4, al. II. *projection, prominence*, ἡ π. τοῦ χείλεος Hp.*Art*.8, etc.; τῆς κεφαλῆς a *prominence* of the skull, Id.*VC*1; τῆς γλώσσης Aret.*SA*1.7; π. ἀπὸ τοῦ χείλεος, of an elephant's trunk, Id.*SD*2.13, cf. Ael.*NA*5.41. 2. *jutting rock, foreland*, or *tongue of land*, S.*Ph*.1455 (anap., prob. for προβλῆς); ἐπὶ προβολῆσι θαλάσσης Q.S.9.378, cf. D.P.1013, Plb.1.53.10; Νειλορύτου δῶρον ἀπὸ π., i.e. from the Delta of the Nile, *AP*9.350 (Leon. Alex.); also the *spur* of a hill, Plu.*Crass*.22. 3. *head of a spear* or κέστρος II, Plb.18.29.3, 27.11.2. 4. *projecting bridge*, Id.3.46.4. 5. *projection* of a weapon from the soldier's body, Ael.*Tact*.14.3. 6. *advanced body* of cavalry, Arr.*Tact*.40.2, al. 7. *rope* for lowering buckets, *PFlor*.153 (iii A.D.), etc. III. *thing held before one as a defence, screen, bulwark*, π. μεγάλη τῆς χώρας X.*Mem*.3.5.27; of the eyebrows, Id.*Cyn*.5.26; τοῦ ὄμματος Arist.*GA*780b23; ὅπως ᾖ π. τοῖς..σπλάγχνοις [τὸ νῶτον] Id.*PA*672a17: c. gen. objecti, *defence against*.., δεῖματος π. καὶ βελέων S.*Aj*.1212 (lyr.); θανάτου E.*Or*.1488 (lyr.); καυμάτων Pl.*Ti*.74b; τοῦ ἡλίου, τῶν ἀνέμων, τοῦ ψύχους, Thphr.*CP*2.7.4, 3.10.4, 5.13.3; πρὸς τοὺς χειμῶνας ib.3.7.2. 2. *protection*, τὰ προβολῆς ἕνεκα εἰργασμένα Pl.*Plt*.288b; π. ἔχειν, of plants, Thphr.*CP*3.20.5; προβεβλημένοι τὴν γαμικὴν π. Dam.*Isid*.160. 3. *front of a horse's hoof*, *Hippiatr*.123. IV. *proposal* of a person's name for election, Pl.*Lg*.765b, *SIG*976.10 (Samos, ii B.C.), *CPR*20.8 (iii A.D.), *Cod.Just*.10.11.8.4, al., Ps.-Ptol.*Centil*.83. V. as law-term, a form of public process by *presentation of a case to the assembly*, D.21.193: pl., ib.11, Lex ib.8,10; τῶν συκοφαντῶν π. ἐποιησάμεθα Aeschin.2.145, cf. X.*HG*1.7.35, Isoc.15.314, Arist.*Ath*.43.5, 59.2, Harp. s.v. καταχειροτονία. VI. *advance, loan*, *PSI*6.666.10 (iii B.C.); π. εἰς τὸ ζῆν financial *provision, means* of livelihood, gloss on ἀφορμή, Sch.E.*Med*.342. **-ιμος,** ον, *liable to a* προβολή V, *IG*5(1).1145.53 (Gythium).

**προβολλεύω,** Aeol. for προβουλεύω I. 2, *IG*12(2).526*d*4 (Eresos).

**προβόλ-ιον,** τό, Dim. of sq. II, *boar-spear*, X.*Cyn*.10.1, Philostr.*Im*.1.2 codd. (προλοβίῳ Benndorf), 28: metaph., Hyp.*Fr*.167. II. *basket*, Hsch. * **-ος,** ὁ, (προβάλλω) *anything that projects*: I. *jutting rock, foreland*, ἐπὶ προβόλῳ Od.12.251: metaph., *boulder in the path, obstacle*, προβόλοις προσπταίειν interpol. in D.8.61; λιμένας προβόλων ἐνέπλησας Id.25.84 (metaph.; also literally, of stones sunk in a harbour, Arr.*An*.2.21.7); τὸν λογισμὸν ὡς π. ἐμποδὼν τῇ γλώττῃ κείμενον Plu.2.510a. 2. πρόβολοι ξύλων *projecting barriers* of wood to break the force of a stream, Id.*Caes*.22. 3. *defence, bulwark*, π. πολέμου, of a fortress, X.*Cyr*.5.3.11 and 23; of a person, *shield, guardian*, π. ἐμός, σωτὴρ δόμοις Ar.*Nu*.1161 (lyr., paratrag.). II. *hunting-spear*, Hdt.7.76; generally, *missile*, Ph.*Bel*.84.11 (pl.). **-ος,** ον, *eligible for nomination* (cf. προβάλλω A. II. 4), *PThead*.17.9 (iv A.D.).

**πρόβονεν·** ἐπέρανεν, Hsch.

**προβόσκ-ημα,** ατος, τό, *plate, dish*, Ph.2.547. **-ίς,** ίδος, ἡ, *means of providing food*: I. elephant's *trunk*, Arist.*PA*659a15, Phylarch.36J., Plb.3.46.12, Agatharch.71, Str.15.1.43. b. fly's *proboscis*, Arist.*HA*528b29. II. pl., *tentacles* of the decapod cephalopoda, ib.523b30, *PA*685a33. **-ός,** ὁ, *assistant herdsman*, Hdt.1.113 (v.l. προβόσκων).

**προβουλ-εία,** ἡ, *office of* πρόβουλος, *Papers of Amer. Sch. at Athens* 3 No.428 (Asia Minor). **-ευμα,** ατος, τό, *preliminary decree of the senate*, to be laid before the Ecclesia, Eup.73 (dub.), D.18.9, 24.11, Aeschin.3.125. II. = Lat. *senatusconsultum*, D.H.6.67, 7.38. **-ευμάτιον,** τό, Dim. of foreg., Luc.*Par*.42, Alciphr.3.22. **-ευσις,** εως, ἡ, *previous deliberation*, Sch.rec.Pi.*O*.7.79. **-εύω,** Aeol. προβολλεύω (q.v.), *contrive* or *concert measures before*, ὅπως μηδὲν δεήσει Th.3.82; ὅπως ἂν ῥῆστα ἐσχηματισμένος ᾖ Hp.*Art*.52; opp. μετανοέω, Democr.66 (Med.); μὴ προβουλεύσας without *premeditation*, Arist.*EN*1135b20:—Med., *debate, consider first*, τι Hdt.1.133: abs., X.*Cyr*.4.3.17, Arist.*EN*1135b10; πρὸς ἕκαστα Hp.*Prog*.1:—Pass., τὸ προβεβουλευμένον Arist.*EN*1112a15. 2. of the βουλή at Athens and elsewh., *frame* or *pass a* προβούλευμα, X.*HG*1.7.7; ἡ βουλὴ ταῦτα προὐβεβουλεύκει D.19.34; ἐξιέναι τοὺς ἱππέας προεβούλευσεν ἡ βουλή Id.21.162; τὴν βουλὴν προβουλεύσασαν ἐξενεγκεῖν εἰς τὸν δῆμον *IG*1².66.17, 110.37; of a board of πρόβουλοι, π. περί τινος Th.8.1, Arist.*Pol*.1298b30; of the Spartan γερουσία, Plu.*Agis* 11; τὸ προβεβουλευμένον, = Lat. *senatusconsultum*, Plb.6.16.2: impers. in Pass., προβεβούλευται ὅπως ἄν.. *it has been decreed* that.., Ar.*Ec*.623; τῇ βουλῇ προβεβ., c. acc. et inf., X.*HG*7.1.2. 3. *award by a* προβούλευμα, τούτων τῶν προβεβουλευμένων..δωρειῶν D.18.53. II. *to have the chief voice in counsel*, X.*Cyr*.8.7.9. III. π. τινός *deliberate for* one, *provide for* his *interest*, Ar.*Eq*.1342, X.*An*.3.1.37; τοῦ δήμου *for* or *before* the people, Arist.*Pol*.1299b33. IV. Med., *make up one's mind beforehand, prejudge* a case, Hp.*Fract*.1. * **-ή,** ἡ, *forethought*, ἐκ προβουλῆς *of malice aforethought*, Antipho 1.5, D.C.47.4, etc. II. *standing committee*, ἡ βουλὴ καὶ ἡ π. dub. in *BCH*26.168 (Syria, i/ii A.D.). **-ιον,** τό, *meeting of* πρόβουλοι, Sch.Il.2.194. **-ομαι,** v. προβέβουλα. **-όπαις,** παιδος, f.l. for προβούλου παῖς, A.*Ag*.386 (lyr.).

**πρόβουλος,** ον, (βουλή) *deliberating beforehand* or *for others*, Ἄτα prob. in A.*Ag*.386 (lyr.): but usu. II. pl., *standing committee to examine measures before* they were formally proposed to the people, Arist.*Pol*.1298b29, 1299b31, 1322b16; at Megara, Ar.*Ach*.755; Corinth, Nic.Dam.60J.; Corcyra, *IG*9(1).682.12; Delphi, *GDI*2642.26; of the ἀμνήμονες at Cnidus, Plu.2.292a; ἀπαγγέλλειν..δήμου προβούλοις A.*Th*.1011. 2. of the *delegates* of the twelve Ionian states at the Panionium, Hdt.6.7; of *delegates* appointed to consult on the mode of meeting Xerxes, π. τῆς Ἑλλάδος Id.7.172. 3. at Athens, *committee of Ten*, appointed after the Sicilian defeat (cf. Th.8.1), Decr. ap.Arist.*Ath*.29.2, Ar.*Lys*.421, Lys.12.65, Arist.*Rh*.1419a28. 4. of the Roman *consuls*, D.H.4.76, 5.1.

**προβρᾰχής,** ές, *shallow*, τὰ π. Plb.1.47.1.

**πρόβρᾰχῠς** (sc. πούς), ὁ, *the foot* ⏑ – – – –, Diom.p.481 K.

**προβρέχω,** *soak beforehand*, Arist.*Pr*.931a14, Thphr.*HP*3.17.2:—Pass., Hp.*Steril*.224: aor. part. προβρᾰχείς Dsc.3.6, *Eup*.2.31.

**πρόβροτος,** ὁ, *former mortal*, dub. in Epigr.ap.D.L.8.45.

**προβύω** [ῡ], fut. -βύσω:—π. λύχνον *push up* the wick of a lamp, *trim* it, cj. in Ar.*V*.250: metaph., π. φορτικὸν γέλωτα *Com.Adesp*.644.

**προβωθέω,** v. προβοηθέω.

**προβώμιος,** ον, (βωμός) *before* or *in front of the altar*, prob. in Pi.*Pae*.9 *Fr*.131; σφαγαί E.*Ion* 376: προβώμια, τά, *space in front of an altar*, Id.*Heracl*.79. II. *placed on the altar beforehand* (as a preliminary sacrifice), *Berl.Sitzb*.1927.161 (Cyrene).

**προγᾰμ-έω,** *live with* a woman *before marriage*, Str.6.1.8:—Pass., of a woman, *to be married before*, τινι App.*Syr*.68. II. *marry first* or *before*, Ph.2.304, Plu.*Alex*.70. 2. *live in wedlock before* or *already*, *BGU*183.6 (i A.D.). * **-ιαῖος,** α, ον, *ante-nuptial*, δωρεά *Cod.Just*.5.1.6, cf. Tz.ad Lyc.547. **-ιος,** ον, = foreg., Ael.*NA*9.66. II. προγάμια (sc. ἱερά), τά, *sacrifice before marriage*, Poll.3.38. * **-ος,** ον, *betrothed*, νύμφαι Tryph.341. II. *before a marriage*: Πρόγαμοι title of a play by Menander, Stob.1.7.2.

**προγᾰνόω,** *cheer* or *comfort beforehand*, Ph.1.104, dub. cj. in 2.416 (Pass., προσ- codd.).

* **προγαργᾰλίζω** (sc. ἑαυτόν), *prepare oneself for tickling*, Arist.*EN*1150b22.

**προγαστ-ρίδιος,** ον, *worn in front of the belly*, ὅπλισις *EM*589.12. II. Subst. προγαστρίδιον, τό, *false paunch worn by actors*, Luc.*Salt*.27, *JTr*.41. **-ρικός,** ή, όν, = προγάστωρ, Alex.Aphr. *in Top*.421.30. **-ριον,** τό, = ὑπογάστριον, Sch.Philostr.*Im*.2.26. **-ωρ,** ορος, ὁ, ἡ, *pot-bellied*, Gerhard *Phoinix* p.6, Str.4.4.6, *App.Anth*.5.11, Luc.*Nec*.11, Gal.10.145, Adam.2.31; of a *pot-bellied* bottle, Antiph.224.6: Comp. προγαστρότερα Hp.*Aër*.24.

**προγελάω,** *smile before*: metaph. of early morning, Ph.1.603.

**προγένειος,** ον, *bearded*, Theoc.3.9, Longus 1.16.

**προγενέτωρ,** ορος, ὁ, = προγεννήτωρ, Pempel.ap.Stob.4.25.52.

**προγενής,** ές, *born before, primeval*, θεοί S.*Ant*.938 (anap.): Comp. προγενέστερος, α, ον, *earlier in birth*, i.e. *older*, Il.2.555, Od.2.29, Theoc.29.10, etc.; γενεῇ π. Il.9.161; τινος 23.789; οἱ π. *those who have gone before us, our predecessors*, Arist.*EN*1181b16, *de An*.403b27, *PA*642a24, Phld.*Ind.Sto*.20: Sup. προγενέστατος, *eldest-born, primordial*, *h.Cer*.110, Arist.*de An*.410b14, Ath.Med.ap.Orib.*inc*.21.21. II. generally, *previous, prior*, συγγραφαί *PSI*8.904.6 (i A.D.); χάρτης *PLond*.1.77.59 (Comp., vi A.D.).

**προγενν-άω,** *beget before*, Thphr.*CP*1.20.3. **-ήτειρα,** ἡ, *ancestress*: *mother*, Lyc.183. **-ήτωρ,** ορος, ὁ, in pl., *forefathers*, E.*Hipp*.1380 (lyr.).

**προγέρων,** οντος, ὁ, *older*, δὶς τῆς σῆς ἡλικίης π. *BMus.Inscr*.829*b*2 (Cnidus).

**προ-γευμᾰτίζω,** *taste before*, τινος Arist.*de An*.422b7. **-γεύσιμον,** τό, *food taken before a meal*, *PKlein.Form*.261.5 (pl., vi A.D.). **-γεύστης,** ου, ὁ, *one who tastes before*, Plu.2.990a, Ath.4.171b: fem. **-γευστρίς,** ίδος, ὀσφρησις Ph.1.170, cf. 603. **-γεύω,** *give a foretaste of*, c. gen., Aristid.Quint.3.27:—Med., *taste before*, Anaxil.10 (prob. cj.), Arist.*PA*690b27, Plu.2.49e; τοῦ μέλλοντος ἀγαθοῦ Ph.1.603.

**προγεωμετρέω,** *measure, survey beforehand*, *PTeb*.151 (ii B.C., Pass.), etc.

**προγεωργ-έω**, *cultivate earlier* or *already*, *BGU*462.18 (ii A.D.), *POxy.*101.8 (Pass., ii A.D.), etc. ⊛ **-ός**, ὁ, *previous cultivator*, *Sammelb.*5672.28 (ii A.D.).

**προγήθω**, *rejoice before*, Ph.1.602.

**προγηράσκω**, *grow old before*, τοῦ χρόνου τοῦ ἱκνευμένου Hp.*Aër.*7: abs., Luc.*Tim.*20. 2. *grow prematurely old*, Id.*Rh.Pr.*10, Sor.1.87; ἐν τοῖς πόνοις Ph.2.287.

**προγήρως**, ων, (γῆρας) *prematurely old*, Poll.2.13.

**προγίγνομαι**, Ion. and later **-γίνομαι** [ῑ]: fut. -γενήσομαι: aor. προὐγενόμην: pf. προγέγονα and -γεγένημαι:—*come forward*, οἱ δὲ τάχα προγένοντο quickly they *came in sight*, Il.18.525, cf. *h.Hom.*7.7; ἄμυδις προγένοντο Hes.*Sc.*345; εἴσω π. Opp.*H.*2.103; κόπρον ἔπι π. Call.*Dian.*178, cf. Theoc.25.134: c. gen., ὠκεανοῖο.. ὁπότε προγένωνται Ἰχθύες Arat.706; ἀστὴρ ὑπὲρ τὸν ὁρίζοντα πρὸ ἁλίου προγενόμενος Ti.Locr.97a. II. *to be born before, exist before*, ἦν..προγεγονότες ἔωσι πρὶν.. Hdt.7.3; οἱ προγεγονότες θεοὶ Id.2.146; οἱ π. ἄνθρωποι *former* men, X.*Mem.*4.8.10; οἱ προγεγενημένοι Id.*Cyr.*8.7.24, etc.; οἱ προγενόμενοι the *previous* crews, Plb.10.17.12. 2. of events, etc., ταὐτά μοι προὐγεγόνει Pl.*Smp.*219e; αἱ ἀκοαὶ τῶν προγεγενημένων reports *of things of old time*, Th.1.20, etc.; τὰ προγεγονότα Hp.*Prog.*1, etc.; προγεγενημένοι [πόλεμοι], καιροί, Th.1.1, Decr.Byz.ap.D.18.90; οἱ προγεγονότες ἡμῖν ἔμπροσθεν λόγοι Pl.*Lg.*699e, cf. *PHib.*1.96.8 (iii B.C.); αἱ διὰ τῆς ψυχῆς ἡδοναὶ πρὸ τῶν διὰ τοῦ σώματος προγίγνοιντ' ἂν Pl.*Phlb.*39d. III. simply, *to be born*, Man.6.255, 336.

**προγιγνώσκω**, Ion. and later **-γῑνώσκω**: fut. -γνώσομαι: Ep. aor. inf. προγνώμεναι *h.Cer.*257:—*know, perceive, learn*, or *understand beforehand*, τι l.c.; τὰ στοιχεῖα Pl.*Tht.*203d: abs., E.*Hipp.*1072; π. ὅτι.. X.*Eq.Mag.*8.12:—Medic., *know before being told, declare unaided*, τά τε παρεόντα καὶ τὰ προγεγονότα καὶ τὰ μέλλοντα ἔσεσθαι Hp.*Prog.*1; τοὺς καιροὺς Id.*Aër.*2. 2. *prognosticate*, π. χειμῶνα αἱ μέλιτται Arist.*HA*627[b]10. 3. *foreknow*, λαὸν *Ep.Rom.*11.2, al. 4. c. gen., π. τῶν θεῶν *learn* things *in advance of*.., Philostr.*VA*8.7. II. *judge beforehand*, ἐς τὸ μέλλον καλὸν π. Th.2.64; *provide*, τι X.*Cyr.*2.4.11:—Pass., παρὰ τῷ διαιτητῇ προεγνωσμένος ἀδικεῖν *judged beforehand* to have done wrong, D.29.58, cf. *Inscr.Délos* 502 A 12 (iii B.C.).

**προγλῠκαίνω**, *sweeten before*, v.l. in Gal.6.546 (Pass.).

**προγλωσσεύομαι**, *to be hasty of tongue*, Hsch. s.v. λαβρεύεαι.

**προγλωσσίς**, ίδος, ἡ, *tip of the tongue*, Poll.2.105.

**πρόγλωσσος**, ον, *hasty of tongue, talkative*, Ptol.*Tetr.*165, Pythag.*Ep.*12.2 (Myia), Polem.*Phgn.*37. II. πρόγλωσσον, τό, = foreg., Ruf.ap.Orib.25.1.23.

⊛ **προγνώμων**, ον, gen. ονος, *discerning beforehand*, c. gen., Orph.*Fr.*49.96.

**προγνωρίζω**, *apprehend before*, Arist.*Top.*141[b]12, Gal.4.764.

⊛ **προ-γνωσία**, ἡ, = sq., Sch.E.*Hec.*1137. **-γνωσις**, εως, ἡ, *foreknowledge*, Lxx *Ju.*9.6, *Act.Ap.*2.23, 1 *Ep.Pet.*1.2. II. *perceiving beforehand*, Plu.2.399d, 982c, Luc.*Alex.*8, etc. b. Medic., *prognosis* of diseases, Κῳακαὶ π. title of work by Hp., cf. Gal.16.490, 18(2).11, *AP*11.382 (Agath.); title of work by Democritus. III. *prediction*, Gem.17.13, al. **-γνώστης**, ου, ὁ, *skilled in prognosis*, of physicians, *Cat.Cod.Astr.*8(4).176. **-γνωστικός**, ή, όν, *foreknowing, prescient*, δύναμις Ph.1.659, 2.164; μόριον..τῆς ψυχῆς Plu.2.433a; of persons, M.Ant.8.25; esp. of astrologers, Vett.Val.37.28, al.: c. gen., π. τῆς κινήσεως τῶν νοσημάτων Gal.17(1).243: τὸ π. *a sign of the future, prognostic*, *Gp.*1.2 tit.: προγνωστικόν, τό, name of a treatise by Hp.; also title of work by Epicurus, D.L.10.28; but -κή, ἡ, name of an antidote, Damocr.ap.Gal.14.134. Adv. -κῶς *Gloss.*

**προγονεῦσαι**· προελθεῖν, Hsch.

⊛ **προγόνη**, ἡ, = *abavia, privigna*, *Gloss.*, v.l. in Ph.2.303.

**προγον-ητικός**, f.l. for sq., Aristid.*Or.*30(10).24. ⊛ **-ικός**, ή, όν, *derived from parentage*, ἀφορμή Metrod.*Herc.*831.15; *ancestral*, πράξεις, δόξα, ἀρετή, Plb.3.64.2, 13.6.3, Ph.2.444; πολιτεία, δυναστεία, Lxx 2 *Ma.*8.17, D.S.17.24; κτήσεις Mitteis *Chr.*31 i 22 (ii B.C.); σορός Judeich *Altertümer von Hierapolis* No.245. ⊛ **-ιος**, α, ον, *showing ancestry*, στέμμα *IG*2².1357.30. ⊛ **-ος**, ον, (γίγνομαι, γέγονα) *early-born*, [ἄρνες], opp. μέτασσαι, Od.9.221, cf. Hermesian.7.74, *SIG*1038.9 (Eleusis, iv/iii B.C.); *first-born*, *IG*2.1301 (dub.). 2. = ἀπόγονος 1, dub. in D.H.7.50. II. *forefather, ancestor*, Pi.*O.*6.59; πατρός σου π. πατήρ E.*Ion* 267, cf. *Hel.*15, Pl.*Euthphr.*11b: freq. in pl., Pi.*P.*9.105, A.*Pers.*405, Hdt.7.150, etc.; οἱ ἄνωθεν π. Pl.*Mx.*236e; οἱ πάλαι π. Id.*Ep.*359d; ἐκ προγόνων Id.*Tht.*173d; also of gods or heroes who are the *authors* or *founders* of a race, A.*Fr.*273, Hdt.4.127, Pl.*Smp.*186e, Isoc.9.14, etc.; Ζεῦ πρόγονε E.*Or.*1242; θεοὶ π. Pl.*Euthd.*302d: also as fem., π. γυνή A.*Supp.*533 (lyr.), cf. 43 (lyr.): metaph., οἱ π. the *fathers* or *founders* of a school, Luc.*Herm.*15; τὸν π. τῆς ἐμαυτοῦ σοφίας Philostr.*VA*8.7; ἰὼ πόνοι π. πόνων troubles *parents* of troubles, S.*Aj.*1197 (lyr.). III. *child by a former marriage, step-son*, E.*Ion* 1329, D.H.*Isoc.*18, *Mon.Anc.Gr.*16.9, Luc.*Cal.*26, *Supp.Epigr.*6.667 (Attalia), *PFay.*48.3 (i A.D.), etc.: fem., *step-daughter*, Stratt.79, Is.12.5, Hyp.*Fr.*10, D.S.4.43, Plu.*Pomp.*9; rarely προγόνη (q.v.): irreg. Sup. προγονέστατος *eldest step-son*, dub. in *TAM*2(1).246.18 (Sidyma).

**πρόγραμμα**, ατος, τό, *public proclamation* or *notice, edict*, *PRev.Laws* 9.7 (iii B.C.), Plu.*Galb.*5, Hdn.4.9.4, D.C.65.1, etc.; *placard, notice*, Luc.*Herm.*11, *POxy.*2108.6 (iii A.D.), *PMasp.*353.4 (vi A.D.). 2. *order of the day, agenda* of βουλή or ἐκκλησία, D.25.9, Arist.*Ath.*44.2. 3. *title* of a prescription, Gal.13.909; *address* of a letter, Procop.Gaz.*Ep.*25. 4. *injunction, advice*, Gal.17(2).141.

**προγραμμός**, ὁ, = foreg., *OGI*441.130 (Lagina, i B.C.), Sch.Ar.*V.*55; ὑπογραμμὸν λέγομεν ἀντὶ τοῦ προγραμμόν Ammon.*Diff.*p.134 V.

⊛ **προγρᾰφή**, ἡ, *public notice, advertisement*, X.*Eq.Mag.*4.9, Plb.25.3.2, *SIG*976.37 (Samos, ii B.C.), *OGI*515.38 (Mylasa, iii A.D.); *edict*, D.C.47.13; ἐκ προγραφῆς by *edict*, Id.56.25. 2. *notice of sale*, Thphr.*Fr.*97.2 (pl.), Plu.2.205c; *public sale of confiscated property*, Str.5.4.11. 3. ἐπὶ θανάτῳ προγραφαὶ *proscriptions*, App.*BC*1.2; σφαγαὶ καὶ π. Plu.*Brut.*27; *warrant* for arrest, *BGU*372.8 (ii A.D., pl.). II. *table drawn up in advance*, of an astronomical cycle, D.S.12.36. III. *heading, preliminary form*, *BGU*780.2 (ii A.D.), Men.Prot.p.16 D., etc.; *title* of a prescription, Gal.13.777:—Dim. **-γράφιον** [ᾰ], τό, *Sammelb.*5273.10 (v A.D.).

⊛ **προγράφω** [ᾰ], *write before* or *first*, τὰς αἰτίας προὔγραψα πρῶτον Th.1.23; *write before* or *above*, *Ep.Eph.*3.3; αἱ προγεγραμμέναι λέξεις Hipparch.1.7.5; κατὰ τὰ -γεγραμμένα *PPetr.*3 p.179 (iii B.C.); ὁ προγεγραμμένος ἀριθμός *before-mentioned*, Plu.2.1018c. 2. *write as a copy*, Poll.4.18. II. *set forth as a public notice*, π. τι ἐν πινακίοις Ar.*Av.*450; π. κρίσιν, δίκην τινί, *give notice of* a trial, D.47.42, Plu.*Cam.*11 (Pass.); *appoint* or *summon by public notice*, ἐκκλησίας Aeschin.2.60, 61; χορηγοὺς π. *appoint* as choregi, Arist.*Oec.*1352[a]1; π. τινὰ [κληρωθησόμενον?] τ]ῆς φυλῆς ἣν ἂν βούληται *Supp.Epigr.*4.183.15 (Halic., iii B.C.); π. τοὺς λειτουργήσοντας *IG*5(1).1390.73, cf. 74 (Pass., Andania, i B.C.); στρατιᾶς κατάλογον Plu.*Cam.*39; φρουρᾶς ἡμῖν προγραφείσης D.54.3; π. ὅσα δεῖ χρηματίζειν τὴν βουλὴν Arist.*Ath.*43.3; ἀπὸ τίνος ἄρχοντος καὶ ἐπωνύμου μέχρι τίνων δεῖ στρατεύεσθαι ib.53.7; οἷς κατ' ὀφθαλμοὺς..Χριστὸς προεγράφη *was proclaimed* or *set forth publicly*, *Ep.Gal.*3.1, cf. *Supp.Epigr.*4.263.13, 15 (Panamara, i A.D.):—Med., περὶ ὧν προεγράψατο εἰς τὴν βουλὴν *Milet.*6.43 (iii B.C.), cf. *SIG*562.3 (Paros, iii B.C.), etc. 2. *give written notice of sale*, παρὰ τῇ ἀρχῇ Thphr.*Fr.*97.1, cf. Plu.2.205c; *sell by auction*, ἐν τῷ πραιτωρίῳ τὰ κτήματα D.C.51.4. 3. = Lat. *proscribere*, π. τινὰς φυγάδας Plb.32.5.12; οἱ προγεγραμμένοι *the proscribed*, ib.6.1; οἱ π. ὑπὸ Σύλλα Str.5.2.6; οἱ προγραφέντες D.C.47.13; οἱ προγραφέντες ἐπὶ θανάτῳ Plu.*Brut.*27: metaph., οἱ προγεγρ. εἰς τοῦτο τὸ κρίμα *those whose names have been registered* for condemnation, *Ep.Jud.*4. III. *write* a name *at the head of a list*, π. τινὰ ἐπὶ τῶν ψηφισμάτων Plu.*Demetr.*10; τῆς βουλῆς π...Μάρκον, of the censor, *name* Marcus *princeps senatus*, Id.*Aem.*38, cf. *Flam.*18:—Pass., προγράφεσθαι τοῦ συνεδρίου Id.2.318c; προγεγραμμένος τῆς βουλῆς Id.*TG*4.

**προγρηγορέω**, *remain awake first*, in aor. part. -ήσαντες Gal.11.311 (written προεγρηγορήσαντες in same context, Id.19.519).

**προγυμν-άζω**, *exercise, train beforehand*, χέρα S.*Fr.*498; ἑαυτὸν ἐς ἄλλον βίον Luc.*Herm.*78, cf. Porph.*VP*47: esp. *train in oratory*, Arr.*Epict.*1.26.13, etc.:—Med., *study, practise oneself*, Gal.*Anim.Pass.*2.3; but also, *act as* προγυμναστής 2, Id.6.177:—Pass., of arguments or passages, *to be prepared beforehand*, οἱ προγυμνασθέντες λόγοι Hermog.*Inv.*4.12. **-ᾰσία**, ἡ, *previous exercise*, βασιλείας Ph.2.90, cf. Iamb.ap.Stob.2.2.6. **-άσιον** [ᾰ], τό, = foreg., f.l. in Gal.6.764. **-ασμα**, ατος, τό, *preparatory exercise*, πολέμου for war, Ath.14.631a; also in Rhetoric, Arist.*Rh.Al.*1436[a]25: in pl., title of works by Aphthonius, etc. **-αστής**, οῦ, ὁ, *trainer*, Arr.*Epict.*3.20.9, 4.4.31. 2. *slave who goes through exercises* with his master, Seneca *Ep.*83.3, Gal.6.187. **-όω**, *keep exposed*, Id.10.416.

**προγωνία**, ἡ, a garment worn by cooks, Hsch. (ante πρόγονοι).

**προδᾰῆναι**, aor. inf. Pass. (with act. sense) from *δάω, *know beforehand*, προϊδὼν ἠὲ προδαεὶς Od.4.396; inf., A.R.1.106: redupl. aor. προδέδαεν· προμεμάθηκεν, Hsch.

⊛ **προδᾰν-είζω**, *lend before* or *first*, D.C.51.17; τῷ Ἀπόλλωνι τὴν χάριν Luc.*Sacr.*3:—Pass., ὁ εἰς τὴν γένεσιν [τῶν ἔργων] τῷ πόνῳ προδανεισθεὶς χρόνος Plu.*Per.*13. II. *advance money* for public objects, ὅσοι ἂν προδανείσωσιν ἄτοκα *OGI*46.5 (Halic., iii B.C.), cf. *IG*7.4254.38 (Oropus, iv B.C.), etc.; τοῖς ἀπόροις χρήματα Arist.*Ath.*16.2:—Med., χρήματα εἰς τὸ θεωρικόν, χρήματα τῷ δήμῳ εἰς τὴν διοίκησιν π., Hyp.*Dem.Fr.*4. ⊛ **-εισμός**, ὁ, *advance of funds* for public purposes, *CIG* (addend.) 2717*b* (Stratonicea); τὸν π. ποιεῖσθαι *Milet.*3 No.138.31 (iii B.C.). ⊛ **-ειστής**, οῦ, ὁ, *one who advances money* for public purposes, *OGI*46.9 (pl., Halic., iii B.C.), *IG*11(2).287 A 122 (Delos, iii B.C.).

⊛ **προδᾰπᾰνάω**, *exhaust beforehand*, τὸ μέγεθος τῆς χάριτος *IG*7.2713.20 (Acraeph., Oratio Neronis):—Pass., ἐξουσία προδεδαπανημένη Luc.*Abd.*11. 2. *defray the expense of beforehand*, ἐπισκευήν *Sammelb.*5232.17 (i A.D.).

**προδείδω**, only aor. 1 part. -δείσας, *fear prematurely*, S.*OT*90.

**προδείελος**, ον, *before evening*, π. ἔστιχεν Theoc.25.223.

⊛ **προδείκνῡμι** (-ύω Hdt.1.209, 7.37), 3 sg. προδίκνυτι [δῐ] Epigr. in *GDI*5112 (Crete): Ion. aor. -έδεξα (v. infr.):—*show by example*, by doing something first, προδέξαντες σχῆμα, οἷόν τι ἔμελλε εὐπρεπέστατον φανέεσθαι ἔχουσα Hdt.1.60; τὸν ζωστῆρα προδέξας *having shown* [the way of] the girdle, Id.4.10. 2. abs., *tell first*, A.*Pr.*779, S.*OT*624. II. *foreshow* what is about to happen, πάντα τὰ ἐπιφερόμενα Hdt.1.209; Ἕλλησι π. ὁ θεὸς ἔκλειψιν τῶν πολίων Id.7.37, cf. 6.27; προφαίνει καρπὸν..μέχρι τοῦ προδεῖξαι μόνον Thphr.*CP*1.13.10: c. acc. et inf., *make known beforehand* that.., Th.3.47; π. ὅτι.. Plu.*Phoc.*28; προδεδειγμένου *it having been already shown*, A.D *Synt.*336.16. III. *point before* one, σκήπτρῳ π. γαῖαν, of a blind man, S.*OT*456; π. τὸ τόξον *put it out before* one, Luc.*Herc.*1, cf. *Herm.*68;

π. δελεάσματα *hold out* baits, Them.*Or.*22.271c; π. χρεῶν ἀποκοπάς ib.7.91c. **2.** as a technical term of pugilists, χερσὶ π. *make feints* with the hands, Theoc.22.102; also in war, X.*Eq.Mag.*8.24; π. τινὰς ἐπιβολάς Plb.2.66.2; of the cuttle-fish, π. εἰς τὸ πρόσθεν Arist. *HA*621$^b$34.

**προδείκτης,** ου, ὁ, *pantomimic actor,* D.S.34/5.34.

**προδειμαίνω,** *fear beforehand,* τι Hdt.7.50, Lyc.276.

**προδειπνέω,** *dine* or *sup before,* Plu.2.226f.

**πρόδειπνον,** τό, f.l. for Πρόδικον, Ath.9.406e.

**προδέκᾰτον,** Adv. *on the tenth day before, GDI*5017 (Crete).

**προδέκτωρ,** ορος, ὁ, Ion. for *προδείκτωρ, *foreshower,* Hdt.7.37.

**προδεξιόομαι,** *begin by saluting,* τινα Hld.10.2 (prob. l. for προσδεξ–).

**προδέρκομαι,** *see beforehand,* μόρον A.*Pr.*250.

**προδεσμέω,** *bind on before, Gloss.*

**προδεύω,** *moisten first,* Dsc.1.43 (Pass.).

**πρόδηλ-ος,** ον, *clear* or *manifest in front* or *beforehand,* Alc.*Oxy.* 1789*Fr.*1 ii 4, D.15.30, etc.; ἐμβολὴ π. ἥτις γίνοιτ' ἂν ἁρμόζουσα Hp. *Art.*30, cf. E.*Or.*190 (lyr.), Hyp.*Epit.*8; οἱ π. [φόβοι] *foreseen,* Arist. *EN*1117$^a$19, cf. Is.3.19, al.; τοῦ μὲν ὄντος π. τοῦ δὲ ἀγνοουμένου Isoc.6. 37; εἰ μὲν ἦν π. τὰ μέλλοντα D.18.196; π. εἵλοντο θανάτους Plb.6.54. 4; πρόδηλον ἤδη ἦν, ὅτι.. X.*HG*6.4.9, cf. Isoc.2.42, Pl.*Phdr.*238b, etc.; *evident,* καὶ τυφλῷ, φασι, πρόδηλον Polystr.p.8 W.; πρόδηλα γάρ [ἐστι], ὅτι..μέλλουσι Hdt.9.17, cf. X.*Eq.*3.3; ἐκ προδήλου from *a place in sight, in full view,* S.*El.*1429 (lyr.). Adv. –λως Aeschin.1.182, Plu.*Oth.*9; θανεῖν π. S.*Aj.*1311. **2.** = προδηλωτικός, c. gen., Vett. Val.92.22, al. **–όω,** *make clear beforehand, show plainly,* Th.6.34; τὰ μέλλοντα Plu.*Pomp.*32:—Pass., Plb.10.46.10, etc.; τὰ προδηλούμενα πρόσωπα the *aforesaid* persons, *IG*12(7).239.23 (Amorgos), cf. *SIG*1234.4 (Lycia), etc. **II.** *give instructions beforehand,* τινι c. inf., Parth.17.3. **–ωσις,** εως, ἡ, *declaring beforehand, prognostication,* Plu.2.398d; *giving notice in advance,* Id.*Mar.*19. **–ωτικός,** ή, όν, *showing beforehand,* τινος Pl.*Def.*414b, Petos.ap.Vett.Val.80.6, Rhetor. in *Cat.Cod.Astr.*8(4).129.

**προδημᾰγωγέω,** f.l. for προσδ– (q.v.).

**προδημιουργέω,** *create before,* Phlp. *in GA*61.14.

**προδια-βαίνω,** *cross before* others, τάφρον, ποταμόν, X.*Eq.*8.3, Plu.2.968e: abs., D.S.18.35, Plu.*Pyrrh.*24, D.C.41.47. **–βάλλω,** *raise prejudices against beforehand,* τινα Th.6.75, Hyp.*Lyc.*10; τὰς ἀντιθέσεις Aps.p.261 H.; *accuse beforehand,* Luc.*Tox.*34:—Pass., τοῖς προδιαβεβλημένοις καὶ ἀνθρώποις καὶ πράγμασιν Arist.*Rh.*1400$^a$22, cf. 1418$^b$14; also, *to be prejudiced,* Plu.2.37b. **–βεβαιόω,** *demonstrate, establish before,* Nicom.*Ar.*1.3 (Pass.). **–βῐβάζω,** *carry across before,* Gal.*UP*9.8. **–βολή,** ἡ, *discrediting in advance,* Aps. pp.242, 247 H. **–βρέχω,** *soak before,* Sor.1.57, Gal.6.821. **–γιγνώσκω,** *perceive* or *understand beforehand,* Th.1.78. **II.** *determine beforehand,* Id.5.38, J.*AJ*8.12.3; μηδὲν π. not *to prejudge* anything, D.C.52.31; προδιεγνωσμένη δίκη J.*AJ*17.5.3. **–γνωσις,** εως, ἡ, *previous recognition* of the imminence of disease, Hp.*Vict.*1.2, 3. 69.

**προδιᾰγόρευσις,** εως, ἡ, *detailed prediction,* Hp.*Aph.*2.19 (pl.).

**προδιαγράφω** [γρᾰ], *portray beforehand,* ἡ φήμη π. τὴν σὴν χάριν Aristaenet.1.26. **II.** *pay beforehand, Inscr.Cos* 28 (dub. rest.).

**προδιᾰγωγή,** ἡ, *previous passing through,* δι' ἀργίλου Plu.2.913c.

**προδιᾰγων-ίζομαι,** *contend previously,* πρός τινα D.S.31.8. **–ιστής,** v.l. for προαγων–, Ph.2.312.

**προδιαδίδωμι,** *disseminate before,* φήμην κατά τινος Plb.38.17.2.

**προδιαζεύγνυμι:** Gramm., σχῆμα προδιεζευγμένον (also called Ἀλκμανικόν), a figure used by Alcman, when a predicate or attribute belonging to two words *is joined to the first,* as ἐγὼ ἤλθομεν καὶ σύ, Sch.Od.10.513.

⊛ **προδιάζω,** of a banker, *pay* or *advance* money, *POxy.*180 (iii A.D.).

**προδια-θερμαίνω,** *warm through before,* in Pass., Gal.7.187. **–θεσις,** εως, ἡ, *predisposition,* Phld.*Mus.*p.63 K. (pl.), Anon.Lond.24.33, S.E. *P.*1.100 (pl.); *previous state,* Dsc.*Alex.Praef.* (pl.).

**προδιαιρ-ετέον,** *one must divide first,* Olymp. *in Phlb.*p.266 S. ⊛ **–έω,** *divide beforehand,* τὰς φλέβας Orib.*Fr.*22. **2.** Med., *warn,* τινὶ ὅπως.. *PCair.Zen.*230.7 (iii B.C.).

**προδῐαιτ-άω,** *prepare by diet,* Ath.Med.ap.Orib.*inc.*7.1 (Pass.), Gal.19.710, *Hippiatr.*14, Alex.Trall.1.17. **II.** Med., *submit a case to arbitration first, SIG*364.87 (Ephesus, iii B.C.). **–ησις,** εως, ἡ, *preparation by regimen,* Luc.*Nec.*7.

**προδια-κᾰθαίρω,** *clear up* a matter *previously,* Sor.1.44 (Pass.). **–καίω,** *burn completely before,* Heras ap.Gal.13.423 (Pass.), Crito ap. eund.13.37 (Pass.). **–κατέχω,** *hold first,* ἐν ταῖς ἀγκάλαις Sor.1. 106. **–κειμαι,** Pass., *to be in a certain condition* or *state before,* τῇ γνώμῃ Arr.*Epict.*3.21.14. **–κενόω,** *evacuate completely first,* Aët.8.50. **–κεντέω,** *make a hole in* a radish *first,* Orib.*Fr.*81 (Pass.), Aët.3.120 (Pass.). **–κῑνέω,** *set in motion before,* τινας J.*AJ*15.5.2; νεῦρα Gal.18(1).441. **–κίνησις** [ῑ], εως, ἡ, *previous setting in motion,* Sor.1.106. **–κλύζομαι,** Med., *wash out one's mouth first,* ἐλαίῳ Aët.13.23.

**προδιᾱκονέομαι,** *serve before,* J.*AJ*18.3.4.

**προδια-κρίνω,** v.l. for προδιευκρινέω (q.v.). ⊛ **–λαμβάνω,** *occupy before,* J.*BJ*4.2.3 (Pass.). **II.** *judge and decide beforehand,* περί τινος, ὑπέρ τινος, Plb.9.31.2, 27.6.3; π. ὅτι.. Id.11.1.3: c. inf., προδιειληφὼς ἀποτρίβεσθαι τὰς διαλύσεις Id.5.29.4: abs., Id.2.2.10:—Pass., προδιειλήφθω *let it be assumed beforehand,* Hipparch.2.1. 15. **2.** *explain beforehand,* ὅτι.. Ptol.*Geog.*1.2.2. **–λέγω,** *discuss before,* Nicom.*Ar.*1.3 (Pass.); ἐν τοῖς προδιειλεγμένοις A.D. *Pron.*37.4. **II.** Med., with aor. Pass., *speak, converse beforehand,* περί τινος Isoc.12.6; τισι *with..*, *PSI*4.360.15 (iii B.C.), D.H.3.71; ταῖς πόλεσι Plu.*Pyrrh.*22: abs., μικρὰ πάνυ προδιαλεχθείς Isoc.12.199, cf. D.S.20.7. **2.** euphem. in mal. part., D.C.*Fr.*87.4. **–λεξις,** εως, ἡ, *conversing beforehand, Gloss.* **–ληπτέον,** *one must presume,* Hipparch.1.3.2, 2.1.23. **–ληψις,** εως, ἡ, *preliminary explanation,* Ptol.*Alm.*1.9.

**προδιαλλάσσω,** *reconcile first,* αὐτοῖς τὴν θεόν Lib.*Ref.*2.2.

**προδια-λογίζομαι,** *discuss previously,* Chrysipp.*Stoic.*3.129. **–λογισμός,** ὁ, *previous casting up of accounts, PTeb.*89.2, al. (ii B.C.). **–λύω,** *dissolve* or *break up before,* τὰς τάξεις Plb.11.16.2; τὴν γῆν Plu.2.640e:—Pass., Arist.*Pr.*934$^b$6. **2.** *relax previously,* λεπτυνούσῃ διαίτῃ Gal.18(2).462. **3.** *dilute previously,* ὕδατι Asclep.(?) ap.Gal.12.586. **4.** *mitigate first,* Gal.14.693. **5.** *refute by anticipation,* Lib.*Decl.*49 *intr.*5. **–μαρτύρομαι** [ῡ], *call to witness* or *invoke beforehand,* τινας Plb.24.10.6 (v.l. προσ–). **–μᾰσάομαι,** *chew first,* Archig.ap.Gal.12.876.

**προδιαναπαύω,** *take an interval of rest beforehand,* Diocl.*Fr.*141.

**προδιανοέομαι,** *think over before, premeditate,* Charond.ap.Stob.4. 2.24; μηδὲν –νοηθείς without *premeditation,* Arist.*MM*1188$^b$30; ὅσα ὁ Ζεὺς π. Plu.2.942a.

**προδιαντλέομαι,** Pass., *to be exhausted beforehand,* λόγος dub.l. in Ath.5.185a.

**προδιᾰνύω** [ῠ], *accomplish beforehand*: Pass., προδιήνυστο D.C.79. 8.

**προδια-πέμπομαι,** Med., *send on as a messenger,* τινα Plb.8.18. 3; *send a message in advance,* πρός τινα Id.16.27.1: abs., Id.21.4. 7. **–πίπτω,** *err through haste, Stoic.*3.147. **–πλάσσω,** *mould, fashion beforehand,* παραδείγματα Him.*Or.*12.2:—Pass., Ph.2. 146. **–πλέω,** *sail across first,* ἐς τὴν ἤπειρον ἐπί τινα D.C.47. 33. **–πονέομαι,** Pass., *to be well trained before,* of dogs, Poll.5.51.

**προδιᾰπορέομαι,** Pass., *to be questioned* or *discussed before,* A.D. *Synt.*229.11.

**προδιαρθρ-όω,** *enucleate beforehand,* Ph.Bybl.ap.Eus.*PE*1.9, S.E. *M.*1.96, 11.18. **–ωσις,** εως, ἡ, *preliminary analysis,* θεωρήματος Simp. *in Cat.*60.3.

**προδιᾰριθμέομαι,** Pass., *to be enumerated before,* Apollon.Cit.1.

**προδιαρπάζω,** *plunder before,* J.*BJ*2.18.8, D.C.37.14.

**προδια-σᾰλεύω,** *shake beforehand,* περιπάτῳ ἢ αἰώρᾳ τὸ σωμάτιον Agathin.ap.Orib.10.7.15. **–σᾰφέω,** *explain beforehand,* A.D.*Synt.* 97.9:—Pass., *to be published* or *made plain beforehand,* J.*BJ*7.5.3, Gal. 13.698; αἱ –ούμεναι χῶραι the *aforesaid..*, Cumont *Fouilles de Doura-Europos* 298, cf. *SIG*685.56 (Magn. Mae., ii B.C.). **–σᾰφηνίζω,** = foreg., Philum.*Ven.*11.1. **–σάφησις** [σᾰ], f.l. for προσ–, Zonae. p.166 S. ⊛ **–σείω,** *stir beforehand*:—Pass., of intuitions, Dam. *Pr.*29. **–σήπω,** *cause to putrefy first,* Gal.17(1).735. **–σκέπτομαι,** *examine well beforehand,* ib.148: aor. inf. –σκέψασθαι Id. *Protr.*9: pf. –εσκέφθαι Id.7.418. **–σκευή,** ἡ, *revision* or *interpolation further back,* Sch.Il.24.109. **–σκοπέω,** = –σκέπτομαι, D.C.*Fr.*70.8. **–σμήχω,** *cleanse thoroughly first,* Gal.15.690 (Pass.). **–σπείρω,** *disseminate beforehand,* λόγον Arist.*Ath.*14. 4. **–στέλλω,** *open out first,* τὸ στόμιον Sor.1.69; *distinguish before,* Tz. in *An.Ox.*3.317:—Med., *forecast,* τὸ ἐκβησόμενον Hp.*Decent.*11; *give an explanation before, premise,* J.*AJ*4.8.4, Dsc.*Eup.*1 *Praef.*, etc.; *make a previous agreement with,* τινι Ath.12.521a; *send a summons previously,* τισὶ ἐκχωρεῖν *PFlor.*55.19 (i A.D.): f.l. for προσ– in Ph.1. 677, A.D.*Synt.*285.17. **–συνίστημι,** *narrate before,* Sch.Il.2. 718. **–σύρω** [ῡ], *pull to pieces, ridicule beforehand,* Arist.*Rh.* 1418$^b$9, *Rh.Al.*1433$^b$9. **–σφίγγω,** *tie up, compress first,* Orib.45. 17.7. **–τάσσομαι,** Med., *arrange beforehand,* prob.l. (for προσ–) in Aen.Tact.16.16. **–τείνω,** *fix in position beforehand,* τὴν κάτω γένυν Gal.18(1).461. **–τέμνω,** *cut through beforehand,* Id.18(2). 438. **–τίθημι,** *arrange beforehand,* ὅπως.. Aristaenet.1.5. **2.** *predispose,* esp. favourably, τινὰ οἰκείως ἔχειν J.*AJ*12.4.3; τὸν ἀκροατήν Men.Rh.p.443 S.; but also of those who *create prejudice,* Suid. s.v. ἀμύνασθαι. **–τρίβω** [ῑ], *spend time on* or *study first,* τῇ ῥητορικῇ Phld.*Rh.*1.223 S. **–ττάω,** *sift beforehand,* πυρόν Gal.18(1). 470. **–τῠπόω,** *express by a type beforehand, prefigure,* Ph.1.103:—Pass., ib.4. **II.** Pass., *to be sketched in outline first,* Ptol.*Tetr.* 16, Olymp. *in Mete.*184.10. **–φθείρω,** *ruin, destroy beforehand,* ναῦς ταῖς ἐμβολαῖς Plb.16.6.13:—Pass., Th.1.119, 6.78: c. gen., Lib.*Or.* 22.32. **II.** *corrupt, demoralize beforehand,* τοὺς κριτάς prob. for προσ– in D.21.18; ἡγεμόνας Plb.5.4.11:—Pass., Isoc.*Ep.*2.8. **2.** Pass., of milk, *go bad beforehand,* Sor.1.88. **–χρίω** [ῑ], *smear, anoint previously,* τὰς ῥῖνας Dsc.3.78. **–χωρέω,** *to have a previous separation* or *difference* with another, Arist.*Rh.*1373$^a$19.

**προδῐδάσκω,** *teach beforehand,* τινά τι S.*Aj.*163 (anap.), Ar.*Nu.* 476; τινα Pl.*Euthd.*302c, *Grg.*489d, *Hp.Ma.*291b: c. acc. et inf., π. τινὰ σοφὸν εἶναι S.*Ph.*1015, cf. D.51.12; [ἀηδὼν] νεοσσὸν ᾄδειν π. Plu.2.973b:—Med., S.*Tr.*681, Ar.*Pl.*687:—Pass., *learn beforehand,* Th.2.40.

**προδίδωμι,** *give beforehand, pay in advance,* X.*HG*1.5.7, *IG*2$^2$.1304. 34; προεδίδου cj. for προσ– in Plb.8.15.7; προδιδούς, opp. ἐπιδιδούς, Gal.12.174; *give first, Ep.Rom.*11.35:—Pass., Arist.*Oec.*1350$^a$36; τῶν –δεδομένων τιμῶν *Inscr.Prien.*107.17, cf. *GDI*5181.34 (Crete); of a menu-tablet, Ath.2.49d. **II.** *give up,* [κλῆρον] *PPetr.*3 p.96 (iii B.C.); *deliver up,* τοὺς ὁμοκωμήτας ἡμῖν *PThead.*17.16 (iv A.D.): most freq., *give up to the enemy, betray*, τοὺς λοιποὺς τοῖσι Σαμίοισι Hdt.6.23; τὸ σὸν θνητοῖσι π. γέρας A.*Pr*.38, etc.; π. τὴν Ποτείδαιαν Hdt.8.128; τὰν φυγάδα A.*Supp*.420 (lyr.); ἱκέτας E.*Heracl*.246; πυργώματα A.*Th*.251; τὰς πύλας, φρούριον, Ar.*Av*.766, *Ra*.362; of a woman, π. τὸ σῶμα Lys.*Fr*.90: c. inf., ὃν σὺ προὔδωκας θανεῖν E.*Or*.1588, cf. *Alc*.659:—Pass., προδοθέντες ὑπὸ Σιτάλκεω ἤλωσαν Hdt.7.137; ἀπόλωλα τλήμων, προδέδομαι S.*Ph*.923. 2. *forsake, abandon*, οἵ με φίλοι προὔδωκαν Thgn.813; π. τὴν Ἑλλάδα Hdt.9.7.β', Ar.*Pax* 408; μηδαμῶς.. προδῷς με Id.*Th*.229; τὴν μητέρα π. Antipho 1.5; τὴν πολιτείαν Pl.*Lg*.762c; σαυτόν Id.*Cri*.45c:—Pass., προδεδόμεθα ὑπὸ τῶν συμμάχων Hdt.9.60, cf. Vett.Val.78.19. 3. abs., *play false, desert*, Hdt.5.113, 6.15, etc.; οὔτοι προδώσει χρησμός *will not prove traitor*, A.*Ch*.269; χάρις.. προδοῦσ' ἁλίσκεται S.*Aj*.1267; ἢν προδιδῶσι πρὸς τοὺς κατιόντας *treat treasonably* with them, Hdt.3.45: c. acc. cogn., προδοσίαν π. *to be guilty of treachery*, Din.1.10. 4. with a thing as subject, *betray, fail* one, [αἱ κάτω πλίνθοι] π. τὰς ἄνω X.*HG*5.2.5; ὁ ὀφθαλμὸς π. τινά D.52.13: intr., *fail*, of wine, Xenoph. 1.5; of a river, *run dry*, Hdt.7.187; of a barricade that has proved useless, Id.8.52. 5. with a thing as object, *surrender, give up*, προδέδοται τὰ κρυπτά E.*IA*1140; χάριν π. to be thankless, Id.*Heracl*.1036; τὰ πράγματα Ar.*Eq*.241; τὸ δοκοῦν ἀληθὲς οὐχ ὅσιον προδιδόναι Pl.*R*.607c; τὸ δίκαιον Id.*Lg*.907a; ἑτέροισι τὴν νίκην ib.906e; καιρὸν τοῖς ἐναντίοις D.19.6; *to be false to, fail to uphold*, ὅρκους X.*Cyr*.5.1.22; τὴν καταχειροτονίαν D.21.120; *give up as lost, bid adieu to*, ἡδονάς S.*Ant*.1166; τὰς ἐλπίδας Ar.*Nu*.1500; τὴν ἐκείνου προαίρεσιν D.60.28; τὸν ἀγῶνα Aeschin.1.115.

**προδιεξ-έρχομαι**, *go out through before*, X.*Cyn*.5.4; of the motions of the bowels, Gal.16.699. II. *go through, explain before*, πρὸς ὑμᾶς ὡς ἔχουσιν οἱ νόμοι Aeschin.1.8. **-οδεύω**, = foreg. II, π. ὅτι.. S.E.*M*.7.188.

**προδι-εορτάζω**, *celebrate a festival beforehand*, D.C.37.54 (Pass.). **-έπω**, *administer beforehand*, v.l. in J.*BJ*2.14.3. **-εργάζομαι**, *prepare beforehand*, in Pass., δεῖ προδιειργάσθαι.. τὴν τοῦ ἀκροατοῦ ψυχήν Arist.*EN*1179$^b$24, cf. *Pr*.931$^a$12, Parth.23.2. **-ερευνάω**, fut. -ήσομαι X.*Cyr*.5.4.4:—*go scouting*, l.c.: c. acc., *search thoroughly*, τὴν ὀροφήν D.S.20.26. **-ερευνητής**, οῦ, ὁ, *spy, scout*, X.*Cyr*.5.4.4 (v.l.), Plu.*Comp.Pel.Marc*.3. **-έρχομαι**, *go through before*, of motions of the bowels, Hp.*Acut*.67, cf. *Coac*.64; Νέστορος προδιελήλυθεν ἀρετὴ τῶν Ἑλλήνων τὰς ἀκοάς X.*Cyn*.1.7. II. *go through* or *narrate before*, ὃν τρόπον γέγραπται Aeschin.2.67; τι D.S.1.9; αἰτίαν J.*AJ*4.2.1; περί τινος D.S.3.11; ὡς.. J.*AJ*12.3.3. III. of time, *precede*, τῷ προδιεληλυθότι ἔτει the year *before last*, *POxy*.1706.15 (iii A.D.); τῷ προδιελθόντι ἔτει *PSI*4.295.7 (iii A.D.). **-ευκρινέω**, *make clear beforehand*, Hermog.*Id*.1.4:—Pass., Plb.6.11.1, S.E.*P*.2.68 (v.l. προδιακρίνεσθαι), prob. in Herm. *in Phdr*.p.63 A. **-ηγέομαι**, *relate beforehand, premise*, Hdt.4.145, D.59.1, Hermog.*Inv*.2.4:—Pass., τὰ προδιηγημένα [ἔθνεα] Hp.*Aër*.13. **-ήγησις**, εως, ἡ, *preliminary exposition* or *narration*, τῆς ἀπολογίας Aeschin.1.117, cf. Arist.*Rh*.1414$^b$14, Hermog.*Inv*.2.1, al.: pl., Aps.p.339 H. **-ηθέω**, in Pass., *filter through before*, cj. for προσ- in Arist.*Pr*.933$^b$37. **-ιδρόομαι**, Pass., *exude before*, Gal.17(1).988. **-ίστημι**, *dilate previously*, Antyll.ap.Orib.6.10.14:—Pass., Sor.1.65. II. Pass., *fall into discord beforehand*, πρό τινος J.*BJ*4.3.2. III. pf. part. Pass. -διεσταμένος *fixed, determined beforehand*, *PRein*.7.11 (ii B.C.).

**προδῐκ-άζω**, *judge beforehand*, Ph.1.603:—Med., Poll.8.24:—Pass., δίκας τὰς προδεδικασμένας *IG*5(2).343.15 (Orchom.Arc., iv B.C.). **-ἄσία**, ἡ, *preliminary proceedings in a prosecution* for murder, Antipho 6.42 (pl.), cf. *AB*186. **-αστής**, οῦ, ὁ, *one who judges before* or *for* another, *Gloss*. II. *advocate*, *SIG*134*b*25,32 (Milet., iv B.C.). **-έω**, (πρόδικος) *to be a patron, advocate*, or *guardian*, τοῦ ἀλλοτρίου ἀπελευθέρου Lys.*Fr*.100, cf. Plu.2.787b, 973a; τῶν τούτου τέκνων Mitteis *Chr*.88 i 15 (ii A.D.); τῶν ἐνύδρων Plu.2.975c. II. *act as advocate*, ὑπέρ.. *GDI*1432*b*5 (Hypata). ® **-ία**, ἡ, *priority of trial*, *SIG*155*a*8 (Delph., iv B.C.), etc.: pl., *decrees granting this privilege*, ib.252.41 (ibid., iv B.C.). II. *office of* πρόδικος, *advocacy*, Plu.2.793e. **-ος**, ον, (δίκη) *judged first*, δίκα π. a cause *which has priority of hearing*, *IG*9(1).334.32 (Locr., v B.C.), cf. *Michel*497.2 (Aerae, iii B.C.), etc. 2. Act., *judging in first instance*, πόλις *Schwyzer*328$^a$ii *B* 8 (Delph., iv B.C.), cf. *GDI*5040.63 (Crete). 3. *decided by arbitration*, ἐθέλω δίκην δοῦναι πρόδικον Ar.*Fr*.267; ἵνα ἀπολάβῃς τὴν τιμὴν τοῦ βάρδου πρόδικον *BGU*276.12 (ii/iii A.D., cf. ii p.355). II. Subst., *defender, avenger*, A.*Ag*.450 (lyr.); *representative in legal proceedings, advocate*, γυναικὸς ἑαυτοῦ *BGU*969.7 (ii A.D.); esp. of *public advocates*, *IG*9(1).694.114 (Corc.): metaph., *advocate, patron*, τῆς ἐναργείας Plu.2.1083c. 2. at Sparta, a young king's *guardian*, X.*HG*4.2.9, Plu.*Lyc*.3.

**προδιοδεύω**, *pass through before*, Sor.2.60 (Pass.).

**προδιοικ-έω**, *regulate, manage beforehand*, D.23.14 (Pass.), Luc.*Hist.Conscr*.52:—Med. in act. sense, Aeschin.1.146, D.H.*Rh*.9.7, al. II. *digest before*, σιτία προδιῳκημένα Antyll.ap.Orib.5.29.10. **-ησις**, εως, ἡ, *setting in due order beforehand*, D.H.*Rh*.10.13: pl., Vett.Val. in *Cat.Cod.Astr*.8(1).165, Sch.Hermog. in Rh.6.124 W. **-ητικός**, ή, όν, *regulating beforehand*, τῶν ἐλαχίστων M.Ant.1.16.

**προδιοικονομέω**, *prepare before*, ἑαυτόν Sch.D.T.p.170 H.

**προδιομολογ-έομαι**, *agree in allowing beforehand*, Pl.*Ti*.78a, Arist.*Top*.108$^b$15; π. τινί c. inf., D.C.38.14; π. ἵνα.. Id.62.21:—Pass., προδιωμολογημένα *points conceded on both sides beforehand*, v.l. for προσ- in Pl.*Sph*.241a; ἐκεῖνο προδιομολογείσθω Arist.*EN*1103$^b$34; τούτου -ομολογηθέντος Ph.1.431. **-ητέον**, *one must grant beforehand*, Arist.*Top*.110$^a$37.

**προδιορθ-όομαι**, Med., *correct, set right by anticipation*, τὰ μέλλοντα Herm. *in Phdr*.p.109 A. **-ωσις**, εως, ἡ, *setting right by anticipation*, Hermog.*Inv*.4.12, Alex.*Fig*.3, Aristid.Quint.2.10, Eust.733.6.

**προδιορ-ίζω**, *limit* or *define beforehand*, D.S.12.2, Alex.Aphr. *in Top*.146.17, al.; βραχέα π. περί τινος D.S.1.4:—Med., ib.5, Ph.1.442, Hermog.*Id*.1.1, Aps.p.247 H. (also, *make arrangements beforehand*, Orib.45.18.17):—Pass., Ph.1.631. **-ισμός**, ὁ, *previous definition* or *distinction*, Gal.6.830, Aps.p.243 H.

**προδιῡλίζω**, *strain beforehand*, Dsc.1.71.

**προδῐ-ώκω**, *get in advance in pursuit*, Th.6.70, f.l. in X.*An*.3.3.10. **-ωξις**, εως, ἡ, expl. of προΐωξις, Sch.Hes.*Sc*.154.

**προδοκάζω**, *lie in wait for*, Hsch.

**προδοκέω**, *seem good, be resolved beforehand*, τὰ προδόξαντα *IG*7.3563 (Thisbe):—mostly in Pass., ὥσπερ προὐδέδοκτο αὐτοῖς *had been before determined*, Th.7.18; τὰ προδεδογμένα Id.3.40; ταὐτά μοι προὐδέδοκτο this *was* my *former opinion*, Pl.*Phd*.88d.

**προδοκή**, ἡ, (δέχομαι II) *place where one lies in wait, lurking-place*, δεδεγμένος ἐν προδοκῇσιν Il.4.107.

**προδοκῐμάζω**, *try, prove beforehand*, Eust.1890.28:—Pass., Ph.2.305.

**πρό-δομα**, ατος, τό, *that which is given in advance, prepayment, advance* of money, *PCair.Zen*.269 (iii B.C.), Plb.29.8.8, 15.25.16 (pl.), *JHS*11.122 (Ceramus), *PTeb*.42.15 (ii B.C.), Hdn.Gr.2.935, Hsch. s.v. ἀρραβών. ® **-δομᾰτικός**, ή, όν, *by way of payment in advance*, μίσθωσις *Sammelb*.5761.26 (i A.D.). **-δομάτιον** [ᾰ], τό, = πρόδοσις I, Hsch.

**προδομ-εύς**, έως, ὁ, *one who builds before*, epith. of certain gods, Paus.1.42.1. **-έω**, *build before*, J.*BJ*1.21.6 (Pass.). **-ος**, ὁ, *chamber entered immediately from the fore-court*, ἐνὶ προδόμῳ πρόσθεν θαλάμοιο θυράων Il.9.473; ἐν προδόμῳ δόμου 24.673, Od.4.302: later, in temples, opp. ὀπισθόδομος, *SIG*247 *I*$^a$27 (Delph., iv B.C.):—also **πρόδομον**, τό, *Inscr.Délos* 370.14 (iii B.C.), *CIG*2754 (Aphrodisias).

**πρόδομος**, ον, *before the house*, ἀοιδαί B.6.14; πυρή *AP*6.285 (Nicarch.): c. gen., Ἑκάτη τῶν βασιλείων πρόδομος μελάθρων (πρόδρομος codd.) A.*Fr*.388 (anap.).

**προδοξ-άζω**, *deem, judge beforehand*, Pl.*Tht*.178e, Arist.*Metaph*.1011$^b$6:—Pass., Id.*Rh*.1356$^a$10. **-ᾰσις**, εως, ἡ, *prejudgement*, censured by Gal.18(2).14. **-ος**, ον, *judging hastily*, Phryn.*PS*p.8 B., Phot.p.140 R., Suid. s.v. ἄνθρωπος π.

**προδόρπια**, τά, *early supper*, *Schwyzer* 725.1 (Milet., vi B.C.).

**προ-δοσία**, Ion. -ίη, ἡ, (προδίδωμι II) *abandonment in need, betrayal*, E.*Hel*.1633: mostly in Prose, *treason*, προδοσίην συντίθεσθαι Hdt.6.88, 8.128; σκευάζεσθαι Id.6.100; προδοσίας ἁλούς D.24.127, cf. Pl.*R*.443a (pl.). **-δοσίκομπος**, ον, f.l. for προδωσ- (q.v.). **-δοσις**, εως, ἡ, *payment beforehand, money advanced*, Lys.*Fr*.1.3 (pl.); δωρεαὶ καὶ προδόσεις D.50.7,12. 2. προδόσει πίνειν to drink *on credit*, Hermipp.83. II. *betrayal, treason*, Pl.*Lg*.856e. **-δοτέον**, *one must betray, abandon*, Id.*Tht*.203e. **-δότης**, ου, Dor. -ας, ὁ, *betrayer, traitor*, Hdt.8.30,144, Timocr.1.5, etc.; π. πατρός, πατρίδος, E.*Or*.1057, *Ph*.996, etc.; ὁ ἐν λέχει π. Id.*Med*.206 (lyr.); π. τῶν ὅρκων *traitor* to his oaths, Lys.*Fr*.71: metaph., τῆς ὑγιείης Democr.234. 2. *one who abandons in danger*, A.*Pr*.1068 (anap.); π. τινὸς καταστῆναι And.2.26. 3. as Adj., irreg. Comp. -ίστερον Phot. **-δοτικός**, ή, όν, *traitorous*, Luc.*Cal*.13; τὸ π. χρυσίον *a traitor's hire*, Plu.2.668a, Ath.8.343e; *treacherous*, π. συνθῆκαι J.*BJ*2.21.3; δῆμος Phalar.*Ep*.77.2. Adv. -κῶς Luc.*Tim*.36. **-δότις**, ιδος, fem. of προδότης, *betrayer*, E.*Hel*.834, 1148 (lyr.), Ar.*Th*.393, *Com.Adesp*.595; γῆς, φίλων, E.*Med*.1332, *Hel*.931. **-δοτος**, ον, *betrayed, abandoned*, Trag. in lyr., S.*El*.126,208,1074; π. ἐκ φίλων E.*Hipp*.595.

**προδουλ-εῖαι**, αἱ, in Law, *servitudes*, *Cod.Just*.1.4.26.8, 10.30.4.11. **-ος**, ον, *serving as a slave*, of a shoe, A.*Ag*.945. **-όω**, *enslave beforehand*, Onos.14.3; τὴν αὐτοῦ πατρίδα Ph.2.322.

® **προδουπέω**, *fall heavily before*, pf. προδέδουπα Nic.*Al*.313.

**προδρομ-εύω**, *to be a mounted skirmisher*, Arist.*Ath*.49.1. **-ή**, ἡ, *running forward*: *sally, sudden attack*, X.*An*.4.7.10: metaph., αἱ σαὶ π. τοῦ λόγου your *lively sallies*, Pl.*Alc*.1.114a. ® **-ος**, ον, *running forward with headlong speed*, π. ἦλθον A.*Th*.211 (lyr.); φυγάδα πρόδρομον S.*Ant*.108 (lyr.), etc.; μόλε π. v.l. in E.*Ph*.296 (lyr.). 2. *running before, going in advance*, π. στρατιῇ Hdt.9.14; κήρυκας π. προπέμπειν Id.1.60; π. ἥκω E.*IA*424; freq. of horsemen *in advance of* an army, Hdt.4.121,122; π. τῶν ἄλλων ἥκειν Id.7.203, cf. Th.2.22; λεὼς π. ἱππότας A.*Th*.80 (lyr.); *mounted skirmishers*, οἱ π. '*guides*', a special corps in the Maced. army, Arr.*An*.1.12.7, cf. D.S.17.17; οἱ ἀμφὶ [τὸν ἵππαρχον] πρόδρομοι X.*Eq.Mag*.1.25; at Athens, Arist.*Ath*.49.1; also, of light ships, Alciphr.1.11. 3. metaph., *precursor*, ἀστέρα.. ἀελίου π. Ion Lyr.10; ἠπίαλος πυρετοῦ π. Ar.*Fr*.332 (anap.); δείπνου π. ἄριστον Eub.75.13; π. τοῦ δοκοῦντος καλλίστου εἶναι Pl.*Chrm*.154a, cf. Plot.6.7.7. 4. π. (sc. οἶνος), v. πρότροπος. II. as Subst., πρόδρομοι, οἱ, 1. v. supr. 1.2. 2. *northerly winds, preceding the etesian winds*, Arist.*Mete*.361$^b$24, *Pr*.941$^b$7, Thphr.*Vent*.11. 3. *early figs*, Id.*CP*5.1.5 sq., cf. Plin.*HN* 16.113.

**προδύνω**, = sq., τοῦ ἡλίου Gem.9.1: abs., *set earlier*, prob. in Ptol.*Tetr*.147 (cf. Sch. ad loc. p.137).

**προδύομαι**, pf. -δέδῡκα, *set before*, τοῦ ἡλίου Arist.*Mete*.343$^b$20.

**πρόδῠσις**, εως, ἡ, *earlier setting*, Gem.16.16 (pl.), Vett.Val.125.26, Man.6.506. II. Astrol., *name of the sixth τόπος* (below the W. horizon), Paul.Al.*M*.1, Procl.*Par.Ptol.*207, Antioch. in *Cat.Cod.Astr.* 8(3).117, Rhetor.ib.8(4).154.

**προδυστῠχέω**, *to be unfortunate before*, Isoc.4.141, 6.104, D.C.48.42.

**προδῠσωπέω**, *cause to be given up for very shame*, π. τὴν ὁρμήν τινος J.*BJ*2.14.7.

**προδωμάτιον**, τό, Att. for προκοιτών, Phryn.227, Hsch.

**προδωρέομαι**, *present before*:—Pass., τὰ προδεδωρημένα J.*AJ*18.8.7.

**προδωσείω**, Desiderat. of προδίδωμι, *wish to betray*, προδωσείοντι ἔοικε Dam.*Isid.*173.

**προδωσέταιρος**, ον, *betraying one's companions*, *Scol.*14, D.C.58.14.

**προδωσίκομπος** [ῐ], ον, *boaster who breaks his word*, Phot., Suid., Eust.710.12: in codd. wrongly written προδοσ-.

⊛ **προέγγονος**, ὁ, *great-grandson*, *CIG*4380b$^1$.7 (Cibyra), *Ephes.*3.17, Just.*Nov.*18.4 *Intr.*: also fem.⊛-εγγόνη, *great-granddaughter*, *Cod. Just.*6.48.1.12.

**προεγγράφομαι** [ᾰ], Pass., *to be inscribed beforehand*, D.C.39.17.

**προεγγύ-άομαι**, *furnish security* or *guarantee*, *Milet.*3 No.138.42 (iii B.C.):—Pass., App.*Fr.*1.1. **-εύω**, only in Dor. form πρωγγυεύω, pf. inf. πεπρωγγυευκῆμεν, = foreg., *Tab.Heracl.*1.155. **-ησις**, εως, ἡ, *furnishing security*, *Milet.*3 No.138.6 (iii B.C.). **-ος**, ὁ, ἡ, Dor. **πρώγγυος**, *surety*, *Tab.Heracl.*1.100, al., *Schwyzer* 394 (Acarnania, iv B.C.), *Milet.*3 No.138.39 (iii B.C.).

**προεγείρω**, *wake up before*, ἑαυτούς Arist.*EN*1150$^b$23. II. προεγρήγορα, intr., *continue awake*, Id.*Pr.*916$^b$2 codd. (dub. l., προσ- cj. Bekker). 2. *watch over*, c. gen., Philostr.*VA*8.7, *Im.*2.17.

**προεγ-κάθημαι**, Pass., *to be implanted before*, αἱ -καθήμεναι αὐτοῖς ὁρμαί Plb.3.15.9. **-κᾰλέω**, *accuse before*: Προεγκαλῶν, name of a play by Menander, Stob.4.19.17. ⊛ **-κειμαι**, Pass., *to be laid* or *lie in before*, τῆς -κειμένης τροφῆς Hdn.1.17.10; *to be interred previously*, *IGRom.*4.1284.31 (Thyatira). **-κελεύομαι**, *urge on before*, Apollon. *Lex.* s.v. προβοῶντε. **-κλῖμα**, ατος, τό, dub. sens. in Vett.Val.354.11. **-κλύζω**, *use a clyster first*, prob. (for προκλύζω) in Dsc.*Eup.*1.231. **-κωμιάζω**, *praise beforehand*, Sch.Aristid. p.31 D.

**πρόεγμα**, ατος, τό, = πρόεχμα, Phot., Eust.1528.26.

**προεγρηγορέω**, v. προγρηγορέω.

**προεγ-χᾰράσσω**, *engrave before*, Ph.2.229. 2. *scarify first*, Aret.*CD*2.13. **-χειρέω**, *attempt before the time*, Plb.2.68.2. II. *test* a matter *beforehand*, Arist.*Top.*160$^b$15:—Pass., τὰ περί τινος προεγχειρημένα S.E.*M.*1.35. **-χειρίζομαι**, in Pass., *to be taken in hand already*, Heph.Astr.3.4. **-χρίω** [ῑ], *rub in* or *on before*, Dsc.*Eup.*2.19 (Pass.), cj. for προσ- in Gal.13.820. **-χῠμᾰτίζω**, *make an infusion first*, *Hippiatr.*129; Subst. **-ισμός**, ὁ, ibid.

**προεδήδοκα**, **προεδεσθῆναι**, v. προεσθίω.

**προεδικ**[ός, ἡ, όν(?)], dub. sens., ἐδάφη *BGU*915.18, al. (i A.D.).

⊛ **προέδρ-α**, ἡ, *front seat* in a theatre, *IG*5(2).113 (Tegea), D.C.59.7 (nisi leg. προεδρία). 2. = *principatus*, *Gloss.* II. *chamber in front*, *IG*14.291 (Segesta), *Not.Scav.*1931.398 (ibid.). ⊛ **-εύω**, *to be* πρόεδρος, *act as president*, Arist.*Ath.*44.3; φυλὴ ἥτις προεδρεύσει Aeschin.1.33; π. τῆς βουλῆς D.22.9; τοῖς ἐναντία τοῖς νόμοις προεδρεύουσι Hyp.*Phil.*5. II. *sit in the front row* in the theatre, Luc. *JTr.*8, 11. ⊛ **-ία**, Ion. -ίη, ἡ, *privilege of the front seats* at public games, in theatres, in the public assemblies, bestowed as an honour on distinguished foreigners, ἀτελείη καὶ π. Hdt.1.54, 9.73, cf. Ar.*Th.*834, X.*Vect.*3.4 (pl.), Decr.Byz.ap.D.18.91; προεδρίην [ῐ] ἐν ἀγῶσιν ἄροιτο Xenoph.2.7; on ambassadors, Aeschin.3.76; on citizens who had deserved well of their country, and (sometimes) on their descendants, Ar.*Eq.*575, 702; freq. in Inscrr., π. ἐν τῷ θεάτρῳ *IG*2$^2$.1214.19, cf. *SIG*1003.13 (Priene, ii B.C.), etc.; π. τῶν ἀγώνων Pl.*Lg.*881b; προεδρίαι ἐν ταῖς πανηγύρεσι ib.946e: hence, generally, *authority*, εἰσὶν ἐν π. Arist.*Pol.*1292$^a$9; *precedence, place*, π. ἀπονέμεσθαί τινι Hdn.1.8.4; ἐκστῆναι τῆς π. Plu.2.535b: in pl., Arist.*Rh.*1361$^a$35: metaph., τὸν αὐλὸν εἰς τιμὴν καὶ π. ἄγοντες Plu.*Pel.*19; προεδρίας ἐτυγχάνομεν we received *attention, respectful treatment*, *PSI*4.380.3 (iii B.C.), cf. *Sammelb.*5942.12 (iii B.C.); later, *care*, τῶν πραγμάτων πολλῆς π. δεομένων *BGU*747 i 15 (ii A.D.); π. τῆς κοιλίης Aret.*CD*1.3. 2. in concrete sense, *front seat*, Δαρεῖον ἐν π. κατήμενον on a *chair of state*, Hdt.4.88; ἐν τοῖσι ἀγῶσι π. ἐξαιρέτους Id.6.57; ἐς τὴν π. πᾶς ἀνὴρ ὠστίζεται Ar.*Ach.*42: esp., at Athens, *seats of the* πρυτάνεις in the Ecclesia, ἡ π. τῶν πρυτάνεων Din.2.13. **-ική** γραφή, impeachment *of a* πρόεδρος, Arist.*Ath.*59.2. ⊛ **-ος**, ὁ, *one who sits in the first place, president*, Th.8.67; ἐν δίκῃ Pl.*Lg.*949a, cf. *PPetr.*3 p.44 (iii B.C.): metaph., ὁ τῆς μαντείας π. ἀετός Arist.*HA*601$^b$2. II. at Athens, in pl., *presiding officers* of the βουλή or ἐκκλησία, Lex ap. D.24.21, Aeschin.2.65, Arist.*Ath.*44.2; οἱ λαχόντες π. *IG*2$^2$.779.11, 1227.23, al.; τοὺς π. οἳ ἂν λάχωσι προεδρεύειν *SIG*158.5 (iv B.C.), etc.; *similar officers* at Mytilene, Th.3.25; ὁ τῶν Αἰτωλῶν π. App.*Mac.*9.1; μέλλοντος τοῦ π. τὸν δῆμον ἐπερωτᾶν Plu.*Arist.*3, cf. ἐπιψηφίζω I. 2; π. Ἑρμοῦ πόλεως *city councillors* of Hermupolis, *BGU*1027 i 10 (iv A.D.).

**προεέργω**, Ep. for *προείργω, *hinder* or *stop by standing before*, c. acc. et inf., πάντας προέεργε ὀδεύειν Il.11.569.

**προεθ-ίζω**, *train beforehand*, ἡμᾶς ἐπὶ τὰ μείζονα Plu.2.531a:—Pass., *to be so trained*, Arist.*Pol.*1337$^a$20; εἰς ὃ δεῖ ἐλθεῖν προειθισμένοι X.*Cyr.*6.2.29. II. *accustom beforehand*, c. dat., Gal.14.256:—Pass., Id.2.223. 2. intr., *become accustomed*, τινι Antyll.ap.Orib.6.36.4. III. εἰ μὴ -είθισται ταῦτα if these things *have* not *been settled beforehand by custom*, Simp.*in Epict.*p.110 D. **-ιστέον**, *one must train beforehand*, ἑαυτὸν πρᾶον εἶναι Plu.*Cat.Ma.*5.

⊛ **προεῖδον**, aor. with no pres. in use, προοράω being used instead, part. προϊδών, inf. προϊδεῖν:—*look forward*, ὀξὺ μάλα προϊδών Od.5.393; *see beforehand, catch sight of*, μή πώς με προϊδών .. ἀλέηται 4.396; ὅτε προΐδωσιν ἰόντα κίρκον Il.17.756, cf. 18.527, Hdt.3.14:—Med., προΐδωνται Od.13.155; χαλεπὸς προϊδέσθαι καπρός Hes.*Sc.*386 (v.l. προσιδ-). 2. *foresee, portend*, κακότητος ἀνάγκας Orac.ap.Hdt.7.140; ἐσσόμενον Pi.*N.*1.27: abs., Pl.*Lg.*691b:—Med., X.*An.*6.1.8, D.9.68, etc. II. *take thought for*, ἡμέων οἰκοφθορημένων Hdt.8.144; καθ' ἡσυχίαν τι αὐτῶν (sc. τῶν ἀποβαινόντων) Th.1.83:—mostly in Med., προϊδόμενος (προειδομένους codd.) αὐτῶν Id.4.64; τοῦ μέλλοντος προϊδέσθαι D.C.45.19; ὅπως μὴ .. D.54.17; προϊδέσθαι ὑπέρ τινος Id.23.134; οὐδὲν τοῦ χωρίου προείδετο *did* not *worry about..*, D.C.56.13.

**προειδωλοποιέω**, *form an idea of beforehand*, Hld.9.25 (Pass.).

**προεικάζω**, *conjecture beforehand*, τὰ μέλλοντα Arist.*Rh.*1358$^b$20.

**πρόειμι**, (εἶμι *ibo*) *go forward, advance*, κατὰ βραχὺ προϊών Th.1.64; ὀλίγα βήματα προϊόντες X.*Cyr.*7.5.6; π. τῆς ὁδοῦ X.Eph.4.3; of the Nile Delta, προϊούσης τῆς χώρης *as it advanced* (by deposit from the water), Hdt.2.15. 2. of Time, προϊόντος τοῦ χρόνου *as time went on*, Id.3.96; προϊούσης τῆς πόσιος, π. τοῦ συμποσίου, Id.6.129, X.*Cyr.*8.4.13; προϊούσης τῆς νυκτός Id.*An.*2.2.19; π. τῆς ἡλικίας, τῆς συνουσίας, Pl.*Phdr.*279a, *Tht.*150d; προϊόντος τοῦ λόγου, τοῦ ᾄσματος, Id.*Phdr.*238d, *Prt.*339c; τοῦ προϊόντος ἔτους the *current* year, *BGU*1126.6 (i B.C.): ἡ ἐργασία κατὰ τοὺς τρεῖς χρόνους π. Hermog.*Prog.*9. 3. *proceed, continue*, προϊὼν καὶ ἀναγιγνώσκων *going on* reading, Pl.*Phd.*98b; πρόϊθί γε ἔτι εἰς τοὔμπροσθεν Id.*Grg.*497a, cf. *Lg.*842a; ὁ λόγος προΐτω Plot.2.4.4. 4. *go first, go in advance*, X.*Cyr.*1.5.14, 2.2.6: c. gen., *go before* or *in advance of*, τῆς ἄλλης στρατιῆς Hdt.1.80: metaph., π. τοῦ καιροῦ X.*Cyr.*6.3.29. 5. *go forth*, θύρασι Ar.*Th.*69; π. ἔξω τῆς φάλαγγος X.*Lac.*12.3 codd.; π. τοῦ οἴκου Hdn.1.17.4; *appear in public*, ἐν ἐρεᾷ ἐσθῆτι *PGnom.*182 (ii A.D.). b. *spring from*, γῆς τε καὶ ὕδατος Aphth.*Prog.*6. 6. π. εἴς τι *pass on to, begin* another thing, X.*Eq.*10.13; π. εἰς ἄπειρον Arist.*EN*1094$^a$20, *Ph.*209$^a$26: hence, *become*, ἐξ οἰκέτου δεσπότης π. Luc.*Nigr.*20. 7. of an action, π. ἐπὶ τὸ λῷον *succeed*, X.*Vect.*6.3.

⊛ **πρόειμι**, (εἰμί *sum*) *to be before*, τά τ' ἐσσόμενα πρό τ' ἐόντα things *which were before*, Il.1.70; οἱ προόντες γεωργοί the *former* cultivators, *PTeb.*379.12 (ii A.D.); αἱ προοῦσαι τάξεις the *previous* positions, Ael.*Tact.*29.10; but, οἱ προόντες those *who were there before* (and still are there), Ath.9.391d; ἀνῳκοδόμησα ἐπὶ προοῦσι θεμελίοις ἀρχαίοις *Sammelb.*5232.19 (i A.D.); τῇ προούσῃ αὐτοῦ γυναικὶ his *present* wife, *PSI*1.36a5, 27 (i A.D.), cf. *PRyl.*154.4 (i A.D.); τὰ προεσόμενα Plu.2.586f (s.v.l.); also τοῖς προοῦσι δίδωμι the *aforesaid*, *POxy.*580 (ii A.D.). II. προεσόμενα, = *profutura*, *Gloss.*

**προεῖπον** (also -εῖπα Plb.3.114.8), aor. with no pres. in use, προλέγω and προαγορεύω being used, part. προειπών, inf. προειπεῖν:—*foretell*, Pl.*Euthphr.*3c, al., Gal.14.601; *premise*, τοῦτο προειπόντα ἐπειπεῖν τὰ ἔμπροσθεν Arist.*Rh.*1394$^b$31. II. *proclaim* or *declare publicly*, ἀλλήλοισι πόλεμον π. Hdt.7.9.β'; ξεινίην τοῖσι Ἀκανθίοισι π. Hdt.7.116; ἀγῶνας ἑκάστοις X.*Cyr.*1.6.18; νικητήρια ταῖς τάξεσι ib.2.1.24; θάνατον αὐτῷ π. μὴ πράξαντι ταῦτα Pl.*Lg.*698c; π. τινὶ φόνου *make proclamation* of murder against him, D.59.9, cf. Lex ap.eund.43.57; π. τοῖς θεοῖς ὅτι.. Pl.*Cra.*401a; ὀνυμάξει αὐτὸν προειπὼν τρὶς ἀμέρας *giving notice of* three days (within which he must answer the call), *Berl.Sitzb.*1927.167 (Cyrene); ἐν ἡμέραις πέντε ἀφ' ἧς ἂν ἀλλήλοις προείπωσιν *BGU*1050.27 (i A.D.). III. c. inf., *order* or *command before*, πρό οἱ εἴπομεν .., μήτ' αὐτὸν κτείνειν Od.1.37, cf. Hdt.1.21, 155, 7.12, S.*OT*351; οἱ νόμοι προεῖπον αὐτῷ μὴ δημηγορεῖν Aeschin.1.3; π. τοῖς καδεσταῖς ἀλλύεθθαι *Leg.Gort.*2.28: c. acc. et inf., π. σῖτον ἐσάγειν τὸν βουλόμενον Th.4.26; π. αὐτῷ ἥσειν *threatened* him that.., And.4.17. 2. *enjoin*, c. acc., π. Λυδοῖσι τὰ ὁ Κροῖσος ὑπετίθετο Hdt.1.156.

**προειρηνεύω**, *pacify beforehand*, J.*BJ*3.1.2, 4.8.1.

**προειρήσομαι**, **προείρηκα**, v. προερέω.

**προεισ-άγω** [ᾰ], *bring in, introduce before* (sc. εἰς τοὺς φράτερας), D.39.32 (Pass.); ἐπὶ τὴν χώραν τἀδελφοῦ *IG*2$^2$.1326.31 (Pass.); τὴν κακίαν τῆς ἀρετῆς Plu.2.1066d; τὰ προεισηγμένα measures *previously introduced*, v.l. in J.*AJ*19.2.2; in writing, *introduce* or *describe first*, τὸν τοῦ πρεσβυτέρου [βίον] Plu.*Dio* 2; ἡ προεισηγμένη σφραγὶς *aforementioned*, *PHamb.*12.20 (iii A.D., prob.), cf. *Stud.Pal.*17 p.25 (iii A.D.). II. intr., ἑαυτοῦ π. *go on the stage before oneself*, Arist.*Pol.*1336$^b$29. ⊛ **-βάλλω**, *throw in a remark before*, περί τινος Socr.*Ep.*36. II. intr., *start, make a beginning*, ἀπὸ τοῦ φόβου Longin.22.2. 2. *supervene, come on before*, τῆς ὥρας Aët.5.23. **-δέω**, *involve in previous ties*: οἱ προεισδεδεμένοι persons *bound by previous alliances*, Plb.9.31.1. **-ελαύνω**, intr., *go in before*, εἰς τὸ ἄστυ Hld.9.1. **-έρχομαι**, *come* or *go in before*, D.28.14, D.S.16.94; τὸ προεισεληλυθὸς πνεῦμα Antyll.ap.Orib.6.10.14. **-ευπορέω**, *contribute in advance*, ἐκ τῶν ἰδίων ἄτοκα τὰ χρήματα *SIG*569.37 (Cos, iii B.C.). **-ηγέομαι**, *introduce previously*, Pass., οἷς ἂν ἀρέσκοιτο τὰ προεισηγημένα J.*AJ*19.2.2 (v.l. προεισηγμένα). **-όδιον**, τό, *introduction, prelude*, Hld.8.17. **-παίω**, *burst in before*, Hsch. **-πέμπω**, *send in before*, X.*Cyr.*5.2.6, J.*AJ*14.11.6, Luc.*Alex.*11, etc. **-πορεύομαι**, *go in before*, Sch.E.*Or.*58. **-πράσσω**, in Pass., of a debtor, *to have* money *prematurely exacted* from him, *PCair.Zen.*367.18 (iii B.C.). **-φέρω**, fut. -οίσω and 1 aor. -ήνεγκα D.50.8:—advance money to pay the εἰσφορά for others, Id.42.25, 50.8; generally, advance money to the State, SIG 344.115 (Teos, iv B.C.); ἀργύριον ἄτοκον π. IG11(4).1055.11 (Delos, iii B.C.), etc. 2. introduce a law before, in Pass., Poll.5.166, Lib. Decl.39.3:—Med., introduce before (in writing), ὄνομα Sch.Ar.Ach. 321. 3. confer previously, χάριν τῇ πόλει Lib.Decl.22.27, cf. Or.12. 37. -φορά, ἡ, money advanced to pay the εἰσφορά for others, D.37. 37, 50.9. 2. advance of money to the State, Inscr.Prien.108.51, 56 (ii B.C., pl.); χρημάτων SIG1003.30 (Priene, ii B.C.). 3. preliminary expenses, Lib.Decl.33.18. -φορος, ὁ, one who contributes to a προεισφορά, Inscr.Prien.108.78 (ii B.C.).

**προεκ-βάλλω**, throw out, eject before, Arist.HA605ᵃ7; squeeze out first, ἰκμάδα Dsc.5.87. II. Astrol., calculate first, τὸν τῆς τύχης κλῆρον Cat.Cod.Astr.1.167. -βᾰσις, εως, ἡ, previous going out, Eust. 1394.14. -βῐβάζω, launch prematurely, εἰς πόλεμον Plb.20.3.2 (leg. προεμ-). -δᾰπᾰνάω, consume, exhaust before, Id.9.43.2 (Pass.). -δέχομαι, intercept before, ὄρη π. ἀνέμους Str.15.3.10; τοὺς κινδύνους J.BJ7.6.4. -δῐδάσκω, teach thoroughly before, Id.AJ17. 6.1 (prob. l. for προσ-), Them.Or.32.358b, Iamb.VP12.58 codd. (leg. προσ-). ⊕ -δίδωμι, publish beforehand, Plb.16.20.7:—Pass., ἐν τοῖς προεκδοθεῖσι ὑπομνηματισμοῖς D.H.Th.1, cf. PTeb.27.59 (ii B.C.), A.D.Synt.3.1, Gal.18(2).1024. II. προεκδοῦσα κοιλία excreting before, Herod.Med. in Rh.Mus.58.100. -δοσις, εως, ἡ, previous edition, Sch.A.R.1.285, etc. -δρομή, ἡ, running out in advance, of troops, Poll.1.164. -ζέω, boil off before, τὰ ὄστρεα Ruf.ap.Orib. 4.2.19. -θερμαίνω, warm thoroughly before, Orib.Syn.1.27 (Pass.). -θεσις, εως, ἡ, introduction, preface, τῆς πραγματείας Plb. 3.1.7, 8.11.2; prefatory account, Scymn.13, D.H.Comp.23, Quint. Inst.9.2.106. -θετέον, one must premise, Str.17.1.1. -θετικός, ή, όν, introductory, prefatory, σχῆμα Eust.20.42, etc. -θέω, run out before, sally from the ranks, rush on, Th.7.30, J.BJ2.16.2, Arr.An.1. 1.12; ἐν τοῖς δρόμοις Jul.Or.2.69d. 2. metaph., outrun, τοῦ λογισμοῦ Plu.2.446d; ὁ λόγος προεκθεῖ Ael.NA13.11. -θρῴσκω, leap out before, Eus.Mynd.34: c. gen., ἡ Ἄρτεμις π. τοῦ Ἀπόλλωνος Sch. E.Hec.458. -κᾰθαίρω, cleanse, purify before, J.AJ18.5.2; γῆν Sor.1.40, cf. Lysis ap.Iamb.VP17.76, Sch.Luc.Cat.24. -καίω, inflame first (sed leg. προσ- (?)), Gal.11.392. -κᾰλέω, Med. -καλεῖται, = procitat, Gloss. -κειμαι, lie before, project beyond, στέρνα τὸ μέτριον π. Philostr.Jun.Im.15: but usu. II. Pass. of προεκτίθημι, to be fixed in advance, ἡ προεκκειμένη ἡμέρα Cic.Att.6.5. 2; to be set forth previously, τὰ -κείμενα Demetr.Lac.Herc.1012.33, etc.; τὰ -κείμενα προστάγματα PTeb.5.224 (ii B.C.); οἱ -κείμενοι λόγοι A.D.Synt.10.24; αἱ -κείμεναι [ἀρεταί] the above-mentioned.., Longin.11.1; to be cited above, Ath.3.105c. 2. τὰ -κείμενα πτωτικά case-forms presupposed by or underlying adverbs, A.D.Adv. 170.26. -κενόω, drain off beforehand, J.AJ3.1.2, Sch.Il.9.223; evacuate first, Gal.15.721: metaph., exhaust a subject, Sch.Hermog. in Rh.4.490 W. -κλύζω, rinse out first, Gal.11.132, Androm. ap.eund.12.631, Apollon.ib.647. -κομίζω, carry out beforehand, Hdt.2.63: metaph., ὑπὸ τῆς τύχης -κομισθεὶς ἀναίμακτος Plu.Tim. 37. 2. Med., remove first, τῇ χειρί Hippiatr.75. -κοπρόω, remove faeces first, Paul.Aeg.3.43. -κόπτω, excise first, τοὺς σπονδύλους Gal.2.682:—Pass., ib.702. II. destroy first, Lib.Or.39. 15. -κρίνω [ῑ], anticipate a crisis, Hp.Hum.13 (dub.l.). II. Pass., -κριθέντων τῶν ὑγρῶν carried off first, Dsc.1.47; to be cleared out first, Sor.2.63 (προκρ- cod.). -κρῐσις, εως, ἡ, previous secretion, interpol. in Artem.4.84. -κρούω, push or drive out before, Vett.Val.337.12, D.C. 43.4. -λάμπω, shine out before, Them.Or.16.201d. -λέγω, collect moneys before or in advance, [τὰ] προεξειλεγμένα D.18.234, 50.9; χρήματα π. ἀπὸ τῆς Ῥόδου App.BC5.2. ⊕ -λείπω, fail to assist, τινα Hp.Ep.10:—Pass., to be evacuated previously, J.AJ17.10.9. -λογίζομαι, calculate before, Ph.2.279, Mithr.Ep.Brut.Praef., Hierocl. in CA12p.447M. -λύω, relax before, τὸν στόμαχον Ath.2.45e; weaken beforehand, in Pass., Chrysipp.Stoic.3.123, Gal.13.566; reduce the force of a blow, Id.UP3.8; π. τὸ ἐνστατικὸν weaken the resistance beforehand, Alex.Aphr. in Top.531.18. 2. release first, τὴν δεξιὰν Sor. 1.111 (προσ- cod.). II. weary before the time, τῷ κόπῳ τὰ σώματα Plb.15.16.3:—pf. part. Pass. προεκλελυμένος Anon.ap.Suid. s. v. ἐκπαθεῖς. 2. metaph. of distance, weaken the force of a projectile, J.BJ3.7.22:—so in Pass., of sounds, Ph.2.140. -μανθάνω, learn by heart before, Theon Prog.3, Sch.D.T.p.18 H. -μάττω, wipe out first, Gal.12.409, 13.665. -μυζάω, suck out first, Sor.1.87 (Pass., προσ- cod.). -νιτρόω, clean beforehand with νίτρον, Dsc. 4.136, 5.1, Cleopatra ap. Gal.12.404:—Pass., Antyll.ap.Orib.7.21. 3, etc. -νιτρωτέον, one must clean beforehand, Id.ib.10.13. 30. -πέμπω, send out before, Ph.2.110, J.AJ13.7.3, Plu.Cam.41, Alc.34; ἐλπίδας περὶ σεαυτοῦ Lib.Or.55.33. -πηδάω, leap out before, Thphr.CP1.19.1, 4.6.7; τῆς τάξεως D.S.12.64: metaph., [πάθος] π. τοῦ λόγου Them.Or.19.232d. -πίνω [ῑ], drink off before, Plu.2.768d, Ath.5.193a. ⊕ -πίπτω, fall or come out before, precede, τὸ κῦμα π. τοῦ πνεύματος Arist.Pr.932ᵇ37: metaph., get abroad before, φήμη Plu.Galb. 5; π. εἰς γένεσιν Id.2.427e. II. go beyond limits, Str.1.2.3; π. τὸ ἀδύνατον Longin.15.8 (προσ- cod.), cf. 38.1. ⊕ -πλέω, sail out before, Plu.Arist.23, Nic.20. -πλήσσω, scare or astound before, J.AJ 18.9.7, Onos.29.2, Plu.Lys.25, Luc.Ind.9, etc.:—Pass., Id.Alex. 16. -ποιέω, alienate before, Just.Nov.159 Praef., 162.1. -πονέω, work out, finish before, Semon.22. -πτωσις, εως, ἡ, going beyond limits, Str.7.3.4 (pl.). -ρέω, aor. inf. -ρυῆναι, flow out first, Orib.45. 3.8. -ρήγνῠμαι, Pass., break out suddenly or prematurely, χειμῶνες π. Hp.Epid.1.4; also of diseases, Id.Hum.13, Gal.9.916. -τείνω, stretch forth, Apollon.Lex. s. v. προτῆλε. -τελέω, bring quite to an end before, Ael.VH13.1. -τέμνω, cut out first, Apollon.Lex. s.v. πρότμησις. -τήκω, melt before: metaph. in Pass., προεξετήκοντο λύπαις Plu.2.107a. -τίθημι, put out or publish before, λόγον ζητήματος ib. 1035b; ἔστιν ἃ εἰς τὸ δημόσιον D.C.53.21. 2. build out, as a salient or projection, Ph.Bel.84.6. II. set forth or expound before or by way of preface, τὸ πρᾶγμα τοῖς ἀκούουσι π. Arist.Rh.Al.1436ᵃ40; δι' ἃ -τεθήκαμεν Demetr.Lac.Herc.1055.23: more freq. in Med., Plb.1. 13.1, Str.1.2.31, J.AJ12.2.5: so in pf. Pass., καθότι -τεθείμεθα SIG 685.56 (Magn. Mae., ii B.C.); καθ' ἣν -τεθείμεθα τήρησιν A.D.Synt.70. 1, cf. Heliod.ap.Orib.49.21.15. 2. Med., secrete and prepare beforehand, τοῖς ἐμβρύοις ἡ φύσις π. τὴν τροφὴν Arist.GA746ᵃ3. -τίκτω, lay before, [τὰ ᾠά] prob. in Id.HA549ᵃ17: abs., πρὸ ἀρκτούρου ib. ᵇ11. -τίλλω, pluck out before, τρίχα Gal.12.742:—Pass., Aët.11. 11. -τίνω, pay before, Them.Or.16.199c (Pass.), Chor. in Lib.4. 85 R. -τρέχω, aor. -έδραμον, run out before, Ph.1.166, al., Plu. Cor.9, Pel.23. 2. shoot out before the season, Thphr.CP2.1.6. 3. to be born before, τινος Lib.Or.5.4. -τρύχω [ῡ], wear out beforehand, App.BC4.108. -τῠπόω, mould or model before, τὸν νοητὸν κόσμον Ph.1.4. ⊕ -φέρω, put out before, τὴν χεῖρα Lxx Ge.38.28. 2. utter, pronounce before, Demetr.Eloc.51. II. Pass., to be carried away headlong, Aristipp.ap.Stob.3.17.17 (s. v.l.); of runners, Chrysipp.Stoic.3.128. -φεύγω, escape before, Plu.2.250e, D.C.Fr.78. 3; ἐπὶ πλοίου Id.38.50. -φλογόω, set on fire before, Olymp. in Mete.31.23 (Pass.). -φοβέω, scare before, Plu.Mar.19, Luc.Salt. 18, D.C.42.14:—Pass., Plu.Mar.26. -φόβησις, εως, ἡ, previous panic, Th.5.11, D.C.Fr.109.18. -φοιτάω, go forth, be announced previously, Id.69.1. b. anticipate a statement, οὐ -φοιτῶν ἀλλ' ἐν τῷ παρόντι ταμιευόμενος Ph.2.294. 2. go forth beyond, c. gen., Stob. 2.7.14. -φράττω, first remove obstruction, Gal.8.375, Orib.Eup. 4.100:—Pass., Gal.15.72. -φωνέω, pronounce one thing before another, τί τινος S.E.M.1.125 (Pass.). -χέω, pour out before, Luc. Pseudol.4:—Pass., Sor.1.57. -χωρέω, go out before, D.C.41.41, v.l. for προσ- in 43.39; τῆς πόλεως Id.50.2.

**προέλ-ᾰσις**, εως, ἡ, riding forward: cavalry charge, X.Eq.Mag.8.3 (pl.). -αύνω, intr., ride on or forward, Id.An.6.3.14(17): c. gen., ride before one, Id.Mem.3.3.1:—also in Pass., of Time, ὡς πρόσω τῆς νυκτὸς προελήλατο as the night was now far advanced, Hdt.9.44.

**προελέγχω**, refute before: pf. part. Pass. -εληλεγμένος Oenom.ap. Eus.PE6.7.

⊕ **προελευθερόομαι**, Pass., to be set free before, D.C.48.34.

⊕ **προέλευσις**, εως, ἡ, issuing forth, Sm.Ex.21.7, al., Olymp. in Mete. 147.23; ἐκ τοῦ παλατίου Tz.H.6.491; progress, procession, π. θριαμβική Eust.1292.16. 2. f.l. for προαίρεσις in Luc.Prom.Es6. 3. παραμύθιον τῆς π. μου a reward for my trouble, PFlor.332.20 (ii A.D.).

**προελκ-ομένως**, prolixe, Gloss. -όομαι, Pass., be ulcerated before, Dsc.Eup.1.150. -υσμένως, = -ομένως, Gloss.

⊕ **προέλκω**, draw, drag forth, Ael.VH4.15: metaph., lead on, entice, τὸ μειράκιον εἰς πότον J.AJ15.3.3:—Med., προελκυσάμενον τὴν ἐσθῆτα having drawn it over his head, Sch.S.Aj.245: metaph., lead on, τοὺς κυνηγέτας π. οἱ κύνες ib.7.

**προελπίζω**, hope for before, Posidipp.27.8, Them.Or.5.65a; προηλπικότες ἐν Χριστῷ Ep.Eph.1.12: generally, anticipate, expect, Gal.16. 822, Dexipp.Hist.32(h) J., Simp. in Epict.p.50 D.

**προεμ-βαίνω**, enter a boat first or before, Plu.Pomp.78; enter a ford first, Philostr.VA2.15. -βάλλω, put in or insert before, ἄμμον εἰς βαλανοδόκην Aen.Tact.18.3; ἐς τὴν ὀπὴν τοὺς πόδας Paus. 9.39.11: metaph., π. τινὶ κατελπισμόν Plb.3.82.8:—Pass., Thphr. Od.18; of words, Arist.Rh.1407ᵃ28; to be applied previously, of bandages, Gal.18(1).801. 2. deposit beforehand, ἀρραβῶνα PCair. Zen.637.6 (iii B.C.). II. abs., προεμβαλλόντων ἐς τὴν γῆν τῶν κερέων the horns butting into the ground in front, of cattle with projecting horns, Hdt.4.183. b. project, be prominent, Philostr. Gym.10, cj. in 34. 2. of ships, make the charge (ἐμβολή) first, Th. 4.25: with acc. expressed, π. [τῇ νηΐ] πληγήν Plb.16.3.2: hence, generally, attack before, τινι D.S.15.81. 3. make an inroad before, εἰς τὴν Γαλιλαίαν, ἐς τὴν Ἀρμενίαν, J.BJ2.20.6, D.C.36.45, cf. 37. 1. -βᾰτήριος, ον, belonging to a προεμβάτης, γέρας π. a reward given one who first boarded the enemy's ship, Hld.5.31. -βάτης [ᾰ], ου, ὁ, one who first boards the enemy's ship, ibid. -βῐβάζω, put in before, π. τινὰς εἰς ἀπέχθειαν make them hated before, Plb.2. 45.4; cf. προεκβιβάζω. -βόλιον, τό, ship's beak, IG2².1613.58: also -βολίς, ίδος, ἡ, Poll.1.85: -βολον, τό, Agath.5.21: -βολος, ὁ, Hsch. -βρέχω, soak first, Asclep.Jun.ap.Gal.13.163.

**προέμεν**, Ep. aor. 2 inf. of προΐημι (q. v.).

**προεμέω**, vomit beforehand, aor. part. -εμέσας Orib.Fr.81: pf. part. fem. -εμημεκυῖα Dsc.5.67, cf. Eup.2.20.

**προεμ-μελετάω**, practise before, τοῖς τοῦ βίου πράγμασι Ph.1. 551. -πίπλαμαι, Pass., to be filled up before, Luc.Cal.8. -πίπρημι, burn first, ἐρύματα D.C.54.5. -πίπτω, fall on or into before, ἡ βολὴ π. τῷ ὕδατι Hld.9.5; attack first, Ael.Tact.37.6; take the first step, εἰς γνῶσιν D.L.4.39. 2. protrude into, c. dat., Gal.UP 7.7; προεμπίπτει τὰ χείλη, of a bear trying to bite a net, Plu.2. 918f. -πνέω, blow into before, τῷ καλάμῳ τὸ μέλος Him.Or.12. 3. -πολεύς, έως, ὁ, previous buyer, AB296. -πολεύω, buy first, ibid. -πορίζω, v. προευπορέω. -φαίνω, insist on, emphasize before, App.BC4.125. -φᾰνίζομαι, Pass., appear before, Longin.17.

2. **-φᾰσις**, εως, ἡ, *previous manifestation*, Dam.*Pr.*118,122 (pl.); τῶν εἰδῶν Simp. *in Ph.*422.6; *foreshadowing*, τινος Id. *in Cat.*246.18. **-φορέομαι**, Pass., *to be filled full before*, κακίας Plu.2.1067f. **-φῡσάω**, *spray first upon*, οἶνον τῷ τόπῳ Aët.15.5.

**προεν-άρχομαι**, *begin before*, 2*Ep.Cor.*8.6,10. **-δείκνῠμαι**, *exhibit oneself* or *make a demonstration before*, τινι Aeschin.3.219. **-δημέω**, *to be in* a place or *among* a people *before*, τοῖς -ενδημήσασι ξένοις Aen.Tact.29.4. 2. *to be prevalent before*, κακά J.*AJ*2.14.4; π. τοῖς πράγμασι *familiarize oneself* with things *beforehand*, Posidon.*Stoic.*3.131. ⊛ **-δίδωμι**, *give way first*, τῶν ὀστέων προενδεδωκότων Hp.*Art.*69; π. ἡ ὁρμή Plu.2.444c. **-έδρα**, ἡ, *ambush*, Hsch. s.v. προδοκῆσι. **-εδρεύω**, *lay an ambush before*, prob. in Aen.Tact.4.8: c. acc., *place in ambush before*, ἱππέας ἐς ὄρος App.*Hann.*20. **-ειμι**, (εἰμί *sum*) *to be in before*, Malch.p.413D.; of one *already interred* in a grave, *BCH*23.167 (Pisidia). **-είρω**, *insert before*, Aen.Tact.31.22. **-εκτέον**, (προφέρω) *one must pronounce*, τὴν πλάγιον πτῶσιν S.E.*M.*1.222, cf. Sch.Ar.*Nu.*1162. **-εργέω**, *practise first*, Arist.*Metaph.*1047$^{b}$33. **-έρχομαι**, *enter in before*, οἷς οὐδὲν προενεληλυθὸς ὑποικουρεῖ πάθος Ph.2.380. **-έχομαι**, Pass., *to be involved in before*, τινι Lxx 2*Ma.*5.18. **-εχῠράζω**, *distrain upon previously*, in Pass., διὰ τὸ προηνεχυράσθαι τοὺς κλήρους *PTeb.*61(*b*).274 (ii B.C.); cf. sq. **-εχῠριάζω**, *bind by pledges before*, τὴν γνώμην Sch.T Il.9.45 (-ράζει Sch. B); προηνεχυριασμένος εὐεργεσίαις Charito 2.7. **-θῡμέω**, *notice before*, τῶν κυνῶν Aen.Tact.24.18. II. aor. Pass. -εθυμήθην in med. sense, *think seriously on before*, Str.2.5.1, Lib.*Or.*14.71. **-θύμησις** [ῡ], εως, ἡ, *previous thought*, Hsch. s.v. πρόνοια. **-ιδρύω**, *set up, establish in* or *among beforehand*, Iamb.*Myst.*5.23 (Pass.). **-ίημι**, *place in* a grave, *inter previously*, pf. part. Pass. -ενειμένος *BCH*23.167, al. (Pisid.). 2. *inject previously*, Orib.*Fr.*55, Aët.15.13. **-ίσταμαι**, Med., *object beforehand*, Arist.*SE*174$^{b}$30.

**προεννέπω, προὐννέπω** (as always in Trag.), *proclaim, announce*, τάδε A.*Eu.*852; π. σοί, εἰ.., θανῇ E.*Med.*351: c. inf., χαίρειν τινὰ π. I *publicly bid* him hail, S.*Tr.*227, cf. E.*Hipp.*1085; π. δ' ὑμῖν ὅτι.. A.*Eu.*98.

**προεν-νοέω**, *conceive* or *consider beforehand*, Plu.2.1072a, Artem.1.3. **-νόημα**, ατος, τό, *previous conception*, Tz.*H.*7.618. **-οικέω**, *dwell in* or *inhabit before*, D.S.5.84, Ph.2.132. **-οίκησις**, εως, ἡ, *dwelling in* a place *before*, ἡ τῶν Φαιάκων π. τῆς Κερκύρας Th.1.25, cf. D.C.53.16, Hld.8.1. **-σείω**, *fling* troops *at before*, τινὰς τῷ Κρατερῷ Plu.*Eum.*6. **-στᾰτέον**, *one must object beforehand*, Arist.*SE*176$^{b}$26. **-τείνω**, *strain, stretch previously*:—Pass., νευραὶ -τεταμέναι Philostr.*VA*4.39. **-τευξις**, εως, ἡ, *previous petition*, *Inscr.Prien.*59.3 (iii/ii B.C.). **-τίθημι**, *insert before*, Phlp. *in GA*202.5. **-τίκτω**, *lay in before*, [τὰ ᾠά] Arist.*HA*526$^{b}$10. **-τυγχάνω**, *encounter, meet first*, Ph.1.363, al., J.*BJ*5.6.5, al.; τῇ ἄγρᾳ Ael.*NA*4.13; *come in contact with first*, τοῖς πράγμασι Plu.2.1122b: pf. part. -εντετυχηκώς *previously acquainted with*, Gal.17(1).501. II. *intercede with first*, Ph.1.547; *have audience of first*, πρέσβεις π. τῇ βουλῇ Plu.*Nic.*10; ὄψις π. αὐτοῦ τῆς φωνῆς an appearance which *spoke for* him *before* he opened his mouth, Id.*Pomp.*2.

**προένωμα**, ατος, τό, *concrete pre-unity*, τῶν διορισθησομένων Dam.*Pr.*54.

**προεξ-αγγέλλω**, *announce beforehand*, D.19.248, J.*BJ*2.21.8, Arr.*An.*6.4.5. **-αγκωνίζω**, as a pugilistic term, *spar before* beginning to fight: hence metaph., of a speaker, οὐδὲν προεξαγκωνίσας οὐδὲ προανακινήσας εὐθὺς ἄρχεται Arist.*Rh.*1416$^{a}$2. **-άγω** [ᾰ], *lead* or *carry out first*, τὴν λῃτὴν ἐς τὸν αἰγιαλόν Hdt.9.106; π. τινὰ ἐκ τοῦ ζῆν Plb.30.7.8, Plu.2.117d:—Pass., *go out first*, π. ναυσί Th.7.70 (προεξαναγόμενοι ap. D.H.*Th.*26); *to be exported previously*, *BGU*802 i 11, al. (i A.D.). **-ᾰδῠνᾰτέω**, *to be already very weak*, Hp.*Prorrh.*1.8, *Coac.*99, Gal.16.531. **-αιθριάζω**, *first expose to the air*, Archig.ap.Gal.13.254. ⊛ **-αιρέω**, *take out before*, Sch.Ar.*Eq.*378 (Pass.); π. τινῶν τὸν φόβον App.*BC*2.64:—Pass., *to be deprived of before*, τι Luc.*Alex.*15. II. *conquer before*, App.*BC*4.76, D.C.46.37. **-αΐσσω**, Att. **-ᾴσσω**, *dart out before*, as out of the ranks in battle, Hdt.9.62; προεξᾴξαντες Th.8.25. **-αιτέω**, *beg off beforehand*, Nicol *Prog.* in Rh.1.321 W. **-ᾰκοντίζω**, *discharge javelins first*, Ael.*Tact.*2.13. **-ᾰλείφω**, *erase, cancel prematurely*, Arist.*Ath.*47.5 (Pass.). **-άλλομαι**, *leap out before*: metaph., of passions, Them.*Or.*1.15d: c. gen., π. τοῦ ἐν τάξει ἀκολουθοῦντος (in thought) Id.*Or.*2.33b. **-αλλοτριόω**, *alienate previously*, *PLond.*2.154.13 (Pass., i A.D.). **-ᾰμαρτάνω**, *do wrong before*, Isoc.4.165; π. τοῦτ' εἰς ὑμᾶς αὐτούς Id.6.38. **-ανάγω**, v. προεξάγω. **-ανᾱλίσκω**, *consume before*, J.*AJ*2.11.2, al. **-ανθέω**, *put forth as flowers first*, ἄτοπα πολλὰ π. αἱ μεγάλαι φύσεις Plu.2.552c. **-άνθημα**, ατος, τό, = προάνθησις, Suid. s.v. κύτταρος. **-άνθησις**, εως, ἡ, *premature growth*, τριχῶν Sch.Pi.*N.*6.104. **-ανίσταμαι**, Pass., with aor. 2, pf. and plpf. Act., *rise before* or *first*, Hdt.9.62; *rouse oneself beforehand*, D.18.163, J.*AJ*18.6.10; π. τῷ πολέμῳ *make war first*, Plu.*Rom.*16: c. gen., π. τοῦ τέλους Lib.*Or.*51.4; *to be roused before*, τὼ χεῖρε π. τῶν ὀφθαλμῶν Them.*Or.*17.216c. 2. in a race, *start before* the signal is given, οἱ προεξανιστάμενοι ῥαπίζονται Hdt.8.59, cf. Plu.*Them.*11; -αναστάντας καταγινώσκειν condemn *hastily*, Ph.2.210. 3. *revolt prematurely*, Plu.2.459e. **-αντλέω**, *empty first*, Sor.1.52 (Pass.). **-αποστέλλω**, *send out before*, Plb.3.86.3, Lxx 2*Ma.*12.21. **-άπτω**, *light up before*, Phlp. *in Mete.*93.25 (Pass.). ⊛ **-ᾰριθμέομαι**, Med., *count up before*, Sch.Pi.*N* 3.129. **-αρτάω**, *hang in front*, ἐκ τῶν ὤμων -ηρτημένον πέλεκυν v.l. in D.S.3.26. **-άρχω**, *to be leader*, τῆς ποίμνης *EM*542.33. **-ασθενέω**, *become quite weak first*, Arist.*Pr.*865$^{a}$36; φυτὰ π. ταῖς ἐνδείαις Ph.2.371: c. gen., αἱ ὄψεις π. τοῦ βάθους J.*BJ*3.7.7. **-εγείρω**, *stir up prematurely*, πρᾶγμα Phryn.*PS* p.101 B. **-έδρα**, Ion. -η, ἡ, *chair of state*, Hdt.7.44, Poll.9.46. **-ειμι**, (εἰμί *sum*) *improve, derive benefit*, Herod.Med. in *Rh.Mus.*58.76. **-ειμι**, (εἶμι *ibo*) *sally forth from*, τῶν ὅπλων Th.3.1. **-ελαύνω**, *ride out in front*, Plu.*Phil.*7, etc.; τῶν ἄλλων ἱππέων Luc.*DMeretr.*13.1. 2. π. πλοίῳ *run out* in a ship *in front*, Plu.*Nic.*24. **-ελκόω**, *exulcerate before*, Philum.ap.Orib.45.29.72 (Pass.). **-εμέω**, *vomit before*, Philagr. ap.Orib.5.22.4. **-επίστᾰμαι**, contr. **προὐξ-**, *know well before*, πάντα A.*Pr.*101; τὸ λοιπὸν ἄλγος π. τορῶς ib.699. **-εργάζομαι**, *work out before*, Nicol.*Prog.* in Rh.1.321 W.: pf. Pass. in pass. sense, ταύτης τῆς πραγματείας τὸ μὲν ἦν προεξειργασμένον Arist.*SE*183$^{b}$35, cf. Paus.1.34.5. **-ερευνάω**, contr. **προὐξ-**, *investigate before*, E.*Ph.*92; τὰ ὑψηλὰ τῶν χωρίων Aen.Tact.15.5. **-ερευνητής**, contr. **προὐξ-**, οῦ, ὁ, *explorer sent before*, E.*Rh.*296. **-έρχομαι**, *go out before*, τῷ πεζῷ Th.7.74; εἰς Σαρδόνα Plb.2.23.6; τῆς πόλεως D.H.1.46; π. τοῦ βίου πρὶν.. J.*AJ*2.7.2 (so abs. -ελθών *previously deceased*, *Supp.Epigr.*6.236 (Phrygia)); φῶς φωτὸς π. Ph.1.603: abs., *anticipate* arrest *by flight*, *SIG*283.11 (Edict. Alex. Magni). **-ετάζω**, *examine beforehand*, τόπους, εἰ βέβηλοι Ph.2.271, cf. Luc.*Merc.Cond.*5, Gal.6.723, S.E.*M.*8.265:—Pass., J.*Ap.*2.1. II. *prefer*, τῆς τοῦ σώματος ἀγχιστείας τὴν τῆς ψυχῆς π. Them.*Or.*5.65c. **-ευκρῑνέω**, *examine carefully before*, Hp.*Aph.*1.24. **-ευρίσκω**, *find out beforehand*, Arr.*Tact.*16.3 (Pass.). **-εφίεμαι**, contr. **προὐξ-**, Med., *enjoin beforehand*, S.*Tr.*759. **-έχω**, *project from*, τοῦ αἰγιαλοῦ Agath.5.22. **-ηγέομαι**, *explain before*, D.H.*Rh.*10.10, Gal.15.774, al. **-ῑλεόομαι**, *propitiate before*, Sostrat.ap. Stob.4.20.72. **-ῑόω**, (ἰός) *free from impurities, refine*, Zos.Alch.p.161 B.:—Pass., *PHolm.*4.24. **-ίστᾰμαι**, Pass., *project forward*, γένυς -εστηκυῖα Arist.*Phgn.*809$^{b}$17. **-ογκόομαι**, *to be made to swell first*, Sor.2.11. **-οδεύω**, *go forth before*, J.*BJ*7.5.4. ⊛ **-οδιάζω**, *expend before*, *IG*5(1).1390.54 (Pass., Andania, i B.C.). **-οδος**, ἡ, gloss on προμολή, *EM*689.34. **-ομᾰλίζω**, fut. -ιῶ, *make level before*, τὴν ὁδόν J.*BJ*3.7.3. ⊛ **-ορμάω**, *set out, start earlier*, μιᾷ ἡμέρᾳ X.*Mem.*3.13.5, cf. D.C.46.37: c. gen., ἐπὶ πόλεμον π. τῆς θεοῦ βουλήσεως J.*AJ*4.1.2. II. *rush out before the time*, Arist.*HA*587$^{b}$1. 2. *to be stimulated first*, εἰς τὴν διαστολήν Gal.9.78:—Pass., prob. ibid. **-υμνέω**, *celebrate first*, τὸ Ἑλληνικόν Olymp. *in Alc.* p.95C.

**προεορτ-άζω**, *celebrate before*, Hdn.1.16.2, Them.*Or.*3.42d. **-ος**, ον, (ἑορτή) of a festival, *preliminary*, ἑτέρας ἑορτῆς Ph.2.294, cf. 481 (v.l. -ιος).

**προεπ-αγγέλλω**, *announce before*, ὡς μαντευσόμενοι D.C.38.13; π. σφίσιν αὐτὸ τοῦθ' ὅπως.. Id.40.32:—Pass., εὐλογία -ηγγελμένη 2*Ep.Cor.*9.5; τὰ -ηγγελμένα *matters on which orders had been issued*, Arr.*An.*6.27.1. II. *canvass for an office before*, D.C.39.31. III. Med., *announce before*, εὐαγγέλιον *Ep.Rom.*1.2:—Pass., *to be promised before*, D.C.42.32, 46.40. **-άγγελσις**, εως, ἡ, *previous announcement*, Id.38.41. **-αινέω**, *praise beforehand*, Th.3.38, *IG*12(5).655.9 (Syros). **-ανασείω**, *raise the hand against before*: metaph., παρασκευὴ προεπανεσείσθη *was threatened before*, Th.5.17. **-αφίημι**, *send forward against* the enemy, Luc.*Tox.*54. **-είγω**, *to be urgent before*, v.l. in Orib.5.30.13:—Pass., -επειχθῆναι Lib.*Decl.*28.2; *hasten before*, ἐπὶ τὴν ναῦν Sch.E.*Tr.*456. **-ειμι**, *advance against*, τῷ ἐρύματι Agath.5.1.

**προεπι-βάλλω**, *lay* or *throw upon before*, τινὶ τὰς χεῖρας Plb.16.9.3; ἐχίδνας ζώσας Gal.14.291:—Pass., Heliod. ap. Orib.50.53.3. **-βουλεύω**, *plot against beforehand*, τινι Th.1.33:—Pass., *to be the object of such plots*, Id.3.83, D.S.19.65 (s.v.l.). **-βουλή**, ἡ, *plot laid beforehand*, D.C.*Fr.*96.2. **-βρέχω**, *foment beforehand*, τὸ τραῦμα Gal.13.384. **-γιγνώσκω**, *recognize* or *observe before*, S.E.*P.*3.22:—Pass., ib.2.119,210. **-γράφω** [ᾰ], *assess before*:—Pass., τὸ -γεγραμμένον ἐκφόριον *PTeb.*60.82, al. (ii B.C.). **-δείκνυμι**, *explain, demonstrate before*, Isoc.3.12, A.D.*Synt.*91.17:—Pass., Gal.13.429. II. Med., *display before*, Ph.1.551:—Pass., τὰ -δειχθέντα θαυματουργήματα Id.2.93. **-δεσμος**, ὁ, *band* or *ligature put on at first*, Gal.18(2).746 (nisi leg. προσ-). **-δέω**, *bind on before*, Id.18(1).814. **-δημέω**, *to be at home before*, Charito 3.4,5.2. **-ζευγνύω**, Rhet., *employ the figure* προεπίζευξις (cf. sq.), Eust.947.57. **-ζευξις**, εως, ἡ, Rhet. figure, = σχῆμα Ἀλκμανικόν (cf. προδιαζευγνύω), Id.606.40, 947.56. **-θεωρέω**, *examine first*, Sor.1.79. **-θῡμία**, ἡ, *condition preceding desire*, Plot.4.4.20. **-κοινόω**, *communicate before*, τι τῇ γερουσίᾳ D.C.55.4. **-κόπτω**, *cut down, trim first*, στήλας *IG*7.3073.68,145 (Lebad.). **-κρίνω** [ῑ], *judge before*, S.E.*M.*8.265 (dub. l.). **-λογίζομαι**, *calculate before*, ib.2.110:—Pass., ἡ προεπιλογισθεῖσα ἀπόδειξις *before-stated*, Ph.2.497. **-λύω**, in Med., *solve previously*, Ammon. *in Porph.*56.22. **-μελέομαι**, *pay attention to before*, τινος Gal.14.298. **-νοέω**, *observe* or *consider before*, Str.2.5.1:—Pass., *to be previously conceived* or *thought of*, Plu.2.1071f: c. gen., ποιητικὴ -νοεῖται βασιλικῆς Ph.*Fr.*63 H., cf. S.E.*M.*11.186, Plot.5.9.8. **-νοια**, ἡ, *previous observation*, Stob.2.7.3f. **-ξενόομαι**, Pass., *to be received as a guest before*, Luc.*Bis Acc.*7. **-πάσσω**, *strew upon before*, Alex.Trall.*Febr.*7. **-πλήσσω**, *to be the first to blame*, prob. in Arist.*Rh.*1408$^{b}$2 (cf. Quint.*Inst.*8.3.37). **-σημαίνω**, *indicate already*, Phld.*Rh.*1.73 S. (Pass.). **-σκεπτέον**, *one must examine first*, Aët.5.115. ⊛ **-σκέπτομαι**, *examine beforehand*, τὰ μέλλοντα Sch.Arat.411, cf. Ptol.*Geog.*1.6.3, Gal.9.525 (s.v.l.): pf. -έσκεμμαι in act. sense, Alex.Aphr. *in Top.*559.16; in pass. sense, Str.8.3.24. **-σκήπτομαι**, bring an action of ἐπίσκηψις first, τοῖς πεπρακόσιν Mitteis Chr.31 vi 7 (ii B.C.). **-σκοπέω**, 1 aor. imper. -σκόπησον Luc.Merc.Cond.3:—inspect, consider before, l.c.

**προεπίστᾰμαι**, know or understand beforehand, Pl.Grg.459e, X. Cyr.4.3.12, Isoc.9.12, Arist.APr.67ᵃ22, Ael.NA7.8, etc.

**προεπι-στέλλω**, dispatch before, PSI4.332.6 (iii B.C.); order by letter before, τινὶ ποιεῖν τι Paus.7.11.3 (Pass., s.v.l.):—Pass., of money, to have been allocated before, Arch.Pap.4.117 ii 13 (iii A.D.). **-τᾰράσσω**, disturb before, Gal.17(1).989 (Pass.). **-τίθεμαι**, Med., attack first, Ph.2.120, Sch.E.Ph.726. **-τροπεύω**, act as ἐπίτροπος before, BGU8 ii 7 (iii A.D.). **-φαίνομαι**, appear first, Sor.1.58. **-χειρέω**, to be the first to attack, Th.6.34, Ph.2.422, Plu. Thes.9, 11, etc. **-χείρησις**, εως, ἡ, attacking first, D.H.3.4, 10. 43. **-χέω**, v. προσ-.

**προεποικέω**, colonize before, τὴν Μυσίαν Str.12.3.3: abs., τὰ τῶν προεποικησάντων γένη Id.5.1.10.

**προερᾰνίστρια**, ἡ, female president of ἐρανισταί, IG2².1292.23.

**προεργ-άζομαι**, Med. with pf. Pass., work beforehand, τῷ βαρβάρῳ Hdt.2.158; work or till beforehand, τῷ σπόρῳ νεόν X.Oec.20.3:—pf. also in pass. sense, to be done before, τὰ προειργασμένα Antipho 2.2. 12, Th.2.89, 8.65; ἡ προειργασμένη δόξα glory won before, X.An.6.1. 21; τὸ ὀψώνιον.. τοῦ -ειργασμένου χρόνου OGI266.8 (Pergam., iii B.C.). **-ᾰσία**, ἡ, previous cultivation, prob. in POxy.1270.47 (ii A.D.).

**προέργου**, v. προὔργου.

**προερεθ-ίζω**, irritate before, Gal.12.590, Sor.ap.eund.12.418 (Pass.); excite, call forth before the time, Heph.Astr.1.25. **-ισμός**, ὁ, previous irritation, v.l. in Gal.15.622.

**προερέσσω**, row forwards, ἐς λιμένα προερέσσαμεν (sc. τὴν ναῦν) Od. 13.279, cf. Ael.NA13.19.

✻ **προερευνάω**, in Med., search out first or before, Onos.6.8; οἱ προερευνώμενοι ἱππεῖς the vedettes, X.Lac.13.6.

**προερέω**, Att. contr. προερῶ, serving as fut. to προεῖπον (q.v.): also pf. προείρηκα, Pass. -ημαι: aor. Pass. προερρήθην, contr. προὐρρήθην:—say beforehand, Pl.Plt.292d, etc.:—Pass., ἐκ τῶν προειρημένων Id. Phd.75b; κατὰ τὰ π. Id.R.408c; τοῖς π. συμφωνεῖν ib.398c; τὰ προρρηθέντα ib.619c; ταῦτά μοι προειρήσθω be said by way of preface, Isoc.4.14, cf. 5.29. II. order beforehand or publicly, συλλέγεσθαι ἐς Σάρδις Hdt.1.77, 81; π. τῷ στρατῷ ὡς.. ἀκουστέα εἴη Id.3.61:—Pass., προὐρρήθη ὅπως.. Pl.Smp.198e; προείρητο αὐτοῖς μὴ ἐπιχειρεῖν Th.2.84, cf. Antipho6.40; ἔχοντες τὸ προειρημένον the prescribed implement, Hdt.1.126; ἀπικέσθαι ἐς τὴν π. ἡμέρην Id.6.128; δεῖπνον.. ἐκ πολλοῦ χρόνου π. ordered beforehand, Id.7.119; πόλεμος προερρήθη was declared, X.Ages.1.17. 2. ὀνυμαστὶ προερεῖ will call him publicly by name, Berl.Sitzb.1927.167 (Cyrene).

**προερμηνεύω**, translate before, Aristeas 314 (Pass.).

**προέρπω**, issue forth, ὡς θηρίον ἐκ φωλεῶν Sor.2.29.

**προερύω**, Ep. aor. -έρυσσα (v. infr.), draw on or forward, in Hom. always of ships, 1. νῆα θοὴν ἅλαδε προέρυσσεν drew the swift ship forward, by hauling her from the beach to the sea, Il.1.308; ἐπὴν ἅλαδε προερύσσω (sc. νῆας) 9.358. 2. move the ship forward, by rowing her towards the shore, αὐτὰς δ' ἐσσυμένως προερύσσαμεν ἤπειρόνδε Od.9.73; τὴν δ' εἰς ὅρμον προέρυσσαν ἐρετμοῖς Il.1.435, Od.15.497 (but προερεσσ- was rightly written by Aristarch. and others).

**προέρχομαι** (πρόειμι serves as fut.), aor. προῆλθον: pf. προελήλυθα Men.113.2:—go forward, advance, Hdt.1.207, 9.14; ἐς τὸ ὁμαλὸν Th. 5.65; ἐς τὸ πλέον Id.2.21; ἐκ τοῦ χωρίου X.HG7.5.25; ἐπὶ τὸ βῆμα D.H.8.58: abs., προελθών, = Att. παρελθών, having come forward to speak, Plb.4.14.7; προελθὼν ὁ κῆρυξ ἐκήρυττε.. Aeschin.3.154; π. εἰς τὸν δῆμον SIG742.49 (Ephesus, i B.C.): c. acc. cogn., π. ἡμερησίαν ὁδόν Pl.R.616b; κατὰ τὴν ὁδὸν X.An.4.2.16. b. come forth, πλάγια π. τὰ ἔμβρυα Arist.HA576ᵃ24; π. μητρός to be born, Olymp. Vit.Pl.p.1 W.: generally, Luc.Tox.25, al.; appear, be published, of a book, Str.13.1.54. c. go away from, leave, ἀπὸ τῆς ἑαυτοῦ [οἰκίας] POxy.472.5 (ii A.D.), cf. Stud.Pal.1.8.10 (v A.D.); οὐδεπώποτε ἐξ Αἰθιοπίας τὸν ἕτερον πόδα προελθών Luc.Herm.32. 2. of Time, προελθόντος πολλοῦ χρόνου Th.1.10, cf. Pl.Plt.273a; π. κατὰ χρόνον Id.Prm.152a; of persons, προεληλυθότες ταῖς ἡλικίαις advanced in years, X.HG6.1.5. 3. go on, proceed, in a story or argument, Pl.Phdr.237c; εἰς τὸ πρόσθεν π. Id.Lg.682a, cf. Prt.339d. 4. metaph., [τὰ Περσέων πρήγματα] ἐς τοῦτο προελθόντα the power of the Persians having advanced to this height, Hdt.7.50; ὥσπερ μαθητὴν εἰς τοὔμπροσθε π. make progress, Isoc.Ep.4.10; ἐνταῦθα π. ὥστε.. Id. 15.82: freq. in bad sense, εἰς πᾶν π. μοχθηρίας D.3.3; οὕτως αἰσχρῶς π. Id.23.204; οἷ προελήλυθ' ἀσελγείας ἄνθρωπος Id.4.9; εἰς τοῦτ' ἀναισθησίας καὶ τόλμης προεληλύθασιν Id.24.182; πόρρω προεληλύθασι φυλακῆς they are far gone in cautiousness, X.Hier.4.4. 5. go before or first, Id.Cyr.6.3.9, etc.; π. τινὸς go before him, ib.2.2.7; π. τινός Ev.Marc.6.33. b. arrive first, Th.8.100: pf., have travelled first, ὁδόν Pl.R.328e. II. take legal proceedings, appear in court, PGiss.8.12 (ii A.D.), etc.

**προερωτάω**, ask before, S.E.P.2.234 (Pass.).

**προεσθίω**, pf. προεδήδοκα Gal.18(1).42: 1 aor. part. Pass. -εδεσθέν Arist.Pr.926ᵇ29:—eat before, πρὸ τοῦ πότου ἀμυγδάλας πικράς Ath.2. 52d, cf. Diocl.Fr.141, Antig.Mir.35; eat before another, to show that the food is not poisoned, Luc.Par.59; τῶν βασιλέων Ath.4. 171b.

**πρόεσις**, εως, ἡ, (προΐημι) sending forth, emission, [τῶν ᾠῶν] Arist. HA550ᵇ12, cf. Ph.1.29, Gal.4.590; οὔρου, οὔρων, Arist.Pr.888ᵇ1, Aret. SD2.4; καταμηνίων, [περιττώματος], Arist.GA765ᵇ21, PA663ᵃ16, cf. Thphr.Metaph.29; φωνῆς voice-production, Anon.Epicureus Herc. 176 p.39 V.; π. ἐκ τῶν νεφῶν Epicur.Ep.2 p.49 U.: pl., δακρύων -έσεις Phld.Mort.25. 2. throwing away, opp. λῆψις, Arist.EN1107ᵇ12.

**προεσκεμμένως**, Adv. with forethought, Antyll.(?) ap.Orib.45.17.9.

**προεστιάω**, feast, entertain before another, Him.Or.10.4.

**προέτειος**, ον, (ἔτος) of the last year, Arist.Pr.924ᵇ6.

**προετέον**, (προΐημι) one must throw away or give up, τινα Din.1.92; τοῖς Δημοσθένους ἐλέοις τὴν ἀπολογίαν ib.108; ἴχνευσιν Epicur.Ep.2 p.42 U.

**προετήσιαι** ἄνεμοι, winds which blow before the ἐτησίαι (q.v.), Olymp.in Mete.180.5.

**προετικός**, ή, όν, (προΐημι) emitting easily, in Comp., opp. καθεκτικώτερος (more retentive), Arist.Pr.963ᵃ21; emitting, βαρέος [ἤχου] Thphr.Fr.89.10; σπέρματος Sor.1.33. II. apt to throw away, profuse, lavish, X.Mem.3.1.6, Arist.EN1120ᵇ15; π. δαπάνης lavish of expense, Pl.Def.416b; χρημάτων Arist.VV1250ᵇ25; π. τινί giving lavishly to.., Id.Rh.1367ᵇ6. Adv. -κῶς Id.EN1122ᵇ8.

**προετοιμ-άζω**, get ready beforehand, Aen.Tact.18.6:—Med., prepare for one's own use or purpose, Hdt.8.24:—Pass., Id.7.22, Ph.2. 252, al., J.AJ17.5.6, Plu.2.230e, Philum.ap.Orib.8.45.7. **-ᾰσία**, ἡ, previous preparation, Eustr.in EN11.7.

**προετῠμολόγησις**, εως, ἡ, explaining a word first, Sch.Opp.H.1. 181.

**προευ-αγγελίζομαι**, bring glad tidings before, Ph.1.7, 602, Sch.S. Tr.335; τῷ Ἀβραὰμ ὅτι.. Ep.Gal.3.8. **-δοκῐμέω**, to be in good repute before, οἱ προευδοκιμηκότες D.H.Rh.5.6; τὸ -δοκιμοῦν καταλύειν D.C.39.25. **-εργετέω**, confer a favour on before, D.S.19.6 (Pass.); -εργετηθεὶς ὑπό τινος Sch.Pi.P.2.32. **-θετίζω**, accommodate, εἰς λόγον A.D.Synt.309.7 (Pass.): c. inf., προηυθέτισται τὰ ἐγκλιτικὰ μόρια ἐπὶ τέλους ἔχειν τὴν ὀξεῖαν ib.134.15. **-κρῑνέω**, pick out carefully before, Aret.CD1.5; judge carefully, ἀμφὶ τῆς δυνάμιος Id.CA1. 10; -κρινηθέντος τοῦ τοιούτου this matter having been cleared up first, A.D.Synt.235.6.

**προευκτικός**, ή, όν, of or for an introductory prayer, κατάστασις Sch. Opp.H.1.73.

**προευ-λᾰβέομαι**, aor. -ηυλαβήθην, take heed, be cautious beforehand, D.25.95. **-λογέω**, praise beforehand, cj. for προσ-, J.AJ4.8.47. **-μενίζομαι**, Med., placate before, Sch.Arat.636. **-πεπτέω**, digest well before, Gal.14.298. ✻ **-πορέω**, provide in advance, prob. (for προεμπορίζω) in SIG344.118 (Teos, iv B.C.):—Pass., to be provided before, v.l. for προσ- in D.24.97. II. solve an ἀπορία, overcome a difficulty beforehand, Arist.Ph.208ᵃ35 (Pass.), Simp.in Ph.523.12. **-τελίζω**, disparage before, Sch.Ar.Av.686:—Pass., Lyd.Mag.2.17 (προσ- cod.). **-τρεπίζω**, adjust, make ready before, παρασκευήν Iamb.Comm.Math.15; prepare, τινὰ ἐπὶ τὸ ἀγαθόν Id.Protr.1; ἕδραν τῷ φωτί Id.Myst.3.14; τι τῇ ζητήσει Hero Deff.136.13:—Med., J.AJ20.4.2; προευτρεπισμένος τι having it ready, Hld.7.24:—Pass., aor. 1 part., Ph.1.212; τῇ δεήσει προευτρεπισθεὶς moved before, J.AJ20.6.3. **-τρεπισμός**, ὁ, previous preparation, Simp.in Epict.p.135 D. **-φραίνω**, delight before, Ph.1.96, Ael.NA10.19, Lib.Or.11.248. **-χρηστέω**, = προδανείζω, διάφορον IG2².1329.16, cf. UPZ110.183 (ii B.C., prob.).

**προεφ-ίημι**, deliver previously, ἀρτάβας PTeb.120.96 (i B.C.). II. Med., c. acc., attack first, λόγους.. τοὺς ἐκκειμένους Phld.Sign. 19. **-ίστημι**, call one's attention to beforehand, π. τοὺς ἀκούοντας ἐπί τι Plb.10.2.1. **-οδεύομαι**, Pass., to be traversed before, Str. 12.8.8. **-οδιάζομαι**, Pass., to be provided, ὄργανα οἷς προεφωδιάσθη Ph.2.03. **-οράω**, survey before, M.Ant.7.49. **-ορμάω**, rush upon first, Hld.9.17.

**προ-εχής**, ές, prominent, coming forward, in paintings, Plu.Fr.13.2 (προσ- codd.). II. = σπουδαῖος, κραταιός, Hsch. ✻ **-εχμα**, ατος, τό, f.l. for πρόβλημα, J.AJ17.10.7. **-εχόντως**, excellently, Phld. Mus.p.52 K.

**προέχω**, contr. προὔχω, as always in Hom., exc. Od.12.11 (v. infr. B), also in S. and Th.: fut. προέξω: aor. προέσχον, Med. προεσχόμην, προὐσχόμην, cf. προΐσχω:—hold before, τὴν ἀσπίδα τῆς κωλῆς Ar.Nu. 989; esp. so as to protect another, τὼ χεῖρε π. X.Cyr.2.3.10:—Med., hold before oneself, προὔχοντο ἑκάστοθι ἐννέα ταύρους Od.3.8; hold out before one, πρὸ δούρατ' ἔχοντο Il.17.355, cf. Hdt.2.42; προὐσχόμην σε held you out as a child (to do your needs), Ar.Nu.1385. 2. metaph. in Med., put forward as a pretext, τάδ' ἂν προὔχοιο S.Ant.80; ὅπερ μάλιστα προὔχονται εἰ καθαιρεθείη, μὴ ἂν γίγνεσθαι τὸν πόλεμον the cancellation of which is the chief consideration in return for which they pretend that war would not occur, Th.1.140. b. hold forth, offer, ἃ προείχοντο αὐτοῖς Id.3.68: προΐσχομαι (q.v.) is more usual in this sense. II. to be possessed or informed of a thing beforehand, π. τῶν Ἀθηναίων οὐ φιλίας γνώμας Hdt.9.4, cf. D.S.31.27, D.C. 43.3. 2. have before, ἃ προεῖχεν μισθῷ ὁ.. Πτολεμαῖος had hitherto on lease, BGU889.9 (ii A.D.), cf. Sammelb.5672.5 (ii A.D.), etc.; εἰς τοῦτο ὑπολόγησον ἃ προέχουσι what they have already received, PPetr.2 p.32 (iii B.C.): abs., ὁ προέχων the first recipient, Arist.EN 1164ᵇ9.

B. intr., jut out, project, in Hom. in a local sense, of headlands, towers, hills, ὅθ' ἀκρότατος πρόεχ' ἀκτή Od.12.11, cf. 10.90; ἐπ' ἠϊόνας προὐχούσας 6.138; πύργῳ ἐπὶ προὔχοντι Il.22.97; ἐπὶ προὔχοντι μελάθρῳ Od.19.544; ἀκτὴ προέχουσα ἐς τὸν πόντον Hdt.4.177, cf. Th. 4.109, 6.97; τὸ προὖχον τῆς ἐμβολῆς Id.2.76: generally, project, c. gen., προέχουσα κάρης εὐρεῖα καλύπτρη Call.Fr.125. II. in running, to be the first, have the start, Il.23.325: c. gen., ἡμέρης ὁδῷ π. τῶν Περσέων *keep ahead* of them by a day's march, Hdt.4.120; προέχων τῶν ἄλλων [ὁ ἵππος] *getting before* the rest, Id.9.22; τῇ κεφαλῇ π. *beat* by a head, in racing, X.*Cyr*.4.3.16: of Time, προεῖχε [ἡ τριήρης] ἡμέρᾳ καὶ νυκτὶ *started first* by.., Th.3.49; π. εἴκοσιν ἔτεσιν Pl.*Lg*.879c: metaph., *have the advantage of*, τινὸς τῷ διπλασίῳ Antipho 3.3.2. 2. of rank, c. gen., δήμου προὔχουσιν *they are the first* or *chief* of the people, *h.Cer*.151; τοῦ Δωρικοῦ, τοῦ Ἰωνικοῦ [γένεος], Hdt.1.56: abs., *to be superior*, Th.1.39, 3.82; ἀνθρωπεία φύσις πολεμία τοῦ προὔχοντος *to all that is eminent*, Id.3.84; οἱ προὔχοντες the *chief men*, Id.5.17; οἱ π. [βίοι] the *principal* kinds of lives, Arist.*EN*1095b18. 3. *surpass, excel*, Th.7.66: freq. c. gen., τὸ Ἄργος π. ἅπασι τῶν ἐν τῇ..χώρῃ in all things, Hdt.1.1, cf. 32; τέχνα γὰρ τέχνας ἑτέρας προὔχει S.*Ph*.138 (lyr.); πολὺ προὔχουσα θεάων Call.*Del*.218; π. αὐτέων τοσοῦτον ὅσον.. Hdt.2.136; πολλῷ π. Id.3.82; π. δυνάμει, πλήθει καὶ ἐμπειρίᾳ, Th.1.18,121; τοσοῦτον ἐκείνων μεγέθει π. Luc.*Musc.Enc*.1: also π. τινὸς τιμήν *to be preferred* to him in honour, S.*Ant*.208; π. ἔν τινος λαμπρότητι Th.6.16; μικρὸν π. ἐν τοῖς μεγάλοις μᾶλλον ἢ πολὺ διαφέρειν ἐν τοῖς μικροῖς Isoc.10.5; κατά τι Luc.*Am*.30. b. rarely c. acc. pers., X.*An*.3.2.19 (nisi secl. [ἡμᾶς]):—Pass., *to be excelled*, οὐδὲν π. ὑπὸ τοῦ Διός Plu.2.1038d; *to be in worse case*, *Ep.Rom*.3.9. III. impers., οὔ τι προέχει *it is of* no *advantage*, c. inf., Hdt.9.27.

**προ-έψημα**, ατος, τό, *savoury meat*, Ph.*Fr*.44 H. (pl.), dub. l. ib. 39 H. **-έψησις**, εως, ἡ, *previous boiling* or *stewing*, Aët.1.130.

**προεψιάω**, = προαγορεύω (προσ- cod.), Hsch.

**προέψω**, *cook* or *dress before*, Hp.*Morb*.3.17, Dsc.5.11, Ath.9.381b. 2. *boil* water *first*, Ruf.*Fr*.66.

**προεωλίζω**, *first make* fish *tender by keeping*, Xenocr.ap.Orib.2.58.30, Gal.13.580 (Pass.), 16.761 (Pass., prob.).

**προζημιόομαι**, Pass., *suffer loss before*, Pl.ap.Lyd.*Mens*.4.7.

**προζητέω**, *search previously*, Arist.*Mem*.451b28:—Pass., *to be inquired into first*, Ph.*Bel*.68.19, S.E.*P*.2.9.

**προζύμια** [ῡ], τά, *ferments* or *reagents* used in alchemy, Zos.Alch. p.160 B.

**προζωννύω**, = *procingo*, *Gloss*.:—Med. -ζώννῠμαι, *gird oneself in front*, as with an apron, φαν λούμενος προζώννυται Pherecr.62.

**προηβάω**, *to be not yet adult*, J.*AJ*4.8.48 (v.l. προβεβηκόσι).

**προηγεμονεύω**, *guide before*, Nonn.*D*.47.268.

**προηγεμών**, όνος, ὁ, *one who goes before as a guide*, Alciphr.3.36. II. *instructor* in the mysteries, D.18.260.

⊛ **προηγ-έομαι**, *go first and lead the way*, Hdt.2.48, 7.40, X.*Lac*.13.2, etc.; τινι *for* a person, i.e. *guide* him, τῷ θεῷ Ar.*Pl*.1195, cf. X.*Cyr*.2.1.1; π. τὴν [ὁδόν] Id.*An*.6.5.10; of troops, *form the van*, Id.*Cyr*.4.2.27; π. πᾶσι [τοῖς ποσίν] *to have* all *in front*, Arist.*IA*714a4. b. *precede logically*, τινος S.E.*P*.1.210. 2. c. gen., *take the lead of*, τῶν προσόδων ἄλλους προσόδους..προηγεῖσθαι X.*Eq.Mag*.4.5; π. τῆς πομπῆς Plb.12.13.11; of the planets in retrograde motion, *get ahead of*, ἀπλανῶν ἀστέρων Gem.12.22: later c. acc., ἀλλήλους π. τῇ τιμῇ *Ep.Rom*.12.10:—c. inf., προήγημαι τὴν τούτων ἐπίδοσιν ποιήσεσθαι *have taken the initiative* in.., *BGU*1193.11 (i B.C.). 3. of things, τὸ πῦρ μὲν ἀπὸ τούτων τῶν ἱερῶν προηγεῖται *goes before, precedes*, X.*Lac*.13.3; ῥάβδοι π. ἑκάστῳ Plb.6.53.8. 4. pres. part. προηγούμενος, η, ον, *going first*, τὸ π. στράτευμα the *van*, opp. οὐρά, X.*Ages*.2.2; *preceding, foregoing*, Phld.*Ir*.p.94 W.; γράμματα Plu.*Pomp*.45. b. Math., τὰ π. *forward* points, i.e. those lying on the same side of the radius vector of a spiral as the direction of its motion, Archim.*Spir*.11 *Def*.6; ἁ π. εὐθεῖα Id.*Spir*.21,23. c. Astron., τὰ π. ζῴδια signs *leading* in the daily movement of the heavens, i.e. *westerly* signs, opp. ἑπόμενα, Gem.1.5, Theo Sm.p.147 H., etc. d. τὰ π. *initial data, premisses*, Plb.16.16.6, Arr.*Epict*.1.20.1; σημεῖα Phld.*Sign*.36; φαντασίαι M.Ant.8.49; π. οὐσία τοῦ ἀγαθοῦ *given*, i.e. external to the soul, Arr.*Epict*.3.7.6; τὸ π., opp. τὸ ἐπιγέννημα, ib.7; τὰ π. *originals* of paintings, Arist.*Mu*.396b14. e. *leading, principal*, κατὰ π. λόγον according to a *guiding* principle, Zeno *Stoic*.1.48; ὁ π. λόγος, τὸ π. ἔργον, Arr.*Epict*.1.20.14, 2.5.4; σύν τινι προηγουμένῳ in conjunction with a *purpose*, Iamb.*VP*27.131, cf. Plot.4.4.8; χειρὸς οὐσία μὲν ἡ σάρξ, προηγούμενα δὲ τὰ χειρὸς ἔργα Arr.*Epict*.3.7.24, cf. 3.22.76; ὑπηρετικὰ ἄλλοις, οὐκ αὐτὰ π. ib.2.8.6; so in Math., π. θεώρημα *leading* theorem, opp. ἀντίστροφον, Procl.*in Euc*.p.254 F. f. Medic., π. αἴτιον *predisposing* cause, Ath.Med.ap.Gal.15.112, cf. 7.10, al.; π. αἰτίαι *antecedent* causes, Chrysipp.*Stoic*.2.264. 5. aor. part., ὁ -ησάμενος the *former* ἡγεμών, *PLips*.63.6 (iv A.D.), etc. ⊛ **-έτης**, ου, ὁ, = προηγητής, δίκης Philem.167. **-ησις**, εως, ἡ, *going before, leading*, Ph.1.697; = ἐπιτολή I, Ptol.*Tetr*.78 (pl.); κατὰ προήγησιν φλεγμονῆς *following on* inflammation, Sor.2.35; π. αἰτίων *sequence* of causes, Simp.*in Ph*.794.10. **-ήτειρα**, ἡ, fem. of sq., A.R.3.1182, Nonn.*D*.35.304. **-ητήρ**, ῆρος, ὁ, = sq., E.*Ba*.1159 (lyr.), Ph.2.107. **-ητής**, οῦ, ὁ, *one who goes before to show the way, guide*, S.*OT*1292, *Ant*.990, Aristid.*Or*.41(4).12. 2. *one who conducts the bride's car in her procession*, ὀρεωκόμον καὶ προηγητὴν ἀκολουθεῖν τῷ ζεύγει Hyp.*Lyc*.5, cf. Hsch. **-ητικός**, ή, όν, *going before*: hence, *initial, fundamental*, σημεῖον Phld.*Sign*.32; *preceding*, περίοδοι Sch. Ar.*Ach*.970. II. Astron., *belonging to* προήγησις, Procl.*Hyp*.5.72,82. **-ήτωρ**, ορος, ὁ, = προηγητής, v.l. in Ph.2.107; *leader* of animals, *Hippiatr*.1. **-μένα**, τά, v. προάγω.

⊛ **προηγορ-έω**, *to be spokesman for* others, X.*An*.5.5.7, Plu.2.386b: c. gen., X.*HG*2.2.22; π. τινί *speak for*, i.e. *in defence of*, another, Plu.*Brut*.6. 2. *to be senior in rank*, of the Roman consul who possesses the *fasces*, *Not.Arch*.4.23 (Cyrene, Aug.). II. Dor. προᾱγορέω, *hold the office of* προάγορος, *IG*14.952 (Agrigentum). **-εών**, v. πρηγορεών. **-ία**, ἡ, *speaking in behalf of* others, Luc.*Pisc*.22. ⊛ **-ος**, ὁ, (ἀγορά) *one who speaks in behalf of* others, *defender, advocate*, Lxx 2*Ma*.7.2, Poll.2.126, Them.*Or*.26.326a, etc.; π. τῆς πατρίδος, τοῦ ἔθνους, *OGI*567.12 (Attalia, ii A.D.), 528.3 (Prusias, ii A.D.). II. Dor. προάγορος [ᾰ], a magistrate at Catana, Cic. *Verr*.4.23.50.

⊛ **προηγουμένως**, Adv. part. of προηγέομαι, *previously*, Dsc.5.75. II. *principally, directly, as the primary* or *initial action*, S.E. *P*.2.240; opp. κατὰ συμβεβηκός, Thphr.*Ign*.14, Plu.*Demetr*.1. 2. *chiefly, first, as the main* or *guiding principle*, Zeno *Stoic*.1.57, Ph.2.6, al., Plu.2.653d, Arr.*Epict*.1.3.1, Jul.*Or*.8.242c; opp. ἑπομένως, Plu.2.569e; *as one's main purpose*, Cleom.2.2, Hermog.*Id*.1.1,7; opp. κατὰ περίστασιν, Arr.*Epict*.3.14.7; *of choice*, ib.3.22.67, Plot.3.8.4, 6.8.10; *preferably*, Archig.ap.Aët.6.8.

**προήδομαι**, Pass., *to be pleased before* or *first*, τῇ ἰδέᾳ with.., Arist. *EN*1167a5.

**προήκης**, ες, (ἀκή A) *pointed*, ἐρετμά Od.12.205.

**προήκω**, *to have gone before, be the first*, ἀξιώσει Th.2.34; χρήμασι X.*HG*7.1.23; χρόνῳ τῶν ἄλλων S.E.*M*.9.1; τοῖς χρόνοις ib.1.204. 2. *to have advanced*, π. ἐς βαθὺ τῆς ἡλικίας Ar.*Nu*.513; τὴν ἡλικίαν Lxx 4*Ma*.5.4; ἡλικίᾳ D.C.58.27; καθ' ἡλικίαν Plu.*Alc*.13; also, ἔχειν ἡλικίαν πλέον προήκουσαν Arist.*Pol*.1336b18 (s.v.l.); [ὁρῶ] τὰ πράγματ' εἰς τοῦτο προήκοντα *have come to this pass*, D.3.1; of Time, τῆς ἡμέρας προηκούσης Plu.*Brut*.15; also ἐπὶ προηκούσῃ τῇ πραγματείᾳ as my work *proceeds*, Gal.2.573. II. *to have come forth*, τοῦ δωματίου Hld.5.2. III. *reach beyond*, τῆς ἄρκυος X.*Cyn*.10.7; *extend* in length, Gal.5.228.

**προηλιάζω**, *expose to sunlight first*, Dsc.2.136 (Pass.).

**προῆλιξ**, ῐκος, ὁ, ἡ, *not having attained to puberty*, Sor.2.6 (Comp. is f.l. for παρ-, Id.1.7).

**προήλιος**, f.l. for παρήλιος, Gal.5.640 codd.

**προηλκυσμένως**, Adv., (προέλκω), = *prolixius*, *Gloss*.

**προῆμαρ**, Adv. *all day*, opp. προνύξ, Semon.7.47.

**προημερινός**, *pridianus*, *Gloss*.

**προηνεμίδες** θύραι, doors *exposed to the wind*, i.e. in the *pronaos*, *IG*11(2).165.4 (Delos, iii B.C.), *BCH*34.501 (ibid.); also **προήνεμος**, ον, τοῖχος, παραστάς, *Milet*.7 p.56, *Rev.Phil*.35.180 (Didyma).

⊛ **προηρόσιος**, α, ον, (ἄροτος) *before the time of tillage*: προηροσία (sc. θυσία), ἡ, a festival *at that time* celebrated by Athens for the whole of Greece, Hyp.*Fr*.75, Lycurg.*Fr*.87 (-όσια cj. Sauppe), Aristid.1.196 J., Lib.*Decl*.1.179, Sch.Ar.*Pl*.1055, Phot., etc.: also προηρόσια (sc. θύματα or ἱερά), τά, *IG*2².1029.16, Hsch., Suid. s.v. εἰρεσιώνη (gen. pl. -ιων is ambiguous in *IG*2².1363.6): sg. **-όσιον** Sch.Ar.*Eq*.725: cf. πληροσία, πρηρoσία. II. θεοὶ προηρόσιοι the gods *in whose honour it was performed*, Plu.2.1119e; π. Δημήτηρ ib.158d.

**προησθησις**, εως, ἡ, *joy beforehand*, Pl.*R*.584c (pl.).

**προησσάω**, Att. -ττάω, *overpower beforehand*, τὸ προηττῆσαν τὰς ψυχάς Plb.2.53.3: but mostly in pf. or plpf. Pass., *to be beaten* or *worsted before*, τοῖς ὅλοις Id.3.90.4, cf. 10.7.6, D.S.13.79, J.*AJ*15.5.2.

**προηχέω**, *cause to resound before*, τινος Pratin.Lyr.1.11 (cj.); ἡ τοιαύτη ἰδέα τῶν προοιμίων εὐγένειαν π. τῶν λόγων Philostr.*VS*1 *Praef*., cf. Them.*Or*.16.201d.

**προθαλής**, ές, (θάλλω) *early growing, precocious*, *h.Cer*.241.

**προθάπτω**, *bury first*, γυναῖκα *Cat.Cod.Astr*.1.150.

**προθεάομαι**, *see before*, Gal.2.701, Nicom.*Ar*.2.6, Hsch.

**προθειλοπεδεύω**, *dry in the sun before*, Dsc.5.28.

**πρόθειος**, ὁ, *great-uncle*, *IGRom*.4.861 (Laodicea ad Lycum), *Ephes*.3 No.72.

**προθέλυμνος**, ον, (θέλυμνον) *from the foundations, from* or *by the roots*, προθελύμνους ἕλκετο χαίτας he tore his hair out *by the roots*, Il.10.15, cf. Q.S.3.411; προθέλυμνα χαμαὶ βάλε δένδρεα he threw to earth trees *uprooted*, Il.9.541; ἐφόρει τὰς δρῦς..προθελύμνους Ar.*Eq*.528; προθέλυμνόν μ' ἀπώλεσας Id.*Pax* 1210, cf. Call.*Del*.134, Q.S.6.331, Tryph.397. II. perh. *close-packed*, of shields *overlapping* in the phalanx, φράξαντες σάκος σάκεϊ προθελύμνῳ Il.13.130; expld. by Gramm. as = ἐπάλληλος, συνεχής, and so used by Nonn.*D*.22.183; also πέτρην προθέλυμνον ἐπασσυτέρῃ θέτο πέτρῃ ib.2.374.

⊛ **πρόθεμα**, ατος, τό, *public notice*, Eun.*Hist*.p.231 D., *IG*4.364.9 (Corinth, iv A.D.). II. *fire-guard* or *fender*, Ph.*Bel*.77.51, dub. in 67.11.

**προθεμελι-όω**, *lay foundations before*, in Pass., Vett.Val.359.19, Ph.2.9. **-ωσις**, εως, ἡ, *previous foundation*, Tz.*H*.2.92 (pl.).

**προθεραπ-εία**, ἡ, Rhet., *preparation for the introduction* of something startling, Hermog.*Inv*.4.12. II. Medic., *preliminary treatment*, Orib.*Fr*.55. **-ευσις**, εως, ἡ, = foreg. I, Donat.ad Ter.*Adelph*.481. **-εύω**, *prepare beforehand*, ἔρια (for dyeing) Pl.*R*.429e; π. ἑαυτῷ τὸν ἀκροατήν Ulp.*Proll.D*.; τῇ ῥητορικῇ Aristid.2.104 J.:—Pass., Thphr.*HP*7.3.5. II. *court beforehand*, τινα J.*AJ*6.14.4; τοὺς δυνατούς Plu.*Alc*.25: metaph., π. ἐλπίδα οἷα πυλωρόν Ph.2.3. III. Medic., *treat first*, Ruf.*Fr*.72 (Pass.).

**προθερίζω**, *reap first*, Lxx *Jd*.15.5 (Pass.).

**προθερμ-αίνω**, *warm first*, Plu.2.725a, Gal.6.90, Procl.*Sacr*.p.149 B.:—Pass., of water, Arist.*Mete*.348b32, *Fr*.216. **-ανσις**, εως, ἡ, *previous warming*, Procl.*Sacr*.p.149 B., Simp.*in Cat*.248.33.

⊛ **πρόθεσις**, εως, ἡ, (προτίθημι) *placing in public*; of a corpse, *laying it out* (cf. προτίθημι II), Pl.*Lg*.947b, 959a, e, D.43.64. 2. *public notice*, αἱ π. τῶν ἀναγεγραμμένων Arist.*Pol*.1322a9. 3. *statement* of a case, Id.*Rh*.1414b8; ὑπέρ τινος τὴν πρόθεσιν ποιήσασθαι Id.*Cat*.

11ᵃ21; *theme, thesis*, Phld.*Rh*.1.36, al. S.: generally, *proposition, statement*, D.H.*Amm*.2.2. 4. πρόθεσιν ποιεῖσθαι ἐπὶ ταῖς.. προσόδοις to make *payment in advance*, *IPE*1².32*A*41 (Olbia, iii B.C.). 5. *offering*, *PCair.Zen*.328.75 (iii B.C.), Gauthier et Sottas *Décret trilingue* (iii B.C.), Call.*Fr*.1.13P., *OGI*90.48 (ii B.C.), *UPZ*149.21,31 (ii B.C.): esp. in *VT* and *NT*, οἱ ἄρτοι τῆς π. the loaves *laid before*, *shew*-bread, Lxx 1*Ki*.21.6(7), *Ev.Matt*.12.4; ἡ π. τῶν ἄρτων *Ep.Hebr*.9.2, cf. Ph. 2.294; ἡ τράπεζα τῆς π. Lxx 2*Ch*.29.18. II. *purpose, end proposed*, ἐπαινῶ σὴν π. *SIG*22.14 (Magn. Mae., Epist. Darei), cf. Philipp. ap.D.18.167, Arist.*APr*.47ᵃ5, Cleanth.*Stoic*.1.131, Plb.5.35.2, Arr. *Epict*.1.21.2, etc.; π. βίων Adam.*Phgn*.1.2; defined as σημείωσις ἐπιτελέσεως, *Stoic*.3.41; κατὰ πρόθεσιν *purposely*, Plb.12.10.6; τὰ κατὰ π. φύντα Ph.2.144; τὰ κατὰ τὴν π. Plb.1.54.1, cf. *PTeb*.27.81 (ii B.C.). 2. *goodwill*, π. ἔχειν πρὸς ἔθνος, ὑπὲρ τῶν πολιτῶν, Plb. 4.73.2, *OGI*765.44 (prob. l., Priene). III. *supposition, calculation*, Plb.6.32.1, 12.21.6. IV. Gramm., *preposition*, Chrysipp. *Stoic*.2.45, D.T.634.5, D.H.*Comp*.2, A.D.*Synt*.305.24, *Pron*.64. 5. 2. *prefixing, placing first*, Id.*Synt*.311.1, *Pron*.58.16. 3. π. καὶ πτῶσις perh. *stem* (or *root*) and ending, Phld.*Po*.2.18. V. = προθεσμία, interpol. in Suid.

**προθεσμ-εύω**, *anticipate the day*, Sch.Ar.*Nu*.1202. **-ία** (sc. ἡμέρα), ἡ, *day appointed beforehand, a fixed* or *limited time*, within which money was to be paid, actions brought, claims made, elections held, etc., and if this period was allowed to expire, no further proceedings were allowed, D.36.25, Aeschin.1.39; ἐὰν ἡ π. ἐξήκῃ is past, *IG*1².41.9; τριετὴς π. Pl.*Lg*.954d, cf. D.38.27, Paus.4.5. 10. 2. generally, *fixed* or *appointed time*, προθεσμίας οὔσης τῷ κινδύνῳ Lys.7.17; π. ἀδικημάτων Id.13.83; μηδεμίαν εἶναι π. τῆς ἐπιλήψεως Pl.*Lg*.954e; τῆς προθεσμίας ὀλίγης εἰς τὴν χειροτονίαν οὔσης App.*BC*1.14, cf. *Ep.Gal*.4.2, *OGI*509.21 (Aphrodisias, ii A.D.); οὐκ ἐτήρησε τὴν π. τῆς θεοῦ *Supp.Epigr*.4.649 (Lydia, ii A.D.); π. φυσικὴ [νόσου] natural *period*, Gal.1.289; ἡ π. τῆς καθάρσεως Sor.2. 10, cf. 1.21, al.: pl., τρεῖς τοῦ μηνὸς ἀρχαὶ καὶ π. (Kalends, Nones and Ides) Plu.2.269b; προθεσμίας ὁριζομένους ἑορτάς Luc.*Nigr*.27. 3. *occasion of delay*, J.*AJ*15.5.1. II. προθέσμιος, α, ον, Adj. *foreappointed*, Ἔφεσος, ἡ π. τῶν γάμων (sc. πόλις) Ach.Tat.5.21. **-ός**, ὁ, in pl., βασιλικοὶ π. royal *privileges* or *prerogatives*, Plu.*Nob*.3.

**προθεσπίζω**, *foretell*, τὸ μέλλον ἢ κραίνοιτο A.*Pr*.213, cf. *IG*12(5). 891.6 (Tenos), Ph.1.511 (Pass.), J.*AJ*10.5.1, Plu.2.421b, Luc.*Alex*. 19, etc.

**προθετικός**, ή, όν, (πρόθεσις II) *setting before itself*, ἡ ἀρετὴ π. [τοῦ τέλους] Arist.*MM*1190ᵃ19; opp. ποιητικός, *connected with planning*, opp. execution, prob. l. ib.21. II. *of* or *for prefixing*, π. μόριον *preposition*, D.H.*Amm*.2.2; *prepositional*, σύνδεσμοι Stoic. ap. A.D. *Synt*.305.24; σύνταξις A.D.l.c.22.

**προθετός**, όν, *proposed, indicated*, τοῖς π. Alex.Trall.*Febr*.3 codd. (fort. προσθετοῖς).

**προθέω** (A), *run before*, Il.10.362; πολὺ προθέεσκε *he was* far *ahead*, 22.459, Od.11.515; opp. ἀπολείπομαι, Pl.*Cra*.412a: c. gen., *outrun*, Ael.*NA*7.26, Jul.*Caes*.315b; βέλη π. τῆς ὄψεως Plu.*Crass*.18. 2. *run forward* or *forth*, X.*An*.5.8.13, A.R.1.314, J.*BJ*3.10.1. II. c. acc., *outrun, outstrip*, X.*Cyn*.3.7.

**προθέω** (B), 3 pl. προθέουσιν, sts. taken as a form of προτίθημι, found once in Hom., τοὔνεκά οἱ προθέουσιν ὀνείδεα μυθήσασθαι; *do they* therefore *appoint* for him revilings to utter? Il.1.291 (but expld. fr. προθέω (A) by Aristarch., with ὀνείδεα as subj.; perh., *do* his insults *dash forward* for utterance?).

**προθεωρ-έω**, *consider before*, Hp.*Ep*.17, v.l. in Arist.*HA*538ᵃ 6. **-ημα**, ατος, τό, *introductory discussion*, Steph. *in Hp*.1.56D. (pl.). **-ητέον**, *one must consider before*, v.l. in Arist.*Cael*.302ᵃ 27. **-ία**, ἡ, *preface*, Them.*Or*.26 tit., *An.Ox*.3.376; *previous exposition*, Sch.Ptol.*Tetr*.66. II. *prophecy*, Hsch. s. v. ἀποκάλυψις.

**προθήκη**, ἡ, *praepositio*, *Gloss*. II. = *nepeta*, dub. in *Gloss*.

**προθηράω**, *hunt before*, Agatharch.52 (Pass.).

**προθησαυρίζω**, *store up, accumulate before*, Arist.*PA*674ᵇ24:— Pass., Pall. *in Hp*.2.27 D.

**πρόθθα**, Cret. = πρόσθε, *Leg.Gort*.4.52.

**προθικάριος**, ὁ, perh. = *προθηκάριος, *sign-painter*, *POxy*.1146.20 (iv A.D.).

**προθλάω**, *crush first*, Gal.14.86 (Pass.).

**προθνήσκω**, *die before*, Th.2.52; π. τῆς μάχης Luc.*Par*.50; π. τῷ δέει Id.*Tox* 60. 2. of hair, *fall off prematurely*, in form προτεθνήσκουσι, Aret.*SD*2.13. II. *die for*, τινος E.*Alc*.383,684, *Heracl*. 590.

**προθρηνέω**, *bewail beforehand*, ζῶντά τινα ἔτι Ph.2.72, cf. Aristid.1. 419 J. (Pass.).

**προθρῡλέω**, *noise abroad beforehand*, Luc.*Patr.Enc*.1.

**προθρώσκω**, *spring forth* or *forward*, Hom. only in Il. and always in aor. part. προθορών, 17.522; μέγα προθορών *springing* far *forward*, 14.363; οὐρανόθεν προθοροῦσα A.R.4.641.

⊕ **πρόθῡμα**, ατος, τό, (προθύω) *preparatory offering*, Ar.*Pl*.660, cf. Sch. ad loc.; τὰ π. τῆς ἑορτῆς *IG*2².1635.37, cf. 47.25: metaph., [ἐμὸν θάνατον] π. ἔλαβεν Ἄρτεμις E.*IA*1311 (lyr.).

**προθῡμ-έομαι**, impf. προυθυμούμην Th.4.12, Pl.*R*.402b; in Hdt. προεθ- (with v. l. προθ-), 5.78,9.38, also in X.*Ages*.2.1, Pl.*Cra*. 395d: fut. προθυμήσομαι X.*Cyr*.2.3.3, Pl.*Men*.74b, *Plt*.262a; προθυμηθήσομαι v.l. in Lys.25.17 and Pl.*Phd*.115c: aor. προυθυμήθην Antipho 1.6, Th.5.17, X.*An*.4.1.22, Pl.*Phd*.69d: pf. προτεθύμημαι *Bull.Soc.Arch.Alex*.7.67:—*to be ready, willing, eager to do a thing*, c. inf., Hdt.1.36,206, al., S.*Tr*.1119, Ar.*V*.1173, Lys.3.9, etc.; ὃς ἂν προθυμεῖσθαι ἐθέλῃ δίκαιος γενέσθαι will *show zeal* in becoming.., Pl.*R*.613a, cf. *Phd*.75b, *La*.186a, etc.; also π. ὅκως.. Hdt.1.91, cf. Pl. *Phd*.91a; π. ὅπως ἂν εὐδαιμονοίης Id.*Ly*.207e; ὡς ὑστερήσειε.., προεθυμεῖτο X.*Ages*.2.1. 2. abs. (though an inf. may commonly be supplied), *show zeal, exert oneself*, A.*Pr*.383, 630, Hdt.8.86, 9.38, Th. 4.81, X.*An*.6.4.22, etc.; *to be of good cheer, in good spirits*, opp. ἀθυμέω, Id.*Cyr*.6.2.13. 3. c. acc. objecti, *to be eager* or *zealous for, desire ardently*, τὴν ξύμβασιν, τὴν ὁμολογίαν, Th.5.17, 8.90: mostly with neut. Adj.. π. τοῦτο, ὅπως.. Antipho l.c.; μηδὲν ἄλλο ἢ τοῦτο Pl.*Phd*.64a, cf. *R*.472e, al., v.l. in 460d; π. περί τι Arist.*HA*581ᵃ 22. **-ητέον**, *one must be eager*, c. inf., Pl.*Phd*.90e, al., Plu.2. 723e: pl. **-τέα**, Pl.*Lg*.770b. **-ία**, Ion. **-ίη**, ἡ, *readiness, willingness, eagerness*, ἧσι προθυμίῃσι [ῑ] πεποιθώς Il.2.588; opp. ἀθυμία, X.*Cyr*.1.6.13; τῶν πέρι καί τινα ἐνάγει π. μαχόμενον ἀποθνήσκειν Hdt.5.49; προθυμίας οὐδὲν ἐλλείπεις A.*Pr*.343; μηδὲν ἀπολείπειν π. Pl.*Lg*.961c; οὐ μὴν ἀνήσω νῦν π. E.*Hipp*.285; π. ἐμβαλεῖν τινι X. *Cyr*.1.6.13, etc.; πάσῃ π. with all *zeal*, Pl.*R*.412e; διὰ τὴν π. Plb.1. 20.15; ὑπὸ προθυμίας by my *eagerness*, Pl.*Phd*.91c: pl., τὰς ἄγαν π. E.*Or*.708. 2. c. gen. pers., ἐκ τῆς Κλεομένεος π. at his *desire*, Hdt. 6.65, cf. E.*Hipp*.1329; κατὰ τὴν τούτου π. as far as his *desire* goes, Hdt.1.124; τοῦ θεοῦ προθυμίᾳ *by the will* of the god, E.*Ion* 1385; also ἡ ἐμὴ π. Lys.12.99. 3. c. gen. objecti, πᾶσαν π. σωτηρίης .. παρεχόμενοι showing the utmost *zeal* to save it, Hdt.4.98; π. ἔργου *readiness* for action, *will* or *purpose* to act, S.*Tr*.669, cf. E. *IT*616; π. τοῦ ἐθέλειν κινδυνεύειν Pl.*Lg*.697d, cf. 935d, etc. 4. π. ἔχειν, = προθυμεῖσθαι, Hdt.7.19,53: c. inf., ἔσχε π. στρατεύσασθαι Id.1. 204, cf. E.*Tr*.689; πᾶσαν π. ἔχειν Pl.*Prt*.327b, cf. 361c: also c. part., ἔφη πᾶσαν π. σχεῖν δεόμενος Id.*Ti*.23d; also π. ἔχειν ὅπως.. Id.*Mx*. 247a. II. *goodwill, ready kindness*, Ἑλλήνων εἵνεκα ἐργον.. ἐργασμαι ὑπὸ προθυμίης Hdt.9.45; εἴς τινας X.*HG*6.5.43; πλείστην π. περὶ ὑμᾶς, π. πολλὴν περί σε, Id.*An*.7.6.11, 7.7.45; ὑπέρ τινων D.1.8; π. ἐδείξαμεν Th.1.74. III. *desire* of natural functions, Sor.1.66, 2. 20,45; πρὸς τὸ κνᾶσθαι Herod.Med.ap.Aët.5.129. **-ιάομαι**, *fumigate before*, v.l. in J.*AJ*3.8.6.

**προθῡμοποι-έομαι**, *make willing* or *ready, encourage*, Steph. *in Hp. Aph*.2.473 D., v.l. in D.S.14.56:—Act. in Eust.1393.43. **-ησις**, εως, ἡ, *encouraging*, Id.1015.3.

**πρόθῡμος**, ον, *ready, willing, eager*, π. εἰμι, c. inf., = προθυμέομαι, Hdt.2.3,6.5, al., E.*Med*.720, Antipho 5.18 (Comp.), etc.; π. ἔα πυθέσθαι I was *eager* to learn, Hdt.2.19; εἶναι ὡς -οτάτοισι συνεξελεῖν Id.1.36; -ότερος ἐγένου ἐμὲ λαβεῖν Pl.*Smp*.220e: with Art. inserted, τὸ προσταλαιπωρεῖν.. οὐδεὶς π. ἦν Th.2.53. 2. c. gen. objecti, *eager for*, ὧν π. ἦσθ' ἀεί S.*El*.3; χάριν.. ὧν πρόθυμοι γεγενήμεθα Th.3.67. 3. with Preps., ἐὰν γένῃ π. ἐς τὰ πράγματα Ar.*Pl*.209; παρέσχεν ἑαυτὸν ..-ότατον ἐς τὴν ὀλιγαρχίαν Th.8.68, cf. 74; προθυμότεροι ἐς τὸ διώκειν X.*Cyr*.1.4.22; ἐπί τι Id.*HG*1.1.34; πρὸς τὸν πόλεμον ib.1.5.2, cf. Pl. *R*.468c, etc. 4. abs., Hdt.9.91, E.*Ba*.829, *Hec*.307, etc.: τὸ πρόθυμον, = προθυμία, Id.*Med*.178 (lyr.), Pl.*Lg*.859b. II. *bearing goodwill, wishing well, devoted*, φύλαξ.. τῇ σῇ π. εἰς ὁδὸν κυναγία S.*Aj*.37; π. εἰχ' ὀφθαλμὸν εἰς Ἰάσονα E.*Med*.1146; π. τῇ πόλει X.*HG*2.3.40; εἴς τινας ib.6.5.42, Lys.20.31. III. Adv. **-μως** *readily, zealously, actively*, Hdt.1.111, 5.13, etc.; π. μᾶλλον ἢ φίλως *with* more *zeal* than kindness, A.*Ag*.1591; π. λέγειν Pl.*Prt*.327b; ἐρωτᾶν D.8.38; μανθάνειν Pl.*La*.201b (Sup.); μάχεσθαι X.*Ages*.2.8 (Sup.); π. ἔχειν πρός τι Pl.*Smp*.176c: Comp. -ότερον Th.6.80, X.*An*.1.4.9, etc.: Sup. -ότατα Hdt.2.59, Th.8.68, etc.

⊕ **προθύρ-αιος** [ῠ], α, ον, also ος, ον (v. infr.): (θύρα):—*before the door*; προθυραία, epith. of Artemis, Orph.*H*.2.4,12, prob. (for -ιδία) in S.E. *M*.9.185; but Ἑκάτη προθύραιε Procl.*H*.6.2,14. II. προθύραια, τά, *front doorway*, *h.Merc*.384. ⊕ **-ον**, τό, *front-door, door-way*, esp. of the entrance to the αὐλή, ἐκ δ' ἔλασε προθύροιο καὶ αἰθούσης Il.24.323, cf. Od.3.493: pl., στῆ δ'.. ἐπὶ προθύροις Ὀδυσῆος, οὐδοῦ ἐπ' αὐλείου 1.103; πρόθυρα δωμάτων A.*Ch*.966 (lyr.), cf. E.*Tr*.194 (lyr.); of the entrance to the μέγαρον, Od.18.10, 101, 386, 21.299. 2. *porch, portico*, παραστάδας καὶ π. βούλει ποικίλα Cratin.42, cf. Dicaearch.Hist.59.8. 3. *space before a door*, whether or not it is a *porch* or *portico*: before the outmost entrance, pl., Od.4.20, 10.220, Hdt.3.140, 6.35; sg., Pl. *Prt*.314c, *Smp*.175a: Ἑρμαῖ.. λίθινοι.. ἐν ἰδίοις προθύροις Th.6.27, cf. Pi.*P*.3.78 (sg.), Ar.*V*.802 (pl.), 875 (sg.), Call.*Epigr*.26 (sg.): before the entrance to the μέγαρον, Od.20.355 (sg.); before the entrance of a νεωκόριον, *IG*2².1672.208. II. metaph., Κόρινθος Ἰσθμίου πρόθυρον Ποτειδᾶνος Pi.*O*.13.5; ἐπὶ τοῖς τοῦ ἀγαθοῦ προθύροις Pl.*Phlb*.64c; πρόθυρα καὶ σχῆμα.. σκιαγραφίαν ἀρετῆς περιγραπτέον Id.*R*.365c; χείλη .. στόματος νεκταρέου πρόθυρα *AP*5.55 (Diosc.). **-ώα**, ἡ, = foreg., Hdn.Gr.1.303. **-ωμα**, ατος, τό, = πρόθυρον 2, *PEnteux*.8.13 (iii B.C.). **-ών**, ῶνος, ὁ, = πρόθυρον 2, Hdn.Gr.1.35, al., *EM*806.4.

⊕ **πρό-θῠσις**, εως, ἡ, *base of an altar*, Paus.5.13.9. ⊕ **-θύτης** [ῠ], ου, Aeol. **προθύτας**, ὁ, *one who offers* προθύματα, τῶν τᾶς πόλιος ἱρῶν *IG* 12(2).484.25 (Hiera); of the *priest* of a θίασος, *BCH*24.386 (Bithynia, iii A.D.).

**προθύω**, fut. -θύσω E.*Ion* 805, *SIG*548.11 (Delph., iii B.C.), *Berl. Sitzb*.1927.160 (Cyrene), -θύσομαι Ar.*Th*.38:—*sacrifice* or *offer first*, πρὸ πάντων θεῶν τῇ Ἑστίᾳ πρώτῃ Pl.*Cra*.401d; π. καὶ προμαντεύεσθαι *Michel* 995*D*40 (Delph., iv B.C.); *act as* προθύτης, *SIG* l.c.: c. acc., τὴν θυγατέρα Plu.2.310d:—more freq. in Med., π. τῷ Διὶ τὰ πέμματα *take care that* they *are offered*, *CIG*3599.24 (Assos); προεθύετο ταῖς Μούσαις ὁ βασιλεύς Plu.*Lyc*.21, cf. *IG*4²(1).121.42 (Epid., iv B.C.), 2.1651: metaph., *to have* a person *sacrificed* or *slaughtered* *before*, J.*BJ*1.19.3, Luc.*Tox.*50, Charito 7.3, Hld.9.24. II. *sacrifice for* or *in behalf of*, παιδός E.*Ion* 805; ὑπὲρ χθονὸς ἀρότου Id.*Supp.* 29. (Both senses in Ar.*Th.*38.)

**προθωράκιον** [ᾱ], τό, *shield*, Str.17.3.7.

**προϊάλλω** [ῐ], *send forth* or *away*, *dismiss*, *discharge*, τινα Il.8.365, 11.3, Od.15.370; σιάλων τὸν ἄριστον 14.18; ὀϊστὸν ἀπὸ νευρῆς Theoc. 25.235.—Ep. word, used by Hom. always in impf. without augm.

**προϊάπτω** [ῐ], *send forth*, *hurl away* to the nether world, ψυχὰς Ἄϊδι προΐαψεν Il.1.3, cf. 6.487; Ἀϊδωνῆϊ 5.190; also, πόλιν.. Ἀΐδᾳ προϊάψαι A.*Th.*322 (lyr.). II. Pass., *project*, Nic.*Th.*723.

**προϊδρόω**, *sweat beforehand*, Antyll.ap.Orib.10.21.4.

**προϊδρύω**, *pre-establish*, in Pass., Dam.*Pr.*13; ἐν τὸ ἑκάστου προϊδρυμένον ib.28 bis.

**προϊερ-άομαι**, *to be deputy priest* or *priestess*, *Milet.*6.22 (iii B.C.), *OGI* 331.14 (Pergam., ii B.C.), *CIG*3657 (Cyzic.). II. *sacrifice on behalf of* another, *SIG*1037.6 (Milet., iv/iii B.C.). **-ᾱτεύω**, Ion. **-ητεύω**, = foreg. I. *BCH*15.204 (Zeus Panamaros), *SIG*1013.11 (Chios, iv B.C.).

**προΐζομαι**, Med., *take the first seat*, Hdt.8.67:—later, in Act., Sch. Ar.*Pax* 1241, dub. l. in Plot.5.8.11.

⊛ **προΐημι**, 3 pres. προΐει Il.2.752; 3 sg. subj. προΐῇ (v.l. 3 opt. προΐοι) *h.Ven.*152: impf. προΐειν, εις, ει, Il.1.326,336, Od.9.88, 10.100, etc.: fut. προήσω: aor. 1 προῆκα, Ep. προέηκα, both in Hom.: aor. 2 ind. 3 pl. πρόεσαν Od.8.399; opt. προεῖεν X.*An.*7.2.15 codd.; imper. πρόες Il.16.241 (on the accent, v. Hdn.Gr.2.931), 3 sg. προέτω 11.796; inf. προέμεν for προεῖναι, Od.10.155:—Med., aor. 1 προηκάμην D.19.78,84, 32.15, etc.: aor. 2 opt. πρόοιντο or προοῖντο Th.1.120, D.18.254, cf. X.*An.*1.9.10:—Pass., pf. προεῖμαι, plpf. προεῖτο, D. (v. infr. II. 1). [On the quantity, v. ἵημι.]:—*send forth*, *send forward*, Il.1.195 (tm.), 326, 336, etc.; esp. *send* troops *forward*, X.*Cyr.*7.1.22,27: also, *send* a thing or person *to* another, ἀγγελίας Od.2.92; ἐπ' Αἴαντα.. κήρυκα Il.12.342; τῷ κῦδος ἅμα πρόες 16.241: in Hom. freq. with inf. added to define the action, Ταλθύβιον προΐει.. ἰέναι Il.3.118; αἰετὼ.. προέηκε πέτεσθαι Od.2.147; [οὖρον] προέηκεν ἀῆναι 3.183; π. τινὰ διδασκέμεναι, μυθήσασθαι, πυθέσθαι, Il.9.442, 11.201,649; ἑτάρους π. πεύθεσθαι Od.9.88; so βασιλευέμεν τοι προήσειν *will allow* thee to.., Pi.*P.*4.166. 2. *dismiss*, *let go*, τινα Il.4.398; τήνδε θεῷ πρόες *let* her *go* to the god, i.e. in reverence to him, 1.127. 3. *let loose*, *let fall*, esp. thoughtlessly, ἔπος προέηκε *let drop* a word, Od.14.466; φήμην 20.105; πηδάλιον ἐκ χειρῶν προέηκε *he let* the helm *slip* from his hands, 5.316: with inf., πόδα προέηκε φέρεσθαι *let slip* his foot so that it fell, 19.468. 4. with direct purpose, *cast*, of a fisherman, ἐς πόντον π. βοὸς κέρας 12.253. 5. of missiles, *discharge*, *shoot*, ἔγχος, βέλος, ὀϊστόν, etc., Il.5.15, 280, 11.270, 13.662, etc.; ἀκόντια π. ἐπὶ τὸν νεβρόν f.l. in X.*Cyn.*9. 6. of a river, ἐς Πηνειὸν προΐει ὕδωρ it *pours* its water into the Peneius, Il.2.752, cf. Hes.*Fr.*37, E.*Hipp.* 124 (lyr.). II. *give up*, *deliver*, *betray* one to his enemy, Hdt.1.159, 3.137; χρήματα μέν σφι π. *offering to give* them.., Id.1.24, cf. Ar.*Nu.*1214; τὰς ναῦς π. τινί Th.8.32: with an inf. added, γυναῖκα.. π. ἀπάγεσθαι Hdt.2.115:—Pass., *to be given* or *thrown away*, εἰ ταῦτα προεῖτ' ἀκονιτεί D.18.200; καιροὶ προεῖνται Id.19.8, cf. 25.10. 2. ἐπὶ τὸ αὐτίκα ἡδὺ π. αὐτούς *devote* themselves to.., X.*Cyr.*7.5.76.

B. in Prose mostly in Med. (not found in Hom.), *send forward from oneself*, *drive forward*, τὸν λαγὼ εἰς τὰς ἄρκυς X.*Cyn.*6.10 (s.v.l.): c. inf., τοὺς ἐρῶντας ἵμερος δρᾶν προΐεται *forces* them *on* to do, S.*Fr.*149.9 codd. Stob. 2. of sounds, *utter*, τὴν φωνήν Aeschin.2.23, etc.; λόγον Ti.Locr.100c; ῥῆμα D.19.118; π. πᾶσαν φωνήν use all sorts of entreaties, Plb.3.84.10, etc.; π. τῶν ἀπορρήτων οὐδὲν οὐδενί Id.3.20.3, etc. 3. *emit*, π. γονήν, σπέρμα, κόπρον, βλαστούς, etc., Arist.*GA*719b3, 721a30, *HA*554b1, Thphr.*CP*1.12.9, etc.; κλημάτια.. προϊέμενα ῥίζας Dsc.4.29. II. *give up*, *let go*, προέμενον αὐτῇ (sc. τὴν χεῖρα) Hdt. 2.121.ε'; *give up* to the enemy, Κέρκυραν τοῖς Κορινθίοις Th.1.44, cf. D.18.72, 21.213; *abandon*, Id.19.152; π. σφᾶς αὐτοὺς *gave* themselves *up as lost*, Th.2.51; αὐτὸν τοῖς πολεμίοις X.*An.*5.8.14; σφᾶς αὐτοὺς καὶ τὰ ὅπλα Polyaen.4.3.4; τὸν βίον Plu.*Ant.*53: abs., *give up hope*, Jul.*Or.*8.250a. 2. *desert*, *abandon*, εἰ τὰ κάτω προοῖντο Th.1.120, cf. 6.78, X.*An.*1.9.10, etc.; οὐδαμῇ προΐενθ' αὑτούς *did* not *lose* themselves (i.e. take bribes), D.19.139; τι τῶν πρὸς τὴν πολιτείαν Arist.*Pol.*1307b4. 3. *give away*, *give freely*, ἔρανον τῇ πόλει Th. 2.43; τὰ ἑαυτῶν D.34.52; ὑμῖν οὐδὲν προεῖνται τῶν σφετέρων Lys. 21.12; ἀπὸ τῶν ἰδίων D.18.114; εὐεργεσίαν ἄνευ μισθοῦ without a stipulated fee, leaving it to one's honour, Pl.*Grg.*520c, cf. *Phdr.* 231c, X.*An.*7.7.47; *give up* without payment received, τὴν ἀλλαγήν Pl.*Lg.*849e. b. *spend lavishly*, μέγεθος χρημάτων οὐδενὶ λόγῳ Procop. *Arc.*26.23. c. *pay*, in kind or in money, *PHib.*1.76.2 (iii B.C.), *UPZ*23.18 and 26, 26.12 (ii B.C.), *PAmh.*61.11 (ii B.C.), *SIG*694.60 (Elaea, ii B.C.). 4. *throw off*, θοἰμάτιον D.21.216 (προϊέμενον χλάμυν is f.l. in Sapph.64). 5. *throw away*, τὰ ἴδια X.*Cyn.*12.11 codd.; π. τὸν καιρόν, τὸ παρόν, Lycurg.126, D.1.9; καθ' ἕκαστον ἀεί τι τῶν πραγμάτων ib.14; πολλὰ τῶν κοινῶν Id.18.134; εἰ οὗτοι χρήματα.. μὴ προοῖντ' ἄν, πῶς ὑμῖν καλὸν τὸν ὅρκον προέσθαι; Id.21.212; μηδενὸς κέρδους τὰ κοινὰ δίκαια π. Id.6.10; τὰ πατρῷα, τὰ τῆς δημοκρατίας ἰσχυρά, Aeschin.3.173,234; πόλεων.. ὧν ἡμέν ποτε κύριοι.. προϊεμένους (gen. by attraction of the relat. ὧν) D.2.2; τὴν ψυχὴν π. Porph.*Abst.* 2.13: abs., *throw away one's advantage*, Arist.*Rh.*1398a2, cf. *EN*1114a17 (less freq. *neglect* a disadvantage, π. κακόν τι Lib.*Or.*21.27); *to be lavish*, Arist.*Rh.*1366b7. 6. with part., inf., or Adj., ἡμᾶς προέσθαι ἀδικουμένους *suffer* us to be wronged, Th.2.73, cf. Plb.30.7.4; προέμενοι ἀπολέσθαι αὐτούς X.*HG*2.3.35; π. τισὶν ὑμᾶς ἐξαπατῆσαι D.16.3, cf. Lys.13.23, etc.; π. τὰ ἴδια ἀνομοθέτητα Pl.*Lg.*780a; also τοὺς Ἕλληνας εἰς δουλείαν π. D.10.25, cf. 5.15. 7. *suffer to escape*, ἐκ τοιούτων τοὺς ὑπεναντίους Plb.3.94.8; τινὰ ἐκ τῆς πόλεως Id.4.4.3; *let pass*, διὰ κενῆς τὸν χρόνον Id.3.70.10; *let slip*, *utter*, μαλθακοὺς λόγους φρενός dub. in E.*Med.*1052. 8. rarely in good sense, *confide*, *entrust* to one, X.*Cyr.* 5.2.9; τὰ τέκνα τισὶν εἰς ὁμηρίαν Plb.28.4.7: abs., X.*An.*7.3.31. 9. *lend* on risk, Pl.*Demod.*384c, D.36.6.

**προῖκα**, v. προίξ II.

**προϊκετεύω** [ῐ], *supplicate before*, Eust.1823.32.

**προικ-ίδιον**, τό, Dim. of προίξ, Plu.2.767c. **-ίδιος**, α, ον, *forming a dowry*, κλῆροι Ph.2.291; θεράπαιναι ib.443. **-ίζω**, *portion*, *give a dowry to*, τινα D.S.16.55, Ph.2.311, etc.:—Προικιζομένη, name of a comedy by Apollod.Car. ⊛ **-ῑμαῖος**, α, ον, *gratuitous*, κτῆσις D.C.47.17. 2. *belonging to a dowry*, πράγματα *POxy.*126.17 (vi A.D.). ⊛ **-ιος**, ον, = foreg. I, π. ἀοιδός, of the cicada, *AP*6.120 (Leon.); π. χάρις, of honey, ib.9.404 (Antiphil.); dub. l. in Call.*Fr.* 542 = *Oxy.*2079.34.

**προϊκνέομαι**, *come before*, *EM*692.20, Hsch.; cf. προΐκω.

**προικοδότης**, ου, ὁ, = ἑεδνωτής, Sch.D Il.13.382.

**προικός**· πονηρός, οἱ δὲ μωρός, Hsch. (leg. πρόκος or πρόκοος); = πτωχός, Id. (leg. προΐκτης).

**προικο-φορέομαι**, Med., *receive as a dower*, τὴν ὕβριν Eust.1851.16. ⊛ **-φόρος**, ἡ, = *dotata*, *Gloss.*

**προΐκτης**, ου, ὁ, (προΐσσομαι) *one who asks a gift*, *beggar*, Od.17.449; ἀνὴρ π. ib.352. II. = γόης or βωμολόχος, Artem.*Praef.*

**προΐκω**, = προικνέομαι, Eust.1823.37.

⊛ **προικῷος**, α, ον, = προικιμαῖος 2, *EM*582.29. *Gloss.*

**προϊλάσκομαι**, Med., *appease beforehand*, Paus.5.13.7.

**πρόϊμος**, f.l. for πρώϊμος, q.v.

⊛ **προίξ**, προικός, ἡ (on the accent v. Arc.125, *An.Ox.*3.243; Ion. accus. πρόϊκα acc. to *EM*495.33), *gift*, *present*, in Hom. only gen. προικός, as Adv., ἀργαλέον ἕνα προικὸς χαρίσασθαι burdensome is it for a single person to give *of his bounty*, *without reimbursement*, Od. 13.15; ἔμελλεν.. προικὸς γεύσεσθαι Ἀχαιῶν was likely to make trial of the Achaeans *with impunity*, 17.413 (unless π. γ. = taste the *gift*). 2. after Hom., *marriage-portion*, *dowry*, Hippon.(?)72, And. 4.14, Lys.19.9, Pl.*Lg.*774c, al.; ἐν τῇ προικὶ τετιμημένα reckoned *as part of the dowry*, D.47.57; ἀποτετιμημένα προικὸς τῇ Διοδώρου θυγατρί *IG*2².2675. II. acc. προῖκα as Adv., *as a free gift*, *freely*, *at one's own cost*, Ar.*Eq.*577,679, *Nu.*1426; π. ἐργάζεσθαι Pl.*R.*346e; ἀρετὴ τὸ π. τοῖς φίλοις ὑπηρετεῖν Antiph.210; π. κρίνειν, πρεσβεύειν, *without a gift*, *unbribed*, D.5.12, 19.232, cf. *IG*3.702, etc.; παῖς.. κακὸν μὲν δρᾶν τι προῖκ' ἐπίσταται *of oneself*, *without a teacher*, [S.]*Fr.*1120.6. 2. π. τῆς δόξης *to say nothing of*, *in addition to*, Plu.2.349e.

**πρόϊξις**, εως, ἡ, *coming forth*, *EM*523.2.

**προϊππ-άζομαι**, aor. -ασάμην, = προϊππεύω, Plu.*Publ.*22. **-ασία**, ἡ, *riding before others*, Polyaen.2.3.14. **-εύω**, *ride before* or *in front*, D.S.17.86, Plu.*Sull.*28, etc.; πρὸ τῆς φάλαγγος, πρὸ τῶν ἄλλων, D.S. 18.30, Arr.*An.*1.15.7; π. τοῦ στρατοῦ Plu.*Cam.*2.

**προΐπτᾰμαι**, *fly before*, *Gloss.*

**προΐσσομαι**, (προίξ) *ask a gift*, *beg*, Archil.130; cf. προΐκτης.

⊛ **προΐστημι**, fut. -στήσω: aor. 1 προὔστησα, part. προστήσας, inf. προστῆσαι. A. Causal in these tenses, as also in pres. and aor. 1 Med., *set before*, once in Hom., προστήσας [σε] πρὸ Ἀχαιῶν Τρωσὶ μάχεσθαι Il.4.156: c. gen., π. τὸ σῶμα τοῦ σκοποῦ *put* his body *in the way*, Antipho 3.2.4 (dub. l.), cf. Plb.1.33.7. 2. *set over*, ὃν ἡ πόλις ἀξιοῖ αὐτῆς προϊστάναι, v.l. for -εστάναι, Pl.*La.*197d. 3. *exhibit publicly*, *prostitute*, π. ἐπ' οἰκημάτων D.Chr.7.133. II. Med., mostly aor. 1, *put* another *before oneself*, *choose as one's leader*, Hdt.1.123, 4.80: c. gen., προΐστασθαι τουτονὶ ἑαυτοῦ *take as one's guardian*, Pl.*R.*565c, cf. 442a (cj.), 599a, D.59.37; σφῶν αὐτῶν προὐστήσαντο τιμωρὸν γενέσθαι Κηφίσιον And.1.139; στρατηγόν τινα τοῦ πολέμου π. D.*Prooem.* 21. 2. *put before one*, *put in front*, σκίπωνα προστήσασθαι Hdt.4.172; τὰ ἅρματα X.*HG*4.1.18; τὴν χεῖρα, so as to shade the eyes, Arist.*Pr.*960a21. 3. metaph., *put forward as an excuse* or *pretence*, *use as a screen*, τί τάδε προὐστήσω λόγῳ; E.*Cyc.*319; τὰ τῶν Ἀμφικτυόνων δόγματα προστήσασθαι D.5.19, etc.: c. gen., [τὴν ἀτυχίαν] τῆς κακουργίας προϊστάμενος Antipho 2.3.1; τοῦ ἀγῶνος τὴν πρὸς ἔμ' ἔχθραν προΐσταται D.18.15. 4. προστησώμεθα Τύρταιον *put* him *forward*, *cite* him *as an authority*, Pl.*Lg.*629a. 5. *prefer*, *value above*, ὦτα τοῦ νοῦ προστησάμενοι Id.*R.*531b. 6. *establish* a thing *before* another, τοὺς ἀριθμοὺς τῆς ὑποστάσεως αὐτῶν (sc. τῶν ὄντων) Plot.6.6.15, cf. Procl.*Inst.*133. 7. *manifest*, ib.195, al.

B. Pass., with aor. 2 Act. προὔστην: pf. προέστηκα, 2 pl. προέστατε Hdt.5.49; inf. προεστάναι, part. προεστώς (v.infr.): fut. pf. προεστήξομαι, v. infr. II. 2:—aor. Pass. προεστάθην, v. infr. II. 3:—*come forward*, v.l. for προσ- in D.60.15. 2. c. acc., *approach* as a suppliant, ἥ σε.. λιπαρεῖ προὔστην χερί S.*El.*1378; προστῆναι μέσην τράπεζαν dub. in *Fr.*660.1 (fort. προσβῆναι):—in Hdt.1.86, προσστῆναι is restored. 3. c. dat., *stand so as to face* another, σοὶ γὰρ Αἴας πολέμιος προὔστη ποτέ S.*Aj.*1133:—in Hdt.1.129, προσστάς is restored. 4. *stand in public*, *be a prostitute*, Aeschin.*Ep.*7.3, Vett.Val.16.7. II. c. gen., *to be set over*, *be at the head of*, τῆς Ἑλλάδος Hdt.1.69, 5.49; τῶν Ἀρκάδων τοὺς προεστεῶτας Id.6.74; esp. *to be chief* or *leader of a party*, τῶν παράλων, τῶν ἐκ τοῦ πεδίου, Id.1.59; τοῦ δήμου Id.3.82, Th.3.70, Lys. 13.7; ἡμῶν Ar.*V.*419; τῆς πόλεως Th.2.65; π. αὐτῶν *to be* their *ring-leader*, X.*An.*6.2.9; π. χοροῦ, στρατεύματος, Id.*Mem.*3.4.3; π. τῶν πολιτειῶν *head* the respective parties in the state, Lys.25.9, etc.: abs., οἱ προεστῶτες, Ion. -εῶτες, *the leading men*, τῶν Σκυθέων Hdt.4.79, cf. Th.3.11, etc.; οἱ προεστηκότες ἐν ταῖς πόλεσι X.*HG*3.5.1; οἱ ἐν ταῖς πόλεσι προστάντες Th.3.82; τῷ προεστῶτι καὶ ἄρχοντι Pl.*R*.428e. 2. in various relations, *govern, direct*, οὐκ ὀρθῶς σεωυτοῦ προέστηκας *you do* not *manage* yourself well, Hdt.2.173; π. τῆς μεταβολῆς Th.8.75; τοῦ ἱεροῦ X.*HG*3.2.31; τοῦ ἑαυτοῦ βίου Id.*Mem*.3.2.2; τοῦ πράγματος D.30.18; προεστήξομαι τῆς χωνεύσεως *PCair.Zen*.481.9 (iii B.C.); ἐργασίας, τέχνης, Plu.*Per*.24, Ath.13.612a; π. ἐνδόξου καὶ καλῆς αἱρέσεως *OGI*219.3 (Ilium, iii B.C.). 3. *stand before* so as *to guard*, οἱ δορυφόροι Μασίστεω προέστησαν Hdt.9.107, cf. E. *Heracl*.306, etc.: hence, *support, succour*, πρόστητ' ἀναγκαίας τύχης S.*Aj*.803; ὁ προστὰς τῆς εἰρήνης *the champion* of peace, Aeschin.2.161; πάντων προστᾶσα [δύναμις] Pl. *Ti*.25b; π. τινός *to be* his *protector*, *GDI*1726.6 (Delph., ii B.C.), *PFay*.13.5 (ii B.C.); τῆς ἐναντίας π. γνώμης Plb.5.5.8; τοῖσιν ἐχθροῖς προὐστήτην φόνου *were the authors of*.., S.*El*.980; π. [νόσου] E.*Andr*.221: abs., βέλεα.. ἀρωγὰ προσταθέντα S.*OT*206 (lyr.).

**προϊστορέω**, *make previous inquiry* or *research*, Ph.*Bel*.71.11, Attal. ap.Hipparch.2.1.6, Marin.*Procl*.24; προϊστορηκότες *having heard of*.., Sosyl.p.32 B. 2. *relate by way of introduction*, τὰς τῶν παλαιοτέρων δόξας Phlp.*in Mete*.75.20. II. Pass., *to be before mentioned*, Arist.*Mu*.393$^b$13; τὰ προϊστορημένα Plb.1.13.9, D.S.11.89, J.*BJ Praef*.5.

**προΐστωρ**, ορος, ὁ, *witness*, in pl., Hsch., Phot.

**προϊσχάνω**, poet. for προΐσχω, Nonn.*D*.11.158.

**προϊσχναίνω**, *become dry* or *lean before*, Arist.*Pr*.874$^a$35.

**προΐσχω**, = προέχω, *hold before, hold out*, of boys playing at ποσίνδα, X.*Eq.Mag*.5.10:—mostly in Med., *hold out before oneself, stretch forth*, χεῖρας Th.3.58,66; of nurse and child, Gal.6.44, al.: c. gen., *hold before*, τῶν ὄψεων τὰς χεῖρας Plu.*Pomp*.71; τὸ ἱμάτιον τοῦ βιβλίου Id.*Cat. Mi*.19. 2. = προέχω B.I, Hp.*Art*.30, *Mochl*.4. II. metaph. in Med., *put forward as a pretext, allege*, π. πρόφασιν ὡς.. Hdt.4.165, cf. 6.137, 8.3; ξυγγένειαν Th.1.26; τὸν νόμον Plu.*Alex*.14, etc. 2. *put forward as a demand*, Hdt.1.3; *propose, offer*, ib.141, 164, Th. 4.87; ξείνι' ἀριστήεσσι A.R.4.1553. 3. *hold out*, ἐλπίδα Porph. *Marc*.4. 4. *prosecute*, *Gloss*.

**προϊτ-έον** [ῐ], *one must advance*, Str.9.5.22. **-ητικός**, ή, όν, *eager to advance*, as etym. of Προῖτος, Eust.631.56.

**Προιτίδες** (πύλαι), αἱ, one of the gates of Thebes, called from Proetus son of Thersander, A.*Th*.377 (cf. 395). 2. *the daughters of Proetus* son of Abas, title of work by Theoc., Suid. 3. = χάριτες, Hsch. (s.v.l.).

**προϊχνεύω**, *trace beforehand*: = θεραπεύω, Hsch.

**προΐωξις** [ῐ], ἡ, *pursuit of the foremost*, opp. παλίωξις, Hes.*Sc*. 154.

⊕ **πρόκἄ**, Ion. Adv. *forthwith, straightway*, Hp.ap.Gal.19.132, A.R. 1.688; in Hdt. πρόκα τε or πρόκατε, 1.111, 6.134, 8.65, 135; so also in Call. in *PSI*9.1092.52.

**προκαδδικάζομαι**, v. προκαταδικάζομαι.

**προκαθαιρέω**, aor. προκαθεῖλον, *conquer before*, App.*Pun*.126.

⊕ **προκἄθαίρω**, *purge first*, Dsc.*Eup*.1.19; *prune, strip off first*, ἐκ πλαγίου τὰ φύλλα *Gp*.5.29.2; τὴν πικρίδα *Sammelb*.6797.14, al. (iii B.C.), cf. *PCair.Zen*.729.4 (iii B.C.): abs., *PLond.ined*.2313$^r$ (iii B.C.): —Med., *discharge prematurely*, τὰ λόχια Hp.*Foet.Exsect*.3.

**προκἄθἄριεύω**, *keep oneself pure before*, Paus.7.26.7.

**προκαθαρπάζω**, *snatch away before*, Sch.D Il.2.302.

⊕ **προκἄθάρσιον**, τό, *previous purification*, Sch. rec. S.*OT*240.

**προκάθαρσις** [κᾰ], εως, ἡ, = foreg., Sch.Ar.*Pl*.846.

**προκαθ-εδρία**, ἡ, = προεδρία, *Et.Gud*.482.43, Mich. *in EN*473. 34. **-έζομαι**, *sit before others, preside over*, οἴκῳ Phintys ap. Stob. 4.23.61$^a$: abs., *preside*, *Mon.Ant*.23.171 (Cilicia), *Jahresh*.15.55 (Notium); ἡ προκαθεζομένη πόλις the metropolis, Sch.rec.S.*El*.4, cf. *OGI*578.10 (Tarsus, iii A.D.). 2. *sit down before and besiege*, τῆς χώρας Alex.Polyh.ap.Eus.*PE*9.27.

**προκαθεύδω**, fut. -ευδήσω, *sleep before* or *first*, Ar.*V*.104. II. *sleep for* or *on behalf of* another, προεγρηγορότας καὶ προκαθεύδοντας Philostr.*VA*8.7.

⊕ **προκαθηγ-εμών**, όνος, ἡ, epith. of Artemis at Ephesus, *Ephes*.2 No. 20; at Iasus, *Rev.Ét.Gr*.6.159. **-έομαι**, *go before and guide*, Plb.3.95. 6; τῆς εὐνοίας ἡγουμένης πρός τινας Id.5.86.10; π. κρίσεων *influence* decisions *beforehand*, Id.3.6.7; τοῖς.. θεοῖς π. τῶν ἀγαθῶν Jul.*Or*.4. 133c; *to be a forerunner, pioneer*, Metrod.*Fr*.33. II. *to be precedent*, opp. consequent or subsequent, S.E.*P*.2.101, 116, etc. ⊕ **-έτης**, ου, ὁ, *leader*, epith. of gods, as Pan, *IG*5(2).93 (Tegea); Hermes, *BSA* 16.107 (Pisidia); Apollo, *Epigr.Gr*.1023.5 (Talmis): fem. ⊕ **-έτις**, ιδος, epith. of Athena, *CIG*4332 (Phaselis); ἀθανάτων π. prob. in *Epic.Alex. Adesp*.9 ii 17; Dor. **-αγέτις** Mesom.*Mus*.6. **-ητήρ**, ῆρος, ὁ, *wedge-shaped instrument for setting the* τόνοι of a torsion-engine, Ph.*Bel*.67. 4. **-ητής**, οῦ, ὁ, *leader*, τοῦ συνεδρίου Hld.10.4.

**προκάθημαι**, Ion. **-κάτημαι**, prop. pf. of προκαθέζομαι:—*to be seated before*, π. τοσοῦτο πρὸ τῆς ἄλλης Ἑλλάδος *lie* so far *in front of* Greece, of the Thessalians, Hdt.7.172. 2. c. gen., *to be seated* or *lie before* a place, so as to defend it, ἐπὶ τῷ στόματι π. τῆς θαλάμης Arist.*HA* 550$^b$5: hence, generally, *protect, defend*, τῶν ἑωυτοῦ, Ἰώνων, Hdt.8.36, 9.106, cf. Th.8.76, X.*HG*5.2.4; τῆς Ῥώμης Plb.2.24.15, al.; αἱ -καθήμεναι θεαὶ τῆς πόλεως *SIG*694.50 (Elaea, ii B.C.): rare in Poets, φυλακὴν.. στρατιᾶς π., of sentinels, E.*Rh*.6 (anap.). II. *preside over*, τὸ προκαθήμενον τῆς πόλεως Pl.*Lg*.758d; τοῦ πλήθους Arist.*Pol*.1322$^b$14: metaph., γεύσεως ὀσφρησις π. Ph.1.603. 2. abs., *sit in public* or *preside*, Plb.5.63.7, etc.; οἱ π. ἄρχοντες Id.12.16.6. b. *sit* at meals, καθ' ἡλικίαν καὶ τιμήν Str.3.3.7.

**προκαθ-ιδρύομαι**, *to be seated before*, ἐπὶ λόφου J.*AJ*1.19.9. **-ιερόομαι**, Pass., *to be consecrated before*, Sch.Pi.*P*.4.361. **-ιζάνω**, *cause to sit down in*, με.. εἰς φρέαρ *Supp.Epigr*.4.573.3 (Notium, ii B.C.). **-ίζω**, Ion. **-κατίζω**, *perch*, of birds, Il.2.463. 2. *sit in public, sit in state*, ἐς θρόνον Hdt.1.14, cf. 97; ἐν τῇ βασιλείῳ ἕδρᾳ Hdn. 1.9.3:—Med., προκατίζεσθαι ἐς τὸ προάστιον Hdt.5.12. 3. *settle before*, εἰς τὸν Ἰσθμόν Plb.20.6.8; ἐπὶ τῆς διαβάσεως Id.*Fr*.43:—Med., Arist.*Pr*.946$^b$36, Plb.10.49.1. 4. c. gen., *sit before, to be chief of*, τῆς Ἠπείρου Id.20.3.3; *have precedence of*, τινος Luc.*JTr*.9. II. trans., π. ἐνέδρας *lay* ambushes *beforehand*, Aen.Tact.15.9. 2. *set as guards*, τινὰς ὡς ἐπὶ Τυρρηνίας Plb.2.24.6. **-ίημι**, *let down beforehand*, εἰς τὴν βαλανοδόκην βρόχον Aen.Tact.18.9: metaph., εἰς ταραχὴν π. πόλιν *plunge* the city into confusion, D.14.5; π. τινὰ ἐξαπατᾶν *put* a person *forward* in order to deceive, Id.19.77; π. τὸν λόγον, τὴν δόξαν, *spread it before*, D.C.58.9 (prob.), Aristid.1.482J.:— Pass., ἐπὶ τῷ ὕδατι τὰ σκεύη προκαθεῖτο D.C.62.15. **-ισις**, εως, ἡ, *sitting in public*, Plu.2.166a (pl.); ἐπὶ θρόνου J.*AJ*17.9.5. ⊕ **-ίστημι**, *appoint beforehand*, ἄρχειν αὐτὸν τῶν σωματοφυλάκων.. προκαταστήσας D.C.58.9. 2. Med., φύλακας προκαθιστάμενοι *causing* them *to be posted in front*, X.*Hier*.6.9. 3. Med., *prepare* or *arrange before*, προκαταστήσασθαι τὸν λόγον D.H.*Rh*.5.2: abs., *establish before*, προκαταστήσασθαι ὅτι.. S.E.*M*.8.379, cf. Anon.Lond.38.55, Theo Sm.p.120 H. II. Pass., with aor. 2 and pf. Act., intr., *to be set before*, φυλακῆς μὴ προκαθεστηκυίας no guard *having been set*, Th.2.2, cf. J. *AJ*15.8.4. 2. *to be established before*, S.E.*M*.11.41. **-οράω**, *examine beforehand, reconnoitre*, νέας ἀπέστειλαν προκατοψομένας Hdt. 8.23. **-οσιόομαι**, Pass., *to be dedicated before*, Hld.10.37; τῇ τοῦ γενέσθαι ἀνάγκῃ J.*AJ*16.11.8.

**πρόκαιρος**, f.l. for προσ– in Lxx 4 *Ma*.15.2. Adv. **-ρως** *prematurely*, *Gloss*.

⊕ **προκαίω**, *burn before*, in Pass., *to be lighted before*, of fires, f.l. in X.*An*.7.2.18; *to be burnt first*, aor. subj. -καῇ (v.l. -καυθῇ) Aët.15. 14.

**προκᾰκόομαι**, Pass., *to be afflicted before*, Lxx 4 *Ma*.17.22, Sch.Ar. *Ra*.33, etc.

**προκᾰκοπᾰθέω**, *suffer before*, Sor.1.88.

**πρόκᾰκος**, ον, *exceeding bad*, κακὰ πρόκακα evils *beyond evils*, A. *Pers*.986 (lyr.), cf. 990 (lyr.).

**προκάλ-εσμα** [ᾰ], ατος, τό, = *irritamentum*, *Gloss*. **-έω**, *call forth*, D.C.44.34:—Pass., Plb.22.9.2; *to be evoked*, Epicur.*Fr*. 411. B. mostly Med., *call out to fight, challenge*, Αἴας δὲ πρῶτος προκαλέσσατο Il.13.809, cf. Od.8.142; ἴθι νῦν προκάλεσσαι.. Μενέλαον ἐξαῦτις μαχέσασθαι Il.3.432, cf. 7.39; προκαλέσσατο χάρμῃ ib.218; so, later, π. εἰς ἀγῶνα X.*Mem*.2.3.17, cf. Luc.*Symp*.20; εἰς μονομαχίαν Ael.*VH*1.24; μάχῃ *Anacreont*.12.7; ταῦτα π. τοὺς συνόντας thus.., X.*Cyr*.1.4.4; *challenge* to drink, Critias *Fr*.6.7 D.; π. τινὰ συμπαίζειν, συγγυμνάζεσθαι, Anacr.14.4, Pl.*Smp*.217c: prov., ἱππέας εἰς πεδίον προκαλῇ, Σωκράτη εἰς λόγους προκαλούμενος, of one who *challenges* another in his own department, Id.*Tht*.183d, cf. Men.268. 2. *invite* or *summon*, τινὰ ἐς λόγους Hdt.4.201, Th.3.34; ἐς σπονδὰς καὶ διάλυσιν πολέμου Id.4.19; ἐπὶ ξυμμαχίαν Id.5.43; ἐπὶ τιμωρίαν D.21.226; πρὸς τὸ συνδειπνεῖν Pl.*Smp*.217c; [ἰχθῦς] πρὸς τὴν θήραν π. *entice* them out, Arist.*HA*534$^a$17; πρὸς αὑτόν τινας *endeavour to attach* them to oneself, Plb.3.77.7. 3. c. acc. et inf., *invite* one to do.., *Trag.Adesp*. 165 (= *Com.Adesp*.1295), etc.; π. τινὰ ἐς λόγον ἐλθεῖν Isoc.5.91; εἰρήνην ποιεῖσθαι X.*HG*2.2.15, cf. Pl.*Euthd*.294b, etc.; προκαλούμεθα ὑμᾶς φίλοι εἶναι καὶ ἐκ τῆς γῆς ἡμῶν ἀναχωρῆσαι Th.5.112; of things, αὐτὰ (sc. τὰ πράγματα) προκαλεῖται παρασκευάζειν τι *invite, admonish*, Arist.*Pol*.1331$^a$22: also π. εἰ βούλοιντο.., c. inf., Th.4.30. 4. abs., αὐτῶν προκαλεσαμένων *at* or *after* their *invitation*, ib.20, cf. Pl.*R*.451c; *appeal*, προκαλεῖσθαι περί τινος ἐπὶ Ῥωμαίους Plb.24.9. 13. II. c. acc. rei, *offer, propose*, δίκην Th.1.39, cf. 2.72, 73, Ar. *Ach*.984, etc.; τὰ εἰρημένα Th.5.37; τὰς σπονδάς Ar.*Eq*.796: with acc. pers. added, προκαλεῖσθαί τινας τὴν εἰρήνην *offer* them peace, Id.*Ach*. 652, cf. Pl.*Euthphr*.5a, *Chrm*.169c. 2. law-term, *make an offer* or *challenge* to the opponent for bringing about a decision, e.g. for submitting the case to arbitration, letting slaves be put to the torture, etc., προκαλοῦνται πρόκλησιν ἡμᾶς D.37.12, cf. 40.44, Antipho 1.6: c. acc. pers., *challenge* him, Id.6.23; π. εἰς πάντα τινάς ib.26; εἰς ἀντίδοσιν Lys.24.9; εἰς ὅρκον D.52.17; εἰς ἐμφανῶν κατάστασιν Is.6.31 (leg. προσ–); π. τινά τι *make* one *an offer*, D.48.4, cf. 37.42: c. acc. et inf., π. τὴν μητέρα ὀμόσαι *offer* that she should take an oath, Id.55.27: c. inf. only, π. ἐθέλειν ἐπιδεῖξαι Id.27.50, cf. 54.27; also π. κατά τινος εἰς μαρτυρίαν Id.29.20 (προσκ- codd.):—Pass., π. περὶ Ἐπιδάμνου ἐς κρίσιν Th.1.34. III. *call up* or *forth*, εὐγένειαν E.*HF*308; τὸν Θησαυρὸν ἐς τοὐμφανὲς Luc.*Tim*.41; τρίχας Dsc.2. 151. ⊕ **-ίζομαι**, Ep. only pres. and impf., *call forth, challenge, defy*, κούρους προκαλίζετο Il.5.807, cf. 7.150; προκαλίζετο πάντας ἀρίστους ἀντίβιον μαχέσασθαι 3.19; ἀλλ' ὅ γ' ἀεθλεύειν προκαλίζετο 4.389; μιν προκαλίζετο τοξάζεσθαι Od.8.228; χερσὶ δὲ μή τι λίην προκαλίζεο *challenge* me not to a pugilistic combat, 18.20.

**προκᾰλινδέομαι**, Pass., *fall prostrate before another*, Lat. *provolvi ad genua*, Isoc.4.151 (v.l. προκυλ–), D.19.338, etc.; τῶν ποδῶν Aristaenet.1.27; τοῦ Καίσαρος Anon.ap.Suid.; ἴχνεσι τοῖς ἐμοῖς Jul.*Ep*. 205.

**προκάλυμμα** [κᾰ], ατος, τό, *anything put before, veil, curtain*, A.*Ag*. 691 (lyr., pl.). 2. *covering*, as a protection, Th.2.75; [σὰρξ ὀστέων] π. Ti.Locr.100b. 3. metaph., *screen, cloak*, ἁμαρτανομένων λόγοι.. π. γίγνονται Th.3.67; τὸ σχῆμα τῆς θείας οἰκίας π. ποιούμενοι *Jahresh*. 23 *Beibl*.285 (Ephesus); τῆς ἐπιβουλῆς J.*BJ*5.3.1; τῆς βδελυρίας Luc.

*Pseudol.*31; π. προβεβλῆσθαι τῆς αὐτομολίας Id.*Merc.Cond.*5; γευμάτων ἀπατηλῶν π. ἡ χολή, in jaundice, Aret.*SD*1.15.

**προκᾰλύπτω**, *hang before* or *put over as a covering*, παραπετάσματα Aen.Tact.32.9:—Med., *put over oneself as a screen* or *cloak*, πέπλων.. προὐκαλύπτετ' εὐπήνους ὑφάς (nisi leg. προὐκάλυπτεν) E.*IT* 312; οὐ προκαλυπτομένα [τι] παρηΐδος *putting* no *veil over one's* face, Id. *Ph.*1485 (lyr.): metaph., π. ποίησιν Pl.*Prt.*316d; π. δόξαν μετριότητος Chio *Ep.*15.1:—pf. Med., πρὸ τῆς ψυχῆς.. ὅλον τὸ σῶμα προκεκαλυμμένοι *having* it *put as a screen*, Pl.*Grg.*523d. II. *cover over*, ἥλιον νεφέλη π. X.*An.*3.4.8 (ἥλιος νεφέλην π. codd.):—Med., προὐκαλύψατ' ὄμματα *veiled her* eyes, E.*Med.*1147:—Pass., *to be covered*, X.*Cyr.*5.4.45.

**προκάμνω**, *work* or *toil before*, Thgn.925. II. *toil for* or *in defence of*, τινος S.*Aj.*1270. III. *grow weary*, *give up*, μὴ πρόκαμνε A.*Eu.*78; μὴ προκάμητε πόδα E.*HF*119 (lyr.); of dogs, Poll.5.64, cf. Porph.*Abst.*3.18. IV. *have a previous illness*, Th.2.49. 2. *to be distressed beforehand*, τοῖς μέλλουσιν ἀλγεινοῖς ib.39: c. gen., Ael.*VH* 14.6.

**προκάμπῠλος**, ον, *bent forward*: προκάμπυλον, τό, = ἀβρότονον, Ps.-Dsc.3.24.

**προκάρδιον**, τό, *pit of the stomach*, Ruf.*Onom.*95, Id.(?) ap.Orib. *inc.*6.27, Poll.2.164, 165.

**προκάρηνος** [ᾰ], ον, *head-foremost*, *AP*7.632 (Diod.), 9.533, Musae.341, etc.

**προκᾰρόομαι**, Pass., *to be affected with drowsiness before*, Hp. *Prorrh.*1.155, *Coac.*25.

**προκάρπιον**, τό, *the part of the hand next the* καρπός, Poll.2.142.

**προκάς**, άδος, ἡ, = πρόξ, *h.Ven.*71.

⊛ **προκατα-βαίνω**, *descend*, of the foetus, Arist.*HA*$583^{b}$31; εἰς τὸν ἀγῶνα D.S.15.85 (s.v.l.); *step* into a bath *first*, Gal.11.606. ⊛ **-βάλλω**, *apply first*, Heliod.ap.Orib.48.35.2 (Pass.):—also in Pass., *to be swallowed first*, Ph.1.320. II. Med., *lay the foundations of before*, Id.2.476; θέατρον, οἰκοδομήματα, D.C.43.49, 57.10: metaph., τὰς ἀρχὰς καὶ τὰς αἰτίας Andronic.Rhod.p.577 M.:—Pass., Ph.1.405, al. III. Pass., *to be previously overcome*, *exhausted*, Gal.19.601. **-βάπτω**, *dip*, *plunge first*, Olymp.Alch.p.94 B.:—Pass., Paul.Aeg.3.70. **-βλάπτω**, *injure first*, App.*Sam.*4.3. ⊛ **-βολή**, ἡ, *payment on account*: in Att. Law, *caution money paid down* by a farmer of the revenue, *AB*193, *EM*148.52, Phot. II. *foundation*: metaph. of medical treatment, π. τῇ θεραπείᾳ Philum.*Ven.*3.1; *condition precedent*, Ammon. *in Int.*145.12. **-βρέχω**, *soak beforehand*, Dsc.3.78.

**προκαταγγ-έλλω**, *announce* or *declare beforehand*, *Act.Ap.*3.18, J.*AJ*2.5.2. **-ελσις**, εως, ἡ, *previous announcement*, Sch.Th.2.1.

**προκατα-γελάω**, *ridicule before*, τινος Jul.*Or.*6.182a codd. (leg. προσκ-). **-γιγνώσκω**, *vote against beforehand*, *condemn by a prejudgement*, τινος D.21.227, Plb.21.42.2, etc.; μὴ προκαταγίγνωσκ'.., πρὶν ἂν γ' ἀκούσῃς ἀμφοτέρων Ar.*V.*919; μὴ προκατεγνωκέναι μηδέν not to *prejudge* in any point, D.18.2: generally, *condemn*, *disapprove of in advance*, Gal.12.260. 2. c. inf., π. ἡμῶν.. ἥσσους εἶναι *prejudge* us and say we are.., Th.3.53; σφῶν αὐτῶν π. ἀδικεῖν Lys.20.21; π. ἀδικεῖν (without τινος) And.1.3; also π. ὡς ἀδικῶ Aeschin.2.7. 3. π. τινὸς φόνον *give a verdict of* murder *against* one *beforehand*, Antipho 5.85; π. τινῶν ἄδικόν τι ib.4; ἀδικίαν τινός Lys.19.10. 4. π. θανατόν τινος *pass sentence* of death *on before*, D.S.18.60; τὴν τιμωρίαν αὐτὸς σαυτοῦ π. D.C.46.11.

**προκατάγνῡμαι**, Pass., *to be broken in pieces before*, Sch.Od.3.296.

**προκατάγομαι** [ᾰγ], Pass., *get into harbour before*, τινος Luc.*Cat.*18.

**προκαταγράφω** [γρᾰ], *write down before* or *in an earlier passage*, Epicur.*Nat.*26 G. (prob. l.), Sor.1.1.

**προκατᾰγωγή**, ἡ, *coming into port before*, Arr.*An.*1.18.5.

**προκατᾰγωνίζομαι**, *overcome*, *defeat first*, πᾶν τὸ ψεῦδος Hierocl. *in CA*12 p.447 M.

**προκατα-δῐκάζομαι**, Pass., *to be condemned before*, Din.*Fr.*89; προκαδδεδικάσθω δύο μνᾶς to pay 2 minae, *Tab.Heracl.*1.171. **-δουλόομαι**, Pass., *to be subdued before*, D.S.12.1. **-δύνω** [ῡ], *set before*, Hipparch.1.5.17; also **-δύομαι**, Gal.9.906, Heph.Astr.2.11: aor. -έδυν Alex.Aphr. *in Mete.*31.25. **-θέω**, *run down before*, v.l. in X.*An.*6.3.10. **-θήγω**, *sharpen at the point before*, Hsch. (Pass.).

**προκατ-αιονάω**, *moisten before*, Gal.10.910, Orib.*Frr.*76, 110, Paul.Aeg.3.81. **-αίρω**, *run in before*, τῶν πέλας ἐς λιμένα Philostr.*Her.*10.4.

**προκατα-καίω**, *burn before*, D.C.60.34; of soldiers, *burn all before them*, X.*An.*1.6.2. ⊛ **-κειμαι**, *lie down before*, at meals, Luc.*Merc.Cond.*26, Hld.4.16. **-κλάω**, *shatter before*, τὰς ψυχάς J.*AJ* 10.7.4. **-κλίνω** [ῑ], *cause to lie down before* others, at meals, ib.15.2.4:—Pass., = προκατάκειμαι, Luc.*DDeor.*13.1; *stoop down before*, J.*BJ*5.6.3. **-κλῐσις**, εως, ἡ, *first place at table*, Id.*AJ*20.3.2. **-κλύζω**, *wash beforehand*, Thphr.*HP*9.11.2. **-κνίζω**, *pick*, *trim first*, ἀλωπεκίας Dsc.2.123 (Pass.), cf. Gal.19.456. **-κόπτω**, *cut up beforehand*, Antiph.230.7: metaph., *cut to pieces*, *massacre first*, πολλούς Eun.*VS*p.480 B. **-κρίνω** [ῑ], *form a prejudgement of*, τῶν ἀνθρωπείων τὴν ἀδηλότητα Plu.2.112d; *reject in comparison with*, f.l. in *AP*12.207 (Strat.). **-λαγχάνω**, *obtain by lot beforehand*, Sch. Pi.*N.*3.129. **-λαμβάνω**, *seize beforehand*, *occupy in advance*, esp. by a military force, Th.2.2, 3.112, X.*An.*1.3.16, etc.:—Med., Plb.2.27.5, *SIG*742.7 (Ephesus, i B.C.), etc.:—Pass., *to be so occupied*, Th.4.89. 2. generally, *preoccupy*, τὸ βῆμα Aeschin.3.71; τὰ κοινὰ καὶ φιλάνθρωπα τῶν ὀνομάτων ib.248; τὰ Φιλίππου ὦτα Id.2.108; πράγματα προκατειλημμένα, by the previous speakers, Isoc.4.74. 3. *apprehend before*, Gal.1.183; -λαμβάνεται τὸ σημεῖον τοῦ σημειωτοῦ S.E.*M.*8.169; -ειλημμένον πρόσωπον A.D.*Synt.*26.13 (-ειλεγμένον is f.l. here and in *Adv.*157.26). 4. Pass., of events, *to be predetermined*, ὑπὸ τῆς εἱμαρμένης Diogenian.Epicur.3.51, cf. 2.20. II. metaph., *prevent*, *anticipate*, *frustrate*, τῶν πόλεων τὰς ἀποστάσεις Th.1.57; π. ὅπως μή.. Id.3.46, 6.18: abs., Id.3.2, etc.; π. καὶ ἀπειλεῖν, of the legislator, Pl.*Lg.*853b; in speaking, π. τὰ ἐπίδοξα λέγεσθαι Arist.*Rh.Al.*$1443^{a}$6, al.; of persons, *anticipate* or *surprise* them, Th.3.3; τοῦ χειμῶνος -λαβόντος [αὐτόν] Plb.38.8.3:—Med., π. τινά Id.5.36.8; π. τὰς νόσους D.S.1.82, cf. Herod.Med. in *Rh.Mus.*58.92:—Pass., τῶν.. προκατειλημμένων κατηγορημάτων the charges *that have been anticipated*, Din.1.1; *to be surprised*, Plb.2.18.6; -ληφθέντες ἀναλαμβάνονται *if taken in time* they recover, Philum.ap.Aët.9.7. III. *overpower first*, π. ἡμᾶς ἐς τὴν ὑμετέραν ἐπιχείρησιν *crush* us *in preparation for* an attack on you, Th.1.33, cf. 36:—Pass., δεσμοῖς Plb.16.34.11: pf. Pass. in med. sense, προκατείλημμαί σ' ὦ Τύχη Epicur.*Sent.Vat.*47 (= Metrod.*Fr.*49). 2. without any notion of force, *win over before*, *preoccupy*, π. καὶ προκολακεύειν τὴν μέλλουσάν τινος δύναμιν Pl.*R.*494c; τὴν ἐκκλησίαν Aeschin.3.67. b. *ensure*, ὑγιείην Hp.*Vict.*3.67. c. Pass., *to be prejudiced*, αἱρέσει τινί Gal.4.705. IV. *fasten securely*, Sor.*Fasc.*1. **-λάμπω**, *illumine in front*, Sch.Il.18.486. **-λέγομαι**, Pass., *to be described beforehand*, Hdt.4.175: pf. part. -λελεγμένος Ath.3.119a; but also ἡ προκατειλεγμένη σύνταξις A.D.*Conj.*213.1, cf. Heph.Astr.2.24. **-λείπω**, *bequeath before*, *PMasp.*3.19 (vi A.D.). **-λήγω**, *terminate beforehand*, Plb.2.14.6; *anticipate cessation*, Gal.19.201. **-ληκτικός**, ή, όν, in Metric, *with anticipated* κατάληξις, τροχαϊκόν Heph.15.18, cf. Sch. ad loc. **-ληξις**, εως, ἡ, *previous cessation*, Gal.19.216. **-ληπτέον**, *one must anticipate*, in speaking, Arist.*Rh.Al.*$1443^{a}$40. **-ληπτικός**, ή, όν, *preventive*, ὀφθαλμίας Gal.12.780, cf. Orib.*Fr.*107, Aët.7.3. ⊛ **-ληψις**, εως, ἡ, *seizing in advance*, τῶν ἐκβολῶν Jul.*Or.*2.74c. 2. *preoccupation*, *anticipation* of an adversary's arguments, Arist.*Rh.Al.*$1428^{a}$8 (pl.), $1432^{b}$11; ἐπὶ -λήψει θέας in *anticipation* of.., J.*AJ*19.1.13. II. *previous apprehension*, ἐκ π. Hsch. s.v. καταφθατουμένη.

**προκαταλλάσσομαι**, Pass., *to be reconciled before*, D.C.55.10a.

**προκατα-λύω**, *break up*, *annul beforehand*, νόμους Th.3.84; τὸν πλοῦν D.56.24; π. τοῦ ἔργου τὸν βίον *before* finishing his work, Plu.*Sol.*32; π. ἑαυτόν *debase* oneself *too low*, J.*BJ*1.6.5; *inhibit*, *check prematurely*, ἀναπνοῆς ἐνέργειαν Gal.1.275:—Med., τὴν ἔχθρην π. *end their mutual* enmity *before*, Hdt.7.6; τὸν πόλεμον *IG*$2^{2}$.127.42, D.H.8.47. II. intr., *rest before*, παρά τινι Ph.1.229. **-μᾰλάσσω**, *soften beforehand*, interpol. post Dsc.*Eup.*1.187. **-μανθάνω**, *learn* or *consider first*, -μεμαθηκέναι Antyll. ap. Orib.8.5.1, cf. D.C.52.33. **-μαντεύομαι**, *divine*, τὰ μέλλοντα D.S.37.19; περί τινων ὅτι... D.H.*Rh.*2.8.

**προκαταναλίσκω**, *squander beforehand*, τὰ ἐφόδια Satyr.20; π. τινὰ ταῖς βασάνοις *use* him *up before* with.., Posidon.36 J.:—Pass., D.H.3.44.

**προκατα-νίζω**, *wash first*, in aor. part. fem. -νίψασα Heraclid.Tar. ap.Gal.13.727. **-νοέω**, *observe beforehand*, ὄψεις Onos.14.4, cf. J.*AJ*17.1.1, Gal.2.606. **-νομή**, ἡ, *previous pasturage*, dub. in *BGU* 636.16 (i A.D.).

**προκαταντλέω**, *give a previous douche*, Dsc.*Eup.*1.168, Gal.13.632, Aët.12.27.

**προκατα-νύσσω**, Att. **-ττω**, *pierce beforehand*, D.C.51.14. **-ξύω**, *scrape first*, Asclep. ap. Gal.12.411 (Pass.), Archig. ap. Aët.6.55. **-παύω**, *cause to cease before*, τινος *from*.., Lib.*Or.*18.99; but π. [τινὰ] τοῦ συμμέτρου *before* the moderate amount, Gal.6.286. **-πέμπω**, *send down in advance*, τὸ Σαρακηνῶν ἱππικόν Eun.*Hist.*p.240 D. **-πίμπρημι**, *burn beforehand*, D.C.66.3. **-πίνω** [ῑ], *swallow beforehand*, J.*BJ*5.10.3. **-πίπτω**, *fall down before*, *sooner*, M.Ant.4.15, D.C.71.7; τοῦ τέλους *collapse before* the end, Plu.2.458d: metaph., π. ταῖς ψυχαῖς *despond beforehand*, D.S.20.9. II. λόγοι προκατέπιπτον εἰς τὴν Ῥώμην rumours *reached* Rome *in advance*, Plu.*Pomp.*43. **-πλάσσω**, *plaster before*, in Pass., Heras ap.Gal.13.547, Herod.Med.ap.Orib.*Fr.*70 (= Aët.5.130). **-πλέω**, *sail down before*, Plb.1.21.4. **-πλήσσω**, *strike with terror beforehand*, τινα D.C.47.34:—Med., Plb.5.70.9:—Pass., D.S.19.106. **-πονέω**, *tire*, *weary first*, τὸ σωμάτιον Agathin.ap.Orib.10.7.14:—Pass., -πεπονημένοι ὀργαῖς, λύπαις, χαραῖς Ruf.ap.Orib.*inc.*9.1.

**προκάτ-αργμα**, ατος, τό, *libation before the sacrifice*, Sch.Ar.*Pl.*660; cf. πρόθυμα. **-ᾰριθμέω**, *reckon up beforehand*, Hierocl.p.57 A. (Pass.), S.E.*M.*7.363 (Pass.). II. *enumerate above*, Herod.Med.ap.Orib.5.30.21 (Pass.). **-αρκτικός**, ή, όν, *initial*, αἰτία ἡ εἱμαρμένη Chrysipp.*Stoic.*2.292; τὰ π. *the immediate exciting causes* of things, S.E.*P.*3.16, cf. Dsc.*Ther.Praef.*, etc.; *predisposing*, αἰτία Sor.2.4. 2. παιὼν π. a paeon *beginning with a long syllable* (– ⏑ ⏑ ⏑), opp. καταληκτικός (⏑ ⏑ ⏑ –), Demetr.*Eloc.*38, 39. 3. Rhet., *prefatory*, ἔννοιαι, νοήματα, Hermog.*Id.*2.9; τὰ π. ib.1.12. **-αρξις**, εως, ἡ, *first beginning*, τῆς δίκης, i.e. *litis contestatio*, *Cod.Just.*1.3.45.4; τοῦ δικαστηρίου *POxy.*67.11 (iv A.D.).

**προκαταρρήγνῡμι**, *break down before*, γεφύρας prob. in D.C.36.7.

**προκαταρτ-ίζω**, *complete beforehand*, *Supp.Epigr.*4.449.13 (Didyma, ii B.C.), 2*Ep.Cor.*9.5:—Pass., προκατηρτισμένος *got ready*, *prepared beforehand*, Hp.*Decent.*8, cf. Ph.*Bel.*95.40. **-ύω**, *prepare* or *temper beforehand*, Plu.2.31d.

**προκατ-αρχή**, ἡ, *origin*, περὶ τῆς τοῦ ἀθρόου π., title of work by Zeno Epicureus, Phld.*Herc.*1005.7. **-άρχης**, ου, ὁ, *founder*, τελετῆς Procl.*Theol.Plat.*4.16 (pl.). ® **-άρχω**, *begin first*, ἡ -άρχουσα χάρις Ph.1.487; ἡ -άρξασα διάθεσις A.D.*Synt.*244.9; π. μιαιφονίας D.S.38.6; χάριτος A.D.*Pron.*40.10. 2. of causes (cf. προκαταρκτικός), τῶν αἰτίων τινὰ μέν ἐστι τὰ προκατάρξαντα Dsc.*Ther.Praef.*, cf. Sor.2.17, Gal.9.1: c. gen., τῆς σωματικῆς ἁπάσης κινήσεως π. Dam.*Pr.*284; προκατάρχοντος αὐτῆς τῆς εἱμαρμένης εἱμαρμένου Plu.2.574d, cf. Iamb.*Myst.*1.7. II. *begin* a thing *before* others, τοῦ πολέμου D.S.2.18, D.C.50.2:—Med., π. [ὀρχήσεως] D.H.7.72; μάχης, εὐποιίας, J.*AJ*1.20.2, 7.15.1; ἔχθρας D.C.*Fr.*40.4; π. τοῦ .. σώματος τὸ στυγνὸν σκότος *Corp.Herm.*1.20 (-έρχεται codd.): abs., *begin hostilities*, Plb.3.31.5, D.C.41.59, Heliod. *in EN*104.9. 2. Med., = *litem contestor*, *Gloss.* III. προκατάρχεσθαί τινι τῶν ἱερῶν *serve* one *with* the *first* or *the best portion of* the victim at sacrifices (one of the privileges of the citizens of the mother-city in their colonies), Th.1.25, cf. App.*BC*1.110.

**προκατα-σείω**, *shake in advance*, τὰς γνώμας τῷ φόβῳ Lib.*Or.*64.96. **-σκέπτομαι**, fut. -σκέψομαι Arr.*An.*1.13.1: aor. -εσκεψάμην D.H.11.26:—*inspect beforehand*, ll. cc.

® **προκατασκευ-άζω**, *prepare beforehand*, εἱρκτὰς ταῦτα π. X.*Cyr.*3.1.19, cf. D.S.15.47 (codd.); νίκην ib.3; φάρμακον D.C.60.34; *fortify in advance*, [εἰσβολάς] Aen.Tact.16.16; π. τινὰ εὔλυτον *put* him into a condition of free bowel-action, Alex.Trall.11.2:—Med., φίλους Plb.4.32.7, cf. Lxx *Si.Prol.*26, Gal.6.180:—Pass., Hp.*Haem.*3, Arist.*Col.*792$^b$5, Plb.1.21.3. II. Rhet., *use the device of* προκατασκευή 3, Hermog.*Inv.*3.2; -σκευαζόμενος στοχασμός Id.*Stat.*3. **-ασμα**, ατος, τό, *preparation*, Sch.Od.1.262 (pl.). **-αστικός**, ή, όν, *preparatory*, f.l. in Aristid.*Rh.*2p.516S. ® **-ή**, ἡ, *preparatory training*, περὶ τοὺς ῥυθμούς Plb.9.20.7; *preparation*, στρατηγήματος v.l. in J.*BJ*2.21.3. 2. *preface*, *introduction*, Plb.1.3.10, 1.13.7, etc. 3. Rhet., *preliminary exposé* of the main points in an argument, Hermog.*Inv.*3.1, al.

**προκατα-σκιρρόομαι**, Pass., *to be hardened beforehand*: metaph., ἀπέχθεια προκατεσκιρρωμένη *inveterate* enmity, Lxx 3*Ma.*4.1. **-σπείρω**, *sow beforehand*, *PMeyer* 12.21 (ii A.D.): metaph., *implant beforehand*, ἐν τοῖς θνητοῖς τὸ ἀθάνατον Aen.Gaz.*Thphr.* p.56 B. **-στᾰσις**, εως, ἡ, *introduction*, D.H.*Rh.*7.4; ἡ π. τῆς διηγήσεως, = προδιήγησις, Hermog.*Inv.*2.1, cf. 1.4. **-στᾰτικός**, ή, όν, *preparatory*, τῶν ζητημάτων νοήματα Sopat. in Rh.8.58 W. **-στέλλω**, *begin by calming* or *moderating*, τὴν διάνοιαν Aristid.Quint.2.15; τὸν θυμόν Eust.104.14. ® **-στοχάζομαι**, *aim at in advance*, σκοποῦ Ptol.*Tetr.*107. **στρέφω**, *subdue*, *overthrow beforehand*, J.*BJ*4.7.3 (Med.). II. (sc. τὸν βίον) *die first*, Phld.*Herc.*1041.8, D.L.2.138: metaph., π. εἰς .. *stop short* at .., Epicur.*Sent.*25. **-στροφή**, ἡ, *predecease*, ib.40. **-σύρω** [ῡ], *plunder completely*, χώραν, τόπους, Plb.4.10.8, 4.19.9. **-σφάζω**, *slay before*, App.*Hisp.*12. **-σχάζω**, *scarify beforehand*, Dsc.3.80.4 (Pass.), Aët.13.23. **-τᾰράσσω**, *disturb beforehand*, Iamb.*Myst.*3.7 (Pass., fort. -καταρχθῇ). **-τᾰχέω**, *to be beforehand*, *get the start* of another, τινος S.E.*M.*10.145 sq.; with v.l. **προκατατᾰχύνω**, ib.153:—Pass., of ships, -ταχούμενα ὑπὸ τοῦ ῥεύματος Gem.12.18. ® **-τίθημι**, in aor. προκατέθηκεν, gloss on ἔθηκεν, Apollon.*Lex.* II. mostly Med., *set down before*, τὸν λόγον *make an introductory* statement, Hp.*Vict.*1.1. 2. *lay up in store*, χάριν J.*AJ*19.1.10; εὐεργεσίαν ἔς τινα D.C.48.30. **-τρίβω** [ῑ], *crush first*, Procop.*Goth.*4.30.

**προκαταυλ-έω**, *soothe beforehand by flute-playing*, Cels.ap.Orig.*Cels.*3.16. **-ησις**, εως, ἡ, *tuning of the flute*, Thphr.*HP*4.11.4.

**προκατα-φέρομαι**, Pass., *fall down* or *sink in first*, Arist.*Pr.*906$^a$32. II. *die first*, Lib.*Or.*40.3. **-φεύγω**, *escape to a place of safety first*, Th.3.78; ἐς τὴν Ναύπακτον Id.2.91; πρὸς τὸ ἱερόν, of suppliants seeking sanctuary, Id.1.134. **-φθείρω**, *destroy first*, τὸν σῖτον Plb.18.20.3. **-φορά**, ἡ, Astrol., name of the sixth τόπος, *Cat.Cod.Astr.*8(4).154. ® **-χέω**, *pour upon first*, f.l. for προσκ- in Gal.13.598 (cf. Paul.Aeg.4.54). **-χράομαι**, *use up beforehand*, τοῖς ἐφοδίοις Plu.*Comp.Dion.Brut.*1, cf. D.H.*Rh.*10.13, Aristid.*Or.*36(48).103: pf., διὰ τὸ προκατακεχρῆσθαι (sc. τὰς ἐκκλησίας), in pass. sense, or (if ταῖς ἐκκλησίαις be supplied) in act. sense, D.19.154. 2. simply, *employ first*, τῷ Καίσαρι ἔς τινα App.*BC*3.51. II. *kill before*, ἑαυτόν D.C.53.23. **-χρίω**, *smear beforehand*, μέλιτι Dsc.1.43, cf. Asclep. ap. Gal.12.411. **-χωρίζω**, *assign before*, Lxx 3*Ma.*2.29. 2. *deposit before*, of deeds, *PTeb.*302.23 (i A.D., Pass.). II. *set down first* (cf. καταχωρίζω III), τὰς λέξεις Apollon.Cit.3. **-ψάω**, *rub first*, σῶμα δι' ὀθονίων Sor.1.49. **-ψύχω** [ῡ], *cool first*, Ptol.*Tetr.*15:—Pass., Procl.*Par.Ptol.*22: pf. part. -εψυγμένος Gal.13.584.

**πρόκατε**, v. πρόκα.

**προκατ-εγγῠάω**, *betroth beforehand*, Tz. ad Lyc.538 (Pass.). **-εισδύνω**, *go in before*, Hero *Spir.Praef.* **-ελίσσω**, *wrap up before use*, δάκεσι προκατειλίχθαι Hp.*Mochl.*38. **-ελπίζω**, *hope beforehand*, περί τινος Plb.14.3.1; ὑπέρ τινος Id.2.4.5. **-επείγω**, *distress first*, J.*BJ*1.19.6. **-εργάζομαι**, *subdue first*, τινα D.C.43.4. 2. *prepare beforehand*, Thphr.*CP*3.20.8, al.; *work up beforehand*, τὸ ψυχικὸν πνεῦμα Gal.*UP*8.10; *do* or *perform beforehand*, χρήσιμον π. ἔργον D.S.30.8:—pf. Pass., Id.4.17; *to be prepared*, J.*AJ*19.1.14, Plu.*Comp.Demetr.Ant.*1: aor. προκατειργάσθην only in pass. sense, ταῖς -ασθείσαις πράξεσι *already performed*, D.S.1.53; -ασθεὶς τῇ μάχῃ *worn out*, *exhausted*, Paus.6.6.5; of food, *digested*, Gal.1.655. **-έρχομαι**, aor. **-κατῆλθον**, *return before*, Hdn.1.10.7, f.l. for -άρχεται in *Corp.Herm.*1.20. **-εσθίω**, *eat up beforehand*, Luc.*Hes.*7. **-εύχομαι**, Med., *pray before* doing a thing, Hld.2.35; π. τῆς τροφῆς J.*BJ*2.8.5. **-έχω**, *hold* or *gain possession of beforehand*, *preoccupy*, τὴν πόλιν Th.4.105; τὸ ἄκρον X.*HG*5.4.59; τὸν διάπλουν Plb.1.61.1; τὰς παρόδους Plu.*Nic.*26; διὰ τὸ προκατεσχῆσθαι φρουρᾷ [τὴν ἄκραν] Plb.8.31.1: simply, *occupy*, ὃν προκατεῖχε τόπον Ael.*Tact.*25.7:—Med., *hold down before oneself*, προκατέσχετο χερσὶ καλύπτρην *h.Cer.*197: metaph. in Pass., *to be prejudiced*, π. εὐνοίᾳ Plb.8.31.3, 27.4.9, cf. 9.31.2; διαβολαῖς Phalar.*Ep.*56. 2. Pass., *to be predetermined*, ὑφ' ἑτέρας αἰτίας Diogenian.Epicur.3.60. II. intr., *to be superior*, ταῖς ἡλικίαις καὶ ταῖς δόξαις Plb.27.15.7; ἀγέλης *to be leaders of* the herd, of bulls, Jul.*Or.*6.200d. **-ηγορέω**, *bring accusations beforehand*, f.l. for προσ- in Th.3.42; περί τινος D.8.23:—Pass., τὰ προκατηγορηθέντα *the accusations so made*, Hyp.*Lyc.*9. II. *to be the first accuser*, Hermog.*Meth.*27. **-ηγορία**, ἡ, *previous accusation*, Th.3.53. **-ηχέω**, *soothe beforehand with sounds*, Cels.ap.Orig.*Cels.*3.16. II. *instruct beforehand*, Hld.9.9. **-ήχησις**, εως, ἡ, *first instruction*, π. ἠθική Simp. *in Cat.*5.29. **-ισχνόομαι**, *to be emaciated already*, Gal.ap.Orib.44.25.24. **-οδύρομαι** [ῡ], *lament beforehand*, τὴν ἐσομένην συμφοράν D.S.37.19. **-οικέω**, *inhabit before*, J.*AJ*1.6.1. **-ονομάζω**, *name beforehand*, Id.*Ap.*1.14. **-οπτάομαι**, *become adust first*, of humours, Gal.15.86. **-οπτεύω**, *observe first*, Hld.7.6:—Pass., Vett.Val.125.22. II. *learn from scouts*, Hld.9.1. **-ορθόω**, *to be successful before*, προκατορθώσας τι D.C.48.42. **-ορρωδέω**, *fear* or *dread beforehand*, Onos.4.2. **-ορυγμός**, ὁ, = *propagatio*, *Gloss.* **-όψομαι**, v. προκαθοράω.

**πρόκαυσις**, εως, ἡ, *heating*, *stoking* of a bath-furnace, *CPHerm.*66.7 (iii A.D.), *IG*14.455 (Catana, v A.D.).

**προκαυτεύω**, *sacrifice as a preliminary burnt-offering*, in Pass., *SIG*1026.12 (Cos, iv/iii B.C.).

**πρόκειμαι**, used as Pass. of προτίθημι, *to be set before one*. ὀνείαθ' ἑτοῖμα προκείμενα the meats *laid* ready, Il.9.91, al.; π. δαίς, δεῖπνον, Hdt.1.211, 5.105; τὰ π. ἀγαθά Id.9.82; ἄρτοι προκείμενοι *shew*-bread, Lxx *Ex.*39.18(36); τράπεζα π. ib.38.9(37.10). 2. *lie exposed*, βρέφω παιδίον προκείμενον Hdt.1.111; of a tuft of wool, S.*Tr.*702; ἄτιμος ὧδε πρόκειμαι, says Ajax of himself, Id.*Aj.*427 (lyr.), cf. E.*Tr.*1179; νομίζετε τὸν παῖδα τουτονὶ ἱκετηρίαν ὑμῖν προκεῖσθαι D.43.83; esp. *lie dead*, A.*Th.*964 (lyr.), S.*Aj.*1059; προκείμενον νέκυν *laid out* for burial, E.*Alc.*1012, cf. S.*Ant.*1101, Ar.*Ec.*537, *Av.*474, Antipho 6.34, Luc.*Luct.*12; opp. ἐξενεχθείς, Lys.*Fr.*23 (also, *to be buried first*, *IGRom.*4.735 (Eumenia), *MAMA*4.357 (ibid., iii A.D.)): metaph., πρὸς ὕβριν π. *to be exposed* to .., D.S.33.15 (dub.l.). 3. *to be set before* competitors, as the prize of a contest, τοῖσι..προὔκειτο μέγας τρίπος Hes.*Sc.*312: hence, b. metaph., *to be set before* one, *proposed*, γνῶμαι τρεῖς προεκέατο three opinions *were set forth*, Hdt.3.83, cf. 7.16.α'; τοσούτων πέρι σκέψις πρόκειτα Pl.*R.*533e, cf. *Phdr.*237c; π. τῷ συμβουλεύοντι σκοπὸς τὸ συμφέρον *is proposed* as a mark, Arist.*Rh.*1362$^a$17; ἡ προκειμένη ξυμμαχία the alliance *which naturally offers*, Th.1.35; freq. of contests, πόνος τε καὶ ἀγὼν ἔσχατος ψυχῇ π. Pl.*Phdr.*247b, cf. *La.*182a; καταγέλαστον.., ὃ πάλαι πρόκειται, τοῦτο πάλιν προτιθέναι Id.*Euthd.*279d; *to be extant*, προοίμια π. Id.*Lg.*722e; freq. in part., ὁ προκείμενος ἄεθλος the task *set*, Hdt.1.126, 4.10, cf. A.*Pr.*259, 755; ἀγῶνος μεγίστου π. Hdt.9.60; ἆθλα π. Lys.1.47, X.*Cyr.*2.3.2, etc.; τὸν π. πόνον E.*Alc.*1149; ἔχειν ἔργον π. Pl.*R.*407a; τὰ προκείμενα, opp. μέλλοντα, S.*Ant.*1334, cf. E.*Rh.*984; so ξυμφορᾶς προκειμένης Id.*Alc.*551; τὸ π. ἐν τῷ λόγῳ or τὸ π., *the question* under discussion, Pl.*Grg.*457d, *La.*184c, etc.; τὸ π. πρῆγμα the matter *in hand*, Hdt.1.207: impers., περὶ σωτηρίας προκειμένου *when the question is* concerning safety, Ar.*Ec.*401; πρόκειται ἡμῖν ζητεῖν Luc.*Par.*54, cf. D.H.*Rh.*7.5. 4. *to be set forth*, *settled*, *prescribed*, *appointed*, ἔργων ὧν νόμοι πρόκεινται S.*OT*865 (lyr.); π. σημήϊα Hdt.2.38; αἱ προκείμεναι ἡμέραι the *prescribed* days, ib.87; ὀγδώκοντα ἔτεα ζόης πλήρωμα ἀνδρὶ προκεῖσθαι Id.3.22; ἀναγκαίη π. Id.1.11; τὸ θανεῖν..πᾶσι πρόκειται prob. in *IG*12(1).146 (Rhodes); of laws, νόμους ὑπερβαίνουσα τοὺς π. S.*Ant.*481; of punishments, στέρεσθαι κρατὸς ἦν προκείμενον A.*Pers.*371; φόνον π. δημόλευστον S.*Ant.*36; πολλῶν [ἁμαρτημάτων] θανάτου ζημίαι π. Th.3.45. 5. *to be first stated*, οὐ πρόκειται τοῦ λόγου τὸ τί ἐστιν Arist.*Top.*142$^b$24. II. *lie before*, *lie in front of*, c. gen., Αἴγυπτος προκειμένη τῆς ἐχομένης γῆς *projecting further than*, Hdt.2.12, cf. 4.99; ᾗ (ᾧ codd.) προὔκειτο μαστῶν περονίς where *was set* a brooch *before* her breasts, S.*Tr.*925; πρὸ τῶν ἀνθρώπων π. τὰ παραφράγματα Pl.*R.*514b; Ἐφέσου τεὰ τόξα πρόκειται Call.*Dian.*258; οἱ προκείμενοι τῶν στοῶν πύργοι Plb.1.48.2: abs., of a cape, island, etc., ἐν τῇ θαλάττῃ π. χωρίον X.*An.*6.4.3; τὰ προκείμενα τῆς χώρας ὄρη Id.*Mem.*3.5.27; παρὰ ἤπειρον νῆσος π. Id.*Ath.*2.13, etc. 2. *bulge*, *project*, ἡ γαστὴρ πρόκειται Hp.*Mul.*1.3. III. *precede*, γράμμα π. an *initial* letter, *AP*11.426; ἐν τοῖς π. in the *preceding pages*, A.D.*Synt.*138.4; ὡς πρόκειται ib.32.17, freq. in Pap., *POxy.*271.15 (i A.D.), etc.; προκείμενον a *preceding* word, A.D.*Pron.*39.25, al.; χρόνος ὁ προκείμενος date *as above*, *PTeb.*397.34 (ii A.D.); τοῦ π. ἔτους in the *aforesaid* year, *PAmh.*50.11 (ii B.C.); ἡ π. βοτάνη *above-mentioned*, *PMag.Par.*1.779, cf. Gal.12.455 (but οἱ π. θεοί *represented* on this monument, *OGI*663.2 (Egypt, i A.D.)). 2. τὸ π. αὐτοῦ μόριον *from which it is derived* (ὧς from ὅς), A.D.*Adv.*171.8.

**προκέλευθος**, ον, *conducting*, ἡμέρα dub. l. in Stratt. 36; ἐμεῖο Mosch.2.151; χρεμέτισμα γάμου π. *AP*5.244 (Maced.); λαμπάδες *Epigr.Gr.*418.7 (Cyrene): abs., of persons, Nonn.*D.*11.419.

**προκελευσματικός** (sc. πούς), ὁ, *proceleusmatic*, a foot consisting of four short syllables, Heph.3.3 (-κελευμ- cod. Ambr.); π. ἁπλοῦς

(⏑⏑), διπλοῦς (⏑⏑⏑⏑), Aristid. Quint.1.15 : -κόν (with or without μέτρον), τό, Heph.8.1, D.L.6.79 ; π. ῥυθμοί D.H.7.72.

**προκελεύω**, *give orders before*, Wilcken *Chr.*14 iii 16 (I A.D.), dub. sens. in Hsch. s. v. **προκελήδης** (corrupt form).

**προκενεαγγέω**, *fast beforehand*, Hp.*Acut.*25,39.

**προκενόω**, *empty beforehand*, J.*BJ*6.7.2 :—Pass., Luc.*Alex.*13, Hdn.2.7.2. II. Medic., *drain* or *evacuate first*, Ruf.ap.Orib.7.26.7, Aret.*CD*1.2, Gal.10.798.

**προκεντ-έω**, *prick first*, [δέρμα] Archig.ap.Gal.12.408. **-ημα**, ατος, τό, *thing pricked* or *traced out beforehand*, *design*, *pattern*, S.E.*M.*7.107 (pl.), Nicom.*Ar.*1.4.

**προκενωτέον**, *one must drain*, *evacuate first*, σῶμα Gal.15.517.

⊛ **προκέφᾰλος**, ον, *with a sugar-loaf head*, *PGrenf.*1.33.8 (ii B.C.), Sch.Ar.*Av.*282. II. of verses, *with a syllable prefixed* (as Il.5.349), Ps.-Plu.*Metr.*2.

**προκηδεύω**, *bury before* oneself, τινα *CIG*3891 (Eumenia) :—Pass., *to be buried before*, ib.3902*f* (ibid.), 3113 (Teos).

**προκήδομαι**, *take care of*, *take thought for*, τινος A.*Pr.*629, S.*Ant.*741, *Tr.*966 (lyr.); in later Prose, ἑαυτοῦ prob. in Phld.*Rh.*2.157 S., cf. J.*AJ*13.16.6.

**προκηραίνω**, *to be anxious for*, τινος S.*Tr.*29.

⊛ **προκήρ-υγμα**, ατος, τό, *previous announcement*, τὸ κομμάτιόν ἐστι π. τῆς παραβάσεως Sch.Ar.*V.*1003. **-ῡκεύομαι**, *have proclaimed by herald*, *give public notice*, Is.*Fr.*162. 2. *negotiate by herald*, περὶ σπονδῶν And.3.3 ; πρός τινας Aeschin.2.172. **-υξις**, εως, ἡ, *proclamation by herald*, Thphr.*Fr.*97.2 (pl.), Wilcken *Chr.*41 iii 37 (iii A.D.). **-ύσσω**, Att. **-ττω**, *proclaim by herald*, *proclaim publicly*, S.*Ant.*461, Is.6.37, etc. : c. inf., π. ὠνεῖσθαι τὸν βουλόμενον Arist.*Oec.*1350$^{a}$20 ; π. οἱ ἔφοροι κείρεσθαι Plu.*Cleom.*9 : c. acc. rei, δρόμον π. S.*El.*684 ; ταῦτα Id.*Ant.*34 ; π. στεφάνους τινί Plb.5.60.3 ; π. ἀγοράν Ael.*VH*4.1 ; *advertise for sale*, κατ' ἀγορὰν τὰ ὤνια Poll.8.103 (v.l.) ; *put up to auction*, γῆν *PEleph.*23.15 (iii B.C.) :—Pass., *POxy.*2112.12 (ii A.D.).

**προκῐθ-άρισμα** [ᾰρ], ατος, τό, *prelude on the lyre*, Hsch. s. v. προαύλια. **-ώνιον** (προκιόνιον cod.), τό, = πρόρινον, Id.

**προκινδῡνεύω**, pf. -κεκινδύνευκα *IG*9(2).531.5 (Larissa) :—*run risk before* others, *brave the first danger*, *bear the brunt of battle*, Th.7.56, D.18.208 ; π. στρατευόμενοι Id.2.24 : c. gen., π. τοῦ πλήθους *brave danger for* the people, And.4.1, cf. X.*Hier.*10.8 ; π. τῷ βαρβάρῳ (sc. τῆς Ἑλλάδος) *braved* him *for* Greece (or, *first of all*), Th.1.73 ; π. ὑπέρ τινος X.*An.*7.3.31, Hyp.*Dem.Fr.*3 ; ὑπὲρ τῆς Ἑλλάδος Isoc.4.75 ; ὑπὲρ τῆς ἐλευθερίας Lys.18.27 ; περὶ τῆς ἐλευθερίας Plb.9.38.4 : c. dat. modi, π. τοῖς μεγίστοις ἀγῶσιν Plu.*Pel.*19 ; π. τοῖς Ἴβηρσι *open the engagement* with them, Plb.3.113.9.

**προκῑν-έω**, *move forward*, τὸ στῖφος X.*Cyr.*1.4.21 ; *urge on*, ἵππον Id.*Eq.*9.3 :—Pass., *come on*, *advance*, Id.*Cyr.*1.4.23 ; *dance before* the eyes, of specks, Hp.*Loc.Hom.*3. II. *excite* or *begin before*, τὴν μάχην D.S.17.19 (nisi leg. προκρίνειν). 2. *excite* or *arouse before*, τὴν τοῦ νέου ψυχήν Plu.2.36d ; τὴν πόλιν J.*BJ*4.4.7. **-ησία**, ἡ, *prior excitement*, Phld.*Ir.* p.77 W.

**προκιόνιον**, v. προκιθώνιον.

**προκῑσηρίζω**, (κίσηρις) *rub with pumice-stone first*, *PLeid.X.*89 B. (Pass., -κεισ- Pap.).

**προκιχράω**, contr. **-χρῶ**, = *praecommodo*, *Gloss.* ; cf. προχράω.

**προκλαίω**, Att. **-κλάω**, *weep beforehand* or *openly*, S.*Tr.*963 (lyr.). II. trans., *lament beforehand*, [τὸν νεκρόν] Hdt.5.8, cf. E.*Alc.*526, *Ph.*1520 (Pap., τοῖσδε (i.e. π. in signf. 1) codd.).

**πρόκλαστος**, ον, *broken off*, of verses apparently defective in metre, Eust.1647.29.

**προκλέπτομαι**, Pass., *to be deceived before*, Sch.S.*Ant.*493.

**προκληδί**, Adv. *by challenge*, Theodos. Gr. pp.74,78 Göttling, Suid. (v.l. -ητί, sine interpr.).

**προκληδονίζομαι**, *deem a favourable omen*, *draw good augury from*, J.*BJ*3.1.3.

⊛ **πρό-κληροι**, οἱ, dub. sens. in *Rev.Ét.Gr.*19.131 (Aphrodisias). **-κληρονομέω**, *inherit before the time*, πλείω τῆς ἰσομοιρίας Ph.2.291. **-κληρόω**, *draw lots first*, Aen.Tact.3.6 (Pass.).

⊛ **προ-κλησία**, ἡ, perh. = προθεσμία, *Docum.Ant.dell' Africa Italiana* 1.86 (Cyrene, iv B.C.). **-κλησις**, εως, Ion. ιος, ἡ, *calling forth*, *challenge*, μουνομαχίη ἐκ προκλήσιος Hdt.5.1, cf. 9.75 ; π. ἔφυγε Plu.*Marc.*2. 2. *sounding of the advance*, opp. ἀνάκλησις, προκλήσεις σάλπιγγος J.*BJ*2.20.7. II. *invitation*, *offer*, *proposal*, τὴν π. ἡμῶν οὐκ ἐδέχεσθε Th.3.64, cf. Arist.*Pol.*1292$^{a}$29, etc. ; π. ποιησάμενοι D.H.7.39 ; προτιθέναι App.*BC*1.4. III. as law-term, *formal challenge* or *wager*, offered by either party to his opponent, for the purpose of bringing disputed points to issue, such as *a challenge* to the opponent to let his slaves be tortured to give evidence against him, or *an offer* of one's own slaves to be tortured, Lys.4.15, D.37.40 ; *challenge* or *offer* to take an oath with respect to the matter at issue, Arist.*Rh.*1377$^{a}$20 ; π. προκαλεῖσθαι to make *such a challenge*, D.59.124 : c. dupl. acc., προκαλοῦνται πρόκλησιν ἡμᾶς ὡς οὐ δεξομένους Id.37.12 ; οὐ δέξεσθαι τὴν π. Id.40.10 ; φεύγειν to decline it, Antipho 6.27 ; μαρτυρεῖν to appeal to it, D.45.15. IV. *titillation*, *stimulation*, Aret.*CA*1.2, al. **-κλητέον**, *one must stimulate*, [ἱδρῶτας] Herod.Med. in *Rh.Mus.*58.85. **-κλητής**, οῦ, ὁ, = *provocator*, *Gloss.* (pl.). **-κλητικός**, ή, όν, *calling forth*, *challenging*, τὸ μέλος π., of the partridge, Ael.*NA*4.16 ; τῇ φωνῇ προκλητικὸν ἐπαλαλάζων Plu.*Marc.*7 : c. gen., π. τοῦ μέλλοντος κεφαλαίου ἐπιχείρημα Hermog.*Inv.*3.13 (also in Comp., ibid.) ; *provocative of*, *stimulating*, οὔρων Dsc.1.115.4, cf. Sor.2.41, Gal.6.624, al. **-κλητος**, ον, *called forth* : *alert*, Hsch.

**προκλίνω** [ῑ], *lean forward*, σῶμα ἐς χέρα φιλίαν S.*OC*201 (lyr.).

**προκλίτης** [ῐ], ου, ὁ, *one who sits in the first place*, Poll.6.12.

**προκλύζω**, *wash out beforehand*, in Pass., Dsc.1.30. II. Medic., *purge beforehand by a clyster*, Id.*Eup.*1.231, Alex.Trall.9.3 (nisi leg. προεγ-).

**πρό-κλῠτος**, ον, (κλύω) *heard formerly*, *of olden time*, ἔπεα Il.20.204. **-κλύω**, *hear beforehand*, interpol. in A.*Ag.*251 (lyr.).

**προκνήμ-ιον**, τό, *inner bone of the leg*, *tibia*, Poll.2.190. **-ίς**, ῖδος, ἡ, *covering for the leg*, Plb.6.23.8, Ascl.*Tact.*1.2, Ael.*Tact.*2.8, Polyaen.6.4.3.

**προκνίς** (or **πρόκνις**), ίδος, ἡ, a sort of *dried fig*, Pamphil.ap.Ath.14.653b, Phot., Eust.1688.30 ; written **πρόκρις** in Poll.6.81.

**προκοθηλῠμᾰνής**, ές, (πρόξ, θηλυμανής) *mad after the female like a* πρόξ, Cerc.5.24.

**προκοιλαίνω**, *hollow out first*, Sor.2.59.

**προκοίλιος**, ον, = *ventrosus*, *Gloss.* : of a verse, *having a syllable too many in the middle*, Ps.-Plu.*Metr.*2 ; π. πάθος Eust.12.34, 52.8.

**πρόκοιλος**, ον, = foreg., *Gloss.*

**προκοιμάομαι**, *go to sleep before*, οἱ προκεκοιμημένοι *those who have died already*, Antioch.Astr. in *Cat.Cod.Astr.*8(3).110.

**προκοιτ-έω**, *keep guard before* a place, J.*BJ*4.5.1, D.C.64.7 : also π. τινός Id.54.15. **-ία**, ἡ, *watch kept before* a place, Id.67.15 : pl., Plb.2.5.6, 6.35.5. **-ος**, ὁ, (κοίτη) *one who keeps watch before* a place : pl., *pickets*, Id.20.11.5 : Adj., τοὺς π. τῆς φρουρᾶς κύνας Plu.2.325c. II. *chamberlain*, D.C.67.15 (but prob. f.l. for πρόκριτος (q.v.) in 78.14). **-ών**, ῶνος, ὁ, *ante-chamber*, Plin.*Ep.*2.17.23 : condemned by Phryn.227, cf. Poll.10.43.

**προκολάζω**, *chastise beforehand*, τῷ λόγῳ Arist.*Rh.*1380$^{b}$19.

**προκολᾰκεύω**, *flatter beforehand*, Pl.*R.*494c, Plu.2.65e.

**προκόλπιον**, τό, (κόλπος) *part of a robe which falls over the breast*, Thphr.*Char.*6.8, 22.7, Luc.*Pisc.*7, etc. ; θεὸς οὐδεὶς εἰς τὸ π. φέρει ἀργύριον Men.201, cf. *Epit.*165. II. *entrance into a gulf*, Ach.Tat.1.1 : dub. sens. in *Sammelb.*676.6 (i A.D.).

**πρόκολπος**, ον, *distended*, of a viper's belly, in Comp., Gal.14.265, Aët.13.23.

**προκομία**, ἡ, = προκόμιον, Ael.*NA*16.10.

⊛ **προκομ-ῐδή**, ἡ, *prolatio*, *Gloss.* ⊛ **-ίζω**, *bring forward*, *produce*, J.*AJ*1.16.2, Luc.*DMeretr.*4.5, Longus 3.20 :—Pass., Gal.18(1).253 ; of a document, *PMasp.*151.55 (vi A.D.), etc. II. Pass., *to be carried on before*, esp. to a place of safety, Hdt.4.122, Luc.*Nav.*19 ; *to be borne in procession*, D.S.31.8.

⊛ **προκόμιον**, τό, (κόμη) *forelock* of a horse, X.*Eq.*5.6 ; τὸ π. [τοῦ βονάσου] *frontal tuft*, Arist.*HA*630$^{a}$35 ; of human beings, τὰ π. ψιλοῦν Str.3.4.17. II. *false hair*, *false front*, Ar.*Fr.*320.2, Arist.*Oec.*1348$^{a}$30, *IG*11(2).203*B*41 (iii B.C.) ; π. πρόσθετον Poll.2.30 ; π. περίθετα Ath.12.523a.

**προκόμισμα**, f.l. for προκόσμημα, *EM*363.28.

**πρόκομμα**, ατος, τό, *progress*, dub. in *Gloss.*

**προκόνδῠλοι**, οἱ, *proximal* or *metacarpo-phalangeal joints* of the fingers, Ruf.*Onom.*84 : also **-κόνδυλα**, τά, Hsch.

**πρόκοος**· πονηρός, Hsch.

⊛ **προ-κοπή**, ἡ, *progress on a journey*, Plu.2.76d. 2. generally, *progress*, *advance*, τὴν οἴησιν ἔλεγε προκοπῆς ἐγκοπήν that opinion-forming was the stoppage of *progress*, Bion ap.D.L.4.50 ; π. σχεῖν, ποιεῖσθαι, λαμβάνειν, Plb.2.37.10, 2.13.1, 8.15.6 ; ἡ ἐπὶ τὸ βέλτιον π. Id.1.12.7 ; opp. ἡ ἐπὶ τὸ χεῖρον π. J.*AJ*4.4.1 ; freq. of *moral progress*, *Stoic.*3.31, al. ; παλίντροπος π. *progress* in a contrary direction, Plb.5.16.9 ; ἐν παιδείᾳ π. Lxx *Si.*51.17 ; *proficiency*, ἐν τοῖς λόγοις Phld.*Piet.*107 ; ἐν φιλοσοφίᾳ D.S.16.6, cf. Cic.*Att.*15.16 ; π. τοῦ εὐαγγελίου *Ep.Phil.*1.12 ; τὸ ἐπιστρέφειν προϊέναι ἐστί, π. γάρ τις, ἀλλ' οὐχὶ ἀπὸ τοῦ αἰτίου Dam.*Pr.*77 ; *improvement* in health, Herod.Med.ap.Orib.10.8.17 : pl., προκοπὰς λαμβάνειν Plb.10.47.12, cf. Phld.*Rh.*2.54 S., Ph.1.83, al., J.*BJ*2.2.5, Plu.2.75b, Luc.*Alex.*22 ; ἐν προκοπαῖς *Epigr.Gr.*321.6, *Arch.Pap.*1.220 (Egypt), cf. *IG*14.1976 (Rome) ; ἐν μείζοσι προκοπαῖς *PRyl.*233.16 (ii A.D.). b. *success*, *prosperity*, δόξα καὶ π. παρά τισιν ὑπάρξει Aristeas 242, cf. *OGI*627.2 (Bostra), Heph.Astr.1.1. 3. *military promotion*, J.*BJ*6.2.6. 4. *process*, κατὰ προκοπήν by *process of time* or *growth*, Sor.1.43. 5. Math., *progression* of numbers, μέχρις ἂν εἰς τετράδα ἡ π. ἔλθῃ *Theol.Ar.*21. **-κοπῐάω**, *labour*, *make effort previously*, *IGRom.*3.739 vi 91 (Rhodiapolis). ⊛ **-κοπος**, v. πρόκωπος. **-κόπτας**, α, ὁ, = Προκρούστης, B.17.28. **-κοπτικός**, ή, όν, *advantageous*, Vett.Val.178.2, al.

⊛ **προκόπτω**, *cut* one's way *forward*, only metaph., π. διὰ τῆς λεωφόρου *advance* by the high-road, Anon.ap.Suid. : c. acc. cogn., τὴν ὁδὸν προκεκοφέναι J.*AJ*2.6.7 : without ὁδόν, ἐπὶ πολὺ προκεκοφότες ib.2.16.3 ; π. τριάκοντα σταδίους Chio *Ep.*4.2 :—Pass. in Hdt., *advance*, *prosper*, ἀνωτέρω οὐδὲν τῶν πρηγμάτων προκοπτομένων 1.190 ; ἐς τὸ πρόσω οὐδὲν προεκόπτετο τῶν πρηγμάτων 3.56. II. with neut. Adjs., προκόψομεν οὐδέν *shall make* no *progress*, *advance* not at all, Alc.35 ; τὰ πολλὰ προκόψασ' *having prepared* most of *the way*, E.*Hipp.*23 ; τί ἂν προκόπτοις ; what *good would you get?* Id.*Alc.*1079 ; οὐδὲν προὔκοπτον εἰς . . *they made* no *progress* towards . ., X.*HG*7.1.6 ; π. οὐδὲν ἐς πρόσθεν E.*Hec.*961 ; ἐν παιδείᾳ προκεκοφότες D.S.17.69 ; π. ἐν Ἰουδαϊσμῷ *Ep.Gal.*1.14 ; ἐν τοῖς μαθήμασι Luc.*Herm.*63 : c. dat. modi, τοῖς πλούτοις -κεκοφότες D.S.34/5.2.26 ; σοφίᾳ καὶ ἡλικίᾳ *Ev.Luc.*2.52. 2. c. gen. rei, τοῦ ναυτικοῦ μέγα μέρος προκόψαντες *having made improvements* in their navy to a great extent, Th.7.56 ; ἡμῶν προκοπτόντων τῆς ἀρχῆς ἐκείνοις *since* we *promote the increase of* their empire, Id.4.60; ἐπὶ πλεῖον π. ἀσεβείας *having advanced* further *in* impiety, 2*Ep.Ti.*2.16: abs., ἐπὶ τοσοῦτο π. Plb.31.23.2; ἐπὶ πλεῖον π. D.S.14.98. **3.** esp. in Philos., of moral and intellectual progress, Zeno *Stoic.*1.56, Chrysipp.ib.2.337, Plu.2.543e, Arr.*Epict.*1.4.1, 3.2.5, etc.; κατὰ φιλοσοφίαν π. Phld.*Mort.*17; ὁ λόγος π. S.E.*P.*2.240; προκοπτούσης τῆς θεραπείας if the treatment *succeeds*, Asclep.ap.Gal.12.413, cf. Herod.Med. in *Rh.Mus.*58.103; εἴωθε προκόπτειν ἡ.. ἀγωγή the treatment is usually *successful*, Heliod.ap.Orib.46.9.1; -κεκοφυίας τῆς νόσου as the disease *improves*, Herod.Med.ap.Aët.9.13. **b.** of Time, προκοπτούσης ὁδοῦ *as* the journey *advanced*, Babr.111.4; ἡ νὺξ προέκοψεν *is far spent*, *Ep.Rom.*13.12, cf. J.*BJ*4.4.6; *to be advanced* in years, τῇ ἡλικίᾳ *SIG*708.18 (Istropolis, ii B.C.); ὁ μὲν -κέκοφεν, ὁ δὲ νέος ἐστίν Herm. *in Phdr.p.*60 A.

**πρόκορμος**, Cret. for *πρόκοσμος, *president of* κόσμοι, *GDI*5009[b]3 (Gortyn).

**προκόσμημα**, ατος, τό, *ornament in front, showy ornament*, Longin. 43.3, D.L.*Prooem.*7; π. κακίας Id.6.72: pl., of a ceiling, J.*BJ*5.4.4.

**προκοσμητεύω**, *to be a deputy*-κοσμητής, *CPR*228.1 (iii A.D.).

**προκόσμ-ιον**, τό, *frontlet* of a horse (nisi leg. προκόμιον), Plu.2.970d. **-ιος**, ον, *existing before the world*, δυνάμεις Jul.*Or.*4.144d, 145c.

**προκόττα**, ἡ, Dor. = προκόμιον, Poll.2.29, Hsch., Phot. (-κόπα cod.). **προκοττίς**· ἡ χαίτη, Hsch. (-κοπίς cod.).

**πρόκουρος**, ον, *shorn in front*, S.*Eurypyl.Oxy.*2081(*b*)*Fr.*3.

**πρόκοψις**, εως, ἡ, = προκοπή, Sapph.*Oxy.*1787*Fr.*1.9. **II.** *outbreak, onset* of an epileptic seizure, Herod.Med. in *Rh.Mus.*58.77 (s.v.l.).

**πρόκρᾱνος**, ον, = προκέφαλος 1, Anatol. in *Cat.Cod.Astr.*8(3).188.

**προκρᾰτέω**, *seize beforehand*, τὰς γεφύρας D.C.40.35.

**προκρεμαννύω**, *hang in front*, σάκκους prob. for προσ- in Aen.Tact. 32.3:—Pass. προκρέμαμαι, *hang forward*, Arist.*Phgn.*811[b]14; part. -κρεμώμενος ib.[a]25.

**πρόκρημνος**, ον, *overhanging, beetling*, ἄκρα LXX 4 *Ma.*7.5.

**πρό-κρῐμα**, ατος, τό, *prejudgement*, 1*Ep.Ti.*5.21, Anon.ap.Suid., Greg.Cor. in Rh.7.1123 W. **2.** = *praejudicium*, *IG*5(1).21 ii 7 (Sparta, ii A.D.), Mitteis *Chr.*88 ii 30 (ii A.D.), *PFlor.*68.13 (ii A.D.), Cod.Just.10.11.8.5. **-κρῐματίζω**, *praerogo*, *Gloss.*:—Pass., *to be punished*, Greg.Cor. in Rh.7.1123 W. ® **-κρίνω** [ῑ], *choose before others, prefer, select*, Th.4.80; πρῶτον τῶν ἀγαθῶν αὐτὸ προκρίνοντες Pl.*Lg.*870b, etc.; προκρίνας οἵπερ ἀλκιμώτατοι E.*Ph.*743, cf. 746, *Hel.*47; π. τινὰς ἐκ πάντων Hdt.1.70:—Med., τούτους ἐκ τῶν προκρίτων προκρινάμενος Pl.*R.*537d:—Pass., *to be preferred before others*, ταῦτα ἦν τὰ προκεκριμένα [γένεα] the *most eminent*, Hdt.1.56, cf. 9.26; εἴ τις δ' ὑμῶν κάλλει προκριθῇ Cratin.28; προκριθῆναι ὑφ' ὑμῶν ἄρχοντα X.*An.*6.1.26, cf. *HG*6.5.34; ὁ προκριθεὶς καὶ ὁ προκρίνων Pl.*Lg.*765e; ἐκ τῶν εἰκοσιετῶν οἱ προκριθέντες Id.*R.*537b; ἄλλους ἀνθ' ἡμῶν προκριθῆναι Isoc.*Ep.*9.17: folld. by inf., τοῦτο προκέκριται κάλλιστον εἶναι X.*Cyr.*2.3.8, cf. *Ap.*21. **b.** *make a preliminary selection* of candidates for office, Arist.*Ath.*8.1, al.:—Pass., προεκρίθην κληροῦσθαι D.57.46, cf. 47, 62. **2.** c. gen., *prefer before*, ῥώμην τῆς σοφίης Xenoph.2.14; τὸ ἐπιεικὲς τοῦ δικαίου Gorg.*Fr.*6; οὓς αὐτοὶ ἑαυτῶν ἐν ταῖς ἀρχαῖς προκρίνουσιν Pl.*Ap.*35b:—Pass., τῶν ἄλλων προκεκρίσθαι Hdt.2.121.ζ; προκρίνονται παντὸς οὑτινοσοῦν οἱ νόμοι Wilcken *Chr.*27.5 (ii A.D.). **II.** *judge beforehand, distinguish*, βαρὺ καὶ κοῦφον ἀφᾷ.. π. Ti.Locr.100d: c. acc. et inf., *judge, decide beforehand that*.., X.*Ap.*15, Isoc.4.4, 11.11, etc.; π. μάχην δι' ἱππέων *decide* the battle by the horse *before* the foot comes up, prob. (for προκινεῖν) in D.S.17.19. **-κρις**, v. προκνίς. **-κρῐσις**, εως, ἡ, *preference, selection*, S.E.*P.*2.45, al.; ἐκ προκρίσεως (προκρίνω 1.1b) Pl.*Plt.*298e. **-κρῐτέος**, α, ον, *to be preferred*, Xenocr.ap.Orib.2.58.66, A.D.*Pron.*108.16, *Gloss.* **II.** προκριτέον *one must prefer*, τὰ πόλεως Ap.Ty.*Ep.*11, cf. Dsc.5.108, Plu.*Nob.*9, etc. **-κρῐτής**, οῦ, ὁ, *one who selects*, *EM* 435.43. **-κρῐτικός**, ή, όν, *of* or *for preference*: προκριτικόν, τό, *ground* or *cause for preference*, Ap.Ty.*Ep.*11. **II.** *heralding a crisis* in disease, παροξυσμός Aët.5.23. **III.** f.l. for Κρητικός, Plu.2.1141a. **-κρῐτος**, ον, *chosen before others, select*, Pl.*R.*537d, *Lg.*945b: esp. of a *preliminary* list of *selected* candidates, κληρωτοὶ ἐκ προκρίτων Arist.*Pol.*1298[b]9, cf. *Ath.*8.1, Decr.ib.30.2; π... *chosen rather than*.., *AP*5.257 (Paul. Sil.). **II.** at Rome, π., = *princeps*, D.C.57.8; π. τῆς γερουσίας, = *princeps senatus*, Id.53.1, cf. 46.20; π. τῆς νεότητος, = *princeps juventutis*, Id.78.17 (also π. τῆς ἱππάδος Id. 71.35); π. (sc. τῶν γραμματοφόρων), = *princeps peregrinorum*, prob. in Id.78.14 (πρόκοιτος codd.).

**πρόκροον**, v. προκρούω 1.2.

**πρόκροσσοι**, αι, α, or οι, α, *ranged in rows* or *ranks*, of ships on a narrow beach, Il.14.35; πρόκροσσαι ὅρμεον τὸ ἐς πόντον καὶ ἐπὶ ὀκτὼ νέας Hdt.7.188; πέριξ αὐτὸ (sc. τὸ χαλκήϊον) γρυπῶν κεφαλαὶ πρόκροσσοί εἰσι Id.4.152; συνδέσεις οὐ περιφερεῖς, ἀλλὰ πρόκροσσαι not round, but *ranged in ranks*, Democr.ap.Thphr.*Sens.*79, cf. Opp.*H.*4.606: metaph., πρόκροσσοι φερόμενοι ἐπὶ τὸν κίνδυνον rushing *in serried ranks* into danger, Agathocl.4. **II.** later in sg., *fringed*, π. περίβλημα Poll.7.52.

**πρό-κρουμα**, ατος, τό, *prelude*, Sch.Pl.*Tht.*176a. **-κρουσις**, εως, ἡ, name of a musical phrase, Anon.Bellerm.p.20. **-κρούω**, *beat out* and so *stretch*, whence the name of the robber Προκρούστης, who stretched all his captives on the same bed, τῶν ἐλαττόνων τοὺς πόδας προέκρουεν D.S.4.59. **2.** *attack*, Dor. impf. πρώκροον (πρόκροον codd.) Ar.*Lys.*1252. **II.** sens. obsc., Id.*Ec.*1017.

**προκρύπτω**, *conceal beforehand*, J.*AJ*18.3.4 (Pass.).

**προκτάομαι**, in pf. and plpf., *possess beforehand*, προεκέκτηντο Str. 8.3.33.

**προκτενίζω**, *comb* the scalp *before* applying hair-restorer, Gal.12.421.

**πρό-κτησις**, εως, ἡ, *title-deed showing previous ownership*, *Sammelb.*4638.10 (pl.), *POxy.*504.13 (pl., ii A.D.), *CPR*187.6 (ii A.D.). ® **-κτητικός**, ή, όν, *relating to previous ownership*, Mitteis *Chr.*159.10 (i A.D.), *PLips.*4.17 (iii A.D.), etc. **-κτήτρια**, ἡ, fem. of sq., *BGU*619.12 (ii A.D.), *POxy.*78.21 (iii A.D.). **-κτήτωρ**, ορος, ὁ, *previous owner*, ib.1636.24 (iii A.D.).

**προκῠβερνάω**, *guide the steerer from the prow*, Poll.1.98.

**προκῡέω**, *to be pregnant before*, αἱ προκεκυηκυῖαι Sor.1.7.

**προκυκλ-έω**, *roll forth* or *out*, παλάθαν ἐκ πίονος οἴκου *Carm.Pop.*41. ® **-ιος**, ον, *of a* προκυκλίς, θάμνη Herod.6.90. **II.** θεοὶ Π., dub. sens., of certain gods at Erythrae, *SIG*1014.130 (iii B.C.). **III.** Προκύκλιος, ὁ (sc. μήν), name of month at Calydon, *IG*9[2](1).137.40 (ii B.C.). **-ίς**, ίδος, ἡ, *procuress*, Herod.1 tit., Hsch.

**προκῠλινδ-έομαι**, Pass., *roll before* or *at the feet of, prostrate oneself before* another, τοῖς ἱκτίνοις Ar.*Av.*501 (cf. Sch.), Luc.*DDeor.*6.2 (v.l. -όμενον); τινος D.19.338 (nisi leg. προκαλ-); τῶν θείων ἰχνῶν Wilcken *Chr.*6.8 (v A.D.); π. ἡ πέρδιξ τοῦ θηρεύοντος Arist.*HA*613[b]18 (προκυλίεσθαι ap.Antig.*Mir.*39); cf. προκαλινδέομαι. ® **-ομαι**, Pass., *roll forward*, of the sea, Il.14.18. **II.** = foreg., *roll at the feet of*, τινος Arat.188: fut. προκυλίσομαι [ῑ] App.*Ital.*5.4: late pres. **προκῠλίομαι**, D.H.8.39; τῶν ποδῶν Onos.14.3.

**προκύλ-ῑσις** [ῠ], εως, ἡ, *prostration before* another, π. καὶ προσκυνήσεις Pl.*Lg.*887e (pl.), Iamb.*Myst.*1.21 (pl.). **-ισμός**, ὁ, = foreg., D.H.9.33.

**προκῡμία**, ἡ, (κῦμα) *breakwater*, J.*BJ*1.21.6; prob. for προκυμάτια (sic) in Id.*AJ*15.9.6.

**προκῠνέω**, (κύων) of a dog, *give tongue too soon*, Poll.5.65.

**προκῠνηγ-ία**, ἡ, *show preliminary to a venatio*, *IGRom.*3.631 (pl., Xanthus); also -ιον, τό, ib.681 (pl., Patara).

**προκύνητος**, prob. f.l. for προσκ-, *Tab.Defix.* in *Rev.Phil.*1930.249 (Egypt).

**προκύπτω**, *point forwards and downwards*, ἄκρος ὁ ποὺς ἧσσόν τι -κύπτειν ἐθέλει ἐς τοὔμπροσθεν (in dislocations) Hp.*Art.*59. **2.** *stick one's head out, peep out*, ἐκ τοῦ δίφρου D.C.64.6; διά τινων ὀπῶν S.E.*M.*7.350, cf. 364: c. gen., τῆς καλύβης Alciphr.3.30; θυρίδων Babr.116.3. **3.** *peep out, emerge*, ἔξω τείχους Ar.*Av.*496; of things, τιτθίον Id.*Ra.*415; γλῶττα Luc.*Alex.*12; κυνίδιον ἐκ τοῦ ἱματίου π. Id.*Merc.Cond.*34; ἐξ ὠδίνων προὔκυψε τὸ βρέφος Porph.*Gaur.*16.5, cf. S.E.*M.*5.65: metaph., τὸ νοητικὸν π. Lysis ap.Iamb.*VP*17.77; ὅσα π. ἀπὸ τῆς συνηρημένης φύσεως Dam.*Pr.*85; ἐπ' ἄκρων τῶν χειλῶν π. τις λόγος (prob. for ὑπερ-) Aristaenet.2.10. **4.** Medic., *suffer from prolapsus*, of the iris, Gal.12.716; of the omentum, Id.18(1).97. **5.** *flow out*, of water, Porph. *in Cat.*104.21. **II.** *stoop before*, of a hunchback, οὐ προεστάναι τῆς πόλεως, ἀλλὰ προκεκυφέναι Plu.2.633d.

**προκῡρόομαι**, Pass., *to be ratified* or *confirmed before*, ἐν τῷ -κεκυρωμένῳ ψαφίσματι *Supp.Epigr.*3.674 *A* 28 (Rhodes, ii B.C.); διαθήκη -κεκυρωμένη ὑπὸ τοῦ Θεοῦ *Ep.Gal.*3.17:—Med., Anon.*Prog.* in Rh.1.605 W.

**πρόκυρτος**, ον, *convex forwards*, Ruf.*Oss.*30.

**πρόκυψις**, εως, ἡ, *peeping out*: *emergence*, of the new-born infant, Porph.*Gaur.*16.6.

® **Προκύων** [ῠ], κυνός, ὁ, the star *Procyon*, Arat.450, Hipparch.2.2.13, etc.; but of Sirius, Gal.17(1).17. **2.** πρόκυνες, οἱ, *winds which precede the rising of Sirius*, Adam.*Vent.*41. **II.** *spaniel-like flatterer*, '*lap-dog*', Phld.*Rh.*1.242 S., prob. l. for πρόσκυνες in Hippias Erythr. 1: but πικροὶ Καλλιμάχου πρόκυνες, a description of the Grammarians, *snappers and snarlers*, *AP*11.322 (Antiphan.).

**προκωδωνίζω**, *sound, test first*, *PMag.Par.*1.89.

**προκώλῡμα**, ατος, τό, *bulwark against*, τινος Hld.9.17.

**προκώμιον**, τό, *prelude sung by a* κῶμος, Pi.*N.*4.11.

**προκωμογραμμᾰτεύς**, έως, ὁ, *deputy*-κωμογραμματεύς, *PTeb.*793 ii 21 (ii B.C.).

**προκώνια** ἄλφιτα, τά, *groats of fresh* or *unroasted barley*, Hp.*Mul.*2.110: without ἄλφιτα, *IG*2[2].1672.280, Lycurg.*Fr.*83, Ar.Byz.ap. Harp., etc.; but expld. as *groats of wheat and barley*, Anticl.*Fr.*17, as πυροὶ μέλιτι κεχρισμένοι, Did.ap.Harp., as κάχρυς κατηριγμέναι μετ' ἀρωμάτων, Demon 22: written **πρόκωνα**, Poll.6.77:—also πυροὶ **προκωνίαι** Hp.*Nat.Mul.*58.

® **πρόκωπος**, ον, (κώπη) of the sword, *grasped by the hilt, drawn*, A.*Ag.*1651 (troch.), E.*Or.*1477 (lyr.), al. **2.** metaph., *ready*, A.*Ag.*1652 (troch.); ἔχειν π. τὴν δεξιάν Hdn.7.5.4. **3.** *elongated*, Aret.*SD*2.4 (πρόκοποι codd.); of the *os uteri*, *advanced*, Sor.1.34 (Comp., προκοπώτερον cod.).

**προλᾰβή**, ἡ, *hilt*, ξίφους Poll.1.136, 10.144.

**προλᾰβόντως**, Adv. *previously*, Aesop.347 (v.l.).

**προλαγχάνω**, *obtain by lot first*, Ar.*Ec.*1159; *obtain as a perquisite*, *SIG*57.10 (Milet., v B.C.).

**προλάζῠμαι**, *receive beforehand* or *by anticipation*, c. gen. partit., τῆς ἡδονῆς E.*Ion* 1027.

® **προλάκκιον**, τό, *ante-chamber*, Arist.*PA*675[a]13.

**προλᾰλ-έω**, *converse first*, Antyll.ap.Orib.6.9.1; *chatter first*, πολλὰ π., of a book, *AP*12.208 (Strat.). **II.** *state, announce before*, Eust. 1382.24:—Pass., J.*AJ*15.3.8. **-ιά**, ἡ, *discourse*, alternative title of Luc.*Bacch.* and *Herc.*, Sch. ad loc.; good Attic (sine expl.) acc. to Thom.Mag.p.224 R. **-ος**, ον, *chattering*, Ael.*Fr.*22, Man.5.337.

* **προλαμβάνω**, fut. -λήψομαι Isoc.6.16: aor. προὔλαβον:—Pass., v. infr. I. 5:—*take* or *receive before*, τὴν πόλιν Lys.26.9 codd.; τὰ χωρία καὶ λιμένας D.2.9; ἀργύριον π. *receive* money *in advance*, Id.50.14, 35; τὰ ἐφόδια Aeschin.1.172; τρία τάλαντα παρά τινος Id.2.166; ἅπαντα ἡμῶν τὰ χωρία D.3.16, etc.; also π. χάριν E.*Ion*914 (lyr.); μισθὸν τῆς ἀγγελίας *for* the message, Luc.*Merc.Cond.*37; γάλα μετὰ μέλιτος *IG*4²(1).126.15 (Epid., ii A.D.); π. τὴν ἡλικίαν Aeschin.1.162; π. τὴν αὔξησιν *begin* their growth *before*, Thphr.*HP*8.1.4:—Pass., *to be contained in advance*, ἐν τῷ ὄντι ἄρα ζωὴ προείληπται καὶ ὁ νοῦς Procl. *Inst.*103. 2. *take* or *seize beforehand*, Aeschin.3.142; τὴν ἀρχήν A.D.*Synt.*40.24; ὅσα τῆς πόλεως π. D.18.26; τοῦτο π., ὅπως σώσομεν *provide* that.., Id.3.2: c. part., προλαβὼν κατεγνωκότας ὑμᾶς *having first procured* your vote of condemnation, Id.24.77:—Pass., σῶμα προειλημμένον ὑπὸ νόσου *Corp.Herm.*12.3. b. *get* or *take as a start*, προειλήφασι πολὺν χρόνον *have had a* long *start*, *PCair.Zen.*60.5 (iii B.C.); π. τῆς νυκτὸς ὁπόσον ἂν δυναίμην Luc.*Gall.*1. 3. *take in preference*, τι πρό τινος S.*OC*1141. 4. *take away* or *off before*, ἐκ γὰρ οἴκων προὔλαβον μόγις πόδα, μὴ θανεῖν E.*Ion* 1253. 5. *assume in advance*, τὴν ὁλότητα προλαβὼν ἐγέννησεν ἀπ' αὐτῆς τὴν παντότητα Dam.*Pr.*253; προειλήφθω.. δισχιλίων σταδίων τὸ βάθος [εἶναι] Plb.34.6.7. II. *to be beforehand with, anticipate*, 1. c. acc. pers., *get the start of*, τὰς κύνας X.*Cyn.*5.19, v. infr. 3; π. τῷ λόγῳ τινάς D.*Prooem.* 29; βραχὺν χρόνον π. ἡμᾶς, i.e. in dying, Plu.2.117e; π. τῇ ῥιζώσει τοὺς χειμῶνας Thphr.*HP*8.1.3, cf. *CP*3.24.3: c. gen. pers., προλαβών μου ὥστε πρότερος λέγειν D.45.6; ἵνα μὴ -λημφθῶμεν (i.e. by death) Diog.Oen.2. 2. c. acc. rei, π. γόους, μαντεύματα, E.*Hel.*339 (lyr.), *Ion* 407; τὸν καιρόν Plb.9.14.12, cf. Plu.*Cam.*34, etc.; τὸν ὄρθρον Luc.*Am.*15; of mental anticipation, π. ὡς οὕτως ἔχον πρὶν γινόμενον οὕτως ἰδεῖν Arist.*GA*765ᵃ28; τὰ συμβησόμενα ταῖς ἐννοίαις Plb.3.112.7, cf. 3.1.7; τὰ πολλὰ εἰκασίᾳ Luc.*Am.*8; π. ὅτι.. Plu.2.102e, etc. 3. c. gen. spatii, π. τῆς ὁδοῦ *get a start* on the way, Hdt.3.105; πολὺ τῆς ὁδοῦ π. Polyaen.7.29.2 (but just above, π. ὡς πλείστην ὁδὸν τοὺς διώξοντας); π. ῥᾳδίως τῆς φυγῆς Th.4.33; π. τῆς διώξεως *get a start* of the pursuers, D.S.16.94: metaph., μύθου προλαβοῦσα *speaking first*, Philicus in *Stud.Ital.*9.44, cf. 46. b. generally, π. τῶν κηρύκων *anticipate* them, Arist.*Rh.*1408ᵇ24; τοῦ χρόνου π. *precede* in point of time, Id.*Metaph.*1050ᵇ5. 4. c. dat. modi, π. τῷ δρόμῳ *get a start* in running, X.*Cyn.*7.7; τῇ διανοίᾳ Arist.*Fr.*660; τῇ φυγῇ Plu.*Alex.*20, *Cic.*47. 5. c. inf., προέλαβε μυρίσαι *Ev.Marc.* 14.8. 6. *detect*, ἐν παραπτώματι *Ep.Gal.*6.1 (Pass.). 7. *anticipate*, τι τῶν μελλόντων Ph.1.620; τὸ μέλλον τοῖς λογισμοῖς D.C.*Fr.* 54.2. 8. abs., προὔλαβε πολλῷ *was* far *ahead*, Th.7.80, cf. X.*Cyn.* 6.19, D.4.31, Plb.31.15.8; *gain an advantage*, D.37.15. b. *anticipate the event, prejudge*, ἐπειδὰν ἅπαντ' ἀκούσητε κρίνατε, μὴ πρότερον προλαμβάνετε Id.4.14; οἱ νόμοι προλαβόντες ἐπιμέλονται ὅπως.. *by anticipation*, X.*Cyr.*1.2.3; *come before the time*, opp. ὑστερίζειν, Gal. 7.353; of corn-buyers, *buy earlier*, *SIG*976.49 (Samos, ii B.C.):—Med., προλαμβάνου Men.701:—Pass., τὸ προειλημμένον that which is *prejudged*, Hermog.*Stat.*1. c. *precede, go before*, ὁ προλαβὼν βίος his *previous* life, Arg.2 D.22.3; τὰ προλαβόντα *what precedes*, Procop. *Vand.*2.16; ἡ προλαβοῦσα τράπεζα the *preceding* meal, Lib.*Or.*57.24; also τῶν προλαβόντων τὴν μνήμην the memory of *the past*, Procop. Gaz.*Pan.*p.495 B. III. *repeat from the origin*, Isoc.6.16; μικρὸν π. Id.16.24. IV. Philos., *form a preconception* (cf. πρόληψις), *prejudge*, οἷα προειλήφαμεν Phld.*D.*3.13, cf. *Sign.*22:—Med., Id.*D.*1.13:—Pass., Id.*Oec.*p.57 J.

**προλάμπω**, *shine forth*, γυμνῷ τῷ κάλλει Chor.p.164 B.; σοφίᾳ π. Procop.Gaz.*Ep.*128. II. trans., *cause to shine forth*, π. τὸ ἐξ αὐτῶν ἀναγωγὸν φῶς Procl. *in Prm.*p.472 S.; τὰ ἀγαθά Hierocl. *in CA*25 p.477 M. III. *illuminate in front*, metaph., τὰς προόδους τῆς ὑμῶν ἐξουσίας *PMasp.*2.1 (vi A.D.). IV. *outshine*, *Gloss.*

**πρόλᾰχος**, εος, τό, *first lot*, Suid. s. v. λάχος.

* **προλεαίνω**, = προλειόω, Aret.*CA*1.6:—Pass., Orib.*Fr.*83.

**προλέγω**, *pick out, choose, prefer*, Ἀθηναίων προλελεγμένοι Il.13.689; ἐξοχώτατοι προλέγονται Pi.*N.*2.18; ἀριστῆες πασᾶν ἐκ πολίων προλελεγμένοι Theoc.13.18. II. *foretell*, Aeol. aor. part. προλέξαις Alc.*Supp.*22.7; *predict*, of an oracle, Hdt.1.53, 8.136; μέμνησθ' ἁγὼ προλέγω A.*Pr.*1071 (anap.), cf. S.*OT*973; π. πρόρρησιν, of a physician, v.l. in Hp.*Prog.*15; τὰ μέλλοντα Pl.*Euthphr.*3c, cf. D. 19.298. b. *say beforehand*, ταῦτα, ὅτι.. Pl.*R.*337a, cf. *Euthd.* 275e, Hyp.*Lyc.*7; ὡς προλέλεκται as *was said above*, Demetr.*Eloc.* 89; ὁ προλεχθεὶς the *aforesaid*, *PMasp.*32.63 (vi A.D.), al. c. προλεγόμεναι (sc. θέσεις) *first principles*, Cic.*Fam.*9.18.3. d. μακρὰ προλεγομένη a long syllable *placed, uttered first*, Demetr.*Eloc.*39. 2. *state publicly, proclaim*, προὔλεγον τὸ ψήφισμα καθελοῦσι μὴ ἂν γίγνεσθαι πόλεμον Th.1.139; προλεγέτω ἁ ἀρχά *Foed.Delph.Pell.*1 *A* 5, cf. *OGI*437.76 (Pergam., i B.C.): c. acc. et inf., A.*Th.*336 (lyr.), etc.: c. acc., ὁ νόμος πέφυκε προλέγειν ἃ μὴ δεῖ πράττειν Lycurg.4; πολέμους ἀλλήλοις Plb.13.3.5. 3. π. τινὶ ἀπιέναι *order* him to.., X.*An.* 7.7.3, cf. Din.1.71; *caution, warn*, π. τινὶ μὴ φεύγειν E.*Fr.*897.9 (anap.); π. τινί, εἰ θεραπεύσοιτο, ὅτι διαφθαρήσοιτο Antipho 4.2.4; ὡς οὐ.. Plb.5.57.2. 4. *denounce* punishment, π. δεσμόν τινι D. 24.60.

**προλειοτρῑβέω**, = sq., Crito ap.Gal.13.799, 800 (Pass.).

**προλειόω**, *pound* or *grind beforehand*, Gal.12.347, Alex.Trall.9. 3:—Pass., Heras ap.Gal.13.756.

**προλείπω**, *forsake, abandon*, νεκρόν Il.17.275; κτήματα... ἄνδρας τε Od.3.314; σε.. οὐ δύναμαι π. δύστηνον ἐόντα 13.331; φεύγει πηοὺς τε προλιπὼν καὶ πατρίδα γαῖαν 23.120; φιλίην Thgn.1102, cf. 351; οὐκ ἔτλη Σπάρτης ἡγεμόνας προλιπεῖν Simon.ap.Hdt.7.228; πατέρα.. ἐν λυγρῷ γήρᾳ S.*Aj.*507; χώραν π. *abandon* one's post, Th.2.87; τὸ τῶν ξυμμάχων κοινόν Id.1.74; simply, *leave*, Ἀρκτοῦρος π. ῥόον Ὠκεανοῖο Hes.*Op.*566; ἄντρον, θᾶκον, ἕδρας σκοτίους, etc., Pi.*P.*9.30, A.*Pr.*282 (anap.), E.*Alc.*124 (lyr.), etc.; ψυχὴ π. τινά Ar.*Av.*1558 (lyr.). 2. *omit to do* a thing, c. inf., π. τόδε μὴ οὐ ποιεῖν S.*El.* 132 (lyr.); π. τὴν μίσθωσιν *fall into arrears of* rent, *BGU*197.15 (i A.D.). 3. rarely of things, *desert, fail* one, σε μήτις προλέλοιπε Od. 2.279, cf. Ar.*Th.*927; ὅταν αὐτὰ τὸ ἄνθος προλίπῃ Pl.*R.*601b: c. gen., ἐφημερίων π. *Epigr.Gr.*321.4. II. intr., *cease, fail*, φονος.. οὐ προλείπει.. Ἀτρείδαις E.*Or.*817 (lyr.); εἴ τῳ προλίποι ἡ ῥώμη Th.7.75; of persons, *faint, fall into a swoon*, E.*Hec.*438.

**πρόλειψις**, prob. f.l. for πρόληψις, Dam.*Pr.*399.

**πρόλεξις**, εως, ἡ, *foretelling*, Hsch. s. v. πρόρρησιν.

**προλεπτύνω**, *make thin, reduce beforehand*, τοὺς τράγους Arist.*GA* 726ᵃ1, cf. Gal.6.90:—Pass., *to be made* or *become thin*, Pl.*Ti.*66a, Arist. *HA*513ᵃ14; of diseases, *to be reduced, mitigated*, Ruf.*Fr.*72.

**προλεσχηνεύομαι**, *hold conversations with* one *before*, προλελεσχηνευμένων αὐτῷ ἀποστάσιος πέρι Hdt.6.4.

**πρόλεσχος**, ον, *forward in talk, eager to begin*, A.*Supp.*200.

**προλευκαίνω**, *whiten beforehand*, Ps.-Democr.ap.Zos.Alch.p.161 B.

**προλεύσσω**, *see before oneself* or *in front*, S.*Ph.*1360.

**πρόλημμα**, ατος, τό, *something taken beforehand, advantage*, π. ποιεῖν τινι Plb.18.10.3, cf. *BGU*775.12 (iii A.D.). II. *prepossession, prejudice*, compared to a *previous disease* of the soul, *Corp.Herm.*12.3 (pl.).

**προλημμᾰτίζω**, *place before*, in Pass., τῶν ἐπιφερομένων A.D.*Synt.* 7.17: pf. προλελημμάτισμαι ib.19.26.

**προλήνιον**, τό, *vat in front of a wine-press*, Lxx *Is.*5.2.

**προ-ληπτέον**, *one must premise*, v.l. in Hipparch.1.3.2; π. κἀκεῖνο Iamb. *in Nic.*p.56 P.; π. ὅτι.. ib.p.100 P. II. *one must anticipate*, S.E.*M.*7.78. **-ληπτικός**, ή, όν, *anticipative*, κίνησις Plu.2. 427e; σχῆμα Anon.*Fig.*p.158 S.; χρόνος π. τοῦ ἀποτελέσματος Vett. Val.244.31. Adv. -κῶς Sch.Ar.*Av.*35, A.D.*Pron.*10.22: Comp. -ώτερον *prematurely*, ib.47.10. 2. Adv. -κῶς *by way of* πρόληψις I. 1, opp. δοξαστικῶς, Phld.*Oec.*p.14 J. II. Medic., of intermittent fevers, *coming before the time*, Gal.7.359. Adv. -κῶς ib.361. * **-ληψις**, εως, ἡ, *preconception, mental picture* or *scheme* into which experience is fitted, εἰς τὴν π. ἐναρμόττειν Epicur.*Sent.*37, cf. 38, *Ep.*1 p.24 U. (pl.), *Ep.*3 p.60 U. (pl.), *Fr.*255, *Nat.*28.4 (p. 7 V., pl.); also in Stoic. philos., ἔμφυτοι π. Chrysipp.*Stoic.*3.17, al.; κοινὴ π. τῶν ἀνθρώπων Id.ib.2. 286, al., cf. Arr.*Epict.*1.22. 2. in common use, *previous notion* or *conception*, Plb.8.27.1; π. ἔχειν πάντων ἀδύνατον Id.10.43.8, cf. A.D.*Conj.*247.22, al., *PFay.*124.16 (ii A.D., -λημψ-). II. Rhet., *anticipation*, ὑπονοίας Hermog.*Meth.*10: generally, Ph.1.425; ζῴων ἐνίοις σεισμῶν καὶ ὑετῶν ἐμπέφυκε π. Iamb.*Myst.*3.26; ἐν προλήψει γεγονέναι Philum.*Ven.*4.5. III. simply, *taking beforehand*, ὅρκου, μισθοῦ, Hld.4.18, 5.8.

**προλῐβᾰνωτίζω**, *fumigate with incense previously*, *PMag.Berol.*2. 19.

**προλιμνάζω**, *form a marsh before* a river, Paus.8.22.3.

**προλιμνάς**, άδος, ἡ, (λίμνη) *stagnant water left by a river overflowing*, ἐν ταῖς προλιμνάσι τῶν ποταμῶν Arist.*HA*568ᵃ20 (cited by *EM*798.15 (ubi προλίμναις)), cf. Poll.9.49.

**προλῑμοκτονέομαι**, Pass., *to be starved beforehand*, Arist.*HA*595ᵃ 22, al.

**προλῐπαίνω**, *anoint beforehand*, ἐλαίῳ -λιπάνασα τὰς χεῖρας Sor.1. 69, cf. Dsc.*Alex.*1, Orib.8.6.27.

**προλιχνεύομαι**, *lick beforehand*, Sch.Ar.*Nu.*1202.

**προλόβ-ιον**, τό, *lower lobe of the ear*, Poll.2.85, Hsch.; cf. προβόλιον. **-ος**, ὁ, = πρηγορεών, *crop* of birds, e. g. of pigeons, Arist. *HA*508ᵇ28, *PA*674ᵇ31, Lxx *Le.*1.16, al.; π. ὀρνιθώδης, of cuttle-fish, Arist.*PA*679ᵇ9, cf. *HA*524ᵇ10. II. *thyroid cartilage, Adam's apple*, Poll.2.207. **-ώδης**, ες, *like the crop of a bird*, Arist.*PA*678ᵇ 31.

**προλογ-έω**, = προλογίζω I. 1, Poll.2.123. * **-ία**, ἡ, = πρόρρησις, Sch.Philostr.*VA*4.24. **-ια**, τά, = θυσία πρὸ τῶν καρπῶν τελουμένη (Lacon.), Hsch. **-ίζω**, *speak a prologue*, Sch.S.*Ph.*1, etc.; *to be the first speaker*, Arg.S.*OC.* 2. *to be spokesman* in a law-court, *PLond.* 5.1708.27 (vi A.D.). II. Med., *consider before*, Phld.*Mus.*p.74 K., Gal.4.815, Simp. *in Epict.*p.26 D. **-ισμός**, ὁ, *previous consideration*, Hierocl. *in CA*18 p.460 M. **-ος**, ὁ, in early Trag. and Com., *prologue of a play*, i.e. the part before the entry of the chorus, Arist.*Po.* 1452ᵇ19; esp. (as in E.) *monologue containing a narrative of facts introductory to the main action*, Ar.*Ra.*1119, etc., cf. Arist.*Rh.*1414ᵇ 20. 2. *one who speaks the prologue*, Luc.*Pseudol.*4. 3. *introduction* in a speech, Lib.*Or.*1.55 (pl.), al. II. Arith., *antecedent*, in ratios *in which the first number is the largest*, as 5:3, Nicom.*Ar.*1. 19, *Theol.Ar.*13, Dam.*Pr.*374; cf. ὑπόλογος.

**πρόλοιπον**, τό, *arrears* of a debt, *Ostr.*1032, al. (i A.D.), *BGU*48. 15 (ii/iii A.D.).

**προλούω**, *wash beforehand*, Hp.*Mul.*1.68, Archig.ap.Gal.13.235:—Pass., Sor.1.65; *bathe beforehand*, Clearch.16.

* **προλοχ-ίζω**, *lay an ambuscade beforehand*, J.*BJ*1.4.4, 4.9.8 (s.v.l.): c. acc. cogn., π. τινὰς ἐνέδρας Hld.6.13:—Pass., αἱ προλελοχισμέναι ἐνέδραι the ambush *that had before been laid*, Th.3.112; but also προλοχίζοιντο αἱ νύκτες ὑπὸ τῶν βαρβάρων J.*BJ*1.13.4 (dub. l.). 2. *place* men *in ambuscade*, Id.*AJ*5.2.11, *BJ*1.2.2. II. *beset with an ambuscade*, πέμπει.. τοῦ στρατοῦ μέρος τι τὰς ὁδοὺς προλοχιοῦντας

Th.3.110, cf. Plu.*Sert.*13; also π. τὰ περὶ τὴν πόλιν ἐνέδραις Th.2.81. **-ισμός**, ὁ, *ambuscade*, ἐνέδραι καὶ -ισμοί Conon 37.3, cf. 5.

**προλῡμαίνομαι**, *destroy beforehand*, Plb.2.68.5.

**προλῡπ-έομαι**, Pass., *feel pain* or *distress before*, Pl.*R.*584b, *Phdr.* 258e, *Phlb.*39d. **-ησις**, εως, ἡ, *previous distress*, Id.*R.*584c (pl.).

**προλυσσάω**, *advance raging*, *PMag.Par.*1.2262.

**προλύται**, οἱ, *law-students who were in their fifth year of study*, Just.*Const.Omnem* 5; cf. λύται.

**προλύω**, *undo*, *refute before*, Ulp.ad D.20.18.

**προλωβάομαι**, *injure before*, Paus.10.35.3.

**προμάδδας**· μάζας προμεμαγμένας, Hsch.

**προμάθεια**, **προμᾱθεύς**, **προμᾱθής**, Dor. for προμηθ-.

**πρόμακρος**, ον, = προμήκης, Hp.*Epid.*6.7.2, *Nat.Mul.*32 (prob. cj. in *Steril.*235), Thphr.*HP*3.10.3.

**προμάλαγγες**, οἱ, Cyprian name for *flatterers*, Clearch.25.

**προμᾰλακ-τήριον**, τό, *the room in which* bathers *were rubbed before* bathing, Gal.12.239 (**προμάλακτον** Sch.Nic.*Al.*111 is f.l.). **-ύνω**, = προμαλάσσω, Alex.Aphr.*Pr.*1.119.

**προ-μάλαξις** [ᾰ], εως, ἡ, *previous softening*, Ps.-Democr.ap.Zos. Alch.p.161 B. **-μᾰλάσσω**, Att. -ττω, *soften beforehand*, *make supple by rubbing* or *kneading*, Arist.*Pr.*869$^b$30 (Pass.), Gal.6.90, 8.287; πρόπολις -ομένη Dsc.*Eup.*1.208. **2.** *relax first*, in Pass., προμαλαχθέντων τῶν σπλάγχνων Alex.Trall.10. **3.** metaph., τὸ θυμούμενον Ph.2.579:—Pass., προμαλαττόμενον τὸν δῆμον Plu.*Caes.* 6; τὰ -μαλαχθέντα τῇ ἑρμηνείᾳ Hermog.*Meth.*10.

⊕ **πρόμᾰλος**, ἡ, an unknown tree with supple springy branches, like ἰτέα, ἄγνος, λύγος, prob. a kind of *willow*, Eup.14.5, Hp.*Nat.Mul.*75, A.R.3.201, Nicaenet.ap.Ath.15.673c.

**προμαλχατεύειν**· μετατροπεύειν, Hsch.

**προμάμμη**, ἡ, *great-grandmother*, Ph.2.565, 588, *IG*14.756*a*, *Gloss.*

**προμανθάνω**, *learn beforehand*, and (aor.) *know beforehand*, ἄγνωμον τὸ μὴ προμαθεῖν Pi.*O.*8.60, cf. *Com.Adesp.*785 (= *Trag.Adesp.*241); οὔτε π. οὐδὲν οὔτ' ἐπιμαθών Th.1.138: c. acc., *learn gradually* or *by rote*, ἄθλους προμαθεῖν E.*Fr.*912.10 (anap.); ᾆσμα Ar.*Nu.*966; μαθήματα Pl.*Lg.*643c: c. gen., dub. in Call.*Fr.anon.*205: c. inf., ἀνάγκῃ προὔμαθον στέργειν τάδε (κακά Sch.) S.*Ph.*538.

**προμαντ-εία**, Ion. -ηΐη (also Delph. -ήα *SIG*292.2 (iv B.C.)), ἡ, *right of consulting an oracle* (freq. of the Delphic oracle) *first*, Hdt.1.54, D.9.32, 19.327; Δελφοὶ ἀπέδωκαν Ναξίοις τὰν προμαντήαν *SIG* l.c., etc. **-ευμα**, ατος, τό, *prediction*, Ael.*Fr.*329. **2.** *presentiment*, Mich.*in PN*77.10. ⊕ **-εύομαι**, *prophesy*, *foretell*, *divine*, abs., Hdt.3.[125]: c. acc., [ψυχή] π. τὰ μέλλοντα Arist.*Fr.*10; *foresee*, E.*Fr.*482; τὸν ὄλεθρόν τινι ἔκ τινος D.C.57.20; π. ὡς.. Luc.*DDeor.*16.1: c. acc. et inf., Id.*DMort.*11.2:—Act. προμαντεύω in Plu.*Cat.Ma.*23. **-ιον**, τό, = προμάντευμα, Cyran.20 (pl.). **-ις**, εως, Ion. ιος, ὁ, ἡ, *prophet* or *prophetess*, ὦ παῖ πρόμαντι Λατοῦς E.*Ion* 681 (lyr.). **2.** = προφήτης, *the representative of the god and the organ of his prophecies*, ἡ π. title of *the Pythia*, Hdt.6.66, 7.111, 141; τὴν π. τὴν ἐν Δελφοῖς Th.5.16; Φοίβου π. Neophr.1.3; also ἡ π. of Apollo at Patara, Hdt.1.182; ὁ π. of Ptoän Apollo, Id.8.135; π. δὲ ὁ ἱερεύς ἐστι (sc. Διονύσου) Paus. 10.33.11; Δωδωναίων αἱ π. Hdt.2.55, cf. Euph.48; οἱ π. of Apollo at Argos, *SIG*735.7 (i B.C.). **II.** Adj., *prophetic*, ἁ π. δίκα justice *giving presage of the issue*, S.*El.*475 (lyr.); θυμὸς π. 'my *prophetic* soul', E.*Andr.*1072: c. gen., τούτων π. οὖσα *prophetic*, *foreboding of* a thing, A.*Ch.*758, cf. E.*Hel.*338 (lyr.), *Or.*1445 (lyr.).

**προμαντίων**, ωνος, ἡ, = Lat. *promotio*, *PGen.*46.9 (iv A.D., cf. *Arch.Pap.*3.398).

**προμάξιμον**, τό, name of a garment, *Sammelb.*7033.42 (v A.D.).

**προμᾰραίνω**, *cause to waste away*: *reduce to nothing*, τὸν φόβον Vett.Val.355.27:—Pass., *die away first*, Arist.*Pr.*932$^b$33; σταφυλὴ -μεμαρασμένη *dried* grapes, Aët.12.55; *to be wasted*, *worn out*, ὑπὸ φόβου Vett.Val.242.2, cf. 252.27.

**προμαρτύρομαι** [ῡ], *bear witness to beforehand*, τὰ εἰς Χριστὸν παθήματα 1*Ep.Pet.*1.11.

**προμᾰσάομαι**, *chew first*, Gal.6.48, 15.395.

**προμάσσω**, *knead first*, Hsch. s.v. προμάδδας (Pass.).

**πρόμαστος**, ον, *with prominent breasts*, Porph.ap.Eus.*PE*3.11.

**προμάτωρ**, v. προμήτωρ.

**προμᾰχ-εῖα**, τά, festival at Sparta, Sosib.4. **-έω**, *fight in front*, ἀπὸ τῶν ἁρμάτων X.*Cyr.*3.3.60, cf. Apollod.*Poliorc.*187.9; Ἑλλήνων προμαχοῦντες *fighting* as their *champions*, Simon.90. **-εών**, ῶνος, ὁ, *breastwork*, *battlement*, in pl., Hdt.1.98, 3.151, X.*An.*7.8.13; π. ἕνα τοῦ τείχεος Hdt.1.164. **-ητικός**, ή, όν, Dor. προμᾰχᾱτ-, *ready to fight in front*, Hippod.ap.Stob.4.1.94. **-ίζω**, *fight before*, Τρωσί *in front of* the Trojans, as their champion, Il.3.16; π. τινός Nonn.*D.*27.265, etc. **2.** *fight as champion with* another, Ἀχιλλῆϊ Il.20.376. **-ιόνιον**, τό, and **-ίων**, ονος, ὁ, = προμαχεών, Sch.E.*Hec.*910 (both pl.). **-ομαι**, *fight before*, *fight in the front rank*, ἁπάντων *before* all, Il.11.217, cf. 17.358, Th.6.69; οἱ προμαχόμενοι Plu.*Ant.*39, v.l. in D.S.18.44. **II.** *fight for* or *in defence of*, σοῦ Ar.*V.*957. **-όρμα**, ἡ, = sq. II, epith. of Athena at Buporthmos, Paus.2.34.8. ⊕ **-ος**, ον, *fighting before* or *in front*: πρόμαχοι, οἱ, *champions*, ἐν προμάχοισι φανέντα Il.3.31; πρώτοισιν ἐνὶ π. μιγέντα Od.18.379, cf. Il.4.354; προμάχων ἀν' ὅμιλον Pi.*I.*7(6).35. **b.** as Adj., π. δόρυ the *champion* spear, i.e. of Heracles (v. Sch.), S.*Tr.*856 (lyr.). **2.** *fighting for*, πόλεως, δόμων, A.*Th.*419 (lyr.), 482 (lyr.); θεσμῶν *IG*3.638. **II.** as a name of tutelary gods, Ἀθηνᾶ Alciphr. 3.51, etc.; παρὰ προμάχῳ Παλλάδι *IG* l.c.; Ἡρακλῆς Paus.9.11.4; Ἑρμῆς Id.9.22.2. **III.** Subst., *bastion*, Procop.*Aed.*5.4. **IV.** in Crete, *cake* made for a seven-days-old child, Hsch. **-ών**, later form of προμαχεών, Lxx*Je.*5.10, al., Ph.*Bel.*91.50, J.*BJ*5.4.2, etc.

**προμεθίημι**, *let go before*, [πελειάδα] νηὸς ἄπο π. A.R.2.329. **II.** c. acc. et dat., *hand over before*, τινὶ στρατόν, στρατιάν, App.*BC*3.8, 36.

**προμεθύσκομαι**, Pass., *to be drunk with wine before*, aor. -μεθυσθείς Plu.2.734a.

**προμείγνυμι**, *mingle beforehand*, only in Pass., παλλακίδι προμιγῆναι *to have intercourse with* her *before*, Il.9.452.

**προμελ-αίνομαι**, Pass., *become black at the tip*, τοῦ.. προμελαίνεται ἄκρη σφόνδυλος Nic.*Th.*797.

**προμελετάω**, *practise beforehand*, ἃ δεῖ λέγειν Ar.*Ec.*117; τὴν μέθοδον Pl.*Sph.*218d: c. inf., π. ἐλαύνειν X.*Ath.*1.20: abs., Ar.*Th.*1177, Plb.10.47.3. **2.** *acquire a habit of*, c. inf., Diocl.*Fr.*27:—Pass., τὸ μὴ -ηθέν that *to which one is* not *accustomed*, Sor.1.26. **II.** Medic., *to be threatening*, of disease (cf. μελετάω II.6), in Med., Ruf.*Fr.*61(2).

**Προμένειος** σίδη, ἡ, a sort of *pomegranate*, Nic.*Al.*490 (ἀπό τινος Προμένου Κρητός Sch.).

**προμερίζω**, *bestow beforehand*, Nech.ap.Vett.Val.291.10.

**προμεριμνάω**, *take thought before*, τί λαλήσητε *Ev.Marc.*13.11.

**προμεσόζευξις**, εως, ἡ, *figure of speech in which the principal verb is placed both at the beginning and in the middle of the sentence*, Sacerd. p.456 K.

**προμεσουράνημα**, ατος, τό, Astrol. name of the ninth τόπος, Paul.Al.*M.*4.

**προμεταβάλλω**, *alter* or *metabolize before*, of food, Gal.6.8:—Pass., of drugs, ὑπὸ τοῦ σώματος Id.11.604. **II.** intr., *change before*, S.E.*M.*5.59.

**προμεταλλαγή**, ἡ, *earlier death*, Vett.Val.102.12.

**προμετρ-έω**, *measure out before*, Poll 4.166; Ὁμήρῳ ἀρκέσει -μετρηθὲν τὸ τῆς τιμῆς Stob.2.7.3$^e$. ⊕ **-ης**, ου, ὁ, = Lat. *mensor*, *camp-surveyor*, Lyd.*Mag.*1.46. **II.** title of magistrate at Ephesus, *CIG* 3028. **-ητής**, οῦ, ὁ, a servant of the μετρονόμοι, *IG*2$^2$.1672.291, Hyp.*Fr.*191, Din.*Fr.*16.4; = *mensor*, *Gloss.* **-ητός**, ή, όν, *measured out beforehand*, Poll.4.166. **-ος**, ον, = μακρός, Sm.2*Ki.*21.20. **II.** πρόμετρον, τό, *previous measure*, of a unit, Syrian.*in Metaph.*134.26.

⊕ **προμετωπ-ίδιος**, ον, *before* or *on the forehead*, τρίχες Ph.2.479, cf. Ael.*NA*14.26; π. τοῖχος *in front*, J.*AJ*15.11.5. **II.** Subst. προμετωπίδιον, τό, *skin of the forehead*, προμετωπίδια ἵππων ἐκδεδαρμένα Hdt.7.70. **2.** *frontpiece*, *frontlet*, esp. for horses, X.*An.*1.8.7, *Cyr.*6.4.1 (but *chest-piece*, Arr.*Tact.*4.1, 34.8); also στέφανος χρυσοῦς.. ἔχων π. prob. in *IG*2$^2$.1652.7. **3.** *skull* of an ox, Thphr.*Char.*21.7; π. βοῶν *Chron.Lind.*C.110 (pl.). ⊕ **-ίς**, ίδος, ἡ, *star on the forehead*, π. χρυσαῖ, ἀργυραῖ, Callix.2. **II.** *front* of a coffin, *Inscr.Magn.*281 (i A.D.). **-ος**, ον, *with prominent forehead*, Erot. s.v. φοξοί.

**προμήθ-εια**, Dor. -μάθεια [μᾱ], Ion. προμηθίη, in Trag. προμηθία (v. sub fin.):—*foresight*, *forethought*, σοφὸν ἡ προμηθίη Hdt.3.36, cf. Pi.*N.*11.46, *I.*1.40, Th.4.62, al.; προμηθίαν λαβεῖν A.*Supp.*178, cf. E.*Hec.*795; πολλὴν προμήθειαν ποιεῖσθαι Pl.*Min.*318e; ἐν πολλῇ προμηθίῃ ἔχειν τινά to hold in great *consideration*, Hdt.1.88; προμηθείην ἔχειν τινός Xenoph.1.24, cf. E.*Alc.*1054, Pl.*Grg.*501b; ἔχειν τὴν ὑπὲρ τῆς ψυχῆς π. Id.*R.*441e: with reference to Prometheus, Luc.*Prom.Es*1. [προμηθία is required by the metre in S.*El.*990, *OC* 332, 1043, *Frr.*302.2, 950.3, E.*Med.*741, *Hec.*1137, *Ph.*1466, *Andr.* 690, *IT*1202, and is admissible in A.*Supp.*178, S.*El.*1036, 1350, *Ph.*557, E.*Alc.*1054, *Ion* 448, whereas προμήθεια is never required.] **-ειος**, α, ον, or ος, ον, *Promethean*, πυρικλοπίη *AP*6.100 (Crin.), cf. Nic.*Al.*273, etc. **2.** βοτάνη Προμήθειος καλουμένη Ps.-Plu.*Fluv.*5.4. **II.** **Προμήθεια**, τά, *festival of Prometheus*, Lys. 21.3, X.*Ath.*3.4: **Προμήθια**, *IG*1$^2$.84.37, 2$^2$.1138.11. ⊕ **-έομαι**, 2 sg. προμήθεσαι Archil.(?) in *PLit.Lond.*54:—*to be* προμηθής, *use forethought*, *take care*, c. gen., σέο, μὴ πλήξω Hdt.3.78; τινὸς ὅπως.. Hierocl.*in CA*26 p.479 M.; ὑπέρ τινος Pl.*Prt.*316c; περί τι Id.*La.* 198e: abs., Hp.*Vict.*3.73, al.: c. inf., Alciphr.1.10: c. acc. rei, Hp.*Fract.*20, Pl.*Cri.*45a: c. acc. pers., *show regard* or *respect for*, ἑωυτόν (v.l. ἑωυτοῦ) Hdt.2.172, cf. 9.108, *Syria* 13.256 (ii B.C.):—neut. part. προμηθεόμενον, abs. in pass. sense, *care being taken*, ὡς μὴ.., ὅπως μὴ.., Hp.*Art.*47, 69.—An Act. form is found in Gal., ἡ φύσις προμηθοῦσα τῷ σώματι 15.277. **-εύομαι**, = foreg., c. acc., Alex.Aphr.*Pr.Praef.* **-εύς**, έως, Ion. έος, ὁ, Dor. **Προμᾱθεύς**, *Prometheus*, opp. Ἐπιμηθεύς (*Forethought* and Afterthought), Hes. *Th.*510, cf. A.*Pr.*85, Pl.*Prt.*320d, *PHib.*1.27.85 (iii B.C.), etc.; Προμαθέος Αἰδὼς [θυγάτηρ] Pi.*O.*7.44; = *Summanus*, *Gloss.*: pl. Προμηθεῖς, οἱ, of workers in clay, Luc.*Prom.Es* 2. **II.** as Appellat., αὐτὸν γάρ σε δεῖ προμηθέως A.*Pr.*86: as Adj., προμᾱθεὺς ἀρχά *provident* rule (prob. προμᾱθίς), Id.*Supp.*700 (lyr.). **III.** Pythag. name for *unity*, *Theol.Ar.*5: for *nine*, ib.57. **-ευτικός**, ή, όν, *using forethought*, Eust.797.39. Adv. -κῶς Id.1375.60. **-ής**, Dor. **προμᾱθής**, ές, *forethinking*, *provident*, μέλλησις Th.3.82; τὸ π., = προμήθεια, Id.4.92; εἰς τὸν ἔπειτα βίον -έστερος Pl.*La.*188b: Sup., -έστατον σόφισμα Hdn.3.2.3 (s.v.l.); *troubling oneself*, *caring about* a thing, τοῦ θανεῖν S.*El.*1078 (lyr.). Adv. -θῶς J.*BJ*1.27.2; ὁ ἀριθμὸς τῶν μυῶν π. ἐξεύρηται Gal.*UP*5.14, etc.: Comp., ἐπὶ τὸ προμηθέστερον ποιεῖν τι Hp.*Art.*69, cf. J.*BJ*1.19.2: Sup. -έστατα Ael.*NA*9.42. **II.** of things, *requiring forethought*, Hp.*Acut.*13 (dub. l.). **-ητέον**, *one must be cautious*, Sch.Th.4.92. **-ία**, -ίη, v.

προμήθεια. -ικῶς, Adv. *shrewdly, warily*, with allusion to the name Prometheus, Ar.*Av.*1511.

**προμήκης**, ες, (μῆκος) *prolonged, elongated*, βέλεα Hp.*VC*11, cf. S. *Ichn.*294; π. ἡ τῶν ὄφεων φύσις Arist.*GA*718ᵃ20; σφῆκες -έστεροι τὴν μορφήν Id.*HA*627ᵇ25, etc.; of Pericles, π. τὴν κεφαλήν Plu.*Per.* 3. 2. *protruding*, γλῶσσα Aret.*SA*1.5. II. *oblong*, σχῆμα Pl. *Tht.*148a; φύλλον προμηκέστερον ἀπίου Thphr.*HP*3.10.1; of right-angled triangles, *having the sides which contain the right angle unequal*, Pl.*Ti.*54a. 2. of numbers, *made up of two unequal factors* (as 8 = 2 × 4, 32 = 4 × 8), opp. τετράγωνος or ἰσόπλευρος, Id.*Tht.* l. c., D.L.3.24; also of solid numbers, *having not more than two out of three factors equal*, Anon. *in Tht.*42.45.

**προμηκικῶς**, Adv. *by the use of unequal factors* (cf. foreg. II. 2), ἵνα ἐπιπεδωθῇ π. πλευρὰ [τοῦ χίλια ἀριθμοῦ] Iamb. *in Nic.*p.89 P.

**προμηλόω**, *probe beforehand*, Hp.*Fist.*5.

**προμην-ηταιος**, = *venerabilis*, *Gloss.* (dub.). -ῦσις, εως, ἡ, *prediction*, τοῦ μέλλοντος Iamb.*Myst.*10.3: in Medicine, = πρόγνωσις II.b, *Hippiatr.Prooem.* -ῡτής, οῦ, ὁ, *one who gives information in advance*, Vett.Val.173.19. -ύτρια, ἡ, *she who indicates before*, Sch.rec. A.*Th.*402. ※ -ύω, *denounce beforehand*, τινί τι S.*Ant.*84, cf. Luc. *Merc.Cond.*3; ἐπιβουλήν Chor.p.97 B.; *indicate before, predict*, τι Lxx *Wi.*18.19, Plu.*Lys.*29, Alex.Aphr.*Pr.Praef.*, Ach.Tat.6.5; τί τινι Plu.*Comp.Cim.Luc.*3.

※ **προμήτωρ**, Dor. **προμάτωρ**, ορος, ἡ, *first mother* of a race, A.*Th.* 140 (lyr.), E.*Ph.*676 (lyr.), 828 (lyr.), Luc.*Am.*19. II. masc., *maternal grandfather*, Hsch. III. epith. of Athena, prob. in Them.*Or.*13.180a (voc. πρόματερ codd.).

**προμηχᾰνάομαι**, *plan, contrive beforehand*, D.H.1.46, 7.13, Luc. *Alex.*38 (v.l. προσ-).

**προμῑαίνω**, *defile beforehand*, J.*BJ*4.6.3.

**προμίγνυμι**, v. προμείγνυμι.

※ **προμικκ(ιχ)ιδδόμενος**, *boy in his second year*, prob. for προκομιζόμενος in Λέξεις Ἡροδότου in Stein Hdt. ii p.465 (Berol.1871).

**προμιμνήσκω**, *remind beforehand*, *Gloss.*

**προμισθ-όομαι**, Pass., *to be hired before*, Plu.*Marc.*5. -ωσις, εως, ἡ, *letting beforehand*, Vett.Val.4.26. ※ -ωτής, οῦ, ὁ, *one who hires out* stage-properties, Ἀρχ. Ἐφ. 1910.371: Lat. *promisthota*, Dessau *ILS*5208 (Philippi).

**προμνάμων** [ᾰ], ονος, ὁ, *president of* μνάμονες in Acarnania, *IG*5(1). 29.5 (Sparta, ii B.C.).

**προμνάομαι**, *woo* or *court for* another, Pl.*Tht.*150a; τινί τινα Luc. *Herod.*6; ἡ προμνησαμένη, = προμνήστρια, X.*Mem.*2.6.36: metaph., Pl.*Tht.*151b; προμνᾶταί τί μοι γνώμα my mind *woos* me to hope, c. inf., S.*OC*1075: c. dat., *woo* themes for others, Pl.*Mx.*239c. 2. generally, *endeavour to obtain, solicit*, τοιαῦτα π. ἑκάστῳ προσιών X. *An.*7.3.18; π. αὐτῷ Κιλικίαν *solicit* it for him, Plu.*Luc.*6; κωφότητα π. Id. 2.38b.

**προμνημονεύω**, *mention before*, *PMasp.*32.66 (Pass., vi A.D.), etc.

**προμνηστ-εύομαι**, = προμνάομαι, Alciphr.1.37:—Pass., -μνηστευθεῖσα τῷ βασιλεῖ App.*Reg.*1. -ικός, ή, όν, *fitted to woo for another*: ἡ -κή (sc. τέχνη) *the art of match-making*, Pl.*Tht.* 150a. -ῖνοι, αι, *one by one, one after the other*, προμνηστῖναι ἐπήϊσαν Od.11.233; προμνηστῖνοι ἐσέλθετε 21.230. -ρια, ἡ, *woman who woos* or *courts for another, matchmaker*, Ar.*Nu.*41, Pl.*Tht.*149d, Luc.*DDeor.*20.16: metaph., ἡ κακῶν π. E.*Hipp.*589; προμνηστρίας is prob. for -ίδας in X.*Mem.*2.6.36.

**πρόμοιρος**, ον, (μοῖρα) *before the destined term*, i.e. *untimely*, of death, Ael.*Fr.*49, Man.1.276. 2. of persons, *doomed to untimely death*, *AP*11.159 (Lucill.); in epitaphs, *dead before their time*, *Epigr. Gr.*418 (Cyrene), *IG*14.1386.3 (Alba), 1521 (Rome). Adv. -ρως ib. 1932 (ibid.), *BMus.Inscr.*794.10 (Cnidus).

**προμοιχεύω**, *procure* a woman *by adultery*, Ποππαίαν Νέρωνι Plu. *Galb.*19.

**προμολεῖν**, v. προβλώσκω.

※ **προμολή**, ἡ, *approach, vestibule*, A.R.1.1174: elsewh. in pl., Call. *Dian.*142, A.R.1.260, 320, 4.1160; of the *foot* of a mountain, *AP*7.9 (Damag.), Call.*Dian.*99; *mouth* of a river, *AP*7.246 (Antip. Sid.), Opp.*C.*2.134.

※ **πρόμος**, ὁ, (πρό) *foremost man*, in Hom. always = πρόμαχος, Il.15. 293, Od.11.493, al.; π. ἀνήρ Il.5.533; π. τινί *opposed to* another *in the front rank*, 7.75, 116, 22.85: later, generally, *chief*, A.*Ag.*200 (lyr.), 410 (lyr.); Ἀχαιῶν..πρόμοι Id.*Eu.*399; γᾶς πρόμοι S.*OC*884 (lyr.); στρατιῆς π. *AP*7.233 (Apollonid.); Ἀθηναίων E.*Tr.*31; τῶν Πανελλήνων πρόμῳ Κίμωνι prob. in Cratin.1; πάντων θεῶν θεὸς π., of the sun, S.*OT*660 (lyr.), cf. *Epigr.Gr.*361 (Phrygia); ἰατρῶν π. prob. ib.352 (Claudiopolis). The forms **πρόμνος**, A.*Supp.*904 (lyr.), and **πράμος**, Ar.*Th.*50, are corrupt.

**προμόσχ-ευσις**, εως, ἡ, *planting out* of cuttings, *Gloss.* -εύω, *plant out* cuttings, Thphr.*HP*6.7.3, *CP*3.5.3.

**πρόμουλον**, τό, or -ος, ὁ, perh. *embankment, quay*, *POxy.*1911.167 (vi A.D.); -ος as gloss on πρόβολος, Hsch.; cf. πρόμωλον.

**προμοχθέω**, *work beforehand*, E.*Supp.*1234 (anap.).

**πρόμοχθοι**, οἱ, in Archit., *beam-ends* projecting over the wall, *SIG*977ᵃ8 (Delos, ii B.C.), Hsch.

**προμῠ-έω**, *initiate beforehand*, in aor. Med., prob. for προθυμησαμένη in Hsch. s.v. προτελειωσαμένη. -ησις, εως, ἡ, *previous initiation*, π. τοῦ θανάτου ὁ ὕπνος Plu.2.107e.

**προμῡθία**, Ion. -ίη, *privilege of speaking first*, π. πρὸς μαντείην, = προμαντεία, Hp.*Ep.*27.

**προμῡθίκτρια**, ἡ, Dor. for προμνήστρια, Poll.3.31.

**προμύθιον** [ῡ], τό, *moral prefixed to a fable*, Aphth.*Prog.*1, Donat. ad Ter.*Eun.*232: title of a work by Sophron, *Cod.Paris.* in Cohn *Zu den Parömiographen* 82.

**προμυκτήριον**, *promunctorium*, *Gloss.*

**προμῠλαία**, ἡ, *goddess who presides over mills*, Poll.7.180; expld. by θεὸς **προμύλιος**, Phot.

**προμυλλαίνω**, *pout the lips*, Hp.*VM*22.

**προμῠρίζω**, *perfume beforehand*, in Pass., Thphr.*Od.*45.

**προμύσσω**, Att. -ττω, *snuff* a lamp, τὸν λύχνον Ar.*V.*249 (prob. for πρόβυσον, cf. Sch. ad loc., Poll.2.72, 6.103), Plu.2.798b. 2. metaph., *extort money from*, τινα Hp.*Praec.*4. 3. λύχνον ἑαυτὸν προμύσσοντα a lamp which *trims* itself, *pushes out* its own *wick*, dub. cj. for προσμύσσοντα in Hero *Spir.*1.34.

**προμύστης**, ου, ὁ, *initiator*, *App.Anth.*3.115c (Eleusis); fem. **πρόμυστις**, *Jahrb.*27.10 (Thasos).

**προμυχθίζω**, *groan* or *roar before*, Hsch., Phot.

**πρόμωλον**, τό, = *promunctorium* (leg. *promontorium*), *Gloss.*; cf. πρόμουλον.

※ **πρόνᾱος**, or **προναῖος**, α, ον, Ion. **προνήϊος**, η, ον, Att. **πρόνεως**: (ναός):—*before a temple*, βωμοὺς προνάους A.*Supp.*494: esp. of gods *whose statues stood before the temple*, Ἀθηνᾶ καὶ Ἑρμῆς πρόναοι at Thebes, Paus.9.10.2; πρόνεως, epith. of Poseidon, Hsch.; freq. of Athena at Delphi, because she had a chapel or statue there *before the great temple* of Apollo, κατὰ τὸ ἱρὸν τῆς Προνηίης Ἀθηναίης Hdt.8. 37, cf. 39; ἐν δὲ Προνηίης τῆς ἐν Δελφοῖσι Id.1.92; Παλλὰς προναία A.*Eu.*21; ἐναγὴς ἔστω τοῦ Ἀπόλλωνος..καὶ Ἀθηνᾶς Προναίας Decr. Amphict.ap.Aeschin.3.110 (Προνοίας codd., so also in 108, al., but cf. Harp.); χὴ Παλλάς, Δελφοί νιν ὅθ' ἱδρύοντο προναίην Call.*Fr.*220; Ἀθηνᾷ Προναίᾳ *SIG*324 (Delph., iv B.C.), cf. *Schwyzer* 323*D* 35 (ibid., iv B.C.). II. Subst. πρόναος, ὁ, *front hall* of a temple, through which one passed to the ναός, *BMus.Inscr.*481*.272, 283 (Ephesus, ii A.D.); Ion. **πρόνηος** Luc.*Syr.D.*30; Att. dat. written προνεοι *IG*1².237.58, προνειοι ib.232.6 (prob. to be understood as πρόνεῳ and πρόνειῳ); Ion. gen. προνηΐου Hdt.1.51: pl. προνήϊα, as Adv., *before the temple*, *AP*6.281 (Leon.): also neut. **πρόναον**, τό, Str.17.1.28, Ph.2. 150, 236, Paus.8.32.2 codd., *OGI*661 (Egypt, i A.D.), 702 (ibid., ii A.D.), *Ath.Mitt.*35.442 (Pergam., ii A.D.), *Milet.*1(7) No.200 (iii A.D.), *Ephes.*2 No.42 (iii A.D.), *IGRom.*4.556 (Ancyra): gender uncertain in προνάοις D.S.14.41; **προνάϊον**, *IG*5(2).515*Ba* (Lycosura, i B.C./i A.D.), 520 (ibid., ii A.D.), 7.225 (Aegosthena), J.*AJ*8.3.2 (v.l. πρόναον); **προνάειν**, *Jahresb.*15 *Beibl.*106 (Dionysopolis, iii A.D.). (The forms Προναια, προναιην, προναιον should perh. be understood as Προνᾴα, προνᾴην, πρόνᾳον: the word is trisyll. in A. and Call. ll. cc.)

**προναυκληρ-έω**, *act for one as shipmaster*, *Bull.Soc.Royale Lund* 1928/9 iv 48 (Prote). -ος, ὁ, *one who acts for a shipmaster*, *IG*12 (8).585 (Thasos); gloss on ἐπίσκοπος, Sch.Od.8.163; = *magister navis*, *Gloss.*

**προναυμᾰχέω**, *fight at sea for* or *in defence of*, Μιλήτου Hdt.6.7; Πελοποννήσου Id.8.60.β'.

**προνέμω**, *assign beforehand*, τινί τι Pi.*I.*8(7).18; καθαρὰς χεῖρας π. *present* unspotted hands, A.*Eu.*313 (anap.). II. Med., *go forward in grazing*: hence, *gain ground, spread*, π. Ἄρης S.*El.*1384 (lyr.).

**προνέομαι**, *go forward*, Opp.*H.*3.238.

**προνεύω**, *stoop* or *bend forward*, προνενευκὼς εἰς τὸ πρόσθεν Pl.*Euthd.* 274b; of a rider, X.*Eq.*8.7; of rowers, Id.*Oec.*8.8, Plb.1.21.2; of horns, Arist.*HA*611ᵇ5; of promontories, Poll.1.115 cod. B, Suid. s.v. πρῆνες; of a wrestler, Gal.6.142 (v.l. προσ-).

**προνέω** (A), *heap up before*, App.*BC*4.80.

**προνέω** (B), *swim before*, Ael.*NA*2.6.

**πρόνεως**, **προνήϊος**, v. πρόναος.

※ **προνήσιον**, τό, *veranda*, *Sammelb.*5231.3 (i A.D.), *PLond.*2.262.1 (i A.D.), etc.

**προνηστεύω**, *fast before*, Hdt.2.40, Hp.*Nat.Mul.*95.

**προνήχομαι**, *swim before*, Plu.2.980f, Ael.*NA*10.8: c. gen., τοῦ στόλου Plu.2.984a.

**προνίζω**, *wash beforehand*, only in 1 aor. part. Med. -νιψάμενος, Aët. 16.17.

**προνῑκάω**, *gain a victory beforehand*, Th.2.89 (Act. and Pass.), Is. 11.18, etc.

**προνιτρόω**, = προεκνιτρόω, Archig.ap.Paul.Aeg.4.6, Thessal.ap. Harpocr. in *Cat.Cod.Astr.*8(3).148.

**προνοετής**, οῦ, ὁ, = προνοητής, *Rev.Bibl.*41.412 (Syria).

※ **προνοέω**, *perceive before, foresee*, δόλον Il.18.526, cf. Pi.*P.*10.63; προνοῆσαι βραδεῖς τὰ..ἀποβησόμενα Th.3.38; τὸ μέλλον ἔσεσθαι Arist. *Cael.*291ᵃ24; προνοῶν ὅτι ἀνάγκη ἔσοιτο *foreseeing* that.., X.*Cyr.*8.1. 13; of divine *foreknowledge*, θεῖος νοῦς νοεῖ μὲν ὡς νοῦς, προνοεῖ δὲ ὡς θεός Procl.*Inst.*134, cf. Plot.4.8.2. b. *preconceive*, Porph.*Sent.* 26. II. *think of* or *plan beforehand, provide*, οὐ..τι πάρα προνοῆσαι ἄμεινον Od.5.364; opp. μετανοέω, Epich.280; π. τὸ παραγγελλόμενον *attend to* it, X.*Cyr.*4.1.6: abs., *to be on one's guard, take precautions*, ὥρα προνοεῖν πρὶν πελάσαι στρατόν E.*Heracl.*289; περαιτέρω π. Th.3.43; π. καὶ προβουλεύεσθαι X.*Mem.*2.10.3: folld. by relat. Adv., π. ὅπως.. *provide, take care* that.., Id.*Eq.Mag.*4.1; π. μή.., or ὡς μή.., *cavere ne*.., Id.*Oec.*9.11, *Cyr.*1.6.24; π. ὅτι.. *pay due regard* to the fact that.., Th.3.58. 2. c. gen., *provide for, take thought for*, τῶν παίδων X.*Cyr.*8.1.1, cf. 8.7.15, etc.; θεὸς π. τῶν ὅλων Arr.*Epict.*2.14.11, Procl.*Inst.*120; μάλιστα δὲ προνόησον Ἀρσινόης *PHal.*1.179 (iii B.C.); opp. ὀλιγωρεῖν, Str.5.3.8:—Pass., Procl.*Inst.*

122. 3. Pass., *to be provided*, τὰ -ούμενα, of a poet's *equipment*, Phld.*Po*.5.3; of a patient, *to be treated*, Gal.2.632; *receive consideration*, *PGiss*.7.23(ii A.D.). III. = προνοητεύω, *CIG*3408(Magn. Sip.).

B. Att. writers (also Inscrr. and Pap., v. infr.) prefer Med. **προνοοῦμαι**, Th.6.9, etc. (so also X.*An*.7.7.33, *Mem*.4.3.12): fut. -ήσομαι D.*Prooem*.43, *IG*2².1035.18, D.H.8.90, etc.: aor. προὐνοησάμην E.*Hipp*.399, Ar.*Eq*.421, Antipho 5.43; in Prose mostly προὐνοήθην, Pl.*Cra*.395c, Lys.3.29, Is.2.46, D.44.64, *PSI*3.166.34 (ii B.C.) (used in pass. sense by S.E.*M*.9.404, Gal.2.632): pf. προνενόημαι Plb.6.48.2, D.S.12.69 (but inf. πεπρονοῆσθαι 17.23), etc.—The sense and constr. are the same as in the Act.: *provide*, ταῦτα Th.4.61, cf. Is. l.c., D.44.64, etc.; οὐδέν Pl. l.c.; οἰκίδιόν τινι D.L.6.23; τὰ συμφέροντα ὑπὲρ τῶν μελλόντων X.*Mem*. l.c.: abs., Lys.3.29, etc.; π. περὶ τούτων ib.37; ὑπὲρ ὑμῶν καὶ τῆς πόλεως Id.26.15, cf. D.14.4: c. inf., *take care to* do, E. l.c., Antipho l.c.; π. μή c. inf., D.23.135; π. ὅπως .. Lys.3.41; ὅτι.. Plb.38.16.1; ἵνα.. *Inscr.Prien*.27.12 (ii B.C.). 2. c. gen., *provide for*, Th.6.9, etc.; τοῦ μέλλοντος And.4.12; τῆς χώρας X.*An*.7.7.33; *superintend*, τῆς οἰκοδομίας Haussoullier *Milet*p.252; τῆς ἀναστάσεως τοῦ ἀνδριάντος *CIG*2930b10 (Tralles).

**προνο-ησία**, ἡ, *office of administrator*, *POxy*.136.9 (vi A.D.). **-ητέον**, *one must provide*, X.*Oec*.7.36, Onos.7.2, Jul.*Or*.2.88a. II. c. gen., *one must take thought for*, Ph.2.318, al., Gal.6.452, Orib.*Fr*.70; ἑαυτῶν Ruf.ap.Orib.*inc*.9.1. III. c. inf., *one must take care to*, Herod.Med.ap.Aët.4.47. **-ητεύω**, *hold the office of* προνοητής, *CIG*2639 (Cyprus). ⊛ **-ητής**, οῦ, ὁ, *supervisor*, *administrator*, πάντων *OGI*660.8(Egypt, i A.D.); of estates, *PLond*.2.214(iii A.D.); ταμίας καὶ π., of Hermes, Herm.ap.Stob.1.49.44; *curator* of public buildings, etc., *CIG*4591 (Palestine); γυμνασίου *PGrenf*.2.67 (iii A.D.). **-ητικός**, ή, όν, *provident*, *cautious*, *wary*, X.*Mem*.1.3.9, Men.*Epit*.344; τὸ πόρρωθεν π. M.Ant.1.16: Comp. -ώτερος Procop.*Arc*.19. Adv. -κῶς X.*Mem*.1.4.6, Aen.Tact.18.11, Ph.1.500, Sor.1.14; π. ἔχειν Aristid.1.377J.; π. ἔχειν τινός J.*AJ*11.5.8: Sup. -ώτατα *most wisely*, A.D.*Pron*.104.13. 2. *taking thought* or *care for*, esp. of divine providence, θεὸς π. κόσμου D.L.7.147, cf. Str.10.3.23, Ph.2.242; φύσις π. τοῦ ζῴου Gal.11.158: abs., ἔχειν π. δύναμιν περὶ τὸν αὐτῶν βίον Arist.*EN*1141ᵃ28, cf. Ph.2.546, Plu.2.1052b, Procl.*Inst*.120: Comp. -ώτερος Chio *Ep*.15.2. II. of things, *showing forethought* or *design*, X.*Mem*.4.3.6.

**πρόνοια**, Ion. -οίη, ἡ, (πρόνοος) *perceiving beforehand*, *foresight*, *foreknowledge*, τοὔπος τὸ θεοπρόπον τᾶς παλαιφάτου π. S.*Tr*.823 (lyr.); προνοίαισι τοῦ πεπρωμένου A.*Ag*.684(lyr.). 2. = πρόγνωσις II.b, Hp. ap.Gal.18(2).8. II. *foresight*, *forethought*, ἐπῄνεσ᾽ .. πρόνοιαν ἣν ἔθου S.*Aj*.536; π. δ᾽ ἐστὶν οὐδενὸς σαφής Id.*OT*978; προνοίας οὕνεκα so far as *foresight*, *caution* is required, Id.*Ph*.774, cf. *El*.1015; ἐκ προνοίης *with forethought*, *purposely*, Hdt.1.120,159, etc.; opp. κατὰ τύχην, Id.8.87, cf. Antipho 5.21, Lys.26.19, Pl.*Phdr*.241e; ἀπὸ προνοίας τινῶν by their *precautions*, Th 8.95; τὴν π. τὴν ἐς ἡμέας ἔχουσαν Hdt. 8.144; προνοίᾳ τῶν συγγενῶν, φίλων, τῆς πόλεως, *by care for*.., And.1.56; esp. of crimes committed *with design* or *malice prepense*, ἐκ προνοίας τραῦμα, ἐκ π. φόνοι, Aeschin.3.212, Din.1.6, etc.; ἐκ π. ἀποθνήσκειν Antipho 1.22, cf. Lys.3.28; τὰ ἐκ π., opp. ἀκούσια, Arist.*Pol*. 1300ᵇ26; so οὐδεμία π. ἐστι τραύματος no *intention* of wounding, Lys.3.41; πρόνοιαν ἔχειν (or ἴσχειν) τινός to take *thought* for.., show *care* for.., E.*Alc*.1061, Th.2.89, etc.; περί τινος S.*Ant*.283; ὑπέρ τινος Isoc.16.9; ἡ τοῦ χόρτου π. *PFlor*.131.7 (iii A.D.), cf. 148.2 (iii A.D.): c. inf., πολλὴν π. εἶχεν εὐσχήμως (fort. εὐσχήμων) πεσεῖν E.*Hec*.569; πολλὴν π. ἔχειν μέλλοντας.. to beware of doing a thing, Antipho 5.91; π. ποιεῖσθαί τινος D.21.97, etc.: pl., X.*Oec*.7.38. 2. *providence*, τοῦ θείου ἡ π. Hdt.3.108; τοῦ θεοῦ S.*OC*1180; θεία π. E.*Ph*.637 (troch.); πρόνοιαι θεῶν Pl.*Ti*.44c: abs., *divine providence*, προνοίας ἔργῳ X.*Mem*.1.4.6, etc., cf. Zeno *Stoic*.1.44, Cleanth.ib.121, Chrysipp. ib.2.168, al. (περὶ προνοίας as title of one of his works, ib.3.203). 3. Pythag. name for *five*, *Theol.Ar*.31. 4. *office of* προνοητής, *POxy*.472.10 (ii A.D.). III. Πρόνοια Ἀθηνᾶ Athena as *goddess of Forethought*, under which name she was worshipped at Delphi, D.25.34, D.S.11.14, Parth.25, Paus.10.8.6, Plu.2.825b, Jul.*Or*.4.149b, etc.; at Delos acc. to Macr.*Sat*.1.17.55, cf. Aristid.1.97J., *Or*.37(2).26; also Ἰουλία θεὰ Σεβαστὴ Π. *IG*3.461: this name of Athena, which is guaranteed by the context in D., Aristid., Jul., Macr. ll. cc., seems to have been a distortion of the name Προναία or Προνάα (v. πρόναος I), but Πρόνοια is f.l. for Προναία (or Προνάα) in Aeschin. (v. πρόναος I), and D.S., Parth., Paus., Plu. ll. cc. shd. perh. be corrected.

**προνομ-αία**, ἡ, = προνομή II, Ph.2.512, Plu.*Alex*.60, Luc.*Zeux*.10, etc.; of a fly's *proboscis*, Id.*Musc.Enc*.6; of a bee's, Philostr.*Im*. 2.12. **-εία**, ἡ, (προνομή I) *going out to forage* or *plunder*, Plb.4.68.3 (v.l. προνομαί): rejected by Thom.Mag.p.275R. **-ευτής**, οῦ, ὁ, *forager*, *plunderer*, Str.15.3.7. **-εύω**, *forage*, *plunder*, Plb.2.27.2, Str.16.1.18, Onos.10.8, Polyaen.3.10.5; [προβοσκίδα] ἔχουσα π., of a fly, Luc.*Musc.Enc*.3. II. trans., *plunder*, *ravage*, τὴν τῶν πολεμίων D.H.8.11 (also in Pass., ibid., D.S.13.109); *pluck*, ὀρμενα Posidipp. 24; *eat greedily*, τὰ δεῖπνα Plu.2.709a. 2. *carry away captive*, Lxx *Nu*.31.9, al.:—Pass., ib.*Si*.48.15. (Rejected by Thom.Mag. p.275R.) ⊛ **-ή**, ἡ, *foraging*, ἐξάγειν εἰς προνομάς X.*Cyr*.6.1.24; *foray*, προνομὴν or προνομὰς ποιεῖσθαι, Id.*HG*1.1.33, 2.4.25, cf. Aen. Tact.31.8; πεδία προνομὰς ἔχοντα suitable for *foraging*, Plu.*Fab*.6; *provision of fodder*, *PFlor*.388.81 (ii A.D.). 2. pl., also, *foraging parties*, σὺν προνομαῖς τὰ ἐπιτήδεια λαμβάνειν X.*HG*4.1.16, *An*.5.1.7, cf. Plb.4.73.4. 3. *plunder*, *booty*, Lxx *Nu*.31.11, al., Phleg.*Mir*. 3. 4. *store*, *provision*, Lxx 3 *Ki*.10.23. II. elephant's *proboscis* (cf. προνομαία), Plb.5.84.3, D.S.17.88 (pl.). III. = sq. I, Luc.*Sat*. 17. **-ία**, ἡ, (νόμος) *privilege*, Ph.1.6, al., Plu.2.279b, 296c (pl.), *PFlor*.382.14 (iii A.D.), Lyd.*Mag*.3.24, etc.; π. διδόναι τινί Str.15.1. 54, Luc.*Abd*.23, etc. II. (νομός) *right of pasturage*, *IG*9(1).442 (Acarn., iv B.C.). **-ιον**, τό, *song sung before the* νόμος (signf. II), Poll.4.53: metaph., Jul.*Or*.2.56d (pl.): also as Adj., π. μέλος Him. *Or*.4.3, cf. 34.1. 2. = ἀρραβών, *earnest-money*. Luc.*Rh.Pr*.17. II. = foreg. I, *privilege*, *POxy*.136.38 (vi A.D.), Suid.

⊛ **προνομοθετέω**, *make a law before*, Suid. s.v. προθεσμία:—Pass., *to be established by law before*, *Milet*.3 No.134.17, D.C.36.39.

**πρόνομος**, ον, (προνέμομαι) *grazing forward*, opp. ὀπισθονόμος (q.v.): generally, π. βοτά *grazing* herds, A.*Supp*.691 (lyr.).

**πρόνοος**, ον, contr. -νους, ουν, *careful*, *prudent*, A.*Supp*.969 (anap.), Hdt.3.36: Comp. -νούστερος S.*Aj*.119.

**προνοσέω**, *to be ill beforehand*, Hp.*Coac*.534.

**προνοτίζω**, *wet*, *moisten beforehand*, in Pass., Dsc.2.83, Archig.ap. Orib.8.2.7.

**προνουμηνία**, ἡ, *the day before a new moon*, Lxx *Ju*.8.6.

**προνύμφιος**, ον, *pre-nuptial*, π. ὕπνον λῦσαι Call.*Aet*.3.1.2.

**προνύξ**, Adv. *all night long*, opp. προῆμαρ, Semon.7.47.

**προνύττω**, *goad on*, Plb.28.17.8.

**προνωπής**, ές, *stooping forwards*, *with head inclined*, στείχει π., of one in deep grief, E.*Alc*.186; π. ἐστι καὶ ψυχορραγεῖ, of one dying, ib.143; π. λαβεῖν to take her *as she fell fainting forward*, of the ministers of the altar taking up Iphigenia, A.*Ag*.234 (lyr.). 2. metaph., *inclined*, *ready*, ἄγαν π. ἐς τὸ λοιδορεῖν φέρῃ E.*Andr*.729. (Cf. νωπέομαι.)

**προνώπια**, τά, *front of a house* (cf. ἐνώπια), ἐς προνώπι᾽ αὐτίχ᾽ ἥξει E.*Ba*.639 (troch.): metaph. in sg., τόδ᾽ ἔσχατον.. χώρας Πελοπίας π., of Troezen, the outer *portal* of Peloponnesus, Id.*Hipp*.374. II. as Adj., πῶς προνώπιος φαίνῃ πρὸς οἴκοις.. ; *in front*, *before the door*, Id. *Ba*.645. 2. ἥρωες π., = *Lares compitales*, D.H.4.14. (Acc. to Eust. for πρό, ἐνώπια, i.e. τὰ πρὸ τῶν ἐνωπίων: but the etym. is doubtful.)

**πρόξ**, gen. προκός, ἡ, *roe deer*, *Cervus capreolus*, αἶγας ἐπ᾽ ἀγροτέρας ἠδὲ πρόκας ἠδὲ λαγωούς Od.17.295; coupled with ἔλαφος by Arist. *HA*506ᵃ22, 515ᵇ34, *PA*676ᵇ27, Dionys.Ath. and Philet.ap.Sch.A.R. 2.279; but expld. as τὸ τέκνον τῆς δορκάδος by Sch.Nic.*Th*.578, cf. Sch. Od. l.c.:—also **προκάς** (q.v.). 2. metaph., *coward*, Archil.188.

**πρόξεινος**, ὁ, Ion. for πρόξενος (q.v.).

⊛ **προξεν-έω**, impf. προὐξένουν (but ἐπροξένει E.*Fr*.1104, Ar.*Fr*. 775): fut. προξενήσω: pf. προὐξένηκα:—*to be* any one's *πρόξενος* (q.v.), διὰ τὸ προξενεῖν ὑμῶν because *he is* your *πρόξενος*, X.*HG*6. 4.24, cf. D.15.15, etc.; π. τῶν πρέσβεων *act as* π. *of* the envoys of a friendly state, Id.18.82. 2. generally, *to be* one's *protector*, *patron*, E.*Med*.724, Ar.*Th*.576. II. from the duties of a πρόξενος (signf. II), 1. *manage* or *effect* anything for another, τἄλλα E.*Ion* 335; θράσος π. *lend* daring, S.*Tr*.726; π. τιμήν, εὐδαιμονίαν τινί, *procure* it for him, Plu.*Caes*.60, Luc.*Vit.Auct*.10; φιλίας βασιλέων Plu.*Sol*.2; ὄψις π. ἡδονήν Aristid.*Or*.53(55).4; γυναῖκας ἐπιπόνους, ἄνδρας συστατικούς, Procl.*Par.Ptol*.255,256; οὐδεμίαν ὠφέλειαν Gal.6.830: in bad sense, π. κίνδυνόν τινι *put* danger *upon* one, X.*An*.6.5.14, cf. Ael.*VH*13.33; π. ὀνείδη, ἀνάγκας τινί, Plu. *Alex*.22, Aristid.1.488J.: c. dat. et inf., ὑμῖν ὧδ᾽ ὁρᾶν τὰ πρόσθε λαμπρὰ προὐξένησαν ὄμματα *have granted* to you to see thus my once bright eyes, S.*OT*1483; π. τινὶ τὸ καταλῦσαι βίον *grant* one to die, X.*Ap*.7; π. τινὶ *guide* one, *give* him *directions*, S.*OC*465. 2. *introduce*, *recommend* one person to another, commonly for purposes of business, μὴ πονηρούς, ὦ πονήρα, προξένει Eup.321; λέγων οἷον ἄνθρωπον προὐξένησέ μοι D.37.11, cf. 53.13; σὺ προξένησον *introduce* me (to the oracle), E.*Hel*.146; π. τινὰ διδάσκαλον, φοιτητήν, *introduce* him as teacher, as pupil, Pl.*La*.180c, *Alc*.1.109d; π. κόρην τινί Longus 3.36, cf. Him.*Or*.1.11; also π. βωμόν Lib.*Ep*.739.1. III. = μαρτυρέω, *give evidence*, Hsch.; π. ἐπὶ κακῷ *IG*9²(1).138.9 (Calydon, iv B.C.); αἱ ψευδέα προξενέοι ib.9(1).333.8 (Locr., v B.C.). **-ησις**, εως, ἡ, *public reception*, Sch.Pi.*O*.3 *Prooem*.(pl.). II. = *conciliatio*, Gloss. ⊛ **-ητής**, οῦ, ὁ, *broker*, *agent*, *CIG*2942 (Tralles); σωμάτων slave-*broker*, *OGI*524.2 (pl., Thyatira); [γάμου] *Cod.Just*. 5.1.6.1. ⊛ **-ητικός**, ή, όν, *of* or *for a broker*, τὸ π. *brokerage*, ib.5.1 tit. (pl., as Lat. word). **-ήτρια**, fem. of προξενητής, = προμνήστρια, Sch.Ar.*Nu*.41. **-ία**, Thess. προξεννία *IG*9(2).258.6,9 (Cierium, ii B.C.): ἡ:—*relation of* πρόξενος, *treaty* or *compact of friendship between a state and a foreigner*, Antipho *Fr*.67, Th.6.89; προξενίᾳ πέποιθα I trust *my public friendship*, Pi.*N*.7.65, cf. *O*.9.83; τινὰ π. ἐξευρήσεις; what *protector* wilt thou find? E.*Med*.359 (anap., v.l.). 2. *status and privileges of a* πρόξενος, π., εὐεργεσία, ἀτέλεια ἁπάντων D.20.60; τὴν παλαιὰν π... ἣν τοῦ πάππου ἀπειπόντος αὐτὸς [sc. ὁ Ἀλκιβιάδης].. διενοεῖτο ἀνανεώσασθαι Th.5.43; τὴν π. ὑμῶν.. πατρὸς πατὴρ πατρῴαν ἔχων παρεδίδου τῷ γένει X.*HG*6.3.4; ἡ πρὸς Θηβαίους π. Aeschin.2.141; freq. in Inscrr., *IG*1².116.40, etc.; coupled with other privileges, e.g. προνομία, προπραξία, ib.9(1).442.4 (Stratos, iv B.C.); πολιτεία, ἀσυλία ib.9(2).62.12 (Lamia, iii B.C.), etc.; ἔγγυος τᾶς π. ib.14; ἔγγυος τᾶν π. ὁ γραμματεύς *SIG*629.31 (Delph., ii B.C.). II. *inscription* or *written instrument in witness of* προξενία, in pl., Arist.*Ath*. 54.3, Plb.12.11.2. **-ίζω**, = προξενέω II.1, *cause*, αὐτῷ λύπην Anon. in *EN*436.24.

⊛ **πρόξενος** (πρόξενϝος *IG*9(1).867 (Corc., vii/vi B.C.)), Cret. πρόξηνος *GDI*5028 *A* 2,6, Schwyzer 187 (ii B.C.), Ion. πρόξεινος Hdt. (v. infr.): ὁ (ἡ, when used of a woman, v. infr. II):—*public ξένος*, *public guest* or *friend*, made so by an act of the State: Alexander I of

Macedon was π. καὶ εὐεργέτης of Athens, Hdt.8.136, cf. 143; πρόξενοι ἀμφικτιόνων Pi.*I*.4(3).8; εἶναι πρόξενον τοῦ δήμου τοῦ Ἀθηναίων Στράτωνα τὸν Σιδῶνος βασιλέα καὶ αὐτὸν καὶ ἐκγόνους *IG*2$^{2}$.141.9; πρόξενοι καὶ πολῖται Lys.28.1; esp. of persons representing the interests of a foreign state in their own community, Pl.*Lg*.642b, etc.; opp. ϝιδιόξενος (q.v.), *IG*9(1).333.11 (Locr., v B.C.); of π. of Athens in other states, Pindar at Thebes, Isoc.15.166; Thucydides at Pharsalus, Th.8.92; π. τῆς πόλεως, i.e. of Athens at Mytilene, Arist.*Pol.* 1304$^{a}$10; of other states at Athens, Cimon and Callias of Sparta, And.3.3, X.*HG*5.4.22; Nicias of Syracuse, D.S.13.27; Thraso of Thebes, Aeschin.3.138; ὅσους γέγραφε προξένους εἶναι καὶ Ἀθηναίους Din.1.45; of other states at Sparta, e.g. Lichas of Argos, Th.5.76; Clearchus of Byzantium, X.*HG*1.1.35; π. of barbarian communities and rulers, Id.*An*.5.4.2, 5.6.11; sts. the function was exercised by a community, εἶμεν τὰν πόλιν τῶν Δελφῶν πρόξενον τᾶς πόλιος τᾶς Σαρδιανῶν.. διὰ τὸ μὴ ὑπάρχειν πρόξενον Σαρδιανοῖς *SIG*548.10 (Delph., iii B.C.). b. later, of *patrons* or *representatives* of guilds, e.g. the σύνοδος τοῦ Διὸς τοῦ Ξενίου at Athens, *IG*2$^{2}$.1012.18, cf. 7.2486 (Thebes), 14.615 (Rhegium). 2. at Sparta, officials appointed by the Kings to entertain foreign guests, Hdt.6.57; also at Delphi, of persons extending public hospitality, E.*Ion* 551, 1039, *Andr*.1103; so in Nephelococcygia, Ar.*Av*.1021. 3. in pl., *witnesses* to a will, *IG*14.636 (Petelia). II. generally, *patron, protector*, A.*Supp*.420 (lyr.), al., Ar.*Th*.602; φίλης γὰρ π. κατήνυσαν at the house of a kind *patroness*, i.e. Clytaemnestra, S.*El*.1451; προξένῳ χρῆσθαί τινι E.*Fr*.721. III. Adj., *assisting, relieving*, c. gen., Alciphr.3.72. 2. *causing, producing*, κακῶν, συμπτωμάτων, νόσων, Ruf.*Fr*.64, Olymp. *in Mete*.3.21, Sch.Ar.*Nu*.243.

**προξενόομαι**, Pass., *to be entertained before*, c. dat. pers., Str.1.2.33.

**προξηραίνω**, *dry first*, Gal.11.701:—Pass., Dsc.5.75.15, Gal.11.600.

**προξηροτρῑβέομαι**, Pass., *to be rubbed dry before*, Crateuas 9, Antyll.ap.Orib.10.21.4.

**προξῠρ-άω**, *shave beforehand*, Heraclid.Tar.ap.Gal.12.402, Crito ib.484, Alex.Trall.1.1. **–ησις**, εως, ἡ, *preliminary shaving*, Antyll. ap.Orib.10.12.3. **–ητέον**, *one must shave first*, Sever.ap.Aët.7.92, Paul.Aeg.6.4. **–ίζω**, = προξυράω, Antyll.ap.Orib.10.12.3 (Pass.).

**προογκάομαι**, *bray beforehand*, Luc.*Asin*.26.

**προόδ-ευσις**, εως, ἡ, *travelling before*, Eust.51.26. **–εύω**, *walk first*, App.*BC*4.43; *travel before*, Luc.*Herm*.73; *emanate*, prob. in Iamb.*VP*17.74; προοδεύει τι τῶν ἐντέρων the patient *has a slight motion* of the bowels, Paul.Aeg.3.71: metaph. in fut. Med., –εύσονται εἰς ἄπειρον *will go on* ad infinitum, Alex.Aphr. *in Metaph*.288.24. **–ηγός**, ὁ, *one who goes before to show the way*, τοῦ πολέμου LXX 2*Ma*.12.36. **–ια**, *praevia*, *Gloss.* **–ικός**, ή, όν, *proceeding, emanating*, Dam.*Pr*.44: Comp., ib.77. Adv. –κῶς ib.221.

**προοδοιπορ-έω**, *travel before*, Luc.*Herm*.27; τινι Id.*DMar*.15.3 (dub.):—Pass., αὐτῷ προωδοιπόρηται he *has gone too far*, D.L.7.176. II. Pass., *to be travelled over before*, J.*AJ*3.1.1. **–ος** (parox.), ὁ, *one who travels before*, Hsch. s.v. ὁδουρός.

**προοδοποι-έω**, aor. προωδοποίησα Arist.*Pr*.867$^{a}$39: pf. προωδοποίηκα Id.*Rh*.1389$^{b}$31:—Pass. προωδοποίημαι Id.*PA*650$^{b}$28, 651$^{b}$10, *GA* 770$^{b}$3, al.; so that the forms προωδο-πεποίηκα, –πεποίημαι in *Pr*.954$^{b}$12, *Pol*.1270$^{a}$4, are prob. corrupt:—*prepare* or *pave the way*, τὸ γῆρας π. τῇ δειλίᾳ Arist.*Rh*. l.c.; πάντα π. πρὸς.. *make* all *preparations* for.., Id.*Pol*.1336$^{a}$32; πρὸς τὴν ἀλήθειαν Jul.*Or*.7.217c: abs., Plu.2.664a:—Med., *make one's way, tend* in a certain direction, πρὸς τὸ ἄνω Arist.*PA*671$^{b}$31, cf. *Pr*.867$^{a}$36, Thphr.*Sud*.28. II. c. acc., *prepare beforehand*, τὸ σῶμα πρὸς τὸ ἱδροῦν Arist.*Pr*.867$^{a}$39; τὴν ψυχὴν εἴς τι S.E.*M*.6.34; πολλὰ αὐτῷ (sc. Σόλωνι) τῆς νομοθεσίας Plu.*Sol*.12, cf. *Lyc*.4:—Pass., αὐτοὺς παρεῖχον τῷ νομοθέτῃ προωδοποιημένους Arist.*Pol*.1270$^{a}$4; π. τῷ πάθει Id.*PA*650$^{b}$28; προωδοποίηται ἕκαστος πρὸς τὴν ἑκάστου ὀργήν Id.*Rh*.1379$^{a}$21, cf. *GA*770$^{b}$3, Epicur.*Nat.Herc*.1420.3. **–ητικός**, ή, όν, *going before to prepare the way*: *directive*, of drugs, Gal.14.759. **–ός**, όν, *preparing the way*, Sch.Ar.*Pl*.1160.

**πρόοδος**, ον, *going before*: οἱ π. *advance-party of soldiers*, X.*Eq.Mag*.4.5. Adv. –ωτέρως *progressively*, Zos.Alch.p.158B.

**πρόοδος**, ἡ, *going on, advance*, Emp.84.1, X.*HG*3.4.15: metaph., *progress*, Plot.5.2.1; ἐκ δυνάμεως εἰς ἐνέργειαν Id.6.3.22. II. *coming out* of a house, Luc.*Nec*.12; *appearance in public*, Id.*Somn*.9. 2. *procession*, J.*AJ*18.4.6, Iamb.post Polem.p.49 Hinck, Hdn.2.4.1, Plot.5.5.3 (pl.), *SIG*900.13 (Panamara, iv A.D.). 3. *proceeding forth, emanation*, Plot.8.5.6, etc.; ἡ ἀφ' ἑνὸς πάντων π. Procl. *in Cra*.p.2P.; opp. μονή, ἐπιστροφή, Dam.*Pr*.72, al.: pl., Porph.*Sent*.24; π. κρύφιοι, opp. ἐγκόσμιοι, Procl. *in Cra*.p.107P. 4. musical *progression*, Iamb.*VP*26.120 (pl.). 5. mathematical *progression*, Plot.6.3.12. 6. = *interrogatio*, *Gloss.*

**προ-όδους**, οντος, ὁ, ἡ, *with prominent teeth*, Poll.2.96 cod. A: also **–όδων**, Phot., Eust.1872.33; written προώδων Phryn.*PS*p.101B.

**προοδῠνάομαι**, Pass., *feel pain before*, Gal.16.557, Sch.Pi.*P*.2.166.

**προοδύρομαι** [ῡ], *lament before*, Sch.E.*Med*.1016.

**πρόοιδα**, inf. προειδέναι, part. προειδώς, pf. (with plpf. προῄδη, –ῄδειν, fut. προείσομαι); late aor. inf. προειδῆσαι Phld.*Rh*.1.286S.:—*know beforehand*, Hdt.1.20, 7.235, 9.41, And.2.21, Lys.16.15, etc.; περὶ τούτων τὴν ἀλήθειαν Pl.*Grg*.459e; τὸν θάνατον ib.523d; ὃν [καιρὸν] οὐ προῄδειν ἐσόμενον Isoc.12.127; π. ὅτι.. D.8.50; π. τίς χορηγὸς [ἔσται] Id.4.36; ἐξ οὐ προειδότος *unforeseen*, D.C.69.4: c. part., μὴ ἐπ' ἀγαθῷ.. κατοικισθησόμενον (sc. τὸ Πελαργικόν) Th.2.17.

**προοικ-ειόομαι**, Med., *make friendly, win over beforehand*, prob. in D.H.5.64. **–έω**, *dwell before*, ἐν τῇ νήσῳ D.S.15.14. **–ία**, ἡ, *the projecting eaves of a house*, Clitodem.25 (pl.).

**προοικο-δομέω**, *build in front*, πρὸ τῶν πύργων τριγώνους Ph.*Bel*.84.13:—Pass., dub. in Luc.*Alex*.14. **–νομέω**, *arrange before*, J.*AJ* 2.5.7:—Med., *get things previously arranged*, Id.*BJ*7.8.2:—Pass., *to be so arranged*, προῳκονόμηται ὑπὸ τοῦ θείου ἑκατέρου ἡ φύσις Arist.*Oec*.1343$^{b}$26. 2. Med., *introduce* into a speech *before, premise*, Cic.*QF* 2.3.6. **–νομία**, ἡ, *prefatory summary*, Hdn.*Fig*.p.103S., Donat.ad Ter.*Eun*.719, Serv.ad Verg.*A*.1.226, al., Eust.16.7 (pl.). **–νομικῶς**, Adv. *by way of preparation*, Sch.S.*El*.448.

**πρόοικος**, ὁ, *major-domo*, *JHS*19.298 (Galatia, misspelt –ηκος), *Supp.Epigr*.2.747 (Pisidia).

**προοιμι-άζομαι**, pf. πεπροοιμίασμαι Luc.*Nigr*.10:—in Trag. contr. **φροιμιάζομαι**: both forms occur in Arist. and later Prose: aor. ἐφροιμιασάμην Arist.*Po*.1460$^{a}$10: pf. πεφροιμίασμαι in pass. sense (v. infr.):—*make a prelude, preamble*, or *preface*, A.*Ag*.1354, X.*Mem*.4.2.5, Pl.*Lg*.723c; π. μακρῶς Arist.*Rh*.1416$^{b}$33, cf. 1415$^{b}$24, Phld.*Rh*.1.56S., al. II. c. acc., *say by way of preface, premise*, τί φροιμιάζῃ νεοχμόν; E.*IT*1162; περὶ οὗ τοσαῦτα προοιμιάζομαι Pl.*La*.179a, cf. Thphr.*Char.Praef*.4; τούτους.. φροιμιάζομαι θεούς *begin by invoking* them, A.*Eu*.20: c. dat. modi, δάκρυσι Them.*Or*.13.173d: pf. in pass. sense, πεφροιμίασται τὰ νῦν εἰρημένα Arist.*Pol*.1325$^{b}$33; ταῦτα ἔστω πεφροιμιασμένα τῷ λόγῳ ib.1323$^{b}$37; πεφροιμιάσθω ταῦτα Id.*EN* 1095$^{a}$12; ἐν τοῖς πεφροιμιασμένοις Id.*Metaph*.995$^{b}$5. 2. *begin*, ἐντεῦθεν Them.*Or*.9.120c: metaph., *inaugurate*, τὴν βασιλείαν τρισχιλίων πολιτῶν φόνῳ J.*BJ*2.6.2, cf. D.S.36.2. **–ᾰκός**, ή, όν, *of* or *for a preface*, ἔννοια Aps.*Rh*.p.238H., cf. Men.Rh.p.438S.; ἐπιχείρησις Longin.*Rh*.p.205H. **–αστέον**, *one must premise*, D.H.*Rh*.2.8, Corn.*Rh*.p.357H.: contr. **φροιμιαστέον**, Arist.*Rh.Al*.1440$^{b}$6, 1445$^{a}$35. **–αστικός**, ή, όν, = προοιμιακός, ἔννοιαι Men.Rh.p.376S. ⊛ **–ον**, τό, Trag. contr. **φροίμιον** (v. infr.): (οἶμος):—*opening, introduction*; in Music, *prelude, overture*, Pi.*P*.1.4; in Ep. poems, *proëm, preamble*, Id.*N*.2.3, Ar.*Eq*.1343; in speeches, *exordium*, Critias 43 tit., Arist.*Rh*.1414$^{b}$19, Phld.*Rh*.1.56S., *Stoic*.2.96, etc.; προοιμίοις ἡδονῆς with *prefaces* about pleasure, X.*Mem*.2.1.27. 2. metaph. of *any prelude* or *beginning*, φροίμιον χορεύσομαι A.*Ag*.31, cf. 829; φροιμίοις ⟨δυσφροιμίοις⟩ ib.1216, cf. *Th*.7; λόγους.. μηδέπω 'ν προοιμίοις only just *beginning*, Id.*Pr*.741; εἴ τι τοῦδε φ. ματᾷ any part of this *presage*, Id.*Eu*.142; δρῶ τάδε φροίμια.. πόνων Id.*Supp*.830 (lyr.), cf. E.*Hipp*.568, X.*Mem*.4.2.3; ἐγχέων π. Pi.*Fr*.78; π. δείπνου Alex.110.3; π. ἔχθρας Plb.22.4.15; ἀρχῆς Id.25.3.8 (pl.); δάκρυά μοι τὰ π. τῆς τέχνης Luc.*Somn*.3; of *premonitory symptoms* of disease, Orib.*Syn*.8.2. II. *hymn* or *short poem*, such as those attributed to Homer, Ἀπόλλωνος Th.3.104, cf. Pl.*Phd*.60d, *R*.531d; φροίμιον Ἀντιλόχου (fort. Ἀρχιλόχου) Call.*Fr*.223.

**προοινοποιέω**, *prepare wine first*, *PRev.Laws* 27.8 (Pass., iii B.C.).

**προοιστ-έον**, (προφέρω) *one must premise, place first*, Arist.*Top*.110$^{b}$29. **–ός**, ή, όν, *pronounced, uttered*, A.D.*Pron*.49.20, *Adv*.124.14.

**προοίχομαι**, *to have gone on before*, X.*Cyr*.7.4.8.

**προολμοκοπέω**, *pound in a mortar first*, in Pass., Orib.*Fr*.93, Aët.12.32.

**προομᾰλύνω**, *make level* or *even first*, Pl.*Ti*.50e.

**προόμνῡμι**, and –ύω (Paus.4.5.8), *swear before* or *beforehand*, D.29.57; τοὺς θεοὺς ἦ μὴν ἐλπίζειν.. by the gods, Pl.*Lg*.954a; π. ὅρκον Paus. l.c.: c. acc. et inf., προυμόσας τό μ' εἰδέναι A.*Ag*.1196; π. τι εἶναι D.29.52.

**προομολογ-έω**, *grant* or *concede beforehand*, δοξαστὸν αὐτὸ δεῖν λέγεσθαι Pl.*R*.479d:—Pass., προωμολόγηταί τι εἶναι Id.*Phd*.93d; τὰ προωμολογημένα *things granted beforehand*, Id.*Tht*.159c:—Med., S.E.*M*.1.9, Gal.4.726. II. Pass., *to be betrothed beforehand*, J.*Ap*.2.24. **–ησις**, εως, ἡ, *previous concession*, Olymp. *in Phd*.p.133N. (pl.). **–ητέον**, *one must concede beforehand*, Arist.*Top*.110$^{b}$3. **–ία**, ἡ, *previous agreement, arrangement*, τοῦ μισθοῦ Plu. *in Hes*.33.

**προονειδίζω**, *reproach before*, Eust.754.47 (Pass.).

**προόντως**, Adv. *in priority to Being*, τὸ π. ὄν Iamb.*Myst*.8.2 (v.l. πρὸ ὄντος).

**προοξῠτονέω**, = παροξυτονέω, in Pass., Phot. s.v. τριακοντούτης.

**προοπτάω**, *roast beforehand*, Alex.149.11.

**προ-οπτέον**, (προοράω) *one must look to, be careful of*, σέο τε καὶ σῆς ἀρχῆς Hdt.1.120. **–όπτης**, ου, ὁ, *scout, vedette*, οἱ π. τῶν ἱππέων Plb.29.17.3, cf. Plu.2.370a. **–οπτικός**, ή, όν, *of* or *for foreseeing*, Προοπτικόν, τό, title of work by Heraclides, D.L.5.88. ⊛ **–οπτος**, Att. contr. **προὖπτος**, ον, *foreseen, manifest*, προόπτῳ θανάτῳ δώσειν τινά Hdt.9.17, cf. Isoc.10.27; ἐς προὖπτον κίνδυνον καταστῆσαι Th.5.99, cf. 111; π. ἀγγέλου λόγος A.*Th*.848 (lyr.); ἐς προὖπτον Ἅιδην S.*OC*1440, cf. E.*Hipp*.1366 (anap.); εἰς προὖπτον.. αὐτὸν ἐνέβαλεν κακόν Aristopho 5; εἰς προὖπτον.. ἐμπεσεῖν κακόν Phoenicid.4.18.

**προόρ-ᾱσις**, εως, ἡ, *foreseeing, prevision*, ἄνευ –οράσεως καὶ προσδοκίας Phld.*D*.1.13; π. θεοῦ Plot.3.2.1, cf. 6.7.1, Simp. *in Ph*.391.32: pl., Them.*Or*.11.146b; Σεβαστὴ Π., = Lat. *Providentia Augusta*, *IG Rom*.4.1593 (Metropolis). **–ᾱτής**, οῦ, ὁ, = καραδοκητής, Sch.E.*Hec*.1135. **–ᾱτικός**, ή, όν, *quick at foreseeing*, Arist.*Div.Somn*.463$^{b}$15; τῶν ἀδήλων Ph.2.176; ἧττον εἶ π. τῆς φύσεως Gal.*UP*5.8; τὸ π. μέρος τῆς τέχνης the *predictive* province of astrology, Id.19.530. **–ᾱτός**, ή, όν, *to be foreseen*, ἀνθρωπίνῃ προνοίᾳ X.*Cyr*.1.6.23. ⊛ **–άω**, fut. προόψομαι: pf. προεόρᾱκα: (cf. προεῖδον):—*see before one, look forward to*, τὰ ἔμπροσθεν Id.*HG*4.3.23; *see what is just before the eyes*, Th.7.44: abs., *look before one* or *forward*, εἰς τὸ πρόσθεν

Arist.*HA*524$^{a}$14; ὀφθαλμοῖς π. X.*Cyr*.4.3.21. 2. *foresee*, τὸ μέλλον γίνεσθαι Hdt.5.24, etc.; π. ὀλίγα περὶ τοῦ μέλλοντος X.*Cyr*.3.2.15; ἑαυτοῖς τὸ ἐπιόν Id.*Smp*.4.5; πρὸ τῶν πραγμάτων π. οὐδέν D.4.41, cf. 54.19 (Pass.): abs., π. διανοίᾳ Arist.*Pol*.1252$^{a}$32. 3. c. gen., *take thought or care, make provision for*.., σεωυτοῦ Hdt.5.39; τοῦ σίτου Id.3.159; ἐκείνων προορῶν, ὅκως..ἔχωσι Id.2.121.α′: abs., τὸ προορᾶν..σευ your *thoughtfulness*, Id.9.79. 4. *see previously*, *Act.Ap*.21.29. II. Med., with pf. and plpf. Pass., *look before one*, δυοῖν ὀφθαλμοῖν προεωρᾶτο X.*Cyr*.4.3.21 (s. v. l.). 2. *foresee*, ἐς οἷα φέρονται Th.5.111; τὸν πόλεμον D.5.24. 3. *provide for*, τὸ ἐφ' ἑαυτῶν Th.1.17; ταῦτα Pl.*R*.499a; πάνθ' ἃ προσήκει D.6.8, etc.; *make provision*, περὶ τῶν μελλόντων Lys.33.7; πρός τι D.S.20.102; π. μή c. inf., *cavere ne*.. D.25.11.

**προοργάζω**, *prepare beforehand* as for reception of a dye, metaph., Dam.*Pr*.427.

**προορ-ίζω**, *determine beforehand*, ἡμέραν Hld.7.24; *predetermine, predestine*, ἡμᾶς εἰς υἱοθεσίαν *Ep.Eph*.1.5; τι γενέσθαι *Act.Ap*.4.28; τινὰς συμμόρφους (sc. γενέσθαι) *Ep.Rom*.8.29. **-ισμα**, ατος, τό, = οὐρός, in pl., Hsch. s. v. οὔρους (οὖρος and οὐρός confused). **-ισμός**, ὁ, *early determination*, Hp.*Praec*.3.

**προορμ-άω**, in Pass., *move forward, push on*, X.*Cyr*.4.3.1. II. intr. in Act., *advance*, ib.1.4.21, *HG*5.2.28; of plants, *advance*, πρὸς αὔξησιν Thphr.*CP*1.12.8, cf. 1.10.7, etc.:—Pass., ib.1.12.6. **-έω**, *sail from an anchorage*, Poll.1.122. **-ίζω**, *moor or anchor in front*, ὁλκάδας πρὸ τοῦ σταυρώματος Th.7.38.

**προορνῑθίαι ἄνεμοι**, οἱ, North winds *that prevail before the spring-birds arrive*, Gem.*Calend*.9.

**προορούω**, *break loose before*, τοῦ λογισμοῦ Them.*Or*.1.7c.

❋ **προορύσσω**, *dig beforehand*, Apollod.*Poliorc*.140.6 (Pass.).

**προορχ-έομαι**, *lead the dance*, *Gloss*. **-ηστήρ**, ῆρος, ὁ, *one who leads the dance*, among the Thessalians = προαγωνιστής, Luc.*Salt*.14.

**προουρέω**, *make water before*, π. αἱματώδεα Hp.*Epid*.4.29.

**πρόουρον**, τό, *first juice from the grapes*, Hsch.

**προούσιος**, ον, *prior to Being*, π. καὶ ἀρχὴ τῆς οὐσίας Iamb.*Myst*.8.2, cf. 10.5; τὸ π. Anon. *in Prm*. in *Rh.Mus*.47.613.

**προοφείλω**, Att. contr. **προὐφ-**, *owe beforehand*, πολλὰ πολλοῖς D.C.47.16: metaph., π. κακόν τινι *owe* one an atonement, i. e. *deserve* evil *at his hands*, E.*IT*523; κακὸν ταῖς πλευραῖς π. *owe* one's ribs a mischief, i. e. *deserve* a beating, Ar.*V*.3; π. τι χρηστὸν τῇ πόλει παραινέσαι Id.*Lys*.648:—Pass., *to be due beforehand*, of debts, ὁ προοφειλόμενος φόρος the *arrears* of tribute, Hdt.6.59, cf. X.*HG*1.5.7; τὸ ληφθὲν προωφείλετο ἱματιοκαπήλῳ Luc.*Merc.Cond*.38: generally, ἔχθρη προοφειλομένη ἐς Ἀθηναίους the hatred *they had long had reason to feel*, Hdt.5.82: εὐεργεσία προὐφειλομένη a kindness *that has long remained as a debt*, Th.1.32; προωφείλετο αὐτῷ κακόν *a debt* of punishment *had long been owing* to him, Antipho 5.61, cf. D.21.77; ἦν μοί τις οὐ μικρὰ π. χάρις Luc.*Abd*.15. II. *to be bound* to do, τὸ προὐφείλειν καλῶς πράσσειν..τούσδε E.*Heracl*.240.

**προοφθαλμ-ίς**, ίδος, ἡ, *first bud* of a young vine, *Gp*.5.3.3. **-ως**, Adv. *before one's eyes*, λαβόντες *PTeb*.28.18 (ii B. C.).

**προοχεύω**, *impregnate before*, Phlp. *in GA*128.13:—Pass., of eggs, Arist.*GA*757$^{b}$2.

**προοχή**, ἡ, *prominent point, eminence*, Plb.4.43.2.

**προόψιος**, ον, *foreseeing*, epith. of Apollo, Paus.1.32.2.

**πρόοψις**, εως, ἡ, *foreseeing*, Th.5.8. II. *seeing before one*, οὐκ οὔσης τῆς προόψεως ᾗ..since there was no *seeing* where.., cj. in Id.4.29 (προσόψεως codd.). III. *provision*, σταθμῶν *SIG*880.15 (Pizus, iii A. D.).

**προπᾰγής**, ὀφθαλμοὶ π. f. l. for προπαλεῖς or προπετεῖς in Luc.*Musc.Enc*.3.

**προπᾰθ-αίνομαι**, of an orator, *to be passionate beforehand*, Sopat. in Rh.8.58 W. **-εια**, ἡ, *preliminary experience, anticipation*, ἐλπίς ἐστι π. τις Ph.*Fr*.17 H.: pl., *anticipations of suffering*, Plu.2.666d; *premonitory symptoms* of disease, ib.127c. 2. *previous experience*, Id.*Fr*.7.10. **-ημα**, ατος, τό, *previous suffering*, f. l. for προμάθημα, Hsch. s. v. προπαιδεύματα. **-ής**, ές, *suffering before*, f. l. for πραϋπαθής in Ph.2.595.

**προπαιδ-εία**, ἡ, *preparatory teaching*, τῆς π., ἣν τῆς διαλεκτικῆς δεῖ προπαιδευθῆναι which they must receive before entering on dialectic, Pl.*R*.536d, cf. Luc.*Rh.Pr*.14. **-ευμα**, ατος, τό, = foreg., ἐγκύκλια π. Ph.1.157. **-ευσις**, εως, ἡ, = foreg., Ascl. *in Metaph*.134.12. **-εύω**, *teach beforehand*, in Pass., Pl.*R*.536d; πρὸς πάσας..τέχνας ἔστιν ἃ δεῖ προπαιδεύεσθαι Arist.*Pol*.1337$^{a}$19; ὑπό τινων S.E.*M*.6.29.

**προπαιδοποιέω**, *generate before*, Herm.ap.Stob.1.49.44.

**προπαίζω**, *sport before*, *Anacreont.App*.2 p.352 Bgk.

❋ **πρόπαις**, παιδος, ὁ, at Sparta, *boy in his fourth year*, Λέξεις Ἡροδότου in Stein Hdt. ii p.465 (Berol. 1871). II. = μαστροπός, Hsch.

**πρόπᾰλαι**, Adv. *very long ago*, π. πάλαι πάλαι Ar.*Eq*.1155, cf. Plu.2.674f, Luc.*JTr*.26; πάλαι καὶ π. Them.*Or*.2.38a.

**προπάλαιος** [ᾰ], ον, *very old*, οἶνος Orib.5.33.1; ἔλαιον Aët.15.14.

**προπᾰλαιόω**, *keep till old*, ἰχθύας Ruf.ap.Orib.4.2.16.

**προπᾰλ-εια** [πᾰ], ἡ, *prominence*, ἡ τῶν ὠτίων (fort. ἀγγείων) π. S.E.*M*.8.219. **-ής**, ές, (πάλλω) *prominent*, ὀφθαλμοί Philostr.*Gym*.25, Adam.*Phgn*.2.2, v. l. in Luc.*Musc.Enc*.3; φάρυγξ Philostr.*Gym*.30; ἀγγεῖα (blood-vessels) προπαλέστατα prob. for ἀ. προπαλειότητα in Herod.Med. in *Rh.Mus*.58.78; τὸ π. the *presenting part* in obstetrics, Sor.2.64: Comp., *more to the front*, Id.1.7; τὸ γένειον προπαλέστερος Poll.4.138. II. Adv. -λῶς, = δαψιλῶς, Hsch.

**προπαππικός**, ή, όν, *like a great-grandfather*, ἀβελτερία Poll.3.18.

❋ **πρόπαππος**, ὁ, *great-grandfather*, And.2.26 codd., Lys.14.39, Pl.*Ti*.20e. 2. *grandfather*, M.Ant.1.4.

❋ **πρόπᾰρ**, (παρά) Prep. with gen., *before, in front of*, Hes.*Th*.518, E.*Ph*.120 (lyr.). 2. *along*, αἰγιαλοῖο A.R.1.454, 4.1288. II. abs. as Adv., *before, sooner, rather*, A.*Supp*.791 (lyr.).

**προπαραβάλλω**, *put beside* one *beforehand*, τί τινι Alex.Trall.11.1:—Med., *do so for oneself*, λίθους προπαρεβάλοντο σφίσιν Th.7.5.

**προπαραγγέλλω**, *announce beforehand*, *GDI*5040.41 (Crete), Hld.9.10: c. inf., D.C.46.41:—Pass., *to be warned before*, Aen.Tact.27.3.

**προπαρα-γίγνομαι**, *to be present before*, Sch.Pl.*Grg*.506d. **-δέχομαι**, *receive before*, *PRyl*.214.10 (Pass., ii A. D.). **-δίδωμι**, *explain or set down beforehand*, Sor.*Fasc*.7 (Pass.), Orib.49.25.5 (Pass.), Sch.Il.6.401, etc. II. *betray beforehand*, Gal.5.310 (Pass.).

**προπαραινέω**, *warn beforehand*, *Gloss*.

**προπαραιτ-έομαι**, *deprecate in advance*, Aps.*Rh*.p.251 H. **-ησις**, εως, ἡ, *deprecation in advance*, ib.pp.258, 280 H. (both pl.).

**προπαρά-κειμαι**, *exist already*, *BGU*243.14 (ii A. D.). **-λαμβάνω**, *receive from* another *before*, D.C.49.18. II. intr., *anticipate* the menstrual period, Sor.1.21 (nisi leg. προλαμβ-). III. προπαραλαμβανόμεναι ὑποθέσεις *previously assumed*.., [Ammon.] *in APr*.67.15. 2. -ληφθεισῶν τῶν..ἐμπλάστρων *previously employed*, Orib.*Fr*.49. **-λήγω**, *to be the antepenultimate*, ἡ προπαραλήγουσα (sc. συλλαβή) the *antepenultimate*, Sch.Ar.*Ra*.1455, Eust.15.34, al.:—Med., π. τῷ ο *have* ο *in the antepenultimate*, *EM*308.49. **-λύομαι**, *to be paralysed first*, τοῦ νεύρου -λυθέντος Gal.2.668. **-μῡθέομαι**, *set forth, expound beforehand*, S.E.*M*.9.293. **-σημαίνομαι**, Pass., *to be noted before*, Eust.1133.14, al.

**προπαρασκευ-άζω**, *prepare beforehand*, ἔρια Pl.*R*.429d, cf. *Plt*.308d; πάντα τινί X.*Mem*.2.2.5; τὰς γνώμας Th.2.88; τι πρὸς τὴν τροφήν Arist.*HA*613$^{a}$4:—Med., *prepare for oneself*, ἐντάφια Is.8.38; ταῦτα περὶ τοὺς Ποτειδεάτας π. Th.1.57; π. τὸν ὅμιλον *for one's purposes*, D.C.38.13: abs., *make one's preparations*, Aen.Tact.11.14, Plu.*Eum*.6:—Pass., ἐκ πολλοῦ προπαρεσκευασμένοι, εἴ ποτε πολεμήσονται Th.1.68. **-αστέον**, *one must prepare before*, Plu.2.124a. **-αστικός**, ή, όν, *preparatory*, Theo Sm.p.16 H., Philagr.ap.Orib.5.17.4. **-ή**, ἡ, *preparation*, Hp.*Acut*.25 (pl.), Sor.1.66, Procl. *in Prm*.p.679 S. (pl.); π. *futurae litis*, Donat. ad Ter.*Eun*.495; of τελετή, opp. μύησις, Herm. *in Phdr*.p.158 A.

**προπαρα-τάσσω**, *post in front*, στρατὸν πρὸ τοῦ στρατοπέδου D.C.49.8. **-τέλευτος**, ον, *antepenultimate*: ἡ π. (sc. συλλαβή), = ἡ προπαραλήγουσα, *Gloss*. **-τήρησις**, εως, ἡ, *previous observation*, Gal.19.396. **-τίθημι**, *set on table before*, in Med., π. τραγήματα Heraclid. Tar.ap.Ath.2.53c, cf. eund.ib.3.120c. **-χωρέω**, *alienate before*, *CPR*22.15 (Pass., ii A. D.).

**προπαρ-εγγυάω**, *guarantee in advance*, Anon.ap.Suid. (Pass.). **-έρχομαι**, *pass already*, τοῦ -ελθόντος ε̄ ἔτους *PLond*.3.1212.5 (iii A. D.). **-έχω**, *offer before*, ἐμαυτόν σοι σύμμαχον X.*Cyr*.5.5.20; *present first*, εἰς ὑπόδησιν τὸν δεξιὸν πόδα Iamb.*Protr*.21.ια′. II. Med., *supply before*, μιᾶς ἡμέρας σῖτον X.*HG*5.1.18.

**προπάροιθε** [ᾰ], before a vowel -θεν (προπάροιθ' Od.24.416, 447, A.*Ag*.1020), Prep. with gen., *before, in front of*, ὑμείων π. μαχοίατο Il.4.348; πάντων δὲ π. 16.218; Ἰλίου π. 15.66; Αἰγύπτου π. Od.4.355; π. ὁμίλου *before* the assembly, Il.23.804; π. ποδῶν *at* one's feet, 13.205; ποδῶν π. Od.17.357; π. ἀνδρός *at* a man's *feet*, A. l. c. (lyr.); π. θυράων *before* the door, i. e. outside, Od.1.107; Σκαιῶν π. πυλάων Il.6.307; π. πόλιος, πόληος, 2.811, Hes.*Sc*.285; πύργων π. B.5.148; ἠϊόνος π. *before*, i. e. *along*, Il.2.92; π. νεός *in front of*, i. e. *beyond* the ship, Od.9.482 (opp. μετόπισθε νεός ib.539): metaph., τῆς ἀρετῆς ἱδρῶτα θεοὶ π. ἔθηκαν Hes.*Op*.289. 2. *before the time of*, νομίμων π. A.*Th*.334 (lyr.). II. as Adv., 1. of Place, *before, in front*, π. κιών Il.15.260, cf. Hes.*Th*.769; οὐδ' εἴ οἱ π.... υἱὸν χαλκῷ δῃόφεν *before his eyes*, Od.4.225. 2. of Time, *before, first*, Il.10.476, Od.17.277; σφι π. φάνη μέγα ἔργον ἐρεῖ that, Il.11.734, cf. Call.*Fr*.182; opp. ὀπίσσω, Od.11.483; τῶν π. εὐγενετᾶν E.*Ph*.1510 (lyr.).

**προπαροξ-υντέον**, *one must place the acute accent on the antepenultimate*, Sch.Ar.*Pax*956. **-υντικός**, ή, όν, *given to placing the acute accent on the antepenultimate*, Αἰολεῖς Eust.75.37. ❋ **-ύνω** [ῡ], *pronounce with the acute accent on the antepenultimate*, Act. and Pass., A.D.*Pron*.30.7, 50.5, al., Hdn.Gr.2.924, 926, Plu.2.845b. II. Pass., *have a premature access of fever*, Gal.16.708.

**προπαροξῠ-τονέω**, = foreg. I, Hsch. s. v. κραταιίς. **-τόνησις**, εως, ἡ, *use of proparoxytone accentuation*, Eust.1361.39. **-τονος**, ον, *with the acute on the antepenultimate*, D.T.p.108 U., Theognost.*Can*.67. Adv. -νως Hermog.*Stat*.2, Phryn.115.

❋ **πρόπᾱς**, πᾶσα, πᾶν, in Hom. and Hes. mostly π. ἦμαρ *all* day *long*, where πρό 'on and on' goes with the verb, Il.1.601, Od.9.161, al.; hence πρόπας becomes merely a strengthd. form of πᾶς, once in Hom., νῆας προπάσας *all* the ships *together*, Il.2.493; freq. in Trag., πρόπασα χώρα, γαῖα, A.*Pr*.407 (lyr.), *Pers*.548 (lyr.); π. δόμος Id.*Ag*.1011 (lyr.); πρόπαντος χρόνου Id.*Eu*.898; π. στόλος, πότμος, S.*OT*169 (lyr.), *Ant*.859 (lyr.); πρόπαντα κακὰ κακῶν Id.*OC*1237 (lyr.); π. γέννα E.*Or*.972 (lyr.); π. ἐσμός *Pae.Delph*.14: neut. πρόπαν as Adv., *utterly*, E.*Ph*.1504 (lyr.).

**πρόπασμα**, ατος, τό, (πάσσω) *salve*, *PMasp*.6 ii 48 (vi A. D.).

**προπαστάς**, άδος, ἡ, *vestibule*, v.l. for παστάς in Sch.A.R.1.789; cf. **προπάστεον** (sic)· τὸν πρὸ τῆς παστάδος τόπον, Hsch.

**προπάσχω**, *suffer first* or *beforehand*, Hdt.7.11, Th.3.82, etc.; τι S.*OC*230 (lyr.), Antipho 2.1.5, Pl.*R*.376a; *to be ill-treated before*, ὑφ' ἡμῶν Th.3.67; π. οὐδὲν ἀγαθόν X.*Mem*.2.2.5: generally, *to be previously affected* or *modified*, Plu.2.725a, Plot.4.5.2.

✱ **προπᾰτέω**, *tread out* corn *before*, *PLond*.1.113.523 (i A.D.).

**προπᾰτήρ**, έρος, ὁ, = sq., *PMag.Par*.1.3122.

**προπάτωρ** [ᾰ], ορος, ὁ, (πατήρ) *first founder of a family, forefather*, Pi.*N*.4.89, Hdt.2.161, 9.122, E.*Or*.1441 (lyr.); ὦ Ζεῦ, προγόνων προπάτωρ S.*Aj*.387 (lyr., s.v.l.); opp. πατήρ, Pl.*Lg*.931d; *ancestor* of a tribe, *OGI*446.3 (Phrygia); θεὸς ὁ π. Herm.ap.Stob.1.49.44, cf. Id.ib.3.11.31, *IGRom*.4.1213, 1215 (Thyatira); Διόνυσος ὁ π. τῆς πόλεως D.Chr.39.8, cf. *BCH*4.157 (Erythrae); *primal god*, *PMag.Par*.1.1988, *PMag.Leid.V*.7.26; π. τῶν ἐν γενέσει δημιουργὸν προτάττουσι Iamb.*Myst*.8.4: in pl., *ancestors, forefathers*, Hdt.2.169, Pl.*Lg*.717e; *founders, inventors* of arts and sciences, Vett.Val.3.22.

**προπαύω**, *stop* a process *before*, π. πρίν.. Hp.*Liqu*.1:—Med., D.S.1.39, Lib.*Or*.2.62.

**προπείθω**, in Pass., *to be persuaded beforehand*, Nausiph.2, Luc.*Alex*.17.

**προπεῖν**, v. προπῖν.

**πρόπειρα**, ἡ, *previous trial* or *venture*, ἐν Ἀθηναίοισι τὴν πρόπειραν ποιέεσθαι, Lat. *periculum facere in..*, Hdt.9.48; π. ποιεῖσθαι εἰ.. Th.3.86; π. τινὸς λαμβάνειν Ael.*NA*8.22; of *a trial* in athletic exercises, *IG*14.1102.16 (pl.).

**προπειρ-άζω**, = sq., -πειράζοντες δικέλλαις ἀνασκάπτειν Ph.*Bel*.100.9; -άσαντες τὸ φάρμακον Herod.Med.ap.Orib.8.3.7. **-άομαι**, Med., with aor. and pf. Pass., *try* or *prove before*, τινος Luc.*Herm*.53, Vett.Val.168.1, D.C.51.11; pf. part. -πεπειραμένος J.*AJ*9.4.4, Gal.13.861.

**προπεμπ-τήριος**, ον, = sq., λόγος Him.*Ecl*.13 tit.; π. ὕμνος a *funeral* hymn, Philostr.*VA*3.49. **-τικός**, ή, όν, *accompanying, escorting, used in escorting*, λαλιά Men.Rh.p.395 S.; λόγοι Him.*Ecl*.10.1; περίοδος Sch.Ar.*Eq*.496. Adv. -κῶς Iamb.*VP*28.145.

**πρόπεμπτος**, ον, only neut. pl. πρόπεμπτα as Adv., *five days before*, Lex.ap.D.43.75, Lys.*Fr*.26 S.: c. gen., *IG*2[2].1237.61.

**προπέμπω**, aor. προέπεμψα, contr. προὔπεμψα, *send before, send forward* or *forth*, πρό μ' ἔπεμψεν ἄναξ Il.1.442; εὖτέ μιν εἰς Ἀΐδαο.. προὔπεμψεν 8.367, cf. Od.17.54, 117, 24.360; π. κήρυκας Hdt.1.60, cf. 4.33 (Pass.), 121, Th.1.29, S.*El*.1158, etc.; π. πρὸ τοῦ στρατεύματος ἄνδρας X.*Cyr*.2.4.23:—Med., ib.5.3.53, *An*.7.2.14:—Pass., impers., προπέπεμπται Th.7.77. b. with a thing for the object, τινὶ φήμας π. S.*El*.1155; ξίφος *afford, furnish*, Id.*Ph*.1205 (lyr.); π. ἄχη *cause*, Id.*Ant*.1287 (lyr.). 2. of things, *send forth*, σποδὸς π. κίονας πλούτου πνοάς A.*Ag*.820; ἰοὺς ἀφύκτους καὶ προπέμποντας φόνον S.*Ph*.105. II. *conduct, escort*, esp. a departing traveller, Hdt.1.111, 3.50, S.*OC*1667, Antipho 1.16, Thphr.*Char*.5.2, etc.; τινὰ ἐς δόμους A.*Pers*.530; νύμφην π. X.*HG*4.1.9, etc.; π. τινὰ χθονὸς *from* the land, E.*Hipp*.1099; π. τινὰ μέλεσιν καὶ μολπαῖσιν Ar.*Ra*.1525 (anap.); π. τινὰ τοῖς ἵπποις X.*An*.7.2.8; τοῖς προπέμπουσι καμήλοις Πολύκαρπον *PFlor*.206.2 (iii A.D.); esp. *follow* a corpse *to the grave*, τινὰ ἐπὶ τύμβῳ A.*Th*.1064 (anap.); Καρικῇ μούσῃ τοὺς τελευτήσαντας Pl.*Lg*.800e; τιμὰς π. θεοῖς *carry* offerings *in procession*, A.*Pers*.622: jocosely, τὸν ἕνα ψωμὸν ἑνὶ ὄψῳ π. *let* one piece of bread *be attended* by one condiment, X.*Mem*.3.14.6:—Pass., Isoc.4.148; of a funeral procession, -πεμφθέντες κοινῇ ὑπὸ τῆς πόλεως Pl.*Mx*.236d; πανδημεὶ προπεμπομένους ἐπὶ θάνατον, of the Minotaur's victims, Isoc.10.27; ὑπὸ ποιητικῆς ἐπὶ φιλοσοφίαν Plu.2.37b. 2. *pursue*, X.*HG*7.2.13.

**προπένθερος**, ὁ, *one's father-in-law's father*, Sch.rec.S.*OT*1494.

**προπεπαίνομαι**, Pass., *to become concocted prematurely*, Hp.*Epid*.4.28.

**προπεραίνω**, *complete before*, ἡ πρὸς ἁπάντων -πεπερασμένη γνῶσις A.D.*Synt*.26.21.

**προπερι-ειλέω**, *wrap round first*, -ειλημένος ἐρίῳ Heliod.ap.Orib.49.9.1. **-ελίσσω**, *twist round first*, Aen.Tact.31.20. **-ζόμενος**· ἀγκαλιζόμενος, Hsch. **-κάθαίρω**, *cleanse all round before*, Dsc.*Eup*.1.196, Aphrodas ap.Gal.12.878. **-κειμαι**, *to be previously applied*, Sor.1.76. **-κλύζω**, *wash round before*, Id.2.86. **-ξύω**, *scrape all round first*, Gal.13.379, Orib.*Fr*.114. **-πᾰτέω**, *take walking exercise first*, Diocl.*Fr*.141, Antyll.ap.Orib.6.9.1, Gal.11.311. **-σπαστέον**, *one must circumflex the penultimate*, Sch.Ar.*Pax*1, etc. **-σπάω**, *circumflex the penultimate*, Gal.18(2).518 (Pass.), Sch.Ar.*Eq*.21, etc.; προπερισπώμενον, τό, *a word circumflexed on the penultimate*, Hdn.Gr.1.10 (pl.). Adv. προπερισπωμένως *circumflexed on the penultimate*, Sch.Ar.*Av*.1655, etc. **-χᾰράσσω**, *incise beforehand round about*, Dsc.3.80 (Pass.), etc.

**προπέρῠσι**, before a vowel -σιν, Adv. *two years ago*, Pl.*Euthd*.272b, D.20.33, 33.25, *PThead*.16.4 (iv A.D.), cj. in Lys.9.4, etc.: but πρωπέρυσιν is Att. acc. to A.D.*Adv*.166.25, Phryn.*PS*p.105 B., and is required by the metre in Pherecr.182.

**προπερῠσινός**, ή, όν, *of the year before last*, καρπός Thphr.*HP*3.12.4: later προπερσυνός, *PSI*1.50.13 (iv/v A.D.).

**προπέσσω**, Att. -ττω, *digest* or *concoct beforehand*, Gal.*UP*7.9:—pf. Pass. -πέπεμμαι ib.14.10; inf. -πεπέφθαι Aret.*CD*1.3.

**προπέτᾰμαι**, *fly before*, in aor. -επετάσθην, Ath.9.395a.

**προπετάννῡμι** and -ύω, *spread out before*, ὑμᾶς αὐτοὺς προπετάσαντες ἡμῶν X.*Cyr*.4.2.23; κυλικείου τοὐθόνιον προπέπταται Ar.*Fr*.104: metaph., σκιαγραφίαν πολιτείας πρὸ τῆς ἀληθείας π. D.C.52.7.

**προπέτασμα**, ατος, τό, *curtain*: metaph., ὁ λόγος μεθέμενος τῶν π. αὐτοπρόσωπος διαλέξεται Them.*Or*.13.165c.

✱ **προπετ-εια**, ἡ, *headlong haste, rashness*, Isoc.5.90, Arist.*EN*1150[b]19; opp. σωφροσύνη, D.19.251; τρόπου π. Id.21.38; π. καὶ θρασύτης Id.22.63, cf. 23.130; π. καὶ ἀπόνοια Id.44.58; *hasty judgement*, Gal.*Anim.Pass*.2.6; *fickleness*, Plb.10.6.2. II. *prominence*, of the nose, Sor.1.103; of the eyes, Gal.18(2).301, Aët.7.2. ✱ **-εύομαι**, *to be hasty*, S.E.*P*.1.20, 205; μηδὲν π. Id.*M*.9.49. **-ηλον**· πεποίηται ἀπὸ τοῦ προπίπτειν, Hsch. **-ής**, ές, (προπίπτω) *falling* or *slipping down* in bed, εἰ π. γένοιτο Hp.*Prog*.3; π. ἐπὶ πόδας Id.*Coac*.487; π. ἂν ἐγίνετο ἡ βάδισις *out of control*, Arist.*IA*712[a]29, cf. Diocl.*Fr*.142. 2. *inclined forward*, κεφαλὴ τοῦ βραχίονος π. ἐς τοὔμπροσθεν Hp.*Art*.1; -έστεραι γένυες *more prominent*, ib.31; ὁ μὲν αὐχὴν.. μὴ π. πεφύκοι X.*Eq*.1.8; *sloping*, of shoulders, Gal.1.623; *stooping*, μὴ ὀρθὸς ἀλλὰ μικρῷ -έστερος Arist.*Phgn*.807[b]31. 3. *thrown away*, κεῖται προπετὲς [τὸ κάταγμα] S.*Tr*.701. 4. *drooping, at the point of death*, ζῇ γὰρ π. ib.976 (anap.); ἡ π. Μοῖρα *untimely*, *IG*5(1).1355 (Messenia, ii A.D.). 5. *prominent*, of the eyes, Poll.1.189, Philum.ap.Orib.*Syn*.8.10, Alex.Aphr.*Pr*.2.22; γνάθοι, ὀφρῦς, Poll.4.68, 134. II. metaph., 1. *being upon the point of*, πολιὰς ἐπὶ χαίτας π. E.*Alc*.909 (lyr.); τύμβου π. παρθένος Id.*Hec*.150 (anap.). 2. *ready for, prone to* a thing, ἐπί or εἴς τι, X.*HG*2.3.15, 6.5.24; πρὸς τὰς ἡδονάς Pl.*Lg*.792d: c. inf., -έστατος μεταστῆσαι X.*HG*2.3.30. 3. *headlong*, π. ἄγειν τὸν ἀκροατήν Arist.*Rh*.1409[b]31. 4. *precipitate, rash, reckless*, π. σώματος ἡδοναί Aeschin.1.191; π. γέλως *uncontrolled* laughter, Isoc.1.15; εἴ τι -έστερον ἔπραττον Hyp.*Dem.Fr*.6, cf. Men.*Pk*.441; ἡ π. ἀκρασία Arist.*EN*1150[b]26; π. βίος Men.382; π. γλῶσσα Alciphr.3.57; of a lot, *drawn at random*, Pi.*N*.6.63. b. of persons, οἱ θρασεῖς προπετεῖς Arist.*EN*1116[a]7; τὰ θήλεα..[τῶν ἀρρένων] -έστερα Id.*HA*608[b]1; μανικὸς καὶ π. ἐπὶ τῶν κινδύνων Theopomp.Hist.268; οἱ π. Arr.*Epict*.4.13.5; οἱ γλώσσῃ προπετεῖς *APl*.4.89 (Gall.); τὸ π., = προπέτεια, opp. τὸ σεμνόν, Hp.*Medic*.1. 5. ἁρμονίαι π. *flowing* rhythms, D.H.*Dem*.40. 6. Medic., *subject to diarrhoea*, Ath.13.584d (Comp.). III. Adv. **-τῶς** *headlong, out of control*, π. εἰς τὸ κάταντες φέρεσθαι X.*Eq*.8.8. 2. metaph., *headlong, hastily*, π. φέρεσθαι εἰς τὴν τυραννίδα Id.*Hier*.7.2; προπετέως ταχυγλωσσότεροι Hp.*Epid*.4.45; ἐπερέσθαι π. X.*Cyr*.1.3.8, cf. Men.*Epit*.306; ἀποκρίνεσθαι, ἀποφαίνεσθαι, etc., Pl.*Phlb*.45a, Isoc.12.272, etc.; π. ἔχειν to be *rash*, X.*Cyr*.1.4.4 (v.l.); μηδὲν.. πράξῃς π. Men.574; *prematurely*, *AP*5.144 (Asclep.); -έστερον χρῆσθαι ταῖς προνομαῖς Plb.3.102.11.

**προπέτομαι**, *fly forwards*, Arr.*An*.3.3.6, Eust.899.56.

**προπεῶντες**· προεστῶτες, Hsch.

**προπή**, ἡ, = Lat. *decus*, *Gloss*. (s.v.l.).

**προπήγνῡμι**, *fix beforehand*, pf. imper. Pass., προπεπήχθω πρίν.. Paul.Aeg.6.120. 2. προπεπηγὸς δάκρυον *congealed before*, Dsc.3.78 (v.l. προσ-).

**προπηδ-άω**, fut. -ήσομαι A.*Fr*.23:—*spring before*, τῶν ἄλλων Luc.*DMort*.19.2. 2. *spring forward*, D.S.17.100, Arr.*Tact*.12.4, App.*Syr*.35: c. gen., χηραμοῦ Babr.107.13; τῆς σκηνῆς Hdn.6.9.1; ἐκ τοῦ ἱεροῦ J.*BJ*4.3.12; ἐκ τῶν πυλῶν ib.5.7.3; ἐς τὴν ἀγοράν Luc.*Alex*.13. **-ησις**, εως, ἡ, *protrusion*, ὀφθαλμῶν Polem.*Phgn*.17. II. *dislocation*, gloss on ἐκπάλεια, Sch.Orib.49.27.

**προπηλᾰκ-ίζω**, Att. fut. -ιῶ Th.6.54: (apparently from πῆλαξ = πηλός, though neither πῆλαξ nor the simple πηλακίζω certainly existed): —*bespatter with mud*, or *trample in the mire*: only metaph., *treat with contumely*, τοὐμὸν στόμα S.*OT*427, cf. Ar.*Th*.386 (Pass.); freq. in Att. Prose, Th. l.c., And.4.16, Pl.*R*.562d, etc.:—Pass., Lys.15.6, etc.; ἰδὼν προπεπηλακισμένην [τὴν φιλοσοφίαν] ἀναξίως Pl.*R*.536c; προπηλακισθέντες λόγοις ἢ καὶ ἀτίμοις ἔργοις Id.*Lg*.866e; ὑβρίζετο καὶ προὐπηλακίζεθ' ὑπὸ τοῦ δήμου D.9.60. II. c. acc. rei, *throw in one's teeth, reproach one with*, εἴ τις πενίαν π. Id.18.256. **-ισις**, εως, ἡ, *contumelious treatment*, τὰς τῶν οἰκείων π. τοῦ γήρως Pl.*R*.329b. **-ισμός**, ὁ, = foreg., Hdt.6.73; ὕβρις καὶ λοιδορία καὶ π. D.18.12; ὁ τῆς δικαιοσύνης π. Aeschin.3.258: pl., προπηλακισμοῖς κολάζειν Pl.*Lg*.855b, etc. **-ιστής**, οῦ, ὁ, *abusive person*, Diog.Oen.27 (pl.). (This word occurred in Hsch., but only the gloss is preserved in the MS.) **-ιστικός**, ή, όν, *contumelious*: Adv. -κῶς D.30.36.

**πρόπηξις**, εως, ἡ, *impact*, f.l. in Orib.50.41 tit.

**προπήχιον**, τό, v. παραπήχιον.

**προπῑ-έζω**, *compress first*, v.l. for προσπ- in Paul.Aeg.1.30 (Pass.). **-εσμός**, ὁ, *previous compression*, Id.6.21 (v.l. προσπ-).

**προπῖν** or **προπεῖν**, contr. aor. inf. of προπίνω used as Subst., a *drink* or *snack* taken *before* a meal, 'cocktail', Mart.12.82.11, Petron.28 (leg. *propin esse*), *CIL*5.5272.13, 25 (Comum), 4449.34 (Brixia).

✱ **προπῖνα**, = *popina*, *Gloss*.

**προπινάριον**, τό, *jug*, ἐλαίου prob. in *POxy*.1297.8 (iv A.D., προ[π]ειν-).

✱ **προπῑνάριος**, = Lat. *popinarius*, *MAMA*3.168 (Corasium, written πρωπ-).

✱ **προπίνω** [ῑ], impf. προὔπῑνον: fut. προπίομαι: aor. προὔπιον: pf. προπέπωκα:—*drink before* or *first*, opp. μεταπίνω, Hp.*Acut*.56 (Pass.), Thphr.*Od*.48 (Pass.), Luc.*Sat*.18, Ath.4.156e. 2. *take a snack before dinner*, Mart.5.78.3. 3. *drink up, drain dry*, ὅκως ἄμυστιν προπίω Anacr.63.3: metaph., ψυχὰν τὰν ἐν ἐμοὶ π. *drink* it *in*, *AP*5.170 (Mel.):—Pass., ἡ προποθεῖσα κύλιξ Call.*Epigr*.37. II. *drink to* another, i.e. *to his health, pledge* him (cf. Ath.5.193a, 10.432d), φιάλαν.. δωρήσεται.. γαμβρῷ π. Pi.*O*.7.4; ᾧ προπιεῖν ἐθέλει Critias *Fr*.6.8 D., cf. 33 D.; π. σοι X.*An*.7.3.26; also π. φιλοτησίας τινί D.

19.128, cf. Alex.291; προπινομένη ποίησις Dionys.Eleg.1. 2. *make a present of* the cup to the person pledged, [ἔκπωμα χρυσοῦν] σοι μεστὸν ἀκράτου προπίομαι Plu.*Alex.*39; τὰ ἐκπώματα.. ἐμπιμπλὰς προὔπινε καὶ ἐδωρεῖτο X.*Cyr.*8.3.35, cf. Sch.Pi. l. c.: hence, 3. simply, *give freely, make a present of*, Anacr.66; ἄλλα τε πολλὰ.., καὶ ἐκπώματ' ἀργυρᾶ καὶ χρυσᾶ προὔπινεν αὐτοῖς D.19.139; π. τὴν ἐλευθερίαν Φιλίππῳ *make* liberty *a drinking-present* to Philip, *give* it *carelessly* to him, Id.18.296; *sacrifice* one's friends, A.*Fr.* 131 (anap.), E.*Rh.*405, *PLond.*3.887.5 (iii B.C.); τούτῳ προέπιεν ὁ βασιλεὺς κώμην τινά Steph.Com.1.1; π. αὐτοῖς τὰς πατρίδας Plu.*Arat.* 14; αὐτῇ πέντε καὶ εἴκοσι μυριάδας ἀργυρίου Id.*Galb.*17; π. σοὶ ἄνδρα Ἕλληνα Philostr.*VA*3.28: c. gen. pretii, προπέποται τῆς παραυτίχ' ἡδονῆς καὶ χάριτος τὰ τῆς πόλεως πράγματα the interests of the state *have been sacrificed* for mere present pleasure, D.3.22, cf. App.*BC*2. 143 (v.l.).

**προπίονι**· εὐθεῖ, Hsch.

**προπῑπίσκω**, aor. -έπῖσα, *give to drink beforehand*, Hp.*Morb.*2.70.

⊛ **προπιπράσκω**, *sell before*, plpf. 3 sg. προεπεπράκει *PMich.Zen.*31. 27 (iii B.C.).

**προπίπτω**, fut. -πεσοῦμαι: aor. προὔπεσον:—*fall* or *throw oneself forward*, as in rowing, προπεσόντες ἔρεσσον Od.9.490, 12.194; π. ἡ κοιλία εἰς τὸ στόμα Arist.*HA*507ᵃ29; of suppliants, *fall prostrate*, E. *Supp.*63 (lyr.); *fall first*, in battle, Plb.1.58.8. II. *rush forward, rush headlong*, ἐν νάπει S.*OC*157 (lyr.); ἐς γαῖαν Theoc.24.113; *burst forth*, π. ἡ λίμνη Str.16.2.44. 2. metaph., *rush headlong*, Hyp.*Fr.* 161; εἰς ἄκαιρον γέλωτα, εἰς κίνδυνον, D.S.13.83, 20.88; *to be precipitate, come to a hasty decision*, *OGI*315.56 (Epist. Attali, ii B.C.): c. inf., π. πλημμελῆσαι M.Ant.1.17: abs., *form a hasty judgement*, Stoic term, Chrysipp.*Stoic.*2.291; π. πρὸ καταλήψεως *Stoic.*3.147, cf. Arr.*Epict.* 2.1.10, etc.; *make a slip of the tongue*, κἂν -πέσωσιν.. τάχιστα διορθοῦσθαι Phld.*Rh.*1.186S. III. *move forwards, advance before* the rest, Plb.1.20.15; οἱ προπίπτοντες, opp. οἱ ἀναχωροῦντες, Id.28.3.4; *project*, of a hill, προπεπτωκυῖα ὀφρύς Id.7.17.1; of an animal's snout, ῥύγχη προπέπτωκε Str.17.3.4; -πεπτωκότες τοῖς μετώποις Id.11.11.8; τὸ προπῖπτον [τοῦ δόρατος] the *projecting part*, Ascl.*Tact.*5.1: c. gen., *project beyond*, τὰ μέσα.. προπέπτωκε τῶν κεράτων Plb.3.115.7, etc.; κλῖμαξ π. τῶν ἐμβόλων Id.8.4.4; ἡ σάρισσα δέκα πήχεις π. πρὸ τῶν σωμάτων Id.18.29.4; ἡ ἄκρα ἔξω τῶν στηλῶν π. Str.2.5.33. 2. Medic., of *prolapse*, ἕδρα -πεσοῦσα Dsc.2.164; μήτρα προπίπτει Sor. 2.84. IV. metaph., *occur, be presented* to sense, Demetr.Lac.*Herc.* 1013.7; π. σημεῖα they *appear*, S.E.*M.*8.219 (προσπ- Bekker): hence, *to be obvious*, ὅσα π. τῶν ἁμαρτημάτων Plu.2.800b.

⊛ **προπιστ-εύω**, *trust* or *believe beforehand*, D.23.127, D.H.11.20, Ph.1.100:—Pass., προεπιστεύθησαν ἄξιοι εἶναι X.*Ages.*4.4. -όομαι, Pass., *to be made credible before*. pf. προπεπίστωμαι S.E.*P.*1.116, *M.*8. 122,261; ἐκ φαινομένου π. τὸ ἄδηλον ib.62.

**προπίτνω**, *fall prostrate*, ἐς γᾶν A.*Pers.*588 (lyr.); of a suppliant, S.*El.*1380.

⊛ **πρόπλασμα**, ατος, τό, *rough draft*, Cic.*Att.*12.41.4; sculptor's *clay model*, Plin.*HN*35.155.

**προπλάσσω**, *mould* or *form before*, τί τινος Ph.1.67.

**προπλέκω**, *wind, apply* a bandage *before*, aor. part. Pass. -πλᾰκείς Heliod.ap.Orib.48.43.1.

**προπλέω**, *sail before*, Th.4.120; cf. προπλώω.

**προπληρόω**, *fill before*, Asclep.ap.Gal.12.586, Ph.1.603, Dsc.*Alex. Praef.* (Pass.).

**προπλήσσω**, *strike first*, τὴν φόρμιγγα Him.*Or.*12.3.

**πρόπλοος**, ον, contr. -πλους, ουν, *sailing before* or *in advance*, τὰς πρόπλους ναῦς Th.6.44; τρεῖς νῆες αἱ πρόπλοι ib.46; αἱ πρόπλοι the *leading ships*, Isoc.4.92, App.*BC*5.85, etc.

**πρόπλοος**, contr. -πλους, ὁ, *sailing before* or *forward*, App.*BC*5. 112 (s.v.l.).

**προπλύνω** [ῡ], *wash clean before*, Dieuch.ap.Orib.4.7.30:—Pass., pf. inf. -πεπλύσθαι Gal.18(1).470; part. -πεπλυμένη Dsc.2.76.

**προπλώω**, Ion. for προπλέω, Hdt.5.98.

**προπνῑγεῖον**, τό, *room before the* πνιγεύς, Vitr.5.11.2, Plin.*Ep.*2. 17.11.

⊛ **προποδ-έω**, perh. *walk in front* as a guide, Call.*Fr.*1.2 P. -ηγός, Dor. -ᾱγός, όν, *going before to show the way, guide*, Plu.2.580c; σκίπωνα προποδαγόν *AP*6.294 (Phan.): fem. -ηγέτις, ιδος, Orph.*A.* 342. -ίζω, (πούς) *advance the foot*, κοῦφα ποσὶ προβιβὰς καὶ ὑπασπίδια προποδίζων Il.13.158, cf. 806; of a horse, Hld.3.3; esp. of the *direct motion* of planets, Sch.Paul.Al.*F.*3; opp. ἀναποδίζω, Vett.Val. 34.21, Simp.*in Cael.*491.24. II. metaph., *advance, progress*, πρόοδος καθ' ὑπόβασιν -ποδίζουσα Dam.*Pr.*56; ὁ προποδίζων ἀπὸ [τῆς μονάδος] ἀριθμός ib.57. -ισμός, ὁ, *process, progression*, ἀπὸ μονάδος Moderat.ap.Stob.1*Coroll.*8; ἀριθμός ἐστι π. πλήθους Theo Sm.p.18H.; π. εἰς τὸ ὂν τοῦ ἑνός Dam.*Pr.*67. II. *direct motion*, of planets, pl., opp. ὑποποδισμοί, Procl.*Hyp.*7.4; opp. ἀναποδισμοί, Nicom.*Ar.*1.5, Alex.Aphr.*in Metaph.*440.7. -ιστικός, ή, όν, *accomplishing its* προποδισμός, of a planet, Vett.Val.338.6.

**προποιέω**, *do before* or *beforehand*, π. χρηστὰ ἔς τινα Hdt.1.41; π. τι, opp. προπαθεῖν, D.C.*Fr.*54.6, cf. Id.38.11: abs., μὴ διαφθαρῆναι.., ἀλλὰ προποιῆσαι *make the first move*, Th.3.13:—Pass., τὰ -πεποιημένα *works already carried out*, *IG*7.3073.27 (Lebad., ii B.C.). II. *make beforehand, prepare*, προεπεποίητο αὐτῷ προεξέδρη Hdt.7.44; ὑγίειαν Gal.5.833.

**προπολεμ-έω**, *make war for* or *in defence of*, τῆς χώρας Isoc.14.33; τῶν ἄλλων Plb.2.48.1, etc.; τισὶ τῆς ἀρχῆς *with*.. *for*.., D.H.6.49; ὑπὲρ [τῆς πόλεως] Pl.*R.*429b, cf. *OGI*56.12 (Canopus, iii B.C.): abs., οἱ προπολεμοῦντες *the guards* or *defenders of a country*, Pl.*R.*423a; τὸ προπολεμοῦν ib.442b, 547d, Arist.*Pol.*1279ᵇ3; τὸ προπολεμῆσον *the body intended to act as guards*, ib.1291ᵃ7. -ητήριον, τό, *bastion, outwork*, π. εἶναι τῆς Ἰταλίας D.S.14.100. -ιος, ον, *customary before war*, ἱερά D.C.46.33; τὰ π. ποιῆσαι, θύειν, Id.50.4, D.H.3.9.

**προπόλεος**, ον, *lying before a city*, κόσμος Anon.ap.Suid.; τὰ π., gloss on προάστεια, Sch. Philostr.*Im.Prooem.* ap. Boissonade ad Marin.*Procl.* p.140.

**προπόλ-ευμα**, ατος, τό, *instrument of service*, π. δάφνας, = πρόπολος δάφνη, E.*Ion* 113 (lyr.). -εύς, έως, ὁ, = πρόπολος, cj. in A.R.1.781 (πρὸ πόληος codd., προπόλοιο *PAmh.*2.16). ⊛ -εύω, *minister to*, θεαῖς *Epigr.Gr.*785 (Cnidus), cf. Phot. s.v. πρόπολος. ⊛ -έω, = foreg., Apollon.*Lex.* s.v. γεραιάς, cj. in S.*Fr.*535.3 (anap.). II. Med., *speak like a prophetess*, Ach.Tat.4.15.

⊛ **προπολι-όομαι**, Pass., *grow grey before*, v.l. in Diod.Cron.ap.S.E. *M.*10.114. -ος, ον, *grey-haired before his time*, Poll.2.12; προπόλιος τὴν κόμην Sch.Pi.*O.*4.32. II. προπόλιον ἐξ ἑρπύλλου *chaplet*, dub. in Semus 20.

**πρόπολις**, εως, ἡ, = προάστιον, Cels.ap.Orig.*Cels.*4.81 (pl.). II. *bee-glue*, Varro *RR* 3.16.24, Dsc.2.84, *PMag.Par.*1.2379, Aët.15. 14,15.

⊛ **προπολῑτεύομαι**, *transact beforehand*, τῶν πάντα τὰ καθήκοντα προπεπολιτευμένων D.C.52.21: pf. also in pass. sense, τὰ προπεπολιτευμένα *the previous measures of his government*, Plb.4.14.7, cf. *IG*5(2). 515.8 (Lycosura). II. *hold chief office*, π. ἰδιώτης κύκλου βασιλικοῦ Them.*Or.*16.205c; πόλεως *POxy.*67.2 (iv A.D.), *PLips.*37.3 (iv A.D.).

⊛ **πρόπολος**, ον, (πέλομαι, τέλλω) *going* or *acting before*: 1. *servant that goes before* one, *attendant, minister*, τυράννων A.*Ch.*357 (lyr.): abs., Xenoph.1.18, E.*Hipp.*200 (anap.), Ar.*Nu.*436; *rower*, Pi.*O.*13.54. 2. *one who serves a god*, esp. *one who interprets his will to men, minister*, [Ἑκάτη] οἱ π. ἔπλετο *h.Cer.*440; ὄνειρος Ἀΐδα π. v.l. in Ar.*Ra.*1333 (lyr.); Ἡσίοδος π. Μουσᾶν B.5.192; Πίνδαρος.. Πιερίδων π. *AP*7.35 (Leon.); Μουσάων π... Ὀρφέα Poet.ap.Alcid.*Od.* 24; αἰθέρος π... πελειαί Simm.ap.Ath.11.491c; of the Κουρῆτες, Str. 10.3.7. b. *temple-servant*, Hdt.2.63; θεοῦ π. Ar.*Pl.*670; Ἐνοδίας E.*Hel.*570, cf. *AP*6.269 (Sapph.), Str.5.3.5, D.H.1.76. II. as Adj., c. dat., *ministering to, devoted to*, ἐπινικίοισιν ἀοιδαῖς Pi.*N.*4.79; θεῷ *IG*1².825.

⊛ **πρόπομα**, ατος, τό, *drink taken before meals*, Phylarch.50J., Plu.2. 734a, Gal.6.828. II. = ἀκράτισμα, Plu.2.624c.—A form **πρόπωμα** is cited by Hdn.Gr.2.935, Choerob. *in Theod.*1.339; cf. προπουματᾶς.

**προπομπ-εία**, ἡ, *escorting in procession, conducting*, *IG*2².2788.8, D.Chr.38.38; written **προπομπία**, Hierocl.p.58A., Dam.*Pr.*81 codd. II. *first place in a procession*, *IG*4²(1).66.65 (Epid., i B.C.), *Delph.*3(2).48.53 (i B.C.), *Bull.Soc.Roy.Lund* 1928/9 iv 17 (Thuria, i B.C./i A.D., -ήα), Hermog.*Id.*2.10; written **προπομπία**, Luc.*Am.* 18. -εύω, *go before in a procession*, Posidon.36J.; βοῦ ἀξίᾳ τῆς θεοῦ *Inscr.Prien.*109.215 (ii B.C.); τινος *before* him or it, Plu.2.765b, Luc. *Merc.Cond.*25, Hdn.5.6.8; Ἥλιον Jul.*Or.*4.154b: abs., Hdn.2.8.6; τὸν θεόν *POxy.*1381.19 (ii A.D.): metaph., πρό τινος Iamb.*Myst.*2. 4. -έω, *conduct as* προπομπός, of Hermes, *IG*14.769 (Naples). -ή, ἡ, *sending forward*, αἱ π. τῶν γραμματηφόρων Plu.*Galb.*8. II. *escort*, π. δόντες μεγαλοπρεπῆ X.*Ages.*2.27, cf. Plb.20.11.8, Plu.*Num.* 14; π. δημοσίᾳ Longin.28.2. -ία, v. προπομπεία. -ός, όν, *escorting*, esp. *in procession*, λόχος X.*Cyr.*4.5.17: c. acc., χοὰς π. *carrying* drink-offerings *in procession*, A.*Ch.*23 (lyr.). II. Subst., *conductor, escort, protector*, Id.*Pers.*1036 (lyr.), X.*Cyr.*3.1.2; of Hermes, Alex.89; of the Furies, A.*Eu.*206; of priestesses of Athena, ib. 1005 (anap.); of *attendants* in a funeral procession, Id.*Th.*1074 (anap.); π. τιράνων *PLips.*35.5 (iv A.D., cf. *Arch.Pap.*3.563).

**προπονέω**, *work* or *labour beforehand*, X.*Cyr.*7.5.80; πολλὰ Luc. *Vit.Auct.*23; τινι for another, Id.*Hist.Conscr.*16. 2. *work for* or *instead of* another, τινος X.*An.*3.1.37, *Cyr.*8.2.2. 3. c. gen. rei, *work for, work so as to obtain*, τῶν εὐφροσυνῶν ib.8.1.32. 4. *obtain by previous labour*, τὰ προπεπονημένα Id.*Mem.*4.2.23, *HG*6.5.40. 5. *elaborate, work up first*, τροφὴν οὐκ ὠμήν, ἀλλὰ προπεπονημένην ὑπὸ τοῦ καυλοῦ καὶ τῶν ῥιζῶν Thphr.*CP*4.6.6, cf. *EM*73.27. II. *suffer pain beforehand*, ἢν -πεπονηκώς τι ᾖ πρὸ τοῦ νοσέειν Hp.*Aph.*4.33; π. τῇ νόσῳ, τοὺς νεφρούς, Ruf.*Fr.*72, Gal.19.597 (Med.); *to be wearied before*, ἐκ τοῦ τραύματος Luc.*JTr.*40; τῷ ἤδη -πεπονηκέναι Agath.3. 27; of a horse, Ael.*NA*14.11. 2. trans., *weary before*, ἑαυτούς Plu. *Oth.*11:—Pass., *to be vexed already*, γᾶς -πονουμένας v.l. in S.*OT*685 (lyr.).

**Προποντίς**, ίδος, ἡ, *the Fore-sea*, a name given to the Sea of Marmora, that leads into the Pontus, A.*Pers.*876 (lyr.), Hdt.4.85, etc.

**προπορ-εία**, ἡ, *those who go in front, advanced guard*, Plb.9.5.8 (pl.). -ευτής, οῦ, ὁ, in pl., *vanguard*, Agath.2.2. -εύω, *cause to go before*, Ael.*NA*10.22:—Pass., with aor. Med., *go before*, Aen.Tact. 23.10, etc.; π. τινός Arist.*Mir.*844ᵇ5, *Act.Ap.*7.40; πρὸ προσώπου τινός Lxx *Ex.*32.34, *Ev.Luc.*1.76; πρὸ τοῦ στρατοῦ Arr.*An.*5.15.1; π. ἐπὶ δύ' ἡμέραις Plb.3.52.8; οἱ προπορευόμενοι the *van*, Id.2.27.2, etc.; ἡ προπορευομένη, = πρόπολος, Seleuc.ap.Ath.6.267c; of a river, *flow onward*, Lxx *Ge.*2.14 (v.l.). 2. *come forward*, Plb.1.80.8, etc. 3. *to be promoted, advance*, πρὸς τὴν στρατηγίαν Id.28.6.9, cf. 2.4.2.

**προπορίζομαι**, Pass., *to be provided beforehand*, Luc.*Salt.*61, prob. in Cyran.43.

**προπόρφῠρος**, ον, *purple-edged*, δελματικομαφόρτης *POxy.*1273.16 (iii A.D.).

⊛ **πρόποσις**, εως, ἡ, (πίνω) *drinking before* or *to* one, προπόσεις πίνειν drink *healths*, Alex.49; πιὼν . . προπόσεις τρεῖς ἴσως ἢ τέτταρας Antiph. 82; π. ἀποδωρεῖσθαι, ὀρέγειν, Critias *Fr.*6.3,7 D., al.; λαμβάνειν Plb.30. 26.6, cf. *AP*5.133 (Posidipp.); προπόσεις ἐν τοῖς συμποσίοις ποιεῖν Ath. 10.432d; δεξιοῦσθαι ἀλλήλους ταῖς π. J.*AJ*6.14.6, cf. Alciphr.*Fr.*6. 18. **2.** *drink* itself, Simon.167.6; Βρομίου νεκτάρεαι π. *BMus. Inscr.*1036 (Caria). **3.** *drinking before* food, ὕδατος ἢ οἴνου Aret. *CD*1.3 (pl.); sg., Aët.9.26.

**προπότ-ης**, ου, ὁ, *one who drinks healths*, προπόται θίασοι bands *of revellers*, E.*Rh.*361 (lyr.). ⊛ **-ίζω**, *present as* or *in a draught*, of physicians, Ruf.*Fr.*118.12:—Pass., Alex.Trall.8.2. **2.** *cause to drink*, τοὺς ἐχιοδήκτους *Gp.*13.8.9; ἵππον *Hippiatr.*1. **-ισμα**, ατος, τό, *draught*, Ruf.*Fr.*114.2, *Hippiatr.*1, al. **-ισμός**, ὁ, = foreg., Dsc.2.160 (pl.), Heraclid.Tar.ap.Gal.11.795 (pl.), Archig. ap.eund.8.153, *Hippiatr.*4. **-ιστέον**, *one must administer a draught*, Herod.Med. in *Rh.Mus.*58.85, Aët.7.51.

**προπουμᾶτᾶς** (sic), ᾶ, ὁ, *seller of* προπόματα, *MAMA*3.698 (Corycus).

**πρόπους**, ποδος, ὁ, *one that has large feet*, Phot., Suid. **II.** *a star in the feet of the Twins* (η Geminorum), Gem.3.4, Ptol.*Alm.*7.5. **III.** *spur* of a mountain, Plb.3.17.2, 8.13.4, Str.9.5.8 (pl.), *AP*7.501 (Pers.), etc.; also τοίχων πρόποδες (πρόσπ- cod.) *buttresses*, Tim.*Lex.* s. v. γεῖσα. **IV.** *sheet* of a sail, Sch.A.R.1.566. **V.** πρόποδα μέλεα *moving forward* in procession, S.*Fr.*240 (lyr.).

**προπραγματεύομαι**, Pass., *to be written* or *published before*, Eun. *VS*p.457 B.; *to be worked out before*, Ptol.*Alm.*13.7.

**προπραξία**, ἡ, *right of precedence in negotiation*, *IG*9(1).442 (Stratos, v/iv B.C.).

**πρόπρᾶσις**, εως, ἡ, *anticipatory sale*: but, in a contract of marriage, *conveyance* of the husband's property to take effect on the dissolution of the marriage by death or otherwise, *PMich.Teb.*121ʳ II ii 1 (i A.D.).

**προπράσσω**, Att. -ττω, *do before*, τὰ συμφέροντα τῷ δήμῳ D.C.52. 13:—Pass., τὰ προπεπραγμένα Arist.*Po.*1455ᵇ30, Luc.*Jud.Voc.*2; τὰ προπραχθέντα Lxx 1*Es.*1.33. **II.** *exact*, χάριτας ὀργᾶς λυγρᾶς A.*Ch.* 834 (lyr.).

**προ-πράτης** [ᾰ], ου, ὁ, = προπώλης, Lys.*Fr.*329:—also **-πράτωρ**, ορος, ὁ, Is.*Fr.*168, *Gloss.*

**προπρεσβεύω**, *accomplish previously as envoy*, *Ephes.*2 No.26.

**προπρεών**, ῶνος, ὁ, ἡ, *friendly*, *kindly*, Pi.*N.*7.86 (προπραόν' cj. Schroeder); προ[πρεόν'] ὡς γενέτην suppl. Herwerden in *BCH*23. 302 (Termessus).

**προπρηνής**, ές, stronger form of πρηνής, *with the face downwards*, ἐν κόνι ἐκτανύσας προπρηνέα Il.24.18; [φασγάνῳ] προπρηνεῖ (v.l. προπρηνέα) τύψας *with the edge of* the sword, Od.22.98: neut. προπρηνές as Adv., *forward*, opp. ὀπίσω, Il.3.218. [Hom. always makes first syll. long.]

**προπρήων**, ωνος, ὁ, sine expl., perh. compd. of πρηών, Choerob. *in Theod.*p.71 Gaisford, Theognost.*Can.*29.

**προπρό**, strengthd. for πρό, Prep. with gen., *before*, A.R.3. 453. **II.** Adv. *on and on*, *thoroughly*, ib.1013, 4.1235, Euph.94. More freq. in compds., v. infr.

**προπροβιάζομαι**, Med., strengthd. for προβιάζομαι, A.R.1.386.

**προπροθέω**, strengthd. for προθέω, Orph.*A.*1257.

**πρόπροθι**, Adv. *forwards*, Opp.*C.*1.530.

**προπρο-κᾰλύπτω**, strengthd. for προκαλύπτω, in Med., Opp.*C.*4. 334. **-κᾰτᾶίγδην**, Adv. *rushing down and onward*, A.R.2. 595. **-κῠλίνδομαι**, Pass., *keep rolling before* another (as a suppliant), *roll at* his *feet*, c. gen., προπροκυλινδόμενος πατρὸς Διός Il.22.221; δεῦρο τόδ' ἵκετο πήματα πάσχων π. *wandering from place to place*, Od.17.525. **-τῐταίνω**, strengthd. for προτείνω, Opp.*H.*4.103 (Med.). **-φεγγής**, ές, *lightening in front*, *PMag.Par.*1.562, 603.

**πρόπρυμνα**, Adv. *away from the stern*, π. ἐκβολὰν φέρει, of jettisoning cargo, metaph. in A.*Th.*769 (lyr.).

**πρό-πταισμα**, prob. f.l. for πρόσπτ-, Gal.12.286. **-πταίω**, dub. for προσπτ- in Luc.*Ner.*5; f.l. in Phalar.*Ep.*38.2.

⊛ **προπτόρθιον**, τό, *projecting branch*, Lex Solonis ap.Hsch.

**προπτύω**, *spit forth* or *out*, Lxx 2*Ma.*6.20.

**πρό-πτωμα**, ατος, τό, = πρόπτωσις I, Gal.14.768. **-πτωσις**, εως, ἡ, *fall forwards*, *prolapse*, ὑστέρας Dsc.1.70 (pl.), cf. Sor.2.84, Gal.12.136 (pl.); τοῦ ῥαγοειδοῦς Id.6.877; of the eyes, Cels.6.6.8; *hernia*, Gal. 10.413. **2.** *falling down before* one, *prostration*, Lxx 2*Ma.*3.21; ἡ τοῦ φθόγγου π. *utterance*, v.l. in S.E.*M.*1.117. **3.** *projection* of spears before the phalanx, Ascl.*Tact.*5.1. **4.** *inclination*, *propensity*, εἴς τι Ath.5.180a. **5.** *hasty judgement*, Gal.*Anim.Pass.* 2.6. **6.** *degeneration*, τῆς ὕλης Iamb.*Myst.*5.14. **-πτωτικός**, ή, όν, *jumping to conclusions*, M.Ant.11.10.

⊛ **προπύλ-αιος** [ῠ], α, ον, (πύλη) *before the gate*, of the statues of gods, Ἀγυιεῦ τοὐμοῦ προθύρου προπύλαιε Ar.*V.*875; π. Ἑρμῆς Paus.1.22.8; Ἄρτεμις Id.1.38.6. **II.** προπύλαια, τά, *gateway*, *entrance*, of Egyptian temples, Hdt.2.63, 101, 121, etc.; on the Acropolis at Athens, *IG*1².92.34, 366.45, Hdt.5.77, Ar.*Eq.*1326, Th.2.13, D.13.28, 22.13, Aeschin.2.105, Plu.*Per.*13; at Eleusis, τὰ π. τῆς Δήμητρος καὶ τῆς Κόρης *IG*2².1187.25; at Epidaurus, ib.4²(1).742.23 (ii/iii A.D., prob.): also in sg., τὸ τοῦ Διονύσου π. And.1.38, cf. *IG*1².363.2, 2².1668.5, D.S.1.67, *AP*6.297 (Phan.). **-ίς**, ίδος, ἡ, arched *opening* in the ἑλέπολις, Bito 53.13. **-ίτης** [ῑ], ου, ὁ, *one who pursues his trade in a* πρόπυλον, ἐργάται π. *CIG*3028.4 (Ephesus). **-ον**, τό, freq. in pl., = προπύλαια, Hdt.2.91, Hp.*Epid.*4.42, S.*El.*1375, E.*HF*523, etc.: in sg., *IG*1².891, Arist.*Ath.*15.4, *AP*6.114 (Simm.), *IG*2².1046. 13, Inscr. in *PFay.*p.32, Plu.2.363f, etc. **-ών**, ῶνος, ὁ, *gateway* of a house, *POxy.*243.15, 21 (i A.D.), Hdn.Gr.1.40.

**προπυνθάνομαι**, pf. -πέπυσμαι, *learn by inquiring before*, *hear beforehand*, τι Hdt.1.21, 5.63, 102; ὅτι.. Th.4.42, etc.

**προπύργιον**, τό, *small outwork*, *BGU*1734.8 (i B.C.).

**πρόπυργος**, ον, *offered for the towers*, i.e. *for the city*, θυσίαι A.*Ag.* 1168 (lyr.).

**προπῡρεταίνω**, *have a fever beforehand*, Hp.*Epid.*4.21.

**προπῡρι-ᾱτέον**, *one must foment previously*, Antyll.ap.Orib.10.27. 15. **-άω**, *foment previously*, Hp.*Superf.*29, al., Antyll.ap.Orib.7.9.6.

**προπῡρόω**, *heat beforehand*, σιδήρια Alex.Trall.9.3.

**πρόπυστος**, ον, *having learnt before*, Phryn.*PS*p.105 B.

**προπωγώνιον**, τό, *moustache*, Ruf.*Onom.*49, Poll.2.80.

**προπωλ-έω**, *negotiate a sale*, Pl.*Lg.*954a, *IG*9(1).374 (Naupactus). ⊛ **-ης**, ου, ὁ, *one who buys for another* or *negotiates a sale*, *broker*, Ar.*Fr.*707a, Poll.7.12, Vett.Val.4.23. ⊛ **-ητής**, οῦ, ὁ, = foreg., *PGrenf.* 1.36.8 (ii B.C.), *PAmh.*2.51.28 (i B.C.). **-ητικός**, ή, όν, *connected with broking*; -κόν, τό, *brokerage*, *PRev.Laws* 55.15 (iii B.C.). **-ήτρια**, ἡ, fem. of προπωλητής, *PGrenf.*2.23(*a*) ii 11 (ii B.C.), *PLips.*2.9 (i B.C.), *BGU*994 iii 6 (ii A.D.).

**πρόπωνα**· εὐκρατῆ, εὔφημα, πρόχειρα, ἑτοῖμα, ἀνεμπόδιστα, Hsch.

**πρόρᾱχος**, ὁ, (ῥαχία) *foreshore*, *Peripl.M.Rubr.*15 (dub.).

**προρέω**, Ep. Verb, *flow forward* or *forth*, *flow amain*, of rivers and streams, Il.21.260, Od.5.444, etc.; ἅλαδε προρέουσι Il.12.19, cf. 5.598; εἰς ἅλαδε Od.10.351; ἐκ πέτρης Hes.*Th.*792. **II.** trans., *pour forth*, *h.Ap.*380; [κρήνη] ὕδωρ προρέεσκε A.R.3.225, cf. Orph.*A.*1132.

**πρόρῑνον**, τό, *inner cuticle*, Hsch.

**προροφάνω**, *swallow first*, Hp.*Morb.*2.54:—also **-ροφέω**, Id.*Mul.* 1.75.

**προρραίνω**, *sprinkle beforehand*, Alex.Trall.12.

**πρόρρευσις**, εως, ἡ, *efflux*, Sch.Nic.*Th.*586 (pl.).

**πρόρρηγ-μα**, ατος, τό, *membrane enveloping the foetus*, Sor.1.57, Paul.Aeg.3.76. **-νῠμαι**, *to be ruptured previously*, Sor.1.57: pf. part. τὰ προερρωγότα Gal.17(2).131.

**προρρ-ηθῆναι**, v. προερέω. **-ημα**, ατος, τό, *prognosis*, Hp.*Art.* 58 (pl.); *prophecy*, Sch.A.R.1.118. ⊛ **-ησις**, εως, ἡ, *prediction*, *prognosis*, Hp.*Prog.*15 (pl.), D.S.12.36, Plot.3.1.2, *AP*11.382.21 (Agath.). **II.** *previous instruction* or *warning*, Th.1.49. **2.** *proclamation*, ἐκ προρρήσεως πολεμεῖν D.9.13; αἱ π. *public notices*, as in case of trials for murder, Antipho 5.88, 6.6, Pl.*Lg.*873b; τὴν π. προαγορεύων ib.871c. **III.** Rhet., *introductory statement*, Arist. *Rh.Al.*1438ᵇ11 (pl.); *comment given beforehand*, opp. ἐπίρρησις, Phld. *Rh.*1.31 S. **-ητέον**, *one must proclaim*, *give notice beforehand*, Pl. *Lg.*854a, 874e. **-ητικός**, ή, όν, *predictive*, δύναμις S.E.*M.*5.1; -κόν, τό, a treatise *on prognosis*, title of two works by Hippocrates, Gal. 14.620, 16.582. **-ητος**, ον, *proclaimed*, *commanded*, S.*Tr.*684.

**πρόρριζος**, ον, (ῥίζα) *by the roots*, *root and branch*, *utterly*, θάμνοι π. πίπτουσιν Il.11.157; ὅθ' . . ἐξερίπῃ δρῦς π. 14.415; [πολλοὺς] ὁ θεὸς προρρίζους ἀνέτρεψε Hdt.1.32; κακῶς ἐτελεύτησε π. Id.3.40; Ζεύς σε . . π. ἐκτρίψειεν E.*Hipp.*684, cf. Hdt.6.86.δ'; π. ἔφθαρται γένος S.*El.*765; [γένος] οἴχεται π. And.1.146; δαιμόνων ἱδρύματα π. ἐξανέστραπται βάθρων A.*Pers.*812; δίφρων π. ἐκριφθεὶς S.*El.*512 (lyr.); π. αὐτὸς.. ἀπολοίμην Ar.*Ra.*587: neut. πρόρριζον as Adv., Arist.*HA*616ᵃ2 (prob.l.), Lyc.214.

**προρριπτω**, f.l. for προσρίπτω in Iamb.*Myst.*3.18.

**προρρυθμίζω**, *regulate before*, Gal.*UP*7.5.

**πρόρῠτος**, ον, (ῥέω) *flowing forth* or *first*, prob. in *Gp.*9.19.8.

⊛ **πρός**, Prep., expressing direction, *on the side of*, *in the direction of*, hence c. gen., dat., and acc., *from*, *at*, *to*: Ep. also **προτί** and **ποτί**, in Hom. usually c. acc., more rarely c. dat., and each only once c. gen., Il.11.831, 22.198:—dialectal forms: Dor. **ποτί** (q. v.) and **ποί**, but Cret. **πορτί** *Leg.Gort.*5.44, etc., Argive **προτ(ί)** *Schwyzer* 84.3 (found at Tylisus, v B.C.), restored in *Mnemos.*57.208 (Argos, vi B.C.), and in Alcm.30; Arc., Cypr. **πός** *SIG*306.11 (Tegea, iv B.C.), *Inscr.Cypr.* 135.19 H., also sts. in Asia Minor in compds., v. ποσάγω, ποσφέρω; Aeol. **πρός** Sapph.69 (προσ-), 109, Alc.20 (s.v.l.); **πρές** Jo.Gramm. *Comp.*3.10; Pamphylian **περτ(ί)** *Schwyzer* 686.7, 686ᵃ4. (With **προτί**, **πρός** cf. Skt. *práti* 'towards, near to, against, back, etc.', Slav. *protivŭ*, Lett. *pret* 'against', Lat. *pretium*: **ποτί** (q. v.) and **πός** are not cogn.)

**A. with Gen.**, **πρός** refers to that *from* which something comes: **I.** of Place, *from*, ἵκετο ἠὲ π. ἠοίων ἢ ἑσπερίων ἀνθρώπων Od. 8.29; τὸν π. Σάρδεων ἤλεκτρον S.*Ant.*1037 (v.l.). **2.** *on the side of*, *towards*, νήσοισι πρὸς Ἤλιδος *towards* Elis, Od.21.347; π. ἁλός, π. Θυμβρης, Il.10.428, 430; εἶναι π. θαλάσσης Hdt.2.154; ἱδρῦσθαι π. τοῦ Ἑλλησπόντου Id.8.120; ἐστρατοπεδεύοντο π. Ὀλύνθου Th.1.62, etc.; φυλακαὶ π. Αἰθιόπων, π. Ἀραβίων, π. Λιβύης, *on the frontier towards* the Ethiopians, etc., Hdt.2.30: freq. with words denoting the points of the compass, δύω θύραι εἰσίν, αἱ μὲν π. βορέαο, αἱ δ' αὖ π. νότου one *on the* north *side*, the other *on the* south *side*, Od.13.110; οἰκέουσι π. νότου ἀνέμου Hdt.3.101; π. ἄρκτου τε καὶ βορέω ἀνέμου κατοικημένοι ib.102; π. μεσαμβρίης ib.107; π. τοῦ Τμώλου τετραμμένον τῆς πόλιος (in such phrases the acc. is more common) Id.1.84; π. Πλαταιῶν Th. 3.21; π. Νεμέας Id.5.59; ἀπὸ τῆσδε τῆς ὁδοῦ τὸ π. τοῦ λιμένος ἅπαν everything *on the* harbour-*ward side* of this road, *IG*1².892: combined with π. c. acc., π. ἠῶ τε καὶ τοῦ Ταναΐδος Hdt.4.122; τὸν μὲν π. βορέω ἑστεῶτα, τὸν δὲ π. νότου Id.2.121, cf. 4.17. **3.** *before*, *in presence of*, μάρτυροι ἔστων π. τε θεῶν μακάρων π. τε θνητῶν ἀνθρώπων Il.1.339; οὐδ' ἐπιορκήσω π. δαίμονος 19.188; ποὶ τοῦ Ἀπόλλωνος..

ὑπίσχομαι prob. in *IG*2$^2$.1126.7 (Amphict. Delph., iv B.C.); ὑποσχομένους πρὸς τοῦ Διός ib.1237.16: hence, b. *in the eyes of*, ἄδικον οὐδὲν οὔτε π. θεῶν οὔτε π. ἀνθρώπων Th.1.71, cf. X.*An*.1.6.6, etc.; ὅσιος π. θεῶν Lex ap.And.1.97; κατειπάτω..ἁγνῶς π. τοῦ θεοῦ if he wishes to be pure *in the sight of* the god, *SIG*986.9, cf. 17 (Chios, v/iv B.C.); ὁ γὰρ καιρὸς π. ἀνθρώπων βραχὺ μέτρον ἔχει Pi.*P*.4.286. 4. in supplication or adjuration, *before*, and so, *in the name of*, σε..γουνάζομαι..π. τ' ἀλόχου καὶ πατρός Od.11.67; π. θεῶν πατρῴων S.*Ant*.839 (lyr.), etc.; ἱκετεύω, ἀντιβολῶ π. παίδων, π. γυναικῶν, etc., D.28.20, etc.: the verb is freq. omitted with π. θεῶν or τῶν θεῶν, E.*Hec*.551, S.*OT*1037, Ar.*V*.760; π. τοῦ Διός Id.*Av*.130: less freq. with other words, π. τῆς ἑστίας E.*Fr*.953.39; π. Χαρίτων Luc.*Hist.Conscr*.14; μὴ π. γενείου S.*El*.1208; μὴ π. ξενίας τᾶς σᾶς Id.*OC*515 (lyr.): sts. in questions, π. θεῶν, τίς οὕτως εὐήθης ἐστίν; *in* heaven's *name*, D.1.15; π. τῆς Ἀθηνᾶς..; Din.1.45; ἆρ' οὖν, ὦ π. Διός,..; Pl.*R*.459a, cf. *Ap*.26e: sts. in Trag. with the pron. σε between prep. and case, π. νύν σε πατρὸς π. τε μητρός..ἱκνοῦμαι S.*Ph*.468; μὴ π. σε γονάτων E.*Med*.324. 5. of origin or descent, *from, on the side of*, γένος ἐξ Ἁλικαρνησσοῦ τὰ π. πατρός *by* the father's *side*, Hdt.7.99; Ἀθηναῖον..καὶ τὰ π. πατρὸς καὶ τὰ π. μητρός D.57.17, cf. Isoc.3.42, *SIG*1015.7 (Halic.); πρόγονοι ἢ π. ἀνδρῶν ἢ γυναικῶν *in* the male or female *line*, Pl.*Tht*.173d; ὁ πατὴρ π. μὲν ἀνδρῶν ἦν τῶν Εὐπατριδῶν Isoc.16.25; οἱ συγγενεῖς τοῦ πατρὸς καὶ π. ἀνδρῶν καὶ π. γυναικῶν D.57.23; οἱ π. αἵματος blood-relations, S.*Aj*.1305; ἢ φίλων τις ἢ π. αἵματος φύσιν Id.*El*.1125. II. of effects *proceeding from* what cause soever: 1. *from, at the hand of*, with Verbs of having, receiving, etc., ὡς ἄν..τιμὴν καὶ κῦδος ἄρηαι π. πάντων Δαναῶν Il.16.85, cf. 1.160, etc.; τιμὴν π. Ζηνὸς ἔχοντες Od.11.302; δίδοι οἱ..χάριν ποτ' ἀστῶν καὶ ποτὶ ξείνων Pi.*O*.7.90; ἄνθεα τιμῆς πρὸς θνητῶν ἀνελέσθαι Emp.4.7; φυλακῆς π. δήμου κυρῆσαι Hdt.1.59; τυχεῖν τινος π. θεῶν A.*Th*.550, cf. S.*Aj*.527; λαχὼν π. δαιμόνων ὄλβον Pi.*N*.9.45; κακόν τι π. θεῶν ἢ π. ἀνθρώπων λαβεῖν Hdt.2.139, etc.; μανθάνειν π. ἀστῶν S.*OC*13: with passive Verbs, προτὶ Ἀχιλλῆος δεδιδάχθαι to have been taught *by*.., Il.11.831, cf. S.*OT*357; ἄριστα πεποίηται.. πρὸς Τρώων Il.6.57; αἴσχε' ἀκούω π. Τρώων ib.525, cf. Heraclit.79; ταῦτα..π. τούτου κλύειν S.*OT*429; οὐ λέγεται π. οὐδαμῶν Hdt.1.47; ἀτιμάζεσθαι, τετιμῆσθαι π. τινῶν, ib.61, 2.75; also λόγου οὐδενὸς γίνεσθαι π. τινῶν Id.1.120; παθεῖν τι π. τινός *at the hand of*, ib.73; π. ἀλλήλοιν θανεῖν E.*Ph*.1269, cf. S.*OT*1237; π. τῆς τύχης ὄλωλεν ib.949; τὸ ποιεύμενον π. τῶν Λακεδαιμονίων Hdt.7.209; αἰτηθέντες π. τινὸς χρήματα Id.8.111; ἱμέρου βέλει π. σοῦ τέθαλπται A.*Pr*.650: with an Adj. or Subst., τιμήεσσα π. πόσιος Od.18.162; ἐπίφθονος π. τῶν πλεόνων ἀνθρώπων Hdt.7.139; ἔρημος π. φίλων S.*Ant*.919; ἀπαθὴς π. ἀστῶν Pi.*P*.4.297; πειθὼ π. τινός S.*El*.562; π. Τρώων..κλέος εἶναι Il.22.514; ἄρκεσις π. ἀνδρός, δόξα π. ἀνθρώπων, S.*OC*73, E.*Heracl*.624 (lyr.); ἐλίπετο ἀθάνατον μνήμην π. Ἑλλησποντίων Hdt.4.144: with an Adv., οἶμαι γὰρ ἂν οὐκ ἀχαρίστως μοι ἔχειν οὔτε π. ὑμῶν οὔτε π. τῆς Ἑλλάδος I shall meet with no ingratitude *at* your *hands*, X.*An*.2.3.18, cf. Pl.*R*.463d. 2. of things, π. τίνος ποτ' αἰτίας [τέθνηκεν]; *from* or *by* what cause? S.*OT*1236; π. ἀμπλακημάτων *by* or *by reason of*.., Id.*Ant*.51. III. of dependence or close connexion: hence, 1. *dependent on* one, *under* one's *protection*, π. Διός εἰσι ξεῖνοί τε πτωχοί τε Od.6.207, 14.57; δικασπόλοι, οἵ τε θέμιστας π. Διὸς εἰρύαται *by commission from* him, Il.1.239; π. ἄλλης ἱστὸν ὑφαίνοις *at the bidding of* another, 6.456. 2. *on* one's *side, in* one's *favour*, Hdt.1.75, 124, S.*OT*1434, *Tr*.479, etc.; π. τῶν ἐχόντων..τὸν νόμον τίθης E.*Alc*.57. IV. of that which is *derivable from*: hence, *agreeable to, becoming, like*, τὰ τοιαῦτα ἔργα οὐ π. τοῦ ἅπαντος ἀνδρὸς νενόμικα γίνεσθαι, ἀλλὰ π. ψυχῆς τε ἀγαθῆς καὶ ῥώμης ἀνδρηΐης Hdt.7.153, cf. 5.12; ἦ κάρτα π. γυναικὸς αἴρεσθαι κέαρ 'tis very *like* a woman, A.*Ag*.592, cf. 1636; οὐ π. ἰατροῦ σοφοῦ θρηνεῖν ἐπῳδάς S.*Aj*.581, cf. Ar.*V*.369, E.*Hel*.950, etc.; π. σοῦ ἐστι Id.*HF*585, etc.; οὐκ ἦν π. τοῦ Κύρου τρόπου X.*An*.1.2.11, etc.: of qualities, etc., π. δυσσεβείας A.*Ch*.704; π. δίκης οὐδὲν τρέμων *agreeably to* justice, S.*OT*1014, cf. *El*.1211; οὐ π. τῆς ὑμετέρας δόξης Th.3.59; ἐάν τι ἡμῖν π. λόγου ᾖ if it be at all *to* our purpose, Pl.*Grg*.459c; εἰ τόδε π. τρόπου λέγω *correctly*, Id.*R*.470c; but π. τρόπου τι ὠνεῖσθαι buy *at a reasonable price*, Thphr.*Char*.30.12; τὰ γενήματα π. ἐλάσσονος τιμᾶς πωλῶν *IG*5(2).515.14 (Lycosura); π. ἀγαθοῦ, π. κακοῦ τινί ἐστι or γίγνεται, it is *to* one's advantage or otherwise, Arist.*Mu*.397$^a$30, Arr.*An*.7.16.5, Hld.7.12; π. ἀτιμίας λαβεῖν τι to take a thing *as* an insult, regard it so, Plu.*Cic*.13; π. δέους λαβεῖν τι Id.*Flam*.7; λαβεῖν τι π. ὀργῆς (v.l. ὀργήν) J.*AJ*8.1.3; μοι π. εὐκλείας γένοιτο ib.18.7.7; τῷ δήμῳ π. αἰσχύνης ἂν ἦν, π. ὀνείδους ἂν ἦν τῇ πόλει, Lib.*Decl*.43.27, 28.

B. WITH DAT., it expresses proximity, *hard by, near, at*, ποτὶ γαίῃ Od.8.190, 11.423; ποτὶ γούνασι Il.5.408; ποτὶ δρυσίν *among* the oaks, 14.398 (nisi leg. περί); πρὸς ἄκμονι χαλκεύειν Pi.*P*.1.86; ποτὶ γραμμᾷ στᾶσαί τινα ib.9.118; ἄγκυραν ποτὶ ναΐ κρημνάντων ib.4.24; δῆσαί τινα πρὸς φάραγγι A.*Pr*.15; νεὼς καμούσης ποντίῳ π. κύματι Id.*Th*.210; π. μέσῃ ἀγορᾷ S.*Tr*.371; π. Ἀργείων στρατῷ Id.*Aj*.95; π. πέδῳ κεῖται Id.*OT*180 (lyr.); θακεῖν π. ναοῖς ib.20, cf. A.*Eu*.855; π. ἡλίου ναίουσι πηγαῖς Id.*Pr*.808; π. τῇ γῇ ναυμαχεῖν Th.7.34; ἐς μάχην καθίστασθαι π. (v.l. ὑπ') αὐτῇ τῇ πόλει Id.2.79; τεῖχος π. τῇ θαλάσσῃ Id.3.105; αἱ π. θαλάττῃ πόλεις X.*HG*4.8.1; τὸ π. Αἰγίνῃ στράτευμα *off* Aegina, Th.1.105; Λίβυες οἱ π. Αἰγύπτῳ *bordering on*.., ib.104; τὸ π. ποσί that which is *close to* the feet, *before* one, S.*OT*130, etc.; θρηνεῖν ἐπῳδὰς π....πήματι *over* it, Id.*Aj*.582; αἱ π. τῇ βάσει γωνίαι the angles *at* the base, Euc.1.5, al.; τὴν π. τῷ..ἱερῷ κρήνην *IG*2$^2$.338.13, cf. *SIG*1040.15 (Piraeus, iv B.C.), al. 2. *before, in the presence of*, π. τοῖς θεσμοθέταις, π. τῷ διαιτητῇ λέγειν, D.20.98, 39.22; ὅσα π. τοῖς κριταῖς γέγονεν Id.21.18; π. διαιτητῇ φεύγειν Id.22.28. 3. with Verbs denoting *motion towards* a place, *upon, against*, ποτὶ δὲ σκῆπτρον βάλε γαίῃ Il.1.245, Od.2.80; με βάλῃ..ποτὶ πέτρῃ 5.415, cf. 7.279, 9.284; νῆας ποτὶ σπιλάδεσσιν ἔαξαν 3.298, cf. 5.401; λιαζόμενον ποτὶ γαίῃ sinking *on* the ground, Il.20.420; ἴσχοντες πρὸς ταῖς πόλεσι Th.7.35. 4. sts. with a notion of *clinging* closely, προτὶ οἷ λάβε clasped *to* him, Il.20.418; προτὶ οἷ εἷλε 21.507; πρὸς ἀλλήλῃσιν ἔχονται Od.5.329; προσπεπλασμένας..π. ὄρεσι Hdt.3.111; π. δμωαῖσι κλίνομαι fall *into the arms of*.., S.*Ant*.1189; π. τινί *close to*, Men.*Epit*.204. II. to express close engagement, *at the point of*, π. αὐτῷ γ' εἰμὶ τῷ δεινῷ λέγειν S.*OT*1169; *engaged in* or *about*, π. τῷ εἰρημένῳ λόγῳ ἦν Pl.*Phd*.84c, cf. *Phdr*.249c, d; ἂν π. τῷ σκοπεῖν..γένησθε D.18.176; ἀεὶ π. ᾧ εἴη ἔργῳ, τοῦτο ἔπραττεν X.*HG*4.8.22; διατρίβειν or σχολάζειν π. τινί, Epicr.11.3 (anap.), Arist.*Pol*.1308$^b$36 (but π. ταῦτα ἐσχόλασα X.*Mem*.3.6.6); ὅλος εἶναι π. τῷ λήμματι D.19.127; π. τῇ ἀνάγκῃ ταύτῃ γίγνεσθαι Aeschin.1.74; τὴν διάνοιαν, τὴν γνώμην ἔχειν π. τινί, Pl.*R*.500b, Aeschin.3.192; κατατάξαι αὐτὸν π. γράμμασιν, i.e. give him a post as clerk, *PCair.Zen*.342.3 (iii B.C.); ὁ π. τοῖς γράμμασι τεταγμένος Plb.15.27.7, cf. 5.54.7, D.S.2.29, 3.22; ἐπιμελητὴς π. τῇ εἰκασίᾳ τοῦ σησάμου *PTeb*.713.2, cf. 709.1 (ii B.C.). III. to express union or addition, once in Hom., ἄασάν μ' ἕταροί τε κακοὶ π. τοῖσί τε ὕπνος and *besides* them sleep, Od.10.68; π. τοῖς παροῦσιν ἄλλα *in addition to*, A.*Pr*.323, cf. *Pers*.531, Xenoph.8.3, Emp.59.3; ἄλλους π. ἑαυτῷ Th.1.90; π. ταῖς ἡμετέραις [τριήρεσι] Id.6.90; δέκα μῆνας π. ἄλλοις πέντε S.*Tr*.45; τρίτος..π. δέκ' ἄλλαισιν γοναῖς A.*Pr*.774; κυβερνήτης π. τῇ σκυτοτομίᾳ *in addition to* his trade of leather-cutter, Pl.*R*.397e: freq. with neut. Adjs., π. τῷ νέῳ ἁπαλός *besides* his youth, Id.*Smp*.195c, cf. *Tht*.185e; π. τῷ βλαβερῷ καὶ ἀηδέστατον Id.*Phdr*.240b; π. τούτοισι *besides* this, Hdt.2.51, cf. A.*Pers*.237 (troch.), etc.; rarely in sg., π. τούτῳ Hdt.1.31, 41; π. τοῖς ἄλλοις *besides* all the rest, Th.2.61, etc.:—cf. the Advb. usage, infr. D.

C. WITH ACCUS., it expresses motion or direction towards an object: I. of Place, *towards, to*, with Verbs of Motion, ἰέναι π. Ὄλυμπον Il.1.420; ἰέναι π. δώματα, etc., Od.2.288, etc.; ἰέναι π. ἠῶ τ' ἠέλιόν τε Il.12.239; φέρειν προτὶ ἄστυ, ἄγειν προτὶ Ἴλιον, etc., 13.538, 657, etc.; ἄγεσθαι πρὸς οἶκον, ἐρύεσθαι ποτὶ Ἴλιον, 9.147, 18.174; ὠθεῖν, δίεσθαι προτὶ ἄστυ, 16.45, 15.681, etc.; ῥίπτασκε ποτὶ νέφεα Od.8.374; βαλεῖν ποτὶ πέτρας 12.71; κυλινδόμενα προτὶ χέρσον 9.147; ἀπῆλθε πρὸς ἑαυτόν returned *to* his home, Lxx *Nu*.24.25; κληθῆναι π. τὸ δεῖπνον (rarer than ἐπὶ δεῖπνον) Plu.*Cat.Ma*.3. 2. with Verbs implying previous motion, *upon, against*, π. τεῖχος, π. κίονα ἐρείσας, Il.22.112, Od.8.66; ἅρματα..ἔκλιναν π. ἐνώπια Il.8.435; ἔγχος ἔστησε π. κίονα Od.1.127; ποτὶ τοῖχον ἀρηρότες 2.342; ποτὶ βωμὸν ἵζεσθαι 22.334; πρὸς γοῦνα καθέζετό τινος 18.395; π. ἄλλοτ' ἄλλον πημονὴ προσιζάνει A.*Pr*.278; τὰ πολλὰ πατρὸς π. τάφον κτερίσματα S.*El*.931; χῶρον π. αὐτὸν τόνδ' dub. in Id.*Ph*.23; later, ἔστη π. τὸν στῦλον Lxx 4*Ki*.23.3; ὁ ὄχλος π. τὴν θάλασσαν ἐπὶ τῆς γῆς ἦσαν *Ev.Marc*.4.1; π. ὑμᾶς παραμενῶ *with* you, 1*Ep.Cor*.16.6; ἐκήδευσαν τὸν..πατέρα..π. τοὺς λοιποὺς συγγενεῖς *beside*, *Supp.Epigr*.6.106 (Cotiaeum). b. of addition, ποὶ τὰν στάλαν ποιγραψάνσθω τάδε *SIG*56.46 (Argos, v B.C.); ἵππον προσετίθει πρὸς τοὔνομα Ar.*Nu*.63, cf. Hdt.6.125, X.*HG*1.5.6, Pl.*Phlb*.33c, Arist.*Rh*.1359$^b$28; προσεδαπάνησε π. τὸ μερισθὲν αὐτῷ εἰς τὸ ἔλαιον ἐκ τῶν ἰδίων *over and above* the sum allotted to him, *IG*2$^2$.1227.9; προσετέθη π. τὸν λαὸν αὐτοῦ was gathered *to* his people, Lxx *Ge*.49.33. 3. with Verbs of seeing, looking, etc., *towards*, ἰδεῖν π. τινά Od.12.244, al.; δρᾶν, ἀποβλέπειν π. τι or τινά, A.*Supp*.725, Ar.*Ach*.291, etc.; ἀνταυγεῖ π. Ὄλυμπον Emp.44; στάντε ποτὶ πνοιήν *so as to face* it, Il.11.622 (similarly, πέτονται πρὸς τὸ πνεῦμα *against* the wind, Arist.*HA*597$^a$32); κλαίεσκε π. οὐρανόν cried *to* heaven, Il.8.364: freq. of points of the compass, π. ζόφον κεῖσθαι lie *towards* the West, Od.9.26; ναίειν π. ἠῶ τ' ἠέλιόν τε 13.240; στάντα π. πρώτην ἕω S.*OC*477; so in Prose, π. ἠῶ τε καὶ ἡλίου ἀνατολάς Hdt.1.201, cf. 4.40; π. βορέην τε καὶ νότον Id.2.149; also ἀκτὴ π. Τυρσηνίην τετραμμένη τῆς Σικελίης Id.6.22 (v. supr. A. I. 2); π. ἥλιον *facing* the sun, and so, *in the* sun*light*, Ar.*V*.772; so π. λύχνον *by* lamp*light*, Id.*Pax* 692, Jul.*Ep*.4; π. τὸ λύχνον Hippon.22 Diehl, cf. Arist.*Mete*.375$^a$27; πὸτ τὸ πῦρ Ar.*Ach*.751; πρὸς τὸ πῦρ Pl.*R*.372d, cf. Arist.*Pr*.870$^a$21; π. φῶς *in open* day, S.*El*.640; but, *by* torch-*light*, Plu.2.237a. 4. in hostile sense, *against*, π. Τρῶας μάχεαι Il.17.471; ἐστρατόωνθ'..π. τείχεα Θήβης 4.378; π. δαίμονα *against* his *will*, 17.98; βεβλήκει π. στῆθος 4.108; γούνατ' ἐπῇδα π. ῥόον ἀΐσσοντος 21.303; χρὴ π. θεὸν οὐκ ἐρίζειν Pi.*P*.2.88; π. τοὐμὸν σπέρμα χωρήσαντα S.*Tr*.304; ἐπιέναι π. τινάς Th.2.65; ὅσα ἔπραξαν οἱ Ἕλληνες π. τε ἀλλήλους καὶ τὸν βάρβαρον Id.1.118; ἀγωνίζεσθαι π. τινά Pl.*R*.579c; ἀντιτάττεσθαι π. πόλιν X.*Cyr*.3.1.18: also in argument, *in reply to*, ταῦτα π. τὸν Πιττακὸν εἴρηται Pl.*Prt*.345c; and so in the titles of judicial speeches, πρός τινα *in reply to*, less strong than κατά τινος *against* or *in accusation*, D.20 tit., etc.; μήτε π. ἐμὲ μήτε κατ' ἐμοῦ δίκην εἶναι Is.11.34. 5. without any hostile sense, π. ἀλλήλους ἔπεα πτερόεντ' ἀγόρευον Il.3.155, cf. 5.274, 11.403, 17.200; π. ξεῖνον φάσθαι ἔπος ἠδ' ἐπακοῦσαι Od.17.584; λέγειν, εἰπεῖν, φράζειν π. τινά, Hdt.1.8, 90, Ar.*V*.335, *Nu*.359; ἀπαγγεῖλαι π. τινάς A.*Ch*.267; μνησθῆναι π. τινά Lys.1.19, etc.; ἀμείψασθαι π. τινά Hdt.8.60 codd.; ἀποκρίνεσθαι π. τινάς Ar.*Ach*.632, Th.5.42; ὤμοσε δὲ π. ἔμ' αὐτόν he swore *to* me, Od.14.331: π. sts. governs the reflex. pron., διαλογίζεσθαι π. ὑμᾶς αὐτούς Is.7.45; ἀναμνήσθητε, ἐνθυμήθητε π. ὑμᾶς αὐτούς, Isoc.6.52, 15.60; π. ἐμαυτὸν..ἐλογιζόμην Pl.*Ap*.21d; μινύρεσθαι, ᾄδειν π.

ἑαυτόν, Ar.*Ec.*880,931; ἐπικωκύω..αὐτὴ π. αὑτήν S.*El.*285. b. π. σφέας ἔχειν δοκέουσι, i.e. they think they are pregnant, Hp.*Nat.Puer.* 30. 6. of various kinds of intercourse or reciprocal action, π... Διομήδεα τεύχε' ἄμειβεν changed arms *with* Diomedes, Il.6.235; ὅσα.. ξυμβόλαια..ἤν τοῖς ἰδιώταις π. τοὺς ἰδιώτας ἢ ἰδιώτῃ π. τὸ κοινόν *IG*1[2]. 116.19; σπονδάς, συνθήκας ποιεῖσθαι π. τινά, Th.4.15, Plb.1.17.6; ξυγχωρεῖν π. τινάς Th.2.59; γίγνεται ὁμολογία π. τινάς Id.7.82, cf. Hdt. 1.61; π. τινὰς ξυμμαχίαν ποιεῖσθαι Th.5.22; π. ἀλλήλους ἡσυχίαν εἶχον καὶ π. τοὺς ἄλλους..εἰρήνην ἦγον Isoc.7.51; π. ἀλλήλους ἔχθραι τε καὶ στέργηθρα A.*Pr.*491; also σαίνειν ποτὶ πάντας Pi.*P.*2.82, cf. *O.*4.6; παίζειν πρός τινας E.*HF*952, etc.; ἀφροδισιάζειν π. τινά X.*Mem.*1.3.14; ἀγαθὸς γίγνεσθαι π. τινά Th.1.86; εὐσεβὴς π. τινὰς πέλειν A.*Supp.*340; διαλέγεσθαι π. τινά converse *with*.., X.*Mem.*1.6.1, Aeschin.2.38,40, 3.219; κοινοῦσθαι π. τινάς Pl.*Lg.*930c; π. τοὺς οἰκέτας ἀνακοινοῦσθαι περὶ τῶν μεγίστων Thphr.*Char.*4.2; διαλογίζεσθαι π. τινά balance accounts *with*.., D.52.3, cf. *SIG*241.127 (Delph., iv B.C.); ἃ ἔχει διελόμενος π. τὸν ἀδελφόν *IG*12(7).55.8 (Amorgos, iv/iii B.C.), cf. D. 47.34. b. in phrases of the form ἡ π. τινὰ εὔνοια (ἔχθρα, etc.), π. sts. means *towards*, as ἡ π. αὐτοὺς φιλία the affection of their wives *towards* or *for* them, X.*Cyr.*3.1.39; ἡ π. ὑμᾶς ἔχθρα Id.*HG*3.5.10; ἡ ἀπέχθεια ἡ π. τοὺς πλουσίους Arist.*Pol.*1305[a]23; τὴν π. τοὺς τετελευτηκότας εὔνοιαν ὑπάρχουσαν D.18.314, cf. *SIG*352.13 (Ephesus, iv/iii B.C.), al.; φυσικαὶ τοκέων στοργαὶ π. τέκνα ποθεινά *IG*12(5).305.13 (Paros): but sts. *at the hands of*, ἡ π. τὸ θεῖον εὐμένεια the favour of the gods, Th.5.105; φθόνος τοῖς ζῶσι π. τὸ ἀντίπαλον jealousy is incurred by the living *at the hands of* their rivals, Id.2.45; τὴν ἀπέχθειαν τὴν π. Θηβαίους..τῇ πόλει γενέσθαι the hostility incurred by Athens *at the hands of* the Thebans, D.18.36, cf. 6.3, 19.85; τῇ φιλίᾳ τῇ π. τὸν τετελευτηκότα the friendship *with* (not 'affection *for*') the deceased, Is.1.17, cf. Pl.*Ap.*21c, 28a, Isoc.15.101, 19.50, Lycurg.135, Din.1.19, etc.; τίνος ὄντος ἐμοὶ π. ὑμᾶς ἐγκλήματος; Lys.10.23, cf. 16. 10; τιμώμενος..διὰ τὴν π. ὑμᾶς πίστιν Din.3.12, cf. Lys.12.67, D.20. 25; τῷ φόβῳ τῷ π. ὑμᾶς the fear *inspired by* you, Id.25.93; τῇ π. Ῥωμαίους εὐνοίᾳ his popularity *with* the Romans, Plb.23.7.5. 7. of legal or other business transacted *before* a magistrate, witness, etc., τάδε ὁ σύλλογος ἐβουλεύσατο..π. μνήμονας *SIG*45.8 (Halic., v B.C.), cf. *IG*7.15.1 (Megara, ii B.C.); γράφεσθαι αὐτὸν κλοπῆς..π. τοὺς ἐπιμελητάς ib.1[2].65.46; ἀτέλειαν εἶναι αὐτῷ καὶ δίκας π. τὸν πολέμαρχον ib.153. 7; λόγον διδόντων τῶν..χρημάτων..π. τοὺς λογιστάς ib.91.27; *before* a jury, ἔστι δὲ τούτοις μὲν π. ὑμᾶς ἀγών, ὑμῖν δὲ π. ἅπασαν τὴν πόλιν Lys. 26.14; ἀντιδικῆσαι τῷ παιδὶ..π. ὑμᾶς Is.11.19 codd. (dub.); *before* a witness to whom an appeal for corroboration is made, Id.3.25; ὀμόσαντες πὸ(τ) τὸν θεόν *Schwyzer* 418.11 (Elis); ϝέρρεν αὐτὸν πὸ(τ) τὸν Δία *in the eyes of* Zeus, ib.415.7 (ibid.); λαχεῖν πρὸς τὸν ἄρχοντα, γράφεσθαι π. τοὺς θεσμοθέτας, D.43.15, Lex ib.21.47, cf. Arist.*Ath.*56. 6; τοῖς ἐμπόροις εἶναι τὰς δίκας π. τοὺς θεσμοθέτας D.33.1; θέντων τὰ ..ποτήρια..π. Πολύχαρμον having pawned the cups *with* P., *IIE*1[2]. 32*A*15 (Olbia, iii B.C.); also διαβάλλειν τινὰ π. τοὺς πολλούς X.*Mem.* 1.2.31, cf. D.7.33. II. of Time, *towards* or *near* a certain time, *at* or *about*, ποτὶ ἕσπερα Od.17.191; ποτὶ ἕσπερον Hes.*Op.*552; πρὸς ἑσπέραν Pl.*R.*328a; ἐπεὶ π. ἑσπέραν ἦν X.*HG*4.3.22; π. ἡμέραν Id.*An.*4.5.21; π. ὄρθρον Ar.*Lys.*1089; ποτ' ὄρθρον (nisi leg. πότορθρον) Theoc.5.126, Erinn. in *PSI*9.1090.48 + 8 (p. xii); πρὸς ἕω Ar.*Ec.*312; π. ἀῶ ἐγρέσθαι, π. ἡμέραν ἐξεγρέσθαι, Theoc.18.55, Pl.*Smp.*223c; π. γῆρας, π. τὸ γῆρας, *in* old age, E.*Med.*592, Pl.*Lg.*653a; π. εὐάνθεμον φυάν *in* the bloom of life, Pi.*O.*1.67; μέχρις ὅτου π. γυναῖκας ὦσι, i.e. of marriageable age, *IG*2[2].1368.41: later, π. τὸ παρόν *for* the moment, Luc.*Ep. Sat.*28, etc.; v. infr. III. 5. III. of Relation between two objects, 1. *in reference to, in respect of, touching*, τὰ π. τὸν πόλεμον military matters, equipments, etc., Th.2.17, etc.; τὰ π. τὸν βασιλέα our *relations to* the King, D.14.2; τὰ π. βασιλέα πράγματα the negotiations *with* the King, Th.1.128; τὰ π. τοὺς θεούς our relations, i.e. duties, *to* the gods, S.*Ph.*1441; μέτεστι π. τὰ ἴδια διάφορα πᾶσι τὸ ἴσον..ἐλευθέρως δὲ τὰ π. τὸ κοινὸν πολιτεύομεν Th.2.37; οὐδὲν διοίσει π. τὸ γενέσθαι..*in respect of*.., Arist.*APr.*24[a]25, cf. Pl.*Phd.*111b; ἕτερος λόγος, οὐ π. ἐμέ that is another matter, and does not *concern* me, D.18.44, cf. 21, 60, Isoc.4.12; τῶν φορέτρων ὄντων π. ἐμέ freightage shall be my *concern*, i.e. *borne by* me, *PAmh.*91.18 (ii A.D.); π. τοῦτον ἦν ἡ τῶν διαφόρων πρᾶξις Lxx 2*Ma.*4.28: ἐάν..βοᾷ καὶ σχετλιάζῃ μηδὲν π. τὸ πρᾶγμα. *nihil ad rem*, D.40.61; οὐδὲν π. τὸν Διόνυσον Prov. ap. Plb.39.2.3, Suid.; οὐδὲν αὐτῷ π. τὴν πόλιν ἐστίν he owes no reckoning *to* the State, D.21.44; λόγος ἐστὶν ἐμοὶ π. Ἀθηναίους Philonid. 1 D.; π. Ἰάσονά ἐστιν αὐτῷ περὶ τῆς τιμῆς *PHamb.*27.8 (iii B.C.), cf. *PCair.Zen.*150.18 (iii B.C.); ἔσται αὐτῷ π. τὸν Θεόν (sc. ὁ λόγος) he shall have to reckon *with* God, *Supp.Epigr.*6.188, cf. 194, al. (Eumenia); without αὐτῷ, ib.236 (Phrygia); ἔσται π. τὴν Τριάδαν *MAMA*1.168, cf. *Supp.Epigr.*6.302 (Laodicea Combusta); ἕξει π. τὸν Θεόν ib.300, al. (ibid.); ἕξει π. τὴν ἐωνίαν κρίσιν ib.4.733 (Eukhaita), cf. 6.841 (Cyprus); π. πολλοὺς ἔχων ἀγωνιστάς Suid. s.v. ὅσα μῦς ἐν πίσσῃ, cf. 2*Ep.Cor.*5.12: with Advbs., ἀσφαλῶς ἔχειν π. τι X.*Mem.*1.3.14, etc.; [τὸ or τὰ] πρός τι the *relative* term or terms, Arist.*Cat.*1[b]25, 6[a]36, al.; τὸ π. τι, Pythag. name for *two*, *Theol.Ar.*8; π. ἡμᾶς *relatively to* us, opp. ἁπλῶς, Arist.*APo.* 72[a]1; ὀρθὸς πρός or ποτί c. acc., perpendicular *to*, Archim.*Sph.Cyl.*2. 3, *Spir.*20; ἁ ΔΖ ποτὶ τὰν ΑΔ ἀμβλεῖαν ποιεῖ γωνίαν ib.16. 2. *in reference to, in consequence of*, πρὸς τοῦτο τὸ κήρυγμα Hdt.3.52, cf. 4.161; π. τὴν φήμην *in view of*.., Id.3.153, cf. Th.8.39; χαλεπαίνειν π. τι Id.2.59; ἀθύμως ἔχειν π. τι X.*HG*4.5.4, etc.: with neut. Pron., π. τί; *wherefore? to what end?* S.*OT*766, 1027, etc.; π. οὐδέν *for* nothing, in vain, Id.*Aj.*1018; π. οὐδὲν ἀναγκαῖον unnecessarily, Sch.Il.9.23; π. ταῦτα *therefore, this being so*, Hdt.5.9,40, A.*Pr.*915, 992, S.*OT*426, etc.; cf. οὗτος c. VIII. 1b. 3. *in reference to* or *for* a purpose, ἕστηκεν..μῆλα π. σφαγάς A.*Ag.*1057; χρήσιμος, ἱκανὸς π. τι, Pl.*Grg.*474d, *Prt.*322b; ὡς π. τί χρείας; S.*OT*1174, cf. *OC*71, *Tr.*1182; ἕτοιμος π. τι X.*Mem.*4.5.12; ἱκανῶς ὡς π. τὴν παροῦσαν χρείαν Arist. *Cael.*269[b]21; ἢν ἀρήγειν φαίνηται π. τὴν σύμπασαν νοῦσον Hp.*Acut.* 60; ποιεῖ π. ἐπιληπτικούς is efficacious *for* cases of epilepsy, Dsc.1.6; ἐθέλοντες τὰ π. τὴν νοῦσον ἡδέα μᾶλλον ἢ τὰ π. τὴν ὑγιείην προσδέχεσθαι Hp.*de Arte* 7. b. *with a view to* or *for* a future time, ὅπως..γράμματα δῷ π. ἣν ἂν ἡμέραν ἑκάτεροι παραγίνωνται *SIG*679.62 (Senatus consultum, ii B.C.); θαυμάζεται τὰ Περικλέους ἔργα π. πολὺν χρόνον ἐν ὀλίγῳ γενόμενα Plu.*Per.*13. c. = πρός B. II, ἐγίνετο π. ἀναχωρήν Plb.3.92.8; ὄντων π. τὸ κωλύειν Id.1.26.3, cf. 1.29.3, al., Plu.*Nic.*5. 4. *in proportion* or *relation to, in comparison with*, κοῖός τις δοκέοι ἀνὴρ εἶναι π. τὸν πατέρα Κῦρον Hdt.3.34; ἔργα λόγου μέζω π. πᾶσαν χώρην Id. 2.35; π. πάντας τοὺς ἄλλους Id.3.94, 8.44; πολλὴν ἂν οἶμαι ἀπιστίαν τῆς δυνάμεως..π. τὸ κλέος αὐτῶν εἶναι Th.1.10, cf. Pi.*O.*2.88, Pl. *Prt.*327d, 328c, *Phd.*102c, etc.; π. τὰς μεγίστας καὶ ἐλαχίστας ναῦς τὸ μέσον σκοπεῖν the mean *between*.., Th.1.10; τὸ κάλλιστον τῶν ἔργων π. τὸ αἴσχιστον συμβαλεῖν Lycurg.68; ἐν π. ἐν συμβάλλειν Hdt.4.50; also ἔχεις π. τὰ ἔτη μέλαιναν τὴν τρίχα Thphr.*Char.*2.3; ἐνδεεστέρως ἢ π. τὴν ἐξουσίαν Th.4.39: also of mathematical ratio, οἷος ὁ πρῶτος (sc. ὅρος) ποτὶ τὸν δεύτερον, καὶ ὁ δεύτερος ποτὶ τὸν τρίτον Archyt.2, cf. Philol.11, Pl.*Ti.*36b, Arist.*Rh.*1409[a]4, al., Euc. 5*Def.*4, etc.; πρὸς παρεόν..μῆτις ἀέξεται ἀνθρώποισι *in proportion to* the existing (physical development), Emp.106: also of price, value, πωλεῖσθαι δὶς π. ἀργύριον sells twice *against* or *relatively to* silver, i.e. for twice its weight in silver, Thphr.*HP*9.6.4; πωλεῖται ὁ σταθμὸς αὐτοῦ π. διπλοῦν ἀργύριον Dsc.1.19; [ἡ μαργαρῖτις λίθος] πωλεῖται..π. χρυσίον *for its weight in* gold, Androsthenes ap.Ath.3.93b: metaph., π. ἀρετήν Pl.*Phd.*69a; ὅπως π. τὰς τιμὰς τῶν κριθῶν τὰ ἄλφιτα πωλήσουσι *on the basis of* the price of barley, Arist.*Ath.*51.3; ἐξέστω αὐτοῦ ἀπογραφὴ τῆς οὐσίας π. τοῦτο τὸ ἀργύριον Ἀθηναίων τῷ βουλομένῳ property *equal in value to* this silver, *IG*2[2].1013.14, cf. *PHib.* 1.32.9 (iii B.C.), *IG*5(1).1390.78 (Andania, i B.C.); τῶν ἐγγύων τῶν ἐγγυωμένων π. [αὐτὰ] τὰ κτήματα *SIG*364.42 (Ephesus, iii B.C.); θέντων τὰ ποτήρια π. χρυσοῦς ἑκατόν *IPE*1[2].32*A*16 (Olbia, iii B.C.); τοὺς ἀπαγομένους εἰς φυλακὴν π. τὰ χρέα imprisoned *for* debt, Plb. 38.11.10, cf. 1.72.5, 5.27.4, 5,7, 5.108.1, *PTeb.*707.9 (ii B.C.); τοὺς π. καταδίκας ἐκπεπτωκότας Plb.25.3.1, cf. *SIG*742.31 (Ephesus, i B.C.); ἐγδίδομεν τὸ ἔργον..π. χαλκόν *IG*7.3073.6 (Lebad., ii B.C.), cf. *PSI*5.356.7 (iii B.C.), *PTeb.*825(*a*).16 (ii B.C.), *Sammelb.*5106.3 (ii B.C.); οἷον π. ἀργύριον τὴν δόξαν τὰς ψυχὰς ἀποδιδόμενοι Jul. *Or.*1.42b; π. ἅλας ἠγορασμένος, i.e. 'dirt cheap', Men.828 (also π. ἅλα δειπνεῖν καὶ κύαμον, i.e. dine frugally, take pot-luck, Plu.2. 684f); so ἡδονὰς π. ἡδονὰς..καταλλάττεσθαι Pl.*Phd.*69a; of measurements of time *by* the flow from the clepsydra, π. ἕνδεκα ἀμφορέας ἐν διαμεμετρημένῃ τῇ ἡμέρᾳ κρίνομαι Aeschin.2.126, cf. Arist.*Ath.*67. 2,3, 69.2; λεγέσθω τὰς δίκας ὁ μὲν πρᾶτος λόγος ἑκατέροις ποτὶ χόας δεκαοκτὼ *SIG*953.17 (Calymna, ii B.C.); λεξάντων πρὸς τὴν τήρησιν τοῦ ὕδατος ib.683.60 (Olympia, ii B.C.); π. κλεψύδραν Eub.p.182 K., Epin. 2; π. κλεψύδρας Arist.*Po.*1451[a]8; π. ὀλίγον ὕδωρ ἀναγκαζόμενος λέγειν D.41.30; hence later, π. ὀλίγον *for* a short time, ἐπανεῖναι π. ὀλίγον τὴν πολιορκίαν J.*BJ*5.9.1, cf. Alex.Aphr.*in Top.*560.2, Hld.2.19, *POxy* 67.14 (iv A.D.), Orib.*Fr.*116, *Gp.*4.15.8; π. ὀλίγον καιρόν, χρόνον, Antyll. ap. Orib.9.24.26, Paul.Aeg.*Prooem.*; π. ὀλίγον ἐστὶ τὸ ζῆν Poet. in *Mus.Script.*p.452 von Jan; μήτηρ δ' ἦν π. μικρόν *Sammelb.* 7288.4 (Ptolemaic); π. βραχύ Jul.*Or.*1.47b (but π. βραχὺ παρηβηκυίας (*by*) a little past their best, *Gp.*4.15.3); π. βραχὺν καιρόν Iamb.*Protr.* 21.κα'; π. τὸ ἀκαρές Porph.*Gaur.*3.3; π. μίαν ἢ δευτέραν ἡμέραν Dsc. 2.101, cf. Sor.1.56; π. δύο ἡμέρας ἐκοίμησα ἐκεῖ *BGU*775.8 (ii A.D.); π. μόνην τὴν ἐνεστῶσαν ἡμέραν *Sammelb.*7299 (ii A.D.), cf. M.Ant.12.4; προστιμάσθω π. χρόνον μὴ εἰσελθεῖν ὅσον ἂν δόξῃ *IG*2[2].1368.89. 5. *in* or *by reference to, according to, in view of*, π. τὸ παρεὸν βουλεύεσθαι Hdt. 1.20, cf. 113, Th.6.46,47, *IG*2[2].1.20, etc.; π. τὴν παροῦσαν ἀρρωστίαν Th.7.47; ἵνα π. τὸν ὑπάρχοντα καιρὸν ἕκαστα θεωρῆτε D.18.17, cf. 314, etc.; εἴ τι δεῖ τεκμαίρεσθαι π. τὸν ἄλλον τρόπον Id.27.22; τοῖς π. ὑμᾶς ζῶσι those who live *with* your *interests in view*, Id.19.226; ἐλευθέρου τὸ μὴ π. ἄλλον ζῆν Arist.*Rh.*1367[a]32; π. τοῦτον πάντ' ἐσκόπουν, π. τοῦτον ἐποιοῦντο τὴν εἰρήνην D.19.63; τὸ παιδεύεσθαι π. τὰς πολιτείας *suitably to* them, Arist.*Pol.*1310[a]14; ὁρῶ..ἅπαντας π. τὴν παροῦσαν δύναμιν τῶν δικαίων ἀξιουμένους *according to* their power, D.15.28; π. τὰς τύχας γὰρ τὰς φρένας κεκτήμεθα *according to*.., E.*Hipp.*701; πρὸς τὰς συνθέσις *in accordance with* the agreements, *IG*5(2).343.41,60 (Orchom. Arc.); τὸν δικαστὰν ὀμνύντα κρίνεν πορτὶ τὰ μωλιόμενα *having regard to* the pleadings, *Leg.Gort.*5.44, cf. 9.30; αἱ ἀρχαὶ..πρὸς τὰ κατεσκευασμένα σύμβολα σηκώματα ποιησάμεναι after making weights and measures *in accordance with*, or *by reference to*, the established standards, *IG*2[2].1013.7; π. τὰ στάθμια τὰ ἐν τῷ ἀργυροκοπίῳ *as measured by* the weights in the mint, ib. 30, cf. *PAmh.*43.10 (ii B.C.); [Σόλων] ἐποίησε σταθμὰ π. τὸ νόμισμα made (trade-)weights *on the basis of* (i.e. *proportional to*) the coinage, Arist.*Ath.*10.2; ὀρθὸν π. τὸν διαβήτην *IG*2[2].1668.9, cf. 95, 7.3073.108 (Lebad., ii B.C.); π. τὸ δικαιότατον *in accordance with* the most just principle, D.C.*Fr.*104. 6. 6. *with the accompaniment of* musical instruments, π. κάλαμον Pi.*O.*10(11).84; π. αὐλόν or τὸν αὐλόν, E.*Alc.*346, X *Smp.*6.3, etc.; π. λύραν..ᾄδειν *SIG*662.13 (Delos, ii B.C.); π. ῥυθμὸν ἐμβαίνειν to step *in time*, D.S.5.34. 7. πρός c. acc. freq. periphr. for Adv., π. βίαν, =

βιαίως, *under* compulsion, νῦν χρή.. τινα π. βίαν πώνην Alc.20 (s.v.l.); π. βίαν ἐπίνομεν Ar.*Ach.*73; τὸ π. βίαν πίνειν ἴσον πέφυκε τῷ διψῆν κακόν S.*Fr.*735; ἥκω.. π. βίαν *under* compulsion, Critias 16.10 D.; *by* force, forcibly, A.*Pr.*210,355, etc.; οὐ π. βίαν τινός not *forced* by any one, Id.*Eu.*5 (but also, *in spite of* any one, S.*OC*657); π. τὸ βίαιον A.*Ag.* 130 (lyr.); π. τὸ καρτερόν Id.*Pr.*214; π. ἀλκήν, π. ἀνάγκαν, Id.*Th.* 498, *Pers.*569 (lyr.); οὐ διαχωρέει [ἡ γαστὴρ] εἰ μὴ π. ἀνάγκην Hp. *Prog.*8,19; π. ἰσχύος κράτος S.*Ph.*594; π. ἡδονὴν εἶναί τινι A.*Pr.*494; π. ἡδονὴν λέγειν, δημηγορεῖν, *so as to* please, Th.2.65, S.*El.*921, D.4.38, cf. E.*Med.*773; οἱ πάντα π. ἡδονὴν ἐπαινοῦντες Arist.*EN*1126ᵇ 13; ἅπαντα π. ἡδ. ζητεῖν D.1.15, cf. 18.4; λούσασθαι τὸ σῶμα π. ἡδ. *as much or little as* one likes, Hp.*Mul.*2.133; πίνειν π. ἡδ. Pl. *Smp.*176e; π. τὸ τερπνόν *calculated to* delight, Th.2.53; π. χάριν *so as to* gratify, μήτε π. ἔχθραν ποιεῖσθαι λόγον μήτε π. χ. D.S.1, cf. S.*OT*1152; π. χάριν δημηγορεῖν D.3.3, etc.: c. gen. rei, π. χάριν τινός *for the sake of*, π. χ. βορᾶς S.*Ant.*30, cf. *Ph.*1156 (lyr.); π. ἰσχύος χ. *by means of*, E.*Med.*538; π. ὀργήν *with* anger, angrily, S.*El.*369, Th.2.65, D.53.16 (v.l.); π. ὀργὴν ἐλθεῖν τινι Id.39.23, etc.; π. τὸ λιπαρές importunately, S.*OC*1119; π. εὐσέβειαν Id.*El.*464; π. καιρόν seasonably, Id.*Aj.*38, etc.; π. φύσιν Id.*Tr.*308; π. εὐτέλειαν cheaply, Antiph.226.2; π. μέρος *in* due proportion, D.36.32; π. ὀλίγον μέρος *Gp.*2.15.1; τέτραπτο π. ἰθύ οἱ straight *towards* him, Il.14.403; π. ὀρθὰς (sc. γωνίας).. τῇ ΑΒ *at* right angles to, Arist.*Mete.*373ᵃ14, cf. Euc.1.11, Archim.*Sph.Cyl.*1.3; π. ὀρθὴν τέμνουσα Arist.*Mete.* 363ᵇ2; π. ἀχθηδόνα, π. ἀπέχθειαν, Luc.*Tox.*9, *Hist.Conscr.*38; γυνὴ π. ἀλήθειαν οὖσα *in* truth a woman, a *very* woman, Ath.15.687a, cf. Luc. *JTr.*48, *Alex.*61: c. Sup., π. τὰ μέγιστα *in* the highest degree, Hdt.8. 20. **8.** of Numbers. *up to, about*, Plb.16.7.5, etc.: cf. πρόσπου.

**D.** ABS. AS ADV., *besides, over and above*; in Hom. always π. δέ or ποτὶ δέ, Il.5.307, 10.108, al., cf. Hdt.1.71, etc.; π. δὲ καί ib.164, 207; π. δὲ ἔτι Id.3.74; καὶ π. Id.7.154,184, prob. in A.*Ch.*301, etc.; καὶ π. γε E.*Hel.*110, Pl.*R.*328a, 466e; καὶ.. γε π. A.*Pr.*73; καὶ δὴ π. Hdt.5.67; freq. at the end of a second clause, τάδε λέγω, δράσω τε π. E.*Or.*622; ἀλογία.., καὶ ἀμαθία γε π. Pl.*Men.*90e, cf. E.*Ph.*610; ἐνενήκοντα καὶ μικρόν τι π. D.4.28, cf. 22.60.

**E.** IN COMPOS., **I.** motion *towards*, as προσάγω, προσέρχομαι, etc. **II.** addition, *besides*, as προσκτάομαι, προσδίδωμι, προστίθημι, etc. **III.** a being *on, at, by*, or *beside*: hence, *a remaining beside*, and metaph. *connexion and engagement with* anything, as πρόσειμι, προσγίγνομαι, etc.

**F.** REMARKS, **1.** in poetry πρός sts. stands after its case and before an attribute, ποίμνας βουστάσεις τε π. πατρός A.*Pr.*653, cf. *Th.* 185, S.*OT*178 (lyr.), E.*Or.*94; ἄστυ πότι (or ποτὶ) σφέτερον Il.17. 419, cf. Pi.*O.*4.5. **2.** in Hom. it is freq. separated from its Verb by tmesis. **3.** sts. (in violation of the rule given by A.D.*Synt.*127.8, *Pron.*42.5) followed by an enclit. Pron., πρός με S.*Aj.*292, Ar.*Pl* 1055, D.18.14 (v.l.), Men.979, *Pk.*77, *Com.Adesp.*15.25 D., 22.68 D., etc.

**προσάββᾰτον,** τό, *eve of the sabbath*, Lxx *Ju.*8.6, *Ev.Marc.*15.42, *Bull.Inst.franç. d'Arch.orientale* 30.5.

**προσᾰγάλλω,** aor. -ήγηλα, *honour besides*, Eup.119.

**προσάγᾰμαι** [ἄγ], *admire besides*, τινα Dam.*Isid.*304 (ap. Suid. s.v. προσηγάσθησαν).

**προσᾰγᾰνακτέω,** *to be angry besides*, Hp.*Ep.*17, D.H.10.24; τινι *at* a thing, J.*AJ*14.8.2, App.*BC*1.46.

**προσαγγ-ελία,** ἡ, *bringing of tidings, message*, *SIG*567.8 (Calymna, iii B.C., Dor. ποτ-), Plb.5.110.11, 14.6.2; τῶν κακῶν προσαγγελίαι Plu.2.504f. **II.** *information laid against* a person, *IG*9(2).1109. 87 (Coropa, ii B.C., pl.), *TAM*2.487 (Patara), *OGI*515.20, al. (Mylasa, iii A.D.). **-έλλω,** *announce, bring tidings*, τινι Pl.*Ep.*362c; τὰ προσηγγελμένα D.18.170; πολέμου προσαγγελθέντος Ὀλατικοῦ *SIG* 707.14 (Olbia, ii B.C.); π. τινά *announce* him, Thphr.*Char.*2.8, cf. Luc.*DDeor.*9.1; π. τὸν λόγον Aristaenet.2.19; freq. in Pap., *PCair. Zen.*481.24 (iii B.C.), *PLille* 6.1 (ii B.C.), etc.:—Pass., also c. part., προσηγγέλλοντο μέλλοντες ἐμβαλεῖν Plu.*Eum.*5. **II.** *denounce*, τῇ βουλῇ τινα Id.*Marc.*2, cf. *OGI*483.39,164 (Pergam.), Luc.*Tox.*32, etc.; ποταγγελλέτω τὸν τούτων τι ποιεῦντα ὁ χρήζων ἐς τοὺς μαστροὺς *SIG*338.33 (Rhodes, iv/iii B.C.); ἑαυτόν *give* oneself *up* to justice, Hermog.*Id.*2.8, cf. *Inv.*4.13; τινὸς οὐσίαν Plu.*Cic.*3:—Pass., *MAMA* 4.297 (Dionysopolis). **-ελμα,** ατος, τό, *report, return, declaration*, *PCair.Zen.*167 (iii B.C.), *PTeb.*71.2 (ii B.C.), etc. **2.** *information laid* against a person, *charge*, *PSI*4.393.1 (iii B.C.), 2.169.8 (ii B.C.). **-ελτής,** οῦ, ὁ, *accuser*, *Gloss.*

**προσᾰγελάζω,** *add to the herd*, *Gloss.*

⊕ **προσάγιος** [ᾰ], ον, (προσ-άγω) *capable of being brought into court*, Mitteis *Chr.*96 iii 5 (iv A.D.).

**προσαγκᾰλίζομαι,** *take in one's arms*, J.*BJ*7.9.1, Aristaenet.1.21, Poll.2.139.

**προσαγκῠλόομαι,** Pass., *to be fastened with a loop*, Hero *Aut.*2.11.

**προσαγλᾰΐζομαι,** Pass., *to be adorned besides*, J.*BJ*5.5.2.

**προσαγνοέω,** *to be ignorant besides*, c. acc. cogn., ἕτερον ἀγνόημα Thphr.*HP*9.4.8, cf. Arist.*Ph.*191ᵇ11.

**προσάγνυμαι,** Pass., *break* or *dash against*, Q.S.3.510, 14.626.

**προσᾰγόρ-άζω,** *buy besides*, *PCair.Zen.*192.9 (iii B.C.), D.S.13.84, *CIG*3385 (Smyrna), 2694*b*6 (Mylasa, Pass.), etc. **-ευμα,** ατος, τό, *appellation, name*, Phld.*Rh.*2.239S., D.H.*Rh.*5.1; of the title 'Imperator', App.*BC*2.44. ⊕ **-ευσις,** εως, ἡ, *address, greeting*, Men.381; ἡ π. τῶν Ἀθηναίων D.H.*Comp.*25, cf. Epict.*Ench.*25.1, Plu.*Fab.*17, etc.; in a letter, Id.*Pyrrh.*6. **-ευτέος,** α, ον, *to be called* or *named*, Pl.*Phd.*104a. **2.** προσαγορευτέον, *one must call*, τινὰ ποιητήν Arist. *Po.*1447ᵇ23, cf. Gal.5.506. **-ευτικός,** ή, όν, *of address* or *greeting*, γράμματα J.*AJ*15.6.3. **II.** as Subst., -κόν, τό, *present given on first meeting*, οὐ δωρεάν, ἀλλὰ τῆς πρώτης ἐς ὑμᾶς ἐντεύξεως προσαγορευτικόν App.*BC*3.44. **2.** Gramm., *vocative case*, *Stoic.*2.61. ⊕ **-εύω,** Att. aor. being προσεῖπον, fut. and pf. προσερῶ, προσείρηκα (but προσαγορεῦσαι occurs in X.*Mem.*3.2.1, προσαγορεύσομεν Pl.*Tht.*147e), aor. Pass. προσερρήθην (but προσηγορεύθην A.*Pr.*834, Anaxil.21.4, Philem.101.6); coupled with προσείποις, προσρητέον in Pl.*Tht.*152d, 182d sq.:—*address, greet*, ἀλλήλους Hdt.1.134, 2.80; δυστυχοῦντες οὐ προσαγορευόμεθα in misfortune *we are* not *spoken to*, Th.6.16; π. τοὺς νέους δι' εὐχῆς Pl.*Lg.*823d; πόρρωθεν π. Thphr.*Char.*5.2; ἐν ταῖς ἐπιστολαῖς τοὺς φίλους π. Pl.*Ep.*315b. **2.** c. dupl. acc., *address* or *greet as* so and so, Δίκαν δέ νιν προσαγορεύομεν βροτοί A.*Ch.*950 (lyr.); τὸν αὐτὸν πατέρα π. X.*Cyr.*8.7.14; βασιλέα π. τινά Plu.*Aem.*8:—Pass., ὑφ' ὧν προσηγορεύθης ἡ Διὸς δάμαρ A.*Pr.*834; -αγορευθεὶς αὐτοκράτωρ, Lat. *imperator consalutatus*, Plu.*Pomp.*8, etc. **3.** simply, *call by name, call* so and so, τὸν Ἀγαμέμνονα π. ποιμένα λαῶν X.*Mem.*3.2.1; τί τὴν πόλιν προσαγορεύεις; Pl.*R.*428d, cf. *Grg.*474e, *Sph.*216c, Lycurg. 26; π. τινὰ ὀνόματι Antipho 6.40, cf. Pl.*Plt.*291e, *Tht.*147e, etc.; ὀνομαστὶ π. X.*Cyr.*5.3.47; τοῦτο τοὔνομα π. σφᾶς αὐτούς Plb.1.8.1:—Pass., *to be called*, Hecat.129 J., etc.; π. ἑταίρα Anaxil. l.c.; λίθος Philem. l.c.; freq. in Pl., *R.*597e, *Phlb.*54a; τῷ τοῦ ὅλου ὀνόματι, ἑνὶ ὂν π., Id.*Smp.*205c, *Sph.*219b, etc. **4.** c. inf., πάσας ἡδονὰς ἀγαθὸν εἶναι προσαγορεύεις Id.*Phlb.*13b, cf. *Prt.*325a; π. τινὰ χαίρειν *bid* one hail or farewell, Ar.*Pl.*323, Pl.*Lg.*771a; also μετὰ τοῦ χαίρειν π. τινά Plu.*Phoc.*17. **II.** *appeal to*, in argument, τὰ τῶν θηρίων ἤθη dub. in Plu.2.493c.

**προσαγρῐαίνω,** *render more savage*, Gal.10.211.

**προσαγρυπνέω,** *lie awake by, sit up over*, οἷς γέγραφε Plu.2.1093c; φιλολογίᾳ Chaerem.ap.Porph.*Abst.*4.8; τοῖς νόμοις ἀλλ' οὐ ταῖς κλοπαῖς Lyd.*Mag.*3.10.

⊕ **προσάγω** [ᾰ], aor. 2 προσήγᾰγον: for aor. 1 προσῆξα v. infr. A. II. 3 fin.: fut. Med. (in pass. sense), Th.4.115: once ποσάγω (q.v.):—*bring to* or *upon*, τίς δαίμων τόδε πῆμα προσήγαγε; Od.17.446, cf. E. *Med.*993 (lyr.); π. δῶρά τινι *h.Ap.*272; ἄστει κόσμον Pi.*I.*6(5).69; θυσίας τινί Hdt.3.24; βοσκήματα S.*Tr.*762; τῷ θεῷν ὕμνους ἢ χορείας Pl.*Lg.*799b; ἱερεῖα τοῖς βωμοῖς Poll.1.27; ποταγόντω.. τὰ ἱερεῖα.. ποτὶ τὸν βωμόν *SIG*1010 (Chalcedon); π. πάντα ἱκανά *furnish, supply*, X.*Cyr.*5.2.5; ἁρμαμάξας ib.4.3.1; λίθους *PCair.Zen.*34.13 (iii B.C.). **2.** *put to, add*, ἅμα ἠγόρευε καὶ ἔργον προσῆγε (v.l. προῆγεν) Hdt.9.92; of exercises and food, ἐξ ὀλίγου π. Hp.*Insomn.*89; cf. προσαγωγή II.5. **3.** *bring to, move towards, apply*, τὴν ἄνω γνάθον π. τῇ κάτω Hdt.2.68; μὴ π. τὴν χεῖρά μοι *lay* it not *on* me, Ar. *Lys.*893; π. κεγχρώμασιν ὀφθαλμόν *apply* it *closely*, E.*Ph.*1386; π. τὴν ῥῖνά τινι Diod.Com.2.39; πρὸς τὸ στόμα τὰς χεῖρας Arist.*HA*587ᵃ27: esp. of medical applications, ἤπια [ἤματα] μετὰ τὰ ἰσχυρά Hdt.3.130; προσαχθέντος φαρμάκου Orib.46.1.125: metaph., [παιδιὰς] π. φαρμακείας χάριν Arist.*Pol.*1337ᵇ41; παρρησίαν καὶ δηγμὸν ἀνθρώπῳ δυστυχοῦντι Plu.2.69a. **4.** of meats, etc., *set before*, βρώματά τινι X.*Cyr.*1.3.4, cf. Plu.2.126a, etc. **5.** metaph., π. ὅρκους σφι *put* oaths *to* them, *make* them *take* oaths, Hdt.6.74. **6.** in military sense, *bring up* for the attack, *move on towards*, π. πύλαις λόχον E.*Ph.*1104; τῇ Ποτειδαίᾳ τὸν στρατὸν Th.1.64; τὸ στράτευμα ἀντίπρῳρον π. X.*HG*7.5.23; [στρατιάν] π. πρὸς πολεμίους Id.*Cyr.*1.6.43; v. infr. II: so also π. μηχανὰς πόλει Th.2.76, cf. X.*HG*2.4.27, etc.; μηχανῆς μελλούσης προσάξεσθαι (in pass. sense) Th.4.115; π. βίαν τοῖς τείχεσι, τῇ πόλει, etc., D.S.11.32, 12.46, etc. **7.** metaph., π. βίαν τοῖς πολεμίοις Id.15.68, cf. *PTeb.*61 (*b*).33 (ii B.C., Pass.), etc.; τὰς ἀνάγκας Th.1.99; συκοφαντίαν π. τοῖς πράγμασι D.19.98; δεινὰν π. τόλμαν *apply* or *put forth* daring, E.*Med.*859 (lyr.); γράψας.. τίνα οἰκονομίαν προσαγήγοχας what steps you *have taken*, *PCair.Zen.*240.10 (iii B.C.); πολλῶν φόβων προσαγομένων X.*An.*4.1.23; π. ἡδονάς Pl.*Lg.*798e. **8.** *bring to* or *before*, τῷ Κύρῳ τοὺς αἰχμαλώτους X.*Cyr.*3.2.12, cf. *HG*2.4.8, etc.; *bring in, bring with one*, Is.8.16; *introduce*, πρὸς τὸν δῆμον Th.5. 61; πρὸς τὴν βουλήν And.1.111, cf. Lys.6.29; π. τοὺς πρέσβεις (i.e. before the assembly) D.18.28, cf. 213; πρεσβείαν ἐλθοῦσαν π. πρὸς βουλὴν καὶ δῆμον *IG*1².39.12; *introduce* at court, X.*Cyr.*1.3.8; *bring* a person *into a law-court* as defendant or as witness, *PHal.*8.5 (iii B.C.), etc. **b.** *introduce* in writing, λόγῳ π. ὅτι.. *introduce* the statement .., Arist.*Cael.*304ᵃ13; π. [ἡλικίαν] πρὸς μάθησιν Id.*Pol.*1336ᵃ24; [παιδάριον] π. πρὸς τὰ μαθήματα *PSI*4.340.24 (iii B.C.); τὰ λοιπὰ μυθικῶς προσῆκται *have been introduced*, Arist.*Metaph.*1074ᵇ4. **9.** *bring hither, lead on*, τίς [σε] προσήγαγεν χρεία; S.*Ph.*236; ἐλπίς μ' ἀεὶ προσῆγε E.*Andr.*27:—Pass., οἴκτῳ καὶ ἐπιεικείᾳ π. Th.3.48; βίᾳ ib.95; ἄκοντες π. ὑπ' Ἀθηναίων ib.63, cf. X.*HG*6.1.7. **10.** Pass., *to be brought over, attached* to the cause of, c. dat., εἴ πως σφίσιν προσαχθείη Th.2.77: abs., προσήγεσθε ὑπ' Ἀθηναίων Id.3.63; cf. B I. **11.** *increase a rent* or *other charge*, *PTeb.*72.187 (Pass.), 200 (ii B.C.); προσηγμένων τοῖς ἀπαιτησίμοις ib.217; ᾧ προσάγω ὑπὲρ ἐπιθέματος ἄλλας δραχμὰς ἑξήκοντα *PRyl.*99.7 (iii A.D.). **12.** = προσαγγέλλω, *announce, report*, *PTeb.*60.69 (ii B.C.), etc. **13.** *debit* a person with an amount, *charge* it to him, συνέβη ναῦλον ἡμῖν προσάγεσθαι τοῦ πλοίου *PCair.Zen.*368.28, cf. 326.16 (iii B.C.). **II.** seemingly intr. (sc. ἑαυτόν, στρατόν, etc.), *draw near, approach*, X.*HG*3.5.22; πρός τινας Lxx 3*Ki.*18.21; esp. in a hostile sense, *advance against, attack*, π. πρὸς τὸ κέρας X.*An.*1.10.9, etc.; κώμῃ τινὶ Arr.*An.*2.3.4; δι' ἀπάτης τοῖς βασιλεῦσι Plu.2.800a; ἐγγυτέρω ταῖς ἐλπίσιν Id.*Galb.*9; τοῖς τετταράκοντα [ἔτεσι] Id.*Pomp.*46; πόταγε (Dor. for πρόσαγε) *come on!* Theoc.1.62, 15.78; μαλακῶς π. [γυναικί] *make advances* to a woman in an effeminate manner, Plu.2.240e; of Time, τῆς προσαγούσης τρύγης the *approaching* vintage, *Sammelb.*5810.16 (iv A.D.). 2. (sc. ναῦν) *bring to, come to land,* τόποις Plb.1.54.5, etc.; Ῥόδῳ Apollod.2.1.4codd. 3. δυσχερῶς προσῆγον πρὸς τὰς εἰσφορὰς dub.l. in Plb.5.30.5 (πως εἶχον πρὸς Hultsch): ὅσων προσῆξαν is f.l. in Th.2. 97 (ὅσωνπερ ἦρξαν Dobree).

B. Med., *bring* or *draw to oneself, attach to oneself, bring over to one's side,* σοφίῃ αὐτούς, οὐκ ἀγνωμοσύνῃ προσηγάγετο Hdt.2.172; ἀνάγκῃ προσάγεσθαί τινα Id.6.25, cf. Th.1.99; τἀρετῇ π. πόσιν E. *Andr.*226; ἀπάτῃ π. τὸ πλῆθος Th.3.43; χρήμασι καὶ δωρεαῖς τὸν δῆμον προσάγεσθαι Pl.*Lg.*695d; τῷ ποιεῖν εὖ π. τὰς πόλεις Isoc.4.80; θεραπείαις Id.3.22; so [ἵππον] ἠρεμαίως π. τῷ χαλινῷ X.*Eq.*9.5; συμμάχους καὶ βοηθοὺς π. Id.*Mem.*3.4.9; τὴν τῶν Ἀθηναίων ξυμμαχίαν Th.5. 82; πάντων π. ὄμματα *draw* all eyes *upon oneself,* X.*Smp.*1.9. 2. abs., *draw to oneself, embrace,* Ar.*Av.*141, X.*Cyr.*7.5.39, Pl.*R.*439b; ἥ γ' ἐμὴν γενειάδα προσῆγετ' ἀεὶ στόματι E.*Supp.*1100. 3. c. inf., ἡ Σφὶγξ τὸ πρὸς ποσὶ σκοπεῖν.. ἡμᾶς.. προσήγετο *put* us *upon* considering, S.*OT*131; προσάξομαι δάμαρτ' ἐάν σε.. *will induce* her to suffer thee.., E.*Ion* 659. II. *take to oneself, take up,* ὅσ᾽τὰ Id.*Supp.*949; τὰ ναυάγια Th.8.106. 2. *get for oneself, procure, import,* ὧν δεῖται X.*Vect.*1.7; τὰ προσαχθέντα *imports,* ib.4.18. 3. αἷς [ταῖς προβοσκίσι] π. εἰς τὸ στόμα τὴν τροφήν with which *they bring* it to their mouths, Arist.*HA*523b31, cf. 526a28, *PA*685b10. 4. μηδὲ προσάγου τῷ πράγματι χειμῶνας ἑτέρους *do* not *add* further troubles, Men.187; π. τὸν χρόνον καὶ τὸν πόνον *employ* it *for one's own advantage,* Plb.29. 17.4. 5. μάρτυρα π. *cite* as witness, Plu.2.1049b.

**προσάγωγ-εῖον**, τό, carpenter's or stonemason's *square,* Pl.*Phlb.* 56c (v.l. -ίῳ), *IG*7.3073.118, 139 (Lebad., ii B.C.) (used for straightening wood acc. to Sch.Pl. l.c.). ⊛ **-εύς**, έως, ὁ, *introducer,* π. λημμάτων *one who hunts for another's profit, jackal,* D.24.161, cf. Aristid.*Or.*28 (49).19, 131. II. *talebearer,* hence 'agent provocateur' of tyrants, Plu.2.522f:—hence fem. **προσαγωγίς**, ίδος, ἡ, Dor. **ποταγωγίς** Arist. *Pol.*1313b13 (but τοὺς καλουμένους -αγωγίδας Plu.*Dio* 28, cf. Id.2. 522f). ⊛ **-ή**, ἡ, *bringing to,* πρὸς τὴν τῆς τροφῆς π. for the purpose of *bringing* the food *to the mouth,* Arist.*PA*687b26; οἰκοδόμῳ εἰς π. πλίνθου *PCair.Zen.*176.14 (iii B.C.). 2. *bringing up,* μηχανημάτων, ὀργάνων, Plb.1.48.2 (pl.), 14.10.9 (pl.); ποιεῖσθαι τὴν π., much like our phrase 'to make *approaches*', Id.9.41.1. 3. *a bringing over, acquisition,* ξυμμάχων Th.1.82; ἐκ π. φίλος a friend under *compulsion,* D.23. 174 (ἐκ προαγωγῆς Harp.). 4. *administering* or *taking* of medicine, Phld.*Ir.*p.44 W. (pl.), Dsc.4.148. II. *solemn approach,* as at festivals or in supplication, Hdt.2.58 (pl.). 2. *approach, access, introduction to* a person, esp. to a king's presence, X.*Cyr.*7.5.45, cf. *Ep.Rom.*5.2, *Ep.Eph.*2.18, etc. 3. π. νεῶν *a place* for ships *to put in,* Plb.10.1.6, cf. D.S.13.46, Plu.*Aem.*13. 4. *attack,* Aen.Tact. 10.23 (pl.). 5. *addition,* of food, opp. ἀφαίρεσις, Hp.*Insomn.*89; ἐκ προσαγωγῆς *by gradual additions, gradually,* Id.*Acut.*11, Thphr. *HP*3.10.5, etc.; opp. ἀθρόος, Arist.*Pol.*1308b16; ἐκ π. καὶ κατὰ μικρόν ib.1306b14, cf. 1315a13; opp. ἐξαίφνης, Id.*Mete.*368a7; τόποι ὑψηλοὶ ἐκ π. *rising gradually* to a height, ib.350b22. III. *accession, addition,* Epicur.*Fr.*190. 2. *increase of rent, PTeb.*72.449 (ii B.C.). IV. *surface* of a stone *intended for application* to another, *IG*2².244.102 (pl.). **-ιον**, v. προσαγωγεῖον. **-ίς** (sc. ναῦς), ίδος, ἡ, *transport, PLille* 21.8 (iii B.C.), *PPetr.*3p.257 (iii B.C., pl.). II. v. προσαγωγεύς. **-ός**, όν, *attractive, persuasive,* τῇ ἀκροάσει Th.1.21 (Comp.); τὸ αὑτοῦ π. Pl.*Def.*415a; προσαγωγὸν μειδιᾶν Luc.*DDeor.*20.11: c. gen., *exciting,* π. ἐπιθυμιῶν αἰσχρῶν τέχναι D.H.2.28. II. Subst., = προσαγωγεύς II, prob. in Anon.Hist. (*FGrH*153) p.825 J.

**προσᾰγωνίζομαι**, *contend besides,* τινι *with* one, Philostr.*Her.*4.2, cf. Poll.3.141.

**προσᾰδῐκέω**, *do* one a *further wrong,* J.*AJ*13.5.4:—Pass., Ph.2. 332. b. *wrong* another person *besides,* Hld.2.5. 2. *injure as well,* τὸ ζῷον εἰς κακοχυμίαν Gal.*UP*5.4.

**προσᾴδω**, *sing to,* τίν ποταείσομαι *to* thee *will I sing,* Theoc.2. 11. 2. π. τραγῳδίᾳ *sing the songs in* a tragedy, Ar.*Eq.*401; π. μέλη Aristaenet.1.2; π. τῇ κιθάρᾳ Ael.*VH*14.23; προσαείσαντος αὐτοῦ τοῦ θεοῦ dub. in *IG*5(2).528 (Lycosura). II. *harmonize, chime in with,* τινι *with* one, S.*Ph.*405: abs., Hp.*Vict.*1.8, Pl.*Phd.*86e, *Lg.* 670b.

**προσαθροίζω**, *gather to,* Gloss.

**προσᾰθῡμέω**, *to be discouraged at,* τινι J.*BJ*4.1.6.

**προσᾰθύρω** [ῠ], = προσπαίζω, Philostr.*Im.*2.2, Hsch.

**προσαιθρίζω**, *send into the air,* προσαιθρίζουσα πόμπιμον φλόγα *Trag. Adesp.*260.

**προσαικάλλω**, *fawn upon,* prob. in Plu.2.974a.

**προσαικίζομαι**, *torment besides,* J.*BJ*4.4.3 (v.l. προ-).

**προσαιον-άω**, *douche besides,* Hp.*Mul.*2.143, *Fist.*4. **-ητέον**, *one must douche besides,* Archig.ap.Orib.47.13.5.

⊛ **προσαιρέομαι**, Med., *choose and associate with,* τινάς τινι ξυμβούλους Th.5.63; ἑωυτῷ π. τινά *take for one's companion* or *ally,* Hdt.9.10; κοινὸν αὐτοῖς [διαιτητήν] D.59.45; σφίσιν αὐτοῖς ἄρχοντας Arist.*Ath.* 35.1; ὁ αἰσυμνήτης τοὺς προσεταίρους -εῖται *SIG*57.7 (Milet., v B.C.), cf. *IG*1².56.27, 84.38. II. *choose in addition to,* τινά τινι X.*HG*6. 2.39; στρατηγοὺς πρὸς τοῖς ὑπάρχουσι ib.2.1.16. III. Act. προσαιρεῖν *appoint* as one's *assistant, POxy.*58.17 (iii A.D.): aor. part. προσελών dub. sens. in *PPetr.*2.20 iii 9 (cf. 3 p.76, iii B.C.).

**προσαίρω**, *bring,* πρόσαιρε τὸ κανοῦν, εἰ δὲ βούλει, πρόσφερε Pherecr. 137; *bring to* a person, *administer,* ἢν.. ἀσθενέοντι προσαίρῃ τις ποτόν Hp.*Acut.*44:—so in Med., *take, consume, eat* or *drink,* Id.*VM*6, *Acut.* 47, Phylotim.ap.Ath.3.81b; π. οἶνον, σιτία, Gal.7.141, *UP*4.7: c.gen., Id.11.336. 2. *raise to a higher level,* τὴν ἠχὼ τῆς διαλέξεως Philostr. *VS*2.5.3. II. προσήραντο is prob. f.l. for συνήραντο, *they took part,* in D.C.43.17.

**προσαισθάνομαι**, *perceive besides,* Arist.*Mem.*450a21.

**προσᾱΐσσω**, Att. -ᾴσσω, *spring* or *rush to,* Od.22.337, 342, 365; ὄσσοις ὁμίχλα π. a cloud *comes over* my eyes, A.*Pr.*145 (lyr.); in Prose, of flames, Aen.Tact.34.2; also of persons, τινι Chio *Ep.*13. 1.

⊛ **προσαιτ-έω**, *ask besides,* οὐδέν Pi.*Fr.*177.6; αἷμα π. *demand more* blood, A.*Ch.*401 (anap.); π. μισθὸν *demand higher* pay, X.*An.*1.3. 21. 2. *demand* or *require for* a purpose, ὅσους.. τὰ ἔργα προσαιτοίη Id.*Vect.*4.39. II. *ask as well as others* (sc. for a share), and so, c. acc. pers., *ask an alms of,* Hdt.3.14, Isoc.7.83, etc.: c. acc. rei, *beg for* a thing, βίοτον, στρατιάν, E.*Hel.*791, Ar.*Lys.*1141: c. dupl. acc., *beg* somewhat *of* one, E.*Hel.*512, X.*An.*7.3.31: c. gen., *beg some of..,* Plu.*Alc.*4: abs., *to be importunate,* E.*Supp.*64 (lyr.), Ar.*Ach.*429, 452; *to be a beggar,* Pl.*Smp.*203b, *PCair.Zen.*493.6 (iii B.C.), prob. in Plu. 2.294a. **-ης**, ου, ὁ, *beggar, Ev.Marc.*10.46, Gal.13.636, Porph. *Antr.*34, dub. l. in Plu.2.294a, Luc.*Nav.*24:—fem. **προσαῖτις**, ιδος, Suid. ⊛ **-ησις**, εως, ἡ, *begging,* ἐφημέρου τροφῆς Plu.2.499c. **-ητής**, οῦ, ὁ, = προσαίτης, Hsch. s.v. προΐκτης. **-ητικός**, ή, όν, *importunate,* Vett.Val.2.5.

**προσαιτιάομαι**, *accuse besides,* τινα Plu.*Fab.*7.

**προσαιωρέομαι**, Med., *raise oneself,* τῇ λόγχῃ by or on one's lance, D.S.33.7.

**προσακές**· ἐγγύς, Hsch.

**προσᾰκοντίζω**, *shoot like a javelin,* Luc.*DMeretr.*12.1.

**προσᾰκούω**, *hear besides,* τι X.*HG*3.4.1. II. as Pass. of προσαγορεύω, τοιαῦτα π. *to be addressed* in such terms, ib.2.4.22, cf. Plu.2. 71e, 812e; ἐπαινέσας προσακούω εἴρων I *am called*.. J.*BJ*1.26.2.

**προσακρῑβόω**, strengthd. for ἀκριβόω, Arist.ap.D.L.5.28 (Pass.), Str.15.1.14.

**προσακροβολίζομαι**, *skirmish with besides,* Plb.3.71.10, 11.22.5.

**προσακτέον**, (προσάγω) *one must bring to* or *near,* Pl.*R.*537a; τὸ κάτω πρὸς τὸ ἄνω Hp.*Art.*14; *one must apply, administer,* of instruments or drugs, Herod.Med.ap.Aët.5.130, Orib.*Fr.*74; [τὴν μουσικήν] Arist.*Pol.*1340b13; παραδείγματα Id.*Rh.Al.*1438b40; τῇ φύσει τοῦ πράγματος π. τὴν τέχνην Hermog.*Stat.*7. II. **προσακτέος**, α, ον, *to be applied,* ἡσυχίη π. Aret.*CA*2.3; *to be administered,* οἶνος οὐ π. Orib.5.31.10.

**προσακτρίδες**, αἱ, prob. *mandibles* of the cockchafer (literally *the bringers-to*), Hsch.

**προσᾰλαζονεύω**, *play the braggart besides,* Hsch. s.v. κομπαλικεύσει.

**προσᾰλείφω**, *rub* or *smear upon,* ἑκάστῳ φάρμακον ἄλλο Od.10. 392. II. *besmear,* τὰ ἄκρα τῶν κερδτων Plu.2.559f:—Pass., ib. 911e.

**προσάλειψις** [ᾰλ], εως, ἡ, *besmearing,* metaph. of a flatterer, Phld. *Herc.*1457.4 (pl.).

**προσᾰλίγκιος**, ον, *like,* Nic.*Th.*739.

⊛ **προσᾰλίζομαι**, f.l. for προαλ-, Aen.Tact.17.4.

**προσᾰλίσκομαι**, *to be cast* in a lawsuit *besides,* Ar.*Ach.*701.

**προσάλληλος**, ον, *one with* or *against another,* X.*Eq.*4.3, Ach.Tat. 2.38. 2. *congenial,* π. καρπὸς τόπῳ prob. in Thphr.*HP*2.2.8. 3. *mutual,* Phld.*D.*3.14; *correlative,* Syrian.*in Metaph.*34.23.

**προσάλλομαι**, *jump up at,* X.*Cyr.*8.4.20, Arist.*HA*612a11, Str. 16.4.19, Plu.2.977c; of a wind, Arist.*Mu.*395a7; π. τῷ στέρνῳ, of the heart, Ruf.*Syn.Puls.*3.6.

**προσαλλοτρι-όομαι**, Pass., *to be alienated* or *averse from,* τινι Phld. *Ir.*p.84 W.; opp. προσοικειόομαι, S.E.*M.*7.140. **-ωσις**, εως, ἡ, *alienation,* dub. in Phld.*Ir.*p.82 W.

**προσάλπιος**, ον, *dwelling near the Alps,* ἔθνη Str.5.4.1.

**πρόσαλσις**, εως, ἡ, (προσάλλομαι) *leaping against,* of the pulse, Agathin.ap.Gal.8.937.

⊛ **προσᾰμαρτάνω**, f.l. in Plu.2.834d.

**προσάμβᾰσις**, ἡ, poet. for προσανάβασις (q.v.).

**προσᾰμείβομαι**, Dor. ποτ-, Med., *answer,* τινα Theoc.1.100.

**προσᾰμέλγομαι**, Dor. ποτ-, Pass., *yield milk besides,* εἰς δύο πέλλας Theoc.1.26.

**προσᾰμιλλάομαι**, *vie with, rival besides,* ταῖς ἑταίραις, τοῖς ὄρεσι, Poll.6.126, 9.20.

⊛ **προσαμπέχω**, *veil besides,* αὐχένα Chaerem.14.8:—Pass., *remain held* or *entangled in,* ἰξῷ *AP*12.93 (Rhian.).

**προσᾰμύνω** [ῡ], *come to aid,* τινι Il.2.238, cf. 5.139, 16.509, Plu. *Them.*9, al.

**προσᾰμύσσω**, *irritate still further,* τόπον φαρμάκῳ Orib.46.30.4.

**προσᾰμφιέννῡμι**, Att. fut. -αμφιῶ, *put on over,* τινά τι Ar.*Eq.*891.

**προσανα-βαίνω**, fut. -βήσομαι X.*Eq.Mag.*1.2:—*go up,* or *mount besides,* l.c.; of water-birds, π. πρὸς τὰς πέτρας Arist.*HA*617a26; π. πρὸς τὸ ὄρθιον D.C.39.45; *rise higher,* as a swollen river, Plb.3.72.4; πόλις προσαναβαίνουσα *lying on a mountain side,* Poll.9.20: metaph., π. τῷ Ῥωμύλῳ *go back as far as* R., Plu.*Thes.*1. II. c. acc. loci, *climb, ascend,* τὸ σιμόν Pl.Com.79. **-βάλλω**, *throw up besides,* Arist.*Mu.*396a6. **-βᾰσις**, poet. **προσάμβ-**, εως, ἡ, *going up, ascent,* Lxx *Jo.*15.3, Bacch.ap.Apollon.Cit.1 (pl.); κλίμακος προσαμβάσεις a ladder's *means of ascent,* A.*Th.*466, E.*Ph.*1173; πηκτῶν κλιμάκων π. ib.489, *Ba.*1213; τειχέων π. *place where* they *may be approached,* Id.*Ph.*744; δωμάτων π. *steps leading* to the house, Id.*IT*97. **-βιβρώσκω**, *corrode,* in Pass., Gal.ap.Orib.51.36.

2. -**γαργᾰρίζομαι**, *use a gargle afterwards*, Heraclid.Tar.ap. Gal.12.984. -**γιγνώσκω**, *read besides*, Aeschin.2.91 (v.l.), J.*BJ* 2.2.4 (v.l.), Gal.18(2).886.

**προσᾰναγκ-άζω**, *force* or *constrain besides*, Th.7.18; *compress too tightly*, of a bandage, Hp.*Off.*8 (Pass.); *force* bones *together*, opp. ἀπαναγκάζω, Id.*Art.*14. II. *increase the severity* of exercises, ἀπὸ κούφων π. Id.*Vict.*3.68; of military training, τῇ ἄλλῃ μελέτῃ Th. 6.72. III. c. acc. et inf., *force* one *to do* a thing, βίῃ με προσηνάγκασσε πάσασθαι *h.Cer.*413; π. τινὰ παρεῖναι, μένειν, ὁμολογεῖν, φιλεῖν, X.*Cyr.*8.1.17, Pl.*Smp.*217d, 223d, *Prt.*346b: the inf. is freq. omitted, τοὺς μὴ δεχομένους τὰς σπονδὰς π. (sc. δέχεσθαι) Th.5.42; π. τινά τι *force* him *also* (to do) something, Pl.*Smp.*181e. IV. *constrain* or *compel* by argument, τῷ λόγῳ τινά Id *Phlb.*13b, cf. Gal.9. 936. 2. π. τι εἶναι *prove that* a thing *necessarily* is, Pl.*Lg.*710a, *Plt.*284b. -**αστέον**, *one must prove*, ibid.

**προσαναγορεύω**, *announce besides*, Pl.*R.*580c; cf. προσανεῖπον.

⊛ **προσαναγράφω** [γρᾰ], *record* or *enter besides*, *IG*2².140.32, 448.71, 12(8).51.8 (Imbros, ii B.C.), *PIand.*27.5 (i/ii A.D., Pass.), Plu.2.243a, Luc.*Macr.*9:—Pass., προσαναγραφέντες προδόται εἰς ταύτην τὴν στήλην Lycurg.118, cf. D.S.5.46. 2. *prescribe as well*, Sor.2.65. 3. Geom., *complete the tracing of*, κύκλον Euc.3.25. II. Med., προσαναγραψάμεναι τὰ λοιπὰ τοῦ χρωτὸς *by tattooing* (cf. Eust.1960.16) *in addition* the rest of *their* skin, Clearch.8.

**προσανάγω** [ᾰγ], Dor. ποτ-, *carry up to*, ἐς φάος ἐκ βυθίας ποτανάγαγον ἰλύος *Hymn.Is.*161:—Pass., *to be drawn up*, πρός τι v.l. for προσαγ- in D.H.*Comp.*14. 2. seemingly intr., *come up to, approach*, f.l. for προσαγαγοῦσαν in Plu.2.564c; π. τῇ γῇ *approached* the land, Id.*Pyrrh.*15.

**προσανα-δέρω**, *strip off further*, Gal.2.719. ⊛ -**δέχομαι**, *expect besides, wait for*, Plb.5.13.8, 21.13.14. -**δῐδάσκω**, *teach in addition*, ὡς.. Ph.2.92 (Pass.). -**δίδωμι**, *distribute* or *give out besides*, Plb. 10.14.3; τινὶ τὴν ἀσπίδα Plu.2.241f. -**ζητέω**, *search out besides*, τοὺς πατρίους νόμους Decr.ap.Arist.*Ath.*29.3. -**ζωγρᾰφέω**, *depict in addition*, Ph.1.684.

**προσαν-αιδεύομαι**, *act impudently besides*, Ar.*Eq.*397 as misquoted by Suid. s. v. ἐρύθημα. -**αιρέω**, *lift up besides*:—Med., *take upon oneself besides*, πόλεμον Th.7.28. II. *destroy besides*, τἀληθές Arist.*EN*1172ᵇ1, cf. *APr.*62ᵃ3 (Pass.). III. of an oracle, *give an answer besides*, Pl.*R.*461e, Plu.2.403c, etc.; π. τινὶ στεφανηφορεῖν D.21.54. -**αισῑμόομαι**, Pass., *to be spent besides*, Hdt.5.34.

**προσανα-κᾰθαίρω**, *purify in addition*, aor. part. Med. -καθηράμενοι Plot.6.7.29. -**καθίζω**, *sit up straighter*, Aët.9.13. -**καίω**, *kindle besides*, Ph.1.428. -**κᾰλύπτω**, *disclose besides*, οὐδέν Str.15.1. 3. -**κάμπτω**, *go backwards and forwards*, πρὸς ἀμφοτέρους Plb.11. 34.8. -**κειμαι**, Pass., *lie hard by*, Sch.Il.15.740. II. *to be wholly given up* or *devoted to*, κυνηγεσίαις Plu.2.314b. -**κεράννῡμαι**, Pass., *to be mixed up*, πίττῃ Ael.*NA*14.4. -**κεφᾰλαιόομαι**, *recapitulate further*, Apollon.Cit.3. -**κλάω**, *bend upwards*, τὰ κῶλα Sor.1.102:—Pass., Id.2.60. -**κλῐμα**, ατος, τό, *that on which one leans*, *AP*7.407 (Diosc.). ⊛ -**κλίνω** [ῑ], *lean against*, δένδρεσιν ἑαυτούς, of elephants, Agatharch.55:—Pass., *lean on*, τινι D.S.17.41, Paus.10.30.6; of a city, τῷ ὄρει προσανακεκλιμένη Str.14.1.43. -**κλῐσις**, εως, ἡ, *leaning* or *lying against*, Luc.*Am.*31. -**κοινόομαι**, Med., *communicate besides*, τινί τι D.S.1.16. -**κόπτω**, *beat up in addition*, τῇ σπάθῃ τὸ φάρμακον Damocr.ap.Gal.13.823. -**κουφίζω**, *hold up, save from falling besides*, J.*Vit.*18 (Pass.). -**κρίνω** [ῑ], *inquire further*, Plu.2. 43e, 592f, S.E.*M*7.426. -**κτάομαι**, *recover besides*, τι Alex.Trall.8. 1. -**κύπτω**, *to be reinvigorated besides*, Anon.Lond.38.19. -**λαμβάνω**, *take in* or *receive besides*, ἐπὶ τὸ κατάστρωμα χιλίας βύρσας D.34. 10; παρὰ τῶν συμμάχων σῖτον Plb.1.52.8, cf. *PPetr.*3 p.227 (iii B.C.); π. ἐσθῆτας περιπορφύρους *assume also*, Plb.6.53.7:—Pass., πλειόνων προσαναλαμβανομένων, of a batch of new senators, Plu.*Rom.*13. 2. *use besides*, Thphr.*HP*5.7.7. II. *recall* to strength, *recruit, restore*, τὴν δύναμιν ἐκ τῆς κακοπαθείας Plb.9.8.7; ἐκ τοῦ πλοῦ αὐτοὺς Id.21.42.6; τὸ στρατόπεδον D.S.17.16. 2. intr., *recover*, Plb.3.60. 8. -**λέγω**, *collect besides*, Ael.*NA*4.39:—Pass., *Sammelb.*4425 v i (ii A.D.). II. Med., *recount besides*, Lxx 2*Ma.*8.19. -**λικμάω**, *winnow besides*, of corn, *Gp.*5.32.2.

**προσᾰν-ᾱλίσκω**, fut. -αναλώσω, *lavish* or *consume besides*, καὶ τὰ τῶν φίλων π. Pl.*Prt.*311d; τὰς ἰδίας οὐσίας D.20.10, cf. D.C.43.18; π. οὐκ ὀλίγα χρήματα *IG*2².834.7; π. χρόνον ἰσοτίς *waste further* time *on*.., D.L.6.98; μισθούς τινι Porph.*Abst.*1.56. -**ἄλλομαι**, *leap up at* a thing, Ath.7.277f.

**προσανα-λογίζομαι**, *consider besides*, Plu.2.115a. -**λύω**, *break up as well*, Steph. *in Hp.*1.104D. ⊛ -**μείγνυμι**, *mix with as well*, in Pass., Gal.18(2).155. -**μένω**, *await besides*, D.S.15.41, 16.85, *PLond.*3.948.9 (iii A.D.). -**μετρέω**, *measure up*, Heliod.ap.Orib.44. 23.65. -**μιμνήσκω**, *remind of*, τινά τινος Plb.4.28.6, al.: abs., Id.4.29. 7:—Med. with aor. 1 Pass., *mention, record as well*, Gal.8.904, 18(2). 434. -**νεόομαι**, Med., *recall afresh to memory*, τι Plb.8.37.2 (v.l. ap.Suid.). -**ξαίνω**, *stimulate as well*, Paul.Aeg.6.49. -**ξηραίνω**, *dry up besides*, Herod.Med.ap.Orib.5.30.12. -**ξύω**, *scrape off besides*, Antyll.ap.Orib.44.23.4. -**παύω**, *cause to rest also* or *beside*, τὴν δύναμιν ἐπὶ τρεῖς ἡμέρας Plb.4.73.3; τὴν χεῖρα τῇ γαστρί τινος J.*AJ* 20.2.1. II. Med. or Pass., *sleep beside*, τῇ γυναικί Nicostr.ap.Stob. 4.23.65. 2. *rest by leaning upon*, δένδροις Str.16.4.10; τοῖς θυρεοῖς Plu.*Sull.*28; *rest upon*, Sor.1.7,100; of a shipwrecked sailor, *cling to* a plank, Favorin. in *PVat.*11.23.36. 3. of words in a sentence, *to be otiose*, D.H.*Dem.*40. 4. *rely on*, τεχνίῳ, τέχνῃ, M.Ant.4.31, S.E.*M.*11.178; τινὶ J.*AJ*6.14.3, Marcellin.*Puls.*227. 5. *find relief in the society of*, [φίλῳ] Arr.*Epict.*3.13.2; also, *find rest in*, τῇ σοφίᾳ Lxx *Wi.*8.16. -**πείθω**, *persuade besides*, D.C.44.34, 46.49 (Pass.). -**πειράομαι**, *attempt* the sea *besides*, Poll.1.123 (s. v.l., cf. προανα-). -**πέμπω**, *send up besides*, *BGU*908.18 (ii A.D.). -**πηδάω**, *leap up on*, τῇ ὄχθῃ Ael.*NA*5.23. -**πίμπλημι**, *fill besides*, τοὺς παρόντας κακοηθείας Plu.2.631f. 2. *infect besides*, Arist.*Pr.*859ᵇ16. ⊛ -**πίπτω**, *recline by* or *with* others at meals, Plb.30. 26.6 (ap.D.S.31.16). -**πλάσσω**, Att. -ττω, *mould upon*, τὸν ὄσχεον ἐκ τῶν συμμηριῶν Sor.1.103. II. *invent besides*, ὅτι.. S.E.*M.*11.158; *ascribe*, αὐχένα τῷ θεῷ Ph.1.226, al.; Διὶ φλύαρον ἦθος Eust.1387.22 (Med.); τὰς γραφὰς ταῖς ἐξηγήσεσι Gal.17(2).257:—Pass., Longin.7. 1, Corn.*ND*34, Palaeph.15. ⊛ -**πλέκω**, *mix in as well*, Alex.Trall.8. 2. -**πληρόω**, *fill up, replenish besides*, τὸν ἐνδεέστατον βίον Arist. *Pol.*1256ᵇ3, cf. D.S.5.71; τὴν λείπουσαν ταῖς βασάνοις κόλασιν Lxx *Wi.*19.4; τὰ ὑστερήματα τῶν ἁγίων 2*Ep.Cor.*9.12, cf. Ph.2.444; τὰ ἐλλείποντα A.D.*Pron.*3.7:—Med., *add so as to fill up*, Pl.*Men.* 84d. -**πτύσσω**, Att. -ττω, *fold back*, hence, *open out, further*, Gal.14.787:—Pass., *to be folded back upon*, Arist.*HA*549ᵇ2.

**προσανάπτω**, *attach, attribute*, Phld.*Vit.*p.12 J.; τὸν λάρον Ἡρακλεῖ Sch.Ar.*Av.*568.

**προσαναπυνθάνομαι**, *inquire besides*, Gal.18(2).57.

**προσανα-ρρήγνῡμι**, *lacerate in addition*, Plu.*Crass.*25; τὸ σῶμα, i.e. caused haemorrhage, Id.*Cleom.*30: metaph., π. τὰς ἀδίκους ἐπιθυμίας *let* them *break out*, Ph.2.372, cf. 479. -**ρριπίζω**, *fan* or *blow up besides*, πόθον ib.442.

**προσαναρτάω**, *hang upon*, τινί τι Luc.*Philops.*11: metaph., *attach, connect*, in Pass., Phld.*Ir.*p.80 W.

**προσανα-σείω**, *shake up* or *about besides*, Hp.*Art.*4: metaph., προσανασείεσθαι λόγοις *to be roused still further*, Plb.1.69.8; δίκαι τῷ Νασικᾷ προσανεσείοντο f.l. for προανεσείοντο in Plu.*TG*21. -**σπάω**, *draw up besides*, Eust.679.62 (Pass.). -**στέλλω**, *hold in, get under control*, τὸν ἵππον Plu.*Alex.*6; *mould* an infant's nostrils, Sor.1. 103. -**τάσσω**, *draw up besides*, ἑαυτά Artem.1.1ᵇ. -**τείνω**, *strain tight beside*, ἱστίον [καρχησίῳ] Sch.Pi.*N.*5.94:—Med., *hold out by way of threat*, τὸν Ῥωμαίων φόβον Plb.24.10.13: abs., *threaten*, τινι Id.18.53.9: so in aor. 1 Pass., βραχέα -ταθεὶς Id.5.87.4. 2. *lift up*, τὴν δεξιάν, τὼ χεῖρε, Aristaenet.1.15, 2.2. II. τῇ ὥρᾳ π. *prolong* the time, *be later*, Plb.11.22.3. III. Pass., *extend along*, Sor. 1.7 cod. -**τέλλω**, poet. προσαντ-, *rise up to*, ἐς οὐρανόν E.*Supp.* 688. -**τέμνω**, *cut off as well*, τὰ γεννητικά Ph.2.128. 2. *incise as well*, τὸ δέρμα Gal.10.391.

**προσανᾰτενίζω**, *gaze at*, c. dat., Tim.Gaz.ap.Ar.Byz.*Epit.*103.27.

**προσανα-τίθημι**, *offer* or *dedicate besides*, δηνάρια πεντακισχίλια *CIG* 2782.44 (Aphrodisias); τῷ θεῷ -τεθεικὼς ἅπαντα Jul. *ad Them.*267b; τὴν παρθενίαν θεῷ Suid. s. v. Πουλχερία:—Med., *take an additional burden on oneself*, X.*Mem.*2.1.8; but π. τινί τι *contribute of oneself* to another, *Ep.Gal.*2.6. 2. *ascribe*, τινί τι Porph.ap.Eus.*PE*3. 11. II. προσανατίθεσθαί τινι *take counsel with* one, Chrysipp. *Stoic.*2.344, Phld.*Vit.*p.31 J., *Ep.Gal.*1.16, Luc.*JTr.*1; τοῖς μάντεσι περί τινος D.S.17.116; *refer* a matter *for consideration*, *PTeb.*99.5 (ii B.C.). -**τρέπω**, *overturn besides*, Lxx *Si.*13.23. -**τρέφω**, *build up, restore by food*, τοὺς ὄγκους D.S.1.43, cf. Cic.*Att.*6.1.2 (Pass.). -**τρέχω**, *run up to*, λόφον D.H.1.56; εἰς τοὺς ὑψηλοτέρους τόπους D.S.5.47; τοῦ λάρυγγος -τρέχοντος τῇ ἐπιγλωττίδι Gal.*UP*4. 8; of iron *approaching* a magnet, Porph.*Abst.*4.20: metaph., π. ταῖς οὐσίαις, i.e. *become suddenly* rich, D.S.16.83. II. *run back, retrace past events*, βραχὺ περί τινος Plb.5.31.8; π. τοῖς χρόνοις περί τινων Id.1.12.8, etc. III. v. προαναστρέχω. -**τρίβω** [ῑ], *rub upon* or *against*, τοῖς δένδροις τὰ κέρατα Ael.*NA*6.1:—Med., *rub oneself upon* or *against* a person, *exercise oneself with* or *against* another, Thphr.*Char.*27.6, Plu.2.751f: metaph., *try a fall*, Pl.*Tht.*169c. II. *rub as well*, ὀθονίῳ Cleopatra ap.Gal.12.404; *massage as well*, Sor.1.103. -**τῡπόω**, *mould further*, Alex. Aphr. *de An.*70.13. ⊛ -**φέρω**, *make a supplementary declaration*, *PPetr.*3 p.195 (iii B.C.):—Pass., *UPZ*14.75 (ii B.C.). 2. *report*, τί τινι Aristeas 29, *PGrenf.*1.11 ii 8 (ii B.C.), *UPZ*119.47 (ii B.C.), etc.:—Pass., Aristeas 30. II. *refer to* any one *for advice*, π. τῇ συγκλήτῳ περί τινος Plb.18.9.10, cf. Phld.*Lib.*p.20 O., D.H.6.56; π. τῇ βουλῇ περί τινος *IG*14.758, cf. 760 (both Naples, i A.D.): abs., Plb.31.11.4; π. τοῖς μάντεσι D.S.17.116. -**φεύγω**, *withdraw, become displaced*, Sor.2.50. -**φθέγγομαι**, *pronounce besides*, Ph.1. 161. -**φλέγω**, *light up, kindle besides*, τὸ πῦρ ib.451: metaph., ἐπιθυμίας Id.2.240. -**φῡσάω**, *play on the flute*, Pl.Com.69.6 (leg. προανα-). -**χᾰλάω**, *relax as well*, Paul.Aeg.6.74. -**χρώννῡμαι**, Med., *communicate by contact*, προσαναχρώννυνται τὸ ψεῦδος ἡμῖν *infect* us *with* the falsehood, Plu.2.16f. II. *associate closely with*, ib. 51f, 490d, 672f, 754c; *follow, imitate closely*, ib.740f. -**χωρέω**, v. προαναχωρέω.

**προσάν-ειμι**, (εἶμι *ibo*) *go up to*, Th.7.44, D.C.56.13; προσανιοῦσα πόλις a city *lying on an ascent*, Poll.9.20. -**εἶπον**, aor. of προσαναγορεύω (q. v.), *declare, publish, order besides*, X.*An.*7.1.11, D.C.49. 14. -**έρομαι**, aor. 2 part. -ερόμενος, *question besides*, J.*AJ*19.4. 1. -**έρπω**, *creep up to*, τῷ τραχήλῳ Plu.*Them.*26. -**ερωτάω**, *ask* or *inquire further*, π. ὁποῖα.. Pl.*Men.*74c, cf. Ruf.*Interrog.*3, Gal. 11.188. -**ευρίσκω**, *find out besides*, τὸ ἄκος Str.15.1.22, Iamb. *in Nic.* p.101 P.:—Pass., -ευρηνται ταύταις ἕτεραι Theo Sm.p.52 H. -**ευρύνω**, *dilate further*, in Pass., Sor.1.10, Heliod.ap.Orib. 50.9.13. -**έχω**, *wait*, ἕως.. Plb.4.19.12, cf. 3.94.3: c. acc., *await*, τὸν καιρὸν τῆς ἐντεύξεως Id.5.103.5. II. *rely on, place one's dependence on*, ἐλπίσι Id.5.72.2, cf.4.60.8, J.*AJ*10.6.2, *BJ*4.2.1, Heliod.(?) in *PMed.Lond.*155.4.5; ταῖς βοηθείαις Plb.1.84.12. III. *devote oneself to*, θεῷ, τοῖς ἡγεμόσι, J.*AJ*10.4.5, 10.7.2; ἔργοις, τέχναις, ib.12.5.5, Id.*Ap.*2.41; Σικελικαῖς τραπέζαις Socr.*Ep.*8; *attend to*, τῇ σκαπάνῃ Alciphr.3.24; τῷ λόγῳ A.D.*Pron.*49.4: in full, π. τὴν γνώμην θεῷ J.*AJ Prooem.*3.

**προσᾱνής**, ές, Dor. for προσηνής (q. v.).

**προσανθέω**, *flower beside, shine beside*, c. dat., Philostr.*Im.*2.5: *add lustre to*, ib.8, 1.29; τὸ αὐτοκίνητον οὐ προσήνθει τῇ πολυμαθίᾳ Dam.*Isid.*74.

**προσαν-ίημι**, fut. **-ανήσω**, *send up in addition*, δακρύοισι πηγήν Philic. in *Stud.Ital.*9.46. II. *slacken, lower the pitch of besides*, τὰς τρίτας Plu.2.1145d. **-ῑμάω**, *draw up* water *besides*, dub. in Aristid.1.155 J. **-ίσταμαι**, Pass., *rise and press against*, τῆς γλώττης τοῖς ὀδοῦσι -ισταμένης D.H.*Comp.*22. 2. *rise in insurrection*, in aor. 2, D.C.39.54 codd. **-οίγνῡμι**, *open besides*, Id.73.9. **-οιδέω**, *swell up besides*, Herod.Med.ap.Orib.6.20.12. **-οιδίσκω**, = foreg., Gal.6.527. ⊛ **-οικοδομέομαι**, Pass., *to be added for edification*, Lxx *Si.*3.14. **-οιμώζω**, *moan* or *sigh at* a thing, Plb.5.16.4.

**πρόσαντα**, Adv. *uphill*, Dicaearch.1.6.

**προσανταποδίδωμι**, *retort, rejoin*, A.D.*Synt.*321.10 (Pass.).

**προσαντάω**, *appear* in court, *BGU*361 ii 8 (ii A. D.).

**προσαντέλλω**, poet. for προσανατέλλω (q. v.).

**προσαντ-επιτάσσω**, *issue an order against in return*, D.C.38.43. **-έχω**, *hold out against still longer*, τοῖς κατὰ γῆν ἔργοις Plb.16.30.5; cf. προσαντίσχω. **-ης**, ες, gen. εος, (ἄντην) *uphill, steep*, κέλευθος, χωρίον, Pi.*I.*2.33, Th.4.43; ἐν ἠρέμα προσάντει Pl.*Phdr.*230c; φορὰ εἰς τὸ π. Arist.*Pr.*889b39, cf. Diocl.*Fr.*142. II. metaph., *arduous, adverse*, ἀλλ' ἕν τί μοι π. E.*Med.*381; κεῖνό μοι μόνον π. Id.*Or.*790 (troch.); σκοπεῖν.., τί π. εἴρηται τῆς νομοθεσίας Pl.*Lg.*746c; πρόσαντές [ἐστι] c. inf., Isoc.8.14; *repugnant, distasteful*, λόγος Hdt.7.160; ζήτησις Arist.*EN*1096a12; εἰ μή τι Μεγίλλῳ π. Pl.*Lg.*702d; of diet, *unsuitable*, Orib.5.31.2. Adv., μήτε ἀκαίρως παρακαλεῖν μήτε ἐκείνῳ προσάντως *in such a way as to encounter* his *opposition*, Nic.Dam.127.8 J. 2. of persons, *adverse, hostile*, τισι E.*Med.*305; π. πρὸς τἆλλα τἀγαθά *setting oneself against*.., X.*Ap.*33. Adv. **-τως** *unwillingly*, D.S.14.1.

**προσαντι-βάλλω**, *collate* a document, *Sammelb.*6298.9 (ii A. D.), *BGU*525.6 (ii A. D.), *POxy.*2131.3 (iii A. D.). **-βολέω**, *supplicate besides*, J.*BJ*6.2.1. **-λαμβάνομαι**, Med., *take hold of one another*, τῶν χειρῶν *by* the hands, Str.3.3.7.

**προσαντίος**, α, ον, = προσάντης, Hsch.

**προσαντίσχω**, = προσαντέχω, Plb.11.21.4.

**προσαντλ-έω**, *draw and pour upon*, Dsc.4.64 (Pass.); *bathe, foment*, Herod.Med.ap.Orib.10.37.11, Antyll.ap.eund.9.23.11. **-ημα**, ατος, τό, in pl., *douches*, Gal.12.505. **-ησις**, εως, ἡ, = foreg., Antyll. l.c. ⊛ **-ητέον**, *one must foment*, Paul.Aeg.3.28.

**προσάνω** [ᾰ], = προσαύξω, Hsch.

**προσαξιόω**, *demand besides*, Plb.3.11.7, 18.8.5; π. τινά c. inf., *ask* one *also* to do a thing, *PCair.Zen.*440.6 (iii B. C.), *PHamb.*25.8 (iii B. C.), *Arch.Pap.*3.134 (Thera, iii/ii B. C.), cf. Lxx 3*Ma.*7.10.

**προσαπ-αγγέλλω**, *announce besides*, X.*HG*4.3.2, D.S.11.4 (Pass.). **-ᾰγορεύω**, *forbid besides*, D.C.38.34, 48.43 (Pass.); cf. προσαπεῖπον. **-άγω** [ᾰγ], *lead off to prison* or *captivity*, *PCair.Zen.*475.15 (iii B. C.), *PEnteux.*83.7 (iii B. C.), Ph.2.33. II. *bring, render in addition*, *Inscr.Magn.*73a22. **-αιτέω**, *require* or *ask besides*, Thphr.*CP*1.16.12, D.H.*Dem.*43, Plu.2.177e, Luc.*Tyr.*13, Alciphr.1.2, Chor. in *Rev.Phil.*1.81. **-αντάω**, *go to meet*, Philostr.*VA*4.5. II. c. acc., *reach*, of a probe, Antyll.ap.Orib.44.20.31.

⊛ **προσάπαξ** [ᾰπ], Adv. *once*, Lib.*Decl.*40.7, Aphth.*Prog.*13.

**προσαπαρτίζω**, *complete as well*, *LW*1583 (Caria).

**προσᾰπᾰτάω**, *deceive besides*, Str.6.1.5.

**προσαπ-αυδάω**, f. l. for προ- in Gal.19.191. **-ειλέω**, τινι *threaten besides*, Test.ap.D.21.93:—Pass., v. l. in Lxx *Si.*13.3. **-εῖπον**, aor. 2 of προσαπαγορεύω, Aeschin.3.45, D.C.54.2. **-εργάζομαι**, *finish off, complete besides*, ἑτέρας [ναῦς] App.*Mith.*13, cf. Archig.ap.Gal.12.410. **-ερείδομαι**, Pass., *press forcibly against*, πρός τι Arist.*Pr.*937b36; *lean on*, αἱ ἐγκλιτικαὶ -ηρεισμέναι προκειμένῳ μορίῳ A.D.*Synt.*131.9: metaph., *rely mainly upon*, ἐπὶ τὰς συνθήκας Plb.3.21.3. **-έχω**, pf. inf. προσαπεσχηκέναι *to have received in addition*, *POxy.*510.21 (i/ii A. D.).

**προσᾰπιστέω**, *to be distrustful besides*, Aristaenet.2.14.

**προσαπο-βάλλω**, *throw away* or *lose besides*, αὐτὰ πρὸς ταῖς δώδεκα f. l. for προσαπολεῖς in Ar.*Nu.*1256; τὰ προϋπάρχοντα χρήματα καὶ τὸ πνεῦμα Plb.33.5.4; τοὺς φίλους τοῖς χρήμασι Plu.*Nic.*5; τὰ ὄντα X.*Mem.*3.6.7. **-βλέπω**, *turn one's eyes and look at*, ἀναθήμασι Ath.5.180b. **-γρᾰφή**, ἡ, *additional registration*, *CPR*225.8 (iii A. D.). **-γράφω** [ᾰ], *denounce besides*, Lys.13.[31], 56. 2. *register besides*, *BGU*52.5 (ii A. D., Pass.), etc.:—Med., ποταπογραφέσθων δὲ καὶ τὰν πατρίδα *they shall register besides* the name of *their* native city, *SIG*1023.41 (Halasarna, iii/ii B. C.). **-δείκνῡμι**, *prove, demonstrate besides*, ἔκ τινων τὸν λόγον A.D.*Synt.*321.9; ὅτι.. Pl.*Phd.*77c, Plu.2.998c:—Pass., Iamb.*Myst.*2.1. II. *appoint besides*, προσαποδειχθῆναι πρὸς ταῖς νῦν ὑπαρχούσαις τέσσαρσι φυλαῖς..καὶ ἄλλην *OGI*56.23 (Canopus, iii B. C.); τοῦ -δειχθέντος [γραμματέως] *Inscr.Prien.*42.17 (ii B. C.); τὸν συνάρξοντα αὐτῷ προσαποδειχθῆναι ἔδει D.C.54.10, etc.; σύνναος τῷ Διὶ προσαπεδείχθη Str.7.7.12. **-διδράσκω**, aor. inf. -δρᾶναι, *run away besides*, D.C.50.33. **-δίδωμι**, *pay as a debt besides*, ἀργύριον Hyp.*Eux.*17, cf. *IG*1$^2$.374.104, 265, D.41.27 (Pass.); ἂν..δέῃ κέρματ' ἀποδοῦναι, προσαπέδωκεν Ἀττικά Diph.66.13: metaph., π. αἰσχύνην τοῖς ἐργασαμένοις Plu.2.20b. 2. Med., *sell besides*, Plb.31.22.4. II. *add by way of completing*, ἐκεῖνο τοῖς εἰρημένοις D.H.*Dem.*54; αἰτίας, ἀποδείξεις, Ph.1.457, 358; τὰ λειπόμενα τῷ λόγῳ π. Plu.2.1100e, cf. Str.12.4.10, J.*Ap.*1.35; *state further*, Thphr.*CP*6.7.2, Demetr.Lac.*Herc.*1055.13; *add* to a remedy, Dsc.1.30, 2.76.9; *finish off* a bandage, Gal.18(1).771, 796, al. **-δοσις**, εως, ἡ, a Rhet. figure, by which when two or more statements follow one another, the reason for each is given (a) after each statement, or (b) after the whole series, Quint.*Inst.*9.2.94, Rutil.1.1. **-δοτέον**, *one must add further*, Arist.*Top.*130b28, Ph.2.145, Ath.9.371d, etc. **-δύομαι**, Med., *put off as well*, τὸν χιτῶνα τῷ ἱματίῳ Plu.2.139d. **-θλίβω** [ῑ], *press against*, τινὰ τῇ θύρᾳ J.*AJ*9.4.4; τοῖς βουβῶσι τὸ κατόπιν τῆς ὀσφύος Alciphr.*Fr.*6.13. **-θνῄσκω**, *die besides* or *with*, Lxx *Ex.*21.29, D.C.53.9. **-κᾰθαίρω**, *cleanse further*, Sor.1.122. **-κειμαι**, *to be stored up as well*, dub. in Aristid.*Or.*50(26).49 (fort. προ-). **-κλύζω**, *wash off as well*, Gal.12.264. **-κόπτω**, v. l. for προ- in Ph.2.306. **-κρέμαμαι**, Pass., *to be suspended from as well*, Procop.*Pers.*1.1. ⊛ **-κρίνομαι** [ῑ], *answer with some addition*, τοῖς ἐρωτωμένοις Pl.*Euthd.*296a, cf. Arist.*SE*175b11. **-κρῐτέον**, *one must answer with some addition*, Id.*Metaph.*1007a17. **-κρούομαι**, Med., *check, inhibit*, Alex.Trall.2. **-κτείνω**, *kill besides*, X.*Cyr.*5.3.6, Plu.*Dio* 58, Palaeph.31. **-λαμβάνω**, *catch, take up as well*, Hp.*Art.*11. II. *receive besides*, dub. in Jul.*Or.*7.228b. **-λαύω**, *reap, share in besides*, ὕβρεως καὶ ἀτιμίας D.H.6.58; ἀνοίας καὶ ἀμαθίας Jul.*Or.*7.228b (prob.): c. acc., κακόν τι *Com.Adesp.*1311; ἕτερόν τι π. *gain* something different *besides*, Pl.*Alc.*2.150c.

**προσαπόλλῡμι** (also **-ύω** Hdt.1.207), *destroy besides*, κἀκεῖνον Id.2.121.β'; προσαπολλύουσι καὶ τὰς μητέρας Id.6.138, cf. E.*Hipp.*1374 (lyr.):—Med. and Pass., *perish besides* or *with others*, ἵνα μὴ προσαπόλωνται Hdt.6.100; τοὺς φίλους προσαπολωλέναι Lys.12.64; ἐλεοῖντ' ἂν δικαιότερον ἢ προσαπολλύοιντο D.57.45. II. *lose besides*, τὴν ἀρχήν Hdt.1.207, cf. 9.23, Ar.*Nu.*1256; τὰ ἀρχαῖα π. πρὸς οἷς ἐκτήσαντο Pl.*Grg.*519a.

**προσαπο-λούω**, *wash further*, τὴν ἕδραν Sor.1.100. **-λύω**, *set free besides*, αὐτὸν τῆς διαβολῆς *Vit.Isoc.*p.255 Westermann. **-νέμω**, *add to*, Hero *Aut.*30.6 (Pass.). **-ξέω**, *erase, expunge as well*: metaph., τὴν τυραννοκτονίαν -απέξεσε τῆς πόλεως Lib.*Decl.*43.45. **-ξύω**, *scrape off in addition*, Dsc.2.76.15. ⊛ **-πέμπω**, *send away* or *off besides*, Ar.*Pl.*999. **-πλύνω** [ῡ], *wash off besides*, Ph.2.333. **-πνίγω** [ῑ], *kill off besides*, Aret.*CA*1.4.

**προσαπορέω**, *propose a further difficulty*, Arist.*Pol.*1275b39, Jul.*Or.*5.171d, Dexipp.*in Cat.*42.32, Iamb.*Myst.*4.5.

**προσαπο-ρραίνω**, *sprinkle besides*, τινος some of.., Ael.*NA*9.63. **-ρρύπτω**, *wash clean besides*, Gal.6.261. **-σείω**, in Med., τὰ ὦτα *close* one's ears *in addition*, dub. in Ph.1.384 (προσαποκλειομένους Mangey, προσαποσαττομένους Cohn). **-σκευάζομαι**, Med., *make away with also*, τινα J.*BJ*4.5.4. **-στέλλω**, *send off* or *dispatch besides*, Th.4.108, *PSI*4.410.25 (iii B. C.), Lxx 2*Ma.*11.14. **-στερέω**, *defraud* or *deprive of besides*, τῆς νίκης D.21.67 (Pass.), cf. Lib.*Or.*17.6. **-στρέφω**, *turn round towards*, τοῖς Ἰουδαίοις τὴν ἕδραν J.*BJ*2.12.1. **-τίθημι**, *lose besides*, τὸ πνεῦμα τῷ χρυσίῳ Plb.13.2.5 (dub. l.). **-τῑμάω**, *estimate besides*, ὧν π. τῷ Λεωκράτει πλεῖν ἢ χιλίας *the value* of which *he set at* more.., D.41.27 (s. v. l.). **-τίνω** [ῐ], fut. -τείσω, *pay besides*, μισθόν Pl.*Lg.*945a, cf. *PEleph.*1.11 (iv B. C.), *Abh.Berl.Akad.*1925(5).29 (Cyrene, i B. C./i A. D.); τόκους Men.235.9; χρήματά τινι Dius ap.J.*AJ*8.5.3; opp. -δίδωμι, Hyp.*Eux.*17. **-τρίβω** [ῑ], *rub off upon*, τινί τι Ael.*NA*9.63. **-φαίνω**, *show* or *prove besides*, Pl.*Plt.*287a:—Med., Arist.*Metaph.*1089b16, Plu.2.152b. **-φέρω**, *carry off besides*, πολλά Posidon.10 J. II. *return as well*, τὰ ὀνόματά τινων Ἀρχ.Ἐφ.1914.168 (iii B. C.):—Pass., προσαπηνέχθη μου τοὔνομα ἐν τριττοῖς δήμοις *was returned besides* as liable to taxation, D.50.8. **-φημι**, *deny besides*, τὴν ἀπόφασιν αὐτήν Dam.*Pr.*22. **-φράσσω**, *block up besides*, D.C.42.38. **-φωνέω**, Dor. ποτ-, *declare besides*, Myro 5 J. **-χρώννῡμαι**, Pass., *to be coloured besides*, θαλασσοειδεῖ χρώματι Hero *Aut.*30.6.

**προσαπτ-έον**, *one must apply* or *attach*, εἰκόνα τισί Pl.*R.*517b; τοῖς τέκνοις ἔγκλημα Porph.*Chr.*71. 2. *one must attribute*, τινί τι Plb.2.60.2. **-ικός**, ή, όν, *fond of touching*, τινος Sch.Luc.*Gall.*27. **-ω**, Ep. **προτιάπτω**, *fasten to* or *upon*, τύμβῳ π. μηδέν S.*El.*432; στέρνοις στέρνα E.*El.*1321 (anap.); κόσμον Πενθεῖ, χλιδὴν τέκνῳ, Id.*Ba.*859, *Ion* 27; τὸ ἀντίγραφον..προσήφαμεν (pf.) *we have attached* the copy, *UPZ*22.11 (ii B. C.). 2. *attach to, bestow upon, grant*, κῦδος Ἀχιλλῆϊ προτιάπτω Il.24.110; π. κλέος τινί Pi.*N.*8.37; τῷ τεθνηκότι τιμάς S.*El.*356; γῇ τῇδε..ἑορτὴν καὶ τέλη E.*Med.*1382; γέρας, ἐγκώμιά τισι, Pl.*Sph.*231a, *Lg.*822b; εὐδαιμονίαν τοῖς φύλαξι Id.*R.*420d; τὸ ὄνομα (sc. πῦρ)..προσάψαι..Ἑλληνικῇ φωνῇ Id.*Cra.*410a; ὠφέλειάν τινι D.61.53; in bad sense, *fix upon, attach*, μή τι..χρέος ἐμᾷ πόλει προσάψῃς S.*OC*236 (lyr.); π. τῇ τύχῃ αἰτίαν Men.1083.4, cf. Porph.*Abst.*1.7:—Pass., *to be bound up with*, σχήματι τοῦ λόγου A.D.*Synt.*232.10. 3. c. acc. only, *apply*, μεῖζον π. τῆς νόσου τὸ φάρμακον S.*Fr.*589, cf. Dsc.*Eup.*1.74 (Pass.), Archig.ap.Gal.12.873 (Med.); π. χεῖρα E.*Supp.*361; γνώμην πρός τι Id.*Fr.*362.10; ἀλγηδόνα τινά Pl.*Plt.*293b; simply, *add*, τό γε εἶναι Id.*Sph.*252a. 4. *deliver, confide to*, ναυτικόν τινι X.*Ages.*1.36. 5. *ascribe, attribute to*, ἐκείνῳ (sc. τῷ Θαλῇ) τὸ κατανόημα προσάπτουσι Arist.*Pol.*1259a8; π. τῷ Ἀπόλλωνι τὴν δάφνην D.S.1.17;

Ποσειδῶνι τὸ τοὺς ἵππους δαμάσαι Id.5.69; τὰ κατορθώματα τῇ τύχῃ Plb.31.30.3, cf. 4.24.3. II. intr., *fasten oneself to*, καί μοι..ἀγχοῦ προσῆψεν..ἐν δισκήματι *came very near* me in the quoit-throw, S.*Fr.* 380 (dub.); *to be added*, εἰ κακοῖς κακὰ προσάψει τοῖς πάλαι Id.*OT*667 (lyr.). III. Med., *fasten oneself upon*, Arist.*Fr.*324; *lay hold of, touch*, τῷ στόματι π. [τινός] X.*Mem.*1.3.12; π. τῆς ἀληθείας Pl.*Ti.*71e; τῶν οὔλων (v.l. τοῖς οὔλοις) Dsc.1.105. 2. *have to do with, meddle with*, ὅτου ἂν π. ἀνδρός Aeschin.3.114; τῶν πραγμάτων ib.133; τοῦ λόγου, τοῦ πολέμου, D.C.60.26, 44.44; πλέω π. τῶν δυνατῶν *attempt* more than is possible, Democr.3. 3. of wrestlers, *come to grips*, Gal.15.197.

**προσαπωθέω**, *push away, reject besides*, Lxx *Si.*13.21.

**προσ-ᾰρακτός**, ή, όν, *dashed against*, Sch.rec.A.*Pr.*713. **-άραξις** [ᾰρ], εως, ἡ, *dashing against*, Sch.rec.A.*Pers.*412 (pl.).

**προσᾰρᾰρίσκω**, *fit to*: pf. 2 προσάρᾱρα, Ion. -άρηρα, intr., *to be fitted to*, ἐπίσσωτρα προσαρηρότα tires *firmly fitted*, Il.5.725; ἠναγκάσθησαν οἱ ἱππεῖς ὥσπερ νυκτερίδες πρὸς τοῖς τείχεσιν -αραρέναι X.*HG*4.7.6: Ep. pf. Pass., προσαρήρεται ἱστοβοῆϊ Hes.*Op.*431.

**προσᾰράσσω**, Att. -ττω, *dash against*, τὰ ὑπομάζια τῇ γῇ D.S.34/5.2.12; πέτρᾳ τὴν κεφαλὴν J.*AJ*14.13.10; π. τινὶ τὰς θύρας, εἰς τὸ μέτωπον τὴν θύραν, *slam* the door *in* one's *face*, Luc.*DMeretr.*15.2, *Nav.*22; esp. of shipwreck, π. ναῦς σκοπέλοις Plu.*Marc.*15; τὸ σκάφος τῷ αἰγιαλῷ Luc.*VH*2.47; ναῦς πρὸς τὴν ἄκραν D.C.48.47; π. τὰς ναῦς *wreck* them, Philostr.*VA*4.32; *shatter*, τὸν οὐρανόν Iamb.*Myst.*6.5:—Pass., *to be dashed against*, αἱμασιαῖς Ph.2.123; τῷ λιθοστρώτῳ J.*BJ* 6.3.2; τῇ γῇ Ael.*NA*12.21; ταῖς πέτραις Alciphr.1.1: also intr. in Act., ἡ τοῦ ποταμοῦ ῥύσις τοῖς ὄχθοις π. D.S.5.27.

**προσάρδω**, *water* or *irrigate besides*, v.l. in J.*BJ*3.3.4 (Pass.).

**προσᾰρήγω**, *assist besides*, τῇ διαίτῃ Aret.*CD*1.4.

**προσάρηρα, προσαρήρεται**, v. προσαραρίσκω.

**προσαρθρόομαι**, Pass., *to be attached by joints*, Hp.*Art.*45.

**προσᾰριθμ-έω**, *pay in* to the bank *in addition*, *PCair.Zen.*22.21 (Pass., iii B.C.). 2. *reckon among*, J.*AJ*7.12.4; *reckon in as well*, τὸ παρεληλυθός Plot.1.5.6:—Pass., Str.17.1.54, Plu.2.1029d. **-ητέον**, *one must reckon in*, Poll.1.138.

**προσᾱριστάω**, *take breakfast as well*, Hp.*Int.*20.

**προσάρκεσις**, εως, ἡ, *assistance*, *CIG*4464 (Syria).

**προσαρκέω**, *give aid, succour, assist*, τινι S.*OT*141; ὡς θέλοντος ἂν ἐμοῦ π. πᾶν ib.12; ὡς ἂν προσαρκῶν σμικρὰ κερδάνῃ μέγα Id.*OC*72; τοῖς πᾶσιν εἶξαι καὶ π. χάριν Id.*Fr.*524.2: abs., E.*Hec.*862:—Pass., *to be satisfied*, c. part., Longin.ap.Porph.*Plot.*20.

**προ-σαρκόω**, *fill with flesh first*, ἐκεῖνα τὰ μέρη τοῦ ἕλκους Gal.10.191.

**προσάρκτιος**, ον, *northerly*, Plb.34.5.9, Str.1.4.5, J.*BJ*1.7.3.

**πρόσαρμα**, ατος, τό, (προσ-αίρω) in pl., *victuals, food*, Hp.*Aph.*1.15, Ruf.*Ren.Ves.*2.26: later in sg., Archig.ap.Aët.8.73.

**προσαρμογή**, ἡ, *fitting together*, στημόνων *Inscr.Délos* 504*A* 9 (pl., iii B.C.).

**προσαρμόζω**, later Att. **-όττω**, *fit to, attach closely to*, μαστῷ τέκνα E.*Ion* 762; τῷ προσαρμόσω στόμα; Id.*HF*486; γυμνὰς ἐκ ⟨πέπλων⟩ ἐπωμίδας κώπῃ π. Id.*IT*1405; τι εἴς τι Pl.*Tht.*193c, cf. 194a:—Pass., δρέπανα περὶ τοῖς ἄξοσι προσήρμοσται X.*Cyr.*6.2.17; προσήρμοσται [τὸ πηδάλιον] τῷ πλοίῳ Arist.*Mech.*850$^{b}$32. 2. metaph., *adapt*, ὄνομα πράγματι Pl.*Cra.*414d; ἕκαστον ἑκάστῳ Id.*Phdr.*271b; π. ἑαυτὸν πρός τινα Plu.2.52b; ῥυθμοὺς π. [μέλει] *set* measures, Pl.*Lg.*669c. 3. c. acc. only, χέρας π. E.*Supp.*816 (lyr.); π. τὴν χεῖρα *fit* it *on to* the stump, X.*Cyr.*7.3.9; π. ξύλα to a broken rudder, Plu.*Brut.*46; ἀντὶ δώρων δῶρα π. *add fitting* gifts, S.*Tr.*494. II. intr., *attach oneself*, Arist.*GA*718$^{a}$28; κύκλος προσαρμόττων κέντρῳ Plot.4.4.16. 2. *suit* or *agree with* a thing, τὸ προσαρμόττον ἑκάστῃ φύσει εἶδος Pl.*Phdr.* 277c; πρός τι X.*Cyr.*8.4.21. III. Med., *fit on to oneself*, Aesar. ap.Stob.1.49.27.

**πρόσαρσις**, εως, Ion. ιος, ἡ, (προσ-αίρω) *administering* or *taking*, ῥυφήματος Hp.*Acut.*26, cf. Aret.*SD*2.6, Gal.ap.Orib.*inc.*6.32.

**προσαρτ-άω**, *fasten* or *attach to*, μόλυβδον πρὸς τοῖς ὀϊστοῖς Arist. *HA*616$^{a}$11; [κυνὶ] κώδωνα Babr.104.2: metaph., *append*, πολλὰ τῇ στρατηγίᾳ Plb.9.20.5; *attach*, ἑνὶ π. ἑαυτούς Arr.*Epict.*1.1.14:—Pass., *to be fastened* or *attached to*, τῷ ὀστέῳ Hp.*Fract.*11; πρὸς τῇσι πλευρῇσι Id.*Art.*13; τῇ μήτρᾳ Porph.*Gaur.*15.1; κατά τι by.., Arist. *HA*550$^{a}$20; δεσμοῖς πρός τι Plb.3.46.8; δεσμά τινα ταῦτα προσηρτήμεθα Arr.*Epict.*1.9.11: abs., π. ὁ καρπός Thphr.*CP*5.4.2: Gramm., of the article, A.D.*Synt.*58.16. 2. metaph. in Pass., *belong to*, ὅσοις νοῦ καὶ σμικρὸν προσήρτηται Pl.*Phlb.*58a; προσηρτημένον τῷ καλῷ τὸ ἀγαθόν X.*Oec.*6.15; λῆμμα προσηρτημένον πρὸς οἷς ἐγὼ πεπολίτευμαι D.5.12; ἡδονῇ προσηρτημένοι *devoted to*.., Luc.*Nec.*5; Τιμολέοντα ὥσπερ ἐκ κρασπέδου..τῇ Σικελίᾳ π. *hanging on*, Plu.*Tim.*11; μειρακίοις Id.*Pomp.*46, cf. M.Ant.12.3, etc. **-έον**, (προσ-αίρω) *one must administer* food, Hp.*Epid.*1.25. **-ημα**, ατος, τό, *appendage*, Gal.5.396. **-ής**, ές, *attached*, opp. προσφυής, Antyll.ap.Orib.45.2.2, cf. 45.17.6, Leonid.ap.Aët.15.5. **-ησις**, εως, Ion. ιος, ἡ, (from Pass.) *attachment*, τῶν καρπῶν Thphr.*CP*2.9.3, 5.4.2, cf. Sor.1.71; opp. σύμφυσις, etc., Gal.2.350 (pl.), *UP*3.3. 2. *place of attachment*, ἄχρι φρενῶν προσαρτήσιος Hp.*Art.*45.

**προσαρτίως**, Adv. *lately*, Lxx 3*Ma.*1.19.

**προσᾰρύομαι**, *draw as well*, [ὕδωρ] Aristid.*Or.*36(48).116.

**προσάρχομαι**, *offer, present*, ταῦτα τῷ ἑταίρῳ σου εἰς βοήθειαν προσηρξάμην Pl.*Tht.*168c: so perh. τὸν Βρασίδαν..ἐταινίουν τε καὶ προσήρχοντο ὥσπερ ἀθλητῇ *paid* him the *tributes* due to an athlete (for which see Plu.*Caes.*30), Th.4.121.

**προσᾰρωγός**, ὁ, *auxiliary*, Iamb.*Comm.Math.*34.

**προσασκέω**, *exercise besides*, τινὰς ἐν ταῖς εἰρεσίαις Plb.5.109.4:—Pass., δόγμα -ασκεῖσθαι ὑπὸ ἐπιστήμης Ph.1.657 (s.v.l.); of land, *to be cultivated*, J.*BJ*3.3.2.

**προσασπάζομαι**, *salute besides*, *EM*260.46.

⊛ **προ-σάσσω**, only aor. Med., προεσάξαντο σιτία ἐτέων κάρτα πολλῶν *stored up* food for many years *in advance*, Hdt.1.190, cf. 8.20 (unless from προεισάγω); cf. σάττω I. 2.

**προσαστεΐζομαι**, *add wittily* to one's words, τι Plb.*Fr.*208 (-αστειασάμενος Suid.).

**προσαστράπτω**, *mingle its radiance with*, τῷ χρυσῷ Philostr.*Im.*1.28.

**προσασφᾰλίζομαι**, Med., *make secure*, Gal.18(1).818, *BMus.Inscr.* 481*.288 (Ephesus, ii A.D.).

**προσασχολέομαι**, *to be engaged in*, c. dat., Simp. *in Epict.*p.19 D.

**προσᾰτῑμόομαι**, Pass., *suffer* ἀτιμία *as well*, Thphr.*Fr.*101.

**προσαυαίνομαι**, Pass., *to be dried* or *wither away upon*, πέτραις A.*Pr.*147 (lyr.), cf. Hp.*Mul.*2.137.

**προσαυγ-άζω**, *look towards*, πόντον Lyc.1082, cf. A.R.1.1231 (tm.): —Med., in Dor. form ποταυγασμένος, Diotog.ap.Stob.4.7.62. II. c. dat., *shine upon*, J.*AJ*12.2.9. III. abs., *gleam*, ἱστία ποικίλως προσαυγάζοντα Philostr.Jun.*Im.*12. 2. = μαρτυρέω II, Antioch. Astr. in *Cat.Cod.Astr.*1.111. **-ᾰσις**, εως, Dor. **ποταύγασις**, ἡ, *gazing at*, τινος Diotog. l.c.

**προσαυδάω**, *speak to, address, accost*, freq. with a part. added, ἀμειβόμενος, ἀπειλήσας, δακρύσασα προσηύδα, Il.14.270, 7.225, Od.1.336; κλαίοντε προσαυδήτην βασιλῆα Il.11.136, cf. 22.90; π. τινὰ ἐπέεσσι, μειλιχίοισι, 5.30, 6.214, etc.; π. τοὺς θεούς A.*Ag.*514; πάντας μύθοισι π. Id.*Pers.*154 (anap.), etc. 2. c. acc. rei, ἔπεα πτερόεντα π. Il.4.203, al.: c. dupl. acc., ἔπεα, ἐλεεινὰ π. τινά, *speak* so and so *to one*, 1.201, 22.37; πολλὰ μειλιχίοισί [τινα] 17.431. 3. c. dat., π. [σοι] ὡς ὄντι μιάστορι S.*OT*353. II. *speak of*, τίνα τύχαν..προσαυδῶν τύχω; E.*Hipp.*827 (lyr.):—Pass., ἀδελφὴ σοὶ προσηυδώμην *was addressed as*.., S.*El.*1148.

**προσαύλειος**, ον, *near a farm-yard, rustic*, E.*Rh.*273.

⊛ **προσαυλ-έω**, *perform on the flute*, μέλος Ar.*Ec.*892, Plu.*Demetr.*53: abs., Arist.*Aud.*801$^{b}$18; *accompany in unison*, Id.*Pr.*921$^{a}$26; τῇ θυσίᾳ Plu.2.632c:—Pass., ib.1140d. ⊛ **-ησις**, εως, ἡ, *accompaniment on the flute*, Poll.4.83.

**προσαυξ-άνω**, and **-αύξω**, *increase, enhance, promote*, προσαυξήσασά τινα τοῖς φιλανθρώποις *honouring* him with.., Plb.32.1.6; π. τὴν ἐκείνων ὑπόθεσιν *confirm* it, Id.28.20.6:—more freq. in Pass., προσαύξομαι Hp.*Vict.*1.7: pf. inf. προσηυξῆσθαι Thphr.*HP*1.8.5, cf. *CP* 1.9.1; τὸ χρυσίον ἐκ τοῦ φορτίου Them.*Or.*23.286a. 2. *add*, ἄλλο..ἀγαθόν *SIG*399.32 (Delph., iii B.C.):—Pass., *to be added*, τινι Philet.3. II. intr. in Act., *wax, increase*, Vett.Val.42.2, 44.9. **-ησις**, εως, ἡ, *additional growth*, Gal.2.744 (pl.), Simp. *in Ph.*600.9. 2. *successive increase* in size of vertebrae, Gal.*UP*13.7. **-ητής**, οῦ, ὁ, voc. -ητά, *giver of increase*, *PMag.Berol.*2.121.

**προσαυρίζω**, *meet with*, νοτὶς προσαυρίζουσα χερσαίᾳ τροχῇ *Trag. Adesp.*261 (ap.Hsch., who also has προσαυρών· προστυχών, and προσηύρετο (Phot. προσαύρετο)· προσέτυχε, προσηγάγετο).

**προσᾰῡτέω**, *call to*, τισι prob. in *Epigr.Gr.*1013 (Egypt).

**προσαυτουργέω**, *make with one's own hands besides*, καινόν τι Them.*Or.*26.319a.

**προσαύω**, *burn against*, πρὶν πυρὶ θερμῷ πόδα τις προσαύσῃ S.*Ant.* 619 (lyr.).

**προσαφαιρέω**, *take away besides*, τὸ δυνατόν τινος Max.Tyr.3.5:—Med., *take away for oneself besides*, D.20.35: c. dupl. acc., τὸν υἱὸν τὴν οὐσίαν π. Is.8.42:—Pass., *to be removed as well*, Gal.2.687; *to be deprived of as well*, τι J.*AJ*7.8.4, Luc.*Am.*36; πολλοὶ ταῖς ψυχαῖς καὶ ταφὴν -αφηρέθησαν Lib.*Or.*19.60. II. Pass. in Gramm., *suffer further aphaeresis* (of ἐθέλω, θέλω, λῶ), A.D.*Adv.*158.17.

**προσᾰφή**, ἡ, (προσάπτω) *touching, handling*, Sor.2.32, *EM* 690.4.

**προσᾰφής**, ές, *touching upon, in communication with*, π. [τῇ κοιλίῃ] ὁ στόμαχος Hp.*Morb.*4.56.

**προσαφ-ίημι**, *let loose against*, λέοντι δύο [κύνας] Str.15.1.31. **-ικνέομαι**, *arrive and join* a force, Th.8.30; *approach*, τινας cj. in *AP*12.185 (Strat.). **-ίστημι**, *cause to revolt besides*, Th.4.117. II. Pass., *become separated from*, c. gen., Heliod.ap.Orib.46.22.5, Archig.ib.46.26.3. **-οδεύω**, *void excrement at* one, Arist.*HA* 630$^{b}$9, *Mir.*830$^{a}$18. **-ορίζω**, *determine and assign besides*, Gal.6.816:—Pass., προσαφορισθῆναι ἑκάστῳ ἐγγράψαι Epist.Antig. in *SIG* 344.99 (Teos, iv B.C.).

**προσαφρίζω**, *foam beside*, Hld.3.3.

**προσβᾰδίζω**, *approach*, gloss on προσέρπει in Pi.*O.*6.83 (i p.380 Boeckh).

**προσβᾰθύνω**, *make still deeper*, Heliod.ap.Orib.46.11.9.

⊛ **προσβαίνω**, Dor. **ποτι-** Sophr. in *Stud.Ital.*10.123: fut. -βήσομαι: aor. 2 προσέβην: aor. Med. προσεβήσατο, Ep. -ετο Il.14.292:—*put one's foot against*, Hom. (who uses only aor. Act. and Med.), λὰξ προσβὰς ἐκ νεκροῦ χάλκεον ἔγχος ἐσπάσατ' Il.5.620; πρὸς τὸ κάτω τοῦ τόξου τῷ ἀριστερῷ ποδὶ π., so as to get a purchase in drawing it, X.*An.*4.2.28; τῷ ποδί Arist.*Mech.*852$^{b}$25. 2. *approach*, c. acc. loci, in Hom. mostly of mountains or heights, Ἥρη..προσεβήσετο Γάργαρον ἄκρον Il.14.292, cf. 2.48, 23.117, Od.21.5, Hes.*Sc.*33, A.*Pr.* 130 (lyr.), E.*Alc.*480, etc.; ἐς ἄλσος, ἐς τὴν Λάκαιναν, S.*OC*125 (lyr.), X.*HG*7.1.29; ποτιβάντες νυν ποτ τὰν ἱστίαν θωκεῖτε Sophr. l.c.;

c. dat., τῷ τείχει π. Pl.*Phdr.*227d, etc. 3. *mount, ascend,* κατά τι Hdt.1.84, cf. Plb.7.17.4; πρὸς λόφον Id.1.30.10, etc.; ὄρει π. *climb up* a mountain, of a town, Philostr.*VA*2.9; τοῦ ποταμοῦ πρὸς πάντα τὰ χώματα προσβαίνοντος *PPetr.*2p.22 (iii B.C.). 4. abs., *walk,* π. μακράν S.*Ph.*42. 5. metaph., *come upon,* τίς σε..προσέβη μανία; Id.*OT*1300(anap.); ἄλλοις ἄλλα π. ὀδύνα E.*IT*195(lyr.). b. *attain* an age, ἐκ παιδὸς τὸν ἄνδρα προσβάς *Sardis*7(1).79c5 (iii A.D.). c. *join* a group, ἐπίκρισις τῶν -βαινόντων εἰς τοὺς ἀπὸ γυμνασίου *POxy.* 257.5 (i A.D.), cf. *Sammelb.*7440.10 (ii A.D.), etc.

**προσβακχεύω,** *send Bacchic rage upon* one, τὸν οἶστρον ταῖς γυναιξί Philostr.*Im.*1.18.

* **προσβάλλω,** Ep. **προτιβάλλω,** Dor. **ποτι-,** *strike, dash against,* ποτὶ σκῆπτρον βάλε γαίῃ Il.1.245; ἀψῖδα πέτρῳ π. *letting* it *dash against..,* E.*Hipp.*1233; τὸν πρὶν ὄλβον ἕρματι π. *having wrecked* his happiness *on* a reef, A.*Eu.*564 (lyr.); π. τινὰς ὥσπερ θηρία τινί *set* them *on* him, D.18.322; of attacking, πύλαισι..π. λόχον A.*Th.*460; π. δόρυ τισί E.*Ph.*728; παισὶ χεῖρα Id.*Alc.*307; but freq. without any notion of violence, *apply,* μαλακὰν χέρα π. [ἕλκει], of a surgeon, Pi.*P.*4.271; of cupping instruments, Hp.*VM*22 (Pass.), Aen.Tact.11.14, Gal.11.93: generally, τὰ μὲν αὐτὰ προσέβαλε S.*Tr.*844 (lyr.); προσβαλοῦσ' ὅσα.. εἶπε *applying, carrying out..,* ib.580; τι πρός τι Pl.*Ti.*36b; τὴν ὄψιν πρός τι Id.*Tht.*193c; mostly τί τινι, παρειὰν π. παρηΐδι E.*Hec.*410; κλιμάκων ὀρθοστάτας πύλῃσιν Id.*Supp.*498; ὄμματα τέκνοις Id.*Med.*860 (lyr.):—Pass., κέρασι χρυσᾶ στόμια προσβεβλημένοις *having* golden mouthpieces *affixed,* A.*Fr.*185. b. Math., *draw a straight line to meet.* ποτί c. acc., Archim.*Spir.*6, al. 2. *assign to, procure for,* κέρδος ἡμῖν Hdt.7.51; [Λακεδαιμονίοισι] Ὀλυμπιάδα *gave* them *the honour of* an Olympic victory, Id.6.70; π. ἄσην τῷ πατρὶ *cause* him distress, Id.1.136; π. μελέταν σοφισταῖς Pi.*I.*5(4).29; κακὸν πόλει A.*Pers.*781; μοι διπλᾶς ὁδούς Id.*Pr.*951; ἐμοὶ ὠδῖνας S.*Tr.*42; εὔκλειαν σαυτῇ τε κἀμοί Id.*El.*974; μή σοί τιν' αἰσχρὰν π. κληδόνα E.*Alc.*315; π. τινὶ ἔγκλημα, αἰτίαν, Antipho 4.2.4, 3.2.4; π. τινὶ αἰσχύνην Pl.*Lg.*878c; π. δεῖμα πατρί, Lat. *incutere timorem alicui,* E.*Ion* 584; ὀργὰς ἀκόρεστα τε νείκη Id.*Med.*640 (lyr.); συμφορὰς καὶ νόσους τισί Lys.*Fr.*53; ὅρκον π. τινί *lay* an oath *upon* him, S.*Tr.*255; π. τὴν ἑαυτῶν μορφήν τισι *contribute* their own form, i.e. be like them, Ael.*NA*14.12. b. *knock down* to a bidder at auction, οἰκίαν *PEleph.*25.4 (iii B.C.):—Med., *UPZ*114 i 24 (ii B.C.). c. *place at* a buyer's *disposal,* αὐτῷ ἱερεῖα *PCair.Zen.*161.5 (iii B.C.):—Med., προσεβαλόμεθα τὰ παρ' ἡμῶν we *accepted an offer for* our crop.., ib.354. 22 (iii B.C.). d. *deliver* corn *as payment,* προσβέβληκεν ἐπὶ θησαυρὸν *PRyl.*200.1 (ii A.D.), cf. *POxy.*1440.1 (ii A.D.), etc.; *pay in* money, *PRyl.*217.1 (ii A.D., Pass.), *PLond.*3.1164(*k*)19 (iii A.D., Pass.). 3. with acc. of the object struck, ἀρούρας π., of the Sun, *strike* the earth with his rays, Il.7.421, Od.19.433; μή σε π. πέμφιξ A.*Fr.*205; of smells, βροτοῦ [ὀσμή] με προσέβαλε Ar.*Pax*180; ὀσμὴ π. τὰς ῥῖνας Ael.*NA*13.21; χρῶμα οὔτε τὸ προσβάλλον οὔτε τὸ προσβαλλόμενον neither *that which strikes* [the eye] nor *that which is struck,* Pl.*Tht.*154a; τοὺς ἄνδρας ἠχὼ π. Philostr.*VA*6.26; π. σε τὸ λιτὸν καὶ αὐτοφυὲς τῆς μούσης Philostr.Jun.*Im.*10. 4. with acc. of the thing thrown, ἀτμὸν βαρὺν π. D.S.2.12 (v.l. προβ-), cf. Ael.*NA*14.22; τράγου ὀσμήν Dsc.4.50; πνοιήν τινι Luc.*Syr.D.* 30; of taste, γευσαμένῳ ὅμοιόν τι μήλῳ π. Dsc.4.6, cf. Gal.*Vict. Att.*1.3: also c. gen., τὰ κρέα ἰχθύων π. *sends* [a smell] of fish, Str.15.2.2; κνίσης π. Ael.*NA*14.27; ἰχθυηρᾶς ὀσμῆς π. ib.20: metaph., *to be redolent of,* τέχνης, Στωικῆς ταλαιπωρίας, Phld.*Rh.* 2.218, 293 S. 5. c. dat., *attend to,* οἷς εἴπαμεν ib.271 S.: abs., Plot.5.5.10. 6. μή μ' ἀνάγκῃ προσβάλῃς τάδ' ἐκλαθεῖν *do* not *drive* me by force to.., S.*OC*1178. 7. *add, throw into the bargain,* Antiph.206.5; *add* an ingredient, Philum.*Ven.*10.2, *Sammelb.*7350.9 (iii/iv A.D.). 8. *throw to,* δράγματα..υἱκοῖς κτήνεσι *BGU*757.18 (i A.D.). II. intr., *strike against, make an attack* or *assault upon,* πύλαις A.*Th.*615; αὐτοῖς, ἀλλήλοις, E.*Ph.*724, Th. 1.49; τῇ Οἰνόῃ, τῷ φρουρίῳ, etc., Id.2.19, 93, etc.; also πρὸς τὸ τεῖχος Hdt.3.155, 9.86; πρὸς τὰ τείχη Lys.14.33; πρὸς τὴν πόλιν Th.2. 56; πρὸς τοὺς ὁπλίτας X.*An.*6.3.6; πρὸς τὸν λόφον ib.4.2.11: abs., *attack, charge,* Hdt.7.211, 9.22, 25; προσβαλὼν αἱρεῖ τὴν πόλιν *by assault,* X.*HG*1.6.13. 2. *put in* with a ship, ἐς τὸν λιμένα Th.8. 101; πρὸς Τάραντα Id.6.44: c. dat., Σικελίᾳ ib.4; Ἰωνίᾳ Id.8.12, cf. *SIG*456.36 (Cos, iii B.C.). 3. generally, *collide,* προσβαλούσης τῆς νεὼς πρὸς ὁλκάδα Pl.*La.*183d; *impinge,* πρὸς ὄψιν ἢ πρὸς ἀκοήν Id.*R.* 401c, cf. Arist.*Col.*$792^a20$; ὀσμὴ π. τινί Thphr.*HP*9.7.1, D.S.2.19; of winds, Arist.*Pr.*$947^a22$; σεισμὸς τῇ Κρήτῃ π. Philostr.*VA*4.34; π. τοῖς ἄρχουσιν *approach* them, Plu.*Nic.*30; ἐκ τῆς Ἀσίας τῇ Ἀττικῇ Id.*Phoc.*21; *light upon,* in argument, Anon.Lond.37.54.

B. Med., ταύτην οὔτ' ἔπεϊ προτιβάλλεαι, οὔτε τι ἔργῳ *payest no heed to,* Il.5.879; but also, *throw oneself upon* another's *protection,* A.R.4.1046; π. γυναικὶ περὶ ἀφροδίτης *make advances,* Sch.Ar.*Eq.* 514; *associate with oneself,* Opp.*H.*5.98.

**προσβάρησις** [ᾰ], εως, ἡ, *lying heavy* or *pressing upon, Gloss.*

**προσβᾰσᾰνίζω,** *torture besides,* Posidon.36 J. cod. A Ath. (where προβασ- is cj.).

* **πρόσβᾰσις,** εως, ἡ, (προσβαίνω) *means of approach, access,* esp. uphill, ὄρεσι, ἔνθα π. οὐδεμίαν εἶναι Hdt.3.111, cf. E.*El.*489, Th.6.96 (pl.), 7.45; προσβάσεις τεκμαίρεται πύργων looks for *means of scaling* them, E.*Ph.*180; τὰς ἐκ θαλάττης π. Plb.4.56.8. 2. *accession,* τοῦ εὖ ζῆν Gal.19.178. 3. *rise,* ἡ τῶν Νειλῴων ὑδάτων π. *PMasp.*2 ii 22 (vi A.D.).

**προσβᾰτός,** ή, όν, *accessible,* ἱππεῦσι X.*An.*4.3.12: abs., ib.4.8.9; χωρίον ἔνθα οὐ προσβατὸν θανάτῳ where was no *point accessible* by death, Id.*Ap.*23.

**προσβεβαιόω,** *confirm besides,* Phalar.*Ep.*23.2.

**προσβῐ-άζομαι,** *compel, constrain,* τινα Ar.*Pl.*16, Pl.*Ep.*331b; π. ταῦτα *push too far,* Id.*Cra.*410a: abs., *use force,* Arist.*GA*$726^b8$; τῇ συνουσίᾳ Sor.1.24 (Pass.). II. π. τόποις προσάντεσι *force* or *storm* heights, D.S.20.39: aor. Pass. προσβιασθῆναι, *to be forced* or *hard pressed,* Th.1.106. III. *assist* parturition *by straining,* Sor.1. 70. IV. *contend in addition,* A.D.*Synt.*258.6. **-ασμός,** ὁ, *forcing, straining,* Antyll.ap.Orib.6.10.14. **-αστέον,** *one must constrain,* τὴν φύσιν Plu.2.125d.

**προσβῐβάζω,** Att. fut. -βιβῶ Ar.*Av.*426 (lyr.), S.*Ichn.*166, Pl.*Phdr.* 229e:—causal of προσβαίνω, *cause to approach, bring near,* π. ἑαυτὸν κινδύνοις *expose..,* Longin.15.5. b. *liken, make to resemble,* τινά τινι Plu.*Pomp.*46. 2. metaph., *bring over, persuade,* εὖ προσβιβάζεις με Ar.*Eq.*35; τὸ τῇδε καὶ τὸ κεῖσε καὶ τὸ δεῦρο προσβιβᾷ λέγων Id.*Av.*426; τῷ λόγῳ προσβιβάζειν [τινάς] X.*Mem.*1.2.17, cf. Aeschin.3.93, Plu.*Cat.Mi.*36:—Pass., προσβιβασθῆναι πρὸς τὴν ἀλήθειαν Luc.*Philops.*33. II. of things, *add,* ἐπὶ τούτοις τὸν κολοφῶνα Pl.*Tht.*153c, cf. Phld.*Mus.*p.73 K. 2. π. κατὰ τὸ εἰκὸς ἕκαστον *reduce* it into accordance with probability, Pl.*Phdr.*229e; τἄλλα π. κατὰ γράμματα καὶ κατὰ συλλαβάς *reduce* to letters and syllables, Id.*Cra.*427c. 3. *prove,* Alex.Aphr.*in Sens.*49.9.

**προσβῐόω,** *live longer* or *after,* χρόνον οὐ πολύν Plu.*Num.*21, cf. *Luc.* 43, Phalar.*Ep.*103.3.

**προσβλᾰβής,** ές, *hurtful,* Phld.*Rh.*1.375 S.

**προσβλάπτω,** *hurt, harm besides,* Hp.*Epid.*3.8:—Pass., Gal.*UP* 7.7.

**προσβλασφημέω,** *abuse, insult besides,* J.*AJ*6.13.6.

**προσ-βλεπτέος,** α, ον, *to be looked upon,* Jul.*Ep.*89b. **-βλέπω,** Dor. **ποτιβλέπω,** also **ποτιγλέπω** Alcm.23.75: Att. fut. -βλέψομαι E.*IA*1192:—*look at* or *upon,* c. acc. pers., S.*OT*1183, etc.; π. σ' ὀρθαῖς κόραις E.*Hec.*972; ὄμμασι τοῖς ὀρθοῖσι ποτιβλέπεν Theoc.5.36; εὐθύς μ' ἐπηρώτησε προσβλέψας μέγα Strato Com.1.5; φίλιόν τι καὶ εἰρηνικὸν π. τινά Luc.*Luct.*4: rarely c. dat., X.*Smp.*3.14, Plu.*Cat. Mi.*65, Luc.*Alex.*42: also ποὶ τὸμ πατέρα..ποτιβλέψας looking *towards* or *at* the father, *IG*$4^2$(1).121.44 (Epid., iv B.C.). 2. c. acc. rei, *look at, regard,* [τοιαῦτα] A.*Pr.*217; τὰ τοῦδε πράγη S.*Aj.*346; τὸ ἀξίωμα τῆς βουλῆς D.*Ep.*3.42. **-βλεψις,** εως, ἡ, *looking at* or *upon,* τινι Plu.2.45c: Dor. **ποτί-,** *aspect, appearance,* Diotog.ap.Stob.4.7.62.

**πρόσ-βλησις,** εως, ἡ, *application,* τῆς σικύης Hp.*Mul.*2.110. II. *momentary impact,* Hierocl.p.19 A. **-βλητέον,** *one must apply,* Herod.Med. in *Rh.Mus.*58.107, Sor.2.32, Gal.13.674. **-βλητός,** ή, όν, *added, affixed,* Lxx *Je.*10.9. II. *subject to momentary impact,* Hierocl.p.23 A.

**προσβλύζω,** *lap against,* of water, ποταμοῦ ὄχθη χλοερῷ λειμῶνι -βλύζουσα Plu.2.320c (s.v.l.).

**προσβοάω,** = *acclamo, Gloss.*:—Med., *call to oneself, call in,* παριόντας προσεβώσατο Hdt.6.35.

**προσβοηθ-εια,** ἡ, *support, aid,* prob. in Dosith.p.397 K. **-έω,** Ion. -βωθέω, *come to aid,* abs., ναυσὶ π. Th.2.25, cf. 6.66, 69, etc.; δέκα ναυσὶν ἐκ τῶν Ἀθηνῶν *with* ten ships.., Id.8.23; στρατιᾷ καὶ ἵπποις v.l. in X.*HG*1.3.5; προσβωθῆσαι ἐς τὴν Βοιωτίην v.l. in Hdt.8. 144; οἱ αὐτοῖς ὁ στρατὸς προσεβεβοηθήκει Th.1.50.

* **προσβολή,** ἡ, (προσβάλλω) *application,* e.g. of the touchstone, A. *Ag.*391 (lyr., pl.); ἡ τῆς σικύας π. Arist.*Rh.*$1405^b3$; ἡ π. τῶν ὀμμάτων πρός τι Pl.*Tht.*153e; φίλιαι π. προσώπων, of kisses, E.*Supp.*1138 (lyr.): abs., *kiss, embrace,* Id.*Med.*1074; τῆς γλώττης προσβολαί, opp. συμβολαὶ τῶν χειλῶν, Arist.*PA*$660^a6$; ἄνευ προσβολῆς (sc. τῆς γλώττης) pronounced without *applying* the tongue to the teeth, etc., Id.*Po.*$1456^b26$: metaph., π. τῆς φαντασίας *Stoic.*2.33: abs., of an act of *intuition,* Porph.*Sent.*43, Plot.2.9.1, 3.8.10, al. 2. in an auction, *document recording the knocking down* of a lot to a purchaser, *PEleph.*23.17 (iii B.C.), *PTeb.*814.28 (iii B.C.). II. (from intr. sense) *falling upon, attack, assault* (expld. by Hsch. as τῶν ἀθητῶν ἡ συναφὴ καὶ κατοχή), π. Ἀχαιῖς A.*Th.*28; προσβολὴν ποιέεσθαι πέριξ τὸ τεῖχος Hdt.3.158: pl., Id.4.128, Th.2.4, 5.61, X.*HG* 1.3.14, etc.; προσβολὰς παρασκευάζεσθαι τῷ τείχει Th.2.18; προσβολῆς γινομένης πρὸς τὸ τεῖχος Hdt.6.101; τὰς π. ἀποκρούεσθαι Id. 4.200; προσβολαὶ ἱππέων Th.3.1, cf. X.*An.*3.4.2; π. *sudden attacks,* opp. ξυσταδὸν μάχαι, Th.7.81; ἐκ προσβολῆς at *the first assault,* Philostr.*Her.*19.3; ἀντιφραττόμενοι ταῖς π. *SIG*780.19 (Epist. Augusti, i B.C.). 2. generally, *attack, visitation,* προσβολαὶ Ἐρινύων A.*Ch.* 283; μιασμάτοιν Id.*Eu.*600; δαιμόνων Ar.*Pax* 39 (with allusion to the stench *striking* one's nose, cf. προσβάλλω I. 3); προσβολὰς κακάς E.*El.*829; ἐκ θεοῦ προσβολῆς ἐμηνάμην Id.*Cret.*9; π. θεῖαι Antipho 3. 3.8; πυρὸς ἢ χειμῶνος προσβολῇ Pl.*Lg.*865b; *attack, fit* of disease, Dsc. 5.113; π. δεισιδαιμονίας Plu.2.43d: but, *beat* of pulse, Ruf.*Syn.Puls.* 7.5. 3. without hostile sense, *impact* of sound, βραδεῖα μὲν γὰρ ἐν λόγοισι π. μόλις δι' ὠτὸς ἔρχεται ῥυπωμένου, i.e. impressions through an old man's ears are slow, S.*Fr.*858; *contact,* π. καὶ ἐπαφή *Stoic.*2. 123; τοῦ ἡλίου αἱ π. αἱ πρῶται Ael.*NA*14.23. 4. *means of approaching, approach,* παρέχειν π. καὶ ἐπαφήν Pl.*Sph.*246a; προσβολὰς ἀφράστους ἔχειν, of a place, Plu.*Caes.*53; π. ἔχειν τῆς Σικελίας to afford *a means of entering* Sicily, Th.4.1; ἡ τοῦ στομάχου π. Arist.*HA*$507^b3$; οὔσης..τραχείας τῆς π. Plb.3.51.4; of ships, *landing-place, harbour, place to touch at,* ὁλκάδων π. Th.4.53; of a place, ἐν προσβολῇ εἶναι τῆς Σικελίας to be *a port of call* on the voyage to Sicily, Id.6.48; *meeting-point,* Pl.*Ti.*36c. 5. Rhet., in pl., *approaches* to a sub-

ject, Philostr.VS1.9.1. III. (from Pass.) *that which is put upon a weapon* or *tool*, *iron point*, D.C.38.49 (pl.), Phryn.PSp.100 B. (nisi leg. προβολή). 2. *point of attachment* of a stake fixed in the ground, Plb.18.18.14 (pl.).

**προσβόρειος**, ον, = sq., opp. καταβόρειος (q. v.), Arist.HA547$^{a}$12, Thphr.HP1.9.2, etc.

**πρόσβορρος**, ον, *towards* or *exposed to the north wind*, E.Ion 11,937, Thphr.HP9.2.3, v.l. in Arist.GA783$^{a}$31 : Sup. -βορρότατος Str.Chr. 11.48.

**προσβοτᾰνίζω**, *weed in addition*, PCair.Zen.286.3 (Pass., iii B.C.).

**προσβράσσω**, *throw up*, *dash against*, in Pass., σῶμα πίτυϊ προσβεβρασμένον ὑπὸ τῆς θαλάττης Plu.2.675e, cf. Zen.4.38, Hsch. s. v. φῦκος.

**προσβρᾰχής**, ές, *somewhat shallow*, Str.6.3.6, al.

**προσβωθέω**, Ion. for προσβοηθέω (q. v.).

**προσβώμιος**, ον, *at the altar*, ἵπποι καὶ βόες Hld.10.39.

**προσβ⟨ωμ⟩ολοχεῖ**· πρὸς χάριν λέγει, Hsch.

**πρόσγειος**, Dor. **ποτίγειος**, ον, (γέα, γῆ) *near the earth*, of the moon, ποτιγειοτάτα Ti.Locr.96d, cf. Stoic.2.196 (Comp.); -ότερος, of a planet, Arist.Mu.392$^{a}$16, cf. Cleom.2.6 (Sup.); -ότατος ἡμῖν ὁ καρκίνος Porph. Antr.21 ; -όταται πτήσεις Ph.2.114, cf. Plu.2.727f ; ψυχαί Ph.1.641 ; τὰ π. *mundane* things, opp. μετάρσια, Placit.3.8.2 ; ἡ π. περὶ τὸν ἀέρα ταχυτής Porph.ap.Eus.PE3.11. II. *keeping inshore*, of fish, opp. πελάγιος, Arist.HA525$^{a}$15, 598$^{a}$2 ; οἱ π. τόποι τῆς θαλάσσης ib.598$^{a}$7 ; τὰ π. ib.597$^{a}$17 ; of islands, Id.Mete.368$^{b}$33 ; of sea-plants, Thphr. HP4.6.2, Dsc.4.179 (Comp.). III. *near the ground*, ταπεινὸς καὶ π. Luc.Prom.1.

**προσγειτνιάω**, *to be neighbouring*, of land, PTeb.441 (i A.D.).

**προσγελάω**, fut. -άσομαι [ᾰ] Ar.Pax600 :—*smile at* one, τινα Hdt. 5.92.γ′, E.Med.1162, Pl.R.566d, etc. ; σὲ..τὰ..φυτὰ προσγελάσεται Ar. l. c. : c. acc. cogn., προσγελᾶτε τὸν πανύστατον γέλων *smile* your last smile *upon* me, E.Med.1041. 2. *greet* the senses, ὀσμὴ βροτείων αἱμάτων με προσγελᾷ A.Eu.253 ; πιστὰ γάρ σε προσγελᾷ θεᾶς ἔπη S.Ichn.291 ; προσγελῶσά τε λοπὰς παφλάζει Eub.109, cf. Diph.33. 5. 3. later c. dat., *smile upon*, δούλοις Arist.Fr.183, cf. Lxx Si. 13.6, Lib.Or.48.10.

**προσ-γένημα**, ατος, τό, *acquisition*, *addition*, OGI669.62 (Egypt, i A.D., pl.), PAmh.2.68.34 (i A.D.), etc. **-γενής**, ές, *akin*, as Subst., *kinsman*, τινος PTeb.380.10 (i A.D.), PStrassb.42.12 (iv A.D.), Suid. s. v. Πίνδαρος : abs., Eust.410.38.

**προσγέννησις**, εως, ἡ, *additional generation*, Eustr. in EN101. 36.

**πρόσγευσις**, εως, ἡ, dub. sens. in CPHerm.27.6 (iii A.D.).

**προσγίγνομαι**, Ion. and later **προσγίν-** [ῑ], *attach oneself to* another, esp. as an ally, τινι Hdt.5.103, Th.7.50, etc. ; οἱ προσγεγενημένοι ξύμμαχοι Id.6.6, cf. Hdt.4.120, Plu.Them.7 : abs., Hdt.4.120, 8.136 ; θαρσεῖν τοῖς προσγιγνομένοις *by the reinforcements*, Th.2.79, cf. X.Cyr.7.5.4 ; μὴ παραγενέσθαι τῇ μάχῃ, ἀλλὰ π. μετὰ τὴν μάχην Plu. Ant.22 ; also in political strife, προσγενομένου τοῦ δήμου αὐτῷ Hdt.6. 136, cf. 110. 2. generally, *to be added*, *accrue*, E.Andr.702, Th.1.142, al. ; ἐκ τῶν σιτίων ταῖς σαρξὶ σάρκες π. Pl.Phd.96d ; τὰ μέν γε τῇ τέχνῃ πράσσειν, τὰ δὲ ἡμῖν ἀνάγκῃ καὶ τύχῃ προσγίγνεται Agatho 8, cf. Pl.R.346d ; opp. ἀπογίγνομαι, χωρίζομαι, Zeno Eleat.2, Pl.Ti. 82b, Arist.GC315$^{a}$16. 3. *come to*, *happen to*, τοῖς γὰρ θανοῦσι μόχθος οὐ π. S.Tr.1173 ; γνώσει..θυμοῦ τελευτήν, ὡς κακὴ π. Id.OC 1198, cf. El.771, Lys.24.8, Pl.Ti.86e, etc. 4. *become in addition*, πρὸς τῷ θυμοειδεῖ ἔτι π. φιλόσοφος Id.R.375e.

**προσγιγνώσκω**, *learn in addition*, τὰ μετὰ ταῦτα -γνωσθέντα βεβρέχθαι the land *of which it has since become known* that.., PLond.3.604. 8 (i A.D.).

**προσγλισχραίνω**, *make more viscid*, Hp.Acut.58.

* **προσγλίχομαι** [ῐ], *desire eagerly besides*, εἴ τι..διέλειπε Arist. Metaph.986$^{a}$7 ; *desire in addition to*, π. ταῖς ἰδέαις τὰ μαθηματικά ib. 1090$^{b}$31.

**προσγομφόω**, *rivet on*, ἀστράγαλον IG1$^{2}$.373.177.

**πρόσγονος**, ον, *after-born*, S.Fr.379 (s. v. l.).

**πρόσγραμμα**, ατος, τό, *heading*, Gal.13.682. II. *additional regulation*, BCH44.78 (Lagina).

**προσγρᾰφ-ή**, ἡ, *enrolment*, Milet.3 No.143 (iii B.C.). II. *adscription of* ι, ἐν π., i. e. written but not pronounced, Eust.1409.47. * **-ος**, ον, *added to a list*, = Lat. *adscripticius*, opposed to the citizens originally enrolled, D.H.2.56 ; Πέρσης τῶν π., a category of persons in Egypt (cf. ἐπιγονή II), PLond.3.879.17 (ii B.C.), cf. Sammelb.1436.9 (i B.C.), etc. II. Subst., πρόσγραφον ἔδωκε τῆς τιμῆς *note* or *bill* of the price, Plu.2.832a : generally, *supplementary document*, POxy. 513.34 (ii A.D.), BGU457.1 (ii A.D.), etc. **-ω**, Dor. **ποτι-** Berl. Sitzb.1927.8 (Locris, v B.C.), **ποι-** SIG56.46 (Argos, v B.C.) :—*write besides*, *add in writing*, And.3.40, IG12(2).645.50 (Nesus), PCair. Zen.696.9 (iii B.C.), SIG723.20 (Rhodes, ii/i B.C., ποτι-), al. ; εἴ τι προσγράψαι ἢ ἀπαλεῖψαι ἐβουλήθη D.46.11 ; π. τῷ τῆς αἰτίας ὀνόματι τιμωρίαν Id.23.26 ; προσγράψαι πρὸς τὸν ὅρκον τὸν τῆς βουλῆς Supp.Epigr.3.713.11 (Lex Attica, v B.C.) :—Pass., τὰ προσγεγραμμένα *conditions added* to a treaty, X.HG7.1.37 ; προσγραφῆναι εἰς στήλην Lys.13.72 : Gramm., *to be added in writing* (instead of being omitted), τὸ ῑ (sc. in νῶι) προσγεγράψεται A.D.Pron.87.10, cf. D.T.639.14. 2. *add to a list* of persons, *enrol*, *register*, π. τινὰ τῇ βουλῇ, τῇ πολιτείᾳ, Plu.Publ.21, Num.8 ; π. τοὺς εὐνούχους εἰς τὰ τῶν σωφρονούντων ἤθη Philostr.VA1.33 :—Med., *cause to be registered besides*, Is.10.2, D.22.71 ; *register*, *enrol oneself*, πρὸς φυλὴν προσγράψασθαι ὁποίαν ἂν βούλωνται IG12(5).821.11 (Tenos), cf. 825. 26 (ibid.), SIG645.60 (Byzantium, ii B.C., ποτι-) :—Pass., ποτιγραφῆμεν ποθ' ἄν κα θέλῃ τᾶν ἑκατοστύων IPE1$^{2}$.79.29 (Olbia, i A.D.); οἱ προσγεγραμμένοι Lxx Da.3.3 : but, of property, *to be marked for confiscation*, εἰ προσγραφήσεται τὰ ἐμά Astramps.Orac.82 p.6 H. (leg. προγρ-). 3. *ascribe*, *attribute*, τὰ ἴδια τοῦ ἀσωμάτου τοῖς σώμασι Porph.Sent.33. 4. *prescribe*, σκορπιοπλήκτοις προσγέγραπται Philum.Ven.14.8. II. *paint together with* or *beside*, τοὺς ποταμίους τῶν ἵππων τῷ Νείλῳ Philostr.Im.1.5, cf. Palaeph.45 :—Pass., Philostr.Im. 1.16.

**προσγυμν-άζω**, *exercise at* or *in* a thing, τινι Pl.Lg.647c :—Med., ὁ -αζόμενος, = sq., Gal.6.177 (v.l. προγ-) ; π. τινί Alex.Aphr. in Top.232. 3 ; πολέμῳ -γεγυμνασμένος Plu.Marc.27. 2. metaph. in Med., *enter into a contest with*, τινι D.Chr.36.27 : abs., M.Ant.6.20. * **-αστής**, οῦ, ὁ, *fellow-wrestler*, Hyp.Lyc.6, Inscr.Prien.111.176 (i B.C., pl.), cj. in Gal.6.177.

**προσδᾰνείζω**, *lend besides*, PFlor.81.1 (ii A.D.) :—Med., *borrow besides*, X.An.7.5.5, Lys.19.55 ; προσδεδανεῖσθαι τοῖς ξένοις *that he had also borrowed* from his friends, ib.26.

**προσδᾰπᾰνάω**, *spend besides*, IG2$^{2}$.949.10, 1227.8, Ev.Luc.10.35, Luc.Ep.Sat.39 :—Med., Them.Or.23.289b.

**προσδᾰτέομαι**, Dor. aor. ποτεδασσάμην, *assign*, τινί τι Tab.Heracl. 2.54, al.

**προσδαψῐλεύομαι**, *spend lavishly besides*, v. l. for προσεπι- in Ph.2. 66.

**πρόσδεγμα**, ατος, τό, *reception*, τὰ τῆς ξένης προσδέγματα S.Tr.628.

**προσδεδοκημένως**, Adv., (προσδοκάω) *as expected*, Dosith. p.412 K.

**προσδεής**, ές, *needing besides*, *yet lacking*, τινος Pl.Ti.33d, Luc. Demon.4, Poll.5.170.

**προσδέησις**, εως, ἡ, *want*, *need*, τῶν πλησίον Epicur.Ep.1 p.28 U.

**προσδείδω**, *fear besides*, ὡς.. D.C.47.4.

**προσδείκνῡμι**, *show besides*, Poll.9.113.

**προσδεικτέον**, *one must prove besides*, ὅτι.. Arist.Top.122$^{a}$24.

**προσδεκ-τέος**, α, ον, *to be admitted*, τινι by one, Pl.Ti.89b. 2. προσδεκτέον, *one must receive*, *admit*, οἴκτους, ὑδροποσίαν, Din.1.92, Plu.2.134e ; *one must accept*, τὴν ἀπόδοσιν Heliod.ap.Orib.48.70. 7. b. *one must expect*, c. acc. et inf., Gal.16.380. * **-τός**, ή, όν, *acceptable*, Lxx Pr.11.20.

**πρόσδενδρος**, ον, *attached to trees*, of creeping plants, Thphr.CP2. 18.2.

**προσδεξιόομαι**, v. προδεξιόομαι.

**πρόσδεξις**, εως, ἡ, *acceptance*, φαντασιῶν Zeno Stoic.1.20, Herill. ib.91.

**προσδέρκομαι**, Ep. **ποτιδέρκομαι** Il.16.10, Od.17.518 : aor. Act. -έδρᾰκον A.Pr.903 (lyr.), Eu.166 (lyr.) :—Pass. -εδέρχθην in act. sense, Id.Pr.53 : pf. -δέδορκα interpol. in E.Ph.144 :—*look at*, *behold*, c. acc., Od.20.385, A. ll. cc., etc. ; προσδέρκεσθέ μ' ὄμμασιν E.Med.1040 ; ἃς οὔθ' ἥλιος π. ἀκτῖσιν.. A.Pr.796. II. *look closely*, S.OC121 (lyr.).

**πρόσ-δεσις**, εως, ἡ, *tying on* or *to*, Gloss. II. *attachment* of a limb, Heliod.ap.Orib.49.25.10. **-δεσμεύω**, *bind on* or *to*, τι πρός τι D.S.4.59 ; κατ' ἀντικρὺ τοῖς ζῶσι νεκρούς Iamb.Protr.8 ; τι περί τι Sch.Ar.V.580 (Pass.) :—Pass., Aët.6.35. **-δεσμέω**, = foreg., τί τινι Sch.Ar.V.1196 ; τι πρός τινι Sch.D Il.1.436 (Pass.). **-δετέον**, *one must bind on*, Gp.5.13.3. **-δετος**, ον, *tied to* a thing, μετώποις, λίθῳ, E.Rh.307, APl.4.147 (Antiphil.). II. *fixed*, Heliod.ap.Orib. 49.2.3.

* **προσδέχομαι**, Ion. **προσδέκομαι** : used by Hom. only in Ep. pres. part. ποτιδέγμενος (v. infr. III) : aor. 1 προσεδέχθην in pass. sense, Arist.Pr.956$^{b}$25, Plb.4.33.9, D.S.15.70 :—*receive favourably*, *accept*, τὸ ἐκ Δελφῶν [χρηστήριον] Hdt.1.48, cf. SIG557.11 (Magn. Mae., iii B.C.), etc. ; π. συμμαχίαν X.HG7.4.2 ; τὴν φιλίαν, τὰς διαλύσεις, Plb.1.16.8, 1.17.1 ; also π. ἑκάστους ἐπὶ.. ὁμολογίαις Id.3.18.7 ; *receive hospitably*, S.OT1428, E.Ph.1706 ; ζῶνθ' Ἡρακλῆ S.Tr. 233. II. *admit*, ἐς τὴν πόλιν Th.2.12 ; *admit into one's presence*, of a king, X.Cyr.7.5.37, HG1.5.9 ; of a demos *receiving* foreign emissaries, SIG561.7 (Chalcis, found at Magn. Mae., iii B.C.). 2. *admit to citizenship*, Pl.Lg.708a, D.57.59 ; so ποία δὲ χέρνιψ φρατέρων προσδέξεται; A.Eu.656 ; τοὺς οἰκέτας π. εἰς τὸ πολίτευμα IG9(2). 517.32 (Epist. Philippi, Larissa, iii B.C.) ; π. τινὰ εἰς τοὺς ἐφήβους Sammelb.7333.40 (Alexandria, ii A.D.) ; ὁ προσδεχθησόμενος εἰς τὴν στιβάδα IG2$^{2}$.1368.52 ; ὅταν τις..προσδεχθῇ εἴς τι τῶν κατὰ τὸ σῶμα ἀθλημάτων Arist. l. c. 3. of the female, ἡ ἵππος π. τὸν ὄνον Id.HA577$^{b}$15, cf. 575$^{b}$17, Hdt.2.121.ε′. 4. *admit* an argument, π. τὸ ψεῦδος, λόγον ἀληθῆ, Pl.R.485c, 561b, cf. SIG685.130 (Magn. Mae., ii B.C.) ; π. πρόφασιν *accept* an excuse, PTeb.27.82 (ii B.C.). 5. *admit*, *be capable of*, μήτε γένεσιν μήτε ὄλεθρον Pl.Phlb.15b ; φθοράν Id.Ti.52a. 6. *undertake*, προσδέχεσθαι μάλα χρὴ τὰ τοιαῦτα ἰήματα Hp.Art.69 ; *take* a liability *upon oneself*, *guarantee*, τὸ ἀνάλωμα IG5(1).501, 555b, al. (Sparta) ; *credit* a sum to a person or an account, PHib.1.58 (iii B.C.), PSI4.372.9 (iii B.C.), PCair.Zen.306.11, 355.69, al. (iii B.C.), Ostr.1089 (ii B.C.), Ostr.Bodl. i 256 (ii B.C.), etc. III. *await*, *expect*, the only sense in Hom., in Ep. part. ποτιδέγμενος *waiting for* or *expecting*, δῶρον Od.2.186 ; σὴν ὁρμήν ib.403 ; σὸν μῦθον 7. 161 ; ἠμέας 9.545 ; λαῶν ὀτρυντύν Il.19.234 ; ἀγγελίην ib.336 ; so later, προσδεκομένους τοιοῦτον οὐδέν Hdt.3.146, cf. S.Tr.15, E.Alc. 131 (lyr.), etc. ; παρὰ ἃ προσεδέχετο Th.4.19 ; τῷ Νικίᾳ προσδεχομένῳ ἦν τὰ παρὰ τῶν Ἐγεσταίων was according to his *expectation*, Id.6.46 ; π. τινός τι *expect* anything from anybody, Antipho Soph.10 : c. acc.

et inf. fut., *οὐδὲν πάντως προσεδέκοντο..τὸν στόλον ὁρμήσεσθαι* Hdt.5.34, cf. 6.100, 7.156, al., Th.4.9; *πολεμίους παρέσεσθαι* X.*Cyr*.4.5.22: c. part. fut., *τοῦτον π. ἐπαναστησόμενον* Hdt.1.89; *πανταχόθεν π. τοὺς πολεμίους* *await* them, Plb.2.69.6, etc. **2.** *wait, ἧατ' ἐνὶ μεγάροις ποτιδέγμεναι* Il.2.137, cf. 9.628, Od.2.205, etc.; *π. ὁππότ' ἄρ' ἔλθοι* Il.7.415; *π. εἰ* c. opt., Od.23.91.

**προσδεχομένως**, Adv., (*προσδέχομαι* I or II. 6) *too accommodatingly, τὰς ἀνεπιτηδείους διδάξαι π.* Sor.1.3.

⊛ **προσδέω** (A), *bind on* or *to, πρὸς ὕπερον τὸ ξύλον* Hp.*Fract*.13; *αὐλίσκον πρὸς κύστιν* Id.*Nat.Puer*.17; *χρυσαῖς σειραῖς τὸ τοῦ Ἀπόλλωνος ξόανον τῇ βάσει* D.S.17.41:—Med., *σιδήριον ὀξὺ -δησάμενος πρὸς τὸν δάκτυλον* Hp.*Morb*.2.28:—Pass., *ἥμισυ ἀσκοῦ οἱ προσδέδεται* Hdt.6.119; *κύνας προσδεδέσθαι νυκτερεύοντας* Aen.Tact.22.14: metaph., *ἡδονῇ π.* J.*AJ*5.2.7. **2.** c. acc. only, *attach, τοὺς κάλους* Hdt.2.36; *ἐπ' ἄκρῳ μυρσίνην* Id.4.195.

⊛ **προσδέω** (B), *need besides*, c. gen. rei, *λύπης τι προσδεῖς;* E.*HF*90; [*τόπους*] *ποτιδέοντας βοαθείας* *SIG*569.7 (Halasarna, iii B.C.); *to be deficient in, ἐὰν δέ του προσδέῃ τόδε τὸ ψήφισμα τῶν περὶ τὸν ἀπόστολον* *IG*2$^2$.1629.264, cf. *Supp.Epigr*.3.674.18 (Rhodes, ii B.C., *ποτι-*). **2.** mostly impers. **προσδεῖ**, *there is still need of*, c. gen. rei, *ὡς ἐκκαυμάτων μή μοι μεταξὺ προσδεήσειεν* S.*Fr*.225; *ναυτικὸν οὗπερ ὑμῖν μάλιστα προσδεῖ* Th.3.13, cf. 1.68, X.*An*.5.6.1, *IG*2$^2$.204.66; *εἴ τινος ἔτι π. τῇ συγκράσει* Pl.*Phlb*.64b; *προσδεῖν ἔφη πρὸς τὸν μισθόν* *that there was wanting* something *to make* it *up*, Lys.19.22; *τὸ ἐπίλοιπον, οὗ προσέδει εἰς τὰς εἴκοσι μνᾶς* D.59.31: c. inf., *οὐκέτι προσδεῖ ἐρέσθαι* Pl.*Smp*.205a; distd. from *ἐνδεῖ*, D.1.19. **II.** more freq. in Med. **προσδέομαι**, Dor. **ποτιδεύομαι** Theoc.5.63: fut. *-δεήσομαι*: aor. *-εδεήθην*:—*to be in want of, stand in need of besides, τινος* Th.1.102, 2.41, Lys.19.21, X.*HG*7.4.2; *ἔτι ταῦτα μαντείας -δεῖται;* Aeschin.1.76, cf. Pl.*Phlb*.63c, etc.: with neut. Adj., *ἤν..τι ποοσδέωμαι* if *I be* at all *in want*, X.*Cyr*.1.3.17: with inf. added, *τοῦ ἱεροῦ προεστάναι οὐδὲν π.* Id.*HG*7.4.35; *desire much, τινος* Id.*An*.5.9.24. **2.** rarely impers., Pl.*Demod*.384b, *Alc*.2.138b, X.*Ages*.1.5, *IG*2$^2$.380.11. **3.** *beg* or *ask of* another, *τί τινος* Hdt.6.35; *οὐδὲν τῶν ἐκεῖνος ἡμέων προσεδέετο* (i.e. *οὐδὲν τούτων ἃ..*) Id.8.144, cf. 3.75: rarely in this sense c. gen. rei, *γυναικὸς οὐ προσδεόμεθά σευ τῆς ἐξέσιος* Id.5.40: c. gen. pers. et inf., Id.1.36, 8.40; *προσδέονται Ἀθηναίων συμπράττειν* *IG*2$^2$.1.46: without gen., *π. λύσαντας..ἀποπλέειν* Hdt.6.41: abs., *προσδεηθήσεται* Lxx *Si*.13.3 (s.v.l.). **4.** *permit, ὁ καιρὸς οὐδεμιᾶς ὑπερβολῆς προσδεῖται* *PPetr*.2p.119 (iii B.C.).

**προσδηλέομαι**, *ruin* or *destroy besides, τι* Hdt.8.68.γ'.

**προσδηλόω**, *make plain besides*, Arist.*APo*.$92^{b}23$:—Pass., Id.*SE* $173^{b}7$.

**προσδημᾰγωγέω**, *win the favour of, τὰ θέατρα* Him.*Or*.7.8.

**προσδια-βάλλω**, *insinuate besides, τὰ ὀρθῶς εἰρημένα π. ἄδικα εἶναι* Antipho 3.4.2. **2.** *bring into greater disfavour, τινα* Plu.*Alc*.28, cf. *Fab*.7; *τινί τινας increase the feeling of..against*, Id.*Cor*.27; *προσδιαβληθῆναι εἴς τι* Id.*Per*.29. **-γράφω** [*γρᾰ*], Dor. **ποτι-** *Supp.Epigr*.3.674.47 (Rhodes, ii B.C.):—*pay in addition*, *PFay*.14.4 (ii B.C.):—Pass., *-γραφόμενα, τά, additional payments*, *Ostr.Strassb*.55 (i A.D.), *PFay*.36.16 (ii A.D.), etc.

**προσδι-αιρετέον**, *one must distinguish further*, Arist.*SE*$175^{a}39$. **-αιρέω**, *apportion, ἐλάχιστα τοῖς ἑστιωμένοις* Suid. s.v. *δαιτρός*. **II.** Med., *divide* or *distinguish further, π. τὴν λέξιν, ὅτι..* Arist.*Rh*.$1414^{a}19$; *π.* [*τινὰς*] *καθ' ἡλικίας* ib.$1369^{a}7$; *subdivide* an estate, *CPR*206.13 (ii A.D.). **-αιτάομαι**, *live beside, τῷ Νείλῳ* Ael.*NA*2.48 codd. (*παρα-* Hercher). **-ακρῑβόω**, *determine precisely in addition*, Phld.*Rh*.1 p.288 S.

**προσδια-κρίνω** [ῑ], *decide as well*, A.D.*Synt*.5.26. **II.** *distinguish in addition*, ib.236.12:—Pass., ib.36.5. **III.** *take into the reckoning, allow for*, Ptol.*Geog*.1.2.4. **-λαμβάνω**, *consider as well*, dub. in Epicur.*Nat.Herc*.996; *προσδιαληφθέντος περὶ αὐτοῦ ἁρμοζόντως* after *a* suitable *declaration* on the subject *has been made*, *BGU*1060.30 (i B.C.). **-λέγομαι**, *answer in conversation* or *disputation, διαλεγομένῳ οὐ προσδιελέγετο* Hdt.3.50, cf. 52, Pl.*Tht*.161b, Eus.Mynd.1; *ὁ προσδιαλεγόμενος* Pl.*Prt*.342e, *Sph*.218a, Arist.*SE*$165^{b}15$. **2.** simply, *hold converse with, θεοῖς π. εὐχαῖς* Pl.*Lg*.887e; *negotiate with, τοῖς ἀνθρώποις* *PSI*4.344.3, 7 (iii B.C.). **-ληπτέον**, *one must hold, consider in addition*, Hierocl. p.48 A., Antyll.ap.Orib.9.3.7. **-λύω**, *relax further*, Ruf.ap.Orib.6.38.8 (Pass.). **-μαρτῠρέω**, *testify in addition*, Is.6.10, Aeschin.2.135. **-μᾰχέω**, *contend with*, Gal.16.390 (dub.).

**προσδιᾰναγκάζω**, *assist in forcing*, Hp.*Art*.6.

**προσδιανέμω**, *distribute besides, λίτραν ἀργυρίου κατ' ἄνδρα* Plu.*Cat.Ma*.10:—Med., *divide among themselves besides*, D.19.168, Plu.*Demetr*.30.

**προσδιανίσταμαι**, Pass., *stand near*: metaph., *exercise vigilance over* one, Simp. *in Epict*. p.31 D.

**προσδια-νοέομαι**, *consider besides*, Pl.*Lg*.857e. **-νοητέον**, *one must consider besides*, ib.740b. **-πολεμέω**, *effect in war besides, τὰ λοιπά* D.C.42.53.

**προσδιᾰπορέω**, *raise questions besides*, Plu.2.42f, 48a, 669f.

**προσδιαπράσσω**, *achieve, obtain besides, ἄλλα σοι -πράξομαι παρὰ Κύρου* X.*Cyr*.8.3.47.

**προσδιαρθρόω**, *detail besides*, Anon. *in Tht*.56.36, Stob.2.7.6$^{a}$.

**προσδι-αρκέω**, *last longer*, Aristid.1.441 J. **-αρπάζω**, *plunder besides*, Plb.4.79.2, D.C.47.14.

**προσδιασᾰφ-έω**, *explain further, proceed to explain*, *Sammelb*.7267.8 (iii B.C.), *PAmh*.2.31.14 (ii B.C.), Plb.3.24.15, Hipparch.2.4.5, Str.10.1.2, Apollon. Cit.3, Plu.2.22b, A.D.*Synt*.184.23, al., S.E.*M*.7.114. **-ησις**, *εως, ἡ, additional explanation*, Alex.*Fig*.2.9.

**προσδια-σείω**, *excite, arouse besides*, Dam.*Pr*.29 (Pass.). **-σταλτέον**, *one must distinguish further*, Alex.Aphr. *de An*.167.6. ⊛ **-στέλλω**, *distend further*, Aret.*CA*1.4. **II.** *add a further condition*, in Med., Posidon.8 J. **2.** *distinguish besides*, Phld.*Rh*.1.104 S., A.D.*Synt*.285.17. **-στρέφω**, *pervert besides*, of persons, Plu.2.61b (Pass.), 697d; also *τὴν αἴσθησιν* ib.1083b. **-σύρω** [ῡ], *satirize* or *ridicule besides*, v.l. for *προδιασ-* (q.v.). **-τᾰράσσω**, *disturb besides*, D.C.36.10. **-τάσσω**, Att. **-ττω**, *ordain besides, τι περί τινος* J.*AJ*4.8.41; *add a clause* to a will, *POxy*.494.26 (ii A.D.):—Med., Ph.2.399, f.l. in Aen.Tact.16.16. **-τείνω**, *distend further, ὑστέραν* Sor.2.29:—Pass., Orib.*Fr*.64. **-τίθημι**, *affect besides*, A.D.*Synt*.290.22, al.:—Pass., *ὑπό τινος* ib.291.25. **-τρίβω** [ῑ], *have intercourse with, οἱ προσδιατρίβοντές σοι* Pl.*Tht*.168a. **2.** *ἐν Ἀλεξανδρείᾳ π. τινὰ χρόνον spend* some time *longer* in A., *PCair.Zen*.217.2 (iii B.C.), cf. Lib.*Or*.31.13. **3.** c. dat. rei, *occupy oneself with, συλλαβαῖς καὶ γράμμασιν* Posidipp.28.4; *spend further time on, τοῖς Ξενοφῶντος οἰκονομικοῖς* Phld.*Oec*.p.25 J.; *ἀκροάμασι* Plu.2.725f; *τῷ λόγῳ* Aristid.1.135 J. **4.** c. dat., *abide by, τοῖς κυήμασι* Plu.2.981f; *πυρὸς ὄγκῳ -τρίβοντος* ib.934b. **II.** abs., *stay yet longer*, Men.481.13. **-φέρομαι**, Pass., *differ besides*, Procl. *in Alc*. p.265 C. **-φθείρω**, *destroy besides, τινα* S.*Ph*.76, cf. Plu.*Cam*.22, Lib.*Ep*.26.1:—Pass., *perish besides*, Isoc.19.29. **II.** *corrupt, spoil besides, τοὺς λοιποὺς ταπιδοφάντας* *PCair.Zen*.484.16 (iii B.C.); *τὴν τροφήν* Sor.1.53; *τὸ χρηστὸν αἷμα* Gal.ap.Orib.51.36.2; *τὸ ὑπάρχον cause abortion of* the existing foetus *as well*, Hp.*Vict*.1.31. **III.** *pervert besides, τινὰ ἐλπίσι* Plu.*Cic*.17, cf. *Luc*.30:—Pass., J.*BJ*4.3.2. **-φορέω**, *act also as a diaphoretic*, Antyll.ap.Orib.9.24.7.

**προσδῐδάσκω**, *teach besides, σμικρὸν π. τινά* Pl.*Chrm*.173d; *π. ἀγαθὰ καὶ προσμανθάνειν* Men.553.4:—Pass., Ph.2.473 codd.

⊛ **προσδίδωμι**, *give* or *pay in addition, ἀεὶ πλείω π.* X.*An*.1.9.19, cf. Isoc.8.23, Men.926, *PMich.Zen*.28.12, 45.18 (iii B.C.), Lxx *Ge*.29.33, Luc.*Macr*.25, *Merc.Cond*.20:—Pass., *to be given* or *paid in addition, προσδίδοσθαι τὸ ἐπιβάλλον τοῦ μισθοῦ* *SIG*578.20 (Teos, ii B.C.), cf. 251 ii 12 (Delph., iv B.C.), *OGI*473.7 (Didyma, i A.D.); *τὸ προσδοθὲν ἐπὶ τὸν λύχνον* (sc. *ἔλαιον*) *Sammelb*.6796.169 (iii B.C.). **II.** *give a share of, οὐ χρή μ' ἀδελφοῖς τοῦδε προσδοῦναι ποτοῦ;* E.*Cyc*.531; *σοὶ μὲν προσεδίδου μικρὸν ὧν ἐλάμβανεν* Ar.*Eq*.1222; *κἀμοὶ πρόσδοτον τῆς ἡδονῆς* E.*Hel*.700; esp. *dole out*, of a sacrificing priest, *τὰ σπλάγχνα τοῦ μάντεως αὐτῷ προσδόντος* Plu.*Crass*.19; *οὐδεὶς προσδώσει* [*μοι*] *τῶν σπλάγχνων;* Ar.*Pax*1111, cf. 955 (lyr.); *τῆς ὑγιίης..οἱ πρόσδος give* him (the sacristan) *some* of the health-offering, Herod.4.94: hence, *dole* or *give* in charity, *βορᾶς μέρος* S.*Ph*.309; *προσαιτεῖν ὥσπερ τοὺς πτωχοὺς ἱκετεύοντα καὶ δεόμενον προσδοῦναι* X.*Mem*.1.2.29. **III.** *concede, permit of*, A.D.*Synt*.324.20. **IV.** *hand* a thing to a person, *δελτάριον τῷ Κάτωνι* Plu.*Cat.Mi*.24, *Brut*.5, cf. *Ant*.83.

**προσδι-εγγῠάω**, *give additional security for, τοῦ ὀφειλήματος* *UPZ*112 vi 8 (iii B.C.). **-ερευνάομαι**, *explore, examine thoroughly besides, ἤθη καὶ τρόπους* Ph.2.333. **-έρχομαι**, *pass through besides*, Hp.*Prorrh*.1.92. **II.** *describe, treat of besides*, Plu.*Them*.28, 2.362e. **-ευκρῑνέω**, *explain accurately as well*, A.D.*Synt*.283.22. **-ηγέομαι**, *narrate besides*, Thphr.*Char*.7.7, Luc.*Per*.43. **-ηθέω**, *filter through besides*, Arist.*Pr*.$933^{b}37$ (Pass.). **-ίστημι**, *separate, dilate, widen further, ἐπὶ μεῖζον πλάτος* Antyll.ap.Orib.6.10.14; *τραύματα* Sor.1.46.

**προσδῐκάζω**, *award as a judge, τινί τι* D.H.11.52. **II.** Med., *make a further claim in a suit, δυοῖν ταλάντοιν* D.37.32.

**προσδι-οικέω**, *settle* business *besides*, *PCair.Zen*.361.37 (iii B.C.). **2.** *manage besides*, D.C.51.18. **-ορθόω**, *correct, set right as well, τοὺς μαθητάς* Anon.*Vit.Pl*. p.6 W.:—Med., Aeschin.2.87. **II.** Med., *pay up, make good in addition, καταγώγιον* *PEleph*.14.10 (iii B.C.), cf. 20.60 (iii B.C.), *CIG*2693*e*.11 (Mylasa). **2.** *restore as well, τὰ προσδεόμενα ἐπισκευῆς* *OGI*90.34 (Rosetta, ii B.C.).

**προσδιορ-ίζω**, *define, specify besides*, D.20.130; *π. διὰ τίν' αἰτίαν..* Arist.*de An*.$407^{b}16$; *ἐν τίνι καὶ ποίῳ..* ib.$414^{a}23$, al.:—Med., Id.*EN* $1139^{b}32$, *Metaph*.$1005^{b}21$, al.:—Pass., *προσδιωρίσθω..τὰ εἰωθότα* ib.$1005^{b}27$, cf. Ph.1.514. **2.** Med., *maintain besides, μηδὲν ἀπαντήσειν* Plb.32.3.10, cf. Plu.*Nic*.7. **-ισμός**, *ὁ, further definition, determination*, or *specification*, Gal.6.826 (pl.), Olymp. *in Mete*.314.17, Dam.*Pr*.38, 237. **II.** *further condition* in a problem, Dioph.1.14, 5.10. **-ιστέον**, *one must define* or *distinguish besides*, Arist.*Top*.$151^{a}24$, *HA*$589^{b}13$, Thphr.*Fr*.97.4, Gal.10.207, Dam.*Pr*.102, 241.

**πρόσδιψος**, *ον, thirsty*, Orib.*Syn*.5.37.

**προσδοκ-άω**, Ion. **-έω** (which is sts. found as f.l., e.g. in Plb.23.7.3): fut. *-ήσω*: aor. *-εδόκησα*: pf. *προσδεδόκηκα* Memn.45.3:—*expect*, whether in hope or fear; mostly c. inf. fut., *expect* that one *will do* or that a thing *will be*, A.*Pr*.930, 988, Hdt.1.42, 7.156, 235, Pl.*Lg*.699b, etc.: c. inf. aor. and *ἄν*, that one *would do* or that a thing *would be*, Ar.*Ra*.556, Pl.*Cra*.438e, X.*Lac*.1.3, etc.: without *ἄν*, *Μενέλεων..προσδόκα μολεῖν* (= *τὸ μολεῖν αὐτόν*) *expect* his arrival, A.*Ag*.675. **2.** c. inf. pres., *think, suppose* that one *is doing* or that a thing *is*, E.*Alc*.1091, Pl.*Lg*.803e, X.*An*.6.1.16: c. inf. pf., *think* that a thing *has been..*, Pl.*Plt*.275a. **3.** c. acc. rei, *expect, look for* a thing, A.*Pr*.1026, S.*Ph*.784, Ar.*V*.56, Antipho 5.19, X.*Eq*.8.14, etc.; *π. τινά expect, wait for* a person, E.*Alc*.363, X.*HG*3.1.20, etc.; *σωτῆρας σφῶν π.* Pl.*Tht*.170b. **4.** abs., *ἰλλὸς γεγένημαι προσδοκῶν from expectation*, Ar.*Th*.846; *μηδεὶς..προσδοκησάτω ἄλλως* (sc. *τοῦτ' ἔσεσθαι*) Pl.*Ap*.17c; *πρᾶγμ' ἔστ' ἐπίπονον τὸ προσδοκᾶν* Men.*Kith.Fr*.7. **5.**

Pass., τὸ προσδοκώμενον, opp. τὰ ἄελπτα, E.*Fr.*550; τὸ π. ὑπὸ τῶν πολλῶν Pl.*Lg.*966e, etc.; ἐλπίδα τῶν δωρειῶν προσδοκᾶσθαι D.*Ep.*2.5; θᾶσσον ἢ προσεδοκήθη Plu.2.204d. **6.** Pass., also, ὁ Νικίου οἶκος προσεδοκᾶτο εἶναι.. ἑκατὸν ταλάντων *was supposed* to be worth.., Lys.19.47; προσεδοκᾶτο ἔχειν ib.48. **7.** *hesitate*, περί τινος J.*BJ*7.8.4. **-έω,** aor. -έδοξα, *to be thought besides*, c. inf., ἀπειρόκαλος προσέδοξεν εἶναι D.22.75, 24.183 (but better divisim πρὸς ἔδοξεν). **-ημα,** ατος, τό, *expectation*, Pl.*Phlb.*32c. **-ητέον,** *one must await* or *expect*, Herod. Med. ap. Orib.10.8.17, Sch.Pi.*N.*2.16. **II.** προσδοκητέος, α, ον, *to be expected*, πάντα.. προσδοκητέ' ἐστὶ καὶ ἀκοῦσαι καὶ ἰδεῖν Din.2.1. **-ητός,** ή, όν, *expected*, πάντα π. μοι A.*Pr.*935; τύχῃ οὐ π. Polystr.*Herc.*346 p.78V. ⊛**-ία,** ἡ, *looking for, expectation*, whether in hope or fear, but more commonly fear, **1.** c. gen., μέλλοντος κακοῦ, δεινῶν, Pl.*La.*198b, *Ti.*70c; π. τοῦ μέλλοντος Arist.*PA*669$^{a}$21; τὸν φόβον ὁρίζονται π. κακοῦ Id.*EN*1115$^{a}$9: in good sense, π. ἀγαθῶν ἐμβάλλειν X.*Cyr.*1.6.19 (pl.); τῆς ἀσφαλείας ἔχειν π. D.18.281; π. μεγάλην ἔχειν ὡς εὖ ἐροῦντος ἐμοῦ Pl.*Smp.*194a; τὰς τῶν ἔργων προσδοκίας ἀπαιτεῖν τινα, i.e. *the fulfilment of the expectations raised*, Aeschin.2.178. **2.** abs., τῶν ὑποκειμένων π. καὶ τῶν ἐλπίδων D.19.24; αἱ ἔσχαται π. D.S.20.78. **3.** folld. by a conjunction, προσδοκία οὐδεμία (sc. ἦν) μὴ ἐπιπλεύσειαν Th.2.93; π. οὔσης μή τι νεωτερίσωσιν Id.5.14; προσδοκίαν παρέχειν ὡς.. Id.7.12; π. ἐμποιεῖν ὡς.. Isoc.8.6. **4.** with Preps., πρὸς προσδοκίαν according to *expectation*, Th.6.63; κατὰ τὴν π. Pl.*Sph.*264b; opp. παρὰ προσδοκίαν, which is used of a kind of joke freq. in Com., e.g. ἔχειν ὑπὸ ποσσὶ—χίμεθλα (where πέδιλα was *expected*), Demetr.*Eloc.*152, Hermog.*Meth.*34, Tib.*Fig.*16: generally, τὸ παρὰ π. ἐξαπίναιον Phld.*Herc.*1251.19. **-ῖμος,** ον, *expected, looked for*, or *to be expected*, π. ὁ θάνατος Hp.*Prog.*9, cf. 24; τοῖσι παρεοῦσί τε καὶ π. κακοῖσι Hdt.8.20. **2.** freq. of persons, *expected*, στρατὸν π. εἶναι Κροίσῳ ἐπὶ τὴν χώρην Id.1.78; π. ἐς τὴν Κύπρον, ἐπὶ Μίλητον π., *expected to come* to Cyprus, against Miletus, Id.5.108, 6.6; κατὰ πόδας ἐμεῦ ἐλαύνων π. ἐστι Id.9.89; τοῦ βαρβάρου π. ὄντος Th.1.14; ἐκ Πελοποννήσου ἄλλη στρατιὰ π. αὐτοῖς Id.7.15, cf. D.6.15; π. ἥξειν D.S.18.64. Adv. -μως *Gloss.*

**προσδοξάζω,** *add to opinion*, Pl.*Tht.*209d. **2.** *import into judgement* an element *additional to* sense-impression, Epicur.*Ep.*1 pp.12, 19 U. (Pass.), *Nat.*10 G. **3.** *imagine further* or *besides*, προσεδοξάσθη περὶ τῆς θαλάττης ταύτης πολλὰ ψευδῆ Str.11.7.4; τὸ -δοξαζόμενον τοῖς ὀνόμασι Gal.10.84.

**προσδόρπιος,** v. ποτιδόρπιος.

**προσ-δόσιμον,** τό, *supplementary order*, *BGU*563 i 9 (ii A.D.). **-δοσις,** εως, ἡ, *additional donation*, *PSI*9.904.2 (i A.D.), Mitteis *Chr.*199.16 (iii A.D.). **2.** f.l. for παράδοσις in Hierocl.p.63 A.

**προσδουλεύω,** *to be a slave besides*, *Gloss.*

**προσδοχή,** ἡ, *reception*, Epicur.*Ep.*2 p.38 U. **2.** *obligation, acceptance, debt*, *POxy.*1223.25 (iv A.D., pl.); dub. sens. in *PTeb.*209 (i B.C.).

**προσδρομή,** ἡ, *charge*, as a military evolution, *IG*9(2).531.16 (Larissa). **2.** *sudden attack*, Ptol.*Tetr.*116: pl., Plu.2.344a.

**προσδύνω,** *to be near setting*, *Cat.Cod.Astr.*8(1).139 (s. v. l.).

**προσδυσκολαίνω,** *to be refractory towards* one, Plu.2.818a.

**προσδυσχεραίνω,** *to be annoyed with*, τοῖς οἰκέταις J.*AJ*6.12.2.

**προσδωρέομαι,** *give besides*, D.S.17.38.

**προσεάω,** *suffer to go further*, μὴ -εῶντος ἡμᾶς τοῦ ἀνέμου *Act.Ap.*27.7. **2.** *permit as well*, *PLond.*5.1790.7 (v/vi A.D.).

**προ-σεβάζομαι,** *reverence*, Ἥραν *Inscr.Magn.*228.10 (ii A.D.).

**προσεγγελάω,** *laugh at*, v.l. for προσγελάω in Aesop.330 (ii p.449 Chambry).

**προσεγγίζω,** *bring near*, Luc.*Am.*53. **II.** intr., *approach*, *AP*7.422 (Leon.), Philum.*Ven.*12.1; τοῖς τόποις D.S.3.16; τοῖς τῆς ἀκμῆς ἰδιώμασι Herod.Med.ap.Orib.5.30.9; τινος Sch.E.*Hec.*585: abs., Plb.38.7.4, Ezek.*Exag.*96:—Med., Sch.E.*Hec.*439; πρός c. acc., *Cat.Cod.Astr.*1.157.

**προσεγγράφω** [ᾰ], *carve on*, or *inscribe, besides*, Hdt.2.102, *TAM*2.247.8 (Paralia, ii A.D.); *add* a name, [ἐν συνθήκαις] Hyp.*Ath.*8. **2.** *add a saving* or *limiting clause*, Aeschin.3.203.

**προσεγγυάομαι,** Med., *become surety besides*, π. τινὰ ὀφλήματος *become* his *surety also for* the sum owed, D.31.11, cf. Aristid.2.204 J.

**προσεγείρω,** *lift up*, στέρνον Philostr.*Gym.*35. **II.** *stimulate, excite*, αὐλῷ τινα ib.55, cf. *VS*2.9.2; cf. προσεγρήγορα.

**προσεγκᾰλέω,** *accuse besides*, ὅτι.. D.S.14.17; ὡς.. D.C.41.6: c. dat. et part., Plu.2.401b: abs., Alex.146.8, D.H.7.46, Gal.*UP*5.4: prov., οἱ φῶρες -καλοῦσι 'Satan rebuking sin', Lib.*Ep.*1134.1.

**προσέγκειμαι,** strengthd. for ἔγκειμαι, Hsch.

**προσεγκελεύομαι,** Med., *exhort besides*, τινι Plu.*Alex.*10. **II.** σαλπιγκταὶ μέλος π. *play a rousing* tune, Id.*Aem.*33.

**προσεγκολάπτω,** *engrave in addition*, *OGI*56.23 (Canopus, iii B.C., Pass.).

**προσεγρήγορα,** intr. pf. of προσεγείρω, *keep awake also*, Arist.*Pr.*916$^{b}$3 (cj. for προ-, q. v.).

**προσεγχέω,** *pour in besides*, Arist.*GA*753$^{a}$20, Diph.17.10; εἰς τὰ ὦτα ἔλαιον Arist.*Pr.*961$^{a}$25; προσεγχέας ἄκρατον Plu.2.149b:—Med., *cause to be poured in*, Arist.*Pr.*961$^{a}$18:—Pass., Id.*GA*723$^{a}$19, Aret.*CA*2.5.

**προσεγχρίμπτω,** *press hard on*, τῇ πτέρνῃ Hp.*Art.*60.

**προσεγχρίω** [ῑ], *besmear besides* or *once more*, τινα *AP*11.117 (Strat.), cf. Ph.2.454.

**προσεγχώννῡμι,** *heap up in besides*, γῆν *Gp.*11.7.2.

**προσεδαφίζω,** ὄφεων πλεκτάναισι περίδρομον κύτος προσηδάφισται the shield is *made fast* or *solid* all round with wreathed snakes, A.*Th.*496.

**προσεδρ-εία,** or **-εδρία** (required by metre in E.*Or.*93 and found in Pap. of Phld. (v. infr.), but -εία *PTeb.* (v. infr.)), ἡ, *sitting by* or *near*: esp., **1.** *besieging, blockade*, Th.1.126, D.C.36.51. **2.** *close attention to* a thing, *assiduity*, *PTeb.*24.39 (ii B.C.), Phld.*Rh.*1.232 S., Longin.ap.Porph.*Plot.*19, Iamb.*Protr.*6; esp. *sitting by a sick-bed*, E.*Or.*93, 304; αἱ τῶν τέκνων π. *attentions* paid by them, Hierocl. p.58 A. **-ευτικός,** ή, όν, *importunate*: Adv. -κῶς Hsch. s.v. λιπαρῶς. ⊛**-εύω,** *sit near, wait* or *watch beside*, πυρᾷ E.*Or.*403; π. τινί *to be always at* his *side, keep watch on* him, D.34.26; τοῖς πράγμασι, τοῖς καιροῖς, Id.1.18, Plb.38.13.9; [τοῖς ἐφήβοις] προσκαρτερῶν ἐπιμελῶς καὶ -εύων, of a κοσμητής, *IG*2$^{2}$.1028.84; π. τῷ θεῷ *wait upon* God, J.*AJ*3.4.1; *attend to*, τοῖς τῆς Ἀσίας πράγμασιν *AJA*18.327 (Sardis, i B.C.), cf. *CIG*2715.18 (Stratonicea); τῇ θεραπείᾳ τοῦ θεοῦ J.*Ap.*1.7; τοῖς ὑπομνήμασι Plb.12.26$^{d}$.5, cf. Phld.*Rh.*2.61 S., al.: abs., Arist.*HA*568$^{b}$15, Plb.11.4.2; *watch* the rise of the Nile, *Sammelb.*6597 (iii A.D.), al.; *persist in*, ταῖς φιλοπονίαις Arist.*Pol.*1338$^{b}$25; τῷ πόθῳ Alex.234; *apply oneself*, λίαν Arist.*Pol.*1337$^{b}$16; πρὸς ἴδιον to one's own affairs, ib.1263$^{a}$29; εἰς τὰ μαθήματα *PSI*1.94.8 (ii A.D.). **2.** *besiege*, ταῖς Συρακούσαις Plb.8.7.11. **3.** *wait*, προσέδρευσα ἐφ' ἡμέρας δύο ἐκδεχόμενός σε *BGU*892.5 (ii A.D.); esp. *attend* at a law-court, παρεῖναι καὶ π. τῷ βήματι *PAmh.*2.81.9 (iii A.D.); *attend regularly, serve*, as clerk of the court, ib.82.3 (iii/iv A.D.), *POxy.*59.10 (iii A.D.). **4.** *to be in service, serve*, πρὸς τῷ διδασκαλείῳ (as a menial), D.18.258; of an apprentice, π. τῷ διδασκάλῳ *POxy.*725.10 (ii A.D.); of a servant, παραμένειν.. καὶ π. *PStrassb.*40.31 (vi A.D.). **-ία,** v. προσεδρεία. **-ικῶς,** *sedulo*, *Gloss.* **-ος,** ον, (ἕδρα) *sitting near*, cj. for πρόεδρος in D.C.57.7 (sed leg. πάρεδρος): metaph., ἐκ προσέδρου λιγνύος S.*Tr.*794. **II.** *assiduous*, Hsch.

**προσεθ-ίζω,** *accustom* or *inure* one *to* a thing, νέους καρτερίαν X.*Ap.*25: c. acc. et inf., Id.*Cyr.*8.1.36, *Eq.Mag.*1.17, Gal.16.142:—Pass., *accustom oneself to* a thing, ἑνὶ ἱματίῳ δι' ἔτους X.*Lac.*2.4, cf. Ael.*Tact.*35.6: c. inf., Luc.*Dem.Enc.*17. **-ισμός,** ὁ, *habituation*, *Gloss.* **-ιστέον,** *one must accustom*, Arr.*Tact.*27.3, Dam.*Pr.*74.

**προσειδ-έναι,** v. πρόσοιδα. **-ής,** ές, (εἶδομαι, cf. sq. II) *similar*, χρυσῷ φυὴν εἰς ὦπα π. Nic.*Fr.*74.3. **-ον,** inf. προσιδεῖν, part. προσιδών, aor. 2 without pres. in use, προσοράω being used instead:—*look at* or *upon*, Hes.*Fr.*93.2, Hdt.1.129, A.*Pr.*553 (lyr.), S.*OT*1372, etc.; π. φάος ἀλίω Sapph.69:—Med. προσιδέσθαι, first in Pi.*P.*1.26, A. *Pers.*48 (anap.), 694 (lyr.) (found as v. l. in Od.13.155, Hes.*Sc.*386). **II.** Pass. προσείδομαι, *to be like*, A.*Ch.*178.

**προσεικάζω,** aor. -ήκασα, *make like, assimilate*, τινί τι Pl.*Ti.*40a, X.*Mem.*3.10.8:—Pass., *to be like, resemble*, τινι Aeschin.3.247. **II.** *liken, compare*, τινί τι A.*Th.*431, *Ch.*12, E.*El.*559, Pl.*R.*473c, J.*BJ*7.8.3; κακῷ δέ τῳ προσεικάζω τάδε *I think* this *looks like* mischief, A.*Ag.*1131. **2.** οὐκ ἔχω προσεικάσαι.. I am not able *to guess by comparison*, ib.163 (lyr.); *conjecture in addition*, Str.3.5.8.

**προσείκελος,** η, ον, *somewhat like*, c. dat., Hdt.2.12, 3.110; γλυκύτητα τοῦ φοίνικος τῷ καρπῷ π. in sweetness, Id.4.177.

**προσεικέναι,** v. προσέοικα.

**προσεικής,** ές, = προσείκελος, Nic.*Th.*292. **II.** = *blandus*, *Gloss.*

**προσειλ-έω,** Ep. προτιειλέω, *press* or *force towards*, αἰεί μιν ἐπὶ νῆας.. προτιειλεῖν Il.10.347; ἃ μὴ προσείλει χεῖρα E.*Hel.*445:—Pass., *to be confined, cooped up*, τοῖς κατὰ μέρος S.E.*M.*9.3, etc. **-ημα,** ατος, τό, *wrapping*, κεφαλῆς, i.e. *turban*, Creon 1.

**προσείλος,** ον, (εἵλη) *towards the sun, sunny, warm*, δόμοι A.*Pr.*451; αὐλή Eup.378; τόποι εὐσκεπεῖς καὶ π. Thphr.*CP*1.13.11, al., cf. Plu.2.649c; τὰ π. Philostr.*VA*2.18; ἡλιούσθων πρόσειλοι Id.*Gym.*58 (πρόσηλος is freq. as f.l.).

⊛**πρόσειμι** (εἰμί *sum*), *to be added to*, τινι Hdt.2.99, 7.173, etc.; ἐὰν.. θερμότης τῷ δίψει προσῇ Pl.*R.*437e; *to be attached to, belong to*, *IG*1$^{2}$.290; ἀνδρὶ χρεὼν μνήμην προσεῖναι S.*Aj.*521; δέος αἰσχύνη θ' ὁμοῦ, δύσνοια ἢ λύπη π. τινί, ib.1079, *El.*654; οὐχ ἅπαντα τῷ γήρᾳ κακὰ π. E.*Ph.*529, cf. Isoc.12.115; δυσβουλία τῇ πόλει π. Ar.*Nu.*588; τῇ βίᾳ π. ἕπεσθαι καὶ κίνδυνοι X.*Mem.*1.2.10; καὶ τὰ προσόντα καὶ τὰ μὴ περὶ ἑκάστου λέγοντες proclaiming each man's virtues, whether he had them or not, Pl.*Mx.*234c; τὰ προσόνθ' ἑαυτῷ one's own *attributes*, D.18.276, cf. *Prooem.*46: c. inf., πρόσεστι γυναιξὶ.. τίκτειν Pl.*Tht.*150a. **2.** abs., *to be present, at hand as well*, τὰ δ' αὖτε χέρσῳ.. προσῆν πλέον στύγος A.*Ag.*558; ὡς ἂν ἀγνοία προσῇ S.*Ph.*129; γνώμη γὰρ εἴ τις κἀπ' ἐμοῦ.. π. Id.*Ant.*720; τοῦ λόγου δ' οὐ χρὴ φθόνον π. Id.*Tr.*251; τύχη μόνον προσείη Ar.*Av.*1315 (lyr.); π. ἡ ὕβρις καὶ ἔθ' ἡ.. αἰσχύνη D.1.27; οὐδ' ὁτιοῦν ἄλλο προσῆν *there was* nothing *else* in the world, Id.21.176; ταῦτα προσέσται this *too will be* ours, X.*HG*3.1.28; τὰς τρισχιλίας καὶ τὸ προσόν and the *surplus*, D.36.15. **3.** *to be adjacent*, εἰ πὸς τᾷ οἰκίᾳ μὴ πόεστι (i.e. πόεστι = πρόσεστι) κᾶπος *SIG*306.12 (Tegea, iv B.C.); τῆς προσούσης αὐλῆς *PStrassb.*87.12 (ii B.C.).

⊛**πρόσειμι** (εἶμι *ibo*), inf. -ιέναι, used in Att. as fut. of προσέρχομαι, and προσῄειν as impf.:—*go to* or *towards, approach*, abs. in Hom. and Hes. in dat. and acc. of part., χάρη δ' ἄρα οἱ προσιόντι Il.5.682; ὡς εἶδον ζωὸν.. προσιόντα 7.308; πρόσιθι E.*Or.*149 (lyr.); σχολαίτερον προσιόντας Th.4.47 codd.; *approach* a person, Id.1.130, cf. And.1.122; of an enemy, βραδέως προσῇσαν X.*An.*1.8.11, etc.; of an adversary at law, πρόσειειν ἐκδικάσων *BGU*361 iii 11 (ii A.D.), cf. *POxy.*1101.15 (iv A.D.): c. dat. pers., *approach* one, Hdt.1.62, etc.; *apply to* a person for help, *PStrassb.*57.6 (ii A.D.), etc.; π. Σωκράτει *visit* him as teacher, X.*Mem.*1.2.47; π. γυναικί *go in to* a woman, Id.*Smp.*4.38 (so abs., Ocell.4.1): c. acc. loci, δῶμα, δόμους, A.*Eu.*242, E.*Cyc.*40: with Preps. governing acc., εἰς.. S.*El.*437, X.*HG*7.5.15, etc.; πρὸς τὰς πύλας, πρὸς τὴν Λάχεσιν, Hdt.8.52, Pl.*R.*620d, etc. 2. in hostile sense, *attack*, καὶ φιλέοντα φιλεῖν καὶ τῷ προσιόντι προσεῖναι Hes.*Op.*353 (cf. Sch.Od.1.406, Apollon.*Lex.* s.v. εἶναι), cf. X.*Cyr.*2.4.12; τῇ πόλει Id.*An.*7.6.24 (dub.); πρὸς τοὺς βαρβάρους Hdt.9.100; ἐπὶ τὸ στράτευμα X.*Cyr.*7.1.24. 3. *come over to the side of*, in war, ἧσσόν τις ἐμοὶ πρόσεισι Th.4.85, cf. 1.39. 4. *come forward* to speak, π. τῷ δήμῳ X.*Mem.*3.7.1; π. τῇ βουλῇ, τοῖς ἐφόροις, *come before*.., D.19.17, Plb.4.34.5; π. πρὸς βουλὴν ἢ δῆμον X.*Ath.*3.3; πρὸς τὰς ἀρχάς Th.1.90; πρὸς τὰ κοινά Aeschin.1.165; πρὸς τὴν πολιτείαν π. Id.3.217 (but π. πολιτείᾳ Plu.2.1033f): abs., *come forward to speak*, περὶ τῶν γεγενημένων And 1.111. 5. of things, *to be added*, σάρκες ἐκ τῆς τροφῆς π. ταῖς σαρξί Arist.*GA*723ᵃ11, cf. *GC*322ᵃ26, al.; τῷ δ' ἐναντίῳ κύτει ἐλπὶς προσῄει χειρὸς οὐ πληρουμένῳ A.*Ag.*817. II. of Time, *come on, be at hand*, ἐπεὰν προσίῃ (v.l. προσῇ) ἡ ὥρη κυΐσκεσθαι τὰς ἵππους Hdt.4.30, cf. 2.41; ἑσπέρα προσῄει X.*Cyr.*3.2.25; προσιόντος τοῦ θερμοῦ *on the approach* of heat, Pl.*Phd.*103d; π. [τῶν ἀνέμων] X.*Mem.*4.3.14. III. *come in*, of revenue, φόροι, ἑπτακόσια τάλαντα π., Hdt.3.89,91, cf. Th.2.13, X.*Vect.*4.1; τῶν τε ὄντων χρημάτων καὶ τῶν προσιόντων τοῖς θεοῖς *IG*1².91.26; τὸν φόρον ἡμῖν ἀπὸ τῶν πόλεων.. προσιόντα Ar.*V.*657; τὰ προσιόντα χρήματα *the public revenue*, Id.*Ec.*712, Lys.30.19; τὰ προσιόντα alone, Ar.*V.*664; τὰ π. τῇ πόλει Lys.21.13.

**προσεῖπον**, used as aor. 2 of προσαγορεύω and προσφωνέω; Ep. **προσέειπον**, always augmented and uncontr. in Hom. and Hes.; Ep. also **ποτιείποι**, Il.22.329 (v.l. προτι-); Att. also **προσεῖπα**, ας, etc., E.*Med.*895, *Cyc.*101, X.*Hier.*8.3:—*speak to* one, *address, accost*, Κάλχαντα.. κάκ' ὀσσόμενος προσέειπεν Il.1.105, cf. Od.4.375, Pi.*I.*1.56, etc.; ἀλλήλας προσέειπον Hes.*Th.*749; π. θεούς A.*Ag.*811, al.; βασιλεῦ, πῶς σε προσείπω; ib.785 (anap.); δός μοι π. αὐτόν S.*Aj.*538, cf. 1221 (lyr.); τινὰς π. ὑστάτοις προσφθέγμασιν E.*Heracl.*573; π. τινὰ φιλικῶς X.*Hier.*8.3; π. σε κατά σε *address* you after your own manner, Pl.*Grg* 467b: c. dupl. acc., τὸν.. πρὸς μῦθον ἔειπεν *addressed* a speech to him, Il.5.632, etc.; τί προσείπω σ' ἔπος; Ar.*Pax* 520: abs., καλὸς μὲν ἰδεῖν, τερπνὸς δὲ προσειπεῖν *IG*1².923. 2. *address as* so and so, τινὰ ὡς ἀλλότριον Pl.*R.*463c; τινὰ αὐτοκράτορα π. *salute* him as.., Plu.*Galb.*5, etc.; χαίρειν τινὰ π. *bid* him greeting, E.*Cyc.*101. 3. *call* so and so, *name*, τί νιν προσείπω; A.*Ch.*983(997); τοῦτο (sc. δύστηνε) γάρ σ' ἔχω μόνον προσειπεῖν S.*OT*1072, etc.; τί ἂν εἰπών σέ τις ὀρθῶς προσείποι; D.18.22; π. αὐτὰς ὀνόματι θυγατέρας Id.59.19; χρῶμα π. τι *apply the name of* colour to an object, Pl.*Tht.*182d; π. οὐδὲν ἄλλο *call* each nothing else, ib.201e; πολλὰς ἐπιστήμας ἑνὶ λόγῳ προσειπεῖν ib.148d, cf. *R.*580d, etc. II. *say* something *further, add*, c. acc. et inf., Id.*Sph.*250b.

**προσείρομαι**, Med., in fut. -ερήσομαι, *ask besides*, Hsch.

**προσείρω**, *annex, attach*, Phot., Suid.

**προσεισ-άγω** [ᾰ], *bring in besides*, τινὰ ἑαυτῷ τύραννον J.*BJ*5.1.3 (v.l.), cf. D.L.9.88:—Med., Arg.D.46:—Pass., Gal.9.432. **-δέχομαι**, *receive in addition*, -δεδέχθαι εἰς τὴν μίσθωσιν ἀρτάβας ν' *PGoodsp. Cair.*7.13 (ii B.C.). **-έρχομαι**, *come in as well*, *PCair.Zen.*730.1 (iii B.C.), Simp. *in Cat.*156.29. ❋ **-ευπορέω**, *aid in procuring*, ἀργυρίου Is.*Fr.*66. **-κρίνω** [ῑ], *introduce in addition into* a vessel, πολὺ προσεισκρινεῖ πνεῦμα Hero *Spir.*1 *Prooem.*:—Pass., ibid. **-οδιασμός**, ὁ, *extra contribution*, ποιεῖσθαι -ασμοὺς ἐκ τῶν ἰδίων *IGRom.*3.739 ii 61 (Lycia, ii A.D.). **-πράσσω**, *exact besides*, *OGI*335.134 (Pergam., ii B.C.): c. dupl. acc., δέκα [τάλαντά] τινα Plu.*Alc.*8, cf. *PCair. Zen.*91.5 (iii B.C.):—Pass., ib.283.3 (iii B.C.), *PRev.Laws* 52.10 (iii B.C.). **-φέρω**, *contribute besides*, Herm.Hist.2; τὰς οὐσίας ὅλας Ph.2.596; ἄλλα τοῖς λόγοις Longin.15.9:—Med. in same sense, *IG*12(3).325.49 (Thera, ii A.D.). II. *propose in addition for election*, ib.5(1).1390.126 (Andania, i B.C., ποτ-). **-φορά**, ἡ, *addition to a story*, J.*AJ*17.7.1.

**προσείω**, *hold out and shake*, π. χεῖρα *shake* it *threateningly*, E.*HF* 1218; προσείειν ἀνασείειν τε [τὸν πλόκαμον] *wave* it up and down, Id.*Ba.*930; π. γυμνὰ τὰ ξίφη Ael.*VH*12.23; θαλλὸν π. *wave* a bough *before* cattle, so as to lead them on, Pl.*Phdr.*230d; π. θήρατρα τοῖς ὄρνισι Ael.*NA*1.29; and metaph., π. Σειρῆνας, αὐλητρίδας, *hold* them *out as a bait*, ib.17.22, *Ep.*16; π. φόβον *hold* a thing *out* as a bugbear, Th.6.86, cf. Ael.*Fr.*22.

**προσεκ-βάλλω**, *cast out besides*, D.21.122, Plu.*CG*14. II. *draw out further, produce*, [γραμμήν] Str.2.1.37:—Pass., Cleom.2.1, Gal.*UP*10.12. 2. = ἐκβάλλω IX. 2, Heph.Astr. in *Cat.Cod.Astr.*1.93. **-βοάω**, *call out at the same time*, D.C.44.20, Paul.Aeg.3.15. **-δεκτέον**, (as if from *προσεκδέχομαι) *one must understand* a thing in a certain sense *besides*, Sch.A.R.3.601. **-δέρω**, *flay besides*, Posidipp.26.14 (Dind. πρὸς ἐκδαρείς). **-διδάσκω**, strengthd. for προσδιδάσκω, D.C.*Fr.*6.6, v.l. in J.*AJ*17.6.1. **-δίδωμι**, *give out by contract as well*, *SIG*245 i 21, 67 (Delph., iv B.C., ποτ-); *let on lease as well*, *GDI*5661.35 (Chios, iv B.C.). **-θλίβω** [ῑ], *squeeze out besides*, Gal.12.238. **-θρώσκω**, *eject semen at*, πέτρᾳ Ps.-Plu.*Fluv.*23.4. **-κᾰθαίρω**, fut. -καθαρῶ, *clear up further*, Epicur.*Nat.*11.13. **-καίω**, *set fire to besides*, D.C.62.17: metaph., *inflame* or *provoke besides*, Phld.*Lib.*p.21 O.; [τινὰς] περὶ τοὺς ἔρωτας Plu.2.60e; φιλοτιμίαν Id.*Cleom.*2; τὰς ὑπολήψεις Porph.*Abst.*2.41:—Pass., S.E.*M.*11.179; ταῖς κακοπραγίαις J.*BJ*3.9.6. **-κᾰλύπτω**, *uncover, disclose besides*, Str.11.6.4. **-κειμαι**, *to be announced, set forth in addition*, dub.l. in *PLille* 4.15 (iii B.C.). **-κόπτω**, *extirpate besides*, καὶ τὰ ἄλλα [δένδρα], καὶ τὸν ἕτερον [ὀφθαλμόν], Teles p.59 H.; τὸν δράκοντα f.l. for προεκκ- in Lib.*Ep.*1385.5. **-λεαίνω**, *triturate as well*, Dsc.2.171, Archig.(?) ap.Gal.12.793. **-λέγω**, *pull out besides*, καὶ τοὺς ἄλλους [ὀδόντας] Teles p.60 H.; τόκους καὶ ἐπιτοκίας Ph.2.596:—Med., *select besides*, οὐραγούς Plb.6.24.2. **-λογίζομαι**, *reckon on besides*, D.C.58.7. **-λοιδορέω**, *revile besides*, J.*AJ*13.13.5. **-λύω**, *relax* or *weaken the more*, Plu.2.143d; f.l. for προσελκύσαντα in J.*AJ* 15.7.1. **-μαίνομαι**, Pass., *become demented besides*, π. τὴν γνώμην Aret.*CA*2.11. **-πέμπω**, *send away besides*, X.*Cyr.*5.3.24. ❋ **-πίπτω**, *fall out besides*, of sinews (as well as flesh) mortifying, τῶν νεύρων -πεσουμένων Hp.*Fract.*27: metaph., πλάσμα εἰς πᾶν -πῖπτον τὸ ἀδύνατον Longin.15.8. **-πλᾰτύνω**, *smooth out further*, Sor.1.103. **-πληρόω**, *fill up* an aperture, ib.68. 2. *make up to the full amount*, τὰς τιμήσεις ( = Lat. *explere census*) *Mon.Anc.Gr.* 19.10. **-πνέω**, *evaporate*, Zos.Alch.p.173 B. **-πονέω**, *work out, finish besides*, Plu.*Nic.*17. **-πορίζω**, *supply besides*, χρηστόν τι Gal.10.433. **-ποτέον**, (as if from *προσεκπίνω) *one must swallow as well*, metaph., τὸ δυσχερές Plu.2.1111c. **-πρῐάμαι**, aor. inf. -πρίασθαι, *purchase besides*, [χώραν] D.C.49.14. **-πῡρόω**, *set on fire besides*, metaph., ἐραστήν Luc.*Tox.*15. **-σπάω**, *draw out besides*, Arist.*Pr.*877ᵃ38 (Pass.). **-τᾰπεινόω**, *humble* or *degrade besides*, Plu.2.814e. **-τᾰράσσω**, *stir up still more*, ib.463f, D.C.61.8. **-τείνω**, *extend further*, Gal.2.367 (Pass.), 18(2).565.

**προσεκτέον**, (προσέχω) *one must apply*, τὸν νοῦν ἡμῖν αὐτοῖς Pl.*Men.*96d, cf. Isoc.*Ep.*2.17: abs., *one must attend*, τινι to a thing, Pl.*Demod.*384e; λόγοις Aeschin.1.119, cf. Plb.1.64.2; Σοφοκλεῖ Plu.*Phoc.*1; *one must notice*, πῶς.. Iamb. *in Nic.*p.69 P. 2. *one must agree with*, τινι Str.7.3.6, cf. Sor.1.56. II. **προσεκτέος**, α, ον, *to be taken into consideration*, π. οἱ τρόποι Vett.Val.332.22.

**προσεκτίθημι**, *exhibit* or *post up publicly in addition*, *Sammelb.*7337.35 (Egypt, i B.C., Pass.):—Med., *set forth besides*, τι Nicom.*Harm.*11, Iamb. *in Nic.*p.38 P.

❋ **προσεκτικός**, ή, όν, (προσέχω) *attentive*, X.*Mem.*3.5.5 (Comp.); ἀκροατής Arist.*Rh.*1415ᵃ36, Ps.-Plu. *Vit.Hom.*163 (Comp.). Adv. -κῶς *assiduously, attentively*, Phld.*Rh.*1.250 S., Gal.4.445: Comp. -ώτερον *more cautiously*, Sor.1.55. II. *capable of holding the attention* of a listener, λόγος Hermog.*Inv.*3.2.

**προσεκ-τίλλω**, *pluck out besides*, τὰ πτερά Ar.*Av.*286. **-τίνω** [ῑ], fut. -τείσω Plu.*Arat.*54:—*pay in addition*, δίκην Pl.*Lg.*934a; ζημίαν Plu.*Phoc.*27; χίλια τάλαντα Id.*Arat.* l.c.; τά τε βλάβη καὶ δαπανήματα *BGU*1113.21 (i B.C.); τόκους Chor.p.246 B. **-τρᾰχηλίζω**, *throw headlong besides*, Arr.*Epict.*3.7.16:—Pass., εἰς πάθος S.E.*M.*11.179. **-τυφλόω**, *blind outright besides*, τινα Plu.2.176f. **-φέρω**, *pay besides*, προσεξενεγκεῖν χίλια τάλαντα Plb.3.27.8. II. Pass., *to be carried too far*, of runners, Chrysipp.*Stoic.*3.127. **-φοβέω**, *terrify besides*, D.C.77.15. **-φυτεύω**, *plant as well*, *BCH*44.79 d 4 (Lagina). **-χλευάζω**, *ridicule besides*, τινα D.24.15.

**προσελ-ᾰσις**, εως, ἡ, *driving up*, τῶν ὄνων Plu.2.866c. II. *assault*, τῶν κοντοφόρων D.C.40.22. **-αύνω**, Att. fut. -ελῶ X.*Cyr.*6.2.18: aor. 1 -ήλᾰσα Th.4.72: Coan non-thematic 3 pl. pres. ind. ποτέλαντι dub. in *SIG*1025.6 (iv/iii B.C.):—*drive* or *chase to* a place, τινὰς πρὸς τὴν Νίσαιαν Th. l.c.; βοῦν *SIG* l.c.; π. τὸν ἵππον Plu.2.755b; π. τινὰ φιλοσοφίᾳ D.L.7.5:—Pass., *to be driven* or *fixed to*, πρὸς τοὔδαφος Plu.*Crass.*25. II. mostly intr., 1. (sc. ἵππον) *ride towards, ride up*, πρὸς τὸ στρατόπεδον Hdt.7.208, cf. 9.20, X.*Cyr.*4.2.17; ἀλλήλοις ib.1.4.23; also π. ἵππῳ Hdt.9.44, X.*HG*4.5.7, cf. *Cyr.*1.4.17; π. ἐπὶ καμήλων ib.6.2.18; οἱ προσελαύνοντες, opp. οἱ προσθέοντες (the infantry), Id.*An.*6.3.7. 2. (sc. στρατόν) *march up*, οὔπω ἧκεν ἀλλ' ἔτι προσήλαυνε ib.1.5.12, etc. 3. of time, *approach*, ἐπὶ τὸν ἀεὶ ἑξῆς καὶ -οντα χρόνον *PMasp.*158.27 (vi A.D.), cf. *PFlor.*294.102 (vi A.D.), etc.

**προσελαφρύνω**, *lighten further*, τῷ ἁλτῆρι τὸν πηδῶντα Philostr.*Gym.*55.

❋ **προσέλευσ-ις**, εως, ἡ, *approach*, Antyll.ap.Orib.6.33.4, *Gp.*9.4.4, Procl. *in Prm.*p.655 S., Phlp. *in GA*178.31; ἡ π. τοῦ περιβόλου *approach, access to*.., Judeich *Altertümer von Hierapolis* No. 336.16. **-τέον**, *one must go in for*, γυμνασίοις Ath.Med.ap.Orib.*inc.*23.5.

**προσελέω**, v. προυσελέω.

**προσεληναῖος**, Dor. -σελᾱναῖος, α, ον, = προσέληνος, *Lyr.Adesp.*84.8. **-ίδες**· αἱ Ἀρκαδικαὶ νύμφαι, Hsch. **-ος**, ον, (σελήνη) *before the moon, older than the moon*, a name given to the Arcadians, as priding themselves on their antiquity, Arist.*Fr.*591, Hippys 2, Plu.2.282a, Sch.A.R.4.264; expld. by other Gramm. as = ὑβριστικός (cf. προυσελέω), cf. *EM*690.11: ὁ **προυσέληνος**, = ὁ Ἀρκάς, Call.*Iamb.*1.121. II. π. ἡμέραι the days *before the new moon appears*, *Gp.*1.6.2.

**προσέλκω**, *draw towards, draw on*, τινα prob. l. in Pi.*O.*6.83; τὰ τόξα *Com.Adesp.*139; πρός τινας.. δόξας αὐτῶν τὰ φαινόμενα π. *wrest* the facts.., Arist.*Cael.*293ᵃ27:—Med., *draw towards oneself, attract*, εἰς φιλότητα Thgn.372; αἱ χεῖρες τὸ τόξον ἀπωθοῦνταί τε καὶ π. Pl.*R.*439b: aor. προσειλκυσάμην *take into one's arms, embrace*, E.*Hipp.*1432, *IA*1451, Ar.*Ec.*910 (lyr.).

**προσελλείπω**, *to be still wanting*, π. τῷ σταδίῳ στάδιον *fail* by the whole length of the course, of a very slow runner, *AP*11.85 (Lucill.); τὰ προσελλείποντα τῶν χρημάτων the sums *still wanting*, D.S.20.101, cf. *IG*4.4.9 (Aegina).

**προσελπίζω**, *hope besides*, Anon.ap.Suid. s.v. σπάδων, Petr.Patr. p.433 D.

**προσελυτρόω,** *sheathe besides,* τὴν γλῶσσαν Ath.1.6c.

**προσελώδης,** ες, *rather marshy,* τόποι Arist.*Pr.*935ª22.

**προσεμ-βαίνω,** *step upon, trample on,* οὐ γὰρ θανόντι καὶ προσεμβῆναί σε χρή; S.*Aj.*1348. II. *step into, enter,* εἴς τι Dsc.5.11. **-βάλλω,** *throw* or *put into besides,* Pl.*Cra.*439c; πίτυρον D.S.3.14; φρουρὰν εἰς τὸ Μουσεῖον Plu.*Demetr.*34; ἀγκύρας εἰς τὸ στόμα τοῦ λιμένος D.C.43.31 codd., cf. *PCair.Zen.*244.1 (Pass.), 423 (Act. and Med., iii B.C.), Dsc.1.56, etc. II. intr., *go into besides,* Plu.2.751f (dub.l.). **-βᾰτεύω,** *continue dalliance,* prob. cj. for προσεμματεύω in Aristaenet.2.22. **-βλέπω,** *look into besides,* ταῖς αὐτῶν ψυχαῖς τὸ ζῆν Plot.4.4.8. **-βρεκτέον,** *one must moisten besides,* Sor.2.10. **-βρέχω,** *moisten besides,* Gal.12.589. **-βρῑμάομαι,** *threaten besides,* Lxx *Si.*13.3. **-μᾰτεύω,** v. προσεμβατεύω. **-παίω,** *sting,* prob. cj. in Aët.13.22 (Pass., -πνυομένοις codd.). **-πάσσω,** *sprinkle upon besides,* ἁλὸς ὀλίγον Dsc.2.76.6, cf. Ruf.ap.Orib.8.47.11. **-πεδόω,** *confirm besides,* Hsch. **-πικραίνομαι,** Pass., *to be yet more angry with,* τινι Hdt.3.146. ® **-πίπρημι,** *set on fire besides,* Lxx *Ex.*22.6, J.*BJ*3.7.36:—Pass., of ulcers, *become still further inflamed,* Aret.*SA*1.9. **-πίπτω,** *fall on besides,* τινι Aristid.*Or.*25(43).22. **-πλάσσω,** *mix in* an ingredient *as well,* Aët.12.67. **-πολάω,** *gain by traffic besides,* Phot., Suid. **-πονέω,** *cultivate besides,* τὴν ἄλλην γῆν *JHS*33.338 (Macedonia, ii A.D.). **-πῡρίζω,** v.l. for προσεμπίπρημι in Lxx *Ex.*22.6. **-φαίνομαι,** *appear to be in* a thing, γραμμῇ τἀναντία πως π. Arist.*Mech.*847ᵇ24, cf. Iamb. *in Nic.*p.72 P. **-φᾰνίζω,** Att. fut. -ιῶ Ph.*Bel.*72.6:—*make clear further,* Phld.*Mus.*p.107 K.; *testify besides,* δωρεαῖς τὴν σπουδὴν J.*AJ*8.7.3. **-φέρεια,** ἡ, *resemblance,* Epicur.*Ep.*1 p.17 U., Phld.*D.*3.12. ® **-φερής,** ές, *resembling,* φυσητῆρες αὐλοῖσι προσεμφερέστατοι Hdt.4.2, cf. E.*Fr.*382.13, X.*Smp.*4.19, Arist.*HA* 629ª31, Thphr.*HP*3.10.1, al., Epicur.*Ep.*1 p.19 U. (Sup.). Adv. -ρῶς D.S.24.3. ® **-φέρω,** *to be like,* Poll.9.131. **-φορέω,** *put in* or *into in addition,* αὐτῷ δείματα καὶ φόβους Plu.2.168a, cf. 547c. **-φορητέον,** *one must put into* people's *minds,* ἐκείνοις τῆς δεισιδαιμονίας ib.1104b. **-φράσσω,** Att. -ττω, *block up besides,* τὰς ὁδοὺς Gal.6.263, cf. 15.633. **-φῡσάω,** *inflate further,* Archig.ap.Orib.*Fr.*59 (Pass.). **-φῡσιόω,** *impress in addition upon* a person, *UPZ*110.69 (ii B.C.). **-φύω,** *implant in addition,* παραγωγάς Phld.*Ir.*p.50 W.:—Pass., *cling yet more closely,* D.S.10.18.

® **προσέναγχος,** Adv. *very lately,* Longin.44.1.

**προσεν-ᾰλείφω,** *smear in in addition,* Philum.ap.Aët.5.78 (Pass.), cj. in Sor.1.122 (Pass.). **-δαψῐλεύομαι,** Med., *give into the bargain,* τι Ph.1.514. **-δείκνῠμαι,** Med., *indicate besides,* D.C.59.13,71.32, Simp. *in Epict.*p.33 D. **-δέχομαι,** *undertake as well,* κατὰ δωρεὰν πρεσβεύσειν *IG*7.2711.64 (Boeotia, i A.D.). **-δίδωμι,** *give way, yield,* Sor.1.70b.

**προσένεγξις,** εως, ἡ, = πρόσοδος, *income,* Thom.Mag.p.306 R.

**προσενεκτέον,** (προσφέρω) *one must apply, administer, offer,* [τῷ σώματι] σιτία Arist.*MM*1199ᵇ29, cf. Ph.2.372, Sor.1.53, Porph.*Abst.*2.61. 2. (προσφέρομαι) *one must deal with,* πρᾴως τοῖς οἰκέταις D.S.34/5.2.33; ὡς συγγενέσιν τοῖς πολίταις Simp. *in Epict.*p.89 D.; δήμῳ Them.*Or.* (i.e. Constant. *pro Them.*) p.20c. II. προσενεκτέος, α, ον, *to be administered,* Alex.Trall.2.

**προσεν-έχομαι,** Pass., *to be holden by, in the grip of,* πολλοῖς ἁμαρτήμασιν Lxx 2*Ma.*5.18. **-εχῠράζω,** *distrain upon in addition,* Σινώπην D.22.56. **-θῡμέομαι,** *consider besides,* Lys.26.13 (better divisim, πρὸς ἐνθ.), Theon *Prog.*5, Lib.*Or.*64.58. **-θυμητέον,** *one must consider further,* Hierocl.p.19 A., Eust.513.11. ® **-ίημι,** *inject as well,* καστόριον Aret.*CA*1.4.

® **προσεννέπω,** impf. προσήνεπον Pi.*P.*4.97, 9.29:—*address, accost,* ll.cc., S.*Aj.*857, E.*Or.*428, etc. 2. c. acc. et inf., *entreat* or *command,* τινὰ σπέσθαι Pi.*I.*6(5).17. 3. π. τινά τι *call* by a name, τοῦτό νιν π. A.*Ag.*162 (lyr.), cf. 1291.

**προσεν-νοέω,** *think of, observe besides,* cj. in X.*Smp.*2.16, cf. Arist.*de An.*430ᵇ1; ὅτι.. Plu.2.640e; *understand in addition,* συμπλεκτικὸν σύνδεσμον Simp. *in Epict.*p.58 D. **-οχλέω,** *disturb* or *offend still more,* τὴν ὄψιν Hp.*Medic.*2; τὴν ἀκοήν Phld.*Po.*2.3.

**προσενόω,** *unite to* or *with,* J.*AJ*8.3.6:—Pass., c. dat., Sor.1.96, *Corp.Herm.*10.11.

**προσέν-στημα,** ατος, τό, *objection,* Phld.*Mort.*16. **-ταξις,** εως, ἡ, *stationing* of light-armed troops on wings of phalanx, Ascl.*Tact.*6.1. **-τάττω,** *insert besides,* Ph.2.536; in a diagram, Ptol.*Alm.*8.6:—Pass., τὸ προσεντεταγμένον ὑπόμνημα *UPZ*26.9 (ii B.C.), cf. *PTeb.*707.3 (ii B.C.). **-τείνω,** *strain still more*: only in phrase π. πληγάς τινι *proceed* or *continue to heap* blows *on* one, D.21.12; π. ἑτέρας Plu.2.237d, cf. Luc.*Tim.*47:—Pass., *become more tense,* Herod.Med. in *Rh.Mus.*58.71. **-τέλλομαι,** *enjoin, command besides,* X.*Cyr.*4.5.34, Plb.14.2.6, *PTeb.*58.52 (ii B.C.), etc. **-τυγχάνω,** *meet with besides,* Gal.10.624. **-τῠπόω,** *mould besides,* of massage, Sor.2.14. **-υβρίζω,** *abuse, maltreat besides,* Plb.4.4.2 (Pass.). **-ῡφαίνω,** aor. inf. -υφῆναι, *weave in besides,* Plu.*Demetr.*12.

**προσεξ-αγριαίνω,** *exasperate yet more,* τὸν θεόν J.*AJ*2.14.3. **-αιρέω,** *capture besides,* φρούριον ib.13.15.3, cf. Lib.*Or.*30.44. II. Med., *choose for oneself besides,* γυναῖκα Hdt.3.150. **-αίρω,** *raise still higher,* τείχη πύργοις J.*AJ*8.6.1. **-ᾰμαρτάνω,** *commit besides,* πρὸς τοῖς ἐξ ἀρχῆς ἀδικήμασι μείζω D.56.43. **-ανδρᾰποδίζομαι,** *enslave besides,* τὸν Ὀρχομενὸν καὶ τὴν Κορώνειαν Id.19.112; γυναῖκας καὶ τέκνα Paus.3.23.4. **-ανίστᾰμαι,** Pass. with aor. -ανέστην, *rise up to,* πρὸς τὰ γόνατά τινος Plu.*Pyrrh.*3; *rise up to meet,* τισι D.C.60.6. **-ᾰπᾰτάω,** *deceive besides,* Hp.*Art.*46; ἑαυτοὺς μείζους ἀπάτας Arist.*LI*969ᵇ5, cf. *Rh.*1412ª19. ® **-απλόω,** *unfold, explain besides,* Erot.*Praef.*, dub. in S.E.*M.*1.56. **-άπτω,** *kindle besides,* J.*AJ*2.16.3 (Pass.): metaph., *inflame yet more,* π. τὴν ὀργήν ib.14.9.4. **-ασκέω,** *practise besides,* Plu.*Caes.*17:—Pass., *to be adorned yet more,* J.*BJ*3.10.7. **-αψις,** εως, ἡ, *continual burning,* Alex.Aphr. *in Mete.*34.34. **-ελαύνω,** intr., *ride forth besides,* D.C.45.16. **-ελέγχω,** *convict besides,* τινὰ πεποιηκότα Id.38.43; αὐτόν, ὅτι.. Id.59.2. **-ελίσσω,** *unrol besides*: of soldiers, *wheel* them *half-round,* Plb.6.40.13. **-εμέω,** *vomit up besides,* Plu.2.524a. **-εργάζομαι,** *work out, accomplish besides,* D.21.109, Macho ap.Ath.13.578d, v.l. for προσεργ- in Hp.*Acut.*65: pf. in act. sense, Plb.12.10.8; in pass. sense, D.21.107. 2. *dress* stone *besides,* π. σφόνδυλον ἑκάστῳ τῷ κίονι *IG*2².1682.19. **-ερεθίζω,** *irritate still more,* J.*Vit.*57. **-ερείδομαι,** Med., aor. inf. -ερείσασθαι, *support oneself by,* ταῖς χερσί Plb.3.55.4. **-έρχομαι,** *come out to meet*: metaph., λόγος π. ὑπαντησόμενος Ph.1.215. **-ετάζω,** *examine* or *search into besides,* D.21.227 (Pass.), 24.69, Gal.6.723, Luc.*Tyr.*11. **-εταστέον,** *one must consider besides,* ὅτι.. Ph.2.416. **-ευπορέω,** *to be still better prepared,* Ammon. *in Int.*116.9. II. *provide further arguments,* Simp. *in Ph.*1203.8. **-εύρεσις,** εως, ἡ, *additional discovery,* Plu.2.1135d (pl.). **-ευρίσκω,** *find out, devise besides,* Hp.*VM*4, Ar.*Eq.*1283, Isoc.4.167, Epicur.*Ep.*1 p.27 U., Plb.1.68.10, *PTeb.*72.113 (Pass., ii B.C.). **-ηγέομαι,** *relate besides,* ὄνειρον Lxx 2*Ma.*15.11. **-ηπειρόω,** *turn still more into dry land,* τὴν θάλατταν τῇ προσχώσει Str.12.2.4. **-ικμάζω,** *draw out moisture besides,* Plu.2.689f.

**πρόσεξις,** εως, ἡ, (προσέχω) *application,* τοῦ νοῦ Pl.*R.*407b: abs., *attention,* Id.*Def.*413d.

**προσεξ-ίστημι,** *cause further disorder,* Plu.2.128e. **-ορκίζω,** *adjure yet again,* προσεξορκίζω ὑμᾶς, δαίμονες *Sammelb.*4324.5, cf. *Tab. Defix.Aud.*242.38 (Carthage, iii A.D.). 2. Dor. **ποτ-,** *administer an additional oath to,* [τινας] *IG*5(1).1390.8 (Andania, i B.C.). **-υβρίζω,** *maltreat besides,* Heraclit.*All.*52 (Pass.). **-ῡφαίνω,** *weave in addition,* τὸ ἄλλο ἱμάτιον *PEnteux.*4.6 (iii B.C.).

**προσέοικα,** pf. with pres. sense, Att. inf. προσεικέναι prob. in E.*Ba.*1283, Ar.*Ec.*1161: Dor. plpf. ποτῴκειν *AP*6.353 (Noss.), part. fem. ποτεοικεῖα prob. in Myia *Ep.*:—Pass. form of pf., προσῄξαι E.*Alc.*1063:—*to be like, resemble,* λέοντι E.*Ba.* l.c., cf. Pl.*Prt.*331d; γεράνῳ Cratin.5; π. ταῖς ἑταίραις τὸν τρόπον in habits, Ar. l.c.; σοὶ τὴν σιμότητα Pl.*Tht.*143e; π. κατὰ τὸ χρῶμα ἱέρακι Arist.*HA*563ᵇ22; ἑορτὴν εἰς τὰ πολλὰ καθαρμῷ -εοικυῖαν Plu.*Num.*19. II. *seem fit,* τὰ μὴ προσεικότα *things* not *fit and seemly,* S.*Ph.*903; ἔξωρα.. κοὐκ ἐμοὶ προσεικότα Id.*El.*618. III. *seem* to do, c. inf., D.20.157.

**προσεοικότως,** Adv. *so as to resemble,* D.Chr.12.55.

**προσεπ-αγγέλλομαι,** Med., *promise besides,* D.S.3.54, 19.86. **-άγω** [ᾰ], *bring besides, add,* ὕβρεως ἀεὶ -αγομένης Plb.15.25.6; π. τῇ ψευδογραφίᾳ *make additions to* it, Ath.5.216b, cf. interpol. in Gal.*Phil.Hist.*1; π. ὅτι.. Jul.*Gal.*358e. II. in Pass., *to be brought before a tribunal,* *PLips.*64.58 (iv A.D.). **-ᾴδω,** *chant over,* Jul.*Or.*7.220c. **-αινέω,** *praise besides,* Aeschin.2.156:—Pass., D.C.47.13. **-αίρω,** *raise besides,* κεφάλιον Sor.1.102:—metaph. in Pass., *to be encouraged yet more,* προσεπήρθη ὑπὸ τῆς ξυμμαχίας δέξασθαι τοὺς Μακεδόνας Arr.*An.*4.5.4, cf. D.C.48.21. **-αιτιάομαι,** *accuse besides,* Plu.*CG*6. **-ανερέσθαι,** aor. of -*είρομαι, *ask besides,* D.C.77.8. **-ᾰπειλέω,** *threaten besides,* Id.38.35, 41.33. **-ᾰράομαι,** *imprecate besides,* ἐξώλειαν ἑαυτῷ ib.38. **-άρχω,** *govern as* ἔπαρχος *besides,* c. gen., J.*AJ*8.2.3. ® **-αυξάνω,** *increase further,* D.C.40.18; τισὶ τὸν φόρον Id.43.39. **-αυρίσκομαι,** Pass., *to be attacked by* disease *besides,* Hp.*Morb.*4.51. **-εῖδον,** aor. of -οράω, *observe besides,* Them.*Or.*25.310b. **-εῖπον,** aor. 2, *say besides,* Plb.4.85.2, Plu.*Caes.*14, M.Ant.8.50. **-εισάγω** [ᾰ], *introduce besides,* Gal.8.575. **-εισφέρω,** = foreg., ἐπεισόδια Longin.9.12. 2. *contribute in addition,* Poll.5.140. **-εισφορέω,** = foreg. 2, Phld.*Mort.*37. **-εκθλίβω** [ῑ], *squeeze out in addition,* Dsc.4.150. **-εκτείνω,** *extend further,* in Pass., Gal.2.742, 18(2).451. **-ελπίζω,** *allure by hope besides,* ἄλλα αὐτοὺς πολλὰ π. D.C.45.6. **-εμβάλλω,** *throw in, add besides,* Gal.6.637, 12.389. **-εξεργάζομαι,** *complete still more perfectly,* Ph.2.203 (dub.), 522. II. Pass., *to be added over and above,* Eust.ad D.P.*Prooem.*p.72 B. **-εξευρίσκω,** *contrive besides,* Th.2.76. **-ερωτάω,** *ask besides,* Aristeas 53, Phld.*Vit.*p.30 J.; *ask a third question,* acc. to Thom. Mag.p.135 R. **-ερωτητής,** οῦ, ὁ, = *adstipulator,* Gloss. **-εύχομαι,** *pray besides,* c. acc. et inf., D.C.55.9. **-ευωνίζω,** *sell additionally cheap,* Ph.2.276 (Pass.). **-έχω,** = *appremo,* Gloss.:—Pass., οἷς προσεπεσχέθη γαστήρ Gal.16.521. **-ηρεάζω,** *abuse besides,* Arist.*Top.*161ª23:—Pass., *to be maltreated as well,* D.C.52.29. **-ηχέω,** *increase resonance,* Gal.*UP*11.12.

**προσεπί,** Prep. c. dat., *in addition to,* *PSI*4.298.13 (iv A.D.), *PMasp.*243.18 (vi A.D.), etc.

® **προσεπι-βάλλω,** *throw upon besides,* τῆς γῆς *throw* some *more* earth upon, Plb.9.38.2, cf. Gal.11.489. II. *impose further burdens,* πλείω π. οἷς ἂν ἐξ ἀρχῆς διανοηθῶσιν Isoc.6.39. III. f.l. for προσπερι-, J.*AJ*5.1.20. **-βλάπτω,** *injure further,* Steph. *in Gal.*1.320 D. **-βλαστάνω,** *blossom besides* or *again,* Thphr.*CP*3.7.7. **-βλέπω,** *look for besides,* Arist.*APr.*45ª21, Str.3.3.6. **-βοάω,** *exclaim besides,* D.C.75.4. **-βοηθέω,** *come to help,* J.*AJ*7.7.1. **-γεννάω,** *produce besides,* Thphr.*CP*1.11.6. **-γίγνομαι,** *to be added, supervene,* Hp.*Morb.*1.19, Plb.4.45.10. II. *become as well, turn out in addition,* π. εὐκλεεῖς Plu.*Nob.*19. ® **-γράφω** [ᾰ], inscribe besides, Thphr.*Char*.13.10. **-δαψῐλεύομαι**, *spend lavishly besides*, Ph.2.66,286, Lib.*Decl*.40.77. **-δείκνῡμι** or **-ύω**, *exhibit, demonstrate besides*, Plb.4.82.5, Phld.*Sign*.36, Ptol.*Geog*.1.2.5, D.C. 54.14; ὡς.. S.E.*M*.1.55. **-δέομαι**, *need besides*, *Gloss*. **-δεσμέω**, = προσεπιδέω, Anon.*Prog*.11 in Rh.1.638 W. (Pass.), *Gloss*. ❀ **-δέχομαι**, *to be liable to besides*, dub. in Ph.*Fr*.63 H. ❀ **-δέω**, *extend a bandage*, Hp.*Fract*.14; *tie on besides*, τι πρός τι Aen.Tact.18.19. **-δημέω**, *visit as a traveller*, J.*BJ*2.11.2 (nisi πρὸς ἐπιδ. scribendum). **-διαιρέω**, *dissect further*, Gal.2.229. **-διακαίω**, in Pass., f.l. for προσέτι διακ., Id.10.786 (ap.Orib.9.21.7). ❀ **-δίδωμι**, *give over and above*, δωρά τισι Pl.*Sph*.222e, cf. *SIG*431.8 (Delph., iii B.C.), J.*AJ*10.2.1, D.C.49.31; f.l. for προσαπ- in D.H.*Th*. 5. **-διίστᾰμαι**, of the pulse, *make another diastole*, Marcellin. *Puls*.421. **-διορίζω**, *distinguish besides*, Gal.11.308. **-δοξάζω**, *confirm by approval*, φαντασίας Epict.*Fr*.9. **-δράσσομαι**, Att. **-ττομαι**, Med., *grasp for oneself*, *appropriate besides*, Plb.21.14.6: metaph., π. φθόνον *draw* envy *on oneself*, Id.9.10.6. **-ζευγνύω**, = *adjungo*, *Gloss*. **-ζητέω**, *demand besides*, ἀεί τι Plb.24.15.11, cf. M.Ant.5.6. **-θεάομαι**, *observe, consider besides*, Longin.30.1. **-θεσπίζω**, *prophesy besides*, Ph.2.170. **-θετέον**, *one must add besides*, τοῖς ῥηθεῖσι Eust.35.11. **-θεωρέω**, = προσεπιθεάομαι, τοὺς πυρετούς Hp.*Coac*.204, cf. Sor.1.108, Gal.9.359; τὸν βίον Socr. *Ep*.6.2: hence **-θεωρητέον**, Longin.9.11. **-θλιπτέον**, *one must press, squeeze besides*, Herod.Med. in *Rh.Mus*.58.109. **-κᾰλέω**, *accuse besides*, τινά τι D.C.42.49. II. Med., *invoke besides*, τινα Id.62.6. **-κατάγω** [ᾰγ], *bring into the calculation*, Vett.Val.275.21. **-καταδέω**, *tie on* or *over besides*, Hp.*Art*.14. **-καταστρέφω**, *overthrow besides*, τὴν δόξαν Vett.Val.87.23. **-κατατείνω**, *strain besides* or *still more*, Lxx 4*Ma*.9.19. **-καταψεύδομαι**, = προσεπιψεύδομαι, Gal.ap. Orib.2.16.1. **-κειμαι**, *to be urgent* or *instant besides*, π. ἡ πόλις ἀξιοῦσα εἰσφέρειν D.27.66. **-κερτομέω**, *jeer at besides*, Heraclid.*Pol*. 36. **-κηρύσσω**, *proclaim besides*, D.C.38.17 (Pass.). **-κοσμέω**, *embellish besides*, Plb.6.22.3 (Pass.), Ph.2.6, Sch.Pi.*P*.5.15. **-κρίνω** [ῑ], *select in addition by* ἐπίκρισις II, *PSI*5.457.15 (iii A.D., Pass.). **-κρούω**, *strike against besides*, λίθους πρὸς τὰ σκεύη D.C.36.49. **-κτάομαι**, *gain, acquire besides*, τιμήν Arist.*Rh*.1367ᵇ14, cf. *PGrenf*.1.21.3 (ii B.C.), J.*AJ*15.6.7; π. Λυδοῖσί [τινας] *add* them to the Lydian realm, Hdt.1.29. **-λαμβάνω**, *bandage something to something else*, ταινίῃ τὸν βραχίονα περὶ τὸ στῆθος περιδέοντα Hp.*Fract*.8:—Med., cj. in Sor.*Fasc*.26. 2. *take* or *require still more*, Thphr.*HP*8.2.7: c. gen., Porph.*Abst*.2.27; *take in, occupy besides*, Plb.10.10.5, Gem. 18.3; *receive in addition*, τὴν ἐποπτείαν Plu.*Demetr*.26; παλάθην ἰσχάδων Luc.*Pisc*.41; τοῦ δημοσίου a piece of public land, Plu.*Publ*. 20: abs., *encroach*, Thphr.*Ign*.50. 3. *extend, increase*, τῷ πλήθει τὴν ἐξουσίαν Arist.*Ath*.41.2. II. Med., *lay hold besides*, [τινὸς] κατὰ τὸ γόνυ Hp.*Fract*.13: metaph., *help in* a thing *besides*, προσεπιλαβέσθαι τοῦ πολέμου Hdt.5.44; τοῦ ἔργου *take part in* it, D.C.75.6: abs., *attack besides*, Pl.*Ti*.65d. 2. *touch on besides*, Paus.3.6.9. 3. *receive part of*, τῶν χωρίων D.S.19.9 (v.l.). **-λεαίνω**, *smooth further*, Heraclid.Tar.ap.Gal.13.718. **-λέγω**, *say still further*, τοῖς εἰρημένοις Thphr.*CP*1.21.7; ὅτι Plb.21.24.14, cf. Phld.*Lib*. p.50 O. II. Med., *pick out* or *choose besides*, D.S.19.6. **-λῐπαίνω**, *enrich yet more*, Eust. ad D.P.*Prooem*.p.71 B. **-λιχμάομαι**, *devour besides*, Ph.2.318. **-λογίζομαι**, *bring further proof*, διότι.. Praef.ad Euc.*Opt*. (*recens. Theonis*) p.144 H.; *consider, take into account besides*, Gal.18(2).62, al. II. abs., *take further consideration*, Ph. *Bel*.57.29. **-λοιμώττω**, *suffer from pestilence besides*, Lyd.*Ost*. 58. **-μανθάνω**, *learn besides*, D.S.4.25, Gal.*Thras*.39. **-μᾰσάομαι**, *chew as well*, Hsch. s.v. ἐπιμάσσεται (-μάσσεται cod.). **-μελέομαι**, *take care of besides*, τινων Pl.*Lg*.755b. **-μερίζω**, *allot, assign in addition, add*, Gem.18.15, Vett.Val.155.35. **-μετρέω**, *give as additional measure, assign over and above*, τισὶ τιμάς Plb.4.51.6, cf. Plu.2.513a, Ath.2.35a, etc. II. *embellish, improve* a story, Luc.*Merc.Cond*.29, *Alex*.30. **-μηχᾰνάομαι**, *contrive besides*, τι Asp. in *EN*91.11: hence **-μηχανητέον**, *one must contrive besides*, Paul.Aeg.2.45. **-μιμνήσκομαι**, Med., *make mention of besides*, τινος Gal.2.227. **-νέμω**, in Pass., of a bandage, *to be further distributed*, Id.18(2).556. **-νεύω**, *bend forward the head towards*, Sch.D II.5.290. **-νοέω**, *think of, devise* or *invent besides*, Plb.20.6 4, *PTeb*.27.80 (ii B.C., Pass.), D.S.1.15, *Supp.Epigr*. 4.418*A* 44 (Nysa), Procl. *in Euc*.p.120 F.; π. αὐτὸς τὰ δυσθεώρητα Ph. 2.84: c. dat., *OGI*475.8 (Epist. Neronis): hence **-νοητέον**, Eust. 1532.64. **-νύσσω**, *prick besides*, Sor.*Fract*.13 (Pass.). **-ορκέω**, *swear a false oath besides*, Ar.*Lys*.1238. **-παρακᾰλέω**, *call in besides*, *BGU*248.4 (Pass.), 249.18 (ii A.D.). **-πάσσω**, *sprinkle upon*, Apollon.ap.Gal.12.649, Aret.*CA*1.7. **-πέμπω**, *send to besides*, λογοθέτας Procop.*Arc*.18. **-πηδάω**, *leap upon besides*: metaph., τῷ λόγῳ Lib.*Decl*.43.22. ❀ **-πλάσσω**, *add by way of fiction*, τινί τι Corn.*ND*17 (Pass., v.l.). II. *work into a plaster*, Sor.ap. Gal.12.495. **-πλέκω**, *add*, ὅτι.. Iamb. *in Nic*.p.19 P. **-πλέω**, *sail towards* or *against*, Poll.1.124. **-πληρόω**, *stuff to repletion*, Gal.6.415. **-πλήσσω**, Att. **-ττω**, *rebuke besides*, δεῖ αὐτὸν αὑτῷ π. Arist.*Rh*.1408ᵇ2 (nisi leg. προεπι-). **-πονέω**, *work still more*: προσεπιπονεῖν ἀκούοντας *take the additional trouble* of listening, Aeschin.2.44. **-ρραίνω**, *continue to pour forth*, τὰ αὐτά Eun.*VS* p.475 B. **-ρρέω**, *flow to besides*, aor. προσεπιρρυῆναι Hp.*Morb*.1.32. **-ρρητορεύω**, *exaggerate rhetorically*, Phld.*Vit*.p.19 J. **-ρρίπτω**, *throw to besides*, ψωμοὺς κυνί Aesop.164. **-ρροφέω**, *gulp down in addition*, Philum.*Ven*.17.6. **-ρρώννῡμι**, *strengthen besides* or *still more*, J.*BJ*1.6.6, Phalar.*Ep*.103:—Pass., *to be strengthened, confirmed*, ταῖς ὁρμαῖς Plb.4.80.3. **-σεμνύνω**, *honour in addition*, τινά τινι D.C.51.21. **-σημαίνω**, *indicate besides*, ὅτι βούλει Men.Rh. p.371 S.:—Med., *show oneself besides*, Phld.*Rh*.1.371 S., Ph.1.16:—Pass., fut. **-σημανθήσεται** Nech.ap.Vett.Val.291.33. **-σῑτίζομαι**, Med., *provide oneself with further supplies of corn*, Plb.1.29.1. **-σκεπτέον**, *one must consider further*, Gal.15.581 (v.l. for -σκέπτου). **-σκέπτομαι**, = προσεπισκοπέω, Id.10.512, al. **-σκευάζω**, *put in repair besides*, J.*AJ*8.6.1:—Pass., *to be enlarged*, of a tomb, *TAM*2.522 (Pinara). ❀ **-σκήπτω**, *entreat besides*, Hld.4.18. **-σκοπέω**, *consider besides*, Gal.*Sect.Intr*.3. **-σκώπτω**, *jest besides*, Plu.*Ages*.15; πολλὰ καὶ μιαρά D.C.47.8. **-σπάομαι**, Med., *draw towards oneself*, Hp.*Acut*.(*Sp*.)59 (v.l.); μάρτυρα Plb.12.13.3; τὴν τῷ στρατηγῷ καθήκουσαν ἐξουσίαν Mitteis *Chr*.31 viii 30 (ii B.C.); τριήρεις D.S.13.77.

**προσεπιστᾰμαι**, *understand* or *know besides*, τι Pl.*Phdr*.268b, *Chrm*.170b.

**προσεπι-στείχω**, *come to* or *upon*, Orph.*A*.538 (s.v.l.). **-στέλλω**, *notify, enjoin besides*, Th.2.85, X.*Cyr*.5.4.2; esp. *by letter*, pf. inf. Pass. -εστάλθαι Th.1.132; τὰ προσεπεσταλμένα *PTeb*.27.95 (ii B.C.). **-στεφᾰνόω**, *crown besides*, *Arch.Pap*.3.134 (Thera, iii/ii B.C.), *Num.Chron*.1905.114 (Abonuteichos, ii B.C.). **-συγκρίνω** [ῑ], *add successively*, ὕλην ἑαυτῷ Ptol.*Tetr*.105. **-συνάπτω**, = *adjungo*, *Gloss*. **-συνετίζω**, *make more intelligible*, Phld.*Po*. 2.40. **-σύρω** [ῡ], *sweep on like a flood*, Ph.1.695; *sweep away as a flood*, λογισμόν Id.2.297. **-σφάττω**, *kill over besides*: metaph., Plu. 2.1104e: also **-σφάζω**, ἑαυτὸν τῇ κόρῃ Arg.3 S.*Ant*. **-σφίγγω**, *press a point home*, Ph.1.291. **-σφρᾱγίζομαι**, *set one's seal to* a thing *besides, testify besides*, τι εἶναι D.*Ep*.4.3; τι S.E.*M*.9.192, Aristid.*Or*.36(48).106.

**προσεπισχῡρίζω**, *strengthen yet more*, D.L.9.77; τὴν τόλμαν D.C. 40.39.

**προσεπι-σωρεύω**, *pile up besides*, Polystr.p.31 W., Arr.*Epict*.1.2.24, Artem.1.16:—Pass., Phld.*D*.1.15, Nicom.*Ar*.1.16. **-τᾰλαιπωρέω**, *endure still longer*, J.*AJ*4.5.2. **-τάσσω**, Att. **-ττω**, *enjoin besides*, D.C.72.2, v.l. in Isoc.6.39:—Med., *take one's appointed post*, Plb.1.50.7. **-τείνω**, *stretch still further*: metaph., *contend more earnestly*, Id.3.24.14. 2. *intensify still more*, τὴν παροῦσαν ἐπιθυμίαν Phld. *Rh*.2.290 S.; τὸ δίψος Plu.2.689e; τὴν καλὴν νεανιείαν Ph.2.306; τὴν ὀργήν J.*BJ*7.3.3:—intr., of fevers, Gal.7.859:—Pass., of wind, Ph. 2.99. II. *impose severer terms upon*, τοὺς Καρχηδονίους Plb.1.63.2: abs., π. ταῖς βασάνοις *use severer* tortures, D.S.10.18. III. intr., *to be prolonged*, Orib.*Fr*.74. **-τελέω**, *complete as well*, Gal. 18(1).822 (Pass.). **-τέμνω**, *chisel away on the surface*, *IG*2². 1682.7. II. *make an incision besides*, Gal.13.607, Paul.Aeg.6. 88. **-τέρπομαι**, Pass., *rejoice in besides*, Ar.*Ra*.231 (lyr.). ❀ **-τεχνάομαι**, *contrive besides*, τι Procop.*Goth*.1.19, al. **-τίθημι**, *lay on besides*, τὸ θέναρ τῆς ἑτέρης χειρὸς [ἐπὶ τὴν ἑτέρην] Hp.*Art*.47; π. δίκην τισί Plb.35.2.7:—Pass., *to be superimposed*, Arist.*HA*549ᵃ33. 2. *add further* by way of qualification, Id.*EN*1148ᵇ6; ὅτι.. Id.*Metaph*.987ᵃ15, J.*Ap*.1.22:—Med., *add to oneself, assume*, ἐπωνυμίαν D.C.37.21; *take*, χρήματα D.Chr.11.60. II. Med., *attack*, σφίσι D.C.53.29. **-τῑμάω**, *reproach besides*, τινι Lxx *Si*.13.22, cf. Plb.22.5.10, D.C.58.19. II. *raise the price of* a thing *still more*, Ael.*Fr*.41. **-τρᾰγῳδέω**, *add with tragic exaggeration*, Anon.ap.Suid. **-τρέπω**, *entrust* or *make over to besides*, στρατόπεδον D.C.38.8; *permit besides*, π. τισί c. inf., Id.77.24. **-τρίβω** [ῑ], *afflict* or *destroy besides*, Plu.2.1048f, Hld.1.14, *Hippiatr*.34. **-τροπεύομαι**, Pass., *to be under guardianship longer*, ἐξ ἔτη ὑπό τινος D.27.63. **-τροπος**, ὁ, *ringleader*, *PAmh*.2.77.31 (ii A.D.). **-τυγχάνω**, *obtain besides*, c. inf., J.*BJ*1.10.3. **-φαίνομαι**, Pass., *appear besides*, St.Byz. s.v. Ἀκραιφία. **-φέρω**, *bear* or *produce besides*, X.*Oec*.5.2. II. *add besides*, J.*AJ*3.9.1; δεσμά τινι Ph.ap.Eus.*PE*8.7. 2. *adduce further*, Phld.*Piet*. p.94 G. **-φημίζω**, *make a response*, τοῖς ἀναγινωσκομένοις Ph.ap.Eus.*PE*8.7:—Pass., *to be quoted by way of reproach*, Str.17.1.19. **-φθέγγομαι**, *exclaim further*, Plb.10.4.7; *declare besides*, Gal.16.744: metaph. of birds, *scream ominously*, οὐδὲν εἰρηναῖον D.C.72.24. **-φθονέω**, *grudge besides*, D.S.34/5.2.48. **-φοιτάω**, *come in besides*, Ph.2.67. **-φωνέω**, *say besides, add*, Plu.*Cat.Ma*. 27. **-φωτίζω**, *throw a light upon as well*, τινας *PLit.Lond*.138 v 36. **-χᾰράσσω**, *engrave on besides*, τῷ πίνακι τὸ πάθος Lib.*Decl*.40. 46. **-χᾰρίζομαι**, *gratify besides*, ἄλλοις θεοῖς X.*Eq.Mag*.3.2. ❀ **-χέω**, *pour on besides*, οἶνον Dsc.2.76.7, Gal.6.670 (nisi leg. προ-), cf. Philum.ap.Orib.8.45.2. **-χώννῡμι**, *heap on, pile on*, Plu.2. 1058a. **-ψεύδομαι**, *lie besides*, Hld.7.2; *exaggerate* (bad qualities), Gal.6.640. ❀ **-ψηφίζομαι**, Att. fut. -ιοῦμαι, *decree by vote besides*, Ph.2.362.

**προσεπ-όμνῡμι**, *swear besides*, D.C.37.38, *Gloss*. **-οφλισκάνω**, *incur besides*, γέλωτα D.C.43.20.

**προσερᾰνίζω**, *contribute besides*, *PSI*6.552.8 (iii B.C.):—Pass., metaph., παραπληρώματι λέξεως προσηρανίσθαι *to be overloaded* with expletives, D.H.*Comp*.9.

**προσεργάζομαι**, *work besides*, μηδὲν τοῖς δεδραμένοις E.*HF*1013; τὸ χρυσίον τῷ ἀγάλματι Plu.*Per*.31; ἀγαθὰ π. τινί *do* good *service* to one *besides*, Hdt.6.61 (nisi leg. προ-); ὠμότατον π. τινά Plu.*CG* 17. 2. *make, earn in addition*, X.*HG*3.1.28, *PCair.Zen*.509.13 (iii B.C.).

**πρόσεργον**, τό, *earnings, interest upon money*, τὸ π. τῶν δέκα ἐτῶν v.l. in D.27.17,35,39. II. *extra work*, i.e. to be paid for when completed, *IG*7.3073.8, al. (Lebad., ii B.C.).—The Adj. πρόσεργος is dub.l. in *AP*6.288 (Leon.).

**⊛ προσέρδω**, *sacrifice to*, Νύμφῃσι θῆλυ καὶ ἄρρεν *IG*12(8).358 (Thasos, v B.C.).

**προσερεθίζω**, *stimulate besides*, Arr.*Epict*.2.2.16; *provoke further*, Lib.*Or*.21.21; *aggravate* a cough, Sor.1.123 (Pass.); τὸν θυμούμενον Choerob.*Trop*.20: prob. f.l. for προ- in Sor.ap.Gal.12.419.

**προσερείδω**, pf. προσήρεικα Plb.1.11.10, προσερήρεικα Plu.*Aem*.19: pf. part. Pass. προσερηρεισμένος Hp.*Art*.78, Arist.*Mech*.853a35: —*plant* or *set firmly against*, κλίμακας τείχει Plb.4.19.3, cf. 5.60.8, Plu.*Arat*.7; πηλὸν τοίχοις Id.2.983b; ἡ φύσις τὸ ἰσχίον εἰς μέσον προσήρεισεν *fixed* it *firmly*, Arist.*PA*695a11; Ὠκεανῷ π. Μακεδονίαν *make* it *bounded by* the O., Plu.2.332a; τὸ βλέμμα π. τινί Hld.1.21:—Pass., of a bandage, Gal.14.793. 2. *thrust violently against*, τὰς λόγχας πρός τι Plb.15.33.4; τὰς σαρίσσας τοῖς θυρεοῖς Plu.*Aem*.19; τῷ τόπῳ ξύλον *POxy*.69.3 (ii A.D.); *give additional force*, Ascl.*Tact*.7.4. II. Med., *lean upon*, τοῖς γόνασι τὴν κεφαλήν J.*AJ*8.13.6. III. intr., *fix itself*, πρὸ τοῦ τὴν ἐπιδορατίδα πρός τι προσερεῖσαι Plb.6.25.5; *press against*, Ph.*Bel*.67.31; π. ταῖς χερσὶ πρὸς τὰ νῶτά τινος Plb.13.7.10; *besiege*, παντὶ τῷ στρατεύματι πρὸς Ἀκράγαντα Id.1.17.8, cf. 1.11.10.

**προσέρεισις**, εως, ἡ, *pressure against*, Hierocl.p.19A.

**προσερέσθαι**, aor. 2 inf., fut. -ερήσομαι Hsch., Phot., Suid.:—*ask besides*, τινά τι Pl.*Prt*.311e, *Demod*.382c.

**προσερέσσω**, f.l. for προ-, Ael.*NA*13.19.

**προσερεύγομαι**, *belch at*: metaph., [κύματα] προσερεύγεται αὐτὴν [πέτρην] *break foaming against* the rock, Il.15.621 (cf. Od.5.438): later προσερυγγάνω (q.v.).

**προσερέω**, Att. contr. **προσερῶ**, used as fut. of προσαγορεύω, προσεῖπον being used as aor.: pf. προσείρηκα, -ημαι, Pl.*Ti*.31a, *Cra*.403a: —Pass., fut. προσρηθήσομαι (v. infr.): aor. προσερρήθην (v. infr.):—*speak to, address, accost*, τινα E.*Alc*.1005 (lyr.), Pl.*Phd*.60a; οὗτις ἦν οὕτω κακός, ὃν οὐ προσεῖπε καὶ προσερρήθη πάλιν E.*Alc*.195, cf. 942; of one who *addresses* a god, Hdt.5.72. 2. c. dupl. acc., *call by a name*, πολίτας ἀλλήλους π. Pl.*R*.463a; ἕνα οὐρανὸν π. Id.*Ti*.31a; τί προσεροῦμεν ὄνομα συμπάσας δυνάμεις; Id.*Sph*.227b; τινὰ ταὐτὸν π. ὄνομα ib.224b:—Pass., βασιλικὸς προσρηθήσεται Id.*Plt*.259b, cf. *Cra*.403a. II. Pass., *to be enjoined, commanded*, Aristid.1.484 J.

**προσερ-ίζω**, Dor. **ποτερίσδω**, *strive with* or *against*, αὐτόθε μοι ποτέρισδε Theoc.5.60, cf. *Lyr.Alex.Adesp*.37.1; τινὶ περί τινος Longus 4.2. II. *provoke to anger*, Aq.*Ex*.23.21, al., Aq.Sm.*De*.9.7, al. **-ιστής**, οῦ, ὁ, *rebel*, Aq., Sm.*Ez*.12.2, Aq.*Is*.30.9, Al.*Ez*.44.6.

**προσέρπω**, Dor. **ποθέρπω** Ti.Locr.97c, Theoc.4.48, 5.37: aor. προσεῖρπυσα Plu.*Pyrrh*.3, Ael.*NA*2.3, etc. 1. abs., *creep* or *steal on, approach*, τύμβου προσεῖρπον ἆσσον S.*El*.900; of animals, Ar.*V*.1509, Plu.2.77f, etc.; of ivy, παντὶ δένδρῳ π. Luc.*Am*.12: metaph., ὁ π. χρόνος, i.e. the time *that's coming*, Pi.*P*.1.57, cf. *N*.7.68 (tm.); πᾶν μοι φοβερὸν τὸ π. every thing *that approaches*, A.*Pr*.127 (anap.); τὸ π., also, *what is coming, the coming event*, S.*Aj*.227 (lyr.); αἱ προσέρπουσαι τύχαι A.*Pr*.274; τοὔργον.. δόλῳ προσέρπον S.*OT*539; προσέρπει.. τόδ' ἐγγύς, of a paroxysm, Id.*Ph*.787. 2. *come to* or *upon*, c. acc. pers., Pi.*O*.6.83 (leg. προσέλκει): c. dat. pers., σοὶ προσέρπον τοῦτ' ἐγὼ τὸ φάρμακον δρῶ, of punishment, S.*Aj*.1255.

**προσερυγγάνω**, aor. -ήρυγον, = προσερεύγομαι, τινι Diod.Com.2.35: abs., Thphr.*Char*.19.4, Ael.*NA*9.11.

**⊛ προσέρχομαι**, impf. -ηρχόμην Th.4.121 (unless fr. προσάρχομαι): fut. -ελεύσομαι Plb.21.14.6 (but the Att. impf. and fut. are commonly προσῄειν, πρόσειμι, q.v.): aor. -ήλυθον, -ῆλθον: pf. -ελήλυθα:—*come* or *go to*, c. dat., A.*Eu*.285, S.*OC*1104, etc.; π. Σωκράτει *visit* him as teacher, X.*Mem*.1.2.47; τινὶ ὥσπερ ἀθλητῇ Th. l.c. (v. προσάρχομαι); αἷς ἂν προσέλθω [γυναιξί] X.*Smp*.4.38: c. dat. loci, δόμοις, ἀκταῖς, A.*Eu*.474, E.*Hel*.1539: c. acc. loci, πεσσούς, δῶμα, βωμούς, Id.*Med*.68, 1205, *Alc*.171: rarely c. acc. pers., ἐπειδὴ τοὺς πρυτάνεις προσήλθομεν Aristomen.4: with Preps. governing acc., π. πρὸς τὸ ἄγγος Hdt.2.121.β'; πρὸς Ἀπολλώνιον *PCair.Zen*.375.4 (iii B.C.): with Advbs., π. δεῦρο S.*Aj*.1171, etc.; πέλας π. μου E.*Andr*.589, cf. S.*Tr*.1076, etc.; ἐγγύθεν, ὄπισθεν, Pl.*Plt*.289d, *R*.327b; ὅπῃ π. χρή ib.493b: abs., *approach, draw nigh*, Hdt.1.86, etc.; opp. ἀπέρχομαι, ib.199; of pain, pleasure, etc., *to be nigh at hand*, S.*Ph*.788, E.*Or*.859. 2. in hostile sense, *attack*, π. πρὸς τοὺς ἱππέας X.*Cyr*.6.2.16. 3. *come in, surrender, capitulate*, Th.3.59. 4. *come forward to speak*, π. τῷ δήμῳ D.18.13; πρὸς τὸν δῆμον Aeschin.3.220; πρὸς ὑμᾶς D.22.69, 24.176; πρὸς τοὺς ἱερομνήμονας *SIG*419.6 (Delph., iii B.C.), cf. 613.24 (ibid., ii B.C.), al.; π. πολιτείᾳ *enter* political life, Plu.*Cat.Mi*.12; π. πρὸς τὰ κοινά *come forward* in public, D.18.257; π. πρὸς τὸ πολιτεύεσθαι, πρὸς τὴν πολιτείαν, Din.1.111 (v.l. εἰς), 2.15; πρὸς τὴν πόλιν D.58.30; π. πρὸς ἓν πρᾶγμα ἴδιον Id.32.32; ὑμῖν (sc. Ἀθηναίοις) Id.25.42; ἐπὶ τοὺς συμμάχους X.*HG*6.3.3. 5. *appear* before a tribunal, προσελθὼν εἶπεν *BGU*587.2 (ii A.D.), cf. *PAmh*.2.66.43 (ii A.D.); π. τῷ δικαστηρίῳ κατ' αὐτοῦ *PSI*1.41.18 (iv A.D.); *approach* an official, π. διὰ βιβλιδίων τῷ λαμπροτάτῳ ἡγεμόνι *BGU*614.12 (iii A.D.); π. τοῖς θεοῖς in supplication, D.C.56.9. 6. π. τῇ φιλοσοφίᾳ, τοῖς νόμοις, *apply oneself to*.., Philostr.*VA*3.18, D.S.1.95; ἐπεὶ προσῆλθον ἀγορασμῷ ἢ καὶ ὑποθήκῃ κλήρου κατοικικοῦ *BGU*650.6 (i A.D.); ἐξ οὗ χρόνου προσῆλθεν ἕκαστος τῇ μισθώσει ib.1047 iv 6 (ii A.D.); π. τῇ τούτου κληρονομίᾳ *enter upon* his inheritance, *POxy*.76.22 (ii A.D.), cf. 907.5 (iii A.D.), etc.; *have recourse to*, τοῖς ἀνασκευαστικωτέροις Sor.2.50. 7. of things, *to be added*, Arist.*GC*321b27, *GA*723a13. II. *come in*, of revenue, Hdt.7.144, Lys.30.20, X.*Mem*.3.6.12. III. *have sexual intercourse*, Hp.*Epid*.6.3.14.

**προσερωτάω**, *question besides*, τινὰ εἰ.. Pl.*Tht*.165d:—Pass., εἰ.. X.*Mem*.3.9.4. 2. c. acc. rei, *ask besides*, Arist.*Rh*.1419a7 (Pass., ib.1); π. τὸ ἐνδεές Id.*SE*169b35.

**προσεσθίω**, *eat besides*, only aor. imper. πρόσφαγε Diog.*Ep*.29.5.

**πρόσεσις**, εως, ἡ, (προσίημι) *putting to* or *into*, π. τῶν σιτίων *a taking* of meals, Arist.*Pr*.957a19.

**προσεσπέριος**, ον, *towards the west, western*, Arist.*Fr*.474, Plb.1.2.6, Scymn.157; τὰ π. τῆς Εὐρώπης D.H.1.13; οἱ π. Λοκροί D.S.14.34, cf. Str.9.5.10.

**προσέσπερος**, Dor. **ποθέσπερος**, ον, *towards evening*: neut. pl. τὰ ποθέσπερα, as Adv., Theoc.4.3, 5.113. II. = foreg., St.Byz. s.v. Ἀντιγόνεια.

**προσεταιρ-ίζομαι**, Med. with pf. Pass., also plpf. προσηταίριστο D.C.58.4:—*take to oneself as a friend, associate with oneself*, τινα Hdt.3.70, Plu.*Cat.Mi*.4; τινὰ κατά τινος Luc.*Pisc*.18; in bad sense, π. ἐς πανδοχεῖον Ps.-Luc.*Philopatr*.9; *take into partnership, secure the approval of*, τὸν δῆμον Hdt.5.66; τὰ πλήθη Porph.*Abst*.2.40. II. Pass., *associate oneself with* another, τινι Pl.*Ax*.369b. **-ιστός**, όν, *joined with as a companion, attached to the same* ἑταιρεία or *club*, ὁπλῖται Th.8.100: as Subst., D.C.42.51. **-ος**, ὁ, *colleague*, *SIG*57.1 (Milet., v B.C., pl.), 633.22 (ibid., ii B.C., pl.), prob. in *IG*1².22.7 (de Milesiis); οἱ π. τοῦ θεοῦ *Milet*.1(7).203a34 (i B.C.).

**προσετέον**, (πρόσειμι) *one must admit*, ἔνια Ph.1.267. II. **προσετέος**, α, ον, *to be admitted*, οὐδὲ π. τἀναντία Chrysipp.*Stoic*.2.90 (prob.).

**προσέτι**, Adv. *over and above, besides*, Hdt.1.41, Ar.*Ach*.984, *Av*.855 (lyr.), Th.1.80, Pl.*Phlb*.30b, etc.; sts. separated by a word, πρὸς δ' ἔτι X.*An*.3.2.2, *Cyr*.6.2.18; προσέτι δέ *SIG*827 iii 4 (Delph., ii A.D.); both orders in X.*Cyr*.2.1.31.

**προσετοιμάζω**, in Med., *make preparations*, *PSI*6.587.6 (iii B.C.).

**πρόσευγμα**, ατος, τό, *votive offering upon the statue of a god*, Eub.96.

**προσευεργετέω**, *do good besides*, τινα to one, D.S.13.22, D.C.41.63.

**προσευθύνω**, *call to account besides*, Arist.*Pol*.1322b9.

**προσευκαιρέω**, *have leisure for*, τοῖς κοινοῖς Arr.*Epict*.3.22.72; ὀρχήσει Plu.2.316a; χορείαις (prob. for χωρίοις) Ps.-Plu.*Fluv*.4.1; τῇ γεωργίᾳ μου, ταῖς λειτουργίαις, *POxy*.487.16 (ii A.D.), 1119.12 (iii A.D.).

**προσευκ-τήριον**, τό, *place of prayer*, Ph.2.168. **-τικός**, ή, όν, *addressed in prayer*, ὕμνοι Men.Rh.p.342 S.

**προσευλαβέομαι**, *guard against as well*, τινας Phalar.*Ep*.67.3.

**προσευλογέω**, *praise besides*, τὴν τοῦ θεοῦ δύναμιν J.*AJ*4.8.47.

**προσευνάζομαι**, Pass., *come to rest upon*, τῇ γῇ, of a wave, Philostr.*Her*.19.12.

**⊛ πρόσευξις**, εως, ἡ, = προσευχή, Orph.*H*.15.2, *Gloss*.

**προσευπορέω**, *procure* or *provide besides*, χρήμαθ' ὑμῖν D.36.57:—Pass., *to be forthcoming*, Id.24.97 (v.l. προ-). II. *solve* a difficulty, or *acquire insight, in addition*, πολλὰ προσευπόρησαν τοῖς πρὸ αὐτῶν Procl. *in Euc*. p.66 F., cf. *Hyp*.7.57.

**προσευρίσκω**, *find besides*, Plb.1.59.6 (Pass.), Ascl.*Tact*.12.10: simply, *find*, ὃν.. μόνον π. πιστόν S.*El*.1352:—Med., Corn.*ND*19.

**προσευσχολέω**, *give one's time to* a thing, τινι J.*AJ*2.9.6, *BJ*4.10.2, Anon.ap.Suid.:—always with v.l. προσασχολέω.

**προσευτελίζω**, *cheapen still more*, Lyd.*Mag*.2.17 cod. (Pass.).

**προσεύτροχος**, ον, τὰ π. βλέφαρα dub. l. in Aret.*CA*1.6 (πρόσθεν εὔτροχα cj. Ermerins).

**προσευφραίνω**, *gladden besides*, f.l. for προ- in Ph.1.230.

**⊛ προσευχή**, ἡ, *prayer*, οἶκος προσευχῆς, of the Temple, Lxx *Is*.56.7; κατὰ τὰς κοινὰς ἡμῶν εὐχὰς καὶ προσευχάς *BGU*1080.5 (iii A.D.). II. *place of prayer, sanctuary, chapel*, *IPE*1².176 (Olbia), 2.52 (Panticapaeum); esp. among the Jews, *synagogue*, *PEnteux*.30.5 (iii B.C.), *OGI*726 (Egypt, iii B.C.), 96.6 (ibid., iii/ii B.C.), al., *PTeb*.86.18 (ii B.C.), Ph.2.523, J.*Vit*.54, Apion ap. eund.*Ap*.2.2, *Act.Ap*.16.13, Juv.3.296.

**προσεύχομαι**, fut. -ξομαι A.*Ag*.317:—*offer prayers* or *vows*, θεοῖς A. l.c., cf. E.*Hipp*.116, al., etc.; τῷ ἡλίῳ Pl.*Smp*.220d; θεῷ π. σωτηρίαν ἡμῖν διδόναι Id.*Criti*.106a, cf. X.*Cyr*.2.1.1. 2. c. acc., π. τὸν θεόν *address* him *in prayer*, Ar.*Pl*.958, cf. E.*Tr*.887. 3. abs., *offer prayers, worship*, Hdt.1.48, A.*Pr*.937, S.*Ant*.1337, etc.; π. γλώσσῃ, πνεύματι, νοΐ, 1*Ep.Cor*.14.14,15. II. c. acc. rei, *pray for* a thing, νίκην πολέμου X.*HG*3.2.22: c. inf., ἕλκειν τὸ βέδυ π. Philyll.20; ζῆσαι προσεύχου *pray* for life, *Epigr.Gr*.1040.11 (Adada): folld. by τοῦ c. inf., *Ep.Jac*.5.17; π. ἵνα.., περί τινων ὅπως, *Ev.Matt*.24.20, *Act.Ap*.8.15.

**προσεφάπτομαι**, Med., *to be connected with, attached to as well*, τινος Gal.2.263.

**προσεφέλκομαι**, Med., *draw after one besides*: metaph., *go so far as to invite persons* (to be citizens), τῶν ξένων Arist.*Pol*.1278a27.

**προσέχ-εια**, ἡ, (προσέχω) *attention*, Procl. *in Euc*. p.208 F., Suid. **⊛-ής**, ές, of Place, *next to*, π. σφίσι ἑστάναι, in battle, Hdt.9.28, cf. 102; νῆσος -εστάτη τῇ ἠπείρῳ Str.14.6.1; ἔπλωον προσεχέες τῇ γῇ *keeping close to*.., Arr.*Ind*.33: c. gen., π. τῶν κρημνῶν (fort. τῷ κρημνῷ) νάπη D.H.1.32; οὐδέν ἐστιν ἑτέρου λίθου π. σιδήρῳ καὶ κόλλῃ *attached* with..., Paus.8.37.3. b. in geogr. sense, *bordering upon, adjoining*, c. dat., Λίβυες οἱ π. Αἰγύπτῳ Hdt.3.91: c. gen., τὸ π. τοῦ κάτω κόσμου Arist.*Mete*.340b12, cf. Paus.8.4.3: abs., οἱ προσεχέες their *next neighbours*, Hdt.3.89,93. 2. *exposed to the wind*, π. ἀκταὶ τοῖς ἐτησίαις Anon.ap.Suid.; π. αἰγιαλὸς Λιβί Str.5.3.6: abs., π. καὶ ἀλίμενος Id.4.6.2, cf. 5.4.4, D.H.3.44. 3. *closely connected*, τὰ -έστατα τῶν εἰδῶν ἐνυπάρχει τῷ γένει Ph.1.17 : Comp., -έστερον νῷ Plot.5.4.2 : hence, *appropriate, suitable, proper*, ὑποθῆκαι π. τῇ πολιτικῇ διοικήσει Phld.*Rh.*2.272 S.; κυριώτατα καὶ -έστατα ὀνόματα D.H. *Comp.*3; ἄγαλμα -έστατον τῇ λύρᾳ Philostr.*Im.*1.10; παραδείγματα Aps.p.280 H.(Comp.). **4.** *proximate, immediate, particular*, κατὰ τὸ π. καὶ ἀκριβές, opp. κατὰ τὸν ἀνωτάτω λόγον, *Placit.*4.4.1; κατὰ τὸ π., opp. κατὰ κοινόν, Sor.2.44, cf. 1.4; τὰ π. καλούμενα μόρια (of the lower limb, viz. thigh, foot, etc.) Gal.7.735, cf. 1.465; τὸ π. τῆς φύσεως αὐτῆς (sc. τῆς ψυχῆς) its *particular* nature, Plot.4.2.1; ἡ π. αἰτία Procl.*Inst.*31; ὁ π. τοῦ κόσμου δημιουργός Jul.*Gal.*99d. Adv. -χῶς *immediately*, Id.*Or.*5.175a, Plot.2.1.5; τὰ π. γεννητικά τινος *proximate* sources or origins, Gal.5.677; π. συνηρτημένος Iamb.*Myst.*5.9, cf. Porph.*Intr.*4.32, Dam.*Pr.*102, al. **5.** *connected by relationship*, Sch.Pi.*N.*3.45 (Comp.). **II.** of Time, *recently*, Paul.Aeg.6.118. **2.** in Dor. form **ποτεχεῖ** (q.v.). **III.** *attentive*, Procl.*in Euc.*p.208 F. (Comp.). Adv. -χῶς Phld.*Rh.*2.259 S.; glossed σπουδαίως, Hsch.: Comp. -έστερον, τὸ γάλα κρίνειν Sor.1.90. **-όντως,** Adv. of προσέχω I.4, *attentively, carefully*, Hp.*Dent.*12, Men.*Mon.*191, Crito ap.Gal.13.884.

⊛ **προσέχω** (Cypr. **ποέχω** (q.v.)) and **προσίσχω**: aor. προσέσχον:—*hold to, offer*, προσέσχε μαζὸν [δράκοντι] A.*Ch.*531; *hold against*, [τὴν ἀσπίδα] προσῖσχε πρὸς τὸ δάπεδον Hdt.4.200; *apply*, χλιάσματα Hp.*Mul.*2.129. **2.** π. ναῦν *bring* a ship *to port*, προσσχόντες τὰς νέας Hdt.9.99; Μαλέᾳ προσίσχων πρῷραν E.*Or.*362; τίς σε προσέσχε.. χρεία; *brought* thee *to land* here? S.*Ph.*236; ⟨ναῦν⟩ πρὸς τὴν γῆν προσσχεῖν D.C.42.4: more freq. without ναῦν, *put in, touch at* a place, προσσχεῖν ἐς Τύρον, ἐς τὴν Σάμον, etc., Hdt.1.2, 3.48, al.; πρὸς τὴν Σίφνον προσῖσχον ib.58: c. dat. loci, π. τῇ γῇ Id.4.156; τῆς νήσου τοῖς ἐσχάτοις Th.4.30; Λιβύῃ κατὰ τὴν Μαυρουσίαν Plu.*Sert.*7: c. acc. loci, τίνι στόλῳ προσέσχες τήνδε γῆν; S.*Ph.*244, cf. Plb.2.9.2: abs., *land*, Hdt.2.182, etc.: with words added, πλέων δι' Ἑλλησπόντου π. ἐς Κύζικον Id.4.76, cf. 6.119; ναυσὶ προσσχεῖν Th.4.11; τῇ νηῒ π. εἰς Ῥόδον D.56.9; ὡς γῇ προσέξων τὸ σῶμα, of a shipwrecked sailor, Plu.2.1103e. **3.** *turn to* or *towards* a thing, π. ὄμμα E.*HF*931: mostly, π. τὸν νοῦν *turn one's mind, attention to* a thing, *be intent on* it, τοῖς ἀναπαίστοις Ar.*Eq.*503; ἐμοί ib.1014, cf. 1064, X.*An.*2.4.2, etc.; π. τὸν νοῦν τινι *give heed* to him, *pay court* to him, Id.*Cyr.*5.5.40; ἑαυτῷ π. τὸν νοῦν to be thinking with himself, in a fit of abstraction, Pl.*Smp.*174d; also πρὸς τὴν ἑαυτοῦ κατηγορίαν π. τὸν νοῦν Antipho 3.4.1; πρὸς τούτοις Ar.*Nu.*1010; π. τὸν νοῦν μὴ .. *take heed* lest.., Pl.*R.*432b, etc.: abs., πρόσεχε τὸν νοῦν Cratin. 284, Pherecr.154, Ar.*Pl.*113, etc.; δεῦρο τὸν νοῦν προσέχετε Id.*Nu.*575, cf. Pl.*Smp.*217b; προσεχέτω τὸν νοῦν *let him take heed*, as a warning, Ar.*Nu.*1122; also τὴν γνώμην π. Id.*Ec.*600, Th.1.95, 2.11, 5.26, 7.15; π. τὴν διάνοιαν ὡς πράξει μεγίστῃ Plu.*Num.*14; but περὶ τούτου τῇ διανοίᾳ π. *IG*7.2225.44(ii B.C.); π. τῇ διανοίᾳ εἰς τὸ ῥῆμα Κυρίου LXX *Ex.*9.21. **4.** without τὸν νοῦν, μὴ πρόσισχε.. βουκόλοις Cratin.286; σαυτῷ π. Ar.*Ec.*294 (lyr.), X.*Mem.*3.7.9; π. ἑαυτοῖς ἀπό τινος *to be on one's guard* against, *Ev.Luc.*12.1; πρόσεχ' οἷς φράζω *attend* to what I shall tell you, Mnesim.4.21 (anap.), cf. D.10.3, etc.; π. τῶν ἐμπείρων.. ταῖς ἀναποδείκτοις φάσεσι Arist.*EN*1143$^b$11; τῷ πολλῷ χρόνῳ Id.*Pol.*1264$^a$2; π. τοῖς νόμοις Id.*Fr.*539; τοῖς χιλιάρχοις *take orders from* them, Plb.6.37.7; also π. ἐπί τινι LXX *Ge.*4.5: abs., πρόσεχε, κἀγώ σοι φράσω Athenio 1.8; προσέχων ἀκουσάτω *attentively*, D.21.8; πρόσσχες *An.Ox.*1.121: also c. acc., προσέχων τε ταῦτα Critias 25.19 D.; οὐ προσέχει τὰ πράγματα Philem.73.4; π. νόμον θεοῦ LXX *Is.*1.11, cf. *Ex.*34.11: also π. ἀπὸ τῶν ἁγίων, τῶν γραμματέων, ib.*Le.*22.2, *Ev.Luc.*20.46; π. τοῦ μὴ φαγεῖν αἷμα LXX *De.*12.23; π. ἵνα μὴ μαστιγωθῇς ib.2*Ch.*25.16. **b.** *devote oneself to* a thing, c. dat., γυμνασίοισι Hdt.9.33; τοῖς ἔργοις Ar.*Pl.*553; τοῖς ναυτικοῖς Th.1.15; τῷ πολέμῳ Id.7.4; πλούτῳ Pl.*Alc.*1.122d; τούτῳ τῷ ἀγῶνι Lycurg.10; τοῖς κοινοῖς, γεωργίᾳ καὶ εἰρήνῃ, Plu.*Cat.Mi.*19, Hdn.2.11.3, etc.:—abs., ἐντεταμένως, προθύμως π., Hdt.1.18, 8.128. **5.** *continue*, ἡ νοῦσος, ἡ ὀδύνη π., Hp.*Int.*11,7. **6.** Med., *attach oneself to* a thing, *cling, cleave to* it, ὅ τι πρόσσχοιτο τοῦ πηλοῦ τῷ κοντῷ Hdt.2.136; ὥσπερ λεπὰς προσεχόμενος τῷ κίονι Ar.*V.*105, cf. *Pl.*1096; τῷ τοίχῳ Arist.*HA*555$^a$1: abs., οἱ πολύποδες οὕτω π. ὥστε μὴ ἀποσπᾶσθαι ib.534$^b$27. **b.** metaph., *devote oneself to the service of* any one, esp. a god, Pi.*P.*6.51 (dub.). **7.** Pass., *to be held fast* by a thing, ὑπό τινος E.*Ba.*756; *to be attached* to it, πρὸς τῷ στήθει Hp.*Art.*14; πρὸς τῷ δένδρῳ προσέχεσθαι, of gum, *stick to*, Thphr.*HP*9.4.4: metaph., *to be implicated in*, τῷ ἄγει Th.1.127. **II.** *have besides* or *in addition*, δεῖ καὶ τοῦτο προσέχειν τὸ μάθημα Pl.*R.*521d, cf. D.31.7, etc.

**προσέψημα,** ατος, τό, late form for προσόψ–, Ph.1.542, Dem.Ophth. ap.Aët.7.33, Philum.ap.Orib.45.29.55.

**προσεψία,** ἡ, *intercourse*, Hsch. (-εψιά cod.).

**προσέψω,** *boil in addition*, τινί τι Orib.*Fr.*93.

**προσεωλίζομαι,** Pass., *become putrefied*, Gal.16.761 (v.l. προ–, q.v.).

**προσεῷος,** ον, *towards the east*, Str.11.8.2.

**προσ-ζεύγνῡμι,** *attach by a yoke*, τὸ ἄροτρον Porph.*Abst.*2.30: metaph., τῇ ὕλῃ τὸν τεχνίτην προσέζευξεν *Placit.*1.3.5:—more freq. in Pass., *to be yoked, harnessed to*, τινι Luc.*Ner.*4: abs., *to be attached*, ᾗ τὸ πηδάλιον προσέζευκται Arist.*Mech.*851$^a$33: metaph., τῷ προσέζευξαι πλάνῳ; E.*Alc.*482, cf. Plot.1.4.16; *to be contiguous*, πύργοις J.*BJ*5.4.4. **-ζευξις,** εως, ἡ, *obtaining, attracting*, τῶν τοῦ βασιλέ[ως δωρεῶν] *Inscr.Prien.*82.17 (iii/ii B.C.).

**προσζημιόω,** *punish besides*, Isoc.1.33; φυγῇ τινα Pl.*Grg.*516d.

**προσζητέω,** *seek besides*, Maxim.ap.Eus.*PE*7.22.

**προσζωννύω,** *gird besides*; and **πρόσζωστος,** ον, *Gloss.*

**πρόσηβος,** ον, (ἥβη) *near manhood*, X.*Cyr.*1.4.4, D.H.2.71, Ael.*VH*3.32, Chor.p.60 B.; τὴν ἡλικίαν π. ὤν Luc.*Somn.*1; also, *near womanhood*, παιδίσκη Clearch.14, cf. Ruf.ap.Orib.*inc.*2.16.

**προσηγορ-έω,** *address*, π. φίλως S.*El.*1471; *console*, τινα E.*Ph.*[989]. **-ημα,** ατος, τό, *object of one's address*, Id.*Supp.*803 (lyr.). **-ητικόν,** τό, *appellative*, *Gloss.* ⊛ **-ία,** ἡ, *friendly greeting, familiarity*, Plu.2.709b, D.L.3.98. **II.** *addressing*, ἡ κατὰ τοὔνομα π. Arist.*Cat.*1$^a$13; τῷ σχήματι τῆς π. ib.3$^b$14: hence, *appellation, name*, Isoc.15.284, *Com.Adesp.*143, D.6.25, Arist.*Pol.*1275$^a$6, Thphr.*HP*3.3.6, Plb.3.49.5, D.H.*Comp.*26, D.S.16.50, Quint.*Inst.*1.4.21; *title*, ἡ τοῦ ἄρχοντος π. *IG*2$^2$.1110. **2.** Gramm., *common noun*, Zeno *Stoic.*1.19, D.H.*Amm.*2.11, etc.; but ἡ π. ὡς εἶδος τῷ ὀνόματι ὑποβέβληται D.T.634.6. **-ικός,** ή, όν, *of* or *for addressing*, π. ὄνομα, = Lat. *praenomen*, opp. *nomen* (τὸ συγγενικόν), D.H.3.65, 4.1; also, = *cognomen*, Plu.*Mar.*1. **II.** Gramm., τὰ π. *appellatives*, opp. τὰ ὀνοματικά, D.H.*Comp.*2, etc.; ὄνομα κύριον ἢ π. A.D.*Adv.*120.23, cf. D.T.636.9; τὰ ἁπλᾶ π. Hermog.*Stat.*1; περὶ τῶν π., title of work by Chrysippus, D.L.7.192. Adv. -κῶς *by* one's *common name*, Ph.1.150; τὰ π. "ἄρμενα" καλούμενα *vulgarly* called 'tackle', Gal.18(2).717. **-ος,** Dor. **ποτάγορος,** ον, (ἀγορεύω) *addressing, accosting*, αἱ π. δρύες the *speaking* oaks, A.*Pr.*832; τί δῆτ' ἐμοὶ.. προσήγορον ἔτ' ἔστ' ἀκούειν; what *word addressing* me, i.e. *addressed to* me..? S.*OT*1338 (lyr.); π. φάτιν ὤρεξε Moschio Trag.9.8: c. gen., Παλλάδος εὐγμάτων προσήγορος *addressing* prayers to her, *addressing* her, S.*Ant.*1185: in late Prose, *conversing*, γνώριμοί τε καὶ π. Iamb.*VP*33.237. **2.** generally, *conversable, mutually agreeable*, φίλοι τι καὶ π. ἀλλήλοις Pl.*Tht.*146a; θεοῖς π. Max.Tyr.11.8; γενόμενος ἐν τοῖς μάλιστα π. his chief *friend*, D.H.1.70; συμπόσιον μηκέτι π. ἑαυτῷ, i.e. too large for general conversation, Plu.2.678d; γνώριμα καὶ π. *familiar*, of ideas, Id.*Cic.*40. **3.** of things, *agreeing*, πάντα π. καὶ ῥητὰ πρὸς ἄλληλα Pl.*R.*546b, cf. Philol.11; ὁμόφρονα καὶ ποτάγορα ἀλλάλοις Polus ap.Stob.3.9.51. **II.** Pass., *addressed*, τῷ π.; by whom *accosted?* S.*Ph.*1353, cf. *OT*1437. **2.** *called*, πόλις δὲ Μυσῶν Μυσία π. Id.*Fr.*411.

**προσήδομαι,** Pass., *to be delighted at* or *in*, aor. Pass. -ήσθην, dub. in Hsch. s.v. ποθήνυτο. **προσήϊξαι,** v. προσέοικα. **προσηκάμην,** v. προσίημι.

**προσηκόντως,** Adv. *suitably, fitly*, π. τῇ πόλει *as beseems* the dignity of the state, Th.2.43, cf. Pl.*Lg.*659b, Isoc.3.27, 6.70, Hyp.*Eux.*17, Men.*Epit.*490, etc.

⊛ **προσήκω** (written προσhεκ-, i.e. προσήκ–, *IG*1$^2$.57.15), Dor. **ποθήκω** *GDI*2151, al. (Delph.), hyperdor. **ποθάκω** Diotog.ap.Stob.4.1.133:—*to have come, be at hand, be present*, χρεία προσήκει A.*Pers.*143 (anap.); ὡς φίλοι προσήκετε S.*Ph.*229, cf. *OC*35, *El.*1142; ἐνταῦθ' ἐλπίδος προσήκομεν E.*Or.*693; π. ὄχθαι ἐπὶ τὸν ποταμόν *reach* to the river, X.*An.*4.3.23; τοῦ πρὸς ταῦτα -ήκοντος θεάτρου Id.*HG*7.4.31. **II.** metaph., *belong to*, εἰ τῷ ξένῳ τούτῳ προσήκει Λαΐῳ τι συγγενές S.*OT*814; τῷ γὰρ προσήκει.. τόδε; whom *does* this *concern?* Id.*El.*909; Πενθεῖ δὲ τί μέρος.. προσῆκε; E.*Ba.*1301; νομίσας ἑορτὴν ἑαυτῷ τι προσήκειν Th.1.126; τῇ βασιλείᾳ π. οὐ ῥᾳδιουργία, ἀλλὰ καλοκἀγαθία X.*Ages.*11.6, cf. Pl.*R.*443a; ὅσα τριήρεσιν προσήκει Id.*Criti.*117d, etc.; γεωργίᾳ, ναυτιλίᾳ π., *appertain* to.., Id.*R.*527d: sts. folld. by πρός, οὐδὲν πρὸς Πέρσας τοῦτο π. τὸ πάθος Hdt.8.100, cf. D.C.58.27. **b.** of persons, *belong to, be related to* (cf. infr. III. 3), τινι E.*IT*550; Τηρεῖ.. ὁ Τήρης οὗτος οὐδὲν π. Th.2.29; αὐτῇ π. Φειδίας *is concerned with* her, Ar.*Pax*616; προσήκετε ἡμῖν τὰ μέγιστα Th.6.84; π. γένει Ar.*Ra.*698: c. inf., οὐ προσήκομεν κολάζειν τοῖσδε *we do* not *belong* to them to punish, i.e. it is not for them to punish us, E.*Or.*771 (troch.). **2.** impers., *it belongs to, concerns*, freq. with neg. and gen. rei (with περί c. gen., Phld.*Rh.*1.202 S.), οὐδέν μοι π. τῆς αἰτίας ταύτης I have nothing *to do with*.., Antipho 6.33, cf. X.*An.*3.1.31, *Cyr.*8.1.37; ἐμοὶ οὐδαμόθεν π. τούτου τοῦ πράγματος And.4.34; οὐδ' ὁτιοῦν π. ἑαυτοῖς οὐδενὸς τῶν Ἁγνίου D.43.20, cf. 35.33; so with a question, τί οὖν π. δῆτ' ἐμοὶ Κορινθίων; Ar.*Av.*969, cf. X.*Mem.*4.5.10, etc.; προσήκει [τισὶ] οἰκείου τινὸς ἀγαθοῦ they *possess* a peculiar excellence, Dam.*Pr.*34. **b.** c. dat. pers. et inf., *it belongs to, beseems*, οἷς προσῆκε πενθῆσαι A.*Ch.*173; οὔ σοι προσήκει τήνδε προσφωνεῖν φάτιν S.*El.*1213; τοὐναντίον δρῶν ἢ προσῆκ' αὐτῷ ποιεῖν Ar.*Pl.*14; ἀγαθοῖς ὑμῖν π. εἶναι X.*An.*3.2.11, cf. Pl.*Phdr.*233a; cf. infr. III. 4: c. acc. pers., οὔ σε προσήκει.. λέγειν '*tis* not *meet* that thou.., A.*Ag.*1551 (anap.), cf. E.*Or.*1071, Pl.*Grg.*491d, X.*An.*3.2.15 (the impf. προσῆκεν is said to be used for προσήκει in 7.7.18, *Eq.*12.14: Att. usage, acc. to Thom.Mag.p.287 R.): sts. the two constructions are combined, προσήκει τοῖς μὲν ἄλλοις.. στέργειν, σὲ δὲ.. νομίζειν Isoc.5.127: sts. the inf. is supplied, ἑκάστῳ (v.l. ἕκαστος) ἀπολοφυράμενοι ὃν π. [ἀπολοφύρασθαι] ἄπιτε Th.2.46; ἐγὼ δὲ πάνθ' ὅσα π. τὸν ἀγαθὸν πολίτην [πράττειν] ἔπραττον D.18.180, cf. 23.164, Isoc.15.119, X.*Mem.*2.1.32. **III.** freq. in Part. as Adj., **1.** *belonging* to one, αἰτία οὐδὲν ἐμοὶ προσήκουσα D.21.110, cf. Antipho 5.2; μηθενὶ μηθὲν ποθήκουσα, of a slave, *GDI* l.c.: c. gen., ἐν τοῖς τοῦ πράγματος ἑκάστοις προσήκουσιν *all that belongs* to his business, Pl.*Lg.*643b: abs., τὰς οὐ προσηκούσας ἁμαρτίας not *his own* faults, Antipho 3.2.10; τὰ μὴ π. (= ἀλλότρια) ἐπικτωμένους Th.4.61; οἱ π. ξύμμαχοι Id.1.40, etc. **2.** *befitting, proper, meet*, π. ἐγκλήματα ibid., Hyp.*Eux.*24; ἡ π. σωτηρία Th.6.83; τὸ π. ἑκάστῳ ἀποδιδόναι Pl.*R.*332c; τιμαί Id.*Lg.*952c, cf. *Epin.*985d; ἔλεος D.21.196, etc.: τὰ π. *what is fit, seemly*, εἰπεῖν περὶ Κύρου τὰ π. X.*Cyr.*3.3.1; τὰ π. πράττειν to do *one's duty*, Id.*Mem.*1.1.12, etc.; τὰ π. ἔργα Id.*HG*3.4.16; also τὸ προσῆκον *fitness, propriety*, ἐκτὸς τοῦ π. E.*Heracl.*214; πέρα τοῦ π. Antipho 5.1; μακρότερα τοῦ π. Pl.*Cra.*413a; μᾶλλον τοῦ π. Id.*Lg.*697c; παρὰ τὸ π. Id.*Phlb.*36d, Thphr.*Char.*17.1; κατὰ τὸ π. Plu.2.

122a; so οὐκ ἐκ προσηκόντων Th.3.67: c. inf., προσήκοντα ἀκοῦσαι σοφίσματα *fit* to hear, Pl.*R*.496a; λόγοι π. ἀκούειν Id.*Lg*.811d. 3. of persons, *akin*, τὸ ἀνέκαθεν τοῖσι Κυψελίδῃσι ἦν προσήκων Hdt.6.128, cf. A.*Ch*.689; γένει προσήκων βασιλεῖ X.*An*.1.6.1; οἱ προσήκοντες γένει E.*Med*.1304, cf. Pl.*Lg*.874a; κατὰ γένος, διὰ συγγένειαν, Plu. *Thes*.19, *Cat.Mi*.14, etc.; οἱ προσήκοντες τῷ νεκρῷ Hdt.4.14, cf. X. *HG*1.7.21, etc.; οἱ προσήκοντές οἱ his *relations*, Hdt.1.216; also οἱ π. τινός Th.1.128, Lys.18.1, Pl.*Ap*.34b; οἱ μάλιστα π. Hdt.3.24; πατέρας καὶ ἀδελφοὺς καὶ ἄλλους τοὺς π. Pl.*Ap*.33d; Dor. οἱ ποθίκοντες Orac.ap.D.43.66: hence αἱ προσήκουσαι ἀρεταί *hereditary* fair fame, Th.4.92. b. οὐδὲν προσήκων *one who has* nothing *to do with the matter*, Pl.*R*.539d; οὐδὲν προσῆκον ἐνίοις *though there is* no *connexion* in some cases, Id.*Cra*.397b: c. inf., θεὸν.. οὐδὲν προσήκοντ' ἐν γόοις παραστατεῖν *having* no *concern* with assisting one in sorrows, A.*Ag*. 1079; πρὸς τοὺς μὴ προσήκοντας (sc. ὀλιγωρίας τυγχάνειν) Arist.*Rh*. 1379b12. 4. abs. in neut., οὐ προσῆκον *though* or *since it is* not *fitting*, Th.3.40; οὐδὲν π... ἐπιτάσσειν Id.6.82, cf. 84: without a neg., prob. in Hyp.*Dem.Fr*.10; ὡς π. αὐτοῖς χρῆσθαι Pl.*Tht*.196e.

**προσηλιάζομαι**, Pass., *to be exposed to the sun*, v.l. for προ- in *Gp*. 6.2.6.

**προσήλιος**, ον, *exposed to the sun, sunny*, τόποι ξηροί, π. X.*Cyn*.4. 6; οἰκίαι Thphr.*Od*.40.

**πρόσηλος**, v. πρόσειλος.

❀ **προσηλόω**, *nail, rivet, fix to*, ['Ιξίονα] τῷ τροχῷ E.ap.Plu.2.19e; σταυρῷ τινα J.*BJ*2.14.9, cf. Luc.*Prom*.2; ἐν δέλτῳ γεγραμμένα π. *IG* 12(2).35b19 (Mytilene): metaph., ψυχὴν πρὸς τὸ σῶμα Pl.*Phd*.83d, cf. Iamb.*Myst*.2.6: c. acc. pers., *crucify*, Plu.2.206a:—Pass., *to be fastened by nails*, *IG* $2^2$.1640.7, 14.759; of persons, = προσπασσαλεύω, D.21.105; τοῖς ζυγοῖς τῶν πλοίων προσηλωμένοι τοὺς τραχήλους Lxx 3*Ma*.4.9: metaph., Herod.Med.ap.Orib.*Fr*.106; of the soul, π. φθαρτικαῖς ὕλαις Ph.1.237; προσηλωθέντα, εἰ χρὴ φάναι, τῷ θεῷ Porph. *Abst*.1.57. II. *nail up*, τὰ παρασκήνια D.21.17:—Pass., τὸ ἐργαστήριον σανιδίοις προσηλοῦσθαι to be boarded up, *SIG*799.26 (Cyzicus, i A.D.).

**προσηλύτ-ευσις** [ῠ], εως, ἡ, *residence as a stranger*, Aq.*Ge*.47. 9. **-εύω**, *live in a place as a stranger*, ἐν τῷ Ἰσραὴλ Lxx *Ez*.14. 7. **-ος**, ον, *one that has arrived at* a place, *stranger, sojourner*, τῷ προσελθόντι προσηλύτῳ ib.*Ex*.12.49, al. II. *one who has come over to Judaism, convert, proselyte*, Ph.2.219, *Ev.Matt*.23.15, *Act.Ap*. 2.10.

**προσήλωσις**, εως, ἡ, *nailing on* or *to*, Apollod.*Poliorc*.155.12, *Gloss*.

**πρόσημαι**, *to be seated at* or *close to*, c. dat., δώμασιν προσήμεναι A. *Ag*.1191; νερτέρᾳ π. κώπῃ ib.1617; βωμοῖσι S.*OT*15: rarely c. acc., καρδίαν προσήμενος A.*Ag*.834: generally, *to be* or *lie near*, νᾶσοι.. τᾷδε γᾷ προσήμεναι Id.*Pers*.881 (lyr.). II. *besiege*, πύργοισι E. *Rh*.390.

❀ **προσημ-αίνω**, *foretell, announce* the future, τινί τι E.*Med*.725; of the gods, τὰ μέλλοντα ἔσεσθαι Hdt.1.45, cf. E.*Supp*.213, *SIG*709.24 (Chersonesus, ii B.C.), etc.; π. ὡς.. Plu.*Nic*.1: abs., Hdt.6.27; of Socrates' δαιμόνιον, X.*Mem*.1.1.4: of medical symptoms, π. θάνατον v.l. in Hp.*Prog*.6; of wind, *give warning*, Arist.*Mete*.367a13, cf. Thphr.*Sign*.31. II. *proclaim* an order, τινί τι, of a herald, Hdt. 6.77: c. inf., [ἡ Πυθίη] π. Λακεδαιμονίοισι ἐλευθεροῦν τὰς Ἀθήνας ib. 123, cf. Aeschin.3.130. III. Pass., ἡ -σημανθεῖσα τιμή the *aforesaid*.., *PMasp*.97.52 (vi A.D.), cf. *PRyl*.156.8 (i A.D.), etc. IV. *mark out beforehand*, μέλανι γραφικῷ Paul.Aeg.6.4 (Pass.). **-αντικός**, ή, όν, *presignifying*, τινος D.S.4.6, Ath.11.490a. **-ασία**, ἡ, *prognostic*, D.S.5.7, Str.7.3.11, Iamb.*Myst*.3.27. **-ειόομαι**, Med., *prognosticate*, τὸν θάνατον Lxx 4*Ma*.15.19. II. Pass., *to be noted before*, Eust.225.15.

**προσημερεύω**, *pass the day with*, τινι Suid. s.v. δράκαυλος, *EM*287. 18.

**προσήμερος**, ον, (ἡμέρα) *happening in one day*, Artem.4.84.

**πρόσημον**, v. πρόσσημον.

❀ **προσήνεια**, ἡ, *mildness, softness*, προσηνείης εἵνεκεν for the sake *of ease* or *comfort*, Hp.*Acut*.21; μετὰ προσηνείας cj. in Herod.Med.ap. Orib.10.18.5; *quietude*, Sm.*Ec*.9.17; of language, ἡ σαφήνεια καὶ ἡ π. τῶν δηλουμένων S.E.*M*.1.194.

**προσήνεμος**, ον, (ἄνεμος) *towards the wind, to windward*, X.*Oec*.18. 6; καθίζειν ἐν προσηνέμῳ καὶ σκιᾷ Arist.*HA*616b14; τὰ π. Id.*GA* 783a32; τὰ εὔπνοα καὶ π. Thphr.*CP*2.9.1, etc.

**προσην-εύομαι**, gloss on σαίνω, Hsch. **-ής**, Dor. **προσᾱνής** ές, *soft, gentle*, Emp.130, etc.; ξενία Pi.*P*.10.64; γλίσχρασμα λεῖον .. καὶ π. Hp.*Acut*.10; προσανέα πίνειν drink *soothing* draughts, Pi. *P*.3.52, cf. Hp.*Acut*.21; αἱ κατὰ σάρκα.. -εῖς κινήσεις Epicur.*Fr*. 411; τὰ -έστατα βρωτὰ καὶ ποτά D.S.17.28; τόπος ἐνδιατρῖψαι.. -έστατος *most pleasant*, Id.3.69; τὰ ἀπήνεμα καὶ π. D.Chr.6.33; π. ὁμιλίαι Plu.2.46e; λεία καὶ π. κίνησις Ph.1.322; π. τι λέγειν speak *smooth things*, Th.6.77; φίλα καὶ π. Plu.2.466d; τὸ μειλιχῶδες καὶ π. Cerc.18 ii 10; τὸ π. τοῦ φθέγματος Luc.*Rh.Pr*.12. 2. c. dat., λύχνῳ π., i.e. *suitable, fit* for burning, Hdt.2.94. 3. of persons, *gentle, kind*, οὐδ' ἀστοῖσι π. Anacr.15; π. ἐγένετο τῇ συγκλήτῳ *IG*5(2).268.29 (Mantinea, i B.C.); τοῖς φίλοις οὐ π. οὐδὲ ἡδὺς Plu. *Nic*.5; εὔνους καὶ π. Id.2.708c; -έστερα.. τὰς ψυχὰς τὰ θήλεα τῶν ἀρρένων Arist.*Phgn*.809a31; τῷ ἤθει -έστατος Plu.*Phoc*.5; π. τὸ βλέμμα Luc.*Pisc*.13; also π. ὄψις Men.584; τὸ π. αὐτοῦ *the enticement* of it, Epict.*Ench*.34: irreg. Sup. προσηνότατος *IPE*2.197.8 (ii A.D.). II. Adv. -νῶς *gently*, εἰς ὕπνον κατενεχθεὶς D.S.2.57; π. λοῦσαι, ἐμβρέξαι, Plu.2.55a,74d; γῆρας π. φέρειν ib.100d; διάγειν D.Chr.32.53, cf. Plot.2.1.7: Comp. -εστέρως, ἡ γεῦσις π. ἀποδέχεται τὰ λιτὰ τῶν ἐδεσμάτων Plb.38.5.7. (Cf. ἀπηνής.) **-ίη**, ἡ, Ion. for προσήνεια, Hp. *Cord*.5.

❀ **προ-σήπω**, *make to rot before*, κρέα Arist.*HA*594b16, Gal.16.761:—Pass., *grow putrid before*, aor. 2 part. προσαπέντα Plu.2.995c.

**προσήρεγε**· προσέθιγεν, Hsch.

**προσηρμοσμένως**, Adv. *fittingly*, Hsch. s.v. ἀραρῶσαι.

**προσηχέω**, *resound* or *re-echo*, Plu.*Alex*.31; θαλάττῃ *with* the sea, Philostr.*Im*.2.16, cf. *VS*1.7; κύματα π. αἰγιαλοῖς Them.*Or*.2.27b: also c. dat. pers., τούτων ῥημάτων ἐμοὶ -ηχούντων Chor. in *Jahrb*.9. 188. II. c. acc., π. μέλος τῇ σύριγγι, τῷ Μουσηγέτῃ, Him.*Ecl*.12. 8, *Or*.14.3.

**προσηχής**, ές, *re-echoing*, prob. f.l. for προσεχής, Plu.*Alex*.17.

**προσηῷος**, α, ον, Hellenistic for προσεῷος, Dor. **ποτᾱῷος**, *towards the East*, καὶ τὸ ποταῷον τὸ Λακίνιον Theoc.4.33; Ἄρτεμις προσηῴα, in Euboea, from the position of her temple, *IG*12(9).1189.5 (Artemisium, ii B.C.), Plu.*Them*.8; Π. δαίμονες D.S.5.55.

**προσθαγενής**, ές (written προσσθ-), *previous*, ϝέργον *IG*5(2).262. 33 (Mantinea, v B.C.).

**προσθᾱκέω**, *sit at* or *near*, π. ἕδραν *sit* here in suppliant guise, S. *OC*1166.

**προσθάλπω**, *comfort, encourage*, τισὶ τὰς γνώμας J.*BJ*4.3.10.

**προσθαρσέω**, *have confidence in*, οἱ ἐπ' αὐτῷ προστεθαρρηκότες Procop.*Arc*.14.

**προσθαυμάζω**, *wonder at*, τι Sch.S.*OC*1119.

**προσθαφαίρ-εσις**, εως, ἡ, Astron., *addition or subtraction as required*, Ptol.*Alm*.5.2, Vett.Val.23.33, Procl.*Hyp*.3.89, *Cat.Cod.Astr*. 8(2).129 (pl.). **-έω**, *add or subtract as required*, Ptol.*Alm*.6.10.

**πρόσθε**, Ion. and poet. for πρόσθεν (q.v.).

**προσθεάομαι**, *behold*, *Supp.Epigr*.6.150 (Phrygia).

❀ **πρόσθεμα**, ατος, τό, = προσθήκη, Ph.1.592, Socr.*Ep*.1; *increase*, Lxx *Le*.19.25, *Ez*.41.7. II. *appendage*: hence, = πόσθη, *AP*12.3 (Strat.), *Gloss*. 2. pl., glossed τὰ πυγιαῖα (dub. sens.), Hsch. III. *pessary*, Hp.*Nat.Mul*.67, *Mul*.1.20, Dsc.1.16. IV. *additional plot* of land, *PPetr*.3 p.39 (iii B.C.), *POxy*.504.12, 45 (ii A.D.).

**προσθεμέλιον**, τό, *additional foundation*, *IG*12(2).11.28 (Mytilene):—hence **-θεμελιόω**, *extend a foundation*, ib.2,8 (Pass.).

❀ **πρόσθεν**, and in Poets **πρόσθε**, also in Ion. Prose (Hdt.1.11, al., cf. ἐπίπροσθε); Dor. and Aeol. **πρόσθα** A.D.*Adv*.153.20, E.M.424. 12 (in elision πρόσθ', Alcm.73, Sapph.*Supp*.1.5); Dor. also **πρόθεν** (cf. ὄπιθεν), Greg.Cor. p.222 S.: Adv.

A. as Prep. with gen.: I. of Place or Space, *before*, στῆ πρόσθ' αὐτοῖο Il.5.170; πεζὸς πρόσθ' ἵππων 13.385, cf. 392, etc.; κατὰ τεύχε' ἔθηκε πρόσθεν Ἀχιλλῆος 19.13; π. ποδῶν Od.22.4, cf. Il.23.877; ἐκ δὲ τὼ ἀΐξαντε πυλάων π. μαχέσθην *before*, i.e. *outside*, 12.145, cf. 9. 473; νῆσος.. π. Σαλαμῖνος τόπων A.*Pers*.447; π. Μυρμιδόνων πολεμιζέμεν *in front of* them, *at their head*, Il.16.220; ἐν τῷ π. τοῦ στρατεύματος *in front of*.., X.*Cyr*.5.3.52; εἰς τὸ π. τῶν ὅπλων ἐκαθέζοντο Id. *An*.3.1.33; εἰς τὸ π. τινῶν θεῖναί τι ἐπὶ τὴν γῆν Pl.*R*.618a: with collat. notion of defence, [σάκος] πρόσθε στέρνοιο φέρων Il.7.224; στὰς πρόσθεν νέκυος 16.321; τάων οὔτοι π. ἵσταμαι I *defend* them not, 4. 54: hence, *for, on behalf of*, π. φίλων τοκέων ἀλόχων τε καὶ υἱῶν 21.587, cf. 16.833; ὅς τε ἑῆς π. πόλιος λαῶν τε πέσῃσιν Od.8. 524. 2. with Verbs of motion, π. ἔθεν φεύγοντα Il.5.56, 80, 20.402; π. δὲ κί' αὐτοῦ 15.307. 3. metaph., οὐδὲν ἐς π. κακῶν E.*Hec*.961: of preference, ἄγειν τινὰ π. τινός Id.*Ba*.225; π. τιθέναι τί τινος Id.*Hec*.129 (anap.), cf. *IG* $2^2$.1299.58; αἰσχρὰ π. τοῦ καλοῦ ζητεῖν E.*Fr*.659.7. II. of Time, *before*, πρόσθ' ἄλλων Il.2.359, cf. S.*Ph*.778; τοῖιν δ' ἔγνω π. *first* of the twain, Il.13.66, cf. Hes.*Th*. 746; ἐμοῦ π. A.*Pers*.529; τοῦ χρόνου π. θανοῦμαι S.*Ant*.462; π. ἑσπέρας X.*Cyr*.7.5.43.—The gen. sts. stands before πρόσθεν, Il.4.54, etc., cf. supr. When it seems to be folld. by a dat., this dat. must be connected with the Verb, and πρόσθεν taken as Adv., v. infr. B. I. 1.

B. as Adv.: I. of Place or Space, *before, in front*, π. λέων ὄπιθεν δὲ δράκων Il.6.181, Hes.*Th*.323; π. δέ οἱ δόρυ τ' ἔσχε καὶ ἀσπίδα Il.5.300, cf. 315; π. δέ οἱ ποίησε γαλήνην Od.5.452; πρόσθ' ὀρόων θάνατον Il.20.481; ὁ π. the *front rank* man, X.*Cyr*.2.2.8; τὰ π. ib.6.3.2; τὰ π. (sc. σκέλη) the *fore*legs (of a horse), Id.*Eq*.1.12; ἡ χώρα ἡ π. Plb. 3.80.3; προῆγε εἰς τὸ π. *on, forward*, Id.4.66.5; ἀεὶ τοῦ π. ὀρεγόμενοι Id. 3.84.12: with collat. notion of defence, π. σάκεα σχέθον Il.4.113; ἦ τοι π. στᾶσα βέλος ἄμυνεν ib.129. 2. with Verbs of motion, *before, in front*, π. ἔφευγε 22.158; ἥ οἱ π. ἰοῦσα 20.95; π. ἡγεμονεύειν Od.22. 400, 24.155; ἵππους π. βαλέειν, v. βάλλω A. II. 5; ἐς τὸ πρόσθε παριέναι *forward*, Hdt.8.89; πάριτ' εἰς τὸ π. Ar.*Ach*.43; εἰς τὸ π. προΐωμεν Pl.*R*.437a, etc.; μηδεμίαν αἰσχύνην π. ποιεῖσθαι allow to stand *in the way*, Id.*Lg*.732b. 3. metaph., εἰς τὸ π. ἔτι ζητήσαντες Id. *Sph*.258c; τοὺς ὄπισθεν εἰς τὸ π. ἄξομεν S.*Aj*.1249. II. of Time, *before, formerly, erst*, οὗ καὶ π. ἀρίστη φαίνετο βουλή Il.7.325, etc.; οὔποτε π. S.*Aj*.318; οὔπω π. X.*An*.5.4.18; ἔτι π. Pl.*Sph*.242d; σμικρῷ π. Id.*Lg*.969b; οἱ π. ἄνδρες the men *of old*, Il.9.524; τοῦ π. Κάδμου τοῦ πάλαι τ' Ἀγήνορος S.*OT*268; ὁ π. γεννηθεὶς Id.*OC*375; ἡ π. the *elder*, E.*Ph*.58; of things, οἱ π. πόνοι the *former, earlier* labours, A.*Supp*.52 (lyr.); ἃ π. ἱππεία S.*El*.504 (lyr.); ὁ π. λόγος Id.*OT*851; ἡ π. ἡμέρα X.*An*.2.3.1, etc.; τὰ π. what was said *above*, Pl.*Phdr*.238b; also τὸ π., as Adv., *formerly*, Il.23.583, Od.4.688; ταὐτὰ τῷ π. the same as *before*, Pl.*Phdr*.241b; τὰ π. A. *Ag*.19.

C. folld. by a Particle, πρόσθεν, πρὶν.. *before*.., mostly with a neg., οὐ πρόσθεν.., πρίν γε..με ἴδηαι Od.17.7, cf. X.*An.*1.1.10, *Cyr.* 1.2.8, etc.; οὐ π. πρὶν ἤ.. ib.1.4.23: without a neg., π. πρὶν τυχεῖν Pi.*P.*2.91: also π. ἤ.. S.*OT*736, *El.*82, 1333; ποτιτάσσει..μὴ π. ἐξελθεῖν ἢ τὰν ματέρα κατακάνῃ Anon.Mythogr. in *PSI*9.1091.3. 2. *sooner, rather*, π. ἂν ἀποθάνοιεν ἢ τὰ ὅπλα παραδοίησαν would die *sooner than*.., X.*An.*2.1.10.

**προσθερμαίνω**, f.l. for προ- in Alex.Aphr.*Pr.*1.54 (Pass.).

⊛ **πρόσ-θεσις**, εως (Dor. **ποτίθεσις** *SIG*569.25 (Halasarna, iii B.C.)), ἡ, (προστίθημι) *application*, ναρθήκων Hp.*Fract.*6; of pessaries, Id. *Mul.*1.11 (pl.), *Nat.Mul.*11; of ladders, π. [κλίμακος] Th.4.135, cf. Plb.5.60.7; of the cupping-instrument, Arist.*Rh.*1405ᵇ3; κόμης προσθέσεις *the use of false* hair, Philostr.*Ep.*22: metaph., Phld.*Sign.* 26. 2. *attachment*, ζῳδίων *IG*1².374.287; of leaf to stem, Thphr. *HP*7.6.2. II. *administration of food, nourishment*, Hp.*Aph.* 1.19 (pl.), Gal.*Nat.Fac.*1.11, 17(2).364. III. *addition*, διὰ τὴν π. τοῦ ἑτέρου τῷ ἑτέρῳ Pl.*Phd.*97a, cf. 101b, c; αὔξησις κατὰ πρόσθεσιν Arist.*GC*333ᵇ1, cf. *Ph.*245ᵃ27; opp. ἀφαίρεσις, ib.190ᵇ6, Hp.*Acut.*38; so in arithmetical sense, ἀριθμεῖσθαι κατὰ π. Arist. *Metaph.*1081ᵇ14, cf. 1092ᵇ31. b. *increase*, Vett.Val.20.17. 2. in the Logic of Aristotle, *addition* of marks (such as properties, accidents, and the like) *to determine a general term*, *Int.*21ᵇ27, *Metaph.* 1029ᵇ30; ἀκρατὴς κατὰ πρόσθεσιν with a *difference*, opp. ἁπλῶς, Id.*EN* 1148ᵃ10; ὁ ἐκ προσθέσεως λόγος, opp. ὁ ἐξ ἀφαιρέσεως, Id.*Metaph.* 1030ᵇ15; hence ἐκ προσθέσεως, of mixed, opp. ἐξ ἀφαιρέσεως, of pure sciences, Id.*Cael.*299ᵃ17; ἡ ἐξ ἐλαττόνων [ἐπιστήμη], opp. ἡ ἐκ π., of arithmetic opp. geometry, Id.*APo.*87ᵃ34, cf.*Metaph.*982ᵃ27. IV. *assignment, provision*, *SIG* l.c. V. Gramm., *addition* of a letter or syllable (as ϝ in ϝ-ρῆξις, ἀ in ἄ-σταχυς), Trypho *Pass.*1.11, 3. 2. VI. π. τοῦ ἡλίου *increase* of the sun's heat, i.e. spring, *PMag.Leid.W.*9.48. VII. in Music, *pause of two time-units*, Aristid.Quint.1.18. VIII. (προστίθεμαι) *assent*, Arr.*Epict.*1.4. 11; ψεύδεσι *Stoic.*3.147. 2. *aid, succour*, π. τοῦ θεοῦ Polyaen.2. 3.8. **-θετέον**, *one must add*, Pl.*Smp.*206a, Arist.*EN*1101ᵃ16. II. *one must assign*, τινί τι X.*Mem.*2.1.2. III. *one must apply*, Orib. *Fr.*1, Aët.16.73, Paul.Aeg.3.66. **-θετέω**, f.l. in Hp.*Nat.Mul.* 8. **-θέτης**, ου, ὁ, of a star, *accelerating*, *Cat.Cod.Astr.*7.119. **-θέτησις**, εως, ἡ, *interposition, occultation*, Epicur.*Ep.*2 p.41 U. codd. (pl., fort. leg. ἐπιπροσθ-). **-θετικός**, ή, όν, *adding*: *repletive*, opp. ἀφαιρετικός, Herod.Med.ap.Orib.7.8.2; *giving additional power, furthering*, δύναμις π. εἰς τὸ τίκτειν Porph.ap.Eus.*PE*3.11; *nutritive*, βοηθήματα Gal.14.694. Adv. -κῶς, θεραπεύειν Herod.Med.ap.Aët.5. 129. II. Astron., *advancing*, of planets, ἡμικύκλιον Ptol.*Alm.*13. 2, cf. *Tetr.*52, Paul.Al.*G.*1. 2. τροπὴ -ωτέρα *adding heat to the sun* (cf. πρόσθεσις VI), *PMag.Leid.W.*10.14. **-θετος**, ον, also η, ον *IG*12(7).62.39 (Amorgos, iv B.C.), Palaeph.12, Luc.*Salt.*27:—*put to, applied*, κλίμακες Aristid.*Or.*51(27).65; πτέρυγες Palaeph. l.c. 2. *put on*, of false hair, X.*Cyr.*1.3.2, Luc.*Alex.*3, etc.; πρόσθετοι (sc. κόμαι or κόσμοι) Ar.*Fr.*321; προκόμιον π. Poll.2.30; π. παχύτης Luc.*Salt.*27. 3. *added, additional*, προσθέτας συκᾶς φυτεύειν *IG* l.c. II. = Lat. *addictus, given up, assigned to* the creditor, of debtors, π. τινὰ ποιήσασθαι D.H.6.59, cf. Plu.*Luc.*20: generally, *assigned, handed over*, [κτήματα] π. ποιήσαντες Μαυσσώλλῳ *SIG*167.12 (Mylasa, iv B.C.), cf. 633.99 (Milet., ii B.C.). III. πρόσθετον, τό, = πρόσθεμα III, *pessary*, Hp.*Superf.*33, Arist.*GA*747ᵃ 8.

**προσθέω**, *run towards* or *to*, τινι Th.4.33 (v.l. for ἐπι-), X.*Cyr.*5.3. 20, etc.; πρὸς τὰ καιόμενα Polyaen.5.8.1: abs., X.*An.*5.7.21.

**προσθεωρ-έω**, *observe besides*, Arist.*HA*538ᵃ6, Epicur.*Nat.*2.9:—Pass., Arist.*Col.*792ᵇ1. 2. *consider besides*, ὅτι.. Id.*Oec.*1344ᵇ 10. **-ητέον**, *one must consider besides*, τίς ὁ τρόπος.. Id.*Cael.* 302ᵃ27 (v.l. προ-).

**πρόσθη**, ἡ, = πρόσθεσις, dub. in Hsch. (fort. προσθή(κη)).

⊛ **προσθήκη**, ἡ, (προστίθημι) *addition, appendage, supplement*, προσθήκας..μοι ὁ λόγος ἐξ ἀρχῆς ἐδίζητο Hdt.4.30, cf. Arist.*Rh.*1354ᵃ14; εὖ γὰρ πρὸς εὖ φανεῖσι π. πέλοι A.*Ag.*500; σμικρὰ π. Pl.*R.*339b, cf. *La.*182c; ἐν προσθήκης μέρει by way of *appendage*, D.11.8 (but ἐν προσθήκῃ μερίς shd. be read in Id.2.14); ἐν ὑπηρέτου καὶ π. μέρει Id. 3.31; ἐν π. μοίρᾳ Luc.*Zeux.*2; προσθήκης μοῖραν ἐπέχειν serve as *auxiliaries*, D.H.5.67; ['Αντώνιος] π. τῆς γυναικὸς ἦν Plu.*Ant.* 62. b. *additional payment*, *PTeb.*296.3 (ii A.D.), etc. 2. *qualification*, ἡ τῆς ἀξίας π. the *additional qualification* of merit, D. *Ep.*3.12; πᾶσίν εἰσι πράγμασι καὶ λόγοις προσθῆκαι δύο, ἡ τοῦ δικαίου καὶ ἀδίκου Id.23.75: hence, *adjective*, Gal.11.74, Dosith. p.398 K. 3. *accident, circumstance*, τὰ δ' ἄλλα προσθήκας ἅπαντα χρὴ καλεῖν Alex.271.5. II. *aid, assistance*, προσθήκη θεοῦ S.*OT*38; ἡ τῶν νόμων π. D.25.24; αἱ λαχάνων π., prov. of what gives no help, Diogenian.2.52. III. *particle*, Longin.21.2; of expletives, π. κεναί Demetr.*Eloc.*55.

**πρόσθημα**, ατος, τό, = foreg. I. 1, E.*El.*193 (lyr.), X.*Mem.*3.10. 13. 2. = πρόσθεμα III, Hp.*Nat.Mul.*32.

**προσθιάζειν**· ἀφελεῖν τὰς ἐκ τῆς ὀσφύος τρίχας, Hsch.

**προσθιγγάνω**, fut. -θίξομαι, *touch*, τινος S.*Ph.*9, E.*IA*339 (troch.); εἰ δὲ τῶνδε προσθίξῃ χερί *with* the hand, Id.*Heracl.*652: abs., προσθιγών *by his touch*, A.*Ch.*1059, cf. S.*Ph.*817, Philum.*Ven.*36.3.

**προσθίδιος**, α, ον, poet. for sq., Nonn.*D.*1.316.

**πρόσθιος**, α, ον, (πρόσθεν) *foremost*, opp. ὀπίσθιος, οἱ π. πόδες (v. l. for ἔμπρ-) the *fore*-feet, Hdt.2.69; π. πούς X.*Cyn.*9.19, etc.; τὰ π. κῶλα (v.l. for ἐμπρ-) Pl.*Ti.*91e, etc.; τὰ π. σκέλη Arist.*PA*688ᵃ3; freq. τὰ π. alone, *the front parts*, opp. τὰ ὀπίσθια, Id.*HA*493ᵃ11, al.; opp. τὰ πρανῆ, Id.*GA*720ᵃ14; βάσιν χερσὶ προσθίαν καθαρμόσας fitting the *fore*-feet to my hands, E.*Rh.*210; οἱ π. ὀδόντες Arist.*HA*501ᵃ13, al.; σιαγόνες δύο, τὸ π. γένειον, τὸ δ' ὀπίσθιον γένυς ib.492ᵇ22; τοῦ χοροῦ (prob. for τοὺς χοροὺς) τοὺς π. the *front* row of teeth, Ar.*Ra.* 548 (lyr.); π. θρίξ Achae.10.2; π. τραύματα wounds *in front*, *AP*9. 279 (Bass.); οἱ κίονες οἱ π., ὁ π. τοῖχος, the *front* row of columns, wall, *IG*2².1682.4, 1668.89.

**προσθλάω**, *squeeze against*, τοῖς κυάθοις τὰ ὑπώπια Sch.Ar.*Pax* 541.

**προσθλίβω** [ῑ], *press* or *squeeze against*, ἑαυτὴν πρὸς τὸν τοῖχον LXX *Nu.*22.25:—Pass., *Placit.*1.4.4.

**πρόσθλιψις**, εως, ἡ, *pressure, oppression*, Aq.*Ps.*42(43).2.

**προσθό-δομος**, ὁ, *chief of a house* or *its former lord*, 'Ατρεῖδαι A.*Ch.* 322 (lyr.). **-φᾰνής**, ές, *showing in front*, Gal.18(1).777.

**προσθροέω**, *address, call by name*, τινα A.*Pr.*595 (lyr.).

**προσθύμιος** [ῡ], poet. **ποτιθύμιος**, ον, *according to one's mind, welcome*, *AP*6.288 (Leon.).

**προσθῠρ-αῖος**, ὁ, *door-keeper*, *PKlein.Form.*84 (vi A.D.). **-εύς**, έως, ὁ, = foreg., *PIand.*37.4 (v/vi A.D.).

**προσῐᾱγών**, όνος, ὁ, = γένειον, *Tab.Defix.Aud.*41.18 (Megara, i/ii A.D.).

**προσιατρεύω**, Ion. **προσιητρ-**, *give extra treatment to*, Hp.*Art.* 14:—Pass., προσιητρεύεται διὰ πλείονος *the cure is prolonged*, Id.*Morb.* 1.21.

**προσιδρύω**, *place near*, ἑαυτοὺς τῷ θεῷ Procl.*in Alc.* p.138C.:—Med., *found in addition* or *near to*, *IG*2.1649:—Pass., βωμὸς -ιδρυμένος Hld.10.18. II. Pass., *to be installed in office*, of a priestess, *IG*2². 1346.19.

**προσίερος**, v. ποθίερος.

**προσιζ-άνω**, *sit by* or *near*: hence, *rest, settle on*, ἡ μέλιττα πρὸς οὐδὲν π. σαπρόν Arist.*HA*535ᵃ2; ἡγοῦντο προσιζάνειν τῷ ὕδατι τὰς ψυχὰς θεοπνόῳ ὄντι Numen.ap.Porph.*Antr.*10; *adhere to*, v.l. for -ίζω in Dsc.5.95: abs., ib.74; ἀπὸ τῶν προσιζανόντων from *all that adheres, dirt*, etc., Paus.5.14.5; of a robe, *sit close*, Luc.*Hist.Conscr.* 10. 2. metaph., κείνῃ μῶμος οὐ προσιζάνει Semon.7.84; πρὸς ἄλλοτ' ἄλλον πημονὴ π. A.*Pr.*278; *cleave to, cling to*, μοι ἀρὰ π. Id.*Th.* 696. **-ησις**, εως, ἡ, *adherence*, Gal.2.903. **-ω**, c. acc., *come and sit near*, πάγον, of suppliants, A.*Supp.*189; Ἄρτεμιν E.*Hec.*935 (lyr.); also π. περὶ τὰ βήματα Pl.*R.*564d; *settle*, ἡ μέλιττα πρὸς οὐδὲν π. σαπρόν Arist.*HA*596ᵇ15; ἐν τοῖς ἄνθεσιν Thphr.*CP*5.10.3; *adhere to*, Dsc.5.95. 2. metaph., *cleave to*, μελέτημα π. τινὶ E.*Fr.*910.9 (anap.); συγγνώμονα ἀλλήλοισι γινώσκει πρὸς ὃ προσίζει· προσίζει γὰρ τὸ σύμφορον τῷ συμφόρῳ Hp.*Vict.*1.6; ἡ προσίζουσα αἰτίη the *inherent* cause, Aret.*SD*1.7.

**προσίημι**, fut. προσήσω, Med. -ήσομαι X.*Cyr.*7.1.13: aor. 1 προσῆκα, Med. -ηκάμην E.*El.*622:—*let come to*, πρὸς τὸ πῦρ τοὺς ὀψίζοντας X.*An.*4.5.5, cf. *Cyr.*7.5.39; *admit*, *POxy.*1070.55 (iii A.D.); *apply*, ἀπειρηκότι τὰ προβόλια X.*Cyn.*10.21. II. more freq. in Med., *let come to* or *near* one, *admit*, προσίεσθαί τινα ἐς ταὐτὸ ἡμῖν αὐτοῖς *admit* one *into* our society, Id.*An.*3.1.30; π. τινὰ εἰς ὁμιλίαν Pl.*Phdr.*255a; ἐγγὺς π. [τοὺς Ἕλληνας] *let* them *approach*, X. *An.*4.2.12; π. τὸν πόλεμον εἰς τὴν χώραν D.9.51; of animals, ἵπποι χαλεπῶς π. ἃ πρόδηλα αὐτοῖς ἐστιν X.*Eq.*3.3; τιθασεύεται καὶ π. τὰς χεῖρας Arist.*HA*608ᵃ26; π. τὰ παιδάρια τῷ μαστῷ Plu.*Cat.Ma.* 20. 2. *admit, allow, believe*, τοῦτο μὲν οὐδὲ προσίεμαι Hdt.1.75; οὐ π. τὴν διαβολήν Id.6.123; προσηκάμην τὸ ῥηθέν E.*El.*622; π. τὰ κεκηρυγμένα *agree to* the proposed terms, Th.4.38, cf. 108; τοῦτον [τρόπον] οὐδαμῇ προσίεμαι Pl.*Phd.*97b. b. *admit, accept, submit to*, ξεινικὰ νόμαια Hdt.1.135; ὀχείαν Arist.*HA*574ᵃ33; ἧττον X.*Cyr.* 3.3.45; τὸ ὑπαίτιον εἶναί τινι οὐ πάνυ π. Id.*Mem.*2.8.5; π. φάρμακον *take* it, ib.4.2.17; ἡ ψυχὴ σῖτον οὐ προσίετο Id.*Cyr.*8.7.4; οἶνον Alex.255.3; προσήκατο ὁ δαίμων ἀντὶ ἀνθρώπου τὸν βοῦν Porph.*Abst.* 2.55. c. *accept, allow, approve*, τὴν προδοσίην Hdt.6.10; τὸ δ' ἄκαιρον.. μὴ προσείμαν E.*Fr.*893 (lyr.); τὰ αἰσχρὰ ἥκιστα προσίεσθαι X.*Mem.*2.6.18; οὐδαμῇ π. οἱ θεοὶ τὸν πόλεμον Id.*An.*5.5.3; πονηρίαν D.25.1; κακὸν οὐδὲν οὐδ' αἰσχρὸν π. X.*Cyr.*7.1.13. d. *accept* a currency, νόμισμα *POxy.*1411.6, 11 (iii A.D.), cf. *PFay.*21.23 (ii A.D.). 3. c. inf., *undertake, venture* to do, Pl.*Lg.*908b, X.*Mem.*2. 7.11; προσεῖτ' ἂν ἀποθανεῖν *would submit* to death, Alex.193; π. κακίονες ἢ πρόσθεν γενέσθαι X.*Cyr.*7.5.83. 4. c. acc. pers., *attach to oneself, attract*, οὐδὲν προσίετό μιν nothing *moved* or *pleased* him, Hdt.1.48; ἓν δ' οὐ προσίεταί με one thing *pleases* me not, Ar.*Eq.*359; τοῦτ' οὐ δύναταί με προσέσθαι Id.*V.*742; προσίεται (sc. Laïs).. καὶ γέροντα καὶ νέον Epicr.3.23.

**προσῐκετεύω**, *supplicate besides*, Ph.2.581.

**προσικνέομαι**, *come to, reach*, δῆγμα δὲ λύπης οὐδὲν ἐφ' ἧπαρ π. A. *Ag.*792 (anap.): also c. gen., *reach so far as, come at*, τόξῳ γὰρ οὔτις πημάτων προσίξεται Id.*Ch.*1033; πρὶν ἐκεῖνον προσικέσθαι σου is f.l. in Ar.*Eq.*761. 2. *approach as a suppliant*, c. acc. loci, A.*Ch.*1035.

**προσ-ίκτης**, ου, ὁ, = sq., *suppliant*, θαλλός Moschio Trag.9. 3. **-ίκτωρ**, ορος, ὁ, *one that comes to a temple, suppliant*, A.*Eu.* 441. II. Pass., *he to whom one comes as a suppliant, protector*, of a god, ib.119 codd. (προσεικότες Weil).

**προσῑνής**, ές, *infestus*, Gloss.

**προσῑνομαι** [ῑ], *hurt, injure before*, Aret.*CD*1.4: also **προσῑνόω**, aor. part. Pass., προσινωθεὶς στόμαχον Vett.Val.168.1 (Hsch. has **προσινάντες**· βλάψαντες).

**προσῑπόω**, *appremo*, Gloss. (προσειπω cod.).

**προσιππ-άζομαι**, = sq., D.S.3.37 (v.l. for προσιππάμενοι), J.*BJ*4.2.2. **-εύω**, *ride up to, charge*, Th.2.79; τῷ ποταμῷ, τῷ στρατοπέδῳ, etc., Plu.*Pyrrh.*16, *Mar.*25, etc.

**προσίπτᾰμαι**, later pres. for προσπέτομαι, Antig.*Mir.*12, D.S.3.37 (cf. προσιππάζομαι).

❋**προσίστημι**, *set against*, πρῷραν βιότου πρὸς κῦμα E.*Tr.*103 (anap.). 2. *weigh out to*, μοι ὀστοῦν Macho ap.Ath.6.243f. 3. *bring together* the edges of a wound, Hp.*Ulc.*10. 4. *check, stop*, τὸ πνεῦμα Arist. l. c., cf. 864ª13. II. mostly Pass. προσίσταμαι, with intr. tenses of Act., *stand near to* or *by*, τινι Hdt.1.129, 5.51; πύλαις A.*Th.*126 (lyr.), cf. Ar.*Ach.*683: also c. acc., with a notion of *approaching*, βωμὸν προσέστην A.*Pers.*203: with a Prep., π. πρὸς τῷ δικαστηρίῳ Aeschin.1.117: c. dat., πλάνος καρδίᾳ προσίσταται E.*Fr.*1038: abs., π. ἀκουσόμενος X.*Cyr.*6.2.13, cf. E.*IA*23 (anap.), Pl.*Ly.*207b, Men.*Pk.*61; *adhere*, c. dat., Archig.ap.Paul.Aeg.4.7. 2. *occur, come on*, of attacks of pain, etc., ᾗ ἂν ὀδύνη π. Hp.*Morb.*2.56, cf. *Epid.*7.96: metaph., κἀμοὶ προσέστη καρδίας κλυδώνιον χολῆς A.*Ch.*183; προσίσταταί μοι *it comes into* my *head, occurs to* me, ὅ σοι προσέστη Pl.*Smp.*175d, cf. *Tht.*173d: c. acc., ὡς δὲ ἄρα μιν προσστῆναι τοῦτο Hdt.1.86. 3. *set oneself against, encounter*, π. ὥσπερ ἀθληταὶ πρὸς τοῦτον τὸν λόγον v.l. for περιιστ- in Pl.*Phlb.*41b. b. more freq. c. dat., *offend, give offence to*, τοῖς ἀκούουσιν D.60.14; προσίστανται ὑμῖν αἱ τοιαῦται εἰσαγγελίαι *you are sick of* them, Hyp.*Eux.*1, cf. Epicur.*Ep.*3 p.61 U.; [πτώσεις] μηκυνόμεναι π. ταῖς ἀκοαῖς *offend* the ear, D.H.*Comp.*12, cf. *Isoc.*2; τοῖς ἀκούουσιν Id.1.8; ἐπαινοῦντες πολλάκις π. Plu.2.629f; π. σοι τὰ ἐν τῷ ἀμφιθεάτρῳ M.Ant.6.46; of food, *go against the stomach*, Pl.Com.95, Plu.2.655f (in Hp.*Mul.*1.11 ὄχλος π. αὐτῇσι (sc. τῇσι γυναιξί) shd. be read).

**προσιστορ-έω**, *narrate besides*, τὸ πῶς Chrysipp.*Stoic.*2.256, cf. Aristeas 314, Str.2.4.1, al.: c. acc. et inf., Plu.*Them.*27, Longin.9.15 (Pass.); with ὅτι.., Asclep.Tragil.3 J., Plu.2.301d; *include in treatment*, Phld.*Rh.*2.108 S. 2. *observe* or *discover besides*, Plu.2.276e. **-ητέον**, *one must narrate further*, Str.8.3.17.

**προσισχύω**, *to be able besides*, c. inf., S.E.*M.*8.368.

**προσίσχω**, = προσέχω (q. v.).

**προσῐτέον**, (πρόσειμι (εἶμι *ibo*)) *one must go to* or *approach*, Pl.*Tht.*179d, X.*Cyn.*10.21, etc.

**προ-σῑτεύω**, *feed before*, τὰ φυτά *Gp.*5.3.1 (Pass.).

**προσῑτητέον**, = προσιτέον, prob. in Aen.Tact.22.13.

**προσῑτός**, ή, όν, *approachable*, of places, Str.6.2.8, J.*BJ*3.7.7; τὸ π. τοῦ τείχους ib.3.7.8. II. of character, ἦθος π. Plu.*Phil.*15.

**προσκαθ-αιρέω**, *pull down besides*, f. l. in Ar.*Eq.*152 ap.Harp. s. v. ἐλεοκόπων; *reduce further*, τὴν δύναμιν *Hippiatr.*1:—Pass., D.C.42.26. **-αίρω**, *purify in addition*, *PLeid.X.*24 B. **-άπτομαι**, Med., *attack besides*, τινος Aristid.2.117 J. **-εδρία**, ἡ, *blockade*, Agath.2.13. ❋ **-έζομαι**, fut. -εδοῦμαι D.1.18, -εσθήσομαι f. l. in Aeschin.3.167: aor. προσκαθεζόμην:—*sit down before* a town, *besiege* it, πόλιν Th.1.26; πόλει Plb.8.7.6, cf. 3.98.7: abs., Th.1.134; πολιορκίᾳ π. ib.11, cf. 61, X.*HG*1.5.21, etc. 2. *watch carefully*, τοῖς πράγμασιν D. l. c. **-έλκω**, aor. part. -ελκύσας, *haul down besides*, πλοῖα Plu.*Cam.*8. **-εύδω**, *sleep by* or *near*, τῇ κορυφῇ Jul.*Ep.*59. **-έψω**, *boil in addition*, Hp.*Vict.*2.52 (Pass., dub. l.). **-ημαι**, Ion. **-κάτημαι**, used as pf. of προσκαθέζομαι, *to be seated by*, Thphr.*Char.*29.5 codd. 2. *rest upon, be close to*, τοῖς ὄρχεσι Arist.*HA*510ª21, cf. Thphr.*HP*7.13.6; *adhere*, [τοῖς ὀδοῦσι] Diocl.*Fr.*141, cf. Orib.*Fr.*76. II. *sit down against* a town, *besiege* it, Hdt.2.157, 5.104, Th.7.48, etc.: metaph., *importune*, Id.6.94; *keep a close watch upon*, D.23.167. 2. *attend diligently to*, ταῖς θεραπείαις ἐπιμελῶς *IG*11(4).1299.12 (Delos, iii B.C.); *devote oneself to*, τοῖς παισί Jul.*Or.*3.110c; of bees, π. [θύμῳ] Plu.2.41f; τέχνῃ π. Lyc.386. III. προσκαθήμενον (dub. sens.) is v. l. for προσκαθεψημένον in Hp.*Vict.*2.52. **-ιδρύω**, *place upon*, περίαπτα ξοάνοις Ph.2.559 (Pass.). **-ιερόω**, *consecrate in addition*, τινί τι *CIG*3080 (Teos). ❋ **-ίζω**, *sit down by* or *near*, c. acc. cogn., θᾶκον οὐκ εὐδαίμονα E.*Hel.*895: abs., *settle*, of gadflies or bees, Pl.*Ap.*31a, Arist.*HA*625ª14:—Med., Pl.*Erx.*397d, Thphr.*Vent.*61. 2. *settle to the bottom of the vessel*, of a mixture, Aët.15.14, cf. Dsc.5.40: metaph., τὸ φυσημάτιον προσεκάθισεν Arr.*Epict.*2.16.10. 3. Med., *sit idle*, Aeschin.3.167. II. *sit down before* a town, προσκαθίσαντα πολιορκεῖν Plb.1.12.4: abs., J.*AJ*12.8.5. **-ίννῡμαι**, *cause to sit down besides*, Hp.*Mul.*1.69. **-ισις**, εως, ἡ, *sitting by* or *near*, v. l. for προκ- in Plu.2.166a (pl.). ❋ **-ίστημι**, *supply* labour *besides*, τὰ ἐλλείποντα σώματα *PPetr.*2 p.7 (iii B.C.); *appoint besides*, στρατηγόν D.S.13.80, cf. Plu.*Num.*7:—also in aor. Med., καινὰ ἕτερα [τέλη] D.C.66.8, etc.; *arrange besides*, τὰ ἐν Πόντῳ προσκατεστήσατο Id.42.46. **-οπλίζω**, *arm besides*, Εἵλωτας Plu.*Cleom.*23. **-οράω**, *behold besides*, τὴν ἐπιστήμην Pl.*Chrm.*172b. **-οσιόω**, *sanctify, consecrate*, δύο ἡμέρας *OGI*383.91 (Nemrud Dagh, i B.C.).

**προσκαινουργέω**, *work some new thing*, πολλά J.*AJ*17.11.2.

**προσκαινόω**, *renew by addition*, prob. l. in Plu.2.273c.

❋ **πρόσκαιρος**, ον, *occasional, extraordinary*, ἑορτή *IG*2².1368.44; αἱ π. ἐπιβολαί the *additional* taxes, *PLond.*3.979.19 (iv A.D.); τὰ δημόσια τέλη κανονικά τε καὶ π. τούτων *PMasp.*168.36 (vi A.D.). 2. *opportune*, ἐκδρομαί Plu.*Pel.*15; θόρυβοι Luc.*Dem.Enc.*31; ῥῆμα Sch.Ar.*Ach.*274. 3. *at the time*, τὰ π. ἄδηλα Gal.1.78. 4. πρόσκαιρον, τό, *agreement having temporary validity*, *Sammelb.*6000ᵛ.35 (vi A.D.). II. *lasting for a time, temporary*, Str.7.3.11; ἀνοχή D.C.*Fr.*46.1; π. ἡ τέρψις, opp. ἀθάνατος, D.H.*Rh.*7.4,6; opp. αἰώνιος, 2*Ep.Cor.*4.18, cf. *OGI*669.14 (Egypt, i A.D.); *transient*, *Ev.Matt.*13.21, Plot.4.8.8. Adv. -ρως Sor.1.31, Ps.-Dsc.4.58, Hdn.4.14.7.

**προσκαίω**, Att. **-κάω**: aor. προσέκαυσα Ar.*V.*828:—*set on fire* or *burn besides*, l. c.; [τὰ ἑψόμενα] Arist.*GA*767ª20; τὴν δᾶδα Thphr.*HP*9.3.4; ὄψον προσκέκαυκε Alex.124.3:—Pass., σκεύη προσκεκαυμένα pots *burnt at the fire*, Ar.*V.*939 (nisi leg. -κεκλημένα), cf. Arist.*Mete.*381ª27: metaph., *to be in love with*.., ἰσχυρῶς προσεκαύθη X.*Smp.*4.23.

**προσκᾰκουργέω**, *do one an ill turn besides*, τινα D.C.45.22.

**προσκᾰκόω**, *injure besides*, Sor.1.49:—Pass., *to be affected besides*, Hp.*Hum.*4.

**προ-σκᾰλεύω**, *dig out first*, τὸν ὀδόντα Pall. *in Hp.*2.174 D.

**προσκᾰλέω**, *call on, summon*, τινας Th.8.98 (v. l.), S.*Aj.*89, Pl.*Men.*82a, etc.; *address, accost*, ὀνόματι D.C.71.34; ἑαυτόν A.D.*Synt.*218.27 (Med.). 2. metaph., *call forth, excite*, ἔκκρισιν Sor.1.26; ἱδρῶτα ib.31. II. Med. with pf. Pass. (v. infr.), *call to oneself, invite, summon*, τινα v. l. in X.*An.*7.7.2, cf. *PCair.Zen.*647.25 (iii B.C.), Plu.2.354d, Luc.*DDeor.*19.1; τὰς κύνας Poll.5.85; esp. *call to one's aid*, τινα Philipp.ap.D.18.166; τινὰ ἐς τὴν πολιτείαν dub. l. in Plu.*Dem.*21: c. dupl. acc., τὸ ἔργον ὃ προσκέκλημαι αὐτούς to which *I have called* them, *Act.Ap.*13.2. 2. as law-term, of an accuser, *cite* or *summon into court*, Telecl.2, Ar.*V.*1334; π. τινὰ ὕβρεως *lay* an action for assault, ib.1417; in full, π. δίκην ἀσεβείας πρὸς τὸν βασιλέα Lys.6.11, cf. 21.19, D.18.150; π. τινὰ πρὸς τὸν πολέμαρχον Lys.23.2; π. σε.. πρὸς τοὺς ἀγορανόμους βλάβης τῶν φορτίων Ar.*V.*1406; π. τινὰ εἰς δίκην δημοσίαν X.*Mem.*2.9.5; π. τινὰ πρὸς τὸν ἄρχοντα εἰς διαδικασίαν D.43.7, cf. 15; τραύματος εἰς Ἄρειον πάγον Luc.*Tim.*46, cf. *Pisc.*39:—Pass., *to be summoned*, λιποταξίου, ξενίας, *on a charge of*.., D.39.17,18; φόνου δίκην Arist.*Ath.*16.8; ὑπομεῖναι προσκληθεὶς δίκην εἰς Ἄρειον πάγον submitted *to be summoned*.. before the Areopagus, Id.*Pol.*1315ᵇ21; προσκληθείς *summoned*, Antipho 5.13, D.49.19, cf. Ar.*Nu.*1277; παρὰ τοῦ.. ἔχοντος τὸν κλῆρον προσκαλεῖσθαι *that citation should be made* of the party in possession, D.43.7; cf. πρόσκλησις. 3. *cite as witness*, Pl.*Lg.*936e codd.; εἰς μαρτυρίαν D.29.20 codd.; μάρτυρα Plu.2.205b.

**προσκᾰλινδέομαι**, *spend one's time among, haunt*, [μνήμασι] Eun.*VS*p.472 B.; τάφοις Jul.*Gal.*335c.

**προσκάμνω**, *work longer*, μικρὸν ἔτι π. App.*Pun.*97. 2. *suffer besides*, Paus.5.13.6.

**προσκάρδιος**, Dor. ποτι-, ον, *at the heart*, ἕλκος Bion 1.17.

❋ **προσκαρτερ-έω**, Dor. ποτι- *IG*4²(1).63.4 (Epid., ii B.C.):—*persist obstinately in*, τῇ πολιορκίᾳ Plb.1.55.4, D.S.14.87; τῇ προφορᾷ Phld.*Rh.*1.158 S.; τῇ προσευχῇ *Act.Ap.*1.14: abs., X.*HG*7.5.14, Ph.*Bel.*101.9, Lxx *Nu.*13.21(20), J.*BJ*6.1.3, Ach.Tat.1.10; καίπερ ἀχθόμενοι τῇ καθέδρᾳ π. J.*AJ*5.2.6. 2. *adhere firmly to* a man, *be faithful to* him, τινι Plb.23.5.3, *Act.Ap.*8.13, 10.7; of servants, *remain in* one's *service*, D.59.120; of a κοσμητής, *IG*2².1028.84. b. *remain in attendance* at a law-court, τῷ βήματι, τῷ κριτηρίῳ, *PHamb.*4.7 (i A.D.), *POxy.*261.12 (i A.D.). c. *devote oneself to* an office or occupation, τῇ στρατηγίᾳ ib.82.4 (iii A.D.); τῇ ἑαυτῶν γεωργίᾳ *PAmh.*2.65.3 (ii A.D.). 3. **Pass.**, ὁ προσκαρτερούμενος χρόνος *time diligently employed*, D.S.2.29. 4. *wait for* a person, Φιλέᾳ *POxy.*1764.4 (iii A.D.): abs., ἕως ἂν Ἑτέαρχος παραγένηται *PSI*5.598.7 (iii B.C.). ❋ **-ησις**, εως, ἡ, *perseverance, patience*, Phld.*Rh.*1.11 S., *Ep.Eph.*6.18. **-ητικῶς**, Adv. *painstakingly*, Phld.*Rh.*1.92 S. **-ία**, ἡ, = προσκαρτέρησις, *Inscr.Prien.*109.101 (ii B.C.).

**προσκαρφόω**, *attach with nails*, Sch. rec. A.*Pr.*56, al., Sch.Ar.*Pl.*944.

**προσκατα-βαίνω**, *descend besides*, Ceb.16, *AP*11.99 (Lucill.); ἐς βόθρον Lxx *Ez.*31.14. 2. *go down to meet*, abs., *UPZ*15.8 (ii B.C.). ❋ **-βάλλω**, *deposit besides*, *PHib.*29.23 (iii B.C.), Sch.Ar.*Nu.*1237. **-βλάπτω**, *damage as well*, Arc. aor. subj. εἰ δ' ἄν τις.. ποσκατυβλάψῃ τι *IG*5(2).6.38 (Tegea, iv B.C.). **-βλημα**, ατος, τό, *that which is paid besides*: in pl., *sums paid in addition to make up a deficiency* in the revenue, D.24.97,98. **-βόλημα**, f.l. for foreg., Suid. **-γελάω**, *laugh at besides*, τοῦ Πλάτωνος Ath.11.508b, cf. Jul.*Or.*6.182b (προκ- codd.). **-γιγνώσκω**, *condemn besides*, Antipho 3.3.4 (Pass.). II. *adjudge, award to*, αὐτοῖς τὰ χωρία -γνώσεται D.55.32. **-γράφω** [γρᾰ], *enrol besides*, στρατιώτας D.S.19.15:—Pass., ib.40; -γραφέντες βουλευταί *enrolled as new* members of the council, D.H.2.47. 2. *describe besides*, τοὺς κύκλους Ptol.*Geog.*1.24.21.

**προσκατάγω** [ᾰγ], *draw back further*, Ph.*Bel.*74.47 (Pass.). 2. *transport down* the Nile *in addition*, ἀγγεῖα *PMich.Zen.*103.11 (iii B.C.).

**προσκατα-δείδω**, *fear besides*, D.C.37.39. **-δείκνῡμι**, *ordain besides*, καινὰ τέλη Id.77.9. **-δεσμέω**, *tie up besides*, Sor.1.83. **-δέω**, *bind down to* or *upon*, τὴν χεῖρα πρὸς τὸ ξύλον Hp.*Art.*7; τὸν βραχίονα πρὸς τὰς πλευράς ib.9.

**προσκαταίρω**, 1 aor. -κατῆρα, τῷ στόλῳ *sail down against*, D.S.11.61.

**προσκαταισχύνω**, *disgrace still further*, Plu.*Phoc.*22.

**προσκατα-κλαίομαι**, Med., *lament one with another*, Plb.38.15.9. **-κλείω**, *shut up besides*, Hsch. s. v. κατακυνῶν:—aor. Pass. -κατεκλείσθην Aesop.349b. **-κλίνομαι** [ῑ], Pass., *recline beside*, Hsch. s. v. πρόσβαλον. **-κλύζω**, *deluge still more*: metaph., τὸν λόγον Plu.2.549e. **-κτάομαι**, *acquire besides*, Plb.15.4.4, D.S.2.32. II. *get made*, Sor.1.4. **-κτείνω**, *kill besides*, v. l. for προσαπο-, Palaeph.31. **-κῡκάω**, *mix, beat up with*, Hp.*Morb.*3.17. **-λᾰλέω**, bring a counter-argument against one, Tab.Defix.Aud.3b8 (Cnidus): —Pass., have a counter-argument brought against one, Arg.3 Ar. Nu. **-λαμβάνω,** fasten down to a thing, τὰς χεῖρας πρὸς τὸ σῶμα Hp.Art.43:—Pass., [ἔναιμα] ῥητίνῃ προσκαταλαμβάνεται are treated with resin, have resin for one ingredient, ib.63. **-λέγω,** enrol besides or in addition to, παρθένοις τέτταρσιν οὔσαις δύο ἑτέρας D.H.3.67, cf. J.AJ12.7.1, Plu.CG5, Arat.14:—Pass., Id.Rom.20. II. reckon as belonging to, τοῖς ἔθνεσιν ἑκάστοις τὰς γειτνιώσας νήσους Str. 6.1.15. **-λείπω,** leave besides as a legacy, ἀρχήν τινι Th.2.36: also, leave or lose besides, τὰ αὐτῶν Id.4.62; σχολήν Plu.2.840e. II. leave over, of surplus material, Lxx Ex.36.7; leave behind, in dissection or operations, Heliod.ap.Orib.50.48.5, Gal.2.531: generally, leave behind one, τὸ ἱμάτιον J.AJ2.4.5.

**προσκατᾰλείφω,** smear besides, πηλῷ Arist.HA552ᵇ28.

**προσκαταλεπτύνω,** reduce, attenuate further, prob. l. in Ruf.Sat. Gon.15.

**προσκαταλλάττομαι,** Pass., become reconciled besides, Arist.Rh. 1372ᵃ19 (v.l. προ-).

**προσκατα-λύω,** undo or dissolve besides, D.C.47.32; complete the ruin of, Lib.Or.28.15. **-μανθάνω,** learn in addition, Hp.Acut. 1. **-μένω,** remain at a place afterwards, αὐτόθι Hyp.Lyc. 17. **-μετρέω,** measure out land in addition, PCair.Zen.745.63 (iii B.C., Pass.). **-νέμω,** allot or assign besides, δευτέραν βουλήν Plu.Sol.19; τὴν Καμπανίαν τοῖς ἀπόροις Id.Cat.Mi.33, cf. D.C.51. 4. **-νοέω,** note in addition, Epicur.Ep.1 p.24U. **-νόησις,** εως, ἡ, perceiving besides, ib.p.29U. **-ξαίνω,** fut. -ξᾰνῶ, cause to pine away, Lyc.173. **-ξύω,** engrave or embroider upon, EM412. 53. **-πήγνυμι,** fasten in besides, τι εἴς τι Ael.NA8.10. **-πίμπρᾰμαι,** Pass., to be burnt down besides, D.C.62.17. **-πλάσσω,** apply as a plaster, Heras ap. Gal.12.819, Paul.Aeg.3.81, Paraphr. Poet.de herb.86. **-πλήσσω,** strike with terror besides, D.C.38.4, 39. 44. **-ποντίζω,** = sq.: metaph., τὴν βουλήν Lib.Or.33.13. **-ποντόω,** sink in the sea beside, ὁλκάδας D.C.42.38 (dub.). **-πράττω,** accomplish besides, Aristid.1.394J. **-πυκνόω,** make still closer, τὴν εὔνοιαν Plu.2.491a.

**προσκατ-ᾰράομαι,** curse besides, Sch.Ar.Pax 248. **-ᾰριθμέω,** reckon in, reckon together with, τὸ μὴ ὂν π. εἰς τὴν τοῦ παντὸς φύσιν Thphr.Metaph.18; τὴν ἀνθύπατον ἀρχὴν ταῖς ὑπατείαις Plu.Marc. 30.

**προσκατα-ρρήγνῡμι,** rend besides, τὴν ἐσθῆτα D.C.78.7:—Med., Id.54.1. **-σήπω,** cause to putrefy besides, Hp.Morb.2.2. **-σκάπτω,** undermine, destroy besides, J.Vit.10. **-σκευάζω,** furnish or prepare besides, ἐμπόριον D.20.33; θησαυρόν another granary, PCair.Zen.509. 9 (iii B.C.); πύλας, τριήρεις, D.S.11.21,43, etc.; δυνάστην π. τινά set him up besides, Plb.21.11.6; build in addition to or beside, οἰκήματα οἰκήμασι, πόλεις πόλεσι, J.AJ8.5.2, 8.6.1:—Med., procure for oneself, ἄλλα τινὰ τῶν καλῶν Arist.Top.118ᵃ13; φρούριον J.AJ15.9.4:—Pass., ὄνειδος -σκευασθῆναι τῇ πόλει D.19.78, cf. 23.189, IG12(8). 51.10 (Imbros, ii B.C.). II. prove in addition, Alex.Aphr. in Metaph.260.32. **-σκευαστικός,** ή, όν, proving in addition, ib. 750.11. **-σπάω,** draw down besides, esp. ships into the sea, launch besides, Plb.4.53.1. II. Pass., to be brought away together, in vomiting, Hp.Coac.626. **-στρέφομαι,** Med., subject to oneself besides, D.H.Isoc.14 (v.l.), D.C.37.5, etc. **-σύρω** [ῡ], pull down besides, χερὶ Ἄδωνιν AP11.174 (Lucill.). **-τάσσω,** append, subjoin, Plb.3.20.1. 2. assign, τὸ γλυκὺ ὕδωρ τῇ γῇ Ph.1.31; τὸ ὑγρὸν τῷ αἰθέρι Corn.ND32. 3. attach, τῷ θεῷ ἑαυτόν Arr.Epict.4.1.98, cf. 89,91:—fut. Pass. τοὺς -ταγησομένους OGI56.27 (Canopus, iii B.C.). **-τείνω,** stretch out or extend besides, Hp.Art.77, v.l. in Lxx 4Ma.9.19. **-τίθημι,** pay down besides or as a further deposit, τριώβολον Ar.Nu.1235; π. ἀργύριον μισθόν Pl.Thg.128a: metaph., add a remark, Gal.6.9. **-τρέχω,** overrun besides, J.AJ13.12.6. **-φθείρω,** destroy besides, Teles pp.59,60H. **-φρονέω,** despise besides, D.C.42.37. **-φῡτεύω,** plant in addition, [ἀρούρας] PCair.Zen. 269.17 (iii B.C.); [γῆν] PEnteux.65.15 (iii B.C.). **-χέω,** pour out still more, Hp.Acut.65 (Pass.). **-χράομαι,** kill besides, τοὺς ἐχθρούς D.C.72.14. **-χρημᾰτίζω,** pf. part. Pass. προσκατακεχρηματισμένην UPZ26.7 (ii B.C.), miscopied from προσκατακεχωρισμένην, cf. *25.11. ⊛ **-χωρίζω,** credit in addition, add in a bank ledger, PRev.Laws 16.9 (iii B.C., prob.). II. enclose or deliver a document with another, PTheb.Bank 2.8, al. (ii B.C., Pass.), UPZ *25.6,11 (ii B.C., Pass.). **-ψεύδομαι,** tell more lies of, τινος Plb. 12.13.3; assert falsely besides, Arr.Epict.3.17.8, D.C.45.31.

**προσκατ-ειλέω,** wrap up against the body, cj. in Sor.1.84 (Pass.). **-εργάζομαι,** accomplish besides, τὰ λοιπά D.C.37.39. 2. acquire besides, μηδὲν ἕτερον Id.56.41. 3. dispatch, kill besides, Id.63.29. **-ερείδομαι,** Pass., to be pressed down besides, πρὸς τὴν γῆν ὑπὸ τῆς χειρός Hp.Art.58. **-ερείπω,** complete the overthrow or ruin of, τὴν Ἑλλάδα Paus.3.7.10. **-εσθίω,** fut. -έδομαι, eat besides, Alex.172.5. **-εύχομαι,** curse besides, v.l. in Thphr.HP 9.8.8. **-έχω,** hold steady against a cushion, τὴν κεφαλήν τινος Hp.Art.30. II. increase the power of retention, Archig.ap.Orib. 8.1.24. **-ηγορέω,** accuse besides, ἐπίδειξιν π. accuse one also of making a display, Th.3.42; π. τινὸς ὅτι.. X.Mem.2.6.34; ὡς.. Plu. Per.32. II. in Logic, use an additional name or predicate, Gal. ap.Orib.44.27.2; predicate besides, Dexipp. in Cat.35.18:—Arist. only in Pass., to be predicated besides, Int.19ᵇ19, Metaph.1054ᵃ16: c. dat., to be predicated of besides, APr.25ᵇ22. **-οικίζω,** remove to another settlement, Arr.An.4.22.5. **-ομνῦμαι,** Med., swear besides, τόδε Paus.5.42.2. **-ορθόω,** set up or establish besides, τινί τι Hld. 6.13. II. achieve besides, τι D.C.49.23.

**προσκαυλέω,** pf. -κεκαύληκα, shoot out like a stalk, Hp.Oss.15.

**πρόσ-καυμα,** ατος, τό, result of burning: hence π. χύτρας soot from the outside of a pot, Lxx Jl.2.6, Na.2.10(11). **-καυσις,** εως, ἡ, burning, of bread, Dieuch.ap.Orib.4.5.2; of food, Plu.2.461c. II. metaph., ardour, passion, Phld.Rh.1.361S. **-καυστικός,** ή, όν, apt to burn the meat, of a cook, Posidipp.1.7.

**προ-σκεδάννῡμι,** scatter before:—Προσκεδαννύμενος, title of a play by Alexis.

⊛ **πρόσκειμαι** (on the Ion. forms v. κεῖμαι), serving as Pass. to προστίθημι, to be placed or laid by or upon, lie by or upon, οὔατα προσέκειτο handles were upon it, Il.18.379; τῇ θύρᾳ πρόσκεισο keep close to the door, Ar.V.142, cf. E.Ph.739; δοκοὶ τῷ τείχει.. προσκείμεναι lying near the wall, Th.4.112; of places, lie near, be adjacent, τῷ καλῷ ἀκρωτηρίῳ Plb.3.24.2, etc.; ὁ προσκείμενος [ἵππος] the inside horse (turning a corner), S.El.722: metaph., πρόσκειται τὸ κάλλος (ὁ καλός ap. Stob.) τῷ ἀγαθῷ X.Oec.6.15. 2. lie beside, cling to, ἀμφὶ μέσσῃ περιπετὴ προσκείμενον S.Ant.1223. 3. of pessaries, to be applied, remain in place, Hp.Nat.Mul.109, Mul.1.37. II. generally, to be involved in or bound up with, εἴ τῳ πρόσκειμαι χρηστῷ S.El.240 (lyr.); ᾧ σὺ πρόσκεισαι κακῷ ib.1040; κακοῖς γὰρ οὐ σὺ πρόσκεισαι μόνη E.Fr.418; cf. infr. III. 2. to be attached or devoted to, τινι Hdt. 6.61; τῷ δήμῳ Th.6.89, etc.: abs., θεραπεύων π. Id.8.52; devote oneself to the service of a god, τῷ Διονύσῳ D.C.51.25; π. διάκονος καὶ ἀκόλουθος ἐκείνῳ (sc. τῷ θεῷ) Arr.Epict.4.7.20; also of things, π. τῷ λεγομένῳ put faith in a story, Hdt.4.11; π. οἴνῳ, τῇ φιλοινίῃ, to be addicted to wine, Id.1.133, 3.34; ἄγραις devote oneself to hunting, S.Aj.407 (lyr.); ταῖς ναυσί Th.1.93, cf. 8.89; τῇ τοῦ ὄντος ἰδέᾳ Pl.Sph.254a; τῇ τοῦ Ὁμήρου ποιήσει Paus.2.21.10; τοῖς Δημοσθένους λόγοις Aristid.2. 315J.; θειασμῷ Th.7.50, Plu.Nic.4. 3. urge, entreat, solicit, Κύρῳ π. δῶρα πέμπων Hdt.1.123; π. αὐτῷ ἀξιοῦντες.. X.HG3.4.7: abs., ἐπηκολούθουν κηντιβόλουν προσκείμενοι with importunity, Ar.Fr.543; προσκείμενος ἐδίδασκε with zeal, Th.7.18; δεόμενοι προυέκειντο Plu. Per.33. b. in military sense, press hard, pursue closely, ἡ ἵππος προσέκειτο πᾶσα Hdt.9.57, cf. 40,60; ᾗ μάλιστα αὐτοῖς προσκέοιντο Th.4.33, etc.; τὸ προσκείμενον the pressure of the enemy, Hdt.9.61; κλύδωνα πολεμίων προσκείμενον E.IT316: metaph., ἀνάγκης ἀεὶ προσκειμένης Pl.Phdr.240e: rarely c. acc., οἵ μ' ἀεὶ προσκείμενοι E.IA814 (s.v.l.). III. to be assigned to, fall to, belong to, τοῖσι θεῶν τιμὴ αὕτη πρόσκειται Hdt.1.118, cf. 2.83, etc.; τῷ πρόσκειμαι δούλα; E.Tr. 185 (lyr.), cf. Hdt.1.196; of qualities, τὴν ἀβουλίαν ὅσῳ μέγιστον ἀνδρὶ πρόσκειται κακόν S.Ant.1243; βραχεῖ λόγῳ δὲ πολλὰ π. σοφά Id.Fr.102; ἡ πόλλ' ἀγρώταις σκαιὰ π. φρενί E.Rh.266; τὸ δ' ἄρσεν αὐτοὺς ὠφελεῖ προσκείμενον Id.Hipp.970; τὸ ῥῆμα πρόσκειται τῇ προτέρᾳ αἰτιατικῇ belongs to.., A.D.Synt.243.20; to be laid upon as a charge, business, προξείνους ἀποδεικνύναι τούτοισι προσκεῖσθαι Hdt.6. 57, cf. 1.119; ἐμοὶ τοῦτο π., μηδένα πελάζειν δόμοις E.Hel.443; ἄλλῳ δ' ἄλλο π. γέρας, σὲ μὲν μάχεσθαι, τοὺς δὲ βουλεύειν καλῶς Id.Rh.107; of punishments, προσκειμένης ζημίας τῷ πωλοῦντι X.Vect.4.21 (sed leg. προκ-). 2. to be added or attached to, ἄλγος ἄλγει π. E.Alc. 1039; ἐπὶ τοῖς πάλαι κακοῖς π. πῆμα Id.Heracl.483; κέρδος πρὸς ἔργῳ Id.Rh.162; π. τῇ πόλει ὑπὸ τοῦ θεοῦ ὥσπερ ἵππῳ Pl.Ap.30e; ἐχθρὰ δὲ τῷ θανόντι προσκείσει thou wilt be for ever hated by.., S.Ant.94; ταῦτα προσκείσθω τοῖς εἰρημένοις Isoc.15.196: abs., ἡ χάρις προσκείσεται S.OT232; εἰ πρόσκειταί τι γράμμα ἢ ἀφῄρηται Pl.Cra.393d; αἱ γραφαὶ (of νῷ) οὐκ ἔχουσι τὸ ῑ προσκείμενον A.D.Pron.86.12; τὰ ἀντίγραφα οὐκ ἔχει προσκείμενον τῷ "φρενιτικοί" τὸ "εἰσίν" Gal.16. 491, cf. 840. 3. Arith. and Geom., to be added, opp. ἀφῃρῆσθαι, Arist.EN1132ᵇ7, cf. 1138ᵃ19, PCair.Zen.707.3, 709.7 (iii B.C.); προσκείσθω ποτί.. Archim.Spir.10; also κοινὸς -κείσθω λόγος let the ratio be multiplied into both, Papp.66.28. 4. in Logic, to be added as a determinant (v. πρόσθεσις III. 2), τὸ προσκείμενον Arist.Int.21ᵃ21; τοῖς ὅροις, ἄλλῳ π., Id.APr.30ᵃ1, Metaph.1029ᵇ31; so later, to be specified or given in a document, ὁ αὐτὸς χρόνος π. BGU388 ii 37 (ii A.D.), cf. PRyl.421.36 (iii A.D.), etc.

**προσκείρομαι,** Med., shave oneself besides, Chrysipp.Stoic.3.198.

**προσκέλλω,** aor. -έκελσα, push to land, land, νήσῳ Orph.A.1050, Opp.H.2.500, cf. Nonn.D.3.47.

**προσκεν-όω,** empty, evacuate besides, Gal.15.727. **-ωτέον,** one must evacuate besides, Id.12.666.

**προσκεπαστής,** οῦ, ὁ, = Lat. protector, Men.Prot.p.115D.

**προσκέπτομαι,** v. προσκοπέω.

**προσκερδαίνω,** aor. προσεκέρδᾰνα Plb.31.28.12, Aen.Gaz.Thphr. p.35B.: pf. -κεκέρδηκα D.56.30:—gain in addition, D. l. c.; ὑγίειαν Plb. l. c.

⊛ **προσκεφᾰλ-άδιον,** τό, Dim. of sq., Dura⁴ 100 (iii A.D.), Eust.1552. 31. **-αιον,** τό, cushion for the head, pillow, Hp.Fract.16, Ar.Pl. 542, Lys.12.18, etc.: generally, any cushion, Cratin.269, Hermipp. 54, Thphr.Char.2.11, PCair.Zen.92.22 (iii B.C.), Lxx Ez.13.18, Ev. Marc.4.38, etc.: Dor. ποτικεφάλαιον IG5(1).1390.23 (Andania, i B.C.); also ποικεφ-, Schwyzer 323 C 30 (Delph.). II. name for a treasure-chamber of the Persian kings, Chares 2 J. **-ίς,** ίδος, ἡ, = foreg. I, Gloss. **-ον,** τό, = foreg., Cyran.25.

⊛ **προσκηδής,** ές, (κῆδος) bringing into alliance or kindred, ξεινοσύνη Od.21.35: but perh. kindly, as in A.R.3.588. II. connected by marriage, τινι Hdt.8.136; προσκηδέες kinsfolk, AP7.444 (Theaet.), A.R.4.717 (but perh. careworn).

**προσκήνιον,** τό, entrance of a tent, Lxx Ju.10.22. 2. porch of a house, *PRyl.*233.4 (pl., ii A.D.). II. *raised platform in front of stage-buildings, stage,* *IG*11(2).153.14, 158 *A* 67 (Delos, iii B.C.), 7.423 (p.745, Oropus, ii/i B.C.), Plb.30.22.4, *TAM*2.408.9 (Patara, ii A.D.), *OGI*510.5 (Ephesus, ii A.D.), Poll.4.123; ἡ τύχη παρελκομένη τὴν πρόφασιν καθάπερ ἐπὶ προσκήνιον Plb.*Fr.*212; Lat. *proscaenium*, Vitr.5.7.1. 2. *painted scenery at the back of the stage,* Duris 14 J.; τὸ προσκάνιον ἱστάτω Ἡρακλείοις *SIG*481 *B* 4 (Delph., iii B.C.).

**προσκήπτω,** *presignify, forebode,* Hsch.

**προσκηρῡκεύομαι,** *send a herald to* one, Th.4.118.

⊛ **προσκηρύσσω,** Att. **-ττω,** *proclaim also,* *CIG*3641 *b* 21 (Lampsacus). II. *summon,* π. τοὺς φιλοσόφους Luc.*Pisc.*39 (v.l. προκ-).

**προσκιγκλίζομαι,** Pass., *wag one's tail,* εὖ ποτεκιγκλίσδευ (Dor. for -ίζου) *didst twist about,* Theoc.5.117.

**προσκῐθᾰρίζω,** Dor. **ποτι-,** *accompany on the lyre,* *SIG*711 *L* 19 (Delph., ii B.C.), prob. in Limen. tit.

**προσκινδῡνεύω,** *expose oneself to danger as well,* D.C.*Fr.*83.2.

⊛ **προσκῑνέομαι,** Pass. with fut. Med., *move to* or *towards,* sens. obsc., of women, Ar.*Pax*903, *Ec.*256, Xenarch.4.23:—in Act. of the man, Pherecr.131.3 (but f.l. in Plb.5.86.10, J.*AJ*2.3.1).

**προσκιχρῶ,** *accommodo, Gloss.*

**προσκλαίω,** *weep at* or *during,* Ael.*VH*9.39.

**προσκλάομαι,** pf. Pass. -κέκλασμαι, *to be shattered* or *shivered against,* X.*Eq.*7.6.

**προσκλείω,** = *accludo, Gloss.*; in Dor. form **ποτικλάιγω** (-**κλᾴγω** or -**κλαΐγω**), *adjoin,* *Tab.Heracl.*2.69, 107.

⊛ **προσκληρόω,** *allot, assign, attribute,* ἀκοσμίαν τινί Phld.*Sto.*339. 16; τούτῳ τῷ βίῳ ἡ τύχη π. σε Luc.*Am.*3:—Med., fut. -ώσομαι, τιμὴν αὐτῷ Ph.1.339:—Pass., *to be assigned,* Id.2.366, 381, J.*BJ*2.20. 4; also, *to be attached to,* Παύλῳ *Act.Ap.*17.4.

⊛ **πρόσ-κλησις,** εως, ἡ, (προσκαλέω) *judicial summons,* Ar.*V.*1041 (pl.), Pl.*Lg.*846c (pl.), 855d (pl.), D.43.16: generally, ἡ τοῦ δίσκου π. *summons* to quoit-throwing, Lxx 2*Ma.*4.14. II. *invocation,* f.l. for -κλισις in Iamb.*Myst.*1.12. **-κλητικός,** ή, όν, *calling, addressing,* φωνή Plu.2.354d; π. ἔχει δύναμιν τὸ κάλλος *that calls men to it,* Ph.2.496. **-κλητος,** ον, *specially summoned,* π. ἐκκλησία Sch. Ar.*Ach.*19; so πρόσκλητος, ἡ, alone, Ἀρχ. Ἐφ.1911.135 (Gonni); ἐν προσκλήτῳ *IG*14.757, 760 (Naples, i A.D.).

**πρόσ-κλῐμα,** ατος, τό, (προσκλίνω) in pl., *inclinations, interests,* *PHerc.*1041.1. **-κλῐνής,** ές, *sloping,* *Gp.*9.3.2. **-κλιντρον,** τό, *easy chair,* *EM*690.29. **-κλίνω** [ῑ], *cause to lean against, place against,* βέλος προσέκλινε κορώνῃ Od.21.138, 165:—Pass., πατρὸς ἐμοῖο θρόνος ποτικέκλῐται (Ep. and Dor. pf. Pass.) αὐτῇ *stands by* her, i.e. hers, or the pillar, 6.308; νῶτον ποτικεκλιμένον his back *thereon reclined,* Pi.*P.*1.28; ὁ ἱερεὺς -κλείνεται (sic) πρὸς με[..] *IG*4$^2$(1).742. 11 (Epid., ii/iii A.D.); προσκλιθείς τινι *turning towards* him, Philostr. *VA*3.30. 2. π. τὴν θύραν *close* the door, J.*AJ*5.4.2. II. *turn* or *incline towards,* τὴν ψυχὴν τοῖς λόγοις v.l. in Plu.2.36d; τὸν νοῦν τῶν θεῶν τοῖς ἀνθρώποις Iamb.*Myst.*1.12. III. seemingly intr. (sc. ἑαυτόν), *incline towards, be attached to* one, *join his party,* τοῖς Ῥοδίοις Plb.4.51.5, cf. 5.86.10 (Reiske for προσκιν(-κυν-)οῦσι); ταῖς Μιθραδάτου ἐλπίσιν Agatharch.*Fr.Hist.*16 J.:—Pass., προσκλιθῆναί τινι Lxx 2*Ma.*14.24, *Act.Ap.*5.36, S.E.*M.*7.324. IV. Gramm., *inflect,* ἔξωθεν -κλιθῆναι A.D.*Synt.*324.18. **-κλῐσις,** εως, ἡ, *leaning against,* ζῴου πρὸς δένδρον D.S.3.27. 2. *genuflexion,* Iamb.*Myst.*1.12 (pl.). II. *inclination, predilection,* τῶν γερόντων Plb.6.10.10; τινι to one, Id.5. 51.8; αἵρεσίς ἐστι π. δογμάτων *Stoic.*2.37; π. δόγμασιν ibid., D.L. *Prooem.*20, S.E.*P.*1.16; μετὰ -κλίσεως Carnead. and Clitomach.ap. eund.ib.230; κατὰ πρόσκλισιν *with partiality,* 1*Ep.Ti.*5.21. **-κλῖτον,** τό, *couch,* *EM*519.42, al., Suid.

**προσ-κλύζω,** Dor. **ποτικλύζω,** *wash with waves,* X.*Cyr.*6.2.22: c. dat., *dash against,* πρίν γε θεοῦ τεμένει κῦμα ποτικλύζῃ Orac.ap. Aeschin.3.112; [ὄρει] προσκλύζει τὸ πέλαγος Plb.5.59.5; πρὸς τὴν ἀκρόπολιν Plu.*Dio* 24: c. acc., *lave,* τοὺς ὀφθαλμοὺς ὕδατι ψυχρῷ Diocl. *Fr.*141:—Pass., *to be washed,* θαλάττῃ by the sea, D.S.1.31, cf. J.*BJ*3. 10.1. 2. metaph., τοῖς ὄμμασι τοῦ κάλλους μονονουχὶ προσκλυζοντος Luc.*Am.*53. II. Pass., *to be used as a wash,* v.l. in Dsc.4.63, cf.*Eup.*1.119. **-κλῠσις,** εως, ἡ, *washing,* τοῦ κύματος D.S.3. 19. II. *fomentation,* Bacch.ap.Erot. s.v. αἰόνησις (prob.). **-κλυσμα,** ατος, τό, *lotion,* Dsc.1.115, Antyll.ap.Orib.9.23 tit.; *mouthwash,* Archig.ap. Orib. 8.1.39; *hair-wash,* Herod.Med.ap.Orib.10. 17.1. **-κλυστέον,** *one must lave,* τὸ πρόσωπον Id.ap.Orib.*Syn.*6. 32.1. **-κλύστιος,** ὁ, *he who dashes against,* of Poseidon, Paus. 2.22.4.

**προσκνάομαι,** inf. -κνῆσθαι, Pass. or Med., *rub oneself against,* τινι X.*Mem.*1.2.30, Plu.2.917d; ἰχθύες π. πρὸς τὸ τραχύ D.Chr.6.18.

**προσκνήθω,** *scratch, tickle,* κάπρον χειρί *Trag.Adesp.*383.

⊛ **προσκνυζάομαι,** *whine to one in a fawning manner,* τινι, of a dog, Philostr.*Her.Prooem.*: metaph. of a person, *fawn upon,* Hld.7.10 (-όμενος is f.l.).

**προσκογχῠλίζομαι,** Med., *gargle* (cf. ἀνακογχυλίζω), Aët.8.44.

**προσκοινόομαι,** Pass., *to be similarly attached,* of rings, J.*AJ*3.7.5.

**προσκοινωνέω,** *to be partaker,* τινος *of* a thing, *share in* it, Pl.*Sph.* 252a; τῶν δρωμένων D.C.66.12; στάσεών τινι *with* one, Pl.*Lg.*757d; τινι *SIG*364.27 (Ephesus, iii B.C.). II. *give* one *a share of..,* π. σφίσι τῶν παρόντων D.C.37.56; π. τούτῳ ἀπὸ τῶν ὑμετέρων χρημάτων D.34.36.

**πρόσκοιτος,** ον, *for the bed* or *bedtime,* Ph.1.635.

**προσκολλ-άω,** *glue on* or *to,* τι πρός τι Hp.*Art.*33:—Pass., generally, *to be stuck to, stick* or *cleave to,* Pl.*Phd.*82e, *Lg.*728b; ὑπὸ τοῦ αἵματος προσκολληθῆναι τὴν ῥομφαίαν αὐτοῦ τῇ δεξιᾷ J.*AJ*7.12.4; of a snail, τοῖς θαμνίσκοις π. Dsc.2.9; of a husband, π. τῇ γυναικί *Ev.Matt.*19.5, cf. Lxx *Ge.*2.24, *Ev.Marc.*10.7, *Ep.Eph.*5.31; τοῖς ἐπαοιδοῖς Lxx *Le.*19.31; ψυχαὶ π. θεῷ Ph.*Fr.*51 H. II. intr. of style, *to be compact,* D.H.*Dem.*43. **-ημα,** ατος, τό, squamous *agglutination,* Gal.2.742, *UP*9.18 (pl.). **-ησις,** εως, ἡ, *a glueing to, affixing,* τινος J.*AJ*8.3.2. ⊛ **-ητός,** ή, όν, gloss on ἀρτίκολλος, Sch.S.*Tr.* 768. **-ίζομαι,** *attach,* dub. in Anthem.p.155 W. ⊛ **-ος,** Dor. **ποτίκ-,** ον, *glued* or *sticking to,* Pi.*Fr.*241; πρόσκολλος τῷ βατανίῳ Zos.Alch.p.222 B.

**προσκομ-ῐδή,** ἡ, *oblation,* Hsch. **-ίζω,** fut. -ιῶ Th.4.115:—*carry* or *convey to* a place, πρὸς Σύβοτα Id.1.50, cf. X.*Cyr.*7.3.4, *Oec.* 11.16; λίθους π., for building, D.55.20; π. τὴν μηχανὴν *bring up* the engine to assault the wall, Th.4.115; τοῖς Ἀχαιοῖς π. τὴν πόλιν *win* it to their side, Plu.*Arat.*25; *bring as a gift,* τί τινι Ael.*VH*1.31:—Med., *bring with one, bring home,* Th.1.54; *procure* necessaries, X.*Cyr.*6.1.23:—Pass., of ships, *to be brought to* a place, Th.1.51, cf. X.*HG*5.1.19 (s.v.l.). **-ιστέον,** *one must administer,* ὕδωρ χλιαρόν Anatolius ap.*Gp.*16.4 (= *Hippiatr.*1). **-ιστικός,** ή, όν, *of* or *for conveyance,* Zonar. s.v. προσαγωγικός.

**πρόσκομμα,** ατος, τό, (προσκόπτω) *stumble,* λίθου πρόσκομμα Lxx *Is.*8.14; ὁ λίθος τοῦ π. *Ep.Rom.*9.33: hence, *offence, obstacle, hindrance,* Lxx *Ex.*23.33, *Ep.Rom.*14.13, etc. II. *result of stumbling, bruise, hurt,* προσκομμάτων ἀπόλυσις Plu.2.1048c, cf. Ath.3.97f.

**προσκοπ-εύομαι,** *intend, look forward to,* c. inf., Democr.92; προεσκοπεύθη εἰς μάχαιραν he *has been chosen out* for the sword, Sm.*Jb.* 15.22. **-έω,** fut. προσκέψομαι: aor. προὐσκεψάμην (no pres. προσκέπτομαι being used in good Att., so that in Th.8.66, Bauer restored προὔσκεπτο as plpf. for προὐσκέπτετο; cf. σκέπτομαι):—*consider beforehand, look to, provide for,* προσκεψάμενος ἐπὶ σεωυτοῦ Hdt.7.10.δ'; ἅπαντα π. ib.177; πάντα προσκοπεῖν S.*Ant.*688, E.*Heracl.*470; τὸ σὸν προσκέψομαι Id.*Andr.*257; τὰ κοινὰ προσκοπεῖν Th.1.120, cf. 4.61; μὴ παθεῖν προὐσκόπουν *were making provision* against suffering, Id.3.83; προσκέψασθε ὅτι.. ib.57; τῆς νυκτὸς προσκόπει, τί σοι ποιήσουσιν X.*Cyr.* 1.6.42; οὐδεὶς εἰς τὰ πάντα προσκοπεῖ *is provident,* Men.*Mon.*486:—Med., τὸ σόν.. προσκοπούμενος E.*Med.*460; πατρὸς δωμάτων προὐσκεψάμην τοὐμόν τε καὶ τοὐδ' *provided for* my share and his in my father's house, Id.*Ph.*473. 2. *watch* (like a πρόσκοπος or *spy*), προσκέψομαι τὸν Παφλαγόνα Ar.*Eq.*154:—Med., προσκοπουμένη πόσιν E.*IA*1098: folld. by indirect question, π. ποῦ εἰσιν οἱ πολέμιοι Thphr.*Char.* 25.4. II. Pass., τῶν.. προειρημένων τε καὶ προεσκεμμένων Pl.*R.* 435d; τὰ ῥηθησόμενα αὐτοῖς προὔσκεπτο Th.8.66 (v. sub init.).

**προ-σκοπή** (A), ἡ, *looking out for,* ἐς π. τῶν Φοινισσῶν νεῶν οἴχεσθαι Th.1.116; ἐς π. πεμφθέντες D.C.36.9.

**προσ-κοπή** (B), ἡ, = πρόσκομμα, *offence taken,* φθόνος καὶ π. Plb.6.7. 8; π. καὶ μῖσος Id.30.29.7; πρός τινα ἀλλοτριότης καὶ π. Id.31.10.4, cf. Phld.*Po.Herc.*994.38, D.S.31.17; νοσήματα κατὰ προσκοπὴν γινόμενα, i.e. antipathies, Chrysipp.*Stoic.*3.102; προσκοπῆς ἄξιος S.E. *M.*1.195: but μηδεμίαν π. διδόναι give no *cause of offence,* 2*Ep.Cor.* 6.3.

**προσκόπησις,** εως, ἡ, = προσκοπή (A), Aq., Sm.*Ez.*7.7.

**προσκοπητέον,** *one must consider beforehand,* Nech.ap.Vett.Val. 291.19.

**προσκόπιον,** τό, *shade for the forehead and eyes, visor,* dub. in Posidon.2 J.

**πρόσκοπος,** ον, *foreseeing, sagacious,* σύνεσις Pi.*Fr.*231 (for A.*Eu.* 105, v. ἀπρόσκοπος). II. as Subst., *outpost, vedette,* X.*Lac.*12.6: pl., *reconnoitring party,* Id.*Cyr.*5.2.6, D.C.40.10, etc.

**προσκοπτικός,** ή, όν, *ready to take offence,* π. καὶ μισητικός Arr. *Epict.*1.18.9, cf. Vett.Val.65.24, 68.22.

**προσκόπτω,** *strike* one thing *against* another, πρὸς λίθον τὸν πόδα Lxx *Ps.*90(91).12; π. τὸν δάκτυλόν που Ar.*V.*275 (lyr). b. intr., *stumble* or *strike against,* τινι X.*Eq.*7.6, Alex.81, Arist.*Pr.*882$^b$18, *GC* 326$^a$27, etc.; π. τῷ ὀφθαλμῷ (sc. ῥίζῃ κυάμου) Thphr.*HP*4.8.8; of liquid, *to be checked by striking against,* c. dat., Plu.*Lyc.*9; πνεῦμα προσκόπτον *broken, interrupted* breathing, Hp.*Aph.*4.68. 2. π. τῷ ἄξονι *encounter friction at..,* Arist.*Mech.*852$^a$32. II. metaph., = προσκρούω III, *offend,* Posidipp.36; τοῖς πολλοῖς Plb.5.49.5; οὐ μόνον δυσαρεστήσειν ἀλλὰ καὶ προσκόπτειν ἔμελλε προφανῶς, of an open *breach,* Id.7.5.6. 2. *take offence at,* ἵνα μή μοι προσκόψῃς *PCair. Zen.*463.11 (iii B.C.); τῇ βαρύτητί τινος Plb.1.31.7, cf. Carneisc.*Herc.* 1027.14; θεοὺς -κόψαντάς τισι D.S.13.59; of things, π. τῷ ζῆν *to be disgusted with* life, Id.4.61:—Pass., δῆμος π. αὐτῷ διά τι *being offended with* him, App.*BC*2.27, cf. Phld.*Piet.*30, M.Ant.9.3.

**προσκορής,** ές, *satiating, palling, tedious,* of a speech, Hermog. *Inv.*3.10; of a person, Id.*Id.*2.11, cf. Luc.*DMort.*26.2, Sch.Ar.*Eq.* 1055, etc. II. Pass., *sated,* Phld.*Mus.*p.109 K.; τινι with.., Hld.3.4. III. Adv. προσκόρως (as if from πρόσκορος) *AP*4.3.3 (Agath.); π. χρῆσθαι κόσμῳ Hermog.*Id.*2.11; λόγος π. κεκοσμημένος ib.1.12.

**προσκορίζομαι,** *annoy, tease,* τινα Sch.Ar.*V.*1332.

**προσκοροδοφᾰγέω,** *eat garlic first,* Dsc.4.184, Id.*Eup.*2.68.

⊛ **προσκοσμ-έω,** *adorn yet more, add ornament to,* ἱερόν J.*BJ*5.13. 6; ξόανα *SIG*798.20 (Cyzicus, i A.D.):—Pass., ἀφειδέσι δαπάναις π. Ph.2.575: also τῶν προσκεκοσμημένων τῷ θεάτρῳ the *adornments added to* the theatre, prob. in Plu.*Caes.*66 (προσκοσμ- is f.l. for πόλεις κοσμ- in Id.2.316d). **-ημα,** ατος, τό, *additional ornament,* Ἑλληνικά 1.18 (Gytheum, i A.D.), *IG*4.203.9 (Corinth, ii A.D.), *CIG* 3080.5 (Teos); π. τῆς Ἀρτέμιδος prob. in *BMus.Inscr.*481*.530

(Ephesus, ii A.D.). **–ησις**, εως, ἡ, *additional decoration*, Keil-Premerstein *Dritter Bericht* No.117 (i A.D.).

**προσκοτέω**, *darken* or *cloud over beforehand*, f.l. for ἐπισκοτέω (cj. Dind.) in Plb.1.48.8.

**προσκουφίζομαι**, Pass., *to be relieved*, Aët.9.30 (fort. προκ–).

**πρόσκοψις**, εως, ἡ, *friction*, Arist.*Mech*.852$^{a}$32, dub. cj. in *Pr*. 940$^{a}$12.

**πρόσκρᾱνον**, v. ποτίκρανον.

**προσκρᾰτύνω**, *strengthen additionally*, Hp.*Art*.58.

**προσκρεμάννῡμι**, *hang* a thing *on* or *to*, ὅταν θήκας προσκρεμῶσι τοῖς στελέχεσι *Gp*.10.5:—Pass., *to be hung up to, hang up*, Ar.*Fr*.131: **προσκρέμᾰμαι**, *to be attached* or *suspended*, πρὸς τὸ ἔμβρυον Hp. *Superf*.8, cf. Arist.*Mech*.856$^{a}$23, Plb.2.10.4.

**προσ-κρίνω** [ῐ], *adjudge* or *award*, τὴν χώραν αὐτῷ *SIG*679.55 (ii B.C.), cf. J.*BJ Prooem*.4, D.L.1.74:—Pass., τῷ θεῷ Ph.1.690, cf. *PAmh*.64.5 (ii A.D.), etc. II. Pass., *to be joined with, assimilated*, opp. ἀποκρίνομαι, Anaxag.14, cf. Gal.8.721; τῷ σώματι Dam.*Pr*. 402. ❋ **–κρῐσις**, εως, ἡ, *accretion, increase, growth by assimilation*, Epicur.*Ep*.2 p.38 U. (pl.), Demetr.Lac.*Herc*.1055.9 (pl.); σωμάτων Artem.4.2 (v.l. –χρησις); *assimilation*, τροφῆς Mich.*in EN*52.14. II. *addictio, judicatio*, *Gloss*.

**πρόσ-κρουμα**, ατος, τό, v. πρόσκρουσμα. **–κρουσις**, εως, ἡ, *dashing against* a thing, Plu.2.696b (pl.). II. *offence*, πρόσκρουσιν προσκροῦσαί τινι give him *offence*, Id.*Cic*.34, cf. 2.138e (pl.), etc. ❋ **–κρουσμα**, ατος, τό, *that against which one strikes, obstacle*, Arist.*PA*658$^{a}$7 (pl.). 2. *knock*, *Hippiatr*.96. II. *stumbling-block, cause of offence* or *friction*, D.54.3 (pl.), J.*BJ*1.26.3 (pl.); πολιτικὰ π. τοῖς δημάρχοις πρὸς τοὺς ὑπάτους συνέστη D.H.10.31, cf. 4.25; τὰ περὶ τὴν σιτοδοσίαν π. Id.7.45.—The form **πρόσκρουμα** (which is preferred by Thom.Mag.p.317 R., citing Aristid.1.455 J.) freq. occurs in the same Mss. as πρόσκρουσμα, cf. Plu.2.137c with 141b, al. **–κρουσμός**, ὁ, = πρόσκρουσις I, *Placit*.3.3.12. **–κρουστέον**, *one must give offence*, Ph.2.401. **–κρουστικός**, ή, όν, *offensive*, τὸ π. τῶν ἐπιτιμήσεων Tib.*Fig*.11, cf. Dam.*Isid*.285, Sch.Ar.*Ach*. 316. **–κρούω**, *knock against*, τὴν κεφαλὴν παρά τι Ant.Lib.8. 7. II. intr., *strike against, collide with*, πυρί Pl.*Ti*.43c, cf. Epicur. *Ep*.2 p.38 U., *Nat*.2.3; πρός τι Zen.3.29: abs., *stumble, fall*, D.18. 254: metaph. of failure or defeat, μικρὰ προσκρούσας Plu.*Sull*.11, cf. *Luc*.17. III. metaph., *have a collision with* another, *give offence*, τὸ π. καὶ φιλονικεῖν περί τινος D.5.25, cf. 21.61: c. acc. cogn., ἃ προσέκρουον Id.19.205; π. τισί Plu.*Them*.20, *Fab*.26, *POxy*.531.10 (ii A.D.). 2. *take offence at, be angry with*, τινι D.24.6; ἀλλήλοις Din.1.99, Arist.*Pol*.1263$^{a}$18; προσκρούσας τι τούτῳ Aeschin.1.110, cf. D.33.7; φιλοσοφίᾳ Plu.*Cat.Ma*.23: abs., Pl.*Phd*.89e; τῶν φίλων οἱ προσκεκρουκότες Arist.*EN*1166$^{a}$6.

**προσ-κτάομαι**, fut. –ήσομαι Hdt.8.136:—*gain, get*, or *win besides*, γῆν ἄλλην π. τῇ ἑωυτῶν Id.3.21; νήσους βασιλέϊ π. *for* him, Id.5.31; Μακεδόνας πρὸς τοῖσι ὑπάρχουσι δούλους Id.6.44; π. ἔθνεα Id.7.8.α'; χώραν π. Th.4.95, cf. 3.28; πόλιν Lys.12.39; π. πρὸς τὴν ἑωυτοῦ μοῖραν *gain and add* to his own portion, Hdt.1.73; βραχύ τι π. αὐτῇ [τῇ ἀρχῇ] *make a* small *addition* to it, Th.6.18, cf. X.*An*.5.6.15; πρὸς τοσούτοις αἰσχροῖς καὶ ἐπιορκίαν π. D.19.219: pf. part. in pass. sense, τὰ προσκεκτημένα v.l. for προκ– in Th.2.62. 2. of persons, *gain* or *win over*, τινὰς π. φίλους Hdt.1.56; π. τὸν Καλλίμαχον *win over* Callimachus *to his side*, Id.6.110; π. τοὺς Ἀθηναίους Id.8.136: c. inf., Καρίης τὴν πολλὴν π. σφίσι σύμμαχον εἶναι Id.5.103. **–κτησις**, εως, ἡ, *increase of fortune*, Artem.3.61; τῆς ἀρετῆς Hierocl.*in CA*11 p.442 M. **–κτητος**, ον, *acquired*, opp. inherited, ἀρχή Hdn.1.5.5.

**προσκτίζω**, *build* or *found besides*, αὐτοῖς ἄλλην πόλιν Str.3.5.3; τὰς Θήβας τῇ Καδμείᾳ Id.9.2.3:—Pass., J.*BJ*5.4.2; ὄρει ib.3.7.7; τῶν προσεκτισμένων αὐτοῦ ἄλλων ἡμερῶν δύο the two *additional* festival-days *founded* in his honour, *Sammelb*.7457.39 (Ptolemaic).

**προσκῠλ-ινδέομαι**, Pass., *roll to*, τῷ ὑγρῷ Clearch.73. **–ίω**, *roll to, roll up*, τὸν ὅλμον..προσκύλιε Ar.*V*.202 codd.: aor. part., προσκυλίσας λίθον *Ev.Matt*.27.60, cf. *Ev.Marc*.15.46. II. metaph. in Pass., *wallow in*, τοῖς ἀφροδισίοις Anon.*in EN*436.7. [ῑ; but προσκυλῐσασα in Man.5.200.]

❋ **προσκύλλω**, *molest before*, Pass. προεσκυλμέναι women *with a past*, Vett.Val.120.6, cf. Heph.Astr.1.1.

**προσκῡμαίνω**, *dash against*, θάλαττα π. τῷ στρατοπέδῳ Philostr. *Her*.19.12.

**πρόσκῠνες**, οἱ, f.l. for πρόκυνες, v. Προκύων.

❋ **προσκῠν-έω**, fut. –ήσω Hippon.32 (tm.), Pl.*R*.469a: aor. προσεκύνησα X.*Cyr*.5.3.18; poet. προσέκῠσα Ar.*Eq*.640, imper. πρόσκυσον ib. 156, S.*Ph*.776, inf. –κύσαι ib.657, part. –κύσας ib.533, 1408 (troch.): pf. –κεκύνηκα Lxx *Ex*.32.8, *OGI*196.2 (Egypt, i B.C.):—**Pass.**, pres. inf. προσκυνεῖσθαι E.*Tr*.1021: aor. προσεκυνήθην Arr.*An*.4.11.9:—*make obeisance* to the gods or their images, *fall down and worship*, c. acc., Hdt.2.121, etc.; γῆν τε π. ἅμα καὶ τὸν θεῶν Ὄλυμπον S.*OC* 1654, cf. A.*Pers*.499, Ar.*Eq*.156: prov., οἱ –κυνοῦντες τὴν Ἀδράστειαν σοφοί, of deprecating the wrath of Nemesis, A.*Pr*.936, cf. Pl.*R*.451a; τὸν φθόνον δὲ πρόσκυσον S.*Ph*.776; στεῖχε προσκύσας χθόνα, to avert divine wrath, ib.1408 (troch.); of sacred places, *do reverence to*, πατρῷα ἕδη θεῶν Id.*El*.1374; τὰς θήκας Pl.*R*.469b; τὴν θόλον D.19.314: abs., Ar.*Eq*.640. 2. esp of the Oriental fashion of *prostrating oneself before* kings and superiors, abs., Hdt.1.119, 8.118: c. acc., π. τὸν Δαρεῖον *make obeisance* to him, Id.3.86; προσκυνεῖν διδάσκονται τὸν βασιλέα [οἱ ἐλέφαντες] Arist.*HA*630$^{b}$20; προσπίπτων π. Hdt.1.134, cf. 7.136; πάντες σε προσκυνοῦμεν οἵδ' ἱκτήριοι S.*OT*327; προσκυνῶ σ', ἄναξ, προσπίτνων E.*Or*.1507 (troch.), cf. X.*Cyr*.5.3.18, 8.3.14, Plu.*Them*. 27, Arr. l.c., etc.; κύψας ὁ λαὸς προσεκύνησεν Lxx *Ex*.12.27; οὐδένα ἄνθρωπον δεσπότην ἀλλὰ τοὺς θεοὺς π. X.*An*.3.2.13; π. τοὺς ὑβρίζοντας ὥσπερ ἐν τοῖς βαρβάροις D.21.106: ironically, π. τινὰ ὡς ἱερὸν καὶ θαυμαστόν Pl.*R*.398a: later c. dat., Lxx *Ge*.24.26, al., *Ev.Matt*.2.2, 11, *Ev.Jo*.4.23, D.C.67.13; τῳ θεῷ J.*AJ*9.13.2. (Orig. perh. *throw a kiss to* the god, cf. Apul.*Met*.4.28: the gesture is probably represented in Sumerian and Babylonian art monuments.) II. later, *kiss*, σοῦ –ήσω τὴν χεῖρα *BGU*423.15 (ii A.D.); τὸ πρόσωπον, τὴν ὄψιν, τοὺς πόδας, *PLond*.3.1244.4 (iv A.D.), *PGiss*.22.5 (ii A.D.), *PGen*. 91.6 (vi/vii A.D.). 2. *greet*, σπουδάζουσα –ῆσαί σε (by letter) *BGU* 615.8 (ii A.D.); ἔλθω πρὸς ὑμᾶς ἵνα ὑμᾶς -ήσω διὰ πολλοῦ χρόνου *PLips*. 110.19 (iii/iv A.D.), cf. *PGiss*.17.11 (ii A.D.). 3. *welcome respectfully, respect*, προσεκύνησά σου τὰ γράμματα *POxy*.237 vi 37 (ii A.D.), cf. *PTeb*.286.22 (ii A.D.), etc.; τὴν θείαν ἀντιγραφὴν ὑπὸ πάντων προσκυνουμένην *OGI*262.27 (Baetocaece, iii A.D.). **–ημα**, ατος, τό, *act of worship*, ib.184.8 (Philae, i B.C.), al., *Epigr.Gr*.1004, 1010 (Egypt); τὸ π. σου ποιῶ παρὰ τῷ κυρίῳ Σαράπιδι *BGU*384.4 (ii/iii A.D.), *PFay*.127.4 (ii/iii A.D.). **–ησις**, εως, ἡ, *adoration, obeisance*, Pl.*Lg*.887e (pl.); τὰ βαρβαρικά, οἷον προσκυνήσεις Arist.*Rh*.1361$^{a}$36, cf. Phld.*Piet*.69 (pl.), Plu.*Alex*.54, Arr.*An*.4.11.8; π. καὶ ἀσπασμός (in a petitioner's letter) *PFlor*.296.57 (vi A.D.). **–ητέον**, *one must worship*, Iamb. *VP*23.105. **–ητέος**, α, ον, in fem., = *adoranda*, *Gloss*. ❋ **–ητήρ**, ῆρος, ὁ, *faldstool*, *Mon.Ant*.23.263 (Adalia). ❋ **–η[τήριον]**, τό, = foreg., dub. rest. in *POxy*.1449.19 (iii A.D.). **–ητής**, οῦ, ὁ, *worshipper*, *Ev.Jo*.4.23, *OGI*262.21 (Baetocaece, iii A.D.), Procop.*Aed*. 5.7. ❋ **–ητός**, ή, όν, *to be worshipped, worshipful*, *Cod.Just*.1.5.20. 1, al., *POxy*.158.6 (vi A.D.); prob. for προκ– in *Rev.Phil*.1930.249 (Egypt, *Tab. Defix*.).

**προσκύπτω**, *stoop to* or *over* one, ὅταν..προσκύψασα φιλήσῃ Ar.*V*. 608; ἔλεγεν ἄττα προσκεκῡφώς Pl.*R*.449b; π. τινὶ πρὸς τὸ οὖς *lean towards* one *and whisper in* his ear, Id.*Euthd*.275e; πρὸς τὸ οὖς cj. in Thphr.*Char*.2.10; π. πρός τινα Ath.5.181f; προσεκεκύφει τῇ γῇ Longin.*Rh*.p.180 H.

❋ **προσκῠρ-έω** and **–κύρω** [ῡ] (v. infr.), aor. προσέκυρσα, *reach, arrive at*, c. dat., προσέκυρσε Κυθήροις Hes.*Th*.198. b. *adjoin*, Herod. Med.ap.Orib.10.5.10; ἕλος παπυρικὸν ὃ προσκυρεῖ (or –κύρει) τῇ λεγομένῃ Βαθείᾳ (place-name) *BGU*1121.8 (i B.C.). 2. *meet with*, τινι Emp.2.5; ναῦς πέτρῃ π. Thgn.1361; ἑωυτοῖσι Hp.*Praec*.8: c. acc. rei, πάντων ὅσ' ἐγὼ προσέκυρσ' ἤδη S.*OT*1299 (anap.): reversely, δόμοισι πῆμα προσκυρεῖ *betides* the house, A.*Ch*.13. 3. *belong, appertain*, or *be attached to*, D.S.16.42, Plu.*Art*.21; τὰ προσκυροῦντα τούτοις Epist.ap.J.*AJ*13.4.9; τὰ προσκύροντα τῷ ἱερῷ *OGI*732 (Egypt, ii B.C.), cf. *Sammelb*.1567.7 (iii B.C.), 4208.7 (ii B.C.); τῶν οἰκοπέδων –κυρόντων *Sardis* 7(1).1 i 11 (iv/iii B.C.); προσκύρουσιν πρὸς τὴν κώμην καὶ ἄλλαι κῶμαι ib.4; οἱ –οντες τόποι *PLond*.2.401.28 (ii B.C.); ᾗ ἔχω αὐλῇ –ούσῃ οἰκίᾳ μου *BGU*275.6 (iii A.D.). **–ησις**, εως, ἡ, *procuring*, ἀκέσιος, i.e. patients, Hp.*Praec*.10.

❋ **προσκῡρ-όω**, *confirm*, Hsch., *Gloss*.:—Pass., τὴν –ωθεῖσάν σοι παρ' ἐμοῦ δεσποτείαν (gift of part of a house) *PLond*.3.1044.15 (vi A.D.): also v.l. for προσηυρῆσθαι in A.D.*Synt*.114.17. **–ωσις**, εως, ἡ, *confirmation*, *Gloss*.

**προσκύσας, πρόσκῠσον**, aor. 1 part. and imper. of προσκυνέω.

**προσκωμάζω**, *burst riotously in upon*, τῇ γῇ Philostr.*VA*4.6.

**πρόσκωπος**, ον, *at the oar, rower*, Th.1.10, Luc.*Cat*.19.

**προσλαγχάνω**, *obtain by lot besides*: δίκην προσείληχεν *has brought* an action *against* us *besides*, D.32.9, cf. Plu.*Per*.36; ῥᾳδίαν τὴν φυγὴν π. Procop.Gaz. p.161 B.

**προσλάζῠμαι**, *take hold of besides*, χειρός E.*Hec*.64 (anap.): also **–λάζομαι**, Pomp.Mac.1.3.

**προσλάκκιον**, τό, *overflow-pit*: metaph. of the kidneys, Gal.19.362.

**προσλᾰλ-έω**, *talk to* or *with*, τινι Antiph.218.3, Henioch.4.3: abs., Thphr.*Char*.7.5, *PMich.Zen*.80.5,7 (iii B.C.); π. ἑαυτῷ τὰ Πινδαρικά Plu.2.602f. **–ιά**, ἡ, *affatus*, *Gloss*.

**προσλαμβάνω**, fut. –λήψομαι X.*An*.7.3.13: aor. προσέλᾰβον Id. *Mem*.3.14.4: pf. –είληφα Id.*An*.7.6.32, Ion. –λελάβηκα Eus.Mynd. 51:—*take* or *receive besides* or *in addition, get over and above*, ἄρτον προσέλαβε (sc. τῷ ὄψῳ) X.*Mem*. l.c.; πρὸς τοῖς παροῦσιν ἄλλα [κακά] A.*Pr*.323; τὸ ἀναίσχυντον τῇ συμφορᾷ E.*IA*1145; π. αἰσχύνην Th.5. 111; ἐμπειρίαν Id.6.18; ὧν μάλιστα δεόμεθα And.3.23; δόξαν γελοίαν ἡμῖν X.*Smp*.4.8; ἄλλην εὔκλειαν πρὸς ἐκείνοις Id.*An*.7.6.32; μισθόν ib.7.3.13; λόγον τῇ ἀληθεῖ δόξῃ Pl.*Tht*.207c; δωρειάς D.19.147; παιδείαν Id.61.42; παιδεύματα [S.] *Fr*.1120.4; ἃ μὴ μεμάθηκας προσλάμβανε ταῖς ἐπιστήμαις Isoc.1.18; in tmesi, τοῦτο πρὸς ζητεῖς λαβεῖν Men.*Epit*.132; καιρούς Pl.*Phdr*.272a: abs., *make gains*, D.2.7; *make progress*, Lib.*Or*.54.16:—Pass., τὸ προσειλημμένον *what has been gained*, opp. τὸ ἀπολειπόμενον, Plu.2.77c. 2. *take in, add* an area to a building site, *PCair.Zen*.193.6 (iii B.C.):—Math., τὸ ποτιλαμβανόμενον or ποτιλᾱφθὲν χωρίον Archim.*Spir.Praef*.; προσλαβών, *plus*, opp. λιπών, minus, Apollon.Perg.*Con*.3.12. b. προσλαβών, *multiplied by*.., Archim.*Sph.Cyl*.2.8.2:—Pass., κοινοῦ –ληφθέντος λόγου if the ratio *be multiplied* into both, Papp.164.22. c. in Music, ὁ προσλαμβανόμενος [τόνος] the *added note* at the bottom of the scale, Ph.1.111, Plu.2.1028f, etc. 3. c. acc. pers., *take to oneself as one's helper* or *partner*, κῆδος καινὸν καὶ ξυνασπιστὰς φίλους S.*OC*378, cf. A. *Pr*.219, E.*Med*.885, *Hipp*.1011; ἱππέας καὶ πελταστάς X.*Cyr*.1.4.16; πόλεις τὰς μὲν βίᾳ τὰς δ' ἑκούσας Id.*HG*4.1.1; τινὰς τῶν πολιτῶν D. 15.14; τὸν δῆμον Arist.*Pol*.1312$^{b}$17; π. ἀδελφοὺς τοῖς παισί, by a second marriage, X.*Lac*.1.9: with a second acc., π. τινὰ σύμμαχον

Id.*An.*7.6.27, cf. Lys.26.16:—Med., πόλεις προσλαβέσθαι Plb.1.37.5; μισθοφόρους Plu.*Pel.*27; π. τινὰ συνεργόν, κοινωνόν, *PFay.*12.10 (ii B.C.), *PAmh.*100.4 (ii/iii A.D.); of *admitting* into the army, π. τὸν.. μου ἀδελφὸν.. εἰς τὴν Δεξειλάου σημέαν *UPZ*14.21 (ii B.C.); προσλαβέσθαι γνώμην τινός *get* his vote *besides*, Plb.3.70.2:—Pass., -ληφθέντες εἰς τὴν κατοικίαν *admitted, enrolled, PTeb.*61(*a*).2, cf. 31, al. (ii B.C.). b. Med., *appropriate* neighbouring land, π. τῇ ἑαυτοῦ οἰκίᾳ ψιλοὺς τόπους *Sammelb.* 5954.5 (i A.D.), cf. *BGU*1060.17 (i B.C.). 4. in Logic, *add by apposition*, ὅρους Arist.*APo.*78a14, cf. Id.*APr.*58b27 (Pass.); *assume as minor premiss, Stoic.*2.85, Muson. *Fr.*1 p.2 H., Procl. *in Prm.*p.855 S.; cf. πρόσληψις. 5. *borrow*, τι κερμάτιον Men.*Her.*32; ἡ σελήνη φέγγος ἴδιον οὐκ ἔχει, ἀλλ' ἀπὸ τοῦ ἡλίου προσλαμβάνει Eudox.*Ars* 11.15. II. *take hold of*, με π. κουφίσας S.*Tr.*1025 (lyr.); π. τὸν ἀγωγέα βραχύτερον *shorten* the rein, Stratt.52:—Med., *take hold of*, c. gen., Ar.*Ach.*1215 sq., *Lys.*202; μικρᾶς ῥοπῆς ἔξωθεν δεῖται προσλαβέσθαι Pl.*R.*556e. 2. *fasten*, Hp. *Art.*78, Arist.*PA*670a14; καταδεῖν καὶ π. v.l. in Thphr.*HP*6.2.2:—Pass., δεσμοῖς π. Arist.*PA*654b27, cf. *HA*497a22; *to be enveloped*, Ruf.*Anat.*32. 3. *lend a hand, help*, X.*An.*2.3.11 and 12; π. τινί *help, assist, IG*1².374.54, cf. Ar.*Pax* 9 (Med.); τῆς ἀποκρίσεως ὑμῖν.. π. *help* you to find an answer, Pl.*Lg.*897d; οἱ ποταμοὶ π. τῇ θαλάττῃ *co-operate with..*, Str.2.5.17, cf. 11.4.2, 13.1.1:—Med., προσελάβετο τοῦ πάθεος he *was partly the author* of what befell, cj. for -εβάλετο in Hdt.8.90:—Pass., π. ὑπό τινος *to be aided by..*, Vett.Val.58.16. III. προσειλήφασιν *have learnt, believe*, ὅτι.. f.l. for προσυπ- in Dsc.2.141.

**προσλάμπω**, *shine upon*, Pl.*R.*617a:—Pass., τοὺς ἀπλανεῖς ἀστέρας ὑπὸ τοῦ ἡλίου προσλάμπεσθαι *Placit.*2.17.1.

**πρόσλαμψις**, εως, ἡ, *shining on*, πρός τι Epicur.*Ep.*2 p.51 U.

* **προσλέγω**, *say in addition*, Luc.*Pseudol.*31:—Med., 1 aor. προσελεξάμην, Dor. ποτ-, τὼς οὐδὲν ποτελέξαθ' *addressed, accosted*, Theoc. 1.92, cf. A.R.4.833: metaph., κακὰ προσελέξατο θυμῷ he *took* evil *counsel with* himself, *meditated* evil, Hes.*Op.*499. II. v. προσλέχομαι.

**προσλειόω**, *grind further*, Gal.13.406.

**προσλείπω**, *leave on*, τῷ μεσογονατίῳ τὸ πρὸς τοὺς βλαστοὺς γόνυ Thphr.*HP*4.11.6. 2. *leave unworked*, π. ἣ συνελεῖν *IG*7.3073.23 (Lebad., ii B.C.). II. intr., *to be lacking*, τὸ προσλεῖπον τῆς φύσεως Arist.*Pol.*1337a2; τὰ προσλείψαντα τοῦ ἔργου *IGRom.*4.845 (Laodicea ad Lycum, i A.D.).

**προσλειτουργέω**, *serve as well*, c. dat., Lyd.*Mag.*3.8.

**προσλεπτύνω**, *extenuo, Gloss.*:—Pass., *become slender besides*, Hp. *Mochl.*5.

**προσλεύσσω**, *look on* or *at*, c. acc., S.*Aj.*546, 1044; ὄψις ἐφίμερος προσλεύσσειν Id.*OT*1376: abs., Id.*Ph.*1068, etc.

**προσλέχομαι**, *lie beside*, only Ep. aor. προσέλεκτο Od.12.34.

**πρόσ-λημμα**, ατος, τό, *upper garment*, τῆς θεοῦ *Michel* 832.20 (Samos, iv B.C.). -**ληπτέον**, *one must add*, ταῦτα Str.10.2.7; ὅτι.. Id.13.1.50. II. *one must assume besides*, Arist.*APr.*59a12. -**ληπτικός**, ή, όν, '*assumptive*', i.e. *belonging to the minor premiss*, σύνδεσμος Stoic.ap.A.D.*Conj.*250.16. -**ληψις**, εως, ἡ, *taking in addition*, λόγου Pl.*Tht.*210a, cf. Hermog.*Id.*1.11; ἀορίστου ib.2.6, Aristid.*Rh.*1 pp.473, 534 S.; τοῦ ἄρθρου, τοῦ ῑ, A.D.*Synt.*170.3, *Pron.*87.13. 2. *acquisition*, δυνάμεως, τοῦ εὐδαίμονος, J.*AJ*17.1.2, 18.9.6; μείζονος τιμῆς Anon.*Trop.*23. b. *rise in rank by acquisition of catoecic land*, προσλήψεως στέφανος *PTeb.*61(*b*).254 (ii B.C.). 3. *enrolment*, εἰς τὸ ταγματικὸν *PTheb.Bank* 8.4 (ii B.C.). II. *additional assumption*, διὰ προσλήψεως Arist.*APr.*58b9 (dub.); κατὰ πρόσληψιν Thphr.ap.Alex.Aphr. *in APr.*378.14, Phlp. *in APr.*416.24; ἐνθύμημα γίνεται.. κατὰ πρόσληψιν Aps.*Rh.* p.288 H.: specifically, π., ἡ, *minor premiss*, Crinis *Stoic.*3.269, Plu.2.387c, A.D.*Conj.*250.21, S.E. *P.*2.149, D.L.7.82; ἐν προσλήψει A.D.*Conj.*250.18.

**προσλῐμενίζομαι**, Pass., *run into harbour*, Sch.rec.A.*Pers.*70.

**προσλῐπαίνω**, *enrich further*, of soil, τοῦ ποταμοῦ -λιπαίνοντος αὐτῇ ἰλὺν γενέσθαι D.H.5.13.

**προσλῐπᾰρ-έω**, *keep close to*, τοῖς χρήμασιν, ὥσπερ κηρίοις μέλιτται Plu.*Aem.*23; π. τοῖς μαχομένοις *stand by* them *to the end*, Id.2.245c: c. part., *persevere*, π. νηχόμενον Agathin.ap.Orib.10.7.25: c. acc., *continue to occupy*, [χώραν] Arr.*Epict.*3.24.33: abs., *persevere*, Luc.*Abd.*16, Ruf.ap.Orib.8.21.15; *to be importunate*, Plu.*Pomp.*13; but, *continue to listen* to a speaker, Id.2.39a: c. acc. et inf., ταῦτα πραχθῆναι Jul.*Or.*7.225a. -**ησις**, εως, ἡ, *perseverance in* a thing, Antyll.ap. Orib.6.10.14; *persistence*, Luc.*Cal.*20.

**προσλογ-εύω**, *exact in addition*, *PHib.*1.66.3 (iii B.C.), *IG*12(7).237.44 (Amorgos, ii/i B.C.):—Pass., *PCair.Zen.*206.66 (iii B.C.). -**ίζομαι**, fut. -ιοῦμαι Luc.*Alex.*1; *reckon* or *count in addition*, Hdt.2.16, Lys.19.44; ὁδὸν ταύτῃ Hdt.5.54:—Pass., *to be reckoned in*, Scyl.113, *PPetr.*3 p.118 (iii B.C.), *PTeb.*61(*b*).190 (ii B.C.), etc. 2. *take into account besides*, Arist.*Cael.*294a4; τῷ πλέον διδόναι π. τὸ αἰσχρόν Plu.*Cam.*28. II. *compare*, τὸ ἑκατέρων ἦθος τῇ πράξει Aristid.1.450 J. III. *consider besides*, ὡς.. Plu.*Demetr.*38. -**ισμός**, ὁ, *encroachment*, *PTeb.*124.29 (ii B.C.). -**ιστέον**, *one must reckon in addition*, Hp.*Hum.*13: also pl. -ιστέα, στράτευμα τούτῳ Hdt.7.185.

**προσλογοποιέω**, *add in narrating*, τινί τι J.*BJ*1.19.3.

**προσλοιδορέω**, *rail at besides*, τινὰ αὐτόν D.C.38.10:—Med., τοῦτο Them.*Or.*23.289b, cf. J.*AJ*7.8.1: aor. 1 Pass. in med. signf., ib.15.7.4.

**πρόσλοιπος**, ον, *left over and above*, *IG*2².1672.239, Eudox.*Ars* 4.13; τὰ π. *the residue*, *PRyl.*66.8 (ii B.C.), cf. Iamb.*VP*3.16. 2. of time, εἰς τὸ π. for the *future*, *Ephes.*2.29 (ii A.D.).

**προσλῡμαίνομαι**, 3 sg. pf. -λελύμανται, *destroy besides*, τινας Aristid.*Or.*25(43).9.

**προσλυσσάω**, *rage against* or *at*, τινι J.*AJ*7.9.4.

**προσμᾰθητέον**, *one must learn besides*, X.*Oec.*13.1.

**πρόσμακρος**, ον, = πρόμακρος (q.v.), Hp.*Steril.*235, *Epid.*6.7.2 codd.

**προσμανθάνω**, *learn besides*, A.*Pr.*697, *Trag.Adesp.*516a, Ar.*V.*1208, *Th.*20: c. inf., ib.24.

**προσμαντεύομαι**, f.l. for προ-, Aristid.2.277 J.

**προσμαρτ-ῠρέω**, *bear witness in addition*, π. τούτους εἶναι κληρονόμους Is.6.45; *confirm by evidence*, τῇ προκλήσει τὴν διαθήκην D.45.12, cf. ib.88; π. ταὐτά τινι Plu.*Arist.*25, etc.: c. dat., *bear additional witness to, confirm* a thing, τὰ πράγματα -εμαρτύρησε τοῖς λογισμοῖς Plb.3.80.4, cf. Plu.2.119e, etc.:—Pass., προσεμαρτυρεῖτο αὐτῷ ὅτι.. *PCair.Zen.*288.7 (iii B.C.), cf. S.E.*M.*7.212. 2. *ascribe*, πάντα τῷ θεῷ J.*AJ*5.8.9. II. Astrol., *to be also in aspect*, Procl.*Par.Ptol.*249, Man.4.384. * -**ύρομαι** [ῡ], *call as witness*, Sch.rec.A.*Pr.*88. -**ῡρος**, ον, Astrol., *in aspect with*, Man.4.161, 176.

**προσμάσσω**, *knead* or *plaster* one thing *against* another: *apply, attach closely to*, χείλεσι χείλη Theoc.12.32; σικύην τύψει the cupping-instrument to the snake-bite, Nic.*Th.*922; π. τὸν Πειραιᾶ [τῇ πόλει] Ar.*Eq.*815:—aor. Med., τηλέφιλον ποτεμάξατο (Dor.) *stuck to* [the arm], Theoc.3.29:—Pass., πλευραῖσι προσμαχθὲν *stuck close* to his sides, of the poisoned robe, S.*Tr.*1053, cf. Lyc.1029; κηλῖδα προσμεμάχθαι τῇ ψυχῇ Philostr.*VA*3.42.

**προσμαστῑγόω**, *whip* or *beat besides*, *PCair.Zen.*631.9 (Pass., iii B.C.).

**προσμάχομαι** [ᾰ], aor. -εμαχεσάμην J.*AJ*20.4.1:—*fight against*, τῇ δειλίᾳ Pl.*Lg.*647c, cf. 830a, Plb.1.28.9; *assault* a town, X.*Cyr.*7.5.7; τοῖς τείχεσιν Plu.*Demetr.*33; κατὰ τὰς κλίμακας X.*HG*7.2.7.

**προ-σμάω**, = προσμήχω, pf. part. Pass. προεζμησμένον *PSI*10.1180.48 (ii A.D.):—aor. Med. dub. in *PRyl.*29(*a*).21 (ii A.D.).

* **προσμείγνῡμι**, Pl.*Lg.*878b, also **προσμίσγω** (v. infr.): fut. -μείξω: aor. -έμειξα:—*make to reach* or *touch*, μακρὰ τείχη τῇ θαλάσσῃ Plu. *Alc.*15; τῷ ποταμῷ τὸ δεξιόν Id.*Art.*8: metaph. of a race-horse, π. κράτει δεσπόταν *lead* him *to sure* victory, Pi.*O.*1.22; reversely, π. κίνδυνον τῇ πόλει Aeschin.3.146. 2. Arith., *add*, *Cat.Cod.Astr.*1.168. 3. *mix in as well*, Zos.Alch.p.142 B. II. intr., *hold intercourse with, approach*, ἐκείνῳ γ' οὐδὲ προσμεῖξαι S.*Ph.*106; Ζηνὶ προσμείξων E.*Fr.*911 (lyr.); of things, ὅρος ὅρῳ προσμειγνὺς Pl.*Lg.*878b; ψυχὴ ἀρετῇ θείᾳ προσμείξασα *having had communion with..*, ib.904d; προσέμειξεν.. τοὔπος ἡμῖν *came suddenly upon* us, S.*Tr.*821 (lyr.); also ἐπειδὴ προσέμειξεν ἐγγὺς τοῦ στρατεύματος *came near..*, Th.4.93, cf. 7.41; ἐγγύτερον ἐπί τινας Pl.*Plt.*290c; αὐτοῖς ἐγγύθεν Id.*Lg.*783b. 2. in hostile sense, *meet in battle, engage with*, προσέμειξαν τοῖσι βαρβάροισι Hdt.6.112, cf. 5.64, etc.; πρὸς ἀταξίαν τοιαύτην.. ὀργῇ προσμείξωμεν Th.7.68: abs., *engage*, ὅπῃ προσμείξειαν X.*Cyr.*5.4.46; [οἱ Σκύθαι] ἄποροι προσμίσγειν difficult *to come to close quarters with*, Hdt.4.46. 3. *come* or *go close up to..*, προσέμειξαν τῷ τείχει τῶν πολεμίων Th.3.22; προσέμισγον τῷ ζεύγματι Id.7.70; προσέμισγον πρὸς τὰς ἐπάλξεις Id.3.22; but πρὸς τὰς ἐντὸς [ναῦς] προσμεῖξαι *form a junction* with them, Id.7.22, cf. X.*Cyr.*2.4.21; ὅπως οἱ τελευταῖοι -μείξειαν Id.*An.*4.2.16: poet. c. acc., μέλαθρα π. E.*Or.*1290 (lyr.). 4. προσέμειξαν (-ξε) τῇ Νάξῳ, τῇ Πελοποννήσῳ, τῇ Ἀσίῃ, *put to shore at, arrived at, landed in*, Hdt.6.96, 7.168, 8.130; τῷ Τάραντι προσμίσγει Th.6.104, cf. 1.46; εἰς Θάψον ταῖς ναυσί Plu. *Nic.*17.

**προσμειδιάω**, *smile upon*, τινι Plu.2.821f, etc.; εὐρησιλογίαις ib.28a; αὐτοῖς ἡ Τύχη -εμειδίασε Chor.*Brum.*6: abs., Luc.*Merc.Cond.*7, 16.

**πρόσμειξις**, εως, ἡ, (προσμείγνυμι II) *coming near to*, and (in hostile sense) *attack, assault*, Th.5.72; ἡ τῶν ἁρμάτων π. D.C.40.2.

**προσμελέομαι**, = ἐπιμελέομαι, Hsch.

**προσμελετάω**, f.l. for προμ-, Ruf.*Fr.*61.

**προσμελῳδέω**, *sing songs to* or *besides*, Semus 10, Aristid.*Or.*21(22).15.

**προσμέμφομαι**, *blame besides*, ὅτι.. J.*AJ*8.1.2.

* **προσμένω**, Dor. ποτι- *SIG*615.7 (Delph., ii B.C.):—*bide, wait*, χρόνον πολλόν Hdt.1.199, cf. 5.19; σῖγ' ἔχουσα πρόσμενε S.*El.*1236, cf. 1399; ἡσυχάζων π. Id.*OT*620; π. χρόνον ὀλίγον ἔστ' ἄν.., π. ἕως.., Hdt.8.4, X.*HG*2.4.7. 2. c. dat., *remain attached to, cleave to*, πάθεα π. τοκεῦσιν A.*Eu.*497 (lyr.); τῷ Κυρίῳ *Act.Ap.*11.23; π. ταῖς δεήσεσιν *continue in..*, 1*Ep.Ti.*5.5; ταῖς ἑαυτῶν ἀγωγαῖς Gal.15.436. II. trans., *wait for, await*, c. acc., Thgn.1144, S.*OT*837, *El.*164 (lyr.), etc.; *face* in battle, *stand one's ground against*, δορίκτυπον ἀλαλάν Pi.*N.*3.60: c. acc. et inf. fut., Ὀρέστην τῶνδε προσμένουσ' ἀεὶ παυστῆρ' ἐφήξειν S.*El.*303.

**προσμερίζω**, *apportion to*, εὐνοιάν τινι Plb.27.9.5, cf. *OGI*455.5 (Aphrodisias, i B.C.), D.S.14.107:—more freq. in Pass., Plb.21.22.15, *Supp.Epigr.*4.246.13 (Panamara, i B.C.), D.H.6.42, Sor.1.42, S.E.*M.*9.284, *PRyl.*209.25 (iii A.D.).

**προσμετα-δίδωμι**, *communicate as well*, *POxy.*68.34 (ii A.D.). -**πέμπομαι**, Med., *send for* or *send to fetch besides*, Th.2.100, 8.71, Aeschin.3.87, *IG*12(5).870.6 (Tenos, ii B.C.), D.H.2.44, D.C.40.2.

**προσμετεωρίζω**, *raise besides* or *further*, Gal.18(2).769.

**προσμετρέω**, *measure out to, join to*, Is.*Fr.*169, Hyp.*Fr.*269; *make additional payments in kind*, ἀρτάβας *PLille* 5.29 (iii B.C.):—Pass.,

*PFay.*81 (ii A.D.), al. 2. *adapt*, τὰν ἑαυτῶ τύχαν τοῖς ἐφίκτοισιν ἀνθρώπῳ *IGRom.*4.1302.13 (Cyme, i B.C./i A.D.).

**προσμηκύνω**, *provide as an extension, add*, δειπνιστήρια προσεμήκυναν δειπνιστηρίοις *IG*5(2).268.36 (Mantinea, i B.C./i A.D.):—Pass., προσεμηκύνετο αὐτοῖς καὶ βαίτης..ἀπόλαυσις ib.48.

**προσμηνύω**, *point out besides*, S.E.*M.*1.273 (v.l. προμ-).

**προσμηχᾰν-άομαι**, Pass., *to be cunningly fastened to* or *upon*, A.*Th.*541,643. II. Med., *contrive* or *procure for oneself*, αὑτοῖς ἀσφάλειαν Pl.*R.*467c; διατριβὴν ἑτέραν D.H.7.37; τούτοις ἄλλα παράδοξα J.*AJ*8.13.1; τιθασεύματα Porph.*Abst.*1.9. **-ητέον**, *one must contrive besides*, Orib.7.12 tit.

**προ-σμήχω**, *rub beforehand*, Archig.ap.Gal.12.407: aor. part. προσζμήξας *PSI*10.1180.64 (ii A.D.):—Pass., οὔρῳ *Gp.*16.15.2; cf. προσμάω.

**προσμίμνω**, f.l. for πυρὸς μένει in Orph.*L.*277.

**προσμίσγω**, v. προσμείγνυμι.

**προσμῑσέω**, *hate besides*, D.39.23, 40.29 (sed melius divisim).

**προσμισθόω**, *let out for hire besides*, π. ἀφορμήν *put* capital *out at interest besides*, D.36.12:—Med., *take into one's pay, hire*, Th.2.33, X.*HG*4.8.7, D.23.132. 2. *give a contract for besides*, *IG*1$^2$.374.127:—Pass., τῶν πετάλων τῶν ὕστερον -ωθέντων ib.370.11.

**προσμοιράζω**, *allot to, assign*, Herm.ap.Stob.1.49.44 (Pass.).

**προσμοιχεύω**, *commit adultery in addition*, Vett.Val.118.35.

**προσμολεῖν**, aor. inf. of pres. *προσβλώσκω, = προσέρχομαι, *come* or *go to, arrive at*, c. acc., S.*Aj.*721: abs., *approach*, ib.72, *Tr.*1109.

**προσμολυβδοχοέω**, *attach by soldering*, Eratosth.ap.Eutoc. *in Archim.*p.94 H. (Pass.).

**πρόσμονος**, ον, *durable*, Antyll.ap.Orib.10.29.1. Adv. -νως Id.ap. eund.9.24.25.

⊛ **πρόσμορος**, ον, *doomed to woe*, corrupt in A.*Th.*576.

**προσμῡθ-έομαι**, Ep. **προτι-**, *address, accost*, Od.11.143: also c. dat., οἱ.. ἔπος π. Theoc.25.66. **-εύω**, *add further fictions*, πλείω Str.1.2.19; τούτοις ib.40; τί τινι Id.10.2.24:—Pass., Plb.34.2.9, Str.1.2.19.

**προσμῡθο-λογέω**, *talk* or *prattle with* one, τινι Luc.*Sat.*7. **-ποιέω**, *invent mythically besides*, τι Str.1.2.40.

**προσμύρομαι** [ῡ], *make tearful lament in answer to*, ποταμῷ π. πηγή *AP*9.362.23.

**προσναυπηγέω**, *build in addition*:—Pass., ἑτέρας [νέας].. ἔδεε -ναυπηγέεσθαι Hdt.7.144:—Med., D.S.17.95.

**προσνεᾱνῐεύομαι**, *add in youthful wantonness*, π. εἰπὼν ὅτι.. D.C. 53.13; *promise wantonly*, χρηστά τινα Id.59.26.

**προσνεμητέον**, *one must allot*, Ptol.*Tetr.*193.

**προσνέμω**, *allot, assign, dedicate to*, γυμνικοὺς [ἀγῶνας]..τοῖς θεοῖς Pl.*Lg.*828c; αὑτούς τινι D.25.43; ταῖς τοῦ δήμου προαιρέσεσιν ἑαυτόν Id.*Ep.*3.2; ὅπου τὸ δίκαιον εἴη τεταγμένον, ἐνταῦθα π. ἑαυτούς Id.60.11; τῷ δικαίῳ ἑαυτούς Plb.6.10.9; μηδεμιᾷ φιλοτιμίᾳ παρὰ τὸ δίκαιον π. τὴν αὑτοῦ γνώμην *SIG*577.39 (Milet., iii/ii B.C.); ἀπώλειάν τινι Alciphr.1.14; *add*, ὀκτακοσίους αὐτοῖς D.14.16; τὰς νήσους ταῖς γείτοσι μοίραις Arist.*Mu.*394$^a$4; πόλιν τοῖς Ἀχαιοῖς Plb.2.43.5:—Pass., *to be assigned, attributed*, οἱ δ' ἄλλοι προσνενέμησθε ὡς τούτους, ὡς ἐκείνους, D.2.29, 13.20; π. ὁ φίλος τοῖς πράγμασι, οὐ τὰ πράγματα τοῖς φίλοις Arist.*EE*1237$^b$33; ὁ ὄχλος ὁ ἐκ τῶν ἀγρῶν προσνεμηθεὶς τῷ κατὰ πόλιν *being added*, D.H.10.48:—Med., *grant on one's own part*, πρόσνειμαί μοι χάριν *grant* me *a further* favour, S.*Tr.*1216; προσνείμασθαί τινα τοῖσι θεοῖσιν *devote* him to the gods, Ar.*Av.*563 (anap.). II. π. ποίμνας *drive* his flocks *to pasture*, E.*Cyc.*36.

⊛ **πρόσνευσις**, εως, ἡ, *'penchant'*, Cic.*Att.*5.4.2. II. Astron., *inclination*, Ptol.*Alm.*5.5, Procl.*Hyp.*1.30 (pl.); *approach*, of a planet, Vett.Val.215.10; *direction of a falling body*, Ptol.*Alm.*1.7 (pl.).

**προσνεύω**, *incline* or *bend towards*, Plu.*Brut.*1. 2. *have an inclination* or *tendency*, οὐ προσνεύσαντος οὐδὲ βουληθέντος Plot.5.1.6. II. *incline, slope towards*, Apollod.*Poliorc.*154.5; *lean towards*, in wrestling, etc., Gal.6.142 (v.l. for προν-), Antyll.ap.Orib.6.32.4; *look towards*, Λιβύη π. ἐπὶ τὸν ἄρκτον Str.2.4.3, cf. 13.1.68; προσνεῦον τὸ ἀπαρέμφατον ἀμφοτέραις ταῖς αἰτιατικαῖς A.D.*Synt.*243.8. 2. Astrol., *approach*, of planets, Vett.Val.7.14, al.

**προσνέω** (A), aor. -ένευσα Th.3.112:—*swim to* or *towards*, l.c.; λιμένι Luc.*Bis Acc.*21.

**προσνέω** (B), *heap up against*, ξύλα ταῖς θύραις Plu.2.775e.

**προσνήχομαι**, *swim towards*, ἐς.. Call.*Del.*47: c. dat., D.S.3.21, Plu.*Mar.*37, etc. II. of water, in Act., *dash upon*, προσένᾱχε θάλασσα Theoc.21.18.

**προσνῑκάω** τῷ χρόνῳ *use* time *as a help in overcoming* an evil, Hp.*Art.*62.

**προσνίσομαι** [ῑ], *come* or *go to*, ἐς.. Il.9.381 (in form ποτινίσ-); οἴκοθεν οἴκαδ' Pi.*O.*6.99; θεοὺς θοίναις ποτινισ. *approach* them with sacrifices, A.*Pr.*530 (lyr.). II. *come against*, S.*Ant.*129 (anap.).

**προσνοέω**, *observe*, ἄλλο τι X.*Smp.*2.16 codd.; τὸ ἐν τοῖς ὕδασι γιγνόμενον.., ὅτι.. D.Chr.21.14; ἱμάτιον *PEnteux.*30.3 (iii B.C.); τινὰ ἐρχόμενον Lxx *To.*11.6: c. dat., ib.*Jd.*3.26: abs., ib.*Is.*63.5; *wait attentively for*, τὸ παραγγελλόμενον X.*Cyr.*6.3.7 codd. II. *think in addition*, φθεγξάμενος τὸ ἀγαθὸν μηδὲν ἔτι προσνόει Plot.3.8.11:—Pass., ἐν τῷ λόγῳ τῆς αὐτογραμμῆς οὐκ ἔνι προσνοούμενον πέρας Id.6.6.17.

**προσνομίζω**, *bring into use* or *practise besides*, Aristid.*Or.*45(8).9, 23:—Pass., *OGI*56.43 (Canopus, iii B.C.).

**προσνομοθετέω**, *ordain by law besides*, *IG*2$^2$.222.43, 7.4254.40 (Oropus, iv B.C.), Ph.2.227, D.C.37.29.

**προσνωμάω**, *approach*, S.*Ph.*717 (lyr.); but εἰς ὕδωρ ἀεὶ προσενώμα *moved himself* to it, Sch. ad loc.

**προσξενολογέω**, *detail* troops *for special service*, *BGU*1231.7 (Pass., iii/ii B.C.).

**προσξηραίνομαι**, Pass., *become dry besides*, *EM*384.55.

**προσξυν-**, v. προσσυν-.

**προσογκέω**, *gain in bulk*, Arist.*Pr.*964$^b$4.

⊛ **προσοδ-άρχων**, οντος, ὁ, *treasurer* of a religious association, *Ath. Mitt.*6.42 (Cyzicus). **-εύω**, *accrue*, καθαρμοὺς ἐκ ποικίλων θεωρημάτων προσοδεύσαντας the *product* of reflection, Iamb.*VP*17.74 (nisi leg. προσδ-). II. Med., *receive income* or *revenue*, ἀπό τινων Str.12.8.16, cf. Ph.2.371,402: c. acc., *convert into a source of revenue, derive profit from*, τὴν ἀθλίων ἀνθρώπων γαστρὸς ἔνδειαν ib.389, cf. 172; τὰς τύχας τοῦ ὁμοφύλου J.*AJ*4.8.25:—Pass., *to be received as revenue*, *IG* 2$^2$.1080, App.*BC*4.5; also, *to be subject to tribute*, J.*AJ*15.5.3.

⊛ **προσοδιάζω**, *receive as income*, ἑκάστης ἡμέρας ἀρτάβην ἀργυρίου Eust.1206.18:—Pass., τὰ προσοδιασθέντα *profits*, Vett.Val.292.30.

**προσοδ-ιακός**, ή, όν, *processional*, χοροί prob. in Democh.2 J. II. π. μέτρον, the metre ‒ ‒ ◡ ◡ ‒ ◡ ◡ ‒ (variously explained), Heph.15.3, Sch.Ar.*Nu.*651, etc., cf. Plu.2.1141a; applied to a different metre, Aristid.Quint.1.17; στίχοι π. D.H.*Comp.*4. **-ικός**, ή, όν, (πρόσοδος II) *productive*, Str.17.3.12 (Comp.). II. *concerning revenue*, τὰ βασιλικὰ καὶ π. καὶ ἰδιωτικά *PAmh.*2.33.9 (ii B.C.); π. κρίσεις ib.30; τὰ π. *accounts of revenue*, *OGI*669.26 (Egypt, i A.D.); ἐδάφη π. lands *belonging to the treasury*, *PRyl.*73.13 (i B.C.). III. προσοδικός, ὁ, *tax-farmer*, *IPE*2.432 (Tanais). IV. Adv. -κῶς dub. in Vett.Val.292.30 (παροδικὸς cj. Kroll).

⊛ **προσόδιος**, ον, *processional*, ὕμνοι Ph.2.484; μέλος π. καὶ πομπικόν Plu.*Aem.*33; π. ᾆσμα Paus.4.4.1: hence προσόδιον (sc. μέλος), τό, *processional ode*, Ar.*Av.*853 (lyr.), *IG*7.1773.6 (Thespiae, ii A.D.), Ath.6.253b; παιὰν καὶ π. εἰς τὸν θεόν *SIG*698*C* I (Delph., ii B.C., = Limen. tit.); Dor. **ποθόδιον** ib.450.5 (iii B.C.).

**προσοδοιπορέω**, *travel to* a place, f.l. in Aret.*SD*2.2.

**προσοδοποιός**, ὁ, *law-court official, summoner*, *BGU*388 i 27, ii 19 (ii A.D.), prob. in 868.3 (ii A.D.).

⊛ **πρόσοδος**, Dor. **πόθοδος** *SIG*1009.27 (Chalcedon, iii/ii B.C.), etc.; Arc. **πόσοδος** *IG*5(2).6.9 (Tegea, iv B.C.): ἡ:—*going* or *coming to, approach*, Pi.*N.*6.45, Th.4.110; ἡ π. μάλιστα ταύτῃ ἐγίνετο *the approach* was most feasible on this part, Hdt.9.21; ἀπείπατο τὴν π. rejected his *advances*, Id.1.205; στυγναὶ π. μελάθρων *to* the halls, E.*Alc.*861 (anap.); π. χαλεπαὶ πρὸς τὸ χωρίον X.*An.*5.2.3; ἐτάμομες κοινὰν πόθοδον..πὸτ τὰν οἰκίαν *Tab.Heracl.*2.43. 2. *onset*, π. ποιέεσθαι Hdt.7.223, 9.101; πρόσοδοι τῆς μάχης *onsets* or *attacks*, Id.7.212; αἱ π. αἱ πρὸς τοὺς πολεμίους X.*Cyn.*12.3. 3. *solemn procession* to a temple with singing and music, π. μακάρων ἱερώταται Ar.*Nu.*307 (lyr.), cf. *Pax* 397 (lyr.); θυσίαι καὶ π. καὶ εὐχαί Lys.6.33; ἐπιτελέων τᾶν εὐχᾶν γενομενᾶν θυσίαν καὶ πόθοδον ποιήσασθαι *SIG*581.6 (Crete, iii/ii B.C.); οἱ ἐπὶ τὰς προσόδους magistrates in charge of the (commissariat of the) *processions*, ib.711*B*21 (Delph., ii B.C.), cf. *IG*2$^2$.1707 (iii B.C.); θεοῖς π. τε καὶ πομπὰς ποιεῖσθαι Pl.*Lg.*796c; αἱ πρὸς τοὺς θεοὺς π. X.*An.*6.1.11, cf. D.18.86. 4. *approach* to an assembly or council, πρόσοδον εἶναι αὐτῷ πρός τε τοὺς πρυτάνεις κτλ...πρώτῳ μετὰ τὰ ἱερὰ ὅταν τι δέηται *IG*1$^2$.59.17; γράψασθαι πρόσοδον πρὸς τὴν βουλήν to petition for *a hearing*, D.24.48; π. ποιεῖσθαι πρὸς τὸν δῆμον Aeschin.1.81, cf. *IG*2$^2$.1012.12, 9(1).694.39 (Corcyra), 12(5).837.20 (Tenos); αἱ πρὸς τὴν βουλὴν αὐτῶν π. Aeschin.2.59; περὶ σωτηρίας τὴν π. ἐποιησάμην Isoc.7.1; *approach* to an official, *PTeb.*326.11 (iii A.D.); π. ποιήσασθαι τῷ δικαστηρίῳ Mitteis *Chr.*96 iii 4 (iv A.D.); τὴν π. πρὸς ὑμᾶς ποιοῦμεν *BGU*1022.18 (ii A.D.); οἱ στραταγοὶ πόσοδον ποέντω shall grant *access* (to the Three Hundred), *IG*5(2) l.c. (unless in signf. II, shall provide *revenue*), cf. *IG*1$^2$.70.15. 5. *sexual intercourse*, Hp.*Epid.*6.3.14 (pl.), Aret.*SA*2.12 (pl.). 6. *visit* of a pupil to his master, Plu.2.1044a. 7. f.l. for πρόοδος in Ph.*Fr.*22 H. II. *income, rent*, opp. stock or principal, πρόσοδον μὲν οὐδεμίαν ἀποφαίνων, ἀπὸ δὲ τῶν ὑπαρχόντων ἀναλίσκων Lys.32.28, cf. 24.6, *SIG*251 iii 29 (Delph., iv B.C.); τοῦ ἐργαστηρίου λαβὼν τὴν π. D.27.18, cf. 21: pl., ἰδίας ἀπὸ τῶν κοινῶν π. κατεσκευάσατο And.4.11, cf. Aeschin.3.173: generally, *returns, profits*, Pl.*Lg.*847a. 2. *public revenue*, φόρων π. ἡ ἐπέτειος Hdt.3.89; ἡ π. ἐγίνετο ἔκ τε τῆς ἠπείρου καὶ ἀπὸ τῶν μετάλλων Id.6.46; χρημάτων π. Th.2.97, 3.13: mostly in pl., *returns, revenue*, ἀπὸ τούτου [τοῦ κλήρου] τὰς π. ποιήσασθαι Hdt.2.109; τοῦ τὰς π. μᾶλλον ἰέναι αὐτῷ that *they* might come in better, Th.1.4; τὰς π. ἀφαιρήσομεν ib.81; αἱ π. ἀπώλλυντο Id.7.28; αἱ π. αἱ ἐξ Ἀμφιπόλεως γιγνόμεναι Isoc.5.5; χρημάτων π. ἐκ πολλῶν μὲν λιμένων ἐκ πολλῶν δ' ἐμπορίων X.*HG*5.2.16; ὑποθεῖναί τινι τὰς δημοσίας π. mortgage *them*, Aeschin.3.104; πόροι ἢ περὶ προσόδων, title of work by X.; ὁ πράκτωρ ὁ ἐπὶ τῶν βασιλικῶν π. τεταγμένος *PPetr.*3 p.56 (iii B.C.); ἡ ἐν προσόδῳ τῶν τέκνων τοῦ βασιλέως [γῆ] land providing *revenue* for the king's children, ib.p.237 (iii B.C.); ἐν προσόδῳ *PTeb.*87.1 (ii B.C.); κεχωρισμένη π. ib.60.56, al. (ii B.C.); τῶν ὄντων ἐν τῇ τῆς Ἀθερνεβενταίγεως προσόδῳ ἀρουρῶν *PGiss.*37 ii 3, cf. 14 (ii B.C.); ὡς αἱ π. according to the *financial* calendar, *PEnteux.*30.2, al. (iii B.C.), *PPetr.*3 p.8, al. (iii B.C.).

⊛ **προσοδύρομαι** [ῡ], *lament beside*, τάφοις Lxx *Wi.*19.3.

**προσόζω**, pf. προσόδωδα, intr., *smell of, be redolent of*, κακοῦ Ar.*Fr.*246; ἡδυσμάτων Philem.41; γλυφάνιο ποτόσδον (Dor. for προσόζον) Theoc.1.28; in late Prose, ἡμερότητος Lib.*Ep.*219.3. 2. abs., *stink*, 3 pl. aor. προσώζεσαν Lxx *Ps.*37(38).6.

**προσοίγνῡμι**, aor. -έῳξα, *shut*, τὴν θύραν Lxx *Ge.*19.6.

**πρόσοιδα**, pf. without pres. in use (cf. *εἴδω), prop. *know besides*: only in phrase χάριν προσειδέναι *be grateful besides*, Pl.*Ap.*20a; χάριν προσείσομαι Ar.*V.*1420.

**προσοικ-ειος**, ον, *suitable*, Orib.8.32.1. **-ειόω**, *assign to*, Ἔφορος Κιμμερίοις προσοικειῶν τόπον Str.5.4.5. **2.** *associate with*, προσῳκείου ἑαυτὸν Ἀντώνιος Ἡρακλεῖ.. Plu.*Ant.*60. **3.** *adapt*, Asp. *in EN*26.11. **II.** Pass., οἱ προσῳκειωμένοι *near relations*, D.S.3.9. **2.** = οἰκειόω II. 1 b, Phld.*D.*3.2; πρὸς τὴν ἡδονήν Gal.4.819. **3.** Astrol., *to be associated in domicile with*, Κρόνος -ωθεὶς τῇ Σελήνῃ Vett. Val.101.33. **-είωσις**, εως, ἡ, = οἰκείωσις 2, Phld.*D.*3.2. **-έω**, *dwell by* or *near*, οἱ προσοικοῦντες *neighbouring tribes*, Isoc.6.46; πόλεσι βάρβαροι -οικοῦντες X.*Vect.*1.8; ποταμοῖς καὶ θαλάττῃ, of towns, *lie by* or *near*, Pl.*Ti.*22d:—also Pass., τῇ πόλει -ῳκημένοι J.*BJ*4.4.3. **b.** π. πρὸς τῷ τοίχῳ *has his house abutting on* the wall, *OGI* 483.105 (Pergam.). **2.** c. acc., *dwell in* or *near*, [Ἐπίδαμνον] Th.1.24; λίμνας καὶ ἕλη Arist.*Pol.*1256$^{a}$37. **II.** Pass., of a place, *to be inhabited*, Plu.2.938d. **-ησις**, εως, ἡ, *dwelling near*, Paus.6.25.6. **-ίζω**, *found near* or *beside*, ἡ προσοικισθεῖσα [πόλις] D.S.13.79; λόφος μέρει πόλεως -ῴκιστο J.*BJ*5.5.8; also of a temple or worship, Porph.ap.Eus.*PE*3.11.

**προσοικο-δομέω**, *build besides*, π. [τεῖχος] *build another* wall, v.l. for ἐσοικ- in Th.2.76; οἰκίαν *PCair.Zen.*642.3 (iii B.C.); τῷ μὲν ἐν τῇ ἀγορᾷ [βωμῷ] προσοικοδομήσας.. μεῖζον μῆκος *having built an additional* length to the altar in the agora, i.e. having added to its length, Th.6.54:—Pass., D.H.1.79; φρούρια π. τῷ τείχει J.*BJ* 5.12.2. **2.** metaph., ἄλλο τε εἶδος.. προσῳκοδόμουν τὸ θνητόν *they also framed*, Pl.*Ti.*69c; τὸ κακῶς -οικοδομημένον ἐν τῇ σαρκί Arist.*Pr.*866$^{b}$17, cf. Thphr.*Sud.*30; πάθη μεγάλα τῇ λύπῃ π. Plu.2.168a. **-δομία**, ἡ, *building of an annexe*, τοῦ ἱεροῦ *IG*2$^{2}$.1282.6. **-νομέομαι**, f.l. for προοικ- (q. v.).

**πρόσοικος**, ον, *dwelling near to, neighbouring*, Hdt.1.144, Th.1.24; οἱ π. *neighbours*, ib.7, Aen.Tact.10.1; τοὺς Λυκίων π. Plu.2.421d; also of places, π. θάλαττα χώρᾳ *abutting upon*, Pl.*Lg.*705a; τὴν π. τῆς Ἰταλίας the *neighbouring* part, Plu.*Fab.*2: c. dat., Jul.*Or.*2.56b.

**προσοιμέομαι**, (οἶμος) *approach*, βηλῷ Keil-Premerstein *Erster Bericht* p.9 (Troketta).

**προσοιμώζω**, *lament*, πάθει J.*BJ*1.17.3. **II.** προσοιμώζειν [μοι] ἔλεγε told me *to 'go to the devil'*, Lib.*Decl.*29.27.

**πρόσοισμα**, ατος, τό, = τὸ προσφερόμενον, *that which is brought to* one, *food* (cf. προσφορά), Hp.*Loc.Hom.*43 (sg. and pl.).

**προσοιστέος**, α, ον, (προσφέρω) *to be added to*, οὐ προσοιστέος ἄλλος [θάνατος] πρὸς ἄλλῳ E.*Hec.*394; στέφανος π. Alex.250. **2.** *to be offered*, [θεῷ] Jul.*Ep.*89b. **II.** προσοιστέον *one must apply*, πρέπουσαν μηχανήν Ar.*Th.*1132, cf. Pl.*Phdr.*272a, etc.; γυμνάσια Arist.*Pol.*1338$^{b}$40. **III.** (προσφέρομαι) *to be administered* (as food or medicine), τὰ π. Hp.*Acut.*3. **2.** προσοιστέον *one must deal with*, τισι Aristid.*Or.*33(51).15.

**προσοίχομαι**, *have gone to* a place, Pi.*P.*6.4.

**προσοκέλλω**, *run* [a ship] *on shore*, D.C.*Fr.*4.4: c. dat., *run ashore on*, Luc.*VH*2.2; so of the ship, Id.*Tim.*3: metaph., π. χρόνῳ v.l. in Aret.*SD*2.10; ἃ εὐμορφία τοῖς ποτοκέλλουσιν ἀδονὰς παρέχει Dius ap. Stob.4.21.17 (Ruhnk. cj. **ποτοπτίλλουσιν**).

**προσολοφύρομαι** [ῠ], *wail to, vent one's griefs to*, τινι Th.8.66; π. ἀλλήλοις *wail to* one another, Plu.*Cic.*47.

**προσόμᾰλος**, ον, *tolerably level*, Diogenian.1.65.

**προσομαρτέω**, *go along with*, ὅτῳ ψεῦδος -ομαρτῇ Thgn.609.

**προσομῑλ-έω**, *hold intercourse with, associate with*, τισι Thgn.31, E.*Med.*1086 (anap.), Pl.*Grg.*502e; προσομιλεῖν ἥδιστος δαίμων θνητοῖς E.*Fr.*897 (anap.); πρός τινα X.*HG*1.1.30; τὰ ἴδια προσομιλοῦντες *conducting* our private *intercourse*, Th.2.37; π. διὰ χάριτος Pl.*Sph.*222e; *converse with*, J.*AJ*4.8.48. **2.** of sexual intercourse, π. γυναικί Hld.4.8, cf. Luc.*Am.*17; ἑτέρῳ γάμῳ π. *PMasp.*153.26, al. (vi A.D.). **3.** *discourse, lecture*, τοῖς γνωρίμοις περί τινος Porph.*VP* 25. **II.** *cling to*, πέτρῃ, of the polypus, Thgn.216; [δίκτυον] ὑφάλῳ πέτρᾳ π. Alciphr.1.14; οἶνος ἀέρι π. *is exposed to* it, *Gp.*7.6.8. **III.** c. dat. rei, *to be conversant with*, πείρᾳ S.*Tr.*591; τῷ πολέμῳ Th.1.122; γυμναστικῇ Pl.*Ti.*88c: metaph., ὕβρει π. Id.*Phdr.*250e. **-ητικός**, ή, όν, *of* or *for intercourse with* others: ἡ -κή (sc. τέχνη) *the art of discourse*, Id.*Sph.*222c. **-ία**, Ion. -ίη, ἡ, *association*, Aret.*CA*1.1; ἡ τοῦ θερμοῦ π. Alex.Aphr.*Pr.*1.115.

**προσόμνῡμι** or -ύω (D.42.18), Dor. **ποτ-** *SIG*953.28 (Calymna, ii B.C.):—*swear besides*, X.*An.*2.2.8, *OGI*5.62 (Scepsis, iv B.C.); ὅρκον D. l.c., *SIG*l.c.; τὸν Δία ib.993.20 (Calaurea, iii B.C.). **2.** *include with in an oath*, ταῖς ἡμέραις τὰς νύκτας Plu.2.223b.

**προσομοι-άζω**, *to be like*, *Gp.*2.21.6. **-ος**, ον, also α, ον Str.3.4.18:—*nearly like, much like*, τινι E.*Ph.*128 (lyr.), Ar.*V.*356, *Av.*685, Amips.19, Pl.*Sph.*267a, etc. Adv. -ως Id.*Lg.*811c. **-όω**, *compare*, τινί τι D.L.7.40. **2.** intr., *to be like, resemble*, τὴν σύνεσιν αὐτοῦ π. ἀνθρώπῳ, τὴν ἀλκὴν δὲ δράκοντι D.60.30:—in pf. Pass., προσωμοιῶσθαι Poll.9.131. **3.** *represent in art*, D.Chr.12.77.

**προσομολογ-έω**, *concede* or *grant besides*, Hyp.*Ath.*8; *agree with*, τοῖσι ὀρθῶς εἰρημένοισι Hp.*Vict.*1.1; *acknowledge a further* debt, π. τριακοσίας δραχμάς Isoc.17.39, cf. D.27.42: c. acc. et inf. with or without dat., *grant also that*.., Pl.*Grg.*461b, *Sph.*248d; ἀληθῆ εἶναι D.48.44. **2.** simply, *concede, allow*, Isoc.9.50; *admit, confess*, πάντων εἶναι δεινότατος Id.15.35; τὴν ἐπιβουλήν J.*BJ*1.25.1:—Pass., ταῦθ' ὑμῖν -ομολογεῖται ἅπαντα And.1.15; παλαιὰ καὶ λίαν προσωμολογημένα Aeschin.3.53 (v.l. προωμ-). **3.** *promise further*, c. inf. fut., D.56.6, *Sammelb.*7421.17 (i B.C.), etc. **4.** *give in, surrender*, X.*An.*7.4.24. **-ία**, ἡ, *further admission*, D.39.41.

**προσομόργνῡμι**, *wipe off upon* another, *impart*, τισὶ τὸ ἄγος Plu. *Crass.*2; τι τῇ ψυχῇ Them.*Or.*21.248d.

**προσόμουρος**, ον, Ion. for *προσόμορος, *adjacent*, τισι Hdt.4.173.

**προσονειδίζω**, *object as a reproach besides*, τὴν ἀταξίαν Sch.Ar.*V.*664; π. ὡς.. J.*BJ*2.2.5:—Pass., ib.2.16.4.

⊕ **προσονομ-άζω**, *call by a name*, θεοὺς π. σφεας ἀπὸ.. *give* them *the name* θεοί, Hdt.2.52; αἰθέρα π. τὸν ἀνωτάτω τόπον Arist.*Cael.*270$^{b}$22; νεὼν π. Διὸς Ὀλυμπίου Lxx 2*Ma.*6.2; ὃν Ἀσφάλειον καὶ Γαιήοχον προσονομάζομεν Plu.*Thes.*36, cf. *OGI*56.22 (Canopus, iii B.C.), 90.39 (Rosetta, ii B.C., both Pass.); Dor. **ποτονομάζω**, -άζοντας Ἀλκεσίππεια *calling* the games A., *SIG*631.5 (Delph., ii B.C.):—Aeol. Pass., εὐεργέταν **προσονῡμάσδεσθαι** *IGRom.*4.1302.7 (Cyme, i B.C./i A.D.). **2.** Pass., *to be surnamed*, Σαρᾶτος Ζωΐλου προσωνομασμένου Ἀμόϊτος *POxy.*1648.68 (ii A.D.). **-ᾰσία**, ἡ, *naming, appellation*, D.L.7.108; Aeol. **προσονῠμᾰσία** *IGRom.*4.1302.17 (Cyme, i B.C./i A.D.). **-αστέον**, *one must apply the name*, λάρκους τούτοις Poll.10.111.

**προσοπτάζω**, v. ποτοπτάζω.

**προσοπτάω**, *bake in addition*, *PCair.Zen.*742.23 (iii B.C., Pass.).

**προσοπτέον**, *one must look for*, τι Hp. *de Arte* 11.

**προσοπτίλλω**, v. ποτοπτίλλω.

**προσοράω**, fut. -όψομαι S.*Ant.*764: Dor. **ποθόρημι** Theoc.6.22 (vv.ll. ποθορῶμαι, -ῆμαι, but prob. ποθορῷμι), inf. ποθορῆν *AP*9.604 (Noss.):—*look at, behold*, Mimn.1.8, Xenoph.2.6, S. l.c., *El.*381, Pl.*Phdr.*250e; προσορῶσα δόμοισι βλάβαν S.*Tr.*842 (lyr.); cf. προσεῖδον:—Med., προσορωμένα Id.*OC*244 (lyr.).

⊕ **προσοργίζομαι**, Pass., *to be angry at*, J.*BJ*2.14.6 (v.l.), Plu.2.13d.

**προσορέγω**, *reach* a thing *to*, ἡμῖν [ἄρτον] Crates *Ep.*34.3:—Med., *hold out as an inducement*, τινι Hdt.7.6.

**προσορέω**, (ὅρος) *border on*, οἱ προσοροῦντες τῇ Μακεδονίᾳ Θρᾷκες Plb.10.41.4; τὰ προσοροῦντα [τῇ Χερσονήσῳ] τῆς Εὐρώπης Id.21.46.9.

**πρόσορθρος**, ον, *towards morning*: Dor. τὸ πότορθρον, as Adv., Theoc.5.126, cf. Erinn. in *PSI*9.1090.48 + 8 (p. xii).

**προσορίζω**, *include within boundaries, add to a dominion*, etc., D.S.2.3; αὐλὴν τῷ μνημείῳ *SIG*1232.6 (Asia Minor, i A.D.):—Med., *add to one's dominion*, τὴν γῆν π. τῇ σφετέρᾳ Paus.2.36.5:—Pass., οἱ προσοριζόμενοι αὐτοῖς Str.4.2.1, cf. *OGI*229.101 (Smyrna, iii B.C.), *POxy.*918 ii 17 (ii A.D.). **2.** *determine* or *fix*, χρόνον πένθους ὀλίγον Plu.*Lyc.*27:—Med. with fut. Att. -ιοῦμαι, *determine* or *define besides*, Arist.*Ph.*252$^{a}$27, *Rh.*1407$^{b}$5:—Pass., ὁ -όμενος χρόνος *PSI* 10.1160.18 (i B.C.). **3.** Med. as Att. law-term, προσωρίσατο τὴν οἰκίαν δισχιλίων *he* (sc. the mortgagee) *had* the house *marked with stones* (v. ὅρος II) *as well* to the amount of 2000 drachmae, D.31.4. **II.** intr., *to be adjacent*, τῇ Συρίᾳ D.S.2.50.

**προσορμ-έω**, *come to anchor at*, τῇ Πεπαρήθῳ Plb.10.42.1; εἰς Μέμφιν *UPZ*81 ii 7 (ii B.C.): abs., *PGoodsp.Cair.*11.4 (iv A.D.). **-ίζω**, *bring* a ship *to anchor at* or *near*, Κνίδῳ προσορμίσαι (sc. τὴν ναῦν) Luc. *Am.*11, cf. *PTeb.*802.11 (ii B.C.); π. τοῖς αἰγιαλοῖς Iamb.*VP*3.14; πρὸς τὴν Σιφνίων χώραν *IG*12(5).653.12 (Syros, perh. i B.C.):—in early writers only Med., *come to anchor near* a place, ἔα τὰς νέας πρὸς τὴν Δῆλον προσορμίζεσθαι Hdt.6.97; πρὸς τούτους (sc. λιμένας) μὴ προσορμίζου D.25.84; ποῖ οὖν προσορμιούμεθα; Id.4.44; προσορμισάμενος τῇ Σαμοθρᾴκῃ Plu.*Aem.*26:—later in Pass., προσορμισθεὶς τῷ αἰγιαλῷ Arr.*An.*6.20.4, cf. Plu.2.601f; τῇ Νάξῳ προσωρμίσθη Ael.*VH*8.5, cf. *Ev.Marc.*6.53: metaph., π. τοῖς μύθοις Philostr.*Her.*11; εὐγένειαι π. τοῖς φαυλοτάτοις Ph.2.38 (nisi leg. προσοριζ-). **-ισις**, εως, ἡ, *coming to anchor* or *to land*, Th.4.10. **-ισμός**, ὁ, = foreg., Sch. Il.1.434. **-ιστήριον**, τό, *anchorage*, Hsch. s.v. ἐπήνιον. **-ος**, ὁ, = foreg., Str.14.3.8.

**πρόσορος**, ον, Ion. **πρόσουρος** Hdt. (v. infr.), once in S., *Ph.*691:—*adjoining, bordering on*, Αἰγύπτου τὰ πρόσουρα Λιβύη Hdt.2.18, cf. 3.97,102; τῇ Ἀραβίῃ, π. ἐούσῃ (sc. τῇ Αἰγύπτῳ) Id.2.12; X. in Att. form, τὰ πρόσορα *Cyr.*6.1.17, cf. D.C.36.53, Poll.1.177, etc.:—in S. l.c., ἵν' αὐτὸς ἦν πρόσουρος οὐκ ἔχων βάσιν, πρόσουρον shd. be read.

**προσορχέομαι**, *dance to*, Luc.*Cal.*16; π. τοῖς λόγοις *to* the words, Plu.2.46b.

**προσοσφραίνω**, *give to smell*, τινά τι *Gp.*19.2.17.

⊕ **προσουδίζω**, (οὖδας) *dash against* or *to the ground*, τὸ παιδίον Hdt.5.92.γ', cf. E.*IA*1151 (Scaliger for προσουρ-), Plu.*Galb.*26, Procop. *Goth.*4.29, al.:—Pass., π. ὑπὸ τοῦ Κύκλωπος Plu.2.506b, cf. D.C.72.13.

**προσουρέω**, *make water upon*, προσεούρουν [τινί] D.54.4, cf. Arist. *Mir.*845$^{a}$33, Thphr.*Fr.*175: metaph., π. τῇ τραγῳδίᾳ *trifle with* it, Ar. *Ra.*95, cf. Porph.*Abst.*3.14.

**πρόσουρος**, v. πρόσορος.

⊕ **προσουσία**, ἡ, perhaps = συνουσία, name of a comedy by Eubulus, Ath.7.301a.

**προσοφείλω**, *owe besides* or *still*, ἔτι πολλά Th.7.48; διακόσια τάλαντα Plu.*Alex.*15; π. σοι ἄλλας χάριτας X.*Cyr.*3.2.16, cf. D.3.31, 23.89, *IG*2$^{2}$.1623.54; τὸ λοιπὸν ὃ προσοφείλεις μοι *PHib.*1.63.14 (iii B.C.), cf. *PCair.Zen.*150.17 (iii B.C.), *OGI*90.13 (Rosetta, ii B.C.), etc.: abs., προσοφείλοντας ἡμᾶς ἐνέγραψεν D.27.38 (divisim):—Pass., *to be still owing*, ὁ προσοφειλόμενος μισθός Th.8.45, cf. *SIG*410.18 (Erythrae, iii B.C.); ἡ ἔχθρη ἡ προσοφειλομένη ἐς Ἀθηναίους ἐκ τῶν Αἰγινητέων the hatred *which was still due* from the Aeginetans to the Athenians, i.e. their ancient feud, Hdt.5.82 (v.l. for προοφ-). **II.** *to be behindhand*, Plb.38.8.6.

**προσοφθαλμιάω**, *look with aching eyes at*, ταῖς μεγάλαις οὐσίαις Ph.2.560.

**προσοφλισκάνω**, fut. -οφλήσω Arist.*EN*1124$^{b}$11: 2 aor. -ώφλον D.35.46, etc.: 1 aor. προσοφλῆσαι Alciphr.3.26:—*owe besides*, πεντακοσίας δραχμάς, ἃς προσώφλεν D.58.19: abs., *incur a debt*, Arist. l.c. 2. as law-term, *lose one's suit and incur a penalty besides*, π. τὰ ἐπιτίμια D.35.46; τὴν ἐπωβελίαν Id.45.6, Aeschin.1.163; χιλίας (sc. δραχμάς) D.23.80: abs., στρατηγήσας προσώφλε *was fined* in his office of στρατηγός, Antiph.204.5. 3. generally, *incur besides*, π. αἰσχύνην D.5.5,8.12; ἀνελευθερίαν τῇ κακοηθείᾳ π. *get a character for* meanness *in addition to*.., Plu.2.856c, cf. 43c; γέλωτα Alciphr. l.c.; π. τὸν λεγόμενον ἰχθύων βίον *deserve to be said* to live like fish, Plb. 15.20.3.

**προσοχή**, ἡ, *attention*, Chrysipp.*Stoic*.3.41, Lxx*Si.Prol*.13, *BMus. Inscr*.888 (Halic., ii B.C.), *PTeb*.27.78 (ii B.C.), D.H.6.85, Hierocl. p.25A., Epict.*Ench*.33.6, D.Chr.34.27, Plu.2.514e, Luc.*Hist.Conscr*. 53; π. νόμων Lxx*Wi*.6.18, cf. Ph.1.474; π. ἀκροατοῦ τῷ λέγοντι Id. 2.342; *diligence*, Ath.Med.ap.Orib.*inc*.21.20; *care*, Leonid.ap.Aët. 15.5, Sor.2.86. 2. *soberness*, Suid. s. v. νηφαλισμός. II. *putting to land*, Iamb.*VP*3.16.

⊛ **προσοχθ-ίζω**, fut. -ιῶ (cf. sq.), *to be wroth with*, τινι Lxx*Ps*.94(95). 10; οὐ μὴ προσοχθίσῃ ὑμῖν (v.l. ὑμᾶς) ἡ γῆ ib.*Le*.20.22; προσώχθικα τῇ ζωῇ μου *I am weary* of.., ib.*Ge*.27.46. 2. Pass., *to be treated with contumely*, ib.2*Ki*.1.21. **-ισμα**, ατος, τό, *object of wrath, offence*, ib.4*Ki*.23.13; προσοχθίσματι προσοχθιεῖς ib.*De*.7. 26. **-ισμός**, ὁ, *offence*, Hsch.

**προσοχλέω**, *annoy* or *vex besides*, Ath.5.180a.

**πρόσοχος**, ον, (προσέχω) *attentive, Gloss*.

**προσοχῠρόω**, *strengthen besides* or *still more*, Lxx 1*Ma*.13.48,52, Sch.Th.4.9.

**προσόψημα**, ατος, τό, *anything eaten with* or *besides* the regular meal, mostly pl., D.S.2.59, Ph.2.483, Dsc.1.84,107, Ath.4.162c, 7. 276e, Sch.Ar.*V*.962 (v.l. προσέψημα).

**προσοψίδιον**, τό, and **προσόψιον**, τό, =*faciale, Gloss*.

**προσόψιος**, ον, *full in view*, πάγος v.l. in S.*OC*1600.

⊛ **πρόσοψις**, εως, ἡ, *appearance, aspect*, ἀνδρὸς αἰδοίου Pi.*P*.4.29 (s.v.l.), cf. Thphr.*HP*7.6.4: periphr., σὴν π. εἰσιδεῖν thy *presence*, thy *person*, thy*self*, S.*Aj*.70, cf. *El*.1286 (lyr.), E.*Or*.952; ὦ φιλτάτη π. Id.*Hel*. 636 (lyr.); νεκρὰν πρόσοψιν..τέκνου, i.e. τέκνον τεθνηκός, *Epigr.Gr*. 376.8 (Phrygia, ii A.D.). II. *seeing, beholding*, E.*Or*.1021; εἰς πρόσοψίν τινος ἐλθών Id.*Andr*.685; μὴ ἔχων τὴν π. τῶν πολεμίων ἐκ πολλοῦ Th.2.89; ἐκ πρώτης π. Luc.*Anach*.29, cf. Corn.*ND*25; *sight*, καταπληκτικὴ π. Plb.3.114.4. III. *look-out, opening*, dub. in Arist. *Pr*.940$^{a}$12.

**προσοψωνέω**, *add to the dishes already mentioned*, Ath.8.331c.

**προσπάθ-εια** [ᾰ], ἡ, *passionate attachment*, πρός τι γένος ἀκρασίας Dicaearch.1.10; defined as ἐπιθυμία δεδουλωμένη, Andronic. Rhod. p.572M.; written **προσπαθία**, Phld.*D*.1.14 (pl.); ἄνευ προσκλίσεως καὶ προσπαθείας S.E.*P*.1.230; γενομένους ἐν π. Heraclit.*Incred*.16; προσπαθείας ⟨ἕνεκα⟩ Zos.Alch.p.118B. II. in later Philos., *clinging* of the soul to the body and its passions, Porph.*Sent*.28; ἡ πρὸς τὸ σῶμα π. ib.29; ἡ θνητὴ π. Hierocl.*in CA*3p.425M., cf. M.Ant. 12.3. **-έω**, *feel passionate love for*, πρὸς ἄλλην χώραν Arr.*Epict*.3. 24.82, cf. Ph.2.48 (s.v.l.); τινι Arr.*Epict*.4.1.77, cf. M.Ant.5.1; *to be affected by contact with, become susceptible to*, τῇ ὕλῃ Dam.*Pr*. 414. **-ής**, ές, (πάθος) *impressionable*, Plot.4.3.11; *warmly attached*, τὸ παρ' ἡμῶν π. our *affection* for them, Hierocl. *in CA*11p.443M., cf. Sch.Pi.*P*.2.165. Adv. -θῶς, λουτροῖς π. ἔχειν Eust.18.41: Comp. -έστερον Pythag.*Ep*.5.5 (Theano). II. Adv. -θῶς *with prejudice*, ἱστορεῖν Gal.1.146.

⊛ **προσπαίζω**, fut. -παίξομαι App.*BC*4.118: aor. προσέπαισα Pl. *Euthd*.283b, Alciphr.3.65; also προσέπαιξα ib.5, Plu.*Caes*.63:—*play* or *sport with*, τινι X.*Mem*.3.1.4, Pl.*Euthd*.278b; of a partridge, Porph.*Abst*.3.4: metaph., προσπαίζουσα τοῖς ὤμοις κόμη *playing over*, Poll.2.25. 2. abs., *sport, jest*, π. ἐν λόγοις Pl.*Phdr*.262d, cf. *Lg*. 653e, 804b; opp. σπουδάζειν, Id.*Euthd*.283b. 3. *laugh at, make fun* or *sport of*, τινι Men.*Epit*.182, Plu.2.197d, *Caes*.63; *satirize*, τινι D.L.4.61,7.164:—Med., App. l.c. II. c. acc., θεοὺς π. *sing to* the gods, *sing in* their *praise* or *honour*, Pl.*Epin*.980b: c. dupl. acc., ὕμνον προσεπαίσαμεν..τὸν..Ἔρωτα *sang* a hymn *in praise of* Eros, Id. *Phdr*.265c. 2. *banter*, τοὺς ῥήτορας Id.*Mx*.235c, cf. *Euthd*.285a; π. τὸν κύνα, τὸν ἄρκτον, *tantalize*, Luc.*Dom*.24, Ael.*NA*4.45.

**πρόσπαιος**, ον, (παίω) *striking upon*: hence, *sudden, fresh*, εἰ π. μὴ τύχοι κακά A.*Ag*.347, cf. Lyc.211; ἐκ π. τινὸς τύχης Plb.6.43.3: ἐκ προσπαίου as Adv., *suddenly, newly*, Arist.*EN*1166$^{b}$35; neut. πρόσπαιον as Adv., S.*Ichn*.119, Nic.*Th*.690. Regul. Adv. -ως Arist.*EN*1167$^{a}$2.

**προσπαιστέον**, *one must amuse oneself with*, τούτοις Plu.2.710e.

**προσπαίω**, =προσπίπτω, Sch.A.*Pr*.885; dub. in S.*Fr*.335.

**προσπᾰλαίω**, *wrestle* or *struggle with*, τινι Pi.*I*.4.53, Pl.*Tht*.162b, *Alc*.1.107e, al.; Ἄτλας οὐρανῷ π. Pi.*P*.4.290; κῆρ π. ψυχῇ Ph.1.654: metaph., ἐν τοῖς λόγοις π. Pl.*Tht*.169b; π. σφαίρᾳ *take wrestling exercise* with a ball, Plu.2.793b; πολλοῖς χρέεσιν π. *wrestle* with debts, *PSI*1.76.6 (vi A.D.).

**προσπάλλομαι**, Med., gloss on πῆλε δὲ χεῖρας, Sch.A.R.2.45.

**Πρόσπαλτα**, τά, name of a deme in the φυλὴ Ἀκαμαντίς, loc. Προσπαλτοῖ Is.11.44: **Προσπάλτιος**, *an inhabitant of P.*, *IG*1$^{2}$.245.153, etc.; Προσπάλτιοι, οἱ, name of a play by Eupolis.

**Προσπαλτόθεν**, Adv. *from Prospalta*, D.43.64.

**προσπαραβάλλομαι**, Med., *dish up as well*, metaph., λόγους prob. in Plu.2.575e:—Pass., *to be put by* the table *besides*, δύο ἄλλαι π. κλῖναι Id.*Cleom*.13.

**προσπαραγγέλλω**, *order* or *enjoin besides*, D.C.56.25.

**προσπαρα-γράφω** [γρᾰ], *write besides, add*, Pl.*Phdr*.257e, D.39.9, 52.4, *PPetr*.3p.267 (iii B.C.). **-δείκνῡμι**, *point out as belonging to*, τί τινος *PFlor*.56.14 (iii A.D.). **-δίδωμι**, *hand over besides*, *IG*2$^{2}$. 1640.9, 7.3498.28 (Oropus).

**προσπαρ-αινέω**, *encourage* or *exhort besides*, D.C.62.8. **-αιρέομαι**, Med., *take away besides*, Id.46.40.

**προσπαρα-κᾰλέω**, *call in besides, invite*, τοὺς ξυμμάχους Th.1. 67, cf. 2.68, 8.98, Luc.*Pseudol*.2. 2. *exhort besides*, τινὰς εἶναι ἑτοίμους Plb.3.64.11; Νίκωνα περὶ τῆς λογείας *PTeb*.58.54 (ii B.C.). **-κειμαι**, Pass., *to be attached* or *appended*, Antig.*Mir*.15, Jul.*Gal*.290c; of landed property, *to be adjacent*, *PFlor*.50.72 (iii A.D.), etc. **-κελεύομαι**, *exhort besides*, J.*AJ*7.9.7. **-λαμβάνω**, *employ as well*, Παῆσιν *PCair.Zen*.500.4 (iii B.C.); *take besides*, D.C. 42.58, Iamb.*Myst*.8.4; *include*, Dsc.1*Praef*.6; ἡ ἔννοια τὴν οὐσίαν οὐ.. π. Plot.6.8.7:—Pass., *to be employed as well*, Sor.1.26. **-ληπτέον**, *one must include*, Heph.Astr. in *Cat.Cod.Astr*.8(1).158, Vett.Val.302. 31. **-ληψις**, εως, ἡ, *taking besides*, ἑτέρου Ph.1.485. II. Gramm., = παραγωγή III. 2, Diom.p.441K. **-μένω**, *abide by*, Aesop. 337, *Cod.Just*.12.37.19.3. **-μῡθέομαι**, Med., *urge* or *exhort besides*, *SIG*762.28 (Dionysopolis, i B.C.):—Pass., *to be argued, urged besides*, Ptol.*Phas*.p.13H. **-μῡθητέον**, *one must urge besides*, Id. *Judic*.p.7B. **-πήγνῡμι**, *fix beside in addition*, χάρακας *Gp*.4.12. 18. **-σκευάζω**, *prepare besides*, ἑτέραν δύναμιν D.8.19, etc.:—Med., *prepare for oneself besides*, ὁρμητήρια Id.19.326. **-τίθημι**, *append, attach*, Antig.*Mir*.15; [ἄρθροις] διάρθρωσιν Gal.*UP*2.17; *add*, ἄρτον ταῖς ἑορταῖς Ath.4.137e, etc.; *put before one besides*, Plb.3. 99.7. **-τρώγω**, *gnaw at the side besides*: metaph., *nibble at one's reputation* or *depreciate besides*, D.L.2.107. **-φύομαι**, Pass. with pf. Act. -πέφῡκα, *to be attached at the side*, Sor.1.12. **-χωρέω**, *give up as well*, *POxy*.271.14 (i A.D.).

**προσπάρ-ειμι**, *to be present with besides*, Petos.ap.Vett.Val.124. 10. **-εισέρχομαι**, *come in besides*, Eun.*VS*p.476B. **-εμβάλλω**, *throw in besides*, Ulp. ad D.20.167. **-έχω**, *furnish, supply besides*, Ἀρκάσι ναῦς Th.1.9, cf. D.C.56.40:—Med., Pl.*R*.437e, *Lg*. 808c. II. *cause besides*, βλάβας Hp.*Art*.47. **-ίσταμαι**, Med., *bring to one's side, subdue besides*, D.C.50.12 (nisi leg. προπ-). 2. *put in one's mind, excite besides*, τόλμαν τινί J.*AJ*19.1.10. II. intr., προσπαρέστη τινὶ νομίζειν *it came into* his *mind*, prob. in D.C. *Fr*.102.9. **-οινέω**, *add a further indignity*, Philostr.*Im*.2. 23. **-οξύνω**, pf. -ώξυγκα D.C.37.29:—*cause additional pain* or *inflammation*, Hp.*Acut*.16: metaph., *provoke besides*, Str.14.2.24, Plu.*Alex*.52, D.C. l.c. **-ορμάω**, *incite besides*, J.*AJ*7.14.10.

**προσπασσᾰλεύω**, Att. **προσπαττ-**, *nail fast to*, σε τῷδε..πάγῳ A.*Pr*.20; [ἐμβάδια] πρὸς τὸ μέτωπον ὥσπερ κοτίνῳ Ar.*Pl*.943; but in Hdt.9.120, σανίδα (or σανίδας) προσπασσαλεύσαντες (sc. αὐτῷ) (nisi leg. σανίδι):—Pass., προσπεπατταλευμένον γράφουσι τὸν Προμηθέα πρὸς ταῖς πέτραις Men.535.1; τὴν Ἀνδρομέδαν ἐπί τινος πέτρας.. προσπεπ. Luc.*DMar*.14.3: metaph., ἀχανής, προσπεπατταλευμένος, ἄφωνος *fixed to the spot*, Hegesipp.Com.1.25. II. *nail up* or *hang upon a peg*, τὸν τρίποδα Hdt.1.144:—Pass., Cratin.164.

**προσπασσᾰλόω**, Att. **προσπαττ-**, = foreg. II, Thphr.*Char*.21.7.

**προσ-πάσσω**, Att. -ττω, aor. προσέπᾰσα Lxx *To*.11.11:—*sprinkle upon*, τί τινι Antyll.ap.Orib.7.21.6, cf. Lxx l.c., Dsc.1.52, Sch.Nic. *Al*.563. **-παστέον**, *one must sprinkle upon*, ἄλευρον Gal.11.318.

⊛ **προσπάσχω**, *experience in addition*, Pl.*Phd*.74a; *suffer as well*, μείζω τῶν πρότερον Aristid.1.156J., cf. Lib.*Or*.12.74; *to be further affected*, τῇ ψυχῇ περί τινων Isoc.10.55. II. *to be devoted* or *addicted to, feel affection for*, c. dat., Plu.2.514a, *Sert*.26, Luc.*Dem.Enc*.40; τῷ καλῷ Cic.*Att*.2.19.1; ᾧ προσπέπονθε Phld.*Lib*.p.6O.; [τῷ θεῷ] μόνῳ Arr.*Epict*.2.16.46; ταῖς κατὰ θάλασσαν ἐργασίαις Dicaearch.1.24: abs., Macho 2.2; τὸ προσπεπονθός *that which has an affinity with* a thing, Plu.2.499e (s.v.l.).

**προ-σπάω**, in Med., *draw on*, εἰς τὸν..ἀγῶνα D.S.18.46.

**πρόσπεινος**, ον, (πεῖνα) *hungry*, Dem.Ophth.ap.Aët.7.33, *Act.Ap*. 10.10.

**προσπειράζω**, *make an attempt besides, Gloss*.

**προσπελ-άζω**, *cause to approach, bring near to*, νέα μέν μοι κατέαξε.. ἄκρῃ προσπελάσας *having driven* her *against* the headland, Od.9.285: —Pass. προσπελασθεὶς is f.l. for πατρὸς πελ. in S.*OT*1101 (lyr.). 2. π. τὴν ἁφήν *apply* touch, Marcellin.*Puls*.130. II. intr., *approach*, τινι Pl.*Smp*.206d, D.S.15.42, etc.; *associate with*, Phld.*Ir*.p.47 W.; also of hostile *approach*, Aen.Tact.22.12, 39.6; *deal with*, in argument, Gal.18(1).278; *visit*, τοῖς αὐτοφυέσι..ὕδασιν Alex.Trall. 8.2. **-ᾰσις**, εως, ἡ, *bringing* or *coming near, Gloss*. **-άτης** [ᾰ], ου, ὁ, =πελάτης, Theopomp.Hist.39(*b*).

⊛ **προσπέμπω**, *send to*, esp. of messengers or envoys, φίλους Ar.*Eq*. 473; κήρυκα Th.7.3; π. τινά τινι *send* or *conduct* one person *to* another, αὐτὸν δεῦρο προσπέμψας ἐμοί S.*OC*1349, cf. 1101, Th.1.53, X.*Cyr*.8.5.18: simply, c. dat., *send* to one (sc. ἄγγελον), Th.7.35, D. 19.167, etc.; π. τινὶ ἵνα.. Arr.*Epict*.1.2.19; also π. λόγους ἔς τινας Th.8.47: abs., Hdt.9.108; ἐς Ὄλυνθον Th.2.79.

**προσπεποιημένως**, *dissimulanter, Gloss*.

**προσπέρδομαι**, with aor. 2 Act. -έπαρδον, *break wind at*, τινι Ar.*Ra*. 1074, Sosip.1.12, Damox.2.39.

**προσπερι-βάλλω**, *put round besides*, of a bandage, Hp.*Fract*.20; περιτείχισμα τῇ πόλει Th.5.2: metaph., ὄγκον τοῖς νοήμασι Ph.1.1: —Med., νεὼς αὐταῖς (sc. εἰκόσι) Id.2.181: also, *throw* or *draw round oneself*, τείχη Isoc.9.47; τὸν πεζὸν στρατὸν ταῖς ναυσὶ π. the land army *in addition to* the ships, Plu.*Them.*7, cf. *Cat.Ma.*13 (Act.); *surround oneself with fresh acquisitions*, D.4.9, Paus.1.10.1; π. πλείονα μολυσμόν Plu.2.831a:—Pass., *to be drawn round*, στρατοπέδῳ ἐρύματος προσπεριβαλλομένου Th.8.40. 2. Pass., κῆπον ἑνὶ περιβόλῳ προσπεριβεβλημένοι *having also* a garden *surrounded* by one fence, Pl.*Criti.* 112b; *to be included in a bandage*, Hp.*Fract.*48. **-γίγνομαι**, *accrue as additional advantage*, D.20.33, Plu.*Ages.*32. **-ειλέω**, *wrap round besides*, Sor.1.50 (Pass.). **-εργάζομαι**, *busy oneself still further, inquire curiously*, Ph.1.12, 2.88, D.C.44.35, etc.; *interfere with the course of nature*, Gal.12.665. **-κειμαι**, *envelope besides*, Orib.*Fr.* 114. **-κόπτω**, *wheedle one out of in addition*, τριακοσίας δραχμάς Hyp.*Ath.*2. **-λαμβάνω**, *embrace* or *include besides*, D.24.44, al., Ph.1.1 (v.l.), Antyll.ap.Orib.44.23.13; π. τινὰ ταῖς συνθήκαις Plb.3. 24.1; π. τι τῷ νῷ Id.5.32.3. **-οδεύω**, *survey and describe besides*, Str.10.5.14. **-ορίζομαι**, Med., *include with besides*, ἔννοιαν τῷ ἐπαίνῳ Longin.28.3. **-ποιέω**, *lay by* or *save besides*, D.27.60.

**προσπερμεία**, ἡ, *ritual sprinkling with corn-seed*, *Abh.Berl.Akad.* 1928(6).21 (Cos, iii B.C.).

**προσπερονάω**, (περόνη) *fasten* or *attach by means of a pin*: generally, *fasten on*, ψυχὴν πρὸς τὸ σῶμα Pl.*Phd.*83d; *nail up*, καρκίνους Thphr.*HP*2.8.3; εἰς τὴν στοὴν Ἀρχ. Δελτ.11.23 (Chios, iv B.C.):—Pass., ἄρτοι προσπεπερονημένοι πρὸς τοῖς κρέασι X.*An.*7.3.21.

**προσπετάμαι**, = sq., Arist.*HA*629ᵃ35: aor. part. προσπετασθέντες D.H.4.63.

* **προσπέτομαι**, fut. -πτήσομαι: aor. -επτάμην [ᾰ], but poet. also with aor. Act. προσέπτην (v. infr.):—*fly to* or *towards*, πόθεν προσέπταντ' (-έπτονθ' Dawes) οἱ βομβαύλιοι; Ar.*Ach.*865; πρός τι Arist. *HA*593ᵃ8; ἐάν τίς σοι φίλος ὥσπερ μυῖα προσπτηται X.*Mem.*3.11. 5. II. generally, *come upon* one *suddenly, come over* one, ὀδμὰ προσέπτα μ' ἀφεγγής A.*Pr.*115 (lyr.); μέλος προσέπτα μοι music *stole over* my sense, ib.555 (lyr.); of evil, misfortune, etc., τίς.. ἀρχὴ τοῦ κακοῦ προσέπτατο; S.*Aj.*282, cf. A.*Pr.*644, E.*Alc.*421.

**προσπεύθομαι**, poet. for προσπυνθάνομαι, S.*OC*122 (lyr.).

**προσπεφῡκότως**, Adv. *clinging to*, *EM*132.53.

**πρόσπηγμα**, ατος, τό, *that which gathers and hardens on a place*, Hp.*Prorrh.*2.23 (pl.). II. *part of a ship*, Hsch. (pl.).

**προσπήγνῡμι**, fut. -πήξω (προσπήξομαι is f.l. for -πτύξομαι in Hsch.):—*fix to* or *on*, τινί [τι] E.*Fr.*679, etc.; τι πρός τι D.C.40.9; ἥλοις [τὸν ἀκινάκην] τῷ κολεῷ προσέπηξε Id.63.2: abs., *crucify*, *Act. Ap.*2.23:—Pass. with pf. Act. -πέπηγα, *to be fixed on*, Heliod.ap. Orib.49.4.72; περί τι D.C.45.17; ἰχθὺς -πεπηγὼς τῷ ἀγκίστρῳ Aristaenet.1.7.

**προσπηδάω**, fut. -ήσομαι Alex.124.16:—*leap against* or *upon*, πρὸς ἑστίαν And.2.15; ἀτμὸς.. π. ταῖς ῥισίν Alex. l. c.; μοι *PEnteux.*75.5 (iii B.C.), cf. *PPetr.*3 pp.57, 65 (iii B.C.); ἐπί τι Arr.*Epict.*1.2.32: abs., D.C.76.4; δόξα π. *sprang up suddenly*, App.*BC*2.45.

**προσπηλόω**, *close with clay*, [χύτραν] Cyran.99.

**προσπήσσω**, late collat. form of προσπήγνυμι, Artem.1.74 (Pass.), *Gloss.*

**προσπηχύνομαι**, Med., *take in one's arms* or *embrace besides*, Call. *Jov.*46; also **ποτιπηχ-**, Rhian.72.3 (tm.).

**προσπῐέζω**, also -πιεζέω Ph.ap.Eus.*PE*8.14:—*press besides*, τι Hp.*Acut.*(*Sp.*)59; *press against*, τοὺς ὀδόντας Archig.ap.Gal.12. 860:—Pass., προσπεπιεσμένη *tight*, of a bandage, Heliod.ap.Orib.47. 14.7. 2. π. τι πρός τι *press to* or *upon*, Arist.*HA*526ᵃ23:—Pass., Ph.2.400.

**προσπικραίνω**, in Pass., *become angry with*, c. dat., *PEnteux.*84.9 (iii B.C.), *PLille* 7.9 (iii B.C.).

**προσπῑλνᾰμαι**, Pass., *approach*, νήσῳ Od.13.95.

**προσπῑλόω**, = προσπιέζω 2, c. dat., Sch.D.T. p.43 H. (Pass.).

**προσπίνω** [ῑ], *drink besides* or *afterwards*, D.C.75.2.

**προσπῑπίσκω**, *give to drink besides*, Hp.*Morb.*2.48, 66.

**προσπιπράσκω**, pf. inf. Pass. -πεπρᾶσθαι, *sell besides* or *at the same time*, Poll.7.13.

* **προσπίπτω**, Dor. **ποτιπίπτω** Archyt.1: fut. -πεσοῦμαι E.*Alc.*350: for ποτιπετηνίαι, v. προσπτήσσω:—*fall upon, strike against*, ἔς τι v.l. in S.*Ant.*855; τινι X.*Eq.*7.6, etc.; πρός τι Arist.*Aud.*800ᵃ2, al.; *fall against*, as a mound against a wall, Th.2.75; but πρὸς τὸ οὖς προσπίπτων is dub.l. in Thphr.*Char.*2.10 (προσκύπτων cj. Valckenaer). 2. *fall upon, attack, assault*, πόλεσιν, ὁπλίταις, Th.1.5, X.*HG*3.2.3, etc.: abs., Th.3.30, 103, X.*Cyr.*7.1.38. 3. simply, *run to*, Hdt.2.2, X. *Cyr.*1.4.4. 4. *fall upon, embrace*, τινι E. l.c., *IA*1191: hence, π. τινί *join the party of* another, X.*HG*7.1.42; also, *fasten on*, in argument, τῇ διαφορᾷ Phld.*Sign.*36. 5. *fall in with, meet with, encounter*, μὴ λάθῃ με προσπεσών S.*Ph.*46, cf. 156 (lyr.), Pl.*Phdr.* 270a: c. dat. rei, Id.*Tht.*154b; *fall in with*, δυστυχεστάτῳ κλήρῳ E. *Tr.*291 (lyr.); αἰσχρᾷ ἐπιθυμίᾳ X.*Ap.*30; μεγίσταις ἡδοναῖς Pl.*Lg.* 637a; δήγματι *to be bitten*, Ael.*NA*6.51: c. acc., μείζω βροτείας π. ὁμιλίας E.*Hipp.*19: with a Prep., πρὸς τὰς τῶν φυλάκων ψυχὰς Pl.*Lg.* 906b; εἰς βράχεα, πρὸς τὰ κοινά, Plb.1.39.3, Plu.2.788c. II. of things, 1. of events, accidents, etc., *come suddenly upon, befall* one, τινι E.*Med.*225, *IT*1229 (troch.), Antipho 3.3.8, Pl.*Cra.*396d; τὰ προσπίπτονθ' ἡμῖν δείματα Id.*Lg.*791c, etc.: abs., ἄτην προσπεσοῦσαν ἐνεῖκαι Hdt.1.32; αἱ συμφοραὶ προσπίπτουσαι misfortunes *by befalling*, Id.7. 46, cf. Isoc.*Ep.*5.4; αἱ π. χρεῖαι *PCair.Zen.*31.7 (iii B.C.); αἱ π. τύχαι Th.1.84; τὰ προσπεσόντα E.*Fr.*505; γενναίως φέρειν τὰ προσπίπτοντα Stob.4.44 tit.; οἱ τὰ π. κρίναντες χρηματισταί *PPetr.*3 p.53 (iii B.C.); ἡ π. ἐπιθυμία Pl.*R.*561c; πρὸς τὰ προσπίπτοντα according to *circumstances*, Arist.*Pol.*1286ᵃ11; οἱ προσπίπτοντες κίνδυνοι Hyp.*Fr.*117; τὰ π. εἰς τὸν ἀνθρώπινον βίον Id.*Epit.*43; ὅ τι ἂν προσπέσῃ ἰχθύδιον Arist. *HA*590ᵃ27, cf. *PCair.Zen.*186.15 (iii B.C.); προσπεσούσης μοι τῆς.. ἐπιστολῆς *when* the letter *came to hand*, *PStrassb.*111.2 (iii B.C.), cf. *PPetr.*3 p.71 (iii B.C.), *PCair.Zen.*240.9 (iii B.C.). 2. of expenses, *to be incurred*, Th.7.28, *PCair.Zen.*60.3 (iii B.C.). 3. of money, *to be paid in* to an account, ib.701.9 (iii B.C.), *PPetr.*3 p.290 (iii B.C.). 4. of rights and duties, etc., *pass to, devolve* or *fall upon*, ὅταν λειτουργία προσπέσῃ ἀπολύειν αὐτούς *PHib.*1.78.4 (iii B.C.); ὥστε μηδεμίαν ὑποψίαν ἐκείνῳ γε προσπεσεῖν *PSI*4.340.12 (iii B.C.); κληρονομίας -πεσούσης μοι *BGU*340.9 (iii A.D.). 5. *come to one's ears, be told as news*, εἴ τισιν ἀπιστότερος προσπέπτωκεν ὁ λόγος Aeschin.3. 59, cf. *PSI*6.614.13 (iii B.C.), *UPZ*9.9 (ii B.C.), Plb.5.101.3, Plu.*Per.* 16, etc.; εἰς τὴν Ῥώμην Plb.9.6.1: impers., προσέπεσε *news came* that.., c. acc. et inf., Id.24.14.10, cf. 31.14.8; προσπέπτωκεν Παῶν ἀναπλεῖν Wilcken *Chr.*10 (ii B.C.); προσπεσόντων τῷ βασιλεῖ περὶ τῶν γεγονότων Lxx 2*Ma.*5.11. b. π. δι' ἑαυτοῦ or αὐτόθεν *to be self-evident*, S.E.*P.*2.168, *M.*1.300; τὰ ποτιπίπτοντα ποτὶ τὰν αἴσθησιν Archyt.1, cf. Thphr.*Sens.*5, 41. 6. *sit* or *fit closely*, of a bandage, προσπεπτωκός, opp. χαλαρόν, Hp.*Fract.*5. 7. Geom., *meet*, πόλος πρὸς ὃν αἱ γραμμαὶ προσπίπτουσιν Arist.*Mete.*376ᵃ19, cf. Archim.*Spir.* 6; of lines, *to be drawn to meet*, πρὸς κύκλον Euc.3.37; π. ἐπὶ.. *pass through* a point, Archim.*Spir.*14. 8. of the pulse, = ὑποπίπτω, Ruf.*Puls.*6.2; of the womb, ἔνθα καὶ ἔνθα π. Hp.*Nat.Mul.*44, cf. *Mul.* 2.125, al. III. *fall down at* another's *feet, prostrate oneself*, προσπίπτων προσκυνεῖ τὸν ἕτερον Hdt.1.134; προσπεσὼν ἔχου S.*Aj.*1181; ἱκέτης προσπίπτω X.*Cyr.*4.6.2: c. dat., π. βωμοῖσι S.*Tr.*904, cf. *OC* 1157; τινὸς γόνασι E.*Or.*1332, *Andr.*860 (lyr.), etc.; προσπεσὼν αὐτῷ..ἱκέτευε Pl.*Ep.*349a; θεῶν πρὸς βρέτας Ar.*Eq.*31; πρὸς γόνυ E. *HF*79: also c. acc., π. βρέτη δαιμόνων A.*Th.*94 (lyr.); cf. προσπίτνω.

**προσπιστεύω**, *believe besides*, ἐκεῖνο, ὅτι.. Aristid.*Or.*36(48).6; ἑαυτῷ dub. in Ph.2.384.

**προσπίτνω**, poet. for προσπίπτω (v. πίτνω), *fall upon* a person's neck, *embrace*, τοῖς φιλτάτοις E.*El.*576; νεκρῷ Id.*Med.*1205; ἀμφὶ γενειάδα Id.*HF*1208 (lyr.). 2. *come in, come upon the scene*, Id.*Ph.* 1429. II. of things, *fall upon*, ἰοὶ προσπίτνοντες ὤλλυσαν A.*Pers.* 461; of passion, σοὶ φρενῶν χόλος π. E.*Med.*1266 (lyr.). III. *fall down to* or *before, supplicate*, abs., αἰτοῦ δὲ προσπίτνουσα S.*El.*453: c. dat., προσπίτνομέν σοι Id.*OC*1754 (anap.): more freq. c. acc., A. *Pers.*152 (anap.), E.*Ph.*924, *Andr.*537 (anap.), *Tr.*762; ἐμὸν γόνυ Id.*Supp.*10; μνῆμα Id.*Hel.*64; προσπίτνω σε γόνασι S.*Ph.*485; γονυπετεῖς ἕδρας π. τινά *fall before* one in kneeling posture, E.*Ph.*293 (lyr.): c. inf., π. σε μὴ θανεῖν I *beseech* thee that I may not die, Id.*El.* 221. IV. *fall upon, attack*, τινα Id.*Ba.*1115.

**προσπλάζω**, *beat* or *knock against, touch*, κῦμα δέ μιν προσπλάζον ἐρύκεται Il.12.285: c. dat., [λίμνη] προσέπλαζε γενείῳ Od.11.583; γαίης.. πεῖρας.. ἠέρι προσπλάζον Xenoph.28.2.

* **προσπλάσσω**, Att. -ττω, *form* or *mould upon*, in Pass., νεοσσιαὶ προσπεπλασμέναι ἐκ πηλοῦ πρὸς ἀποκρήμνοισι ὄρεσι nests *formed* of clay *and attached to* precipitous mountains, Hdt.3.111; *to be applied as a plaster*, Hp.*VM*15; *to be smeared upon*, prob. in Aen.Tact.22. 25; *adhere to*, Alex.Trall.7.7:—Act., τέφραν προσπλάττουσι τῷ βωμῷ Plu.2.433b: metaph., τοὺς τόκους ib.831a. II. *increase*, in Pass., of the body, *increase by continued growth*, Gal.4.541: metaph., *to be added*, ποτεπλάσθη, of Berenice as a fourth Χάρις, Call.*Epigr.*52.

**προσ-πλαστικός**, ή, όν, *sticking on*, Dsc.5.75. **-πλαστός**, ή, όν, = foreg., Gal.17(1).902.

**πρόσπλᾰτος**, ον, (προσπίλναμαι) *approachable*, ξένοις A.*Pr.*716 (Elmsl. for πρόσπλαστοι).

**προσπλεκ-τέον**, *one must add, mix in*, Herod.Med.ap.Aët.5.130, Archig.ib.6.3. * **-ω**, *connect with*, τινί τινα M.Ant.10.7; *mix with* a medicine, Archig.ap.Gal.12.645:—Pass., *cling to, attach oneself* or *be attached to*, Plb.5.60.7, Plu.2.796b; εἴδει ἑτέρῳ Dam.*Pr.*84; in hostile sense, *attack*, τῷ Διονύσῳ Arg.1 Ar.*Ra.*; *fasten upon*, in argument, λέξει Gal.1.176; *to be mixed up with*, μυθώδη τινὰ -πέπλεκται τοῖς λεγομένοις Str.1.1.10; of astrological relationship, Vett.Val.119.27.

**προσπλεονάζω**, *to be specially frequent* or *prevalent*, ἐν θέρει Dem. Ophth.ap.Aët.7.14.

**προσπλέω**, fut. -πλεύσομαι: Ion. pres. **προσπλώω** only as v.l. in Hdt.8.6: aor. προσέπλωσα Arr.*Ind.*39.4:—*sail towards* or *against*, Hdt. l. c., 9.96, al., Th.1.47, X.*Cyr.*6.2.10, etc.; τινι *against* one, Th. 2.83; ἐν πλοίῳ π. D.23.78; of ships, X.*HG*6.2.33.

**προσπληρόω**, *fill up* or *complete* a number, ἱππέας π. εἰς δισχιλίους v.l. in X.*Cyr.*5.3.24, cf. *HG*1.6.3, prob. in *PCair.Zen.*421.8 (iii B.C.): esp. *man and equip* ships *besides, man still more* ships, Th.6.104, 7. 34:—Med., ἐκ Κερκύρας ἄλλας π. X.*HG*5.4.66, cf. 5.1.27.

**προσπλήσσω**, Att. -ττω, *strike*, Procop.Gaz.p.171 B.: fut. -πλήξω Hsch.

* **προσπλοκ-ή**, ἡ, *close embrace*, αἱ π. τοῦ κισσοῦ Artem.1.77, cf. Aq. *Ex.*28.32. 2. *admixture*, Alex.Trall.1.15. * **-ος**, ον, θεῷ, = θεόπλοκος, Rhetor. in *Cat.Cod.Astr.*8(4).148.

**πρόσπλους**, ὁ, *access by sea*, App.*BC*4.102, D.C.37.53, Hld.9.5.

**προσπλωτός**, ή, όν, *accessible from the sea*, i.e. *navigable*, ποταμοὶ π. ἀπὸ θαλάσσης Hdt.4.47, cf. 71.

**προσπλώω**, v. προσπλέω.

**πρόσ-πνευμα**, ατος, τό, *inspiration*, Plb.*Fr.*202. **-πνευσις**, εως, ἡ, *breathing on*, Plot.2.9.14 (pl.). II. *fragrance*, D.S.2.49. III. *rough breathing, aspiration*, Phld.*Po.*2.5, 18, Jul.*Or.*2.72a. **-πνέω**, poet. -πνείω Theoc.17.52: fut. -πνεύσομαι:—*blow* or *breathe upon, inspire*, ἔρωτας l.c.; τῷ σώματι ζωήν Hierocl. *in CA*26 p.478 M.:

—Pass., *to be blown upon*, προσπνείσθω τόπος ἀπὸ βορρᾶ *Gp*.2.27.1. 2. intr., *blow to* or *over*, τόποις Thphr.*Vent*.27; ἡμῖν..π. αὖραι Luc.*Am*.12: impers., c. gen., ὡς ἡδύ μοι προσέπνευσε χοιρείων κρεῶν a sweet *savour* of pork *is wafted to* me, Ar.*Ra*.338. II. Gramm., *pronounce with the rough breathing*, A.D.*Pron*.55.23:—Pass., Id. *Synt*.141.4, Seleuc.ap.Ath.9.398b.

προ-σπογγίζω, *sponge beforehand*, Aët.9.1.

προσποθέω, *desire to know besides*, τόδε Pl.*Chrm*.174a.

* προσποι-έω, *make over to, add* or *attach to*, π. τισὶ τὴν Κέρκυραν Th.1.55, cf. 2.2, 3.70, etc.; Λέσβον π. τῇ πόλει X.*HG*4.8.28, etc.; χάριν D.60.14, cf. Plot.6.1.21. 2. μνημείῳ κακὸν π. *do* damage *to*, *MAMA*4.27. 3. = προσποιέομαι II. 3, ὡς εἴη X.Eph.1.5. II. mostly in Med., with aor. Pass. in Plb. (v. infr. 5), D.S.15.46, 19.6:—*procure for oneself*, ξύλινον πόδα Hdt.9.37; *include in one's purview*, Plot.6.1.19, 6.3.8, 6.3.19: most freq. of persons, *attach to oneself, win* or *gain over*, ἑταιρηΐην Hdt.5.71, cf. 6.66, Th.4.77, etc.; τὸν δῆμον Ar.*Eq*.215; [θεούς] X.*Vect*.6.3; c. dupl. acc., φίλους π. τινάς *as* friends, Hdt.1.6; εὔνουν π. τινά E.*Hel*.1387; ὑπηκόους τὰς πόλεις Th.1.8; π. χωρίον ἐς τὴν ξυμμαχίαν Id.2.30. 2. *take to oneself what does not belong to one, pretend to, lay claim to*, c. acc., τὴν τῶν γεφυρῶν οὐ διάλυσιν Id.1.137; φήμην Aeschin.2.166; μείζω τῶν ὑπαρχόντων Arist.*EN*1127ᵇ9: c. gen. partit., π. τῶν χρημάτων *claim some of*.., Ar.*Ec*.871, cf. Is.4.3,7. 3. generally, *pretend, affect*, ὀργὴν Hdt.2.121.δ'; τὸ δεῖσθαι Isoc.1.24; π. ἔχθραν *use it as a pretence, allege*, Th.8.108; π. Ἀριστοτέλην Luc.*Pisc*.50: c. acc. part., προσποιούμενος τὸν ἡδόμενον Ph.2.531. 4. c. inf., *pretend* to do or to be, Hdt.3.2, Antipho 2.4.2, Lys.1.13; ὅσοι πολιτικοὶ π. εἶναι *profess* to be, Pl.*Grg*.519c, cf. *Alc*.1.108e, etc.; π. μὲν εἰδέναι, εἰδότες δὲ οὐδέν Id.*Ap*.23d, cf. 26e; ὅρα μὴ τούτων μὲν ἐχθρὸς ᾖς, ἐμοὶ δὲ προσποιῇ (sc. εἶναι) D.18.125; μὴ ἀποκτείνας π. (sc. ἀποκτεῖναι) Lys.13.75: aor. Pass., -ποιηθεὶς στρατεύειν D.S.19.6: c. inf. fut., *make as if one* would, X.*An*.4.3.20, etc. 5. with a neg., *pretend the contrary*, δεῖ δέ, εἰ καὶ ἠδίκησαν, μὴ προσποιεῖσθαι one must *make as if it were* not *so*, Th.3.47, cf. Thphr.*Char*.1.5; τούτων οὐ προσποιουμένων D.47.10; οὐδὲν πέπονθας δεινόν, ἂν μὴ προσποιῇ Men.*Epit*.*Fr*.8, cf. Philem.23: aor. Pass., σαφῶς εἰδὼς.., οὐ προσποιηθεὶς δέ Plb.5.25.7, cf. 31.14.1. -ημα, ατος, τό, *that which one takes to oneself unduly, pretence, assumption* of a thing, Arist.*EN*1127ᵃ20; τῆς καλοκἀγαθίας, δικαιοσύνης, Heraclid.Pont.ap.Ath.14.625a, Plu.2.858f. 2. *deception, illusion*, Epicur.*Nat*.11.7. 3. *disguise*, ἐν π. φίλων D.H.10.13, cf. App.*BC*3.64. * -ησις, εως, ἡ, *taking something to oneself, acquisition*, ξυμμαχίας Th.3.82; ἐρώτων J.*AJ*17.4.1. 2. *pretension* or *claim* to a thing, Th.2.62: c. gen., Id.6.16, Pl.*La*.184c; εἰρωνεία is defined as π. ἐπὶ χεῖρον πράξεων καὶ λόγων *affectation* of.., Thphr.*Char*.1.1, cf. Jul.*Or*.3.129b; ἡ εἰς οὐσίαν π. *pretension* to real existence, Plot.6.6.18. 3. *pretension, affectation*, Arist.*EN*1165ᵇ10, Porph.*Marc*.3. -η(σί)σοφος [ῐ], ον, *making a pretence of wisdom*, Ptol.*Tetr*.163. -ητής, οῦ, ὁ, = *simulator*, *Gloss*. * -ητικός, ή, όν, *making pretence to* a thing, c. gen., ἀνδρείας Arist.*EN*1115ᵇ30; ἀλαζονεία ἕξις π. ἀγαθοῦ Pl.*Def*.416a. -ητός, όν, or ή, όν Demarat.ap.Plu.2.309d, or προσποίητος:—*taken to oneself, assumed, affected, pretended*, ἐρασταί Pl.*Ly*.222a; ἔχθραι D.58.39; ἡ π. καλοκἀγαθία Din.3.18; φιλανθρωπία Arist.*VV*1251ᵇ3; φυγή Demarat. l.c. Adv. -ητῶς or -ήτως, opp. τῷ ὄντι, Pl.*Tht*.174d, cf. D.C.44.47, etc.: neut. pl. προσποιητά as Adv., Babr.103.5,106.17. 2. *to be adopted*, *Stoic*.1.57.

προσπολεμ-έω, *carry on war against*, τινα X.*An*.1.6.6; τινι Aeschin.1.64: abs., Pl.*R*.332e; ξυμφορώτατοι προσπολεμῆσαι Th.8.96, cf. 7.51; χαλεπὸς προσπολεμεῖν Isoc.4.138, cf. D.2.22. -όομαι, Med., *make one's enemy besides, go to war with besides*, τινα Th.3.3. II. = foreg., D.C.37.20, 48.49.

προσπολέω, *attend, serve*, τινι E.*Tr*.264; δόμοις Id.*Alc*.1024. II. Pass., *to be escorted by a train of attendants*, S.*OC*1098.

προσπολῑτεύομαι, Med., *oppose in public life*, Phalar.*Ep*.93.2 codd.

πρόσπολος, ὁ, *servant, attendant*, S.*OC*897, 1553, E.*Or*.106, etc.; *ministering priest*, A.*Eu*.1024, S.*OC*1053 (lyr.); π. θεᾶς E.*Supp*.2; π. φόνου *minister* of death, A.*Th*.574; Λητοῖ π. *App.Anth*.1.193 (Egypt): not in Prose, exc. as v.l. for πρόπολος, Hdt.2.63. 2. fem., Ἀθάνας π. B.14.2; Βάκχου πρόσπολοι, = Βάκχαι, Limen.46; *handmaid*, S.*OT*945, *OC*746, etc.

προσπονέομαι, *labour, toil*, App.*BC*2.81, 4.128; γεωργίᾳ *at* husbandry, Id.*Pun*.87 (v.l.).

* προσπορεύομαι, Dor. ποτιπορ- *SIG*338.15 (Rhodes, iv/iii B.C.):—*go to, approach*, Arist.*HA*625ᵃ13, cf. *PSI*4.403.16 (iii B.C.), etc.; *apply* for a loan, *PMich.Zen*.46.5 (iii B.C.); for hire of a boat, ib.60.9 (iii B.C.); π. πρὸς τὰς προσοδικὰς κρίσεις *take up* revenue cases, of advocates, *PAmh*.33.17 (ii B.C.); π. πρὸς ταῦτα καὶ πρὸς τὰ λοιπὰ μαθήματα *PCair.Zen*.60.6 (iii B.C.); π. πρὸς τὰ γενήματα *make a start* or *get on with* the crops, ib.132.4 (iii B.C.); π. πρὸς τὴν ἀγορανομίαν *go in quest of* the office of aedile, *be candidate for* it, Plb.10.4.1; of a writer, π. πρὸς πᾶν παρὰ τὴν κοινὴν ἔννοιαν λεγόμενον *hunt for* paradoxes, Id.10.27.8: c. gen., π. τῶν μὴ καθηκόντων αὐτῷ *encroach on* what does not belong to him, *PEnteux*.69.7 (iii B.C.). 2. of a certain day, *draw near, approach*, προσπορευομένης τῆς νουμηνίας Arist.*Oec*.1353ᵇ1. II. *attach oneself to*, ἀνδρὶ ἁμαρτωλῷ Lxx *Si*.12.14; of proselytes, ib.*Nu*.1.51, al., *Jo*.9.1 (8.35); also ὅταν -πορεύωνται πρὸς τὸ θυσιαστήριον λειτουργεῖν ib.*Ex*.30.20. III. of revenue, *come in*, *SIG*344.112 (Antig.Epist.).

* προσπορ-ίζω, Att. fut. -ιῶ, *procure* or *supply besides*, X.*Mem*.3.6.5, D.4.29; αὐτοὶ παρ' αὑτῶν ἕτερα (sc. κακά) -πορίζομεν Men.534.8; π. τινὶ τὴν ἀγωγὴν καὶ ἐνοχὴν *acquire* for one the *actio* and *obligatio* of the transaction, *POxy*.133.6 (vi A.D.):—Pass., Aen.Tact.11.3 (sed leg. προπ-); τὰ -ιζόμενα ἐκ τοῦ λουτροῦ the *income* from.., *PFlor*.384.35 (v A.D.). 2. Math., *add*, in Pass., Arist.*Mete*.376ᵃ14, Iamb. *in Nic*. p.47 P. -ισμα, ατος, τό, *corollary*, David *Proll*.160.27.

προσπορπᾱτός, ή, όν, *fastened on* or *to with a* πόρπη, *pinned down*, δεσμῷ A.*Pr*.142 (lyr.).

πρόσπου, *about*, of round numbers, *Mon.Anc.Gr*.14.1, al.

προσπράσσω, Att. -ττω, *exact* or *demand besides*, τινά τι Ar.*Fr*.286 (dub.):—Med., ἕτερα τοσαῦτα π. And.4.13:—Pass., *have something exacted from one*, D.C.66.8; *to be exacted besides*, *PSI*3.234.21 (ii A.D.).

προσπρίασθαι, aor. of προσωνέομαι, *buy besides*, τι παρά τινος *CIG* 2693e (Mylasa).

πρόσ-πταισις, εως, ἡ, *striking, stumbling against*, λίθου D.H.1.79. 2. *collision*, Olymp.*in Mete*.204.15. -πταισμα, ατος, τό, *stumble*, Arist.*EN*1138ᵇ3, Ph.*Fr*.58 H.; ἕλκη ἐκ προσπταισμάτων Gal.12.286 (προπτ- codd.): metaph., προσπταίσματα τοῦ βίου *misfortunes*, Agatharch.49. II. *whitlow*, Thphr.*Char*.19.3 (pl.), Luc.*Peregr*.45; π. δακτύλου Gal.7.136. -πταίω, Ep. ποτιπταίω Q.S.7.81:—*hurt by striking against* a thing, *injure*, τὸ γόνυ Hdt.6.134; τὸν πόδα Plu.*Ages*.3: abs., *bump oneself*, Pl.*R*.604c; *hurt one's foot*, X.*HG*3.3.3; *stumble*, Ar.*Pl*.121; πρὸς τὸν οὐδόν Plu.*TG*17; ἐν τῇ ὁδῷ Thphr.*Char*.15.8; πόδεσσι Q.S. l.c. 2. c. dat. objecti, *stumble upon, strike against*, τισὶν ὥσπερ προβόλοις D.10.63; τῷ νόμῳ Porph.*Chr*.30. 3. generally, *to be checked*, πνεῦμα προσπταῖον ἐν τῇ ἄνω φορῇ Hp.*Acut*.42; of the tongue, Arist.*Pr*.905ᵇ30; προσπταίειν..ποιεῖ τὸν ἀκροατήν Id.*Rh*.1409ᵇ19. II. metaph., *suffer check* or *disaster*, opp. εὐτυχέω, Hdt.3.40; of shipwreck, π. περὶ τὸν Ἄθων Id.7.22; esp. *fail in war, suffer defeat*, ναυμαχίῃ Id.9.107; προσπταίσας μεγάλως Id.1.16, cf. 2.161, 5.62; πρὸς Τεγεήτας *lost battles* against them, Id.1.65; τῷ πεζῷ π. πρὸς τοὺς Βρύγους Id.6.45. III. c. dat., *offend, clash with*, τῷ δήμῳ Plu.*Per*.32, cf. *Cat.Mi*.30.

προσπτῆναι, aor. inf. of προσπέτομαι.

προσπτήσσω, *crouch* or *cower towards*, ἀκταὶ λιμένος ποτιπεπτηυῖαι (Ep. pf. part. for προσπεπτηκυῖαι) headlands *verging towards* the harbour, i. e. shutting it in, Od.13.98.

πρόσ-πτυγμα, ατος, τό, *object of embraces*, E.*Or*.1049, *Tr*.782 (anap.). -πτυγμάτιον, τό, Dim. of foreg., *small compress* or *pad*, Heliod.ap.Orib.48.34.1.

προσπτύσσω, *embrace*, βρέτας, σῶμα, E.*El*.1255, 1325 (anap.); Ep. ποτιπτ- Orph.*L*.322. B. mostly Med. προσπτύσσομαι, Ep. ποτιπτ- (but in Od.2.77 προτιπτ-, acc. to Sch.): fut. -πτύξομαι Od.11.451, etc.: aor. -επτυξάμην, Ep. -πτυξάμην 4.647, etc.: pf. -έπτυγμαι Pi.*I*.2.39:—*cling close to*, προσπτύσσεται πλευραῖσιν ἀρτίκολλος ὥστε τέκτονος χιτὼν ἅπαν κατ' ἄρθρον S.*Tr*.767; ὁρμῇ λαγόνας π. *presses its* flanks *against* the line, Opp.*H*.3.151. II. commonly of persons, 1. *clasp to one's bosom, embrace*, πατέρα Od.11.451, E.*Ba*.1319, cf. Theoc.3.19, Luc.*DDeor*.7.3, etc.; στόμα γε σὸν προσπτύξομαι *will press* it *to my lips*, E.*Ph*.1671, cf. *Med*.1400 (anap.):—Pass., c. dat., *cling to*, παρθένῳ προσπτύσσεται S.*Ant*.1237. 2. metaph., *greet warmly, welcome*, τινα Od.8.478: c. dupl. acc., π. τινά τι *address* a friendly greeting *to* one, ὄφρα τί μιν -πτύξομαι 17.509; οὐδέ τιν' οὔτ' ἔπεϊ προσπτύσσετο οὔτε τι ἔργῳ *greeted* no one either with word or gesture, *h.Cer*.199; π. μύθῳ *entreat* warmly, *importune*, Od.2.77, 4.647. 3. θεῶν δαῖτας προσπτύσσεσθαι *welcome* the feasts of the gods, i. e. *honour* or *celebrate* them, Pi. l. c.—Poet. and late Prose.

πρόσπτυστος, ον, *spat on*: *degraded*, Plu.2.565b.

προσπτύω, fut. -πτύσω, but -πτύσομαι Luc.*DMort*.20.2:—*spit upon*, τινι Thphr.*Char*.19.11, Luc. l. c., etc.; π. τῇ ὄψει in his face, D.L.2.75; πρὸς τὸ πρόσωπον Hyp.*Fr*.98: rarely c. acc., π. τὸν Ζηνόθεμιν Luc.*Symp*.33, cf. Plu.*Luc*.18: abs., Id.*Phoc*.36:—Pass., οἱ προσεπτυσμένοι ὑπὸ τῆς πτυάδος Philum.*Ven*.16.4. 2. metaph., π. τῷ καλῷ Epicur.*Fr*.512; ταῖς ἐκ πολυτελείας ἡδοναῖς ib.181. II. trans., *spit forth*, ἰόν Hierocl. p.13 A.; [τὴν γλῶτταν] αὐτῷ D.L.9.59; τὸ σωμάτιον ὅλον προσπτύσας τινὶ ἀπελθεῖν Arr.*Epict*.3.24.71.

πρόσπτωσις, εως, ἡ, *falling* or *lying against*, Hp.*Nat.Mul*.44; *impact*, αἱ τοῦ ῥοῦ π. D.S.3.44; πνεύματος *Placit*.4.16.1; φωνῆς Phld.*Mus*. p.50 K., cf. Thphr.*Vent*.21, Sor.*Fract*.3 (πρόπτ- cod.), Gal.8.712, etc.; *pressure* of bandages, Id.18(1).770.

προσπυνθάνομαι, *inquire* or *ascertain besides*, Arist.*SE*173ᵇ12, Macho ap.Ath.8.349a, *PCair.Zen*.513.6 (iii B.C.), *OGI*90.35 (Rosetta, ii B.C.), Plb.5.16.3, Plu.*Alex*.60, etc.; cf. προσπεύθομαι.

προσπῡριάω, *foment as well*, Archig.ap.Aët.16.100(90).

προσπῡρόω, *kindle* or *incense still more*, τινα Lxx 2*Ma*.14.11.

προσπωλέω, *sell besides*, ἑαυτοὺς τοῖς Ῥωμαίοις J.*BJ*4.4.3:—Pass., *Delph*.3(5).16.30, 76 (iv B.C.).

προσραίνω, fut. -ρᾰνῶ Lxx *Le*.4.6: Dor. ποτιρραίνω *Abh.Berl.Akad*.1928(6).12 (Cos, iv B.C.):—*sprinkle, throw about*, π. μίλτον κύκλῳ Ar.*Ec*.379. 2. *sprinkle on* one, τινί τι Lyc.684; π. πολὺ τῇ θύρᾳ Str.14.5.14; τινὶ ὕδατος (partit. gen.) Gal.11.418: abs., Arist.*HA*620ᵃ14. 3. Pass., *to be sprinkled*, ἅλμῃ with salt, ib.596ᵃ26, cf. *Mir*.835ᵇ35; ταῖς φλοξὶ *upon* flames, Plu.2.627c.

πρόσραμμα, ατος, τό, *patch*, Phot. s.v. ὀχθοίβους.

προσραντέον, *one must besprinkle*, ὕδατος ⟨κόχλαξι⟩ Herod.Med.ap.Orib.10.4.1.

προσραντίζω, = προσραίνω, Sch.Ar.*Nu*.410.

πρόσραξις, εως, ἡ, *dashing against*, *PCair.Zen*.534.23 (iii B.C.), Ph.2.489.

**προσραπτέον**, *one must sew on*, Plu.*Lys.*7, al.

**προσράπτω**, poet. impf. ποτιρράπτεσκον prob. in Eratosth.9:—*stitch* or *sew on*, τι πρός τι Hp.*Art.*62; τί τινι Sor.*Fasc.*42, D.L.6.91:—Pass., Hp.*Cord.*4, J.*AJ*3.7.5, Sor.*Fasc.*41; τρίβωνες προσερραμμένοι *patched*.., Plu.*Ages.*30.

**προσράσσω**, *dash against*, ταῖς Σηπιάσι [ναῦς] Paus.8.27.14:—Pass., πέτραις -ραχθέντες D.S.31.45, v.l. in Ph.2.123.

**προσρέπω**, *incline towards*, τινι J.*AJ*18.6.5; ἐπὶ τὸ μελάντερον Olymp.*in Mete.*218.27.

* **προσρέω**, aor. Pass. προσερρύην (v. infr.), *flow towards a point, stream in, assemble*, Hdt.1.62; *steal* or *creep towards*, τινὸς προσρυέντος τῇ τραπέζῃ Plu.2.760a; also, *rush up to*, αὐτῷ προσρυείς Id.*Brut.*16, cf. Parth.7.1, Luc.*Am.*8, Philostr.*VS*2.30. II. Med., ὅταν γυνὴ κύουσα προσρέηται *has losses*, Hp.*Superf.*42.

**προσρήγνῡμι**, *dash* or *beat against*, παιδία πέτραις J.*AJ*9.4.6. II. intr. in Act., προσέρρηξεν ὁ ποταμὸς τῇ οἰκίᾳ *Ev.Luc.*6.48. III. *burst*, τὰς φλέβας Aret.*CA*2.2.

**πρόσρημα**, ατος, τό, *address, greeting*, Pl.*Chrm.*164e; τὸ Δελφικὸν π. (sc. γνῶθι σεαυτόν) D.Chr.67.3; ἑωθινὸν π. τὸ "χαῖρε" D.C.69.18. II. *name, designation*, Pl.*Phdr.*238b, D.23.30, etc.; τὰ τῶν Μοιρῶν π. Pl.*Lg.*960c.

**πρόσρηξις**, εως, ἡ, (προσρήγνυμι) *dashing against*, Sm.2*Ki.*5.24, Sch.D Il.1.34.

**πρόσρησις**, εως, ἡ, *addressing*, διδοὺς πρόσρησιν ἑξῆς πᾶσι *accosting* them, E.*IA*341; π. τοῦ θεοῦ τῶν εἰσιόντων Pl.*Chrm.*164d, cf. X.*Hier.*8.3; ἡ οἰκέτου π. *address to*.., Pl.*Lg.*777e; ἐπ' ἐξόδοισι γὰρ ἔθαψα.. σ' ἕνεκ' ἐμῆς π. to enable me *to address* thee, E.*Hel.*1166; so ὁ σὸς δὲ τύμβος..τοῖς ἐμπόροις π. ἔσται πανταχοῦ Pl.Com.183. 2. *advice, recommendation*, Gal.12.2. II. *naming*, Pl.*Plt.*258a; *designation*, ib.306e: c. gen., Hierocl.*in CA*4 p.425 M. III. in Logic, καθ' ἑκάστην πρόσρησιν according to *the mode added* in each case, Arist.*APr.*25ᵃ3.

**προσρήσσω**, = προσρήγνυμι, M.Ant.4.49 (Pass.).

**προσρητέος**, α, ον, (προσερῶ) *to be addressed, called*, Pl.*R.*428b, *Lg.*812b. II. προσρητέον, *one must call*, Id.*R.*431d, *Lg.*689d, al.

**προσρητός**, ή, όν, (προσερῶ) *accosted, belonging to salutations*, Poll.5.137 (v.l.).

**προσρῑγόω**, *shiver besides*, Hp.*Epid.*7.107.

**πρόσριζος**, ον, *at the root*, v.l. for πρόρριζος in Arist.*HA*616ᵃ2 and App.*Fr.*11.

**προσριζόφυλλος**, ον, *with sessile leaves*, Thphr.*HP*6.6.2.

**προσριζόω**, *root, plant firmly*, τὰς βάσεις γῇ Ph.1.207; τὰ ἀμείνω τῷ ἡγεμονικῷ ib.334:—Pass., μένωμεν ὡς τὰ φυτὰ -ερριζωμένοι Arr.*Epict.*3.24.8, cf. Gal.19.181: c. dat., Meno *Iatr.*6.19.

**προσριπτέω**, = sq., Plu.*Luc.*35, cf. Hsch. (Pass.).

**προσρίπτω**, *throw to*, ἐπιστόλιόν τινι Plu.*Cat.Mi.*24; κυνιδίοις ἄρτων ἢ ὀστέων Ath.3.114a; of a wet-nurse, μὴ ἐξέστω τῇ Φιλωτέρᾳ προσρείπτειν τὸ σωμάτιον τῷ Παποντῶτι, i. e. she shall not give up her post, *PSI*3.203.7 (i A. D.): metaph., στρατηγοὺς τοῖς πολεμίοις γυμνοὺς π. Plu.*TG*7, cf. *Alex.*71; π. ὀνειδός τισι Plb.18.14.1; *throw in* a remark or argument, Iamb.*Myst.*3.18:—Med., τὰ μοσχάρια προσερρίφθαι τῷ κυάμῳ *throw* the young calves *upon* the beans (as feeding-stuff), *PTeb.*759.6 (iii B. C.):—Pass., ἡ προσριφεῖσα τῷ Κοπωνίῳ φωνή Plu.*Crass.*27; προσερριμμένον ἐνὶ σκάφει Id.*Pomp.*74; *to be thrown in casually*, of remarks, Gal.15.10, al.; τὰ προσερρειμένα (sic), opp. τὰ ὁμολογούμενα, Phld.*Rh.*2.94 S.; *to be added*, τὰ ἄλλα σαφηνείας ἕνεκα προσέρριπται Dam.*Pr.*290.

**προσρυθμίζω**, *adapt, accommodate*, τὴν κρᾶσιν Gal.15.415.

**προσσαίνω**, *fawn upon, coax*, prop. of dogs, S.*Fr.*1082, Arr.*Cyn.*7.2; ταῖς κέρκοις Ph.2.422: mostly metaph., οὐκ ἂν Ἀργείων τόδ' εἴη φῶτα προσσαίνειν κακόν A.*Ag.*1665 (troch.): c. dat., π. τοῖς συνδείπνοις Ath.3.99e. 2. of things, *please*, τῶνδε προσσαίνει σέ τι; A.*Pr.*835, cf. E.*Hipp.*863.

**προσσαίρω**, prop. *grin* or *snarl at*: metaph., ῥόδα προσσεσηρώς *grinning* roses, Pherecr.131.2; τὸ προσσεσηρός M.Ant.1.15, cf. Poll.6.123; δέρτροισι -σεσηρότες, of shipwrecked sailors, Lyc.880.

**προσσέβω**, *worship, honour besides*, A.*Th.*1028.

**προσσεύω**: pf. part. Pass. προσεσσυμένος *rushing upon*, Q.S.8.166.

* **προσσημ-αίνω**, *signify* or *indicate besides, connote*, Arist.*Int.*16ᵇ6, *Rh.*1374ᵃ13, *Po.*1457ᵃ17. * **-ειόω**, *brand in addition*, ἐπὶ ποδὸς *Supp.Epigr.*4.512.13 (Ephesus, ii A. D.):—Med., *annotate, Gloss.*

**προσσῐελίζω**, *spit upon*, Lxx *Le.*15.8.

**προσσῑτέω**, *feed also on*, Philum.ap.Orib.45.29.10 (Pass.).

**προσσίτια** [σῐ], τά, gloss on ποτιδόρπια, Hsch.

**προσσκᾰλεύω**, in Pass., *to have one's teeth scraped*, Hp.*Epid.*6.6.13.

**προσσκάπτω**, *throw up earth about*, δένδρεα ποτισκαψεῖ (Dor. fut.) *Tab.Heracl.*1.173.

**προσσκέλλω**, lit. *grow dry in* a thing: metaph. in intr. pf. προσέσκληκα, *to be importunate*, *EM*384.54, Phot., Suid. s. v. ἐσκληκότα.

**προσσκηνέω**, *to be adjacent*, ἐν Αἰθιοπίᾳ καὶ τοῖς -οῦσιν αὐτὴν τόποις prob. for προσκυνοῦσιν in Nech. in *Cat.Cod.Astr.*7.140.

**προσσκοπέω**, *consider besides*, Str.8.3.3 (v.l. προσκοπεῖν).

**προσσκώπτω**, *jeer besides*, J.*AJ*6.9.4:—Pass., D.L.2.120.

**πρόσσοθεν**, Adv., Ep. for πρόσθεν, read by Aristarch. in Il.23.533.

**προσσοτέρω**, Adv., poet. for προσωτέρω.

**προσσπαίρω**, *pant after*, c. dat., Plu.*Oth.*2.

**προσσπάομαι**, Pass., *to be contracted*, Arist.*Phgn.*807ᵇ1 (sed leg. κατεσπ-).

**προσσπένδω**, *pour besides*, οἶνον κατὰ τῶν ἁγνιζομένων D.H.7.72.15.

* **προσσπεύδω**, *to be eager besides*, Teles p.43 H. codd. (fort. πρὸς σπεύδει).

**προσσπουδάζω**, *to be deeply engaged in*, τοῖς βιβλίοις Philostr.*VA* 6.3.

**προσστάζω**, Dor. ποτιστ-, *drop on, shed over*, τοῖς αἰδοίᾳ π. Χάρις μορφάν Pi.*O.*6.76; πραῢν..ποτιστάζων ὄαρον *letting fall* mild words, Id.*P.*4.137.

**πρόσσταλ-σις**, εως, ἡ, *reduction, contraction*, τῆς γαστρός Paul. Aeg.1.97. **-τικός**, ή, όν, *reducing*, π. τῶν ὄγκων φάρμακα Aët.12.49.

**προσστᾰσιάζω**, *stir up to sedition*, τινας D.C.38.37:—Pass., *to have a sedition stirred up against one*, Id.44.10.

**πρόσστᾰσις**, εως, ἡ, *adhesion*, Hp.*Loc.Hom.*13 (written προστ-): pl., in concrete sense, *things which touch* the tongue, Id.*Epid.*6.5.10 (written προστ-). II. in Dor. forms ποίστασις, ποτίστασις (qq. v.).

**προσστάτης**, written for προστάτης in *SIG*546*B*33 (Delph., iii B. C.).

**προσσταυρόω**, *draw a stockade along* or *before* a place, c. acc., π. τὰς τριήρεις Th.4.9; τὰς τάφρους App.*BC*5.33.

**προσστείχω**, *go* or *come towards*, προσέστῐχε μακρὸν Ὄλυμπον Od.20.73; δεῦρο π. S.*OC*30, cf. 320, *OT*79 (in codd. of S. always προστ-).

**προσστέλλω**, *bring close to*, καρχησίῳ τὸ κέρας Luc.*Am.*6:—Med., *keep close to*, τοῖς ὀρεινοῖς, of a general, Plu.*Sull.*19. 2. *tuck in*, τοὺς μηρούς prob. in Arist.*IA*713ᵃ22. II. Pass., *to be tight-drawn, close tucked in*, προσεσταλμένος, of an abscess *which does not project*, Hp.*Prog.*7; προσστέλλεται τῷ χρωτὶ τὸ δέρμα Gal.18(2).599; ἰσχία ἔνδοθεν προσεσταλμένα loins *drawn* or *tucked up*, of dogs, X.*Cyn.*4.1, cf. Poll.5.58; κοιλία πλατεῖα καὶ π., ἰσχίον π., Arist.*Phgn.*807ᵃ34, 37; ἡ [τοῦ βονάσου] θρὶξ τῆς τοῦ ἵππου..προσεσταλμένη μᾶλλον *lying closer to the skin*, Id.*HA*630ᵃ25; αἱ σάρκες αὐτοῖς ὀστέοις π. Luc.*Am.*14; αἰδοῖον, τιτθοὶ π., Gal.8.451,452; φύλλα Dsc.4.88; προστείλας (leg. προσστ-) τὰ ἄρθρα *reducing* swellings in the joints, Philagr.ap.Aët.12.49. 2. metaph., *to be orderly, modest*, ἐπιστήμη προσεσταλμένη καὶ κοσμία Pl.*Grg.*511d. III. v. προστέλλω.

* **προσστερνίζομαι**, Med., *clasp to one's breast*, J.*AJ*2.9.7, Sor.1.106, Longus 4.23; aor. inf. written προστερνίσασθαι in Poll.2.162.

**προσστοχάζομαι**, *venture further experiments*, τὰ ὅμοια Demetr.*Eloc.*256 (s. v.l.).

**προσστρᾰτοπεδεύω**, *encamp near*, [πόλει] Plb.1.42.8, al., cf. D.S.14.17.

**προσστρώννῡμι**, *place additional foundation-courses in*, [τόπον] πώροις *IG*7.3073.65 (Lebad., ii B. C.).

**προσσυγχρίω** [ῑ], *anoint besides*, Alex.Trall.*Febr.*7.

**προσσυγχωρέω**, *agree in addition*, *BGU*1098.45 (i B. C.).

**προσσῡκοφαντέω**, *slander besides*, D.55.29 (sed leg. divisim).

* **προσσῡλάω**, *steal* or *carry off in addition*, *UPZ*6.19 (ii B. C.).

**προσσυλλαμβάνω**, *join* or *add to*, Porph.*in Ptol.*192:—Med., *take part in besides, contribute to*, προσξυνελάβοντο..τῆς ὁρμῆς αἱ νῆες Th.3.36 (v.l. -εβάλετο); *help to confirm*, λόγου D.C.43.47.

**προσσυμ-βάλλομαι**, Med., *contribute to besides* or *at the same time*, abs., Hp.*Fract.*27; πρός τι Id.*Art.*30; cf. foreg. **-βιόω**, f.l. in Ph.*Fr.*51 H. **-πλέκω**, *entangle besides*:—Pass., προσσυμπλᾰκήσομαι v.l. in Thd.*Da.*11.10.

**προσσυν-άγω** [ᾰ], *collect in addition*, *Yale Classical Studies* 2.6 (Dura, ii A. D., Pass.). **-αποβάλλω**, *lose besides*, τὰ ὄντα Ph.2.284. **-άπτω**, *add besides*, τῷ ἐνεστῶτι τὸν παρῳχημένον [χρόνον] S.E.*M.*9.46; στίχους Ath.5.180c. **-εργέω**, *work with as well*, Ruf.*Ren.Ves.*13.5. **-θερμαίνω**, *warm besides*, Hp.*Morb.*4.51:—Pass., ib.46. **-ίημι**, *understand besides*, Id.*Acut.*52, *Fract.*8; π. τὴν ἕξιν, τὰ χωρία, Aret.*SD*1.9. **-ίστημι**, *recommend further*, D.61.31. **-οικέω**, *settle with* others in a place, *join with* others *in a settlement*, c. dat. pers., Th.6.2. **-οικίζω** τὴν θυγατέρα, *give* one's daughter *in marriage besides*, D.C.60.5. II. Pass., *to be settled in addition*, [ψυχαὶ] -οικιζόμεναι cj. for προσυν- in M.Ant.4.21. **-τελέω**, *finish in addition*, *PSI*5.547.13 (Pass., iii B. C.). **-τίθεμαι**, Med., *concert* or *agree besides*, c. inf., D.C.46.56.

**προσσῡρίζω**, *give a signal to*, Plb.8.29.5; cf. προσυρίζω.

**προσσύρω** [ῡ], *drag on* or *along*, τὰ σκέλη Gal.6.155.

**πρόσσφαγμα**, v. πρόσφαγμα.

**προσσφάζω**, *slay at*, Ὀρτήσιον τῷ μνήματι Plu.*Brut.*28.

**προσσφίγγω**, *bind tightly*, οἱ -σφίγγοντες τὸ ἄρθρον μύες Gal.18(1).350:—Pass., Arr.*Tact.*34.7 (cj.).

**προσσφρᾱγίζω**, *seal as well*, Dor. pf. part. Pass. **ποτεσφραγισμέναν** *Delph.*3(2).120 (ii B. C.).

**προσσχεδιάζω**, *add besides*, τοῖς πεπραγμένοις τὰ μὴ γενόμενα J.*BJ* 3.9.5.

**προσσχητέον**, *one must attend*, τοῖς ἀριθμοῖς dub. cj. for προσσχηστέον in Vett.Val.244.18.

**πρόσσω**, v. πρόσω.

**προσσώρ-ευσις**, εως, ἡ, *piling up*: in Arith., name for the *series* 1+2+3+4, Nicom.*Ar.*2.8. * **-εύω**, *heap up beside*, λίθους τοῖς Ἑρμαῖς Corn.*ND*16. II. *store up*, Luc.*Anach.*25, *Gloss.*

**πρόστα**, Delph., = πρόσθεν, *Schwyzer* 323*C*39 (iv B. C.).

**προσ-τᾰγή**, ἡ, = sq., Lxx *Da.*3.28(95), *Sammelb.*3924.15 (i A. D.), Diog.Oen.11, Ps.-Plu.*Fluv.*6.4, 10.2; κατὰ -ταγήν τινος J.*AJ*1.7.1, al.; προσταγῇ *IG*4²(1).497 (Epid., ii/iii A. D.). **-ταγμα**, ατος, Dor. ποτίταγμα *SIG*569.28 (Cos, iii B. C.): τό: (προστάσσω):—*ordinance, command*, Pl.*R.*423c, al., Isoc.4.176, etc.; ἐκ προστάγματος D.17.

16; κατὰ πρόσταγμα D.S.14.41, cf. *OGI*225.37 (Didyma, iii B.C.), *PEnteux.*6.11, al. (iii B.C.), *PTeb.*5.206 (ii B.C., pl.), *UPZ*112 i 7 (ii B.C., pl.), etc.; κατὰ τὸ π. τοῦ παιδαγωγοῦ ζῆν by his *prescription*, Arist.*EN*1119$^b$13, cf. *PCair.Zen.*426.7 (iii B.C.), Ael.*VH*9.23; = Lat. *edictum*, *OGI*665.3 (Egypt, i A.D.), etc. 2. *order to pay* or *deliver*, *PCair.Zen.*8.3, 375.8 (iii B.C.). II. military *command*, as division of the army, ὑπηρέτης προστάγματος *PRein.*15.30 (ii B.C.), unless an error for τάγματος.

**προστάδιον** [ᾰ], τό, Dim. of προστάς, *PSI*5.546 (iii B.C.).

**προσ-τακτέον**, *one must order*, X.*Hier.*9.3; π. ὅπως.. Pl.*R.* 527c. **-τακτικός**, ή, όν, *of* or *for commanding*, *imperative*, *imperious*, τὸ π. [ἡ ψυχή], opp. τὸ ὑπηρετικόν (of the body), Arist.*Top.*128$^b$19; π. τινῶν Corn.*ND*16; λόγος Plu.2.1037f; Προστακτικός (sc. λόγος), title of work by Protagoras, D.L.9.55; βραχυλογία Plu.*Phoc.*5; also of persons, ἄρχων Max.Tyr.13.2 (Sup.). II. Gramm., ἡ -κὴ ἔγκλισις the *imperative* mood, D.T.638.7, A.D.*Synt.*31.20; π. ἐκφορὰ τῶν ῥημάτων ib.69.20; τὸ π. σχῆμα Anon.*Fig.*24; also τὸ -κόν D.L. 7.66,67, Ps.-Plu.*Vit.Hom.*53. Adv. -κῶς *in the imperative mood*, D.H.4.18, Sch.Ar.*Av.*1163.

**προστᾰλαιπωρέω**, *hold out*, *persevere*, ἔτ' ὀλίγον χρόνον Ar.*Lys.*766; π. τῷ δόξαντι καλῷ *persevere* in.., Th.2.53, cf. Plu.*Arat.*27: abs., Id. *Ant.*40.

**πρόσταμα·** κοιτών, Hsch.

**πρόσταξις**, εως, ἡ, *posting of additional troops on the wings of a phalanx*, Ael.*Tact.*24.3, Arr.*Tact.*20.3. II. *ordinance*, *command*, Pl.*Lg.*631d (pl.), 673c; προστάξεις προστάττοντες ἀνίσους ib.761e; τινὶ τὴν πρόσταξιν ποιεῖσθαι to *command* him, Arist.*Top.*103$^a$35, cf. Lys.2.1; ἐκ προστάξεως τοῦ κυρίου μου κτλ. *POxy.*1204.7 (iii A.D.), cf. 1252$^r$.19 (iii A.D.); *requisition*, τὴν π. ταῖς πόλεσιν ἑκατὸν νεῶν τῆς ναυπηγίας ἐποιοῦντο Th.8.3. III. at Athens, ἄτιμοι κατὰ προστάξεις citizens deprived of their rights *in certain specified particulars* (opp. παντάπασιν ἄτιμοι), And.1.75.

**προστᾰράσσω**, *trouble further*, Lxx *Si.*4.3.

**προσταργᾰνόω**, *fasten to*, Lyc.748 (Pass.).

**προ-στάς**, άδος, ἡ, (προΐστημι) prop. *part between the two antae* (or *wall-ends*) of a building, Vitr.6.7.1, cf. *EM*688.35. II. *vestibule*, *porch*, *portico*, Callix.1, Lxx *Jd.*3.23, *GDI*3723.5 (Cos), *OGI*51.22 (Egypt, iii B.C.), *PSI*4.396 (iii B.C.), *PCair.Zen.*445.3, al. (iii B.C.), *UPZ*77 i 22 (ii B.C.), *PTeb.*793 xii 25, al. (ii B.C.). **-στᾰσία**, Ion. **-ίη**, ἡ, *standing in front*, κατὰ τὴν τῶν θηρίων π., i.e. opposite the animals which were posted in front, Plb.11.1.3. II. *standing before* or *at the head of*, *leadership*, τοῦ δήμου Th.2.65; τοῦ πλήθους Id. 6.89: abs., *chieftainship*, *presidency*, ἐπ' ἐτησίῳ π. v.l. for προστατείᾳ in Id.2.80; *leadership*, *authority*, οἱ προστασίας ἀξιούμενοι D.19.295; ἡ ἰατρικὴ π. *authority* or *dignity* of a physician, Hp.*Praec.*10, cf. *Medic.* 1; ἡ τοῦ ξυγγραφέως π. Plb.12.28.6, cf. Chrysipp.*Stoic.*3.43, Plot.3. 4.3. b. *governorship*, Ph.2.63; = Lat. *praefectura*, Id.1.675. c. *superintendence*, *care*, *charge*, δι' ἣν ποιεῖται ἡμῶν π. *UPZ*20.28 (ii B.C.); πρὸ τῆς π., of a midwife, before *taking up a charge*, Sor.1.4 cod. (nisi leg. πρὸς ταῖς π.); τοῦ σωματίου π. ποιησαμένη, of a wet-nurse, *PSI*3. 204.8 (i A.D.), cf. *PStrassb.*40.25 (vi A.D.); *management*, εὐθηνίας *PTeb.*397.28 (ii A.D.); of a temple, *PTheb.Bank* 2.6 (ii B.C.); ἡ τοῦ θεοῦ π. καὶ ὅλου ἡμῶν τοῦ οἴκου *OGI*331.22 (Pergam., ii B.C.). 2. *outward dignity*, *pomp*, *show*, etc., οὐ μόνον π. βασιλική, ἀλλὰ καὶ δύναμις Plb.4.2.6, cf. 5.43.3, D.S.18.23 (leg. βασιλείων); π. τῶν ἱερῶν Plb.1.55.8. III. *patronage*, *protection*, *SIG*685.97 (Magn. Mae., ii B.C.), *IPE*1$^2$.79.9 (Olbia, i A.D.), J.*AJ*16.2.4, etc. 2. = Lat. *patronatus*, Plu.*Rom.*13; = Lat. *patrocinium*, Lib.*Or.*47.7 (pl.), al. 3. in bad sense, *partisanship*, D.10.52 (pl.); *collusion*, *champerty*, ταῦτ' οὐχ ὁμολογουμένη π.; Id.30.30; προστασίᾳ (-σίαι codd.) τινὲς ὠνοῦνται καὶ πωλοῦσι Thphr.*Fr.*97.3. IV. *place before a building*, *court* (= προστάς, Did.ap.Harp.), τὰ τῆς Ἀθηναίων Ἀκροπόλεως Προπύλαια μετενεγκεῖν εἰς τὴν προστασίαν τῆς Καδμείας Aeschin.2.105; τῆς περὶ τὸ Διονυσιακὸν θέατρον προστασίας Plb.15.30.4; in this sense oxyt. προστασιά acc. to Hdn.Gr.1.294. ⊛**-στάσιμον** [ᾰ], dub. sens. in *Gloss.Oxy.*1801.11 (i A.D.). **-στάσιος** [ᾰ], α, ον, = προστατήριος II, Δημήτηρ π. Paus.2.11.3. ⊛**-στᾰσις**, εως, ἡ, *outward dignity*, Pl. *R.*577a; τοῦ ἱεροῦ *Delph.*3(4).43.7 (ii B.C.). II. = προστάς II, *IG*1$^2$.372.58,62, al., *SIG*245.32 (Delph., iv B.C.), al. III. v. πρόσστασις I. IV. dub. sens. in *BGU*432 ii (2).7 (ii A.D.).

**προστάσσω**, Att. -ττω; Dor. **ποτιτάσσω** *IG*12(1).155.91 (Rhodes), Anon. in *PSI*9.1091.1, also **ποιτάσσω** *IG*4$^2$(1).122.39, al. (Epid.): pf. προστέταχα Lxx *Da.*2.8:—Pass., 1 aor. προσετάχθην (v. infr.), also 2 aor. προσετάγην ib.*Si.*3.22: I. c. acc. pers., 1. *place* or *post at* a place, χωρεῖτε οἷ προστάσσομεν (sc. ὑμᾶς) E.*Or.*1678:—Pass., προσταχθέντα.. πύλαις A.*Th.*527, cf. S.*Ant.*670; ᾗ ἄν τις προσταχθῇ Th.2.87, cf. 7.70. 2. *attach to*, πρὸς τοῖσι ἔθνεσι τοὺς πλησιοχώρους π. *attaching* to certain tribes their next neighbours, Hdt.3.89; π. τινάς τινι *assign* them *to* his command, Th.5.8, cf. X. *Cyr.*7.1.20:—Pass., Ἰνδοὶ προσετετάχατο.. Φαρναζάθρῃ Hdt.7.65; κατὰ τέλη στρατηγῷ τινι προστεταγμένοι Th.6.42. 3. reversely, ἐπὶ μὲν τῇ [μοίρῃ] ἑωυτὸν π. *appointed* himself to the one part as their head, Hdt.1.94; π. ἄρχοντά τισι *appoint* as commander over them, Th.6.93: with dat. omitted, Id.3.16, 8.23:—Pass., ib.8. II. c. acc. rei, *command*, *prescribe*, *enjoin*, περὶ βοηθείας ἢ ἄλλο τι προστάττοντες τῇσι πόλεσι *IG*1$^2$.57.43; ἑκάστῳ ἔργον π., αὐτῷ πόνον π., Hdt. 1.114, E.*Ion* 1176, cf. X.*Cyr.*4.5.25; πολὺ ἔργον π. ὡς τηλικῷδε Pl.*Prm.* 136d, etc.; πολλὰς ἐπιμελείας Arist.*Pol.*1299$^b$8; π. μνᾶς ἕξ *prescribe* 6 minae, Id.*EN*1106$^b$2; τισὶ περί τινος π. D.19.71:—Pass., τοῖσι δὲ ἵππος προσετέτακτο to others *orders had been given* to supply cavalry, Hdt.7.21, cf. A.*Eu.*208; τὰ προσταχθέντα *orders given*, Hdt.2.121.δ', cf. Isoc.3.13; τὸ προστεταγμένον Hdt.9.104; τὸ προσταχθέν Id.1.114, S.*Ph.*1010; τὰ προσταχθησόμενα X.*Mem.*3.5.6: abs., προσταχθὲν αὐτῷ *the order having been given* him, Lys.30.2, cf. D.50.12; πλείω τῶν ὑπὸ τῆς πόλεως προσταττομένων δαπανᾶσθαι Lys.25.13. 2. c. dat. pers. et inf., *command*, *order* one to do, Hdt.5.105, 9.99, S. *OC*1018, Th.7.29, X.*Cyr.*8.6.3, *PEnteux.*6.4 (iii B.C.), etc.; the dat. must be supplied in Hdt.1.80, S.*OC*494, etc.:—Pass., impers., ἐκέλευε τοῖσι προσετέτακτο ταῦτα πρήσσειν διαταμεῖν Hdt.7.39; ὁ βασιλεὺς.. ἢ ἄλλος τις οἷς προστέτακται περὶ τούτων *IG*1$^2$.94.19. 3. c. acc. et inf., E.*Hel.*890; both usages in successive clauses, ὅσα οἱ νόμοι π. τοὺς προσήκοντας ποιεῖν, ἡμῖν π. καὶ ἀναγκάζουσι ποιεῖν D.43. 59:—Pass., *to be ordered* to do, τέσσερες.. κῶμαι.. τοῖσι κυσὶ προσετετάχατο σιτία παρέχειν Hdt.1.192, etc.; ὥσπερ προσετάχθησαν (sc. ἐξεργάσασθαι) Th.5.75. 4. abs., *command*, *order*, opp. ὑπηρετέω, Arist.*Top.*129$^a$12:—Pass., *receive orders*, ib.14; οἱ προστεταγμένοι Th.1.136. III. Astrol., correl. of ἀκούω V, Ptol.*Tetr.*35, Heph. Astr.1.9, Serapio in *Cat.Cod.Astr.*8(4).226.

**προστᾰτ-εία**, ἡ, (προστάτης) = προστασία II, Th.2.80 (cf. προστασία II. 1), X.*Mem.*3.6.10, *Oec.*2.6 (pl.), *Supp.Epigr.*3.468.16 (Thess., i B.C.), *IG*2$^2$.1099.23 (Epist.Plotinae, ii A.D.), D.C.41.34, Porph. *Abst.*4.18, etc. **-ευτικός**, ή, όν, *of* or *for exercising authority*, Poll. 1.178. **-εύω**, *to be leader* or *ruler of*, εἴτε χοροῦ εἴτε οἴκου εἴτε πόλεως εἴτε στρατεύματος X.*Mem.*3.4.6, cf. *Hier.*11.5,7; [θυσίας] *IG*4$^2$(1). 73.34 (Epid., iii B.C., prob.): abs., *exercise authority*, X.*HG*3.3.6, *Vect.*5.6; ἐν ταῖς πόλεσιν Id.*Mem.*2.8.4. II. π. ὅπως.. *to have authority for providing* that.., *provide* or *take care* that.., Id.*An.* 5.6.21, *Cyr.*1.2.5: with gen. added, π. ἀνθρώπων ὅπως ἕξουσιν.. ib. 1.6.7; cf. sq. III. *hold office of* προστάτης II. 3, *SIG*241 *A* 39 (Delph., iv B.C.), *IG*14.208 (Acrae). IV. *to be guardian of*, *regent for*, τῶν βασιλέων App.*Syr.*52. **-έω**, = foreg.: *rule over*, *lord it over*, χθονός E.*Heracl.*206; αἰσχρὸν προστατεῖν γε δωμάτων γυναῖκα Id. *El.*932; τῆς πόλεως Pl.*Grg.*519c; τῶν μεγίστων Id.*La.*197e; π. τοῦ ἀγῶνος *to be steward* of the games, X.*An.*4.8.25; π. νούσου, of a physician, *to be in charge*, Hp.*Praec.*13; τοῦ λύχνου τῶν ἱερῶν *POxy.* 1453.14 (i B.C.): abs., ὁ προστατῶν *he that acts as chief*, v.l. in X.*Cyr.* 8.3.25; ὅταν δημοκρατουμένη πόλις ἐλευθερίας διψήσασα κακῶν οἰνοχόων προστατούντων τύχῃ Pl.*R.*562d; = προστατεύω II, X.*Mem.*2.7. 9; π. τοῦ θεμελιωθῆναι τὴν σύνοδον *IG*2$^2$.1343.14:—Pass., προστατεῖσθαι ὑπό τινων *to be ruled* or *led* by them, X.*Hier.*5.1. b. *to be president*, ἐκκλησίας Ἀρχ.Ἐφ. 1914.180 (Gonni); βουλᾶς *IG*14.612 (Rhegium). II. *stand before* as a defender, *to be guardian* or *protector of*, πυλῶν A.*Th.*396; Ἥρα π. [Ἀργείων] E.*Heracl.*349; ἁ διὰ παντὸς Χερσονασιτᾶν προστατοῦσα Παρθένος *IPE*1$^2$.352.23 (ii/i B.C.); ἀναίδειαν, ἥπερ μόνη π. ῥητόρων Ar.*Eq.*325 (lyr.); πολιτῶν π. αἱρούμενον Men.578. 2. π. περὶ τοῦ ἀνατεθέντος ἀργυρίου *bring forward a measure* respecting.., *IG*9(1).694.106 (Corc.). III. ὁ προστατῶν χρόνος the time *that stands before*, i.e. *is close at hand*, S.*El.*781 (cf. Sch. ad loc.), unless rather *tyrannous*. ⊛**-ήριος**, α, ον, *standing before*, δεῖμα π. καρδίας fear *hovering before*, or *lording it over*, my heart, A.*Ag.*976 (lyr.). II. *standing before*, *protecting*, of Artemis, Id.*Th.*449; of Apollo as the tutelary god or (acc. to Hsch., Phot.) from his statue *standing before* the doors, S.*El.*637, Orac.ap.D.21.52, *IG*2$^2$.674.6, al.; π. θεοί *CIG*3530 (Cyme). III. ὁ Π. (sc. μήν), a Boeot. month, Plu.2.655e. ⊛**-ης**, ου, ὁ, (προΐστημι) *one who stands before*, *front-rank man*, f.l. for πρωτοστάτης in X.*Cyr.* 3.3.41, *Eq.Mag.*2.2,6:—but elsewh., II. *leader*, *chief*, esp. of a democracy, προστάτεω ἐπιλαβέσθαι Hdt.1.127, 5.23; οἱ π. τοῦ δήμου Th.3.75, 4.46,66; οἱ τῶν δήμων π. Id.3.82; ὁ π. Κλέων Ar.*Ra.*569, cf. *Eq.*1128 (lyr.); μεταβολὴ ἐκ προστάτου ἐπὶ τύραννον Pl.*R.*565d; [Σόλων] πρῶτος τοῦ δήμου π. Arist.*Ath.*2.2, al. 2. generally, *ruler*, opp. ἀστοί, A.*Supp.*963; Καδμείων Id.*Th.*1031; Κνωσίων Arr.*Epict.*3. 9.3; Μολοσσῶν *GDI*1334 (Epirus, iii B.C.); χώρας, χθονός, E.*Heracl.* 964, *IA*373 (troch.); τῆς Ἑλλάδος προστάται, of the Spartans, X.*HG* 3.1.3, cf. Isoc.4.103, D.9.23; π. τοῦ ἐμπορίου, of Greeks in Egypt, Hdt. 2.178; τοῦ πολέμου X.*Cyr.*7.2.23; προστάται τῆς εἰρήνης its *chief authors*, Id.*HG*5.1.36; τῆς πρὸς τοὺς θεοὺς ἐπιμελείας π. D.22.78; *administrator*, τῆς κεχωρισμένης προσόδου *PTeb.*81.19 (ii B.C.); [τοῦ ἱεροῦ] *OGI*531.3 (Bithynia, iii A.D.); θεᾶς ib.209.4 (Philae, iii A.D.), cf. *Ostr.*412, al. (i A.D.): metaph., ἔρως π. τῶν ἀργῶν ἐπιθυμιῶν Pl.*R.* 572e. 3. *president* or *presiding officer*, π. τοῦ γυμνασίου *CIG*2881. 16 (Branchidae), cf. *OGI*130.16 (Egypt, ii B.C.), *Supp.Epigr.*4.598. 37 (Teos, i B.C.), *IG*2$^2$.1368.13; π. συνεδρίου ib.9(2).205.33 (Aetolian League); προβούλων ib.9(1).694.116 (Corc.); [γερουσίας] ib.7.2808 (Hyettus, iii B.C.); δαμιοργῶν ib.5(1).1425.16 (Messene); [βουλᾶς] ib.14.256.5 (Phintias); τῆς μέσης Ἀκαδημίας S.E.*P.*1.232: freq. in pl., = πρυτάνεις, *SIG*194.15 (Amphipolis, iv B.C.), etc.; γνώμα προστατᾶν ib.187.1 (Cnidus, iv B.C.), cf. *IG*12(8).264.13 (Thasos, iv B.C.). III. *one who stands before and protects*, *guardian*, *champion*, πυλωμάτων A.*Th.*408, cf. 798; πόλεως Pl.*Grg.*519b; [τῆς ποιητικῆς] Id.*R.*607d; τῆς πάντων ἐλευθερίας D.15.30, etc.; epith. of gods, as Apollo, S.*Tr.*209 (lyr.), *IPE*1$^2$.89 (ii A.D.). 2. at Athens, etc., *patron* who took charge of the interests of μέτοικοι, etc.: hence ἐπὶ προστάτου οἰκεῖν live under protection of *a patron*, Lys.31.9, 14, Lycurg.145; προστάτην ἐπιγράφειν τινά choose as one's *patron*, Luc. *Peregr.*11; αὑτῷ πονηρὸν προστάτην ἐπεγράψατο Ar.*Pax* 684; ἔχειν Id.*Pl.*920, cf. S.*OT*882 (lyr.); νέμειν π. Arist.*Pol.*1275$^a$13; also γράφεσθαι προστάτου to be entered *by one's patron's name*, be attached to *a patron*, οὐ Κρέοντος προστάτου γεγράψομαι S.*OT*411. **3.** = Lat. *patronus*, Plu.*Rom.*13, *Mar.*5, *IG*3.687, 14.1078 (Rome, iii A.D.), *OGI*549.6 (Ancyra, iii A.D.), etc. **IV.** θεοῦ π. *one who stands before* a god to entreat him, *suppliant*, S.*OC*1278, cf. 1171. **V.** Medic., *prostate gland*, Herophil.ap.Gal.*UP*14.11 (v.l.). **-ικός**, ή, όν, *of* or *for a* προστάτης II. 1, ἐκ π. ῥίζης ἐκβλαστάνει [τύραννος] Pl.*R.* 565d. **2.** *magnificent*, τὸ τῆς τιμῆς σεμνὸν καὶ π. Plb.6.33.9, al. Adv. -κῶς, σεμνῶς καὶ π. Id.5.88.4. **3.** *ready to champion* or *protect*, π. καὶ βοηθητικός Plu.*Thes.*36. **4.** -κόν, τό, name of a charge included in a lease, *POxy.*590 (ii A.D.). **-ίνα**, ή, = sq., title of priestess at Messene, *IG*5(1).1447.13 (iii/ii B.C.). **-ις**, ιδος, fem. of προστάτης, ἐὰν..θέληθ' ὁμοῦ προστάτισι ταῖς σεμναῖσι..θεαῖς (Dind. for ἐὰν..θέλητέ μου πρὸς ταῖσι ταῖς σ.) S.*OC*458; προστάτιν ἐπιγράφεσθαί τινα Luc.*Bis Acc.*29; ὁ δῆμος ἀρχὴν ἑαυτοῦ π. ἀπέφηνε καὶ ἐκάλεσε δημαρχίαν App.*BC*1.1; νύμφαις ὑδάτων προστάτισιν Porph. *Antr.*12, cf. 18, Luc.*Charid.*10; τὴν ἰδίαν π., of Rhea, prob. in *CIG* 6835 (inc. loc.); π. τοῦ Ἀνούβεως *PMag.Osl.*1.338.

**προστάτρια**, ή, = foreg., *Lex.Havn.*ap.Schmidt Hsch. s. v. ταῖη.

**προσταυρόω**, *draw a stockade in front of* or *along*, τὴν θάλασσαν Th.6.75:—Pass., πυλίδα, ἣ προεσταύρωτο σταυροῖς App.*BC*4.79.

**προστᾰφῐδόομαι**, Pass., of grapes, *to be converted into raisins before*, Dsc.5.3.

**προστᾰχή**, ή, = προσταγή, *SIG*707.5 (Olbia, ii B.C.).

**προστέγ-ασμα**, ατος, τό, *projecting roof, penthouse*, Apollod.*Poliorc.* 154.6. **-αστήρ**, ῆρος, ὁ, *provisional roofing*, *Delph.*3(5).26 i *A* 36 (iv B.C.).

**προστέγιον**, τό, = προτέγιον, Plu.*Caes.*17.

**προστεγνόω**, *stop up before*, Gal.11.480 (Pass.).

**πρόστεγον**, τό, (πρός, στέγη) *house-rent*, *PLond.*5.1708.40 (vi A.D., pl.).

**προστειχίζω**, *include in the city-wall*, ἡ ἔξω -τειχισθεῖσα πόλις Th.6. 3; π. τῇ πόλει τὸν λόφον D.H.3.1.

⊛ **προστείχω**, f.l. for προσστείχω.

**προστεκμ-αίρομαι**, *judge of by further symptoms*, Hp.*Art.*50 (v.l. for προτεκμ-). **-αρτέος**, α, ον, *to be noticed besides*, Id.*Acut.*38.

**προστεκταίνομαι**, Med., *add of one's own device*, Plu.*Lys.*26.

**προστελέω**, *pay besides*, μισθόν X.*An.*7.6.30, cf. *BGU*1115.8 (i B.C.), *PGiss.*48.22 (iii A.D., Pass.); f.l. for προ- in Th.6.31.

**προστέλλω**, in Med., Δίκη δ' ὁμαίμων κάρτα νιν προστέλλεται *sends him forth as a champion*, A.*Th.*415:—Pass., μακρὰν γὰρ ὡς γέροντι προὐστάλης ὁδόν *hast travelled* far.., S.*OC*20. **II.** διὰ τὸ.. προστέλλειν τὰ γυμνὰ ἕκαστον..τῇ τοῦ ἐν δεξιᾷ παρατεταγμένου ἀσπίδι *protect, shield*, Th.5.71, cf. D.C.40.23 (unless f.l. for προσστ-, = *draw close to*, in both).

**προστέμνω**, *cut also*, ἀλλᾶντος προστετμημένον *a slice* of sausage *also*, Antiph.71: Dor. 2 aor. ποτέταμε $IG4^2$(1).110 *C* 9 (Epid.).

**προστένω**, *sigh* or *grieve beforehand*, A.*Ag.*253 (lyr.).

**προστερᾰτεύομαι**, = ἐπιτερατεύομαι, Ph.2.189, Dam.*Isid.*88.

**προστερν-ίδιον** [ῐδ], τό, *covering* or *ornament for the breast* of horses, X.*Eq.*12.8, *An.*1.8.7, *Cyr.*6.4.1. **II.** *padding for the chest*, Luc.*Salt.*27. **-ίζομαι**, v. προσστ-. **-ος**, ον, *before* or *on the breast*, στολμοί A.*Ch.*29 (lyr.).

**προστέρπω**, Ep. **ποτιτέρπω**, *delight* or *please besides*, Il.15.401.

**προστεφᾰνόω**, *crown beforehand*, τινά τινι Ath.4.128c.

**προστεχνάομαι**, *devise besides*, Plu.*Sert.*11, Iamb. *in Nic.* p. 101 P.

**προστήθ-ειος**, ον, = πρόστερνος, Eust.1328.32. ⊛ **-ίδιος**, ον, = foreg.: προστηθίδιον, τό, *breast-ornament*, of horses, Plb.21.6.7 (pl.), Poll.2.162 (pl.). **-ίς**, ίδος, ή, *ball of the foot* (cf. στῆθος), ib.198.

**προστήκομαι**, Pass., with pf. προστέτηκα, *stick fast to, cling to*, προστᾰκέντος ἰοῦ, of the poisoned robe *clinging to* Heracles, S.*Tr.* 833 (lyr.); ὕδρας προστετᾱκὼς φάσματι ib.836 (lyr.): metaph., *to be given up to, engrossed by*, πορισμῷ Plu.2.524d; τοῖς ἀνιαροῖς ib.600c; τέχνῃ Ael.*VH*3.31; τῷ Κριτίᾳ Philostr.*VS*2.1.14; δόξῃ Jul.*Or.*7. 226a; ταῖς αἱρέσεσι Gal.8.657.

**πρόστηξις**, εως, ή, *attachment, devotion*, τῆς ψυχῆς Plu.2.1089c.

**προστηρέω**, *keep watch*, Phleg.*Fr.*36.1 J.

**προστιβάζεται**· μερίζεται, προσπορεύεται, Hsch.

**προστιβάς**, f.l. (ap.Suid.) for στιβάς in D.S.17.85.

**προστίζιος**, α, ον, = πρυσθίδιος, *former, earlier*, *Schwyzer* 410 (Elis).

⊛ **προστίθημι**, Dor. **ποτι-**, also aor. inf. ποιθέμεν $IG4^2$(1).121.17 (Epid.); ποτθέμειν prob. in Epich.170.8: late pres. **προστιθῶ** Ps.-Luc.*Philopatr.*18, 27; imper. προστίθει A.*Pr.*83: fut. προσθήσω: aor. προσέθηκα, pl. -έθεμεν, subj. προσθῶ Th.4.86, Ion. προσθέω Hdt.1.108:— **Med.**, fut. προσθήσομαι Lxx *Ex.*14.13: aor. 1 προσεθηκάμην Hdt.4.65: more freq. aor. 2 προσεθέμην, subj. προσθῶμαι (not πρόσθωμαι), 3 sg. opt. προσθεῖτο D.6.12, but πρόσθοιτο Id.11.6; Dor. part. ποτθέμενος, Πρακτικά 1931.89 (Dodona): pf. -τέθειμαι Lxx *De.*23.15:—**Pass.**, aor. 1 προσετέθην Th.3.82: fut. -τεθήσομαι Lxx *Nu.*27.13, al. (-τεθήσεσθαι is f.l. ib.*Ex.*5.7): but the pf. Pass. is chiefly supplied by πρόσκειμαι:—*put to*, χερσὶν ἀπώσασθαι λίθον ὃν προσέθηκεν Od.9. 305; π. τὰς θύρας, τὴν θύραν, *put to*, *close* the door, Hdt.3.78, Lys.1. 13; τὰς πύλας Th.4.67; κλίμακας [τοῖς πύργοις] Id.3.23; κόμη προσθεῖσα βόστρυχον *holding* it *close* to.., A.*Ch.*229; χέρα ἐλάτῃ E.*Ba.* 1110; γόνασιν ὠλένας Id.*Andr.*895, cf. S.*Ph.*942; τοῖς καλλίστοις τοῦ ζῴου τὰ κάλλιστα φάρμακα Pl.*R.*420c; π. μύωπας *apply* the spur, Plb.11.18.4; π. χεῖρ' ἐπὶ πρόσωπα E.*Ph.*1699; *apply* a pessary, Hp. *Nat.Mul.*32, Sor.1.62, al.; [κύαθον] Arist.*Pr.*$890^b24$:—Pass., of pessaries, Dsc.1.76, al., Sor.1.35, al. **2.** *hand over, deliver to*, θεῶν γέρα..ἐφημέροισι προστίθει A.*Pr.*83, cf. *h.Merc.*129; τινὶ γυναῖκα π. *give* her to him as wife, Hdt.6.126; but π. γυναικὶ τάλαντον, as a dower, Hyp.*Lyc.*13; π. τινὰ ἄλλῳ πατρί E.*Ion* 1545; Ἅιδῃ ἐμὸν δέμας Id.*Hec.*368, cf. *IA*540; π. τινὰ πυρί Id.*Supp.*948; σφαγέντα παῖδα π. πόλει Id.*Ph.*964; τισὶ π. πόλιν Th.4.86; τὴν διοίκησιν τῶν κοινῶν ἑαυτῷ D.C.52.14; also νᾶσον εὐκλέϊ π. λόγῳ Pi.*N.*3.68. **3.** *give besides* or *also*, φερνάς E.*Hipp.*628; προῖκα D.19.195; χρήματα Id. 18.239, etc.; πίστιν ὑμῖν Id.54.42; τὰ ἴδια τοῖς ἀλλοτρίοις Men.557: abs., *spend money*, οὐ μόνον ἄνευ μισθοῦ, ἀλλὰ καὶ προστιθεὶς ἂν ἡδέως Pl.*Euthphr.*3d, cf. Arist.*EN*$1130^a25$, Iamb.*Protr.*9. **II.** *impose upon*, πρῆγμα τὸ ἄν τοι προσθέω Hdt.1.108, cf. 3.62: c. inf., π. τινὶ πρήσσειν Id.5.30; π. μέτρον *impose* measure or bounds, A.*Ch.*796 (lyr.); π. τινὶ ἀτιμίην *impose, inflict* disgrace upon him, Hdt.7.11; π. ⟨φθόρον⟩ A.*Ch.*482; ἐπ' ἐμαυτῷ ἀράς S.*OT*820; ὄκνον Id.*Ant.*243; αὐτὸς αὑτῷ τὴν βλάβην Id.*Fr.*350; λύπην, πόνους, E.*Supp.*946, *Heracl.* 505; ἀναλώματα *IG*14.830.12 (Puteoli, ii A.D., Pass.); π. τινὶ ἔκπληξιν ἀφασίαν τε strike him dumb with fear, E.*Hel.*549; ἐνθύμιον τοῖς ζῶσι Antipho 3.1.2; τισὶ ζημίας Th.3.39; π. φιλανθρωπίαν εἰς τὰ τῆς πόλεως πράγματα *employ* it on.., D.19.140. **2.** *attribute* or *impute to*, τῷ θεῷ τὴν αἰτίαν E.*Ion* 1525, cf. Th.3.39 (Pass.); π. θράσος μοι *impute* boldness to me, E.*Heracl.*475; θεοῖσι π. ἀμαθίαν Id.*Hipp.*951; ἀπληστίαν λέχους γυναιξί Id.*Andr.*219; τὸ ἐμπλήκτως ὀξὺ ἀνδρὸς μοίρᾳ προσετέθη Th.3.82. **III.** *add*, τάδε τούτοισι Hdt.1.20, al.; πρὸς [τῇ γνώμῃ] ἔργα Id.4.139; ἄλλον πρὸς ὧν ἔθηκαν χρυσόν ib.196; χάριτι χάριν E.*HF*327; νοσοῦντι νόσον Id.*Alc.*1048; π. τῷ νόμῳ τὸν λόγον τόνδε Th.2.35, cf. Hdt.2.136 (Pass.), Pl.*R.*468b; προσθεῖναι τῷ δικαίῳ ἢ ὡς ἐλέγομεν (for πλέον ἢ..) ib.335a; ἄγγελλε δ' ὅρκον π. S.*El.*47 (Reiske for ὅρκῳ codd., cf. ὅρκου προστεθέντος *Fr.*472; ὀμόσας..προσθείς τε χεῖρα δεξιάν *Ph.*942); τὴν στήλην ὕστερον προσέθηκε $IG1^2$.374. 174; τοῖς εὖ ἔχουσιν ἔργοις οὔτ' ἀφελεῖν ἔστιν οὔτε προσθεῖναι Arist.*EN* $1106^b11$; ἐάν τι ἀφέλωμεν ἢ προσθῶμεν ἢ μεταθῶμεν Pl.*Cra.*432a; π. γράμματα ib.418a, cf. 431c; also π. ἐπὶ τοῖσδε χάριν S.*Tr.*1253; ἵππον πρὸς τοὔνομα Ar.*Nu.*63; πρὸς τὸν μισθὸν ἑκάστῳ ὀβολόν X.*HG*1. 5.6, cf. Pl.*Phlb.*33c: abs., *make additions*, Th.3.45; πρὸς τὰ ὑπάρχοντα -τιθέντες πλουσιώτεροι γίνονται Arist.*Rh.*$1359^b28$; *make additions* to a story, *improve* it, Id.*Po.*$1460^a18$; also of actors, ib.$1461^b30$: esp. of adding articles to statements or documents, προσθεῖναι οὐδὲν εἶχον τοῖς εἰρημένοις οὐδ' ἀφελεῖν Isoc.12.264, cf. *POxy.*1062.4 (ii A.D.), etc.; π. καὶ ἀφελεῖν τι περὶ τῆς ξυμμαχίας Foed.ap.Th.5.23, cf. 29; π. τὶ πρὸς τοῖς ξυγκειμένοις Foed.ib.47; πρὸς τὰς συνθήκας Foed.ap. Plb.21.43.27; π. ὅτι..D.18.231; of entries in accounts, προσετέθη τὰ τέλη τῷ κυριακῷ λόγῳ *PAmh.*77.15 (ii A.D.), cf. *BGU*620.15 (iv A.D.), etc.; π. τινὶ [ἀργύριον] *pay*, *PMich.Zen.*28.24 (iii B.C.), cf. *PCair.Zen.*647.56 (iii B.C.), *PRyl.*153.27 (ii A.D.); πρόσθες εἰς ὄνομα Ἐπωνύχου *credit* to account of E., *Ostr.*1159 (ii/iii A.D.); *pay in, deposit* gold in a bank or mint, *PCair.Zen.*23.32 (iii B.C.). **2.** c. acc. pers., τίνα τῇδε προστιθῶ στάσει; A.*Ch.*114; Ἀθηναίοις π. σφᾶς αὐτούς *join* their party, Th.3.92; π. ἑαυτόν τινι ἐς πίστιν, ἐπὶ ἰδίοις κέρδεσι, Id. 8.46, 50. **3.** Math., *add*, πὸτ ἀριθμόν..ψᾶφον Epich.170.8 (prob.); [χωρίον] ἕτερον αὐτῷ τουτὶ ἴσον Pl.*Men.*84d; πρὸς πεπερασμένον ἀεὶ π. Arist.*Ph.*$266^b2$:—Pass., εἴ κα..ποτὶ τὸ ἕτερον τῶν βαρέων ποτιτεθῇ,.. ῥέπειν ἐπὶ τὸ βάρος ἐκεῖνο ᾧ ποτετέθη Archim.*Aequil.*1 *Def.*2, cf. Euc. 1 *Ax.*2, etc.; κοινοῦ -τεθέντος Papp.742.15. **4.** in Logic, *add some determining word*, opp. ἀφαιρεῖν, Arist.*APo.*$91^b27$, cf. *EN*$1147^b$ 33. **5.** in Lxx and *NT*, *continue* or *repeat* an action, c. inf., προσέθηκεν ἔτι λαλῆσαι Lxx *Ge.*18.29; οὐ προσθήσω ἔτι πατάξαι ib.8.21; οὐ μὴ προσθῶ πεῖν I will not drink *again*, *Ev.Marc.*14.25 (v.l.); also προσθεὶς Ἰὼβ εἶπεν Job *continued* and said, Lxx *Jb.*27.1; προσθεὶς εἶπε παραβολήν *Ev.Luc.*19.11; προσθεῖσα ἔτεκεν υἱόν she bore *another* son, Lxx *Ge.*38.5:—also in Med., v. infr. B. III.

**B.** Med., *side with* one, οἷς ἂν σὺ προσθῇ S.*OC*1332, cf. Th.3. 11, 8.48, 87, D.6.12, 11.6, 52.25; τῷ ἀστῷ π. *to be favourable, well-inclined* to him, Hdt.2.160, cf. D.43.34; τῇ ἡδονῇ *side with* pleasure, Arist.*MM*$1201^a2$: abs., *come in, submit*, Epist.Phil.ap.D.18.39. **2.** *assent, agree*, οὔ οἱ ἔγωγε π. τῇ γνώμῃ Hdt.1.109, cf. 3.83, Th.6.50, X. *An.*1.6.10; τῷ λόγῳ τῷ λεχθέντι Hdt.2.120; τῷ Καρχηδονίων νόμῳ Pl. *Lg.*674a: later c. inf., *consent, bring oneself to*, J.*AJ*19.1.8. **3.** ψῆφον δ' Ὀρέστῃ τήνδ' ἐγὼ προσθήσομαι *will deposit* this vote *in favour of* Orestes, i.e. will vote in his favour, A.*Eu.*735; ἡμῖν ἂν προσθέμενοι τὴν ψῆφον εὐορκοίητε D.57.69; so μὴ μιᾷ ψήφῳ π. (sc. τὴν γνώμην), ἀλλὰ δυοῖν Th.1.20; ψῆφον π. ἐναντίαν τινί ib.40; ψῆφον π. ὥστε ἀποκτεῖναι *OGI*218.102 (Ilium, iii B.C.). **4.** Math., *add*, *Sammelb.* 6951 ii 30, al. (ii A.D.). **II.** c. acc. pers., *associate with oneself*, i.e. *take to one as a friend, ally*, or *helper, win over*, π. τὸν δῆμον πρὸς τὴν ἑωυτοῦ μοῖραν Hdt.5.69, cf. Th.6.18; εἰ στρατὸν προσθέοιτο φίλον Hdt. 1.53, cf. 69, S.*OC*404; ταύτην προσθοῦ δάμαρτα *take* her to wife, Id. *Tr.*1224: also in bad sense, πολέμιον π. τινά X.*Cyr.*2.4.12. **2.** c. acc. rei, *apply to oneself*, βάλανον Hp.*Epid.*1.26.α', cf. 4.30 (abs., ib.1.26.δ'); ὀξύβαφον προσθοῦ λαβών Ar.*Av.*361; πατρὸς στέρνα προσθέσθαι θέλω E.*HF*1408: metaph., *put on*, τῇ ὄψει ἀχθηδόνας Th.2. 37; *add to oneself, gain*, τί ἂν προσθείμην πλέον; what should I *be profited?* S.*Ant.*40; π. χάριν, = ἐπιχαρίζεσθαι, Id.*OC*767; esp. of evils, *bring* or *take upon oneself*, πρὸς κακοῖσι κακόν A.*Pers.*531; μέριμναν S. *OT*1460; κακά E.*Heracl.*146; ἄχθος ἐπ' ἄχθει π. διπλοῦν Id.*Andr.*396; οἰκεῖον πόνον, κινδύνους αὐθαιρέτους, Th.1.78, 144; ἔχθρας ἑκουσίους πρὸς ταῖς ἀναγκαίαις π. Pl.*Prt.*346b. **b.** *bring upon* others, οἱ..πόλεμον προσεθήκαντο *made* war *upon* him, Hdt.4.65; οὐκ ἄν σφι Σπαρτιήτας μῆνιν οὐδεμίαν προσθέσθαι *vented* any wrath upon.., Id.7.229. **III.** in Lxx and *NT*, *continue* or *repeat* an action (cf. supr. A. III. 5), οὐ προσθήσεσθε ἔτι ἰδεῖν αὐτούς Lxx *Ex.*14.13; προσέθετο πέμψαι ἕτερον *Ev.*

*Luc.*20.11; προσέθετο συλλαβεῖν καὶ Πέτρον he *caused* Peter *also* to be arrested, *Act.Ap.*12.3; also Φαραὼ προσέθετο τοῦ ἁμαρτάνειν Lxx *Ex.*9.34; οὐ προσέθετο τοῦ ἐπιστρέψαι ib.*Ge.*8.12.

**προστίκτω,** *bring forth besides*, v.l. in Arist.*HA*549$^{a}$17.

**προστῖλάω,** *befoul with dung*, Ar.*Nu.*411:—Pass., Artem.2.26.

⊛ **προστῑμ-άω,** *award further penalty* (cf. ἀτίμητος), in Act. of the court, π. τοὺς κρίναντας τὴν δίκην ὅ τι χρὴ πρὸς τούτῳ παθεῖν Pl.*Lg.*767e, cf. 943b, Arist.*Ath.*63.3; πρὸς τῷ ἀργυρίῳ π. δεσμὸν τῷ κλέπτῃ D.24.114, cf. 103; π. τῷ δημοσίῳ *adjudge* to the treasury *as a debt*, Id.21.44; τὸ ἴσον τῷ δημοσίῳ π. ὅσονπερ τῷ ἰδιώτῃ ibid.:—Med., of the individual δικαστής who proposed the additional penalty, ἐὰν προστιμήσῃ ἡ ἡλιαία (sc. τὸ δεδέσθαι), προστιμᾶσθαι δὲ τὸν βουλόμενον Lex ap. D. 24.105, cf. Legem ap.Lys.10.16:—Pass., impers., εἴ τινι τῶν ὀφειλόντων δεσμοῦ προστετίμηται if *the further penalty of* imprisonment *has been laid on* him, D.24.46, cf. 60, 207; εἴκοσι δραχμῶν προστιμηθῆναι Id.47.43; προστιμάσθω πρὸς χρόνον μὴ εἰσελθεῖν ὅσον ἂν δόξῃ $IG2^{2}$.1368.88. **–ημα,** ατος, τό, *additional penalty* or *fine*, D.24.2, Poll.6.180, 8.21,149. **–ησις,** εως, ἡ, *infliction of a further penalty*, Ael.*VH*14.7. **II.** *valuation*, τῶν ὀθονίων *PTeb.*5.63 (pl., ii B.C.). ⊛ **–ον,** τό, *penalty, fine*, Hp.*Lex* 1, *PHib.*1.41.9 (iii B.C.), *SIG*976.76 (Samos, ii B.C.), Plb.1.17.11, *IG*7.2872 (Coronea), *BMus.Inscr.*481*.245 (Ephesus, ii A.D.); τὰ π. τῆς ὑπερηφανίας Lxx 2*Ma.*7.36; τοιάδε τοῖς κακῶς βουλευομένοις δίδωσι τὰ π. ἡ δίκη Ael.*Fr.*237 (glossed by ἐπίχειρα ap. Suid.). **2.** π. μεταφυτείας *licence-fee* for alteration of crop, etc., *Ostr.Bodl.*1.89 (ii B.C.), cf. *PAmh.*2.31.3 (ii B.C.), *POxy.*1032.12 (ii A.D.).

**προστῑμωρέω,** *assist besides*, ὅσων δεῖται.. Hp.*Acut.*16; *promote*, πνιγί Aret.*CA*1.7:—Med., *promote*, νοσήματι Gal.*Nat.Fac.*1.13.

**προστῑνάσσω,** *shake at*, *AP*12.67 (tm.).

**προστοιχειόω,** *place first as elementary*, S.E.*M.*1.104 (Pass.).

**προστομ-ιαῖον,** τό, name of a chamber in the Erechtheum at Athens, $IG1^{2}$.372.71. **–ιον,** τό, *mouth*, esp. of a river, A.*Supp.*3 (anap., pl.). **II.** *joining of the lips*, Ruf.*Onom.*41, Poll.2.90. **–ίς,** ίδος, ἡ, *mouthpiece*, Apollod.*Poliorc.*152.4. **–ος,** ον, *pointed*, Eub. 107.10; ξίφος Poll.2.101. **2.** *with protruding lips*, *PCair.Zen.*76.11 (iii B.C.).

**πρόστοον,** τό, v. προστῷον.

**προστοχάζομαι,** *predict*, τὸ μέλλον *Cat.Cod.Astr.*8(1).245.

⊛ **προστρᾰγῳδέω,** *exaggerate in tragic style*, τούτοις, ὅτι.. Str.17.1.43. **II.** τὸ ἔξωθεν –τραγῳδούμενον *external trappings, parade*, Longin.7.1.

**προστρᾰτ-εύω,** *serve as soldiers before*, in pf. part., Hsch. s.v. ἀμοιβοί. **–ηγέω,** *hold office of* στρατηγός *before*, *BGU*250.4 (ii A.D.).

**προστρᾰχηλίζω,** *wrench the neck in wrestling*, Plu.2.234d.

**προστρεβλόω,** *torture first*, in Pass., v.l. in J.*BJ*4.5.3.

**προστρέπω,** *turn towards*, esp. *towards a god* as a suppliant, *approach with prayer, supplicate*, τοσαῦτά σ', ὦ Ζεῦ, προστρέπω S.*Aj.*831: c. acc. pers. et inf., *entreat* one to do, μή μ' ἀτιμάσῃς.., ὧν (= τούτων ἃ) σε προστρέπω φράσαι Id.*OC*50: c. acc. rei et inf., *pray that*.., ὀλέσθαι πρόστρεπ' Ἀργείων χθόνα E.*Supp.*1195:—Med., with aor. προσετραπόμην Hom.*Epigr.*15.1; π. δῶμα, δόμους, Hom. l.c., A.*Eu.*205; τὴν Διὸς.. Ἐργάνην S.*Fr.*844: in late Prose, Plu.*Cleom.*39, Ael. *NA*15.21, etc.; *reverence, celebrate*, τινα Plu.2.1117a. **2.** *approach* (as an enemy), Ἰαωλκὸν πολεμίᾳ χερὶ προστραπών Pi.*N.*4.55 codd. **II.** Med., *make a matter of supplication, appeal to*, τοῦ παθόντος προστρεπομένου τὴν πάθην Pl.*Lg.*866b.

**προστρέφω,** *bring up in*, ἱερεύς τις ἄτας δόμοις προσεθρέφθη A.*Ag.*736 (lyr.). **2.** *feed up*, Ruf.*Fr.*68 (Pass., prob. cj.). **II.** *feed in addition* to oneself, Teles p.40 H.

⊛ **προστρέχω,** fut. –δρᾰμοῦμαι D.21.224:—*run to* or *towards, come to* one, πρὸς τοὺς νεκρούς Pl.*R.*440a; τινι Ar.*Ach.*1084, *Av.*759, X.*An.* 4.3.10, etc.: abs., *run up*, Id.*HG*3.1.18, *Cyr.*7.1.15, D. l.c., etc. **2.** in hostile sense, *make a sally*, πρός τι X.*Cyr.*5.4.47. **3.** of things, *happen to* one, τινι D.S.13.37 codd.; προστρέχει πολλαχοῦ τὸ "γίγνεται" *occurs* frequently, Dam.*Pr.*401. **II.** metaph., *join* or *side with*, [τῇ συγκλήτῳ] Plb.24.10.4, etc.; πρὸς τὴν τῶν πολλῶν γνώμην Id.28.7.8; πρὸς τὴν ἀλήθειαν Id.18.15.2. **2.** *approach*, –τρέχων τῇ ἐννόμῳ ἡλικίᾳ, i.e. not quite of age, *POxy.*247.12 (i A.D.). **3.** *resemble*, c. dat., Corn.*ND*32.

**προσ-τρίβω** [ῑ], *rub on* or *against*: abs., προστρίβοντα *by friction*, Arist.*HA*535$^{b}$23:—Med., *rub oneself against*, τῷ τοίχῳ $IG4^{2}$(1).126.10 (Epid., ii A.D.):—Pass., *to be rubbed on*, Dsc.4.153; προστετριμμένος *worn away, dulled*, πρὸς ἄλλοισιν οἴκοις A.*Eu.*238. **II.** *attribute*, πᾶν τὸ ἀνθρώπειον πάθος τοῖς θεοῖς D.L.*Prooem.*5. **III.** more freq. in Med., mostly in bad sense, *inflict* or *cause to be inflicted*, πληγάς τισι Ar.*Eq.*5; ὑμῖν τὸ μήνιμα τῶν ἀλιτηρίων προστρίψομαι Antipho 4.2.8; τινὶ συμφορὰν ἢ βλασφημίαν ἢ κακόν D.25.52; τὴν ὑποψίαν τῆς προδοσίας Plu.2.89f:—Pass., γλώσσῃ ματαίᾳ ζημία προστρίβεται A.*Pr.*331, cf. *Sammelb.*5273.12 (v A.D.), *PMonac.*6.66 (vi A.D.). **2.** in good sense, πλούτου δόξαν προστρίψασθαι τοῖς κεκτημένοις *attach to* them the reputation of wealth, D.22.75, 24.183. **3.** *impart*, [χροιᾶς] φάντασμα τοῖς ὁρατοῖς Gal.7.96. **–τριμμα,** ατος, τό, *that which is rubbed on*: metaph., *that which is inflicted upon* one, esp. a *brand, disgrace*, πόλει π. ἄφερτον ἐνθείς A.*Ag.*395 (lyr.). **II.** pl., *tooth powders*, Gal.12.875, Aët.5.25. **–τριψις,** εως, ἡ, *rubbing, galling*, ἀστράβης interpol. in Arist.*Col.* (v. ἀστράβη).

**προστρόπ-αιος,** Dor. **ποτιτρόπαιος** (A.*Supp.*362, *Eu.*176, both lyr.), ον, (προστροπή) prop. *turning oneself towards*: hence, **1.** of one who has incurred pollution by committing a crime and *turns to a god* or *man to obtain purification, suppliant for purification*, τὸν προστρόπαιον, τὸν ἱκέτην S.*Ph.*930, cf. A.*Supp.*362, *Eu.*234,445, S.*Aj.* 1173, E.*Heracl.*1015, etc.: as Adj., ἕδραν ἔχοντα π. A.*Eu.*41; προστρόπαιοι λιταί S.*OC*1309. **b.** *suppliant for vengeance*, A.*Ch.*286, *Ag.* 1587, Antipho 2.3.10. **2.** of one who has not yet been purified after committing crime, *polluted person*, E.*HF*1259; π. τῆς πόλεως *bringing pollution* on the city, prob. in Eup.120; αὐτοῦ π., μὴ γὰρ δὴ τῆς πόλεως Aeschin.2.158. **3.** of pollution incurred, π. αἷμα blood *that cries for vengeance*, E.*Ion* 1260, *HF*1161; οὐδενὶ οὐδὲν π. καταλείψει Antipho 3.4.9: neut. as Subst., *guilt*, προστρόπαιον ἑαυτοῖς προσέθεντο D.C.42.3. **II.** Pass. (= ᾧ ἄν τις προστρέποιτο δεόμενος, Eust.1807.11), the god *to whom the murdered person turns* for vengeance, *avenger*, οἱ τῶν θανόντων π. Antipho 4.1.4, cf. 4.2.8, Plb.23.10.2 (pl.), Paus.2.18.2. **–ή,** ἡ, *turning* of a suppliant (ἱκέτης) *to* a god or man to implore protection or purification, *supplication*, A.*Eu.*718 (pl.); λιταὶ καὶ π. Plu.2.560e: hence, **2.** *any address to a god, solemn invocation*, θεοὺς.. προστροπαῖς ἱκνουμένη A.*Pers.*216, cf. E.*Alc.*1156, *IG*5(1).26.10 (Amyclae, ii/i B.C.); ἱκεσία ξένων π. E.*Heracl.*108 (lyr.); π. καὶ ἀρὰν ὑπὲρ τούτων ἐποιήσαντο Aeschin.3.110; θεᾶς ἔχω προστροπήν discharge *the duty of ministering* to the goddess, E.*IT*618; but πόλεως προστροπὴν ἔχειν address a *petition* to the city, S.*OC*558; of libations, A.*Ch.*85. **3.** π. γυναικῶν *suppliant band* of women, ib.21. ⊛ **–ιος,** ον, poet. for προστρόπαιος, Orph.*A.*1225. ⊛ **–ος,** ὁ, = προστρόπαιος 1.1, *suppliant*, τινος S.*Ph.*773: abs., Id.*OT*41. **II.** *accursed*, Phot. s.v. προστρόπαιος.

**προστρουθίζω,** *clean beforehand with* στρουθίον, *PLeid.X.*100 (Pass.).

**προστροχ-άζω,** *run to*, τοῖς καθηγηταῖς Phld.*Lib.* p.25 O. **–αστής,** οῦ, ὁ, *obsequious person, sycophant*, Id.*Herc.*1457.4.

**πρόστροχος,** ον, *round*, Hsch.

**προστρωννύω,** *prosterno*, *Gloss.*

**προστυγχάνω,** *obtain one's share of*, and generally, *obtain*, προστυχόντι τῶν ἴσων S.*Ph.*552; ἐμοῦ κολαστοῦ προστυχών Id.*El.*1463: c. dat., *meet with, hit upon*, Pl.*Lg.*844b, 893e, *Plt.*262b, *Sph.*246b. **2.** of events, *befall* one, κακότας π. τινί Pi.*Fr.*42.5. **3.** = πρόσειμι, φασι τῷ ἐμβρύῳ προστυγχάνειν ἕτερον χιτῶνα Sor.1.58. **4.** abs., ὁ προστυγχάνων *the first person one meets, anybody*, Pl.*Lg.*914b; πᾶς ὁ π. ib. 808e; οἱ αἰεὶ –τυγχάνοντες Th.1.97; ὁ προστυχὼν Φρύξ Herod.3.36: so in neut., τὰ προστυχόντα ξένια *whatever* fare *there was*, E.*Alc.*754; ἐρρύφεον τὸ προστυχόν *anything that came handy*, Hp.*Acut.*39; but τὸ προστυχόν *casualness*, Pl.*Ti.*34c; πράξει τὸ π. ἑκάστοτε will act *offhand*, Id.*Lg.*962c; ἐκ τοῦ προστυχόντος *offhand, ex tempore*, Plu.2.150d, 407b; so κατὰ τὸ π. D.H.7.1.

**πρόστῡλος,** ον, *with pillars in front*, ναός Vitr.3.2.1, 7 *Praef.* 17. **II.** πρόστυλον, τό, *portico*, *IG*7.2808.10 (Hyettus, iii B.C.), perh. to be read in ib.$2^{2}$.204.27.

**πρόστυμμα,** ατος, τό, (προστύφω) *mordant*, τῆς πορφύρας Hsch. s.v. μήλωθρα.

**προστῠπ-ής,** ές, *adherent*, ὑμένες Archig. ap.Gal.8.91, cf. Sor.2.41, Gal.14.710: c. dat., Ruf.*Anat.*4; θρόνῳ π. J.*AJ*3.6.5; cf. sq. **–ος,** ον, *executed in low relief*, opp. ἔκτυπος (in high relief), Callix.2, Plin. *HN*35.152. **2.** Subst., πρόστυποι, οἱ, of the Cherubim, J.*AJ*3.6.5. **II.** *lying flat*, φύλλα Dsc.4.10. **–όω,** *mould to the shape of* a thing, τὸν πνεύμονα τῷ θώρακι Gal.2.700 (Pass.), cf. Orib.46.17.3; τοῖς τοίχοις Herod.Med.ap.eund.10.10.4:—Pass., Dsc.2.105. **–ωσις,** εως, ἡ, *shaping by pressure*, Paul.Aeg.6.117.

**προστύφω** [ῡ], *thicken beforehand*, τὰ ἀρώματα Thphr.*Od.*24; τὸ ἔλαιον Dsc.1.39. **II.** *apply a mordant*, *PHolm.*3.30, prob. in *PLeid.X.*100.

**προστῠχής,** ές, *engaged in* or *acquainted with*, ταῖς τιθασείαις τῶν ἰχθύων Pl.*Plt.*264c; π. [τῇ στερεομετρίᾳ] γεγονότες Id.*Epin.*990e; τῷ βίῳ ib.973c, etc.; π. γίνεται, = προστυγχάνει, Id.*Lg.*955d. Adv. –χῶς *by chance*, Numen.ap.Eus.*PE*14.5.

⊛ **προστῷον** (on the accent v. Hdn.Gr.1.377), τό, *portico*, Pl.*Prt.* 314e, 315c, $IG2^{2}$.1675.3, 1680.1, Plu.2.838d, etc.; written **πρόστοον** in *IGRom.*3.690.8 (Aperlae, i A.D.).—As Adj., τόποι πρόστῳοι Sch. Il.20.11.

**προσυβρίζω,** *maltreat besides*, D.21.32, J.*AJ*12.4.5:—Pass., D. 54.40, J.*AJ*6.13.7, D.C.69.3.

**προσυγ-γίγνομαι,** old Att. **προξυγγ–,** *have an interview with* one *before*, τισι Th.8.14; *become acquainted with before*, τοῖς ἤθεσι καὶ βουλεύμασί σου D.C.52.33. **–γράφομαι** [γρᾰ], Med., *write out before*, Sch.Pl.*Grg.*448c. **–κειμαι,** Pass., *to be arranged, agreed beforehand*, Aen.Tact.18.18, al., J.*AJ*18.3.2; τὸ προσυγκείμενον Aen. Tact.31.16; τὰ π. J.*AJ*19.2.5. **–χέω,** *throw into disorder before*, τὰς τάξεις Plb.5.84.9. **–χρίω,** *anoint beforehand*, Orib.*Fr.*74.

**προσυδρεύω,** misspelling of προσεδρεύω, *PMasp.*328 i 10, al. (vi A.D.).

**προσυζεύγνῡμι,** *yoke together beforehand*:—Pass., ἑτέρῳ εἰς γάμον π. Eust.61.29.

**προσῠλακτ-έω,** *bark at*, τινι D.H.*Th.*2, Them.*Or.*16.205d. **–ησις,** εως, ἡ, *carping*, Simp.*in Ph.*1182.38.

**προσυλ-λέγομαι,** Pass., *assemble before*, D.C.37.33, al., Hsch. s.v. πρηγορεών. **–λογίζομαι,** *conclude by a prosyllogism* (cf. sq.), Arist. *APr.*66$^{a}$35, *Top.*156$^{a}$7. **–λογισμός,** ὁ, *prosyllogism*, i.e. *a syllogism the conclusion of which forms the major premiss of another*, Id. *APr.*44$^{a}$22: pl., ib.42$^{b}$5. **–λογιστέον,** *one must use a prosyllogism*, Id.*Top.*148$^{b}$8.

**πρόσῡλος,** ον, (ὕλη) *conjoined, connected with matter*, Procl. *in Cra.* p.71 P., Dam.*Pr.*265, Eustr.*in EN*284.14.

**προσυμ-βαίνω**, *happen before*, Agath.5.15; τὰ -βεβηκότα Sch.Od. 7.243. **-βῐβάζω**, *accommodate beforehand*, v.l. for προσβιβάζω in Hierocl. *in CA* 14 p.450 M. **-βολέω**, dub.l. et sens. in *PTeb.*348.2 (i A.D.). **-βολον**, τό, *prognostic*, or perh. *preliminary contribution*, ταῦτα μὲν εἰρήσθω προσύμβολα, ὥς φασι Anon.ap.Suid. **-μίσγω**, *intermix first*, τὸ ὕδωρ ἐς τὠυτό Hdt.7.129.

**Προσυμναῖος**, α, ον, *of Prosymna*, St. Byz.; epith. of Hera at Argos, Timoth.Hist. et Agatho Samius ap.Ps.-Plu.*Fluv.*18.3; Προσυμναίᾳ θεῷ, i.e. Δήμητρι **Προσύμνῃ** (Paus.2.37.1), *IG*4.666.1 (Lerna); Προσυμναῖος λεώς prob. ib.666.7; ἁ πάτρα τῶν Π. ib.5(2).493 (Megalopolis).

**προσυμνέω**, *sing besides*, gloss on ποταείσομαι, Sch.Theoc.2. 11. II. *celebrate in song as well*, τινας Lxx 2*Ma.*15.9.

**προσυμ-πάσσω**, *besprinkle first*, Agathin. ap. Orib. 10.7.22. **-πλέκομαι**, fut. -πλᾰκήσομαι, v.l. for συμπροσ- in Thd.*Da.*11. 10. **-φύομαι**, Pass. with aor. 2 Act. -εφύην, *grow together before*, ἣν προσυμφύῃ τὸ ἔξω τῷ ἔσω Hp.*Morb.*1.21. **-φωνέω**, *harmonize beforehand*, S.E.*M.*8.183 (Pass.).

**προσυν-άγω** [ᾰ], *arrive at a total beforehand*:—Pass., ὁ προσυναχθεὶς ἀριθμός Vett.Val.32.3. **-αθροίζομαι**, Pass., *assemble together beforehand*, J.*Vit.*27, *AJ*18.4.1. **-αίρεσις**, εως, ἡ, *antecedent aggregation*, Dam.*Pr.*96. **-αιρέω**, in Pass., *to be antecedently aggregated*, ibid. **-απάντησις**, εως, ἡ, a rhet. figure, in which when two nouns are placed first the words belonging to the second precede those belonging to the first (as in Il.4.450), Alex.*Fig.*2.27. **-εδρεύω**, *take counsel beforehand*, Hippod.ap.Stob.4.1.94:—Pass., *to be settled beforehand*, τὰ προσυνηδρευμένα ibid.

**προσύν-ειμι**, *to be cohabiting with already*, ᾧ προσύνεστι ἀνδρί *PSI*5. 450.9 (ii/iii A.D.), cf. *POxy.*1473.25 (iii A.D.). **-ίστημι**, *recommend* or *praise before*, D.H.*Rh.*10.5, Plu.2.19b; *mention before*, Sch. Od.9.187. **-οικέω**, *cohabit* or *live as wife with before*, τινι Hdt.3. 88, Plu.*Demetr.*14. **-οικίζω**, f.l. for προσσυνοικίζω (q.v.). **-τάσσω**, *arrange beforehand*, στρατιώτην ἐσδραμεῖν Polyaen.4.6.19:—Med., *arrange before*, τὰς δυνάμεις J.*BJ*5.1.1. II. *compose before*, in Pass., -τεταγμέναι βίβλοι Vett.Val.330.8, cf. 173.28. **-τελέω**, *complete before*, in Pass., Aristeas 55, 77. **-τίθεμαι**, *agree upon, arrange beforehand*, Aen.Tact.18.13; οὐδὲν προσυνθέμενος J.*BJ*5.13. 1. II. *contract beforehand*, φιλίαν τινὶ ἐπὶ τοῖς αὐτοῖς D.C.36. 45. **-τρίβω** [ῑ], *break in pieces before*, ῥάβδους Id.59.20.

**προσυπ-ᾰκουστέον**, *one must understand, supply in thought*, Phld. *Po.*5.32, Sch.E.*Alc.*10, Sch.Pi.*P.*9.42, Sch.Luc.*Tim.*48. **-ᾰκούω**, *listen to as well*, τι Pl.*Lg.*898d. II. Gramm., *understand something not expressed, supply in thought*, Gal.16.740, Alex.Aphr.*in Sens.* 105.13, Hierocl. *in CA* 3 p.423 M.:—Pass., Phld.*Po.*5.10 (dub.), Ph. 1.443, Sch.Luc.*Anach.*17. **-αναπτύσσω**, *unfold besides*, τὰ γράμματα Lib.*Decl.*43.61. **-αντάω**, *meet with*, Ph.2.186, *PSI*4. 292.10 (iii A.D.). **-αρκτέον**, *one must prescribe besides*, Sor.1.53 (s.v.l.). **-άρχω**, *exist besides*, δεῖ τὴν τρίτην ἔτι -ειν Arist.*GC* 335ᵃ31; καὶ μηδὲ [ἂν] ταφῆναι προσυπῆρχεν οἴκοι μοι and *it would further have been my fate* not even to be buried at home, D.21. 106. **-ειμι**, *underlie in addition*, c. dat., Eustr. *in EN* 113.10. **-εμφαίνω**, *indicate besides*, Sch.A.*Th.*495 (Pass.).

**προσυπερβάλλω**, *surpass*, τινὰς ὠμότητι Ph.2.44, cf. 190; ἀλλήλους ἐν ἀσεβείαις J.*BJ*7.8.1. II. *exceed, transgress*, τοὺς ἐπιεικείας ὅρους Ph.2.393 (s.v.l.): abs., *go beyond what is right* or *necessary*, Id.1.276, 2.262, al.

**προσυπεργάζομαι**, *prepare the ground for* another, Plu.*Sol.*12.

**προσυπερέχω**, *project beyond*, Hp.*Epid.*5.49.

**προσυπ-έχω** (sc. λόγον), *to be answerable also for*, τῆς τύχης D.*Prooem.*25 (v.l. πρὸς ὑπ-); also π. δίκην τῆς ὕβρεως Aristid.2. 429 J. **-ισχνέομαι**, *promise besides*, Plu.*Demetr.*10, D.C.38.31, 40. 60, Ant.Lib.41.6. 2. *make a higher bid*, Wilcken *Chr.*167.20 (ii B.C.).

**προσυπο-βάλλω**, *place under, submit besides*, Plu.2.814f:—Pass., Gal.18(2).454. **-γράφω** [ᾰ], *sketch out besides*, τι τῇ διανοίᾳ Longin. 14.2, cf. Ph.1.577, D.L.6.103: abs., Ph.1.590. II. *subjoin*, Ptol. *Phas.*p.10 H.; *add below in writing*, *PMag.Lond.*121.804. **-δείκνῡμι**, *show besides*, τινί τι Plb.22.10.4, cf. Aristeas 136; διότι.. Id. 168. **-δεικτέον**, *one must show besides*, τι ἀκριβέστερον Ph.1. 11. **-θήγω**, *whet upon*, τινί τι Ael.*NA*9.16. **-κειμαι**, Pass., *lie under besides*, v.l. for προϋπ- in Gal.*UP*3.8. 2. *to be mortgaged besides*, *OGI*46.17 (Halic., iii B.C.). 3. *to be assumed besides*, Gal. 6.246, 10.351. **-κλίνω** [ῑ], *place underneath*, τοῖς μηροῖς τὰ γόνατα Paul.Aeg.3.76. **-λαμβάνω**, *suppose besides*, Arist.*Cael.*308ᵃ27; *imply, import in addition*, Phld.*Mus.*p.74 K. (Pass.), f.l. for προϋπ- in D.H.*Th.*35. **-λογίζω**, *subtract besides*, Ptol.*Geog.*1.13.7. **-μένω**, pf. -μεμένηκα *Jahresh.*15 *Beibl.*96 (Thrace, iii B.C.):—*endure further*, *PPetr.*2 p.22 (iii B.C.), Ph.2.531. **-μιμνήσκω**, *remind* one *of* a thing *besides*, τινά τι Plb.38.8.2: abs., Id.22.18.7:—Pass., aor. part. -μνησθέντος Phld.*Ir.*p.19 W. **-μνηστέον**, *one must mention besides*, Str.17.3.1. **-νοέω**, *suspect besides*, τι τῶν ἀληθῶν Eun.*VS* p.501 B. **-νοητέον**, *one must note besides*, Procl.*Chrest.* p.101 Allen.

**προσυποπτεύω**, *suspect besides*, Phld.*Ind.Sto.*4, D.C.*Fr.*40.46ᵃ; π. μή.. Id.*Fr.*40.46: c. inf. fut., Id.*Fr.*111.3.

**προσυπο-στρώννῡμι**, *spread underneath*, τὰ χλωρά Bilabel Ὀψαρτ. p.10. **-τάσσω**, *subjoin besides*, *PTeb.*38.26, al. (ii B.C.), Ar.Byz. *Epit.*35.19, Vett.Val.96.24, S.E.*M.*11.1. ※ **-τίθημι**, *put underneath besides*, Dsc.1.68.7, v.l. in *Hippiatr.*74. II. Med., *assume besides*, Gal.6.127. **-τοπέω**, *suspect besides*, D.C.58.18, 66.5.

**προσυπουργέω**, *assist in besides*, J.*AJ*15.6.2.

**προσῡριγγόομαι**, Pass., *to be channelled, provided with a cavity beforehand*, D.S.32.10.

**προσῡρίζω**, f.l. for προσσυρ- in Plb.8.20.5, 8.25.10.

**προσύστᾰσις**, εως, ἡ, *preliminary exposition*, Aps.*Rh.*p.242 H.

**προσυστέλλομαι**, Pass., *to be drawn up beforehand*, ἡ προσυνεσταλμένη αὐθεντία Lxx 3*Ma.*2.29.

**προσῠφαίνω**, 1 aor. inf. -υφᾶναι Sever.ap.Eus.*PE*13.17:—*interweave with*, ἀθανάτῳ θνητόν Pl.*Ti.*41d, cf. Sever. l.c.; τὸ ἀκόλουθον τῇ γραφῇ Ph.1.511, cf. 536 (Pass.), Jul.*Gal.*178b; καινόν τι τοῖς ἀρχαίοις Them.*Or.*26.316a; προσυφάνθη τὸ χόριον (sc. τῷ σώματι) Porph.*Marc.* 32: metaph. of buildings, οἰκίας προσυφαίνουσι ταῖς γωνίαις (in a painting) Philostr.*Im.*2.28; [στοαὶ] αἷς ἱππόδρομός τε προσύφανται καὶ θέατρον Lib.*Or.*11.218.

**προσυφ-άπτω**, *fix on beneath*, Theo Sm. p.180 H. (Pass.). **-ίσταμαι**, fut. -στήσομαι, *reply, rejoin*, Phld.*Lib.* p.6 O.; *present itself to the mind from without*, in pf. part., τὰ προσυφεστῶτα *external objects*, M. Ant.5.19.

**προσυψόω**, *raise still higher*, Lxx 1*Ma.*12.36, J.*BJ*3.7.30, etc.

**προσφάγημα** [φᾰ], ατος, τό, = sq., Aesop.64, Moer. p.274 P.

**προσφάγιον** (A) [ᾰ], τό, (φαγεῖν) = ὄψον 1.1, *Ev.Jo.*21.5, Aesop.325, *PLond. ined.*2687 (iv A.D.); ἄρτον ἕνα καὶ π. *POxy.*498.33 (ii A.D.), cf. 736.89, 739.10 (i B.C./i A.D.): metaph., of an illicit commission or agio, τὸ καλούμενον παρ' αὐτοῖς π. *OGI*484.26 (Pergam.).

**προσφάγιον** (B) [ᾰ], τό, (προσφάζω) *victim sacrificed beforehand*, *IG*12(5).593.12 (Iulis, v B.C.).

※ **πρόσφαγμα**, ατος, τό, *victim sacrificed for* others, τύμβῳ πρόσφαγμα E.*Hec.*41; θεᾷ π. Id.*IT*243, cf. Plu.*Comp.Thes.Rom.*1 (2): pl., of a single victim, E.*Hec.*265; of the victim's blood, Id.*Alc.*845. II. *sacrifice, slaughter*, A.*Ag.*1278, E.*Tr.*628 (pl.).

**προσφάζω**, Att. -σφάττω Pl.*Min.*315c:—*sacrifice beforehand*, τινι E.*Hel.*1255 (Pass.). Pl. l.c. 2. *kill first*, dub. l. in Plu.*Phoc.*30.

**προσφαίνομαι**, Pass., *appear besides*, π. κοινωνὸς τινος Aristid.*Or.* 45(8).24; f.l. for προφ- in X.*Cyr.*4.5.57 codd.; cf. ποτιφαίνω.

**προσφᾰνής**, ές, dub. sens., προσφανῆ· Θεόφραστος ἐν Μεταλλικῷ χρυσίου συρροάς, Hsch.

**προσφάσθαι**, v. πρόσφημι.

**προσφάτης**· πλάγιος πεσών, Hsch.

**πρόσφᾰτος**, ον, *fresh, not decomposed*, of a corpse miraculously preserved, νῦν δέ μοι ἑρσήεις καὶ π. ἐν μεγάροισιν κεῖσαι Il.24.757; νεκρὸς π. Hdt.2.89, 121.ε'; τροφὴ ἔτι π. (sc. before digestion begins) Arist.*PA*675ᵇ32; [ζῷα] τὰ πεπωκότα πόμα π. which have taken a *recent* drink, Id.*HA*520ᵇ31; πορφύρας .. πρόσφατον τὸ ἄνθος ἔτι φυλαττούσης Plu.*Alex.*36; of fish, Antiph.218.1, Men.462.4, *PMich. Zen.*72.8 (iii B.C.); ἐχῖνοι Posidipp.14; of poultry, Gal.*Vict.Att.*8; [κρέα] Hp.*Acut.*(*Sp.*)49, cf. Sor.2.15, al.; δέλεαρ Arist.*HA*534ᵃ12; ζῷα π., opp. salted, D.S.3.31, cf. Gal.6.728; ἄλφιτα καὶ ἄλητα Hp. *Vict.*2.44, gloss on ποταίνια in *Acut.*37; καρποί, ἔλαιον, Arist.*Pr.*926ᵃ 30, 927ᵃ29; ῥίζαι [σιλφίου] Thphr.*HP*6.3.5; σταφυλή Lxx *Nu.*6.3, Sor. 1.51; φῦκος Agatharch.35; νάρδος Dsc.1.7; χιών Plb.3.55.1; παγάν Pi.*P.*4.299 (unless πρόσφατον ξενωθεὶς = *recently* entertained); ὕδωρ *newly-drawn* well-water, Plu.2.690c; ποτόν Porph.*Marc.*4; αἷμα *uncoagulated*, opp. πεπηγότες θρόμβοι, Hp.*Epid.*7.10; [καταμηνίων ῥύσις] -ωτέρα Arist.*GA*764ᵃ6; σπέρμα, οὖρον, Id.*Pr.*924ᵇ28, 907ᵇ 25. 2. of events and actions, *recent*, δίκαι A.*Ch.*804 (lyr.); ἐπιστολαί S.*Fr.*128; ὀργή Lys.18.19; ὀχεία Arist.*HA* 509ᵇ31; φόβος Aen.Tact.3.1; φθόνος Plu.*Them.*24; θεωρίαι καὶ μαθήσεις Arist.*EE* 1237ᵃ24; φαντασία Id.*MM*1203ᵇ4; λύπη defined as δόξα πρόσφατος κακοῦ παρουσίας Zeno *Stoic.*1.52; ἀτύχημα Plb.1.21.9; εὐεργεσίαι Id. 2.46.1; [πράγματα] Plu.2.146b; ὄγκοι (= οἰδήματα) Gal.18(2).145; βήξ, i.e. not yet chronic, Sor.1.123, cf. 2.46; γάλα, i.e. lately begun to be secreted, Id.1.89; of persons, *recent in date*, of Homer, Arist. *Mete.*351ᵇ35; μάρτυρες.. οἱ μὲν παλαιοὶ οἱ δὲ π. Id.*Rh.*1375ᵇ27: used predicatively, χρόνοι [τοῖς πλουσίοις] τοῦ δίκην ὑποσχεῖν .. δίδονται, καὶ τἀδικήμαθ' ἕωλα.. ὡς ὑμᾶς καὶ ψυχρ' ἀφικνεῖται, τῶν δ' ἄλλων ἡμῶν ἕκαστος π. κρίνεται the cases of us poor men are served up *fresh*, D.21.112; νεαλὴς καὶ π. *fresh* (because recently imprisoned), Id.25. 61. 3. *new*, οὐκ ἔστι πᾶν π. ὑπὸ τὸν ἥλιον Lxx *Ec.*1.9; οὐκ ἔσται ἐν σοὶ θεὸς π. ib.*Ps.*80(81).10; ὁδὸν π. καὶ ζῶσαν *Ep.Hebr.*10.20; ἀεὶ ἡδίων ἡ π. ἀφροδίτη Alciphr.1.39. II. Adv. -τως *newly, lately*, π. ἠγγελμένων Aen.Tact.16.2, cf. Lxx *De.*24.5, *OGI*315.23 (Pessinus, ii B.C.), Parth.28.1, D.S.14.115, J.*BJ*1.6.2, Babr.30.3, Anon.Hist. (*FGrH* 153) p.826 J. (Orig. = νεωστὶ ἀνηρημένος (cf. πέφαται, etc.) acc. to Phot.; perh. *slaughtered for* (the occasion).)

**προσφερής**, ές, (προσφέρω) *similar, like*, c. dat., Hdt.2.105, 4.33, A. *Ag.*1218, *Ch.*176, E.*Hel.*591, Ar.*Ec.*67, Th.1.49, etc.; προσφερέστατοι [τῇ θεῷ] ἄνδρες Pl.*Ti.*24d; τὸ σῶμα προσφερὴς τῇ ψυχῇ Id.*R.*494b, cf. *Phlb.*51d; βίος οἴνῳ π. Antiph.240; προσφερέστερον δέμας E.*Hel.*559: rarely c. gen., πατρὸς προσφερεῖς ὀμμάτων αὐγαί Id.*HF*131 (lyr.). Adv. -ρῶς, c. dat., *Placit.*4.4.4, etc. II. = πρόσφορος, *conducive, useful*, τινι Hdt.5.111 (v.l. προφερέστερον).

※ **προσφέρω** (once ποσφέρω, q.v.), Dor. ποτιφέρω Prov.ap Plu.2. 239a: fut. προσοίσω E.*Andr.*257: Ion. aor. προσένεικα Hdt.3.87: Ion. aor. Pass. προσηνείχθην Id.9.71:—*bring to* or *upon, apply to*, π. πύργοισι κλιμάκων προσαμβάσεις E.*Ph* 488; πῦρ σοι Id.*Andr.*257; μηχανὰς [τοῖσι τείχεσι] Hdt.6.18, cf. Th.2.58 (and so metaph., Hdt.6.125 (unless in signf. A. I. 2); π. νόμον, ψήφισμα πρὸς τὴν συγγραφὴν *bring to bear against*.., D.35.39); τὴν χεῖρα πρὸς τοὺς μυκτῆρας Hdt.3.87; but χέρα τινὶ προσενεγκεῖν *lay hands upon*.., Pi.*P.*9.36; π. τὰς χεῖρας αὐτοῖς, in hostile sense, Plb.3.79.4, cf. *PCair.Zen.*18.8 (iii B.C.), *PPetr.*2 p.10 (iii B.C.) (but also in a friendly relation, X.*Mem.*2.6.31 sq., and in supplication to the gods, *hold out* one's hands *to*, *UPZ*106.12, 107.14 (ii B.C.)); ἀνάγκην or ἀναγκαίην τισὶ π. Hdt.7.136, 172, cf. A.*Ch.*76 (lyr.); βίην τισί Hdt.3.19; τινὶ βάσανον Pl.*Phlb.*23a; so of surgical or medical treatment, Hp.*Ulc.*24; πταρμὸν [τῇ λυγγί] Pl. *Smp.*189a (Pass.), cf. 187e; τὰς τομὰς καὶ τὰς καύσεις τινί D.C.55.17; κλύδωνα σαυτῷ αὐθαίρετον *bring upon* thyself, *Trag.Adesp.*568: without dat., *apply, employ, use*, καινὰ σοφὰ E.*Med.*298, Ar.*Th.*1130 (cf. infr. 3); ἴαμα Th.2.51; τεχνήματα A.*Fr.*322; πάσας μηχανὰς E.*IT* 112; πάντας ἐλέγχους Ar.*Lys.*484; π. τόλμαν *bring* it *to bear*, Pi.*N.* 10.30; also π. πόλεμον Hdt.7.9.γ′ (v.l.); ἔρωτα Pl.*Smp.*187e. 2. *add*, μηδὲ π. μέθυ S.*OC*481 (or in signf. A. I. 3a); εἰ κακὸν προσοίσομεν νέον παλαιῷ E.*Med.*78 (or perh., *bear in addition*); π. τι πρός τι Hdt. 6.125 (or in signf. A. I. 1). 3. *present, offer*, ἄεθλον, of a triumphal ode, Pi.*O.*9.108; λουτρὰ πατρί S.*El.*434; [τόξα] Id.*Ph.*775; τὴν δᾷδά τινι Ar.*Pl.*1052; τὴν χεῖρά τινι ἄκραν Id.*Lys.*436; δῶρα Th.2.97 (Pass.); οὐθὲν κολοβὸν προσφέρομεν πρὸς τοὺς θεούς Arist.*Fr.*101; οἶνον μὴ π. *Schwyzer* 696 (Chios); σφάγια καὶ θυσίας Lxx *Am.*5.25, al., cf. *Ep.Hebr.*11.4; τὸ δῶρόν σου *Ev.Matt.*5.24, etc. b. esp. of food, drink, or medicine, θαλλὸν χιμαίραις S.*Fr.*502; π. τὰ ῥυφήματα καὶ τὰ πόματα Hp.*Acut.*26, cf. Pl.*Phdr.*270b, Pl.Com.55, Alex.189, etc.; π. τὸ φάρμακον τῇ κεφαλῇ Pl.*Chrm.*157c; ἑαυτῷ π. φάρμακον *administer* poison to oneself, *POxy.*472.6 (ii A.D.); *set* food *before* one, X.*Mem.*3.11.13 and 14, Pl.*Lg.*792a: c. inf., π. τινὶ ἐμπιεῖν καὶ φαγεῖν X.*Cyr.*7.1.1; also διψῶντι γάρ τοι πάντα προσφέρων σοφὰ οὐκ ἂν πλέον τέρψειας ἢ 'μπιεῖν διδούς S.*Fr.*763; χυμὸς ἐπιτήδειος προσφέρειν Hp.*VM*24; ὁ προσφέρων Id.*Epid.*1.23:—Pass., τὰ προσφερόμενα ibid., X.*Cyn.*6.2; ἡ προσφερομένη τροφή Pl.*Sph.*230c. 4. *address* proposals, an offer, etc., π. λόγον τινί Hdt.3.134, 5.30, cf. 40; περὶ σπονδῶν Th.3.109; ὅτι.. D.48.6; λόγους π. τισί Th.3.4; λόγους π. περὶ ξυμβάσεως τοῖς στρατηγοῖς Id.2.70, cf. Hdt.8.52; λόγους τισὶ ξυναποστῆναι Th.1.57. 5. *convey* property *by deed of gift* or *by bequest*, *Arch.Pap.* 4.130 (ii A.D.):—Pass., *PAmh.*2.71.6 (ii A.D.). II. *contribute, pay*, ἑκατὸν τάλαντα π. Hdt.3.91, cf. Th.1.138; π. μετοίκιον *pay* an alien-tax, X.*Vect.*2.1, cf. *OGI*13.20 (Samos, iv B.C., Med.), *PGiss.*50.12 (iii A.D.); *bring in, yield*, X.*Vect.*4.15, D.27.9. III. intr., *resemble*, c. acc. of respect in which, π. νόον ἀθανάτοις Pi.*N.*6.4; θηρὸς χρωτὶ νόον προσφέρων Id.*Fr.*43; π. τρόπους παιδί *Trag.Adesp.*453; cf. infr. B. I. 5. IV. *bear in addition*, v. supr. A. I. 2.

B. Pass., with fut. προσοίσομαι Th.6.44, D.48.22: aor. προσηνεγκάμην, = προσηνέχθην, D.S.16.8:—*to be borne towards*, and of ships, *put in*, εἰς λιμένα X.*Cyr.*5.4.6: hence, 2. *attack, assault*, πρός τινας Hdt.5.34, 111, 112, 7.209, X.*HG*4.3.20, etc.; τινι Hdt.5.109, Th.4.126, etc.; κατὰ τὸ ἰσχυρότατον προσηνείχθησαν *attacked* where the enemy was strongest, Hdt.9.71, cf. 5.101, Th.7.44, Pl.*R.*422b; προσφέρεσθαι ἄποροι difficult *to engage*, Hdt.9.49, cf. Pl.*Ly.*223b. 3. without any sense of hostility, *go to* or *towards, approach*, ἐκ τοῦ Ἰκαρίου πελάγεος προσφερόμενοι *sailing*, Hdt.6.96; π. τοῖσι Κορινθίοισι Id.8.94; τῷ σκοπέλῳ, τῇ Τρῳάδι, Luc.*JTr.*15, *DMort.*19.2; πόλεμος ἀπὸ Πελοποννήσου -φερόμενος Plu.*Per.*8; τὰ -όμενα πρήγματα matters *that were brought* to him, Hdt.2.173. 4. *deal with, behave oneself* in a certain way *towards* a person, ἀπὸ τοῦ ἴσου ὑμῖν π. Th.1.140; τοῖς κρείσσοσι καλῶς Id.5.111, cf. X.*Cyr.*7.2.16; τισὶν οὐ μετρίως D. 9.24, cf. *PTeb.*750.2 (ii B.C.), *Sammelb.*5675.6 (ii B.C.); φιλανθρώπως [τῇ Ποτειδαίᾳ] D.S.16.8, cf. *SIG*807.13 (Magn. Mae.); ὀρθότατα ἵπποις π. X.*Eq.*1.1; also τίνα τρόπον προσφέρῃ πρὸς τὰ παιδικά Pl.*Ly.* 205b, cf. *Phdr.*252d; ἄριστα π. πρὸς τοὺς ἀμφισβητοῦντας D.48.22; also of circumstances, ταῖς ξυμφοραῖς εὐξυνετώτερον *meet* them with intelligence, Th.4.18; πρὸς τὰ πράγματα ἄριστα π. Id.6.44; πρὸς τὰς τύχας Pl.*R.*604d; πρὸς λόγον *answer* it, X.*Cyr.*4.5.44: abs., χρησμῳδέων π. Hdt.7.6; ὀλιγώρως π. Lys.9.17. 5. προσφέρεσθαί τινι *come near, be like*, ὁ χαρακτὴρ τοῦ προσώπου προσφέρεσθαι ἐδόκεε ἐς ἑωυτόν Hdt.1.116; cf. supr. A. III, and v. προσφερής. II. *to be added*, Longin.*Proll.Heph.* p.89 C.

C. Med., with fut. -οίσομαι Phld.*Sign.*8: 3 sg. aor. 1 subj. -ενέγκηται Epicur.*Ep.*3 p.64 U.:—προσφέρεσθαί τι *take*, of food or drink, *assimilate*, π. σῖτον, ποτόν. X.*Cyr.*4.2.41, cf. Aeschin.1.145, Thphr. *HP*8.4.5, Epicur. l. c., Plu.*Dem.*30, *Cic.*3, etc. 2. *exhibit*, ὑμῖν φιλοτιμίαν Epist.Phil.ap.D.18.167, cf. Epicur.*Ep.*1 p.14 U., *Inscr.Prien.*42.14, 108.221 (ii B.C.), etc.; also π. ἑαυτόν ib.111.294 (i B.C.). 3. like the Act., *apply*, κἂν ὁτιοῦν δουλείας Pl.*R.*563d; πᾶσαν σπουδὴν καὶ μηχανήν Plb.1.18.11, cf. *Supp.Epigr.*2.663.5 (Prusa, ii B.C.), *PTeb.*27.14, al. (ii B.C.). 4. *contribute*, πλεῖστα πρός τι Athenio 1.2 (s. v. l.); *bring with one* as dowry, εἱματισμὸν καὶ κόσμον *PEleph.*1.4 (iv B.C.), cf. *PGiss.*2.12 (ii B.C.), etc.; cf. supr. A. II. 5. *declare*, μὴ εἰδέναι γράμματα *PHamb.*39.63 (ii A.D.), cf. *POxy.*237 vii 26 (ii A.D.), etc. 6. = προσορίζω, *add* land *by deed of conveyance*, κυρία ἔσται -ομένη πρὸς πόλιν ἣν ἂν βούληται *OGI*225.10 (Didyma, iii B.C.), cf. 221.44 (Ilium, iii B.C.), al. 7. *convey* property, π. ἐν προσφορᾷ [μέρος οἰκίας] *PRyl.* 155.7 (ii A.D.), etc.

**προσφεύγω**, *flee for refuge to*, c. dat., Plu.*Pomp.*46, *Cic.*3, *POxy.* 488.23 (ii A.D.), cf. J.*AJ*1.19.8, Sm.*Ez.*29.16.

**προσφευκτέον**, *one must be liable to a prosecution besides*, D.37.38 (or divisim).

*πρόσφημι, mostly 3 sg. aor. προσέφη (Dor. aor. προσέφᾱσεν Call. *Lav.Pall.*79), *speak to, address*, τινα Il.1.84, Hes.*Sc.*77, etc.; in a parody of Homer, Cratin.68: c. dupl. acc., τὸν δ' οὔ τι π. Il.4.401: abs., 13.768, Od.11.565:—also inf. Med., προσφάσθαι ἔπος 23.106.

**προσ-φθέγγομαι**, Dor. ποτιφθ- *AP*7.656 (Leon.):—*call to, address*, τινα E.*Alc.*331, *Hipp.*1097, *Or.*481, etc.; *salute*, σῆμα *AP* l. c. 2. *call by a name, call* so and so, καὶ πάγον Κρόνου προσεφθέγξατο Pi.*O.*10(11).50; π. μιᾷ κλήσει Pl.*Plt.*287e. II. intr., *sound to, accompany*, [αὐλοί] π. χοροῖς Poll.4.81. **-φθεγκτήριος**, α, ον, *accosting*; δῶρα π. gifts *brought* to a bride *with a salutation*, Id. 3.36. **-φθεγκτός**, ή, όν, Dor. ποτιφθ-, *addressed, saluted*, σοῦ φωνῆς by thy voice, S.*Ph.*1067, cf. *AP*7.649 (Anyt.). **-φθεγμα**, ατος, τό, *address, salutation*, mostly in pl., A.*Ag.*903, *Ch.*876, E.*Ion* 401, etc.: sg., S.*Aj.*500, *Ph.*235; *epithet*, Σαπφοῦς τὸ ἡδὺ π. Philostr. *Im.*2.1.

**προσφθείρομαι**, *meet to one's own* or *another's hurt, meet in an evil hour*, ἥν σοι λοιδορῆται προσφθαρείς if he, *curse him, meet* and insult you, Ar.*Ec.*248; θεούσῃ νηὶ προσφθαρεὶς *mischievously meeting* a ship in full course, Ael.*NA*2.17; θηρίῳ (of a person) προσέφθαρσαι Alciphr.1.32, cf. 34; also, *make an acquaintance in an evil hour*, Plu. 2.482b:—dub. sens. in *POxy.*1100.20 (iii A.D.).

**πρόσφθογγος**, ον, *addressing, saluting*, μῦθοι π. words *of salutation*, A.*Pers.*153 (anap.); π. σοι νόστου βοά ib.935 (lyr.).

**προσφθονέω**, *oppose through envy*, Plu.*Cam.*36; *regard with envy*, Id.*Alex.*33.

**προσφίγγω**, f.l. for προσσφ- in Gal.18(1).350.

**προσφίλ-εια** [ῐ], ἡ, *kindness, goodwill*, δαιμόνων A.*Th.*515. **-έω**, *approach so as to kiss*, οἱ προσφιλοῦντες the *kissers*, late phrase for οἱ ἀμείβοντες the *rafters*, Eust.1327.1. *-ής, ές, (φιλέω) *dear, beloved*, τῶν ἡλίκων.. προσφιλεστάτῳ Hdt.1.123, cf. Th.5.40: c. dat., *dear* or *friendly to*.., Hdt.1.163, S.*Ichn.*78, Pl.*Grg.*507e, etc.: of things, *pleasing, agreeable*, ἔργον θεοῖσι π. A.*Th.*580; στολή, χάρις, S.*Ph.*224 (Sup.), 558; πάσαις ἡλικίαις.. ἡ χρῆσις αὐτῆς (sc. τῆς μουσικῆς) ἐστὶ π. Arist.*Pol.*1340$^a$5; π. ἑκάστῳ.. τὸ κατὰ φύσιν Id.*HA*590$^a$10; τῇ αἰσθήσει Thphr.*Od.*45; also of actions, *lovely*, ὅσα π. *Ep.Phil.*4.8. Adv. -λῶς *agreeably*, c. dat., *OGI*331.9 (Pergam., ii B.C.). II. Act., of persons, *kindly affectioned, well-disposed*, ὥς μ' ἔθεσθε προσφιλῆ S.*Ph.*532, cf. Th.1.92, 7.86. Adv. -λῶς *kindly*, S.*El.*442, Pl.*Lg.*822b; π. ἡμῖν ἔχειν to be *kindly affectioned* to us, X.*HG*2.3.44; π. χρῆσθαί Id.*Mem.*2.3.16: Comp. -έστερον Pl.*Mx.*248d: Sup. -έστατα X.*Eq.Mag.*1.1, -εστάτως Isoc. (s. v. l.) ap. Poll.3.63: poet. προσφιλέως *IG*9(1).235 (Larymna). **-ία**, ἡ, = προσφίλεια, Aq.*Ps.*44 (45).1.

**προσφῐλο-κᾰλέω**, *add from a love of splendour*, ἀναθήματα Str.13. 4.2, cf. 17.1.8. II. abs., of artists, *have a love of beauty*, Ph.1. 495. **-νεικέω**, *vie with* another *in* anything, τισὶ πρός τι Plb.2.19. 6. 2. *cling stoutly to*, τῇ δόξῃ τῇ αὐτοῦ Arist.*Mete.*343$^b$25; *persist in*, πολέμῳ Charito 5.1. 3. *insist, contend*, c. inf., Hld.10.19. 4. abs., J.*BJ*5.11.3, Plu.2.648d. **-πονέω**, *maintain obstinately*, τῇ ἰδίᾳ δόξῃ Phlp. *in Mete.*88.20. **-σοφέω**, *speculate further upon*, ἔτι τῷ λόγῳ Plu.2.669c; ταῦτα π. Luc.*Sat.*9. II. *philosophize in company with* another, c. dat. pers., Id.*Gall.*11, Philostr.*VS*2.1.9: metaph., τῇ ἐρημίᾳ καὶ τῇ δικέλλῃ Luc.*Tim.*6. **-τεχνέω**, *employ further art*, Athenio 1.25; *add by art*, τοῖς καταπήροις ὀνείροις παρ' ἑαυτοῦ τι π. Artem.1.11, cf. Iamb. *in Nic.* p.116 P. (Pass.): c. inf., Arr.*Epict.*2.20.21. II. abs., *cavil*, Ph.2.509. **-τῑμέομαι**, *lavish money* or *enthusiasm upon*, τῇ ῥαθυμίᾳ Ael.*VH*9.9: abs., Ph.1.451, *Ephes.*2.20 (ii A.D.), *IGRom.*4.881.7 (Tacina, iii A.D.), Phalar.*Ep.* 142.2. **-φρονέομαι**, *make affectionate overtures to* a woman, Nic. Dam.47.7 J.

**προσφλεγμαίνω**, *inflame as well*, Paul.Aeg.3.78.

**προσφοιτάω**, *go* or *come to frequently, resort to*, τὸ κουρεῖον, ἵνα οἱ Δεκελεῖς π. Lys.23.3, cf. Id.24.20, D.25.52, Hyp.*Ath.*6, *IG*2$^2$.1237.64; π. τισὶ *associate with*, Str.14.1.32; esp. *go to* a master, D.H.*Rh.*9.11, etc.; τοῖς παλαιοῖς λόγοις Plu.2.653b. II. metaph., *visit*, τὰ κακὰ π. πρὸς τὸ γῆρας Antiph.240.

**προσφορ-ά**, ἡ, (προσφέρω) *bringing to, applying*, τῶν κλιμάκων Plb. 5.16.7; *application, use*, Pl.*Lg.*638c. 2. *presenting, offering*, ib. 792a; οἱ ἄρτοι τῆς π. *shewbread*, Lxx 3*Ki.*7.48. II. (from Pass.) *that which is added, increase*, τῶν ἡμαρτημένων ἄκη μέν ἐστι π. δ' οὐκ ἔστ' ἔτι S.*OC*1270; *bounty, benefit*, ib.581; wedding *present*, Thphr. *Char.*30.19; *offering*, Lxx *Ps.*39(40).7, al., *Act.Ap.*21.26: pl., ib.24. 17, J.*AJ*11.4.1, *Stud.Pal.*1.7.27 (v A.D.), etc.; *offerings* for the dead, *PMonac.*8.5,23 (vi A.D.), *PLond.*5.1708.62 (vi A.D.); *deed of gift*, esp. of *donatio propter nuptias*, Mitteis *Chr.*288.8 (ii A.D.), *PTeb.*351.1 (ii A.D.), *PRyl.*155.20 (ii A.D.). 2. *income, revenue*, Antipho *Fr.* 31, J.*AJ*19.8.2. III. (from Med.) *taking* of food, Arist.*Somn.Vig.* 458$^a$22, *Metaph.*1000$^a$14, Thphr.*HP*7.9.4, 8.4.4, *Od.*5; ἡ τοῦ ὑγροῦ π. Arist.*PA*671$^a$13; πόσεις καὶ -φοραί Plu.2.129e. 2. *food, victuals*, Hp.*Aph.*2.33 (pl.), Thphr.*CP*4.9.6, Orph.*Fr.*49.87. 3. *flavour*, Thphr.*HP*4.8.11, Ath.1.33f; *bouquet*, Thphr.*HP*9.19.1. **-έω**, *bring to, bring in*, τὰ ὅπλα Hdt.1.82; [τὰ δράγματα] X.*HG*7.2. 8. **-ημα**, ατος, τό, = προσφορά III. 2, E.*El.*423. **-ία**, ἡ, Astrol., *approach*, τῶν δεσποτῶν Vett.Val.5.16 (s. v. l.). * **-ος**, Dor. ποτίφ- (q. v.), ον, *serviceable, useful*, τὰ π. τῇ στρατιῇ Hdt.7.20, cf. S.*OC* 1774 (anap.), etc.: abs., ἐκπορίζεσθαι ἃ πρόσφορα ἦν Th.1.125, cf. 7.62. 2. *suitable, fitting*, κόσμος, κόμπος, Pi.*N.*3.31, 8.48, cf. E. *Heracl.*480, etc.; π. καὶ οἰκεῖον Epicur.*Fr.*250 (= Metrod.*Fr.*1 K.): c. dat., Pi.*N.*7.63, E.*Supp.*338, *Hec.*1246, Ar.*V.*809, *Av.*124 (Comp.), prob. in Pi.*N.*9.7; τροφαί Antiph.62; οὐχὶ πρόσφορος ἁμερίῳ γέννᾳ *suitable to, agreeing with*, E.*Ph.*129 (lyr.): c. inf., οὐ πρόσφορον μολεῖν 'tis not *fit* or *meet* to go, A.*Eu.*207, cf. Pi.*O.*9.81, Ocell.4.12; ζῴοις πρόσφορα ἐσθίειν J.*BJ*6.3.3. 3. πρόσφορον, τό, *what is fitting* or *suitable*, Arist.*EN*1180b12; ἡ φύσις αὐτὴ ζητεῖ τὸ π. Id.*HA*615a26: c. gen., μακρᾶς κελεύθου..τὰ π. *attendance meet* after a long journey, A.*Ch*.711, cf. 714; τὰ π. τῆς νῦν παρούσης ξυμφορᾶς E.*Hel*.509: abs., τὰ πρόσφορα *things meet* or *due*, esp. for the dead, Hdt.4.14, E.*Alc.* 148; τὰ π. πάντα Ar.*Pax* 1025 (lyr.): τὰ π. as Adv., *fitly*, E.*Hipp*.112, cf. 1361 (anap.): regul. Adv., -ρως ἔχειν τινί Thphr.*CP*4.7.2, cf. Phld. *Herc*.1457.7. II. πρόσφορα, τά, *that which is taken* or *eaten*, f.l. in Hp.*VM*24; cf. προσφορά III.2. III. πρόσφορα, τά, *revenues, rents*, *PTeb*.88.15 (ii B.C.), *POxy*.1208.22 (iii A.D.), 1829.4 (vi A.D.), etc.; τὰ Ἀριστίππου λεγόμενα π. the place called Aristippus's *Rents*, *PPetr*. 2 p.56 (iii B.C.).

**προσφρᾱγίζω**, *seal beforehand*, *IG*2².1013.66.

**προσ-φῠγή**, ἡ, *refuge, asylum*, *POxy*.135.25 (vi A.D.). 2. = *clientela*, *Gloss.* **-φύγιον** [ῠ], τό, *refuge*, Al. 2*Ki*.19.42(43). **-φῠγος**, ον, *fleeing for refuge*, Aesop.417, v.l. in Hdn.5.3.10.

❋**προσ-φυή**, ἡ, (προσφύω) = πρόσφυσις II, dub. in Arist.*HA*528a 33. 2. pl., *supernumerary teeth*, *Hippiatr*.95. **-φυής**, ές, *firmly attached by growth*, Thphr.*CP*1.6.3; λοβοὶ ὤτων προσφυεῖς *PPetr*.3 p.25; ὄνυχες π. τῇ σαρκί Adam.2.4; opp. προσαρτής, χοιράς Antyll. ap.Orib.45.2.2. 2. *fixed* or *attached to*, θρῆνυν..προσφυέ' ἐξ αὐτῆς [τῆς κλισίης] Od.19.58; τοῖς ὀστέοις Diog.Oen.39: metaph., *inseparable from*, Epicur.*Fr*.200: Comp., *more akin to*, Pl.*Phlb*.64c,67a. Adv. -ῶς, of kissing, Luc.*DMeretr*.3.2. 3. π. τινί *attached* or *devoted to*, ἐδωδαῖς καὶ..ἡδοναῖς Pl.*R*.519b. II. *naturally belonging to*, *suitable* or *fitted for* a thing, τῶν δικαίων π. καὶ συγγενεῖς Id.*Ep.* 344a; τοῖς πράγμασι π. λέξις D.H.*Th*.5; π. τῷ θεῷ ἄγαλμα Hierocl. *in CA* 1 p.421 M.: c. inf., οἰκτίσασθαι -έστατος *most adapted* to move pity, Longin.34.2. Adv. -ῶς, Ion. -έως, προσφυέως λέγειν speak *suitably, ably*, Hdt.1.27, cf. Ph.2.421, al.

**προσφῠλακή**, ἡ, f.l. in Plb.3.75.4, for προφυλ-.

**πρόσφῡμα**, ατος, τό, *excrescence*, of expletives, Demetr.*Eloc*.55 (pl.).

**πρόσφυξ**, ῠγος, ὁ, *one who seeks* or *is under protection*, π. θεοῦ Ph.1. 187, al., Hdn.5.3.10; *client*, Procop.Gaz.*Ep*.72, Sch.Il.9.640; gloss on πρόπολος, Sch.Ar.*Nu*.435.

**προσφῡράω**, *mix in*, Asclep.ap.Gal.13.248.

**προσφύρω** [ῡ], *bedabble*, αἵματι προσέφυρεν αὐτὸν ἡ σφαγὴ τῆς κόρης D.H.11.37.

**προσφῡσάω**, *blow upon*, πρὸς τὰ πρόσωπα Arist.*Mir*.845a22:—Pass., πόλεμος -φυσώμενος ὥσπερ ὑπ' ἀνέμων Plb.11.4.5.

**πρόσφῠσις**, εως, Ion. ιος, ἡ, (προσφύομαι) *growing to*: *clinging to*, of a rider, ἰσχυροτέρα π. a firmer *seat*, X.*Eq*.1.11; of vine to tree, D.H.19.2. II. *ongrowth, attachment* or *point of attachment*, e.g. of the legs to the body, Diog.Apoll.6, Hp.*Art*.45; of the diaphragm to the spine, τῶν φρενῶν ibid.; of the navel in embryos, Arist.*GA* 745b24; of the caudal vertebrae in birds, Id.*IA*710a4; of flowers to spray, leaves to stem, Thphr.*HP*3.16.4, al., 1.10.8, al.: freq. in Arist. of all *after* or *adventitious growths* which do not form part of the organism, ἐν γενέσθαι..προσφύσει *Ph*.227a17; ἡ τοῦ ᾠοῦ π. *GA* 754b12; of zoöphytes, *HA*548b8; *assimilation*, τῆς τροφῆς *Pr*.866b21 (prop., *adhesion* of food to tissues, Gal.*Nat.Fac*.1.11, 3.1); in trees, *growth of new wood*, Thphr.*HP*9.2.6; of a fungus, Id.*Fr*.168.

**προσφῠτεύω**, Dor. fut. 3 sg. ποτιφυτευσεῖ, *plant besides*, *Tab.Heracl.* 1.174.

**πρόσ-φῠτος**, ον, *adherent*, τόνοι Hp.*Art*.45. **-φύω**, with fut. and aor. 1, *cause to grow to*: metaph., καὶ ταῦτ' ἀληθῆ..προσφύσω λόγῳ *will make sure, confirm*, A.*Supp*.276; τοῦτο τῷ νῦν λόγῳ εὖ προσέφυσας Ar.*Nu*.372. II. mostly in Pass., with aor. 2 and pf. Act. and fut. Med., *grow to* or *upon*, σῷ κέρατα κρατὶ προσπεφυκένα E.*Ba*.921, cf. Pl.*R*.611d, *Ti*.45a; σοι ταῦτα προσφύσεται *will accrue*, Id.*Ep*.313d: freq. in Arist. of any *after* or *adventitious growth* which does not form part of the organism, π. τῇ ὑστέρᾳ τὸ ᾠόν, πρὸς τῇ ὑστέρᾳ, *GA*752a11, 754b17; τὰ κέρατα π. μᾶλλον τῷ δέρματι *HA*517a27, cf. Lxx *Da*.7.20; προσπέφυκεν ὥσπερ τὰ φύματα Arist.*GA*772b29; of zoöphytes, *HA*487b11, 588b13; π. ταῖς πέτραις *PA*681b6; of tapeworms, *HA*551a11; of food, *to be assimilated*, *Pr*.864b8, 927a20. b. *to be attached*, πλευραὶ προσπεφύκασι [τοῖς σφονδύλοις, sc. by joints] Hp.*Art*.45. 2. *hang upon, cling to*, τῷ προσφὺς ἐχόμην Od.12.433: abs., προσφῦσα Il.24.213; προσφὺς ὅπως τις ἀναρίτης Herod.*Fr*.11; of a fish, τὠγκίστρῳ ποτεφύετο Theoc.21.46; of leeches, Gal.8.265: metaph., π. τοῖς τοιούτοις *consorts constantly with*, Pl.*Lg*.728b; προσφύντες ἔχονται τοῦ χρυσίου they *cling fast* to it, Luc.*Pisc*.51, cf. *Musc. Enc*.3, etc.

❋**προσφων-έω**, *call* or *speak to, address*, pres. first in A.*Supp*.236: used by Hom. only in impf., the Ep. aor. being προσέειπον, τινα Il.2.22, Od.4.69: abs., 5.159, 10.109, al.: later c. dat. pers., Lxx 1*Es*.2.21, Antig.Rex ap.D.L.7.7, *Ev.Matt*.11.16, *Act.Ap*.22.2: c. dupl. acc., *address* words *to* a person, οὐδέ τί μιν προσεφώνεον Il.1.332, cf. A.*Fr.* 159, E.*Med*.664. 2. *call by name*, ποδαπὸν ὅμιλον τόνδε..προσφωνοῦμεν; A.*Supp*.l.c.; ὀνόματι π. τινά E.*Tr*.942; π. τινὰ βασιλέα *salute* him king, Plb.10.38.3, etc. 3. *issue directions* or *orders*, τινι *PTeb*.27.109 (ii B.C.): abs., folld. by ὅπως, ib.124.21 (ii B.C.):—Pass., *UPZ*106. 20 (ii B.C.). II. c. acc. rei, *pronounce, utter*, τήνδε π. φάτιν S.*El.* 1213; τὰ ὑπογεγραμμένα *IG*7.2713.7 (Acraeph., i A.D.); *address* or *dedicate* a book, τινι Cic.*Att*.16.11.4, Plu.*Luc*.1, Ath.7.313f, etc. 2. *make a report*, *POxy*.475,476 (ii A.D.); περί τινος Wilcken *Chr*.27.15 (ii A.D.): abs., *OGI*572.43 (Myra, ii/iii A.D.). **-ήεις**, Ep. ποτιφωνήεις, εσσα, εν, *addressing, capable of addressing*, Od.9.456. **-ημα**, ατος, τό, *that which is addressed to* another, *address*, S.*OC*891: pl., ib. 325, E.*Alc*.1144. **-ημᾰτικός**, ή, όν, *usual in addressing*, λόγος π. a public oration or address, D.H.*Rh*.5 tit., cf. Sch.E.*Hec*.299. **-ησις**, εως, ἡ, *addressing, address*, Parmenisc.ap.Ath.4.156d (pl.), Phld.*Mort.* 37, D.H.*Rh*.5.1; αἱ πρὸς ἑαυτὸν π. Longin.26.3. 2. *dedication*, Cic.*Att*.13.12.3; συνταγμάτων Onos.*Praef*.1; γραμμάτων Plu.*TG*8 (pl.). 3. *assignment* of property, *PGot*.2.1 (ii A.D.). 4. *report, declaration*, *BGU*647.1 (ii A.D.), etc.; ἔγγραφος π. *PAmh*.2.142.13 (iv A.D.); *official intimation*, *PGrenf*.1.35.6 (ii/i B.C.). **-ητέον**, *one must address*, τί τινι S.E.*M*.1.132. ❋**-ητικός**, ή, όν, = προσφωνηματικός, only in Adv. -κῶς Eust.1410.27.

**προσχαίρω**, *rejoice at*, τινι Lxx *Pr*.8.30, Plu.*Ant*.29.

**προσχάραιος** [ᾰ], ον, Dor. contr. for προ-εσχ-, *offered before the hearth*, θυσία *IG*12(1).792 (Rhodes, iv B.C.).

**προσχᾰρακτηρικῶς**, Adv. *as extension of character*, dub. in Phld. *Lib*. p.6 O.

**προσχᾰρ-ίζομαι**, *gratify* or *satisfy*, τῇ γαστρί X.*Oec*.13.9; *stretch a point in* one's *favour*, *BGU*1141.30 (i B.C.), Luc.*DMeretr*.9.5; *concede the truth of*, τοῖς Θετταλοῖς μυθώδεις λόγους Str.7.7.12. II. *gratify besides*, Ath.Naucr.ap.Ath.5.211b. III. *sacrifice* something *for the sake of* something, τῶν πτερυγωμάτων τι τῇ μήτρᾳ Sor. 2.89. **-ισμός**, ὁ, = Lat. *arrogatio*, *Gloss.*

**προσχάσκω**, aor. προσέχᾰνον: pf. in pres. sense προσκέχηνα:—*gape*, or *stare open-mouthed at* one, μηδὲ..χαμαιπετὲς βόαμα προσχάνῃς ἐμοί *fall* not prostrate before me *with loud cries*, A.*Ag*.920. 2. *gape eagerly at, be greedy for*, τῷ λεγομένῳ προσκεχηνέναι παιδικῶς Plb.4.42.7; τῷ εἴδει τινός J.*AJ*11.3.5, cf. Ph.2.560.

❋**προσχεθεῖν**, aor. of προέχω (v. σχέθω), *hold before*:—Med., *ward off from oneself*, βέλεμνα χειρὶ προεσχεθόμην Theoc.25.254.

**προσχειμάζω**, *winter*, of an army, ἐν.. Polyaen.4.6.11.

**πρόσχειρος**, ον, = πρόχειρος, Phld.*Ir*. p.62 W.

**προσχειρουργέω**, *accomplish in addition*, π. ταῖς εὐχαῖς πολλὰ ἐξ ἐπιστήμης J.*BJ*4.8.3.

**πρόσχερος**, ον, dub. sens., πρόσχερα δὲ ἑκάστῳ δύο κρέα Harmod. 1; προσχέρων β πήχεις νς two πρόσχερα = 56 cubits each, in an account for plastering or whitewashing a bath, *POxy*.2145.7, cf. 10, al. (ii A.D.); cf. πρόσχορος II.

**πρόσχεσις**, *obtentus* (v.l. *obtutus*), *Gloss.*: f.l. for ὑπόσχεσις in Lxx 4*Ma*.15.2.

**προσχέω**, fut. -χεῶ Lxx *Le*.1.5:—*pour to* or *on*, Lxx l.c., al., Luc. *Sacr*.9 (s. v.l.):—Med., *pour* water *on oneself*, Hp.*Steril*.230, Diocl. *Fr*.139; *have poured on one*, τὸ θερμόν Arist.*Somn.Vig*.457b14, cf. *Pr*.875a9:—Pass., Ph.2.242; προσεχύθη πρὸ τῶν οὔρων αἷμα Aret.*SD* 2.3. II. metaph. in Pass., ὑπὸ τοῦ Χρυσίππου προσχυθεὶς ἀδολεσχίας *deluged*, Gal.5.318.

❋**πρόσχημα**, ατος, τό, (προέχω) *that which is held before*: hence, I. *that which is held before to cover, screen, cloak*, τὸ σῶφρον τοῦ ἀνάνδρου π. Th.3.82; *pretence, pretext*, πατὴρ..σοὶ π. ἀεί, ὡς ἐξ ἐμοῦ τέθνηκεν S. *El*.525; τοῦτο π. ποιούμενος Lys.6.37; also π. τοῦ λόγου in the same sense, Hdt.4.167, cf. 6.133: c. gen., αὗται [αἱ πόλεις] π. ἦσαν τοῦ στόλου ib.44; Φίλιππος γίγνεται π. τοῦ πολέμου Plb.11.5.4; τῷ τῆς τέχνης π. *on the ground* of.., D.5.6; π. ποιεύμενος ὡς ἐπ' Ἀθήνας ἐλαύνει making *a pretence* or *show* of marching against Athens, Hdt.7. 157: c. inf., π. ποιούμενοι τοὺς ἐπὶ Θρᾴκης μὴ προδώσειν *pretend* that they will not.., Th.5.30; π. ἦν ἀμύνεσθαι Id.1.96; also π. ποιεῖσθαι or ποιήσασθαί τι to put forward *as a screen* or *disguise*, Pl.*Prt*.316d, e, cf. 317a: πρόσχημα, as acc. abs., *by way of pretext*, Hdt.9.87; καλῶν ὀνομάτων καὶ προσχημάτων μεστή full of fair words and *appearances*, Pl.*R*.495d. 2. *preface*, π. καὶ ἀρχὴ τοῦ λόγου Id.*Hp.Ma*.286a. II. *ornament*, τῆς Ἰωνίης π., of Miletus, Hdt.5.28, cf. Plb.3.15.3; τῆς Ἑλλάδος Str.10.2.3, cf. 11.11.1, Plu.*Alex*.17; τὸ κλεινὸν Ἑλλάδος π. ἀγῶνος, of the Pythian games, S.*El*.682; μετὰ προσχήματος ἀξίου τῆς πόλεως with a *dignity*, D.18.178; τὸ τοῦ γένους π. the *nobility* of his birth, *OGI*470.23 (i B.C./i A.D.); Ἀχιλλέα τιν' ἢ Νιόβην.., π. τῆς τραγῳδίας *the pomp* or *show* of tragedy, Ar.*Ra*.913; Δαρείου τὸ π. his *pomp*, Arist.*Mu*.398a12; of a person, π. ἑαυτῆς (sc. τῆς πόλεως) *IG* 12(7).395.17 (Amorgos). 2. *outward appearance* of a wound, f.l. in Hp.*Ulc*.24; *aspect*, τῆς ὅλης θεουργίας διττόν ἐστι π., τὸ ἱερατικὸν τῶν θεῶν π., Iamb.*Myst*.4.2. 3. *costume, uniform*, *PMasp*.334.12, *PFlor*.288.9 (both vi A.D.).

**προσχημᾰτ-ίζομαι**, Med., *make a pretext*, Apostol.3.33. II. Pass., *to be protruded, become apparent*, of haemorrhoids, Dsc.*Eup*.1. 204. **-ισμός**, ὁ, *outward show*, τιμῆς ἕνεκεν ἢ καὶ π. Gal.*Anim. Pass*.2.2 (nisi leg. πρὸς χρηματισμόν, cf. *Protr*.14).

**προσχίζω**, *slit before* or *in front*, *Gloss.*

**πρόσχισμα**, ατος, τό, a kind of shoe, *slit in front* (ἐσχισμένον ἐκ τῶν ἔμπροσθεν Hsch.), Ar.*Fr*.842. II. *the forepart* of the shoe, *from its being slit*, Arist.*Rh*.1392a31, *Pr*.956b4.

**προσχλευάζω**, *mock* or *jeer besides*, Plb.4.16.4.

**προσχολάζω**, pf. -εσχόλακα, *study formerly with*, τινι Phld.*Ind. Sto*.46.

**προσχόλιον**, τό, *ante-room of a school*, *Gloss.*

❋**πρόσχολος**, ὁ, *assistant schoolmaster*, Aus.*Prof*.22 tit., Aug.*Serm.* 178 No.8, prob. in *Gloss.*

**πρόσχορδος**, ον, (χορδή) *attuned to a stringed instrument*: generally, *in unison with*, ἀποδιδόναι πρόσχορδα τὰ φθέγματα τοῖς φθέγμασι bring voices *into unison with* voices, Pl.*Lg*.812d, cf. Poll.4.58,63.

**προσχορεύω**, *dance to the sound of*, αὐλοῖς Poll.4.81.

**προσχορηγέω**, *supply in addition*, in Pass., *PTeb*.27.57, 61 (*b*).360, al. (ii B.C.).

**πρόσχορος**, ον, *belonging to a chorus*, Ar.*Fr*.843. II. οἶκοι π. perh. *outer, external* rooms, Gal.13.570 (fort. πρόσχεροι).

**προσχόω**, v. προσχώννυμι.

**προσχράομαι**, *use* or *avail oneself of* a thing *besides*, τινι Arist.*Rh*. 1358ᵇ19; but more freq. simply, *use*, τινὶ εἴς τι Pl.*Cra*.435c; χάριν τοῦ σίτου Id.*Criti*.115a; τούτοις ταῦτα Id.*Phlb*.44d: c. dupl. dat., ὥσπερ μάντεσι π. τισί ib.c; [θεράπουσι] πρὸς τὰς διακονίας Arist.*Pol*.1263ᵃ20, cf. *Ph*.200ᵇ19, Lxx *Es*.8.13(16.17), etc.; νόμῳ *BGU*1127.21 (i B.C.):—Pass., τὰ -χρησθέντα *CPHerm*.92.11 (iii A.D.). II. *abuse*, [παιδίσκῃ] dub. sens. in *PSI*4.406.7 (iii B.C.).

**προσχρῄζω**, Ion. -χρηΐζω, *require* or *desire besides*, c. gen., τυραννίδος οὐδεμιῆς π. Hdt.5.11, cf. 18; οὐδὲ σοῦ προσχρῄζομεν S.*Ph*.1055: c. gen. pers. et inf., προσχρηΐζω ὑμέων πείθεσθαι Μαρδονίῳ I *request* you *to* listen to him, Hdt.8.140.β′: c. inf. only, τί προσχρῄζων μαθεῖν; S.*OT*1155, cf. *OC*1168: in poetry with inf. understood, πᾶν ὅπερ προσχρῄζετε (sc. πυθέσθαι) πεύσεσθε A.*Pr*.641, cf. 787, S.*OC*520, 1160, 1202.

**πρόσχρησις**, εως, ἡ, *use in addition*, τοῦ ἡγεμονικοῦ M.Ant.7.5, cf. Procl.*Sacr*. p.149 B.

**προσχρηστέον**, (προσχράομαι) *one must use besides*, μύθῳ Pl.*Lg*. 713a; ἀναλογίᾳ Plu.2.931d.

**προσχρίμπτω**, Ep. ποτι-, *touch, graze*, Orph.*L*.53 (Med.).

**προσχρίω** [ῑ], *apply as salve*, Hp.*Morb*.2.30.

**πρόσχρωμον**, τό, *sample of colour*, *POxy*.1153.23 (i A.D.).

**προσχρώννυμι**, *spread upon*, τοῖς ἐδέσμασι D.S.19.33 (Pass.). II. metaph., Λακεδαιμονίους ὑποπεσόντας..τῷ γραφείῳ προσέχρωσε 'painted them black', Plu.2.859e.

**προσχρῶτα**, Adv. *body to body* (cf. συγχρῶτα), Artem.1.79 (πρόσχρωτα Hercher: v.l. πρὸς χρῶτα).

**πρόσ-χῠσις**, εως, ἡ, *pouring upon, sprinkling*, τοῦ αἵματος *Ep.Hebr*. 11.28. **-χύτης** [ῠ], *profusor*, *Gloss*.

**πρόσχωμα**, ατος, τό, *alluvial deposit*, π. Νείλου, of the Delta of the Nile, A.*Pr*.847; ποταμῶν Str.13.1.36. II. *mound raised for attacking* a city, Lxx 2*Ki*.20.15, al.

**προσχώννῡμι** (Plb.9.41.4, J.*BJ*5.5.1) and -ύω (Thphr.*HP*2.5.5): aor. προσέχωσα Hdt.2.10,99: pf. προσκέχωκα D.S.1.39:—pf. Pass. -κέχωσμαι Thphr.*HP*5.8.3, Palaeph.28: aor. Pass. -εχώσθην *Gp*.2.24. 2:—also **προσχόω**, 3 sg. pres. προσχοῖ Th.2.102:—Pass., impf. προσεχοῦτο ib.75: part. προσχούμενος Arist.*Mete*.351ᵇ7; inf. προσχοῦσθαι ib. 353ᵃ8:—*heap upon*, esp. of water, *deposit* mud, silt, etc.: hence, 1. ταῦτα τὰ χωρία π. *form* these *new* lands *by deposition*, of rivers, Hdt. 2.10: abs., ὁ ποταμὸς προσχοῖ ἀεί continually *forms fresh deposits*, Th. l.c.:—Pass., *to be joined to the land by deposits* of rivers, Thphr.*HP*5.8.3. 2. *choke with mud, silt up*, π. τὰς ἀνωμαλίας *fill up* hollows, *level*, Plb. l.c., cf. Str.6.2.10:—Pass., ἡ θάλαττα ἐξηραίνετο προσχουμένη Arist.*Mete*.351ᵇ7, cf. 353ᵃ8. II. *throw earth upon*, J. l.c.; ἵνα αἱ ῥίζαι προσχωσθῶσι *Gp*.2.24.2; also, *raise mounds against*, μέρη τῆς πόλεως Dius ap.J.*AJ*8.5.3; *form by a dam*, τὸν.. ἀγκῶνα τοῦ Νείλου Hdt.2.99:—Pass., ᾗ προσεχοῦτο where *earth was being raised up against it*, Th.2.75. III. generally, *heap up*, in Pass., ὄρος ἐξ οὗ ἡ..ὕλη -κέχωσται Palaeph.28.

* **προσχωρ-έω**, fut. -ήσω Th.2.2,79; also -ήσομαι Id.8.48, X.*HG*7.4. 16, Pl.*R*.539a:—*go to, approach*, c. dat., προσεχώρεον πλησιαιτέρω τὸ στρατόπεδον τῷ στρατοπέδῳ Hdt.4.112, cf. Th.3.32, Epicur.*Nat*.2.3: abs., opp. ἀπιέναι, X.*Mem*.4.3.8. II. *come* or *go over to, join*, [τῷ Ἑλληνικῷ ἔθνεϊ] Hdt.1.58, cf. 7.235; τῷ Μήδῳ Th.1.74, cf. 2. 2, etc.; πρός τινα Hdt.4.120, Th.3.61, D.13.20: abs., Th.2.79, 3.7, 52, al.; also π. ἐς ὁμολογίην Hdt.7.156; ὁμολογίᾳ Th.1.117, 2.100; π. Ἀθηναίοις ἐς ξυμμαχίαν Id.1.103; πρὸς ὁποῖον βίον ἄλλον..προσχωρήσεται to what other sort of life *he will give himself up*, Pl. l.c. 2. *side with, support*, οὐκ ἐθέλει οὐδὲ ὁ θεὸς προσχωρέειν πρὸς τὰς ἀνθρωπηΐας γνώμας Hdt.8.60.γ′; πρός τινας Id.9.55; τούτοισι Id.5.45; *comply with*, τοῖσδε π. λόγοις S.*Ph*.964; π. πόλει E. *Med*.222. 3. *approach*, i.e. *agree with, be like*, τὰ νόμαια Θρήϊξι προσκεχωρήκασι Hdt.4.104; γλῶσσαν πρὸς τὸ Καρικὸν ἔθνος Id.1. 172. 4. of funds, *to be applied*, εἰς συνωνὴν πυροῦ *POxy*.909.20 (iii A.D.). 5. μὴ προσχωρηθέντος written in error for μήποτε χωρισθέντος in *UPZ*35.17 (ii B.C., cf. 36.15). **-ησις**, εως, ἡ, *approach*, v.l. for προχ- in Pl.*Ti*.40c (pl.). II. *surrendering, joining*, Men.Prot.p.102 D. **-ιος**, ον, = πρόσχωρος, Str.15.1.70, J.*AJ*11.4. 1, Paus.2.18.1. **-ος**, ον, (χώρα) *lying near, neighbouring*, τόπος A.*Pers*.273, S.*OT*1127; ξένοι Id.*OC*493; τοῖχοι *OGI*483.120 (Pergam.). II. Subst., *neighbour*, Hdt.9.15, S.*OC*1065 (lyr.), Th.8. 11, Pl.*Lg*.737d, Arist.*Pol*.1269ᵇ6, *IG*2².1364 (i A.D.). 2. πρόσχωρος, ἡ, *frontier*, *BCH*55.43 (Odessus, i B.C.).

**πρόσχωσις**, εως, ἡ, = πρόσχωμα I, αἱ νῆσοι..τῆς π. σύνδεσμοι γίγνονται Th.2.102; πᾶσα [Αἴγυπτος]..π. οὖσα τοῦ Νείλου Arist.*Mete*.351ᵇ 30, cf. 352ᵃ4, 353ᵃ2, Str.1.2.30, *BGU*656.7 (ii A.D.). 2. *process of silting up*, Str.1.2.29: pl., Id.7.3.6. II. *mound raised against* a place, Th.2.77. 2. *ramp of earth*, π. [τῷ βωμῷ] κατὰ πρανοῦς γενομένης J.*AJ*4.8.5, cf. *PRein*.52ᵇ.26 (iii A.D.).

**πρόσ-ψαυσις**, εως, ἡ, *touching*, Steph. *in Hp*.1.98 D. **-ψαύω**, Dor. and poet. ποτι-, *touch upon, touch*, τιμαῖς Pi.*Fr*.121.3: c. gen., Ael.*NA*1.57: abs., S.*Ph*.1054, *OC*329; ὅσον γ' ἂν αὐτὸς μὴ ποτιψαύων χεροῖν Id.*Tr*.1214:—Pass., Dsc.*Eup*.1.167.

**προσψεύδομαι**, *add falsely*, D.S.14.65, J.*BJ*4.4.1; πλάσματα τῇ Λιβυκῇ παραλίᾳ Str.17.3.3.

**προσψηφ-ίζομαι**, Dor. ποτιψᾱφ- *Supp.Epigr*.3.674 *A* 18 (Rhodes, ii B.C.):—*vote besides*, τινὰ εἴργεσθαι τῆς ἀγορᾶς Lys.6.24; Καίσαρι πενταετίαν App.*BC*2.18, cf. D.C.37.31, etc.: c. inf., π. τὴν σύγκλητον ὀμόσαι πᾶσαν Plu.*Cat.Mi*.32:—Pass., προσεψηφίσθη *it was also voted*, c. acc. et inf., D.C.56.28; τὰ προσεψηφισμένα, τὰ προσψηφισθησόμενα, *Inscr.Magn*.92ᵇ.15, 101.89. **-ισμα**, ατος, τό, *addition, rider to a decree*, Sch.Hermog. in Rh.4.818 W. (pl.).

**προσψῐθῠρίζω**, *whisper, chirp, whistle to*, τί τινι *AP*5.151 (Mel.), cf. Plu.2.505c, Porph.*VP*24.

**προσψύχω** [ῡ], of wind, *blow cold*, f.l. in Hp.*Mul*.2.133. II. *shiver at* or *beside*, τί μάτην κενεῷ προσψύχετε (or πρὸς ψ.) τύμβῳ; *Epigr.Gr*.292.5 (Heraclea ad Latmum).

**πρόσω**, Ep., Ion., Pi., Trag. (but f.l. for πρὸ ἔω in Th.4.103); poet. **πρόσσω**; also **πόρσω**, Pi., Trag.; later Att. **πόρρω** Pl., X., Com., Oratt. (πρόσω should be restored in S.*Fr*.858.3 and πόρσω in E.*Rh*.482): Th. never uses the word.—Regul. Comp. and Sup. προσωτέρω, πορρωτέρω, προσωτάτω, πορρωτάτω, v. προσωτέρω: poet. Comp. πόρσιον Pi.*O*.1.114: Sup. πόρσιστα Id.*N*.9.29. Adv.: (πρό).

A. abs.: I. of Place, generally with a notion of motion, *forwards, onwards*, π. ἄγειν, φέρειν, Il.18.388, Od.9.542, etc.; [δοῦρα] ὄρμενα πρόσσω Il.11.572; ἵπποι πρόσσω μεμαυῖαι ib.615; πρόσω ἵεσθε 12.274, etc.; π. πᾶς πέτεται 16.265; π. κατέκυψε ib.611; π. ἀΐξας 17. 734; π. τετραμμένος αἰεί ib.598; νέμεσθαι π. Hdt.3.133; παραγγεῖλαι, πέμψαι π., A.*Ag*.294,853; βῆναι, ἕρπειν π., S.*Tr*.195,547; μὴ πόρσω φωνεῖν speak no *further*, Id.*El*.213 (lyr.); μηκέτι πάπταινε πόρσιον Pi.*O*.1.114: with Art., πορεύεσθαι αἰεὶ τὸ πρόσω Hdt.7.30, cf. 9.57; also ἰέναι τοῦ π. X.*An*.1.3.1; ᾔιε αἰεὶ ἐς τὸ π. Hdt.3.25. II. of Distance, *far off*, παπταίνειν τὰ πόρσω Pi.*P*.3.22; ἐγγὺς παρεστὼς καὶ πρόσω δ' ἀποστατῶν A.*Eu*.65; ὡς ἀπ' ὀμμάτων, πρόσω S.*OC*15; πρόσω λεύσσειν to see *at a distance*, Id.*Fr*.858.3; πόρρω ποι ἀπεσκοποῦμεν Pl.*R*.432e; ἐγγύς, οὐ πρόσω βεβηκώς E.*Ph*.596; ἡ δέ γ' Εὔβοια.. παρατέταται μακρὰ πόρρω πάνυ Ar.*Nu*.212; εἴτ' ἐγγύς, εἴτε πόρρω Pl. *Prt*.356e; πόρρω που ἐκτὸς ὄντι Id *R*.499c, etc.; πόρρω ποιεῖν τι leave *at a distance*, Anaxil.22.18, cf. Herod.6.90 (dub.); πάνυ π. γενέσθαι X.*Cyr*.4.3.16; τὰ σκέλη κινεῖν ταχὺ καὶ π., of a runner, Arist.*Rh*. 1361ᵇ24; οἱ πόρρω βάρβαροι Id.*EN*1149ᵃ11. 2. *too far*, καὶ νῦν ἴσως πόρρω ἀποτενοῦμεν [τὸν λόγον] Pl.*Grg*.458b; οὐ πόρρω ἐθελήσαιμ' ἂν πιεῖν Id.*Smp*.176d. 3. *in front*, τὰ π. μέρη Gal.16.680, cf. 15.141, 18(2).265. III. of Time, *forward*, πρόσσω καὶ ὀπίσσω, v. ὀπίσω II; χρόνος..ἰὼν πόρσω Pi.*O*.10(11).55; of continuance, A. *Eu*.747; *hereafter*, Pi.*P*.3.111; ἀναβάλλομαι ὡς πόρσιστα *as late as possible*, Id.*N*.9.29; ἤδη πόρρω τῆς ἡμέρας οὔσης *far spent*, Aeschin.3. 122; μέχρι πόρρω till *late*, Arist.*HA*581ᵃ26.

B. c. gen.: I. of Place, *further into*, π. τοῦ ποταμοῦ προβαίνειν X.*An*.4.3.28, cf. Hp.*Mul*.1.2: esp. metaph., προβήσεσθαι πόρρω μοχθηρίας will go *far* in wickedness, X.*Ap*.30; π. ἀρετῆς ἀνήκειν to have reached *a high point* of virtue, Hdt.7.237; οὕτω πόρρω σοφίας ἥκεις Pl.*Euthd*.294e; πόρρω σοφίας ἐλαύνειν Id.*Euthphr*.4b, cf. *Grg*.486a, *Cra*.410e, *Ly*.204b; π. τέχνης a *past* master, Ar. *V*.192 (v. infr. II); π. πάνυ ἐλάσαι τῆς πλεονεξίας X.*Cyr*.1.6.39: also with Art., προβήσομαι ἐς τὸ π. τοῦ λόγου Hdt.1.5; ἐς τὸ π. οὐδὲν προεκόπτετο τῶν πρηγμάτων Id.3.56; ἐς τὸ π. μεγάθεος τιμῶνται are honoured *to a high point* of greatness, i.e. very greatly, ib. 154. II. of Distance, *far from*, οὐ π. τοῦ Ἑλλησπόντου Id.5. 13; οὐ π. Σπάρτης πόλις E.*Andr*.733; στάντες οὐ πόρρω τῶν βωμῶν Pl.*Lg*.800d, cf. X.*An*.3.2.22, etc.: metaph., π. δικαίων A.*Eu*.414; πόρρω τέχνης, = οὐκ ἀπὸ τέχνης, i.e. φύσει, Ar.*V*.192 (acc. to Sch., sed v. supr. B. I); π. τοῦ χειρίσματος Hp.*Art*.11; οὐκέτι πόρρω διθυράμβων φθέγγομαι Pl.*Phdr*.238d; πόρρω που τῶν ἐμαυτῷ πεπολιτευμένων *far below* them, D.18.299; πόρρω εἶναι τοῦ οἴεσθαι Pl.*Phd*.96e; πόρρω τῶν πραγμάτων Isoc.4.16; πόρρω τοῦ διαφθείρειν Id.15.240; πόρρω λίαν τῆς ὑποθέσεως ἀποπλανηθῆναι Id.7.77; π. σαρκός *very far* (i.e. different) *from*, Arist.*HA*504ᵇ11, cf. Pl.*R*.581e: also folld. by ἀπό, ἐξαναχωρέειν π. ἀπὸ τῶν φορτίων Hdt.4.196; πάνυ πόρρω ἀπὸ τῆς θαλάσσης Antipho 5.27; ἀπὸ τοῦ τείχους X.*Cyr*.5.4.49; also οὕτω πόρρω εἶ περὶ τοῦ δικαίου so *far out* in your notions of right, Pl.*R*. 343c. III. of Time, ὡς πρόσω ἦν τῆς νυκτός *far into* the night, Hdt.2.121.δ′; ὡς π. τῆς νυκτὸς προελήλατο Id.9.44; διαλέγεσθαι πόρρω τῶν νυκτῶν Pl.*Smp*.217d; λίαν π. ἔδοξε τῶν νυκτῶν εἶναι Id. *Prt*.310c; ἐκάθευδον μέχρι π. τῆς ἡμέρας X.*HG*7.2.19; βιότου πόρσω E.*Alc*.910 (lyr.); π. ἤδη ἐστὶ τοῦ βίου, θανάτου δὲ ἐγγύς Pl.*Ap*.38c; ὀψὲ καὶ π. τῆς ἡλικίας Plu.*Dem*.2. 2. οὐ π. ἑπτὰ ἡμερέων not *longer than*.., Hp.*Epid*.4.38.

**προσώδης**, ες, (ὄζω) *smelling, stinking*, Hp.ap.Gal.19.133 (Comp.).

**προσῳδής**, ές, (οἰδάω) *swollen*, cited fr. Hp.*Int*. by Gal.19.133 (Comp.).

**προσῳδία**, ἡ, (ᾠδή) *song sung to instrumental music*, = ᾠδὴ πρὸς κιθάραν, Critias 57, cf. Choerob. in Sch.D.T.p.124 H., Hsch., Phot., etc. 2. = προσφώνησις I, A.*Fr*.299. II. *variation in pitch* of the speaking voice, φθόγγοι καὶ π. tones and *voice-modulations*, Pl.*R*.399a. 2. *pronunciation* of a syllable *on a certain pitch*, Arist.*SE*166ᵇ1, 177ᵇ3 (where Uhlig ad D.T. (index) cj. ὀρός for ὅρος, cf. infr. 3), *Po*.1461ᵃ 22; τὸ δασύνειν ἢ ψιλοῦν ἢ ταῖς π. ἑτέρως τῆς συνηθείας ἐκφέρειν Phld. *Rh*.1.155 S., cf. Str.9.2.20, D.H.*Comp*.11,19, Plu.2.439d, Hermog. *Stat*.2; ἀναγνωστέον κατὰ προσῳδίαν D.T.629.15; Dionysius..Thrax ..tres [prosodias]..tradidit.., βαρεῖαν ὀξεῖαν περισπωμένην *Gramm. Lat*. iv p.529 K.; prosodiam ibi esse dicimus ubi aut sursum est aut deorsum, ib.p.531 K.; περὶ καθολικῆς π., title of work by Hdn.Gr., Hdn.Gr.2.924. 3. more generally, to include other normally unwritten differences of pronunciation, viz. quantity and breathing, οὐ δύο μόνον ὑπειλήφασιν εἶναι προσῳδίας γραμματικῶν παῖδες, τὴν τε μακρὰν καὶ βραχεῖαν, ἀλλὰ καὶ ὀξεῖαν βαρεῖαν περισπωμένην δασεῖαν ψιλὴν S.E.*M*.1.113, cf. Theon.*Prog*.13, Choerob. in Sch.D.T.p.124 H.; so Gal.14.583,591 understands Arist.*SE*177$^b$3. **4.** written marks indicating the above differences of pronunciation, αὐτὸς ὁ χαρακτὴρ τῶν τόνων καὶ τῶν χρόνων καὶ τῶν πνευμάτων, οἷον ´ ` ^ ‒ ˘ ⊢ ⊣, Choerob. l. c. **5.** improperly of the πάθη (cf. πάθος IV. 2c), Id.ib.p.125 H.

**προσῳδιακός**, f.l. for προσοδιακός in D.H.*Comp*.4 (v.l. -ῳδικός), Ath.14.631d, Sch.Ar.*Nu*.651.

**προσῴδιον**, f.l. for προσόδιον in Procl.ap.Phot.*Bibl*.p.320 B.

**προσῳδός**, όν, (ᾠδή) *singing* or *sounding in accord, harmonious*, μέλος E.*Fr*.631 (lyr.); ὑμνεῖτο δ' αἰσχρῶς.. οὐ προσῳδὰ *Com.Adesp*. 1203.6, cf. Plu.2.443a, Poll.4.58. **2.** metaph., π. στοναχὰ E.*Ph*. 1498 (lyr.): c. dat., π. ἡ τύχη τὠμῷ πάθει Id.*Ion* 359; τῷ νόμῳ π. Plu. 2.138b.

**πρόσωθεν**, Att. **πόρρωθεν**, Dor. **πόρσωθεν** Archyt.1, Ep. **πρόσσοθεν** Il.23.533: Adv. (πρόσω):—*from afar*, opp. ἐγγύθεν, ἐλαύνων πρόσσοθεν ἵππους Il. l. c.; πρόσωθεν βαλεῖν, προσδέρκεσθαι, A.*Ag*.947, 952; κλύειν Id.*Eu*.297, cf. 397; στείχειν S.*Aj*.723; οὐ ταὐτὸν εἶδος φαίνεται τῶν πραγμάτων, πρόσωθεν ὄντων ἐγγύθεν θ' ὁρωμένων E.*Ion* 586; πόρρωθεν ἀσπάζεσθαι, ἀναγνῶναι, etc., Pl.*Chrm*.153b, *R*.368d, etc.:—Comp. **πορρωτέρωθεν**, *from a more distant point*, σκοπεῖν Isoc. 4.23, cf. 6.16, 12.120, 16.4, Thphr.*Sud*.4. **2.** *distantly*, in sense, D.L.7.16. **II.** of Time, *from long ago*, E.*Hipp*.831 (lyr.), Pl. *Chrm*.155a, D.10.46, etc.

**προσωθέω**, *push to* or *towards*, Hp.*Morb*.1.8 (v.l. προ-), Lxx 2*Ma*. 13.6, *Gp*.17.19.4; freq. v.l. for προωθέω, as in Plb.1.48.8, D.S.20. 95.

**προσωνέομαι**, *buy besides*, X.*Vect*.4.7; f.l. for πρὸς ὠνεῖσθαι in D. 27.32.

⊛ **προσωνῠμ-ία**, Ion. -ίη, ἡ, *surname*, Hp.*Morb.Sacr*.1, Dsc.2.142, 3.3, Plu.*Per*.8,39, Gal.6.778, D.C.41.39, etc. **II.** *right of placing one's name at the head of an order*, *BCH*51.220 (Thasos, pl.). **-ος**, ον, = ἐπώνυμος, *IG*4$^2$(1).84.29 (Epid., i A.D.).

**προσωπαιδοῦντες**· ἐπιβεβαιοῦντες, Hsch. (leg. προσεμπεδοῦντες).

**προσώπ-ατα**, v. πρόσωπον. **-εῖον**, τό, *mask*, Thphr.*Char*.6.3, Dsc.3.144 (v.l. -ποις), Lxx 4*Ma*.15.15, Arr.*Epict*.1.29.41, al., Luc. *Nigr*.11, *Tim*.27; τὸ γῆρας φέρει π., i.e. wears an *ugly aspect*, *CIG* 3902r (Eumenia); ἐν τῷ Σόλωνος π. to do a thing under the *mask*, in the *person*, of Solon, Plu.2.857f. **-η**· πρόσοψις, Hsch. **-ιάς**, v. προσώπιον. **-ίδιον**, τό, Dim. of πρόσωπον, Ar.*Fr*.264, *Stud.Pal*. 22.56.23 (iii A.D.), Maria ap.Zos.Alch.p.157 B. ⊛ **-ικῶς**, Adv. *in respect of grammatical person*, Choerob. *in Theod*.2.29 H. ⊛ **-ιον**, τό, = προσωπεῖον, *IG*7.303.68 (Oropus, iii B.C.). **II.** = ἄρκιον, Dsc. 4.106: also fem. **προσωπίς**, ίδος, ibid.; **προσωπιάς**, Id.*Eup*.2.119 (s.v.l.); ⊛ **προσωπῖτις**, *Gp*.5.48.4.

**προσωπο-ληπτέω**, (v. πρόσωπον I. 1) *to be a respecter of persons*, *Ep.Jac*.2.9. **-λήπτης**, ου, ὁ, *respecter of persons*, *Act.Ap*.10. 34. **-ληψία**, ἡ, *respect of persons*, *Ep.Rom*.2.11, *Ep.Col*.3.25, *Ep. Jac*.2.1 (pl.).

⊛ **πρόσωπον**, τό: pl. πρόσωπα, Ep. (Aeol. acc. to Sch.Il.7.212) προσώπατα Od.18.192, *AP*5.230 (Maced.), Opp.*C*.1.419, etc.; dat. προσώπασι Il.7.212: a masc. nom. πρόσωπος is cited from Pl.Com.250:—*face, countenance* (cf. μέτωπον), Hom., always in pl., even of a single person, Il.7.212, 18.414, Od.19.361, al. (exc. Il.18.24), and so in Hes. *Op*.594 (v.l. -πον), S.*Fr*.871.6 (v.infr.), *El*.1277 (lyr.), *OC*314, X.*An*. 2.6.11 (dub.), *AP*9.322 (Leon.): sg. in *h.Hom*.10.2, 31.12, and usu. in later writers; π. κλιθὲν προσώπῳ Simon.37.12; εἰς π. βλέπειν E. *Hipp*.280; ἐς π. τινὸς ἀφικέσθαι come before him, ib.720; π. πρός τινα στρέφειν Id.*Ph*.457; οὐκ ὄψεσθε τὸ π. μου Lxx *Ge*.43.3, cf. *UPZ* 70.5 (ii B.C.); κατὰ πρόσωπον *in front, facing*, Th.1.106, X.*Cyr*.1.6. 43, etc.; τὴν κατὰ π. τῆς ἀντίας φάλαγγος τάξιν ib.6.3.35; κατὰ π. Αἰγύπτου *facing, fronting* Egypt, Lxx *Ge*.25.18; opp. κατὰ νώτου, Plb. 1.28.9; κατὰ π. ἄγειν, opp. κατὰ κέρας ὑπεραίρειν, Id.11.14.6, etc.; κατὰ π. *in person*, ἡ κατὰ π. ἔντευξις Plu.*Caes*.17; κατὰ π. παραμυθήσασθαι, opp. διὰ τοῦ ψαφίσματος, *IG*4$^2$(1).86.22 (Epid.); so κατὰ πρόσωπα Eudox.*Ars* 11.21; also πρὸς τὸ π. X.*Cyn*.10.9; ἐπὶ προσώπου Ἰεριχώ *in front of* Jericho, Lxx *De*.34.1; ἔρρ' ἐκ προσώπου Herod. 8.59; ἀπὸ π. τῆς γῆς Lxx *Am*.9.8; βλέπειν εἰς π. τινὸς regard his *countenance*, *Ev.Matt*.22.16: usu. of the face of man or God, as λειτουργῶν τῷ π. Κυρίου Lxx 1*Ki*.2.11; οἱ ἄρτοι τοῦ π., of shewbread, ib.21.6: of the ibis, Hdt.2.76; of dogs, ἀπὸ τῶν π. φαιδραί X.*Cyn*.4. 2; of horses, Arist.*HA*631$^a$5; of deer, ib.579$^a$2; of fish, Anaxandr. 30,33.16; *face* of the moon, S.*Fr*.871.6 (pl.), Plu.2.920b: metaph., ἀργυρωθεῖσαι πρόσωπα.. ἀοιδαί Pi.*I*.2.8. **2.** *front, façade*, Id.*P*.6. 14, cf. E.*Ion* 189 (lyr., pl.); κατὰ π. τοῦ ἱεροῦ, τῆς νεώς, *PPetr*.3 p.2 (iii B.C.), Ach.Tat.3.1, 2; τιθέναι τὰς φιάλας ἐπὶ πρόσωπον Asclep.Myrl. ap.Ath.11.501d. **II.** *one's look, countenance*, A.*Ag*.639,794 (anap., pl.), *Eu*.990 (anap., pl.), etc.; οὐ τὸ σὸν δείσας π. S.*OT*448: metaph., φαίνοισα π. Ἀλάθεια Pi.*N*.5.17. **2.** Astrol., decan considered as the *domain* of a planet, ἐν ἰδίοις π. Vett.Val.62.21, Paul. Al.*C*.2. **III.** = προσωπεῖον, *mask*, D.19.287 (-εῖον is v.l.), Arist. *Po*.1449$^a$36, $^b$4, *Pr*.958$^a$17, Dsc.3.144 (v.l.), Poll.2.47; π. ὑπάργυρον κατάχρυσον *IG*1$^2$.276.6, cf. 4$^2$(1).102.58,68 (Epid., iv B.C.), *Clara Rhodos* 6/7.428; ὀθόνινον π. prob. in Pl.Com.142; π. περίθετον Aristomen.5; of the Roman *imagines*, Plb.6.53.5; *bust* or *portrait*, *Sammelb*.5221, *OGI*432.1 (Naksh-i-Rustam, iii A.D.). **2.** *dramatic part, character*, Phld.*Rh*.1.199 S., Arr.*Epict*.1.29.45 and 57; κωφὸν π. Cic.*Att*.13.19.3; *character* in a book, τὸ τῆς Ἑλλάδος ὄνομα καὶ π. Plb.8.11.5; τὸ τοῦ Ὀδυσσέως π. Id.12.27.10, cf. Phld.*Po*.5.32; also ἀστοχεῖν τοῦ π., of an author, Callisth.44 J.; ἐπὶ προσχήματι καὶ π. δικαστῶν Ael.*Fr*.168. **IV.** *person*, Phld.*Rh*.1.52 S. (pl.); ἀδίκως μὴ κρῖνε πρόσωπον Ps.-Phoc.10; προσώπῳ, οὐ καρδίᾳ *in person*, *in bodily presence*, 1*Ep.Thess*.2.17, cf. 2*Ep.Cor*.5.12; ποιεῖν or πληροῦν τὸ π. τινός to represent a *person*, *PRein*.56.30 (iv A.D.), *Sammelb*. 6000 ii 12 (vi A.D.); λαμβάνειν π. τινός admit a *person* to one's presence, εἰ προσδέξεταί σε, εἰ λήψεται πρόσωπόν σου Lxx *Ma*.1.8; hence, = προσωποληπτεῖν, *Ev.Luc*.20.21, *Ep.Gal*.2.6; μὴ ἀποστρέψῃς τὸ π. μου, i.e. do not reject my prayer, Lxx 3*Ki*.2.20; θαυμάσαι π. ἀσεβοῦς ib.*Pr*.18.5; ὁ θεὸς ὁ μέγας.., ὅστις οὐ θαυμάζει π. οὐδὲ οὐ μὴ λάβῃ δῶρον ib.*De*.10.17. **2.** *legal personality*, Bion Borysth.ap.D.L.4. 46. **3.** Gramm., *person*, D.T.638.4, A.D.*Pron*.3.12, etc.; γυναικεῖα π. Alex.Trall.2. **4.** π. πόλεως a *feature* of the city, of a person, Cic.*Fam*.15.17.2. **5.** f.l. in Zeno *Stoic*.1.23 (cf. Nicol.*Prog*. p.4 F.).

**προσωπο-ποιέω**, *compose by means of* πρόσωπα III. 2, διάλογον π. *dramatize* a dialogue, D.H.*Th*.37. **2.** Med., *identify* a person, Olymp.Alch.p.80 B. **-ποιία**, ἡ, *dramatization, the putting of speeches into the mouths of characters*, Phld.*Po*.5.12 (pl.), D.H.*Vett. Cens*.3.1, Demetr.*Eloc*.265, Marcellin.*Vit.Thuc*.38, Herm. *in Phdr*. p.182 A.; opp. ἠθοποιία, Hermog.*Prog*.9. **II.** *the putting of imaginary speeches into one's own* or *another's mouth* ('I should have said..', 'your father would have said..'), Id.*Inv*.3.10,15, Charis. p.284 K., Rutil.2.6. **III.** *change of grammatical person*, A.D. *Adv*.131.16. **-ποιός**, ὁ, *mask-maker*, *Com.Adesp*.332.

**πρόσωπος**, ὁ, = πρόσωπον, τό (q. v.).

**προσωποῦττα**, ἡ, contr. for προσωπόεσσα, *vessel with a face*, Polem. Hist.94, Poll.2.48.

⊛ **προσωρεύω**, *heap up before*, App.*BC*1.69 (Pass.).

**προσωτέρω**, Att. **πορρωτέρω** (πορρώτερον v.l. in Arist.*Mu*.397$^b$ 35; late **προσώτερον**, Iamb.*Myst*.5.9), Comp. of πρόσω, *further on*, ἔτι π. Hdt.2.175, 4.7; ἐπιδιώκειν ἔτι π. Id.8.111; π. ἀπεῖναι Hp.*Art*. 46; αἱ πορρ. πόλεις the *more distant*, Plb.5.34.8: c. gen., *further than*, Hdt.4.16, etc.; πορρ. τοῦ καιροῦ X.*HG*7.5.13; π. εἰπεῖν τούτων Hdt. 6.124; πορρ. τοῦ δέοντος Pl.*R*.562d; πορρ. τῶν τριτείων Id.*Phlb*.22e: also with the Art., τὸ προσωτέρω πορεύεσθαι, πλέειν, Hdt.1.105, 3.45, etc.; τὸ π. τούτων Id.2.103. **2.** *further from*, τῶν πυλῶν Plu. *Cam*.4. **II.** Sup. **προσωτάτω** (**προσώτατα** Hdt.2.103, S.*El*.391), Att. **πορρωτάτω**, *furthest*, ἀποπτύουσιν ὡς δύνανται πορρωτάτω X. *Mem*.1.2.54; ὅτι π. ταχθέντες Id.*Cyr*.2.1.11; τὰ προσωτάτω *when furthest distant*, Hdt.4.43; προσώτατα ἀπικέσθαι Id.2.103; δραμοῦσα τοῦ προσωτάτω S.*Aj*.731; ὅπως ἀφ' ὑμῶν ὡς προσώτατ' ἐκφύγω *as far as possible*, Id.*El*.391. **2.** c. gen., *furthest from*, ὅτι πορρωτάτω τοῦ βουλευομένου κατοικοῦν Pl.*Ti*.70e; ἐμαυτὸν ὡς πορρωτάτω ποιῆσαι τῶν ὑποψιῶν Isoc.3.37; also ὡς πορρ. ἀπὸ τῆς πόλεως Id.17.19.

**προσωφελ-έω**, *help, assist besides, contribute to assist*, τινας Hdt.9. 68; σε *PSI*4.400.5 (iii B.C.): c. dat., Hdt.9.103, E.*Alc*.41, *Heracl*. 330: abs., ib.34, D.H.8.74; μέγα π. ἐς τὸ εὔσαρκον *contribute to* it, Hp.*Art*.53:—Pass., ὁ βραχίων τι προσωφελεῖται ἐς εὐσαρκίην *gains* something towards it, ibid. **-ημα**, ατος, τό, *help* or *aid in* a thing, c. gen., παισὶν.. π. χρημάτων E.*Med*.611. **-ησις**, εως, ἡ, *help, aid*, S.*Ph*.1406 (troch.). **-ητέον**, *one must assist*, X.*Ages*.11.8.

**πρόταγμα**, ατος, τό, *the van*, D.S.19.27, Plu.*Luc*.27.

**προταινί** [ῑ], Adv. *in front of*, π. τάξεων E.*Rh*.523 (Boeot. acc. to Parmeniscus ap.Sch.): Boeot. **προτηνί**, = πρότερον, *IG*7.1739.14 (Thespiae, iv/iii B.C.), 2406.6 (Thebes).

**προταίνιον**· πρὸ μικροῦ, Hsch.; also, = παλαιόν, Id.

**προ-τακτέον**, (προτάσσω) *one must place in front* or *before*, X.*Mem*. 3.1.10; π. τῆς τριάδος τὸ ἕν Dam.*Pr*.44. **2.** *one must prefer*, τί τινος Aeschin.3.170. **-τακτικός**, ή, όν, *used as prefix*, φωνήεντα D.T.631.7; στοιχεῖα, συλλαβή, A.D.*Synt*.7.5,7; σύνδεσμος, opp. ὑποτακτικός, ib.306.6; ἄρθρον π. the *prepositive* article, ὁ, ἡ, τό, Trypho ap. eund. *Synt*.306.15; π. θέσις A.D.*Adv*.180.7. Adv. -κῶς, opp. ὑποτακτικῶς, Id.*Synt*.227.15, cf. Syrian. *in Metaph*.164.22. **-τακτος**, ον, or **προτακτός**, όν, *posted in front*, οἱ π. *the van*, Plu.*Cam*.41, *Crass*. 23, etc.

**προτᾰλαιπωρέομαι**, *suffer beforehand*, Poll.6.139:—Act. is v.l. in Th.2.53.

**προτᾰμιεῖον**, τό, *room before a storeroom*, X.*HG*5.4.6.

**προτᾰμιεύω**, *lay in beforehand*, Luc.*Salt*.61.

**προτάμνω**, Ion. for προτέμνω.

**προτᾰν-εία**, ἡ, alternative Attic form of πρυτανεία, *IG*2$^2$.1672.6,8; also **προτανέα**, ib.11. **-εύω**, alternative Attic form of πρυτανεύω, ib.656.6. **-ήϊον**, Aeol., = πρυτ-, *Milet*.3 p.371 (ii B.C.). ⊛ **-ις**, Aeol. for πρύτανις, *IG*12(2).1.19, al. (Mytilene), 11(4).1064a1; perh. to be restored (as Attic) in Ar.*Th*.936 (pun on προτείνειν).

**πρόταξις**, εως, ἡ, *posting in front*, [ψιλῶν] Ascl.*Tact*.6.1. **II.** *prefixing*, ἐν π. εἶναι τοῦ ῥήματος, opp. ἐν ὑποτάξει, A.D.*Adv*.125.7, al.: pl., dub. in Id.*Synt*.199.8.

**προτᾰράσσω**, *disturb beforehand*, ἡ γαστὴρ προεταράχθη Hp.*Epid*. 4.25, cf. Them.*Or*.4.50b (Pass.).

**προταρβέω**, *fear beforehand*, βαρείας τύχας A.*Th*.332 (lyr.); θάνατον E.*Fr*.360.25, cf. *HF*968. **II.** *fear* or *be anxious for one*, τινος S.*Tr*.89, *Ant*.83.

**προτᾰρῑχεύω**, *salt* or *pickle beforehand*, Hdt.2.77. **II.** *reduce* a patient *first by fasting*, Hp.*Acut*.26. **III.** *macerate* chemicals *beforehand*, *PHolm*.17.7:—Pass., Zos.Alch.p.166 B.

⊛ **πρότᾰσις**, εως, ἡ, (προτείνω) *putting forward*: in concrete sense, *that which is put forward*; hence, **1.** in Logic, *proposition*, π.

ἐστι λόγος καταφατικὸς ἢ ἀποφατικός τινος κατά τινος Arist.*APr.*24ᵃ16: esp. *premiss* of a syllogism, ἐκ δύο προτάσεων [πᾶς συλλογισμός] ib. 42ᵃ32; ἡ ἑτέρα, ἡ τελευταία π., the minor *premiss*, Id.*EN*1143ᵇ3, 1147ᵇ9; = ἀξίωμα, Plu.2.1009c, al. b. Math., *enunciation* of a proposition, Autol.2.6, al., Archim.*Sph.Cyl.*2*Praef.* (pl.), *Eratosth. Praef.* (pl.), Dioph.1*Def.*11 (pl.), Procl.*in Ti.*2.190d. 2. Gramm., *hypothetical clause* of a sentence, answered by the ἀπόδοσις, D.L.3.52. 3. *question proposed, problem*, Sor.1.27, Plu.2.736e, Ath.6.234c, etc. 4. *the earlier part of a dramatic poem*, opp. ἐπίτασις (in which the action begins) and καταστροφή, Donat. in *CGF* p.69 K. 5. *proposal*, *Milet.*7.67 (perh. i B.C.), *PMonac.*6.80 (vi A.D.): pl., *proposals* for peace, App.*Mac.*9.3. II. *stretching out, 'urge'*, αἱ τοῦ πάθους π. Plot.4.4.44.

* **προτάσσω**, Att. -ττω, 2 aor. Pass. προετάγην [ᾰ] A.D.*Synt.*306.16:—*place* or *post in front*, σφᾶς αὐτοὺς π. πρὸ τῶν Ἑλλήνων *put* themselves *in front of* them, so as to defend them, And.1.107; π. σφῶν αὐτῶν Ἀστύμαχον *put* him *at their head*, as speaker, Th.3.52:—Med., προετάξαντο τῆς φάλαγγος τοὺς ἱππέας *posted* the horse *in front* of it, X.*HG*6.4.10:—Pass., *stand before* one, so as to protect, ἄναξ, προτάσσου A.*Supp.*835 (lyr.); τὸ προταχθέν *the front rank, van*, X.*Cyr.*5.3.37; οἱ προτεταγμένοι Id.*HG*2.4.15, Ar.*Pax* 1340; προταχθέντες ὑπὲρ ἁπάντων Isoc.4.99; also in documents, ὁ -τεταγμένος the *aforesaid*, *POxy.*1112.18 (ii A.D.), etc. 2. *class as prior*, Plot.6.1.25; *prefer*, τί τινος Sch.Ar.*Ra.*546. 3. Gramm., *prefix*, D.T.631.7 (Pass.), etc.; προτάσσεται τῷ ῥήματι καὶ ὑποτάσσεται A.D.*Pron.* 116.6. II. *appoint* or *determine beforehand*, χρόνον S.*Tr.*164; ἆθλον Arist.*Pr.*956ᵇ17, 20 (Act. and Pass.):—Pass., προτεταγμένοι Aen.Tact.1.5. III. Med., *set before oneself, take as an example*, Pl.*Sph.*218e; *propose to oneself*, ἐκ τούτου τὸ ζῆν ib.224d.

**προτᾰτ-έον**, *one must use as a* πρότασις (I. 1), Arist.*Top.*155ᵇ30, 161ᵃ29. * -ικός, ή, όν, *capable of advancing a proposition*, ib.164ᵇ3. Adv. -κῶς *in the form of a premiss*, ἐρωτᾶν Id.*SE*174ᵇ39.

**προτέγγω**, *wet* or *moisten before*, Ath.15.692b.

**προτέγιον**, τό, = sq., Poll.7.120.

**προτέγισμα**, ατος, τό, in pl., *eaves*, Poll.1.81.

* **προτείνω**, *stretch out before, hold before*, τὸν χαλινόν X.*Eq.*6.11 (Pass.); [ὁ ναυτίλος] π. τὰς πλεκτάνας Arist.*HA*525ᵃ28. 2. *expose to danger*, ψυχὴν.. προτείνων S.*Aj.*1270. 3. metaph., *hold out* as a pretext or excuse, π. πρόφασιν Hdt.1.156; σκῆψιν E.*El.*1067; θεούς S.*Ph.*992; παιδὸς θάνατον E.*Andr.*428:—Med., π. τὴν ἡλικίαν Pl.*Ep.*317c. II. *stretch forth, hold out*, χεῖρα, as a suppliant, Archil.130; τὰς χεῖρας Hdt.1.45, 7.233 (for punishment, Ps.-Callisth. 2.2); φύλλον οἱ ἱκέται προτείνουσι Call.*Iamb.*1.275a (προτιμῶσι 275); also προτείνει χεὶρ ἐκ χερὸς ὀρέγματα (Herm. for ὀρεγόμενα) A.*Ag.* 1110 (lyr.); π. ἑαυτόν *leaning forward*, Pl.*R.*449b: hence intr., *stretch forward*, προτείνουσα εἰς τὸ πέλαγος [ἄκρα] Id.*Criti.*111a, cf. Plb.1.29.2, etc. 2. π. χεῖρα δεξιάν *offer, tender* it as a pledge, S.*Ph.* 1292, cf. *Tr.*1184, E.*Alc.*1118, etc.; π. πίστιν D.23.117. 3. *hold out, offer*, μεγάλα π. ἐπ' οἷσι ὁμολογέειν ἐθέλουσι Hdt.8.140.β'; κέρδος A.*Pr.*777; τελετάς E.*Ba.*238; κάλλος Id.*Hel.*28; φάντασμα Pl.*R.* 382a; ἐλπίδα E.*Fr.*131; δραχμὰς εἴκοσιν Ar.*Pl.*1019; ἐλευθερίαν Antipho 5.50; δέλεαρ π. τὴν ἡδονήν Plu.2.13a; ἐμοὶ λόγους Pl.*Phdr.*230d: c. inf., π. τινὶ λαβεῖν ὅ τι χρῄζει X.*Oec.*5.8:—Med., Hdt.5.24, 7.161; ἔρωτα Pl.*Phdr.*266b; φιλίαν προτενεῖται D.14.5; τὴν ἀειλογίαν Id.19.2:—Pass., δυοῖν προτεινομένοιν ἀγαθοῖν Isoc.6.37, cf. 12.117. 4. *put forward, propose*, π. ζητήματα, ἐρωτήματα, Plu.2.737d, Arr.*Epict.* 3.8.1; αἴνιγμά τινι D.L.2.70, etc.:—Med., *offer* or *put forward* as instances, Pl.*Grg.*518b:—Pass., Sor.2.1, Iamb.*Myst.*1.3. 5. Med., μισθὸν προτείνασθαι *stipulate for* as a reward, Hdt.9.34. III. *put forward as a proposition* (πρότασις I. 1), Arist.*APr.*47ᵃ15, *Top.* 104ᵃ5, al.:—Med., ib.164ᵇ4:—Pass., ib.7.

**προτειχ-ίζω**, *protect by a wall*, Str.5.3.7 (Pass.), *Gloss.* -ισμα, ατος, τό, *advanced fortification, outwork*, Th.4.90, 6.100 (pl.), Lxx 2*Ki.* 20.15, Plb.2.69.6, etc.

**προτεκμαίρομαι**, v. προστεκμαίρομαι.

**προτεκνόω**, pf. -τετέκνωκα, *have issue previously*, *PGnom.*45 (ii A.D.).

**προτέλ-εια**, ἡ, *previous payment, advance*, *PFlor.*296.47 (vi A.D.). * -ειος, ον, (τέλος) *before a ceremony of initiation*, etc.: Subst. προτέλεια (sc. ἱερά), τά, *sacrifice offered before any solemnity*, θυτὴρ γενέσθαι.., προτέλεια ναῶν *as an offering in behalf of*.., A.*Ag.*227 (lyr.); π. Ἐλευσινίων restd. in *IG*1².5.2; *before the marriage-rite*, π. δ' ἤδη παιδὸς ἔσφαξας θεᾷ; E.*IA*718, cf. Pl.Com.174.5; π. γάμων Pl.*Lg.* 774e, cf. Men.1058, Ael.Dion.p.61 Schwabe: rarely in sg., Aristid. Quint.3.27. 2. generally, *beginning*, ἐν προτελείοις κάμακος in the *preliminary* conflicts, A.*Ag.*65 (anap.); ἐν βιότου π. ib.720 (lyr.). b. metaph., *introduction*, τὰ π. τῆς φιλοσοφίας Ph.1.294, cf. Gal.*Phil. Hist.*16; π. γράφων τῆς ἀκροάσεως Procl.*in Prm.* p.541 S.: rarely in sg., Them.*Or.*20.235d. -ειόω, *perform preliminary initiation*, in Med., Hsch.:—Pass., of a deed, *to be executed previously*, *PFlor.*56.11 (iii A.D.). -εσις, εως, ἡ, Astrol., *prognostication*, Ptol.*Phas.* p.11 H. (pl.), *Tetr.*7. * -εσμα, ατος, τό, = foreg., ib.77. -εσματικός, ή, όν, *belonging to a* προτέλεσμα, Procl.*Par.Ptol.*48.

**προτελευτ-αῖος**, ον, *second-last*, Steph. *in Hp.*2.249 D. * -άω, *die before*, τινος Philoch.169, cf. D.S.1.91, Plu.2.113e, Hdn.1.15.8, Artem.2.57 (interpol.), etc. -ή, ἡ, *earlier death*, Vett.Val.101.2, Paul.Al.*M.*4. -ησις, εως, ἡ, = προτέλεσις (nisi hoc legend.), Id. *Q.*2. -ος, ον, *penultimate*, Simp.*in Ph.*68.12.

**προτελ-έω**, *pay* or *expend beforehand*, τι ἡμῖν X.*An.*7.7.25, cf. *Ages.*1.18; ἀφ' οὗ ἂν π. εἰς τὴν ἀφορμήν Id.*Vect.*3.9; τι πρὸς τὰς θυσίας Luc.*Philops.*14: *lend*, c. dat., Democr.255:—Pass., *POxy.*279.12 (i A.D.), etc. II. *initiate* or *instruct beforehand*, Luc.*Rh.Pr.*14 (Pass.); ψυχὴ ὥσπερ ἐν ἱεροῖς -τελεῖται Aristid.1.97 J. III. *accomplish before*, κάθαρσίν τινα Alciphr.2.4; τὰ -τετελεσμένα ἔργα Ph.Byz. *Mir.*4.5. -ής, ές, (τέλος) = προτέλειος, θυσία sacrifice *offered before a marriage*, Agathocl.2. -ίζω, *initiate* or *consecrate by a ceremony preliminary to marriage*, νεάνιδα Ἀρτέμιδι E.*IA*433:—Pass., *to be prepared for the mysteries*, Cratin.180, v.l. in Poll.3.38.

**προτεμένισμα**, ατος, τό, (τέμενος) *precincts* or *entrance of a* τέμενος, Th.1.134, Chor.p.85 B.; *vestibule* or *outer court of a temple*, Hld.5.15, etc.

* **προτέμνω**, aor. προὔτᾰμον, *cut off beforehand*, [ὦμον] προταμών Il.9.489. II. *cut off in front, cut short*, κορμὸν ἐκ ῥίζης προταμών Od. 23.196; *prune* vines, *PLond.*1.131.375, al. (i A.D.). III. Med., *cut forward* or *in front* of one, εἰ ὦλκα διηνεκέα προταμοίμην if in ploughing I *cut* an unbroken furrow *before me*, Od.18.375; but προταμέσθαι ἀρούρας *mow* them *before*, A.R.3.1387.

**προτενής**, ές, (προτείνω) *fore-stretching*, ἄκρα Dion.Byz.53; ἀκρεμόνες, of horns, Opp.*C.*2.304; of feelers, Id.*H.*2.122; of a spear, *in rest, couched*, A.R.1.756.

**προτενθ-εύω**, *forestall, receive too soon*, προὐτένθευσαν ἡμέρᾳ μιᾷ [τὰ πρυτανεῖα] Ar.*Nu.*1200. 2. Med., χαίνει δὲ [ὁ λέων] ὡς οἷον εὐόμενος λιχνότερον κατὰ τοῦ βαλόντος greedily *anticipating his bite*.., Eust. 1202.3. -ης, ου, ὁ (ἡ, Ael.*NA*15.10), in pl., *those who celebrated the* Δορπία (q. v.), ἀφεῖσθαι τοὺς βουλευτὰς.. ἀπὸ τῆς ἡμέρας ἧς οἱ π. ἄγουσι πέντε ἡμέρας Decr.Att.ap.Ath.4.171e; τίς εἰμ' ἐγώ; ἡ τῶν π. Δορπία καλουμένη Philyll.8. 2. *forestaller, regrater*, in pl., Ar.*Nu.*1198 (ubi v. Sch.), Pherecr.7. 3. Adj., *greedy*, Ael.*Fr.*39; ἡ μάλιστα π. [πηλαμύς] Id.*NA* l. c. (Glossed προγεύστης by Artemidor.ap.Ath. 4.171b, cf. ib.c.)

* **προτερ-αῖος**, α, ον, (πρότερος) *previous to*, qualifying ἡμέρα, c. gen., τῇ π. ἡμέρᾳ τῆς μάχης on the day *before* the battle, Th.5.75: more freq. alone, τῇ π. (sc. ἡμέρᾳ) Hdt.1.84, 126, etc. (in full, τῇ π. ἡμέρᾳ (s.v.l.) Pl.*Phd.*59d): c. gen., τῇ π. τῆς.. καταστάσιος μελλούσης ἔσεσθαι *the day before* the audience, Hdt.9.9; τῇ π. τῆς θυσίας And. 4.29, cf. Pl.*Phd.*58a; τῇ π. ᾗ ἀνήγετο Lys.19.22; τῇ π. ὅτε ταῦτ' ἔλεγεν D.21.119; κραιπαλῶντα ἔτι ἐκ τῆς π. Pl.*Smp.*176d. II. *former*, ἡ τῶν γονέων π. ὄψις the *former* condition.., *PMasp.*2 iii 6 (vi A.D.). III. προτεραίτερος, Com. Comp. of πρότερος, *'soonerer'*, Ar.*Eq.*1165. * -άσιος [ᾱ], α, ον (Dor. for *-ήσιος), *on the previous day*, *Schwyzer* 345.9 (Delph.). -εία, ἡ, = προτεραία, *Tab.Heracl.* 1.101. -εύω, = sq., Simp.*in Cat.*420.36. -έω (irreg. augm. προετέρουν, προετέρησα, *PSI*4.422.34 (iii B.C.), D.S.11.73, 15.53, al.), *to be before, be in advance*, Hdt.9.57; π. τῆς ὁδοῦ *to be forward* on the way, ib.66. 2. of Time, *to be beforehand with, get the start of, precede*, opp. ὑστερέω, π. τῇ γενέσει τί τινος Arist.*GA*741ᵇ35, cf. 775ᵃ26; ἡ ὄψις π. τῆς ἀκοῆς Id.*Mete.*369ᵇ9; π. ἀστραπὴ βροντῆς Epicur. *Ep.*2 p.46 U.; of abnormally precocious animals, Arist.*HA*544ᵇ21; π. τοῖς χρόνοις *to be earlier* in date, D.S.3.52, etc.; of plants, *to be early*, opp. ὑστερέω, Thphr.*CP*3.24.2; π. εἰς τὴν φθοράν perish *first*, ib.4.2.1; of constellations, π. ἐν ταῖς ἀνατολαῖς τῶν κατ' αὐτὰ δωδεκατημορίων Hipparch.2.4.4. 3. *to be beforehand, take the lead*, Th.1.33; οὐδὲν προτερήσετε *you will gain* no *advantage*, Philipp.ap.D.18.39; ὁ πατήρ μου προετέρησε παρὰ πάντας τοὺς ἐκεῖ *outstripped* them all (as a farmer), *PSI* l. c.; of soldiers, *to be superior, have the advantage*, Plb. 11.14.4, al.; κατὰ τὴν συμπλοκήν Id.3.110.6; ταῖς εὐκινησίαις ἐν τοῖς διωγμοῖς D.S.3.49; π. τῆς γνώμης *carry* one's motion, Id.15.53: c. gen., *have the advantage over*, τὰ κακὰ τῶν ἀνὰ μέσον π. Chrysipp. *Stoic.*3.188; πλοῦτον -οῦντα πενίας Phld.*Rh.*1.236 S.; οὐδὲ τὸ παρὰ φύσιν π. τῆς φύσεως Sallust.17 (cj. for πρότερον ἔχει):—Pass., *to be defeated*, ἐπροτερήθης διὰ τοῦ δικαστηρίου *IG*5(2).443.35 (Megalopolis). II. c. acc., *go beyond, surpass*, στοργᾷ φύσιν ἐπροτέρησεν *IPE*2.299.9 (Panticapaeum). -ηγενής, ές, *born sooner, older*, Antim.42, Call.*Jov.*58, A.R.4.268. * -ημα, ατος, τό, *advantage, superiority*, in pl., Plb.1.51.3, 16.20.6, al.; π. φυσικά Phld.*Rh.*2.87 S., D.S.15.39, cf. Longin.44.3, M.Ant.1.16: less freq. in sg., ἐπὶ μηδενὶ ἐπαρθῆς ἀλλοτρίῳ π. Epict.*Ench.*6. 2. in war, *advantage gained, success*, Plb.1.9.7, 2.10.6, D.S.2.19, al.; ἐπὶ τοῦ π. γίγνεσθαι Id.3.54; οὐκ ἔσται τὸ π. σου Lxx *Jd.*4.9, cf. Onos.13.1. II. *privilege*, τὰ τῆς βασιλείας π. D.S.31.19, cf. Hsch. -ησις, εως, ἡ, *superiority*, π. τισὶ παρασχεῖν give them a *'longer start'*, Hld.4.20. * -ικόν, τό, *prior claim*, *BGU*820.20 (i A.D.). -ιος, α, ον, prob. f.l. for πρότερος in *Tab.Defix.Aud.*50.13 (iv B.C.).

* **πρότερος** and **πρῶτος**, Comp. and Sup. formed from πρό, opp. ὕστερος, ὕστατος.

A. Comp. **πρότερος**, α, ον, I. of Place, *before, in front*, π. πόδες the *fore*-feet, Od.19.228; π. ἵπποι horses *in front*, B.5.43:—but mostly, II. of Time, *former, earlier*, ἄνδρες Il.21.405; ἄνθρωποι 5.637, 23.332; οἱ π. *men of former times*, 4.308 (rarely without Art., A.*Ag.*1338 (anap.), etc.); οὗτος δὲ προτέρης γενεῆς π. τ' ἀνθρώπων Il.23.790: also, *older*, opp. ὁπλότερος, 2.707, etc.; γενεῇ π. 15.182; but παῖδες π. children *by the first* or *a former marriage*, Od.15.22; παῖδες ἐκ τῆς π. γυναικός Hdt.7.2; τῇ προτέρῃ (sc. ἡμέρᾳ) *on the day before*, Od.16.50; ἠοῖ τῇ π. Il.13.794 (in Prose more freq. τῇ προτεραίᾳ, cf. προτεραῖος); τοῦ π. ἐνιαυτοῦ the year *before*, *IG*1².352.11; τοῖς π. Παναθηναίοις the *preceding* P., ib.57.8; τὰ π. what has *preceded*, Plot.3.2.8:—freq. used predicatively, sts. where we should expect the Adv. (which is never used by Hom.), ὅ με π. κάκ' ἔοργε Il.

3.351, cf. 16.569, Hes.*Op.*708, etc.; σπονδὰς οὐ λύσετε πρότεροι Th.1.123; οἱ π. ἐπιόντες ibid.; τοῖς π. μετὰ Κύρου ἀναβᾶσι X.*An.*1.4.12, cf. *IG*2².1.7; εἰ μὴ π. ἑωράκη αὐτὸν ἢ ἐκεῖνος ἐμέ Pl.*R.*336d, cf. 432c, etc.; ὅτι εἴη π. ὑπὸ ἐκείνων ἠδικημένος *PCair.Zen.*288.9 (iii B.C.). 2. as regular Comp., c. gen., ἐμέο πρότερος Il.10.124; π. τούτων Hdt.1.168, cf. Pl.*Phd.*86b, *Hp.Ma.*282d; τὰς γυναῖκας μὴ ἀπιέναι προτέρας τῶν ἀνδρῶν *IG*12(5).593.19 (Iulis, v B.C.); τῇ π. ἡμέρᾳ τῆς τροπῆς the day *before*.., Arist.*Pol.*1316ᵃ16; προτέρᾳ εἰδυῶν Ὀκτωμβρίων *IG*7.2225.14 (Thisbe, Senatus Consultum, ii B.C.); τῷ π. ἔτει Παναθηναίων τῶν μεγάλων ib.2².212.27; τῷ π. ἔτει τῆς ἥττης Plb.2.43.6: folld. by ἤ, τῷ προτέρῳ ἔτεϊ ἢ τὸν κρητῆρα [ἐλη̣ί̣σαντο] Hdt.3.47. III. of Rank, Worth, and generally of Precedence, *superior*, τῷ γένει, τῇ δυνάμει, Is.1.17, D.3.15; π. τινὸς πρός τι *superior to* him in.., Pl.*La.*183b; π. τι ἄγειν, π. ποιήσασθαι τὰ σὰ πράγματα, Lib.*Or.*58.36, 52.1. IV. after Hom., neut. πρότερον freq. as Adv., *before, earlier*, Pi.*O.*13.31, Hdt.4.45, *IG*1².374.265, etc.; ὀλίγον π. Pl.*Prt.*317e: c. gen., π. φήμης A.*Th.*866 (anap.); ὀλίγῳ τι π. τούτων Hdt.8.95; πολλοῖσι ἔτεσι π. τούτων ib.96; ἐνιαυτῷ π. τῆς ἁλώσεως D.9.60; also πρὸ τῶν Περσικῶν δέκα ἔτεσι π. Pl.*Lg.*642d, cf. *Criti.*112a; τούτου π. Paus.1.1.2: most freq. folld. by ἤ, π. ἢ κατὰ τὴν προσδοκίαν Pl.*Sph.*264b; also μὴ π. ἀπαναστῆναι ἢ ἐξέλωσι Hdt.9.87, cf. 7.54, Antipho 2.1.2, Th.7.63, etc.: with inf., π. ἢ βασιλεῦσαι Hdt.7.2, cf. Th.1.69, etc.: folld. by πρίν, Hdt.1.82; by πρὶν ἄν, ib.140; by πρὶν ἤ with vb. in Indic., Id.6.45, 8.8, or Subj., 7.8.β′ (v.l. πρὶν ἂν ἤ), 9.93; also οὐ π. εἰ μή.. Plu.*Lys.*10, etc.; οὐ π. ἕως.., or ἕως ἄν.., Lys.12.71, Ath.14.640c; μὴ π., ἀλλ' ὅταν.. Plb.9.13.3: also used with the Art., τὸ π. Pl.*R.*522a, X.*An.*4.4.14, etc. (τὸ π., also, *for the first time*, *Ep. Gal.*4.13): c. gen., τὸ π. τῶν ἀνδρῶν τούτων Hdt.2.144: the Adv. is freq. put between Art. and Subst., ὁ π. βασιλεύς Id.1.84; τὰ π. ἀδικήματα Id.6.87; αἱ π. ἁμαρτίαι Ar.*Eq.*1355, etc.

B. Sup. **πρῶτος**, η, ον, Dor. **πρᾶτος** (q.v.): I. as Adj., 1. of Place, *foremost*, πρώτοισιν ἐνὶ προμάχοισι μιγέντα Od.18.379; ἐν πρώτοις, μετὰ πρώτοισι alone, Il.19.424, 11.64; πρώτῃ ἐν ὑσμίνῃ, ἐνὶ πρώτῳ ὁμάδῳ, 15.340, 17.380; τῆς πρώτης τάττειν (sc. τάξεως) Isoc.12.180, cf. Lys.16.15, etc.; ἐν π. ῥυμῷ at the *front* or *end* of the pole, Il.6.40, 16.371; πρώτῃσι θύρῃσιν at the *outermost* doors, 22.66; π. ξύλον the *front* bench, Ar.*Ach.*25, Poll.4.121, etc.; οἱ π. πόδες, like πρόσθιοι, Id.1.193. 2. of Time, στάντα πρὸς π. ἕω looking towards *first* dawn, S.*OC*477; περὶ π. νύκτα Poll.1.70. 3. of Order, serving as ordinal to εἷς, ἄεθλα θῆκε.. τῷ πρώτῳ· ἀτὰρ αὖ τῷ δευτέρῳ.., αὐτὰρ τῷ τριτάτῳ.., κτλ., Il.23.265, cf. 6.179; opp. ὕστατος, 2.281, 5.703, etc.; opp. τελευταῖος, A.*Ag.*314; opp. πανύστατος, Od.9.449; πρῶτοι πάντων ἀνθρώπων Hdt.2.2; τὰ π. τῶν ὀνομάτων Pl.*Cra.*421d; τῇ π. τῶν ἡμερέων Hdt.7.168, etc.; π. ἄξων *IG*1².115.10; ἐπὶ τοῦ π. [ἱερείου] *first-offered*, X.*An.*4.3.9; ἐν τοῖς π. λόγοις in the *earlier* books, Arist.*Ph.*263ᵃ11, al.; ἐν πρώτοις among *the first*, Is.7.40; hence, *above all, especially*, Hdt.8.69, Pl.*R.*522c; in Att., ἐν τοῖς πρῶτοι (v. ὁ, ἡ, τό A. VIII. 6):—freq. used predicatively of being the first to do something, Νέστωρ πρῶτος κτύπον ἄϊε Il.10.532; πρῶτος ἀνατέλλει Eratosth.*Cat.*42; εἴθε π. σοι ἐνέτυχον Luc.*Tyr.*21. b. Philos., *first in order of existence, primary*, αἱ π. οὐσίαι Arist.*Cat.*2ᵇ26, cf. *Metaph.*1032ᵇ2; π. ὕλη, π. φιλοσοφία, ib.1015ᵃ7, 1061ᵇ19; *primitive, simple*, οἰκία π., ἡ π. πόλις, Id.*Pol.*1252ᵇ10, 1291ᵃ17; ἡ π. κοινωνία ib.1257ᵃ19; ἡ π. ὀλιγαρχία ib.1293ᵃ14; ὁ π. συλλογισμός *normal, typical*, Id.*Rh.*1357ᵃ17; τὰ π. σώματα, μόρια, = τὰ ὁμοιομερῆ, Gal.5.673, 674; πρῶτα κατὰ φύσιν, e.g. health, perception, *Stoic.*3.34; τὰ π. πάθη ib.92; αἱ π. ἀρεταί ib.64. c. Math., πρῶτοι ἀριθμοί *prime* numbers, Euc.7 *Def.*11, 12; but also, *first* numbers (= 1 to 100,000,000) in the notation of Archim., *Aren.*3.2. d. πρῶτος is sts. used where we should expect πρότερος, Αἰνείας δὲ πρῶτος ἀκόντισεν Il.13.502, cf. 18.92: in late Greek folld. by gen., πρῶτός μου ἦν *Ev.Jo.*1.15, 30, cf. 15.18; οἱ πρῶτοί μου ταῦτα ἀνιχνεύσαντες Ael.*NA* 8.12; πρώτη εὕρηται ἡ περὶ τοὺς πόδας κίνησις τῆς διὰ τῶν χειρῶν Ath.14.630c; γεννήτορα πρῶτον μητέρος εἰς ἀΐδην πέμψει Man.1.329, 4.404; ἀλόχου πρῶτος *before* his wife, *IG*12(5).590.5 (vi (?) A.D.). 4. of Rank or Dignity, μετὰ πρώτοισιν among *the first men* of the state, Od.6.60, etc.; νομίσαντες πρῶτοι ἂν εἶναι Th.6.28; διαβάλλειν τοὺς π. X.*An.*2.6.26, cf. Arist.*Pol.*1266ᵃ18; αἱ π. πόλεις Th.2.8; ὁ π. ἄρχων *IG*12(3).481.10 (Thera), *CIG*2837 (Aphrodisias); ὁ π. τῆς πόλεως, as a title, *IG*12(5).292.2 (Paros); ὁ π. τῆς νήσου *Act.Ap.*28.7; τῶν π. φίλων, title at the Ptolemaic court, *PTeb.*31.15 (ii B.C.), etc.; τῶν π., as military title, *PHib.*1.110.72 (iii B.C.), *PPetr.*3 p.23 (iii B.C.), *PTeb.*815 *Fr.*4.23, al. (iii B.C.): c. gen., ἐν πρώτοισι Μυκηναίων Il.15.643; οἱ π. στρατοῦ S.*Ph.*1305, cf. E.*Hec.*304, etc.: c. dat. modi, ἀρετῇ π., οἱ π. καὶ χρήμασι καὶ γένει, πλούτῳ π. τῶν Ἑλλήνων, etc., S.*Ph.*1425, Th.3.65, Isoc.16.31, etc.; π. ἐν συμφοραῖς βίου S.*OT*33. 5. of Degree, *first, highest*, μοῖρα Id.*OC*145 (anap.), etc. II. as Subst. in neut. pl. πρῶτα, τά, 1. (sc. ἆθλα), *first prize*, τὰ π. λαβών Il.23.275; τὰ π. δόρει κρατύνων S.*OC*1313; ἔχειν πρῶτα κυναγεσίας *AP*6.118 (Antip.); τὰ π. φέρεσθαι D.C.42.57, etc. 2. *first part, beginning*, τῆς Ἰλιάδος τὰ π. Pl.*R.*392e; ἐν τοῖς π. Id.*Smp.*221d; τὸ π. τοῦ ᾄσματος Id.*Prt.*343c. 3. *first, highest*, in degree, τὰ π. τᾶς λιμῶ (Dor.) the *extremities* of famine, Ar.*Ach.*743 (nisi leg. ἄπρατα); ἐχέτωσαν τὰ π. τῆς εὐδαιμονίας Luc.*Cont.*10; ἐς τὰ π. τιμᾶσθαι Th.3.39, cf. 56; φρενῶν ἐς τὰ ἐμεωυτοῦ π. οὔκω ἀνήκω I have not yet come to the *highest development* of my judgement, Hdt.7.13, cf. D.C.38.22; of persons, ἐὼν τῶν Ἐρετριέων τὰ π. Hdt.6.100; Λάμπων.. Αἰγινητέων ⟨ἐὼν⟩ τὰ π. Id.9.78, cf. E.*Med.*917; ἐστὶν τὰ π. τῆς ἐκεῖ μοχθηρίας (of a person) Ar.*Ra.*421. 4. Philos., *primary things, elements*, Emp.38.1, Arist.*GC*335ᵃ29; τὰ π. αἴτια Id.*Mete.*338ᵃ20; also τὸ π. ἐνυπάρχον ἑκάστῳ Id.*Ph.*193ᵃ10. 5. in Logic, *the first undemonstrable propositions*, on which all future conclusions rest, Id.*Top.*100ᵇ18; τὰ π. ἀναπόδεικτα Id.*APo.*71ᵇ26. III. in Adverbial phrases, 1. τὴν πρώτην (sc. ὥραν, ὁδόν) *first, for the present, just now*, Hdt.3.134, Ar.*Th.*662, D.3.2, Arist.*Metaph.*1038ᵃ35, etc.; τὴν πρώτην εἶναι Hdt.1.153. 2. with Preps., ἀπὸ πρώτης (sc. ἀρχῆς) Antipho 5.56, Th.1.77; ἀπὸ τῆς π. εὐθὺς Luc.*Hist.Conscr.*1; ἐκ π. Babr.45.14; κατὰ πρώτας Pl.*Plt.*292b, D.C.52.19; κατὰ τὴν π. εὐθὺς Id.62.3; παρὰ τὴν π. *the first time*, opp. ἐπὶ τῆς δευτέρας, Philostr.*VA* 1.22. 3. freq. as Adv. in neut. sg. and pl., πρῶτον, πρῶτα, a. *first, in the first place*, πρῶτόν τε καὶ ὕστατον (vulg. ὕστερον) Hes.*Th.*34; π. μὲν.., δεύτερον αὖ.., τὸ τρίτον αὖ.. Il.6.179; τί π. τοι ἔπειτα, τί δ' ὑστάτιον καταλέξω; Od.9.14; Κύπριδα μὲν πρῶτα.., αὐτὰρ ἔπειτ'.. Il.5.458; οὐρῆας μὲν π. ἐπῴχετο.., αὐτὰρ ἔπειτα.. 1.50; π. μὲν.., ἔπειτα δὲ.. S.*OC*632, X.*Cyr.*2.1.2, 23, *An.*5.6.7–8, *Hier.*11.8, etc.; π. μὲν.., ἔπειτα.. Pl.*Phd.*89a, etc.; π. μὲν.., ἔπειτα δεύτερον.., τρίτον δὲ.. Aeschin.1.7; π. μὲν.., εἶτα.. Pl.*Phlb.*15b; π. μὲν.., εἶτα δὲ.. X.*An.*1.2.16; π. μὲν.., εἶτα.., ἔτι δὲ.. Id.*Mem.*1.2.1; π. μὲν.., ..δὲ αὖ.. Pl.*Lg.*935a; π. μὲν.., ἔτι δὲ.. Lys.4.10, etc.; π. μὲν.., ἔτι τοίνυν.. D.44.57; freq. answered only by δέ, Id.9.48, etc.; sts. the answering clause must be supplied, A.*Ag.*810, D.7.7, etc.: also πρῶτον μὲν.. δεύτερον μήν.. Pl.*Phlb.*66a: also πρῶτα μὲν.., ἔπειτα.. S.*Tr.*616, Ar.*Pl.*728; πρῶτα μὲν.., ἔπειτα.., εἶτα.. E.*Med.*548; πρῶτα μὲν.., ..δὲ.. A.*Pr.*447; πρῶτα μὲν.., ἔπειτα δὲ.. X.*HG*7.1.7, cf. S.*Ph.*919; ἐπεί σε πρῶτα κιχάνω since my *first* meeting is with you, Od.13.228, cf. 7.53, Il.8.274: also τὸ πρῶτον, *first, in the first place, at the beginning*, ὡς τὸ π. ὑπέστην καὶ κατένευσα 4.267; οὕνεκά σ' οὐ τὸ π., ἐπεὶ ἴδον, ὧδ' ἀγάπησα Od.23.214. cf. Il.3.443, 6.345, Pi.*P.*9.41, *N.*3.49; τὸ μὲν οὖν π. Pl.*Prt.*333d, etc.; τὸ π..., μετὰ ταῦτα.. D.1.12: also τὰ π., Il.1.6, Od.1.257, etc.; πόντῳ μὲν τὰ π..., αὐτὰρ ἔπειτα.. Il.4.424; τὰ π. μὲν.., ὡς δὲ.. A.*Pers.*412; τὰ π..., τέλος δὲ.. S.*Fr.*149.5, cf. 966. b. *too early, before the time*, ἦ τ' ἄρα καὶ σοὶ πρῶτα (v.l. for πρωΐ) παραστήσεσθαι ἔμελλε Μοῖρ' ὀλοή Od.24.28. c. = πρότερον, *before*, ἦν.. πρῶτον ἀπόλωμαι κακῶς Ar.*Ec.*1079; π. οὐδ' ὑφ' ἑνὸς.. κρατηθέντες X.*HG*5.4.1; θάλασσα π. ἦν ἢ γενέσθαι γῆν v.l. in Heraclit.31; λόγῳ π. ἢ τοῖς ἔργοις Arist.*Rh.Al.*1420ᵇ28; οὐ π. αὐτὴν ἀπέκτειναν πρὶν ἢ ἀπεκύησεν Ael.*VH*5.18; π. συμμελετᾶν ἢ μελετᾶν μαθέτω *AP*12.206 (Strat.). d. *first, for the first time*, οὐ.. νῦν πρῶτα ποδώκεος ἄντ' Ἀχιλῆος στήσομαι Il.20.89; οὐ νῦν πρῶτον, ἀλλὰ καὶ πάλαι S.*Ph.*966; ἐνταῦθα πρῶτον ἔφαγον X.*An.*2.3.16. e. πρῶτον, πρῶτα are used after the relat. Pron. and after relat. Advbs., like Engl. *once* (= *at all*), οὐδ' ἐνοσίχθων λήθετ' ἀπειλάων, τὰς.. Ὀδυσῆϊ π. ἐπηπείλησε Od.13.127, cf. 3.320, 10.328, 13.133, Il.1.319, 19.136; μοῖραν δ' οὔ τινά φημι πεφυγμένον ἔμμεναι ἀνδρῶν.. ἐπὴν τὰ π. γένηται when *once* he is born, 6.489, cf. Od.3.183, 4.13, 414; οὔτε.. Λυκίους ἐδύναντο τεῖχος ῥῆξ ὤσασθαι, ἐπεὶ τὰ π. πέλασθεν Il.12.420, cf. Od.11.106, 221; also ἐπεὶ τὸ (or τὰ) π. *now that*.., ἀλλ' ἐπεὶ οὖν τὸ π. ἀνέκραγον, οὐκ ἐπικεύσω *now that* I have spoken up, 14.467; τὸ μὲν οὔ ποτε φύλλα καὶ ὄζους φύσει, ἐπεὶ δὴ πρῶτα τομὴν ἐν ὄρεσσι λέλοιπε Il.1.235, cf. 276, 19.9: c. part., τῷ ῥ' Αἴας τὸ π. ἐφεζόμενος μέγ' ἀάσθη (the rock) on which *once* seated A. blasphemed, Od.4.509: the sense *as soon as* is never necessary in Hom., but is possible in Od.4.414, 19.355; δινέμεν εὖτ' ἂν πρῶτα φανῇ σθένος Ὠαρίωνος when *once* (or perh., *as soon as*), Hes.*Op.*598; ὅπως τις πρῶτα γένοιτο πάντας ἀποκρύπτεσκε *as soon as* each was born, Id.*Th.*156; ὡς τὸ π. X.*An.*7.8.14; τότ' εὐθύς.., ὅτε πρῶτον εἶδον D.18.141; αὖθίς με ἀνερέσθαι ὅταν ἐντύχῃς πρῶτον the *first time* you meet me, Pl.*Ly.*211b; ἐὰν μάθω γε πρῶτον.. τί λέγεις Id.*R.*338c. IV. Adv. πρώτως *primarily*, first in Arist., π. καὶ κυρίως *EN*1157ᵃ30; opp. δευτέρως, ib.1158ᵇ31; π. καθ' αὑτό, opp. κατὰ συμβεβηκός, Id.*Ph.*192ᵇ22, cf. Gal.1.692, al., Jul.*Or.*5.168b. 2. ὅτε π. ἐπεδήμησεν.. when he *first* visited.., *BSA*27.228 (Sparta, ii A.D.).—(From πρῶτος was formed a new Sup. πρώτιστος, q.v.)

**προτέρ-ω**, Adv. *further, forwards*, ἴθυσαν δὲ πολὺ π. Il.4.507; τὼ δὲ βάτην π. 9.192; ἀλλ' ἕπεο π. 18.387; μερμήριξε δ'.. ἢ π... διώκοι 5.672; μαίεσθαι π. Od.14.356; ἔτι π. Il.23.526, Od.5.417; καί νύ κε δὴ π. ἔτ' ἔρις γένετ' the quarrel would have gone *further*, Il.23.490; ἦ πῄ με π. ἄξεις; wilt thou carry me *further away*? 3.400; ἔτ' οὐ π. no *further*, no *more*, A.R.1.919: c. gen. loci, D.P.923. II. of Time, *sooner*, Call.*Dian.*72. **-ωθεν**, Adv. of foreg., = ἐκ τοῦ προτέρου, Theognost.*Can.*156; **προτέρωθε**, *EM*385.49. **-ωσε**, Adv. *toward the front, forward*, *h.Hom.*32.10, A.R.1.306, etc.; π. κελεύθου ib.1241.

⊛**προτέταρτον**, Adv. *on the fourth day before*, *Leg.Gort.*11.53.

**προτεύχω**, in pf. inf. Pass. προτετύχθαι, *to have happened beforehand, to be past*, τὰ μὲν π. ἐάσομεν Il.16.60, 18.112. II. *to be brought to light*, πρὸ γάρ τ' ἀναφανδὰ τέτυκται A.R.4.84.

**προτεχνολογ-έω**, *treat technically before*, in Pass., Ammon. *in Porph.*21.7, Sch.Hermog. in Rh.7.551 W.; προτετεχνολογημένον ἡμῖν περί τινος Nicom.*Ar.*1.17, cf. Alex.Aphr. *in Top.*124.33. **-ημα**, ατος, τό, *preliminary technical treatment*, τῶν ἐθνικῶν St.Byz. s. v. Αἰθίοψ (pl.).

**προτεχνόομαι**, Pass., *to be trained already*, pf. inf. προτετεχνῶσθαι Gal.13.656.

**προτήθη**, ἡ, *great-grandmother*, Poll.3.18, D.C.59.2.

**προτήθυς**, υος, ἡ, *born before Tethys*, comic name of an old woman with a play on foreg., Cratin.438.

**προτήκω**, *melt beforehand*, στέαρ *Hippiatr.*34, cf. Archig.ap.Orib. *Fr.*133.

**προτηνί**, v. προταινί.

**προτήνιον**· ἡλικία τις αἰγός· ἐν Καμειρέων ἱεροποιίᾳ τράγον π. θύειν νόμος, Phot.; cf. πρατήνιον, πρητήν.

**προτηρέω**, *watch carefully*, dub. in *PFlor.*262.13 (iii A.D.).

**προτί**, v. πρός.

**προτιάπτω, προτιβάλλομαι, προτιειλεῖν, προτιείποι**, v. προσ-.

**προτῐθᾰσεύω**, *soothe, conciliate first*, Olymp. *in Alc.*p.87 C.

***προτίθημι** (also thematic forms, 3 sg. προτιθεῖ Hdt.1.133, 3 pl. προτιθεῖσι Id.7.197), fut. -θήσω Th.3.67: aor. προὔθηκα Il.24.409, etc. (for προθέουσι v. προθέω (B)):—**Med.** (v. infr.):—**Pass.**, aor. 1 προὐτέθην E.*Ph.*803, Pl.*Phd.*90b, etc.; but pres. and impf. Pass. are usu. supplied by πρόκειμαι:—*set before, set out*, esp. of meals, τραπέζας νίζον καὶ πρότιθεν (Ep. for προὐτίθεσαν) Od.1.112; βοῦν Hes.*Th.*537; τούτοισι προθεῖναι δαῖτα Hdt.1.207, cf. S.*Aj.*1294, *Ant.*775, *Ph.*274, etc.; ξείνια στρατῷ Hdt.7.29:—Med., *set before oneself, have set before one*, δαῖτα Id.1.133, 4.26; κλίνας καὶ τραπέζας Plu.2.99e; also προτίθεσθαί τισι ἄριστον *cause* it *to be set before* them, Chionid.7. **b.** π. τινὰ κυσίν *throw* him to the dogs, Il.24.409; τινὰ θηρσὶν ἁρπαγὴν π. E. *El.*896. **c.** *hand over for burial*, τινά τινι S.*El.*1198, cf. 1487. **2.** *expose* a child, Hdt 1.112; π. τινὰ ἔρημον S.*Ph.*268:—Pass., ὁ θανάτῳ προτεθεὶς E.*Ph.*803 (lyr.). **3.** *set up, institute, propose*, esp. of contests, ἅμιλλαν λόγων E.*Med.*546; λόγων τοὺς ἀγῶνας Th.3.67; εἰ πονηρίας ἀγὼν προτεθείη Pl.*Phd.*90b; ἄπορον αἵρεσιν *offer* a choice, Id. *Tht.*196c (but also προτίθεσθαί τινι αἵρεσιν Id.*Lg.*858a); π. νόμον E. *Hipp.*1046. **b.** *set up as a mark* or *prize*, στέφανόν τισι τῶν ἀγώνων Th.2.46; σκοπὸν κάλλιστον ἐν τῷ ζῆν Plb.7.8.9:—Pass., προὐτέθην ἐγὼ ἆθλον.. δορὸς E.*Hel.*42. **c.** *set as a penalty*, θάνατον ζημίαν π. Th.3.44; τιμωρίας ἔτι μείζους οὐ μέχρι τοῦ δικαίου ib.82; τῶν νόμων τὰ ἔσχατα ἐπιτίμια προτεθηκότων D.34.37; τοῖσι ἐκείνου ἀπογόνοισι ἀέθλους τοιούσδε Hdt.7.197. **4.** *fix, set*, ἐς ἑβδομήκοντα ἔτεα οὖρον τῆς ζόης ἀνθρώπῳ π. Id.1.32:—Med., οὖρον π. ἐνιαυτόν ib.74. **5.** *appoint as a task* or *duty*, τινί τι S.*Tr.*1049; νεωτέρῳ τοῦτο βαστάζειν πρόθες Id.*Ant.*216; δμωαῖς π. πένθος οἰκεῖον στένειν ib.1249, cf. Hdt. 9.94:—Med., *propose to oneself* as a task or object, ὅπερ προὐθέμεθα σκέψασθαι Pl.*Phdr.*259e, *R.*352d, cf. *Sph.*221a, *Tht.*169c; π. ψέγειν αὐτὸ ἢ ἐπαινεῖν Id.*Lg.*638c, cf. Arist.*EN*1142ᵇ19 (dub.), Hipparch. 1.1.6, Luc.*Nec.*19. **b.** Med., c. fut. inf., *propose to oneself, intend*, προτεθειμένου κατοικήσειν ἐνταῦθα *Syria* 13.256 (Seleucia in Pieria, ii B.C.). **6.** Med., also, *put forth on one's own part, display, show*, εὐλάβειαν S.*El.*1334; ἀνδραγαθίαν Th.3.64; ἔχθραν Id.8.85. **7.** Med., θνητοὺς ἐν οἴκτῳ προθέμενος *setting before oneself* in pity, feeling compassion for, A.*Pr.*241. **8.** *advance* money, *IPE*1².32 *B*30, 63 (Olbia, iii B.C.); τὸ διδόμενον ἆθλον ὑπὸ τοῦ δήμου αὐτὸς προέθηκεν ἐκ τοῦ ἰδίου *IG*12(9).234.18 (Eretria, i B.C.); τισὶν τῶν πολιτῶν εἰς λύτρα προτιθεὶς *SIG*708.15 (Istropolis, ii B.C.). **II.** π. νεκρὸν *lay out* a dead body, *let it lie in state*, Hdt.5.8:—Med., E.*Alc.*664, *Supp.*53 (lyr.), Ar.*Lys.*611, Th.2.34, Lys.12.18, etc.; ποτήρια χρύσεα προθεῖτο Hdt.3.148. **2.** *set out* wares *for show* or *sale*, Luc.*Nigr.*25, al. **3.** *display* a public notice, τὸ λεύκωμα πρὸ τοῦ ναοῦ *IG*9(2). 1109.35 (Coropa, ii B.C.); ἐπ' αὐτῆς τῆς οἰκίας π. ἐν λευκώματι *UPZ* 106.20 (ii B.C.); τὸ ὑπογεγραμμένον ἔκθεμα *OGI*664.4 (Egypt, i A.D.), cf. *POxy.*2108.8 (Pass., iii A.D.); *notify publicly*, τοὺς [προέδρους] προτιθέναι περὶ ὧν δεῖ βουλεύεσθαι *IG*4²(1).68.80 (Epid., iv B.C.); περὶ ὧν.. οἱ ἄρχοντες προτίθεισι 'Αρχ.Δελτ.9 παρ.53 (Eresus), cf. *IG* 12(2).526 *a*21 (ibid., iv B.C.), 645 *b*35 (Nesus, iv B.C.); τὰς πράξεις (exactions).. τῶν προτιθεμένων (Pass.) κατὰ τὰς ἐγγραφὰς Arist.*Pol.* 1321ᵇ42; *call* a case *for trial by means of a public notice*, τῶν κατ' αὐτοὺς προτεθέντων *UPZ*118.18 (ii B.C.); οἱ προτεθέντες ἐπ' ἐμὲ καὶ μὴ ὑπακούσαντες ἴστωσαν ὅτι.. *PHamb.*29.6 (i A.D.); *advertise* for sale or other purpose, *BGU*992 i 7 (Pass., ii B.C.), *PLips.*64.44 (iv A.D.), etc.; τοῖς συλλημψομένοις ὑμῖν γέρα προτιθέντα *advertising* rewards to those of you who apprehend (robbers), *POxy.*1408.16 (iii A.D.). **4.** *propose, bring forward* a thing to be examined and debated, also *give an opportunity for* debate, voting, ἐς μέσον σφι π. πρῆγμα Hdt.1.206; π. τὸν λόγον Id.8.59; γνώμας σφίσιν αὐτοῖς Th. 1.139; π. λόγον (sc. εἰς ἐκκλησίαν) Aeschin.2.65; λόγον περί τινος X.*Mem.*4.2.3; γνώμας π. αὖθις 'Αθηναίοις, of the Prytanes, Th.6.14, cf. 3.36; π. τὴν διαγνώμην αὖθις περὶ Μυτιληναίων ib.42, cf. Isoc.8. 15; π. βουλὴν εἴτε.. εἴτε.. D.H.6.15; τὸν ἐπιμήνιον, ἣν μὴ προθῇ, ἑκατὸν στατῆρας ὀφείλειν *SIG*58.10 (Milet., v B.C.), cf. 141.12 (Corc. Nigra, iv B.C.), 167.13 (Mylasa, iv B.C.), al.; προθεῖναι αὖθις περὶ Μυτιληναίων λέγειν *propose* a discussion about.., Th.3.38; τὸ συμφέρον ἡ πόλις προὐτίθει σκοπεῖν D.18.273, etc.; π. αὐτοῖς κρίσιν *appoint* a trial for them, Lys.27.8; π. αὐτοῖς ἀγορὰν δικῶν Luc.*Bis Acc.*4; προέθηκε.. λέγειν τὰ ἑκατέροισι.. κατέργασται *has proposed* (or *initiated*) a recital of what each has done, Hdt.9.27: c. dat. pers. et inf., Id.3.38: c. acc. et inf., π. γνώμην ἀποφαίνεσθαι τὸν βουλόμενον Id.8. 49:—Med., ἥν τις προθῆται ψῆφον, ὥστε μὴ εἶναι τὸν νόμον τοῦτον *SIG*45.33 (Halic., v B.C.):—Pass., οὐ προὐτέθη σφίσι λόγος speech *was not allowed* them, X.*HG*1.7.5; ψῆφος περὶ ἡμῶν ὑπὲρ ἀνδραποδισμοῦ προτεθεῖσα D.19.65. **5.** *convene* a meeting, προὔθεσαν οἱ πρυτάνεις ἐκκλησίαν Luc.*Nec.*19:—Med., σύγκλητον τήνδε γερόντων προὔθετο λέσχην S.*Ant.*161 (anap.). **III.** *put forward*, as one foot before the other, βραδύπουν ἤλυσιν ἄρθρων E.*Hec.*67 (anap.). **2.** *hold out* as a pretext, αἰτίαν S.*Aj.*1051:—Med., τὴν συγγένειαν Plb. 2.19.1, etc. **IV.** *put before* or *first*, προτιθέντι ἀνάγκη.. λέγειν, opp. ἐπιλέγοντι, Arist.*Rh.*1394ᵃ15, cf. ᵇ28; π. τοῦ λόγου προοίμιον Pl. *Lg.*723c; *set down first* in writing, προθεὶς ἄρχοντα Νικόμαχόν φησιν οὕτως· "ἐπὶ τούτου κτλ." Did. *in D.*1.19, cf. 8.17, al., Gal.19.183:—Med., *put in front*, τοὺς γροσφομάχους Plb.1.33.9; *premise*, λόγον Id.3.118.11; τὰς προειρημένας αἰτίας Id.4.25.6:—Pass., τὸ μὴ καὶ τὸ οὐ προτιθέμενα τῶν ἐπιόντων ὀνομάτων Pl.*Sph.*257c: metaph., Th.2. 42. **2.** *put before* or *over*, πρόσθεν ὀμμάτων πέπλον π. E.*IA*1550:—Med., E.*IT*1218, etc. **3.** *prefer* one to another, τί τινος Hdt.3.53, E.*Med.*963; ἡδονὴν ἀντὶ τοῦ καλοῦ Id.*Hipp.*382:—Med., πάρος τοὐμοῦ πόθου προὔθεντο τὴν τυραννίδα S.*OC*419.

**προτίκτω**, 2 aor. προέτεκον, *bring forth prematurely*, Hp.*Superf.* 17:—Pass., *Cat.Cod.Astr.*2.167. **2.** pf. part. προτετοκυῖα *having had a child*, Sor.1.4.

**προτῑμ-άω** (Ion. -έω Heraclit.55; Phocian dat. pl. part. προτιμέοντοις *Supp.Epigr.*3.416.6 (Elatea, ii B.C.)), *honour* one *before* or *above* another, *prefer* one to another, τὴν σωτηρίαν τοῦ κέρδους, δίκην πλούτου, Antipho 2.2.5, Pl.*Lg.*913b, etc.; also π. ὑὸν ἀντὶ τῶν χρημάτων Id.*Ly.*219d; πρὸ ἀρετῆς κάλλος Id.*Lg.*727d; πλέον αὐτῶν ib.777d; βραχυλογίαν μᾶλλον ἢ μῆκος ib.887b. **2.** c. acc. only, *prefer in honour* or *esteem*, ταῦτα ἐγὼ π. Heraclit. l. c.; οὐ π. τι A.*Eu.*739, etc., cf. *Ag.*1415; τὴν αὐτονομίαν οὐ π. v.l. in Th.8.64; π. τὴν ἀλήθειαν Arist.*EN*1096ᵃ16; π. τὸν ἄνδρα ἀξίως τῆς ἡμετέρας κρίσεως *OGI*244.34 (Daphne, ii B.C.):—Pass., *to be so preferred*, Th. 6.9, Lys.6.50, *OGI*754 (Cilicia), etc.; μᾶλλον προτετίμηται τὸ κάλλος παρ' ἐκείνοις ἢ παρ' ἡμῖν Isoc.10.60; προτιμηθῆναι μάλιστα τῶν 'Ελλήνων X.*An.*1.6.5; προτιμᾶσθαι ἀποθανεῖν *to be selected* as a victim to be put to death, Th.1.133; προτιμᾶσθαι ἐς τὰ κοινά *to be preferred* to public honours, Id.2.37:—Med., τὸν δ' οὐδ' ἂν ἡμιμναίου προτιμησαίμην X.*Mem.*2.5.3: fut. Med. in pass. sense, Id.*An.*1.4.14. **3.** c. inf. folld. by ἤ.., *wish rather, prefer*, προτιμῶντες καθαροὶ εἶναι ἢ εὐπρεπέστεροι Hdt.2.37: c. inf. only, π. πολλοῦ ἐμοὶ ξεῖνος γενέσθαι *valuing* at a great price the privilege of becoming my friend, Id.3. 21: c. acc. et inf., τὸν ἂν ἐγὼ πᾶσι τυράννοισι προετίμησα μεγάλων χρημάτων ἐς λόγους ἐλθεῖν the man for whom I *should have wished, though it might cost me* much money, the opportunity to address all princes, Id.1.86. **II.** *take heed of, reck of*, with neg., μὴ προτιμήσῃς ὑλαγμάτων A.*Ag.*1672 (troch.); τῶν ἐν 'Αδμήτου κακῶν οὐδὲν προτιμῶν E.*Alc.*762; οὐδὲν προτιμῶ σου Ar.*Pl.*883, cf. D.7.16: c. part., χὠπότερον ἂν νῷν ἴδῃς ... -ήσαντά τι τυπτόμενον Ar.*Ra.*638, cf. 655: c. inf., *care* to do or be, ζῆν.. κακῶς κλύουσαν οὐκ ἀνασχετὸν ἥτις π. μὴ κακὴ πεφυκέναι S.*Tr.*722; οὐδὲν π. μηχανήσασθαι τέκνοις E.*Med.* 343: with ὅπως, εἰρήνη δ' ὅπως ἔσται προτιμῶσ' οὐδέν Ar.*Ach.* 27. **-ησις**, εως, ἡ, *honouring before* or *above* others, *preference*, Th. 3.82; pl., Poll.8.140; *assigning a higher value to*, τῶν αὐτῶν ἡ π. καὶ ἡ αἵρεσις Plot.6.7.20; κατὰ προτίμησιν in order of *importance*, τὸ κ. π. σχῆμα (sc. μάλιστα μέν.. κτλ.) Hermog.*Id.*1.11. (Dor. προτίμᾱσις is dub. in *SIG*943.13 (Cos, iii B.C.).) **-ητέον**, *one must prefer before*, τί τινος Pl.*Lg.*726a, Iamb.*Protr.*9; *one must prefer*, c. inf., Pl.*Criti.*109a. **-ία**, ἡ, *preferring in honour, high honour*, Max.Tyr. 2.5; εἰς τὸ θεῖον paid to.., *SIG*601.17 (Teos, ii B.C.). **-ος**, ον, *most honoured*, Xenoph.2.17: abs., π. λίθοι *precious* stones, v.l. in Pl.*Lg.*947d; προτιμότερον τῶν χρημάτων Id.*Erx.*393d (v.l.), cf. J.*AJ* 6.10.2, Luc.*DDeor.*5.3, Ael.*NA*8.4 (s.v.l.), D.C.47.31.

**προτιμῡθέομαι**, Ep. for προσμυθέομαι.

**προτῑμωρέω**, *help beforehand* or *first*, τινι Th.1.74:—Med., *revenge oneself before*, Id.6.57.

**προτῑνάσσω**, *set in movement first*, Archig.ap.Orib.8.1.1 (Pass.).

**προτιοπτος**, ον, Ep. for *πρόσοπτος, *which can be looked at*, Man.2.31.

**προτιόσσομαι**, Ep. Verb, only pres. and impf., and never in the form προσόσσομαι:—*look at* or *upon*, μηδέ τιν' ἀνθρώπων προτιόσσεο Od.7.31, cf. 23.365. **II.** of the mind, *forebode*, κραδίη προτιόσσετ' ὄλεθρον 5.389; θάνατον προτιόσσετο θυμὸς ἀγήνωρ 14.219, cf. A.R.1. 895, al.; so, prob., ἦ σ' εὖ γιγνώσκων προτιόσσομαι from thorough knowledge of thee *I divine* my fate, Il.22.356, cf. A.R.4.1372.

**προτιτλόω**, *entitle* a book, Eust.888.17.

**προτιτρώσκω**, *wound beforehand*, Gal.18(1).86 (Pass.).

**προτῑτύσκω**, *prepare before*, δαῖτα *IGRom.*4.360.34 (Pergam., ii A.D.).

**προτίω** [ῐ], fut. -τίσω [ῑ], *prefer in honour, prefer*, τι A.*Ag.*789 (anap.), *Eu.*546 (lyr.); τάφου.. τὸν μὲν προτίσας.. ἔχει *has deemed* the one *more worthy* of burial, S.*Ant.*22.

**πρότμησις**, εως, ἡ, (προτέμνω) *waist* or *loins*, where the body is drawn in, Il.11.424, Q.S.6.374; = ὀσφῦς, Poll.2.179, *SIG*1017.7 (Sinope, iii B.C.); but cf. *EM*691.18 (πρότμητιν is a variant in Sch.T Il. l.c., cf. προτμῆτις Hsch., πρότμηστιν Phot.); προτμητόν· τὸν ὀμφαλόν, Hsch.

**προτόλημα**, perh. = πρωτόληνον, *PLond.*5.1881.5 (vi A.D.).

**προτολμάομαι**, Pass., *to be first ventured* or *risked*, ἐν Κερκύρᾳ τὰ πολλὰ προτολμήθη Th.3.84; τὰ προτετολμημένα Hdn.6.7.10; τὰ προτολμηθέντα D.C.47.4.

**προτομᾰφόρος**, ὁ, (cf. sq. 3) = Lat. *imaginifer*, *BGU*241.3 (ii A.D.); also **προτομοφόρος**, *Gloss.*

***προτομή**, ἡ, (προτέμνω) *front part cut off*: esp., **1.** *head and face of a decapitated animal* (rarely *of a decapitated man*, Lxx 2 *Ma.* 15.35, and of a boar with human head, Ps.-Plu.*Fluv.*21.4), γλαύκου Antiph.132.4; γρυπὸς *IG*1².280.15; λέοντος *Inscr.Délos* 442 *B*108 (ii B.C.); ἐλάφου *OGI*214.41 (Didyma, iii B.C.); λύκου D.S.1.18; λεόντων, ταύρων, δρακόντων, ib.62; Κερβέρου ib.96; Γοργόνος Corn. *ND*20; χηνίσκων Orib.49.4.28; of a dolphin as figurehead, *AP*7. 215 (Anyt.); π. ἵππου, name of the asterism Equuleus, Gem.3.8,

Ptol.*Alm.*7.5. 2. *cup* in shape of animal's face, Philox.5, *IG* 11(2).287*B*34,134 (Delos, iii B.C.). 3. *bust*, ib.14.1518; *αἱ π. τοῦ Καίσαρος* the *imagines* or *busts* of the Emperor on the Roman standards, J.*AJ*18.3.1, cf. *IG*2$^2$.1108.6, *Ostr.*178 (ii A.D.), al.; *π. τῆς ἀρχῆς* Lyd.*Mag.*3.21.

**προτομίζεσθαι** (–*τολμ*– Suid.)· *προάρχεσθαι* (*προέρχ*– Suid.), Phot.

® **προτον-ίζω**, *haul up with πρότονοι*, *AP*10.2 (Antip. Sid.). ® **–ιον**, *τό*, *piece of temple-furniture*, Poll.10.191; = *ὕφασμα*, Hsch. ® **–οι**, *οἱ*: heterocl. pl. *πρότονα Et.Gud.*483.13, Eust.130.44:—two *ropes from the masthead to the forepart of a ship, forestays* (opp. *ἐπίτονος* 'backstay'), *κατὰ δὲ προτόνοισιν ἔδησαν* [*τὸν ἱστόν*] Od.2.425; *ἱστοῦ δὲ προτόνους ἔρρηξ' ἀνέμοιο θύελλα ἀμφοτέρους, ἱστὸς δ' ὀπίσω πέσεν* 12.409; *ἱστὸν προτόνοισιν ὑφέντες* Il.1.434, cf. Alc.*Supp.*12.10: in sg., *σωτῆρα ναὸς πρότονον* A.*Ag.*897, cf. E.*Fr.*773.42 (lyr.), *PCair.Zen.*754.4 (iii B.C.), Luc.*Nav.*5: metaph., of an old woman's hair, *AP*5.203 (Mel.). II. *halyards*, E.*Hec.*112 (anap.), *IT*1134 (lyr.); *κατὰ προτόνων ἱστίον ἐκπετάσας Epigr.Gr.*779, cf. Call.*Epigr.*6.

**προτρᾰγῳδέω**, *indulge in tragic declamation before*, *ἐπί τι* Sch.E.*Hipp.*601:—Pass., Lyd.*Mag.*2.21.

**προτρᾱχύνω**, *roughen, scrape first*, Gal.17(1).901:—Pass., Sor.1.36.

**προ-τρέπτης**, *ου*, *ὁ*, *one who admonishes* or *exhorts*, Olymp.*in Alc.* p.31 C., *Gloss.* **–τρεπτικός**, *ή*, *όν*, *hortatory*, *λόγοι* Isoc.1.3, cf. Phld.*Po.*5 *Fr.*1, *IG*2$^2$.2291a.4, etc.; *ἡ π. σοφία* skill *in oratory*, Pl.*Euthd.*278c, cf. Chrysipp.*Stoic.*3.189; *π.* (sc. *λόγος*), *ὁ*, title of works by Aristotle, Epicurus, Cleanthes, etc.: Comp., *οὐδὲν –κώτερον* Arr.*Epict.*3.23.36: Sup., *κήρυγμα –κώτατον πρὸς ἀρετήν* Aeschin.3.154. Adv. *–κῶς encouragingly*, Luc.*Somn.*3. 2. generally, *exciting, stimulating*, *ἐς οὔρησιν* Hp.*Acut.*59; *γάλακτος Gp.*12.13.2.

**προτρέπω**, *urge forwards*; used by Hom. only intr. in Med. or Pass., *turn to flight*, *προτρέποντο μελαινάων ἐπὶ νηῶν* Il.5.700; of the sun, *ὅτ' ἂν ἂψ ἐπὶ γαῖαν ἀπ' οὐρανόθεν προτράπηται* Od.11.18, cf. 12.381: metaph., *ἄχεϊ προτραπέσθαι give myself up* to grief, Il.6.336. II. later, in Act., *urge on, impel*, *τίς σ' ἀνάγκη τῇδε προτρέπει;* S.*El.*1193; *π. τινά* Isoc.5.123; opp. *κωλύω*, Arist.*EN*1113$^b$26: c. acc. pers. et inf., *urge on, impel, persuade* one to do a thing, Hdt.9.90, S.*Ant.*270; *π. τὰ δέοντα ποιεῖν ὑμᾶς* D.2.3, cf. *BGU*164.17 (ii/iii A.D.), etc.; *π. τοὺς δικαστὰς ὀργίζεσθαι* Aeschin.2.3; *ὁ καλῶς προτρέπων ἐρᾶν* Pl.*Smp.*181a; *προτρέψαι* (or *–τρέψασθαι*) *τινὰ ὥστε πειρᾶσθαι* Th.8.63: folld. by a Prep., *π. τινὰ εἰς* or *ἐπὶ φιλοσοφίαν*, Pl.*Euthd.*275a, 307a; *ἐπ' ἐλευθερίαν τὰ πλήθη* Id.*Lg.*699e; *ἐπ' ἀρετήν* Isoc.2.8, Lycurg.10, etc.; *ἐπὶ τὰς ἀδικίας* Isoc.7.46; *πρὸς τὸ παρέπεσθαι* Pl.*Phd.*89a, etc.; *συμβουλεύει ἢ προτρέπων ἢ ἀποτρέπων* Arist.*Rh.*1358$^b$15:—Med., c. acc. pers. et inf., A.*Pr.*990, S.*OT*358, etc.; *προτρέπεσθαι ἀνθρώπους ἐπ' ἀρετήν, τοὺς συνόντας πρὸς ἐγκράτειαν*, X.*Mem.*1.4.1, 4.5.1; *νόμοι πολίτας ἐς δικαιοσύνην π.* Id.*Cyr.*2.2.14; *προὐτράπετο εἰς τὸ διαλέγεσθαι* Pl.*Prt.*348c; *πρὸς ἀρετῆς ἐπιτηδεύματα π. τοὺς πολίτας* Id.*Lg.*711b; *ὡς.. προετρέψατο ὁ Σόλων τὸν Κροῖσον εἴπας.., ἐπειρώτα..*, as Solon's story *led* Croesus *on*, he asked, Hdt.1.31; *προτρέψομαι I will lay an injunction on thee*, S.*OT*1446 (v.l.); *prescribe*, *ἐν τῇ φαρμακείῃ* Hp.*Nat.Hom.*9, but cf. Gal.15.122, 19.133:—Pass., *to be persuaded* or *influenced*, *ὑπὸ τῶν ὀρνίθων ἀποτρέπεσθαι καὶ π.* X.*Mem.*1.1.4, cf. Luc.*Icar.*29: c. inf., *ὑπ' ἐκείνων –τραπήσεσθαι ὅ τι ἂν κελεύωνται ποιεῖν* Phld.*Mus.* p.87 K.; *ὑπὸ τῆς ἐλπίδος π. SIG*1073.37 (Olympia, ii A.D.); *προετράπη γράψαι* Ach.Tat.*Vit.Arat.* p.77 Maass. III. *promote*, *οὖρα, χυμόν*, Gal.11.32; *γάλα, σπέρμα*, ib.771:—Pass., *ἢν προτρέπηται ὁποῖα δεῖ* if *stimulated* in the right way, Hp.*Acut.*51. IV. in Med., *outstrip, outdo*, *πάντας ἐν τῷ πίνειν* Plu.2.624c. V. *search out, discover*, E.*Hipp.*715 (acc. to Sch.; dub.l.).

**προτρέφω**, *nourish, feed before*, Alex.Trall.9.3.

® **προτρέχω**, aor. *προὔδρᾰμον* Antipho 3.2.8, X.*An.*1.5.2:—*run forward* or *forth*, ll. cc.; *ἀπὸ τοῦ δένδρου δύο βήματα* X.*An.*4.7.10; [*ἕλμινθες*] *τῷ στομάχῳ προτρέχουσαι* Herod.Med.ap.Aët.9.37. II. *run in advance of, outrun*, *στάδια πέντε τῶν ὁπλιτῶν* X.*An.*5.2.4; *πολλοῖς ἡ γλῶττα προτρέχει τῆς διανοίας* Isoc.1.41; *π. τὰ κοπριζόμενα τῶν ἀκόπρων* Thphr.*HP*8.7.7. III. *ἡ προτρέχουσα εἰκασία* the *foregoing* simile, Heraclit.*All.*5.

® **προτρῐᾱκάς**, *άδος*, *ἡ*, *29th day of the month*, *IG*7.531 (Tanagra).

**προτριβεῖς**· *δριμεῖς καὶ ὀξεῖς*, Hsch.

**προτρίβω** [ῑ], *rub up* or *powder beforehand*, Hp.*Mul.*2.133, Dsc.1.98. 2. *rub first*, *τὰς δᾷδας ἐν τῇ τέφρᾳ* Sch.Arat.1035 (*προστρ*– codd.).

® **πρότρῐτα**, Adv., (*τρίτος*) *for three days before*, or *for three successive days*, Th.2.34, *CIG*3641*b*22 (Lampsacus); *προγράψας π. εἰς τὴν ἡμέραν ταύτην* Aristid.*Or.*51(27).34.

**πρότροπα**· *θυσίας εἶδος*, Hsch.

® **προτροπ-άδην** [ᾰ], Dor. **–δᾱν**, Adv., (*προτρέπω*) *turned forwards*, i.e. *headforemost, with headlong speed*, *π. φοβέοντο* Il.16.304; *π. σπεύδειν* Pi.*P.*4.94; *φεύγειν* Pl.*Smp.*221b, Arr.*An.*3.28.3; *φέρεσθαι* Plb.12.4.4; *π. ὤσασθαι* to drive *headlong*, Plu.*Ages.*18; *φήμαις ψευδέσι π. πεσοῦνται* Ph.2.432. **–ή**, *ἡ*, *exhortation, encouragement*, Democr.181, Ti.Locr.104a (pl.), S.E.*M.*1.98, etc.; opp. *ἀποτροπή*, Arist.*Rh.*1358$^b$8, Phld.*Rh.*1.65 S., cf. *Stoic.*2.287 (pl.); *ἡ Σωκράτους π. ἡμῶν ἐπ' ἀρετήν* Pl.*Clit.*408d; *ἡ εἰς ἀδοξίαν π.* Plu.2.1128b; *εἰς προτροπὴν ἀρετῆς* Onos.1.13, cf. *IG*5(1).1331.10 (Cardamyle); *incitement* to virtue, Diogenian.Epicur.3.6 (pl.); concrete, of persons, *ἵνα τοῖς λοιποῖς προτροπὴ ὦσι Supp.Epigr.*3.583.24 (Olbia, ii/iii A.D.). 2. *urgent invitation, behest*, *κατὰ τὴν π. τῆς βουλῆς POxy.*1252$^v$.27 (iii A.D.), cf. 1415.23 (iii A.D.), *BGU*618.19 (iii A.D.). II. *impulse*, Pl.*Lg.*920b (ed.Ald. for *ῥοπή*), Herod.Med.ap.Orib.6.20.14, Corn.*ND*27. III. *driving force*, *διὰ τὴν τῆς θαλάττης π.* Dion.Byz.3. **–ίς**· *σπυρίς*, Hsch. **–ος** (sc. *οἶνος*), *ὁ*, (*τραπέω*) a sweet Mytilenean wine, that flowed from the grape *before the treading* (cf. Poll.6.17, Moer.p.305 P.), Dsc.5.6, Androm.ap.Gal.13.30, Xenocr.ap.Orib.2.58.114, Ath.1.30b, 2.45c.

® **πρότροχος**, *ὁ*, (*τροχός*) *fore-wheel*, Ath.Mech.34.7.

**προτρύγ-αιος** [ῠ], *ον*, (*τρύγη*) epith. of Dionysus, *presiding over the vintage*, Ach.Tat.2.2, Ael.*VH*3.41; *θεοὶ π.* Poll.1.24. 2. *προτρύγαια*, *τά*, festival of Dionysus and Poseidon, Hsch. **–άω**, *gather the vintage in advance*, *PRev.Laws* 26.11, 17 (iii B.C.). **–ησις**, *εως*, *ἡ*, *early vintage*, Sch.Arat.150 (pl.). **–ητήρ**, *ῆρος*, *ὁ*, *harbinger of the vintage*, name of the star *Vindemiatrix* (ε Virginis), interpol. in Arat.138, cf. Hipparch.2.5.5, 3.1.4, Gem.3.6, Ptol.*Tetr.*24: pl., Plu.2.308a. **–ητής**, *οῦ*, *ὁ*, = foreg., *PHib.*1.27.130 (iv/iii B.C.), Ptol.*Alm.*7.5 codd.

**προτρώγω**, *eat beforehand*, Hp.*Morb.*2.15, 70; *σκόρδον Gp.*12.30.4.

**προτυγχάνω**, *happen* or *be before* one, *προτῠχὸν ξένιον the first* gift *that came to hand*, Pi.*P.*4.35. II. *obtain first*, c. gen., pf. part. *–τετυχηκότες* D.C.47.34: abs., *οἱ προτυχόντες* App.*BC*1.53 (v.l. *προσ–*).

**προτυμβίδιος**, *α, ον*, *before the tomb*, *σῆμα BCH*28.192 (Dorylaeum).

**προτῠπόω**, *form* or *mould beforehand*, *θεὸς π. τὸν γενικὸν ἄνθρωπον* Ph.1.69, cf. Gal.5.418:—Med., *form for oneself*, Hld.9.25; *figure to oneself, conceive*, Luc.*Par.*40:—Pass., *ἐς ἀρετὴν π.* Phld.*Mus.* p.77 K.; *οὕτως τῆς τάξεως –τετυπωμένης ἵνα.. OGI*458.15 (i B.C.).

**προτύπτης**, *ου*, *ὁ*, sine expl., Hdn.Gr.2.898.

® **προτύπτω**, intr., *press forward*, *Τρῶες δὲ προὔτυψαν ἀολλέες* Il.13.136, al.; *ἀνὰ ῥῖνας δριμὺ μένος προὔτυψε rushed forward*, Od.24.319; *Ἀργὼ προὔτυψεν ἐπειγομένη ἀνέμοισιν pressed onward*, A.R.1.953, cf. 3.1397, etc.; *Νεῖλος.. προὔτυψε πόντῳ rushed forward to..*, Nic.*Th.*176, cf. *Al.*499; *πηλαμύσι προὔτυψεν dashed against* them, Opp.*H.*4.545; *ἐς θάλαμον π.* ib.392. II. *forge beforehand*, *προτυπὲν στόμιον μέγα Τροίας* A.*Ag.*132 (lyr.). III. *strike first* or *before another*, Procop.*Vand.*1.18.

**προτύπ-ωμα** [ῠ], *ατος*, *τό*, *pattern*, *π. ἑαυτῷ χρὴ προτιθέναι Σωκράτην* Simp.*in Epict.* p.121 D. **–ωσις**, *εως*, *ἡ*, *prefiguration, preformation*, *παρασκευὴ πρὸς τὰ ὄντα καὶ π.* Plot.6.6.10, cf. Hdn.*Epim.*126.

**προῦ**· *προσέρχου*, Hsch. **προυγελέω**, v. *προυσελέω*.

**προϋγραίνω**, *moisten first*, *σώματα τροφῇ* Hp.*Aph.*4.13, cf. Gal.11.346.

**προϋδροποτέω**, *drink water first*, Antyll.ap.Orib.7.16.2.

**προυεσμένη**· *ἀναβαλλομένη, προϊοῦσα*, Hsch.

® **προϋιωνός**, *ὁ*, *great-grandson*, *Abh.Berl.Akad.*1932(5).51 (Pergam., ii A.D.).

**προύκας**· *δορκάδας*, Hsch.; cf. *πρόξ*.

**προϋλακτέω** [ῠ], *bark in defence of*, *τῶν τρεφόντων* Alciphr.3.62 (prob. for *προσ–*).

**προυλέσι**· *πεζοῖς ὁπλίταις*, Hsch.; cf. *πρυλέες*.

**προϋλίζω**, v.l. for *προδιυλίζω* in Dsc.1.71.5 (ap.Orib.).

**προύμνη**, *ἡ*, *plum-tree, Prunus*, Thphr.*HP*9.1.2.

**προῦμνον**, *τό*, *plum*, Lat. *prunum*, Gal.12.33, Aët.1.214, Alex.Trall.4.

**προῦμορ**· *εἶδος σικύου* or *σύκου* (*οἴκου* cod.), Hsch. (prob. for *πρού⟨ι⟩μορ*, = *πρώϊμος*).

**προύνεικος** or **προύνῑκος** (**προυνικός**, Hsch.), *ὁ*, (*ἤνεικα*) *one who bears burdens out of* the market, *hired porter*, *Com.Adesp.*333, 1343, Hdn.Gr.2.445, Ael.Dion.*Fr.*284 (as pr. n., *IG*3.1100.12, 12(8).484): Byz., acc. to Poll.7.132; used as a term of abuse, *low fellow*, Herod.3.12, 65, D.L.4.6; *ἀνδράσι π.* prob. in Epic.ap.Ath.14.639d: as Adj., *lewd*, *φιλήματα AP*12.209 (Strat.). (Derived fr. *πρό, ἐνείκω* by Ael.Dion. l.c., cf. *AB*1415, Phot.; also expld. by *πρό, νεῖκος EM*691.19.)

**προυνῑκία**, *ἡ*, *lewd conduct*, Hsch. s.v. *σκίταλοι*. **προὐννέπω**, v. *προεννέ*–. **προύνους**· *βουνούς*, Id.

**προϋπ-άγομαι** [ᾰ], Med., *lead on*, *εἰς ἔρωτά τινος προϋπῆκτο* D.C.58.28. **–ᾰκουστέον**, *one must understand* (*supply*) words *before*, Sch.Ptol.*Tetr.*79, 122. **–ᾰκούω**, *obey before*, *Ῥωμαίων* App.*Ill.*15. **–ᾰλείφω**, *anoint beforehand*, Gal.11.103. **–αλλάττω**, *mortgage previously*, *POxy.*1034.3 (ii A.D.):—Pass., ib.907.18 (iii A.D.). **–αντάω**, *advance to meet*, J.*AJ*8.1.2, *BJ*2.5.2, Hld.9.22; *δίκῃ π. τινί* Ph.2.532: abs., ib.13. **–αντιάζω**, = foreg., ib.22, Olymp.Hist.p.456 D. **–αρχή**, *ἡ*, *previous service*, *τὴν π. ἀμείψασθαι* Arist.*EN*1165$^a$5. **–άρχω**, *take the initiative in* a thing, c. gen., *ἀδικίας* Th.3.40; *τῶν εὐεργεσιῶν, τῆς ἔχθρας*, Isoc.5.36, 125: c. dat., *π. τῷ ποιεῖν εὖ* D.20.46: with neut. Adj., *π. τι ἔς τινα* D.C.38.34:—Pass., *τὰ προϋπηργμένα εἰς αὐτόν benefits formerly received*, D.49.25, cf. *OGI*244.8 (Daphne, ii B.C.), Hierocl.*in CA*7 p.429 M.; but also *προϋπηργμένα ἀδικήματα* Iamb.*Myst.*4.5. II. intr., *exist before, be pre-existent*, Th.2.85, 4.126, Pl.*Prt.*317d, *PLille* 1$^v$4 (iii B.C.), etc.; *οἱ νόμοι οἱ προϋπάρχοντες* Arist.*Pol.*1292$^b$20, cf. *SIG*526.31 (Itanos, iii B.C.); *ἡ τῶν σωμάτων αὔξησις ἐκ προϋπαρχόντων ἐστίν* from *pre-existent materials*, Arist.*Rh.*1419$^b$22; *πᾶσα μάθησις ἐκ προϋπαρχούσης γίνεται γνώσεως* Id.*APo.*71$^a$1; *προϋπάρξαντα things that happened before, past events*, v.l. for *πρὶν ὑπ.* in D.1.11; *τὰ προϋπάρχοντα former possessions*, Ceb.31, D.C.38.38; *οἱ π. ὕπατοι* the *previous* consuls, Plb.3.106.2: pf. Pass., *τὰ προϋπηργμένα antecedents*, D.18.262, Arist.*Rh.*1367$^b$13; *οἰκειότης, χάρις προϋπηργμένη*, J.*Ap.*1.29, A.D.

Synt.132.21. 2. c. gen., προϋπάρχειν δεῖ τὸ κινοῦν τοῦ κινουμένου must exist before.., Arist.MA700$^b$1; π. ἑαυτοῦ S.E.M.10.208; to be logically prior, μέθοδος πασῶν προϋπάρχουσα καὶ κυριωτέρα Nicom.Ar.1.4. -ειμι, exist before, νόσος ἀργαλεωτέρα τῆς προϋπούσης Ph.1.282. II. precede, προϋπόντα μόρια, προϋποῦσα εὐθεῖα, A.D.Synt.17.22, 93.20, cf.18. -εκλύω, loosen or weaken beforehand, Hld.9.17. -εξέρχομαι, go out secretly before, D.C.48.13. ⊛-εξορμάω, rush out before, Luc.DMort.27.3. -εργάζομαι, prepare beforehand, D.S.3.16:—Pass., προϋπείργαστο ἡ ψυχὴ πρὸς πειθαρχίαν Ph.2.94. -εργᾰσία, ἡ, preparation, previous defence of what one is going to say, Lat. praemunitio, as a form of Rhetoric, like προπαρασκευή, Rufinianus 32 (Rhet.Lat.Min.p.46 Halm). -ερείδομαι, Pass., to be sustained (by food) beforehand, Aret.CA2.3.

**προϋπεροχή**, ἡ, protuberance above the eye, Aët.13.35 (pl.).

**προϋπ-έρχομαι**, to be moved first, of the bowels, Gal.18(2).271. -εύθῡνος, ον, previously subject or liable, c. dat., Keil-Premerstein Dritter Bericht No.55 (ii/iii A.D.). -ηρετέω, serve previously, Gal.14.74. -ισχνέομαι, promise before, διηγήσασθαι (leg. -εσθαι) Plb.31.23.2: c. inf. fut., J.AJ20.7.1: τι D.C.60.25:—Pass., προϋπεσχημέναι δραχμαί App.BC3.74. II. bid before, Sammelb.5673.7 (Pass., ii A.D.).

**προϋπο-βάλλω**, put under first, Gal.11.138, 18(2).568:—Med., put under as a foundation, Plu.2.966d, Them.in de An.49.6, al.:—Pass., to be prepared or ready as material, Luc.Hist.Conscr.51. -βρέχω, moisten beforehand, Hippiatr.58 (Pass.). -γρᾰφή, ἡ, previous sketch, outline, Plot.6.7.7. -γράφω [ᾰ], sketch out, indicate before, ὅτι.. Clearch.39, cf. Plot.6.7.7; π. ἑαυτῷ καὶ προελπίζειν Simp.in Epict.p.50D.:—Med., σχῆμα πόλεως Plu.Luc.31. II. subscribe, sign first, συνθήμασι Lyd.Mag.2.10. -δείκνῡμι, explain beforehand, Aristid.2.226J., Hierocl.in CA20p.466M.; ἐκεῖνο, ὅτι.. Ph.1.480:—Pass., προϋποδεδειγμένων τῶν ὅσα.. Longin.43.6, cf. S.E.M.2.71. -θετέον, one must assume in advance, Iamb.Comm.Math.4, al. -κατασκευή, ἡ, foretaste, Simp.in Cat.249.33. ⊛-κειμαι, serving as pf. Pass. to προϋποτίθημι, to be put under before, Dsc.1.8, Sor.1.68, Gal.6.289; subsist before, τὰ -κείμενα parts already founded, of a city, Str.5.3.7; -κειμένης ὥσπερ ἐδάφους τῆς ἐν τῷ λέγειν δυνάμεως Longin.8.1; χώραν ἔδει καὶ τόπον -κεῖσθαι τοῖς γενομένοις Plu.2.678f; τὸ δεξόμενον π. σώματι Ph.2.490, cf. S.E.P.3.94; προϋπόκειται τοῦ ἀνδριάντος τὸ ἐργαστήριον Id.M.10.218, cf. Hierocl.in CA10p.436M.; -κειμένη γνῶσις A.D.Synt.29.19; σῶμα -κείμενον Dam.Pr.14. 2. to be assumed first, Nicom.Ar.1.4. II. to be mortgaged before, Plu.Sol.15, PMasp.97.34, al. (vi A.D.). -λαμβάνω, assume beforehand, Arist.APo.71$^a$12; ἀλόγως π. make an improbable presumption, Id.Po.1461$^b$1. 2. hold an opinion previously, Id.Rh.1395$^b$6. -μνημᾰτίζομαι: οἱ -σάμενοι previous commentators, Sch.Pi.I.2 Arg., Sch.E.Med.209. -πάσσω, strew under before, κόπρον Gp.12.14.1.

**προϋποπτεύω**, suspect before, J.BJ7.7.4, Hld.7.2; τι ἔς τινα D.C.38.15.

**προϋπο-ρρίπτω**, cast under first, Sor.2.13 (Pass.). -σπείρω, sow beforehand, metaph. in Pass., π. φιλίαι καὶ ἐλπίδες Vett.Val.269.30. ⊛-στᾰσις, εως, ἡ, = προϋπαρξις, Dsc.Ther.Praef., Procl.Inst.11, Dam.Pr.118. -στέλλομαι, Med., use abstinence first, Archig.ap.Orib.8.2.17. II. Pass., to be placed beneath, προϋπέσταλται τοῖς ὑποχονδρίοις ὁ σπλὴν καὶ τὸ ἧπαρ Ruf.Anat.28. -στικτέον, one must punctuate before, Sch.Il.2.155 cod.A. -στρώννῡμι, strew or put under before, in Pass., Gp.4.15.5, 5.8.5. II. Pass., constitute a prior foundation, ἡ ὕλη ζῳογονία -στρώννυται τῆς μεριστῆς Dam.Pr.341, cf. Ammon.in Porph.120.13. -στῡφή, ἡ, astringent, hardening process: metaph. in pl., οἱ πόνοι π. τινὲς τοῖς παισίν εἰσι..ἀρετῆς Theano Ep.4.4. -σχεσις, εως, ἡ, previous promise, Sch.Hermog. in Rh.6.184W. -τάσσω, place under one before, Lxx 3Ma.1.2 (Pass.). -τέμνω, cut away from under before, Hld.4.18. -τίθημι, set under before, Hp.Acut.21; σπόνδυλον [θύρᾳ] Aen.Tact.36.2 (Pass.); προϋποθεὶς τὸν Ἄτλαντα τοῖς βάρεσι Ph.Byz.Mir.6.2. 2. Pass., to be laid as a foundation before, θεμέλιον ἢ οἷον ἔδαφος -τιθέμενον Dam.Pr.121; -τιθεμένην ἀρχήν ibid. II. Med., assume as preliminary, πολλά Arist.Pol.1325$^b$38, cf. Plu.2.1013b. 2. premise, ὡς.. Longin.1.3; ταῦτα Str.1.2.11, Cleom.1.10. 3. mortgage before, PFlor.81.6 (ii A.D.). -τοπέω, suspect before, τινα D.C.39.57, 46.49. -τρέφω, bring up before:—Pass., ἐν συγγενείᾳ καὶ φιλίᾳ -τεθραμμένοι Inscr.Prien.109.46 (ii B.C.). -τῡπόομαι, Pass., to be sketched in outline before, τούτων προϋποτυπωθέντων Ph.1.493, cf. Alex.Trall.8.2. -φαίνω, indicate beforehand, Plu.2.583b. -φεύγω, escape secretly before, Suid. s.v. διώκειν. -χέω, pour under before, Dsc.Eup.1.235. ⊛-χρίω [ῑ], smear underneath before, Asclep.ap.Gal.13.743, Aët.7.43.

**προϋπτιάζω**, elate first, αὐτοὺς τῷ.. ἐπαίνῳ Sch.D.Chr.33.17 (A. Sonny AdD.Chr.Analecta p.117).

**προϋπτος**, ον, contr. for πρόοπτος.

**προὔργου**, contr. for πρὸ ἔργου (as it is written in Arist.Rh.1354$^b$27, PA674$^b$2, Arr.Fr.163J.), serving for or towards a work, serviceable, τι τῶν προὔργου something useful, Th.4.17, Ar.Pl.623; οὐδὲν π. [ἐστί] it's no good, And.2.21; τῶν π. τι δρᾶν Ar.Ec.784; φαίνεταί μοι π. τι ἂν γενέσθαι Pl.Tht.197a, cf. Isoc.4.19, etc.; ἆρά τι π. ἡμῖν ἐστιν αὐτὸ σκοποῦσι πρὸς τὸ κατιδεῖν; Pl.R.376c; εἴς τι ib.d; π. τι ποιῆσαι εἴς τι ib.498d; π. τι πεποιηκέναι πρός τι Id.Men.84b, cf. X.HG7.1.10; ὑπόθεσιν π. ἔχειν πρὸς.. Pl.Men.87a: c. gen., τί ὑμῖν π. τῆς ξυνόδου ταύτης ἂν εἴη; Id.Demod.380c; οὐδὲν αὐτοῖς ἦν π., c. inf., Id.Alc.2.149e, cf. D.5.1: as Adv. serviceably, conveniently, π. πεσόντα E.IT309, cf. Hel.1379. II. Comp. προὐργιαίτερος, α, ον, more serviceable, important, ἕτερα ἦν προὐργιαίτερα αὐταῖς Ar.Lys.20, cf. D.19.228; χάριν προὐργιαιτέραν Din.1.114: mostly in neut., τῷ μὲν οὐδὲν προὐργιαίτερόν ἐστιν ἢ σκοπεῖν Isoc.4.134, cf. PSI4.380.7 (iii B.C.); π. ποιεῖσθαί τι deem of more consequence, Th.3.109, Isoc.6.35 (also Posit. in Comp. sense, οὐδὲν ἔστι μοι προὔργου ἤ.. Hp.Ep.17); οὐδὲν π. ποιεῖσθαι τούτου Plb.2.7.10, etc.; π. τι γενέσθαι Pl.Grg.458c.—Sup. προὐργιαίτατος, η, ον, Hsch., Suid.; προὐργιέστατος Hsch. s.v. προκαδέστατον: Adv. Sup. προυργιαίτατα cj. in Hp.Liqu.6; -ιαίτατον Paul.Aeg.3.61.

**προυρός**, ὁ, = φρουρός, official title at Clazomenae, Schwyzer 709$^a$16 (iii B.C.); in Thessaly, ib.600 (iii B.C.).

**προυσελέω**, treat with contumely, outrage, maltreat, δρῶν ἐμαυτὸν ὧδε προυσελούμενον A.Pr.438 (προσηλούμενον with ε written over η, cod.Med.; προσελούμενον cett.); οὓς μὲν ἴσμεν εὐγενεῖς..προυσελοῦμεν Ar.Ra.730 cod.Rav. (προσ- cett., προυγελοῦμεν Stob.): προσηλούμενον is written in codd. of Ael.Ep.3; Hsch. has προσέλει· προπηλακίζει, προυγελεῖν· προπηλακίζειν, ὑβρίζειν; cf. προυσελεῖν λέγουσι τὸ ὑβρίζειν EM690.11; προσελοῦμεν· προπηλακίζομεν, ἐλαύνομεν, εἰσβάλλομεν, Suid.—The etym. is unknown.

**προυσέληνος**, v. προσέληνος.

**προυστέλλιον**, = Lat. armo, dub. in Gloss.

**προὐφ-αιρέω**, snatch, π. τὰς ἐκκλησίας, i.e. have them held before the proper time, Aeschin.2.61. -αρπάζω, snatch beforehand, Sch.Ar.Pax 289, Sch.S.Aj.1; τὴν σημασίαν EM401.2.

⊛**προυφῆτις**, ιδος, ἡ, = προφ- (metri gratia), Hymn. in Inscr.Perg.324.17.

⊛**προϋφίσταμαι**, fut. -υποστήσομαι A.D.Synt.14.12:—presuppose, Phld.Sign.16: but usu. in aor. 2 and pf. Act., exist before, Lxx Wi.19.7, Plu.2.636d, etc.; προϋφεστῶσα γνῶσις A.D.Pron.7.2; τὰ προϋφεστῶτα antecedents, Aen.Gaz.Thphr.p.43B.; π. ἔν τινι Dam.Pr.23; ἀριθμὸν -στάντα ἐν τῇ τοῦ θεοῦ διανοίᾳ Nicom.Ar.1.6: c. gen., πέφυκε τὸ δυνατὸν -εστάναι τοῦ ἐνδεχομένου Plu.2.570f; τὸ ὁλόκληρον π. παντὸς πεπονθότος A.D.Synt.142.25.

**προφᾰγεῖν**, aor. inf. of προεσθίω, eat before, Theopomp.Hist.177(a), S.E.P.1.110, etc.

**προφαίνω**, poet. 2 aor. Pass. προφάνη B.5.77:—bring to light, show forth, manifest, τοῖσι θεοὶ τέρας προὔφαινον Od.12.394; οὐρανῷ σκέλη π. let them be seen, S.El.753; ὡς τέρατα π. Thphr.CP2.17.4; display, τὰς πορφυρίδας Luc.Nigr.21: metaph., Ἀχιλεὺς..Αἴγιναν π. brought it into light, made it illustrious, Pi.I.8(7).61:—Pass., to be shown forth, come to light, appear, προὐφαίνετο πᾶσα [νῆσος] Od.13.169; προφάνητε Κάστορ καὶ Πολύδευκες Alc.Supp.12.3, cf. Hp.Aër.8, Superf.4, S.Ant.1149 (lyr.), OT163 (lyr.), E.Hipp.1228; ψυχὰ προφάνη Μελεάγρου B.l.c.; προπέφανται ἅπαντα is all open to view, Il.14.332; ἱππέων τάξις μεγάλη ἐν τῷ πεδίῳ π. X.Cyr.6.3.12: c. inf., οὐδὲ προὐφαίνετ' ἰδέσθαι there was not light enough for us to see, Od.9.143: aor. part. Pass. προφᾰνείς, εῖσα, coming forward and appearing, 24.160; προφανέντε (v.l. -εῖσα) ἀνὰ πτολέμοιο γεφύρας Il.8.378; ἐς πόλεμον, ἐς πεδίον προφανέντε, 17.487, 24.332; ὥς τις ἀφ' αἵματος ὑμετέρου προφανεῖσα S.OC246 (anap.); appear to the mind, ἄτοπα π. Pl.Chrm.172e; πολλά γέ μοι π. τοιαῦτα πρὸ τῆς ψυχῆς dawn upon, Id.Hp.Ma.300c, cf. 303c; of sound, to be plainly heard, προὐφάνη κτύπος S.Ph.202; δεινὰ προὐφάνη λέγων Id.OT790 (sed leg. προὔφηνεν). 2. show forth by word, indicate or declare, οὔτε μείζον' οὔτ' ἐλάσσονα Id.Tr.324; οἱ ἐφ' ἑκάστης μαντείας προφαινόμενοι θεοί indicated by the oracle, D.21.54; ὁ νῦν π. λόγος Pl.R.545b. 3. = προτίθημι 1.3, offer, ἆθλα X.Cyr.2.1.23. II. show beforehand, foreshow, esp. of oracles and divine revelations, Hdt.7.37, S.Tr.849 (lyr.), X.Cyr.4.5.15; π. πολὺν καρπόν have a great promise of fruit, Thphr.HP4.14.9: folld. by a relat. clause, ὁ δαίμων π. ὡς αὐτὸς μὲν τελευτήσειν..μέλλοι Hdt.1.210; ὅκως στρατιὴν πέμψεις.., οὐ προφαίνεις holdest out no hope that.., Id.7.161: c. inf., τόν μοι ὁ δαίμων π. ἐν τῇ ὄψει ἐπαναστήσεσθαι Id.3.65. III. seemingly intr. (the cogn. acc. φάος or φῶς being understood), give forth light, shine forth, οὐδὲ σελήνη οὐρανόθεν προὔφαινε Od.9.145, cf. Antioch.Astr. in Cat.Cod.Astr.1.110; hold a light before one, Plu.Cic.22; of a torch, λύχνου -φαίνοντος Id.Sol.21; ὁ προφαίνων torch-bearer, Id.Cat.Mi.41.

**προφάν-εια** [φᾱ], ἡ, eminence, distinction, Vett.Val.181.33 (pl.), al. ⊛-ής, ές, foreseen, ὁ π. ἔχθιστος φόνων B.3.51; τὰ π. Arist.EN1117$^a$21. II. seen clearly or plainly, conspicuous, φῶς τῷ Κύρῳ ἐκ τοῦ οὐρανοῦ π. γενέσθαι X.Cyr.4.2.15; τὰ προφανέστατα εἴδη Thphr.HP3.18.8. 2. metaph., plain, clear, ἡμῖν προφανῆ Pl.R.530d; ἀπὸ τοῦ προφανοῦς openly, Th.1.35,66, 2.93, etc.; ἐκ τοῦ π. Id.3.43, 6.73, etc.; ἐκ τοῦ προφανεστάτου D.S.12.39. Adv. -νῶς Lxx Si.51.13, PTeb.25.5 (ii B.C.), Plb.1.21.9, Lysis ap. Iamb.VP17.77, Gal.1.643, al. 3. metaph., famous, renowned, Man.2.362; conspicuous, extraordinary, of a disaster, IG12(8).92.2 (Imbros, ii/i B.C.): irreg. Comp. -ώτερος Ptol.Tetr.167 (s.v.l.). III. στομάτων προφανέων f.l. in Hp.Mul.1.17. -τᾰσιόομαι, Pass., to be already enabled to conceive or imagine, τοῖς ὑπὸ Εὐκλείδου γεγραμμένοις ἤδη Papp.678.9. -τις, ιδος, ἡ, = προφῆτις, Trag.Adesp.425. -τος, ον, appearing at a distance, far seen, hence far-famed, π. σοφία καθ' Ἕλλανας Pi.O.1.117. II. foreshown, esp. by an oracle, ἐμοὶ γὰρ ἦν π. ἐκ πατρός S.Tr.1159; ὡς τὸ θεῖον ἦν π. as the divine oracle ran, ib.1163; ὥς σφι αἰεὶ τὠυτὸ π. ἐγίνετο Hdt.5.63; πρόφαντα δέ σφι..ἐγίνετο oracles were delivered to them, Id.9.93; σημεῖον π. J.AJ18.6.9.

⊛**προφᾰσ-ίζομαι**, impf. προὐφασιζόμην Th.1.90: Att. fut. προφασιοῦμαι Aeschin.3.24, later -ίσομαι Sch.Ar.Ec.1019: aor. προὐφασισάμην Th.5.54, X.Cyr.2.2.30, etc.; προεφ- D.C.59.26:—allege by way *of excuse, plead in excuse*, c. acc., τὸν αὐλητήν Thgn.941; τὸν μῆνα Th.5.54; ἀεί τι D.48.20: c. inf., *allege as an excuse that..*, ἀρρωστεῖν Id.19.124; so π. ὅτι οὐκ ἐπίστανται X.*Oec.*20.14: c. acc. cogn., πάσας προφάσεις π. Pl.*R.*474e, cf. Lys.8.16: abs., *make excuses*, Ar.*Lys.*756, Th.1.90; οὐκ ἔφη χρῆναι π. οὐδὲ διαμέλλειν Id.6.25; π. ὑπέρ τινος Isoc.4.13: aor. in pass. sense, ὡς εὗρον ἅπαν..προφασισθέν that all *was used as a pretext*, all *was a mere pretence*, Th.8.33, cf. D.C.*Fr.*57.72. II. *allege* (by way of accusation) *that..*, Σάρδεσιν ἐπιβουλεῦσαι [ἡμᾶς] π. Pl.*Mx.*240a. III. *seek a quarrel against*, τινι Lxx 4*Ki.*5.7. ※ **-ις**, εως, ἡ, (προφαίνω) *motive* or *cause alleged*, whether truly or falsely: then, *actual motive* or *cause*, whether alleged or not: I. *alleged motive, plea*, without implication of truth or falsity, ἐπὶ σμικρῇ π. Thgn.323; νόστου π. γλυκεροῦ κώλυεν μεῖναι Pi.*P.*4.32; κατὰ θεωρίης πρόφασιν ἐκπλώσας Hdt.1.29; π. ἔχων, ὡς.. Id.6.133; καὶ ἐπὶ μεγάλῃ καὶ ἐπὶ βραχείᾳ π. whether the *plea put forward* be a trifle or a weighty matter, Th.1.141; τῆς αἰτίας τὴν π. the *plea* in the case, the *basis* of the charge, Lys.9.7; τοιαύτας ἔχοντες π. καὶ αἰτίας *pleas* and motives, Th.3.13; π. ἐπιεικής ib.9; ἀναγκαῖαι Is.4.20, D.54.17; προφάσεις ἀληθεῖς λέγοντος *pleading* what was in fact true, And.4.17. 2. *falsely alleged motive* (or *cause*), *pretext, pretence, excuse*, π. ἰδίης ἀβουλίης an *excuse* for.., Democr.119; οὔτε τιν' ἔχων π. οὔτε λόγον εὐτράπελον Ar.*V.*468 (lyr.); καλλίστην εἶναι π., τιμωρεῖσθαι μὲν δοκεῖν, ἔργῳ δὲ χρηματίζεσθαι Lys.12.6: abs. in acc., πρόφασιν *in pretence, ostensibly*, στενάχοντο γυναῖκες Πάτροκλον π., σφῶν δ' αὐτῶν κήδε' ἑκάστη Il.19.302, cf. Hdt.5.33, E.*IA*362 (troch.), Ar.*Eq.*466, etc.; opp. τὸ ἀληθές, Th.6.33: in dat., προφάσει Id.3.86; προφάσει τῶν δημοσίων on the *pretence* that public debts are owing, *OGI*669.15 (Egypt, i A.D.); προφάσιος [εἵνεκεν], προφάσεως ἕνεκα, Hdt.4.135, Antipho 6.14; προφάσεως χάριν Arist.*Pol.*1297ᵃ14; ἐκ μικρᾶς π. Plb.2.17.3; ἐπὶ προφάσιος Hdt.7.150: folld. by an inf., αὕτη γὰρ ἦν σοι π. ἐκβαλεῖν ἐμέ for casting me out, S.*Ph.*1034; οὔτε..ἔστιν οὐδεμία π. τοῦ μὴ δρᾶν Pl.*Ti.*20c; π. τοῖς δειλοῖς ἔχει μὴ ἰέναι gives them an *excuse* or *plea* for not going, Id.*R.*469c; οὐδεμία σοι π. ἐστιν ὡς.. X.*Cyr.*2.2.15; εὑρὼν π. *BGU*1024 vi 21 (iv A.D.). b. phrases, πρόφασιν διδόναι, ἐνδοῦναι, allow, afford an *excuse*, D.43.53, 18.158; οὐκ ἐνδώσομεν π. οὐδενὶ κακῷ γενέσθαι Th.2.87; π. μηδεμίαν θέμενος making no *excuse*, Thgn.364; π. προτεῖναι put forward a *pretext*, Hdt.1.156; π. τὴν Παυσανίεω ὕβριν προϊσχόμενοι Id.8.3; προφάσεις παρέχειν Ar.*Av.*581, cf. D.10.35, 18.156; προφάσιας εἷλκον kept making *pretences*, Hdt.6.86; πάσας π. ἕλκουσιν Ar.*Lys.*726; π. δέχεσθαι Pl.*Cra.*421d (cf. ἀγών III. 5); π. εὑρίσκειν τοῦ ἀδικήματος Antipho 5.65; π. καλῶς εὑρημένη Archipp.36; ἔχθρας π. ζητήσουσιν Pl.*Phdr.*234a, cf. *PCair.Zen.*270.9 (iii B.C.); π. τινὰ πρεσβείας πορισάμενοι Pl.*Ep.*350a; π. κατασκευάσαι X.*Cyr.*2.4.17; ἔχει προφάσεις it is excusable, ib.3.1.27; πρόφασιν ταύτην τῆς διαφορᾶς ποιούμενος Pl.*Ep.*349d; προφάσεις εὐλόγους εἰλήφεσαν D.18.152; ἐχόμενος προφάσιος Hdt.6.94; ἐπιλαβέσθαι Id.3.36, 6.49; τὰς π. ἀφελεῖν D.2.27; προφάσεως δεῖσθαι Arist.*Rh.*1373ᵃ3: personified, τὰν Ἐπιμαθέος ὀψινόου θυγατέρα Π. Pi.*P.*5.28. c. elliptically, μή μοι πρόφασιν no *excuse*, no *shuffling*, Ar.*Ach.*345; μὴ προφάσεις ἐνταῦθά μοι Alex.127.1. II. *the actual motive, purpose*, or *cause*, whether alleged or not, οὔτ' εὐνῆς προφάσιν κεχρημένος οὔτε τευ ἄλλου Il.19.262; ἐπ' αὐτομολίας προφάσει ἀπέρχονται Th.7.13; τὸ ἐκ προφάσεως τῶν.. στρατιωτῶν δηληγατευθὲν μέτρον ἐλαίου for the *purpose* of.., *PLips.*64.2, cf. 8 (iv A.D.); τὴν ἀληθεστάτην π., ἀφανεστάτην δὲ λόγῳ Th.1.23, cf. 6.6, D.18.156, *SIG* 888.138 (Scaptopara, iii A.D., pl.): esp. as a medical t.t., *external exciting cause*, ἐκ πάσης π. ἐκτιτρώσκουσι they miscarry on any *provocation*, Hp.*Aph.*3.12, cf. *Epid.*3.3, 3.17.ια', *Acut.*(*Sp.*)6; τοὺς δ' ἄλλους ἀπ' οὐδεμιᾶς π...τῆς κεφαλῆς θέρμαι..ἐλάμβανε Th.2.49: pl., Hp.*Aër.*16, *Fract.*15, al.: generally, *cause*, σμικρὰ π. ἔξωθεν Pl.*R.*556e; βραχεῖα π. Hp.*Coac.*477; ἀπὸ μηδεμιᾶς π. ἔξωθεν ἀξιολόγου Diocl.*Fr.*82; φανερὴ π. Hp.*Aph.*2.41, cf. X.*HG*6.4.33; ἐπεὶ δέ οἱ ἔδεε κακῶς γενέσθαι, ἐγένετο ἀπὸ προφάσιος τὴν ἐγὼ..ἀπηγήσομαι Hdt.2.161, cf. 4.145, 7.230; ἄνθρωπός εἰμι, τοῦτο δ' αὐτὸ τῷ βίῳ π. μεγίστην εἰς τὸ λυπεῖσθαι φέρει Diph.106, cf. Men.230, 811, Philem.194; βραχείας προφάσεως ἔδει μόνον ἐφ' ᾗ..δεξόμεθα.. it needed but a little *to move* us to.., E.*IA*1180. 2. *occasion*, θοἰμάτιον δεικνὺς τοδὶ πρόφασιν ἔφασκον, ὦ γύναι, λίαν σπαθᾷς I said *à propos*, ..I *took occasion* to say.., Ar.*Nu.*55; ἐπὶ τῇ ἐμῇ π. *à propos* of me, Lys.6.19; ἐπὶ τῇ π. τῆς ἐμαυτοῦ ἀρχῆς on the *occasion* of my accession, *PFay.*20.11 (iii/iv A.D.). III. *persuasion, suggestion*, dub. l. in S.*Tr.*662 (lyr.). IV. *preface*, τὰς σημειώσεις ὑπὸ μίαν ἐκθησόμεθα π. Dsc.*Ther.*3. **-ιστέον**, *excuses must be made*, τῷ νέῳ ἐκ τῶν τοιούτων π. Arist.*Rh.Al.*1437ᵇ7. ※ **-ιστικός**, ή, όν, *reproachful*, Lxx *De.*22.14, 17; εὑρεσιλογίαι Ph.2.448.

**προφάσκω**, gloss on προχαίνω, Eust.1109.40.

**προφᾱτεύω, προφάτας**, Dor. for προφητ-.

**πρόφᾰτος**, ον, = πρόφαντος, *shown forth, renowned*, Pi.*O.*8.16 (s. v. l.; πρόφαντον codd. vett., contra metrum).

**προφάω**, *shine forth*, Max.280.

**προφερής**, ές, (προφέρω) poet. Adj., *carried before, placed before, excelling*, c. gen., ἀλλάων προφερὴς τ' ἦν πρεσβυτάτη τε Hes.*Sc.*260: Hom. only Comp. (exc. Sup., ἅλματι..πάντων προφερέστατος Od.8.128), *more excellent*, τῶν δ' ἄλλων ἐμέ φημι πολὺ προφερέστερον εἶναι Od.8.221: c. dat. rei, βίῃ προφερέστερος 21.134: c. inf., [ἡμίονοι] βοῶν προφερέστεραί εἰσιν ἑλκέμεναι Il.10.352: Sup., προφερεστάτη ἐστὶν ἁπασέων Hes.*Th.*79, 361 (where it is commonly interpreted *eldest*); ἀνὴρ προφερέστατος ἀνδρῶν *IG*14.935, cf. Theoc.17.4; ἡνιόχων π. *IG*14.1628, cf. *Epigr.Gr.*435 (Trachonitis); also Comp. and Sup., προφέρτερος, προφέρτατος in the sense of *older, eldest*, S.*Fr.*447, *OC* 1531. II. *looking older than one is, well-grown*, Pl.*Euthd.*271b, cf. Aeschin.1.49; of plants and young persons, *forced, premature, precocious*, τὰ π. Aristox.ap.Stob.4.37.4, cf. Iamb.*VP*31.209.

**προφέρ-ιστος**, ον, *surpassing, excellent*, Dioscorus in *PLit.Lond.* 100 C 1. **-τερος, -τατος**, v. προφερής I.

※ **προφέρω**, Ep. and Ion. impf. προφέρεσκον, Q.S.4.275, *IG*14.1747.6 (Rome): fut. προοίσω: aor. 1 προήνεγκα: aor. 2 προήνεγκον Th.5.17: Hom. only pres.; 3 sg. pres. subj. προφέρῃσι Il.9.323:—*bring before* or *to* one, *present*, ὡς ὄρνις..νεοσσοῖσι προφέρῃσι μάστακα Il. l. c.; νέκυν Ἀχιλλῆϊ 17.121; μάντεις σφάγια προὔφερον Th.6.69; προενέγκας τὴν ἐπιστολὴν *BGU*1141.11 (i B.C.), cf. *PTeb.*291.43 (ii A.D.), etc. 2. of words, σφιν ὀνείδεα π. *cast* reproaches *in* their *teeth*, Il.2.251; π. τινί *throw in* one's *teeth, bring forward, allege*, esp. in the way of reproach or objection, μή μοι δῶρ' ἐρατὰ πρόφερε χρυσέης Ἀφροδίτης 3.64, cf. Hdt.1.3, 8.61, 125, Isoc.4.100; π. τοὔνομα τοῦθ' ὡς ὄνειδος D.21.190; δικαιώσεις ἀλλήλοις Th.5.17: abs., *reproach* (folld. by words quoted), Hdt.3.120:—also in Med., τὴν ἐν Δωδώνῃ ἀσέβειαν Plb.5.11.2; εἶναι βασιλικὴν γῆν *PTeb.*81.17 (ii B.C.), cf. *PAmh.*2.30.7 (ii B.C.), etc. 3. *utter*, μῦθον E.*Med.*189 (anap.):—Med., ζῷα ἀνθρωπίνας π. φωνάς S.E.*P.*1.73, cf. 15, Jul.*Or.*7.218c. b. π. Αἴγιναν πάτραν *proclaim* it as their country, Pi.*I.*5(4).43; π. εἰς μέσον or εἰς τὸ μ. *publish*, Pl.*Lg.* 812c, 936a:—Med., ὁπόσσω κα προφέρηται for whatever sum [the priest] *lays down*, *Berl.Sitzb.*1927.169 (Cyrene). 4. *bring forward, cite*, μὴ π. τὴν τότε γενομένην ξυνωμοσίαν Th.3.64, cf. 5.26 (Pass.), Pl.*Sph.*259d; προφέρων Ἄρτεμιν *putting forward* her *authority*, A.*Ag.* 201 (lyr.); π. τὰς ἐπονειδίστους τῶν ἡδονῶν *citing by way of example*, Arist.*EN*1173ᵇ21, cf. *Pol.*1288ᵃ20:—also in Med., Pl.*Phlb.*57a, X.*Oec.*14.6; ἀναμνήσεως χάριν π. Plb.4.66.10; αὐτοῦ -ομένου τὴν περὶ τὸ σῶμα γεγενημένην ἀσθένειαν *pleading*.., *OGI*244.10 (Daphne, ii B.C.); *cite*, Plu.*Lyc.*21; *recite*, ποιήματα D.S.14.109, cf. 16.92; ἀριθμοὺς τῶν ἀρχαίων ποιητᾶν *SIG*703.7, cf. 660.3 (Delph., ii B.C.). 5. of an oracle, *propose as a task*, τοῖσι Θηραίοισι προέφερε ἡ Πυθίη τὴν ἐς Λιβύην ἀποικίην Hdt.4.151; ἡ Πυθίη προφέρει σφι, τὰς Ἀθήνας ἐλευθεροῦν Id.5.63:—Pass., δόμοισι προὐνεχθέντος ἐν χρηστηρίοις (gen. abs.) *it having been commanded* to do so, A.*Ag.*964. II. *bring forward, display*, π. κρατερὸν μένος Il.10.479; σπουδήν Lxx *Si.Prol.*22; ἔριδα π. *show*, i. e. engage in, rivalry, Od.6.92; ἀντιώσεσθαι πόλεμον προφέρων Hdt.7.9.γ':—Med., ξεινοδόκῳ ἔριδα προφέρεσθαι *challenge* one's host *to* rivalry, Od.8.210, cf. Il.3.7. 2. *bring out*, ἐντεῦθεν ὥσπερ ἐκ ταμιείου π. Isoc.1.44; ἤνοιξα τὸν τόπον τῶν οἰναρίων καὶ προενήνεχα (sic) οἴνου κεράμια να' *POxy.*1288.12 (iv A.D.); ἠξίωσαν προενεχθῆναι αὐτὸν ἀπὸ τοῦ δεσμωτηρίου that he *should be produced*.., *BGU*1024 vii 4 (iv A.D.). III. *carry off, sweep away*, of a storm, Il.6.346, Od.20.64; of death, π. σώματα τέκνων E.*Med.*1111 (anap.). IV. *put* or *move forward*, πόδα Id.*Tr.*1332 (lyr.); *carry forward, pass on*, σκυταλίδα Aen.Tact.22.27: hence, *promote, further*, ἠώς τοι προφέρει μὲν ὁδοῦ, π. δὲ καὶ ἔργου *furthers* one on the road and in the work, Hes.*Op.*579: without gen., *AP*9.344 (Leon. Alex.); μέγα π. εἴς τι *conduce, help* towards gaining an object, Th.1.93; μεγάλη τύχη πρὸς πάντα π. D.C.78.38:—Pass., *move forward*, προενεχθέντος τοῦ σώματος Arist.*IA*711ᵃ29. 2. intr., *surpass, excel* another, δόξας ἔργα πολὺ προφέρει Simon.161, cf. Theoc.12.5: c. dat. rei, εἴρια καλλονῇ τε προφέροντα καὶ ἀρετῇ τῶν ἀπὸ τῶν ὀΐων (tree) wool *surpassing* sheep's wool in beauty and goodness, Hdt.3.106; πλούτῳ καὶ εἴδεϊ προφέρων Ἀθηναίων Id.6.127; ἡ Νάξος εὐδαιμονίῃ τῶν νήσων π. Id.5.28; π. εἰς εὐτυχίαν τινῶν E.*Med.*1092 (anap.): abs., ἐν πάντα νόμον εὐθύγλωσσος ἀνὴρ π. Pi.*P.*2.86; πλούτῳ καὶ ἐξουσίᾳ, εὐψυχίᾳ, Th.1.123, 2.89, cf. Q.S.4.275; ἔν τινι D.C.77.11. V. *bring forth* children, *IG*14.1747.6 (Rome). VI. *carry before*, λύχνον τινί D.C. 39.31:—Pass., τὸ ῥόπαλον προεφέρετο αὐτοῦ Id.72.17.

**προφεύγω**, Hom. only in aor. προὔφυγον, *flee forwards, flee away*, Il.11.340, A.*Fr.*69.5 (lyr.). II. c. acc., *flee from, shun, avoid*, μένος καὶ χεῖρας Ἀχαιῶν Il.6.502, cf. 7.309; κακόν 14.81; προφυγὼν ἰοειδέα πόντον Od.11.107; οὐκ ἂν θάνατον..προφύγοισθα (Ep. opt.) 22.325, etc.; π. χρέα *avoid* debts, Hes.*Op.*647.

**πρόφημι**, *say before*, ὡς προέφην *PMasp.*151.44, cf. 2 ii 11 (vi A.D.).

**προφημίζω**, *spread a report*, D.C.41.41.

**προφητ-άζω**, = προφητεύω, Man.4.217. **-εία**, ἡ, *gift of interpreting the will of the gods, gift of prophecy*, διδασκαλίαν ὡς π. ἐκχεῶ Lxx *Si.*24.33; ἡ δὲ προφητείη δίης φρενός ἐστιν ἀπορρώξ Orac.ap.Luc.*Alex.*40. 2. concrete, *prophecy* or *oracular response*, Lxx 2*Ch.*15.8, Hld.2.27. II. *office of* προφήτης 2, εἴ τοι μέμηλεν ἔμπεδος π. *BMus.Inscr.*921 b 7 (Branchidae), cf. *CIG*2869 (Didyma), 2880 (Branchidae), *OGI*494.8 (Milet.); in Egypt, προφητειῶν καὶ γραμματειῶν καρπεῖαι *PTeb.*6.34 (ii B.C.). III. in *NT, gift of expounding scripture*, or *of speaking and preaching, under the influence of the Holy Spirit* (cf. προφήτης), *Ep.Rom.*12.6, 1*Ep.Cor.*12.10, 1*Ep.Ti.*1.18, 4.14, al. **-ευμα**, ατος, τό, *prophecy, oracular utterance*, Phot. and Suid. s. v. θεοπροπία. ※ **-εύω**, Dor. **προφᾱτ-** Pi.*Fr.*150 and Inscrr. (v. infr.):—in impf. and aor. 1 the augm. is sts. placed after the prep., προ-εφήτευον, -εφήτευσα, as Lxx 3*Ki.*22.12 (v. l.), *Act.Ap.*19.6 (v. l.), Lxx *Si.*46.20 (but ἐπροφήτευσαν ib.*Nu.*11.25, al.):—*to be a* προφήτης or *interpreter* of the gods, μαντεύεο, Μοῖσα, προφατεύσω δ' ἐγώ Pi. l. c.; τίς προφητεύει θεοῦ; who *is* his *interpreter*? E.*Ion*413; οἱ προφητεύοντες τοῦ ἱροῦ Hdt.7.111; ἡ ψυχὴ τὰ θεῖα καταλαβομένη τοῖς τε ἀνθρώποις προφητεύουσα Arist.*Mu.*391ᵃ16; οὗ [μαντείου] προειστήκει προφητεύων Luc.*VH*2.33, cf. Plu.2.412b; οὐκ ἔστιν ὅστις σοι προφητεύσει τάδε *will be* thy *intermediary in asking* this, E.*Ion*369; ἡ μανία..προφητεύσασα *with* *oracular power*, Pl.*Phdr.*244d:—Pass., τὰ προφητευθέντα Sch.Od. 12.9. II. *expound, interpret, preach, under the influence of the Holy Spirit*, *Ev.Luc.*1.67, *Ev.Jo.*11.51, *Act.Ap.*2.17, 19.6, 1*Ep.Cor.* 11.4, 13.9, al.: also δημιουργῶν χεῖρες π. τὰ ποιήματα Callistr.*Stat.* 2. III. *hold office of* προφήτης, Θεοδώρου προφατεύοντος *IG*7. 4155 (Ptoön), cf. 12(1).833.6 (Lindus), *PGnom.*211 (ii A.D.). IV. *to be a quack doctor*, Gal.15.172. -ης, ου, Dor. and Boeot. **προφάτας** [ᾱ], α, Pi. (v. infr.), Corinn.*Supp.*2.68: ὁ: (πρό, φημί):— prop. *one who speaks for a god and interprets his will* to man, Διὸς π. *interpreter, expounder of the will* of Zeus, of Tiresias, Pi.*N.*1.60; Βάκχου π., perh. of Orpheus, E.*Rh.*972; [Διονύσου] π., of the Bacchae, Id.*Ba.*551 (lyr.); Νηρέως π., of Glaucus, Id.*Or.*364; esp. of the Delphic Apollo, Διὸς π. ἐστι Λοξίας πατρός A.*Eu.*19; of the *minister* and *interpreter* at Delphi, Hdt.8.36,37; at the Ptoön, ib. 135, *IG*7.4135.13 (ii B.C.); cf. προφῆτις. 2. title of official *keepers of the oracle* at Branchidae, *CIG*2884, al., *Supp.Epigr.*1.426 (Milet., i A.D.); elsewhere, *IG*14.961,1032,1084,2433 (Massilia), 9(2).1109. 22 (Coropa, ii/i B.C.), etc. b. in Egyptian temples, *member of the highest order of the clergy, priest*, π. θεῶν Εὐεργετῶν *PTeb.*6.3 (ii B.C.), cf. *OGI*56.59 (Canopus, iii B.C.), etc. 3. *interpreter, expounder* of the utterances of the μάντις (q.v.), Pl.*Ti.*72a: hence, of Poets, Πιερίδων π. Pi.*Pae.*6.6; Μουσᾶν π. B.8.3, cf. Pl.*Phdr.*262d. 4. *possessor of oracular powers*, of Amphiaraus, A.*Th.*611, cf. *Ag.*409 (lyr.); of Pseudo-Bacis, Ar.*Av.*972; of Epimenides, *Ep.Tit.*1.12. 5. generally, *interpreter, declarer*, ἐγὼ π. σοι λόγων γενήσομαι E.*Ba.*211; π. ἀτόμων, of the Epicureans, Ath.5.187b; τῶν Πύρρωνος λόγων, of Timon, S.E.*M.*1.53; *spokesman*, Lxx *Ex.*7.1. b. metaph., *proclaimer, harbinger*, κώμου προφάτας, of the wine-bowl, Pi.*N.*9.50; δείπνου π. λιμός Antiph.217.23; φθόης π. Pl.Com.184.4; τέττιξ.. θέρεος γλυκὺς π. *Anacreont.*32.11. II. *herald* at the games, B.9. 28 (pl.). III. in Lxx, *revealer of God's will, prophet*, 1*Ki.*9.9, al.:— hence, 2. in *NT*, *inspired preacher and teacher, organ of special revelations from God*, 1*Ep.Cor.*12.28, 14.32; and (as comprised in this), b. *foreteller, prophet of future events*, *Act.Ap.*2.30, 3.18,21, 2*Ep.Pet.*3.2. 3. *herbalist*, Ps.-Dsc.1.10, al.; *quack doctor*, Gal. 16.761. -ίζω, = προφητεύω, Hp.*Prorrh.*2.1. -ικός, ή, όν, *oracular, prophetic*, ἀνήρ Ph.1.515; λόγος ib.95, 2*Ep.Pet.*1.19; νοῦς Ph.*Fr.*66 H. (Sup.), cf. Luc.*Alex.*60. 2. εἰκὼν χαλκῆ π. *in the official robes of a* προφήτης, *Rev.Phil.*44.38 (Didyma); so ἠμφιεσμένος π. σχήματι, στολίσας σεαυτὸν π. σχήματι, *PMag.Par.*1.933, *PMag. Berol.*1.278.

**προφῆτις**, ιδος, fem. of προφήτης, esp. of the Pythia, E.*Ion* 42,321, Pl.*Phdr.*244a, Phld.*Acad.Ind.*p.26 M.: generally, *CIG*3796 (Chalcedon), Lxx *Ex.*15.20, *Jd.*4.4, *Schwyzer* 633.20 (Eresus, ii/i B.C.): metaph., π. τῆς ἀληθείας D.S.1.2. 2. *prophet's wife*, Lxx *Is.* 8.3.

**προφητοτόκος**, ον, *bearing prophets*, Ph.1.658.

**προφήτωρ**, ορος, ὁ, poet. for προφήτης, Man.2.317, 4.227.

® **προφθάνω** [ᾰ], *outrun, anticipate*, c. acc., προφθάσασα καρδία γλῶσσαν A.*Ag.*1028 (lyr.); ἐγὼ.. σε προφθάσας λέγω.. Pl.*R.*500a, cf. *PCair.Zen.*520.2 (iii B.C.): c. part., προὔφθης με παρακύψασα Ar.*Ec.* 884, cf. Th.7.73, Lxx 1*Ki.*20.25, al.: c. gen., προέφθασα τοῦ φυγεῖν ib.*Jn.*4.2, cf. 1*Ma.*10.4. 2. abs., *to be beforehand*, στόματι E.*Ph.* 1385, Theo Sm.p.160 H.: aor. Med., προφθάμενος A.R.4.913.

**προφθάσία**, ἡ, *anticipation*, name of a festival, D.S.15.18 (leg. -φθάσια, τά).

**πρόφθεγξις**, εως, ἡ, *a speaking before*, Poll.2.118.

**προφθείρω**, *seduce before*, Heph.Astr.1.1 (Pass.).

® **προφθίμενος** [ῐ], η, ον, *dead* or *killed before*, *AP*7.184 (Parmen.).

**προφῐλιόομαι**, *to be treated as a friend first*, Plu. *in Hes.*31.

**προφῐλοσοφητέον**, *one must begin philosophy*, ἐν ποιήμασι Plu.2. 15f.

**προφλεβοτομέω**, *open a vein before*, Posidon.ap.Gal.19.711, Gal. 10.786 (Pass.), Alex.Trall.7.9.

**προφοβ-έομαι**, Pass., *fear beforehand*, πολέμους αἱματόεντας A. *Supp.*1044 (lyr.); π. μή.. X.*Cyr.*1.6.24 (v.l.): abs., τὸ προφοβηθῆναι D.C.55.18. -ητικός, ή, όν, *apt to fear beforehand*, c. acc., πάντα π. Arist.*Rh.*1389b29.

**προφοιβάομαι**, Med., *predict the future*, *Cat.Cod.Astr.*8(4).137, prob. in 147.

**προφοινίσσω**, *redden, stimulate beforehand*, Sor.ap.Gal.12.419, Archig.ib.407, v.l. in Alex.Trall.1.1.

**προφοιτάω**, *precede, arrive before*, ἡ προφοιτήσασα ἤδη δόξα Iamb. *VP*2.12.

**προφορ-ά**, ἡ, (προφέρω) *pronunciation, utterance*, D.H.*Dem.*22, Ph. 1.50; λέξις καὶ π. Plu.2.41a; π. καὶ γραφῇ Phld.*Rh.*1.159 S.; τῶν φωνῶν, τοῦ λόγου, S.E.*P.*1.15,203; ῥημάτων Hdn.1.8.6; ὁ κατὰ προφορὰν λόγος, ἐν προφορᾷ λόγος, = ὁ προφορικὸς λ., Ph.1.232, Plu.2. 777b. II. '*procession*', *going forth*, Plot.2.9.1; π. καὶ ἐνέργεια Id.4.3.2. III. *front end* of a battering-ram, Ath.Mech.25.3. IV. *public reproach, rebuke*, Plb.9.33.12. V. *decision* of a court, *CPR* 18.40 (ii A.D.). -έομαι, Med., in weaving, *carry on the web by passing the weft to and fro* across the warp (the setting up of which is διάζεσθαι), Poll.7.32, Hsch., Phot., Suid., prob. in Call.*Fr.*244: hence, of a spider, τὴν ὁδὸν προφορεῖσθαι *run to and fro*, Call.Com. 2, cf. Ar.*Av.*4; of dogs, π. παρὰ τὰ αὐτά X.*Cyn.*6.15. -ικός, ή, όν, *of* or *for utterance, uttered*, opp. ἐνδιάθετος (v. λόγος fin.), Ph.2. 154, al., *Stoic.*2.43,74, Plu.2.777c, 973a. -ος, ον, *put forward*, προφόρῳ ποδί Il.Pers.6.2. II. πρόφορος, ὁ, *the fluid in which the foetus floats, discharged before parturition, forewaters*, Arist.*HA*586a 30.

**πρόφραγμα**, ατος, τό, (προφράσσω) *fence placed in front*, Arist.*Oec.* 1347a5, D.S.19.30: metaph., εἰ μὴ Μακεδόνας εἴχομεν π. Plb.9.35.3.

**προφράζω**, *tell* or *announce beforehand*, Hdt.1.120 (unless = προειπεῖν, προερεῖν, *speak out boldly*): pf. part. Pass., προπεφραδμένα.. ἄεθλα Hes.*Op.*655, cf. A.R.3.1315. II. Pass., *to be explained above* or *previously*, Nicom.*Ar.*1.19.

**πρόφρακτος**, ον, *with a barrier* or *membrane in front*, of a shellfish, cj. in Xenocr.ap.Orib.2.58.107.

**πρόφρασσα**, Ep. fem. of πρόφρων, *kindly, gracious*, or, *having forethought*, Il.10.290, Od.5.161, al. (Formed from πρόφρων on analogy of ἑκών: ἕκασσα.)

**προφροντίζω**, *consider before*, Hp.*Aër.*2 (vv. ll. πρόφροντις ᾖ, πρόφρων τις ᾖ). 2. *do mental work*, Gal.17(2).175.

**προφρύγω** [ῡ], *toast, parch before*, aor. part. Pass. -φρῠγείσης v.l. for προφωχθείσης in Dsc.2.90 (ap.Gal.6.517).

® **πρόφρων**, ονος, ὁ, ἡ, (φρήν, φρονέω): poet. Adj.: prop. *with forward mind*, i.e. *of one's free will*, οὐδέ τί πώ μοι π. τέτληκας εἰπεῖν ἔπος Il.1.543; π. κεν δὴ ἔπειτα Δία Κρονίωνα λιτοίμην I should be *fain* to entreat Zeus, Od.14.406: hence, *kindly, gracious, willing*, usu. predicative (as always when used of persons in Hom.), ὄμοσσον π. ἔπεσιν καὶ χερσὶν ἀρήξειν Il.1.77; π. κατένευσε Κρονίων 8.175; ὁ δέ με π. ὑπέδεκτο 9.480, cf. Od.2.387; π. Δαναοῖσιν ἄμυνεν Il.14.71, cf. Sapph.118; π. τελεῖν, ἀείδειν, Pi.*P.*5.117, *N.*5.22; προφρόνων Μοισᾶν τύχοιμεν Id.*I.*4(3).43; καί σε.. π. θεὸς φυλάσσοι A.*Ch.*1063; γενοῦ π. ἡμῖν ἀρωγός S.*El.*1380; π. σε.. Ἑρμῆς Ἅιδης τε δέχοιτο E.*Alc.* 743 (anap.). 2. *earnest, zealous*, ὅτε δὴ.. π. ἐθέλοιμι ἐρύσσαι *in earnest*, Il.8.23; οὔ νύ τι θυμῷ πρόφρονι μυθέομαι ib.40; εἰ δὴ πρόφρονι θυμῷ.. ἀνώγει 24.140; ἀμύνειν π. θ. Od.16.257; βοῦν π. θ. δασσάμενος προέθηκε Hes.*Th.*536; also π. κραδίῃ Il.10.244. II. Ep. Adv. προφρονέως *willingly, readily, earnestly*, π. μάχεσθαι 5.810, cf. 7.160; νήπια τέκνα π. ῥύοισθε 17.224; π. μιν τῖεν ἄναξ 6.173: later προφρόνως, φιλεῖν, φιλῆσαι, Thgn.786, Pi.*P.*2.16; ἐπιδεῖν A.*Supp.*1 (anap.), cf. *Ag.*173 (lyr.), *Ch.*478 (anap.), *Eu.*927 (anap.), 968 (anap.).

**προφυάς**, άδος, ἡ, = *racemus*, σταφυλῆς *Gloss.*

**προφυλ-αγμα** [ῠ], ατος, τό, *outpost*, Hsch. s.v. φρούριον. -ακή, ἡ, *guard in front*; in pl., *outposts, vedettes, piquets*, X.*Cyr.*3.3.25, *Eq. Mag.*7.13, Plu.*Caes.*39: sg., ἡ π. αὐτοῦ his *advanced guard*, X.*HG*4. 1.24, cf. Plb.5.3.2; ἀριστοποιεῖσθαι διὰ προφυλακῆς with *an advanced guard*, with *outposts*, Th.4.30. II. *guarding, guard*, τῶν πόλεων Plb.5.95.5, cf. D.S.11.2 (pl.). III. *watch, vigil*, Lxx *Ex.*12.42, al. IV. *caution*, προφυλακῇ χρῆσθαι περί τι Ph.1.283. 2. *precaution*, c. gen., against.., Id.2.368, al., cf. Epicur.*Oxy.*215 iii 14: Medic., προφυλακῆς χάριν as a *precaution*, Sor.1.118, cf. Dsc.2.47. -ακίς ναῦς, ἡ, *look-out* ship, Th.1.117 (pl.). -ακτέον, *one must use precaution*, Plu.2.127c. -ακτέος, α, ον, *to be guarded against*, Vett. Val.292.4. -ακτήριον, τό, *outpost, guard*, Hsch. s.v. φρούριον, Tz. *H.*7.147. -ακτικός, ή, όν, *prophylactic*, π. ἰοβόλων Dsc.3.146, cf. Gal.1.296; π. ἐπιμέλεια Id.10.877. -αξ, ἄκος, ὁ, *advanced guard*: οἱ π., = αἱ προφυλακαί, Th.3.112, X.*An.*2.4.15, etc. II. *officer on guard*, Aen.Tact.22.9, and so prob. in *IGRom.*4.455 (Pergam.).— Also fem., Eratosth.*Cat.*22. III. epith. of Apollo, *IG*12(7). 419. -άσσω, Att. -ττω, *keep guard before* a place or house, c. acc., νηόν *h.Ap.*538 (in Ep. imper. form προφύλαχθε, for προφυλάσσετε), cf. X.*Mem.*2.7.14: c. gen., Id.*Hier.*6.10: abs., *to be on guard, keep a look-out*, τὴν προφυλάσσουσαν (sc. νέα) ἐπὶ Σκιάθῳ Hdt.8.92, cf. 7.179, Ar.*Ach.*1146 (anap.), Th.2.93:—Med., *to be on one's guard, take precautions*, προεφυλάξατο ὅσα ἐδύνατο μάλιστα Hdt.1.185, cf. Th.6.38: c. acc., *to be on one's guard* or *take precautions against*, Hdt.7.176, cf. 9.99, X.*HG*5.3.5, *Mem.*1.4.13. II. later Act. is used like Med., *take precautions against*, τὰ τοῦ σώματος κινήματα Plu.2.129a.

**πρόφυξ**, ῠγος, ὁ, *fugitive*, Hdn.Gr.2.744.

**προφύομαι**, Pass., with aor. 2 and pf. Act., *to be born before*, ὃς προὔφυ πατήρ S.*Aj.*1291; προπεφυκυῖα φλεγμονή *previously existing*, Gal.18(2).642.

**προφύρ-āμα** [ῡ], ατος, τό, *dough kneaded before*, Eratosth.ap.Ath. 4.140a. -άω, *knead beforehand*:—Pass., μᾶζα προφυρηθεῖσα Hp. *Vict.*2.40; also, *to be steeped beforehand*, οἴνῳ, ὕδατι, Thphr.*Od.* 23. II. metaph., προπεφύραται λόγος the speech *is all ready concocted*, Ar.*Av.*462; ἔστιν κακόν μοι προπεφυραμένον there's a mischief *ready brewed* for me, Id.*Th.*75. -ητός (Ion. for *-φυρατός), ή, όν, *kneaded beforehand*, π. μᾶζα a *well-kneaded* barley-loaf, Hp.*Vict.*3.68, 81.

**προφύσιον** [ῡ], τό, *case for the pipe of a bellows*, Hsch. (pl.).

**πρόφῠσις**, εως, ἡ, (προφύομαι) *germ, bud*, Hp.ap.Gal.19.133.

**προφῠτεύω**, *plant before*, *Gp.*5.11.4 (Pass.): metaph., *engender*, S.*El.*198 (anap.).

**προφώγνῡμι**, *parch first*, ζέας -φωχθείσης Dsc.2.90 (cf. προφρύγω).

® **προφωνέω**, *utter, declare beforehand*, Ζηνὸς κότον A.*Supp.*617; πήματα, ἄλγη, Id.*Ag.*882, *Eu.*466: c. inf. fut., *AP*5.20 (Rufin.); *utter before all*, ἠχώ S.*El.*109 (anap.); πᾶσιν π. τόνδε ναυάρχοις λόγον *gives* this order *beforehand* to all, A.*Pers.*363. II. *order beforehand* or *before all*, c. dat. et inf., καί σοι προφωνῶ τόνδε μὴ θάπτειν S.*Aj.*1089, cf. E.*Hipp.*956, *El.*685: without inf., ὑμῖν προφωνῶ τάδε S.*OT*223.

**προχάζω**, *advance*, Hsch., Phot. 2. = ἀναποδίζω, Hsch.

**προχαίνω**, = προφασίζομαι, etym. of προχάνη in Eust.1109.39; f.l. in Procl.*Theol.Plat.*5.37.

**προχαίρω**, *rejoice beforehand*, Pl.*Phlb.*39d; προχαρέντες Orph.*H.* 85.9. II. προχαιρέτω *far be it from me! away with it!* A.*Ag.*252 (lyr., s. v. l.).

**προχᾰλάω**, *relax beforehand*, Aret.*CD*1.5, *Hippiatr.*43:—Pass., *to be loosed beforehand*, προκεχάλασται ἡ γλῶσσα Lxx 4*Ma.*10.19 (v.l.).

**προχαλκεύω**, *forge beforehand*, A.*Ch.*647 (lyr.).

**προχάνη** [ᾰ], ἡ, Dor. -χάνα, *pretext*, Call.*Cer.*74 (where -χανά codd.): pl., Id.*Fr.*26; cf. προχαίνω; but Sch.S.*Ant.*80 derives it from προέχομαι.

**προχάρ-αγμα** [χᾰ], ατος, τό, = προκέντημα, *outline, pattern*, Nicom. *Ar.*1.6, Eustr. *in EN* 41.18 (pl.). **-άσσω**, Att. -ττω, *engrave before*: hence, *make an outline, sketch*, Ph.1.609.

**προχᾰρής**, ές, *given as a thankoffering*, ἄρτος *IG*5(1).364.13 (Lacon.).

**Προχᾰρισία**, ἡ, a name of Thetis, Hsch. [Perh. -ῑσ-, cf. χαρίσιος.]

**προχᾰριστήρια**, τά, *thanksgiving to open the year*, a festival of Athena, celebrated by all Athenian magistrates at the beginning of spring, Lycurg.*Fr.*53 (προσχ- ap.*AB*295).

**προχειλίδιον**, τό, *projecting part of the lip*, Poll.2.90 (pl.).

**πρόχειλος**, ον, *with prominent lips*, Str.2.2.3:—also -ής, ές, Luc. *Philops.*34. II. πρόχειλα, τά, = τὰ ἄκρα [τῶν χειλῶν] Ruf.*Onom.* 41.

**προχειμ-άζω**, of the weather, *to be stormy before*, Arist.*Pr.*941ᵃ17. 2. *to be prematurely stormy*, Plin.*HN*18.207; of the moon, *cause premature storms*, Vett.Val.188.27, *Cat.Cod.Astr.*2.146, 5(1). 174. **-ᾰσις**, εως, ἡ, *premature stormy weather*, Veget.4.40 (s. v. l.).

**προχειρ-άριος**, ὁ, = *amanuensis*, *Gloss.* **-ίζω**, *make* πρόχειρος, *deliver up*, -κεχειρικέναι τινὰ ἐπὶ τὸ (fort. τῷ) τὴν τιμωρίαν δοῦναι Din.3.14:—Pass., mostly in part., *taken in hand, undertaken*, τὸν προκεχειρισμένον λόγον Pl.*Lg.*643a; προκεχειρισμένα καὶ ἑτοῖμα ἀγαθά D.7.33. 2. *produce*, ὡς ἴδια αὐτοὶ ἀφ' ἑαυτῶν π. Iamb.*Comm.Math.* 11. II. more freq. in Med. προχειρίζομαι, fut. -χειριοῦμαι Ar.*Ec.* 729:—*make ready for oneself, mobilize*, προχειριοῦμαι κἀξετάσω τὴν οὐσίαν Ar. l. c.; δύναμιν, στρατόπεδα, D.4.19, Plb.1.16.2, 3.107.10; ἐσθῆτα Luc.*Merc.Cond.*14; τὴν μαλάχην Id.*VH*2.46; τὰς ῥήσεις, τοὺς λογισμούς, Plu.2.396c, 813d; βιβλίον Gal.6.555. 2. *choose, select*, δημαγωγούς Isoc.8.122; τοὺς τὴν πίστιν.. τηρήσοντας *OGI*339.46 (Sestos, ii B. C.); γραμματέα κοινὸν ἐκ περιόδου Plb.2.43.1, cf. Lxx *Jo.* 3.12, al.; τινὰ ἐπί τι D.25.13; ἐπί τινι Plu.*Caes.*58; πρός τι τοὺς ἐπιτηδείους Plb.3.44.4; *appoint*, τινὰ δικτάτορα D.C.54.1, cf. *IG*2².1110.14:—Pass., -ισθεὶς.. ἀγωνοθέτης *OGI*268.4 (Nacrasa, iii B. C.), cf. Lxx *Da.*3.22, Plb.3.106.2, D.H.4.27, D.C.58.20; ὑπὸ τοῦ βασιλέως Str.2.3.4, cf. Wilcken *Chr.*12.13 (i B. C.); -ισθεὶς θεωρός *PCair.Zen.* 341(a).25 (iii B. C.), cf. 42.3 (iii B. C.); ὑπὸ τῶν πολιτῶν ἐπὶ τὴν στρατηγίαν D.S.16.66, cf. *BMus.Inscr.*1044 (Attaleia), *PTeb.*27.22 (ii B. C.), etc. b. *allot, assign*, in Pass., διὰ τὸ -κεχειρίσθαι αὐτῷ τὴν γῆν *PCair.Zen.*132.3 (iii B. C.); τὰ Ποπλίῳ -κεχειρισμένα στρατόπεδα Plb. 3.40.14; τὸν -κεχειρισμένον ὑμῖν Χριστὸν Ἰησοῦν *Act.Ap.*3.20. 3. *prefer*, οἱ Δημοσθένην -χειρισάμενοι D.H.*Din.*8. 4. c. inf., *determine* to do, Plb.3.40.2: c. acc. et inf., *decide*, τῆς πόλεως -κεχειρισμένης τὸν ἀγῶνα.. στεφανίτην εἶναι *SIG*457.14 (Thespiae, iii B. C.). 5. *discuss* or *examine*, τὰς ἄλλας κατηγορίας Arist.*Cat.*10ᵇ19; τὰς πάντων δόξας Id.*Top.*105ᵃ35; also π. περί τινος Id.*Cael.*271ᵇ25, cf. *Ph.* 200ᵇ23; περὶ ἕκαστον γένος (v.l. ἑκάστου γένους) Id.*Mete.*378ᵇ6. 6. ἐπὶ παραδείγματος π. *propose* by way of example, Id.*Pr.*953ᵃ33:—Pass., Id.*Cat.*2ᵃ36; ὁ περὶ τῶν -χειρισθέντων λόγος Phld.*D.*3.14. **-ιον**, τό, *hand-bag* or *-box, hold-all*, *PTeb.*413.10 (ii/iii A. D.): pl., *POxy.* 741.14 (ii A. D.). **-ῐσις**, εως, ἡ, *utterance*, Plot.3.8.6; *taking in hand, execution*, Porph.*Sent.*16; *handling*, τῶν θεωρημάτων Phlp. *in de An.*165.1; *exercise, actualization*, ib.227.26, Eustr. *in EN*37. 16. **-ισμός**, ὁ, = foreg., τῆς δημιουργίας Dam.*Pr.*270. II. οἱ ἐν π., perh. *recruits in training*, *PAmh.*2.39 (ii B. C.). III. *appointment* of an official, *PTeb.*711.7 (ii B. C.). **-ιστέον**, *one must deal with, treat*, Nicom.*Ar.*1.19; π. τί σοι τῶν ἀπορρήτων Them. *Or.*25.311a. **-ογράφος** [ᾰ], ὁ, perh. = προχειράριος, *PTeb.*112. 116 (ii B. C.). **-ον**, τό, = προχείριον, *Stud.Pal.*20.67.39 (ii/iii A. D.). 2. *crutch* used in moving and flattening wool in the dye-bath, *PHolm.*26.2,5. **-όομαι**, Pass., *to be subdued before*, J.*BJ*4.8. 1. **-ος**, ον, (χείρ) *at hand*, Hp.*Art.*11; π. ψάλια (v. l. ψέλια) δέρκεσθαι πάρα *ready*, A.*Pr.*54; π. ἄχθος a *handy* burden, S.*El.*1116; of a drawn sword or knife, Id.*Ph.*747, E.*Hel.*1564, *El.*696, X.*Cyr.*4.2.32; ἔβαλλον λίθοις καὶ.. ἀκοντίοις, ὡς ἕκαστός τι π. εἶχεν Th.4.34; ἁρπάζει μου ἀεὶ τὸ π. τῶν σκευῶν *whatever* furniture *he can lay his hands on*, *PEnteux.* 25.8 (iii B. C.); [τὴν ἐπιστήμην] π. οὐκ εἶχε τῇ διανοίᾳ Pl.*Tht.*198d; οὓς π. εἶχον μύθους Id.*Phd.*61b; τὰ κατὰ πάντων τῶν φιλοσοφούντων π. Id.*Ap.*23d; εἰ οὖν σοι πρόχειρον, εἰπέ Id.*Min.*313b; ἔστι τις π. λόγος D.20.112; ὃ ἔχω προχειρότατον εἰπεῖν Id.24.1; τὸ προχειρότατον ποιεῖν Isoc.11.9; τὰ π. τῶν ἀπόρων *obvious* difficulties, Arist. *Metaph.*982ᵇ13, cf. 1054ᵇ12; τὰ προχειρότατα Id.*Pr.*924ᵃ12, cf. Demetr.Lac.*Herc.*1012.35; ταῦτα γὰρ ὧν ἐστι προχειρότερον (sc. εὔξασθαι) Xenoph.1.16. b. *readily accessible, external* parts of the body, Sor.1.17,69: Comp., Id.2.64,85. 2. *common, ordinary*, φαῦλα καὶ π. Pl.*Tht.*147a; αἱ π. τῶν ἡδονῶν Id.*Phlb.*45a. b. πρὸς τῷ ἰδίῳ λόγῳ καὶ τοῖς π., official title in Egypt, *Sammelb.*7455 (i B. C.), *BGU*1756.8 (i B. C.), al. 3. πρόχειρόν [ἐστι] it is *easy*, c. inf., Pl. *Sph.*251b, Philem.24; ψεύδεσθαι προχειρότατον τοῖς ἁμαρτάνουσιν Lys. *Fr.*86; ἐν προχείρῳ [ἐστί], c. inf., Arist.*Mete.*356ᵇ19; ἐκ προχείρου *easily, lightly*, S.E.*M.*6.19, Gal.1.241. II. of persons, *ready* to do, c. inf., S.*El.*1494; τῇ φυγῇ π. *ready for* flight, E.*HF*161; also ἡ σπάνις π. εἰς τὸ δρᾶν κακά Philem.157; π. γλῶττα Poll.6.120. 2. *of a ready wit*, ἐν ταῖς ὁμιλίαις εὔχαρις καὶ π. Plb.23.5.7; *glib*, Phld. *Po.*5.14; τὸ προπετὲς καὶ π. Hp.*Medic.*1. 3. *hasty*, σφοδρὸς καὶ π. Plu.*Brut.*34; πνεῦμα οἷον τοῖσι πνιγομένοισι πρόχειρον Hp.*Prorrh.* 1.25 (unless *perceptible, obvious* breathing, cf. πρὸς χεῖρα *Epid.*7. 17). III. Adv. -ρως *offhand, readily*, ἀποκρίνασθαι Pl.*Smp.* 204d; περί τι π. ἔχειν Arist.*Top.*163ᵇ25; π. εἰς τὰ ἑαυτῶν σώματα ἐξαμαρτάνοντες Aeschin.1.22; ἐπὶ τὰ πράγματα ὁρμᾶν π. Amphis 33.7; *hurriedly, rashly*, Theopomp.Hist.217(a), Plb.5.7.2; *bluntly*, εἰπεῖν Demetr.*Eloc.*281; *ordinarily* or *obviously*, δηλούσης Phld.*Rh.* 2.268 S. Comp. -οτέρως Pl.*Alc.*2.144d; -ότερον τοῦ δέοντος Plb.1. 21.5. **-ότης**, ητος, ἡ, *readiness*, ἡ ἐπὶ τοσοῦτον π. τινῶν Corn.*ND* 35, cf. Arr.*Epict.*3.21.18: pl., -τητες συκοφαντικαί Phld.*Rh.*1. 119 S. 2. ἡ π. τῆς ἀμεθόδου ὕλης *that which is given* in the unworked matter, i. e. the *subject-matter* of literary works, S.E.*M.*1. 249.

**προχειροτον-έω**, *choose, elect before*, Pl.*Lg.*765b (Pass.); μάρτυρες -κεχειροτονημένοι ὑπὸ θεοῦ *Act.Ap.*10.41; ἐς ὑπατείαν D.C.50.4 (Pass.). 2. *take a preliminary* or *previous vote*, περὶ ἱερῶν Aeschin. 1.23, cf. D.24.11. ⊛ **-ία**, ἡ, *preliminary vote*, ἄνευ -τονίας Arist.*Ath.* 43.6; περὶ τῆς ὀστρακοφορίας π. δίδοσθαι, εἰ δοκεῖ ἢ μή Id.*Fr.*436.

**προχειρουργέω**, *perform before*, J.*BJ*4.8.3.

⊛ **προχειροφόρος**, ὁ, = *amanuensis*, *Gloss.*

**πρό-χευμα**, ατος, τό, (προχέω) *that which is poured forth, silt, deposit*, Arist.*PA*647ᵇ4 (pl.). **-χεύω**, poet., = sq., οἶδμα D.P.52.

**προχέω**, *pour forth* or *forward*, π. ῥόον εἰς ἅλα δῖαν, of a river, Il. 21.219, cf. *h.Ap.*241; ποταμοὶ δ' ἁμέραισι μὲν προχέοντι ῥόον καπνοῦ Pi.*P.*1.22; τρὶς ὕδατος προχέειν *pour in* three parts of water *first*, Hes.*Op.*596; σπονδὰς προχέαντες Hdt.7.192; πλημοχόας Critias 17 D.: metaph., π. τὰ γλυκεῖαν Pi.*P.*10.56, cf. *IG*3.713.4; λίγειαν ὀμφήν *Anacreont.*41.10:—Pass., *pour on* or *forth*, metaph. of large bodies of men *pouring over* a plain, ἐς πεδίον προχέοντο Il.2.465, cf. 15.360, 21.6, A.R.1.635, etc.; θυσία.. προχυθεῖσα cj. in E.*Fr.*912.5 (anap.); προχεῖται τὰ λεγόμενα Longin.19; τὰς προκεχυμένας ἄκρας *far-projecting*, Ph.1.14: later in literal sense, ἱδρῶτες προχυθήσονται Antyll.ap.Aët.9.40; αἷμα προχυθέν D.C.42.26, cf. Opp.*C.*2.39.

**προχθές**, Adv. *the day before yesterday*, *PLips.*37.12 (iv A. D.), Sch. Philostr.*Her.*p.578 B.

**προχθεσῐνός**, ή, όν, *of the day before yesterday*, *EM*691.56.

**προχία**, ἡ, ἀπὸ προχίας (for προνοίας), = *ex praecelato*, dub. in *Gloss.*

**προχλῐαίνω**, *warm first*, in Pass., Sor.2.62, Aët.12.55.

**πρόχλωρος**, ον, *greenish*, Sch.Ar.*Pl.*204 (fort. ὑπόχλ–).

⊛ **πρόχνῠ**, Adv. *utterly*, ὥς κε.. ἀπόλωνται π. κακῶς Il.21.460; so ὀλέσθαι π. Od.14.69. II. *with the knees forward*, π. καθεζομένη, i. e. kneeling or crouching, Il.9.570 (where *πρόγνυ shd. perh. be restd., cf. γνύπετος, Skt. Adj. *prajñú-* (dub. sens.)). III. dub. sens. in Antim.Col.2 P.: later, simply = πάνυ, A.R.1.1118, 2.249.

**προ-χοή** (A), ἡ, (προχέω) poet. noun, almost always pl., *outpouring*, i. e. *mouth*, of a river, ἐπὶ προχοῇσι διιπετέος ποταμοῖο Il.17.263; ἐς ποταμοῦ προχοάς Od.5.453; ἐν προχοῇς ποταμοῦ 11.242; ἐν προχοῇς ..Ὠκεανοῖο 20.65; Τριτωνίδος ἐν προχοαῖς λίμνας Pi.*P.*4.20, cf. Anacr. 28 codd., B.6.3, A.*Supp.*1025 (lyr.), Ar.*Nu.*272, Theoc.Chius in *FHG* ii 86, Call.*Fr.*480, etc.; θερμαῖς ὕδατος μαλακοῦ π. A.*Fr.*192.8 (anap.); ὕδατος προχοὰς χειμερίους *AP*9.147 (Antag.): sg. is dub. l. in Hes.*Op.* 757; προχοὴ τῶν ὑδάτων *discharge* of amniotic fluid, *Cat.Cod.Astr.*8(4). 127. 2. *overflow, flood*, A.R.4.271 (pl.). 3. = πρόχωσις, *promontory*, Archestr.*Fr.*40 codd.Ath. (sed leg. προβολαῖσι). II. *libations*, *IG*14.1595, Porph.*Marc.*23, *Epigr.Gr.*312.16 (Smyrna). **-χοή** (B), ἡ, = πρόχοος 1, A.R.1.456, *AP*6.292 (Hedyl.), Alciphr.3.47. **-χοΐδιον**, Att. **προχοίδιον**, τό, Dim. of πρόχοος, Cratin.193, Stratt.22, Str.17.1. 38, etc. ⊛ **-χοΐς**, ἴδος, ἡ, Dim. of πρόχοος, = ἀμίς, *chamber-pot*, X.*Cyr.* 8.8.10, cf. Ath.11.496c. II. = ἐπίχυσις, *AB*294. ⊛ **-χοος**, Att. contr. **πρόχους**, ἡ: acc. sg. written πρόχουν *SIG*1121 (Naucratis, vii/vi B. C.): nom. pl. πρόχοι ib.1026.25 (Cos, iv/iii B. C.); dat. pl. πρόχουσι is f. l. in E.*Ion* 435; acc. pl. πρόχους X.*Cyr.*5.2.7, Ael.*NA*5. 23: (προχέω):—*vessel for pouring out, jug*, esp. *ewer for pouring water upon the hands* of guests, Il.24.304, Od.1.136, 4.52, 15.135, Hes. *Th.*785, S.*Ant.*430, E. l.c., Anaxandr.41.27 (anap.), Xenarch.7.14, etc. 2. *wine-jug* from which the cupbearer pours into the cups, Od.18.397. 3. Thessal. for λήκυθος, Clitarch.ap.Ath.11. 495c. II. a liquid measure, *IG*14.422 ii 10, al. (Tauromenium).

⊛ **προχορεύω**, *go* or *dance before in a chorus*, κῶμον π. *lead a* κῶμος or festive band, E.*Ph.*791 (lyr.).

**προχορηγέω**, *provide beforehand*, τὸ ἀνάλωμα παρ' ἑαυτοῦ *SIG*679. 30 (Magn. Mae., ii B. C.).

**προχόω**, collat. pres. of προχώννυμι, *pile in front, heap up*, χῶμα Pl. *Criti.*111b (nisi leg. προσχοῖ), cf. Aristid.1.128 J.

**προ-χράω**, *lend, advance*, aor. inf. -χρῆσαι *PCair.Zen.*477.4 (iii B. C.), cf. *Supp.Epigr.*1.366.35,39 (Samos, iii B. C.), *SIG*976.92 (ibid., ii B. C.), *PRyl.*229.13 (i A. D.), *CIG*2927.7 (Tralles, ii A. D.): pf. inf. -κεχρηκέναι *PCair.Zen.*326.191 (iii B. C.):—Med., *borrow*, ib.150.12 (iii B. C.), *PSI*5.526.12 (iii B. C.), *Inscr.Délos* 442 *A* 25 (ii B. C.):—Pass., ib.43; τὰ ὑπ' ἐμοῦ -χρησθέντα.. τελέσματα the tax-payments *advanced* by me, Mitteis *Chr.*69.20 (iv A. D.). II. Med., *use before*, Arist.*Xen.*974ᵇ11, Gal.11.365 (nisi leg. προσχρ-); this sense and sense I are equally possible in *SIG*976.89 (Samos, ii B. C.). **-χρεία**, ἡ, *payment in advance, loan*, *BGU*14 iv 8, al. (iii A. D.), *PHamb.*39 (ii A. D.), *PTeb.*353.26 (ii A. D.), etc.; = ἀφορμή, *working capital*, *AB*472;

*plant*, *POxy*.907.13 (iii A.D., pl.). **-χρημᾰτίζω**, *transact business before*, ἄλλο δὲ π. τούτων μηδέν *IG*1².57.55. II. *to be formerly styled* so-and-so, -ισάσης ἀπὸ κώμης Τεπτύνεως *PTeb*.333.3 (iii A.D.), cf. *BGU*614.3 (iii A.D.). III. of a name, *to be mentioned at the beginning*, προχρηματίζειν τὸ τοῦ Διὸς Παναμάρου ὄνομα *Supp.Epigr*.4.263.17 (Panamara, i A.D.). **-χρησις**, εως, ἡ, *use by preference*, σχήματος dub. in Longin.27.2. II. *loan*, *PCair.Zen*.4.70, 326.9, al. (iii B.C.), *POxy*.640 (ii A.D.), etc.

**προ-χριστέον**, *one must anoint first*, Ruf.ap.Orib.8.39.7. **-χρίω** [ῑ], *smear, anoint before*, Gal.13.514; τινι with a thing, S.*Tr*.696, cf. Luc.*Alex*.21.

**προχρονέω**, *precede in time*, c. gen., Ptol.*Phas*.p.8 H., al.

⊛ **πρόχρονος**, ον, *anticipatory*, πράγματα μετάχρονα ἢ π. Luc.*Salt*.80.

**προχῡλόω**, *emulsify first*, Crito ap.Gal.13.788.

**πρό-χῠμα**, ατος, τό, (προχέω) *wine that flows from the grape* without pressing, *Gp*.6.16.1. II. = ψυκτήρ (expld. as a *vessel in which cups are washed*), Moer.p.422 P. (s.v.l.). III. in building, *projection*, π. ἔχειν Apollod.*Poliorc*.166.10. **-χῠσις**, εως, ἡ, *pouring out*, οὐλὰς κριθέων πρόχυσιν ἐποιέετο, = προέχεε, Hdt.1.160. II. π. τῆς γῆς *deposition* of mud by water, alluvial soil, Id.2.5; π. ἐξ Αἰθιοπίης κατενηνειγμένην ὑπὸ τοῦ ποταμοῦ ib.12, cf. A.R.2.964; Ἀσσυρίης π. χθονός D.P.772; π. ἰλυόεσσα Opp.*H*.1.116. 2. of sweat, ἡ δι' ὅλου τοῦ σώματος ἐν ἱδρῶτι π. Ph.1.29. III. metaph., *pouring forth*, τῶν παθῶν Longin.9.13, cf. Dam.*Pr*.84. **-χύται** [ῠ] (sc. κριθαί), αἱ, = οὐλοχύται, E.*El*.803, *IA*1112, 1471, A.R.1.425. II. *flowers* or *wreaths thrown* to popular persons in token of honour, Plu.*Dio* 29. **-χῠταῖος**, α, ον, *consisting in a libation*, θυσία cj. in E.*Fr*.912.5 (anap.). **-χῠτήριον**, τό, = *fusorium*, *Gloss*. **-χύτης** [ῠ], ου, ὁ, = πρόχοος, *jug*, *pitcher*, Ion Lyr.2, Alexand.Com.4, Simaristus et Philet.ap.Ath.11.496c. **-χῠτικός**, ή, όν, *of* or *for pouring*, ἀγγεῖον Sch.Od.1.136. **-χῠτός**, ή, όν, *poured out in front*, πέτρησι προχυτῇσιν with *a shower of* stones, *h.Ap*.383. II. Προχύτη νῆσος the island of *Procida* in the Gulf of Naples, formed by eruption from Vesuvius, D.H.1.53, Str.5.4.9.

**πρόχωλος**, ον, *very lame* or *halt*, Luc.*Ocyp*.146.

**πρόχωμα**, ατος, τό, *earth thrown up before* a place, *dam*, *IG*7.3170.5 (Orchom.Boeot.); v.l. for πρόσχωμα in Lxx 2*Ki*.20.15, Str.13.1.36.

**προχῶναι**, αἱ, = γλουτοί 1, Archipp.41.

**προχωνεύω**, *smelt before*, *PLeid.X*.19 (Pass.), 30.

**προχωννύω**, pf. -κέχωκα, *form by deposition before*, τὰς νήσους Arist.*Mir*.836ᵃ30. II. *dam back*, [τὴν θάλατταν] Aristid.*Or*.46(3).17.

⊛ **προχωρ-έω**, *go* or *come forward, advance*, πρὸς ἐμὴν χεῖρα as my hand guides thee, S.*Ph*.148 (anap.), etc.; of troops, Th.2.12, 3.111, etc.; of excrement, *to be voided*, Arist.*HA*594ᵇ22 (later Pass., Alex. Trall.9.3); οἶκος εἰς Βορρᾶν προκεχωρηκώς, Lat. *vergens ad*.., Luc.*Hipp*.7: of Time, τοῦ αἰῶνος προκεχωρηκότος X.*Cyr*.8.7.1, cf. Hdn.2.2.2, etc.; προὐχώρει ὁ πότος X.*An*.7.3.26, cf. Luc.*DMeretr*.15.2: of Degree, προχωρεῖ καὶ οὐ μένει τό τε θερμότερον ἀεὶ καὶ τὸ ψυχρότερον ὡσαύτως Pl.*Phlb*.24d. 2. of coin, *pass current*, *Peripl.M.Rubr*.47, S.E.*M*.1.178; of funds, *to be allocated* or *expended*, εἰς τὴν τῶν τειρώνων συντέλειαν *IGRom*.4.1763 (Tira), cf. *IG*4²(1).91.10 (iii A.D.), *PSI*4.285.4 (iv A.D.). 3. *to be imported*, *Peripl.M.Rubr*.6, al. b. *find a market, sell*, οὐ προχωρεῖ ὁ πυρὸς εἰ μὴ ἐκ δραχμῶν ἑπτά *PAmh*.2.133.18 (ii A.D.). II. metaph., of states, wars, enterprises, etc., *proceed*, freq. with some word denoting a good or bad issue, δόξας εὖ προχωρῆσαι δόμος E.*Heracl*.486 (nisi leg. δρόμος); τὰ Περσέων πρήγματα ἐς ὃ δυνάμιος προκεχώρηκε Hdt.7.50; Ἴωσι προχωρησάντων ἐπὶ μέγα τῶν πραγμάτων Th.1.16; οὕτως ὠμὴ ⟨ἡ⟩ στάσις π. Id.3.81; αὐτῷ π. τὰ πράγματα ᾗ ἐβούλετο Id.1.74; τούτων προκεχωρηκότων ὡς ἐβούλοντο X.*HG*5.2.1, cf. 7.2.1, *Cyr*.2.3.16: abs., *go on well, prosper*, οὔ τι προχωρέειν οἷόν τε ἔσται τῶν πρηγμάτων Hdt.8.108; ἐπεί τέ σφι.. οὐ προεχώρεε [κάτοδος] Id.5.62; ἤν τινά γε προχωρῇ Hp.*Fract*.15 (v.l. προσ-); τὸ ἔργον π. Th.8.68; τὰ πλείω αὐτοῖς προὐκεχωρήκει Id.4.73, cf. 6.103; τὰ νῦν προχωρήσαντα your present *successes*, Id.4.18; of auguries and the like, τὰ διαβατήρια αὐτοῖς οὐ π. Id.5.54; ἴσως ἂν τὰ ἱερὰ μᾶλλον προχωροίη ἡμῖν X.*An*.6.4.21: rarely of ill success, *turn out*, παρὰ δόξαν αὐτοῖς π. τῶν πραγμάτων Plb.5.29.1; τὸ δ' ἐς τοὐναντίον π. Luc.*Alex*.36. 2. impers., προχωρεῖ μοι *it goes on well* for me, *I have success*, commonly with neg., ὥς οἱ δόλῳ οὐ προεχώρεε when he *could* not *succeed* by craft, Hdt.1.205, cf. 84, Th.1.109, etc.; οὐ προὐχώρει ᾗ προσεδέχοντο *things did* not *succeed* as.., Id.3.18: c. inf., ἢν μὴ προχωρήσῃ ἴσον ἑκάστῳ ἔχοντι ἀπελθεῖν if *it be* not *possible*.., Id.4.59; ἐὰν τοῖς γεωργοῖς προχωρῇ πωλεῖν κτλ. *PCair.Zen*.723.8 (iii B.C.); ῥίψαντες, ὡς ἑκάστοις προὐχώρει (sc. ῥῖψαι).. Arr.*An*.1.1.12; ἡνίκ' ἂν ἑκάστῳ π. X.*Cyr*.1.2.4; ὁπόσα σοι προχωρεῖ as much as *is convenient*, ib.3.2.29, cf. *An*.1.9.13: abs. in part., προκεχωρηκότων τοῖς Λακεδαιμονίοις ὥστε.. *when things went on so well* for them that.., Id.*HG*5.3.27. 3. later, of persons, *advance*, ἐπὶ μέγα π. Luc.*DMort*.12.2; of excess, ἐς πᾶν τρυφῆς π. D.C.39.37, cf. 48.1; ἐς τοῦτο, ὥστε.. Id.73.3; ἐς τοσοῦτον μανίας, ὡς.. Hdn.1.15.8. III. *come forward to speak*, π. τῶν ἄλλων *come out in front of* the rest, v.l. in Din.3.14. **-ημα**, ατος, τό, *excrement*, Lxx *Ez*.32.6. ⊛ **-ησις**, εως, ἡ, *going forth*, ἐς ἄφοδον Hp.*Fract*.16 (pl.). II. *advance* of the tide, Thphr.*Metaph*.29 (pl.); *progress*, τὴν π. ποιουμένη [φιλοσοφία] Iamb.*Protr*.21.κ′; musical *progression*, Id.*VP*26.121; arithmetical *series*, Id. *in Nic*. p.63 P. **-ητέον**, *one must advance*, Gal.19.667. **-ητικός**, ή, όν, = προφορικός, λόγος Numen.ap.Lyd.*Mens*.4.80.

**πρόχωσις**, εως, ἡ, *promontory, embankment, mole*, Aristid.*Or*.46(3).17, Philostr.*VS*2.23.3.

**προψᾰλάσσω**, *assail*, S.*Ichn*.241 (lyr.).

**πρόψαλμα**, ατος, τό, sine interpr., *Gloss*.

**προψηλᾰφ-άω**, *massage beforehand*, Paul.Aeg.4.1 (Pass.). **-ημα**, ατος, τό, = προοίμιον in music, *prelude*, Procl.*in Ti*.1.355 D. (pl.).

**προψηνίζω**, *inoculate figs beforehand* (cf. ψηνίζω), *EM*818.29 (Pass.).

**προψηφίζομαι**, *decree before*, esp. in pf. Pass., *Inscr.Prien*.105.54 (i B.C.), *IG*12(2).26.6 (Mytilene), *CIG*3597*b* (Ilium), 4380*n*³ (add.) (Termessus Minor), D.C.43.14. II. Act., *reckon beforehand*, *PMag.Leid.W*.1.4:—Pass., Vett.Val.312.35.

**προψυχρίζω**, = sq., of wine, Gal.6.813 (Pass.).

**προψύχω** [ῡ], *cool before*, Gal.11.480, *PLeid.X*.82:—Pass., Plu.2.690f (nisi leg. περιψ-), Gal.6.690.

**προῳδικός**, ή, όν, *of* or *for a prelude*, Sch.Ar.*Ach*.1142, Heph.*Poëm*.4.

**προωδίνω** [ῑ], *to be in travail with antecedently*, τὴν κοσμικὴν ἰδέαν Dam.*Pr*.106.

**προῳδός**, ἡ, (ᾠδή) *prelude, overture*, Sch.Ar.*Av*.1372, *EM*691.48. II. *a short verse before a longer one*, opp. ἐπῳδός, Heph.*Poëm*.7.

**προώδων**, = προόδους (q.v.), Phryn.*PS* p.101 B.

**προωθέω**, aor. προέωσα, contr. part. πρώσας Hp.*Nat.Mul*.3, *AP*12.206 (Strat.), Luc.*Asin*.9; imper. πρῶσον prob. in Hsch.:—*push forward, propel*, Pl.*Phd*.84d (metaph.), Arist.*HA*611ᵇ32, al., Agatharch.5, *PPetr*.2 p.59 (iii B.C.); βιαίως π. τινὰ ἐπί τι Chrysipp.*Stoic*.3.95; π. αὐτόν *rush on*, X.*Cyn*.10.10. 2. simply, *push*, ὀπίσω Hp.*Mul*.1.69, cf. 2.145, Herod.Med. in *Rh.Mus*.58.106 (Pass.), Antyll.ap.Orib.46.27.6; κάτω Hp.*Nat.Mul*. l. c. II. *thrust forward*, sens. obsc., Luc. l. c. III. Pass., *to be pushed forward*, Thphr.*HP*3.6.2; τὸ στῆθος ἔξω προεωθεῖτο, in tetanus, Aristid.*Or*.49(25).17.

**προώλης**, ες, (ὄλλυμι) *utterly destroyed* or *ruined*, ἐξώλης καὶ π. D.19.172, cf. 18.324, Ael.*Fr*.325, Ἀρχ. Δελτ. 11 παρ. 20 (Lesbos, πρωώλ-).

**προωμοσία**, ἡ, *prosecutor's affidavit*, Poll.8.55.

⊛ **προωνέομαι**, *buy beforehand*, *IG*12(3).169.9, 170.8 (Astypalaea), Gal.14.68.

**προωνύμιον** [ῠ], τό, (ὄνομα) = Lat. *praenomen*, *Gloss*.

**προώνῠμος**, ον, *called by a name previously*, Nonn.*D*.17.397.

**προώριος**, ον, *dying untimely*, Nonn.*D*.33.53.

⊛ **πρόωρος**, ον, (ὥρα) *before the time, untimely*, πένθος Ph.2.314; πολιοί Aret.*SD*2.13; γῆρας Luc.*Am*.21, cf. *AP*7.643 (Crin.), Ath.Med.ap.Orib.*inc*.21.8, Plu.2.101f; of a person, = foreg., *AP*13.27 (Phal.), *IGRom*.4.616 (Temenothyrae): Comp., Sor.1.33.

**πρό-ωσις**, εως, ἡ, (προωθέω) *pushing forward, propulsion*, Arist.*Cael*.297ᵇ13, *Mu*.396ᵃ8, Thphr.*HP*3.6.3, etc.; *extrusion* of calculi, Aret.*CA*2.8; contr. πρῶσις, prob. in Hsch. **-ωσμός**, ὁ, = foreg., Hero *Aut*.8.3. **-ώστης**, ου, ὁ, *projecting beam, swing-beam*, Aen.Tact.32.5 (pl.). **-ωστικός**, ή, όν, *propellent, expulsive*, δύναμις Gal.*Nat.Fac*.3.3, cf. *UP*4.7. Adv. -κῶς S.E.*M*.10.83.

**προωφελέω**, *assist before*, Ph.1.186 (v.l. προσ-).

**πρόωφος**· πρόσκοπος, Hsch. **προωχής**· ἵππος· ὁ ἐκ τῶν ὄπισθεν μετέωρος καὶ τῷ ἀναστήματι καὶ τῇ ἱππασίᾳ, Id. **πρύανος**· νέος, Id.

**πρῠλέες**, έων, οἱ, *men-at-arms, soldiers*, αὐτοὶ δὲ π. σὺν τεύχεσι θωρηχθέντες, opp. chiefs fighting from chariots, Il.11.49; πρώτοισι μετὰ πρυλέεσσι 21.90; Λαοδάμαντα, ἡγεμόνα πρυλέων 15.517; κυνέην ..ἑκατὸν πολίων πρυλέεσσ' ἀραρυῖαν 5.744; Ἄρης..πρυλέεσσι κελεύων Hes.*Sc*.193: dat. pl. (Boeot. or Lacon.) προυλέσι (q.v.). 2. later as Adj., *close, in masses*, like foot-soldiers, Opp.*C*.3.125.

**πρυλεύσεις**· ἐπὶ τῆς ἐκφορᾶς τῶν τελευτησάντων παρὰ τῷ ἱερεῖ, Hsch.

⊛ **πρύλῐς** [ῠ], εως, ἡ, *dance in armour, armed dance*, Call.*Jov*.52, *Dian*.240; Cret., = πυρρίχη, acc. to Arist.*Fr*.519.

⊛ **πρύμν-ᾰ**, acc. -ᾰν Th.1.50, al., *PCair.Zen*.54.8 (iii B.C.); Ion. and Ep. πρύμνη (also in S.*Ph*.482, Ar.*V*.399 (anap.); both forms in Phryn.*PS* p.114 B.): ἡ:—prop. fem. of πρυμνός (sc. ναῦς), *stern, poop*, in Hom. mostly πρύμνη νηῦς in full, νηῒ πάρα πρύμνῃ, νηὸς ἄπο πρύμνης, Il.7.383, al., 15.435; ἐπὶ πρύμνῃ..νηΐ 11.600; νηῒ ἐνὶ π. Od.2.417: pl., νηυσὶν ἔπι πρύμνῃσι Il.12.403; ἐπὶ π. νέεσσι 13.333; ἐπὶ πρύμνῃσιν (ναῦφι going before) 8.475; but also τῆς (sc. νηός) πρύμνη Od.13.84, cf. Pl.*Phd*.58a, c; π. alone, Il.1.409, al.:—Phrases: πρύμνην ἀνακρούεσθαι Hdt.8.84; also metaph. of a man, Ar. l. c.; χωρεῖν πρύμναν *retire, draw back*, E.*Andr*.1120; ἐπείγει κατὰ πρύμναν, of a fair wind, S.*Ph*.1451 (anap.); κατὰ π. ἵσταται τὸ πνεῦμα Th.2.97; ἄγειν ἑαυτὴν ἐκ πρύμνης, metaph. of the soul, Dam.*Pr*.400.—Ships were generally drawn up on land by the stern, [νῆας] πεδίονδε εἴρυσαν, αὐτὰρ τεῖχος ἐπὶ πρύμνῃσιν ἔδειμαν Il.14.32; κατὰ πρύμνας καὶ ἀμφ' ἅλα ἔλσαι Ἀχαιούς 1.409; πρύμνας λῦσαι E.*Hec*.539. 2. metaph., π. πόλεος *the Acropolis*, A.*Supp*.345; also of *the vessel* of the State, Id.*Th*.2, 760 (lyr.); so ἐκ πρύμνης φρενός, prob. in Id.*Supp*.989. II. *bottom, foot*, π. Ὄσσας dub. in E.*El*.445 (lyr.). **-ᾰδε**, Adv. *towards the stern*, Hsch. **-αῖος**, α, ον, *of a stern*, πείσματα A.R.4.208, Tryph.139, cf. *AP*10.16.9 (Theaet.), Opp.*H*.1.191. ⊛ **-ηθεν**, Dor. -ᾱθεν, *from the stern*, Il.15.716, A.*Th*.209, E.*IT*1349; πομπεύσαις πρυμνᾶθεν, of a fair wind, Erinn.1. **-ήσιος**, α, ον, *of a stern*, κάλως E.*HF*479. II. mostly neut. pl. πρυμνήσια (sc. δεσμά), *stern-cables*, κατὰ..π. ἔδησαν Il.1.436; ἀνάψαι Od.9.137; ἀνὰ..π. λῦσαι 9.178, cf. 2.418, al.: metaph., ἐν σοὶ τἀμὰ βίου πρυμνήσι' ἀνῆπται *AP*12.159 (Mel.), cf. *PMag.Berol.*1.346. **-ήτης**, ου, ὁ, *steersman*: metaph., χώρας τῆσδε π. ἄναξ '*the pilot*' of the State, A.*Eu.*16; ἄνδρα..π. χθονός ib. 765. II. as masc. Adj., =foreg., π. κάλως E.*Med.*770. 2. of a fair wind, v.l. for ἀργέστης, A.R.4.1628. **-ητικός**, ή, όν, = πρυμνήσιος, ἄφλαστα Callix.1. II. -κή, ἡ, *poop-awning*, *PCair. Zen.*54.4,19 (iii B.C.). ⊛ **-όθεν**, Adv. = πρύμνηθεν, A.R.4.911, Arat. 343, etc. II. *from the bottom*: hence, *utterly*, *root and branch*, ὀλλύναι A.*Th.*71,1061 (anap.). **-όν**, τό, *lower part*, *end*, π. θέναρος Il.5.339: pl., πρυμνοῖς ἀγορᾶς ἔπι at the *far end* of the agora, Pi.*P.* 5.93.—Prop. neut. of sq. **-ός**, ή, όν, Ep. Adj. *hindmost*, *undermost*, *end-most*, π. βραχίων *the end of* the arm (where it joins the shoulder), Il.13.532, 16.323; π. γλῶσσα, κέρα, σκέλος, ὦμος, *the end* of the [limb] *next the body*, 5.292, 13.705, 16.314, Od.17.504; ὕλην π. ἐκτάμνειν cut off *at the root*, Il.12.149; δόρυ π. *the lowest part* of a spear-head (where it joins the shaft), 17.618; [λᾶας] πρυμνὸς παχύς broad *at base*, opp. ὕπερθεν ὀξύς, 12.446; πέτραι τε [πρ]υμναί *broad-based* rocks, prob. in E.*Antiop.*p.21 A.: Sup. πρυμνότατος Od.17.463; cf. πρύμνα, πρυμνόν; Hsch. has πρυμνός· κάτωθεν βαρύς, ἢ πλοῦτος. **-οῦχος**, ον, (ἔχω) *holding the ship's stern*, κάλος *AP*7.374 (Marc. Arg.). II. *detaining the ships* (because they were anchored *by the stern*), Αὖλις E.*El.*1022. **-ώρεια**, ἡ, (ὄρος) *lower slope*, *foot of a mountain*, Il.14. 307, Pisand.Larandensis ap. St.Byz. s.v. Νιφάτης.

**πρῠτᾰν-άρχης**, ου, ὁ, *president of a board of* πρυτάνεις, *Ath.Mitt.*6. 42 (Cyzicus). ⊛ **-εία** (A), Ion. **-ηΐη**, ἡ, *presidency*, at Athens the period during which the πρυτάνεις of each φυλή in turn presided in the βουλή and ἐκκλησία, Antipho 6.45, And.1.73; ἑνδεκάτῃ τῆς πρυτανείας (sc. τῆς Πανδιονίδος) Decr.ap.D.24.27, cf. Lex ib.39, *IG*1$^2$.57.53, al., 2$^2$.212.4, 223 *A* 4, al.: also κατὰ πρυτανείαν by *presidencies*, i.e. every 35 or 36 days, Lys.30.5, D.59.27; ὁ γραμματεὺς ὁ κατὰ π. *IG*2$^2$.120.16, al.; καθ' ἑκάστην π. Aeschin.3.25. II. *office* or *government of* πρυτάνεις, at Miletus, Arist.*Pol.*1305$^a$17; at Rhodes, Plu.2.813d (pl.); at Halicarnassus, *SIG*1015.2; at Mytilene, *IG* 12(2).68. 2. *any public office held by rotation* for given periods; π. τῆς ἡμέρης the *chief command* for the day, held by each general in turn, Hdt.6.110. **-εία** (B), ἡ, fem. of πρυτάνειος, title of Ἑστία at Syros, *IG*12(5).659.10. ⊛ **-εῖον**, Ion. **-ήϊον** (also **βρυτανεῖον**, *Schwyzer* 183.15 (Crete, iii B.C.), cf. Sch.Pi.*N.*11.1, and v. πρυτανεύω), τό, *the magistrates' hall*, *town hall*, Hdt.1.146, 3.57, 7.197, Ar.*Ach.*125, Th. 2.15, D.19.32, etc.; ἐν πρυτανείῳ δειπνεῖν, σιτεῖσθαι, Ar.*Pax* 1084, Pl. *Ap.*36d, cf. *IG*1$^2$.77.4,13; ἐπὶ δεῖπνον εἰς τὸ π. καλεῖν τινα D.50.13, Aeschin.2.46, cf. Ar.*Eq.*1404; καλέσαι ἐπὶ ξένια εἰς πρυτανεῖον prob. in *IG*1$^2$.19; εἰς π. ἐκάλεσα D.19.234; οὗ γὰρ μὴ τίθενται συμβολαί, π. ταῦτα πάντα προσαγορεύεται are called *free tables*, Timocl.8.18, cf. *SIG*4 (Cyzicus, vi B.C.): metaph., τῆς Ἑλλάδος αὐτὸ τὸ π. τῆς σοφίας Pl.*Prt.*337d, cf. Theopomp.Hist.267. II. *a law-court* at Athens, τὸ ἐπὶ πρυτανείῳ δικαστήριον, οἱ ἐκ πρυτανείου καταδικασθέντες, D.23. 76, Decr.ap.And.1.78, cf. Plu.*Sol.*19. 2. πρυτανεῖα, τά, *sum deposited by each party to a lawsuit before the suit began*, π. τιθέναι, κατατιθέναι, *IG*1$^2$.22.33, 28.5, cf. Ar.*Nu.*1136,1180, *V.*659, etc.; ἄνευ πρυτανείων *IG*1$^2$.3.29; π. τιθέτω ὁ διώκων τοῦ αὐτοῦ μέρους Lex ap.D.43. 71; ἵν' αἱ θέσεις γίγνοιντο τῇ νουμηνίᾳ (sc. τῶν πρυτανείων) Ar.*Nu.* 1191; δέχεσθαι τὰ π. to receive *this deposit*, i.e. to allow the action to be brought, ib.1197; π. ἐκτίνειν to pay *this deposit*, D.47.64. ⊛ **-ειος**, α, ον, *of* or *belonging to the prytanes*, Aristid.*Or.*50(26).88; cf. πρυτανεία (B). ⊛ **-ευμα**, ατος, τό, *principate*, i.e. *prince*, Epigr. in *Rev. Phil.*19.178 (i B.C.). **-εύς**, έως, ὁ, = πρύτανις, *IG*12(1).49.12 (Rhodes), f.l. in Harp. s.v. πρυτανεύοντα. ⊛ **-εύω** (also **βρυτανεύω**, *IG*9(1).111 (Elatea), cf. πρυτανεῖον), *to be* πρύτανις or *president*, *hold sway*, ἀθανάτοισι *among* them, *h.Ap.*68; so of God, Ph.2.595. 2. *to be chairman* of a board, D.21.87; of a βουλή, *POxy.*2130.7 (iii A.D.), etc. II. at Athens, *hold the presidency*, prop. of the tribe in order of πρυτανεία in βουλή and ἐκκλησία, ἔτυχεν..ἡ φυλὴ ['Αντιοχὶς] πρυτανεύουσα Pl.*Ap.*32b, cf. *Grg.*473e; Ἀκαμαντὶς ἐπρυτάνευε *IG*1$^2$.16, Th.4.118, etc.: sts. of an individual member of the πρυτανεία, *IG*1$^2$. 39.14, al., Antipho 6.45; οἱ τότε πρυτανεύσαντες And.1.46. b. generally, of the *mover* of a motion, ὁ πρυτανεύσας ταῦτα καὶ πείσας D.15.3. 2. π. περὶ εἰρήνης *put the question on a motion for* peace, this being the duty of the Prytanes, Ar.*Ach.*60; εἰρήνην πρυτανεῦσαι Isoc.4.121: hence, 3. π. τινὶ εἰρήνην *obtain* peace for another, Luc.*Demon.*9, cf. *PStrassb.*5.8 (Pass., iii A.D.); φιλίαν τισί D.C.46. 11; πᾶσι τὰ ἀγαθά Aristid.*Or.*26(14).109; [αἱ Πλειάδες] τὸ ἔαρ ἡμῖν π. *herald* the spring, Procop.Gaz. p.141 B. III. generally, *control*, *regulate*, joined with διοικεῖν, D.5.6:—Pass., πρυτανεύεσθαι παρά τινος *to suffer oneself to be guided* by one, Id.9.60. 2. metaph., δεῖπνον χαριέντως πεπρυτανευμένον *served* daintily, Alex.110.4; of persons, *to be entertained*, χορηγίᾳ βασιλικῇ Plu.2.602a. **-ηΐη, -ήϊον**, Ion. for πρυτανεία, -νεῖον. **-ῐκός**, ή, όν, *of* or *for a* πρύτανις, ἡ π. ἐξουσία *IG*12(7).396.5 (Amorgos), cf. *Inscr.Perg.*254.7; π. γραφή action *against a* πρύτανις, Harp. s.v. ῥητορικὴ γραφή; ἐσθῆτες Herm.Hist.2: -κόν, τό, = πρυτανεῖον, στῆσαι ἐν τῷ π. *IG*2$^2$.915, al.; also, *receipts from* πρυτανεῖα (?), ib.11(2).287 *A* 13 (Delos, iii B.C.). 2. *having the rank of ex-*πρύτανις, Wilcken *Chr.*27.16 (ii A.D.), etc. **-ις**, also **πρότανις** (q.v.), gen. εως, *ruler*, *lord*, π. κύριε..ἀγυιᾶν καὶ στρατοῦ Pi.*P.*2.58, cf. B.18.43; στεροπᾶν κεραυνῶν τε π., of Zeus, Pi.*P.*6.24; ἵππων, of Poseidon, Stesich.49; ἀγορῆς π., of Apollo, Simon.164; μακάρων π., of Zeus, A.*Pr.*170 (anap.); Κρόνιε πρύτανι Φρύγιε E.*Tr.* 1288 (lyr.); π. συμποσίων, i.e. Dionysus, Ion Lyr.1.14; οἶνον..ἀνθρώπων π. Id.9.3; δυσαμεριᾶν π., of the Sphinx, A.*Fr.*236; Ἡρόδοτον.. ἱστορίης πρύτανιν *App.Anth.*2.21; πλούτου καὶ σοφίης π., of Periander, Epigr.ap.D.L.1.97; π. ὕμνων (sc. ἡ ᾠδή) *Lyr.Adesp.*80; μούσης ὑψινόου π. *Epigr.Gr.*440.10 (Batanaea); τέχνας ὁ π. πέλεκυς *AP*6.205 (Leon.); πρυτάνεις κόσμου, of the stars, Lxx *Wi.*13.2; ὅρκος..ἀληθείας γενόμενος ἡμῖν π. Hierocl. *in CA* 2 p.422 M. II. at Athens, *member of the tribe presiding in* βουλή or ἐκκλησία, τοὺς πρυτάνεις τοὺς τότε πρυτανεύσαντας And.1.46, etc.; in other states, οἱ π. οἱ πρυτανεύοντες τὸν μῆνα *SIG*1015.19 (Halic.), cf. *IG*12(3).169 (Astypalaea); at Calynda in Caria, *PCair.Zen.*341(*a*).23 (iii B.C.). 2. πρυτάνεις τῶν ναυκράρων, *officials of the* ναύκραροι (q.v.). 3. in other Greek states title of a *chief magistrate*, *IG*12(1).53, al. (Rhodes); in Lycia, Ephipp.5.19 (anap.); at Miletus, Arist.*Pol.*1305$^a$18; as title of a *chief priest*, ib.1322$^b$29: rarely of a woman, *IGRom.*4.1325 (Phocaea), *CIG* 3953*d* (Trapezopolis). b. pl., title of a board of magistrates, *SIG* 581.91 (Hierapytna, ii B.C.), 976.3 (Samos, ii B.C.), etc. c. *president* of a council, *POxy.*77.2 (iii A.D.), etc. **-ῖτις**, ιδος, as title of Ἑστία, = πρυτανεία (B), Herm.Hist.2.

**πρώ** or **πρῴ**, **πρῳαίτερον**, **πρῳαίτατα**, v. πρωΐ. **πρωγγυ-εύω**, **-ος**, v. προεγγυ-εύω, -ος. ***πρώειρα**, v. πρῷρα. **πρῳζός**, v. πρωϊζός. **πρωή**, ἡ, = Lat. *mane*, *Gloss.*

⊛ **πρώην**, Dor. **πρώᾱν** Theoc.5.4,15.15; contr. **πρῶν** Call.*Fr.*84, Herod.5.62; **πρᾶν** Theoc.2.115:—*lately*, *just now*, Il.5.832, 24.500, Ar.*Fr.*408, Alex.258, Herod. l.c., *UPZ*42.25 (ii B.C.), Cic.*Att.*6.4.3, etc.; in a book, *above*, Arist.*EN*1104$^b$18. 2. *long ago*, Procop.Gaz. *Pan.*p.505 B.; Ἀγησίλαος ὁ π. ib.p.514 B. II. more definitely, *the day before yesterday*, οὐ..χθές, ἀλλὰ π. Th.3.113; μέχρι οὗ π. τε καὶ χθές till yesterday or *the day before*, i.e. till *very lately*, Hdt.2.53; π. καὶ χθές D.44.42; χθές τε καὶ π. Ar.*Ra.*726; χθὲς καὶ π. Pl.*Lg.*677d; τὰ ἐχθὲς καὶ π. Id.*Grg.*470d; ἐχθὲς καὶ π. Isoc.6.27; ἄρτι καὶ π., ὀψὲ καὶ π., Plu.*Brut.*1, 2.394b. (The first syll. of πρώαν is short in Theoc. ll.cc.; πρόαν is written in 15.15 (codd. opt.), v.l. in 4.60.)

**πρωθ-ευρετής**, οῦ, ὁ, *first discoverer*, Nicom.*Harm.Exc.*1. ⊛ **-ήβης**, ου, ὁ, *in the prime of youth*, παῖδας πρωθήβας Il.8.518; κοῦροι π. Od.8. 263, cf. Epigr. in *BpW.*32.480 (Delph.): in late Prose, Luc.*DMort.* 5.2, App.*Hisp.*65:—fem. πρωθήβη only Od.1.431; also **-ῆβις**, *IG*14. 2122, Hdn.Gr.2.67. **-ηβος**, ον, = foreg., B.17.57. ⊛ **-ύπνιον**, τό, v. πρωτοΰπνιον. **-ύστερος**, ον, *hindmost foremost*, *last first*, π. ὁ τρόπος Sch.E.*Or.*702: neut., = ὕστερον πρότερον, Sch.E.*Ph.*887, etc.

⊛ **πρωΐ** [ῐ], Att. **πρῴ** (Hdn.Gr.1.494, Sch.Ar.*Av.*132, etc.), though codd. commonly give πρῶϊ, πρωΐ, or πρῷ: Adv.: (πρό):—*early in the day*, *at morn*, opp. ὀψέ (acc. to Thphr.*Sign.*9, *the forenoon*, *between* ἀνατολή *and* μεσημβρία), πρωΐ (v.l. πρῶϊ) ὑπηοῖοι Il.8.530, al.: c. gen., πρωῒ ἔτι τῆς ἡμέρης Hdt.9.101; ἑκάστης ἡμέρας τὸ πρῴ X.*HG.*1.1.30, cf. *PSI*3.402.10 (iii B.C.): also πρῴ πάνυ Ar.*V.*104; πρῴ τῇ ὑστεραίᾳ *early* next morning, X.*Cyr.*1.4.16; τὸ πρωΐ Lxx *Ge.*19.27; ἅμα πρωΐ *Ev.Matt.*20.1; ἀπὸ πρωῒ ἕως ἑσπέρας *Act.Ap.*28.23. 2. generally, *betimes*, *early*, Hes.*Op.*461, *Fr.*204, Ar.*Av.*132, etc.: c. gen., πρωῒ τοῦ ἦρος, τοῦ θέρεος, Hp.*Epid.*1.1,2. 3. = πρὸ καιροῦ (Phryn.*PS* p.106 B.), *too soon*, *too early*, πρῴ γε στενάζεις (v.l. πρό) A.*Pr.*696; δέδοικα γὰρ μὴ πρῴ λέγοις ἂν S.*Tr.*631; πρῴ ἐσβαλόντες, καὶ τοῦ σίτου ἔτι χλωροῦ ὄντος Th.4.6, cf. Pl.*Prm.*135c.—Comp. and Sup. πρωΐτερον (or πρῴτερον), πρωΐτατα (or πρῴτατα) are found in Th.7.19,39, 8.101, Arr.*Ind.*26.4, Aristid.*Or.*47(23).35, 51(27).51, v.l. in Hp.*Epid.* 2.1.6, 2.3.2, 6.8.13, al.; but usu. πρωϊαίτερον (or πρῳαίτερον), πρωϊαίτατα (or πρῳαίτατα), Hp. ll.cc. (v.l.), Pl.*Phd.*59d, e, *Tht.*150e, *Prt.* 326c, X.*Cyr.*8.8.9, etc.

**πρωΐα**, v. πρώϊος.

**πρωϊανθής**, ές, *flowering early*, Thphr.*CP*5.1.12.

**πρωϊβλαστ-έω**, *sprout early*, Thphr.*HP*1.9.6, *CP*5.6.6, etc. **-ής**, ές, (βλάστη) *budding* or *sprouting early*, Id.*HP*1.14.3, *CP*1.10.7: also neut. pl. -βλαστα, Id.*HP*3.4.2, cf. *CP*5.1.6 (cj.). **-ία**, ἡ, *early budding*, ib.1.21.3.

⊛ **πρωϊζός**, Att. **πρῳζός**, όν, dub. sens. in Call.*Fr.*63 P.; = προχθεσινός, ὑπόγυος, *EM*691.56. II. neut. pl. πρωϊζά as Adv., = πρώην, χθιζά τε καὶ π. yesterday or *the day before*, Il.2.303, cf. Pl.*Alc.*2.141d. 2. οὕτω δὴ π. κατέδραθες so very *early*, Theoc.18.9; πρωϊζὸν ὁδεύων dub. sens. in *Epic.Alex.Adesp.*4.6. (In codd. freq. written proparox., but cf. Hdn.Gr.1.144.)

⊛ **πρωΐθεν**, Adv., (πρωΐ) *from morning*, ἀπὸ π. Lxx *Ex.*18.13, *Ru.*2.7; ἐκ π. ib.3 *Ki.*18.26; cf. Hdn.Gr.1.501.

**πρωϊκαρπ-έω**, *bear fruit early*, Thphr.*CP*1.13.9. **-ία**, ἡ, *fruiting early*, ib.1.17.8. **-ος**, ον, *fruiting early*, Id.*HP*1.14.3, *CP*1.10.7.

⊛ **πρώϊμος**, ον, Ion. **πρόϊμος** cj. in Call.*Fr.*482 (*Hermes* 24.453):—*early*, of fruits, X.*Oec.*17.4, Arist.*Pr.*924$^b$5, *OGI*56.68 (Canopus, iii B.C.); of winter, *Cat.Cod.Astr.*1.172; ὥρῃ Call. l.c.; also, *born early*, ἄρνες *PCair.Zen.*771.10 (iii B.C.). 2. metaph., *precocious*, π. πονηρία Metrod.*Fr.*56. Adv. Comp. -ώτερον *PTeb.*27.25 (ii B.C.).

**πρωϊνός** [ῐ], ή, όν, later form of πρώϊος (for wh. it is f.l. in Thphr. *CP*3.24.2), *PCair.Zen.*207.36 (iii B.C.), Lxx *Ge.*49.27, *Ex.*29.41, al.; ἐδωδή Plu.2.726f, cf. Ath.1.11c; ἔργα Babr.124.17. Adv. -νῶς interpol. in Suid. s.v. πρώϊμος.

⊛ **πρώϊ-ος**, Att. **πρῷος**, α, ον: (πρωΐ, πρῴ):—*early*, I. *early in the day*, *at early morn*, Il.15.470 (neut. πρώϊον as Adv. = πρωΐ); π. ἐμπολέα *AP*6.304 (Phan.); π. ῥόδον Call.*Lav.Pall.*27; also περὶ δείλην πρωΐην Hdt.8.6; δείλης πρωΐας Philem.210. 2. Subst. πρωΐα, ἡ, *early morning*, ἅμα τῇ π. Aristeas 304; ἦν δὲ πρωΐα *Ev.Jo.*18.28; πρωΐας γενομένης *Ev.Matt.*27.1: gen. πρωΐας as Adv. = πρῴ, ib.21.18: with Preps., καθ' ἑκάστην πρωΐαν J.*AJ*7.8.1; ἀπὸ πρωΐας ἄχρις ἡλίου δύσεως *IG*4.597.16 (Argos), cf. *PLond.*3.1177.66 (ii A.D.). II. *early in* *the year*, πρώϊος [ὁ στρατὸς] συνελέγετο Hdt.8.130; τῶν καρπίμων ἅττα μὴ 'στι π. Ar.*V.*264; σικύων πρῴων Id.*Pax* 1001, cf. 1164 (lyr.), Thphr.*CP*4.11.1; π. χειμών an *early* winter, Id.*Sign.*40; τὸν πρώϊον (or πρῷον) σῖτον *PCair.Zen.*155.2 (iii B.C.); διὰ τὸ τὰ μὲν πρώϊα, τὰ δ' ὄψια προΐεσθαι (sc. ᾠά) Arist.*HA*543ᵃ9; π. τόπος an *early* place, i.e. producing early fruits, Thphr.*HP*8.2.9: Comp. πρωΐτερος Id.*CP* 5.6.5 codd. **-ότης**, ητος, ἡ, *earliness*, of fruits, ib.4.11.9.

**πρωϊ-σπορέομαι**, *to be sown early*, Thphr.*HP*8.1.2. **-σπορος**, ον, *sown* or *to be sown early*, ib.8.1.3 (Posit. and Comp.).

**πρωΐτερον, πρωΐτατα**, v. πρωΐ 3.

**πρώκεα**· δῶρα, Hsch. (leg. προίκια).

⊕ **πρώκῐος** or **πρώκῖνος**, η, ον, (πρώξ) *dewy*, εἶδαρ restd. in Call.*Aet.Oxy.*2079.34 (= *Fr.*542).

**πρωκτίζω**, = Lat. *paedico*, Ar.*Th.*1124.

**πρωκτοπεντετηρίς**, ίδος, ἡ, *quinquennial debauchery*, Ar.*Pax*876.

⊕ **πρωκτός**, ὁ, *anus*, Ar.*V.*604, etc.; π. καμήλου Id.*Pax*758; π. κυνός Id.*Ach.*863.

**πρωκτοτηρέω**, *to be a watcher of* πρωκτοί, Ar.*Eq.*878.

**πρωλυθίαι**· παρειμένοι, παραλελυμένοι, and **πρωλύθιον**· ὁ ἐπιφερὴς καὶ ἐπὶ στόμα, Hsch.

**πρῷμος**, ον, Att. for πρώϊμος, Ar.*Fr.*373.

**πρών**, ὁ, gen. πρῶνος (as pr. n., Paus.2.34.11 codd.), πρωνός Id.2.35.4, al. codd., *AP*9.328 (Damostr.); Ep. dat. pl. πρώνεσσι Q.S.4.520:—*foreland, headland*, Hom. only in Il., πρὼν ἰσχάνει ὕδωρ ὑλήεις 17.747: elsewh. in pl. πρώονες, 8.557, 12.282, 16.299; later, πρώονές τε καὶ χαράδραι Alcm.60.2, cf. Q.S.2.120; πρῶνες ἔξοχοι Pi.*N.*4.52; Λοκρῶν πρῶνες S.*Tr.*788; Πόσειδον, ὃς Αἰγαίου μέδεις πρῶνας Id.*Fr.*371 (lyr.); ἔρημοι πρῶνες ἀνθρώπων E.*Cyc.*116; πορθμοῦ κάτοπτον πρῶνα, of Geraneia, A.*Ag.*307; ἀμφοτέρας ἅλιον πρῶνα κοινὸν αἶας, *forelands* on both sides of the Hellespont, Id.*Pers.*132 (lyr.); π. ἅλιος, of the Troad, ib.879; Δελφὸς π., of Parnassus, *Pae.Delph.*7:—Ep. also **πρηών**, ῶνος, ὡς δ' ὅτ' ἀπὸ μεγάλου πέτρη πρηῶνος ὀρούσῃ Hes.*Sc.*437, cf. Nic.*Al.*104, D.P.116, Coluth.14,102: dat. pl. πρηόσιν Call.*Dian.*52: in later Prose, Ant.Lib.11.1, 23.5; also **πρεών**, όνος, *AP*6.253 (Crin.). (Orig. πρηών, όνος, whence πρεών, όνος and ῶνος, also (contr.) **πρών**, πρῶνος, pl. πρῶνες (then, by 'distraction' of ω and its accent, πρώονες).)

**πρῶν**, v. πρώην.

**πρώξ**, ἡ, gen. πρωκός, *dewdrop*, only pl., πρῶκας σιτίσδεται ὥσπερ ὁ τέττιξ Theoc.4.16, cf. Call.*Ap.*41, Hsch.

**πρῷος**, v. πρώϊος. **πρωπέρῠσι**, v. προπέρυσι.

⊕ **πρῷρ-α** [ᾰ in nom. and acc. sg., A.*Supp.*716, S.*Ph.*482, *Fr.*726, E.*Hel.*1563, 1582, *Or.*362, *IT*1134 (lyr.); nom. πρῷρ' with elision in *IG*2.2836; acc. πρῴρᾱν is f.l. in A.R.1.372; πρῴρην is found in codd. of Hdt.1.194, 7.180], ἡ, *forepart of a ship, prow*, εἰς ἴκρια νηὸς πρῴρης Od.12.230 (here prob. adjectival with νηός), cf. Hdt. ll.cc., etc.; πνεῦμα τοὐκ πρῴρας a contrary wind, opp. κατὰ πρύμναν, S.*Ph.*639. 2. metaph., πρῷρα βιότου *the prow* of life's vessel, i.e. early youth, E.*Tr.*103 (anap.); ὦ πρῷρα λοιβῆς Ἑστία *thou who art first entitled to* it, S.*Fr.*726; πάροιθεν πρῴρας . . καρδίας before my heart's *prow*, in front of my heart, A.*Ch.*390 (lyr.). 3. *end* of a vine-branch, Thphr.*HP*2.1.3 (cj. in *CP*3.14.7). (Written πρῶρρα in Plb. 8.6.1, al., but πρωιρ- in *PSI*4.382.2 (iii B.C.), cf. πρῳρατικός; κυανοπρωΐρους [⏑⏑– – – –] is cited by *EM*692.32 from Hom., and κυανοπρῴϊραν from Simon.241: hence πρῷρα is prob. contr. from a word of the form – – ⏑, but whether from *πρώειρα, as inferred by Hdn. Gr.2.410, is doubtful; perh. from *πρώαιρα, cf. νείαιρα; -πρωϊρ- in Hom. and Simon. may have arisen by 'distraction' of the contracted form.) **-άζω**, metaph., = κροτέω, in aor. part. πρῳράσαντες, Hsch. **-ᾱθεν**, Ion. -ηθεν, in Poets before a consonant -θε: Adv. *from the ship's head, from the front*, Pi.*P.*4.22, 10.52, Th.7.36, etc.; ἐκ πρῴρηθεν, opp. κατὰ πρύμναν, Theoc.22.11; ἀπὸ π. Q.S.14.378. **-ᾱτεύω**, *to be a* πρῳράτης, Ar.*Eq.*543, Demad.ap. Plu.*Cleom.*27, Alciphr.2.4; of a naval officer, *SIG*1225.3 (Rhodes, iii B.C.), *Supp.Epigr.*4.178.7 (Caria, ii B.C.); π. τριηρέων *GDI*3779.20 (Rhodes). ⊕ **-άτης** [ᾰ], ου, ὁ, = πρῳρεύς, opp. πρυμνήτης, X.*Ath.*1.2, Poll.1.95: metaph., π. στρατοῦ S.*Fr.*524.1. **-ᾱτικός**, ή, όν, *of* or *for a* πρῳράτης, ἑδώλιον Poll.1.89. II. Subst. -κή, ἡ, *prow-awning*, *PCair.Zen.*54.13,27 (iii B.C., πρωιρ-). **-αχθής**, ές, *laden at the prow*: metaph., *bowed forwards*, Hsch. **-εύς**, έως, ὁ, *officer in command at the bow*, as the κυβερνήτης at the stern (= πρῳράτης), X.*An.*5.8.20, *Oec.*8.14, D.32.7, Arist.*Pol.*1253ᵇ29, *GDI*4335 (Rhodes), *OGI*674.11 (Egypt, i A.D.). **-ηθεν**, v. πρῴραθεν. **-ήσια**, τά, = κόρυμβα, *EM*177.47.

**πρωρός**, = φρουρός, *IG*7.4249 (loc. incert.), *Documenti antichi dell' Africa Italiana* 1.88 (Cyrene, ii B.C.); as pr. n., *Schwyzer* 234.20 (ibid.).

**πρώσας, πρῶσον, πρῶσις**, v. προωθέω, πρόωσις.

**πρωτάγγελος**, ὁ, *harbinger*, c. gen., *AP*9.383.8, Nonn.*D.*27.14. II. = ἀρχάγγελος, *PMag.Berol.*1.302.

**Πρωτᾰγόρειος**, α, ον, *of Protagoras*, μέτρον Pl.*Tht.*162c; μῦθος ib.164d.

**πρωτάγριον**, τό, *first fruits of the chase*, Call.*Dian.*104: mostly pl., *first fruits, first prize*, *AP*9.656.8, Nonn.*D.*19.196, 37.467.

⊕ **πρωτᾰγωνιστ-έω**, *to be* πρωταγωνιστής, Plu.*Lys.*23: mostly metaph., *play first fiddle, take the lead*, Arist.*Pol.*1338ᵇ30, Plu.2.1141d; πράξεως in an action, ib.332d. **-ής**, οῦ, ὁ, on the stage, *one who plays the first part, chief actor*, ib.816f; π. τοῦ δράματος Luc.*Cal.*7: metaph., [ὁ Αἰσχύλος] τὸν λόγον π. παρεσκεύασεν Arist. *Po.*1449ᵃ18: generally, *leader*, π. τῆς ὑπηρεσίας Clearch.25; τοῖς μαθηματικοῖς, of king Antiochus, Ps.-Diocl.ap.Paul.Aeg.1.100: expl. of πρόμαχος, *EM*612.51.

**πρωτ-αίτιος**, α, ον, *first author*, Sch.Hermog. in Rh.6.412W., Sch. Th.3.36. **-αίχμεια**, τά, = πρωτόλεια, Lyc.469. **-ανακλίτης** [ῑ], ου, ὁ, *he who reclines first at table*, title of president of an association, *JHS*32.159, 163, al. (Asia Minor).

⊕ **πρωταπογράφομαι** [ᾰ], *register for the first time*, *PFay.*31.18 (ii A.D.).

**πρωταρχ-έω**, *to be chief magistrate*, *Supp.Epigr.*2.410.9 (Thessalonica, ii/iii A.D.), 3.509 (Philippopolis, iii A.D.). **-ης**, ου, *commander*, Man.1.324 (cj. for πλωτ-), 4.399. **-οντεύω**, = πρωταρχέω, *IPE*4.105 (Chersonesus). **-ος**, ον, *primal*, ἄτη A.*Ag.*1192. **-ων**, οντος, ὁ, = πρῶτος ἄρχων, *IG*12(3).326 (Thera), *Ath.Mitt.*48.114 (Nicopolis ad Istrum); π. στρατηγός *IG*12(5).724 (Andros).

⊕ **πρωτ-αύλης**, ου, ὁ, *chief flute-player*, *SIG*1257 (Ephesus); π. Διὸς Οὐρυδαμηνοῦ *Rev.Arch.*12(1888).223 (Yeni-Ali). **-αυράριος**, ὁ, *head of the guild of goldsmiths*, *MAMA*1.281 (Laodicea Combusta), 3.351 (Corycus). **-έγγρᾰφος**, ον, *first inscribed*, *IG*3.1092, al.; cf. ἐπέγγραφος. **-εῖον**, τό, (πρωτεύω) *chief rank, first place*, τὸ π. ἔχειν D.10.74, cf. 18.321, D.S.1.2, etc.: mostly pl., *first prize* or *place*, Pl.*Phlb.*22e, 33c, D.18.66, Longin.34.1; τὰ π. τῆς ἀγωγῆς Phld.*Sto.* 339.11; τὰ π. φέρεσθαι D.H.*Comp.*24; τῶν π. ὀρέγεσθαι D.S.17.54; τινὶ τὰ π. τῆς ἡγεμονίας παρασχέσθαι Agath.3.2. ⊕ **-ειος**, α, ον, *of the first quality*, μέταξα Lyd.*Mag.*2.4; οἶνος Orib.5.33.4, cf. Aët.12.55, *PLond.*5.1764 (vi A.D.). **-είρης**, ου, ὁ, (εἴρην) *Spartan youth in his 20th year*, Hsch., Phot. s.v. κατὰ πρωτείρας (s.v.l.). **-ελληνοδίκης** [ῑ], ου, ὁ, *chief* Ἑλληνοδίκης, π. Ὀλυμπίων (at Ephesus) *IG*14.739 (Naples). **-ενίαυτος** [ῐ], ον, *of the first year*, *POxy.*1413.17 (iii A.D.). **-ενσῑτεύω**, *to be first on the list of those receiving free maintenance*, *IG*5(1).1314, 1315 (Thalamae, ii A.D.). **-εξάδελφος** [ᾰ], ὁ, = αὐτανέψιος, Thom.Mag.p.361 R.

**πρωτερική** συκῆ, ἡ, a kind of *early fig*, Seleuc.ap.Ath.3.77d, Eust. 225.44; π. παιδίον (πεδίον cod.) a *precocious* child, Hsch.

**Πρωτεσί-λᾱος** [ῐ], ὁ, Dor. **-λας**, α, Pi.*I.*1.58; Ion. and Att. **-λεως**, εω:—*First of the people*, name of the hero who *first* leaped ashore at Troy, Il.2.698 (so understood by Hom., ib.702, but the name may be a corruption of *Πορθεσίλαος, cf. Cret. Πορθεσίλας and Πορτεσίλας):—**Πρωτεσιλάειον**, τό, *his monument*, Str.13.1.31: **Πρωτεσιλάεια**, τά, *his festival*, Sch.Pi.*I.*1.11.

**Πρωτεύρυθμος**, ὁ, name of a divinity worshipped by the Iobacchi, *IG*2².1368.125.

**πρωτεύς**, έως, ὁ, = πρώτιστος, λαός Tim.*Pers.*248. II. v. πρᾱτεύς. III. name of an *eyesalve*, Aët.7.106.

⊕ **πρωτεύω**, (πρῶτος) *to be the first, hold first place*, And.4.41 (s.v.l.), Pl.*Lg.*692d, Arist.*EN*1124ᵇ23; οἱ πρωτεύοντες *the primates* or *chief men* in a city, Hdn.8.7.2, cf. Isoc.5.68; *hold position of* πρῶτος (q.v.), *MAMA*4.151 (Apollonia); π. τοῦ ἔθνους *OGI*563.6 (Cadyanda). II. with a modal word added, *to be first in* a thing, καρτερίᾳ X.*Ages.*10.1; βδελυρίᾳ Aeschin.1.192; γένει Is.1.21; ἐν ἕδρᾳ X.*Cyr.*8.4.5; περὶ κακίαν Aeschin.2.159; φιλίᾳ π. παρὰ τῷ Κύρῳ X.*Cyr.*8.2.28, cf. Isoc.3.60; ἐν τούτοις (sc. ἐπιτηδεύμασιν) Id.7.48. 2. c. gen. pers., *to be first of* or *among*, Ἑλλήνων ib.6; τῶν ῥητόρων Aeschin.1.171, cf. X.*Ages.*1.3; π. Ἑλλάδος εἰς ἀρετήν *Epigr.Gr.*489: also π. ἐν τοῖς Ἕλλησι Isoc.8.24; ἐν τῷ δήμῳ D.19.297. III. = προτερέω, *excel*, π. τῆς Ἀρτέμιδος ταῖς κυνηγεσίαις D.S.4.81.

⊕ **πρωτηρότης**, ου, ὁ, (ἀρόω) *one who ploughs earliest* or *first*, Hes. *Op.*490 (nisi leg. πρῳηρότης).

**πρωτιστ-εύω**, *to be the very first*, M.Ant.7.55; Dor. **πρᾱτιστεύω** (q.v.). **-ος**, η, ον, also ος, ον *h.Cer.*157:—poet. and late Prose Sup. of πρῶτος, *the very first*, Il.2.228, 16.656, Od.19.447; πολὺ π. Il.2.702, Od.14.220, etc.; ὁ π. χρόνος, opp. ὁ ἐνεστώς, *PEleph.*10.4 (iii B.C.); *principal, primal*, θεὰ π. Νύξ Phld.*Piet.*14; αἰτία Procl.*Inst.*12; τῶν φύσει κρειττόνων π. ὁ δημιουργός Hierocl. in *CA* 3 p.424 M., cf. Iamb.*Comm.Math.*4, al., Dexipp.*Fr.*32(b) J., Agath.3.2: neut. πρώτιστον as Adv., *first of all*, Od.10.462, 20.60, al., Pi.*N.*5.25, B.8.11, Ar.*Lys.*555, D.43.75, Antiph.98: also pl. πρώτιστα Il.1.105, Od.3.419, Hes.*Op.*109, A.*Fr.*195, S.*OT*1439, *El.*669, Ar.*Pl.*792; ἐπειδὴ π. *now that*, Alc.15.7; ὅτε π. when *aforetime*, Call.*Aet.Oxy.*2079.21; *especially, principally*, π. ἁλίσκεται ἐνταῦθα τὸ ὗψον Str.12.3.19: also τὸ π. E.*Supp.*430; τὰ π. Od.11.168.

**πρωτό-ἀλος**, ον, (ἅλς) = πρωτόπλοος, Hsch. **-βαθρέω**, *place* a man's *seat in front of* others, Lxx *Es.*3.1. **-βαθρος**, ον, *taking the first seat*, Pherecr.226. **-βοιος**, α, ον, = βούπρῳρος, δωδεκής *Delph.*3(2).63. **-βολέω**, *throw first, take the first shot*, Plu.2.173d. 2. *shed the first teeth*, *Hippiatr.*95, *Gp.*16.1.13. 3. *bring forth new fruit*, τῆς καινότητος αὐτοῦ -βολήσει Lxx *Ez.*47.12: metaph., π. χάριτας *AP*5.123 (Phld.). **-βολία**, ἡ, *shedding of first teeth*, Phlp. in *GA*128.22. ⊕ **-βόλος**, ον, (βάλλω) *budding, fresh*, ἥβη *AP*7.217 (Asclep.); βλέφαρα ib.5.61 (Rufin.). 2. *in course of shedding the first* or *milk teeth*, of horses (intermediate between ἄβολος and παντιβόλος), *PPetr.*2 p.115 (iii B.C.), *Anatolian Studies* 204 (Pisidia), *Hippiatr.*20; κάμηλος, ὄνος, *BGU*468.9 (ii A.D.), *PFay.*92.23 (ii A.D.). II. proparox. πρωτόβολος, ον, Pass., *first struck*, τέρμονα π. ἁλίῳ E.*Tr.*1068 (lyr.). **-γᾰλα**, ακτος, τό, = πυός, Gal.19.131; = *colostra*, *Gloss.* **-γᾰμία**, ἡ, Jewish *preliminary marriage-festival*, *CIL*8.25045 (Carthage). **-γᾰμος**, ον, *just married*, Orph.*L.*256. **-γένεια**, ἡ, *first-born*, pecul. fem. of πρωτογενής, Id.*H.*10.5; as pr. n. in Pi., etc. II. = Lat. *Primigenia*, Plu.2.289b; Ἴσιδι

Τύχη Π. *SIG*1133 (Delos, ii B.C.). **-γένειος**, ον, *with the first beard, in the bloom of youth*, as a stage of life, between μειράκιον and νεανίας, Ph.1.159, al. **-γενέσια**, τά, *celebration of the first birthday*, *PCair. Preis.*31.23 (ii A.D.). **-γέννημα**, ατος, τό, *firstfruits*, Ph.2.294: but usu. in pl., LXX *Ex.*34.26, al., Ph.1.172. **-γενής**, ές, (γενέσθαι) *first-born, primeval*, κτῆμα, εἶδος, Pl.*Plt.*288e, 289b; of persons, LXX *Ex.*13.2, Orph.*H.*25.2; epith. of Τύχη, *Historia* 5.231 (Itanus); Τύχη π., = *Fortuna Primigenia*, *Gloss.* **-γεννάω**, = πρωτοβολέω 3, Al. *Ez.*47.12. **-γέννητος**, ον, = *primo genitus*, *Gloss.* **-γεύστης**, ου, ὁ, *first taster*, ib. II. name of an Indian animal, Alex. Aphr.*Pr.*2.60. **-γλῠφής**, ές, *first* or *newly carved*, *AP*5.35.8 (Rufin.). ⊕ **-γνᾰφος**, ον, *fresh from the fuller's*, *PTeb.*406.14 (iii A.D.), *PMasp.*6 ii 97 (vi A.D.). **-γονία**, ἡ, *first birth*, name of a work by Clidemus, Ath.14.660a. **-γονον**, τό, = ἀείζωον, Ps.-Dsc. 4.88. ⊕ **-γονος**, ον, also η, ον Paus.1.31.4:—*first-born, firstling*, ἄρνες, ἔριφοι, Il.4.102, Hes.*Op.*543; φοῖνιξ π. *first-born, first-created*, E.*Hec.*458 (lyr.); τὰ π. LXX *Mi.*7.1; of the tissues, = ὁμοιομερῆ, Pl. ap.Gal.4.773; of a child, π. θάλος E.*IT*209 (lyr.); π. τῶν τέκνων *IG Rom.*4.539 (Cotiaeum); π. λόγος, υἱός, Ph.1.427,308; ὄρχησις Luc. *Salt.*7; of the τριάς (= 1 + 2), Adam.*Vent.*46. 2. of rank, π. οἶκοι *high-born* houses (εὐγενεῖς, Sch.), S.*Ph.*180 (lyr.). 3. epith. of gods, Dam.*Pr.*123 bis; so Πρωτογόνη, ἡ, name of Persephone, Paus. l.c. II. parox. πρωτογόνος, ἡ, *bringing forth first*, implied by Poll.4.208. **-γύναικες** [ῠ], οἱ, *persons married for the first time*, or *who still have their first wife*, Hsch. **-δαής**, ές, *having learnt for the first time*, Opp.*H.*4.323. **-δαμνος**, ον, *first-tamed*, Hsch. s.v. ἄδαμνον. **-δέκᾱνος**, ὁ, = *primus virgariorum*, *Gloss.* **-δεύτεροι**, οἱ, *first two*, σπόνδυλοι Pall. *in Hp.*2.107 D. **-δημότης**, ου, ὁ, *chief townsman*, *POxy.*1730.4 (iv A.D.). **-διάκονος** [ᾱ], ὁ, *first deacon*, *Supp.Epigr.*6.243 (Phrygia, v A.D.). **-εδρία**, ἡ, *first seat*, Tz.*H.*4.569. **-ζευκτος**, ον, *newly married*, *EM*17.54. **-ζῠγον**, τό, *front rank* of a squad of cavalry, Afric.*Cest.*p.58 V. **-ζύμιον** [ῡ], τό, *prime ferment*, Zos.Alch.p.113 B. **-ζυξ**, ῠγος, = πρωτόζευκτος, Κύπρις *AP*9.245 (Antiphan.). **-θοινία**, ἡ, (θοίνη) *the first part of a meal*, Poll.1.34. **-θρόνιος**, α, ον, = sq., epith. of Artemis, Paus.10.38.6. **-θρονος**, ον, *filling the first seat*, Call.*Dian.* 228, Nonn.*D.*8.166, Coluth.153: heterocl. pl. πρωτόθρονες *IG*14.1389 i 35. **-θῠτος**, ον, gloss on πρωτόσφακτος, Sch.Lyc.329. **-καθεδρία**, ἡ, *the first seat* in a public place, *Ev.Matt.*23.6 (pl.). **-καιρία**, ἡ, *favourable opportunity*, *POxy.*1678.6 (iii A.D.). **-καρπος**, ον, *yielding the first harvest*, Ἀτθίς Limen.12. **-κατασκεύαστος**, ον, *of primitive construction*, *Gloss.* **-κλήσια**, τά, = ἀνακλητήρια, LXX 2*Ma.*4.21. **-κλίναρχος** [ῐ], ὁ, *president of a* κλίνη (i.e. religious association), *Arch.Pap.*1.413 (v A.D.). ⊕ **-κλισία**, ἡ, *first seat at table*, *Ev.Matt.*23.6, etc.; cf. πρωτοκαθεδρία. **-κολλον**, τό, *the first* κόλλημα of a papyrus-roll, bearing the official authentication and date of manufacture of the papyrus (as in *POxy.*1928[r]), Just.*Nov.*44. 2. **-κόμης**, ου, ὁ, *with unshorn locks*, Sch.Pi.*P.*4.145. **-κοπος**, ον, = πρωτόκουρος, *Sammelb.*4496.18 (vi A.D.), al. ⊕ **-κοσμέω**, *to be* πρωτόκοσμος, *Riv.Fil.*61.489 (Crete, ii/iii A.D.). **-κοσμος**, ὁ, in Crete, *president of* κόσμοι, *SIG*524.3 (iii B.C.), *Historia* 5.226, etc. **-κουρία**, ἡ, *first shearing*, prob. in LXX *To.*1.6. **-κουρος**, ον, (κείρω) *first cut*, of clover, Arist.*HA*595[b]28. **-κτίστης**, ου, ὁ, *original founder*, *PMasp.*96.34 (vi A.D.). ⊕ **-κτιστος**, ον, *first created*, *PMag.Leid.W.*5.16, *Gloss.* **-κτόνος**, ον, *of first homicide*, προστροπαὶ Ἰξίονος A.*Eu.*718. **-κύμων** [ῡ], ονος, ὁ, ἡ, (κῦμα II) *pregnant for the first time*, ἔρωτος *with* love, Ach.Tat.1.10. **-κύων** [ῠ], κυνος, ὁ, *first dog*, i.e. *chief of the Cynics*, *AP*11.154 (Lucill.). **-κωμήτης**, ου, ὁ, *head man of a village*, Keil-Premerstein *Zweiter Bericht* No.152 (ii A.D.), *JHS*22.358 (near Konia), *PSI*2.279.6 (ii A.D.), *POxy.*1835.2 (v/vi A.D.), etc. **-λεια**, τά, (λεία) *first spoils* in war, and, generally, *firstfruits*, Lyc.298, f.l. for προτέλεια in J.*AJ*4.8.22; τὰ π. τῶν ἐμαυτοῦ σώστρων Jul.*Ep.*184; τῶν σῶν δὲ γονάτων πρωτόλεια θιγγάνω, *as the first act* of my supplication, E.*Or.*382: sg., = ἀπαρχή, Phot.:—as Adj., τὸ πρωτόλειον στέφος Lyc.1228. **-λεχής**, ές, *bringing forth first*, Opp.*H.*4.197. **-λήδεσθαι**· τὸ πρῶτον ἀποπειρᾶσθαι, Hsch. **-ληνα**, τά, *wine from the first vat*, *Ostr.Strassb.* 653 (iii A.D., -λινα ostr.), *PHamb.*23.34 (vi A.D.). **-λογία**, ἡ, *right of speaking first* in a law-court, *part of the prosecutor*, Demad.3; δίκαιος ἑαυτοῦ κατήγορος ἐν π. LXX *Pr.*18.17. II. *right* of the leading advocate *to speak first*, Arg.2 D.20. **-λόγιμος**, ον, *of the highest repute*, as a title, *POxy.*1256.15 (iii A.D.). **-λόγος**, ον, *speaking first*, and so = πρωταγωνιστής, Teles p.5 H. II. ὁ π. ἄρχων the chief magistrate at Aphrodisias, *CIG*2760, al.; at Iconium, ib.3992. ⊕ **-λοχία**, ἡ, *the first line of the* λόχοι, Ascl.*Tact.*2.5, Arr. *Tact.*8.1, Suid. s.v. μῆκος φάλαγγος. **-μαντις**, εως ὁ, ἡ, *first prophet* or *seer*, τὴν π. Γαῖαν A.*Eu.*2, cf.*EM*455.49. **-μᾰχος**, ον, *fighting in the first rank*, Ath.4.154e, cf. *AP*5.70 (pr. n. with pun, Pall.). **-μηνία**, only in Dor. form **πρᾱτομηνία** (q.v.). **-μισθος**, ον, *serving for hire first*, Lyc.1384. **-μορος**, ον, *dying* or *dead first*, A.*Pers.*568 (sed leg. -μοιρ- metri gr.), dub. in *Epigr.Gr.*369 (Cotiaeum). **-μῠσής**, ές, *first defiled*, Sch.A.*Eu.*718. **-μύστης**, ου, ὁ, *one just initiated*, *IG*5(1).1390.50 (Andania, i B.C.), Ach.Tat.3.22.

**πρωτόμφᾰλον**, τό, *the very centre* of a shield, Hsch.

**πρωτό-νεως**, gen. ω, *going by ship for the first time*, Phot., Suid. **-νύμφευτος**, ον, *just married*, Callicrat.ap.Stob.4.28. 18. **-πᾰγής**, ές, (πήγνυμι) *just put together, new-made*, δίφροι, ἅμαξα, Il.5.194, 24.267; τὰ π. στοιχεῖα τῆς φύσεως Heraclit.*All.* 23, cf. A.D.*Adv.*137.12; τὸ π. σχῆμα, of incipient cataract, Cass. *Pr.*19: metaph., ἀοιδὰν -παγεῖ σοφίᾳ διαποίκιλον *Lyr.Alex.Adesp.* 20.5.

**πρωτοπάθ-εια** [πᾰ], ἡ, *primary affection* or *symptom*, opp. συμπάθεια, Gal.8.31. **-έω**, *to be primarily affected*, Heliod.ap.Orib.46.7. 4. Sor.2.38, Archig.ap.Gal.8.138, etc. **-ής**, ές, *affected first*, ἀήρ Eust.41.22. Adv. -θῶς, f.l. for ἀνθρωποπ- in Id.38.8.

⊕ **πρωτό-πᾰλος**, ὁ, *a member of the* πρῶτος πάλος (v. πάλος II), of a gladiator, π. σεκουτόρων D.C.72.22. **-πατρίκιος**, ὁ, *first patrician*, as a title, *POxy.*1898.9, al. (vi A.D.). **-πειρία**, ἡ, = *rudimentum, tirocinium*, *Gloss.* **-πειρος**, ον, (πεῖρα) *making the first trial, a novice*, of a bride, Theopomp.Com.94; π. τῆς τέχνης Alex.98.4; πάσης κακοπαθείας Plb.1.61.4; less freq. εἴς τι, Ach.Tat.2.37,38; πρός τι *An.Ox.*3.175. **-πήμων**, ονος, ὁ, ἡ, (πῆμα) *first cause of ill*, A.*Ag.*223 (lyr.). **-πλαστος**, ον, *first-formed*, of Adam, LXX *Wi.* 7.1, 10.1, Ph.*Fr.*61 H. **-πλοια**, ἡ, *first voyage*, *Gloss.* **-πλοος**, ον, Att. contr. **-πλους**, ουν, *going to sea for the first time*, νηῦς Od.8.35, cf. E.*Hel.*1531; π. πλάτα the *first-plied* oar (of the ship Argo), Id.*Andr.* 865 (lyr.), cf. S.E.*M.*9.32: metaph., π. νεότης *just embarking on the sea* of love, Pl.*Epigr.*30 (v.l. πρωτοπόρος). II. *sailing first* or *foremost*, X.*HG*5.1.27: pr. n. of Athenian warship, H.E.K. Schmidt *Die Namen der attischen Kriegsschiffe* 7 (v B.C.). **-ποιητικὸς αἴτιος**, ὁ, the *Prime Cause* (personified), Zos.Alch.p.132 B. ⊕ **-πολις**, εως, ὁ, ἡ, *first in the city*, Τύχη Plu.2.322c. ⊕ **-πολίτης** [ῑ], ου, ὁ, *first citizen, princeps civitatis*, *Gloss.*: pl., *optimates*, ib. ⊕ **-πορεία**, ἡ, *advanced guard* of an army, *vanguard*, Plb.1.76.5, Onos.6.3,6. **-πόρος**, ον, *taking one's first voyage*, cf. πρωτόπλοος. **-ποσις**, εως, ἡ, *a woman who still has her first husband*, Themiso Hist.1, Poll.3.39. **-πραξία**, ἡ, *right of first payment*, belonging to preferential creditors, *OGI* 669.19,26 (Egypt, i A.D.), *BGU*970.11 (ii A.D.), Plin.*Ep.Traj.*108; = *privilegium*, *Gloss.* ⊕ **-πρεσβύτερος**, ὁ, *chief elder*, *MAMA*3.670 (Corycus). **-ραβδοῦχος**, ὁ, *chief lictor*, *Gloss.* **-ρριζος**, ον, *being the first root* or *origin*, Luc.*Am.*19. **-ρρῠτος**, ον, (ῥέω) *flowing first*, Gal.13.626, Opp.*C.*4.238.

**πρῶτος**, η, ον, v. πρότερος B.

**πρωτός**, ή, όν, (πέπρωμαι) *destined*, Hdn.Gr.1.215.

**πρωτο-σέληνος**, ον, = προσέληνος, of old, worn-out men, Ar.*Fr.* 55 D. **-σπόρος**, ον, *sowing* or *begetting first*, Luc.*Am.*32; μόθου π. ἀρχή Coluth.62. II. proparox. πρωτόσπορος, ον, Pass., *first sown* or *generated*, Theodect.18, Nonn.*D.*9.142, etc. **-στακτος**, ον, *first drawn off*, π. κονία a lye made of lime and ashes, Alex.Trall.3.7, cf. Paul.Aeg.7.17, *Hippiatr.*82. **-στᾰσία**, ἡ, *office of* πρωτοστάτης II, as a λειτουργία, *Cod.Theod.*11.23.1, *Cod.Just.*10.42.8, 10.62.3; = *principatus*, *Gloss.* **-στάσιον** [ᾰ], τό, *foundation*, metaph., Paul.Al.*L.* 1. **-στᾰτέω**, *stand first* or *in the first rank*, Ph.2.109, Ael.*Tact.*3. 2,28.2: generally, of the first-born in Egypt, Ph.2.291. ⊕ **-στάτης** [ᾰ], ου, ὁ, (ἵστημι) *one who stands first*, esp. *the first man on the right* of a line, *right-hand man*, ὁ π. τοῦ δεξιοῦ κέρως Th.5.71; but also οἱ π. *the front-rank men*, X.*Cyr.*3.3.57, 6.3.24, *Lac.*11.5, etc.; either sense possible in Teles p.4 H. 2. = λοχαγός, Ael.*Tact.*5.1, Arr. *Tact.*5.6. 3. *man in the uneven rows in a* λόχος, opp. ἐπιστάτης, Ascl.*Tact.*2.3, etc. II. metaph., *chief* or *leader* of a party, *Act.Ap.* 24.5; π. τοῦ χοροῦ τῶν μαθητῶν Porph.*Chr.*26.1; π. τοῦ θητικοῦ καὶ οἰκετικοῦ Men.Prot. p.28 D. ⊕ **-στολιστής**, οῦ, ὁ, *chief of the* στολισταί, *PGrenf.*1.44 ii 2 (ii B.C.), *CIG*4945 (Philae, v A.D.), etc. **-στρᾰτηγία**, ἡ, *office of chief* στρατηγός, Μουσ. Σμυρν.1875.131 (Philadelphia). **-σφακτος**, ον, *slaughtered first*, Lyc.329. **-σχεδής**, ές, and **-σχέδιος**, ον, *written offhand, improvised*, Tz.*H.*11.987, 10. 366. **-τευκτος**, ον, *first-fashioned*, Ezek.*Exag.*172. **-τμητος**, ον, = πρωτόκουρος, *IG*12(5).173 iv (Paros).

**πρωτοτοκ-εῖα**, v. πρωτοτόκια. **-εύω**, *invest with the privilege of primogeniture*, LXX *De.*21.17. **-έω**, *bear* one's *first-born*, ib. 1*Ki.*6.7, al. **-ία**, ἡ, = sq., Aq.*Ge.*25.34, *De.*21.17. **-ια**, τά, with v.l. **-τοκεῖα**, *rights of the first-born, birthright*, LXX *Ge.*25.32, *Ep.Hebr.*12.16. **-ος** (parox.), Dor. **πρᾱτοτόκος**, ον, *bearing* or *having borne her first-born*, μήτηρ π., of a heifer, Il.17.5; αἴξ Theoc. 5.27; ὗς, ταῶς, Arist.*HA*546[a]12, 564[a]30; κύων Dsc.2.70.6; of women, Pl.*Tht.*151c, 161a; νύμφη Orph.*L.*193. II. proparox. πρωτότοκος, ον, Pass., *first-born*, LXX *Ge.*22.21, al., *Ev.Luc.*2.7, *PLips.* 28.15 (iv A.D.), Man.3.9; τὰ π. τῶν προβάτων LXX *Ge.*4.4, cf. *PMag. Osl.*1.312; π. ἐγὼ ἢ σύ LXX 2*Ki.*19.43. 2. metaph., π. πάσης κτίσεως *Ep.Col.*1.15; of Homer, opp. Nicander, *AP*9.213.

**πρωτό-τομος**, ον, *first cut*, Thphr.*HP*4.14.6; κράμβη *AP*9.412 (Phld.); καυλός Archig.ap.Gal.13.331. **-τροφος**, ον, *first-reared*, κριός *PMag.Par.*1.1093, 1102, cf. Man.3.9, Ptol.*Tetr.*119.

**πρωτοτῠπ-έω**, *to be primitive* or *original*, A.D.*Pron.*66.1. **-ία**, ἡ, *original form*, Eust.50.38. ⊕ **-ος**, ον, *original, primitive*, esp. in Gramm. sense, Gal.18(2).167, Longin.*Proll.Heph.*p.86 C.; π. ἀντωνυμίαι, of personal pronouns, opp. κτητικός, A.D.*Synt.*62.15; opp. παράγωγος, Id.*Adv.*166.5. 2. *archetypal*, Simp.*in Cael.*277.4, Dam. *Pr.*340. II. Subst. πρωτότυπος, ὁ, *principal party* to a contract, *POxy.*136.11 (vi A.D.), etc. 2. πρωτότυπον, τό, *archetype, original*, Poll.5.102. III. Adv. -πως *originally, chiefly, in the first instance*, *POxy.*902.13 (v A.D.), Lyd.*Mag.*3.37, Anon.*in Cat.*48.7, Hsch.

**πρωτοϋδρέω**, *have the first claim on water for irrigation*, *PHamb.* 65.24 (ii A.D.).

**πρωτουργός**, όν, *primary*, κινήσεις Pl.*Lg.*897a, cf. Iamb.*Myst.*1.5, al.; ἔρωτος ἀρχή Procl.*in Alc.* p.32 C.; ζωή Iamb.*Protr.*3, cf. Jul.*Or.* 4.150b.

**πρωτο-ΰφαντος** [ῠ], ον, *fresh from the loom, unused*, or perh., *of* *first-quality weaving*, λεντίον *PSI*8.971.20 (iii/iv A.D., -υφαντον Pap.). **-φαής**, ές, *first shining*, σελήνη the *new* moon, Tryph.517, Suid. s. v. βοῦς ἕβδομος, *PMag.Leid.W.*7.5. **-φανής**, ές, *appearing first, first visible*, Sch.E.*Hec.*451: Sup., *Theol.Ar.*16. II. metaph., π. καλύκων, of a girl, *IG*9(2).649.3 (Thess.). **-φορέω**, *bear first*, corrupt in Ath.13.565f. **-φόρημα**, ατος, τό, *first-fruits of the earth*, ἦρος π. Longus 3.12. **-φυής**, ές, *first-produced, first-born*, A.R.3.851. **-φύλαξ** [ῠ], ακος, ὁ, *chief of* φύλακες, *PKlein.Form.*24 (vi A.D.). **-φῦτος**, ον, = πρωτοφυής, *AP*4.2.2 (Phil.). **-χνοος**, ον, contr. **-χνους**, ουν, *with the first down*, Luc.*Am.*53. **-χορος**, ὁ, *the first chorus*, name of plays by Alexis (Ath.7.287f) and Antidotus (Id. 6.240b). II. *leader of a chorus*, *IG*1[2].187.15, 17 (pl.). **-χρονέω**, *precede in time*, c. gen., Diog.Oen.26. **-χρονος**, ον, = *primaevus*, *Gloss.* **-χῠτος**, ον, *first-flowing*, οἶνος *AP*6.44 (Leon.(?)). **-ψάλτης**, ου, ὁ, *chief harpist*, *MAMA*3.649 (Corycus).

**πρωτρίς**, ίδος, ἡ, dub. sens. in *PGiss.*90.8 (ii A.D.).

**πρωτώλη**· πρώτη ἡ πτερόν, Hsch. **πρώτως**, Adv. of πρῶτος, v. πρότερος B. IV. **πρώνδᾶν**, v. προανδάω. **πρώων**, ονος, ὁ, Ep. lengthd. form for πρών (q. v.).

**πτάζω**, Aeol. for πτήσσω, Alc.27.

⊛ **πταῖμα**, ατος, τό, = πταῖσμα, *SIG*456.40 (Cos, iii B.C.).

**πταίρω**, *Hippiatr.*38 (v. l. πτέρεται, v. πτέρομαι), also **πτείρω**, Hdn. Gr.1.191 codd. (pres. in use in early writers **πτάρνυμαι**, Hp.*Morb.*2.54, X.*An.*3.2.9, Philem.100.4, Arist.*Pr.*962$^b$8 (also πτάρνεται *Gloss.*), impf. ἐπταρνύμην Diog.*Ep.*35.3): aor. 2 ἔπτᾰρον Od.17.541, etc.: rarely aor. 1, part. πτάραντες Arist.*Pr.*963$^a$33 (s. v. l.):—Pass., v. sub fin.:—*sneeze*, μέγ' ἔπταρεν he *sneezed* aloud, Od. l. c. (taken for a good omen, cf. Ar.*Ra.*647, etc.); but also as a bad omen, λυπούμεθ' ἂν πτάρῃ τις Men.534.9; ἔπταρον εἰς ἀνέμους *AP*11.375 (Maced.); οὐδὲ λέγει "Ζεῦ σῶσον", ἐὰν πτάρῃ ib.268; ἀναλαβὼν τοιοῦτόν τι, οἵῳ κνήσαις ἂν τὴν ῥῖνα, πτάρε Pl.*Smp.*185e: metaph. of a lamp, *sputter*, *AP*6.333 (Marc. Arg.):—also in aor. Pass., part. πταρείς Hp.*Epid.*5.14, Arist.*Pr.*887$^b$35.

⊛ **πταῖσμα**, ατος, τό, (πταίω) *stumble, trip, false step, mistake*, Thgn. 1222 (pl.); of a horse, Plu.2.549c, etc.; in writing, Longin.33.4 (pl.). 2. *error, fault*, J.*AJ*7.7.1; τῆς ἀνοσιουργίας ἀσεβῆ π. Iamb. *Myst.*3.31. II. *failure, misfortune*, euphem. for *defeat*, ἢν σφέας καταλάβῃ π. πρὸς τὸν Πέρσην Hdt.7.149; συμβαίνει π. [τινί] D.10.13, cf. Aeschin.3.164; ἄν τι γένηται π. D.*Ep.*3.18; τὸ τῆς τύχης π. Phld. *Vit.*p.22 J.; περὶ τὴν ναυμαχίαν D.S.11.15.

**πταιστός**, ή, όν, *liable to fail*, Eust.48.24 (prob.).

⊛ **πταίω**, Th.1.122, etc.: fut. πταίσω D.2.20: aor. ἔπταισα Hdt.9.101, etc.: pf. ἔπταικα Men.675, Bato 1, Plb.3.48.4, (προσ-) Isoc.6.82:—Pass., v. infr. I: I. trans., *cause to stumble* or *fall*, σύνθεσιν ποτὶ ψεύδει Pi.*Fr.*205, cf. Lxx 1*Ki.*4.3:—Pass., *to be missed*, of things, Ael. *NA*2.15; τὰ πταισθέντα *failures, errors*, Luc.*Demon.*7; ἃ ἐπταίσθη his *failures*, Plu.*Comp.Dion.Brut.*3. II. intr., *stumble, trip, fall*, π. πρός τινι *stumble against, fall over*, π., ὥσπερ πρὸς ἕρματι, πρὸς τῇ πόλει Pl.*R.*553b, cf. A.*Pr.*926, Theoc.7.26; πρὸς τὰς πέτρας cj. in X. *An.*4.2.3; prov., μὴ δὶς πρὸς τὸν αὐτὸν λίθον πταίειν Plb.31.11.5; also π. περί τινι, μὴ περὶ Μαρδονίῳ πταίσῃ ἡ Ἑλλάς lest Hellas *should get a fall* over him, i.e. be defeated by him, Hdt.9.101. 2. metaph., *make a false step* or *mistake*, Th.2.43, D.2.20, Men.672, etc.; ἐὰν πταίωσί τι when *they make a blunder*, of medical men, Philem.75.5; οὐκ ἐλάττω, ἐλάχιστα, τὰ πλείω π., Th.1.122, 4.18, 6.33; ἔν τισι D. 18.286; λογισμοῖς Men.380; τῇ μάχῃ, τοῖς ὅλοις, τοῖς πράγμασι, etc., Plb.18.14.13, 3.48.4, 1.10.1, etc.; ἀψευδὴς ὢν καὶ μὴ π. τῇ διανοίᾳ περὶ τὰ ὄντα Pl.*Tht.*160d; also π. ὑπ' ἀνάγκας S.*Ph.*215 (lyr.); ὑπό τινος π. τῇ πατρίδι Plb.5.93.2; ἐκ τύχης Id.2.7.3. 3. π. τῆς ἐλπίδος *to be baulked of*.., Hdn.8.5.1. 4. ἡ γλῶττα π. *stutters*, Arist.*Pr.*875$^b$19.

**πτᾰκάδις** [κᾰ], Adv., (πτάξ) *timidly*, Theognost.*Can.*163.

**πτακάλα** or **πτανάκα**, *boat-mat*, dub. in Poll.10.166.

**πτάκ-ις** [ᾰ], ιδος, ἡ, pecul. fem. of πτάξ, *Com.Adesp.*1127. **-ισμός**, ὁ, *shyness, timidity*, ib.1128. **-ωρέω**, = πτήσσω, πτώσσω, Hsch.

**πταλόν**· ἐφ' ᾧ ἡ σταφυλὴ πατεῖται, Hsch. (leg. πύαλον).

**πτάξ**, gen. πτᾰκός, ὁ, ἡ, (πτήσσω) = πτώξ, A.*Ag.*137 (lyr.).

**πταρ-μική**, ἡ, *sneezewort, Achillea ptarmica*, Dsc.2.162, Gal.12.108. **-μικός**, ή, όν, *causing to sneeze*, φάρμακα Id.2.883; π., τά, *sternutatories*, Hp.*Epid.*7.112: sg., Id.*Aph.*5.49, Arist.*Pr.*962$^b$4, Diog.*Ep.*35.3. **-μός**, ὁ, *sneezing*, Hp.*Aph.*6.13 (pl.), Th.2.49, Pl. *Smp.*189a, Arist.*Pr.*961$^b$9; πταρμόν τ' ὄρνιθα καλεῖτε Ar.*Av.*720, cf. Arist.*HA*492$^b$6; as a bad omen, Polyaen.3.10.2. **-νῠμαι**, v. πταίρω:—Act. inf. πταρνύναι Cass.*Pr.*44.

**πταώτην**· κατεπτηχότα, Hsch. **πτείρω**, v. πταίρω.

**πτεκάς**, άδος, ὁ, ἡ, = πτάξ, Phot.

**πτέλας**, ὁ, *wild boar*, Lyc.833; cf. **πτελέα**, Lacon., = σῦς, Hsch.

⊛ **πτελέ-α**, Ion. -η, ἡ, *elm*, *Ulmus glabra*, Il.6.419, 21.242, 350, Hes.*Op.*435, Ar.*Nu.*1008, Thphr.*HP*3.14.1, Dsc.1.84, etc. II. v. foreg. **-άδες**· πτελεῶδες, Hsch. **-ῐνος**, η, ον, *of elm*, ξύλα, σανίς, *IG*1[2].313.27, 133, cf. Thphr.*HP*5.3.5, *IG*2[2].1672.307, al., *Inscr. Délos* 504 *A* 15 (iii B.C.): written πτελείινος, *IG*2[2].1672.151, al. **-ών**, ῶνος, ὁ, *elm-grove*, *Gloss.*

**πτέον**, τό, Att. for πτύον (q. v.).

**πτερᾰφόρος**, ὁ, = πτεροφόρας, *BGU*1849.4 (i B.C.), *PTeb.*298.21 (ii A.D.): written **πτερλαφόρος** (sic), *BGU*1196.37 (i B.C.).

**πτερ-ίδιος**, α, ον, *feathered*, *EM*783.23. **-ῐνος**, η, ον, also ος, ον, (πτερόν) *made of feathers*, κύκλος *feather*-fan, E.*Or.*1429 (lyr.); ῥιπίς *AP*6.306 (Aristo); στέφανος Plb.6.23.12; ναός Str.9.3.9, Eratosth. *Cat.*29, Porph.ap.Stob.3.21.26. 2. *feathered, winged*, Ar.*Av.* 903. **-ιον**, τό, Dim. of πτερόν, Hdn.Gr.1.356. II. = πτερίς, Ps.-Dsc.4.184; = καλλίτριχον, ib.134; = τριχομανές, ib.135. ⊛ **-ίς**, ίδος, or πτέρις, εως, ἡ, acc. πτέριν Dsc.4.185: nom. pl. πτέρεις Plb.3.71.4:—*male fern, Aspidium Filix-mas*, Thphr.*HP*1.10.5, 8.7.7, 9.20.5, Theoc.3.14, etc. II. = πολυπόδιον, Ps.-Dsc.4.186. III. νυμφαία π., = θηλυπτερίς, Dsc.4.185: = δρυοπτερίς, Ps.-Dsc.4.187. **-ίσκος**, ὁ, Dim. of πτερόν, Babr.118.5. **-ισμα**, v. πτερύγισμα. **-ισμός**, ὁ, dub. sens. in *PCair.Zen.*418.4 (iii B.C.).

⊛ **πτέρνη** (Hp.*Art.*3, *Epid.*5.48, Phot.), later **πτέρνᾰ** (Lyc.500, Lxx *Ge.*3.15, etc.), ἡ, *heel*, Il.22.397, Hp. ll. cc., Arist.*HA*494$^b$7; *under part of the heel*, A.*Ch.*209 (pl.); *heel-bone*, Gal.2.776, al.: prov., εἴπερ τὸν ἐγκέφαλον.. μὴ ἐν ταῖς π. φορεῖτε D.7.45. 2. *hoof*, Lxx *Jd.*5.22. 3. *heel* of a shoe, Herod.7.21, Phryn.*PS*p.69 B. 4. *footstep*, Lxx *Ca.*1.8. II. metaph., *foot* or *lower part* of anything, πύργων Lyc.442; τῆς μηχανῆς Plb.8.6.2; of a mast, Asclep.Myrl.ap. Ath.11.474f (but, *waist* of a ship, Hero *Stereom.*2.52). 2. *butt-end* of the ἀγκών of a torsion-engine, Ph.*Bel.*59.30, 66.2; of a surgical machine, Orib.49.4.9, al. III. *ham* (mock Epicism formed from Lat. *perna*), Batr.37; f.l. for πέρνα in Aët.15.15, Paul.Aeg.7.17.74 (πέρνα correctly in 4.32).

⊛ **πτερν-ίζω**, fut. -ιῶ Lxx*Je.*9.4(3): pf. ἐπτέρνικα ib.*Ge.*27.36:—*strike with the heel*, *Hippiatr.*40, Suid. 2. *trip up, supplant*, Lxx *Ge.*27.36, Ph.1.125. II. *heel an old shoe*, *Com.Adesp.*46. **-ιξ**, ῑκος, ὁ, *stem of the* κάκτος, Thphr.*HP*6.4.11. **-ίς**, ίδος, ἡ, *bottom* of a dish, Alex.329, Ael.Dion.*Fr.*289. **-ις**, ὁ, a kind of *hawk*, Arist.*HA*620$^a$19. **-ισμα**, ατος, τό, = sq., Tz.*H.*9.179. ⊛ **-ισμός**, ὁ, *supplanting*, Lxx *Ps.*40(41).10: generally, *craft, subtlety*, ib.4*Ki.*10.19. **-ιστής**, οῦ, ὁ, *one who strikes with the heel* or *trips up*, Ph.1.84, Tz.*H.*9.181; *supplanter*, Ph.1.55, al.; f.l. for φροντιστής in Polem.*Phgn.*21.

**πτερνο-βᾰτέω**, *walk on one's heels*, Paul.Aeg.6.118. **-βάτης** [ᾰ], ου, ὁ, *one who walks on his heels*, Hp.*Art.*60. II. *surgical bandage*, Hsch. **-γλύφος** [ῠ], ὁ, *Ham-scraper*, name of a mouse in Batr.224. **-κοπέω**, *stamp with the heels* in a theatre, to show disapprobation, Poll.2.197, 4.122. **-κόπις**, ἡ, nickname of a certain Philoxenus, Men.276, Axionic.6.2. (Origin unknown; not from πτέρνη III, since πέρνα first occurs in Roman times.)

**πτέρνος**, ὁ, = *culdex*, *Gloss.*

**πτερνοτρώκτης**, ου, ὁ, *Ham-nibbler*, name of a mouse in Batr.29; also **-φάγος** [ᾰ], ὁ, *Ham-eater*, ib.227.

**πτερο-βάμων** [ᾰ], ονος, ὁ, ἡ, *moving on wings*, κύμβαι Emp.20.7. **-δόνητος**, ον, (δονέω) *moved by flapping wings*: metaph., *high-soaring, high-flown*, Ar.*Av.*1390, 1402. **-είμων**, ονος, ὁ, ἡ, (εἷμα) *feather-clad*, Opp.*C.*2.190, Orac.ap.Phleg.*Fr.*37.5 J. (πτερο- cod.). ⊛ **-εις**, εσσα, εν: contr. forms, πτεροῦσσα E.*Hipp.*733 (lyr.), *Ph.*1019 (lyr.); πτεροῦντος Id.*Ion* 202 (lyr.); πτεροῦντα A.*Supp.*1000:—*feathered, winged*, ὀϊστοί, ἰοί, Il.5.171, 16.773; πέδιλα Hes. *Sc.*220; αἰετός, Πάγασος, Pi.*P.*2.50, *I.*7(6).44; π. κόρα, of the Sphinx, S.*OT*508 (lyr.); π. ἵππος, of Pegasus, E.*Ion* 202 (lyr.); ἵπποι π., of the horses of the Sun, Id.*El.*466 (lyr.); κεραυνός Ar.*Av.*576 (anap.); *fluttering*, λαισήϊα Il.5.453, 12.426. II. metaph., esp. in Ep., in phrase ἔπεα πτερόεντα *winged* words, Il.1.201, al.; also π. ὕμνος Pi. *I.*5(4).63; πτερόεντι τροχῷ Id.*P.*2.22; φυγὰ πτερόεσσα E.*Ion* 1238 (lyr.); θυμός A.R.4.23: applied by Call. to the τέττιξ, *Aet.Oxy.*2079.32. **-ιππος**, ον, *riding a winged horse*, Tz.*H.*3.164. **-κοπέω**, metaph., *clip the wings of*, τὴν ἐλευθερίαν *Com.Adesp.*25 a 3 D.

**πτέρομαι**, = πταίρω (q. v.), *Gloss.*, v. l. in *Hippiatr.*38.

⊛ **πτερόν**, τό, (πέτομαι, πτέσθαι) mostly in pl., *feathers*, Od.15.527, Hdt.2.73, etc.: in sg., *feather*, E.*Rh.*618, Ar.*Ach.*584, 1105; πτεροῦ σῦριγξ *quill*, Hp.*Fist.*6; τὰ ὦτα πτερῷ κνωμένοις Luc.*Salt.*2; ἀντὶ τριχῶν πτερὰ φύειν Pl.*Ti.*91d (cf. Ar.*Av.*106); ἡ τῶν π. ἀποβολή Pl.*Phdr.*246d: prov., πόνου δ' ἴδοις ἂν οὐδαμοῦ ταὐτὸν π. misery is of varied *plumage*, i. e. manifold, A.*Supp.*329; τοῖς αὑτῶν π. ἁλίσκεσθαι to be shot with an arrow feathered from one's own plumes, 'hoist with one's own petard', Id.*Fr.*139; ἀλλοτρίοις π. ἀγάλλεσθαι pride oneself on 'borrowed *plumes*', Luc.*Pro Merc.Cond.*4; κεῖρευ πτερά 'have your *wings* clipped', Call.*Epigr.*47.8. 2. = πτέρυξ, *bird's wing*, freq. in pl., *wings*, Il.11.454, Od.2.151, etc. (sg., A.*Fr.*304.4); οἷμον αἰθέρος ψαίρει πτεροῖς Id.*Pr.*396; Παλλάδος ὑπὸ πτεροῖς ὄντας, metaph. from chickens under the hen's wings, Id.*Eu.*1001 (lyr.); τὰ τέκν' ἔχων ὑπὸ πτεροῖς E.*Heracl.*10, etc.: as an emblem of speed, ὡσεὶ π. ἠὲ νόημα Od.7.36; πόδα τιθεὶς ἴσον πτεροῖς E.*IT*32; δοκεῖτε πηδᾶν τἀδικήματ' εἰς θεοὺς πτεροῖσι; Id.*Fr.*506; also τῷ δ' εὖτε πτερὰ γίγνετο he got as it were *wings*, i.e. spirit, courage, Il.19.386; νωμᾷ δ' ἐν οἰωνοῖσι τοὐκείνης (sc. Ἀφροδίτης) πτερόν, ἐν θηρσίν, ἐν βροτοῖσιν, ἐν θεοῖς her *uplifting influence*, S.*Fr.*941.11. 3. *wings* of a bat, Hdt.2.76; of insects, Arist.*HA*532$^a$25, *PA*682$^b$18, al. II. *any winged creature*, as the Sphinx, E.*Ph.*806 (lyr.); a beetle, Ar.*Pax*76. 2. *omen*, πιστὸν ἐξ ὑμῶν π. S.*OC*97. III. *anything like wings* or *feathers*: as 1. *oars*, ἐρετμά, τά τε πτερὰ νηυσὶ πέλονται Od.11.125; νηὸς πτερά Hes.*Op.*628 (unless *sails*, cf. πτίλον III. 2); ὅπῃ νεὼς στείλαιμ' ἂν οὔριον π. E.*Hel.*147; σκάφος ἀΐσσον πτεροῖσι Id.*Tr.*1086 (lyr.): hence conversely, of birds, πτεροῖς ἐρέσσει Id.*IT*289; πτερῶν εἰρεσία, of Hermes, Luc.*Tim.*40. 2. ἀέθλων πτερά, i.e. *the crown of* victory, which lifts the victor to heaven, Pi.*O.*14.24, cf. *P.*9.125. 3. sg., *wings* of the wind, dub. in S.*Fr.*23.3. 4. *fan* or *parasol*, *Com. Adesp.*1129. 5. π. ἱέρακος a hawk's *wing*, worn by the ἱερογραμματεύς in Egypt, D.S.1.87. 6. *feathered arrow*, E.*Hel.*76. 7.

*ploughshare*, Lyc.1072. **8.** *side-walls* of Egyptian temples, Str.17.1.28, Plu.2.359a. **b.** *battlements*, Procop.*Aed.*2.8. **c.** *portcullis*, or *drawbridge*, in gateways, Sch.E.*Ph.*114. **9.** πτερὰ Θετταλικά were the *fluttering corners* of a χλαμύς (v. πτέρυξ II. 4), Poll.7.46.

**πτερο-νόμος,** *ον*, *plying the wings*, Hsch. **-ποιέω,** = πτεροφυέω, Suid. s.v. νύμφαι:—Pass., Lyd.*Mens.*4.11. **-ποίκῐλος,** *ον*, *motley-feathered*, Ar.*Av.*249 (lyr., s.v.l.), 1410. **-πους,** *ποδος*, *ὁ*, *wing-footed*, of Hermes, *APl.*4.234 (Phld.). **-ρρῠέω,** (ῥέω) *shed the feathers, moult*, Ar.*Av.*106, Pl.*Phdr.*246c, *Com.Adesp.*172, Arist.*HA* 564$^{a}$32, 600$^{a}$23: metaph., *to be plucked, fleeced, plundered*, Ar.*Av.*284; π. τὸν πλοῦτον Philostr.*VA*6.36 (πτερορροεῖν is interpol. in Arist.*GA*783$^{b}$17). **-ρρύησις** [ῠ], *εως*, *ἡ*, *moulting*, Hierocl. *in CA*24 p.470 M., Syrian. *in Metaph.*82.18.

**πτερότης,** *ητος*, *ἡ*, *wingedness*, Arist.*PA*642$^{b}$27.

**πτερό-φοιτος,** v. πτεροφύτωρ. **-φόρᾱς,** *ου*, *ὁ*, a name of certain sacred officers in Egypt, so called from the hawk's *wing worn* on their heads, nom. pl. -φόραι *OGI*56.4 (Canopus, iii B.C.), 90.7 (Rosetta, ii B.C.): also -φόροι, Hsch.; cf. sq. III, and πτεραφόρος. **II.** dat. sg. -φόρᾳ χιλιάρχῳ, perh. name of a military rank, or = πτεροφόρος II, Men.*Pk.*104, cf. Hsch. s.v. πτεροφόροι. ® **-φόρος,** *ον*, *feathered, winged*, δέμας A.*Ag.*1147 (lyr.); θεαί E.*Or.*317 (lyr.); φῦλα the *feathered* tribes, Ar.*Av.*1757 (lyr.): metaph., π. Διὸς βέλος the *winged* bolt of Zeus, ib.1714. **II.** under the Roman Emperors, as Subst., *courier*, Plu.*Oth.*4; cf. πτεροφόρας II. **III.** πτεροφόρου, gen. sg. of this or the foreg. word, dub. sens. in *PCair.Zen.*512 (iii B.C.). **-φῠέω,** *grow feathers* or *wings*, Pl.*Phdr.*251c, 255d, Plu.2.751f, Luc.*Icar.*10, Them.*Or.*26.324d, Lib.*Or.*59.148. ® **-φῠής,** *ές*, *growing feathers* or *wings*, Pl.*Plt.*266e. **-φύησις** [ῠ], *εως*, *ἡ*, = sq., Herm. *in Phdr.* p.160 A., *Gp.*15.2.33. **-φῠΐα,** *ἡ*, *growing feathers*, Hierocl. *in CA*26 p.479 M. **-φῠτος,** *ον*, = πτεροφυής, Sch.Ar.*Eq.*1341. **-φύτωρ** [ῡ], *ορος*, *ὁ*, *ἡ*, *feather-producing*, διὰ πτεροφύτορ' ἀνάγκην Poet.ap.Pl.*Phdr.*252b (-φυτον or -φοιτον codd., -φύτορ' Stob.).

**πτερόω,** (πτερόν) *furnish with feathers* or *wings*, τινα Ar.*Av.*1334, 1361, *Ra.*1437, Pl.*R.*467d; for πτεροῦν βυβλίον, v. γλυφίς:—Pass., *to be* or *become feathered, to be fledged*, Ar.*Av.*804, 1382, 1446 (with a play on signf. II), Pl.*Phdr.*249a, al., *Com.Adesp.*172; ἔπος ἐπτερωμένον Ar.*Ra.*1388. **b.** *represent as winged*, τὰς Μούσας καὶ τὰς Σειρῆνας Porph.*Abst.*3.16. **2.** ναῦν π. *have the oars spread like wings* ready to dip into the water, Plb.1.46.11 (intr. in pf., ναῦς ἐπτερωκυῖα ib.9), cf. Plu.*Ant.*63, Charito 1.9; ταρσῷ κατήρει πίτυλος ἐπτερωμένος E.*IT*1346. **II.** metaph., *set on the wing, excite*, Ar.*Av.*1446 (v. supr. I. 1):—Pass., *to be excited*, ἐπὶ τὸν Πυθαγόρου βίον Philostr.*VA*1.7; ἐς χορείην *Anacreont.*51.4; πρὸς τὴν τοῦ πολέμου ἐπιθυμίαν Luc.*Dom.*4; τοῖς ἔξωθεν πλεονεκτήμασιν Jul.*Or.*7.235b: abs., Plu.*Art.*24.

**πτερῠγ-ίζω,** Att. fut. -ιῶ Ar.*Av.*1466: (πτέρυξ):—*flutter with the wings*, like young birds trying to fly, ib.795, 1466; *flap the wings*, like a cock crowing, metaph. of a man, Id.*Pl.*575; of sea-birds, Thphr.*Sign.*28:—in Ar.*Eq.*522 the word alludes to the play Ὄρνιθες by Magnes. ® **-ιον,** *τό*, Dim. of πτέρυξ, Arist.*HA*615$^{b}$30. **II.** *anything like a wing*. **1.** in pl., *fins* of fish, ib.489$^{b}$24, 504$^{b}$30, *IA*714$^{a}$11; of the *tail-flaps* of a lobster, Id.*HA*490$^{a}$3, cf. 525$^{b}$27, *PA*684$^{a}$13, *GA*720$^{b}$12; of certain *sea-slugs*, Id.*HA*532$^{b}$22, 24; *fins* of the sepia and other cuttle-fish, πτερύγι'.. σηπίας ὠπτημένα Sotad.Com.1.16, cf. Alex.187.3, Arist.*HA*524$^{a}$31, *PA*685$^{b}$16. **2.** *horns* of the horned owl, Id.*HA*597$^{b}$22. **3.** *end* or *tip* of the rudder, Poll.1.90; of a pole, Hsch. **4.** in a building, *turret* or *battlement*, or (as others) *pointed roof, peak*, *Ev.Luc.*4.9; cf. πτέρυξ II. 7. **5.** *flap, fold* (cf. πτέρυξ II. 4), Arist.*Aud.*802$^{a}$39, Lxx *Nu.*15.38, *Ru.*3.9, Poll.7.62; *flap* of a cuirass, Aen.Tact.31.8; π. κρανῶν *IG*2$^{2}$.1424a.399 (pl.). **6.** in the body, *part of the shoulder-blade*, Poll.2.177; of the ear, *parts joining the temples*, ib.85, Hsch.; of the nose, *parts joining the cheeks*, Poll.2.80, Sor.1.71, Gal.*UP*11.12. **7.** Medic., disease of the eye when a *membrane grows over it from the inner corner*, Hp.*Prorrh.*2.20, Cels.7.7.4, Dsc.1.108, Gal.7.732. **8.** *fleshy excrescence* on the nails, Cels.6.19.1, Dsc.1.110, Paul.Aeg.6.85. **9.** pl., = τοῦ πνεύμονος τοῦ λοβοῦ τὰ ἄκρα, Hsch. **10.** pl., *flanges* holding the projector of a torsion-engine, Ph.*Bel.*54.23; on a κέστρος II, Plb.27.11.4. **-ισμα,** *ατος*, *τό*, *flapping of the wings*, cj. for πτέρισμα in Longin.*Proll.Heph.* p.83 C. (pl.); τερετίσματα cj. Nauck (*Hermes* 24.467).

® **πτερῠγο-ειδής,** *ές*, *like a wing*, only Adv. -δῶς Thphr.*HP*3.12.7, *PMag.Berol.*2.2. **-ομαι,** v. πτερυγόω. **-ποίκῐλος,** *ον*, *with parti-coloured wings*, ἀτταγᾶς prob. cj. in Ar.*Av.*249 (lyr.). **-τομέω,** *excise a* πτερύγιον II. 7, Aët.7.59 (Pass.). **-τόμος,** *ὁ*, *instrument for this purpose*, ibid., Paul.Aeg.6.18 (also -τόμον, *τό*, *Hermes* 38.283). **-τύραννος** [τῠ], *ὁ*, name of an Indian bird presented to Alexander, Hsch. **-φόρος,** *ον*, *attracting feathers*, ἤλεκτρον Dsc.2.81.3. **-ω,** dub. sens., εἰ ἐπτερύγωσεν (as cause of hoarseness) Pall. *in Hp.*2.183 D. **II.** Pass., *fly*, πεδὰ μάτερα πεπτερύγωμαι Sapph.32.

**πτερῠγ-ώδης,** *ες*, = πτερυγοειδής, Thphr.*HP*3.12.7; ὦτα π., of elephants, Aret.*SD*2.13. **2.** οἱ π. *emaciated persons whose shoulder-blades stick out like wings*, Hp.*Epid.*3.14, 6.3.10, cf. Gal.1.623, etc. **-ωκής,** *ές*, (ὠκύς) *fleet of wing*, A.*Pr.*288 (anap.). **-ωμα,** *ατος*, *τό*, *the wings*, Horap.2.118. **II.** *anything that spreads like a wing*:—*flap of the ear*, Gal.14.701. **b.** *part of the pudenda muliebria*, Sor.1.16, al., Gal.19.114, Poll.2.174. **III.** *part of a ballista*, prob. in Vitr.10.11.7. **IV.** *group of letters* written so as to resemble a wing, *PMag.Leid.W.*20.26. **V.** = συκὴ ἐν πτέρναις, in horses, v.l. in *Hippiatr.*82. **-ωτός,** *ή*, *όν*, *winged*, Arist.*PA*659$^{b}$7, 693$^{b}$7: metaph., χρησμὸς π. Ar.*Eq.*1086.

® **πτέρυξ** (πτερύξ Aristarch. ap. Hdn.Gr.1.45), *ῠγος*, *ἡ*: Ep. dat. pl. πτερύγεσσι: (πτερόν):—*wing* of a bird, Il.2.316; mostly pl., ib.462, Od.2.149, Hes.*Sc.*134, A.*Ag.*52 (anap.), etc.; λευκὴ πτεροῖσι, πλὴν.. ἄκρων τῶν πτερύγων white in its plumage, save..the tips of the *wings*, of the ibis, Hdt.2.76; of Eros and Nike, Aristopho 11.8: metaph., κινοῦντα πτέρυγας ἤδη 'trying your *wings*', Lib.*Ep.*155.2. **2.** *winged creature, bird*, *AP*6.12 (Jul.). **3.** *flight, augury, omen*, ποίων (sc. ὀρνίχων) οὐκ ἀγαθαὶ πτέρυγες Call.*Lav.Pall.*124. **II.** *anything like a wing*, **1.** in pl., = πτερύγια, *fins* of fish, Arist.*HA*505$^{b}$21, *Mir.*835$^{b}$10, Ael.*NA*11.24; *flippers* of seals, Arist.*PA*697$^{b}$5; of dolphins and whales, Id.*HA*537$^{b}$3; of the tortoise, Nic.*Al.*559. **2.** pl., *feathery foliage*, Thphr.*HP*3.9.6. **b.** = ἄσπληνος I, Dsc.3.134. **3.** *blade* of the steering-paddle, *IG*2$^{2}$.1607.74: hence, *rudder*, S.*Fr.*1083; ἐξήρετμοι π., of oars, *Epigr.Gr.*337.2 (Cyzicus). **4.** *flap* of a cuirass, X.*An.*4.7.15 (v.l.), cf. *Eq.*12.4, 6; of the Doric χιτών, Ar.*Fr.*325, Men.*Epit.*187, *Com.Adesp.*17.1 D., Plu.*Comp.Lyc.Num.*3, Poll.7.62. **5.** *broad edge* of a knife or hunting-spear, Plu.*Alex.*16, Poll.5.21; *beak* of the sword-fish (v.l. ῥύγχος), Ael.*NA*9.40. **6.** *lobe* of the lungs, Hp.*Coac.*394. **7.** *point* of a building, Poll.7.121. **8.** *front frame* of a torsion-engine, Hero *Bel.*101.8. **9.** *shoulder-blade*, Philostr.*Gym.*30. **10.** in pl., title of poem whose lines form a pattern like wings, *AP*15.24 (Simm.). **11.** pl., *sails*, *Com.Adesp.*9 D., *Lyr.Alex.Adesp.*20.9. **III.** *anything that covers* or *protects* like wings, π. πέπλων E.*Ion* 1143; κολπώδη πτέρυγ' Εὐβοίας, i.e. Aulis, Id.*IA*120 (lyr.); νεοσσὸς ὡσεὶ πτέρυγας εἰσπίτνων ἐμάς Id.*Tr.*751; of a mountain, Λιβάνου πτέρυγες Musae.48. **2.** *fence, wall*, Lyc.291. **IV.** metaph., πτέρυγες γόων the *wings*, i.e. the *flight* or *flow*, of grief, S.*El.*242 (lyr.); π. Πιερίδων Pi.*I.*1.64.

**πτερύσσομαι,** Att. **-ττομαι,** fut. -ξομαι, *flutter, flap the wings* like a cock crowing, Babr.65.6, Luc.*VH*2.41, Ael.*NA*7.7, etc.; ἐπτερύσσετο shd. perh. be restd. for ἀπτ- in Archil.49 Diehl. **II.** metaph., *triumph, exult*, Diph.61.6. **2.** *become full-fledged, spread one's wings for flight*, of the soul, Ph.2.32, al.

**πτέρ-ωμα,** *ατος*, *τό*, *that which is feathered*, e.g. *feathered arrow*, A.*Fr.*139, Lyc.56. **2.** π. βραγχίων the *fin* by the gills of fishes, Ael.*NA*16.12. **3.** *colonnade* of a temple, Vitr.3.3.9, 4.8.6. **4.** πτερώματα πετάσου *awnings*, *Ephes.*2.41 (iii A.D.). **II.** *plumage*, τὸ τῆς ψυχῆς π. Pl.*Phdr.*246e; in literal sense, Porph.ap.Eus.*PE*3.12: pl., Arist.*Col.*792$^{a}$24, $^{b}$28. **2.** οἷον..π. τῆς κινήσεως motive *wing-power*, Gal.7.586. **-ων,** *ωνος*, *ὁ*, *a bird* of some kind, *Com.Adesp.*592 (on the accent v. Hdn.Gr.1.35). **-ώνῠμος,** *ον*, *named from its feathers* or *wings*, Pl.*Phdr.*252c. **-ως,** *ωτος*, *ὁ*, *the winged god*, a play on the name of Ἔρως, Poet.ap.eund.ib.252b. **-ωσις,** *εως*, *ἡ*, *plumage*, Ar.*Av.*94, 97; ἀπολαμβάνειν τὴν π., opp. πτερορρυεῖν, Arist.*HA*564$^{b}$2, cf. 601$^{b}$6, *PA*642$^{b}$24. **2.** *feathering* of arrows, Aen.Tact.31.27. **3.** pl., names of parts of surgical machines, Orib.49.4.9, al. **II.** metaph., λόγων πτέρωσις (cf. πτερόεις II) Jul.*Ep.*193. **-ωτικός,** *ή*, *όν*, *of* or *for plumage*, καθαρότης Hierocl. *in CA*25 p.477 M. **-ωτός,** *ή*, *όν*, also *ός*, *όν* S.*OC*1460:—*feathered*, Hdt.2.76; τοξεύματα E.*HF*571, cf. *Or.*274; [ἡ ψυχὴ] ἦν τὸ πάλαι π. Pl.*Phdr.*251b; προσκεφάλαια π. *stuffed with feathers*, Poll.6.10. **II.** *winged*, ὄφιες Hdt.2.75; ὄχος, ἅρματα, A.*Pr.*135 (lyr.), E.*IA*250 (lyr.), etc.; Διὸς βροντή S. l.c.; Ἅιδας E.*Alc.*261 (lyr., dub. l.); ὄνειροι Luc.*VH*2.34: metaph., π. ἰξὸς ὀμμάτων Ἔρως Tim.Com.2. **2.** π. φθόγγος a sound *as of wings* in the air, Ar.*Av.*1198. **3.** π. χιτωνίσκοι tunics *with flaps*, Plu.2.330b. **4.** Astrol., epith. of certain signs, Vett.Val.10.9, Heph.Astr.1.1, *Cat.Cod.Astr.*1.104, al. **5.** πτερωτοί (sc. ὄρνιθες) *winged* creatures, *birds*, E.*Ba.*257; gen. πτερωτῶν A.*Supp.*510, E.*Hel.*747; π. γένος Arist.*HA*490$^{a}$12; τὰ π. τῶν ζῴων, οἷον τὰς ὄρνιθας ib.518$^{b}$35; ἔντομα, καὶ ἄπτερα καὶ π. ib.523$^{b}$18; sts. of birds, as a sub-division of τὰ πτηνά, opp. τὰ πτιλωτά, τὰ δερμόπτερα, ib.490$^{a}$6.

**πτέσθαι,** v. πέτομαι. **πτῆμα,** *ατος*, *τό*, *flight*, Suid. **πτήν,** πτηνός, *ὁ*, *ἡ*, *winged*, Hdn.Gr. in *An.Ox.*3.243, *EM*694.7. **πτῆναι,** v. πέτομαι.

**πτηνοβόλος,** *ον*, *striking birds*, ἰοί cj. in Orph.*H.*12.16.

**πτην-ολέτις,** *ιδος*, *ἡ*, *bird-killing*, νεφέλη, of a net, *AP*6.185 (Zos.).

® **πτηνοπέδῑλος,** *ον*, *with winged sandals*, Orph.*H.*28.4.

**πτηνός,** *ή*, *όν*, Dor. **πτανός,** *ά*, *όν*; also *ός*, *όν* Pl.*Prt.*320e: (πτῆναι, πέτομαι):—*flying, winged*, Διὸς π. κύων, i.e. eagle, A.*Pr.*1022, cf. *Ag.*136 (lyr.); π. ὄφις Id.*Eu.*181; ὄρνις, οἰωνός, S.*Ph.*955, *Ant.*1082; Ἔρως, ἵπποι, E.*Hipp.*1275 (lyr.), *IT*193 (lyr.); ἅρμα Pl.*Phdr.*246e; also of arrows, π. ἰοί S.*Ph.*166 (anap.); βέλη E.*HF*179; π. φυγή, of birds, Pl.*Prt.*320e. **2.** τὰ π. *winged creatures, birds*, A.*Ch.*591 (lyr.), S.*Aj.*168 (anap.), E.*Ion* 504 (lyr.), etc.; πτηνὸν ὀρνίθων γένος Ar.*Av.*1707; πτηνῶν γένη Id.*Th.*46; opp. τὰ πεζά, Pl.*Smp.*207a; opp. τὰ πεζά and τὰ πλωτά, Arist.*HA*488$^{a}$1, cf. 542$^{a}$23: hence πταναὶ θῆραι the pursuit *of winged game*, S.*Ph.*1146 (lyr.); ἡ [θήρα] τῶν π. Pl.*Lg.*823b: of young birds, *fledged*, E.*Tr.*146 (lyr.). **3.** *swift-footed*, παρδάλεις, κάμηλοι, Lib.*Ep.*219.5, 1402.3. **II.** metaph., πτηνοὶ μῦθοι, Homer's ἔπεα πτερόεντα, E.*Or.*1176: but κοῦφοι καὶ π. λόγοι *fleeting, idle* words, Pl.*Lg.*717d; π. ὄνειροι E.*IT*571; πτηνὰς διώκεις ἐλπίδας *fleeting* hopes, Id.*Fr.*271. **2.** πτανὰ ἰσχύς *soaring, aspiring* strength, Pi.*Fr.*107.3.

**πτῆξις**, εως, ἡ, (πτήσσω) *terror*, Aq., Sm., Thd.*Pr.*18.7.

**πτήσιμος**, ον, *able to fly, winged*, λόγοι Jul.*Ep.*191.

**πτῆσις**, εως, ἡ, (πτῆναι) *flight*, A.*Pr.*488, Arist.*PA*639ᵇ2, *EN*1174ᵃ31, Q.S.12.5 (pl.): metaph. of rapid reading, ἡ περὶ τὴν ἀνάγνωσιν π. Lib.*Ep.*949.2.

**πτήσσω** (never -ττω), Ar.*V.*1490, X.*Cyr.*3.3.18: fut. πτήξω *AP* 12.141 codd. (Mel.): aor. ἔπτηξα E.*HF*974, etc., Dor. ἔπταξα Pi.*P.* 4.57, Ep. πτῆξα Il.14.40: aor. 2 ἔπτᾰκον in compd. καταπτακών A.*Eu.* 252; Ep. 3 dual καταπτήτην Il.8.136: pf. ἔπτηχα Isoc.5.58, (κατ-) Lycurg.40, D.4.8; later ἔπτηκα (κατ-) Them.*Or.*24.309b; Ep. part. πεπτηώς, ῶτος (v. infr. II. 2). I. Causal, *scare, alarm*, πτῆξε θυμὸν ἐνὶ στήθεσσιν Ἀχαιῶν Il.14.40; ἐχθροὺς πτῆξαι Thgn.1015. II. intr., *crouch* or *cower for fear*, of animals, ἅπερ πτηνῶν ἀγέλαι τάχ' ἂν σιγῇ πτήξειαν ἄφωνοι S.*Aj.*171 (anap.); πτήξας δέμας παρεῖχε A.*Pers.*209; [πῶλος] π. αἰσχύνησιν S.*Fr.*659.9, cf. Ar.*Av.*777; of human beings, ἔπταξαν ἀκίνητοι σιωπᾷ Pi.*P.*4.57; ὑπὸ φόβῳ π. E.*Ba.*1035 (lyr.); πτῆξαι ταπεινήν Id.*Andr.*165; π. θυμόν S.*OC*1466 (lyr.); κακῶς πάσχων π. Pl.*Smp.*184b; δοκεῖ μοι τοῦ αὐτοῦ ἀνδρὸς εἶναι καὶ εὐτυχοῦντα ἐξυβρίσαι καὶ πταίσαντα.. πτῆξαι X.*Cyr.*3.1.26; ἐκποδὼν π. Ar.*Th.*36: with Preps., π. ἐν μυχοῖς πέτρας E.*Cyc.*408; εἰς ἕνα χῶρον Ar.*Lys.*770; πόλις πρὸς πόλιν π. E.*Supp.*269; βωμὸν ὄρνις ὣς ἔπτηξ' ὕπο Id.*HF* 974: c. acc. loci, βωμὸν π. Id.*Ion* 1280. 2. *crouch*, of men in ambush, νῶν εἰς ἐρημίαν ὁδοῦ Id.*Andr.*753; ὑπὸ τεύχεσι πεπτηῶτες Od.14.474. 3. c. acc. rei, *crouch for fear of*.., ἀπειλάς A.*Pr.*175 (anap.); φοβούμενοι πτήσσομεν αὐτούς X.*Cyr.*3.3.18; ταῖς διανοίαις μὴ πτήξαντες τὸν τῶν ἐπιόντων φόβον Lycurg.49; δόρυ Lyc.280, *IG*14. 1296: abs., ὁ λέων.. δρώμενος.. οὐδέποτε φεύγει οὐδὲ πτήσσει Arist. *HA*629ᵇ13.

**πτητικός**, ή, όν, *able to fly*, τὰ π. *strong fliers*, Arist.*HA*504ᵇ8, cf. 614ᵃ32; τὸ π. Id.*PA*693ᵇ13; βάρεα (βραχέα codd. Ath.) καὶ μὴ π. Thphr.*Fr.*180. Adv. -κῶς Plu.2.405b.

**πτίλλος**, v. πτίλος. **πτῖλοβάφος** [ᾰ], ὁ, = *plumarius*, *Gloss.* (ψιλ- codd.).

※ **πτίλον** [ῐ], Dor. ψίλον (q.v.), τό: (πέτομαι, πτέσθαι): prop. of *soft feathers* or *down* under the true feathers (πτίλα· πτερὰ ἁπαλά, Hsch., cf. Phot., Suid.), π. κύκνειον [S.]*Fr.*1127.3, cf. Clytus 1, Ael.*NA*12. 4, etc.; κνεφάλλων ἢ πτίλων σεσαγμένος Pl.Com.97, cf. Eub.5; burned in order to spread pungent smoke, Plb.21.28.12; *down on a youth's chin*, D.H.*Dem.*51. 2. Com., of the *plume* of a helmet, φέρε νῦν ἀπὸ τοῦ κράνους μοι τὸ πτερόν. Ans. τουτὶ πτίλον σοι Ar.*Ach.*585, cf. 588; π. τὸ μέγα κομπολακύθου ib.1182. II. *wing*, prop. of insects, Arist.*IA*713ᵃ10; of *the wing-like membrane* in a kind of serpents, π. οὐ πτερωτά Hdt.2.76. III. *anything like a feather* or *wing*, 1. *leaf*, Nic.*Th.*524. 2. pl., *sails* of a ship, Lyc.25.

**πτῖλόνωτος**, ον, *with downy back*, κάμπη *AP*9.256 (Antiphan.).

**πτίλ-ος** [ῐ], η, ον, *suffering from* πτίλωσις II, π. τοὺς ὀφθαλμούς Lxx *Le.*21.20; π. alone, Gal.10.1017, 12.799; also π. βλέφαρα Dsc.1.69. 3: **πτίλλος**, = *lippus*, *Gloss.* **-όω**, *furnish with feathers*, πτηνὰ ἐπτίλωσε (sc. ἡ φύσις) Herm.ap.Stob.1.49.69:—Pass., *to have wings*, ἐπτιλῶσθαι Philostr.*VA*3.48. **-ωσις**, εως, ἡ, (πτίλον) = πτέρωσις, Ael.*NA*16.4. II. *a disease of the eyelids* in which their edges become swollen and inflamed, and the eyelashes fall off, Gal. 10.1004, Aët.7.80. **-ώσσω**, *have sore eyes*, Archyt.ap.Simp.*in Cat.*395.35. ※ **-ωτός**, ή, όν, *winged*, esp. πτιλωτά, opp. πτερωτά, δερμόπτερα, *membrane-winged creatures*, Arist.*HA*490ᵃ6. 2. *stuffed with feathers*, of a cushion, Poll.6.10.

**πτῐσάν-η** [ᾰ], ἡ, (πτίσσω) *peeled barley*, Nicopho 15; πτισάνης χυλός Hp.*Acut.*6. II. *barley-gruel*, π. παχεῖα, opp. χυλός (barley-water), ib.7,10; both opp. ποτόν, ib.68; πτισάνην ἕψειν Ar.*Fr.*159, cf. 412, Alex.142.3, *PCair.Zen.*710.76 (iii B.C.). ※ **-ης**, ου, Dor. **-ας**, ὁ, *one who shells* or *peels*, dub. l. in *AP*11.351.6 (Pall.); πτιστής Scaliger. **-ον**, τό, poet. for πτισάνη, Nic.*Th.*590.

**πτῖσᾰνορρῠφία**, Ion. -ίη, ἡ, *drinking of gruel*, Hp.*Acut.*16.

**πτίσις** [ῐ], εως, ἡ, *winnowing of grain*, Gal.19.115: pl., *Gp.*2.34.1.

**πτίσμα**, ατος, τό, *peeled* or *winnowed grain*, Str.17.1.34.

**πτισμός**, ὁ, *winnowing*, προσαυλεῖν πτισμόν to sing a *winnowing-song*, Nicopho 17.

**πτίσσω**, Pherecr.183, Ar.*Fr.*339, Att. **πτίττω** ib.271 (prob. l.), Luc.*Herm.*79, v.l. in Pherecr. l.c.: aor. ἔπτισα Hdt.2.92:—**Pass.**, aor. ἐπτίσθην *Gp.*12.23.2, (περι-) Thphr.*HP*4.4.10: pf. ἔπτισμαι Hp.*VM*14, Arist.*HA* 595ᵇ10:—*winnow grain*, Hp. l.c. (Pass.), Pherecr. l.c., etc.; πτισσουσῶν ᾠδή the song *of women winnowing*, Ar.*Fr.*339. II. *bray in a mortar*, τὸ ἐκ μέσου τοῦ λωτοῦ Hdt. l.c., cf. D.L.9.59, Luc. l.c. (Cf. Lat. *pinso*, Skt. *pináṣṭi* 'pound'.)

**πτισ-τέον**, *one must winnow*, ζειάς, σῖτον, *Gp.*3.7.1,8. **-τής**, οῦ, ὁ, cj. for πτισάνης (q.v.). **-τικός**, ή, όν, *fitted for winnowing*, πτιστικὸν τερετίζειν Phryn.Com.14.

**πτόα**, v. πτοία.

※ **πτοέω** and **πτοιέω**, fut. -ήσω *AP*7.214 (Arch.): Ep. aor. ἐπτοίησα, Aeol. ἐπτόαισα (v. infr.):—Pass., Ep. aor. ἐπτοιήθην Call.*Dian.*191: pf. ἐπτόημαι, Ep. ἐπτοίημαι (v. infr.):—*terrify, scare*, *AP* l.c.:—Pass., *to be scared, dismayed*, φρένες ἐπτοίηθεν Od.22.298; ἐξ ὕπνου κέκραγεν ἐπτοημένη A.*Ch.*535; ἐπτοημένας δεινοῖς δράκουσιν by serpents, E.*El.* 1255 (s.v.l.); ἔβαλλε χεῖρας ἐπτοημένας Id.*Tr.*559 (lyr.); πτοηθεὶς ἐπὶ τοῖς ἠγγελμένοις Plb.31.11.4, cf. Lxx *Ex.*19.16, al., *Ev.Luc.*21.9, 24.37; περὶ δ' ἂν τύχῃ Polystr.p.29 W.; of animals, Q.S.11.48, 13. 457. II. metaph., *flutter, excite* by any passion, τό μοι καρδίαν.. ἐπτόαισεν Sapph.2.6, cf. eand.*Supp.*14.6; τὴν δὲ φρένας ἐπτοίησεν Κύπρις A.R.1.1232; Κύπρις ἐπ' Αἰακίδῃ κούρῃ φρένας ἐπτοίησεν Poet. ap.Parth.21.2:—Pass., *to be passionately excited*, Mimn.5.2 (= Thgn. 1018); ἐπτοημένοι φρένας A.*Pr.*856; ὡς ἐπτόηται E.*Ba.*214, cf. *IA* 1029; ἔρωτι ἐπτοάθης ib.586 (lyr.); πτοιηθεὶς ὑπ' ἔρωτι Call. l.c.; τὸ περὶ τὰς ἐπιθυμίας μὴ ἐπτοῆσθαι Pl.*Phd.*68c, cf. *R.*439d, Epicur.*Fr.* 465; περὶ τὴν ὀχείαν Arist.*HA*614ᵃ26, cf. 571ᵇ10; περὶ τὰ ὄψα Plu. 2.1128b; περὶ τὸ κέρδος Onos.1.20; ἐς γυναῖκας Luc.*Am.*5; ἐπὶ τὸ νέον ib.23; ἐπὶ γυναικί Parth.4.2; πρὸς τὰς αἶγας Plu.2.989a; τῇ γνώμῃ πρὸς τὸν πόλεμον Id.*Sull.*7; *to be distraught*, μεθ' ὁμήλικας ἐπτοίηται *he gapes like one distraught* after his fellows, Hes.*Op.*447; τὸ πτοηθέν *distraction*, E.*Ba.*1268. (πτοι- only in dactylic verse, perh. metri gr.; the -άω inflexion only in Thgn. l.c., E.*IA*586 (lyr.); Lesb. -αισ(ε) may have -αι- for -η- as αἰμίονος, etc.)

**πτόη**, v. πτοία.

**πτό-ησις**, or **πτοίησις** (so in Pl.), εως, ἡ, *vehement emotion* or *excitement*, Pl.*Prt.*310d; περί τι Id.*Smp.*206d; ἡ τοῦ σώματος π. Id.*Cra.* 404a, cf. Arist.*GA*774ᵃ5 (dub.), Clearch.(?) ap.Ath.15.670c, Agatharch.5, Ph.1.509; μὴ φοβούμεναι μηδεμίαν πτόησιν 1*Ep.Pet.*3. 6. **-ητός**, only in the form **πτοιητός**, ή, όν, *scared*, Nic.*Al.*243, Max.164.

**πτοιά**, Ep. **πτοίη** Opp.*H.*3.431, Nic.*Al.*212: rarely **πτόα**, *EM* 695.1, v.l. in Ph.1.531; and **πτόη**, Lxx 1*Ma.*3.25, 3*Ma.*6.17: ἡ: (πτοέω):—*terror, fright*, Onos.6.5; ταραχῇ καὶ π. Plu.*Fab.*11, cf. Ph.2.204, al.; ἀμυδραὶ καὶ φαντασιώδεις π. Philostr.*VA*7.14, cf. Plb. 1.39.14, 1.68.6. II. *excitement*, πάθος ἐστὶ πτοία ψυχῆς Zeno *Stoic.* 1.51, cf. Chrysipp.ib.3.127; π. περὶ τὰ ἀφροδίσια, εἰς ἀφρ., Epicur. *Fr.*458, Ael.*NA*10.27; ἡ περὶ φιλοσοφίαν π. Procl.*in Alc.*p.43 C., cf. Plu.2.83d: pl., Ti.Locr.103b.

**πτοιᾰλέος**, α, ον, *scared*, Opp.*H.*3.431.

**πτοιέω, πτοίησις, πτοιητός**, v. πτο-. **πτοίνα**, v. κτοίνα. **πτοῖος**, ὁ, = πτοία, Hsch. (s.v.l.).

**πτοιώδης**, ες, (πτοία) *scared, shy*, Hp.*Epid.*6.2.20, cf. Erot.; ὁρμαί, ἄγνοια, *Stoic.*3.166.

**Πτολεμ-άεῖον**, τό, precinct dedicated to the Ptolemies at Rhodes, D.S.20.100. **-αῖα**, τά, festival at Athens, *IG*2².891.14; at Alexandria, *IG*5(2).118.12 (Tegea, iii B.C.); at Delos, **Πτολεμαίεια** *Inscr.Délos* 320*B*60 (iii B.C.); also **Πτολεμαίεα**, ib.57; of a festival in the island of Hiera, *PSI*4.364 (iii B.C.). ※ **-αϊκός**, ή, όν, *of Ptolemy* or *the Ptolemies*, ὅπλα Lxx 3*Ma.*1.2; νόμισμα *BGU*713.23 (i A.D.), Poll.9.85: hence Πτολεμαϊκά, τά, *Ptolemaic* coins, *IG*7.303. 91 (Orop.). 2. οἱ Π. βασιλεῖς kings *of the Ptolemaic dynasty*, Str. 2.5.12. **-αῖος**, ὁ, *Ptolemy*, name of the Kings of Egypt in the period after Alexander: also of a month at Methymna, dub. in *IG*12 (2).500. **-αΐς** (also -αιίς), ΐδος, ἡ, with or without φυλή, name of an Att. tribe, named after Ptolemy Euergetes I, ib.2².957.28, 964.16, al., Poll.8.110; ἐπὶ τῆς Πτολεμαΐδος.. πρυτανείας *IG*2².897, al. II. name of several cities, esp. of one in Phoenicia, now *Acre*, Str.2.5.39, etc.:—**Πτολεμ-αΐτης**, ου, or **-αιεύς**, έως, ὁ, *a citizen thereof*, St.Byz.

**πτολεμίζω, πτολεμιστής, πτόλεμόνδε**, Ep. for πολεμ-.

**πτόλεμος**, ὁ, Ep. for πόλεμος (q.v.).

**πτολίαρχος**, Ep. for πολίαρχος, Call.*Jov.*73; also **-άρχης**, ου, ὁ, *Epigr.Gr.*1036 (Nicomedia).

**πτολίεθρον** [ῐ], τό, Ep. lengthd. form for πόλις (πτόλις), Il.2.133, Od.1.2, Hes.*Sc.*81, etc.

**πτολί-οικος** [ῐ], ὁ, *dweller in the city*, on Cretan coins, *BMus.Cat. Coins Crete* p.8 (Aptera, iv B.C.). **-πόρθης**, v. πτολίπορθος. **-πόρθιος**, ον, = sq., of Odysseus, Od.9.504. **-πορθος**, ον, (πέρθω) *sacking* or *wasting cities*, epith. of Ares, Il.20.152, Hes.*Th.*936; of Odysseus and Oïleus, Il.2.278,728; of Achilles, 15.77, etc.; also of Heracles, *Tab.Defix.* in *Stud.Ital.*2(1922).394 (Cret., iv/iii B.C.); π. μάχαι Pi.*O.*8.35; πτολίπορθον στίχα Μήδων Epigr.ap.D.S.11.14:—also **-πόρθης**, ου, ὁ, A.*Ag.*472 (lyr.); as pr. n. of a son of Odysseus, Paus.8.12.6:—the form πολίπορθος never occurs, for πτολίπορθ' (voc.) is rightly restored in A.*Ag.*783 (lyr.); cf. sq.

※ **πτόλις**, ἡ, Ep., = πόλις, Il.2.130, etc. (not Aeol., but an Epicism in Sapph.*Supp.*20a.12); also in Trag. (not S.) lyr., A.*Th.*114,843, E.*Tr.*556, (in dialogue) A.*Th.*6, *Eu.*79, E.*Hec.*767, *Andr.*699; found in Cypr., *Inscr.Cypr.*135.1 H., cf. Heraclid.ap.Eust.842.63, Sch.Il. 23.1; also Arc. as the old name of Mantinea, Paus.8.12.7; once in Ion. Prose, Hp.*Medic.*14; in ll. cc. only nom. and acc. sg. (πτόλις, πτόλιν) are found; gen. sg. πτόλεως Hermesian.7.72 cod.; Cypr. dat. sg. πτόλιϝι *Inscr.Cypr.*135.6 H.—Expld. by ναῦγος ἢ πόλις, Hsch.

**πτόλισμα**, = πόλισμα, Phot., Suid.

**πτορθάκανθος** [ᾰκ], ον, *with spinous shoots*, Thphr.*HP*6.1.3.

**πτορθ-εῖον**, τό, = πτόρθος, Nic.*Al.*267. ※ **-ιος**, ὁ, epith. of Poseidon, *IG*1².190.16. **-ος**, ὁ, *young branch, shoot, sucker, sapling*, Od.6.128; ὥς τις π. ηὐξόμην E.*Hec.*20; πτόρθοισι δάφνης Id. *Ion* 103 (anap.); μαλάχης Ar.*Pl.*544; οἱ π. καὶ οἱ νέοι κλῶνες Pl.*Prt.* 334b, cf. Thphr.*CP*5.1.3; πτόρθους ἁπαλοὺς ἀποτρώγουσαι Eup.14.2: generally, *branch*, Arist.*PA*687ᵃ2, etc.; π. μέγας, of Heracles' club, *APl.*4.103 (Tull. Gem.). II. *sprouting, budding*, Hes.*Op.*421.

**πτορθοφορέω**, cj. for πρωτοφορέω in Ath.13.565f.

**πτόρμος**, ὁ, Aeol. for πταρμός, Jo.Gramm.*Comp.*3.47.

**πτόρος**, ὁ, = πταρμός, Hdn.Gr.1.191.

**πτῠᾰλ-ίζω** or **πτῠελίζω**, (πτύαλον) *salivate*, Hp.*Prorrh.*1.31 (-ελ-), *Coac.*555 (-αλ-). **-ισμός** or **πτῠελισμός**, ὁ, *salivation*, Id.*Prog.*17 (-ελ-), *Acut.(Sp.)*40 (-αλ-), al. **-ον** or **πτύελον**, τό, (πτύω) *sputum, saliva*, Id.*Aph.*1.12 (-ελ-), *Prog.*15 (-ελ-), *Acut.*66 (-αλ-), al., Arist.*HA*607ᵃ30, *GA*747ᵃ10:—also **πτύελος**, ὁ, Id.*EE*1235ᵃ38,

Lxx *Jb.*7.19, Hsch. s.v. σίαλος.—The forms in πτυαλ- and πτυελ- are found in codd. of Hp. (v. Kuehlewein i p.cvi) and of later writers; in those of Arist. the latter only is found. **-ώδης**, ες, *secreting saliva freely*, Diogenian.8.71. 2. *like spittle*, Hp. *Coac.*571 (-αλ-).

**πτῠάριον**, τό, Dim. of πτύον, Hdn. *Epim.*117, *EM*562.43.

**πτῠάς**, άδος, ἡ, (πτύω) *spitter*, a kind of *asp*, Hierocl. p.11 A., Gal. 14.235, Philum. *Ven.*16, interpol. in Porph. *Abst.*3.9.

**πτύγμα**, ατος, τό, (πτύσσω) *fold* or *anything folded*. πέπλοιο π. Il.5.315, cf. *AP*6.271 (Phaedim.); π. τοῦ δέρματος *fold* of skin, Antyll.ap.Orib.45.15.8; τῆς ὑστέρας, = *fundus* uteri, Paul.Aeg.3.64. **II.** Medic., *piece of lint folded up to stop a wound, pledget*, Antyll.ap.Orib.10.13.27; of a bandage, Gal.18(1).826.

**πτυγμάτιον**, τό, Dim. of foreg. II, Heliod.ap.Orib.44.10.17, Sor.1.82, Leonid.ap.Aët.7.71.

**πτύγξ**, πτυγγός, ὁ, *eagle-owl*, = ὕβρις, dub. l. in Arist. *HA*615ᵇ11.

**πτυελ-ίζω, -ισμός, -ον, -ώδης**, v. πτυαλίζω, etc.

**πτῠΐδιον**, τό, Dim. of πτύον, Sch.Ar. *Av.*1150.

**πτυκτός**, ή, όν, (πτύσσω) *folded*, πίναξ π. *folding* tablet, Il.6.169, cf. Aristid. *Or.*17(15).22 (pl.), Hdn.7.6.5 (pl.). 2. generally, *capable of being folded* or *doubled up*, κλῖμαξ, πύργος, App. *Hisp.* 94, *BC*5.36. **II.** **πτυκτόν**, τό, *folded bandage*, Paul.Aeg.6.90.

**πτύξ**, ἡ (nom. only Gramm., Hdn.Gr.1.396, Hsch.), dat. πτῠχί Il. 20.22: pl. πτύχες, πτύχας, 7.247, al., Hes. *Sc.*143, etc.: after Hom. **πτῠχή**, ῆς, which prevails in Pi. (v. infr. II) and Trag.; the metre requires acc. sg. πτύχα in E. *Supp.*979 (lyr.), but acc. pl. πτυχάς in S. *Fr.*144; in other places either πτύχας or πτυχάς will suit the metre:—poet. word, *layer, plate*, mostly in pl., σάκεος πτύχες *plates* of metal or leather, in strong shields, Il.18.481, cf. 7.247, 20.269, Hes. *Sc.*143. 2. *fold* (i.e. *folded piece*) of a garment, in pl., first in *h.Cer.*176, then in S. *Fr.*494, E. *Supp.*979 (lyr.); of the entrails, κατὰ σπλάγχνων πτυχάς ib.212; εἰς τὰς πτυχάς Arist. *HA*549ᵃ17; *coats* of the stomach, Gal.2.556; *layers* of muscles, Id.18(2).944. 3. writing *tablets*, ἐν πτυχαῖς βίβλων κατεσφραγισμένα A. *Supp.*947; γραμμάτων πτυχὰς ἔχων S. *Fr.*144; ἐν δέλτου πτυχαῖς E. *IA*98, cf. *IG*9(1).880.10 (Corc.). **II.** in hilly country, *folds, glens*, κατὰ πτύχας Οὐλύμποιο Il.11.77; πτύχες ἠνεμόεσσαι (from the wind that rushes down narrow mountain-clefts), Od.19.432; also in sg., πτυχὶ Οὐλύμποιο, Παρνησοῖο, Il.20.22, *h.Ap.*269, *h.Merc.*555; πτυχαὶ Κρισαῖαι, Πίνδου, Πέλοπος, Pi. *P.*6.18, 9.15, *N.*2.21; ἐν Κιθαιρῶνος πτυχαῖς S. *OT* 1026, cf. E. *Supp.*757, *Ba.*62, *Andr.*1277; Αὐλίδος κατὰ πτυχάς Id. *IT*1082, cf. 9: also of the sky, πτυχαὶ αἰθέρος, οὐρανοῦ, Id. *Or.*1631, *Hel.*44, *Ph.*84: sg., μέχρις οὐρανοῦ πτυχός Ezek. *Exag.*69. **III.** metaph., ὕμνων πτυχαί *folds* of song, i.e. sinuous songs, Pi. *O.*1.105. **IV.** acc. pl. πτυχάς or πτύχας *leaves* of a folding door, metaph., ὁ κλείσας οὐρανοῦ δισσὰς π. *PMag.Par.*1.190; nom. πτύχες, = θύραι, σανίδες, Poll.10.24. **V.** πτυχή, ἡ, the part of a ship on which her name was inscribed, Sch.A.R.1.1089; cf. πτυχίς.

**πτύξαγρις** and **πύξαγρις**, ὁ, name of the crab *which extracts* the flesh of the oyster from its shell by putting a small stone between the *valves* (πτύχες or πυξία), Zonar.

**πτύξις**, εως, ἡ, *folding*, Hsch., Eust.633.19; π. ὑστερῶν *corrugation*, dub. in Hp. *Coac.*515. **II.** *fold*, Lxx *Jb.*41.4(5). **III.** a military evolution, Arr. *Tact.*9.4 (pl.).

❀ **πτύον** [ῠ], τό, *winnowing-shovel, fan*, Il.13.588 (in poet. gen. πτυόφιν), A. *Fr.*210, S. *Fr.*1084, Theoc.7.156, Porph. *Antr.*35:—**πτέον** is Att. acc. to Ael.Dion. *Fr.*288, Poll.1.245, etc.

**πτυρμός**, ὁ, *consternation*, Hsch. s.v. πτοία (πτοιρμός cod.), Phot. s.v. πτοίαν, Eust.795.29.

❀ **πτύρομαι** [ῡ], aor. 2 ἐπτύρην [ῠ] Plu. *Fab.*3, inf. πτυρῆναι Pl. *Ax.* 370a:—Pass., *to be scared* or *frightened*, Hp. *Mul.*1.25; of the soul, M.Ant.8.45; esp. of horses, *shy, start*, D.S.2.19, Plu. l.c.; τινι at a thing, Id. *Marc.*6; φωνῇ π. ὥσπερ θηρίον Id.2.800c; πρός τι Ph. Bybl. ap. Eus. *PE*1.10: c. acc., π. τὸν θάνατον *start at, be alarmed at* death, Pl. l.c.; ἔν τινι *Ep.Phil.*1.28.

**πτυρτικός**, ή, όν, *timorous*, Arist. *Mir.*846ᵇ35, Str.6.1.13, Eust. ad D.P.373.

**πτύσις** [ῠ], εως, ἡ, *spitting*, αἵματος Hp. *Aph.*3.29 (pl.), Arist. *Ph.* 243ᵇ13, etc.

**πτύσμα**, ατος, τό, *sputum*, Hp. *Aph.*5.11: more freq. in pl., Id. *Acut.*42, *Coac.*401, Plb.8.12.5. **II.** serpent's *venom*, Porph. *Abst.* 3.9.

**πτυσμός**, ὁ, = πτύσις, Hp. *Epid.*7.25.

**πτύσσω** (never -ττω), (ἀνα-) S. *Fr.*301: fut. πτύξω (ἀνα-) E. *HF*1256: aor. ἔπτυξα (v. infr.):—**Med.**, Od.2.77 (ποτι-), etc.: fut. πτύξομαι (προσ-) 3.22: aor. ἐπτυξάμην Ar. *Nu.*267:—**Pass.**, Il.13.134, etc.: aor. ἐπτύχθην (ἀν-, δι-) X. *Cyr.*7.5.5, S. *Ant.*709: aor. 2 ἐπτύγην [ῠ], (ἀν-) Hp. *Int.*48: pf. ἔπτυγμαι App. *BC*4.72, etc., (ἀν-) E. *El.*357; πέπτυκται Arist. *HA*536ᵃ11: plpf. ἔπτυκτο (προσ-) Pi. *I.*2.39:—*fold, double up*, χιτῶνα, εἵματα πτύξαι, *fold up* garments and put them by, Od.1.439, 6.111, 252; σπλῆνα Hp. *Fract.*8; χεῖρας πτύξαι ἐπί τινι *fold* one's arms over or round another, S. *OC*1611; βιβλίον *fold, close* a book, *Ev.Luc.*4.20. **II.** Pass., of the foetus, Hp. *Mul.*1.69; of bandages, Gal.18(1).826; γραμματεῖα ἐπτυγμένα Hdn.1.17.1; πύργοι ἐπτ. App. l.c.; ἔγχεα δὲ πτύσσοντο perh. *were interlaced*, Il. l.c. 2. *fold* or *cling round*, χιτὼν.. ἀμφὶ μηρὸν πτύσσεται S. *Fr.*872.3 (lyr.). **III.** Med., *fold round oneself, wrap round one*, τι Ar. *Nu.*267.

**πτύσχλοι** and **πτύχλοι**, οἱ, = ὑποδημάτιόν τι, Phot.; πτύσχλον (leg. πτύσχλον), = ὑπόδημα ἀνδρεῖον, Hsch.: cf. ἔπτυσχλοι (quod fort. legend.).

**πτῠχ-ή**, ἡ, v. πτύξ. ❀ **-ιον**, τό, *folding tablet*, Hdn.Gr.1.356, *PMag.Lond.*121.740, Zen.5.82. **II.** *pendant* of an ear-ring, *PLond.*5.1719.15 (vi A.D.). ❀ **-ιος**, α, ον, = πτυκτός, *EM*64.28. **-ίς**, ίδος, ἡ, *slab*, in sg. as collective, μαρμάρων πτυχίς Procop.Gaz. *Ecphr.* p.151 B.; = ἀκροστόλιον, the part of a ship on which the name was inscribed, Poll.1.86; cf. πτύξ v. **-ώδης**, ες, *in folds* or *layers*, Arist. *HA*541ᵇ27.

**πτύω**, Il.23.697, etc.: fut. πτύσω [ῠ] Hp. *Prorrh.*2.40; πτύσομαι Id. *Morb.*1.28: aor. ἔπτῠσα ib.22, S. *Ant.*653, etc.: pf. ἔπτῠκα S.E. *M.*8.252, Gal.10.374, 11.281:—Pass., fut. πτυσθήσομαι (ἀνα-) Id.9.686, 15.700, (ἐμ-) *Ev.Luc.*18.32: aor. ἐπτύσθην Hp. *Morb.*1.28: aor. 2 part. πτυέντα Id. *Epid.*2.3.4. [ῡ in pres. and impf.; later Ep. have ῠ in impf. before a short syll., Nonn. *D.*10.171, but mostly in compds., (ἀνα-) A.R.2.570, (ἀπο-) 4.925, (ἐξ-) Theoc.24.19; ῠ always in aor.):—*spit out* or *up*, αἷμα Il. l.c., Hp. *Art.*49: abs., *spit*, Hdt.1.99, X. *Cyr.* 8.1.42: c. dat., πτύσας προσώπῳ *spat* in his face, S. *Ant.*1232. 2. of the sea, *disgorge, cast out*, με.. τηλόσ' ἀπὸ.. ᾐϊόνος *AP*7.283 (Leon.), cf. Opp. *H.*5.596: metaph., στοργὰν ἔπτυσας εἰς ἀνέμους *AP*7.468 (Mel.): abs., ἐπ' ἀϊόνι πτύοντα, of waves, Theoc.15.133; ἱστὸς ὅλισθεν εἰς ἅλα πτύσας *with a splash*, *AP*9.290 (Phil.). b. of fish, *spawn*, Babr.6.8. c. prov., πρὶν πτύσαι 'before you can say Jack Robinson', Men. *Pk.*202. 3. metaph., πτύσας *with loathing*, S. *Ant.*653; ἰδεῖν ῥᾴδιόν ἐστι καὶ πτύσαι Epicr.3.20. 4. εἰς κόλπον π., to avert a bad omen, disarm magic, etc., which was done three times, ὡς μὴ βασκανθῶ δὲ τρὶς εἰς ἐμὸν ἔπτυσα κόλπον Theoc.6.39, cf. 20.11; φρίξας εἰς κόλπον πτύσαι Thphr. *Char.*16.15, cf. Luc. *Nav.*15, etc.; ὑπὸ κόλπον π. *AP*12.229 (Strat.). **II.** *promote the flow of spittle*, of certain wines, in Pass., Hp. *Vict.*2.52. (Cf. Goth. *speiwan* 'spit', Lat. *spuo*, etc.)

**Πτωϊεύς**, έως, ὁ, = sq., *IG*7.2729 (Acraeph.), al.

**Πτώϊος**, contr. **Πτῷος**, ον, a name of Apollo from Mt. Ptoön in Boeotia, *IG*7.2712: τὰ Πτώϊα *the festival of Apollo* Πτώϊος, ib. 2170, al.

**πτωκάς**, άδος, ἡ, (πτώξ, πτώσσω) *timorous*, πτωκάσιν αἰθυίῃσι Hom. *Epigr.*8.2; π. κύπειρος *crouching, low*, Simm.12. **II.** pl. as Subst., *timorous ones*, i.e. *birds*, S. *Ph.*1093 (lyr., dub. l.).

❀ **πτῶμα**, ατος, τό, (πίπτω) *fall*, πεσεῖν.. πτώματ' οὐκ ἀνασχετὰ A. *Pr.* 919; πίπτουσι.. πτώματ' αἰσχρὰ S. *Ant.*1046; π. θανάσιμον πεσῇ E. *El.* 686; ἡ πόλις οὐκ ἂν ἔπεσε τοιοῦτον π. Pl. *La.*181b. b. *fall* in wrestling, Call. *Iamb.*1.274, *AP*9.391 (Diotim.): metaph., *booby-trap*, π. φιλοσόφων ἀπαλαιστρότατον Phld. *Rh.*1.88S.; *lapse, blunder*, Gal. 10.124. 2. metaph., *misfortune, calamity*, τά γ' ἐκ θεῶν πτώματα *calamities* sent by the gods, E. *HF*1228. 3. pl., *injuries due to falls, bruises*, Dsc.1.128, 3.1, 5.117. **II.** *fallen body, corpse, carcase*, freq. with gen., πτῶμα Ἑλένης, Ἐτεοκλέους, E. *Or.*1196, *Ph.*1697, cf. Lxx *Jd.*14.8, D.H.4.70, etc.; πτώματα νεκρῶν E. *Ph.*1482 (anap.): without a gen., A. *Supp.*662 (s. v. l., lyr.), Plb.15.14.2, *Sardis* 7 No. 165, Plu. *Alex.*33, etc.: collective in sg., *SIG*700.17 (Maced., ii B.C.), *Apoc.*11.8, Polyaen.6.18.1. 2. of buildings, *ruin*, οἰκίας, κρηνῖδος, *IG*11(2).161 A 120, 163 *Ba* 21 (Delos, iii B.C.); ἐπὶ τοῦ π. on the *ruins* (of the wall), Plb.16.31.8, cf. 5.4.9, 5.100.6, Aristid. *Or.*25(43).27; *breach* in a city-wall, D.S.16.8, al.: pl., *ruins*, *IG*11(2).199 *A* 103 (Delos, iii B.C.), Ph. *Bel.*100.45, Plb.21.28.2; π. οἴκων Phryn.351; π. ἐλαιῶν *fallen* olive-trees or fruit, Lys. *Fr.*203 S.; *windfall fruit*, of the φοῖνιξ, Dsc.1.109. **III.** *payment which falls due*, *PEleph.*11.4 (iii B.C., pl.), *PLond.*1.3.37 (ii B.C.).

**πτωμᾰτ-ίζω**, *make to fall*, Aq. *De.*25.2, al., *Tab.Defix.Aud.*16 (Syria, iii A.D.):—Pass., οἱ πτωματιζόμενοι *those who have the falling sickness, epileptics*, Apollon. *Mir.*36, Paul.Al. *L.*4. **II.** intr., *fall* or *be ready to fall*, *IG*2².463.47, Theano *Ep.*4.3. **-ικός**, ή, όν, *subject to epilepsy*, Vett.Val.113.1; -κά, τά, = πτωματισμοί, Procl. *Par.Ptol.* 215. **-ιον**, τό, Dim. of πτῶμα II, *corpse*, *CIG*2801 (Aphrodisias). **-ίς**, ίδος, ἡ, *tumbler*, i.e. cup that will not stand upright, and therefore must be emptied at once, Mosch.ap.Ath.11.485e. ❀ **-ισμός**, ὁ, *epilepsy*, Ptol. *Tetr.*153, *Cat.Cod.Astr.*2.179 (pl., but in both places perh. distinguished from epilepsy).

**πτώξ**, ὁ, gen. πτωκός, (πτώσσω) *cowering animal*, i.e. *hare*, Il.17.676, Thphr. *HP*4.3.5, Theoc.1.110; also πτῶκα λαγωόν Il.22.310, cf. Babr.102.10: metaph. of a person, A. *Eu.*326. **II.** as Adj., *cowering*, πτῶκα δ' ἐν κλόνῳ δορὸς Lyc.944.

**πτώσῐμος**, ον, (πίπτω) *having fallen, fallen*, στρατός A. *Ag.*639; σταγών ib.1122 (lyr.).

❀ **πτῶσις**, εως, ἡ, (πίπτω, πέ-πτωκα) *falling, fall*, κύβων Pl. *R.*604c, cf. Chrysipp. *Stoic.*2.282 (pl.); κεραυνῶν Arist. *Mete.*339ᵃ3, Plu.2.1005b (pl.); Φαέθοντος Plb.2.16.13: metaph., π. τῆς ψυχῆς, opp. ἔπαρσις, Zeno *Stoic.*1.51 (pl.): abs., *calamity*, ἐν καιρῷ πτώσεως Lxx *Si.*3.31, cf. *Ex.*30.12; πτώσεις ἀνθρώπων Orph. *Fr.*251, al.; *death*, Lyd. *Ost.*12, 14, 20. **II.** Gramm., *mode* or *modification* of a word, Arist. *Po.* 1457ᵃ18, al.; applied to cases, including nom., ib.20, *Int.*16ᵇ1: to genders, Id. *SE*173ᵇ27: to Sup. of Adjs., Id. *Top.*136ᵇ30: to Advbs., ib.15, *Rh.*1397ᵃ20: to Adjs. derived fr. nouns, e.g. χαλκοῦς, ib.1410ᵃ 32: to tenses (exc. the pres.), Id. *Int.*16ᵇ17: so by the Stoics to variety of flexion, *Stoic.*3.263, but most freq. to cases of the Noun, περὶ τῶν πέντε π., title of work by Chrysipp., cf. D.T.634.16, etc.; κατὰ μίαν πτῶσιν *indeclinable*, A.D. *Adv.*165.10. **III.** in the Logic of Arist., *mood* of syllogisms, *APr.*42ᵇ30. b. *arrangement of terms* in a syllogism, Id. *APo.*94ᵃ12.

**πτωσκάζω,** poet. for sq., *crouch* or *cower for fear,* Il.4.372.

**πτώσσω,** only pres., *shrink from, shrink,* of birds or other animals, π. ὥστε πέρδικα Archil.106; [ἀκρίδες] πτώσσουσι καθ' ὕδωρ *flee* into.., Il.21.14; also of men, πτῶσσον ὑπὸ κρημνούς ib.26; τί πτώσσεις; 4.371; τίς τοι ἀνάγκη πτώσσειν..; 5.634; πτώσσοντας ὑφ' Ἕκτορι 7.129; κατὰ λαύρας.. πτώσσοντι *skulk, slink,* Pi.*P.*8.87; εἰς ἐρημίαν π. *flee cowering* into.., E.*Ba.*223; π. ὑπ' ἀσπίδος *crouch* beneath it, without any notion of fear, Tyrt.11.36:—poet. Verb, once in Hdt., πτώσσοντας [ὑμέας εὕρομεν] 9.48. **2.** *cringe* like a beggar, *go begging* (cf. πτωχός), κατὰ δῆμον Od.17.227, 18.363: c. acc. loci, π. ἀλλοτρίους οἴκους Hes.*Op.*395. **II.** c. acc. pers., οὐδ' ἂν (v.l. ἄρ) ἔτι δὴν ἀλλήλους πτώσσοιμεν *we can* no longer *shirk* one another, Il.20.427; ποῖ καί με φυγᾷ πτώσσουσι μυχῶν; to what corners have they fled *to shun* me? E.*Hec.*1066 (lyr.): c. acc. rei, [ὄρνιθες] νέφεα πτώσσουσαι *shrinking from* the clouds, Od.22.304; π. δόρυ, βροντήν, Q.S.5.300, 7.531.

⊛ **πτωτικός,** ή, όν, (πτῶσις) *capable of inflexion,* ἄρθρον ἐστὶ στοιχεῖον λόγου π. Diog.Bab.*Stoic.*3.214; ὄνομά ἐστι μέρος λόγου π. D.T.634.11, cf. A.D.*Pron.*9.5, al.; τὸ π. τὸ "Σωκράτης" the *case-form* Σ., S.E.*M.*8.84; *connected with cases,* π. σχῆμα, when several cases of the same Noun follow one another, Simp.*in Cat.*359.9. Adv. -κῶς, ἀντωνυμίαι κάτωθεν μὲν π. κινοῦνται ἄνωθεν δὲ προσωπικῶς Choerob.*in Theod.*2.418H. **2.** Math., πτωτικόν, τό, *special case* of a problem, Papp.850.19, al.

**πτωτός,** ή, όν, *apt to fall, fallen,* Hdn.Gr.2.943, Hsch.

**πτωχ-ἄλαζών,** όνος, ὁ, *braggart beggar,* of Midias, Phryn.Com.4, cf. Ath.6.230c. **-εία,** Ion. **-ηΐη,** ἡ, *beggary, mendicity,* ἐς πτωχηΐην ἀπῖκται Hdt.3.14; εἰς ἐσχάτην π. ἐλθεῖν Pl.*Lg.*936b; εἰς π. καταστάντες Lys.32.10: pl., Pl.*R.*618a: prov., πτωχείας πενία ἀδελφή Ar.*Pl.*549. **II.** *poor relief, Cod.Just.*1.3.41.23. **-εῖον,** τό, *poorhouse,* ib.1.2.15.1 (pl.), Procop.*Aed.*5.9, *EM*187.22; written **πτωχῖον,** *MAMA*3.783; Lat. *ptochium, Cod.Just.*1.3.48.1. **-ελένη,** ἡ, *beggar-Helen,* i.e. *prostitute,* Ath.13.585b. **-εύω,** fut. -σω Od.15.309: Ep. impf. πτωχεύεσκον 18.2:—*to be a beggar, go begging,* ll.cc.; ἀνὰ δῆμον 19.73, cf. Tyrt.10.4, Ar.*Nu.*921 (anap.), etc.; ἐπὶ ξενίας Antipho 2.2.9. **2.** *to be as poor as a beggar,* Antiph.322, Pl.*Erx.*394b. **3.** metaph. c. gen., *to be badly off for,* πραγμάτων, of historians, Plb.7.7.6. **II.** trans., *beg (for),* δαῖτα Od.17.11, 19. **2.** c. acc. pers., *ask an alms of,* φίλους Thgn.922. **-ηΐη,** v. πτωχεία. **-ίζω,** *make poor,* Κύριος πτωχίζει καὶ πλουτίζει Lxx 1*Ki.*2.7. **-ικός,** ή, όν, *of* or *fit for a beggar, beggarly,* στολή E.*Rh.*503, Lycurg.86; ἐπιθυμίαι Pl.*R.*554c; π. βακτήριον a *beggar's* staff, Ar.*Ach.*448; ὀνόματα π. *fit for beggars,* Luc.*Hist.Conscr.*22. **-ίστερος,** v. πτωχός.

**πτωχό-μουσος,** ον, *living* (or rather *starving*) *by his wits,* κόλαξ Gorg.*Fr.*15 (πτωχομουσοκόλακας cj. Vahlen). **-ποιός,** όν, *drawing beggarly characters,* of a poet, Ar.*Ra.*842. **2.** *making poor,* δικαιοσύνη Plu.*Comp.Arist.Cat.*3.

⊛ **πτωχός,** ή, όν, also ός, όν A.*Ag.*1274, S.*OC*444,751:—*beggar,* Od.14.400, 18.1, Hdt.3.14, etc.; πρὸς γὰρ Διός εἰσιν ἅπαντες ξεῖνοί τε πτωχοί τε Od.6.208, cf. 17.475; πτωχὸς πτωχῷ φθονέει Hes.*Op.*26; π. ἀνὴρ ἀλαλήμενος ἐλθών Od.21.327; π. καὶ ἀλήμονες ἄνδρες 19.74; πτωχοὺς ἀλᾶσθαι E.*Med.*515; πτωχοῦ βίος ζῆν ἐστιν μηδὲν ἔχοντα, τοῦ δὲ πένητος ζῆν φειδόμενον Ar.*Pl.*552: prov., πτωχοῦ πήρη οὐ πίμπλαται Call.*Fr.*360: πτωχή *beggar-woman,* Ath.10.453a (so πτωχός (fem.), S.*OC*444); χήρα πτωχή *Ev.Marc.*12.42. **2.** metaph., οἱ π. τῷ πνεύματι *Ev.Matt.*5.3, cf. *Ev.Luc.*6.20. **II.** as Adj., *beggarly,* πτωχῷ διαίτῃ S.*OC*751; π. στοιχεῖα *Ep.Gal.*4.9: c. gen., *beggared of, poor in,* [πηγή] π. νυμφῶν *AP*9.258 (Antiphan.). **2.** Comp. πτωχότερος Timocl.6.10; prov., π. κίγκλου 'as poor as a church mouse', Men.221; irreg. πτωχίστερος Ar.*Ach.*425: Sup. πτωχότατος *AP*10.50 (Pall.). **3.** Adv. -χῶς *poorly, scantily,* ἠροτρία π. μέν, ἀλλ' ἀναγκαίως Babr.55.2.

**πτωχότης,** ητος, ἡ, *poverty,* dub. in *Ostr.Strassb.*794.

**πτωχοτροφ-εῖον,** τό, *poorhouse, Cod.Just.*1.2.19, 7.37.3.3 (as Lat. word), Suid. **-ος** (parox.), ον, *supporting the poor, Cod.Just.*1.3.41.13, Just.*Nov.*120.6.2.

⊛ **πτωχοφᾰνής,** ές, *like a beggar,* Thd.*Pr.*13.7.

**πυᾰλίς, πύᾰλος,** v. πυελ-.

**πυᾰλίτης** [ῑ], ου, ὁ, *a throw of the dice,* Eub.57.4.

**πῠάνιον** [ᾰ], τό, Dim. of πύανος, *mixture of various kinds of pulse,* cooked sweet, Sosib.ap.Ath.14.648b.

**πῠάνιος,** ον, *made of beans,* πόλτος Alcm.75 (otherwise expld. by Sosib., v. foreg.).

⊛ **πύᾰνος** [ῠ], ὁ, = ὀλόπυρος, Heliod.Hist.3, cf. Poll.6.61; but Lacon. **πούανοι,** = κύαμοι ἑφθοί, Hsch.; neut. pl. **πύανα,** Hp.*Mul.*2.113 (one cod.); cf. sq.

**Πῠᾰνόψια** (sc. ἱερά), τά, an Athenian festival in the month Πυανοψιών, in honour of Apollo, Lycurg.*Fr.*84: elsewh. written **Πυανέψια** (cf. sq.) and expld. fr. πύανον ἕψειν, of a dish of beans cooked and offered, Plu.*Thes.*22, Ath.10.408a, etc.; acc. to Lycurg. l.c. the other Greeks called it **Πανόψια** (**Πανοψίαν** codd.).

**Πῠᾰνοψιών,** ῶνος, ὁ, the fourth month of the Att. year, named from the festival Πυανόψια, corresponding to the latter part of October and former of November, *IG*1$^{2}$.6.64, 2$^{2}$.1014.4, etc.; also at Priene, Miletus, etc., *SIG*282.19 (iv B.C.), 588.90 (ii B.C.), etc.: freq. written **Πυανεψιών,** Thphr.*HP*4.2.10, etc.; but not in Att. Inscrr. (exc. **Ποιανεψιών** *IG*2$^{2}$.2239.82 (iii A.D.)); cf. **Κυανοψιών.**

**πῦαρ,** gen. and dat. not found, τό, = πυός, *first milk after calving, beestings,* Ael.Dion.*Fr.*290 (where πύαρ), Hsch. (where πύας (sic) is glossed πιτύα (leg. πυτία)).

**πυαρίτης,** f.l. for πυριάτη, Eust.1626.5.

⊛ **πύας,** v. πόα.

**πῡγ-αῖος,** α, ον, (πυγή) *of* or *on the rump*: **I.** τὸ π., = ἡ πυγή, Hp.*Art.*57,78, Arist.*HA*620$^{a}$15: pl., Archipp.41 (s.v.l.), Sor.1.102, Dsc.*Eup.*2.56, Hsch., Phot.; τὸ π. ἄκρον, of a bird, Hdt.2.76. **II.** πυγαῖα, τά, in Architecture, = σπεῖρα, *base of a column,* Hsch. **III.** = κατάπυγος, Suid. **IV.** v. πυγλίον. **-αλγίας,** ὁ, *suffering pain in the buttocks,* Democles Pygelensis (?) ap.Str.14.1.20 (Lobeck; πυγαλίας codd., -αλγής Schneid.). **-αργος,** ὁ, *white-rump,* name of a kind of antelope, Hdt.4.192, Lxx *De.*14.5, Ael.*NA*7.19. **II.** a kind of *eagle,* perh. *Circus cyaneus,* Arist.*HA*618$^{b}$19; opp. ὁ μελάμπυγος, Archil.189, cf. Lyc.91 (et ibi Sch.): metaph. of a coward, S.*Fr.*1085. **III.** a water-bird, perh. *dipper, Cinclus aquaticus,* Arist.*HA*593$^{b}$5.

***πῡγᾰρίζω,** v. πυδαρίζω.

**πῡγ-εών,** ῶνος, ὁ, dub. sens. in Hippon. in *PSI*9.1089.2. **-ή,** ῆς, ἡ, heterocl. acc. πῦγα Arist.*Phgn.*810$^{b}$1 (τὸ πυγή is a barbarism in Ar.*Th.*1187):—*rump, buttocks,* Archil.91, Ar.*Eq.*365, Sor.2.60, etc.; pl., Luc.*Peregr.*17; ποτὶ πυγὰν ἅλλεσθαι to kick up the heels so as to strike *the buttock* in dancing, *dance the fling,* a girls' exercise at Sparta, Ar.*Lys.*82, cf. Antyll.ap.Orib.6.31.2; πρὸς π. πηδῆσαι Hp.*Nat.Puer.*13 (cited as πρὸς πυγὰς πηδᾶν by Sor.1.60). **2.** metaph. of *fat, swelling land,* Eust.310.2. **II.** = οὐρά, *EM*513.14. **-ηδόν,** Adv. *tail foremost,* ὑποχωρεῖν πάλιν π., of certain oxen, Arist.*PA*659$^{a}$20 (nisi leg. παλιμπ.). **II.** *rump to rump,* Id.*HA*539$^{b}$22. **-ίδιον,** τό, Dim. of πυγή, Ar.*Ach.*638, *Eq.*1368. ⊛ **-ίζω,** *paedico,* Id.*Th.*1120, Theoc.5.41: 3 pl. impf. ἐπυγίζοσαν *Sammelb.*6840 (Karnak, ii B.C.): pf. πεπύγικα *AP*9.317:—Pass., *Sammelb.*7452.9. **-ισμα,** ατος, τό, *paedicatio,* Theoc.5.43. **-ιστί,** Adv., dub. sens. in Hippon. in *PSI*9.1089.2.

**πυγλίον** or **πυγαῖον,** τό, dub. sens., part of an ἀκινάκης, different from λαβή and κολεόν, *IG*2$^{2}$.1421.30, 1425.77, 1424a.80.

**Πυγμαιομάχος** [ᾰ], ον, *fighting with pygmies,* Hecat.328 J.

**πυγμαῖος,** α, ον, (πυγμή II) *a* πυγμή *long* or *tall.* ἀκρόθινα π. κολοσσῷ ἐφαρμόζων Philostr.*VS*1.19.2. **2.** of men, *dwarfish,* Hdt.3.37, Arist.*Pr.*892$^{a}$12, Phld.*Sign.*2. **II.** pr. n. Πυγμαῖοι, οἱ, the *Pygmies,* a fabulous race of dwarfs on the upper Nile, said to have been warred on and destroyed by cranes, Il.3.6, Arist.*HA*597$^{a}$6, cf. Hdt. l.c.

**πυγμᾰχ-έω,** *practise boxing, be a boxer,* Hexam.ap.Hdt.5.60, A.R.2.783. **-ία,** Ep. **-ίη,** ἡ, *boxing,* Il.23.653,665, Pi.*O.*11(10).12, etc.: pl., Pratin.Lyr.1.8, Opp.*C.*2.20. ⊛ **-ος,** ὁ, *one who fights with the fist, boxer,* Od.8.246, Pi.*I.*8(7).68, Luc.*JTr.*33.

**πυγμ-ή,** ἡ, (πύξ) *fist,* Hp.*Art.*71, E.*IT*1368; τῇ π. θενών Ar.*V.*1384; πυγμῇ πατάξαι Lxx *Ex.*21.18, cf. *Is.*58.4. **2.** *boxing,* as an athletic contest, πυγμῇ νικήσαντα Il.23.669; πυγμὴν νικᾶν E.*Alc.*1031; ἄνδρας πυγμὰν ἐνίκα Ὀλύμπια *AP*6.256 (Antip.); πυγμᾶς ἄποινα Pi.*O.*7.16, cf. 10(11).67; πυγμὴν or τὴν π. ἀσκεῖν, Pl.*Lg.*795b, D.61.24; freq. in Inscrr., e.g. πυγμὴν Ζωΐλος (sc. ἐνίκησε) *IG*7.1765 (Thespiae), etc. **b.** generally, *fight,* π. μονομάχων καὶ θηρίων Edict.Caes.ap.J.*AJ*14.10.6, cf. Artem.5.58; εἰς π. καθίστασθαι, τρέπεσθαι, of partridges, *Gp.*14.20.1,2. **3.** in *Ev.Marc.*7.3, πυγμῇ νίψασθαι is interpr. *diligently* (v.l. πυκνά, *often*). **II.** a measure of length, *the distance from the elbow to the knuckles,* = 18 δάκτυλοι, Thphr.*HP*9.11.5, Poll.2.147,158. **-ικός,** ή, όν, *of* or *for boxing, An.Ox.*3.223.

**πυγμομᾰχία,** ἡ, f.l. for πυγμαχία, *EM*695.55.

**πῡγολαμπίς,** ίδος, ἡ, (πυγή) *fire-tail,* i.e. *glow-worm, Lampyris noctiluca,* Arist.*HA*523$^{b}$21 (v.l. πτερόποδες), 551$^{b}$24 (v.l. πυρολαμπίδες); cf. πυριλαμπίς.

**πῡγονιαῖος,** α, ον, *a* πυγών *long,* Hp.*Morb.*2.33, Thphr.*HP*3.17.6 (-γων- codd.), Menesth.ap.Ath.11.494b.

**πῡγό-ριζα,** ἡ, *short, stumpy root,* Hsch. **-σκελίς,** ίδος, ὁ, waterbird *with legs set far back,* like the grebe or puffin, Id. **-στόλος,** ον, epith. of a woman, *decorating the* πυγή, with collat. notion of *lewd,* Hes.*Op.*373.

**πῡγούσιος,** α, ον, poet. for πυγονιαῖος, *of the length of a* πυγών, Od.10.517, 11.25, Arat.896.

**πῡγών,** όνος, ἡ, *the distance from the elbow to the first joint of the fingers,* = 20 δάκτυλοι or 5 παλαισταί, Hdt.2.175, X.*Cyn.*10.2, Archestr.*Fr.*29, Hero *Geom.*4.10.

**πῡγωνιαῖος,** α, ον, v. πυγονιαῖος.

**πῡδᾰρίζω** (**πυδαλ-** Suid.), *dance the fling,* ὄνον ἐπάραντα τὰ σκέλη πυδαρίζειν *App.Prov.*4.25: hence **ἀποπῡδᾰρίζειν** μόθωνα *kick up* (i.e. dance) *a* μόθων, Ar.*Eq.*697: **διαπῡδᾰρίζει** (-πονδ- cod.), = διαναβάλλεται, διαναρρίπτεται, *Com.Adesp.*977. (Falsely expld. as Aeol. for *ποδαρίζω (from πούς) or from *πυγαρίζω (from πυγή) by Irenaeus ap. *EM*696.2 = Sch.Ar. l.c.): hence **πῡδᾰρισμός,** ὁ, = δυσχέρεια, Zonar.

⊛ **πῠέλ-ιον,** τό, Dim. of πύελος: prov., ἀστραπὴ ἐκ πυελίου 'when pigs begin to fly', Diogenian.3.7. ⊛ **-ίς,** ίδος, ἡ, in a seal-ring, *setting, socket of the stone,* Ar.*Fr.*315, Lys.*Fr.*106S. **2.** *bearing* or *axlebox,* Hero *Aut.*5.3, Apollod.*Poliorc.*148.8. **3.** *eye-socket,* Ruf.*Anat.*9 (sg.), *Oss.*4 (pl.). **4.** *cup* of the flowers of τιθύμαλλος, Dsc.4.164. **II.** (mostly in form πυαλίς), *sarcophagus,* dat. πυαλίδι *TAM*2(1).249 (Lycia): acc. πυαλεῖδα *IGRom.*4.1285 (Thyatira): but πυελεῖδα *TAM*2(1).342 (Lycia). **2.** (πυαλίς), *reservoir, basin, IG*4.823.9,43 (Troezen). ⊛ **-ος** (so Phld.*Mort.*33) or **πύᾰλος,** ἡ, *trough,* for feeding animals, Od.19.553. **2.** *bathing-tub,* Hp.

Acut.65, Ar.Eq.1060, Pax 843, Th.562, Crates Com.15.5, Eup.256, PEnteux.83 (iii B.C.). 3. vat, kitchen-boiler, Ar.V.141. 4. sarcophagus, Thphr.Lap.6, Arr.An.6.29.9, CIG3785, al. (Nicomedia), 4164 (Sinope); πύαλος, ib.2050 (Philippopolis), 3777 (Nicomedia), IGRom.1.624 (Tomi), Supp.Epigr.4.106 (Rome, ii A.D.). 5. = πυελίς 1.1, Poll.7.179. 6. infundibulum of the brain, Gal.2.709, UP8.3, 9.3. 7. a surgical instrument, Hermes 38.283. [ῡ Od. l.c., perh. metri gr., ῠ Att.] -ώδης, ες, like a trough, hollow, Arist.HA 547$^{b}$27.

**πῡετία**, Ion. -ίη, ἡ, also **πῡτία** (q.v.), curdled milk obtained from an animal's stomach, containing (and used as) rennet, Arist.HA522$^{b}$5, PA676$^{a}$6, GA739$^{b}$22, Nic.Al.68,323.

**πύη** [ῠ], ἡ, = φθίσις, prob. f.l. for φθόη in Aret.SD1.8.

**πυήρ**· ἀναπεπλησμένον, Hsch.; **πυηρόν**· ἀναπεπλασμένον, Theognost.Can.23.

**πύ-ησις** [ῠ], εως, ἡ, suppuration, ἣν ἐς π. τρέπηται Aret.CA1.7. -ητικός, ή, όν, of suppuration, δύναμις Gal.10.887.

**Πῡθᾰγόρ-ας**, ου, Ion. -ης, εω, ὁ, Pythagoras, Hdt.4.95, etc. ⊕ -ειος, ον (Str.6.3.4), of P. or Pythagorean, Pl.R.530d, Arist.Metaph.985$^{b}$23. -ίζω, to be a disciple of Pythagoras, Antiph.226.8, Alex.220.1. ⊕ -ικός, ή, όν, = Πυθαγόρειος, μῦθοι Arist. de An.407$^{b}$22; βαθύτης Hierocl. in CA26 p.480 M.; τὰ Π., title of work by Zeno the Stoic, D.L.7.4. Adv. -κῶς in the Pythagorean manner, Plu.2.728e, Iamb.Comm.Math.22: Comp. -κώτερον S.E.M.4.11, Iamb.Protr.21.ιη'. -ισμός, ὁ, Pythagorean doctrines, Alex.220.7 (pl.). -ιστής, οῦ (Dor. -ικτάς, ᾶ, Theoc.14.5), ὁ, follower of Pythagoras, Antiph.160; title of play by Aristopho, Ath.4.161e: applied only to exoteric followers, acc. to Iamb.VP18.80: fem. -ίδες γυναῖκες ib.36.267.

⊕ **Πῡθᾰ-εύς**, έως, ὁ, epith. of Apollo at Lindus, IG12(1).820,834; also at Corinth, Sparta, etc., Paus.2.35.2, 3.10.8, etc.: hence -εῖα, and **Πυθαῆα**, τά, his festival at Sparta and Megara, IG5(1).659, 7.48. ⊕ -ίζω, consult his oracle, Eust.274.16.

**Πῡθαῖος**, ὁ, epith. of Apollo, τὸ ἱερὸν (at Chalcedon) τοῦ Ἀπόλλωνος τοῦ Π. SIG550.4 (Delph., iii B.C.), cf. St.Byz. s.v. Πυθώ; also ῥόος Π. IG9(1).699.

**Πῡθα-ΐς**, ΐδος, ἡ, sacred mission or θεωρία sent to Delphi, Is.7.27, SIG696 A 6 (Delph., ii B.C.), prob. ib.296 (iv B.C.). ⊕ -ϊστής, οῦ, ὁ, member of such a mission, ib.696 B 19 (ii B.C.), Str.9.2.11; also as Adj., Πυθαϊστὴς χορός Call.Iamb.1.229.

**Πῡθαύλης**, ου, Dor. -ας, α, ὁ, = ὁ τὰ Πύθια αὐλῶν, one who plays the νόμος expressing the battle between Apollo and the Python, IG5(1).758 (Sparta), 7.1773.18 (Thespiae), 14.737 (Naples), Seneca Ep.76.4, Diom. p.492 K.

**πῡθεδών**, όνος, ἡ, (πύθω) putrefaction, Eratosth.18 (pl.), Nic.Th.466 (pl.).

**πῡθεῖον**, τό, = μαντεῖον, Zonar.

⊕ **Πῡθία** (sc. ἱέρεια), Ion. **Πυθίη** Hdt.1.13, al., Call.Iamb.1.222: ἡ:—Pythia, priestess of Pythian Apollo at Delphi, who uttered the responses of the oracle, Hdt. l.c., etc.; cf. προφήτης. II. Πυθίη, epith. of Artemis at Branchidae, CIG2866, 2885.

⊕ **Πύθια** (sc. ἱερά), τά, the Pythian games, celebrated at Delphi in honour of Pythian Apollo, ἐν Πυθίοισι νικᾶν Pi.N.2.9; Π. ἀνελόμενος Hdt.6.122; ἐνίκα τὰ Π. τῷ τεθρίππῳ D.59.33: also of festivals elsewhere, IG3.129, etc.

**πῡθιάζω**, to be inspired by Apollo, prophesy, St.Byz. s.v. Πυθώ.

**Πῡθιακός**, ή, όν, of the Pythian games, περίοδοι Gal.7.476.

**Πῡθιάς**, άδος, pecul. fem. of Πύθιος, Π. βοά a song to Apollo, S.Fr.490; νίκη Pl.Lg.807c. II. as Subst., 1. (sc. ἱέρεια), = Πυθία, the Pythian priestess, Plu.2.295d; Π. προφῆτις, one of the dramatis personae in A.Eu. 2. (sc. ἑορτή), the celebration of the Pythian games, Pi.P.1.32, 5.21, IG14.747 (Naples); ἁ Πυθιὰς ἁ ἱαρά, ἁ ἱερομηνία ἁ Πυθιάς, ib.2$^{2}$.1126.38,44. 3. (sc. νίκη), Pythian victory, ἐνίκησε.. Πυθιάδας ἓξ Paus.6.14.10, cf. 10.7.4. 4. (sc. πομπή), sacred mission from Athens to Delphi, Ephor.31 J., dub. in SIG296 (Delph., iv B.C.): leg. Πυθαΐς. 5. (sc. ὁδός), sacred way from Delphi to Tempe, Ael.VH3.1.

⊕ **Πῡθιασταί**, οἱ, = Πυθαϊσταί, Hsch. s.v. ἀστραπὴ δι' Ἅρματος.

⊕ **Πῡθικός**, ή, όν, of or for Pytho, Pythian, χρηστήρια, ἑστία, A.Th.747 (lyr.), E.Andr.1067; μαντεῖον S.El.32, Th.2.17; ἆθλα S.El.49; δάφνη Ar.Pl.213; τὸ Π. (sc. χρηστήριον) Id.Eq.220; Π. αὐλητής, κιθαριστής, IG7.1776 (Thespiae); νικήσαντα παίδων Πυθικῶν πάλην IGRom.4.244 (Alexandria Troas), cf. 1064.7 (Cos), Supp.Epigr.3.335.7, al. (Thespiae, ii A.D.). II. Πυθικόν, τό, name of a work on tooth- and mouth-washes by Democrates, Gal.12.889.

⊕ **Πύθιον** [ῠ], τό, temple of the Pythian Apollo at Athens, IG1$^{2}$.188.64, Th.2.15, Str.9.2.11, Paus.9.35.7; at Poeessa, IG12(5).1100 (v/iv B.C.).

⊕ **Πῡθιο-νίκης** [ῑ], ου, Dor. -ας, α, ὁ, conqueror in the Pythian games, Pi.P.9.1, Hdt.8.47, PLond.3.1178.67 (ii A.D.), Hld.5.19:—fem. -νίκη, ἡ, pr. n. of a ἑταίρα, afterwards deified as Π. Ἀφροδίτη, Python 1.8, Antiph.26.20, Timocl.17, Philem.16, Theopomp.Hist.244,245, Paus.1.37.2; called **Πυθονίκη** in D.S.17.108, Plu.Phoc.22 (so, of another woman, IG3.3823). II. Πυθιονίκη = Pythian victory, Hld.5.19. -νῖκος, ον, of or belonging to a Pythian victory, Pi.P.6.5, etc.

⊕ **Πύθιος** [ῠ; ῑ metri gr. in h.Ap.373], α, ον, (Πυθώ) Pythian, i.e. Delphian, epith. of Apollo, l.c., Pi.O.14.11, etc. (Π. alone is f.l. in E. Ion 285); ἐν Πυθίου in his temple, Th.6.54 (citing Πυθίου ἐν τεμένει from IG1$^{2}$.761), IG2$^{2}$.17.10, prob. in Pl.Grg.472b; also οἱ Πύθιοι, αἱ Πύθιαι, the gods and goddesses worshipped at Pytho or Delphi, Ar.Th.332, cf. IG14.2436 (Massilia). 2. = Πυθικός, ἆεθλα, στέφανοι, μαντεύματα, Pi.P.3.73, 10.26, I.7(6).15; ἀκταί S.OC1047 (lyr.); ἀστραπαί E.Ion 285; κύκνος Ar.Av.870. II. οἱ Πύθιοι, at Sparta, four persons whose office it was to consult the Delphic oracle on affairs of state, Hdt.6.57, X.Lac.15.5, etc.; cf. Πυθία, Πύθια, Πύθιον.

**πυθμεν-έω**, (πυθμήν III) of a number, to be a base of a series, prob. in Iamb. in Nic. p.117 P. (-μένειν codd.). -ικός, ή, όν, basic, first in a series (cf. πυθμήν III), ὁ δύο ῥίζα τῆς π. τοῦ μείζονος σχέσεως Theol.Ar.13; π. ὅροι Iamb. in Nic. p.49 P., al.; of the τριάς, Adam.Vent.46: Comp., Nicom.Ar.2.2: Sup., Theol.Ar.11. Adv. -κῶς ib.34. -ιον, τό, Dim. of πυθμήν, BGU781 ii 15 (i A.D.), Gp.4.4, Hsch. s.v. πτερνίς. -όθεν, Adv. from the foundation, π. οὐκ ἴσασιν not at all, Hp.Acut.40, cf. Erot.

⊕ **πυθμήν**, ένος, ὁ, bottom, of a cup or jar, δειλὴ δ' ἐνὶ πυθμένι φειδώ Hes.Op.369 (so prov. ἐν τῷ πυθμένι τοῦ πίθου Lib.Ep.127.2); τὼ δὲ πίθω πατάγεσκ' ὁ πύθμην Alc.Supp.25.9, cf. Arist.Pr.936$^{a}$32, Sor.1.91; distd. from πύνδαξ, Arist.Pr.938$^{a}$14; φιάλη.. ἡ ἐπὶ τὸν π. καὶ τὸ στόμα τιθεμένη Asclep.Myrl.ap.Ath.11.501d, cf. Apollod. ib. a; this sense is doubtful in Il.11.635 (cf. infr. 4 and Ath.11.488f), and in IG1$^{2}$.282.111, 11(2).161 B 120, 287 B 89,131,143 (Delos, iii B.C.); ἐν τῷ π. ἐπιγραφὴν ἔχουσα Inscr.Délos 313 a 102, cf. 320 B 45, al. (iii B.C.). 2. generally, base, foundation, χθόνα ἐκ πυθμένων κραδαίνειν A.Pr.1046 (anap.); π. γαίης, πέτρης, Orph.A.92, L.162; foot of a mountain, Arat.989. 3. of the sea, bottom, depth, π. θαλάσσης, πόντου, λίμνης, Hes.Th.932, Sol.13.20, Thgn.1035; τοῦ πελάγους Pl.Phd.109c, cf. 112b; also Ταρτάρου, abyss, Pi.Fr.207. 4. support under a cup's handle, δύω δ' ὑπὸ πυθμένες ἦσαν Il.11.635 (cf. supr. 1); legs of a tripod, 18.375. 5. pl., sockets, ἐκ πυθμένων ἔκλινε κλῇθρα S.OT1261. 6. in Anatomy, fundus of univalves, Arist.HA529$^{a}$6, PA680$^{a}$23; lower parts of the testes, Ruf.Onom.105 (but, upper part of the uterus, Sor.1.7, Gal.2.889); also γενειάδος π. A.Fr.27; distal end of a quince, Aët.1.111. 7. metaph., Δίκας ἐρείδεται π. the base of Justice is firmly set, A.Ch.646 (lyr.); π. κακῶν Orph.A.893; πυθμένες λόγων fundamental principles, Protag.ap.D.L.9.54; Ζεὺς π. γαίης τε καὶ οὐρανοῦ Orph.Fr.168.4. II. stock, root of a tree, παρὰ πυθμέν' ἐλαίης Od.13.122,372, cf. 23.204; ἐν π. φηγοῦ Hes.Fr.134.8; π. δρυὸς Ion Trag.28; ὁ π. τῆς ῥίζης Dsc.4.104, cf. 3.126; σεύτλον πυθμένες beet-roots, BGU1118.17 (i B.C.); ἀλικακκάβων π. ib.1120.37 (i B.C.); ἀμπέλου Str.2.1.14, cf. PPetr.1 p.78 (iii B.C.); ἐπὶ τοῦ αὐτοῦ π. Thphr.HP2.2.9, cf. CP3.13.3: metaph., ἐκ νεάτου π. ἐς κορυφήν Sol.13.10. 2. stem, stalk, πυροῦ, κριθῶν, Arist.GA728$^{b}$36, D.S.1.14; σύκων Poll.2.170; τυτθὸν.. ἐν χθονὶ πυθμένα τείνει Nic.Th.639. b. metaph., stem, stock of a family, A.Ch.260, Supp.106 (lyr.); σμικροῦ γένοιτ' ἂν σπέρματος μέγας π., i.e. great things might come from small, Id.Ch.204; πυθμένες θάλλουσιν ἐσθλῶν B.5.198; π. δικῶν, of a litigious person, Com.Adesp.896. III. in Arithmetic, base of a series, i.e. lowest number possessing a given property, π. ὁ δέκα (of the numbers such that the previous integers contain an equal number of primes and non-primes) Speus. ap. Theol.Ar.62; ἐπίτριτος π. the first couple of numbers giving the ratio 4:3, Pl.R.546c, cf. Nicom.Ar.1.21, 2.19. [ῠ in A. ll.cc.; ῡ by position in Ep., etc.] (Cf. Skt. budhnás 'bottom, base', Lat. fundus, OE. botm.)

**Πῡθόθεν**, Adv., (Πυθώ) from Pytho or Delphi, St.Byz.

**Πῡθοῖ**, Adv., (Πυθώ) at Pytho or Delphi, Pi.O.7.10, P.11.49, Simon.153, E.Fr.923, Ar.Lys.1131, Th.5.18, Pl.Ly.205c, etc. 2. to Pytho or Delphi, Πυθοῖ καὶ Ὀλυμπίαζε Plu.Demetr.11.—The trisyll. form Πυθόϊ is cited by Choerob. in Theod.1.310 H. from Pi., cf. I.7(6).51.

**Πῡθοῖδε**, = Πυθώδε, Hes.Sc.480, Aristocl.ap.Eus.PE14.18.

**Πῡθοῖος**, ὁ (sc. μήν), name of month at Halos, IG9(2).109 a 13.

**Πῡθό-κραντος**, ον, (κραίνω) confirmed by the Pythian god: τὰ Π. the Pythian oracles, A.Ag.1255. -κτόνος, ον, slaying the serpent Python, Orph.H.34.4.

**Πῡθολέτης**, ου, ὁ, dragon-slayer, epith. of Apollo, PMag.Lond.47.32.

**Πῡθό-ληπτος**, ον, seized with Pythian frenzy, Hsch., Phot. -μαντις, εως, ὁ, ἡ, the Pythian prophet, Π. Λοξίας A.Ch.1030. II. Π. ἑστία the prophetic seat at Pytho, S.OT965. -νίκη, v. Πυθιονίκη. ⊕ -νῖκος, ον, = Πυθιόνικος, Pi.P.11.43. -χρήστης, ου, Dor. -τας, ὁ, (χράω) sent by the Pythian oracle, φυγάς A.Ch.940 (lyr., sed leg. -τος). ⊕ -χρηστος, ον, (χράω) delivered by the Pythian god, μαντεύματα ib.901; νόμοι X.Lac.8.5; Πυθόχρηστον ἔσχον c. inf., Phld.Mus. p.85 K.; μαντεῖον Arist.Pol.1331$^{a}$27; κατὰ Πυθόχρηστον Arg.S.OC. II. declared or appointed by the Pythian oracle, ὁ Π. Λοξίου νεανίας E.Ion1218; ἀποικίας ἡγεμὼν Plu.2.163b; ἐξηγητὴς SIG697 E 9 (Delph., ii B.C.), IG3.241, Tim.Lex. s.v. ἐξηγηταί; θυσία Clitodem.14. 2. epith. of Aphrodite, SIG1014.74,160; of Dionysus, ib.145; of Kore, ib.90 (Erythrae, iii B.C.).

**πύθω** [ῡ], Ep. impf. πύθεσκον A.R.4.1530: fut. πύσω Il.4.174: aor. ἔπῡσα (κατ-) h.Ap.371, Ep. πῦσα ib.374 (but πύσε [ῠ] Call.Fr.313):—Pass., only used in pres. and impf.:—cause to rot, σέο δ' ὀστέα πύσει ἄρουρα Il.4.174; σέ γ' αὐτοῦ πύσει γαῖα h.Ap.369; αὐτοῦ πῦσε πέλωρ μένος Ἠελίοιο ib.374, cf. Hes.Op.626:—Pass., become rotten, decay, moulder, ὁ δέ θ' αἵματι γαῖαν ἐρεύθων πύθεται Il.11.395; ὀστέα π. ὄμβρῳ Od.1.161, cf. Hes.Sc.153; ὀστεόφιν θὶς ἀνδρῶν πυθομένων Od.12.46; πυθομένοισιν ἐφ' ἕλκεσι A.R.4.1405; ἐπύθετό μοι ὁ ὀφθαλμός *PSI*4.299.5 (iii A.D.). (Cf. Skt. *pū́yati* 'putrefy', Lat. *pūs*, etc.)

**Πῡθώ**, gen. οῦς, dat. οῖ, ἡ, *Pytho*, the region in which lay the city of Delphi, Πυθοῖ ἔνι πετρηέσσῃ Il.9.405; Π. ἐν ἠγαθέῃ Od.8.80, Hes. *Th.*499, etc.; of Delphi itself, Pi.*P.*4.66, 10.4, Hdt.1.54, etc. (Acc. to the legend, derived from the *rotting* of the serpent, *h.Ap.*372.)

✻ **Πῡθώδε** (better **Πυθὼ δέ**, cf. A.D.*Pron.*87.30), Adv., (Πυθώ) *to Pytho*, Od.11.581, S.*OT*603,788, Ar.*Av.*189, *SIG*56.9 (Argos, v B.C.), Pl.*Lg.*950e.

✻ **Πῡθῶθεν**, Adv., (Πυθώ) *from Pytho*, Pi.*I.*1.65, St.Byz.

**Πύθων** [ῠ], ωνος, ὁ, (cf. Πυθώ) the serpent *Python*, slain by Apollo, Ephor.31(b) J., Apollod.1.4.1, Plu.2.293c. **II.** παιδίσκη ἔχουσα πνεῦμα Πύθωνα a spirit *of divination*, *Act.Ap.*16.16. **2.** pl. Πύθωνες, *ventriloquists*, Plu.2.414e, cf. Hsch.

**Πῡθών**, ῶνος, ἡ, = Πυθώ, Il.2.519, *h.Merc.*178, Simon.125, Pi.*O.*6.48, S.*OT*152 (lyr.), Ar.*Ra.*659, al.

**Πῡθωνάδε**, Adv. = Πυθώδε, Pi.*O.*9.12.

**πυθώνιον**, τό, = ὑοσκύαμος, Ps.-Dsc.4.68; = *dracontea*, *symphoniaca*, *Gloss.*

**Πῡθωνόθεν**, Adv. = Πυθῶθεν, Tyrt.4.1, Pi.*P.*5.105.

**Πῡθῷος**, α, ον, = Πύθιος, St.Byz.

**πύϊον**· τὸ γάλα, Hsch.; cf. πυός.

**πύκᾰ** [ῠ], poet. Adv., v. πυκνός B. III.

**πυκάεις**, v. πευκήεις II.

**πῠκ-άζω**, Od.12.225, Dor. **πυκάσδω** Theoc.3.14: impf. ἐπύκαζον Id.20.22: Ep. aor. inf. πυκάσαι Od.11.320; part. πυκάσσας Hes.*Op.*542; ind. ἐπύκασσα Sapph.89:—**Med.**, Cratin.98.7, etc.: Ep. fut. πυκάσσομαι Max.513: aor. subj. πυκάσωμαι *AP*11.19 (Strat.):—Pass., aor. ἐπυκάσθην Hdt.7.197, etc.: pf. πεπύκασμαι Od.22.488, Hes.*Op.*793; Aeol. part. πεπυκάδμενος Sapph.56: (πύκα):—poet. Verb (also in Hdt., v. supr., and later Prose, D.S.5.13), *cover closely*, freq. with collat. notion of *protection*, νεφέλῃ πυκάσασα ἓ αὐτήν Il.17.551; πύκασεν κάρη ἀμφιτεθεῖσα [ἡ κυνέη] 10.271; νῆα π. λίθοισι *surround* a ship with stones, *so as to protect* it while lying up, Hes.*Op.*624: generally, *cover thickly*, of a youth's chin, π. γένυς εὐανθέϊ λάχνῃ Od.11.320; πέδιλα πίλοις ἔντοσθε π. *lining* them *with thick* felt, Hes.*Op.*542; π. στεφάνοις *cover thick* with crowns, Orac.ap.D.21.52, Theoc.2.153, cf. *IG*3.758: —also Med., μελιλώτῳ κάρα πυκάζομαι Cratin. l.c.; στεφάνοις κεφαλὰς πυκασώμεθα *AP* l.c.: without στεφάνοις, *crown*, *deck with garlands*, πύκαζε κρᾶτ' ἐμὸν νικηφόρον E.*Tr.*353:—also Med., λουσάμενοι ..πυκασώμεθα *let us put on crowns*, *AP*5.11 (Rufin.):—Pass., στέμμασι πᾶς πυκασθεὶς Hdt. l.c., cf. E.*Alc.*796; δάφνῃ πυκασθεὶς (v.l. σκιασθεὶς) Id.*Andr.*1115; βωμὸς ἄνθεσι πεπύκασται Xenoph.1.11; ὄρεξιν ἥβης (cf. ἥβη I.4) πυκαζομένης Ps.-Democr. in Hp.*Ep.*23 (s.v.l.):—Pass. is used by Hom. only in pf. part. πεπυκασμένος *thickly covered*, ὄζοισιν Il.14.289; ἅρματα δὲ χρυσῷ πεπυκασμένα κασσιτέρῳ τε 23.503; but ἅρματα εὖ πεπ. well *covered over* (i.e. stowed away), 2.777; ῥάκεσιν πεπυκασμένος ὤμους Od.22.488, cf. E.*Rh.*713 (lyr.); ὄρος πεπυκασμένον a hill *well-clothed* with wood, Hes.*Th.*484; χώρα πεπυκασμένη δρυμοῖς D.S. l.c.; Aeol. πεπυκάδμενος, *covered*, *hidden*, Sapph.56:—Med., κόσμῳ πυκάζου τῷδε *cover thyself*, E.*Heracl.*725; π. τεύχεσιν δέμας Id.*Rh.*90 (v.l. -αζε). **2.** metaph., Ἕκτορα δ' αἰνὸν ἄχος πύκασε φρένας *threw a shadow over* his soul, Il.8.124, 17.83:—Pass., παρθενίης αἰδοῖ πεπυκασμένος *Epigr.Gr.*875.2 (Sinope); also νόον πεπυκασμένος *close*, *cautious* of mind, Hes.*Op.*793. **II.** *close*, *shut up*, ἐντὸς πυκάζοιεν σφέας αὐτοὺς *shelter* themselves *closely* within, Od.12.225; πύκαζε θᾶσσον (sc. τὸ δῶμα) *shut* it *close*, S.*Aj.*581. **-ασμα**, ατος, τό, *that which is close*, *covered*, or *thick*, Sm.*Ps.*117(118).27.

**πῠκῐμηδής**, ές, (πύκα, μῆδος) *of close* or *cautious mind*, *shrewd*, Od.1.438: also written parox. πυκιμήδης, *h.Cer.*153, Q.S.7.189.

**πῠκῐνά**, neut. pl. used as Adv., v. πυκνός B. II.

**πῠκῐνό-θριξ**, τρῐχος, ὁ, ἡ, = πυκνόθριξ, Nonn.*D.*7.322, al. ✻ **-κίνητος** [ῑν], ον, *moving frequently*, Hp.*Art.*14. **-ρριζος**, ον, (ῥίζα) = πυκνόρριζος, Id.*Oss.*16.

**πῠκῐνός**, **πυκινῶς**, v. πυκνός.

**πῠκῐνόφρων**, ὁ, ἡ, gen. ονος, = πυκιμηδής, βουλή, ῥήτρη, *h.Merc.*538, *AP*11.350 (Agath.); of a person, Hes.*Fr.*143, Q.S.5.98.

**πυκνά**, neut. used as Adv., v. πυκνός B. II.

**πυκν-άζω**, *to be frequent*, *EM*442.21, *Gloss.* **-αία**, ἡ, = πνύξ (q.v.), Ion *Trag.*65. **-άκις** [ᾰ], Adv. *oft-times*, Arist.*Pr.*872ᵃ22, 874ᵃ9. **-άρμων**, ονος, ὁ, ἡ, *close-fitted*, Democr.ap.*Placit.*3.3.11. **-ί̄της** [ῑ], ου, ὁ, *assembled in the Pnyx*, δῆμος π. Ar.*Eq.*42: fem. -ῖτις, *from the Pnyx*, [κονία] *IG*2².1672.199.

**πυκνό-βλαστος**, ον, *covered with buds*, Thphr.*CP*3.7.11. **-γόνᾰτος**, ον, (γόνυ II) *with frequent knots* or *joints*, Dsc.1.18, al.

**πυκνόδους**, ὁ, ἡ, gen. -όδοντος, *with teeth close together*, Sch.Opp. *H.*1.170.

**πυκνό-θριξ**, τρῐχος, ὁ, ἡ, *thick-haired*, Nonn.*D.*36.302 (leg. πυκιν-). **-καρπος**, ον, *thick with fruit*, Luc.*Am.*12. **-κίνδῡνος**, ον, *ever in dangers*, v.l. for μικροκίνδυνος in Arist.*EN*1124ᵇ7. **-κοκκον**, τό, name of a plant with purgative properties, Ruf.ap.Orib.7.26.37 (v.l. -κολον: -κομον cj. Daremberg). **-κομον**, τό, *motherwort*, *Leonurus Cardiaca*, Dsc.4.174, Plin.*HN*26.57; cf. foreg.

**πυκνομμᾰτέω**, *to be riddled with holes*, of a shield, S.*Fr.*35.

**πυκνόν**, neut. Adj. used as Adv., v. πυκνός B. II.

**πυκνο-νεφής**, ές, *covered with thick clouds*, Sch.Arat.412. **-πλοέω**, *sail constantly*, f.l. for νυκτοπλοέω, Hipparch.1.7.1. **-πνεύμᾰτος**, ον, *having rapid respiration*, Hp.*Epid.*6.4.4. **-πνοια**, ἡ, *rapid respiration*, Gal.17(2).128. **-ποιέω**, *make thick*, Eust.1546.44. **-πορος**, ον, *with close* or *narrow pores*, Alex.Aphr.*Pr.*2.76. **-πτερος**, ον, *many and feathered*, ἀηδόνες S.*OC*17. **-ρράξ**, ᾶγος, (ῥάξ) *thick with berries*, *AP*6.22 (Zon., ap.Suid., but πυκνόρρωγα or πυκνορρῶγα codd. as in Str.15.2.14). **-ρριζος**, ον, (ῥίζα) *with matted roots*, Thphr.*HP*3.11.4, al., Dsc.1.1. **-ρρώξ**, ῶγος, (ῥώξ) v. πυκνορράξ.

✻ **πυκνός**, ή, όν, poet. also **πῠκῐνός**, ή, όν, both forms in Ep. (v. infr.) and Lyr., Pi.*O.*13.52 (Sup.), B.*Fr.*1; Aeol. **πύκνος** Sapph.1.11, Alc.*Supp.*14.9 (πύκινος is dub. l. Id.82); Trag. **πυκνός**, exc. S. in lyr., *Aj.*1208, *Ph.*854; πυκινός once in Com., Eub.38 (s.v.l.): Lacon. Sup. πουκότατος is corrupt in Simm.26.17:—*close*, *compact*. **I.** of a thing with reference to the close union of its parts, *close*, *firm*, *solid*, πυκινὸς θώρηξ Il.15.529; χλαῖναν πυκνὴν καὶ μεγάλην Od.14.521; πυκινὸν νέφος Il.5.751; πυκινὸν λέχος *well-stuffed*, *firm* bed, 9.621, Od.7.340; πυκνὸν καὶ μαλακὸν Il.14.349; Ἁρμονίης πυκινῷ κρυφῷ Emp.27.3; σπάρτα πυκνὰ ἐστραμμένα X.*An.*4.7.15; π. δέμας Parm.8.59; of a sponge, Hp.*Ulc.*2; π. ὀστοῦν Pl.*Ti.*75b, cf. Hp.*VM*22; [σάρκες] Pl.*Ti.*74e; χρυσοῦ πυκνότερον ib.59b; ἔβενος Thphr.*HP*1.5.5; πλεύμων Plu.2.698b; χωρία ib.650d; πυκινὴν νάπαις Ἄζιλιν Call.*Ap.*89; [ὁ ἐλαιὼν] πυκνός ἐστι τοῖς φυτοῖς *overgrown* with plants, *PFay.*113.8 (i/ii A.D.); ξοῖς χαρακτῇ π. *IG*7.3073.104 (Lebad., ii B.C.); of a woman, *thick-set*, *stocky*, Sor.1.34. **2.** *narrow*, *constricted*, οὐ διέρχεται..ἀρκέουσα ἰκμάς.., πυκνῆς τῆς ὁδοῦ ἐούσης Hp.*Mul.*1.73; πυκνοὺς ἔχουσι τοὺς πόρους τοῦ σώματος Alex.Aphr.*Pr.*1.6. **II.** of the parts of a thing, *close-packed*, *crowded*, πυκιναὶ κίνυντο φάλαγγες Il.4.281; τῶν δὲ στίχες ἥατο πυκναί 7.61, etc.; πυκινὸν λόχον εἷσαν 4.392, etc. (v. infr. III. 1); πυκνὰ καρήατα λαῶν 11.309; πυκνοὶ ἐφέστασαν ἀλλήλοισιν 13.133, cf. Od.5.480; σταυροῖσιν πυκινοῖσι Il.24.453; σταυροὺς..πυκνοὺς καὶ θαμέας Od.14.12; of *thick* plumage, πυκινὰ πτερά 5.53; πτερὰ πυκνά Il.11.454, 23.879; but πύκνα πτέρα *fast-beating* wings, Sapph.1.11 (and so perh. Hom. ll. cc.); freq. of thick foliage, ὕλη, λόχμη, θάμνοι, ὄζοι, ῥωπήϊα, δρυμά, πέταλα, Il.18.320, Od.19.439, 5.471, Il.21.245, Od.14.473, 10.150, 19.520; π. νέφεα Hes.*Op.*553; πυκινοῖσι λίθοισι with *close-laid* stones, Il.16.212; πυκινοῖσι..βελέεσσι with *a thick shower of* darts, 11.576; πυκνῇσιν λιθάδεσσιν Od.14.36; τοξεύματα πολλὰ καὶ π. Hdt.7.218; πυκνοῖς ὄσσοις δεδορκώς, of Argus, A.*Pr.*678; πεπλεκτανημέναι π. δράκουσιν, of the Furies, Id.*Ch.*1050; of *thick-falling* rain, snow, etc., πυκνῆς ἀκοῦσαι ψακάδος S.*Fr.*636; πυκιναῖς δρόσοις Id.*Aj.*1208 (lyr.); πυκνῇ νιφάδι E.*Andr.*1129; π. ῥόος a *dense* current, Emp.100.14; π. θρίξ X.*Cyn.*4.6; π. τρίχες Pl.*Prt.*321a; [δένδρεα] Hdt.4.22, cf. X.*An.*4.8.2; τὰ μὲν π...τὰ δὲ μανὰ κατὰ τὴν φυτείαν Thphr.*HP*1.8.2. **b.** in Tactics, *in close order*, opp. ἀραιός, Ascl.*Tact.*4.1 (Sup.), Arr.*Tact.*11.1 (Comp.). **2.** of a repeated action, *frequent*, *numerous*, πυκνοὺς θεοπρόπους ἴαλλε A.*Pr.*658; τῶν π. φιλημάτων Id.*Fr.*135; ὀδύναι πυκνόταται Hp.*VM*22; πυκινῶν κρεγμῶν ἀκροαζομένα Epich.109 (anap.); π. ὀδοὺς ἐλθόντα E.*Tr.*235; π. βαίνων ἤλυσιν, of a blind man, Id.*Ph.*844; ἐν πυκνῷ θεοῦ τροχῷ κυκλεῖται on the *oft-revolving* wheel, S.*Fr.*871.1; μεταβολαὶ πυκνόταται Hp.*Aër.*13; πνεῦμα πυκνότερον *quicker* breathing, Id.*Acut.*16; π. σφυγμὸς ἢ μανός Plu.2.136f; *continuous*, *constant*, φῶς *Corp.Herm.*16.10; ἐρωτήμασι πυκνοῖς χρώμενοι Th.7.44; ἠ..εἰωθυῖά μοι μαντικὴ..πάνυ πυκνὴ ἦν Pl.*Ap.*40a; ἐπιθυμίαι π. τε καὶ σφοδραί Id.*R.*573e; τὰς ἐντεύξεις π. ποιεῖσθαι Isoc.1.20: c. inf., πυκνοτέραν εἰσαφικνεῖσθαι πᾶσιν ἀνθρώποις ποιεῖν τὴν πόλιν *more frequently* visited by.., X.*Vect.*5.1 codd. **III.** of artificial union, *well put together*, *compact*, *strong*, πυκινὸς δόμος, χηλός, θύραι, θάλαμος, κευθμῶνες (v. infr. B. III. 1), Il.10.267, Od.13.68, Il.14.167, Od.23.229, 10.283; ἀσπὶς ῥινοῖσιν πυκινή Il.13.804; π. δῶμα Xenoph.17: hence, *close*, *concealed*, πυκινὸς δόλος Il.6.187; and so perhaps π. λόχος, v. supr. II. 1. **2.** in Music, πυκνόν, τό, part of the tetrachord in which the intervals are small, defined as τὸ ἐκ δύο διαστημάτων συνεστηκὸς ἃ συντεθέντα ἔλαττον διάστημα περιέξει τοῦ λειπομένου διαστήματος ἐν τῷ διὰ τεσσάρων Aristox.*Harm.* p.24 M., cf. Plu.2.1135b, etc. **IV.** generally, *strong* of its kind, *sore*, *excessive*, ἄτη Il.24.480; μελεδῶναι Od.19.516; ἄχος Il.16.599. **V.** metaph. of the mind, *shrewd*, *wise*, πυκιναὶ φρένες 14.294, cf. Alc.*Supp.*14.9, B. l.c.; νόος Il.15.461; μήδεα 3.208; βουλή 2.55; ἐφετμή 18.216; μῦθοι Od.3.23; ἔπος Il.11.788; θυμός, βουλαί, Pi.*P.*4.73, *I.*7(6).8; φρήν E.*IA*67; μήτιδι πυκνῇ Orac.ap.Hdt.7.141, cf. *IG*3.1320: in Prose, πυκνὴ διάνοια Pl.*R.*568a; τὸ π. *terseness* of expression, D.H.*Th.*24. **2.** of persons, *sagacious*, *shrewd*, *crafty*, *cunning*, Σίσυφος πυκνότατος παλάμαις Pi.*O.*13.52; κύων πυκινώτατον ἑρπετὸν Id.*Fr.*106; πυκινοί *the wise*, S.*Ph.*854 (lyr.); πυκνότατον κίναδος Ar.*Av.*430 (lyr.); πυκνός τις καὶ σοφὸς γνώμην ἀνήρ Critias 25.12.

**B.** Adv. πυκινῶς, and after Hom. πυκνῶς, θύραι or σανίδες πυκινῶς ἀραρυῖαι *close* or *fast shut*, Il.9.475, Od.2.344, etc. **2.** *sorely* (v. supr. A. IV), πυκινῶς ἀκαχήμενος Il.19.312, cf. Od.19.95, al.; *constantly*, ὅταν π. διάττωσι X.*Cyn.*6.22. **3.** *sagaciously*, *shrewdly*, π. ὑποθήσομαι Od.1.279, cf. Il.21.293; πυκνῶς ἀνευρεῖν Ar.*Th.*438 (lyr., s.v.l.). **II.** neut. sg. and pl., πυκνόν, πυκνά, πυκινόν, πυκινά as Adv., esp. in the sense *much*, *often*, πήρην πυκνὰ ῥωγαλέην a *much* torn wallet, a wallet full of holes, Od.13.438, 17.198; πυκινόν περ ἀχεύων 11.88; τέττιξ..καταχεύετ' ἀοιδὴν πυκνόν Hes.*Op.*584: in Prose, πυκνὰ ἐκπίπτει ὦμος Hp.*Art.*2; πυκνὰ ἀποβλέπειν Pl.*R.*501b; πυκνὰ στρέφεσθαι X.*An.*6.1.8; πυκνὸν ἀναπνεῖν Arist.*Rh.*1357ᵇ19; πυκνότερον ἰέναι, παρέρχεσθαι, Pl.*R.*328d, D.41.24; πυκνότερα ἐπάγειν Pl.*Cra.*420d. Adv. -οτέρως Lesb.Gramm.23, *PLond.*5.1929 (iv A.D.): Sup. πυκνότατα X.*Eq.*11.11. **2.** πυκινὰ φρονεῖν (v. supr. A. V) Od.9.445. **III.** poet. Adv. **πύκα** [◡◡], *thickly*, *solidly*, θαλάμου πύκα ποιητοῖο 1.436; π. π. δόμοιο 22.455; σάκεος π. π. Il.18.

608; Λυκίων π. θωρηκτάων 12.317, cf. 15.689,739; πύλαι π. στιβαρῶς ἀραρυῖαι 12.454. **2.** θάλαμος πύκ' ἐβάλλετο with *thick-falling* darts, 9.588. **3.** *wisely*, π. φρονεῖν ib.554, 14.217, Q.S.1.449, al.; τρέφειν rear *carefully*, Il.5.70.

**πυκνός**, gen. of πνύξ (q.v.).

**πυκνό-σαρκος**, ον, *with solid flesh*, Hp.*Vict.*3.78, *Mul.*1.73, al., Arist.*Pr.*861$^b$29. **-σπορέω**, *sow thick*, Thphr.*HP*8.6.2:—Pass., κύαμοι πυκνοσπορούμενοι ib.8.7.2, cf. *CP*4.14.2. **-σπορος**, ον, *thick-sown*, ib.3.21.5. **-στικτος**, ον, *thick-spotted, dappled*, ἔλαφοι S.*OC*1092 (lyr.). **-στῦλος**, ον, *with the pillars close together*, i.e. at a distance of 1½ diameters, opp. ἀραιόστυλος, Vitr.3.3.1. **-σύγκρῐτος**, ον, Medic., *of a constricted habit of body*, *BKT*3 p.20. **-σφυξία**, ἡ, *a frequent pulse*, Marcellin.*Puls.*260.

**πυκνότης**, ητος, ἡ, *closeness, thickness, denseness, solidity*, [νεφελῶν] Ar.*Nu.*384,406; [χρυσοῦ] Pl.*Ti.*59b; π. ἡ κάτω Epicur.*Nat.*11.10; π. νοητή Phld.*D.*3.11; of flesh, opp. μανότης, Hp.*VM*22, Arist.*EN* 1129$^a$23, etc.; opp. ἀραιότης, Id.*Ph.*260$^b$10 (pl.); ἡ π. τῆς ξυγκλήσεως Th.5.71. **2.** Medic., π. κοιλίης *costiveness*, Hp.*Epid.*6.3.1. **3.** *closer spacing* of notes in music, opp. μανότης, Pl.*Lg.*812d. **4.** in Tactics, *close formation* of the phalanx, Arr.*Tact.*11.1, 12.11; ἡ συνέχεια καὶ π. τῶν Ῥωμαίων Plu.*Crass.*24. **II.** *frequency*, μεταβολῶν Isoc.4.116; μέγεθος καὶ πλῆθος καὶ πυκνότητες [λυπῶν] Pl.*Lg.*734a; ἡ π. τῶν ἐννοιῶν Hermog.*Id.*2.10 (pl.), Longin.ap.Porph.*Plot.*19, cf. Arist.*SE*175$^b$34. **III.** metaph., *sagacity, shrewdness*, π. ἔνεστ' ἐν τῷ τρόπῳ Ar.*Eq.*1132 (lyr.); πιθανότης καὶ π. τοῦ ἀνδρός Plu.*TG*15.

**πυκνόφθαλμος**, ον, *with thick-set eyes*, π. κόραι E.*Fr.*1063.14. **II.** of plants, *with too many leaf-buds*, Thphr.*CP*3.15.3: Comp., Id.*HP* 5.4.1.

**πυκνόφυλλος**, ον, *with thick foliage*, Arist.*Pr.*927$^a$3 (Comp.).

**πυκν-όω**, *make close* or *solid*, τὴν σάρκα Arist.*Pr.*865$^b$18, cf. Phld. *Mort.*8; of winds, νέφεσι π. τὸν οὐρανόν *thickens* it, Arist.*Mete.*364$^b$24:—Pass., of vapour and air, ib.342$^a$21, 344$^b$4; νεφῶν πυκνουμένων Epicur.*Nat.*14 *Fr.*6. **2.** *contract, condense*, opp. μανόω, Arist.*Spir.* 485$^a$31; of the effect of cold, Id.*GA*783$^b$1:—Pass., of frozen water, Antipho Soph.29, Arist.*Metaph.*1042$^b$28, *Mu.*394$^a$33; ὁ σίδηρος ὑπὸ τοῦ ψυχροῦ πυκνοῦται *is contracted*, Plu.*Alc.*6; of steam, ὁ ἀτμὸς -οῦται καὶ σταγόνες ἀποπίπτουσι Hp.*Flat.*8. **II.** *pack close*, ἑωυτούς *close* their ranks, Hdt.9.18, cf. Ascl.*Tact.*10.4, Ael.*Tact.*11.2 (Pass.); τὸ βάθος ἐπὶ τὸ δεξιόν Plb.18.24.8; τὴν τάξιν εἰς βάθος Plu.*Flam.*8; σαυτὸν στρόβει πυκνώσας spin yourself round *and concentrate your thoughts*, Ar.*Nu.*701 (lyr.):—Pass., *to be compressed*, εἰς ἐλάττω τόπον Arist.*Cael.*296$^a$18; [τὴν διάνοιαν] πυκνοῦσθαι εἰκός Plu.2.715c; τῷ πνεύματι πυκνουμένῳ, i.e. without taking breath, Id.*Dem.*11. **b.** in Logic, πυκνοῦται τὸ μέσον *is compressed, becomes closer* in signification, Arist.*APo.*84$^b$35; also πεπύκνωται [ὁ Λυσίας] τοῖς νοήμασι, of a *terse* style, D.H.*Lys.*5. **III.** *close, shut up*, π. τοὺς πόρους Thphr.*Sud.*27; τὸν στόμαχον Plu.2.687d; φλέβες πυκνωθεῖσαι Hp.*Salubr.*7. **IV.** Pass., *to be thickly covered*, ἡ γῆ τῶν [ἰχνῶν] πυκνοῦται with traces, X.*Cyn.*5.7. **V.** intr., *become dense*, Arist. *Mete.*344$^a$30, *Pr.*934$^b$15: in Tactics, πεπυκνωκότες ἀπὸ τῶν κεράτων ἐπὶ τὰ μέσα Plb.3.115.6, cf. Ascl.*Tact.*4.4, Ael.*Tact.*11.6. **-ωμα**, ατος, τό, *thick cloth*, A.*Supp.*235 (nisi leg. ἀμπυκώμασι). **II.** *dense mass, concentration*, Epicur.*Ep.*1 p.4 U., al.; *crowded detail*, π. στερέμνιον Phld.*D.*3.11; *compression*, Sor.2.41; *close order*, τὸ π. τῶν πολεμίων J.*BJ*6.1.3; τῶν σαρισῶν Plu.*Aem.*20, cf. *Phil.*9. **2.** *close planting* or *growth*, τῶν κυάμων Str.17.1.15; τῶν δένδρων, τῶν ὄζων, Alciphr.3.37,55; τῶν τριχῶν ib.66, etc. **3.** in pl., = πυκνόν (v. πυκνός III. 2), Pl.*R.*531a. **-ωσις**, εως, ἡ, *condensation*, opp. μάνωσις, Arist.*Ph.*260$^b$8; opp. ἀραίωσις, Epicur.*Nat.*14*Fr.*11, Plu.2.695b; π. ὑδατώδης, of the air, Arist.*Mete.*372$^b$31; τὸ νέφος π. ἀέρος Id. *Top.*146$^b$29; ἡ διὰ ψῦχος π. S.E.*P.*1.238. **II.** (from πυκνόομαι) *condensed matter*, Arist.*Mete.*344$^a$16, Plu.2.721a (pl.). **2.** *frequency* of the pulse, Marcellin.*Puls.*228. **III.** in Tactics, *close order*, κατὰ τὰς ἐναγωνίους π. Plb.18.29.2; τῶν σαρισῶν Id.18.30.3, cf. Onos.10.2 (pl.); esp. of the phalanx, Ascl.*Tact.*4.1,3, Ael.*Tact.*11.3, Arr.*Tact.* 11.3. **IV.** Rhet., *aggregation*, τῶν ἐκλελεγμένων Longin.10.1. **-ωτικός**, ή, όν, *serving to close the pores*, δύναμις π. τῶν σωμάτων Dsc.3.22, cf. Sor.1.50, Aret.*CA*2.1; ψυχροὶ τε καὶ π., of N. winds, *bracing*, Ptol.*Tetr.*30.

⊛ **πυκτᾰλ-εύω**, = πυκτεύω, Sophr.111. ⊛ **-ίζω**, = foreg., Anacr.62.4.

**πυκτ-εῖον**, τό, *boxing-ring*, Suid. **II.** (*πυκτός = πτυκτός) *book-case*, Zonar. **-ευσις**, εως, ἡ, *boxing, Gloss.* **-ευτής**, οῦ, ὁ, *boxer*, ib. ⊛ **-εύω**, Boeot. πουκτ-, *box, spar*, X.*Lac.*4.6, D.4.40; οὕτω πυκτεύω ὡς οὐκ ἀέρα δέρων 1*Ep.Cor.*9.26; π. καὶ παγκρατιάζειν Pl.*Grg.*456d; περὶ τεοῦς Ἑρμᾶς ποτ' Ἄρευα π. Corinn.11; ἐς σὸν κρᾶτα π. *strike with the fist* on the head, E.*Cyc.*229: generally, *fight*, ξιφήρη π. Hld.10.31; of gladiators, *Rev.Arch.*30(1929).24 (Gortyn):—Med., πεπύκτευται αὐτόν Philostr.*Im.*2.19.

**πυκτή**, ἡ (for πτυκτή), *tablets, diptych*, *Cod.Just.*4.21.16*Intr.*, Just. *Edict.*13.15. **II.** *codex*, *Cod.Just.*4.21.22.10.

**πύκτης**, ου, ὁ, *boxer*, Xenoph.2.15, Pi.*O.*10(11).16, S.*Tr.*442, Pl. *Grg.*460d; opp. παλαιστής, Id.*Lg.*819b; freq. in Inscrr., *IG*1$^2$.846.7, 2$^2$.2311.32,47, 3.128.4, 743.14, etc., and Papyri, *PLond.*3.1158.6 (iii A.D.), etc. **II.** epith. of Apollo, Plu.2.724c.

**πυκτίζω**, as if πτυκτίζω, *fold*, Suid.

⊛ **πυκτικ-ός**, ή, όν, *skilled in boxing*, Pl.*Grg.*456d, *Alc.*2.145d, etc.; opp. παλαιστικός, Arist.*Rh.*1361$^b$25: ἡ -κή (sc. τέχνη) *the art of boxing*, Pl.*Grg.*460d, *Alc.*2.145d; π. ἐπιστήμη Arist.*Cat.*10$^b$3. Adv. -κῶς Sch.Theoc.22.67: Comp. -ώτερον Philostr.*Gym.*35. **2.** *of* or *for boxers*, μάχη Pl.*R.*333e; πόνοι, γυμνάσιον, Ruf.*Sat.Gon.*34, Gal.19.690; ἡ -κή *plaster for boxers*, Id.13.509. **-ότης**, ητος, ἡ, *skill in boxing*, Simp. *in Cat.*214.18.

**πυκτίον**, τό, *tablet*, Sch.Ar.*Pl.*39, Suid.; = βιβλίον, Zonar.; parox. acc. to Sch.D.T.p.195H.

**πυκτίς** (A), ίδος, ἡ, as if πτυκτίς, *picture*, *AP*9.346 (Leon. Alex.). **II.** *parchment codex*, Gal.12.423.

⊛ **πυκτίς** (B), ίδος, prob. ἡ, an unknown animal, perhaps the *badger*, v.l. in Ar.*Ach.*879 (sed leg. πικτίδας).

**πυκτομᾰχέω**, = πυκτεύω, Suid. s. v. παγκρατιασταῖς.

**πυκτοσύνη**, ἡ, (πύκτης) *the art of boxing*, Xenoph.2.4.

**Πῠλᾱγόρ-ας**, ου, ὁ, (Πύλαι, ἀγείρω) *delegate sent to the Amphictyonic Council at Pylae*, ἥκειν..φασι τοὺς Πυλαγόρας Ar.*Fr.*322:—also **Πυλᾱγόρος** or **Πυλάγορος**, Hdt.7.214, D.18.149 (v.l. -γόρας), Decr. Amphict.ib.154, Aeschin.3.113,114 (v.l. -γόρας), 122, al., Str.9.3.7 (both forms); Π. διὰ βίου *SIG*795*B*5 (Delph., i A.D.); cf. Πυληγόρος. **-έω**, *to be a* Πυλαγόρας, D.18.155, Aeschin.3.126.

**Πῦλαι**, αἱ, v. πύλη II. 2.

⊛ **Πῠλαία**, Ion. -αίη (sc. σύνοδος), ἡ, fem. of πυλαῖος, *meeting of the Amphictyons at Pylae*, Hdt.7.213, Thphr.*HP*9.10.2, etc.; π. ἠρινά *SIG*230.27 (Delph., iv B.C.); ἐαρινή Decr.Amphict.ap.D.18.154; ὀπωρινά *SIG*239*C*32 (Delph., iv B.C.); μετοπωρινή Str.9.3.7. **2.** *right of sending deputies to the Amphictyonic Council*, D.5.23, 6.22. **3.** *place where the Amphictyons met*, *GDI*2507.5, 2524.11 (Delph., iii B.C.), Plu.2.409a. **II.** *promiscuous crowd*, such as was found at these meetings: hence μύθων ἀπιθάνων..πυλαία *farrago*, Id.*Art.*1, cf. 2.924d. **III.** a place (perh. in Arcadia, cf. St.Byz.) considered undesirable for Spartan youths, Id.2.239c.

**πυλαιασταί**, οἱ, *buffoons, mountebanks*, such as flocked to Pylae and Delphi during the Amphictyonic assembly, Phot., Suid. **II.** *liars* (Rhod.), Hsch.

**πῠλᾰϊκός**, ή, όν, *silly*, ὀχλαγωγία Plu.*Pyrrh.*29.

**πῠλαιμάχος** [ᾰ], *fighting at the gate*, prob. in Stesich.48 (-λαμ- codd. Ath., -λεμ- Sch.Il.), Call.*Fr.*503 (-λεμ- codd.). **II.** epith. of Athena in Ar.*Eq.*1172, with a play on Pylos, as the scene of Cleon's triumph.

⊛ **πῠλαῖος**, α, ον, *at* or *before the gate*, Ἑρμῆς Anon.ap.D.L.8.31, Sch. Il.2.842; π. Ὀρθώσιος, = *Janus Geminus*, *Gloss.* (v. πυλεύς). **2.** (Πύλαι) *at Pylae*, Δημήτηρ ἡ Πυλαίη Call.*Epigr.*40.

**πῠλαῖτις**, ιδος, ἡ, (πύλη) *door-keeper*, epith. of Athena, Lyc.356.

**πῠλᾰμάχος**, f. l. for πυλαι- (q.v.).

**πῠλάοχος** [ᾱ], ον, = πυλοῦχος, epith. of Dionysus, Plu.2.364f.

**πῠλάρτης**, ου, ὁ, (ἀραρίσκω) *gate-fastener, he that keeps the gates of hell*, epith. of the god who held this office, Ἀΐδαο πυλάρταο Il.8.367, cf. 13.415, Od.11.277 (expld. by Apion as ὁ ταῖς πύλαις προσηρτημένος).

**Πῠλᾶτις**, ιδος, poet. fem. of Πυλαῖος 2, ἀγοραί S.*Tr.*639 (lyr.).

**πῠλαυρός**, ὁ, = sq., Hsch.

⊛ **πῠλᾰωρός**, ὁ, Ep. for πυλωρός, *gate-keeper*, Il.21.530, 24.681, A.R. 3.747; of Odysseus in the Wooden Horse, Tryph.201; [κύνας] πυλαωρούς Il.22.69 (quoted ap. Arr.*Epict.*3.22.80, but θυραωρούς Aristarch.); π. Πλούτωνος Κέρβερος *AP*7.319. (πυλᾰ-*sorwó*- (cf. ἐρύω (B)) became πυλᾰ-(*h*)ορ(ϝ)ό-, πυλᾱορό-, πυλωρό-, then Ep. πυλᾰωρό- (with -ω- taken from the contr. form): πυλᾰ-(*h*)ορ(ϝ)ό- also became πυλαυρός, πυλευρός (qq. v.), and πυλαουρός (v.l. in Il.24. 681), πυλαορός (v.l. in 21.530).)

**πῠλευρός**, ὁ, = foreg., Hsch.

**Πῠλεύς**, έως, ὁ, Π. Ὀρθώσιος, = *Janus Geminus*, *Gloss.* (nisi leg. Πυλαῖος).

⊛ **πῠλεών**, ῶνος, ὁ, = πυλών, Democr.288*, Opp.*C.*3.419, *AP*5.241 (Eratosth.), 7.70 (Jul. Aegypt.), Nonn.*D.*3.136, etc. **II.** Lacon. for a *wreath*, Alcm.16, Call.*Fr.*358, Pamphil.ap.Ath.15.678a.

⊛ **πύλη** [ῠ], ἡ, prop. *one wing of a pair of double gates*, ὀλίγον τι παρακλίναντες τὴν ἑτέρην π. Hdt.3.156: mostly in pl., *gates of a town* (whereas θύρα = house-door), Σκαιαὶ π. Il.3.145, etc.; π. εὖ ἀραρυίας 7.339; πύκα στιβαρῶς ἀραρυίας 12.454; πεπταμένας ἐν χερσὶ π. ἔχετε 21.531; ἄνεσάν τε π. καὶ ἀπῶσαν ὀχῆας ib.537; π. ἀνοῖξαι A.*Ag.*604; π. κλῇσαι Pl.*R.*560c (the Art. is freq. omitted even in Prose): pl. of several *gates*, A.*Th.*125; ἐν πύλαις in or at *the gates*, ib.160, 213 (both lyr.), al.; πρὸς πύλαις ib.377,457; ἐπὶ ταῖς πύλαισιν, οὗ τὸ τάριχος ὤνιον Ar.*Eq.*1247. **2.** in Trag. sts. of the *house-door*, δωμάτων πύλαι A.*Ch.*732, cf. 561; γυναικείους π. *gate* or *door* leading to the women's apartments, ib.878; πύλαις διπλαῖς ἐνήλατο S.*OT*1261; ἐκτὸς αὐλείων πυλῶν Id.*Ant.*18: also in sg., ib.1186, *El.*818; of the *door* of a tent, Id.*Aj.*11; πύλης ἄναξ θυρωρέ Id.*Fr.*775. **3.** πύλαι Ἀΐδαο the *gates of the nether world*, periphr. for *hell*, Il.5.646, 9.312, Od.14.156; Ἅιδου πύλαι A.*Ag.*1291, cf. *Ev.Matt.*16.18, etc.; also σκότου πύλαι E.*Hec.*1; νερτέρων π. Id.*Hipp.*1447. **4.** *custom-house*, *PTeb.*5.34 (ii B.C.); τετελώνηται διὰ πύλης has paid the *customs*, *BGU*1592 (iii A.D.), etc.; τὸ σύμβολον τῆς ἱερᾶς Συηνιτικῆς π. *PStrassb.*79.10 (i B.C.); μισθωταὶ ἱερᾶς π. Σοήνης *Ostr.*106 (ii A.D.), al., cf. *Ostr.Bodl.*v C1 (ii A.D.). **II.** generally, *entrance, orifice*, ἀμφὶ πύλας ἰσθμοῖο Emp.100.19; ἀναπεπταμένας ἔχω τῶν ὤτων τὰς π. Ath.4.169a; πύλας τοῖς ὠσὶν ἐπίθεσθε Pl.*Smp.*218b; ἡλίου πύλαι, Pythag. name for the eyes, D.L.8.29; *portal fissure* of the liver, π. καὶ δοχαὶ χολῆς E.*El.*828, cf. Hp.*Epid.* 2.4.1, *Anat.*1, Pl.*Ti.*71c, Arist.*HA*496$^b$32, Gal.15.145; *portal vein* of the liver, Ruf.*Onom.*179, Gal.2.785, 5.542. **b.** pl., of the *carceres* in the circus, Aristid.1.124J. **c.** metaph., πύλας ὕμνων ἀναπιτνάμεν Pi.*O.*6.27; ἐπέων π. B.*Fr.*4; ἐν πύλαις γήρως D.C.57. 24, cf. 76.7. **2.** *entrance into a country through mountains, pass*,

Hdt.5.52: hence, Πύλαι, αἱ, the common name for Θερμοπύλαι, *the Gates* of Greece, Id.7.201, etc.: of other *passes*, π. τῆς Κιλικίας καὶ τῆς Συρίας X.*An*.1.4.4; αἱ Σύριαι π. ib.5; αἱ Κάσπιαι π. Str.11.12.1; π. Λύδιαι Id.13.1.65; Ἀμανίδες π. Id.14.5.18, 16.2.8 (αἱ Ἀμανικαὶ καλούμεναι Arr.*An*.2.7.1): these *passes* were sometimes really barred by *gates*, Hdt.7.176, cf. 3.117, 5.52, X. l.c.: the Isthmus is called πόντοιο πύλαι, Pi.*N*.10.27; Κορίνθου π. Id.*O*.9.86; αἱ π. τῆς Πελοποννήσου X.*Ages*.2.17; Πέλοπος νάσου θεόδματοι π. B.p.437 J. **3.** of *narrow straits*, by which one enters a broad sea, Πύλαι Γαδειρίδες the *Straits* of Gibraltar, Pi.*Fr*.256; ἐπ' αὐταῖς στενοπόροις λίμνης π., of the Thracian Bosporus, A.*Pr*.729; ἐν πύλαις, of the Euripus, E.*IA*803.

**Πῠληγενής**, = Πυλοιγενής, *h.Ap*.398, 424 codd., Euph.63.

**Πῠληγόροι·** τελῶναι, καὶ οἱ τῶν πανηγύρεων ἐπιμεληταί, Hsch.; cf. Πυλαγόρος.

**πῠληδόκος**, ὁ, *watching at the door*, of Hermes, *h.Merc*.15.

**πυλιάς**, άδος, ἡ, an unknown precious stone, f.l. (in gen. pl.) for πολυειδῶν, Aristeas 66.

**πύλιγξ**, ιγγος, ἡ, *hair about the posteriors*, Hsch. (pl.); also, *curls*, Id. (Cf. Skt. *pulakas* 'bristling hairs', Ir. *ulcha* 'beard'.)

**πῠλίς**, ίδος, ἡ, Dim. of πύλη, *little gate, postern*, Hdt.1.180, 186, Th.4.110, *SIG*813*B*6 (Delph., i A.D.), etc.; ὁ Ἑρμῆς ὁ πρὸς τῇ π. D.47.26; π. χάρακος Onos.10.20; τὸν..τοῖχον σὺν τῇ π. *CIG*1948 (inc. loc.). **II.** pl., a disease of the anus, prob. *multiple fistula*, Gal.15.329.

**πυλλεῖ·** θραύει, λέγει, διαβοᾷ, θρυλλεῖ, Hsch.

**Πῠλόθεν**, Adv. *from Pylos*, Od.16.323.

**Πῠλοιγενής**, ές, (Πύλος) *born in Pylos*, Il.2.54, 23.303; cf. Πυληγενής.

⊛ **πῠλοκλειστής**, οῦ, ὁ, *shutter*, i.e. *warden, of the gate*, *Documenti antichi dell' Africa italiana* 2.101 (Cyrene, i A.D.).

**Πύλονδε** [ῠ], Adv. *to* or *towards Pylos*, Il.11.760, Od.3.182.

**πύλος** [ῠ], ὁ, = πύλη, only ἐν πύλῳ Il.5.397 Aristarch. ap. Sch.; better ἐν Πύλῳ Paus.6.25.3.

⊛ **Πύλος** [ῠ], ὁ and ἡ, *Pylos*, ἐν Π. ἠγαθέῃ Il.1.252; Πύλου ἱερῆς Od.21.108, cf. Pi.*P*.5.70, Ar.*Eq*.1058, Th.4.39, etc.; but Π. ἠμαθόεντος Il.2.77, al., Hes.*Sc*.360; λέγεται καὶ θηλυκῶς καὶ ἀρσενικῶς St.Byz.: masc. in Str., 8.3.26 (sg. and pl.), al.

**πῠλ-ουρός**, ὁ, = πυλωρός, Hdt.3.72, 77, 118, 140, 156 (with v.l. πυλωρός in 72, 156), Baur and Rostovtzeff *Second Report on Dura-Europos* 138 (ii A.D.), *Gloss.*: as fem., ib. ⊛ **-οῦχος**, ὁ, *beam supporting gates*, J.*AJ*3.6.2 (pl.). **-όω**, *furnish with gates*, τὸν Πειραιᾶ X.*HG*5.4.34:—Pass., *to be so furnished*, ἅπαντ' ἐκεῖνα πεπύλωται πύλαις Ar.*Av*.1158.

**πυλωλάκτας·** κακῶν μεστούς, Hsch.

**πύλ-ωμα** [ῠ], ατος, τό, *gateway*, in pl., A.*Th*.408, 799, E.*Hipp*.808, *Ph*.1113, etc. ⊛ **-ών**, ῶνος, ὁ, *gateway*, Arist.*Mu*.398a16 (pl.), *PCair. Zen*.193.9 (iii B.C.), *PEnteux*.74.3 (iii B.C.), *Sammelb*.6157 (ii B.C.), *IG*3.398 (pl.); freq. separated from the house or temple to which it gave entrance, *gate-tower, gate-house*, *IPE*1$^{2}$.32*B*48 (Olbia, iii B.C.), Plb.4.18.2, Luc.*Hipp*.5, etc.; of a temple, Plu.*Tim*.12; τετράθυρος π. Callix.1; π. τὸ μῆκος δίπλεθρος D.S.1.47, cf. Luc.*Nigr*.23; ἡ θύρα τοῦ π. *Act.Ap*.12.13.

**πῠλωνοφύλαξ** [φῠ], ἄκος, ὁ, *warder, gate-keeper*, *BGU*14v2 (iii A.D.).

**πῠλωρ-έω**, *keep the gate*, Luc.*DMort*.20.1, etc.; ὁ πινοτήρης π. τὴν κόγχην Plu.2.980b: metaph., γλῶσσα π. τὴν γεῦσιν Ps.-Democr. ap. Hp.*Ep*.23, cf. *PMag.Par*.2.158 (dub.). **-ικός**, ή, όν, *of a warder*, Aen.Tact.28 tit. ⊛ **-ιον**, τό, *porter's lodge*, Poll.1.77. **-ός**, ὁ, *gate-keeper, warder, porter*, A.*Th*.621; π. πύργων, ναῶν, E.*Tr*.956, *IT*1227 (troch.); Ἅιδου κύων Id.*HF*1277: as fem., ἡ π. δωμάτων γυνή Id.*IT*1153: in Prose, Aen.Tact.28.2, al., Lxx *Ne*.7.1, al., Ph.2.216; of the guards of the Propylaea at Athens, *IG*2$^{2}$.2297: metaph., τοῖον πυλωρὸν φύλακα..τροφῆς such a *watchful* guardian of thy life, S.*Aj*.562; κακοὺς π. ὑμᾶς, ὦ Κορίνθιοι, ἡ Πελοπόννησος ἔχει Prov. ap. Plu.2.221f. **II.** Medic., *pylorus* or *lower orifice of the stomach*, οἷον π. τις Gal.*UP*4.7, cf. *Nat.Fac*.3.4, Cels.4.1.7, Ruf.*Onom*.169, Id. ap. Orib.7.26.34. **2.** π., ἡ, *os uteri*, Ps.-Democr. ap. Hp.*Ep*.23. (Cf. πυλαωρός.)

**πύμᾰτος** [ῠ], η, ον, Ep. Adj. = ἔσχατος, *hindmost, last*, Il.4.254; ἐν πυμάτοισι, opp. μετὰ πρώτοισι, 11.65; also, *outmost*, ἄντυξ ἣ π. θέεν ἀσπίδος 6.118, cf. 18.608; ῥινὸς ὕπερ π. above *the root of* the nose, 13.616; πυμάτῃ (sc. Ὕδρῃ) δ' ἐπίκειται εἴδωλον κόρακος Arat.448; *nethermost*, φάρος Pl.*Epigr*.12.2; π. Ταρτάρου βάθη Luc.*Trag*.295; *remotest*, φωλειοί Opp.*C*.3.451. **2.** of Time, *last*, ἄνδρα κτείνας π. Il.11.759; Οὖτιν ἐγὼ πύματον ἔδομαι Od.9.369; ἀργειφόντῃ πυμάτῳ σπένδεσκον 7.138; π. τέλεον δρόμον..ἵπποι Il.23.373; π. δ' ὁπλίσσατο δόρπον Od.2.20; Trag. only in lyr., π. γῆρας S.*OC*1236: neut. πύματον and πύματα as Adv., *at the last, for the last time*, πύματόν τε καὶ ὕστατον Il.22.203; ὕστατα καὶ πύματα Od.4.685, 20.13; ἐν πυμάτῳ S.*OC*1675 (lyr.). **3.** of Degree, ὅ τι πύματον ὀλοίμαν by whatever is *the last, worst* fate, Id.*OT*661 (lyr.).

**πύνδαξ**, ἄκος, ὁ, (cf. πυθμήν) *bottom* of a jar, cup, or other vessel, τὸν πύνδακα εἰσκρούειν knock in the *bottom* so as to make the cup hold less, a trick of wine-sellers, Pherecr.105; μέτρῳ τὸν πύνδακα εἰσκεκρουμένῳ μετρεῖν prob. in Thphr.*Char*.30.11 (ἐκκεκρ- codd., and so ἐκκρουσαμένους τοὺς π. Ar.*Fr*.270 codd. Poll.), cf. Arist.*Pr*.938a13; *bottom* of a ship, *Mim.Oxy*.413.103. **II.** = λαβή, *sword-hilt*, S.*Fr*.311.

**πυνθάνομαι**, Od.2.315, etc.; poet. also **πεύθομαι** (q.v.): Ep. impf. πυνθανόμην 13.256: fut. πεύσομαι Il.18.19, etc., Dor. πευσοῦμαι Theoc.3.51 (so cod. Med. in A.*Pr*.988): aor. ἐπῠθόμην Il.5.702, etc., Ep. and Lyr. πυθόμην Od.4.732, B.15.26; imper. πυθοῦ, Ion. πυθεῦ Hdt.3.68; Ep. opt. πεπύθοιτο Il.6.50, al. (subj. πεπύθωνται is f.l. for γε πύθωνται, 7.195); 3 pl. πυθοίατο S.*OC*921: pf. πέπυσμαι Od.11.505, etc.; 2 sg. πέπῠσαι Pl.*Prt*.310b, Ep. πέπυσσαι Od.11.494; inf. πεπύσθαι Th.7.67, etc.; part. πεπυσμένος Pl.*Smp*.179e: plpf. ἐπεπύσμην Ar.*Pax*615, *Av*.470; 3 sg. ἐπέπυστο Il.13.674, Ep. πέπυστο ib.521; 3 dual πεπύσθην 17.377:—*learn*, whether *by hearsay* or *by inquiry* (ἐξιστορήσαντες τὰ ἐβούλοντο πυθέσθαι Hdt.7.195): constr. **1.** π. τί τινος *learn* something *from* a person, Il.17.408, Od.10.537, A.*Ag*.599, Ar.*Ra*.1417, etc.; also π. τι ἀπό τινος A.*Ch*.737; ἐξ ἄλλων S.*OC*1266; ἐκ τοῦ παρατυχόντος Th.1.22; freq. παρά τινος, Hdt.2.91, etc.; παρ' ἄλλων (v.l. ἄλλων) X.*Cyr*.4.1.3. **2.** c. acc. rei only, *hear* or *learn* a thing, Od.2.411, A.*Ch*.765, Antipho 5.25, etc.: abs., αἰσχρὸν τόδε γ' ἐστὶ καὶ ἐσσομένοισι πυθέσθαι Il.2.119, cf. Pi.*P*.7.7, etc.; ὡς ἐγὼ πυνθάνομαι Hdt.1.22, etc. **3.** c. gen. objecti, *hear* or *inquire concerning*, πυθέσθαι πατρός, ἀγγελιάων, μάχης, Od.1.281, 2.256, Il.15.224, cf. S.*El*.35, Pl.*Lg*.635b. **4.** π. τινά τινος *inquire about* one person *of* or *from* another, τὸν ἄνδρα τῶν ὁδοιπόρων Ar.*Ach*.204; so π. περί τινος Hdt.2.75; πᾶσαν πυθέσθαι τῶνδ' ἀλήθειαν πέρι S.*Tr*.91: c. acc. pers. only, *inquire about* a person, Ar.*Th*.619. **5.** c. part., πυθόμην ὁδὸν ὁρμαίνοντα that he was starting, Od.4.732, cf. Hdt.9.58, S.*Aj*.692; π. τὸ Πλημμύριον ἑαλωκός Th.7.31, cf. X.*An*.1.7.16, etc.; οὔ πω..πεπύσθην Πατρόκλοιο θανόντος they *had* not yet *heard of* his being dead, Il.17.377, cf. 427, 19.322, A.*Ch*.763; ὡς ἐπύθοντο τῆς Πύλου κατειλημμένης Th.4.6: with acc. rei added, εἰ σφῶϊν τάδε πάντα πυθοίατο μαρναμένοιιν Il.1.257. **6.** c. acc. et inf., *hear* or *learn that*.., Hdt.1.62, 5.15, S.*Tr*.103 (lyr.), Th.7.25, etc. **7.** folld. by an interrog. clause, ὡς πυθώμεθα ὅπου ποτ' ἐσμέν S.*OC*11; αὐτοῦ π. τί ποτε νοεῖ *inquire* or *learn* from him what.., Pl.*La*.196c, cf. X.*An*.6.3.25, Plb.3.107.6; π., ὅτεῳ..συνοικέει Hdt.3.68; π. εἰ.. *inquire* whether.., S.*OC*993, *IG*4$^{2}$(1).121.18 (Epid., iv B.C.); τοῦ ξένου ἡδέως ἂν π., τί ταῦθ' ἡγοῦντο Pl.*Sph*.216d; π. τινῶν, ὅτι.. X.*An*.4.6.17; π., ὅπως ἂν κάλλιστα πορευθείη ib.3.1.7, cf. *Cyr*.1.4.7. **II.** Act., aor. 1 part. fem. πεύσασα *having learned*, *PMasp*.5.7 (vi A.D.). **2.** v. πεύθω.

**πυνικοί**, οἱ, *boiled beans*, Hsch. **πυννιάζω**, = πουνιάζω, Id.

**πύξ**, Adv. *with the fist*, π. ἀγαθὸς Πολυδεύκης good *with the fist*, i.e. *at boxing*, Il.3.237; πολὺ φέρτατος..π. Od.8.130; οὐ γὰρ π. γε μαχήσεαι Il.23.621; π. μὲν ἐνίκησα Κλυτομήδεα ib.634; περιγιγνόμεθ' ἄλλων π. τε παλαισμοσύνῃ τε Od.8.103; πειρηθήτω..ἢ π. ἠὲ πάλῃ ib.206; οἱ δὲ μάχοντο π. τε καὶ ἑλκηδόν Hes.*Sc*.302; ἄνδρα π. ἀρετὰν εὑρόντα *by boxing*, Pi.*O*.7.89; Ἴσθμι' ἑλὼν π. Simon.158, cf. 154; πὺξ πεπληγέμεν Il.23.660; πατάσσειν, παῖσαι, παίεσθαι, Ar.*Ra*.547 (lyr.), X.*An*.5.8.16, Lys.4.6, etc.; π. ἐπὶ κόρρας ἤλασα Theoc.14.34; τοὺς δακτύλους π. ἔχειν to have one's fist *clenched*, Hp.*Morb*.3.13. (Cf. Lat. *pug-nus*.)

**πύξ**, πῦγός, ἡ, later form for πυγή (q.v.). **πύξαγρις**, v. πτύξαγρις.

**πυξ-άκανθα** [ᾰκ], ἡ, *thorn like the box-tree*, = λύκιον, Dsc.1.100: also **πυξάκανθος**, Lat. *pyxacanthus*, Plin.*HN*12.31, 24.125, Gal.12.63. **-εών**, ῶνος, ὁ, (πύξος) *grove of box-trees*, *Gloss.* ⊛ **-ίδιον**, τό, = πυξίον I, Ar.*Fr*.846, *Gloss.* **II.** Dim. of πυξίς, *PRyl*.125.14 (i A.D.), *Sammelb*.4324.18, Sch.Ar.*Eq*.902. **-ίζω**, *to be yellow like box-wood*, Xenocr. ap. Orib.2.58.63.

**πυξίνεος** [ῐ], α, ον, = πύξινος, *AP*6.309 (Leon.).

**πυξῐνόπους**, πουν, gen. ποδος, *with feet of box-wood*, κλίνη Roussel *Cultes Égyptiens* 221 (Delos, ii B.C.).

**πύξῐνος**, η, ον, (πύξος) *made of box-wood*, ζυγόν Il.24.269; πλαισίω (dual) *IG*1$^{2}$.373.203; κλίνη Pl.Com.34; πόδες κλίνης *PGrenf*.1.14.7 (ii B.C., cf. 2 p.211); ἁλία Archipp.13; φόρμιγξ Theoc.24.110; κτένα *AP*6.211 (Leon.). **2.** **-ινον**, τό, *box-wood tablet*, *PGrenf*.1.14.12 (ii B.C., pl.). **II.** *yellow as box-wood*, Χαιρεφῶν ὁ π. Eup.239, cf. Philostr.*VS*1*Praef*., Sch.Ar.*V*.1399, etc.; *pyxinum* [*collyrium*], Cels.6.6.25.

**πυξ-ίον**, τό, *tablet of box-wood* for painting on, Anaxandr.13, Amphis 51; for writing on, Ar.*Fr*.845, Luc.*Ind*.15. **II.** *list*, hence *section, division*, τῷ ὀγδόῳ π. τῆς γερουσίας Judeich *Altertümer von Hierapolis* No.278.3, cf. 209.7 (prob.), 234.4 (pl.). **-ίς**, ίδος, ἡ, *box of box-wood*: generally, *box* (cf. A.D.*Synt*.249.1), *PRyl*.125.26 (i A.D.), *Sammelb*.4324.17, Luc.*Asin*.12, *Philops*.21, etc.; π. χαλκῆ Trypho *Trop*.1.2; π. ἰατρικαί Ph.*Bel*.77.28, cf. Dsc.3.11; for poison, J.*BJ*1.30.7; so Lat. *pyxis*, Cic.*Cael*.25.61, Juv.13.25. **II.** *cylinder* in which a piston works, Hero *Spir*.1.28. **III.** = πυξίον I, Eust.632.57. **IV.** name of a *plaster*, Aët.12.63, 15.15, Paul.Aeg.3.78.

**πυξο-γρᾰφέω**, *write* or *draw on a tablet*, Artem.1.51. **-ειδής**, ές, *like box-wood*, χρόα D.S.3.35, cf. Dsc.4.183.

**πύξος**, ἡ, *box*, *Buxus sempervirens*, Thphr.*HP*3.15.5, Arist.*Mu*.401a3, *Mir*.831b23, etc. (Hom. only has Adj. πύξινος): prov., πύξον εἰς Κύτωρον ἤγαγες 'carry coals to Newcastle', Eust.88.3. **2.** *box-wood*, *IG*4$^{2}$(1).102.45 (Epid., iv B.C.), Nic.*Al*.579, *Th*.516.

**πυξ-ώδης**, ες, = πυξοειδής, τὴν χρόαν π. Dsc.1.16. **-ών**, ῶνος, ὁ, = πυξεών, Ps.-Hdn.Gr. in Greg.Cor. p.225 S.

**πῠοειδής**, ές, (πύον) *like purulent matter*, γάλα Arist.*HA*573a24.

**πύον** [ῠ], τό, *discharge from a sore, matter*, Hp.*Aph*.2.47, Arist.*GA*777a11, etc.: pl. πύα Hp.*Int*.2, Aret.*SD*1.10, etc.: also **πύος**, εος, τό, Hp.*Morb*.1.15, al., *IG*4$^{2}$(1).122.55, 58 (Epid., iv B.C.), Aret.*SA*2.1; cf. πύον τὸ ἔμπυον τὸ καὶ πύος Hdn.Gr.1.376 codd. Arc. **II.** = πυός, Emp.68.

® **πῡο-ποιέω**, *make pus*, Dsc.2.155. **-ποίησις**, εως, ἡ, *making of pus*, Alex.Trall.3.7. **-ποιός**, όν, *making pus*, Dsc.2.72, Aret.*CA*2.6; π. ἀγωγή, θεραπεία, Aët.15.5,7. **-ρροέω**, (ῥέω) *discharge matter*, Hp.*Epid.*7.5, Dsc.1.64.4, 2.151, Ruf.ap.Orib.8.24.67. **-ρροια**, ἡ, *discharge of matter*, Dsc.5.113.

**πύος**, τό, = πύον (q. v.).

® **πῡός**, ὁ, *first milk after the birth*, whether of women or cattle (*beestings*), Cratin.142, Pherecr.108.19, Ar.*V.*710, *Pax*1150, *Fr.*318.5, *Fr.*16 D. [ῡ Ar., but πῠον Emp. (v. supr.); on the accent cf. Hdn.Gr.1.111.]

**πῡ-ουλκός**, ὁ, (πύον, ἕλκω) *surgical instrument for drawing off pus*, Hero *Spir.*2.18, Afric.*Cest.*p.27 V., Gal.11.125, *Hermes* 38.283. **-όω**, *cause to suppurate*, Eust.464.27:—Pass., *suppurate*, Arist.*Resp.*479b30.

**πυππάζω**, *cry* πύππαξ, Cratin.52.

**πύππαξ**, an exclamation of admiration, *bravo!* Pl.*Euthd.*303a, *Com.Adesp.*1130.

® **πῦρ** (once **πύυρ** [⏑⏓] by 'distraction', Simon.59 codd. Hdn.Gr. (*Rh.Mus.*35.101, 38.378)), τό, gen. πυρός; not used in pl., v. πυρά, τά:—*fire*, π. καίειν or δαίειν to kindle *fire*, Il.8.521, Od.7.7, etc.; π. ἀνακαίειν, ἅπτειν, ἐξάπτειν, αἴθειν, ἐναύειν, v. sub vocc.; π. ποιεῖν, ποιήσασθαι, Anaxipp.1.12, X.*An.*5.2.27; οἴσετε π. Il.15.718; π. προσέφερον X.*An.*5.2.14; π. ἐμβαλεῖν νηυσί, κλισίῃσι, Il.15.597, Od.8.501 (tm.); π. φυσητέον, ῥιπίζειν, Ar.*Lys.*293, Plu.*Flam.*21; as exclam., "πῦρ" βοᾷ Men.*Sam.*208. **b.** π. τεχνικόν, v. τεχνικός. **2.** *funeral-fire* (cf. πυρά), ὄφρα πυρός με.. λελάχωσι θανόντα Il.7.79, 22.342, cf. 15.350, 23.76; ζῶντα διδόναι τινὰ πυρί *burn* one alive, Hdt.1.86. **3.** *sacrificial fire*, ἐν πυρὶ βάλλε θυηλάς Il.9.220, cf. Od.3.341,446; κατὰ τοῦ π. σπένδειν Pl.*Criti.*120a; διὰ τοῦ π. ὀμνύναι D.54.40. **4.** *hearth-fire*, πυρὸς ἐσχάραι Il.10.418, cf. Od.5.59; ἕως ἂν αἴθῃ πῦρ ἐφ' ἑστίας ἐμῆς A.*Ag.*1435; πυρὶ δέχεσθαί τινα E.*Or.*47; τὸ π. τὸ ἀθάνατον *the fire* of Vesta, Plu.*Num.*9, etc.; deified, Πῦρ ἀθάνατον *SIG*826 ii 14 (Delph., ii B.C.). **5.** *lightning*, κεραυνὸς ἀενάου πυρός Pi.*P.*1.6; πῦρ πνέοντος κεραυνοῦ Id.*Fr.*146; πυρὸς ἀμφήκης βόστρυχος A.*Pr.*1044 (anap.); πυρὶ καὶ στεροπαῖς S.*OT*470 (anap.); παλτῷ ῥιπτεῖ πυρί Id.*Ant.*131 (anap.); θείῳ πυρὶ παμφαής Id.*Ph.*728 (lyr.). **b.** *fire, light*, or *heat* of the sun, θερινὸν π., opp. χειμών, Pi.*P.*3.50, cf. Pl.*Lg.*865b; of the stars, π. πνείοντα ἄστρα S.*Ant.*1146 (lyr.); *summer solstice*, Alcm.79, Paul.Al.*A.*3. **6.** *flame* of torches, S.*Ant.*964 (lyr.), etc.; π. εὐάγγελον, ἄγγαρον, πομπόν, of the beacon fire, A.*Ag.*21,282,299. **7.** *fever heat, violent fever*, πῦρ ἔλαβέν [τινα] Hp.*Epid.*1.26.η', al.; ὁ δ' ἔχων θέρμαν καὶ π. ἧκεν Ar.*Fr.*690; τεταρταίῳ πυρί Call.*Aet.*3.1.17; π. ἄγριον Hp.*Epid.*7.20 (of erysipelas acc. to Gal.19.134). **II.** phrases, ἐν πυρὶ γενέσθαι to be consumed, come to nothing, Il.2.340; φεύγων καπνὸν εἰς πῦρ δεσποτείας ἐμπεπτωκώς 'out of the frying pan into the *fire*', Pl.*R.*569b, cf. Prov.ap.Simp.*in Epict.*p.72 D.; ἦν ἄρα πυρός γ' ἕτερα θερμότερα Ar.*Eq.*382; πῦρ ἐπὶ πῦρ ἐγχεῖν, ἄγειν, φέρειν, ἐπεισφέρειν, Cratin.18, Ar.*Fr.*453, Arist.*Pr.*880a21, Plu.2.61a; εἰς π. ξαίνειν 'plough the sands', Pl.*Lg.*780c; βασανίζειν χρυσὸν ἐν πυρί Id.*R.*413e, cf. Plb.21.20.7: as a type of things *irresistible* or *terrible*, ἀντίος εἶμι, καὶ εἰ πυρὶ χεῖρας ἔοικε Il.20.371; μάρναντο δέμας πυρὸς αἰθομένοιο 11.596, al.; Ἕκτωρ πυρὸς αἰνὸν ἔχει μένος 17.565, cf. 6.182; so τὸ πεπρωμένον οὐ π. σχήσει Pi.*Fr.*232; κρεῖσσον ἀμαιμακέτου πυρός S.*OT*177; οὐδὲν θηρίον γυναικὸς ἀμαχώτερον, οὐδὲ π. Ar.*Lys.*1015; ἀναρχία κρείσσων πυρός E.*Hec.*608; ἐχίδνης καὶ πυρὸς περαιτέρω Id.*Andr.*271; so διὰ πυρὸς ἰέναι (as we say) to go through *fire and water*, dash through any danger, X.*Smp.*4.16, cf. *Oec.*21.7, Ar.*Lys.*133; but διὰ πυρὸς ἦλθε ἑτέρῳ λέχεϊ she *raged furiously* against the other partner of the bed, E.*Andr.*487 (lyr.); διὰ πυρὸς ἔμολον ματρί Id.*El.*1183 (lyr.); σωθήσεται οὕτω δὲ ὡς διὰ πυρός 1*Ep.Cor.*3.15; εἰς π. ἅλλεσθαι X.*Mem.*1.3.9; κἂν εἰς π. ἐμβαίεν Lib.*Ep.*314.3; π. διέρπειν S.*Ant.*265; of persons, ὦ π. σύ.. Id.*Ph.*927; of Hannibal, Plu.*Flam.*21: metaph. of anxious hope, θάλπει τῷδ' ἀνηκέστῳ πυρί S.*El.*888; of love, ἀρσενικῷ θέρεται π. Call.*Epigr.*27.5, cf. 45.2. (Cf. Arm. *hur*, OE. *fyr* 'fire', etc.)

® **πῡρά**, ῶν, τά, *watch-fires*, in Hom. only nom. and acc., καίωμεν πυρὰ πολλά Il.8.509, cf. 554, 9.77, 10.12; ἐκκαύσαντες π. Hdt.4.134; πύρ' αἴθει(ν) prob. for πυραίθει(ν) in E.*Rh.*41 (lyr.), 78,823 (lyr.) and for πύραιθεῖν (sic) in Call.*Fr.*1.13 P.; πυρὰ δαίεται E.*Rh.*136 (lyr.); ὡς.. ᾐσθάνοντο τὰ πυρὰ.. φανέντα the *beacon-fires*, Th.8.102; π. κατασβεννύναι X.*An.*6.3.25; dat., ἐπιτυγχάνει πυροῖς ἐρήμοις ib.7.2.18, cf. *Cyr.*4.2.16; of volcanic *fires*, Arist.*Mir.*833a1; πυρὰ.. εὔδηλα πᾶσι Scymn.258: metaph., δῆμος π. ἐς τὸν Τίβεριν πολλὰ ἐνέβαλε D.C.55.13. (A sg. πυρόν is cited by Hdn.Gr.2.944, but rejected by Eust.729.63: the accent, as well as dat. πυροῖς, shows that πυρά does not belong to πῦρ.)

® **πῡρά**, ᾶς, Ep. and Ion. **πῡρή**, ῆς, ἡ, (πῦρ) *funeral-pyre*, πυραὶ νεκύων καίοντο θαμειαί Il.1.52, etc.; πυρῆς ἐπιβάντ' ἀλεγεινῆς 4.99, etc.; ἐν δὲ πυρῇ ὑπάτῃ νεκρὸν θέσαν 23.165, 24.787, cf. Pi.*N.*9.24, S.*Tr.*1254, etc.; ποίησαν δὲ πυρὴν ἑκατόμπεδον Il.23.164; πυρὴν νῆσαι, συννῆσαι, to raise *one*, Hdt.1.50,86; πυρῆς ἀμμένης ibid.; τινὰ πυρᾷ κέαντες S.*El.*757; σκῦλα πρὸς πυρὰν ἐμὴν κόμιζε Id.*Ph.*1432; ἐπὶ τῇ π. κείμενος Pl.*R.*614b; αἱ τῶν ζωγρηθέντων σφαγαὶ εἰς τὴν π. ib.391b. **b.** *mound raised on the place of the pyre, tumulus*, Pi.*I.*8(7).63, S.*El.*901, E.*Hec.*386, *IT*26. **2.** *altar for burnt sacrifice*, Hdt.7.167, E.*Ion* 1258 (troch.); ἑρκεῖος π. Id.*Tr.*483; *fire burning thereon*, dub. l. in Hdt.2.39. **3.** *burning mass*, ib.107, Zos.2.13; λαμπάδων π. *a mass of burning* torches, D.S.17.36.

**πυράγηρα**· τὰ θωράκια, Hsch.

® **πῠρ-άγρα**, ἡ, *pair of fire-tongs*, Il.18.477, Od.3.434, Call.*Del.*144. **2.** *forceps*, Gal.2.635. **-αγρέτης** καρκίνος, = πυράγρα, *AP*6.92 (Phil.).

**πῠράζω**, *singe*, coined as etym. of πυρακτέω, *EM*697.16.

**πύρᾰθος** [ῠ], ὁ, poet. for σπύραθος, Nic.*Th.*932 (pl.).

**πῠραίθει(ν)**, v. πυρά, τά.

**πῠραιθής**, ές, *fiery*, Aglaïas 11.

**πῦρ-αιθοι**, οἱ, (αἴθω) *the Persian fire-worshippers*, Str.15.3.15: hence **-αιθεῖον**, τό, *their temple*, ibid.

**πῠραίθουσα**, ἡ, *furnace*, dub. in Hom.*Epigr.*14.11.

**πυραῖνος**, = πύρινος, *fiery*, dub. in *PMag.Lond.*121.801. **II.** πύραινος, written for πύραυνος, Hsch.

**πῠρ-άκανθα** [ᾰκ], ἡ, = ὀξυάκανθα, Nic.*Th.*856, Dsc.1.19,118; acc. πυρακάνθην ib.93. **2.** = σκόλυμος, Ps.-Dsc.3.14. **-άκμων**, ονος, ὁ, = *forfex*, *Gloss.* (πυραρμων cod.).

**πῠρακτ-έω**, *turn in the fire*: hence, *harden in the fire, char*, Od.9.328. **II.** *burn*, Nic.*Th.*688. **-όω**, = foreg. 1, βέλη, ξύλα, Plu.2.624b,762b; ξύλα, τόξα, βέλη πεπυρακτωμένα, D.S.3.25, Str.17.2.3, Scyl.112; πυρακτωθεὶς τὸν μηρόν *wounded by such a weapon*, dub. l. in Luc.*Tox.*55; πεπυρακτῶσθαι, opp. ἐψύχθαι, S.E.*M.*10.164,165. **2.** *heat* a cautery-iron, in Pass., Leonid.ap.Paul.Aeg.6.44, Gal.14.280. **II.** metaph. in Pass., *to be inflamed*, ζήλῳ Hld.2.9.

**πῠρᾰλίς** or **πῠραλλίς**, ίδος, ἡ, an unknown *bird*, perh. a kind of *pigeon*, Arist.*HA*609a18, Call.*Fr.*100c4, Ael.*NA*4.5; **πυρραλίς**, Hsch. **2.** an *insect* said to live in fire, Plin.*HN*11.119. **II.** ἐλαῖαι πυραλλίδες, a *red* kind of olive, Phylotim.ap.Orib.2.69.9.

**πῠράμη** [ᾰ], ἡ, = ἄμη, Sch.Ar.*Pax* 298 (pl.); = *vatillum*, *Gloss.*; written **πυράμμη**, ib.

**πῠρᾱμητός**, ὁ, (πυρός, ἀμητός) *the time of the wheat-harvest*, Arist.*HA*571a26, Thphr.*HP*7.6.2, 9.9.2, Democr.ap.Gal.14.94.

**πῠρᾰμῐδ-ῐκός**, ή, όν, *pyramidal*, Iamb. *in Nic.* p.72 P., al. Adv. **-κῶς** prob. cj. in *Theol.Ar.*22. **-οειδής**, ές, = foreg., Epicur.*Nat.*14.5.

**πῠράμῐνος** [ᾰ], η, ον, (πυρός) poet. for πύρινος, as κριθάμινος for κρίθινος, *wheaten*, ἀθέρες Hes.*Fr.*117; ἄλευρα Polyaen.4.3.32; cf. σπυραμινός.

® **πῠρᾰμίς**, ίδος, ἡ, *pyramid*, Hdt.2.8,124, D.S.1.63, Str.17.1.33, *OGI*666.13 (Egypt, i A.D.), etc.; as a sepulchral monument, *PLips.*30.14 (iii A.D.). **2.** *pyramid*, as a geometrical figure, Pl.*Ti.*56b, Arist.*Cael.*304a12, etc. **b.** *pyramidal number*, Speus.ap.*Theol.Ar.*62. **3.** name of a farm-building, *IG*2².2776.16; of a fountain, *Arch.Anz.*26.233 (Panticapaeum). **II.** a sort of *cake*, Ephipp.13.5 (anap.); different from πυραμοῦς, acc. to Iatrocl.ap.Ath.14.647c codd. (but dub., cf. πυραμοῦντα· τὴν πυραμίδα, Hsch.); ἡ ἐκ πυρῶν καὶ μέλιτος, ὥσπερ σησαμὶς ἡ ἐκ σησάμων καὶ μέλιτος, *EM*697.27. (Expld. by Gramm., etc., fr. πῦρ because pointed, Amm.Marc.22.15.29, cf. Pl. l. c.; from πυρός, St.Byz.: it is suggested that the pyramids were named from resembling a πυραμίς II in shape; but the shape of a π. II is unknown: the derivation from Egypt. *pr-m-wś* 'the height of a pyramid' is doubtful.)

**πῠρᾰμοειδής**, ές, *pyramidal*, Thphr.*Ign.*52; σχῆμα Ph.1.11, cf. Arr.*An.*5.7.3; τὸ π. S.E.*M.*10.280; of the human heart, *Corp.Herm.*5.6.

**πῠραμός**, ὁ, = sq., Artem.1.72 (pl.).

**πῠρᾰμοῦς**, οῦντος, ὁ, contr. fr. πυραμόεις, (πυρός) *cake of roasted wheat and honey*, Ephipp.8.3, cf. Trypho ap.Ath.3.114b; given to him who kept awake best during a παννυχίς, Call.*Fr.*2.6 P.: hence, generally, *meed of victory, prize*, τοῦ γὰρ τεχνάζειν ἡμέτερος ὁ π. for stratagem 'we take the *cake* (*or biscuit*)', Ar.*Th.*94, cf. *Eq.*277.

**πύραστρον**, τό, prob. = πυράγρα, πυραύστρα, Herod.4.62 [ῠ, cf. πυραύστης].

® **πῠραυγής**, ές, (αὐγή) *fiery bright*, *h.Mart.*6, *AP*12.41 (Mel.), Luc.*Nav.*5, Nonn.*D.*2.536, al.

® **πύραυνος** [ῠ], ὁ, (αὔω (A)) *pan of coals*, Poll.6.88: neut. sg. πύραυνον Id.10.104. **II.** = ὁ πῦρ ἐναυόμενος, Phot., Eust.1547.64.—Name of plays by Alexis and others.

**πῠραύστης**, ου, ὁ, (αὔω (A)) *moth that gets singed in the candle*, δέδοικα μῶρον κάρτα πυραύστου μόρον A.*Fr.*288, cf. Arist.*HA*605b11, Ael.*NA*12.8.

® **πῠραύστρα**, ἡ, = πυράγρα, *IG*2².47.18 (iv B.C.); cf. πύραστρον.

**πυράφλεκτος**, ον, *unburnt by fire*, interpol. in Suid.

**πυρβόλος**, ον, (βάλλω) *casting fire*, Man.5.93.

**πυργ-αλίδαι**, οἱ, name of a guild at Camirus, *IG*12(1).701.11. **-ειος**, α, ον, *like a tower*, σκοπή Ion Trag.47. **-ηδόν**, Adv. *towerwise*, Aret.*SD*2.13; of soldiers, *in masses* or *columns*, *in close array*, Il.12.43, 13.152, 15.618, D.H.6.33; also of clouds, Nonn.*D.*32.76. ® **-ηρέομαι**, Pass., *to be shut up as in a tower, beleaguered*, A.*Th.*22,184, E.*Or.*762 (troch.), 1574, *Ph.*1087. **-ήρης**, ες, of a place, *furnished with towers, fortified*, κώμη Orac.ap.Paus.10.18.2. **-ίδιον** [ῐδ], τό, Dim. of πύργος, Ar.*Eq.*793; as a farm-building, *IG*2².2776.15,24. **-ῖνος**, η, ον, *tower-like*, πολίσματα (prob. for νομίματα cod. Med.) π. A.*Pers.*859 (lyr.). ® **-ίον**, τό, Dim. of πύργος, *IG*11(2).287 *A* 154 (Delos, iii B.C.), *PTeb.*780.11 (ii B.C.), Str.3.5.5, 12.3.18 (pl.), *BGU*889.10 (ii A.D.), Luc.*Pseudol.*19, *Vit.Auct.*9. **-ίς**, ῖδος, ἡ, *cupboard, cabinet*, Herod.7.15. **-ισκάριον**, τό, Dim. of πύργος, *Gloss.* **-ίσκιον**, τό, = foreg., Sch.rec.A.*Th.*158. ® **-ίσκος**, ὁ, Dim. of πύργος, *burial-vault*, *CIG*4207.13,4212 (Telmissus), al. **2.** *cupboard, cabinet*, Ael.*VH*9.13, Artem.1.74, S.E.*M.*7.102,9.

78. ⊛ -ίτης [ῑ], ου, ὁ, of a tower, στρουθὸς π. house-sparrow, Gal. 6.435. II. fem. πυργῖτις, ιδος, ἡ, a plant, Hsch. -ιτρον, τό, = πυργίσκος 2, π. ἰατρικόν PMasp.6ii65 (vi A.D.).

**πυργό-βᾶρις**, εως, ἡ, (βᾶρις 2) battlemented house, fortress, Lxx Ps. 121(122).7. -δάϊκτος [ᾰ], ον, (δαΐζω) destroying towers, πόλεμοι A.Pers.104 (lyr.). -δόμος, ον, building towers, κιθάρη Nonn.D.5. 67; μόσχος ib.44.41. -ειδής, ές, like a tower, J.BJ5.5.8, D.C.74. 5. -κάστελλον, τό, fort, Procop.Aed.2.5. -κέρᾶτα, metapl. acc., with towering horns, B.Fr.31. -μαγδῶλ, (τό?), watch-tower, BGU282.13, 542.6 (ii B.C.). -μᾰχέω, assault a tower, X.Cyr.6.4. 18, An.7.8.13, Plu.2.228d. II. fight from a tower, Plb.5.84. 2. -μάχος [ᾰ], ον, fighting from a tower, Ath.4.154f. ⊛ -ποιία, ἡ, building of a tower, Ph.Bel.82.43.

⊛ **πύργος**, ὁ, tower, esp. such as were attached to the walls of a city, Il.7.219, al., Hes.Sc.242, Hdt.3.74, al., Th.2.17, al., Plb.5.99. 9, etc.: in pl., city walls or ramparts with their towers, Il.7.338, 437; in sg., ἧντ' ἐπὶ πύργῳ 3.153, cf. 22.447; πόλιος ἦν πέρι πύργος ὑψηλός Od.6.262; πέριξ δὲ πύργος εἶχ' ἔτι πτόλιν E.Hec.1209; πύργους ἐπὶ τῶν γεφυρῶν ἐπιστῆσαι Pl.Criti.116a. b. movable tower for storming towns, X.Cyr.6.1.53, 6.2.18; π. ὑπότροχοι Onos. 42.3. c. tower on the back of war-elephants, Arr.Tact.2.4. d. Ζανὸς π., Pythag. name for the central fire of the universe, Arist. Fr.204. 2. metaph., tower of defence, τοῖος..σφιν π. ἀπώλεο, of Ajax, Od.11.556; ἄνδρες πόλιος π. ἀρεΐοις Alc.Supp.1a.10; παῖς ἄρσην πατέρ' ἔχει π. μέγαν E.Alc.311, cf. Med.390; ἅπας μοι π. Ἑλλήνων πατρίς Trag.Adesp.392; θανάτων δ' ἐμᾷ χώρᾳ π. ἀνέστα a tower of defence from deaths, S.OT1201 (lyr.). 3. the part of a house (prob. a separate building) in which the women lived and worked, αἱ ἄλλαι θεράπαιναι ἐν τῷ π. ἦσαν, οὗπερ διαιτῶνται D.47. 56; esp. if unmarried, as Hero in her tower, Musae.32,187, cf. Philostr.Jun.Im.1; of the workman's hut of Timon the misanthrope (which also became his tomb, cf. Luc.Tim.42), Paus.1.30.4, cf. AP 7.402 (Antip.); outbuildings, esp. if used in industry, Lxx Is.5.2, Mi.4.8, PStrassb.110.6 (iii B.C.), BGU1194.9 (ii B.C.), 650.8 (i A.D.), POxy.243.15 (i A.D.), Ev.Marc.12.1, Ev.Luc.14.28, PGiss.67.16 (ii A.D.), IG2$^{2}$.2776.65 (ii A.D.); π. ἐν ᾧ βαφεῖον καὶ ἕτερα χρηστήρια PLond.2.371.3 (i A.D.). II. part of an army drawn up in close order, column, Il.4.334,347. 2. at Teos, a division of the people, CIG3064, 3081, al. III. dice-box, AP9.482.24 (Agath.); cf. Lat. pyrgus.

**πυργο-σείστης**, ου, ὁ, tower-shaker, an engine of war, Anon. in Rh.3.580W. -σκάφος [ᾰ], ον, undermining towers, Lyc. 469.

**πυργοῦχος**, ὁ, (ἔχω) tower-bearer: in ships of war, platform which bore towers for defence, Plb.16.3.12, Poll.1.92.

**πυργο-φορέω**, bear a tower or towers, Luc.Syr.D.15. -φόρος, ον, bearing a tower, of Rhea, AP5.259 (Paul. Sil.); of Demeter, Lyd. Mens.4.63, Suid. s.v. Δημήτηρ; ἐλέφαντες Plu.2.307b, Hld.9. 16. -φύλαξ [ῠ], ἄκος, ὁ, tower-guard, warder, A.Th.168 (lyr.), PFlor.297.469 (vi A.D.), etc.

**πυργ-όω**, gird or fence with towers, Θήβης ἕδος ἔκτισαν..πύργωσάν τε Od.11.264, cf. Hom.Epigr.4.3, Orac.ap.Hdt.1.174, E.Ba.172:—Med., fortify, ὀχυρὰ X.Cyr.6.1.20; ἄστη MoschioTrag.6.27:—Pass., κορυφαὶ πεπυργωμέναι Str.12.3.39. 2. metaph., fence, protect, δέμας ἀσπίδι Nonn.D.30.52, etc. 3. πυργωθεὶς furnished with a tower, of an elephant, AP9.285 (Phil.). II. metaph., raise up to a towering height, πυργωθέντα πλοῦτον B.3.13; πρῶτος..πυργώσας ῥήματα σεμνά the first..'to build the lofty rhyme', Ar.Ra.1004; τέχνην..ἐπύργωσ' οἰκοδομήσας ἔπεσιν μεγάλοις κτλ. Id.Pax749; so ἀοιδὰς εὐδαιμονίας ἐπύργωσε E.Supp.998 (lyr.), cf. AP7.39 (Antip. Thess.): hence, exalt, lift up, π. ἄνω τὸ μηδὲν ὄντα E.Tr.612; Τροίαν ib.844 (lyr.); ⟨ὑμᾶς⟩..τυραννίσι πατὴρ ἐπύργου Id.HF475; of doctors, πυργοῦντες αὑτοὺς magnifying themselves, Men.497 (= Mimn.Trag.2); π. χάριν exalt, exaggerate it, E.Med.526; δὶς τόσα π. τῶν γιγνομένων Id.Heracl. 293 (anap.); τὴν τέχνην Lib.Ep.834.5; καθαροῖς λουμασι adorn (the city) with.., Epigr.Gr.903: also intr., declaim, μάταιον τὸ πυργοῦν λέγοντα .. Phld.Mort.33:—Pass., exalt oneself, τῇδ' ἐπυργοῦτο στολῇ, of a horse, A.Pers.192; πεπύργωσαι θράσει, λόγοις, E.Or.1568, HF 238. -ώδης, ες, = πυργοειδής, towering, S.Tr.273. -ωμα, ατος, τό, that which is furnished with towers, fenced city, Orac.ap.Hdt.7.140 (pl.), E.Ph.287: pl., fenced walls, A.Th.30,251,469, E.Cyc.115, Hel. 51. -ῶτις, ιδος, fem. of sq., π. ὀρκάνα A.Th.346 (lyr.). -ωτός, ή, όν, made like a tower, ἐμπετάσματα π. curtain-hangings edged with a pattern like battlements, Callix.2; χιτωνίσκος π. IG2$^{2}$.1514.26,46; πίλημα Str.15.3.19; π. στέφανος, = Lat. corona muralis, OGI560.11 (Tlos, i A.D.), cf. Corn.ND6.

**πυρδαής**, ές, (δαίω (A)) burning with fire, incendiary, πυρδαῆ τινα πρόνοιαν (πυρδαῆτιν πρόνοιαν cj. Hermann), of Althaea burning Meleager's fatal torch, A.Ch.606 (lyr.).

**πύρδαιον**, τό, = sq. II, IG4$^{2}$(1).108.146 (Epid.): pl., ib.109 ii 149; Lacon. πούρδαιν (q.v.); cf. πυροδάνσιον.

⊛ **πύρδᾰλον** or **πύρδᾰνον**, τό, small wood for burning, = φρύγανον, Hsch.; the latter form in Lyr.Alex.Adesp.31. II. kitchen or stove for cooking, Hsch.; perh. to be read in Men.Per.2.

⊛ **πύρεθρον** [ῠ], τό, pellitory, Anacyclus Pyrethrum, Nic.Th.938, Gal. 12.110, etc.; πύρεθρος (v.l. -ον) Dsc.3.73; cf. πυρῖτις II.

**πῠρεῖον**, Ion. -ήϊον, τό, mostly in pl., firesticks, h.Merc.111, S.Ph. 36, Thphr.HP5.3.4, D.S.5.67, etc.; τάχ' ἂν..τρίβοντες, ὥσπερ ἐκ πυρείων, ἐκλάμψαι ποιήσαιμεν τὴν δικαιοσύνην Pl.R.435a; πυρεῖά τε χερσὶν ἐνώμων Theoc.22.33; ἀμφὶ πυρήϊα δινεύεσκον A.R.1.1184; πυρεῖα συντρίψαντες Luc.VH1.32; the stationary piece was called ἐσχάρα, the drill τρύπανον, Thphr.Ign.64. II. sg., earthen pan for coals (= θυμιατήριον, Hsch. (πυρίον), Phot., Suid.), Lxx Ex.27.3; pl., ib.2Ch.4.11,21.

**πύρειος**, = πύριος, Olymp. in Mete.17.15.

**πῡρεκβολ-ίτης** [ῑ] λίθος, ὁ, stone yielding fire, Sch.Luc.VH1. 32. -ος, ον, neut. (?) pl. as Subst., fire-throwing machines, Alex. Aphr.Pr.1.38.

**πῡρεκτικός**, ή, όν, (πυρέσσω) feverish, Gal.16.491, Theol.Ar.51. Adv. -κῶς Paul.Aeg.3.43.

**πῡρεσσός**, ὁ, = πυρετός, PFay.248 (100 A.D.).

**πῡρέσσω**, E.Cyc.228; Att. -ττω Ar.V.813, Pl.Tht.178c: fut. πυρέξω Hp.Mul.1.2: aor. ἐπύρεξα Id.Prog.16, Epid.3.17.α', 4.26, al., Arist.Ph.228$^{a}$28: pf. πεπύρεχα Id.Pr.901$^{b}$10, M.Ant.8.15:—Pass., pf. πεπύρεγμαι Gal.4.447: (πυρετός):—to be feverish, fall ill of a fever, Hp.Aph.2.28, E. l.c., Ar.V.813, Aeschin.3.115, Artem.4.30, Sallust.9.

**πῡρεστία**, ἡ, hearth, PMasp.2 iii 11 (vi A.D.).

**πῡρετ-αίνω**, = πυρέσσω, Hp.VM17, Epid.4.7, etc.:—Med., ὅσα συνεχῆ πυρεταίνηται f.l. in Id.Fract.11. ⊛ -έω, = foreg., dub. in PGurob 5.6 (iii B.C.). -ιάω, = πυρέσσω, Gp.11.23.2, Cyran. 44. -ικός, ή, όν, = πυρεκτικός, Ptol.Tetr.85. -ιον, τό, Dim. of sq., slight fever, Hp.Epid.3.17.α': pl., POxy.896.33 (iv A.D.). ⊛ -ός, ὁ, (πῦρ) burning heat, fiery heat, φέρει πυρετὸν δειλοῖσι βροτοῖσιν (sc. Sirius) Il.22.31. II. fever, Hp.Aph.2.26, Ar.V.1038 (pl.), etc.; θνήσκειν ἐκ π. Epigr.Gr.247 (Mysia); π. ἀμφημερινοί, τριταῖοι, τεταρταῖοι, quotidian, tertian, quartan fevers, Pl.Ti.86a, etc. (v. sub vocc.); διαλείποντες Arist.Pr.866$^{a}$23.

**πῡρετοφόρος**, ον, causing fever, Sch.S.OT27.

**πῡρέττω**, Att. for πυρέσσω.

⊛ **πῡρετώδης**, ες, feverish, ῥίγεα Hp.Fract.34; inflamed, ἕλκος ib.25 (v.l. πυρῶδες). 2. subject to fever, κύστις Id.Aër.9. 3. of a sickly season, π. θέρος ib.10; π. νότοι Arist.Pr.862$^{a}$17, etc. Comp. -έστερος Hp.Art.49.

**πῡρ-εύς**, έως, ὁ, (πῦρ) one who lights fire or burns, Hsch. (pl.); πυρις (sic), = flamines, Gloss. (fort. ἱερεῖς). II. fire-proof vessel, cj. in AP13.13. -ευτής, οῦ, ὁ, one who fishes by torchlight, Poll.1. 96. -ευτικός, ή, όν, of or for fishing by torchlight, πυρευτική (sc. θήρα) Pl.Sph.220d; cf. πυρία II. II. for burning, χρεία Thphr.HP 5.1.12. -εύω, light a fire, Pl.Lg.843e.

**πῡρή**, ῆς, ἡ, Ion. and Ep. for πυρά. **πῡρήϊον**, τό, Ion. for πυρεῖον.

⊛ **πῡρήν**, ῆνος, ὁ, stone of stone-fruit, as of the olive, Hdt.2.92, Thphr.CP5.18.4, etc.; of the pomegranate, Hp.Aff.54, Thphr.HP 1.11.6; of the medlar, ib.3.12.5; of the date, Arist.Mete.342$^{a}$10, Thphr.CP1.19.2 (where ἐλάας is prob. cj. for ἰτέας); of the elder, Hp.Mul.2.133; of the myrtle and grape, Arist.Pr.925$^{b}$26; of the wild cherry, Hdt.4.23. 2. an edible nut, the kernel of κῶνος I. 2, Mnesith.ap.Ath.2.57b, IG2$^{2}$.1013.21. II. hard bone of fishes, implied by ἀπύρηνος Archestr.Fr.8.9. III. grain of frankincense, Hp.ap.Gal.19.134. b. an unknown aromatic, PMag.Par.1.2874, al. c. = ὀξυάκανθα, Dsc.1.93. IV. round head of a probe, Gal.UP15.7. 2. = ὀδούς III, Id.2.462. V. name of a gem, Plin.HN37.188; as a votive offering, IG7.3498.17 (Oropus). VI. growth under the chin of an animal, Str.4.6.10. (Sts. misspelt πυρρ- in codd.; the quantity of υ is inferred from ἀπῡρηνος Archestr. l.c. and Lat. apȳrinus.)

**πῡρηνάδες**, αἱ, knob-turners, guild at Ephesus, Ephes.2.79.

**πῡρήνεμος**, ον, (ἄνεμος) fanning fire, AP6.101 (Phil., s.v.l.).

**πῡρην-ίδιον**, τό, Dim. of πυρήν, knob, IG11(2).223B19,36 (Delos, iii B.C.), BGU781 iii 9 (i A.D.). -ίζειν, prob. for πιρην-, sine expl., Hsch. -ιον, τό, Dim. of πυρήν I, Thphr.HP3.7.4, Porph.Abst. 2.7. II. = πυρηνίδιον, π. χρυσᾶ IG11(2).161B116 (Delos, iii B.C.). *-ίς, only in Boeot. form πουρεινίς (q.v.).

**πῡρηνο-ειδής**, ές, shaped like a stone in fruit, of the ὀδούς III, Gal.2.756, UP12.7; καυτῆρας π. provided with knobs, Paul.Aeg.6. 2. -σμίλη, f.l. for πυρῆνος μήλης in Id.6.9,21.

**πῡρηνώδης**, ες, like a fruit-stone, σπέρματα Thphr.HP1.11.3, al.; ὀφθαλμοί dub. in Arist.HA568$^{a}$1.

**πῡρητόκος**, ον, (πῦρ) producing fire, AP6.90 (Phil., dub.).

**πῡρή-φᾰτος**, ον, (πυρός) formed like μυλήφατος, π. Δάματρος λάτρις wheat-pounding servant of Demeter, i.e. a millstone, AP7.394 (Phil., πυρηφάτου cod. P). -φόρος, ον, poet. for πυροφόρος, wheat-bearing, πεδίον Od.3.495, h.Ap.228.

⊛ **πῡρί-α**, Ion. -ίη, ἡ, (πῦρ) vapour-bath, made by throwing odorous substances on hot embers confined under a cloth, Hdt.4.75; πυρίαις χρῆσθαι ἐκ λίθων διαπύρων Str.3.3.6; τὰ σώματα ταῖς π. εὖ διατίθησι Plu.2.658d; πυρίαν ἐφεῦρεν [Μήδεια] Palaeph.43: metaph., γίνονται οἷον πυρίαι ἐν τῷ αἵματι Arist.PA651$^{a}$1. 2. generally of all forms of external application of heat, ξηραὶ π. Hp.Acut.21; ὑγραί, ξηραί, Gal.15.519, cf. Hp.Aph.5.28, 6.31; of cauteries, πυρίῃσι καυτήρων Aret.CD1.2. 3. = πύελος 2, Moschio ap.Ath.5.207f; so perh. in AP11.243 (Nicarch.). 4. = εἰσώστη, CIG3108, 3113 (Teos); tomb-chamber, Keil-Premerstein Dritter Bericht No.108, al., Supp. Epigr.4.548.4 (Ephesus), 594.11 (Colophon). II. fishing by torchlight, Arist.HA537$^{a}$18 (pl.). -ᾱλωτος [ᾰ], ον, caught by fire, of sea-birds, Philostr.Im.2.17. -ᾱμα, Ion. -ημα, ατος, τό, = πυρία I. 2, Hp.Flat.9, Philist.63, Arist.Pr.866$^{a}$24; = πυρία I. 1, Palaeph.

43. ❋-ᾱσις, εως, ἡ, *warming by a vapour bath*, Thphr.*Ign.*37 (pl.), Dsc.1.16 (pl.). -αστέον, *one must warm*, Herod.Med. in *Rh. Mus.*58.109; κατάπλασμα Antyll.ap.Orib.10.13.18 (v.l. -ᾱτέον, and so Apollon.ap.Gal.12.654). -άτη [ᾰ], ἡ (Poll.1.248, 6.54, Phot., who says, πυριάτη θηλυκῶς, οὐχὶ πυρίατος, οὐδὲ πυριατὴ ὀξυτόνως), *beestings curdled by heating over embers*, ἐμπιπλάμενοι πυριάτη Cratin.142; πυῷ καὶ πυριάτῃ Ar.*V.*710, cf. Eub.74.5, Luc.*Lex.*3, Gal. 6.694, Poll.1.248, Phot.; cf. πυριατόν. -ᾱτήρ, ῆρος, ὁ, *hot-water bottle* or *warming-pan*, Sor.2.10. -ᾱτήριον (Ion. -ητήριον Hp.*Steril.*230), τό, *vapour-bath*, heated by a furnace, Eup.128, Arist.*Pr.*869a19, *IG*5(1).938 (Cythera, iii B.C.), Plu.*Cim.*1; τὸ π. τὸ Λακωνικόν, Lat. *Laconicum*, D.C.53.27; π. τὸ ἐκ τῆς σικύης Hp. l.c. 2. π. φακωτά bean-shaped *hot-water bottles*, Archig.ap.Aët. 9.28. -ᾱτός, ή, όν, *heated in* or *for a bath*, κέραμος Gal.19. 86; but **πυριατόν**· τὸ ἑφθὸν πυρί, ὃ γίνεται ἐκ τοῦ πρώτου γάλακτος, Hsch. ❋-άω, Ion. inf. -ιῆν Hp.*Nat.Mul.*107, but -ιᾶν Id.*Morb.*2. 14: aor. ἐπυρίησα ib.19, -ίᾱσα *Hippiatr.*100:—Med., inf. -ιῆσθαι Hp.*Vict.*1.35: aor. ἐπυριησάμην Id.*Nat.Mul.*7,107, etc.:—Pass., aor. ἐπυριήθην Id.*Int.*1:—*put* persons *in a vapour-bath*, c. acc., Id. *Art.*47, Palaeph.43, etc.: metaph., τὸν λάρυγγ' ἥδιστα π. τεμαχίοις Crobyl.8:—Pass., *take a vapour-bath*, Ath.12.519e. 2. c. dupl. acc., π. αὐτὴν ὅσον τριήκοντα πυρίας Hp.*Mul.*1.75. 3. generally, *foment*, τὰ ἕλκη σαρξὶν ὑείαις Str.15.1.43:—Pass., πυριῶνται διά τινος οἱ ὀδόντες Dsc.3.9. 4. Pass., *to be used for vapour-baths*, [κύπερος] πρός τι πυριωμένη ἁρμόζει Id.1.4.

**πῡρῐ-βήτης**, ου, poet. εω, ὁ, (βαίνω) *standing over a fire*, τρίπους Arat.983. -βῐος, ον, *living in fire*, ζῷα D.L.9.79. -βλητος, ον, *struck by fire*, Nonn.*D.*8.355: metaph., *fevered*, Nic.*Th.*774. II. Act., = πυροβόλος, ἀκίδες *AP*12.76 (Mel.), cf. Nonn.*D.*30.91. -βόλος, ον, *fiery*, πλαγαί E.*Fr.*781.69 (lyr.). II. proparox. -βολον, τό, = *malleolus*, *Gloss.* -βουλος, ον, *of fiery counsel*, Ἑκάτη *PMag.Par.* 1.2752. -βρεμέτης, v. πυριγενέτης. -βρῑθής, ές, (βρίθω) *laden with fire*, Orac.ap.Procl. *in Ti.*2.54 D. -βρομος, ον, *roaring with fire*, ἥλιος Orph.*A.*1122 (nisi leg. -δρομος); Ζεύς Id.*H.*20. 2. -βρωτος, ον, (βιβρώσκω) *devoured by fire*, Str.17.1.27. -γενέτης, ου, ὁ, = sq., *fire-wrought*, χαλινοί A.*Th.*207 (lyr., πυριβρεμετᾶν Dind., cf. Timachid.ap.Hsch. s.v. πυριβρεμέτας). -γενής, ές, = foreg., *born in* or *from fire*, δράκων E.*Fr.*943 (lyr.); Διόνυσος Str.13.4. 11. 2. of instruments, *wrought* or *forged by fire*, στόμια E.*Hipp.* 1223; κώθων Henioch.1; π. παλάμα, i.e. a weapon, E.*Or.*820 (lyr.). -γληνος, ον, *fiery-eyed*, Opp.*C.*3.97, Orph.*L.*657, etc. -γλώχῑν, ὁ, ἡ, gen. ῖνος, *barbed with fire*, Opp.*C.*2.166 (v.l. περι-), Nonn.*D.*1.151. -γόνος, ον, *producing fire*, Plu.*Alex.* 35. II. proparox. πυρίγονος, ον, Pass., *fire-engendered*, Ael.*NA*2. 2; τὰ π. Ph.1.263, 2.500. -δαπτος, ον, (δάπτω) *devoured by fire*, A.*Eu.*1041 (lyr.). -δειπνος, ον, = foreg., prob. to be written divisim in Call.*Fr.*346. -δίνης [ῑ], ὁ, voc. -δῖνα, *whirling fire*, *PMag.Par.*1.598.

**πῡρίδιον**, τό, Dim. of πῦρ, *spark*, Thphr.*Fr.*33.

**πῡρίδιον**, τό, Dim. of πυρός, Ar.*Lys.*1206 (pl.), *PSI*6.611.2 (pl., iii B.C.).

**πῡριδρᾰκοντόζωνος**, ον, *girt with fiery serpents*, *PMag.Par.*1.1404.

**πῡρί-δρομος**, ον, *fiery in its course*, ἥλιος Orph.*H.*8.11, prob. in *A.* 1122. -έθειρα, ἡ, *with tresses of fire*, ἀστραπά B.16.56. -εφθον, τό, = πυριάτη, Philippid.10 (as cited by Poll.6.54, but τοὺς πυριέφθας Ath.14.658d cod. A, and Hsch. has πυρὶ ἕφθαι (sic)· τὸ πρῶτον γάλα, and πυριεφθής as gloss on ξηροπυρίτας, s.v. ψηροπυρίτας), cf. Gal.6.694, Poll.1.248, Eust.1626.6 (ubi vulg. πύρεφθον), Phot., etc. -ηκής or -ήκης, ές or ες, (ἀκή A) *with fiery point*, μοχλός Od.9.387. -θαλπής, ές, *heated in the fire*, A.R.4.926, Nic.*Th.*40, *AP*7.742 (Apollonid., s.v.l., prob. περι-). -θῡμος, ον, *fiery-spirited*, *PMag.Par.*1. 592. -κᾰής, ές, = πυρίκαυστος, *AP*6.281 (Leon.); πυρετός Gal. 16.709. [ᾱ metri gr. in *AP* l.c.] -καοι, οἱ, *fire-burners*, of the Delphians, Orac.ap.Plu.2.406e. -καυστος, ον, *burnt in fire*, Il. 13.564, Plu.2.922a, Vett.Val.127.32; in late Ep. -καυτος, Epic. in *Arch.Pap.*7.4, Nonn.*D.*10.74, al. 2. *caused by a burn* (or *scald*, cf. Gal.13.384), φλυκταινίδες ὥσπερ π. Hp.*Epid.*2.1.1; π. [ἕλκη] Dsc. 1.68.2, cf. Hp.*Fract.*27, Arist.*Pr.*866a6; later πυρίκαυτα ἕλκεα Aret. *SA*1.9. 3. πυρίκαυστον, τό, *plaster for a burn*, Thphr.*HP*9.19.3, *Ign.*38; ἡ π. ἔμπλαστρος Asclep.ap.Gal.13.525. II. *inflammatory*, in the form -καυτος, Pl.*Ti.*85c, Luc.*Asin.*6, etc. 2. *inflamed*, ὑπερῴα πυρίκαυτος Aristid.*Or.*49(25).30. -καύτωρ, ορος, ὁ, *burning with fire*, σφαίρης πυρικαύτορα κύκλον Timo 67.7. -κλόνος, ον, *fire-thronging*, *PMag.Par.*1.597. -κλοπία, v. πυροκλοπία. -κμητος, ον, (κάμνω) *wrought at* or *with fire*, λέβης Call. *Del.*145, cf. *Fr.anon.*50; *scorched*, χρώς Nic.*Th.*241; *cooked*, κρέα Porph.*Abst.*1.13. -κοίτης, ου, Dor. -ᾱς, ὁ, *wherein fire lies asleep*, νάρθηξ π., of the cane of Prometheus, *AP*6.294 (Phan., dub.).

**πῡρικός**, ή, όν, *of* or *from wheat*, φόρος *BGU*920.30 (ii A.D.); γόμος *OGI*629.86 (Palmyra, ii A.D.): -κά, τά, *wheat*, *PLond.*3.924.9 (ii A.D.).

**πῡρι-κρότᾰφος**· ὁ μετὰ πυρὸς κεκροτημένος σίδηρος, Hsch. -κτῐτος, ον, (κτίζω) *made in* or *with fire*, ἐν πυρικτίτῳ στέγᾳ in an earthen pot, restored by Kock (for πυρικτίτοισι γᾶς) in Tim.*Fr.*23. -λαμπής, ές, *bright with fire*, ἀστέρες *AP*5.15 (Marc. Arg. cod. Plan., περιλάμπει cod. Pal.), cf. Arat.1040, *Hymn.Is.*8, Opp.*C.*3.72, al. -λαμπίς, ίδος, ἡ, = πυρολαμπίς, Phot. (s.v.l.). -ληπτος, ον, *seized by fire*, πεδία π. *volcanic* country, Str.12.2.7; πέτραι Id.16.2.44. -μᾰνέω, *break out into a furious blaze*, Plu.*Alex.*35. -μάρμᾰρος, ον, *sparkling like fire*, ἀστήρ Man.4.93,391, *Cat.Cod.Astr.*1.173. -μᾰχέω, *to be fire-resisting*, Zos.Alch.p.252 B. -μάχος [ᾰ], ον, *resisting fire*, of a fire-proof stone, Arist.*Mete.*383b5, *Mir.*833b27. II. *fiery in fight*, Hsch.

❋ **πυρίνη**, ἡ, f.l. for πυρήν in Hp.*Mul.*2.133, Hsch.

**πυρινίζειν**, sine expl., Hsch.; prob. = πυρηνίζειν.

**πῡρῐνόθριξ**, ὁ, ἡ, gen. τρῐχος, *with fiery hair*, *PMag.Par.*1.636.

**πύρινον**, τό, = πύρεθρον, Ps.-Dsc.3.73.

**πύρῐνος** [ῠ], η, ον, (πῦρ) *of fire*, *fiery*, σῶμα Arist. *de An.*435a12, cf. *GC*326a31; εἰ.. ὁ ἀὴρ μὴ πῦρ, ἀλλὰ π. Id.*Metaph.*1049a26; ἄστρα Id. *Cael.*289a16; δοκίς D.S.15.50; θώρακες *Apoc.*9.17; π. κλῆθρα *PMag. Par.*1.589; π. νύμφαι *hot* springs, *AP*14.52; π. φάρμακον *fiery* drug, prob. arsenic, Maria ap.Zos.Alch.p.201 B. II. metaph., π. πόλεμος *bitter*, *obstinate* war. Plb.35.1.6, D.S.31.40. 2. π. ἀσπαστικόν *fiery* greeting, *PMag.Par.*1.638.

**πύρῐνος** [ῠ], η, ον, (πυρός) *of wheat*, *wheaten*, ⟨στάχυς⟩ E.*Fr.*373; prob. for πυρίμου ib.350; ἄρτοι X.*An.*4.5.31; σῖτος *PEleph.*5.26 (iii B.C.), Babr.26.2; πτισάνη Arist.*Pr.*863a35; ἄχυρον, ἄλευρον, Thphr.*HP*8.4.1, Dsc.3.102; γράστις *PSI*3.351.7 (iii B.C.), *Hippiatr.* 68; ἡ πυρίνη, name of a plaster containing bread, Paul.Aeg.7.17.15.

**πυρίον**, τό, f.l. for πυρεῖον, Corn.*ND*19, Anthem.p.153 W.

**πύριος** [ῠ], α, ον, = πύρινος (πῦρ), Iamb.*Myst.*2.7, Dam.*Pr.*9. Adv. -ίως Iamb.*Myst.*2.4 (s.v.l.).

**πῡρί-παις** [ῐ], παιδος, ὁ, *Son of fire*, of Dionysus, Opp.*C.*4. 287. -πηγάναξ, ὁ, *lord of the fount of fire*, *PMag.Osl.*1.155 (s.v.l.); written -άνυξ (sic) ib.344 (παγ-), *PMag.Par.*1.3177 (prob. corrected fr. -άναξ), *Rev.Phil.*1930.249 (Tab. defix., Egypt), *Tab.Defix.Aud.*38.29 (ibid., iii A.D., prob.), etc. -πληθής, ές, *full of fire*, Orac.ap.Eus.*PE*4.9. -πλοκος, ον, *wreathed with fire*, σειρή Nonn.*D.*30.83. -πνευστος, ον, = πυρίπνοος, ὀϊστοί Musae.88 (v.l.). II. *breathed on by fire*, λέβητες Nonn.*D.*33.6, cf. *IPE*1².274 (Olbia, i A.D., dub.). -πνέων, Ep. -πνείων, ουσα, ον, part. with no Verb in use, *fire-breathing*, Musae.41; πῦρ πνέουσαν must be read in E.*Ion* 203 (lyr.). -πνοος, ον, contr. -πνους, ουν, (πνέω) *fire-breathing*, Lyc.1314, *PMag.Par.*1.592, etc.; *fiery*, π. τόξα [Ἔρωτος] *AP*5.179 (Mel.); ζάλος ib.7.354 (Gaet.). -πολος, ον, = πύρπολος, *PMag.Par.*1.590. -ρραγής, ές, = πυρορραγής, Poll.7. 164, Phot. ❋-ρρόθιος, ον, *surging with fire*, ἀστέρες cj. in Orph. *H.*7.4. -σθενής, ές, *mighty with fire*, Διόνυσος Nonn.*D.*24.6; πολιῆται ib.29.193, cf. *PMag.Berol.*2.90. -σμάρᾰγος [ᾰρ], ον, *roaring with fire*, Theoc.*Syrinx* 8 (v.l. -σφάραγος). -σπαρτος, ον, *sowing fire*, *inflaming*, δῆγμα *APl.*4.208 (Gabriel.). -σπόρος, ον, = foreg., *PMag.Par.*1.596. II. proparox. πυρίσπορος, ον, *gendered in fire*, Orph.*H.*45.1, Opp.*C.*4.304. -σσοος, ον, (σώζω) for πυρί-σοος, *plucked from the burning*, Agamestor ap. Sch. Lyc.178. -στακτος, ον, *fire-streaming*, πέτρα π., of Etna, E.*Cyc.* 298. -στάτης [ᾰ], ου, ὁ, *tripod to stand on the fire*, Sch.Ar.*Av.* 436; also **πυρίστατος** and **πυροστάτης**, Eust.1827.56; **πυρίστατος** and -ον, *Gloss.* -στεφής, ές, *fire-wreathed* or *crowned*, Nonn.*D.*8. 289. -σφάραγος, v. πυρισμάραγος. -σφρήγιστος (Ion. for *πυρισφρᾱγ-), ον, *sealed with fire*, ib.13.328. -σχησίφως [σῐ], ωτος, ον, *maintaining light by fire*, *PMag.Par.*1.601. -σώμᾰτος, ον, *with body of fire*, ib.595.

**πῡρίτης** [ῑ], ου, ὁ, (πῦρ) *of* or *in fire*, π. τὴν τέχνην, i.e. a smith, Luc.*JConf.*8, cf. *Sacr.*6. II. π. λίθος, a mineral *which strikes fire*, *copper pyrites*, Dsc.5.125, Plin.*HN*36.138; other varieties of uncertain nature, ib.137, *PHolm.*11.38, Zos.Alch.p.120 B., al., Suid. s.v. ἄφαντον φῶς; of a zinc ore, Dsc.5.74.

**πῡρίτης** [ῑ] ἄρτος, ὁ, *wheaten loaf*, Aët.2.263 (pl.), Suid.

❋ **πῡρῖτις** (sc. βοτάνη), ιδος, ἡ, = πύρεθρον, Nic.*Th.*683, *Al.*531. 2. = ὀρεινὴ νάρδος, Dsc.1.9. II. (sc. λίθος), an unknown gem, Plin. *HN*37.189.

**πῡρί-τοκος** [ῐ], ον, *gendered in fire*, of Dionysus, Lyd.*Mens.*4. 160. -τρεφής, ές, *fire-fed*, *PMag.Berol.*2.94, Nonn.*D.*2. 486. -τρόφος, ον, *cherishing fire*, ῥιπίδες *AP*6.101 (Phil.). -τροχος, ον, *fiery in its course*, Nonn.*D.*14.292. -φᾰνής, ές, *appearing in fire*, *PMag.Par.*1.3023. -φᾰτος, ον, (θείνω II) *slain by fire*, A.*Supp.* 633 (lyr.). -φεγγής, ές, *fire-blazing*, *fiery*, Orph.*A.*214, *PMag. Par.*1.960. -φερής, ές, *fire-borne*. ib.3244 (dub.). ❋ -φευκτος, ον, *volatile*, *vaporizable*, Ps.-Democr.ap.Zos.Alch.p.122 B. -φλεγέθης, ες, = πυριφλεγής 2, κοιλίη Hp.*Mul.*1.52, cf. 2.178. ❋ -φλεγέθων, ουσα, ον, *blazing like fire*, ἔσοπτρον Agesianax ap.Plu.2.921b. II. pr. n. *Pyriphlegethon*, one of the rivers of hell, Od.10.513, Pl.*Phd.* 114a. ❋-φλεγής, ές, *flaming with fire*, *blazing*, Plu.2.948c; f.l. for περι- in X.*HG*5.3.19. 2. *violently inflamed*, ὑστέραι Hp.*Mul.*1. 64; π. δίψαι *burning* thirst, Aret.*SD*2.2. -φλέγων, οντος, ὁ, = foreg. 1, E.*Ba.*1019 (lyr.). -φλεκτος, ον, (φλέγω) *burnt* or *blazing with fire*, κάμακες A.*Fr.*171 (anap.); πανός E.*Ion* 195 (lyr.); *fiery*, βλάβαι Lyc.218; πόθοι *AP*12.151; βοστρύχια ib.11.66 (Antiphil.). -φλογος, ον, *flaming with fire*, Emp.*Sphaer.*113. -φοιτος, ον, *walking in fire*, epith. of Persephone, *Hymn.Mag.*3.25. -φόρος, ον, *holding heat*, prob. in Sor.1.76. -χαλκον, τό, *cupping-instrument*, Anon. *in Rh.*170.11. -χᾰρής, ές, *rejoicing in fire*, *PMag. Par.*1.593.

**πῡρίχη** [ῐ], ἡ, poet. for πυρρίχη, *AP*12.186 (Strat.).

**πῡρίχρως**, ωτος, ὁ, ἡ, *fire-coloured*, ὄψις Alcid. ap. Arist.*Rh.* 1406a2.

❋ **πυρ-καεύς** [prob. ᾰ], έως, ὁ, *fire-kindler*, Ναύπλιος π. title of play by S. ❋ -καϊά, Ep. and Ion. -ϊή, ἡ: trisyll. πυρκαιά E.*Supp.*1207;

(καίω) :—*funeral pyre*, νεκροὺς πυρκαϊῆς ἐπενήνεον Il.7.428; πυρκαϊὴ ἐμαραίνετο 23.228; κατὰ πυρκαϊὴν σβέσαν αἴθοπι οἴνῳ quenched *the burning pyre*, ib.250; πυρκαιὰς νεκρῶν E.l.c.; χλωρίωνι, ὃν.. μυθολογοῦσι γενέσθαι ἐκ πυρκαϊᾶς Arist.*HA*609$^b$10. 2. *conflagration*, πυρκαϊῆς γινομένης Hdt.2.66, cf. Arist.*Mu*.400$^a$29 (pl.); *arson*, Lex ap.D.23.22; πυρκαϊᾶς γραφή, δικάζειν, Poll.8.40,117. 3. metaph., *flame of love*, δι' ὅσης ἤλθετε πυρκαϊῆς *AP*7.217 (Asclep.). 4. *burnt ruins*, D.S.16.45. II. *olive-tree which has been burnt down to the stump*, and grows up again *a wild olive*, Lys.7.24 (s. v.l.). -καϊός, ά, όν, *for burnt-offerings*, ἐσχάραι *IG*11(2).145.58 (Delos, iv B.C.), 161*B*124 (ib., iii B.C.). -κόος, ον, (κοέω) *one who watched a sacrificial fire* (at Delphi) to draw omens from it, Hsch.

**πυρν-αῖος**, α, ον, *fit for eating*, σταφυλαί Theoc.1.46 (nisi leg. Πυρν- as pr. n.). -ηται· ἐσθίηται, Hsch. -ον, τό, *wheaten bread*, Od.15.312, 17.12,362; esp. of bread with the bran in it, Philem.Gloss.ap.Ath.3.114d. II. generally, *food, meat*, φήγινον π. *acorns* or *mast*, Lyc.482 (pl.), cf. 639: pl., Hsch. -ος, ὁ, = ψωμός, Id.: pl., expld. by ζειαὶ κνηστώδεις, ὁ κατειργασμένος σῖτος, χόρτος or μαγίς, Id.

**πυρνοτόκος**, ον, *food-producing*, ἄρουρα *Hymn.Is.*45.

**πῡροβολέω**, *sow wheat*, *PLond.*1.131.278,285 (i A.D.).

**πῡροβόλος**, ον, *fire-darting*, τὰ πυροβόλα *bolts* or *arrows tipped with fire*, Lxx 1*Ma*.5.61, Plu.*Sull*.9, *Ant*.66; gloss on πυρεῖα, Sch.S.*Ph*.36.

**πῡροβόρος**, ον, *eating wheat*, Q.S.2.197.

**πῡρογενής**, ές, (πῦρ) *fire-born*, of Dionysus, Aus.*Epigr*.49.3.

**πῡρογενής**, ές, (πυρός) *made from wheat*, *AP*9.368 (Jul.).

**πῡροδάνσιον** (sic cod.), = μαγειρεῖον, Hsch.; cf. πύρδανον.

**πῡροδόκος**, ον, (πυρός) *receiving wheat*, στεφάνη Opp.*H*.4.501.

**πῡρό-δρομον**, τό, = *vaporalis*, *Gloss*. -ειδής, ές, *fiery*, Pl.*Lg*.895c, Arist.*GC*330$^b$24; φύσεις Epicur.*Ep*.2 p.39 U.; of the planet Mars, Eudox.*Ars* 5.13. Adv. -δῶς *Placit*.2.13.9 (v.l.). ❋-εις, εσσα, εν, *fiery*, κεραυνός Cleanth.1.10; ἀστήρ A.R.3.1377; μύκητες Call.*Fr*.47; ὄμματα, πόθος, *AP*5.14 (Rufin.), 9.132; κάπρος Opp.*C*.1.389, al.; βέλος Nonn.*D*.2.436. 2. ὁ Π. *the planet Mars*, from its *fiery* colour, Arist.*Mu*.399$^a$9, *IG*12(1).913 (Rhodes, i B.C.), Cic.*ND*2.20.53, Alex.Eph.ap.Theon.Sm.p.139 H., Ph.1.504, Cleom.1.3, etc. 3. as epith. of divinities, freq. in Nonn.*D*., as Ares, 41.348; Dionysus, 21.222; Hephaestus, 2.225; Zeus, 6.218. II. πυροῦντες, οἱ, a sort of *trout*, Mnesith.ap.Ath.8.358c. -εργής, ές, *working at the fire*, Man.1.78.

**πῡροκάπηλεύω**, *deal in wheat*, Poll.7.18.

**πῡρο-κλοπία**, ἡ, *theft of fire*, *AP*6.100 (Crin., v.l. πυρι-). -λᾰβίς, ίδος, ἡ, (λαμβάνω) *pair of fire-tongs*, *Gloss*. -λαμπίς, v. πυγολαμπίς.

**πῡρολόγος**, ον, (πυρός) *reaping wheat*, *AP*6.104 (Phil., v.l. πυριλ-).

**πῡρο-μαντεία**, ἡ, *divination from fire*, *PMag.Leid.W*.17.4 (dub.), Isid.*Etym*.8.9.13. -μαντις, εως, ὁ, and ἡ, *fire-diviner*, v.l. for τυρ-, Artem.2.69. -μᾰχέω, = πυριμαχέω, Zos.Alch.p.168 B. -μάχος [ᾰ], ον, = πυριμάχος, Thphr.*Lap*.9.

**πῡρο-μέτρης**, ου, and -μετρητής, οῦ, ὁ, *one who measures wheat*, and -μετρέω, *measure wheat*, Poll.7.18.

*πῦρόν, τό, v. πυρά, τά. πυρόξανθος, v. πυρρόξανθος.

**πῡροπεμψίφλογος**, ον, *sending flames of fire*, *PMag.Par*.1.1362.

**πῡροπίπης** [ῐ], ου, ὁ, (ὀπιπεύω) *corn-ogler*, Com. word for σιτοφύλαξ, Ar.*Eq*.407 (cf. Sch. ad loc., Suid. s. v. πυροπίπας), Cratin.340.

**πῡροπωλ-εῖον**, τό, *wheat-market*, Poll.7.18 (v.l.). -έω, *deal in wheat*, D.19.114. -ης, ου, ὁ, *wheat-merchant, corn-merchant*, Poll.7.18.

**πῡρορρᾰγής**, ές, (ῥήγνυμι) *bursting in the fire*, Cratin.253. II. of sound, ψοφεῖ λάλον τι καὶ π. *cracked*, Ar.*Ach*.933 (lyr.).

**πῡρός** (in dialects also **σπυρός** (q.v.)), ὁ, *wheat, Triticum vulgare*, μελίφρονα, μελιηδέα πυρόν, Il.8.188, 10.569; κατὰ πυρὸν ἄλεσσαν ground *it*, Od.20.109; given to geese, 19.536: pl., with other grains, πυροί τε ζειαί τε ἰδ' εὐρυφυὲς κρῖ λευκόν 4.604; πυροὶ καὶ κριθαί 9.110, 19.112, cf. Il.11.69, *IG*1$^2$.76.38, al., Hdt.2.36, 4.33, Ar.*V*.1405, *Pax* 1145, *Av*.580, Th.6.22, D.19.145, Thphr.*HP*8.4.3, Dsc.2.85, etc. 2. *a grain of wheat*, ἐξ ἑνὸς πυροῦ εἷς πυθμήν Arist.*GA*728$^b$35, cf. Plu.*in Hes*.84. 3. π. ἄγριος, = χελιδόνιον τὸ μικρόν, Dsc.2.181. (Cf. Lith. *pūraĩ* (pl.) 'wheat', and perh. πυρήν.)

**πῡροσῑτόχροος**, ον, *wheat-coloured*, *Sammelb*.7365.110 (ii A.D.).

❋ **πῡροσπορέω**, *sow with wheat*, *POxy*.1628.11 (i B.C.).

**πῡρό-σπορος**, ον, *born of fire*, epith. of Dionysus, Orph.*H*.52.2. -στάτης, v. πυριστάτης. -στρόφον, τό, = *ignitabulum*, *Gloss*.

**πῡρότης**, ητος, ἡ, *fieriness*, Gal.19.442, Plot.2.6.1.

**πῡρο-τομία**, ἡ, (πυρός, τέμνω) *reaping of wheat*, Thphr.*HP*9.8.2. -φθόρος, ον, *wheat-destroying*, νοῦσος *IG*3.171.

**πῡροφοβέω**, *fear fire*, in Med., Hp.*Ep*.19 (*Hermes* 53.70).

**πῡροφορέω**, *bear wheat*, App.*BC*2.40.

**πῡρο-φορέω**, *to be* πυροφόρος II, *IG*4$^2$(1).227 (Epid.); π. Ἀσκληπιοῦ ib.384.8 (ibid.). -φορικός, ή, όν, *of* πυροφόροι (= πυρφόροι), δεῖπνα ib.5(2).269.25 (Mantinea). -φόρος, ὁ, (πῦρ) in pl., *inflammatory missiles*, Ph.*Bel*.91.41, 94.8; *engines* which discharge such missiles, ib.95.20. II. sg., *bearer of sacrificial fire*, at Epidaurus, *IG*4$^2$(1).400, al.; at Argos, *SIG*735.13 (i B.C.); written πουροφόρος, πυρωφόρος, *IG*5(1).997, 1021 (Laconia). 2. v.l. for πυρφόρος II. 2b (q.v.).

**πῡροφόρος**, ον, (πυρός) *wheat-bearing*, ἄρουρα Il.12.314; ἄρουραι 14.123, Simon.15; πεδίον, πεδία, Il.21.602, E.*Ph*.644 (lyr.); πεδιάς Ph.2.117; Λιβύα Pi.*I*.4(3).54; γῆ Sol.24.2, Thphr.*CP*3.21.2, *PSI*4.432.4 (iii B.C.); Γέλα A.*Eleg*.4; cf. πυρηφόρος. II. ἀὴρ π. air *promoting the growth of wheat*, Hes.*Op*.549 (nisi leg. πυροφόροις.. ἐπὶ ἔργοις).

**πῡρόχρους**, ουν, = πυρίχρως, Gal.19.495.

**πῡρόω**, (πῦρ) *burn with fire, burn up*, τὰς Ἀθήνας Hdt.7.8.β', 8.102; στέγην A.*Fr*.281; ναούς S.*Ant*.286; *burn as a burnt sacrifice*, ὀσφῦν A.*Pr*.497; πυροῦτε σώματα E.*HF*244; *burn on a pyre*, ἣν πεπύρωκαν (sic) ἐγώ *Supp.Epigr*.1.569 (Egypt); π. Κύκλωπος ὄψιν *burn out* his eye, E.*Cyc*.594, cf. 600:—Med., παῖδα πυρωσαμένη *having placed my* son *on the pyre*, *AP*7.466 (Leon.):—Pass., *to be set on fire, to be burnt*, πυρωθέντων Τρώων Pi.*P*.11.33; Ἴλιον πυρούμενον E.*Andr*.400, cf. *Tr*.1283; πυρωθῆναι δέμας Id.*IT*685, cf. *Med*.1190, Parth. in *PLit.Lond*.64.6, Ph.1.256. b. π. τὴν γεῦσιν, τὴν γλῶσσαν, *seem hot to* the taste or tongue, Dsc.1.16, 4.170. c. ἡ ζεστολουσία.. πυροῦσα τὴν ἐπιφάνειαν *reddening* or *warming up* the surface, Theon ap.Gal.6.208. 2. metaph., *set on fire, inflame*, Ἔρως σὺ δ' εὐθέως με πύρωσον *Anacreont*.10.15:—Pass., *to be inflamed* or *excited*, παραγγέλμασιν.. πυρωθεὶς καρδίαν A.*Ag*.481 (lyr.); τινι by a person (with love), *AP*12.87; εὐχαριστίᾳ Ph.1.60, cf. 2*Ep.Cor*.11.29. II. abs., *produce fire*, Arist.*PA*649$^b$5:—Pass., *to become fire, to be ignited*, Pl.*Ti*.51b, 52d, Arist.*Cael*.307$^a$24, al. III. *treat with fire*: *roast, grill*, Hp.*Vict*.2.56; *bake*, πλίνθους Ph.1.420; τὸ σταῖς Arist.*Pr*.927$^b$39, cf. 929$^b$12 (Pass.); *warm on the fire*, Agatharch.61 (Pass.); *melt*, [ἀργυρώματα] *IG*7.303.15 (Oropus, iii B.C.); *make red hot*, Ph.1.625 (Pass.); *fumigate*, δῶμα θεείῳ Theoc.24.96; *cauterize*, Arist.*HA*515$^b$18 (Pass.). 2. Pass., *to be affected by fire*, ὁ χρυσὸς μόνος οὐ πυροῦται Id.*Mete*.378$^b$4. 3. of gold, *to be proved* or *tested by fire*, χρυσίον πεπυρωμένον ἐκ πυρός *Apoc*.3.18: metaph., *proved by fire, approved*, Lxx *Ps*.17(18).31, 118(119).140, Ph.1.57. 4. *to be affected by heart-burn*, Herod.Med.ap.Aët.9.2.

**πυρπᾰλᾰμ-άομαι**, = κακοτεχνέω, Eust.513.30 (expl. of *h.Merc*.357, wrongly divided). -ος, ον, *cunningly wrought from fire*, π. βέλος, of the thunderbolt, Pi.*O*.10(11).80. II. πυρπαλάμης· πυρπαλάμους ἔλεγον τοὺς διὰ τάχους τι μηχανᾶσθαι δυναμένους, καὶ τοὺς ποικίλους τὸ ἦθος, Hsch., cf. Eust.513.30; πυρπαλάμην· ὁ ταχέως τι ἐπινοῶν καὶ παλαμώμενος ἴσα πυρί, Phot.; cf. foreg.

**πυρπερέγχει**, f.l. for πῦρ πῦρ ἔγχει in Cratin.18.

**πύρπνοος**, ον, contr. -πνους, ουν, = πυρίπνοος, *fire-breathing*, Τυφών A.*Th*.511, cf. 493; ταῦροι, λέαινα, E.*Med*.478, *El*.473 (lyr.); χίμαιρα Anaxil.22.3, Epin.2.10; π. βέλος, of lightning, A.*Pr*.917; βέλεσι πυρπνόου ζάλης, of Etna, ib.373.

❋ **πυρπολ-έω**, *light and keep up a fire, watch a fire*, Od.10.30, X.*Cyr*.3.3.25; π. τοὺς ἄνθρακας *stir up, fan* the fire, Ar.*Av*.1580. II. *burn with fire*, Id.*Th*.727; τινα, of the bull of Phalaris, Phalar.*Ep*.66.2:—Pass., Phld.*Piet*.89. 2. *waste with fire, burn and destroy*, τὴν οἰκίαν Ar.*Nu*.1497; πόλιν Id.*V*.1079; π. καὶ καίουσι καὶ σφάττουσι Luc.*Cal*.19:—Med., πᾶσαν πυρπολέεσθαι [τὴν Ἀττικήν] *cause it to be burnt with fire*, Hdt.8.50. 3. *assail with fiery missiles*, τοὺς ἐπὶ τῷ πύργῳ τοξότας Palaeph.38, cf. 40. 4. metaph., ὥσπερ ἡ χίμαιρα π. τοὺς βαρβάρους, of a ἑταίρα, Anaxil.22.9, cf. Men.*Mon*.195; also of disease or pain, Nic.*Th*.245,364; of love, Ach.Tat.1.11. -ημα, ατος, τό, *watch-fire, beacon*, E.*Hel*.767. -ησις, εως, ἡ, *wasting with fire*, J.*BJ*3.7.11 (pl.). -ητής, οῦ, ὁ, gloss on πυρεύς, Hsch. -ος (parox.), ον, *wasting with fire, burning*, κεραυνός E.*Supp*.640. II. Pass., ἄστη δέ τε π. θήσει *wasted by fire*, Orac.ap.Phleg.*Fr*.36.3 J.

**πυρρᾶ**, ἡ, (πυρρός) *a red-coloured bird*, Ael.*NA*4.5.

**πυρρ-άζω**, *to be fiery red*, of the sky, *Ev.Matt*.16.2. -αία, ἡ, *red robe* (?), *Supp.Epigr*.4.188 (Halic., iii B.C.). -άκειος [ᾰ], ὁ, *red-haired man*, prob. for *porracius* in *Gloss*. -άκης [ᾰ], ου, ὁ, *red, ruddy*, Lxx 1*Ki*.16.12, al., *PPetr*.3 p.1 (iii B.C.), *PCair.Zen*.76.11 (iii B.C.): acc. sg. written πυρράκη ib.374.5; also **πυρράκων**, Suid. -ίας, ου, ὁ, *red-coloured serpent*, Hsch. II. *Redhead*, common name of a slave, prop. of the *red-haired slaves from Thrace*, Ar.*Ra*.730, etc.; cf. πυρρός II. -ιάω, *to be* or *become red*: *blush*, Ach.Tat.2.11, Hld.3.5. II. *to be of a ruddy complexion*, Procop.*Arc*.8. -ίζω, *to be red* or *ruddy*, Lxx *Le*.13.19, al.

**Πυρρῑκός**, ή, όν, *named after Pyrrhus*, of a certain breed of sheep, Arist.*HA*522$^b$24; prob. for πυρρίχας ib.595$^b$18.

❋ **πυρρίχ-η** [ῐ] (sc. ὄρχησις), ἡ, *war-dance*, Ar.*Ra*.153, X.*An*.6.1.12, Pl.*Lg*.816b; called from one Πύρριχος the inventor, acc. to Aristox.*Fr.Hist*.46, Str.10.3.8, 10.4.16; but acc. to Arist.*Fr*.519, from its being first used at the funeral of Patroclus (from πυρά); as a prize-contest, *CIG*2758 IV (Aphrodisias), 3089 (Teos). 2. generally, δειναὶ π. strange *contortions*, E.*Andr*.1135: prov., πυρρίχην βλέπειν 'to look daggers', Ar.*Av*.1169. -ιακός, ή, όν, *pyrrhic*, [μέτρον] Heph.8.8; [λέξις] Hdn.Gr.1.562. ❋ -ίζω, *dance the* πυρρίχη, Arist.*Fr*.519, Plu.2.554b, Luc.*DDeor*.8.1. -ιοανάπαιστος, ὁ, *the foot* ⏑⏑⏑⏑–, Diom.p.481 K. ❋ -ιος, ὁ, *of* or *belonging to the* πυρρίχη, π. [εἶδος], ὄρχησις, the *Pyrrhic* dance, Luc.*Salt*.9, Hld.3.10; π. δρόμος Hdn.4.2.9. II. in Metric, ποὺς π. *a pyrrhic*, i.e. a foot consisting of two short syllables, used in the πυρρίχη, Longin.41.1, Heph.3.1, Aristid.Quint.1.15. ❋ -ισμός, ὁ, *dancing of the* πυρρίχη, J.*AJ*19.1.14 (pl.). ❋ -ιστής, οῦ, ὁ, *dancer of the* πυρρίχη: οἱ π. *the chorus of Pyrrhic dancers*, Lys.21.1, Is.5.36, *IG*2$^2$.2311.72. -ιστικός, ή, όν, *of* or *like a* πυρριχιστής, Poll.4.73. -ος, Dor. for πυρρός, *red*, ταῦρος ὁ π. Theoc.4.20.

**πυρρό-γειος**, ον, *of* or *with red earth*, Antyll.ap.Orib.9.11.6. -γένειος, ον, *red-bearded*, *AP*7.707 (Diosc.). -θριξ, gen. τρῐχος, ὁ, ἡ, *red-haired*, Sol.22 (v.l.), Arist.*Pr*.966$^b$33. -κόμης, ου, ὁ, = foreg., Sch.D Il.2.642. -κόραξ, ἄκος, ὁ, *Alpine chough*,

Corvus pyrrhocorax, Plin.*HN*10.133. **-μάκρεια** μοσχεύματα, dub. sens. in *PCair.Zen.*196.9 (iii B.C.). **-ξανθος**, ον, *reddish-yellow*, prob. for πυρό- in Pall.*in Hp.*2.15 D.

**πυρρόομαι**, Pass., *become red*, Arist.*Pr.*966b32, Aq., Sm., Thd.*Ex.*25.5; Act. and Pass. dub. in Plu.2.1081b.

**πυρρο-ποίκῐλος**, ον, *red-spotted*, of red granite, Plin.*HN*36.157, Tz.*H.*6.610. **-πτέρυξ**, ῠγος, ὁ, ἡ, *red-winged*, prob. cj. in *Com. Adesp.*1 D. (anap.).

⊛ **πυρρός**, ά (Ion. ή), όν, but Trag. and Dor. **πυρσός**, ἡ (Dor. ά), όν, E.*Ph.*32, *HF*361 (lyr.), Mosch.2.70, cj. in A.*Pers.*316; rare in Prose, Plu.*Pel.*22: (πῦρ):—*flame-coloured, yellowish-red* (πυρρὸν ξανθοῦ τε καὶ φαιοῦ κράσει γίγνεται Pl.*Ti.*68c, cf. Arist.*Metaph.*1054b13, Gal.9.600), ᾠοῦ τὸ π. the *yolk* of an egg, Hp.*Mul.*2.171, *PLit.Lond.*170 (i A.D.); ἡ λευκότης γίγνεται πυρρή Hp.*Aër.*20; of sediment in urine, Id.*Epid.*6.1.5. **2.** esp. of persons *with red hair*, Xenoph.16.2, Hdt.4.108; π. τὸ Σκυθικὸν γένος Hp.*Aër.*20; οἱ ἁλιεῖς π. Arist.*Pr.*966b26; π. τρίχες Id.*GA*785a19; of the colour of the first beard, γενειάς A.l.c.; γένυες E.*Ph.*32; [θρίξ] Theoc.15.130, cf. 6.3. **3.** generally, *tawny*, λέων E.*HF*l.c., Arist.*GA*785b17, *AP*6.263 (Leon.); βοῦς *PLond.*3.890.5, 10 (i B.C., written πυραί), Plu.2.363b; ἵππος *Apoc.*6.4; [πῶλον] ἡ χρόα στίλβουσα τῆς χαίτης πυρσότατον Plu.*Pel.*22; αἶγες *PHib.*1.120.6 (iii B.C.); τὰ χρώματα τῶν κυνῶν X.*Cyn.*4.7. **4.** of more positive colour, *red*, χλανίς Hdt.3.139; ῥόδον Mosch.2.70; ἕψημα Lxx *Ge.*25.30; τὸ π. *redness*, Ar.*Ec.*329:—Ep. Comp. (for πυρρότερα), πυρώτερα φοινίσσεσθαι to be of a *brighter* red, Arat.798. **5.** *blushing*, Ar.*Eq.*900; also κύων..πύρσ' ἔχουσα δέργματα glaring with *bloodshot* eyes, E.*Hec.*1265. **II.** parox. Πύρρος, ὁ, *Pyrrhus*, as pr. n.; also Πύρϝος, name of a horse, *GDI*3119*h*50 (Corinth); cf. Πυρϝίας *IG*4.492.5 (Mycenae, vi B.C.), Πυρϝαλίων ib.517.4 (Argos). (Prob. from *πυρσϝός.)

**πυρρόστυφον**, = *babylonicum*, dub. in *Gloss.*

⊛ **πυρρότης**, ητος, ἡ, *redness*, of hair, Arist.*GA*785a20, Gal.6.21.

**πυρρότρῐχος**, ον, = πυρρόθριξ, Theoc.8.3.

**πυρρούλας**, ου, ὁ, a *red-coloured bird* (cf. πύρρα), perh. the *bullfinch, Pyrrhula vulgaris*, Arist.*HA*592b22 (v.l. πυρρουρός, etc.).

**πυρρόχροος**, ον, contr. -χρους, ουν, *red-coloured*, Plu.2.363b, 364b, *PRyl.*134.16 (i A.D.).

**πυρρώδης**, f.l. for ῥυπώδης, Hsch. s.v. σκεῖρος.

**Πυρρώνειος**, ον, *of Pyrrho* the Sceptic, Gal.1.589, D.L.*Praef.*20, al.; σοφίσματα Arr.*Epict.*1.27.2; ὑποτυπώσεις, title of work by S.E.; also Subst. **Πυρρωνιαστής**, οῦ, ὁ, *follower of P.*, *IGRom.*4.1740 (Cyme).

**πυρσ-αίνω**, (πυρσός B) *tinge with red*, ξανθὰν χαίταν π. E.*Tr.*227 (lyr.), cf. Sotion p.191 W.; τὸ πρόσωπον φύκει π. Poll.5.102; ἡ πυρσαίνουσα μίλτος τὰ χείλη Philostr.*Ep.*40. **-ανίδες**· οὕτω Νύμφαι καλοῦνται, Hsch. ⊛ **-αυγής**, ές, *fiery bright*, Orph.*H.*19.1. **-εία**, ἡ, *communication by means of* πυρσοί, Plb.10.43.1 (pl.); ἀποδιδόναι τὴν π. ἀλλήλοις ib.45.8. **-ευτήρ**, ῆρος, ὁ, *one who heats a bath*, Aret.*SD* 1.11. **-ευτής**, οῦ, ὁ, *fire-signaller*, Aen.Tact.6.7. **-εύω**, *light up, kindle*, πυρσεύσας.. σέλας Εὔβοιαν *having lit it up* with beacon-fires (σέλας combining with the notion of the Verb), E.*Hel.*1126 (lyr.); γαῖαν πᾶσαν, of the Sun, *Lyr.Alex.Adesp.*35.16: metaph., π. ἔχθραν D.S.11.64; τὸ κάλλος Philostr.*Ep.*12:—Pass., *blaze*, μαρμαρυγῇ Hld.7.5; ὥρα τις εἰαρινὴ π. *beams forth*, Id.5.13. **2.** *set on fire*, τρίχα Opp.*C.*1.327. **II.** *communicate news by means of* πυρσοί, *signal by beacon-fires*, X.*An.*7.8.15, Onos.25.3, etc.; τισι to others, D.S.12.49; τῶν φρυκτωρῶν (or -ίων) κατὰ διαδοχὰς πυρσευόντων ἀλλήλοις Arist.*Mu.*398a33; πυρσεύετε κραυγὴν ἀγῶνος *give* a shout *in signal* of battle, E.*El.*694:—Pass., ἄν τι πυρσευθῇ Aen.Tact.15.1; δόξα ὥσπερ ἀπὸ σκοπῆς τῆς Ἑλλάδος εἰς τὴν οἰκουμένην πυρσεύεται Plu.2.182f: impers., πυρσεύεται *fire-signals are made*, Luc.*Hist.Conscr.*62.

**πυρσο-βολέω**, *shoot forth fire*, π. ἀκτῖνας Man.4.214. **-βόλος**, ον, *shooting forth fire*, ἀκτῖνες *AP*12.196 (Strat.), Man.4.438. **-γενής**, ές, (γενέσθαι) *fire-producing*, Nonn.*D.*2.495. **-δυνάστης**, ου, ὁ, = *ignipotens, Gloss.* **-έλικτος**, ον, *writhing in fire*, Procl.ap.Marin.*Procl.*28. **-θριξ**, τρίχος, ὁ, ἡ, = πυρρόθριξ, Poll.4.144, prob. (for πυρρό-) in E.*IA*225 (lyr.). **-κορσος**, ον, *red-maned*, λέων A.*Fr.*110. **-λοφοι**, οἱ, *straps of leather dried at the fire*, Antim.93; cf. Hsch. s.vv. πυρσολεῖφοι ἢ πυρσόλειφθοι. **-νωτος**, ον, *red-backed*, δράκων E.*HF*397 (lyr.).

**πυρσός** (A), ὁ, heterocl. pl. πυρσά E.*Rh.*97: (πῦρ, πυρρός):—*fire-brand, torch*, Il.18.211 (pl.), E.*Ph.*1377, etc.: pl., *fires*, λίθος μήτηρ πυρσῶν *AP*6.28 (Jul. Aegypt.); ἠελίοιο Opp.*H.*4.353; of lightning, Orac.ap.Eus.*PE*6.3: metaph., ἅψαι πυρσὸν ὕμνων Pi.*I.*4(3).43, cf. *AP*5 *Praef.*; πυρσὸν ἄναπτε κακῶν *IG*12(5).229.14 (Paros): pl., of the *fires* of love, Theoc.23.7, *AP*12.17. **II.** *beacon* or *signal-fire* (= Att. φρυκτός), Hdt.7.183, 9.3, Aen.Tact.6.7, Plb.10.44.10, etc.: metaph., πυρσὸν ὡς Ἕλλᾶσι φαίνων B.12.82. **2.** pl. πυρσά, *watch-fires*, E.*Rh.*97, cf. 43 (lyr.).

**πυρσός** (B), ή, όν, v. πυρρός.

**πυρσοτόκος**, ον, *fire-producing*, π. λίθος a flint, *AP*6.27 (Theaet.); λάϊγξ Nonn.*D.*37.59; π. Ἄρης Man.4.467.

**πυρσούρ-ιον**, τό, = φρυκτώριον, Poll.9.14 (-ούργια codd.). **-ίς**, ίδος, ἡ, = foreg., Anon.ap.Suid. **-ός**, ὁ, = φρυκτωρός, *PGurob* 22.1 (iii B.C.), prob. in Polyaen.3.9.55.

**πυρσο-φόρος**, ον, *carrying fire*, νάρθηξ Nonn.*D.*7.340, al., dub. in D.S.20.48. **II.** Subst., *torch-bearer*, Hsch.; *large brazier*, Id. **-χαιτος**, ον, *red-haired*, κάρα B.17.51.

**πυρσ-ώδης**, ες, *like a firebrand, bright-burning*, φλόξ E.*Ba.*146 (lyr.). **-ωπός**, όν, (ὤψ) *fiery-eyed*, Opp.*C.*1.181; *red*, Marc.Sid.49.

⊛ **πυρφορ-έω**, *to be a torch-bearer*, E.*Tr.*348: c. acc., π. λαμπάδιον Hld.4.1. **b.** esp. *to be a* πυρφόρος or *bearer of sacred fire*, *IG*7.1776 (Thesp.); ὁ παῖς ὁ τῷ θεῷ πυρφορῶν ib.4²(1).121.43 (Epid., iv B.C.). **2.** *carry fire*, θεωρὶς ναῦς ἐκ Δήλου π. Philostr.*Her.*19.14. **II.** *set on fire*, A.*Th.*341 (lyr.): metaph., ψυχήν Charito 2.4. ⊛ **-ος** (parox.), ον, *fire-bearing*, esp. of lightning, π. κεραυνός Pi.*N.*10.71, A.*Th.*444, S.*OC*1658; ἀστραπαί Id.*OT*200 (lyr.); Διὸς ἔγχος Ar.*Av.*1749 (lyr.); πυρφόρος αἰθέρος ἀστήρ Id.*Th.*1050 (lyr.). **b.** π. οἰστοί arrows *with combustibles tied to them*, so that they may set fire to woodwork, Th.2.75, Arr.*An.*2.21.3; τοῖς μὲν π... τοῖς δ' ἄλλοις βέλεσι D.S.20.96; οἱ π. ibid.; πυρφόρα, τά, ib.88; πυρφόρος, ὁ, *engine for throwing fire, fire-dart*, Plb.21.7.1 (dub.), Jul.*Or.*2.62d. **II.** in special senses, **1.** epith. of several divinities, as of Zeus in reference to his *lightnings*, S.*Ph.*1198 (anap.); of Demeter, prob. in reference to the *torches* used by her worshippers, E.*Supp.*260; similarly π. θεαί of Demeter and Persephone, *IG*4.666.9 (Lerna), E.*Ph.*687 (lyr.); π. Ἀρτέμιδος αἴγλας S.*OT* 206 (lyr.); Προμηθεὺς π. the *Fire-bringer*, title of a satyric play of A., cf. S.*OC*55; also of Capaneus, A.*Th.*432, S.*Ant.*135 (lyr.); of Eros, *AP*5.87 (Rufin.); but, θεὸς π. *the fire-bearing* god, the god *who produces plague* or *fever*, S.*OT*27. **2.** *bearer of sacred fire* in the worship of Asclepius, Ἀσκληπιοῦ δμῶα π. *IG*3.693; of the Syrian Goddess, Luc.*Syr.D.*42. **b.** πυρφόρος, ὁ, in the Spartan army, *the priest who kept the sacrificial fire*, which was never allowed to go out, X.*Lac.*13.2: hence prov. of a total defeat, ἔδει δὲ μηδὲ πυρφόρον..περιγενέσθαι Hdt.8.6, cf. D.C.39.45; οὐκ ἔσται π. (v.l. πυροφόρος) τῷ οἴκῳ Ἠσαῦ Lxx *Ob.*18. **3.** π. ἡ ἐκ Δελφῶν *bearer of sacred fire* from Delphi, *SIG*711 *D*22 (ii B.C.), cf. 728 *I* (i B.C.); Φοίβου πυρφόροι *IG*4.666.15 (Lerna); also in a Bacchic thiasos, *AJA*37.253 (Latium, ii A.D.).

**πῡρώδης**, ες, *cereal*, καρποί Str.2.2.3.

⊛ **πῡρώδης**, ες, = πυροειδής, *like fire, fiery*, ὄμματα Emp.ap.Arist.*GA* 779b15; Διὸς ἀστεροπαί Ar.*Av.*1746 (anap.); μαρμαρυγαί Pl.*Criti.*116c; ἀρχὴ π. Arist.*Mete.*344a17; ἀναθυμίασις ξηρὰ καὶ π. ib.372b33; στεφάνη Parm.ap.*Placit.*2.7.1; χωρίον Ph.1.39: Sup., -εστάτη αὐγή J.*BJ*5.5.6; τὸ π. *fiery* or *hot substance*, Parm. l.c., Arist.*MA*703a24, Plu.2.19f, etc.: metaph., π. λόγος Ph.1.144; τὸ π. *fiery nature*, of Achilles, Ath.14.624a. Adv. -δῶς v.l. for πυροειδῶς in Diog.Apoll.ap.*Placit.*2.13.9: neut. as Adv., πυρῶδες ὑποβλέπειν Poll.5.79. **II.** *flame-like, bright*, Arist.*Mete.*342b8, *de An.*419a3; ἐρύθημα Plu.*Demetr.*38. **III.** Medic., *inflamed, betokening inflammation*, ἕλκος Hp.*Fract.*25 (v.l. πυρετῶδες): metaph., ἔνθερμος ἡ ψυχὴ γενομένη καὶ π. Plu.2.432e.

**πύρωθρον**, τό, = πύρεθρον, Ps.-Dsc.3.73.

**πύρωμα** [ῠ], ατος, τό, *inflammation*, Ptol.*Tetr.*152, *Cat.Cod.Astr.* 8(1).182.

**πυρών**, ῶνος, ὁ, dub. sens. in *Inscr.Délos* 444 *B* 107 (ii B.C.).

**Πῡρωνία**, ἡ, *presiding over the purchase of wheat*, epith. of Artemis, Paus.8.15.9.

**πῡρ-ώπης**, ες, = sq., Opp.*C.*2.317; fem. **-ῶπις**, ιδος, Nonn.*D.*5.221. ⊛ **-ωπός**, όν, (ὤψ) *fiery-eyed, fiery*, κεραυνός A.*Pr.*667; γλήνος Id.*Fr.*300.4; δι' ἀστέρων διῆλθε τὰν π. κέλευθον *IG*9(1).880.7 (Corc.); [ῥόδον] τῇ ὄψει π. Plu.2.648a; τὸ λαμπρὸν καὶ π. ib.404d: neut. as Adv., πυρωπὸν ἐμβλέπειν Ph.2.331. **II.** Subst. *pyropus*, a kind of *red bronze*, Plin.*HN*34.94. **-ωσις**, εως, ἡ, *firing, burning*, Thphr.*HP*5.9.1. **2.** *exposure to the action of fire*, as in cooking, Arist.*Pr.*928a24, Thphr.*HP*7.7.2, *Lap.*4, al.; ἡ ἐν τῷ ὑγρῷ π. *boiling*, Arist.*Mete.*380b28; μαλακὴ π. Mnesith.ap.Ath.8.357d. **3.** *proving by fire*, Lxx *Pr.*27.21, 1*Ep.Pet.*4.12, Hsch. **4.** *cautery*, Antyll.ap.Orib.44.23.42. **5.** *destruction by fire*, γῆν πυρώσει ἀφανίζων J.*AJ*1.11.4. **II.** *flame*, Arist.*Mete.*369b6. **III.** metaph., *burning desire*, Sch.Ar.*Pl.*975. **IV.** *fever*, S.E.*P.*2.240: pl., *feverish states*, Hp.*Loc.Hom.*27. **2.** *inflammation*, Epicur.*Fr.*60; στομάχου Dsc.2.124. **-ώτερος**, α, ον, poet. Comp. of πυρρός (q.v.). **-ωτής**, οῦ, ὁ, *one who works with fire, smith*, Lxx *Ne.*3.8 (v.l.), Aq., Sm.*Is.*41.7, *Je.*6.29. **-ωτικός**, ή, όν, *heating*, δύναμις Dsc.2.171; ἄκοπον τὸ π. *Hippiatr.*103; τὸ π. τῶν σωμάτων Corn.*ND*30. **-ωτός**, ή, όν, *fiery*, Antiph.217.21; epith. of the planet Mars, Vett.Val.249.5.

**πῦς**, Dor. for ποῖ, Sophr.75, prob. in Id.5.

**Πύσιος**, = Βύσιος (q.v.), Plu.2.292e.

**πύσμα**, ατος, τό, (πυνθάνομαι) *question*, Ph.1.99, al., Plu.2.408c (pl.): distd. fr. ἐρώτημα, as requiring an explanatory answer, and not merely assent or dissent, S.E.*P.*1.189, Alex.*Fig.*1.23, Anon.*Fig.* 18 p.179 S. **II.** *interrogative particle*, A.D.*Synt.*307.12, al.

**πυσμᾰτικός**, ή, όν, *interrogative*, A.D.*Synt.*72.23, al.; χρεῖαι Hermog.*Prog.*3; σχῆμα Tib.*Fig.*13, S.E.*M.*1.315: τὰ -κά *interrogative particles*, *EM*67.6; distd. fr. πευστικά, ib.759.29. Adv. -κῶς A.D.*Pron.*27.16, Sch.S.*OC*3.

**πύσσᾰχος**, ὁ, *muzzle* put on calves' noses to prevent their sucking, Hsch.; also **πύσσακος**, cj. in *Lyr.Adesp.*46 A.

**πυστιάομαι**, *inquire*, as of a god, Plu.2.292e, Phot.: impf. in Hsch.

**πύστις**, εως, ἡ, (πυνθάνομαι) = πεῦσις, *inquiry*, τὰς π. ἐρωτῶντες, εἰ ..introducing the *questions* whether.., Th.1.5; κοινὴ..ἡ π. ὑπὲρ ἐμοῦ τε καὶ σοῦ Pl.*La.*196c. **II.** *that which is learnt by asking, tidings, news*, A.*Th.*54 (Stob. read πίστις), E.*El.*690; π. κατ' ἐσθλὴν ὕδατος *AP*6.203 (Laco or Phil.); κατὰ πύστιν ᾗ χωροίη *according as they learnt* which way he was gone, Th.1.136; κατὰ π. τοῦ τρέφοντος *by information received* from the foster-father, D.H.1.81; πύστει τῶν προγενομένων *by hearing* of what was done before, Th.3.82; τὰ ὑπὸ πύστιν ἐρχόμενα J.*AJ*5.2.3.

**πυστός**, ή, όν, (πυνθάνομαι) *learnt*, *EM*323.49, Eust.1684.37.

**πυτά**· τὰ ἐρυθρὰ ἱμάτια (Lacon.), Hsch.

**πῡτία**, ἡ, = πυετία, Arist.*GA*729ᵃ12 (v.l. πιτύα), *Mete.*381ᵃ7 (v.l. πυετία), *Mir.*835ᵇ31 (v.l. πιτύα), *UPZ*149 ii 38 (ii B.C.); πιτύα is written in Thphr.*HP*9.11.3, Dsc.2.75, Erot. s.v. τάμισος, Plu.2.700d; φώκης Thphr., Dsc. ll.cc., Plu.2.552f, cf. Arist.*Mir.*835ᵇ31: prov., αὐτὸς γὰρ εὗρε τοῦ κακοῦ τὴν πιτύαν (codd. πητ-) 'he asked for trouble', Diogenian.3.18, Suid. s.vv. αὐτός, πητύα. II. *a sort of junket*, Alciphr.*Fr.*6.10 (pl.).

⊛ **πῡτίζω**, *spit frequently*, *spurt* water from one's mouth, *EM*697.57: hence Lat. *pȳtissare*, *spit out wine after tasting*, Ter.*Heaut.*457; *pytisma*, *spittle*, Vitr.7.4.5, Juv.11.175.

**πῡτῑναῖος**, α, ον, *of a* πυτίνη, πτερά Ar.*Av.*798.

⊛ **πῡτίνη** [ῑ], ἡ, *flask covered with plaited osier*, Poll.7.175; name of a comedy by Cratinus. II. = ἀμίς, Hsch. (Cf. βυτίνη.)

**πῡτῑνοπλόκος**, ὁ, *manufacturer of* πυτῖναι, Sch.Ar.*Av.*1442.

**πύτῑνος** [ῡ], ὁ, name of a *fish*, prob.l. in Numen.ap.Ath.7.327f (written πίτυνος ib.304e); cf. *Gloss.*

**πῡ-ώδης**, ες, (πύον) *like pus*, πτύελον, οὖρον, Hp.*Prog.*18,19; οὐρήσιες v.l. (ap.Gal.16.754) for ἀφρώδεες in *Prorrh.*1.113; θρόμβοι Aret. *SD*2.3, cf. *Hippiatr.*6, al.: metaph., M.Ant.3.8. **-ωσις**, εως, ἡ, *suppuration*, Gal.19.433.

**πῶ**; Adv., Dor. for ποῦ; *where?* Hsch.; for πόθεν; Sophr.125, A.*Ag.*1507 (lyr.), Orph.*Fr.*32(b).3, cf. A.D.*Adv.*185.15, *EM*773.19. II. πῶ μάλα; or πώμαλα; *where in the world? how in the name of fortune?* or, without a question, = οὐδαμῶς, *not a whit*, Pherecr.9, Ar.*Pl.*66, *Fr.*346, Lys.*Fr.*254S., D.19.51.

**πω**, Ion. κω, enclit. Particle, *up to this time*, *yet*, in early Ep. always with a neg., with which it sts. forms one word, cf. οὔπω, μήπω, etc.; sts. a word is interposed, οὐδ' ἄρα πώ τι ᾔδεε Il.17.401; μὴ δή πω.. λυώμεθα.. ἵππους 23.7, cf. A.*Pr.*27,511, S.*OT*105, *Tr.*591,1061, etc.; μὴ συναλλάξαντά πω Id.*OT*1110. II. *at all*, with neg. in Ep., οὐδέ τί πω ἴδμεν (που Ar.Byz.) Il.1.124; οὔ πω τλήσομ' 3.306; μὴ δή πω χάζεσθε 15.426: after Hom. sts. with questions which imply a negative, ἦ ξυναλλάξας τί πω; S.*OT*1130 (v.l. που); πόλις ἀφισταμένη τίς πω τούτῳ ἐπεχείρησε; has *ever* a city meditating revolt..? Th.3.45.

⊛ **πῶ**, = πῖνε, *drink!* Alc.54*A*: Cypr. **πῶθι**, *Inscr.Cypr.*144H.

⊛ **πώγων**, ωνος, ὁ, *beard*, πώγωνα μέγαν ἴσχει Hdt.1.175; φύει π. grows *a beard*, Id.8.104; πώγωνα καθεῖναι to let *it* grow, Ar.*Ec.*99; ὑποκαθιεὶς ἄτομα πώγωνος βάθη Ephipp.14.7; βαθὺν π. καθειμένος Luc.*Philops.*5, cf. *Pisc.*11, Plu.*Ant.*18; π. ποδήρης καθεῖται Id.2.52c; πώγωνος ἤδη ὑποπιμπλάμενος just beginning to have *a beard*, Pl.*Prt.*309a; τὸν π. ξύρεσθαι, κατακείρειν, Chrysipp.*Stoic.*3.198, Plu.2.52c (Pass.). 2. of animals, π. [ἱππελάφου] Arist.*HA*498ᵇ34; of the fish τράγος, Clearch.73; *beard* of the cock sparrow, Arist.*HA*613ᵃ31, cf. Clytus 1, etc.; *wattles* of a cock, Ammon.*Diff.* s.v. κάλλαια; growth under the chin of a serpent, Philum.*Ven.*30.2. 3. in plants, Gal.12.420, dub.l. in Thphr.*HP*6.4.5; γεραὸν πώγωνα, = τραγοπώγωνα, Nic.*Fr.*74.71. 4. *barb* of an arrow, Poll.7.158, Nonn.*D.*29.100 (pl.), Hsch. s.v. ὄγκους, etc. 5. πώγων φλογός, πυρός, *beard* or *tail* of fire, A.*Ag.*306, E.*Fr.*836. 6. name of a harbour at Troezen, Hdt.8.42 (whence prov. πλεύσειας εἰς Τροιζῆνα, of those wearing false beards, Eust.287.14; also εἰς Τ. δεῖ βαδίζειν, Suid.).

**πωγων-ιαῖος**, α, ον, *bearded*, *Gloss.* **-ίας**, ου, ὁ, *bearded*, Cratin.439, Procop.*Pers.*2.4; ἀλεκτρυόνες Ptol.*Geog.*7.2.23. II. π., with or without ἀστήρ, *bearded* star, i.e. comet, Arist.*Mete.*344ᵃ23, *Stoic.*2.201, *Placit.*3.2.5, etc. **-ιάτης** [ᾰ], ου, ὁ, = πωγωνίτης, epith. of Zeus, in Ion. form -ιήτης, *EM*698.8, Suid. **-ικός**, ή, όν, *bearded*, *Gloss.* **-ιον**, τό, Dim. of πώγων, Luc.*Par.*50, *AP*11.157 (Ammian.). **-ίτης** [ῑ], ου, ὁ, *bearded*, Hdn.*Epim.*112, Sch.Theoc.6.2, *EM*698.8.

**πωγωνο-κουρία**, ἡ, = *barbatoria*, *Gloss.* **-τροφέω**, *let the beard grow*, Str.15.1.71, D.S.4.5, Plu.2.230b. **-τροφία**, ἡ, *letting the beard grow*, ib.352c (pl.). **-φόρος**, ον, *wearing a beard*, Scyl.112, Xenocr.ap.Orib.2.58.42, Luc.*Epigr.*46.

**πώεα**, τά, v. πῶϋ. ⊛ **πῶθι**, v. πῶ.

⊛ **πωλ-άριον**, τό, Dim. of πῶλος, *young foal*, Pl.ap.D.L.5.2, Ar.Byz.*Epit.*145.1, Sch.Ar.*V.*195. **-εία**, ἡ, *breeding of foals*, *stud*, X.*Eq.*2.2; *breed*, Str.5.1.4; written πωλέα, *BGU*563 i 10, al. (ii A.D.). **-ειος**, α, ον, *of a foal*, χαίτη Suid.

⊛ **πωλέομαι**, Ion. πωλεῦμαι, used by Hom. in 2 sg. πώλεαι Od.4.811; part. πωλεύμενος 2.55 (also in A.*Pr.*645): impf. πωλεύμην Od.22.352, πωλεῖτο 9.189; Ion. impf. πωλέσκετο Il.1.490, Od.11.240: fut. πωλήσομαι *h.Ap.*329, Ep. 2 sg. πωλήσεαι Il.5.350:—Ep. Verb, prop. Frequentat. of πολέομαι, *go up and down* or *to and fro*: hence, *go* or *come frequently*, οὔτε ποτ' εἰς ἀγορὴν πωλέσκετο.., οὔτε ποτ' ἐς πόλεμον Il.1.490, cf. 5.350,788; εἰς ἡμέτερον [δῶμα] πωλεύμενοι ἤματα πάντα Od.2.55, cf. 22.352; πωλεῖταί τις δεῦρο 4.384; ἐνθάδε *h.Ap.*170; ἔνθα καὶ ἔνθα *h.Ven.*80; μετ' ἄλλους Od.9.189; εἰς εὐνὴν *h.Ap.*329; ἐπ' Ἐνιπῆος ῥέεθρα Od.11.240; π. μετὰ πᾶσι τετιμένος Emp.112.5; περὶ πόλιν πωλεύμενος Archil.46; ἀγγελίην (prob.) πωλεῖται ἐπ' εὐρέα νῶτα θαλάσσης *she goes* on a message, Hes.*Th.*781; ὄψεις ἔννυχοι πωλεύμεναι ἐς παρθενῶνας A. l.c.

**πώλ-ευμα**, ατος, τό, *colt*, Max.Tyr.7.8. **-ευσις**, εως, ἡ, *horsebreaking*, X.*Eq.*2.1. **-ευτής**, οῦ, ὁ, *horsebreaker*, Max.Tyr.7.8: generally, *trainer* of animals, *keeper*, ἐλέφαντος Ael.*NA*7.41, cf. 8.17, 13.8. **-ευτικός**, ή, όν, *skilled in horsebreaking*, ib.11.36. **-εύω**, *break in a young horse*, X.*Eq.*2.1, Poll.1.182, Him.*Ed.*13.36:—Pass., ib.21.4: generally, *to be trained*, of elephants, ὀσμῇ πωλευθησόμενοι Ael.*NA*13.8; ἐκ νηπίων πεπωλευμένοι ib.16.36.

⊛ **πωλ-έω**, Ion. impf. πωλέεσκε Hdt.1.196: fut. -ήσω Ar.*Fr.*543, X.*Cyr.*6.2.38; Dor. 3 pl. πωλησεῦντι *IG*12(1).3.2 (Rhodes, i A.D.): aor. ἐπώλησα Plu.*Phil.*16:—Pass., fut. in med. form πωλήσεται Eub.74.1: 2 fut. πεπωλήσεται Aen.Tact.10.19: aor. ἐπωλήθην Pl.*Plt.*260d, prob. in *IG*1².60.10:—*sell* or *offer for sale*, opp. ὠνεῖσθαι, Hdt.1.165, 196, etc.; opp. ἀποδίδοσθαι (of the actual sale), X.*Smp.*8.21, cf. *Mem.*2.5.5 (Pass.); μετ' ἀβακίου καὶ τραπεζίου π. ἑαυτόν *sell* oneself across the counter, Lys.*Fr.*50: c. gen. pretii, ἐπώλεε ἐς Σάρδις χρημάτων μεγάλων *sold* at a high price for exportation to Sardis, Hdt.8.105, cf. Ar. l.c.; πωλέω οὐδενὸς χρήματος refuse *to sell* it at any price, Hdt.3.139; τὰ ξύμπαντα τούτου ἑνὸς ἂν πωλοῖτο Th.2.60; τῶν πόνων π. ἡμῖν πάντα τἀγάθ' οἱ θεοί Epich.287; ἀργυρίου π. τι X.*Mem.*1.6.13, etc.; τὰ σφῶν αὐτῶν μικροῦ λήμματος π. D.11.18; ἔρωμαι ὁπόσου πωλεῖ; ask what he wants for it, X.*Mem.*1.2.36; π. δὶς πρὸς ἀργύριον Thphr.*HP*9.6.4 (Pass.); τὴν Ἀσίην πωλῶ πρὸς μύρα *AP*11.3; π. τινί τι Stratt.13.1, cf. X.*Hier.*1.13 (Pass.); τι πρός τινας Hdt.9.80, Pl.*Lg.*741b; ὑπὸ κήρυκος π. τὰ κοινά D.51.22: abs., *carry on business*, *trade*, ἐν τῇ πόλει *OGI*629.83 (Palmyra, ii A.D.); π. πρός τινα *deal with* one, Ar.*Ach.*722; π. πάλιν *retail*, Pl.*Plt.*260d:—Pass., *to be sold* or *offered for sale*, ἐν ἀγορῇ πωλεύμενα Hom.*Epigr.*14.5, cf. *Berl.Sitzb.*1927.160 (Cyrene), Hdt.8.105; of a person, *to be sold up*, *POxy.*1477.3 (iii/iv A.D.). 2. π. τέλη *let out* the taxes, Aeschin.1.119; μέταλλα Arist.*Ath.*47.2; ὠνὰς *SIG*284.28 (Erythrae, iv B.C.). b. *sell* or *farm out* offices, priesthoods, etc., [τὰς ἀρχάς] Arist.*Ath.*62.1; ἐπὶ τοῖσδε πωλοῦμεν τὴν ἱερωσύνην τοῦ Διονύσου *SIG*1003.2 (Priene, ii B.C.). 3. *sell*, i.e. *give up*, *betray*, τὰς γραφὰς D.58.35; τὰ τῆς πόλεως Id.19.141; τὰ οἴκοι Id.7.17:—Pass., of persons, *to be bought and sold*, *betrayed*, Ar.*Pax* 633. **-η**, Dor. **πώλα**, ἡ, = πώλησις, Sophr.71 (pl.), Hyp.*Fr.*12. **-ημα**, ατος, τό, *thing sold* or *sale*, *IG*14.426 i 9, 430 ii 23 (Tauromenium), X.ap.Poll.3.127, 7.8. **-ης**, ου, ὁ, *seller*, *dealer*, found only in compds., exc. in Ar.*Eq.*131, 133, 140 (used comically, as the last part of an intended compd.). **-ησις**, εως, ἡ, *selling*, *sale*, X.*Oec.*3.9, Arist.*EE*1232ᵃ3, *BGU*184.1 (i A.D.). ⊛ **-ητήρ**, ῆρος, ὁ, = πωλητής, Ph.1.161; τοὶ π. τᾶν δεκατᾶν *SIG*241.195 (Delph., iv B.C.). **-ητήριον**, τό, *place where wares are sold*, *auction-room*, *shop*, Hermipp.93 (nisi leg. πωλητῆρα), X.*Vect.*3.13 (pl.), App.*BC*3.23 (pl.). II. τὸ π. τοῦ μετοικίου the *office of the* πωληταί, *who farmed out* the metic-tax, D.25.57, cf. Hyp.*Fr.*270. **-ητής**, οῦ, ὁ, prop. *seller*, Plu.*Galb.*24: but, 2. at Athens and elsewhere, *officials who farmed out taxes and other revenues*, *sold confiscated property*, and *entered into contracts for public works*, *IG*1².36.7, al., Antipho 6.49, Arist.*Ath.*7.3, 47.2; also at Rhodes, *SIG*581.97 (ii B.C.); τοὶ π. μισθωσάντω ἀναγράψαι τὸ ψάφισμα ib.398.49 (Cos, iii B.C.); they also *sold up the metics* who failed to pay their tax, D.25.58. 3. at Epidamnus, an official *who regulated commercial dealings* with the neighbouring barbarians, Plu.2.297f. ⊛ **-ητικός**, ή, όν, *offering for sale*, τὸ τῆς.. ἀρετῆς π. *the trade of offering* excellence *for sale*, Pl.*Sph.*224d. **-ητός**, ή, όν, *for sale*, ἱερωσύνα *SIG*1006.6 (Cos, iii B.C.). **-ήτρια**, ἡ, fem. of πωλητήρ, Poll.3.80.

**πωλιείτης**, perh. for πωλητής, *Sammelb.*5220.14.

⊛ **πωλικός**, ή, όν, (πῶλος) *of foals*, *fillies*, or *young horses*, π. ἀπήνη a chariot *drawn by young horses*, or (generally) *by horses*, S.*OT*802; so π. ἄντυγες, ὄχημα, ζυγά, ὄχος, E.*Rh.*567,621, *IA*619,623, etc.; π. διώγματα pursuit *in a chariot drawn by young horses*, Id.*Andr.*992; in races, π. τέθριππον, opp. τέλεον τέθριππον, *IG*5(2).549 (Arc., iv B.C.); ἵππων πωλικῷ ζεύγει ib.2².2311.52; συνωρὶς π. ib.4²(1).101.46 (Epid., i A.D.), *Supp.Epigr.*1.380b (Samos, ii B.C.); ἅρμα π. *IG*4²(1).101.48. 2. *of any young animal*, -κὸν ζεῦγος βοῶν a team of *young* oxen, Alc.Com.14. 3. poet., π. ἑδώλια *the girls'* apartments, A.*Th.*454 (lyr.).

**πώλιμος**, ον, *for sale*, *PCair.Zen.*225.6 (iii B.C.).

⊛ **πωλίον**, τό, Dim. of πῶλος, *pony*, Ar.*V.*189, *Pax*75, And.1.61, Arist.*GA*748ᵃ29; also, *a young elephant*, Ael.*NA*3.46. II. *the membrane round the foal* in the uterus, Arist.*HA*605ᵃ6.

**πωλο-δαμαστής**, οῦ, ὁ, = πωλοδάμνης, *PMich.Zen.*71.4 (iii B.C.), D.S.17.76. **-δαμαστική**, ἡ, = πωλοδαμνική, St.Byz. s.v. Ἄχναι.

**πωλοδαμν-έω**, *break young horses*, E.*Rh.*187,624, X.*Oec.*3.10; ἵπποι πωλοδαμνηθέντες Plu.2.2e. 2. metaph., *train*, αὐτὸν ἐν νόμοις πατρὸς δεῖ πωλοδαμνεῖν S.*Aj.*549; π. τὴν νεότητα Luc.*Am.*45; νεότης πωλοδαμνεῖται Plu.2.13e. **-ης**, ου, ὁ, *horsebreaker*, X.*Eq.*2.2,3, Porph.*Abst.*3.6. **-ία**, ἡ, *horsebreaking*, *Hippiatr.*115,116. **-ικός**, ή, όν, *of* or *for horsebreaking*, λέξις Eust.743.64: ἡ -κή (sc. τέχνη) *the art of horsebreaking*, Ael.*NA*6.8.

**πωλομάχος** [ᾰ], ον, *won in the chariot-race* (cf. πωλικός 1), νίκη *AP*15.50.

⊛ **πῶλος**, ὁ and ἡ, *foal*, whether *colt* or *filly*, Il.20.222 (fem.), Od.23.246 (masc.); ἵππους.. πάσας θηλείας, πολλῇσι δὲ πῶλοι ὑπῆσαν Il.11.681; ἐδάμασσε πώλους Pi.*P.*2.8; νεοζυγὴς π. A.*Pr.*1010; κριθῶντα π. Id.*Ag.*1641; ὁ ἔτι ἀδάμαστος π. X.*Eq.*1.1; ἵπποι π., opp. ἵπποι τέλειοι, *IG*9(1).12.18 (Ambryssus, iii A.D.): freq. used by Poets generally for ἵππος, A.*Fr.*326, S.*OC*313, 1062 (lyr.), *El.*705 sq.: in races, πώλων ἀβόλων ἅρμα *IG*2².2326.11; πώλοις τε ἀβόλοις καὶ τελείων τε καὶ ἀβόλων τοῖς μέσοις Pl.*Lg.*834c: metaph., π. Κύπριδος, of courtesans, Eub.84.2. 2. *any young animal*: of the elephant,

Arist.*HA*610ª33; camel, ib.630ᵇ34; κάμηλος π. *BGU*768.2 (ii A.D.); of the dog, *AP*12.238 (Strat.); *ass*, *Ev.Marc.*11.2; ὄνοι π. *PLille* 8.9 (iii B.C.); *pullet*, Alex.Trall.5.6; πῶλοι βουβαλίδων Ael.*NA*7.47. 3. in Poets, in fem., *young girl, maiden*, Anacr.75.1, E.*Hec.*142 (anap.); πῶλον ἄζυγα λέκτρων Id.*Hipp.*546 (lyr.), cf. *Fr.*781.21 (lyr.), Cratin.87, Epicr.9; κακῆς γυναικὸς πῶλον E.*Andr.*621: less freq. masc., *young man*, Id.*Rh.*386 (anap.), *Ph.*947; ἀνδρὸς φίλου πῶλον.. ζυγέντ' ἐν ἅρμασιν πημάτων A.*Ch.*794 (lyr.). II. *a Corinthian coin*, from the figure of Pegasus upon it, E.*Fr.*675, cf. Poll.9.76. III. ἱερὸς π. Ἴσιδος, title of priest in Egypt, *OGI*739.8 (ii B.C.), *PGrenf.*2.20.5 (ii B.C.), *PRein.*10.5, al. (ii B.C.); π. alone, of a priest of Demeter and Persephone, *IG*5(1).1444 (Messene, iv/iii B.C.).

**πωλοτροφ-έω**, *rear* or *breed horses*, *Gp.*16.1.1. **-ία**, ἡ, *horse-breeding*, Diotog.ap.Stob.4.1.96. **-ικός**, ή, όν, *of* or *for horsebreeding*: ἡ -κή (sc. τέχνη), = foreg., Ael.*NA*4.6. **-ος** (parox.), ον, *rearing young horses*, Θεσσαλίη *AP*9.21. 2. generally, οἱ π. τῶν ἐλεφάντων their *trainers*, Ael.*NA*16.36.

**πωλύπιον**, τό, Dim. of πώλυπος, Hp.*Epid.*2.6.29.

**πώλυπος, πῶλυψ**, v. πολύπους.

* **Πωλώ**, οῦς, ἡ, epith. of Artemis at Thasos, *Jahrb.*27.8,9.

**πωλωνεῖα**, τά, *buying of colts*, dub. in *IG*1².462.

**πῶμα** (A), ατος, τό, *lid, cover*, φαρέτρης Il.4.116, cf. Od.9.314, B.5.76; χηλοῦ Il.16.221, cf. Od.8.443; πίθου, πίθοιο, Hes.*Op.*94,98; κάδων Archil.4; κεραμίων *PCair.Zen.*481.26 (iii B.C., pl.); [κιβωτοῦ] Plu.*Rom.*28; σιδηροῦν Plb.22.11.16; ἔχει ἡ ἀρτηρία (the windpipe) οἷον π. τὴν ἐπιγλωττίδα Arist.*Resp.*476ª34, cf. *HA*530ª21, al.; ἐπέθηκα τῇ θύρᾳ τὸ π. the stone *that closed* the entrance, Luc.*DMar.*2.2; π. λάϊνον, of a tomb, *IG*12(8).93 (Imbros); *operculum* of univalves, πορφύρας πώματα Dsc.2.7, cf. 8, *Eup.*2.63; of the Egyptian bean, Id.2.106.

* **πῶμα** (B), ατος, τό, (πίνω, πέπωκα) *drink, draught*, A.*Eu.*266 (lyr.), S.*Ph.*715 (lyr.), E.*Hec.*392 (prob.), *Ba.*279 (prob.), Pl.*R.*406a, etc.; τὰ ἀναγκαῖα π. *drinking water*, Id.*Lg.*844b: pl., εὐτρεφέστατον πωμάτων, of Dirce, A.*Th.*308 (lyr.):—the short form **πόμα** occurs in Pi.*N.*3.79 (metaph.), and in later Poets, Call.*Fr.*8.20 P., Nic.*Al.*105,299, Man.3.71 (poet. dat. pl. πομάτεσσι Hsch.); also in Ionic and later Prose, Hp.*VM*5 (opp. ῥόφημα), Hdt.3.23, Phld.*Mus.*p.51 K., cf. Poll.6.15; but only as v.l. in correct Attic writers, as Pl.*Phd.*117b, *Phlb.*34e:—for **ποματίον** in *EM*578.8 Dind. restores πόμα τι from Hsch. s. v. μελίτιον. II. *drinking-cup*, Hsch.

**πωμάζω**, *furnish with a lid* or *cover*, Arist.*HA*627ᵇ8, *Pr.*899ᵇ26, Dsc.1.8, Babr.58.2; *cover up, seal*, ἀγγεῖα γύψῳ *Gp.*6.16.1; *stop up*, τρῆμα τῷ δακτύλῳ ib.7.15.2: generally, *cover*, ὄψιν 1*Enoch* 10.5.

**πώμαλα**, v. πῶ.

* **πωμάρ-ιον** [ᾰ], τό, Lat. *pomarium*, *orchard*, *PFlor.*50.12 (iii A.D.), etc. **-ίτης** [ῑ], ου, ὁ, *fruiterer*, *POxy.*1917.75 (vi A.D.), *BGU*643 (v/vi A.D.), etc.: fem. **-ίτισσα** [ῐτ], ἡ, *PKlein.Form.*809 (vi A.D.).

**πωμ-αστέον**, *one must cover up*, τι *Gp.*7.15.1,9.11.3. **-ατίας**, ου, ὁ, (πῶμα A) *a snail, which* in winter *shuts up its shell with a lid*, *Helix pomatia*, Dsc.2.9. **-ατίζω**, = πωμάζω, Gal.*UP*4.8 (Pass.), 14.291, v.l. in Dsc.2.76.9 (Pass.). **-άτιον** [ᾰ], τό, Dim. of πῶμα A, *little lid*, Sor.1.71, *Gloss.* II. = πωματίας, *Gp.*20.29.

**πωνίω**, v. φωνέω. **πῶννα**· γραφίον, λύπη, Hsch.

**πώνω**, Dor. and Aeol., = πίνω, Alc.20,52, Eub.12; μαστὸς τὸν ἔπωνε Call.*Cer.*96.

**πωολογία**, written for ποιολογία, *PLille* 5.2, al. (iii B.C.).

**πῶπαι**· φοραί (Dor.), Hsch. (fort. ἐπωπᾷ· ἐφορᾷ).

* **πώποκα**, Dor. for sq., οὐ πώποκα Epich.170¹.

* **πώποτε**, (πω, ποτέ) *ever yet*, in early Ep. always with neg. and best written divisim, οὐ γάρ πώ ποτέ μ' ὧδέ γ' ἔρως φρένας ἀμφεκάλυψεν Il.3.442, cf. Hes.*Op.*650, etc. (referring to fut., οὐκ ἂν πώ ποτ' ἐγὼ.. ἐλθοίμην Batr.178); usu. preceded by neg. in post-Hom. writers, but πώ ποτ' οὐδαμοῖ Ar.*V.*1188: c. fut. in later Gr., κακία οὐχ εὑρεθήσεται ἐν σοὶ π. LXX 1*Ki.*25.28; οὐ μὴ διψήσει π. *Ev.Jo.*6.35, cf. *PMag.Par.*1.291; also οὐ μὴ γένωνται καθαροὶ π. *UPZ*78.27 (ii B.C.); μηδ' ὄψον.. μετὰ τούτου π. δαίσῃ Cratin.Jun.8: with pres., *PMag.Leid.V.*11.30; cf. οὐ π., μὴ π., οὐδεπώποτε, μηδεπώποτε. II. sts., later, without a neg., 1. with questions which imply a neg. (cf. πω II), τοῦ γὰρ π. ἄνευ νεφελῶν ὗοντ' ἤδη τεθέασαι; Ar.*Nu.*370; ἤδη π. του ἤκουσας; Pl.*R.*493d, cf. X.*Mem.*2.2.7, etc.: c. fut., τίς γὰρ ἁλώσεται π.; D.45.45 (s.v.l.). 2. with a conditional clause, εἴ που ξένον τις ἠδίκησε πώποτε Ar.*Ra.*147, cf. *V.*556, *Ach.*405, Pl.*Tht.*196a, etc. 3. after Relatives, οὓς φαμεν πώποτέ τι.. πρᾶξαι Id.*R.*352c; ἄλλον ὅστις πώποτέ τι γέγραφεν ἢ γράψει Id.*Phdr.*258d; ὅσοι ἐμοῦ π. ἀκηκόατε Id.*Ap.*19d, cf. D.2.5, 4.50, al. 4. with the Art. and Part., οἱ π. γενόμενοι who *ever yet* existed, Isoc.10.38, cf. 16.33, Pl.*Phd.*116c, etc.: the Part. may be omitted, οἱ π. προδόται Lycurg.134; μεγίστους τῶν π. X.*HG*3.5.14, cf. *PLips.*119ʳ.ii 4 (iii A.D.).

**πωρεία λίθος**, = πώρινος λίθος, Str.17.1.34.

**πωρ-έω**, = πενθέω, Hsch.; Elean, acc. to Sch.S.*OC*14, Suid. s. v. ταλαίπωρος. **-ητύς** [ῡ], ύος, ἡ, *misery, distress*, Antim.56, Hsch.

**πωρίασις**, εως, ἡ, *callus on the eyelid*, Gal.14.767.

**πωρίδιον** [ῐδ], τό, Dim. of πῶρος 4, Ruf.*Ren.Ves.*3.1.

**πώρῐνος λίθος**, = πῶρος 1, Hdt.5.62, Ar.*Fr.*510 (pl.), Paus.6.19.1; λατόμια.. π. *SIG*1182.12 (Ephesus, iii B.C.); λιθουργοῖς τῶν π. *IG*1².336.10.

**πωρίον**, τό, Dim. of πῶρος, *small callus*, Heliod.ap.Orib.45.5.3.

**πωρο-ειδής**, ές, *like* πῶρος 1, λίθος Aret.*SD*2.3; of gall-stones, Gal.8.384. **-κήλη**, ἡ, *hard tumour of the testicle*, Id.19.448, Poll.4.203, Paul.Aeg.6.63. **-λυτικός**, ή, όν, *softening callosities*, ib.109.

**πωρόμφᾰλον**, τό, *stony concretion in the navel cavity*, Gal.19.445.

**πωροποιέομαι**, Pass., = πωρόομαι, πεπωροποιημένης τῆς οὐρήθρας Antyll.ap.Orib.50.3.3.

* **πῶρος**, ὁ, a *stone* used in building, described by Thphr.*Lap.*7 (where πόρος), Plin.*HN*36.132, as *a kind of marble*, like the Parian in colour and solidity, but lighter; but ἐπιχώριος π., of the local *conglomerate* of Olympia, Paus.5.10.2; πώρου cj. for πόρου in Gal.6.57 (= Orib.5.1.4); cf. πώρινος λίθος: pl., of stone used for substructures, *IG*7.3073.9, al. (Lebad., ii B.C.); τῶν εἰς τὰν στοιβὰν π. ib.4²(1).106 i 17 (Epid., iv B.C.); τῶν εἰς τὰ ἀντιθέματα π. τομᾶς ib.71. 2. *stalactite* in caverns, Arist.*Mete.*388ᵇ26. 3. *chalkstone*, formed in the joints, Id.*HA*521ª21, Dsc.5.93. 4. *stone* in the bladder, Hp.*Nat.Hom.*14, Ruf.*Ren.Ves.*13. 5. metaph., πῶροι γῆς τὰ μάρμαρα M.Ant.9.36.

**πωρός**, ά, όν, etym. of ταλαίπωρος in Gramm.; *miserable*, Hsch.; *blind*, Suid.

**πωρ-όω**, (πῶρος) *petrify*, λίθος πεπωρωμένος Ael.*NA*10.13. II. *cause a stone* or *callus to form*:—Pass., of *a stone forming* in the bladder, Hp.*Aër.*9. 2. *unite fractured bones by a callus*, Id.*Fract.*47 (Pass.), Dsc.1.70,84:—Pass., *become hard*, Arist.*Aud.*802ᵇ8, Thphr.*HP*4.15.2; *become thickened, coagulated*, Hp.*Steril.*222. III. in Pass., *become insensible*, of the flesh, ὑπὸ τῆς πεπωρωμένης ἐκ τοῦ στέατος σαρκός Nymphis 16: metaph., *become insensible, obtuse*, or *blind*, of the heart, *Ev.Marc.*6.52, 8.17, *Ep.Rom.*11.7; πεπώρωνται γὰρ ἀπὸ ὀργῆς οἱ ὀφθαλμοί μου LXX *Jb.*17.7. **-ώδης**, ες, *like* πῶρος, Gal.6.760, Hsch. s. v. σπῖδος. **-ωμα**, ατος, τό, *hardened part, callus*, Hp.*Fract.*47, Poll.4.203. **-ωσις**, εως, ἡ, *process by which the extremities of fractured bones are reunited by a callus*, Hp.*Fract.*23 (pl.), *Art.*15, Gal.1.387. II. metaph., *obtuseness, blindness*, τῆς καρδίας *Ev.Marc.*3.5, *Ep.Eph.*4.18: abs., *Ep.Rom.*11.25.

* **πῶς**, Ion. κῶς, interrog. Adv. of Manner, *how?* Il.1.123, etc.; sts. to express displeasure, 4.26, S.*OT*391, *Ph.*1031, *Tr.*192; to express astonishment or doubt, π. εἶπας; A.*Pers.*798, S.*El.*407, etc.; π. λέγεις; Id.*Ph.*1407; π. φῄς; A.*Ag.*268, E.*El.*575; π. τοῦτ' ἔλεξας; A.*Pers.*793; π. τοῦτ' εἶπες αὖ; Pl.*Plt.*309c; also π. μὴ φῶμεν..; surely we must, Id.*Tht.*161e. b. in dialogue, to ask explanation, with a repetition of a word used by the previous speaker, δίκαια—Answ. π. δίκαια; S.*OC*832; μὴ δίκαιος ὤν—Answ. π. μὴ δίκαιος; Id.*Tr.*412; συμβολάς—Answ. π. συμβολάς; Alex.143; πῶς alone, *how so*, π., ὅς γε..; S.*Ph.*1386. 2. with a second interrog. in the same clause, π. ἐκ τίνος νεὼς ποτε.. ἤκετε; *how* and by what ship..? E.*Hel.*1543; τί τἀμὰ—π. ἔχει—θεσπίσματα; ib.873; π. τί τοῦτο λέγεις; *how* say you and what? Pl.*Ti.*22b, cf. *Tht.*146d, 208e, etc. 3. c. gen. modi, π. ἀγῶνος ἥκομεν; *how* are we come off in it? E.*El.*751; π. ἔχει πλήθους ἐπισκοπεῖ Pl.*Grg.*451c. 4. with Verbs of selling, *how? at what price?* π. ὁ σῖτος ὤνιος; Ar.*Ach.*758, cf. *Eq.*480; τὰ δ' ἄλφιθ' ὑμῖν π. ἐπώλουν;—Answ. τεττάρων δραχμῶν.. τὸν κόφινον Stratt.13. II. with other Particles, π. ἄν..; π. κε(ν)..; *how possibly..?* π. ἂν ἔπειτ' ἀπὸ σεῖο.. λιποίμην οἶος; Il.9.437, cf. Od.1.65, etc.; π. ἂν γένοιτ' ἂν.. ποδῶν ἔκμακτρον; E.*El.*534: so with indic., Il.22.202, E.*Alc.*96 (lyr.), etc. b. in Trag., π. ἄν c. opt. is freq. used to express a wish, *O how might it be?* i. e. *would that* it might..! π. ἂν θάνοιμι; π. ἂν ὀλοίμην; etc., S.*Aj.*388 (lyr.), E.*Supp.*796 (lyr.), cf. *Hipp.*208 (anap.), 345; rare in Com., Ar.*Th.*22 (a trace of this usage appears in Hom., Od.15.195): in later Prose, π. ἂν γένοιτο ἑσπέρα; LXX *De.*28.67; also with aor. subj. (without ἄν), π. κοιμηθῶ; M.Ant.9.40; π. μή μοι μέγας λέων ἐπιφανῇ; Arr.*Epict.*4.10.10; with pres., π. μὴ χρῄζω; M.Ant. l. c. 2. π. ἄρα..; in reply, *how then?* π. τ' ἄρ' ἴω..; Il.18.188, cf. Od.3.22, *h.Ap.*19,207. 3. π. γάρ..; also in reply, as if something had gone before, [*that cannot be*], *for how can..?* Il.1.123, Od.10.337, etc.; π. γὰρ κάτοιδα; S.*Ph.*250, cf. 1383; v. infr. III. 1. 4. π. δέ..; to introduce a strong objection, π. δὲ σὺ νῦν μέμονας, κύον ἀδδεές..; Il.21.481, cf. Od.18.31; δόξει δὲ π.; A.*Pr.*261. 5. π. δή; *how in the world?* π. δὴ φῂς πολέμοιο μεθιέμεν; Il.4.351, cf. 18.364, A.*Ag.*543, etc.; also π. γὰρ δή..; Od.16.70; π. δῆτα..; A.*Ag.*622,1211, Ar.*Nu.*79, etc. 6. π. καί..; *just how..?* E.*Hec.*515, *Ph.*1354, etc.; π. δὲ καί..; A.*Pers.*721, v. καί B.6; but καὶ π...; to introduce an objection, E.*Ph.*1348, v. καί A. II. 2: hence καὶ π.; *alone, but how? impossible!* Pl.*Alc.*1.134c, *Tht.*163d, etc. 7. π. οὐ..; *how not so..?* i. e. *surely it is so..*, π. οὐ δεινὰ εἴργασθε; Th.3.66, cf. Ar.*Nu.*398, D.18.273. 8. π. οὖν..; like π. ἄρα..; A.*Supp.*297,340, S.*OT*568, etc.; π. ἂν οὖν.. with opt., A.*Pers.*243, E.*IT*98. 9. π. ποτε..; *how ever..?* S.*OT*1210 (lyr.), *Ph.*687 (lyr.). III. πῶς folld. by several of the abovenamed Particles is freq. used in elliptical sentences, as, 1. π. γάρ; inserted parenthet. in a negative sentence, *for how is it possible? how can* or *could it be?* hence in emphatic denial, κἀγὼ μὲν οὐκ ἔδρασα, τοῦτ' ἐπίσταμαι, οὐδ' αὖ σύ· π. γάρ; Id.*El.*911; οὐκ ἀπορῶν (π. γάρ;), ὅς γε.. D.18.312, cf. 21.217, Pl.*Sph.*263c, etc.; οὐδ' ἐπὶ τὴν ἑστίαν καταφυγὼν (π. γὰρ ἄν;), ὅστις.. Lys.1.27; π. γὰρ οὔ; *how can it but be?* i. e. *it must be so*, A.*Ch.*754, S.*El.*1307, Pl.*Tht.*160c, al.; π. γάρ; (sc. ἄλλως ἔχει) is so used in S.*Aj.*279. 2. π. δή; *how so?* A.*Eu.*601, Ar.*Nu.*664,673, etc.; π. δῆτα; Pl.*Grg.*469b; π. δαί; Ar.*V.*1212. 3. π. δ' οὔ; like π. γὰρ οὔ; (v. supr. 1), Pl.*Tht.*153b, *R.*457a; π. δ' οὐχί; S.*OT*1015, Ar.*Pax* 1027; parenthetically, S.*OT*

567; π. δ' οὐκ ἄν..; A.*Pr.*759. **4.** π. οὖν; *how* then? *how* next? E.*Med.*1376, *Hipp.*598, 1261, D.19.124; π. οὖν ἄν..; X.*Mem.*1.2.64. **5.** π. δοκεῖς; parenthet., in conversation, *how* think you? hence (losing all interrog. force), = λίαν, *wonderfully*, Ar.*Pl.*742, *Nu.*881, *Ach.*24; also π. οἴει σφόδρα Id.*Ra.*54; cf. δοκέω I. 2. **IV.** π. in indirect questions for ὅπως, A.*Eu.*677, S.*Tr.*991 (anap.), Ar.*Eq.* 614, X.*Mem.*1.2.36, etc.; ἐθαύμαζον ἂν π... ἔδεισαν *IG*12(3).174.28 (Cnidus, Epist. Aug.); ζητηθήσεται π. ὅτι καὶ τοῦτο ἀληθές ἐστι S.E. *M.*8.16. **V.** in exclamations, ὦ π. πονηρόν ἐστιν ἀνθρώπου φύσις τὸ σύνολον Philem.2; π. παραχρῆμα ἐξηράνθη..! *Ev.Matt.*21.20; π. δυσκόλως..! *Ev.Marc.*10.23.

**πως**, Ion. **κως**, enclit. Adv. of Manner, *in any way, at all, by any means*, οὐ μέν π. ἅλιον πέλει ὅρκιον Il.4.158, cf. Od.20.392; ἀλλὰ μή γένοιτό π. A.*Ag.*1249; cf. οὕπως, μήπως: freq. after other Advbs. of Manner, ὧδέ π. *somehow* so, X.*Cyr.*3.3.7; ἄλλως π. *in some* other *way*, Id.*An.*3.1.20; τεχνικῶς π. ib.6.1.5; εὐσχημόνως π. Id.*Cyr.*1.3.9; sometimes merely to qualify their force, when it cannot be always rendered by any one English equivalent, ἀεί π. Il.12.211; μάλα π. 14.104, X.*Cyr.*4.5.54; μόγις π. Pl.*Prt.*328d, etc.: with Verbs, καὶ ἔτυχέ κως τοῦ μάγου Hdt.3.78, cf. 150; τὸ γὰρ κάταγμα τυγχάνω ῥίψασά π. S.*Tr.*695; ἠθάς εἰμί π. τῶν τῆσδε μύθων Id.*El.*372; πράσσοντές π. ταῦτα Th.2.3; ἀπώκνησάν π. Id.3.20; freq. after γάρ, ἔνεστι γάρ π... τῇ τυραννίδι νόσημα A.*Pr.*226, cf. *Ch.*958 (lyr.), etc.: most freq. after hypothet. Particles, εἴ πως Od.14.460; ἐάν π. S.*OC*1770 (anap.), *Tr.*584; ἤν π. Ar.*V.*399: expressing uncertainty, *I suppose*, Hdt.1.95, 3.108. **II.** πως, πῶς, or πώς, *in a certain way*, opp. ἁπλῶς, Arist.*Pol.*1275$^b$16; οὐδ' ὁ ἁπλῶς ὀργιζόμενος, ἀλλ' ὁ πῶς Id.*EN*1106$^a$1; ἀλλὰ πῶς πραττόμενα καὶ πῶς νεμόμενα δίκαια ib. 1137$^a$12. **2.** πὼς μὲν.., πὼς δὲ.. *in one way.., in another..*, Iamb.*Comm.Math.*13, Them. *in de An.*4.25–28, al.; πῶς μὲν.., ὅλως δὲ.. Arist.*Pol.*1263$^a$26. (πῶς is Adv. of stem πο- (I.-E. *q*$^w$*o*-), whence ποῦ, ποί, πῇ, etc.)

**πωτ-άομαι**, Ep. impf. πωτῶντο Il.12.287: Dor. fut. πωτάσομαι [ᾱ] Ar.*Lys.*1013: aor. ἐπωτήθην *AP*7.699, (ἐξ-) Babr.12.1:—poet. Frequentat. of ποτάομαι, *fly about*, λίθοι πωτῶντο Il. l. c.; σπινθαρίδες *h. Ap.*442; ψυχαὶ ἀσεβέων.. πωτῶνται ἐν ἄλγεσι Pi.*Fr.*132.1 (sed leg. ποτῶνται); πωτῶντο.. μέλισσαι Theoc.7.142; [αἰετὸς] πωτᾶτ' ἔνθα καὶ ἔνθα Q.S.5.437; Ion. impf. πωτάσκετο ἄμβροτος αἴγλη Orac.ap. Marin.*Procl.*28. **-ήεις**, εσσα, εν, *flying*, Nonn.*D.*8.177, al.; of the sun, *PMag.Berol.*2.91. **-ημα**, v. πότημα (A).

❀ **πῶυ**, εος, τό, pl. πώεα, τά, Ep. Noun, *flock*, in Hom. of sheep, in phrases, οἰῶν μέγα πῶυ Il.3.198, cf. 11.696, al.; οἰῶν πώεα Od.11.402; opp. βοῶν ἀγέλαι, 12.129, cf. Il.11.678, al.; πώεσι μήλων Od.4.413, etc.; πώεα abs., Hes.*Op.*516; apptly. of goats, Opp.*H.*2.500; later πώεα παίδων Nonn.*D.*3.302; ἁλίτροφα π. λίμνης, of fish, ib.41.33, cf. Opp.*H.*1.66, 2.547.

**πῶυξ**, ἡ, perh. a kind of *heron*, Arist.*HA*617$^a$9 (v.l. φῶυξ, θῶυξ), cf. Hsch.; **πῶυγξ**, Ant.Lib.5.5, *EM*699.10.

# M

M (Greek name prob. σάν (v. Σ σ B. 2), eighteenth letter in the Etruscan abecedaria (*IG*14.2420) and probably in the oldest Gr. alphabets, occupying the same serial position as the Hebrew Tsade (ϒ, Phoenician ϟ ϻ *Syria* 6.103), with which it may be identified. In many of the oldest Gr. alphabets it represents the sound *s*, for which ϟ and Σ (twenty-first letter in the Etruscan abecedaria) is an alternative representation preferred in other Gr. alphabets.

It is uncertain whether the letter Ͳ (name and serial position unknown), which represents the sound σσ in *Schwyzer* 707 (Ephesus, vi B.C.), 701 *A*17 (Erythrae, v B.C.), *SIG*4.6 (Cyzicus, vi B.C.), 45.2, al. (Halic., v B.C.) and the third sound (σσ?) in the name of Mesambria in *BMus.Cat.Coins Thrace* p.132, is to be identified with M.

It is also uncertain whether the numerical symbol ϻ (= 900), described by Gal.17(1).525, which has this form in *PEleph.*1 (iv B.C.), *PCair.Zen.*22.5 (iii B.C.), *Rev.Phil.*35.138 (Thessaly, iii B.C.), *Milet.*6.39 (ii B.C.), where it forms part of a symbol for thousands, and later the forms Ͳ *JHS*26.287 (Athenian tesserae of iv B.C.), 25.342 (papyri of ii B.C.), *SIG*695.83 (Magn. Mae., ii B.C.), *IG*12(1).913 (Rhodes, i B.C.), ϡ ib.2².2776.11, al. (ii A.D.), and ϡ (medieval Mss., called παρακύισμα in Sch.D.T. p.496 H.), is to be identified with either of the foregoing. The numerical symbol, in the form ⋒, follows ω in an Attic abecedarium, *Bullettino dell' Inst. di corrisp. archeol.* 1867.75, and that position tallies with its numerical value, since ω = 800. The extended alphabet used by Archim.*Spir.*11, *Aequil.*2.3 for a diagram ends with ω ϡ ϙ.

# Ϙ

Ϙ ϙ, **κόππα** (q.v.), nineteenth letter in the Etruscan abecedaria (*IG*14.2420), occurring in *IG*9(1).334.1, al. (Locr., v B.C.), etc.; as numeral = 90, *PCair.Zen.*22.21 (iii B.C.), *PHib.*1.27.55 (iii B.C.), etc.

# P

P ρ, **ῥῶ**, τό, indecl., twentieth (later seventeenth) letter of the Gr. alphabet: as numeral ρ' = 100, but ͵ρ = 100,000: reckoned as a semivowel by Arist.*Po.*1456$^b$28: the name ῥῶ occurs in Ar.*Th.* 781, Callias ap.Ath.10.453d, Pl.*Cra.*426c, *BCH*29.483 (Delos), etc.

**ῥά** [ᾰ], enclit. Particle, Ep. for ἄρα (q. v.), freq. in Hom. and Pi.; less freq. in Trag. (lyr.), ἤ ῥα A.*Pers.*633, S.*Aj.*172; ἤ ῥα ib.177, B. 18.33.—This and κα are the only monosyll. Particles not ending in ε which allow elision.

**ῥᾶ**, Adv. *easily*, Alcm.42, S.*Fr.*1086, Ion Trag.66. [Codd. vary between ῥᾶ and ῥᾷ; only ῥᾷ (ῥᾴι) seems to be admitted by A.D.*Adv.* 156.8, Eust.163.20, but ῥᾶ is prob. correct Attic and Dor. for *ῥᾶα whence Ep. *ῥῆα (written ῥεῖα in Hom. but ῥῆα in Alc.*Supp.*12.7), later Ion. ῥέα (q. v.); cf. Aeol. βρᾶ.]

**ῥᾶ**, τό, *rhubarb*, *Rheum officinale*, Dsc.3.2; growing near the river *Rha* (mod. *Volga*), whence its name acc. to Amm.Marc.22.8.28; cf. ῥῆον.

**ῥάας**· ῥεύματα, Hsch.

**ῥᾰβάσσω**, Att. -ττω, = ῥάσσω, ἀράσσω, *make a noise*, esp. *by dancing or beating time with the feet*, Hsch., Phot.; cf. ἀρραβάσσω.

**ῥαββί**, *O my Master*, Hebr. word in *Ev.Matt.*23.7, al.; also **ῥαββονί** or **ῥαββουνί**, *Ev.Marc.*10.51, *Ev.Jo.*20.16.

**ῥαβδεύομαι**, *angle as with a rod*, v. ῥαβδίον I. 2.

**ῥαβδηφόρος**, ον, poet. for ῥαβδοφόρος, = θυρσοφόρος, Lyc.1140.

**ῥαβδίδα**· τὰ διδασκαλεῖα, Hsch.

**ῥαβδ-ίζω**, *beat with a rod* or *stick*, *cudgel*, Ar.*Lys.*587, Pherecr.50, 2 *Ep.Cor.*11.25 (Pass.); ῥ. δένδρα *thresh* trees, to bring down the fruit, Thphr.*CP*1.19.4 (Pass.), cf. *PRyl.*148.20 (i A.D.); ἐλάας Thphr.*CP* 5.4.2; ῥ. [κριθάς] *thresh out* barley, Lxx *Ru.*2.17; σῖτον ib.*Jd.*6.11. ❀ **-ίον**, τό, Dim. of ῥάβδος, *little rod* or *shoot*, Thphr.*HP*3.17.6, Dsc.1.14; *the wand* of Hermes, Babr.117.9, Arr.*Epict.*3.20.12; ἀπὸ ῥαβδίου οἰακίζεσθαι, of horses, Str.17.3.7. **b.** *divining-rod*, Lxx *Ez.*21.21(26) (cod. A). **2.** *barbel* or *filament appended to the lips of certain fishes*, which are said ῥαβδεύεσθαι τοῖς ἐν τῷ στόματι, ἃ καλοῦσιν οἱ ἁλιεῖς ῥαβδία Arist.*HA*620$^b$32. **3.** *iron stile*, used in encaustic painting, Plu.2.568a, Ath.15.687b. **4.** ῥαβδία ἀκοντίων perh. javelin *shafts*, *BCH*35.16 (Delian inventory). **5.** teacher's *pointer* (or = ῥάβδος I. 7), Eudem.ap.Simp.*in Ph.*732.32. **II.** = ἅλιμον, Ps.-Dsc.1.91. ❀ **-ισμός**, ὁ, *winnowing, threshing*, *PTeb.*119.46 (ii B.C.). ❀ **-ιστής**, οῦ, ὁ, *thresher*, *BGU*115 i 15 (ii A.D.), *Sammelb.* 5124.103 (ii A.D.), al.

**ῥαβδο-δίαιτος** [ῐ], ον, *living by the painter's stile* (ῥαβδίον I. 3), epith. of Parrhasius, a parody on ἁβροδίαιτος, Ath.12.543d, 15.687c. **-ειδής**, ές, *striped*, πόα Dsc.3.97; ἄνθος *Gp.*12.37; γόμφοι v.l. for λαβδ- in *Hippiatr.*96. ❀ **-μαντεία**, ἡ, *divination by a wand*, *Gloss.* **-μᾰχία**, ἡ, *fighting with a staff* or *foil*, Plu.*Alex.*4. **-νομέω**, *to be ῥαβδονόμος, sit as umpire*, S.*Tr.*516 (lyr.). **-νόμος**, ον, (νέμω) *wielding a rod* or *wand*: hence of the Roman *lictors*, Plu.*Aem.*32; *umpire*, Hsch. **-ομαι**, Pass., *to be striped* (cf. ῥάβδος III), Lyd. *Mag.*1.7.

❀ **ῥάβδος**, ἡ, *rod, wand*, Hom. (v. infr.), etc.; lighter than the βακτηρία or walking-stick, X.*Eq.*11.4 (but = βακτηρία, *Ev.Matt.*10.10, al.).—Special uses: **1.** *magic wand*, as that of Circe, Od.10.238, 319, etc.; that with which Athena touched Odysseus, to restore his youthful appearance, χρυσείῃ ῥάβδῳ ἐπεμάσσατο 16.172; that with which Hermes overpowers the senses of man, Il.24.343; that with which Hades rules the ghosts, Pi.*O.*9.33; *divining-rod*, Hdt.4.67. **2.** *fishing-rod*, Od.12.251. **3.** *limed twig*, for catching small birds, Ar.*Av.*527. **4.** *shaft* of a hunting-spear, X.*Cyn.*10.3, 16. **5.** *staff of office*, like the earlier σκῆπτρον, Pl.*Ax.*367a, Lxx *Ps.*44(45).7, 109(110).2; carried by a βραβευτής, Phld.*Vit.* p.25 J.:—dub. in A.*Supp.*248 for ῥαβδοῦχος. **6.** *wand borne by the* ῥαψῳδός, τὸν ἐπὶ ῥάβδῳ μῦθον ὑφαινόμενον Call.*Fr.*138 (= *Fr.*3.10 P.), cf. Paus. 9.30.3: hence κατὰ ῥάβδον ἐπέων according to the *measure* of his (Homer's) verses, Pi.*I.*4(3).38(56). **7.** *rod for chastisement*, ῥ. κοσμοῦσα Pl.*Lg.*700c; μάστιξ ἢ ῥ. *riding-switch*, X.*Eq.*8.4; ῥ. βοηλάτις ox-goad, *APl.*4.200 (Mosch.); ξαίνεσθαι ῥάβδοις Plu.*Alex.*51, cf. *AP* 11.153 (Lucill.): of the *fasces* of the Roman lictors, Plb.11.29.6, D.H.4.11, Str.5.2.2, Plu.*Publ.*10, *Luc.*36; πρὸς πέντε ῥάβδους, = Lat. *at* (i. e. *ad*) *quinque fasces* (*CIL*8.7044 (Numidia)), *OGI*543.18 (Ancyra, ii A.D.), *IGRom.*3.175 (ibid., ii A.D.); cf. ῥαβδονόμος, ῥαβδοῦχος. **8.** *shepherd's staff* or *crook*, Lxx *Ps.*22(23).4, *Mi.*7.14. **9.** ῥ. κληρονομίας *measuring-rod*, ib.*Ps.*73(74).2. **10.** *stitch*, ἔντοσθεν δὲ βοείας ῥάψε θαμειὰς χρυσείῃς ῥάβδοισι διηνεκέσιν περὶ κύκλον Il.12.297 (unless it means *rivets, studs*). **II.** *young shoot* of some trees, Ion Trag.40, Thphr.*HP*2.1.2. **III.** *streak* or *stripe* on the skin of animals, διαποίκιλα ῥάβδοις Arist.*HA*525$^a$12; of fish, Clearch.73; of clothes, Poll.7.53; *fluting* of a column, *Supp.Epigr.*4.448.7 (Didyma, ii B.C., pl.); of minerals, *vein*, Thphr.*CP*4.12.6, D.S.5.37; *streak* or *shaft* of light, Arist.*Mete.*377$^a$30, *Mu.*395$^a$31, Thphr.*Sign.*11. **IV.** in Gramm., **1.** *line, verse*, Sch.Pi.*I.*4.63. **2.** *a critical mark*, like ὀβελός, Hsch. **3.** *stroke* forming a letter, Theodect.6.6.

❀ **ῥαβδουχ-έω**, *to be a* ῥαβδοῦχος, *carry a rod* or *wand*, esp. as a badge of office, Hippias Erythr.ap.Ath.6.259d; of the Roman lictors, *bear the fasces*, D.C.48.43:—Pass., *have the fasces borne before one*, Plu. *Num.*10. **-ία,** ἡ, *office* or *duties of a* ῥαβδοῦχος, *BGU*244.14 (iii A.D.), *POxy.*1626.21 (iv A.D.): at Rome, *the insignia of the lictor, fasces*, Plu.*Fab.*4, *Cic.*16. ⊛ **-ος** (properisp.), ὁ, *one who carries a rod* or *staff of office*: 1. *judge, umpire at a contest*, Pl.*Prt.*338a. 2. *magistrate's attendant, staff-bearer, beadle*, Ar.*Pax* 734, *UPZ*3.6 (ii B.C., prob.), *IG*9(2).735 (Larissa, iii B.C.), 1109.24 (Coropa, ii B.C.), *Act.Ap.*16.35; so, prob., in Th.5.50: esp. at Rome, of the *lictors who carried the fasces*, Plb.5.26.10, etc.: also ῥαβδοῦχοι, αἱ, *female attendants* on Oenanthe, mother of Agathocles, Id.15.29.13.

**ῥαβδοφορ-έω,** *carry a wand* or *stick*, Str.16.4.25. **-ία,** ἡ, *office of* ῥαβδοφόρος, *IG*2².1368.131 (ii A.D.). **-ικόν,** τό, a tax in Egypt, prob. *police-tax*, *Ostr.Bodl.*i.14,17 (iii B.C.). **-ος** (parox.), ον, *carrying a rod* or *staff*: 1. = ῥαβδοῦχος 2, at Athens, a sort of *beadle* or *constable*, Sch.Ar.*Pax* 733 (pl.); in Egypt, *PSI*4.332.11 (iii B.C.), *PPetr.*3 p.340 (iii B.C.), *PCair.Zen.*753.73 (pl., iii B.C.); of officials at games, *IG*7.3078 (Lebad., i B.C.); in the mysteries, ib.5(1).1390.41 (Andania, i B.C.); at Rome, *lictor*, Plb.10.32.2. 2. Astrol., of *the planets* (ἥλιος being the βασιλεύς), Sch.A.R.4.262, cf. S.E.*M.* 5.31.

**ῥαβδ-ῳδία, -ῳδός,** v. ῥαψῳδός. **-ωμα,** ατος, τό, *rod* or *bundle of rods*, Hsch. s.v. σκυτάλια. **-ωσις,** εως, ἡ, *fluting* of columns, etc., *IG*1².374.194, al., Arist.*EN*1174ᵃ24 (misunderstood by Mich. *in EN* 552.3), *Rev.Phil.*50.67 (Didyma, ii B.C.), Aristeas 64,74, J.*AJ*12.2.9. II. = *virgultum*, dub. in *Gloss.* ⊛ **-ωτός,** ή, όν, (as if from ῥαβδόω, cf. ῥάβδος) *made* or *plaited with rods*, ῥ. θύραι *wicker hurdles*, D.S.3.22. II. (ῥάβδος III) *striped*, ἱμάτια X.*Cyr.*8.3.16; of shells, *ribbed, fluted, keeled*, Arist.*HA*528ᵃ25, *Fr.*304; so of a cup, *ribbed*, *IG*11(2).162*B* 26 (Delos, iii B.C.), Polem.Hist.60.

**ῥάγα·** ἀκμή, βία, ὁρμή, Hsch.; but **ῥαγή** is similarly glossed in Erot.*Fr.*31.

**ῥᾰγάδιον,** τό, Dim. of ῥαγάς, Cels.6.18.7.

**ῥάγανον·** ῥᾴδιον, Θούριοι, Hsch.

⊛ **ῥᾰγάς,** άδος, ἡ, (ῥαγῆναι, ῥήγνυμι) *fissure* in soil, Ephor.65(e) J.; *chink, crevice*, Lxx *Is.*7.19, *AP*11.407 (Nicarch.), Zos.Alch.p.186 B.; *crack* or *chap* of the skin, Dsc.1.72, cf. Sor.1.60, Gal.19.446, D.L.1.81, *EM*810.27; *fistula* and *haemorrhoids*, *Gloss.* II. = σταφυλίς, ῥωγάς, Hsch. III. = *rima*, γυναικεία φύσις, *Gloss.*

**ῥαγδ-αῖος,** α, ον, (ῥάγδην) *furious, violent*, of rain-storms, Arist. *Mete.*349ᵃ6, *Aud.*803ᵃ5, Plu.*Tim.*28, Luc.*Tim.*3; of lightning, Philostr.*Im.*1.14. Adv. **-αίως** Aristid.Quint.2.11. 2. of persons, *raging, furious*, Telecl.30, Ar.*Fr.*243, Antiph.7; ὡς ῥ. ἐξελήλυθεν Diph.67; ῥ. ἐν τοῖς ἀγῶσι Plu.*Pel.*1: τὸ ῥ. *violence*, Id.2.447a, 456c. Adv. **-αίως** *violently*, ἀναχεῖν Dsc.2.74; ὕειν, metaph. of a talkative woman, Lib.*Decl.*26.22. **-αιότης,** ητος, ἡ, *violence, fury*, Poll.4.22. **-ην,** Adv., (ῥάσσω) *in torrents*, Plu.2.418e codd. (βράγδην Wyttenbach).

**ῥᾰγή,** ἡ, = ῥαγάς, ῥῆγμα, Hp.*Nat.Puer.*12, al.; cf. ῥάγα.

**ῥᾱγ-ίζω,** (ῥάξ) *gather grapes*, Theoc.5.113. **-ικός,** ή, όν, *of berries* or *grapes*, Thphr.*HP*3.18.12. **-ίον,** τό, Dim. of ῥάξ, *EM* 705.52 (Gaisf. ῥαγί). II. a poisonous *spider*, Philum.*Ven.*15.1, Aët.13.20; cf. ῥώξ.

**ῥᾱγοειδής,** ές, *like berries* or *grapes*: ῥ. χιτών in the eye, *the choroid membrane*, but including the iris, Herophil.ap.[Ruf.]*Anat.*13, Ruf. *Onom.*153, Gal.*UP*10.4, Poll.2.70.

**ῥᾰγόεις,** εσσα, εν, (ῥαγή) *torn, rent, burst*, δέρος Nic.*Th.*821.

**ῥᾱγολογ-ία,** ἡ, *gathering of berries* or *grapes*, Suid. s.v. ἐπιφυλλίδα. **-ος** (parox.), ον, *gathering berries* or *grapes*, ἐχῖνος *AP* 6.45.

**ῥᾰγόπους,** ποδος, ὁ, ἡ, *with chapped feet*, *EM*810.28.

**ῥάγος,** τό, = ῥάκος, *PStrassb.*21.24, al. (ii A.D.).

**ῥᾰγόω,** only in *EM*703.3, and Suid., ῥαγῶσαι· τεμεῖν, prob. f.l. for ῥακῶσαι.

**ῥᾱγώδης,** ες, = ῥαγοειδής, Thphr.*HP*6.2.9, 7.15.4.

**ῥᾰγώδης,** ες, *rimosus*, *Gloss.*

⊛ **ῥᾰδᾰλός,** ή, όν, v. ῥοδανός. **ῥαδαμεῖ·** βλαστάνει, Hsch. **ῥάδαμνος,** v. ὀρόδαμνος. **ῥᾰδαμνώδης,** ες, *like a young shoot*, Sch.Nic. *Th.*543. **ῥαδανᾶται·** πλανᾶται, Hsch. **ῥαδάνη·** κρόκη, ὁμοίως ῥοδάνη, Id. ⊛ **ῥᾰδᾰνίζω,** v. ῥοδανίζω. **ῥᾰδᾰνός,** v. ῥοδανός. **ῥαδανῶροι·** οἱ τῶν λαχάνων κηπουροί, Ταραντῖνοι, Id. **ῥαδές·** τὸ ἀμφοτέρως ἐγκεκλιμένον, Id.

**ῥάδια,** τά, a kind of *easy shoes*, Pherecr.227, Pl.Com.251.

**ῥαδινάκη,** ἡ, Persian name for *a black strong-smelling petroleum*, found at Ardericca near Susa, Hdt.6.119.

⊛ **ῥᾰδῐνός,** ή, όν, Aeol. **βράδῐνος** [ᾰ], α, ον, poet. Adj. *slender, taper*, ἱμάσθλη Il.23.583; ἄκοντες Stesich.53; κίονες Ibyc.58; of plants, ὄρπαξ Sapph.104; φοῖνιξ Thgn.6; κυπάρισσοι Theoc.11.45, 27.46. 2. of the limbs or body, *taper, slim, slender*, πόδες *h.Cer.*183, Hes.*Th.*195; χεῖρες Thgn.1002, cf. *Ath.Mitt.*17.272 (Athens, ii A.D.); μηροί Anacr. 66; πῶλοι Id.165 (unless in signf. 3); βραδίναν Ἀφροδίταν Sapph.90; παῖς Theoc.10.24; σώματα X.*Lac.*2.5; ῥ. τῷ μήκει τοῦ σώματος Plu.2.723d; of the neck, Aret.*SD*1.8; τράχηλος *AP*5.131 (Phld.); πτέρυγες (of a cicada) ib.7.200 (Nic.). 3. generally, *soft, tender*, ῥαδινῇ τῇ κόμῃ, of ivy, Ach.Tat.1.15; δέρμα προβάτου ὡς ὅτι ῥαδινώτατον Id.3.21: metaph., *tender* or *mobile*, ὄσσε A.*Pr.*401 (lyr.); and the Gramm. (Sch.A. l. c.) give εὐκίνητος among other interpretations.

**ῥάδιξ** [ᾰ], ῑκος, ὁ, *branch*, Nic.*Th.*378, 533, *Al.*57,331; of the palm, *frond*, D.S.2.53. (Cf. Lat. *radix.*)

⊛ **ῥᾴδιος** (ῥαιδ- correctly in early texts, *PCair.Zen.*367.20 (iii B.C.), etc., later ῥαδ-, Diog.Oen.10, etc.), α, ον: Ep. and Ion. **ῥηΐδιος** [ῐδ], η, ον, as always in Hom.; **ῥήδιος,** η, ον, Thgn.574,577 (v. infr. B):—Degrees of Comparison: ῥᾳδιώτερος is cited from Hyp. by Poll.5.107, perhaps by error for ῥᾳδιέστερος, which occurs in Hyp. *Fr.*86, Arist.*Pr.*870ᵇ37 (as Adv.), Plb.11.1.1, 16.20.4. Adv. **-έστατα** Ph.*Bel.*96.33:—but the form ῥᾴων, ῥᾷον is more common, Th.5.36, etc.; Ion. ῥηΐων, ῥήϊον, (v. infr. B); Ep. ῥηΐτερος Il.18.258, 24.243, etc.; contr. ῥήτερος Thgn.1370; Dor. ῥᾴτερος Pi.*O.*8.60 (ῥαΐτερον codd.); a form ῥάσσων in *EM*158.15: ῥᾴτερον, gloss on εὐπετέστερον, Erot.p.35 N.: Sup., Att. ῥᾷστος, η, ον; Dor. ῥάϊστος Theoc.11.7 (Adv.); Ion. and Ep. ῥήϊστος Od.4.565; contr. ῥῆστος Timo 67.2 (Adv.); Ep. ῥηΐτατος, v. infr. B. III fin.: (v. ῥᾶ, ῥέα, ῥεῖα):—*easy, ready*, and so *easy to make* or *do*, opp. χαλεπός (Arist.*Rh.*1363ᵃ23); ῥηΐδιόν τι ἔπος a word *easy to understand and follow*, Od.11.146, cf. *h. Ap.*534; οἶμος ῥηιδίη an *easy* road, Hes.*Op.*292; ταχὺς γὰρ Ἅιδης ῥᾷστος ἀνδρὶ δυστυχεῖ, i.e. least painful, E.*Hipp.*1047: c. inf., τάφρος περῆσαι ῥηϊδίη *easy* to pass over, Il.12.54; ῥηΐτεροι πολεμίζειν ἦσαν Ἀχαιοί *easier* to fight with, 18.258; ῥηΐτεροι.. Ἀχαιοῖσιν ἐναιρέμεν *easier* for them to slay, 24.243; οὐ ῥηΐδι' ἐστὶ θεῶν ἐρικυδέα δῶρα ἀνδράσι γε θνητοῖσι δαμήμεναι 20.265; ῥᾴονι ἂν ἐχρώμεθα τῷ Φιλίππῳ we should have found P. *easier* to resist, D.1.9. 2. ῥᾴδιόν ἐστι it is *easy*, c. inf., ῥᾴδιον πόλιν σεῖσαι καὶ ἀφαυροτέροις Pi.*P.*4.272; τοῖς γὰρ δικαίοις ἀντέχειν οὐ ῥᾴδιον S.*Fr.*78, cf. *Ph.*1395, Ar.*Th.*68, Th. 6.21, etc.: c. acc. et inf., τύραννον εὐσεβεῖν οὐ ῥᾴδιον S.*Aj.*1350, cf. X.*HG*6.2.10; χαλεπὸν τὸ ποιεῖν, τὸ δὲ κελεῦσαι ῥ. Philem.27; τὸ ἐπιτιμᾶν ῥ. καὶ παντὸς εἶναι D.1.16; ῥᾷον παραινεῖν ἢ παθόντα καρτερεῖν Men.*Mon.*471, etc.: ῥᾷστοί εἰσιν ἀμύνεσθαι, = ῥᾴδιόν ἐστιν αὐτοὺς ἀμύνεσθαι, Th.4.10; ῥᾷσται ἐς τὸ βλάπτεσθαι (sc. αἱ νῆες) Id.7.67. b. also ῥᾴδιόν ἐστι it is *a light matter*. *you think little* of doing, παρ' ὑμῖν ῥ. ξενοκτονεῖν E.*Hec.*1247. 3. Adv. phrase, ἐκ ῥᾳδίας *easily*, Plot. 4.8.1. II. *easy-going, adaptable*, ῥ. ἤθεα E.*Hipp.*1116 (lyr.); in bad sense, *reckless, unscrupulous*, ῥ. τὸν τρόπον Luc.*Merc.Cond.*40, cf. *Alex.*4; ῥ. τὼ ὀφθαλμώ *having a roving* eye, Alciphr.1.6; cf. B. I. 2, ῥᾳδιουργός. 2. ῥᾴων γενέσθαι to be *easier*, get *better*, of a sick person, Hp.*Loc.Hom.*34; ὥσπερεὶ ῥ. ἔσομαι shall feel *easier, better*, D.45.57; ταῦτ' ἢν ποιῇς, ῥ. ἔσει Theopomp.Com.62; Εὐριπίδου μνήσθητι, καὶ ῥ. ἔσει Philippid.18.

B. Adv. ῥᾳδίως, Aeol. βραϊδίως Theoc.30.27; Ep. and Ion. ῥηϊδίως, as always in Hom.; ῥηδίως Herod.7.69:—*easily, readily*, Il.4.390, al., Hes.*Op.*43, Hdt.9.2, etc.; in Trag. and Att. freq. ῥᾳδίως φέρειν bear *lightly* or *with equanimity*, make *light* of a thing, E.*Andr.*744, etc.; ῥ. προσίσταται ib.232; ῥ. ἀπολείπειν to leave *not unwillingly*, Th. 1.2; ῥᾳδίως ἀπαλλάττοιντο αὐτῶν Pl.*Phd.*63a. 2. in bad sense, *lightly, recklessly*, ῥ. περὶ μεγάλων βουλεύεσθαι Th.1.73, cf. Pl.*Lg.*917b; ῥᾳδίως οὕτως *in* this *easy, thoughtless way*, Id.*R.*377b, 378a; ῥ. τολμῶσι λέγειν Lys.19.49. 3. of things, ταλάντου ῥᾳδίως ἄξιος *easily, fully* worth a talent, Is.8.35; οὐ ῥ. *hardly, scarcely*, Plu.*Lyc.*31, cf. 2.39b. II. Comp., ῥᾷον φέρειν Th.8.89; ῥ. ὀμνύναι κἀπιορκεῖν ἢ ὁτιοῦν nothing so *easy*, D.54.39; Ion. ῥήϊον Hp.*Int.*12; also ῥηϊτέρως, Id.*Mul.*1.1,26. III. Sup. ῥᾷστα, esp. in phrases, ῥᾷστα φέρειν S.*OT*983; ὡς ῥᾷστα φέρειν A.*Pr.*104, E.*Hel.*254, cf. *Supp.*954, etc.; ῥ. τε καὶ ἥδιστα βιοτεύειν X.*Mem.*2.1.9; later, ἐκ τοῦ ῥᾴστου D.H. *Comp.*25, Plu.*Fab.*11: Ep. ῥηΐτατα Od.19.577.

**ῥᾳδιουργ-έω,** *do things with ease* or *offhand*, οἷα πολλὰ ὁ θεὸς (sc. Εὐχή) ῥ. Luc.*Herm.*71. 2. *act thoughtlessly* or *recklessly, do wrong, play the rogue*, κλέπτει, τελωνεῖ, ῥᾳδιουργεῖ Apollod.Com.13.13, cf. Plu.2.602a; ῥ. ἐν ταῖς ἐφημερίσι *make fraudulent entries*, ib.829d; of writers on Alexander the Great, Str.11.6.4: c. acc., ἐπιστολάς J. *Vit.*65:—Pass., *PTeb.*42.16 (ii B.C.), διαθήκη ἐρᾳδιουργημένη *PVat.* 11ʳ.7.41 (ii A.D.). II. *live a lazy life, take things easily*, opp. προνοεῖν, φιλοπονεῖν, X.*Cyr.*1.6.8, 2.1.25, 8.4.5, *Oec.*20.17, *Hier.*8.9, etc.:—Pass., γνοὺς πλεῖστα (v.l. πλείστους) ῥᾳδιουργεῖσθαι Id.*Lac.*5.2. III. c. acc., *treat slightingly, neglect*, τὴν ἀλήθειαν Philostr. *Im.*1.12. **-ημα,** ατος, τό, *misdeed, villany*, D.H.1.77, *Act.Ap.*18.14, Plu.*Pyrrh.*6. ⊛ **-ία,** ἡ, *self-indulgence*, X.*Cyr* 1.6.34 (prob. the interpr. εὐκολία in Phot., Suid., etc., refers to this passage). 2. *laziness, sloth*, ib.7.5.74, *Mem.*2.1.20. II. *knavery*, *PEnteux.*30.11 (iii B.C.), Plb.12.9.5, 13.4.4; δόλος καὶ ῥ. *Act.Ap.*13.10, etc.; of historians, Plb.12.25ᴱ.2; *fraud*, Plu.*Cat.Mi.*16. ⊛ **-ός,** όν, prop. *doing things easily*, only in bad sense, *unscrupulous, reckless*, ῥ. εἶναι ἐν τοῖς λόγοις καὶ ἐν τοῖς ἔργοις Arist.*VV*1251ᵃ20: as Subst., *knave, rogue*, Plb.4.29.4, *Supp.Epigr.*2.292.9 (Delph., i B.C.), Plu.2.602a, Arr.*Epict.*3.22.93; esp. for πλαστογράφος, *forger*, Hsch., Phot., Suid. 2. of things, opp. ἁγνός, *impure*, θυσίαι **-ότεραι** X.*Smp.* 8.9: Adv. Comp. **-ότερον** in this sense, Arr.*An.*2.5.4.

**ῥάδις,** ὁ, (Lat. *radius*) *spoke* of a wheel, ῥ. τορονευτός *Edict.Diocl.* 15.5.

**ῥάζω,** = ῥύζω (q.v.), *snarl*, as a dog, metaph. of men, Cratin. 25.

**ῥᾰθᾰγ-έω,** *make a noise*, Hsch. s.v. ἐρραθάγει. **-ος,** ὁ, = ῥόθος, Sch.Nic.*Th.*194, Hsch.

**ῥᾰθαίνω,** = ῥαίνω, Hsch. (Pass.); but in Phot., = σπείρω, as Hsch. expl. ῥανάω (v. ῥανᾶται). **ῥαθάμη·** ῥαστώνη, ῥαθυμία, Hsch.

**ῥᾰθάμιγξ** [θᾰ], ιγγος, ἡ, *drop*, Il.11.536, Hes.*Th.*183, Pi.*Pae.*7.9, Zos.Alch.p.175 B. II. of solids, *grain, bit*, κονίης ῥαθάμιγγες Il.23.502. III. *spot, speckle*, Opp.*C.*2.559, 3.299.

**ῥᾰθᾰμίζω,** = ῥαίνω, Opp.*H.*5.657 (Pass.), Nonn.*D.*6.256.

**ῥᾰθᾰπῡγίζω,** (πυγή) *give one a slap on the buttocks*, Ar.*Eq.*796;

written **ῥοθοπυγίζω** in Suid. and Thom.Mag. p.325 R.; the latter also cites **ῥοθοπῡγισμός**, ὁ.

**ῥᾰθάσσω**, = ῥαίνω, in Pass., Hsch., Phot. II. = πλήσσω, Hsch. (Pass.). **ῥαθμίζεσθαι**· ῥαίνεσθαι, Id.

* **ῥᾰθῡμ-έω**, *leave off work, take holiday*, Plb.10.20.2, Plu.*Sull.*26. 2. mostly in bad sense, *to be remiss, be idle*, X.*An.*2.6.6, Isoc.1.9, *PHib.*1.46.12 (iii B.C.), etc.; ῥ. ἐπί τινι D.19.270; περί τινος Plb.2.49.9; τὰ περὶ τὰς φυλακάς D.S.2.18; περὶ τὴν φυλακήν Id.14.88. 3. trans., *neglect*, ἀμπεχόνη οὐκ ἐρραθυμημένη Lib.*Or.*11.154, cf. 60.5, *Descr.*29.4. [Freq. written ῥαθ- in codd., but ῥαθ- correctly in *PCair.Zen.*57.6 (iii B.C.), *PHib.* l. c., Phld.*Lib.* p.24 O.; καταρ(ρ)αθ- *PCair.Zen.*408.11 (iii B.C.), *PHib.*1.44.4 (iii B.C.).] **–ητέον**, verb. Adj. *one must be careless*, Lib.*Decl.*47.38. **–ία**, ἡ, *easiness of temper, taking things easily*, Th.2.39. 2. *recreation, relaxation, amusement*, E.*Cyc.*203, Ael.*VH*9.9: in pl., αἱ ῥ. καὶ αἱ ἀπονίαι καὶ αἱ ἀμέλειαι Arist.*Rh.*1370ᵃ14, cf. Isoc.9.42, 45, Plb.10.19.5. II. mostly in bad sense, *indifference, sluggishness, laziness*, Lys.10.11, X.*Mem.*3.5.5, al., cf. D.9.5; ἐκτήσαντο ῥ. get *a name for laziness*, E.*Med.*218. 2. *heedlessness, rashness*, τοῦ λόγου Pl.*Phd.*99b. [Written ῥαθ- correctly in Phld.*Rh.*2.31 S., *Ir.* p.60 W., *Hom.* p.28 O., *IG*5(1).1208.33 (Gythium, i A.D.); Ion. ῥαθυμίη is dub. in Hp.*Acut.*47 (cf. i p. lxxviii K.); this group of words is not found in Hdt. or other Ionic texts.] * **-ος**, ον, (ῥᾶ, θυμός) *light-hearted, easy-tempered, frivolous, careless*, ὦ -ότατε Pl.*Tht.*166a. 2. mostly in bad sense, *taking things easy, indifferent*, S.*El.*958, Isoc.9.35; οὐδεὶς γὰρ ὢν ῥ. εὐκλεὴς ἀνήρ E.*Fr.*237. 3. *slipshod*, of literary style, Cic.*QF*2.15(16).5 (Comp.). II. of things, *care-free, easy*, βίος Isoc.4.108; -οτάτη καταφυγή Id.11.45; τὰ -ότατα αἱρεῖσθαι Pl.*Cri.*45d, cf. Arist.*Rh.*1368ᵇ18. III. Adv. -μως *carelessly*, Pl.*Lg.*659b, etc. 2. much like ῥᾳδίως, *lightly, with equanimity*, ῥ. φέρειν And.4.23, Pl.*R.*549d; ὑποφέρειν Id.*Lg.*879c; ῥ. ἔχειν Isoc.12.17; περί τι Plb.4.7.6: Comp. -ότερον Isoc.6.56, 7.10; -οτέρως διάγειν Arist.*Pol.*1335ᵇ17; διακείμενοι Aen.Tact.26.2. [ῥαθυμότερος correctly in *PSI*5.522.4 (iii B.C.), but ῥαιθυμότατε wrongly in cod. B of Pl.*Tht.* l.c. (fol. 93ᵛ).]

**ῥαθώδημα**· ψεῦσμα, Hsch. **ῥαῖαν**· ὑγείαν, Id.; v. ῥαΐζω.

**ῥαιβηδόν**, Adv., (ῥαιβός) *as if crooked*, Euph.20.

**ῥαιβίας**· ἀζήμιος δῆμος, Hsch. (cf. ῥαμβάς).

**ῥαιβο-ειδής**, ές, *crooked-looking*, Hp.*Art.*45, *Mochl.*1 (Sup.); cf. ῥοικοειδής. **–κρᾶνος**, ον, *with crooked head*, κορύνα *AP*6.35 (Leon.).

**ῥαιβ-ός**, ή, όν, *crooked, bent*, esp. of *bandy* legs (cf. sq.), τὸ ῥαιβόν Arist.*SE*182ᵃ2; cf. βλαισός, ῥοικός; also ῥ. γυῖα Nic.*Th.*799; πάγουροι ib.788; νηρῖται, δράκων, Lyc.238, 917; μηρός Gal.*UP*3.9. **–οσκελής**, ές, (σκέλος) *bandy-legged*, πάγουρος *AP*6.196 (Stat. Flacc.). **–ότης**, ητος, ἡ, *crookedness*, Eust.914.47. **–όω**, *make crooked, bend*, Lyc.563, prob. in 262:—Pass., Gal.*UP*3.9.

* **ῥαίδ-α**, ἡ, = Lat. *rhaeda*, *Edict.Diocl.*15.33: gen. pl. written **ῥεδῶν** (v.l. ῥαιδῶν) in *Apoc.*18.13. **–ιον**, τό, Dim. of foreg., *Gloss.*; written **ῥέδιον** in Hsch.

**ῥᾱΐζω**, Ion. **ῥηΐζω**, (ῥᾶ, ῥᾴων) *grow easier, more endurable*, of ailments, Hp.*Epid.*2.3.18, 4.56, etc. 2. of persons, *find relief from pain, recover from illness*, Id.*Fract.*5, 19, Pl.*R.*462d, D.1.13; *take one's rest*, X.*Cyr.*7.5.68 (as v.l.): sts. c. gen., ῥ. πόνων *rest* from toil, Memn.4; ῥ. ἐκ νόσου Ach.Tat.4.16; cf. ῥᾴδιος II. 2. II. trans., *make easier, alleviate* an illness, Hp.*Aph.*5.25. [ῥαΐσαι τρισυλλάβως Ἀττικοὶ τὸ ἐκ νόσου ἀναλαβεῖν, Hsch.; 3 sg. aor. subj. ῥαείσηι (sic) *PCair.Zen.*263.3 (iii B.C.), ῥαΐσηι *PHamb.*27.8 (iii B.C.).]

* **ῥαικακερεῖς**· στρεβλοκέρατοι, Hsch. **ῥαίκερος**· χαλεπός, Id.

**ῥαίνω**, Pi.*I.*8(7).50, Xenarch.7.7: fut. ῥᾰνῶ Antiph.217.12, Lyc.1104, but Att. also ῥᾱνῶ (like φᾱνῶ) acc. to A.D.*Adv.*187.27: aor. ἔρρᾱνα Arched.2.5, E.*Rh.*73, *Cyc.*402 (ἐξ-), *Trag.Adesp.*90; Ion. ἔρρηνα Hp. (v. infr.); ἔρηνα Opp.*H.*2.100: pf. ἔρραγκα (δι-) Lxx *Pr.*7.17:—Med., aor. ἐρρᾰνάμην (περι-) Aristobul.6 J., Plu.*Arist.*20, Longus 3.28:—Pass., aor. ἐρράνθην Pi.*P.*5.100, Arist.*Pr.*938ᵃ35: pf. ἔρραμμαι Persae.ap.Ath.4.140f; later ἔρρασμαι Sch.D Il.12.431.—Ep. aor. imper. ῥάσσατε Od.20.150, 3 pl. pf. Pass. ἐρράδαται ib.354, plpf. ἐρράδατο Il.12.431 [ᾰ] are formed as if from pres. ῥάζω, cf. περιρραίνω I. I. *sprinkle, besprinkle*, with acc. of the object besprinkled, 1. prop. with liquids, ῥάσσατε (sc. δῶμα ὕδατι) Od.20.150; ῥᾶνον δόμους *Com.Adesp.*1211, cf. Thphr.*CP*4.3.3; ὕδατι τοὺς λειποψυχοῦντας Id.*Fr.*10.6; φόνῳ πεδίον Pi.*I.* l. c.; ἐλαίῳ ῥῆνας Hp.*Fract.*21; ἐκ καλπίδων μύροις ῥ. Plb.30.25.17:—Pass., πύργοι καὶ ἐπάλξιες αἵματι φωτῶν ἐρράδατ' Il.12.431; αἵματι δ' ἐρράδαται τοῖχοι Od.20.354; αἵματι βωμὸς ἐραίνετ' E.*IA*[1589]; τὰ πρόσωπα διὰ τὸ ῥαίνεσθαι μέλανα γίνεται Arist.*HA*579ᵃ2. 2. also of solids, *bestrew, besprinkle*, [ἵπποι] ῥαίνοντο κονίῃ Il.11.282; ῥ. χθόνα καρπῷ Nonn.*D.*2.65. 3. metaph., ῥ. τινὰ ὕμνῳ, νᾶσον εὐλογίαις, Pi.*P.*8.57, *I.*6(5).21; θεῶν..ὅμιλον ἀμβρότᾳ ῥαίνοισα μοίσᾳ *IG*4²(1).130.24. II. *sprinkle, scatter*, with acc. of the thing scattered or sprinkled, ῥανῶ τε πεδόσ' ἐγκέφαλον *will scatter* it on the ground, E.*Fr.*384 (dub. l.); ῥαίνειν *sprinkle* (water) on the fish, Xenarch. l. c.; ῥαίνειν ὄξιδας ἐς τὰ βλέφαρα *sprinkle* vinegar in their eyes, Ar.*Ra.*1441; ῥ. πυρούς Opp.*H.*2.100; χοάς Lyc.1185. III. abs., *sprinkle water*, Arist.*HA*620ᵃ12; ῥανίσι ῥ. *let water fall* in drops, Id.*Mete.*374ᵇ1.

**ῥαιξία**· τόπος ἴδιος ἰατροῦ ἐν Ταραντίνοις, Hsch.

**ῥάϊος** [ᾰ], α, ον, Ion. **ῥήϊος**, η, ον, = ῥᾴδιος, Opp.*C.*1.101 (unless ῥήϊον is neut. Comp.).

**ραιστάζει**· πονεῖ, ὠθεῖ, Hsch.; cf. ῥαστάζει.

**ῥαισ-τήρ**, ῆρος, ὁ and ἡ, (ῥαίω) *smasher*, i.e. *hammer*, Il.18.477 (fem.), A.*Pr.*56, Call.*Dian.*59; masc. in *AP*6.117 (Pancrat.); με χρύσειον ἀπὸ ῥαιστῆρος στήσητε set up a statue of me in *beaten* gold, ib.7.5:—found in late Prose, Iamb. *in Nic.* p.121 P. (pl.). 2. generally, *destroyer*, δαλὸς ῥ. μεγάρων Opp.*H.*5.120. **–τήριος**, α, ον, *smashing, hammering*, ῥ. ἱδρώς *the blacksmith's* sweat or toil, ib.2.28; ἄκμοσι.. ῥ. *hammered* upon the anvil, ib.5.153. II. generally, *destructive, pernicious*, ῥ. φάρμακα, opp. ἐσθλά, A.R.3.803: c. gen., ῥ. φάρμακα θυμοῦ ib.790; νηῶν 4.921. **–τηροκοπία**, ἡ, *working with a hammer*, Ph.Byz.*Mir.*42.

**ῥᾴϊστος**, α, ον, Dor. for ῥήϊστος; v. ῥᾴδιος.

**ῥαιστότῠπος**, ον, *struck with the hammer*, ἄκμονες Man.1.289, 4.124.

**ῥαίστωρ**· κραντήρ, Hsch. **ῥαιφάσσει**· ἁγνεύει, Id.

* **ῥαίω**, poet. subj. ῥαίησι Od.5.221: fut. ῥαίσω (διαρ-) 2.49; Ep. inf. ῥαισέμεναι (v.l. ῥαίσεσθαι) 8.569: aor. ἔρραισα, subj. ῥαίσῃ 23.235:—Pass., fut. (in med. form) ῥαίσομαι (διαρ-) Il.24.355: aor. ἐρραίσθην 16.339:—*break, shiver, shatter*, ῥ. νῆα *wreck* a ship, Od.8.569, 13.151, 23.235; ῥ. τινά *cause* one *to suffer shipwreck*, 5.221:—in Pass., ῥαιόμενος *suffering shipwreck*, 6.326; νηῦς ῥαισθεῖσα A.R.2.1112; also φάσγανον ἐρραίσθη it *was shivered*, Il.16.339; τῷ κέ οἱ ἐγκέφαλός γε διὰ σπέος..ῥαίοιτο πρὸς οὔδεϊ his brain *would be dashed* on the ground throughout the cavern, Od.9.459; so αἰὼν δι' ὀστέων ἐρραίσθη the marrow *spurted* through the bones, Pi.*Fr.*111. II. generally, *destroy*, A.R.1.617:—Pass., *to be broken down, crushed by suffering*, ὅταν..ῥαισθῇ A.*Pr.*191, *AP*7.529 (Theodorid.), etc. (anap.), cf. S.*Tr.*268.

* **ῥακά**, Hebr. word expressive of contempt, *Ev.Matt.*5.22.

* **ῥάκανα** or **ῥακάνη**, ἡ, name of a garment, *Edict.Diocl.*7.60, 22.4.

**ῥάκελος** (and **ῥακλεός**), = σκληρός, Hsch.

**ῥᾰκενδύτης** [ῠ], ου, ὁ, = ῥακοδύτης, *Cat.Cod.Astr.*8(4).165.

**ῥᾰκετρίζω**, = ῥαχετρίζω, Pl.Com.252.

**ῥάκετρον**, τό, *butcher's cleaver*, Poll.7.25 (v.l. ῥάχ-): Hsch. has **βράκετρον** (Aeol.?), *pruning-hook*.

**ῥάκ-ῐνος** [ᾰ], η, ον, *ragged*, *Michel* 832.17, al. (Samos, iv B.C.), *Schwyzer* 462 *B* 37 (Tanagra, iii B.C.). 2. -ον, τό, a substance used in alchemy, Zos.Alch. p.185 B. (s. v. l.). * **–ιον**, τό, Dim. of ῥάκος, mostly in pl., *rags*, Ar.*Ach.*412, *V.*128, al.: in sg., ῥάκιόν τι τοῦ παλαιοῦ δράματος Id.*Ach.*415; of a tattered flag, Them.*Or.*16.210b. [ῥᾰκ- in *BCH*51.326 (Athens), pl.]

**ῥᾰκιοσυρραπτάδης** [ᾰ], ου, ὁ, *rag-stitcher*, of Euripides, *who tricked out his heroes in rags*, Ar.*Ra.*842.

**ῥακίς**, pl. ῥακῖδες, = ὀρόδαμνοι, κλάδοι, Hsch. II. ῥάκις, perh. Ion. for ῥάχις, Herod.3.50.

**ῥακίωσις**, v. ῥάκωσις. **ῥακκίζω**, v. ῥαχίζω. **ῥακκόδυτος**, v. ῥακόδυτος. **ῥακλεός**, v. ῥάκελος.

**ῥᾰκο-δύτης** [ῠ], ου, ὁ, *wearer of rags*, ἐν ἱεροῖς Rhetor. in *Cat.Cod.Astr.*8(4).148. **–δῠτος**, ον, *ragged*, στολά E.*Rh.*712 (lyr.); written **ῥακκό–** in Hsch. s. v. κακοείμονας.

**ῥᾰκόεις**, εσσα, εν, *ragged, torn, tattered*, *AP*6.21. II. (ῥάκος II) *wrinkled*, χρώς ib.11.66 (Antiphil.).

* **ῥάκος** [ᾰ], εος, τό, *ragged, tattered garment*, δὸς ῥ. ἀμφιβαλέσθαι Od.6.178, cf. 13.434, 14.342, 349 (never in Il.); ἀνθ' ἱματίου μὲν ἔχειν ῥ. Ar.*Pl.*540; ῥ. φορεῖ Antiph.204.6, *PPetr.*3 p.115 (iii B.C.), cf. Philem.146: freq. in pl. ῥάκεα, Att. ῥάκη, *rags, tatters*, Od.14.512, 18.67, 74, 19.507, al., Hdt.3.129, S.*Ph.*39, 274; ἐν ῥάκεσι περιφθείρεσθαι Isoc.*Ep.*9.10. 2. generally, *strip of cloth*, ῥάκεα φοινίκεα Hdt.7.76, cf. *Ev.Matt.*9.16, Arr.*Tact.*35.3: even a *strip* of flesh, σώματος ῥ. A.*Pr.*1023. 3. collectively, *rag, lint*, Hp.*Morb.*2.36; ῥάκη λινᾶ Dsc.5.75.15. II. in pl. also, *rents in the face, wrinkles*, Ar.*Pl.*1065. III. metaph., *rag, remnant*, εἰκάσαι τὸ ἐρείπιον ῥάκει οἰκίας Anon.ap.Arist.*Rh.*1413ᵃ6; of an old seaman, ἁλίοιο βίου ῥ. *AP*9.242 (Antiphil.), cf. 7.380 (Crin.), Luc.*Tim.*32.—The Aeol. form βράκος (q. v.), used of a garment, lacks the sense 'ragged'.

**ῥᾰκο-φορέω**, *wear rags* or *tatters*, Sch.Ar.*Pax* 739. **-ω**, in Pass., *become ragged* or *wrinkled*, of skins of dead animals, Plu.2.642e; ἐρρακωμένα πρόσωπα *wrinkled* faces, Dsc.5.87.12. 2. in Pass., *to be dispersed all about*, τὸ χολῶδες..ῥακούμενον ἐντῷ σώματι Hp.*Morb.*4.49.

**ῥακ-τήριος**, α, ον, (ῥάσσω) *fit for striking with*, κέντρα S.*Fr.*802. II. μέλη βοῶν ἄναυλα καὶ ῥ. *broken, discordant* (ψοφώδη καὶ θορυβώδη Hsch.), Id.*Fr.*699. III. **ῥακτήριον**· ὄρχησίς τις, Hsch. IV. **ῥακτήρια**· τύμπανα, Id. **–τός**, ή, όν, *broken, rugged*, βούσταθμα Lyc.92. II. Subst. -τός, ἡ, *ravine*, Hsch. **–τρια**, ἡ, *pole for beating fruit-trees*, esp. *olives, with*, Poll.7.146, 10.130: **ῥάκτριον**, τό, is dub. in Hsch. and Phot.

**ῥακχίζω**, v. ῥαχίζω.

* **ῥᾰκ-ώδης**, ες, *ragged*, χιτωνίσκος D.C.65.20. 2. *wrinkled*, *AP*5.20 (Rufin.), Sor.1.88; of the *worn and chafed* skin of bedridden people, Gal.11.132. **–ωλέον**· ῥάκος, Hsch. **–ωμα**, ατος, τό, in pl., = ῥάκη, *rags*, Ar.*Ach.*432. * **–ωσις**, εως, ἡ, *a becoming ragged* or *wrinkled*, of the skin, when the flesh under it is shrunk, Sor.2.40, Zen.6.42 (written ῥακίωσις in Diogenian.8.70).

**ῥάματα**· βοτρύδια, σταφυλίς (Maced.), Hsch. **ῥαμβάς**· ὁ δήμιος, Id. (cf. ῥαιβίας).

**ῥάμμα** (A), ατος, τό, f. l. (ῥάμα, ῥᾶμα codd.) for ῥεῦμα in Apollod.*Poliorc.*183.7.

* **ῥάμμα** (B), ατος, τό, (ῥάπτω) *anything sewn* or *stitched, seam, hem*, Pi.*Fr.*85, Hermipp.48, Pl.Com.36, J.*AJ*3.7.5. 2. *fastening* of a bandage *by sewing* (as ἅμμα by a knot), Hp.*Off.*8. 3. *thread*, D.S.1.87, Dsc.*Eup.*1.200, Gal.*UP*10.12. 4. *suture* of a wound, *Hippiatr.*71.

**ῥαμμάτ-ινος**, η, ον, *of suture-thread*, ἀγκτῆρες Heliod.ap.Orib.44.10.4. ⊛ **-ώδης**, ες, *like a thread*, Hsch. s. v. κροσσούς.

**ῥάμνος**, ἡ, name of various *prickly shrubs*, Eup.14.5, Theoc.4.57, 21.36, Plb.12.2.2, *IG*14.352 ii 32 (Halaesa); *Box-thorn, Lycium europaeum*, Dsc.1.90, Paus.3.14.7; ῥ. λευκή (λευκοτέρα Dsc. l. c.) *Stone buckthorn, Rhamnus graeca*, Thphr.*HP*3.18.2; ῥ. μέλαινα *Black buckthorn, R. oleoides*, ibid.

**Ῥαμνοῦς**, οῦντος (contr. from ῥαμνόεις), ὁ, *Rhamnus*, a deme in Attica (named from the ῥάμνοι growing in it), ἡ ἐν Ῥ. θεός, i.e. Nemesis, Paus.1.33.2, cf. Str.9.1.17 and 22; Ῥαμνοῦντι, not ἐν Ῥ., *at Rhamnus*, Lys.19.28, etc.—Hence ⊛**Ῥαμνούσιος**, α, ον, *Rhamnusian*, Aeschin.1.157, etc.; ἡ **Ῥαμνουσία**, epith. of Nemesis from her temple at Rhamnus, Hsch., etc.; also **Ῥαμνουσίς**, ίδος, ἡ, Call.*Dian.*232; **Ῥαμνουσιάς**, άδος, ἡ, *IG*14.1389 ii 2.

**ῥαμοσαίτης**· κατάρατος, Hsch. **ῥαμφαδέκται**· τὸ πυκτεύειν, Id.

**ῥαμφάζη**· ῥυγχωθήσῃ, Id., cf. Phot.

**ῥαμφ-ή**, ἡ, *hooked knife, bill*, Plb.10.18.6, Hsch. II. = ῥάμφος, Id. **-ηστής**, οῦ, ὁ, a fish, prob. = βελόνη, Id. **-ιον**, τό, Dim. of ῥάμφος, Sch.D.T. p.196 H. **-ιος**, ὁ, = πελεκανός, Cyran.96. **-ίς**· νεὼς εἶδος, Hsch. ⊛ **-ος**, εος, τό, *crooked beak* of birds of prey: generally, *beak, bill*, Ar.*Av.*99, Pl.Com.138, Plu.2.980e; cf. ῥύγχος. **-ώδης**, ες, *beak-shaped*, Philostr.*VS*2.6.

**ῥαμψός**, ἡ, όν, = ῥαιβός, Hsch. **ῥᾶνα**· ἄρνα, Ῥωμαῖοι δὲ βάτραχον, Id. (cf. ῥήν, also ϝρᾶνον [cod. τρανόν]· ἐξαμηνιαῖον πρόβατον, Id.). **ῥανᾶται**· πλανᾶται, σπείρεται, Id.

⊛**ῥᾰν-ίζω**, = ῥαίνω, Poll.10.30. **-ίς**, ίδος, ἡ, (ῥαίνω) *drop*, πέτρην κοιλαίνει ῥ. ὕδατος ἐνδελεχείῃ Choeril.10, cf. Acus.4 J.; ὑγραὶ ῥ. E.*Ion* 106 (anap.); δρόσου Id.*Andr.*227, Lxx *Wi.*11.22; ῥ. βέβληκέ με a rain-*drop*, Ar.*Ach.*171, cf. Arist.*Mete.*349$^b$31, 374$^a$9. 2. *semen virile*, *AP*10.45 (Pall.). 3. metaph., *drop, spot*, τὰ πτίλα ἔχει ῥανίδας Ael.*NA*17.23, cf. 38; αἱ τοῦ χρυσοῦ ῥ. Philostr.*VA*3.48.

⊛**ῥαν-τήρ**, ῆρος, ὁ, (ῥαίνω) *one who wets*, esp. of *the inner corner of the eye*, Nic.*Th.*673, cf. Poll.2.71. II. *sprinkler*, *Mon.Ant.*23.150 (Adanda). **-τήριος**, α, ον, *of* or *for sprinkling*, πέδον ῥ. *besprinkled, reeking*, with blood, A.*Ag.*1092; Pors. read πέδου ῥαντήριον (as Subst.) *defilement*; and, in the same sense, Dobree suggested the compd. πεδορραντήριον. II. ῥαντήριον, τό, = περιρραντήριον, *BCH* 35.286 (Delos, ii B.C.), 54.98 (ibid., ii B.C.). ⊛ **-[της]**, ου, ὁ, *sprinkler*, *POxy.*1050.17 (ii/iii A.D.), dub. in *IG*5(1).197 (Sparta). **-τίζω**, = ῥαίνω, *Ep.Hebr.*9.13,19,21:—Pass., *to be sprinkled*, Lxx *Le.*6.27, al., Ath.12.521a, Alex.Trall.*Febr.*4. II. of the effect, *purify*, Lxx *Ps.*50(51).7; ἐρραντισμένοι τὰς καρδίας ἀπὸ συνειδήσεως πονηρᾶς *Ep.Hebr.*10.22. III. ῥαντίζει· σκώπτει, Hsch. **-τισμα**, ατος, τό, name of a skin affection, περὶ τὰς ὄψεις Vett.Val.110.17. **-τισμός**, ὁ, *sprinkling*, ὕδωρ ῥαντισμοῦ Lxx *Nu.*19.9 sq.; αἷμα ῥαντισμοῦ *Ep.Hebr.*12.24, cf. 1*Ep.Pet.*1.2. ⊛ **-τός**, ή, όν, *sprinkled*: hence, *speckled* or *spotted*, μᾶζα Hp.*Vict.*2.40, 3.82; ἄρτος *Supp.Epigr.*4.518 (Ephesus, i/ii A.D.); of animals, *PSI*6.569.10 (iii B.C.), v.l. in Lxx *Ge.*30.32; of *veined* marble, σκούτλη ῥ. *Ephes.*3 No.65 p.148. **-τρίς**, ίδος, ἡ, = περιρραντήριον, *IG*7.3498.18 (Oropus).

⊛ **ῥάξ**, ῥᾶγός, ἡ, Ion. and later Gr. ῥώξ (v. ῥώξ (B)):—*grape*, S.*Fr.*398; κατὰ ῥᾶγα βοτρύων for each *grape* in the bunch, Pl.*Lg.*845a; ῥᾶγες βότρυος Arist.*HA*550$^a$28, cf. *Pr.*925$^b$15; ἐν αὐτῷ τῷ βότρυϊ ῥᾶγας Thphr.*CP*5.5.1, cf. 1.21.1, *HP*3.17.6; τὰς σταφυλὰς καὶ ὡς κατὰ μίαν αἱ ῥᾶγες Philostr.*Im.*1.31. 2. generally, *berry*, Dsc.4.51; ῥ. γλυκυσίδης *seed* of peony, Id.*Eup.*2.117; *clove* of garlic, Id.2.152. 3. *a venomous kind of spider, malmignatte*, so called from its shape, Ael.*NA*3.36. 4. pl., *finger-tips*, Ruf.*Onom.*85, Sor.1.3, Poll.2.146. 5. ῥάξ = θηλή, 'in common speech', Eust.1485.59. [In Nic.*Al.*184, ῥάγεσσι should be read for ῥαγέεσσι.]

⊛**ῥάπα**· τὴν καλάμην, καὶ τοὺς ἐν αὐτῇ αὐλοῦντας ῥαπαύλους, Hsch. (ῥαπατὴν κ. and ῥαπάλους cod.).

**ῥάπαλος**, ὁ, = ῥάφανος, *PJena* 3.12 (v A.D.), cf. sq. II. v. foreg.

**ῥαπάνιον**, = ῥαφ-, *UPZ*89.15 (ii B.C.).

**ῥαπατήν**, v. ῥάπα.

**ῥαπαύλης**, ου, ὁ, *player on a reed-pipe*, Amerias ap.Ath.4.176e (where ῥαππαύλας), Eust.1157.39 (where ῥαπταύλης); cf. ῥάπα.

**ῥαπεύς**, έως, ὁ, = *rupiam* (*rapium* cj. Salmasius), *Gloss.*

**ῥᾰπιδήϊον**, τό, synon. of λεοντοπέταλον, Ps.-Dsc.3.96; *rapadion* (with vv.ll.), Plin.*HN*27.96.

**ῥαπιδοποιόν**· τὸν ποιητήν, Δωριεῖς, ἢ ποικιλτήν, ἢ τὰς κρηπῖδας ποιοῦντα, Hsch.

⊛ **ῥᾰπίζω**, (ῥαπίς) *strike with a stick, cudgel, thrash*, τινα Xenoph.7.4, Hippon.64 (Pass.), Hdt.7.35,223, D.25.57, Lxx *Jd.*16.25, Plb.8.6.6, Phld.*Ir.* p.40 W.; τινὰ ῥάβδῳ *Anacreont.*29.2:—Pass., ῥ. ἐκ τῶν ἀγώνων *to be flogged* off the course, Heraclit.42, cf. Hdt.8.59: Ion. pf. part., ῥεραπισμένα νῶτα Anacr.166. II. *slap in the face* (later for Att. ἐπὶ κόρρης πατάξαι), ἐπὶ κόρρης ῥ. (metaph.) Plu.2.713c; κατὰ κόρρης Ach.Tat.2.24; εἰς τὴν σιαγόνα *Ev.Matt.*5.39:—Pass., ῥαπισθῆναί τε καὶ πληγὰς λαβεῖν ἁπαλαῖσι χερσίν Timocl.22.5; ἐρραπίσθη τὴν γνάθον Hyp.*Fr.*97, cf. *AB*300; ῥαπίζειν distd. from κολαφίζειν, *Ev.Matt.*26.67. III. generally, *strike, beat*, [τὸν ἀέρα] Arist.*de An.*419$^b$23:—Pass., Id.*Mete.*368$^a$16, 370$^a$14, Epicur.*Fr.*398.

**ῥᾰπίς**, ίδος, ἡ, *rod*, Hsch., Phot. II. *a kind of shoe*, = κρηπίς, Hsch., *EM*702.33. III. = γογγυλίς, Hsch.; cf. ῥάπυς, ῥάφυς.

**ῥάπ-ισμα** [ᾰ], ατος, τό, *stroke*, ἀνθράκων ῥαπίσμασι (Abresch ῥιπ-) Antiph.217.21. 2. *slap on the face*, *Ev.Marc.*14.65, *Ev.Jo.*18.22; in Lat. form *rhapismata*, *Cod.Just.*8.48.6; ῥ. λαμβάνειν Luc.*DMeretr.*8.2; ῥ. ἀμφὶ πρόσωπα *AP*5.288 (Agath.). 2. *weal*, *Arch.Pap.*3.418.30 (vi A.D.). **-ισμός**, ὁ, *striking, beating*, Corn.*ND*16, Sor.2.31,37. **-ιστέον**, *one must beat*, Aët.9.8.

⊛ **ῥάπ-της**, ου, ὁ, (ῥάπτω) *one who stitches, clothes-mender*, Anub. in *Cat.Cod.Astr.*8(4).208, *PHamb.*56v7 (vi/vii A.D.), *Gloss.* **-τικός**, ή, όν, *of* or *for stitching*, Gal.*Thras.*5, Sch.Philostr.*Her.*2.19 (p.464 Boissonade). ⊛ **-τός**, ή, όν, *stitched, patched*, χιτών, κνημῖδες, Od.24.228,229; ἐν σκυταρίοις ῥ. Anaxil.18.6; πλοῖα boats *made of hides sewn together*, Str.7.4.1. 2. metaph., *strung together, continuous*, ῥαπτῶν ἐπέων ἀοιδοί Pi.*N.*2.2; cf. ῥαψῳδός. II. *worked with the needle*: hence ῥαπτά, τά, *embroidered carpets*, X.*HG*4.1.30; ῥαπτὴ σφαῖρα a ball *of divers colours*, *AP*12.44 (Glauc.). ⊛ **-τρια**, ἡ, fem. of ῥάπτης, Eust.1764.60.

⊛ **ῥάπτω**, Od.16.422, etc.: fut. ῥάψω (ἀπορ-) Aeschin.2.21: aor. 1 ἔρραψα Hdt.9.17, E.*Andr.*911; Ep. ῥάψα Il.12.296: aor. 2 ἔρρᾰφον (συν-) Nonn.*D.*7.152: plpf. ἐρραφήκει (συν-) X.Eph.1.9:—Med., aor. ἐρραψάμην Ar.*Eq.*784, etc.:—Pass., fut. ῥαφήσομαι (συν-) Androm.ap. Gal.13.685: aor. ἐρράφην [ᾰ] D.54.41, v. infr.: pf. ἔρραμμαι Ar.*Ec.*24, D.54.35: poet. plpf. ἔραπτο (συν-) Q.S.9.359:—*sew together, stitch*, βοείας Il.12.296: abs., Ar.*Pl.*513:—Med., ῥαψάμενον δερμάτων ὀχετόν *having made himself* a pipe of leather, Hdt.3.9; ῥαψάμενός σοι τουτί (sc. τὸ προσκεφάλαιον) *having got it stitched* or *made*, Ar.*Eq.*784; also, *sew on* or *to one*, Id.*Nu.*538:—Pass., ἐρράφθαι τὸ χεῖλος *to have* one's lip *sewed up*, D.54.35, cf. 41; ἔχειν πώγωνας ἐρραμμένους to have beards *sewed on*, Ar.*Ec.*24; ἐν μηρῷ ποτ' ἐρράφθαι Διός *was sewn up* in.., E.*Ba.*243; ἐρραμμένα *stitched work, a cushion* or *pad*, Alex.98.11; χρὴ τὸ ἔποχον τοιοῦτον ἐρράφθαι ὡς.. X.*Eq.*12.9. II. metaph. c. dat., *devise, contrive, plot*, σφιν κακὰ ῥ. Od.3.118, cf. Il.18.367; φόνον, θάνατόν τε μόρον τε ῥ., Od.16.379,422; ῥάψαι μόρον σοι E.*IT*681; also ἐπ' Ἕλλησι φόνον ῥ. Hdt.9.17; εἴς τινα E.*Andr.*911; ἐπιβουλὰς ῥ. τινί, Lat. *suere dolos*, Alex.98.2: prov., τοῦτο τὸ ὑπόδημα ἔρραψας μὲν σύ, ὑπεδήσατο δὲ Ἀρισταγόρης you *sewed* the shoe but A. put it on, Hdt.6.1. 2. generally, *string* or *link together, unite*, ἀοιδήν Hes.*Fr.*265. 3. ῥάψαντα διὰ βίου τοῖς αὐτοκράτορσι, perh. f.l. in *JHS*42.168 (iii A.D.). 4. ῥάπτουσα, ἡ, name of a plaster, Cels.5.19.6, 5.26.23.

**ῥάπυς** [ᾰ], ἡ, = ῥάφυς, Glauc.ap.Ath.9.369b, prob. cj. in Gal.6.622.

**ῥάριον**, τό, Dim. of ῥάρος, Hsch., *EM*702.37, Suid.

**Ῥᾶρος**, ὁ, *Rarus*, father of Triptolemus, Paus.1.14.3, Hsch., Suid.; in Phot. **Ῥάρ**:—τὸ **Ῥάριον** πεδίον the field *of Rarus*, where tillage was first practised, and which was sacred to Demeter, Paus.1.38.6, St.Byz.; (without πεδίον) **Ῥάριον**, τό, *h.Cer.*450; ⊛**Ῥαρία**, ἡ (sc. γῆ), Plu.2.144b; whence the goddess was herself called **Ῥαριάς**, ἡ, St.Byz. [α is long, *h.Cer.* l. c., so that the accent is prob. not Ῥάρος, as in most codd.:—for the smooth breathing, v. Hdn.Gr.2.402, 940.]

**ῥάρος**, ὁ, a word found only in Gramm., expld. as = γαστήρ in *EM* 702.37, Suid.; as Aeol. for ἔμβρυον in Sch.D.T. p.143 H.; as = ἀμβλωθρίδιον βρέφος in *Lex. de Spir.* p.215 Valck.; as = ἰσχυρός (cf. ῥωρός), Hsch., Phot., Suid. [The breathing is smooth, as in Ῥᾶρος, Sch.D.T. and *Lex. de Spir.* ll. cc.]

**ῥάσδον**, or -ος, name of an ingredient of nard, Aët.1.130,132.

⊛ **ῥάσμα**, ατος, τό, (ῥαίνω) *shower*, μύρων Duris 10 J. (pl.); *sprinkling*, θαλαμίων Crito ap.Gal.12.447.

**ῥάσσατε**, v. ῥαίνω.

⊛ **ῥάσσω**, Att. -ττω, (κατα-) Plb.10.48.7, (συρ-) D.H.8.18: fut. ῥάξω Lxx *Is.*9.11(10), (ξυρ-) Th.8.96: aor. ἔρραξα D.54.8, Apollod. Com.22, (συν-) X.*HG*7.5.16:—Pass., fut. (in med. form) ῥάξομαι (καταρ-) Plu.*Caes.*44: aor. ἐρράχθην Lxx *Da.*8.10, (ἐπι-) D.H.8.18:—like ἀράσσω, *strike, dash*, τινὰ εἰς τὸν βόρβορον D. l. c.; *overthrow*, τινας Lxx *Is.* l. c. 2. in Ion. form ῥήσσω, of dancers, *beat the ground, dance*, ῥήσσοντες ἁμαρτῇ μολπῇ τ' ἰυγμῷ τε ποσὶ σκαίροντες ἕποντο Il.18.571; οἱ δὲ ῥήσσοντες ἕποντο *h.Ap.*516; for which A.R. 1.539 has in full, ὥστε..πέδον ῥήσσωσι πόδεσσι:—so also αἴρησιν ὅτε ῥήσσοιτο σίδηρος Euph.51.9; ῥήσσειν τύμπανα *beat* them *violently*, *AP* 7.709 (Alexander). [ῥάσσω (ῥάττω) prob. has ᾱ by nature, as shown by Ion. ῥήσσω: cf. ἀράσσω:—the Ion. form is found also in the κοινή, as Lxx *Wi.*4.19, *Ev.Marc.*9.18, *Ev.Luc.*9.42, Arr.*Epict.*1.20.9.]

**ῥαστάζει**· πονεῖ, ὠθεῖ, ταράττεται, Hsch.; cf. ῥαιστάζει.

**ῥᾷστος**, v. ῥᾴδιος.

**ῥαστών-ευσις**, εως, ἡ, = ῥαστώνη, Ael.*Fr.*110, cf. 321. ⊛ **-εύω**, = ῥαθυμέω, *to be idle, listless*, τῇ ψυχῇ X.*Oec.*20.18, D.C.38.39:—Med., Zen.1.23, Diogenian.1.21, Hsch., dub. l. in Ael.*Fr.*281:—pf. Pass. in med. sense, [Aristid.]*Or.*54 p.652 Dind., Thom.Mag.p.325 R. **-έω**, *grow easy, become less painful*, Hp.*Prorrh.*1.52, Gal.9.703. **-η**, Ion. ῥηστώνη, ἡ, (ῥᾷστος) *easiness of doing* anything, Pl.*R.*460d, *Lg.*684d; opp. χαλεπότης, Id.*Criti.*107c; ῥαστώνῃ or μετὰ ῥαστώνης *with ease, easily, lightly*, Id.*Epin.*991c, *Lg.*625b; ῥαστώνην παρασκευάζειν τινός find *an easy way of doing* a thing, ib.720c; πολλὴ ῥ. γίγνεται, c. inf., one has great *ease* in doing, Id.*Grg.*459c; ὄχλῳ ῥαστώνην φυγῆς παρέσχον afforded an *easy opportunity* of escape, Plu.*Cam.*20; πρὸς τὰς ῥ. for the *conveniences* of getting food, Arist.*Pol.*1256$^a$26. II. *easiness of temper, good nature, mildness*, c. gen. objecti, ἐκ ῥηστώνης (dub. l.) τῆς Δημοκήδεος from *kindness to* Democedes, Hdt.3.136; χάριτι καὶ ῥ. Plb.38.11.11. III. *relief from anything unpleasant*, μηδεμίαν διδόντα ῥ. [τοῖς ἀδικοῦσι] D.24.69, cf. Lys.13.85; *relief from pain*, Hp.*Epid.*3.17.θ'; ῥ. τῆς πόσεως *recovery from* the effects of drinking, Pl.*Smp.*176b; ἐκ τῶν πόνων Id.*Lg.*779a; ἀσφάλεια καὶ ῥ. τισὶ ἀπὸ Λακεδαιμονίων Plb.18.14.15. 2. abs., *rest, leisure, ease*, ἐμαυτῷ ῥᾳστώνην ἐξηῦρον found *recreation*, Lys.24.10, cf. Pl.*Plt.*310c, etc.; ὀλίγοις πόνοις πολλὰς ῥ. κτώμενος Isoc.9.45; ἔχει τινὰ ῥᾳστώνην τὸ λέγειν it brings a certain *relief*, D.*Ep.*3.44; ἀναπνοὴν καὶ ῥ. ἐν τῷ καύματι παρέχειν Pl.*Ti* 70d; διὰ ῥᾳστώνην for the sake of *resting*, X.*An.*5.8.16; πρὸς ῥ. καὶ διαγωγήν Arist.*Metaph.*$982^{b}23$. b. *luxurious ease, indolence*, τῆς ῥ. τὸ τερπνόν Th.1.120; ῥ. καὶ ῥαθυμία *nonchalance, carelessness*, D.10.7, cf. 18.45 (interchanged with ῥαθυμία in Isoc. l.c.). c. *resting-time, season of calm and tranquillity*, ἐν ἀπεριστάτοις ῥ. σφάλλεσθαι Plb.6.44.8. [Ῥαιστώνη as name of an Athenian trireme, $IG2^{2}$.1608.52; ῥαιστ– also in Phld.*D.*3.8.]

**ῥάστωρ·** κρατήρ, Hsch. (cf. ῥαίστωρ). **ῥατάναν·** τορύνην, Id. (cf. βρατάναν, also ῥοταρία). **ῥᾴτερος,** α, ον, Dor. Comp. of ῥᾴδιος (q. v.). **ῥατίζει·** πρεσβεύει, Id. **ῥατιχεύειν·** καταρᾶσθαι, Id. **ϝράτρα,** Elean for ῥήτρα. **ῥατῶνα·** ῥεκτῆρα, σφαγέα, Hsch. **ῥαυλόν·** ἄγραυλον, ἄγροικον, Id.

**ῥᾰφᾰν-έλαιον,** τό, *oil of radishes*, Dsc.1.37 (as v.l.), in lemmate; written **ῥεφαναιέλαιον,** *POxy.*155.8 (vi A.D.). **–η,** ἡ, = ῥάφανος, Batr. 53 (as v.l.), *Hippiatr.*33, Hsch. **–ηδόν,** Adv. *radish-like*, of fractures, Erot. s. v. ἀτρεκέως, Gal.10.424, Sor.*Fract.*10; cf. καυληδόν. ⊛ **–ίδῐον** [ῐδ], τό, Dim. of ῥαφανίς, Pl.Com.171. **–ῑδόω,** *thrust a radish up the fundament*, a punishment of adulterers in Athens, Ar.*Nu.*1083, cf. Luc. *Peregr.*9:—hence **ἀποράφᾰνίδωσις,** εως, ἡ, Sch.Ar.*Pl.*168. **–ῑδώδης,** ες, *like a radish*, Thphr.*HP*7.6.2. ⊛ **–ῐνος,** η, ον, *of radish*, ἔλαιον Dsc.1.37, *PAmh.*2.93.10 (ii A.D.), Gal.11.750: ῥαφάνινον alone, *PFay.*240 (i B.C.). **–ιον,** τό, Dim. of ῥάφανος II, *PHib.*1.34.18 (iii B.C.), *UPZ*89.4 (ii B.C.); cf. ῥαπάνιον. **–ίς,** ῖδος, ἡ, *radish, Raphanus sativus*, Ar.*Nu.*981, *Pl.*544, *Fr.*253, Cratin.313, Eup.312, Thphr.*HP*1.2.7, Dsc.2.112, etc.: later **ῥεφανίς,** Philum.*Ven.*18.4, *Gloss.*; cf. ῥάφανος. II. ῥ. ἀγρία *charlock, Raphanus raphanistrum*, Dsc.2.112, Plin.*HN*19.82. [–ῖs, ῖδος in all known passages, though Ath.2.56e says that ι is common.] **–ῖτις,** ιδος, ἡ, = ἶρις Ἰλλυρική, Plin.*HN*21.41. ⊛ **–ος,** ἡ, Att. for κράμβη, *cabbage, Brassica cretica*, Ar.*Fr.*109; οἶδ' ὅτι καλοῦμεν ῥάφανον, ὑμεῖς δ' οἱ ξένοι κράμβην Apollod. Car.27; τῆς ῥ., ἣν καλοῦσί τινες κράμβην Arist.*HA*$551^{a}15$, cf. Thphr. *HP*1.6.6, al.; it was boiled for use, Nicoch.15, Alex.286; distd. fr. –ίς by Phryn.11, Hsch. 2. ῥ. ἀγρία, = κράμβη ἀγρία, Thphr.*HP*7.6.2. b. = ῥαφανὶς ἀγρία, ib.9.15.5. c. *tuberous spurge, Euphorbia Apios*, Dsc.4.175; also ῥ. ὀρεία, ὀρεινή, Thphr.*HP*9.12.1, Ps.-Dsc.4.175. II. also, = ῥαφανίς, Arist.*Pr.*$924^{a}34$, *PTeb.*79.22 (ii B.C.), Poll.1.247. (Ion.(?) and late Gr. **ῥέφανος** Hp.*Mul.*2.115, *Gloss.*: v. ῥάπυς.) **–ουρός,** ὁ, *cabbage-watcher, gardener*, like κηπουρός, Hsch.

**ῥαφάσσει·** πλανᾶται, Hsch.

**ῥᾰφ-εύς,** έως, ὁ, (ῥάπτω) *stitcher, patcher, cobbler*, Poll.7.42. 2. metaph., ῥ. φόνου *planner* of murder, A.*Ag.*1604. **–ή,** ἡ, *seam*, ἱμάντων Od.22.186; [χιτῶνος] Plu.*Cleom.*37. 2. *suture* of the skull, κεφαλὴ οὐκ ἔχουσα ῥαφήν Hdt.9.83, cf. Hp.*VC*1 (pl.), Pl.*Ti.*76a, Arist.*HA*$491^{b}2$, $516^{a}15$; also of the heart and other parts, Id.*PA* $667^{a}7$, $677^{b}19$; ῥαφαὶ ὀστέων E.*Ph.*1159, *Supp.*503. II. *stitching, sewing*, τρήσει καὶ ῥαφῇ χρωμένη σύνθεσις Pl.*Plt.*280c; αἱ ῥ. τοῦ τραύματος, of a wound *that had been sewn up*, D.C.43.11.

**ῥάφη** [ᾰ], ἡ, Dor. **ῥάφα,** *a large kind of radish*, Trypho ap.Hsch., dub. in Epich.204.

⊛ **ῥᾰφῐδ-ᾶς,** ᾶ, ὁ, *embroiderer*, *PWürzb.*$15^{v}$ (iv A.D.). **–εια,** ἡ, fem. of sq., in Delph. acc. sg. ῥαφίδηαν, *Delph.*3(3).26.6 (ii B.C.). ⊛ **–εύς,** έως, ὁ, = ῥαφεύς, *AP*11.288 (Pall.). **–ευτής,** οῦ, ὁ, *stitcher, embroiderer*, Lxx *Ex.*27.16. **–ευτός,** ή, όν, = ῥαπτός, ib.37.21.

**ῥᾰφῐδο-θήκη,** ἡ, *needle-box*, *Gloss.* ⊛ **–ποιός,** ὁ, *needle-maker*, ib.

⊛ **ῥᾰφίς,** Dor. **ῥᾰπίς** (Epich.51), ίδος, ἡ, (ῥάπτω) *needle*, Hp.*Morb.* 2.66 (where Gal.19.134 read ῥαφίῳ, al. γραφίσι), Archipp.38, Ph.*Bel.* 61.14, Hero *Bel.*109.1 (ῥανίδα codd.), *AP*11.110 (Nicarch.), *Hermes* 38.283; διὰ τρυπήματος (v.l. τρήματος) ῥαφίδος διελθεῖν (v.l. εἰσελθεῖν) *Ev.Matt.*19.24:—in Att. replaced by βελόνη, Phryn.72. II. *garfish, Belone acus*, Epich. l.c., Arist.*Fr.*294, Opp.*H.*1.172, *C.*2.392.

**ῥάφοι·** ὄρνεις τινές, Hsch.

**ῥάφυς** [ᾰ], υος, ἡ, = βουνιάς, Speus.ap.Ath.9.369b; perh. to be read (for ῥάφιν) in Numen.(?) ib.371c; cf. ῥάπυς.

**ῥᾰχάδην·** ἐπὶ τῆς ῥάχεως, Hsch. **ῥᾰχάς,** άδος, ἡ, *wooded ridge*, Id., Phot., but **ῥάχας,** ὁ, gen. τοῦ ῥάχα, *IG*14.352 ii 25,66 (Halaesa).

**ῥᾰχετρ-ίζω,** (ῥάχις) *cut through the spine*, Poll.2.136; cf. ῥακετρίζω. **–ον,** τό, = ῥάχις, Hsch.; acc. to Phot. *the beginning of the spine*, acc. to Poll.2.136 *the middle*; = πλευρόν, Did.ap.Phot. II. *butcher's knife* or *chopper*, Poll.7.25; Hsch. cites βράκετον (leg. –τρον) = δρέπανον.

**ῥάχη** [ᾱ], ἡ, v.l. for ῥάχος, = ῥαχός I. 1, Poll.1.225 (ῥάχην ἢ ῥάχον). **ῥάχι·** τὸ στέμφυλον, Hsch.

**ῥᾱχία,** Ion. **ῥηχίη,** ἡ, *flood-tide*, opp. ἄμπωτις, Hdt.2.11, 7.198; joined with πλημυρίς (s. v.l.), Id.8.129, cf. Hp.ap.Gal.19.135. 2. *the roar of the breakers*, metaph. of a crowd of people, ὄχλου τοιούτου ῥαχίαν ἠθροισμένην Posidipp.27.11; ῥ. ποιεῖν ἐν δήμῳ Plu.2.789d, cf. 791a: prov., ῥαχίας λαλίστερος Diogenian.7.99. II. *rocky shore* or *beach* (πᾶς πετρώδης αἰγιαλός Hsch.), ἁλίστονοι ῥ. A.*Pr.*713; παρ' αὐτὴν τὴν ῥ. Th.4.10, cf. Plb.3.39.4, Str.16.4.23. 2. = ῥάχις II. 1, S.*Fr.*1088; = ῥάχις I, Nonn.*D.*11.182, 39.334 (v. ad fin.). [ῥᾰ– metri gr. only in late Poets, as *AP*7.393 (Diocl.); in sense II. 2, Nonn. ll.cc.] (Cogn. with ῥάσσω, ῥήσσω, and ἀράσσω; = τὸν τόπον ᾧ προσαράττει τὸ κῦμα, Ael.Dion.*Fr.*427: not cogn. with ῥήγνυμι, which has pan-Hellenic η.)

**ῥᾰχ-ιαῖος,** α, ον, (ῥάχις) *of the spine*, μύες Hp.*Aph.*7.36, Gal.*UP* 12.10. ⊛ **–ίζω,** *cut through the spine*, esp. in sacrifices (Hsch.), *cleave in twain*, of persons and animals, A.*Pers.*426, S.*Aj.*56,299, E.*Fr.*1105, *Hippiatr.*22. II. *play the braggart, boast*, Din.*Fr.*80, Hsch. ⊛ **–ις,** ιος, Att. εως, ἡ (but ὁ $IG4^{2}$ (v. infr.)), *the lower part of the back, the chine*, συὸς ῥ. Il.9.208. 2. *spine* or *backbone*, σύγκειται ἡ ῥ. ἐκ σφονδύλων, τείνει δ' ἀπὸ τῆς κεφαλῆς μέχρι πρὸς τὰ ἰσχία Arist.*HA*$516^{a}11$, cf. *PA*$654^{b}12$, al.; ὑπὸ ῥάχιν παγέντες impaled, A.*Eu.*190, cf. S.*Fr.*20, E.*Cyc.*643; μυελὸς κοίλης ῥάχεως Archel.ap. Antig.*Mir.*89, cf. Pl.*Ti.*77d, 91a. II. *anything ridged like the backbone*: 1. *ridge* of a hill or mountain, Hdt.3.54, 7.216, $IG4^{2}$(1).71.14 (Epid., iii B.C.), Plb.3.101.2, D.H.5.44, Str.3.2.3 (pl.); ἂν ῥάχιν along the *ridge*, *GDI*5075.69 (Crete, i B.C.); so Archil.21 likened Thasos to an ὄνου ῥάχις. 2. ῥ. ῥινός *bridge* of the nose, Poll.2.79, Ruf.*Onom.*35. 3. ῥ. φύλλου *mid-rib* of a leaf, Thphr.*HP*3.7.5, al. 4. *the sharp projection on the middle of the shoulder-blade*, Gal. *UP*13.10, Ruf.*Onom.*71. 5. *outer edge* of the arm of the polypus, Arist.*HA*$524^{a}7$. 6. *trunk*, of Dagon, Lxx 1*Ki.*5.4. ⊛ **–ιστής,** οῦ, ὁ, *he who cuts the victim through the spine*, Phot. II. *boaster, braggart*, Theopomp.Com.43: also **ῥαχιστήρ,** ῆρος, ὁ, Hsch. **–ιστός,** ή, όν, *cut up, cleft*, Amphis 16. **–ίτης** [ῑ], ου, ὁ, (ῥάχις) *in* or *of the spine*, μυελὸς ῥ. the *spinal* marrow, Hp.*Coac.*499, Arist.*PA*$651^{b}32$; without μ., ib.$652^{a}30$, cf. ῥάχις I; ῥ. μύες Gal.*UP*12.8.

**ῥᾱχιώδης,** ες, *with surf* or *breakers*, αἰγιαλός, ἀκταί, Str.5.4.4, 12.3.11; παραλία Id.16.2.13.

⊛ **ῥάχνος,** εος, τό, perh. *cloak*, *PGen.*80.7 (iv A.D.), *PKlein.Form.*407 (vi A.D.).

⊛ **ῥᾱχ-ός,** ἡ (in codd. freq. ῥάχος, but the Ion. form **ῥηχός** Hdt.7.142, and the compd. εὔρρηχος show that it must be either ῥᾱχός or ῥᾶχος:—in *EM*703.1 ῥάχος, ὁ):—*thorn-hedge*, S.*Fr.*812 (pl.), X.*Cyn.*10.7, cf. Poll.1.225; in Hdt. l.c., ῥηχός is prob. *palisade* or *wattled fence*; *brushwood*, ῥαχὸς (Dor. acc. pl.) καὶ φρύγανα *GDI*5027 (Crete). 2. generally, *twig, branch*, of the vine, Thphr.*CP*3.7.3; of the tamarisk, Hsch., Phot., dub. in Orph.*Fr.*31 ii 10. II. at Troezen, *wild olive tree*, Paus.2.32.10. **–όω,** *cover with wattle-work*, prob. in $IG2^{2}$.463.82.

**ῥαψαϝυδός,** late Boeot. for ῥαψῳδός, *IG*7.3195 (Orchomenos).

**ῥάψις,** εως, ἡ, (ῥάπτω) *stitching together*, ἐπῶν Eust.6.36.

**ῥαψῳδ-έω,** *recite poems*, esp. those of Homer, τί δή ποτ' οὖν..ῥαψῳδεῖς..περιιών; Pl.*Ion* 541b; ἅ τε εὖ ῥαψῳδεῖ καὶ ἃ μή ib.533c, cf. Isoc. 12.33; of the poems of Archilochus, Clearch.61; τι περί τινος Luc. *JConf.*1:—Pass., of the poems, *to be recited*, Lycurg.102. 2. abs., Arist.*Po.*$1462^{a}6$; of Homer and Hesiod, ῥ. περιιόντας *reciting* or *declaiming*, Pl.*R.*600d; Ξενοφάνης..ἐρραψῴδει τὰ ἑαυτοῦ D.L.9.18; ἐμμέτρως ἐρρ. πρὸς ἄνδρας φίλους Luc.*Nec.*1. 3. in contemptuous sense, *repeat by heart* or *rote, declaim*, οὐδὲν..ἀλλ' ἢ ῥαψῳδήσουσιν οἱ πρέσβεις περιιόντες D.14.12, cf. 25.2, Luc.*DMort.*15.2; [λόγοι] ῥαψῳδούμενοι ἄνευ ἀνακρίσεως καὶ διδαχῆς Pl.*Phdr.*277e, cf. Phld.*Rh.*2.39S. II. c. acc. pers., *sing of* one, *celebrate*, τοὺς ἀνδρείους Ar.*Ec.* 679. **–ία,** ἡ, *recitation of Epic poetry*, Pl.*Ion* 533b; ἆθλα..οἱ πατέρες ἔθεσαν ῥ. Id.*Ti.*21b. 2. *Epic composition*, opp. lyric (κιθαρῳδία), ἐπιδεικνύναι ῥ. Id.*Lg.*658b; ἐπι(v.l. ἀπο-)τελεῖν Clearch.62: generally, of all kinds of poetry, ποιεῖν μικτὴν ῥ. ἐξ ἁπάντων μέτρων Arist. *Po.*$1447^{b}22$. II. *portion of an Epic poem fit for recitation at one time*, e.g. a *book* of the Iliad or Odyssey, Plu.2.186e, Luc.*DMort.* 20.2, *Cont.*7. III. contemptuously, *rigmarole*, Plu.2.514c (pl.). **–ικός,** ή, όν, *of* or *for a rhapsodist*: ἡ –κή (with and without τέχνη) *the rhapsodist's art*, Pl.*Ion* 538b, 540a, al. Adv. –κῶς Eust. 3.55. **–ός,** ὁ, *reciter of Epic poems*, sts. applied to the *bard who recited his own poem*, as to Hesiod, Nicocl.ap.Sch.Pi.*N.*2.2 (v. infr.); but usu., *professional reciters*, esp. *of the poems of Homer*, Hdt.5.67, Pl.*Ion* 530c, etc.: also ῥ. κύων, ironically, of the Sphinx who *chanted* her riddle, S.*OT*391. (Prob. from ῥάπτω, ἀοιδή; Hes.*Fr.* 265 speaks of himself and Homer as ἐν νεαροῖς ὕμνοις ῥάψαντες ἀοιδήν, and Pi.*N.*2.2 calls Epic poets ῥαπτῶν ἐπέων ἀοιδοί: not from ῥάβδος (cf. ῥάβδος I. 6) as if ῥαβδῳδός (Eust.6.24, ῥαβδῳδία ib.16).)

**ῥᾴων, ῥᾷως,** v. ῥᾴδιος.

**ῥέᾰ,** Ep. Adv. of ῥᾴδιος, *easily, lightly*, Il.5.304, 8.179, etc.; cf. ῥεῖα, ῥᾶ. [⏑⏑ or –, ll.cc.; but as one long syll. in 12.381, 13.144, Hes. *Op.*5.]

⊛ **Ῥέᾱ,** ἡ, Ep. **Ῥείη** Il.14.203 (in gen. Ῥείης, v.l. Ῥείας), *h.Cer.*442, *h.Ap.*93 (Ῥέη codd.), *h.Ven.*43, Hes.*Th.*625 (Ῥείαν ib.135); Ῥεῖα δ' ὑποδμηθεῖσα ib.453 (but with v.l. Ῥείη δ' αὖ δμηθεῖσα); gen. Ῥείας *AP*6.219.20 (Antip.); the common form Ῥέα is found in Il.15.187, as a monosyll.; contr. Ῥῆ Pherecyd.Syr.9; Ῥέη *h.Cer.*459, Hes. *Th.*467:—*Rhea*, daughter of Uranos and Gaia, wife of Cronos, mother of Zeus and the gods, ll.cc. [Derived by Chrysipp.*Stoic.*2. 318 from ῥέω, because rivers flow from Earth.] II. Pythag. name for 2, Anatolius ap.*Theol.Ar.*12; also for $2^{3}$ or 8, ib.55.

⊛ **ῥέανσις,** εως, ἡ, prob. = λέανσις, *polishing* with wine as a cleanser (cf. Varro *RR*2.11.7, Juv.5.24), *Stud.Pal.*22.183.109 (ii A.D.).

⊛ **ῥεαντής,** οῦ, ὁ, prob. = *λεαντής, *polisher*, *BGU*185.10 (ii A.D.).

**ῥεγεύς,** έως, ὁ, *dyer*, *EM*703.28 (vv.ll. ῥαγεῖς, ῥηγεῖς); also **ῥεγιστής,** οῦ, ὁ, Hsch.; cf. ῥογεύς.

**ῥεγεών,** ῶνος, ἡ, = ῥεγιών, *BCH*24.337 (Caria).

**ῥεγεωνάρχης,** ου, ὁ, *president of a regio*, in pl., Lyd.*Mens.*4.138.

**ῥεγιών,** ῶνος, ἡ, Lat. *regio*, *CIG*3436 (Philadelphia).

**ῥέγκ-ος**, εος, τό, *snoring, stertorous breathing*, Hp.*Acut*.17, *Epid*. 5.55; also **ῥέγχη**, ἡ, Erot. s. v. διαρόγχας, and **ῥέγχος**, τό, Hp.*Epid*. 5.104, 7.77; cf. sq. **-ω**, *snore*, A.*Eu*.53, Eup.267, Ar.*Nu*.5, al.; of horses, *snort*, E.*Rh*.785; of a dolphin asleep, Arist.*HA* 537b3, 566b15:—in Ar.*Eq*.115 also in Med. ῥέγκεται, but (as Sch. observes) only to balance πέρδεται; but cf. ll. cc. infr.—The form **ῥέγχω** occurs in Hp.*Aph*.6.51, Arist. ll. cc., Men.*Mon*.711, Herod.8.2, Lxx *Jn*.1.5,6, Orph.*Fr*.148: Med., τῆς πλευρᾶς ῥέγχομαι *I am wheezing* from my lung, *POxy*.1414.26 (iii A. D.), cf. *AP*11.343. **-ώδης**, ες, *as if snoring*, only in form ῥεγχ-, Hp.*Epid*.5.105, 7.14.

**ῥέγμα**, ατος, τό, (ῥέζω (B)) *that which is dyed*, Ibyc.10B; cf. ῥέγος.

**ῥέγξις**, εως, ἡ, (ῥέγκω) *stertorous breathing*, Hp.*Acut*.17.

**ῥέγος**, εος, τό, = ῥῆγος (q. v.), *rug, coverlet*, Anacr.138.

**ῥέγχος, ῥέγχω, ῥεγχώδης**, v. ῥεγκ-. **ῥέδα, ῥέδιον**, v. ῥαῖδα, ῥαίδιον. **ῥέδδω**, v. ῥέζω (A). **ῥέεθρον**, Ion. and poet. for ῥεῖθρον (q. v.).

⊛ **ῥέζω** (A), freq. in Ep. and Trag. (v. infr.), but rare in Att. Prose and Com. (Pherecr.152 is mock heroic): impf. ἔρεζον Il.2.400, Ep. ῥέζον Od.3.5, Ion. ῥέζεσκον Il.8.250: fut. ῥέξω Od.11.31, A.*Eu*.788 (lyr.), al.: aor. ἔρρεξα Il.9.536, 10.49, Pl.*Lg*.642c; poet. also ἔρεξα Hom. (v. infr.), Hes.*Fr*.174, S.*OC*538 (lyr.), etc.; Aeol. part. ῥέξαις Pi.*O*.9.94:—Pass., aor. 1 opt. ῥεχθείη Hp.*Epid*.7.11; part. ῥεχθείς Il.9.250, 20.198. (ῥέζω from ϝρέγ-yω, cogn. with ἔρδω from ϝέργ-yω [through ϝέρσδω]: Dor. and Boeot. **ῥέδδω** Eust.226.8, 984.1, Hsch.; aor. part. ϝρέξαντα *IG*4.1607 (Cleonae).) I. *do, act, deal*, opp. εἰπεῖν, Od.4.205, 22.314; opp. παθεῖν, v. infr.:—Constr., 1. abs., ὧδε δὲ ῥέξαι Il.2.802; οὐ κατὰ μοῖραν ἔρεξας Od.9.352, etc. 2. more freq. trans. c. acc. rei, *do, accomplish, make*, ὅσ' ἂν πεπνυμένος ἀνὴρ εἴποι καὶ ῥέξειε 4.205; μέρμερα ἔργα, ὅσσ' ἄνδρες ῥέξαντες.. Il.10.525, cf. Od.22.314; τί ῥέξομεν; Il.11.838; μέγα ῥέξας τι καὶ ἐσσομένοισι πυθέσθαι 22.305, cf. 2.274; ὅ τι ποσσίν τε ῥέξῃ καὶ χερσίν Od.8.148; so in Lyr. and Trag., ῥέζοντά τι καὶ παθεῖν ἔοικε Pi.*N*.4.32; τί ῥέξω; A.*Eu*.788, cf. *Th*.104 (both lyr.); τί ῥέξας τύχοιμ' ἄν..; Id.*Ch*.316 (lyr.):—Pass., οὐδέ τι μῆχος ῥεχθέντος κακοῦ ἔστ' ἄκος εὑρεῖν for the mischief *if once done*, Il.9.250; ῥεχθὲν δέ τε νήπιος ἔγνω 17.32. 3. c. dupl. acc. pers. et rei, *do* something *to* one, κακὰ ῥέξαι τινά 3.354, Od.2.73; ἀγαθὰ ῥ. τινά 22.209, cf. Il.9.647; οὐδέν σε ῥέξω κακά 24.370, cf. 4.32, Od.2.72: with Adv., κακῶς μιν ἔρ. *wronged* him, 23.56; so ἡ πόλις ἡμᾶς οὐ καλῶς ἔρρεξε Pl.*Lg*.642c: but c. dat. pers., μηκέτι μοι κακὰ ῥέζετε *do* me (ethic dat.) no more mischiefs, Od.20.314; ὅσα βροτοῖς ἔρεξας κακά E.*Med*.1292 (lyr.). 4. with strengthd. signf., εἴ τι νόος ῥέξει if it *shall avail* aught, *be of* any *service*, Il.14.62. II. in special sense, *perform* sacrifices, ἱερὰ ῥ. Od.1.61, 3.5; ῥ. ἑκατόμβας ἀθανάτοις *offer* a hecatomb to the gods, Il.23.206, cf. Od.5.102, Pi.*P*.10.34; ῥ. θαλύσια τινι Il.9.535; θύματα Ζηνὶ τῆς ἁλώσεως S.*Tr*.288: abs., *do sacrifice*, ῥ. θεῷ Il.2.400, 8.250, etc.: sts. with the victim in acc., σοὶ..ῥέξω βοῦν ἦνιν *will sacrifice* it, 10.292, cf. Od.9.553, 10.523.

**ῥέζω** (B), Dor. Verb, = βάπτω, *dye*, Phot., *EM*703.27, cf. Epich.107. (Cf. ῥέγος, ῥεγεύς, ῥεγιστής, and lengthd. ῥῆγος, ῥηγεύς, also ῥογεύς:—cogn. with Skt. *rajyate* 'is coloured or red'.)

⊛ **ῥεθομᾱλίδας**, α, ὁ, (μῆλον (B)) *with cheeks like apples*, Alc.150.

⊛ **ῥέθος**, εος, τό, *limb*, usu. in pl. ῥέθεα, *limbs*, ψυχὴ δ' ἐκ ῥεθέων πταμένη Il.16.856; ῥεθέων ἐκ θυμὸν ἕληται 22.68, cf. Theoc.23.39. II. in sg., *face, countenance*, S.*Ant*.529 (anap.), E.*HF*1204 (anap.), Theoc.29.16: Aeol. in this sense acc. to Eust.1090.27; it occurs in broken context, Sapph.*Supp*.11.3. 2. *body*, Lyc.173.

**ῥεῖα**, Ep. for ῥέα, ῥᾶ (qq. v.), (sts. elided, Il.15.356, Od.17.273), Adv. of ῥᾴδιος, *easily, lightly*, freq. in Hom. (v. infr.) and Hes. (*Op*.6, al., but ῥέα ib.5); θεοὶ ῥεῖα ζώοντες the gods who live *at ease*, Il.6.138, Od.4.805; τούτοισιν μὲν ταῦτα μέλει, κίθαρις καὶ ἀοιδή, ῥεῖ' *lightly, pleasantly*, 1.160; strengthd. ῥεῖα μάλ' Il.3.381, 15.362, etc.; ὡς ῥεῖα κυβιστᾷ *easily, deftly*, 16.745, cf. 749.

**Ῥείη**, ἡ, Ep. and Ion. for Ῥέα.

**ῥεῖθρ-ον**, τό, Att. contr. from Ion. and Ep. **ῥέεθρον**, which is used by Trag. once in dialogue, A.*Pers*.497, freq. in lyr.: (ῥέω):—*that which flows, a river, stream*, ποταμοῖο ῥέεθρα *the streams, waters of*.., Il.14.245; ἐρατεινὰ ῥ. 21.218; Στυγὸς ὕδατος αἰπὰ ῥ. 8.369, cf. *h.Hom*.19.9, etc.; παρθενοσφάγα ῥ. *streams* of a maiden's blood, A.*Ag*.210 (lyr.): sg., ἐκτρέψασα τοῦ ποταμοῦ τὸ ῥέεθρον πᾶν ἐς τὸ ὤρυξε χωρίον Hdt.1.186, cf. 179, Th.7.74; Ἀλφεοῦ ῥέεθρον Pi.*O*.9.18; ῥέεθρον ἁγνοῦ Στρυμόνος A.*Pers*.497; ὅταν περάσῃς ῥεῖθρον Id.*Pr*.790; esp. of *rivulets, brooks*, X.*Cyn*.5.15, Plb.3.71.4, Jul.*Or*.3.126d. II. *bed* or *channel of a river*, ἄψορρον..κῦμα κατέσσυτο καλὰ ῥέεθρα Il.21.382; ποταμοῦ ῥ. ἀπεξηρασμένον Hdt.7.109; ποταμὸν ἐκτραπέσθαι ἐκ τῶν ἀρχαίων ῥ. Id.1.75; παρατρέψας [τὸν ποταμὸν] δι' ὧν νῦν ῥέει ῥεέθρων, i.e. ἐκ τῶν ῥεέθρων δι' ὧν νῦν ῥέει, Id.7.130, cf. 127:—signf. I and II are sts. hard to distinguish, cf. Hdt.1.191, 2.11, 9.51. **-ώδης**, ες, *full of streams, Gloss*.

**ῥεῖος**, Cypr. for ἀσθενής, *EM*539.30.

**ῥειτά**, τά, name of sacred *streams* at Eleusis, S.*Fr*.1089; also **ῥειτοί**, οἱ, Paus.1.38.1, Hsch.; sg. in *SIG*86.5 (Eleusis, v B. C.); ῥῖτοι Hdn.Gr.2.577, wrongly, as shown by the spelling Ῥετόν *SIG* l. c.

**ῥείτης**, ὁ, only in Gramm., as part of the compds. βαθυρ-, εὔρ-ρείτης, Choerob. in *An.Ox*.2.256, etc.

**ῥεῖτος** or **ῥειτός**, ὁ, dub. sens., name of an object in a gymnasium, ῥείτους ἐπιχρύσους δύο *BCH*54.101 (Delos, ii B. C.). II. v. ῥειτά.

**ῥείω**, Ep. for ῥέω. **ῥέκος** (gender unknown), expld. in Theognost. *Can*.11 by ζώνη.

**ῥέκ-τειρα**, ἡ, fem. of sq., Man.1.212. **-τήρ**, ῆρος, ὁ, (ῥέζω) *worker, doer*, like Homer's πρηκτήρ, κακῶν Hes.*Op*.191. 2. c. gen. objecti, *worker in* a thing, χρυσοῖο Man.1.297, cf. 4.149. **-τήριος**, α, ον, *active, busy*, Ion Hist.1. ⊛ **-της**, ου, ὁ, = ῥεκτήρ, *active*, Plu.*Brut*.12, Aret.*SD*1.6. **-τικός**, ή, όν, *able to do*, τῶν ἐφ' ἡμῖν μόνων ῥεκτικὸς ὁ σπουδαῖος Porph.ad Od.1.5.

⊛ **ῥεμβ-άς**, άδος, pecul. fem. of ῥεμβός, v.l. in Lxx *Si*.26.8. **-ασμός**, ὁ, *roaming about*: metaph., *wavering, anxious turn of mind*, ib.*Wi*.4.12. **-εύω**, = ῥέμβομαι, ib.*Is*.23.16. **-η**, ἡ, *wandering*, metaph., κατὰ φωνὴν ἣν ἐν τῇ ῥέμβῃ Hp.*Epid*.7.17 (restored for ῥεμβίῃ from Gal.19.134).

**ῥεμβοειδής**, ές, f. l. in Hp.*Art*.45 and Erot. ad loc. (*Fr*.41) for ῥαιβοειδής.

**ῥεμβονάω**, = ῥυμβονάω, Hsch.

⊛ **ῥεμβ-ός**, όν, *roaming, roving*, of a slave, prob. in *BGU*887.5,16 (ii A. D.); of a lecturer on tour, Aristid.*Or*.33(51).28; ῥ. τῇ διανοίᾳ Antyll.ap.Orib.9.14.7; ψυχή M.Ant.2.17 (v.l.). **-ος**, ὁ, *roving*, Plu.2.603e, Aret.*SD*2.6. ⊛ **-ω**, *turn round and round*, Act. ῥέμβει· πλανᾶται, Gal.19.134:—Pass., aor. inf. ῥεμφθῆναι Hsch. II. Med. **ῥέμβομαι**, *roam, rove, roll about*, Men.481.15, *PCair.Zen*.447.10 (iii B. C.), Ptol.Euerg.3J., *POxy*.1581.6 (ii A. D.), D.Chr.62.7; ἔξω ῥ. Lxx *Pr*.7.12; ἀπὸ τοῦ στρατοπέδου Plu.*Fab*.20; ἐν Πειραιεῖ Id.*Dem*.6; εἰν ἁλί *AP*9.415 (Antiphil.); ὄμμασι ib.5.288 (Agath.): metaph., *to be unsteady, act at random*, ἐν τοῖς πράγμασι Plu.*Pomp*.20; ἐν εἰδώλοις καὶ σκιαῖς Id.2.80f; of food eaten without an appetite, ib.664a; ῥέμβεται ἡ λέξις *is vague*, S.E.*M*.2.52. (Cf. Lith. *reñgtis* 'bend, curve (intr.)'.) **-ώδης**, ες, *roving, rolling*, βλέμμα Plu.2.45d. 2. metaph., *desultory, remiss*, πολιορκία Plb.16.39.2; διατριβαί *idle*, Plu.*Dio*7; τὸ ῥ. (ῥομβ- codd.) καὶ ἀκόλαστον Id.2.715c; ῥ. πυρετοί *irregular*, opp. περιοδικοί, Chrysipp.ap.Gal.5.433 (ῥομβ- codd.). Adv. -δῶς Hsch. s. v. σκαλαπάζειν (-αδῶς cod.).

**ῥέμφος**, εος, τό, Aeol. for ῥάμφος, Hsch. **ῥέμω**, = πειρῶμαι, δύναμαι, Theognost.*Can*.11, Suid., but = ὀδυνᾷ, σήπει, Hsch., Phot.

**ῥέον**, οντος, τό, (ῥέω) = ῥυτόν (ῥυτός II), Astyd.3.3.

**ῥέον**, τό, = ῥῆον, Aët.1.347, Alex.Trall.5.5, 9.2, 12, Paul.Aeg.7.11.59.

**ῥέος**, εος, τό, (ῥέω) like ῥεῦμα, *anything flowing, stream*, A.*Ag*.901, *Pr*.676, 812; also of tears, δακρυσίστακτον ῥ. ib.401.

**ῥεπ-τέον**, *one must incline*, ἐπί τι Archig.ap.Orib.8.2.22. **-τικός**, ή, όν, *inclining*, ὄρεξις ῥ. πρός τι *Stoic*.3.108. ⊛ **-ω**, mostly used in pres. and impf.: fut. ῥέψω Hdt.7.139, Paus.9.37.8: aor. ἔρρεψα Hp.*Art*.38,48, Pl.*Phlb*.46e; poet. ἔρεψα Cerc.4.32:—*turn the scale, sink*, ἐτίταινε τάλαντα, ἕλκε δὲ μέσσα λαβών, ῥέπε δ' αἴσιμον ἦμαρ Ἀχαιῶν, implying defeat and death, Il.8.72; ῥέπε δ' Ἕκτορος αἴσιμον ἦμαρ 22.212; τὸ τοὐδέ γ' αὖ ῥέπει Ar.*Ra*.1393; τοῦ ταλάντου τὸ ῥέπον κάτω βαδίζει τὸ δὲ κενὸν πρὸς τὸν Δία Id.*Fr*.488.4, cf. Cerc. l. c.; τὸ μὲν κάτω ῥέπον.., βαρύ· τὸ δὲ ἄνω, κοῦφον Pl.*Just*.373e; ἀεὶ τοὐναντίον ῥ. Id.*R*.550e, cf. Archim.*Aequil*.1 *Praef*. 2. more generally, of things, *incline one way or the other*, ὃ τι πολλᾷ ῥέποι what *is always shifting, never steady*, Pi.*O*.8.23; βλεμμάτων ῥέπει βολή *inclines downward, falls*, of a young girl's eye, A.*Fr*.242; ὕπνος ἐπὶ γλεφάροις ῥέπων sleep *falling* upon the eyes, Pi.*P*.9.25; ἐς τὸ λορδόν, κυφόν, Hp.*Art*.48; ῥ. πρὸς τὴν γῆν Arist.*PA*686a32, etc. 3. of one of two contending parties, *preponderate, prevail*, ἐπὶ ὁκότερα [οἱ Ἀθηναῖοι] ἐτράποντο, ταῦτα ῥέψειν ἔμελλε Hdt.7.139; μοι σκοπουμένῳ ἔρρεψε δεῖν on consideration [the opinion] that it was necessary *prevailed*, Pl.*Ep*.328b; ἠθῶν.., ἃ ἂν ὥσπερ ῥέψαντα τἆλλα ἐφελκύσηται Id.*R*.544e. 4. of persons, εὖ ῥέπει θεός *is favourably inclined*, A.*Th*.21; ἐπὶ τὸ πρηνὲς the doctor should *incline towards* (*prefer*) pronation, Hp.*Fract*.1 (unless in signf. 2, the subject being τὴν χεῖρα); ῥ. ἐπὶ τὸ πείθεσθαι Isoc.15.4; ἐπὶ τὸ λῆμμα D.18.298; πρὸς τὴν ἀνδρείαν Pl.*Plt*.308a, cf. *Lg*.802e; also ῥ. ταῖς γνώμαις ἐπὶ τοὺς Ῥοδίους Plb.33.16.2; εἴς τινα Luc.*Bis Acc*.6; but νομίζων τούτους πλεῖστον ῥέπειν ἐπὶ τὸ ἀγαθὸν τῇ πόλει *avail* most, *have* the greatest *influence*, X.*Lac*.4.1, cf. Isyll.24; so also εἰς ἕν τι αἱ ἐπιθυμίαι σφόδρα ῥέπουσιν Pl.*R*.485d, cf. *Phlb*.46e; ῥ. πρὸς [τὴν ἡδονήν] Arist.*EN*1172a31; ῥ. πρὸς τὴν ὀλιγαρχίαν Id.*Pol*.1293b20. 5. ῥ. εἴς τινα *fall to, be directed towards*, τὸ μητρὸς ἔς σέ μοι ῥέπει στέργηθρον A.*Ch*.240; τοὔργον εἰς ἐμὲ ῥέπον that this deed *points* to me, S.*OT*847. 6. of events, *fall, happen*, in a certain way, φιλεῖ τοῦτο μὴ ταύτῃ ῥέπειν Id.*Ant*.722; τῇδε or ἐκείνῃ ῥ. Pl.*Lg*.862c, *Ti*.79e; ῥ. εἴς τι *turn* or *come* to something, συμφορὰν..κακῶν ῥέπουσαν ἐς τὰ μάσσονα A.*Pers*.440; τὸ μηδὲν εἰς οὐδὲν ῥ. naught *comes* to naught, E.*Fr*.532; ὁ χρησμὸς ἐς τοῦτο ῥ. Ar.*Pl*.51; ὁ γρῖφος ἐνταῦθα ῥ. Antiph.124.11. II. trans., *cause* the scale *to incline* one way or the other, only in compds. ἐπιρρέπω, καταρρέπω, exc. that A. uses the Pass., τῶνδ' ἐξ ἴσου ῥεπομένων *being* equally *balanced*, *Supp*.405 (lyr.):—in B.16.25, ὅ τι μὲν ἐκ θεῶν μοῖρα παγκρατὴς ἄμμι κατένευσε καὶ Δίκας ῥέπει τάλαντον, ῥ. is prob. intrans. (sc. ἐπ' αὐτό). (Perh. cogn. with Lith. *virpti* 'quiver'.)

**ῥερῠπωμένος**, v. ῥυπόω.

**ῥεῦμα**, ατος, τό, (ῥέω) *that which flows, current, stream*, A.*Pr*.139 (anap.), X.*HG*4.2.11; μειλιχίων ποτῶν ῥ. S.*OC*160 (lyr.); ἐλαίου ῥ. ἀψοφητὶ ῥέοντος Pl.*Tht*.144b; ῥεῦμα μελισσῶν *AP*9.404 (Antiphil.): metaph., ῥ. αὔξης καὶ τροφῆς, ὄψεως, Pl.*Ti*.44b, 45c; τὸ ἀκούειν γίνεται ῥεύματός τινος φερομένου ἀπὸ τοῦ φωνοῦντος Epicur.*Ep*.1 p.13U. 2. *stream* of a river, Hdt.2.20, 24; ῥ. Διρκαῖον E.*Supp*.637, cf. *IT*401 (lyr.); τὸ τοῦ Νείλου ῥ. Pl.*Ti*.21e; also, *eruption of lava*, Th.3.116, Carc.5.7: metaph., *stream* or *flood of men*, μεγάλῳ ῥ. φωτῶν A.*Pers*.88 (anap.); ῥ. Περσικοῦ στρατοῦ ib.412, cf. E.*IT*1437; πολλῷ ῥ. προσνισσόμενοι S.*Ant.*129 (anap.); so ῥεύματα ἐπῶν Cratin.186; κλαυθμῶν καὶ ὀδυρμῶν Plu.2.609b. **3.** *flood*, κατελθόντος αἰφνιδίου τοῦ ῥ. Th. 4.75, cf. Hdt.8.12; φερομένῳ συναπενεχθῆναι τῷ ῥ. Demad.15. **II.** *that which is always flowing* or *changing*, τὸ τῆς τύχης..ῥ. μεταπίπτει ταχύ the *ebb and flow* of fortune, Men.*Georg.Fr.*2. **III.** Medic., *humour* or *discharge* from the body, *flux, rheum*, διὰ τῶν ῥινῶν Hp. *VM*18; ῥ. εἰς τοὺς πόδας κατεληλύθει Luc.*Philops.*6; ῥ. νοσηματικά Arist.*Sens.*444$^a$13; στομάχου καὶ κοιλίας ῥ. Dsc.1.83; κατασκῆψαι ῥ. εἰς τὰ νεῦρα Paus.6.3.10: abs., *POxy.*1088.1 (i A.D.), Plu.*Mar.*34, etc.

**ῥευμᾰτ-ίζομαι**, Pass., *flow as a current*, Str.1.3.7. **II.** *suffer from a flux*, Ti.Locr.103a, Dsc.2.126, 4.40, Plu.2.902a; so also in Act. ῥευματίζω, Porph.*Abst.*1.28. **-ικός**, ή, όν, (ῥεῦμα III) *subject to a discharge* or *flux*, εἰς τοὺς ὀφθαλμούς Arist.*Pr.*957$^b$25; ἕλκη ῥ. Dsc.2.126; τραῦμα Plu.2.131b. **-ιον**, τό, Dim. of ῥεῦμα III, Arist. *Pr.*901$^a$3. **2.** *rivulet*, Plu.*Thes.*27. **-ισμός**, ὁ, = ῥεῦμα (signf. III), Hp.*Coac.*567, Dsc.1.82, 4.64, Gal.14.276, *Arch.Pap.*4.270 (iii A.D.), etc. **-ώδης**, ες, *like a flux*, Hp.*Epid.*7.5: Comp., Gal.19.535. **II.** *in flood, swollen*, ποταμοί Tz.*H.*3.122.

**ῥεῦσις**, εως, ἡ, *flowing*, Epicur.*Ep.*1 p.11 U., Hero *Spir.*1.3, Diog. Oen.4, Dsc.2.151 (interpol.).

**ῥευσ-τᾰλέος**, α, ον, *liquid, fluent*, Orac.ap.Eus.*PE*4.9. **-τικός**, ή, όν, *flowing, liquid*, Plu.*Aem.*14, 2.905e. Adv. -κῶς ib.878f. **-τός**, ή, όν, *in a state of flux, flowing*, ἔργα Emp.121.3; ἡ ὕλη Arist.*Fr.*207, S.E.*P.*1.217, Porph.*Antr.*5; of time flowing away, Ath.Mech.3.10. **2.** metaph., *fluctuating, unsettled*, οὐσία Plu.2.268d; ὀλισθηρὰν καὶ ῥ. εἰς ἅπαντα τὴν πολυπραγμοσύνην ποιοῦντες ib.522a.

**ῥεφᾰνίς**, v. ῥαφανίς. **ῥέφᾰνος**, v. ῥάφανος.

⊛ **ῥέω**, Il.22.149, etc.; Ep. **ῥείω** Hes.*Fr.*263 (dub.), D.P.1074, *AP*7.36 (Eryc.), but not in Hom.: impf. 3 sg. ἔρρει Il.17.86, Telecl.1.4, but elsewhere in Hom. ἔρρεε or ῥέε: fut. ῥεύσομαι Thgn.448, E.*Fr.*384, Crates Com.15.4, Pherecr.130.5, Hp.*Haem.*5; also ῥευσοῦμαι, Arist.*Mete.*356$^a$16, 361$^a$33; later ῥεύσω, *AP*5.124 (Bass.): aor. ἔρρευσα Ar.*Eq.*526 (anap.), Hp.*Loc.Hom.*11, *Int.*23, Mosch.3.33, *AP*5.32 (Parmen.), Plb.5.15.7 (ἀπ-), Paus.5.7.4, etc.:—but the Att. fut. and aor. are of pass. form, ῥυήσομαι Isoc.8.140, cf. Hp.*Nat.Hom.*5; ἐρρύην [ῠ] Th.3.116, X.*Cyr.*8.3.30, Pl.*Ti.*84c, etc., as also in Hdt.8.138; Dor. ἐξ-εῤῥύα, v. ἐκρέω; 3 sg. subj. ἐ[γ]ρυᾷ *GDI*3591a51 (Calymna); Ep. 3 sg. ῥύη Od.3.455: pf. ἐρρύηκα Hp.*Loc.Hom.*10, Pl.*R.*485d, Isoc.8.5; later ἔρρυκα, Gal.5.398.—A pres. Med. **ῥέομαι** occurs also in Orac.ap.Hdt.7.140 (v. infr.), Plu.*Cor.*3, Luc.*Salt.*71, Philostr. *VS*1.25.9, etc.; so ἐρρεῖτο E.*Hel.*1602, Philostr.*VA*8.31, etc.—This Verb does not contr. εη, εο, εω:—*flow, run, stream, gush*, Od.19.204, Il.3.300, 17.86, etc.: with dat. of that which flows, [πηγὴ] ὕδατι ῥέει the fountain *runs with* water, 22.149, cf. Od.5.70, *IG*1².54.7; ῥέε δ' αἵματι γαῖα Il.8.65, etc.; φάραγγες ὕδατι..ῥέουσαι E.*Tr.*449 (troch.); ῥεῖ γάλακτι πέδον ῥεῖ δ' οἴνῳ Id.*Ba.*142 (lyr.); οἴνῳ..ἔρρει χαράδρα Telecl. l.c. (v. sub fin.); (also in Med., ἱδρῶτι ῥεούμενοι (metri gr. for ῥεόμενοι, cf. μαχεούμενοι) Orac.ap.Hdt.7.140; φόνῳ ναῦς ἐρρεῖτο E. *Hel.*1602); πόλιν χρυσῷ ῥέουσαν Id.*Tr.*995: so metaph., πολλῷ ῥ. ἐπαίνῳ Ar.*Eq.*527: rarely with acc. in the same sense (v. infr. II. 2): also with gen., ἀσφάλτου Str.7.5.8; πολλοῦ ὕδατος Arr.*An.* 5.9.4: sts. with nom., Ζεὺς χρυσὸς ῥυεὶς Isoc.10.59, cf. *AP*5.32 (Parmen.). **b.** the post-Hom. expression for *a full stream* is μέγας ῥεῖ, ῥέουσι μεγάλοι Hdt.2.25; μέγας ἐρρύη Id.8.138, cf. Th.2.5; ῥ. οὐδὲν ἧσσον ἢ νῦν Hdt.7.129; also πολὺς ῥεῖ, metaph. of men, ῥεῖ πολὺς ὅδε λεώς A.*Th.*80 (lyr.); Κύπρις ἢν πολλὴ ῥυῇ E.*Hipp.*443 (cf. infr. 2); so ῥ. μου τὸ δάκρυον πολύ Ar.*Lys.*1034; also ἐς ἔρωτα ἅπας ῥ. Ps.-Phoc.193; πρὸς τὸν Ἀλκιβιάδην ὁ δῆμος ὅλος ἐρρύη Plu.*Alc.* 21. **c.** of a river, also ῥ. ἀπὸ τηκομένης χιόνος *derive its stream* from melted snow, Hdt.2.22. **d.** prov., ἄνω ῥεῖν *flow* upwards, of inversion of the usual or right order, E.*Supp.*520; ἄνω ποταμῶν ἐρρύησαν οἱ..λόγοι D.19.287; cf. ἄνω (B) I. **e.** ταῦτα μὲν ῥείτω κατ' οὖρον (v. οὖρος (A)) S.*Tr.*468. **2.** metaph. of things, ἐκ χειρῶν βέλεα ῥέον from their hands *rained* darts, Il.12.159; ῥεῖ μάλιστα ὁ ἀὴρ ῥέων ἐν τοῖς ὑψηλοῖς Arist.*Mete.*347$^a$34, cf. 349$^a$34; φλὸξ ῥυεῖσα Plu.*Brut.*31; so τὴν Αἴτνην ῥυῆναι Ael.*Fr.*2; esp. of a *flow* of words, ἀπὸ γλώσσης μέλιτος γλυκίων ῥέεν αὐδή Il.1.249, cf. Hes.*Th.*39, 97; ἔπε' ἐκ στόματος ῥεῖ μείλιχα ib.84: abs., of the tongue, *run glibly*, A.*Th.*557; so θρασυνομένῳ καὶ πολλῷ ῥέοντι καθ' ὑμῶν D.18.136: hence, of words or sentiments, *to be current*, κληδόνος καλῆς μάτην ῥεούσης S.*OC* 259. **3.** *fall, drop off*, e.g. of hair, Od.10.393, Hes.*Fr.*29, Theoc. 2.89, etc.; of ripe fruit, Plb.12.4.14, *Gp.*9.12; of over-ripe corn, ἤδη ῥέοντα τὸν στάχυν Babr.88.14; *wear out*, εἰ ῥέοι τὸ σῶμα καὶ ἀπολλύοιτο Pl.*Phd.*87d; of a house, *to be in a tumble-down condition*, Gorg.ap.Stob.4.51.28, Teles p.27 H.; ῥέουσαν σύγκρισιν στῆσαι to stay a *collapse* of the system, Herod.Med.ap.Orib.5.27.1. **4.** of molten objects, *liquefy, run*, ῥεῖ πᾶν ἄδηλον S.*Tr.*698; τήκεται ὁ λίθος..ὥστε καὶ ῥεῖν Arist.*Mete.*383$^b$6, cf. Thphr.*Lap.*9. **5.** *to be in perpetual flux and change*, ἅπανθ' ὁρῶ ἅμα τῇ τύχῃ ῥέοντα μεταπίπτοντά τε *Com.Adesp.*200; ὡς ἰόντων ἁπάντων ἀεὶ καὶ ῥεόντων Pl.*Cra.* 439c, cf. 411c; κινεῖται καὶ ῥεῖ..τὰ πάντα Id.*Tht.*182c: hence οἱ ῥέοντες, of the Heraclitean philosophers, opp. οἱ τοῦ ὅλου στασιῶται, ib.181a. **b.** '*run*', of ink, etc., metaph., στιγμῆς ῥυείσης γραμμὴν φαντασιούμεθα.., γραμμῆς δὲ ῥυείσης πλάτος ἐποιήσαμεν S.E.*M.*7.99; cf. ῥυίσκομαι II. **6.** of persons, ῥ. ἐπί τι *to be inclined, given* to a thing, Isoc.8.5; πρός τι Pl.*R.*485d; οἱ ταύτῃ ῥυέντες ib.495b. **7.** *leak*, of a ship, opp. στεγανὸν εἶναι, Arist.*Fr.*554, cf. Paus.8.50.7; λύχνοι ῥέοντες prob. in Roussel *Cultes Égyptiens* p.222 (Delos, ii B.C.); of a roof, Men.*Sam.*248; [ἀγγεῖον] ῥέον Plu.2.782e; οἰνοχόαι ῥέουσαι *Michel* 815.131 (Delos, iv B.C.). **8.** *to have a flux*, τὰς κοιλίας τὰς ῥεούσας D.S.5.41. **9.** impers., ἐκ ῥινῶν ἐρρύη Hp.*Epid.*1.19. **II.** very rarely trans., *let flow, pour*, ἔρρει χοὰς E.*Hec.*528 (as v.l. for αἴρει):—this differs from the usage **2.** c. acc. cogn., ῥείτω γάλα, μέλι, *let* the land *run* milk, honey, Theoc.5.124, 126; αἷμα ῥυήσεται, of the Nile, Ezek.*Exag.*133; οἶνον ῥέων Luc.*VH*1.7, cf. Lxx *Jl.*3(4).18, Sch.Ar.*Pl.*287:—in place of this acc. the best writers commonly used the dat., v. supr. I. 1. **III.** v. ῥέον. (Cf. ῥόϝος, Skt. *sravati*, Lith. *sravēti* 'flow': I.-E. *srĕw-* alternating with *srŏw-* and *srŭ-*.)

**ῥῆα**, v. ῥᾶ, ad fin.

⊛ **ῥηγεύς**, έως, ὁ, (ῥῆγος) *dyer*, Sch.Il.9.661, Hsch.

**ῥηγή**, prob. f.l. for ῥαγή, Gal.19.134.

**ῥῆγ-μα**, ατος, τό, (ῥήγνυμι) *breakage, fracture*, joined with σπάσμα, Hp.*Aër.*4, cf. D.18.198, Dsc.3.74; with στρέμμα (a strain), D.2.21, 11.14. **2.** *laceration, rupture*, Gal.10.160, 18(2).882, cf. Arist.*HA* 635$^a$4. **3.** *rent, tear*, in clothes, Archipp.38. **4.** *cleft, chasm*, ῥ. τῆς γῆς Arist.*HA*628$^b$29; *chink*, ἐν τοίχοις Plb.13.6.8; *breach* in a dyke, *PLond.*1.131$^r$.45, 60 (i A.D.). **II.** *lesion* or *rupture* of tissue, ὅταν ὑπὸ βίης διαστέωσιν αἱ σάρκες ἀπ' ἀλλήλων Hp.*Flat.*11, cf. Gal.1. 238, 10.232; esp. of lung, Hp.*Loc.Hom.*14, *Morb.*1.20: hence **ῥηγμᾰτίας**, ου, ὁ, *one who has such a rupture*, Id.*Aër.*4, Dsc.3.146, 4.10; τοὺς ἐκ βηχὸς ῥηγματίας *Hippiatr.*22; but ῥηγματίας πλεύμονος perh. = *pleurisy*, Hp.*Morb.*2.53; **ῥηγμᾰτώδης**, ες, Id.*Epid.*7.26. ⊛ **-μίν** or **-μίς** (neither form is found, unless [ῥηγμῖ]ν is to be restd. in *IGRom.*4. 272.1 (Elaea, cf. *Wiener Sitzb.*214(4).26)), gen. ῖνος, ἡ, *sea breaking on the beach, surf* (v. ῥήγνυμι B.1), ἄκρον ἐπὶ ῥηγμῖνος ἁλὸς..θέεσκον Il.20. 229; κώπῃσιν ἁλὸς ῥηγμῖνα βαθεῖαν τύπτετε, of the *broken sea* between Scylla and Charybdis, Od.12.214; with the Prep. ἐπί, it may be rendered *at the sea's edge*, ἐκ..βαῖνον ἐπὶ ῥηγμῖνι θαλάσσης Il.1.437, cf. Od.9.150; κοιμήθημεν ἐπὶ ῥηγμῖνι θαλάσσης ib.169, cf. Pi.*N.*5.13; ἄκραις ἐπὶ ῥηγμῖσιν ἀξένου πόρου E.*IT*253; also λαοὶ δὲ παρὰ ῥ. θαλάσσης δίσκοισιν τέρποντο Il.2.773, cf. Od.4.449; ὅταν κυμαίνουσα ἐκβάλλῃ [ἡ θάλαττα],..παχεῖαι καὶ σκολιαὶ γίνονται αἱ ῥ.· ὅταν δὲ γαλήνη ᾖ,.. λεπταὶ εἰσι καὶ εὐθεῖαι Arist.*Mete.*367$^b$14. **2.** metaph., ῥ. βίοιο *verge* of life, i.e. *death*, Emp.20.5; ὥσπερ ῥηγμῖνα οὖσαν ἀέρος τὴν νεφέλην Arist.*Mete.*367$^b$19. **II.** τὰ ἀπορπύματα (fort. ἀπορρήγματα) τῆς πέτρας, Hsch. **-μός**, ὁ, *fissure*, γῆ ῥηγμῶν πλήρης *PSI*4.422. 15 (iii B.C.). **II.** = foreg., Hsch.

⊛ **ῥήγνῡμι** or **-ύω** (ἀναρ- Hp.*Flat.*10: impf. κατ-ερρήγνυε D.21.63, etc.); later **ῥήσσω**, Gal.10.640, Orib.*Fr.*93, *Gloss.*; ῥήσσεσθαι *PHolm.*6.3, cf. 4.22; ἀπο-, δια-ρρήσσεσθαι, Hp.*Int.*17, 42; **ῥήττω**, Str.11.14.8, Dsc.4.150 (v.l. ῥήσσει), (περι-) Id.2.98, 3.18 (v.l. περιρρήσσει); ῥήττεσθαι Bito 45.8, Str.7.3.18: Ep. impf. ῥήγνυσκε Il.7. 141: fut. ῥήξω Il.12.262, Hdt.2.2, (ἐκ-) S.*Aj.*775: aor. ἔρρηξα Il.3.348, Pi.*N.*8.29, Ar.*Nu.*960; ῥῆξα Il.6.6: pf. ἔρρηχα (δι-) Lxx 2*Ki.*14.30, 15.32:—**Med.** ῥήγνῠμαι, fut. ῥήξομαι, aor. ἐρρηξάμην, all in Il. (12.257, 224, 291), pres. also in Hp.*VC*4.12: aor. ἐρρηξάμην E.*Heracl.*835, (κατ-) X.*Cyr.*3.1.13; Ep. 3 pl. ῥήξαντο Il.11.90:—**Pass.**, subj. ῥήγνυται Hippon.19.4: Ep. 3 sg. impf. ῥήγνυτο Arat.817: fut. ῥαγήσομαι Plu.2.668a, (διαρ-, ἐκ-) Ar.*Eq.*340, A.*Pr.*369, etc.: aor. ἐρράγην [ᾰ] S.*Fr.*578, Ar.*Nu.*583, etc.; later ἐρρήχθην, Tryph.11; δια-ρρηχθῇ (v.l. -ῥαγῇ) Hp.*Int.*29: pf. ἔρρηγμαι (συν-) Od.8.137; but intr. pf. ἔρρωγα is more freq., v. infr. C. 1; pf. part. fem. ἐρρηγεία, v. infr. C. 2; masc. pl. κατ-ερρηγότας Hsch. The word is hardly used by correct Att. Prose-writers, exc. in Pass.:—*break asunder, rend, shatter*, τεῖχος Il.12.198; πύλας 13.124; σάκος 21.165; θώρηκας 2.544; ἱμάντα 3.375; νευρὴν 8.328; ὀστέον 20.399; χρόα 23.673; only once in Od., προτόνους ἔρρηξ' ἀνέμοιο θύελλα 12.409:—later, esp. *rend* garments, in sign of grief, ῥ. πέπλους A.*Pers.*199, 468; ῥ. ἕλκεα *make grievous* wounds, Pi.*N.*8.29; ῥ. ὀστᾶ, σάρκας, E.*HF*994, *Ba.*1130; ἀρότροις γῆς δάπεδον Ar.*Pl.*515: in Ion. and later Prose, ῥήγνυσι..τὸν ἀμφὶ τὴν ὄψιν χιτῶνα Hp.*VM*19; ῥήττειν νευράν Str.15.1.57; τὰ δεσμά Luc.*DDeor.*17.1; τὰς πύλας Id.*Par.*46; μὴ στραφέντες ῥήξωσιν ὑμᾶς *Ev.Matt.*7.6:—Med., *break for oneself, get broken*, ὄρνυσθ'..ῥήγνυσθε δὲ τεῖχος Il.12.440, cf. 224, 257, 291:—Pass., v. infr. B. **2.** *break* a line of battle or body of men, ῥ. φάλαγγα, ὅμιλον, στίχας ἀνδρῶν, Il.6.6, 11.538, 15.615; τὸ μέσον ῥῆξαι *break through* the centre, Hdt. 6.113: abs., ἐρρηξάτην ἐς κύκλα..ὅπλων *broke through*, S.*Fr.*210.9:—Med., ῥήξασθαι φάλαγγας, στίχας, *break oneself a way through* the lines, Il.11.90, 13.680, cf. E.*Heracl.*835; ῥηξαμένῳ θέσθαι παρὰ νηυσὶ κέλευθον Il.12.411. **3.** *let break loose*, ἔριδα ῥ. 20.55 (Med.). **4.** after Hom., ῥῆξαι φωνήν *let loose* the voice, of children and persons who have been dumb or silent, *break into* speech, *speak out*, Hdt.1.85, 2.2, 5.93, cf. Ar.*Nu.*357, 960; ῥῆξαι αὐδὴν E.*Supp.*710; later ῥήξασθαι φωνήν, θρόον αὐδῆς, φθόγγον, *utter*, *AP*5.221 (Agath.), 7.597 (Jul.), 9.61: abs., ῥῆξον καὶ βόησον *cry aloud*, Lxx *Is.*54.1; v. infr. C. **5.** also δακρύων ῥήξασα..νάματα *having let loose, having burst into* floods of tears, S.*Tr.*919; κλαυθμὸν ῥ. Plu.*Per.*36; ῥ. τὰ ὄρη εὐφροσύνην Lxx *Is.*49.13; ῥήγνυσι πηγὰς ὁ χῶρος Plu.*Mar.*19; ῥ. νεφέλην ἔς τινας Philostr.*Im.*2.27; v. infr. B.

**B.** Pass., *break, break asunder, burst*, κῦμα ῥήγνυτο Il.18.67; κῦμα..χέρσῳ ῥηγνύμενον 4.425, Hes.*Sc.*377; of clouds, Ar.*Nu.*378; ῥαγῆναί τι τῆς γῆς, as in an earthquake, Pl.*R.*359d; ῥαγεῖσα Θηβαίων κόνις S.*Fr.*958; ἱμάτια ῥαγέντα X.*Cyr.*1.6.16; ὀστέον ῥήγνυται τιτρωσκόμενον Hp.*VC*4; ῥήττονται ὑδρίαι (by the cold) Str.7.3.18; τοῖς βασκάνοις εἶναι ῥήγνυσθαι may the envious *burst*, Aristid.*Or.*50 (26).69; τοῖς εἴ τις εὐδοκιμήσειεν ἐπί τῳ ῥηγνυμένοις Lib.*Or.*29.13, cf. *Or.*1.207. **2.** *burst forth*, like lightning, βροντὴ δ' ἐρράγη δι' ἀστραπῆς S.*Fr.*578, Ar.*Nu.*583, cf. Plu.2.919b; so καταμηνίων ῥαγέντων Hp.*Aph.*5.32, cf. *Nat.Mul.*13, Arist.*HA*582$^{b}$10, etc. 3. of ships, *to be wrecked*, D.56.21: metaph., πολλῶν ῥαγεισῶν ἐλπίδων A.*Ag.*505. 4. of a stone, γράμματι ῥηγνύμενον *scored* with lettering, i.e. inscribed, Puchstein *Epigr.Gr.*p.76 (Memphis, i B.C.).

C. intr., like Pass., *break* or *burst forth*, ἔρρηξεν ἔμετος Hp.*Epid.* 4.24; τὸ πνεῦμα ῥήγνυσι Id.*Nat.Puer.*12; εἰ ἐθελήσει ῥήξας ὑπερβῆναι ὁ ποταμός Hdt.2.99: metaph., ὁποῖα χρῄζει ῥηγνύτω S.*OT*1076 (in answer to the words δέδοιχ' ὅπως μὴ.. ἀναρρήξει κακά): freq. in this signf. in pf. ἔρρωγα, *to have broken out*, ἔρρωγε παγὰ δακρύων Id.*Tr.* 852 (lyr.): metaph., κακῶν πέλαγος ἔρρωγεν A.*Pers.*433; τάδ' ἐκ δυοῖν ἔρρωγεν..κακά S.*OT*1280; σοὶ τάδ' ἔρρωγεν κακά E.*Hipp.*1338; ἐρρωγότες λόγοι *broken, disjointed*, *Com.Adesp.*661. 2. in lit. sense, γῆ ἐρρηγεῖα (= -υῖα) *broken, arable*, opp. ἄρρηκτος, *Tab.Heracl.*1.18, al. (ϝρηγ- (cf. Aeol. aor. Pass. εὐράγη Hdn.Gr.2.640, ϝρῆξις, αὔρηκτος), cogn. with Lith. *rėžti* 'cut, notch, furrow', *rúožas* 'stripe, streak, strip'.)

**ῥῆγος**, εος, τό, *rug, blanket*, in Hom. mostly in pl. (sg. in Il.9.661, Od.13.73,118); ῥ. καλά, πορφύρεα, Il.24.644, Od.4.297; σιγαλόεντα 6.38, 11.189, etc.: used as covering of a bed, Il.9.661, 24.644, Od.3. 349, etc.; or of a seat, 10.352; prob. a garment, 6.38: since, in 13.73,118, Hom. distinguishes ῥῆγος and λίνον, it is prob. that the ῥῆγος was of wool. (From ῥῆξαι, = βάψαι, acc. to Eust.782.20, but elsewhere this verb is written ῥέξαι, v. ῥέζω (B).)

**ῥήδην**, Adv. only in A.D.*Adv.*198.15, *EM*363.42, as part of the compd. διαρρήδην. **ῥῄδιος**, v. ῥᾴδιος. **ῥηδίων**· καρούχων, ῥαιδίων, Hsch. **ῥηθῆναι, ῥηθήσομαι**, v. ἐρῶ. **ῥήΐδιος**, v. ῥᾴδιος. **ῥηΐζω**, v. ῥαΐζω. **ῥήΐστος, ῥηΐτατος, ῥηΐτερος**, v. ῥᾴδιος.

**ῥήκ-της**, ου, ὁ, (ῥήγνυμι) *breaker, render*; of an earthquake *that breaks the earth into fissures*, Arist.*Mu.*396$^{a}$5, Lyd.*Ost.*54. **-τικός**, ή, όν, *apt to burst*, τὸ ψυχρὸν φλεβῶν ῥηκτικόν Hp.*Epid.*6.3.6. 2. *causing* abscesses *to break*, Aët.15.17. ⊛**-τός**, ή, όν, *that can be broken* or *rent, penetrable*, [ἀνὴρ].., χαλκῷ τε ῥηκτὸς μεγάλοισί τε χερμαδίοισιν Il.13.323.

**ῥῆμα**, ατος, τό, (ἐρῶ) *that which is said* or *spoken, word, saying*, Archil.50, Thgn.1152, Simon.37.14,92 (where perh. it = ῥήτρα II. 2), Pi. (v. infr.), etc.; in Prose first in Hdt. (s. v. l.), ὁ νόος τοῦ ῥ. 7.162; τὰ λεγόμενά τινων [ῥήματα] 8.83; τοῦ Πιττακοῦ..περιεφέρετο τοῦτο τὸ ῥ. Pl.*Prt.*343b; τὸ δόγμα τε καὶ ῥ. Id.*R.*464a; opp. ἔργματα, Pi.*N.*4.6; opp. ἔργον, Th.5.111; opp. τὸ ἀληθές, Pl.*Phd.*102b: prov., ῥήματα ἀντ' ἀλφίτων 'fine words butter no parsnips', ap.Suid.; ῥήματα πλέκων Pi.*N.*4.94; ῥήματα θηρεύειν catch at one's *words*, And.1.9; ῥ. ἱπποβάμονα, ῥ. μυριάμφορον, Ar.*Ra.*821, *Pax* 521; ῥήματος ἐχόμενον depending on the *word*, Pl.*Lg.*656c; τῷ ῥ. τῷ τόδε προσχρώμενοι *the word* τόδε, Id.*Ti.*49e; τῷ ῥ. λέγειν, εἰπεῖν, say *in so many words*, Id.*R.* 340d, *Grg.*450e, cf. *Tht.*166d; κατὰ ῥῆμα ἀπαγγεῖλαι *word for word*, Aeschin.2.122. 2. *phrase*, opp. ὄνομα (a single word), Pl.*Cra.*399b, Aeschin.3.72; λέγοντες ἐν μύθοις τε καὶ ἐν ῥήμασιν Pl.*Lg.*840c. b. *verse, line*, Ar.*Ra.*1379, cf. 97. 3. *subject of speech, matter*, Hebraism in LXX and *NT*, *Ge.*15.1, 22.1, *De.*2.7, *Ev.Luc.*1.37,65, 2.15; cf. ῥητός IV. 2. II. Gramm., *verb*, opp. ὄνομα (noun), Pl. *Sph.*262a sq., *Cra.*425a, al., Arist.*Po.*1457$^{a}$14, Diog.Bab.*Stoic.*3.213: —from the fact that a Verb usually forms *the predicate* (Arist.*Int.* 16$^{b}$6), ῥῆμα is applied to an Adj. *when used as a predicate*, ib.16$^{a}$13, 20$^{b}$1.

**ῥημ-ᾰτικός**, ή, όν, *of* or *for a verb*: τὸ ῥ. *a verbal form*, D.H.*Comp.* 22, S.E.*M.*1.195; *derived from a verb*, A.D.*Adv.*135.14. Adv. -κῶς Eust.381.22. ⊛**-άτιον**, τό, Dim. of ῥῆμα, *pet phrase, phrasicle*, Ar. *Ach.*444,447, *Nu.*943:—also **ῥημᾰτίσκιον**, τό, Pl.*Tht.*180a, Them. *Or.*21.253c. **-ων**, ονος, ὁ, = ῥήτωρ, acc. to Plu.2.675a, an old v.l. in Il.23.886, for καί ῥ' ἥμονες ἄνδρες.

⊛ **ῥήν**, ἡ, *sheep, lamb* (not found in nom.), ῥήνεσσι A.R.4.1497; ῥῆνα Nic.*Th.*453. (From ϝρήν, old nom. of ϝάρνα, ϝαρνός, etc., v. ἀρήν, and cf. πολύ-ρρην:—also ῥᾶνα· ἄρνα, Hsch. (perh. Elean); τρανόν [i.e. perh. ϝρᾶνον]· ἑξαμηνιαῖον πρόβατον, Id.)

**Ῥηνειοεργής**, ές, *made at* Ῥήνεια, τράπεζα Critias 35 D.; ἔμβαθρα Ῥηνιουργῆ Poll.7.93.

**ῥηνικός**, ή, όν, *of a sheep*, Hp.*Epid.*5.58, etc.

**ῥῆνιξ**, ικος, ἡ, = ἀρνακίς, Hp.*Mul.*1.58 (ap.Gal.19.135), cf. Hsch.

**ῥηνοφορεύς**, έως, ὁ, *clad in sheepskin*, of Dionysus, *AP*9.524.18.

**ῥηξην-ορία**, ἡ, *might to break through armed ranks*, Od.14.217. **-ωρ**, ορος, ὁ, *breaking armed ranks*, in Hom. always epith. of Achilles, Il.7.228, Od.4.5, etc., cf. Hes.*Th.*1007; of Apollo, *AP*9.525.18.

**ῥηξί-[ζῠγ]ος**, ον, *breaking the thwarts*, πλαγά Tim.*Pers.*10 (prob.). **-κέλευθος**, ον, *opening a path*, of Apollo, *AP*9.525.18. **-νοος**, ον, *breaking the wits*, of Dionysus, ib.524.18.

**ῥῆξις**, εως, ἡ, Aeol. ϝρῆξις Alc.149:—*breaking, bursting*, φλεβίου Hp.*Aph.*4.78; sc. ὀστέου Id.*VC*12; πλευμόνων Phld.*Ir.*p.28 W. (pl.); ἐμπύρους τ' ἀκμὰς ῥήξεις τε, i.e. both the pointed flames and the *broken* (the former a good omen, the latter bad), E.*Ph.*1256; κατὰ ῥῆξιν νέφους Arist.*Mu.*394$^{b}$17, cf. *Stoic.*1.34; ἀέρος ῥ., as the effect of a mighty shout, Plu.*Flam.*10. 2. *breaking forth*, τῶν καταμηνίων Hp.*Aph.*3.28 (pl.); αἵματος ῥ. διὰ ῥινῶν Id.*Prog.*7; *discharge*, Id. *Aph.*5.15, *Epid.*6.6.12. II. *rent, cleft*, Plu.2.935c (pl.); ῥήξεις ἐν τοῖς τείχεσιν Ph.*Bel.*84.22.

**ῥηξί-φλοιος**, ον, *with cracked, split bark*, Thphr.*HP*1.5.2. **-φρων**, ονος, ὁ, ἡ, (φρήν) = καταβαλὼν τὴν φρένα, Hsch. ⊛ **-χθων**, ονος, ὁ, ἡ, *bursting forth from the earth*, Orph.*H.*52.9, *PMag.Par.*1.2722, al., *PMag.Lond.*121.692, 123.3, *Tab.Defix.Aud.*38.11 (Alexandria, iii A.D.); written **ῥησίχθων** in *PMag.Leid.V.*9.10, *Tab.Defix.Aud.*23. 13 (Cyprus, iii A.D.); **ῥηξίκθων** *Tab.Defix.* in *Rh.Mus.*55.261.

⊛ **ῥῆον**, τό, = ῥᾶ, *rhubarb*, Gal.12.112.

**ῥησί-αρχος** [ῐ], f.l. in Suid. for ῥησός· ἀρχός, v. ῥησός. **-διον**, τό, Dim. of ῥῆσις, *short speech* or *saying*, Gal.16.795, Hsch.: also **ῥησείδιον**, Ath.11.510a, Simp.*in Ph.*31.3, etc. **-κοπέω**, *to be a phrase-monger*, Polystr.p.11 W., Plb.12.25$^{i}$.9, Poll.6.119. **-μετρέω**, *measure one's words*, Luc.*Lex.*9, *Pseudol.*24.

**ῥῆσις**, εως, Ion. ιος, Arc. ϝρῆσις (*IG*5(2).343.19, Orchom., iv B.C.), ἡ, (ἐρῶ) *saying, speech*, μύθων καὶ ῥήσιος Od.21.291; ῥ. ἀγγελῶν Pi.*N.* 1.59; καταπλέξαι τὴν ῥῆσιν end one's *speech*, Hdt.8.83; ῥ. βραχεῖα S.*Fr.*64; ξυνεχὴς Th.5.85; μακρὰν ῥ. οὐ στέργει πόλις A.*Supp.*273; εἰπεῖν ῥ. οὐ θρῆνον θέλω Id.*Ag.*1322; ῥ. λέγειν ἀμφί τινος Id.*Supp.*615, cf. S.*Fr.*142.20; περὶ σμικροῦ πράγματος ῥ. παμμήκεις ποιεῖν Pl.*Phdr.* 268c; μακρὰν ῥ. ἀποτείνειν Id.*R.*605d, Luc.*Prom.*6; ἡ ἀπὸ Σκυθῶν ῥ. the Scythian *answer*, Hdt.4.127 (a phrase that became proverbial, cf. Plu.*Prov.*1.62; prob. interpol. in Hdt.). 2. *resolution, declaration*, Λακεδαιμονίων ῥ. Hdt.1.152, cf. Crates Com.56, *IG* l.c. 3. *speaking*, opp. reading (ἀνάγνωσις), D.H.*Isoc.*2 (Wolf, for χρήσεως). II. *tale, legend*, ἀνθρώπων παλαιαὶ ῥ. Pi.*O.*7.55. III. *expression* or *passage* in an author, esp. *speech in a play*, Ar.*Nu.*1371, *V.*580, *Ra.* 151, Men.*Epit.*585: pl. in Ephipp.16.3, D.18.267; ῥ. τινὲς τῶν Ἀριστοφανείων Plu.2.712d; esp. of the dramatic parts of epic poetry, Phot. IV. *manner of speaking, style*, ἡ κατὰ πεζὸν ῥ. *prose*, Longin. *Proll.Heph.*1.3.

**ῥησιχθόνη**, ἡ, epith. of a Chthonian goddess, *Tab.Defix.Aud.*22. 31, al. (Cyprus, iii A.D.); cf. ῥηξίχθων.

**ῥησκομένων**· λεγομένων, Hsch., cf. Phot.

**ῥησός**, ὁ, = ἀρχός, ὃς αἱρέσει (dub. l.) τὰ θέσφατα, Epich.205.

**ῥήσσω**, v. ῥήγνυμι. II. v. ῥάσσω. **ῥηστώνη**, v. ῥαστώνη.

⊛ **ϝρήτ-α**, ᾶ, *treaty, agreement*, *Inscr.Cypr.*135.28 H. (pl.). ⊛**-άομαι**, *make a treaty* or *agreement with*, ib.4,14.

**ῥητέον**, *one must say, mention*, τι Pl.*Lg.*730c, *Sph.*227d; *one must pronounce*, Id.*Cra.*410c. II. **ῥητέος**, α, ον, *to be spoken* or *mentioned*, D.22.62, Hermog.*Stat.*7.

**ῥήτερος**, Ion. for ῥηΐτερος, v. ῥᾴδιος. **ϝρητεύω**, v. ἀρητεύω.

**ῥητήρ**, ῆρος, ὁ, (ἐρῶ) = ῥήτωρ, *speaker*, μύθων τε ῥητῆρ' ἔμεναι πρηκτῆρά τε ἔργων Il.9.443, cf. Hippon.63 (s. v. l.), *AP*7.579 (Leont.), *IG*3.625, *Milet.*1(9).341.

**ῥητιάριος**, ὁ, = Lat. *retiarius*, Artem.2.32, *IGRom.*3.44 (Nicaea); also **ῥητιᾶρις**, ib.43 (ibid.), 1438 (Amasia).

**ῥητίν-η** [ῐ], ἡ, *resin of the pine*, Hp.*Art.*63, Arist.*HA*617$^{a}$19, Thphr.*HP*9.2.1, al., Nic.*Al.*300,554, Dsc.1.71, etc. (Prob. a foreign word.) **-ίζω**, *to be resinous, smell* or *taste of resin*, Id.3.74. **-ίτης** [ῑτ], ου, ὁ, *that tastes of resin*, οἶνος ῥ. Id.5.34.

**ῥητῑνόκηρον**, τό, *wax dissolved in resin*, Crito ap.Gal.13.879, Orib. *Fr.*97.

**ῥητῑν-όω**, *flavour with resin*, Dsc.*Eup.*2.65: pf. part. Pass. ἐρρητινωμένος, *mixed with resin*, κηρωτή Hp.*Art.*62. **-ώδης**, ες, *resinous*, Id.*Mochl.*32, Thphr.*HP*3.15.3, Diph.Siph.ap.Ath.2.57c.

**ῥητορ-εία**, ἡ, *oratory*, Pl.*Plt.*304a, Phld.*Rh.*2.231 S., Plu.2. 975c. II. *piece of oratory, set speech*, Isoc.5.26, 12.2, Arist.*Rh.* 1356$^{b}$20 (pl.). **-ευτέον**, *one must practise oratory*, Hermog.*Prog.* 11. **-εύω**, *to be a public speaker, practise oratory*, Isoc.*Ep.*8.7, Pl. *Grg.*502d, Arist.*Rh.Al.*1444$^{a}$33; οἱ μετὰ γαστέρα -εύοντες after-dinner *speakers*, Ph.1.156; ῥ. καὶ πολιτεύεσθαι Chrysipp.*Stoic.*3.175; opp. πολιτεύεσθαι, Nausiph.2:—Pass., of the speech, *to be spoken*, τοὺς μὲν [λόγους] ῥητορεύεσθαι, τοὺς δὲ γεγράφθαι Isoc.5.25:—later in Act. c. acc., τὴν ἐπεσταλμένην πρεσβείαν ἐρρητόρευε *was setting forth*, Luc.*Laps.*2. II. *teach oratory*, Str.14.1.48. **-ίζω**, = foreg. I, Satyr.*Vit.Eur.Fr.*1. ⊛ **-ικός**, ή, όν, *oratorical*, ἡ ῥητορική (sc. τέχνη) *rhetoric*, Pl.*Phdr.*266d, Phld.*Rh.*1.187 S.; τὸ ῥ. Pl.*Phdr.*266c, *Plt.*304e; τὰ ῥ. D.L.4.49, etc.; οἱ δειλίαν ὁ δημόσιος καιρὸς οὐκ ἀναμένει *an orator's* timidity, Aeschin.3.163; ῥ. γραφή an indictment *against an orator* (παρανόμων), Is.*Fr.*64 S. Adv. -κῶς Pl.*Grg.*471e, Aeschin. 1.71, Arist.*Po.*1450$^{b}$8, Phld.*Rh.*2.134 S.: Comp., -ώτερον λέγεσθαι D.H.*Is.*8. 2. of persons, *skilled in speaking, fit to be an orator*, Isoc.3.8, Pl.*Phdr.*260c, 272d, al.; φύσει ῥ. ib.269d, etc.; σχολαστικὸς ῥ. *OGI*693 (Egypt). b. *student*, Lib.*Or.*14.62. 3. *belonging to a* ῥήτωρ, δοῦλος *Stud.Pal.*1.67.289 (i A.D.). **-ίσκος**, ὁ, contemptuous Dim. of ῥήτωρ, 'spouter', *PUniv.Giss.*20 ii 14 (ii A.D.); in Lat. form, Gell.17.20.4.

**ῥητορο-μάστιξ**, ῑγος, ὁ, *the Rhetoricians' scourge*, as Aeschines of Mytilene was called, D.L.2.64. **-μυκτος**, ου, ὁ, (μύσσομαι) μυκτὴρ ῥ. a nostril (= nose = sneerer) *blown* (i.e. trained) *by rhetoricians*, of Socrates, Timo 25.3. **-πρεπής**, ές, *befitting an orator*, dub. in Phld. *Rh.*1.165 S.

⊛ **ῥητ-ός**, ή, όν, (ἐρῶ) *stated, specified, covenanted*, μισθῷ ἔπι ῥ. Il.21. 445; παρεῖναι ἐς χρόνον ῥ. Hdt.1.77, cf. Aeschin.3.124; ἐν ἡμέραις ῥ. Th.6.29; ἐπὶ ῥητοῖς γέρασι πατρικαὶ βασιλεῖαι Id.1.13; ῥ. ἀργύριον a *stated* sum, Id.2.7, 4.69; ἐπὶ ῥητοῖσι, Att. ἐπὶ ῥητοῖς, on *stated terms*, on *certain conditions*, according to *covenant*, Hdt.5.57, E.*Hipp.*459, Th.1.122, And.3.22, al.; παρέσεσθαι εἰς ῥ. ἡμέραν X.*HG*3.5.6; ῥ. ἀπόκρισις a *distinct, definite* answer, Plb.32.6.7: ῥητόν, τό, *fixed date* for a lawsuit, *PSI*4.463.14 (iii B.C.), etc.; so perh. ἀπὸ ῥητῶν *IG*12 (9).1273 (Euboea, vi B.C.). Adv. -τῶς *expressly, distinctly*, Plb.3.23.5, *SIG*685.77 (ii B.C.), Phld.*Rh.*1.105 S., 1 *Ep.Ti.*4.1, Gal.17(2).427: Sup. ῥητότατα S.E.*M.*7.16. 2. *spoken of, famous*, ῥητοί τ' ἄρρητοί τε Hes.*Op.*4. 3. of language, *in common use* (= συνήθης), A.D.*Pron.*

113.18; φράσις Id.*Synt.*39.15. Adv. -τῶς Phld.*Rh.*1.161 S. II. *that may be spoken* or *told*, εἰ ῥητόν, φράσον A.*Pr.*765; ἦ ῥητόν; ἢ οὐχὶ θεμιτὸν ἄλλον εἰδέναι; S.*OT*993; αὐδῶν ἀνόσι' οὐδὲ ῥητά μοι ib. 1289; ῥ. ἄρρητόν τ' ἔπος Id.*OC*1001; δεινὸν γάρ, οὐδὲ ῥ. Id.*Ph.*756; cf. ἄρρητος III. 3. 2. *that can be spoken* or *enunciated*, συλλαβή Pl.*Tht.*202b, cf. 205d, e; διάλεκτοι Phld.*Rh.*1.110 S.; οὐ ῥ. κατ' ἰδίαν αἱ ἐγκλιτικαί A.D.*Pron.*36.30; *communicable in words*, Pl.*Ep.* 341c. III. Math., *rational*, of magnitudes, opp. surds (ἄλογα), ῥητὰ πρὸς ἄλληλα Id.*R.*546c, *Hp.Ma.*303b, cf. Euc.10 *Deff.*3 and 4, Hero *Deff.*128; in Metric, ῥ. πούς, opp. ἄλογος, Aristid.Quint.1.14; v. ἄρρητος IV. IV. τὸ ῥ. *the precise, literal contents* of a document, *the letter* of the law, S.E.*M.*2.36, etc.; ῥητός *literal*, opp. allegorical, Ph.1.69, al. V. = ῥῆμα I. 3, even of *a living thing*, Hebr. *dāvār*, Lxx *Ex.*9.4. **-ότης**, ητος, ἡ, *rationality*, of numbers, Iamb. *in Nic.* p.91 P.

❋ **ῥήτρ-α**, ἡ, Ion. **ῥήτρη**, Elean **Ϝράτρα**, v. infr.: (ἐρῶ):—*verbal agreement, bargain, covenant*, ἀλλ' ἄγε νῦν ῥήτρην ποιησόμεθ' Od.14. 393; παρὰ τὴν ῥ. X.*An.*6.6.28; ῥ. πρὸς αὐτὸν καὶ ὁμολογία γίνεται Ael.*VH*2.7, cf. 10.18; ποιοῦνται ῥήτρας ἐπὶ χρυσίῳ παμπόλλῳ they lay *wagers*, Id.*NA*15.24. II. in the Doric and Elean dialects, *compact, treaty*, ἁ Ϝράτρα τοῖρ Ϝαλείοις καὶ τοῖς Ἑρϝαοίοις (i.e. ἡ ῥήτρα τοῖς Ἠλείοις καὶ τοῖς Ἡραιεῦσι) *SIG*9 (Elis, vi B.C.). 2. of *the laws* of Lycurgus, which assumed the character of *a compact between the Law-giver and the People*, Plu.*Lyc.*6, cf. 13; later, *decree, ordinance*, of the Spartan kings, as of Agis, Id.*Agis* 8; εὐθείαις ῥ. ἀνταπαμειβομένους (perh. in reference to the σκολιά (sc. ῥήτρα) mentioned in the addition made to the original ῥήτρα, Plu.*Lyc.*6), Tyrt.2.8. 3. at Byzantium, = προβούλευμα, ἐκ τᾶς βωλᾶς λαβὼν ῥήτραν Decr.Byz. ap.D.18.90 (unless, *leave to speak*, cf. infr. III). 4. generally, *law*, X.*Cyr.*1.6.33; *ordinance* of a festival, *IG*5(1).1498.12 (Messenia). III. *speech*, ῥ. παραλαβεῖν take up *the word*, Luc.*Pro Merc. Cond.*2; παραδιδόναι Id.*Tox.*35: pl., *speeches*, Lyc.470,1037, Nic. *Al.*132. **-εύω**, *pronounce, declare*, δίκας Lyc.1400.

**ῥητροφύλαξ** [ῠ], ἄκος, ὁ, *keeper of archives*, Phot., Suid., *EM*703. 46.

**ῥήττω**, v. ῥήγνυμι.

**ῥήτωρ**, ορος, ὁ, also ἡ Ar.*Fr.*945 (cf. *Th.*292): (ἐρῶ):—*public speaker*, μύθων ῥήτορες E.*Hec.*124 (anap.), cf. *Fr.*597.4, Isoc.8.129, Arist. *Top.*149b25, Phld.*Rh.*2.272 S., Plu.2.131a, etc.; esp. at Athens, οἱ ῥήτορες the *public speakers in the ἐκκλησία*, Ar.*Ach.*38,680, *Eq.*60, 358, al., Th.8.1, And.3.1, Lys.30.22, etc.; sg. prob. in *IG*1².45.21; οἱ δέκα ῥ. the Ten Attic Orators, Luc.*Am.*29; ὁ ῥ. 'par excellence' = Demosthenes, Hermog.*Inv.*4.1, al. 2. *one who gives sentence, judge*, S.*Fr.*1090. 3. *advocate*, *POxy.*37.4 (i A.D.), etc. 4. later, *teacher of eloquence, rhetorician*, *OGI*712 (Egypt), etc. II. as Adj., ῥ. λόγος *oratory*, *IG*2.1386.7.

**ῥηχιάδης** or **ῥηχάδης**, ου, ὁ, *one who threw convicts into the sea*, Hsch., Suid. **ῥηχίη, ῥηχός**, Ion. for ῥαχία, ῥαχός.

❋ **ῥηχμός**, ὁ, = ῥηγμός, *Mnemos.*42.332 (Argos).

**ῥηχώδης**, ες, *thorny, rough*, Nic.*Al.*230.

**ῥίαινα**· πηγή, λιβάς, Hsch. **ῥίγα**· σιῶπα, Id. (fort. Cypr. ἴγα, i.e. σίγα).

**ῥῑγ-ᾰλέος**, α, ον, (ῥῖγος) *cold, chilling*, ὄμβρος Emp.21.5. **-εδᾰνός**, ή, όν, *making one shudder*, ῥιγεδανὴ Ἑλένη *at whose name one shudders, horrible*, Il.19.325; so ῥ. γῆρυς A.R.4.1343, cf. Opp.*H.*5.37; μοῖραν ῥιγεδανοῦ βιότου *IG*12(3).869.10 (Thera). 2. *shivery, cold*, ῥ. πηγυλίς *AP*9.384.24. Adv. -νῶς Tryph.558. **-είω**, = ῥιγέω, *EM* 620.46. **-εσίβῐος** [σῐ], ον, *living in the cold*, Poll.4.186, Phryn.*PS* p.106 B. ❋ **-έω**, Pi.*N.*5.50: fut. -ήσω Il.5.351: aor. ἐρρίγησα, Ep. ῥίγησα (also in S.*OC*1607), Il.5.596: pf. (with pres. sense) ἔρρῑγα 17.175 (prob. f.l. in Thphr.*Ign.*74); Dor. 3 pl. ἐρρίγαντι Theoc.16. 77; Ep. subj. ἐρρίγῃσι Il.3.353; Ep. dat. part. ἐρρίγοντι (for ἐρριγότι) Hes.*Sc.*228: plpf. 3 sg. ἐρρίγει Od.23.216:—*shudder* or *bristle* with fear or horror, ἰδὼν ῥίγησε Il.5.596, etc.; ἐρρίγησαν ὅπως ἴδον 12.208; once in Trag., αἱ δὲ παρθένοι ῥίγησαν (the augm. being omitted although in an iambic verse) S. l. c.: c. inf., *shudder to do, shrink from doing*, ὄφρα τις ἐρρίγῃσι. . ξεινοδόκον κακὰ ῥέξαι Il.3.353, cf. 7.114; cf. ἀπορριγέω: folld. by a clause, θυμὸς ἐρρίγει μή. . Od.23.216. 2. *cool* or *slacken in zeal*, Pi.*N.*5.50. 3. *bristle* with arms, Φοίνικες. . ἐρρίγαντι Theoc. l. c. II. trans., *shudder at* anything, ῥιγήσειν πόλεμον Il.5.351; ἔρριγα μάχην 17.175 (in 16.119 ῥίγησέν τε is best taken parenthetically). (Cf. Lat. *frīgeo*, from *srīg-*.) **-ηλός**, ή, όν, *making to shudder, terrible*, ὀϊστοί Hes.*Sc.*131; ὑλαγμός Nic.*Al.*220; ὄνειδος *AP*7.351 (Diosc.); ἀγών Nonn.*D.*37.149; ῥ. ναύταις ἐρίφων δύσις *AP*7.640 (Antip.). 2. of persons, *susceptible to cold*, Anon. ap.Suid. Adv. -λῶς Poll.5.111. **-ιον**, Comp. neut. Adj. formed from ῥιγέω, *more horrible* or *miserable*, τό οἱ καὶ ῥ. ἔσται Il.1.325, cf. 563, 11.405; τὸ δὲ ῥ. . . ἄλγεα πάσχειν Od.20.220; [γυναικὸς] κακῆς οὐ ῥ. ἄλλο Hes.*Op.*703; cf. Semon.6. II. *colder*, ποτὶ ἕσπερα ῥ. ἔσται Od. 17.191.—The masc. ῥιγίων is not found. **-ιστος**, η, ον, Sup. Adj. formed from ῥιγέω, *most horrible*, ῥίγιστα θεοὶ τετληότες εἰμέν Il.5.873; [Ζεὺς] ῥίγιστος ἀλιτροῖς A.R.2.215, cf. 292; ὃ δὴ ῥίγιστον ὄδωδεν Nic.*Th.*64.

**ῥιγίτανον**, τό, name of a plant, *Gp.*12.1.2.

**ῥιγνόομαι**, = ῥικνόομαι, Phot. **ῥιγνός**, ή, όν, = ῥικνός, Hsch.

**ῥῑγό-λῠτον**, τό, *hot bath administered to an epileptic patient*, cj. in Cael.Aur.*TP*1.93 (*pygolithon* codd.). **-μάχης**, or **-χος** [ᾰ], ου, ὁ, *fighting with cold*, *AP*11.155 (Lucill.). **-πύρετος** [ῠ], ὁ, *fever with shivering fits, ague*, Gal.19.560,567, Ptol.*Tetr.*115, Vett.Val.210.5; also **-πύρετον**, τό, Phryn.*PS* p.73 B.; Dim.❋ **-τίον**, τό, Hsch. s.v. ἠπιόλιον.

**ῥῖγ-ος**, εος, τό, *frost, cold*, Od.5.472, Hdt.6.44, etc.; ὑπὸ λιμοῦ καὶ ῥίγους Pl.*Euthphr.*4d; λιμῷ καὶ ῥίγει μαχόμενος X.*Cyr.*6.1.15: pl., ῥίγη καὶ θάλπη Id.*Oec.*7.23. 2. *shivering*, Pl.*Ti.*62b; *shivering fit*, as in ague, Hp.*VM*16, *Aph.*4.29, *BGU*956.2 (iii A.D.); ῥ. πυρετώδη Hp.*Fract.*34. **-όω**, fut. -ώσω X.*Mem.*2.1.17, Ep. inf. -ωσέμεν Od. 14.481: aor. ἐρρίγωσα Hp.*Epid.*3.1.ς', (ἐν-) Ar.*Pl.*846: pf. ἐρριγωκότες Thphr.*Ign.*74 (vv.ll. ἐρριγότες, ἐρριγνωκότες), Gal.11.556.—Like ἱδρόω, has an irreg. contr. into ω, ῳ, for ου, οι, 3 sg. subj. ῥιγῷ Pl.*Grg.* 517d, cj. in *Phd.*85a; opt. ῥιγῴη Hp.*Int.*10, Plu.2.233a; inf. ῥιγῶν Ar.*Ach.*1146, *V.*446, *Av.*935, Pl.*R.*440c, X.*Cyr.*5.1.11; part. fem. ῥιγῶσα Semon.7.26, but acc. masc. ῥιγοῦντα Phld.*Vit.* p.22 J.:—*to be cold, shiver*, Od.14.481, Hdt.5.92.η', Hp.*VM*16, etc.; though several forms may belong either to this word or to ῥιγέω, as ῥιγῶν τε καὶ πεινῶν Ar.*Ach.*857, cf. *Nu.*416, Crates Com.33, Pl.*Grg.*517d. **-ώδης**, ες, *provocative of shivering*, Hp.*Coac* 609, Gal.19.146. **-ωσις**, εως, ἡ, *shivering*, prob. cj. for ῥάσιν in Thphr.*Vent.*23.

❋ **ῥίζ-α**, ης, ἡ: Ion. nom. ῥίζη Hp.ap.Erot., acc. ῥίζην Marc.Sid.89 (before a vowel), but ῥίζαν Il.11.846 (whence Ion. nom. ῥίζα may be inferred):—*root*, Od.10.304, 23.196, etc.; used as a medicine, Il.11. 846; ῥ. ἐλατήριος, of a purgative medicine, Hp.*Epid.*5.34: mostly in pl., *roots*, Il.12.134, Od.12.435, etc.; δένδρεα μακρὰ αὐτῇσιν ῥίζῃσι Il.9.542: hence 2. metaph., *roots of the eye*, Od.9.390 (but ῥίζας ἐν ὄσσοις αἱματώπας in E.*HF*933 prob. bloodshot *streaks*); the *roots* or *foundations* of the earth, Hes.*Op.*19; χθόνα. . αὐταῖς ῥ. πνεῦμα κραδαίνοι A.*Pr.*1047 (anap.); ἰπούμενος ῥίζαισιν Αἰτναίαις ὕπο ib.367; of feathers, hair, etc., Pl.*Phdr.*251b, Arist.*HA*518b14; of the teeth, Id.*GA*789a13; γαστρὸς ῥ. ὀμφαλός Id.*HA*493a18, etc. 3. τὸν πόλεμον ἐκ ῥιζῶν ἀνῄρηκε 'root and branch', Plu.*Pomp.*21, cf. Heraclid.Pont.ap.Ath.12.523f; ἐκ ῥιζῶν ἀπώλεσεν Lxx *Jb.*31.12; cf. ῥιζόθεν, πρόρριζος. II. *that from which anything springs as from a root*, ῥίζαν ἀπείρου τρίταν a third continental *foundation*, of Libya, Pi.*P.*9.8; ἀστέων ῥ., of Cyrene, as the *root* or *original* of the Cyrenaic Pentapolis, ib.4.15; *root* or *stock* from which a family springs, ῥ. σπέρματος Id.*O.*2.46, cf. *I.*8(7).61, A.*Ag.*966, S.*Aj.*1178, etc.; so, *race, family*, A.*Th.*755 (lyr.), E.*IT*610, *OGI*383.31 (Nemrud Dagh, i B.C.), etc.; συκοφάντου. . σπέρμα καὶ ῥ. D.25.48; *sect, party*, Jul. *Gal.*106e; also ῥ. κακῶν E.*Fr.*912.11 (anap.); ἀρχὴ καὶ ῥ. παντὸς ἀγαθοῦ Epicur.*Fr.*409, cf. 1*Ep.Ti.*6.10; πηγὴ καὶ ῥ. καλοκἀγαθίας Plu. 2.4c; ἀρχαὶ καὶ ῥ. γῆς καὶ θαλάττης Arist.*Mete.*353b1, etc.; cf. ῥίζωμα II. 2. *base, foundation*, ῥ. πάντων καὶ βάσις ἃ γᾶ ἐρήρεισται Ti. Locr.97e, cf. Pl.*Ti.*81c; *base* of a vertical pillar, Procl.*Hyp.*3.23; τῶν λόφων Onos.10.6. 3. Math., *root* or *base* of a series, Anatolius ap.*Theol.Ar.*9. (Aeol. **βρίζα** (q.v.): cf. Goth. *waúrts*, Lat. *radix*.) **-άγρα**, ἡ, *instrument for extracting the roots* of a tooth, Cels.7.12.1, Paul.Aeg.6.88. **-αῖος**, α, ον, *forming a base* (cf. ῥίζα II. 2), ῥ. λίθος, of a column, opp. σπεῖρα, *Sardis* 7(1) No.181 (prob. i A.D.). **-εῖον**, τό, = ῥίζιον, Nic.*Al.*265: a pl. form ῥίζεα ib.69, 145,588, *Th.*646,940 (ῥιζία is a freq. v.l.). **-ηδόν**, Adv. *like roots*, Hld.1.29. **-ηθεν**, Adv. *from the roots*, A.R.3.1401. **-ίας**, ου, ὁ, *made from the root* of a plant, ὀπὸς ῥ., opp. καυλίας, Thphr.*HP*6.3. 2, 9.1.7, cf. Plin.*HN*19.43. **-ικός**, ή, όν, *of* or *for the root*, λόγος Plu. *in Hes.*84. **-ινος**, η, ον, *made from a root* (viz. of ἐρευθέδανον), πορφύρα *PHolm.*26.29. **-ιον** or **ῥιζίον**, τό, Dim. of ῥίζα, *little root*, Ar.*Av.*654, Antiph.45, Thphr.*CP*2.18.2, *HP*4.2.3, etc.; πορφύρα ῥιζίου *vegetable* purple (cf. ῥίζινος), *POxy.*1051.13 (iii A.D.). **-ίς**, ίδος, ἡ, poet. for ῥίζα in Nic.*Al.*403,531 (v.l. ῥιζάς).

❋ **ῥίζις**, ὁ, an Ethiopian animal of the elephant kind, Str.17.3.5.

**ῥιζο-βολέω**, *strike root*, Dsc.3.38, *AP*11.246 (Lucill.), S.E.*M.*5.57. **-βόλος**, ον, *striking root*, Nic.*Th.*69. **-θεν**, Adv. = ῥίζηθεν, *by, from the roots*, Id.*Al.*257, *Th.*307, Luc.*Tyr.*13, Q.S.6.381; ᾧ τὸ δίκαιον στήρικτο ἐγ γνώμῃ ῥ. ἐκ φύσεως *Supp.Epigr.*2.482 (Kertch):—also **-θι**, Nic.*Fr.*27. ❋ **-κέφᾰλος**, ον, of plants, *of which the flower grows straight from the root*, Thphr.*CP*1.10.5. **-λογέω**, *root out*, τυράννους D.S.16.82 (s. v.l.). **-πᾰγής**, ές, (πήγνυμι) *firmly rooted*, Nonn. *D.*2.247. **-πώλης**, ου, ὁ, *dealer in roots*, Poll.7.196 (= Critias 70 D.). **-σημος**, ον, *with a stripe of vegetable purple* (cf. ῥίζιον), *POxy.*1051.3 (iii A.D.).

**ῥιζοτομ-έω**, *cut* or *prune the roots* of a tree by digging round it, συκῇ ῥιζοτομηθείσῃ Thphr.*CP*1.17.10, etc. II. *cut up by the roots, extirpate*, D.S.32.4: esp. for Medic. purposes, ῥ. βοτάνας *cut and gather* their *roots*, Hp.*Ep.*16, cf. Thphr.*HP*4.5.1; *gather roots* for food, Str.16.4.9: metaph., Philostr.*VA*7.26. **-ία**, ἡ, *cutting and gathering of roots*, Thphr.*HP*6.3.2, 9.8.2: pl., books *on roots, herbals*, Ruf.ap.Orib.7.26.31. **-ικός**, ή, όν, *of* or *for the cutting and gathering of roots*: ῥιζοτομικόν, τό, botanical work of Amerias, Ath. 15.681f. **-ος** (parox.), ὁ, *one who cuts* or *gathers roots*, esp. for purposes of medicine or witchcraft, *herbalist*, Hp.*Ep.*16, Thphr.*HP* 9.1.7, 9.8.1, Dsc.*Prooem.*, Luc.*DDeor.*13.1, Phot., etc.; Ῥιζοτόμοι, αἱ, title of play by Sophocles, Macr.*Sat.*5.19.9, etc. 2. as Adj., ῥ. ὥρα the time *for cutting roots*, Nic.*Th.*494. II. ἡ ῥ., name of a kind of *iris*, Plin.*HN*21.41.

**ῥιζοτροφέω**, *grow, nourish roots*, Poll.1.235; v.l. for δρυζοτροφέω in Str.17.3.23 in Cod. in *Sitzb.Heidelb.Akad.*1931/2.23.

**ῥιζουχία**, ἡ, *root, origin of a family*, Tz.*H.*4.330 (pl.).

**ῥιζοῦχος**, ον, (ἔχω) *upholding the roots* or *foundation*, epith. of Poseidon, Call.*Fr.*285: generally, *upholding*, θεμείλια ῥ. Opp.*H.*5. 680.

**ῥιζοφᾰγ-έω**, *eat roots*, Str.3.2.6, 11.8.7. **-ος** (parox.), ον, *eating roots*, Arist.*HA*595$^a$16, *PA*662$^b$14; οἱ Ῥ. *Root-eaters*, name of an Ethiopian tribe in D.S.3.23, Str.16.4.9.

**ῥιζο-φοίτητος**, ον, *coming from a root*, φλέβες φοίνικος Chaerem. 39. **-φόρος**, ον, *bearing roots*, *EM*515.10. **-φῠέω**, *put out roots*, Thphr.*CP*1.2.1. ✻ **-φῠής**, ές, *putting out roots*, ib.1.8.1. II. *growing from a root*, Id.*HP*7.10.1. **-φῠΐα**, ἡ, *putting out of roots*, Sch.Hes.*Th*.304. **-φυλλος**, ον, *with leaves from the root*, Thphr. *HP*6.4.9, 7.11.3. **-φῠτος**, ον, *growing from a root*, Ocell. 1.13.

**ῥιζ-όω**, *cause to strike root*: metaph., *plant, fix firmly*, ὅς μιν [τὴν ναῦν] λᾶαν θῆκε καὶ ἐρρίζωσεν ἔνερθεν Od.13.163; [νήσους] κατὰ βυσσὸν πρυμνόθεν (s. v.l.) Call.*Del*.35:—Pass., of trees and plants, *take root, strike root*, X.*Oec*.19.9, Thphr.*CP*1.2.1:—Med., ἄριστον ῥιζώσασθαι, of the fig, Id.*HP*2.5.6; so αἱ πίνναι ἐρρίζωνται, opp. ἀρρίζωτοι, Arist. *HA*548$^a$5; ῥ. ἐπί τινος *AP*6.66 (Paul.Sil.); ὀδὸς βάθροισι γῆθεν ἐρριζωμένος *made fast* or *solid*, S.*OC*1591; of a bridge, αἰώνιος ἐρρίζωται *Epigr.Gr.*1078.7 (Adana). 2. metaph., ἐρρίζωσε τὴν τυραννίδα Hdt.1.64:—Pass., τυραννὶς ἐρριζωμένη ib.60, cf. Pl.*Lg*.839a; ἐξ ἀμαθίας πάντα κακὰ ἐρρ. *have their root* in.., Id.*Ep*.336b, cf. S.E. *M*.1.271; ἐν ἀγάπῃ ἐρρ. *Ep.Eph*.3.18. II. Pass. also of land, *to be planted with trees*, ἀλωὴ ἐρρίζωται Od.7.122. **-ώδης**, ες, *like a root*, Thphr.*HP*7.2.1, Hero *Metr*.2.20. **-ωμα**, ατος, τό, *the mass of roots* of a tree, Thphr.*CP*3.3.4. II. *element*, τέσσαρα μὲν πάντων ῥιζώματα πρῶτον ἄκουε Emp.6.1; ἀενάου φύσεως ῥ. Pythag.15. 2. *stem, race*, A.*Th*.413; θείων δ' ἀπ' ἀμφοῖν ἔκγονον ῥιζωμάτων, i.e. on the side of both parents, Theodect.3. **-ωνῠχία**, ἡ, *root of the nail*, Poll.2.145 (pl.), cf. Paul.Aeg.6.85:—in Ruf.*Onom*.85, **-νύχια**, τά; but -ίαι Id.ap.Orib.25.1.32. **-ωρῠχέω**, *dig up roots*, Plu.2. 473a. **-ωρύχος** [ῠ], ον, *root-grubbing*, of grammarians, *AP*11.322 (Antiphan.). **-ωσις**, εως, ἡ, *taking root*, Thphr.*CP*2.12.5, 8.1.3; ῥ. λαμβάνειν Plu.*Publ*.8: metaph., of the formation of the embryo, ὀμφαλὸς -ώσιος ἀρχά Philol.13; ἡ τῶν γεννωμένων ῥ. Plu.*Lyc*.14; *origin* of veins and arteries, Hp.*Alim*.31.

**ῥικάζεται**, v. ῥιξικάζεται.

**ῥικν-ήεις**, εσσα, εν, poet. for ῥικνός, Nic.*Th*.137. **-όομαι**, Pass., *grow stiff* or *be shrivelled* by frost, heat, or old age, Arist.*HA*553$^a$13, Opp.*H*.5.593, Sor.1.15. II. *dance with unseemly contortions*, S.*Fr*.316, cf. Luc.*Lex*.8. III. later Act., *have sexual intercourse*, πρὸς ἄνδρα, πρὸς γυναῖκα, *PMag.Leid.W*.6.28. ✻ **-ός**, ή, όν, *shrivelled with cold*, = πεφρικώς, S.*Fr*.1091; *shrivelled* by old age or disease, *shrunk, contracted*, Hp.*Prog*.2 (s. v.l.), Xenarch.4.8, Cerc.2, Call.*Fr*. 49, etc.: generally, *withered, shrivelled, crooked*, Ἥφαιστος ῥικνὸς πόδας *h.Ap*.317; ἅψεα Opp.*C*.2.346; ῥικνοὶ πόδες A.R.1.669, cf. *APl*. 4.306 (Leon.); ῥ. καὶ κώδιον *shrivelled* and (like) leather, *IG*14.1363. 15 (Rome, iv A.D.). **-ότης**, ητος, ἡ, *shrivelledness*, Hsch. s.v. διερρικνοῦντο.

**ῥικνοφῠής**, ές, *shrivelled* or *crooked-shaped*, Hsch.

✻ **ῥικν-ώδης**, ες, *shrivelled-looking*, of gooseflesh, Hp.*Epid*.6.3.14; of a person, γήραϊ ῥ. *AP*5.272 (Agath.). ✻ **-ωσις**, εως, ἡ, *shrivelling* of the skin, Hp.*Epid*.6.3.16.

**ῥίμβαι**· ῥοιαὶ μεγάλαι. ἄμεινον δὲ διὰ τοῦ ξ ξίμβαι, Hsch. (cf. ξίμβραι). **ῥίμβησις**· ἀγκύλη τοῦ ὤμου, οἱ δὲ τὸν βραχίονα τοῦ ἱερείου, Id.

✻ **ῥῖμμα**, ατος, τό, (ῥίπτω) *throw, cast*, ποδῶν ῥίμματα Arion 6; = ἡ ῥῖψις καὶ τὸ βέλος, Hdn.*Epim*.118.

**ῥίμφ-ᾰ**, Adv. *lightly, swiftly*, ῥίμφα ἑ γοῦνα φέρει Il.6.511, cf. Hes. *Sc*.342; τοὶ δὲ πέτοντο ῥ. μάλ' Il.13.30; ῥ. μάλα τρωχῶσι 22.163; δεῖπνον ἕλοντο..ῥ. 8.54; ῥ. τοξεύειν ὕμνους Pi.*I*.2.3; βέβακεν ῥ. A.*Ag*. 407 (lyr.), cf. A.R.1.387, 1194. **-ᾰλέος**, α, ον, *light, swift*, *EM*135. 24, 262.7. **-άρμᾰτος**, ον, *of a swift chariot*, διφρηλασία Pi.*O*.3.37; ῥ. ἁμίλλαις with the *swift* racing *of chariots*, S.*OC*1063 (lyr.).

**ῥίν**, v. ῥίς. **ῥῖνα**, ἡ, Hellenistic for ῥίνη I, Moer.p.338P.

**ῥῑνάριον**, τό, *small file*, Aët.8.82. 2. a sort of *eye-salve*, Id.7. 115, Paul.Aeg.3.22, 7.16.

**ῥῑν-αυλέω**, (ῥίς) *blow through the nose, snort*, from anger, cj. for ῥιναυστέω in Luc.*Lex*.19 (cf. Sch.). **-άω** (A), *lead by the nose*, Pherecr.23, Men.895:—Pass., ἐρρινώμεθα *we were chaffed*, Alciphr. *Fr*.6.2 (unless metaph. use of sq.). ✻ **-άω** (B), (ῥίνη) *file, fine down*, Arist.*Aud*.802$^a$38, 803$^a$2, Ph.*Bel*.70.15, Ael.*NA*6.3; ψῆγμα ῥινηθέν *filings*, *AP*9.310 (Antiphil.): metaph. of literary work, D.H. *Th*.24.

**ῥινέαι**· αἱ μέλαιναι ἰσχάδες, Hsch.

**ῥῑν-εγκᾰτᾰπηξῐ-γένειος**, ον, (ῥίς, ἐγκαταπήγνυμι) *with a nose reaching to the chin, with a nutcracker nose and chin*, Epigr.ap.Hegesand. 1. **-εγχυσία**, v.l. for ῥινὸς ἔγχυσιν, Dsc.2.181. **-εγχῠτέω** or **-όω**, *inject at the nose*, ib.179, in Pass. **-εγχύτης** [ῠ], ου, ὁ, *instrument for passing such injections*, Cael.Aur.*TP*2.4, Aët.6. 52. **-έγχῠτον**, τό, *injection for the nose*, Gal.12.582. **-έγχῠτος**, ον, *injected at the nose*, Crateuas *Fr*.8.

**ῥῑν-έω**, = ῥινάω (B), Sch.Ar.*Ra*.931. ✻ **-η**, ἡ, *file, rasp*, X.*Cyr*.6.2. 33, Arist.*Aud*.803$^a$2, Aen.Tact.18.5, *IG*11(2).173.11 (Delos, iii B.C.), etc.; χαρακταὶ ῥῖναι *AP*6.205 (Leon.). II. *shark with a rough skin*, used (like shagreen) for polishing wood and marble, *Rhina squatina, angel-fish*, Hp.*Int*.1, Epich.59, Archipp.25, Anaxandr.41. 53, Arist.*HA*540$^b$11, al. (ῥινή I, ῥίνη II acc. to Hdn.Gr.1.333.)

**ῥῑνηλ-ᾰσία**, ἡ, (ἐλαύνω) *tracking by the nose, hunting by scent*, Anon. Lond.33.16, Longus 1.21. **-ᾰτέω**, *track by scent*, ἴχνος κακῶν ῥ. A.*Ag*.1185, cf. S.*Ichn*.88, Ph.1.628, Longus 2.13. ✻ **-άτης** [ᾰ], ου, ὁ, *one who tracks by scent*, κύων ῥ. Poll.2.74. **-ᾰτος**, ον, *tracked by the scent*, ἴχνος Opp.*H*.2.290.

**ῥίν-ημα** [ῑ], ατος, τό, (ῥινέω) *that which is filed off, filings*, in sg. and pl., χαλκοῦ Hp.*Mul*.1.78, Herod.7.81; ἀργύρου S.E.*P*.1.129; ἐλέφαντος τοῦ ὀδόντος Aret.*CD*2.13; πριστοῖσι λόγχης..ῥινήμασιν E.*Fr*. 724. II. an eyesalve, Gal.12.778. **-ησις**, εως, ἡ, *filing*, of teeth, ib.872; of bones, Id.14.782. **-ητήριον**, τό, = ῥίνη I, *Gloss*. **-ητής**, οῦ, ὁ, *one who files*, ib. **-ίζω**, *file*, *POxy*.1066.19 (iii A.D.), *Gloss*.:— Pass., Aët.8.32. **-ίον**, τό, Dim. of ῥίνη I, *small file*, Gal.12.871, Hdn.*Epim*.119. 2. = ῥινάριον 2, Cels.6.6.30, Gal.12.736. II. Dim. of ῥίς, in pl. ῥινία, *nostrils*, Arist.*Phgn*.808$^a$34. **-ισμα**, ατος, τό, = ῥίνημα I, Ctes.*Fr*.57.25 (p.101 Dind.), Antyll.ap.Orib.10.19.7, Ruf.*Fr*.75.

✻ **ῥῑνό-βᾰτος**, ὁ, *a rough-skinned fish*, between the species ῥίνη (signf. II) and βάτος (B), perh. *Rhinobatus Columnae*, Arist.*HA*566$^a$ 28; also **-βάτης**, ου, ὁ, Id.*GA*746$^b$6. **-βόλος**, ον, *striking the nose*, of smells, Hsch. II. proparox. **ῥῑνόβολος**, Pass., *emitted through the nose*, of a snorting sound, *AP*9.769 (Agath.).

**ῥῑνοδέψης**, ου, ὁ, (ῥινός) *leather-dresser*, Hsch.

✻ **ῥῑνόκερως**, ωτος, ὁ, (ῥίς) *the Rhinoceros* or *Nose-horn*, Callix.2, Str. 16.4.15, Ael.*NA*17.44, *IG*14.1302 (Praeneste); ῥ. λίθος, of its horn, Cyran.36. 2. *wild bull*, Aq.*Jb*.39.9, *Ps*.28(29).9. 3. = ποιὸς ὄρνις ἐν Αἰθιοπίᾳ, Hsch. (perh. *hornbill*).

**ῥῑνοκόλλητος**, ον, *made of glued hides*, S.*Ichn*.366 (lyr.).

**ῥῑνο-κολοῦρος**, ον, (κολούω) = *mutilatis naribus*, Erasistr.ap.Gal. 19.142. **-κολούστης**, ου, ὁ, *nose-clipper*, of Heracles, Paus.9.25. 4. **-κοπέω**, *cut off the nose*, ῥ. τινά Suid. **-λᾰβίς**, ίδος, ἡ, *instrument for taking hold of the nose*, Id.

**ῥῑνόν**, τό, = ῥινός II. 1, *hide*, Il.10.155, *AP*9.328 (Damostr.). 2. = ῥινός II. 2, *shield*, Od.5.281, v. Sch.

**ῥῑνοπύλη** [ῠ], ἡ, *side-gate, wicket*, Plb.8.25.8, 8.29.5, 15.31.10.

✻ **ῥῑνός** (v. sub fin.), *skin* of a living person, Il.5.308, Od.5.426, 435, etc.; rarely of a corpse, Od.14.134, Hes.*Sc*.152. II. *hide* of a beast, esp. *ox-hide*, Od.1.108, al.; also ῥ. πολιοῖο λύκοιο Il.10.334; ῥ. λέοντος Pi.*I*.5(6).37; not in Hom. of the skin of a live beast, but so used by Hes.*Op*.515, *Sc*.427; πωλικῆς ῥινοῦ E.*Rh*.784. 2. *ox-hide shield*, σὺν ῥ' ἔβαλον ῥινούς Il.4.447 (imitated by Ar.*Pax* 1274); cf. Il.16.636 and ῥινόν 2. 3. pl., *thongs of boxing-gloves*, A.R.2. 58. 4. *leather* of a sling, *AP*7.172 (Antip. Sid.).—The gender is fem. in Il.7.248, 20.276, Od.22.278 (v.l.), Hes.*Sc*.152, E.l.c., Nic. *Th*.361, A.R.4.174; masc. in Nic.*Al*.476, Opp.*C*.3.277: cf. ῥινόν, τό. (Ϝρινός, as shown by γρῖνος· δέρμα, Hsch., γρίντης· βυρσεύς, Id.: cf. ταλαύρινος.)

**ῥῑνό-σῑμος**, ον, (ῥίς) *snub-nosed*, Luc.*Bacch*.2. **-σπάθιον** [ᾰ], τό, a surgical instrument, *Hermes* 38.283.

**ῥῑνο-τομέω**, = ῥινοκοπέω, Eust.1839.16. **-τόμος**, ον, (ῥινός) *piercing shields* or *hides*, dub.l. for -τόρος in Nonn.*D*.21.87. **-τορίνιον**, τό, dub. in *Hermes* 38.283 as name of surgical instrument (cod. Laur. ῥινη το ῥινιον; cod. Par. *rinotorine*). **-τόρος**, ον, (ῥινός) *hide-piercing, shield-piercing*, of Ares, Il.21.392, Hes.*Th*.934; θύρσος Nonn.*D*.45. 288, etc.

**ῥῑνουλκέω**, (ῥίς) *inhale*, Thessalus in *Cat.Cod.Astr*.8(3).138.

✻ **ῥῑνοῦχος**, ὁ, (ῥίς II) *sewer*, Str.14.1.21, *Gloss*.

**ῥινόχοος**· χώνη, Hsch.

**ῥῑν-ώλεθρος**, ον, (ῥίς I) *nose-plaguing*, ὀσμή *Com.Adesp*.899. ✻ **-ωτηρία**, ἡ, = ἐφολκίς (q.v.), Poll.1.86.

**ῥιξικάζεται**· ῥικάζεται, στροβεῖται, Hsch.

✻ **ῥίον** [ῐ], τό, *any jutting part* of a mountain, whether upwards or forwards; hence, 1. *peak*, περὶ ῥίον Οὐλύμποιο Il.8.25, cf. 14.154, 225, etc.; ῥ. ὀρέων Od.9.191; ῥ. οὔρεος *h.Ap*.139. 2. *headland*, Od.3.295; hence as pr. name of several places, esp. Ῥ. Μολυκρικόν and Ῥ. Ἀχαϊκόν at the mouth of the gulf of Corinth, Th.2.86 (cf. 84). 3. later, *bay formed by a foreland*, Ael.*NA*15.3. (Perh. akin to ῥίς, cf. *Ness, Naze* with *nose*.)

**Ῥῖπαι**, αἱ, name of a fabulous range of mountains in the far North, Alcm.58 (leg. Ῥιπᾶν), Arist.*Mete*.350$^b$7 (for S.*OC*1248, v. ῥιπή I): hence **Ῥιπαῖος**, α, ον, *Rhipaean*, ὄρη Hellanic.*Fr*.187(b) J., Damastes *Fr*.1 J., Str.7.3.1, 6.

**ῥῑπάριος**, ὁ, = Lat. *riparius*, police official in Egypt, Wilcken *Chr*. 469.2 (iv A.D., pl.), *POxy*.2110.23 (iv A.D.), 904.3 (v A.D.), etc.

**ῥῑπ-ή**, ἡ, (ῥίπτω) poet. Noun, *swing* or *force with which anything is thrown*, ὅσση δ' αἰγανέης ῥιπὴ..τέτυκται as far as is the *flight* of a javelin, Il.16.589; λᾶος ὑπὸ ῥιπῆς 12.462, Od.8.192; πέτριναι ῥ. E. *Hel*.1123 (lyr.); βελέων ῥ. Pi.*N*.1.68; ὑπὸ ῥιπῆς..Βορέαο *the sweep* or *rush* of the N. wind, Il.15.171, 19.358, cf. B.5.46; κυμάτων ῥιπαὶ ἀνέμων τε Pi.*P*.4.195, cf. *Parth*.2.20, *Fr*.88.2; ῥ. ἀνέμων Id.*P*.9.48, S.*Ant*.137 (lyr., here metaph. of *gusts* of passion, cf. 930); ῥ. Διόθεν τεύχουσα φόβον *storm*, A.*Pr*.1089 (anap.), cf. A.R.1.1016; ῥ. πυρός *rush* of fire, Il.21.12; ἀνδρός 8.355; ἀθανάτων Hes.*Th*.681, 849; κεραυνῶν, χαλάζης, Opp.*H*.3.21, Q.S.14.77; ὑπὸ ῥιπῆς Ἀφροδίτης, of love, Opp.*H*.4.141; νυχιᾶν (ἐννυχιᾶν Lachm.) ἀπὸ ῥιπᾶν from the night *storms*, i.e. from the *North*, the land of darkness and storms, S.*OC*1248 (lyr., but Sch. understands Ῥιπᾶν, v. Ῥῖπαι). 2. πτερύγων ῥιπαὶ *flapping* of wings, A.*Pr*.126 (anap.), cf. E.*Fr*.594. 4; *buzz* of a gnat's wing, A.*Ag*.893; of the lyre's *quivering notes*, Pi.*P*.1.10. 3. *quivering, twinkling light*, ῥιπαὶ ἄστρων S.*El*.106 (anap.). b. of any *rapid movement*, ῥ. ποδῶν E.*IT*885 (lyr.); ῥ. ὠκυάλῳ, of a dolphin, Opp.*H*.2.535; of a bird's wing, οὐδὲ τινάσσει ῥιπήν A.R.2.935; ἐν ῥ. ὀφθαλμοῦ the *twinkling* of an eye, 1*Ep.Cor*.

15.52. 4. *a strong smell*, ῥ. οἴνου Pi.*Fr.*166. **-ημα**, ατος, τό, = foreg., Hsch. s.v. ἐν ἀτόμῳ. ⊛ **-ίδιον**, τό, Dim. of ῥιπίς, *small bellows*, Hdn.*Epim.*118. **-ίζω**, (ῥιπίς) *blow up* or *fan* the flame, πολέμου ἔριν Cypr.*Fr.*1; στάσιν ἀνεγείρει καὶ ῥιπίζει Ar.*Ra.*360; ῥ. πῦρ Plu.*Flam.*21; φλόγα *AP*5.121 (Diod.):—Pass., τεμάχη ῥιπίζεται the fish *is fanned to boiling-point*, Ar.*Ec.*842. 2. *fan* a person, in Med., *fan oneself*, Hp.*VM*16:—Pass., ῥιπίζεσθαι ὑπὸ τῶν περιστερῶν Antiph.202.5; *to be fanned* or *blown about*, ὑπ' ἀνέμου *Com.Adesp.*1324, cf. Arist.*Pr.*$967^{a}$21; πρὸς ἀνέμων Ph.2.511; κλύδων ἀνεμιζόμενος καὶ ῥιπιζόμενος *Ep.Jac.*1.6; ῥιπιζομένη ἄχνη D.C.70.4: metaph., ῥ. ταῖς ἐλπίσι Alciphr.3.47. 3. *hurl*, Hld 10.32, cf. 30 (Pass.). ⊛ **-ίς**, ίδος, ἡ, (ῥίψ) *fan for raising the fire*, Ar.*Ach.*669,888; ῥ. δ' ἐγείρει.. Ἡφαίστου κύνας, i.e. the slumbering flames, Eub.75.7; πτερίνα ῥ. *AP*6.306 (Aristo). II. *lady's fan*, Stratt.56, *AP*6.290 (Diosc.), D.H.7.9. III. = ῥίψ, Crates Com.13. IV. ῥιπίρ (prob. Elean)· ῥιπίς, τὸ πλέγμα, ἢ ἐκ σχοίνου πέτασος. Ἀττικοὶ δὲ ῥιπίδα, ᾧ τὸ πῦρ καίουσι· καὶ τραπέζας οὕτω λέγουσι, Hsch.; Elean ῥιπίρ also in *Inscr. Olymp.*718, perh. = δίσκος, *quoit*, unless it is a pr. n. V. ῥιπίς· τοῦ σκέλους τὸ ἀκροκώλιον, Hsch. [The acc. ῥιπῖδα occurs in *AP*6.306 (Aristo); but ῥιπίδα, -ίδι in Ar., etc.] **-ῐσις**, εως, ἡ, *blowing with a bellows* or *fan*, Thphr.*Ign.*36 (dub. rest.), Gal.8.416, Alex. Aphr.*Pr.*1.113. **-ισμα**, ατος, τό, *air of a fan*, etc., ῥ. λώπης *AP*5.293 (Agath.). **-ισμός**, ὁ, *fanning*, Herod.Med. in *Rh.Mus.*58.100,101 (written ῥυπ-). **-ιστής**, οῦ, ὁ, *fan*, *Gloss.* **-ιστός**, ή, όν, *ventilated*, *airy*, ὑπερῷα Lxx *Je.*22.14.

⊛ **ῥῖπος**, εος, τό, = ῥίψ, *mat* or *hurdle*, ῥίπεϊ καλάμων v.l. in Hdt.2.96; ἀχύρων ῥ. *Docum.Ant.dell' Africa Italiana* 1.86, al. (Cyrene, iv B.C.): also **ῥῖπος**, ὁ, Aen.Tact.29.6 (pl.), *PPetr.*3 p.328 (pl.), Agatharch.63, Dsc.1.45.

⊛ **ῥιπτ-άζω**, Frequentat. of ῥίπτω, *throw to and fro*, *toss about*, ῥιπτάζων κατὰ δῶμα θεούς Il.14.257; ὀφρύσι ῥιπτάζεσκε *moved* the eyebrows *up and down*, *h.Merc.*279:—Pass., *toss about*, esp. in bed, Hp.*Epid.*4.31 (so ῥιπτάζειν ἑαυτόν *Morb.*2.69; and ῥιπτάζειν alone, *Acut.*(*Sp.*)18); πρᾶγμα πολλαῖσι..ἀγρυπνίαισιν ἐρριπτασμένον Ar.*Lys.*27; ὕφη γυναικῶν..ἐρριπτάζετο S.*Fr.*210 iii 12; τῇ γνώμῃ πολλὰ ῥιπτασθεὶς ἐπ' ἀμφότερα Plu.*Cic.*37; ῥιπτάσαι περιδεῶς *BCH*48.518 (Palestine). II. Pass. also, = ῥίπτομαι, *AP*5.164 (Mel.). **-ασμός**, ὁ, *throwing* or *tossing about*, τῶν μελέων Hp.*Acut.*54: abs., *tossing about* in bed, Id.*Coac.*81, Plu.2.455b; ἄσῃ λύπῃ μετὰ ῥιπτασμοῦ *Stoic.*3.100. **-αστικός**, ή, όν, *tossing to and fro*: τὸ ῥ., = ῥιπτασμός, M. Ant.1.16. **-έω**, used only in pres. and impf., collat. form of ῥίπτω, first in Od., ἀν-εῤῥίπτουν ἅλα πηδῷ 13.78, where it suits the metre (but not the Ion. dialect); so in Ar., ῥιπτεῖτε χλαίνας *Ec.*507; διαρριπτοῦντε Id.*V.*59; in Trag. ῥιπτέω is never either guaranteed or disproved by the metre, ῥιπτείσθω A.*Pr.*1043 (anap., cod. Med.), ῥιπτεῖ S.*Aj.*239 (anap.), *Ant.*131 (anap.), *Tr.*780, ῥιπτεῖν E.*Tr.*734 cod. P, ῥιπτοῦνθ' *Hel.*1096 cod. L, ῥιπτοῦντες *Heracl.*149 codd. LP; ῥίπτετ' and ἔρριπτον are guaranteed by the metre in E.*HF*941, *Ba.*1097, so that ῥίπτων, ῥίπτει may be accepted in E.*Ba.*150 (lyr.), *Hel.*1325 (lyr.); ῥιπτέω is found also in Prose, ῥιπτεῦσι Hdt.4.94 (v.l.); ῥιπτέουσι ib.188, cf. 7.50 (ἀνα-), 8.53, Th.4.95 (ἀνα-), Pl.*Ti.*80a, Arist.*Ph.*$266^{b}$30, *Mu.*$396^{a}$2, Plb.1.47.4, al., Agatharch.26; ῥειπτουμένων *OGI*629.158 (Palmyra, ii A.D.), etc. **-ίζομαι**, Pass., = ῥιπίζομαι (perh. f.l. for it), Arist.*Pr.*$866^{a}$18. **-ικός**, ή, όν, *capable of throwing*, Simp.*in Ph.*1228.37. **-ός**, ή, όν, *thrown*, *cast*, *hurled*, ῥ. μόρος death *by throwing down* (a precipice), S.*Tr.*357. ⊛ **-ω**, also **ῥιπτέω**, and (in frequentat. sense) **ῥιπτάζω** (qq. v.):—Ion. Iterat. ῥίπτασκον Il.15.23, Od.11.592, -εσκον Nic.*Fr.*26: fut. ῥίψω Il.8.13, etc.: aor. ἔρριψα 23.842, etc. (ἔριψα Arion 18, Mosch.3.32, ἀπέριψα Pi.*P.*6.37), Ep. ῥῖψα Il.3.378; also 3 sg. aor. 2 ἔρρῐφε Opp.*C.*4.350: pf. ἔρριφα Lys.10.9:—**Med.**, aor. ῥίψαντο Man.6.10, ἀπο-ρίψασθαι Gal.16.146:—**Pass.**, fut. ῥιφθήσομαι (ἀπορ-) S.*Aj.*1019; ῥῐφήσομαι Lxx *Ez.*7.19, Plu.*CG*3 (v.l. in S. l.c.); 3 fut. ἐρρίψομαι Luc.*Merc.Cond.*17: aor. ἐρρίφθην A.*Supp.*484 (ἀπο-), E.*Andr.*10 (v.l.), Pl.*Lg.*944d; also ἐρρίφην [ῐ] E.*Hec.*335, *Fr.*489, Pl.*Lg.*944a, Sosith.3, etc.; poet. ἐρίφην *AP*12.234 (Strat.): pf. ἔρριμμαι Orac. ap.Hdt.1.62, E.*Med.*1404 (anap.), Ar.*Ec.*850, etc.; poet. redupl. ῥερίφθαι Pi.*Fr.*318, cf. *PMag.Par.*1.194,2039 (ἀπο-): plpf. ἔρριπτο Luc.*Nec.*17. [ῑ by nature, Hdn.Gr.2.10; freq. written with ει in later Inscrr. (cf. ῥιπτέω, καταρρίπτω) and Papyri, as Phld.*Ir.* p.38 W., (προσ-) *Rh.*2.94 S.; the Ep. aor. 1 is ῥῖψα, not ῥίψα: ῐ in fut. 2 and aor. 2 Pass.]:—*throw*, *cast*, *hurl*, σόλον, σφαῖραν, Il.23.842, Od.6.115; χερσί Pi.*P.*3.57; ῥ. ἀπὸ βηλοῦ Il.1.591, etc.; ἤ μιν ἑλὼν ῥίψω ἐς Τάρταρον 8.13, cf. A.*Pr.*1051 (anap.); ἐς τὸ δυστυχές Id.*Ch.*913; ἐς φλόγα S.*Tr.*695; ποτὶ νέφεα Od.11.592; χθονὶ ῥ. ἑαυτόν *throw* on the ground, S.*Tr.*790, cf. E.*IA*39 (anap.); ἐς ὕδωρ ψυχρόν Th.2.49: abs., ἐρριμμένος *prostrate*, ἐρριμμένους καὶ μεθύοντας Plb.5.48.2; ἔτι τῶν νεκρῶν..ἐρριμμένων ἐπὶ τῆς ἀγορᾶς *lying*, Plu.*Galb.*28; κλῶνας ἔχουσα ἐπὶ γῆς ἐρριμμένους Dsc.1.29, cf. 4.169; ἔρριπται νεκροῖς ὅμοια, of hibernating animals, Aët.16.67; τὰ μελίσσεια ἐν ἀγρῷ ἔριπται *have been deposited*, *PCair.Zen.*467.5 (iii B.C.); *cast* a net, ἔρριπται ὁ βόλος the cast *has been made*, Orac.ap.Hdt.1.62; αὐτοῦ χερμάδας..ἔρριπτον *threw* stones *at* him, E.*Ba.*1097, cf. *Cyc.*51 (lyr.); ῥ. τινὰ πρὸς πέτραν *throw* him against a rock, S.*Tr.*780; but κατὰ στύφλου πέτρας down from a rock, E.*IT*1430, cf. A.*Pr.*748; κατὰ κρημνῶν down a precipice, Th.7.44, Pl.*Lg.*944a (Pass.); ὠλένας πρὸς οὐρανόν E.*Hel.*1096. II. like ῥιπτάζω, ῥ. ἑωυτήν *toss* oneself *about*, as in a fever, Hp.*Mul.*1.2; ἐπὶ λαιὰ καὶ ἐπὶ δεξιὰ σαυτόν *AP*5.118 (Crin.): generally, *throw about*, πλοκάμους E.*IA*758, cf. *Ba.*150 (both lyr.); *winnow*, Gal.6.541. III. *cast out* of house or land, S.*OT*719, *Ph.*265, etc.; μὴ ῥιφθῶ κυσὶν πρόβλητος Id.*Aj.*830. IV. *throw off* or *away*, of arms, E.*El.*820; of clothes, Pl.*R.*474a, Lys.3.12; so ἔρριψε Πάγασος δεσπόταν *threw* him, Pi.*I.*7(6).44; esp. ῥ. ἀσπίδα (cf. ῥίψασπις), Lys.10.9, etc.; βιβλίον *PUniv.Giss.*20.12 (ii A.D.). V. ῥ. λόγους *cast* them *forth*, *hurl* them, A.*Pr.*314, E.*Alc.*680; τὸ προειρημένον ἀναποδείκτως ἐρρίφθαι Phld.*Rh.*1.57 S.; also, *throw* them *away*, *waste* them, A.*Ag.*1068, cf. E.*Med.*1404 (anap., Pass.); λόγοι μάτην ῥιφέντες Id.*Hec.*335; so οἴχεται..ταῦτ' ἐρριμμένα *set at naught*, S.*Aj.*1271. VI. ῥ. ἐπὶ πάντας τοὺς κλήρους, as in a scramble, Pl.*R.*617e; ῥ. πάντα κύβον κεφαλῆς ὕπερθεν ἐμῆς *AP*5.24 ([Phld.]): hence ῥ. κίνδυνον *make a bold throw*, *run a risk*, E.*Fr.*402.7. VII. ῥ. ἑαυτόν *throw* or *cast* oneself *down*, X.*Cyr.*3.1.25: abs., *fling oneself*, ἐς πόντον Thgn.176; ἐς ἅλμην E.*Cyc.*166; τάφρον ἐς κοίλην Id.*Alc.*897 (anap.); ῥ. ἐν πένθει κατὰ δρία Id.*Hel.*1325 (lyr.), cf. Men.312, Vett.Val.126.22; cf. βάλλω A. III. VIII. dub. l. in Orph.*Fr.*264.

⊛ **ῥίς**, ἡ, gen. ῥῑνός, acc. ῥῖνα, pl. ῥῖνες:—*nose* or *snout* of men and beasts, Il.5.291, Od.4.445, Hdt.3.154, Ar.*Pax* 21, Pl.*Prt.*329d, etc.; ἕλκειν τινὰ τῆς ῥινός lead him by the *nose*, Luc.*Herm.*73; ἕλκεσθαι τῆς ῥ. ib.68; μὴ τὴν χολὴν ἐπὶ ῥινὸς ἔχ' εὐθύς Herod.6.37. 2. in pl. *nostrils*, but freq., like Lat. *nares*, *nose*, Il.16.503, Od.5.456, al., Hes.*Sc.*267, S.*Aj.*918, Ar.*Nu.*344, etc.; στόμα τε ῥῖνές τε Il.14.467, cf. 23.395, al., Pl.*Ti.*79e. II. prob. *brow* of a hill or projecting *spur of land*, *IG*14.352 ii 36, al. (Halaesa).—A later nom. form is **ῥίν**, Hp.*Vict.*1.23 (prob. f.l. for ῥῖνες), Aret.*CA*1.2, Luc.*Asin.*12; as name of a bandage, Sor.*Fasc.*11. [ῑ, but ῐ in *AP*11.418 (Trajan).]

**ῥισῆς**, ὁ, *superintendent of the lake*, title of Egyptian priest, *Sammelb.*5231.2 (i A.D.), al.; also ⊛ **ῥισηγέτης**, ου, ὁ, ibid.

⊛ **ῥίσκος**, ὁ, *coffer*, *chest*, esp. for plate or money, Antiph.130, Phylarch.10 J., Posidipp.10, Phleg.*Fr.*36.1 J., *PLond.ined.*2312.11, *PSI* 4.428.45, cf. 411 (both iii B.C.), Phot.; *travelling-trunk*, *portmanteau*, *PCair.Zen.*92.1 (iii B.C.). II. *sarcophagus*, *IG*14.1934 *f* 3. III. ῥίσκοι· εἶδός τι μυῶν, Hsch. (Phrygian word acc. to Donat. ad Ter. *Eun.*754.)

⊛ **ῥισκο-φῠλάκιον** [ᾰ], τό, *treasury*, Aristeas 80. **-φύλαξ** [ῠ], ᾰκος, ὁ, *treasurer*, ῥ. ἐν Περγάμῳ *Sardis* 7(1).4 (ii B.C.), cf. Aristeas 33.

**ῥῐφή**, ἡ, = ῥῖμμα and ῥῖψις, Lyc.235,1326.

**ῥίψ**, ῥῑπός, ἡ (later also ὁ, Arist.*Pr.*$911^{b}$11), *plaited work* of osiers or rushes, *wicker-work*, *mat*, φράξε δέ μιν [σχεδίην] ῥίπεσσι διαμπερὲς οἰσυΐνῃσι, κύματος εἶλαρ ἔμεν, evidently as a kind of *bulwark* (cf. παράρρυμα), Od.5.256; ῥιψὶ καταστεγάζειν Hdt.4.71; πάρεξις ῥιπῶν *SIG*57.32 (Milet., v B.C.): prov., θεοῦ θέλοντος κἂν ἐπὶ ῥιπὸς πλέοις E.*Fr.*397, cf. Ar.*Pax* 699, Luc.*Herm.*28, Favorin. in *PVat.*11.7.27; cf. ῥῖπος.

**ῥιψ-ασπία**, ἡ, (ῥίπτω, ἀσπίς) *throwing away of the shield*, Sch. Hermog. in Rh.4.253 W. **-άσπῐδος**, ον, = sq., χείρ Eup.*Oxy.*1087.46. ⊛ **-ασπις**, ιδος, ὁ, ἡ, *throwing away one's shield in battle*, *craven*, Ar.*Nu.*353, *Pax* 1186, Pl.*Lg.*944b. **-αύχην**, ενος, ὁ, ἡ, *tossing the neck* (or *head*), properly of horses: metaph., ῥιψαύχενι σὺν κλόνῳ Pi.*Dith.Oxy.*1604 ii 13.

**ῥῖψις**, εως, ἡ, *throwing*, *hurling*, τοξικὴ καὶ πᾶσα ῥ. Pl.*Lg.*813e, cf. Arist.*Ph.*$243^{a}$20, $257^{a}$3, Str.6.1.1. 2. pl., *glances*, ῥίψεις ὀμμάτων Plu.*Sull.*35; but ῥῖψις ὄμματος *drooping* of eyelid, read by Gal.(17(1).895) for ἔρριψις in Hp.*Epid.*6.1.5. II. *being thrown* or *hurled*, Ἡφαίστου ῥίψεις ὑπὸ πατρός Pl.*R.*378d; ῥ. καὶ πτῶσις οὐρανίων σωμάτων Plu.*Lys.*12; *throwing oneself*, ῥίψεις ἐπὶ πρόσωπον Id.2.166a.

**ῥιψοκινδῡν-ευσία**, ἡ, *fool-hardiness*, Ptol.*Tetr.*182. **-έω**, *to be fool-hardy*, Hp.*Ep.*17, D.C.66.8. **-ία**, ἡ, = -ευσία, *Cat.Cod.Astr.*2.173. **-ος**, ον, *fool-hardy*, *reckless*, ἔργον X.*Mem.*1.3.9; ναυτιλία Alciphr.1.3; of persons, Id.3.52, Poll.1.179; τὸ ῥ. Ph.1.326, App.*BC*5.84. Adv. -νως ib.1.103, *POxy.*2131.16 (iii A.D., ῥειψ-).

**ῥιψολογέω**, *utter rashly*, Plb.12.8.5, 32.2.8.

**ῥίψ-οπλος**, ον, *throwing away one's arms*, ἄτη ῥ., of a panic flight, A.*Th.*315. **-οφθαλμία**, ἡ, = ταχυτὴς περὶ τὸ ἰδεῖν τὸ ποθούμενον, *Stoic.*3.97. ⊛ **-όφθαλμος**, ον, *casting the eyes about*, Ptol.*Tetr.*164, 171.

⊛ **ῥόα**, ἡ, Ion. and Ep. **ῥοιή**; later **ῥοιά**, Arist.*Col.*$796^{a}$21, *Pr.*$923^{b}$25, al., Thphr.*HP*1.6.3, al., *PHib.*1.121.57 (iii B.C.), Gal.6.605:—*pomegranate-tree*, *Punica Granatum*, Od.7.115, *IG*11(2).287 *A* 147 (ῥοαν), 155 (ῥοην) (Delos, iii B.C.). II. the fruit, *pomegranate*, *h.Cer.*372, 412, A.*Fr.*363, Ar.*V.*1268, Hermipp.36, Pl.*Lg.*845b, Thphr.*HP*7.13.4, *IG*11(2).161 *B* 44 (Delos, iii B.C.), Dsc.1.110. 2. *knob shaped like a pomegranate*, ῥοιαὶ χρύσεαι, ἀργύρεαι, Hdt.7.41; *tassel* of like shape, = ῥοΐσκος, Lxx 3*Ki.*7.18, J.*AJ*3.7.4, *BJ*5.5.7.—Cf. σίδη. [Both ῥοά and ῥοιά are oxyt. acc. to Hdn.Gr.1.301, 2.271.]

**ῥοά**, ἡ, Dor. for ῥοή (q.v.).

**ῥοάς**, άδος, ἡ, (ῥέω) *shedding of fruit*, a disease of vines, f.l. for ῥυάς, Thphr.*HP*4.14.6.

**ῥόβα**, ἡ, *dress*, *garment*, ῥάπτης ῥοβον (i.e. ῥοβῶν) *MAMA*3.581 (Corycus). (Cf. French *robe*.)

**ῥοβδεῖ**· ἀναρριπτεῖ μετ' ἤχους, Hsch. (cf. ῥοιβδέω). **ῥόβιλλος**· βασιλίσκος ὄρνις, Id. **ῥοβλεῖ**· ῥοφεῖ, πνεῖ, Id. **ῥοβοπώλης**, v. ῥωποπώλης. **ῥόγαν**· τὸν φονέα, τὸν αὐτόχειρα, Id. **ῥόγαν**· ῥῶγα, Id. **ῥογεῖ**· ὀργᾷ, ἀκμάζει, δαμάζει, Id.

**ῥογεύς**, έως, ὁ, *dyer*, *IG*5(1).209.27 (Sparta), Hsch.; cf. ῥεγεύς, ῥέζω (B).

**ῥογή**, ἡ, = ῥογίον, Ps.-Democr.Alch.p.55 B.

**ῥογία**· ἀκέστρια, Hsch.

**ῥογίον**, τό, *receiver* of a still, Zos.Alch.p.142 B.

**ῥογκιάω**, = ῥέγκω, Dor. inf. ῥογκιῆν Epich.197.

**ῥογμός**, v. ῥωχμός.

**ῥογός**, ὁ, in Sicily and Magna Graecia, *granary, barn*, Epich.22, *Tab.Heracl.*1.102, Hsch. (Cf. Lat. *rogus.*)

**ῥογχάζω**, = ῥυγχιάζω, Hsch. s.h.v. 2. = *runcino, Gloss.*

**ῥογχᾰλίζω**, *snore*, Gloss. ad Theoc.6.30, *Gloss.*

**ῥογχασμός**, ὁ, = ῥέγχος, Gal.10.467 (pl.).

**ῥογχαστής**, οῦ, ὁ, = *nasator, Gloss.*

**ῥογχός**, v. ῥωχμός.

**ῥοδ-άκανθα**, ἡ, *wild rose, Gloss.* **-ἀκινον**, τό, *nectarine*, Alex. Trall.7.1, *Febr.*1; also **ῥοδακινέα** Id.*Verm.*(2 p.595 P.). **-ᾰλός**, ή, όν, = ῥόδινος, παρειαί Opp.*C.*1.501. **-αμνος**, v. ῥόδαμνος.

**ῥοδάν-η** [ᾰ], ἡ, (ῥοδανός) like κρόκη, *spun thread, woof* or *weft*, Batr. 183, cf. Eust.1527.60, Sch.Ar.*V.*1137, etc.; Hsch. gives ῥαδάνη, but (s.v. τολύπη) ῥοδάνη. **-ίζω**, = τὸ συνεχῶς τὴν κρόκην τινάσσειν, Sch. B Il.18.576, cf. Eust.1527.60; **ῥαδανίζω**, Id.1165.22, cf. Heracleon ap.*EM*702.8, Hsch. (Pass.). **-ιστήριον**, τό, = *tramarium, Gloss.*

**ῥοδᾰνός**, ή, όν, perh. *wavering, flickering*, παρὰ ῥοδανὸν δονακῆα Il. 18.576:—this is the reading of most codd., but ancient critics differed as to the form; Zenod. gave διὰ ῥαδαλόν (which he derived from κραδαλόν); the reading of Aristoph. and Aristarch. is uncertain, perh. παρὰ ῥαδινόν, v. Sch. ad loc.; cf. also ῥαδινός (Apollon. *Lex.*, who reads ῥαδινόν, absurdly interprets as λεπτόν, οἱονεὶ ῥαδονόν, παρὰ τὸ ῥᾳδίως δονεῖσθαι).

**ῥοδ-άριον**, τό, Dim. of ῥόδον, as an ornament, *BGU*781 iii 19 (pl., i A.D.); cj. for ῥοιδάριον in Hsch. s.v. ἄφυκα. **-έα**, ἡ, contr. ῥοδῆ (q.v.). **-ειος**, ον, = sq., Suid. ❀ **-εος**, α, ον, *of roses*, ἄνθεα, πέταλα, Ibyc.5, E.*Med.*841 (lyr.), *Hel.*244 (lyr.); λίπος Nic.*Al.* 155. II. *like a rose, rosy*, σταφυλή *AP*6.102 (Phil.); μαζοί Nonn.*D.* 9.296. **-εών**, ῶνος, ὁ, *rose-bed*, *BGU*1119.11 (i B.C.), *Anacreont. App.*2.57 p.353 Bgk. (Constant. Sic.). **-ῆ**, ἡ, contr. for ῥοδέη = ῥοδέα, *rose-bush*, Archil.29, Asclep.Myrl.ap.Ath.2.50e, Pamphil.ib. 52f; Ion. ῥοδέη A.R.3.1020 (but v. ῥόδον init.).

**ῥοδία**, v. Ῥόδιος. II. **ῥοδιή**, ἡ, = ῥοδεών, *Schwyzer* 719.9 (Theb. ad Mycalen, iv B.C.).

**Ῥοδιᾰκός**, ή, όν, *of Rhodes*, Str.2.5.14:—Ῥοδιακόν (sc. σκύφος), τό, *a kind of cup made at Rhodes*, Epig.5, Diph.5, *IG*11(2).110.21,27 (Delos, iii B.C.), etc.; also called Ῥοδιακὴ χυτρίς, Arist.*Fr.*110; **Ῥοδιακή** alone, *IG*11(2).110, al. (Delos, iii B.C.), 7.3498.6 (Orop.); and **Ῥοδιάς**, άδος, ἡ, Ath.11.496e, Phot.

❀ **ῥοδίζω**, (ῥόδον) *to be like the rose*, Ath.15.677e; τῇ ὀσμῇ Dsc.1.13; in colour, *Gp.*14.16.2. II. trans., *scent with roses*, τὰς συνθέσεις Thphr.*Od.*47; τὸ δέρμα Alex.Aphr.*Pr.*1.12. 2. *deck* a person's grave *with roses*, *BCH*24.415 (Bithynia):—Pass., *to have one's grave decked with roses*, *CIG*3754 (Nicaea).

❀ **ῥοδῖνοπορφῠροῦς**, ᾶ, οῦν, *rose-purple*, *Stud.Pal.*20.245.11 (vi A.D.).

❀ **ῥόδῐνος**, η, ον, (ῥόδον) *made of* or *from roses*, στέφανος Anacr.83; ἄλειφα Hippon.58; μύρον Cephisod.3; μύρον is understood in Thphr. *Od.*25, al., *PPetr.*2 p.114 (iii B.C.), Dsc.1.43; sc. ἔλαιον, *Edict.Diocl. Delph.*6, *SIG*1172.8 (Lebena). II. *pink*, *POxy.*496.4 (ii A.D.), *Cod.Just.*11.9.3, etc.

**Ῥόδιος**, α, ον, (Ῥόδος) *Rhodian, of* or *from Rhodes*, Il.2.654, etc.; Ῥ. τέχνη the art of *painting*, *Anacreont.*15.3; ἡ Ῥ. (sc. χώρα) Str.2. 4.3, etc.; ῥ. (sc. δραχμή) *Rhodian drachma*, Roussel *Cultes Égyptiens* p.236 (Delos, ii B.C.), *Inscr.Délos* 442 *B* 204 (pl., ii B.C.): **Ῥόδια**, τά, a kind of shoes, Hsch.: **Ῥόδιον**, τό, sc. μέτρον, *Ostr.Bodl.* iii 369, *Ostr. Strassb.*615–617 (ii A.D.), *Ostr.*i p.765:—cf. Ῥοδιακός.

**ῥοδ-ίς**, ίδος, ἡ, *pastille made from roses*, Dsc.1.90.3, Damocr.ap.Gal. 14.133. **-ίσια**, τά, = sq., *Jahresh.*26 *Beibl.*17 (Ephesus). ❀ **-ισμός**, ὁ, *ceremony at which graves were decked with roses*, *Inscr.Perg.*374 *B* 8 (ii A.D.), *Supp.Epigr.*1.330 *B* 8 (Istria, ii A.D.), *BCH*24.425 (Bithynia). **-ίτης** [ῑ] οἶνος, ὁ, wine *flavoured with roses*, Dsc.5.27, *Gp.*8.2 tit. **-ῖτις**, ιδος, ἡ, name of a gem, Plin.*HN*37.191.

**ῥοδο-βᾰφής**, ές, *rose-coloured*, *PHolm.*19.31. ❀ **-δάκτῠλος**, ον, Aeol. **βροδοδάκτυλος** (q.v.), *rosy-fingered*, as epith. of Ἠώς in Hom. and Hes., Od.2.1, Hes.*Op.*610, etc.; Ἰνάχου ῥοδοδάκτυλος κόρα B.18. 18; Κύπρις Coluth.99. **-δάφνη**, ἡ, *rose-laurel*, i.e. prob. *Nerium Oleander*, or perh. *rhododendron*, Dsc.4.81, cf. Plin.*HN*16.79, Luc. *Asin.*17, *Pseudol.*27, Artem.1.77, 2.25. **-δενδρον**, τό, = foreg., Dsc.4.81, Plin.*HN*16.79. **-ειδής**, ές, *rose-like, rosy*, Musae.114, *AP*15.40.18 (Cometas); χιτών f.l. for ῥαγοειδής in Poll.2.70; -ές, τό, name of a remedy for nose-bleeding, Orib.*Fr.*15. ❀ **-εις**, εσσα, εν, *of roses*, ἔλαιον Il.23.186; ἄνθεα E.*IA*1298 (lyr.); ῥ. χάρις *as of roses*, *AP*5.80 (Dionys.), cf. Dsc. in *PLit.Lond.*99.6. 2. ἐπὶ ῥοδόεντι Λυκόρμᾳ on the *rose-clad* banks of L., B.15.34. II. *rose-coloured*, εἴρια *AP*6.250 (Antiphil.). **-κολπος**, ον, *rosy-bosomed*, Εὐνομία *Lyr.Adesp.*140. **-μᾶλον**, v. ῥοδόμηλον. **-μελι**, ιτος, τό, *rose-honey*, Dsc.5.27, Philagr.ap.Orib.5.17.5, *Edict Diocl.Delph.*14, Aët.3.104. **-μηλον**, Dor. **-μᾶλον**, τό, *rose-apple*: metaph. of *a plump rosy cheek*, Theoc.23.8 (ῥοδομάλλον codd., ῥόδα μάλων Ahrens). II. *a confection of roses and quinces*, Alex.Trall.1.10.

❀ **ῥόδον**, τό, metaplast. dat. pl. ῥοδέεσσι v.l. in A.R.3.1020:—*rose*, first in *h.Cer.*6, cf. Thgn.537, Pi.*I.*4(3).18(36), Hdt.8.138, *IG*1².289; Aeol. **βρόδον** (q.v.); mostly of *Rosa gallica, red rose*, Thphr.*HP*6.6. 4, etc.; ῥ. ἑκατοντάφυλλον, *Rosa centifolia, cabbage rose*, ibid.; ῥ. ἄγριον, *Rosa dumetorum, wild rose*, ib.6.2.1: metaph., ῥόδα μ' εἴρηκας you've spoken *roses* of me, have said *all things sweet and beautiful*, Ar.*Nu.*910; πάττε πολλοῖς τοῖς ῥόδοις ib.1330: prov., ὗς διὰ ῥόδων 'a bull in a china shop', Crates Com.4. 2. = ῥοδωνιά, Coluth.348. II. **Ῥόδα**, τά, = ῥοδισμός, *Rev.Hist.Rel.*97.275 (Bulgaria). III. *pudenda muliebria*, Pherecr.108.29.

**ῥοδό-πεπλος**, ον, *with roseate veil* or *robe*, Q.S.3.608. **-πηχυς**, Dor. etc. **-πᾶχυς**, Aeol. **βροδόπαχυς** (q.v.), υ, gen. εος, *rosy-armed*, *h.Hom.*31.6, Hes.*Th.*246,251, B.12.96, Theoc.2.148, *Anacreont.*53. 21. **-πῐτῠΐνη**, ἡ, *rose-pine resin*, *Hippiatr.*35. **-πνοος**, ον, *breathing of roses*, Ephipp.26. **-πῡγος**, ον, *rosy-rumped*, *AP*5.54 (Diosc.). **-πώλης**, ου, ὁ, *rose-seller, Gloss.*

❀ **Ῥόδος**, ἡ, the island (also the city) of *Rhodes*, Il.2.654, etc.

❀ **Ῥοδοσκάρφα**, title of a deity in Cyprus, *Berl.Sitzb.*1911.639 (Rantidi); cf. σκαρφάσθαι.

**ῥοδό-σταγμα**, ατος, τό, (στάζω) *extract of roses prepared with honey*, like ῥοδόμελι, Sch.Ar.*Pl.*529; also **-στακτον**, τό, Paul.Aeg.7. 15. **-στερνος**, ον, *with rosy breast*, epith. of Isis, *CIG*5115 (Nubia). **-στεφής**, ές, (στέφω) *rose-crowned*, Nonn.*D.*48. 681. **-σφῠρος**, ον, *rosy-ankled*, Q.S.1.138; Χάριτες Him.*Or.*1. 19; Ἀντολίη *PMag.Berol.*2.93.

**ῥοδουντία**, ἡ, *dish flavoured with roses*, Ath.9.403d; cf. ῥοδωνιά IV.

**ῥοδο-φεριστής**, οῦ, ὁ, dub. sens. in *PRyl.*224(*a*)Intr. (ii A.D.). **-φόρια**, τά, = ῥοδισμός, prob. in *Supp.Epigr.*2.432 (Macedonia, iii A.D.). **-φόρος**, ον, *bearing roses*, name of Ptolemaïs (Acre), Lxx 3*Ma.*7.17 (v.l. -φόνος); dub. sens. in *Sammelb.*4425 v 6 (ii A.D.). **-φυλλον**, τό, *rose-leaf*, v.l. in Paul.Aeg.3.66. **-χειρ**, χειρος, ὁ, ἡ, = ῥοδόπηχυς, Sch.Theoc.2.148. **-χροος**, ον, contr. **-χρους**, ουν, (χρόα) *rose-coloured*, *AP*5.55 (Diosc.), Dsc.1.111, 2.106, Opp.*H.*1. 130, *Anacreont.*53.22. **-χρως**, ωτος, ὁ, ἡ, = foreg., Theoc.18.31.

**ῥοδ-ών**, ῶνος, ὁ, *rose-bed*, *AP*5.35 (Rufin.), *POxy.*729.32 (ii A.D.). II. pl. ῥοδῶνες, = ἄνεμοι ὀρνιθίαι, λευκόνοτοι, at Alexandria, Olymp. *in Mete.*177.21. **-ωνιά**, ἡ, *rose-bed, garden of roses*, Hecat. 37 J., D.53.16, etc.; *the rose*, Thphr.*HP*2.2.1, 6.1.1, Ael.*NA*14. 24. II. *vine with rose-coloured grapes*, Phot. III. = ῥοδοδάφνη, Id., *AB*299. IV. = ῥοδουντία, Aemilian.ap.Ath.9.406a. V. = ῥόδον III, Cratin.109. VI. gloss on Ἀφροδίτης ἀκάνθη (sic), prob. = ῥοδάκανθα, Cyran.27. **-ωπός**, όν, (ὤψ) *rosy-faced, rosy*, Dsc.5. 113; poet. fem. **ῥοδῶπις**, ιδος, Nonn.*D.*10.176. **-ωτός**, ή, όν, as if from ῥοδόω: τὸ ῥ. *rose-water, Gloss.*

**ῥοείδιον**, τό, Dim. of ῥόος, *conduit* or *brook*, *IG*14.352 i 36, al. (Halaesa).

**ῥόζω**, = ῥύζω, *snarl*, of dogs: metaph. of men, Phot., Suid.

**ῥοή**, ἡ, Dor. **ῥοά** (dat. pl. ῥhoϝαῖσι, *IG*9(1).868 (Corc., vii/vi B.C.)), (ῥέω) *river, stream*, freq. in Hom., always in pl., and mostly with gen. added, ἐπ' Ὠκεανοῖο ῥοάων Il.3.5; Μαιάνδρου τε ῥοάς 2.869; ποταμοῖο ῥοῇσι Od.6.216; ὕδατος καλῇσι ῥ. Il.16.229, cf. *Schwyzer* 289.107 (Priene, ii B.C.); Ὠκεανοῦ ῥ. Hes.*Th.*841; also Σκαμάνδριοι ῥ. S.*Aj.* 419 (lyr.); τεναγέων ῥ. Pi.*N.*3.25; ἀμπέλου ῥ. *the juice* of the grape, E.*Cyc.*123; μέλιτος Id.*Ba.*711; αἵματος Id.*Supp.*690: rarely in sg., παρ' Ἰσμηνοῦ ῥοάν Pi.*N.*11.36 codd. (but ῥοαῖν is prob.); ἀμπέλου ῥοή E.*Ba.*281: in Dor. Prose, *SIG*1183 (Gort.): metaph., *stream* of song or poesy, ῥοαὶ Μοισᾶν, ἐπέων, Pi.*N.*7.12, *I.*7(6).19; ἡ διὰ τοῦ στόματος ῥ. Pl.*Tht.*206d; προμαθείας ῥοαί Pi.*N.*11.46; also ῥοαί *streams of events, tide of affairs*, Id.*O.*2.33. 2. *flowing* of sap, Thphr.*CP*1. 13.5 (pl.). 3. *flux*, as a philosoph. term, Pl.*Tht.*152e, v. *Cra.* 402a; cf. ῥέω I.5. Cf. ῥόος II, ῥοία I.

**ῥοητόκος**, ον, *producing streams*, Jo.Gaz.*Ecphr.*2.311.

**ῥοθ-έω**, (ῥόθος) *make a rushing noise*: hence, of a *roaring* fire, ἐν ῥοθοῦντι κριβάνῳ A.*Fr.*309. 2. of any confused *noise*, ταῦτα.. ἐρρόθουν ἐμοί such *clamours they raised* against me, S.*Ant.*290; λόγοι ..ἐρρόθουν κακοί *there was a noise of* angry words, ib.259. **-ιάζω**, strengthd. form of foreg., *ply the dashing oar*, Cratin.345, Hermipp. 54; also of the ship, ἐκ πιτύλων ῥ. Ar.*Fr.*84. 2. of pigs eating, *make a guttling noise*, Id.*Ach.*807; cf. ῥόθιος I. 2. **-ιάς**, άδος, ἡ, poet. fem. of ῥόθιος, *dashing*, κώπη A.*Pers.*396. **-ιον**, τό, v. sq. II. **-ιος**, ον, also α, ον *AP*9.32, 10.2 (Antip.Sid.):—*rushing, roaring, dashing*, esp. of waves, ἀμφὶ δὲ κῦμα βέβρυχεν ῥόθιον Od.5.412; of oars, ῥ. πλᾶται E.*IT*1133 (lyr.); of a ship *dashing through the waves*, *AP*10.2 (Antip. Sid.); μετὰ ῥοθίου βίας Arist.*Mu.*396ᵃ14: metaph. of an orator, Poll.6.147; of a horse, J.*BJ*6.2.8. Adv. -ίως Poll.4.24 codd., Vett.Val.345.33. 2. of fishes, *guttling*, Numen.ap.Ath.7.306d; cf. ῥοθιάζω 2. 3. *swift*, πόδες Leonid.*Oxy.*662.45. II. Subst. ῥόθια, τά, *waves dashing on the beach, breakers, waves*, S.*Ph.*688 (lyr.); ἀνέμων εὐαέσσιν ῥοθίοις E.*Fr.*773.36 (lyr.); cf. οὐτιδανός II; and collectively in sg., *surf, surge*, A.*Pr.*1048 (anap.), E.*IT*426 (lyr.), Th.4.10: esp. of *the dash and sound of oars*, ῥοθίοις..κώπας E.*IT*407 (κώπαις codd., lyr.), cf. *Cyc.*17; so in sg., Th. l. c. (acc. to Sch.), Hyp.*Fr.*157, Str.15.2.12, D.S.13.99, etc.; γλυκερὰ ῥ., of wine, *AP*11.64 (Agath.): generally, of *rushing, dashing motion*, τῆς ἵππου τὸ ῥ. ἀνέχεσθαι D.H. 6.10, cf. Arr.*Frr.*164, 165 J.; so τῆς ὁρμῆς, τοῦ θυμοῦ, Luc.*Tox.*19,55: metaph., ἀοιδᾶν ῥόθια Pi.*Pae.*6.129; ῥοθ[ίῳ τινὶ] ἥκω τύχης prob. in Men. *Pk.*353. 2. *loud shout*, esp. of applause, ῥ. αἴρεσθαί τινι Ar.*Eq.*546: generally, *tumult, riot*, ἐχώρει ῥ. ἐν πόλει κακόν E.*Andr.*1096. **-ιότης**, ητος, ἡ, *impetuosity, vehemence*, of language, v.l. in Poll.4.22.

**ῥοθοπῡγ-ίζω**, **-ισμός**, v. ῥαθαπυγίζω.

**ῥόθος**, ὁ, *rushing noise, roar of waves, dash of oars*, ἐξ ἑνὸς ῥ. with one *stroke*, i.e. all at once, A.*Pers.*462. 2. of any confused, inarticulate sound, Περσίδος γλώσσης ῥ. the *noise* of the Persian (i.e. barbarian) tongue, ib.406; τῆς δὲ Δίκης ῥ. ἑλκομένης, ᾗ κ' ἄνδρες ἄγωσι δωροφάγοι but there is *tumult* or *confusion*, when Justice is dragged whithersoever bribed judges lead her, Hes.*Op.*220. 3. of any *rushing motion*, πτερύγων ῥ. Opp.*H.*5.17. 4. Boeot., = *mountain path*, Plu. *in Hes.*13; αἰγὸς ῥ. a goat-*track*, Nic.*Th.*672.

**ῥοία**, ἡ, (ῥέω) *flow*, *flux*, Hp.*Loc.Hom.*9(pl.). II. = κυλίστρα τῶν ἵππων παρὰ τῷ ποταμῷ καὶ ψάμμῳ, Hsch. (cf. ῥοαί·..ἱππόδρομος, Id.).

**ῥοιά**, ἡ, later Att. for ῥόα. **ῥοίαγξ**· φάραγξ, Hsch. **ῥοιαδικός**, v. ῥυαδικός.

**ῥοιάς**, άδος, ἡ, v.l. for ῥυάς III. 2, Gal.*UP*10.11. II. *corn poppy*, *Papaver Rhoeas*, Thphr.*HP*9.12.4, Dsc.4.64.

**ῥοιβδ-έω**, *move with a whistling* or *rustling sound*, ῥοιβδοῦσα κόλπον αἰγίδος *letting* the swelling aegis *rustle* (as she flies), A.*Eu.*404: intr., of wind, *whistle*, ῥοιβδήσας Εὖρος *AP*7.636 (Crin.). II. *suck down*, of Charybdis, Od.12.106; κῦμα δ' ἐρροίβδει μέγα σύνεγγυς ἡμῶν Ezek.*Exag.*237, cf. Aristid.*Or.*46(3).38. 2. *cause to gush forth*, ὅταν..κρηναῖον ἐξ ἄμμοιο -ήσῃ γάνος Lyc.247. (In signf. II ῥυβδέω shd. perh. be written, cf. ἀναρροιβδέω; signf. I is found also in ἀπορροιβδέω, ἐπιρροιβδέω.) **-ηδόν**, = ῥοιζηδόν, Q.S.5.381; also **ῥοίβδειν** (sic), Phot.; cf. ῥύβδην. **-ημα**, ατος, τό, *rustling sound*, S.*Ichn.*107. **-ησις**, εως, ἡ, *whistling*, *piping*, βουκόλων E.*IA*1086 (pl., lyr.).

**ῥοῖβδος**, ὁ, *any rushing noise* or *motion*, πτερῶν ῥ. *whirring* of wings, S.*Ant.*1004; [ἀνέμου] ῥ. καὶ ῥύμη *rushing* of the wind, Ar.*Nu.*407. (Cogn. with ῥοῖζος.)

**ῥοιβδῳδέω**, 3 sg. pres. ῥοιβδῳδεῖ, glossed μετὰ ῥοίζου σαλεύει, ᾀδεῖ (sic), Theognost.*Can.*24; ῥοιβδῳδεῖ (-ώδει cod.)· μετὰ ἤχου ᾄδει (ἀηδεῖ cod.) ὡς οἱ ποιμένες, Hsch. **⟨ῥο⟩ιδαμός**· ὁ ἀσπάραγος, Id.

**ῥοιδάριον** or **ῥοϊδάριον**, τό, a cosmetic (*rouge*?) containing ἄγχουσα, Aët.2.68, dub. in Hsch. s.v. ἄφυκα (v. ῥοδάριον); cj. in Orib.*Fr.*15.

⊛ **ῥοΐδιον**, τό, Dim. of ῥοιά, ῥόα, *small pomegranate*, Men.146, *POxy.*1757.11 (ii A.D., written ῥοΰδιον). 2. *rind of pomegranate*, *Gloss.*

**ῥοιδμός**· ποιὸς ψόφος, Hsch. **ῥοίδνας**· δάκνας, and **ῥοιλιαῖς**· δάκναις, Id.

**ῥοιζ-αῖος**, α, ον, = ῥοιζήεις, *Orac.Chald.*300. ⊛ **-έω**, Ion. and Ep. impf. ῥοίζεσκε Hes.*Th.*835: aor. ἐρροίζησα Opp. (v. infr.), Ep. ῥοίζησα Il.10.502:—**Pass.**, v. infr.: (ῥοῖζος):—*whistle*, Il. l.c.; of a snake, *hiss*, Hes. l.c., A.R.4.129, etc.; ἑὸν νόμον ἐρροίζησε Opp.*H.*1.563; of birds, *rush* or *whirr through the air*, Luc.*Am.*22, cf. Arist.*HA*$535^{b}$27: in late Prose, *shoot an arrow*, Lxx 4*Ki.*13.17 (cod. A); of a stream, ib.*Ca.*4.15:—so in Pass., ἰῶν τηλόθεν ῥοιζουμένων Lyc.1426, cf. 1325, Orac. in *App.Anth.*6.140.10; τάχ' ἂν ἐρροίζητο δι' αἰθέρος *AP*11.106 (Lucill.); of a stream, *Orac.Chald.*109. **-ηδά**, Adv. *with rushing sound* or *motion*, Nic.*Al.*182,498; also **-ηδόν**, Id.*Th.*556, Lyc.66, 2*Ep.Pet.*3.10, Aesop.30, Aret.*CA*1.7. **-ήεις**, εσσα, εν, *whizzing*, *rushing*, λόγχας ἀκωκή *IG*12(7).115.7 (Amorgos, ii/i B.C.); συριγμός Nonn.*D.*6.191. **-ημα**, ατος, τό, *rushing*, *whirring noise* or *motion*, as of birds, Ar.*Av.*1182 (pl.), cf. Luc.*Musc.Enc.*2; στεροπᾶς Id.*JTr.*1; of the planetary spheres, Iamb.*VP*15.65 (pl.); τραγικῷ -ήματι ῥήξατο φωνήν *AP*5.221 (Agath.). **-ησις**, εως, ἡ, *whizzing*, *hurtling*, *Theol.Ar.*37; *shot* of an arrow, Aq.*Ex.*19.13. ⊛ **-ήτωρ**, ορος, ὁ, ἡ, *one who moves with a rushing sound*, Orph.*H.*6.5, 8.6. **-ος**, ὁ, Ion. ἡ, *whistling* or *whizzing* of an arrow, Il.16.361, cf. Plu.*Marc.*15, Onos.19.3, etc.; of a scourge, Opp.*H.*2.352: any *whistling* or *piping sound*, as of a shepherd, πολλῇ ῥ. Od.9.315; πνευμάτων ῥ. Plu.2.18c; *rush* of wings, Lxx *Wi.*5.11, Ael.*NA*2.26; of a stream, Lxx *Ez.*47.5, Ael.*NA*17.17; of the sea, *Hymn.Is.*150; of the *noise* of a falling tree, Q.S.1.251; *hissing* of a serpent, A.R.4.138, 1543; used of the sound made by filing, Arist.*Aud.*$802^{a}$39; of the letter ρ, Phld.*Po.Herc.*994.29, D.H.*Comp.*14, S.E.*M.*1.102. II. *rushing motion*, *rush*, *swing*, Plu.*Marc.*15, *Demetr.*21, Epic. in *Arch.Pap.*7 p.4. **-όω**, = ῥοιζέω, Hsch.; also **ῥοίζομαι**, Iamb.*Myst.*3.2 (codd.), 3.9 (as v.l. for ῥοιζουμένας).

**ῥοΐζω** ἵππον, (ῥοή) *water a horse*, *ride* him *in a pond*, ῥοΐσαντα εἰς ὕδωρ γλυκύ *Hippiatr.*87.—The form ῥοϊζομένους is dub.l. in Str.14.5.12.

**ῥοιζώδης**, ες, *like* or *with a rushing noise*, of the pulse, Archig.ap. Gal.8.647; of emission of breath, Id.5.231: τὸ ῥ. *rapid*, *whizzing motion*, Plu.2.923c.

**ῥοιή**, v. ῥόα.

**ῥοικοειδής**, ές, *crooked-looking*, Gal.18(1).537; cf. ῥαιβοειδής.

**ῥοικός**, ή, όν, *crooked*, κορύνα, λαγωβόλον, Theoc.7.18, 4.49; περὶ κνήμας ῥοικός *bow*-legged, Archil.58.4 (v. l. ῥαιβός, q.v.); ῥ. μηροί Hp.*Mochl.*22; τὸ ῥ. *curvature* of the leg, Arist.*SE*$181^{b}$38.—Ion. word, acc. to *EM*242.2 (cod. Leid., where ῥυκός).

**ῥοϊκός**, ή, όν, (ῥέω, ῥόος) *fluid*: hence, *flabby*, σώματα Hp.*Aër.*20. II. *suffering from a flux*, of women, Dsc.1.68.5 (leg. -καῖς), 5.34, al.; γυναῖκες ῥ. Id.1.117.

**ῥοικώδης**, ες, = ῥοικοειδής, ὀστέα Hp.*Mochl.*30 (f.l. for ῥοιώδης, cf. ῥοώδεα ὀστέα ap.Erot.); = γαῦσος καὶ στρεβλός, Hp. (*Art.*86) ap.Erot. (ῥοιώδη codd. Hp., v. ῥοιώδης).

**ῥοιλιαῖς**, v. ῥοίδνας.

**ῥόϊνος**, η, ον, *of the* ῥόα, *of pomegranate*, μοσχεύματα *PCair.Zen.*162 (iii B.C.); ῥάβδος *An.Ox.*3.226.

**ῥοΐσκος** (A), ὁ, Dim. of ῥόα, *small pomegranate*: hence, *knob* or *tassel shaped like a pomegranate*, Lxx *Ex.*28.29(33), al., J.*AJ*3.7.4.

**ῥοΐσκος** (B), ὁ, Dim. of ῥοή, *rivulet*, *brook*, *IG*14.352 i 16, al. (Halaesa).

**ῥοϊσμός**, ὁ, (ῥοΐζω) = ὁ τῶν ἵππων ῥισμός (sic), Hsch.

**ῥοΐτης** [ῑ] οἶνος, ὁ, (ῥόα) *pomegranate*-wine, Dsc.5.26: also **ῥοϊτικός** (sc. οἶνος), *POxy.*1142.16 (iii A.D.).

**ῥοιώδης**, ες, = ῥοώδης, *watery*, ὀφθαλμός Gal.17(1).967. II. of bones, *unjointed*, held together only by ligaments, Hp.*Art.*86, *Mochl.*30: cf. ῥοικώδης.

**ῥομβ-έω**, *cause to spin like a* ῥόμβος, *whirl*, gloss on **ῥυμβέω** (Pl.*Cra.*426e codd.), Tim.*Lex.*, cf. Hsch. s.v. βεμβικίζει. **-ηδόν**, Adv. *like a* ῥόμβος, Man.4.108. **-ητής**, οῦ, ὁ, *one that spins like a* ῥόμβος, Orph.*H.*31.2. **-ητός**, ή, όν, *spun round like a* ῥόμβος, *whirled about*, ῥομβητοὺς δονέων πλοκάμους *AP*6.219 (Antip.), cf. 218 (Alc.). **-ίζω**, = ῥομβέω, εἴ σε κλωστὴρ Μοιρέων ἐρόμβισεν *Mélanges Nicole* 308 (Panticapaeum). **-ίον**, Att. **ῥυμβ-**, τό, Dim. of ῥόμβος I. 2, Sch.A.R.4.143 (ῥυμβ-).

**ῥομβοειδής**, ές, *rhombus-shaped*, *rhomboidal*, Hp.*Art.*35, Str.2.1.22, etc.; ῥ. σχῆμα *rhomboid*, i.e. a four-sided figure with only the opposite sides and angles equal, Euc.1 *Def.*22, Ph.*Bel.*52.30, Ptol.*Alm.*7.5, cf. Hegesand.37; τὸ ῥ. στερεόν (v. ῥόμβος B.1 b) Simp.*in Cael.*410.5:—τὸ ῥ., a place at Megara, Plu.*Thes.*27.

⊛ **ῥόμβος** or **ῥύμβος**, ὁ, (ῥέμβω) *bull-roarer*, instrument whirled round on the end of a string, used in the mysteries, ῥόμβου θ' εἱλισσομένα κύκλιος ἔνοσις αἰθερία E.*Hel.*1362, cf. Archyt.1, Theoc.2.30; as a boy's toy, *AP*6.309 (Leon.), Orph.*Fr.*31.29, *Fr.*34, M.Ant.5.36; defined as ξυλήφιον, οὗ ἐξῆπται τὸ σπαρτίον, καὶ ἐν ταῖς τελεταῖς ἐδονεῖτο, ἵνα ῥοιζῇ, Sch.Clem.Al.*Protr.*2.17.2, cf. Hsch. 2. *magic wheel*, spun alternately in each direction by the torsion of two cords passed through two holes in it, used as a love-charm, Luc.*DMeretr.*4.5; called ἴυγξ in Theoc.2.17, *AP*5.204; Lat. *rhombus*, Prop.2.28.35, Ov.*Am.*1.8.7. b. τροχίσκος ὃν στρέφουσιν ἱμᾶσι τύπτοντες, καὶ οὕτως κτύπον ἀποτελοῦσι Sch.A.R.1.1134; ὦ ῥύμβε μαστίξας ἐμέ (dub. sens.) Eup.72. 3. *tambourine* or *kettle-drum*, used in the worship of Rhea and of Dionysus, Ar.*Fr.*303, Diog.Ath.1.3, A.R.1.1139, *AP*6.165 (Phal.); ῥύμβος ξύλινος ἐπίχρυσος *IG*$2^{2}$.1456.49, cf. 1517.207. 4. *membrum virile*, *PLond.*1821.164. II. *whirling motion*, as of a bull-roarer, ἀκόντων ἱέντα ῥόμβον shooting forth *whirling* darts, Pi.*O.*13.94; αἰετοῦ ῥ. the eagle's *swoop*, Id.*I.*4(3).47(65); ῥ. τυπάνων Id.*Dith.Oxy.*1604 *Fr.*1 ii 9; ἐν αἰθερίῳ ῥύμβῳ Critias 19.2 D.; ῥόμβου ἀπειρεσίου δινεύμασιν οἶμον ἐλαύνων, of the Sun, Orph.*H.*8.7: metaph., Νέμεσις καὶ ῥ. ἀλάστωρ *IG*14.1389 ii 34 (perh. an Adj., = ῥεμβός).—The Gramm. hold ῥύμβος to be Att., ῥόμβος Hellenic, Sch.Theoc.2.30, Ath.7.330b.

B. *rhombus*, *lozenge*, i.e. a four-sided figure with all the sides, but only the opposite angles, equal, Arist.*Mech.*$854^{b}$16, Euc.1 *Def.*22. b. ῥ. στερεός, a figure composed of two cones on opposite sides of the same base, Archim.*Sph.Cyl.*1.26, al. 2. a species of fish, of which *turbot* and *brill* are varieties, so called from its rhomb-like shape, Nausicr.2.13; Ῥωμαῖοι καλοῦσι τὴν ψῆτταν ῥ. Ath.7.330b, cf. ψῆττα. 3. *surgical bandage*, so called from its shape, Hp.*Off.*7, Heliod.ap.Orib.48.20.14. 4. *pattern of the same shape*, in weaving cloth, Democr.Eph.1; διαπλοκὴ ῥόμβων Aristeas 74.

**ῥομβοτετράγωνον** σχῆμα, the figure *of a rhombus*, Tz.*H.*8.581.

**ῥομβ-όω**, *bring into the shape of a rhombus*, Hero *Bel.*102.12 (pf. Pass.). **-ώδης**, ες, f.l. for ῥεμβώδης, Plu.2.715c. ⊛ **-ωτός**, ή, όν, *made in the shape of a rhombus*, *panelled in lozenges*, Callix.1, *AP*6.111 (Antip.), Aristeas 67, J.*AJ*12.2.10.

**ῥόμιξα**· εἶδος ἀκοντίου, Hsch. (Lat. *rumex*.)

**ῥόμμα**, ατος, τό, (ῥόφω) = ῥόφημα, Hp.ap.Gal.19.135.

**ῥόμος**, ὁ, *wood-worm*, Arc.59.24; **ῥόμοξ**, Hsch. (s.v.l.).

**ῥομφάζω**, = βαστάζω, Hsch.

**ῥομφαία**, ἡ, *large*, *broad sword*, used by the Thracians, ὀρθὰς ῥ. βαρυσιδήρους ἀπὸ τῶν δεξιῶν ὤμων ἐπισείοντες Plu.*Aem.*18, cf. Phylarch.*Fr.*57 J., Arr.*Fr.*103 J.: generally, *sword*, Lxx *Ge.*3.24, al., *Ev.Luc.*2.35, *Apoc.*6.8, Jul.*Ep.*89b; of the *sword* of Goliath, Lxx 1*Ki.*17.51, J.*AJ*6.12.4. II. = νυκτερίς, Cyran.36.

**ῥομφεῖς**· ἱμάντες οἷς ῥάπτεται τὰ ὑποδήματα, Hsch. (cf. ὁρμοί).

**ῥοόκοκκα**, τά, *pomegranate seeds*, Steph.*in Hp.*1.222 D.

**ῥόον**, τό, only in pl. ῥόα, = τὰ ἐκ τῆς συκαμίνου μόρα τὰ ἄωρα ξηρανθέντα, Hp.ap.Gal.19.135: but in sg., ὁ **ῥοῦς** ὁ ἐκ τῶν συκαμίνων Diocl.*Fr.*140, cf. Hp.*Mul.*1.31.

⊛ **ῥόος**, ὁ, Cypr. **ῥόϝος** *Inscr.Cypr.*135.19 H., Att. contr. **ῥοῦς**: Ion. and later writers have the heterocl. dat. ῥοΐ (like νοΐ from νοῦς), Hellanic.28 J., Ach.Tat.3.20; also gen. ῥοός *Peripl.M.Rubr.*46: (ῥέω):—*stream*, *flow of water*, *current*, Hom. only in sg., freq. with gen., ῥ. Ἀλφειοῖο, Ὠκεανοῖο, etc., Il.11.726, 16.151, al.; κῦμα ῥόοιο 21.263; προχέειν ῥόον εἰς ἅλα ib.219; ποταμοὺς ἔτρεψε νέεσθαι κὰρ ῥόον to flow in *their own bed*, 12.33; κατὰ ῥόον down, i.e. with, the *stream*, Od.5.327.461, Hdt.2.96, etc.: metaph., φέρεσθαι κατὰ ῥοῦν Pl.*R.*492c; ταυτὶ κατὰ ῥ. προχωρεῖ Luc.*JTr.*50; πρὸς ῥόον against *it*, Il.21.303; Βόσπορος, ῥ. θεοῦ A.*Pers.*746 (troch.); *current* at sea, ὑπό τε τοῦ ῥοῦ καὶ ἀνέμου Th.1.54; εἰκῇ κατὰ ῥοῦν πλέοντας Phld.*Rh.*1.381 S.: also, *current of air*, Emp.100.14; ῥόος καπνοῦ Pi.*P.*1.22. II. *flux*, *discharge* of morbid humours, Hp.*Aph.*5.56, Arist.*HA*$521^{a}$28, Thphr.*HP*9.12.1. III. = ῥοή 3, Pl.*Cra.*411d. IV. v. ῥόον.

**ῥοπᾰλ-ίζει**· στρέφει, κινεῖ ὡς ῥόπαλον, Hsch. **-ικός**, ή, όν, *like a club*, i.e. *thicker towards the end*: hence, *versus rhopalicus*, a verse *in which each word is one syllable longer than that before* (such as Il.3.182), Serv. in *Gramm.Lat.*4.467 K. (*rhopalius* Sacerd.ib.6.505 K.). **-ιον**, τό, Dim. of ῥόπαλον, *PPetr.*3 p.59 (iii B.C.), Promathid.ap.Ath.11.489b; part of a κύλιξ, *Inscr.Délos* 442 *B* 146 (ii B.C.); part of a σκύφος, Roussel *Cultes Égyptiens* p.217 (Delos, ii B.C.). **-ισμός**, ὁ, *priapism*, Ar.*Lys.*553 (pl.).

**ῥοπᾰλο-ειδής**, ές, *like a club*, ῥίζα Dsc.3.132. **-μάχος** [μᾰ], ον, = κορυνήτης, Hsch. sub h.v.

**ῥόπᾰλον**, τό, *club, cudgel*, used to beat an ass, Il.11.559,561; to walk with, Od.17.195; *club* of the Cyclops, 9.319; of Heracles, S.*Tr.*512 (lyr.), Ar.*Ra.*47,495; *war-club* or *mace*, shod with metal, παγχάλκεον Od.11.575, cf. X.*HG*7.5.20; ῥόπαλα ξύλων τετυλωμένα σιδήρῳ Hdt.7.63; a hunter's *staff*, X.*Cyn.*6.11,17: as votive offering, *SIG*1106.124 (Cos, iv/iii B.C.): metaph., Πειθόλαος τὴν Πάραλον ῥ. τοῦ δήμου ἐκάλει Arist.*Rh.*1411$^a$13. II. *membrum virile*, *APl.*4.261 (Leon.). III. v.l. for ῥόπτρον III, X.*HG*6.4.36. IV. = νυμφαία, Plin.*HN*25.75.

**ῥοπᾰλοφόρος**, ον, *club-bearing*, of Heracles, Eust.1699.31.

**ῥοπᾰλ-ώδης**, ες, t. t. of the pulse, invented by Archig., Gal.8.943. **-ωσις**, εως, ἡ, name of a disease of the hair, Id.19.430. **-ωτός**, ή, όν, as if from ῥοπαλόω, *club-shaped*, κύλιξ D.C.72.18.

⊛ **ῥοπ-ή**, ἡ, (ῥέπω) *turn of the scale, fall of the scale-pan, weight*, Arist.*Cael.*307$^b$33; μέχρι τοῦ μέσου τὴν ῥ. ἔχειν *gravitate* to.., ib.297$^a$28; *downward momentum*, τῷ μείζονι βάρει καὶ ῥ. πλείων παρέπεται Ph.*Bel.*69.21; ῥ. ποιεῖν make (counter-)*weight*, Thphr.*CP*5.4.7; ἁ γᾶ ἐρήρεισται ἐπὶ τᾶς αὐτᾶς ῥ. *in equilibrium*, Ti.Locr.97e; διαστρεφόντων τὴν ῥ. disturbing the *balance*, Plu.*Cam.*28. 2. metaph., *balancing, suspense*, ἁ δ' (sc. ἁ πόλις) ἔχεται ῥόπας Alc.25; ῥ. Δίκας A.*Ch.*61 (lyr.); ἐν οὖν ῥ. τοιᾷδε κειμένῳ S.*Tr.*82; ποντοναῦται.. λεπταῖς ἐπὶ ῥοπῇσιν ἐμπολὰς μακρὰς ἀεὶ παραρρίπτοντες staking distant ventures on nice *balancings*, Id.*Fr.*555 (= *Philol.*88.2); ῥ. βίου μοι the *turning-point* or *sinking-point* of life, i.e. death, Id.*OC*1508; ῥ. 'στιν ἡμῶν ὁ βίος ὥσπερ ὁ ζυγός Men.*Mon.*465. b. *turn of the scale*, ποιεῖν ῥ. *turn the scale*, Arist.*Pol.*1295$^b$38; τοῦ πολέμου Isoc.12.50; πολλάκις μικραὶ δυνάμεις μεγάλας τὰς ῥ. ἐποίησαν Id.4.139; μεγάλην ἔσεσθαι τὴν ῥ., εἰ.. Id.14.33; εἰς ἑκάτερα τὰ μέρη ῥοπὰς λαμβάνοντα τὸν πόλεμον Plb.1.20.7, cf. *Trag.Adesp.*102: hence, *decision, outcome*, βλέπω δύο ῥ.· ἢ γὰρ θανεῖν δεῖ μ'.. ἢ.. E.*Hel.*1090; ἀσθενεῖς καὶ ἐπὶ ῥ. μιᾶς ὄντες at the mercy of a single *weighing in the scales*, Th.5.103. II. *weight* placed in the scale-pan, Arist.*Mech.*850$^a$13; esp. *small additional weight, make-weight, casting weight*, *IG*2$^2$.1013.35, al.; ὡς ῥ. ἐκ πλαστίγγων Lxx *Wi.*11.22; ὡς ῥ. ζυγοῦ ἐλογίσθησαν 'as *dust* in the balance', ib.*Is.*40.15; οὐδ' ὅσον ῥ. Herod.7.33. 2. metaph., σμικρὰ παλαιὰ σώματ' εὐνάζει ῥ. *casting weight*, S.*OT*961; σῶμα νοσῶδες σμικρᾶς ῥ... δεῖται προσλαβέσθαι πρὸς τὸ κάμνειν Pl.*R.*556e; δέδορκε φῶς ἐπὶ σμικρᾶς ῥ. E.*Hipp.*1163, cf. Plu.*Art.*30. b. δεῖ ῥ. διδόναι ταῖς αὑτῶν πατρίσι τοὺς συγγραφέας give the *casting weight* to.., Plb.16.14.6. c. *weight, decisive influence*, ὡς τοῖσδε καὶ δὶς ἀντισηκῶσαι ῥοπῇ A.*Pers.*437; μεγάλη γὰρ ῥ., μᾶλλον δὲ ὅλον, ἡ τύχη παρὰ πάντα τὰ πράγματα D.2.22; ῥ. ἔχειν have *influence*, Id.11.8, cf. *SIG*761.5 (Delph., i B.C.); ἔχει τι βρῖθος καὶ ῥ. πρὸς τὸν βίον Arist.*EN*1101$^a$29, cf. 1094$^a$23, 1172$^a$23; πλείστην παρέχεται ῥ. εἰς τὸ νικᾶν Plb.6.52.9. III. *decisive moment, crisis* (i.e. *victory*), καὶ τὸν Βαλαάμ.. ἀπέκτειναν ἐν τῇ ῥ. Lxx *Jo.*13.22: so generally, *moment*, πρὸς μίαν ῥ... διεφθάρη in one *moment*, ib.*Wi.*18.12; ὑστάτην βίου ῥ. αὐτοῖς ἐκείνην δόξαντες εἶναι ib.3*Ma.*5.49; ἐν ῥοπῆς καιρῷ βραχεῖ *AP*11.289 (Pall.). IV. *discount* deducted from a payment, *PLond.*3.780.4 (vi A.D.), *POxy.*143.3 (vi A.D.), etc.; perh. *illicit commission*, *Cod. Just.*4.59.1.1. **-ικός**, ή, όν, *inclined*, πρὸς τὴν συνουσίαν Antig.*Mir.*115 (Comp.).

**ῥοπτίον**· κλειδίον, Hsch.

⊛ **ῥόπτον**, τό, *operating-table*, *IG*4$^2$(1).122.41 (Epid., iv B.C.).

**ῥοπτός**, ή, όν, (ῥόφω) = ῥοφητός, Hp.ap.Gal.19.136.

⊛ **ῥόπτρον**, τό, (ῥέπω) *the wood in a trap* which falls when touched and catches the mouse, Archil.90, Poll.7.115: metaph., δίκης ἔπαισεν αὐτὸν ῥ. E.*Hipp.*1172. II. *musical instrument* of the Corybantes, *tambourine* or *kettle-drum*, Corn.*ND*30, Luc.*Trag.*36, Orph.*Frr.*105,152, *AP*6.74 (Agath.); ῥ. βυρσοπαγῆ καὶ κοίλα περιτείναντες ἠχείοις χαλκοῖς Plu.*Crass.*23; cf. ῥόμβος A.I.3. III. *knocker* on a door, E.*Ion* 1612 (troch.), Ar.*Fr.*39, Lys.6.1, X.*HG*6.4.36; cf. ῥόπαλον III.

**ῥοσᾶτον**, τό, = Lat. *rosatum*, *Edict.Diocl.*2.19 (ῥοσσ-), Alex.Trall.1.16.

⊛ **ῥοταρία**· τορύνιον, Hsch. (cf. ῥατάναν, βρατάναν).

**ῥούα**, ἡ, *road*, *SIG*1231.11 (Nicomedia, iii/iv A.D.). (Lat. *ru(g)a*, Fr. *rue.*)

**ῥουβοτός**· ῥόφημα, Hsch. **ῥουγός**· πρόσωπον, Id. (perh. **ῥύγχος** or a dialectal form **ῥούγχος**).

⊛ **ῥούδιον**, τό, = κλύσμα πρὸς βοῦν γυναικεῖον, Aët.16.64.

**ῥουδόν**, v. ῥυδόν. **ῥουμάζεται**· φρίττει, Hsch. **ῥοῦς**, ὁ, Att. contr. for ῥόος. II. v. ῥόον.

⊛ **ῥοῦς**, ὁ and ἡ: uncontr. acc. sg. masc. ῥόον Hp.*Mul.*1.31; dat. sg. fem. ῥόῳ ib.78; gen. ῥοῦ Id.*Nat.Mul.*32,34, Thphr.*HP*3.18.5 (fem.), etc.; but ῥοός Hp.*Mul.*2.181, Dsc.1.108; dat. ῥοΐ interpol. in Dorio ap. Ath.7.309f:—*sumach, Rhus coriaria*, Dsc. l.c. 2. *its fruit*, Sol.41, Antiph.142.2, Alex.127.6, *PCair.Zen.*83.4, 702.29 (iii B.C.); used in medicine, Hp. ll. cc.:—the fruit of one kind (ῥ. Συριακή Gal.19.741; ῥ. ἐρυθρός Hp.*Mul.*1.31, Gal.12.353, cf. 922) was used as a spice:—of another, in tanning, ῥ. βυρσοδεψική Hp.*Mul.*1.78; σκυτοδεψικός Ruf.ap.Orib.8.24.3. II. *red ray, Lolium perenne*, Dsc.4.43.

**ῥουσίζω**, *to be reddish*, *Gp.*11.23.1.

⊛ **ῥούσιος**, ον, *reddish*, Lat. *russus, russeus*, Dsc.4.130 (interpol.), *Stud.Pal.*20.245.18 (vi A.D.). II. οἱ ῥ. the *Red* faction in the Circus, Lyd.*Mens.*4.30: sg., τοῦ ῥουσσέου *Tab.Defix.Aud.*242.53 (Carthage, iii A.D.); τοῦ ῥωσέου ib.160.80 (Rome, iv/v A.D.); ῥόσεον Σιλουανόν ib.237.23 (Carthage, i A.D.):—cf. *APl.*5.386.

**ῥουσιόστᾰχυς**, = ῥοῦς II, Ps.-Dsc.4.43.

**ῥουσιώδης**, ες, *of a reddish colour*, Sch.Od.9.125.

**ῥουσσᾶτοι**, οἱ, = ῥούσιοι II, Lyd.*Mens.*4.30.

**ῥοῦτο**· τοῦτο, Μακεδόνες, Hsch. **ῥούφισμα**, gloss on βρόγχος, Id.

⊛ **ῥοφ-έω**, A.*Eu.*264, Ar.*V.*906, etc.; also **ῥοφάνω** (ῥῡφ-), Hp.*Morb.*2.12,19, etc.; **ῥοφάω**, *PMag.Lond.*121.182 (ῥοφωμένην together with ῥοφοῦντι Colot. *in Ly.*7 [col. 9]), Sch.Tll.5.126:—fut. ῥοφήσομαι Ar.*V.*814; whence Elmsl. alters ῥοφήσεις into -ήσει in *Ach.*278, *Eq.*360 (ἐκ-), *Pax* 716: aor. ἐρρόφησα Hp.*Morb.*2.42, Ar.*Eq.*51, (ἐπεκ-) ib.701, (ἀπ-) X.*Cyr.*1.3.10:—Pass., aor. part. ῥοφηθείς Nic.*Al.*389:—a form **ῥῡφέω** (Ion. acc. to Phot.) occurs in Hippon.132; aor. ῥυφῆσαι Ar.*Fr.*450; Med. ῥυφήσασθαι Hp.*Epid.*7.11:—*sup greedily up, gulp down*, ἀπὸ ζῶντος ῥ. ἐρυθρὸν.. πελανόν A.*Eu.*264 (lyr.), cf. Ar.*V.*812,814, etc.; τινος *some of* a thing, Luc.*Lex.*5; ῥοφοῦντα πίνειν ὥσπερ βοῦν X.*An.*4.5.32: abs., Ar.*Eq.*51, *V.*906,982; of Charybdis, Arist.*Mete.*356$^b$15. 2. *drain dry, empty*, τρύβλιον Ar.*Ach.*278, *Eq.*905; so ῥ. ἀρτηρίας, of the poison on the robe of Heracles, S.*Tr.*1055. II. *live on slops*, opp. ξηρὸν σιτίον, Hp.*VM*6. (Cf. Lat. *sorbeo*, Lith. *srebiù* 'sip', etc.) **-ημα**, Ion. **ῥύφ-**, ατος, τό, *that which is supped up, thick gruel* or *porridge*, opp. πόμα, Hp.*Aph.*7.68, *VM*5, *Fist.*7, Arist.*Pr.*863$^b$6. **-ημάτιον**, τό, Dim. of foreg., A.D.*Conj.*219.26. **-ημᾰτώδης**, ες, *of the nature of a* ῥόφημα, *gruel-like*, Gal.6.247, Sor.1.98. **-ησις**, εως, ἡ, *supping up*, opp. ἐδωδή, Arist.*Mete.*381$^a$2. **-ητικός**, ή, όν, *drawing in, absorbing*, τινος Str.15.1.38. **-ητός**, ή, όν, *that can be* or *is supped up*, Id.15.1.53, Dsc.5.107, Gal.6.706, Sor.2.11; cf. ῥοπτός.

**ῥόφια**· κύματα, ἢ ῥόθια, Hsch.

**ῥόφισμα**, ατος, τό, = ῥόφημα, Cyran.9.

**ῥόφω**, collat. form of ῥοφέω, *EM*705.26: hence ῥόμμα, ῥοπτός.

**ῥόχᾰνον**, τό, *strickle*, Hsch.

**ῥοχθ-έω**, *dash with a roaring sound*, of the sea, ῥόχθει γὰρ μέγα κῦμα ποτὶ ξερόν Od.5.402; προτὶ δ' αὐτὰς [πέτρας] κῦμα μέγα ῥοχθεῖ 12.60; ὑπὸ κύματι πέτραι ῥόχθεον *sounded with the dashing* of the waves, A.R.4.925; ῥοχθεῦσιν δὲ κάλωες Opp.*H.*1.228.—Cf. ὀρεχθέω. **-ος**, ὁ, *roaring*, of the sea, Lyc.402,696,742, Nic.*Al.*390.

**ῥοχμός**, v. ῥωχμός.

**ῥοώδης** (A), ες, *with a strong stream, running violently*, of a sea *in which there are strong currents*, Th.4.24, Arist.*Mete.*366$^a$25; τὸ μάλιστα ῥ. τοῦ πελάγους Ael.*NA*7.24: hence, of rocks, promontories, etc., *exposed to such seas*, κρημνός Str.8.5.1; ἄκραι Ael.*NA*14.24; τόποι ῥ. regions *of rapid currents*, Arist.*HA*621$^a$16, cf. Thphr.*CP*3.?.4. II. Medic., *running*, ὀφθαλμίαι Hp.*Epid.*1.5: of persons, *affected with diarrhoea* or *other fluxes*, Id.*Aër.*3; αἱ ὑπέρλευκοι -έστεραι Id.*Mul.*2.111; ῥ. νόσος ibid. (but metaph. in Ph.1.698, cf. 2.428); πυρετοὶ ῥ. Dsc.5.26; πυρετὸς ῥ. Gal.19.399. Adv., ῥοωδῶς πυρέσσειν Cass.*Pr.*70. b. as Methodic t.t., ῥ. νόσημα, opp. στεγνόν, Gal.*Sect.Intr.*6; πάθος Sor.1.29, 2.45. III. *falling off*, καρπός Thphr.*CP*5.9.10.

**ῥοώδης** (B), ες, *like a pomegranate*, Thphr.*HP*3.18.13.

**ῥοών**, ῶνος, ὁ, (ῥόα) *pomegranate-orchard*, Lxx *Za.*12.11.

**ῥυά**, v. ῥυῆαν.

**ῥῠᾰδικός**, ή, όν, (ῥυάς) *like diarrhoea*, Paul.Aeg.6.70. II. of persons, *suffering from incontinence of urine*, Gal.14.787, Heliod.(?) ap.Orib.45.7.5. 2. *suffering from epiphora* or *running from the eyes without external cause*, Dem.Ophth.ap.Aët.7.46 (where ῥοιαδ-).

**ῥῠᾰκώδης**, ες, *abounding in streams*, *Gloss.*

**ῥύαξ** [ῡ], ᾱκος, ὁ, (ῥέω) *rushing stream, mountain torrent*, Th.4.96, Dsc.3.51, prob. in *OGI*335.111 (Pergam., ii B.C.). 2. esp. *stream of lava* from a volcano, ὁ ῥ. τοῦ πυρὸς ἐκ τῆς Αἴτνης Th.3.116, cf. Pl.*Phd.*111e, 113b, Arist.*Mir.*833$^a$17, Thphr.*Lap.*22; ὁ καλούμενος ῥ. D.S.14.59. 3. metaph., ῥ. ἀργύρου γενέσθαι Id.5.35. 4. of dolphins, etc., ἔχει οἷον ῥ. δύο ἐξ ὧν τὸ γάλα ῥεῖ two *flow-holes*, Arist.*HA*504$^b$24.

**ῥυάς**, άδος, ὁ, ἡ, τό, (ῥέω) *fluid, flaccid, flabby*, ῥυάδος σώματος γενομένου Arist.*PA*668$^b$7. II. *falling off*, ῥ. θρίξ hair *that is shed*, Id.*Pr.*898$^a$32; ῥ. ἄμπελος a vine *that sheds its grapes*, Thphr.*HP*4.14.6 (cod. Urb., v.l. ῥοάς), *Gp.*5.39.1. III. as Subst., ῥυάδες, οἱ, fishes *that go in shoals with the currents*, like herrings, Arist.*HA*534$^a$27, 543$^b$14, Ael.*NA*9.46, al. 2. ῥυάς, ἡ, *a disease of the eye causing a continual weeping discharge*, Cels.7.7.4, Gal.10.1002. 3. *urinary fistula*, Heliod.ap.Orib.45.7.5, 50.4 tit., Aret.*SD*2.4 (ῥοι- codd.).

**ῥύᾰτο**, v. ἐρύω (B).

**ῥυάχετος** [ᾱ], ὁ, Lacon. word in Ar.*Lys.*170, ὁ τῶν Ἀσαναίων ῥ. the *unstable crowd* of the Athenians; expld. by Hsch. and Phot. as ὁ ῥέων ὀχετός; cod. Rav. gives ῥυγχάχετος, other codd. and Suid. ῥυχάχετος.

**ῥύβδην**, Adv. = δαψιλῶς, ῥύβδην θυννίδα (θύνναν codd.).. δαινύμενος Hippon.35 (ῥύδην codd., em. Bgk.; ῥοίβδην· δαψιλῶς, Phot. post ῥυάχετον); κηφῆνες προσφέρονται ῥύβδην (v.l. ῥύδην) ἄνω πρὸς τὸν οὐρανόν Arist.*HA*624$^a$24.

**ῥυβός**, = ῥαιβός, τὸ ἐπικαμπές (Aeol.), Hdn.Gr.1.187.

**ῥυγχ-άζω**, = μυκτηρίζω, Phot. **-αινα**, ἡ, *with a large nose* or *snout*, Lat. *nasuta*, *Gloss.* **-άχετος**, v. ῥυάχετος. **-ελέφας**, αντος, ὁ, *with an elephant's trunk*, *AP*11.204 (Pall.). **-ιάζω**, = ῥογχάζω, ῥέγχω, Hsch. **-ίον**, τό, Dim. of ῥύγχος, Ar.*Ach.*744, Theophil.8.2, *POxy.*108.5 (ii A.D.). **-όομαι**, Pass., = ῥαμφάζομαι, Hsch. and Phot. s.v. ῥαμφάξῃ (s.v.l.). ⊛ **-ος**, εος, τό, *snout, muzzle*, of swine, Stesich.14, Pherecr.102, Anaxil.11, Arist.*HA*595$^a$18, cf. Sch.Ar.

*Av.*347 ; of dogs and other quadrupeds, Theoc.6.30, Arist.*PA*658[b] 30, Thphr.*Char.*4.10 : of birds, *beak, bill*, Ar.*Av.*348,364, al., Arist. *HA*504[a]21, *PA*659[b]22, 693[a]16. **2.** Com., of a man's face, Cratin. 440, Archipp.1 ; of a god's face, Arar.1.

**ῥυδεῖ·** περιπλέκεται, Hsch.

**ῥύδην** [ῠ], Adv., (ῥέω) *flowingly*, i.e. *abundantly, lavishly*, Cratin. 441, Plu.*Sull.*21, *Caes.*29, *Luc.*39, Eun.*VS* p.489 B., etc. : cf. ῥύβδην.

**ῥυδία·** ῥόα, ἡ ῥοιά, Hsch. (fort. ῥοΐδια).

⊛ **ῥῠδόν**, Adv. = ῥύδην, ῥυδὸν ἀφνειός *abundantly* rich, Od.15.426 : ῥουδόν (Lacon.?)· ῥευστικῶς, Hsch.

**ῥυδωμένην·** ῥοφωμένην, Hsch.

**ῥύεινα·** ἄρνα, Κύπριοι, Hsch. (from Ϝρῆνα? ; v. ἀρήν).

**ῥυζέω** or **ῥύζω**, like ῥάζω, *growl, snarl*, like an angry dog (Poll.5. 86), ῥύζων Hermipp.24 (ῥυζῶν ap.Suid., cf. Hsch.) ; also of hawks, Poll.5.89.

**ῥυῆαν·** κάτοχον πιπάζεσθαι, καὶ ῥυὰ ὁ ἵππος, Hsch.

**ῥύημα** [ῠ], ατος, τό, (ῥέω) a kind of *honey-cake*, Gal.4.526 (printed ῥύμματα), 6.492.

**ῥῠηφεν-ής**, ές, (ῥέω, ἄφενος) *flowing with riches, abounding*, D.P. 337, Nonn.*D.*10.152. **-ίη**, ἡ, *affluence*, Call.*Jov.*84.

⊛ **ῥυθμ-ίζω**, *bring into a measure of time* or *proportion*, περιόδους Plu. 2.350e ; *repeat* a verse *in proper time* or *rhythm*, i.e. *scan* it, D.H.*Comp.* 18 :—Pass., ἐν δυσὶ τετραχόρδοις ῥ. τὰ μέρη (sc. τοῦ οὐρανοῦ) Arist. *Fr.*47 ; λιθοῦται καὶ -ίζεται Philostr.*VA*3.57. **II.** generally, *order, arrange, compose*, Arist.*Metaph.*1075[b]12, *Spir.*485[b]2 :—Pass., Id.*Ph.*245[b]9. **2.** of persons, *educate, train*, τὰ παιδικά Pl.*Phdr.* 253b, cf. X.*Cyr.*8.8.20 ; τὰν ψυχάν Ti.Locr.103d ; τὸ πρόσωπον Luc.*Merc.Cond.*30 ; τὰς γνώμας Id.*Anach.*22 ; [δένδρα] ῥ. ὥστε πρὸς μεσημβρίαν βλέπειν *train* them, Thphr.*CP*3.7.9 ; ῥ. τινάς *bring* them *to order, correct* them, *GDI*5075.35 (Crete) ; ῥ. καὶ διδάσκει τινὰς κινεῖσθαι κινήσεις *Stoic.*2.28 ; ῥ. λύπην ὅπου *define* the place of grief (referring to the line before), S.*Ant.*318 :—Med., πλόκαμον μίτραισι E. *Hec.*924 (lyr.) : metaph., πρός τι *prepare oneself* for.., Hld.10.10 :—Pass., νηλεῶς ὧδ' ἐρρυθμισμαι thus ruthlessly *am I brought to order*, A. *Pr.*243 ; ὄρνιθες ἐρρυθμισμένοι τὴν γλῶτταν *taught* to speak, Philostr. *VA*1.7. **3.** *shape* by massage, Sor.1.83, Ruf.ap.Orib.*inc.*20. 6. **-ικός**, ή, όν, *set to time, rhythmical*, κίνησις Pl.*Plt.*307a, etc. : of a man, Plu.2.1014c. **2.** *of* or *for rhythm*, ποικιλία ib.1138b, cf. 1144d ; ἡ ῥ. λέξις, opp. ἡ πεζή, D.H.*Comp.*11 ; ῥυθμικοί, οἱ, *rhythmicians*, ib.17 : ἡ -κή, opp. ἡ μετρική, Aristox.*Harm.* p.32 M. **-ιος**, α, ον, = ῥυθμικός, Hdn.Gr.2.443,853. **-ισις**, εως, ἡ, *shaping, ordering*, ἡ τοῦ λόγου ῥ. Eustr. *in EN*257.30.

**ῥυθμο-γρᾰφία**, ἡ, *noting down of the time* or *rhythm*, *CIG*3088 (Teos). **-γράφος** [ᾰ], ον, *writing on rhythms*, of Hephaestion, Tz. in *An.Par.*1.95. **-ειδής**, ές, *rhythmical*, D.H.*Isoc.*2, Aristid.Quint. 1.14. **-ποιία**, ἡ, *making of time* or *rhythm*, Aristox.*Harm.* p.34 M., *Rhyth.*2 p.8 W., Plu.2.1135c (pl.), Aristid.Quint.1.5.

⊛ **ῥυθμός**, Ion. **ῥυσμός** (v. infr. III, IV), ὁ : (ῥέω) :—*any regular recurring motion* (πᾶς ῥ. ὡρισμένῃ μετρεῖται κινήσει Arist.*Pr.*882[b]2) : **I.** *measured motion, time*, whether in sound or motion, Democr.15[c] ; = ἡ τῆς κινήσεως τάξις, Pl.*Lg.*665a, cf. 672e ; ὁ ῥ. ἐκ τοῦ ταχέος καὶ βραδέος, ἐκ διενηνεγμένων πρότερον, ὕστερον δὲ ὁμολογησάντων γέγονε Id.*Smp.*187b, cf. Suid. s.v. ; *rhythm*, opp. μέτρον and ἁρμονία, Ar. *Nu.*638 sq., Pl.*R.*397b, 398d, 601a, Arist.*Rh.*1403[b]31 ; λόγοι μετὰ μουσικῆς καὶ ῥυθμῶν πεποιημένοι Isoc.15.46 ; of Prose rhythm, Arist.*Rh.*1408[b]29, D.H.*Comp.*17 : defined by Aristox.*Rhyth.Fr.*1, Aristid.Quint.1.13. **2.** special phrases : ἐν ῥυθμῷ *in time*, of dancing, marching, etc., βαίνειν ἐν ῥ. Pl.*Lg.*670b, cf. X.*An.*5.4. 14 ; ὀρχεῖσθαι Id.*Cyr.*1.3.10 ; ἐν τῷ ῥ. ἀναπνεῖν respire *regularly*, Arist.*Pr.*882[b]1 ; so σωζόμενος ῥ. A.*Ch.*797 (lyr.) ; μετὰ ῥυθμοῦ βαίνοντες Th.5.70 ; ῥυθμὸν χορείας ὑπάγειν keep *time*, Ar.*Th.*956 (lyr.) ; θάττονα ῥυθμὸν ἐπάγειν play in quicker *time*, X.*Smp.*2.22 ; πυρριχίῳ δρόμῳ καὶ ῥυθμῷ Hdn.4.2.9, cf. Plb.4.20.6 : pl., *paces*, Alcid.*Soph.* 17. **II.** *measure, proportion* or *symmetry* of parts, at rest as well as in motion, κατὰ τὸν αὐτὸν ῥ. Pl.*Lg.*728e. **III.** generally, *proportion, arrangement, order*, ῥυθμῷ τινι E.*Cyc.*398 (codd., but θ' ἑνί is prob.) ; οὐκ ἀπὸ ῥυσμοῦ εἰκάζω not without *reason*, Call. *Epigr.*44.5. **IV.** *state* or *condition* of anything, *temper, disposition*, Thgn.964 (coupled with ὀργή and τρόπος) ; οἷος ῥυσμὸς ἀνθρώπους ἔχει Archil.66.7 ; ὅσοι χθονίους ἔχουσι ῥυσμοὺς καὶ χαλεπούς Anacr. 74 ; μένει..χρῆμ' οὐδὲν ἐν ταὐτῷ ῥ. Eup.356. **V.** *form, shape* of a thing, Democr.5[1] ; identified by Arist. with σχῆμα, *Metaph.*985[b]16, 1042[b]14 ; μετέβαλον τὸν ῥ. τῶν γραμμάτων changed the *form* or *shape* of the letters, Hdt.5.58 ; of Chian boots, Hp.*Art.*62 ; of the *shape* of a cup, Alex.59 ; of a breastplate, X.*Mem.*3.10.10 ; [τοῦ θυσιαστηρίου] Lxx 4*Ki.*16.10 ; Αὐτονόας ῥ. αὐτός Theoc.26.23 ; so of the natural *features* of a country, D.P.271,620 ; *structure* of a substance, κεγχροειδὲς τῷ ῥ., τῷ ῥ. σπογγῶδες, Dsc.5.77,118. **VI.** *manner, fashion* of a thing, Ἕλλην ῥ. πέπλων E.*Heracl.*130 ; τίνι ῥ. φόνου ; by what *kind* of slaughter ? Id.*El.*772, cf. *Supp.*94 ; ἐν τριγώνοις ῥυθμοῖς triangular-*wise*, A.*Fr.*78. [ῠ by nature, A.*Ch.*797 (lyr.), E.*Supp.*94, etc. ; ῡ by position in Thgn.964, etc.]

**ῥυθμόω**, *shape*, Sm.*Is.*44.12 :—Pass. **ῥυθμόομαι**, Ion. **ῥυσμ-**, *to be moulded*, κέρδεσιν Democr.197.

**ῥῠΐσκομαι**, (ῥέω) *have diarrhoea*, Hld.2.19 :—prob. *flow* (metaph.) in Archil.142. **2.** *suffer from falling hair*, Orib.*Eup.*4.6. **II.** Math., ἡ αὐτὴ στιγμὴ ῥυϊσκομένη ποιεῖ τὸ μέγεθος ἀλλ' οὐ παρατιθεμένη πρὸς ἄλλην στιγμήν *flowing*, Simp. *in Ph.*722.30 ; cf. ῥέω I. 5b, ῥύσις III.

⊛ **ῥῠκάν-η** [ᾰ], ἡ, *plane*, *AP*6.204 (Leon.). **-ησις**, εως, ἡ, *planing*, Bito 54.2 (where ῥυχ-). **-ίζω**, *plane*, *Gloss.*

**ῥύμα** [ῠ], ατος, τό, (ῥέω) = ῥεῦμα, *anything that flows, stream*, *IG*9 (1).692.5 (Corc.) : metaph., θοὸν ῥ. δινεύουσα Orph.*H.*10.22 ; ἁρμονίης ῥ. Procl.*H.*1.4.

**ῥῦμα** (A), ατος, τό, (ἐρύω (A)) *that which is drawn* : **1.** τόξου ῥ., i.e. the Persian *archers*, opp. λόγχης ἰσχύς, i.e. the Greek spearmen, A.*Pers.*147 (anap.) ; ἐκ τόξου ῥύματος from the distance of a bow-*shot*, X.*An.*3.3.15 ; ἐς τόξου ῥ. Eun.*Hist.* p.271 D. **2.** *towing-line*, Plb. 1.26.14, 3.46.5, al., D.H.3.44.

⊛ **ῥῦμα** (B), ατος, τό, (ἐρύω (B)) *defence, protection*, βωμὸς φυγάσιν ῥ. A. *Supp.*85 (lyr.) ; ἅπασι κοινὸν ῥ. δαιμόνων ἕδρα E.*Heracl.*260 ; πύργου ῥ. a tower of defence, S.*Aj.*159 (anap.) : c. gen. objecti, *defence against*, [θάνατος] μέγιστον ῥ. τῶν πολλῶν κακῶν A.*Fr.*353 ; ῥύματα, = βοηθήματα, Hp.ap.Gal.19.136 ; cf. ῥύσιον.

**ῥῡμ-άρχης**, ου, ὁ, *chief officer of* ῥύμη (II), Aen.Tact.3.4. **-αρχος**, ὁ, = *magister vici*, *Gloss.*

**ῥυμβέω, ῥυμβίον**, Att. for ῥομβ- (q.v.).

**ῥυμβονάω**, (ῥυμβών) *swing round*, Phld.*D.*3.10 (Pass.). **2.** metaph., *swing round and throw away*, ῥ. τὰ τιμιώτατα '*to make ducks and drakes*' *of money*, Ael.*Fr.*146.

**ῥύμβος**, v. ῥόμβος.

**ῥυμβών**, όνος, ἡ, *coil* of a serpent, A.R.4.144 (pl.).

**ῥῡμεῖος**, α, ον, *of the form of* ῥυμοί I. 2, neut. pl. ῥυμεῖια and ῥυμεῖα, *IG*2[2].1672.307.

**ῥύμ-η** [ῠ], ἡ, *force, swing, rush* of a body in motion, ῥύμῃ ἐμπίπτειν with *a swing*, Th.2.76 ; πτερύγων ῥύμη *rush* of wings, Ar.*Pax* 86, cf. *Av.*1182 ; τροχοῦ ῥύμαισι τευκτὸν..κύτος formed by the *whirl* of the potter's wheel, Antiph.52.2, cf. Ar.*Ec.*4 ; ἡ ῥ. τοῦ αἵματος the *flow* of blood in the veins, Hp.*Medic.*6 ; ἡ ῥ. τῆς ἐκκρούσεως X.*Cyn.*10.12 ; τῆς ῥ. τῆς ἁλιάδος ὁ ψόφος, of the noise made by a boat in motion, Arist.*HA*533[b]19 : metaph., εὐτυχεῖ ῥύμῃ θεοῦ E.*Rh.*64 ; ἡ ῥ. τῆς τύχης Plu.*Caes.*53 ; ἡ ῥ. τῆς ὀργῆς κτλ. the *vehemence* of passion, D.21.99 ; γλώσσης ῥ. *Lyr.Alex.Adesp.*35.11, cf. Eun.*Hist.* p.245 D. **2.** abs., *rush, charge*, of soldiers, Th.2.81 ; of ships, Id.7.70 ; τῶν ἵππων X.*Cyr.*7.1.31, cf. Polyaen.4.3.5, al., Ach.Tat.1.12 ; ὑπὸ τοῦ ῥοίβδου καὶ τῆς ῥ. Ar.*Nu.*407. **3.** = ῥοπή, Chrysipp.ap.Sch.T Il. 22.212. **II.** *street*, Aen.Tact.2.5, 3.4 ; τὴν ῥ. ὁδοιπορεῖν Philippid. 13, cf. Lxx *Is.*15.3, al. ; of a Roman camp, Plb.6.29.1 ; *lane, alley*, *PCair.Zen.*764.142 (iii B.C.), *PStrassb.*86.19 (ii B.C.), *Act.Ap.*9.11 ; *slit, chink*, dub.l. in Hp.*Cord.*2. **-ηδόν**, Adv. *with a swing* or *rush*, Polyaen.4.3.5.

⊛ **ῥύμμα**, ατος, τό, (ῥύπτω) *anything used for washing, soap, lye*, Hp. *Morb.Sacr.*1, Ar.*Lys.*377, Pl.*R.*429e sq. **II.** *sediment, dirt remaining from washing*, Gal.6.795, Sch.Nic.*Al.*95, Hsch.

**ῥῡμοπύλιον**, *portella*, *Gloss.*

⊛ **ῥῡμός**, ὁ, (ἐρύω (A)) *pole of a chariot* or *car*, Il.10.505, 23.393, 24. 271, Hdt.4.69 ; ἐν πρώτῳ ῥ. at the front end of the *pole*, Il.6.40, 16.371 ; ἀρτήματα ῥυμοῖς *pole*-chains, *IG*1[2].314.40, cf. 313.21,22,28, 2[2].1672. 307. **b.** *three stars* in the Bear, the *pole* of the Wain, Suid. **2.** *log* or *block* of wood for fuel, *SIG*975.1, al. (Delos, iii B.C.), *IG*11 (2).154 *A* 18 (ibid., iii B.C.) ; ξύλα καὶ κληματίδες καὶ ῥυμοὶ τὰ ἱερεῖα ἑψῆσαι ib.203 *A* 51 (ibid., iii B.C.) ; ῥυμὸς εἰς βωμόν ib.144 *A* 32 (ibid., iv B.C.) ; ῥυμοὶ εἰς τοὺς χορούς *Inscr.Délos* 442 *A* 186, cf. 189 (ii B.C.). **II.** *trace*, Ael.*NA*10.48. **III.** *trail* of a shooting star, Arat.927. **IV.** perh. *shelf* or *row*, πρῶτος ῥ., δεύτερος ῥ., etc., *IG*2[2].1388.16,19, al., *Michel* 832.63 (Samos, iv B.C.), etc. ; αἱ ..ἐν τῷ πρώτῳ ῥ. φιάλαι *Inscr.Délos* 442 *B* 21 (ii B.C.) ; ἐκ τοῦ πρώτου ῥ. τοῦ ἐκ τῆς κιβωτοῦ φιάλη ἡ περιγενομένη ἀπὸ τοῦ ῥ. τοῦ παραδοθέντος τοῖς ἀνδράσιν ib.25. **V.** a *weight* at Rhodes, Suid. **VI.** = τάξις, ἡ ἐμμέλεια, Hsch. (sed leg. ῥυθμός).

**ῥῡμοτομ-έω** πόλιν, (ῥύμη II) *divide* a town *by streets*, D.S.17.52, J.*BJ*3.5.2 :—Pass., πόλις κακῶς, καινῶς, ἐρρυμοτομημένη Dicaearch. 1.1,12 ; τετράπυλος ἐρρυμοτομημένος πρὸς ὀρθὰς γωνίας Str.12.4.7, cf. Cleom.2.1. **-ία**, ἡ, *division* of a town or camp *by streets*, Plb.6. 31.10, D.S.17.52, Str.14.1.37.

**ῥῡμουλκέω**, (ῥῦμα (A) 2, ἕλκω) *draw by a line, tow*, Lat. *remulcare* or *remulco agere*, ναῦς Plb.1.27.9, cf. Str.5.3.6, D.S.20.74, *Peripl.M. Rubr.*44, etc.

**ῥυντάκης**, ὁ, *an Indian bird* of the size of a pigeon, Ctes.*Fr.*45 ; **ῥυνδάκη**, Hsch.

**ῥύομαι**, v. ἐρύω (B). **ῥύπα**, τά, heterocl. pl. of ῥύπος (q.v.).

**ῥῠπαίνω**, fut. ῥῠπᾰνῶ (καταρ-) Isoc.12.63 :—Pass., aor. ἐρρυπάνθην Plu.2.434b : (ῥύπος) :—*defile, disfigure*, ῥ. τὸ μακάριον Arist.*EN*1099[b] 2 ; τὸν ἐμὸν βίον Aristaenet.2.17 ; *abuse, disparage*, Pherecr.228, Arist. *Rh.*1405[a]25 :—Pass., *to be* or *become foul*, opp. λαμπρύνεσθαι, X.*Lac.* 11.3, cf. *Apoc.*22.11 ; of a garment, *get dirty*, Thphr.*Char.*10.14. **2.** metaph., *contaminate, infect*, τοὺς πλησιάζοντας Gal.1.254.

**ῥυπαπαῖ**, v. ῥυππαπαῖ.

**ῥῠπᾰρ-εύομαι**, Pass., = ῥυπαίνομαι, v.l. in *Apoc.*22.11. **-ία**, ἡ, *dirt, filth*, Dsc.1.56 (prob. in 5.74, pl.), Plu.2.142a, Sor.1.122, Porph. *Abst.*1.42. **2.** metaph., *sordidness*, Critias 56 D., Teles pp.33, 37 H., Plu.2.60d ; οἰκονομικὸς χωρὶς ῥυπαρίας D.C.74.5.

**ῥῠπᾰρό-βιος**, ον, *of sordid life*, Vett.Val.16.22. **-γράφος** [γρᾰ], ον, *painting sordid subjects*, Plin.*HN*35.112 ; cf. ῥωπογράφος. **-κέρᾰμος**, ον, *of a dirty earthenware colour*, Alex.Mynd ap.Ath.9.395e (ῥυποκέραμος codd.). **-μέλᾱς**, αινα, αν, *of a dirty black*, ib.d.

⊛ **ῥῠπᾰρός**, ά, όν, *filthy, dirty*, κόλυθρον Telecl.3 ; δάπιδες Pherecr. 185 ; ῥ. εἴριον *greasy*, Hp.*Fract.*21 ; γαστέρας Id.*Prorrh.*2.23 (s.v.l.) ;

*unpurged*, σῶμα Alex.Trall.*Febr.*7. 2. metaph., *sordid, mean*, ἤδη χορηγὸν πώποτε -ώτερον τοῦδ' εἶδες; Eup.306; *uncultured*, ῥ. τρόποι Philetaer.18; βίος δουλοπρεπὴς καὶ ῥ. Arist.*VV*1251$^b$13; ῥ. πολῖται, ὄχλος, D.H.7.8, 9.44; of style, Longin.43.5. Adv. -ρῶς Men. 142, Epicur.*Sent.Vat.*43, Arr.*Epict.*2.9.4, *AP*10.48 (Pall.): Sup. -ώτατα D.C.59.4. 3. of coins, *made of base metal, gold* or *silver alloy*, ἀργυρίου ῥυπαρὰς δραχμάς *BGU*214.12 (ii A.D.), cf. *Ostr.Bodl.* ii 32 (ii A.D.), al. 4. κροτὼν ῥ., prob. = ἀδειγμάτιστος, *PCair.Zen.* 670.6 (iii B.C.); σῖτος ῥ. *unwinnowed*, *PFay.*16.10 (i B.C.); κριθὴ ῥ. *POxy.*1542.7 (iv A.D.).

**ῥῠπᾰρότης**, ητος, ἡ, = ῥυπαρία 2, βίου Ath.5.220a.

**ῥῠπᾰρο-φάγος** [φᾰ], ον, *foul-feeding*, Tz. ad Lyc.513. **-φορέω**, v. ῥυποφορέω. **-φόρος**, ον, *wearing dirty clothes*, Steph. *in Hp.*2.251 D.

**ῥύπ-ασμα** [ῠ], ατος, τό, *dirt, filth, pollution*, Apollon.*Lex.* s. v. λύματα: but **ῥῠπασμός**, ὁ, is f. l. in Eust.1849.12. ❋ **-άω**, Ep. **ῥῠπόω**, *to be filthy, slovenly*, μάλα περ ῥυπόωντα καθῆραι Od.6.87; ῥωγαλέα, ῥυπόωντα 13.435; ἦ ὅτι δὴ ῥυπόω 19.72; νῦν δ' ὅττι ῥυπόω 23.115; ῥυπόωντα δὲ ἕστο χιτῶνα 24.227; ῥυπῶντα, κυφόν, ἄθλιον Ar.*Pl.*266; of the habits of Spartans and philosophers, ἐρρύπων, ἐσωκράτων Ar.*Av.*1282; τοὺς Πυθαγοριστὰς.. ῥυπᾶν ἑκόντας Aristopho 9.2, cf. Luc.*Nec.*4; τὰ ῥυπῶντα τῶν τραυμάτων Ael.*NA* 14.4. II. Pass., *to be filled with wax*, of the ear, prob. in S.*Fr.* 858. **-έλαιον**, τό, *foul, dirty oil*, Paul.Aeg.7.17.

**ῥῠπό-εις**, εσσα, εν, = ῥυπαρός, Nic.*Al.*470; ὅλπη *AP*6.293 (Leon.); πίνος ib.11.158 (Antip.). **-κέραμος**, v. ῥυπαροκέραμος. **-κιβδοτόκων**, ωνος, ὁ, *miser*, '*dirty usurer*', Cerc.4.10. **-κόνδῦλος**, ον, *with dirty knuckles*, esp. of one who imitates the Laconians, Pl.Com.124, Ar.*Fr.*718.

**ῥύπον** [ῠ], τό, = ὀρός, *whey*, Phot.

❋ **ῥύπος** [ῠ], ὁ, *dirt, filth*, used by Hom. once in heterocl. pl., κάθηράν τε ῥύπα πάντα Od.6.93: later in sg., Semon.7.63, A.*Fr.*82 (cf. Ar.*Fr.*892), Pl.*Prm.*130c, Eup.252, Alex.197, etc.; ὁ ἐν τοῖς ὠσὶ ῥ. Arist.*Pr.*960$^b$18, cf. Artem.1.24, *PMag.Osl.*1.332; ῥ. ὁ ἀπὸ τῶν ἐν τοῖς γυμνασίοις ἀνδριάντων Gal.12.116; τὸν ἀπὸ τῶν ὀνύχων ῥύπον Suid. s. v. γρύ; ἅπαν ῥύπον all of it *filth* (acc.), Theoc.15.20; of a person, πρὸς τὸ μὴ λοῦσθαι ῥύπος Aristopho 10.4:—also ῥύπος, εος, τό, of cheese-*parings*, Hp.*Mul.*1.64. 2. metaph., *sordidness, meanness*, ὁ ῥ. τοῦ χαμαὶ βίου M.Ant.7.47. II. *sealing-wax*, τοὺς ῥ. ἀνασπάσαι Ar.*Lys.*1198.

**ῥῠπο-φορέω**, *wear dirty clothes*, Sch.Ar.*Av.*1554, where Hemsterhuis cj. ῥυπαροφ-. **-ω**, *make foul and filthy, befoul* (cf. ῥυπάω):—Pass., *to be foul and filthy*, Ep. pf. part. Pass., εἵματα.. τά μοι ῥερυπωμένα κεῖται Od.6.59, cf. Hp.*Mochl.*33, *Mul.*1.66; ἐρρυπωμένος Sch.Ar.*Ach.*425; ῥυπωθῆναι Ph.*Fr.*9 H.:—Act., dub. l. in Thphr.*Char.* 15.6.

**ῥυππάπαῖ**, a cry of the Athenian rowers, *yoho!* Ar.*Ra.*1073: hence comically, τὸ ῥ. the *crew, one's messmates*, Id.*V.*909; also **ῥυππαπαῖ** *AB*446.—Cf. ἱππαπαῖ.

**ῥύπ-τειρα**, as if fem. of ῥυπτήρ (which is only f.l. for ἀρυτήρ in Dsc. 2.74), *that cleanses from dirt*, ῥ. κονίη *soap, lye*, v. l. for θρύπτειρα in Nic.*Al.*370. **-τήριον**· καθαρτήριον, Suid. (post ῥύσιον). **-τικός**, ή, όν, *fit for cleansing from dirt*, ῥυπτικωτάτη κόνις Plu.2.697a; -κὴ δύναμις *detergent*, Gal.10.565: c. gen., ῥ. τοῦ φάρυγγος *cleansing* or *clearing* the throat, Arist.*Pr.*903$^b$29, cf. Pl.*Ti.*65d, Thphr.*CP*6.1.3: but c. gen. objecti, ῥ. ξηρότητος *fit for cleaning* it *off*, Arist.*Sens.*443$^a$1. 2. *purgative*, Id.*Pr.*873$^b$1. **-τω**, (ῥύπος) *cleanse, wash*, esp. with soap or lye, ῥ. τὰ ἱμάτια Id.*Mete.*359$^a$22; τὰν γλῶτταν Ti.Locr.100e; τὰς χεῖρας Phylotim.ap.Ath.3.79c:—Med., *wash oneself*, Antiph.148.3, Thphr.*HP*9.9.3, f.l. in Nic.*Al.*530; aor. ἐρρύψαντο Ph.1.613; λουομένη τὰς τρίχας ἐρρύπτετο Polyaen.8.27: prov., ἐξ ὅτου 'γὼ ῥύπτομαι ever since I *began to wash*, i.e. from my childhood, Ar.*Ach.* 17. **-ώδης**, ες, *filthy, dirty*, Dsc.1.73, Artem.2.4, al., Vett.Val. 249.25; [ἔμπλαστροι] μελάγχλωροι καὶ ῥ. ὠνομασμέναι Gal.13.460, cf. Cels.5.19.15, al.

**ῥῡσ-ά**, = ῥυσή, Phot., Suid. **-αίνομαι**, Pass., *to be wrinkled*, Nic.*Al.*78, *AP*14.103. ❋ **-ᾰλέος**, η, ον, *wrinkled*, ὀπώρη Nic.*Al.* 181. **-άω**, = ῥυσαίνομαι, Hsch. s. v. ῥυσοῖσι. **-ή**, ἡ, *withering, decay*, dub. in Suid. **-ημα**, ατος, τό, *wrinkle*, in pl., Phot., Suid.

**ῥῦσθαι**, v. ἐρύω (B).

**ῥῡσῐ-άζω**, Dor. **ῥῡτιάζω** *IG*4$^2$(1).77.11, al. (Epid., ii B.C.):—*treat as a* ῥύσιον, *seize, distrain upon*, οὐ ῥυσιάζω, τἀμὰ δ' εὑρίσκω φίλα E.*Ion* 523, cf. *SIG*629.20 (Delph., ii B.C.), al., Ph.1.638; of *plundering* a city *as reprisal* for stolen property, τὴν πόλιν D.S.8.7:—Pass., *to be so treated*, A.*Supp.*424 (lyr.), E.*Ion* 1406, *IG* l. c.; τί ῥυσιασθείς; *robbed of* what? cj. in E.*Heracl.*163; of debtors at Rome, Plu.*Cor.*5: metaph., ψευδόδειπνα.. μαργώσης γνάθου ἐρρυσιάσθη cj. in A.*Fr.* 258. **-βωμος**, ον, *defending altars*, Id.*Eu.*920 (lyr.). **-διφρος**, ον, *preserving the chariot*, of a charioteer, Pi.*I.*2.21.

**ῥύσιλλα**, ἡ, = ῥυτίς, Hsch.

**ῥύσῑμον** [ῠ], τό, f.l. in Nic.*Al.*607.

**ῥύσιον** [ῠ], Dor. **ῥύτιον** *SIG*56.41 (Argos, v B.C.): **τό**: (ἐρύω (B)): —*surety, pledge*. I. *property held* or *seized as a pledge* or *compensation*, ῥύσι' ἐλαυνόμενος driving off his cattle *in distraint*, Il.11. 674; ῥύσια δόντες Sol.11.3 (v.l. ῥύματα *protection*); μεῖζον ῥύσιον πόλει θήσεις· ἐφάψομαι γὰρ οὐ ταύταιν μόναιν, i.e. Oedipus shall himself be seized, not his daughters alone, as a *pledge* or *surety* to Thebes, S.*OC*858; ἐπαγέτω ῥύτιον δέκα στατήρων shall impose a *pledge* of ten staters, *SIG* l. c.; ῥύσιον θεὶς τὸν παῖδα J.*BJ*1.14.1; ῥύσια κατὰ τῶν πολεμίων ἄγων ib.1.19.2; ῥύσια τῶν χρημάτων καὶ τῶν παρ' ἐκείνοις λῃστῶν ἐποιεῖτο Id.*AJ*16.9.2; τῆς προθεσμίας παρελθούσης ῥύσια λαμβάνειν ib.16.10.8; ῥύσια καθέξοντες ἀνθ' ὧν.. ἀφείλοντο.. Ῥωμαῖοι χρημάτων D.H.5.33. 2. *stolen property taken back as compensation for the theft*, τοῦ ῥυσίου θ' ἥμαρτε A.*Ag.*535; ῥυσίων ἐφάπτορες laying hands on *alleged stolen property*, Id.*Supp.*728, cf. 412. II. *reprisals*, φόνον φόνου ῥύσιον τείσω suffer death as *reprisals* for death, S.*Ph.*959; ῥύσια κατήγγειλαν τοῖς Ῥοδίοις proclaimed *reprisals*, Plb.4.53.2; κατὰ ῥρύσιον *by way of distraint* or *reprisals*, *IG*12(2). 15.19 (Mytil., iii B.C.); but κατὰ ῥύσιον prob. *in search of persons to seize and hold to ransom*, ib.12(5).653.11 (Syros, i B.C.). 2. ῥύσια, τά, the *right of reprisals*, ᾐτοῦντο ῥύσια τοὺς Ἀχαιοὺς οἱ Δήλιοι κατὰ τῶν Ἀθηναίων Plb.32.7.4; ἀπέδωκε τοῖς αἰτουμένοις τὰ ῥ. κατὰ τῶν Βοιωτῶν granted the *right of reprisals* against.., Id.22.4. 13. III. ῥύσια, τά (cf. ῥύσιος), *restitution, deliverance*, Ἔπαφος ἀληθῶς ῥυσίων ἐπώνυμος A.*Supp.*315. 2. *offerings for deliverance*, ῥ. ἀνάγουσιν D.P.527; ὠδίνων ῥ. *AP*6.274 (Pers.).

**ῥύσιος** [ῠ], ον, (ἐρύω (B)) *delivering, saving*, A.*Supp.*150 (lyr.); ῥύσια ψυχῆς δῶρα *AP*7.605 (Jul. Aegypt.). II. (ἐρύω (A)) ῥυσίαν βολάν· τὴν τῶν τόξων τάσιν, Hsch.

**ῥῡσί-πολις** [ῐ], εως, ὁ, ἡ, *saving the city*, A.*Th.*129 (lyr.); ῥ. Δαναῶν, opp. περσέπολις Τρώων, Poet.ap.Hld.3.2. **-πονος**, ον, *setting free from trouble*, *AP*9.525.18. ❋ **-πτολις**, poet. for ῥυσίπολις, *Epigr.Gr.* (add.) 888a (Ephesus).

**ῥῦσις**, εως, ἡ, (ἐρύω(B)) *deliverance*, θανάτου from death, *Epigr.Gr.* 200 (Cos), Lxx *Si.*51.9.

**ῥύσις** [ῠ], εως, ἡ, (ῥέω) *flow*, ὕδατος Pl.*Lg.*944b; εἰς τὸ κοιλότατον ἡ ῥ. Arist.*Mete.*355$^b$17; opp. ἄμπωτις, ib.366$^a$19; ἐκ ῥινῶν αἵματος -ιες Hp.*Aph.*3.27; κοιλίης ib.2.14; [ἐλαίου], i.e. *yield* of oil, Thphr.*HP*4.14.10, *PRev.Laws* 60.16 (iii B.C.); φλεβῶν Arist.*PA*668$^a$11; of fire, Thphr.*Ign.*54; *shedding*, τριχῶν Dsc.2.120, Gal.19.431; used for γονόρροια, Lxx *Le.*15.2 sq. II. *course of a river, stream*, ποταμὸς ποιεῖται τὴν ῥ. Plb.2.16.6, cf. D.H.1.9, D.S.4.35, Str.6.2. 4. III. Math., [στιγμῆς] ῥύσιν φασὶν εἶναι οἱ γεωμέτραι τὴν γραμμήν (cf. ῥυΐσκομαι, ῥέω 1.5b) Iamb. *in Nic.* p.57 P., cf. Plot.3.7.3, Procl. *in Euc.* p.97 F.; οἷον ἀστρου ῥ. Arist.*Mu.*395$^b$8.

❋ **ῥῡσίς**, ίδος, ἡ, = ῥυτόν, v.l. for χρυσίς in Cratin.124.

**ῥύσκομαι**, v. ἐρύω (B). **ῥυσμός, ῥυσμόω**, v. ῥυθμός, ῥυθμόω.

**ῥῡσόκαρφος**, ον, *with shrivelled branches*, Dsc.1.14, Anon.Lond.32. 46.

**ῥῡσός**, ή, όν, *shrivelled, wrinkled*, Il.9.503, E.*El.*490, Ar.*Pl.*266, Pl.*R.*452b; ῥυσὰ σαρκῶν πολιὰν καταδρύμματα the tearing of old *wrinkled* flesh (cf. ῥυτίς), E.*Supp.*49 (lyr.); ῥ. βουλευτήρια, prob. = ῥυσοὶ βουλευταί, Theopomp.Com.75; μαστός Sor.1.88; ἕλκος Gal.10.404; ῥυσότερον βαλλαντίων πρόσωπον Alciphr.3.55; ῥ. ἐπισκύνιον *AP*6.64 (Paul. Sil.); also of fruits, etc., [ἀκρόδρυα] ἰσχνὰ καὶ ῥ. Plu.2.735d; ἐλαῖαι Archestr.*Fr.*7; σῦκα Philostr.*Im.*1.31.—The forms ῥυσσός, ῥυσσαίνομαι, etc., are freq. in codd.

**ῥῡσό-της**, ητος, ἡ, *wrinkledness, wrinkles*, Plu.*Galb.*13, Antyll.ap. Orib.44.8.2. **-χίτων** [ῐ], ωνος, ὁ, ἡ, *with shrivelled coat* or *skin*, κόκκος Orph.*L.*721 (prob. for χρυσ-).

**ῥῡσόω**, (ῥυσός) *make wrinkled, shrivel*, Dsc.5.92, *Hippiatr.*11, Sch. Od.13.401:—Pass., *to be* or *become wrinkled, shrivel*, δέρμα Arist.*Pr.* 937$^a$9; ῥερυσωμέναι, of skins *hung loosely* on χελῶναι, opp. προτεινόμεναι, Apollod.*Poliorc.*142.4; of fruits, Dsc.5.6.14, *Gp.*7.18.3, 10. 38.10.

**ῥυσσαίνομαι, ῥυσσός, ῥυσσόομαι**, etc., v. ῥυσός.

**ῥύσ-ταγμα**, ατος, τό, *dragging away, maltreatment*, in pl., Lyc. 1089. ❋ **-τάζω**, Frequentat. of ἐρύω (A), *drag about*, πολλὰ ῥυστάζεσκεν.. περὶ σῆμα *he dragged* it many times round the grave of Patroclus, Il.24.755; δμῳὰς.. ῥυστάζοντας ἀεικελίως κατὰ δώματα Od.16. 109; cf. sq. **-τακτύς**, ύος, ἡ, *dragging about, rough handling*, 18. 224. ❋ **-τήρ**, ῆρος, ὁ, rare and late form for ῥυτήρ (B), *deliverer*, Tryph.266. II. *rein*, Phot.; cf. βρύτηρ. 2. perh. to be read for ῥηστήρ, *ladle* of an irrigating-machine, *PLond.*1821.210. **-της**, ου, ὁ, (ἐρύω (B)) *saviour, deliverer*, Lxx *Ps.*17(18).2, al., Ps.-Luc. *Philopatr.*6. **-τικός**, ή, όν, *protective, saving*, [πρᾶξις] *PMag. Berol.*1.197; χαρακτῆρες ib.266, cf. *PMag.Par.*1.9.

**ῥυστόν**· δόρυ, Κρῆτες, Hsch.

**ῥῡσ-ώδης**, ες, *wrinkled-looking*, *AP*5.75 (Rufin.), Dsc.5.79. **-ωσις**, εως, ἡ, *wrinkling*, an eye-disease, Gal.14.767.

**ῥῡτά**, τά, v. ῥυτός (B) 2.

**ῥῡτᾰγωγεύς**, έως, ὁ, *rope of a horse's halter*, X.*Eq.*7.1, Poll.10.55; cf. ῥυτήρ (A) 2b.

❋ **ῥύτειρα** [ῠ], ἡ, fem. of ῥυτήρ (B), Suid.

**ῥυτή**, ἡ, Peloponnesian word for πήγανον, *rue*, Nic.*Al.*306, *Th.* 523, Aret.*CD*2.5, *Hippiatr.*130; ῥυτέων f.l. for βρυτέων in Aret.*SD*2.9.

**ῥῡτήρ** (A), ῆρος, ὁ, (ἐρύω (A)) *one who draws* or *stretches*, ῥ. βιοῦ, ὀϊστῶν, *drawer of the bow, of arrows*, Od.21.173, 18.262. 2. *strap by which one holds a horse, rein*, Il.16.475 (pl.); σπεύδειν ἀπὸ ῥυτῆρος *with loose rein, at full gallop*, S.*OC*900; ἀπὸ ῥ. ἐλαύνειν τοὺς ἵππους D.H.4.85, cf. 11.33, D.S.19.26 (Phryn.*PS* p.41 B. expl. ἀπὸ ῥ. by ἄνευ χαλινοῦ): ῥυτῆρα χαλινόν Pancrat.*Oxy.*1085.4; χαλινὸν.. ἔχον ῥυτῆρας *PCair.Zen.*659.11 (iii B.C.). b. *strap* to flog with, D.19.197, Aeschin.2.157, cf. S.*Aj.*241 (anap.), *Fr.*501.

❋ **ῥῡτήρ** (B), ῆρος, ὁ, (ἐρύω (B)) *saviour, guard, defender*, σταθμῶν ῥ. Od.17.187, 223; ῥυτῆρες Διός Opp.*C.*3.13: fem. abs., Id.*H.*1. 669; cf. ῥύτειρα. (Cf. ῥυστήρ I.)

**ῥυτιάζω**, v. ῥυσιάζω.

**ῥῡτῐδόφλοιος**, ον, *with shrivelled rind*, σῦκον *AP*6.22 (Zon.).

**ῥῠτῐδ-όω**, *make wrinkled, shrivel up*, Arist.*Pr*.936$^{b}$10 :—Pass., *to be wrinkled*, ῥυτιδούμενοι [ὀφθαλμοί] Hp.*Epid*.6.1.13 ; δέρμα ἐρρυτιδωμένον Arist.*HA*578$^{a}$9, cf. *GA*780$^{a}$32 ; φύλλα Thphr.*HP*3.10.3 ; μῆλον Dsc.1.115 ; τὴν ὄψιν ἐρρυτιδωμένος Luc.*Luct*.16 ; of bandages, Sor.1. 83. **-ώδης**, ες, *wrinkled-looking*, γαστέρες Hp.*Prorrh*.2.23, cf. Arist.*HA*604$^{a}$28 ; τὰ ῥ. τῶν προσώπων Id.*Phgn*.808$^{a}$8 ; φύλλον -έστερον Thphr.*HP*4.6.6. **-ωμα**, ατος, τό, *wrinkle*, Sch.Ar.*Pl*. 1052, 1066. **-ωσις**, εως, ἡ, *wrinkling, contraction*, e.g. of the eye, Gal.10.171 (pl.), Ruf.*Fr*.78.

**ῥύτιον**, v. ῥύσιον. II. v. ῥῠτός.

**ῥῠτίς**, ίδος, ἡ, Aeol. **βρῠτίς** (q.v.), *pucker, wrinkle*, Ar.*Pl*.1051, Pl. *Smp*.190e, 191a.

**ῥύτις** [ῠ], εως, ἡ, = ῥύσις, in a play on words, Ps.-Democr.ap.Zos. Alch. p.119 B.

**ῥύτισμα** [ῠ], ατος, τό, *darn* or *patch*, Men.1059 (pl.).

**ῥῡτόν**, τό, = πήγανον, Cratin.270 ; cf. ῥυτή.

**ῥῠτόν**, τό, v. ῥῠτός II.

**ῥῡτός** (A), ή, όν, *quarried*, ῥυτοῖσιν λάεσσι Od.6.267, 14.10. (Cf. Lat. *rūta caesa*.)

**ῥῡτός** (B), ή, όν, (ἐρύω (A)) *dragged, hauled*, σανίδες Ph.*Bel*.95.48 (s.v.l.). **2.** Subst. neut. pl. ῥῡτά, τά, *reins* (cf. ῥυτήρ (A) 2a), ῥυτὰ χαλαίνειν Hes.*Sc*.308.

⊛ **ῥῠτός**, ή, όν, (ῥέω) *flowing, fluid, liquid*, ῥυτᾶς ἐξ ἁλός A.*Ag*.1408 (lyr.) ; ῥ. πόροι (v. πόρος I.3) Id.*Eu*.452 ; ῥυτῶν ὑδάτων λουτρά S.*OC* 1598 ; παγά E.*Hipp*.123 (lyr.) ; ὑγρὸν ῥ., opp. πακτόν, Ti.Locr.99c ; [ὕδατα] ῥ. distd. fr. στάσιμα, Arist.*Mete*.353$^{b}$19, cf. Thphr.*CP*2.6.3 ; distd. fr. φρεατιαῖα, Plu.2.954c. II. ῥῠτόν, τό, *drinking-cup* or *horn*, running to a point, where was a small hole, through which the wine ran in a thin stream, S.*Fr*.772, D.21.158, *PPetr*.3 p.113 (iii B.C.), *Inscr.Délos*442 *B*27 (ii B.C.), Plb.14.11.2, Plu.*Alex*.67 ; made in the form of an elephant, a trireme, the god Βησᾶς, Damox.1.2, Epin.2.1, Hedyl.ap.Ath.11.497d ; *funnel* used as a filter, Ps.-Democr.ap.Zos. Alch.p.155 B. ; v. κρουνίζω :—Dim. **ῥύτιον** [ῠ], τό, only in Lat. form *rhytium*, Mart.2.35.2.

**ῥῦτρα**· λυτήρια, σωτήρια, σῶστρα, Hsch.

**ῥύτρος**, εος, τό, a plant with prickles at the ends, *globe-thistle*, *Echinops viscosus*, Thphr.*HP*6.4.4.

**ῥύτρυς**· χύτας, Hsch.

⊛ **ῥύτωρ** (A) [ῡ], ορος, ὁ, (ἐρύω (A)) *one who draws*, χρυσέων ῥ. τόξων, of Apollo, Ar.*Th*.108 (lyr.).

**ῥύτωρ** (B) [ῡ], ορος, ὁ, (ἐρύω (B)) *saviour, deliverer, defender*, πόλεως A.*Th*.318 (lyr.) ; σωφροσύνης ῥ. καὶ βιότου *IG*3.1171.6 ; ῥ. βουκολίων *AP*6.37 ; ῥ. χαίτας κεκρύφαλος ib.207 (Arch.) : c. gen. objecti, *one who saves* or *delivers from*, λιμοῦ καὶ θανάτου ib.9.351 (Leon.Alex.). III. ῥύτορας· τοὺς θαλλοὺς τοὺς καθαρτηρίους, Hsch.

**ῥῠφάνω, ῥῠφέω, ῥύφημα**, Ion. for ῥοφάνω, -έω, -ημα (qq.v.).

***ῥύφω**, in aor. inf. ῥύψαι·..ῥοφῆσαι, and fut. ῥυψόμεθα·..ῥοφησόμεθα, Hsch. **ῥυχάνησις**, v. ῥυκάνησις. **ῥυχάχετος**, v. ῥυάχετος.

**ῥύψις**, εως, ἡ, (ῥύπτω) *cleansing, purifying*, Pl.*Ti*.65e, Ti.Locr.100e.

**ῥῠώδης**, ες, (ῥέω) *running, flowing* ; of persons, ῥ. τὰ οὖρα *incontinent* of urine, Hp.*Art*.48 ; σπέρμα πολὺ καὶ ῥ. *flowing freely*, Pl.*Ti*. 86c, cf. d ; of fevers, *continuous* or *frequent*, Gal.19.552 (nisi ῥοώδης legend.).

**ῥῶ**, v. Ῥ ῥ.

⊛ **ῥωβίδας**, α, ὁ, at Sparta, *boy of less than one year old*, Λέξεις Ἡροδότου in Stein *Herodotus* ii p.465 (Berol.1871).

**ῥωβικός**, ή, όν, *unable to pronounce the letter* ῥῶ, ῥωβικώτερος D.L. 2.108.

**ῥωγ-ᾰλέος**, η, ον, (ῥώξ A) *broken, cleft*, χιτὼν χαλκῷ ῥ. Il.2.417 ; ῥ. πήρη *torn, ragged*, Od.17.198 ; ῥάκος .. ἠδὲ χιτῶνα, ῥωγαλέα 13. 435. ⊛ **-άς**, άδος, ὁ, ἡ, = foreg., *ragged*, πήρη Babr.86 ; ῥ. πέτραι *cloven* rocks, *clefts in* the rocks, Theoc.24.95, cf. A.R.4.1448, Nic. *Th*.389 ; κάπετος ῥ. Posidipp.ap.Ath.8.414e. **-ή**, ἡ, in pl. ῥωγαί· ῥήξεις, Hsch. **-μᾰτίας**, ου, Ion. -ίης, ὁ, = ῥηγματίας, Hp.ap.Gal. 19.136. **-μή**, ἡ, = ῥωγή, *fracture*, Hp.*VC*3 ; ῥ. ξύλου *cleft*, Arist.*HA* 614$^{b}$15, cf. 556$^{a}$5. **-μοειδής**, ές, *like a fracture*, ῥαφαί Hp.*VC*12.

**ῥωγμός**, v. ῥωχμός (B). **ῥώδιγγες**· πληγαὶ ὕφαιμοι διακεκομμέναι, οἱ δὲ μώλωπες, Hsch. (also **ῥώτιγγες** Id.). **ῥῳδιόν**· τὸν ἐρῳδιόν, Id., cf. Hippon.63.

**ῥώθων**, ωνος, ὁ, *nose*, Heraclid.Tar.ap.Gal.12.692, *Hippiatr*.21 : mostly in pl., *nostrils*, Nic.*Th*.213, *Al*.117, D.H.*Comp*.14, 22, Str.7. 4.8, Poll.2.72, Horap.2.68 :—**ῥώθυνες**· μυκτῆρες, Hsch. (Aeol. ?).

**ῥώκομαι**· ὀργίζομαι, λυποῦμαι, Λάκωνες, Hsch. :—**ῥώκωσα** (ῥωκῶσα cod.)· πρίουσα τοὺς ὀδόντας, Id. (Cf. ῥώχω.)

**ῥῶμα**· ῥώμην, ἰσχύν, ὅρμημα, ὡς γνῶμα γνώμην, Hsch.

**Ῥωμᾰ-ΐζω**, *speak Latin*, App.*Hann*.41, Philostr.*VA*5.36. **2.** *hold with Rome, be of the Roman party*, App.*Pun*.68, *Mac*.7, al. ⊛ **-ϊκός**, ή, όν, *Roman*, Plb.30.18.3, al. ; δακτυλίδιον *BCH*29. 537 (Delos, ii B.C.) : Sup. -κώτατος *AP*9.502 (Pall.). Adv. -κῶς *in Latin*, ibid. ; *in Roman fashion*, Ptol.Euerg.7 J., Plu.*Aem*.13 : Comp., J.*BJ*2.20.7.

⊛ **Ῥωμ-αῖος**, α, ον, *a Roman*, Plb.10.36.3, etc. ; τὰ Ῥωμαῖα *ludi Romani*, D.C.37.8. **-αιότης**, ητος, ἡ, *Roman citizenship*, *Notiz. Arch*.4.20 (Cyrene, i B.C.). **-ᾰΐς**, ΐδος, ἡ, fem. of Ῥωμαῖος, παιδεία Dam.ap.Suid. s.v. Μαρκελλῖνος.

⊛ **Ῥωμᾰ-ϊστής**, οῦ, ὁ, *actor of Latin comedies*, *IG*11(2).133.81 (Delos, ii B.C.). **-ϊστί**, Adv. *in Latin*, App.*Mith*.2, Plu.2.318d, etc.

**ῥωμᾰλ-εόομαι**, Pass., *to be endued with strength*, Arist.*Phgn*.809$^{a}$ 32. ⊛ **-έος**, α, ον, (ῥώμη) *strong of body*, ῥ. τῷ σώματι Pl.*Ax*.365a ; ἡλικίᾳ Aen.Tact.1.8 (Sup.) ; κάμηλοι *PFlor*.278 ii 6, al. (iii A.D.) ; κατὰ χεῖρα Plu.2.597e ; ῥ. ὦμοι Arist.*Phgn*.809$^{b}$27 ; -ώτατος ἐν τῷ λέγειν Plu.*CG*4. **2.** of things, *strong*, ῥωμαλεώτεραι πέδαι Hdt.3. 22 ; ῥίζαι Dsc.1.16 (Sup.) ; βίοτος *robust, virile*, *AP*7.413 (Antip.). Adv. -έως Gal.6.139, Them.*Or*.21.249c.

**ῥώμη**, ἡ, (ῥώομαι) *bodily strength, might*, Xenoph.2.11, Hdt.1.31, 8.113 ; γυίων ῥ. A.*Pers*.913 (anap.) ; μεῖζον ἢ κατ' ἐμὰν ῥώμαν S.*Tr*. 1019 (lyr.) ; ἐπ' ἀσθενοῦς ῥώμης ὀχούμεθ' E.*Or*.69 ; ἀκμαζούσῃ τῇ ῥώμῃ τῶν χειρῶν χρώμενος Antipho 4.3.3, cf. Agatho 27 ; εἴ τῳ..προλίποι ἡ ῥ. καὶ τὸ σῶμα, i.e. his bodily *strength*, Th.7.75 ; ὁ μετὰ ῥώμης γιγνόμενος θάνατος in the *full strength* or *vigour* of life, Id.2.43 ; ὑγίειαν καὶ ῥ. Pl.*Phdr*.270b ; τὴν ἰσχὺν δεινὰ καὶ τὴν ῥ. Id.*Smp*.190b ; ῥ. καὶ τόλμη D.18.220 ; ῥώμης ἀκμή Eub.7.6 : pl., πιστεύοντες ταῖς αὑτῶν ῥ. Lys.24.16 ; ταῖς τῶν σωμάτων ῥ. X.*Cyr*.3.3.19. **2.** of nations, armies, and the like, τὴν παροῦσαν νῦν ῥ. πόλεως Th.4.18. **3.** of things, *strength, force, might*, δορός E.*Supp*.26 ; πνίγους Pl.*Lg*. 633c ; πνεύματ' ἀνέμων οὐκ ἀεὶ ῥώμην ἔχει E.*HF*102 ; also ῥ. ψυχῆς X.*Cyr*.4.2.14 ; ἡδονῶν Pl.*Lg*.841a ; τοῦ λέγειν ib.711e ; λόγου Id. *Phdr*.267a ; ἡ τῶν λόγων ῥ. Cratin.Jun.7.3. **4.** οὐ μιᾷ ῥώμῃ not single-handed, S.*OT*123 : *a force*, i.e. *army*, X.*An*.3.3.14, *HG*7.4. 16. **5.** *confidence*, τοῖς Λακεδαιμονίοις ἐγεγένητό τις ῥ., διότι τοὺς Ἀθηναίους ἐνόμιζον διπλοῦν τὸν πόλεμον ἔχοντας.. εὐκαθαιρετωτέρους ἔσεσθαι Th.7.18, cf. 42, 4.29.

⊛ **Ῥώμη**, ἡ, *Roma, Rome*, first mentioned in Gr. literature by Arist. *Fr*.610 ; deified in Inscrr., θεὰ Ῥώμη *IG*3.63, *CIG*2696 (Mylasa), *SIG*893 (Olympia, iii A.D.), etc.

**ῥώμσιν** (acc. sg.), v. ῥώψ (B). **ῥώνιξις**, v. ῥώψ (B). **ῥώνιος**· ἄξιος, πλούσιος, Hsch. (fort. ϝώνιος).

⊛ **ῥώννῡμι**, Hp.*Alim*.2 ; **ῥωννύω**, Ti.Locr.103e, Gal.6.581 : fut. ῥώσω (ἐπιρ-) Plu.2.9e : aor. ἔρρωσα Arat.335, Plu.*Pomp*.76, (ἐπ-) Hdt.8. 14, Th.4.36 :—Pass., ῥώννῠμαι Plu.*Rom*.25, *Cor*.24, etc. : fut. ῥωσθήσομαι Apollod.1.6.3, (ἐπιρ-) Luc.*Somn*.18 : aor. ἐρρώσθην Th.4.72, Pl.*Phdr*.238c, (ἐπ-) S.*OC*661 : pf. ἔρρωμαι (v. infr.) :—*strengthen*, τροφὴ ῥώννυσι Hp. l.c. ; ῥ. τὰν ψυχὰν ποτ' (= πρὸς) ἀλκάν Ti.Locr. 103b ; ὁρμάν ib.e ; τὰς πόλεις Plu.*Per*.19 : but II. mostly in pf. Pass. (with pres. sense) ἔρρωμαι, and plpf. ἐρρώμην (as impf.) :—*have strength* or *might*, γέροντές ἐσμεν κοὐδαμῶς ἐρρώμεθα E.*Heracl*.636 ; ἐρρῶσθαι τὴν ψυχήν X.*HG*3.4.29 ; so ἐρρώσθη χρήμασιν Plu.*Publ*. 23. **2.** *to be eager, enthusiastic*, glossed by προθυμεῖσθαι, Cratin. 411 ; ἔρρωντο ἐς τὸν πόλεμον Th.2.8, cf. 8.78, 4.72 : c. inf., *to be eager* to do, ἔρρωτο πᾶς ξυνεπιλαμβάνειν Id.2.8, cf. Lys.13.31, Pl.*Smp*. 176b. **3.** *to be in good health*, Th.7.15 : freq. in imper. ἔρρωσο, *farewell*, the usual way of ending a letter, as in X.*Cyr*.4.5.33, and at the close of Pl.*Ep*.1, 2, and 10 ; ἔρρωσο πολλά Men.*Georg*.84 ; ἔρρωσθε Id.*Pk*.50 ; also φράζειν τινὶ ἐρρῶσθαι Pl.*Phd*.61b, D.18.152, 19.248 ; εἰ ἔρρωσαι..καλῶς ἂν ἔχοι, ἐρρώμεθα δὲ καὶ αὐτοί *PPetr*.2 p.27 (iii B.C.) ; εἰ ἔρρωσθε εὖ ἂν ἔχοι *IG*7.413 (Oropus, Senatus consultum, i B.C.), cf. *SIG*768 (Epist. Aug.). **4.** freq. in part. ἐρρωμένος (q.v.).

**ῥώξ** (A), ῥωγός, ἡ, (ῥήγνυμι) *breach* : in Od.22.143, ἀνὰ ῥῶγας μεγάροιο, the sense is dub. ; it seems to mean *narrow entrances* or *passages leading to* the hall.

**ῥώξ** (B), ῥωγός, ἡ (ὁ in Lxx *Is*.65.8), = ῥάξ 1, Archil.191 ; τοῦ ἀμπελῶνος Lxx *Le*.19.10, cf. Ph.2.390 (v.l.) ; ἐλαίας Lxx *Is*.17.6. **2.** = ῥάξ 4, in pl., Ruf.ap.Orib.25.1.32. **3.** = ῥάξ 3, Nic.*Th*.716.

**ῥώομαι**, Ep. Verb, of which Hom. uses 3 pl. impf. ἐρρώοντο, Ep. ῥώοντο, and 3 pl. aor. ἐρρώσαντο (v. infr.) ; aor. subj. ῥώσονται or -ωνται Call.*Del*.175 : Nic. has also ῥώετο, *Th*.351 ; later in pres., Orph.*L*.707 (prob.), D.P.518 codd. :—*move with speed* or *violence*, *rush on*, esp. of warriors, Il.11.50, 16.166, cf. Hes.*Sc*.230 ; τεύχεσιν ἐρρ. πυρὴν πέρι *ran* round it, Od.24.69 ; Νυμφάων, αἵ τ' ἀμφ' Ἀχελώϊον ἐρρώσαντο *dance*, Il.24.616 (cf. ἐπιρρώομαι I.2) : c. acc. cogn., χορὸν ἐρρώσαντο *they ply* the dance, *h.Ven*.261 ; ὑπὸ ῥώοντο ἄνακτι *they moved* supporting their lord, Il.18.417 ; κνῆμαι ῥώοντο, γούνατα ἐρρώσαντο, ib.411, Od.23.3 ; also of horses' manes, ἐρρώοντο μετὰ πνοιῇς ἀνέμοιο *waved streaming* in the wind, Il.23.367.

**ῥῷον**, τό, = Τρώων οἶνος, Theognost.*Can*.148 (who derives it from ῥώω). ⊛ **ῥώπαες**, τό, sine expl., ib.131.

**ῥωπ-άκιον**, τό, Dim. of sq., Suid. **-άς**, άδος, ἡ, = ῥώψ (A), Opp.*C*. 4.393 ; so **ῥῶπαξ**, ἄκος, ὁ, Suid. **-εῖον**, τό, v. ῥωπήϊον. ⊛ **-εύω**, *cut down underwood*, *AP*6.226 (Leon., but ῥωπεῖον is prob.). II. (ῥῶπος) = ῥωποπωλέω, Hsch. **-ήεις**, εσσα, εν, *grown with underwood*, ἄγκος Q.S.7.715. **-ήϊον**, τό, Ep. word (Att. form ῥωπεῖον dub., v. ῥωπεύω I), only used in pl., *bushes, brushwood, underwood*, ῥωπήϊα πυκνά Il.13.199, 23.122, etc. ; κατά τε ῥωπήϊα δύω 21.559.

**ῥωπ-ίζω**, (ῥῶπος) perh. *deal in petty wares*, but variously glossed, Ion Trag.31. **-ικός**, ή, όν, *of* or *for petty wares, trumpery*, Plu.*Lyc*. 9 ; δῶρον *AP*6.355 (Leon.) ; of persons, Plb.23.5.5 ; ῥωπικὰ γράψασθαι paint *poorly, coarsely*, *AP* l.c. ; [ἡ φύσις] οὐδὲν ἔχουσα ῥ. Erasistr. ap.Plu.2.495c : τὸ ῥ. *tawdry ornaments* in writing, *claptrap*, Longin. 3.4.

**ῥωπίον**, τό, (ῥώψ A) = ῥωπεῖον, *bush, twig, bough*, D.C.63.28.

**ῥωπο-γρᾰφία**, ἡ, '*artificial prettiness*' of scenery, Cic.*Att*.15. 16b. ⊛ **-γράφος** [γρᾰ], ον, (ῥῶπος) *one that paints petty subjects* (ῥῶπες, glossed as ὕλη καὶ ὑλώδη φυτά), such as *still life*, like the Dutch masters, *EM*705.55, perh. to be read in Donat.ad Ter.*Eun*. 253 ; cf. ῥυπαρογράφος. **-περπερήθρα**, ἡ, (πέρπερος) *empty braggart talk*, *Com.Adesp*.294 (restored fr. Plu.*Dem*.9). **-πωλέω**, *deal in small wares* or *frippery*, Hsch. s.v. ῥωπεύειν. ⊛ **-πώλης**, ου, ὁ, *dealer in petty wares, huckster*, Lxx *Ne.*3.31 (written **ῥοβο–**, v.l. **ῥοπο–**), Gal.12.252, al., prob. in *Jahresh.*23 *Beibl.*172 (Thrace); written **ῥοπο–**, Maiuri *Nuova Silloge* 634 (Cos). **–πώλιον·** *rimentarium* (fort. *pimentarium*, cf. ῥῶπος 2 and πιμεντάριος), *Gloss.*

**ῥῶπος**, ὁ, *petty wares*, ὅστις ῥῶπον ἐξάγει χθονός A.*Fr.*263; ὁ ῥ. ὃν σὺ περιφέρεις Diph.55; ἄπρατον εἶναι τὸν ῥ. D.34.9; ἔλαιον καὶ ἄλλον ναυτικὸν ῥ. Arist.*Mir.*844ᵃ19; ὑαλᾶ σκεύη καὶ ἄλλος ῥ. τοιοῦτος Str.4.5.3, cf. 8.6.16. **2.** = μεῖγμα χρώματος, Sch.Porph.*Abst.*4.3.

**ῥωρός**, ά, όν, (ῥώννυμι) *strong, mighty*, Hsch.; cf. ῥάρος.

**ῥῶσις**, εως, ἡ, (ῥώννυμι) *strengthening, strength*. ῥ. καὶ θρέψις σωμάτων S.E.*M.*11.97; ῥῶσιν εὔξασθαί τινι *OGI*206 (Nubia, ii or iii A.D.); κοινὴν ἅπασι πορίζεται ῥῶσιν Chor. in Lib.4p.524R. **2.** *encouragement*, τοῦ Ἕκτορος Sch.Il.*Oxy.*1087 i 13. **3.** *violence*, τοῦ πάθους Porph.*Abst.*1.38; *preponderance*, τοῦ χείρονος ἤθους Plot.3.4.3.

❋ **ῥωσκομένως**, Adv. pres. part., as if from a Verb ῥώσκομαι = ῥώννυμαι, *strongly*, Hp.*Cord.*1.

**ῥῶσταξ**, ακος, ὁ, *stand for putting anything on*, Tz.*H.*11.612.

**ῥωστήρ·** σφῦρα, Hsch. (cf. ῥαιστήρ).

❋ **ῥωσ-τήριον**, τό, = παρορμητήριον, Phot. **–τικός**, ή, όν, *strengthening*, Dsc.5.6.10, Gal.6.604 (interpol.), Philagr.ap.Orib.5.17.6. **II.** *strong*, Gal.17(1).43.

**ῥῶστρον·** ἔμβολον, Hsch. (i.e. Lat. *rostrum*). **ῥωτακίζω**, *make overmuch* or *wrong use of* the letter ρ, Suid. **ῥώτιγγες**, v. ῥώδιγγες.

❋ **ῥωχ-μή**, ἡ, = sq. (A), in pl., *fissures*, Marc.Sid.79. **–μός** (A), ὁ, (ῥώξ A) *cleft*, ῥ. ἔην γαίης *a runnel* or *gutter* scooped out by heavy rains, Il.23.420, cf. A.R.4.1545, Bion *Fr.*1, Opp.*C.*3.323; τῆς πέτρας Plu. *Crass.*4; οἱ ἀπὸ τῶν σεισμῶν ῥ. Str.8.5.7. **–μός** (B), ὁ, *wheezing*, Aret.*SD*1.11 (written **ῥωγμός**), Aët.6.3 (written **ῥοχμός**); gloss on ῥέγχος, Erot.; written **ῥογμός** in Cael.Aur.*CP*2.27; **ῥογχός**, ib. 10. **–ω**, *wheeze*, Sor.1.123; but **ῥώχειν**, = βρύχειν τοῖς ὀδοῦσι, Hsch.

**ῥώψ** (A), ἡ, gen. ῥωπός, *shrub, bush*, sg. only in Hsch., who has ῥώψ· βοτάνη ἁπαλή: elsewh. only in pl., *underwood, brushwood*, Od.10.166, 14.49, 16.47; ῥῶπες εἰς σκέπην Lib.*Or.*11.254; ἱμαντώδη φυτά, acc. to Eust.1750.2.

**ῥώψ** (B), πλοῖον παπύρινον, ὃ καλεῖται Αἰγυπτιστὶ ῥώψ *UPZ* 81 ii 7 (ii B.C.); ἐὰν δὲ μὴ ἔχητε πλοῖον, συνεμβήσητε ἅμα ἡμῖν εἰς ῥῶμσιν *PPar.* in *Glotta* 2.150; corrupted to ῥώνιξις· ποταμίας νεὼς εἶδος, in Hsch. [ῥώψ from *ρωμς; Egyptian *rms.*]

**ῥώω**, v. ῥῴον.

# Σ

**Σ σ, σίγμα** or **σῖγμα** (both accents are found in codd.), τό, twenty-first letter of the Etruscan abecedaria, *IG*14.2420, and prob. of the oldest Gr. alphabets (corresponding to the twenty-first Hebrew letter *shin* ש, Phoenician W, *Syria* 6.103), but eighteenth of the Ion. alphabet: as numeral σʹ = 200, but ͵σ = 200,000: a semi-vowel, Arist.*Po.*1456ᵇ28, cf. Pl.*Tht.*203b.

**A.** the oldest forms expressing this sound were M (which is however the old eighteenth letter, q.v.), also Σ and ϟ; compared to a twisted curl, E.*Fr.*382.7, Theodect.6; to a Scythian bow, Agatho 4; after this, but yet early, it took the shape of a semicircle C, whence Aeschrio (*Fr.*1) calls the new moon τὸ καλὸν οὐρανοῦ νέον σῖγμα: hence the orchestra is called τὸ τοῦ θεάτρου σῖγμα, Phot., *AB* 286: and Lat. writers used *sigma* of a *semicircular couch*, Mart.10.48.6, etc.; cf. σιγμοειδής. The rare form Ǝ is used in the numbering of building-stones in *Berl.Sitzb.*1888.1234, 1242 (Pergam.). From final ς must be distinguished the character ς = 6, v. Ϝ ϝ (sixth letter).

**B.** the name **σίγμα** (**σῖγμα**) was usu. indeclinable, τοῦ σίγμα Pl. l.c., *Cra.*402e, 427a, Ath.10.455c, Lyd.*Mens.*1.21 (v.l. σίγματος); τῷ σῖγμα Gal.*UP*2.14, al.; τῶν σῖγμα Pl.Com.30; τὰ σίγμα τὰ ἐπὶ τῶν ἀσπίδων X.*HG*4.4.10, cf. Hellad.ap.Phot.*Bibl.* p.532 B.; later declined, τοῦ σίγματος Eust.1389.15; σίγμασιν Id.905.7. **2.** we also hear of another name **σάν** [ᾰ], τό, τὰ οὐνόματά σφι (sc. τοῖσι Πέρσῃσι) τελευτῶσι πάντα ἐς τὠυτὸ γράμμα, τὸ Δωριέες μὲν σὰν καλέουσι, Ἴωνες δὲ σίγμα Hdt.1.139, cf. Pi.*Dith.Oxy.*1604 *Fr* 1 ii 3, Ath.11.467a; as name of the fourth and tenth letters in Θρασύμαχος, and of the sixth in Διονύσο(υ), Epigr.ap.Ath.10.454f, Achae.33.4; cf. the compd. σαμ-φόρας: σάν and σίγμα were evidently pronounced alike; it is conjectured that σάν is originally the name of the old eighteenth letter.

**σ'**, by apostr. for σέ; also, though rarely, for σοί; v. σύ. **II.** for σά, but in Hom. only in phrases τὰ σ' αὐτοῦ, τὰ σ' αὐτῆς, Od.14.185, Il.6.490, al.; so, in Trag. and later Poets, τὰ σ' S.*OT*329, 405, *Ph.*339, *El.*1499, E.*Supp.*456.

**σᾶ**, fem. sg. and neut. pl. of σῶς.

**σά μάν;** Doric (Megarian) for τί μήν; Ar.*Ach.*757, 784; Boeot. **τά** Pi.*O.*1.82. (From *τya (*qʷya), neut. pl. of τίς, cf. ἅ-σσα, ἄ-ττα, Lat. *quia.*)

**σαάμον**, τό, Lacon. for σήσαμον (q.v.).

❋ **Σᾰβαζιασταί**, οἱ, *worshippers of Sabazius*, *IG*2².1335.4 (ii B.C.).

❋ **Σᾰβάζιος**, ὁ, (Σαβός) a Phrygian deity, whose mysteries resembled the τελεταί of Dionysus, Thphr.*Char.*27.8 (but **Σαβαδίου** [acc.] ib.16.4, cf. Dessau *Inscr.Lat.Sel.*2189), Nymphis 11; hence afterwards taken as a name of Dionysus himself, Ar.*V.*9, *Av.*875, *Lys.*388; θεῷ Σαβαζίῳ παγκοιράνῳ *CIG*3791 (Bithynia), cf. *IG*12(5).27 (Sicinus); Δὶ Σαβαζίῳ *BMus.Inscr.*1100 (Italy, iii A.D.); Διὶ **Σεβαζίῳ** (sic) *Supp.Epigr.*1.302 (Thrace): also **Σαόαζος** *AJA*3(1887).363 (Phrygia); τοῦ Διὸς **Σαουάζου** *IGRom.*4.889 (ibid.); **Σαβάδιος**, *Gloss.* **II.** Adj. Σᾰβάζιος, α, ον, *Bacchic*, θύσθλα cj. in Opp.*C.*1.26; τὰ Σαβάζια Str.10.3.18.

**Σᾰβάζω**, = εὐάζω, Nymphis 11; written **σαββάζειν** in Sch.Patm. D. in *BCH*1.145.

**σᾰβάζω**, *shake violently, scatter*, in aor. part. σαβάξας, Hsch., Phot.

**σαβαῖ**, a Bacchanalian cry, like εὐαί, εὐοῖ, Eup.84.

**σᾰβᾰκάθιον** [κᾰ], τό, = σάβανον, Hsch. s.v. κεκρύφαλος, *POxy.* 2002ᵛ.4 (vi A.D.); [σα]βακάτια (pl.) prob. in *PCornell* 29.2 (prob. ii A.D.): also **σαββακάθιον**, Phot. s.v. κεκρύφαλον, **σᾰβάκᾰνον**, Hsch. s.v. κρύφαλον.

❋ **σᾰβᾰκός**, ή, όν, = σαθρός (Chian), Hsch. **2.** *feeble*, Hp.*Morb.* 1.31; *effeminate*, σαβακῶν σαλμακίδων *AP*7.222 (Phld.): neut. sg. written σαβακουν, = *quassum*, *Gloss.*

❋ **σᾰβάκτης**, ου, ὁ, (σαβάζω) *shatterer, destroyer*, of a mischievous goblin who broke pots, Hom.*Epigr.*14.9: fem. pl. **σαβακτίδες·** ὀστράκινα ζῴδια, Hsch.

**σᾰβάν-ιον** [βᾰ], τό, Dim. of sq., *POxy.*1729.7 (iv A.D.), *PGen.*80 (prob. iv A.D.), *Gloss.* ❋ **–ον**, τό, *linen cloth* or *towel*, *Hippiatr.*97, al., *Sammelb.*7033.40 (pl., v A.D.), *PKlein.Form.*83 (vi A.D.), Alex. Trall.*Febr.*4, *Cat.Cod.Astr.*6.64; cf. σαβακάθιον.

**σᾰβᾰνοφᾰκιάριον**, τό, *face-cloth*, *POxy.*921.11 (iii A.D.).

**σαβαρίχις**, ἡ, *pudenda muliebria*, Telecl.64; also **σαβαρίχη**, Hsch., Phot., or **σαμαρίχη**, Theognost.*Can.*118; **σάραβος**, Phot.

**Σᾰβασμός**, ὁ, (Σαβάζω) *feast of Sabazius* or *Dionysus*, Nymphis 11.

**Σαβάτ**, ὁ, v. Σάββατον 3.

❋ **σαβαύτια**, τά, an unknown agricultural product, dub. in *PRyl.*172.25 (iii A.D.).

**Σαββᾰτ-εῖον**, τό, *a house in which the Sabbath service was held*, perhaps a *synagogue*, Decr.ap.J.*AJ*16.6.2. **–ίζω**, fut. –ιῶ Lxx 1*Es.*1.58:—*keep Sabbath*, ib.*Ex.*16.30, al.; ἡ γῆ σ. τὰ σάββατα αὐτῆς *keeps Sabbath by resting untilled*, ib.2*Ch.*36.21. **–ικός**, ή, όν, *Sabbatical*, J.*AJ*14.10.6, *BJ*7.5.1; σ. ἡμέρα Vett.Val.26.12; Σ. πόθος love *for a Jew*, *AP*5.159 (Mel.). **–ισμός**, ὁ, *a keeping of days of rest*, *Ep. Hebr.*4.9, cf. Plu.2.166a (codd., βαπτισμούς Bentley). **–ιστής**, οῦ, ὁ, member of a religious sect of *sabbath-keepers*, *OGI*573 (Cilicia, i B.C./i A.D.). **–ον**, τό, the Hebrew *Sabbath*, i.e. *Rest* (δηλοῖ δὲ ἀνάπαυσιν..τὸ ὄνομα J.*AJ*1.1.1), Lxx *Ex.*16.23, al., *Ev.Marc.*6.2, al.: freq. in pl. of the single day, *PCair.Zen.*762.6 (iii B.C.), Lxx 4*Ki.*4.23; ὀψὲ σαββάτων *Ev.Matt.*28.1; ἡ ἡμέρα τῶν σ. Lxx *Nu.*15.32, *Ev.Luc.*4.16, al. (but ἡ ἡμ. τοῦ σ. ib.13.14): heterocl. dat. pl. σάββασι(ν) Lxx 1*Ma.*2.38, J.*BJ*1.7.3, al., *Ev.Marc.*2.23, al., freq. with v.l. σαββάτοις; but σάββασι is certain in *AP*5.159 (Mel.). **2.** *period of seven days, week*, εἰς μίαν σαββάτων toward the first day *of the week*, *Ev.Matt.*28.1; κατὰ μίαν σαββάτου 1*Ep.Cor.*16.2; πρώτῃ σαββάτου *Ev.Marc.*16.9; τῇ μιᾷ τῶν σ. ib.2, *Ev.Jo.*20.1; δὶς τοῦ σ. *Ev.Luc.*18.12. **3.** **Σαβάτ**, the 11th month of the Hebr. year, nearly = February, Lxx 1*Ma.*16.14.

**σαββάτωσις**, εως, and **σαββώ**, οῦς, ἡ, a *disease of the groin* in Egypt, Apion ap.J.*Ap.*2.2.

**σάβειρος·** σάβειρος, σάβειος, κόραξ, Hsch. **σαβῆρον·** τὸ δακτύλιον, Id. **σάβηττοι·** κώνωπες, Id.

**Σαβίνα** (or **Σαβῖνα**, Hdn Gr.1.258 [as woman's name]), ἡ, = βράθυ, *Hippiatr.*22; ἕρβα Σ. Ps.-Dsc.1.76. (In both places given as Latin.)

**Σαβῖνον** ἔλαιον, oil *from over-ripe olives*, opp. ὠμοτριβές, Gal.11.872, Aët.1.99, Alex.Trall.1.12; *old oil*, Paul.Aeg.7.3.

**σᾰβοῖ**, *cry of the* Σάβοι *at the feast of Sabazius*, εὐοῖ σαβοῖ D.18.260, Str.10.3.18, cf. Men.1060.

❋ **Σάβος** or **Σαβός**, = Σαβάζιος, Orph.*H.*49.2, Phot.; σάβος· βακχεία, Hsch.:—hence **Σάβοι**, οἱ, *persons dedicated to the service of Sabazius*, *Bacchanals*, Plu.2.671f; Phrygian word, acc. to St.Byz. s.v. Σάβοι.

❋ **σάβουρος**, ον, *without ballast*, of a ship, *AB*401.

❋ **σάβυττος**, ὁ, *a fashion of cutting hair*, Hsch.; **σαβύττης**, Phot. **II.** *pudenda muliebria*, Id.; **σάβυττα**, ἡ, *Com.Adesp.*1134.

❋ **σαγάλινος**, η, ον, emended by Salmasius to σαντάλινος, *of sandal-wood* (in view of Skt. *candanam* 'sandal-wood' and Gr. σάνδανον, q.v.), in *Peripl.M.Rubr.*36.

❋ **σάγανα·** σκεπάσματα, περιβόλαια, Hsch. (cf. ἄγανα and σαγήνη).

**σαγανάριος**, ὁ, perh. an error for σαργανάριος, *basket-weaver*, *MAMA*3.46 (Cilicia).

**σᾰγάπηνον**, τό, a plant, prob. *Ferula persica*, Gal.12.117; also its *gum*, Dsc.3.80, 81; and as Adj., ὀπὸς σαγαπηνός Gal. l.c., 13.567:—hence **σαγᾰπηνίζω**, *smell* or *taste like it*, Id.14.55.

**σάγᾰρις**, εως Ion. ιος, ἡ; pl. σαγάρεις Ion. –ῑς:—a weapon used by the Scythian tribes, Hdt.1.215, 4.5; ἀξίνας σαγάρις εἶχον Id.7.64; by the Amazons, Aristarch. in *PAmh.*2.12 ii 10; by the Persians, Amazons, Mossynoeci, etc., X.*An.*4.4.16, 5.4.13:—acc. to Hsch. single-edged, and joined by X. with κοπίς and μάχαιρα, *Cyr.*1.2.9, 2.1.9, 4.2.22; double-edged acc. to *AP*6.94 (Phil.).

**σαγγάδης** or **σαγγάνδης**, ου, ὁ, Persian word for *messenger*, Gramm. post Phot. (ed. Pors.) s.v. Ὀροσάγγης.

**σάγγαθον**, τό, or **σάγγαθος**, ὁ or ἡ, name of some commodity, *Ostr.Bodl.* iii 262 (i A.D.).

❋ **σαγγαικόν**, τό, dub. sens., σ. βεβλημένον κ[όκ]κιν[ον ἐν] κ[ιβ]ωτ[ί]ωι Roussel *Cultes Égyptiens* p.224.

**σαγγάριος**, ὁ, *maker of* τζάγγαι (a kind of shoe), Hsch. s. v. σκυτεύς; cf. τσαγγάριος.

**σάγγαρον**, τό, a kind of *boat* or *canoe*, *Peripl.M.Rubr.*60.

**σάγδας** or **σαγδᾶς**, ὁ, v. ψάγδας.

**σαγείρετον**· μετακλέπτην, Hsch.

⊛ **σαγεσφ[όρος**, ὁ, dub. in *Sammelb.*5224.62 (Fayum).

**σᾰγή**, ἡ, a man's *pack, baggage*, αὐτόφορτος οἰκείᾳ σαγῇ, i.e. carrying his own baggage, etc., A.*Ch.*675; *scrip, wallet, knapsack*, Ion Trag.7: then, generally, *harness, furniture, equipment*, παντελῆ σαγὴν ἔχων A.*Ch.*560, cf. E.*Rh.*207; τοξήρης σ. Id.*HF*188; esp. *armour, harness*, S.*Fr.*1092 (prob.), cf. Ar.*Fr.*848, Men.1061, Lxx *2Ma.*3.25; also in pl., φεράσπιδες σαγαί A.*Pers.*240 (troch.), cf. *Th.* 125 (lyr.), 391. II. later, = σάγμα II, *pack-saddle*, *PGoodsp.Cair.*30 xxxviii 16 (ii A.D.), Babr.7.12, Poll.1.185, 10.54; καμήλου J.*AJ*1.19. 10; also the *padding* of a saddle, Str.15.1.20. (From σάττω: hence πανσαγία or πασσαγία.—On the accent, v. Hdn.Gr.1.309.)

**σᾰγην-αῖος**, α, ον, *of a* σαγήνη, *AP*6.23,192 (Arch.). **-εία**, ἡ, *hunting and taking with the* σαγήνη, Plu.2.730b, Him.*Or.*2. 19. **-εύς**, έως, ὁ, = sq., D.S.9.3, *AP*7.276 (Hegesipp.), 295 (Leon.), Plu.*Pomp.*73; gen. sg. written σαγινέος *MAMA*3.411 (Corycus). **-ευτήρ**, ῆρος, ὁ, *one who fishes with the* σαγήνη: hence, of a comb, πλατὺς τριχῶν σ. *AP*6.211 (Leon.). **-ευτής**, οῦ, ὁ, = foreg., Plu.2.966f, *AP*9.370 (Tib. Ill.). **-εύω**, *surround and take fish with a drag-net* (σαγήνη), Lib.*Or.*11.258: metaph., *sweep* the whole population off the face of a country by forming a line and marching over it, a Persian practice, σ. ἀνθρώπους Hdt.6.31, Str.10. 1.10, cf. D.L.3.33 (Pass.); ὥσπερ ἐν δικτύοις σεσαγηνευμένοι Hdn.4.9. 6; σ. Σάμον *sweep* it *clear* of men, Hdt.3.149; so [ὡς] συνάψαντες..τὰς χεῖρας σαγηνεύσαιεν πᾶσαν τὴν Ἐρετρικὴν οἱ στρατιῶται τοῦ Δάτιδος Pl.*Lg.*698d, cf. App.*Mith.*67, Philostr.*VA*1.23. 2. generally, *catch as in a net*, [σοφισταί] σ. τοὺς νέους Lysis ap.Iamb.*VP*17.76, cf. Luc.*Tim.*25; σαγηνευθεὶς ὑπ' ἔρωτι *AP*11.52, cf. Hld.1.9; of Ares and Aphrodite, Luc.*Gall.*3, *DDeor.*15.3. **-η**, Cypr. **ἀγάνα** (v. ἄγανα and cf. σάγανα), ἡ, *large drag-net* for taking fish, *seine*, Ital. *sagena*, Lxx *Hb.*1.15, al., *Ev.Matt.*13.47, Plu.2.169c, Luc.*Tim.*22, *Pisc.*51, etc.; σαγήνην βάλλειν Babr.4.1, 9.6; *hunting-net*, Id.43. 8. 2. = ἐπίπλοος (c), Poll.2.169.

**σᾰγηνο-βόλος**, ὁ, *one who casts the* σαγήνη, *fisherman*, *AP*6.167 (Agath.), 10.10 (Arch. Jun.). **-δετος**, ον, *bound* or *attached to a net*, ἅμμα ib.9.299 (Phil.).

**σᾰγηφορέω**, (σάγος) *wear a cloak*, Str.4.4.3.

**σαγινεύς**, v. σαγηνεύς.

⊛ **σαγίον** (not σάγιον, Sch.D.T. p.195 H.), τό, Dim. of σάγος, *PFlor.* 76.32 (iii A.D.), *PSI*4.481.10 (v/vi A.D.).

**σᾰγίς**, ίδος, ἡ, *wallet*, Hsch. **σαγλῶδες**· πλαδαρὸν σῶμα, Id.

⊛ **σάγμα**, ατος, τό, (σάττω) mostly in pl., *covering, clothing*, esp. like σάγος, *large cloak*, Ar.*V.*1142; *covering of a shield*, E.*Andr.*617, Ar. *Ach.*574. II. later, like σαγή II, *pack-saddle*, *Ostr.Bodl.* i 321 (ii B.C.), Str.15.1.20, *POxy.*326 (i A.D.); τὰ σ. τῶν ὑποζυγίων Plu. *Pomp.*41, cf. *Arat.*25; τῆς καμήλου Lxx *Ge.*31.34; cj. in A.*Pr.* 463. III. *pile*, ὅπλων Plu.*Cat.Ma.*20.

**σαγμᾰτᾶς**, ᾶ, ὁ, *saddler*, *PFlor.*376.8 (iii A.D.).

**σαγμάτιον**, τό, Dim. of σάγμα I, Arr.*Epict.*4.1.80.

**σαγμᾰτογήνη**, ἡ, *an Indian stuff*, *Peripl.M.Rubr.*14, cf. 6 (pl.).

**σαγμᾰτο-ποιός**, ὁ, *saddler*, *Stud.Pal.*3.119 (vi A.D.), *Gloss.* **-ράπτης**, ου, ὁ, *saddler*, *POxy.*1883.3 (vi A.D.). **-ράφος** [ρᾰ], ὁ, = foreg., *PGoodsp.Cair.*30 xxxvii 19 (ii A.D.).

**σαγολαίφεα**, τά, *sails*, οἱ κοινότεροι ap.Eust.1890.9.

**σάγος** [ᾰ], ὁ, *coarse cloak, plaid*, used by the Gauls, Plb.2.28.7, 2.30.1, D.S.5.30; by the Spaniards, App.*Hisp.*42; *soldier's cloak*, Lat. *sagum*, Plu.2.201c; σ. Ἀρσινοϊτικοί *Peripl.M.Rubr.*8; σ. Γαλλικός, Ἄφρος, *Edict.Diocl.*19.60,61; simply *cloak* or perh. *blanket*, *POxy.*1051.20 (iii A.D.); *horse-cloth*, *Hippiatr.*99 (so Lat. *sagum*, *Cod.Theod.*8.5.50, al.).

**σάγουρον**· γυργάθιον, Hsch. **σαγροῖς**· κοπίς, ἢ πέλεκυς, Id. **σαγύριον**· ἄρτου κλάσμα, Id.

**Σαδδουκαῖοι**, οἱ, *Sadducees*, name of a Jewish sect, *Act.Ap.*23.8, J.*AJ*13.5.9, etc.

⊛ **σαθαρυγά**· ταραχή, Hsch.

**σᾰθέριον**, τό, prob. a kind of *beaver*, Arist.*HA*594$^b$31 (v.l. σαθρίον).

**σάθη** [ᾰ], ἡ, *membrum virile*, Archil.97 (prob.), Ar.*Lys.*1119.

**σάθραξ**· φθείρ, Hsch.

**σαθρ-ός**, ά, όν, *unsound*, σκυτέες τὰ σ. ὑγιέα ποιέουσι Hp.*Vict.*1.15; of diseased or unsound parts of the frame, τὰ σ. ὑπὸ τῶν ἰητρῶν ὑγιαίνονται ibid.; γάλλοι καὶ σ. *impotent*, *PGnom.*244 (ii A.D.). 2. of a vessel, *cracked*, opp. ὑγιής, εἴ πῄ τι σαθρὸν ἔχει, πᾶν περικρούωμεν Pl.*Phlb.*55c; εἴτε ὑγιὲς εἴτε σ. φθέγγεται Id.*Tht.*179d; ἀγγεῖα τετρημένα καὶ σ. Id.*Grg.*493e; πίθοι σαθροί prob. in *IG*1².326.7; [φωναί] σαθραὶ καὶ παρερρυηκυῖαι Arist.*Aud.*804$^a$32: metaph., ἡ κολακεία σαθρὸν ὑπηχεῖ Plu.2.64e. 3. metaph., σ. κῦδος *unsound* fame, Pi. *N.*8.34; πρίν τι καὶ σαθρὸν μετεξετέροισι ἐγγενέσθαι before any *unsound thought* comes into their heads, i.e. before they prove traitors, Hdt.6.109; σ. λόγοι E.*Hec.*1190, *Rh.*639; τί τοῦτ' αἴνιγμα σημαίνεις σ.; Id.*Supp.*1064; τοῦτ' ἐς γυναῖκας δόλιόν ἐστι καὶ σαθρόν Id.*Ba.*487; σ. μετάβασις Pl.*Lg.*736e; σ. ἐστι..πᾶν ὅ τι ἂν μὴ δικαίως ᾖ πεπραγμένον D.18.227; εὕροιμ' ἂν ὅπῃ σαθρός ἐστι Pl.*Euthphr.*5c; εὑρήσει τὰ σαθρὰ τῶν ἐκείνου πραγμάτων ὁ πόλεμος D.4.44; τὰ σ. τῆς τυραννίδος Plu.*Dio* 23. Adv., σαθρῶς ἱδρυμένος built on *unsound* foundations, Arist.*EN*1100$^b$7. **-ότης**, ητος, ἡ, *unsoundness, weakness*, Plot.3.6.2, *Corp.Herm.*18.2, Eust.187.39. **-όω**, *make unsound* or *feeble*, Lxx *Jd.*10.8 (cod. A):—Pass., οἰκίας δύο μέρη ἐσαθρώθησαν *PLond.*5.1708.77 (vi A.D.), cf. *Gloss.* **-ωμα**, ατος, τό, *that which is unsound, flaw*, Hsch. s. v. σαπρία. **-ωσις**, εως, ἡ, *ruin*, διαρπαγὴ καὶ σ. *PLond.*5.1677.34 (vi A.D.).

⊛ **σάθων**, ωνος, ὁ, from σάθη, like πόσθων from πόσθη, a coaxing word of nurses to a boy-baby, Telecl.65.

**σαικίς**· δειλός, Hsch.

**σαικωνέω** or **-ίζω**, *move*, Ar.*Fr.*849; cf. σαλακωνίζω.

**σαινί-δωρος** [ῐ], ον, *coaxing by presents*, Epicurus' nickname for Antidorus, cj. for Σαννίδωρος in Epicur.*Fr.*4.

**σαινικρίζει**· ἐκτρέφει, Hsch.

**σαιν-ουρίς**, ίδος, fem. of sq., Hsch. **-ουρος**, ον, (οὐρά) *wagging the tail*, as a dog, Phot., Eust.1821.51.

**σαίνω**, Hes.*Th.*771: Ep. impf. σαῖνον Od.10.219: aor. ἔσηνα 17. 302; Dor. ἔσᾱνα Pi.*O.*4.6, *P.*1.52:—Pass., A.*Ch.*194:—prop. of dogs, *wag the tail, fawn*, ὅτ' ἂν ἀμφὶ ἄνακτα κύνες..σαίνωσι Od.10. 217; νόησε δὲ δῖος Ὀδυσσεὺς σαίνοντάς τε κύνας 16.6; σαίνεις δάκνουσα καὶ κύων λαίθαργος εἶ S.*Fr.*885; ἡ κύων ἔσηνε καὶ προσῆλθ' Apollod. Com.14.5: with the dat. added, οὐρῇ μέν ῥ' ὅ γ' ἔσηνε, of the dog Argus, Od.17.302; σ. οὐρῇ τε καὶ οὔασι Hes. l. c.; ἔσαινεν οὐρᾷ με S. *Fr.*687 (ἔσαινεν οὐράν *wagged* his tail, Hemsterhuis, cf. Sch.rec.A. *Th.*704, Sch.rec.Theoc.2.109). II. metaph. of persons, *fawn, cringe*, ὑδαρεῖ σ. φιλότητι A.*Ag.*798 (anap.), cf. *Pers.*97 (lyr., s. v. l.); also σ. ποτὶ πάντας Pi.*P.*2.82; σ. ποτὶ ἀγγελίαν greet it with joy, Id. *O.*4.6. III. c. acc. pers., *fawn upon*, κέρκῳ τινά Ar.*Eq.*1031, cf. *AP*9.604 (Noss.); so of fishes, σαίνοντες οὐραίοισι τὴν κεκτημένην S. *Fr.*762. 2. *fawn on, pay court to, greet*, τινα Pi.*P.*1.52; ὅτ' ἐλεύθερος ἀτμένα σαίνει Call.*Aet.*1.1.19; σ. μόρον *cringe to* it, *seek to avert* it, A.*Th.*383,704; παιδός με σαίνει φθόγγος *greets* me, S.*Ant.*1214; φαιδρὰ γοῦν ἀπ' ὀμμάτων σαίνει με *greets* me gladly from her eyes, Id. *OC*320. 3. *gladden*, esp. with hope or conviction, ἐλπίδι κέαρ B.1.55; οὐ γάρ με σ. θέσφατα E.*Ion* 685 (lyr.); τὰ λεγόμενα..σ. τὴν ψυχήν Arist.*Metaph.*1090$^a$37; so σ. τὴν ὑπόσχεσιν *receive it with marks of gladness*, Luc.*Merc.Cond.*20 (dub., σαίνει τῇ ὑποσχέσει is prob. cj.):—Pass., σαίνομαι δ' ὑπ' ἐλπίδος A.*Ch.*194. 4. *beguile, cozen, deceive*, ἡ δ' ἄρ' ἐν σκότῳ λήθουσά με ἔσαιν' Ἐρινύς S.*Fr.*577; σ. μ' ἔννυχος φρυκτωρία *seeks to deceive* me, E.*Rh.*55 (or in signf. III. 3). 5. in 1*Ep.Thess.*3.3, σαίνεσθαι ἐν ταῖς θλίψεσι seems to mean *to be shaken, disturbed*; σαινόμενοι τοῖς λεγομένοις ἐδάκρυον D.L.8.41 (or in signf. III. 4); σαίνεται· κινεῖται, σαλεύεται, ταράττεται, Hsch.; but cf. σιαίνω.

**σαιρός**· σαρός, Hsch.

**σαίρω** (A), only found in pf. with pres. sense σέσηρα, *part the lips and show the closed teeth* (cf. Gal.18(2).597), *grin*, σέσηρεν ἄν τε βούλητ' ἄν τε μή Alex.98.26; Σάτυροι ἀπὸ τοῦ σεσηρέναι Ael.*VH*3.40; but mostly in part., ἄπληστον σεσᾱρυῖα (Ep. for σεσηρυῖα) Hes.*Sc.*268; οἷον σεσηρὼς ἐξαπατήσειν μ' οἴεται Ar.*V.*901; ἠγριωμένους ἐπ' ἀλλήλοισι καὶ σεσηρότας Id.*Pax* 620; σ. καὶ γελῶν *Com.Adesp.*606; γελῶντα καὶ σ. Plu.2.223c; σιμὰ σ. *AP*5.178 (Mel.); but also without any such bad sense, εἶπε σεσᾱρὼς ὄμματι μειδιόωντι *smiling*, Theoc. 7.19 (cf. προσσαίρω). 2. transferred to *grinning* laughter, σεσηρόσι μειδιήμασι Hp.*Gland.*12; σεσηρότι γέλωτι Luc.*Am.*13: the neut. is used in Adv. sense, σεσᾱρὸς γελᾶν Theoc.20.14; σεσηρὸς αἰκάλλειν, of a fox, Babr.50.14, cf. Ps.-Luc.*Philopatr.*26. 3. of a wound or sore, ἕλκος σεσηρὸς καὶ ἐκπεπλιγμένον *gaping*, Hp.*Fract.*32, cf. Aret.*CA*2.2; also σ. χάσμημα, of a metrical hiatus, Eust.840.43.

**σαίρω** (B), aor. 1 ἔσηρα (v. infr.), *sweep, clean*, σαίρειν τε δῶμα E. *Hec.*363; σαίρειν στέγας Id.*Cyc.*29, cf. *Hyps.Fr.*1 ii 17 (lyr.); μυρσίνας ἱερὰν φόβαν, ᾇ σαίρω δάπεδον θεοῦ Id.*Ion* 121, cf. 115 (both lyr.). 2. *sweep up* or *away*, πᾶσαν κόνιν σήραντες S.*Ant.*409: metaph., τὰμ.. πορτ' ἀλλάλους διαφορὰν καὶ ἀμειξίαν σᾶραι *BCH*29.204 (Crete).

**σαῖς**· κοῦρος, κάρος, Hsch. **Σαισαρία**· ἡ Ἐλευσὶν πρότερον, Id. ⊛ **σαιστός**· ἐλαία θλαστή, Id.

**σαΐτης**, ου, ὁ, *a liquid measure*, = 22 ξέσται, Epiphan.ap.Hultsch *Metrol.Script.* i p.264, al.: also Dim. **σαΐτιον**, τό, *Arch.Pap.*3.448, *POxy.*1658.1 (iv A.D.):—**σαΐτις**, ἡ, name of a *plaster*, Orib.*Fr.*88. (Named from Σάϊς in Egypt.)

**σᾰκάδιον**, τό, a kind of *musical instrument*, Hsch. (Prob. named after the musician Sacadas of Argos.)

**σᾰκάλιον** [κᾰ], τό, = *saccus*, *Gloss.*

**σάκ-ανδρος** [ᾰ], ὁ, *pudenda muliebria*, Ar.*Lys.*824:—so **σάκας**, ὁ, Hsch.; **σάκτας**, ὁ, Phot. s. v. σάραβον (= *Com.Adesp.*1135).

**σακελίζω**, Byz. form for σακίζω, Sch.Ar.*Pl.*1088; also **σακέλισμα**, gloss on ἠθμοῦ, D.S.5.28, and **σακελιστήριον**, τό, used to explain ἠθμός, Sch.Ar.*Pl.*1088, Tz.*H.*13.420.

**σακέλλιον**, τό, Dim. of σάκος, Hsch. (-έλιον cod.), Phot.

**σάκελλος** [ᾰ], ὁ, = foreg., σάκελλοι διὰ πιτύρων bran *poultices*, Aët. 8.76.

**σᾰκέσ-πᾰλος**, ον, (πάλλω) *wielding a shield, warlike*, Il.5.126, Call. *Jov.*71; σ. πορείη Nonn.*D.*23.140, cf. 8.178. ⊛ **-φόρος**, ον, *shield-bearing*, of Ajax, S.*Aj.*19; σακεσφόροι γὰρ πάντες Αἰτωλοί E.*Ph.* 139. II. (σάκκος or σάκος III) *beard-bearer*, epith. of the demagogue Epicrates, Pl.Com.122, cf. Plu.*Pel.*30.

**σάκ-εύω**, *strain, filter*, quoted by Ael.Dion.*Fr.*296, Phot., Suid. from Hdt.4.23, where codd. have σακκέουσι ἱματίοισι (v. σάκκος). ⊛ **-ηφόρος**, ὁ, = σακκοφόρος I, Διονύσου..σ. μύσται *Supp.Epigr.* 4.522 (Ephesus, ii A.D.). **-ίζω**, = σακεύω, Lyc.ap.Phot.; **σακκίζω** in Thphr.*CP*6.7.4 (Pass.), Crito ap.Gal.12.437. **-ίον**, v. σακκίον.

**σᾰκίτας**, ὁ, v. σηκίτης.

**σακκ-ᾶς**, ᾶ, ὁ, *sack-maker* or *-carrier*, *MAMA* 3.470 (Corycus), *PLond*.2.427v.2,8 (iv A.D.). **-έω**, = σακεύω (q.v.). **-ηγέω**, *transport sacks*, *PTeb*.585 (ii A.D.). ❀ **-ηγία**, ἡ, *transport of sacks*, ib.356.5 (ii A.D.), etc. **-ηγός**, ὁ, *sack-transporter*, *PFlor*.364.17 (iii A.D.). **-ίας** (or **σακίας**) οἶνος, *strained* wine, Poll.6.18. **-ίδιον**, τό, Dim. of σάκκος, *PLond.ined*.2167 (ii/iii A.D.). **-ίζω**, v. σακίζω. **-ῐνος**, η, ον, *of sackcloth*, ὑλιστήρ Sch.Ar.*Pl*.1088. **-ῑνόσῡκοι**· δασύπρωκτοι, Hsch. **-ίον**, Att. **σᾰκίον**, τό, Dim. of σάκκος or σάκος, *small bag*, σ. θερμά *poultices*, Hp.*Loc.Hom*.39, cf. X.*An*.4.5.36, *Ostr.Bodl*. i 321 (ii B.C., -κκ-), Dsc.5.109; σακίον, ἐν οἷσπερ τἀργύριον ταμιεύεται a *bag*, such as those in which.., Ar.*Fr*.328. 2. later, *sackcloth*, *mourning*, Men.544.4, J.*AJ*2.3.4, Plu.2.168d.

**σακκο-γενειοτρόφος**, ον, (σάκκος III) *cherishing a huge beard*, Epigr. ap.Hegesand.1. **-πήρα**, ἡ, *knapsack*, *wallet*, rejected by Poll.10.161, who cites it from Apollod.Car.1: found in *PEnteux*.32.7 (iii B.C.), *PLond*.2.402v.16 (ii B.C.). ❀ **-πλόκος**, ον, (πλέκω) *sack-weaver*, *PGiss*.10.5,19 (ii A.D.); = *saccarius*, *Gloss*. **-ράφιον** [ᾰ], τό, *packing-needle*, *EM*46.31, Sch.Luc.*DMort*.14.1.

❀ **σάκκος** or **σάκος**, ὁ, v. sub fin.:—*coarse cloth of hair*, esp. of goats' hair, σάκκος τρίχινος *Apoc*.6.12, cf. Lxx *Is*.50.3, *Si*.25.17. II. *anything made of this cloth*: 1. *sack*, *bag*, Hdt.9.80, Ar.*Ach*.745, *Lys*.1209, Gal.2.559,8.672:—as a measure, *Ostr*.1096, al. 2. *sieve*, *strainer*, esp. for wine, Hippon.57, Poll.6.19; σ. τρίχινοι *PHamb*.10.39 (ii A.D.). 3. *coarse garment*, *sackcloth*, worn as mourning by the Jews, Lxx *Ge*.37.34, *Ev.Luc*.10.13, J.*BJ*2.12.5, cf. Plu.2.239c. III. *coarse beard*, like rough hair-cloth, σάκον πρὸς ταῖν γνάθοιν ἔχειν Ar.*Ec*.502; cf. σακεσφόρος II.—The form σάκος is said to be Att., Ael.Dion.*Fr*.296, Phryn.229, Moer. p.354P., Thom.Mag. p.344R., etc.; while σάκκος is called Dor. by Phryn. l.c., Hellenic by Moer. and Thom.Mag. ll.cc., Comic by Poll.7.191. In Ar.*Ach*. 822, *Ec*.502, σάκος is required by the metre, as is σάκκος in *Ach*. 745 (Megarian), and in Hippon. l.c.; codd. of Hdt. give σάκκος. Inscrr. have σάκος *IG*2².1672.73,74,108 and σάκκος ib.198: Papyri have σάκος *PCair.Zen*.753.27 (iii B.C.), *UPZ*84.52 (ii B.C.), but oftener σάκκος *PSI*4.427.1,14 (iii B.C.), *PTeb*.116.3 (ii B.C.), etc. (Prob. the word, like the thing, was borrowed from Phoenicia, cf. Hebr. *saq*.)

**σακκούδιον**, τό, dub. sens. in pl., perh. articles of jewellery or feminine apparel, *POxy*.937.29 (iii A.D.), *POsl*.46.14 (iii A.D.).

**σακκο-ῡφάντης**, ου, ὁ, *saccarius*, *Gloss*.; cf. σακχυφάντης. **-φορέω**, *to be a porter*, Aristarch. in *PAmh*.2.12 ii 1 (where σακοφ-). ❀ **-φορικός**, ή, όν, *of a porter*, μισθοί *PFlor*.75.21 (iv A.D.). **-φόρος**, ον, *wearing coarse hair-cloth*, Plu.2.239c: -φόροι, οἱ, name of a religious sect, *MAMA*1.171 (Laodicea Combusta, iv A.D.), *Cod.Just*.1.5.5; cf. σακηφόρος. 2. *porter*, *PTeb*.39.26 (ii B.C.), 141 ii 7 (iii A.D.): **σακοφ-**, *Sammelb*.3939.7.

**σακκώνυμος**, ον, *named from a sack*, Sch.Lyc.183.

**σακνός**, ή, όν, *broken*, *leaky*, πίθοι *IG*12(5).572.16 (Ceos, iii B.C.), cf. 11(2).154*B*23, 161*C*17 (Delos, iii B.C.).

**σακοδερμηστής**, οῦ, ὁ, *eating through leather shields*, of a worm, prob. in S.*Fr*.635.

**σάκοιτοι**· οἱ ἱστῶντες τὸν κέραμον, Hsch.

**σάκος** [ᾰ], ὁ, v. σάκκος. B. **σᾱκός**, ὁ, v. σηκός.

**σάκος** [ᾰ], εος, τό, Ion. gen. σάκευς Hes.*Sc*.334 (Cretan word acc. to *AB*1096):—*shield*, Il.7.222, 18.478, 20.268, Hdt.1.52, etc.: it was concave, and hence sts. used as a vessel to hold liquid, A.*Th*. 540. 2. metaph., *shield*, *defence*, βωμός, ἄρρηκτον σ. A.*Supp*.190. (Prob. cogn. with Skt. *tvác-* 'skin, hide'.)

**σάκουτος**, ὁ, a kind of *fish*, *Gp*.20.7.1.

**σᾰκοφόρος**, ον, = σακεσφόρος, Hsch.; dub. in *Ath.Mitt*.10.208 (Cyzicus). II. = σακκοφόρος (q.v.).

**σᾰκόω**, v. σηκόω.

❀ **σάκρα**, ἡ (Lat. *sacer*), in pl., *imperial archives*, *PSI*4.481.13 (v/vi A.D.).

**σάκταρον**· τοῦτο ἐμφερές ἐστι κόμμει, γεννώμενον ἐν τῇ Ἰνδικῇ, διαλυτικόν, Hsch.

**σάκ-τας** (A), ου, ὁ, (σάττω) *sack*, Ar.*Pl*.681, Poll.3.155, 10.64, Ael.Dion.*Fr*.206. II. v. σάκανδρος. **-τας** (B), ὁ, Boeot. for ἰατρός, Stratt.47.5. **-τήρ**, ῆρος, ὁ, *sack*, Hsch. **-τός**, ή, όν, *crammed*, *stuffed*, Antiph.132.3, *POxy*.1760.9 (ii A.D.). II. *strained* (cf. σακεύω), Eup.439. **-τρα**, ἡ, = φορμός, Phot. **-τωρ**, ορος, ὁ, *packer*, Ἅιδου σάκτορι Περσᾶν *who fills* the nether world with Persians, of death, A.*Pers*.924 (unless Περσᾶν be taken with ἥβαν).

**σακυνδάκη**· ἔνδυμα Σκυθικόν, Hsch.

**σάκχᾰρ**, αρος, τό, Gal.12.71: also **σάκχᾰρι**, *Peripl.M.Rubr*.14, Orib. *inc*.12.6; **σάκχᾰρις**, ἡ, Dsc.*Eup*.1.40; and **σάκχᾰρον**, τό, Id.2.82, 107, 112:—*sugar*, *Saccharum officinarum*, ll.cc. (Eastern word, cf. Skt. *śarkarā*, Malay *jagara*.)

**σακχῠφάντης**, ου, ὁ, (ὑφαίνω) *one who weaves sackcloth*, *sailmaker*, D.48.12, *IG*2².2403 (iv B.C.), Poll.10.191, Hsch.; cf. σακκοϋφάντης.

**σάλα**, v. σάλη. **σαλαβάρ**· μάγειρος (Lacon.), Hsch. **σαλάβη**, ἡ, v. σαλάμβη; also **σάλαβος**, Id.

❀ **σᾰλᾰγέω**, = σαλάσσω (cf. παταγέω = πατάσσω), Opp.*C*.4.74 (where, however, there is a tmesis of ἐπισαλαγέω), 3.352. 2. trans., sens. obsc., = *subagito*, Orac.ap.Luc.*Alex*.50.

❀ **σᾰλάγη** or **σᾰλᾰγή** (cf. σελαγή), ἡ, *noise*, *outcry*, Hsch. **σάλαγξ**· ἰχθῦς ἀγαθός, καὶ μεταλλικὸν σκεῦος, Id. (Cf. σάλαξ, σηλαγγεύς.)

**σαλαΐδιον**, τό, in pl. -ια, dub. in *GDI*3707 (Cos), cf. *Supp.Epigr*.1 p.139:—perh. σιαλίδιον.

**σᾰλᾰ-ΐζω**, *cry out in distress*, Anacr.167 (glossed by κόπτεσθαι in Hsch.). **-ϊσμός**, ὁ, cj. for σαλαΐς (= κωκυτός) in Hsch.

**σαλακύρων**· εὐήθων, Hsch.

**σᾰλάκ-ων** [λᾰ], ωνος, ὁ, *pretentious person*, Arist.*Rh*.1391a3, *EE* 1221a35, *MM*1192b2. **-ωνεία**, ἡ, *pretentiousness*, ib.a37; **-ωνία**, ἡ, *snobbery*, Alciphr.2.3. **-ωνίζω** or **-ίζομαι**, and **-ωνεύομαι**, *behave snobbishly* or *pretentiously*, Hsch., Phot., Suid.; σεσαλακωνισμένη is prob.l. in Hermipp.71; cf. διασαλακωνίζω.

**σᾰλᾰμάνδρ-α**, ἡ, *salamander*, *S. vulgaris*, a kind of newt, supposed to be a fire-extinguisher, Arist.*HA*552b16, Thphr.*Ign*.60, *Sign*.15, Dsc.2.62, Ael.*NA*2.31, Philum.*Ven*.34. **-ειος**, ον, *of* or *like a salamander*, σ. δάκος Nic.*Th*.818.

**σᾰλάμβη**, ἡ, *vent-hole*, *chimney*, S.*Fr*.1093, Lyc.98:—**σαλάβη** Hsch., Phot., but in Lyc. l.c. the metre requires σαλάμβη.

**Σᾰλᾰμίν**, v. Σαλαμίς.

**Σᾰλᾰμῑν-ἀφέτης**, ου, ὁ, *betrayer of Salamis*, Sol.2.4. ❀ **-ιος**, α, ον, also ος, ον, *Salaminian*, *of* or *from Salamis*, Hdt.5.104, etc.: also **-ιακός**, ή, όν, Str.8.2.2; and fem. **-ιάς**, άδος, A.*Pers*.965 (lyr.). II. Σαλαμινία (sc. ναῦς or τριήρης), ἡ, Ar.*Av*.144, Th.3.33; v. πάραλος III.

❀ **Σᾰλᾰμίς** (also in Gramm. **Σᾰλᾰμίν**, Hsch., Eust.ad D.P.498), gen. ῖνος, ἡ, *Salamis*, an island and town of the same name, between Athens and Megara, Il.2.557, etc. II. a town of Cyprus founded by Teucer of Salamis, *h.Hom*.10.4, Hdt.4.162, etc.; **Σαλαμίνη**, Suid. s.v. Ἐπιφάνιος.

**σαλάννη**· φαρέτρα, Hsch.

**σάλαξ** [σᾰ], ακος, ὁ, (σαλάσσω) *miner's sieve* or *riddle*, Thphr. or Arist.(*Fr*.261) ap.Poll.10.149; **σάλαγξ**, Hsch.

❀ **σαλάριον**, τό, Lat. *salarium*, *salary*, *POxy*.473.45 (ii A.D.), etc.: Adj. **σαλάριος**, μέτρον *PMasp*.100.20 (vi A.D.).

**σάλασσα**, **σαλασσομέδοισα**, Dor. for θάλ-.

❀ **σᾰλάσσω**, = σαλεύω, τινα Nic.*Al*.457. II. *overload*, *cram full*, σεσαλαγμένος οἴνῳ *AP*6.56 (Maced.), cf. 11.57 (Agath.), *APl*.4.306 (Leon.); cf. σαλεύω.

**σαλέη**, v. σάλη. **σάλεσσι**, v. θάλεα.

**σάλ-ευμα** [ᾰ], ατος, τό, *oscillation*, in pl., Artem.1.79 (in marg.); σ. πολεμικὸν ἵππου D.Chr.63.4. **-ευομένως**, Adv. *shakily*, opp. βεβαίως, Phld.*Rh*.1.260S. **-ευσις**, εως, ἡ, *oscillation*, Arist.*Mech*. 857a8. ❀ **-ευτός**, ή, όν, *tottering*, *unsteady*, *AP*5.174 (Mel.). ❀ **-εύω**, fut. σαλεύσω Lxx *Wi*.4.19: aor. ἐσάλευσα Isoc.8.95, *AP*11.83:—Pass., fut. σαλευθήσομαι Lxx *Si*.16.18, *Ev.Luc*.21.26: aor. ἐσαλεύθην Lxx 1*Ma*.9.13, *Act.Ap*.4.31, 2*Ep.Thess*.2.2, v.l. in Isoc. l.c.: pf. σεσάλευμαι (v. infr.): (σάλος):—*cause to rock*, *make to vibrate* or *oscillate*, c. acc., [τὰς ἀγκύρας] οὐδεὶς χειμὼν σαλεύει Pythag.ap.Stob.3.1. 29; σ. τρικυμίᾳ πέδον, of the sea, Lyc.475; of an earthquake, *AP*11. 83 (Lucill.), cf. 259 (Id.): metaph., δόξαν σ. Plu.2.1123f, cf. S.E.*M*. 8.56, 337, etc.; σ. τινὰ ἐκ θεμελίων Lxx *Wi*.4.19; ἐπιστολαὶ δυνάμεναι λίθον σαλεῦσαι *heartrending*, *POxy*.528.12 (ii A.D.); σ. τοὺς ὄχλους *stir* them *up*, *Act.Ap*.17.13, cf. Lxx *Si*.28.14:—Pass., *to be shaken to and fro*, *waver*, *totter*, *reel*, χθὼν σεσάλευται A.*Pr*.1081; κύκλος σαλευόμενος Pl.*Ti*.79e, cf. Arist.*Mech*.857a7, Thphr.*Lass*.11; of teeth or nails, *to be loosened*, Gal.12.871, Dsc.5.3; of persons, ἐκ Βρομίου γυῖα σαλευόμενον *AP*11.26 (Marc.Arg.), cf. 12.31 (Phan.); ὑφ' ἡδονῆς σαλευομένη κορώνη Sch.Arat.1009 (wrongly attributed to Archil., *Fr*. 102); later simply, *stir*, *move*, κατεσχέθην νόσῳ.. ὡς μὴ δύνασθαι μηδὲ σαλεύεσθαι *PSI*4.299.4 (iii A.D.). 2. *shake in measuring*, so as to give good measure, μέτρον σεσαλευμένον *Ev.Luc*.6.38; cf. σαλάσσω II. II. intr., *move up and down*, *roll*, *toss*, esp. of ships in a stormy sea or persons in them, σ. ἐν πλοίοις X.*Oec*.8.17, cf. Hld.10.4, etc.: generally, *put out to sea*, App.*Mith*.77: metaph., *toss like a ship at sea*, *to be tempest-tossed*, *be in sore distress*, πόλις γὰρ.. ἄγαν ἤδη σαλεύει S.*OT*23; πρόδοτος δὲ.. σ. Ἠλέκτρα Id.*El*.1074 (lyr.); ὅταν.. σαλεύῃ πόλις E.*Rh*.249 (lyr.), cf. *OGI*515.47 (Mylasa, iii A.D.); ἐν νόσοις ἢ γήρᾳ σ. Pl.*Lg*.923b, cf. Arist.*Pr*.883a34; ἐν κινδύνῳ σ. D.H.10.11; σ. ὑπὲρ ἑαυτοῦ Ael.*Fr*.48; *to be unstable*, Poll.6.121; *flicker*, of the eye-balls in nystagmus, Gal.18(2).68; *oscillate*, of the λόγος ἐνδιάθετος, ἐν τούτοις S.E.P.1.65. 2. of ships also, ἐπ' ἀγκυρῶν *ride* at anchor, Polyaen.2.2.7: metaph., ὡς ἐπ' ἀγκύρας τῆς φύσεως σ. Plu.2.493d; σ. ἐπὶ τῶν ἐλπίδων Hld.1.26; also δρῶν ἡμᾶς ἐπὶ τούτῳ μόνῳ (sc. τῷ υἱῷ) σαλεύοντας Plu.*Demetr*.38; γραῦν ἐπὶ ἑνὶ γομφίῳ σ. Alciphr.3.28, cf. *POxy*.472.50 (ii A.D.); ἐπὶ τοιούτοις παραγγέλμασιν S.E.*M*.2.12 (hence later in a causal sense, σ. ἐπί τινι τὰς ἐλπίδας *anchor* them upon.., Hld.2.33). 3. metaph., *roll like a ship*, *roll in one's walk*, of persons with the hip-joints far apart, Hp.*Art*.56.

**σάλη**, Dor. **σάλα**, ἡ, = φροντίς (cf. σάλος II. 2), Hsch., Phot., *EM* 151.47: also **σαλέη**, Hsch. II. both σαλέη and σάλη = βλάβη, Id. **σαλητόν**, v. σάρητον.

**σᾰλία**· πλέγμα καλάθῳ ὅμοιον, ὃ ἐπὶ τῆς κεφαλῆς φοροῦσιν αἱ Λάκαιναι, οἱ δὲ θολία, Hsch.

**σᾱλ[ία]**, Dor. for τηλία, *sifter*, dub. in *Supp.Epigr*.1.414 (Crete, v/iv B.C.).

**σαλιᾷ** (or **σάλω**), = ἀρκεῖ, Rhinth.22 (s.v.l.).

**σαλιούγκα**, ἡ, = *saliunca*, Κελτικὴ νάρδος, Dsc.1.8, Plin.*HN*21.42.

**σαλκᾶ** (gen. sg.), *a fragrant oil*, Aët.1.135, 12.49.

**σάλκαθον** (?), τό, dub. sens. in *Stud.Pal*.20.96.7 (iv A.D.).

**σαλκόν**, τό, dub. sens. in *PLond*.5.1904.5 (v/vi A.D.).

**σάλλω**, Dor. for θάλλω, Alcm.76.4.

**Σαλμᾰκίς**, ίδος, ἡ, a district in Halicarnassus, *SIG*46.24 (v B.C.); also a fountain there, said to cause sexual weakness and associated with Hermaphroditus, Str.14.2.16, Vitr.2.8.11, Ov.*Met*.4.286: hence **σαλμᾰκίδες**, αἱ, a name for ἑταῖραι (so Suid.) or effeminate men, *AP*7.222 (Phld.).

**σᾰλόομαι**, Pass., *go delicately*, *EM*270.40.

**σάλος** [ᾰ], ὁ, *tossing motion*, of an earthquake, χθονὸς νῶτα σεισθῆναι σάλῳ E.*IT*46; esp. *rolling swell* of the sea, πόντου σ., πόντιος σ., Id.*Hec*.28, *IT*1443: pl., πόντιοι σ. Id.*Or*.994 (lyr.). 2. *open roadstead, roads*, opp. a harbour, ἐν σάλῳ στῆναι, = σαλεύειν II. 2; ἀλίμενον μὲν σάλους δὲ ἔχον Plb.1.53.10; οὔτε λιμὴν οὔτε σ. ἐπ' ἀγκύρας D.S.3.44, cf. Agatharch.92, *Peripl.M.Rubr*.7 (pl.), 55. II. of ships or persons in them, *tossing on the sea*, ἐκ πολλοῦ σ. εὕδοντ' ἐπ' ἀκτῆς S.*Ph*.271; σάλον εἶχεν ἡ θάλασσα Plu.*Luc*.10; καρηβαρεῖν ὑπὸ σ. Luc.*Herm*.28; ἐν τοσούτῳ σ. ναυτιάσαντα Id.*Tox*.19: metaph. of the ship of the state, τὰ μὲν δὴ πόλεος θεοὶ πολλῷ σ. σείσαντες ὤρθωσαν πάλιν S.*Ant*.163; πόλις..σαλεύει κἀνακουφίσαι κάρα βυθῶν ἔτ' οὐχ οἵα τε φοινίου σάλου Id.*OT*24; ἐν σάλῳ πόλις γενομένη Lys.6.49; ἔσχε..ὁ ἀγὼν ὑποτροπὴν καὶ σ. began to *waver*, Plu.*Alex*.32, cf. *Aem*.18; cf. σαλεύω II. 1. 2. *distemper, restlessness, perplexity*, Lxx *Si*.40.5, Gal.9.816; τῆς ψυχῆς Max.Tyr.1.1.

**σαλός**, ή, όν, *silly, imbecile*, Hsch. s.v. ὑσθλός, Sch.Ar.*Nu*.397.

**σαλούσιον**, τό, ὀρτύγων σ. dub. sens. in *PSI*4.428.55 (iii B.C.), cf. *PCair.Zen*.12.44, 672.4 (pl.).

**σάλπη**, ἡ, a sea-fish, the *saupe*, *Box salpa*, Epich.63, Arist.*HA* $543^{a}8$, al. (ὃν καὶ βοῦν [leg. βῶκα] καλοῦσιν, Hsch.): also **σάλπης**, ὁ, Archipp.19; **σάλπος** is v.l. in Arist.*HA* $534^{a}16$; **σάρπη**, ib.$534^{a}9$, $621^{b}7$; **σάλπιγξ**, ib.$543^{a}8$.

**σαλπίγγιον**, τό, Dim. of σάλπιγξ, *tube*, Gal.2.707; prop. *a little trumpet*, Hsch. s.v. ἰσκάνδιον. 2. name of a plant, = ἵππουρις, *Gp*.2.6.27.

**σαλπιγγο-ειδής**, ές, *trumpet-like*, Ruf.*Anat*.38. **-λογχ-ῠπηνάδαι**, οἱ, *lancer-whiskered trumpeters*, Ar.*Ra*.966.

⊛ **σαλπ-ιγγωτός**, ή, όν, *trumpet-shaped*, λυχνία *CIG*3071.8 (Teos), Hsch. s.v. ἰσκανδωτόν. **-ιγκτής**, οῦ, ὁ, *trumpeter*, Th.6.69, X.*An*.4.3.29, Ascl.*Tact*.2.9, 6.3, etc.; this spelling has the best MS. authority and occurs in Phld.*Rh*.2.299S., but has not been found in Att. Inscrr.; **σαλπικτής**, *SIG*153.68 (Delos, iv B.C.), *IG*3.1288, *POxy*.519.16 (ii A.D.), etc.; Boeot. **σαλπικτάς** *IG*7.1773 (Thespiae, ii A.D.), **σαλπιγκτάς** ib.3195 (Orchom., i B.C.); later **σαλπιστής**, ib.9(2).525.4 (Thessaly, ii B.C.), 3.1285 (Attica, i A.D.), 7.3196 (Orchom. Boeot.), *Sammelb*.4591.3, etc.; also in Plb.1.45.13, D.H.4.17, *Apoc*.18.22, etc. 2. = ὄρνις ὁμοίως σάλπιγγι φθεγγόμενος, Phot.; = ὀρχίλος, Hsch. ⊛ **-ιγξ**, ιγγος, ἡ, *war-trumpet*, ὅτε τ' ἴαχε σάλπιγξ Il.18.219; σ. ἡ ἱερά Artem.1.56, cf. Lyd.*Mens*.4.73:—on various σάλπιγγες, v. Poll.4.85 sq., Sch.Il. l.c.:—σ. Τυρσηνική A.*Eu*.568, E.*Ph*.1378, *Heracl*.831; ὑπαὶ σάλπιγγος by sound *of trumpet*, S.*El*.711, cf. Ar.*Ach*.1001; also ἀπὸ σ. X.*Eq.Mag*.3.12, Plb.4.13.1. 2. metaph., Πιερικὰ σ., of Pindar, *AP*7.34 (Antip. Sid.); οὐρανίη σ. *thunder*, Tryph.327, Nonn.*D*.2.558. II. = σάλπισμα, ap.Arist.*Rh*.$1408^{a}9$. III. σ. θαλασσία, = στρόμβος 2, Archil.192; cf. σάλπη. IV. name of a *bird*, Hsch. (perh. = σαλπιγκτής 2). V. a kind of comet, Ptol.*Tetr*.90. VI. epith. of Athena at Argos, Lyc.915,986, Paus.2.21.3. ⊛ **-ίζω**, fut. -ιῶ Lxx *Nu*.10.4: aor. ἐσάλπιγξα X.*An*.1.2.17, Archipp.19; Ep. σάλπιγξα (v. infr.):—later, fut. σαλπίσω 1*Ep.Cor*.15.52: aor. ἐσάλπισα Lxx *Jo*.6.13, Luc.*Ocyp*.114, Ath.4.130b, etc.:—Pass., pf. σεσάλπιγκται (περι-) Eudamidas ap. Stob.4.13.65:—**σαλπίσσω** is Tarentine, Eust.1654.24, *An.Ox*.1.62; **σαλπίττω** Att., ap.Phot., Luc.*Jud.Voc*.10, v.l. in Poll.4.86; **σαλπίδδω** Boeot., *An.Ox*.4.325:—*sound the trumpet*, σάλπιγξι ῥυθμοὺς σ. X.*An*.7.3.32: c. acc. cogn., σ. πολέμου κτύπον Batr.200; σ. ἀνακλητικόν *AP*11.136 (Lucill.); λιγὺν ἦχον Hedyl.ap.Ath.11.497d; τὸ.. δείπνου σημεῖον Ath.4.130b: abs., ὅταν ποιῇς ἐλεημοσύνην, μὴ σαλπίσῃς ἔμπροσθέν σου *Ev.Matt*.6.2: metaph., ἀμφὶ δὲ σάλπιγξεν μέγας οὐρανός heaven *trumpeted* around, Il.21.388: impers., ἐπεὶ ἐσάλπιγξε (sc. ὁ σαλπιγκτής) when *the trumpet sounded*, X.*An*.1.2.17, cf. 1*Ep.Cor*.15.52. 2. c. acc., ἡμέραν σ. *proclaim, announce* day, of the cock, Luc.*Ocyp*.114. **-ικτής**, v. σαλπιγκτής. **-ισμα**, ατος, τό, *trumpet-call*, Poll.4.86; **σαλπισμός**, ὁ, Thd.*Nu*.23.21. **-ίσσω**, v. σαλπίζω. **-ιστής**, v. σαλπιγκτής. **-ιστικός**, ή, όν, *of* or *for a trumpet*, κρούματα Poll.4.84. **-ίττω**, v. σαλπίζω.

**σάλπος**, ὁ, v. σάλπη.

⊛ **σαλτάριος**, ὁ, = Lat. *salt(u)arius*, *IGRom*.4.634 (Phrygia), 1186 (Lydia), prob. in *Rev.Arch*.1904 i 20 (Thrace, iii A.D.).

**σαλύγη**, ἡ, *constant motion*, as of the spindle, Hsch.

**σάλυξ**, ἡ, f.l. for κάλυξ, Ps.-Dsc.4.23.

**σάλω**, v. σαλιᾷ.

**σαλώμη**, ἡ, *a medicine* (prob. from the pr. n.), Androm.ap.Gal.13.507.

**σαλῶος**· ὁ πεφροντισμένος, Hsch.

⊛ **σαλώτια**, pl., dub. sens. (in list of eatables, etc.), *POxy*.920.5 (ii/iii A.D.); ῥίζια δύο σαλωτίων *Sammelb*.1.25 (iii A.D.); cf. σαλούσιον.

**σᾶμα**, τό, Dor. for σῆμα (q.v.).

**σαμαγόρειος** οἶνος, ὁ, a kind of wine, Arist.*Fr*.109.

⊛ **σάμαθον** (?), dub. sens. in *POxy*.1290.1 (v A.D.).

**Σάμαινα** [Σᾰ], ἡ, (Σάμος) *a ship of Samian build*, Plu.*Per*.26; used as a stamp on Samian coins, Duris 66 J., cf. Hsch. s.v. Σαμιακὸς τρόπος (= Cratin.13), Head *Hist.Num*.[2] p.603.

**σᾱμαίνω**, Dor. for σημαίνω.

**σαμάκιον**, τό, an article of female attire, *Com.Adesp*.1136.

**σάμαξ** [σᾰ], ᾰκος, ὁ, *rush-mat*, used as a bed in war, Chionid.1; also, = τοξικὸς κάλαμος, Lysipp.10.

**Σᾰμάρεια** [ᾰρ], ἡ, *Samaria*, a city of Palestine, called Sebaste by Herod, Str.16.2.34, etc.; also as name of a region, *Ev.Luc*.17.11, etc.; of a village in Egypt, *PEnteux*.8.6, al. (iii B.C.), *PPetr*.2 p.14, al. (iii B.C.):—**Σᾰμᾰρίτης** [ῑ], ου (Dor. **-ίτας** *IG*12(8).439 (Thasos, ii B.C.)), ὁ, *Samaritan*, *Ev.Matt*.10.5, etc.; fem. **-ῖτις**, ιδος, *Ev.Jo*.4.9, *IG*3.2892 (**-εῖτις** ib.2891):—also **Σᾰμᾰρεύς**, έως, St.Byz., Suid.

**Σαμάτης**, v. Σαρμάτης.

**σαμβά**· ὀσφῦς, ὀφρῦς, Hsch.

**σάμβαλον, σαμβαλίσκος**, v. σάνδαλον, σανδαλίσκος.

**σαμβᾰλούχη**, ἡ, *shoe-case*, Herod.7.19; also **-χίς**, ίδος, ἡ, ib.53.

⊛ **σαμβύκ-η** [ῡ], ἡ, *a triangular musical instrument with four strings*, Arist.*Pol*.$1341^{b}1$, Neanth.5 J., Juba 73; of barbaric origin, Str.10.3.17. (Aramaic *sabbᵉkhā* (perh. not Semitic), with *m* inserted, as in Ἀμβακούμ = *Habakkuk*, etc.). 2. = σαμβυκίστρια, Plb.5.37.10; with pun on signf. II, Id.8.6.6. II. *an engine of like form* used in sieges, Id.8.4.8, al., Bito 57.1, Plu.*Marc*.15, Ath.Mech.27.7, App.*Mith*.26.—Cf. σάμβυξ. [Penult. long in *sambūca*, Pers.5.95.] **-ιστής**, οῦ, ὁ, *player on the* σαμβύκη, Euph.ap.Ath.4.182e:—fem. ⊛ **-ίστρια**, Philem.44.5, Plu.*Cleom*.35, *Ant*.9.

**σάμβυξ**, ὁ, = σαμβύκη, Plb.5.37.10, as cited by Suid.

**σάμεα**, ων, τά, *marks on the edge of the dress* (Lacon.), Hsch.

**σᾱμεῖον**, τό, Dor. for σημεῖον, Archyt.1.

**σαμένορα**· τὸν βραβευτὴν τῶν σφαιριζόντων, Hsch.

**σάμερον**, v. σήμερον. **Σάμη**, v. Σάμος. **σαμία**, v. ζημία. **σαμίθη**· ῥόφημά τι, ὡς Γλαυκίας ὁ ἰατρός, Hsch. **σαμινά**, Lacon. for θαμινά, Id. **σάμμα**· ὄργανον μουσικὸν παρὰ Ἰνδοῖς, Id.

**Σᾰμοθρᾴκη**, Ion. **-θρηΐκη**, ἡ, *Samothrace*, Hdt.6.47; the seat of the mysteries of the Cabeiri, Id.2.51; called Σάμος Θρηϊκίη in Hom., Il.13.12, *h.Ap*.34; and simply Σάμος, Il.24.78,753. Adj. ⊛ **Σᾰμόθρᾳξ** (not Σαμοθρᾷξ), Hdn.Gr.1.42, Choerob.*in Theod*.1.187 H., etc.; Ion. pl. Σαμοθρήϊκες Hdt.2.51, 8.90; also **Σᾰμοθρᾴκιος**, Ion. **-θρηΐκιος**, η, ον, Id.7.59,108.

**Σαμοθρᾳκιασταί**, οἱ, *celebrators of Samothracian mysteries*, *IG*12(1).43, al., *Michel* 1307 (Teos), *Supp.Epigr*.4.168 (Caria).

**Σαμοθρᾴκιον**, τό, *temple of the gods of Samothrace*, *Jahresh*.26 *Beibl*.54 (Ephesus, i A.D., in form -κιν).

**Σάμος** [ᾰ], ἡ, *Samos*, the name of several Greek islands: 1. old name for Κεφαλληνία (q.v.), Il.2.634, Od.4.671; also called Σάμη, 1.246, *h.Ap*.429; though this, acc. to others, is a town on the island: hence Adj. **Σαμαῖος**, α, ον, Str.10.2.13. 2. Σάμος Θρηϊκίη, v. Σαμοθρᾴκη. 3. *Samos*, the large island over against Ephesus, first in *h.Ap*.41: hence Adj. **Σάμιος**, α, ον, Hdt.1.70, etc.; ἡ Σαμία (sc. γῆ) ibid., Thphr.*Lap*.62; also Σ. ἀστήρ, clay with medicinal properties, Gal.12.178:—**Σαμιακός**, ή, όν, Cratin.13. (Acc. to Str.8.3.19, 10.2.17, σάμος was an old word signifying *a height*.)

**σαμοῦχος** λίθος, name of a kind of stone, *PMag.Par*.2.200.

**σαμσειρα**, v. σαμψήρα.

**σαμυλίς**· ἡ πρόπολις ὑπὸ τῶν μελισσουργῶν, Hsch.

**σαμφαριτικὴ** νάρδος, ἡ, *camel-hay*, *Cymbopogon Schoenanthus*, Dsc.1.7.

**σαμφόρας**, ου, ὁ, (φέρω) *horse branded with the letter* σάν (v. Σ σ B. 2), Ar.*Eq*.603, *Nu*.122,1298, Eust.785.30.

**σαμψήρα**, ἡ, a kind of *sword of state*, J.*AJ*20.2.3, cf. Suid.; written **σαμσειρα**, *PGiss*.47.11 (ii A.D.). (Persian *šamšīr*.)

**σαμψουχ-ίζω**, *resemble marjoram*, τῇ ὀσμῇ Dsc.3.38. 2. *flavour* or *scent with marjoram*, in Pass., Id.2.76.14. **-ῐνος**, η, ον, *of marjoram*, Dsc.1.48, Gal.6.291, Aët.4.42. (Written -ψιχ- in Aët. l.c., cf. sq.) ⊛ **-ον**, τό, foreign name of ἀμάρακος or *marjoram*, *Origanum majorana*, Nic.*Th*.617, Dsc.3.39, Paus.9.28.3, *IG*14.2508 (Nemausus); written -ψυχ- in Aret.*CA*2.6, cf. 10; gender indeterm. in Poll.6.107.

**σαμώσῃ**· κεραυνώσῃ, Hsch. **σάν**, v. Σ σ B. 2. **σάναπτιν**· τὴν οἰνώτην, Σκύθαι, Hsch. **σανδαία**· τροπὴ ἀπὸ γῆς, ἔνιοι δὲ τὸν λίβα ἄνεμον, Id.

⊛ **σανδάλ-ιον** [ᾰ], τό, Dim. of σάνδαλον, mostly in pl., *sandals*, Hdt.2.91 (sg.), Cratin.131, Cephisod.4, Lxx *Jo*.9.5. 2. *horseshoe*, σ. ὀνικά *POxy*.741.10 (ii A.D.). II. a surgical bandage, Heliod. (?) ap.Orib.49.35.3, as v.l. for **σανδάλιος**, ὁ, which is found also in Heraclas ap. eund.48.4. III. v. σάνδαλον II. **-ίς**, ίδος, ἡ, a kind of *date*, Plin.*HN*13.43. ⊛ **-ίσκος**, ὁ, Dim. of σάνδαλον, Ar.*Ra*.406 (s.v.l., τὸ -κον Blass):—also **σαμβᾰλίσκος**, ὁ, heterocl. pl. -ίσκα, Hippon.18.

⊛ **σανδᾰλοθήκη**, ἡ, *sandal-case*, Men.333.

⊛ **σάνδᾰλ-ον**, τό, *sandal*, Eup.295; mostly in pl., *sandals*, *h.Merc*.79,83,139, etc.; Aeol. **σάμβᾰλον** Eumel.13 K., Sapph.98, *AP*6.267 (Diotim.). II. *a flat fish*, Matro *Conv*.76; also **σανδάλιον**, identified by Hsch. with ψῆττα, but distinguished from it by Alciphr.1.7. **-ώδης**, ες, *sandal-like*, Sch.E.*Or*.1370.

**σάνδανον**, τό, perh. *sandal-wood*, *Santalum album*, in pl., Aët.16.142 (dub. sens., cf. σαγάλινος).

**σανδᾰράκ-η** [ρᾰ], ἡ, *red sulphide of arsenic, realgar*, Arist.*HA*$604^{b}28$, Plin.*HN*34.177, *Peripl.M.Rubr*.49; written **σανδαράχη** in Hp.*Morb*.2.14 (but -κη *Superf*.32), Dsc.5.105, Gal.17(1).834, Alciphr.1.33, etc. 2. *an orange pigment* made therefrom, Thphr.*Lap*.40, 50. (Assyr. *šindu arḳu* 'green paint', i.e. *yellow sulphide of arsenic*, orpiment, cf. ἀρσενικόν.) II. bee-bread, Arist.*HA*626$^a$7. **-ίζω**, v.l. -χίζω, to be bright red, Dsc.5.104. **-ῖνος**, η, ον, of orange colour, Hdt.1.98, Ael.*NA*17.23, Philostr.*VA*3.14:—also **σανδᾰρᾰχώδης**, ες, Ruf.*Fr.*67.4, Gal.17(1).834. **-ούργιον**, τό, pit whence σανδαράκη is dug, Str.12.3.40.

**σανδύκ-ινος**, η, ον, (σάνδυξ) red, ζώνη *POxy.*496.4 (ii A.D.). ✱ **-ιον**, τό, = sq. I. 1 or 3, σαντοικίου (sic) καὶ ψιμυθίου *PLips.*102 ii 2 (iv A.D.).

✱ **σάνδυξ**, υκος, ἡ, a bright red colour, also called ἀρμένιον, Str.11.14.9 (prob. cj.); obtained by heating ψιμύθιον (= cerussa), Dsc.5.88, cf. Plin.*HN*35.40; though a like colour was made from a plant of the same name, red sandalwood, Pterocarpus santalinus, Sosib.21, Verg.*Ecl.*4.45, Plin. l. c., Lyd.*Mag.*3.64. **2.** pl., flesh-coloured women's garments dyed with this colour, in Lydia, ibid. **3.** a kind of salve, prob. a pink mixture of zinc oxide and carbonate, Dsc. l. c., Gal.12.244, Hsch. **II.** casket, Id. [ῠ in genit., Prop.2.19.81; but ῡ in Grattius *Cyn.*86.] (Assyr. sâmtu, sându 'red stone', prob. cinnabar.)

**σανδών**, όνος, ὁ, transparent robe (cf. foreg. I. 2), Lyd.*Mag.*3.64.

**σανθείς**· αἰσθόμενος, γνούς, Hsch.

**σᾰνίδ-ιον** [ῐδ], τό, Dim. of σανίς, small board or plank, Ar.*Pax* 202, Hippias (?) in *PHib.*1.13.30, Men.202, Str.17.1.50. **II.** tablet, public register, ἐκ σανιδίου Lys.16.6, cf. Aeschin.3.200,201, *IG*1$^2$.313.161, 2$^2$.1237.124. **III.** small splint, Heliod.ap.Orib.44.23.74, Gal.18(2).888; foot-prop, Id.10.444. **-όω**, board over, *Supp.Epigr.*4.449.22 (Didyma, ii B.C.); σεσανιδωμένον πλοῖον decked vessel, *PLond.*3.1164h 7 (iii A.D.), cf. Ath.Mech.22.9 (Pass.), Sch.Th.1.10. ✱ **-ώδης**, ες, like a plank, flat, Aret.*SD*1.8, Plu.2.896e. **-ωμα**, ατος, τό, planking, framework, Ath.Mech.17.14, Plb.1.22.6, 6.23.3, Lxx 3*Ma.*4.10; τῶν μακρῶν πλοίων Thphr.*HP* 5.7.5 (pl.); of a gateway, Hld.9.3; sloping table, Agatharch.27. ✱ **-ωτός**, ή, όν, planked, boarded over, Lxx *Ex.*27.8, al.

✱ **σᾰνίς**, ίδος, ἡ, board, plank, timber, σ. πτελεΐνη *IG*1$^2$.313.133, cf. 2$^2$.1672.168, Plb.1.22.9, *AP*9.269 (Antip.Thess.), *Act.Ap.*27.44, etc.; σ. ἄξοος Call.*Fr.*105:—hence anything made thereof, **1.** door, Hom. always in pl., folding doors, Il.12.453,461, Od.22.128, etc.; κολληταὶ σ. Il.9.583; σ. πυκινῶς ἀραρυῖαι, δικλίδες Od.2.344, cf. Il.21.535; πύλῃσιν ἐπικεκλιμέναι σ. 12.121: rarely in sg., E.*Or.*1221. **2.** wooden platform, scaffold, or stage, ἐφ' ὑψηλῆς σ. Od.21.51. **3.** wooden floor, esp. ship's deck, E.*Hel.*1556, Archimel.ap.Ath.5.209c, Luc.*JTr.*48. **4.** bench, seat, *SIG*244*B*61 (Delph., iv B.C.), Herod.7.5. **5.** lid of box, v.l. in Lxx 4*Ki.*12.9. **6.** in pl., wooden tablets for writing on, E.*Alc.*967 (lyr.): esp. at Athens and elsewh., tablets covered with gypsum, on which were written all sorts of public notices, esp. the causes for hearing in the law-courts, Ar.*V.*349,848; laws to be proposed, Decr.ap.And.1.84; laws corrected by the Thesmothetae, Aeschin.3.39; lists of officers, Lys.26.10; accounts, *IG*1$^2$.374.190; names of debtors, D.25.70 (in sg.), Isoc.15.237: sg. also in *SIG* 975.30 (Delos, iii B.C.); at Rome, of the tables on which the laws were written, D.C.42.32. **b.** pl., painted panels, pictures, *SIG* 977$^a$10 (Delos, ii B.C.). **7.** plank to which offenders were bound or nailed, ζῶντα πρὸς σανίδα διε- (v. l. προσδιε-) πασσάλευσαν Hdt.7.33; σανίδι προσπασσαλεύσαντες Id.9.120, cf. Cratin.341; ἐν τῇ σ. δῆσαι, πρὸς τῇ σ. δεῖν, Ar.*Th.*931,940; σανίσι προσδῆσαι Duris 67 J.

✱ **σανίσκη**, ἡ, Dim. of foreg. 6b, picture, Herod.4.36.

**σάνιτρα**· τροφός, τιθήνη, Hsch. ✱ **σαννάδας**· τὰς ἀγρίας αἶγας, Id.

**σαννάκιον** [ᾰκ] or **σάννᾰκρον**, τό, a kind of cup, Philem.87.

✱ **σάννας**, ου, ὁ, zany, Cratin.337.

**Σαννίδωρος**, ὁ, Epicurus' nickname for Antidorus, Epicur.*Fr.*4.

**σάννιον**, τό, membrum virile, Eup.440:—**σαννιόπληκτος**, ον, = αἰδοιόπληκτος, Hsch.

**σαννίς**· δρυοσάνδραξ (Thurii), Hsch.

**σαννίων**, ὁ, = σάννας, Arr.*Epict.*3.22.83.

**σάννορος**, = μωρός, Rhinth.23.

**σαννυρίζω**, jeer, mock, prob. in Hsch. s. v. ἐσαθνύριζεν· ἤκαλλεν.

**σαντάλινος**, v. σαγάλινος. **σαντοίκιον**, v. σανδύκιον.

**σαντονικόν**, τό, a kind of wormwood found in the country of the Santones in Gaul, worm-seed, Artemisia maritima, Dsc.3.23 (with vv. ll.; σαντονίον in lemmate), Gal.11.804.

**σάξις**, εως, ἡ, (σάττω) cramming, Arist.*Pr.*938$^b$29, cf. 928$^b$34.

**σαξίφρᾰγον**, τό, saxifrage, = κέστρον I. 2, Gal.6.339 (gender uncertain), Ps.-Dsc.4.16; σαξίφραγος, ὁ or ἡ, Ps.-Gal.19.694; cf. σαρξίφαγον.

**σαό-μβροτος**, ον, preserving mortals, Procl.*H.*7.40. ✱ **-πτολις**, ιος, ὁ, ἡ, protecting cities, *Supp.Epigr.*1.405*B*1 (Samos, iii A.D.), *IG* 5(2).153 (Tegea, iv A.D.), Nonn.*D.*41.395, Coluth.142.

✱ **σάος**, as Posit. only in the contr. form σῶς, σᾶ (v. σῶς), exc. in Alc.32 and as v.l. in Il.1.117 ap.A.D.*Conj.*223.10; but Comp. σαώτερος in Il.1.32, X.*Cyr.*6.3.4, Theoc.25.59: Comp. Adv. σαώτερον *AP*9.788: cf. σάως.

**σᾰοσίμβροτος**, ον, = σαόμβροτος, Hsch.

**σᾰοστρέω**, make thank-offering (σῶστρα) for safety, *IG*9(1).610 (Cephallenia).

**σᾰοφρονέω, σᾰοφροσύνη, σᾰόφρων**, poet. for σωφρ-· σαόφρων also in Aret.*SD*1.6.

**σᾰόω**, = σῴζω (q. v.).

**σᾰπέρδ-ης**, ου, ὁ, the fish κορακῖνος, prob. the great Nile-perch, Tilapia nilotica, Hp.*Int.*25, Ar.*Frr.*414,686, Archipp.26; a Pontic fish acc. to Archestr.*Fr.*38.3; σ. τῶν ἐκ τῆς λίμνης *PCair.Zen.*680.33 (iii B.C.); found in the Maeander, Porph.*Abst.*3.5; both the κορακῖνος and the πλατίστακος were called σ. acc. to Parmeno ap. Ath.7.308f; cf. σαπερδίς. **-ιον**, τό, Dim. of foreg.; nickname of Phryne, Apollod.ap.Ath.13.591c. **-ίς**, ἡ, prob. = σαπέρδης, Arist. *HA*608$^a$2.

**σᾰπή(η)**, v. σήπω. **σάπιθος**· θυσία (Paphian), Hsch.

**σαπουλανᾶς**, ᾶ, ὁ, perh. wool-cleaner (cf. σάπων, Lat. lana), *MAMA* 3.224 (Corycus).

**σαππείριον**, v. σαπφ-.

✱ **σαπρ-ία**, ἡ, decay, decayed matter, Lxx *Jb.*2.9, al., Dsc.1.84, *AP* 15.38 (Cometas). **-ίας** οἶνος, ὁ, old, mellow wine (v. σαπρός II. 3), Hermipp.82.6. **-ίζω**, fut. -ιῶ, make rotten or stinking, Lxx *Ec.*10.1:—Pass., rot, decay, σεσάπρισται τὰ ὀστέα Hp.*Fract.*33.

**σαπρό-ζωος**, ον, living in filth, *Cat.Cod.Astr.*8(4).144. **-κνημος**, ον, rotting the legs, ἕλκη Dsc.4.182. **-πλουτος**, ον, stinkingly rich, perhaps a parody on ἀρχαιόπλουτος, Antiph.224.1 (Dobree suggested σατραπόπλουτος, rich as a satrap). **-πωμάριος**, ὁ, perh. seller of preserved fruits, or cider-maker, *MAMA*3.760 (Corycus).

✱ **σαπρός**, ά, όν, (σήπω) rotten, putrid, Hippon.23, Hp.*Oss.*13; of the lungs, diseased, Id.*Morb.*1.13; of bone, carious, Id.*Fract.*33; of wood, etc., rotten, ἱστίον Ar.*Eq.*918; βύρσα Id.*V.*38; πινακίσκος, φορμός, σχοινίον, Id.*Pl.*813,542, *V.*1343; ἱμάς Men.109.4; τοῦ διατειχίσματος ἀνελόντι τὰ σ. *IG*2$^2$.1672.24; of a house, σ. καὶ ῥέουσα καὶ καταπίπτουσα Teles p.27 H.; ἐλαῖαι Thphr.*HP*4.14.10: prov., σαπροῦ πείσματος ἀντιλαβέσθαι Thgn.1362: esp., of fish that have been long in pickle, stale, rancid, τάριχος Ar.*Ach.*1101; opp. πρόσφατος, Antiph.218.4, cf. 125.6; of withered flowers, D.22.70. Adv., -ρῶς λούει τὰ βαλανεῖα so as to leave one filthy, Arr.*Epict.*2.21.14. **II.** generally, stale, worn out, ἀρχαῖον καὶ σαπρόν Ar.*Pl.*323; of clothes, *PGiss.*26.6 (ii A.D.). Adv., -ῶς (perh. misspelt for -ός) περιπατῶ I am walking about in rags, *BGU*846.9 (ii A.D.). **2.** of persons, γέρων ὢν καὶ σ. Ar.*Pax*698; ὦ σαπρά, to an old woman, Id.*Ec.*884, Hermipp.10; so εἶναι σαπρὸν κοὐδὲν δύνασθαι Ar.*V.*1380; οὐδὲν ἐσμεν οἱ σ. Eup.221; σ. γυναῖκα.. ὁ τρόπος εὔμορφον ποιεῖ Philem.170. **3.** of wine, mellow (cf. σαπρίας), Eup.442, cf. Philyll.24; τρὺξ παλαιὰ καὶ σαπρά Ar.*Pl.*1086; of old wine, ὀδόντας οὐκ ἔχων, ἤδη σαπρὸς.., γέρων γε δαιμονίως Alex.167.4. **4.** εἰρήνη σαπρά, a joke παρὰ προσδοκίαν, Ar.*Pax*554. **5.** metaph., unsound, bad, λόγος *Ep.Eph.*4.29; opp. καλός, Vett.Val.36.30, cf. *PSI*4.312.13 (iv A.D.); ἄρουραι *PGiss.*13.22 (ii A.D.); τὰ σ. ταῦτα Arr.*Epict.*3.16.7; ὡς σ. καὶ κίβδηλος ὁ λέγων.. M.Ant.11.15, cf. *Sammelb.*5761.23 (i A.D.), *PSI*6.717.4 (ii A.D.); τὴν σ. εἱμαρμένην the evil fate, *PMag.Leid.W.*14.38. **III.** of sound, αὐλεῖ γὰρ σαπρὰ.. κρουμάτια Theopomp.Com.50 (perh. f.l. for σαθρά, v. σαθρός 2).

✱ **σαπρό-στομος**, ον, with foul breath, Arist.ap.Stob.3.5.42. **-της**, ητος, ἡ, rottenness, putridity, Pl.*R.*609e, Arist.*Mete.*379$^a$6, al., Thphr.*Od.*2. **-φᾰγέω**, eat stinking food, Mart.3.77.

**σαπρ-όω**, = sq., in Pass., Sch.Ar.*Pl.*1086, Sch.Nic.*Al.*468. **-ύνομαι**, Pass., become rotten or stinking, Nic.*Al.*468.

**σαπύλλειν**, = σαίνειν, Rhinth.24.

**σαπφείρ-ινος**, η, ον, of or like lapis lazuli, Philostr.*VA*1.25, Ps.-Callisth.3.8, Sch.A.R.2.395 codd.; δελματική σαπιρίνη (sic) *PTeb.*405.10 (iii A.D.). **-ιον** (written **σαππείριον**), τό, pigment made from lapis lazuli, *Sammelb.*2251 (iv A.D.); (written **σαππίριν**) *POxy.*1739.1 (ii/iii A.D.), *PHolm.*4.2. **-ος** (proparox.), ἡ, lapis lazuli, of which two chief kinds, κυανῆ and χρυσῆ, are mentioned by Thphr.*Lap.*23,37, D.P.1105; cf. Lxx *Ex.*24.10, al., J.*AJ*3.7.5, *Peripl. M.Rubr.*39. (Cf. Hebr. sappīr, perh. not Semitic.)

**Σαπφώ**, οῦς, acc. οῦν Greg.Cor. p.427 S., voc. οἶ, ἡ:—Sappho, Alc.55, etc.; Aeol. **Ψάπφω** Sapph.1.20, Sapph.*Supp.*23.5, *BMus.Cat. Coins* (Troas, etc.) p.200 (Mytil.); sts. **Σάφφω**, Head *Hist.Num.*$^2$ p.560 (Eresus):—Adj. **Σαπφῷος**, α, ον, Posidipp.ap.Ath.13.596d; or **Σαπφικός**, ή, όν, of Sapphic measure, Heph.14.1.

**σᾰπών**, v. σήπω.

**σάπων** [ᾱ], ωνος, ὁ, Lat. sapo, soap, τῷ Γερμανικῷ σμήγματι (καλεῖται δὲ σ.) Ruf.ap.Orib.45.29.59, cf. Asclep.ap.Gal.12.586, Aret.*CD* 2.13:—a Gallic invention (hair-dye) adopted by the Germans acc. to Plin.*HN*28.191. [ᾱ, Seren.Sammon.153.] (The Germanic forms (OHG. seifa, OE. sāpe, etc.) come fr. prim. Germanic *saipjō, whence also Finn. saippio; cf. σήπων.)

**σᾱπων-αρικός**, ή, όν, saponaceous, soapy, Zos.Alch. p.226 B., Paul. Aeg.6.9; -αρικὴ τέχνη art of making soap, Zos.Alch. p.142 B. **-ιον**, τό, Dim. of σάπων, Sch.Theoc.3.17, Zos.Alch. p.143 B.; cf. σαφώνιον.

**σαράβᾰρα**, τά, loose trousers worn by Scythians, Antiph.201; also = Aramaic sarbālīn, Lxx, Thd.*Da.*3.27 (cf. 21). (Prob. Persian shalvâr or shulvâr (braccae).)

**σάραβος**, ὁ, pudenda muliebria, *Com.Adesp.*1137.

**σαράγαρον**, τό, a kind of wagon, *Edict.Diocl.*15.32,36; = rheda, *Gloss.*

**σάραγος**· ὑπηρέτης ὁ σαρῶν τὰς δημοσίας στοάς, Hsch.

**σαρακνον**, apptly. name of a bird, *Sammelb.*5301.13.

**σάραξ** (A), ακος, ὁ, a long, flowing garment, Lyd.*Mag.*1.12.

**σάραξ** (B), = tinea, *Gloss.*

✱ **σᾰρᾱπιακός**, ή, όν, of Sarapis, φαυλον σ. name of a plaster, Gal.12.744.

**σαραπιάς**, = σερ-, Dsc.*Eup.*2.39.

**σαραπίους**· τὰς μαινίδας (Pergaean), Hsch.

✱ **Σάρᾱπις** [Σᾰ], ιδος, ὁ, later also **Σέρᾱπις**, dat. sg. Σαράπι and Σεράπι *Milet.*1(7).283, 205b:—Sarapis or Serapis, an Egyptian god, Osiris-Apis (introduced from Sinope under Ptol. I acc. to Tac.*H.*4.83–84),

Men. in *POxy.*1803.8, Call.*Epigr.*38.3, D.S.1.25, Plu.2.362a; freq. in Inscrr., *OGI*16 (Halic., iii B.C.), al., *SIG*664.25 (Delos, ii B.C.), al., *CIG*4042 (Ancyra), al., and Papyri, *UPZ*32.38 (ii B.C.), etc.:—hence **Σᾰρᾱπιεῖον**, τό, *temple of Sarapis*, *SIG*663.14 (Delos, iii/ii B.C.), *PCair. Zen.*34.13 (iii B.C.), *UPZ*122.6 (ii B.C.), Plb.4.39.6; contr. **Σᾰρᾱπεῖον** or **Σερᾱπεῖον**, τό, *CIG*4401, Plu.*Alex.*76, D.C.66.24; **Σαράπιον** or **Σερ-**, Str.17.1.10, *CIG*2715*b*.4 (Caria):—***Σᾰρᾱπιεῖα**, τά, festival at Tanagra, *IG*7.540:—**Σᾰρᾱπιασταί**, οἱ, *guild of worshippers of Sarapis*, ib.2².1292, *SIG*1114 (Rhodes, ii B.C.). **II.** a plant, *PMag.Osl.*1.363. [Inscrr. and Papyri show Σαρ- almost without exception in iii and ii B.C.; Σερ- becomes common in the Roman period.]

**σάρᾱπις**, εως or ιος, ὁ, *a white Persian robe with purple stripes*, Democr.Eph.1, Ctes.*Fr.*43.

**σάρᾰπους**, ποδος, ὁ, ἡ, acc. σαράπουν and, in Alc.37B, σάραπον:—*splay-footed*, Alc. l.c., Gal.19.136. (From σαίρω (B), = ἐπισύρων τὼ πόδε, D.L.1.81; from σαίρω (A), = διασεσηρότας καὶ διεστῶτας ἔχουσα τοὺς δακτύλους τῶν ποδῶν, Gal. l.c.)

**σαραχηρώ**· ἡ κοσμήτρια τῆς Ἥρας, Beros.ap.Hsch.

**σάργαλος**, ὁ, *the place in a chariot where the whip was kept*, Poll.7.116.

***σαργάν-η** [γᾰ], ἡ, = ταργάνη, *plait, braid*, A.*Supp.*788 codd. (lyr.). **2.** *basket*, Aen.Tact.29.6, Timocl.21.7, 2*Ep.Cor.*11.33, Luc.*Lex.*6, *PFlor.*269.7 (iii A.D.), *PLond.*2.236.11 (iv A.D.):—v. σάρκινος III. **-ίδιον**, τό, Dim. of foreg., *BGU*1095.21 (i A.D.), *PGoodsp.Cair.*30 xxii 13 (ii A.D.). **-ιον**, τό, = foreg., ἀχύρου σ. ἕν *PLips.*21.18 (iv A.D.). **-ίς**, ίδος, ἡ, = σαργάνη, Cratin.40.7.

**σάργανος**· ὁ ἀγροῖκος, Hsch.

**σαργῖνος**, ὁ, a kind of gregarious fish, Epich.56, Arist.*HA*610ᵇ6.

**σαργίον**, τό, = sq., *Gp.*20.7.1.

**σαργός** (on the accent, v. Hdn.Gr.1.139), ὁ, a sea-fish, the *sargue, Sargus Rondeletii*, Epich.55, Philyll.13, Diocl.*Fr.*135, Arist.*HA* 543ᵃ7, ᵇ15, 570ᵃ32, 591ᵇ19.

**σάρδα**, ἡ, = σαρδίνη, Diph.Siph.ap.Ath.3.120f, Xenocr.ap.Orib.2.58.142, Gal.6.729,746.

**σαρδάζω**, v. sq.

**σαρδάνιος** [δᾰ], α, ον, an Adj. used of *bitter* or *scornful* smiles or laughter, μείδησε δὲ θυμῷ σαρδάνιον μάλα τοῖον Od.20.302; so ἀνεκάγχασε μάλα σαρδάνιον Pl.*R.*337a; ὑπομειδιάσας σαρδάνιον Plb. 18.7.6; τί μάταια γελᾷς..; τάχα που σαρδάνιον γελάσεις *AP*5.178 (Mel.); πεφύλαξο σίνεσθαι, μὴ καὶ σ. γελάσῃς *APl.*4.86; *ridere* γέλωτα σαρδάνιον Cic.*Fam.*7.25.1. (Perh. connected with σεσηρώς, *grinning, sneering*, Sch.Pl. l.c.; cf. **σαρδάζων**· μετὰ πικρίας γελῶν, Phot., Suid. —The common expl. given of this laugh was that it resembled the effect produced *by a Sardinian plant* (*Ranunculus Sardoüs, Sardinian crowfoot*, called **σαρδάνη** by Tz. ad Hes.*Op.*59, **σαρδόνιον** by Ps.-Dsc.2.175, D.Chr.32.99) which when eaten screwed up the face of the eater, Paus.10.17.13, Sch.Pl. l.c., Phot., Serv. ad Verg.*Ecl.*7.41; whence later authors wrote σαρδόνιον or σαρδώνιον (from Σαρδώ) for σαρδάνιον, Ps.-Dsc. l.c., D.Chr. l.c., Luc.*Asin.*24, etc., σαρδώνιος γέλως and -ωνία πόα Dsc.*Alex.*14, and σαρδόνιον appears as a v.l. in Hom. and Pl.; hence our form *sardonic*; this and other explanations are given in Timae.29, Zen.5.85, Tz. ad Lyc.796, Sch. Pl. l.c.)

**σαρδανάφαλλος**· γελωτοποιός, Hsch.

**Σάρδεις**, εων, αἱ, *Sardes*, the capital of Lydia, A.*Pers.*45 (anap.); dat. Σάρδεσι ib.321:—Ion. **Σάρδιες** *AP*7.709 (Alexander), etc. (**Σάρδῖς** is only f.l. in Hdt.5.102); gen. Σαρδίων, dat. Σάρδῖσι, Hdt.1.7, 5.101, etc.; acc. Σάρδιας Call.*Dian.*246, or Σάρδῖς Hdt.1.27:—Adj. **Σαρδιᾱνός**, Ion. **-ηνός**, ή, όν, ib.22,80, E.*Fr.*630, Call.*Iamb.*1.172 (-ηνευς Pap.); οἱ Σαρδιανοί X.*Cyr.*7.2.3:—**Σαρδιᾱνικός**, ή, όν, Ar.*Ach.*112, *Pax* 1174, Pl.Com.208; v. βάπτω I. 2.

**σαρδίνη** [ῑ], ἡ, *pilchard* or *sardine, Clupea pilchardus*, Gal.6.746 (pl., v.l. -ῆναι); also **σαρδῖνος**, ὁ, Arist.*Fr.*329 (s.v.l.), Epaenet. ap.Ath.7.329a.

**σάρδιον**, τό, *the Sardian stone*, Pl.*Phd.*110d, Thphr.*Lap.*8,23, J. *BJ*5.5.7, *Apoc.*4.3, al., *PHolm.*3.36; as a seal, *IG*2².1408.9 (iv B.C.), *Inscr.Délos* 442 *B* 3 (ii B.C.); σάρδια, of female ornaments, Ar.*Fr.*320. 13, cf. Men.373.—This stone was of two kinds, the transparent-red or female being our *carnelian*, the transparent-brown or male our *sardine*, Thphr.*Lap.*30:—later λίθος ***σάρδιος**, Phlp. *in de An.*321.10 (pl.); **σάρδινος** λ., *An.Ox.*4.229; **σαρδόνιον**, Hsch. s. v. σαρδώ.

***σαρδισμός**, ὁ, *mixture of dialects*, Quint.*Inst.*8.3.59 (from the mixed population of Sardis).

**σαρδόνιον**, τό, = σαρδών, X.*Cyn.*6.9. **II.** v. σάρδιον.

**σαρδόνιος**, v. σαρδάνιος. **σάρδοντα**· διαπίπτοντα, Hsch.

**σαρδόνυξ**, ῠχος, ὁ, (σάρδιον) *sardonyx*, Philem.216, Gal.5.46, *AP*1. 116, J.*AJ*3.7.5, *BJ*5.5.7, *Apoc.*21.20, Ps.-Plu.*Fluv.*20.4, etc. The stone was called ὄνυξ when the dark ground was simply spotted or streaked with white, but σαρδόνυξ if the different colours were disposed in layers.

**Σαρδώ**, ἡ, gen. όος contr. οῦς, dat. οῖ, *Sardinia*, Hdt.1.170, Ar.*V.* 700; the obl. cases are sts. Σαρδόνος, -όνι, -όνα (as if from Σαρδών), Plb.1.24.5 sq., 1.79.1, etc.; Σαρδῶνος is f.l. in Str.2.4.3: a nom. **Σαρδώνη** in Hsch.(s.v.l.).—Hence Adj. **Σαρδόνιος**, Hdt.1.166, Theoc. 16.86; cf. σαρδάνιος (hence *Σαρδονία = Σαρδώ, *CIG*2509.14):—also **Σαρδονικός**, Hdt.2.105, Arist.*Mete.*354ᵃ21, Poll.5.26: **Σαρδώνιος**, Str.2.4.3, 2.5.19, etc.; **Σαρδωνικός**, Lyc.796; **Σαρδῷος**, ῴα, ῷον, Plb. 1.42.6, etc.:—**Σαρδοί**, οἱ, *the Sardinians*, D.S.21.16; **Σαρδῷοι** Plb.1. 88.9; γῆς τῆς λεγομένης **σάρδης**, = Lat. *Sarda*, a kind of fuller's earth from Sardinia, Gal.13.734, cf. Plin.*HN*35.196. **II.** *a precious stone*, prob. = σάρδιον or σαρδόνυξ, Luc.*Dom.*15, Philostr.*Im.*1.6.

**σαρδών**, όνος, ἡ, *the rope sustaining the upper edge of a hunting-net*, Poll.5.31, Hsch.; cf. σαρδόνιον.

***σαρήσιον**, τό, a garment, *PMasp.*6 ii 85 (vi A.D.).

**σάρητον**, τό, = σάραπις (garment), S.*Fr.*135 (v.l. σαλητόν).

**σάρι**, τό, pl. σάρια, an Egyptian water-plant, *Cyperus auricomus*, Thphr.*HP*4.8.5: called *sari pha* in Plin.*HN*13.128.

**σαρίν**, ὀρνέου εἶδος, ὅμοιον ψάρῳ, Hsch.; cf. ψάρ. **σαρίρ**· κλάδος φοίνικος (Lacon.), Id.

**σάρῖσα**, ἡ, *sarissa*, a long pike used in the Macedonian phalanx, Thphr.*HP*3.12.2, Plb.2.69.9, 18.29.2, etc. (Freq. written σάρισσα, Ovid.*Metam.*12.466, Lucan.8.298; but σάρισα appears in most of the best codd. of Plb.2.69, etc., and is recognized by Hdn.Gr.1.267.)

**σᾰρῑσο-φόρος**, ον, *armed with the sarissa*, Plb.12.20.2, Arr.*An.*1. 14.1; v. foreg. Hence **-φορέω**, Zonar.

**σαρκ-άζω**, (σάρξ) *tear flesh like dogs*, Ar.*Pax* 482, ubi v. Sch.; cf. σαρκοκύων. **2.** *pluck grass with closed lips*, as grazing horses do, Hp.*Art.*8. **II.** *bite the lips in rage*, Gal.19.136: hence, *speak bitterly, sneer*, εἰρωνεύεσθαι μετ' ἐπισυρμοῦ τινος Stob.2.7.11ᵐ; σαρκάζων..καὶ σεσηρώς Ph.2.597; cf. Sch.Ar.*Ra.*966, Eust.1083.32. **-ασμο-πῐτῠοκάμπτης**, ου, ὁ, *sneering-pinebender*, Comic word in Ar.*Ra.* 966. **-ασμός**, ὁ, *mockery, sarcasm*, Hdn.*Fig.* p.92 S., Phryn.*PS* p.16 B.

**σαρκάω**, v. σαρκοκύων.

**σάρκ-ειος**, α, ον, *fleshy*, Ps.-Alex.Aphr. *in Metaph.*542.23. **-ελάφεια** [λᾰ] (sc. σῦκα), τά, *venison-figs*, a kind so called, Ath.3. 78a. **-ήρης**, ες, *of, consisting of flesh*, στάχυς *Trag.Adesp.* 263. **-ίδιον**, τό, Dim. of σάρξ, *a bit of flesh*, Arist.*GA*746ᵃ20, *Fr.* 334, Plu.*Cat.Ma.*23, Archig.ap.Orib.8.1.39; τὰ δύστηνά μου σαρκίδια, Arr.*Epict.*1.3.5. **II.** = νύμφη IX, Sor.1.18, Gal.14.706; of the urethral orifice, Sor. l.c. **-ίζω**, *scrape clean of flesh*, Hdt.4.64. **-ικός**, ή, όν, = sq. I, χρώς, δέρμα, Sotad.19; = sq. 3, 1*Ep.Cor.*9.11, *Ep.Rom.* 7.14 (v.l.), *Cod.Just.*1.3.41.4. **-ῐνος**, η, ον, *of* or *like flesh, fleshy*, σ. ὄζος (v. ὄζος); σ. [μέρη] *fleshy* parts, such as the gums, Arist.*HA* 493ᵃ1; *made of flesh* (and blood), Id.*EN*1117ᵇ5; ἄνθρωποι θνατοὶ καὶ σ. Hipparch.ap.Stob.4.44.81, cf. Phld.*D.*3*Fr.*6, *Sign.*34; σ. ἰχθῦς (opp. a dream) Theoc.21.66; τοῖς τὸ χρήσιμον καὶ σ. καὶ ὠφέλιμον [ἔχουσι τῶν λόγων] *substantial*, Plu.2.79c. **2.** *made of gut*, σχοινία *PLond.*3.1177.169 (ii A.D.). **3.** *fleshly, of the flesh*, *Ep. Hebr.*7.16, v.l. in *Ep.Rom.*7.14. **II.** *fleshy, corpulent*, Ar.*Fr.*711, Eup.387; σώματα Pl.*Lg.*906c. **III.** σάρκινος ἤτοι γυργαθός, perh. = σαργάνη 2, *Edict.Diocl.*32.18. **-ίον**, τό, Dim. of σάρξ, *bit of flesh*, Hp.*Aph.*4.76, al., Diph.14, Arist.*HA*503ᵇ13, Plu.*Brut.*8; ὠμὰ σ. Jul.*Or.*6.190c; σαρκία φορῶν, of Heracles, Id.*Or.*5.167a. **II.** = νύμφη IX, Sor.1.18. **-ίς**, ίδος, ἡ, *meat*, *Stud.Pal.*20.250.5 (vi/vii A.D.).

**σαρκῖτις**, ἡ, name of a precious stone, Plin.*HN*37.181.

**σαρκο-βλαστάνω**, *grow flesh*, Paul.Aeg.6.7 (v.l. σάρκα βλ.). **-βορέω**, *eat flesh*, Sch.Th.2.50. **-βόρος**, ον, (βορά) *eating flesh, carnivorous*, ἄνθρωποι Ph.1.665; [ζῷα] Plu.2.956c; θῆρες Man.5.193; also βουβρωστις σ. *MAMA*4.140 (Apollonia). **-βρώς**, ῶτος, ὁ, ἡ, = foreg., Moschio Trag.6.14. **-γονία**, ἡ, (γενέσθαι) *formation of flesh*, ἐξ αἵματος Porph.*Antr.*14. **-δακής**, ές, (δάκνω) *biting* or *eating flesh*, βίος Orph.*Fr.*292. **-ειδής**, ές, *flesh-like, fleshy*, φύσις Pl.*Ti.*76a; σ. ὢν τὴν φύσιν Arist.*HA*495ᵇ22: Comp., -ειδέστερα νεῦρα Hp.*Loc.Hom.*4, cf. Aret.*SA*2.6: cf. σαρκώδης. **-επιπλοκήλη**, ἡ, prob. *omental hernia with tumour of the spermatic cord*, Gal.14. 788. **-θλασμα**, ατος, τό, *bruise of the flesh*, Orib.*Syn.*7.14 tit., Paul.Aeg.4.30. **-κήλη**, ἡ, *sarcocele, a fleshy excrescence on the testicles*, Cels.7.18.10, Poll.4.203, Gal.7.729. **-κηλικός**, ή, όν, *afflicted with sarcocele*, Id.14.789. **-κόλλα**, ας, ἡ, a Persian gum, *Astragalus fasciculifolius*, Dsc.3.85, Gal.12.118, Plin.*HN*13.67, 24.128. **2.** = ἀργεμώνη ἑτέρα, Ps.-Dsc.2.178. (Named from its power of healing wounds.)

**σαρκοκύων** [ῠ], κῠνος, ὁ, prob. f.l. in Hippon.133: Schneid. and Dind. (Sch.Ar.*Pax*481) read σαρκῶν κύων, from **σαρκάω**, = σαρκάζω (cf. σαρκῶν· σεσηρώς, Hsch.).

**σαρκο-λᾰβίς**, ίδος, ἡ, *surgeon's forceps*, Dsc.3.80, *Hippiatr.*20:—also **-λάβος**, ὁ, Antyll.ap.Orib.45.10.2; and **-λάβον**, τό, *Hermes* 38. 283. **-λῐπής**, ές, *forsaken by flesh*, πλευρά *AP*7.383 (Phil.).

**σαρκ-όμφᾰλον**, τό, *fleshy excrescence on the navel*, Gal.19.445.

**σαρκο-πᾰγής**, ές, (πήγνυμι) *compact of flesh*, *APl.*4.134 (Mel.). **-ποιέω**, *make of flesh*, τὸν ἄνθρωπον ὅλον Plu.2.1096e. **-ποιία**, ἡ, *making of flesh*, Porph.*Antr.*14. **-ποιός**, όν, *making flesh, nourishing, fattening*, Dsc.5.6, Plu.2.771b. **-πτερος**, ον, *with fleshy wings*, Simp. *in Cat.*183.21. **-πῦον**, τό, *purulent flesh*, Hp. *Coac.*615. **-πυώδης**, ες, *like purulent flesh*, Id.*Epid.*4.8. **-ρριζος**, ον, *with a fleshy root*, Thphr.*HP*7.12.1, *Od.*63. **-τᾰκής**, ές, (τήκω) *wasting the flesh*, νοῦσοι Procl.*H.*7.44. **-τοκέομαι**, Pass., *to be born like lumps of flesh*, of young bears, opp. ζῳο-, ᾠο-τοκέομαι, S.E. *P.*1.42: **σαρκοτίκτω**, Suid. (interpol.). **-τῠπής**, ές, *smiting on the flesh*, Orac.ap.Phleg.*Fr.*37 J.

**σαρκοφᾰγ-έω**, *eat flesh, be carnivorous*, Arist.*HA*628ᵇ33, *PA*662ᵇ 1, al. **II.** c. acc., *eat the flesh of*, ἀνθρώπους D.S.1.89; σ. τὰς ζῴων σάρκας Id.5.39; σ. μέλη *eat the flesh of* my limbs, *AP*5.150 (Mel.). **-ία**, ἡ, *flesh-diet*, Arist.*HA*594ᵇ4: in pl., Ph.2.355: Plu. wrote a treatise περὶ σαρκοφαγίας, 2.993a sq., cf. *Stoic.*3. 91. **-ος** (parox.), ον, *eating flesh, carnivorous*, τὰ σ. (sc. ζῷα)

Arist.*HA*488$^a$14; ἔντομα ib.556$^b$21; ὄρνεον σ. Plu.*Cleom.*39; ταῦροι οἱ καλούμενοι σ. Ael.*NA*17.45. 2. *cannibal*, J.*AJ*13.12.6: metaph., ζῷον ὁ βασιλεὺς σ. Plu.*Cat.Ma.*8. II. λίθος σ. a limestone (of which the best kind was quarried at Assos in the Troad), remarkable for *consuming the flesh* of corpses laid in it, Erastus ap.Poll.10.150, Dsc.5.124, Cels.4.31.7, Plin.*HN*2.211, 36.131, Aët.7.41: hence **σαρκοφάγος**, ἡ, *coffin*, *IG*14.1472, cf. Juv.10.172.

**σαρκο-φᾰνής**, ές, *with a fleshy outside*, S.E.*P.*1.50. II. Subst., *open-work garment*, ἄρτι μοι πέμψον σαρκοφανὴν ἔχοντα κτλ. *POxy.*936.26 (iii A.D.). **-φθόρος**, ον, *flesh-consuming*, αἴγλη Orph.*H.*70.7. **-φῠέω**, *produce flesh, cause it to grow*, Hp.*Aff.*38. **-φῠΐα**, ἡ, *growth of flesh*, σ. τάχισται Id.*Fract.*33. **-φυλλος**, ον, *with fleshy leaves*, Thphr.*HP*1.10.4, 4.6.7.

* **σαρκ-όω**, *make fleshy* or *strong*, Hp.*Off.*13, Arist.*HA*603$^b$30, cf. Plu.2.54e:—Pass., *grow fleshy*, Aret.*SD*1.8; σεσαρκωμένος *fleshy*, Hp.*Art.*8, Arist.*PA*656$^b$10. II. *make* or *produce flesh*, *flesh up a wound*, ἀνάτριψις σαρκοῦσα Hp.*Off.*24:—Pass., θᾶσσον σαρκοῦται Id.*Fract.*27. III. *make flesh of*, χαλκὸν σ., of a sculptor, *AP*9.742 ([Phil.]). **-ώδης**, ες, = σαρκοειδής, *fleshy*, Hp.*VM*22, *Aër.*19, X.*Cyn.*4.1, 5.30, etc.; θεοὶ ἔναιμοι καὶ σαρκώδεες gods *of flesh* and blood, Hdt.3.29; τὸ σ. the *fleshy part*, Arist.*HA*508$^b$33; or *flesh-like substance*, ib.519$^b$29: also of plants, σ. ἔχουσι τὸ φύλλον Thphr.*HP*1.10.4, al.; of timber, ib.5.1.5; of wine, *of a full body*, Ath.1.27c. **-ωμα**, ατος, τό, *fleshy excrescence*, esp. in the nose, Dsc.3.80, Gal.19.439, etc. * **-ωσις**, εως, ἡ, *growth of flesh*, Herod.Med. ap.Orib.10.9.1, Aret.*CD*1.2: also, = foreg., Dsc.5.117, Gal.10.446; *fleshiness*, Id.1.342. **-ωτέον**, *one must fatten*, Id.10.180. **-ωτικός**, ή, όν, *making flesh grow*, Id.1.261, 11.799; πληγῶν σ. interpol. in Dsc.1.126; κόλπων σ. Id.1.1.2.

**σάρμα**, ατος, τό, (σέσηρα, σαίρω (A)) *chasm in the earth*, *EM*709. II. (σαίρω (B)) *sweepings, refuse*, Rhinth.25, prob. l. in Heraclit.124.

**Σαρμάτης**, ου, ὁ, = Σαυρομάτης (q.v.); poet. **Σᾶμάτης**, D.P.304.

**σαρμεύω**, perh. *dig sand*, *Tab.Heracl.*1.136; cf. sq.

* **σαρμός**, ὁ, = σωρὸς γῆς, καὶ κάλλυσμα, ἄλλοι ψάμμον, ἄλλοι χόρτον, Hsch.

* **σάρξ**, gen. σαρκός, ἡ, Aeol. **σύρξ** *EM*708.31:—*flesh*, Hom. always in pl., exc. Od.19.450, cf. Hes.*Sc.*364,461; κορέει κύνας .. δημῷ καὶ σάρκεσσι Il.8.380; ἔγκατά τε σάρκας τε καὶ ὀστέα Od.9.293, cf. 11.219; σάρκες περιτρομέοντο μέλεσσιν 18.77, cf. Hes.*Th.*538, Pi.*Fr.*168, etc.; τούτου σάρκας λύκοι πάσονται A.*Th.*1040; ὀπτὰς σάρκας Id.*Ag.*1097; σάρκες δ' ἀπ' ὀστέων .. ἀπέρρεον E.*Med.*1200; sts. to represent the whole body, μήτε γῆ δέξαιτό μου σάρκας θανόντος Id.*Hipp.*1031, cf. 1239, 1343 (anap.): sg. later in same sense, τοῦ αἵματος .. πηγνυμένου σ. γίνεται (of the foetus) Hp.*Nat.Puer.*15, cf. *Steril.*233; κορέσαι στόμα πρὸς χάριν ἐμᾶς σαρκὸς αἰόλας S.*Ph.*1157 (lyr.); ἔδαπτον σάρκα E.*Med.*1189, cf. *Ba.*1136, *Cyc.*344, etc.: also collectively, of the *body*, γέροντα τὸν νοῦν, σάρκα δ' ἡβῶσαν φέρει A.*Th.*622; σαρκὶ παλαιᾷ Id.*Ag.*72 (anap.); σαρκὸς περιβόλαια, ἐνδυτά, E.*HF*1269, *Ba.*746:—Pl. uses sg. and pl. in much the same manner, ταῖς σαρξὶ σάρκες προσγένωνται *Phd.*96d, cf. *Smp.*211e, *R.*556d, *Grg.*518c, etc.; τῆς σαρκὸς διαλυτικόν *Ti.*60b, cf. 61c, 62b, etc.: *portions of meat*, usu. in pl., σάρκας τρεῖς *IG*12(7).237.17 (Amorgos) (sg., ib.12(2).498.16 (Methymna, iii B.C.)); but, *pieces of flesh* or *membrane*, βήσσοντα .. ὥστε σάρκας ἐνπτύους .. ἀποβάλλειν *SIG*1171.5 (Lebena). b. εἰς σάρκα πημαίνειν to the *quick*, Phld.*Herc.*1289 p.60 V. 2. ἡ σ. τοῦ σκύτεος the *inner* or *flesh-side* of leather, Hp.*Art.*33. 3. *fleshy, pulpy substance of fruit*, Thphr.*CP*6.8.5, *HP*1.2.6, 4.15.1, al. II. the *flesh*, as the seat of the affections and lusts, *fleshly nature*, ἐν τῇ σ. ἡ ἡδονή Epicur.*Sent.*18, cf. *Sent.Vat.*33; ἀδούλωτον (prob. l.) τῇ σαρκὶ καὶ τοῖς ταύτης πάθεσι Plu.2.107f, cf. 101b; freq. in *NT*, *Ep.Gal.*5.19, al. 2. in *NT* also, the *body*, τῆς σαρκὸς πρόνοια *Ep.Rom.*13.14; οὔτε ἡ σ. αὐτοῦ εἶδεν διαφθορὰν *Act.Ap.*2.31, etc.: hence (partly as a Hebraism) πᾶσα σάρξ, = *everybody*, Lxx *Ge.*6.12, al., *Ev.Luc.*3.6, etc.; οὐ .. πᾶσα σάρξ *nobody*, *Ev.Matt.*24.22, etc. 3. the *physical* or *natural order* of things, opp. the spiritual or supernatural, σοφοὶ κατὰ σάρκα 1*Ep.Cor.*1.26; ἐν Χριστῷ Ἰησοῦ καὶ οὐκ ἐν σαρκὶ πεποιθότες *Ep.Phil.*3.3; τὸν κύριον τῶν πνευμάτων καὶ πάσης σ. *SIG*1181.3 (ii B.C., Jewish). (Perh. I.-E. *twrk-* 'portion', cf. Avest. *θwarəs-* 'cut'.)

**σαρξι-φᾰγές** and **-φάγον**, τό, in Paul.Aeg. (3.45, 7.3) and other Medic. writers, prob. merely corruptions of the Lat. *saxifragus, saxifrage*: Gal. writes correctly **σαξίφραγος** or **-ον**, exc. in 14.228.

* **σάρον** [ᾰ], τό, (σαίρω (B)) *broom, besom*, *IG*4$^2$(1).122.48 (Epid., iv B.C.), Pythagorei ap.Plu.2.727c, *AP*11.207 (Lucill.). II. *sweepings, refuse, rubbish*, τὸ σ. ἄνελε Sophr.160, cf. Thphr.*Metaph.*15 (prob. cj.); of sea-weed, Call.*Del.*225: Com., of *an old woman*, παλαιὸν οἰκίας σάρον Ion Trag.9.—The Atticists (Phryn.63) rejected the word, but cf. Poll.6.94, 10.29. III. σ. σιδαροῦν dub. in *Supp.Epigr.*6.171 (Acmonia).

* **σαροννύω**, prob. late form of σαρόω, *sweep*, φύλλα *PLond.*1.131$^r$.385, al. (i A.D.).

**σάρος** or **σαρός**, ὁ, a Babylonian *cycle of years* (3600), Abyd.1, cf. Hsch. 2. Babylonian *cycle of* 222 *months*, Suid.

**σᾰρόω**, = σαίρω (B), *sweep clean*, τὴν οἰκίαν *Ev.Luc.*15.8, Artem.2.33, cf. A.D.*Synt.*253.7:—Pass., οἶκος σεσαρωμένος *Ev.Matt.*12.44, etc.: metaph., *to be swept clean, exhausted*, *PGiss.*11.19 (ii A.D.). II. Pass., of the thing *swept*, κῦμα .. μεταξὺ χοιράδων σαρούμενον Lyc.389. Rejected by Phryn.63.

**σάρπη**, ἡ, and **σαρπίον**, τό, = σάλπη (q.v.), Sch.D.T.p.195 H.: **σαρπίς** is expld. by **σαρπός** in *An.Ox.*2.466.

**Σαρπηδών**, όνος, ὁ, *Sarpedon*, Il.16.327, al.: also gen. Σαρπήδοντος, dat. -οντι, 12.379,392, voc. Σαρπῆδον 5.633, as if from nom. Σαρπήδων:—**Σαρπηδονεῖον**, τό, *his shrine* at Xanthos, App.*BC*4.78:—Adj. **Σαρπηδόνιος**, α, ον, A.*Supp.*869 (lyr.).

**σάρπους**· κιβωτούς, Βιθυνοὶ δὲ ξυλίνους οἰκίας, Hsch.; cf. σάρπη. **σαρρυφθεῖν**· μωραίνειν, Id. **σάρσαι**· ἅμαξαι, Id. **σαρσίτει**· χορὸς πρὸς μύλον ποιούμενος τὴν χορείαν, Id.

**σάρωμα** [ᾰρ], ατος, τό, (σαρόω) *sweepings*, *AB*434, *An.Ox.*2.453, Suid.

**σάρων**· λάγνος, τινὲς δὲ τὸ γυναικεῖον, Hsch. **σαρῶνες**· τὰ τῶν θηρατῶν λινά, Id. (cf. σαρδών). **σαρωνίζω**, = διασαρωνίζω, Id. (σαρκ- cod.).

* **σᾰρωνίς**, ίδος, ἡ, *an old hollow oak*, Call.*Jov.*22, Poet.ap.Parth.11.4, *Eleg.Alex.Adesp.*1.10; Hsch. cites also **σορωνίς**· ἐλάτη παλαιά.

**σάρ-ωσις** [ᾰ], εως, ἡ, (σαρόω) *sweeping away*, φύλλων *POxy.*1692.11 (iii A.D.). 2. = σάρωμα, Suid. **-ώτης**, ου, ὁ, *sweeper*, *IPE* 2.342.21 (Phanagoria, pl.). **-ωτρον**, τό, *broom*, Eust.1887.35, Thom.Mag. p.201 R.

**σάσαι**· καθίσαι (Paph.), Hsch.; cf. θάσσω (nisi leg. σᾶσαι· καθαρίσαι). * **σάσαμον**, **σασαμόπαστος**, etc., v. σησαμ-. **σᾶσις**, v. σῆσις. **σάσσω**, v. σάττω.

* **σαστήρ**, ῆρος, ὁ, dub. sens. (cf. *Supp.Epigr.*3.602), τὸν σαστῆρα τῷ δάμῳ διαφυλαξῶ *SIG*360.24 (Chersonesus Taurica, iii B.C.).

**Σᾰτάν** or **Σατᾶν**, ὁ, *Satan*, Hebr. word for *adversary, opponent*, Lxx 3*Ki.*11.14,23; transl. by ἐπίβουλος in Lxx 1*Ki.*29.4; also *accuser*, transl. by ὁ διάβολος in *Jb.*1.6 sq., *Za.*3.1:—hence as *chief of the evil spirits, the Devil*, 2*Ep.Cor.*12.7 (indecl., as gen.); also **Σᾰτᾰνᾶς**, ᾶ, ὁ, Lxx *Jb.*2.3 (cod. A), *Si.*21.27, freq. in *NT*, *Ev.Matt.*4.10, al.:—Adj. **Σατανικός**, ή, όν, *PLond.*5.1731.11 (vi A.D.).

**σατάνειος**, name of a kind of μεσπίλη, *medlar*, Thphr.*HP*3.12.5.

**σαταρίς** and **σαταρνίς**, ίδος, ἡ, woman's *head-dress*, Hsch.

**σᾶτες**, v. σῆτες. **σατήραι**· σκαφαὶ βοτρύων, Hsch.

**σᾰτίνη** [ῑ], ἡ, *chariot*, ποιῆσαι σατίνας καὶ ἅρματα *h.Ven.*13; ἐπιβαίνει σατινέων Anacr.21.12; σατίναις ὑπ' εὐτρόχοις ἄγον αἰμιόνοις Sapph.*Supp.*20a13; ζυγίους ζευξάσα θεᾷ σατίνας E.*Hel.*1311 (lyr.): only found in pl. (sg. in E. l. c. codd.).—Hsch. cites **σάτιλλα**, = Πλειάς, the constellation being regarded as *a car*.

**σᾱτινός**, ή, όν, = τητινός (σητινός is not found), ἀρνία *PCair.Zen.*406.11 (iii B.C.); [πυροί] *EM*711.48 (where σατίνους, v. l. σατινούς).

**σάτον**, τό, a Hebrew measure, $\frac{1}{30}$ of a κόρος, = about a modius and a half or 24 *sextarii*, Lxx *Hg.*2.17(16), *Ev.Matt.*13.33, al., J.*AJ*9.4.5. (Hebr. *ṣeah*.)

**Σατορνάλια**, τά, = Lat. *Saturnalia*, Arr.*Epict.*1.25.8.

**σάτρα**, Comic Persian for *gold*, Ar.*Ach.*100.

**σᾰτρᾰπ-εία**, Ion. **-ηΐη**, ἡ, *satrapy, office* or *province of a satrap*, Hdt.1.192, 3.89, X.*HG*3.1.10, *OGI*221.28 (Ilium, iii B.C.), Lxx *Jo.*13.3 (-ίαις), J.*AJ*11.3.2:—**ξατραπ-**, Arr.*Fr.*10 J., cf. σατράπης. **-εῖον**, τό, *palace of a satrap*, in Hld.8.12 (bis). * **-εύω**, *to be a satrap, exercise the authority of one*, δεῖ τὴν γυναῖκα σατραπεύειν X.*HG*3.1.12, cf. *SIG*302 (iv B.C.), al., *PEleph.*1.1 (iv B.C.); **ξατραπ-**, Arr.*Fr.*10 J., cf. σατράπης. 2. c. gen., *rule as a satrap*, σ. τῆς χώρας X.*HG*3.1.10, *An.*3.4.31, cf. Plu.*Them.*30: also c. acc., τὰ ἐν μέσῳ σ. X.*An.*1.7.6; Αἴγυπτον Hld.2.24: metaph. in Pass., Philostr.*VA*1.27. * **-ης**, or **σατράπητης** *CRAcad.Inscr.*1931.241 (Susa, i A.D.), ου, ὁ, *satrap*, title of a Persian *viceroy* or *governor of a province*, X.*Cyr.*7.4.2, 8.6.3, *SIG*182.3 (iv B.C.), Men.897, etc. (in form **σαδράπας**, *IG*12(2).645.18 (Nesus, iv B.C.); dat. pl. σαδράπησιν [⏑⏑–⏑] Ἐφ. Ἀρχ. 1907.27 (Aranda)); of the five lords of the Philistines, Lxx *Jd.*16.5, al.; of a Roman Governor, Philostr.*VS*1.22.3. (In Theopomp.Hist.103 J. also **ἐξατράπης**, and in Carian Inscrr. ἐξαιθραπεύω, ἐξαιτραπεύω (qq. v.); in Arr.*Fr.*10 J. **ξατράπης** (cf. **ζατράπης** (leg. ξα-)· ὁ βασιλεύς, Hsch.), which is nearer to the OPers. *xšaθrapāvan-* lit. 'kingdom-protector'.) 2. cant word for *a rich man*, '*nabob*', Alex.116.8 (pl.); σ. ἐκ πένητος Luc.*Nigr.*20. 3. as cult-title of a god, *IGRom.*3.1059 (Maad, i B.C.), Paus.6.25.6. * **-ικός**, ή, όν, *of a satrap*, ἡ σ. οἰκονομία, opp. ἡ βασιλική, Arist.*Oec.*1345$^b$13; αὐλὴ Plu.*Agis* 3. II. *like a satrap, luxurious*, Id.*Comp.Cim.Luc.*1; δωρεαί Alciphr.1.38; οἱ -ώτεροι τῶν φιλοσόφων Phld.*Oec.*p.74 J.; *formal, stately*, συμπόσιον Plu.2.616e:—irreg. fem. **-ίς**, ίδος, ναῦς Philostr.*VA*2.17.

**σατραπόπλουτος**, v. σαπρόπλουτος.

**σάτρης**, ὁ, = σατράπης, Phot. (pl.).

**σάττα**, ἡ, *a woman's head-dress*, Hsch.

**σάττω**, Ion. **σάσσω** Hp.*Morb.*2.14: impf. ἔσαττον Pherecr.78: aor. ἔσαξα Hdt.3.7, X.*Oec.*19.11, Alex.133.6:—Med., v. infr. I. 1,4: —Pass., aor. ἐσάχθην, v. infr. II: pf. σέσακται Cerc.3; imper. σεσάχθω Antiph.222.8; part. σεσαγμένος and 3 pl. plpf. ἐσεσάχατο (v. infr.):—*fill quite full, pack, stuff*, πᾶς δ' ἀνὴρ ἔσαττε τεῦχος ἢ κόϊκ' ἢ κωρύκους Pherecr. l. c.; ἔσαττον τὰς γνάθους Eub.42.3: c. gen., σ. τῶν ἀρωμάτων (sc. τὴν κοιλίην) Hp.*Steril.*230; τὸ δέρμα κνεφάλλων σ. Theopomp.Com.45: c. dat., τυρῷ τε σάξον ἁλσί τ' (sc. τὸν σαῦρον) Alex. l. c., cf. Luc.*Herm.*65, *Syr.D.*48:—Med., ἵνα δῷς αὐτῷ τῶν τε γιγάρτων καὶ στεμφύλου κεράμια β' σάξασθαι prob. in *PCair.Zen.*527 (iii B.C.); χρυσῷ σαξάμενος πήρην Orac.ap.Luc.*Peregr.*30, cf. D.L.6.9:—Pass., τὴν γαστέρ' ἥων κἀχύρων σεσαγμένος Pherecr.161; ὁ σπλὴν σεσάχθω Antiph. l. c.; τὰ ἀγγεῖα σαττόμενα οὐδὲν μείζω γίνεται Arist.*Pr.*928$^b$29. 2. τὸν καρπὸν .. σ. εἰς ἀγγεῖα *pack* it into jars, Plb.12.2.5. 3. *press close, compress*, σ. τὴν γῆν περὶ τὸ φυτὸν X.*Oec.*19.11:—Pass., Arist.*Mete.*365$^b$18, *Pr.*938$^b$30. 4. τὰ σιδάρια δ[εσμὰ . . .]σαι καὶ σάξαι dub. sens., perh. *strengthen*, *SIG*247 $I^2$17 (Delph., iv B.C.) :—Med., τὸ τεῖχος ἐσάξαντο they *strengthened their* wall, Hdt.5.34. II. metaph., *load*, σάττει καὶ πληροῖ τὴν ἐπιθυμίαν (compared to an ἀγγεῖον) Arist.*Pr.*928$^b$32 :—Pass., τριήρης σεσαγμένη ἀνθρώπων *manned*, X.*Oec.*8.8; πημάτων σεσαγμένος *laden* with woes, of a messenger, A.*Ag.*644; σεσαγμένος πλούτου τὴν ψυχὴν *laden* with spiritual riches, X.*Smp.*4.64; τρυφῆς ὑφ' ἡδοναῖσι σαχθέντες κέαρ Diog.Sinop.1.2 (prob.cj.); ἀνέρες ὧν τὸ κέαρ παλῷ σέσακται Cerc. l.c.; σὺν πορδακοῖσιν εἵμασιν σεσαγμένοι (σεσαγμένοις codd. Sch. Ar., om. codd. Str.) *weighed down*, Semon.21. III. *equip, provide with a store*, σάξαντες ὕδατι [τὴν ἐσβολὴν] *equipping* the entrance to Egypt *with a store of* water, Hdt.3.7 :—Pass., Ὑρκάνιοι κατά περ Πέρσαι ἐσεσάχατο *were equipped*, Id.7.62, cf. 70,73,86; ἀσπιδιῶται χαλκῷ μαρμαίροντι σεσαγμένοι Theoc.17.94.

**σᾰτῡρι-ακή**, ἡ, name of an *antidote*, Orib.*Fr.*67, Id. ap. Aët.11.35, Paul.Aeg.7.11 :—Adj. **-ακός**, ή, όν, *producing satyriasis*, ἀγγεῖα Ruf.*Sat.Gon.*15. **-ᾱσις**, εως, Ion. **-ησις**, ἡ, (Σάτυρος) *satyriasis*, Aret.*SA*2.12, Gal.19.426. II. *disease in which the bones near the temple become prominent, like Satyrs' horns*, Id.7.22; this and σ. I are combined in the early stage of elephantiasis, Ruf.ap.Orib.45.28.2, Aret.*SD*2.13. 2. *swelling of the glands about the ear*, Hp.*Aph.*3.26. **-ασμός**, ὁ, v.l. for foreg. in Hp. l.c. 2. = foreg. I, Ruf.*Sat. Gon.*49. **-άω**, *suffer from* σατυρίασις, Arist.*GA*768$^b$34 (sense II), Ruf.*Sat.Gon.*7 (sense I).

**Σᾰτῠρ-ίδιον** [ῐδ], τό, Dim. of Σάτυρος, Stratt.66.4. **-ικός**, ή, όν, *suiting a Satyr, like a Satyr*, Σωκράτης . . σ. καὶ ὑβριστὴς φαινόμενος Plu.*Cat.Ma.*7, cf. Pl.*Smp.*221e; ἐφήμεροι καὶ σ. τοῖς βίοις Plu.*Galb.*16, cf. *Per.*13. 2. *of* or *resembling the Satyric drama*, Pl.*Smp.*222d; ποίησις Arist.*Po.*1449$^a$22; ὄρχησις D.H.7.72; δρᾶμα Id.*Rh.*9.6, etc.: abs., σατυρικόν, τό, *Satyric drama*, X.*Smp.*4.19, Arist.*Po.*1449$^a$20, *IG*2$^2$.2320.16; also σατυρική Tz.*Proll.Com.*p.21 K., cf. Σάτυρος II.

⊛ **σᾰτύριον** [ῠ], τό, *man orchis, Acera anthropophora*, Dsc.3.128, Plu.2.126a, Gal.12.118. 2. = ὄρχις, Ps.-Dsc.3.126. 3. = ὀξυλάπαθον τὸ μέγα, Id.2.114. II. σ. ἐρυθραϊκόν *fritillary, Fritillaria graeca*, Dsc.3.128.2, *Eup.*2.101, Plin.*HN*26.97; called σ. ἐρυθρόνιον, Ps.-Dsc.3.128. III. a water animal of the rodent kind, perh. *sorex moschatus*, Arist.*HA*594$^b$31.

**Σᾰτύριος** [ῠ], η, ον, = Σατυρικός I, ὠτάρια, of ornaments, *BGU*781 ii 1 (i A.D.).

⊛ **Σᾰτῠρίσκος**, ὁ, Dim. of Σάτυρος I. 2, Theoc.4.62, 27.3,49, Heph. Astr.1.1. II. σατυρίσκος, ὁ, = σατύριον II, Ps.-Dsc.3.128.

**σᾰτῠρισμός**, ὁ, = σατυρίασις, Hp.ap.Gal.19.136 (but prob. f.l. for -ιασμός, cf. Hp.*Aph.*3.26, Gal.7.728).

**Σᾰτῠριστής**, οῦ, ὁ, *player of Satyric dramas*, Σατυριστῶν χοροί D.H.7.72; also Σατυρισταὶ χ. (as Adj.) ibid. (codd., corr. Salmasius).

**Σᾰτῠρογράφος** [γρᾰ], ον, *writing Satyric dramas*, D.L.5.85, *IG*7.1773.29 (Thespiae).

⊛ **Σάτῠρος**, ὁ, Dor. **Τίτυρος** (q.v.), *Satyr*, first in Hes. (γένος οὐτιδανῶν Σατύρων καὶ ἀμηχανοεργῶν *Fr.*198.2), cf. X.*An.*1.2.13, Paus.1.23.5, Sch.Theoc.4.62; of Dionysus himself, *AP*9.524; Σατύρων πρόσωπα as ornaments, Lys.*Fr.*34. 2. *lewd, goatish fellow*, Jul.*Caes.*309d; βασιλεὺς Σατύρων, of Pericles, Hermipp.46; σατύρα, ἡ, of a courtesan, *Com.Adesp.*1352 :—Socrates is called ὅδε ὁ Σ. from his appearance, Pl.*Smp.*216c. 3. from their supposed likeness, *a kind of tailed ape*, Paus.1.23.5sq., Ael.*NA*16.21. b. a fabulous people in Ethiopia, D.S.1.18. 4. = ἡ ἔντασις, Hsch. II. in pl., *a play in which the Chorus consisted of Satyrs, Satyric drama*, forming the fourth piece of a Tragic tetralogy, ὅταν Σατύρους ποιῇς Ar.*Th.*157; ποηταὶ σατύρων *SIG*711 *L*35 (Delph., ii B.C.); ἐν τοῖς Σ. οὓς Μενέδημον ἐπέγραψεν [Λυκόφρων] D.L.2.140; ἐν Ὀμφάλῃ Σατύροις Str.1.3.19. [Σᾰτῠρος; so that when the 1st syll. is long, Dor. Τίτυρος (q.v.) should prob. be restored.]

**Σᾰτῠρόφηρ**, ηρος, ὁ, *wild creature like a Satyr*, Hdn.Gr.1.48.

**Σᾰτῠρώδης**, ες, *Satyr-like*, ὦτα Luc.*Zeux.*6; γένειον Ael.*NA*16.10; σώματα *Cat.Cod.Astr.*8(4).240.

**σαυᾶδαι**· σαῦδοι; Macedonian name for Sileni, Amerias ap.Hsch.

**σαυκός**, ή, όν, *dry* (Syrac.), Hsch. ⊛ **σαυκρός**, ά, όν, = ἁβρός, and ⊛ **σαυκρόπους**, ὁ, ἡ, = ἁβρόπους, Id.

**σαυλόομαι**, Pass., (σαῦλος) *swagger, dance affectedly*, ἀοιδαῖς βαρβίτων σαυλούμενοι E.*Cyc.*40, cf. Luc.*Lex.*10.

⊛ **σαυλοπρωκτιάω**, *walk in a swaggering way*, so as *to make the hinder parts sway to and fro*, Ar.*V.*1173.

**σαῦλος**, η, ον, an Adj. descriptive of gait and carriage, defined as τὸ φαῦλον καὶ διερρυηκός by Sch.Ar.*V.*1169; σαῦλα ποσὶν βαίνουσα, applied to the gait of the tortoise, *straddling, waddling*, *h.Merc.*28; of the *loose, wanton* gait of courtesans or Bacchantes, σ. βαίνειν Anacr.168; σαῦλαι Βασσαρίδες Id.55; also of a *prancing* horse, σ. βαίνειν, ἵππος ὡς κορωνίης Semon.18.

**σαύλωμα**, ατος, τό, *effeminacy*, Hsch.

**σαυνάκα**, a specimen of Triballian jargon in Ar.*Av.*1628.

**σαυνι-άζω**, *hurl a javelin at*, τοὺς ἐναντίους D.S.5.29. ⊛ **-αστής**, οῦ, Dor. **-τάς**, ὁ, *javelin-thrower*, or perh. *fish-spearer, leisterer*, *Lyr. Alex.Adesp.*31.25.

**[σαυ]νιοθήκη**, ἡ, *javelin-case*, dub. in *IG*11(2).161 *C*75 (Delos, iii B.C.), cf. 199 *B*84.

**σαύνιον** or **σαυνίον**, τό, *javelin*, Men.508, Str.15.1.66, 15.3.18, D.S.14.27, D.H.4.17, prob. in *IG*2$^2$.1641.55. II. *membrum virile*, Cratin.443.

**Σαυνῖται**, οἱ, *Samnites*, *GDI*2000.4 (Delph., ii B.C.), Str.5.4.11, 12 (v.l. Σαυν-): so **Σαυνῖτις**, ιδος, ἡ, *Samnium*, Plb.3.90.7, and Σαυνίτιδες [πόλεις] Str.5.4.11. (Osc. *Safinim* (from *Sabniom*); Fest. p. 437 L. wrongly derives Lat. *Samnites* from σαύνιον.)

**σαύρ-α**, Ion. **σαύρη**, ἡ, *lizard*, A.*Fr.*146 codd. Ath., Hdt.4.192 (cf. 183), Arist.*HA*488$^a$24, 489$^b$21, Theoc.2.58; cf. σαῦρος. 2. = σαλαμάνδρα, Thphr.*Sign.*15. II. = κάρδαμον, Nic.*Fr.*74.72 :— also as Dim. **σαυρίδιον**, τό, Hp.*Ulc.*11, Gal.19.136, etc. III. *membrum virile*, esp. of boys, *AP*12.3 (Strat.), 242 (Id.). IV. αἱ σ. αἱ ἐκ φοινίκων πεπλεγμέναι plaited *cases* of palm-bark, used in setting dislocated fingers, Hp.*Art.*80, Diocl.*Fr.*188. **-ήτης**, ου, ὁ, *keeper of crocodiles*, *PTeb.*57.4 (ii B.C.). **-ίγγη**, ἡ, = σαύρα, Hsch. II. = ποα τις, Id. **-ίδιον**, v. σαύρα II. **-ιεῖον**, τό, *crocodile-pond*, dub. in *BGU*1216.126 (ii B.C.). **-ίς**, ίδος, a kind of fish, Suid. **-ίτης** [ῑ], ου, ὁ, a kind of *serpent*, Hsch. 2. precious stone found in the belly of the lizard, Plin.*HN*37.67. II. fem. **σαυρῖτις**, ιδος, ἡ, = ἀναγαλλὶς ἡ φοινικῆ, Ps.-Dsc.2.178.

**σαυρο-βρῑθής**, ές, *with a heavy* σαυρωτήρ, *Trag.Adesp.*264. **-ειδής**, ές, *like a lizard*, Arist.*HA*503$^a$16. **-κτόνος**, ον, *lizard-killer*, epith. of Apollo, as represented in a famous statue by Praxiteles, Plin.*HN*34.70.

⊛ **Σαυρομάτης** [ᾰ], ου, ὁ, *Sarmatian*, Hdt.4.21,110, etc.; also **Σαρμάτης**, Scymn.876, and **Σαμάτης** (q.v.) :—fem. **Σαυρομάτις**, Pl.*Lg.*804e, etc.; as fem. Adj., Hdt.4.123; **Σαρμάτισσα**, *GDI*2274.4, al. (Delph., ii B.C.) :—**Σαρμᾰτία**, ἡ, *Sarmatia*, *IPE*1$^2$.54 (Olbia) :—Adj. **Σαυροματικός**, ή, όν, Arist.*GA*783$^a$14; **Σαρματικός**, Str.7.4.8, Ptol. *Geog.*5.8.5, al.

**σαῦρος**, ὁ, = σαύρα, Hdt.4.183 (as v.l.), cf. Hp.*Morb.*3.11, Arist.*HA*503$^a$22, Nic.*Th.*817. II. *horse-mackerel*, = τραχοῦρος, Alex.133.1, Arist.*HA*610$^b$5, Gal.6.720.

**σαυρ-ωτήρ**, ῆρος, ὁ, *ferrule* or *spike* at the butt-end of a spear, by which it was stuck into the ground, Il.10.153, Hdt.7.41, Plb.6.25.6, 11.18.4, *AP*6.110 (Leon. or Mnasalc.), Sch.Th.*Oxy.*853 v 30. **-ωτός**, ή, όν, *furnished with a* σαυρωτήρ, Hsch. II. *spotted like a lizard*, Id.

**σαῦσαξ**, ᾱκος, ὁ, *a leguminous plant*, *Com.Adesp.*1375. 2. *a mild kind of cheese*, Hsch.

**σαυσαρισμός**, ὁ, *paralysis of the tongue*, Arist.*Pr.*947$^b$35; cf. **σαυσαρός**· ψιθυρός, Hsch.

**σαυσιαλεῖ**· μαστιγᾶται, Ἠλεῖοι, Hsch. **σαυτορία**· σωτηρία, Amerias ap.Hsch. **σαυτοῦ**, v. σεαυτοῦ. **σαυχμόν**· σαχνόν, χαῦνον, σαθρόν, ἀσθενές, Hsch.

**σάφα** [σᾰ], poet. Adv. of σαφής, *clearly, plainly, assuredly*, in Hom. esp. with Verbs of knowing, most freq. σάφα οἶδα, σάφα εἰδώς, etc., like εὖ οἶδα, εὖ εἰδώς, etc., to *know assuredly, of a surety*, followed by interrog., Il.2.192,252, al.; by εἰ, 5.183; c. acc. and interrog. clause, Od.17.373; abs., 2.108; c. gen., ὃς σάφα θυμῷ εἰδείη τεράων Il.12.228, cf. Od.1.202; c. inf., Il.15.632; freq. in Trag., σάφ' οἶδα, σάφ' ἴσθι, etc., A.*Supp.*740, *Pers.*337, etc.; Com., σάφ' ἴσθ' ὅτι Ar.*Pl.*889; less freq. in Prose, Antipho 6.18, X.*Cyr.*4.5.21; also ἐπιστάμεναι σ. θυμῷ Od.4.730; σ. ἐπίστασθαι Hp.*Art.*64; σ. δαείς Pi.*O.*7.91: also with Verbs of speaking, *clearly* or *with certainty*, σ. εἰπεῖν Od.2.31, Pi.*O.*8.46; σ. φράζειν Hp.*Acut.*3; μυθήσασθαι Theoc.25.198; σ. εἰπεῖν speak *truly*, opp. ψεύδεσθαι, Il.4.404.

**σάφ-ανής**, v. σαφηνής. **-εια**, ἡ, coinage to expl. σοφία, Ascl. *in Metaph.*3.30. **-έω**, = σαφηνίζω, Gal.14.596, Suid.; elsewhere only in compds., δια-σαφέω, etc. **-ηγορίς**, ίδος, pecul. fem. of *σαφήγορος, *speaking clearly* or *truly*, Σίβυλλα Epigr.ap.Paus.10.12.6.

**σᾰφήν-εια**, ἡ, *clearness, distinctness*, Pl.*Phdr.*277d; opp. ἀσάφεια, Id.*R.*478c; πάσῃ σ. λαβεῖν τι Id.*Sph.*254c; σ. τινός Id.*R.*524c; τῶν χορδῶν Id.*Lg.*812d; τὴν τοῦ στόματος σ. Isoc.15.189; τῶν πραχθέντων τὴν σ. πυθέσθαι to learn *the plain truth*, Antipho 1.13; σαφηνείᾳ λόγου εἰδώς τι A.*Th.*67; *clear knowledge*, σ. θεοὶ ἔχοντι Alcmaeon 1. **-έω**, = σαφηνίζω, cj. in A.*Ch.*197. **-ής**, Dor. **-ᾱνής**, ές, = σαφής, Id.*Pers.*635 (lyr.), 738 (troch.), S.*Tr.*892; τὸ σ. the *plain truth*, Pi.*O.*10(11).55: σαφηνῆ is corrupt in A.*Ch.*197, cf. foreg. Adv. -νῶς Thgn.963 (but -νέως is the better reading); Ion. -νέως Hdt. (who never has the Adj.), with the Verbs εἰπεῖν, λέγεσθαι, ἐξαγγέλλεσθαι, 1.140, 3.122, 6.82; τὰ λοιπά σοι φράσω σ. A.*Pr.*781. **-ίζω**, *make clear* or *plain*, τοῦτο δὴ σαφηνιῶ ib.227, cf. 621; ἐξιστορήσας καὶ σαφηνίσας ὁδόν Id.*Ch.*678; σ. τοὺς κρατιστεύοντας X.*Cyr.*8.4.5; τὴν παιδείαν Id.*Lac.*2.1, cf. *Mem.*4.3.4, 4.7.6; σ. τὴν βασιλείαν *determine* the succession, Id.*Cyr.*8.7.9. 2. abs., *articulate clearly*, Hp.*Carn.*18; τῇ φωνῇ Arist.*HA*633$^a$12, cf. *Pr.*888$^b$10, 902$^a$6. **-ισμός**, ὁ, *explanation, distinction*, D.H.1.66, Corn.*ND*32. **-ιστέον**, *one must explain*, Pall. *in Hp.*2.107 D., Tz. ad Hes.*Op.*382. **-ιστικός**, ή, όν, *explanatory*, τινος of a thing, Luc.*Salt.*36; τὸ -κόν Procl. *in Prm.* p.534 S.; σ. πρόβλημα dub.l. in Gal.18(2).891.

⊛ **σᾰφής**, ές, gen. έος, contr. οῦς, *clear, plain, distinct*, of things heard, perceived, or known, σαφὲς δ' οὐκ οἶδα *h.Merc.*208 (Hom. only has Adv. σάφα, q.v.); μῦθος A.*Pr.*641; λόγος Id.*Ag.*1047; χρησμός Ar.*Lys.*777; κτύπος S.*OC*1501; φθέγματ' ὀρνίθων Id.*El.*18; γράμματα *distinctly legible*, *OGI*665.12 (Egypt, i A.D.); τὰς κλεῖς ἔχουσι σαφεῖς *prominent* collar-bones, Gal.17(2).97: generally, *clear* or *manifest* to the mind, σ. ἀρετά Pi.*I.*1.22; τέκμαρ Id.*N.*11.43; σημεῖα S.*El.*23; πρόνοια Id.*OT*978; τεκμήριον E.*Hipp.*926; πίστις Th.1.35 (Sup.); βάσανος Pl.*Lg.*957d; σ. τοῦτο παντὶ ὅτι . . *it is manifest* that . ., Id.*Phdr.*239e; σ. τι . . λέξον A.*Pers.*705; σαφῆ δ' ἀκούεις Id.*Supp.*948; σαφῆ τἀκεῖθεν ἐκ στρατοῦ φέρων Id.*Th.*40; σαφὲς καταστῆσαί τι to make it *quite clear*, Th.1.140, cf. 3.40; τῶν γενομένων τὸ σ. the *clear* *truth*, Id.1.22 ; σοφόν τοι τὸ σ., οὐ τὸ μὴ σ. E.*Or*.397. 2. of persons (mostly Trag.), σ. ἄγγελος A.*Th*.82 (lyr.) ; φίλος E.*Or*.1155 ; μηνυταί Pl.*Lg*.918a ; esp. of seers, oracles, prophets, *sure, unerring*, S. *OT*390,1011, *OC*623 ; *accurate*, γραμματεύς A.*Fr*.358. II. Adv. σᾰφῶς, Ion., etc. -έως, *h.Cer*.149, and freq. in Hdt., esp. (like σάφα) with Verbs of saying, hearing, knowing, *clearly, plainly, distinctly*, σαφέως φράσαι 2.31 ; δηλοῦν ib.44 ; ἐπίστασθαι 8.88 ; δεῖξαι A.*Pr*. 914 ; εἰδέναι S.*El*.660 ; σαφέως μαρτυρήσω Pi.*O*.6.20 ; φράσσατέ μοι σ. Id.*P*.4.117 ; ἤκουον σ. S.*Ph*.595, etc. ; εὖ γὰρ οἶδ' ἐγὼ σ. Ar.*Pax* 1302. 2. *clearly, manifestly*, σ. μ' ἐς οἶκον σὸς λόγος στέλλει πάλιν A.*Pr*.389 ; πρὸς γυναικὸς ἦν σ. Id.*Ag*.1636 ; κατοικεῖ τούσδε τοὺς τόπους σ. S.*Ph*.40 ; σ. φρόνει be well assured of it, ib.810 ; σ. ἤρετο ἡ δύναμις Th.1.118 ; σ. ἀπολωλέναι to be *undoubtedly* dead, X.*Cyr*.3. 2.15 ; πήγνυμαι σ. Antiph.166.7 ; ὡς κεχρημένη σ. σιδήρῳ καὶ φοροῦσα τοὔνομα (sc. Σιδηρώ) S.*Fr*.658 ; τῶν σ. ἀποχειροβιώτων X.*Cyr*.8.3.37, cf. *Smp*.4.32. 3. in affirmative answers, *yes obviously*, ib.60. 4. Comp. -έστερον A.*Ch*.735,767, Pl.*Prt*.352a, al. ; -εστέρως Arist. *Metaph*.986$^{b}$30 (as v.l.) : Sup. -έστατα A.*Ag*.38, S.*OT*286, Ar.*Pl*. 46, Pl.*Phd*.58d.

⊛**σᾰφήτωρ**, ορος, ὁ, (as if from σαφέω) *explainer, interpreter*, Hsch. ; perh. a variant for ἀφήτωρ, Il.9.404.

**Σάφφω**, v. Σαπφώ.

⊛ **σαφώνιον**, τό, *soap* (cf. σάπων), *POxy*.1924.4 (v/vi A.D.).

**σάχματα·** φορτία, and **σαχμίς·** ἡτοιμασμένος, prob. to be restored in Hsch. (σαγμ- cod. extra ordinem).

**σαχνός**, ή, όν, *tender*, κοέα Gal.16.761, cf. Hsch. s.vv. σαυχμόν, σαχνόν.

**σαχρός**, ά, όν, *thin*, Gloss.ap.Zonar.

**σαψίς·** ὁ ἀγαθὸς δαίμων παρὰ Ἀράβοις (sic), Hsch.

**σάω**, = σήθω, *sift, bolt*, Hdt.1.200, in 3 pl. σῶσι.

⊛ **σάω**, pres. imper. Med., and Ep. 3 sg. impf. Act. of σαόω. **σαώσω**, fut. of σαόω.

**σαω-τήρ**, ῆρος, ὁ, v. σωτήρ. **-της**, ου, ὁ, (σαόω) poet. for σωτήρ, epith. of Dionysus, *AP*9.603 (Antip.), Paus.2.37.2. **-τωρ**, ορος, ὁ, = σωτήρ, Maiist.4 (pl.).

**σβέννῡμι**, Hdt.2.66, Pl.*Lg*.835e, etc. ; **σβεννύω**, Pi.*P*.1.5, Hp.*Acut*. 54, Thphr.*Ign*.19, etc. : impf. ἐσβέννυον Paus.4.21.4 : fut. σβέσω App.*BC*2.68, (κατα-) A.*Ag*.958, E.*IT*633 ; Ep. σβέσσω Orac.ap.Hdt. 8.77, Theoc.23.26 : aor. ἔσβεσα Il.16.293 (tm.), S.*Aj*.1057, Ar.*Av*. 778 (lyr.) ; Ep. inf. σβέσσαι Il.16.621 ; Ion. inf. κατα-σβῶσαι Herod. 5.39 : pf. and aor. 2, v. infr. :—**Med.**, fut. σβήσομαι (ἀπο-) Pl.*Lg*. 805c : aor. σβέσαντο Q.S.1.795 :—**Pass.**, Hes.*Op*.590 : fut. σβεσθήσομαι Gal.7.17 : aor. ἐσβέσθην Hp.*Acut*.(*Sp*.)26, (κατ-) X.*HG*5.3. 8 ; Ep. συν-έσβετο Opp.*H*.2.477, etc. : pf. ἔσβεσμαι Longin.21.1, Ael.*NA*9.54, etc., (ἀπ-) Hp.*Int*.43 :—besides these, aor. 2 and pf. and plpf. Act. are used intr., ἔσβην Il.9.471, (ἀπ-) E.*Fr*.971, (κατ-) Hdt.4.5 ; imper. σβῆτε (trans.) Sophr. in *Stud.Ital*.10.123 ; part. ἀπο-σβείς Hp.*Epid*.4.31 : pf. ἔσβηκα (ἀπ-) X.*Cyr*.8.8.13, (κατ-) A.*Ag*. 888 : plpf. ἐσβήκει (ἀπ-) Pl.*Smp*.218b :—*quench, put out*, used by Hom. in the literal sense only in compd. κατα-σβέννυμι (q.v.) ; σ. τὸ καιόμενον Hdt.2.66 ; κεραυνόν Pi.*P*.1.6 ; φλόγα Th.2.77, A.R.4. 668. 2. of liquids, *dry up*, ἡ Μηδικὴ πόα σ. τὸ γάλα Arist.*HA*522$^{b}$ 25, cf. *AP*9.549 (Antiphil.). 3. generally and metaph., *quench, quell, check*, κεῖνός γ' οὐκ ἐθέλει σβέσσαι χόλον Il.9.678 ; ἀνθρώπων σβέσσαι μένος 16.621 ; ὕβριν Simon.(132) ap.Hdt.5.77, cf. Orac.ap. eund.8.77, Heraclit.43, Pl.*Lg*.835e ; εἰ μὴ θεῶν τις τήνδε πεῖραν ἔσβεσεν S.*Aj*1057 ; ὡς φόνῳ σβέσῃ φόνον E.*HF*40 ; ἔσβεσε κύματα νήνεμος αἴθρη Ar.*Av*.778 ; σ. αὔξην καὶ ἐπιρροήν Pl.*Lg*.783b ; τὸν θυμόν ib.888a ; καῦμα (in the bowels) Hp.*Acut*.54 ; ὁ βορέας σ. τὴν θερμότητα Arist.*Mete*.347$^{b}$4 ; λιθάργυρον ὄξει ἢ οἴνῳ σ. *cooling* it, Dsc.5.87 ; ὕδατι δίψαν σ. A.R.3.1349 ; σ. τυραννίδα Epigr.ap.Plu.*Lyc*.20 ; κλέος *AP*9.104 (Alph.) ; Ἑλλάδα φωνήν ib.451 ; *regard as extinguishable*, ταύτας τὰς δυνάμεις Plot.6.4.10. II. Pass. σβέννυμαι (with intr. tenses of Act., v. supr.), *to be quenched, go out*, of fire, οὐδέ ποτ' ἔσβη πῦρ Il.9.471 ; of inflamed pustules, *go down, disappear*, Hp.*Acut*. (*Sp*.)26 ; ἰχθύων..ᾠὰ μετὰ ἁλῶν σβεσθέντα (s.v.l.) καὶ ἐποπτηθέντα Diph.Siph.ap.Ath.3.121c : metaph. of men, *become extinct, die*, *AP* 7.20 (Simon.?) ; of a city, ib.9.178 (Antiphil.). 2. of liquids, *run dry*, γάλα Arist.*HA*587$^{b}$28 ; πηγαί *AP*9.128 ; αἷμα Plu.2.49d ; αἶγες σβεννύμεναι goats *which are going off their milk*, Hes.*Op*. 590. 3. generally, *to be quelled* or *lulled*, of wind, οὐδέ ποτ' ἔσβη οὖρος Od.3.182 ; of sound, σβέννυτο θωρήκων ἐνοπή Tryph.10 : metaph., τὸ μάχιμον σβεννύμενον ὑπὸ γήρως Plu.*Pomp*.8 ; ἐσβέσθη Νίκανδρος his charm *is quenched*, *AP*12.39 ; of an orator, D.H.*Pomp*. 4 ; ἐσβέσθη τὰ φίλτρα *AP*7.221, cf. Philostr.*VA*1.33, Longin.21.1 ; of legal proceedings, *to be cancelled*, διὰ τὸ ἐσβέσθαι πᾶν σπέρμα δίκης *PMonac*.1.43 (vi A.D.). (I.-E. *zgʷes-*, cf. ζείναμεν· σβέννυμεν, Hsch., Lith. *gèsti* 'to be extinguished'.)

**σβέσ-ις**, εως, ἡ, *quenching, putting out*, or (from Pass.) *extinction*, πυρὸς σ. καὶ μάρανσις Arist.*Resp*.474$^{b}$14, cf. *Juv*.469$^{b}$23, Thphr.*Ign*. 60, D.H.2.67 ; opp. διάλαμψις, Arist.*Mete*.370$^{a}$24 ; κατὰ τὴν σ. while *cooling*, Dsc.1.100. II. metaph., *cancellation*, δίκης *PLond*.5. 1708.248 (vi A.D.). ⊛ **-τήρ**, ῆρος, ὁ, *extinguisher*, Plu.2.1059c (pl., codd., σβεστηρίων Cobet). **-τήριος**, α, ον (ος, ον Ph.1.350), *serving to quench* or *put out*, κωλύματα [πυρὸς] σ. Th.7.53 : as Subst., σβεστήρια τοῦ πυρός D.H.3.56, cf. Plu.*Cam*.34, etc. : metaph., σ. κακοῦ φάρμακον Heraclit.*All*.20 ; σ. ἰάματα (for a fever) Orib.*Eup*. 3.6. **-τικός**, ή, όν, = foreg., Arist.*Pr*.933$^{a}$23, Lxx *Wi*.19.20, Dsc. 1.128 : Comp. and Sup., Thphr.*Ign*.59. **-τός**, ή, όν, *quenched, extinguished*, Nonn.*D*.28.189.

**σγάλη**, ἡ, = σκάλη (Lat. *scala*), dub. in *PFay*.122.16 (i/ii A.D.), cf. *Edict.Diocl*.14.6 (*IG*5(1).1115).

**σγουρός**, ά, όν, *curly*, Tz.*H*.12.801.

**σδεύγλα**, ἡ, Aeol. for ζεύγλη, Melinno ap.Stob.3.7.12.

**-σε**, adverbial Suffix, denoting *motion towards*, e.g. ἄλλοσε *to some other place*, ἀμφοτέρωσε, etc.

**σεαγών**, v. σιαγών.

**σεαυτοῦ**, -ῆς, also **σαυτοῦ**, -ῆς, Ion. **σεωυτοῦ**, ῆς, reflexive Pron. of 2nd pers., *of thyself*, etc., in masc. and fem. of gen., dat., and acc. sg., first in Alc.87, Pi.*Fr*.97, Hdt.1.45,108 ; ἐν σαυτοῦ (v.l. -ῷ) γενοῦ contain thyself, S.*Ph*.950 : rarely in neut., φίλον ξύλον, ἔγειρέ μοι σεαυτὸ καὶ γίγνου θρασύ E.*Fr*.693 :—the Trag. use the longer form (but not so freq. as the shorter), S.*Ant*.547, *OT*312, etc. :—in pl. always separated, ὑμῶν αὐτῶν, etc. : and orig. separated in sg., as in Hom., who always has σοὶ αὐτῷ, σ' αὐτόν ; and so τὰ σ' αὐτοῦ, τὰ σ' αὐτῆς for τὰ σά αὐτοῦ, etc., v. σός I. 3.—The separated forms, σοῦ αὐτοῦ, αὐτοῦ σοῦ, etc., were used in Att., not as reflexive, but as emphat. personal pronouns, cf. Pl.*Grg*.472b, A.*Th*.632.

⊛**σεβ-άζομαι**, Ep. aor. σεβάσσατο Il.6.167,417 ; ἐσεβάσθην *AP*7.122, *Ep.Rom*.1.25 :—*to be afraid of*, c. acc., σεβάσσατο γὰρ τό γε θυμῷ Il. ll. cc. 2. later, = σέβομαι, ξεῖνον θανόντα Orph.*A*.550 ; θεόν Jul. *Gal*.354b. ⊛ **-ας**, τό, only nom., acc., and voc. sg. ; pl. σέβη A. *Supp*.755, as if from σέβος, τό : (σέβομαι) :—*reverential awe*, which prevents one from doing something disgraceful (cf. σέβομαι), σ. δέ σε θυμὸν ἱκέσθω Πάτροκλον Τρῳῇσι κυσὶν μέλπηθρα γενέσθαι Il.18.178 ; αἰδώς τε σ. τε *h.Cer*.190 ; also *awe* with a notion of *wonder*, σ. μ' ἔχει εἰσορόωντα Od.3.123, 4.75, cf. 142, etc. : generally, *reverence, worship, honour*, σ. ἀφίσταται A.*Ch*.54 (lyr.) ; σ. τὸ πρὸς θεῶν Id.*Supp*.396 (lyr.) : c. gen. objecti, Διὸς σέβας *reverence for* him, Id.*Ch*.645 (lyr.) : c. gen. subjecti, πάγος ἄρειος, ἐν δὲ τῷ σ. ἀστῶν Id.*Eu*.690 ; so εἴ περ ἴσχει Ζεὺς ἔτ' ἐξ ἐμοῦ σ. S.*Ant*.304. II. after Hom., *the object of reverential awe, holiness, majesty*, σ. Τροΐας Sapph.*Supp*.5.9 ; δαιμόνων σ. A.*Supp*. 85 (lyr.) ; γᾶ, πάνδικον σ. ib.776 (lyr.) ; θεῶν σέβη ib.755, cf. E.*Med*.752 ; Ἥλιε, . . Θρῃξὶ πρέσβιστον σ. (as Bothe and Lob. for σέλας) S.*Fr*.582 ; σ. ἐμπόρων, of a funeral mound serving as a land-mark, E.*Alc*.999 (lyr.) : hence periphr. of reverend persons, ὦ μητρὸς ἐμῆς σ. A.*Pr*.1091 (anap.) ; σ. κηρύκων, of Hermes, Id.*Ag*.515 ; σ. ὦ δέσποτ' Id.*Ch*.157 (lyr.), cf. E.*IA*633 ; Πειθοῦς σ. A.*Eu*.885 ; τοκέων σ. ib.546 (lyr.) ; Ζηνὸς σ. S.*Ph*.1289 ; of things, σ. μηρῶν A.*Fr*.135 ; χειρός E.*Hipp*. 335 ; σ. ἀρρήτων ἱερῶν Ar.*Nu*.302. 2. *object of awestruck wonder*, σ. πᾶσιν ἰδέσθαι *h.Cer*.10 ; πᾶσι τοῖς ἐκεῖ σέβας, of Orestes, S.*El*.685 ; of the arms of Achilles, Id.*Ph*.402 (lyr.). **-ᾰσις**, εως, ἡ, *reverence*, Epicur.*Fr*.141 (pl.). ⊛ **-ασμα**, ατος, τό, *that for which awe is felt, an object of awe* or *worship*, D.H.1.30, *Act.Ap*.17.23, etc. II. = σέβασις, D.H.5.1.

**Σεβάσμ-εια**, τά, v. Σεβάσμιος II. 2. **-ιάζω**, = εὐσεβέω, Zonar. ⊛ **-ιος**, ον, Vett.Val.242.26, also ος, α, ον ib.14, Hdn.7.5.3 : (σέβας) :—*reverend, venerable, august*, Plu.2.764b, Luc.*Am*.19, etc. ; τὸ σ. Orph.*H*.27.10 ; τὸ πρὸς θεοὺς σ. *reverence* for . ., Hdn.2.10.2. Adv. -ίως Ptol.Ascal. p.395 H. II. as epith. of the Roman Emperor, = Σεβαστός, *Augustus*, *SIG*834.6 (Sup., ii A.D.), Hdn.2.3.3 (v.l. σεβαστόν) ; οἱ -ώτατοι Καίσαρες *CPR*37.15 (iii A.D.) ; σ. ὅρκος, oath taken by the genius of the Emperor, *PSI*1.40.19 (ii A.D.), etc. 2. Σεβάσμια, τά, *games in honour of the Emperor*, *IG*3.129 (iii A.D., in form Σεβάσμεια, but perh. rather Σεβασμεῖα, contr. from *Σεβασμιεῖα) ; also on coins, Head *Hist.Num.*[2] 717,784. **-ιότης**, ητος, ἡ, *Reverence*, as a title, *PMasp*.1.28 (vi A.D.). **-ός**, ὁ, = σέβασις, *OGI*383.80 (Commagene, i B.C.), cf. D.S.1.83 ; σεβασμὸν ἀποδοῦναι Aristeas 179 ; τὸν περὶ τῶν θεῶν σ. *Placit*.1.6.9, cf. *SIG*867.36 (ii A.D.) ; περὶ τοὺς βασιλέας Str. 11.13.9 ; σ. τοῦ σοφοῦ Epicur.*Sent.Vat*.32 ; τὸν σ. τοῦ λόγου M.Ant. 4.16 ; ἀρχὴ σεβασμοῦ μεστή *of majesty*, D.H.6.81 : pl., Orph.*H*.17. 8 bis, D.H.2.75. 2. *ritual*, Gal.12.173.

⊛ **Σεβαστ-εῖον**, τό, *temple of* Σεβαστός, i.e. *Augustus*, Ph.2.567 (vulg. -άστιον) ; also **Σεβάστειος** ναός *CIG*2839 (Aphrodisias). II. Σεβαστεῖα, τά, *games in honour of the Emperor*, *SIG*802 *A* 14 (Delph., i A.D.), *IG*4.795 (Troezen, ii A.D.) ; so in sg., *Sardis* 7(1).79 *C* 21 (iii A.D.). **-εύω**, = σεβάζομαι, Manetho ap.J.*Ap*.1.26 (Pass.). **-ιάς**, ἡ, = Lat. *Augusta*, *AP*9.355 (Leon.). ⊛ **-ικός**, ή, όν, *reverent*, Iamb. *Protr*.21.κε', Pythagorei ap.Phot.*Bibl*.p.438 B. Adv., -κῶς διακεῖσθαι πρός τινα *have reverence* for him, D.H.*Pomp*.1, cf. Iamb.*VP*3. 17. **-ιος** ὅρκος, ὁ, an oath *by the genius of the Emperor*, *IG*9(1). 643 (Cephallenia, ii A.D.).

**Σεβαστό-γνωστος**, ον, *known to the Emperor, amicus Caesaris*, γένους γενόμενος λαμπροῦ καὶ -ου *IPE*1[2].43 (Olbia, iii A.D.) : paraphrased by μέχρι τᾶς τῶν Σεβαστῶν γνώσεως προκόψαντος ib.79.6. **-δώρητος**, ον, *authorized by Imperial grant*, of games, θέμις *MAMA*4.154 (Apollonia, iii A.D.). **-κρᾰτέω**, *rule as Augustus* or *Augusta*, Tz. *H*.11.45. **-λόγος**, ὁ, and ⊛**-νέως**, ὁ, names of officials, coupled with ἀρχινεώκορος, *Milet*.7.65. ⊛ **-ν(ε)ίκης**, ου, ὁ, *victorious in Imperial games*, *Supp.Epigr*.6.58.12 (Ancyra) ; also ⊛**-νεικηφόρια**, τά, *Imperial games*, *Abh.Berl.Akad*.1932(5).43 (Pergam.).

⊛**σεβαστός**, ή, όν, *venerable, reverend, august*, πρᾶγμα D.H.2.75 ; θεοί, prob. of deified Emperors, *IG*7.2233 (Thisbe), cf. *SIG*820.6 (Ephesus, i A.D.). II. = Lat. *Augustus*, Str.3.3.8, 12.8.16, *Act. Ap*.25.21, Paus.3.11.4, Hdn.2.10.9, etc. ; Καίσαρος Σ. θεοῦ Luc. *Macr*.21, cf. 17 ; ἐπὶ τοῦ πρώτου Σ. in the time of the first *Emperor*, Id.*Laps*.18 ; κατὰ τὸν Σ. μάλιστα Id.*Salt*.34, etc. ; fem. Σεβαστή, = *Augusta*, Wilcken *Chr*.14 ii 7 (i A.D.), etc., cf. Σεβαστιάς ; joined with Αὔγουστος, -ούστη, *CIG*3770 (Nicomedia). 2. name of month,

*Augustus*, in Egyptian calendars, = Thoth, *Yale Classical Studies* 2. 242; in Phrygia and elsewhere, *IGRom.*4.536, etc. 3. σεβαστή, ἡ (sc. ἡμέρα), the *Emperor's day*, the day on which his birthday or accession day was celebrated every month, *OGI*658 (Egypt, i B.C.), *POxy.*288.32 (i A.D.), *PMich.Teb.*123ʳ iv 30 (i A.D.), etc. 4. Σεβαστά, τά, = Σεβαστεῖα II, *CIG*2810*b*.13 (p. 1112) (Aphrodisias), cf. *IG* 3.129, 14.748, *SIG*1065.5 (Cos, i A.D.).

**Σεβαστο-φαντέω**, *to be flamen Augusti*, *OGI*544.20 (Ancyra, ii A.D.), *Ath.Mitt.*30.324 (Prusa, ii A.D.), etc. ❋ **-φάντης**, ου, ὁ, *priest of Augustus*, Lat. *flamen Augusti*, *OGI*479.6 (Dorylaeum, ii A.D.), *IGRom.*3.22 (Bithynia), *Sardis* 7(1).62, etc.; fem. **-φάντις**, ιδος, *OGI* 479.13. **-φαντικός**, ή, όν, *pertaining to the flamen Augusti*, χρήματα *funds collected by him*, ib.544.21 (Ancyra, ii A.D.). **-φορικός**, ή, όν, *pertaining to the* Σεβαστοφόροι, *IG*3.1145 iii 15 (ii/iii A.D.); μετὰ τὰς -κὰς νομάς ib.1184 (iii A.D.). ❋ **-φόροι**, οἱ, perh. *priests in the cult of the Roman Emperor*, Lyd.*Mens.*4.138: later (sg.), an *official in Egypt*, *Sammelb.*4663 (vi A.D.).

❋**σεβένιον** and **σεβέννιον**, τό, *palm-fibre*, *PLond.*1.131*.1 (i A.D.), Archig. ap. Gal.12.574, *PHolm.*13.43, Hsch.: Adj.❋**σεβένινος** or **σεβέννινος**, *made of palm-fibre*, *PLond.*1.131ʳ.610 (i A.D.), *PMag. Par.*1.903,1342; written **συμβεννίων**, *PCair.Zen.*438 (iii B.C.).

❋ **σέβερος**· εὐσεβής, δίκαιος, Hsch., cf. Theognost.*Can.*11.

**σέβ-ημα**, ατος, τό, *act of worship*, Orph.*Fr.*49 i 7; v.l. for σέβασμα in Lxx *Wi.*15.17. **-ίζω**, mostly used in pres.: fut. σεβιῶ D.C.52.40: aor. ἐσέβισα S.*Ant.*943 (anap.), Ar.*Th.*106 (lyr.):—**Med.** and **Pass.**, v. infr.:—*worship, honour*, τινα Pi.*P.*5.81, A.*Eu.*12; σὸν κράτος Id.*Ag.* 258, cf. 785 (anap.); σ. τινὰ τιμαῖς, λιταῖς, S.*OC*1007,1557 (lyr.); εὐχαῖσι θεούς E.*El.*196 (lyr.); σ. τινὰ πλούτου *honour* or *admire* one *for* it, ib.994 (anap.); καινὰ λέχη σ. *devote oneself to* a new wife, Id.*Med.*156 (lyr.); εὐσεβίαν σεβίσασα S.*Ant.*943 (anap.); σ. βάρη *paying my tribute* (prob. a dirge) *to*.., A.*Pers.*945 (lyr., dub. l.):—Pass., σεβιζόμενοι ἐν θυσίαις Pi.*I.*5(4).29; σ. ἀνδράσιν ἠδὲ γυναιξίν Emp.112.8:—also Med. in sense of Act., σ. ἱκέτας A.*Supp.*815 (lyr.); δαίμονας ib.922; οὐδὲν σεβίζει γενεθλίους ἀράς *standest* not *in awe of* them, Id.*Ch.*912; ἁγὼ σεβισθείς S.*OC*636.

**σέβις**· πυξίς, Hsch.; cf. σεβίτιον.

❋ **σέβ-ισμα**, ατος, τό, = σέβασμα, Sch.A.*Eu.*92. **-ιστός**, ή, όν, = σεβαστός, Hsch.

**σεβίτιον**, τό, perh. Dim. of σέβις, *BGU*1558 (iii B.C.), *UPZ*121.22, 149.26 (ii B.C.), *POxy.*919.8 (ii A.D.).

❋ **σέβομαι**, mostly used in pres.: impf. in Hdt.7.197: fut. σεβήσομαι *POxy.*1381.202 (ii A.D.): aor. ἐσέφθην S.*Fr.*164, Pl.*Phdr.*254b, Porph.*Plot.*12:—*feel awe* or *fear* before God, *feel shame*, οὔ νυ σέβεσθε; Il.4.242, cf. Ar.*Nu.*293; τιμῶν καὶ σεβόμενος Pl.*Lg.*729c; σεφθεῖσα *awe-stricken*, Id.*Phdr.* l.c.: rarely c. inf., *dread* or *fear to do* a thing, σ. προσιδέσθαι.., ἀντία φάσθαι A.*Pers.*694 (lyr.); μιαίνειν τὸ θεῖον Pl.*Ti.*69d; σέβεται καὶ φοβεῖται..τό τι κινεῖν τῶν καθεστώτων Id.*Lg.* 798b: so c. acc. rei, *to fear to do* it, Antipho 2.4.12: c. part., σ. προσορῶν Pl.*Phdr.*250e. 2. after Hom., c. acc. pers., *revere, worship*, Κρονίδαν Pi.*P.*6.25; θεούς A.*Supp.*921, etc.; πάντων ἀνάκτων κοινοβωμίαν ib.223; Λατώ Ar.*Th.*123; Λυκοῦργον σέβεσθαι *worship* him *as a hero*, Hdt.1.66, cf. 7.197; προσορῶν ὡς θεὸν σ. τινά Pl.*Phdr.*251a; *do homage to* Zeus, A.*Pr.*937: generally, *pay honour* or *respect to*.., θνατοὺς ἄγαν σ. ib.543 (lyr.); τὸ φίλον S.*OC*187 (lyr.), cf. *Ph.*1163 (lyr.), etc.; σ. τινὰ τύχης μάκαρος E.*IT*648. b. esp. of Jewish proselytes, σεβομένη τὸν θεόν *Act.Ap.*16.14, cf. J.*AJ*14.7.2; σεβόμενοι προσήλυτοι, Ἕλληνες, *Act.Ap.*13.43, 17.4; σεβόμεναι γυναῖκες ib.13.50. 3. of things, τὰ βυβλία σεβόμενοι μεγάλως Hdt.3.128; ὄργια Ar.*Th.*949; ὦ Πιερία, σέβεταί σ' Εὔιος E.*Ba.*566 (lyr.); τὸ σῶφρον αἰδούμενος ἅμα καὶ σ. Pl.*Lg.*837c. II. Act. σέβω is post-Hom., used only in pres. and impf., *worship, honour*, mostly of the gods, σ. Δήμητρος πανήγυριν Archil.120; πατρὸς Ὀλυμπίοιο τιμάν Pi.*O.*14.12; θεούς A.*Th.*596; Νύμφας Id.*Eu.*22; Ἅιδην S.*Ant.*777; τὰν Ἅιδου ib.780; θεῶν θέσμια Id.*Aj.* 713 (lyr.), etc.; rare in Prose, νομίζεται θεοὺς σέβειν X.*Mem.*4.4.19, cf. Ar.*Nu.*600; but also of parents, S.*OC*1377, cf. *Ant.*511; of kings, Id. *Aj.*667, etc.; of suppliants, A.*Eu.*151 (lyr.); λέγω κατ' ἄνδρα, μὴ θεόν, σέβειν ἐμέ Id.*Ag.*925; αἰχμὴν..μᾶλλον θεοῦ σ. Id.*Th.*530; σ. ὀνείρων φάσματα Id.*Ag.*274; τὰς ἐμὰς ἀρχὰς σ. S.*Ant.*744 (εὖ σέβουσι is dub. cj. for εὐσεβοῦσι in A.*Ag.*338, cf. E.*Ph.*1320, *Tr.*85); σέβειν ἐν τιμῇ c. acc., A.*Pers.*166, Pl.*Lg.*647a: c. inf., ὑβρίζειν ἐν κακοῖσιν οὐ σέβω, i.e. τὸ ὑβρίζειν, I do not *respect, approve* it, A.*Ag.*1612; τὸ μὴ ἀδικεῖν σέβοντες Id.*Eu.*749: rarely of a god, Ποσειδῶν..τὰς ἐμὰς ἀρὰς σέβων E.*Hipp.*896:—σέβομαι as Pass., *to be reverenced*, ἡ δ' οἶκοι [πόλις] πλέον δίκῃ σέβοιτ' ἄν S.*OC*760; τὸ σεβόμενον *reverence*, Plu. 2.1101d. 2. less freq. abs., *to worship, to be religious*, τὸν σέβοντ' εὐεργετεῖν A.*Eu.*725, cf. 897; οὐ γὰρ σέβεις S.*Ant.*745; κρίνοντες ἐν ὁμοίῳ καὶ σέβειν καὶ μή Th.2.53; but in all these places an object shd. perh. be supplied from the context. (σέβομαι prob. orig. '*I shrink from*..', of which σοβέω is the causal; perh. cogn. with Skt. *tyajati* 'desert, let go'.)

**σεβομένως**, Adv. = σεβασμίως, Ammon.*Diff.* p.8 V., but σεβασμίως should be restd. from Ptol.Ascal. p.395 H.

**σεγάνιον**· γυργαθῶδες πλέγμα (Rhod.), Hsch. (cf. σαργάνη).

❋ **σέγεστρον**, τό, *blanket* or *counterpane*, *Edict.Diocl.*8.42.

**σέδας**· καθέδρας, Hsch.

**σέδετον**, τό, = Lat. *sedes*, in pl., *Cod.Just.*1.4.18.

**σέθεν**, v. σύ. **σεῖα**· ἐδίωξα (Boeot.), Hsch. (Boeot. spelling of *σῆα, prob. aor. of σεύω). **σειεύς**, ὁ, v. σείσων. **Σειληνικός**, **Σειληνός**, **Σειληνώδης**, v. Σιλ-.

**σεῖν**, Dor. for θεῖν, *run*, Hsch. II. *a whistling sound* used by nurses to induce young children to make water, Ar.*Fr.*850.

**σεῖναι**· θεῖναι (Cret.), Hsch.

**σειναρμόστρια**, v. θοιναρμόστρια.

❋ **σείνιοι τόποι**, prob. *winnowing floors*, *PStrassb.*45.11 (iv A.D.).

**σεῖο**, v. σύ.

**σεῖος**, α, ον, Lacon. for θεῖος, Arist.*EN*1145ᵃ29, cf. Pl.*Men.*99d.

❋ **σειρά**, Ion. **σειρή**, Dor. **σηρά** Choerob. in *An.Ox.*2.260, *Et.Gud.* 497.47: ἡ:—*cord, rope*, σειρὰς τ' εὐπλέκτους Il.23.115; σειρὴν δὲ πλεκτήν Od.22.175; σ. χρυσείη *cord* of gold, Il.8.19, cf. Pl.*Tht.* 153c: metaph., σειραῖς.. ἁμαρτιῶν σφίγγεται Lxx *Pr.*5.22; σειραὶ ζόφου v.l. in 2*Ep.Pet.*2.4: v. also σαύρα IV. 2. *trace* (cf. σειραφόρος), Poll.1.141. 3. *cord* or *line with a noose, lasso*, used by the Sagartians and Sarmatians, Hdt.7.85, Paus.1.21.5: hence the Parthians are called σειραφόροι, Suid. 4. a bandage, Gal.18(1). 777; σ. μονομερής, διμερής, κτλ. Sor.*Fasc.*23,24, al. 5. ἡ σ. τοῦ βίρρου, = *cimussatio* (prob. *edge, border*), Dosith. p.435 K. II. metaph. of an animal's *tail*, Nic.*Th.*119,385. III. σειραὶ τῆς κεφαλῆς *locks* of hair, Lxx *Jd.*16.13; σ. τριχῶν Poll.2.30. IV. metaph., *line, lineage*, Tz. ad Lyc.481, Sch.Il.1.176. V. *series*, Dam.*Pr.*45,95. VI. pl., *a disease of horses*, *Hippiatr.*52. VII. *the front part of the perineum*, Aët.6.34.

**σειρ-ᾰγωγεύς**, έως, ὁ, *cord for leading* (cf. ῥυταγωγεύς), Poll.1. 216. **-άδιον**, τό, Dim. of σειρά, Eust.1291.31, 1923.55.

**σειράζω**, *strike*, of lightning, Ael.Dion.*Fr.*430.

❋ **σειραίνω**, (Σείριος) *dry up by heat, parch*, Orus ap. *EM*710.22; cf. σειριάω, σειρεόω, and σειρόω.

❋ **σειραῖος**, α, ον, (σειρά) *joined by a cord* or *band*, ἵππος σ., = σειραφόρος, S.*El.*722; δυσὶ γὰρ ἵπποις..τρίτος παρείπετο σ..ῥυτῆρσι συνεχόμενος D.H.7.73; νῶτα σειραίου (sc. ἵππου) cj. for σειρίου in E.*Fr.*779. 8; σ. ἱμάς *the attaching* trace of the horse, Poll.1.148; cf. ὑποσειραῖος. 2. *of cord, twisted*, βρόχοι E.*HF*1009; μήρινθος Orph.*A.*241.

**σειρᾱφόρος**, Ion. **σειρηφ-**, ον (sc. ἵππος), a horse *which draws by the trace only* (being harnessed by the side of the pair under the yoke, οἱ ζύγιοι), *trace-horse*: hence metaph., sts. *yoke-mate, coadjutor*, A.*Ag.*842; sts. *one who has light work*, ib.1640, cf. Ar.*Nu.*1300; σ. [κάμηλος] *attached like a trace-horse*, Hdt.3.102. II. *carrying a lasso*, v. σειρά I. 3.

**σειράω**, (σειρά) *bind* or *draw with a rope*, Phot.

**σειρεόω**, *drain dry*, v.l. (vulg.) in Hp.*Hum.*8; cf. sq. and σειρόω.

**σειρέω**, *empty, drain dry*, Hp.*Hum.*8, *EM*710.25.

**Σειρηδών**, όνος, ἡ, late form of sq., Sch.Il.24.253, Aus.*Id.*11.20 (p.201 P.).

❋**Σειρήν**, ῆνος, ἡ, *Siren*; in pl., Σειρῆνες, αἱ, *Sirens*, Od.12.39, al., cf. Sch. ad loc.; Ep. dual gen. Σειρήνοιιν ib.52,167; πτεροφόροι νεανίδες ..Σειρῆνες E.*Hel.*169 (lyr.), cf. *Fr.*911 (lyr.); Σειρὴν..τὰ σκέλη δὲ κοψίχου Anaxil.22.20; cf. ἀρπυιόγουνος; σειρῆνα κόμπον..ὃς Ζεφύρου σιγάζει πνοάς Pi.*Parth.*2.13, cf. Hes.*Fr.*69; ἐπὶ τῶν κύκλων [τοῦ ἀτράκτου]..ἐφ' ἑκάστου βεβηκέναι Σειρῆνα..φωνὴν μίαν ἱεῖσαν Pl.*R.*617b (hence σειρῆνες· τὰ ἄστρα, *Lex.Rhet.* ap. Eust.1709.54, cf. Theo Sm. p.146 H.); as a grave-ornament, στᾶλαι καὶ Σειρῆνες ἐμαί *AP*7.710 (Erinna), cf. 491 (Mnasalc.). II. metaph., *Siren, deceitful woman*, E.*Andr.*936: also, *the Siren charm* of eloquence, persuasion, and the like, Alcm.7, Aeschin.3.228, Alex.Aet.7 (pl.); ποικίλη σ., of philosophy, Phld.*Rh.*2.145 S.; λόγων σ. καὶ χάρις Plu.*Mar.*44, cf. D.H. *Comp.*26, Jul.*Or.*2.52d; ὤλετο παρθενίη σ. ἐμή *Supp.Epigr.*1.567.7 (Fayum), cf. *IG*14.1942 (Rome); σειρῆνα θεάτρων, of Menander, ib.1183; ἔνθεον σειρῆνα χεύῃ ib.4²(1).130.17 (Epid.). III. ὁ, a kind of *solitary bee* or *wasp*, Arist.*HA*623ᵇ11. IV. a small *singing-bird*, Hsch. 2. prob. *ostrich*, Lxx *Is.*13.21, al., 1*Enoch* 19.2. V. as name of Zeus, dub. in Antim.94 (σείρινα acc. sg., codd. *EM*). VI. *a light garment*, Harp. s.v. σείρινα, Phot. (Correctly written with -ει-, as name of a ship, *IG*2².1629.687.)

**Σειρήνειος**, ον, *Siren-like*: metaph., *bewitching*, Lxx 4*Ma.*15.21, Hld.5.1:—in codd. freq. σειρήνιος. Also fem. Adj. **Σειρηνίς**, ίδος, D.P.360, Tz.*H.*1.341, and Σειρηνίδες, = Σειρῆνες, ib.9.19; Dor. **Σηρηνίδες** dub. in Alcm.23.96.

**σειρηφόρος**, ον, Ion. for σειραφόρος.

**σειρι-άζω**, *sparkle, twinkle*, given as etym. of Σειρῆνες used as name of the planets, Anon. ap. Theon.Sm. p.146 H. **-ᾱσις**, εως, ἡ (not σιρ-), *heat-stroke*, Sor.1.124, Orib.*Syn.*5.13, Paul.Aeg.1. 13. **-άω** (not σιρ-), (σείριος) *to be hot and scorching*, of the Dog Star, Arat.331. II. *suffer from* σειρίασις, Dsc.4.70, *Eup.*1.9, Alex. Aphr.*Pr.*1.98; = φλεγμαίνει, καροῦται, Ael.Dion.*Fr.*430; σ. τοὺς πόδας, of horses (v. σειρά VI), *Hippiatr.*52.

**σειρικάριον**, v. σηρικάριος.

**σειρικόν**, τό, = σέρις, Suid. **σειρικός**, v. σηρικός.

**σείρῖνα**, τά, *light summer clothes*, Lycurg.*Fr.*28.

**σειριό-εις**, εσσα, εν, (Σείριος) *scorching*, ἥλιος Opp.*C.*4.338; ἀτμός Nonn.*D.*12.289. **-καυτος**, ον, *scorched by the dog-star*, *AP*9.556 (Zon.).

❋ **σείριος**, ὁ, name of the *dog-star, Sirius*, whose visible heliacal rising marked the season of greatest heat (cf. Gem.17.39), Hes.*Op.* 587,609, *Sc.*153,397, Alc.39, E.*Hec.*1104 (lyr.); Σείριος κύων A.*Ag.* 967, S.*Fr.*803; Σείριος ἀστήρ Hes.*Op.*417:—of the *sun*, acc. to Hsch., in Archil.61, cf. ἀκτὶς Σειρία Lyc.397 and Sch. ad loc.; σ. ἥλιος Orph.*A.*120; of *stars*, Ibyc.3, Alcm.23.62, cf. E.*Fr.*779. 8 cod. Longin., of a bright *planet*, Id.*IA*7 (acc. to Theo Sm. p.146 H., dub., anap.). 2. Adj. *destructive*, σείριαι νᾶες Tim.*Pers.*

192. 3. σείριον πάθος, = σειρίασις, Sor.1.124. 4. σείριον (sc. ἱμάτιον), *a light summer garment*, Harp. s. v. σείρινα, Phot. s. v. σειρῆνα. (Suid. derives it from a form σείρ gen. σειρός, = ἥλιος, which is suspect.)

**σειρίς**, ίδος, ἡ, Dim. of σειρά I. 3, X.*Cyn*.9.13,14,15,19.

**σειρομάστης**, v. σιρ-. **σειρόν**· τὸ ἀνδρεῖον θέριστρον (Sicyonian), Hsch.; cf. ζειρά. **σειρός**, v. σιρός.

**σειροφόρος**, ον, = σειραφόρος, only in Ps.-E.*IA*223 (signf. I), and Suid. (signf. II).

**σειρ-όω**, *strain, filter*, Cleopatra ap. Paul.Aeg.3.2, *PFay*.134.6 (iv A. D.), Aët.1.102; but σειρώσουσιν is prob. f.l. for στρώσουσιν in Sm.*Je*.48.12. (Cf. σειρεόω and σειρέω.) II. σειρῶ, = *cimusso, provide* a garment *with a border*, Dosith. p.435 K. **-ωσις**, εως, ἡ, (σειρά) *binding, fastening*, Phot. II. *filtering*, Hsch. s. v. διηθήσεως. **-ωτός**, ή, όν, *bound*, Sm., Thd.*Ex*.28.32.

**σεισάχθεια**, ἡ, (σείω, ἄχθος) *shaking off of burdens*, Plu.*Luc*.20: a name for *the disburdening ordinance* of Solon for the relief of debt, Arist.*Ath*.6.1, D.S.1.79, Plu.*Sol*.15; so of Caesar, σεισαχθείᾳ τινὶ τόκων ἐκούφιζε τοὺς χρεωφειλέτας Id.*Caes*.37.

**σεῖσις**, εως, ἡ, (σείω) *shaking*, Aret.*CA*2.2; *concussion* of the spine, Gal.18(1).496, al.

**σεισίφυλλος**, gloss on εἰνοσίφυλλος, Eust.1613.42.

**σεισίχθων**, ονος, ὁ, *earth-shaker*, epith. of Poseidon, Pi.*I*.1.52, D.H.2.31, etc., cf. ἐνοσίχθων; of Zeus, Orph.*H*.14.8.

**σεῖσμα**, ατος, τό, (σείω) *shaking*, κοσκίνου Lxx *Si*.27.4. 2. pl., metaph., *extortions* (cf. σείω I. 4), *PTeb*.41.22 (ii B. C.), *PMasp*.58 ii 11 (vi A. D., σῖσμ(α)).

**σεισμᾰτίας**, ου, ὁ, of earthquakes, *shaking, tremulous*, D.L.7.154: Σ., name of a tomb of certain victims of an earthquake, Plu.*Cim*.16.

**σεισμοποιός**, όν, *causing earthquakes*, Ptol.*Tetr*.94, Vett.Val.8.25.

✱ **σεισμ-ός**, ὁ, (σείω) *shaking, shock*, γῆς σ. *earthquake*, E.*HF*862, Th.3.87; χθονός E.*IT*1166: abs., Hdt.4.28, 5.85, 7.129, S.*OC*95, Ar.*Ec*.791, Th.1.23, etc. 2. generally, *shock, agitation, commotion*, σ. τοῦ σώματος Pl.*Phlb*.33e, cf. *Ti*.88d; ἔξωθεν..προσφέρειν τοῖς.. πάθεσι σεισμόν *a shock*, Id.*Lg*.791a; σ. τῆς οὐρᾶς Poll.5.61; σ. ἐν τῇ θαλάσσῃ *Ev.Matt*.8.24. 3. *blackmail, extortion*, *Sammelb*.5675.13 (ii B. C.); συκοφάντεια καὶ σ. *PPar*.15.67 (ii B. C.). **-οσκοπικά**, τά, title of a work *on earthquakes* by Tages, Lyd.*Mens*.4.79. **-ώδης**, ες, *indicative* or *productive of an earthquake*, Ptol.*Tetr*.94, Vett.Val.6.25, Anon.ap.Lyd.*Ost*. p.174 W.

**σεισο-κέφᾰλος**, ον, *shaking the head*, Dsc.*Eup*.1.9, Id.ap.Orib.*Syn*.8.21. **-λοφος**, ον, *shaking the crest*, Hsch. s. v. τινακτοπήληξ. **-πῡγίς**, ίδος, ἡ, = ἴυγξ (cf. κιναίδιον), Cyran.97, Suid. s. v. κίγκλος, Sch.Theoc.2.17:—Dim. **-πύγιον**, τό, Cyran. l. c., Tz.*H*.11.577.

**σεισόφελος**· τὸ τῶν τροχίλων εἶδος, Hsch.

**σεισόφυλλος**, ον, gloss on εἰνοσίφυλλος, Eust.1613.42.

**σεισ-τής**, οῦ, ὁ, (σείω) *earth-shaker*, a kind of earthquake, Lyd.*Ost*.53. **-τός**, ή, όν, *shaken*, Ar.*Ach*.346. II. *pendant*, of earrings, ἐνώτια χρυσᾶ σειστὰ ἐγ κιβωτίῳ *IG*11(2).203*B*69 (Delos, iii B. C.), cf. 287*B*28 (iii B. C.), *Inscr.Délos* 442*B*4 (ii B. C.).

**σεῖστρον**, τό, (σείω) *rattle* used in the worship of Isis, *Inscr.Délos* 385*a*5 (ii B. C.), Plu.2.376c sq., Philostr.*Im*.1.5, Lib.*Or*.64.97.

**σεῖστρος**, ὁ, *yellow-rattle, Rhinanthus major*, growing in the Scamander, Arist.*Mir*.846ᵃ34, cf. Ps.-Plu.*Fluv*.13.2 (οἶστρ- codd.).

**σειστροφόρος**, ον, *bearing the sistrum*, Βούβαστις *Hymn.Is*.3.

**σείσων**, ονος, ὁ, (σείω) *earthen vessel* in which beans were *shaken* while being roasted, Alex.134, Axionic.7. Also **σειεύς**, έως, ὁ, Poll.7.181 (s. v. l.).

**σεῖφα**· σκοτία (Cret.), Hsch.

**σείφαρος**, ὁ, *awning in a theatre*, *OGI*510.6 (Ephesus), *Ephes*.2.39; cf. σίφαρος.

**σείω**, Il.5.563, etc., poet. **σίω** Anacr.49: Ep impf. σεῖον Od.3.486; Ion. σείασκον (ἀνασ-) *h.Ap*.403 (v.l. ἀνασσείσασκε): fut. σείσω Lxx *Is*.10.14, (δια-) Hdt.6.109, (ἐπι-) E.*Or*.613: aor. ἔσεισα S.*El*.713, Ar.*Ach*.12, etc.; Ep. σεῖσα Il.15.321: pf. σέσεικα (κατα-) Philem.84, (ἐν-) Luc.*Merc.Cond*.30:—Med., aor. ἐσεισάμην (ἀπ-) Thgn.348, Hdt.7.88, Ar.*Nu*.287, Pl.*Grg*.484a; Ep. σείσατο Il.8.199, ἐσείσατο Call.*Ap*.1, etc.:—**Pass.**, aor. ἐσείσθην Hdt.6.98, etc.: pf. σέσεισμαι Pi.*P*.8.94, Ar.*Nu*.1276:—*shake, move to and fro*, Hom. (esp. in Il.); σ. ἐγχείας, ἔγχεα, μελίην, *shake the poised* spear, Il.3.345, 13.135 (Pass.), 22.133, etc.; αἰγίδα 15.321; σανίδας σ. *shake* the door, 9.583; of chariot horses, σεῖον ζυγὸν ἀμφὶς ἔχοντες Od.3.486; σ. λόφον, of a warrior, Alc.22, A.*Th*.385; ἡνίας χεροῖν σ. S.*El*.713; χαλινούς E.*IA*151 (anap.); σ. χαίτην, etc., Anacr.40, E.*Cyc*.75 (lyr.), *Med*.1191; εὔπτερον δέμας Id.*Ion* 1204; κάρα σ., as sign of discontent, S.*Ant*.291; but of one dancing, E.*Ba*.185; ἄκρᾳ τῇ οὐρᾷ σ. X.*Cyn*.3.4. 2. of earthquakes, which were attributed to Poseidon (cf. Pl.*Cra*.403a), ὅστις νομίζει Ποσειδέωνα τὴν γῆν σείειν Hdt.7.129; without τὴν γῆν, αὐτοῖς ὁ Ποσειδῶν σείσας ἐμβάλοι οἰκίας Ar.*Ach*.511, cf. *Lys*.1142; βρονταῖς χθόνα σ. Id.*Av*.1752; ἔσεισεν ὁ θεὸς X.*HG*4.7.4: also impers., ἔσεισεν *there was an earthquake*, Th.4.52. 3. metaph., *agitate, disturb*, πόλιν Pi.*P*.4.272; τὰ πόλεος..θεοὶ πολλῷ σάλῳ σείσαντες ὤρθωσαν πάλιν S.*Ant*.163; σ. τὴν καρδίαν *turn* the stomach, Ar.*Ach*.12; σ. τὴν κεφαλήν *cause a concussion of*.., Hp.*Prorrh*.1.143, v. infr. II. 2:—Pass., ἐσείσθη τὴν καρδίαν Philostr.*VS*2.1.11. 4. in Att., *accuse falsely* or *spitefully*, so as to extort hush-money, *blackmail*, σ. καὶ ταράττων Ar.*Eq*.840, cf. Telecl.2; ἔσειον τοὺς παχεῖς καὶ πλουσίους Ar.*Pax*639; ἑτέρους τῶν ὑπευθύνων ἔσειε καὶ ἐσυκοφάντει Antipho 6.43, cf. *BGU*428.9 (ii A. D.); so perh. σείειν κατ' ἀγοράν Alciphr.3.70 (s. v. l.):—Pass., *to be extorted*, *POxy*.1252ʳ.37 (iii A. D.). II. Pass., *shake, heave, quake*, of the earth, ἐσσείοντο πόδες Ἴδης Il.20.59; Δῆλος..πρῶτα καὶ ὕστατα..σεισθεῖσα Hdt.6.98: metaph., *to be shaken to its foundation*, τὸ τερπνὸν πιτνεῖ..σεσεισμένον Pi.*P*.8.94; οἷς..ἂν σεισθῇ θεόθεν δόμος S.*Ant*.584 (lyr.). 2. generally, *move to and fro*, Il.14.285; φαεινὴ σείετο πήληξ 13.805; κόμαι σείονται Ar.*Lys*.1312; ὄρχος σειόμενος φύλλοισι an orchard *waving* with foliage, Hes.*Sc*.[299]; ὀδόντων οἱ πλεῦνες ἐσείοντο his teeth *were loose*, Hdt.6.107; σεισθῆναι σάλῳ E.*IT*46; τὸν ἐγκέφαλον σεσεῖσθαι Ar.*Nu*.1276; ὁκόσων ἂν σεισθῇ ὁ ἐγκέφαλος Hp.*Aph*.7.58; σελεῖσθαι τὴν ὄψιν Thphr.*Vert*.8. III. Med., *shake* something *of one's own, from oneself*, etc., σεισαμένας πτερὰ ματρός Theoc.13.13; σ. γυίων ἄπο νήχυτον ἅλμην A.R.4.1367; σ. πλοκαμῖδας *AP*5.272 (Agath.). 2. *shake oneself, shake, stir*, Ἥρη σείσατο εἰνὶ θρόνῳ Il.8.199; ἐσείσατο δάφνινος ὄρπηξ Call.*Ap*.1.

**σεκάνες**· πόρρωθεν, Hsch.

**σέκουα**, = σικύα, and **σεκουάνη**, a kind of olive (Lacon.), Hsch.

✱ **σεκουνδαρούδης**, ὁ, of a gladiator, *secunda rude insignis*, *TAM*2.117 (Lycia).

**σεκουνδοκέριος** and **-κήριος**, ὁ, = Lat. *secundocerius*, *Cod.Just*.12.17.5, 4.59.1.1.

**σεκούριον**, τό, (Lat. *securis*) *axe*, *IG*5(1).1406.8 (Edict. Diocl.).

✱ **σελᾰγ-έω**, (σέλας) *enlighten, illuminate*, ἀκτὶς ἀελίω σελάγεσκε.. γαῖαν *Hymn.Is*.9:—Pass., *beam brightly*, σελαγεῖτο δ' ἀν' ἄστυ πῦρ E.*El*.714 (lyr.); ὄμμα αἰθέρος σελαγεῖται Ar.*Nu*.285, cf. 604; also, *to be in a blaze*, Id.*Ach*.924 sq. II. intr., *shine, beam*, Opp.*C*.1.210, 3.136. **-ή**, ἡ, *flashing*, ξιφέων dub. in Tryph.428 (σελάγη cod. F); v. σέλαγος. **-ησις**, εως, ἡ, = λαμπηδών, Zonar. ✱ **-ίζω**, = σελαγέω II, Hymn. in *PRoss.-Georg*.1.17 (iii A. D.), Nonn.*D*.7.195, al. **-ισμα**, ατος, τό, *lightning*, Man.4.189. **-ος**, εος, τό, *ray*, μήνας..σελάγεσσι *Hymn.Is*.30: nom. pl. dub. in Tryph.428 (v. σελαγή).

**σελᾱη-γενέτης**, ου, ὁ, *father of light*, of Apollo, *AP*9.525.19. **-φόρος**, ον, *light-bringing*, Ἑρμῆς Man.4.333.

**σέλαιναι**· λαμπάδες, Hsch.

**σέλ-ας**, αος, τό: Hom. uses (besides nom.) dat. σέλαϊ Il.17.739, contr. σέλᾳ Od.21.246; gen. σέλαος Plot.6.7.33, σέλατος Conon 49.2: pl. σέλᾱ Arist.*Mu*.395ᵃ31, al., Plu.*Caes*.63, *AP*9.289 (Bass.); gen. σελάων Arist.*Mu*.395ᵇ4 codd. (σελῶν ap. Stob.):—*light, brightness, flame*, πυρός Il.19.366, al.; καιομένοιο πυρός, π. αἰθομένοιο, ib.375, 8.563; ἐν σέλαϊ μεγάλῳ, without any word added, 17.739; δαΐδων σ. Od.18.354, Hes.*Sc*.275; σ. λάβρον Ἡφαίστου Pi.*P*.3.39; ἀπὸ..λάμπε γυίων σ. ὥτε πυρός B.16.104; Ἥφαιστος..λαμπρὸν ἐκπέμπων σ., of a beacon fire, A.*Ag*.281, cf. 289; Ἡφαιστότευκτον, of a volcano, S.*Ph*.986; καμίνου A.*Fr*.281; ἐφέστιον σ. S.*Tr*.607; of the heavenly bodies, σ. γένετ' ἠΰτε μήνης Il.19.374; ἁλίου σ. A.*Eu*.926 (lyr.), S.*El*.17, Ar.*Av*.1711; of day*light*, καθαρὸν ἁμέρας σ. Pi.*Fr*.142.4, cf. S.*Aj*.856; πρὶν θεοῦ δῦναι σ. E.*Supp*.469; τὸ σ. καὶ τὸ φῶς ταὐτόν Pl.*Cra*.409b; *lightning, flash of lightning*, δαιόμενον σ. Il.8.76, cf. Democr.152; Διὸς σ. S.*OC*95; σ. ἐκ τοῦ οὐρανοῦ Hdt.3.28; *meteor*, Arist.*Mu*.395ᵃ31; *torchlight*, *h.Cer*.52, A.R.4.808, cf. *AP*9.46, etc., *the flash* of an angry eye, ἐξ ὀμμάτων ἤστραπτε γοργωπὸν σ. A.*Pr*.358, cf. E.*Cyc*.663 (so in Hom., ὄσσε λαμπέσθην ὡς εἴ τε πυρὸς σ. Il.19.366; ὄσσε δεινὸν ὑπὸ βλεφάρων ὡς εἰ σ. ἐξεφάανθεν ib.17): metaph. of love, Theoc.2.134, cf. *AP*12.93 (Rhian.). ✱**-άσκω**, *shine*, Theognost.*Can*.11. **-ασμα**, ατος, τό, *shining*, Man.4.601: — also **-ασμός**, ὁ, ib.36, etc.; also f.l. for σελλισμός (q. v.). **-άσσομαι**, *glow*, Nic.*Th*.46.

**σελασφόρος**, ον, *light-bearing, light-bringing*, λαμπάδες A.*Eu*.1022; ἅρμα prob. in *Epic.Alex.Adesp*.9 x 11; name of Ἄρτεμις (cf. πυρφόρος), Paus.1.31.4; of the moon, *Cat.Cod.Astr*.1.173.

**σελάτης**, ου, ὁ, *snail*, Hsch.

**σελάχ-ιον** [ᾰ], τό, Dim. of σέλαχος, Eup.1, Pl.Com.56, Luc.*Lex*.6:—poet. **σελάχειον**, τό, Opp.*H*.1.643. **-ιος**, α, ον, of fishes, *cartilaginous, having no scales*, Artem.2.14, Ar.Byz.*Epit*.1.21, 111.10. ✱ **-ος**, εος, τό, mostly in pl. σελάχη, τά, *the cartilaginous* or *elasmobranch fishes, sharks* and *rays*, Arist.*HA*505ᵃ1, 511ᵃ5, al.; ἰχθύσι σελάχεσι Hp.*Morb*.2.50, etc. (Some derived the name from σέλας, because fishes of this kind emit a phosphorescent light, Gal.6.737.) **-ώδης**, ες, *of* or *like the tribe of* σελάχη, ἰχθύες Arist.*HA* 540ᵇ15, *PA*669ᵇ36, 696ᵇ26, al.

**σελάω** (σέλας), intr., *shine*, Nic.*Th*.691.

**Σελεύκ-ειος**, α, ον, *of Seleucus*, δίδραχμον *IG*11(2).203*B*22 (iii B. C.); name of a month at Ilium, *OGI*212.11 (iv/iii B. C.), *Supp.Epigr*.4.664.3 (i B. C.): Σελεύκεια, τά, *festival of S.*, *IG*12(1).6.3 (Erythrae). **-ίζω**, *side with S.*, Polyaen.8.57. **-ίς**, ίδος, ἡ, a kind of *woman's shoe from Seleucia* in Syria, Poll.7.94, Hsch. II. *a drinking-cup, so named after Seleucus*, Polem.Hist.57, *Inscr.Délos* 443*Bb*72 (ii B. C.), Plu.*Aem*.33. III. σ. τριήρης, a kind of *ship*, Id.*Pomp*.77. IV. the realm of Seleucus, *OGI*219.4 (iii B. C.), 229.2 (iii B. C.), Str.16.2.4. 2. Adj. of part of Cappadocia, Κ. τῆς Σελευκίδος λεγομένης App.*Syr*.55. V. *a bird which eats locusts*, the *Rose-coloured Pastor, Pastor roseus*, Plin.*HN*10.75, Gal.8.397, Ael.*NA*17.19, Zos.1.56.3, Hsch.

**σεληνάζω**, *to be moonstruck*, Man.4.217, prob. cj. for -ιάζω ib.81. **-αίη**, ἡ, Ion. and Ep. for σελήνη, Emp.43, Ar.*Nu*.614, A.R.1.500, *IG*14.1389 i 27, etc., and in later Prose, Luc.*Astr*.3, 17; prov., ἡ Ἀκέσεω σ. 'the Greek Kalends', Herod.3.61; Dor. **σελᾱναία** E.*Ph*.176 (lyr.), Pl.*Cra*.409c. **-αῖος**, α, ον, *lighted by the moon*, σ. νύξ a *moonlight* night, Orac.ap.Hdt.1.62; *of the moon*, αἴγλη

A.R.4.167; τοῦ σεληναίου [κύκλου] D.L.1.24 (v. Diels *Vorsokr.* i p.1). ❀ **-άριον**, τό, *crescent-shaped ornament*, *BGU*162.1 (iii A.D.). **-η**, ἡ, Dor. **σελάνα** [λᾱ] Pi.*O.*10.75, Aeol. **σελάννα** Sapph. 3,53; cf. also σεληναίη:—*the moon*, σ. πλήθουσα the full-*moon*, Il.18.484; σ. ἀεξομένη, ὀλίγη κεράεσσι, Arat.780,733; *a moon's breadth*, measure used by early astronomers, Ptol.*Alm.*9.10; νουμηνία κατὰ σελήνην, i.e. by the *lunar* month, Th.2.28, cf. *SIG*683.44 (ii B.C.); τὰς ἡμέρας κατὰ σ. ἄγειν D.L.1.59, cf. *PHib.*1.27.42 (iii B.C.); πρὸς τὴν σ. ὁρᾶν by *moonlight*, And.1.38, cf. X.*HG*5.1.9; ἐν σελήνῃ Ach.Tat.3.2; ἡ ἐκ τῆς σ. νόσος, = σεληνιασμός, Ael.*NA*14.27; τὴν σ. καθελεῖν, of Thessalian witches, Ar.*Nu.*750, cf. Pl.*Grg.*513a, Sosiph. 1. **b.** *month*, δεκάτῃ σελήνῃ in the tenth *moon*, E.*El.*1126, cf. *Alc.*431, *Tr.*1075 (lyr.); πολλὰς σ. Id.*Hel.*114; τὰς ἡμέρας τῆς σ. Astramps.*Orac.*p.3 H.; ὁρῶν ἄγουσαν τὴν σ. εἰκάδας Ar.*Nu.*17. **2.** *a moon-shaped wheaten cake*, E.*Fr.*350, cf. Alciphr.2.4, Poll.6. 76. **3.** *a round table*, or *tripod*, Ath.11.489d. **4.** name of a plant, Ps.-Plu.*Fluv.*18.5; cf. σελήνιον II. **II.** as fem. pr. n., *Selene, the goddess of the moon* (never in Hom.), Hes.*Th.*371, *h.Merc.*100, etc. (σελήνη (σελάνα, σελάννα) fr. *σελάσ-νᾱ, cf. σέλας.) **-ιάζομαι**, Pass., *to be moonstruck*, i.e. *epileptic*, *Ev.Matt.*4.24, 17.15, Vett.Val.113. 10. **2.** *to be sublunar*, i.e. subject to change and decay, -ομένης τῆς φύσεως Zos.Alch.p.107 B., cf. *Cat.Cod.Astr.*8(3).146. **-ιακός**, ή, όν, *lunar*, ἐνιαυτός Plu.*Num.*18; σφαῖρα Id.2.376d; ζῴδιον *that in which the moon is situated*, Vett.Val.19.22. Adv. -κῶς *by lunar reckoning*, Procl. *in Prm.*p.631 S. **II.** *epileptic*, Alex.Trall.1.15, cf. Orph.*L.*50. **III.** κάνθαρος σ. *a species of beetle* (cf. ἡλιοκάνθαρος), *PMag.Par.*1.2456, 2688. **IV.** distinguishing epith. of a kind of κῦφι, Paul.Aeg.3.28, 7.22. **-ιασμός**, ὁ, *epilepsy*, Vett.Val.127.6, al. **-ιάω**, poet. for σεληνιάζομαι, Ep. part. -ιόωντα (φῦλα βροτῶν) Man.4.546. **-ιεῖα**, τά, the *moon-festival*, Σεληνειήοις (sic) *UPZ*77 i 15 (ii B.C.). **-ιον**, τό, Dim. of σελήνη, *moonlight*, πρὸς τὸ σ. Ath.7.276e; ἅμα τῷ σ. with the *moon's phases*, Arist. *Mir.*834$^b$4; *the outline of the moon*, Thphr.*Sign.*38; *little moon*, D. Chr.7.70. **II.** = γλυκυσίδη, Ps.-Dsc.3.140; cf. σελήνη I. 4. **-ίς**, ίδος, ἡ, *ivory crescent* on the boots of Roman senators, Plu.2. 282a. **2.** *an amulet worn by children*, Hsch. **3.** = σελήνη I. 2, Phot. **-ίσκος**, ὁ, *crescent*-shaped gold ornament worn on the belt, Lyd.*Mag.*2.13. **-ίτης** [ῑ] λίθος, ὁ, *moon*-stone, *selenite*, i.e. foliated sulphate of lime, so called because it was supposed to wax and wane with the moon, Dsc.5.141, Procl.*Sacr.*p.149 B. **2.** οἱ Σεληνῖται *the men in the moon*, Luc.*VH*1.18: fem. -ίτιδες, γυναῖκες Herodor.21 J. **b.** *a people of Arcadia*, Dionys. Chalcidensis ap. Sch.A.R.4.264. ❀ **-ῖτις**, ιδος, ἡ, = χαμαίκισσος, Ps.-Dsc.4.37.

❀ **σεληνό-βλητος**, ον, *moonstruck*, *epileptic*, Sch.Ar.*Nu.*397. **-γονος**, ἡ, or **-γονον**, τό, *peony*, Ps.-Dsc.3.140, Aët.12.63. **-ειδής**, ές, *like the moon*, *crescent-shaped*, Cleom.2.1, Porph.*Sent.*29, Suid. s.v. μηνοειδής. **-πληκτος**, ον, = σεληνόβλητος, Sch.Ar.*Nu.*397, Suid. s.v. βεκκεσέληνος. **-ρύτιον**, τό, = βάτος, Ps.-Dsc.4.37 codd. (-τρόπιον Wellm.). **-τρόπιον**, τό, name of *a mystic plant*, formed after ἡλιοτρόπιον, Procl.*Sacr.*p.148 B. **-φως**, ωτος, τό, *moonlight*, *moonshine*, Chaerem.14.

**σελίαρ**· φοῖνιξ, Hsch. **σελίγνιον, σέλιγνις**, v. σιλίγνιον, σίλιγνις.

**σελῐδηφάγος** [ᾰ], ον, (σελίς) *devouring leaves of books*, of a bookworm, *AP*9.251 (Even.).

**σελίδ-ιον**, τό, Dim. of σελίς, *column of a papyrus* or *mathematical table*, Plb.5.33.3 (v.l.), Ptol.*Geog.*2.1.3, *Alm.*6.7, al., Vett.Val.303. 26, Suid. **-ωμα**, ατος, τό, *a broad plank*, Sch.A.R.1.528.

**σελῑν-ᾶτον**, τό, = Lat. *apiatum*, Philagr.ap.Orib.5.23 tit., *Gloss.* **-ῐνος**, ον, *of celery*, τράπεζας σελινίνους Tz. ad Lyc.1232 (but σελιγνίας *wheaten* (acc. pl.) seems prob.: vv.ll. σελινίας, σελινίνας); σ. [ἔλαιον] cj. in Sor.2.24 (σελήνου cod.). **-ίτης** [ῑτ] οἶνος, ὁ, wine *flavoured with celery*, Dsc.5.74. **II.** **-ῖτις**, ιδος, ἡ, = χαμαίκισσος, Ps.-Dsc.4.125.

**σελῑνοειδής**, ές, *like celery*, Thphr.*HP*3.12.5.

❀ **σέλῑνον**, τό, Aeol. **σέλιννον** Choerob. in *An.Ox.*2.258:—*celery*, *Apium graveolens*, Il.2.776, Od.5.72, Batr.54, Ar.*Nu.*982, Eub.36 (pl.), Thphr.*HP*1.2.2, *CP*6.11.10, Nic.*Th.*649; σελίνου σπέρμα Hdt.4. 71; it had curly leaves, v. οὖλος (B), and grew in marshy spots, Il. l.c., Thphr.*HP*9.11.10; σελίνων στεφανίσκοι Anacr.54, cf. Theoc.3.23, *AP*4.1.31 (Mel.); of the chaplets with which the victors at the Isthmian and Nemean games were crowned, Pi.*O.*13.33; Κορίνθια σ. Id.*N.*4.88, cf. *I.*2.16, *Com.Adesp.*153, D.S.16.79; such chaplets were also hung on tombs, τὸ σ. πένθεσι προσήκει Duris 33 J.: hence persons dangerously ill were said δεῖσθαι τοῦ σ., Plu.2.676d, cf. *Tim.* 26; σελίνων στέφανος νοσοῦντας ἀναιρεῖ Artem.1.77; mostly planted in garden borders (cf. σ. κηπαῖον Dsc.3.64), hence prov., οὐδ' ἐν σελίνῳ σοὐστὶν οὐδ' ἐν πηγάνῳ "'tis scarcely begun yet", Ar.*V.*480. **2.** σ. ἄγριον, = βατράχιον, Dsc.2.175; = σμύρνιον, Ps.-Dsc.3.67; = ἐλεοσέλινον, ib.64. **II.** *pudenda muliebria*, Phot., cf. Sch.Theoc.11. 10. [ῐ only in *AP*7.621.]

**σελῑνόσπερμον**, τό, *celery seed*, *Gp.*8.30.

**Σελῑνοῦς**, οῦντος, ὁ, *Selinus*, in Sicily, Th.6.4:—Adj. **Σελινούντιος**, α, ον, *of Selinus*, Id.8.26, Str.6.2.9; cf. sq. II.

**σελῑνούσιος**, α, ον, *celery-leaved*, κράμβη Eudem.ap.Ath.9.369e, Hsch.; but σελινοῦσσα is cj. **II.** in Thphr.*CP*3.21.2, Σ. πυρός is prob. wheat *of Selinus* in Sicily; γῆ Σ. earth used in adulterating indigo, Dsc.5.155, Plin.*HN*35.46, 194.

❀ **σελῑνοφόρος**, ὁ, *one who conveys celery*, *Jahresh.*18 *Beibl.*287 (Ephesus, i B.C.).

❀ **σελίς**, ίδος, ἡ, *cross-beam* of stone in ceiling-construction, *IG*1$^2$. 374.58, al., 4$^2$(1).103.163, al. (Epid., iv B.C.), *SIG*244 i 39 (Delph., iv B.C.). **2.** *junction*, *cross-piece* left unexcavated in excavation-works, διαλείπων σελίδας δι' ὅλου τοῦ πλάτους *PPetr.*3 p.124 (iii B.C.). **3.** *block* or *sector* of seats in a theatre, *BMus.Inscr.*481*. 157, 440 (Ephesus, i A.D.), Phryn.*PS* p.108 B.: pl., *theatre seats*, *JHS*22.123 (Pisidia). **4.** *rowing-bench*, Poll.1.88, Hsch., Eust. 1041.27. **II.** *column of writing* in a papyrus-roll, σελίδων κανόνισμα φιλόρθιον *AP*6.295 (Phan.); σελίδων σημάντορα πλευρῆς, of a lead pencil, ib.62 (Jul.); κολλήματα ϛε, σελίδες ρλζ *PHerc.*1414 (*Riv. Fil.*37.361); ἀρχόμενος πρώτης σελίδος Batr.1, cf. Lxx *Je.*43(36).23, Plb.5.33.3, *AP*6.227 (Crin.), 7.117 (Phil.), 594 (Jul.), al., *Sammelb.* 5217.10 (ii A.D.), *PFlor.*297.438, al. (vi A.D.): more generally, *writing*, *page*, freq. in pl., Σαπφῷαι..σελίδες Posidipp.ap.Ath.13.596d; σελίδες Μουσῶν *CIG*2237 (Chios): sg., σ. Ἰλιάδος *AP*7.138 (Acerat.); Ὁμηρείη σ. *App.Anth.*3.186. **2.** = πτυχίον, καταβατὸν βιβλίου, Hsch. **b.** ἐν τοῖς βιβλίοις, = τὰ μεταξὺ τῶν παραγραφῶν, Id. s.v. σελίδες; *the unwritten space between two* καταβατά, Suid.

**σελιων** (gen. pl.), dub. sens. in *PMich.Zen.*84.7 (iii B.C.), *POxy.* 520.30 (ii A.D.).

**σέλκες**, = ἀλεκτορίδες, Hsch. s.v. σέρκος.

**σέλλα**, ἡ, *seat*, Lat. *sella*, *POxy.*1146.6 (iv A.D.), Tz.*H.*9.860. **II.** *saddle*, *Hippiatr.*26, Lyd.*Mag.*1.32.

**σελλάστρωσις**, εως, ἡ, *sellisternium*, *Gloss.*

**σελλίζομαι**, Pass., *imitate Aeschines* ὁ Σέλλου, *affect to be wealthy*, Phryn.Com.10; but also σελλίζεσθαι· ψελλίζεσθαι (v. ψελλός), τινὲς δὲ σελλίζει· ἀλαζονεύει, Hsch.

**σελλίον**, τό, Dim. of σέλλα, *PMasp.*6 ii 88 (vi A.D.).

**σελλισμός**, ὁ, = ἀλαζονεία, prob. l. for σελασμός in Theognost. *Can.*11.

**Σελλοί**, οἱ, *Selli*, ancient inhabitants of Dodona, guardians of the oracle of Zeus, ἀμφὶ δὲ Σελλοὶ σοὶ ναίουσ' ὑποφῆται ἀνιπτόποδες χαμαιεῦναι Il.16.234; τῶν ὀρείων καὶ χαμαικοιτῶν..Σελλῶν S.*Tr.*1167; ἐν ἀστρώτῳ πέδῳ εὕδουσι, πηγαῖς δ' οὐχ ὑγραίνουσιν πόδας E.*Fr.*367, cf. Arist.*Mete.*352$^b$2, Str.7.7.10. (Pi. (*Fr.*59) understood ἀμφὶ δέ σ' Ἑλλοί in Il. l.c., but this is an error acc. to Aristarch., cf. Hsch. s.v. Σελλήεις, though countenanced by Id. s.v. Ἕλλα and Ἕλα, where it is apparently derived from Lacon. ἕλλα *seat* (sc. of Zeus at Dodona).)

❀ **σέλμα**, ατος, τό, *the upper planking of a ship*, *deck*, *h.Bacch.*47 (Hom. has only the compd. ἐύσσελμος): metaph., γεμισθεὶς ποτὶ σ. γαστρὸς ἄκρας E.*Cyc.*506: generally, *ship*, Lyc.1217, Archimel.ap.Ath.5. 209c. **2.** pl. σέλματα, *rowing-benches* (in Hom. ζυγά), Archil.4, A.*Pers.*358, *Ag.*1442, S.*Ant.*717, E.*Or.*242. **3.** generally, *seat*, *throne*, A.*Ag.*183 (lyr.). **II.** any *timberwork*, σέλματα πύργων, prob. *scaffolds behind the parapet*, on which the defenders of the wall stood, Id.*Th.*32. **2.** *logs of building timber*, Str.5.2.5.

**σελμίς**, ίδος, ἡ, *angler's noose made of hair* (ὁρμιὰ τριχίνη), Hsch. **2.** = ἴκρια, Id.:—also **σελμῶν**· σανίδων, Id. **σέλπιδες**· σχεδίαι, Id. **σέλπον**, τό, = σίλφιον, Id.

**σέλω**, Lacon. for θέλω, Ar.*Lys.*1080.

**σεμαλία**· ῥάκη, Ἀργεῖοι, Hsch.

**σεμέλη**· τράπεζα, παρὰ δὲ Φρυνίχῳ (Phryn.Trag.23) ἑορτή, Hsch.

**σεμεληγενέτης**, ου, ὁ, *born of Semele*, epith. of Dionysus, *AP*9. 524.

**σέμελος**, ὁ, Lacon. for κοχλίας, Apollas ap.Ath.2.63d, cf. Hsch.: **σεμελοιρίδαι**· οἱ ἄνευ κελύφους, οὓς ἔνιοι λίψακας, Id.

**σεμίαρ**· χιτών, ἢ πλὰξ ἀντὶ στέγης ἐπικείμενος, ὡς Λάκωνες, Hsch.

**σεμιδάλιν**, τό, v. sq.

❀ **σεμίδᾱλις** [ῐ], εως or ιος (εος in Archestr.*Fr.*4.14), ἡ, *the finest wheaten flour*, Hp.*Vict.*2.42, *Acut.*(*Sp.*)53, Ar.*Fr.*412, Hermipp.63. 22, Stratt.2 (who has gen. -ιδος), Lxx *Ge.*18.6, al., *Apoc.*18.13, etc.; σεμιδάρεως is an error in *POxy.*736.82 (i A.D.):—hence **σεμῐδᾱλίτης** [ῑ] ἄρτος, ὁ, *bread made of* σεμίδαλις, Hp.*Vict.*2.42, *PPetr.*3 p.179 (iii B.C.), Diph.Siph.ap.Ath.3.115c, Trypho ib.109c, Ath.Med.ap.Orib. 1.2.2, etc.:—also **σεμιδάλιν** (= -ιον), τό, *PLond.*2.190.45 (iii A.D.), *Gloss.* (Cf. Assyr. *samīdu*, Aram. *semīdā* in same sense.)

❀ **σεμνεῖον**, τό, (σεμνός) in Egypt, οἴκημα ἱερόν, ὃ καλεῖται σ. καὶ μοναστήριον, Ph.2.475, cf. Suid., *Gloss.*

**σεμνηγορ-έω**, = σεμνολογέω, περὶ τῆς χώρας Ph.2.164; τὰ καλά ib. 154; τι Hld.9.9. **-ία**, ἡ, = σεμνολογία, Timo 57.

**σεμνο-βάσκᾰνος**, ον, *jealous of what is majestic*, Τύχη *IG*12(7).52 (Arcesine). **-δότειρα**, ἡ, *giver of glorious gifts*, Φήμα B.2. 1. **-θεοι**, οἱ, *Druids*, Arist.*Fr.*35. **-κομπέω**, *vaunt*, *boast highly*, A.*Fr.*124 (prob.). **-κοπέω**, *affect a grand style*, ὥσπερ ῥήτορες Phld.*Rh.*2 p.159 S. **-κόπος**, ον, *affecting grandeur*, Id.*Vit.*p.36 J.

**σεμνολογ-έω**, *speak solemnly*, *use fine phrases*, ὡς οὐκ εἰδόσι Aeschin. 2.94; ἀμφί or περί τινος App.*Hisp.*18, *BC*1.9; τι περί τινος Luc.*Sacr.* 5:—also Med. σεμνολογέομαι, *talk in solemn phrases*, D.19.255; νεανικῶς σ. τι Luc.*Am.*50; τὸν Θησέα καὶ τὰ Μηδικὰ σ. Plu.*Sull.* 13. ❀ **-ημα**, ατος, τό, = sq., *pride*, S.E.*P.*3.201. **II.** *anything that one may be proud of*, τὰ πάτρια σ. D.C.50.27, cf. Him.*Ecl.*16. 1. **-ία**, ἡ, *boasting*, Chrysipp.*Stoic.*3.50; *impressiveness*, D.H. *Comp.*11, *Th.*23, 50, App.*Syr.*10. **-ικός**, ή, όν, *of* or *for grave*, *solemn speech*, in Adv. -κῶς, Suid. **-ος** (parox.), ὁ, *one who speaks solemnly* or *affectedly*, D.18.133. Adv. -γως App.*Mith.*70.

**σεμνό-μαντις**, εως, ὁ, *grave and reverend seer*, S.*OT*556. **-μῡθέω**, = σεμνολογέω, E.*Hipp.*490, *Andr.*234, Phld.*Vit.*p.36 J. (dub.), Ph. 1.151:—also Med. σεμνομυθέομαι, ib.233. **-μῡθία**, ἡ, = σεμνολογία, Suid. s.v. Ἀδάμ.

**σεμνόν**, τό, = ἄγνος, Ps.-Dsc.1.103.

**σεμνο-πᾰνοῦργος**, ὁ, *solemn rascal*, Anon.*in EN*200.8. **-παρά-σῖτος**, ον, *pompous parasite*, Alex.116. **-ποιέω**, *make august, magnify*, τὸ θεῖον Str.10.3.9, J.*AJ*16.5.3; τὰ τῆς πόλεως ἔθιμα *Inscr.Prien.*112.94:—Pass., -ποιεῖται τὸ πῦρ *is reverenced*, Eust.748.49. **-ποιία**, ἡ, *worship*, ἡ ἐπ' ἀσέμνοις πράγμασι σ. Ph.2.194. **-ποτος**, ον, *costly to drink*, of Lesbian wine, Antiph.174. ❀ **-πρέπεια**, ἡ, *grave, solemn bearing*, D.L.8.36. ❀ **-πρεπής**, ές, *solemn-looking, dignified*, D.C.42.34, D.L.8.11 (both Sup.); τὸ σ., = σεμνοπρέπεια, D.C.68.31. Adv. -πῶς Hdn.2.10.3. **-προσωπέω**, *assume a grave, solemn countenance*, ἐπί τινι Ar.*Nu.*363, cf. *AP*11.382.14 (Agath.).

**σεμνός**, ή, όν, (σέβομαι) *revered, august, holy*: I. prop. of gods, e.g. Demeter, *h.Cer.*1, 486; Hecate, Pi.*P.*3.79; Thetis, Id.*N.*5.25; Apollo, A.*Th.*800; Poseidon, S.*OC*55; Pallas Athena, ib.1090 (lyr.); at Athens the Erinyes were specially the σεμναὶ θεαί, Id.*Aj.*837, *OC* 90, 458, Ar.*Eq.*1312, *Th.*224, Th.1.126, Autocl.ap.Arist.*Rh.*1398$^{b}$26; or simply Σεμναί, A.*Eu.*383 (lyr.), 1041 (lyr.), E.*Or.*410; τὸ σ. ὄνομα their name, S.*OC*41; σ. βάθρον the threshold of their temple, ib.100; σ. τέλη their rites, ib.1050 (lyr.). 2. of things divine, ὄργια σ. *h.Cer.*478, S.*Tr.*765; θέμεθλα δίκης Sol.4.14; ὑγίεια Simon.70; θυσία Pi.*O.*7.42; σ. ἄντρον the cave of Cheiron, Id.*P.*9.30, cf. *O.*5.18; σ. δόμος the temple of Apollo, Id.*N.*1.72; παιάν A.*Pers.*393; σέλμα σ. ἡμένων, of the Olympian gods, Id.*Ag.*183 (lyr.); σ. ἔργα, of the gods, Id.*Supp.*1037 (lyr.); μυστήρια S.*Fr.*804, E.*Hipp.*25; τέρμων οὐρανοῦ ib.746; σ. βίος *devoted to the gods*, Id.*Ion* 56; σεμνὰ φθέγγεσθαι, = εὔφημα, A.*Ch.*109 (v.l.), cf. Ar.*Nu.*315, 364; ἦ πού τι σ. ἔστιν ὃ ξυναμπέχεις; A.*Pr.*521; τὸ σ. *holiness*, D.21.126. II. of human or half-human beings, *reverend, august*, ἐν θρόνῳ σεμνῷ σεμνὸν θωκέοντα Hdt.2.173, cf. A.*Ch.*975, E.*Supp.*384, al.; σ. θάλος Ἀλκαϊδᾶν Pi.*O.*6.68; τὸ σχῆμα σεμνὸς κοὐ ταπεινός E.*Fr.*688; αἱ φαυλότεραι ..παρὰ τὰς σεμνὰς καθεδοῦνται beside *the great ladies*, Ar.*Ec.*617, cf. Isoc.3.42; οἱ σεμνότατοι ἐν ταῖς πόλεσιν Pl.*Phdr.*257d; ἄνθρωπος οὐ σ., i.e. a nobody, Ar.*Fr.*52D.; opp. χαῦνος, Pl.*Sph.*227b (Comp.); opp. κομψός, X.*Oec.*8.19; σεμνὸς οὐ προσώπου συναγωγαῖς ἀλλὰ βίου κατασκευαῖς Isoc.9.44: c. dat., *revered by*.., σ. πόλει *Riv.Fil.*57.379 (Crete); also, *worthy of respect, honourable*, 1*Ep.Ti.*3.8, 11, *Ep.Phil.*4.8. 2. of human things, *august, stately, majestic*, θᾶκοι A.*Ag.*519; ἱμάτια Ar.*Pl.*940, cf. *Ra.*1061 (Comp.); ταφή X.*HG*3.3.1; πράγματα, ἔργα, Ar.*V.*1472, Isoc.12.213; σεμνοτέραν τὴν πόλιν ποιῆσαι Is.5.45; οἰκία τοῦ γείτονος οὐδὲν σεμνοτέρα D.3.26, cf. 29; ψεύδεσι [τοῦ Ὁμήρου] σ. ἔπεστί τι Pi.*N.*7.22; λεγόντων..περὶ αὐτοῦ σ. λόγους Hdt.7.6; of Tragedy, Pl.*Grg.*502b; of style, Arist.*Po.*1458$^{a}$21, cf. *Rh.*1404$^{b}$8 (Comp.); of certain metres, ib.1408$^{b}$32; ἐπὶ τὸ σ. μιμεῖσθαι to imitate it in its *noble qualities*, Pl.*Lg.*814e; σ. τι λέγειν, πράσσειν, Id.*R.*382b, E.*Tr.*447; σεμνὰ ἄττα μεμαθηκότας Pl.*Ep.*342a; οὐδὲν σ. nothing *very wonderful*, Arist.*EN*1146$^{a}$15; so τί ἂν εἴη τὸ σ. (sc. τοῦ νοῦ); Id.*Metaph.*1074$^{b}$18; *worthy of respect*, E.*IA*996; σεμνόν ἐστι, c. inf., 'tis a *noble, fine* thing to.., Pl.*Cra.*392a, Isoc.*Ep.*9.5. 3. metaph., σ. βρῶμα a *noble* dish, Aristopho 7, cf. Archestr.*Fr.*20; σ. ὀσμή Mnesim.4.60, etc. III. in bad sense, *proud, haughty*, τὰ σέμν' ἔπη S.*Aj.*1107; σεμνότερος καὶ φοβερώτερος And.4.18; τὸ σ. *haughty reserve*, E.*Hipp.*93, cf. *Med.*216. 2. in contempt or irony, *solemn, pompous*, σ. καὶ ἅγιον Pl.*Sph.*249a; τί σεμνὸν καὶ πεφροντικὸς βλέπεις; look *grave and solemn*, E.*Alc.*773; τὸ σ. ἄγαν καὶ τραγικόν Arist.*Rh.*1406$^{b}$7: very freq. in Com., ἀνελκτοῖς ὀφρύσι σεμνός Cratin.355; ὡς σ. οὑπίτριπτος how *grand* the rascal is! Ar.*Pl.*275; ὡς σ. ὁ κατάρατος Id.*Ra.*178; λόγοι σ. Id.*V.*1175; σεμνὸς σεμνῶς χλανίδ' ἕλκων Ephipp.19. IV. Adv. -νῶς A.*Supp.*193, E.*Ion* 1133, Ar.*V.*585, etc.; ὥσπερ κοχλίας σεμνῶς ἐπηρκὼς τὰς ὀφρῦς, of Plato, Amphis 13; σεμνῶς κεκοσμημένος X.*Cyr.*6.1.6, etc.; περὶ εὐτελῶν σ. λέγειν Arist.*Rh.*1408$^{a}$13: Comp. -ότερον X.*Mem.*3.5.20: Sup. -ότατα Plb.15.31.7.

**σεμνό-στομος**, ον, *solemnly spoken, haughty*, in sarcastic sense, μῦθος A.*Pr.*953. Adv. Comp. -ώτερον Tz.*H.*6.35. **-της**, ητος, ἡ, *solemnity, dignity*, σεμνότητ' ἔχει σκότος E.*Ba.*486, cf. X.*Cyr.*8.3.1, Isoc.12.242, Pl.*Mx.*235b; ἡ σ. τοῦ ῥήματος D.*Prooem.*45; [τῆς λέξεως] Arist.*Rh.*1408$^{b}$35; ἡ τοῦ τόπου σ. *Milet.*1(9).368; also of persons, *seriousness, dignity*, ἐπὶ τῆς σ. αὐθάδεις ὑπολαμβάνεσθαι D.61.14, cf. Arist.*Rh.*1391$^{a}$28, *Ep.Tit.*2.7, 1*Ep.Ti.*2.2: in pl., σ. οὐκ ἀληθιναὶ ἀλλὰ πεπλασμέναι Isoc.6.98. II. of a girl, *reserve* or *shyness*, E.*IA* 1344. **-τῖμος**, ον, *reverenced with awe*, A.*Ch.*356 (lyr.), *Eu.*833. ❀ **-τροπία**, ἡ, *gravity of manner*, Ptol.*Tetr.*206. **-τῡφία**, ἡ, (τῦφος) *empty solemnity, grave airs*, M.Ant.9.29.

**σεμν-όω**, *make solemn* or *grand, exalt, magnify*, τὰ περὶ Κῦρον Hdt.1.95; ἄλλως αὐτὰ σ. Id.3.16:—Med., *hold the head high, give oneself airs*, dub. cj. in Call.Com.12. **-ύνω**, = foreg., *exalt, magnify*, τὸν σαυτοῦ θεόν Pl.*Phlb.*28b; τῷ ῶ Id.*Phdr.*244d; ἑαυτούς Id.*Phlb.*28c, cf. *Plt.*263d; ὑμᾶς D.19.238; τὰ παρ' αὑτοῖς Id.23.212; ταῦτα περὶ ἑωυτὸν ἐσέμνυνε thus *did he throw a cloak of majesty* about himself, Hdt.1.99. II. Med. with aor. ἐσεμνυνάμην, *to be grave, solemn*, esp. *affect a grave and solemn air*, E.*Fr.*924 (lyr.); μηδ' αὐθάδως σεμνυνόμενος χαλέπαινε Ar.*Ra.*1020, cf. *Av.*727; δικανικὴ καὶ ἰατρικὴ σεμνύνονται Pl.*R.*405a; πρὸς σέ Id.*Thg.*130b: *to be reserved*, of a girl, E.*IA*996: with part., σεμνύνεσθαι ὥς τι ὄντε Pl.*Phdr.*243a; οὐ σεμνύνεται ἐσχηματισμένη ὡς ὑπερήφανόν τι διαπραττομένη Id.*Grg.*511d; σ. πολίτης ὤν Luc.*Patr.Enc.*2; also σ. ἐπὶ πέντε καὶ εἴκοσι καταλόγῳ προγόνων *to be proud* of.., *pique oneself* on it, Pl.*Tht.*175a, cf. Isoc.16.29, D.19.235; ἔν τινι Id.18.258: also c. dat., ταῖς ἐξουσίαις Sosiph.3.2; τῷ σπανίως δρᾶσθαι σ. X.*Ages.*9.1, cf. 2, Hdn.1.5.5: rarely c. acc., σ. τὴν μοιχείαν Id.5.7.3: c. dupl. acc., μητρόπολιν Ὑπάταν Hld.2.34; σ. διότι Plb.9.35.1. **-ωμα**, ατος, τό, *dignity, majesty*, Epicur.*Ep.*1 p.28 U., echoed in *SIG*834.19 (Epist. Plotinae, ii A.D.), cf. Epicur.(?) *Oxy.*215 i 30: in pl., *grand words*, Eust.18.25.

**σέμπαδα**· ὑποδήματα, Hsch. (Cf. σάμβαλα.)

**σεμσέλλιον, σεμψέλλιον**, v. συμψέλια.

**σενδούκη**, ἡ, Dim. **σενδούκιον**, τό, = κιβώτιον or σκευάριον, Sch. Ar.*Pl.*711, 809.

**σεννίον**, τό, dub. sens. (connected with *winnowing*, cf. σινίον), *PRyl.*139.9 (i A.D.).

**Σεξτίλιος** [τῐ], ον, = Lat. *Sextilis*, Σ. μήν *August*, D.H.9.25, Lyd.*Mens.*4.71.

**σέο**, v. σύ. **σέος**, v. σέως.

**σεπτάς**, άδος, ἡ, (ἑπτά, σέβομαι) = ἑπτάς, in Pythagorean philosophy, *Theol.Ar.*43.

**Σεπτέμβριος**, α, ον, = Lat. *Septembris*, D.H.6.49, etc.

**σεπτ-εύω**, (σεπτός) = σέβομαι, Hsch. **-ήρια**· καθαρμός, ἔκθυσις, Id. (Perh. f.l. for στεπτήρια.) **-ικός**, ή, όν, *reverential*, of words, Id. s.v. ἠθεῖος, Suid. s.v. πάππα. **-ός**, ή, όν, *august*, ἵησι σ. Νεῖλος ῥέος A.*Pr.*812: in late Prose, D.C.53.16, *Cod.Just.*1.5.16.

**σερᾱπιάς** (also **σᾰρᾱπιάς** Ps.-Dsc.3.127), άδος, ἡ, *Salep, Orchis longicruris*, Dsc.3.127, Plin.*HN*26.95.

**Σέρᾱπις, Σεραπεῖον**, v. Σάραπις.

**Σεραφείμ**, οἱ, Hebr. *Seraphim*, Lxx *Is.*6.2.

**σεργοί**· ἔλαφοι, Hsch. (Fort. Lat. *cervi*.) **σερήτιον**· ἡ σερίς, Id.

**σέρῐς**, ἡ, gen. ιδος (εως *Gp.*12.28 tit.), pl. σέρεις Diog.*Ep.*32.1 and 3:—*endive* or *chicory* (σ. ἀγρία, = *Chicory, Cichorium Intybus*, σ. κηπευτή, = *Endive, Cichorium Endivia*, Dsc.2.132), Epich.161, *AP* 11.413 (Ammian.); cf. πικρίς I. 2.

**σέρῑφον**, τό, a kind of *wormwood*, = σαντονικόν (q.v.), Dsc.*Prooem.* 8, Id.3.23, Gal.11.804. II. γραῦς σέριφος or σερίφη, an insect, = μάντις II, a name used for *an old maid*, Zen.2.94, Suid.

**σερός**· χθές, Ἠλεῖοι, Hsch. **σέρτης**· γέρανος, Πολυρρήνιοι, Id.

**σέρφος**, ὁ, a small winged insect, prob. a kind of *gnat* or *winged ant*, Ar.*V.*352 (ubi v. Sch.), *Av.*82, 569, Nicopho 1, dub. in Phld.*Mort.*34: prov., ἔνεστι κἀν μύρμηκι κἀν σέρφῳ χολή 'even the gnat has its sting', Sch.Ar.*Av.*82, *V.*352, cf. *AP*10.49 (Pall.):—written **συρφός** in Hsch.

**σεσᾰρυῖα, σεσᾱρώς**, v. σαίρω (A).

**σέσελις**, εως, ἡ, *hartwort, Tordylium officinale*, Arist.*HA*611$^{a}$18, Plu.2.383e:—also **σέσελι**, τό, Hp.*Acut.*23, Alex.127.8, Thphr.*HP* 9.15.5; σ. κρητικόν Dsc.3.54; other kinds, σ. μασσαλιωτικόν *Massilian hartwort, Seseli tortuosum*, ib.53; σ. αἰθιοπικόν *hare's ear, Bupleurum fruticosum*, ibid.; σ. ἐν Πελοποννήσῳ *golden cow-parsnip, Malabaila aurea*, ibid.; σ. Κύπριον, = κίκι, Id.4.161.

**σεσερῖνος**, ὁ, a sea-fish, Arist.*Fr.*294.

**σεσηρότως**, Adv. of σέσηρα (σαίρω (A)), *with a grin*, Poll.3.132.

**σέσῑλος**, ὁ, *snail*, [Epich.] ap.Ath.2.63c; σέσιλον ἢ **σεσέλιτα** καλοῦσι Dsc.2.9:—also **σέσηλος**, Hsch.; cf. σέμελος.

**σεσοβημένως**, Adv. *hurriedly, excitedly*, Antyll.ap.Orib.10.3.9 (ἐσοβ- codd.), Anon. *in Tht.*10.34.

**σεσοφισμένως**, Adv. *cunningly*, X.*Cyn.*13.5.

**σέσοψ**· ποιὸς ἰχθῦς, Hsch.

**σεσσιών**, ῶνος, ἡ, (Lat. *sessio*) *seat* in a carriage, *Edict.Diocl.*15.7.

**σέσυφος**· πανοῦργος, Hsch.

**σεσωφρονισμένως**, Adv. pf. part. Pass. *temperately*, A.*Supp.*724.

**σέτω**, Lacon. for θέτω (v. τίθημι), Ar.*Lys.*1081.

**σεῦ**, Ion. for σοῦ, v. σύ. **σεῦα**, v. σεύω.

❀ **Σευήρεια**, τά, *games in honour of Severus*, *IG*3.129 (iii A.D.).

**Σευίδαι**, οἱ, *attendants on Dionysus* (ἀπὸ τοῦ σεύειν), Corn.*ND*30.

**σεῦμαι**, v. σεύω.

**Σευτλαῖος**, ὁ, (σεῦτλον) *Beety*, name of a frog in Batr.209.

**σεύτλιον, σευτλίς**, ἡ, v. τευτλ-.

**σευτλομόλοχον**, τό, *leaf-beet, Beta cicla*, *Gp.*12.1.4.

**σεῦτλον**, τό, Ion. and Hellenistic for τεῦτλον (q.v.).

❀ **σεύω**, B.17.10, Opp.*H.*2.445, Q.S.7.487, Ep. inf. σευέμεν A.R.2.296; with σ doubled after the augm., as always in Hom. (exc. in ἐξεσύθη (Zenod. and most codd. for -λύθη) Il.5.293): Ep. impf. σεύεσκε Q.S.2.353: aor. ἔσσευα Il.5.208; Ep. also σεῦα 20.189; 3 sg. subj. σεύῃ 11.293:—Med., aor. subj. σεύωνται (v.l. -ονται) ib.415: impf. or aor. ἐσσεύοντο 2.808: aor. ἐσσεύαντο 11.549 (v.l. -οντο); Ep. σεύατο 6.505:—Pass., B.*Scol.Oxy.*1361 *Fr.*1.7: aor. ἐσύθην [ῠ] E.*Hel.*1302 (lyr.) (ἐξ- Il., v. supr.). ἐσσύθην S.*Aj.*294, also σύθην A.*Pr.*135 (lyr.); subj. 3 sg. συθῇ Hp.*Mul.*1.36, 2.138; part. συθείς A.*Th.*941, *Pers.*866, S.*OC*119 (all lyr.); in iamb., Id.*OT*446: pf. (with pres. sense) ἔσσῠμαι Il.13.79; part. ἐσσύμενος (not -μένος) 11.554, al., Adv. ἐσσῠμένως 3.85, al.: σεσύανται· ὡρμήκασιν, Hsch.: poet. aor. 2 ἐσσύμην [ῠ], 2 sg. ἔσσυο Il.16.585, Od.9.447; 3 sg. ἔσσῠτο, Ep. σύτο Il.21.167, ἐπ-έσυτο E.*Hel.*1162, *Ph.*1065 (both lyr.); part. σύμενος A.*Ag.*747, *Eu.*1007, cf. 786, 816 (all lyr.): also σεῦται, 3 sg. pres. Pass., S.*Tr.*645 (σοῦται is prob. cj.), σοῦμαι (Dor. σῶμαι Epil.3), σοῦνται A.*Pers.*25 (anap.); imper. σοῦ Ar.*V.*209, σούσθω S.*Aj.*1414 (anap.), σοῦσθε A.*Th.*31, Ar.*V.*458, etc.; inf. σοῦσθαι Plu.2.362c: Hsch. cites imper. σύθι or σῦθι:—poet. Verb (also in Ion. Prose, Hp. and Aret. (v. infr.)), *put in quick motion, drive*: esp. 1. *hunt, chase*, Διωνύσοιο τιθήνας σεῦε κατ' ἠγάθεον Νυσήϊον Il.6.133; *drive away*, σεῦεν κύνας ἄλλυδις ἄλλον πυκνῇσιν λιθάδεσσιν Od.14.35; σεύοντ' (3 pl.) ἀγέλας βίᾳ B.17.10: more freq. in Med., ὡς δ' ὅτε κάπριον ἀμφὶ κύνες σεύωνται Il.11.415, cf.

549, 3.26; ὥς τ᾽..ἄγριον αἶγα ἐσσεύαντο κύνες 15.272, cf. 20.148: metaph., σ. κακότητα ἀπὸ καρήνου *h.Hom.*8.12; θάμβος με σ. Orph.*L.* 531. 2. *set on, let loose at*, ὅτε πού τις θηρητὴρ κύνας..σεύῃ ἐπ᾽ ἀγροτέρῳ συΐ Il.11.293. 3. *drive* or *hurry away to* or *from a place*, Αἰνείαν δ᾽ ἔσσευεν ἀπὸ χθονός 20.325; ἵππους ἐκ πεδίοιο 15.681; [τινὰ] κατ᾽ Ἰδαίων ὀρέων 20.189: c. inf., [ἡμιόνους] σεῦαν ποταμὸν παρὰ δινήεντα τρώγειν..*drove*, Od.6.89. 4. *set in swift motion*, ὅλμον δ᾽ ὣς ἔσσευε [Πείσανδρον] κυλίνδεσθαι *sped* him so that he rolled, Il.11. 147; στρόμβον δ᾽ ὣς ἔσσευε βαλών 14.413; also αἷμ᾽ ἔσσευα *shed* blood, 5.208; v. infr. II. 1. II. Pass. and Med., *to be put in quick motion*, and so, *run, rush, dart* or *shoot along*, ἐπὶ τεύχεα to arms, 2.808; ἐπὶ κοῖτον Od.14.456; νέρθε δὲ ποσσὶν ἔσσυμαι Il.13.79; σεύατ᾽ ἔπειτ᾽ ἀνὰ ἄστυ 6.505; σεύατ᾽ ἔπειτ᾽ ἐπὶ κῦμα Od.5.51, cf. Il.14.227; κατ᾽ ἀμαξιτόν 22.146; παρ᾽ ἐρινεόν 11.167; ἀμφ᾽ Ὀδυσῆα ib.419; ἰθὺς Λυκίων 16. 585; διὰ σπέος Od.9.447; so in Trag., ἐκτόπιος συθεὶς *having gone, departed*, opp. παρών, S.*OC*119; ἀφ᾽ ἑστίας A.*Pers.*866; ἐκ ναοῦ E.*IT* 1294; σύθην δ᾽ ἀπέδιλος ὄχῳ πτερωτῷ A.*Pr.*135; κατὰ γᾶς σύμεναι Id. *Eu.*1007, cf. *Ag.*747; ἀνὰ νάπη E.*Hel.*1302; of things, αἷμα σύτο *gushed out*, Il.21.167; ψυχὴ κατ᾽..ὠτειλὴν ἔσσυτο 14.519; ἐκ πυρὸς συθεὶς σίδηρος A.*Th.*941; ἐσύθη ἔξω πῦον Aret.*SD*1.9; so of *flux*, ἣν πολλὰ συθῇ Hp.*Mul.*1.36; of the *eruption* of disease, ὅταν τὰ παρέοντα συθῇ νοσήματα ib.2.138. 2. c. inf., *hasten, speed*, ὅτε σεύαιτο διώκειν when *he hasted to* pursue, Il.17.463; ὄφρα ὕλη σεύαιτο καήμεναι that the wood *might begin* (cf. Engl. *start*) to burn, 23.198, cf. 210; ἔσσυται κελαδῆσαι *is eager* to sing of, Pi.*I.*8(7).67. 3. metaph., *to be eager, have longings*, θυμὸς ἔσσυται Od.10.484; esp. in pf. part. ἐσσύμενος used as Adj., v. sub voce. (σεϝ-: σῡ-, from I.-Eur. *k̑yew-*: *kyū-*, cf. Skt. *cyávati* 'set in motion', part. Pass. *cyutás*:—σοῦμαι, etc., perh. contr. fr. *σοομαι (= *σοόομαι, fr. σό(ϝ)ος, q.v.).)

**σεφθείς**, v. σέβομαι. **σέω**, Dor. for θέω. II. etym. of σύω and σόος, A.D.*Adv.*198.11. **σέων**, gen. pl. of σής.

**σέως**, ὁ, = σεισμός, dub. in Alc.26; v.l. σέος.

**σεωυτοῦ**, fem. σεωυτῆς, etc., Ion. for σεαυτοῦ (q.v.). **σῆ·** τρέχε, Hsch. (Lacon., = θεῖ). **σηδόν·** γλαυκὸν ἔλαιον, Id. **σηδρακεῖ·** κτυπεῖ, Id.

**σήθω**, *PCair.Zen.*761.3,4 (iii B.C.), Asclep.ap.Gal.13.244,342, *BGU*952.2 (ii/iii A.D.): aor. part. σήσας Hp.*Mul.*1.64:—Pass., aor. ἐσήσθην or ἐσήθην, Aret.*CA*1.4, *Gp.*3.7.2 (interpol. in Dsc.2.96): pf. σέσησμαι Hp.*Morb.*3.11, *Int.*3, *Nat.Mul.*34, Dsc.1.68; cf. ἐττημένος (also ἐσσημένος *Inscr.Délos* 500*A* 9 (iii B.C.)):—*sift, bolt*, ll.cc.

**σῆκα**, Adv. *into the fold* (σηκός), a shepherd's call to his flocks, Hsch.

**σηκάζω**, (σηκός) *shut up in a pen*, καί νύ κε σήκασθεν (for ἐσηκάσθησαν) κατὰ Ἴλιον ἠΰτε ἄρνες Il.8.131; ὥσπερ ἐν αὐλῷ σηκασθέντες X.*HG* 3.2.4; σηκάζειν πυρούς τε καὶ ἀστάχυας κατ᾽ ἀλωάς Orph.*Fr.*268.

**σήκαλιν** (acc. sg.), perh. = Lat. *secale*, Aët.15.11.

**σηκηκόρος**, ὁ, ἡ, = σηκοκόρος, cj. for βόκορος in Poll.7.151, v.l. in Suid.

® **σηκ-ίς**, ίδος, ἡ, (σηκός) *female house-slave, housekeeper*, Ar.*V.*768, Pherecr.10 (where however it seems to be a pr. n.), cf. Poll.3.76, Phot. **-ίτης** [ῑ], ου, Dor. **σᾱκίτας**, α, ὁ, *kept in the fold, weaned*, of a young lamb, Theoc.1.10, *Ep.*4.18; ἔριφος Longus 3.18.

**σηκο-βάτης** [ᾰ], ου, ὁ, a religious official, θεοῦ Ἑρμανούβιδος *BCH* 37.94 (Thessalonica). **-κόρος**, ὁ, ἡ, (κορέω) *cleaner of a stable, byre*, or *pen, herdsman*, Od.17.224, Poll.7.151, Suid.; cf. σηκηκόρος. II. *chapel-keeper*, Zonar.

**σηκολόαι·** λῃσταί, Hsch.

® **σηκ-ός** (neut. pl. σῆκα (q.v.) as Adv.), Dor. **σᾱκός** (*IG*4²(1).102.29 (Epid., iv B.C.)), ὁ, *pen, fold*, esp. for rearing lambs, kids, calves, Od. 9.219,227,319,439, 10.412, Il.18.589, Hes.*Op.*787; εἰς τὸν σ. οἴσουσιν, metaph. of young children, Pl.*R.*460c; σηκὸν νομίζειν τὸ τεῖχος Id. *Tht.*174e; σ. δράκοντος the dragon's *den*, E.*Ph.*1010; οἱ πέρδικες δύο ποιοῦνται τῶν ᾠῶν σ. *nests*, Arist.*HA*564ᵃ21. II. *sacred enclosure, precinct*, Hdt.4.62 (v.l.), S.*Ph.*1328, E. (v. infr.), *IG*l.c., *SIG*247*K*¹ 1155 (Delph., iv B.C.), Maiist.23, Lxx 2*Ma.*14.33; ὁ σ. τοῦ ἱεροῦ *OGI* 702.4 (Egypt, ii A.D.): acc. to Ammon.*Diff.*p.94 V. (cf. Call.*Fr.*38 P. (ap. Sch.Oxy.Th.2.17), Plu.*Cim.*8, *Epigr.Gr.*781.7 (Cnidus)), the σηκός was sacred to a hero, the ναός to a god, a distinction not observed (v. Poll.1.6) by the Poets, cf. *Trag.Adesp.*424, E.*Ph.*1751 (lyr.), *Rh.*501, with *Ion* 300, etc. 2. *sepulchre, burial-place*, enclosed and consecrated, ἀνδρῶν ἀγαθῶν ὅδε σ. Simon.4.6, cf. *TAM* 2(1).207.6,208.7 (Sidyma). 3. *library building*, Gal.15.24 (pl.). 4. *bedroom*, σ. ἐπίπεδος Aret.*CA*2.2. III. *stump of an old olive-tree*, περὶ τοῦ σ., title of speech by Lysias. IV. *weight*, in the balance, Eust.1625.26. **-όω**, *weigh, balance*, *IG*2². 1407.41, Plu.2.928d (Pass.). II. Dor. σάκωσε· κατέκλεισεν, Hsch. **-ύλη**, ἡ, = σηκίς, Ael.Dion.*Fr.*297, Hsch., Phot. **-ώδης**, ες, (σηκός II) *chapel-like*, Ael.*NA*10.31. ® **-ωμα**, Dor. **σάκωμα** [ᾰ], ατος, τό, (σηκόω) *a weight in the balance, standard weight*, *IG*2².1013. 8, Hyp.*Fr.*271 (ap.Poll.4.172); σμικρὸν τὸ σὸν σ. προστίθης slight is the *weight* that you throw into the scale, E.*Heracl.*690; σ. μολίβδινα leaden *weights* or *counterpoises*, Plb.8.5.9; τὸ κατόπιν σ. τῆς προβολῆς, of the spear, Id.18.29.3; *makeweight*, Id.18.24.5. b. a standard *measure*, [κρότωνος] *PCair.Zen.*670.7 (iii B.C.); σ. σιτηροῦ ἡμεδίμνου *SIG*²588 (Delos, i B.C.); *jar* or *measure* of wine, *POxy.*1720.5 (iv A.D.), 1896.19 (vi A.D.), *PLond.ined.*2115 (vi A.D.). 2. *momentum*, Ael.*Tact.*13.2. 3. *return, recompense*, Phalar.*Ep.*134. II. = σηκός II, *sacred enclosure*, E.*El.*1274, *IG*3.1979. **-ωτήρ**, ῆρος, ὁ, (σηκόω) *the beam of a balance*, Hsch. **-ωτός**, *loculatus*, *Gloss.*

® **σηλαγγεύς**, έως, ὁ, *gold refiner*, Agatharch.27,28; cf. σάλαγξ and σῆραγξ II.

**σηλία**, ἡ, = Att. τηλία, *AB*382.

**σήλια·** τὰ μικρὰ πιθάρια (i.e. Lat. *seria*), καὶ σκεῦος ἀρτοποιητικόν, Hsch.

® **σῆμα**, Dor. **σᾶμα** *Berl.Sitzb.*1927.161 (Cyrene), etc.: ατος, τό:—*sign, mark, token*, Il.10.466, 23.326, Od.19.250, etc.; of the star on a horse's forehead, Il.23.455; ἥβης σήματα γεινομένης Sol.27.4; νέφος σ. χειμῶνος Archil.54; esp. 1. *sign from heaven, omen, portent*, in phrases, σήματα φαίνω Il.2.353, cf. 308; κτύπε Ζεύς, σ. τιθεὶς Τρώεσσι 8.171; δεικνὺς σ. βροτοῖσι 13.244; θεοῦ σάμασιν πιθόμενοι Pi. *P.*4.200, cf. 1.3; φλογωπὰ σ. A.*Pr.*498, cf. *Ch.*259; of things heard as well as seen, ἔπος φάτο σ. ἄνακτι Od.20.111. 2. generally, *sign to do* or *begin something*, τόδε σ. τετύχθω 21.231; σ. ἀροτοῖο Hes. *Op.*450; esp. *watchword*, τί τὸ σῆμα; θρόει E.*Rh.*12 (anap.), cf. 688; *battle-sign, signal*, σ. μάχης Id.*Ph.*1378. 3. *sign by which a grave is known, mound, cairn, barrow*, Il.2.814, etc.; τοῦ δὲ τάφον καὶ σῆμ᾽ ἀΐδες ποίησεν Ἄναυρος Hes.*Sc.*477; ἐπὶ σῆμ᾽ ἔχεεν raised *a mound*, Il.6.419, etc.; σ. κυνός E.*Hec.*1273: c. dat. pers., σῆμά τέ οἱ χεύω Od. 2.222; σῆμά τέ μοι χεῦαι..ἀνδρὸς δυστήνοιο 11.75; σάματι πὰρ Πέλοπος Pi.*O.*10(11).24; *grave, tomb*, Hdt.1.93, 4.72, *Berl.Sitzb.* l.c., etc.; τὸ δημόσιον σ. Th.2.34; στῆλαι ἀπὸ σημάτων Id.1.93, cf. Ar.*Th.*886,888, etc.; ἤδη του..ἤκουσα τῶν σοφῶν ὡς τὸ μὲν σῶμά ἐστιν ἡμῖν σ. Pl.*Grg.* 493a, cf. *Cra.*400c. 4. *mark to show the cast of a quoit* or *javelin*, ὑπέρβαλε σήματα πάντων Il.23.843; ὑπέρπτατο σ. πάντων Od.8.192; also, *boundary*, D.P.18. 5. *token* by which any one's identity or commission was certified, μιν ἐρέεινε καὶ ᾔτεε σ. ἰδέσθαι Il.6.176, cf. 178; σ. λυγρά, of written characters or symbols, ib.168; *mark, token* on the lot of Ajax, 7.189; so, *device* or *bearing* on a shield, by which a warrior is known, freq. in A.*Th.*, as 387, 404, E.*El.*456 (lyr.); of the *seal* set on a box, τῶνδ᾽ ἀποίσεις σ. S.*Tr.*614; *mark* made by an illiterate person, *PMasp.*163.37 (vi A.D.). 6. *constellation*, mostly in pl., *heavenly bodies*, S.*Fr.*432; also λαμπρότατος μὲν ὅ γ᾽ ἐστί, κακὸν δέ τε σῆμα τέτυκται, of Sirius, Il.22.30. (Perh. cogn. with Skt. *dhyāti* 'thinks'.)

**σημάδιον**, τό, gloss on ἐνέχυρον, Sch.Ar.*Pl.*451, cf. Eust.1675. 46. II. *ensign, flag*, [Polyaen.]6.38.10.

**σημαία**, v. σημεία. **σημαιαφόρος**, v. σημειοφόρος.

® **σημαίνω**, Il.10.58, etc.; **σᾱμαίνω**, *Schwyzer* 686.23 (Pamphylia): Ion. impf. σημαίνεσκον Q.S.4.193: fut. σημᾰνῶ A.*Ag.*497, Th.6.20, Ion. -ανέω Od.12.26, Hdt.1.75: aor. ἐσήμηνα ib.43, Th.5.71, Ep. σήμηνα Il.23.358; but in codd. of X.(*HG*1.1.2, al.) and later writers (Str.13.3.6, *Act.Ap.*25.27, Polyaen.1.41.3, Arr.*An.*1.6.2) ἐσήμᾱνα, and so in Mitteis *Chr.*29.8 (ii B.C.): pf. σεσήμαγκα Aristobul.ap.Eus. *PE*13.12, Arr.*Epict.*3.26.29:—Med., fut. σημᾰνοῦμαι, Ion. -έομαι Hp. *Prog.*3, etc.: aor. ἐσημηνάμην Il.7.175, etc.:—Pass., fut. σημανθήσομαι S.E.*M.*8.267, (ἐπι-) E.*Ion* 1593: fut. Med. in pass. sense, Hp. *Int.*44: aor. ἐσημάνθην D.47.16: pf. σεσήμασμαι Hdt.2.39, Lys.32. 7, Pl.*Lg.*954a, etc.; 3 sg. σεσήμανται Hdt.2.125, inf. σεσημάνθαι Ar. *Lys.*1196: (σῆμα):—*show by a sign, indicate, point out*, τέρματα Il.23. 358; δείξω ὁδὸν ἠδὲ ἕκαστα σημανέω Od.12.26; τοῦτον σημήνας *after indicating* the person, Hdt.1.5; τέκμαρ A.*Ch.*667; θησαύρισμα S.*Ph.* 37; σ. τι περί τινος Pl.*Lg.*682a; σ. ὅ τι χρὴ ποιεῖν X.*Ap.*12; σ. εὔδια πάντα (sc. εἶναι) Theoc.22.22:—Med., πάντα σημαίνει *you have* all things *shown you*(?), *Epigr.Gr.*1039.11 (Limyra). 2. abs., *give signs*, φθόγγος, φῶς σ., A.*Supp.*245, *Ag.*293; ὁ λόγος σημαινέτω S.*Tr.*345; σ. καπνῷ *make signal*, A.*Ag.*497: freq. in E. in fut. with αὐτός, πλοῦς αὐτὸς σημανεῖ *Hel.*151; τὸ δ᾽ ἔργον αὐτὸ σημανεῖ *Andr.*265; αὐτὸ σημανεῖ (without Subst.) *Ph.*623; τἄλλα δ᾽ αὐτὸ σημανεῖ *Ba.* 976. 3. of the Delphic oracle, οὔτε λέγει οὔτε κρύπτει ἀλλὰ σημαίνει Heraclit.93; so of omens, X.*Mem.*1.1.2, etc.; σ. ἐν τοῖς ἱεροῖς Id. *An.*6.1.31; περί τινος Id.*Mem.*1.1.19; ἐπὶ τοῖς μέλλουσι γενήσεσθαι Th.2.8; πρὸ τῶν μελλόντων X.*HG*5.4.17:—Pass., σημαίνεσθαι διὰ τῶν ἐμπύρων Plu.2.222f, etc. 4. in later Prose intr., *appear, be manifest*, Arist.*HA*533ᵃ11 (but Pass. in same sense, ib.588ᵇ18); σ. ἐκ τῶν εἰρημένων Pl.*Epin.*989a; cf. δηλόω II. b. σημαίνει impers., *signs appear*, Arist.*Pr.*941ᵇ2, 944ᵃ4. II. *give a sign* or *signal to do* a thing, or *bid* one do it, c. dat. pers. et inf., Hdt.1.116, 6.78, A.*Ag.*26, S.*Aj.*688, X.*An.*6.1.24; *give orders to, bear command over*, c. dat., πᾶσι δὲ σημαίνειν Il.1.289, cf. 10.58, 17.250; c. gen., στρατοῦ Il.14.85; also σ. ἐπὶ δμῳῇσι γυναιξίν Od.22.427: abs., *give orders*, ὁ δὲ σημαίνων ἐπέτελλεν Il.21.445, cf. Od.22.450: in part., σημαίνων, = σημάντωρ, S.*OC*704 codd. 2. in war or battle, *give the signal* of attack, etc., Th.2.84, etc.; in full, σ. τῇ σάλπιγγι And.1.45, X.*An.* 4.2.1, Achae.37.3; σ. τῷ κέρατι ὡς ἀναπαύεσθαι X.*An.*2.2.4: c. acc., σ. ἀναχώρησιν *give a signal for* retreat, Th.5.10; ἐπειδὰν ὁ σαλπικτὴς σημήνῃ τὸ πολεμικόν X.*An.*4.3.29, cf. 4.3.32; τὸ ἀνακλητικόν Plu.2. 236e: c. inf., X.*Cyr.*1.4.18, etc.: impers. σημαίνει (sc. ὁ σαλπικτής), *signal is given*, as τοῖσι Ἕλλησι ὡς ἐσήμηνε when *signal was given* for the Greeks to attack, Hdt.8.11: c. inf., ἐσήμαινε παραρτέεσθαι πάντα *signal was given* to make all ready, Id.9.42, cf. E.*Heracl.*830; also σ. ἐπὶ πλόον πῦρ *gives the signal* for sailing, Tryph.145. 3. generally, σ. [τῷ ἵππῳ] τι, προχωρεῖν σ. τῷ ἵππῳ, X.*Eq.*9.4, 7.10. 4. *make signals*, εἰς τὴν πόλιν Id.*HG*6.2.33; σ. ὡς πολεμίων ἐπιόντων ib.7.2. 5:—Pass., ἐσημάνθησαν προσπλέουσαι ib.6.2.34: abs., σημανθέντων τῷ Ἀστυάγει ὅτι.. Id.*Cyr.*1.4.18. III. *signify, indicate, declare*, φόνον E.*HF*1218; τινί τι Hdt.7.18, 9.49, S.*OT*226: folld. by ὡς.., Hdt.1. 34; by ὅτι.., S.*OC*320, Pl.*Phd.*62c; σ. ὅστις A.*Pr.*618; σ. ὅ τι χρή σοι συμπράσσειν ib.297 (anap.); σ. ὅπῃ γῆς πεπλάνημαι ib.564 (anap.);

σ. ὅπου.. S.El.1294; σ. ὅτου τ' εἶ χὠπόθεν Id.Fr.104; σ. εἴτε.. Id. Ph.22; σ. ποίῳ θανάτῳ.. Ev.Jo.12.33, 21.19: c. part., *signify that* a thing is, φρυκτοῦ φῶς..σημαίνει μολόν A.Ag.293; Κρέοντα προσστείχοντα σημαίνουσί μοι S.OT79, cf. OC1669; ταῦτα ὡς πολέμου ὄντος σημαίνει Pl.Lg.626e, cf. 722e:—Pass., ὁ σημαινόμενος δοῦλος the *above-mentioned* slave, POxy.283.12 (i A.D.): abs., σημανθέντος *it having been reported*, PAmh.2.31.8 (ii B.C.), cf. supr. II. 4. **2.** *interpret, explain*, Hdt.1.108; *tell, speak*, Id.3.106: abs., σήμαινε *tell*, S.OC51, cf. OT1050; οὐ στηλῶν μόνον σ. ἐπιγραφή Th.2.43. **3.** of a writer, *signify, indicate*, ὅτι.. Str.8.6.5; of words, sentences, etc., *signify, mean*, ταὐτὸν σημαίνει Pl.Cra.393a, cf. 437c, Phdr.275d, Arist.Ph. 213$^{b}$30, etc.; σημαίνοντα *significant sounds*, opp. ἄσημα, Id.Po.1457$^{a}$32 sq.:—Pass., τὸ σημαινόμενον the *sense, meaning* of words, Id.Rh. 1405$^{b}$8, D.H.Th.31, A.D.Pron.12.27, al.; opp. τὸ σημαῖνον, Chrysipp. Stoic.2.38 (pl.).

**B.** Med. σημαίνομαι, *give oneself a token*, i.e. *conclude from signs, conjecture*, τὰ μὲν σημαίνομαι, τὰ δ' ἐκπέπληγμαι S.Aj.32; ἄστροις σ. [τὰς πόλεις], prov. in Ael.NA7.48; σ. τι ἔκ τινος ib.2.7; of dogs hunting, μυξωτῆρσι σ. τι Opp.C.1.454. **II.** *provide with a sign* or *mark, seal*, σημαίνεσθαι βύβλῳ (sc. βοῦν), i.e. by sealing a strip of byblus round his horn, Hdt.2.38, cf. Pl.Lg.954c, X.Cyr.8.2.17, Is. 7.1,2, Hyp.Ath.8:—Pass., εὖ σεσημάνθαι *to be* well *sealed up*, Ar.Lys. 1196; τὰ σεσημασμένα, opp. τὰ ἀσήμαντα, Pl.Lg.954a, cf. Lys.32.7, D.39.17, Ath.Mitt.7.368. **2.** *mark out, choose for oneself*, τοὺς εὐρωστοτάτους Plb.3.71.7.

**σημαιοφόρος**, v. σημειοφόρος.

**σημᾰλέος**, α, ον, (σῆμα) *giving a sign*, epith. of Zeus, *who sends signs by thunder*, Paus.1.32.2.

**σήμαν-σις**, εως, ἡ, (σημαίνω) *notation*, Nicom.Ar.2.6. **-τέος**, α, ον, *to be noted*, τόποι Aret.SA2.2. **-τήρ**, ῆρος, ὁ, = σημάντωρ, *herdsman*, A.R.1.575; κλήρου σ. its *owner*, Id.3.1403. **II.** *seal, signet*, J.AJ11.6.12, SIG880.33 (Pizus, iii A.D.); σ. δακτύλιος J.AJ20.2. 2. **-τήριον**, τό, *mark* or *seal upon anything* to be kept, A.Ag.609; dub. sens. in S.Fr.432.9. **II.** *place for coining* money, *mint*, Harp. s.v. ἀργυροκοπεῖον. **-τικός**, ή, όν, *significant*, opp. ἄσημος, ὄνομά ἐστι φωνὴ σ. κατὰ συνθήκην ἄνευ χρόνου Arist.Int.16$^{a}$19; ῥῆμα.. φωνὴ συνθετὴ σ. μετὰ χρόνου Id.Po.1457$^{a}$14; λόγος..ἐστι φωνὴ σ. κατὰ συνθήκην Id.Int.16$^{b}$26, cf. Stoic.2.48: c. gen., σ. ὑγιείας Arist. Top.106$^{b}$36; σ. πάσης κακίας D.S.3.4; σ. ὄρη mountains *giving signs* of the weather, Thphr.Sign.51; σ. παρωτίδων *indicative* of mumps, Gal.17(1).405; -κά *significant symptoms*, Hp.Praec.11. Adv. -κῶς Arist.Top.106$^{b}$37: c. gen., M.Ant.10.7: Sup. -ώτατα Longin.31.1. **-τός**, ή, όν, *marked*, τροχαῖος a trochee consisting of 8 + 4 time-units, Plu.2.1140f, Aristid. Quint.1.16. ⊛ **-τρια**, ἡ, fem. of σημαντήρ, Iamb.VP24.109. 2. **σᾱμάντριαν** (Dor.)..πυρᾶς ἰωάν *sign*, Call.Fr.1.40 P. **-τριον**, τό, in pl., *sign*, εἰς θ' ἕω σημάντρια dub. cj. in S.Fr.432. **-τρὶς** γῆ, clay *used for sealing*, like our wax, Hdt.2.38. ⊛ **-τρον**, τό, = σημαντήριον, *seal*, σημάντρων σόων unbroken *seals*, Hdt.2.121.β'; σ. ἀνείς, ἀνοίξαντες, E.IA325, X.Lac.6.4: metaph., δεινοῖς σημάντροισιν ἐσφραγισμένοι, i.e. wounded, E.IT1372. ⊛ **-τωρ**, ορος, ὁ, (σημαίνω II) *one who gives a signal, leader, commander*, Il.4.431, cf. Od.19.314; of a horse, *driver*, Il.8.127; of a herd, *herdsman*, 15.325, Q.S.13.74; θεῶν σ., of Zeus, Hes.Sc.56; σ. ἄνδρες h.Ap.542; ἐθνέων ἦσαν ἄλλοι σ., of the *subordinate officers*, Hdt.7.81. **2.** *informer, guide*, S.OT 957 (v.l. σημῆνας); παγίδων σημάντορα φελλόν *indicator* of the nets, AP6.27 (Theaet.); μόλιβον, σελίδων σ. πλευρῆς (v. σελίς II), ib.62 (Phil.), cf. 64 (Paul. Sil.). **II.** later as Adj., even in fem., σημάντορι φωνῇ Nonn.D.37.551; σ. καπνῷ Tryph.237.

⊛ **σημᾰσία**, ἡ, (σημαίνω II) *the giving a signal* or *command*, Lxx Nu.29. 1; αἱ ἀπὸ τῶν ἄρκτων σ. D.S.2.54. **II.** *indication*, αἱ πράξεις ἤθους σ. ἐστίν Arist.Pr.919$^{b}$36; *designation*, Str.8.6.5. **2.** *meaning, signification*, πρὸς τὸ περὶ σημασιῶν Φίλωνος, title of work by Chrysippus, Stoic.2.5, cf. Phld.Sign.34: freq. in Gramm., A.D.Pron.14.3, al., Ael.Tact.24.4, Iamb.Protr.4, etc. **3.** *notation* in Music, Gaud. Harm.20. **III.** *the decisive appearance* of a disease, Aret.SA1.5, al. **IV.** *mark*, ἐν δέρματι χρωτός Lxx Le.13.2; of the Nile-flood, ἀνῆλθεν ἡ τοῦ Νείλου σ. κατὰ τὸ ἱερατικὸν σημεῖον Bull.Soc.Arch.Alex. 5.55 (v/vi A.D.). **V.** *address* of a correspondent, POxy.1678.28 (iii A.D.). **VI.** βασιλικὴ σ. royal *insignia* or *appearance*, Sor. Fasc.8.

**σημᾰτ-ίζομαι**, = σημαίνομαι, Sch.S.Aj.32. **-ιον**, τό, Dim. of σῆμα, Eust.1675.44. **-όεις**, εσσα, εν, (σῆμα 3) *full of tombs*, χθών AP7.628 (Crin.).

**σ]ημᾰτοποικίλος** [ῐ], perh. *motley*, dub. rest. in Lyr. in Philol. 80.338.

**σημᾰτουργός**, ὁ, *one who makes devices for shields*, A.Th. 491.

**σημεαφόρος**, v. σημειοφόρος.

⊛ **σημεία**, ἡ, *military standard*, Plb.2.32.6, Lxx Is.30.17, Mon.Anc. 15.23, 16.3. **b.** = Lat. *vexillum*, as a decoration, OGI560.13 (Tlos, i A.D.). **2.** *a body of troops under one standard*, the Roman *manipulus*, UPZ14.23, al. (ii B.C.), Sammelb.1436.10 (ii B.C.), Plb.1.33.9, 3.113.3, 6.24.5, etc.; cf. σημεῖον I. 4 b. **II.** *image* of Emperor on standard, J.BJ2.9.2. **III.** = σῆμα 5 (on shield), Sch.Ar.Ra. 963. **IV.** = σημεῖον, διαξέσας σημείας (on stone) IG7.3073.138 (Lebadea). (The spellings σημεία as in IG l.c., UPZ18.5 (ii B.C.), and good Mss. of Plb. (v. vol.4 p.xxi B.-W.), D.H.8.64, 9.13, al., D.S.20.90, and σημέα as in UPZ14.23, Sammelb. l.c., Mon.Anc. ll. cc., Abh.Berl.Akad.1932 (5).41 (Pergam., ii A.D.), are prob. the only early spellings: σημαία which is found in Plu.Fab.12 and as v.l. in Plb., D.H.8.65, al., is prob. f.l. for σημέα.)

**σημειογράφος** [ᾰ], ὁ, (σημεῖον II. 5) *shorthand writer*, Plu.Cat. Mi.23, Stud.Pont.3.3a (Amisus), CIG3902d (Eumenia), POxy.724.2 (ii A.D.).

⊛ **σημεῖον**, τό, Ion. **σημήϊον**, Dor. **σᾱμήϊον** IG12(3).452 (Thera, iv B.C.), **σᾱμεῖον** IPE1$^{2}$.352.25 (Chersonesus, ii B.C.), IG5(1).1390.16 (Andania, i B.C.), **σᾱμᾶον** CIG5168 (Cyrene):— = σῆμα in all senses, and more common in Prose, but never in Hom. or Hes.: *mark* by which a thing is known, Hdt.2.38; σημεῖα τῶν δεδικασμένων.., σημεῖα πάντων ὧν ἔπραξαν Pl.R.614c; *sign* of the future, τυραννίδος σ. A.Ag.1355; σ. λαβεῖν ἔκ τινος E.Hipp.514; *trace, track*, σημεῖα δ' οὔτε θηρὸς οὔτε του κυνῶν..ἐξεφαίνετο S.Ant.257, cf. El.886; τῆς καταβάσεως X.An.6.2.2; of a cork on a buoy, Paus.8.12.1. **b.** Dor., *tomb*, IG12(3).452 (iv B.C.), CIG l.c. **2.** *sign from the gods, omen*, S.OC94; τὰ ἀπὸ τῶν θεῶν σ. γενόμενα Antipho 5.81, cf. Pl.Phdr. 244c, Ap.40b, X.Cyr.1.6.1; *wonder, portent*, Lxx Ex.4.8, al.; σ. καὶ τέρατα Plb.3.112.8, Ev.Matt.24.24, Ev.Jo.4.48, cf. IPE l.c., D.S.17. 114; φόβηθρα καὶ σ. ἀπ' οὐρανοῦ Ev.Luc.21.11; esp. of *the constellations*, regarded as *signs*, δύεται σημεῖα E.Rh.529 (lyr.), cf. Ion 1157. **3.** *sign* or *signal* to do a thing, made by flags, ἀνέδεξε σημήϊον τοῖσι ἄλλοισι ἀνάγεσθαι he made *signal* for the rest to put to sea, Hdt.7.128; *signal for battle*, τὰ σ. ἤρθη, κατεσπάσθη, Th.1.49,63, etc.; καθαιρεῖν τὸ σ. to take *it* down, strike the *flag*, as a *sign* of dissolving an assembly, And.1.36; τὸ τῆς ἐκκλησίας σ. Ar.Th.278; ὕστερος ἐλθεῖν τοῦ σ. Id.V.690: generally, *signal*, σ. ὑποδηλῶσαί τινι ὅτι.. Id.Th.1011; τὰ σ. αὐτοῖς ἤρθη Th.4.42; τὸ σ. τοῦ πυρός, ὡς εἴρητο, ἀνέσχον ib.111; *signal* to commence work, [ἡ] τοῦ σημείου ἄρσις Ath.Mitt.35.403 (Pergam.); σημείῳ ἀβαστάκτῳ, σημείοις ἀβαστάκτοις with unremoved *signal(s)*, of gymnasia, i.e. never closed, IG Rom.4.446 (ibid.), Abh.Berl.Akad.1932(5).44 (ibid., ii A.D.). **4.** *standard* or *flag*, on the admiral's ship, Hdt.8.92; on the general's tent, X.Cyr.8.5.13; ἔξω τῶν σ. out of the *lines*, ib.8.3.19. **b.** *body of troops* under one standard or flag, PAmh.2.39.2 (ii B.C.); cf. σημεία I. 2. **5.** land*mark, boundary, limit*, ἔξω τῶν σ. τοῦ ὑμετέρου ἐμπορίου out of the *limits* of your commercial port, D.35.28; of milestones, Plu.CG7, Hdn.2.13.9. **6.** *device* upon a shield, Hdt.1.171, E.Ph.1114; upon ships, *figure-head*, Ar.Ra.933, Th.6.31, E.IA255 (lyr.). **7.** *signet* on ring, etc., Ar.Eq.952, V.585, Pl.Tht.191d, al., X.HG5.1.30, D.42.2, PRev.Laws 26.5 (iii B.C.); *figure, image*, Διὸς κτησίου Anticl.13; *badge*, τρίαιναν σ. θεοῦ A.Supp.218: pl., *written characters*, γράψαι σημήϊα..φωνῆς IG14.1549 (Rome). **b.** pl. (Dor.) σαμεῖα, *stripes*, ib.5(1).1390.16 (Andania, i B.C.); *clavi*· σημεῖα, Gloss. **8.** *watchword, war-cry*, Plb.5.69.8; ἀπὸ σ. ἑνὸς ἐπιστρέφειν τὰς ναῦς Th.2.90, cf. X.HG6.2.28. **9.** *birthmark* or *distinguishing feature*, Wilcken Chr.76.14 (ii A.D.), Sammelb.15.27 (ii A.D.), etc. **II.** *sign, token, indication* of anything that is or is to be, S.OT1059, E.Ph.1332; σ. φαίνεις ἐσθλὸς..γεγώς S.El.24, cf. OT710; τέχνης σ. τῆς ἐμῆς Id.Ant.998; so later τὰ σ. τῶν καιρῶν Ev.Matt.16.3, etc. **2.** in reasoning, a *sign* or *proof*, Ar.Nu.369, Th.1.6,10, And. 2.25, etc.; τούτων ὑμῖν σημεῖα δείξω Aeschin.2.103, cf. 3.46; τάδε τὰ σ. ὡς.. X.Ages.1.5; σ. εἰ.. Pl.Grg.520e; ὅτι ἀγαθὸς ἦν.., τοῦτο μέγιστον σ. Id.Min.321b; τὸ μὴ ἐκδυθῆναι οὐδὲν σ. ἐστι is no *proof* to the contrary, Antipho 2.2.5; also, *instance, example*, Hp.VM 20; σημεῖον δέ· to introduce an argument, D.21.149, Isoc.4.86,107, etc. **3.** in the Logic of Arist., *a sign* used as *a probable argument* in proof of a conclusion, opp. τεκμήριον (a demonstrative or certain proof), APr.70$^{a}$11, SE167$^{b}$9, Rh.1357$^{a}$33. **b.** in Stoic and Epicurean philos., *sign* as observable basis of inference to the unobserved or unobservable, Epicur.Ep.2 p.43 U., Phld.Sign.27, al., S.E.M.8.142, al.; περὶ σημείων (dub. sens.), title of work by Zeno, Stoic.1.14. **4.** Medic., *symptom*, Hp.Morb.3.6,15, Aret.SD1.9, Gal.1.313, 18(2).306. **b.** = Lat. *lenticula*, a kind of skin-eruption, Cels.6.5.1. **5.** pl., *shorthand symbols*, Plu.Cat.Mi.23, Gal. Libr.Propr.1, POxy.724.3 (ii A.D.), Lib.Or.42.25. **6.** *critical mark*, Heph.Poëm.p.73 C., D.L.3.65. **III.** = στιγμή, *mathematical point*, Arist.APo.76$^{b}$5, Ph.240$^{b}$3, Euc.Def.1, al.; also σ. (with or without χρόνου) *point* of time, *instant*, Arist.Cael.283$^{a}$11, Ph.262$^{b}$2 sq. **2.** in Prosody and Music, *unit of time*, Aristid.Quint.1.14, Longin.Proll. Heph.5.

**σημειο-σκόπος**, ὁ, *one who observes omens, diviner*, Al.1Ki. 28.3,9. **-σκοποῦμαι**, *divine*, Sm.De.18.10. **-φόρος**, ὁ, *standard-bearer*, Sammelb.599.7, al. (Ptolemaic), D.H.8.65, Plu. Brut.43:—also **σημεαφόρος** BGU600.10,12 (ii/iii A.D.), PFlor.278 iii 30 (iii A.D.), IGRom.3.57 (Prusias), CIG4957e (Egypt); **σημηαφόρος** Sammelb.979.7 (Alexandria, i A.D.), CIL3.6026 (Syene), Stud.Pal.22.92 (iii A.D.); **σημιαφόρος** Supp.Epigr.6.535 (Isauria), Judeich Altertümer von Hierapolis No.153; **σημιαφώρος** PHamb. 39 No.16; **σιμιαφόρος** ib.No.45 (ii A.D.); **σημαιαφόρος** (with v.l. **σημαιοφόρος**) Plb.6.24.6, J.BJ6.1.7; σημαιοφόρος also in Plu.Galb. 22. **II.** = σημεία I. 1 b, in form σημιαφόρος, Jahresh.13.201 (Alabanda, ii A.D.). **III.** *signaller*, Ascl.Tact.2.9, 6.3.

⊛ **σημει-όω** (Dor. **σᾱμ-** IG5(1).1390.71 (Andania, i B.C.)), = σημαίνω, *mark* (by milestones), Plb.3.39.8 (Pass.), cf. 1.47.1; *seal*, ἐπιστολὰς -ωμένας σφραγῖδι D.H.4.57:—Pass., *to be marked* or *stamped*, IG l.c. **2.** *give a signal*, impers. in Pass., ὅταν σημειωθῇ Aen. Tact.22.23 (cod. M). **II.** Med., *mark for oneself, note down*, ὅτι.. Thphr.CP1.21.7; τόπον Plb.21.28.9: abs., Δυμᾶς σεσημείωμαι (*signed*) Δυμᾶς, Ostr.Bodl. iii 280 (i A.D.), cf. ii 25 (i A.D.), etc.;

*take notice of, pay honour to*.., ὅπως ὁ δῆμος φαίνηται τοὺς καλοὺς κἀγαθοὺς τῶν ἀνδρῶν σημειούμενος *Inscr.Perg.*252.28. 2. *interpret* anything *as a sign* or *portent*, Plb.5.78.2, Str.9.2.11; *infer as from a sign*, ὁ ἐκ τῆς ἐναργείας -ούμενος περὶ τῶν ἀδήλων Phld. *Sign.*15, cf. Epicur.*Ep.*2 p.47 U., S.E.*M.*8.271:—Medic., *diagnose*, Antyll.ap.Orib.45.2.1, Gal.18(2).851; later, *examine*, σημειωσόμεθα κοπαρίῳ Paul.Aeg.6.77; οἱ τοῦ -ουμένου δάκτυλοι ib.96. 3. in Gramm., of marginal marks, σημείωσαι, = *nota bene*, Hdn.Gr.1.87, al., freq. in Sch.:—in Pass., σημειοῦται δὲ ὅτι.. Sch.Il.*Oxy.*1086 i 17; τὰ σεσημειωμένα *noted as exceptions*, A.D.*Pron.*115.11, Choerob. *in Theod.*1.406 H.: fut. σεσημειώσεται A.D.*Adv.*166.14. **-ώδης**, ες, *remarkable, conspicuous*, Str.8.1.3 (Sup.); of language, *peculiar, singular*, ὀνόματα D.H.*Isoc.*2. II. *significant* of something to come, ἄλφ Arist.*Mete.*373ᵃ30, cf. Thphr.*Vent.*35; τὰ ἐνύπνια ἔχει τι σ. Arist. *Div.Somn.*462ᵇ15, cf. Phld.*Sign.*19, Plu.2.286b. Adv. -δῶς *remarkably*, Str.16.2.28. **-ωμα**, ατος, τό, in pl., *records*, *Vit Philonid.* p.11 C. ⊕ **-ωσις**, εως, ἡ, *indication, notice*, Plu.2.961c. II. *inference from a sign*, Phld.*Sign.*2, al.; ὁ καθ' ὁμοιότητα τρόπος τῆς σ. ib.1; ὁ κατ' ἀνασκευὴν τρόπος τῆς σ. ib.31. 2. Medic., *remarking, observing* of symptoms, Gal.19.394; used by the νεώτεροι for διάγνωσις acc. to Heliod.ap.Orib.45.16.4; later, *examination*, ἡ διὰ τοῦ πυρῆνος σ. Paul.Aeg.6.77. III. *visible sign* or *token*, as a banner, Lxx *Ps.* 59(60).6. **-ωτέος**, α, ον, *to be noted* as an exception, A.D.*Pron.*54. 14, etc. 2. σημειωτέον, *one must note*, Sor.2.8, Sch.Ar.*Av.*417, etc. **-ωτικός**, ή, όν, *observant of signs*, ὁ ὄντως φιλόσοφος σ. Porph. *Abst.*2.49. Adv. -κῶς S.E.*M.*8.158. II. **-κόν**, τό, the *science of symptoms* in medicine, *diagnosis*, Gal.14.689; name of treatise on diagnosis, Sor.1.124. ⊕ **-ωτός**, ή, όν, *signified, inferred from a sign*, S.E.*P.*2.101, *M.*8.166.

**σημερῖνός**, ή, όν, *of to-day*, Call.*Sos.*vi 2, Ammon.*in Int.*32.5, Sch. Ar.*Nu.*699, Dosith.p.397 K., *Gloss.*

**σήμερον**, Adv. *to-day*, Il.7.30, Od.17.186, E.*Rh.*683, *PHib.*1.65.13 (iii B.C.), *SIG*1181.11 (Rhenea, ii B.C.), *Ev.Matt.*27.19, etc.; Dor. **σάμερον** [ᾰ] Pi.*O.*6.28, *P.*4.1; Att. **τήμερον** Cratin.123, Ar.*Eq.*68, etc., cf. Moer.p.364 P. (though σήμερον is sts. found in Com., Hermipp.80, Philem.121); εἰς τ. Pl.*Smp.*174a; τὸ τ. ib.176e; τὸ τ. εἶναι *to-day*, Id.*Cra.*396e; ἡ τ. ἡμέρα D.4.40; also in the form **τήμερα** Ar.*Fr.*401 (s.v.l.), cf. 296. (Prob. fr. κyāμερον, containing stem *kyo-* 'this', cf. Lith. *šis* 'this', Lat. *ci-tra*: σήμερον (τήμερον) is to ἡμέρα as σῆτες (τῆτες) to ἔτος.)

⊕ **σημήϊον**, τό, Ion. for σημεῖον. **σημιαφόρος**, v. σημειοφόρος.

**σημῑκίνθιον** (written **σιμικίνθιον**), τό, Lat. *semicinctium, apron* or *kerchief*, *Act.Ap.*19.12.

**σημοδιαῖος**, α, ον, *holding six modii*, *Edict.Diocl.*15.51.

⊕ **σημόθετος**, ον, poet. σᾱμο-, *placed as a mark*, *AP*6.295 (Phan.).

**σημοφόριον**, τό, dub. rest. in Ἀρχ. Ἐφ.1913.27 (Gonni, iii B.C.).

**σημύδα**, ἡ, *Judas-tree, Cercis Siliquastrum*, Thphr.*HP*3.14.4, 5.7.7.

**σημών**, ὁ, Lacon. for θημών, *EM*711.16.

**σηνίκη**· ἄτροχος ἅμαξα, καὶ τὸ τετράπουν ζῷον, σαύρᾳ παραπλήσιον. καὶ ζῷον πολύπουν, ὅμοιον τοῖς κατοικιδίοις ὄνοις, Hsch. ⊕ **σηνοῦροι**· ταῖς οὐραῖς σαίνοντες, Id.

**σηπεδον-ικός**, ή, όν, *causing putrefaction*, Heliod.ap.Orib.47.16.1. Adv. -κῶς ibid. **-ώδης**, ες, *inclined to putrefy*, ἕλκεα Hp.*Mul.*1.36, Paul.Aeg.6.45; ἀήρ Alex.Aphr.*Pr.*1.88.

**σηπεδών**, όνος, ἡ, (σήπομαι) *decay, putrefaction*, in animal bodies or wood, or even stone, Hp.*Epid.*3.4, Antipho Soph.15, Pl.*Phd.*110e, Thphr.*CP*6.1.5; σηπεδόνα λαβεῖν Pl.*Phd.*96b. 2. of live flesh, *mortification*, of two kinds, σ. χλωρή (v. σῆψις) when a humour discharges, and ξηρή when it is dry, Hp.*Epid.*5.4. II. pl., *putrid humours*, Id.*Aph.*3.16 (sg. in 7.20), Plb.1.81.7, *Com.Adesp.*344, etc. III. *a serpent whose bite causes putrefaction*, Nic.*Th.*327, Ael. *NA*15.18.

**σήπειον**, τό, v. σήπιον.

**σηπ-ετός**, ὁ, = σηπεδών, Hsch. **-εύω**, *cause to putrefy*, Man.4. 269. **-η**, ἡ, = σηπεδών, Aq.*Jb.*17.14, 21.26, dub. l. in Lxx *Si.*19.3.

⊕ **σηπία**, ἡ, *cuttle-fish, sepia*, Hippon.68 B, Epich.61, Ar.*Ach.*351, al., Antipho Soph.78, Arist.*HA*524ᵃ25, al.; a dainty at Athens, Ar. *Ach.*1040, etc.

⊕ **σηπιάς**, άδος, ἡ, = foreg., Nic.*Al.*472.

**σηπῐδ-άριον**, τό, = sq., Philyll.13. **-ιον**, τό, Dim. of σηπία, Hp. *Mul.*2.133, Ar.*Fr.*247, Ephipp.15.4, Arist.*HA*550ᵃ16.

**σήπιον** (or **σηπίον**), τό, *bone of the sepia* or *cuttle-fish, pounce*, Arist.*HA*524ᵇ24, 532ᵇ1, *APo.*98ᵃ21 (where σήπειον).

**σηπιοπουλῠπόδειος**, ον, *of cuttle-fish and polypus*, prob. in Philox. 2.13.

**σηποιαλίς**· εἶδος ἀμπέλου, Hsch.

**σηποποιός**, όν, = σηπτικός, Alex.Aphr.*Pr.*1.66.

**σηπ-τικός**, ή, όν, *putrefactive, septic*, -κὴ κοιλίη *digestive* stomach, opp. oesophagus, Hp.*Anat.*1; τὸ σ. (sc. φάρμακον) Arist.*HA*607ᵃ22, Thphr.*HP*9.16.5; σ. φάρμακον D.S.4.38: so **-τήριον** φ. Hp.*Loc. Hom.*38. **-τός**, ή, όν, *converted into excrement*, of food, τὸ σ. περίττωμα τοῦ πεφθέντος ἐστίν Arist.*GA*762ᵃ15; cf. σῆψις II. II. Act., = σηπτικός, ⟨δυνάμεις⟩, i.e. medicines, Dsc.2.62 (δ. expressed in 3.9); φάρμακον Meges ap.Orib.44.24.10.

⊕ **σήπω**, A.*Ch.*995, Pl.*Ti.*84d, etc.: fut. σήψω A.*Fr.*275: aor. ἔσηψα (δι-) Ael.*NA*9.62:—*make rotten* or *putrid*, A.*Fr.*l.c., Pl.l.c.; of a serpent's poison, A.*Ch.*l.c.; of the sting of the σήψ, Ael.*NA*16.40. b. *soak* hides, δέρματα σ. *Supp.Epigr.*3.18 (Athens, v B.C.). 2. metaph., *corrupt, waste*, αἱ ἡσυχίαι σήπουσι καὶ ἀπολλύασι Pl.*Tht.*153c; σ. τὰ τῆς πόλεως πράγματα D.H.11.37. II. mostly in Pass. (pf. σέσηπα being used in pass. sense, Il.2.135, E.*El.*319, (κατα-) Ar. *Pl.*1035, (ἀπο-) X.*An.*4.5.12), fut. σᾰπήσομαι Gal.7.397, (κατα-) Pl. *Phd.*86b, (ἀπο-) Hp.*Prorrh.*2.1: aor. ἐσάπην [ᾰ] Hes.*Sc.*152, Hdt.2. 41, 3.66, Pl.*Phd.*80d; σαπῇ (κατα-), Ep. subj. for σαπῇ, Il.19.27: pf. σέσημμαι prob. in *POxy.*1449.51 (iii A.D.):—*rot, moulder*, of dead bodies, χρὼς σήπεται Il.24.414, cf. 19.27, Hdt.2.41; περὶ ῥινοῖο σαπείσης Hes.*Sc.*152; of wood, δοῦρα σέσηπε Il.2.135; τριήρης ὑπὸ τερηδόνων σαπεῖσα Ar.*Eq.*1308. 2. of live flesh, *mortify*, ὁ μηρὸς ἐσάπη Hdt.3.66; σφακελίσαντος τοῦ μηροῦ καὶ σαπέντος Id.6. 136, cf. Pl.*Phd.*80d; αἷμα σέσηπεν E.*El.*319; *promote coction* or formation of 'laudable' pus, in Act., Hp.*Morb.*1.6, 28. 3. of water, Id.*Aër.*8; οἶνος.. σαπὲν ἐν ξύλῳ ὕδωρ Emp.81. 4. of the food rejected after digestion, Arist.*Mete.*381ᵇ12, al.; cf. σηπτός, σῆψις II. 5. metaph., σ. ὑπὸ τῆς ἡδονῆς Men.23; ὁ πλοῦτος ὑμῶν σέσηπε *Ep.Jac.*5.2.

**σήπων**, ωνος, ὁ, = *sapo*, *Gloss.*; cf. σάπων.

**Σήρ**, ὁ, gen. Σηρός, mostly in pl. Σῆρες, *Seres*, the people from whom silk was obtained (i.e. the Chinese), Str.11.11.1, 15.1.34, D.P.752, etc.; interpol.(?) in Ctes.*Fr.*p.86 M. (cod. Monac.):—Adj. **Σηρικός** (q.v.). II. *silkworm*, Paus.6.26.6.

⊕ **σήρ**, ὁ, Lacon. for θήρ, Hsch.; cf. σηροκτόνος.

**σηρά**· σκῦλα, ἢ δεσμὸς πλεκτός (v. σειρά), Hsch.

**σηράγγ-ιον**, τό, Dim. of σῆραγξ, a place in the Piraeus, where was a bath, Ar.*Fr.*122, Lys.*Fr.*17 S., Is.6.33, Alciphr.3.43. **-όομαι**, Pass., *to be* or *become hollow*, Dsc.5.121, Hld.1.28:—Act. **-όω**, *make spongy* or *porous*, τίς ὁ τὸν πνεύμονα -ώσας; *Corp.Herm.*5.6.

**σήραγγος** ἢ **σήραγξ**· ἐπιθυμία, Hsch.; cf. **σηράγγων**· σπηλαίων, ἐπιθυμιῶν, Id.

**σηραγγώδης**, ες, *full of holes* or *caverns*, Ἴδη Paus.10.12.4, cf. D.C.48.51, Agath.2.15, Lyd.*Ost.*53. 2. *porous, spongy*, Hp.*VC* 1, al.; θηλαί Sor.1.88; νεῦρον Gal.10.968.

**σῆραγξ**, αγγος, ἡ (ὁ, Agath.5.6), *cave hollowed out by water, hollow rock*, S.*Fr.*549, Pl.*Phd.*110a, Arist.*HA*548ᵃ24, al.; of a lion's *den*, Theoc.25.223; of the sponge-like *pores* of the lungs, Pl.*Ti.*70c, Ps.-Democr. in Hp.*Ep.*23; of the *bronchi*, Ruf.*Onom.*159; *medullary cavity* of a bone, Antyll.ap.Orib.44.20.11. II. = σανίδωμα *used by* σηλαγγεύς (q.v.), Agatharch.27. III. v. σήραγγος.

**σήραμβος**· εἶδος κανθάρου, Hsch.

**σηρικάριος**, ὁ, *silk-worker* or *silk-mercer*, *IG*3.3513 (written σιρ-), *Edict.Diocl.*20.9, al. (written σειρ-).

**σηρῐκο-διαστής**, οῦ, ὁ, *silk-weaver*, Ps.-Callisth.3.12. **-ποιός**, v. σιρικοποιός.

**σηρῐκός**, ή, όν, (Σήρ) *Seric, silken*, ἐσθής Luc.*Salt.*63; παραπετάσματα, σκευή, D.C.43.24, 59.26; νῆμα Gal.10.942 (pl.), Hld.2.31; τὰ σ. τῶν ὑφασμάτων Plu.2.396b; written **σειρικός**, Gal.5.46:—as Subst., **σηρικόν**, τό, *silken robe, silk*, *Apoc.*18.12 (v.l. σιρικόν), *Peripl.M. Rubr.*49; in pl., Nearch.ap.Str.15.1.20. 2. σηρικά, τά, *jujubes*, Gal.6.614, Paul.Aeg.1.81. 3. σηρικόν (fort. συρικόν), τό, *a red pigment*, Olymp.Alch.p.76 B., Zos.Alch.p.248 B.; *Syricum pigmentum, quod Syrii Phoenices in Rubri maris litoribus colligunt*, Isid.*Etym.*19. 17.6 (where it is distd. from *Sericum*).

**σηροκτόνος**, ον, Lacon. for θηροκτ-, Ar.*Lys.*1262.

**σής**, ὁ, gen. σεός (as if fr. σεύς, which is given as nom. by Choerob. *in Theod.*1 p.406 H.); pl., nom. σέες Moer.p.339 P.; gen. σέων Hermipp.94, Ar.*Lys.*730, Ph.2.461 (not σεῶν, v. Choerob. l.c.); acc. σέας Luc.*Ind.*1:—the forms σητός, σῆτες, σητῶν, etc., were later, as in Men.540.5, Arist.*HA*557ᵇ3, Thphr.*HP*9.11.11, Ph.2.361 (and v.l. in 2.461), cf. Moer. l.c., etc.:—*moth*, [χρυσὸν] οὐ σ. οὐδὲ κὶς δάπτει Pi.*Fr.*222, cf. Ar. l.c., Str.13.1.54, *Ev.Matt.*6.19, *Ev.Luc.*12. 33; attacking books, Luc. l.c. 2. metaph., σῆτες ἀκανθοβάται or -λόγοι, of the Grammarians, *bookworms*, *AP*11.322 (Antiphan.), 347 (Phil.).

**σησᾰμ-αῖος**, α, ον, *made of sesame*, πλακοῦς Luc.*Pisc.*41; μουστάκια σ. (σησαμᾶτα in codd., perh. rightly) *seasoned with sesame*, Chrysipp. Tyan.ap.Ath.14.647d. **-εία**, ἡ, *sowing* (or *planting*) *of sesame*, *PSI*5.500.3 (iii B.C., in pl.), *PLille* 26.1 (iii B.C.). **-εύω**, *cultivate sesame*, *PSI*4.432.3, *PTeb.*815 *Fr.*3ʳ ii 10 (both iii B.C.). **-η**, ἡ, *sesame, Sesamum indicum*, *Gp.*3.2.4. **-ῆ**, ἡ, contr. from σησαμέα (which occurs in Hdn.Gr.2.425), *a mixture of sesame-seeds, roasted and pounded with honey*, an Athenian delicacy, given to guests at a wedding, Ar.*Pax* 869, Men.938; in pl., Amphis 9.3; wrongly written σησάμη in Hp.*Int.*42, etc. ⊕ **-ικός**, ή, όν, *pertaining to sesame*; -κά, τά, *accounts relating to sesame*, *PCair.Zen.*314. 4 (iii B.C.). ⊕ **-ῖνος**, η, ον, *made of sesame*, σ. ἔλαιον *sesame-oil*, *PRev.Laws* 40.10 (iii B.C.), *PPetr.*3 p.218 (iii B.C.), Str.16.4.26, Dsc.1.34; δοκοί *Peripl.M.Rubr.*36; σ. χρῖμα X.*An.*4.4.13 (σ. ξύλα is prob. f.l. for συκάμινα in Dsc.1.98). **-ιον**, τό, Dim. of σησαμῆ, Hdn.*Epim.*125. **-ίς**, Dor. **σᾱσᾰμίς**, ίδος, ἡ, = σησαμῆ, Stesich.2, Eup.162, Antiph.78. II. = σησαμοειδὲς τὸ μέγα, Ps.-Dsc.4.149. **-ίτης** [ῑ] (sc. ἄρτος or πλακοῦς), ου, ὁ, bread or a cake *made with sesame seeds*, Poll.6.72, Ath.3.114a: fem. Adj. **-ῖτις**, ιδος, *planted with sesame*, γῆ *PSI*5.522.1 (iii B.C.); so ἡ σ. alone, ib.503. 28, 522.11 (iii B.C.); *of sesame*, sc. κράστις (?), ib.4.351.16 (iii B.C.). II. σησαμῖτις, ιδος, ἡ, = foreg. II, Ps.-Dsc.4.149.

**σησᾰμο-ειδής**, ές, *like sesame* or *sesame-seeds*, Thphr.*HP*3.13.6; of bones, Gal.*UP*2.12. II. σησαμοειδές, τό, *fruit of* ἐλλέβορος μέλας, Dsc.4.162; used medicinally, Hp.*Acut.*(*Sp.*)60, *Ep.* 21; hellebore from Anticyra acc. to Diocl.*Fr.*152; also σ. φάρμακον

Str.9.3.3. 2. σ. τὸ μικρόν, *purple rock-cress, Aubrietia deltoidea*, Dsc.4.163 (also called σ. τὸ λευκόν, Ps.-Dsc. ibid.). 3. σ. τὸ μέγα, *bastard rocket, Reseda alba*, Dsc.4.149. **-εις, εσσα, εν**, *of sesame*, ἐδέσματα Hp.*Aff.*47; σησαμοῦς ἄρτος Sor.1.115. II. as Subst. (contr.) σησαμοῦς (sc. πλακοῦς) *sesame-cake*, Ar.*Ach.*1092, *Th.*570.

**σήσᾰμον**, τό, Lacon. **σάᾰμον** *IG*5(1).364.9:—*seed* or *fruit of the sesame-plant*, Hippon.36 (pl.), Sol.40 (pl.), Hdt.1.193, 3.48, 117, Ar.*V.*676 (pl.), Thphr.*HP*8.1.1, *OGI*55.16 (Telmessus, iii B.C.), *PCair. Zen.*787.21 (iii B.C.), etc.: σ. ἄγριον, = κίκι, Ps.-Dsc.4.161. 2. τὰ σ. the *sesame-market*, Moer.p.351 P. II. = σησάμη, *sesame plant*, Ar.*Av.*159 (pl.), X.*An.*1.2.22, etc.; ἀλείφεσθαι ἐκ τοῦ σ., i.e. *with sesame-oil*, Str.16.1.20; cf. σήσαμος.

**σησᾰμό-παστος** (Dor. σασ-), ον, *sprinkled with sesame-seeds*, Philox.3.18. **-πώλης**, ου, ὁ, *sesame-seller*, *IG*2[2].1561.23; fem. **-πωλις**, ιδος, ib.1554.40.

**σήσᾰμος**, ὁ, = σήσαμον I. 1, *Gp.*9.18.2, Suid.

**σησᾰμό-τῡρον**, τό, *mess of sesame and cheese*, Batr.36. **-τῡρο-πᾰγής**, ές, *compounded of sesame and cheese*; or **-ρῡτο-πᾰγής**, *compounded of sesame and rue*, Philox.3.18.

**σησᾰμούντιος**, α, ον, *made of sesame*, Sch.Ar.*Pax* 869.

**σησᾰμοῦς**, v. σησαμόεις.

**σησᾰμο-φόρος**, ον, *sesame-bearing*, γῆ *PMich.Zen.*96.3 (iii B.C.). **-φωκτος** (Dor. σασ-), ον, *toasted with sesame*, Philox.3.16 (corr. Meineke for -φλωκτα).

**σησᾰμώδης**, ες, = σησαμοειδής, σπέρμα, καρπός, Thphr.*HP*6.5.3, 9.9.2.

**σῆσις**, εως, ἡ, (σήθω) *sifting*, Suid.: Dor. **σᾶσις**, τοῦ κονίματος τᾶς γᾶς τὰν σᾶσιν Ἄσανδρος [sc. ἐπρίατο] *BCH*23.566 (Delph.).

**σηστέον**, (σήθω) *one must sift*, Dsc.5.88, *Gp.*3.7.1.

**σηστέρτιος** νόμος, = Lat. *sestertius nummus*, *SIG*674.69 (Thessaly, ii B.C.); σ. νοῦμμος *BGU*326 ii 4 (ii A.D.). II. **σηστέρτιον**, τό, = Lat. *sestertium*, *PGnom.*84, al. (ii A.D.).

**Σηστιώδης**, ες, *in the style of Sestius*: Adv. Comp., Σηστιωδέστερον *scriptum*, Cic.*Att.*7.17.2.

**σηστός**, ἡ, (σήθω) nickname of the courtesan Phryne, *the sifter*, because she drained her lovers of money, Herodic.ap.Ath.13.591c. II. σηστὸν καρύων Ποντικῶν, perh. name of a measure, *PCair.Zen.*13.22, cf. 12.9 (iii B.C.).

**Σηστός**, ἡ, Hdt.7.78, 9.115, and Att. acc. to St.Byz.; also ὁ, X.*HG*4.8.5,6, Ephor.155 J.:—*Sestos*, a town on the European side of the Hellespont, over against Abydos, Il.2.836, etc.:—Adj. **Σήστιος**, α, ον, *IG*1[2].203.10, al.; poet. fem. **Σηστιάς**, άδος, Musae.24, 189.

**σηστρίδιον**, τό, Dim. of sq., *PFay.*118.20 (ii A.D.).

**σῆστρον**, τό, (σήθω) *sieve*, Hsch.

**σητάνειος** [ᾰ], ον, Plu.2.466d, Favorin. et Orus ap.*EM*711.49,50; **σητάνιος**, α, ον, Hp. (v. infr.), Dsc. (v. infr.), etc.; Att. **τητάνιος** v.l. for σητ- in Poll.6.73; Dor. **σᾱτάνιος** Sch.Ar.*Nu.*624:—*of this year*, σ. πυροί *this year's*, i.e. *spring*-wheat, Hp.*Acut.*(*Sp.*)53, Dsc.2.85 (v.l. σιτ-), cf. 101 (v.l. σιτ-); ἐν πυρῶν κρίμνοις..σητανίοις Hp.*Mul.*1.50 (v.l. σιτ-), *Nat.Mul.*57; πυροὶ σιτάνιοι (v.l. σητ-) καὶ ἀλευρῖται, opp. σεμιδαλῖται, Ath.Med.ap.Orib.1.2.2; σ. κρόμυα Thphr.*HP*7.4.7; μῆλα Diph.Siph. ap.Ath.3.81a; σ. ἄλευρον Hp.*Acut.*(*Sp.*)63, Dsc.2.85 (pl.); σ. ἄλητον Hp.*Acut.*(*Sp.*)70, *Art.*36; ἄρτος Plu.2.466d (v.l. σιτ-), Anon.*in EN* 449.10:—cf. σητινός. (Derived by Gal.18(1).469, Sch.Ar. l.c. from σῆτες = τῆτες, by Suid., Eust.1792.4, Zonar. from σήθω, as if 'sifted, bolted'; the exact meaning and spelling of σητάν(ε)ιος are uncertain; Plin. has *sitanius HN*22.139, *setania* ib.19.101; σ. ἄρτος is opp. αὐτόπυρος ἄρτος in Plu. l.c., Anon.*in EN* l.c.; σατάνειος (q.v.) is prob. not cogn.)

**σητάνιον** [ᾰ], τό, = ἐπιμηλίς, Dsc.1.118; also **σιτάνιον** Gal.19.99; cf. σατάνειος.

**σητᾰνώδης**, ες, = σητάνιος, Hp.ap.Gal.19.137. (Spelt σιταν-.)

**σητάω**, (σής) *fret*, of moths, Suid.

**σήτειος**· νέος, Hsch. (fort. σητάνειος).

**σῆτες** (Ion. acc. to *EM*711.44), Dor. and Hellenistic **σᾶτες** *IG* (v. infr.), *PCair.Zen.*346.6 (iii B.C.), *EM*711.45:—*this year*, ἐς τὸν σᾶτες ἐνιαυτόν *IG*14.256.9 (Gela); mostly found in the Att. form τῆτες (q.v.).

*σητινός, v. σατινός.

**σητό-βρωτος**, ον, *eaten by moths*, Lxx *Jb.*13.28, *Ep.Jac.*5.2. **-δόκιδες**· ψυχαί, ἢ πτηνὰ ζῷα, Hsch. **-κοπος**, ον, (κόπτω) = σητόβρωτος, Dsc.2.182, *AP*11.78 (Lucill.), Damocr.ap.Gal.14.127.

**σήψ**, gen. σηπός, ἡ, (σήπω) *putrefying sore*, Hp.*Epid.*3.7, Dsc.1.58, al. II. σήψ, ὁ, Arist., Thphr. (v. infr.), Lucan.9.723:—*a serpent, the bite of which causes intense thirst*, Arist.*Mir.*846[b]11, Thphr.*HP*9.11.1 (cj.), etc.; δίψιος Nic.*Th.*147; mortification followed, Ael.*NA*16.40. 2. a kind of *lizard*, Nic.*Th.*817; also called σαύρα Χαλκιδική, Dsc.2.65.

**σηψῐδάκης**, ές, *causing mortification by its bite*, φαλάγγιον Pl.ap. Arist.*Top.*140[a]4.

**σῆψις**, Dor. **σᾶψις**, εως, ἡ, (σήπομαι) *fermentation, putrefaction, decay*, αὐχμηραί τε νόσοι καὶ σήψιες Emp.121; ὑγρῶν σάψιες Ti.Locr. 102c, cf. Arist.*HA*569[a]28; τὸ τέλος τῆς κατὰ φύσιν φθορᾶς σ. ἐστιν Id.*Mete.*379[a]8; σ. χλωρή Hp.*Prorrh.*1.99; σ. ὀστέων, = σφάκελος, Moer.p.342 P. II. (σήπω) *the process by which the intestines reject that part of food which is not nutritious*, opp. πέψις, Arist.*GA*762[a]14, cf. Ath.7.276d, and v. σήπω II. 4. (Acc. to Gal.19.373 Empedocles said that πέψις took place σῆψει.)

**σθεν-ᾰρός**, ά (Ion. ή), όν, poet. and Ion. Adj. *strong, mighty*, Ἄτη Il. 9.505; βραχίων E.*El.*389; σιδήρια Hp.*Fract.*31; *intense*, καρδιωγμός Id. *Mul.*2.126: Comp., ἵππων σθεναρώτερον φυγᾷ πόδα νωμᾶν S.*OT*467. Adv. **-ρῶς** *violently* Phld.*Sign.*20; ἀπωθεῖν Ph.1.553. **-εια**, τά, *a trial of strength*, an ἀγών at Argos, Plu.2.1140c, Hsch. II. σθένεια, ἡ, *the strong one*, of Athena, Lyc.1164; cf. σθένιος. **-ής**· ἰσχυρός, κρατερός, Hsch. **-ιος**, ὁ, = σθεναρός, epith. of Zeus in the Argolid, Paus.2.32.7, 2.34.6: fem. **σθενιάς**, άδος, of Athena, Id.2.30.6, 2.32.5.

**σθενοβλᾰβής**, ές, *hurting the strength, weakening*, Opp.*C.*2.82.

**σθένος**, εος, τό, *strength, might*, esp. *bodily strength*, freq. in Il., less freq. in Od.; κάρτεΐ τε σθένεΐ τε Il.17.329; ἀλκῆς καὶ σθένεος ib. 499; χερσίν τε ποσίν τε καὶ σθένεϊ 20.361; ποδῶν χειρῶν τε σ. Pi.*N.*10.48; opp. φρήν, ib.1.26; γνῶμαι πλέον κρατοῦσιν ἢ σθένος χερῶν S.*Fr.*939: c. inf., ἐν δὲ σ. ὦρσεν ἑκάστῳ..πολεμίζειν *strength* to war, Il.2.451; σ. ποιεῖν εὖ φερέγγυον A.*Eu.*87; σ. ὥστε καθελεῖν E.*Supp.*66 (lyr.): less freq. of the *force* of things, as of a stream, Il.17.751; σ. ἀελίου Pi.*P.*4.144; [ἄρουραι] σθένος ἔμαρψαν Id.*N.*6.11: σθένει *by force*, S.*OC* 842 (lyr.), E.*Ba.*953; λόγῳ τε καὶ σθένει both by right and *might*, S.*OC*68; ὑπὸ σθένους E.*Ba.*1127; παντὶ σθένει with all *one's might*, freq. in treaties, *SIG*122.6, al., Foed.ap.Th.5.23, Pl.*Lg.*646a—the only phrase in which early prose writers use the word (cf. infr. III); found in Lxx, *Jb.*4.10, al. 2. later, generally, *strength, might, power*, moral as well as physical, ἀνάγκης A.*Pr.*105; τῆς ἀληθείας S.*OT*369; ἀγγέλων σ. their *might* or *authority*, A.*Ch.*849: c. gen. obj., ἀγωνίας σ. *strength* for conflict, Pi.*P.*5.113 (s.v.l., -ίαις Bgk.); εἰ σ. λάβοιμι if I should gain *strength* enough, S.*El.*333, cf. 348, etc. II. *a force* of men, Il.18.274; ἐπελθὼν οὐκ ἐλάσσονι σ. S.*Aj.*438: but in both places sense I. 1 is more prob. 2. metaph., *quantity, profusion*, σ. πλούτου Pi.*I.*3.2; ὕδατος, νιφετοῦ, Id.*O.*9.51, *Fr.*107.11. III. periphr., like βίη, ἴς, μένος, σ. Ἰδομενῆος, Ὠρίωνος, Ὠαρίωνος, etc., for Idomeneus, Orion, etc. themselves, Il.13.248, 18.486, Hes.*Op.*598, etc.; σ. ἵππων, ἵππιον, Id.*Sc.*97, Pi.*P.*2.12, etc.:—in Pl. *Phdr.*267c, Χαλκηδονίου σ. is ironical.

**σθενόω**, *strengthen*, 1*Ep.Pet.*5.10, Hsch. (in fut.).

**σθένω**, used only in pres. and impf., Trag.Verb, found also in late Ep., and in later Prose, Lxx 3*Ma.*3.8, Ael.*NA*11.31: (σθένος):—*to have strength* or *might, be strong* or *mighty*, οὐ γὰρ ἂν σθένοντά γε εἷλέν με *in my strength*, S.*Ph.*947; σθενόντων βραχιόνων E.*HF*312: c. dat. modi, σ. χερί, χειρί, ποσίν, *to be strong* in hand, in foot, S.*El.*998, E. *Cyc.*651, *Alc.*267 (lyr.); also σ. μάχῃ, χρήμασι, Id.*Fr.*1048.5, *El.*939; σθένοντος ἐν πλούτῳ S.*Aj.*488: freq. with a neut. Adj., μέγα, μεῖζον σ., A.*Ag.*938, *Pr.*1013; οὐδὲν σ. S.*OC*846; ὅσον σ. how *strong* it *is*, A. *Eu.*619; σ. τοσοῦτον S.*Aj.*1062; ὅσονπερ ἂν σ. Id.*El.*946, cf. *Tr.*927; εἰς ὅσον σ. Id.*Ph.*1403. 2. *to have power*, εἴ τις ἄλλος ἐν πόλει σ. Id.*OC*456; πόλις σθένουσα ib.734; οἱ κάτω σθένοντες *they who rule* below, the gods below, E.*Hec.*49. 3. of things, σθένουσα λαμπὰς A.*Ag.*296; ἀστραπαῖσι λαμπάδων σθένει Id.*Fr.*386. 4. c. inf., *to have strength* or *power* to do, *be able*, mostly with a neg. οὐδέπω μακρὰν πτέσθαι σ. S.*OT*17, cf. A.R.1.62, Lxx l.c.; προσβλέπειν γὰρ οὐ σ. S.*OT*1486; οὐ γὰρ ἂν σθένοι δέμας ἕρπειν Id.*OC*501, cf. 256, 1345, *Aj.* 165 (anap.), etc.; τὸ σιγᾶν οὐ σ. E.*IA*655: with inf. understood, τόδ', εἴπερ ἔσθενον, ἔδρων ἂν S.*El.*604; εἶμι..ὅποιπερ ἂν σ. Id.*Aj.*810, etc. 5. c. acc., βάρος οὐκέτι χεῖρες ἔσθενον *AP*6.93 (Antip.).

**σιά**, Lacon. for θεά, Ar.*Lys.*1263, 1320.

**σῐᾱγ-όνιον**, Ion. **σιηγ-**, τό, in pl., *the parts under* or *near the jaw*, Hp.*Morb.*2.26, Lxx *De.*18.3. II. *cheek-piece, side-piece*, in military engines, Ath.Mech.35.5, Apollod.*Poliorc.*183.3, 188.4. **-ονίτης** [ῑτ] μῦς, ὁ, the muscle *of the jaw-bone*, Alex.Trall.1.16, Steph.*in Hp.* 1.99 D.

**σῐᾱγών**, Ion. **σιηγών**, όνος, ἡ, *jaw-bone, jaw*, Hp.*Epid.*3.17.β', S.*Fr.*112, Ar.*Fr.*287, *PCair.Zen.*76.12 (iii B.C.), Lxx *Jd.*15.14, al.; of an ox, Cratin.163; of a camel, prob. in *PLond.*3.909(*a*).7 (ii A.D.); κινεῖται δὲ τοῖς..ζῴοις ἅπασιν ἡ κάτωθεν σ., κτλ., Arist.*HA*516[a]24, cf. 492[b]22; *cheek*, Cerc.5.6, *Ev.Matt.*5.39:—written **συαγών**, *BGU* 100.5 (ii A.D.), cf. Ath.3.94f; also **σεαγών**, *BGU*153.17,35 (ii A.D.), *Sammelb.*5167.11.

**σιάδες**· θυσία παρὰ Λάκωσιν, Hsch. **σίαι**· πτύσαι, Πάφιοι, Id.

**σῐαίνω**, *cause loathing* or *disgust to* a person, c. acc., Sch.Luc. *DMort.*20.9:—Pass. with aor. ἐσιάνθην, *feel loathing*, *Gloss.*, Hsch. s.v. ἀπεκάκησεν; σιαίνεται· αἰτιατική, Suid.; τὸ λάχανον ὅδε σαπρόν ἐστι καὶ σιαίνομε (sic) *POxy.*1849.2 (vi/vii A.D.).

**σῐᾰλενδρίς**, ίδος, ἡ, perh. = σιαλίς I, Call.*Fr.*100[c]6.

**σῐᾰλ-ίδιον**, τό, v. σαλαΐδιον. **-ίζω** or **σιελ-**, (σίαλον) *slaver, foam*, Archig.ap.Gal.13.170 (σιελ-); ἦχοι..σιελίζοντες noises in the throat *with expectoration*, Hp.*Prorrh.*1.114, cf. Hsch.

**σιᾰλίς**, ίδος, ἡ, a kind of *bird*, Did.ap.Ath.9.392f. II. σιαλίς· βλέννος, Ἀχαιοί, Hsch.

**σῐᾰλ-ισμός** or **σιελ-**, ὁ, *flow of saliva*, Gal.7.470 (-ελ-), 16.146 (-αλ-), Ruf.ap.Orib.8.24.64 (-ελ-), Archig.ib.8.2.6 (-ελ-). **-ιστήριον** or **σιελ-**, τό, a *bridle-bit*, which is *apt to be covered with foam*, *Gp.*16.1.11 (where -ελ-). **-ον** or **σίελον**, τό, *spittle, saliva*, Hp. *Aph.*7.16, Pherecr.69, X.*Mem.*1.2.54; σιάλῳ παιδία παραλείφειν Democrates ap.Arist.*Rh.*1407[a]8. II. *synovial fluid*, Hp.*Carn.* 10. [Att. σίαλον, τό, Hellenic σίελος, ὁ, acc. to Moer.p.347 P.; the latter occurs Lxx *Is.*40.15 (neut. σίελον cod. A), Aret.*SD*2.2, *PMag. Par.*1.132: pl. τὰ σίελα Lxx 1*Ki.*21.13.]

**σιαλοπάλλαγος**· ὁ παράληρος, καὶ ἀνόητος, Hsch.

**σῐᾰλοποιός**, in form **σιελοπ-**, όν, *producing saliva*, Xenocr.ap. Orib.2.58.78.

**σιαλόρ**· θαλίς, Λάκωνες, Hsch.

⊛ **σῖᾰλος** [ῐ], ὁ, *fat hog*, Il.21.363, Od.2.300, 20.163, Q.S.11.170; also σῦς σ. Il.9.208, Od.14.41,81, etc., where σίαλος is the specific Subst., added as in ἴρηξ κίρκος, σῦς κάπρος, etc. :—also in Prose, Thphr.ap.Porph.*Abst.*2.25. 2. *fat, grease*, Hp.*Acut.*(*Sp.*)37 codd. MV, but λάσιον is prob. to be restored fr. Erot. and Gal. II. = σίαλον, *EM*712.3.

**σῐᾰλοχόος**, ον, (χέω) *letting the spittle run*, Aret.*SA*1.7, *SD*2.6; σ. ἀδένες the *salivary* glands, Gal.16.508: hence **σῐᾰλοχοέω**, *secrete saliva*, Hp.*Vict.*2.47; *slaver*, Id.*Morb.*3.10.

**σῐᾰλ-όω**, (σίαλος) *fatten*, in Pass. σιαλοῦται, Hsch.:—Act. σιαλῶσαι· ποικῖλαι, Id. **-ώδης**, ες, (σίαλον) *like slaver, slavering*, Hp.*Morb. Sacr.*5, D.P.791. II. (σίαλος) *fat*, σκυλάκια Hp.*Steril.*217. **-ωμα**, ατος, τό, *ornamental shield-rim*, Plb.6.23.4; cf. σιγάλωμα.

**σῐαντ-ία**, ἡ, (σιαίνω) *nuisance*, ἀπαλλαγῆναι τῆς σ. ταύτης *POxy.* 1855.13 (vi/vii A.D.); = *fastidium*, *Gloss.* **-ός**, ή, όν, *taeter*, ib.; cf. sq.

**σῐαντόφρικτος**, ον, *horridus*, *Gloss.* (fort. σιαντός· φρικτός).

**σιβαία**· ἡ σίβδα, πήρα, Hsch. **σίβδη**, ἡ, Dor. **-δā**, v. σίδη. **σιβδία**· σιδία, Id. **σίβληθρα**· πόπανα τὰ περικεκνισμένα, Id.

⊛ **Σίβυλλ-α** [ῐ], ἡ, *Sibyl*, Heraclit.92, Ar.*Pax* 1095,1116, Pl.*Phdr.* 244b. Early writers only recognize *one* Sibyl (Σίβυλλαι καὶ Βάκιδες, Arist.*Pr.*954ᵃ36, is no exception), first localized at Erythrae or Cumae, Id.*Mir.*838ᵃ6; later, others are mentioned, cf. Str.14.1.34, Paus.10.12.1 sqq., Sch.Pl.l.c., Buresch *Klaros* p.120. [Σίβιλλα *IG*2². 1534.85 (iv B.C.).] **-αίνω**, *foretell like a Sibyl*, D.S.4.66. **-ειος**, ον, *Sibylline*, Σ. βίβλοι, at Rome, Plu.*Fab.*4; τὰ Σ. D.H.6.17, Plu. *Marc.*3, etc.; also **-ιακός**, ή, όν, D.S.34/5.10. **-ιάω**, *want the Sibyl*, = χρησμῶν ἐρᾶν (Sch. l. c.), Ar.*Eq.*61. **-ιστής**, οῦ, ὁ, *believer in the Sibyl*, Cels.ap.Orig.*Cels.*5.61; *seer, diviner*, Plu.*Mar.*42.

⊛ **σῐβύνη** [ῠ], ἡ, and **σῐβύνης** [ῠ], ου, ὁ, Alex.131 (fem.), *AP*7.421 (Mel.), 6.93 (Antip., masc.):—*hunting spear*, and generally, *spear, pike*, D.S.18.27, 20.33:—also written **ζιβύνη** (q. v.), **συβίνη**, *PCair. Zen.*362.34 (iii B.C.), cf. συ[μ]βίνη[ς] (post συβήνη)· καπροβόλον, ἐμβόλιον, Hsch., but σιγύνης [ῡ] is prob. not related. (Illyrian acc. to Fest.p.453 L., citing Ennius.)

**σῐβύνιον** [ῠ], τό, Dim. of foreg., Plb.6.23.9.

**σῖγα**, Adv., (σιγή) *silently*, used in Trag. (and late Ep., A.R.1.267), σῖγ' ἔχοντες S.*Ph.*258; σῖγ' ἔχουσα πρόσμενε Id.*El.*1236; ἀλλὰ σ. πρόσμενε ib.1399; ἄκουε σ. Id.*Fr.*815; κάθησο σ. Ar.*Ach.*59: also as an exclam., σῖγα *hush! be still!* A.*Ag.*1344; so οὐ σ.; Id.*Th.*250; οὐ σῖγ' ἀνέξει; S.*Aj.*75; the public crier proclaiming *silence* said σ. πᾶς (sc. ἔστω), Ar.*Ach.*238, cf. E.*Hec.*532; σ. κηρῦξαι στρατῷ Id.*Ph.* 1224. 2. *under one's breath, in a whisper, quietly, secretly* (cf. σιγή II), τὰ δὲ σ. τις βαΰζει A.*Ag.*449; σῖγ' ἐπέρχεται φάτις S.*Ant.*700; σ. σήμαινε Id.*Ph.*22; σ. μὲν ἡρώεσσιν ἐκέκλετο Orph.*A.*702; πῶς αἱ πατρῷαί σ' ἄλοκες φέρειν.. σῖγ' ἐδυνάθησαν; S.*OT*1212.

**σίγα**, imper. of σιγάω (q. v.):—**σιγά**, Dor. for σιγή.

**σῑγᾷ**, 3 sg. of σιγάω; or Dor. dat. of σιγή.

**σῑγ-άζω**, *bid* one *be silent, silence* him, Ζεφύρου πνοάς Pi.*Parth.*2. 16; τινα(ς) X.*An.*6.1.32, D.C.64.14; τύμπανα Opp.*C.*3.286:—Pass., D.C.39.34. **-ᾰλέος**, α, ον, *silent, still*, *AP*7.597 (Jul.), Orph.*A.* 1003, etc.

**σῑγᾰλόεις**, εσσα, εν, *glossy, glittering*, Ep. Adj.: 1. of apparel, σ. χιτών Od.15.60, 19.232; εἵματα Il.22.154, Od.6.26; ῥήγεα ib. 38; δέσματα Il.22.468; cf. νεοσίγαλος. 2. of horses' reins, *glittering* with colour or metal work, Od.6.81, Il.5.226, etc.; of house-furniture, θρόνος Od.5.86; of a queen's chamber, ὑπερῷα σιγαλόεντα 16.449, 18.206, etc.; νηὸν [σιγ]αλόεντα *IG*14.1026 (iii/iv A.D.). II. *fatty, oily*, ἀμύγδαλα Hermipp.63.20; μνία Numen. ap.Ath.7.295c.

**σῑγᾰλός**, Dor. for σιγηλός (q. v.).

⊛ **σῑγᾰλ-όω**, (σιγαλόεις) *make smooth, polish*, Apollon.*Lex.* s. v. σιγαλόεντα. ⊛ **-ωμα**, ατος, τό, *instrument for smoothing* or *polishing*, esp. of shoemakers for smoothing leather, ibid., Hsch. s. v. σιγαλόεντα. II. *border, edging* of a dress, Id.; v. σιάλωμα.

**σιγᾶς**, i. e. perh. Dor. contr. from *σιγάεις ( = *σιγήεις), *silent*, dub. in A.*Ag.*412 (lyr.).

⊛ **σῑγάω**, Dor. 2 sg. σιγῇς Ar.*Ach.*778; Cyrenaic inf. σιγέν *Berl.Sitzb.* 1927.170; 1 sg. opt. σιγῷμ(ι) E.*Hipp.*336: fut. **-ήσομαι** S.*OC*113, 980, E.*Ba.*801, Ar.*Av.*1684, etc.; later **-ήσω** *AP*9.27 (Arch. or Parmen.), D.Chr.37.42, Charito 1.10: pf. σεσίγηκα Aeschin.3.218:—**Pass.**, fut. σιγηθήσομαι E.*IT*1076; σεσιγήσομαι Pl.*Ep.*311c: aor. ἐσιγήθην E.*Supp.*298, Aeschin.2.86: pf. σεσίγημαι (v. infr.): (σιγή):—*keep silence*, used by Hom. only in imper. σίγα, *hush! be still!* Il.14. 90, Od.17.393; σιγᾶν *h.Merc.*93, Hdt.8.61,110; but freq. in Pi., Trag., and Att., as Pi.*N.*10.29, A.*Pr.*200, etc.; σ. περί τινος E.*Hipp.*312; πρὸς οὓς δεῖ Pl.*Phdr.*276a; πρὸς τοῦτο, ἐν τούτῳ, X.*Cyr.*5.5.20, *An.*5. 6.27. 2. metaph. of things, σιγῶν δ' ὄλεθρος καὶ μέγα φωνοῦντ'.. ἀμαθύνει A.*Eu.*935 (anap.); σύριγγες οὐ σιγῶσιν Id.*Supp.*181; σίγησε δ' αἰθήρ E.*Ba.*1084; σ. πόντος, σ. ἀῆται, ἁ δ' ἐμὰ οὐ σ. ἀνία Theoc.2. 38:—in E.*Fr.*781.13, τὰ σιγῶντ' ὀνόματ'.. δαιμόνων seems to be = τὰ ἄρρητα, *secret, mystical*:—Pass., μέμψομαι σιωπὴν ὡς ἐσιγήθη κακῶς I shall impute as a fault that silence *was kept*, Id.*Supp.*298; also τί σεσίγηται δόμος Ἀδμήτου; why is it *all silent?* Id.*Alc.*78; σιγῶντα λέγειν, λέγοντα σιγᾶν, phrases illustrating a logical fallacy, Pl.*Euthd.* 300b, Arist.*SE*166ᵃ13. II. trans., *hold silent, keep secret*, Pi.*Fr.* 81, A.*Pr.*106,441, *Ag.*36, Hdt.7.104 (s. v. l.), etc.:—Pass., *to be kept silent* or *secret*, σεσιγαμένον χρῆμα Pi.*O.*9.103; ὁ θάνατος.. ἐσιγήθη Hdt.5.21; σιγώμενος S.*Fr.*653; ἐσιγάθη δ' ἂν ὑφορβός *would never have been heard of*, Theoc.16.54.

⊛ **σιγγλάριος**, ὁ, = Lat. *singularis*; εἴλη Σιν[γ]λαρίων, = *ala Singularium*, *IGRom.*4.1213 (Thyatira, iii A.D.); **σιγγουλάριος**, Lyd. *Mag.*3.7, *PLond.*5.1797.6 (vi A.D.), etc.; written **σινγουλάρις** or **-ιος**, Baillet *Inscriptions des tombeaux des rois à Thèbes* 1473, 1688. II. ἱππεὺς σινγλάρις, = *eques singularis*, *IGRom.*3.394 (= 503) (Pisidia, iii A.D.).

**σιγγρίᾰσις**, εως, ἡ, = ἄφθα (A), in horses, *Hippiatr.*97 (v.l. **σιγρίασις**).

**σῑγεῖν**, Lacon. for θιγεῖν, Ar.*Lys.*1004, cf. Hsch. s. v. σίγε.

**σῑγέρπης**, ου, ὁ, (ἕρπω) *one that steals silently to* a place, Call.*Epigr.* 45.6 (cj. Bentl., for σειγάρνης cod. Pal., cf. σιγέρπης· λαθροδάκτης, Hsch.).

**σῑγ-ή**, Dor. **σιγά**, ἡ, *silence*, σ. ἔχειν keep *silence*, Hdt.1.86; σ. ποιήσασθαι make *silence*, Id.6.130; παρέχειν S.*Tr.*1115, etc.; σ. φυλάσσετε E.*IA*542; σ. τῶνδε θήσομαι πέρι Id.*Med.*66; γύναι, γυναιξὶ κόσμον ἡ σ. φέρει S.*Aj.*293; κόσμος ἡ σ. τε καὶ τὰ παῦρ' ἔπη Id.*Fr.*64; ὦ παῖ, σιώπα· πόλλ' ἔχει σ. καλά Id.*Fr.*81; πολλῶν φάρμακον κακῶν σ. Carc. 7.2; δυσμενὴς τῇ σ. Hdt.7.237; ἡ ἄγαν σ. S.*Ant.*1251, cf. 1256: pl., σιγαὶ ἀνέμων E.*IA*10 (anap.); σιγαί.. τῶν νεωτέρων παρὰ πρεσβυτέροις Pl.*R.*425b. b. in a mystical or religious sense, Aristeas 95, *Apoc.*8.1; σ. σύμβολον θεοῦ ζῶντος *PMag.Par.*1.559. II. σιγῇ, as Adv., *in silence*, the only case used by Hom., πάντες ἥατο σιγῇ Il. 19.255, cf. 3.8, al.; also διὰ σιγῆς, μετὰ σ., Pl.*Grg.*450c, *Sph.*264a; σὺν σιγῇ Critias 25.22: like σῖγα, as an exclam., σιγῇ νῦν *be silent now!* Od.15.440. 2. *in an undertone, in a whisper, secretly* (cf. σῖγα 2), σ. λόγον ἐποιέετο Hdt.8.74; τὰ σ. βουλευόμενα X.*Mem.*1.1. 19; σιγῇ ἔχειν τι keep it *secret*, Hdt.9.93; σιγᾷ καλύψαι, σιγῇ στέγειν, κεύθειν, Pi.*N.*9.7, S.*OT*341, *Tr.*989 (anap.). 3. c. gen., σιγῇ τινος *unknown to* him, Hdt.2.140, E.*Med.*587. **-ηλός**, ή, όν, Dor. **σῑγᾱλός**, όν, Pi.*P.*9.92:—*silent*, Hp.*Acut.*65, S.*Ph.*741, Nicopho 27; *disposed to silence*, S.*Tr.*416; of animals, Arist.*HA*488ᵃ 34; τὰ ἐκ ποδῶν σιγηλὰ σῴζοντες E.*Ba.*1049. Adv. **-λῶς** Poll.5. 147. **-ημονᾶς**· σιγᾶς, Hsch. **-ηρός**, ά, όν, less Att. form for σιγηλός, Men.*Mon.*167, Hp.*Ep.*12; opp. talkative, γυνή Lxx *Si.* 26.14. Adv. **-ρῶς** Hsch. **-ητέον**, *one must be silent*, E.*Hel.* 1387. ⊛ **-ητής**, οῦ, ὁ, *one who keeps silence*, of Bacchic initiates, in pl., *AJA*37.262 (Latium, ii A.D., σειγ-). **-ητικός**, ή, όν, = σιγηλός, Hp.*Decent.*3.

**σῑγιλλάρια**, τά, = Lat. *sigillaria, puppets*, M.Ant.7.3.

**σίγιον**, τό, a kind of cicada, Sch.Ar.*Av.*1095.

**σίγιστρον**, τό, = ζύγαστρον, Eust.956.6, 1604.16.

**σιγιστροπύλη** [ῠ], ἡ, *cupboard door*, *POxy.*1923.5 (v/vi A.D.).

**σίγκηρες**· ὑπηρέται βάρβαροι, Hsch.

⊛ **σίγλα**, ἡ, *ear-ring*, *PMasp.*340ᵛ77 (vi A.D.), Hsch.; Aeol. acc. to Poll.5.97.

⊛ **σίγλος** or **σίκλος** (the latter form in Lxx, J., and S. (v. infr.)), ὁ, = Hebr. *shekel*, a weight (Lxx *Ex.*30.23, al.) or coin (ib.*Le.*5.15); δραχμὴ μία τὸ ἥμισυ τοῦ σ. ib.*Ex.*39.2 (38.26); but ὁ σ... Ἀττικὰς δέχεται δραχμὰς τέσσαρας J.*AJ*3.8.2, cf. Hsch. s. v. σίκλος. 2. the Persian σ. was the $\frac{1}{3000}$th part of the Babylonian silver talent, half the silver stater of Asia Minor, and = 7½ Att. ὀβολοί, X.*An.*1.5.6; or 8 ὀβολοί, acc. to Phot., quoting S.*Fr.*1094 (perh. erroneously, instead of for sense II). II. *ear-ring*, Phot., cf. sq. III. in Plb.34.8.7, prob. corrupt for Σικελικός.

**σιγλοφόρος**, ον, *wearing ear-rings*, *Com.Adesp.*792.

⊛ **σίγμα** or **σῖγμα**, the letter *sigma*, v. Σ σ. II. *a* ⊂ *shaped portico*, *Princeton Exp.Inscr.* III A No.560 (v A.D.), *JHS*28.195 (Aspendus, written σίμμα). 2. Lat. *sigma, crescent-shaped dining-table*, Mart. 10.48.6, etc.

**σιγμᾰτίζω**, *write with sigma*, διπλῶς σιγματίζεται *is written with double* σ, Eust.1389.15.

**σιγμᾰτοειδής**, ές, = sq., Onos.21.6, Zos.3.11.3; ἐκκοπή Apollon. Cit.ap.Erot. s. v. ἄμβην (v.l. σιγμο-). Adv. **-δῶς** Sch.Il.9.5.

**σιγμοειδής**, ές, *of the shape of sigma* (⊂), *crescent-shaped, semicircular*, ἀπόφυσις Gal.*UP*13.12; of the moon, Cleom.2.5. Adv. σιγμοειδῶς Heliod.ap.Orib.49.8.6.

**σιγμός**, ὁ, (σίζω) *hissing*, as of tortoises, Arist.*HA*536ᵃ7; as a signal, Plu.2.593b; in Magic, Plot.2.9.14; in Gramm., of sibilants, D.T.631.18, Phld.*Po.Herc.*994.33, S.E.*M.*1.102.

⊛ **σίγνον**, τό, = Lat. *signum, statue*, *IG*14.971 (Rome, iii A.D.). II. pl., *the place where the standards were set up* in a camp, used as a *store, prison*, etc., *PLond.*2.413.12 (iv A.D.), *PLond.ined.*2487.18 (iv A.D.).

**σιγνοφόρος**, ὁ, = Lat. *signifer*, of begging priests (μηναγύρται), Tz.*H.*13.245.

**σῖγος**, εος, τό, = σιγή, *An.Ox.*2.319.

**σίγραι**, οἱ, a kind of *wild swine*, βραχεῖς καὶ σιμοί, Hsch.

**σιγρίασις**, v. σιγγρίασις.

**σιγύνης** [ῡ], ου, ὁ, *spear*, Hdt.5.9, Opp.*C.*1.152; also **σίγῡνος**, ὁ, A.R.2.99, *AP*6.176 codd. (Maced.); **σίγῡνον**, τό, Arist.*Po.*1457ᵇ6, *AP*7.578 (Agath.); and in Lyc.556, **σίγυμνον** (in dat. -ῳ).—Cyprian acc. to Hdt. and Arist. ll. cc., Scythian acc. to Sch.Par.A.R.4.320 (cf. III). II. σιγύνης among the Ligyes near Marseilles was used for κάπηλος, Hdt. l. c. III. Σιγύνναι, οἱ, a people on the Middle Danube, Hdt. l. c.; in A.R.4.320, Σίγυννοι; in Str.11.11.8, Σίγιννοι. [In A.R. and Opp., ῡ; freq. written with double ν, σιγύννης, etc.]

**σίγχος**, ὁ, v. σκίγγος.

**σίδαιον**· ἑτεροκλινές, Hsch. (fort. σκαιόν). **σίδᾱρος**, Dor. for σίδηρος; for all forms in σιδαρ–, v. σιδηρ–.

**σίδειος** [ῐ], α, ον, (σίδη) *of the pomegranate*, Hdn.Gr.1.135.

**σιδεύνης**, ου, ὁ, Lacon. word, *a boy in his fifteenth* or *sixteenth year*, Phot. s. v. συνέφηβος.

❀ **σίδη**, ἡ, = ῥόα, *pomegranate* tree and fruit, Emp.80, Hp.*Nat.Mul.* 32, *Ulc.*11: Boeot. **σίδα** for Att. ῥόα, Epaminond.ap.Agatharch.*Fr. Hist.*8 J.; **σιδέα**, *IG*14.352 i 54 (Halaesa, pl.); **σίβδα**, Call.*Lav.Pall.* 28. II. a water-plant growing near Orchomenos in Boeotia, = νυμφαία, Thphr.*HP*4.10.1, Nic.*Th.*887. [ῑ in signf. I, ib.72,870, etc.; but ῐ in signf. I, Emp. l. c., and in signf. II, Nic.*Th.*887; cf. σίδιον, σιδόεις.]

**σῐδηρ-ᾰγωγός**, όν, *attracting iron*, of the magnet, S.E.*M.*1. 226. **-εία**, ἡ, *working in iron*, X.*An.*5.5.1. **-εῖα**, τά, *iron-mines*, Arist.*Pol.*1259ᵃ25, Thphr.*HP*5.9.2, *Lap.*52, Str.1.2.39: sg. **-εῖον**, τό, *IG*11(2).161 *A* 19 (Delos, iii B.C.). **-ένδετος**, ον, *iron-banded*, *Edict.Diocl.*15.50(Megalop.). **-εόεις**, εσσα, εν, = sq., βρόχοι *Epic.Alex.Adesp.*9 ix 12. ❀**-εος**, α, Ion. and Ep. η, ον, Att. contr. **σιδηροῦς**, ᾶ, οῦν *SIG*144.14, etc.; Ep. also **σιδήρειος**, η, ον, v. infr.; also late, *Stud.Pal.*20.217.9 (vi A.D.) (fem. -ειος Theognost.*Can.* 56); Dor. **σιδάρεος** [ᾱ] *IG*4²(1).103.114 (Epid., iv B.C.), and v. infr. II, also **σιδάριος** *SIG*246 ii 67 (Delph., iv B.C.); Aeol. **σιδάριος** Theoc.29.24:—*made of iron* or *steel*, ἄξων Il.5.723; σιδηρείη κορύνη 7.141; πύλαι 8.15; ὑποκρητηρίδιον Hdt.1.25; σκύταλον Theoc.17. 31; χεὶρ σ. *grappling-iron*, Th.4.25, 7.62: also σ. ὀρυμαγδός, i.e. the clang *of arms*, Il.17.424; σ. οὐρανός the *iron* sky, the firmament, which the ancients held to be of metal, Od.15.329 (cf. χάλκεος); σ. γένος, of the *Iron* age, Hes.*Op.*176. 2. metaph., ἦ γὰρ σοί γε σ. ἐν φρεσὶ θυμός a soul *of iron*, i.e. *hard, stubborn as iron*, Il. 22.357, cf. Od.23.172; οὐδέ μοι.. θυμὸς ἐνὶ στήθεσσι σ., ἀλλ' ἐλεήμων 5.191; οὐδ' εἴ οἱ κραδίη γε σ. ἔνδοθεν ἦεν 4.293; σιδήρειόν νύ τοι ἦτορ Il.24.205,521; ἦ ῥά νυ σοί γε σ. πάντα τέτυκται thou art *iron* all! Od. 12.280; πυρὸς μένος.. σ. the *iron* force of fire, Il.23.177; of Heracles, the *ironsided*, Simon.8; of men, Ar.*Ach.*491; σὰρξ σ. Theoc.22.47; ὦ σιδήρεοι O ye *ironhearted!* Aeschin.3.166; εἰ μὴ σιδηροῦς ἐστιν, οἴομαι ἔννουν γεγονέναι Lys.10.20; σ. λόγοι Pl.*Grg.*509a. II. σιδάρεοι, οἱ, *Byzantine iron coins*, always used in Dor. form, even at Athens, Ar.*Nu.*249, Pl.Com.96, Stratt.36. **-εύς**, έως, ὁ, *worker in iron, smith*, X.*Ages.*1.26, *Vect.*4.6, Aret.*SD*1.11, Them.*Or.*20.236 d. **-εύω**, *work in iron*, Poll.7.105. **-ήεις**, εσσα, εν, poet. for σιδήρεος, Nic.*Al.*51, Man.1.313. **-ίζω**, *to be like iron*, of the magnet, Gal.11.612; of chalybeate baths, etc., Antyll.ap.Orib.10.3.1, Paul.Aeg.1.52, 6.21. **-ιον** (Dor. **σιδάριον** *Schwyzer* 180.5 (Crete)), τό, *implement* or *tool of iron*, *IG*1².313.128 (v B.C.); θερμοῖσι σ. ἐκκαίειν τοὺς ὀφθαλμοὺς *with* hot *irons*, Hdt.7.18; ἐπαΐοντες σιδηρίων feeling *iron*, not being proof against it, Id.3.29; of a *knife*, Id.9.37, cf. Lys.1.42; σ. εἰς κρεονομίαν *PCair.Zen.*720.3 (iii B.C.); σ. λιθουργά, of a stonemason's *tools*, Th.4.4, cf. Thphr.*Lap.*41; σιδηρίων μισθός *IG*2².1656; λίθους καὶ ξύλα καὶ σ. Pl.*Euthd.*300b; σ. πλατέα Arist. *Cael.*313ᵃ17. II. *iron*, Daimachus 4 J. (v.l. σίδηρον). **-ιουργός**, ὁ, *faber ferrarius*, *Gloss.* ❀ **-ίσκος**, Dor. σιδᾱρ–, ὁ, a medical instrument, perh. *spatula*, *Supp.Epigr.*1.414 (Crete, v/iv B.C.). ❀ **-ίτης** [ῑτ], ου, ὁ, fem. **-ῖτις**, ιδος: Dor. **σῐδᾱρίτας**, α, ὁ:—*of iron*, σ. πόλεμος *iron* war, Pi.*N.*5.19; σ. τέχνη the *smith's* art, Eup.263; σ. πέτρα rock *with iron ore* in it, D.S.5.13; σ. γῆ Arist.*Fr.*326 ed. Berol., Poll.3.87. 2. σιδηρῖτις, with or without λίθος, *loadstone*, Phld. *Sign.*9, Str.15.1.38, Plu.2.1005c, etc. 3. *a precious stone*, Plin. *HN*37.58, al.; used as remedy for snake-bite, Orph.*L.*361,390, 419. II. σιδηρῖτις, ἡ, *ironwort*, *Sideritis romana*, Dsc.4.33, Plin. *HN*25.43, Aret.*CD*2.12; also σ. πόα Hsch.; βοτάνη ἡ σ. J.*AJ*3.7.6, Gal.12.885. 2. also applied by Dsc. to *burnet*, *Poterium Sanguisorba*, 4.34; *Cretan fig-wort*, *Scrophularia lucida*, ib.35; *Achilles' woundwort*, *Achillea tomentosa*, ib.36. 3. = ἑλξίνη, ib.85. 4. = χαμαίπιτυς, Id.3.158. 5. = περιστερεὼν ὕπτιος, Ps.-Dsc.4.60.

**σῐδηρο-βαστᾰγή**, ἡ, *provision, supply of iron*, *PMasp.*57.12 (vi A.D.), *PFlor.*297.41 (vi A.D.). **-βᾰφος**, ον, *of ferruginous colour*, Lyd.*Mens.*4.30. **-βόλιον**, τό, *anchor*, Sch.Luc.*Lex.*15. **-βόρος**, ον, = σιδηροβρώς, σ. σίδηρος *a file*, Opp.*C.*2.174. **-βρῑθής**, ές, *iron-loaded*, ξύλον E.*Fr.*531. **-βρώς**, ῶτος, ὁ, ἡ, (βιβρώσκω) *iron-eating*, θηγάνη S.*Aj.*820; where the Sch. has a fem. form **-βρῶτις**, ιδος. **-δάκτῠλος**, ον, *iron-fingered*, κρεάγρη *AP*6.101 (Phil.). **-δέσμος**, ον, *with bonds of iron*, ἀνάγκαι Lxx 3*Ma.*4.9. **-δετέω**, (δέω) *bind in iron*, Heraclit.*Ep.*7.8 (Pass.). ❀ **-δετος**, ον, *iron-bound*, πόρπακες B.*Fr.*3; ἐδέδετο ἐν ξύλῳ σ., of stocks, Hdt.9.37; μόχλοι J.*BJ* 6.5.3. **-εις**, εσσα, εν, gloss on μελάνδετος, *EM*551.40. **-θήκη**, ἡ, *armoury*, Hsch. s. v. ὀγκίαι. **-θώραξ**, ᾶκος, ὁ, ἡ, *with iron breastplate*, Sch.D Il.2.47, 3.131. **-κατάδῐκος**, ον, *condemned to the iron*, i.e. *mutilated*, Suid. s. v. σπάδων. **-κμής**, ῆτος, ὁ, ἡ, (κάμνω) *slain by iron*, i.e. *by the sword*, used with neut. dat. βοτοῖς, S.*Aj.*325; cf. ἀνδροκμής. **-κόλεος**, ον, *iron-sheathed*, μάχαιρα *PCair.Zen.*54.41 (iii B.C.). ❀ **-κόντρα**, ἡ, in pl., perh. gladiatorial contest *with barbed iron spears*, *Ausonia* 6.9* (Gortyn); sg. in *IGRom.*3.360 (Sagalassus); cf. κοντροκυνηγέσιον. **-κόπος**, ὁ, *faber ferrarius*, *Gloss.* **-κωπος**, ον, *armed with iron*, Ἕλλαν Tim.*Pers.*155. **-μήτωρ**, ορος, ἡ, *mother of iron*, αἶα A.*Pr.*303.

**σίδηρον**, τό, v. σίδηρος.

**σῐδηρο-νόμος**, ον, (νέμω) *distributing with iron*, i.e. *with the sword*, χεὶρ A.*Th.*788 (lyr.). **-νωτος**, ον, *iron-backed*, ἀσπίδος τύποι E.*Ph.* 1130. **-πέδη**, ἡ, *iron fetter*, Eust.1411.32. **-πλαστος**, ον, *moulded of iron*, Luc.*Ocyp.*164. ❀ **-πληκτος**, Dor. **-πλακτος**, ον, *smitten by iron*, A.*Th.*911 (lyr.). **-πλοκος**, ον, *plaited of iron*, Hld.9.15. **-πλύτης** [ῠ], ου, ὁ, *one who washes iron*, dub. cj. in Hsch. s. v. σάλαγξ. **-ποίκῐλος**, ὁ, name of *a variegated stone*, Plin. *HN*37.182. **-πους**, ουν, gen. ποδος, *iron-footed*, ἵπποι Nonn.*D.*29. 212. **-πτερος**, ον, *iron-winged*, Sch.A.R.2.1031,1090. **-πώλης**, ου, ὁ, *ironmonger*, Critias(?) [*Fr.*70] ap.Poll.7.196, *IG*2².1673.16.

**σίδηρος** [ῐ], Dor. **σίδᾱρος** *IG*4²(1).102.61 (Epid., iv B.C.), etc.: ὁ; also ἡ, Nic.*Th.*923: neut. **σίδηρον**, τό, Sch.D Il.4.151, v.l. in Hdt.7. 65 and Daimachus 4 J. (but prob. f.l. for σιδήριον in Gal.19.72, cf. Hsch. s. v. Ἀκίς): pl. σίδηρα Aret.*SD*2.12, *EM*26.36, Tz. (v. infr.): —*iron*, σ. πολιός Il.9.366, Od.24.168; ἰόεις Il.23.850; μέλας Hes.*Op.* 151; αἴθων Il.4.485, al.; πολύκμητος 6.48, al., cf. Od.9.393; as an article of traffic, οἰνίζοντο.. Ἀχαιοί, ἄλλοι μὲν χαλκῷ, ἄλλοι δ' αἴθωνι σ. Il.7.473; πλέων.. μετὰ χαλκόν· ἄγω δ' αἴθωνα σίδηρον Od.1.184; χαλκός τε χρυσός τε πολύκμητός τε σ., of treasures, Il.11.133, al.; as a prize, 23.261,850; Σκύθης σ., because brought from the Euxine, A.*Th.*818; ὁ πόντιος ξεῖνος.. θηκτὸς σ. ib.942 (lyr.). 2. freq. as a symbol of *hardness* (cf. σιδήρεος I. 2), or of *stubborn force*, Il.20.372, Od.19.494; ὀφθαλμοὶ ὡσεὶ κέρα ἕστασαν ἠὲ σ. ib.211; οὔ σφι λίθος χρὼς οὐδὲ σ. Il.4.510; ἐκ σ. κεχάλκευται.. καρδίαν Pi.*Fr.*123.4, cf. S. *Fr.*658; ἦσθα πέτρος ἢ σ. E.*Med.*1279 (lyr.), cf. Pl.*Lg.*666c; also of *firmness, steadfastness*, πέτρης ὅ γ' ἔχων νόον ἠὲ σ. Mosch.4.44, cf. Ach.Tat.5.22. II. *anything made of iron, iron tool* or *implement*, for husbandry, Il.4.485, cf. 23.834: also of weapons, *arrow-head*, 4. 123; *sword* or *knife*, 18.34, 23.30; αὐτὸς γὰρ ἐφέλκεται ἄνδρα σ. Od. 16.294, cf. E.*Or.*966 (lyr.); *axe-head*, Od.19.587: generally, *arms*, οἱ Ἀθηναῖοι σ. κατέθεντο Th.1.6; ὅπλοις τε καὶ σιδήρῳ διώξειν *OGI*532. 25 (Galatia, i B.C.): also, *knife, sickle*, Hes.*Op.*387: pl., *fishing-hooks*, Theoc.21.49; *irons, fetters*, Aret.*SD*2.12, Tz.*H.*13.302; cf. σιδήριον. III. *place for selling iron, smithy* or *cutler's shop*, ἀγαγόντα εἰς τὸν σ. X.*HG*3.3.7.

**σῐδηρό-σπαρτος**, ον, *sown* or *produced by iron*, Luc.*Ocyp.*100. **-σφᾰγία**, ἡ, *slaying with the sword*, Vett.Val.128.2. **-τέκτων**, ονος, ὁ, *worker in iron*, A.*Pr.*714. **-τευκτος**, ον, *wrought of iron*, βέλος Epicr.8. **-τόκος**, ον, *producing iron*, *AP*9.561 (Phil.). **-τομέω**, *cut* or *cleave with iron*, ib.311 (Id.). **-τροχος**, ον, *with iron wheels*, ἅμαξαι Suid. s. v. περίγρα. **-τρύπᾰνον** [ῠ], τό, *iron borer*, Daimachus 4 J. **-τρωτος**, ον, *wounded with iron*, Sch.D Il.13. 323.

**σῐδηρουργ-εῖον**, τό, *iron-mine*, Str.4.2.2, 5.1.8, 17.2.2. **-ία**, ἡ, *working in iron*, Poll.7.105. **-ός**, ὁ, *iron-worker, smith*, Thphr. *HP*4.8.5, *PPar.*5.31.6 (ii B.C.), *Ostr.Bodl.*1.319 (ii B.C.), *PLond.*3. 1207.17 (i B.C.).

**σῐδηροῦς**, ᾶ, οῦν, v. σιδήρεος.

❀ **σῐδηρο-φάγος** [ᾰ], ον, *eating into iron*, ῥίνη *BGU*40.6 (ii/iii A.D.). **-φορέω**, *bear iron*, i.e. *go armed*, Th.1.6: c. acc. cogn., σ. πελέκεις D.S.5.39:—in Med., Th.1.5, Arist.*Pol.*1268ᵇ40. 2. *wear iron rings*, App.*Pun.*104. II. *go with an armed escort*, Plu. *Cic.*31 (Med.). **-φόρος**, ον, *producing iron*, γαῖα σ., of the Chalybes, A.R.2.141, cf. 1005. II. *bearing arms* or *tools*, Nonn.*D.* 46.2, *AP*8.203. **-φρων**, ον, gen. ονος, *of iron heart*, A.*Pr.*244; σ. θυμός Id.*Th.*52; φόνος E.*Ph.*672 (lyr.). **-φυής**, ές, (φύω) *of iron nature*, dub.l. in Poll.7.106, where Bekker (after cod. A, -φύσσα) reads **σιδηροφῦσα**, *forge-bellows*. **-χαλκεύς**, έως, ὁ, *smith*, *POxy.*84.3 (iv A.D.). **-χαλκος**, ον, *of iron and copper*, τομή Luc. *Ocyp.*96, cf. Zos.Alch.p.214 B. **-χάρμης**, ου, ὁ, *fighting* (or perhaps *exulting*) *in iron*, epith. of mailed war-horses, Pi.*P.*2.2; cf. χαλκοχάρμης. **-χίτων** [ῑ], ωνος, ὁ, ἡ, *with iron tunic*, Nonn. *D.*31.162. ❀ **-ψῡχος**, ον, *iron-hearted*, *PMag.Par.*1.1366.

**σῐδηρ-όω**, *overlay with iron*, σιδηρώσας ἐπὶ πολὺ τῆς ὁρμιᾶς Luc. *Pisc.*51:—mostly Pass., ἐσεσιδήρωτο ἐπὶ μέγα καὶ τοῦ ἄλλου ξύλου *iron had been laid* over a great part of the rest of the wood, Th.4. 100, cf. Aen.Tact.20.2, al.; ῥυμοὶ σεσιδηρωμένοι *IG*1².313.21; δράκοντα σεσιδηρωμένον Posidipp.26.8. II. *put in irons, fetter*, *PLond.* 2.422.1 (iv A.D.). **-ώδης**, ες, *of iron*, Sch.rec.A.*Pr.*64. **-ωμα**, ατος, τό, in pl., *iron fittings*, *PFlor.*325.11 (v A.D.). **-ωρῠχεῖον**, τό, *iron-mine*, Ptol.*Geog.*2.11.11. **-ωσις**, εως, ἡ, *iron-work*, *IG*2². 1672.205, Bito 49.7: in concrete sense, = σιδηρώματα, *POxy.*1208.14 (iii A.D.). **-ωτός**, ή, όν, *iron-bound*, *Edict.Diocl.*15.50 (Geronthrae).

**σῐδιοειδής**, ές, *of pale yellow colour, like pomegranate-peel, jaundiced*, Hp.*Dieb.Judic.*9.

**σίδιον**, τό, (σίδη) *pomegranate-peel*, Hp.*Nat.Mul.*33, *Ulc.*12, Thphr.*CP*5.6.1: pl., Ar.*Nu.*881, Dsc.1.110, Alciphr.3.60. [σῐ– Ar. l.c.; σῑ– Luc.*Trag.*156.]

**σιδιωτόν**, τό, *medicine prepared from* or *with* σίδιον, Paul.Aeg.6. 22.

**σῐδόεις**, εσσα, εν, *of the pomegranate*, καρπεῖον Nic.*Al.*276.

**Σῑδονίηθεν**, Adv. *from Sidon*, Il.6.291.

**Σῑδονῠφής**, ές, *from the Sidonian loom*, cj. for σινδον– in Philox. 2.42.

**Σῐδοῦς**, οῦντος, ὁ, *Sidus*, a place near Corinth, where pomegranates grew, X.*HG*4.4.13, Rhian.2; also **Σιδόεις**, Euph.11, Nic.*Fr.*50: Adj. **Σῐδούντιος**, α, ον, St.Byz.; fem. **-τιάς**, άδος, Hsch.

**σίδριμνον**· εὔζωνον, Hsch.

**Σῑδών**, ῶνος, ἡ, *Sidon*, Od.15.425, Hdt.2.116, etc.: hence Adj. **Σῑδόνιος**, α, ον, Il.6.290, A.*Supp.*122; later **Σιδώνιος**, Phryn.Trag.9 (lyr.), Hdt.7.44, S.*Fr.*909, Sopat.16, etc.; fem. **Σιδωνιάς**, άδος, E.

*Hel.*1451 (lyr.):—**Σῑδόνες,** *οἱ, men of Sidon,* Il.23.743; also **Σιδόνιοι,** Od.4.84,618; Σιδονίη (sc. γῆ) 13.285. [ῐ in Il.23.743, prob. in Sopat. 16, elsewh. ῑ.]

⊛ **σῑειδής,** ές, = θεοειδής, Alcm.23.71; cf. σιός.

**σιελίζω, σίελον,** etc., v. σιαλ-.

**σιζεύς·** ἄγναφος, Hsch.

**σίζω,** mostly used in pres. and impf.: aor. 1 σίξα prob. in Theoc.6. 29:—*hiss,* esp. of the noise made by plunging hot metal into cold water, to which is compared the hissing of the Cyclops' eye when the burnt stake was thrust into it, ὣς τοῦ σίζ' ὀφθαλμὸς ἐλαϊνέῳ περὶ μοχλῷ Od.9.394; so of pancakes, Magn.1; τάγηνον σίζον Ar.*Eq.* 930; of fish frying, Id.*Ach.*1158, cf. *Com.Adesp.*140; σ. καὶ ψοφεῖν, of fire quenched, Arist.*APo.*94$^{b}$33; σίζει δὲ ταῖς ῥίνεσσι κινεῖ δ' οὔατα, of Heracles snorting as he eats, Epich.21; of the note of the κόψιχος, Poll.5.89.

**σιηγόνιον, σιηγών,** v. σιαγόνιον, σιαγών.

**σιθιλεσαδέ,** African word, = ἱεράκιον τὸ μέγα, Ps.-Dsc.3.64, vv.ll. σιθιλαισαδε, σιθιλεσας.

**Σῑθωνία,** Ion. **-ίη,** *Sithonia, land of the Sithones,* a part of Thrace, Hdt.7.122: **Σῑθώνιος,** α, ον, *Sithonian,* St.Byz.; **Σῑθών,** όνος and ῶνος, ὁ, *a Thracian,* Lyc.1357,583; **Σῑθωνίς,** ίδος, ἡ, *a Thracian woman,* Nonn.*D.*13.336. [Some forms in ο are used by Poets, **Σῑθονίη** Euph.58, **Σῑθονίς** Nonn.*D.*48.113.]

**σίκα·** ὗς (Lacon.), Hsch.  **σῖκα,** v. σίκη.

**Σῐκᾰνία,** Ion. **-ίη,** ἡ, *Sicania,* old name of Sicily as inhabited by Σικανοί (afterwards of the part they inhabited, St.Byz.), Od.24.307; Σ. ἡ νῦν Σικελίη καλευμένη Hdt.7.170:—**Σῐκᾰνός** [ῐκᾰ Call.*Dian.*57], ὁ, *a Sicanian,* Th.6.2, Philist.3, etc.: Adj. **Σῐκᾰνικός,** ή, όν, Th.6. 62; ἐν τῇ Σ. τῆς Σικελίας Arist.*Mete.*359$^{b}$15 (v.l. Σικάνῃ).

**σικανός,** = πονήρευμα ἐνεδρευτικόν, αἴτιον κεκρυμμένον, Hp.ap.Gal. 19.138 (dub. l.).

**σῑκάριος** [ᾰ], ὁ, = Lat. *sicarius, Act.Ap.*21.38, J.*AJ*20.8.10, al.

⊛ **Σῐκελ-ία,** Ion. **-ίη,** ἡ, *Sicily,* Pi.*P.*1.19, al., Hdt.1.24, etc.: hence **Σῐκελίδης,** ου, ὁ, Dor. Σικελίδας, name given by Theoc. (7.40) to Asclepiades, and variously expld. in Sch. ad loc. [Σῐ- in dactylics, as ἄρχετε Σῐκελικαί.., Mosch.3.8, etc.; Σικελίδας Theoc. l.c.]  **-ίζω,** *do like the Sicilians*: hence, 1. = ὀρχέομαι, Thphr.*Fr.*92 (from one Andron of Catana, a flute-player). 2. *play the rogue,* dub. in Epich. 206.  **-ικός,** ή, όν, *Sicilian,* Ar.*V.*838, etc.; Σ. ποικιλία ὄψου, for the Sicilian banquets were proverbial, Pl.*R.*404d, cf. Luc.*DMort.*9. 2, Philostr.*Gym.*44(74). Adv. **-κῶς** Ephipp.22.  II. Σικελικόν, τό, a liquid measure, *PBaden*54.6 (v A.D.).  **-ιώτης,** ου, ὁ, *a Sicilian Greek,* as distinguished from a native Σικελός, Th.7.32, etc.:—Adj. **-ιωτικός,** ή, όν, Dsc.3.24; neut. **-κόν,** τό, = ψύλλιον, Ps.-Dsc.4.69; fem. **-ιῶτις,** ιδος, συγγραφή, title of work by Antiochus of Syracuse, Paus.10.11.3.  ⊛ **-ός,** ή, όν, *Sicel,* later *Sicilian, of* or *from Sicily,* γυνὴ Σ. Od.24.211, cf. 389; ἀμφίπολος ib.366; γαῖα Thgn.783; πάγος, πόντος, E.*Cyc.*95,703, etc.: rare in Prose, πυροὶ Σ. Thphr.*HP*8.4.3; Σ. ἔλαιον a liquid form of asphalt, Dsc.1.73.  **II. Σικελοί,** οἱ, *Sicels,* Od.20.383, Hdt.6.22, Th.6.2, etc.

**σίκεον·** ὡς Ἴστρος, Hsch.

**σίκερα,** τό, *fermented liquor, strong drink,* Lxx *Le.*10.9, *Is.*24.9, *Ev.Luc.*1.15, Gal.19.693. (Cf. Hebr. *šēkār.*)

**σικερίτης** [ῑτ] οἶνος, *cider,* Zos.Alch.p.184 B.

**σίκη** or **σῖκα,** ἡ, = Lat. *sica,* in dat. pl. σίκαις, mentioned as Latin by J.*AJ*20.8.10.

**σίκινν-ῐς** [σῐ], or **σίκῑνις** (E.*Cyc.*37), ιδος, ἡ, acc. Σίκιννιν D.H.7. 72:—*Sicinnis,* a dance of Satyrs used in the Satyric drama, S.*Fr.*772, E. l.c., D.H. l.c., Luc.*Salt.*22: named from its inventor *Sicinnus,* Ath.1.20e, cf. Scamon 1; or from *Sicinnis,* a nymph of Cybele, although originally danced in honour of Sabazios, Arr.*Fr.*106 J.—Also written **Σίκιννον,** τό, Suid.; **Σίκιννα,** *AB*267.  **-ιστής,** οῦ, ὁ, *Sicinnis-dancer,* Ath.1.20e.

**σῐκιννοτύρβη,** ἡ, a common *air on the flute,* Trypho ap.Ath.14. 618c.

**σίκκα·** κούφη, Hsch.  **σίκλαι,** = σίγλαι, Id.

**σίκλος,** ὁ, = σίγλος (q.v.):—Dim. **σικλίον,** τό, Ps.-Gal.19.773.

**σῐκύ-α** [ῠ], Ion. **-ύη,** ἡ, *bottle-gourd, Lagenaria vulgaris,* Arist.*HA* 616$^{a}$22, Thphr.*HP*1.13.3, *CP*1.10.4.  2. σ. Ἰνδική, = κολοκύντη, Euthyd.ap.Ath.2.58f, cf. Menodor.ib.59a: but σ. distd. fr. κολοκύντη in Hellespontian dialect, Ath.2.59a.  3. = κολοκυνθίς, Hp.*Mul.*1. 37; σ. πικρά Dsc.4.176.  4. *gourd* used as a calabash, *Sammelb.* 7202.20 (iii B.C.).  II. *cupping-instrument,* because it was shaped like the gourd, Crates Com.41, Hp.*VM*22, *Aph.*5.50, Pl.*Ti.*79e, Arist.*Rh.*1405$^{b}$3, *IG*2$^{2}$.47.8,11.  **-άζω,** (σικύα II) *to cup,* Arr.*Epict.* 2.17.9:—hence **-ᾰσις,** εως, ἡ, *cupping,* Paul.Aeg.6.41 tit.; **-ασμός,** ὁ, Aët.7.50.  **-αστέον,** *one must cup,* Gal.12.560.  **-αστήριον,** τό, *cupping-instrument,* prob. for σηκυιαστήριον in Zonar.

**σῐκύδιον,** τό, Dim. of σικύα or σίκυος, Phryn.Com.25, *POxy.*117.11 (ii/iii A.D.).

**σῐκῠ-ηδόν,** Adv., (σίκυος) *cucumber-like,* esp. of a fracture, when the bone breaks smoothly off without splinters, Sor.*Fract.*10, Paul. Aeg.6.89; cf. καυληδόν, ῥαφανηδόν.  **-ήλᾰτον,** τό, *cucumber-bed,* Hp.*Genit.*9:—also ⊛**-ήρᾰτον,** τό, *PPetr.*2 p.143 (iii B.C.), *PEnteux.*73. 5 (iii B.C.), Lxx *Is.*1.8.

**σῐκυοπέπων,** ονος, ὁ, = σίκυος πέπων (v. πέπων I. 2), Gal.6.565.

**σίκῠος** [ῐ] or **σῐκῠός,** ὁ (also **σίκυς,** ἡ, Alc.151, Dsc.2.135, Gal.19.89 (s.v. βουβάλιος)), *cucumber, Cucumis sativus,* Ar.*Ach.*520, *Pax* 1001, Thphr.*HP*7.4.1, Diocl.*Fr.*49, al., *PCair.Zen.*176.4, al. (iii B.C.); σίκυς ἥμερος Dsc. l.c.; eaten unripe and raw, Hp.*Vict.*2.55; but also σ. πέπων, v. πέπων I. 2 (πέπων alone is condemned by Phryn.230); also called σ. σπερματίας, seeding, i.e. ripe *cucumber,* Cratin.136.  2. σ. ἄγριος *squirting cucumber, Ecballium Elaterium,* Hp.*Nat.Mul.*95, *Mul.*1.77, Thphr.*HP*9.15.6; also σίκυς ἄγριος Dsc.4.150.

**σίκυς,** v. foreg.  II. σικύς· ὁ γναφεύς, Hsch.

**σῐκῠ-ώδης,** ες, *like the* σικύα or σίκυος, φύλλον Thphr.*HP*7.13.1, cf. Hp.*Morb.*3.17.  ⊛ **-ών,** ῶνος, ὁ, *cucumber-bed,* Eust.291.36, etc.  II. as pr. n. **Σῐκῠών,** ῶνος, ἡ, *Sicyon,* Pi.*N.*9.53, etc.; also ὁ, X.*HG*4.2.14, 7.2.11; gender indeterm. in Il.2.572, 23.299; as Adj., γῆ Σ. Arist. *Fr.*640.26:—regul. Adj. **Σῐκῠώνιος,** α, ον, *Sicyonian,* Th.1.28, etc.; Σ. ἔλαιον *Sicyonian* olive oil, Dsc.1.30, Gal.11.739 (but **σικυώνιον** ἔλαιον *oil of* σίκυς, Aët.1.122, Alex.Trall.*Febr.*3, Paul.Aeg.3.77, 7.20); **Σῐκῠωνικός** or **-ιακός,** ή, όν, Callix.2, Ath.6.271d.—Adv. **Σῐκῠώνοθε,** *of* or *from Sicyon,* Pi.*N.*9.1.—The people themselves called their town **Σεκυών,** A.D.*Adv.*144.20, cf. **Σεκυώνιοι** *GDI*2581.273 (Delph., ii B.C.); its oldest name was Αἰγιαλεῖς and then Μηκώνη, acc. to Str. 8.6.25.  **-ώνη,** ἡ, = σίκυος 2, Hp.*Steril.*221.  2. *cupping instrument,* ib.222.  **-ωνία,** Ion. **-ίη,** ἡ, = κολοκύντη, Hp.*Loc.Hom.*47, Plu.2.154c; Megalopolitan word acc. to Ath.2.58f.

⊛ **Σῐκῠώνια** (sc. ὑποδήματα), τά, a kind of *women's shoes,* Herod.7.57, Luc.*Rh.Pr.*15, Poll.7.93.

**Σῐκῠωνιουργής,** ές, *manufactured at Sicyon,* ξύστραι *PCair.Zen.* 488.3 (iii B.C.).

**Σῐκύωνος,** ὁ, *name of a stone used in ritual,* Ps.-Plu.*Fluv.*23.3.

⊛ **σικχάζομαι,** *mock,* Hsch.  **σίκχαι·** κράσπεδα, Id.

**σικχ-αίνω,** (σικχός) *loathe, dislike,* c. acc., σικχαίνω πάντα τὰ δημόσια Call.*Epigr.*30.4: abs., Plb.38.5.7, Arr.*Epict.*3.16.7, M.Ant.5.9, etc.  II. Med., Aq.*Ex.*1.12, prob. cj. in Euph.21: aor. ἐσικχάνθην Sch.Ar.*Ra.*442.  **-αντός,** ή, όν, *disgusting, loathsome,* M.Ant.8. 24.  **-ᾰσία,** ἡ, and **-ασμός,** ὁ, *loathing,* Gloss.  **-ός,** ὁ, a *squeamish, fastidious person,* esp. in eating, opp. παμφάγος, Arist.*EE*1234$^{a}$ 6, cf. Plu.2.87b, Ath.6.262a.  II. *sickening, offensive,* = ἀηδής, Hsch.  **-ος,** εος, τό, = βδέλυγμα, Sm.*Ez.*7.19, al.:—also **σικχότης,** ητος, ἡ, Eust.972.35.

**σίλβαι·** ῥοιαί, Hsch.  **σίλβη,** ἡ, *cake made of barley, sesame, and poppy-seed,* Id.  **σιλβία,** = σιδία, Id.  **σίλγης·** κολυμβητής, Id.

⊛ **Σῑλεντιάριος,** ὁ, = Lat. *Silentiarius,* an officer *who looked to the quiet* of the Palace at Constantinople, having the rank of senator, Procop. *Pers.*2.21, Agath.5.9.

**σιλήνει·** μυ⟨λ⟩λίζει, σκώπτει, σιωπᾷ, Hsch.

**Σῑληνικός,** ή, όν, *of* or *like Silenus,* σατυρικὸν δρᾶμα καὶ σ. Pl.*Smp.* 222d.

**Σῑληνόκοσμος,** ὁ, title of official in a Dionysiac thiasos, *AJA*37. 244 (Latium, ii A.D., Σειλ-).

⊛ **Σῑληνός,** ὁ, *Silenus,* companion of Dionysus, Pi.*Fr.*156 (s.v.l.), Hdt.7.26, 8.138, etc.; father of the Satyrs, E.*Cyc.*13,82,269: the older Satyrs were called Σιληνοί, *h.Ven.*262, D.S.3.72; but S. was distinguished by prophetic powers, Ael.*VH*3.18.  2. *a figure of Silenus,* used as a casket for precious pieces of sculpture, Pl.*Smp.* 215a,b. (Freq. written Σειλ-, but Σιλ- in early Inscrr., *IG*1$^{2}$.51 (v B.C.), Kretschmer *Griech.Vaseninschr.*p.132.)

**Σιληνώδης,** ες, *like Silenus,* Pl.*Smp.*216d.

⊛ **σιλη-πορδέω,** Dor. **σιλᾱ-,** (πέρδομαι) *behave with vulgar arrogance,* Sophr.164, Posidon.36 J.:—Subst. ⊛**-πορδία,** ἡ, Luc.*Lex.*21. (The first part of the compd. is dub.:—the word remains in modern Gr.)

**σίλι,** τό, = κροτών, Plin.*HN*15.25.  II. = σέσελι, ib.20.36, Fest. s.v. silatum.

**σῐλιγν-άριος,** ὁ, *seller of* σιλίγνιον, *MAMA*3.700 (σηληγ-), 727, *PKlein.Form.*765 (vi A.D.): also written **σιλιγινάριος,** ib.182 (vi A.D.), and **σιλιγνιάριος,** ib.957 (v/vi A.D.).  ⊛ **-ιον,** τό, = Lat. *siligo, winter wheat,* ibid. (pl.); written **σελ-** in *PMag.Lond.*46.295; also **σίλιγνον,** *PLond.*1.266.112 (ii A.D.).  **-ις,** εως, ἡ, *flour from siligo,* still finer than σεμίδαλις (q.v.), Gal.6.483, Eust.1753.6, *EM*793.8; written σελ- in Chrysipp.Tyan.ap.Ath.14.647e.  **-ίτης** [ῑτ] ἄρτος, ὁ, bread *made therefrom,* Gal. l.c.: written **-είτης,** *Supp.Epigr.*4.518 (Ephesus, i/ii A.D.); and **-ίας,** ου, ὁ, Eust.1753.7.  **-οπώλιον,** τό, perh. f.l. for **σιλιγνοπάλιον** (from πάλη (B)) *siligo-flour,* in Zos.Alch. p.221 B.

**σιλλαίνω,** (σίλλος) *insult, mock,* Herod.1.19, Ael.*VH*3.40, Poll. 2.54, D.L.9.111, Sch.Il.2.212, etc.

**σιλλέα·** τρίχωμα, ἢ λεῖον (Ἠλεῖοι cj. Guyet), Hsch.  **σιλλεῖ·** ἀναξαίνει, λυπεῖ, Id.

**σιλλικύπριον,** τό, = σέσελι Κύπριον, Hdt.2.94.

**σιλλογρᾰφ-έω,** *write* σίλλοι, Zonar.  **-ία,** ἡ, *writing of* σ., Eust. 1850.33.  **-ος** (parox.), ὁ, *writer of* σ., esp. of Timo of Phlius, called ὁ σ., Ath.1.22d, Procl.*in Alc.*p.256 C.: generally, *satirical poet,* Jul.*Or.*7.207c.

**σιλλοποιός,** ὁ, = σιλλογράφος, Sch.Luc.*DMort.*20.2.

**σίλλος** (not σιλλός, Hdn.Gr.2.918), ὁ, *squint-eyed,* ἐγὼ..σ. γεγένημαί σε περιορῶν Luc.*Lex.*3 (ἰλλός cj. Hemsterhuis).  II. *satirical poem* or *lampoon* in hexam. verse, such as those written by Timo of Phlius (cf. σιλλογράφος), D.L.9.111; applied to the poems of Xenophanes of Colophon by Str.14.1.28, Sch.Ar.*Eq.*406, Procl. ad Hes. *Op.*284, Sch.Il.2.212, Eust.204.22: in general, τὸν σ. ψόγον λέγουσι μετὰ παιδιᾶς δυσαρέστου Ael.*VH*3.40, cf. Poll.2.54, Sch.Luc.*Prom.* 8.

**σιλλόω,** = σιλλαίνω, Gal.19.213, Poll.9.148, Hsch.; expld. by Phot. (who cites Archipp.52) as τοὺς ὀφθαλμοὺς ἠρέμα παραφέρειν.

**σιλλῠβιάω**, = τὸ τοὺς κροσσοὺς ἀποσείεσθαι, Hsch. (corr. Bentl. for σιβυλλιᾶν, q.v.).

⊛ **σίλλῡβον**, τό, *milk thistle, Silybum marianum*, Dsc.4.155, Ruf.ap. Orib.7.26.38, Hsch.

**σίλλῠβος**, ὁ, *parchment-label*, appended to the outside of a book, Cic.*Att.*4.4a.1, 4.8.2, dub. in 4.5.3 (v. infr.): pl. **σίλλυβα**, τά, = θύσανοι, Poll.7.64. (In Cic.*Att.*4.5.3 the vv.ll. *sit tybis* and *sic tu iubes* are perh. traces of *sittybis*; but σιττύβαι (q.v.) has an inappropriate meaning, unless it can mean *leather case* of a book.)

**σιλόδουροι**, οἱ, a Gallic word translated by εὐχωλιμαῖοι, *vassals who have vowed to live and die with their lord*, Nic.Dam.*Fr.*80J.: Lat. *soldurii*, Caes.*BG*3.22.

**σῖλουρ-ισμός**, ὁ, *eating of a* σίλουρος, *serving it up* at table, Diph. 17.11. **-ος**, ὁ, a river fish, Lat. *silurus*; it was so large as to require to be drawn out by horses or oxen, Ael.*NA*14.25; prob. *sheatfish, Silurus glanis*, Diph.17.9, Diod.Com.2.36, Sopat.15, *PCair.Zen.*680.36 (iii B.C.), Gal.12.377; used in Magic, *PMag.Osl.* 1.362.

**σιλφαῖος**, v. σιφαῖος.

**σίλφη**, ἡ, *cockroach, Blatta germanica*, Arist.*HA*601ᵃ3, Gal.12. 366,641, Ael.*NA*1.37, Luc.*Gall.*31; also, *book-worm*, Id.*Ind.*17 (in form τίλφη), *AP*9.251 (Even.). II. a kind of *boat*, Sch.Ar.*Pax* 143, Suid. (acc. to Phryn.268, τίφη (q.v.) is the correct form).

**σιλφιόεις**, εσσα, εν, *of silphium*, μοιρίδα λίτρην Nic.*Al.*329.

**σίλφιον**, τό, *laserwort, Ferula tingitana*, the juice of which was used in food and medicine, Sol.39; ὀπὸς σιλφίου Hp.*Acut.*23; σ. ἢ ὀπὸς ἢ καυλός ib.37, Gal.12.123, cf. S.*Fr.*603, Antiph.88, Alex. 127.5, Thphr.*HP*6.3.1, Nic.*Al.*309, Dsc.3.80, Poll.6.67; freq. in Ar. as an eatable, esp. mashed with cheese, *Av.*534, 1579; having a strong flavour, *Eq.*895sq.: largely grown in and exported from Cyrene, hence prov., τὸ Βάττου σ., of rare and precious commodities, Id.*Pl.*925, Arist.*Fr.*528; γαλαῖ ἐν τῷ σ. γινόμεναι in the *silphium-region*, Hdt.4.192, cf. 169: of other plants, σ. κατὰ Μηδίαν, *Ferula Assafoetida*, Dsc. l.c.; σ. κατὰ Συρίαν καὶ Ἀρμενίαν, *Prangos ferulacea*, ibid.; σ. ἐν Καυκάσῳ, *Ferula alliacea*, Aristobul.ap.Arr.*An.*3.28.6.

**σιλφιοπώλης**, ου, ὁ, *silphium-seller*, Critias*Fr.*70D.

**σιλφιοφόρος**, ον, *bearing silphium*, Str.2.5.37, Eust.ad D.P.791.

**σιλφι-όω**, *prepare with silphium*, σεσιλφιωμένος, = sq., Philox.2. 31. **-ωτός**, ή, όν, *prepared with silphium*, Ar.*Fr.*130.

**σίμαι**, v. σιμός II. 1.

**σῑμαίνω**, *to be* σιμός (q.v.), *An.Ox.*1.138; μὴ σίμαινε do not *turn up your nose*, Call.*Iamb.*1.104 (*Hermes* 69.168): cf. σιμοποιέω.

**σῑμάριον**, τό, Dim. of σῖμος II, a Nile fish, *POxy.*1857.1 (vi/vii A.D.): but Dim. **σιμαρίδιον**, τό, appears to be part of a horse's trappings, ib.1289.9 (v A.D.).

**σιμβλ-εύω**, (σίμβλος) *shelter as in a hive*, σ. κηρότροφα δῶρα μελισσᾶν *AP*6.236 (Phil.). **-η**, ἡ, = σίμβλος, Hsch. **-ήϊος**, η, ον, *of* or *from the hive*, σ. ἔργα μελισσέων *honey*, A.R.3.1036:—pecul. fem. **σιμβλητ̆ς**, ῖδος, πέτρη σ. *a hole* in a rock *used by bees as a hive*, Id.1.880; also σιμβλητ̆δες μέλισσαι *AP*9.226 (Zon.):—written **σιμβλίδες** in Hsch. (s.v.l.). **-ιος**, α, ον, *of a hive, found in one*, dub. in Dsc.2.82: prob. f.l. for Λιλυβαῖον or Ὑβλαῖον, cf. Ruf.ap.Orib. 2.63.3. **-ος**, ὁ, *beehive*, Hes.*Th.*598, Arist.*HA*627ᵃ6, Theoc.19. 2, A.R.2.132. 2. metaph., *any store* or *hoard*, σ. χρημάτων Ar. *V.*241:—later **-ον**, τό, pl. σίμβλα, Opp.*C.*1.128, Alciphr.3.23 (v.l. -ους). **-ωσις**, εως, ἡ, a disease of the eyes in horses, *Hippiatr.*11.

**Σιμιακόν** (sc. μέτρον), τό, *metre named after Sim(m)ias*, Heph. 10.6.

**σιμικίνθιον**, τό, v. σημικίνθιον.

**σιμίκιον**, τό, *a musical instrument of thirty-five strings*, Poll.4.59 (v.l. **σιμικόν**).

**σίμιον**· αἰγιαλός, Hsch.

**Σῐμόεις**, εντος, ὁ, the river *Simois*, Il.4.475, al.; contr. **Σῐμοῦς**, οῦντος, Hes.*Th.*342:—Adj. **Σιμοέντιος**, contr. **Σιμούντιος**, α, ον, E. *Or.*809 (lyr.), *IA*767 (lyr.); also ος, ον Id.*Hel.*250 (lyr.); poet. fem. **Σιμοεντίς**, ίδος, Id.*Andr.*1019 (lyr.); **Σιμουντίς**, Ar.*Th.*110; also **Σιμοείσιος**, ον, Str.13.1.34, Tryph.326 (as pr. n., Il.4.474).

**σῑμο-ποιέω**, *make* σιμός, gloss on σίμαινε, Sch.Call. in *PSI*9.1094*b* 37. **-πρόσωπος**, ον, *snub-nosed, dish-faced*, ἵππος Pl.*Phdr.*253e; μέλισσαι *Lyr.Alex.Adesp.*7.12.

**σῑμός**, ή, όν, *snub-nosed, flat-nosed*, of the Ethiopians and their gods, Xenoph.16; of the Scythians, Hdt.4.23, cf. Ar.*Ec.*617 (Comp.), 705, Theoc.3.8; represented as giving an arch, pert look, σιμός, ἐπίχαρις κληθεὶς Pl.*R.*474d; Arist. says that all children are σιμοί, *Pr.*963ᵇ15; of dolphins, Arion 1.7; of dogs, X.*Cyn.*4.1; of the hippopotamus, Hdt.2.71, Arist.*HA*502ᵃ11; of the ponies of the Sigynnae, Hdt.5.9; of bees and goats, Theoc.7.80, 8.50. 2. of the nose, *snub, flat*, opp. γρυπός, Pl.*Tht.*209c; τὸ σ. τῆς ῥινός, = σιμότης, X.*Smp.*5.6, cf. Arist. *Pol.*1309ᵇ24.—As this kind of nose gives a *pert* expression, we find σιμὰ γελῶν *AP*5.176 (Mel.); σιμὰ σεσηρὼς μυχθίζεις ib.178 (Id.); cf. σιμόω I. II. metaph., *bent upwards*, like the slope of a hill-side: hence, *up-hill*, opp. κατάντης, χωρίον Ar.*Lys.*288, ubi v. Sch.; πρὸς τὸ σ. διώκειν pursue *up-hill*, X.*HG*4.3.23; πρὸς τὸ σ. ἀνατρέχειν Dionys.Com.4, cf. Arist.*Pr.*870ᵃ30; σ. [ὁδός] X.*Cyn.*6.5; ὑπερβάλλειν τὰ σ. ib.5.16; σίμαι (sic cod.) the *ends* of the lyre, Hsch.; also, *parts of the cornice*, Id., cf. Vitr.3.5.12. 2. generally, *hollow, concave*, opp. κυρτός, ἡ γαστὴρ τῶν ἀδείπνων σ. X.*Cyr.*8.4.21; τὰ σ. τοῦ ἥπατος the *bottom* of the liver, Poll.2.213, Gal.11.93; χεὶρ σ. Ath.14.630a; of splints, νάρθηκες σ. Hp.*Off.*12, acc. to Gal.18(2).833 *rounded and tapering off towards the end*, so as gradually to diminish the pressure; also, of a kind of bandage, Hp.*Off.*7. III. σιμός· τυφλός, Hsch.

⊛ **Σῖμος**, ὁ, pr. n. *Flat-nose*, Call.*Epigr.*49, etc.; used as name of a Satyr, Kretschmer *Griech. Vaseninschr.*pp.63, 64:—**Σιμύλος** is a dim. form. II. an unknown *fish*, Opp.*H.*1.170, Artem.2.14, Ath.7.312b.

**σῑμότης**, ητος, ἡ, *the shape of a snub nose*, opp. γρυπότης, Pl.*Tht.* 143e, 209c, X.*Cyr.*8.4.21. II. metaph., τὴν σ. τῶν ὀδόντων the *upward curve* of the tusks of a wild boar, Id.*Cyn.*10.13.

**σῑμο-τομέω**, (τέμνω) perh. *cut short off*, *Gp.*5.17.6. **-τράχηλος** [ᾰ], ον, *with concave neck*, so that the face is turned upwards, Tz.*H.* 11.100.

**Σῐμοῦς**, οῦντος, ὁ, contr. for Σιμόεις.

**σῑμόω**, (σιμός) *turn up the nose*, and metaph., = μέμφομαι (cf. σιμός I. 2), Hsch. II. generally, *bend upwards*, τὴν ἰγνύαν Hld.10.31; τὸν αὐχένα, τὰ νῶτα, Ach.Tat.1.12:—Pass., *become* σιμός, Hp.*Art.* 35; of the nose, Id.*Epid.*6.1.3; πόδες σεσιμωμένοι *upturned* feet, as of some wading birds, Arist.*PA*693ᵃ7, cf. Hp.*Art.*60.

**Σιμύλος**, v. Σῖμος.

**σῑμ-ῳδία**, ἡ, *a loose song, named from one* Σῖμος, its inventor, Str. 14.1.41. **-ῳδός**, ὁ, *one who sings such songs*, Aristocl.Hist.7.

**σίμωμα** [ῑ], ατος, τό, *anything turned up*: *the upturned bow* of a ship, Plu.*Per.*26, cf. Sch.Pi.*O.*7.35.

**Σίμων** [ῑ], ωνος, ὁ, *Simon*, one of the Telchines (v. Τελχίν), used prov. of *a confederate in evil*, οἶδα Σίμωνα καὶ Σ. ἐμέ Zen.5.41. II. name of a throw of the dice, Eub.57.

**Σῑμωνίδης**, ου and Ion. εω, ὁ, voc. -ίδη *AP*6.213 (Simon.):—*Simonides*, Hdt.5.102, Pl.*Prt.*339a, etc.:—Adj. **Σιμωνίδειος**, ον, *of* or *like Simonides*, τρόπος Plu.2.1137f.

⊛ **σίμωρ**, *a kind of fur-bearing field-mouse* (Parthian), Hsch. (Cf. Arab. *sammur* 'mustela scythica'.)

**σίμωσις** [ῑ], εως, ἡ, *snubness* of nose, Gal.14.778.

**σῐνᾰμώρ-ευμα**, ατος, τό, *a stolen dainty*, Pherecr.230. **-έω**, *ravage* or *destroy wantonly*, τῆς Ἑλλάδος μηδεμίαν πόλιν σιναμωρέειν Hdt.1. 152, cf. 8.35: intr., Phld.*Herc.*1457.12; σ. ἔς τι Paus 2.32.3:—Pass., *to be treated wantonly*, γυνὴ σιναμωρουμένη χαίρει Ar.*Nu.*1070. **-ία**, ἡ, *mischievousness*, joined with ὕβρις, Arist.*EN*1149ᵇ33; *greediness*, Sch.Ar.*Av.*1690; *extravagance*, Them.*Or.*23.294a. **-ος**, ον, *mischievous, hurtful*, ὀλέθρια καὶ σ. Hp.*Art.*48; *wantonly mischievous*, Anacr.52; of a dog, Plu.2.3a: c. gen. rei, τῶν ἑωυτοῦ σ. *destructive of* his own property, Hdt.5.92.ζ'. Adv. -ρως, ἐπέδακνεν τὸν Εὐριπίδην Satyr.*Vit.Eur.Fr.*39 xvi 23. 2. *wanton*, ἀπάτη Ach.Tat.2.38 (s.v.l.). (σίνομαι: for the termin. -μωρος, cf. ἰόμωρος.)

**σῐνᾱπ-έλαιον**, τό, *mustard-oil*, Dsc.1.38 lemma. **-ηρός**, ά, όν, *flavoured with mustard*, ὀψαρίδιον *POxy.*2148.14 (i A.D.). **-ῐ**, τό, Anaxipp.1.45, *PFay.*122.4,12 (i/ii A.D.); gen. εως *PTeb.*9.13 (ii B.C.), *Ev.Matt.*13.31, *POxy.*920.2 (ii/iii A.D.), Alex.Trall.1.12; ιος *PMich.Zen.*72.9 (iii B.C.), *PStrassb.*102.9 (iii A.D.); ις *PLond.*2. 453.6 (iv A.D.); dat. ι *PFlor.*20.21 (ii A.D.); also **σίνᾱπυ**, Diocl. *Fr.*120, *PCair.Zen.*608.31, 703.12 (iii B.C.); gen. υος Sor.2.15 cod.; **σίνηπι**, Archig.ap.Gal.12.813, Crito ib.817, Dsc.2.154, Artem.5.5, etc.; gen. εως Asclep.ap.Gal.13.248, Dsc.1.38, *PLips.*97 xxxiii 4 (iv A.D.), etc.; ιος Aret.*CD*1.2, v.l. in Polyaen.4.3.32, etc.; **σίνηπυ**, Nic. *Fr.*84, Dsc.*Eup.*1.14; also **σίνηπυς**, acc. υν, ὁ, Nic.*Al.*533, and **σίνᾱπις**, ἡ, Herod.Med. in *Rh.Mus.*58.88:—*mustard, Sinapis alba*:—in early Att. and Ion. none of these forms appear, but νᾶπυ, Hp.*Vict.*2.54, *Morb.*3.15, *Mul.*1.13, cf. Ath.9.367a, Phryn.255. II. σίνηπι ἄγριον or Περσικόν, = θλάσπι, Ps.-Dsc.2.156. III. σ. κηπαῖον, *Brassica nigra*, ib.154. **-ίδιον**, τό, Dim. of σίναπι, Alex.Trall.5.6. II. = μίλτος, as if = σινωπίδιον (q.v.), Eust. ad D.P.1178. **-ίζω**, pf. σεσινάπικα, *apply a mustard-blister* to one, τινα Xenarch.12 (but dub. sens.), Antyll.ap.Orib.10.13.6 and 10:—Pass., *have a mustard-blister applied*, τὰ σεσιναπισμένα [μέρη] Id.ib.8. **-ινος**, η, ον, *of mustard*, Dsc.1.38, Gal.11.870. ⊛ **-ιον**, τό, Dim. of σίναπι, *EM*713.38, *Gloss.* **-ισμός**, ὁ, *use of a mustard-blister*, Sor.2.28, Archig.ap.Aët.3.181, Philum. *Ven.*4.9. **-ιστέον**, *one must put on a mustard-blister*, ib.3.5, Antyll.ap.Orib.10.13.7.

**σινάπυξ**· γογγυλίς, Hsch.

**σῐνᾰρός**, ά, όν, (σίνομαι) *hurt, damaged*, χείρ, ὀδόντες, σκέλος, Hp. *Art.*3, 34, 52; τὸ σ. Id.*Fract.*33, *Art.*60.

**σῐνάς**, άδος, ἡ, *destructive*, Hsch.

**σινδαρωνεύομαι**, perh. corrupt for σιναμωρέω in *App.Prov.*4.71 (cf. Pherecr.230).

**σίνδιον**, prob. an error for σινδόνιον, *PMasp.*6 ii 87 (vi A.D.).

**σίνδις**· γέρων, Hsch.

**Σινδογενής**, ές, *Indus-produced*, Aglaïas 18.

**σινδοκόθορνοι**, a kind of foot-gear, Hsch. (-κύθ- cod.).

⊛ **σινδόν-η**, ἡ, f.l. for σινδόνιον in Gal.19.117 s.v. λάσιον. **-ιάζω**, *wrap in muslin*, *PMag.Par.*1.88; σινδο]νιάσας prob. rest. in *Inscr. Perg.*264.6. **-ιον**, τό, *curtain, garment*, etc., *made of* σινδών, *IG* 4²(1).118.67 (Epid., iii B.C.), Gal.*Protr.*10, Poll.7.73, D.C.79.13, *POxy.*921.15 (iii A.D.), *Sammelb.*7033.40 (v A.D.). **-ιος**, ον, Adj. *of* σινδών, ῥάκος Str.15.3.19. ⊛**-ίσκος**, ἡ, Dim. of σινδών, *Michel* 832.24 (Samos, iv B.C.). **-ίτης** [ῑ], ου, ὁ, *wearing clothes of* σινδών, Str.15.1.71; *a garment made of* σινδών, *IG*2².1525.6, Men. *Sam.*163, *PHib.*1.121.16 (iii B.C.); Dor. **-ίτας** *IG*5(1).1390.17 (Andania, i B.C.); *made of* σινδών, τελαμών Poll.4.181; χιτών Phot.

**σινδονο-ειδής**, ές, *like* σινδών, σκέπασμα Eust.782.21, cf. *An.Par.* 3.75. **-πώλης**, ου, ὁ, *seller of cambrics*, *Tab.Defix.*87. **-φορέω**, *wear clothes of* σινδών, Str.15.1.59. **-φόρος**, ὁ, σινδών*-wearing* *priest*, *IG*11(4).1253 (Delos). II. *bath-attendant who bore the* σινδών, ib.5(2).48.29 (Tegea).

**σινδονῠφής**, ές, *woven like* or *of* σινδών, Philox.2.42; v. Σιδονυφής.

**σίνδρων**, ωνος, ὁ, *mischievous*, glossed by πονηρός, Phot.; also = δουλέκδουλος, Seleuc.ap.Ath.6.267c:—Hsch. also cites **σινδρός**, ὁ, in gen. pl.

❋ **σινδών**, όνος, ἡ (ὁ, A.*Fr.*153; acc. pl. in Hsch. σινδοῦς, as εἰκοῦς from εἰκών), *fine cloth*, usually *linen*, Hdt.1.200, 2.95, A.l.c., S.*Fr.*210. 67; βρόχῳ μιτώδει σινδόνος Id.*Ant.*1222; σ. βυσσίνης τελαμῶνες, used for mummies, Hdt.2.86; of surgeons' bandages, Id.7.181 (but also ἐξ ἐρίου τὰς σ. ὑφαίνουσιν Thphr.*HP*4.7.7, cf. Str.15.1.20). 2. *anything made of such cloth*, *garment of linen* (sts. *muslin*), *Michel*832.19 (Samos, iv B.C.), *PCair.Zen.*176.255 (iii B.C.), *SIG*²754.5 (Pergam.), *PTeb.*182 (ii B.C.), *UPZ*84.4 (ii B.C.), Luc.*Deor.Conc.* 10; ἐν εὐτελεῖ σ. Plu.2.340d; *napkin*, Alciphr.3.66; *ship's sail*, E.*Fr.*773.42 (lyr.), Luc.*Epigr.*39, Alciphr.1.12; *flag*, *standard*, Plb.2.66.10; *cloth* or *sheet*, σ. καθαρά *PLond.*1.46.206 (iv A.D.) (so of a winding-sheet, *Ev.Matt.*27.59, cf. *PPar.*18^bis 10); σ. κοιτάριαι *sheets*, *Edict.Diocl.* 28.16, cf. Th.2.49; ἐντὸς σινδόνος within the *veil*, *esoteric*, Iamb.*VP* 17.72; ἔξω σ. *exoteric*, ib.18.89.

**σινδώνιον**, τό, = σινδόνιον, *PGen.*80.8 (iv A.D.).

**σῑνέομαι**, dub. Ion. form for σίνομαι (q.v.).

**σίνηπι**, Ion. for σίναπι.

**σινι-άζω**, (σινίον) = σήθω, *sift*, *winnow*, *Ev.Luc.*22.31, Hsch., Phot., *Gloss.* **-ασμα**, ατος, τό, *detrimentum*, *recrementum*, *retrimentum*, σ. ἡ ῥυπαρία τοῦ σίτου, ib. **-ᾱτήριον**, τό, = sq., Hsch. **-ον** (parox.), τό, late word for *sieve*, Id. (cf. σεννίον).

❋ **σίνις** [σῐ], ιδος, ὁ, acc. σίνιν, (σίνομαι) *ravager*, *plunderer*, Αὐτόλυκον πολέων κτεάνων σίνιν Antim.(?)ap.Sch.S.*OC*378; ἔθρεψεν λέοντα σίνιν δόμοις (λέοντος ἶνιν Conington) A.*Ag.*718, cf. Call.*Ap.*92, Lyc.539: as Adj. *destroying*, σ. ἀνήρ, as an example of a γλῶσσα, Poet.ap.Arist. *Rh.*1406^a8. II. pr. n. Σίνις, *the Destroyer*, a famous robber of the Isthmus of Corinth, E.*Hipp.*977, *Marm.Par.*36, X.*Mem.*2.1.14, etc.; cf. Πιτυοκάμπτης. (Freq. misspelt σίννις in codd., as Arist. l.c.)

**σῑν-όδους**, οντος, ὁ, ἡ, *hurting with the teeth*, Hsch. (cf. συνόδους). **-όδων**, οντος, ὁ, a kind of *sea-bream*, prob. *Dentex vulgaris*, Epich.69, Arist.*HA*591^a11, 610^b5, Antiph.43, Archestr.*Fr.*17, Dorio ap.Ath.7.322c (codd. vary between σινόδων, σινώδων, συνόδων).

❋ **σίνομαι**, Aeol. **σίννομαι** dub. in Sapph.12; 2 sg. pres. or aor. subj. σίνηαι Od.12.139: Ion. impf. σινέσκετο, -οντο, Hes.*Fr.*117, Od.6.6: fut. σινήσομαι f.l. in Hp.*Mul.*1.52: aor. 3 pl. ἐσίναντο Hdt.8.31, -έατο Id.7.147 codd.:—codd. give a form **σινέομαι** in Hdt.4.123, 5.81, Hp. *Morb.*4.41, 53, etc.; but σίνομαι is the only form in Hom., and prob. should be restored everywhere:—Act. σίνω Ion. for βλάπτω acc. to Gal.15.662; σίνομαι Pass., *IG*2².1126.42 (Amphict. Delph.), Orph. *A.*211. [ῑ in the Verb (exc. perh. in Sapph.12); ῐ in σίνις, σίνος, ἀσῐνής.] I. *harm*, *hurt*, *do* one *harm* or *mischief*, Hom., only in Od. (but v. infr. II, and cf. σίντης), of plunderers and marauders, οἵ σφεας σινέσκοντο, of the Cyclopes who *used to plunder* the Phaeacians, Od.6.6; ὅτε μοι σίνοιτό γ' ἑταίρους, of Scylla *destroying* Odysseus' comrades, 12.114; εἰ δέ κε σίνηαι (sc. Ἠελίου βόας) 11.112, cf. ἀσινής; οὐ σινέσκετο καρπόν Hes.*Fr.*117; in later Ep., ἀλώπηξ.. σινομένα τὰν τρώξιμον *plundering* the grapes, Theoc.1.49; σ. ἔπαυλα καὶ.. ἄνδρας *AP*6. 262 (Leon.), cf. A.R.1.951, 1260, etc.; in Prose, *pillage*, *waste* a country, Hdt.5.74, 6.97, 8.31; τὴν Μηδικήν X.*Cyr.*5.5.4; *waste*, *destroy* the crops, Hdt.1.17, 4.123; αἰ δέ κα σίνηται [τοὺς καρπούς], ἀποτεισάτω τὰ ἐπιτίμια ὁ σινόμενος *GDI*5040.28 (Crete), cf. *Tab.Heracl.*1.129, X.*Cyr.* 3.3.15; ἐὰν ὑποζύγιον.. σίνηταί τι τῶν πέλας Pl.*Lg.*936e. II. generally, *injure*, αἰδώς, ἥ τ' ἄνδρας μέγα σίνεται Hes.*Op.*318 (interpol. in Il.24.45, v. Sch.), cf. Phld.*Piet.*p.93 G.; [ὁ κροκόδειλος] οὐδὲν σ. τὸν τροχίλον Hdt.2.68; τὴν ἕδραν τοῦ ἵππου μὴ σ. not *to hurt* his back, X. *Eq.*12.9, cf. Thphr.*HP*9.18.3; αἰ δὲ σίναιτο ἀφακεσάσθω if he *damages* the utensils, he must make it good, *Mnemos.*57.208 (Argos, vi B.C.); esp. in war, *injure*, *harass*, σ. τὸν στρατόν Hdt.5.27; τοὺς πολεμίους μέγα σ. Id.7.147, cf. 9.49, X.*An.*3.4.16; opp. ὠφελεῖν, Id.*Lac.*12. 5.—Never in Trag., once in Pl., freq. in X.; once in non-literary Pap., *BGU*248.17 (i A.D.).

**σῑνοποιός**, όν, *hurtful*, ζῴδια, ἀστήρ, *Cat.Cod.Astr.*1.147, 2.163.

**σίνος**, εος, τό, *hurt*, *lesion*, in pl., Hp.*Fract.*10, *Acut.*54, al.: generally, *mischief*, *injury*, Hdt.8.65; *blemish*, *PGnom.*205 (ii A.D.). II. of things, *mischief*, *bane*, *plague*, used by A. alone of Trag., πρέπει σ. *the mischief* is revealed, *Ag.*389 (lyr.); σ. ἐσθημάτων *ruin* to them, ib.561; σ. πολυκτόνον, of Helen, ib.734 (lyr.); *pest*, of the ἀστήρ (star-fish), Arist.*HA*548^a9; σ. πρὸς εὐκαρπίαν Thphr.*CP* 2.7.5.—Ion. word, very rare in Att. Prose, Isoc.*Ep.*4.11. [σῐ, A. ll. cc., Nic.*Th.*1, 653; but σῖνεα Id.*Al.*231.]

**σῑνότης**, ητος, ἡ, *faultiness*, *Gloss.*

**σῑνόω**, late form of σίνομαι, Man.6.552, Olymp.Hist.p.454 D.:—Pass., σεσινωμένα Paul.Al.*L.*2, cf. Vett.Val.77.6, al.

❋ **σινπλαρία**, ἡ, *simple* (*money*), Lat. *simplaria*, *SIG*901.14 (Delph., iv A.D.).

❋ **σίντης**, ου, ὁ, (σίνομαι) poet. word, = σίνις, *ravening*, of the lion, Il. 11.481, 20.165; of the wolf, 16.353: with a fem. Subst., σίνταο φάλαγγος Nic.*Th.*715. 2. Subst., = ἔχις, ib.623. 3. *spoiler*, *thief*, Opp.*H.*4.602, *Cat.Cod.Astr.*7.115. 4. *hoopoe*, Hsch. s. v. μακεσίκρανος (σιήτην cod.).

**Σίντιες**, οἱ, the *Sintians*, a name (variously expld. in Eust.158.4 sq.) of early inhabitants of Lemnos, Il.1.594, Od.8.294, Hellanic.71(*a*), (*c*) J.:—hence **Σιντηΐς**, ΐδος, ἡ, old name of Lemnos, A.R.1.608, 4.1759:—Adj. **Σιντιακός**, ή, όν, Orph.*A.*471.

**σίντωρ**, ορος, ὁ, = σίντης, *Tab.Defix.* in *Rh.Mus.*55.85 (Crete, iv B.C.): c. gen., *AP*6.45.

**σινώδων**, v. σινόδων.

**σίνων**, ωνος, ὁ, *stone parsley*, *Sison Amomum*, Dsc.3.55 (v.l. σίσων, as in Gal.12.123), Plin.*HN*27.136, Aret.*CA*2.5 codd. II. σ. ἄγριος, = πευκέδανον, Ps.-Dsc.3.78.

**Σινώπη**, ἡ, *Sinope*, Hdt.1.76, etc.; **Σινωπεύς**, έως, ὁ, *an inhabitant thereof*, Simon.118, X.*An.*5.3.2, etc.; **Σινωπίτης** [πῑ], D.P.255; **Σινωπίς** or **Σινωπῖτις**, ἡ, *the country*, Str.12.3.40, 12.3.12; but Σινωπίς, *a compound medicine* in Heras ap.Gal.13.785:—Adj. **Σινωπικός**, ή, όν, St.Byz. II. **Σινωπική** (sc. μίλτος), ἡ, *a red earth* found in Cappadocia, imported into Greece from Sinope, Thphr.*Lap.*52, Dsc.5.96, Str.12.2.10, etc.:—also **Σινωπίς**, Aret.*CA*1.8; **Σινωπῖτις**, *PSI*10. 1180.55 (ii A.D., σινοπ-); also **σινωπίδιον**, τό, Tz.*H.*13.44; cf. σιναπίδιον.

**Σῐνωπίζω**, *behave like the courtesan Sinope*, Hsch.

**σῑνωτικός**, ή, όν, (σινόω) *mischievous*, *baneful*, Ptol.*Tetr.*148, Vett. Val.17.25, al., Sch.Nic.*Al.*231.

**σίξις**, εως, ἡ, (σίζω) *hissing*, such as is made by plunging hot metal in water, Arist.*Mete.*369^b17.

❋ **σῐοειδής**, ές, *like* σίον, coined by *EM*134.24.

❋ **σῐο-κόμος**, ον, Lacon. for *θεο-κόμος, *with hair like the gods*, Eup.444 (Meineke for σιωκολλος). **-κόρος**, ὁ, Lacon. for θεο-κόρος, = νεωκόρος (q.v.), Hsch.

**σίον** [ῐ], τό, *water parsnip*, *Sium angustifolium*, Speus.ap.Ath.2. 61c, Theoc.5.125, Dsc.2.127; read by Ptol.Euerg.(*Fr.*11 J.) in Od.5. 72. 2. *water pimpernel*, *Veronica Anagallis*, Crateuas(?)ap.Dsc. l.c. 3. = σισύμβριον, Dsc.2.128. 4. = ἄνησσον, Ps.-Dsc.3.56.

❋ **σιός**, Lacon. for θεός, Ar.*Lys.*81, 174, al., Foed.ap.Th.5.77, *IG*5 (2).510 (near Megalopolis, iii/ii B.C.); **σιόρ**, Hsch.; acc. σίν *IG*5(1). 210.55, 211.51.

**σιοφόρος**, Lacon., = θεοφόρος, *IG*5(1).212.57 (Sparta).

**σῐπᾰλός**, ή, όν, *purblind*, *ugly*, Call.*Fr.anon.*106, Eust.972.29; glossed by χαλεπός, ἀκάθαρτος, ἄμορφος, Hsch., Zonar.; also by ἐπάρχεμος κτλ., Hsch.; cf. σιφλός.

❋ **σιππινόμεστος**, ον, *stuffed with tow*, προσκεφάλαια *PMasp.*6 ii 60 (vi A.D.).

**σίππιον**, τό, = στυππεῖον, *BGU*1080.18 (iii A.D.), *POxy.*1130.12 (v A.D.), etc.

**σιππουργός**, ὁ, *worker in tow*, *CPR*19 *a* 17 (iv A.D.).

**σίππα**· σιῶπα (Messapian), Hsch.

**σιπταχόρας**, ου, ὁ, *lac-tree*, *Schleichera trijuga*, Ctes.*Fr.*57.22 and *Fr.*74:—written *psitthachoras*, Plin.*HN*37.39.

**σιπτῶναι**· ἀπεικάσαι, Hsch. (Cf. θισπῶσαι: both perh. ff.ll. for ϝισϝῶσαι.)

**σίπυδνος** [ῐ], ἡ, collat. form of sq., Orac.ap.Luc.*Alex.*25.

**σῐπύ-η** [ῠ], ἡ, *meal-tub*, Ar.*Eq.*1296, *Pl.*806, Pherecr.142, *AP*6.302 (Leon.); spelt **συπύη**, *PCair.Zen.*14.14 (iii B.C.); the Att. form σιπύα, though cited by Harp.(= Lys.*Fr.*165 S.) and Hsch. s.v. σίφνον, is not found exc. in Poll.10.162; cf. ἰπύα. **-ηθεν**, Adv. *from the meal-tub*, Call.*Fr.*454. ❋ **-ΐς**, ΐδος, ἡ, = σιπύη, *jar*, Hp.*Steril.*235, cf. Gal.19.138.

**σίραιον** [ῐ], τό, *new wine boiled down*, Ar.*V.*878, Antiph.142, Alex. 127.8, 188, Nic.*Al.*153 (where ι, written ει), Gal.10.403; also of figs, Id.13.8, 9:—also οἶνος **σίραιος**, Dsc.5.6, Aret.*CA*1.1; **σίρινος**, Eust.1385.14.

**σίραμφος**· τὸ ῥύγχος, Hsch. **σίρβηνον**, τό, *cake offered to Aphrodite*, Id. **σιρία**· ἀσφάλεια, Λάκωνες, Id. **σιρίασις**, **σιριάω**, **σίριος**, v. σειρ-. **σῑρῐκόν**, v. σηρικός.

**σῑρῐκοποιός**, ὁ, *silk-manufacturer*, *IG*14.785 (Naples).

**σῖρις** or **σίρις**, ιδος, ἡ, = ξυρίς, *EM*209.35. II. σίρις· ἀπαίδευτος, Hsch.

**σῑρομάστης**, ου, ὁ, prop. *pit-searcher*, i.e. a *probe* or *gauge*, with which tax-gatherers searched corn-pits and magazines, used in war to try whether there were pits in the ground, Ph.*Bel.*100.5, cf. Ph. 1.135. II. *barbed lance* of the same shape, Lxx 3*Ki.*18.28, al., J. *AJ*7.2.2. 2. *use of the* σ. II. 1, Steph. *in Hp.*2.255 D.

**σιρόν**, τό, or **σῖρος**, ὁ, in acc. sg., = θεῖον ἄπυρον, Gal.12.903.

**σιρός**, ὁ, *pit* for keeping corn in, *IG*1².76.10, S.*Fr.*276, E.*Fr.*827, Anaxandr.41.28 (anap.), D.8.45, 10.16, *PLond.*2.216.11 (i A.D.). II. *pitfall*, Longus 1.11. [ῐ, E. l.c., Anaxandr. l.c., Eratosth.35.4, ῑ in Xenoph.(?)41 D.: later written σειρός, D.S.19.44, 2*Ep.Pet.*2.4, *PLeid.X.*50 B. (iii/iv A.D.).]

❋ **σίρωμα**, ατος, τό, *sediment*, Aët.1.135.

❋ **σιρωτής**, ὁ, *simussator*, i.e. *cimussator*, οἴνου ἢ ἄλλου τινὸς ὑγροῦ, *Gloss.*

**σιρω(τόν?)**, *vessel for holding wine* or *vinegar*, *Sammelb.*1960. (Coptic word.)

**σιρώτρια**, ἡ, *ornatrix*, *Gloss.*

❋ **σισακικία**, ἡ, a garment (?), *PGen.*80.12 (iv A.D.).

**σισαμίς**· τὸ παρὰ τοῖς ἰατροῖς λεγόμενον σέσελι, Hsch. **σίσανον**· τὸν ὀξίνην οἶνον, Id.

**σισάριον**, τό, *a woman's ornament of gold*, Poll.5.101, Hsch., Phot.

**σίσᾰρον**, τό, *parsnip*, *Pastinaca sativa*, Epich.3, 27, Diocl.*Fr.*122, *Sammelb.*6801.23 (iii B.C.), Dsc.2.113, Sor.1.51.

**σισέλεος**, ὁ, = *siselium*, *Gloss.*

**σισίλαρος**· πέρδιξ, Περγαῖοι, Hsch.

**σισῐλισμός** or **-ιγμός**, ὁ, = σισμός, Sch.Od.9.394, Eust.1636.17.

**σίσιλλος**· *νόσημα, καθάπερ σκωληκίασις, καὶ ζῷόν τι*, Hsch. **σισίνδιος**· *γέρων*, Id.

**σίσμα**, *ατος, τό*, written for *σεῖσμα* (q.v.), *PMasp*.58 ii 11 (vi A.D.).

**σισμός**, *ὁ*, (*σίζω*) = *σίξις*, *hissing*, Suid. s.v. *σεισμός*.

**σισόη**, *ἡ*, *roll of hair*, Lxx *Le*.19.27; Phaselite word acc. to Hsch.

**σισορβάκος**· *τράχουρος ὁ ἰχθῦς*, Hsch.

**σίστρος**, v. *σεῖστρος*.

**σίσῠβος**, *ὁ*, in pl., glossed by *κροσσοί, ἱμάντες*, and *θύσανοι*, Phot., Eust.976.28.

**σῐσύμβρ-ινος**, *η, ον*, *of σίσυμβρον*, *μύρον* Antiph.106.5, Thphr.*Od*. 27. ⊛**-ιον**, *τό*, *bergamot-mint*, *Mentha aquatica*, Cratin.98, Ar. *Av*.160, Arist.*Fr*.367, Thphr.*HP*2.1.3, al. (distd. fr. *μίνθα* 2.4.1), Dsc.3.41; *ὀσμηρὸν σ.* Nic.*Fr*.74.57. 2. *water-cress*, *Nasturtium officinale*, Dsc.2.128, Plin.*HN*20.247. II. *a woman's ornament*, Poll.5.101. **-ον**, *τό*, = foreg. I. 1, *AP*4.1.19 (Mel., *σῐ-*), Nic.*Th*. 896 (pl., *σῑ-*).

**σῐσύρα** [ῠ], *ἡ*, *goat's-hair cloak*, used as a garment by day and a coverlet by night, Ar.*Ra*.1459, *V*.738, *Ec*.347, *Lys*.933, *Av*.122; *ἐν πέντε σ. ἐγκεκορδυλημένος* Id.*Nu*.10; *σ. δερματίνη* Pl.*Erx*.400e; cf. *σίσυρνα, σίσυς*.—Tz. (ad Lyc.634) distinguishes *σισύρα* as made *ἐκ δέρματος ἐντρίχου* from *σίσυρνα* = *ἄτριχον δερμάτιον*.

**σῐσῠριγχίον**, *τό*, *Barbary nut*, *Iris Sisyrinchium*, Thphr.*HP*1.10.7.

**σίσυρνα** [ῐ], *ἡ*, = *σισύρα* (q.v.), *garment of skin*, Alc.128 Diehl, Hdt.4.109, 7.67; *τῆς σ. τῆς λεοντέας* A.*Fr*.109; also **σίσυρνος**, *ὁ* (a kind of *bandage*, cf. *σίσυρος*), and **σίσυρνον**, *τό*, Hsch.:—Dim. **σισύρνιον**, *τό*, to be read in Sch.Theoc.5.15.

**σῐσυρνο-δύτης** [ῡ], *ου, ὁ*, *one who wears a σίσυρνα*, Lyc. 634. **-φόρος**, *ον*, *wearing a σίσυρνα*, Hdt.7.67.

**σῐσυρνώδης**, *ες*, *like a skin* or *fur*, *στόλος* S.*Fr*.413.

**σῐσῠροποιός**, *ὁ*, *blanket-maker*, *GDI*4957.3 (Eleutherna).

**σίσυρος**· *γράμματος* (leg. *ῥάμμ-*) *εἶδος*, Hsch.; cf. *σίσυρνος*.

**σῐσῠρωτός**, *ἡ, όν*, *shaped into a σισύρα*, *SIG*1259.7 (Athens, iv B.C.).

⊛ **σίσυς**, *ὁ*, = *σισύρα*, Hsch.; *any coarse* or *cheap garment*, Tz. ad Lyc. 634.

**σῐσῠφίζω**, *act like Sisyphus*, i.e. *slily and unscrupulously*, Phryn. *PS*p.110 B.

**Σίσῠφος** [ῑ], *ὁ*, *Sisyphus*, Il.6.153, Od.11.593: prov., *πλείονα δ' εἰδείης Σισύφου* Thgn.702; *μηχαναὶ Σισύφου* Ar.*Ach*.391; nickname of the Spartan Dercyllidas, X.*HG*3.1.8:—Adj. **Σῑσύφειος**, *α, ον*, E.*Med*. 405, etc.; ⊛**Σισυφία** *χθών*, i.e. *Corinth*, Epigr.ap.Paus.5.2.5; **Σισυφὶς** *ἀκτή, αἶα*, Theoc.22.158, *AP*7.354 (Gaet.); **Σισύφειον**, *τό*, *temple of S.*, D.S.20.103, Str.8.6.21.

**σίσων**, v. *σίνων*. **σῖτα**, v. *σῖτος*.

**σῑτᾰγέρτης**, *ου, ὁ*, (*ἀγείρω*) *collector of corn* for state purposes, *commissary*, *Tab.Heracl*.1.102, 177.

**σῑτᾰγωγ-έω**, *convey corn*, c. acc. cogn., *σ. σιταγωγίαν* Luc.*Nav*. 14: abs., D.C.47.37, 49.27:—Med., *import corn*, *IG*2$^2$.28.18. **-ία**, *ἡ*, *conveyance of corn*, *PTeb*.57.12 (ii B.C.), Luc.*Nav*.14. **-ός**, *όν*, (*ἄγω*) *conveying corn*, *πλοῖα provision*-ships, Hdt.7.147; *ἄκατοι* ib. 186; *νῆες* And.2.21, Th.8.4; *ὁλκάδες* Id.6.30; cf. *σιτηγός*.

**σιταῖα**, *τά*, *corn-rents*, *LW*331 (Olymos).

⊛ **σῑτᾰλετικός**, *ή, όν*, *for grinding corn*, *μηχανή BGU*405.7 (iv A.D.).

**Σιτάλκας**, *ὁ*, epith. of Apollo at Delphi, Paus.10.15.2.

**σῑτανίας** *πυρός*, *ὁ*, a branching cereal, Thphr.*HP*8.2.3; formed like *κριθανίας*. II. v. *σητάνειος*.

**σῑτ-αποδέκτης**, *ου, ὁ*, *corn-collector*, *PFlor*.43.9 (iv A.D.), *PLips*. 98 iii 11 (iv A.D.). ⊛ **-αποδοχεῖον**, *τό*, *granary*, Partsch *Sandschak Berat* 200 (Epirus, ii A.D.). **-ᾰποχία**, *ἡ*, (*ἀπέχω*) *abstinence from food*, Hsch. s.v. *βουβίλιξ*. **-άριον**, *τό*, Dim. of *σῖτος*, *a little corn* or *bread*, *a bit of corn* or *breadstuff*: sg., *PCair.Zen*.160.10 (iii B.C.), Plu.2.1097d: pl., Philem.98.3, *PTeb*.750.16 (ii B.C.), Plb.16.24.5; *bits of food*, Hp.*Epid*.3.17.α'.

**σῑταρκ-έω**, *supply with provisions*, *ὁ τὸ σιταρκεῖν φάμενος σῖτον ἐπαρκεῖν* Eust.626.55. **-ησις**, *εως, ἡ*, = *τὸ ἀρκοῦν βρῶμα*, Zonar. **-ία**, v. *σιταρχία*. **-ισμός**, *ὁ*, *supply of food*, Al.*Ge*.43.2.

**σῑταρχ-έω**, *pay* an army, etc., *τοὺς στρατιώτας IG*9$^2$(1).3 *A* 35 (Thermum, iii B.C.), *PMich.Zen*.32.5 (iii B.C.), D.S.10.33:—Pass., *BGU*1190.6 (prob. i B.C.), Str.14.2.5, 17.3.15. **-ημα**, *ατος, τό*, a soldier's *rations*, Antiph.80.12. **-ης**, *ου, ὁ*, (*ἄρχω*) *commissary-general*, *victualler*, Ph.2.69: also ⊛**-ος**, *ὁ*, Harmod.1. **-ία**, *ἡ*, *commissariat*, *victualling department*, *IG*5(2).266.36 (Mantinea, i B.C.), Ph.2.64, etc. II. *a soldier's pay in money*, Arist.*Oec*.1350$^a$36 (v.l. *-αρκία*), 1351$^b$16, 1353$^b$2, *IG*9$^2$(1).3 *A* 38 (Thermum, iii B.C.); opp. *σιτομετρία* (pay in kind), *PHal*.1.159 (iii B.C.), cf. *PAmh*.2.29.22 (iii B.C.), *PTeb*.729.2 (ii B.C.), *UPZ*16.7 (ii B.C.). 2. *pay in kind*, *provisions*, Ph.*Bel*.101.51 (pl.); *τὰ σύμβολα τῶν σ., ἐξαρτίσας αὐτὸν ταῖς σ.*, *BGU*1755.5, 10, cf. 1749.15 (both i B.C.), etc. 3. generally, *provision*, *maintenance*, ib.948.14 (iv/v A.D.); *ἡ ἀναγκαία τροφὴ ἤτοι σ.* *PLond*.5.1708.118 (vi A.D.). **-ώ**, *οῦς, ἡ*, *female commissariat officer*, *IG*5(2).266.37 (Mantinea, i B.C.).

**σῑτ-εία**, *ἡ*, *feeding*, *fattening*, *ὀρτύγων PLips*.97 xi 17 (iv A.D.), *Gloss.*: pl., *σ. ἄρτων BGU*1067.14 (ii A.D.). **-ένδεια**, *ἡ*, *shortage of food*, *BSA*23.73 (Macedonia, ii A.D., pl.). ⊛ **-εύσιμος**, *η, ον*, *of* or *for feeding*: *τὸ σ. a fowl stuffed for the table*, Lemma to *AP*9. 484 and 486. **-ευσις**, *εως, ἡ*, = *σιτεία*, *PMich.Zen*.48.2 (iii B.C.), *Gloss*. ⊛ **-ευτάριος**, *ὁ*, *altor*, *τροφεύς*, *Gloss*. (written *-αρις*). **-ευτής**, *οῦ, ὁ*, *one who feeds up cattle*, etc., Plu.2.750c. **-ευτός**, *ή, όν*, *fed up*, *fatted*, *παῖδες* X.*An*.5.4.32; of beasts, *PCair.Zen*.350.4 (iii B.C.), Lxx *Jd*.6.25 (cod. A), Plb.38.8.7, *Ev.Luc*.15.23, al.; *σ. χήν* Epig.2, *PGrad*.2.9 (iii B.C., pl.), *PCair.Zen*.26(*a*).4 (iii B.C.). **-ευτώριος**, *ὁ*, *poultry-fattener*, Hierocl.*Facet*.59 (s.v.l.). **-εύω**, *feed*, *fatten*, *σιτεύεσκον κτήνεα* (Ion. impf.) Hdt.7.119, cf. *PCair.Zen*.375.2 (iii B.C.), Plu.2.661b:—Pass., Id.*Luc*.40, Sor.1.109, Gal.6.675, Philostr.*VA* 4.3 (*πιαίνω* is Att., Moer.p.332 P.). 2. *supply with corn*, *τὰς [ἱερὰ]ς τραπέζας GDI*3529 (Cnidus). II. Pass., *feed on*, *eat*, c. acc., Plb. 12.2.5 (v.l. *σιτέομαι*); cf. *σιτέω*. ⊛ **-ευωνέω**, *buy corn and sell it cheap*, *'Αρχ.Δελτ*.2.148 (Beroea). **-έω**, part. gen. *σιτεόντων* Hp.*Nat. Hom*.9 (v.l. *σιτευμένων*): aor. 1 part. *σιτήσας* Hsch.:—elsewh. **σιτέομαι**, Ion. impf. *σιτέσκοντο* Od.24.209: fut. *σιτήσομαι* Ar.*Nu*.491, *Pax* 724, Arist.*Mu*.400$^b$19: aor. *ἐσιτήθην IG*5(1).51.1 (Laconia); poet. *σιτήθην* Theoc.9.26: (*σῖτος*):—*take food*, *eat*, *κλίσιον ἐν τῷ σιτέσκοντο* Od. l.c., cf. Hdt.1.94, 133, Pl.*Ap*.36d; *οἱ ἐν τῷ Μουσείῳ σιτούμενοι BGU*73.4 (ii A.D.), etc. 2. c. acc., *feed on*, *eat*, *ἰχθῦς*, *καρποὺς σιτέεσθαι*, Hdt.1.200, 202, cf. 71; *ἐλπίδας* A.*Ag*.1668; *ἀπομαγδαλιάς* Ar.*Eq*.414; *τὴν σοφίαν* Id.*Nu*. l.c.; *ὅπως, οἷς αὐτὸς σιτοῖτο σίτοις, τούτοις ὅμοια παρατίθοιτο αὐτῷ* X.*Cyr*.8.2.3; *κρέας σ.* Theoc. l.c. 3. *eat of*, *ἀπό τινος* Hld.2.23; *τινι* Scymn.854.

**σῑτηβόρος**, *ον*, (*βορά*) *eating corn*, Nic.*Al*.115.

**σῑτηγ-έω**, = *σιταγωγέω*, *convey* or *transport corn*, *'Αθήναζε εἰς τὸ 'Αττικὸν ἐμπόριον* D.34.36, cf. Lycurg.27; *import corn*, *παρά τινος* D. 20.34; *ὀνηλάτῃ σιτηγοῦντι PCair.Zen*.176.113 (iii B.C.). **-ήσια**, *τά*, *right of importing* or *exporting corn*, *SIG*344.81 (Teos, Epist. Antig.). **-ία**, *ἡ*, *conveyance* or *importation of corn*, *ἡ σ. ἡ εἰς 'Ρόδον* D.56.11.

**σῑτήγονος**, *ον*, *produced for food*, f.l. for *χιλήγ-*, Nic.*Al*.424.

**σῑτηγός**, *όν*, (*ἄγω*) = *σιταγωγός*, *σ. πλοῖα* D.50.20, D.S.20.5; *σ. τι* (sc. *πλοῖον*) *PCair.Zen*.31.2 (iii B.C.); *τὰ σ.* (sc. *πλοῖα*) Plu.*Galb*.13.

**σῑτηρεσι-άζω**, *pay* a ship's crew, *εἰς δίμηνον* Arist.*Oec*.1353$^a$ 22. ⊛**-ον**, *τό*, *provision-money*, X.*An*.6.2.4; *δέκα τοῦ μηνὸς ὁ στρατιώτης δραχμὰς σ. λαμβάνει* D.4.28; *ἐδίδου τοῖς ναύταις σ.* Id.50.53; *ἐργώναις σ. IG*4$^2$(1).103.168 (Epid., iv B.C.): generally, *allowance*, *pension*, *PLond*.3.955.10 (iii A.D.); *annuity purchased*, *Milet*.3.147.44 (iii B.C.); at Rome, *σ. ἔμμηνον* a monthly *allowance of grain* to the poorer citizens, Lat. *frumentatio*, Plu.*Caes*.8, cf. 57, *Crass*.2, *Cat. Mi*.26; cf. *σιτοδοτέω*.

**σίτηρις**, Eretr. for *σίτησις*, *IG*12(9).187.5, 15.

⊛ **σῑτ-ηρός**, *ά, όν*, *of corn*, *τὰ σ. γεύματα* food *made from corn*, Hp. *Acut*.10; *σ. μέτρα corn* measures, Arist.*EN*1135$^a$2; *μέδιμνος σ. IG*2$^2$. 1013.27; *σιτηρά, ἡ*, *tax on corn*, ib.1707.6, *BGU*1742.16, 1743.13 (i B.C.). II. *fit for food*, *eatable*, Xenocr.ap.Orib.2.58.47. III. *καρπὸς ὁ σ. cereals*, Thphr.*Vent*.13; so *τὰ σ.*, = *τὰ σιτώδη*, opp. *ζῷα, λάχανα*, Id.*HP*1.10.7, 8.2.3, Dsc.3 *Prooem*. **-ησις**, *εως, ἡ*, *eating*, *feeding*, *ἐπὶ σιτήσι* for *home consumption*, opp. *πρῆσις*, Hdt.4.17; *σ. καὶ δίαιτα* Pl.*R*.404d; *σ. ἐν Πρυτανείῳ public maintenance* in the Prytaneum, Ar.*Ra*.764, cf. *IG*1$^2$.77, And.4.31, Pl.*Ap*.37a, *OGI*49.12 (Ptolemais, iii B.C.): abs., *σίτησιν αἰτῆσαι* Ar.*Eq*.574; *γέρα..δίδοται..σ.* Timocl.8.18: pl., D.20.107. II. *food*, *σίτησιν εἶναι κρέα ἑφθά* Hdt. 3.23, cf. Thphr.*HP*8.4.3.

**σῑτηφάγος** [ᾰ], *ον*, (*φαγεῖν*) = *σιτηβόρος*, *ἀκρίς An.Ox*.1.210.

**σῑτ-ίζω**, aor. *ἐσίτισα* X.*Smp*.4.9:—Med., fut. Att. *-ιοῦμαι* (*ἐπι-*) Pherecr.32.1; Ion. *-ιεῦμαι* (*ἐπι-*) Hdt.9.50: aor. *ἐσιτισάμην* (*ἐπ-*) Th. 6.94, D.50.53: pf. *σεσίτισμαι* (v. infr.):—*feed* an infant, Hdt.6.52, Ar. *Eq*.716, Mnesith.ap.Orib.*inc*.19.3; *κύνας* Isoc.1.29; *τοὺς ἀλεκτρυόνας σκόροδα σ.* X.*Smp*.4.9:—Pass., *to be fattened*, *PCair.Zen*.464.4 (iii B.C.); = *σιτέομαι*, *eat*, c. acc., *πρῶκας σιτίζεται* Theoc.4.16, cf. Philostr.*VA*3.26: metaph., *τὸν 'Ισαῖον ὅλον σεσίτισται* (of Demosthenes), Pytheas ap.D.H.*Is*.4. ⊛ **-ικός**, *ή, όν*, *of wheat* or *corn*, (sc. *λόγος*) *PCair.Zen*.292.2 (iii B.C.); *σ. ἐξαγωγή* exportation *of corn*, Plb.28.16.8; *οἱ σ. καρποί* Aristeas 112, D.S.5.21, etc.; *σ. τροφή* Str. 5.4.3; *ὁ σ. νόμος*, Lat. *lex frumentaria*, Plu.*CG*5; *σ. πρόσοδοι, τελέσματα*, *OGI*90.11 (Rosetta, ii B.C.), 669.47 (Egypt, i A.D.); *πράξας τὸ σ.*, *πράκτωρ σιτικῶν*, *POxy*.2120.4 (iii A.D.), *Ostr.Bodl*. iv 74 (iii A.D.), etc. (cf. *πράκτωρ* II. 2); *σ. ἐδάφη, ἄρουραι*, lands *subject to corn-tax*, *PSI*6.704.17 (ii A.D.), Wilcken *Chr*.115.14 (iii A.D.), etc. **-ινος**, *η, ον*, = foreg., Gal.12.666, *Gp*.2.23.9, *OGI*200.21 (Axum, iv A.D.); *ἄχυρον PLips*.92.7 (ii/iii A.D.), etc. **-ίον**, *τό*, mostly in pl. *σιτία* (sg. in Hp.*Acut.*(*Sp.*)44, *de Arte* 10, *VM*6, Pl.*R*.338d, *Phdr*.241c, and later Prose, as Archig.ap.Orib.8.1.15, Pythagorei ap.Plu.2.12f, Porph. *Abst*.1.27); only used in Prose and Comedy: I. *grain*, *corn*, *ἦλουν ὄρθριαι τὰ σ.* Pherecr.10. II. *food made from grain*, *bread*, *τούτοισι δὲ* (sc. *ὀσπρίοισι*) *μὴ χρῆσθαι εἰ μὴ μετὰ σιτίων* Hp.*Acut.*(*Sp.*) 47; *ἀπὸ ὀλυρέων ποιεῦνται σιτία* make *bread* from spelt, Hdt.2.36; *σ. σφί ἐστι ἱρὰ πεσσόμενα* ib.37. 2. generally, *victuals*, *provisions* for men, opp. *χόρτος* (fodder for cattle), Id.1.94, 188, etc.; *σιτί' ἡμερῶν τριῶν* three days' *provision*, of soldiers, Ar.*Ach*.197, *Pax* 312, cf. Th.1.48, 3.1; *σ. καὶ ποτά food* and drink, Pl.*Grg*.490b: so in sg., X.*An*.1.10.18, etc.; *ἐν τοῖς σ. τε καὶ ὄψοις* Pl.*Prt*.334c; opp. *ῥόφημα*, Hp.*Acut*.13. 3. *τὰν Πρυτανείῳ σ.* public *maintenance* in the Prytaneum, Ar.*Eq*.709. 4. rarely, *food* for dogs, X.*Cyn*.7. 11. III. *faeces*, Ar.*Ec*.355. **-ῐσις**, *εως, ἡ*, freq. f.l. for *σίτησις*, e.g. in Str.15.3.7, 17.1.40. ⊛ **-ισμός**, *ὁ*, *feeding*, *fattening*, Sch.Nic.*Al*.424, abbrev. in *PLips*.97 xxi 17 (iv A.D., nisi leg. *σι(τείας)*). **-ιστής**, *οῦ, ὁ*, = *fartor*, *Gloss*. **-ιστός**, *ή, όν*, = *σιτευτός*, *Ev.Matt*.22.4, J.*AJ*8.2.4, Ath.14.656e.

⊛ **σίτλα**, *ἡ*, = Lat. *situla*, *bucket*, *pail*, Ulp. ad D.21.133, Alex.Trall.1. 2: hence Dim. ⊛**σιτλίον**, *τό*, *POxy*.1290.9 (v A.D.), Hsch. s.v. *κρατῆρες*.

**σιτνίδες**· *θυσία τις Νύμφαις ἐπιτελουμένη*, Hsch.

**σῖτο-βολών**, ῶνος, ὁ, (βάλλω) *place for storing corn, granary*, *IG*11(2).287 *A* 170 (Delos, iii B.C.), *PSI*4.358.9 (iii B.C.), Lxx *Ge*.41.56, Ph.*Bel*.87.9, *Gp*.2.25.4; cf. βολεών:—also **-βολεῖον**, τό, *IG*2².1281 (iii B.C.); **-βόλιον**, τό, Men.193, Plb.3.100.4; **-βολον**, τό, *IPE*1².32 *B* 48 (Olbia, iii B.C.). **-βόρος**, ον, = σιτοφάγος, read by *EM* 216.9 in Nic.*Th*.802. **-γεωργός**, ὁ, *corn-grower*, Vett.Val.76.10. **-δεία**, Ion. -είη, ἡ, *want of food, famine*, Hdt.1.22,94, Th.4.36, *IPE*1².32 *A* 23 (Olbia, iii B.C.), Lxx *Le*.26.26, Plb.1.18.10, *OGI* 194.10 (Egypt, i B.C.). **-δόκη**, ἡ, *granary*, Poll.6.36. **-δόκος**, ον, *receptive of corn* or *bread*, πήρα, γαστήρ, *AP*6.95 (Antiphil.), 11.60 (Paul. Sil.); later **-δόχος** (q.v.). II. Subst. σιτοδόκος, ὁ, *keeper of corn*, Hp.*Epid*.4.25. **-δοσία**, ἡ, *gratuitous distribution of corn*, D.H.7.45, Poll.8.103 (pl.). 2. *allowance of corn*, ὁ ἀγορασμὸς τῆς σ. Lxx *Ge*.42.19.

**σῖτοδοτ-εία**, ἡ, = σιτοδοσία, Lxx *Ne*.9.15. **-έω**, *furnish corn*, Poll.6.36, Them.*Or*.23.289b. II. *furnish with provisions* or *victuals*, δραπέτας *IG*5(1).1390.81 (Andania, i B.C.), cf. Them.*Or*.23.292d:—Pass., *to be provisioned, victualled*, Th.4.39, *PCair.Zen*.620.14 (iii B.C.); esp. at Rome, of the recipients of the corn-dole, ὁ σιτοδοτούμενος ὄχλος or δῆμος, D.C.43.21, 55.10. **-ης**, ου, ὁ, *furnisher of corn*, *CIG*2804 (Aphrodisias), Man.5.308.

**σῖτο-δοχεῖον**, τό, = σιτοδόκη, Sm.*Jl*.1.17. **-δόχος**, ον, = σιτοδόκος, κοιλία Pall. *in Hp*.2.144 D.; γαστήρ Steph. *in Hp*.2.279 D. **-ενδεία**, ἡ, = σιτοδεία, Dsc.1.127 (pl.). **-θήκη**, ἡ, *granary*, Them.*Or*.18.221b (pl.). **-καπηλεύω**, *deal in corn*, Poll.7.18. * **-κάπηλος** [ᾰ], ὁ, *dealer in corn, corn-factor*, *PTeb*.120.125 (i B.C.), Ap.Ty.ap.Philostr. *VA*1.15, Poll.7.18. **-κεντρον**, τό, dub. sens. in *PFay*.348 (ii/iii A.D.). **-κλονέομαι**, Pass., *to be in want of corn*, Hsch. **-κοπικός**, ή, όν, *for pounding corn*, ἐργαστήριον *PFlor*.50.103 (iii A.D.); λίθος σ. σὺν θυείῃ *POxy*.1890 (vi A.D.). **-κόπτης** λίθος, stone *for pounding corn*, *BGU*405.7 (iv A.D.). **-κουρος**, ον, (κείρω) *consuming bread and doing nothing else, wastrel*, Alex.177, Men.244, 420. * **-κρῖθον**, τό, *mixture of wheat and barley*, *POxy*.1253.15 (iv A.D.), *PSI*1.78.6 (v A.D.), etc.

**σῖτ-όλεθρος**, ὁ, *pest of corn, destruction of corn*, Hdn.*Epim*.203.

**σῖτολογ-έω**, *collect corn, forage*, Plb.1.17.9, App.*BC*2.42, al.: c. acc., σ. τὴν χώραν Plb.3.101.2. II. *discharge the office of* σιτολόγος, *PSI*4.412.3 (iii B.C.), etc.: c. acc., τινὰς τόπους *PGoodsp.Cair*.7.5 (ii B.C.); also σ. τὸν ἱππικόν *PTeb*.798.2 (ii B.C.). **-ία**, ἡ, *collecting of corn, foraging*, Plb.3.100.6, D.S.20.42, Plu.*Fab*.8:—also **-ιον**, τό, Hdn.*Epim*.237. II. *office of* σιτολόγος, *PTeb*.24.63 (ii B.C.), etc. **-ικός**, ή, όν, *of a* σιτολόγος, διάγραμμα *Sammelb*.7450.13 (iii B.C.): Subst. **-ικόν**, τό, *fee paid to the* σιτολόγος, *POxy*.740.22 (ii/iii A.D.). **-οπράκτωρ**, ορος, ὁ, *collector of dues for* σιτολόγοι, dub. in *CPR*243.26 (iii A.D.). **-ος** (parox.), ὁ, *collector of corn, keeper of the public granary*, *PHib*.1.42.4 (iii B.C.), *Sammelb*.4512.12 (ii B.C.), *Ostr*.295, *PAmh*.2.59 (ii B.C.), *PTeb*.123.5 (i B.C.), etc.

**σῖτομεταβόλος**, ὁ, *corn-merchant*, *Gloss*.

* **σῖτομετρ-έω**, *deal out portions of corn* or *provisions*, Plb.*Fr*.75; τινι D.S.13.58: c. acc. cogn., σ. σῖτον Lxx *Ge*.47.12; *hold office of* σιτομέτρης, *IGRom*.3.516 (Cadyanda). 2. trans., σ. δύναμιν *supply* a force *with provisions, victual* it, Plb.4.63.10, etc.; τὸν δῆμον *IG*12(7).389.15 (Aegiale, ii B.C.):—Pass., οἱ πεζοὶ σιτομετροῦνταί τι they *have it served out as rations*, Plb.6.39.13, cf. *IGRom*.3.679 (Tlos).—Phryn.360, Thom.Mag.p.335 R., object to the word, preferring σῖτον μετροῦμαι. * **-ης**, ου, ὁ, *one who measures and deals out corn* or *provisions*, *PTeb*.701.296 (iii B.C.), *Sammelb*.4623 (ii/i B.C.). 2. *magistrate who inspected corn-measures*, Hyp.*Fr*.271a, Arist.*Pol*.1299ᵃ23. **-ία**, ἡ, *measured allowance of corn, rations*, *PCair.Zen*.292.63 (iii B.C.), Plb.1.68.9, *Mélanges Glotz* 904 (Iasos, ii B.C.), D.S.2.41, Plu.*Cat.Ma*.8, *OGI*533.29 (Ancyra), Polyaen.4.12.1: so **-ιον**, τό, *Ev.Luc*.12.42; ἔπαρχος -μετρίου δήμου Ῥωμαίων, = Lat. *praefectus annonae*, *IGRom*.3.667 (Patara); **-μετρον**, τό, Plu.2.313b. **-ικόν**, τό, *fee for measuring corn*, *PHib*.1.110.14 (iii B.C.), *POxy*.740.23 (ii/iii A.D.).

**σῖτόμετρος**, ὁ, = σιτομέτρης, *BGU*509.11 (ii A.D.).

**σῖτομετροσακκοφόρος**, ὁ, *one who carries sacks for the* σιτομέτραι, Frisk *Bankakten* 1 xxii 3 (ii A.D.).

**σῖτομνημονέω**, (μνήμων) = σιτομετρέω, Phryn.*PS*p.107 B., Hsch.

**σῖτον**, v. σῖτος.

**σῖτονόμος**, ον, (νέμω) *dealing out corn* or *food*, σ. ἐλπίς the hope *of getting food*, S.*Ph*.1091 (lyr.).

**σῖτοπαραλήμπτης**, ου, ὁ, *receiver of corn-dues*, *BGU*81 (ii A.D.), etc.

**σῖτοποι-εῖον**, τό, *room for grinding corn*, *Sammelb*.6796.129 (iii B.C., -ποεῖον), *PCair.Zen*.193.9 (iii B.C.), *PLond*.1.50.12 (iii/ii B.C., -ποεῖον). **-έω**, *prepare corn for food, make bread*, E.*Tr*.494; τὸ πτίσσειν καὶ ἀλήθειν καὶ σ. Sor.1.93; σ. τισί *give victuals* to.., X.*Cyr*.4.4.7:—Pass., *to be made into bread*, ἀπὸ τοῦ -ηθέντος σίτου *PCair.Zen*.4.23 (iii B.C.). II. Med., *prepare food for oneself*, X.*Cyr*.6.2.31; *take food*, ib.1.6.36. **-ητικός**, ή, όν, = σιτοποιικός, Gal.*Thras*.44. **-ητρα**, τά, *payment for baking bread*, *POxy*.739.4 (i B.C./i A.D.). **-ία**, ἡ, *bread-making, preparation of food*. X.*Oec*.7.21, *BGU* 1552.3 (Ptolemaic). **-ικός**, ή, όν, *for bread-making*, ὄργανα, σκεύη, X.*Cyr*.6.2.31, *Oec*.9.9; μηχανήσεις Plb.1.22.7. **-ός**, όν, ἀνάγκη σ. the task *of grinding and baking*, E.*Hec*.362. II. Subst., *one that ground the corn in the hand-mill, miller*, σ. ἐκ τῶν μυλώνων Th.6.22; Λαμέδοντι σιτοποιῷ *PCair.Zen*.4.41 (iii B.C.); ἐπίστειλον..πόθεν δεῖ λαβόντα σῖτον καὶ πόσον δοῦναι Ἀμμωνίῳ τῷ σ. ὅπως ἑτοιμασθῇ σεμίδαλις *PMich.Zen*.28.32 (iii B.C.); ἔργον σιτοποιοῦ *bake-meats*, Lxx *Ge*.40.17; mostly fem., *baking-woman*, Hdt.3.150, Thphr.*Char*.4.7; γυναῖκες σ. Hdt.7.187, Th.2.78; opp. ὀψοποιός (a cook), Pl.*Grg*.517e, X.*Cyr*.5.5.3; opp. μάγειρος, Plu.*Alex*.23 (pl.), cf. *Ostr.Bodl*. i 304 (pl., ii B.C.).

**σῖτοπομπ-εῖον**, τό, *conveyance of corn*, in pl., Str.7.4.6. **-ία** (in codd. freq. -εία), ἡ, *conveyance, transport of corn*, D.18.87, 241, 301, 23.155, *IG*2².1629.220. II. *supply of corn*, τῆς σ. ἐπιλιπούσης D.S.14.55, cf. *SIG*839.12 (Ephesus, ii A.D.). **-ός**, ὁ, *transporter of corn*, σειτ. ἀπὸ τῆς Αἰγύπτου *Ephes*.3 p.106 No.16.

**σῖτοπον-έω**, = σιτοποιέω, Ph.2.233,467. **-ία**, ἡ, = σιτοποιία, Hierocl. p.62 A. **-ος** (parox.), ὁ, ἡ, = σιτοποιός, Ph.1.131, al.

**σῖτοπωλ-έω**, *deal in corn*, Poll.7.18. * **-ης**, ου, ὁ, *corn-merchant, corn-factor*, κατὰ τῶν σ., title of Lys.22, cf. Arist.*HA*578ᵃ1 (v.l. -πώλους), *SIG*589.62 (Magn. Mae., ii B.C.): fem. Adj. **-πωλις**, ιδος, ἀγορά *BMus.Inscr*.413.6 (Priene).

* **σῖτος**, ὁ, heterocl. pl. σῖτα, τά, Xenoph.2.8, Hdt.4.128, 5.34 (neut. sg. σῖτον only *Delph*.3(5).3 ii 19 (iv B.C.)):—*grain*, comprehending both wheat (πυρός) and barley (κριθή), ἐν [Ἰθάκῃ] σ. ἀθέσφατος ἐν δέ τε οἶνος γίγνεται Od.13.244; περὶ σίτου ἐκβολήν about the shooting of *the corn* into ear, Th.4.1; τοῦ σ. ἀκμάζοντος at *its* ripening, Id.2.19; πρὶν τὸν σ. ἐν ἀκμῇ εἶναι Id.4.2; τὸν νέον σ. σὺν τῇ καλάμῃ ἀποκείμενον X.*An*.5.4.27; σ. ἀληλεσμένος or -εμένος ground *corn*, Hdt.7.23, Th.4.26; σ. ἀπηλοημένος D.42.6; σῖτον ἐσαγαγεῖν Th.2.6, etc.; σ. ἐπείσακτος D.18.87; σίτου εἰσαγωγή, ἐξαγωγή, Arist.*EN*1133ᵇ9, *IG*1².57.35; συγκομιδή X.*HG*7.5.14; ἐγδοχεία *PMich.Zen*.23 (iii B.C.); comprehending πυρός, κριθή, ὄλυρα, and φακός, *PTeb*.66.41 (ii B.C.); περὶ τοῦ σ. καὶ τοῦ σησάμου *PMich.Zen*.43.3 (iii B.C.); ὁ σ. καὶ τὰ λάχανα as examples of πόα, Thphr.*HP*1.3.1. 2. *food made from grain, bread*, opp. flesh-meat, σ. καὶ κρέα Od.9.9, 12.19, cf. Hdt.2.168; σῖτον ἔδοντες, a general epith. of men as opp. to beasts, ὅσσοι νῦν βροτοί εἰσιν ἐπὶ χθονὶ σ. ἔδ. Od.8.222, cf. 9.89; of savages, who eat flesh only, οὐδέ τι σῖτον ἤσθιον Hes.*Op*.146; of civilized men, σῖτον καὶ σπείρουσι καὶ σιτέονται Hdt.4.17; σωρὸν σίτου κεχυμένον Id.1.22; ἐσθίειν ἐπὶ τῷ σ. ὄψον X.*Mem*.3.14.2; κάρδαμον ἔχειν ἐπὶ τῷ σ. Id.*Cyr*.1.2.11; πίνειν ὕδωρ ἐπὶ τῷ σ. ib.6.2.27, cf. Plu.*Them*.29, with Id.2.328f. 3. in a wider sense, *food*, as opp. to drink, σ. ἠδὲ ποτῆς Od.9.87, cf. Il.19.306; σ. καὶ οἶνος Od.3.479, Il.9.706; σ. καὶ μέθυ Od.4.746, etc.; even of porridge (κυκεών), 10.235; σῖτα καὶ ποτά Hdt.5.34, X.*An*.2.3.27; σ. ποιεῖν καὶ οἶνον Pl.*R*.372a; ἄκμηνος σίτοιο Il.19.163, cf. A.*Fr*.182; εὐνὴ καὶ σ. Od.20.130, cf. Il.24.129; ὕπνον καὶ σ. αἱρεῖσθαι Th.2.75; *provisions*, σῖτα ἀναιρέεσθαι Hdt.4.128; παρέχειν σῖτα καὶ νέας Id.7.21; παρέχειν μέχρι τριάκοντα ἡμερῶν σ. Foed.ap.Th.5.47. 4. rarely of beasts, *fodder*, Hes.*Op*.604, E.*HF*383 (lyr.), X.*Eq*.4.1.—In the general sense of *food*, Prose writers prefer the dim. form σιτία, τά. II. in Att. Law, *allowance of grain* made to widows and orphans, σῖτον διδόναι, ἀποδιδόναι, D.27.15, 28.11, Arist.*Ath*.56.7. 2. δίκην σίτου δικάσασθαι, bring an action under the Athen. Corn-law against regraters and monopolists, Is.3.9, cf. D.59.52. 3. *allowance* made to the Ἱππεῖς, *IG*1².304.4, al. 4. *public distribution of corn* in Rome, Lat. *frumentatio*, τὸν ἐπὶ τοῦ σίτου ὄντα ἐν Ῥώμῃ Arr.*Epict*.1.10.2.

**σῖτό-σπελλος**, ὁ, = αἰγίλωψ 1, Ps.-Dsc.4.137. **-σπορος**, ον, *sown with corn*, D.H.4.56, Heph.Astr.3.37 (in *Cat.Cod.Astr*.8(1).154).

**σῖτουργ-ία**, ἡ, = σιτοποιία, Sch.Call.*Cer*.22. **-ός**, όν, = σιτοποιός, Pl.*Plt*.267e.

**σῖτοφᾰγ-έω**, *feed on bread*, etc., Eust. ad D.P.310. **-ος** (parox.), ον, *eating corn* or *bread*, Od.9.191, Hdt.4.109, Hecat.335 J.

**σῖτοφορ-έω**, *grow corn upon*, [ἄρουραν] *PSI*4.400.7 (iii B.C.). **-ικός**, ή, όν, *corn-bearing*, ib.2.240.8 (ii A.D.). **-ος** (parox.), ον, *carrying corn* or *provisions*, of beasts of burden, Hdt.1.80, 3.153, 7.125. II. *producing corn*, Thphr.*HP*8.2.8, *PCair.Zen*.723.23 (iii B.C.), Ph.2.390, *POxy*.45.11 (σειτ-, i A.D.), etc.

**σῖτοφῠλᾰκ-εῖον**, τό, *granary*, Suid. * **-ες**, οἱ, *corn-inspectors*, Athenian officers *who registered imports of corn, and superintended the sale of corn, flour, and bread*, Lys.22.16, D.20.32, Arist.*Ath*.51.3. II. similar officers at Tauromenium, *IG*14.423 i 25, al. (in metaplast. dat. σιτοφυλάκοις). **-έω**, *act as corn-inspector*, App.*Pun*.47.

**σῖτό-χροος**, ον, contr. **-χρους**, ουν, (χρόα) *of the colour of ripe wheat*, Opp.*C*.1.435; βοῦς, μόσχος, *PFlor*.51.12 (ii A.D.), *BGU*986.10 (ii A.D.); of horses, *PFay*.301 (ii A.D.).

**σίττᾰ**, a cry of drovers to urge on or guide their flocks (Hsch.), *st!* σίττα, νέμεσθε Theoc.8.69; σίτθ', ὁ λέπαργος Id.4.45; when ἀπό follows, to drive them off, οὐκ ἀπὸ τᾶς κράνας σίττ', ἀμνίδες; Id.5.3; σίττ' ἀπὸ τᾶς κοτίνω ib.100; when πρός follows, to lead them on, σίτθ', ἁ Κυμαίθα, ποτὶ τὸν λόφον Id.4.46: cf. ψίττα, ψύττα.

**σιττακός**, ὁ, = ψιττακός, Phld.*Po*.2.20, Arr.*Ind*.15.8: also **σίττας**, Hsch.

**σίττη**, ἡ, *nuthatch*, *Sitta europaea*, Arist.*HA*609ᵇ11, 616ᵇ22, Call.*Fr*.173, Sch.Ar.*Av*.705; αἰσίῳ σίττῃ Call.*Iamb*.1.121, cf. *Lyr.Adesp*.27: also **σίττος**, ὁ, variously identified, Hsch.

**σιττύβαι**· δερμάτιναι στολαί· τὰ μικρὰ ἱμαντάρια, Hsch.: cf. σίττυβα χιτὼν ἐκ δέρματος Poll.7.70; σίττυβα· δερμάτια, Phot.; σίττυβον τὸ μικρὸν δέρμα Hdn.Gr.1.378: cf. σίλλυβος.

**σίττῠβος**, ὁ, = κάκκαβος, Antiph.182.7.

**Σιτώ**, οῦς, ἡ, epith. of Demeter, Polem.Hist.39, Ael.*VH*1.27.

**σῖτ-ώδης**, ες, *like corn*, τὰ σ. *cereals*, Thphr.*HP*8.1.1, Muson.*Fr*.18ᴬ p.95 H.; τροφὴ σ. Sor.1.46, cf. Archig.ap.Orib.8.1.17, Aret.*CA* 2.3, *CD*1.3; διαχωρήματα σ. καὶ ἄπεπτα Hp.*Salubr*.7. **-ωμα**, ατος, τό, in pl., *provisions*, *Sammelb.*4425 iv 1 (ii A. D.). ⊛ -ών, ῶνος, ὁ, *cornfield*, Plu.2.524a. * -ωνέω, *buy corn*, *IG*11(4).1055.12 (Delos, iii B. C.), *PCair.Zen.*723.13, *PLond.ined.*2316, *PSI*5.525.4 (all iii B. C.). -ώνης, ου, ὁ, (ὠνέομαι) *public buyer of corn*, an officer in many Greek states, as at Athens, D.18.248, *IG*2$^2$.792.11; at Samos, *SIG*976.45 (ii B. C.); in Laconia, *IG*5(1).551.4 (iii A. D.); at Thyatira, *IGRom.*4.1228. -ωνία, ἡ, *purchase of corn*, D.34.39, *IPE*1$^2$.32 *A* 68 (Olbia, iii B. C.), *PCair.Zen.*326.33 (iii B. C.), Ph.2.64; *office of* σιτώνης, *Cod.Just.*1.4.17. ⊛ -ωνικόν, τό, *wheat-fund*, *Inscr.Délos* 399 *A* 73 (ii B. C.), *IG*4.2.8 (Aegina, i B. C.): pl., ib.2$^2$.1272.3 (Eleusis, iii B. C.), 1708 (ii B. C.), *IGRom.*4.580 (Aezani); -κὰ χρήματα *Papers of Amer. School at Athens* 3.612 (Ilias). -ώνιον, τό, *public granary, storehouse*, or *wheat-fund*, = σιτωνικόν, *IG*14.423 i 37, al. (Tauromenium, ii/i B. C.). 2. *money for the purchase of corn, corn-money*, as part of a soldier's pay, *UPZ*14.74 (ii B. C.), *PTheb.Bank* 6.3, 7.3, al. (ii B. C.). 3. name of a tax, prob. levied to provide corn-money, *BGU*1846.5 (i B. C.).

**σιφαῖος** ἄρτος, ὁ, dub. in Luc.*Lex.*6; σιλφαῖος Suid.

**σίφᾰρος** [ῐ], ὁ, *top-sail*, ἐπαίρειν τοὺς σ. Arr.*Epict.*3.2.18, cf. Hsch. s. v. ἐπίδρομον (prob.): cf. σείφαρος. (The Lat. forms are *sīparum*, *sīpharum*, from which *supparus* pl. *suppara* (name of a garment) is to be distinguished.)

**σιφθείριον**, Egypt. word for καλάμου ἐπιφάνεια, Gal.12.408.

⊛ **σιφλός**, ή, όν, *crippled, maimed*, πόδα σιφλός A.R.1.204: metaph., *mad*, of Glaucus the Lycian (Il.6.234), *Eleg.Alex.Adesp.*1.2; of fish, *mad on food, greedy*, πλωτῶν σ. γένος Opp.*H.*3.183. II. *soft, spongy*, νάρθηξ τὰ ἐντὸς σ. quoted as Lycian by Eust.972.38; of persons, Lycian for ῥάθυμος καὶ οὐκ ἐνεργής, ib.36.—The Adj. is late, but v. σιφλόω: Hsch. has **σιφνός**· κενός; cf. σιπαλός.

**σίφλος**, ὁ, *defect, blemish*, μορφῆς Lyc.1134.

**σιφλ-όω**, *maim, cripple*, Il.14.142. -ωμα, ατος, τό, *sponginess, loose structure*, Eust.972.41.

**σίφνα**· ποιὸς ἰχθῦς, Hsch.

**σιφνεύς**, έως, ὁ, = ἀσπάλαξ, Lyc.121.

**σιφνιάζω**, *play the Siphnian*, Ar.*Fr.*912, cf. Poll.4.65, Hsch.

**σίφνις**, ἡ, acc. sg. σίφνιν, = σιπύα, Hymn.Att.ap.Poll.10.162.

**Σίφνος**, ἡ, *Siphnus*, Hdt.3.57, etc.: Adj. **Σίφνιος**, α, ον, Str.10.5.1; οἱ Σίφνιοι Hdt. l. c., etc.

**σιφνός**, v. σιφλός. **σιφνύει**· κενοῖ, Hsch. **σιφῶμαι**· τήκομαι, Id.

**σίφων**, ωνος, ὁ, = ἡ καλάμη τοῦ ἀγρίου καλάμου, *Gloss.*: hence, *tube, pipe*, Aen.Tact.18.10, Anon.Lond.26.51; καλάμινος σ. Dsc.*Eup.*2.35; esp., 1. *siphon*, used for drawing wine out of the cask or jar, Hippon.56, *PEleph.*5.4 (iii B. C.); καμπύλος σ., τουτέστι σωλὴν Hero *Spir.*1.1. b. *drainage-tube* for hydrocele, Gal.10.988. c. *pump*, *PLond.*3.1177.129 (ii A. D.). 2. *fire-engine*, Apollod.*Poliorc.* 174.5, Hsch.: generally, *service-pipe for water in houses*, Str.5.3.8. 3. *water-spout*, Olymp. *in Mete.*13.15, Sch.Arat.785. 4. αἵματος ἀνδρῶν σίφωνες *blood-suckers*, i. e. mosquitoes, *AP*5.150 (Mel.). 5. sens. obsc. for τὸ αἰδοῖον, E.*Cyc.*439 (s. v. l.). 6. = ῥυπαρὸς ἄνθρωπος, ἢ λίχνος, Hsch. 7. εἶδος θηρίου μυρμηκοειδές, Id. 8. ὄργανον σκόλοπι ὅμοιον, ἐν ᾧ τοὺς μαρσίππους ἐπισκοποῦσι, Id. (perh. = σιρομάστης 1). [ῑ in *AP* l. c., Juv.6.310; but ῐ E. l. c. (s. v. l.).]

**σῑφων-ίζω**, *draw off* wine *with a siphon*, οἶνον Ar.*Th.*557. -ιον, τό, Dim. of σίφων, Hsch. II. = αἰγίλωψ 1, Ps.-Dsc.4.137.

**σῑφωνολογία**, ἡ, *weeding of* σιφώνιον II, in pl., *Sammelb.*7373.22 (i A. D.), *BGU*538.16 (i/ii A. D.), 918.16 (ii A. D.).

**σίω**, v. σείω.

**σιώ**, Lacon. dual of θεός, Ar.*Lys.*142; **σιῷ**, dat. for θεῷ, ib.174.

**σῑωπ-άω**, inf. σιωπᾶν Il.2.280: fut. -ήσομαι in early writers, S.*OT*233, Ar.*Pax* 309, *Av.*225, *Lys.*364, Pl.*Phdr.*234a, etc.; later -ήσω Aeschin.*Ep.*10.1, D.H.11.6, Plu.2.240e, etc. (cf. σιγάω): aor. (ἐ)σιώπησα Il.23.568, etc.: pf. σεσιώπηκα Ar.*V.*944, D.6.34:—Med. and Pass., v. infr.: Dor. **σωπάω** (q. v.):—*keep silence*, σιωπᾶν λαὸν ἀνώγει Il.2.280, cf. 23.568, Od.17.513, Hdt.7.10, etc.; Σιμωνίδης τὴν ζωγραφίαν ποίησιν σιωπῶσαν προσαγορεύει Plu.2.346f; φησὶν σιωπῶν *his silence is an admission*, E.*Or.*1592, cf. *IA*1245; πονηρῶν ἔργων δόξει κοινωνεῖν τῷ σιωπῆσαι D.19.33; σ. τινί *keep silence for* or *at the behest of* . ., Ar.*Ra.*1134, *Lys.*530; σ. πρός τινα Pl.*Phdr.*234a; πρὸς τοῦτο X.*Cyr.*5.5.20; ὑπέρ τινος E.*Fr.*796; imper. σιώπα *hush! be still!* S.*Fr.*81, Ar.*Lys.*529, etc. 2. of bees, *to be still*, opp. βομβέω, Arist.*HA*627$^a$24. II. trans., *keep secret, speak not of*, τὰ δίκαια E.*Fr.*1037, cf. Ar.*Th.*27, X.*Smp.*6.10, etc.; σ. ὅτι . . *PMasp.*295.21 (v A. D.):—Pass., ἂν σιωπηθῇ τὰ παρὰ τῶν πολεμίων D.*Prooem.*21, cf. Isoc.1.22, etc.; τί σιγῶσ' ὧν σιωπᾶσθαι χρεών; E.*Ion* 432; σιωπώμενον καὶ ἀβασάνιστον ἐᾶσαι Antipho 1.13; οὐ τὸ αἰσχρὸν σιωπηθήσεται Aeschin.3.155; ταῦτα σιωπᾶσθαι συνέφερεν D.19.42; ἡ σιωπωμένη ἀλήθεια D.H.1.76. III. Med., *silence*, σιωπησάμενος τὰ πλήθη Plb.18.46.4. ⊛ -ή, rarely σωπή (q. v.), ἡ, *silence*, S.*OT*1075, *Fr.*928, E.*Hipp.*911; σ. ὑπεσημάνθη Th.6.32; σ. ποιεῖν, ποιεῖσθαι, X.*HG*6.3.10, Isoc.12.234; ἦν σ. *there was a hush* or *calm*, S.*OC*1623, Aeschin.2.35: pl., τῶν ἀπειράτων ἄγνωστοι σ. inglorious *silence* is their lot who make no venture, Pi.*I.*4(3).30 (48). 2. *the habit of silence*, ἐκ τῆς σ. τὴν τῆς σωφροσύνης δόξαν θηρᾶσθαι D.61.21, cf. Plu.2.39b, etc. II. dat. σιωπῇ as Adv., *in silence*, the only case used by Hom., ἀκὴν ἐγένοντο σιωπῇ Il.3.95, etc.; σ. ἧσο 4.412; ἐπ' ὀφρύσι νεῦσε σ. made a sign *without speaking*, 9.620; σ. πίνειν Od.1.339; σ. πάσχειν ἄλγεα 13.309, cf. Pi.*P.*4.57; στῆναι, πορεύεσθαι, καθῆσθαι σ., E.*HF*930, X.*Cyr.*5.3.43, D.48.31; *secretly*, Il.14.310; σιωπῇ τοῦτ' ἀκύρωτον μένει E.*Ion.*801, cf. Ar.*Eq.*1212. -ηλός, ή, όν, *silent*, E.*Med.*320, Arist.*Pr.*953$^b$1, Plu.2.47d; σιωπηλότερος τῶν Πυθαγόρᾳ τελεσθέντων Prov.ap.Suid. s. v. σιωπή; τὸ σ. *taciturnity*, Plu.*Fab.*1: of things, σ. κίθαρις Call.*Ap.*12; θάλασσα *calm*, Gal.6.709. Adv. -λῶς Poll.5.147. II. σιωπηλόν, τό, = κατακάλυμμα, Sm.*Is.*47.2; cf. σιώπησις. ⊛ -ηρός, ά, όν, = foreg., *AP*7.199, 211 (both Tymn.); σιωπηρότερος (-ηλότερος as cited in Ath.5.188a) X.*Smp.*1.9. Adv. -ρῶς *Gloss.* -ησις, εως, ἡ, *taciturnity*, Sch. Ptol.*Tetr.*160 (pl.): metaph., *veil, covering*, LXX *Ca.*4.1,3, 6.6(7); cf. σιωπηλός II. -ητέος, α, ον, *to be passed over in silence*, Luc.*Hist. Conscr.*27. II. σιωπητέον, *one must pass over in silence*, ib.6.

**σκάζω**, only pres. and impf., *limp, halt*, Il.19.47; ἐκ πολέμου 11.811, cf. *Com.Adesp.*610, Plu.2.317e: metaph., ἀκέσασθαι τὸ σκάζον make good *the damage*, Men.Prot.p.22 D.; δρῶ τὰ ἡμέτερα σκάζοντα, of parasites, Alciphr.3.50; σ. ἀμφοτέροις ἡ κρίσις Chor. in *Rh.Mus.* 49.504; πρὸς τὴν θεραπείαν Luc.*Merc.Cond.*39. II. σκάζων, οντος, ὁ, = χωλίαμβος, the iambic verse of Hipponax, with a spondee in the last place, σκάζοντα μέτρα *AP*7.405 (Phil.). (Cf. Skt. *khañjati* 'limp', Germ. *hinken*.)

**σκαιο-βᾰτέω**, *walk* or *dance awkwardly*, Eust.1468.65; **σκαιεμβατέω**, Phot., Suid. -θεν (parox.), Adv. *from the left*, Id. -λογέω, *speak amiss*, Id. s. v. ῥάζειν. -λ]όγος, ον, *speaking recklessly*, dub. in *Supp.Epigr.*4.512 (Ephesus, ii A. D.).

**σκαι-ός**, ά, όν, *left, on the left hand*, poet. for ἀριστερός (used by Prose writers in metaph. sense, and once by Pl. in literal sense, *Phdr.*266a; also in Dor. Prose, ἐν σκαιάν, = ἐς ἀριστεράν, *SIG*636.22 (Delph., ii B. C.; σκαγαν lapis)); τὸ σ. ὄμμα παραβαλών A.*Fr.*308 (cf. Ath.7.303c); in Hom. always in dat. σκαιῇ (sc. χειρί), *with the left hand*, Il.1.501, al.; χειρὶ σ. Hes.*Th.*179:—hence, II. *western, westward* (for the Greek diviner always turned his face northward, and so had the West on his left): hence Σκαιαὶ πύλαι the *West*-gate of Troy, Il.3.145, al., cf. Hsch. (otherwise expld. by Sch. ad loc.); σ. ῥίον either, *on the left*, or *west* headland, Od.3.295; σ. λιμὴν Orac. ap.D.S.8.21; πόρος D.P.161,481,541. 2. *unlucky, ill-omened, mischievous* (cf. δεξιός II), ἡ φιλοτιμίη κτῆμα σ. Hdt.3.53; σεσιγαμένον οὐ σκαιότερον χρῆμ' ἕκαστον a thing is none *the worse* for remaining unsaid, Pi.*O.*9.104; σ. ἐκλύσων στόμα about to speak *mischief*, S.*Aj.* 1225. III. metaph. of persons, *lefthanded, awkward, clumsy, stupid*, -ότατος καὶ ἀδικώτατος Hdt.1.129; σ. ἰητροί Hp.*Art.*42; σκαιοῖσι πολλοῖς εἷς σοφὸς διόλλυται S.*Fr.*921, cf. 771; ὅπου δ' Ἀπόλλων σ. ᾖ, τίνες σοφοί; E.*El.*972, cf. *Heracl.*258, *HF*283; ὦ σκαιὲ κἀπαίδευτε Ar.*V.*1183, cf. 1266; ἐπιλησμότατον καὶ -ότατον γερόντιον Id.*Nu.*790; οὕτω σ. ὥστε μαθεῖν οὐ δύνασθαι Lys.10.15, cf. Pl.*Euthd.*295d; σ. καὶ βάρβαρος τὸν τρόπον D.26.17; σ. καὶ ἀναίσθητος Id.18.120; σ. ἢ ἀνήκοος Id.19.312. Adv., σκαιῶς λέγειν Ar.*Ec.*644, cf. *Pl.*60: Comp., Phld.*Acad.Ind.*p.7 M. 2. of words, thoughts, or actions, -ότατον ἔπος Ar.*Av.*174, cf. Arist.*Rh.Al.*1430$^b$7; σ. καινουργία *OGI*569.18 (Arycanda, iv A. D.).—In these senses σκαιός is opp. to δεξιός (q. v.). IV. *aslant, crooked*, of serpents, Nic.*Th.*266; cf. σκοιός. (Prob. σκαιϝός, cf. Lat. *scaevus*.) -οσύνη, ἡ, = sq., S.*OC*1213 (lyr.). -ότης, ητος, ἡ, (σκαιός III) *awkwardness*, ἀγνωμοσύνη καὶ σ. Hdt.7.9.β'; αὐθαδία τοι σκαιότητ' ὀφλισκάνει S.*Ant.*1028; ἐν ἀμαθίᾳ καὶ σ. Pl.*R.*411e; σ. πλουσία, opp. σοφὴ πενία, Critias 29 D.; σ. τῶν τρόπων D.6.19. -ουργέω, *behave amiss*, περὶ γονέας towards one's parents, Ar.*Nu.*994. -ούργημα, ατος, τό, *ill-behaviour*, Tz.*H.*3.255.

**σκαίρω**, only pres. and impf., Ion. impf. σκαίρεσκε A.R.4.1402:—*skip, dance, frisk*, of calves, Od.10.412, cf. Theoc.4.19, Call.*Dian.* 100; οὐρῇ σ. A.R.4.1402; of dancers, ποσὶ σκαίρειν Il.18.572, cf. Arist.*Pr.*869$^b$9. (Hence σκαρθμός, σκαρίζω, cf. ἀσκαρίζω:—σκιρτάω is prob. Frequentat.)

**σκαίωμα**, ατος, τό, *zig-zag slope*, Plb.5.59.9 (s. v. l.).

**σκαιωρ-έω**, = πανουργέω, *devise mischievously*, ἐπιβουλήν τινι Procop.*Aed.*1 *Prooem.*, cf. Sch.S.*OT*673. -ημα, ατος, τό, *mischievous device*, Poll.6.182, Procop.*Arc.*28, Sch.A.*Ch.*730. ⊛ -ία, ἡ, *mischief*, Tz.*H.*8.903. (Cf. σκευωρός fin.)

**σκάλα**, ἡ, = Lat. *scala*, *stairs, gangway* of a ship, etc., Poll.1.93, Hsch.

**σκᾰλᾰβώτης**, ου, ὁ, later form for ἀσκαλαβώτης, Orac.ap.Eus.*PE* 5.12 (s. v. l.).

**σκαλαθάρβα**· τύρβη, ἀπὸ τοῦ σκαλεύειν, Hsch.

**σκαλαθαρβία**· ἀκηδία, Hsch.

**σκᾰλᾰθυρμάτιον**, τό, Dim. of **σκαλάθυρμα** (cited in Hsch. and Phot.), *trifling subtlety* or *technicality, petty quibble*, Ar.*Nu.*630.

**σκᾰλᾰθύρω** [ῠ], (σκάλλω) *dig*, Hsch.: sens. obsc., Ar.*Ec.*611.

**σκαλαπάζει**· ῥέμβεται, Hsch. (Cf. σκαλπάζειν, καλπάζω, ἀνακαλπάζω.) **σκάλατος**· ὁ σκαφιτός (i. e. -τρός), Id.

**σκᾰλαυθρ-ῖτις**, ιδος, ἡ, name of a kind of λιθάργυρος, prob. cj. in Dsc.5.87. -ον, τό, *oven-rake*, gloss on σπαύλαθρον, Hsch.; on σπάλαυθρον, Phot.; cf. σκάλευθρον, σπάλαθρον.

**σκᾰλ-εία**, ἡ, *hoeing*, *Gp.*2.24 tit. -ευθρον (v. l. -εθρον), τό, later form for σπάλαθρον, Poll.7.22. -ευμα, ατος, τό, *that which is hoed*, Sch.Ar.*Nu.*630, Hsch. s. v. σκαλαθυρμάτια (-ύματα cod.). -εύς, έως, ὁ, *hoer*, X.*Oec.*17.12,15. -ευσις, εως, ἡ, *poking, scratching up*, Aq.*Ps.*63(64).7. ⊛ -εύω, = σκάλλω, *stir, poke*, ἄνθρακας Ar. *Pax* 440; πῦρ μαχαίρᾳ μὴ σ., i. e. don't provoke an angry man, Pythag. prov. in Arist.*Fr.*197, cf. Plu.*Num.*14, Luc.*VH*2.28, D.L. 8.17; σ. τὰ ὦτα, τὸ οὖς, Arist.*Pr.*960$^b$35, 961$^a$37: abs., of poultry, *scratch*, Plu.2.516d: prov., αἰγὸς τρόπον μάχαιραν ἐσκάλευσά (μοι), i.e. I have unearthed the weapon for my own destruction, *Com. Adesp.*47 D.

**σκᾰλην-ής**, ές, = σκαληνός, Arist.*APo.*74$^a$27, *Ph.*224$^a$5 (in both places with v.l. σκαληνόν). **-ία**, ἡ, *unevenness*, σχημάτων Plu.2.697a. **-οειδής**, ές, *oblique*, σ. ὀχετός, of the ureter, Hp.*Anat.*1; σχήματα, of Sicily, Agathem.5.20. **-όομαι**, Pass., *have the conception* or *impression of something unequal* or *crooked*, τὴν ὄψιν Plu.2.1121b. **-ός**, ή, όν, also ός, όν Leon.ap.Stob.4.52.28:—*uneven, unequal, rough*, Democr.ap.Thphr.*Sens.*66, Epicur.*Ep.*2 p.50 U.; ἀταρπὸς σ. a *rugged* path, Leon. l.c.; σ. φλέψ a *slanting* vein, Hp.*Anat.*1; ἀριθμὸς σ. *odd* number (v. ἰσοσκελής), Pl.*Euthphr.*12d, cf. Nicom.*Ar.*2.16; τρίγωνον σ. a triangle *with unequal sides*, Ti.Locr.98b, cf. Call.*Iamb.*1.125; τὸ σ. Arist.*APo.*84$^b$7; κῶνος σ. *oblique* cone, Apollon.Perg.*Con.*1 *Def.*1.3; cf. σκαληνής. (Prob. akin to σκολιός.)

**σκᾰλίας**, ου, ὁ, *fond d'artichaut*, Thphr.*HP*6.4.11; cf. ἀσκάληρον.

**σκᾰλῐδεύω**, (σκαλίς) = σκαλίζω, σκάλλω, *scalpo*, *Gloss.*

**σκαλίδρις**, ἡ, a speckled waterbird, prob. *redshank*, *Scolopax calidris*, Arist.*HA*593$^b$7 (v.l. καλίδρις).

**σκᾰλ-ίζω**, = σκάλλω, *hoe*, Att. ἀσκαλ-, Phryn.*PS*p.42 B. ⊕ **-ίς**, ίδος, ἡ, *instrument for hoeing, hoe* or *shovel*, *IG*2$^2$.1424*a*391, 1548, Str.3.2.9, J.*BJ*2.8.9. **-ισμός**, ὁ, *hoeing*, *POxy.*1692.18 (ii A.D.). II. a form of torture, Eun.*VS* p.478 B. **-ιστήριον**, τό, = σκαλίς, Sch. rec.Theoc.10.14.

**σκαλλίον**, τό, *small cup, bowl*, Philet.ap.Ath.11.498a, Hsch.

⊕ **σκάλλω**, *stir up, hoe*, Hdt.2.14, Arist.*Mir.*837$^b$22, cf. Thphr.*HP*2.7.5, etc.: metaph., *search, probe*, σ. τὸ πνεῦμά μου Lxx *Ps.*76(77).7.

**σκάλμη**, ἡ, (σκάλλω) *knife, sword*, S.*Fr.*620, M.Ant.11.15. On the accent, v. Hdn.Gr.1.324.

**σκαλμίδιον** [μῐ], τό, Dim. of sq., *Com.Adesp.*607.

**σκαλμός**, ὁ, *pin* or *thole* to which the Greek oar was fastened by the τροπωτήρ, *h.Hom.*7.42, A.*Pers.*376, E.*Hel.*1598, *IT*1347; ὑπομόχλιον ὁ σ. γίνεται Arist.*Mech.*850$^b$11; κατὰ σκαλμὸν ἐρέσσειν (opp. *paddle*) Arr.*Ind.*27.5:—of the πριαπίσκος in the βάθρον Ἱπποκράτους, Ruf.ap.Orib.49.26.6. II. σ. θρανίτης *a bank* or *bench* of rowers, Plb.16.3.4. III. = σκαλισμός I, *POxy.*1631.12 (iii A.D.).

**σκᾰλο-βάτης** [βᾰ], ὁ, (σκάλα) *one who goes up a ladder, funambulus*, *Gloss.*: hence **-βᾰτέω**, *go up a ladder*, Hsch.

**σκᾰλοπιά**, ἡ, *blind-rat's run*, Thphr.*HP*7.12.3 (v.l. σκολοπ-).

**σκάλοψ** [ᾰ], οπος, ὁ, = σπάλαξ, Ar.*Ach.*879: Phot. cites σκάλωψ (σκάλοψ?) from Cratin.93.

**σκαλπάζειν**· ῥεμβωδῶς βαδίζειν, Hsch. (σκαλαπ- cod., post σκάλοψ).

**σκάλσις**, εως, ἡ, (σκάλλω) *hoeing, digging*, Thphr.*CP*3.20.6, 4.13.3.

**σκαλτωμίζειν**· λαμπυρίζειν, Hsch. **σκάμαια**· κύων, Id.

**Σκάμανδρος**, ὁ, *Scamander*, the river of Troy, ὃν Ξάνθον καλέουσι θεοί, ἄνδρες δὲ Σκάμανδρον Il.20.74:—Adj. **Σκᾰμάνδριος**, ον, *Scamandrian*, 2.465, S.*Aj.*418 (lyr.), E.*Tr.*374, etc.; pr. n. of Hector's son, Il.6.402. [Σκᾰ-; Hom. leaves a short vowel short before the Σκ-, cf. σκέπαρνον.]

**σκαμβάλυξ**, = σκαμβός, στρεβλός, Hsch. **σκαμβηρίζοντες**· ὀλισθαίνοντες, Id.

**σκαμβόπους**, πουν, gen. ποδος, *bow-legged*, Ps.-Archyt.ap.Simp. *in Cat.*396.1.

**σκαμβ-ός**, ή, όν, *crooked, bent*, σ. ξύλον οὐδέποτ' ὀρθόν 'there's no straightening a *crooked* billet', Macar.7.69; of a cow's horns, dub. rest. in *PBaden* 19.5 (ii A.D.); esp. *bent asunder, bow*, of the legs, opp. βλαισός, *Gp.*19.2.1 (Comp.), cf. Gal.14.793, *Hippiatr.*102: metaph., καρδία σ. Lxx *Ps.*100(101).3. **-όω**, *twist*, in Pass., Aq., Thd.*Is.*59.8.

**σκάμβυκες**· σκόλοπες, χάρακες, Hsch.

**σκάμμα**, ατος, τό, (σκάπτω) *that which has been dug, trench, pit*, Pl.*Lg.*845e. 2. *action of digging*, οὕτω τὸ σ. ποιοῦσι Apollod.*Poliorc.*145.5. II. *place dug up and sanded*, on which wrestlers practised, *CIG*2758 III col.3 D (Aphrodisias), cf. *IG*14.1102.16 (Rome), 1107.10 (ibid.), Gal.*Thras.*46: prov., ἐπὶ τοῦ σ. ὤν at a *crisis*, time of trial, Plb.38.18.5; εἰς τοσοῦτο σ. προεκαλεῖτο πάντα ὁντιναοῦν to such *trials*, Arr.*Epict.*4.8.26. 2. *place dug up*, on which athletes landed in the long jump, *AB*224. 3. *furrow* marking the length of a jump, Sch.Pi.*N.*5.34a; cf. σκάπτω II. 3.

**σκαμμάδες**· πόρναι, Hsch.

**σκαμμων-ία** (and **σκαμωνία**), ἡ, *scammony, Convolvulus Scammonia*, from the roots of which the purgative medicine *scammony* is extracted, Eub.19, Arist.*Pr.*864$^a$4, $^b$13, Thphr.*HP*4.5.1, 9.1.3, al., Dsc.4.170; also **σκαμμώνιον**, τό, Nic.*Al.*565; **σκαμώνειον**, Anon.Lond.37.19; cf. ἀσκαμωνία, κάμμων. [σκᾰμωνία Eub. l.c.; the spelling with one μ is found also in Thphr.*HP*9.1.4 codd., 9.9.1 codd., Sor.1.125, Hsch., and as v.l. in Dsc. l.c.; cf. σκαμώνειον; but σκαμμώνιον is corroborated by the metre in Nic. l.c.] **-ίτης** οἶνος [ῑ], wine *prepared with* σκαμμωνία, used as a purgative, Dsc.5.73, Plin.*HN*14.110.

⊕ **σκάμνος**, ὁ, = σκίμπους, Sch.Ar.*Nu.*633 (Lat. **scamnum**).

**σκαμφυσεῖ**· μεμψιμοιρεῖ, ἀγανακτεῖ, Hsch.

**σκαμωνία, σκαμώνειον**, v. σκαμμωνία.

**σκᾱνά**, Dor. for σκηνή, *IG*14.352 I 39 (Halaesa), etc.

**σκανάω**, v. σκανέω.

**σκανδᾰλάριος**, ὁ, *shingler* of roofs, *IGRom.*4.1646 (Philadelphia), Rhetor. in *Cat.Cod.Astr.*8(4).215; cf. Lat. **scandularius**.

**σκανδάλ-η** [ᾰ], ἡ, = sq., Alciphr.3.22. **-ηθρον**, τό, *stick in a trap* on which the bait is placed, and which, when touched by the animal, springs up and shuts the trap, Poll.7.114, 10.156: metaph., σκανδάληθρ' ἱστὰς ἐπῶν setting word-*traps*, i.e. throwing out words which one's adversary will catch at, and so be caught himself, Ar.*Ach.*687, ubi v. Sch., cf. Cratin.457; cf. σκάνδαλον. **-ίζω**, *cause to stumble, give offence* or *scandal* to any one, τινα *Ev.Matt.*5.29, 17.27, etc.:—Pass., *to be made to stumble, take offence*, ib.26.33, etc.; ἔν τινι Lxx *Si.*9.5, al., *Ev.Matt.*11.6, 26.31, etc. **-ιστής**, οῦ, ὁ, prob. *acrobat who performed on a trapeze* (σκάνδαλον), *SIG*847.5 (Delph., ii A.D.), v. *Supp.Epigr.*2.328. **-ον**, τό, *trap* or *snare* laid for an enemy, Lxx *Jo.*23.13, 1*Ki.*18.21, *Ep.Rom.*11.9, 1*Ep.Pet.*2.7; prob. laid for animals, *PCair.Zen.*608.7 (iii B.C., written σκανδάνων, gen. pl.): metaph., *stumbling-block, offence, scandal*, *Ev.Matt.*18.7, *Ev.Luc.*17.1; σκάνδαλα ποιεῖσθαι *PMasp.*4.9 (vi A.D.). II. v. σκανδαλιστής. **-ος**, ὁ, = σκάνδαλον, Hsch. **-όω**, = σκανδαλίζω, Aq.*Is.*8.15, al.

**σκανδεία**· εἶδος περικεφαλαίας, Hsch. (prob. misunderstanding of Il.10.268).

⊕ **σκανδῐκοπώλης**, ου, ὁ, *dealer in wild chervil*, as Ar. called Euripides, Hsch., Phot.

**σκανδῐκώδης**, ες, *like, of the nature of wild chervil*, Thphr.*HP*7.11.1.

**σκάνδιξ**, ῐκος, ἡ (Sch.Ar., v. infr.), *wild chervil, Scandix Pecten-Veneris*, Ar.*Ach.*478, And.*Fr.*4, Thphr.*HP*7.7.1, 7.8.1, Dsc.2.138.

**σκάνδυξ**, ῠκος, ἡ, = foreg., v.l. in Dsc.2.138.

**σκανεύεσθαι**· ἐπαρι⟨σ⟩τερεύεσθαι, Hsch.

**σκᾱνέω**, = σκηνοποιέω, *IG*9(1).129 (Elatea), unless inf. **σκανεν** is to be understood as σκανῆν, from σκᾱνάω.

**σκάνθαν**· κράββατον, Hsch.

**σκανθαρίζω**, = σκινθαρίζω, Poll.9.122, 126.

**σκάνθος**, a bird-name, written *scanthos*, dub. in *Gloss.*

**σκάνιξ**, ικος, ὁ, ἡ, = σκαιός, Hsch.

**σκᾱνο-θήκα**, ἁ, Dor. for σκηνοθήκη, *IG*5(1).879.2, al. (Sparta), 5(2).469.5 (Megalopolis). **-πᾰγέομαι**, = σκανέω, *SIG*1000.1, al. (Cos, i B.C.).

**σκᾶνος**, Dor. for σκῆνος, Ti.Locr.101c, al., Ocell.ap.Stob.1.13.2: but **σκάνος**· αἰτία, κώλυμα, Hsch., cf. Gal.19.138 (σικανός cod.).

**σκᾱνόω**, *make a tent*, *BCH*26.268 (Delph., iii B.C.).

⊕ **σκᾰπᾰν-εύς**, έως, ὁ, *digger*, Lyc.652, Phld.*Rh.*1.189 S., Str.2.5.1, 3.4.4, Luc.*Tim.*7, *Vit.Auct.*7. **-εύω**, *dig up*, χώραν *SIG*22.25 (Epist. Darei), cf. Phld.*Rh.*2.55 S. ⊕ **-η**, ἡ, (σκάπτω) *digging tool, spade, mattock*, Alciphr.3.24, *AP*5.239 (Maced.), 9.644 (Agath.); used by athletes for exercise, Theoc.4.10; cf. σκεπάρνη. II. *spadework*, Thphr.*HP*2.7.1. **-ήτης**, ου, ὁ, = σκαπανεύς, Zonar.

⊕ **σκαπέρδα**, ἡ, *tug-of-war at the Dionysia*: a rope was passed through a hole in a post, and boys at the ends (placed back to back) tried each to pull the other up, Poll.9.116, Hsch.: playing at this game was called σκαπέρδαν ἕλκειν, Poll. l.c.

**σκαπερδεύω**, in Hippon.1, expld. by Tz. (*An.Ox.*3.351, where -παρδ-) συμμαχῆσαι: but by Hsch., λοιδορῆσαι: cf. σκαρπαδεῦσαι· κρῖναι, and καπαρδεῦσαι· μαντεύσασθαι, Id.

**σκάπετ-ος** [ᾰ], ἡ, (σκάπτω) *trench*, *SIG*241*A*15 (Delph., iv B.C.), *Klio* 16.170 (Delph.), *IG*4.823.47 (Troezen), Hsch.; **σκάπεδος**, *IG*7.17 (Megara):—mostly in form κάπετος (q.v.). **-ωσις**, εως, ἡ, *trenching*, dub. in *IG*4.823.50 (Troezen).

**σκᾶπος** (σκάπος cod.)· κλάδος, καὶ ἄνεμος ποιός, Hsch.: cf. Lat. *scapus*.

**σκάπ-τειρα**, ἡ, fem. of σκαπτήρ, σ. δίκελλα *AP*6.21. **-τέον**, *one must dig*, *Gp.*5.21.3: pl. -έα, Poll.1.226. **-τήρ**, ῆρος, ὁ, *digger*, Margites 2, X.ap.Poll.7.148.

**σκᾶπτον**, τό, Dor. for σκῆπτρον.

**σκαπτός**, ή, όν, (σκάπτω) *dug*: *that may be dug*:—Σκαπτὴ Ὕλη a district in Thrace, named after a forest, ἐκ Σκαπτῆς Ὕλης Hdt.6.46; ἐν τῇ Σ. Ὕλῃ Plu.*Cim.*4; ἐν Σ. Ὕ. Marcellin.*Vit.Thuc.*25, 47:—the form Σκαπτησύλης (gen. sg.) is found in Thphr.*Lap.*17; nom. Σκαπτησύλη St.Byz.; Lat. *Scaptensula* Lucr.6.810:—hence **Σκαπτησῡλικός**, ή, όν, *IG*1$^2$.301.103, 116; **Σκαπτησῡλῖται**, St.Byz.

**σκαπτοφόρος**, ον, Dor. for σκηπτροφόρος.

**σκάπτω**, *h.Merc.*90, etc.: fut. σκάψω Pl.*Lg.*778e, (κατα-) E.*HF*566: aor. ἔσκαψα Hp.*Art.*12, (κατ-) Hdt.7.156, etc.: pf. ἔσκαφα (κατ-) Isoc.14.7, 35:—Pass., fut. σκᾰφήσομαι (ἀπο-) Polyaen.5.10.3, (κατα-) J.*AJ*20.6.1: aor. ἐσκάφην [ᾰ] Lxx *Is.*5.6, *Gp.*12.5.1, (κατ-) E.*Hec.*22, etc.: pf. ἔσκαμμαι Pl.*Cra.*413a, Luc.*Gall.*6:—*dig*, abs., Hp.*Art.*12, Pl.*Lg.*778e; σ. τἄλλά τε μοχθεῖν Ar.*Pl.*525: prov., σ. οὐκ ἐπίσταμαι Id.*Av.*1432, cf. *Fr.*221, *Ev.Luc.*16.3:—Med., σ. δικέλλῃ Ps.-Phoc.158. II. c. acc., 1. *dig, delve*, for cultivation, σκάπτων, ἀρῶν γῆν, ποιμνίοις ἐπιστατῶν E.*Fr.*188, cf. X.*Oec.*16.15; τοὺς ἀμπελῶνας D.S.4.31; ὑπόλιθον γήδιον Luc.*Tim.*31. 2. *dig about, cultivate by digging*, φυτὰ σ. (as we say *to hoe* turnips) *h.Merc.*90, cf. X.*Oec.*20.20: metaph., σκάπτει, μοχλεύει θύρετρα *digs about* them, *digs* them *up*, E.*HF*999. 3. of the result, σ. τάφρον *dig* a trench, Th.4.90; σ. βαθεῖαν (sc. τάφρον) Thphr.*CP*3.20.4; θεμελίους Luc.*Alex.*10:—Pass., τὰ ἐσκαμμένα, = σκάμμα II. 2, hence, metaph., ὑπὲρ τὰ ἐσκαμμένα ἅλλεσθαι to leap *too far*, or *further than seemed possible*, Pl.*Cra.*413a, cf. Luc.*Gall.*6, Lib.*Ep.*438, *Or.*64.69 (v.l. ὑπὲρ τὸ σκάμμα); cf. σκάμμα II, ὑποσκάπτω.

**σκάραιβον**· αἱμοποιόν, Hsch.

**σκαρδᾰμ-υγμός**, ὁ, *blinking*, Antyll.ap.Orib.47.27.5. **-υκτέω**, = σκαρδαμύσσω, Luc.*Lex.*4 (v.l. -ύττω); τοὺς ὀφθαλμοὺς Porph. ad

Il.13.443. **-υκτής**, οῦ, ὁ, *one who blinks* or *winks*, Arist.*Phgn.* 813ᵃ20. **-υκτικός**, ή, όν, *given to winking, blinking*, of the eye, Id.*HA*492ᵃ10, *Phgn.*807ᵇ37. **-ύσσω**, Att. **-ττω**, *blink, wink*, Hp.*Coac.*77, E.*Cyc.*626, X.*Cyr.*1.4.28, *Smp.*4.24; σ. τοῖσιν ὀφθαλμοῖσι Hp.*Int.*43; of birds, σ. ὑμένι Arist.*PA*657ᵃ29, 691ᵃ22, cf. *HA*504ᵃ25; of the eyes, Id.*Phgn.*807ᵇ7, 808ᵃ1; cf. ἀσκαρδάμυκτος, καρδαμύσσω.

**σκαρθμός**, ὁ, (σκαίρω) *leaping, leap*, A.R.3.1260, Nic.*Th.*139; ἵππου σ. the *prancing* horse, Arat.281; of a ship, Lyc.101, but corrupt in *AP*7.215 (Anyt.) ap.Suid.

**σκαρία**· παιδιά, Hsch.

**σκᾰρίζω**, (σκαίρω) *jump, throb, palpitate*, *Gp.*20.7.4: cf. ἀσκαρίζω, σπαρίζω.

**σκάριον** [ᾰ], τό, Dim. of σκάρος, ὁ, *PCair.Zen.*82.8 (iii B.C.).

**σκᾰρίς**, ίδος, ή, = ἀσκαρίς, Hsch.

⊕ **σκᾰρισμός**, ὁ, *jumping, palpitation*, Eust.1164.31: pl., Hsch. s.v. σκαρθμοί.

**σκᾰρῖτις**, ιδος, ή, *stone coloured like the fish* σκάρος, Plin.*HN*37.187.

**σκᾰρῖφ-άομαι**, *scratch an outline, sketch lightly*: hence, *do anything perfunctorily*, Sch.Ar.*Ra.*1545, cf. Hsch.; also **σκᾰρῖφεύω**, Sch. Ar.l.c. **-ησμός**, ὁ, *a scratching up*, σκαριφησμοὶ λήρων *petty quibbles*, Ar.*Ra.*1497, ubi v. Sch.(1545), prob. cj. in Numen.ap.Eus.*PE*14.5 (for σκαρφηθμοῖς codd.); also **σκαριφήματα**, Sch.Ar.*Nu.*630, Phot. s.v. σκαλαθύρματα; **-εύματα**, Suid. s.v. σκαλαθυρμάτια; **-ίσματα**, Hsch. s.v. σκαλαθυρμάτια. ⊕ **-ος**, ὁ, = κάρφος, φρύγανον, γραφίς, Sch.Ar.*Ra.*1545; = ξέσις, γραφή, μίμησις ἀκριβὴς τύπου (τόπου cod.), Hsch.; also **σκάριφον**, τό, *EM*273.33.

**σκάρος**, ὁ, a sea-fish, the *parrot-wrasse*, *Scarus cretensis*, supposed by the ancients to chew the cud, Epich.54, Arist.*HA*508ᵇ11, Archestr.*Frr.*13,41 (where σπάρον is dub. cj.), *PCair.Zen.*83.2 (iii B.C.), Gal.*Vict.Att.*8. (Prob. from σκαίρω, Arist.*Fr.*332.) [ᾰ, ll. cc.; ᾱ dub. in Philem.79.20.]

**σκάρος** [ᾰ], εος, τό, = σκαρθμός, *EM*723.2. **σκαρπαδεῦσαι**, v. σκαπερδεύω. **σκάρτας**· ταχύς, Hsch. **σκαρφᾶσθαι**· σκεδάννυσθαι, Id. (Cf. Ῥοδοσκάρφα.) **σκάρφος**, v. κάρφος.

**σκασμός**, ὁ, (σκάζω) *limping, halting*, Aq.*Ps.*34(35).15.

**σκαταμίζω**, v. ἐσκατάμιζεν. **σκατός** and **σκάτους**, gen. of σκῶρ.

⊕ **σκᾰτοφᾰγ-έω**, *eat dung* or *dirt*, Antiph.126.4. **-ος** (parox.), ον, *eating dung* or *dirt*, Epich.63, Crobyl.7, Men.825, *Sam.*205, *Pk.*204; as epith. of Asclepios, with allusion (cf. Sch.) to a foul practice of Hippocrates, Ar.*Pl.*706, cf. Arg.Metr.*Eq.*

**σκᾰτοφόροι**, οἱ, *dung-carriers*, Poll.7.134.

⊕ **σκαῦρος**, ὁ, Lat. *scaurus*, *with deviating hoof*, πόδες *Hippiatr.*14,104.

**σκάφαλος**· ἀντλητήρ, Hsch.

**σκᾰφ-εία**, ή, *digging, hoeing*, Suid. **-είδιον**, τό, Dim. of sq. (not = σκαφίδιον), Hdn.*Epim.*239, Suid. **-εῖον**, τό, *spade, hoe, mattock*, Hyp.*Dem.Fr.*7, Clearch.65, *IG*11(2).144*A*84 (Delos, iv B.C.), *PPetr.*3 p.109, al. (iii B.C.), *PCair.Zen.*164.2, al. (iii B.C.), Ph.*Bel.*90. 2, D.S.4.31, *IG*2².1631.409; cf. σκάφιον (A) IV. 2. prob. *basin*, ib.1².314.132, 2².1425.353. 3. *concave mirror*, used as a burning-glass, Plu.*Num.*9: Lat. *scaphium*, Mart.Cap.6.597. **-ετός**, ὁ, *hoeing*, *Gloss.* **-εύς**, έως, ὁ, (σκάπτω) *digger, delver*, E.*El.*252, Archipp. 44, *BGU*1538 (Ptolemaic), *Arch.Pap.*5.381 (i A.D.). II. = σκαφηφόρος, *Com.Adesp.*1144. **-ευσις**, εως, ή, = σκαφεία, Suid. II. *a cruel method of execution* (cf. σκαφεύω), Eun.*VS*p.478 B., Tz.*H.*10. 883. **-ευτής**, οῦ, ὁ, *fossor*, *Gloss.* **-εύω**, (σκάφη) *lay* a person *in a trough* with head, arms, and legs hanging out, and expose him in the heat of the sun, until he dies eaten by insects, a Persian mode of torture, Ctes.*Fr.*29.30, Plu.*Art.*16. ⊕ **-η**, ή: I. *trough, tub, basin*, or *bowl* (Hom. only in Dim. σκαφίς), Hdt.4.73, Ar.*Ec.*742, etc.; *kneading-trough* or *baker's tray*, Timocl.33, cf. Poll.10.102; *wash-tub, bath*, A.*Fr.*225, Hp.*Steril.*234; *bowl* or *tray* on which offerings were carried by metoeci at the Panathenaea, etc., *IG*1².844.6, 2².1388.46, al., Semus 5; cf. σκαφηφόρος: prov., τὰ σῦκα σῦκα, τὴν σκάφην σκάφην λέγει Apostol.15.95b, cf. Plu.2.178b, Luc.*Hist.Conscr.*41, Jul.*Or.* 7.208a. 2. *light boat, skiff*, Ar.*Eq.*1315 (with a pun on signf. 1), *PCair.Zen.*25.5 (iii B.C.), Plb.1.23.7; used for cargo, *BGU*1742.9 (i B.C.); *boat-load*, ξύλων *PGrad.*9.5 (iii B.C.). 3. child's *cradle*, Arist.*Po.*1454ᵇ25, Phylarch.36 J., Plu *Rom.*3, Sor.1.106, al., Sch. Ar.*Lys.*138 (prob.). 4. *grave*, *BCH*24.394 (Bithynia). II. *concave sun-dial*, Vitr.9.8.1, Cleom.1.10, cf. Poll.6.110. (Prob. orig. *something dug* or *scooped out*, fr. σκάπτω.) **-ή**, ή, *digging*, *PSI*6. 595.3 (iii B.C.), Procl. ad Hes.*Op.*569, cf. Hdn.Gr.1.345. **-ητός**, ὁ, = σκαφετός, σκάπετος, *hoeing* or *digging*, Thphr.*CP*3.16.2, *SIG*963.10 (Amorgos, iv B.C.), *PMich.Zen.*62.8 (iii B.C.), Str.3.4.17. **-ητρός**, ὁ, = σκαφητός, *PFay.*112.2,16 (pl., i A.D.), etc.

⊕ **σκᾰφηφορ-έω**, *carry a tray* of offerings at the Panathenaea, as the μέτοικοι did, Ael.*VH*6.1. **-ία**, ή, performance of this service, *AB*280, *Gloss.* **-ος** (parox.), ὁ, *carrier of* such *trays*, Din.*Fr.*16, Poll.3.55, Phot.

**σκᾰφ-ιά**, ή, Sicil. for σκάφος (A), *trench, pit*, *IG*14.352 i 64 (Halaesa). **-ίδιον**, τό, Dim. of σκάφη I. 1, σ. χαλκοῦν τετρυπημένον ib. 11(2).161 *C*80 (Delos, iii B.C.). 2. Dim. of σκαφίς (B), *small skiff*, Plb.34.3.2, Str.1.2.16, Luc.*Cont.*8. II. *boat-load*, *POxy.*1068.7 (iii A.D.). III. = κάρδοπος, Sch.Ar.*Nu.*669.

**σκᾰφῖδοποιός**, ὁ, *alvearius*, *Gloss.*

**σκᾰφιόκουρος**, ον, *one with his hair cut in the fashion* σκάφιον (A) II. 1, *Com.Adesp.*34 D.

**σκαφιόλια**, gloss on κυάθους, Hsch.

⊕ **σκάφιον** [ᾰ] (A) (not σκαφίον), τό, Dim. of σκάφη, *small bowl* or *basin*, Thphr.*CP*4.16.3, *PLond.*2.402 ii 13 (ii B.C.), *PHamb.*10.36 (ii A.D.), etc.; used in baths, Lyc.ap.Ath.11.501f; *small cup*, Phylarch.44 J., *Inscr.Délos* 442 *B* 43, al. (ii B.C.). 2. *woman's chamber-pot* or *nightstool*, Ar.*Th.*633, Eup.46. II. *a fashion of haircutting* (borrowed from the Scythians), *in which the hair was cut close off round the head*, so as to leave it only on the crown, which then looked like a *bowl*, σκάφιον ἀποκεκαρμένη Ar.*Th.*838; σ. ἀποτετιλμένος Id.*Av.*806: hence, 2. *crown* of the head, ἵνα μὴ καταγῇς τὸ σ. Id.*Fr.*604. b. *occiput*, Ruf.*Oss.*2. c. name of a bandage for the head, Sor.*Fasc.*3. III. in pl., = ἰσχία, τά, Poll.2.183. IV. = σκαφεῖον 1, Hp.*Fract.*8.

**σκάφιον** [ᾰ] (B), τό, Dim. of σκάφος (B), *small boat*, Str.17.1.50, Hld.10.4.

**σκᾰφ-ίς** (A), ίδος, ή, Dim. of σκάφη; esp. I. *bowl*, ἄγγεα πάντα, γαυλοί τε σκαφίδες τε *small milk-pails*, Od.9.223; mentioned among *bakers' vessels* in Ar.*Fr.*417; later, *drinking vessel* or *measure*, Hp.*Mul.*1.86, cf. *Morb.*2.64; *pot* for honey, Theoc.5.59. II. *spade, shovel*, σ. εἰς παλαίστραν *Inscr.Délos* 290.76 (iii B.C.); used in dredging, Ph.*Bel.*98.27: ῥαπτὰς γειοφόρους σκαφίδας perh. *baskets* for carrying earth, *AP*6.297 (Phan.). **-ίς** (B), ίδος, ή, Dim. of σκάφος (B), *boat, skiff*, ib.7.214 (Arch.), Palaeph.12. ⊕ **-ιστήριον**, τό, *vas in quo triticum mundatur*, *Gloss.* **-ίτης** [ῑ], ου, ὁ, (σκαφίς (B)) *one who guides a skiff, steersman*, Anon.ap.Demetr.*Eloc.*97, Str.17.1. 49. **-λεύς**, έως, ὁ, prob. misspelling of σκαφεύς, *Supp.Epigr.*3. 207 (Athens, iv B.C.).

⊕ **σκᾰφο-ειδής**, ές, *like a bowl, hollow*, Eudox.*Ars* 12.9, D.S.2.31, *Placit.*2.22.2, al., Gal.*UP*3.6, Ach.Tat.*Intr.Arat.*19; τὸ σ. *bowl-shaped body*, *Placit.*2.24.3. **-λουτρέω**, *bathe in a tub*, Alex.Trall.*Febr.* 2. **-πάκτων**, ωνος, ὁ, a kind of boat or *raft*, *POxy.*1554.7 (iii A.D.). ⊕ **-πλωρος**, ὁ, a kind of *boat*, *BGU*812 ii 2 (ii/iii A.D.), *PCair.Preis.*34.16 (iv A.D.).

**σκάφος** [ᾰ] (A), ὁ, *digging, hoeing*, τότε δὴ σ. οὐκέτι οἰνέων *the time for hoeing* vines, Hes.*Op.*572; ὁ δεύτερος σ. τῶν νέων ἀμπέλων *Gp.* 3.4.5.

**σκάφος** [ᾰ] (B), εος, τό, *hull of a ship*, Hdt.7.182, Th.1.50; ἐν μέσῳ σκάφει S.*Tr.*803; ὑπτιοῦτο δὲ σκάφη νεῶν A.*Pers.*419; ναυτικὰ σ. S.*Aj.*1278; Ἀργοῦς σκάφος E.*Med.*1; ναὸς or νεὼς σ., poet. = ναῦς, Id.*IT*1345, al.: generally, *ship*, οὐδ' ἐπόντισε σ. A.*Ag.*1013 (lyr.), cf. *Supp.*440, Ar.*Ach.*541, D.9.69, *BGU*1755.4 (i B.C.), etc.; σκάφευς ἀνάσσων Alcm.72 (nisi leg. Καφεύς = Κηφεύς): metaph., πόλεως σ. *the ship* of the state, Ar.*V.*29. b. τὸ ἴδιον κυβερνῆσαι σ. 'paddle one's own *canoe*', Phld.*Rh.*2.294 S. 2. *hollow of the* external *ear*, Poll.2.85. II. = σκαφεῖον, *AP*6.21.7.

**σκᾰφώδης**, ες, = σκαφοειδής, ὀστέον *PLit.Lond.*167.27.

**σκᾰφώρη**, ή, = καφώρη, *bitch-fox, vixen*, Ael.*NA*7.47.

⊕ **σκεδάννῡμι**, Thphr.*CP*3.6.4, etc.:—also **σκεδάω**, Nic.*Al.*583: fut. σκεδάσω [ᾰ] Thgn.883 (ἀπο–), J.*BJ*4.9.6, Plu.*Cor.*12, etc.; Att. σκεδῶ A.*Pr.*25, 925, (ἀπο–) S.*OT*138, (δια–) Ar.*V.*229, *Av.*1053 (also in Hdt.8.68.β'), (συσκ–) Ar.*Ra.*903: aor. ἐσκέδασα, Ep. σκέδασα, the only tense used by Hom. (v. infr.):—Med., aor. ἐσκεδασάμην (συγκατ–) X.*An.*7.3.32, (ἀπ–) Pl.*Ax.*365e:—Pass., fut. σκεδασθήσομαι M.Ant.6.4, Gal.6.6: aor. ἐσκεδάσθην, pf. ἐσκέδασμαι (v. infr.):—*scatter, disperse*, ἀπὸ πυρκαϊῆς σκέδασον [λαόν] Il.23.158, cf. 19.171; λαὸν σκέδασεν κατὰ νῆας 23.162; also of things, σκέδασον δ' ἀπὸ κήδεα θυμοῦ Od.8.149; ἠέρα μὲν σκέδασεν Il.17.649, cf. Od.13.352; τῶν νῦν αἷμα.. ἐσκέδασ' ὀξὺς Ἄρης *shed* the blood *all round*, Il.7.330; πάχνην.. ἥλιος σκεδᾷ πάλιν A.*Pr.*25; ὅσα φαίνολις ἐσκέδασ' αὔως Sapph.95; τρίαιναν.. σκεδᾷ *will shiver* it, A.*Pr.*925; μὴ σκεδάσαι τῷδ' ἀπὸ κρατὸς βλεφάρων θ' ὕπνον (sleep being conceived of as a cloud over the eyes) S.*Tr.*989 (anap.); *scatter abroad*, of Pandora opening the fatal casket, Hes.*Op.*95. II. Pass., *to be scattered, disperse*, σκεδασθῆναι ἀνὰ τὰς πόλιας Hdt.5.102; of a routed army, Th.4.56, 112, 6.52; σ. καθ' ἁρπαγήν, of plundering parties, X.*An.*3.5.2; ἐπὶ τὰ ἐπιτήδεια Id.*Eq. Mag.*7.9; of the rays of the sun, πρὶν σκεδασθῆναι θεοῦ ἀκτῖνας *to be shed abroad*, A.*Pers.*502; of a rumour, *to be spread abroad*, ἐσκεδασμένου τοῦ λόγου ἀνὰ τὴν πόλιν Hdt.4.14; also ὄψις ἐσκεδασμένη vision *not confined to one object*, X.*Cyn.*5.26.

**σκέδ-ᾰσις**, εως, ή, *a scattering*, σκέδασιν θεῖναι, = σκεδάσαι, Od.1. 116, 20.225, cf. Ph.1.686; ὕδατος Hp.*Vict.*1.10; σ. τοῦ ζοφώδεος Aret. *CD*1.3. ⊕ **-ασμός**, ὁ, = σκέδασις, Epicur.*Nat.Herc.*908.2, Ph.1. 686, J.*AJ*1.1.3, M.Ant.7.32. **-αστής**, οῦ, ὁ, *scatterer*, Ph.1.135, Phot. **-αστικός**, ή, όν, *able to disperse*, φασμάτων, of the laurel, Lyd.*Mens.*4.4. **-αστός**, ή, όν, *that may be scattered*, οὐσία σ. *dissoluble* substance, Pl.*Ti.*37a; τὸ τῆς ὕλης σ. Plu.2.430f.

**σκεθρός**, ά (Ion. ή), όν, *exact, careful*, γνώμῃ σ. βασανίσας Hp.*Mul.* 1.11; ἴησις σκεθροτέρη Id.*Art.*50; δίαιτα Gal.18(2).403; τάλαντον τρυτάνης Lyc.270. Adv. **-ρῶς**, προὐξεπίστασθαι A.*Pr.*102, cf. 488; ὁρᾶν E.*Fr.*87.

**σκειρός, σκεῖρος, Σκείρων**, etc., incorrect forms of σκῑρός, etc. (q.v.).

**σκελεᾱγής**, ές, (ἄγνυμι) *with broken legs*, σκελεαγεῖς ποιήσω, gloss on γυιώσω, Porph. ad Il.8.402 p.300 S.; τὸ σ. *fracture* of the legs, *Gloss.* (σκελι–).

**σκέλεαι**, αἱ, (σκέλος) *breeches*, Critias 38 D., Antiph.36.

**σκελετά**· σκίλλα, Hsch.

**σκελετ-εία**, Ion. -ίη, ή, *a being withered*, Gal.19.139, Aret.*CD*2.13, prob. in 2.6, for -ίνην. **-ευμα**, ατος, τό, *anything withered*, Sch. Nic.*Th.*695. **-εύω**, = σκέλλω, Poll.2.194, Zonar.:—Pass., *wither* or *waste away*, Ar.*Fr.*851, Gal.6.126. II. *dry* or *salt* flesh, Dsc.2.2 (Pass.); σ. δι' ἁλός ib.25 (Pass.); *dry* fruit, Gal.6.558; also, *embalm* a corpse, Telesp.31 H. **-ίζω**, = σκελετεύω, Zonar. (Pass.). **-ός**, ή, όν, (σκέλλω) *dried up, withered*, Κινησίας σ., ἄπυγος Pl.Com.184.3; σ. δάκος Nic.*Th.*696. II. Subst. σκελετός, ὁ, *dried body, mummy*, Λάμπρος .. Μουσῶν σ. Phryn.Com.69, cf. Str.17.3.8, Plu.2.148a,735f; ἡμιθανῆ σ. *AP*11.392 (Lucill.); τῶν ὑπὸ γῆν σ. λεπτότατος ib.92 (Id.); κείσεται σ. καὶ τὸ μηδὲν γενόμενος Plu.*Ant.*75. 2. *skeleton*, Phld. *Mort.*30, Gal.2.221,222,734, al. III. v. σκελετά. **-ώδης**, ες, *like a dried corpse*, Luc.*Salt.*75, Erot. s. v. σκελιφρούς.

**σκέλεφερ·** βόλου ὄνομα, Λάκωνες, Hsch. **σκελεφρός**, v. σκελιφρός.

**σκελήπερον**, = νήπιον, Archil.193.

**σκελίδιον**, τό, Dim. of σκελλίς, σκελίς, Sch.Nic.*Al.*432.

**σκελ-ίζω**, = ὑποσκελίζω, Lxx *Je.*10.18, S.E.*M.*1.159: metaph., Plu.*Fr.inc.*30. **-ίς**, ίδος, ή, later form for σχελίς (q.v.). II. v. σκελλίς. **-ίσκος**, ὁ, Dim. of σκέλος, Ar.*Ec.*1167. **-ισμα·** τὸ ἀείμνημα, Hsch. **-ισμός**, ὁ, *snare*, Aq.*Je.*14.14.

**σκελιφρός** (in Erot. with v.l. **σκελεφρός**), ά, όν, *dry, parched, lean, dry* or *lean looking*, Hp.*Aër.*4, v.l. in *Art.*8; Att. σκληφρός (q.v.).

**σκελλίς**, ίδος, ή, = ἀγλίς, Plu.2.349a; σκελίς Alex.Trall.8.2.

**σκελλός**, ή, όν, (σκέλος) *crook-legged*, Sch.Il.16.234, Hsch.; used in common speech for ῥαιβός, *EM*701.10.

**σκέλλω**, aor. 1 ἔσκηλα, opt. σκήλειε Il. (v. infr.), ἔσκειλα Zonar.:—Pass., v. infr. II:—*dry up, parch*, μὴ μένος ἠελίοιο σκήλει' ἀμφὶ περὶ χρόα ἴνεσιν ἠδὲ μέλεσσιν Il.23.191; cf. ἐνσκέλλω. II. Pass. σκέλλομαι (κατα- A.*Pr.*481): fut. σκελοῦμαι Hsch.: intr. pf. Act. ἔσκληκα in pres. signf. (in compds. also with intr. aor. 2 Act. σκλῆναι, cf. ἀποσκλῆναι):—*to be parched, lean, dry*, ἐσκληκότα καπνῷ smoke-*dried*, Choeril.4, cf. Nic.*Th.*718; χρὼς ἐσκλήκει A.R.2.201; Ep. part. nom. pl. ἐσκληῶτες ib.53.

**σκελό-δεσμον**, τό, *garter, crurarium*, Gloss. **-κοπία**, ή, (κόπτω) *fracture of a leg*, ib. **-πέδη**, ή, *fetter*, ib.

⊛ **σκέλος**, εος, τό, *leg* from the hip downwards, only once in Hom., πρυμνὸν σκέλος the ham or buttock, Il.16.314; κάμηλος ἐν τοῖσι ὀπισθίοισι σ. ἔχει τέσσερας μηροὺς καὶ γούνατα τέσσερα Hdt.3.103, cf. 7.61,88; τὰ σκέλη τε καὶ τὰ ἰσχία πρὸς τὴν γῆν ἐρείσας Pl.*Phdr.*254e, cf. Arist.*HA*494ᵃ4; of dancers, τὸ σ. ῥίψαντες, αἴρειν, Ar.*Pax*332, *Ec.*265; σ. οὐράνιον ἐκλακτίζων Id.*V.*1492, cf. 1526; οὐρανῷ σκέλη προφαίνων, of one thrown head foremost, S.*El.*753; βαδιοῦνται ἐπὶ δυοῖν σκελοῖν, ἐφ' ἑνὸς πορεύσονται σκέλους, Pl.*Smp.*190d; ὁ δεινός, ὁ ταλαύρινος, ὁ κατὰ τοῖν σκελοῖν he *with the legs, the strider*, Ar. *Pax*241 (but expld. by Sch. ἀπὸ τῶν διὰ δειλίαν ἀποτιλώντων, cf. Men. *Per.*18); dual, τὼ σκέλει Ar.*Pax*325, al., cf. Luc.*Tim.*26, *Anach.*1; σκέλε (i.e. prob. σκέλει) δύο *IG*2².1388.24, cf. 1502.5; but σκέλη (pl.) δύο in Att. Inscrr. from 390 B.C., ib.1425.15, cf. 57, etc.; and so τὰ σ. Luc.*Ind.*9: sg., *leg* of sacrificial victim, *IG*1².190.32, al., 4²(1).40.10 (Epid., v B.C.). 2. as a military phrase, ἐπὶ σκέλος πάλιν χωρεῖν, ἀνάγειν, retreat with the face towards the enemy, retire leisurely, E.*Ph.*1400, Ar.*Av.*383; cf. πούς I. 6 b. 3. κατὰ σκέλος βαδίζειν, of the lion and the camel, *with the hind foot following the fore on the same side* (not crosswise), Arist.*HA*498ᵇ7, cf. 629ᵇ14. 4. παρὰ σκέλος ἀπαντᾷ it meets one *across*, i.e. crosses one's path, thwarts one, Arr.*Epict.*2.12.2 (v.l. π. μέλος). II. metaph., τὰ σ. the *legs*, i.e. the *two long walls* connecting Athens with Piraeus, Str.9.1.15, Plu.*Cim.*13; τὰ μακρὰ σ. D.S.13.107, Plu.*Lys.*14; of the long walls between Megara and Nisaea, τὰ Μεγαρικὰ σ. Ar.*Lys.*1170; between Corinth and Lechaeum, Str.8.6.22. b. *side-wall* of a temple, *SIG* 247*K*¹iii3,11 (Delph., iv B.C.); of other structures, *PPetr.*3p.88 (iii B.C.), etc. 2. *side-poles* or *frames of an engine*, Orib.49.4.4. 3. *tails of a surgical bandage*, Heliod.ap.Orib.48.20.5; of the *ends* of the Persian head-dress, Plu.2.820d. 4. *members* of a sentence, Sch.rec.A.*Th.*94. (Written **σχέλος** *IG*11(2).161*B*61 (Delos, iii B.C.).)

**σκελοτύρβη**, ή, *lameness in the leg*, such as to make one totter about, frequent in Arabia, Str.16.4.24; acc. to Gal.19.427, *a kind of paralysis*.

**σκελύδριον**, τό, Dim. of σκέλος, Herod.4.89, Arr.*Epict.*1.12.24.

**σκελύθριον**, **σκέλυθρος**, f. ll. for σκολύθριον, -θρος (qq. v.).

**σκέμμα**, ατος, τό, (σκέπτομαι) *subject for speculation* or *reflection, problem*, Hp.*Acut.*9, Pl.*R.*435c, 445a, Phld.*Rh.*1.202 S. II. *speculation*, Pl.*Cri.*48c; τὸ σ. περὶ δυοῖν ἐστίν Arist.*Pol.*1285ᵇ37. III. *scheme, plot*, J.*BJ*1.24.6.

**σκεμμός**, ὁ, late form for σκέψις, Anon.ap.Suid. (pl.).

**σκενδύλη**, ή, v. σχενδύλη:—Dim. **σκενδύλια**, τά, *pincers*, Hero *Bel.*76.11.

**σκέπᾰ**, v. σκέπας.

**σκεπ-άζω**, fut. -άσω Lxx *Ex.*40.3: (σκέπω) prose form of σκεπάω:—*cover, shelter*, σ. τὰ δεόμενα σκέπης X.*Mem.*3.10.9, cf. *Eq.*12.8, Arist. *IA*711ᵇ32, *PA*658ᵇ6; σ. [τινὰ] ἱματίοις cover him with blankets, *POxy.*1088.47 (i A.D.):—Med., aor. 1, Gal.4.549:—Pass., ὁκόσα ὑπὸ τοῦ ἱματίου ἐσκέπασται Hp.*Aër.*8, cf. X.*Cyr.*8.8.17, Arist.*GA*785ᵃ27; esp. of armour, Plb.1.22.10, etc.; δοραῖς τὸ σῶμα σ. *POxy.*1241 iv 18 (ii A.D.); ἐσκεπασμένην σκοπαῖς *guarded, watched*, Lyc.1311; σ. ἀπὸ καύματος Lxx *Si.*14.27. 2. *protect* or *shelter*, esp. by patronage, τοὺς πλινθουλκούς, οὓς ἔδει λειτουργεῖν *PSI*4.440.14 (iii B.C.):—Pass., *PHib.*1.35.10 (iii B.C.), *UPZ*110.15 (ii B.C.). b. *exercise unauthorized patronage over*, τὰς ἱερὰς ἀρούρας Wilcken *Chr.*65.60 (ii B.C.). II. c. acc. rei, *keep off*, καῦμα τῶν Ἐρώτων *Anacreont.*17.9. **-ᾰνον**, τό, *covering*, κεφαλῆς *AP*6.298 (Leon.). **-ᾰνός**, ή, όν, *sheltered* or *sheltering*, κευθμῶνες Opp.*H.*3.636; ὑφόρμισις *AP*7.699, cf. Dion. Byz.1.

**σκέπᾰνος**, ὁ, prob. a kind of tunny, Opp.*H.*1.106; **σκέπινος**, Dorio ap.Ath.7.322e.

⊛ **σκεπαρν-ηδόν**, Adv. *like a* σκέπαρνον II, Hp.*Fract.*29. **-ίζω**, *hew with an adze*, Hero *Aut.*1.5. **-ιον**, τό, Dim. of σκέπαρνον, Archit., *pier*, '*piedroit*', *Rev.Phil.*44.249 (Didyma, ii B.C.). ⊛ **-ον**, τό, or **σκέπαρνος**, ὁ (the Homeric passages and Lxx 1*Ch.*20.3, *Is.* 44.12, leave the gender uncertain, masc. in Hp.*Art.*35, S.*Fr.*797, *PCair.Zen.*753.33 (iii B.C.); later mostly neut., *Peripl.M.Rubr.*6, *AP*6.205 (Leon.), Luc.*JConf.*11, Poll.10.146, cf. Phot.):—*carpenter's axe, adze*, for hewing and smoothing the trunks of trees, different from the πέλεκυς (felling-axe or hatchet), Od.5.237, 9.391; ἀμφίξουν *AP*l.c. II. from a likeness in the shape, *a slightly oblique surgical bandage*, Hp.*Off.*7 (neut.): but masc. in pl., [ἐπίδεσις] πλείστους σκεπάρνους ἔχουσα with many *oblique turns*, Id.*Art.*35. III. used, as a sort of pun, of a *sheepskin*, as if σκέπ-αρνον, Dionys.Trag. 12, cf. Sch.D.T.p.11 H., interpol. in Artem.4.22. [Hom. does not lengthen a short vowel before σκ-, cf. Σκάμανδρος.]

**σκέπ-ας**, gen. -αος Arat.857: τό: (σκέπω):—*covering, shelter*, Hom., only in Od.; κὰδ δ' ἄρ' Ὀδυσσῆ' εἷσαν ἐπὶ σκέπας placed him in or under *shelter*, 6.212, cf. 210; σ. ἀνέμοιο *shelter* from the wind, 5.443, 12.336: abs. in poet. nom. and acc. pl. σκέπᾰ, Hes.*Op.*532; σκέπας ὄρμων Lyc.736; of clothes, χλαίνης λιτὸν σ. *AP*9.43 (Parmen.); of the Maced. hat (καυσία), ib.6.335 (Antip. Thess.): pl., ζωσάμενοι σκέπασι λινοῖς Porph.*Abst.*4.12 codd. (σκεπάσμασι is prob. l.): metaph. in sg., *pretext, pretence*, E.*Antiop.* iv *B* 2 Arnim.—In Prose commonly σκέπη (q. v.), or σκέπασμα. **-ᾰσις**, εως, ή, *protection*, Lxx *De.*33.27. **-ασμα**, ατος, τό, *a covering*, τῶν σ. ὑποπετάσματα μὲν ἄλλα, περικαλύμματα δὲ ἕτερα Pl.*Plt.*279d; of a cap or shoe, Id.*Lg.*942d; of clothing generally, Arist.*Pol.*1336ᵃ17; also ὄνυχες σ. τῶν ἀκρωτηρίων εἰσίν Id.*PA*687ᵇ24; *covering membrane*, Id.*GA*780ᵇ28; τὸ φύλλον περικαρπίου σ., in plants, Id. *de An.*412ᵇ2; οἰκία σ. ἐκ πλίνθων καὶ λίθων Id. *Metaph.*1043ᵃ32. **-ασμός**, ὁ, = foreg., *EM*531.11. **-αστέον**, *one must cover*, Sor.2.11, Antyll.ap.Orib.10.13.21. **-αστήριος**, α, ον, *fitted for covering, defensive*, δοραῖς χρῆσθαι σ. D.S.1.24; ὅπλον Id.5.18; τὰ σ. ὅπλα D.H.2.38,39; also τὰ σ. (without ὅπλα) Id.8.89; of a cloak, Ph.1.20; of a shield for the eyes, Herod.Med.ap.Orib. 10.8.5. **-αστής**, οῦ, ὁ, *shelterer, protector*, Lxx *Ex.*15.2, 3*Ma.*6.9, al. **-αστικός**, ή, όν, = σκεπαστήριος, Arist.*GA*719ᵇ17; ἀγγεῖον σ. σωμάτων Id.*Metaph.*1043ᵃ16; σ. ὅπλα Ath.5.193c. Adv. -κῶς Hp. *Medic.*4. 2. metaph., *sheltering*, *BGU*1185.8 (i B.C.), *OGI*665.40 (Egypt, i A.D.). **-αστός**, ή, όν, *covered*, σ. (sc. κλισία), ή, *shed, covered sheep-fold*, Eust.1165.52, 1957.57: σκεπαστόν, τό, *tilted wagon*, Aq.*Nu.*7.3, *Is.*66.20. **-άστρα**, ή, *surgical bandage*, Gal.18(1).777. **-αστρον**, τό, = σκεπαστήριον, *veil*, Sm.*Jb.*24.15; *hood*, Gloss. **-άω**, = σκέπω, *cover, shelter*, ἀνέμων σκεπόωσι κῦμα (Ep. for σκεπάουσι, σκεπῶσι) *they ward off* (*provide shelter against*) the sea raised by the wind, Od.13.99; κόρυν σκεπάουσιν ἔθειραι Theoc. 16.81 (v.l. σκιάουσι). **-εινός**, ή, όν, = σκεπανός, σκεπεινὴν νῆα καταγωγὴν ἔχει Scymn.336; ἐν τοῖς σ. in the *sheltered places*, Lxx *Ne.*4.13(7): written **σκεπηνός** in Ath.Med.ap.Orib.*inc.*23.2, Archig.ap.Orib.46.25.7; **σκεπινός** *PHolm.*11.39. ⊛ **-η**, ή, = σκέπας, *covering, shelter, protection*, Hp.*VM*16; σ. ἄκαπνος Id.*Acut.*65; of clothes, Id.*Aër.*8; of arms, Plb.6.22.3, etc.; of the flesh as *the covering* of bones, Ti.Locr.100b; of the hair, σκέπης χάριν αἱ τρίχες Arist. *PA*658ᵃ18; δεῖσθαι σκέπης ib.20; σ. δερματική Id.*GA*719ᵇ4; σ. φλοιῶτις, = φλοιός, Lyc.1422. II. *shelter, protection*, τὰ δεόμενα σκέπης the parts of the body needing *protection*, X.*Mem.*3.10.9; σκιὰν καὶ σ. παρέχειν Pl.*Ti.*76d; ἐν σκέπῃ εἶναι Arist.*PA*689ᵇ29; σ. ἔχειν D.S.5.65. 2. c. gen., σ. πνευμάτων *shelter from* them, Hp. *Aër.*3; so ἐν σκέπῃ τοῦ πολέμου Hdt.7.172,215; τοῦ φόβου Id.1.143; τοῦ κρύους Ael.*NA*9.57: but ὑποστέλλειν ἑαυτὸν ὑπὸ τὴν Ῥωμαίων σ. under their *protection*, Plb.1.16.10; ὄντα αὐτοῦ ὑπὸ σκέπην being under his *protection*, *PTeb.*34.12 (ii/i B.C.); ἀντέχεσθαι τῆς σῆς σ. ib.40.9 (ii B.C.); ἔξω ἱεροῦ .. καὶ πάσης σ. *Sammelb.*5680.19 (iii B.C.), cf. *PHib.*1.93.5 (iii B.C.).

**σκεπηνός**, **σκεπινός**, v. σκεπεινός. **σκέπινος**, v. σκέπανος. **σκέπος**, εος, τό, = σκέπη, *EM*597.19.

**σκεπ-τέον**, (σκέπτομαι) *one must reflect* or *consider*, Ar.*Eq.*35, Th. 1.72; οὐ ταύτῃ σ. ὃ ζητοῦμεν Pl.*Tht.*188c; περί τινος Id.*Ti.*28b; τόδε, εἰ.. X.*Eq.*3.4; τίς κτῆσις δικαία ἐστί Id.*Cyr.*1.3.17; ποῖά ποτε.. Id. *Smp.*8.39; ὅπως.. Id.*An.*1.3.11; *one must pay attention to*, τὸ χωρίον Hp.*Liqu.*2. 2. σκεπτέος, α, ον, *to be considered, examined*, ἡ ἀλήθεια σ. αὐτῶν Antipho 3.4.2. **-τήριον**, τό, = τεκμήριον, *proof*, Man.4.165. **-τικός**, ή, όν, *thoughtful, reflective*, Phld.*Rh.*1.191 S.: οἱ σ. (also ἀπορητικοί, ἐφεκτικοί) the *Sceptics* or *philosophers who asserted nothing positively*, followers of Pyrrho, Luc.*Vit.Auct.*27, D.L.*Prooem.* 20,9.69 sq., Gell.11.5; ἡ σ. φιλοσοφία or ἀγωγή S.E.*P.*1.5,7, etc. Adv., -κῶς ἔχειν to profess *the Sceptical philosophy*, D.L.9.71: Comp. -ώτερον S.E.*M.*9.194, etc. ⊛ **-τομαι**, Il.17.652, Thgn.1095, and Ion., Hdt.3.37, al., Hp.*Prog.*2, Herod.7.92; but Att. writers (before Arist.) hardly ever have the pres. and impf. σκέπτομαι, ἐσκεπτόμην (exc. Pl.*La.*185b, *Alc.*2.140a; in Th.8.66, Bauer restored plpf. προὔσκεπτο), but use σκοπῶ or σκοποῦμαι as pres., and take the other tenses from σκέπτομαι, fut. σκέψομαι Ar.*Pax*29, Th.6.40, etc.; aor. ἐσκεψάμην A.*Ch.*229, S.*Aj.*1028, E.*Ion* 206 (lyr.), Th.6.38, etc.; pf. ἔσκεμμαι E.*Heracl.*147, Hp.*VM*24, etc.: cf. σκοπέω:—but the pf. is used also in pass. sense, as also some other tenses, v. infr. II. 4. I. *look* *about carefully*, *spy*, σκεψάμενος δ' ἐς νῆα θοὴν ἅμα καὶ μεθ' ἑταίρους Od. 12.247; so σκέψασθε δ' ἐς τόνδ' E.*Hipp.*943: c. acc., σκέπτετ' ὀϊστῶν τε ῥοῖζον καὶ δοῦπον ἀκόντων *he looked after* the whistling of the darts (so as to shun them), Il.16.361; σκέπτεο δὴ νῦν ἄλλον Thgn.1095; σκεπτόμενος τοὺς νεκρούς Hdt.3.37; σκέψαι.. βόστρυχον τριχός *look well at* it, A.*Ch.*229; τὴν ἔγχελυν Ar.*Ach.*889; κλόνον E.*Ion* 206 (lyr.); τὰ ἔνδον X.*HG*4.4.8; τιν' ἐς σὲ μωρίαν ἐσκεμμένοι *looking into you and seeing*.., E.*Heracl.*147: folld. by an Interrog., σκέπτεο νῦν.., αἴ κεν ἴδηαι Il.17.652; σ. πόθεν ἡ στάσις, ἢ τίς ὁ θρύλλος Batr.135; τί εἴη τὸ κωλῦον X.*An.*4.5.20; εἰ εἴη ἴχνη ἀνθρώπων ib.7.3.42: abs., *look at*, *examine*, Hdt.4.196; σκέψασθε, παῖδες *look*, lads! Ar.*Eq.*419. **2.** *examine*, τῷ δακτύλῳ τι Hp.*Nat.Mul.*7. **II.** later of the mind, *view*, *examine*, *consider*, σκέψασθε.. τὴν τύχην δυοῖν βροτοῖν S.*Aj.*1028; σκέψαι δὲ τοῦτο πρῶτον Id.*OT*584; ὃ πολλάκις ἐσκεψάμην Th.6.38, etc.; τὸ δίκαιον E.*Or.*494; μηδὲν ἐσκέφθαι δίκ. D.21.192; πρὸς ἑαυτόν τι Pl.*Phd.*95e; ἐκ τῶνδε σκέψαι *from* these facts, X.*Mem.*2.6.38, cf. D.2.17; περί τινος Pl.*La.*185c, *Cra.*401a; σκέψασθαι ἀπὸ τῶν παίδων *judge* by what children do, Ar.*Pl.*576; ἐν σοὶ σκεψώμεθα Pl.*Sph.* 239b: abs., σκέψασθέ νυν ἄμεινον E.*Or.*1291; σκεψώμεθα δή Ar.*Th.* 802; σκέψασθε δέ· *only consider*, to call people's attention to a point, Antipho 6.41, Th.1.143: folld. by a clause with οἷος, ὁποῖος, ὡς, A. *Pr.*1014, S.*Tr.*1077, E.*IA*1377, etc.; by ὅτῳ τρόπῳ, Th.1.107; by πῶς.., πόθεν.., πότερον.. ἤ.., X.*An.*4.5.22, 5.4.7, 3.2.20, etc.; by εἰ, *consider* whether or no, S.*El.*442, Ar.*Pax* 29, *Eq.*1141, X.*An.*3. 2.22; in full, σ. τοῦτο, εἰ.. S.*OT*584; τί ἐστιν ἡ ἀρετὴ σκεπτόμεθα Arist.*EN*1103$^b$28. **2.** rarely, *think* or *deem* a thing to be so and so, καλλίω θάνατον σκεψάμενος Pl.*Lg.*854c. **3.** *think of beforehand*, *provide*, σκεπτόμεθα τἀναγκαῖ' ἑκάστης ἡμέρας Philem.120; τὸ συμφέρον Pl.*R.*342a; *prepare*, *premeditate*, λόγους D.24.158; εἴ τι χρήσιμον ἐσκεμμένος ἥκει Id.1.1: c. inf., *plan*, Th.8.63. **4.** pf. in pass. sense, πάντα ἐσκεμμένα ἡτοίμασται *with consideration*, Id.7.62; σκοπεῖτε οὖν. Answ. ἔσκεπται Pl.*R.*369b, cf. X.*HG*3.3.8, D.21.191, 61. 7: also 3 fut. Pass. ἐσκέψεται Pl.*R.*392c; aor. ἐσκέφθην, ες τὸ σκεφθῆναι for *observation*, Hp.*de Arte* 11; aor. 2 and fut. 2 ἐσκέπην (ἐπ-), σκεπήσομαι (ἐπι-), Lxx *Nu.*1.19, 1*Ki.*20.18. **-τοσύνη**, ἡ, poet. for σκέψις, Timo 59.4, Cerc.9.9.

⊛ **σκέπω**, = σκεπάζω, only in pres. and impf., Hp.*Art.*11, Plb.16.29. 13; freq. in later Prose, Luc.*Tim.*21, *Pisc.*29, al., Diog.Oen.10, Hdn.3.3.2, 5.3.6, Jul.*Or.*2.57b, 5.165b, Lib.*Or.*57.17; of a ship, = στέγειν, D.Chr.34.24.

**σκεραός**· οἶδος, Hsch. **σκέρᾰφος** and **σχέραφος**, = λοιδορία, βλασφημία, Id.; cf. κέραφος.

**σκερβόλλω**, *scold*, *abuse*, σ. πονηρά 'talk Billingsgate', use foul abuse, Ar.*Eq.*821, Hsch.; cf. κερβολέω.

**σκέρβολος**, *scolding*, *abusive*, Call.*Fr.*281, Hsch.

**σκερολίγγες**· λαικασταὶ ἢ ὠπισταί, Hsch. **σκερός**· αἰδοιολείκτης, Id.

⊛ **σκευᾰγωγ-έω**, (σκεῦος) *pack up and carry away goods*, ἐκ τῶν ἀγρῶν σ. *pack up one's chattels* and remove into the city, Aeschin.2.139, 3. 80, D.18.36:—Med., Sch.Ar.*Pax*631. **-ός**, όν, *conveying goods*, ἅμαξαι Poll.10.14; σκευαγωγά *baggage-trains*, Plu.*Pomp.*6; also, *transport vessels*, *transports*, Str.16.4.23. **II.** as Subst., *one who looks to the baggage of an army*, *baggage-master*, X.*Cyr.*8.5.4.

⊛ **σκευάζω**, fut. -άσω Ar.*Eq.*372: aor. ἐσκεύασα Id.*Ach.*739, etc.; Dor. -αξα (κατ-) Ti.Locr.99a: pf. ἐσκεύακα Men.*Sam.*254:—Med., aor. ἐσκευασάμην Din.*Fr.*89.31: pf., v. infr.:—Pass., fut. -ασθήσομαι Gal.6.501 as cited by Orib.4.1.16 (σκευασθῇ codd. Gal.), (κατα-) D.19. 219: pf. ἐσκεύασμαι, Ion. 3 pl. ἐσκευάδαται Hdt.4.58, and so of plpf. -ατο, Id.7.62; used in med. sense, E.*Supp.*1057, Lys.*Fr.*54: (σκεῦος, σκευή):—*prepare*, *make ready*, esp. *prepare* or *dress* food, [πρόβατα] Hdt.1.207, cf. 73; ὅ τι ἂν τις.. σκευάσῃ Ar.*Eq.*53; ἄλφιτα ib.1104 (Pass.); ὄψον Alex.49, Philem.79.2, Thphr.*Char.*20.9; τὸ δεῖπνον Pl.Com.46.2; θοίνη Pl.*Tht.*178d (Pass.); σ. ἐλλέβορον μετὰ φαρμάκου Str.9.3.3; κρέα ὀπτὰ σ. D.S.2.59: metaph., ἐπίστασαι τὸν σαῦρον ὡς δεῖ σκευάσαι; Alex.133.1; περικόμματ' ἐκ σοῦ -άσω *make* mincemeat of you, Ar.*Eq.*372; ὑμᾶς.. φρυκτοὺς σκευάσω Id.*V.*1331:—Med., *prepare for oneself*, and then much like the Act., θοίνην E.*HF*956; ἄλφιτα Pl.*R.*372b. **2.** generally, *make ready*, *arrange*, Hdt.1.80; *make* a barrier, *IG*1$^2$.44.9; κέραμον σ. ib.313.164; χαλινὸν.. χαλκεῖ ἐκδιδόντα σκευάσαι giving it him *to make*, Pl.*Prm.*127a; σ. ἡδονάς *provide*, *procure*, Id.*R.*559d:—Med., σ. τόξ' ἑαυτοῦ παισί *made his* arrows *ready for* (i.e. *against*) them, E.*HF*969; *contrive*, *bring about*, πόλεμον, προδοσίην σ., Hdt.5.103, 6.100. **3.** *collect* σκεύη, of a burglar, *h.Merc.*285:—Med., c. acc., Lys.*Fr.*54, Din.*Fr.*89.31. **II.** of persons, *furnish*, *supply*, only in Pass., σιτίοισι εὖ ἐσκευασμένος καὶ προβάτοισι Hdt.1.188; ποταμοῖσι οὕτω Σκύθαι ἐσκευάδαται Id.4.58; ἐς πρᾶγμα νεοχμὸν ἐσκευάσμεθα E.*Supp.*1057. **2.** *dress up*, τὴν γυναῖκα σ. πανοπλίῃ Hdt.1.60; ἄνδρας τῇ τῶν γυναικῶν ἐσθῆτι Id.5.20; τὴν ἀδελφεὴν ὡς εἶχον ἄριστα ib.12; σ. τινὰ ὥσπερ γυναῖκα Ar.*Th.*591; χοίρως ὑμὲ -άσας Id.*Ach.*739; σ. [αὐτὴν] ὡς ἐδύνατο κάλλιστα X.*An.* 6.1.12; οὕτω σκευάσαντες ἑαυτούς Plu.*Caes.*31; also σ. τοὺς θεράποντας ἐς ὑπηρέτας, ἐς στρατιώτας, App.*BC*4.45,46; σ. εἴδωλόν τινι *dress up* an effigy of him, Hdt.6.58:—Pass., ἐσκευασμένοι *accoutred*, Th.4.32; εὐνοῦχος ἐσκευασμένος *dressed up* as.., Ar.*Ach.*121; rarely of things, τὰ προπύλαια τύποισι.. ἐσκευάδαται *are decorated* with.., Hdt.2. 138. **III.** *cheat*, *cozen*, Men.*Sam.*254. (From iii B.C. sts. written **σκεα-**, as παρασκεαστέον *PTeb.*703.248.)

**σκευάκας**· εὐωνύμους, Hsch. (Perh. σκεϝ- for σκαιϝ-.)

**σκευ-άριον**, τό, Dim. **I.** (σκεῦος) *small vessel* or *utensil*, mostly in pl., Ar.*Ach.*451, *Ra.*172, *Pl.*809, Pl.Com.121, etc.: sg., Ar.*Pl.* 1139. **2.** *implements of gaming*, Aeschin.1.59. **II.** (σκευή) *paltry garment*, Pl.*Alc.*1.113e. **-ᾰσία**, ἡ, *preparing*, *dressing*, esp. of food, ὄψου Id.*Ly.*209e, *Alc.*1.117c, *Min.*316e; abs., ἐὰν ἡ σ. καθάρειος ᾖ Men.*Phasm.Fr.*2; φαρμάκων D.S.5.74; πυρός Aen.Tact.33.2, 34.1: pl., *modes of dressing*, *recipes*, Alex.110.24: metaph., σ. τῆς μουσικῆς Astyd.4 = *Com.Adesp.*1330. **II.** *furniture*, ὄνων Callix.2; *furnishing*, *Stoic.*1.68. **-ᾰσις**, εως, ἡ, = foreg., dub. in Alex.110. 24, Lxx *Ec.*10.1 (v.l. -ασίαν). **-ασμα**, ατος, τό, *preparation*, *dish* of food, Sch.Ar.*Lys.*664; of Deianira's φίλτρον, Sch.S.*Tr.*594. **II.** in pl., *furniture*, Lxx *Ju.*15.11. **-αστέον**, *one must prepare* to do a thing, c. inf., Ar.*Pax* 855. **II.** *one must prepare*, *compound* a medicine, Dsc.2.76, Gal.13.814. **-αστής**, οῦ, ὁ, *preparer*, Aq.*Is.* 32.5; φαρμάκων Tz.*H.*8.920 (pl.). **-αστός**, ή, όν, *prepared by art*, *artificial*, opp. φυτευτός, Pl.*R.*510a; τὰ σ. ib.515c, Arist.*Metaph.* 1013$^b$18; of a drug, σ. ἐκ.. Luc.*Alex.*21; *medicated*, ἅλες Gal.6. 549,573; θυμιάματα Dsc.1.23; σκεῦος σ. Lxx *Is.*54.17. **-ή**, ἡ, *equipment*, *attire*, *apparel*, Hdt.7.15, S.*OC*555, E.*Ba.*180, etc.; σ. Μηδικὰς ἐνδυόμενος Th.1.130; σκευήν τινα περιθέσθαι Pl.*Cri.*53d; σκευῆς ἀνάθεσις, of the chorus, Lys.21.4; esp. of the *dress* of a singer or actor, ἐνδὺς πᾶσαν τὴν σ. Hdt.1.24, cf. Ar.*Ra.*108; τραγικὴ σ. Pl. *R.*577b; of soldiers, σ. ψιλή Th.3.94; ἡ σ. τῶν ὅπλων Id.1.8; of *horse-trappings*, Id.6.94; of the *dress* of priests and public officers, And.1.112, Eub.71. **2.** *fashion*, *style of dress* or *equipment*, Μηδικὴ αὕτη ἡ σ. ἐστι Hdt.7.62; τὴν αὐτὴν σ. ἔχοντες ib.66, cf. 73, al.; ἐπὶ πολὺ αὕτη ἡ σ. κατέσχεν Th.1.6. **II.** *tackle*, as of a net, Pi.*P.*2.80; of a ship, D.S.14.79, *Act.Ap.*27.19. **2.** = αἰδοῖον, *AP*5.241 (Eratosth., where σκεϋήν ⏑⏑–, dub.l.); cf. σκεῦος III.

**σκευηφορέω**, = σκευοφ-, Sch.Ar.*Ra.*14.

**σκευο-γρᾰφία**, ἡ, *inventory* of furniture, etc., *PLond.*2.191.1 (ii A.D.). **-γρᾰφικός**, ή, όν, *descriptive of tools* or *utensils*: τὸ σ. title of a work by Eratosthenes, Poll.10.1. ⊛**-θήκη**, ἡ, *chest for all kinds of* σκεύη, A.*Fr.*274, Ath.11.460d. **2.** *arsenal*, *IG*2$^2$.1668.2, al. (iv B.C.); σ. ᾠκοδόμουν Aeschin.3.25, cf. *IG*2$^2$.505.13 (iv B.C.), Philoch.135, Phld.*Rh.*1.192 S.; late Dor. **σκεοθήκα** *IG*9(1).692.12 (Corc., ii B.C.). **-πλᾰσία**, ἡ, *moulding of pots*, *pottery*, Suid. s.v. Κωλιάδος κεραμῆες. **-πλαστικὸς** τροχός, ὁ, *potter's* wheel, Id.ibid.

**σκευοποι-έω**, *fabricate*, [ὄργανα] Plu.*Marc.*16 (Pass.); ῥυτόν Ath. 11.497b (Pass.). **II.** esp. *prepare by art* or *cunning*, σ. τὰς ὄψεις, of women painting their faces, Alex.98.[27]; σ. διαθήκας *forge* a will, Is.*Fr.*8, cf. *Fr.*89, Hyp.*Fr.*124:—Pass., *to be tricked out*, *disguised*, τοῖς τοῦ φίλου ἐπισήμοις Plu.2.59b. **-ημα**, ατος, τό, in pl., *mask and dress* of a tragic actor, Id.*Crass.*33. **II.** *trick*, Hyp.*Fr.* 93. **-ία**, ἡ, *preparing of masks and other stage-properties*, Philostr.*VA*6.11, Poll.10.15. **-ός**, ὁ, *maker of masks and other stage-properties*, Ar.*Eq.*232, Arist.*Po.*1450$^b$20, *OGI*51.66 (Ptolemais, iii B.C.), Plu.2.1123c, Ath.14.621e.

**σκευοπώλης**, ου, ὁ, *one who sells* σκεύη, Critias 70 D., *PLond.*3. 1177.101 (ii A.D.).

⊛ **σκεῦος**, εος, τό, *vessel* or *implement of any kind*, in sg., Ar.*Th.*402, Th.4.128; in dual, σκεύη δύο χρησίμω Ar.*Eq.*983, cf. Pl.*R.*596b; and in pl., κλῖναι καὶ.. τἆλλα σκεύη ib.373a, al.:—but the pl. is freq. used in a collective sense, *all that belongs to a complete outfit*, *house-gear*, *utensils*, *chattels*, opp. live-stock and fixtures, Ar.*Pax* 1318, Lys.19. 31, etc.; σ. γεωργικά farming *implements*, Ar.*Pax* 552; ἱερὰ σ. sacred *vessels and implements*, Th.2.13, cf. *IG*1$^2$.313.20; a druggist's *stores*, Thphr.*HP*9.17.3; σ. τὰ ἐπιτράπεζα table-*furniture*, Id.*Lap.*42; military *accoutrements*, *equipment*, τὰ περὶ τὸ σῶμα σ. Th.6.31; τὰ τῶν ἵππων σ. X.*Cyr.*4.5.55; *baggage* of an army, and, generally, *baggage*, *luggage*, Ar.*Ra.*12,15, X.*Mem.*3.13.6; ὄνοι αὐτοῖς σκεύεσι *packs* and all, Id.*HG*5.4.17; *tackle*, *gear* of ships, *naval stores*, etc., *IG*1$^2$.74.14, 2$^2$.1611.10, Pl.*Criti.*117d, *La.*183e, X.*Oec.*8.11, Arist. *Ath.*46.1; σ. τριηρικά D.47.19; τὰ σκέα (= σκεύη) τοῦ πλοίου *PSI*4. 437.2 (iii B.C.) (so, collectively, in sg., *Act.Ap.*27.17): various kinds of σκεύη catalogued by Pollux (10). **2.** *inanimate object*, *thing*, opp. ζῷον, σῶμα, Pl.*R.*601d, *Grg.*506d; opp. ὄργανον, Democr. 159; Protagoras gave the name of σκεύη to neut. nouns, ἄρρενα καὶ θήλεα καὶ σκεύη Arist.*Rh.*1407$^b$8; ὑπηρετικὸν σ. a subordinate *person*, *a mere tool* or *chattel*, Plb.13.5.7; σ. ἀγχίνουν καὶ πολυχρόνιον Id.15. 25.1: in *NT*, in good sense, σ. ἐκλογῆς a chosen *instrument*, of Paul, *Act.Ap.*9.15. **II.** τὸ σ. the *body*, as the *vessel* of the soul, a metaph. clearly expressed in 2*Ep.Cor.*4.7, ἔχομεν δὲ τὸν θησαυρὸν τοῦτον ἐν ὀστρακίνοις σκεύεσιν, cf. 1*Ep.Thess.*4.4, 1*Ep.Pet.* 3.7. **III.** = αἰδοῖον, *APl.*4.243 (Antist.), Ael.*NA*17.11. **IV.** *sarcophagus*, *Jahresh.*26 *Beibl.*13 (Ephesus, ii A.D.).

**σκευότριψ**, ῐβος, ὁ, ἡ, (τρίβω) *one who breaks vessels*, Hdn.Gr.1. 246.

**σκευουργία**, ἡ, *making of tools*, *implements*, or *gear*, Pl.*Plt.*299d: also **σκευουργική** (sc. τέχνη), ἡ, Poll.7.210.

**σκευοφορ-εῖον** or **-φόριον**, τό, *yoke resting on the shoulders for carrying pails*, = ἀνάφορον, Pl.Com.50 (-φόριον): -φορεῖον is prescribed by Theognost.*Can.*129. **-έω**, *carry* σκεύη or *baggage*, X.*An.*3.2. 28, *Cyr.*3.1.43, v.l. in 8.3.7:—Pass., σκευοφορεῖσθαι καμήλοις *have one's baggage carried* by camels, Plu.*Crass.*21. **-ικός**, ή, όν, *of* or *for baggage-carrying*, στρατὸς σ. the body of σκευοφόροι, X.*Lac.*13.4; σ. βάρος the load *usually packed on one animal*, *a beast's* load, Id.*Cyr.* 6.1.54. **-ιον**, τό, v. σκευοφορεῖον. **-ιώτης**, ου, ὁ, comic form of σκευοφόρος, formed after εἰραφιώτης, Eup.264. **-ος** (parox.), ον, *carrying* σκεύη, σ. κάμηλοι *baggage*-camels, Hdt.1.80; ὑποζύγια X. *HG*4.1.24; ὄνος Poll.1.139; τὰ σ. (sc. κτήνη) *pack-animals*, Th.2.79, X.*Cyr*.5.4.45, *An*.1.3.7, al.: collectively in sg., πᾶν τὸ σ. Plb.3.79.2, cf. 3.51.6, 12.19.5. II. Subst., of persons, *baggage-carrier, porter*, Ar.*Ra*.497, *IG*4$^{2}$(1).121.79 (Epid., iv B.C.), *PAmh*.2.62.13 (ii B.C.); οἱ σ. *sutlers, camp-followers*, esp. *the servants of the* ὁπλίτης, who carried his baggage and shield, οἱ σ. τε καὶ τὰ ὑποζύγια Hdt.7.40.

**σκευοφῠλ-ᾰκέω**, *guard the baggage*, Plu.*Alex*.32. **–άκιον** [ᾰ], τό, *storehouse*, *PPetr*.2 p.16 (iii B.C.). **–αξ**, ᾰκος, ὁ, *storekeeper*, ib. p.39 (iii B.C., written σκεο–), Poll.10.16.

**σκευόω**, = σκευάζω, Hsch.: cf. κατασκευόω.

**σκευύφιον**, τό, Dim. of σκεῦος, Lyd.*Mag*.2.7.

**σκευωρ-έομαι**, aor. ἐσκευωρησάμην D.45.47: pf. ἐσκευώρημαι Id.32.9, 11:—Act. σκευωρέω Ph.2.569; and pf. ἐσκευώρημαι in pass. sense, D.45.5:—prop. *look after the baggage* or *utensils* (σκεύη), but only found in general sense, *inspect, examine thoroughly*, τοὺς τάφους Str.16.1.11; σ. τὴν Πομπηΐου οἰκίαν *ransack* it, Plu.*Caes*.51, cf. *Cam*.32, 2.587f. II. *contrive, manage, fabricate*, D.32.9, 11, 45.47, 46.17, Diog.Oen.24; with a sense of *fraud* or *intrigue*, τὰν Πελοποννήσῳ D.9.17; σ. ὑποκρίσεις *contrive* dramatic effects, Plu.2.711e. III. intr., σ. περὶ τὰς νεοττιάς *to be busy* about them, Arist.*HA*619$^{a}$24. 2. *act knavishly*, περί τι D.17.20. 3. abs., *plagiarize*, D.L.2.61. **–ημα**, ατος, τό, *fabrication, fraud*, D.36.33, 41.24. **–ία**, ἡ, *care of baggage*, etc., Poll.10.15: generally, *great care, excessive care*, σ. ποιεῖσθαι περὶ τοὺς νεοττούς Arist.*HA*631$^{b}$15, etc.; ἡ περὶ ταῦτα σ. Id.*GA*718$^{a}$33; σ. γίγνεται περί τι Philem.61; *critical nicety* or *elaboration*, D.H.*Comp*.25; σ. διθυραμβική Id.*Th*.29; τεχνική ib.5, cf. Phld.*Rh*.1.65 S. II. *knavery, intrigue*, D.55.2, Plu.*Lys*.25, *Dio* 30. **–ός**, όν, = σκευοφύλαξ, Cratin.159. (In late Gr. written **σκαιωρ-έω, –ία**, etc. (qq. v.) with –αι– representing –ε– (cf. παρασκεάζω, σκεοθήκα, σκεοφύλαξ, etc.).)

**σκέψ**, = σκοπός, Hdn.Gr.1.404.

⊛ **σκέψις**, εως, ἡ, (σκέπτομαι) *viewing, perception by the senses*, ἡ διὰ τῶν ὀμμάτων σ. Pl.*Phd*.83a; *observation* of auguries, Hdn.8.3.7. II. *examination, speculation, consideration*, τὸ εὕρημα πολλῆς σκέψιος Hp.*VM*4, cf. Pl.*Alc*.1.130d; βραχείας σ. Id.*Tht*.201a; νέμειν σ. take *thought* of a thing, v.l. in E.*Hipp*.1323; ἐνθεὶς τῇ τέχνῃ σ. Ar.*Ra*.974; σ. ποιεῖσθαι Pl.*Phdr*.237d; σ. προβέβληκας Id.*Phlb*.65d; σ. λόγων Id.*R*.336e; σ. περί τινος *inquiry into, speculation on* a thing, Id.*Grg*.487e, etc.; περί τι Id.*Lg*.636d; ἐπὶ σκέψιν τινὸς ἐλθεῖν X.*Oec*.6.13. 2. *speculation, inquiry*, ταῦτα ἐξωτερικωτέρας ἐστὶ σκέψεως Arist.*Pol*.1254$^{a}$34; ἔξω τῆς νῦν σ. Id.*Ph*.228$^{a}$20; οὐκ οἰκεῖα τῆς παρούσης σ. Id.*EN*1155$^{b}$9, etc. 3. *hesitation, doubt*, esp. of the Sceptic or Pyrrhonic philosophers, *AP*7.576 (Jul.); *the Sceptic philosophy*, S.E.*P*.1.5; οἱ ἀπὸ τῆς σ. the Sceptics, ib.229. 4. in politics, *resolution, decree*, συνεδρίου Hdn.4.3.9, cf. Poll.6.178.

**σκηκός**· πόας εἶδος καὶ ζῴου, Hsch. (v. σκίγκος). **σκῆλαι**, v. σκέλλω. **σκήλημα**, v. σκλῆμα. **σκῆν**· ὅ τινες μὲν ψυχήν, τινὲς δὲ φάλαιναν, Hsch.; i.e. *butterfly* or *moth*.

**σκηναρχέω**, *to be camp-captain*, *Supp.Epigr*.1.378 (Samos, ii/i B.C.), *IG*3.1096.8, 1124.44 (Athens, ii A.D.).

**σκην-άω**, = σκηνέω, v.l. in X.*An*.7.4.12; τοῖς σκηνῶσιν the *banqueters*, ib.5.3.9. II. elsewh. in Med., with pf. and plpf. Pass., *encamp*, σκηνᾶσθαι παρὰ τὸν ποταμόν Pl.*R*.621a; σκηνησάμενος ἐν θαλάττῃ Id.*Lg*.866d; ἐσκηνημένοι, prob., *in covered carriages* (v. σκηνή III), Ar.*Ach*.69; τὰ.. ἱερά, ἐν οἷς ἐσκήνηντο in which *they found harbourage*, Th.2.52. 2. c. acc., σκηνησαμένου καλύβην *having built him* a hut or cottage, Id.1.133. **–εῖον**, τό, *tent-pole*, *PCair.Zen*.353.2 (iii B.C.). **–εύομαι**, *pretend, feign*, εὐήθειαν Lyd.*Mag*.1.31 (s.v.l.): v. σκηνικεύομαι. **–ευτής**, οῦ, ὁ, = σκηνίτης, *EM*743.15; *tent-dweller* or *tent-maker*, *AB*304. **–έω**, Dor. **σκᾱνέω** (q.v.), *to be* or *dwell in a tent, encamp*, also generally, *to be quartered* or *billeted*, οἰκίαι.. ἐν αἷς αὐτοὶ ἐσκήνησαν (v.l. –ωσαν, –ουν) Th.1.89; ἐν τῇ οἰκίᾳ –οῦντι *PSI*4.340.13 (iii B.C.); αἱ κῶμαι ἐν αἷς ἐσκήνουν X.*An*.1.4.9; κατὰ ναῦν ἔμελλον οἱ ναῦται –ήσειν Id.*HG*5.1.20; ἐσκήνησαν εἰς κώμας *went* to villages *and quartered themselves there*, Id.*An*.7.7.1; πρὸς τῷ ὄρει –οῦντος Id.*HG*4.6.7; ἐν τῷ ὄρει, ἔνθαπερ ἐσκήνουν Id.*An*.4.8.25; ἐσκήνουν ἐν τῷ αἰγιαλῷ ib.6.4.7, etc.; οἴκοι –οῦντας, ἔξω –οῖεν, *have one's meals* at home, abroad, Id.*Lac*.5.2, 15.4: hence, *banquet*, κατελάμβανον κἀκείνους –οῦντας ἐστεφανωμένους κτλ. Id.*An*.4.5.33.—For the Med. forms, v. σκηνάω (σκηνᾶσθαι is certainly found in Pl., and the other Med. forms *may* belong to it; cf. σκηνόω I. 2). **–ή**, Dor. **σκᾱνά**, ἡ (not in Hom., who uses κλισίη (q.v.)). I. *tent, booth*, *IG*1$^{2}$.314.110, E.*Hec*.1289; ἐπὶ σκηναῖς.. ναυτικαῖς S.*Aj*.3; σκηνῆς ἔνδον ib.218 (anap.); ὑπὸ σκηναῖσι ib.754; σκηνῆς ὕπαυλος ib.796; σκηνὴν ποιήσαντες Th.2.34; πηξάμενοι Hdt.6.12, cf. And.4.30; ἵστασθαι X.*Cyr*.8.5.3; τὰς σ. καταλύειν, διαλύειν, strike *camp*, Plb.6.40.2, Paus.10.25.3; σ. δερματίνη *PCair.Zen*.13.14 (iii B.C.); but also σ. μάλα ἰσχυρῶν ξύλων *hut*, D.Chr.7.23; *booth* in the market-place, Ar.*Th*.658, D.18.169 (both pl.), Theoc.15.16; σκανὰν ἐμ Πυλαίᾳ τὰν πρώταν ὑπάρχειν αὐτῷ *SIG*422.11 (Delph., iii B.C.): pl., *camp*, A.*Eu*.686, Ar.*Pax*731, X.*An*.3.5.7. 2. σκηνὰς ἐς ἱεράς to the holy *tabernacle*, E.*Ion* 806, cf. 1129, Lxx *Ex*.26.1, al. II. *stage-building* as background for plays, Pl.*Lg*.817c, Poll.4.123 sqq., Vitr.5.6.1; τῆς σ. τὸ τέγος *IG*11(2).161 *A* 115, cf. *D* 127 (Delos, iii B.C.), 153.14 (ibid.); τραγικὴ σ. *a sort of* πῆγμα, such as that from which the prologue of A.*Ag*. is perhaps spoken, X.*Cyr*.6.1.54, Plu.*Demetr*.44, Suid. s.v. τραγικὴ σ. 2. οἱ ἀπὸ τῆς σ. [ἥρωες] *heroes represented on the stage*, D.18.180; οἱ ἀπὸ σκηνῆς *actors, players*, opp. χορός, Arist.*Pr*.922$^{b}$17; also οἱ περὶ σκηνήν Plu.*Galb*.16; οἱ ἐπὶ σκηνῆς Alciphr.3.65 codd., cf. Luc.*Nec*.16; cf. σκηνικός and v. infr. III. 1b. 3. τὸ ἐπὶ τῆς σκηνῆς μέρος that which is *actually represented on the stage*, Arist.*Po*.1459$^{b}$25; τὰ ἀπὸ τῆς σκηνῆς (sc. ᾄσματα), *songs* or *odes sung by one of the actors standing on the stage* (not by the chorus), ib.1452$^{b}$18; τὰ μὲν ἀπὸ τῆς σ. οὐκ ἀντίστροφα, τὰ δὲ τοῦ χοροῦ ἀντίστροφα Id.*Pr*.918$^{b}$27. 4. metaph., *stage-effect, acting, unreality*, σκηνὴ πᾶς ὁ βίος 'all the world's a *stage*', *AP*10.72 (Pall.); ἡ σ. τοῦ βίου Max.Tyr.7.10; *theatrical trick, deception*, J.*BJ*2.21.2, Hdn.3.12.3. III. *tented cover, tilt of a wagon* or *carriage*, X.*Cyr*.6.4.11, D.S.20.25, Plu.*Them*.26; σ. τροχήλατοι A.*Pers*.1000 (lyr.); also, *bed-tester*, D.41.11. b. metaph., τὸν ὑπὸ (prob. cj. for ἐπὶ) σκηνῆς βίον the *hidden* life, Luc.*Icar*.21. 2. in large ships, *state-cabin* on the poop, Poll.1.89, Palaeph.29; τῶν συριῶν ὑπὲρ τὴν σ. οὐσῶν *PHib*.1.38.7 (iii B.C.); ἀποκαταστήσω [τὸν σῖτον] ἐπὶ σκηνήν ib.86.8 (iii B.C.). IV. *entertainment given in tents, banquet*, X.*Cyr*.2.3.1, 4.2.34, etc.; σ. δημοσία Id.*Lac*.15.4. **–ημα**, Dor. **σκάναμα** *IG*4$^{2}$(1).109 i 128, al. (Epid., iii B.C., pl.), ατος, τό, = σκηνή, X.*HG*5.3.19; *camp*, Anon.ap.Suid.: pl., *nest*, A.*Ch*.251. **–ήτης**, v. σκηνίτης. **–ίδιον**, τό, Dim. of σκηνή, Th.6.37.

**σκηνῐκ-εύομαι**, prop. *play a part as an actor*: metaph., ἐκείνοις ταῦτα ἐσκηνικεύετο *in* this he *was play-acting* to them, Memn.51.3; prob. cj. for σκηνεύομαι in Lyd.*Mag*.1.31. **–ός**, ή, όν, (σκηνή II) *of the stage, theatrical*, Plu.2.1142c; ἀγών *CIG*2820 *A* 15 (Aphrodisias), cf. *SIG*704 *E* 17 (Decret.Amphict., ii B.C.), 711 *L* 5 (Delph., ii B.C.), *BGU*1074.16 (iii A.D.); σ. φιλόσοφος, of Euripides, Ath.13.561a. Adv. –κῶς Eust.6.11. 2. Subst. σκηνικός, ὁ, *actor* (whereas θυμελικοί are, or include, musicians and dancers, Vitr.5.7.2), Plu.*Oth*.6.

**σκηνίπτω**, = διαφθείρω, Hsch.; cf. διασκηνίπτω.

**σκην-ίς**, ίδος, ἡ, = σκηνή III.2, Plu.*Luc*.7. ⊛ **–ίτης** [ῑ] (in codd. sts. misspelt σκηνήτης, which is accepted by Eust.70.29), ου, ὁ, *dweller in tents* or *booths*, of nomad tribes, Str.2.5.32, 11.2.1, etc.; *one who keeps a stall*, *IG*2$^{2}$.1672.15, 171, 7.2712.72 (Acraephia). 2. *a low fellow*, Isoc.17.33. II. Adj. *in* or *belonging to a tent*, βίος D.S.2.40; κισσός *AP*7.36 (Eryc.).

**σκηνοβᾰτέω**, *tread the stage*, metaph., *act a part*, Vett.Val.238.29. II. *bring on the stage, exhibit publicly*, τὴν μοχθηρίαν Heraclit.*Ep*.8.3:—Pass., ποιήματα σκηνοβατεῖται *are brought upon the stage*, Str.5.3.6, cf. Heraclit.*All*.30, Ph.2.597.

**σκηνογρᾰφ-έω**, *show as in a theatre, stage-manage*, Hld.10.38. **–ία**, ἡ, *scene-painting*, Arist.*Po*.1449$^{a}$18 (who ascribes its introduction to Sophocles): pl., Plb.12.28$^{A}$.1. 2. metaph., *illusion*, τραγῳδία καὶ σ. Plu.*Arat*.15, S.E.*M*.7.88. **–ικός**, ή, όν, *for* or *in the manner of scene-painting*, ὄψις Str.5.3.8; θαυματουργία Hld.7.7. **–ος** (parox.), ὁ, *scene-painter*, D.L.2.125.

**σκηνο-θήκη**, ἡ, *tent-store*, *Inscr.Délos* 444 *B* 103, 104 (ii B.C.); cf. σκανοθήκα. **–πᾰγής**, ές, (πήγνυμι) *put together like a tent*, θαλάμαι f.l. for κηροπαγεῖς in *AP*6.239 (Apollonid.) ap.Suid. s.v. θαλάμη. **–πηγέω**, *put up a tent*, σ. τὰ καπηλεῖα *set* them *up like tents*, Damon 1. 2. *keep the feast of tabernacles*, J.*AJ*13.11.1:—Med. in Dor. form **σκᾱνο–** (q.v.). **–πηγία**, ἡ, *setting up of tents*: *nest-building*, ἡ τῆς χελιδόνος σ. Arist.*HA*612$^{b}$22. 2. *feast of tents* or *tabernacles*, Lxx *De*.16.16, 2*Ma*.1.9, *Ev.Jo*.7.2, J.*AJ*11.4.1, al.; σύλλογος τῆς σ. *CIG*5361 (Egypt, Jewish).

**σκηνοποι-έω**, *make a tent* or *booth*, Sm.*Is*.13.20, 22.15:—Med., *form a canopy*, Dsc.2.146:—but Med. in prop. sense, *make oneself a tent* or *booth*, Arist.*Mete*.348$^{b}$35, Clearch.9, Plb.14.1.7, D.S.3.27. **–ία**, ἡ, *tent-making*: *pitching of tents*, Aen.Tact.8.3, *Rev.Arch*.3(1934).40 (Amphipolis, iii/ii B.C.), Plb.6.28.3; *building of a theatre*, D.C.67.2; *nest-building*, of swallows, Antig.*Mir*.37: metaph., σ. τῆς τύχης *theatrical, dramatic stroke* of fortune, Hld.10.16. II. *theatrical display*, Jul.*Or*.7.216d. **–ός**, ὁ, *tentmaker*, *Act.Ap*.18.3. II. *maker of stage-properties*, *Com.Adesp*.98. III. (σκῆνος II) *making bodies*, Herm.ap.Stob.1.49.69.

**σκηνο-ρρᾰφεῖον**, τό, *workshop of a tentmaker*, Zonar.:—in Isoc.15.287, f.l. for σκιραφεῖον. ⊛ **–ρράφος** [ᾰ], ον, (ῥάπτω) *sewing tents*: as Subst., *tentmaker*, Ael.*VH*2.1.

**σκῆνος**, Dor. **σκᾶνος**, εος, τό, = σκηνή, *hut, tent*, *CIG*3071 (Teos). II. *the body* (as the *tabernacle* of the soul), Hp.*Cord*.7, *Anat*.1, Democr.37, 187, 223, al., Pl.*Ax*.366a, Ti.Locr.100a, 101c, e, 2*Ep.Cor*.5.1; σ. [μελίσσης] *AP*9.404 (Antiphil.). 2. *dead body, corpse*, *IG*3.1330, 12(5).591 (Ceos), *CIG*3123 (Teos), etc.; of an animal, μόσχου, ταύρων, Nic.*Al*.447, *Th*.742 (pl.).

**σκηνοφύλαξ** [ῠ], ᾰκος, ὁ, ἡ, *guard of tents, of a camp*, X.*HG*3.2.5, D.H.10.44, Plu.*Pomp*.72.

**σκην-όω**, *pitch tents, encamp*, ἐσκήνωσαν v.l. for –ησαν in X.*An*.2.4.14; σκηνοῖεν v.l. for σκηνῷεν (cj.) in ib.7.4.12. 2. = σκηνέω (q.v. sub fin.), *live* or *dwell in a tent*, ἐν τῷ ὁμοῦ σκηνοῦν prob. cj. in Id.*Cyr*.2.1.25: generally, *settle, take up one's abode*, κατὰ τὰς κώμας σκηνοῦν Id.*An*.4.5.23; –οῦν ἐν ταῖς οἰκίαις ib.5.5.11; ἐν τῇ ἀκροπόλει, οὗπερ αὐτὸς ἐσκήνου Id.*HG*5.4.56, cf. Lxx *Jd*.5.17, al., J.*AJ*3.12.6: metaph., ὁ λόγος.. ἐσκήνωσεν ἐν ἡμῖν *Ev.Jo*.1.14:—hence in pf. Pass., *live* or *be*, πόρρω ἐσκήνωται (v.l. ἐσκήνηται) τοῦ θανάσιμος εἶναι Pl.*R*.610e. II. trans., *pitch* a tent, σκηνὰς.. σκηνώσας Polyaen.7.21.6. 2. τὸν τόπον τὸν νῦν σκενοῖ (sic) the place which he now *inhabits*, dub. in *PCair.Zen*.499.89 (iii B.C.). **–ύδριον**, τό, Dim. of σκηνή, Plu.*Mar*.37. **–ωμα**, ατος, τό, = σκήνημα, mostly in pl., E.*Hec*.616, *Ion* 1133, *Cyc*.324, Lxx 2*Ki*.7.23, al., Agatharch.43, etc.;

soldiers' *quarters*, X.*An*.7.4.16 : sg., *tent*, Lxx 1*Ki*.4.10, al. 2. in sg. metaph., = σκῆνος II, 2*Ep.Pet*.1.13 ; τὸ σ. τῆς ψυχῆς Sext.*Sent*. 320. 3. *temple*, Lxx *Ps*.14(15).1, al. : name of a building at Sparta, Paus.3.17.6. 4. = *papilio*, *Gloss*. (perh. in both senses, *pavilion* and *butterfly*, cf. σκῆν). -ωσις, εως, ἡ, *construction of a tent* or *house*, Agatharch.47 (pl.). II. *dwelling in one*, Lxx 2*Ma*. 14.35, D.S.3.19, *Sammelb*.3924.7 (i A.D.). -ωτής, οῦ, ὁ, *comrade in a tent*, Hsch. -ωτός, ή, όν, *represented on the stage, scenic*, Lyd. *Mag*.1.40.

**σκηπάνη** [ᾰ], ἡ, *staff*, Sch.D.T.p.196 H. ; Dim. **σκηπάνιον** [ᾰ], τό, Il.13.59, 24.247, Call.*Fr.anon*.48, *AP*6.83 (Maced.); Dor. **σκᾱπάνιον** Hsch., Phot. s. v. σκίπων.

**σκηπῆίον·** πτύον, Hsch. **σκηπήνιον·** βακτηρία, τρίαινα, βάκτρον, κηρύκ⟨ε⟩ιον, ῥάβδος, Id. **σκῆπτον**, τό, = σκῆπτρον, only in Dor. form σκᾶπτον, and compds. σκηπτοῦχος, σκηπτουχία, σκηπτοφόρος.

⁎**σκηπτός**, ὁ, (σκήπτω) *thunderbolt* (σκηπτοὶ [λέγονται τῶν κεραυνῶν] ὅσοι κατασκήπτουσιν εἰς τὴν γῆν Arist.*Mu*.395$^{a}$28), X.*An*.3.1. 11 ; τάρβος..ὡς ἀπὸ σ. Aret.*SD*1.6 : metaph. also of a dust-*storm*, S.*Ant*.418 ; *hurricane*, D.18.194, Jul.*Or*.1.35b ; λοιμοῦ σ. A.*Pers*. 715 (troch.) ; of war, E.*Andr*.1046 (lyr.), *Rh*.674 ; καλοῦσί μ' οἱ νεώτεροι..σκηπτόν, says a parasite, Antiph.195.11 ; σ. πόθος *falling like a thunderbolt*, Aspasia ap.Ath.5.219e.

**σκηπτουχία**, ἡ, *bearing of a staff* or *sceptre* as the badge of command, hence *military command*, esp. of the Persians, ἐπὶ σκηπτουχίᾳ ταχθεὶς A.*Pers*.297 ; technically, *rank* or *province of a Persian* σκηπτοῦχος (v. sq. 2), Str.11.2.18. 2. generally, *command, power*, Lyc.111.

⁎**σκηπτοῦχος**, Dor. **σκαπτ-**, ον, (σκῆπτον, ἔχω) *bearing a staff, baton*, or *sceptre* as the badge of command, σ. βασιλεύς *a sceptred* king, Il.2.86, Od.2.231, etc. ; ὅς τις σ. εἴη Il.14.93 : c. gen., θεῶν σ., of Aphrodite, Orph.*H*.55.11 ; [Ἄρης] ἠνορέης σ. *h.Mart*.6. 2. Subst., *wand-bearer*, a great officer in the Persian court, generally a eunuch, ἡ τύραννος ἢ σ. Semon.7.69, cf. X.*Cyr*.7.3.15, 8.1.38, 8.3. 15, *An*.1.6.11 ; of Scythian princelings, *IPE*1$^{2}$.32 *A* 42 (Olbia, iii B.C.) ; later, of *beadles* at Ephesus, *BMus.Inscr*.4.481⁎.300, *Ephes*. 4(1) No.4.

⁎**σκηπτοφόρος**, Dor. **σκᾱπτο-**, ον, = σκηπτροφόρος, *AP*7.428 (Mel.).

**σκηπτρισμός**, ὁ, dub. sens. in *Cat.Cod.Astr*.8(1).257.

**σκηπτροβάμων** [ᾱ], ον, gen. ονος, *sitting on the sceptre*, ὁ σ. αἰετός, κύων Διός S.*Fr*.884.

⁎**σκῆπτρον**, τό : Dor. **σκᾶπτον** (Pi.*O*.7.28, *P*.1.6, etc.), later **σκᾶπτρον** (*AP*7.428 (Mel.)), but σκῆπτρον in lyr. passages of Trag., as S.*Ph*.140 : (σκήπτω) :—*staff* or *stick*, used by the lame or aged, Il.18. 416, Od.13.437, 14.31, 17.199, 18.103 ; ἰσχὺν..νέμοντες ἐπὶ σκήπτροις A.*Ag*.75 ; σκήπτρῳ προδεικνύς, of a blind man feeling his way, S.*OT* 456 ; πρεσβῦται..σκήπτροισιν ἄκασκα προβῶντες Cratin.126 : metaph. of the daughters of Oedipus, ὦ σκῆπτρα φωτός his *staffs* or *supports*, S.*OC*1109, cf. 848 :—the Prose word is βακτηρία. II. *staff* or *baton*, esp. as the badge of command, *sceptre* : in Hom. borne by kings and chiefs, and transmitted from father to son (whence Il.2. 101 sqq. is called ἡ τοῦ σκήπτρου παράδοσις, Th.1.9), Il.9.156, Od. 11.569 : also borne by heralds, Il.7.277, al. ; by speakers, who on rising to speak received it from the herald, 1.234, 18.505, 23. 568, Od.2.37 ; by priests and soothsayers, Il.1.15, A.*Ag*.1265 ; later by minstrels, first in Hes.*Th*.30 ; σ. χρύσεον Il.1.15, 2.268, Od.11. 91, 569 ; wrought by Hephaestus, Il.2.101 ; χρυσείοις ἥλοισι πεπαρμένον 1.245. In oaths or protests it was held up, the gods being called to witness, ib.234, 7.412, 10.321, 328 ; ὁ δ' ὅρκος ἦν τοῦ σ. ἐπανάτασις Arist.*Pol*.1285$^{b}$12 ; used as a *stick* or *cudgel* to punish the refractory, Il.2.199, 265, Pi.*O*.7.28, S.*OT*811. 2. as a symbol of *royalty, kingly power*, etc., Il.6.159, 9.38 ; τοι Ζεὺς ἐγγυάλιξε σκῆπτρόν τ' ἠδὲ θέμιστας ib.99, cf. 156, 298, A.*Pr*.172 (anap.) ; τὸ θεῖον Διὸς σ. S.*Ph*.140 (lyr.) : freq. in pl. in this sense, Hdt.7.52 ; τύραννα σ. A.*Pr*.761, cf. *Eu*.626 ; ὃς..σκῆπτρα καὶ θρόνους ἔχει S.*OC*425, cf. 449, etc. ; σκῆπτρα χώρας E.*HF*1167. III. = Hebr. *Shevet*, of the tribes (φυλαί) of Israel, Lxx 3*Ki*.11.13, al. (but in 1*Ki*.10.20 sq., φυλή is a sub-division of σκῆπτρον). IV. = λυχνὶς στεφανωματική, Ps.-Dsc.3.100.

**σκηπτρο-φορέω**, *rule over*, γῆς *AP*12.56 (Mel.) : abs., Ph.2. 363. ⁎**-φόρος**, ον, *sceptre-bearing*, πατήρ (prob. Zeus) *Delph*.3(1). 510.3 (iv B.C.) ; *kingly*, σοφία *AP*12.101 (Mel.) ; cf. σκηπτοφόρος.

⁎**σκήπτω**, A.*Ag*.310 : fut. σκήψω (ἐπι-) Pl.*Tht*.145c (s.v.l.) : aor. ἔσκηψα E.*Hel*.834 : pf. ἔσκηφα (ἐπ-) D.L.1.117 :—Med., fut. σκήψομαι Hdt.7.28, Ar.*Ec*.1027 : aor. ἐσκηψάμην D.6.13 :—Pass., aor. ἐσκήφθην *IG*2$^{2}$.1629.746, (ἐπ-) Pl.*Lg*.937b : pf. ἔσκημμαι (ἐπ-) Is. 3.12. I. *prop, stay* one thing *against* or *upon* another :—Pass. and Med., *prop oneself* or *lean upon a staff*, of an aged beggar, πτωχῷ ..ἐναλίγκιον ἠδὲ γέροντι, σκηπτόμενον Od.17.203 ; of a wounded man, αὐτῷ σκηπτόμενον (sc. τῷ ἄκοντι) Il.14.457 ; βάκτρῳ A.R.2.198 : metaph., *lean* or *depend upon* a person or thing, μάρτυρι D.34.28, 47. 2. c. acc. rei, *put forward by way of support, allege by way of excuse*, τὴν βίαν σκήψασ' ἔχεις, = σκήπτεις, E.*Hel*.834 :—in this signf. most freq. in Med., *allege on one's own behalf*, τὸ σκηπτόμενον οἱ Πέρσαι ... Hdt.5.102 ; σ. τὸ μὴ εἰδέναι Id.7.28 ; σκήπτεσθαί τι πρός τινας Th. 6.18, Pl.*Sph*.217b ; σ. ἀσθένειαν *allege, pretend* illness, Plb.39.1.11 ; simply *pretend, simulate*, προσποιητὴν χαρὰν σκηψαμένη prob. l. in Ps.-Plu.*Fluv*.16.1 : c. inf., *pretend to be*, ἔμπορος εἶναι σκήψομαι Ar.*Ec*. 1027, cf. *Pl*.904, D.6.13, etc. ; σ. εἶναι [φυλῆς τινος] Lys.23.2 ; καθ' ἥντινα πρόφασιν ἐσκήψατο εἰς θήρας ἰέναι Ant.Lib.41.2 : c. acc. et inf., *allege* or *pretend that*.., σ. [τινὰ] παίζοντα λέγειν Pl.*Tht*.145c, cf. Is. 6.13 ; σ. τοῦτο, ὡς.. Aeschin.3.242 ; σ. ὅτι.. Pl.*Smp*.217d : abs., σ. ὑπέρ τινος *make a defence* for another, Id.*Lg*.864d. II. *let fall* or *hurl upon*, βέλος A.*Ag*.366 (anap.) : metaph., σ. ἀλάστορα εἴς τινα E.*Med*.1333 :—Med., σκήψασθαι κότον τῇ γῇ A.*Eu*.801 (s.v.l.) :—Pass., τῶν τριήρων..τῶν σκηφθεισῶν κατὰ χειμῶνα *which were fallen upon* (i.e. caught) in the storm, *IG* l.c. 2. intr., *fall*, πέδοι σκήψασα *having fallen* on the plain below, A.*Pr*.749 ; Διὸς ἔριν πέδοι σκήψασαν Id.*Th*.429 ; of plague, ὁ πυρφόρος θεὸς σκήψας ἐλαύνει..πόλιν S. *OT*28 ; λίμνην ὑπὲρ Γοργῶπιν ἔσκηψεν φάος *shot down* across.., of the beacon-light, A.*Ag*.302, cf. 308, 310.

**σκήπων**, v. σκίπων.

**σκηρίπτω**, *prop, fix, plant firmly*, ἐνὶ γαίῃ χηλὰς A.R.2.667. II. Hom. only in Med., δὸς δέ μοι [ῥόπαλον], . . σκηρίπτεσθ' *to support myself withal*, Od.17.196 ; σκηριπτόμενος χερσίν τε ποσίν τε *pressing, pushing against* it, with hands and feet, 11.595 ; so φρίκη ἐν ῥέθεϊ σ. Nic. *Th*.721 ; ἐπί τινος Ph.2.274 ; βακτηρίᾳ ib.317 : abs., πῦρ σκηριπτόμενον ὀρθοῦται *sustained*, ib.512. (Found only in pres. ; formed by assimilation of σκήπτω (Ep. only in pres.) to ἐστήρικτο, στηρίξασθαι, etc. (Ep. only in tenses other than pres.).)

⁎**σκῆψις**, εως, ἡ, (σκήπτω I. 2) *pretext, plea, excuse*, τοιάδε μέντοι σ. οὐ δόλον φέρει A.*Ag*.886 ; μή σ. οὐκ οὖσαν τίθης S.*El*.584 : c. gen., κατὰ φόνου τινὰ σ. pleading some murder as an *excuse*, Hdt.1.147 ; σ. τοῦ μὴ τὰ δέοντα ποιεῖν a *plea, excuse* for not doing, D.1.6 ; σ. ἡ νόσος..ἔδοξεν *pretence*, Luc.*Merc.Cond*.31 ; σκῆψιν ποιεῖσθαί τι to use as an *excuse*, Hdt.5.30 ; πρὸς Ἕλληνάς σφι σ. ἐπεποίητο Id.7.168 ; ἔχω σ. εὐπρεπεστάτην Id.3.72 ; ἐς ἄνδρα σ. εἶχ' ὀλωλότα (sc. τὰ τέκνα) E.*El*.29 ; σ. προτείνειν, δεικνύναι, ib.1067, *Med*.744 ; φέρειν *PCair. Zen*.110.5 (iii B.C., pl.) ; τοῖς νέοις σκῆψιν φέρει E.*IT*122 ; σκήψεις καὶ προφάσεις ἐρεῖ D.19.100 ; opp. σ. ἐσδέχεσθαι, Ar.*Ach*.392 ; σ. παραδέχεσθαι Hyp.*Eux*.7 ; εὑρίσκειν D.21.81 ; διδόναι Arist.*Top*. 131$^{b}$11 ; προβαλέσθαι, πορίσασθαι, etc., Plb.5.56.7, 5.2.9, etc. : acc. as Adv., σκῆψιν..ἐλήλυμεν, ὡς.. Cratin.235. 2. *plea* in a law-court, ὅπως ἂν αἱ σ. εἰσαχθῶσι *IG*2$^{2}$.1629.205. II. σκῆψις or σκέψις, ἡ, = ἀπόσκηψις, Hp.*Epid*.6.3.23, cf. Gal. ad loc.(17(2).110) and 19.138.

⁎**σκιά**, ᾶς, Ion. **σκιή**, ῆς, ἡ, *shadow*, Od.11.207 ; σκιὰ ἀντίστοιχος ὥς like the *shadow* that is one's double, E.*Andr*.745 ; ὑπὸ κίονος σκιὰν ἔπτηξεν Id.*HF*973 : prov., τὴν αὑτοῦ σ. δέδοικεν Ar.*Fr*.77, cf. Pl.*Phd*.101d. 2. *reflection, image* (in a bowl of oil), Sch.Il.17. 755. 3. *shade* of one dead, *phantom*, Od.10.495, A.*Th*.992 (lyr.), S.*Aj*.1257 ; σποδόν τε καὶ σκιάν Id.*El*.1159 ; κατθανὼν δὲ πᾶς ἀνὴρ γῆ καὶ σ. E.*Fr*.532 ; σκιᾷ τινι λόγους ἀνέσπα S.*Aj*.301 ; also, of *one worn to a shadow*, A.*Eu*.302 ; κακωθεὶς δ' οὐδὲν ἄλλ' εἰμ' ἢ σ. Id.*Niob*. in *Bull. Soc.Arch.Alex*. No.28 p.110 ; φωνὴ καὶ σ. γέρων ἀνήρ E.*Fr*.509 : freq. in proverbs of man's mortal estate, σκιᾶς ὄναρ ἄνθρωπος Pi.*P*.8.95 ; εἴδωλον σκιᾶς A.*Ag*.839, cf. S.*Fr*.659.6 ; ὁρῶ γὰρ ἡμᾶς οὐδὲν ἄλλο πλὴν εἴδωλα..ἢ κούφην σ. Id.*Aj*.126 ; ἄνθρωπός ἐστι πνεῦμα καὶ σ. μόνον Id.*Fr*.13 ; οὐδὲν ἐσμεν πλὴν σκιαῖς ἐοικότες Id.*Fr*.945 ; of human affairs, εὐτυχοῦντα μὲν σκιά τις ἂν πρέψειεν A.*Ag*.1328 (dub.l.) ; οὐδὲν μᾶλλον ἢ καπνοῦ σ. Id.*Fr*.399 ; καπνοῦ σκιὰν δέδοικεν *Com.Adesp*.692 ; of worthless things, τἄλλ' ἐγὼ καπνοῦ σκιᾶς οὐκ ἂν πριαίμην S.*Ant*. 1170, cf. *Ph*.946 ; καπνοὺς καὶ σκιάς Eup.51 ; ὅσ' ἂν γένηται ταῦτα πάντ' ὄνου σκιά S.*Fr*.331 ; περὶ ὄνου σκιᾶς [μάχεσθαι] Ar.*V*.191, cf. Pl.*Phdr*.260c ; Archipp. wrote a Com. entitled Ὄνου σκιά ; ἡ ἐν Δελφοῖς σ. that *phantom* at Delphi, of the Amphictyonic council, D.5.25 ; αἱ τοῦ δικαίου σ. *mere shadows* of.., Pl.*R*.517d ; σκιαὶ καὶ ἐν ὕδασιν εἰκόνες ib.510e ; σκιαὶ τῶν ὄντων, ἀλλ' οὐκ εἰδώλων σ. ib.532c ; στιγμὴ ἢ σ. τούτων D.21.115 ; ἂν ἔχῃ φίλου σκιάν Men. 554. 4. *evil spirit*, Hippiatr.130, *PMasp*.188.5 (vi A.D.). II. *shade* of trees, etc., as a protection from heat, πετραίη τε σκιή the *shade* of a rock, Hes.*Op*.589 ; ἐν σκιῇ ἑζόμενος ib.593 ; ἐν συμμιγεῖ σκιᾷ Pl.*Phdr*.239c ; εἰ ὑπὸ σκιῇ ἔσοιτο ἡ μάχη Hdt.7.226 ; ὑπὸ σκιᾶς E.*Ba*.458 ; εἰσελθὼν ὑπὸ τὴν σκιὰν καθέζεσθαι And.1.38 ; θέρους σκιὰν παρέχειν Pl.*Ti*.76d ; ἐν σκιᾷ, i.e. indoors, X.*Smp*.2.18, cf. *Cyr*.3. 3 ; σκιὰν ὑπερτείνασα Σειρίου κυνὸς *shade* from its heat, A.*Ag*.967 : pl., αἱ τῶν δένδρων, αἱ τῶν πετρῶν σ., X.*Cyr*.8.8.17 ; ὑπὸ σκιαῖς Id. *Oec*.20.18, cf. 5.9. III. *shadow in painting*, τὰ λαμπρὰ τῇ σκιᾷ τρανότερα ποιοῦσι Plu.2.863e, cf. 407a, D.H.*Is*.4, Longin.17.3 ; ἀνθρώπων πρῶτος ἐξευρὼν φθορὰν καὶ ἀπόχρωσιν σκιᾶς, of the painter Apollodorus, Plu.2.346a, cf. Hsch. 2. *silhouette, profile*, Διόδωρος σ. Ἀντιφίλου ἐποίησεν *Sammelb*.344 (Alexandria, ii B.C.). 3. perh. *coloured border* on a garment, καλάσηριν ἢ ὑπόδυμα μὴ ἔχον σκιάς *IG*5(1).1390.19, cf. 24 (Andania, i B.C.), cf. Men.561, *BGU*1141. 41, 43 (i B.C.). IV. *an uninvited guest, introduced by another* (Lat. *umbra*), Plu.2.707a, Ael.*Fr*.110. (Cf. Skt. *chāyā* 'shadow'.)

⁎**σκῐᾱγρᾰφ-έω**, *paint with the shadows*, so as to produce an illusion of solidity at a distance, Pass., τὰ πόρρωθεν..φαινόμενα..καὶ τὰ ἐσκιαγραφημένα Pl.*R*.523b ; οἷον -ημένα ἀποστάντι πάντα ἓν φαινόμενα Id.*Prm*.165c : metaph., -ημένη ἡδονή *deceptive, unreal*, opp. παναληθής, καθαρά, Id.*R*.583b, cf. 586b, *Lg*.663c, Ph.1.589. 2. *surround with a border, outline*, βέλεσι σ. τινά, of a juggler, Philostr. *VA*2.28 :—Pass., *to be outlined*, ἐσκιαγραφημένοις ἐπιβαλὼν χρώματα ib.1.2. -ημα, ατος, τό, *painting with the shadows*, ἐπειδὴ ἐγγὺς ὥσπερ σκιαγραφήματος γέγονα τοῦ λεγομένου, συνίημι οὐδὲ σμικρόν Pl. *Tht*.208e ; κενὰ -ήματα τῆς διανοίας *figments* of the imagination, Diog.Oen.7. -ία, ἡ, *painting with the shadows* (cf. σκιαγραφέω), so as to produce an illusion of solidity at a distance, *scene-painting*, σ. ἀσαφεῖ καὶ ἀπατηλῷ χρώμεθα Pl.*Criti.*107d; σκιαγραφίαν ἀρετῆς περιγραπτέον Id.*R.*365c, cf. 602d, *Phd.*69b, Numen.ap.Eus.*PE*14.5, 26; ἡ σ. καὶ τὰ ἐνύπνια, compared as being both illusory, Arist.*Metaph.*1024b23; ἡ δημηγορικὴ λέξις ἔοικε τῇ σ., i.e. in being calculated for effect, Id.*Rh.*1414a8, cf. D.C.52.7. **-ικός**, ή, όν, *illusively painted*, Procl.*in Alc.*p.155 C. **-ος** (parox.), ὁ, *perspective-painter, scene-painter* (cf. σκηνογράφος), Lxx *Wi.*15.4, Hsch., Phot.—The forms in σκιογρ- are later, v.l. in Lxx l.c., etc.

**σκῐάδειον** [ᾰ], τό, (σκιά) *sunshade, parasol*, ἐξεπετάννυτο ὥσπερ σ. καὶ πάλιν ξυνήγετο Ar.*Eq.*1348, cf. *Av.*1508, 1550, Thphr.*HP*9.12.2; as a sign of effeminacy, καθήμενον ὑψηλῶς ὑπὸ σκιαδείῳ Pherecr.64, cf. Eup.445, Stratt.56. 2. a sort of *broad-brimmed hat*, like θολία, Sch.Theoc.15.38, Hsch. s.v. θολία. 3. *carriage with a tilt* or *hood*, Phot., Eust.613.43; *the tilt* itself, Lxx *Is.*66.20. 4. *umbel* of umbelliferous plants, Dsc.2.139; also, *flower-head* or similar part of other plants, Id.3.27, 49, 4.36, 173. 5. perh. *arbour*, Str.15.1.21. 6. perh. Dim. of σκιά, *shade*, Id.3.4.17.—The Mss. wrongly give σκιάδιον in Pherecr., Thphr., Dsc. ll. cc., Dem.Phal.*Fr.*5 J., etc.

**σκῐάδεύς**, έως, ὁ, = σκίαινα, Numen.ap.Ath.7.322f, Ruf.ap.Orib.*inc.*4.18, Hsch.

**σκῐᾱδηφορ-έω**, *carry a sunshade*, Ael.*VH*6.1: later σκιαδοφ-, Poll. 7.174. **-ος** (parox.), ον, (σκιάς) *carrying a sunshade*, of the daughters of μέτοικοι at Athens, who *carried sunshades* for the κανηφόροι in the Panathenaic procession, v.l. ib.134 (but σκιαδοφόροι ib.174). II. generally, *shading, shady*, Ael.*NA*16.18.

**σκῐᾰδίσκη**, ἡ, Dim. of σκιάδειον, παῖς Κύκης.. σ. φορεῖ γυναιξὶν αὔτως Anacr.21.13.

**σκῐᾰδο-φορέω, -φόρος**, v. σκιαδη-φορέω, -φόρος.

⊛ **σκῐάεις** [ᾰ], εσσα, εν, = σκιόεις, Hdn.Gr.1.239: contr. σκιᾶς, ᾶντος, Id.2.618.

⊛ **σκῐάζω**, S.*Fr.*776, etc.: fut. Att. σκιῶ (κατα-) Id.*OC*406: aor. ἐσκίασα Il.21.232, Hes.*Op.*613 (συ-), Luc.*Zeux.*5:—Pass., ἐσκιάσθην E.*Andr.* 1115 (v.l.), Arist.*Col.*792a22: pf. ἐσκίασμαι Semon.7.66: (σκιά):—*overshadow, shade, darken*, εἰς ὅ κεν ἔλθῃ δείελος ὀψὲ δύων σκιάσῃ δ' ἐρίβωλον ἄρουραν Il.21.232; Ἄθως σκιάζει νῶτα Λημνίας βοός S.*Fr.* 776; σ. τὰ ἡλιούμενα X.*Oec.*19.18; σ. ἔθειραν, with a chaplet, Simon. 148.4, cf. Semon.7.66; φάρεα.. περιβαλλομένα γένυσιν ἐσκίαζον E.*IT*1151 (lyr.), cf. *Hipp.*134 (lyr.): metaph., εὐθυμίᾳ σκιαζέτω νόημ' ἄκοτον Pi.*Pae.*1.2: abs., of the sun, *cast a shadow*, Arist.*Mete.*374b3; of the sun-dial, ὁ γνώμων σκιάζει τὴν ἕκτην *marks it by its shadow*, Alciphr.3.4:—Pass., *to be in shadow*, Arist.*Col.* l.c.; σκιάζεσθαι τοῖς ποσί, of the Σκιάποδες, Ctes.*Fr.*89. II. generally, *overshadow, cover*, κατὰ δ' ἐσκίασαν βελέεσσι Τιτῆνας Hes.*Th.*716; τὸ γένειον τὴν ἀσπίδα πᾶσαν σ. Hdt.6.117; σκιάσαι γένυν εὔξατο, i.e. prayed for a beard, *AP*12.26 (Stat. Flacc.):—Pass., ἐπεὶ δὲ τέκνων γένυς ἐμῶν σ. E.*Ph.*63. III. *shade* in painting, Luc.*Zeux.*5: metaph., Lib.*Or.* 13.17. IV. καῦμα σ. *keep off* the sun's heat, Alciphr.3.12.

**σκῐᾰθίς**, ίδος, ἡ, an unknown fish (perh. = σκίαινα), Epich.44.

⊛ **σκίαινα** [ῐ], ἡ, a sea-fish, prob. either *Corvina nigra* or *Umbrina cirrosa*, Arist.*HA*601b30.

**σκιαινίς**, ίδος, ἡ, = foreg., Gal.6.720, 724 (v.l. σκινίδες, etc.).

**σκῐᾰκός**, ή, όν, *shady*, Hdn.*Epim.*126. II. σ. ὡρολόγιον sun-dial, *IGRom.*4.293.35 (Pergam., ii B.C.).

**σκῐᾰμᾰχ-έω**, *fight against a shadow*, i.e. an imaginary opponent, and so, *spar*, Posidon.16 J., Plu.2.130e, Paus.6.10.3: πρὸς τὸν οὐρανὸν σκιαμαχῶν *sparring* with the sky, 'baying at the moon', Cratin. 17 (lyr.). II. metaph., Pl.*Ap.*18d; πρὸς ἀλλήλους Id.*R.*520c; πρὸς ἡμᾶς αὐτοὺς Id.*Lg.*830c; πρὸς τὸν οὐκέτι ἐν ζῶσιν ὄντα Πλάτωνα ἐσκιαμάχει Numen.ap.Eus.*PE*14.6:—Pass., ἔπη μάτην σκιαμαχούμενα *thrown out at random in disputations*, Luc.*Pisc.*35.—**σκιομαχέω** is a later form in codd. of Ph.1.356, Antyll.ap.Orib.6.29.3. **-ία**, ἡ, *a fighting against a shadow*: esp. *a form of exercise with hands and feet*, Ph.1.153. 2. metaph., *fighting with a shadow, mock-fight*, '*beating the air*', Cic.*Fam.*11.14.1 (pl.), Plu.2.514d, Eust.663.16; title of satire by Varro, Non.p.190 L.—**σκιομαχία** is a later form, Gal.6.146. **-ος** (parox.), ὁ, *one who fights against a shadow*, opp. ἀγωνιστής, Ph.1.199.

⊛ **Σκῐά-ποδες** [ᾰ], οἱ, *Shade-footed* or *Shady-feet*, a fabulous people in the hottest part of Libya, *with immense feet which they used as sunshades* as they reclined, Ar.*Av.*1553, cf. Sch. ad loc., Archipp.53, Ctes.*Fr.*89.

**σκῐᾰρόκομος**, ον, *with shading leaves*, ὕλη E.*Ba.*875 (lyr.).

**σκῐᾰρός**, ά, όν, v. σκιερός.

**σκῐ-άς**, άδος, ἡ, (σκιά) *canopy* or *arbour* (in form like a *sunshade*), Eup.445, Theoc.15.119, Demetr.Sceps.ap.Ath.4.141f, *AP*9.488 (Trypho, pl.), Plu.*Them.*16; of Dionysus (cf. σκιάδειον), Poll.7.174, Hsch. 2. esp. the θόλος at Athens, *IG*2².1013.39; ἐπὶ Σκιάδος warden of the Σ., ib.3.1041 (ii A.D.), 1051.22 (ii/iii A.D.), etc., cf. Ammon.ap.Harp. s.v. θόλος: also, *a rotunda* at Sparta in which the assemblies of the people were held, Paus.3.12.10. II. *umbel* of plants, Phanias ap.Ath.9.371d (σκίλλα cj. Wilamowitz). III. = ἀναδενδράς, Hsch. **-ᾰσις**, εως, ἡ, *shadowing, shade*, Strato Lampsacen.ap.Simp. *in Ph.*790.14. **-ασμα**, ατος, τό, *shadow cast*, τῆς γῆς, of eclipses, Gem.11.1, D.S.2.31, *Placit.*2.29.6, Vett.Val. 343.18. 2. *reflected image, shadow* in water, Callistr.*Stat.* 5. **-ασμός**, ὁ, = foreg. 1, Sch.Arat.872, Vett.Val.241.27. 2. a disease, perh. *specks before the eyes*, Id.210.5. 3. *visitation by a ghost* (σκιά), *PMag.Par.*1.2701. **-αστής**, οῦ, ὁ, Laconian epith. of Apollo, of dub. sense, Lyc.562. **-αστικός**, ή, όν, *shading, covering*, Sch.S.*OC*313. Adv. -κῶς Eust.1703.13. **-αστός**, ή, όν, *shaded*, γραμμαί Zos.Alch.p.233 B.

**σκῐᾱτρᾰφ-έω**, = σκιατροφέω (q.v.). **-ής**, ές, *brought up in the shade*, i.e. *leading a sedentary life*, Agath.1.7. **-ία**, ἡ, *a being brought up in the shade, sedentary, effeminate life*, Plu.*Aem.*31: pl., *effeminate habits*, Id.2.209c, D.S.20.62: **-τροφία** in Plu.*Thes.*23, *Lyc.*14 (v.l. -τραφ-), *Ages.*9 (vv.ll. -τραφ-, σκιοτροφ-), Poll.6.185 (v.l. -τραφ-), Gal.13.949.

**σκῐᾱτροφ-έω**, Ion. **σκῑητροφέω**; Att. also **σκιᾱτρᾰφέω** (v. infr.): (σκιά, τρέφω):—*rear in the shade* or *within doors*, i.e. *bring up tenderly*, σκιατροφοῦντες [τὰ σώματα] Max.Tyr.28.3:—Pass., *keep in the shade, shun heat and labour*, σκηνὰς πηξάμενοι ἐσκιητροφέοντο Hdt.6. 12; μὴ σκιατραφούμενος *Trag.Adesp.*546.8 (v.l. -τροφ-); καθῆσθαι καὶ σκιατραφεῖσθαι X.*Oec.*4.2, cf. Muson.*Fr.*11 p.59 H. (-τροφ-, v.l. -τραφ-); ἐσκιατραφημένη (v.l. -τροφ-) σωμάτων ἕξις Plu.2.8d; ὁπλίτας ἐσκιατροφημένους Max.Tyr.30.7; of a plant, σκιατροφούμενος *growing in the shade*, Thphr.*CP*2.7.4. II. intr. in Act., *wear a shade, cover one's head*, σκιητροφέουσι,.. τιάρας φορέοντες Hdt.3.12: hence also, like Pass., πλούσιος ἐσκιατροφηκώς a rich *effeminate* man, opp. πένης ἡλιωμένος one who bears all the heat of the day, Pl.*R.*556d. III. ἐσκιοτροφημένα f.l. for ἐσκιαγραφημένα in Suid. **-ία**, v. σκιατραφία. **-ίας**, ου, ὁ, = σκιατραφής, Poll.4.147, 6.185.

**σκιαυγέω**, (σκιά, αὐγή) *have dim sight, to be purblind*, from having as it were shadows before the eyes, Hp.*Int.*48 = *Dieb.Judic.*3.

**σκῐάω**, = σκιάζω, *overshadow, make shady*, Λῆμνον.. ἀκροτάτῃ κορυφῇ σκιάει A.R.1.604, cf. Arat.864, Nic.*Th.*30:—Pass., *to be shaded* or *dark*, δύσετό τ' ἠέλιος σκιόωντό τε πᾶσαι ἀγυιαί (Ep.3 pl. impf.) Od. 2.388, al., cf. Arat.600.

**σκίγγος** or **σκίγκος**, ὁ, *skink*, a kind of lizard found in Africa and the East, used in medicine, Dsc.2.66, cf. Aret.*CA*2.8 (κοσκίνου codd.), *CD*2.5 (σόγχος codd.). II. = μυρσίνη ἀγρία, Ps.-Dsc.4.144.

**σκιδαρόν**· ἀραιόν, Hsch.

**σκιδαφή**· ἀλώπηξ, *An.Ox.*2.302.

**σκίδνημι**, collat. form of σκεδάννυμι (q.v.), *disperse*, Heraclit.91, Aret.*SD*1.5, Plu.2.933d; used by Hom. in compd. διασκίδνημι. II. mostly Pass. σκίδναμαι, only pres. and impf., *to be spread* or *scattered, disperse*, freq. of a crowd or assembly, αὐτοὶ δ' ἐσκίδναντο κατὰ κλισίας τε νέας τε Il.1.487; ἐπὶ σφέτερα σκίδνασθαι Od.1. 274; ἐσκίδναντο ἑὴν ἐπὶ νῆα ἕκαστος Il.19.277; ἐπὶ νῆας ἕκαστοι ἐσκίδναντ' ἰέναι 24.2; σκίδνασθ' ἐπὶ ἔργα ἕκαστος Od.2.252; ἐσκίδναντο ἑὰ πρὸς δώμαθ' ἕκαστος ib.258; of foam or spray, ὑψόσε δ' ἄχνη σκίδναται Il.11.308; of a cloud of dust, ὕψι δ' ἀέλλη σκίδναθ' ὑπὸ νεφέων 16.375; of a stream, ἀνὰ κῆπον ἅπαντα σκίδναται Od.7.130; also ὀδμὴ σκίδνατο *h.Cer.*278; ὄψ σκιδναμένη Hes.*Th.*42; σκιδναμένα Simon.41 codd.Plu. (f.l. for κιδν-); σκιδναμένης ἐν στήθεσιν ὀργῆς f.l. in Sapph.27; σκιδναμένης Δημήτερος, i.e. at seedtime, in spring, Orac.ap.Hdt.7.142; ἅμα ἡλίῳ σκιδναμένῳ as the sun *began to spread his light*, i.e. soon after sunrise, Id.8.23; in Hp. of an odour, *to be dissipated*, *Loc.Hom.*2; of the distribution of τὸ πνεῦμα through the system, *Morb.Sacr.*7; also of the pupils, *to be dilated*, αἱ κόραι σκίδνανται Id.*Int.*48 = *Dieb.Judic.*3; elsewh. rare in Prose, Thphr. *Sens.*55, 56; εὐωδία ἐκ πηγῆς -αμένη Plu.2.941f (not found in good Att., except compd. ἀποσκίδναμαι in Th.6.98).

**σκιερός** or (less freq.) **σκιᾰρός**, ά, όν, (σκιά) *shady, giving shade*, ἐν νέμεϊ σκιερῷ Il.11.480; ἄλσος ὕπο σκιερόν Od.20.278; σκιαρόν τε φύτευμα Pi.*O.*3.18; σκιεροῖσιν ὑφ' ἔρνεσιν Ibyc.1.5; σκιερᾷ δάφνᾳ E.*IT*1246 (lyr.); ὦ σκιερὰ φυλλάς Id.*Fr.*308 (anap.); ὄρος σκιερόν Ar.*Av.*349 (lyr.); σκιεροῖσι πόθοισι longings *for the shade*, Opp.*H.*4.438. 2. *shady, in the shade*, σκιεροὺς θώκους Hes.*Op.*574; ἀπὸ σκιαρᾶν παγᾶν Pi.*O.*3.14; ἀνάπαυλαι σκιαραί Pl.*Lg.*625b. 3. *dark-coloured*, Gal.17(1).655; τὸ σ. μέλαν φαίνεται Arist.*Col.*791a23; σκιερῆς ἄνθος ὀπώρης *AP*6.154 (Leon. or Gaet.); φρίκῃ σ. θάλαττα Alciphr.1.17; κεῖται ὑπὸ σκιερὰν Σύρου κόνιν *IG*12(5).675.5 (Syros), etc. 4. *faint*, ἀστήρ Vett.Val. 6.9.

**σκιή, σκιητροφέω**, v. σκιά, σκιατροφέω.

**σκιθακός**, ὁ, a fish, = τράχουρος, Hsch.

**σκίλλα**, ης, ἡ, *squill, Urginea maritima*, Thgn.537, Arist.*HA*556b4, Thphr.*HP*7.9.4, Theoc.7.107, Dsc.2.171; used in purificatory rites, Hippon.5, Diph.126.3, Thphr.*Char.*16.14, *SIG*968 vi (Mytil., iii B.C.), D.Chr.48.17.

**σκιλλῑτικός**, ή, όν, (σκίλλα) *of squills*, ὄξος σ. vinegar *of squills*, Dsc.2.171, Archig.ap.Orib.44.26.11, etc.; sts. wrongly written σκιλλητικός:—also **σκιλλητικώδης**, ες (leg. σκιλλιτ-), = σκιλλιτικός, Gal.13.242; **σκίλλινος**, η, ον, Dsc.*Eup.*1.75, Archig.ap.Orib.8.1.32.

**σκιλλοκρόμμῠον**, τό, = σκίλλα, Sch.Theoc.5.121.

**σκιλλομᾰχία**, ἡ, *a fight with* σκίλλαι, name of a contest of ἔφηβοι, *Inscr.Prien.*112.91, 95 (i B.C.).

**σκίλλος**· ἰκτῖνος, Hsch.

**σκιλλώδης**, ες, *like squills*, φύλλον Thphr.*HP*9.18.3, cf. *CP*1.7.4, Dsc.2.170; of taste, Hices.ap.Ath.3.87c: Comp. -έστερος Diph. Siph.ib.121a.

**σκιμᾰλίζω**, *jeer at, flout*, τινα Ar.*Pax* 549; ῥηματίοις Id.*Ach.*444; σ. ποδί *kick*, D.L.7.17; expld. as Att. for καταδακτυλίζω by Moer. p.360 P., Phryn.*PS* p.83 B., cf. Sch.Ar. ll. cc.; also expld. by Sch.Ar. *Pax* l.c. as *to hold up the middle finger* (sens. obsc.). [The quantity of σκι- is not determined.]

**σκίμαλλος**, ὁ, *middle finger* (?), *PLond.*1821.308.

**σκιμβάδες**· ὕλη εὔθετος εἰς τοίχων ἐπίθεσιν, Hsch.

**σκιμβάζω**, *halt, limp*, Ar.*Fr.*853; cf. κιμβάζω, δκιμβάζω.

**σκιμβασμός·** φιλήματος εἶδος, Hsch. **σκιμβόλος·** ἠλίθιος, Id.

**σκιμβός**, ή, όν, *halt*, Hsch., cf. Sch.Ar.*Nu.*254.

**σκίμβρον**, τό, = σισύμβριον, *Gp.*12.35.

**σκιμπόδιον**, τό, Dim. of σκίμπους, Philem.26, Luc.*Asin.*3, etc.

⊛ **σκίμπους**, ποδος, ὁ, *small couch, pallet*, Ar.*Nu.*254,709, Pl.*Prt.*310c, X.*An.*6.1.4. II. a kind of *hammock* used by invalids travelling, Gal.6.150.

⊛ **σκίμπτομαι**, = σκήπτω, *press forward*, ἄροτρον σκίμψατο καὶ βόας Pi.*P.*4.224; cf. ἀποσκίμπτω. II. Pass., ἢν [τὸ ῥῆγμα] ἐς τὴν φλέβα σκιμφθῇ *fall* upon it, Hp.*Morb.*1.20. III. metaph., ἄστυ Λινδόθεν ἀρχαίῃ σκιμπτόμενον γενεῇ *boasting* its ancient descent from Lindus, Call.*Aet.Oxy.*2080.49.

**σκίμπων**, v. σκίπων.

**σκίναξ** [ῐ], ἄκος, ὁ, ἡ, *quick, nimble*, epith. of hares, σ. νεαροῖο λαγωοῦ Nic.*Th.*577; so ὁ σ., = λαγώς, Id.*Al.*67; cf. κίνδαξ.

**σκίνᾰρ** [ῐ], ἄρος, τό, *body*, Nic.*Th.*694; cf. σκῆνος II.

**σκινδάλᾰμος** [ᾰλ], Att. **σχινδάλᾰμος**, ὁ, *splinter*, in form **σχινδαλμός** Hp.*Mul.*2.133 (σκινδαλαμός, σχιδαλαμός, etc. in codd.); **σκινδαλμός**, Dsc.1.18. II. metaph., λόγων ἀκριβῶν σχινδάλαμοι *straw-splittings, quibbles*, Ar.*Nu.*130, cf. *Ra.*819, Luc.*Hes.*5; so σκινδαλμούς Alciphr.3.64:—cf. ἀνασχινδυλεύω.

**σκινδᾰλᾰμοφράστης**, ου, ὁ, *straw-splitter*, *AP*11.354 (Agath.).

**σκινδᾰλεύω**, = ἀνασταυρόω, Phot.

**σκινδάριον**, τό, an unknown fish, Anaxandr.27 (anap.).

**σκίνδᾰρος**, ὁ, *an indecent gesture*, Hsch., Phot.: hence the verbs **σκινδᾰρεύομαι, σκινθᾰρίζω, σκινθίζομαι**, Hsch.

**σκινδᾰφός**, ἡ, *she-fox, vixen*, Ael.*NA*7.47; cf. κίδαφος, σκιδαφή.

**σκινδαψ-ίζομαι**, βλιτυριζόμενον ἐρῶ σφυγμὸν καὶ -ιζόμενον coined as examples of meaningless jargon, Gal.8.662; cf. sq. **-ός**, ὁ, *a four-stringed musical instrument*, Anaxil.15, Theopomp.Coloph.ap. Ath.4.183a, cf. 14.636b. 2. *a word without meaning*, a '*what d'ye call it*', '*so-and-so*', Artem.4.2, S.E.*M.*8.133, Gal.7.348, Herm.*in Phdr.*p.180 A., St.Byz. s.v. Γαληψός:—in mock-heroic form, νοῦν δ' εἶχεν ἐλάσσονα **κινδαψοῖο** Timo 38. 3. = οἰκέτης, or name of an οἰκέτης, Gal.8.662. II. *an ivy-like tree*, Clitarch.17 J. III. κινδαψοί· ὄρνεα, καὶ ὄργανα κιθαριστήρια, καὶ Ἰνδοί, Hsch.

**σκίνδιον**, τό, = λεύκωμα, Lat. *album*, Theognost.*Can.*15.

**σκινδύλιον**, τό, *small piece of wood, shingle*, *SIG*671 *B*17 (Delph., ii B.C.): cf. σχινδύλη.

**σκινθαρίζω, σκινθίζομαι**, v. σκίνδαρος.

**σκινθός**, ὁ, *diver*, Thphr.*HP*4.6.9 (s.v.l.); rendered *naufragus* by Plin.*HN*13.137.

**σκινίς**, v. σκιαινίς. **σκιογράφος**, v. σκιαγράφος.

**σκῐο-ειδής**, ές, *shadowy*, σκιοειδέα φῦλ' ἀμενηνά Ar.*Av.*686 (mock-heroic); σ. φαντάσματα Pl.*Phd.*81d. 2. of colours, *dark*, καρποί Arist.*Col.*$795^{a}33$; cf. σκιώδης. **-εις**, εσσα, εν (neut. σκιόειν metri gr., A.R.2.404):—*shady, shadowy*, οὔρεα, ὄρεα σ., *shady*, i.e. *thickly wooded*, mountains, Il.1.157, Od.7.268, Pi.*P.*9.34; μέγαρα σ. *dark chambers*, Od.1.365, 4.768; ὄρθρον ὑπὸ σκιόεντα the morning twilight, Tryph.236. 2. Act., νέφεα σ. *overshadowing* clouds, Il.5.525, Od.8.374, etc. II. *unsubstantial*, of a reflection in a mirror, and of the shadow on a sun-dial, τύπος *AP*6.20 (Jul.), 9.807; κέρδος ὀνείρου ib.11.366 (Maced.).

**σκῐοθηρ-έω**, *observe shadows*, of astronomers, Hsch. s.v. φρέαρ ὀρύττειν. **-ης**, ου, ὁ, *sun-dial*, Vitr.1.6.6. **-ικός**, ή, όν, *of a sun-dial*, γνώμονες Str.2.5.24; διὰ τῶν σ. (sc. ὀργάνων) *sun-dials*, Cleom.1.8. **-ιον**, τό, Dim. of sq., Sch.Luc.*Lex.*2. **-ον**, τό, = σκιοθήρης, Plu.*Marc.*19, D.L.2.1: as Adj., ἀπὸ τῶν . . σ. ὀργάνων Ptol.*Geog.*1.2.2.

**σκῐό-θρεπτος**, ον, *nurtured in the shade*, φῦλα Cerc.6.8. **-μαντεία**, ἡ, *invocation of departed spirits*, *Gloss.* **-μαχέω, -μαχία**, v. σκια-. **-ποιέω**, = σκιάω, Sch.D Od.2.388. **-πρυμνον**, τό, *tent* or *awning on the stern*, *PSI*5.533.19 (iii B.C.). **-πρῳρον**, τό, *tent* or *awning on the prow*, ibid. **-τροφέω, -τροφία**, v. σκια-.

**σκίουρος** [ῐ], ὁ, (οὐρά) prop. *shadow-tail*, i.e. *squirrel*, Opp.*C.*2.586; cf. Plin.*HN*8.138.

**σκῐο-φᾰνής**, ές, *shadowy, phantom-like*, Eust.1699.8. **-φόρος**, ον, *shadow-bringing*, *Gloss.* **-φως**, ωτος, τό, *twilight*, formed like λυκόφως, Hld.5.27. **-ψυκτος**, ον, *cooled* or *dried in the shade*, Sch. Nic.*Th.*97,692, Maxim.ap.Lyd.*Mens.*4.14.

**σκίπτω**, given as etym. of σκίφος and ξίφος, Sch.Il.1.220; cf. **σκίπει·** νύσσει, Hsch.; **σκίψαι·** ὀκλάσαι, Ἀχαιοί, Id.

⊛ **σκίπων**, ωνος, ὁ, (σκίμπτομαι) = σκῆπτρον, *staff*, Hdt.4.172, E.*Hec.*65 (anap.), Cratin.239, Ar.*V.*727; *crutch*, Hp.*Art.*52, $IG4^{2}$(1).121.111 (Epid., iv B.C.); σ., γεροντικὸν ὅπλον Call.*Epigr.*1.7, cf. *Iamb.*1.134.—The form **σκίμπων** occurs as v.l. in Hdt. l.c., E. l.c., etc.; **σκήπων** v.l. in *AP*6.293 (Leon.), 294 (Phan.), 7.65 (Antip.), Call.*Epigr.* l.c., etc., recognized also by Hdn.*Epim.*127, Theognost.*Can.*34.

**Σκίρα** [ῐ], τά, *festival of Athena celebrated by Athenian women on the 12th of* Σκιροφοριών, Ar.*Th.*834, *Ec.*18,59, Pherecr.231, Philoch.204, Men.*Inc.*p.99 Koerte, $IG2^{2}$.1177.10, 1358 ii 30,51, Polyaen.3.10.4; τῇ δωδεκάτῃ τῶν Σ. on the twelfth of Σκιροφοριών, $IG2^{2}$.2773.13; prob. = Σκιροφόρια (q.v.); confused with Ὠσχοφόρια by Aristodem.ap.Ath.11.495f.

**Σκιράδιον** [ᾰ], τό, name of a promontory on Salamis, Plu.*Sol.*9.

**σκῑραίνω**, *harden* iron by tempering, Sch.S.*Aj.*651 (Pass.).

**Σκιράς**, άδος, ἡ, old name of Salamis, Str.9.1.9. II. title of Athena in Salamis, Hdt.8.94; in Phalerum, Str. l.c., Paus.1.1.4, 1.36.4; at Σκῖρον or Σκίρον, Poll.9.96.

⊛ **σκῑρᾰφ-εῖον** (in codd. sts. σκιράφιον), τό, *gambling-house*, Isoc.7.48, 15.287, Theopomp.Hist.221. **-ευτής**, οῦ, ὁ, *dice-player*, Amphis 25. ⊛ **-ος**, ὁ, *dice-box*, *EM*717.28: metaph., *trickery, cheating*, Hippon.86. **-ώδης**, ες, *tricky, swindling*, *AB*101 (where σκιραπ-).

**σκῑρία**, ἡ, = σκῖρος 2, Aret.*CD*1.14 (τῆς σκιρρίης codd.).

**Σκιρίδαι** [ῐδ], οἱ, *worshippers* or *priests of Artemis* Σκιρίς, *GDI*5498.3 (Milet., iii B.C.).

**σκῑρίδιον**, τό, a name of the fish βασιλίσκος, Sch.Opp.*H.*1.129.

**Σκιρίς**, ίδος, ἡ, title of Artemis at Miletus, *GDI*5498.3 (iii B.C.).

**Σκῑρῖται**, οἱ, *the Scirites*, a light-armed division of the Spartan army, named from the town Σκῖρος in Arcadia, Th.5.67,68,71, X.*HG*5.2.24, *Lac.*12.3, etc.: also **Σκιρίτης** λόχος D.S.15.32. II. Σκῑρῖται, οἱ, *inhabitants of* Σκιρῖτις II, St.Byz.

**σκῑρίτης**, ὁ, (σκῖρος) *worker in stucco*, Zonar. (σκιρρ-).

**Σκῑρῖτις** (sc. γῆ), ιδος, ἡ, *the district of Laconia near the Arcadian town* Σκῖρος, Th.5.33, X.*HG*7.4.21, *SIG*665.31 (Olympia, ii B.C.). II. = ἡ δωδεκάπολις τῆς Καρίας, St.Byz.

**σκίρον** [ῐ], τό, *the large white sunshade* which was held by the Eteobutadae over the heads of the priestess of Athena and the priests of Poseidon and Helios in the procession from the Athenian Acropolis to a place called Σκῖρον or Σκίρον (q.v.) in a festival of Athena (cf. Σκίρα), Lysimachid.23; *white parasol* carried by the priest of Erechtheus in the festival of Athena Σκιράς on the 12th of Σκιροφοριών, Sch.Ar.*Ec.*18.

**Σκῖρον** or **Σκίρον**, τό, a suburb of Athens, Ἀθηναῖοι τρεῖς ἀρότους ἱεροὺς ἄγουσι, πρῶτον ἐπὶ Σκίρῳ Plu.2.144a; named after the seer Σκῖρος, Paus.1.36.4, cf. Hsch. s.v. Σκειρόμαντις; ἐπὶ Σκίρῳ ἱεροποιία Str.9.1.9; ἐκύβευον ἐπὶ Σκίρῳ ἐν τῷ τῆς Σκιράδος Ἀθηνᾶς νεῴ Poll.9.96, cf. Eust.1397.25; a district of brothels and the like, Alciphr.3.8,25, St.Byz.; cf. foreg.

**σκῖρον**, τό, *rind* of cheese, Eup.277, Ar.*V.*925 (also = λατύπη, used as cement, acc. to Sch.Ar. l.c. (921)). 2. *ingrained dirt*, Cratin.444. II. *scar*, glossed by σκίρρον, Tz.*H.*5.702.

**σκῑρόομαι**, Pass., *to be* or *become indurated*, Hp.*Mul.*2.155,156, *Nat.Mul.*24,36, Sor.2.39; *to be ingrained*, πρὶν τὰν νόσον εἰς τὸν μυελὸν σκιρωθῆναι (-θῆμεν Ahrens) Sophr.33; νοσήματα ἐσκιρωμένα χρόνῳ D.Chr.7.137 (σκιρρ-, σκυρ- are vv.ll. in Hp. and Sor. ll.cc.).

**σκῑρός**, ά, όν, *hard*, of tempered iron, Sch.S.*Aj.*651; *cancerous*, νοσήματα Them.*Or.*8.110c: metaph., σκιροὺς θεούς (v.l. for σκληρούς) Plu.2.421d (ap.Eus.*PE*5.5, σκιρρούς ap.Theodoret.); σ. γέροντες dub. cj. for σκληροί in Longus 2.14.

**σκῖρος**, ὁ, *hard* (perh. *chalk*) *land overgrown with bushes, scrub*, *Tab.Heracl.*1.19; τῶν ξύλων . . τῶν ἐν τοῖς σ. ib.144; = πυρρώδης (ῥυπώδης cj. Mein.) γῆ acc. to Philet.ap.Hsch.; σκ[ε]ίρα (leg. σκῖρα)· . . χωρία ὕλην ἔχοντα εὐθετοῦσαν εἰς φρύγανα, Hsch.; σκ[ε]ῖρος· . . ἄλσος καὶ δρυμός, Id. (but opp. δρυμός, *Tab.Heracl.* ll.cc.); ἠὲ σ. ἔην, νῦν αὖ θέτο τέρματ' Ἀχιλλεύς Il.23.332,333 as shortd. into one line by Aristarch. (here = ῥίζα, διὰ τὸ ἐσκιάσθαι acc. to Sch.T ad loc.). 2. *hardened swelling* or *tumour, induration*, Hp.*Mul.*1.18 (τὸν σκῖρον [σκίρρον codd.] σκῦρον ὀνομάζει Erot. s.v. σκυρωθῶσι), Sor.2.7 (σκύρου cod.), 9 (σκύρον cod.), 56, Gal.11.736, Aret.*CD*1.14 (σκίρρος codd.). 3. **σκίρρος**, = γύψος, Suid. (cod. A in marg.); also **σκίρρα**, = γῆ λευκή, ὥσπερ γύψος, Id. (written **σκίρα** Id. s.v. σκίρος); γῆ **σκιρράς**, Sch.Ar.*V.*921.

⊛ **Σκίρος** or **Σκῖρος**, ὁ, name of a μάντις, Philoch.42. II. Σκῖρος, ἡ, a town in Arcadia, St.Byz.; cf. **Σκιρῖται, Σκιρῖτις**.

**Σκῐροφόρια**, τά, name of a festival, prob. = Σκίρα, Hsch., Phot., Suid. s.v. Διὸς κῴδιον; written **Σκιρροφορία**, Sch.Luc.*DMeretr.*2.1.

**Σκῐροφοριών**, ῶνος, ὁ, *Scirophorion*, the 12th Attic month, the latter part of June and former part of July, so called from the festival Σκιροφόρια, $IG1^{2}$.304.81, Antipho 6.42, Arist.*HA*$543^{b}7$, $575^{b}16$, Thphr.*HP*4.11.5, $IG2^{2}$.1358 ii 30,51, etc.

**σκιρράς, σκίρρος**, v. σκῖρος 3. **σκίρρον, -ρρός, -ρρόομαι, -ρρων, -ρρωσις**, v. σκιρ-.

**σκιρτ-άω**, Ion. -έω Opp.*C.*4.342:— Frequentat. of σκαίρω, *spring, leap, bound*, of young horses, αἱ δ' ὅτε μὲν σκιρτῷεν ἐπὶ ζείδωρον ἄρουραν . ., ἀλλ' ὅτε δὴ σ. ἐπ' εὐρέα νῶτα θαλάσσης Il.20.226,228; πῶλοι ἐσκίρτων φόβῳ E.*Ph.*1125; of goats, Theoc.1.152; of the Bacchae, E.*Ba.*446; ὀρχεῖσθε καὶ σ. καὶ χορεύετε Ar.*Pl.*761, cf. *V.*1305; ἄλλεσθαι καὶ σ. Pl.*Lg.*653e: also of wind, σκιρτᾷ δ' ἀνέμων πνεύματα πάντων A.*Pr.*1085 (anap.). 2. metaph., *to be skittish, unruly*, E.*Fr.*362.31, Pl.*R.*571c, etc. **-ηδόν**, Adv. *by leaps* or *bounds*, *Orac.Chald.*298. **-ηθμός**, ὁ, = σκίρτησις, Orph.*L.*220. **-ημα**, ατος, τό, *bound, leap*, esp. of restive or frightened animals, ἐμμανεῖ σ. ᾖσσον A.*Pr.*675, cf. 599 (lyr.); ποδῶν σκιρτήματα ἔλαυνε E.*HF*836, cf. *Hec.*526, etc. **-ηματικῶς**, Adv. *skittishly*, Sch.E.*Ph.*1127. **-ησις**, εως, ἡ, *bounding, leaping*, Plu.*Cleom.*34, 2.1091d. 2. *rioting, uproar*, σκιρτήσεις ἐθνῶν ib.341f. **-ητής**, οῦ, ὁ, *leaper*, Σάτυρος Mosch.*Fr.*2.2; Πάν Orph.*H.*11.4; Κουρῆτες ib.31.1; of Dionysus, *AP*9.524.19. **-ητικός**, ή, όν, *skittish, unruly*, Plu.2.12b, Corn.*ND*20.

**σκιρτο-πόδης**, ου, ὁ, *spring-footed*, Σάτυρος *APl.*1.15*. **-ποιέω**, *make to leap*, Quint.*Ps.*28(29).6; Aq. σκιρτώσει.

⊛ **Σκίρτος**, ὁ, *Leaper*, name of a Satyr, *AP*7.707 (Diosc.), Nonn.*D.*14.111; Σκίρτοι, attendants of Dionysus, Corn.*ND*30.

**σκιρτών**, ῶνος, ὁ, *wanton*, ἄνδρες Eun.*Hist.*p.259 D.

⊛ **σκῑρ-ώδης**, ες, *of a hard nature, callous*, Poll.4.203, Gal.6.527. II. 'obstinate', of epilepsy, Id.11.374. **-ωμα**, ατος, τό, = σκῖρος 2, Dsc.1.1 (σκιρρ-); f.l. for σκλήρωμα in Poll.4.198.

**Σκίρων** [ῑ], ωνος, ὁ, Attic name for the wind *which blew from the Scironian rocks* in the Isthmus of Corinth, Arist.*Vent.*973b19 (written Σκίρρων), Thphr.*Vent.*62, Str.1.2.20, 9.1.4, *CIG*518 (i B.C.); but it is *a north-west wind*, like Ἀργέστης, in Arist.*Mete.*363b25. II. a mythical robber who haunted the rocks between Attica and Megara, killed by Theseus, X.*Mem.*2.1.14, Pl.*Tht.*169a, etc.; Σκίρωνος ἀκτή or ἀκταί the coast near these rocks, S.*Fr.*24.6, E.*Hipp.*1208; the adjacent sea was **Σκιρωνικὸν** οἶδμα θαλάσσης, Simon.114.3; the rocks themselves **Σκιρωνίδες** πέτραι, E.*Hipp.*979, *Heracl.*860, Str.1.2.20, 9.1.4; without πέτραι, Plb.16.16.4; written Σκιρρωνίδες in Arist.*Vent.* l.c.; Σκιρωνὶς ὁδός the road from Athens to Megara, Hdt.8.71. (Σκίρων is thus written on vases, Kretschmer *Griech. Vaseninschr.*p.133; Σκειρ– (codd. Simon., etc.) and Σκιρρ– are misspellings.)

**σκίρωσις**, εως, ἡ, *induration, cirrhosis*, Sor.2.36 (σκίρρ–), Gal.11.726 (σκίρρ–); *scirrosis*, = *duritia sine dolore, Gloss.*

**σκῑτᾰλίζω**, *to be lustful*, ἐσκιτάλιζε prob. cj. for ἐσκυτ– in Longus 3.13.

**Σκίτᾰλοι** [ῐ], οἱ, name of demons of lewdness (perh. fictitious, cf. Σκίτων) in Ar.*Eq.*634, cf. Sch. ad loc. (631), Hsch.

**Σκίτων**, ὁ, *Feeble*, Pherecr.232; name of a fuller said to be ridiculed by Ar.*Eq.*(634), Sch.Ar.*Eq.*631.

**σκιφᾱτόμος**, ὁ, *cutter of palms for* ψίλινοι στέφανοι (cf. ψιλινοποιός), *IG*5(1).212.63 (Sparta, i B.C.): cf. σκιφίνιον and κίφος.

**σκίφη** [ῐ], ἡ, (σκιφός) = κνιπεία, Crantor ap. D.L.4.27:—also **σκιφία**, ἡ, Hsch. s.v. κιμβεία.

**σκῐφίας**, ου, ὁ, Dor. for ξιφίας, *sword-fish*, Epich.58, Hsch.

**σκῐφίζω**, Dor. for ξιφίζω, Hsch.

**σκῐφίνιον**· πλέγμα ἐκ φοίνικος, Hsch.

**σκίφος** [ῐ], εος, τό, dialectal form of ξίφος, *sword*, Sch.D.T. p.203 H., Sch.Il.1.220, *EM*718.11, etc. 2. = τὸ αἰδοῖον, Hsch.

**σκιφός**, ἡ, όν, = κνιπός, Suid. (s.v.l.).

**σκῐφύδριον**, τό, Dor. for ξιφύδριον, Epich.42.

**σκῐώδης**, ες, *shady*, πέτρα E.*Supp.*759; χωρία Thphr.*HP*9.18.2. 2. of weather, *dark, gloomy*, Hp.*Epid.*3.2; of colours, *dark*, Arist.*Col.*793b5. Adv. –δῶς Ps.-Alex.Aphr. *in Metaph.*440.9, Eustr. *in EN*104.6.

**σκιώδιον**, perh. neut. of **σκιώδιος**, α, ον, = foreg. 2, στρῶμα σ. ἕν *Sammelb.*7033.38 (v A.D.).

**σκῐωτός**, ή, όν, *striped*, cf. σκιά; σ. ζώνη *Peripl.M.Rubr.*24, cf. *POxy.*921.15 (iii A.D.).

**σκλῆμα**, ατος, τό, *dryness, hardness, induration*, Gal.19.139 (prob. cj. for σκήλημα).

**σκλῆναι**, v. σκέλλω.

**σκληρᾰγωγ-έω**, *bring up hardy*, Andron 4 J.; ἑαυτόν J.*AJ*10.10.2; τὰς θυγατέρας Luc.*DMar.*6.1:—Pass., Nic.Dam.*Fr.*103 (aa) J., Anon.Vat.64. 2. metaph., σ. τὴν λέξιν *make it harsh* or *austere*, D.H.*Th.*30. **–ία**, ἡ, *hardy training*, Λακωνική Ph.2.482, cf. Hsch.

**σκληρ-άργιλλος**, ον, *of* or *with hard clay*, *Gp.*9.4.5. **–ᾱσία**, ἡ, *hardening*, κασσιτέρου *PLeid.X.*81. **–αύχην**, ενος, ὁ, ἡ, *stiff-necked, unmanageable*, prop. of horses, Ph.1.114, Plu.2.2f: metaph., Ph.2.528. **–ευνία**, Ion. **–ίη**, ἡ, *the use of a hard bed*, v.l. for σκληροκοιτίη, Hp.*Vict.*3.68. **–ία**, ἡ, = σκληρότης, *hardness*, Plu.2.376c codd.; opp. μαλακία σώματος, Phld.*Mus.*p.30 K. 2. *an induration*, Dsc.2.72, Herod.Med.ap.Orib.5.27.3, Aret.*SD*1.13, etc. **–ίᾱσις**, εως, ἡ, *induration of the eyelid*, Gal.14.770.

**σκληρό-βῐος**, ον, *leading a hard life*, Tz.*Proll.Hes.*p.13 G.; **–βίοτος**, ον, Phryn.*PS*p.107 B. **–γεως**, ων, *with a hard soil*, ἡ σ. (sc. γῆ) Thphr.*Fr.*30. **–γνώμων**, ον, gen. ονος, *hard-hearted*, Sch.Hes.*Op.*146 (Moschop.). **–δερμος**, ον, *with hard skin*, Arist.*HA*558a4, al.: τὰ σ. *crustacea*, ib.490a2, *PA*657b30, al. **–δίαιτος** [ῐ], ον, *of a hard, austere way of life*, Ph.2.163. **–ειδής**, ές, *of hard nature* or *kind*, Hsch. s.v. ἶπες. **–θριξ**, ὁ, ἡ, gen. τρῐχος, *with hard, coarse hair*, opp. μαλακόθριξ, Arist.*Phgn.*806b16; πρόβατα Id.*GA*783a14. **–καρδία**, ἡ, *hardness of heart*, Lxx *Je.*4.4, *Ev.Marc.*16.14. **–κάρδιος**, ον, *hard-hearted, stubborn*, Lxx *Pr.*17.20, *Ez.*3.7. **–κέφᾰλον**, τό, a kind of *spider*, Philum.*Ven.*15.4. **–κηρος**, ον, *overlaid with hard wax*, δέλτοι Zeno *Stoic.*1.67. **–κοίλιος**, ον, *costive*, Dsc.5.19, Aët.7.10. **–κοιτέω**, (κοίτη) *sleep on a hard bed*, Hp.*Salubr.*4. **–κοιτία**, Ion. **–ίη**, ἡ, = σκληρευνία, Thphr.*Lass.*2, and v.l. for σκληρευνίη (q.v.) in Hp. **–κοκκος**, ον, *with hard seeds*, ῥόαι Antiph.59. **–λέκτης**, ου, ὁ, *harsh-speaking*, Sch.Ar.*Nu.*1370. **–πᾰγής**, ές, *firmly put together, hard*, Xenocr.ap.Orib.2.58.18. **–παίκτης**, ου, ὁ, (παίζω) *clown*, Hippoloch.ap.Ath.4.129d (–πέκται cod.). **–ποιέω**, *harden*, Xenocr.ap.Orib.2.58.53 (Pass.). **–ποιός**, όν, *making hard, hardening*, Plu.2.953c. **–πους**, πουν, gen. ποδος, ὁ, ἡ, *hard-footed, Gloss.* **–πρόσωπος**, ον, *hard, bold of face*, Lxx *Ez.*2.4 cod.A (also Thd.ibid.).

**σκλῆρος**· νόσημά τι ἀραχνίδων ἐν τοῖς σμήνεσι, πρὸς τὸ σήπεσθαι τὰ κηρία, Hsch.

**σκληρός**, ά, όν, also Dor., Pi.*O.*7.29, Epich.[288], hyperdor. **σκλᾱρός** Ti.Locr.104c:—*hard*, opp. μαλακός in all senses: I. *hard* to the touch, ξύλον σ. ἢ μαλακόν Thgn.1194; ἐλαία Pi. l.c.; γῆ A.*Pers.*319, cf. X.*Oec.*16.11; κοίτη Pl.*Lg.*942d, etc. 2. of sound, *harsh*, σκληρὸν ἐβρόντησε Hes.*Th.*839; βρονταί Hdt.8.12; ἡ φωνὴ σκληροτέρα Arist.*Aud.*801b38, al. 3. of taste and smell, *harsh, bitter*, σ. ὕδατα (springing from a rocky soil) Hp.*Aër.*1; so σκληρότατος ἀὴρ καὶ τόπος Plb.4.21.5; of wine, *dry*, Ar.*Fr.*579, Dsc. *Alex.Praef.*; ὀσμαί Thphr.*CP*6.14.12 (Comp.): metaph., σ. φράσις D.H.*Pomp.*2. 4. *stiff, unyielding*, opp. ὑγρός (lithe and supple), τιτθία σ. καὶ κυδώνια Ar.*Ach.*1199; σκληρότεροι μαστοί Arist.*PA*688a27; σκέλη X.*Eq.*1.6; τί τὸ ὑγρὸν τοῦ χαλινοῦ καὶ τί τὸ σ. ib.10.10; of the hair (cf. σκληρόθριξ), Arist.*HA*517b11 (Comp.), al.; σ. δέρμα, σάρξ, Id.*PA*665a2, *Phgn.*806b22, etc.; of persons, Pl.*Tht.*162b, *Smp.*196a, Plu.*Ages.*13, Luc.*Salt.*21; of dogs, X.*Cyn.*3.2; τράχηλος ib.5.30; οἱ τὸ σῶμα σ. Arist.*Pr.*873a34, al. 5. κοιλίη σ. *costive*, Hp.*Aph.*3.25, cf. Arist.*PA*670b9. 6. of light, *strong*, ἐν σ. αὐγῇ ἢ μαλακῇ Id.*Col.*793b17. 7. of a wind, *strong*, *Ep.Jac.*3.4, Poll.1.110, Ael.*NA*9.57. II. metaph., 1. of things, *hard, austere*, μὴ τὰ μαλακὰ μῶσο, μὴ τὰ σ. ἔχῃς Epich. l.c.; τροφή S.*OC*1615; δίαιται E.*Fr.*525.5; βίος Men.522; τὰ σ. *hard words*, S.*OC*1406; σ. συμφοραί E.*Fr.*684.3; σκληρὰ μαλθακῶς λέγων S.*OC*774; τόνος ἀπηνὴς καὶ σ. Plu.*Phoc.*2; τὸ σ. = σκληρότης, ἡ δίαιτα.. ὑπερβάλλει ἐπὶ τὸ σ. Arist.*Pol.*1270b33. 2. of persons, *harsh, austere, cruel, stubborn*, S.*Fr.*24.7, Pl.*Tht.*155e, Ti.Locr. l.c.; σ. ἀοιδός, of the Sphinx, S.*OT*36; σ. γὰρ αἰεί E.*Alc.*500; ὦ σ. δαῖμον Ar.*Nu.*1264; τοὺς τρόπους σκληρός Id.*Pax*350; ἄγροικοι καὶ σ. Arist.*EN*1128a9; σ. ψυχή S.*Aj.*1361, *Tr.*1260 (anap.); σ. ἄγαν φρονήματα Id.*Ant.*473; ἦθος Pl.*Smp.*195e; σ. θράσος *stubborn courage*, E.*Andr.*261. III. Adv., –ρῶς καθῆσθαι, i.e. *on a hard seat*, Ar.*Eq.*783; εὐνάζεσθαι X.*Cyn.*12.2. 2. *hardly, with difficulty*, E.*Fr.*282.9. 3. *harshly, obstinately*, σ. διαμάχεσθαι Pl.*Lg.*629a; ἀπειλεῖν ib.885d; τὰ μαλακὰ σ. καὶ τὰ σκληρὰ μαλακῶς λέγειν Arist.*Rh.*1408b9; σ. αὐλεῖν Id.*Aud.*803a20. (Prob. cogn. with σκέλλω.)

**σκληρό-σαρκος**, ον, *with hard flesh*, Arist.*HA*486b9, *de An.*421a25, Phylotim.ap.Gal.6.727, Xenocr.ap.Orib.2.58.24, al. **–στομος**, ον, *hard-mouthed*, of horses, Poll.1.197, Sch.S.*El.*724. II. *hard to pronounce*, σῖγμα Aristox.ap.Ath.11.467a.

**σκληρ-όστρᾰκος**, ον, *hard-shelled*, Arist.*HA*528b2.

**σκληροσωμᾰτος**, ον, *with a hard body*, Alex.Aphr.*Pr.*1.120.

**σκληρότηρ**, Eretrian for σκληρότης acc. to Pl.*Cra.*434c: but final –ς is preserved in Eretrian inscrr., only medial –σ– becoming –ρ–.

**σκληρότης**, ητος, ἡ, *hardness*, opp. μαλακότης, Pl.*R.*523e, Arist.*PA*644b14, al. 2. of taste, *harshness*, οἴνου Thphr.*CP*6.14.12. 3. *stiffness, rigidity*, Arist.*Pr.*881a10. 4. ἡ τῆς κοιλίης σ. *costivity*, Hp.*Aër.*7. II. of persons, *harshness, austerity*, τοῦ δαίμονος Antipho 3.3.4; σ. καὶ ἀγροικία Pl.*R.*607b, cf. 410d; παράδειγμα σκληρότητος Arist.*Po.*1454b14.

**σκληροτράχηλος** [ᾰ], ον, *stiff-necked*, Lxx *Ex.*33.3, al., Aesop.318, *Act.Ap.*7.51; cf. σκληραύχην:—hence **σκληροτρᾰχηλέω**, Hsch. s.v. Τελχιτένοντες, Phot. s.v. Τελχιταίνει, *EM*751.36.

**σκληρό-τρῐχος**, ον, = σκληρόθριξ, πρόβατον Gal.4.605. **–τῠχής**, ές, *having hard luck*, Vett.Val.89.12, Salač and Škorpil *Několik Archeol.Památek z Východního Bulharska* 57 (Mesembria).

**σκληρουργ-ία**, ἡ, *work in hard materials*, Vett.Val.12.2, 48.32. **–ός**, ὁ, apparently, *one of a corps of masons* in the Roman army, *Sammelb.*4411, cf. Vett.Val.3.7; = *silicida, Gloss.*

**σκληρ-ουχία**, ἡ, f.l. for σκληροῦ λίαν in J.*AJ*8.8.2. **–οφθαλμία**, ἡ, *hardness of the eyes, blepharitis marginalis*, Dem.Ophth.ap.Aët.7.76, *PMed.Strassb.* p.6, Paul.Aeg.3.22. **–όφθαλμος**, ον, *having hard dry eyes*, opp. ὑγρόφθαλμος, Arist.*HA*505b1, *PA*648a17, al., Thphr.*Sens.*36; also σ. ὄμματα Arist.*HA*526a9.

**σκληρό-φῠής**, ές, *of hard, harsh nature, tough*, Xenocr.ap.Orib.2.58.16. **–φυλλος**, ον, *with hard leaves*, Thphr.*HP*3.9.2 (Comp.). **–ψῡχος**, ον, *hard-hearted*, Sch.rec.A.*Pr.*242.

**σκληρόω**, *harden*, in Pass., Xenocr.ap.Orib.2.58.28.

**σκληρ-υντικός**, ή, όν, *hardening*, Dsc.1.39, Gal.11.710. **–ύνω**, *harden*, opp. μαλάσσω, Hp.*Acut.*45, Arist.*HA*548b23:—Pass., with pf. ἐσκλήρυσμαι Hp.*Liqu.*6, and –υμμαι, *to be hardened, grow hard*, Id.*VM*22, Thphr.*Lap.*11. 2. metaph., σ. τὴν καρδίαν τινός *harden his heart*, Lxx *Ex.*7.3, al., *Ep.Hebr.*3.8, cf. *Ep.Rom.*9.18:—Pass., Lxx *Si.*30.12. **–υσμα**, ατος, τό, = σκλήρωμα, Hp.*Coac.*559. **–υσμός**, ὁ, *hardening, induration*, Id.*Prorrh.*1.19, cf. *Coac.*98, Antyll.ap.Orib.45.15.5. **–ώδης**, ες, contr. for σκληροειδής, Man.4.325, cj. for ὀχληρώδης in Lucil.ap.Gell.18.8. **–ωμα**, ατος, τό, *induration*, Hp.*Epid.*4.38, Poll.4.198 (v.l. σκίρωμα), Orib.45.7.1. **–ωσις**, εως, ἡ, *hardening*, μολίβου *PLeid.X.*1 (σλ– Pap.); κασσιτέρου ib.24.

**σκληφρός**, ά, όν, (prob. from σκέλλω) *slender, slight, thin*, Pl.*Euthd.*271b, and prob. l. in Arist.*Somn.Vig.*457a29, *Pr.*954a7; of a woman, Theopomp.Com.58.

**σκλοιός**, ά, όν, = σκολιός, Hdn.Gr.1.109.

**σκνήφη**, ἡ, = ἀκαλήφη, Hsch. s.v. κνίδαι.

**σκνῑπαῖος**, α, ον, (σκνιπός (B)) v.l. for σκνιφαῖος in Theoc.16.93.

**σκνῑπολογέω**, *catch fleas*, Ar.Byz.*Epit.*120.16 (prob. cj., συνιπ– cod. D).

**σκνῑπός** (A), ή, όν, *niggardly, stingy*, Anon. *in EN*182.27, Hsch.; **σκνιφός**, Phryn.376, cf. Moer.p.387 P.

**σκνῑπός** (B), ή, όν, *dim-sighted*, ἢ τυφλὸς ἤ τις σκνιπός Semon.19; **σκνιφός**, Hsch. (who also cites **σκνίφος**· τὸ σκότος); cf. ὑπόσκνιφος, –σκνιπος.

**σκνῑποφάγος** [ᾰ], ον, *eating* σκνῖπες, Arist.*HA*593a3.

**σκνίπτω**, *pinch, nip*, Hsch. (Akin to σκνίψ; cf. σκηνίπτω.)

**σκνῑφαῖος**, α, ον, (cf. σκνιπός (B)) *dark*, σ. ὁδίτας a wanderer *in the twilight*, Theoc.16.93 (v.l. σκνιπαῖος).

**σκνῑφός**, ή, όν, v. σκνιπός (A); **σκνίφος**, v. σκνιπός (B).

**σκνίψ**, ὁ, gen. σκνῑπός: nom. pl. σκνῖφες Lxx *Ex.*8.16(12), al., but σκνῖπες *Ps.*104(105).31; acc. σκνίπας [ῑ] Ezek.*Exag.*135:—an insect found under the bark of trees, eaten by the woodpecker, Arist.*HA* 614b1, *Sens.*444b12 (in both places with v. l. κνίψ, which is the form used by Thphr.), Plu.2.636d: from its quick jump comes the prov., ὁ σκνὶψ ἐν χώρᾳ '*a flea* at home!' Stratt.70, Zen.5.35:—an insect which attacks vines, Gal.12.186. (Cf. Slav. *sknipa* 'gnat'.)

**σκοβαδές**· ἔδεσμά τι, Hsch. **σκογχούλας**· γογγυσμούς, τονθ⟨ο⟩ρυσμούς, Id. **σκοίδιον**, τό, = σκιάδειον, Id.

❀ **σκοῖδος** (for which **κοῖδος** is wrongly given by codd. of Arc.47), ὁ, Maced. for διοικητής or ταμίας, Poll.10.16, Hsch., Phot.: as epith. of Dionysus, Men.*Kith.Fr.*9.

**σ[κ]οίθης**· διάβολος, Ἀττικοί, λάλος, στωμύλος, Hsch.: cf. σοίθης and ψοίθης.

**σκοίκιον**, τό, a *vessel* or *receptacle* of some kind, *Riv.Fil.*1928.263 (Cyrene, iv B.C.), *PTeb.*45.41 (ii B.C.), *UPZ*89.17 (ii B.C.), *PUniv. Giss.*10 i 19 (ii/i B.C.).

**σκοιός**, ά, όν, *shady*, restd. by Schneid. in Nic.*Th.*660, from the Sch. (who explains the vulg. σκαιοῖς by σκιεροῖς, ἀνηλίοις) and Hsch.

**σκοῖπος**, ὁ, *wall-plate* of a building, Hsch. **σκοίψ**· ψώρα, Id. **σκόλακες**, οἱ, (σκολιός) in Lat. form *scolaces*, = *funalia*, *Gloss.* ❀ **σκόλεφραι**· κατακεκαυμέναι τὰς τρίχας, Hsch.

**σκολῐ-άζω**, *to be crooked*, σ. ταῖς ὁδοῖς *walk in crooked* ways, Lxx *Pr.*14.2. **-αίνομαι**, Pass., *grow crooked*, -αίνεται ῥάχις Hp.*Art.*47 (cf. Gal.18(1).553); ἐς τὸ ἔσω σ. οἱ σφόνδυλοι ib.48.

**σκολῐό-βουλος**, ον, *of crooked counsel*, *AB*329, Suid. s. v. ἀγκυλομήτης. **-γραπτος**, ον, *marked with oblique lines*, Arist.*Fr.*297. **-δ[ει-ρ]ος**, ον, *with crooked neck*, dub. rest. in *IG*5(2).443.43 (Megalop., ii/i B.C.). ❀ **-δρόμος**, ον, of the moon, *going in an oblique orbit*, Orph.*H.*51.4, Man.4.478. **-θριξ**, τρῐχος, ὁ, ἡ, *with curled hair*, Nonn.*D.*15.137; *with crisp leaves*, ἄκανθα *AP*4.1.37 (Mel.). **-καυλος**, ον, *with crooked* or *slanting stalk*, Thphr.*HP*7.8.2.

❀ **σκόλιον**, τό, prop. neut. of σκολιός (sc. μέλος), *song which went round crookedly at banquets*, being sung to the lyre by the guests one after another in irregular order, the singer holding a myrtle-branch (μυρρίνη) passed to him by the previous singer, ᾆσον δή μοι σ. τι λαβὼν Ἀλκαίου Ἀνακρέοντος Ar.*Fr.*223, cf. Arist.*Pol.*1285a38, Ath.15.694a; the word first in Pi.*Fr.*122.11 (cf. Aristox.*Fr.Hist.*66, Ath.13.573f); examples in B.*Scol.Oxy.*1361, Bergk *PLG* iii pp.643 sqq., cf. Ar.*Ach.*532, *Ra.*1302, *V.*1222, Pl.*Grg.*451e (cf. Sch. ad loc.); τὰ Ἀττικὰ ἐκεῖνα σ. Ath.15.693f. (The name was variously expld.: (a) from σκολιός *crooked*, because of the *crooked* order of the singers, the bad singers being passed over, or the couches being crookedly arranged, Dicaearch.Hist.43, Aristox.*Fr.Hist.*59, Plu.2.615c, Sch. Pl. l. c. (b) later, the omission of the bad singers being ascribed to the difficulty or non-social character of the songs (cf. Plu.2.615b), σκόλιον was derived from δύσκολον or δυσκολία, Hsch., Sch.Ar.*V.* 1217; or it was said that the songs were easy, but appeared difficult to drunken revellers, Procl. in Phot.*Bibl.*p.321 B.; or were called difficult κατ' ἀντίφρασιν, Procl. l. c., Suid.)

**σκολῐόομαι**, Pass., *to be bent*, *crooked*, Hp.*Art.*41; of plants with crooked roots, Thphr.*HP*1.6.4; of the pulse, ἐσκολιωμένος Gal.19. 410.

**σκολῐο-πλᾰνής**, ές, *darting aslant*, κεράσται Nic.*Th.*318. **-πλόκᾰμος**, ον, *with twisted locks* or *curls*, Nonn.*D.*26.65. **-πόρος**, ον, *with winding passages*, ὦτα S.E.*P.*1.126.

**σκολιός**, ά, όν, *curved*, *bent* (opp. ὀρθός, εὐθύς), σ. σίδηρος Hdt.2.86; σ. σκίπωνι E.*Hec.*65 (anap.); of rivers and paths, *winding*, ποταμός Hdt. 1.185, cf. 2.29; Μαίανδρος σ. εἰς ὑπερβολήν Str.12.8.15; οἶμος, ἀτραπός, etc., A.R.4.1541, Nic.*Th.*478, etc.; ῥηγμῖνες Arist.*Mete.*367b14; λαβύρινθος Call.*Del.*311; πλέγμα ἕλικος *AP*7.24 (Simon.); πλοκαμῖδες Nonn.*D.*14.182; *twisted*, *tangled*, βάτος *AP*7.315 (Zenod. or Rhian.), cf. 11.33 (Phil.); ἐς τὸ σ. Hp.*Art.*37. 2. *bent sideways*, δουλείη κεφαλὴ σκολιή Thgn.536; γένυες Pi.*Fr.*203; ἵππος σ. *crooked made* or *going askew*, Pl.*Phdr.*253d. II. metaph., *crooked*, i.e. *unjust*, *unrighteous*, θέμιστες Il.16.387; μῦθοι, δίκαι, Hes.*Op.*194,221; αἱ σκολιὰν (sc. ῥήτραν) ὁ δᾶμος ἕλοιτο, Spartan law ap.Plu.*Lyc.*6; λόγος Thgn.1147; ἀπάται Pi.*Fr.*213; πατέων ὁδοῖς σκολιαῖς Id.*P.*2.85; *riddling*, *obscure*, ῥημάτια Luc.*Bis Acc.*16; τὸ σ. τῆς εἰσόδου (into true science) Vett.Val.250.23: rarely of men, ἰθύνει σκολιόν makes *the crooked one* straight, Hes.*Op.*7; σ. καὶ φοβερός Plu.2.551f: with Verbs, σκολιὰ φρονεῖν, opp. εὐθὺς ἔμμεν, *Scol.*16; σ. πράττειν Pl.*Tht.* 173a; τυφλὰ καὶ σ. Id.*R.*506c, cf. *Grg.*525a; σκολιά, τά, *indirect methods*, Cic.*Att.*13.39.2. Adv. σκολιῶς Hes.*Op.*258,262; σ. ἔχοντος τοῦ χρησμοῦ D.S.16.91; εἰς πλάγια καὶ σκολιά Pl.*Tht.*194b. III. σκολιόν, τό, *intestine*, σπλάγχανα καὶ νεφρὸν καὶ σκολιόν *SIG*1002.5 (Milet., v/iv B.C.), cf. *Schwyzer* 721.23 (Mycale, iv B.C.), al.

**σκολῐότης**, ητος, ἡ, *crookedness*, σ. τῆς καμπῆς, of a Parthian bow, Plu.*Crass.*24: in pl., *the windings* of a stream, Str.10.2.19; of *windings* generally, Id.12.8.15. II. metaph., *inequality*, σκολιότητα ἔχειν *to be unequally affected*, Hp.*Acut.*(*Sp.*)22. 2. of men, *crookedness*, *dishonesty*, Lxx *Ez.*16.5.

**σκολῐό-φρων**, ὁ, ἡ, gen. ονος, (φρήν) *of crooked mind*, Hp.*Ep.*17; cf. σκολιόβουλος. **-χειλος**, ον, gloss on ἀγκυλόχειλος, *AB*329.

**σκολῐ-ώδης**, ες, *crooked-looking*, Apollon.*Lex.* s.v. παιπαλόεντος. **-ωμα**, ατος, τό, *bend*, *curve*, Str.2.4.4, 4.3.3. **-ωπός**, όν, (ὤψ) *looking askew*, and generally *oblique*, Max.3: neut. pl. as Adv., Man.4.78. **-ωσις**, εως, ἡ, *obliquity*, ῥινός, τραχήλου, Sor.*Fract.*11, Gal.17(2).709 (pl.), etc.

**σκολλέ**· σκυμμόν, Hsch.

**σκόλλυς**, υος, ὁ, *fringe of hair*, Dsc.*Eup.*2.97, Poll.2.30, *Lex.Rhet.* ap.Eust.1528.20, Hsch., cj. in Alcm.44; σκόλλυν ἀποκείρειν Pamphil. ap.Ath.11.494f.

**σκολλῡφόρος**, ον, *wearing a* σκόλλυς, Hsch. s. v. κοννοφόρων. **σκολοβράω**, *to be displeased*, *vexed*, Id. **σκολοῖς**· δρεπάνοις, Id.

**σκολόπαξ**, ᾰκος, ὁ, prob. = ἀσκαλώπας, Arist.*HA*614a33, prob. cj. for σπάλακα in Thphr.*Sign.*49. [*scolŏpax* in Nemesian.*Aucup.*21.]

❀ **σκολόπενδρ-α**, ἡ, *scolopendra*, *millepede*, Arist.*HA*489b22, 532a5, al.; classed with ἴουλος, ib.523b18, cf. Gal.*UP*3.2, Dsc.*Eup.*2. 128. 2. *the sea-scolopendra*, perh. an animal of the genus Nereïs or Aphrodite, Arist.*HA*505b13, 621a6, Ael.*NA*7.26, Gal.12.366, Opp. *H.*2.424. **-ειος**, α, ον, *of* or *like the scolopendra*, dub.l. in Nic.*Th.*684 (where -δρῖοιο from -δριον, lengthd. metri gr., is prob.). **-ιον**, τό, = ἄσπληνος (v. ἄσπληνον I; so called from a fancied likeness to the scolopendra), Dsc.3.134, cf. 4.50. 2. = σαξίφραγον, Ps.-Dsc.4.16 p.182 Wellm. 3. = πολυπόδιον, ib.186. **-ον**, τό, *hart's tongue*, *Scolopendrium officinale*, Thphr.*HP*9.18.7. **-ώδης**, ες, *like a scolopendra*, of a hill that throws out a number of spurs (πρόποδες), Str.13.1.5.

**σκολοπ-ηΐς** μοῖρα, ἡ, the fate *of one impaled*, Man.4.198. **-ιά**, v. σκαλοπιά. **-ίζω**, *protect by palisades*, νησία ἐσκολοπισμένα *Stad.* 115. **-ιον**, τό, Dim. of σκόλοψ I. 3, Antyll.ap.Orib.50.5.4. ❀ **-ισμός**, ὁ, *impaling*, Vett.Val.127.26.

**σκολοπο-ειδής**, ές, *pointed like a pale*, ἄκανθα Dsc.1.101. **-μᾰχαίριον**, τό, *a pointed surgical knife*, Gal.2.682, 10.1011, Paul.Aeg.6.74.

**σκολοπώνυμον**· τὸν στ(αυ)ρώσιμον, Hsch. ❀ **σκολοφρή**· κατακεκαυμένη, Id. **σκόλοφρον**· θρανίον, Id.

**σκόλοψ**, οπος, ὁ, *anything pointed*: esp. *pale*, *stake*, κεφαλὴν πῆξαι ἀνὰ σκολόπεσσι Il.18.177; for impaling, E.*IT*1430, *El.*898; ἐπὶ σκόλοψι ἀναρτᾶσθαι D.S.33.15: pl. σκόλοπες, *palisade*, τείχεα.. σκολόπεσσιν ἀρηρότα Od.7.45; freq. in Il., ἐν δὲ [τάφρῳ] σκόλοπας κατέπηξαν 7.441; διά τε σκόλοπας καὶ τάφρον ἔβησαν 8.343, cf. 12.63, 15. 344; σκόλοπας περὶ τὸ ἕρκος κατέπηξαν Hdt.9.97, cf. E.*Rh.*116, X. *An.*5.2.5 (Att. usually σταύρωμα). 2. *thorn*, *IG*4²(1).121.92 (Epid., iv B.C.), Lxx *Nu.*33.55, al., Dsc.4.49, Babr.122; σκόλοπες φοίνικος *PMag.Osl.*1.270, al., cf. 2 *Ep.Cor.*12.7. 3. *an instrument for operating on the urethra*, Heliod.ap.Orib.50.9.4. 4. *point of a fishing-hook*, Luc.*Merc.Cond.*3. II. *tree*, E.*Ba.*983 (lyr.).

**σκόλυβος**· ὁ ἐσθιόμενος βολβός, Hsch. **σκολύβρα**· ἡ σκυθρωπή, Id.; cf. σκολοβράω, σκολύφρα.

**σκολύθριον**, τό, *stool*, cj. for κόλυθρον in Telecl.3:—Dim. **σκολύθριον**, τό, Pl.*Euthd.*278b, Poll.3.90, 10.48.

**σκόλυθρος**, ον, *low*, *mean*, *shabby*, Phot., Suid.

**σκόλῠμ-ος**, ὁ (ἡ Numen.ap.Ath.9.371c; σκόλυμον, τό, Zonar.), *golden thistle*, *Scolymus hispanicus*, Hes.*Op.*582, Alc.39, *Com. Adesp.* in *PTeb.*693.21, Thphr.*HP*6.4.3, Arist.*Pr.*879a28. 2. = κυνόγλωσσον, Ps.-Dsc.4.127. **-ώδης**, ες, *like a* σκόλυμος, φύλλον Thphr.*HP*7.4.5, cf. 9.12.2.

**σκολύπτω**, = κολούω, κολοβόω, ἐκτίλλω, Hsch. ❀ **σκολύφρα**· σκυθρωπή, σκληρά, ἐργώδης, δυσχερής, Id.; cf. σκολύβρα. **σκομβρίζω**, = γογγύζω, Id., Phot.; also, = ῥαθαπυγίζω, Hsch.

**σκομβρίς**, ίδος, ἡ, Dim. of sq., Hsch.; v.l. for σκορπίς, Arist.*HA* 543b5.

**σκόμβρος**, ὁ, *mackerel*, *Scomber scomber*, Epich.62, Arist.*HA*571a 12, 597a22, 610b7, *PCair.Zen.*6.1 (iii B.C.); caught in the Hellespont, Hermipp.63.5, cf. Ar.*Eq.*1008.

**σκόμιον**, τό, *projecting coping*, *eaves*, Sch.Arat.971.

**σκονδάμνα**, = ῥάφανος, Hsch. **σκόνδρον**· δρυπτόν, ἢ δρύπτει, Id. **σκονθύλλω**, *murmur*, *mutter*, Phot.

**σκόνυζα**, ἡ, Att. for κόνυζα, Pherecr.167. **σκοπαῖος**, v. σκωπαῖος.

**σκοπ-άρχης**, ου, ὁ, *chief scout*, *leader of a reconnoitring party*, X. *Cyr.*6.3.6. **-άω**, = σκοπιάζω, Ar.*Fr.*854. **-εῖα**, τά, Astron., *instruments of observation*, Procl.*Hyp.*4.48.

**σκοπελίζω**, *plant boundary-stones* on a man's land to warn him against tilling it, Ulp. in *Dig.*47.11.9:—hence **-ισμός**, ὁ, ibid.

**σκοπελο-δρόμος**, ον, *running over rocks*, βασσαρίς *AP*6.74 (Agath.). **-ειδής**, ές, *rocky*, νησίδια Sch.Pi.*P.*4.370.

**σκόπελ-ον**, τό, *mound*, Lxx 4*Ki.*23.17. **-ος**, ὁ, prop. *lookout-place*: hence *peak*, *headland*, *promontory*, Hom., esp. in Od., 12.73, 80,430, al.; προβλὴς σ. Il.2.396; φάραγγος σ. ἐν ἄκροις A.*Pr.*143 (lyr.); σ. πέτρας E.*Ion* 274; Θηβᾶν σ., of the Theban acropolis, Pi. *Fr.*196; ἐμοὶ (sc. Κρεούσης) σ., of the Athenian, E.*Ion* 871 (anap.), cf. 1434,1578; σ. νιφόεντα Μίμαντος Ar.*Nu.*273 (anap.). II. *watch-tower*, *PLips.*70.2 (ii A.D.), etc. **-ώδης**, ες, = σκοπελοειδής, νησίδιον Sch.Theoc.13.22.

**σκόπ-ευσις**, εως, ἡ, *look-out*, Aq.*Ho.*5.1. **-ευτής**, οῦ, ὁ, = σκοπός I. 2, Id.*Is.*52.8, al., Eust.810.25. **-εύω**, = σκοπέω, X.*Eq.Mag.*7.6, Lxx *Jb.*39.29, al., D.S.3.25, Str.11.11.8; v.l. in Hdt.1.8: the correct word is ἀποσκοπεῦσθαι acc. to *AB*435. **-έω**, used by early writers only in pres. and impf. Act. and Med. (v. infr. II), the other tenses being supplied by σκέπτομαι (q. v.):—but in later writers we find fut. σκοπήσω, Anon.*Prog.* in Rh.1.615 W., Gal.*UP*3.10 (f. l.), (ἐπι-) Babr. 103.8, (κατα-) Hld.5.4: aor. ἐσκόπησα Thphr.*Sign.*1 (προ-), Plb. *Fr.*54 (s. v. l.) (περι-), Lib.*Or.*12.28, etc.: and of Med., aor. ἐσκοπησάμην (περι-) Luc.*VH*1.32: pf. ἐσκόπημαι (προαν-) J.*AJ*17.5.6: (cf. σκέπτομαι):—*behold*, *contemplate* (rather of particulars than of universals, of which θεωρέω is more commonly used, but οἱ τὸν ἥλιον ἐκλείποντα θεωροῦντες καὶ σκοπούμενοι Pl.*Phd.*99d), ἄστρον Pi.*O.*1.5; πλοῦν μὴ 'ξ ἀπόπτου μᾶλλον ἢ 'γγύθεν σκοπεῖν S.*Ph.*467, cf. E.*IA*490;

τὰ πόρρω Id.*Rh*.482; τὰ ἔμπροσθεν X.*An*.6.3.14(17); *examine, inspect*, καταθεῖναί τι..σκοπεῖν τῷ βουλομένῳ *IG*12(5).480 (Athenian law, v B.C.); σ. παραγραφάς *PLips*.38 ii 2 (iv A.D.): abs., ἄλλοσε σ. S.*El*.1474; σκοπεῖτε *look out, watch*, A.*Supp*.232, etc.: folld. by a clause, σ. ὅπου.. S.*Ph*.16; σ. ποῦ.. X.*Cyr*.3.2.1, etc.: folld. by a Prep., σ. εἰς.. E.*Fr*.812.6, Pl.*Plt*.305b. **2.** metaph., *look to* or *into, consider, examine*, τὰ ἑωυτοῦ σ. *look to* one's own affairs, Hdt.1.8; τὸ σεαυτοῦ Pl.*Phdr*.232d; τὸ ὑμέτερον Antipho 4.2.8; καιρόν Th.4.23; τὸ συμφέρον Pl.*R*.342b sq.; τὸ πρὸς ποσί S.*OT*130; τοὺς νόμους πρὸς τοὺς τῇδε with reference to the laws here, Pl.*Ti*.24a; τι πρὸς ἐμαυτόν Id.*Euthphr*.9c: abs., σκοπῶν εὕρισκον ἴασιν S.*OT*68, cf. *Ph*.282: folld. by an acc. and interrog. clause, or μή.., σ. τὴν τελευτὴν κῇ ἀποβήσεται Hdt.1.32, cf. S.*Ph*.506, *OT*407: folld. by an interrog. clause alone, σ. πόθεν χρὴ ἄρξασθαι And.1.8; σ. εἰ.. S.*Ant*.41, Pl.*Lg*.862a (Med.); ὅπως.. X.*Cyr*.2.2.26: sts. c. gen. pers. as well as acc. or clause, σκόπει δὴ τόδε αὐτῶν Pl.*Tht*.182a; πρῶτον αὐτῶν ἐσκόπει πότερα.. X.*Mem*.1.1.12: folld. by a Prep., ἐξ ὧν ἀγγέλλουσι σκοποῦντες λογιεῖσθε τὰ εἰκότα Th.6.36, cf. 1.1, X.*An*.3.1.13; πρὸς τὸ ἄρχειν σκοπῶν λογίζομαι Id.*Cyr*.1.6.8; σ. τὰ λοιπὰ πρὸς ὑμᾶς αὐτούς Antipho 1.31; ἀνομολογούμενοι πρὸς ἀλλήλους Pl.*R*.348b; τόδε περὶ αὐτοῦ ib.351b, etc.; τὴν ὀρθολογίαν περί τι Id.*Sph*.239b: with Adv., abs., ὀρθῶς σ. E.*Ph*.155; καιρίως Id.*Rh*.339; ἄμεινον Pl.*Smp*.219a. **3.** *look out for*, παῦλαν X.*An*.5.7.32; τι ἀγαθόν Id.*Hier*.9.10; νεώσοικον Ar.*Ach*.96; ἐσκόπει γυναῖκά μοι Is.2.18, cf. D.*Ep*.2.11; σ. ὄνομα κάλλιον αὐτῇ Plu.2.991f. **II.** Med., used like Act. I.1 (perh. implying a more deliberate consideration), c. acc., E.*IT* 68, *Hel*.1537; τένοντ' ἐς ὀρθὸν ὄμμασι σκοπουμένη Id.*Med*.1166. **2.** = I.2, S.*OT*964; σ. τύχας βροτῶν E.*Fr*.262: folld. by relat., σ. τίνι τρόπῳ.. Pl.*Smp*.176b, cf. Th.8.48: περί τινος Pl.*Prt*.353a, X.*Hier*.1.10: abs., ἔνεστι τοῖσιν εὖ σκοπουμένοις ταρβεῖν.. S.*Tr*.296. **3.** = I.3, ὅτανπερ ἀδικεῖν ἐπιχειρῶσιν, ἅμα καὶ τὴν ἀπολογίαν σκοποῦνται Isoc.21.17. **III.** rarely in Pass., σκοπῶν καὶ σκοπούμενος ὑπ' ἄλλων *considering and being considered*, Pl.*Lg*.772d; ὁ λόγος..αἰσχρὸς τοῖς σκοπουμένοις is disgraceful *in the very matter considered*, D.20.54 (s.v.l., τοῖς σ. secl. Dobree). ⊛ **-ή**, ἡ, = σκοπιά, *lookout-place, watch-tower*, A.*Supp*.713: pl., Id.*Ag*.289,309, X.*Cyr*.3.2.11, etc.; *observatory*, Str.2.5.14, 17.1.30; = θυννοσκοπεῖον, σ. δαμοσία *SIG*1000.10 (Cos, ii B.C.). **II.** *look-out, watch*, πατρὸς σκοπαί A.*Supp*.786 (lyr.), cf. Lyc.1311; σκοπὰς ποιεῖσθαι ἀπὸ δένδρων D.S.3.26, cf. Luc.*Hist.Conscr*.29. **-ήσεις**· σκέψεις, Hsch. **-ητέον**, *one must examine* or *consider*, *Gp*.7.15.1, Sever.*Clyst*.p.17 D., Aët.7.9. **-ιά**, Ion. **-ιή**, ἡ, *lookout-place*, in Hom. esp. a *hill-top*, σκοπιὴν εἰς παιπαλόεσσαν Od.10.97; ἀπὸ σκοπιῆς εἶδεν Il.4.275, Od.4.524; ἥμενος ἐν σκοπιῇ Il.5.771; ὀπτῆρας δὲ κατὰ σκοπιὰς ὤτρυνα νέεσθαι each to his *lookout-place*, Od.14.261; ἄγγελος..ἀπὸ τηλαυγέος φαινόμενος σ. Thgn.550; *watch-tower*, Hdt.2.15; ὥσπερ ἀπὸ σ. μοι φαίνεται Pl.*R*.445c. **2.** *peak, height*, of Cithaeron, Simon.130; of Athos, S.*Fr*.237 (anap.); Ἰλιὰς σ., of the Trojan acropolis, E.*Hec*.931 (lyr.), cf. *Ph*.233 (lyr.), Ar.*Nu*.281 (lyr.), etc.; Θάσου σκοπιαί *JHS*29.93: metaph., Pi.*N*.9.47:—σκοπιαί personified as women (Oreads), Philostr.*Im*.2.4. **II.** *look-out, watch*, σκοπιὴν ἔχειν to keep *watch*, Od.8.302; οὔ κῃ πρόσω σ. ἔχοντες τούτων Hdt.5.13; κρυπταὶ σ. X.*Eq.Mag*.4.10; σκοπιὴν φυλάσσειν Arat.883. ⊛ **-ιάζω**, (σκοπιά) poet. Verb, almost always pres. and impf., *spy from a high place* or *watch-tower*, Il.14.58, Q.S.2.6: generally, *spy, watch*, even on a plain, Od.10.260. **2.** *watch for shoals of fish*, applied to certain members of a guild of Isis-worshippers, *IGRom*.1.817.8 (Callipolis). **II.** trans., *spy out, watch*, c. acc., Il.10.40, *AP*9.606, etc.:—Med., *look out for, watch*, τὼς θύννως Theoc.3.26; νῆα A.R.2.918, etc.: aor. σκοπιασάμενος Callicrat.ap. Stob.4.28.18. **-ιήτης**, ου, ὁ, (σκοπιά) *highlander*, epith. of Pan, *AP*6.16 (Arch.), 34 (Rhian.), 109 (Antip.). (Glossed κατάσκοπος by Suid.) **-ιμος**, ον, (σκοπός II) *suitable to a purpose*, Iamb.*Comm. Math*.7, Procl. *in Alc*. p.9 C., *in Prm*. p.487 S., Simp. *in Ph*.882.2 (all Sup.). **-ιωρέομαι**, *look out for, watch*, Hermipp.95, Ar.*V*.361, X.*Cyn*.9.2, Philostr.*Im*.1.13. **-ιωρός**, ὁ, *watcher*, ibid., restd. in Alciphr.1.17. **-ός**, ὁ (also ἡ, Od.22.396, Call.*Del*.66): (σκέπτομαι): —*one that watches, one that looks about* or *after* things, παρὰ δὲ σκοπὸν εἷσεν Il.23.359; γυναικῶν δμῳάων σ. ἐσσι, of a housekeeper, Od. l. c.: in Pi., of gods and kings, c. gen. loci, *guardian, protector*, Ὀλύμπου σ. *O*.1.54; Δάλου 6.59; Μαγνήτων σ., of Peleus, *N*.5.27; τὸν ὑψόθεν σ., φύλακα βροτῶν A.*Supp*.381 (lyr.); also σκοποὶ τῶν εἰρημένων S.*Ant*.215. **b.** *one who watches* or *looks out* to take advantage, Od.22.156; *watchful, jealous master*, S.*Aj*.945. **2.** mostly, *lookout-man, watcher*, stationed in some high place (σκοπιά) to overlook a country, esp. in war, Il.2.792, Od.16.365, X.*Cyr*.3.2.1, 4.1.1, etc.; hence Ἠέλιον..θεῶν σ. ἠδὲ καὶ ἀνδρῶν *h.Cer*.62: also, *game-watcher*, X.*Cyr*.1.6.40. **3.** *spy, scout*, Il.10.324, 526, 561 (later κατάσκοπος); σ. καὶ κατοπτῆρας στρατοῦ ἔπεμψα A.*Th*.36, cf. E.*Tr*.956; of *a messenger who has been sent to learn tidings*, S.*OC*35, cf. *Ph*.125; σκοπός, ναῶν κατόπτας E.*Rh*.557 (lyr.). **II.** *mark* or *object on which one fixes the eye*, σκοπὸν ἄλλον, ὃν οὔ πώ τις βάλεν ἀνήρ, εἴσομαι αἴ κε τύχωμι Od.22.6; ἀπὸ σκοποῦ away from *the mark*, 11.344; ἀπὸ σ. εἰρηκέναι, εἰρῆσθαι, Pl.*Tht*.179c, X.*Smp*.2.10; παρὰ σκοπόν Pi.*O*.13.94; σκοπῷ ἐπέχειν τόξον to aim at *it*, ib.2.89; σκοποῦ ἄντα τυχεῖν Id.*N*.6.27; ἔκυρσας ὥστε τοξότης..σκοποῦ A.*Ag*.628; ὥστε τοξόται σκοποῦ, τοξεύετ' ἀνδρὸς τοῦδε S.*Ant*.1033; ἄθλιον σκοπὸν ἐμοὶ ἀκοντίσας Antipho 3.3.6; ἐπὶ σκοπὸν βάλλειν X.*Cyr*.1.6.29; παραλλάξαι τοῦ σ. καὶ ἁμαρτεῖν Pl.*Tht*.194a; ἀποτυγχάνω τοῦ σκοποῦ Id.*Lg*.744a. **2.** metaph., *aim, end, object*, οὗτος...δοκεῖ ὁ σ. εἶναι πρὸς ὃν βλέποντα δεῖ ζῆν Id.*Grg*.507d; τὴν ἡδονὴν σ. ὀρθὸν πᾶσι ζῴοις γεγονέναι Id.*Phlb*.60a; στοχάζεσθαι σκοποῦ Id.*R*.519c; σ. τυραννικὸς τὸ ἡδύ Arist.*Pol*.1311$^a$4, etc.; σκοπός .. *nihil praebere* 'his little game' is to make no allowance, Cic.*Att*.15.29.2, cf. Arg. II Ar.*Eq*. **b.** Medic., of healing, ἐπὶ τῷ πρώτῳ σ. by first *intention* (i.e. direct union), κατὰ δεύτερον σ. by second *intention* (i.e. granulation or scar tissue), Gal.1.387, cf. 10.162. **3.** *contest in shooting at a mark*, σ. ἱππέων, πεζῶν, *IG*9(2).527.16,18 (Larissa). **III.** name of *a dance*, Eup.446.

⊛ **σκοραδᾶν** (gen. pl.), prob. = σκόρδων, *Docum. Ant. dell'Africa Italiana* 1.139 (Cyrene).

**σκορᾰκ-ίζω**, *bid* one *go* ἐς κόρακας (cf. κόραξ), *dismiss contemptuously*, Phld.*Vit*.p.15 J., Luc.*Rh.Pr*.16:—Pass., *to be treated contemptuously*, D.11.11, Plu.*Art*.27; σ. εἰς χῶρον ἀσεβῶν Ph.1.139. **-ισμός**, ὁ, *contumely*, Lxx *Si*.41.19, Plu.2.467e. **-ιστέον**, *one must reject with contempt*, Ph.1.267.

**σκορδάζειν**· σπᾶσθαι, Hsch. **σκορδαμυκτέω**, = σκαρδ- (so cod., but out of order), Id.

⊛ **σκορδᾶτον**, *alliatum, Gloss.*

⊛ **σκορδ-ευτής**, οῦ, ὁ, *worker in the garlic fields*, *BGU*1504.6 (iii B.C.). **-ίζω**, *to be like garlic*, τῇ ὀσμῇ Dsc.3.111.

**σκορδῑν-άομαι**, Ion. **-έομαι**, Med., *stretch one's limbs, yawn, gape*, properly of men or dogs half roused from sleep, Hp.*Superf*.20, cf. Poll.5.168; hence also of a person tired or bored, στένω, κέχηνα, σκορδινῶμαι Ar.*Ach*.30; σ. καὶ δυσφορεῖς Id.*Ra*.922, cf. *V*.642. **-ημα**, ατος, τό, *stretching*, Hp.*Epid*.2.3.1; also **-ησμός**, ὁ, ib.6.5.1 (**-ισμός** codd., as in Gal.17(2).244).

⊛ **σκόρδ-ιον**, τό, *garlic germander, Teucrium Scordium*, Dsc.3.111, Gal.12.125. **2.** σ. μέγα, = σίνηπι ἄγριον, Ps.-Dsc.2.154. [ῐ, Androm.ap.Gal.14.39.] **-οειδής**, ές, *like garlic*, Dsc.3.47. **-ον**, τό, = σκόροδον, Crates Theb.4.5 D., *IG*$2^2$.1184.15 (iv B.C.), *PSI*4.332.6 (iii B.C.), *PTeb*.717.5 (ii B.C.), Lxx *Nu*.11.5, Phld.*Po*.2.52, Dsc.2.152, *IG*3.73.10, *Edict.Diocl*.6.23, *Gp*.12.8.8, etc.: prov., μὴ σκόρδου (sc. φάγω) 'anything for a quiet life', prob. in Cic.*Att*.13.42.3; cf. σκόροδον: codd. of Thphr. have both σκόρδον (*HP*1.10.7, al.) and σκόροδον (1.6.9, al., *Od*.63):—Dim. **σκορδόνιον**, τό, Dsc.*Eup*.2.119; **-ονίαν** καλοῦσιν οἱ Ῥωμαῖοι Orib.ap.Aët.11.10 (s.v.l.). **II.** ἡ ἀνθρωπίνη κόπρος ἐστὶν τὸ λεγόμενον σκόρδον *PHolm*.9.26.

**σκορδό-πρᾰσον, -φᾰγία, -φόρος**, v. σκοροδ-.

**σκορδύλη** [ῡ], ἡ, *a young tunny-fish*, Arist.*HA*571$^a$16; cf. κορδύλη III.

**σκόρθοι**· τόρνοι σκορωβροί, Hsch. **σκόρνος**· κόρνος, μυρσίνη τὸ φυτόν, Id. **σκορόβυλος**· κάνθαρος, Id.

**σκοροδ-άλμη**, ἡ, *sauce* or *pickle composed of brine and garlic*, Cratin.143, Ar.*Eq*.199, 1095, *Ec*.291. **-ίζω**, *dose with garlic*, prop. of game-cocks *which were primed with garlic* before fighting, φάσκων φιλεῖν μ' ἐσκορόδισας Id.*Eq*.946:—Pass., ἐσκοροδισμένος *primed with garlic*, ib.494, *Ach*.166. **II.** *flavour with garlic*, κάθαλα ποιήσας.. κἀσκοροδισμένα Diph.17.13. **-ιον**, τό, Dim. of σκόροδον, in pl., Ar.*Pl*.818, Antiph.62.

**σκοροδο-ειδής**, ές, v.l. for σκορδο-, Dsc.3.47. **-μάχοι**, οἱ, *Garlic-fighters*, Luc.*VH*1.13. **-μίμητος** [ῐ], ον, *resembling garlic*, φύσις Ar.*Fr*.5.

⊛ **σκόροδον**, τό, contr. **σκόρδον** (q.v.), *garlic, Allium sativum*, Hdt.2.125, 4.17, Gal.12.126: pl., *Schwyzer*725.5 (Milet., vi B.C.), Hp.*Acut*.37; σκορόδων κεφαλαί Ar.*Pl*.718, cf. *V*.679; σκορόδοις ἀλείφειν, = σκοροδίζειν, Id.*Pax* 502; ἵνα μή ποτε σκόροδα φάγῃ μηδὲ κυάμους μέλανας if he doesn't want to eat *war-rations*, Id.*Lys*.690 (on κυάμους in this phrase cf. *App.Prov*.3.27, Suid.); cf. σκόρδον. **II.** τὰ σ. the *garlic-market*, Eup.304.

**σκοροδο-πανδοκευτριαρτόπωλις**, ιδος, ἡ, *garlic-bread-selling hostess*, Com. word in Ar.*Lys*.458. **-πρᾰσον**, τό, *garlic-leek, Allium descendens*, Dsc.2.153, in form σκορδ-. **-πώλης**, ου, ὁ, *garlic-seller*, Sch.Ar.*V*.678, Poll.7.198. **-φᾰγέω**, *eat garlic*, Anon.Lond.33.54 (σκορδ-), Hsch. s.v. ἐσκοροδισμένος. **-φᾰγία**, ἡ, *eating of garlic*, Dsc.*Eup*.2.122; σκορδ-, Orib.*Fr*.58.

**σκοροδ-όφθαλμος**, ον, *with eye elongated antero-posteriorly* (a cause of short sight), Aët.7.47.

**σκοροδοφόρος**, ον, *garlic-bearing*, Sch.Ar.*Pl*.718, *Pax* 245; σκορδ-, Eust.ad D.P.525.

**σκοροδόω**, inf. -οῦν· συνουσιάζειν, Hsch.

**σκόρπαινα**, ἡ, a kind of fish, Ath.7.320f; fem. of σκορπίος II, acc. to Eust.1129.24.

**σκόρπειος**, α, ον, Ion. **-ήϊος**, η, ον, *of the scorpion*, Orph.*L*.510 (-ήϊα), 622 (-είην), Man.1.35.

⊛ **σκορπέρως**, dub. sens., as emblem on a shield, *BCH*2.323 (Delos).

**σκορπ-ιαίνομαι**, Pass., *to be enraged*, ἔς τινας Procop.*Arc*.9, cf. Suid. **-ιακός**, ή, όν, *of* or *for a scorpion*, -κὴ ἀντίδοτος Claud. Abascant.ap.Gal.14.177. **-ιᾱνός**, ή, όν, *born under* or *belonging to Scorpio*, οἱ σ. Antioch.Astr. in *Cat.Cod.Astr*.7.112; σ. κλίμα Harp. Astr.ib.8(3).138. **-ίδιον**, τό, Dim. of σκορπίος V, Plb.8.5.6, Lxx 1*Ma*.6.51, restd. in Ph.*Bel*.73.39. ⊛ **-ίζω**, fut. -ιῶ Lxx *Jb*.39.15:—*scatter, disperse*, Ion. word, Hecat.366 J. (Pass.); elsewh. only in later writers, Lxx 2*Ki*.22.15, al., Str.4.4.6, *Ev.Matt*.12.30, Dsc.4.134, Philum.*Ven*.12.2; ἐσκορπισμέναι μύξαι *CPHerm*.7 ii 18 (iii A.D.). **2.** *disintegrate, reduce to powder*, Zos.Alch.p.177 B. **3.** *dissipate*, τὸν πατρικὸν βίον *Cat.Cod.Astr*.2.162.

⊛ **σκορπιό-δηκτος**, ον, *stung by a scorpion*, Dsc.1.4 codd. (-πληκτος Wellm., cf. cap.6), *Gp*.12.13.6. **-ειδής**, ές, *scorpion-like*, only in form σκορπιώδης (q.v.). **II.** σκορπιοειδές, τό, *scorpion-wort* (so called because of the likeness of its seed to a scorpion's tail), *Scorpiurus sulcata*, Dsc.4.192; cf. σκορπίουρος. **-εις, εσσα, εν,** *of a scorpion*, τύμμα Nic.*Th*.654. II. *of* σκορπίουρον, ῥίζεα Id.*Al.* 145. **-θεν** (parox.), Adv. *by a scorpion*, σ. βεβολημένος Orph.*L.* 761. **-κτόνον,** τό, = ἡλιοτρόπιον τὸ μέγα, Ps.-Dsc.4.190 p.338 Wellm. **-μάχος** [ᾰ], ον, *fighting with scorpions*, [ἀκρίς] Arist.*Mir.* 844$^b$24.

**σκορπίον,** τό, = τράγος (the plant), Dsc.4.51. 2. = σίκυς ἄγριος, Ps.-Dsc.4.150. 3. = *heliotropium* (i.e. σκορπιοκτόνον), *Gloss.*

**σκορπιό-ομαι,** = σκορπιαίνομαι, Hsch. **-πληκτος,** ον, = σκορπιόδηκτος (q.v.), Dsc.4.192, Philum.*Ven*.10.1, al.

⊕ **σκορπί-ος,** ὁ, *scorpion*, A.*Fr*.169, Pl.*Euthd*.290a, *Sammelb*.1267.7 (i A.D.), etc.; σ. ὁ χερσαῖος (v. infr. II) Arist.*HA* 555$^a$23: prov., ὑπὸ παντὶ λίθῳ σκορπίον φυλάσσεο Praxill.4; ἐν παντὶ σ. φρουρεῖ λίθῳ S. *Fr*.37; also σκορπίον ὀκτώπουν ἐγείρεις 'let sleeping dogs lie', Hsch.; ὥσπερ ἔχις ἢ σ. ἠρκὼς τὸ κέντρον D.25.52. II. a sea-fish, prob. *Scorpaena scrofa*, Alex.261.9, Diocl.*Fr*.135, Arist.*HA* 508$^b$17, Plu.2.977f; used (like the *mugilis* in Catull.15.19, Juv.10.317) to punish adulterers, Pl.Com.173.21; dub. sens. in Lxx 3*Ki*.12. 11. III. *scorpion furze, Genista acanthoclada*, Thphr.*HP*6.1.3, 6.4.1. 2. *scorpion root, Doronicum caucasicum*, ib.9.13.6. 3. = θηλυφόνον, ib.9.18.2. IV. the constellation *Scorpio*, Cleostrat.1, Arat.85, Eudox.ap.Hipparch.1.2.20, Eratosth.*Cat*.7. V. an engine of war for discharging arrows, Hero *Bel*.74.6, Plu.*Marc.* 15; σκορπίων σωλῆνες *IG*2$^2$.1627.333. VI. a stone, Orph.*L*.500, cf. 494. **-ουρος,** ον, (οὐρά) *scorpion-tailed*: neut. as the name of a plant, = σκορπιοειδές, Sch.Nic.*Al*.146. 2. = ἡλιοτρόπιον τὸ μέγα, Dsc.4.190. 3. = σκορπιοκτόνον, Ps.-Dsc.4.190. 4. = ὠκιμοειδές, Ps.-Dsc.4.28.

**σκορπιοφόρος,** ον, *producing scorpions*, Ptol.*Geog*.6.17.3.

**σκορπίς,** ίδος, ἡ, a sea-fish, prob. *Scorpaena porcus*, Arist.*HA* 543$^b$5 (cited by Ath.7.320f); cf. σκομβρίς.

**σκόρπ-ισις,** εως, ἡ, *reduction to powder*, Zos.Alch.p.178B. ⊕ **-ισμός,** ὁ, *scattering*, Ph.1.82, Artem.2.30, Aq., Sm., Thd.*Je*.25.34 (32.20), Dam.*Pr*.394; φλεγμονῶν *Hippiatr*.70. **-ιστής,** οῦ, ὁ, *scatterer, spendthrift*, Lyd.*Mag*.1.42, *Cat.Cod.Astr*.8(4).154, al. **-ιστικός,** ή, όν, *dissipative*, φυμάτων Gal.14.242, cf. Simp.*in Ph*.1186.2.

**σκορπῖτις,** ιδος, ἡ, *scorpion-like*, name of a stone, Plin.*HN*37.187.

**σκορπιώδης,** ες, metaph., *scorpion-like*, Ph.2.576; *malignant*, Poll.6.125, Procop.*Arc*.1, Eust.851.52. II. τὸ σκορπιῶδες, *Chelifer cancroïdes*, an insect found in books, Arist.*HA* 532$^a$19, cf. 557$^b$10.

**Σκορπιών,** ῶνος, ὁ, name of a month at Alexandria, Ptol.*Alm*.9.10.

**σκορωβροί,** v. σκόρθοι.

**σκοτ-άζω,** *grow dark*, Lxx *Ez*.31.15, al.:—Pass., *to be darkened*, *Cat.Cod.Astr*.7.124, v.l. in Sch.Pi.*N*.4.64. **-αῖος,** α, ον, also ος, ον D.S.3.48, Plu.*Fab*.7:—*in the dark*, joined with a Verb, of persons, 1. before morning, ἐλείπετο τῆς νυκτὸς ὅσον σκοταίους διελθεῖν τὸ πεδίον X.*An*.4.1.5, cf. 10; ἔτι σ. παρῆλθεν Id.*HG*4.5.18; or, 2. after nightfall, ἤδη σ. ἀναγαγών Id.*Cyr*.7.1.45; σκοταῖοι προσιόντες Id.*An*.2.2.17: cf. κνεφαῖος. II. of things, *dark*, χωρίον Hp.*Mul*.1.11; νὺξ D.S. l.c.; ἐνέδραι *in the dark*, Plu. l.c. **-αρία·** ζόφος, Ἀχαιοί, Hsch. **-ασμός,** ὁ, *a being* or *becoming dark*, Aq. *Is*.59.9, Sm.*Ca*.1.5; ὀφθαλμῶν Dsc.*Ther*.7. **-άω,** = σκοτάζω: Ep. 3 pl. σκοτόωσι *their sight is darkened*, Nic.*Al*.35. **-εία,** ἡ, v.l. for σκοτία, Lxx *Mi*.3.6.

**σκοτεινο-ειδής,** ές, = ἀχλυώδης, Sch.Opp.*H*.3.163. **-λογία,** ἡ, *obscure utterance*, Vett.Val.260.29.

**σκοτειν-ός,** ή, όν, (σκότος) *dark*, νυκτὸς ἄρμ' ἐπείγεται σ. A.*Ch*.661; σ. τῶν ἐνερτέρων βέλος ib.285; σ. περιβολαί, of a scabbard, E.*Ph*.276; [ὁδοί] X.*Cyn*.6.5; τὰ σ. θεάσασθαι Pl.*R*.520c; ἀνὰ τὸ σ. προϊδεῖν *in the darkness*, Th.3.22; of a person, *blind*, καίπερ σ. S.*OT*1326; σ. ὄμμα E.*Alc*.385; τὰ σ. the *dark shadows* in a picture, X.*Mem*.3.10.1, Plu.2.57c: neut. as Adv., σκοτεινὸν ζῆν to live *in privacy*, Pl.*Lg*. 781c. II. metaph., *dark, obscure*, opp. ἐλλόγιμος καὶ φανός, Id. *Smp*.197a; τόπος σ. καὶ δυσδιερεύνητος Id.*R*.432c; Heraclitus was called ὁ σκοτεινός, Arist.*Mu*.396$^b$20, Cic.*Fin*.2.5.15; σ. προοίμιον Aeschin.2.34; σ. ἀκοαί *obscure* reports, Pl.*Criti*.109e; σ. μηχανήματα *dark, secret*, E.*Fr*.288; ὀρχεῖσθαι Id.*Ba*.611; σκοτεινὸς ὀργήν *Trag. Adesp*.345, cf. Procop.*Arc*.1. Adv., -νῶς διαλέγεσθαι Pl.*R*.558d, cf. D.H.*Th*.32. III. prob. f.l. for κοτ- in Pi.*N*.7.61. **-ότης,** ητος, ἡ, *darkness, obscurity*, Pl.*Sph*.254a. **-ώδης,** ες, = σκοτώδης, Hsch. s.v. νυθῶδες.

⊕ **σκοτερός,** ά, όν, = σκότιος, ὄρφνη Orph.*A*.1042 (s.v.l.).

**σκοτεύει·** δραπετεύει, Hsch.

⊕ **σκοτί-α,** ἡ, (σκότος) *darkness, gloom*, A.R.4.1698, Lxx(*Mi*.3.6, al.), *NT*(*Ev.Matt*.10.27, al.), cf. Moer.p.354P. II. in Architecture, *scotia, cavetto*, a sunken moulding, so called from *the dark shadow* it casts, Vitr.3.5.2, Hsch. III. **Σκοτιά,** epith. of Aphrodite in Egypt, Id. **-αῖος,** α, ον, v.l. for σκοταῖος in Poll.1.69. **-ας·** δραπέτης, Hsch.

**σκοτίζω,** *make dark*, τὸν θεὸν τὸν φωτίζοντα καὶ σκοτίζοντα τὸν κόσμον *Tab.Defix.Aud*.242.13 (Carthage, iii A.D.); *get in the light of*, ἐνέργειαν Gal.18(2).698: metaph., λαβὼν δισσὰς ἐσκότισας χάριτας Ἀρχ.Δελτ.11.57 (Larissa), cf. D.H.*Th*.33, Them.*Or*.11.153a; *stupefy*, σκορπίους Dsc.*Eup*.2.133:—Pass., *to be darkened*, Plu.2. 1120e; *to be blinded*, σκοτισθήτωσαν οἱ ὀφθαλμοὶ αὐτῶν Lxx *Ps*.68(69). 24; τῇ διανοίᾳ *Ep.Eph*.4.18 (v.l.); χολῇ τὰς φρένας Tz.*H*.8.929; *to be dizzy*, Aesop.247b.

**σκοτιοέρεβος,** ον, *inhabitant of dark Erebos*, *PMag.Par*.1.1361, *PMag.Lond*.121.354 (written σκοτιοερέμβους).

⊕ **σκότ-ιος,** α, ον, also ος, ον E.*Alc*.125 (lyr.), J.*AJ*19.7.1:—*dark*, I. of persons, *in the dark, in secret, secret*, σκότιον δέ ἑ γείνατο μήτηρ, i.e. not in open, lawful wedlock, Il.6.24; so prob. καὶ θεῶν σκότιοι φθίνουσι παῖδες ἐν θανάτῳ (the Sch. expl. it οἱ μὴ γνήσιοι ὄντες τῶν θεῶν παῖδες), E.*Alc*.989 (lyr.); also σ. εὐναί *clandestine* loves, Id.*Ion* 860 (lyr.); σ. λέχος, opp. a wedded wife, Id.*Tr*.44; λέκτρων σκότια νυμφευτήρια ib.252; λέχη σ. νυμφεύειν Eub.67.1; σ. Κύπρις *AP*7.51 (Adaeus): rare in Prose, παῖς σ. *bastard*, Charax 6, cf. Hsch.: metaph., γνώμη σ., of sense-perception, opp. γνησίη, Democr.11. 2. in Crete the boys were called σκότιοι, because they lived in the women's apartment, Sch.E.*Alc*.988. II. of things, *dark*, νύξ E.*Hec*.68 (anap.), *Alc*.269 (lyr.), etc.; θάλαμοι Id.*Ph*. 1541 (lyr.); ἕδραι, of the nether world, Id.*Alc*.125 (lyr.). 2. metaph., *dark, obscure*, of dithyrambs, Ar.*Av*.1389. Adv. -ίως, μηνύειν, opp. τηλαυγῶς, Ph.1.659. **-ισμός,** ὁ, *darkening*, σ. καὶ φωτισμοὶ ἀέρος Cleom.1.7, cf. Eust.849.23; = σκοτοδινία, Ptol.*Tetr*. 116, Vett.Val.193.9, Hsch. s.v. ἴλιγγος. **-ίτας** [ῑ], ου, ὁ, epith. of Zeus, whether as bringer of *dark* clouds (cf. κελαινεφής), or as a god of the nether world, or from the *dark* oak-forest surrounding the shrine (v.l. Σκοτινᾶς ap.St.Byz.), Paus.3.10.6.

**σκοτο-βῑνῐάω,** (βινέω) Com. word formed after σκοτοδινιάω, *in tenebris concumbere cum aliqua gestio*, Ar.*Ach*.1221. **-δᾰσῠπυκνόθριξ,** τρῐχος, ὁ, ἡ, *dark with shaggy thick hair*, κυνῆ σ. 'cap of darkness', ib.390. **-δειπνος,** ον, *eating in the dark*, Hsch. s.v. ζοφοδερκίας.

**σκοτοδῑν-έω,** = σκοτοδινιάω, Ps.-Luc.*Philopatr*.1. **-ία,** Ion. -ίη, ἡ, *dizziness, vertigo*, Hp.*VM*10, *Coac*.157, *Morb*.2.4, Pl.*Sph*.264 c. **-ίᾰσις,** εως, ἡ, = foreg., Ecphant.ap.Stob.4.7.64 (pl.), Poll.2.41, 4.184. **-ιάω,** *suffer from dizziness* or *vertigo*, Ar.*Ach*.1219, Pl.*Tht*. 155c, *Lg*.663b, etc. **-ος,** ὁ, = σκοτοδινία, Hp.*Aph*.4.17, *Prorrh*.2. 30, Aret.*SD*1.2.

**σκοτο-ειδής,** ές, *dark-looking*, Hsch. s.v. ζοφοειδές. **-εις,** εσσα, εν, poet. for σκότιος, *dark*, νέφος Hes.*Op*.555; ζόφος A.R.2.1105; νύξ Nic.*Al*.188: metaph., σκοτόεσσα θεῶν πέρι δόξα a *dark, doubtful* opinion, Emp.132. II. **Σκοτοῦσσα,** ἡ, a town in Thessaly, *IG* 5(2).11.4 (Tegea, iii B.C.), etc.; in codd. written **Σκοτοῦσα,** Plb.10. 42.3, Str.9.5.20; uncontr. **Σκοτόεσσα,** Poet.ap.Paus.7.27.6: Adj. **Σκοτουσσαῖος,** *IG*9(2).519 iii 9 (Larissa), al. **-εργός,** όν, *working in the dark*, κλιβανεύς Man.1.80.

⊕ **σκοτοιβόρος,** ον, (βορά) *devouring in the dark*: metaph., *malicious, mischievous*, Eust.1496.38, cf. Hsch.

**σκοτό-μαινα,** ἡ, = σκοτομήνη, *AP*13.12 (Hegesipp.): metaph., Aristid.*Or*.22(19).11: Att. acc. to Hsch. **-μᾰχέω,** *fight in the darkness*, *Corp.Herm*.1.23. **-μήδης,** ες, *of dark counsel, wily*, Eust.1496.37. **-μήνη,** ἡ, *moonless night*, Lxx *Ps*.10(11).2, Aristid.*Or*.24(44).51 (f.l. for -μαίνη), Democr.(?) ap.*Et.Gen.* s.v. γλαύξ. **-μηνία,** ἡ, = foreg., Chrysipp.*Stoic*.2.212, Aq.*Jb*.3. 6. ⊕ **-μήνιος,** ον, *dark and moonless*, νύξ Od.14.457. **-ποιός,** όν, *making darkness*, Prisc.Lyd.8.15, Sch.E.*Ph*.950: hence **-ποιέω,** Sch. Il.20.38.

**σκότος,** ὁ, more rarely **σκότος,** εος, τό (v. sub fin.), *darkness, gloom*, Od.19.389, Emp.121.4, Pi.*Fr*.142, etc.; opp. φάος, A.*Ch*.319 (lyr.), E.*Hipp*.417, etc.; opp. ἡμέρα, Pl.*Def*.411b. 2. in Il. always of the *darkness* of death, mostly in phrase τὸν δὲ σ. ὄσσε κάλυψεν 4.461, al.; στυγερὸς δ' ἄρα μιν σ. εἷλεν 5.47, 13.672; so in Trag. and Com., σκότῳ θανεῖν E.*Hipp*.837 (lyr.); ἤδη με περιβάλλει σ. Id.*Ph*.1453; σ. γίγνεται Pherecr.40; σκότον εἶναι τεθνηκότος (sc. Αἰσχύλου) Ar.*Fr*. 643. 3. of the nether world, Pi.*Fr*.130; σκότον νέμονται Τάρταρόν τε A.*Eu*.72, cf. *Pers*.223; τὸν ἀεὶ κατὰ γᾶς σ. εἱμένος S.*OC*1701 (lyr.); παῖδες ἀρχαίου Σκότου ib.106; ἰὼ σ., ἐμὸν φάος Id.*Aj*.394 (lyr.); γῆς σκότῳ κέκρυπται E.*Hel*.62; σκότου πύλαι Id.*Hec*.1. 4. the *darkness* of the womb, φυγόντα μητρόθεν σκότον A.*Th*.664: pl., ἐν σκότοισι νηδύος τεθραμμένη Id.*Eu*.665. 5. of blindness, σκότου νέφος S.*OT* 1313 (lyr.); ὁθούνεκ'.. ἐν σκότῳ.. ὀψοίατο, i.e. οὐκέτι ὀψοίατο, ib.1273; βλέποντα νῦν μὲν ὀρθ', ἔπειτα δὲ σκότον, i.e. μηδέν, ib.419; σκότον δεδορκώς E.*Ph*.377, cf. *HF*563. b. *dizziness, vertigo*, Hp.*Epid*. 5.23; σκότοι πρὸ τῶν ὀμμάτων Arist.*HA* 584$^a$3; cf. σκοτόδινος, -δινιάω. 6. metaph., σκότῳ κρύπτειν hide in *darkness*, S.*El*.1396 (lyr.), cf. Pi.*Frr*.42.5, 228; σκότον ἔχειν to be in *darkness, obscurity*, Id.*N*.7.13, E.*Fr*.1052.8; ἀπορία καὶ σ. Pl.*Lg*.837a; περικαλύψαι τοῖσι πράγμασι σκότον E.*Ion* 1522: with Preps., διὰ σκότους ἡ ὁδός it is dark and uncertain, X.*An*.2.5.9; ἐν σ. καθήμενος Pi.*O*.1.83; μηδὲν ἐν σ. τεχνωμένων S.*Ant*.494; κατὰ σκότον Id.*Ph*.578; ὑπὸ σκότου Id. *Ant*.692, E.*Or*.1457 (lyr.), X.*Cyr*.4.6.4; ὑπὸ σκότῳ A.*Ag*.1030 (lyr.), E.*Ph*.1214. 7. of a person, Μητρότιμος ὁ σ., like ὁ σκοτεινός, the *mystery-man*, Hippon.78; also, *darkness*, i.e. *ignorance*, D.19.226; *deceit*, σ. καὶ ἀπάτη Pl.*Lg*.864c. 8. pl., σκότη *shadows* in a picture, Paus.Gr.*Fr*.300, Suid. s.v. ἀπεσκοτωμένα, Eust.953.51.—Ael.Dion. *Fr*.217 regarded the masc. as the Att. form: the neut. never occurs in Ar., and is nowhere required by the metre in Trag., though it sts. occurs in codd., E.*Hec*.831, *HF*1159, *Fr*.534, v.l. in S.*OC*40, dub. l. in A.*Fr*.6; it is found, however, without v.l., in Pi.*Fr*.42.5 and Att. Prose, Pl.*R*.516e, *Cra*.418c, D.18.159, etc.; also in Hdt.2.121. έ, X.*An*.2.5.9, 7.4.18; the word is always neut. in Lxx and *NT*.

**σκοτο-φεγγής,** ές, perh *darkly glimmering*, κλίμακες Zos.Alch. p.108B. **-φρων,** ὁ, ἡ, gen. φρονος, *dark-minded*, gloss on the pr.n. Λυκόφρων, Sch.Lyc.1 p.9 Bachmann.

®σκοτ-όω, *darken, blind*, σκοτώσω βλέφαρα καὶ δεδορκότα S.*Aj.*85; *stupefy*, Sor.1.125 (Act. and Pass.); *make dizzy*, τὰς ὄψεις Ph.Byz. *Mir.*2.5: metaph., *Ep.Eph.*4.18:—Pass., *to be in darkness, suffer from vertigo*, like σκοτοδινιάω, Pl.*R.*518a, *Prt.*339e, *Tht.*209e, Thphr. *Vert.*7, Plb.10.13.8; ἕλμινθες -ωθεῖσαι *stupefied*, Herod.Med.ap.Aët. 9.37, cf. Gal.16.657. **-ώδης**, ες, *dark*, Pl.*Phd.*81b, *R.*518c. 2. *obscure*, Id.*Cra.*412b (Comp.). II. *dizzy*, Hp.*Prorrh.*1.71; τὰ -ώδεα περὶ τὰς ὄψιας Id.*Epid.*1.12; νόσος σ. *vertigo*, Nic.Dam.*Fr.*130. 23J. **-ωδία**, ἡ, *darkness*, Nicom.ap.Phot.*Bibl.* p.143B., *Theol.Ar.* 6. **-ωμα**, ατος, τό, *dizziness, vertigo*, Plb.5.56.7 (pl.), Plu.2.137d, Gal.6.324 (pl.). **-ωματικός**, ή, όν, *causing dizziness*, Dsc.5.34. 2. *suffering from it*, Id.2.70; -κὸν πάθος Gal.8.201, Alex.Aphr.*Pr.*2.71, etc. **-ωσις**, εως, ἡ, *darkening, eclipse*, μαντικῶν δυνάμεων σκοτώσεις Plu.2.414d. II. *dizziness, vertigo*, *Stoic.*3.57, Erot. s. v. δῖνος, Gal. 19.417: metaph., ἄγνοια καὶ σ. Porph.*Sent.*29.

**σκοῦτα**, ἡ, (Lat. *scutum*) *shield*, Hero *Mens.*14:—Dim. **σκουτάριον**, τό, *POxy.*1839.4 (vi A.D.), Sch.Luc.*DMort.*12.2, Just.*Nov.*85.4.

®**σκουτάριος**, ὁ, = Lat. *scutarius*, *PCair.Preis.*39.4 (iv A.D.), etc.

**σκουτέλλιον**, τό, and **σκούτλιον**, τό, Dim. of Lat. *scutella*, *dish*, *Stud.Pal.*20.151.4, al. (vi A.D.), *PLond.*2.191.10 (ii A.D.).

**σκούτλα**, ἡ, *lozenge*, Hero *Stereom.*2.18; = Lat. *scutula, chequer-work*, σκουτλῶσαι τοίχους σ. ῥαντῇ *Ephes.*3 No.65.

®**σκουτλ-άριος**, ὁ, *maker of scutulae for chequer-work* or *mosaic flooring*, *SIG*1124 (Pergam., prob. i A.D.). ®**-όω**, *decorate with mosaics*, *Ephes.*3 No.65 (cf. σκούτλα); λίθῳ ποικίλῳ στοὰν *BCH*44.88, 90 (Lagina), cf. 28.45 (Panamara). ®**-ωσις**, εως, ἡ, *chequered work*, as a *border*, Hero *Geom.*23.3 (pl.); σ. οἴκου βασιλικοῦ *IGRom.*4.1290 (Thyatira), cf. *Jahresh.*7 *Beibl.*42 (Ephesus, ii A.D.), $IPE\,1^2$.174.7 (Olbia, ii A.D.), *Sardis* 7(1) No.63.

®**σκουτουλᾶτος**, ον, Lat. *scutulatus, chequered*, of dresses, *Peripl. M.Rubr.*24, cf. Lyd.*Mag.*1.10.

**σκριβλίτης** [λῑ], ου, ὁ, a kind of cheese-cake, Chrysipp.Tyan.ap. Ath.14.647d.

®**σκρῑνιάριος**, ὁ, *secretary*, *MAMA*4.34 (Afion Karahisar, v/vi A.D.), Just.*Nov.*30.7.1, *PLond.*5.1714.13 (vi A.D.).

**σκρίνιον** [ῐ], τό, = Lat. *scrinium, dossier*, Dosith. p.391 K., Lyd. *Mag.*1.34; *office*, *Cod.Just.*1.2.24.11, al., *PMasp.*131.13, al. (vi A.D.). II. *box, chest*, *BGU*40.10 (ii A.D., σκρήν-), 388 ii 24 (ii A.D., σκρείν-).

**σκύβα** or **σκοῦβα**· λάχανον, ἡ λαψάνη, Hsch.

**σκῠβᾰλ-ίζω**, *look on as dung, reject contemptuously*, D.H.*Orat.Vett.* 1, cf. σκυβλίζω:—Pass., opp. λαμπρίζομαι, Pempel.ap.Stob.4.25.52, cf. Lxx *Si.*26.26:—later **-εύω**, Sch.Luc.*Nec.*17 (Pass.). **-ικός**, ή, όν, *dirty, mean*, ἀργυρίοισι σκυβαλικοῖσι, of bribes, Timocr.1.6 vulg., contra metrum; κυβαλικοῖσι Bgk. **-ισμα**, ατος, τό, = σκύβαλον, Ps.-Phoc. 156. **-ισμός**, ὁ, *contemptuous rejection*, Plb.30.19.12, Hsch. **-ον**, τό, *dung, excrement*, Plu.2.352d, Alex.Aphr.*Pr.*1.18: pl., σ. λευκὰ καὶ ἀργιλώδεα Aret.*SD*1.15, cf. Str.14.1.37, J.*BJ*5.13.7, etc.; *manure*, *PFay.*119.7 (i/ii A.D.). 2. *refuse, offal*, *Ep.Phil.*3.8, Jul.*Or.*5. 179c; ἀποδειπνίδιον σ. *AP*6.302 (Leon.); ἄνδρα, πολύκλαυτον ναυτιλίης σ. ib.7.276 (Hegesipp.); τέφρης λοιπὸν ἔτι σ. ib.382 (Phil.); opp. τὸ χρήσιμον, Ath.Med.ap.Orib.1.2.8; σ. τοῦ σησάμου *PCair.Zen.* 494.16 (iii B.C.); σ. χόρτου *PSI*3.184.7 (pl., iii A.D.): pl., δεῖπνον ἀπὸ σκυβάλων *AP*6.303 (Aristo); σ. ἀνθρώπου Lxx *Si.*27.4. **-ώδης**, ες, *refuse-like*, Anon.Lond.29.39, Suid. s. v. ἐραία.

**Σκυβελίτης** [ῑ] οἶνος, ὁ, wine *from* Σκύβελα in Pamphylia, Aret. *CA*2.9, *CD*1.5, Gal.*Vict.Att.*12, 6.337, 10.405, 13.8, Hsch. s. v. Κέσκος; grown in Galatia, Plin.*HN*14.80.

**σκυβλίζω**, = σκυβαλίζω, *defile, desecrate*, τὸ πτῶμά μου *Sardis* 7(1) No.165 (iii/iv A.D.).

**σκυδά**· σκιά, Εὔκλος, Hsch. **σκυδίζω**, = λακτίζω, Id. **σκύδμαινος**, ον, = σκυθρωπός, Id.

**σκυδμαίνω**, = σκύζομαι, μή μοι, Πάτροκλε, σκυδμαινέμεν Il.24.592.

**σκύζ-α**, ἡ, *lust*, Philet.ap.Hsch.: as a term of abuse applied to a woman, *Supp.Epigr.*4.47 (Messana, Defixio). **-άω**, *to be in heat*, of dogs, Arist.*HA*$572^b$26; of women, Phryn.*PS* p.18 B., cf. Phryn. Com.6 D. II. *bark during sleep*, Poll.5.86. **-ησις**, εως, ἡ, *breeding season* of dogs, Ar.Byz.*Epit.*78.1.

®**σκύζομαι**, Ep., used mostly in pres.: impf. ἐσκύζοντο, σκύζοντο, Q.S.3.133, 5.338: Ep. aor. opt. σκύσσαιτο (ἐπι-) Od.7.306:—*to be angry with* one, σκυζομένη Διὶ πατρί Il.4.23; σκύζεσθαί οἱ εἶπε θεούς 24.113; μή μοι σκύζευ Od.23.209: abs., *to be wroth*, ὅσ σευ ἔγωγε σκυζομένης ἀλέγω Il.8.483, cf. 9.198. (Cf. σκυδ-μαίνω and prob. σκυθρός.)

**Σκύθ-αινᾰ** [ῠ], ἡ, fem. form of Σκύθης, Ar.*Lys.*184, Alex.331. ®**-άριον**, τό, *Scythian wood*, i.e. θάψος, Sch.Theoc.2.88. ®**-ης**, ου, ὁ: voc. Σκύθα Thgn.829, Ar.*Th.*1112, etc.:—*Scythian*, first in Hes. *Fr.*55: prov., Σκυθῶν ἐρημία, of a desert, Ar.*Ach.*704: metaph., *rude, rough person*, ἐν λόγοις Σ. Plu.2.847f, cf. Men.533.13. 2. Adj. *Scythian*, Σ. ἐς οἶμον A.*Pr.*2; Σ. ὅμιλος ib.417 (lyr.); σίδηρος Id.*Th.* 818 (cf. Χάλυψ); κύανος Thphr.*Lap.*55. II. at Athens, *one of the city police*, which was mainly composed of Scythian slaves, Ar.*Th.* 1018, 1026, *Lys.*451; cf. τοξότης III. 2. = ἱπποτοξότης, Ael.*Tact.*2. 13. ®**-ία**, ἡ, *Scythia*, Call.*Dian.*174; **Σκυθίηνδε**, ib.256: **Σκυθιάς**, ἄδος, ἡ, a name of Delos, Nicanor ap.St.Byz. **-ίζω**, *behave like a Scythian*, i.e., 1. *drink immoderately*, Hieronym.Rhod.ap.Ath.11. 499f; cf. ἐπισκυθίζω. 2. from the Scythian practice of scalping slain enemies, *shave the head*, ἐσκυθισμένος ξυρῷ E.*El.*241; so [χαίτην] ἐσκύθιξε φασγάνῳ *cut* it *off* in mourning, *Epigr.Gr.*790.8 (Achaea): cf. ἀποσκυθίζω. 3. *talk Scythian*, Him.*Or.*30.1. ®**-ικός**, ή, όν, *Scythian*, A.*Ch.*161 (lyr.), etc.; of persons *with a ruddy complexion*, Alc.48 B, Cratin.336: τὸ -κόν the *Scythian race*, Zos.4. 20, cf. Luc.*Tox.*54; -κὸν ξύλον, = θάψος, Sapph.167:—fem. **Σκύθις**, -ιδος, acc. -ιν, Aeschin.3.172: as name of a gem, Mart.Cap.1. 75. II. **Σκυθικαί**, αἱ, *a kind of shoes*, like Περσικαί, Σικυώνια, etc., Alc.103, Lys.*Fr.*60S. III. **Σκυθική** (sc. ῥίζα), ἡ, = γλυκύρριζα, Thphr.*HP*9.13.2. IV. Adv. -κῶς Str.11.8.7, Plu.*Crass.* 24. **-ιον**, τό, = Σκυθικός III, prob. in Dsc.3.5. **-ισμός**, ὁ, *shaving of the head*, *Trag.Adesp.* in *PLit.Lond.*78.25. **-ιστί** [τῑ], Adv. *in Scythian fashion*, Σ. χειρόμακτρον ἐκκεκαρμένος, with reference to the use of scalps as napkins (cf. Hdt.4.64), S.*Fr.*473. 2. *in the Scythian tongue*, Hdt.4.27, 59, Parmeno 1.2.

**σκυθόπομα**, ατος, τό, = βούγλωσσος, Cyran.104.

**σκύθος** [ῠ], ὁ, Aeol. for σκύφος, Parmeno ap.Ath.11.500b.

**Σκῠθοτοξότης**, ου, ὁ, *Scythian bowman*, f. l. in X.*An.*3.4.15.

**σκυθράζω**, *to be angry, peevish*, E.*El.*830.

**σκύθραξ**· μεῖραξ, ἔφηβος, Hsch.

**σκυθρός**, ά, όν, *angry, sullen*, Men.10, Arat.1120.

**σκυθρωπ-άζω**, *look angry* or *sullen, be of a sad countenance*, Ar. *Lys.*7, *Pl.*756; ὡς οὐδὲν ᾔσθα πλὴν σκυθρωπάζειν μόνον Amphis 13, cf. Antiph.218.3, *PCair.Zen.*481.30 (iii B.C.): aor. 1, ἐσκυθρώπασαν ἀκούσαντες X.*Cyr.*6.2.21; σφόδρα πάνυ σκυθρωπάσας Aeschin.2.36, cf. Thphr.*Char.*14.7: pf. ἐσκυθρωπακέναι Pl.*Alc.*2.138a; ἐσκυθρωπακώς D.45.68. 2. *to be of a sad colour*, Philostr.*Im.*1. 28. **-ασμός**, ὁ, *sadness of countenance*, [τῶν φιλοσόφων] Plu.2.43f, cf. 378f. **-ός**, όν, also ή, όν Hp.*Epid.*3.17.ιδ', Ephor.*Fr.*96 J., Plu. 2.417c, etc.: (σκυθρός, ὤψ):—*of sad* or *angry countenance, sullen*, E. *Med.*271, *Hipp.*1152; ὄμμα καὶ πρόσωπον Id.*Ph.*1333; σ. τοῖς ξένοις Id.*Alc.*774; ἐπὶ τοῖς κακοῖς X.*Mem.*3.10.4; opp. ἱλαρός, φαιδρός, ib. 2.7.12, 3.10.4; also of affected gravity, D.45.68, Aeschin.3.20: τὸ σ., = sq., E.*Alc.*797, cf. Pl.*Smp.*206d. Adv., -πῶς ἔχειν X.*Mem.*2.7. 1: Comp. -ότερον *with greater severity*, J.*BJ*6.2.7. II. of things, *gloomy, sad, melancholy*, γῆρας E.*Ba.*1252; ὁδὸς Archyt.ap.Stob.3.1. 105 (Comp.); μέλη Paus.10.7.5; ἡμέρα Plu.*Dem.*30 (Sup.). 2. of colour, *sad-coloured, dark and dull*, of the river Μέλας, Him.*Or.*23. 22; of wine, ib.9.4. **-ότης**, ητος, ἡ, *sullenness*, Hp.*Coac.*210, D.H.*Rh.*11.8.

**σκῠλᾰδέψης**, ου, or **-ος**, ὁ, = σκυλοδέψης, Eust.450.6.

**σκυλαίας**· τὰ σκῦλα καὶ λάφυρα, οἱ δὲ τὰς πανοπλίας, Hsch.

**σκῠλᾰκ-ᾰγέτις**, ιδος, ἡ, (σκύλαξ, ἡγέομαι) *leader of dogs* (at the chase), epith. of Hecate, prob. cj. in *PMag.Par.*1.2722 (-άγεια Pap.). ®**-αινα**, ἡ, poet. fem. of σκύλαξ, *AP*9.604 (Noss.). **-εία**, ἡ, *breeding of dogs*, Plu.*Cat.Ma.*5, Poll.5.51. **-ειος**, α, ον, *of puppies*, κρέα Hp.*Int.*9, S.E.*P.*3.225. ®**-ευμα**, ατος, τό, *whelp, cub*, contemptuously of a boy, Epigr.ap.Plu.2.241a, *AP*3.7 (Inscr. Cyzic.). **-εύς**, έως, ὁ, = σκύλαξ, Ep. gen. -ῆος, -ήων, Opp.*C.*4.227, 1.481. **-ευτής**, οῦ, ὁ, *dog-trainer*, Him.*Ecl.*21.4. **-ευτικός**, ή, όν, *of* or *for puppies*, Ph.1.202. **-εύω**, *pair dogs for breeding*, c. acc., X.*Cyn.*7.1, Arr. *Cyn.*31.3:—Pass., ὑπὸ λυκαίνης σκυλακεύεσθαι *to be suckled* by a she-wolf, Str.5.3.2; *to be trained from puppyhood* (cf. πωλεύεσθαι, παιδεύεσθαι), Max.Tyr.1.1. **-η**, ἡ, = σκυλάκαινα, Orph.*A.*979. **-ιον**, τό, Dim. of σκύλαξ, *young puppy*, Hp.*Steril.*217, Pl.*R.*539b, X.*Cyn.* 7.3, *Abh.Berl.Akad.*1925(5).33 (Cyrene, iv B.C.), Ph.1.318. 2. of other young animals, Poll.5.15. 3. name of an *eye-salve*, Gal.12. 755, 776, Aët.7.112. ®**-ῖτις**, ιδος, ἡ, *protectress of dogs*, of Artemis, Orph.*H.*36.12.

**σκῠλᾰκο-δρόμος** ὥρη, *of the dog-days*, Poet.*de herb.*140. ®**-κτόνος**, ον, *dog-killing*, Glycon ap.Heph.10.2.

**σκῠλᾰκοτροφ-ία**, Ep. -ίη, ἡ, *breeding, rearing of dogs*, Opp.*C.*1. 436. **-ικός**, ή, όν, *of* or *for the breeding and rearing of dogs*: ἡ σ. (sc. τέχνη) *this art*, Ael.*NA*6.8. **-ος** (parox.), ον, *breeding* or *rearing dogs*, εὐνή Opp.*H.*1.719; θεά *TAM*2.174 E16 (Oracle, Sidyma).

®**σκῠλᾰκώδης**, ες, *like a young dog*: τὸ σ. *puppyish character*, X.*Cyr.* 1.4.4.

**σκύλαξ** [ῠ], ᾰκος, ὁ, and (as always in Hom. and Hes.) ἡ, *young dog, puppy*, Od.9.289, 12.86, Hes.*Th.*834; κύων ἀμαλῇσι περὶ σκυλάκεσσι βεβῶσα Od.20.14; in full, σ. κυνός Hdt.3.32: generally, *dog*, masc. in Pl.*R.*375a, 537a; fem. in Sophr. in *Stud.Ital.*10.123, E.*Ba.* 338, Pl.*Prm.*128c, X.*Cyn.*7.6; ᾄδου τρίκρανος σ., of Cerberus, S.*Tr.* 1098. 2. of other young animals, *whelp, cub*, ὀρεσκόων σκυλάκων πελαγίων τε E.*Hipp.*1276 (lyr.); ἄρκτου Luc.*DMar.*1.5; γαλέης Nic. *Th.*689; of a dolphin, Arion 1.8: metaph., of grammarians, Ζηνοδότου σκύλακες *whelps* of his litter, *AP*11.321 (Phil.). II. *chain*, Pl.Com.23; *collar for the neck*, Plb.20.10.8. III. σχῆμα ἀφροδισιακόν, Hsch.

®**σκῠλ-άω**, = σκυλεύω, dub. in *AP*3.6 (Inscr. Cyzic.), Eust.1072. 64. **-εία**, ἡ, *despoiling, plundering*, Lxx 1 *Ma.*4.23. **-ευμα**, ατος, τό, usu. in pl., *arms stripped off a slain enemy, spoils*, E.*Ph.*857, *Ion* 1145, Th.4.44. **-ευμός**, ὁ, = sq., Eust.1080.32. **-ευσις**, εως, ἡ, = σκυλεία, τάφου *SIG*1233 (Cilicia), cf. Heb.*Jb.*15.21. **-ευτής**, οῦ, ὁ, *one who strips a slain enemy*, Aq.*Ez.*23.15. **-ευτικός**, ή, όν, *stripping a slain enemy*, Ἀθηνᾶ Tz.ad Lyc.853. ®**-εύω**, *strip* or *despoil a slain enemy*, esp. of his arms (taking off the clothes also is condemned by Pl., *R.*469c), not in Hom.; c. acc. pers. et rei, Κύκνον σκυλεύσαντες ἀπ' ὤμων τεύχεα Hes.*Sc.*468; σ. τοὺς τελευτήσαντας πλὴν ὅπλων *strip* of anything but arms, Pl. l. c.; [ἀμφίσβαιναν] δέρματος Nic.*Th.*379: c. acc. pers. only, σ. τοὺς νεκρούς Hdt.1.82, Th. 4.44, 97, cf. *BCH*51.148 (Salamis Cypr.); σ. τὰς πόλεις Plb.9.10. 13. 2. c. acc. rei et gen. pers., *strip* the arms *off* an enemy, ὅπλα τῶν πολεμίων σ. Lys.12.40, cf. X.*An*.6.1.6, *HG*2.4.19; ἀπὸ τῶν.. νεκρῶν σ. ψέλια κτλ. Hdt.9.80. ⊛ -ήτρια, ἡ, *she who strips a slain enemy*, παρθένος Lyc.853 codd. (dub. l.). -ηφόρος, ον, poet. for σκυλοφόρος, *AP*9.428 (Antip. Thess.).

**σκύλιον**, τό, *dog-fish*, Arist.*HA* 565ᵃ16 sq.

**Σκύλιος**, ὁ, epith. of Zeus at Rhytion, *Riv.Ist.Arch.*2.64 (ii A.D.).

**Σκύλλᾰ**, ης, ἡ, A.*Ag*.1233, Ep. **Σκύλλη**, *Scylla*, Od.12.85, al., cf. A. l.c., etc.; Σκύλλαν αὐλεῖν, in allusion to a composition bearing that name, Arist.*Po*.1461ᵇ32; ταῖς λεγομέναις Ἐχίδναις καὶ Σκύλλαις Plu. *Crass*.32 (as v.l. for σκυτάλαις). (Derivation fr. σκύλαξ (prob. erroneous) is implied in Od.12.86.)

**Σκυλλανίς**· ἡ πολεμική, ἴσως ἀπὸ τοῦ σκυλεύειν, Hsch.

**σκύλλᾰρος**, v.l. for κύλλαρος in Arist.*HA*530ᵃ12.

**σκυλλίς**· κληματίς, Hsch.

**Σκυλλίτας** [ῑ], α, ὁ, god *of the* σκυλλίς, epith. of Dionysus, *SIG* 1025.58,63 (Cos, iv/iii B.C.).

**σκυλλοπνίκτης** or σκυλο-, ου, ὁ, *dog-throttler, choke-dog*, as interpr. of the Lydian name *Can-daules*, Tz.*H*.6.482.

**σκύλλος** or **σκύλος**, ὁ, = σκύλαξ, *EM*720.19, Hsch.

⊛ **σκύλλω**, *Ev.Marc*.5.35, aor. ἔσκῡλα Hdn. (v. infr.):—Pass., v. infr.; aor. ἐσκύλθην Eust.769.41, 1516.57; also ἐσκύλην [ῠ] (v. infr.): pf. ἔσκυλμαι (v. infr.):—= τοῖς ὄνυξι σπᾶν, Hsch.; aor. inf. σκοῦλαι (perh. Lacon.), = κνῆσαι, Id.:—Pass., σκύλλονται, of dead bodies *torn* by fish, A.*Pers*.577 (lyr.); ἔσκυλται.. κίκιννος *is dishevelled*, *AP*5.174 (Mel.); ἔσκυλται δὲ κόμη ib.258 (Paul. Sil.). 2. *maltreat, molest*, τοὺς ἐν [τοῖς ἱεροῖς] ἀποτεταγμένους *Sammelb*.6236.22 (i B.C.); ὃς δὲ ἂν σκύλῃ [τὸ μνῆμα] *IG*14.1901 (Rome), cf. *AP*3.6 (Inscr. Cyzic.), *CIG*3757 (Nicaea), 4077 (Ancyra):—Pass., *UPZ*107. 8,16 (ii B.C.). 3. *trouble, annoy*, τὴν ἀσθενοῦσαν Sor.2.11; σκύλας καὶ ὑβρίσας Hdn.7.3.4; σ. τὸν στρατόν Id.4.13.3; τί σκύλλεις τὸν διδάσκαλον; *Ev.Marc*. l.c., cf. *Ev.Luc*.8.49; σκῦλον σεαυτὸν πρὸς ἡμᾶς φέρων..τὴν ὕαλον *bestir* yourself (i.e. *hurry*) to us with.., *PFay*.134.2 (iv A.D.):—Pass. and Med., μὴ σκύλλου *trouble* not *thyself*, *Ev.Luc*.7.6; σκυλῆναι πρὸς Τιμόθεον *take the trouble to go* to T., *POxy*.123.10 (iii/iv A.D.); σκυλῆναι ἀνέξεται; will he *trouble to come?* Phoeb.*Fig*.p.44 S.; σκῦλαι (imper. Med.) σεαυτὸν καὶ κτλ. *PBaden* 33.6 (ii A.D.); ἐσκυλμένοι *Ev.Matt*.9.36; σκύλλεται καὶ καταπονεῖται Diog.Oen.1. II. Med., σκύλαιο κάρη *shave* the patient's head, Nic.*Al*.410.

**σκύλ-μα**, ατος, τό, *hair plucked out*, κόμης σκύλματα *AP*5.129 (Maec.); σκύλμα κόμης ib.247 (Paul. Sil.). -μός, ὁ, *rending, mangling*, Sch.Il.17.62. 2. *irritation*, of purgatives or plasters, Sor.2.41,42, Archig.ap.Orib.8.2.8, Orib.*Fr*.74. 3. *annoyance, vexation*, freq. in pl., Lxx 3*Ma*.3.25, 4.6, Artem.2.30, Man.4.364, Ptol.*Tetr*.206, Petos.ap.Vett.Val.96.6; of a lover's *violence*, *AP*5. 198 (Hedyl.): sg., *PTeb*.41.7 (ii B.C.), *PFay*.111.5 (i A.D.), al., Vett.Val.180.7. 4. *expenditure of effort, trouble*, *POxy*.941.5 (vi A.D.). -μώδης, ες, *troublesome, bringing trouble*, Vett.Val. in *Cat.Cod.Astr*.8(1).171.

**σκῡλοδεψ-έω**, *tan hides*, Ar.*Pl*.514 (Bentl. for σκυτοδεψεῖν). -ης, ου, ὁ, (δέφω, δέψω) *tanner of hides*, Ar.*Av*.490, *Ec*.420. -ος, ὁ, = foreg., D.25.38, prob. in *IG*2².1556.34: σκυλοδεσφ[, ib.1².645.

**σκῦλον**, τό, mostly in pl. σκῦλα, *arms stripped off a slain enemy, spoils*, S.*Ph*.1428,1431, E.*IT*74, *El*.7,1000, Th.4.134, *SIG*61 (Olympia, v B.C.); σκῦλα γράφειν to write one's name on *arms gained as spoils*, which were then dedicated to a deity, E.*Ph*.574; σκῦλ' ἔδειξα Βακχίῳ Id.*Cyc*.9, cf. Th.2.13, 3.57: less freq. in sg., *booty, spoil, prey*, σκῦλον οἰωνοῖσιν E.*El*.897, cf. *Rh*.620, D.Chr.64.24; τὰς πτέρυγας.. τῇ Νίκῃ φορεῖν ἔδοσαν, ..σκῦλον ἀπὸ τῶν πολεμίων Aristopho 11.9; σκῦλον τὴν ὑπατείαν φέρεσθαι Plu.*Mar*.9.

**σκύλος** [ῠ], εος, τό, *animal's skin, hide*, τὸ δὲ σ. ἀνδρὶ καλύπτρῃ, of a lion's skin, Call.*Fr*.142, cf. Theoc.25.142, *AP*6.35 (Leon.), 165 (Phal.); *outer husk* of a nut, Nic.*Al*.270: heterocl. pl. σκύλα Id.*Th*. 422: σκυλος is f.l. for σκῦτος in Herod.3.68.

**σκῦλο-φόρος**, ον, *bearing the spoil*, *AP*6.161 (Crin.); Ζεὺς σ., = Lat. *Jupiter Feretrius*, D.H.2.34. -χᾰρής, ές, *delighting in spoils* or *booty*, Ἔρωτες *APl*.4.214 (Secund.).

**σκῦλω**, (σκύλος) *veil, cover*, Hsch. **σκύλσις**, εως, ἡ, (σκύλλω) = σκυλμός, Id.

⊛ **σκυλτικός**, ή, όν, *vexatious*, Vett.Val.236.25.

**σκυμν-ᾰγωγέω**, *lead about whelps*, Eust.1098.49, Sch.Il.17. 133. -ειος, α, ον, *belonging to whelps*, Suid. -εύω, *rear*, νεβροὺς τῇ Γαλατείᾳ Philostr.*Im*.2.18. -ίον, τό, Dim. of σκύμνος, σ. τῆς φώκης, τῆς ἄρκτου, Arist.*HA*608ᵇ25, 611ᵇ32. -ος, ὁ (and ἡ, E.*Or*. 1493 (lyr.)), *cub, whelp*, esp. *lion's whelp*, Il.18.319; in full, σ. λέοντος Hdt.3.32, E.*Supp*.1223, Ar.*Ra*.1431, cf. *Eq*.1039; λεαίνης S.*Aj*.987; also of other animals, σ. λύκων E.*Ba*.699; λυγγός Lasus 3; τῆς ἄρκτου, τῆς ἐλέφαντος, Arist.*HA*571ᵇ30, 578ᵃ22; ἀλώπεκος Plu.*Lyc*. 18. 2. in poets also of men, Ἀχίλλειος σ. E.*Andr*.1170 (anap.), cf. *Rh*.381 (anap.); of women, Id.*Or*.1213,1387 (lyr.).

**σκυμνοτοκέω**, *to be viviparous*, of certain selachia, Arist.*Fr*.324.

**σκυνίζει**· λακτίζει, Hsch.

**σκύνιον** [ῠ], τό, *skin above the eyes*, Nic.*Th*.177,443, Poll.2.66 (all pl.); cf. ἐπισκύνιον.

**σκυξιφόν**· σκύφον, Hsch.

**σκύπφειος, σκύπφος**, v. σκύφειος, σκύφος.

**σκῡράω**, *go mad* (from eating the herb σκύρον), Nic.*Th*.75.

**σκύρβια**· κρόμμυα, Hsch. **σκυρθάκια**· μειράκια, ἔφηβοι, Id. **σκυρθαλιάς**· Θεόφραστος τοὺς ἐφήβους οὕτω φησὶ καλεῖσθαι· Διονύσιος δὲ τοὺς μείρακας, Id. **σκυρθάλιος**· νεανίσκος, Id. **σκυρθάνια**· τοὺς ἐφήβους οἱ Λάκωνες, Phot. **σκυρίττω**, = κυρίττω, Suid.

**σκύρον** [ῠ], τό, = ἄσκυρον I, Nic.*Th*.74; cf. σκυράω.

**σκῡρόομαι**, in aor. Pass. -ωθῶσι, = λιθωθῶσι, Hsch. (prob. = Hp. *Mul*.1.18 et ap.Gal.19.139); cf. σκιρόομαι.

⊛ **σκῦρ-ος**, ὁ, = λατύπη, *chippings of stone*, used as road-metal, *IG*4² (1).102.27 (Epid., iv B.C.), Sch.Pi.*P*.5.124, Hsch., cf. Poll.9.104; cf. σκῖρος. -ώδης, ες, *stony*, Eust.ad D.P.521. -ωτός, ή, όν, *paved*, ὁδὸς Pi.*P*.5.93; τὰ σκυρω[τά] *road-metal*, prob. rest. in *IG*11(2).199*A* 40 (Delos, iii B.C.).

**Σκῦρος**, ἡ, the island of *Scyros*, Σ. αἰπεῖα Il.9.668:—Adj. **Σκύριος**, α, ον, *of* or *from Scyros*, Pi.*Fr*.106; ἀρχὴ Σ., prov. of a useless acquisition, Lib.*Ep*.1200, Eust.782.52: **Σκύριος**, ὁ, a *Scyrian*, Hdt. 7.183, etc.; Σκυρία δίκη, a lawsuit in which the defendant pleaded absence in Scyros, *Com.Adesp*.902: **Σκῡρόθεν**, Adv. *from Scyros*, Il.19.332.

**σκυσμός**, ὁ, (σκύζομαι) *anger*, Tz.*H*.9.133.

⊛ **σκῠτάλη** [ᾰ], ἡ, *staff, cudgel, club*, D.S.3.8; σ. ἀγριέλαιος, of Heracles' *club*, *AP*9.237 (Eryc.); cf. σκύταλον:—Special usages: 1. at Sparta, *staff* or *baton*, used as a cypher for writing dispatches, a strip of leather being rolled slantwise round it, on which the dispatches were written lengthwise, so that when unrolled they were unintelligible: commanders abroad had a staff of like thickness, round which they rolled these strips, and so were able to read the dispatches:—hence σκυτάλη came to mean *a Spartan dispatch*, Th.1.131, X.*HG*3.3.8, Ar.*Lys*.991, Plu.*Lys*.19, Gell.17.9.15; and, generally, *dispatch, message*, as Pi. calls the bearer of his ode σκυτάλα Μοισᾶν *O*.6.91, where the Sch. quotes ἀχνυμένη σκυτάλη (dub. sens.) from Archil. (*Fr*.89.2); ἡ σκυτάλης περιτροπή, of labour in vain (cf. ὕπερος), Pl.*Tht*.209d. 2. *pole* or *staff*, like those of a sedan-chair, Lxx *Ex*.30.4. 3. *strickle for levelling grain* piled up in a measure, σ. δικαία *PTeb*.823.15, *PAmh*.2.43.10 (both ii B.C.), cf. Poll.4. 170. 4. *wooden tally* or *ticket* on a money-bag, etc., Diosc.Hist.4, D.S.13.106. 5. *strip* or *rod of metal* or *ivory*, κασσιτέρου *Inscr. Délos* 442 *B*170 (ii B.C.); ἐλέφαντος ibid.; cf. Hld.9.15. 6. *scourge, whip*, Moer.p.346 P. 7. *handle* or *lever* in a machine, Orib.49.3.3; *handspike* for turning a wheel, Ph.*Bel*.68.6, 85.2, Hero *Bel*.86.12 (pl.). II. *sucker* from a stem, *Gp*.9.11.4, al. III. *cylinder* or *roller* wherewith weights are moved, Arist.*Mech*.852ᵃ16, cf. *CPHerm*. 95.16 (iii A.D.). IV. *a serpent*, of uniform roundness and thickness, Nic.*Th*.384, Sor.ap.Philum.*Ven*.27.3 (for Plu.*Crass*.32 v. Σκύλλα). 2. *a fish* of like shape, Opp.*H*.1.184. V. *finger-bone, phalanx*, Paul.Aeg.6.43, Tz.*H*.9.126.

**σκῠτᾰληφορέω**, *carry a club*, Str.15.1.8: -φόρος, ον, Id.16.4.17.

**σκῠτᾰλ-ίας**, ου, ὁ, *cudgel-shaped*, σίκυος a *long* cucumber, Thphr. *HP*7.4.6; αὐλός Juba ap.Ath.4.177a (-είας). ⊛ -ιον, τό, Dim. of σκύταλον, *little staff, baton*, σκυτάλι' ἐφόρουν Ar.*Av*.1283, where the Sch. remarks on the exceptional quantity σκυτᾱλι' ἐφόρουν, quoting *Fr*. 422 (where it may well be short), Nicopho 2, and other examples; ἐσκυτᾰλιοφόρουν Porson. 2. *little pipe, flute*, Poll.4.82, and perh. so in Thphr.*HP*4.4.12. 3. *lever, handle* for turning a windlass, etc., Hero *Spir*.1.43; *support*, Orib.49.4.41. 4. *cog, tooth*, on a wheel, Hero *Dioptr*.34 (pl.). 5. dub. sens., σφαιρίον σ. οὐκ ἔχον *BCH*29.546 (Delos, ii B.C.). II. = κοτυληδών 5, Dsc.4.91. -ίς, ίδος, ἡ, Dim. of σκυτάλη, *stick*, Hdt 4.60. 2. = σκυτάλιον I. 3, esp. as used by fishermen for drawing the net to land, Ael.*NA*12.43. 3. = σκυτάλη I. 2, J.*AJ*3.6.3. 4. = σκυτάλη I. 1, Aen.Tact.22.27, D.S. 8.27, etc. 5. = σκυτάλη I. 5, ἐλέφαντος, κασσιτέρου, *Inscr.Délos* 443*Bb*94,95 (ii B.C.). 6. *engine for hurling fire*, Suid. 7. *finger-bone* (cf. σκυτάλη v), J.*AJ*3.7.6, Poll.2.144, Sor.*Fract*.22, Gal.2.250; of the neck, σ. τοῦ αὐχένος dub. in Id.19.139. 8. = σκυτάλη I. 4, *ticket*, Polyaen.1.17. 9. = σκυτάλη I. 7, *handspike*, Hero *Bel*.86.11. II. = σκυτάλη II, *Gp*.4.3.11: hence, *withy, willow wand*, Str.17.1.50. 2. Dim. of σκυτάλη III, διὰ -ίδων ἐβενίνων λείων ἐξομαλίζονται τὰ σώματα Id.15.1.54, cf. 55. III. *small crab*, of the καρίς kind, Hsch. 2. a kind of *caterpillar*, *EM* 720.45. -ισμός, ὁ, the *reign of club-law* at Argos, D.S.15.57, Plu.2.814b, Hellad.ap.Phot.*Bibl*. p.534 B. -ον, τό, = σκυτάλη, *cudgel, club*, Pi.*O*.9.30, Hdt.3.137, Ar.*Ec*.76, X.*An*.7.4.15: also ⊛ **σκύταλος**, ὁ, Tz.*H*.9.130. II. v. σκύτη. -όω, *cudgel*, in Pass., *EM*720.47, Hsch. -ωσις, εως, ἡ, = ῥάβδωσις, prob. in *IG*4.742.3 (Troezen). -ωτός, ή, όν, *cogged, toothed*, τύμπανον, τροχοί, Hero *Dioptr*.34, *EM*720.42.

**σκῦτ-άριον**, τό, Dim. of σκῦτος, Anaxil.18.6, *POxy*.936.23 (iii A.D.). II. *little shield* (Lat. *scutum*), Hsch. s.v. ἀσπίδα. -εία, Ion. -είη, ἡ, *shoemaking*, Hp.*Art*.53 (σκυτίης cod. B), Poll.7.80; also σ. τέχνη Man.4.321. -εῖον, τό, *shoemaker's workshop*, Hp. *Epid*.4.20, Teles p.46 H., *Vit.Hom*.9. -εύς, έως, ὁ, = σκυτοτόμος, Ar. *Av*.491, Pl.*Grg*.491a, X.*Ages*.1.26, Archipp.30, *PPetr*.2 p.108 (iii B.C.), etc. -ευσις, εως, ἡ, = σκυτεία, Arist.*EE*1219ᵃ21. -εύτρια, ἡ, fem. of σκυτεύς, prob. in Hsch. s.v. πεσσοσύπτη. -εύω, *make shoes*, X. *Mem*.4.2.22, Artem.1.51; also -έω, *PGen*.75.7 (iii A.D.).

**σκύτη**· κεφαλή, Hsch.; also **σκύτα**· τὸν τράχηλον, Σικελοί, Id.; freq. in Hp. acc. to Psell.ap.Zonar.1 p.cxviii.8 Tittm.; cited fr. Hp. by Erot. and expld. as *part of the neck* or *spinal marrow* or *scalp*, citing Archil.122; τὰ σκύταλα (leg. σκύτα).., ὅ ἐστι τοὺς τραχήλους, Sch. Ar.*Av*.1283 (ascribed to Epich.(173a) by Kaibel *CGF*p.vii).

**σκυτίζω**, = σπαράττω, Hsch.

**σκῦτ-ικός**, ή, όν, (σκῦτος) *skilled in shoemaking*, Socr.*Ep*.13: ἡ -κή (sc. τέχνη), = σκυτοτομία, Pl.*R*.374b, al., Arist.*Pr*.956b4: **-κὴ** πλατεῖα *Street of Cobblers*, *IGRom*.4.790 (Apamea); παντοπωλεῖα σ. *OGI*629.78 (Palmyra, ii A.D.). **-ῖνος**, η, ον, *leathern, made of leather*, μάστιξ Anacr.21.10; ἀναξυρίδες, ἐσθής, σκευή, Hdt.1.71, 4.189, 7.71; πλοῖα Id.1.194; ἁμαξίδες Ar.*Nu*.880; χύτρα Crates Com.29; ὑποκεφάλαιον Hp.*Art*.30; κράνη X.*An*.5.4.13; σκύτινον καθειμένον a *leathern* phallus, Ar.*Nu*.538 (v.l. -ίον); so σκυτίνη ἐπικουρία Id.*Lys*. 110; a phrase which is used by Strattis (*Fr*.54) to denote the *feebleness* of Sannyrio; prob. both writers meant to pun upon the proverb συκίνη ἐπικουρία, v. σύκινος. **2.** metaph., *of skin and bone, gaunt*, σ. δαιμόνια *AP*11.361 (Autom.). **-ίον**, τό, v. σκύτινος. ® **-ίς**, ίδος, ἡ, Dim. of σκῦτος, D.L.4.56; *leather amulet*, τοῦ Σαράπιδος τὸ ὄνομα ἐγγεγραμμένον λεπίδι χαλκῇ περὶ τὸν τράχηλον δεδέσθαι ὥσπερ σκυτίδα Artem.5.26, cf. Afric.*Cest*.p.39 V.

**σκῦτο-βρᾰχίων** [ῑ], ονος, ὁ, ἡ, *with the leathern arm*, nickname of Dionysius the historian, Ath.12.515e, cf. Suet.*Gramm*.7. **-βυρσεύς**, έως, ὁ, *leather-worker*, *OGI*495.6 (Cibyra).

**σκῡτοδεψ-έω**, *dress leather*, Poll.7.81. **-ης**, ου, ὁ, *leather-dresser, currier*, Thphr.*Char*.16.6, *HP*3.18.5, Plu.*Num*.17 (gen. pl.), Luc.*Vit.Auct*.11; cf. σκυλοδέψης. **-ικός**, ή, όν, *of* or *for curriers* or *currying*, ῥοῦς Hp.*Liqu*.5: **-κή**, ἡ (sc. κόπρος), Thphr.*CP*3.17.5, 5.15.2. **-ός**, ὁ, = σκυτοδέψης, Pl.*Grg*.517e, v.l. in Luc.*Vit.Auct*.11.

**σκῡτοκόλεος**, ον, *leather-sheathed*, μάχαιραι *PCair.Zen*.54.42 (iii B.C.).

**σκύτον**, τό, v. σκύτη.

**σκῡτο-π[ωλεῖον]**, τό, *leather-seller's shop*, dub. in *PSI*6.678.3 (iii B.C.). **-πώλης**, ου, ὁ, *leather-seller*, *IG*2².2403 (Piraeus, iv B.C.), Poll.7.80. **-ρράφος** [ᾰ], ὁ, (ῥάπτω) *shoemaker* or *leather-worker*, Orib.47.17.2.

**σκῦτος**, εος, τό, *skin, hide*, esp. *dressed* or *tanned hide*, Od.14.34, Hp.*Art*.33, Ar.*Eq*.868; ὁ νοῦς γὰρ ἡμῶν ἦν τότ' ἐν τοῖς σκύτεσι (with a reference to Cleon the tanner) Id.*Pax* 669; εἰ ἐμβάται γένοιντο σκύτους X.*Eq*.12.10; τῶν σκυτῶν ῥυτίδες Pl.*Smp*.191a; σκυτῶν τομή Id.*Chrm*.173d. **II.** *leather thong, whip*, D.21.180, Plu.*Pomp*.18, etc.; σκύτη βλέπειν to look like a whipped cur, Eup.282, Ar.*V*. 643; σ. τέμνειν εἰς νουθεσίαν ἀνθρώπων ἀφρόνων Socr.*Ep*.12. (Cf. Skt. *skunoti* 'cover', Lat. *ob-scū-rus*.) [σκῦτος with ῠ occurs in codd.; but in Ar.*Pl*.514 Bentl. restored σκῠλοδεψεῖν; so in Theoc. 25.142 σκύλος is the better reading, and in Lyc.1316 Scheer conjectures σκύλος.]

® **σκῡτοτομ-εῖον**, τό, *shoemaker's shop*, Lys.24.20, Macho ap.Ath. 13.581d (v.l. -ιον). **-έω**, *cut leather* for shoes, *to be a shoemaker*, Ar.*Pl*.162,514, Pl.*R*.454c, al.; ὑποδήματα σ. Id.*Chrm*.161e. **-ία**, ἡ, *shoemaking*, Id.*R*.397e. **-ικός**, ή, όν, *of* or *for a shoemaker*, τὸ σ. πλῆθος Ar.*Ec*.432; ὁ σ., = ὁ σκυτοτόμος, Pl.*R*.443c; ἡ **-κή** (sc. τέχνη), = foreg., ib.333a, etc.; ἡ σ. τέχνη Aeschin.1.97. **-ος** (parox.), ὁ, *leather-cutter, worker in leather*, Il.7.221, Pl.*R*.601c, X. *Cyr*.6.2.37, etc.; esp. *shoemaker, cobbler*, Ar.*Eq*.740, *Lys*.414, Pl. *Grg*.447d, al., *IG*2².2403 (Piraeus, iv B.C.).

**σκῦτο-τρᾰγέω**, *gnaw leather*, κύων Luc.*Ind*.25, Alciphr.3. 47. **-φάγος** [ᾰ], ον, f.l. for σκατ-, Poll.6.40.

**σκῡτ-όω**, *cover* or *guard with leather*, in Pass., τένοντε(?) ἐσκυτωμένω *IG*1².313.121, 314.135; τόξα ἐσκ. ib.2².1631.223, cf. *Chron.Lind.* B 25; ξύλιναι ἐσκυτωμέναι μάχαιραι Plb.10.20.3. **-ώδης**, ες, *like leather*, Arist.*HA*622a21.

**σκύφ-ειος** [ῠ], α, ον, *like a σκύφος*, σκύπφειον δέπας Stesich.7 (σκυφίον codd. Ath.; σκύπφειον Casaubon). ® **-ίον**, τό, Dim. of σκύφος, Ath.11.477f:—also **-ίδιον**, prob. in *EM*549.13; **-άριον**, *Gloss*. **II.** Medic., *skull*, Paul.Aeg.3.22.5.

**σκῠφο-ειδής**, ές, *like a σκύφος*, Ath.11.499a. **-κώνακτος**, ον, *carried round in cups*, Epich.93.

® **σκύφος** [ῠ], ὁ, and **σκύφος** [ῠ], εος, τό:—*cup, can*, esp. used by peasants, Od.14.112 (where Aristarch. read δῶκε σκύφον, Ar.Byz. σκύφος): neut. in Epich.83, E.*Cyc*.390,411, *Fr*.146, Epig.3, Alex. 130, Archipp.7, *PCair.Zen*.327.26, al. (iii B.C.); masc. in Alcm.34, Anacr.82 (where **σκύπφον**), Simon.246, B.*Fr*.17, Sophr.15, E.*Cyc*. 256,556, Arist.*Pol*.1324b17, *OGI*214.54 (Didyma, iii B.C.), etc.:—of wooden milk-vessels, Theoc.1.143; κισσοῦ σ., κίσσινον σ., = κισσύβιον, E.*Cyc*.390, *Fr*.146. **2.** perh. *skull* (cf. σκυφίον II), *PMag.Par*. 1.1996, al. [ῠ:—but **σκύπφος** in Hes.*Frr*.165,166, Anaximand. Hist.1 J., Panyas.4, *IG*11(2).110 (Delos, iii B.C.), al.]

**σκύφ-ωμα** [ῠ], ατος, τό, = σκύφος I, A.*Fr*.184. **-ών**, ῶνος, ὁ, prob. *valve, cover*, in περιστερεῶνες, Gal.2.582.

**σκῶ·** πεδίσκη, Hsch.

**σκωληκ-ίᾰσις**, εως, ἡ, = σκωλήκωσις, Sm., Thd.*Jb*.17.14. **-ιάω**, *breed worms, be worm-eaten*, *Gp*.10.90.5, Hsch. s.v. εὐλάζει; -ιῶντα πόρον, of the ear, Orib.*Fr*.10. **-ίζω**, *wriggle like a worm*, Hsch. (Med.). **2.** of the pulse, *beat feebly and irregularly*, Gal.8.553, al. **-ιον**, τό, Dim. of σκώληξ, Arist.*HA*552a24, 570b9, Thphr.*HP* 9.5.3, Dsc.1.66. **II.** A kind of *spider*, Philum.*Ven*.15. **-ίτης** [ῑ], ου, ὁ, *worm-like*, κηρός Dsc.1.66.

**σκωληκό-βορος**, ον, *worm-eaten*, καρπός Thphr.*HP*3.12.8. **-βρωτος**, ον, *worm-eaten*, of a tree, ib.3.12.6, *CP*5.9.1; γῆ *PTeb*.701.81 (iii B.C.), *PSI*5.490.14 (iii B.C.). **2.** *eaten of worms*, of a man, *Act. Ap*.12.23. **-ειδής**, ές, *worm-shaped*, Arist.*HA*553a4, Dsc.1.101, Gal.2.730. **-ομαι**, Pass., *to be infested by worms* or *grubs, be worm-eaten*, Thphr.*HP*.4.14.2, *CP*4.14.4, al. **-τοκέω**, *produce grubs*, of animals that produce their young in this shape, Arist.*GA*729b32, al.:—Pass., *to be born in this shape*, ib.733b28, al. **-τόκος**, ον, *producing by grubs*, Id.*HA*538a25, al. **-φάγος** [ᾰ], ον, *eating worms* or *grubs*, ib.592b16.

**σκωληκ-ώδης**, ες, contr. for σκωληκοειδής, ᾠά Arist.*GA*733a30; τὰ σ. the *grubs* or *larvae* of insects, ib.763a18. **-ωσις**, εως, ἡ, *a being worm-eaten*, Thphr.*HP*7.5.6.

® **σκώληξ**, ηκος, ὁ, *worm*, esp. *earthworm*, ὥς τε σκώληξ ἐπὶ γαίῃ κεῖτο ταθείς Il.13.654. **2.** pl., *grubs* or *larvae* of insects, Ar.*V*.1111, *Fr*. 583, Nicopho 1, Thphr.*HP*8.10.4; ἐξ οὗ ὅλου ὅλον γίνεται τὸ ζῷον, opp. the egg (ᾠόν), Arist.*HA*489b8, cf. *GA*733a1, *HA*506a26, 551b2, al. **3.** pl., *worms in dung, in decayed matter, in trees and wood*, Thphr.*HP*3.12.6, 5.4.4, etc. **4.** metaph., οἱ κόλακές εἰσι..οὐσίας σκώληκες Anaxil.33.1. **5.** *aerugo vermicularis*, Dsc.5.79, Androm. ap.Gal.13.806. **II.** *thread twisted* from the distaff, Epig.7. **III.** Aeol. for κολόκυμα, Pl.Com.25, cf. Phryn.*PS* p.108 B., Hsch., Phot. **IV.** *worm-shaped cake*, Alciphr.*Fr*.6. **V.** *heap of threshed corn*, Hsch.

**σκωλο-βάτης** [ᾰ], ου, ὁ, *weevil*, Hsch. **-βᾰτίζω**, *walk on stilts*, Epich.112; cf. ἀσκωλιάζω.

® **σκῶλον**, τό, = σκῶλος, *EM*155.37, Hsch. (pl.). **II.** *stumbling-block, hindrance*, like σκάνδαλον, Lxx *Ex*.10.7, al.:—whence **σκωλόομαι**, Pass., *to be offended*, Aq.*Ho*.9.8, Al.*De*.7.25.

**σκῶλος**, ὁ, = σκόλοψ, *pointed stake*, ὥς τε σ. πυρίκαυστος Il.13.564: also, *thorn, prickle*, Ar.*Lys*.810, Call.*Fr*.7.1 P. **2.** metaph., *evil, ruin*, Lxx 2*Ch*.28.23. **3.** = δρέπανον, Hsch.

**σκῶλος**, εος, τό, dub. sens. in *BGU*40.13 (ii/iii A.D.).

**σκωλύπτομαι**, *wave to and fro*, νεάτην (-ον codd.) σ. οὐρήν Nic.*Th*. 229.

**σκῶμμα**, ατος, τό, (σκώπτω) *jest, gibe*, Eup.159.15,244, Ar.*Nu*.542, *Pax* 750, *Pl*.316, Pl.*R*.452b, etc.; ἐν σκώμματος μέρει by way of a *joke*, Aeschin.1.126; εἰς γέλωτα καὶ σκώμματ' ἐμβαλεῖν D.54.13; εἰς σ. καταστῆναι Lys.*Fr*.75; σ. παρὰ γράμμα a *pun*, Arist.*Rh*.1412a29; it generally implies scurrility, but not necessarily, v. *EN*1128a30, cf. Thphr.ap.Plu.2.631e.

**σκωμμάτιον** [ᾰ], τό, Dim. of σκῶμμα, Ar.*V*.1289.

**σκωπαῖος**, v.l. σκοπ-, ὁ, among the Sybarites, a *dwarf*, Timae.ap. Ath.12.518e; cf. στίλπων.

**σκωπᾰλέος**, α, ον, cited as a parox. word in -αλεος, sine expl., by Hdn.Gr.2.908.

**σκώπ-ευμα**, ατος, τό, = σκώψ 2, A.*Fr*.79. **-ίας**, ου, ὁ, = foreg., Poll.4.103.

**σκωπ-τηλός**, όν, = σκωπτικός, Zonar. **-της**, ου, ὁ, *scoffer*, Archig.ap.Aët.6.8, *EM*593.7, Suid. ® **-τικός**, ή, όν, *given to mockery, jesting*, Plu.*Luc*.27; σ. τι ἐπειπεῖν Luc.*Dem.Enc*.33. Adv. -κῶς Poll.5.161, 9.149.

**σκωπτιλλιο**[, dub. in Cerc.9.2.

® **σκωπτόλης**, ου, ὁ, *mocker, jester*, Ar.*V*.788, D.C.46.18, etc.

**σκωπτολόγος**, ον, = σκωπτικός, Sch.Ar.*Ach*.854.

**σκώπτρια**, ἡ, fem. of σκώπτης, Procop.*Arc*.9.

**σκώπτω**, Ar.*Pl*.973, etc. (not in Hom., but παρα- *h.Cer*.203): fut. σκώψομαι Ar.*Ach*.854, whence Elmsl. restores σκώψει for -ης in *Nu*. 296: aor. 1 ἔσκωψα Hdt.2.121.δ', Pl.*Men*.80a, etc.:—Med., aor. ἐσκωψάμην Alciphr.3.57:—Pass., aor. ἐσκώφθην X.*Cyr*.5.2.18: pf. ἔσκωμμαι, imper. ἐσκώφθω (ἀπ-) Luc.*Bacch*.8:—*mock, jeer, scoff at*, τινας Ar.*Nu*.540,992, *Ra*.421, etc.; σ. τὴν μανίαν τινός Id.*Nu*.350, cf. *Pax* 745; τινὰ τῆς ἀμεριμνίας for his want of thought, Ach.Tat.1.7; τινὰ εἰς μαλακίαν D.18.245; τὰς Λακωνικὰς μαχαίρας εἰς τὴν μικρότητα Plu.*Lyc*.19; also σ. ἐς τὰ ῥάκια *jest* at them, Ar.*Pax* 740; εἴς τινα Aeschin.2.41 (v.l.); πρός τινα Pl.*Thg*.125e:—Pass., *to be mocked*, Nicol.Com.1.31. **b.** in good sense, *joke with*, τινα Hdt.2.121.δ'. **2.** abs., *jest, joke*, Cratin.308, Ar.*Eq*.525, *Nu*.296, etc.; σκώψαντα εἰπεῖν X.*Cyr*.1.3.8; σ. καὶ κωμῳδεῖν Ar.*Pl*.557; σ. ἀγροίκως Id.*V*.1320; χλευάζειν καὶ σ. Arist.*Rh*.1379a29; ὥσπερ Ἀναξανδρίδης ἔσκωψεν according to the *joke* of An., Id.*EN*1152a22; *to be in fun*, opp. to be in earnest, E.*Cyc*.675, X.*Smp*.9.5: sts. in a good sense, εὖ σκώπτειν Arist.*EN*1128a25; ἐμμελῶς σ. Id.*Rh*.1381a36. (Cf. σκώψ fin.)

**σκῶρ** (in Att., but σκώρ in Dor. acc. to Hdn.Gr.1.394), τό; gen. σκᾰτός Pl.Com.5.91, σκάτους in Sophr.12 (s.v.l.): nom. **σκάτος** and gen. σκάτους condemned by Phryn.261:—*dung, ordure*, Epich.54 (codd., rightly), Ar.*Ra*.146, *Pl*.305, Stratt.9. (σκῶρ: σκατός [fr. *σκῃ-τ-ός] is a stem in *r* alternating with *n*(-τ-), cf. ὕδωρ, ὕδατος, etc.: Skt. *apa-(ava-)skaras* 'excrement', ONorse *skarn* 'dung', Lat. *mūscerda*.)

**σκωρᾰμίς**, ίδος, ἡ, *night-stool*, Ar.*Ec*.371.

**σκωρ-ία**, ἡ, (σκῶρ) *dross of metal, slag*, Arist.*Mete*.383b1, *Sens*.443a 19, Herod.6.83, Str.9.1.23, Dsc.5.80, Simp.*in Cael*.667.15; written **σκωρέα**, Zopyr.ap.Orib.14.62.1. **-ιάζω**, *become dross*, Zos.Alch. p.235 B. **-ίδιον**, τό, *small dross*, ibid., Olymp.Alch.p.88 B.

**σκωριο-ειδής**, ές, *like dross*, Dsc.5.85. **-ποιία**, ἡ, *making of dross*, prob. for σκοροπ- in Zos.Alch.p.214 B.

**σκωρνυφία**, ἡ, = σκάνδαλον, Epich.94; = τὰ δσιώδη χρέα (i.e. ὀστώδη κρέα) Id.129.

® **σκωρσελεινα**, ἡ, dub. in *POxy*.936.16 (iii A.D.).

**σκώψ**, ὁ, gen. σκωπός, nom. pl. σκῶπες, a small kind of *owl* (γλαῦξ being the generic name), *the little horned owl*, *Strix scops*, Od.5.66, Epich.166, Theoc.1.136, cf. Arist.*HA*592b11, 617b31. **2.** *a dance* in which the dancers mimicked an owl, Ael.*NA*15.28, Poll.4.103, Ath.9.391a, 14.629f:—in the last place it is explained (as if = σκοπός) *of shading the eyes with the hand* so as to see better; so also Hsch. s.v. σκωπευμάτων: cf. ὑπόσκοπος. **3.** a kind of *fish*, Nic.*Fr*.18. (In

Ael. l. c., Ath.9.391a,b, σκώπτω (as if = *mimic*) is expld. fr. σκώψ, the owl being captured by means of its tendency to mimic one who danced in front of it; other explanations in Sch.Theoc.1.136.)

**σκῶψις**, εως, ἡ, (σκώπτω) *mockery, scoffing, banter*, Alex.156.3.

⊛ **σλιφομαχος**, ὁ, *weigher of silphium* (?), dub. in *Schwyzer* 230 (Cyrenaic vase, vi B.C.).

**σμᾰλερός**, ά, όν, = μαλερός, Poet.*de herb.*101.

**σμάλλεος**, α, ον, κολόβια σμάλλεα perh. *woollen* shirts, dub. in *POxy.*921.6 (iii A.D.).

**σμᾶμα**, v. σμῆμα.

**σμᾰράγδ-ειος**, α, ον, *of smaragdus*, μέταλλα Hld.2.32, etc. **-ίζω**, *to be of a smaragdus green*, D.S.2.52, Dsc.5.142. **-ῖνος**, η, ον, *of smaragdus*, [λίθος] *Apoc.*4.3, cf. Jul.*Or.*2.101c. II. *smaragdus-green*, Cels.5.19.4, *CPR*27.8 (ii A.D.); written ζμ- in *PHamb.*10.25 (ii A.D.). ⊛ **-ιον**, τό, Dim. of σμάραγδος, M.Ant.4.20, prob. in Palaeph. 30. **-ίτης** [ῑ], ου, ὁ, *of the kind* or *colour of the smaragdus*, λίθος Phoen.6.9, Lxx *Es.*1.6; *mons Smaragdites*, Plin.*HN*37.73.

⊛ **σμάραγδος** [μᾰ], ἡ (ὁ, Str.16.4.20, Orph.*L.*614), name of several green stones, including the *emerald*, Hdt.2.44, 3.41, Pl.*Phd.*110d, Thphr.*Lap.*23, al., Lxx *Ex.*28.9, al., Str.l. c., 17.1.45, Plin.*HN*37.62, al., Hld.2.30, Olymp.Hist. p.466 D., *PMag.Lond.*46.239; also **μάραγδος**, Men.373, Com. in *PSI*2.143.3, Orph. l. c., Nonn.*D.*5.178, 18.80; σφραγὶς μαράγδου *IG*11(2).161 *B*44 (Delos, iii B.C.), 199 *B*59 (ibid.), but σφραγὶς σμαράγδου 203 *B*87 (ibid., iii B.C.); **ζμάραγδος** implied in Luc.*Jud.Voc.*9. II. Σμάραγδος, ἡ, name of the emerald mines in Egypt, ἀρχιμεταλλάρχου τῆς Ζμαράγδου *Proc.Soc.Bibl.Arch.* 31 (1909).323 (i A.D.); μεταλλάρχη (gen. sg.) Ζμαράκτου *OGI*660.2 (Egypt, i A.D.); also Σμάραγδος ὄρος Ptol.*Geog.*4.5.8.

**σμᾰραγδοχαίτᾱς**, *emerald-haired*, epith. of πόντος, Tim.*Pers.*32.

**σμᾰραγδώδης**, ες, *like smaragdus*, Sch.Nic.*Th.*444.

**σμᾰρᾰγ-έω**, *crash*, ὅτ' ἀπ' οὐρανόθεν σμαραγήσῃ, of Zeus (= thunder), Il.21.199; σμαραγεῖ πόντος 2.210; σ. λειμών *resounds with the screaming* of cranes, ib.463; of the battle of the Titans, Hes.*Th.* 679; of the bowels, Hp.*Mul.*2.154; of Ares, ὑψόθι δ' ἐσμαράγησε Call.*Del.*136. (Onomatop., cf. σφαραγέω.) **-ή**, ἡ, *crashing, roar*, Opp.*H.*5.243. **-ίζω**, = σμαραγέω, Hes.*Th.*693.

**σμάραγνα** [μᾰ], ἡ, *sounding scourge*, Hsch.; cf. μάραγνα.

⊛ **Σμάρᾰγος** [μᾰ], ὁ, *Smasher*, a lubber-fiend in Hom.*Epigr.*14.9.

**σμᾰράσσω**, = μαράσσω, σμαραγέω, *EM*721.1.

**σμάρδικον**· στρουθίον, and **σμαρδικοπῶλαι**· οἱ τοὺς στρουθοὺς πωλοῦντες, Hsch.

**σμᾰρίλη** [ῑ], ἡ, = μαρίλη, Arist.*Mir.*833ᵃ25.

**σμᾰρίς**, ίδος, ἡ, a small poor sea-fish, *Smaris vulgaris*, Epich.29, 60, Arist.*HA*607ᵇ22, Opp.*H.*1.109, etc. [ᾰ: ᾱ only in Marc.Sid.97.]

**σμαρκόν**· καθαρόν, βρωτικόν, δριμύ, Hsch.

**σμάω**, 3 sg. contr. σμῇ (ἐπι-) Cratin.90, Ar.*Th.*389; inf. σμῆν Luc.*Lex.*3; 3 sg. Pass. σμῆται Antiph.148.4; but in Ion. and late Prose σμᾷ, σμᾶται, Hdt.9.110, Luc.*Anach.*29 (ἀπο-σμᾷ):—impf. ἔσμων (ἐξ-) Hdt.3.148: aor. ἔσμησα Alex.187.5:—**Med.**, pres. part. σμώμενος Ar.*Fr.*360: aor. part. σμησάμενοι Hdt.4.73; Dor. part. σμᾱσαμένα Call.*Lav.Pall.*32; inf. ζμήσασθαι *PEnteux.*82.3 (iii B.C.): —**Pass.**, pf. part. προ-εξμησμένος *PSI*10.1180.48 (ii A.D.). (Hence σμή-χω, cf. ψάω ψήχω, νάω νήχω):—*wipe* or *cleanse with soap* or *unguent* (σμῆμα), ἀποπλύματι τὰς τρίχας D.S.5.28: metaph., σμήσας τε λεπτοῖς ἁλσί (sc. τὴν σηπίαν) Alex. l. c.:—Act. mostly found in compds. δια-, ἐκ-, ἐπι-σμάω:—more freq. in Med., σμησάμενοι τὰς κεφαλάς Hdt.4.73, cf. 9.110; λιπαρὸν σμασαμένα πλόκαμον Call. l. c.: abs., κατέλιπον αὐτὴν σμωμένην ἐν τῇ πυέλῳ Ar.*Fr.*360, cf. Antiph. l. c.—σμῆσαι and σμῆμα are said by Phryn. (228) to be more Att. than σμῆξαι, σμῆγμα; but Moer. (p.336 P.) cites ῥύπτομαι, ῥύμμα as the true Att. words. II. *wipe, wipe clean*, τὴν κάρδοπον Luc.*Lex.*3.

**σμερδ-ᾰλέος**, α, Ion. η, ον, Ep. Adj. (Ar.*Av.*553 is mock-heroic), *terrible to look on, fearful*, δράκων Il.2.309; of Odysseus when cast up by the sea, Od.6.137; σ. κεφαλή, of Scylla, 12.91; χαλκὸς σ. bronze *dire-gleaming*, Il.12.464, 13.192; of armour of all kinds, σάκος, αἰγίς, ἀορτήρ, 20.260, 21.401, Od.11.609; οἰκία σ., of Hades, Il.20.65; ἔρις Hes.*Th.*710; πόλισμα Ar. l. c. 2. *terrible to hear*, esp. in neut. as Adv., σμερδαλέον δ' ἐβόησε Il.8.92, etc.; σ. κονάβησαν, κονάβιζε, 2.334, Od.10.399: pl., σμερδαλέα κτυπέων, of Zeus, Il.7. 479; σ. ἰάχων 5.302. (Prob. cogn. with Skt. *márdati* 'crush, crumble', Lat. *mordere*, OHG. *smerzan*, Engl. *smart*.) **-νός**, ή, όν, = foreg., Γοργείη κεφαλή Il.5.742; σμερδναῖσι γαμφηλαῖσι συρίζων φόνον A.*Pr.*357; μυγαλέη Nic.*Th.*815:—as Adv., σμερδνὸν βοόων Il. 15.687; δέρκεται *h.Hom.*31.9.

**σμέρδ[ν]ος**· λῆμα, ῥώμη, δύναμις, ὅρμημα, Hsch. **σμέρδος**, a kind of *fish*, Id.

**σμῆγμ-α**, ατος, τό, = σμῆμα (v. σμάω 1 fin.), Hp.*Acut.*65, Dsc.5. 118, *Eup.*1.102, Plu.*Demetr.*27; for sheep, *PLond.*1.113(4).18 (vi A.D.). **-ᾰτοπώλης**, ου, ὁ, *one who sells soap and the like*, *Gloss.* **-ᾰτώδης**, ες, *like a σμῆγμα, fatty*, Hp.*Acut.*53; τροφή Aret.*CA*1.10, cf. 2.1; χυλοί Id.*CD*1.13.

**σμήκ-της**, ου, ὁ, *one who rubs* or *cleanses*, *Gloss.* **-τικός**, ή, όν, *purgative*, of medicines, Diphil.Med.ap.Ath.2.55b, 64b; *detersive*, ὀδόντων σ. δύναμις Dsc.2.4, cf. Luc.*Am.*39. **-τός**, ή, όν, *smeared*, κεράμια *POxy.*1735.3 (iv A.D.). **-τρίς**, ίδος, ἡ, γῆ a kind of *fuller's earth*, Eup.380, Nicoch.4, Cephisod.6, Hp.*Mul.*2.189, *Fist.*3.

**σμῆλαι**· ῥίψαι, Hsch. (fort. ἐνῆλαι). **σμηλακεῖ**· φωνεῖ, Id.; cf. σμιλακτεῖ. **σμηλίον**, v. σμιλίον.

**σμῆμα**, Dor. σμᾶμα Theoc.15.30, ατος, τό, (σμάω) *soap, unguent*, Antiph.136, Philox.2.40, Theoc. l. c., Aristid.*Or.*49(25).36; written ζμῆμα *PRyl.*230.8 (i A.D.), *PLond.*2.243.23 (iv A.D.); cf. σμάω 1 fin.

**σμημᾰτο-δοκίς**, ίδος, ἡ, *box of unguents*, Hsch. s.v. ῥύμμα. **-δόχος**, ον, *for holding unguents*, perh. to be read for σαματοδόχος in Id. s. v. λιτρίς. ⊛ **-θήκη**, ἡ, = σμηματοδοκίς, Id. s. v. ῥύμμα. **-φορεῖον**, τό, = foreg., Ar.*Fr.*17, *IG*2².1485.49.

**σμήν-η**, ἡ, f. l. for μήνη in Hdn.Gr.2.923 codd. II. pl., = τῶν μελισσῶν οἱ κηροδόχοι ἤτοι αἱ θῆκαι, Hsch. **-ηδόν**, Adv., (σμῆνος) *in swarms*, Hdn.*Epim.*127. **-ίον**, τό, Dim. of σμῆνος, Dsc.2. 84. II. = ἡ πρόπολις, Hsch. **-ιών**, ῶνος, ὁ, *stand of beehives*, Apollon.*Mir.*44.

**σμηνο-δόκος**, ον, *keeping bees*, *AP*9.438 (Phil., s. v. l.). **-κόμος**, ὁ, (κομέω) *bee-keeper*, Hsch.

**σμῆνος**, Dor. σμᾶνος Theoc.1.107, εος, τό, *beehive*, σμήνεσσι κατηρεφέεσσι Hes.*Th.*594, cf. *IG*1².326.15, Pl.*R.*552c, Arist.*HA*624ᵃ6 sq. II. *swarm of bees*, σ. ὣς μελισσᾶν A.*Pers.*128 (lyr.), cf. Pl.*Plt.* 293d, Arist.*HA*627ᵇ15, al.; of wasps, Ar.*V.*425; of ἀνθρῆναι, Arist. *HA*629ᵃ7. 2. generally, *swarm, crowd*, βομβεῖ δὲ νεκρῶν σ. S.*Fr.* 879; οἷον σοφιστῶν σ. Cratin.2; σ. θεῶν, of the clouds, Ar.*Nu.*297: metaph., τὸ τῶν ἡδονῶν σ., σ. τι ἀρετῶν, Pl.*R.*574d, *Men.*72a; ἀποικιῶν σμήνη Aristid.1.115 J.: heterocl. pl., σμῆνα μελισσάων Orac.ap.Plu. 2.96b. [pl. written ζμήνη, *PCair.Zen.*151.4 (iii B.C.).]

**σμηνουργ-έω**, *to be a bee-master*, Suid. II. Pass., of bees, *swarm*, ἐν τοῖς δένδρεσι Str.11.7.2, cf. 2.1.14. **-ία**, ἡ, *beekeeping*, Poll.7.101. **-ός**, ὁ, *bee-master*, ibid., Ael.*NA*5.13.

**σμῆξις**, εως, ἡ, *cleansing*, τῶν ὀδόντων Str.17.3.7, Dsc.2.4; *washing* of the hair, Diocl.*Fr.*141. 2. *wash, salve*, σ. ψωρικαί Dsc.5. 109.

**σμηρέα**, ἡ, prob. f.l. for σπειραία (q.v.) in Thphr.*HP*6.1.4; but Hsch. has **σμηρία**· κισσός.

**σμηρεύς**, v. σμιρεύς.

**σμῆριγξ**, ιγγος, ἡ, *hair*, Lyc.37, Poll.2.22; esp. on the thighs and necks of dogs, Hsch. II. σμῆρι⟨γ⟩ξ· πόα, καὶ εἶδος ἀκάνθης, Id.; cf. μῆριγξ.

**σμηρίζω**, *smooth* a metal surface, Hero *Spir.*1.11, 28.

**σμήρινθος**, ἡ, = μήρινθος, Pl.*Lg.*644e. II. a bird, Hsch.

**σμήρισμα**, ατος, τό, *air-tight fitting*: I. *tube with another inside it as in a siphon or syringe*, Hero *Spir.*1.6, 2.17. II. *tube with another passing through it at right angles, tap, stopcock*, ib.2.10: Dim. **σμηρισμάτιον**, τό, ib.1.6.

**σμήχη**, ἡ, = σεύτλιον, Hsch.

**σμήχω**, Hp *Acut.*65, impf. ἔσμηχον Od.6.226: aor. ἔσμηξα Aret. (v. infr.), Nonn.*D.*25.331, etc.:—**Med.** and **Pass.**, σμήχομαι Hp. *Acut.* l. c.: aor. ἐσμήχθην (δι-) Ar.*Nu.*1237: ἐσμηξάμην Hp.*Steril.*219, *Superf.*25: pf. part. ἐσμηγμένος Dsc.5.79:—lengthd. form of σμάω, *wipe off* by help of soap or unguent (cf. σμῆμα, σμῆγμα), *wash off*, ἐκ κεφαλῆς δ' ἔσμηχεν ἁλὸς χνόον Od. l. c. 2. *clear off* by help of lotions or salves, ἀχῶρας, λέπρας, Dsc.1.33, 2.9, etc. b. *purge away*, φλέγμα Aret.*CA*1.10. II. *soap* a person, *wash* him *with soap* or *unguent*, Hp.*Acut.* l. c.; *wipe clean*, Lyc.876; ἀσπίδα Babr.76. 12: prov., Αἰθίοπα σ. '*wash* a blackamoor white', Luc.*Ind.*28, Zen. 1.46, Diogenian.1.45:—Med. and Pass., *wash oneself* or *get oneself washed with soap* or *unguent*, Hp.*Acut.* l. c.; σμηξάσθω τὴν κεφαλήν Id.*Steril.* l. c., *Superf.* l. c.; σμηχομένα κρόταφον *wiping her* brow *clean*, *AP*6.276 (Antip.); τοὺς ὀδόντας Str.3.4.16; of hair, οὔρῳ κυνείῳ σμῆχου Archig.ap.Gal.12.443.

**σμῑκρ-ασπις**, v. μίκρασπις. **-ίζω**, *sift* or *bolt very small*, Hsch. (Pass.).

**σμῑκρο-**, for all words beginning thus v. μικρο-. (σμικρολογέομαι, = μικρ- 1, Gal.*UP*11.15; σ[μικρο]λόγος is dub. in *Supp.Epigr.*4.512 (Ephesus, ii A.D.).)

**σμῑκρός, σμῑκρότης, σμῑκρόφθαλμος**, v. μικρ-.

**σμῑκρύνω**, *think meanly of*, τὰς προτάσεις App.*Mac.*9.3; cf. μικρύνω.

**σμῖλα**, ἡ, = σμίλη, *AP*6.62 (Phil.), 295 (Phan.).

**σμῑλάκ-ῐνος** [ᾰ], η, ον, *of the* σμῖλαξ, ξύλον Poll.5.32:—also **-ειος**, α, ον, Theognost.*Can.*55.

**σμιλακτεῖ**· φωνὴν ἀποτελεῖ, Hsch.; cf. σμηλακεῖ.

**σμῖλαξ**, older Att. μῖλαξ, ᾰκος, ἡ (but τοῦ μίλακος Thphr.*HP*1.10. 5):—in Arcadia, *holm-oak, Quercus Ilex*, ib.3.16.2; *milax*, Plin.*HN* 16.19. II. = σμῖλος, μῖλος, *yew, Taxus baccata*, Pl.*R.*372b, Dsc.4. 79, Plu.2.647f; *milax*, Plin.*HN*16.51. III. σμ. κηπαία, *kidney-bean, Phaseolus vulgaris*, Dsc.2.146. IV. *bindweed*, μῖλαξ in Thphr.*HP*1.10.6, Plin.*HN*24.83, σμῖλαξ Thphr.*HP*3.18.11, 7.8.1; μ. τραχεῖα rough *bindweed, Smilax aspera*, Dsc.4.142; σμ. τραχεῖα Ps.-Dsc.4.142; μ. λεία *great bindweed, Convolvulus sepium*, Dsc.4. 143; σμ. λεία Ps.-Dsc.4.143.—The σμῖλαξ or μῖλαξ of Trag. and Com. is prob. *Smilax aspera* (No. IV), cf. E.*Ba.*108 (lyr.), 703, Ar.*Nu.* 1007; σμ. ἡ πολύφυλλος Eup.14.3, cf. Ar.*Av.*216 (anap.).

**σμῑλ-άριον**, τό, Dim. of σμίλη, Heliod.ap.Orib.44.7.5, Gal.14. 785. **-εία** and **-ευσις**, εως, ἡ, *carving*, Hdn.*Epim.*127. **-ευμα**, ατος, τό, *a piece of carved work*: metaph., σμιλεύματα ἔργων finely carved works, Ar.*Ra.*819. **-ευτός**, ή, όν, *cut, carved*, *AP*7.411 (Diosc.). **-η**, ἡ, *knife for cutting* or *carving*, Ar.*Th.*779, Pl.*R.*353a, Babr.98.13; *graving tool, sculptor's chisel*, *AP*7.429 (Alc.); *surgeon's knife* or *lancet* (cf. φλεβοτόμος), Luc.*Ind.*29, Poll.4.181; *shoemaker's knife*, Pl.*Alc.*1. 129c, Herod.7.119; *vinedresser's pruning-knife*, *Gp.*5.35.1 (but v. Pl. *R.*353a); *penknife*, *AP*6.67 (Jul.), etc.: cf. σμῖλα.

**σμῑλιγλύφος** [ῠ], ον, *chiselling*, τέχναι *Epigr.Gr.*402.3 (Galatia).

**σμίλῖνος** [μῑ] τροχίσκος, pill *that acts like a scalpel*, Androm.ap. Gal.13.835.

**σμῑλίον**, τό, Dim. of σμίλη, ἰατρικὸν σ. *scalpel*, Plu.2.60a, cf. S.E. *M*.9.207, Dsc.*Eup*.1.44; of a *drug* producing the same effect, Paul. Aeg.3.23.13, 7.17.12; of an *eye-salve*, written *zmilion*, Cels.6.6. 18. 2. *shoemaker's knife*, Luc.*Gall*.26; *penknife*, written **σμηλίον**, *POxy*.326 (i A.D.).

**σμῑλιωτός**, ή, όν, *shaped like a* σμιλίον, Heliod.ap.Orib.46.11.17; written **μηλιωτός** in Paul.Aeg.6.90. II. = κοπίσκος, a kind of λίβανος, Dsc.1.68.

**σμῖλος**, ἡ, = μῖλος, σμῖλαξ II, *yew*, Call.*Fr*.100f.48, Nic.*Al*.611, Dsc.4.79.

**σμινδῠρίδια** (sc. ὑποδήματα), τά, a kind of *women's shoes*, Poll.7. 89, Hsch. (Named after *Smindyrides* of Sybaris, Hdt.6.127.)

⊛ **Σμινθεύς**, έως, ὁ, epith. of Apollo, Il.1.39; either (from **Σμίνθος** or **Σμίνθη** a town in the Troad, Hsch., St. Byz.) *the Sminthian*; or (from σμίνθος) *mouse-killer*, Sch. ad loc., cf. Str.13.1.48 and 64:—also **Σμίνθιος**, ὁ, Ael.*NA*12.5, Sch.Il. l.c.; Σμίνθιος, ὁ (sc. μήν), name of a month at Rhodes, *IG*2[2].1131,12(1).1068.2, al.; written Ζμ–, ib.1149. 8, al. ⊛ **Σμίνθεια**, τά, *games at festival of Apollo* Σμινθεύς, Μουσ. Σμυρν. 1876 p.125 (Troad).

**σμίνθος**, ὁ, *mouse* (Mysian word, Sch.Il.1.39), A.*Fr*.227, Lyc. 1306, *AP*9.410 (Tull. Sab.), Str.13.1.48 (where codd. σμίνθιοι):—also **σμίνθα**, ἡ, Hsch.—Cf. Σμινθεύς.

**σμίνθουροι**· τὰ(ς) οὐρὰς οἱ σαίνοντες, Hsch. **σμίντα**· παλίουρος, Id.

**σμῐνύη** [ῠ], ἡ, *two-pronged hoe* or *mattock*, *IG*1[2].313.128, al., Ar. *Nu*.1486,1500, *Av*.602, *Pax* 546, Pl.*R*.370d; σμινύδας in Ar.*Fr*.402b (Poll.10.173) is prob. an error for σμινύας.

**σμίνῠον** [ῐ], τό, = foreg., prob.l. in Nic.*Th*.386.

⊛ **σμιρεύς**, a measure of wine in the Libyan Pentapolis, also **σμηρεύς**, Hsch.

**σμιρινηα**, ἡ, prob. = σμυρναία, in a list of colours, *POxy*.1739.6 (ii/iii A.D.).

**σμίρις, σμιρίς, σμιρίτης, σμιριτος**, v. σμύρις. **σμίς**· μῦς, Hsch.

⊛ **Σμισιών**, ῶνος, ὁ, name of a month at Antioch in Pisidia or at Magnesia on the Maeander, *Inscr.Magn*.81.7, cf. *Schwyzer* 687 *D* 1 (Chios, vii/vi B.C.).

**σμογερόν**· σκληρόν, ἐπίβουλον, μοχθηρόν, Hsch. **σμοιός**, ά, όν, Hdn.Gr.1.109; σμοιῷ προσώπῳ Anon. (fort. A.*Ag*.639, ubi στυγνῷ) ap.Hsch.; and **σμοῖος**, α, ον, Theognost.*Can*.49, = σκυθρωπός; as pr. n., Ar.*Ec*.846; also **μοιος** and **σμυός**, Hsch. **σμοκορδοῦν**· τὸ σχηματίζεσθαι τὰς γυναῖκας, Id. **σμοκόρδους**· τοὺς τὰς ὀφρῦς ἐγκοίλους ἔχοντας, Id. **σμορδοῦν**· συνουσιάζειν, Id. ⊛ **σμόρδωνες**, = πόσθωνες, Id. **σμόω**, = σμώχω, *EM*721.22, *An.Ox*.2.407.

**σμῠγερός**, ή, όν, poet. for μογερός, *with pain, painful*, A.R.4.1065: Comp., Id.2.374: Adv., Id.4.380; σμυγερὸν σμυγερῶς S.*Ph*.166 (anap.), as Brunck for στυγερὸν στυγερῶς; cf. Sch. ad loc., Hsch., Eust.1463.44:—Hom. has only the compd. Adv. ἐπισμυγερῶς (q. v.).

**σμυδρός**· διάπυρος σίδηρος, Hsch. (i. e. = μύδρος). **σμυκτήρ**· ὁ μυκτήρ, Id.

**σμύλη**, ἡ, a fish, Alex.Trall.12; gen. pl. σμύλων (implying **σμύλος**, ὁ, s. v. l.) *Gp*.20.7.1: **σμύλλα**· σαύρα, Hsch.

**σμυλίχη**, ἡ, *the hole in the yoke in which the pole was inserted*, Hsch.

**σμύξων**, ὁ, = μύξων, Arist.*HA*543[b]15 (v.l. μύξ–). **σμυός**, v. σμοιός.

**σμύραινα** [ῠ], ἡ, = μύραινα, Pl.Com.151, Mnesim.4.39, Arist.*HA* 504[b]34, Agatharch 33; cf. σμῦρος.

⊛ **σμυρίζω**, poet. for μυρίζω, κόμας Archil.30 (Pass.).

⊛ **σμύρις**, ιδος, ἡ, *emery-powder*, used by lapidaries, Dsc.5.147; **σμίρις** v.l. in Dsc. l.c., Orib.13 λ 24, Paul.Aeg.7.3 s. v. λίθοι; **σμιρίς**, ἡ, Hsch., Aët.2.26; gen. σμίρεως Orib.15.1.20 codd.; cf. ζμιρριεῖα:—also **σμιρίτης** [ῑτ] λίθος, ὁ, Lxx *Jb*.41.7 (v.l. **σμιριτος**).

⊛ **σμύρνα**, freq. written **ζμύρνα** as in *PSI*4.328.2 (iii B.C.), *PTeb*.35.4 (ii B.C.), *PMag.Par*.1.781, etc., ἡ, = μύρρα, *myrrh*, the gum of an Arabian tree, *Balsamodendron Myrrha* (itself called σμύρνα Apollod. 3.14.4, Ant.Lib.34.5), used for embalming the dead, Hdt.2.40,86, cf. 73, *Ev.Jo*.19.39; called σμύρνης ἱδρώς by E.*Ion* 1175; burnt as incense, βωμὸς ἀτμίζων πυρὶ σμύρνης σταλαγμούς S.*Fr*.370; ὑποθυμιῆν σ. Hp.*Nat.Mul*.6; used as an unguent or salve, σμύρνῃ κατάλειπτος Ar.*Eq*.1332; σμύρνῃ ἰώμενοι τὰ ἕλκεα Hdt.7.181; cf. Thphr.*HP*9.1. 2, 9.4.3 and 10, Dsc.1.64, etc. II. *Indian bdellium, Balsamodendron Mukul*, Arr.*An*.6.22.4. (The orig. form must have been μύρρα, from Phoen. *môrâh*; cf. κιννάμωμον.)

**Σμύρνα**, Ion. –νη, ἡ, *Smyrna*, in Ionia, Hom.*Epigr*.4.6, Mimn.9.6 (where it is called Aeolic, cf. Hdt.1.149):—**Σμυρναῖος**, α, ον, *of Smyrna*, Pi.*Fr*.204; **Σμυρναϊκός**, ή, όν, Dorio ap.Ath.7.319d, etc.—In Inscrr. and Coins freq. written **Ζμύρνα, Ζμυρναῖος**, *IG*3.128.14, *IGRom*.4.1545 (Erythrae), Head *Hist.Num*. p.593.

**σμυρν-αῖος**, α, ον, *of myrrh*, *AP*4.1.29 (Mel.). **–εῖον**, τό, = σμύρνιον, Nic.*Th*.848, *Al*.405. **–ιάζω**, = sq. 1, dub. in Alex.Trall. 8.2. **–ίζω**, *flavour* or *drug with myrrh*, ἐσμυρνισμένος οἶνος *Ev. Marc*.15.23. 2. intr., *to be like myrrh*, Dsc.1.66. **–ῐνος**, η, ον, *of myrrh, made from it*, ἔλαιον Lxx *Es*.2.12; μύρον *PMag.Lond*.46. 224. 2. *myrrh-coloured*, παλλίον ζμ. *POxy*.1584.18 (ii A.D.). **–ιον**, τό, *Cretan alexanders, Smyrnium perfoliatum*, Dsc.3.68, Gal.6.637, Ael.ap.Ar.Byz.*Epit*.138.16. **–ισις**, εως, ἡ, *embalming with myrrh*, Aët.16.143(153).

**σμυρνό-μελαν**, ανος, τό, a mixture of *ink and myrrh* used in magic, only in form **ζμυρνό–**, *PMag.Par*.1.815, al., *PMag.Osl*.1.103: Dim. **–μελάνιον**, ib.257 (–μέλανον ib.3.2). **–φόρος**, ον, *bearing myrrh*, (sc. γῆ), Str.16.4.4; βασιλεία Id.16.4.25.

**σμυρνόω**, *embalm with myrrh*, Cyran.97.

**σμῦρος**, ὁ, a kind of *eel*, different from σμύραινα, Arist.*HA*543[a]24.

**σμυρτή**· σμυρτός, Hsch. **σμυστία**· ἡ πρόπολις, Lysicrates ap. Hsch.

**σμύχω** [ῡ], aor. ἔσμυξα (κατ–) Il.9.653, *AP*5.253 (Paul.Sil.) (simple σμῦξαι Hsch.):—Pass., aor. 1 ἐσμύχθην (κατ–) Theoc.8.90; aor. 2 ἐσμύγην [ῠ] (ἀπ–) Luc.*DMort*.6.3: pf. ἔσμυγμαι (κατ–) Hld.7.21:—*burn in a slow, smouldering fire, make* a thing *smoulder away* (cf. κατασμύχω): metaph. of grief, τεῖρ' ὀδύνη σμύχουσα A.R.3.762; κῆρ ἄχεϊ σμύχουσα ib.446:—Pass., *smoulder away*, Ἴλιος πυρὶ σμύχοιτο Il.22.411; by the fires of love, Mosch.*Fr*.2.4; by suspicion, Hld. 1.16; πυρετὸς –όμενος Gal.11.25; σμύχονται σάρκες *are shrivelled*, Aret.*SD*1.8.

**σμώφ**· ῥανίς, τὸ τυχόν, Hsch.: also, = βούγλωσσον, Amerias, ib.

**σμώγω**, *smite*, cited as etym. of σμῶδιξ, *EM*721.23.

**σμωδικός**, ή, όν, *belonging to weals* or *bruises*, φάρμακον a plaster *for them*, Gal.19.139.

⊛ **σμῶδιξ**, ιγγος, ἡ, *weal, swollen bruise*, caused by a blow, σ. αἱματόεσσα μεταφρένου ἐξυπανέστη Il.2.267; πυκναὶ δὲ σμώδιγγες.. αἵματι φοινικόεσσαι ἀνέδραμον 23.716, cf. Opp.*H*.2.428.

**σμώνη**, ἡ, *squall of wind*, Hdn.Gr.1.336, *EM*721.28, al.

**σμώχω**, *rub down, grind down*, καὶ σμώχετ' ἀμφοῖν τοῖν γνάθοιν Ar. *Pax* 1309; σμώξας Nic.*Th*.530. 2. metaph., *attack with abuse*, Diodorus ap.Sch.Ar.*Th*.396.

⊛ **σοβᾰρ-εύομαι**, *bear oneself pompously, give oneself airs*, *AP*5.272, 279, 11.382.14 (all Agath.). **–ητικός**, ή, όν, = σοβαρός, σφοδρός, Hsch.

**σοβᾰροβλέφᾰρος**, ον, *with haughty upraised eyebrows, supercilious*, *AP*5.216 (Paul.Sil.).

⊛ **σοβ-ᾰρός**, ά, όν, (σοβέω) *rushing, violent*, ἄνεμος.. φέρεται σ. Ar.*Nu*. 406; σ. κατέχει αὔρα Id.*Pax* 944; ὡς σ. εἰσελήλυθεν ὁ συκοφάντης Id. *Pl*.872; ὁ σ. ἡμῖν ἀρτίως καὶ πολεμικός.. κλάει κατακλινείς Men.*Pk*.52; λίαν ἦν θρασὺς καὶ σ. [ὁ Ἔρως] Aristopho 11.5. Adv. –ρῶς, opp. ἥσυχος, ἠρέμα, Ar.*Pax* 83. II. *swaggering, pompous, haughty*: of a horse, = γαῦρος, X.*Eq*.10.17; σ. καὶ ὀλίγωρος D.59.37; σ. αὐχένες, ὀφρύες, *AP* 5.27,91 (both Rufin.); σοβαρὸς τῇ χαίτῃ Luc.*Zeux*.5; σοβαρὸν γελᾶν Pl.*Epigr*.4.1, Theoc.20.15. Adv. –ρῶς Plb.3.72.13, Plu.*Alc*.4. b. *proud*, λόγοι ἀδεεῖς καὶ σ. Id.*Pyrrh*.18; *fearless*, dub. in Epicur. *Sent.Vat*.45. 2. of things, σ. μέλος a *rousing* tune, Ar.*Ach*.674; *imposing*, [στολή] Plu.*Alex*.45; of a triumphal procession, Id.*Sull*. 34; σοβαρωτέρα τιμή at a *more impressive* price, Ael.*NA*16.32; σ. ἀναθήματα Id.*Fr*.67. Adv. –ρῶς ib.70. **–άς**, άδος, ἡ, poet. fem. of σοβαρός, of bacchanals and courtesans, *insolent, capricious*, Eup.344, cf. Ph.1.568, 2.266. II. ἡ σοβάς, a kind of *dance*, Ath.14.629f. **–έω**, *scare away* birds, ἡμεῖς δὲ.., οὐ σοβοῦντος οὐδενὸς ἀνεπτόμεσθ' Ar.*Av*.34; ἐπειδὴ τουτονὶ σεσοβήκαμεν (just above he had been called στροῦθος) Id.*V*.211; σ. τὰς ἀλεκτρυόνας Pl.Com. 20; οὐ σοβήσετ' ἔξω τὰς ὄρνιθας ἀφ' ἡμῶν; Men.167; τέττιγας Arist. *HA*556[b]14; μυίας Thphr.*Char*.25.5; *drive along*, ὥσπερ αἰπόλιον.. αὐτοὺς τῇ ῥάβδῳ σ. Luc.*Cat*.3; ἔχοντες ξύλα σοβοῦσι τὴν ὕλην they *scare* the wood (i. e. *beat* it so as to put up the birds), Arist.*HA*620[a] 35. 2. generally, *drive away, clear away*, τὴν κόνιν X.*Eq*.5.5:—Pass., τὰς ἄλλας φροντίδας.. σεσοβῆσθαι Hp.*Ep*.12. II. *move rapidly* or *violently* (cf. σοβαρός I and κυκλοσοβέω), σ. τὴν κύλικα *push about* the bottle, Philostr.Jun.*Im*.3. 2. metaph., ὁ παῖς σοβείτω τοῖς ποτηρίοις *let* him *ply* [the guests] with cups (cf. πατάσσω II. 2), Amphis 18. 3. metaph. also in Pass., *to be agitated, excited*, Philostr.*VS*1.21.5; σεσόβηται ἐρωτικῶς Id.*Im*.1.8; γυνὴ σεσοβημένη 'forward' (of Opinion personified), Hp.*Ep*.15; σεσοβημένος οἴστρῳ *AP*6.219 (Antip.); σεσ. πρὸς δόξαν *all in a fever* for glory, Plu.*Pomp*. 29; σεσ. περί τι Ph.1.131; ῥυθμὸς σεσ. *hurried, wild*, Longin.41.1; σεσ. κίνησις Ph.2.267. III. intr.. *walk in a pompous manner, strut, swagger*, διὰ τῆς ἀγορᾶς σοβεῖ D.21.158; σοβοῦντες ἐν ὄχλῳ προπομπῶν Plu.*Sol*.27; μεθ' ὅσης θεραπείας καὶ παρασκευῆς ἐσόβει Alciphr.1.38; σόβει ἐς Ἄργος *off with you!* Luc.*DDeor*.24.2; σ. παρὰ τὸν Δρύαντα Longus 3.29. (Causative of σέβομαι, q. v.) **–η**, ἡ, *the solid part of a horse's tail*, *Hippiatr*.55; *of a bull's tail*, Sch. Ptol.*Tetr*.2. 2. *horsehair plume* of a helmet, Suid. **–ησις**, εως, ἡ, *agitation, excitement*, Plu.2.671f; περί τι ib.286c. 2. v. sq. **–ητρον**, τό, *fly-flap*, οὐρά, σ. τῶν ἐπιποτωμένων v. l. for σόβησις in Ph.2.428.

**Σόβος**, ὁ, (σοβέω) = Σάτυρος, Ulp. ad D.21.158 (pl.).

**σόγκος**, ὁ, = σόγχος I (q. v.). II. in Lat. form, *soncus niger*, = σόγχος II, Plin.*HN*22.88.

**σογκώδης**, ες, *like the plant* σόγκος, Thphr.*HP*6.4.5.

**σογχίτης** [ῑ], ου, ὁ. = ἱεράκιον τὸ μέγα, Ps.-Dsc.3.64 p.75 Wellm.

⊛ **σόγχος**, ὁ, *sow-thistle, Sonchus aspera*, Antiph.226.4; also written **σόγκος**, Matro *Fr*.2.1, Thphr.*HP*4.6.10,6.4.3,8, Nic.*Fr*.71, Hegesand. 9 (where ἐξογκοῖτ' is a pun on ἐκσογκοῖτ'). II. σ. τρυφερός, *milk-weed, Sonchus oleraceus*, Ps.-Dsc.2.131.

**σοέω**, = σεύω, impf. σόει B.16.90: pf. part. Pass. ἐσσοημένον Hsch.; σεσοῆσθαι restored for σεσοβεῖσθαι in Id. s. v. σοιδηύδεις.

**σοί**, v. σύ. **σοιδηύδεις**· βάκχαι.., Hsch. **σοίθης**· ψίθυρος, ἀλαζών, διάβολος, Id. **σοίκιδες**· κώνωπες, Id. **σοῖο**, Ion. gen. of σός, σόν.

**σόκκος**, ὁ, *lasso*, Olymp.Hist. p.457 D.

**σολῖνος** or –ον, prob. a kind of *shoe*, *IG*2[2].1120 (Edict.Diocl.).

⊛ **σόλιον**, τό, *slipper*, Lat. *solea*, *POxy*.741.8 (ii A.D.), *PSI*3.206.9 (iii A.D.); ζεῦγος σολίων *Bull.Soc.Arch.Alex*.6.280; σ. παπύρινα

*POxy.*1742.6 (iv A.D.). 2. *seat, stool,* Lat. *solium, Sammelb.*1.10 (iii A.D.), *POxy.*1288.16 (iv A.D.); σ. σιδηροῦν *PMasp.*6 ii 47 (vi A.D.).

**σολοειδής,** ές, perh. = θολοειδής, *dome-shaped,* δάφνη *IG*5(1).258 (Sparta, metr.).

**σολοικ-ία,** ἡ, = σολοικισμός, Luc.*Salt.*80; περὶ σολοικίας, title of treatise by Ammonius. **-ίζω,** fut. -ιῶ A.D.*Synt.*199.14:—*speak* or *write incorrectly, commit a solecism,* φωνῇ Σκυθικῇ σ. *speak bad* Scythian, Hdt.4.117; σ. τῇ φωνῇ D.45.30, cf. Arist.*SE*173ᵇ20, *Rh.*1407ᵇ18; defined as τῇ λέξει βαρβαρίζειν, Id.*SE*165ᵇ20; coupled with βαρβαρίζειν, Phld.*Rh.*1.154 S., Plu.2.59f. 2. *to be guilty of an absurdity,* σ. ἐν δόξαις Epicur.*Nat.*14.9, cf. 10; περὶ σολοικιζόντων λόγων, title of treatise by Chrysippus, *Stoic.*2.6. II. *err against good manners* or *propriety* in any way (in speech, thought, dress, eating, etc.), *behave boorishly,* Zeno *Stoic.*1.23; περί τι Plu.2.45e; τῇ χειρί Philostr.*VS* 1.25.9. **-ισμός,** ὁ, *incorrectness in the use of language, solecism,* Arist.*SE*173ᵇ17; σολοικισμοὶ καὶ βαρβαρισμοί Phld.*Rh.*1.159 S., cf. Plu.2.731f, Luc.*Vit.Auct.*23; but βαρβαρισμός, incorrectness in the use of words, is distd. fr. σολ., *incorrectness in the construction of sentences,* A.D.*Synt.*198.8, cf. Phld.*Rh.*1.159 S. 2. of incorrect reasoning, περὶ σολοικισμῶν, title of work by Chrysippus, *Stoic.*2.6; cf. foreg. 1.2. II. *awkwardness,* Plu.2.520b (pl.). ⊛ **-ιστής,** οῦ, ὁ, *one who speaks incorrectly, commits solecisms,* title of a dialogue by Luc.

**σολοικοειδής,** ές, *solecistic,* Serv.Dan. ad Verg.*A.*10.10, Eust.1752.43:—also **-ώδης,** ες, Gal.16.511.

**σόλοικος,** ον, *speaking incorrectly, using broken Greek,* φθόγγος Anacr.79; οἱ σόλοικοι *foreigners,* Hippon.46; βάρβαρον ἢ σ. τι M.Ant. 1.10. II. metaph., *erring against good manners, awkward, in bad taste,* τῷ τρόπῳ X.*Cyr.*8.3.21 (Comp.), cf. Arist.*Rh.*1391ᵃ4, Cic.*Att.* 14.6.2, Plu.2.817b; σολοικότερον, c. inf., it would be *clumsy, absurd,* Hp.*Fract.*15. Adv. **-κως** *rudely,* σ. κεκομμένοι, of coins, Zeno *Stoic.* 1.23. (Said to come from the corruption of the Attic dialect among the Athenian colonists of Σόλοι in Cilicia, Str.14.2.28, D.L.1.51.)

**σολοικοφανής,** ές, *like a solecism,* σχηματισμοί D.H.*Din.*8, cf. Gal. 16.512, Serv. ad Verg.*A.*4.355. Adv. **-νῶς** Eust.630.46.

⊛ **σολοιτύπος** [ῠ], ον, *hammering a mass of iron* (σόλος), Hsch. II. *forged at Soli* in Cyprus, χαλκός Id.

**σολόμη,** corrupt word in Hp.*Mul.*1.109 (γολόμης (gen.) cod. θ).

**Σολομωνιακὸς** λίθος, ὁ, *Solomon's* stone, ingredient in a prescription, *Hippiatr.*130.135.

**σόλος,** ὁ, *mass* or *lump of iron,* used in throwing, σόλον αὐτοχόωνον Il.23.826, cf. 839, 844, Eumel.9, *CIG*1541 (Olympia), Sosith.3. 2; distinguished (but not clearly) from the δίσκος by Sch.Il.2.774, 23.826; in μέγαν περιηγέα πέτρον,..σόλον Ἄρεος, A.R.3.1366, σόλος seems = δίσκος, cf. Nic.*Th.*905 (et Sch.), Q.S.4.436.

**Σόλων,** ωνος, ὁ, *Solon,* Hdt.1.29, etc. II. a throw at dice, Eub.57.6.

**σομφ-όομαι,** *become spongy,* Aët.7.6. **-ός,** ή, όν, *spongy, porous,* σ. οἷον σπογγιά Hp.*Loc.Hom.*2; of pumice-stone, Alex.124.10; ἡ γλῶττα σὰρξ μανὴ καὶ σ. Arist.*HA*492ᵇ33; freq. of the lungs, ib.496ᵇ3, *Resp.*478ᵃ13, al., cf. Clidem.ap.Thphr.*Sens.*38; σομφὴ σάρξ, of fish, Archestr.*Fr.*14; of ground, χώρα σ. καὶ ὕπαντρος Arist.*Mete.* 366ᵃ25, cf. 352ᵇ10. II. metaph. of sound, *unresonant,* σομφὸν φθέγγεσθαι, of persons with polypus in the nose, Hp.*Morb.*2.33; σομφὸν ἐμπνεύσας, of a flute-player, blowing *thickly, huskily,* D.H. *Comp.*11, cf. Alex.Aphr. *in Top.*329.28; half-way between λευκός and μέλας in sounds, as φαιός is in colours, Arist.*Top.*106ᵇ7. III. σομφός, ὁ, = κολοκυνθίς, Plin.*HN*20.13. **-ότης,** ητος, ἡ, *sponginess, porosity,* τοῦ πλεύμονος Arist.*PA*669ᵃ16. **-ώδης,** ες, *of spongy, porous nature,* Thphr.*HP*9.14.1: Comp., Pall. *in Hp.Fract.*12.283 Chart.

**σοναρόν·** ῥωμαλέον, Hsch. (fort. σοβ- vel σθεν-). **σόος,** η, ον, Ep. and Ion. form of σῶος, σῶς: v. σῶς. **σορδισμός·** τὸ μὴ καθαρῶς διαλέγεσθαι ἤτοι ἑλληνίζειν, Id.; cf. σαρδισμός. **σορεῖον** or **σόρειον,** v. σορίδιον.

**σορέλλη,** nickname of an old man, *with one foot in the grave* (cf. σοροδαίμων, σορόπληκτος), Ar.*Fr.*198.

⊛ **σορίδιον,** τό, Dim. of σορός, Hierocl.*Facet.*97: also **σορεῖον** or **σόρειον,** τό, *IG*12(8).553, 556 (Thasos); ⊛ **σόριον,** τό, *CIG*2846.10 (Aphrodisias).

**σόρνιξα·** εὔζωμον, Hsch. **σορόα·** παλιούρου εἶδος, Id. (παλινούρου cod.).

**σορο-δαίμων,** ονος, ὁ, ἡ, a nickname of *one on the brink of the grave, an old ghost, Com.Adesp.*1151, cf. Plu.2.13b. **-εργός,** όν, *coffin-making,* τέχνης κανονίσματα Man.4.191. ⊛ **-πηγός,** ὁ, (πήγνυμι) *coffin-maker,* Ar.*Nu.*846, *AP*11.122 (Callicter?), 123 (Hedyl.):— **-πήγιον,** τό, *his workshop,* Poll.7.160. ⊛ **-πληκτος,** ον, and **-πλήξ,** πλῆγος, ὁ, ἡ, = σοροδαίμων, Eust.1431.43. **-ποιός,** ὁ, *coffin-maker,* Poll.10.150.

⊛ **σορός,** ἡ, *vessel for holding* human remains, *cinerary urn,* ὡς δὲ καὶ ὀστέα νῶϊν ὁμὴ σ. ἀμφικαλύπτοι Il.23.91; *coffin,* Hdt.1.68, 2.78, Ar.*Ach.*691, *Lys.*600, etc.; of stone, Thphr.*Ign.*46, Dsc.5.124: prov., τὸν ἕτερον πόδα ἐν τῇ σ. ἔχειν Luc.*Herm.*78; *bier, Ev.Luc.*7.14, *PLond.*1.121.236 (iii A.D.). II. as nickname of an old man or woman, Ar.*V.*1365, Macho ap.Ath.13.580c. III. αἱ δημόσιαι σ. dub. sens. in *PLips.*86.11 (iv A.D.).

⊛ **σορῷον,** τό, *cerecloth, PHib.*1.67.14, al. (iii B.C.).

**σορωνίς·** ἐλάτη παλαιά, Hsch. (fort. σαρωνίς).

**σός,** ή, όν, possessive Adj. of 2 pers. sg. (σύ), the alternative Ep. and Dor. form being τεός (q.v.), *thy, thine,* Il.8.420, etc.; Ep. gen. σοῖο Od.15.511; σ. δέμας, σ. ἔργον, λέχος σ., etc., A.*Pr.*146 (lyr.), 635, 557 (lyr.), etc.: σ. ἑταῖρος a friend *of yours,* Pl.*Ly.*204a, etc.: with the Art., τὸ σὸν γέρας Il.1.185, cf. 207, al., and so freq. in Att., δέμας τὸ σ., τὸ σ. κάρα, etc., A.*Pr.*1019, *Ag.*1615, etc. (but never so when it serves as predicate, οὐ σ. τόδ' ἐστὶ τοὔργον S.*El.*296; πάτερ, σός εἰμι Id.*Ant.* 635); σ. ἔργον c. inf., 'tis *thy* business to.., ἔργον ἤδη σ. τὰ λοίφ' ὑπηρετεῖν Id.*Ph.*15; σόν [ἐστι] alone, σ. δ' αὖ τὸ σιγᾶν A.*Th.*232, cf. S.*El.*1470; σὴ μὲν ἐγώ, σὰ δὲ πάντα *thine* am I, *thine* are all things, Call.*Del.*219. 2. without a Subst., *thine,* εἰ ἐτεόν γε σός εἰμι *thy son,* Od.9.529, cf. E.*Hel.*226 (lyr.); σὺ μὲν ἀπάγου τὴν σ. X.*Cyr.*3.1.37; οἱ σ. *thy kinsfolk, people,* S.*OT*1448, etc.: also sg., *your agent* or *servant, PFay.*123.5 (i/ii A.D.): τὸ σ. *what concerns thee, thy interest, advantage,* S.*El.*251, *Aj.*1313; *thy words, thy purpose,* ib.99, 1401, etc.; τὰ σ. *thy property,* ἐπὶ σοῖσι καθήμενος Od.2.369, cf. X.*Mem.*2.3.12, *Ev.Luc.*6.30; εὖ φρονῶ τὰ σ. *thy interests,* S.*Aj.*491; καὶ σὲ καὶ τὰ σ. Id.*El.*522, etc. 3. with a gen. added, τὰ σ' αὐτῆς ἔργα Il.6.490; τὰ σ' αὐτοῦ κήδε(α) Od.14.185; σῷ δ' αὐτοῦ κράατι 22.218; τοῖς σοῖσιν αὐτοῦ S.*OT*416; τὸ σὸν μόνης δώρημα Id.*Tr.*775; τὸν σ. τοῦ πρέσβεως [ὀφθαλμόν] Ar.*Ach.*93. II. objective, *of* or *for thee,* σῇ ποθῇ Il.19.321; σ. τε πόθος σ. τε μήδεα Od.11.202; σῇ προμηθίᾳ S.*OC*332; προνοίᾳ τῇ τε σ. κἀμῇ E.*Andr.*660; εὐνοίᾳ τῇ σ. Pl.*Grg.*486a.

**σόσσος·** ἡ διόπτρα, καὶ τὸ σταδιαῖον διάστημα, Hsch.

**σοῦ,** gen. of σύ; also of σός. (In Hom. only the latter.)

**σοῦ, σοῦ,** *shoo! shoo!,* a cry to scare away birds, Ar.*V.*209.

**σουβίτυλλος,** ὁ, a kind of *cake,* Lat. *savillus,* Chrysipp.Tyan.ap. Ath.14.647d.

**σουβλ-ίζω,** *pierce,* Suid. s.v. πείρω. **-ίον,** τό, and **-ίν,** τό, = Lat. *subula, Gloss.*

⊛ **σοῦβος,** ὁ, an unknown animal, Opp.*C.*2.382, *An.Ox.*4.267.

⊛ **σουβρίκιον,** *subricula, Gloss.*

**σουβρῐκομᾰφόρτιον,** τό, *outer veil, POxy.*905.7 (ii A.D.).

**σουβρῐκοπάλλιον,** τό, *outer cloak, BGU*327.7 (ii A.D.); written **σουρικο-,** *POxy.*921.4 (iii A.D.).

⊛ **σουβρικός,** *superaria, Gloss.*

**σουγχῖνος,** ὁ, = *sucinum, amber, Gp.*15.1.29: cf. σούκινος.

**σουδάριον,** τό, = Lat. *sudārium, towel, napkin, Ev.Luc.*19.20, *Ev. Jo.*11.44, *CPR*1.27.7 (ii A.D.), *Supp.Epigr.*7.417 (Dura), Poll.7.71; σ. ὀλόλιτον *PMag.Osl.*1.269 (iv A.D.).

**σούκῐνος,** η, ον, *made of amber* (Lat. *sucinum*), Artem.2.5 (v.l. σούχιχοι): cf. σουγχῖνος, σούχινον. II. σούκινος· εὐνοῦχος, Hsch.

**σοῦκλαι·** φοινικοβάλανοι, Hsch. **σοῦμαι,** v. σεύω: cf. ἀπεσσούα.

**σουμμαρούδης,** ου, ὁ, = Lat. *summarudis, Supp.Epigr.*6.60 (Ancyra).

**σούμωρος·** κεχορτασμένος, πλήρης, Hsch.

**σοὔνεκα,** Att. crasis for σοῦ ἕνεκα, S.*Ph.*554 (Aurat. σοῦ νέα).

**σουνεπτᾶσθαι·** συνακολουθῆσαι, Hsch.

**Σουνῐάρᾱτος** [ἄρ], ον, (Σούνιον) *worshipped at Sunium,* Ποσειδῶν Ar.*Eq.*560 (lyr.); parodied in *Av.*868, **Σουνιέρᾱκος** *Hawk of Sunium.*

**Σούνιον,** τό, *Sunium,* the southern headland of Attica, Od.3.278, etc.:—Adj. **Σουνιακός,** ή, όν, Hdt.4.99; pecul. fem. **-ιάς,** άδος, D.P. 511:—⊛ **Σουνιεύς,** έως (ῶς), ὁ, pl. Σουνιεῖς (ῆς), *a man of Sunium,* Pl. *Tht.*144c, Anaxandr.4.

**σουρίζει,** Att. crasis for σοι ὀρίζει, A.*Ch.*927.

**σοῦς,** ὁ, *upward motion,* a Democritean term, Arist.*Cael.*313ᵇ5; Lacon. for ἡ ταχεῖα ὁρμή, acc. to Pl.*Cra.*412b. (From *σόϝος, cf. σεύω, σοῦμαι.)

**σοῦσθαι, σοῦσθε, σούσθω,** v. σεύω.

**Σουσῐ-γενής,** ές, *born at Susa,* A.*Pers.*644 (lyr.).

**σούσῐνος,** η, ον, (σοῦσον) *of lilies,* [ἔλαιον] Hp.*Nat.Mul.*32, 74; with ἔλαιον expressed, *Edict.Diocl.Delph.*13; cf. Thphr.*Od.*27, Dsc. 1.52, Antyll.ap.Orib.10.25.2:—σούσινον, = κρίνον, Dsc.3.102.

**σοῦσον,** τό, *lily,* = κρίνον, Aristobulus and Chares ap.Ath.12.513f, dub. in Arist.*Mir.*838ᵃ23 (Phoen. and Phrygian word, acc. to Zonar.; cf. Hebr. *shûshan*; σασά Syrian acc. to Ps.-Dsc.3.102). II. **Σοῦσα,** τά, *Susa,* in the province of Susiana or Shushan, Hdt.1.188; the winter and spring residence of the King of Persia, Id.5.52, X.*Cyr.*8. 6.22, *An.*3.5.15:—**Σούσιος,** ὁ, *a man of Susa,* Id.*Cyr.*5.1.2:—**Σουσίς,** ίδος, ἡ, *the province of Susa,* A.*Pers.*119, 557 (s.v.l.) (Σ. γυνή a woman *of Susa,* X.*Cyr.*4.6.11); also **Σουσιάδες** πέτραι D.S.17.68; and **Σουσιανή,** ἡ, Id.2.2. (Derived from σοῦσον acc. to St.Byz. (σοῦσαν codd.).)

**σουστί,** Att. crasis for σοι ἐστί, A.*Eu.*913, Ar.*Ach.*339. **σοῦται, σοῦνται,** v. σεύω.

**σούχινον,** τό, *amber,* Aët.2.35: cf. σούκινος.

⊛ **σοῦχος,** ὁ, name of the *crocodile* in one part of Egypt, Str.17.1. 38, Dam.*Isid.*99; as pr.n. of the crocodile god of the Fayûm, *PTeb.* 60.9 (ii B.C.), etc.: **Σουχιεῖον,** τό, *his temple,* ib.86.35 (ii B.C.), al.

⊛ **σοφία,** Ion. -ίη, ἡ, prop. *cleverness* or *skill* in handicraft and art, as in carpentry, τέκτονος, ὅς ῥά τε πάσης εὖ εἰδῇ σ. Il.15.412; of the Telchines, Pi.*O.*7.53; ἡ ἔντεχνος σ., of Hephaestus and Athena, Pl.*Prt.*321d; of Daedalus and Palamedes, X.*Mem.*4.2.33, cf. 1.4.2; in music and singing, τέχνῃ καὶ σ. *h.Merc.*483, cf. 511; in poetry, Sol.13.52, Pi.*O.*1.117, Ar.*Ra.*882, X.*An.*1.2.8, etc.; in driving, Pl. *Thg.*123c; in medicine or surgery, Pi.*P.*3.54; in divination, S.*OT* 502 (lyr.); δυσθανατῶν ὑπὸ σοφίας εἰς γῆρας ἀφίκετο Pl.*R.*406b; σ. δημηγορική, δικανική, ib.365d; ἡ περὶ Ὁμήρου σ. Id.*Ion* 542a; οὐ σοφίᾳ ἀλλὰ φύσει ποιεῖν Id.*Ap.*22b; σημαίνοντες τὴν σ..., ὅτι ἀρετὴ τέχνης ἐστίν Arist.*EN*1141ᵃ12: rare in pl., Pi.*O.*9.107, Ar.*Ra.*676 (lyr.), *IG*1².522 (vase, v B.C.). 2. *skill* in matters of common life, *sound judgement, intelligence, practical wisdom,* etc., such as was attributed to the seven sages, like φρόνησις, Thgn.790, 876, 1074, Hdt.1.30, 60; ἡ τῶν δεινῶν σ., opp. ἀμαθία, Pl.*Prt.*360d; τὴν τότε καλουμένην σ., οὖσαν δὲ δεινότητα πολιτικὴν καὶ δραστήριον σύνεσιν Plu.*Them.*2; also, *cunning, shrewdness, craft*, Hdt.1.68, etc.; τὸ λοιδορῆσαι θεοὺς ἐχθρὰ σ. Pi.*O.*9.38. **3.** *learning, wisdom*, μείζω τινὰ ἢ κατ' ἄνθρωπον σοφίαν σοφοί Pl.*Ap.*20e; opp. ἀμαθία, ib.22e; freq. in E., e.g. μόρσιμα..οὐ σοφίᾳ τις ἀπώσεται *Heracl.*615 (lyr.); τὸ σοφὸν οὐ σοφία (v. σοφός I.3) *Ba.*395 (lyr.), etc.; freq. in Arist., *speculative wisdom*, *EN*$1141^{a}19$, *Metaph.*$982^{a}2$, $995^{b}12$ (pl.), $1059^{a}18$; defined as θείων τε καὶ ἀνθρωπίνων ἐπιστήμη, *Stoic.*2.15; but also of *natural philosophy and mathematics*, σ. τις καὶ ἡ φυσική Arist.*Metaph.*$1005^{b}1$, cf. $1061^{b}33$. **4.** among the Jews, ἀρχὴ σοφίας φόβος Κυρίου Lxx *Pr.*1.7, cf. *Jb.*28.28, al.; Σοφία, recognized first as an attribute of God, was later identified with the Spirit of God, cf. Lxx *Pr.*8 with *Si.*24sq. **5.** later as a title, ἡ ὑμετέρα, ἡ ὑμῶν σ., *POxy.*1165.6, *PSI*7.790.14 (both vi A.D.).

**σοφῐβόλος**, *ον*, *stupid*, τὴν κεφαλὴν σοφιβόλον (–βωλον Pap.) ἔχω *POxy.*1873 (v A.D.).

**σοφ-ίζω**, *make wise, instruct*, Lxx *Ps.*18(19).8; τινὰ εἰς σωτηρίαν 2 *Ep.Ti.*3.15. **2.** Pass., *become* or *be clever* or *skilled in* a thing, c. gen. rei, ναυτιλίης σεσοφισμένος *skilled in* seamanship, Hes.*Op.*649; Μοῖσαι σεσοφισμέναι Ibyc.*Oxy.*1790.23; so ἐν τοῖς ὀνόμασι σ. X.*Cyn.*13.6: abs., *to become* or *be wise*, freq. in Lxx, *Ec.*7.24(23), al.; βέλτερος ἀλκήεντος ἔφυ σεσοφισμένος ἀνήρ Ps.-Phoc.130. **3.** Med., *teach oneself, learn*, ἐσοφίσατο ὅτι.. he *became aware* that.., Lxx 1*Ki.*3.8. **II.** Med. **σοφίζομαι**, with aor. Med. and pf. Pass. (v. infr.), *practise an art*, Thgn.19, *IG*$1^{2}$.678; *play subtle tricks, deal subtly*, E.*IA*744, D.18.227, etc.; οὐδὲν σοφιζόμεσθα τοῖσι δαίμοσι *we use* no *subtleties* in dealing with the gods, E.*Ba.*200; *to be scientific, speculate*, περὶ τὸ ὄνομα Pl.*R.*509d, cf. *Plt.*299b, Muson.*Fr.*3 p.12 H., etc.; σοφιζόμενος φάναι to say *rationalistically*, Pl.*Phdr.*229c; καίπερ οὕτω τούτου σεσοφισμένου though he *has dealt* thus *craftily*, D.29.28; σοφίσασθαι πρός τι *to use fraud* for an end, Plb.6.58.12; οἱ ἰητροὶ σοφιζόμενοι ἔστιν οἳ ἁμαρτάνουσι *when they deal in subtleties*, Hp.*Fract.*1; οἱ μυθικῶς σοφ. Arist.*Metaph.*$1000^{a}18$, cf. *HA*$582^{a}35$, D.35.56; σ. πρὸς τὸν νόμον *evade* it, Plu.*Dem.*27. **2.** c. acc. rei, *devise cleverly* or *skilfully*, Hdt.2.66, 8.27, cf. 1.80; καινὰς ἰδέας σοφίζεσθαι Ar.*Nu.*547; χαρίεντα καὶ σοφά Id.*Av.*1401; ἀλλότρια σ. *meddle with* other men's *craft*, Id.*Eq.*299; with internal acc., ἀνόητα σ. *exercise one's skill* without νοῦς, Pl.*Hp.Ma.*283a, cf. X.*Mem.*1.2.46; ὅσα ..σοφίζονται πρὸς τὸν δῆμον Arist.*Pol.*$1297^{a}14$; ἀλλ' αὐτὸ τοῦτο δεῖ σοφισθῆναι this is the very thing one must *gain by craft*, S.*Ph.*77; οἶνον ἀπὸ τῶν φοινίκων σ. *make spurious* wine, Philostr.*VA*2.6; πορφύραν παρὰ τῆς κόχλου Id.*Her.*19.15:—Pass., σεσοφισμένοι μῦθοι *craftily devised*, 2*Ep.Pet.*1.16. **b.** σ. νόμον *evade* it, Philostr.*VA*2.40, cf. Ael.*VH*2.41, Palaeph.50, *OGI*383.208 (Commagene, i B.C.). **3.** c. acc. pers., *deceive*, τὸν Τίτον J.*BJ*4.2.3; μή με σοφίζου *AP*12.25 (Stat. Flacc.); τὸν δῆμον Hdn.7.10.7; also σ. τὴν αἴσθησιν Aret.*SD*1.15. **4.** '*counter*' by a device, σοφίζεται τὴν βίαν τοῦ μηχανήματος J.*BJ*3.7.20. **–ισμα**, *ατος*, *τό*, *acquired skill, method*, in medicine, Hp.*Loc.Hom.*41. **II.** *clever device, ingenious contrivance*, Pi.*O.*13.17 (pl.); σ. μηχανᾶσθαι Hdt.3.85; σ. καὶ μηχαναί ib.152; ἀριθμὸν ἔξοχον σοφισμάτων A.*Pr.*459; οὐκ ἔχω σ. ὅτῳ..πημονῆς ἀπαλλαγῶ ib.470; μὴ..κἀκχέω τὸ πᾶν σ. S.*Ph.*14; τὸ Θεσσαλὸν σ. *a trick* in fighting, v. Θεσσαλός; πολλαῖσι μορφαῖς οἱ θεοὶ σοφισμάτων σφάλλουσιν ἡμᾶς E.*Fr.*972; τέχναι..καὶ σ. Ar.*Pl.*160; τὸ γὰρ σ. δημοτικόν Id.*Nu.*205; πρὸς μὲν Σωκράτη..τὸ σ. μοι οὐδέν Pl.*Smp.*214a; τὸ σ. τὸ τοῦ δρεπάνου Id.*La.*183d. **2.** in less good sense, *sly trick, artifice*, δίκην δοῦναι σ. κακῶν E.*Ba.*489, cf. *Hec.*258; ἐφ' ἡμᾶς ταὐτὰ παρόντα σ. Th.6.77, cf. D.35.2; *stage-trick, claptrap*, Ar.*Ra.*17, 872, 1104; of *tricks* in government, Arist.*Pol.*$1297^{a}35$, $1308^{a}2$; in cookery, X.*Hier.*1.23 (pl.). **3.** *captious argument, quibble, sophism*, Pl.*R.*496a, D.25.18, Epicur.*Nat.*28.9, etc.; περὶ σοφισμάτων, title of work by Chrysippus; σ. τῆς ῥητορικῆς Longin.17.2; opp. a true logical argument (φιλοσόφημα, ἐπιχείρημα), Arist.*Top.*$162^{a}16$:—Ar. calls a person σόφισμ' ὅλον, *Av.*431, cf. Ath.1.11b. **–ισμᾰτικός**, *ή*, *όν*, *sophistical*, of a person, Gell.18.13 (v.l.). **–ισμάτιον**, *τό*, Dim. of σόφισμα, Arr.*Epict.*2.18.17, Luc.*Par.*43. **–ισμᾰτώδης**, *ες*, *sophistical*, Arist.*Top.*$158^{a}35$, Procl.*in Prm.* p.954 S. **–ισμός**, *ὁ*, = σόφισμα, Simp.*in Ph.*1020.11.

**σοφισ-τεία**, *ἡ*, *sophistry*, D.S.12.53, Plu.2.78f, D.L.2.113, etc.; opp. σοφία, Ph.1.10; σ. μαντική, of Balaam, ib.609; title of work by Hermagoras of Amphipolis, *Stoic.*1.102: acc. to Poll.4.50, a barbarism. **–τέον**, *one must contrive*, ὅπως ἂν.. Arist.*Pol.*$1319^{b}25$. **–τευμα**, *ατος*, *τό*, = σόφισμα, Oenom.ap.Eus.*PE*6.7. **–τεύω**, *play the sophist, deal* or *argue as one*, D.61.48, Arist.*SE*$165^{a}28$, Epicur.*Nat.*14.6; *occupy oneself with academic pursuits*, Cic.*Att.*2.9.3, 9.9.1; *practise the profession of sophist*, Epicur.*Fr.*172. **2.** *give lectures*, as the Sophists did, esp. in Rhetoric, Plu.*Luc.*22, *Caes.*3, etc.; ἐπ' ἀργυρίῳ Id.2.1047f: c. acc. cogn., σ. τὰ ῥητορικά *lecture in* rhetoric, Phld.*Rh.*1.223 S., Str.13.1.66. **II.** trans., *devise artfully*, τι Hld.6.9: also, *conceal artfully, dissemble*, τὸν ἔρωτα Id.1.10. **–τήριον**, *τό*, *school of sophistry*, Oenom.ap.Eus.*PE*5.25. **–τής**, *οῦ*, *ὁ*, *master of one's craft, adept, expert*, of diviners, Hdt.2.49; of poets, μελέταν σοφισταῖς πρόσβαλον Pi.*I.*5(4).28, cf. Cratin.2; of musicians, σοφιστὴς..παραπαίων χέλυν A.*Fr.*314, cf. Eup.447, Pl.Com.140; σοφιστῇ Θρῃκί (sc. Thamyris) E.*Rh.*924, cf. Ath.14.632c: with modal words added, οἱ σ. τῶν ἱερῶν μελῶν Ael.*NA*11.1; of the Creator of the universe (ὁ δημιουργός), πάνυ θαυμαστὸν λέγεις σ. Pl.*R.*596d; of cooks, εἰς τοὺς σ. τὸν μάγειρον ἐγγράφω Alex.149.14, cf. Euphro 1.11; οἱ τὴν ἱππείαν σ. *skilled in..*, Ael.*NA*13.9: metaph., σ. πημάτων *deviser, contriver* of pains, E.*Heracl.*993:—then, **2.** *wise, prudent*, or *statesmanlike man*, in which sense the seven Sages are called σοφισταί, Hdt.1.29, cf. Isoc.15.235, Arist.*Fr.*5, D.61.50; of Pythagoras, Hdt.4.95; of natural philosophers, Hp.*VM*20; of Isocrates and Plato, D.H.*Comp.*25; of the Βραχμᾶνες, Arr.*An.*6.16.5, cf. γυμνοσοφισταί; freq. with a slightly iron. sense, ἵνα μάθῃ σ. ὢν Διὸς νωθέστερος A.*Pr.*62, cf. 944; ψυχὴ..κρείσσων σοφιστοῦ παντὸς εὑρέτις S.*Fr.*101, cf. E.*Hipp.*921: prov., μισῶ σοφιστὴν ὅστις οὐχ αὑτῷ σοφός Id.*Fr.*905: of the philosophic *sage*, Aristid.2.311 J. **II.** from late v B.C., *a Sophist*, i.e. *one who gave lessons* in grammar, rhetoric, politics, mathematics, *for money*, such as Prodicus, Gorgias, Protagoras, τὴν σοφίαν τοὺς ἀργυρίου τῷ βουλομένῳ πωλοῦντας σοφιστὰς ἀποκαλοῦσιν X.*Mem.*1.6.13, cf. *Cyn.*13.8, Th.3.38, Pl.*Prt.*313c, *Euthd.*271c, *La.*186c, *Men.*85b, Isoc.15.148, Arist.*SE*$165^{a}22$; σ. ἄχρηστοι καὶ βίου δεόμενοι Lys.33.3; but sts. even of Socrates (though he did not teach for money), Aeschin.1.173; so of Christ, Luc.*Peregr.*13: hence (from the ill repute of the professed sophists at Athens), **2.** *sophist* (in bad sense), *quibbler, cheat*, Ar.*Nu.*331, 1111, al., Pl.*Sph.*268d; γόητα καὶ σοφιστὴν ὀνομάζων D.18.276. **3.** later of the ῥήτορες, *Professors of Rhetoric*, and *prose writers* of the Empire, such as Philostratus and Libanius, Suid.; Ἀπολλωνίδῃ σοφιστῇ *PLips.*97 x 18 (iv A.D.); freq. as a title in epitaphs, *IG*3.625, 637, 680, 775, 14.935. **–τιάω**, *play the sophist*, Eubulid.1, Plu.2.42a, 545c. ⊛**–τικός**, *ή*, *όν*, *of* or *for a sophist*, βίος Pl.*Phdr.*248e; τὸ σ. γένος the class *of sophists*, Id.*Sph.*224c; ἡ –κή (sc. τέχνη) *sophistry*, ib.224d, al. **2.** *sophistical*, μὴ σ. ποιεῖν ἀλλὰ σοφούς X.*Cyn.*13.7; ἐροῦμεν σοφὸν ἢ σ.; Pl.*Sph.*268b; σ. λόγος *fallacy*, Arist.*Pol.*$1307^{b}36$; περὶ σ. ἐλέγχων, title of work by Arist. Adv. –κῶς Pl.*Tht.*154e, Arist.*Rh.*$1419^{a}14$.

**σοφιστορήτωρ**, *ορος*, *ὁ*, = σοφιστὴς καὶ ῥήτωρ, Tz.*H.*11.189.

⊛**σοφίστρια**, *ἡ*, fem. of σοφιστής, coined by Pl.*Euthd.*297c.

**Σοφοκλέης**, Ar.*Ra.*787, *Pax* 695, contr. **Σοφοκλῆς**, *IG*$1^{2}$.202.36, $2^{2}$.2325.5, Th.4.3, ὁ; gen. *έους* Ar.*Pax* 697; poet. also *έος* *AP*7.22.1 (Simm.), 37.1 (Diosc.); acc. *έα* ib.21.1 (Simm.); ἦ (v.l. ἦν) Epigr. in *Vit.Soph.*:—*Sophocles*:—Adj. **Σοφόκλειος**, *α*, *ον*, D.H.*Comp.*9.

**σοφόνοος**, *ον*, contr. **–νους**, *ουν*, *wise-minded*, Luc.*Rh.Pr.*17.

**σοφός**, *ή*, *όν*, *skilled in any handicraft* or *art, clever*, ἁρματηλάτας σ. Pi.*P.*5.115, cf. *N.*7.17; κυβερνήτης A.*Supp.*770; μάντις Id.*Th.*382; οἰωνοθέτας S.*OT*484 (lyr.); of a sculptor, E.*Fr.*372; even of hedgers and ditchers, Margites *Fr.*2; but in this sense mostly of poets and musicians, Pi.*O.*1.9, *P.*1.42, 3.113; ἐν κιθάρᾳ σ. E.*IT*1238 (lyr.), cf. Ar.*Ra.*896 (lyr.), etc.; τὴν τέχνην –ώτερος ib.766; περί τι Pl.*Lg.*696c; γλώσσῃ σ. S.*Fr.*88.10; σοφὸς ὁ πολλὰ εἰδὼς φυᾷ, μαθόντες δὲ λάβροι Pi.*O.*2.86. **2.** *clever in practical matters, wise, prudent*, ὁ χρήσιμ' εἰδώς, οὐχ ὁ πόλλ' εἰδώς, σ. A.*Fr.*390; esp. *statesmanlike*, in which sense the seven Sages were so called, Dicaearch. ap.D.L.1.40: hence, *shrewd, worldly-wise*, Thgn.120, Pi.*I.*2.12, Hdt.3.85; σ. ἄνδρες εἰσὶ Θεσσαλοί Id.7.130; σ. παλαιστής..., ἀλλὰ χαὶ σοφαὶ γνῶμαι..ἐμποδίζονται S.*Ph.*431, cf. 440, *Aj.*1374; πολλὰ σ. A.*Ag.*1295; ἃ δεῖ σ. E.*Ba.*655 sq.; τῶν λεγομένων πονηρῶν μέν, σοφῶν δέ Pl.*R.*519a: also σοφαὶ πραπίδες Pi.*O.*11(10).10; φύσις Ar.*V.*1282: even of animals, X.*Cyn.*3.7 (Comp.), 6.13 (Sup.); σ. πειθώ Pi.*P.*9.39 codd. (σοφοῖς Bgk.); εὐβουλία A.*Pr.*1038: τὸ σ. my little *trick*, Pl.*R.*502d; your *clever notion*, Id.*Euthd.*293d; τἀπ' ἐμοῦ σοφά, δάκρυα my tears, *all the resources that I have*, E.*IA*1214; εἰ δίκαια, τῶν σοφῶν κρείσσω τάδε better *than all craft*, S.*Ph.*1246; σοφόν [ἐστι] c. inf., E.*Hec.*228. **b.** more generally, *learned, wise*, τὸ μὲν σ. [αὐτὸν] καλεῖν ἔμοιγε μέγα εἶναι δοκεῖ καὶ θεῷ μόνῳ πρέπειν Pl.*Phdr.*278d, cf. 279c, *Prt.*329e, *Ap.*21a (Comp.), 22c (Sup.); opp. ἀμαθής, ib.25d (Comp.); of sophists, ib.20a, *Prt.*309d, X.*Mem.*2.1.21, etc.; *universally and ideally wise*, ὁ σ., τουτέστιν ὁ τὴν τοῦ ἀληθοῦς ἐπιστήμην ἔχων Chrysipp.*Stoic.*2.42, cf. 3.167, al.: later σοφώτατος as a title, esp. of lawyers or professors, *PIand.*16.4 (v/vi A.D.), *POxy.*126.6 (vi A.D.). **3.** *subtle, ingenious*, opp. ἀμαθής (1445) and σαφής, Ar.*Ra.*1434 (Adv.); σοφόν τοι τὸ σαφές, οὐ τὸ μὴ σαφές E.*Or.*397; τὸ σοφὸν οὐ σοφία *wisdom overmuch* is no wisdom, Id.*Ba.*395 (lyr.); τί οὖν ἦν τοῦτο; οὐδὲν ποικίλον οὐδὲ σοφόν nothing curious or *recondite*, D.9.37.—For the senses of σ., v. Arist.*EN*$1141^{a}10$.—mostly abs., but c. acc. rei, E.*Ba.*655, Pl.*Phlb.*17c, etc.; also ἐν οἰωνοῖς, κιθάρᾳ, E.*IT*662, 1238 (lyr.); εἴς τι Id.*Fr.*162 (Sup.); περί τι or τινος, Pl.*Smp.*203a, *Ap.*19c: rarely c. gen., σοφὸς κακῶν A.*Supp.*453: also c. inf., πῶς δῆτ' ἔγωγ' ἂν..Διὸς γενοίμην εὖ φρονεῖν σοφώτερος; S.*Fr.*524.7. **II.** of things, *cleverly devised, wise*, νόμος Hdt.1.196 (Sup.); νοήματα, ἔπεα, Pi.*O.*7.72 (Sup.), *P.*4.138, etc.; γνῶμαι S.*Aj.*1091; νοῦς Id.*El.*1016; πάντα προσφέρων σοφά all *wise sayings*, Id.*Fr.*763, cf. *Ph.*1245; χρόνου τε διατριβὰς σοφωτάτας ἐφηῦρε Id.*Fr.*479; σοφώτερ' ἢ κατ' ἄνδρα συμβαλεῖν ἔπη E.*Med.*675; σ. φυγή Id.*Supp.*151; οὐδὲν σοφὸν εἶναι shows no great wisdom, Arist.*EN*$1137^{a}10$. **III.** Adv. σοφῶς *cleverly, wisely*, etc., first (?) in S.(?)*Fr.*1122; then in E.*Alc.*699, *Ba.*1271 codd., *Heracl.*558, Ar.*Ra.*1434, etc.: Comp. –ώτερον E.*Hec.*1007: Sup. –ώτατα Id.*Hel.*1528, Ar.*Nu.*522:—σοφῶς, as an exclamation of applause, Plu.2.45f, Mart.3.46.8, etc. (Not in Ep., exc. in Margites l.c. and as ancient v.l. (Eust.1023.14) in Il.23.712; but v. σοφία, σοφίζομαι.)

**σοφοτέχνης**, *ου*, *ὁ*, *skilled in art*, in nom. pl. σοφοτεχνήϊες (sic), *Epigr.Gr.*841.3 (Thrace, ii A.D.).

**σοφόω**, = σοφίζω, Lxx *Ps.*145(146).8.

**σο-ωδίνη** [ῑ], *ἡ*, *saving in travail*, epith. of Artemis, *IG*7.3407 (Chaeronea).

**σοω-ναύτης**, *ου*, *ὁ*, *saver of sailors*, of a harbour, A.R.2.746, cf. Sch.

**σπάδακες**· κύνες, Hsch.; cf. σπάκα.

**σπᾱδίζω**, (*σπάδιξ* III) *strip off*, *σπαδίξας τὸ δέρμα* Hdt.5.25.

**σπᾱδῑκοφόρος**, *ὁ*, written **σπαδεικ-**, *palm-branch bearer*, *IG*5(2).50.83 (Tegea, ii A.D.).

**σπάδιξ** [ᾰ], *ῑκος*, *ἡ*, (*σπάω*) *bough* or *branch torn off*, esp. *palm-branch* or *frond*, = *βάϊς* (cf. *σπάθη* 7), *σ. φοίνικος* Porph.*Abst*.4.7: abs., Plu.2.724a: pl. in Lat. *spadica* (Amm.Marc.24.3.12); applied to other plants, e.g. *ῥυτῆς* Nic.*Al*.528; *ποῖσω ἀργυρέ[α]ν σ*. *Supp.Epigr*.4.61 (Centuripae, i (?) A.D., but perh. in signf. II). **2.** as Adj., *palm-coloured*, i.e. *bay*, only Lat. *spadix*, Verg.*G*.3.82, Gell.2.26.9. **II.** *a stringed instrument like the lyre*, with high notes, Nicom.*Harm*.4, Poll.4.59; condemned by Quintilian as effeminate, *Inst*.1.10.31. **III.** *rind stripped from the root of the πρῖνος*, *Λέξεις Ἡροδότου* in Stein *Herodotus* ii p.469 (Berol. 1871), cf. Hsch. s.v. *σπᾶ*.

**σπάδιον** [ᾰ], *τό*, Dor. for *στάδιον*, *IG*4.561 (Argos), Hsch., *EM*743.25, Greg.Cor.p.364 S.

**σπᾰδοειδής**, *ές*, *eunuch-like*, Hp.*Ep*.19 (*Hermes* 53.69).

**σπᾰδον-ίζω**, (*σπάδων*) *make flaccid*, *περὶ τοῖς ὀδοῦσι..τὰς τῆς πιμελῆς κτηδόνας* Sor.1.118. **2.** metaph. in trans. sense, *σ. τὸν ἦχον curtail*, *cramp*, *emasculate* their sound, of the short vowels, D.H.*Comp*.14 (as v.l. for *σπανίζει*). **-ισμα**, *ατος*, *τό*, *flaccidity*, *μαστῶν AP*5.203 (Mel., pl.). **-ισμός**, *ὁ*, *weakening*: metaph., *ἤχων σπαδονισμοί impediments* to sound, *arrested* sounds, caused by harsh clashings of consonants, D.H.*Dem*.40.

**σπάδος**, *ὁ*, *eunuch*, St. Byz. s.v. *Σπάδα* (v.l. *σπάθοι*).

⊛ **σπάδων** [ᾰ], *ωνος* (and *οντος* Lxx, Plu., and Artem., v. infr.), *ὁ*: (*σπάω*):—*eunuch*, Lxx *Ge*.37.36, *Is*.39.7, Plb.28.21.5, D.S.30.17, Ph.1.604, Plu.*Demetr*.25, Artem.2.69. Hence **σπᾰδωνισμός**, *ὁ*, *castration*, Zonar.

**σπᾰδών**, *όνος*, *ἡ*, (*σπάω*) *convulsion*, *cramp*, *spasm*, Hp.*Morb*.1.15, Nic.*Al*.317. **2.** generally, *tear*, *rent*, *rag*, Hsch. (Sts. less accurately written *σπάδων*.)

**σπάζει**, Achaean, = *σκυζᾷ* (*σκύζαι* cod.), Hsch.

**σπᾰθ-ᾰρία**, *ἡ*, *a match at sword-play*, *EM*212.10. ⊛ **-ᾰρικόν**, *τό*, *thin upper garment*, Sm.*Is*.3.23. **-άριος** [ᾱρ], *ὁ*, (*σπάθη* 5) *guardsman*, Lyd.*Mens*.4.28, *BCH*33.120 (Cappadocia), etc. **-ᾰρίσκος**, *ὁ*, = *σπαθαρικόν*, Al.*Ge*.38.14 (s.v.l.). **-ᾱτός**, *ά*, *όν*, Dor. for *σπαθητός*, Hsch. ⊛ **-άω**, in weaving, *strike the woof with the σπάθη* (q.v.), *σ. τὸν ἱστόν make* the web *close and strong*, Philyll.12, cf. Poll.7.36:—Pass., metaph., *συλλαβαὶ πολλοῖς γράμμασιν ἐσπαθημέναι close-packed*, Phld.*Po*.2.41. **II.** *θοἰμάτιον δεικνὺς τοδὶ πρόφασιν ἔφασκον "ὦ γύναι, λίαν σπαθᾷς"* you *are laying it on* too *thick*, a cant phrase for 'playing ducks and drakes with' money (perh. with a play on signf. I), Ar.*Nu*.55; *τὰ πατρῷα βρύκει καὶ σ*. Diph.43.27; *σ. τὰ χρήματα* Plu.*Per*.14; *τάλαντα σ*. Luc.*Cat*.20, cf. Philostr.*VA*5.38, Alciphr.3.34; *ἐσπαθᾶτο ταῦτα καὶ ἐδημηγορεῖτο*, expld. by Sch. as = *ἐδαψιλεύετο*, these *were the prodigalities indulged in*, thus *were all advantages squandered away*, D.19.43. **2.** = *ἀλαζονεύομαι*, Men.347. **III.** *σ. τὰ μεγάλα τῶν φυτῶν prune* plants, Philostr.*Im*.2.17. ⊛ **-η**, *ἡ*, *any broad blade*, of wood or metal: **1.** *flat wooden blade used by weavers* in the upright loom (instead of the comb (*κτείς*) used in the horizontal), for striking the threads of the woof home, so as to make the web close, A.*Ch*.232, Philyll.12, Pl.*Ly*.208d; Dor. acc. pl. *σπάθᾶς AP*6.288 (Leon.). **2.** *spattle* for stirring anything, Alex.60; esp. for medical purposes, Gal.13.378, Heraclid.Tar.ap.eund.13.812. **3.** *blade of an oar*, Lyc.23. **4.** pl., *broad ribs*, Poll.2.181, Ruf.*Oss*.25, and so prob. in Hp.*Gland*.14, *PMag.Par*.1.3116, Paul.Aeg.3.78. **5.** *broad blade of a sword*, *Χαλκίδικαι σπάθαι* Alc.15.6; *σπάθη κολούων φασγάνου* E.*Fr*.373; *σπάθην παραφαίνων..χρυσένδετον* Philem.70; *χλαμὺς καὶ σ*. (cf. Ital. *capa e spada*) Men.*Pk*.165, *Sam*.314, cf. Thphr.*Char*.25.4. **6.** *scraper for currying horses*, *PSI*4.430.6 (iii B.C.), Poll.1.185. **7.** *stem of a palm-frond*, Hdt.7.69: also *spathe of the flower* in many plants, esp. of the palm kind, Thphr.*HP*2.6.6, 2.8.4, Poll.1.244. **8.** pl., *flukes* of an anchor, *PLond*.3.1164(*h*).9 (iii A.D.). **9.** pl., = *ἀγκῶνες* II.1, in machines, Orib.49.4.10. **-ημα**, *ατος*, *τό*, *web made close by striking*, Hsch. **II.** metaph., *σ. φρενῶν shrewd fellow*, Phot., Suid. **-ησις**, *εως*, *ἡ*, *striking the web with the σπάθη*, Arist.*Ph*.243$^b$6. **II.** *squandering*, Suid. **-ητός**, *ή*, *όν*, *struck with the σπάθη*, *compactly woven*, A.*Fr*.365, Democr.Eph.1. **-ηφόρος**, *ὁ*, *a σπάθη-bearer*, a police-officer at Alexandria, Ph.2.528. **-ίας**, *ου*, *ὁ*, *like a σπάθη*, *σπαθίην κτένα the broad ribs*, Opp.*C*.1.296. ⊛ **-ίζω**, (*σπάθη* 2) *stir with a spatula*, *ἰατρικῶς* Ps.-Democr.Alch. p.56 B.:—Pass., Orib.*Fr*.85:—Med., *use one in anointing oneself*, Hsch. **2.** (*σπάθη* 5) *play with the sword*, v.l. in Cratin.219. **II.** = **σπαθάω** II, in Pass., *to be squandered*, i.e. *destroyed*, Lyd.*Mag*.2.1. **-ίνης** [quantity of ι unknown], *ου*, *ὁ*, (*σπάθη*) *a young deer*, so called from the shape of its horns, Hsch. (*-ήνης* cod.), Eust.711.38: also in pl. *σπαθιναῖοι*, Sch.A.R.4.175. **-ίον**, *τό*, Dim. of *σπάθη* (signf. 1), *AP*6.283; (signf. 5), *POxy*.1839.4 (vi A.D.); (signf. 2), Gal.2.724, al.; *knife*, *scalpel*, Sor.2.63; *blade* of a scalpel, *Hippiatr*.20; *small blade* in a machine, Hero *Spir*.1.42; name of a measure of capacity, *ἐλαίου σ. ἓν ἐσφραγισμένον PLond*.2.236.5 (iv A.D.), cf. 3.1266(*a*).7 (ii A.D.), etc. **-ίουρος** [ῐ], *ὁ*, *sword-tail*, name of an animal (tapering towards the tail) that kills mice, Philum.*Ven*.32.2 (= Aët.13.32). **-ίς**, *ίδος*, *ἡ*, = *σπάθη* 2, *spatula*, Ar.*Fr*.205, Eub.100; *σ. ἀργυρ[ᾶ] IG*1$^2$.386.17 (unless in signf. II). **II.** *garment of closely-woven cloth* (v. *σπάθη* 1), ib.2$^2$.1469.131, 1517.201, cf. Poll.7.36, Hsch. **-ισμα**, *ατος*, *τό*, = *σπαδόνισμα*, Id. **-ίτης** [ῑ] *οἶνος*, *ὁ*, *palm*-wine, Alex.Trall.2.

**σπᾰθο-μήλη**, *ἡ*, *flat broad probe*, Sor.2.11, Gal.2.724. **-ποιός**, *ὁ*, *gladiarius*, *Gloss*.

⊛ **σπαίρω**, *gasp*, *pant*, *quiver*, of dying fish, Arist.*Resp*.471$^a$30 (v.l. *ἀσπαρίζουσιν*), cf. A.R.4.874, Plb.15.33.5, D.H.4.39, *AP*6.30 (Maced.) (more freq. *ἀσπαίρω*, q.v.).

**σπάκα**, Median for *κύνα*, Hdt.1.110; hence Gramm. (Hdn.Gr.2.8, al.) formed *σπάξ*, *ακός*, *ἡ*: cf. *σπάδακες*.

**σπάλαγμα**, *ατος*, *τό*, in form *spalagma*, = *compositio et ordinatio*, *Gloss*. (dub.).

**σπάλαθρον**, *τό*, v. *σκάλευθρον*.

**σπᾰλᾰκ-ία**, *ἡ*, *dim-sightedness*, Hsch. **-ορύπαινα** [ῠ], *ἡ*, *dirty mole-coloured*, prob. to be read in *PPetr*.2 p.117 (iii B.C.). **-ός**, *ή*, *όν*, perh. *mole-coloured*, *BGU*1283.16 (iii A.D.), dub. in *PHib*.1.120.15 (iii B.C.).

**σπάλαξ** [σπᾰ], *ᾰκος*, *ἡ*, also *ἀσπάλαξ* (q.v.), *blind-rat*, *Spalax typhlus*, Arist.*de An*.425$^a$11, Lxx *Le*.11.30; masc. in Ael.*NA*11.37:—also written **σφάλαξ**, Paus.7.24.11. **II.** *ἵππων εἶδος οἱ σ*. (perh. *mole-coloured*), Hsch.: cf. *σπαλακός*. **III.** *meadow-saffron*, *Colchicum parnassicum*, Thphr.*HP*1.6.11 (s.v.l.).

⊛ **σπάλαυθρον**, v. *σκάλαυθρον*: **Σπάλαυθρα**, *τά*, a town in Thessaly, *IG*9(2).1111.34.

**σπᾰλείς**, Aeol. for *σταλείς*, part. aor. Pass. of *στέλλω*, Jo.Gramm.*Comp*.3.14.

**σπαλίς**, old form for *ψαλίς*, Sch.D.T. p.320 H.

**σπᾰλίων**, *ωνος*, *ὁ*, *wicker-roof* to shelter soldiers (Lat. *vinea*), Agath.3.5, 4.20.

**σπαλύσσομαι**, = *σπαράσσομαι*, Hsch.

**σπᾰνᾰδελφ-έω**, *to have few brothers* or *sisters*, Ptol.*Tetr*.119. **-ία**, *ἡ*, *fewness of brothers* or *sisters*, ibid., Antigonus in *Cat.Cod.Astr*.6.71. **-ος**, *ον*, *with few brothers* or *sisters*, Vett.Val.17.10, S.E.*M*.5.101, Man.4.390, etc.

**σπάνακα** (cod. *σπάρν-*)· *ὀρίγανον*, Hsch.

**σπᾰνανθρωπέω**, *to be short of men*, *Sammelb*.7330.2 (ii A.D.).

**σπᾰν-ία**, *ἡ*, = *σπάνις*, E.*Rh*.245 (lyr.), D.S.24.1, Phot. **-ιάκις**, Adv. = *ὀλιγάκις*, Luc.*Rh.Pr*.17, Hermog.*Inv*.3.5, A.D.*Pron*.47.3, Ar.Byz *Epit*.30.10. **-ίζω**, of things, *to be rare*, *scarce*, [*καλὰ ἔργα*] *Βασσίδαισιν οὐ σ*. Pi.*N*.6.31; *τοὐλαίου σπανίζοντος* Ar.*V*.252; *τὰ παρ' ἀμφοτέροις σπανίζοντα* D.S.2.54, etc.; of books, Gal.17(1).605. **2.** of persons, *lack*, *be in want of*, c. gen., *ὑδάτων* Hdt.2.108; *χρημάτων*, *βίου*, Id.1.187, 196; *οὐ σπανίζοντες φίλων* A.*Ch*.717; *πέπλων*, *πομπῆς*, *βωμοῦ*, etc., E.*Med*.960, *IA*352 (troch.), *Hel*.800, etc.; *νεῶν μακρῶν* Th.1.41; *τροφῆς* Id.4.6, etc.; of a country, *σ. πεύκης* Thphr.*HP*5.7.1: rarely c. dat., *σίτῳ* Dicaearch.1.23 cod., cf. III fin. **II.** trans., *exhaust*, *use up*, *τὰ μέταλλα* Ph.Byz.*Mir*.4.1; *spend*, *PFlor*.99.7 (i/ii A.D.), *Sammelb*.4317.7 (iii A.D.):—Pass., *ἐσπανίσθη πᾶν ὕδωρ* Lxx *Jb*.14.11. **III.** Pass., = Act. (signf. I.2), *to be in want of*, *ἐσπανίσμεθ' ἀρωγῶν* A.*Pers*.1024 (lyr.); *ὁρᾷς..φίλων ὡς ἐσπανίσμεθα* E.*Or*.1055; *πάντων σπανιζόμενοι* X.*HG*7.2.16: abs., *to be in want*, *μὴ σπανιζοίμεσθα* E.*Med*.560: rarely c. dat., *οἴνῳ σπανίζονται* Str.3.3.7. ⊛ **-ιος**, *α*, *ον* (also *ος*, *ον* Arist.*HA*608$^b$21, Thphr.*Lap*.3, Plb.4.16.3, etc.), of persons and things, *rare*, *scarce*, *scanty*, Hdt.2.67, 5.29, etc.; *σ. θήρευμα..λαβεῖν* a *rare* catch, E.*IA*1162; of persons, *rarely seen*, *aloof*, *δυσπρόσιτος*, *ἔσω τε κλήθρων σπάνιος* ib.345 (troch.); *σ. σεαυτὸν παρέχειν* Pl.*Euthphr*.3d, cf. Plu.*Crass*.7; *τῷ ὕδατι σ. χρώμενοι* having a *scanty* supply of water, Th.7.4; in an Adv. sense, *σπάνιος ἐπιφοιτᾷ* he *seldom* visits, Hdt.2.73; so *τοὺς σπανίους ἰδεῖν στρατηγούς seldom* seen, X.*Cyr*.7.5.46, cf. Pl.*Lg*.953c; *σπάνιοι περιπεπλεύκασι* Str.15.1.4; *σπάνιόν ἐστι*, c. inf., it is *seldom* that.., X.*Cyr*.1.3.3, Isoc.10.13; opp. *ῥᾴδιον*, Archyt.3; *σπάνιον εἴ τις..it is rare* for one to.., Str.7.3.4: *τὸ σ*. Aeschin.3.180, Arist.*Mete*.372$^a$23; *ὁ ταὼς διὰ τὸ σ. θαυμάζεται* Eub.114. **II.** Comp. *σπανιώτερος* Hdt.8.25, Th.1.33, etc.: Sup. *-ώτατος* Id.7.68, *Lyr.Adesp*.138.1, Pl.*Cra*.389a, etc. **III.** Adv. *-ίως seldom*, X.*Ages*.9.1, Arist.*HA*488$^b$6, Plb.2.15.6 (so *σπάνιον* Str.3.5.1, Plu.*Cic*.8, etc., but *σπανίᾳ* is Adj. in Pl.*Phdr*.256c, and *σπάνιον* in Arist.*Mete*.372$^a$14): Comp. *-ιώτερον* Th.1.23; *-ιαίτερον* Thphr.*HP*3.7.5 codd.—Rare in Poets, as Ion Eleg.3.4.

**σπᾰνιό-σπερμος**, *ον*, gloss on *σπανότεκνος*, Sch.Paul.Al.*O*.4. **-της**, *ητος*, *ἡ*, = sq., *lack*, *γῆς* Isoc.4.34, 132: pl., *rarities*, J.*BJ*7.5.5.

**σπάν-ις** [ᾰ], *ἡ*, gen. *εως*, dat. *ει*, Ion. *ι*:—*scarcity*, *dearth*, *lack*, *τόλμης* E.*Or*.942; *ἀνδρῶν* D.25.31; *ὕδατος* Arist.*GA*746$^b$10, cf. Lxx *Ju*.8.9; *θηρίων* Str.2.5.26; *νεκύων AP*9.53 (Nicod. or Bass.); *οὐ σπάνις..ἔχειν*, = *οὐ σπάνιον*, *there is* no *lack*, no *difficulty*, in getting, E.*IA*1163; *οὗ σ. ἀνδρὶ τυχεῖν* which 'tis *rare* for a man to get, *IG*2.2753, cf. 3577: abs., *dearth*, *τροφὰς ἐν τῇ μεγάλῃ σ. παρέσχε* ib.3.687. **II.** *unsatisfied need*, *want*, c. gen., *ἐν σπάνι βύβλων* Hdt.5.58; *σ. σχεῖν τοῦ βίου poverty*, S.*OT*1461; *βίου* E.*Hec*.12; *ἦν δέ του σπάνιν τιν' ἴσχῃς* S.*OC*506, cf. Pl.*Lg*.678d; *σ. τῶν ἀναγκαίων* Antipho 4.1.2; *τῇ τῶν χρημάτων σ*. Th.1.142; *ἀργυρίου* Lys.19.11; *ἡ..σ. πρόχειρος εἰς τὸ δρᾶν κακά want*, *poverty*, Philem.157. **2.** *craving*, defined as *ἐπιθυμία ἀτελής*, *Stoic*.3.97; *ἐν σ. χρημάτων* D.19.153, cf. Phld.*Lib*. p.45 O. **-ισιτία**, v. *σπανοσιτία*. **-ιστικός**, *ή*, *όν*, *lacking*, *poor*, Vett.Val.15.12, 18.8, al. **-ιστός**, *ή*, *όν*, of things, *scanty*, *δωρήματα* S.*OC*4; *scarce*, *ἄρωμα* Philostr.*VS*2.25.5; *ἐν σπανιστοῖς ἔκειτο* ib.2.21.3. **II.** of a country, *σπανιστὴ καρποῖς stinted of*.., Str.15.3.1.

**σπᾰνο-καρπία**, *ἡ*, *lack of fruit*, D.S.5.39. **-πώγων**, *ωνος*, *ὁ*. *with scanty beard*, Ion Hist.10, *PPetr*.3 p.25 (iii B.C.), Suid. s.v. *εἰς Τροιζῆνα*.

⊛ **σπᾰνός**, ή, όν, = σπάνιος, *rare, uncommon*, Hsch.; *lacking*, mostly in compds.; esp., = σπανοπώγων, Ptol.*Tetr.*144, Polem.*Phgn.*2.35; = *malebarbis*, *Gloss.* Adv. -νῶς, *rariter*, ib.

⊛ **Σπᾶνός**, ή, όν, = Ἱσπανός, Plu.*Sert.*11, etc. (v. Ἱσπανός). **2.** *grey*, = Lat. *pullus*, *PHamb.*10.17 (ii A.D.), Nonius p.882 L.

**σπᾰνο-σῑτία**, ἡ, *lack of corn* or *food*, X.*HG*4.8.7, *IG*2².360.9, Arist.*Mir.*832ᵃ20, Ἀρχ.Ἐφ.1912.61 (Gonni, iii/ii B.C.): also **σπανισιτία**, *IG*11(4).1049 (Delos, iii B.C.). **-τεκνος**, ον, *with too few children*, S.E.*M.*5.101, Vett.Val.15.7, al., Paul.Al.*O.*3. **-φῐλία**, ἡ, *shortage of friends*, prob. in Phld.*Herc.*1251.21. **-φυλλος**, ον, *lacking in leaves*, of the fir, pine, etc., Thphr.*HP*1.10.4 codd.; v. ἀκανθόφυλλος.

**σπάν-υδρος**, ον, *lacking water*, Diph.Siph.ap.Ath.3.80c.

⊛ **σπαπιρώτας**, dub. sens. in *GDI*1267.24 (Pamphylian word).

**σπαραβάραι**· οἱ γερ(ρ)οφόροι, Hsch.

**σπάραγ-μα**, ατος, τό, *piece torn off, shred, fragment*, ὅσων σπαράγματα all whose *mangled corpses*, S.*Ant.*1081; σπάραγμα κόμας E.*Andr.*826 (lyr.); γίνεται τὰ μὲν ἀπὸ σπέρματος τὰ δ' ἀπὸ σπαραγμάτων others from *slips*, Arist.*GA*761ᵇ28: pl., σ. κρημνῶν jagged *fragments*, Plu.*Mar.*23; σ. στεφάνων *fragments* of.., Id.2.463a, etc.; γραμμάτων σπαράγμασι..οἱ σπεύδοντες γράφουσι ib.1011d. **II.** *tearing, rending*, δαμάλας διεφόρουν σπαράγμασιν E.*Ba.*739. **III.** collect. in sg., = λατύπη, *SIG*996.31 (Smyrna, prob. i A.D.). **-μᾰτώδης**, ες, *convulsive*, Plu.2.130d. **-μός**, ὁ, *tearing, rending, mangling*, δαιμον ὄνυχα τιθεμένα σπαραγμοῖς E.*Hec.*656 (lyr.); σ. Βακχῶν *by* them, Id.*Ba.*735; but σπαραγμοὶ χαίτας, χρωτός, etc., *rending of* them, Id.*Ph.*1525 (lyr.), *Tr.*453 (troch.), cf. Phld.*Piet.*87, etc. **II.** *convulsion, spasm*, A.*Fr.*169, S.*Tr.*778,1254; *agony*, Anon.*Prog.* in Rh.1.613 W. (pl.). **-μώδης**, ες, f.l. for σπαραγματώδης in Plu.2.130d, and for σπασμώδης in Hp.*Epid.*7.18.

**σπᾰρακ-τέον**, *one must irritate*, τὸν στόμαχον Gal.17(1).434, cf. Sor.2.16; ἐμέτοις Antyll.ap.Orib.7.12.5. **-τόν**, τό, *rubble*, Hero *Stereom.*2.33.

**σπάραξις** [ᾰ], εως, ἡ, *retching*, Alex.Aphr.*Pr.*2.57; = *carptus*, *Gloss.*

**σπᾰράσσω**, Att. -ττω Ar.*Ach.*688, etc., fut. -ξω A.*Pr.*1018: aor. ἐσπάραξα Babr.95.40, (κατ-) Ar.*Eq.*729:—Med., fut. -ξομαι E.*Andr.*1209 (in *IA*1458 σπαράσσεσθαι is restored for σπαράξεσθαι in pass. sense):—Pass., pf. ἐσπάρακται (δι-) Eub.15.3:—*tear, rend*, esp. of dogs, carnivorous animals, and the like, σάρκας ἐσπάρασσ' ἀπ' ὀστέων E.*Med.*1217; σ. τὰς γνάθους Ar.*Ra.*428:—Med., σπαράσσεσθαι κόμαν *tear one's* hair, E.*Andr.*1209 (lyr.). **2.** *rend asunder*, φάραγγα βροντῇ..πατὴρ σπαράξει A. l. c. **3.** metaph., *pull to pieces, attack*, ἄνδρα σπαράττων καὶ ταράττων καὶ κυκῶν Ar.*Ach.*688; σ. τινὰς τῷ λόγῳ ὥσπερ σκυλάκια Pl.*R.*539b; τὰς ἀρχάς D.25.50, cf. Ar.*Pax*641, *PPetr.*2 p.57 (iii B.C.), Herod.5.57, Teles p.19 H.:—Pass., λώβαισι.. ἐσπαραγμένους Lyc.656. **4.** Medic., σ. τὸ στόμα τῆς κοιλίας provoke sickness, Gal.11.57; cf. σπαρακτέον:—Pass., σ. ἀνημέτως *retch* without being able to vomit, Hp.*Coac.*546. **b.** *convulse*, of an evil spirit, *Ev.Marc.*1.26.

**σπαργᾰν-άω**, = σπαργανόω, Pl.*Lg.*789e. **-ίζω**, = foreg., Hes.*Th.*485. **-ιον**, τό, Dim. of σπάργανον, *bur-reed*, *Sparganium ramosum*, Dsc.4.21. **2.** = *quinquefolii radix*, Plin.*HN*25.109. **3.** v. σπάργανον II. **-ιώτης**, ου, ὁ, *child in swaddling-clothes*, *h.Merc.*301. **-ον**, τό, (σπάργω) *band for swathing infants*, ib.151,306, Pi.*N.*1.38: mostly in pl., *swaddling-clothes*, *h.Merc.*237, Pi.*P.*4.114; παῖς ἔτ' ὢν ἐν σπαργάνοις A.*Ch.*755, cf. 529,759, *Ag.*1606; εἰς σπάργανά μ' αὐτὸς ἔθηκεν *Epigr.Gr.*314.6 (Smyrna, iii A.D.); ἐκ πρώτων σ. *ab incunabulis*, S.E.*M.*1.41; τὰ τῆς γεννήσεως εὐτελῆ σ. a mean *origin*, Hdn.7.1.2:—hence, in Trag. and Com., *objects left with an exposed child, the marks by which a person's true birth and family are identified* (Lat. *crepundia, monumenta*), S.*OT*1035, Men.*Pk.*15, Donat. ad Ter.*Eun.*753; so prob. τούτου (sc. τοῦ Τηλέφου) δὸς..μοι τὰ σ. Ar.*Ach.*431. **II.** a plant, = ὠκιμοειδές, f.l. for σπαργάνιον, Ps.-Dsc.4.28. **-όω**, = σπάργω, *wrap in* σπάργανα (whether I.1 or I.2), σπαργανώσαντες πέπλοις [τὸν παῖδα] E.*Ion*955; *swathe*, Arist.*HA*584ᵇ4, Sor.1.83, al.: metaph., Clearch.*Fr.*26; θρίοισι ταύτην (sc. τὴν ἀμίαν) ἐσπαργάνωσα Sotad.Com.1.28; ἀχύροις σ. [τὴν χιόνα] Plu.2.691c:—Pass., Hp.*Aër.*20, *Fract.*22; βρέφος ἐσπαργανωμένον *Ev.Luc.*2.12. **-ωμα**, ατος, τό, = σπάργανον, *AB*304, Phot. **-ωσις**, εως, ἡ, *swathing*, Sor.1.83, Orib.*Syn.*9.9. **-ωτέος**, α, ον, *to be swathed*, Sor.1.78.

**σπαργ-άω**, = ὀργάω, *to be full to bursting, swell, be ripe*, μαστὸς σπαργῶν E.*Ba.*701, cf. *Cyc.*55 (lyr.); of nursing mothers, *swell* with milk, Pl.*R.*460c (metaph., Id.*Smp.*206d); σ. τοὺς μαστοὺς ὑπὸ γάλακτος or γάλακτι, D.H.1.79, Plu.2.320d. **2.** *swell with humours*, τὰ ἄνω..σ. Hp.*Epid.*2.6.21, cf. Gal.19.82. **3.** of plants, Poll.1.230. **II.** metaph., *swell with desire* or *passion*, Pl.*Phdr.*256a; πρὸς δόξαν Plu.2.1100a, cf. 585c; ἐπὶ τὴν βασιλείαν Id.*Art.*3: abs., *wax wanton, be insolent*, σπαργῶσαν..τὴν ἀρχὴν ὁρῶν Pl.*Lg.*692a; ὀλιγαρχία -ῶσα Plu.*Lyc.*7; -ῶντι τῷ δήμῳ Id.*Comp.Per.Fab.*1. **-έω**, = foreg., Hsch., v.l. in Q.S.14.283. **-ή**, in pl. σπαργαί· ὀργαί, ὁρμαί, Hsch. **-ησις**, εως, ἡ, *swelling, distention*, μαστῶν Dsc.3.34, cf. 2.107 (v.l. σπαργανώσεις), Sor.1.76. **-ω**, only in Ep. aor. 1, = σπαργανόω, σπάρξαν ἐν φάρεϊ λευκῷ *h.Ap.*121. **-ωσις**, εως, ἡ, f.l. for σπάργησις, μαστῶν Dsc.3.34.

**σπᾰρίζω**, = σκαρίζω, but formed from σπαίρω, acc. to *Lex.Rhet.*ap. Eust.416.37, cf. 947.13.

**σπάρνιοι**· ἐνθαλάττιοι πέτραι, Hsch. **σπαρνοπόλιος**, v. σπαρτοπόλιος.

⊛ **σπαρνός**, ή, όν, poet. for σπανός, σπάνιος, A.*Ag.*556, Pl.Com.253, Call.*Dian.*19.

**σπάρος** [ᾰ], a sea-fish, a sort of *bream*, *Sargus annularis* or *Rondeletii*, Epich.54, Matro *Conv.*81, Arist.*HA*508ᵇ17.

**σπαρταγενής**, ές, *producing the shrub spartos*, App.*Hisp.*12.

**Σπαρτάκειος**, α, ον, *of Spartacus*, Plu.*Pomp.*31.

**σπαρτέον**, (σπείρω) *one must sow*, *Gp.*2.13.2.

**σπάρτη**, ἡ, = σπάρτον, *rope* or *cord* (v. σπάρτος, ὁ), Ar.*Av.*815 (with a play upon *Sparta*), cf. Cratin.110; μαντεύεσθαι..τῇ τῶν σπαρτῶν διατάσει dub. l. in Alciphr.2.4.15. **2.** = σπαρτίον III, Gal.12.129. **II.** = στάθμη, *plumbline*, Hsch.: cf. σπάρτος II.2.

**Σπάρτη**, Dor. **Σπάρτα**, ἡ, *Sparta* in Laconia, Il.2.582, etc.:—hence Advbs., **Σπάρτηθεν**, *from Sparta*, Od.2.327; **Σπάρτηνδε**, *to Sparta*, 1.285:—**Σπαρτιάτης** [ᾱ], ου, ὁ, *a Spartan*, E.*Or.*457, Th.1.128, etc.; Ion. **-ιήτης**, εω, Hdt.1.65:—fem. **-ᾶτις**, ιδος, ἡ, *a Spartan woman*, E.*Andr.*596, etc.; also (sc. χώρα) *Laconia*, Plu.2.219f; also as Adj., Σ. γυνή, χθών, E.*Hel.*115, *Or.*537, etc.; also **Σπαρτιάς**, άδος, St. Byz.:—Adj. **Σπαρτιᾶτικός**, ή, όν, *Spartan*, Paus.6.4.10, Luc.*Salt.*46, etc.

**σπαρτικός**, ή, όν, *vegetative*, of souls embedded in the body, Pl.ap. Anon.*Proll.Plat.*10 (vi p.206 Hermann).

⊛ **σπαρτίνη**, ἡ, = σπάρτη I.1, Ael.*NA*12.43.

**σπάρτῐνος**, ον, *made of* σπάρτος, Cratin.110; η, ον, Poll.7.181.

**σπαρτίον**, τό, Dim. of σπάρτον, *small cord*, Ar.*Pax*1247, Aeschin. Socr.41 D., Philippid.12, Lxx *Ge.*14.23, *Jo.*2.18; of the *cord(s)* of a bedstead, Arist.*Mech.*856ᵇ11,18, Poll.10.36: pl. of one *rope*, Arist.*Pr.*888ᵃ21. **II.** *cord* by which the beam of a balance is suspended, *Mech.*850ᵃ3, 852ᵃ20. **2.** = σπάρτον I.2, Lxx *Jb.*38.5, *Ez.*40.3. **III.** *Spanish broom, Spartium junceum*, Dsc.4.154; cf. λινόσπαρτον.

**σπαρτιοχαίτης**, ου, ὁ, *with ropy hair*, Pl.Com.124.

**σπαρτόδετος**, ον, (δέω A) *bound with* σπάρτος, Opp.*C.*1.156, 4.415.

**σπαρτομέταξα**, ἡ, = *vermix*, dub. cj. for *partus metaxa* in *Gloss.*

**σπάρτον**, τό, *rope, cable*, Il.2.135, Hdt.5.16; of bedstead-cords, Th.4.48. **2.** *measuring cord*, Call.*Fr.*158. **3.** = λίνον I.1, *thread*, Aen.Tact.18.17,19. **II.** = σπαρτίον II, Arist.*Mech.*849ᵇ23,35. **III.** = σπάρτος I, Id.*HA*627ᵃ9. **IV.** *esparto*, *Stipa tenacissima*, Liv.22.20.6, Plin.*HN*19.26, 24.65. (In signf. I.1 not from σπάρτος I.1 acc. to Varro ap.Gell.17.3.4, cf. Plin.*HN*24.65.)

**σπαρτο-πλόκος**, ον, *making ropes of* σπάρτος, Poll.7.181. **-πόλιος**, ον, *with a sprinkling of grey hairs*, Men.979 (nisi leg. -όπωλις), Poll.4.133,134,151; **σπαρνο-** in Hsch. **II.** name of a gem, Plin.*HN*37.191. **-πώλης**, ου, ὁ, *dealer in ropes* or *mats of* σπάρτος, Poll.7.181.

**σπαρτός**, ή, όν, also ός, όν E.*Supp.*578: (σπείρω):—*sown, grown from seed, cultivated*, Thphr.*HP*6.8.2, Dsc.3.37, etc. **2.** of men, οἱ..σπαρτοί τε καὶ αὐτόχθονες Pl.*Sph.*247c; σπαρτῶν γένος children *of men*, A.*Eu.*410. **b.** esp. at Thebes, **Σπαρτοί**, οἱ, *the Sown-men*, those who sprang from the dragon's teeth *sown* by Cadmus, and their descendants, Pi.*I.*1.30, 7(6).10; Σπαρτῶν στάχυς E.*HF*5; Ἐχίων σπαρτός *IG*14.1285 ii 9, 1292 i 3, cf. E.*Ba.*1274; λόγχη σπαρτός the *Theban* spear, Id.*Supp.*578. **II.** *scattered*, of the limbs of a corpse, *AP*7.383 (Phil.).

**σπάρτος**, ὁ and ἡ, = σπαρτίον III, Pl.*Plt.*280c, X.*Cyn.*9.13, Ps.-Dsc.4.154. **2.** = σπάρτον IV, Str.3.4.9. **II.** σπάρτος, ἡ, = σπάρτη I.1, Hero *Spir.*1.17, al. **2.** = σπάρτη II, Hsch. s.v. στάθμη, Sch.Pl.*Chrm.*154b; masc. in Sch.Il.*Oxy.*1086.23; τὸν λίθον ποτὶ τὰν σ. ἄγοντας Dor. prov. ap. Basil. in Migne *Patrol.Graec.*31.569.

**σπαρτό-τονος**, ον, *slung on ropes*, κλίνη *PTeb.*793 vi 3 (ii B.C.), *PUniv.Giss.*10 ii 6 (ii/i B.C.). **-φόρος**, ον, *bearing the shrub* σπάρτος, Str.3.4.9.

**σπάσις** [ᾰ], εως, ἡ, (σπάω) *drawing up, traction*, Arist.*Pr.*882ᵇ27. **II.** *drawing in, suction*, ἡ τῆς τροφῆς σ. Id.*PA*693ᵃ17; σπάσει πίνειν, opp. λάψει, κάψει, Id.*HA*595ᵃ9; cf. σπάω III.1. **III.** = ἀντίσπασις, cj. for στάσις in Sor.2.11.

**σπάσ-μα**, ατος, τό, *sprain* or *rupture of muscular fibre*, Hp.*Aph.*5.25, cf. Pl.*Ti.*87e, D.18.198, Thphr.*HP*9.9.2, Gal.1.239. **2.** *spasm, convulsion*, Arist.*Pr.*885ᵃ6. **II.** *that which has been torn off, fragment, shred*, Plu.*Lys.*12, *Sull.*21; τῆς φρονήσεως μόρια καὶ σ. Id.2.99c. **2.** σ. ξίφους *sword-blade*, as *drawn from the scabbard*, Id.*Oth.*17. **-μᾰτώδης**, ες, = σπασμώδης, Arist.*Pr.*880ᵇ18 (v.l. σπερματώδης), Thphr.*Lass.*15. **-μός**, ὁ, = σπάσμα I.2, *convulsion, spasm*, Hdt.4.187, Hp.*Aph.*2.26, Th.2.49, Sor.1.46, al.; βρυχώμενον σπασμοῖσι S.*Tr.*805; *fit of epilepsy*, Hp.*Coac.*350; ἐπιληπτικοὶ σ. Sor.1.96: metaph., ἔθαλψεν ἄτης σ. S.*Tr.*1082. **II.** *priapism*, Ar.*Lys.*845. **III.** *violent agitation*, as of the sea, D.S.3.44, Plu.*Cic.*32, App.*BC*5.90. **IV.** *drawing*, μαχαιρῶν Lxx 2*Ma.*5.3. **-μώδης**, ες, *convulsive, spasmodic*, Hp.*Prorrh.*1.28, Sor.2.26; *suffering from convulsions*, Id.1.88; τὰ σ. *attacks of cramp*, Hp.*Coac.*100; ἀλγήματα σ. pains which are *premonitory symptoms of* σπασμοί, Id.*Prorrh.*1.114. Adv. -δῶς Gal.17(2).750, Alex.Trall.7.9. **-τέος**, α, ον, *to be pulled*, of weeds, Thphr.*HP*6.5.4. **-τικός**, ή, όν, *drawing in, absorbing*, τῆς τροφῆς Arist.*PA*683ᵃ22, cf. *Pr.*881ᵇ15; σ. ζῴδια *Cat. Cod.Astr.*1.166, 4.152, 8(3).100.

**σπατάγγης**, ου, ὁ, a kind of *sea-urchin*, Sophr.102, Ar.*Fr.*409, Arist.*HA*530ᵇ4; πάταγγας acc. pl., Poll.6.47 (v.l. πάταγα, παταγας).

**σπαταγγίζω**, = ταράσσω, Hsch.

**σπᾰτᾰλ-άω**, *live softly* or *in excessive comfort* or *indulgence*, Plb.36.17.7, *IG*14.2002 (Rome), Lxx *Si.*21.15, 1*Ep.Ti.*5.6, *Ep.Jac.*5.5; τὰ σπαταλῶντα τῶν παιδίων *spoilt* children, Theano in Pythag.*Ep.*4.4, cf. Diog.*Ep.*28.7. **-η**, ἡ, *wantonness, luxury*, LxxSi.27.13, *AP*11.17 (Nicarch.); χρυσομανὴς σ. ib.5.301.2 (Agath.); of a dainty feast, Luc.*Epigr.*50, *AP*7.206 (Damoch.); of ornaments, ταρσῶν χρυσοφόρος σ., i.e. anklets, ib.5.26 (Rufin.), cf. 270 (Maced.). II. *bracelet*, *SIG*1184.1 (Cnidus, iii B.C.), cf. *AP*6.74 (Agath.). **-ημα**, ατος, τό, = foreg., of delicacies eaten, ib.9.642.1 (Id.). **-ιον**, τό, in Lat. form *spatalium*, = σπατάλη II, Juba ap.Plin.*HN*13.142, *CIL*2.2060.12, 3386.12 (Spain), 14.2215.8 (Nemi).

**σπᾰτᾰλοκίναιδος** [ῑ], ὁ, *lascivious* κίναιδος, Petron.23.3.

**σπᾰτᾰλ-ος** [σπᾰ], ον, *wanton, lascivious*, κλέμματα *AP*5.17 (Rufin.); of persons, Bardesan.ap.Eus.*PE*6.10, Eust.1437.22, etc., cf. Sm.*De.*28.54, *AP*5.26 (Rufin.). [Oxyt. in Eus. and Sm. ll. cc.] **-ώδης**, ες, *soft, self-indulgent*, Sor.2.54.

**σπάτειος** [ᾰ], ον, (σπάτος) *of a skin* or *leather*, Hsch.

**σπατίακτον**· διεσπασμένον, καὶ εὔχροον, Hsch.

**σπᾰτίζω**, (σπάω) *draw, suck*, Hsch.

**σπᾰτίλη** [ῐ], ἡ, *thin excrement*, as in diarrhoea, Hp.*Acut.*28: generally, *ordure*, Ar.*Pax*48, D.C.46.5 (pl.). II. (σπάτος) *parings of leather*, Sch.Ar. l.c.; also **πατίλη** *An.Ox.*2.303; **παστίλη** Hdn.Gr.1.322.

**σπᾰτίλουρος** [ῐ], ὁ, (οὐρά) *foul-tailed, filthy*, Hsch.

**σπᾰτολειαστής**, οῦ, Dor. **-ληστάς**, ὁ, *leather-dresser*, restored in *IG*4.581 (Argos).

**σπάτος** [ᾰ], εος, τό, *hide, leather*, Boeot. word ap. Sch.Ar.*Pax* 48.

**σπαύλαθρον**, v. σκάλαυθρον.

**σπαύονθες**· Σαλαμίνιοι, Hsch. (cf. ἐναύω (A) fin., fort. ἔπαυον· ἐπίθες).

❋ **σπάω**, S.*Ant.*1003, Ar.*Pax* 498, etc.: fut. σπάσω [ᾰ] Lyc.484, (δια-) Hdt.7.236, (ἐπι-) S.*Aj.*769: aor. ἔσπᾰσα Il.13.178 (tm.), Ep. σπάσα 5.859 (tm.), etc.: pf. ἔσπᾰκα Arist.*Pr.*930a21, (ἀν-) Hp.*Superf.*22, Ar.*Ach.*1069:—Med., fut. σπάσομαι Hp.*Vict.*2.38, etc.: aor. ἐσπᾰσάμην Il.19.387, Hdt.3.29, Philostr.*VA*7.42, Ep. σπασάμην Od.10.166, Ep. also σπάσσασθε, σπασσάμενος (v. infr.):—Pass., fut. σπασθήσομαι Gal.16.760, (δια-) X.*An.*4.8.10: aor. ἐσπάσθην Il.11.458, etc.: pf. ἔσπασμαι Hp.*Morb.*1.20, (δι-) Th.6.98, etc.; also in med. sense, X.*An.*7.4.16, *Cyr.*7.5.29. Mostly poet. (ἕλκω being preferred in Prose):—*draw*, hence, I. of a sword, *draw*, mostly in Med., φάσγανά τε σπάσσασθε Od.22.74; σπασσάμενος.. ἄορ παχέος παρὰ μηροῦ Il.16.473; ἐκ δ' ἄρα σύριγγος.. ἐσπάσατ' ἔγχος 19.387; σπασαμένων τὰς μαχαίρας *PTeb.*48.19 (ii B.C.), cf. 138 (ii B.C.): in Act., ξίφος σπάσαντα E.*Or.*1194; φάσγανον σπάσας χερί Id.*IT*322:—Pass., ἐσπασμένοι τὰ ξίφη *having their* swords *drawn*, X.*An.*7.4.16; ἐσπασμένον ὃν εἶχεν ἀκινάκην Id.*Cyr.*7.5.29; ἐσπασμένοις τοῖς ξίφεσι D.S.4.52. 2. of other things, ἐκ χειρὸς χεῖρα σπάσατο Od.2.321; σπασάμην ῥῶπάς τε λύγους τε 10.166; ὡς ἕκαστος ἔσπασεν τύχης πάλον *drew* the lot (out of the helmet), A.*Ag.*333:—Pass., σπασθέντος (sc. ἔγχεος ἔξω χροός) Il.11.458. 3. abs., σπᾶτ' ἀνδρείως *pull, hoist away*, like men, Ar.*Pax* 498. II. of violent actions, *pluck off* or *out*, κόμην S.*OT*1243; λάχνην Id.*Tr.*690; cf. σπαστέος. 2. *tear, rend*, esp. of ravenous animals, S.*Ant.*258, 1003; λαιμοτόμους κεφαλὰς dub. l. in E.*IA*776 (lyr.); σ. τοῖς ὄνυξιν [τοὺς νεοττούς], of the eagle, Arist.*HA*619b31:—Pass., φλέβιον, σάρκα σπασθῆναι, Hp.*Morb.*1.17. 3. *wrench, sprain*, τὸ σκέλος ἔσπασε Plu.*Arat.*33:—Pass., τὸν μηρὸν σπασθῆναι Hdt.6.134; τοὺς πόδας E.*Cyc.*639. 4. *snatch, tear* or *drag away*, πῶλον παρὰ συννόμων Pl.*Lg.*666e; ὑπὸ πτερῶν E.*Andr.*441:—Pass., ἔλαφον ἀπ' ἐμῶν γονάτων σπασθεῖσαν Id.*Hec.*92 (lyr.); ἐκ βραχίονος σπασθεὶς ib.408. 5. metaph., *carry away, draw aside*, ἀλλά σ' ἔσπασεν πειθὼ S.*El.*561; τὰ πάθη οἷον νεῦρα σ. ἡμᾶς Pl.*Lg.*644e. 6. Medic., *cause convulsion* or *spasm*, v.l. in Hp.*Art.*67:—Pass., *to be convulsed*, σπασθεὶς ἀποθνήσκει Id.*Aph.*5.5, Thphr.*HP*4.4.13, etc.; ἐσπᾶτο γὰρ πέδονδε καὶ μετάρσιος, of Heracles in his agony, S.*Tr.*786, cf. σπάσμα, σπασμός: metaph., *to be harassed, anxious*, Arr.*Epict.*1.1.16. III. *draw in, suck in*, θρόμβον αἵματος A.*Ch.*533; ἔσπασεν ἄμυστιν ἑλκύσας E.*Cyc.*417; συνεκθανεῖν σπῶντα χρὴ τῷ πώματι ib.571; μεστὴν ἀκράτου Θηρίκλειον ἔσπασεν Alex.5, cf. 285; opp. λάπτω, κάπτω, Plu.2.699d, cf. σπάσις II; σ. τὸν μαστὸν *suck* it, Arist.*HA*587a33; σ. ἀμυστί Ael.*NA*6.51; and in Med., ταυρείου σπασάμενος αἵματος Apollod.1.9.27:—Pass., of the female, *to be sucked*, Arist.*HA*576b11 (τὸ ἄγαν σπᾶσθαι prob. l.); cf. ἕλκω A. II.4. 2. σ. τὸ πνεῦμα *draw* breath, Id.*Resp.*473a2; τὸν ἀέρα τὸν κοινόν Men.531.7; *absorb*, ἕκαστον τῶν τοῦ σώματος τὸ αὑτῷ οἰκεῖον ἐσπακέναι Arist.*Pr.*930a21. 3. metaph., *derive*, τροφήν, of winds, Hp.*Vict.*2.38; πειθώ τε καὶ ἵμερον ἔσπασε ἐκ.. *drew, derived*.., *IG*14.889 (Sinuessa); σ. ἔρωτα *enjoy* it, Opp.*H.*4.270; ὀλίγον ὕπνου σ. *snatch* a little sleep, Hld.5.1:—Med., Id.2.16. IV. *draw tight, pull* the reins, χαλινῷ τὸ στόμα τοῦ ἵππου X.*Eq.*7.1, cf. 9.5; but τὸν χαλινὸν ἐκ τῶν ὀδόντων ἵππου Pl.*Phdr.*254e. 2. of angling, ἡ μήρινθος οὐδὲν ἔσπασεν Ar.*Th.*928: hence prov., οὐκ ἔσπασεν ταύτῃ γε 'he took nothing by his motion', Id.*V.*175. V. *derive*, ἐπωνυμίαν παρά τινων Philostr.*VS*2.10.6, cf. Ael.*NA*14.15 (Med.); ἀρχὴν λυρικῆς καὶ πέρας σ. *AP*9.184 (s.v.l.); ῥίζαν σ. τινός *derive* one's origin from.., Lyc.623; σ. τὴν κλῆσιν ἀπό τινος S.E.*M.*1.46; ἔννοιαν θεοῦ ἐκ τῶν κατὰ τοὺς ὕπνους φαντασιῶν Epicur.*Fr.*353.

**σπεῖμα**· σχοινίον, Hsch. **σπεῖο**, v. *ἕπω (B). **σπεῖος**, v. σπέος.

❋ **σπεῖρα**, ἡ, *anything twisted* or *wound*, ποιεῖν τι οἷον σπεῖραν twist it into *a ball*, Hp.*Morb.*2.33. 2. pl., *coils* or *spires* of a serpent, S.*Fr.*535 (anap.), Ar.*Fr.*500; πολύπλοκοι σ. E.*Med.*481, cf. *Ion* 1164: so in sg., Nic.*Th.*156, A.R.4.151, Arat.47, 89, etc. 3. *rope, cord*, Nic.*Fr.*74.21, f.l. in Hp.*Steril.*235; σπείραισι δικτυοκλώστοις with the net's meshy *folds*, S.*Ant.*346 (lyr.); *ship's cable*, Plu.2.507b; *padded circle* used by women carrying weights on their head, Aët.12.55; so by Atlas, Apollod.2.5.11; as a lamp-stand, ἀρτεμισίας σ. ἐπὶ τὸν λύχνον *PMag.Lond.*121.601 (cf. σπειρίον III); *round cushion*, *IG*5(1).1390.24 (Andania, i B.C.). 4. *a mode of dressing the hair*, Poll.2.31, 4.149. 5. σ. βόειαι *thongs* or *straps* of ox-hide to guard and arm a boxer's fist, Theoc.22.80. 6. *knot* or *curl in wood*, Thphr.*HP*5.2.3, Plin.*HN*16.198. 7. a kind of *cheesecake* (al. σπῖρα), Chrysipp. Tyan.ap.Ath.14.647d. 8. *rounded moulding* in the base of an Ionic or Corinthian column, *torus*, *IG*1².372.64, *Sardis* 7(1) No.181 (i A.D.), *CIG*2713-14 (Labranda), Poll.7.121, Vitr.3.5.3. 9. Geom., *anchor-ring, tore*, produced by revolution of a circle about a line in its plane but not passing through the centre, Hero *Deff.*97, Procl. *in Euc.* p.119 F. II. Milit., *tactical unit*, in the Ptolemaic army, *BGU*1806.4 (i B.C.); used to translate the Roman *manipulus*, Plb.11.23.1, al., Str.12.3.18, Plu.*Aem.*17; κατὰ σπείρας, = Lat. *manipulatim*, Plb.3.115.12; later, *cohort*, *Act.Ap.*10.1, J.*BJ*3.4.2, *IGRom.*1.10 (Massilia), 1373 (Egypt), al., *OGI*208.2 (Nubia, ii A.D.), al. (gen. in this sense always σπείρης, *Act.Ap.* l.c., *POxy.*477.3 (ii A.D.), *BGU*73 (ii A.D.), *OGI* l.c., etc.). 2. = θίασος, *religious college* or *guild*, gen. σπείρης *IG*14.925 (Portus Trajani); dat. σπείρῃ ib.977 (Rome), *Inscr. Perg.*319, 320; nom. σπεῖρα *AEM*14.28 (Roumania); Lat. *spira*, *CIL*6.261 (Rome), al. (cf. σπειράρχης).

**σπειραία**, ἡ, *privet*, *Ligustrum vulgare*, Thphr.*HP*1.14.2, 6.1.4.

❋ **σπειρ-ᾱμα**, Ion. **-ημα**, ατος, τό, *coil, convolution*, ἐχίδνης A.*Ch.*248; ὄφεων Arist.*Mir.*843a32, cf. D.S.3.36, Plu.2.972f, etc.; σ. περισφυρίοιο δράκοντος, of a serpent-shaped ornament, *AP*6.207 (Arch.): metaph., αἰῶνος σπειρήματα *periods, cycles*, *App.Anth.*3.186. 2. = σπάργανον, Nic.*Al.*417. 3. *twisted thread*, Hsch. and Phot. s.v. μήρυμα. 4. *rolled bandage*, Gal.18(1).788, 809, al. **-αντικός**, ή, όν, perh. *with wavy blade*, μάχαιραι *PLond.*2.402v.21 (ii B.C.). ❋ **-άομαι**, (σπεῖρα) Pass., *to be coiled* or *folded round*, πέντε ζῶναι ἐσπείρηντο Eratosth.16.3; πέριξ.. σπειρηθεὶς [δράκων] Nic.*Th.*457; δράκοντα.. ἐσπειραμένον περὶ τὸ ἀγγεῖον Paus.10.33.9; σχοινίου ἐσπειραμένου S.E.*P.*1.227: c. dat., ὄφεις ἐσπειρημένους τοῖς παισίν *coiled round* them, f.l. in Sch.Lyc.p.5 S. for ἐπῃωρημένους. 2. metaph., λόγος ἐσπειραμένος πρὸς δεινότητα Demetr.*Eloc.*8. ❋ **-άρχης**, ου, ὁ, *leader of a* σπεῖρα II. 2, in Lat. form *spirarches*, *CIL*6.2251 (Rome), 3.870 (Dacia). **-ᾱσις**, εως, ἡ, *being coiled up, compressed*, Plu.2.1077b. **-αχθής**, ές, *with heavy coils*, κνώδαλα Nic.*Th.*399. **-ηδόν**, Adv. *in coils*, Opp.*H.*1.516, Philum.*Ven.*22.2; *in a ring*, *AP*9.301 (Secund.); *in zig-zag lines* (= σπυριδόν, q.v.), γράφειν Sch.D.T. p.484 H. II. (σπεῖρα II) of troops, *in maniples, manipulatim*, Plb.5.4.9, Lxx 2*Ma.*5.2; ἡ σ. μάχη Str.3.3.7. **-ημα**, v. σπείραμα. **-ικός**, ή, όν, *pertaining to a* σπεῖρα I. 9, *spiric*, Procl. *in Euc.* p.112 F., Hero *Deff.*74. **-ίον**, τό, Dim. of σπεῖρον, *light summer garment*, X.*HG*4.5.4. II. Dim. of σπεῖρα I. 8, *base-moulding of a column*, Hero *Aut.*3.1. III. (cf. σπεῖρα I. 3 fin.) *ring-shaped mat*, ἐξ ἀρτεμισίας *PMag.Par.*1.1088, cf. 1096. **-ίτης** [ῑ], ου, ὁ, sc. λίθος, *stone forming the base of a column* (σπεῖρα I. 8), *Supp.Epigr.*2.569.13, 23 (Didyma, ii B.C.); Lat. *spirita*, in abl. pl. *spiritis*, *CIL*8.15497 (Africa).

**σπειρο-δρᾰκοντόζωνος**, ον, *girt with coils of snakes*, *An.Ox.*3.182. **-ειδής**, ές, *coiled*, σῶμα Hermes Trism. in *Rev.Phil.*32.258. Adv. **-δῶς** *spirally*, f.l. for πιοειδῶς in Ruf.*Anat.*45. **-κέφᾰλον**, τό, (σπεῖρα I. 8) *base and capital of a column*, *CIG*3148.19, 29 (Smyrna), *Rev.Phil.*44.74 (Aphrodisias), prob. in *AJA*9.307 (Sinope).

**σπεῖρον**, τό, *piece of cloth*, Hom. (only in Od.), εἴλυμα σπείρων a wrapping *cloth*, 6.179; σπεῖρα κακά sorry *wraps*, of a beggar, 4.245; αἴ κεν ἄτερ σπείρου κεῖται without a *cerecloth* or *shroud*, 2.102, cf. 19.147, 24.137; σπεῖρον καὶ ἐπίκριον *sail* and sailyard, 5.318; πείσματα καὶ σπεῖρα [where the ult. is long in arsi] 6.269 (v.l. σπείρας):—later, *garment*, νυμφιδίου σπείροιο καλύπτρῃ Euph.107; cf. σπειρίον.

**σπειρόπωλις**, ιδος, ἡ, *for the sale of old clothes*, σ. ἀγορά *the old clothes market*, Poll.7.78.

**σπεῖρος**, εος, τό, = σπεῖρον: metaph., βολβῶν σπείρεα the *coats* of onions, Nic.*Th.*882.

**σπειροῦχος**, ον, (ἔχω) *circle-holding, ring-holding*, *AP*6.295 (Phan.).

**σπειρο-φόρος**, ὁ, *bearer of a* σπεῖρον, i.e. *garment of image of Artemis*, *Jahresh.*18 *Beibl.*287 (Ephesus). **-φύλαξ** [ῠ], ακος, ὁ, *spirale*, a kind of gold ornament, *Gloss.*

**σπειρόω**, (σπεῖρον) = σπαργανόω, Call.*Del.*6, *Jov.*33. II. Pass., *to be coiled*, of a blood-vessel, περί τι Hp.*Oss.*15.

❋ **σπείρω**, Aeol. **σπέρρω** Sch.D.T.p.117 H., *EM*300.19: Ion. impf. σπείρεσκον Hdt.4.42: fut. σπερῶ E.*El.*79, Pl.*Phdr.*276d; Aeol. σπέρσω Sch.E.*Hec.*202: aor. ἔσπειρα A.*Th.*754 (lyr.), Hdt.7.107, Pl.*Ti.*41c: pf. ἔσπαρκα Polyaen.2.1.1, etc.:—Med., aor. inf. σπείρασθαι A.R.3.1028; aor. 2 σπαρέσθαι dub. l. in Polyaen.8.26:—Pass., fut. σπᾰρήσομαι Lxx *Na.*1.14, (δια-) D.S.17.69: aor. ἐσπάρην [ᾰ] S.*OT*1498, Th.2.27: pf. ἔσπαρμαι E.*HF*1098, Ar.*Ra.*1206, Pl.*Lg.*693a, etc.:—*sow*, I. *sow* seed, c. acc., [κέγχρους] Hes.*Sc.*399; σῖτον Hdt.4.17; στάχυν E.*Cyc.*121; of Cadmus, σ. γηγενῆ στάχυν Id.*Ba.*264 (so in Med., σπείρασθαι ὀδόντας A.R.3.1028): abs., *sow*, Hes.*Op.*391; opp. θερίζω, Ar.*Av.*710, etc.: metaph., θερ. καὶ σ. ταῖς γλώσσαις, of corrupt orators, ib.1697 (lyr.); καρπὸν ὃν ἔσπειρε θερίζειν Pl.*Phdr.*260d; αἰσχρῶς μὲν ἔσπειρας κακῶς δὲ ἐθέρισας Gorg.16: prov., εἰς πέτρας τε καὶ λίθους σ. Pl.*Lg.*838e; σ. κατὰ πετρῶν, i.e. εἰς πέλαγος (cf. σπέρμα I. 1), Luc.*Am.*20. 2. *engender, beget* offspring (cf. II. 2), S.*Aj.*1293, *Tr.*33, E.*Ion*

49, etc.; οἱ σπείραντες the *parents*, *IG*3.1339, cf. 14.1794 (Rome); ἄθυτα παλλακῶν σπέρματα σ. Pl.*Lg*.841d:—Pass., *spring* or *be born*, ὅθενπερ αὐτὸς ἐσπάρη S.*OT*1498, cf. E.*Ion* 554 (troch.), Pl.*R*.460b; πρὸ τοῦ Ζήνωνα..σπαρῆναι before Z. *was begotten*, Phld.*Rh*.2.110S. **3.** *scatter like seed, strew*, χρυσὸν καὶ ἄργυρον Hdt.7.107; σ. φλόγα *Trag.Adesp*.85; of liquids, *scatter* or *sprinkle*, ἐκ τευχέων σ. δρόσον E.*Andr*.167; *spread abroad, extend*, σ. ἀγλαΐαν νάσῳ Pi.*N*.1.13; *spread* rumour, σ. ματαίαν βάξιν S.*El*.642; μὴ σπεῖρε πολλοῖς τὸν παρόντα δαίμονα *do* not *speak of* it *indiscriminately*, Id.*Fr*.653:—Pass., *to be scattered* or *dispersed*, ἐσπαρμένος κατὰ..πόλιν, of the ashes of Solon *scattered* over Salamis, Cratin.228; τόξα δ' ἔσπαρται πέδῳ E.*HF*1098; of persons, ἐσπάρησαν καθ' Ἑλλάδα Th.2.27; ἐσπαρμένοι εἰς ἁρπαγήν X.*HG*3.4.22; κατὰ χώραν ib.6.2.17; ἔσπαρται λόγος E.*Fr*.846 ap.Ar.*Ra*.1206. **II.** *sow* a field, νειόν Hes.*Op*.463; γῆν, τέμενος, πεδιάδα, Hdt.4.42, 9.116, 122; ἄρουραν A.*Fr*.158; ἡ σπειρομένη Αἴγυπτος *the arable part of* Egypt, Hdt.2.77; τυχεῖν μὲν ἤδη 'σπαρμένα Ar.*Pax* 1140; ἀροῦται καὶ σπείρεται τὸ Θηβαίων ἄστυ Din.1.24: prov., πόντον σπείρειν, of lost labour, Thgn.106, 107: metaph., καινοτάταις σ. διανοίαις Ar.*V*.1044; σ. εἰς ἀρετῆς ἔκφυσιν Pl.*Lg*.777e; τοὺς ἐν γράμμασι κήπους Id.*Phdr*. 276d. **2.** of procreation, ματρὸς..σ. ἄρουραν A.*Th*.754; σ. τέκνων ἄλοκα E.*Ph*.18; σ. λέχη Id.*Ion* 64; ἣν ἔσπειρε, i.e. his wife, Lib.*Or*. 37.9; v. supr. I. 2.

**σπειρ-ώδης**, ες, (σπεῖρος) *with many coats*, κόρση, of σκίλλα and ῥάφανον, Nic.*Al*.253, 527. **-ωσις**, εως, ἡ, = σπείραμα, Sch.Arat.86, 697.

**σπεῖσαι, σπείσασκε, σπείσω**, v. σπένδω.

**σπεῖσις**, εως, ἡ, (σπένδω) = σπονδή, Zonar.

**σπειστέον**, (σπένδω) *one must pour a drink-offering*, Poll.10.65.

⊛ **σπεκλάριον**, τό, = sq. 2, *PHolm*.4.28: hence **σφεκλαράριος**, ὁ, = Lat. *speculararius*, *Supp.Epigr*.7.197 (Berytus, v/vi A.D.).

⊛ **σπέκλον**, τό, = Lat. *speculum, mirror*, Alex.Aphr. *in Sens*.29.7. **2.** = Lat. *lapis specularis*, i.e. *mica* or *talc*, *Hippiatr*.70, 130, 150: hence **σπεκλοποιός**, ὁ, *specularius*, *Gloss*.

**σπεκλόω**, v. σπλεκ-.

⊛ **σπεκουλάτωρ**, ορος, ὁ, = Lat. *speculator*, prop. *scout*: but in the Roman Imperial army, **1.** one of the *principales* or head-quarters' staff of a legionary commander or provincial governor (whose duties included the carrying out of executions), *Ev.Marc*.6.27, *POxy*.1193.1 (iv A.D.), etc. **2.** one of the Imperial body-guard (*speculatores Augusti*), = δορυφόρος, Suid.

**σπεκούλιον**, τό, *small mirror*, *PGoodsp.Cair*.30 vii 31 (ii A.D.).

**σπέλεθος**, f.l. for πέλεθος in Ar.*Ec*.595; cf. σπέληξ.

**σπέλεκτος**· πελεκάν, Hsch. **σπέληξ**· γυναικεῖον ἱμάτιον, ἡμιδιπλοΐδιον, Suid.; but σπέλληξι· σπελέθοις, Hsch. **σπέλιον** or **σπέλλιον**, τό, Aeol. for ψέλιον, Sch.D.T.pp.203, 504 H., *An.Ox*.4.326. **σπελλάμεναι**· στειλάμεναι, Hsch. (Aeolic). **σπένδαμνον**· ξύλον, Id. (= σφ.). **σπενδαυλέω, σπενδεῖον, σπενδοποιέω**, f.ll. for σπονδ-.

⊛ **σπένδω**, Il.11.775, etc.; Ep. subj. 2 sg. σπένδησθα Od.4.591: Ion. impf. σπένδεσκον Il.16.227, Od.7.138: fut. σπείσω Lxx *Nu*.28.7, (κατα-) Hdt.2.151, E.*Or*.1187: aor. ἔσπεισα Od.13.55, S.*Fr*.42, etc.; Ep. σπεῖσα Il.9.177, σπείσασκε Od.8.89; Ep. subj. σπείσομεν, for -ωμεν, 7.165, 181: pf. ἔσπεικα (κατ-) Plu.*Sert*.14:—**Med.**, aor. ἐσπεισάμην Hdt.3.144, etc.:—**Pass.**, aor. ἐσπείσθην Plu.*Rom*.19: pf. ἔσπεισμαι, v. infr. II fin.:—*make a drink-offering* (because before drinking wine a portion was poured on the table, hearth, or altar), σπεῖσάν τ' ἔπιόν θ' ὅσον ἤθελε θυμός Il.9.177; ἐπὴν σπείσῃς τε καὶ εὔξεαι Od.3.45, cf. Xenoph.1.15, S.*Ph*.1033, E.*Ba*.313, etc.: c. dat. of the god to whom the libation was made, δέπας ἑλὼν σπείσασκε θεοῖσιν Od.8.89; ὡς σπείσῃς Διὶ πατρὶ καὶ ἄλλοις ἀθανάτοισι Il.6.259, cf. 16.227, Od.3.334, etc.; τὴν (sc. κύλικα) δὲ θεοῖς σπένδεις Thgn.490; κρητῆρας σπενδέτω prob. *let* him *dedicate* them *by pouring an offering from* them, *SIG*57.13 (Milet., v B.C.):—the liquid poured is mostly in acc., σ. οἶνον *pour* wine, Il.11.775, Od.18.151; λοιβάς S.*El*.270; σπονδάς, χοάς, E.*El*.512, *Or*.1322; ellipt., σ. ἀγαθοῦ δαίμονος (sc. σπονδήν) Ar.*Eq*.106; σ. οἴνου (partit. gen.) Hdn.5.5.7: rarely c. dat. rei, ὕδατι σ. *make a drink-offering with* water, Od.12.363; Ὀλυμπίῳ σ. ἀοιδαῖς *make libations with* songs to Zeus, Pi.*I*.6(5).9: also c. dat. instrumenti, σ. δέπαϊ, δεπάεσσι, Il.23.196, Od.7.137; χρυσίδι Cratin.124; χαλκέῃ φιάλῃ Hdt.2.147; ἐκ χρυσέης φιάλης Id.7.54: c. gen., σ. βαιᾶς κύλικος S.*Fr*.42:—Pass., οὗτος θεοῖσι σπένδεται θεὸς γεγώς E.*Ba*.284: so metaph. of a person, σπένδομαι ἐπὶ τῇ θυσίᾳ *I am offered* (*as a drink-offering*) upon it, *Ep.Phil*.2.17, cf. 2*Ep.Ti*.4.6. **2.** rarely without the religious sense, simply *pour*, τράγου οὖρον, as remedy for convulsions, Hdt.4.187: metaph., σ. δάκρυα *AP*7.555b (Joann.), *IG*14.1957, al.; ξίφος αἷμα τυράννων ἔσπ. *AP*9.184. **II.** Med., *pour libations one with another*, and, as this was the custom in making treaties or agreements, *make a treaty, make peace*, Hdt.3.144, Ar.*Ach*.199, *Av*.1534, Th.4.99, 119, X.*An*.1.9.7, etc.; τὰ μὲν σπενδόμενοι τὰ δὲ πολεμοῦντες Th.1.18:—Constr., σπένδεσθαί τινι *make peace with* one, Ar.*Ach*.225, Th.5.5, etc.; in full, σπένδεσθαί τινι σπονδάς ib.14 (but σ. τῇ πρεσβείᾳ *give* it *pledges* of safe conduct, Aeschin.3.63, cf. 2.109; so σ. τινί *obtain a truce for* one, X.*An*.2.3.7); σ. πρός τινας, for τισι, Th.5.17, 30, X.*An*.3.5.16; of a person, σπείσασθαι *cum Bruto et Cassio*, Cic.*Att*.15.29.2: metaph., σ. συμφοραῖς καὶ θεσπίσμασιν E.*Or*.1680 sq.; σ. ἐπὶ τοῖσδε *on these terms*, Id.*Ph*.1240; ἐφ' ᾧ.. X.*An*.4.4.6; also σ. ὥστε μὴ ἀδικεῖν Th.6.7; σ. ἦ μὴν ἐμμενεῖν ἐν ταῖς σπονδαῖς Id.4.118: c. inf. alone, Id.7.83: less freq. c. acc., εἰρήνην σπεισάμενοι Λακεδαιμονίοισι *having concluded a peace* with them, Hdt.7.148; νεῖκος ἐσπεῖσθαι *make up* a quarrel, E.*Med*.1140; πόλεμον D.H.9.36; σ. ἀναίρεσιν τοῖς νεκροῖς *obtain a truce* for taking up the dead, Th.3.24; σ. σφίσιν ἡμέραν τοὺς νεκροὺς ἀνελέσθαι Id.4.114; σ. ἀναχώρησίν τινι Id.3.109; σ. περὶ τῶν τέκνων Plu.2.494d:—pf. ἔσπεισμαι is used in med. sense in E.*Med*. l.c.; τοῖς ἐχθροῖς ἐσπείσμην Luc.*Phal*.1.3; but in pass. sense, ἐσπεῖσθαι τὰς σπονδάς Th.4.16; οἷς ἔσπειστο Id.3.111: aor., ἐσπείσθησαν ἀνοχαί Plu.*Rom*.19. (In Th.4.98, τοὺς νεκροὺς σπένδουσιν ἀναιρεῖσθαι, emphasis is laid on the act of one of the parties, and in *AP*9.422 (Apollonid.), σπεῖσαι δεύτερα φίλτρα γάμου, Reiske cj. σπεύσῃς.) (Cf. Hittite š(*i*)*pand*- 'pour a libation', Lat. *spondeo*.)

⊛ **σπέος**, Ep. **σπεῖος**, τό, Ep.Noun (also in *Inscr.Cypr*.98 H.), *cavern, grotto*, Od.5.57, etc.; ὑπὸ σ. ἤλασε μῆλα Il.4.279; [Κύκλωπες] οἴκεον ἐν σπήεσσι Od.9.400; ἐν σπέσσι γλαφυροῖσι ib.114; νῆα..ὡρμίσαμεν κοῖλον σ. εἰσερύσαντες 12.317.—Hom. uses only the following forms: nom. and acc. sg. σπέος, Il.13.32, ll. cc.; irreg. dat. σπῆϊ 18.402, Od.2.20, al., cf. Hes.*Th*.297 (σπέϊ in Opp.*C*.4.246): of the Ep. form σπεῖος, acc. sg. only in Od.5.194; gen. σπείους only in Od.(5.68, al.): of the pl., only dat. σπέσσι and σπήεσσι, only in Od. (1.15, al., 9.400, al.); gen. σπείων *h.Ven*.263; irreg. dat. pl. σπεάτεσσι, as if from σπέας, in Xenoph.37.

**σπέρᾰδος**, εος, τό, = σπέρμα, Nic.*Th*.649, *Al*.330; Ep. dat. pl. σπεράδεσσι ib.134.

**σπεργανῆσαι**· σπαράξαι, Hsch. **σπέργδην**, Adv., (σπέρχω) *hastily*, Id. **σπέργουλος**· ὀρνιθάριον ἄγριον, Id. **σπέργυς**· πρέσβυς, Id., *EM*723.17. **σπερηδών**· εἴλησις, περιπλοκή, Hsch.

⊛ **σπέρμ-α**, ατος, τό, (σπείρω) *seed*, only once in Hom., in metaph. sense, v. infr. I. 2: **I.** mostly, *seed* of plants, σ. ἀνιέναι, κρύπτειν, *h.Cer*.307, cf. Hdt.3.97: pl., Hes.*Op*.446; σ. τῇ γῇ διδόναι, ἐμβαλεῖν, X.*Oec*.17.8, 10: prov., εἰς πέλαγος σ. βαλεῖν *Epigr.Gr*.1038.8 (Pamphylia); of fruit, Antiph.58.4; τοῖς γαίης σπέρμασι with *the products* of earth, of corn-stalks, *AP*9.89 (Phil.). **2.** metaph., *germ, origin* of anything, σ. πυρός Od.5.490; φλογός Pi.*O*.7.48, cf. *P*.3.37; σπέρματα, = στοιχεῖα, *elements*, Anaxag.4, cf. Epicur.*Ep*.2 p.38 U., *Fr*.250; ὁ τὸ σπέρμα παρασχών, οὗτος τῶν φύντων αἴτιος D.18.159; συκοφάντου σ. καὶ ῥίζαν οἴεται δεῖν ὑπάρχειν τῇ πόλει Id.25.48; σ. τῆς στάσεως Plu.*Mar*.10; τοῦ ὅρκου Longin.16.3. **3.** *seed-time, sowing*, Hes.*Op*.781. **II.** of animals, *seed, semen*, φέροισα σ. θεοῦ pregnant *by* the god, Pi.*P*.3.15; but σ. φέρειν Ἡρακλέους to be pregnant *of* Heracles, Id.*N*.10.17; μυελὸν..εἰς σ. καὶ γόνον μερίζεσθαι Ti.Locr.100b, cf. Pl.*Ti*.86c; σ. παραλαβεῖν E.*Or*.553; σπέρματος πλῆσαι Plu.*Lyc*.15: pl., κατ' ἀμφότερα τὰ σ. θεῶν ἀπόγονος Hp.*Ep*.2. **2.** *race, origin, descent*, τοὐμὸν..σπέρμ' ἰδεῖν βουλήσομαι S.*OT*1077; τίνος εἶ σπέρματος πατρόθεν; Id.*OC*214 (lyr.); γένεθλον σπέρμα τ' Ἀργεῖον A.*Supp*.290, cf. *Ch*.236; σ. ἄντασ' Ἐρεχθειδᾶν S.*Ant*.981 (lyr.), cf. Pi.*O*.7.93, etc. **3.** freq. in Poets, *seed, offspring*, τὸ βρότειον σ. A.*Fr*.399; σ. Πελοπιδῶν Id.*Ch*.503; σ. [τοῦ Ἀβραάμ] *Ev.Luc*.1.55, etc.; sts. of a single person, Pi.*O*.9.61, A.*Pr*.705, S.*Ph*.364, Orac.ap.Th.5.16, Lxx *Ge*.4.25, etc.: pl., A.*Eu*.803, 909, S.*OT*1246, *OC*600, *Ep.Gal*.3.16; once in Pl., ἀνθρώπων σπέρμασι νουθετοῦμεν *Lg*.853c. **-ᾰγοραιολεκῐθο-λᾰχᾰνό-πωλις**, ιδος, ἡ, *green-grocery-market-woman*, Ar.*Lys*.457. ⊛ **-αίνω**, *sow with seed, fertilize*, of the Nile, Plu.2.366a; of the male, Horap.2.115: c. acc. cogn., σ. σπέρμα Aq., Thd.*Ge*.1.29. **2.** metaph., *procreate*, σ. γενεήν Hes.*Op*.736, cf. Call.*Fr*.207: abs., Arist.*Pr*.876$^b$39:—Med., Nonn.*D*.3.295. **-ᾰτία**, ἡ, *seed*, Sm.*Ps*.64.10 (v.l. πανσπερμία). **-ᾰτίας** σικυός, ὁ, a cucumber or gourd *left to ripen for seed*, opp. εὐνουχίας, Cratin.136. **-ᾰτίζω**, *sow*, τι εἰς γῆν Herm.ap.Stob.1.21.9:—Pass., of a woman, *conceive, become pregnant*, Lxx *Le*.12.2. **2.** ἐξ Ἀπόλλωνος αὐτὸν σ. *make* him *son* of A., Eust.1348.52. **II.** intr., of plants, *to be in seed*, Lxx *Ex*.9.31. **-ᾰτικός**, ή, όν, *of* or *for seed* or *generation, seminal*, πόροι, ὄργανα, Arist.*GA*716$^b$17, 717$^a$12; περίττωμα ib.717$^a$30; ἀπόκρισις Id.*PA*681$^b$35; *fruitful in seed*, ζῷον Thphr.*CP*1.16.4; σ. γένεσις *from seed*, ib.1.2.1; τὸ -κόν *the seed-vessel*, Id.*HP*6.4.3. **b.** *capable of procreating*, Arist.*Pr*.876$^b$38, *GA*750$^a$13; δυνάμεις Sor.1.41; πόρος, of the Fallopian tubes, Herophil.ap.Gal.4.597; τὸ σ. the *procreative* faculty, Zeno *Stoic*.1.39, cf. *Stoic*.2.258. **2.** metaph., *generative*, esp. in Stoic Philosophy, σ. λόγοι *generative* principles, v. λόγος III. 7b: in Arith., ἡ δυὰς σ. Iamb. *in Nic*. p.31 P., al. Adv. -κῶς *Theol.Ar*.3, 4. **II.** *general, summary*, Ulp. ad D.9 init., Syrian. *in Hermog*.2.91 R. Adv. -κῶς, [εἴρηται] Gal.7.764. **-άτιον**, τό, Dim. of σπέρμα, Thphr.*HP*9.20.1, *BGU*1861.4 (i B.C., pl.), Dsc.2.180, M.Ant.12.26. **-ᾰτισμός**, ὁ, *production of seed*, μεταφυτεύουσι πρὸς τοὺς σ. (sc. τὰ λάχανα) Thphr.*HP*7.5.3, cf. 7.4.3. **II.** *copulation*, Lxx *Le*.18.23. **-ᾰτῖτις**, ιδος, ἡ, fem. Adj. *spermatic*, φλέβες σ. (v.l. σπερματίδες) Diog.Apoll.6. **II.** masc., **σπερματίτης** λόγος, = σπερματικός I. 2, Nicom.ap.Phot.p.143 B.

**σπερμᾰτο-λογέω**, metaph., *glean, pick up little by little*, μελέτας ὥσπερ ἐσπερματολογῆσθαι Philostr.*VS*1.22.2. **-λόγος**, ον, = σπερμολόγος, τέτραγες Epich.45, 46. **-ομαι**, Pass., *to be sown*, of land, Thphr.*CP*3.2.2. **2.** of plants, *come to seed, bring seed to perfection*, Id.*HP*6.8.2. **-ποιέω**, in Med., *convert into semen*, Porph.*Gaur*.7.2. **-πώλης**, ου, ὁ, *seedsman*, Nicopho 19, Critias 70.

**σπερμᾰτοῦχος**, ον, (ἔχω) *seed-holding, fruitful*, δύναμις Porph.ap.Eus.*PE*3.11, Lyd.*Mens*.4.137.

**σπερμᾰτοφάγος** [φᾰ], ον, *eating seeds*, D.S.3.24.

**σπερμᾰτ-ώδης**, ες, *like seed*, Sch.Nic.*Al*.253; σ. κίνησις the action *of a sower*, v.l. for σπασματώδης (q.v.). **II.** *germinant*, metaph.,

Charond.ap.Stob.4.2.24 (Sup.); *in the germ, undeveloped*, Artem.4 Prooem. (Comp.). **-ωσις**, εως, ἡ, *a bearing of seed, seeding*, Phan. Hist.25.

**σπερμ-εῖον**, τό, = σπέρμα, Nic.*Al*.201, *Th*.599,894, al. **-εῖος**, ὁ, *presiding over seeds*, epith. of Apollo, Orph.*H*.34.3; fem. Σπερμείη, of Demeter, ib.40.5.

**Σπέρμιος**, ὁ, name of month at Cnossus, *SIG*712.6 (ii B.C.).

**σπερμο-βολέω**, *emit semen*, Horap.1.46. **-βόλημα**, ατος, τό, *seminarium*, Gloss. **-βολία**, ἡ, *sowing*, *POxy*.133.13 (vi A.D.); *seed-corn* (?), *PLond*.1821.397. **-βόλος**, ὁ, *sower*, Poet. in *BKT* 5(1) p.122. **-γονέω**, *bear seed*, Thphr.*HP*7.14.3. **-γόνος**, ον, *bearing seed*, Sch.Lyc.352. **-λογέω**, *pick up seeds*, like birds, Hp.*Vict*.2.47, Plu.2.473a. 2. *to be a* σπερμολόγος III, *gossip*, Philostr.*VA*5.20. **-λογία**, ἡ, *babbling, gossip*, Plu.*Alc*.36, 2.65b, etc. **-λογικός**, ή, όν, *like a* σπερμολόγος III, *frivolous*, περίεργα καὶ σ. Id.2.664a. **-λόγος**, ον, (λέγω) *picking up seeds*, of birds, Id. *Demetr*.28, Alex.Mynd.ap.Ath.9.388a: as Subst., *rook*, Arist.*HA*592[b] 28; glossed κολοιῶδες ζῷον, Hsch.; σπερμολόγων τε γένη Ar.*Av*.232 (lyr.), cf. 579. 2. τὰ σπερμολόγα τῶν παιδαρίων *guttersnipes*, Ath.3. 85f. II. *picking up scraps, gossiping*, ἄνθρωπος D.H.19.5 (Sup., ib.4); also πικρὰ καὶ σ. ῥήματα Plu.2.456c. III. as Subst., *one who picks up and retails scraps of knowledge, an idle babbler, gossip*, D. 18.127, *Act.Ap*.17.18, Ath.8.344c. **-νόμος**, ον, = foreg. I, Hsch., Eust.1547.54. **-ομαι**, Pass., *bear seed*, Thphr.*HP*3.18.8. **-τοκέω**, *produce seed*, cj. in Id.*HP*6.4.8.

**σπερμο-φάγος** [ᾰ], ον, = σπερματοφάγος, S.E.*P*.1.56. **-φορέω**, *bear seed*, Thphr.*HP*1.2.2, 6.7.1. **-φόρος**, ον, *bearing seed*. Id.*CP* 1.21.1, *AP*6.104 (Phil.). **-φυέω**, *produce seed*, Thphr.*HP*7.4.7, *CP*1.16.4. **-φυής**, ές, *growing from seed*, Id.*HP*7.10.1.

**σπερύνειν**· σπείρειν, θυμοῦσθαι, ἀπειλεῖν, διώκειν, Hsch.

**σπερχνός**, ή, όν, (σπέρχω) *hasty, hurried*, ἄγγελοι A.*Th*.286; of diseases and pains, *violent*, Hp.*Morb*.2.64, *Nat.Mul*.35, al.: neut. as Adv., σπερχνὸν κοτέων Hes.*Sc*.454, al. II. Act., *hastening, pressing*, Hsch. (glossed by **σπερχνοποιός**). III. εἶδος ἱέρακος, Hsch. (cf. περκνός II).

**σπερχυλλάδην**, Adv., (σπέρχομαι) *hastily, vehemently*, κέκραγας *Com.Adesp*.30.

**σπέρχω**, Il.13.334, etc. (Act. only in pres. and impf.):—**Med.**, fut. σπέρξομαι, aor. ἐσπερξάμην, Hsch.:—**Pass.**, Il.19.317, etc.: aor. part. σπερχθείς Pi.*N*.1.40, Hdt.1.32:—poet. Verb (used also in Ion. Prose, cf. περισπέρχω; Att. only in compds. ἐπι-, κατα-σπέρχω), *set in rapid motion*, only late, c. inf., τρέχειν Luc.*Trag*.236: more freq. in Pass., *to haste, be in haste*, c. inf., ὁπότε σπερχοίατ' Ἀχαιοὶ.. φέρειν Ἄρηα Il. 19.317, cf. A.R.4.211; ὁπότε σ. ἐρετμοῖς Od.13.22; σ. μετά, ποτί τι, A.R.1.1255, Orph.*L*.706; of the sea, *rage*, *Hymn.Is*.151: in Hom. mostly part. pres. Pass. σπερχόμενος *in haste, hurriedly*, σ. δ' ὁ γεραιὸς ἑοῦ ἐπεβήσετο δίφρου Il.24.322, cf. 23.870, Od.9.101, al.; [νηῦς] ἐπέκελσεν σπερχομένη 13.115, cf. E.*Alc*.257 (lyr.). 2. metaph., *to be hasty of temper*, σπερχομένοιο γέροντος Il.24.248, cf. Hdt.3.72; σπερχθείς Id.1.32; σπερχθεῖσα θυμῷ *in haste and heat*, Pi.*N*.1.40; μὴ σπέρχου *be* not *hasty*, E.*Med*.1133; σ. μέγα δή τι καὶ οὐ φατόν Call.*Del*.60; σπέρχεσθαί τινι *to be angry with* one, Hdt.5.33, Call.*Del*. 158. II. intr., = Pass., ὅθ' ὑπὸ λιγέων ἀνέμων σπέρχωσιν ἄελλαι *are driven rapidly*, Il.13.334, cf. *h.Hom*.33.7; ὁπότε σπέρχοιεν ἄελλαι (v.l. σπερχοίατ') Od.3.283; ἵππος σπέρχων Opp.*C*.1.342; εἰρεσίη σ. Id.*H*.5.295. (Cf. Skt. *sprhayati* 'desire'.)

**σπές**, aor. imper. of *σπῶ, = λέγω, *EM*740.11 (mentioned without expl. by A.D.*Adv*.147.1): pl. σπέτε, = εἴπατε, Hsch. **σπέσθαι**, v. *ἕπω (B). **σπευδόντως**, Adv. *in haste*, Id. s. v. ἠπειγμένως.

⊛ **σπεύδω**, Ep. inf. σπευδέμεν Od.24.324: fut. σπεύσω E.*Med*.153 (lyr.), Ar.*Eq*.926, etc.; Cret. σπευσίω *SIG*527.42 (iii B.C.): aor. ἔσπευσα E.*Supp*.161, Pl.*Cri*.45c, etc.; Ep. σπεῦσα Od.9.250; subj. σπεύσομεν, for -ωμεν, Il.17.121: pf. ἔσπευκα *Annuario* 8/9.375 (Perga, ii B.C.), Paus.7.15.11:—**Med.**, A.*Ag*.151 (lyr.): fut. σπεύσομαι Il.15.402:—**Pass.**, pf. ἔσπευσμαι Luc.*Am*.33, Gal.12.895. I. trans., *set going, urge on, hasten*, ταῦτα δ' ἅμα χρὴ σπεύδειν Il.13.236; οἱ δὲ γάμον σπεύδουσιν Od.19.137, cf. Hdt.1.38; παῦσαι σπεύδων τὰ σπεύδεις ib.206; σ. ἀθλίαν ὁδὸν E.*Ion* 1226; σ. οἱ μὲν ἴγδιν, οἱ δὲ σίλφιον, οἱ δ' ὄξος *procure quickly, get ready*, Sol.39; κλίμακας E.*IT*1352; σπευσίω ὅτι κα δύναμαι κακὸν τᾷ πόλει *SIG* l. c. (in Hdt.8.46, Δημοκρίτου σπεύσαντος, an acc. must be supplied). b. *seek eagerly, strive after*, μηδὲν ἄγαν σ. Thgn.335,401; σ. βίον ἀθάνατον, μακροτέραν ἀρετάν, Pi.*P*.3.62, *I*.4(3). 13(31); εὐψυχίαν ἀντ' εὐβουλίας E.*Supp*.161; τὴν ἡγεμονίαν Th.5.16; χάριν E.*Hec*.1175; πόλεμον τέκνοις Id.*HF*1133. c. *promote* or *further zealously, press* or *urge on*, τι τῶν φέρει φρὴν A.*Supp*.599 (lyr.); τὸ σὸν σ. ἅμα καὶ τοὐμὸν S.*El*.251; τὸ σὸν ἀγαθὸν E.*Hec*.120 (lyr.); τὸ ἐφ' ἑαυτὸν ἕκαστος σ. Th.1.141; σ. ἀσπούδαστ' ἐπὶ σοὶ δαίμων E.*IT*201 (lyr.); τὰ ἐναντία τῇ ἑαυτῶν ὠφελείᾳ σ. And.2.2; in arguing, σεαυτῷ τὰ ἐναντία σ. Pl.*Prt*.361a; σ. τοῦτο, ὅπως.. Id.*Lg*.687e; μὴ σπεῦδ' ἃ μὴ δεῖ, μηδ' ἃ δεῖ σπεύδειν μένε Men.*Mon*.344: c. dat., οἱ Χαιρέᾳ σπεύδοντες *the partisans of* Chaereas, Charito 6.1: ἐς τὰ Ἑλλήνων σ. Philostr.*VA*5.8: folld. by a conj., εἰς τοὺς πλουσίους σπεύσω σ' ὅπως ἂν ἐγγραφῇς Ar.*Eq*.926:—Med., σπευδομένα θυσίαν A.*Ag*.151 (lyr.):—Pass., ξυνὸν πᾶσι ἀγαθὸν σπεύδεται Hdt.7.53; ἐσπευσμέναι χρεῖαι *pressing* needs, Luc.*Am*.33. 2. c. acc. et inf., σπεύσατε.. Τεῦκρον ἐν τάχει μολεῖν *urge* him to come quickly, S.*Aj*.804; σπεῦσον.. κάπετόν τιν' ἰδεῖν *hasten* to look out for.., ib.1165 (anap.). II. more freq. intr., *press on, hasten*. διὰ δρυμὰ πυκνὰ καὶ ὕλην σπεύδουσ' Il.11. 119, cf. 8.191, 23.414, Hes.*Sc*.228; σ. ἀπὸ ῥυτῆρος with loose rein, S.*OC*900; δρόμῳ E.*Ion* 1556; πεζῇ X.*An*.3.4.49, etc.; *exert oneself, strive eagerly* or *anxiously*, of warriors fighting, Il.4.232, cf. 8.293, etc.; of a smith at work, 18.373; of beasts of draught, 17.745; of bees working, Hes.*Th*.597: prov., ὅταν σπεύδῃ τις αὐτὸς χὠ θεὸς συνάπτεται A.*Pers*.742 (troch.); σπεῦδε βραδέως *festina lente*, Gell.10.11.5; σ. τινί *exert oneself for* another, Alex.309:—Construct., 1. c. part., σπεῦσε πονησάμενος τὰ ἃ ἔργα (for σπουδαίως ἐπονήσατο) Od.9.250, cf. S.*El*.935, E.*Med*.761 (anap.), Ar.*Ach*.179: reversely, σπεύδων *in haste, eagerly*, τὼ δὲ σπεύδοντε πετέσθην Il.23.506; ἵκετο σπεύδων Pi. *P*.4.95; εἰς ἀρθμὸν ἐμοὶ.. σπεύδων σπεύδοντί ποθ' ἥξει A.*Pr*.193 (anap.); σ. ἐβοήθει X.*HG*4.3.1. 2. c. inf.. *to be eager to*.., Hes *Op*.22,673, Pi.*O*.4.11(14), *N*.9.21, A.*Ag*.601, Hdt.8.41; σῴζειν θέλοντας ἄνδρα γ' ὃς σπεύδῃ θανεῖν S.*Aj*.812:—Med., σπευδομένα ἀφελεῖν A.*Eu*.360 (lyr.). 3. c. acc. et inf., *to be anxious that*.., εἰρήνην ἑωυτοῖσι γενέσθαι Hdt.1.74; ἔσπευδεν εἶναι μὴ μάχας Ar.*Pax* 672, cf. Pl.*Prt*.361a; τὸ λεκτικοὺς γίγνεσθαι τοὺς συνόντας οὐκ ἔσπ. X.*Mem*.4.3.1: also ἔσπευσεν τοῦ διατηρηθῆναι τὴν εὐφημίαν αὐτοῖς *IG*2[2].1028.83. 4. folld. by ὡς, ὅπως, etc., σ. ὡς Ζεὺς μήποτ' ἄρξειεν A.*Pr*.205; σ. ὅπως μὴ .. Pl.*Grg*.480b; ἵνα.., ἵνα μή.., Id.*Plt*.264a, Isoc.4.164; ὥστε μή, c. inf., Thphr.*Od*.57. 5. folld. by a Prep., σ. μάχην ἐς *show eagerness for*.., Il.4.225 (Med., σπεύσομαι εἰς Ἀχιλῆα, ἵνα.. *hasten*, 15.402); εἰς ἄφενος σπεύδειν Hes.*Op*.24; εἰς ἀρετήν Thgn.403; ἐς θαλάμους E. *Hipp*.182 (anap.); ἐς τὰ πράγματα Id.*Ion* 599, etc.; εἰς τὸ αὐτὸ ἡμῖν X.*Cyr*.1.3.4; δώματος εἴσω E.*Med*.100 (anap.); ἐπί τι Lycurg.57; περὶ Πατρόκλοιο θανόντος *struggle* for him, Il.17.121; ὑπέρ τινος *IG*12(9).903 (Chalcis, ii B.C.); πρός τινα Ar.*V*.1026, etc.; also σ. ὁδόν *IG*14.1729. 6. with Adv., σ. οἷ θέλεις S.*Tr*.334; δεῦρο Ar.*Ach*.179; ἔνθα X.*An*.4.8.14, etc. 7. *to be troubled in mind, harassed*, Lxx *Ex*.15.15, 1*Ki*.28.21, al. (Cf. σπουδή, σπούδαξ, Lith. *spáudžiu* 'press'.)

**σπεῦσδος**, ὁ, an official at Gortyn, *Annuario* 8/9.33 (i B.C.).

**σπευσίνιοι**, οἱ, = Σκύθαι, τοξόται, *policemen*, said to be named after Σπευσῖνος (Suid. s. v. τοξόται) the founder of the force, Poll.8.132.

**σπεῦσις**, εως, ἡ, *festinatio*, Gloss.

**σπευσ-τέον**, *one must hasten*, Ar.*Lys*.320, Plb.4.30.5. **-τικός**, ή, όν, *hasty*, Arist.*EN*1125[a]14. Adv. -κῶς *EM*738.27. **-τός**, ή, όν, *to be done* or *pursued eagerly*, Phryn.*PS* p.108 B.

**σπήεσσι, σπῆϊ**, v. σπέος.

**σπηλάδιον** [ᾰ], τό, Dim. of σπήλαιον, Theopomp.Com.46 (leg. -ᾴδιον).

**σπηλαιοειδής**, ές, = σπηλαιώδης, Eust.892.33.

⊛ **σπήλαιον**, τό, *grotto, cavern*, Pl.*R*.514a, 515a, 539e, Moschio Trag. 6.5, Satyr.*Vit.Eur.Fr*.39 ix 6, *Apoc*.6.15, etc.; σ. λῃστῶν *den* of robbers, Lxx *Je*.7.11, *Ev.Matt*.21.13; of a *grave*, *Supp.Epigr*.7.160 (Palmyra, i A.D.), 166 (ibid., ii A.D.), *Ev.Jo*.11.38. 2. *privy parts*, Lxx *Hb*. 2.15 (pl.). 3. *place behind the scenes* in a theatre, Poll.4.124.

**σπηλᾱ̈́της** [ῑ], ου, ὁ, *worshipped in grottos*, of certain gods, Paus. 10.32.5.

**σπηλαιώδης**, ες, *cavern-like*, κατάγειος οἴκησις σ. Pl.*R*.514a, cf. Dsc.5.91.

**σπηλεῦσαι**, written σπιλευσε, = *antruare*, Gloss.

**σπηλόν**· σκληρόν, Hsch.

**σπηλυγγώδης**, ες, = σπηλαιώδης, *EM*724.3:—also **σπηλυγγοειδής**, ές, Sch.Od.5.405.

**σπῆλυγξ**, υγγος, ἡ, = σπήλαιον, *cave*, οἰκεῖ σπήλυγγας Arist.*HA*616[b] 26, cf. Theoc.16.53, A.R.2.568; Νυμφῶν ὑπὸ σ. αὐτόστεγον Dionys. Trag.1; πόντος ἐνὶ σπήλυγξι βαθείαις *Hymn.Is*.151.

**σπίγγος**, ὁ, = σπίνος I, Hsch.; also a fish, Id. **σπιγνόν**· μικρόν, βραχύ, Id.

**σπῑδής**, ές, gen. έος, only in διὰ σπιδέος πεδίοιο Il.11.754, which is expld. by the authorities cited in Sch.A as meaning either *vast, broad*, or *rugged, difficult*: the former interpr. is confirmed by other forms, viz. **σπίδιον** μῆκος ὁδοῦ A.*Fr*.378 (which is expld. in *EM*271. 18 by μακρόν); **σπῑδόθεν**, = μακρόθεν, Antim.77; **σπιδνός**, = πυκνός, συνεχής, πεπηγώς, and **σπιδόεις**, = μέλας, πλατύς, σκοτεινός, μέγας, πυκνός, Hsch.; and **σπίζω**, = ἐκτείνω, Sch.Ar.*V*.18, Eust.996.22 sq. (Ptol. Asc. and others read δι' ἀσπιδέος π., expld. either as *round like a shield* or *covered with shields*.)

**σπίζα**, ἡ, (σπίζω (A)) *chaffinch, Fringilla caelebs*, S.*Fr*.431, Arist. *HA*592[b]17, 613[b]3; ἤϋτε γλαῦκα πέρι σπίζαι Timo 34:—Dim. **σπιζίον**, τό, Hsch.

**σπιζίας**, ου, ὁ, *sparrow-hawk, Accipiter nisus*, Arist.*HA*592[b]2, 620[a]20.

**σπιζίτης** [ῑ], ου, ὁ *great tit, ox-eye, Parus major*, Arist.*HA*592[b]18.

**σπίζω** (A), *pipe, chirp*, of the shrill note of small birds, = πιππίζω, Arat.1024, Thphr.*Sign*.39.

**σπίζω** (B), *extend*, v. σπιδής.

**σπῐθαμ-ή**, ἡ, *space one can embrace between the thumb and little finger, span* (*EM*647.34), as a fixed measure, = 3 παλαισταί (Hero *Deff*.131), first in Hdt.2.106, Hp.*Mochl*.38 (though the compd. τρισπίθαμος occurs in Hes.*Op*.426); also in Pl.*Alc*.1.126d, Arist.*HA*606[a] 14, *Pol*.1302[b]38, Chrysipp.*Stoic*.2.47, *POxy*.669.32 (iii A.D.), etc.: metaph., σ. τοῦ βίου Diogenian.8.17. **-ιαῖος**, α, ον, *a span long, broad*, etc., Hp.*Art*.72, Arist.*HA*630[a]33, *Pol*.1326[a]40, Plb.6.22.4, etc.

**σπιθίαι**· σανίδες νεώς, Hsch. **σπίκανον**· σπάνιον, Id.

**σπικᾶτα**, τά (sc. χρίσματα), embrocations *of spikenard*, Gal.6.427, 8.292, 10.574 (prob. Lat. *spīcāta*).

**σπίλα**, v. σπίλον.

**σπῑλᾰδώδης**, ες, *rocky*, Str.16.4.18.

**σπίλαξ·** μῶλος ὁ πλατανώδης, Hsch.

⊛ **σπῐλάς** (A), άδος, ἡ, *rock over which the sea dashes* (opp. ὕφαλοι πέτραι in *AP*11.390 (Lucill.)), νῆάς γε ποτὶ σπιλάδεσσιν ἔαξαν κύματα Od.3.298; δοῦπον ἄκουσε ποτὶ σπιλάδεσσι θαλάσσης 5.401 (v. πάγος); ἐφ' ὑψηλαῖς σπιλάδεσσι S.*Fr.*371 (lyr.); πλαγκταὶ σ. A.R.4.932; σ. εἰν ἁλὶ πέτρῃ Id.3.1294; ῥεῖθρον ἀπὸ σ. Theoc.*Ep.*4.6: generally, *slab*, S.*Tr.*678; ὧδ' ὑπὸ τὸ σπιλάδος μέλαθρον, i.e. under this *tombstone*, *Sammelb.*6160 (Egypt); *hollow rock, cave*, Simon.(?)179. **II.** as Adj., *stony*, or perh. *marly*, sc. γῆ, Thphr.*CP*2.4.4.

**σπῐλάς** (B), άδος, ἡ, = σπίλος (ὁ), *spot*, κατάστικτον σπιλάδεσσι πυρσῇσιν Orph.*L.*620:—in *Ep.Jud.*12, σπιλάς *spot* is prob. in view of 2*Ep.Pet.*2.13; cf. also σπιλάς (C).

**σπῐλάς** (C), άδος, ἡ, *storm, squall*, Plu.2.476a; ἐκραγείσης ὥσπερ ἐν εὐδίᾳ σπιλάδος ib.101b; ἄνδρας αἰφνιδίῳ σπιλάδι κατασεισθέντας Hld.5.31, cf. *AP*7.382.4 (Phil.): cf. κατασπιλάζω II.

**σπίλη,** ἡ, = σπίλος (B), Hsch. **σπίλον,** τό, only in pl., *strings of gut*, Id. **II.** = στέμφυλα, Id.

**σπίλος** [ῐ] (A), ἡ, = σπιλάς (A), *rock, cliff*, Ion Trag.19, Arist.*Mu.* 392$^{b}$30, Lyc.188,374, *Peripl.M.Rubr.*20, etc.: τὸν σπῖλον is f. l. for τὸν πηλόν in Plu.*Sert.*17. [ῐ in Lyc. ll. cc.]

**σπίλος** [ῑ] (B), ὁ, *spot, fleck, blemish*, Hp.*Ep.*16, Dorio ap.Ath.7. 297c; σ. αἵματος J.*AJ*13.11.3 (pl.); on the moon, Plu.2.921f; on the face or body, Dsc.1.33, Luc.*Am.*15, Artem.5.67, Lib.*Decl.*26.19, *Gp.*12.26.2: metaph., *stain* of impurity or vice, Lysis ap.Iamb.*VP* 17.76, *Ep.Eph.*5.27; of persons, D.H.4.24 (cj.), 2*Ep.Pet.*2.13. (Att. use κηλίς acc. to Phryn.21.) [σπῖλος Hdn.Gr.2.920; but ῐ in the equiv. σπιλάς (B) and in the compd. ἄσπιλος.]

**σπῐλ-όω,** *stain, soil*, D.H.9.6, *Ep.Jac.*3.6; *mark*, λευκαῖς (with leucodermia) *Cat.Cod.Astr.*8(4).174:—Pass., εἶδος σπιλωθὲν χρώμασι, of a painting, Lxx *Wi.*15.4: pf. part. ἐσπιλωμένος *soiled*, *Ep. Jud.*23, cf. Luc.*Am.*15: simply, *to be marked*, Hld.10.15. **-ώδης,** ες, (σπιλάς (A), σπίλος (A)) *rocky*, Arist.*HA*548$^{a}$2, Plb.10.10.7; cf. σπιλαδώδης. **-ωμα,** ατος, τό, *defilement, stain*, Aq.*Is.*13.12 (Auct. p.29 Field); = *refined gold* in Aq.*Is.*13.12. **II.** *mole, birthmark*, Hld.10.15. **-ωτός,** ή, όν, *stained*, *Gloss.*

**σπίνα,** ἡ, = σπίνος I, Hsch. **II.** a fish, Alex.84.

**σπίνδαλος,** ὁ, an Indian bird, akin to the ἀτταγᾶς, Ael.*NA*13.25.

**σπινδεῖρα·** ἄροτρον, Hsch.

**σπινθ-ᾰρίς,** ίδος, ἡ, = σπινθήρ, *spark*, *h.Ap.*442; **σπινθάρυξ,** ῠγος, ἡ, A.R.4.1544. **-εύω,** in form ἐσπινθέυετο, glossed by ἠξήροντο (dub. sens.), Hsch. ⊛ **-ήρ,** ῆρος, ὁ, *spark*, Ar.*Pl.*1053, Arist.*Ph.* 205$^{a}$12, *Cael.*276$^{a}$4; of a meteor, τοῦ δέ τε πολλοὶ ἀπὸ σπινθῆρες ἵενται Il.4.77: metaph., ἐμβαλὼν σ. Μεγαρικοῦ ψηφίσματος ἐξεφύσησεν πόλεμον Ar.*Pax*609; ἐκ τούτου τοῦ σ. ἐξεκαύθη πόλεμος Plb.18.39.2; ὀφθαλμοὺς σπινθῆρας ἔχεις *AP*12.196 (Strat.), cf. Lxx *Wi.*11.18. ⊛ **-ηρίζω,** *emit sparks*, Thphr.*HP*3.8.7. **II.** *cause the emission of sparks*, Id.*Sign.*19, Plu.2.893d.

**σπινθηρο-βολέω,** *scintillate*, of the planet Venus, *PMag.Par.*1. 2941. **-ειδής,** ές, *like a spark*, Alex.Aphr.*Pr.*1.72.

**σπινθίον,** τό, = σπίνος I, Hsch.

**σπίνθραξ,** ακος, ὁ, = σπινθήρ, Sext.*Ca.*8.6.

**σπῑνίδιον** [ῐδ], τό, Dim. of σπίνος I, Ar.*Fr.*387.7; also **σπῑνίον,** τό, Eub.123.

**σπίνος** [ῑ], ὁ, = σπίζα, Ar.*Av.*1079, *Pax* 1149, Eub.150.5, Thphr. *Sign.*39; σ. ἠῷα σπίζων Arat.1024; also **σπίννος,** *Gloss.*; cf. σπίγγος, σπίνα, σπινθίον. **II.** a kind of *stone*, which blazes when water touches it, Arist.*Mir.*832$^{b}$29, Thphr.*Lap.*13.

⊛ **σπῑνός,** ή, όν, = ἰσχνός, Procl.*Par.Ptol.*202; also **σπῑνώδης,** ες, Ptol.*Tetr.*143.

**σπιοέλης,** = *babylonicum*, *Gloss.* (prob. f.l. for ψιλή, name of a garment).

**σπῖρα,** v. σπεῖρα.

**σπλαγχν-εύω,** *eat the inwards* (σπλάγχνα) *of a victim* after a sacrifice, Ar.*Av.*984, cf. D.C.37.30, Doroth.ap.Ath.9.410b; dub. sens. and constr. in *IG*4.4.6 (i A.D.):—Pass., ἐσπλαγχνευμένων τῶν ἱερῶν D.H.1.40. **II.** *prophesy from the inwards* (cf. σπλαγχνοσκοπία), Str.7.2.3:—Med., Id.3.3.6, Poll.1.27. **-ίδιον,** τό, Dim. of σπλάγχνον, in pl., Diph.14. **-ίζω,** = σπλαγχνεύω, Lxx 2*Ma.*6.8:—Pass., *Abh.Berl.Akad.*1928(6).12 (Cos, iv B.C.). **II.** Med. (with aor. Pass. -ίσθην), *feel pity, compassion*, or *mercy*, Lxx *Pr.*17.5; ἐπί τινα *Ev.Marc.*6.34, 8.2, etc.; περί τινων *Ev.Matt.*9.36; οὐκ ἐσπλαγχνίσθη *had* no *mercy*, *PFlor.*296.23 (vi A.D.). **-ικός,** ή, όν, *of* or *for the bowels*, φάρμακα Dsc.1.68.3. **II.** metaph., *tender*, ἔρως *PMag.Osl.* 1.149. **-ίς,** ίδος, ἡ, acc. pl. σφλανγνίδης (sic), *inwards*, *UPZ*89.3 (ii B.C.). **-ισμός,** ὁ, *a feeding on the inwards of a sacrifice*, Lxx 2*Ma.* 6.7, al.

⊛ **σπλάγχνον,** τό, mostly in pl. σπλάγχνα (σπλάγχανα *SIG*1002), *inward parts*, esp. the heart, lungs, liver, kidneys, which in sacrifices were reserved to be eaten by the sacrificers at the beginning of their feast (distd. from ἔντερα, κοιλίη, A.*Ag.*1221, Hdt.2.40, cf. Arist. *PA*667$^{b}$3); σπλάγχνα πάσαντο Il.1.464, Od.3.9; δῶκε δ' ἄρα σπλάγχνων μοίρας ib.40; σπλάγχνα δ' ἄρ' ὀπτήσαντες ἐνώμων 20.252, cf. Ar. *Pax*1105 (hex.): hence, *sacrificial feast*, Id.*Eq.*410, *V.*654, *SIG*1002.4 (Milet., v/iv B.C.), 1044.39 (Halic., iv/iii B.C.), *Test.Epict.*6.17, etc.; also as used in divination, σπλάγχνων τε λειότητα A.*Pr.*493, cf. E. *Supp.*212, *El.*828,838, Aeschin.3.160. **2.** *any part of the inwards*, ὑπὸ σπλάγχνων ἐλθεῖν to come from the *womb*, of a babe, Pi.*O.*6.43, cf. *N.* 1.35; τῶν σῶν..ἐκ σπλάγχνων ἕνα S.*Ant.*1066; μητρὸς ἐν σπλάγχνοις *IG*14.1977: so in sg., τὸ κοινὸν σ. οὗ πεφύκαμεν A.*Th.*1036; of the lungs, μόχθοις ἀνδροκμῆσι φυσιᾷ σ. Id.*Eu.*249; τοῦ γείτονος αὐτῷ (sc. τῷ ἥπατι) σπλάγχνου, of the spleen, Pl.*Ti.*72c. **3.** οἱ παῖδες (*children*) σπλάγχνα λέγονται Artem.1.44, cf.5.57. **II.** metaph. (like *heart*), *the seat of the feelings, affections*, esp. of anger, σ. θερμῆναι κότῳ Ar.*Ra.*844; τὰ σ. ἀγανακτεῖ ib.1006; μομφὰς ὑπὸ σπλάγχνοις ἔχειν E. *Alc.*1009: generally, of anxiety, A.*Ag.*995 (lyr.); σπλάγχνα δέ μου κελαινοῦται Id.*Ch.*413 (lyr.); of love, ἐκύμηνε τὰ σ. ἔρωτι καρδίην ἀνοιστρηθείς Herod.1.56; παιδὸς ὑπὸ σπλάγχνοισιν ἔχει πόθον Theoc. 7.99, cf. D.H.11.35, *AP*5.55 (Diosc.), etc.; of pity, Lxx *Pr.*12.10, *Ep.Phil.*1.8, 2.1, etc.; ὑπὲρ σπλάχνου 'for *pity's* sake', *BGU*1139.17 (i B.C.); so S.*Aj.*995, E.*Or.*1201, *Hipp.*118; ἀνδρὸς σ. ἐκμαθεῖν to learn a man's '*heart*', Id.*Med.*220; ἀνδρὸς πονηροῦ σ. οὐ μαλάσσεται Men.*Mon.*31; σ. σιδηροῦν, of Epaminondas, Epicur.*Fr.*560. **III.** = βρύον, Dsc.1.21.

**σπλαγχνόπτης,** ου, ὁ, *one who roasts* σπλάγχνα, only as pr. n. of a slave of Pericles, Plin.*HN*22.44, 34.81.

**σπλαγχνο-σκοπία,** ἡ, *examination of the entrails of a victim*, for purpose of prophecy, Herm. *in Phdr.*p.109A. **-τόμος,** ον, *cutting up the* σπλάγχνα, epith. of Zeus in Cyprus, Hegesand.30. **-φάγος** [ᾰ], ον, *eating the* σπλάγχνα, ἀετός Ps.-Plu.*Fluv.*5.3, cf. Lxx *Wi.*12.5.

**σπλαχρός·** μεμιασμένος, Hsch.

**σπλεκόω,** *have sexual intercourse* (whence διασπλ-), also written πλεκόω, σπεκλόω, Ar.*Lys.*152, cf. Poll.5.93.

**σπλέκωμα,** ατος, τό, *sexual intercourse*, Sch.Ar.*Pl.*1082.

**σπληδός,** ἡ (?), = σποδός, Lyc.483, Nic.*Th.*763:—**σπληδώ,** ἡ, Hsch.

**σπλήν,** ὁ, gen. σπληνός:—*milt, spleen*, Hdt.2.47, Hp.*VM*22, Ar. *Fr.*506.4, Antiph.222.8; τὸν σ. ἐκβαλεῖν, of one dying with anxiety, Ar.*Th.*3. **2.** pl. σπλῆνες, *affections of the spleen*, Hp.*Aph.*3. 22. **3.** αἰγὸς σ., = μολόχη, *mallow*, Ps.-Dsc.2.118. **II.** = σπληνίον I, Hp.*Off.*12. (Prob. cogn. with σπλάγχνον and with Skt. *plīhán-*, Lat. *lien*, Slav. *slězena*, Lith. *blužnìs*.)

**σπλην-άριον,** τό, = σπληνίον I, Dsc.2.63, *Eup.*1.51. **-ιάω,** *to be splenetic, have enlarged spleen*, Arist.*PA*670$^{b}$9, *Pr.*890$^{a}$10, Plu.*Pyrrh.* 3, *Hippiatr.*40. **-ικός,** ή, όν, *of the spleen*, τρόπος Hp.*Epid.*2. 2.23; ἀρτηρία *An.Ox.*3.120, cf. Ptol.*Tetr.*198: τὰ -κά *affections of the spleen*, Dsc.1.87. **II.** of persons, *diseased in the spleen, splenetic*, Macho ap.Ath.8.348e, Aristo *Stoic.*1.88, Apollon.*Mir.*42, Vett.Val. 127.27, *Gp.*11.30.4. **-ίον,** τό, *pad* or *compress of linen* laid on a wound, Hp.*Fract.*27, Philem.113. **II.** = ἄσπληνος (v. ἄσπληνον I), Dsc.3.134; = ἡμιονῖτις, ib.135; = περικλύμενον, Id.4.14; = κυνόγλωσσον, Ps.-Dsc.4.127.—On the accent, v. Hdn.Gr.1.360. **-ίσκος,** ὁ, Dim. of σπληνίον I, Hp.*Morb.*2.18:—also **σπληνίσκον,** τό, *Michel* 832.24, al. (Samos, iv B.C.). **-ίτης** [ῑ], ου, ὁ, *of* or *due to the spleen*, ὑδρωπισμός Diocl.*Fr.*47: fem. **-ῖτις,** ιδος, ἡ, φλέψ a blood-vessel *of the spleen*, Diog.Apoll.6, Hp.*Morb.*1.26, Ruf.*Onom.* 200. **II.** *disease of the spleen*, οἱ παλαιοί ap.Gal.18(1).145. **-όομαι,** (σπληνίον I) Pass., *have a compress applied*, Heliod.ap.Orib.46.9. 3. **II.** *to be distended*, [τὸ αἷμα] ὑφ' οὗ σπληνοῦται τὸ ἧπαρ Philostr. *VA*8.7. **-όπεδον,** prob. f.l. for σφην-, Hermipp.70. **-ώδης,** ες, = σπληνικός, Hp.*Aph.*6.43, Herod.Med.ap.Orib.10.8.9.

**σπογγ-άριον** [ᾰ], τό, Dim. of σπόγγος, M.Ant.5.9, Sor.2.41. **II.** *a kind of eye-salve*, Alex.Trall.2. **-εῖον,** τό, *penicillum*, *Gloss.* **-εύς,** έως, ὁ, = σπογγοθήρας, Arist.*HA*620$^{b}$34, *Pr.*960$^{b}$21. **-ιά** (also **σφογγιά,** Ar.*Ra.*482,487), Ion. **σπογγιή,** ἡ, = σπόγγος, *sponge*, Ar. ll. cc., Arist.*HA*616$^{a}$24, Aret.*SD*1.10; σπογγιᾶς μαλακώτερον τὸ πρόσωπον *Com.Adesp.*125; σπογγιᾶς ἔπαινος, said of a toper, Aeschin.2. 112. (οἱ Ἀττικοὶ τὴν σπογγίαν σπογγιάν (καλοῦσι) Greg.Cor.p.148 S., cf. Suid.) **-ίας,** ου, ὁ, = foreg., Ar.*Fr.*856. **-ιεύς,** έως, ὁ, dub. form for σπογγεύς in Thphr.*HP*4.6.4. **-ίζω** or **σφ-,** *wipe with a sponge*, Ar.*Th.*247; τὰ βάθρα D.18.258; τὰ ὑποδήματα Arr.*Epict.*2.22.31, Ath.8.351a (Pass.). **II.** *wipe away*, τὸν ἱδρῶτα..ἀπ' ἐμοῦ σπόγγισον Pherecr.53. **-ίον,** τό, Dim. of σπόγγος, Ar.*Ach.*463 (σφογγίον), Dsc.*Eup.*1.197. **II.** an ἐπίθεμα of this name, Paul.Aeg.3. 48. **-ιστικός,** ή, όν, *of* or *for sponging*: ἡ -κή (sc. τέχνη) Pl.*Sph.* 227a. ⊛ **-ίτης** [ῑ], ου, ὁ, *of, in*, or *like a sponge*: only fem. **-ῖτις,** ιδος, ἡ, of a stone, Plin.*HN*37.182; βοτάνη Aët.4.25, prob. in 6.80, 9.41.

**σπογγο-δετέω,** *fasten a sponge over* the eye, Paul.Aeg.3.22. 22. **-ειδής,** ές, *sponge-like, spongy*, Hp.*VM*22, *Oss.*4, Gal.*UP*7.8, al.; cf. σπογγώδης. Adv. -δῶς Epicur.ap.*Placit.*2.20.14. **-θήρας,** ου, ὁ, *diver for sponges*, Plu.2.950b, 981e:—hence ἡ -**θηρική** (sc. τέχνη) Poll.7.139. **-κολυμβητής,** οῦ, ὁ, = foreg., Lycurg.*Fr.*85.

**σπόγγος,** ὁ, *sponge*, σ. πολυτρήτοισι τραπέζας νίζον Od.1.111, cf. 22. 439; σπόγγῳ ἀμφὶ πρόσωπα καὶ ἄμφω χεῖρ' ἀπομόργνυ Il.18.414; ὑγρώσσων σ. ὤλεσεν γραφήν A.*Ag.*1329; used at the bath, Ar.*Fr.*55, Crates Com.15.7; for cleaning shoes, Ar.*V.*600 (cf. σπογγίζω); cf. Arist.*HA*487$^{b}$9, 588$^{b}$20, *Ev.Matt.*27.48, etc. **II.** *any spongy substance*, σικυώνης σ. Hp.*Steril.*221; οἱ σ. the *glands* in the throat, *tonsils*, from their *spongy* nature and liability to swell, Id.*Epid.*4.7, Gal.19. 140. **III.** = νήριον, Ps.-Dsc.4.81. (**σφόγγος** is found in *IG*11(2). 144*A*37 (Delos, iv B.C.), *PSI*6.558.7 (iii B.C.), *POxy.*1384.25 (v A.D.); cf. σπογγιά, σπογγίον.)

**σπογγο-τήρας,** ου, ὁ, *sponge-watcher, a small creature like a spider which inhabits sponges*, Plu.2.980b; cf. πινοτήρης. **-τόμος,** ὁ, *one that cuts sponges from the rocks*, Opp.*H.*2.436, 5.612, Sch.A.*Supp.* 408.

**σπογγώδης,** ες, = σπογγοειδής, Hp.*Gland.*1, Arist.*Pr.*875$^{b}$22, Dsc. 5.118.

**σπόδειος,** v. σπόδιος.

**σποδεύνης,** ου, Dor. **-νας,** ὁ, *lying on ashes*, Dosiad.*Ara* 3.

**σποδέω**, *pound, smite, crush*, τοὺς καδίσκους συγκεραυνώσω σποδῶν Cratin.187, cf. Ar.*Nu.*1376, *Ra.*662, *Av.*1016; σ. τοῖς κονδύλοις Id. *Lys.*366, cf. ἀπο-, κατα-σποδέω:—Pass., νιφάδι.. σποδούμενος *pelted* by the storm, E.*Andr.*1129; σ. πρὸς πέτρας *dashed* against the rocks, Id.*Hipp.*1238: abs., στρατὸς κακῶς σ. *handled roughly, in sorry plight*, A.*Ag.*670. II. = βινέω, Ar.*Ec.*942, 1016:—Pass., of the woman, ib. 908, *Th.*492; of boys, Id.*Ec.*113. III. *eat greedily, devour*, Id.*Pax* 1306; ὀβελίαν Pherecr.55; cf. παίω III. (There is no indication of any connexion of this Verb with σποδός, except perh. in Cratin. l.c.)

* **σποδησίλαυρα**, ἡ, *street-walker*, Com.*Adesp.*1352.

**σποδ-ιά**, Ion. -ιή, ἡ, *heap of ashes, ashes*, Od.5.488, E.*Cyc.*615 (lyr.), Pl.Com.173.9, Lxx *Le.*4.12; σ. οἰναρέη *ashes* of vine-twigs, Hp.*Mul.* 2.195; σποδιῇ κεχριμένος prob. in Call.*Dian.*69; freq. in Epitaphs, *AP*7.279, 435 (Nicand.); διψὰς σ. ib.9.549 (Antiphil.); *scoria, dross* of metals, Dsc.5.126. **-ιαῖος**, α, ον, = *gilvus*, Gloss. **-ιακός**, ή, όν, *made from* σπόδιον, Orib.*Syn.*3.129, Aët.7.23, Paul.Aeg.3.22.6, 7.16.17. **-ιάς**, άδος, ἡ, *bullace, Prunus insititia*, Thphr.*HP*3.6.4; quoted in form **σπονδίας** by Ath.2.50b (codd. epit.). **-ίζω**, *roast* or *bake in ashes*, μύρτα καὶ φηγοὺς πρὸς τὸ πῦρ σ. Pl.*R.*372c; ἥ με κεραυνῷ.. σπόδισον *burn* me *to ashes*, Ar.*V.*329; σ. τὰς τρίχας *singe*, D.S.3.25. II. intr., *to be ash-coloured*, Dsc.5.152. III. dub. l. in Cratin.219 (σπύρθιζε cj. Kock). **-ιον**, τό, = σποδός III, Posidon. 52 J., Dsc.1.105, 5.75. **-ιος**, α, ον, *ash-coloured, grey*, ὄνος Semon. 7.43 (sed leg. σποδεῖης); αἶγες *PHib.*1.120.9 (iii B.C.); χρῶμα, of a dove, Arist.*Fr.*347. 2. *of the ashes*, epith. of Apollo, Paus.9.11.7, 9.12.1 (vulg. Σπόνδιος). **-ίτης** [ῑ] ἄρτος, ὁ, bread *baked in hot ashes*, Hp.*Mul.*2.118, Diph.26: **σποντίτης** (sic), = *libum*, Gloss. **-ιώδης**, ες, = sq., Erot. s. v. τροφιωδέων.

**σποδο-ειδής**, ές, *ashy, ash-coloured*, Hp.*Epid.*7.92, Arist.*HA*592b 6, 617b4, Lxx *Ge.*30.39, al. **-κράμβη**, ἡ, *cabbage-ash*, -ης ὕδωρ *crude potash* water, Zos.Alch. p.226 B. **-νιτροποιός**, ὁ, *maker of soap from potash*, dub. in *MAMA* 3.546 (Corycus, σπονδῶν lapis).

**σποδόομαι**, Pass., *to be burnt to ashes*, Hp.*Mul.*2.191, Lyc.178, *AP*10.90 (Pall.). II. Med., ἐσποδώσαντο τὰς κεφαλάς *strewed their* heads *with ashes*, Lxx *Ju.*4.11.

**σποδόρχης**, ου, ὁ, (σποδέω I) *eunuch*, Eust.1431.47.

**σποδός**, ἡ, *wood-ashes, embers*, Od.9.375, *h.Merc.*238: generally, *ashes*, Hdt.2.140; ἐπ' Ἰσμηνοῦ τε μαντείᾳ σ., *of the ashes* of an altar, S.*OT*21, cf. *Ant.*1007, Hdt.4.35; σ. ἱερὰ ἡ ἐκ τοῦ βωμοῦ *SIG*1171.18 (Lebena); of the dead, A.*Ag.*435, 443 (both lyr.), *Ch.*687, S.*El.*758, etc.; ἀμφὶ σποδὸν κάρα κεχύμεθα, in sign of mourning, E.*Supp.*827 (lyr.), cf. 1160; σποδὸς δὲ τἆλλα, Περικλέης, Κόδρος, Κίμων Alex.25. 12:—death by plunging into a room filled with ashes, αὐτήν μιν ῥῖψαι ἐς οἴκημα σποδοῦ πλέον Hdt.2.100; as a Persian punishment (cf. Val. Max.9.2.6), εἰς τὴν σποδὸν ἐμβάλλεται Ctes.*Fr.*29.48, cf. 51, al., Lxx 2*Ma.*13.5 sq.—There seems to be no difference in sense between σποδός and τέφρα: both occur in Trag., the latter alone in Att. Prose. II. *dust*, τῆς χαμᾶθεν σποδοῦ Hdt.4.172; μετρεῖν τὴν σ., of labour in vain, Arr.*Epict.*3.26.17. III. *oxide* of certain metals, σ. Κυπρίη copper *oxide*, Hp.*Mul.*1.104; σ. Ἰλλυριῶτις Id. *Ulc.*13; σ. χρυσῖτις Id.*Mul.*1.103, cf. Dsc.5.75. IV. metaph., κυλίκων, πίθων σ., of a bibulous old woman, 'soaker', 'sponge', *AP* 6.291, 7.455 (Leon.). V. *lava*, Str.6.2.3.

**σποδώδης**, ες, = σποδοειδής, App.*BC*5.114; of taste, τὸ σ. Gal.14.293.

**σπολά**, ἡ, Aeol. for στολή, Sapph.55 (dub.).

**σπολάς**, άδος, ἡ, *leathern garment, jerkin*, S.*Fr.*11, Ar.*Av.*933, 935, 944, X.*An.*3.3.20, 4.1.18 (with v.l. στολάς).

**σπολεῖσα**· σταλεῖσα, Hsch. (Aeol.).

**σπολεύς**, έως, ὁ, a kind of *loaf*, Philet.ap.Ath.3.114e (σποδέα cj. Schw.).

**σπόλια**· τὰ παρατιλλόμενα ἐρίδια ἀπὸ τῶν σκελῶν τῶν προβάτων, Hsch.

**σπόλος**, ὁ (Aeol. for στόλος), *stake* used in palisading, *IG*9(2) p.xi (Achaea Phthiotis, ii B.C.).

**σπόμενος**, v. *ἕπω (B).

**σπονδ-ἄγωγός**, όν, *offering a truce*, Phryn.*PS* p.108 B. **-άριον**, τό, Dim. of σπονδή III, *POxy.*525.7 (ii A.D.). **-αρχέω**, *begin the drink-offering*, *SIG*1003.17 (Priene, ii B.C.), Poll.6.30. **-αρχία**, ἡ, *right of beginning the drink-offering*, Hdt.6.57. **-αρχος**, ον, *beginning the drink-offering*, Phryn.*PS* p.107 B. * **-αυλέω**, *play the flute at a* σπονδή, Artem.1.56. **-αύλης**, ου, ὁ, *playing the flute at a* σπονδή, *CIG*2915 (Magn.Mae.), 2983 (Ephesus), *IG*14.617 (Rhegium).

**σπονδει-άζω**, *employ* σπονδειασμός, ὁ σπονδειάζων τρόπος Plu.2.1137b. 2. σπονδειάζων (sc. στίχος) *hexameter with a spondee in the fifth foot*, Cic.*Att.*7.2.1. **-ακός**, ή, όν, *of the kind used at libations*, τρόπος (in Music) Plu.2.1137b; αὐλοί Poll.4.81; μέλος Iamb.*VP*25.112; ῥυθμοί, i.e. *spondaic*, Hermog.*Id.*2.12; συνθῆκαι ib.1.6. Adv. -κῶς Eust.546.16. II. σπονδειακός (sc. πούς), ὁ, *antispastic*, Sch. Heph. p.303 C. **-ασμός**, ὁ, in Music, *rise of pitch by an interval of three quarter-tones* (διέσεις), Aristid.Quint.1.11, cf. Plu.2.1135a,b.

**σπονδειοκατάληκτος**, ον, *ending with a spondee*, Sch.Ar.*Ra.*243.

* **σπονδεῖον** (sc. σκύφος), τό, *cup from which the* σπονδή *was poured*, Clitarch.ap.Ath.11.486a, Lxx *Nu.*4.7, al., *PCornell* 33.9 (iii B.C.), Ph.2.157; Ion. **σπονδήϊον** *IG*12(5).123b (Paros). 2. *bowl* for offerings, *Sammelb.*5252.20 (i A.D.), *BGU*590.9 (ii A.D.). 3. a *pouring-cup* used by doctors, Plu.2.377e. II. part of the νόμος Πυθικός, Demetr.Lac.*Herc.*1014.53 (written σπονδήον).

**σπονδειο-παράληκτος**, ον, of a verse *with a spondee before the last syllable*, Tz. in *An.Ox.*3.311. **-πύρρῖχος**, ὁ, *a foot consisting of spondee and pyrrhic*, i.e. *Ionicus a majore*, Id.ib.305.

**σπονδεῖος**, α, ον, *used at a libation*, αὔλημα, μέλος, D.H.*Dem.*22, Poll.4.79, etc.; ὁ σ. (sc. νόμος) a piece of music used at libations, Plu.2.1135a. II. σπονδεῖος (sc. πούς), ὁ, in metre, *spondee*, foot consisting of two long syllables used in melodies accompanying σπονδαί, D.H.*Comp.*17, Heph.3.1, etc. 2. metaph. of the pulse διὰ ἴσου, Ruf.*Syn.Puls.*4.

**σπονδειοτρόχαιος**, ὁ, *a foot consisting of spondee and trochee*, Tz. in *An.Ox.*3.315.

* **σπονδ-ή**, ἡ, (σπένδω) *drink-offering*, of wine poured out to the gods before drinking, σπονδῇσι θύεσσί τε ἱλάσκεσθαι Hes.*Op.*338; οὐ σπονδῇ χρέωνται [οἱ Πέρσαι] Hdt.1.132; ἣν δὲ κἀμπέλου σπονδή S.*Fr.*398; σπονδὴ θεοῦ a *drink-offering* to a god, E.*Cyc.*469; ἔγχει δὴ σπονδήν Ar. *Pax*1102, cf. Antipho 1.19, *Berl.Sitzb.*1927.169 (Cyrene); σ. ἐγκανάξαι Ar.*Eq.*106; σπονδὰς θεοῖς λείβειν, σπεῖσαι, A.*Supp.*982, E.*El.*511; Διοσκόρων μέτα σπονδῶν μεθέξεις Id.*Hel.*1668, cf. *Ba.*45; σπονδὰς ποιεῖσθαι, ποιεῖν, Antipho 1.18, Men.273, etc.; τρίτας σπονδὰς ποιήσαντες (where pl. is used of a single libation) X.*Cyr.*2.3.1, cf. τριτόσπονδος; σπονδὴ σπονδή· εὐφημεῖτε εὐφημεῖτε Ar.*Pax* 433; σπονδῶν μετεῖχε καὶ εὐχῶν D.19.128; περὶ σπονδὰς καὶ κύλικας εἶχον were engaged in feasting, Hdn.4.11.4; of the rites of hospitality, D.19.189. II. pl., σπονδαί *a solemn treaty* or *truce* (because *solemn drink-offerings* were made on concluding them, D.S.3.71 [here in sg.]; σπονδαὶ τ' ἄκρητοι καὶ δεξιαὶ ᾗς ἐπέπιθμεν Il.2.341; distd. fr. εἰρήνη, And.3.11); σ. τοῦ πολέμου Aeschin.2.172; αἱ Λακεδαιμονίων σ. the *truce with* them, Th.1.35; αἱ πρός τινα σ. ib.44, etc.; σπονδὰς φέρειν to offer *a truce*, E.*Ph.*97; παραδιδόναι Ar.*Eq.*1389; προκαλεῖσθαι ib.796; δέχεσθαι Th.5.21, 30; ἄγειν πρός τινας δεχημένους σπονδάς Id.6.7; σ. εἵλετο X.*HG*3.2.1; σπονδῶν τυχεῖν Id.*An.*3.1.28; σ. ποιήσασθαί τινι make *a truce* with any one, Hdt.1.21; πρός τινας Ar.*Ach.*52, 131; less freq., σ. ποιεῖν Th.5.76; σ. σπένδεσθαι (v. σπένδω); ὀμνύειν Foed.ib.5.23; σ. γενέσθαι Hdt.7.149; ἐπὶ τούτοις on these conditions, Th.4.16; σπονδέων ἐουσέων Hdt.7.149; τῶν σ. προκεχωρηκυιῶν Th.1.87; αἱ σ. μενόντων X.*An.*2.3.24; σπονδὰς τέμωμεν (on the false analogy of ὅρκια τ.) E.*Hel.*1235; τὰς σ. μέλλειν ἀπορρηθήσεσθαι Lys.22.14; ξυγχέαι Th.5.39, cf. 1.146; λύειν ib.78, etc.; παραβῆναι Ar.*Av.*461, cf. X.*An.*4.1.1, D.19.191; σπονδῶν σύγχυσις Pl.*R.*379e; ἐμμενῶ ταῖς σπονδαῖς Foed.ap.Th.5.18; σπονδὰς ποιησαμένους τὰ περὶ Πύλον, = σπεισαμένους τὰ π. Π., having made *a truce* as regards.., Id.4.15; σ. τοῖς σώμασιν, ὥστε ἀπελθεῖν a *safe-conduct*, Aeschin.2.141. 2. esp. *the Truce of God* during the Olympic games, etc., αἱ Ὀλυμπιακαὶ σ. Th.5.49; λέγοντες μὴ ἐπηγγέλθαι πω ἐς Λακεδαίμονα τὰς σ. ibid.; during the Eleusinian mysteries, Aeschin.2.133, *IG*1².6.48, 68, al. 3. *document embodying a treaty*, εἴρηται ἐν [ταῖς σ.] Th.1.35, cf. X.*HG*2.4.36. III. *money payment* in addition to rent in kind, *POxy.*101.19 (ii A.D.), etc. 2. *douceur, gratuity*, σ. παιδαρίοις ib.1207.10 (ii A.D.), etc. 3. *fee* paid to officials, ib.1284.16 (iii A.D.), etc. **-ήσιμος**, η, ον, *of* or *for a drink-offering*, σοὶ φέρω σπονδήσιμα Philem.67 (σπονδὴν ἅμα cj. Mein.). **-ηφορέω**, = σπονδοφορέω, Luc. *Syr.D.*42 (v.l. σπονδὴν φορ-). **-ιάς**, άδος, ἡ, f.l. for σποδιάς (q.v.). **-ικός**, ή, όν, *for libations*, of wine, *PSI*8.948.9, al. (iv A.D.). **-ιξ**, ικος, ὁ, *one who offers a* σπονδή, Hsch. (pl.). **-ιοφόροι**, *fetiales*, Gloss. **-ῖτις**, ιδος, ἡ, *making a* σπονδή, *AP*6.190 (Gaet.).

**σπονδο-ποιέομαι**, *pour a libation*, *IG*7.303.10 (Oropus), Chares *Fr.*4 J., Nic.*Fr.*1. II. *represent as making libations*, τινας Ath.5.179c. **ποιία**, ἡ, in pl., *offering of libations*, *IGRom.*4.293a ii 25 (ii B.C.). * **-ποιός**, ὁ, *offerer of libations*, *IG*5(1).112.12 (Sparta, ii A.D.). **-φορέω**, *offer a* σπονδή, Poll.8.139. **-φορία**, ἡ, = ἐπαγγελία σπονδῶν, *SIG*1019.6 (Eleusis, iii B.C., pl.). **-φόρος**, ὁ, *one who offers libations*, Ph.1.683:—hence, *one who brings proposals for a truce* or *treaty of peace*, Ar.*Ach.*216. II. *herald* or *officer who published the* σπονδαί of the Olympic and other games, σπονδοφόροι Ζηνὸς Ἀλείοι Pi.*I.*2.23; οἱ σ. οἱ τὰς μυστηριώτιδας σπονδὰς ἐπαγγέλλοντες Aeschin.2.133, cf. *SIG*1021.7 (Olympia, i B.C.), al. 2. = Lat. *fetialis*, D.H.1.21, Plu.2.279b. **-χόη**, ἡ, *vessel for offering libations*, *IG*11(2).110 (Delos, iii B.C.), al. **-χοΐδιον**, τό, Dim. of foreg., ib.122.59, 124.62 (Delos, iii B.C.). **-χους**, ὁ, = σπονδοχόη, ib.11(4).1307.16 (Delos, ii B.C.).

**σπονδύλη, -ύλιον, -ύλιος, -υλώδης, -υλος**, v. σφονδ-.

**σποντίτης**, v. σποδίτης.

**σπόπια**· πέμμα, ὅ τινες σταιτίας, Hsch.

* **σπορ-ά**, ἡ, (σπείρω) *sowing* of seed, σπερμάτων Pl.*Amat.*134e: hence metaph., μαθημάτων εἰς ψυχήν ibid. b. of children, σπορᾶς γε μὴν ἐκ τῆσδε from this *origin*, A.*Pr.*871; τοιοῦτος ὢν τοιῷδ' ὀνειδίζεις σποράν; his *origin, birth*..? S.*Aj.*1298; *procreation*, παίδων, γένους, Pl.*Lg.*729c, 783a; τὴν Ῥωμύλου σ. *begetting*, Plu.2.320b, cf. Ptol.*Tetr.*103, 105. 2. *seed-time, sowing-time*, ἀπὸ τῆς σ. Thphr.*HP* 8.2.6; δεκέτεσιν σποραῖσιν in the tenth *seed-time*, i.e. *year*, E.*El.*1152 (lyr.). II. *seed*, 1*Ep.Pet.*1.23, *PLeid.W.*11.50; *field sown*, ξηρὰ σ. dry land, dub. l. in E.*Andr.*637; σ. δράκοντος *ground sown* with the dragon's teeth, S.*Ant.*1125 (lyr.). b. of persons, *seed, offspring*, Id.*Tr.*316, 420; γυναῖκα καὶ τέκνων.. σποράν Men.598: pl., *young ones*, dub. in E.*Cyc.*56: generally, θῆλυς σ. the female *race*, Id.*Hec.* 659; θήλεια σ. Id.*Tr.*503. **-άδην** [ᾰ], Adv. *scatteredly, here and there*, σ. ἀπώλλυντο Th.2.4 (v.l. for σποράδες); οἰκεῖν, i.e. not in communities, Pl.*Prt.*322b, Isoc.4.39; τὰ λεγόμενα σ. Arist.*Pol.*1259a 4; σ. τὸ πρὶν ἀειδόμενος, of Homer before Peisistratus, *AP*11.442; σ. ἀναγέγραπται Plu.2.629e; οἱ σ., opp. οἱ ἐλλόγιμοι Πυθαγορικοί, D.L. 8.91. **-ἄδικός**, ή, όν, *scattered*, i.e. not living in communities, θηρία, ζῷα, Arist.*Pol.*1256a23, *HA*488a3; σποραδικοὶ ἀπολώλασι Th.

2.4 as loosely cited by Gal.17(1).2. **-άζω**, *scatter, tear asunder*, τἀμὰ θέλων σποράσαι (sc. μέλη), of a lion, *IG*2.2836. ⊛ **-αῖος**, α, ον, = σπόριμος :—σποραῖα, τά, *seeds*, Babr.13.2. **-άς**, άδος, ὁ, ἡ, mostly pl., *scattered*, Hdt.4.113 ; of ships *scattered* by a storm or a defeat, Th.1.49, 3.69,77 ; βουκολικαὶ Μοῖσαι σ. ποκά, i.e. *not collected* into a volume, *AP*9.205 (Artemid.) ; νησιώτης σ. βίος a *vagrant* life, E.*Rh.* 701 (lyr.) ; so of men, σποράδες.. τὸ ἀρχαῖον ᾤκουν, i.e. not in communities, Arist.*Pol.*1252b23 ; of birds, opp. ἀγελαῖος (cf. σποραδικός), Id.*HA*617b21 ; σ. ἀστέρες Id.*Mete.*344a15, cf. 346a20 ; λόγοι σ. *unconnected*, Plu.2.431d ; σ. νᾶσοι *scattered, not in a group*, Pi.*Pae.*5.38, cf. D.S.3.44 ; hence αἱ Σποράδες the islands off the west coast of Asia Minor, opp. αἱ Κυκλάδες, A.R.4.1711, Str.2.5.21 ; of diseases, *sporadic*, opp. endemic, Hp.*Acut.*5 (Littré σποράδεες, with cod. M).

**σποργαί**· ἐρεθισμοὶ εἰς τὸ τεκεῖν, Hsch.

**σπορ-εύς**, έως, ὁ, *sower*, X.*Oec.*20.3, *PFlor.*20.22 (ii A.D.). II. *father, begetter*, Them.*Or.*6.77b. **-ευτής**, οῦ, ὁ, = foreg., Hsch. **-ευτός**, ή, όν, *sown*, χώρα *seed*-land, Thphr.*CP*3.20.6. ⊛ **-ητός**, ὁ, *sown corn, growing corn*, A.*Ag.*1392. 2. *sowing of corn*, τὸν σ. διακωλύειν X.*HG*4.6.13 ; also σ. ὀσπρίων Thphr.*HP*8.2.8. 3. *seed-time*, Hp.*Hebd.*4 (σποράτος cod.).

**σπόρθυγγες**· αἱ συνεστραμμέναι μετὰ ῥύπου τρίχες, Hsch. **σπορθύγγια**· τρίβολα, τὰ διαχωρήματα τῶν αἰγῶν, ἅ τινες σπυράδας καλοῦσιν, Id.

⊛ **σπόρῐμος**, ον (ᾱ, ον *Hymn.Is.*162 ; η, ον, v. infr. I. 3), (σπείρω) *sown, to be sown, fit for sowing*, αὖλαξ Theoc.25.219 ; γῆ σ. *seed*-land, X.*HG*3.2.10, etc. ; so ἡ σ. (sc. γῆ) Thphr.*HP*6.5.4 ; σ. ἄρουραι *PGiss.*28.4 (ii A.D.), etc. ; τὰ σ. the *corn-fields*, *Ev.Matt.*12.1, *Gp.*1.12.37 ; γένοιτο αὐτῷ τὰ σ. ἄσπορα Tab.Defix. in *BCH*51.149 (Salamis Cypr.) ; πεδίων σποριμᾶν βάσιν, i.e. solid corn-fields, *Hymn.Is.* l.c. 2. σ. σπέρμα *fit for sowing* or *bearing seed*, Lxx *Ge.*1.29. 3. μὴν σ. a month *for sowing*, Plu.2.378e : metaph., σπορίμη ἡμέρα day *of conception*, Vett.Val.50.31, Paul.Al.*R.*1 ; σπόριμος γένεσις *Cat.Cod.Astr.*8(1).244. 4. μέτρον σ. a measure *of seed-corn*, *AP*6.95 (Antiphil.). II. Act., αἰδὼς σ., = τὸ αἰδοῖον, Man.3.396.

**σπόριον**, τό, Sabine word, = τὸ τῆς γυναικὸς αἰδοῖον, Plu.2.288f.

**σπόριος**, v. σπούριος.

**σπορολογέομαι**, Pass., *to have its produce gathered*, of land, D.H.15.2(3).

⊛ **σπόρος**, ὁ, (σπείρω) *sowing*, Hdt.8.109, X.*Oec.*7.20, Theoc.16.94, etc. ; μετὰ τὸν σ. Pl.*Ti.*42d : metaph., ὁ γαμήλιος σ. καὶ ἄροτος Plu.2.144b : pl., Thphr.*HP*7.5.5. 2. *seed-time*, X.*Oec.*17.4 ; ἀπὸ σπόρω Theoc.10.14. II. *seed*, λίνου σ. Hp.*Epid.*7.65 ; σ. ἐν νειοῖσιν βάλλοντες Theoc.25.25, cf. A.R.3.413, *Ev.Marc.*4.26, etc. 2. *harvest, crop*, Hdt.4.53, *PGrenf.*2.36.16 (i B.C.), etc. ; ὁ πρώϊμος σ. *OGI*56.68 (Canopus, iii B.C.) ; γᾶς σ. S.*Ph.*706 (lyr.). 3. *offspring*, Lyc.221,750. 4. *semen genitale*, v.l. for γονή in Hp.*Vict.*2.54.

**σπορτηληνοί**, οἱ, dub. sens. in *Bull.Inst.Arch.Bulg.*4.319.

**σπορτία**· ἑορτὴ ἀγομένη.., Hsch.

**σπόρτουλον**, τό, = Lat. *sportula*, *Cod.Just.*1.4.26.15, al., Lyd.*Mag.*3.59, *PMasp.*32.44 (vi A.D.).

**σποῦ**, in Scythian, *eye*, Hdt.4.27.

**σπουδάζω**, S.*OC*1143, Ar.*Pax*471 (lyr.), etc. : Att. fut. -άσομαι Pl.*Euthphr.*3e, D.21.213, later -άσω Plb.3.5.8, D.S.1.58, etc. : aor. ἐσπούδασα E.*HF*507, Pl.*Phd.*114e : pf. ἐσπούδακα Ar.*V.*694, Pl.*Phdr.*236b, etc. :—Med., fut. v. supr. :—Pass., fut. σπουδασθήσομαι Ael.*NA*4.13 : aor. ἐσπουδάσθην Str.17.3.15, Plu.*Per.*24 : pf. ἐσπούδασμαι Pl.*Ly.*219e (v. infr.) : I. intr., 1. *to be busy, eager* to do a thing, c. inf., S.*OC*1143, E.*Hec.*817, Pl.*Euthd.*293a, etc. ; σπούδασον ἐλθεῖν..ταχέως *make haste*.., 2*Ep.Ti.*4.9 ; ὅτ' ἐσπούδαζες ἄρχειν *wast eager* to rule, E.*IA*337 (troch.) : c. part., ἐσπ. διδάσκων X.*Oec.*9.1 : freq. σ. περί τινος or τι, Id.*Mem.*1.3.8, Pl.*R.*330c, etc. ; ὑπέρ τινος D.59.77 ; εἰς τὰ σά Id.21.195 ; πρός τι Id.22.76 ; ἐπί τισι X.*Mem.*1.3.11, cf. D.21.2 : c. dat., σ. γάμῳ Aristaenet.2.3 ; σ. ὅπως.. *endeavour that*.., D.43.12, *SIG*312.10 (Samos, iv B.C.) : abs., ἐσπουδακυῖα *in haste, hurriedly*, Ar.*Th.*572 ; ἐσπουδακώς *eagerly*, Men.562. b. c. acc. et inf., σπουδάσαντες τοῦτ' αὐτοῖς παραγενέσθαι Pl.*Alc.*2.141d, cf. 2*Ep.Pet.*1.15, *BGU*1080.14 (iii A.D.), etc. 2. of persons, σ. πρός τινα *pay* him *serious attention*, Pl.*Grg.*510c, etc. ; εἴς τινα *AP*9.422 (Apollonid.) ; σ. περί τινα *to be anxious* for his success, Isoc.1.10, X.*Cyr.*5.4.13, etc. (distd. fr. πρός τινα by Luc.*Sol.*10) ; περί τινος X.*Lac.*4.1 ; ὑπὲρ τῶν οἰκετῶν Aeschin.1.17 ; ὑπέρ τινος D.21.213, etc. ; σ. τινί *be a partisan* or *backer of*, Plu.*Art.*21, Arr.*Epict.*1.11.27, *PGiss.*71.6 (ii A.D.) ; ἀπό τινος Philostr.*VS*2.27.6. 3. *to be serious* or *earnest*, Ar.*Ra.*813 ; opp. σκώπτειν καὶ κωμῳδεῖν, Id.*Pl.*557 ; freq. in Pl., σπουδάζει ταῦτα ἢ παίζει ; *Grg.*481b, etc. ; ἐσπούδακας, ὅτι ἐπελαβόμην ἐρεσχηλῶν σε ; *did you take it seriously*, that I..? *Phdr.*236b ; σπουδάζοντα τοῖς πράγμασι τοῖς ὀνόμασι παίζειν D.H.*Lys.*14 ; ἐσπουδάκατον *they have worked hard*, Ar.*V.*694 ; μάλα ἐσπουδακότι τῷ προσώπῳ with a very *grave* face, X.*Smp.*2.17. 4. *study*, Philostr.*VS*1.7.2 ; *lecture, teach*, ib.1.21.5. II. trans., 1. c. acc. rei, *do* anything *hastily* or *earnestly, be earnest about*, τὸ αὑτοῦ E.*HF*507 ; τὰς περὶ τὸ μανθάνειν ἡδονάς Pl.*Phd.*114e, etc. ; opp. παρέργοις χρῆσθαι, Id.*Euthd.*273d, cf. *Ti.*21c ; τὰ ἑαυτοῦ ἤθεα X.*Smp.*8.17 ; σ. τοῦτο, ὅπως..Id.*Eq.*11.10 :—Pass., σπουδάζεταί τι *is zealously pursued*, πᾶν ὅ τι σ. E.*Supp.*761 ; σ. ἀγών X.*Lac.*10.3 ; χρήματα μετὰ πολλῆς δαπάνης σ. Pl.*R.*485e ; ἡ κωμῳδία διὰ τὸ μὴ σπουδάζεσθαι..ἔλαθεν because it *was* not *taken up seriously*, Arist.*Po.*1449b1 ; οὐ πάνυ σπουδάζεται ὑπ' αὐτῶν is not much *valued*, Luc.*Cont.*11 : esp. freq. in pf. part., πᾶσα ἡ τοιαύτη σπουδὴ οὐκ ἐπὶ τούτοις ἐστὶν ἐσπουδασμένη Pl.*Ly.*219e ; προοίμια θαυμαστῶς ἐσπουδασμένα elaborately *worked up*, Id.*Lg.*722e, cf. 659e ; so τὰ μάλιστα ἐσπ. σῖτα καὶ ποτά the *choicest*, X.*Cyr.*4.2.38 ; τὰ ἐσπ., of writing tablets, the *best quality*, Thphr.*HP*3.9.7 (also κλίνας καὶ δίφρους καὶ τὰ ἄλλα τὰ σπουδαζόμενα ib.5.3.2) ; εἰ ταῦτ' ἐσπουδασμένα ἐν γράμμασιν ἐτέθη if those pains were *seriously* bestowed on letters, Pl.*Ep.*344c ; αἱ ἐσπουδασμέναι παιδιαί Arist.*Rh.*1371a3, cf. *Pol.*1336a34. 2. Pass., of persons, *to be treated with respect*, opp. καταφρονεῖσθαι, Id.*Rh.*1380a26 ; *to be courted*, Str.17.3.15, Plu.*Them.*5, D.L.5.75 ; of women, Plu.*Cim.*4, *Art.*26. b. in Lxx, *trouble, disturb* any one, *Jb.*22.10, 23.16.

**σπουδαιο-γέλοιος**, ον, = σπουδογέλοιος, *IG*12(8).87 (Imbros). **-λογέω**, *speak seriously, talk on serious subjects*, X.*Smp.*8.41, Ph.1.218 :—Med., X.*An.*1.9.28 :—Pass., ὁ λόγος ἐσπουδαιολογήθη the matter *was treated seriously*, Id.*Smp.*4.50. **-λογία**, ἡ, *serious talk* or *conversation*, *An.Ox.*2.318. **-λόγος**, ον, = sq., Phot.*Bibl.* p.205 B. **-μῦθος**, ον, *able to speak seriously*, Democr.104. **-πάρῳδος**, ὁ, *composer of half-serious burlesques*, Phld.*Ind.Sto.*74.

**σπουδ-αῖος**, α, ον, (σπουδή) prop. *in haste, quick*, σ. τοὺς πόδας Poll.1.197, 3.149 ; τὸ σ. τῆς πορείας Polyaen.6.24 :—but in ordinary use denoting *energy* or *earnestness* : I. of persons, *earnest, serious*, X.*Cyr.*2.2.16 (Sup.), cf. *Smp.*8.3 ; *active, zealous*, in canvassing, Plu.*Aem.*1. 2. *good, excellent* in their several kinds, Hdt.8.69 ; opp. φαῦλος, Pl.*Lg.*757a, 814e, Arist.*Po.*1448a2 ; ἀκροαταὶ -ότεροι Isoc.12.271 ; σ. αὐλητής, opp. ἄνθρωπος μοχθηρός, Antisth.ap.Plu.*Per.*1 ; κιθαριστής Arist.*EN*1098a9 ; σκυτεύς Id.*EE*1219a22 ; ἀνδράποδον D.9.31 ; σ. τὴν τέχνην X.*Mem.*4.2.2 ; περί τι Pl.*Lg.*817a. 3. in moral sense, *good*, opp. πονηρός, X.*HG*2.3.19 ; opp. φαῦλος, Id.*Cyr.*2.2.24, Zeno *Stoic.*1.52 ; οἱ σ. Λακεδαιμονίων X.*HG*3.1.9 ; σ. τὰ ἤθη Isoc.1.4 ; τῷ ἀρετὴν ἔχειν σ. λέγεται Arist.*Cat.*10b8, cf. *EN*1166a13, *Top* 131b2 ; σπουδαῖον = ἀγαθόν, Id.*EN*1136b8, 1137b4 : generally, of all *virtuous* objects or qualities, Id.*Metaph.*1021b24, 1051a4, *EN* 1151a27, al. II. of things, *worth serious attention, weighty*, χρῆμα, πρῆγμα, Thgn.65,70,116, etc. ; τὰ -έστερα (-έστατα) τῶν πρηγμάτων Hdt.1.8,133 (v.l. -ότερα, -ότατα), cf. Isoc.2.50 ; ταῦθ' ὑμῖν σπουδαιότατ' ἐστίν D.24.4 ; opp. γελοῖος, Ar.*Ra.*392 (lyr.) ; τί γελᾷς ἐπὶ σπουδαίοις πράγμασιν ; Pl.*Euthd.*300e. 2. *good* of its kind, *excellent*, σ. νομαί Hdt.4.23 ; ἡ σπουδαιοτάτη [τῶν ταριχεύσεων] *the most elaborate, costliest*, Id.2.86, cf. *PSI*4.413.26 (iii B.C.) ; ἡ ἰσηγορίη χρῆμα σ. Hdt.5.78 ; λόγος σ. Pi.*P.*4.132 ; μουσική Pl.*Lg.*668b ; τιμαί Id.*R.*519d ; σπέρματα X.*Mem.*4.4.23 ; δῶρον οὐ σ. εἰς ὄψιν not *goodly* to look on, S.*OC*577 ; τραγῳδία σ. Arist.*Po.*1449b17 ; σ. ὑπόδημα Id.*EE*1219a22 :—a play on senses II. 1 and II. 2 in Arist.*EN*1176b25, 1177a3 ; ironically, σ. χρῆμα a *fine* thing, *h.Merc.*332. III. Adv. σπουδαίως *with haste* or *zeal, seriously, earnestly, well*, X.*Cyr.*1.3.9, Pl.*Cra.*406b, etc. : Comp. -ότερον X.*Cyr.*2.3.20 ; -οτέρως Plu.*Nob.*15 : Sup. τὰ -ότατα *most carefully, in the best way*, Hdt.2.86.—Besides the regul. Comp. and Sup., we find in Ion. the forms -έστερος, -έστατος, Hdt.1.8,133, Hecat.ap.Eust.1441.15, Eus.Mynd.4. ⊛ **-αιότης**, ητος, ἡ, *earnestness, seriousness, goodness*, ἤθους Pl.*Def.*412e, cf. D.S.1.93, Lxx 3*Ma.*1.9.

**σπούδαξ**· ἀλετρίβανος, Hsch.

**σπουδαρχ-αιρεσίας**, ου, ὁ, *a busy electioneerer*, Hsch. **-έω**, = σπουδαρχιάω, D.C.36.27, al., Them.*Or.*8.103c. ⊛ **-ης**, ου, ὁ, *one who is eager for offices of state, placeman*, X.*Smp.*1.4 ; but σπουδαρχίας is restored from Hsch. and Phryn.*PS* p.109 B. **-ία**, ἡ, *eagerness to gain offices of state, canvassing* for them, Lat. *ambitus*, Ph.1.290, Plu.*Aem.*38, D.C.52.15. **-ίας**, v. σπουδάρχης. **-ιάω**, *to be eager for offices of state, canvass for them*, Arist.*Pol.*1305a31, D.C.36.39, 55.5, Them.*Or.*18.224a. **-ίδης**, ου, ὁ, comic Patronymic of σπουδαρχίας, *Son of a Placeman*, Ar.*Ach.*595.

**σπουδασ-μα**, ατος, τό, *thing* or *work done with zeal, pursuit*, τὰ ἀνθρώπινα σ. Pl.*Phdr.*249d, cf. Metrod.*Herc.*831.15 ; of material works, Arr.*An.*7.7.7 ; of literary work, Ph.1.298, S.E.*P.*3.279. **-μάτιον**, τό, Dim. of foreg., *short treatise*, Phot.*Bibl.* p.99 B. **-μός**, ὁ, *zeal*, Thd.*Ez.*27.36. **-τέος**, α, ον, *to be sought for zealously*, X.*Lac.*7.3. II. σπουδαστέον, *one must bestir oneself, be earnest* or *anxious*, περί τινος E.*IA*902 (troch.) ; ἐπί τινι Pl.*R.*608a ; ὑπέρ τινος Isoc.6.91 ; ὅπως.. Arist.*EN*1098b5 : so pl., -αστέα περί τι Hierocl. p.62 A. ⊛ **-τής**, οῦ, ὁ, *one who wishes well to another, supporter, partisan*, Plu.*Caes.*54, *Art.*26. **-τικός**, ή, όν, *zealous, earnest*, opp. φιλοπαίσμων, Pl.*R.*452e ; σπουδαστικώτεροι Arist.*Rh.*1391a25. Adv. -κῶς, ἔχειν Plu.2.613a. **-τός**, ή, όν, *that deserves to be sought* or *tried zealously*, Pl.*Hp.Ma.*297b, Arist.*EN*1163b25.

⊛ **σπουδή**, ἡ, (σπεύδω) *haste, speed*, σπουδὴν ἔχειν *make haste*, Hdt.9.89 ; σ. ἔσται τῆς ὁδοῦ *haste* on the journey, Th.7.77 ; ὅκως ἂν αὐτὸν δρῶσι σπουδῆς ἔχοντα Hdt.9.66 ; χωρίον.., οἷ σπουδὴν ἔχω whither *I am hastening*, Ar.*Lys.*288 ; τοῖς μήτε σχολὴν μήτε σπουδὴν διαγινώσκουσιν Thphr.*Char.*3.6 ; σπουδῇ *in haste*, v. infr. IV ; σὺν σπουδῇ ταχύς S.*Ph.*1223 ; σὺν πάσῃ σ. with all *dispatch*, *POxy.*63.5 (ii/iii A.D.) ; διὰ σπουδῆς E.*Ba.*212, X.*HG*6.2.28, etc. ; ἐκ σπουδῆς Arist.*Mir.*837a15 ; μετὰ σ. *Ev.Marc.*6.25, cf. Hdn.6.4.3, etc. ; κατὰ σπουδὴν Th.1.93, 2.90, X.*An.*7.6.28, etc. (but this sense freq. runs into the next). II. *zeal, pains, trouble, effort*, ἄτερ σπουδῆς Od.21.409 ; σῆς ὑπὸ σ. A.*Th.*585 ; σπουδῆς οὐκ ἀξία S.*OT*778, cf. Pl.*R.*604c, etc. ; freq. in dat. σπουδῇ, *zealously*, v. infr. IV. 3 ; so σὺν σπουδῇ Id.*Lg.*818c ; σὺν πολλῇ σ. X.*An.*1.8.4 ; ἐπὶ μεγάλης σ. Pl.*Smp.*192c ; μετὰ πολλῆς σ. Id.*Chrm.*175e ; σπουδὴν ποιεῖσθαι *exert oneself, take pains, be eager*, Th.4.30 ; c. inf., Hdt.3.4, 7.205 ; σ. πολλὴν ποιέεσθαι Id.6.107 ; πᾶσαν σ. ποιήσασθαι ὅπως.. *PHib.*1.71.9 (iii B.C.) ; σ. ποιεῖσθαι περί τινος Pl.*Smp.*177c; περί τινα ib.179d; ἐπί τινι Luc.*Salt.*1: c. gen., σπουδήν τινος ποιήσασθαι make *much ado about..*, Hdt.1.4; σπουδαὶ λόγων κατατεινομένων *zeal for* the conflicting arguments, E.*Hec.*130 (anap.); πρός τι D.S.17.114; ἀμφὶ Κυράνας θέμεν σ. ἅπασαν Pi.*P.*4.276; ὅτου χάριν σ. ἔθου τήνδ' S.*Aj.*13; σ. ἔχειν, c. inf., *to be eager*, Hdt.6.120; c. acc. et inf., Id.7.149; σ. ἔχειν τινός E.*Alc.*778,1014; περί τινος Pl. *Amat.*136c; εἴς τι E.*Med.*557; ὅπως τι γένηται D.H.*Comp.*22; σ. γίγνεται περί τι Pl.*Phdr.*276e; σ. ἐστι περὶ πραγμάτων D.8.2; σπουδῆς καὶ βουλῆς τὰ πράγματα προσδεῖσθαι Id.9.46; ἡ σ. τῆς ἀπίξιος my *zeal* in coming, Hdt.5.49, cf. S.*Fr.*257; ὅπλων σπουδῇ *with great attention to* the arms, Th.6.31, cf. Pl.*Lg.*855d: pl., ἐπιμέλειαι καὶ σ. πλήθους γεννημάτων *eagerness for..*, ib.740d; *zealous exertions*, E.*Ion* 1061 (lyr.), Arist.*Rh.*1370$^a$12. **b.** in a religious sense, *zeal*, πρὸς τὴν θεὰν *Inscr.Magn.*85.12 (ii B.C.), cf. *Ep.Rom.*12.11; ἐνδείκνυσθαι σ. *Ep. Hebr.*6.11. **2.** *esteem, regard* for a person, διὰ τὴν ἐμὴν σ. Antipho 6.41; πάνυ πολλῆς σ. ἄξιος X.*Smp.*1.6; *good will, good offices*, σ. ὑπέρ τινος 2*Ep.Cor.*8.16, cf. *PTeb.*314.9 (ii A.D.); *support* in political life, Plu.*Crass.*7: pl., *party feelings* or *attachments, rivalries*, σ. ἰσχυραὶ φίλων περί τινος Hdt.5.5; κατὰ σπουδάς Ar.*Eq.*1370, Ael.*VH*3.8; σπουδαὶ ἐρώτων erotic *enthusiasms*, Pl.*Lg.*632a. **3.** *disputation*, Philostr.*VA*4.27,34 (in pl.). **III.** *earnestness*, σ. ἔχειν, ποιεῖσθαι, = σπουδάζειν, E.*Ph.*901, Ar.*Ra.*522; σπουδῆς μὲν μεστοί, γέλωτος δὲ ἐνδεέστεροι X.*Smp.*1.13, cf. 2*Ep.Cor.*7.11, etc.: freq. with a Prep., in adv. sense, ἀπὸ σπουδῆς ἀγορεύεις *in earnest, seriously*, Il.7.359, 12.233; μετὰ σπουδῆς, opp. ἐν παιδιαῖς, X.*Smp.*1.1; μετά τε παιδιᾶς καὶ μετὰ σ. Pl.*Lg.*887d; οὐ σπουδῆς χάριν ἀλλὰ παιδιᾶς ἕνεκα Id.*Plt.*288c, cf. *Smp.*197e; καὶ χωρὶς σπουδῆς καὶ μετὰ σπουδῆς ἐπαινεῖν Arist.*Rh.*1366$^a$29. **2.** *object of attention, serious engagement* or *pursuit*, σπουδὴν ἐπ' ἄλλην Ἡρακλῆς ὁρμώμενος E.*Supp.*1199: pl., ἔν τε παιδιαῖς καὶ ἐν σπουδαῖς Pl.*Lg.*647d, cf. 732d, al. **IV.** σπουδῇ as Adv., *in haste, hastily*, προερέσσαμεν Od.13.279; ἀνάβαινε 15.209; στρατιὴν ἄγειν Hdt.9.1, cf. 89; Dor., σπουδᾷ ἐξελθοῦσα *IG*4$^{2}$(1).121.21 (Epid., iv B.C.); freq. in Att., σ. πάνυ Th.8.89, etc.; σπουδῇ ποδός E.*Hec.*216. **2.** *with great exertion and difficulty*, and so, *hardly, scarcely*, σπουδῇ ἕζετο λαός Il.2.99, cf. 5.893, Od.3.297; σ. παρπεπιθόντες Il.23.37, Od.24.119. **3.** *earnestly, seriously, urgently*, τί με καλεῖς σπουδῇ; E.*Ph.*849; σπουδῇ ἀκούειν Pl.*R.*388d; σ. χαριεντίζεσθαι Id.*Ap.*24c; πάνυ σ. *attentively*, Id.*Phd.*98b; πολλῇ σ. very *busily*, Hdt.1.88, Ar.*Th.*791, X.*Cyr.*4.5.12, etc.; πάσῃ σ. μανθάνειν Pl.*Lg.*952a, etc.

**σπουδο-γέλοιος**, ον, *blending jest with earnest*, Str.16.2.29, D.L. 9.17: also -γελως, ων, *Cat.Cod.Astr.*7.92.

**σπούριος**, ὁ, = Lat. *spurius, bastard*, *PFlor.*5.16 (iii A.D.); spelt **σπόριος**, Plu.2.288e.

**σπύγγας**· ὄρνις, Hsch.

⊛ **σπύλιον**, in pl. σπύλια, dub. in *IG*2$^{2}$.1358 (iv B.C.).

⊛ **σπύλων** (gen. pl.), dub. in Hsch. s.v. σπεῖρα.

**σπύραθ-ος** [ῠ], ὁ or ἡ, = σπυράς, only in pl., Hp.*Nat.Mul.*32, 34, Dsc.2.80; so -ιον, τό, prob. cj. for σπυρίθιον in Id.*Ther.*19 (pl.); **σφυραθία**, ἡ, Poll.5.91: also **σπύρδαρα** ibid. (v.l. -δανα). **-ώδης**, ες, *like sheep's* or *goats' dung*, τὰ σ. Hp.*Prorrh.*1.41, cf. *Coac.*591, etc.; σ. κοιλίαι ib.471.

⊛ **σπυράμινος**, η, ον, = πυράμινος, *Docum. ant. dell' Africa Italiana* 1.88 (Cyrene, iv B.C.); cf. σπυρός.

⊛ **σπῠράς**, Att. **σφῠράς**, άδος, ἡ, *ball of dung*, such as that of sheep or goats: hence in pl., σφυράδων ἀποκνίσματα scraps of *sheep's* or *goats' dung*, Ar.*Pax* 790, cf. Sch., Hsch. s.v. σφυράδες. **2.** Medic., *pill*, τρεῖς σπυράδας Hp.*Mul.*2.147.—Cf. σπύραθος.

**σπυρθίζω**, = πυδαρίζω, Ar.*Fr.*857; cf. σποδίζω III.

**σπῠρίδιον** [ῐδ], τό, Dim. of σπυρίς, Ar.*Ach.*453,469, Pherecr.52, *PSI*4.428.26 (iii B.C.): later **σφῠρίδιον**, *Arch.Pap.*6.220 (iii B.C.), *PTeb.*120.77 (i B.C.).

**σπῠρῐδόν**, Adv. *in the form of a* σπυρίς, γράφειν Sch.D.T. p.190 H.; cf. σπειρηδόν.

**σπῠρῐδοφόρος**, ον, *basket-carrying*, παιδάρια *BGU*1290.25 (ii B.C.).

**σπῠρῐδώδης**, ες, *of the nature of a* σπυρίς, Sch.Ar.*Ach.*1096.

**σπυρίθιον**, v. σπυράθιον.

⊛ **σπῠρίς**, ίδος, ἡ; also **σφυρίς**, Hp.*Art.*78 (v.l. σπυρίς), *IG*11(2).287*A* 43 (Delos, iii B.C.), *PCair.Zen.*754.15 (iii B.C.), *PTeb.*796.7 (ii B.C.), *IG*12(5).663.15, al. (Syros, ii A.D.), *Sammelb.*4425 iii 9 (ii A.D.), v.l. in *Ev.Matt.*15.37, al.:—*large basket, creel*, Hdt.5.16, Ar.*Pax* 1005, *Frr.*415,545, Antiph.34, *Ev.Matt.* l.c., etc.; σ. σίτων *PTeb.* l.c.; used for transport of money, *UPZ*112 v 18 (ii B.C.); ταῖς φιάλαις *IG*11(2) l.c. **2.** used to translate the Lat. *sportula*, σπυρίσι δειπνίσαι Arr.*Epict.*4.10.21; τὸ ἀπὸ σπυρίδος δεῖπνον, *cena e sportula*, Ath.8.365a; σφυρίδος δηνάρια πέντε *IG*12(5) l.c.

**σπῠρίχνιον**, τό, Dim. of σπυρίς, Poll.6.94.

⊛ **σπῡρός**, ὁ, Syracusan form for πυρός, *An.Ox.*1.362, cf. *EM*724.33; found at Cyrene, *Docum. ant. dell' Africa Italiana* 1.86, al. (iv B.C.); at Cos, *SIG*1026.9, 1027.11; at Thera, *IG*12(3).450.18; at Epidaurus, ib.4$^{2}$(1).40.8, 66.38.

**στάβαρον**, τό, *stake*, Sch.Lyc.290.

**σταβατίνης**, ου, ὁ, and **σταβεύς**, έως, ὁ, = κωπεών, κωπεύς, Hsch.

⊛ **σταβλάριον**, τό, Dim. of στάβλον, *POxy.*1676.38 (iii A.D.).

**Σταβλησιᾶνοί**, οἱ, = Lat. *equites Stablesiani*, *Supp.Epigr.*6.187 (Phrygia).

⊛ **σταβλίτης** [ῑ], ου, ὁ, *official in the posting service*, *POxy.*140.7 (vi A.D.), etc.

⊛ **στάβλον**, τό, = Lat. *stabulum, stable, posting-station*, *POxy.*2115.9 (iv A.D.), *Hippiatr.*34, etc.

**σταβόλιχον**· εὔστραβον, Hsch.

**στάγδην**, Adv., (στάζω) *in drops, drop by drop*, Hp.*Epid.*6.3.1, Aret.*SA*2.2.

**στάγες**, v. σταγών I fin.

**στᾰγετός**, ὁ, (στάζω) *drop*, Aq.*Pr.*19.13.

**στάγην**· κάρδοπον, Hsch.

**στάγιον**, τό, = δηνάριον α', Gal.19.763; = κεράτια κδ', ib.764.

**Στάγῑρος**, ἡ, a city in Chalcidice, Hdt.7.115, etc.; also **Στάγιρα**, τά, Arist.*Fr.*669, etc.:—**Σταγιρίτης** [ῑτ], ου, ὁ, *a Stagirite*, *IG*1$^{2}$.195.27 (pl.), etc.; esp. of Aristotle, *SIG*275 (Delph., iv B.C.), St. Byz.:—**Σταγιρόθεν**, *from Stagira*, Tz. in *An.Ox.*4.131. (In codd. usu. misspelt **Σταγειρ-**).

**στάγμα**, ατος, τό, *that which drips*, τῆς ἀνθεμουργοῦ σ., i.e. honey, A.*Pers.*612; μίλτειον σ., v. μίλτειος; *perfume, aromatic oil*, *Ostr. Bodl.* i 346 (ii/i B.C.), *POxy.*155.3 (vi A.D.); τὸ ἀπὸ τῶν φοινίκων σ. Aët.8.22, cf. 23.

⊛ **σταγματοπώλης**, ου, ὁ, *seller of aromatic oils*, *MAMA*3.307 (Corycus).

**σταγμός**, ὁ, dub. sens. in *PMasp.*6$^{v}$.13 (vi A.D.).

**στᾰγον-ιαῖος**, α, ον, *in drops* or *grains*, *PMag.Par.*1.215. **-ίας**, ου, ὁ, *running in drops, drop by drop*, λίβανος Dsc.1.68. **-ῖτις**, ιδος, ἡ, = χαλβάνη, Plin.*HN*12.126.

**στᾰγονόθαλπος**, ὁ, *one who melts and purifies metals*, Hsch.

**σταγρόν**· ξηρόν, θερμόν, ἀκμαῖον, Hsch. (cf. σταιρόν).

**στᾰγών**, όνος, ἡ, (στάζω) *drop*, κροκοβαφὴς σ., of blood, A.*Ag.*1122 (lyr.), cf. *Ch.*400 (anap.); φόνου S.*OT*1278, cf. E.*Ba.*767; ὡς ἐκ πέτρας ὑγρὰ ῥέουσα σταγών, of water, Id.*Supp.*81 (lyr.); σ. ἀποπίπτουσιν Hp.*Flat.*8; δίψιοι σ., of tears, A.*Ch.*186, cf. *Ag.*888; οἴνου χλωραὶ σ. E.*Cyc.*67 (lyr.); Λεσβία σ., of wine, Ephipp.29; τῆς.. ἀπὸ Λέσβου ..σταγόνος Antiph.174.5; σ. σπονδῖτις *AP*6.190 (Gaet.); σ. μαζῶν, of milk, ib.7.552 (Agath.); σ. πίσσης Str.16.2.44; σ. τοῦ κόσμου, the sea, M.Ant.6.36; ψυχραῖσιν σταγόνεσσι *with dew-drops*, *IG*14.1942; σταγόσι κατέστικται is covered *with spots, bespeckled*, Ael. *NA*12.24; κατὰ σταγόνα *drop by drop*, S.E.*M.*7.90 (irreg. nom. pl. στάγες as if from στάξ, A.R.4.626). **II.** *a metal*, = ὀρείχαλκος or ἄσπρον χάλκωμα, Ti.Locr.99c, v. Sch. (p.22 ed.Gelder).

**στᾰδ-αῖος**, α, ον, (στάδην) *standing erect* or *upright*, Ζεὺς σ., in act to hurl his bolt, A.*Th.*513; ἔγχη σ. pikes *for close fight*, opp. missiles (cf. στάδιος I.1), Id.*Pers.*240; σ. σῶμα *firm, steady*, of the cube, Ti. Locr.98c; βάθος βραδὺ καὶ σ., of water, Aristid.Quint.2.9; σταδαία πάλη, μάχη, prob. l. in Philostr.*VS*1.22.4, J.*BJ*6.2.6, for σταδιαία; μάχη σ. v.l. in Th.4.38, for σταδία. **-ην**, Adv., (ἵστημι) *in standing posture*, σ. ἑστῶτες standing *stock-still*, Pl.Com.130; cf. στήδην.

**σταδία**· ἡ λυχνία, Hsch.

**στᾰδιᾱδρομέω, -δρόμος**, v. σταδιοδρ-.

**στᾰδι-αῖος**, α, ον, (στάδιον) *a stade long, deep*, or *high*, σ. βάθος Plb. 34.11.14; ὁ σ. δρόμος D.H.7.73; πυραμίδες σταδιαῖαι τὸ ὕψος D.S.1.52; διφθέραι σ. τοῖς μεγέθεσιν Ath.12.539c:—v. σταδαῖος. **-ασμός**, ὁ, *measuring by stades*, Str.1.3.2, 2.1.17; in title of a lost geographical work, *IGRom.*4.1445 (Smyrna); also of an extant work (*GGM* i p.427). **2.** *conjecture*, Victorin. *in Cic.Rhet.* p.180 Halm. **-εύς**, έως, ὁ, = σταδιοδρόμος, Plb.16.28.9, 38.14.1, *AP*9.557 (Antip.); παῖς σ., in the title of Pi.*O.*14, cf. Sch.Id.*N.*8. **-εύω**, *run as in the stadium*, δρόμους Arist.*Fr.*11; βίον Ph.1.328; δόλιχον βιότου *Epigr. Gr.*311.4 (Smyrna). **-η**, ἡ, v. στάδιος.

**σταδινόν**· παρὰ Δίωνι πολίτην, Hsch.

**στᾰδιοδρομ-έω**, *run in the stadium, race*, Pl.*Thg.*129a, D.59.121 (στάδια δραμοῦμαι shd. be read for σταδιοδρομοῦμαι (-ᾶδρ- cod. L) in E.*HF*863). **-ης**, ου, ὁ, = sq., Ar.*Fr.*858. **-ος** (parox.), ὁ, *one who runs in the stadium, one who runs for a prize*, Simon.125, Pi. *O.*13 tit., Stratt.62, Pl.*Lg.*833a, Aeschin.1.157:—the collat. form **σταδιαδρ-** is found in *IG*4$^{2}$(1).99.17 (Epid., iii/ii B.C.), 7.1772.3 (Thespiae, ii A.D.), *CIG*2758 iii i 4, al. (Aphrodisias), Paus.6.20.9, etc.

⊛ **στάδιον** [ᾰ], Argive **σπάδιον** (q.v.), τό: pl. στάδια and heterocl. στάδιοι; Hdt. uses both, στάδιοι 1.26, 2.149,158, al., στάδια 4.101, 5.53, 9.23, al.; so Th. in the same chapter (7.78) has στάδια once and σταδίους twice; στάδια E.*Ion* 497 (lyr.), Ar.*Av.*6, Antiph.100, Pl.*Phdr.*229c; στάδιοι Ar.*Ra.*1319, Pl.*Criti.*113c,117e, *PCair.Zen.*388.6 (iii B.C.), etc.; the sg. masc. is not found: **I.** as a standard of length, *stade*, = 100 ὀργυιαί or 6 πλέθρα (Hdt.2.149), i.e. 600 Greek, $606\frac{3}{4}$ English feet, about $\frac{1}{8}$ of a Roman mile, Plb.3.39.8, 34.12.4, cf. Plin.*HN*2.85, Hero *Deff.*131; a longer *stade*, of which there were $7\frac{1}{2}$ in a Roman mile, is implied by D.C.52.21. **2.** metaph., ἑκατὸν σταδίοισιν ἄριστος 'best by a hundred miles', Ar. *Nu.*430; πλεῖν ἢ σταδίῳ λαλίστερα Id.*Ra.*91. **II.** *race-course*, *IG*2$^{2}$.677.3, etc. (because the most noted, that of Olympia, was exactly a stade long): prop. *a single course*, opp. δίαυλος, Pi.*O.*13.37, *IG*2$^{2}$.2313.23, *SIG*1067.9 (Rhodes, ii B.C.), etc.; σταδίου δρόμος Pi.*O.*13.30; γυμνὸν σ., opp. ὁπλίτης δρόμος, Id.*P.*11.49; ὠκύτερον σταδίου Thgn.1306; ἀγωνίζεσθαι σ. run a *race*, Hdt.5.22; ἁμιλλᾶσθαι Pl.*Lg.*833a; νικᾶν X.*HG*1.2.1, cf. Pi.*N.*8.16; ἀσκεῖν Pl.*Thg.*128e; of the building, *IG*2$^{2}$.351.16, 677.3, *PRyl.*93.16 (iii A.D.), etc.; ἐν σταδίοις, i.e. in the amphitheatre, *CIG*4377 (Sagalassos). **2.** *any area*, e.g. for dancing, E.*Ion* 497 (lyr.); ξύλινον σ., of a board for playing πεσσοί, *AP*15.18. **3.** *walk* in a garden, *IG*14.1853 (pl.).

**στάδιος** [ᾰ], α, ον, (ἵστημι) *standing fast and firm*, σ. ὑσμίνη *close fight, fought hand to hand*, Il.13.314,713, cf. Th.4.38; ἐνὶ σταδίῃ (sc.

ὑσμίνη) Il.7.241, cf.13.514; ἡ σ. μάχη Ath.6.273f, cf. σταδαῖος; [πῖδαξ] σταδίη μένει, of a spring from which no water flows, Opp.*C*.4.326. 2. *firm, fixed*, θάλαμοι Pi.*O*.5.13: τὸ σ. *immobility*, D.C.39.43. 3. *standing upright* or *straight*, σ. χιτών, = ὀρθοστάδιον, an ungirt tunic *hanging in straight plaits*, Call.*Fr*.59, cf. στατός; θώραξ σ. a *stiff* breastplate, plate-armour, opp. στρεπτός or ἁλυσιδωτός, A.R.3.1226 (v. Sch.). II. (ἵστημι A. IV) *weighed*, Nic.*Al*.402 (στήδην cj. Bentley).

⊛ **στάζω**, Hippon.57, etc.: fut. στάξω Lxx *Je*.49(42).18, Aeol. 3 pl. στάξοισι Pi.*P*.9.63, Dor. 1 pl. σταξεῦμες Theoc.18.46: aor. ἔσταξα E.*HF*1355, Ep. στάξα Il.19.39, Pi.*N*.10.82:—Pass., (ἐν-) Dsc.2.179: aor. 1 ἐστάχθην (ἐπ-) Hp.*Ulc*.21: aor. 2 ἐστάγην (ἐπ-, ἐν-) Dsc.1.19, 2.35: I. c. acc. rei, *drop, let fall* or *shed drop by drop*, [Θέτις] Πατρόκλῳ..νέκταρ στάξε κατὰ ῥινῶν Il.19.39, cf. 348,354; σπέρμα θνατὸν ματρὶ τεᾷ στάξεν Pi.*N*.10.81; ἐξ ὀμμάτων σ. αἷμα A.*Ch*.1058; ἱδρῶτα σώματος ἄπο E.*Ba*.620 (troch.), cf. *Tr*.1199; βότρυν Id.*Ph*.230 (lyr.); ὕδωρ σ. πέτρα Id.*Hipp*.122 (lyr.); esp. of tears, σ. δάκρυ Id.*IA*1466; ἀπ' ὀμμάτων ἔσταξα πηγάς Id.*HF*1355; and metaph., κατ' ὀμμάτων σ. πόθον Id.*Hipp*.526 (lyr.); μυριάδας χαρίτων *AP*5.12 (Phld.); ἵμερον ἐξ ὀμμάτων Callistr.*Stat*.14. 2. c. dat. rei, αἵματι στάζοντα χεῖρας *having* one's hands *dripping* with blood, A.*Eu*.42; κάρα στάζων ἱδρῶτι S.*Aj*.10; ἀφρῷ γένειον E.*IT*308: also without acc., the part affected being in the nom., στάζουσι κόραι δακρύοισι Id.*Ion* 876 (anap.); χέρ' αἵματι στάζουσαν Id.*Ba*.1163 (lyr.): rarely c. gen., χεὶρ στάζει θυηλῆς Ἄρεος S.*El*.1423. 3. abs., *leak*, τῶν νεωρίων ἐπεσκευάσθαι τὰ στάζοντα Aen.Tact.11.3. II. *fall in drops, drip, trickle*, ὕδωρ σ. Hdt.6.74; στάζει..φοίνιον τόδ'..αἷμα S.*Ph*.783: metaph., σ. δ' ἐν ὕπνῳ πρὸ καρδίας..πόνος A.*Ag*.179 (lyr.); ψόφος σ. δι' ὤτων E.*Rh*.566; στάζω λισσάδος ὡς πέτρας λιβὰς ἀνήλιος Id.*Andr*.533 (lyr.): c. gen., ὀπὸν στάζοντα τομῆς *dripping from* the cut, S.*Fr*.534 (anap.); αἷμα ἐξ ἄκρου ἔσταζε κρατός E.*Med*.1199, etc.; σμικρὸν ἀπὸ ῥινῶν ἔσταξεν Hp.*Epid*.1.14. 2. of dry things, as ripe fruit, *drop off*, A.*Supp*.1001 (dub. l.).

**στάθεν, στᾰθέν**, v. ἵστημι.

**στᾰθερ-ός**, ά, Ion. ή, όν, *standing fast, firm, fixed*, γαῖα, opp. ἄστατος, Opp.*C*.2.412; of the sea, *calm, still*, σ. χεῦμα A.*Fr*.276; βύθος D.H.1.71; σταθερῆς (sc. θαλάσσης) *AP*10.17 (Antiphil.), cf. 7.393 (Diocl., dub. sens.), Poll.1.106; σ. ὕδωρ *stagnant*, App.*Pun*.99; σ. μέλαν, of ink, *AP*6.66 (Paul. Sil.). 2. σ. μεσημβρία *high* noon, when the sun as it were *stands still* in the meridian, Pl.*Phdr*.242a; σ. ἦμαρ *mid*-day, A.R.1.450; νυκτὸς τὸ -ώτατον Eun.*VS* p.485 B.; θέρος σ. *mid*-summer, Antim.95. 3. *steady, settled*, of weather, ἀὴρ εὔδιος καὶ σ. D.H.*Dem*.7; εὐδία σ. Plu.*Dio* 38, cf. M.Ant.12.22; οὐ σ. φῶς οὐδ' ἠρεμοῦν Plu.2.934e. 4. metaph., σ. κάλυξ ἥβης Ar.*Fr*.467; σ. ἡλικία J.*BJ*3.1.3; ἡ ἀρετὴ σ. τι *AP*10.74 (Paul. Sil.); σαοφροσύνη *IG*3.776; σ. βάδισμα, βλέμμα, Ph.2.267,26; ἀνάληψις Id.1.179 (Sup.); of speech, *calm, deliberate*, τὸ βραδὺ καὶ σ. D.H.*Comp*.23. 5. not used, properly, of persons, Phryn.189, Thom.Mag.p.110 R., but v. *EM*277.49. 6. Adv. -ρῶς *constantly*, Cratin.206; *firmly*, Procl.*Inst*.156. Adv. Comp., -ώτερον ὁ νοῦς ἵδρυτο Ph.1.372. **-ότης**, ητος, ἡ, *steadiness, firmness*, ib.515; cf. σταθηρότης.

**στάθ-ευσις** [ᾰ], εως, ἡ, *scorching*, Arist.*Mete*.379$^b$14, 381$^b$16 (where some codd. στάτευσις, and so some codd. of Alex.Aphr. *in Mete*.186.4). **-ευτός**, ή, όν, *scorched, burnt*, A.*Pr*.22. **-εύω**, *scorch, roast, fry*, Ar.*Ach*.1041, *Ec*.127, Arist.*HA*534$^a$24, Thphr.*HP*7.13.3; σ. τινὰ τῇ λαμπάδι Ar.*Lys*.376.

**στᾰθηρός, στᾰθηρότης**, late forms of σταθερός, σταθερότης, the former in Ph.1.244, Iamb.*Comm.Math*.34 (Adv. -ρῶς Mich. *in EN* 592.24), the latter in Eustr. *in EN*98.33.

**στᾶθι**, Dor. for στῆθι, aor. 2 imper. of ἵστημι.

⊛ **σταθμ-άω**, Ion. **-έω** Hdt.2.150 (Med.), Hp.*Nat.Puer*.30 (Pass.):—*measure by rule* (στάθμη), πλέθρου σταθμήσας μῆκος εἰς εὐγωνίαν (sc. τὴν σκηνήν) E.*Ion* 1137; σ. τὸ ὕδωρ *measure* or *weigh* it, Ath.2.43b; *certify as containing full measure*, *PTeb*.5.86 (ii B.C.):—Pass., *to be measured* or *weighed*, σταθμεόμενα Hp. l.c., cf. Lxx 3*Ki*.6.23: fut. Med. in pass. sense, ταλάντῳ μουσικὴ σταθμήσεται Ar.*Ra*.797: pf. Pass., ἐπὶ τρισὶν ἐστάθμηται Δελτωτὸν πλευρῇσιν Arat.234. II. more freq. in Med. **σταθμάομαι**, Ion. σταθμόομαι (q.v.), *measure*, σταθμᾶτο..ἄλσος πατρί Pi.*O*.10(11).45; τὰς τράφας (i.e. τάφρους) ὀρύξει..ὅπου ἂν σταθμήσωνται οἱ νεωποῖαι *SIG*963.28 (Amorgos, iv B.C.); *calculate, estimate* distance or size, without actual measurement, Hdt.2.150; σ. ὅκως ἐξελεύσεται.. Id.9.37; μετρεῖν ἢ σ. Pl.*Lg*.643c; σταθμήσασθαι τοὺς ἀστερίσκους Call.*Iamb*.1.119. 2. metaph., *measure, estimate*, τινι *by* some criterion, σ. ταῖς χάρισι Pl.*Grg*.465d; [ταύτῃ τῇ στάθμῃ] Luc.*Hist.Conscr*.63: abs., *conjecture*, S.*OT* 1111. 3. *attach weight to* a thing, *take* it *into account*, τούτων τι σ. ὧν ὅδε λέγει Pl.*Ly*.205a; εἴ τι δεῖ σταθμᾶσθαι τοῦτο Thphr.*HP*9.4.9. **-εία**, ἡ, *composition by weight*, ἐμπλάστρου Gal.13.413. **-εύω**, (σταθμός) *have* or *take up quarters*, *BGU*1006.14 (iii B.C.), App.*Mith*.20; ἐπὶ τοῦ ῥεύματος Anon.ap.Suid.; ἐπὶ λίμνῃ App.*Pun*.99. **-η**, ἡ, *carpenter's line* or *rule*, ξέσσε δ' ἐπισταμένως καὶ ἐπὶ στάθμην ἴθυνεν [δοῦρα] Od.5.245, cf.23.197; [πελέκεας] ἐπὶ σ. ἴθ. 21.121; also στάθμη δόρυ νήϊον ἐξιθύνει Il.15.410; τόρνου καὶ στάθμης καὶ γνώμονος..ἰθύτερον Thgn.805; ἐπὶ σ. θεῖναι μίαν on a *level*, Arist.*PA*657$^a$10: prop. στάθμη was *the line rubbed with chalk* or *red ochre*, being distd. from the rule (κανών) by Pl.*Phlb*.56c, X.*Ages*.10.2; κανόσι καὶ στάθμαις Plu.2.807d, etc.; λευκὴ σ., v. λευκός II. 1a: metaph., ἀτεχνῶς λευκὴ σ. εἰμὶ πρὸς τοὺς καλούς a white *measuring-line*, i.e. unable to discriminate, Pl.*Chrm*.154b, cf. Plu.2.513f. 2. παρὰ στάθμην *by the rule*, εἶμι παρὰ σ. ὀρθὴν ὁδόν Thgn.945, cf. 543; τέκτονος παρὰ σ. ἰόντος S.*Fr*.474; for A.*Ag*.1045 v. παρά C. II. 2; κατὰ στάθμην ἵστασθαι, c. gen., *in a straight line with*, Democr.ap.Plu.2.929c; κατὰ σ. ἐνόησας you guessed *aright*, Theoc.25.194; ὡς ἂν ἀπὸ στάθμης D.H.*Comp*.23; στάθμῃ Aret.*SD*2.11; πρὸς στάθμῃ πέτρον τίθεσθαι, μή τι πρὸς πέτρῳ στάθμην, i.e. when facts are obstinate, do not relax your standard, Com. (?) ap.Plu.2.75f (cf. Bergk *PLG*3.740); στάθμα πατρῴα perh. the *measure* [of piety] towards his father, Pi.*P*.6.45; στάθμας ἑλκόμενοι περισσᾶς perh. straining at an over-exact *measure*, ib.2.90. 3. *verification, certification*, τὰς σ. τῶν μέτρων ἀπὸ τοῦ βελτίστου ποιεῖσθαι prob. in *PTeb*.5.88 (ii B.C.). II. *plummet* or *plumbline*, μολιβαχθής *AP*6.103 (Phil.); ῥιπτεῖσθαι ἄνω κατὰ στάθμην to be thrown perpendicularly upwards, Arist.*Cael*.296$^b$24. III. like γραμμή, *the line which bounds the race-course, goal*, δραμεῖν ποτὶ στάθμαν, metaph. of man's life, Pi.*N*.6.7; παρ' οἵαν ἤλθομεν σ. βίου E.*Ion* 1514. 2. *starting point*, 'scratch', στάθμης ὁρμηθέντες ἀπόσσυτοι Opp.*H*.4.102, cf. Eust.1023.5. IV. metaph., *law, rule*, ὑπὸ στάθμᾳ νέμεσθαι Pi.*Fr*.1.4; Ὑλλίδος στάθμας ἐν νόμοις, i.e. according to laws of Dorian *rule*, Id.*P*.1.62. V. δοράτων στάθμαι *butt-ends*, like σαυρωτῆρες, D.S.17.35, cf. *PCair.Zen*.782(*a*).49 (iii B.C.). **-ηλάται**· ἐξῶσται νεῶν, Hsch. **-ημα**, ατος, τό, *calculation, estimate*, τὰ τῆς ἑκάστου ψυχῆς σ. Ph.1.614. **-ησις**, εως, ἡ, *measuring* or *weighing*, Nausiph.2. **-ητέα**, *perpendenda*, Gloss. **-ητικός**, ή, όν, *of* or *for measuring*, σ. τῆς ἰσότητος S.E.*M*.7.442; σ. λέξις *used of weighing*, Eust.81.17. **-ητός**, ή, όν, *to be measured*, ἐμοὶ οὐδὲν σ. 'I am nothing to judge by', Pl.*Chrm*.154b, cf. Poll.4.93; οὔτε πλῆθος οὔτε μέγεθος σ. Arr.*Peripl.M.Eux*.8, cf. *Fr*.166 J.

⊛ **Σταθμία**, ἡ, epith. of Athena, Hsch.

**σταθμ-ίδιον**, τό, prob. *a small box*, Musa ap.Gal.12.956. **-ίζω**, = σταθμάω, *weigh*, literally or metaph., Aq.*Jb*.28.25, al., Sm.*Jb*.6.2, *IG*2$^2$.1121.12 (iv A.D.), Elias *in Porph*.75.21, Suid., Eust.114.6. **-ικός**, ή, όν, *by weight*, οὐγγία Gal.13.417,894. **-ίον** or **στάθμιον**, τό, Dim. (in form) of σταθμός III, *weight of a balance*, v.l. in Hp.*Fract*.8. 2. a specific weight of wool, *PTeb*.116.23, 26 (ii B.C.), 117.17 (i B.C.). II. *standard weight*, σ., ἃ ὁ δῆμος σηκῶσαι ἐψηφίσαντο *IG*2$^2$.1388.46, al., cf. Lxx *Le*.19.35, al.; *balance*, Luc.*Vit.Auct*.27, S.E.*M*.7.27 (and so perh. in ll.cc. supr.). III. *plummet*, Lxx 4*Ki*.21.13. **-ιστής**, οῦ, ὁ, *one who weighs*, Gloss. **-ιστί**, Adv. *by weight*, *PSI*5.459.11 (i A.D.). **-ιστικός**, ή, όν, *for weighing*, ὄργανον Simp. *in Ph*.1110.3.

**Σταθμίτας** [ῑ] οἶνος, wine from οἱ Σταθμοί near Sparta, Alcm.117.

**σταθμο-δοσία**, ἡ, *billeting*, τῶν στρατιωτῶν *PHal*.1.167 (iii B.C.), cf. *PEnteux*.11.3, 12.9 (iii B.C.). **-δοτέω**, *billet* a soldier, σταθμοδοθείς (by error for -δοτηθείς) ib.13.2 (iii B.C.), cf. *PLond*.1.106.6 (iii B.C.). **-δότης**, ου, ὁ, *quartermaster*, Plu.*Demetr*.23.

**σταθμόν**, τό, = σταθμός III. 2, *weight*, *IG*1$^2$.301.21, 2$^2$.1627.296: pl., μέτρα..καὶ σταθμά Gorg.*Pal*.30, Pl.*Lg*.746e; and so in gen. and dat., *SIG*87.12 (Attic Law, v B.C.); ἐφηῦρε..σταθμῶν ἀριθμῶν καὶ μέτρων εὑρήματα S.*Fr*.432, cf. Decr.ap.And.1.83, X.*Mem*.3.10.10, etc.; μέτρα..καὶ μέρη σταθμῶν E.*Ph*.541, cf. Ar.*Av*.1041, Pl.*Lg*.757b, Arist.*Ath*.10.1, etc. 2. *standard weight* kept under public authority, in pl., *IG*2$^2$.1013.10, al. (ii B.C.); σ. τὰ ξυληρά *SIG*975.2 (Delos, iii B.C.). 3. = σταθμός II, *PTeb*.804.13 (ii B.C.).

**σταθμόνδε**, Adv. *to the stall, homewards*, Od.9.451.

**σταθμόομαι**, = σταθμάομαι, *form an estimate, judge* or *conclude by* or *from* a thing, freq. in Hdt. in aor. 1, c. dat., 7.11,214; σ. τινὶ ὡς.., ὅτι.., *conclude* by a thing that.., 3.15,38, 4.58 (codd. have σταθμησάμενοι (-ος) in 2.2, 9.37, σταθμεόμενοι 2.150, σταθμώμενος 7.237, σταθμεύμενοι 8.130); cf. σταθμάομαι.

⊛ **σταθμός**, ὁ, in Trag., etc., with heterocl. pl. σταθμά, S.*Ph*.489, *OT* 1139, E.*HF*999, X.*Eq*.4.3, etc.; σταθμοί however occurs not only in Hom. (v. infr.), but in E.*Andr*.280, *Or*.1474 (both lyr.):—*standing-place* for animals, *farmstead, steading*, τὼ μὲν (the lions) ἄρ', ἁρπάζοντε βόας καὶ ἴφια μῆλα, σταθμοὺς ἀνθρώπων κεραΐζετον Il.5.557, cf. 12.304; κατὰ σταθμοὺς δύεται 5.140; κατὰ σ. ποιμνήϊον 2.470; σταθμῷ ἐν οἰοπόλῳ 19.377, cf. Hes.*Th*.294; sts. including the human dwelling, Od.14.504; of a swineherd's steading, ib.32; of a sheep-station, Il.5.140, 18.589, cf. E.*Rh*.293; of the *stable* of the griffin of Oceanus, A.*Pr*.398; of a deer's *lair*, Arist.*HA*578$^b$21, 611$^a$20. 2. of men, *dwelling, abode*, Pi.*O*.5.10 (pl.), *P*.4.76 (pl.); Ἀΐδα Id.*O*.10(11).92; οὐρανοῦ Id.*I*.7(6).45; Εὐβοίας σταθμά S.*Ph*.489, cf. *PCair.Zen*.344.2 (iii B.C.), *BGU*1185.13 (i B.C.), etc. 3. *quarters, lodgings* for travellers or soldiers, Hdt.7.119, X.*An*.1.8.1, al., *SIG*880.15 (Pizus, iii A.D.), etc.; soldier's *billet*, *PStrassb*.92.4 (iii B.C.), etc. 4. *quarter* of a town, *PRyl*.102.8 (ii A.D.). 5. in Persia, of *stations* or *stages* on the royal road, where the king rested in travelling, σ. βασιλήϊοι Hdt.5.52, cf. 6.119, Plu.*Art*.25: hence in reference to Persia, of distances, *a day's march* (about 5 parasangs or 150 stades), X.*An*.1.2.10; *posting-station* in the desert, σ. καὶ φρούρια *OGI*701.13 (Egypt, ii A.D., pl.). 6. *station* for ships, E.*Rh*.43 (lyr.), Lyc.290. II. *upright standing-post*, freq. in Hom.; sts. of the *bearing pillar* of the roof, παρὰ σταθμὸν τέγεος Od.1.333, 8.458, 18.209; παρὰ σ. μεγάροιο 17.96, cf. 22.120,257: in pl., E.*IT*49; also *door-post*, Od.4.838, 17.340: pl., ἀργύρεοι σ. ἐν χαλκέῳ ἕστασαν οὐδῷ 7.89, cf. 10.62, Il.14.167, Hdt.1.179, S.*El*.1331, E.*Or*.1474 (lyr.): later, pl. σταθμά in this sense, Id.*HF*999, Ar.*Ach*.449, *IG*2$^2$.1672.70, 173, 4$^2$(1).103.94 (Epid., iv B.C.); σ. θυράων Theoc.24.15: σταθμός alone, = *threshold, door*, Lxx 4*Ki*.12.9, al. III. (ἵστημι A. IV) *balance*, γυνὴ..σταθμὸν ἔχουσα Il.12.434; ἱστᾶσι σταθμῷ πρὸς ἀργύριον τὰς τρίχας weigh them against silver, Hdt.2.65; ἐπὶ τὸν σ. ἀγαγεῖν Ar.*Ra.*1365; ἐς τὸν σ. ἐμβάς ib.1407; ἕλκειν σ. *weigh* so much, Hdt.1.50, cf. Eup.116. 2. *weight*, σίτου σ. Hdt.2.168; σ. ἔχοντες τριήκοντα τάλαντα Id.1.14; διαφέρειν ἐν τῷ σ. Hp.*Aër.*1: abs., in acc., ἀναθήματα ἴσα σταθμὸν τοῖσι.. equal *in weight* to.., Hdt.1.92; ἡμιπλίνθια σταθμὸν διτάλαντα two talents *in* or *by weight*, ib.50; Βαβυλώνιον σταθμὸν τάλαντον a talent, Babylonian *weight*, Id.3.89, cf. Th.2.13; ᾧ πλείω παρὰ τὸν σ. excess resulting from difference of *standard*, *PCair.Zen.*782(*a*).141 (iii B.C.); μυρίος χρυσοῦ σ. E.*Ba.*812; σ. [θύννου] ἦν τάλαντα ιε' Arist.*HA*607ᵇ32; νόμισμα..ὁρισθὲν μεγέθει καὶ σταθμῷ Id.*Pol.*1257ᵃ39. 3. *fixed standard* of health, Hp.*VM* 9, *Steril.*230.

**σταθμ-οῦχος**, ὁ, (ἔχω) *keeper of a house, landlord*, A.*Fr.*226, Antiph.171. II. *quartermaster*, Polyaen.7.40. 2. *householder on whom a soldier is billeted*, *PEnteux.*13.1, *PPetr.*3 p.39, *PStrassb.*92.5 (all iii B.C.). 3. *billeted soldier*, *BGU*1247.6 (ii B.C.); = σύσκηνος, Sm.*Ex.*3.22. **-ώδης**, ες, *full of dregs* or *sediment*, τὸ -έστατον [τοῦ ὕδατος] Hp.*Aër.*8. **-ών**, όνος, ἡ, = σταθμός II, Hsch.

**σταῖμεν, σταῖτε, σταῖεν**, Att. 1, 2, and 3 pl. aor. 2 opt. of ἵστημι.

**σταινίον**· τὸ ἱερὸν ὀστοῦν, καὶ τὸ ὑπογάστριον, Hsch.; cf. στέρνιον.

**σταιρόν**· ξηρόν, θερμόν, ἄκρατον, Hsch. (cf. σταγρόν, σταθερός).

**σταῖς** or **σταίς** (not στᾶς), τό, gen. σταιτός, *flour of spelt mixed and made into dough*, Hdt.2.36, Hp.*Art.*38, Arist.*Mete.*386ᵇ14, *Pr.*927ᵇ23, Thphr.*Od.*51, Lxx *Ex.*12.34; εἰ μὴ κόρη δεύσειε τὸ σ. Eup.332; also of *dough* in general, Gal.6.482,510,597. II. = στέαρ, οἷος σταῖς dub. l. in Hp.*Nat.Mul.*103 (οἰσύπην Littré); ἐν σταιτὶ τρίβειν Id.*Mul.*1.84 (perh. in sense I).

**σταιτήϊα**· πέμματος εἶδος, Hsch. **στα⟨ι⟩τίας**· ἄρτου εἶδος, Id.

**σταιτῑνοκογχομᾱγής**, ές, *moulded into a boss of dough*, prob. cj. in Philox.3.14.

**σταίτ-ῑνος**, η, ον, *of flour* or *dough of spelt*, Hdt.2.47, Plu.*Luc.*10. **-ίον**, τό, *piece of dough*, *PMag.Par.*1.2945. **-ίτης** [ῐ], ου, ὁ, = σταίτινος, Epich.52, Sophr.28. **-ουργός**, ὁ, *one who makes dough of spelt*, *Ostr.Bodl.* iii 334 (misspelt στετ-). **-ώδης**, ες, *like dough*, τὸ ἐν τῷ ἄρτῳ σ. the *soft, crumby* part of the loaf, Poll.6.93.

**στακ-τερία**, ἡ, *vessel containing aromatic oil*, *Stud.Pal.*20.233 (vi/vii A.D.). **-τή**, ἡ, (στάζω) *oil of myrrh*, Antiph.223, Lxx *Ge.*37.25, Plb.13.9.5, Dsc.1.60: metaph., ἡ τῶν φρενῶν σ. Men.*Per.*16. **-τικός**, ή, όν, *for filtering*, ἀγγεῖα Hsch. **-τός**, ή, όν, *oozing out in drops, trickling, distilling*, μύρα Ar.*Pl.*529; σμύρνη Hp.*Ulc.*12, cf. Thphr.*HP*9.4.10, *Od.*29, *Edict.Diocl.Delph.*22; χυλοί Pl.*Criti.*115a; σ. ἔλαιον oil *that runs off without pressing, virgin*-oil, *Gp.*7.12.20; σ. ἅλμη *brine*, ib.20.46.5; σ. κονία lime-*water*, ib.6.7.1 (but = *lye* from wood-ashes in Gal.13.569). 2. στακτά, τά, perh. *filtering vessels*, Ath.Med.ap.Orib.5.5.1. **-τώδης**, ες, *ash-coloured, ashy*, Sch.Opp.*H.*1.214.

**στάλα**, Dor. for στήλη.

**σταλαγεῖ**· μαρμαρύσσει, Hsch. (fort. σελαγεῖ).

**σταλαγ-μα** [στᾰ], ατος, τό, (σταλάσσω) *that which drops, a drop*, A.*Eu.*802; ῥοὴ φοινίου σταλάγματος S.*Ant.*1239; πώματος Philostr.*VA*3.25: dub. sens. in *BGU*531 ii 16 (i A.D.). **-μιαῖος**, α, ον, *as measured by the water-clock*, ὥρα Paul.Al.*K.*4; τὰς λεπτομερεῖς ἡμέρας καὶ σ. ὥρας Vett.Val.274.2. **-μίας**, ου, ὁ, *dropping, trickling*, of a kind of χάλκανθος, Plin.*HN*34.124. **-μιον**, τό, Dim. of στάλαγμα: in pl., *ear-drops, ear-rings*, Plaut.*Men.*542. **-μός**, ὁ, *dropping, dripping*, from the mouth of horses and hunted animals, A.*Th.*61, *Eu.*247, cf. 783 (lyr.); φόνου E.*Hec.*241 (pl.); αἵματος Id.*Ion* 351, 1003 (pl.); of a profuse sweat, Hp.*Aph.*7.85, cf. Gal.19.140; ὁ σ. καταρτρίβει τοὺς λίθους Arist.*Ph.*253ᵇ15; κίονες πεπήγασιν ἀπό τινων σ., of stalactites, Id.*Mir.*834ᵇ32; also σμύρνης S.*Fr.*370 (pl.): metaph., σ. εἰρήνης *the least drop* of.., Ar.*Ach.*1033; τύχης σ. Diog.Sinop.2; contemptuously of a little man, Anaxandr.34.3. (σταλαγμοὺς is unmetrical in Arat.966: σταλαημοὺς cj. Koechly, cf. σταλεηδόνες.)

**στᾰλ-άζω**, = σταλάσσω, Aq.*Mi.*2.6, Plu.2.317d. **-ακτικός**, ή, όν, *dropping, dripping*, χάλκανθον interpol. in Dsc.5.98; cf. σταλαγμίας. **-ακτός**, ή, όν, = foreg., ibid. **-άσσω**, late -ττω (Porph. *in Harm.*p.195.10 W.): aor. ἐστάλαξα Lyc.37, Lxx *Mi.*2.11: I. *let drop*, δάκρυ σ. E.*Hel.*633 (lyr.); σ. ἐς οἶδμα..δακρύων..αὐγάς Id.*Hipp.*738 (lyr.); σκηπτὸς σ...φόνον Id.*Andr.*1046 (lyr.); ἡμιτύβιον σταλάσσον a napkin *dripping wet*, Sapph.116: metaph., τοὺς ἐν τῷ διαλέγεσθαι δυσφόρους καὶ κατ' ὀλίγας λέξεις σταλάττοντας Porph. l. c. II. *drop, drip*, E.*Ph.*1388. **-άω**, = σταλάσσω, I. *let drop, let fall*, δάκρυ Maiist.43, *AP*7.552 (Agath.), A.R.4.1064; αἴγειροι τὸ ἤλεκτρον ἐπ' αὐτέῳ δάκρυον σταλάουσιν Luc.*Astr.*19; of snakes, λοίγια σταλάουσι σὺν αἵματι Androm.ap.Gal.14.37; σταλάοντα ὄμματα, with δάκρυα unexpressed, cj. in *AP*5.236 (Agath.). II. *drop, drip*, Arat.962.

**σταλεηδόνες**· σταλαγμοί, Hsch. **στάλη**· ταμεῖον κτηνῶν, Id. **σταλίζομαι**· ἐπὶ τῆς στήλης τρόπον ἕστηκας (sic), Id.

**στάλιξ** [ᾰ], ῐκος, ἡ, (στέλλω) *stake to which nets are fastened*, Theoc.*Ep.*3, *AP*6.109 (Antip.), Plu.*Pel.*8, Tryph.222, etc.; distd. from σχαλίς, Opp.*C.*1.151,157, Poll.5.19,31, 10.141.

**στᾰλίς**, ίδος, ἡ, = foreg., Hsch.; f.l. for σχαλίς in X.*Cyn.*2.8.

**στᾰλῖτις**, ιδος, ἡ, Dor. for στηλῖτις.

**στάλλα**, Aeol. and Thess. for στήλη, *IG*12(2).67.13 (Mytil., ii A.D.), 9(2).517.21 (Larissa, iii B.C.).

**στᾱλουργός**, όν, Dor. for στηλ-, *with a* στήλη or *gravestone*, τύμβος *AP*7.423 (Antip. Sid.); but **σταλοῦχος** is prob. l., cf. στηλοῦχος.

**στάλ-σις**, εως, ἡ, (στέλλω) *checking* of a flow, Gal.*Sect.Intr.*6. **-τέον**, *one must check*, ib.7. **-τικός**, ή, όν, *capable of staunching*, Arist.*Pr.*863ᵃ14; *capable of checking, astringent*, οἶνος κοιλίας -ώτατος Str.5.3.10, cf. Diocl.*Fr.*141, Dsc.2.90 (Comp.); δύναμις σ. τῶν ἐκσαρκούντων Id.5.87; καρκινωμάτων Id.1.68; ὑποσάλων ὀδόντων ib.105 (v.l. στατικόν).

**στάλυξ**, ἡ, = σταλαγμός, prob. l. for στάληξ, Zonar.:—hence νεοστάλυξ, and perh. (through σταλύζω, which is not found) ἀσταλύζω, ἀνασταλύζω.

**στᾱμᾰγορίς** or **-ᾰγορίς**, ίδος, ἡ, Dor. for *στημηγ- or *στημᾰγ-, (στήμων I, ἀγείρω) *twisting of several threads of the warp into one*, Hsch.

**στᾶμεν**, Dor. for στῆναι, v. ἵστημι.

**στᾰμίν** or **στᾰμίς**, ὁ, nom. pl. σταμῖνες Poll.1.92, Hsch.; acc. pl. σταμῖνας Moschio (v. infr.); Ep. dat. pl. στᾰμίνεσσι: (ἵστημι):—in pl., *the ribs* or *frame-timbers* of a ship, *which stand up* from the keel (expld. as ὀρθὰ ξύλα, οἷον στήμοσιν ἐοικότα, Aristarch.ap.*EM*724.56), Od.5.252, Poll. l. c., Nonn.*D.*40.446: but = ἐπηγκενίδες in Moschio ap.Ath.5.206f, 207b.

**σταμν-άριον**, τό, Dim. of στάμνος, *wine-jar*, Eup.204, Ephipp.24. **-ίας**, ου, ὁ, Com. pr. n., *Wine-jar*, prob. formed like Καππίας, Διόνυσος, υἱὸς Σταμνίου Ar.*Ra.*22. **-ίον**, τό, = σταμνάριον, Id.*Lys.*196,199, Men.129, *PSI*4.413.19 (iii B.C.), *Inscr.Délos* 399 *A* 40 (ii B.C.). 2. = ἀμίς, S.E.*M.*1.234, cf. Phryn.377. **-ίσκος**, ὁ, = foreg. I, *Inscr.Délos* 372 *B* 24, al. (200 B.C.), Poll.7.162. **-ος**, ὁ, also ἡ Hermipp.82.7, Eratosth.ap.Ath.11.499e, *Ep.Hebr.*9.4:—*earthen jar* or *bottle for racking off wine* (cf. κατασταμνίζω), Ar.*Pl.*545, *Fr.*531, Hermipp. l. c., D.35.32: generally, *jar*, Hp.*Epid.*7.89; σ. μέλιτος Lxx 3*Ki.*12.24h; σ. χρυσῆ ἔχουσα τὸ μάννα *Ep.Hebr.* l. c.; used to keep money in, *IG*11(2).287 *A* 76 (Delos, iii B.C.), *PTeb.*46.35 (ii B.C.); as a ballot-box, *Jahresh.*23 *Beibl.*75 (Pygela, iv/iii B.C.); as a measure, τοῦ ἐλαίου *SIG*900.27 (Panamara, iv A.D.): ἀμφορέα· τὸν δίωτον στάμνον, Ἀττικῶς, στάμνον, Ἑλληνικῶς, Moer. p.44 P. **-οῦρος**, ὁ, *keeper of oil-jars* in the palaestra, Hsch.

**στάν**, Ep. 3 pl. aor. 2 of ἵστημι. 2. neut. of part. aor. 2. **στάνει**· τείνεται, συμβέβυσται, Hsch. **στάνης**· δύστηνος, Id.

**στανύω**, Cret. for ἵστημι:—Med., πόλιν στανυέσθων *let them appoint* an umpire city, *GDI*5040.66.

**στάξ**, v. σταγών.

**στάξις**, εως, ἡ, (στάζω) *dropping, dripping*, e.g. of blood from the nose, in pl., Hp.*Coac.*57, cf. 588, *Prorrh.*1.59,148; in sg., σ. ἀπὸ ῥινῶν αἵματος Id.*Coac.*399.

**σταρεῖ**· βάπτει, Hsch.

**σταρταγέτας**, ὁ, = στρατηγός, *GDI*4985.4 (Crete).

**σταρτός**, ὁ, Cret., = στρατός, a division of the people, *GDI*4985.7 (Crete), *Riv.Fil.*61.489 (ibid.), *Leg.Gort.*5.5; cf. στάρτοι· αἱ τάξεις τοῦ πλήθους, Hsch.

**στασάνη**, ἡ, (ἵστημι) *pledge given*, Hsch.

**στᾰσι-άζω**, fut. -άσω Hdt.8.3: (στάσις B. III): I. intr., *to be at variance*, τινι *with* one, X.*An.*2.5.28, etc.; πρός τινα ib.6.1.29, Pl.*R.*545d, etc. 2. in the Greek states, *form a party* or *faction, be at odds* (defined by Arist. as happening ὅταν ἑκάτερος ἑαυτὸν [ἄρχειν] βούληται, *EN*1167ᵃ34), Hdt.1.59, 7.2, al., Cratin.54; ἀλλήλοις X.*Mem.*2.6.17; ἐπ' ἀλλήλοισι Hdt.1.60; περὶ τῆς ἡγεμονίης Id.8.3; ὑπὲρ τῆς δημοκρατίας Lys.2.61; πρὸς τοὺς τυράννους ὑπὲρ τοῦ δήμου And.2.26: generally, *quarrel*, τοῖσι ἑωυτοῦ ἀδελφεοῖσι Hdt.4.160; τάξιος εἵνεκα Id.9.27; διά τι Pl.*R.*464e; ἐν ἑαυτοῖς ib.465b; τοῖς ἐχθροῖσι μεθ' ἡμῶν σ. *side* with us *against* them, Ar.*Eq.*590; σ. κατ' ἀλλήλους περί τινος Th.4.84; πρὸς ἀλλήλους περί τινος Pl.*R.*488b, cf. Phld.*Rh.*2.220 S. 3. of the states themselves, *to be distracted by factions and party strife*, Ar.*Av.*1014, Th.4.1,66, Pl.*Ep.*336e, etc. 4. generally, *to be in a state of discord, disagree*, περί τινος Id.*Euthphr.*8d, al. 5. σῶμα σ. αὐτὸ αὑτῷ Id.*R.*556e, cf. 352a; ἡ ψυχὴ σ. ib.586e, Arist.*EN*1166ᵇ19. II. trans., *revolutionize, throw into confusion*, τὴν πόλιν Lys.18.18; τὰ πράγματα D.11.18; οἴκους Anon.ap.Stob.4.31.84; τὴν Ἀντιόχειαν Philostr.*VA*6.38:—Pass., in signf. I. 3, διὰ τὸ τὰ ἐν τῇ Ῥώμῃ στασιάζεσθαι D.C.40.32; τὸ ἐστασιασμένον S.E.*M.*7.346.—This trans. sense is expressed by στασιάζειν ποιῶ in Isoc.4.134. **-άρχης**, ου, ὁ, = στασίαρχος 2, D.C.60.31. **-αρχία**, ἡ, *leadership in sedition*, *BCH*50.18 (Delph., iv B.C.). **-αρχος**, ὁ, (στάσις B. II) *chief of a band* or *company*, A.*Supp.*12 (anap.). 2. *head of a party, leader in sedition*, App.*BC*1.2, D.C.*Fr.*96. **-ᾰσις**, εως, ἡ, = sq., *IG*5(2).20.15 (Tegea). **-ασμός**, ὁ, *raising of sedition*, Th.4.130, 8.94, Men.1066, *Hell.Oxy.*11.1. **-αστής**, οῦ, ὁ, *one who stirs up sedition*, D.H.6.70, *Ev.Marc.*15.7, J.*AJ*14.1.3, Ptol.*Tetr.*162. II. (στάσις A. II) *weigher* in a wool-factory, *PCair.Zen.*484.4, 499.87 (iii B.C.). **-αστικός**, ή, όν, *seditious, factious*, opp. πολιτικός, Pl.*Plt.*303c; λόγοι Aeschin.3.208; πράττειν οὐδὲν σ. Plu.*Cor.*6. Adv., -κῶς ἔχειν to be *factious*, πρός τινας D.9.21, 18.61; σ. χρῆσθαι τοῖς ὀστρακισμοῖς *in a factious spirit*, Arist.*Pol.*1284ᵇ22.

**στᾰσίζω**, = στασιάζω, *foment civil strife*, *SIG*527.62 (Crete, iii B.C.).

**στᾰσῐμοποιός**, όν, *creating stability*, Dam.*Pr.*298.

**στάσῐμος** [ᾰ], ον, (στάσις): I. Act., *checking, stopping*, τὰ σ. τοῦ αἵματος *styptics*, Hp.*Mul.*2.110; of foods, = στατικός I, Id.*Vict.*2.54,55. II. Pass., *brought to a stand, standing, station-*

*ary*: of water, *stagnant*, Id.*Aër*.7, X.*Oec*.20.11, Aen.Tact.8.4, etc.; -ώτατος ποταμῶν Id.*Aër*.15; σ. αἷμα Id.*Acut*.(*Sp*.)9; σ. ὕδατα, opp. ῥυτά, Arist.*Mete*.353b19. b. *stable, steadfast*, opp. ὑγρός and ῥοώδης, Hp.*Mul*.2.111, cf. *Nat.Mul*.1, Diog.Apoll.5 (Comp.); τὸ ψυχρὸν ἔοικε σ. εἶναι, opp. κινητικόν, Plu.2.945f; σ. κίνησις Pl.*Sph*.256b, cf. *Tht*.180b, Arist.*GA*717a30 (Comp.); πνεῦμα Thphr.*CP*5.12.11; βίος *BCH*51.148 (Salamis Cypr.); σ. ἄστρα *fixed*, Poll.4.156; σ. ὄργανα defined in Orib.49.2.6. Adv. -μως Hp.*Acut*.29: Comp. -ωτέρως Pl.*Ti*.55e. 2. of men, *steadfast, steady*, φύσεις κόσμιοι καὶ σ. Id.*R*.539d; τὰ σ. γένη ἐξίσταται εἰς νωθρότητα Arist.*Rh*.1390b30; φρόνιμος καὶ σ. ἄνθρωπος Plb.27.15.10; -ώτερος, opp. τολμηρότερος, Id.21.7.5: τὸ σ. *steadiness*, Id.6.58.13; τὸ σ. τῆς ἵππου the *heavy* cavalry, Id.3.65.6; οἱ -ώτατοι τῶν ἀνδρῶν Id.15.16.4. 3. of music, ἡ Δωριστὶ -ωτάτη καὶ μάλιστα ἦθος ἔχουσα ἀνδρεῖον Arist.*Pol*.1342b13, cf. 1340b9, *Pr*.922b15; μέτρον -ώτατον, of heroic verse, Id.*Po*.1459b34; λέξις σ. Id.*EN*1125a14:—but, b. στάσιμον, τό, in Tragedy, *choral song*, distd. by Aristotle fr. πάροδος and defined as μέλος χοροῦ τὸ ἄνευ ἀναπαίστου καὶ τροχαίου, *Po*.1452b23, cf. S.E.*M*.6.17, Poll.4.53, Ath.13.592b; expld. as sung by the chorus when *stationary*, σ. μέλος ὃ ᾄδουσιν ἱστάμενοι οἱ χορευταί Sch. Ar.*Ra*.1314, cf. Arg.A.*Pers*., Sch.Ar.*V*.270, Sch.S.*Tr*.216, *EM*690.49, 725.2; cf. στάδην. 4. ἀργύριον σ. money *out at interest*, Lex Solonis ap.Lys.10.18. III. (στάσις A. II) *weighed, weighable*: τὰ σ., = σταθμία, Cephisod.13; θεωρῶν..τὸν ἄνδρα..ἕλκοντα τὸ τῆς πράξεως σ. Plb.8.19.2.

**στᾰσίνχαλκον**, τό, *stand for a copper vessel*, *PCair.Zen*.14(*b*).17 (iii B.C., pl.).

**στᾰσιοποι-έω**, *stir up sedition*, J.*AJ*17.5.5. **-ία**, ἡ, *stirring up of sedition*, Olymp. *in Grg*. p.251 J. (pl.). **-ός**, όν, *causing sedition*, J.*Vit*.27.

❋ **στάσις** [ᾰ], εως, ἡ, (ἵστημι) *placing, setting*, (sc. δικτύων) X.*Cyn*.2.8, 9.16; τῶν κλιμάκων Plb.5.60.7; *erection* of a statue, εἰκόνος *IG*7.411.34 (Oropus, ii B.C.); στήλης ib.2$^2$.654.59 (iii B.C.), 11(4).1023 (Delos, iii B.C.). 2. *standing stone, pillar*, Lxx *Jd*.9.6. 3. *erection, building*, *PPetr*.3 p.139 (iii B.C., pl.); = ἐργαστήριον, Hsch.; so perh. in *BGU*1122.18,21 (i B.C.). II. (ἵστημι A. IV) *weighing*, αὕτη 'στὶ λοιπὴ σφῷν στάσις Ar.*Ra*.1401; βολίμου *SIG*241 *A* 28 (Delph., iv B.C.); στάσις μισθοῦ the *paying* of the doctor's fee, Hp. *Praec*.4; ἀπὸ τᾶν κοινᾶν ποθόδων..ἐπιλυθῆμεν τοὺς ἐρρυτιασμένους στάσι *IG*4$^2$(1).77.13 (Troezen, ii B.C.).

B. (ἵσταμαι) *standing, stature*, A.*Eu*.36 (marg. M βάσιν); *standing still, stationariness*, defined as ἀπόφασις τοῦ ἰέναι, Pl.*Cra*.426d; opp. φορά, κίνησις, ib.437a, 438c, *Sph*.250a, 251d, Arist.*Metaph*.1025b21, al.; *rest*, as a category of the intelligible, Plot.6.2.8; opp. ἠρεμία, Id.6.3.27; ὀμμάτων στάσιες *fixed stare*, Hp.*Acut*.(*Sp*.)6; σ. ὤτων *pricking* of the ears, Poll.5.61; σ. τῆς γαστρός *constipation*, Orib.*inc*.13.6; [τοῦ αἵματος] *sluggishness*, Hp.*Acut*.(*Sp*.)7; τοῦ ἀέρος, = νηνεμία, Thphr.*Vent*.18, Gal.9.908. 2. *the place in which one stands* or *should stand, position, posture, station*, ἔχοντες σ. ταύτην ἐς τὴν ἔστημεν Hdt.9.21; λέβης..φυλάσσων τὴν ὑπὲρ πυρὸς σ. A.*Fr*.1; ἰδέσθαι.., τίν' ἔχει σ. E.*Fr*.308 (anap.), cf. Ar.*Pl*.954; τὴν Ἰνοῦς σ. ἑστάναι E.*Ba*.925; τῆς αὐτῆς ἠξιοῦτο σ. D.19.272; σ. ἵππων, = ἱππόστασις, σταθμός, *stable, stall*, E.*Fr*.442; ὄνων ἵππων τε στάσεις Ephipp.18; τῆς σ. παρασύρων..τὰς δρῦς Ar.*Eq*.527; κατὰ τὴν σ. δὴ στάντες standing each in his *place*, Antid.2; of military formation, κατάπυκνος σ. close *order*, Ascl.*Tact*.5.1; *row*, ἀμπέλων *Tab.Heracl*.2.77, al., cf. *BGU*1122.18,21 (i B.C., unless in signf. A. I. 3). b. *position in relation to the compass*, ἡ σ. ἤλλακτο τῶν ὡρέων Hdt.2.26; ἡ σ. τοῦ νότου καὶ τῆς μεσαμβρίης ibid.; *setting* of a wind from a quarter, τῶν ἐτησίων ἤδη στάσιν ἐχόντων having *set in*, Plb.5.5.3; γίνεταί τις ἀνέμου σ. Id.1.48.2, cf. Arist.*Mete*.362b33, Thphr.*Sign*.35 (pl.); v. infr. III. 4. c. of planetary connexion, Vett.Val.38.17. d. metaph., from a boxer's *position*, ὥσπερ..ὁρᾶτε τοὺς πύκτας περὶ τῆς σ. ἀλλήλοις διαγωνιζομένους, οὕτω καὶ ὑμεῖς..ὑπὲρ τῆς πόλεως περὶ τῆς σ. (τάξεως codd., but cf. Quint.*Inst*.3.6.3) αὐτῷ μάχεσθε Aeschin.3.206: hence, *position* taken up by a litigant (esp. defendant), Cic.*Top*.25.93; ἐπ' ἀδίκου σ. ἱστάμενος *PRein*.18.16 (ii B.C.); *issue*, σ. ὁρική, νομική, λογική, etc., Hermog.*Stat*.2, cf. Syrian. *in Hermog*.2.55 R. e. *position, opinion* of a philosopher, Plu.*Cic*.4, S.E.*P*.2.48, 3.33,37, al., Marcellin.*Puls*.234. 3. *position, state, condition* of a person, ἐν τῇ καλλίονι στάσει εἶναι Pl.*Phdr*.253d; esp. of moral, social, political *position*, μειρακιώδης Plb.10.33.6; ἰδιώτου Epict.*Ench*.48; φιλοσόφου Arr.*Epict*.3.15.13; σ. ἔχειν ἐν τῷ βίῳ ib.1.21.1; *state of affairs*, *Ostr*.1151.3 (iii A.D.); ἡ σ. τῆς νόσου Hp.*Dieb.Judic*.10, cf. *Mochl*.21 (pl.). 4. στάσις μελῶν, expld. by Sch. as = στάσιμον (q.v.), Ar.*Ra*.1281. II. *party, company, band*, A.*Ag*.1117 (lyr.), *Ch*.114, 458 (lyr.), *Eu*.311 (anap.). III. esp. *party formed for seditious purposes, faction*, Thgn.51, Hdt.1.59,60; ἐπεκράτησε τῇ στάσι ib.173; αἱ τῶν Μεγαρέων σ. Th.4.71. 2. *faction, sedition, discord*, Thgn.781, Sol.4.19, Democr.245, Th.2.65; οἴκων Pi.*N*.9.13, al., cf. Hdt.5.28, al.; σ. ἀντιάνειρα Pi.*O*.12.16; σκεπτομένων πόθεν ἡ σ. how the *row* began, Batr.135; στάσις ἐν ἀλλήλοισιν ὠροθύνετο a *contest*, A.*Pr*.202; ὅστις..στάσιν ποιέοι περὶ γαδαισίας *Berl.Sitzb*.1927.8 (Locr., v B.C.); εἰς λόγου στάσιν ἐπελθών S.*Tr*.1180; σ. γλώσσης Id.*OT*634; στάσει νοσοῦσα πόλις E.*HF*34; τὰς σ. ἐποιοῦντο πρὸς ἀλλήλους Isoc.4.79; στάσεις παύω X.*Mem*.4.6.14; καταλύειν Ar.*Ra*.359; πόλιν εἰς στάσιν ἐμβάλλειν X.*Mem*.4.4.11; τὴν πόλιν εἰς στάσεις κατέστησαν Lys.25.26; κατὰ στάσιν ἀποκτείνειν Id.30.13; opp. πόλεμος, Pl.*R*.470b, cf. *Phd*.66c, Sol. l.c.; στάσεις καὶ διαστάσεις Arist.*Pol*.1296a8. 3. *division, dissent*, στάσιν ἐνέσεσθαι τῇ γνώμῃ Th.2.20; οὐδ' ἔνι σ. there's no *disputing* it, A.*Pers*.738 (troch.). 4. metaph., τὰν ἀνέμων σ. Alc.18 (unless in signf. B. I. 2b); ἀνέμων πνεύματα..στάσιν ἀντίπνουν ἀποδεικνύμενα A.*Pr*.1087 (anap.); σ. κυμάτων Ach.Tat.3.2. IV. στάσεις, = τὰ πεφυκότα σπέρματα, Ar.*Fr*.859. V. *statute, decree*, Lxx *Da*.6.7(8), 1 *Ma*.7.18.

**στᾰσι-ώδης**, ες, *factious, seditious*, Arist.*Pr*.956b29; τὸ κινητικὸν καὶ σ. τῆς δυνάμεως Plb.1.9.6; οἱ -έστατοι τῶν δημοτικῶν D.H.8.15. Adv. -δῶς, ἔχειν Paraphr.Lyc.128. 2. *quarrelsome*, X.*Mem*.2.6.4; πρὸς τοὺς γονεῖς *Cat.Cod.Astr*.2.187. **-ωρός**, ὁ, (ὤρα) *watcher of the station* or *fold*, E.*Cyc*.53 (lyr.). **-ωτεία**, ἡ, *state of faction*, formed after πολιτεία, And.4.8, Pl.*Lg*.832c, f.l. in 715b. **-ώτης**, ου, ὁ, (στάσις B. III) mostly in pl., *members of a party* or *faction in a state, partisans*, οἱ τοῦ Μεγακλέος σ. Hdt.1.60, cf. 59,173, al.; acting as *a body-guard*, Antipho *Fr*.1. 2. metaph. (with punning allusion to στάσις B. I. 1), οἱ τοῦ ὅλου σ. the *partisans* of 'The Whole', opp. οἱ ῥέοντες, Pl.*Tht*.181a; σ. τῆς φύσεως καὶ ἀφυσίκους, of Parmenides and Melissus, who denied motion, Arist.ap.S.E.*M*.10.46. **-ωτικός**, ή, όν, *inclined to faction, seditious*, κατὰ τὸ σ. Th.4.130; καιροί Id.7.57; λόγοι Id.8.92; -κὸν τὸ μὴ ὁμόφυλον Arist.*Pol*.1303a25. Adv. -κῶς Pl.*Phdr*.263a, Arist.*Pol*.1306a38 (v.l. for -αστικῶς).

**στάσκε**, Ion. 3 sg. aor. 2 of ἵστημι.

**στατά**· μακρά (fort. μάκρα, cf. στάγην and v.sq.), Hsch. **στατή**· πάρνη (leg. πόρνη, cf. στρατή), κάρδοπος, Id.

**στατάριον**, τό, *slave-market*, *OGI*524 (Thyatira), *Inscr.Magn*.240 (i B.C.).

**στᾰτέον**, (ἵστημι) *one must appoint*, ἄρχοντα Pl.*R*.503a.

**στάτευσις**, v. στάθευσις.

**στᾰτήρ**, ῆρος, ὁ, (ἵστημι A. IV, cf. *EM*725.11) a weight, = λίτρα, κρόκης πέντε σ. Eup.252, cf. *IG*1$^2$.314.42, Poll.4.173, *BGU*953.2 (iii/iv A.D.), Phot.; σ. Αἰγιναῖος as a weight, Hp.*Mul*.1.78. II. *standard coin*, struck in various materials, whether gold, electrum, or silver: 1. gold, σ. χρυσοῖ, σ. χρυσοῦ, Ar.*Pl*.816, Pl.*Euthd*.299e; of various standards, e.g. σ. Δαρεικός (cf. Δαρεικός) Hdt.7.28, Th.8.28; Δαρεικοῦ χρυσίου στατῆρες *IG*1$^2$.310.103; σ. Κροίσειος Plu.2.823a, Poll.3.87, Hsch.; χρυσοῦ στατῆρες Λαμψακηνοί *IG*1$^2$.339.32, al., cf. 7.2425, al. (Thebes, iv B.C.); σ. Φιλίππειος, Ἀλεξάνδρειος, Poll.9.59, cf. *SIG*285.12 (Erythrae, iv B.C.); Πτολεμαϊκὸς σ. *Inscr.Délos* 442 *B* 190 (ii B.C.). 2. electrum (cf. χρυσός I. 1a), struck at Cyzicus, χρυσίου Κυζικηνοῦ σ. *IG*1$^2$.302.12, al., cf. Lys.32.6; Κύζικος πλέα στατήρων Eup.233; at Phocaea, σ. Φωκαῖται, Φωκαῆς, Th.4.52, D.40.36; Φωκαϊκὼ στατῆρε *IG*2$^2$.1388.42. 3. silver, σ. Αἰγιναῖοι ib.1$^2$.310.111, 2$^2$.1126.17, 1388.70, X.*HG*5.2.22; σ. Κορκυραῖοι *IG*1$^2$.310 add.; σ. Κορίνθιος *SIG*421.39 (Aetolia, iii B.C.), Poll.4.175; in Sicily called δεκάλιτρος σ., Epich.10; σ. πάτριος *SIG*976.8 (Samos, ii B.C.); later applied to the Attic τετράδραχμον, Phot., Suid.; also to the Ptolemaic τ., *PCair.Zen*.567.4, 734.3, *PRev.Laws* 58.7 (all iii B.C.), *BGU*1846.8 (i B.C.), Hero *Geom*.23.55,56; also of the Jewish *shekel*, *Ev.Matt*.17.27. III. *one who owes money, debtor*, πολλοὶ σ., ἀποδοτῆρες οὐδ' ἂν εἷς (οὐδαμεῖ cj. Kaibel) Epich.116.

**στᾰτηρ-ιαῖος**, α, ον, *worth a* στατήρ, Theopomp.Com.21, *PTeb*.406.15 (iii A.D.); *weighing a* στατήρ, *IG*2$^2$.1184.14 (iv B.C.). **-ίσκος**, ὁ, or **-ισμός**, ὁ, name of a tax, *BGU*1843.10 (i B.C.).

**στατιαῖον**· τὸ πενταμνοῦν, Hsch. **στατίδας**· ναύτας εἰς πόλεμον, Id.

**στᾰτ-ίζω**, poet. for ἵστημι, *place*, πόδα S.*Inach*. in *PTeb*.692 iii 12: —Pass., = ἵσταμαι, *stand*, E.*Alc*.89 (lyr.). II. Act. intr., *stand*, Id.*El*.316. 2. = στατιωνίζω, *POxy*.2130.23 (iii A.D.), 65.1 (iii/iv A.D.). III. Med., *establish, prove*, ὅτι.. Phld.*Sign*.26. **-ικός**, ή, όν, (ἵστημι) *causing to stand, bringing to a stand-still*, Arist.*Pr*.908a24; ἀρχὴ σ. principle *of rest*, opp. κινητική, Id.*Metaph*.1049b8, cf. 1019a35, *Top*.127b16; ἄρτου γένος σ. κοιλίας Str.17.2.5 (nisi σταλτ- legend.), cf. Philistion ap.Ath.3.115d: hence, *astringent*, Diph.Siph.ap.Ath.3.80f (Comp.); ἡ -κή an *astringent* herb, *thrift*, *Armeria canescens*, Dsc.*Eup*.2.87; σ. πόα ib.1.110. 2. περὶ σ. ποιήσεως, composition of στάσιμα (q.v.), title of work by Ptolemaeus, *An.Boiss*.4.458. II. (ἵστημι A. IV) *skilled in weighing*, Pl.*Just*.373c,e: ἡ -κή (sc. τέχνη) the *art of weighing*, Id.*Chrm*.166b; opp. μετρητική, Id.*Phlb*.55e. Adv. -κῶς Poll.4.171.

**στατίνη**· ἡ ἐκ στέατος πεποιημένη καὶ ἁπ⟨α⟩λή, Hsch.

❋ **στᾰτἰών**, ῶνος, ἡ (ὁ, *OGI*755.4 (Milet.)); acc. στατιῶναν *IGRom*.3.748.4 (Olympus):— = Lat. *statio*, *IG*14.830.5, al. (Puteoli, ii A.D.), *BGU*326 ii 10 (ii A.D.), *Ostr*.145 (ii A.D.), al., *IGRom*.3.883 (Tarsus, ii/iii A.D.), Hsch. s.v. συνέδρα, Just.*Nov*.44.1.1: hence ❋**στᾰτιωνάριος**, ὁ, = *stationarius*, *IG*14.830.32 (Puteoli, ii A.D.), Ruppel *Der Tempel von Dakke* 3 No.81 (ii A.D.); and **στᾰτιωνίζω**, *to be on duty*, *PAmh*.2.80.12 (iii A.D.); cf. στατίζω II. 2.

**στᾰτός**, ή, όν, (ἵστημι) *placed, standing*, σ. ἵππος a *stalled* horse, Il.6.506; σ. ὕδωρ *standing* water, S.*Ph*.716 (lyr.); στατοῖς λίκνοισι *set up* as votive offerings, Id.*Fr*.844; λίθος σ. *set up*, *AP*9.806. 2. of wine-coolers, bowls, etc., perh. *intended to stand*, i.e. not to be lifted, ψυκτηρίσκον τε στατὸν χωροῦντα χοᾶ καὶ μικρῷ πλέον καὶ.. *PCair.Zen*.38.8, cf. 44.32 (iii B.C.); ψυκτήριον στατόν *Inscr.Délos* 320 *B* 70 (iii B.C.); στατοὺς δύο ψυκτῆρας prob. cj. in Diox.5: as Subst., στατός, ὁ, *large bowl*, σ. καὶ κάδος *Inscr.Délos* 448 *B* 15 (ii B.C.), cf. *IG*11(2).126.12 (Delos, iii B.C.), *Inscr.Délos* 320 *B* 72 (iii B.C.), 442 *B* 93,156 (ii B.C.), *IG*7.3498.12,51 (Orop.); στάτος· σκάφη, ἄλλοι δὲ τὰς πέντε μνᾶς, Hsch. 3. στατός (sc. χιτών), = ὀρθοστάδιον or στάδιος χιτών (cf.

στάδιος I. 3), Duris 70 J., Arr.*Epict.*2.16.9; σ. θώραξ, = στάδιος, Sch. Ar.*Pax* 1227. **4.** σ. αὐτόματα *standing*, forming tableaux, with restricted movements, opp. ὑπάγοντα, Hero *Aut.*1.7, 20.1. **II.** Στατοί, οἱ, officials at Sparta, *IG*5(1).145.2 (iii B.C.); compared with the Ἀγαθοεργοί, *AB*305; στατῶν is cj. for ἀστῶν in Hdt.1.67. **III.** σ. ἱερεῖς, at Rhodes, *permanently appointed* priests, *SIG*725*a* (i B.C.), cf. *IG*12(1).786.9.

**στάτρια**· ἐμπλέκτρια, Hsch.

**στάτωρ**, ορος, ὁ, = Lat. *stator*, *usher* in a law-court, *OGI*665.23 (Egypt, i A.D.), *IG*14.991.6, *Supp.Epigr.*7.525,526 (Dura).

**σταυνίξ**· ἱέραξ, Hsch.

**σταυρ-ικός**, ή, όν, *of* or *by a cross*, θάνατος Tz.*H.*4.220. **-ίον**, τό, Dim. of σταυρός, Theognost.*Can.*122.

® **σταυρο-ειδής**, ές, *like a cross*, Aët.7.37. Adv. -ειδῶς Hsch. s.v. σταυροτύπως. **-κόμιστος**, = *furcifer*, *Gloss.*

**σταυρός**, ὁ, *upright pale* or *stake*, σταυροὺς ἐκτὸς ἔλασσε διαμπερὲς ἔνθα καὶ ἔνθα πυκνοὺς καὶ θαμέας Od.14.11, cf. Il.24.453, Th.4.90, X. *An.*5.2.21; of *piles* driven in to serve as a foundation, Hdt.5.16, Th.7.25. **II.** *cross*, as the instrument of crucifixion, D.S.2.18, *Ev.Matt.*27.40, Plu.2.554a; ἐπὶ τὸν σ. ἀπάγεσθαι Luc.*Peregr.*34; σ. λαμβάνειν, ἆραι, βαστάζειν, metaph. of voluntary suffering, *Ev. Matt.*10.38, *Ev.Luc.*9.23, 14.27: its form was represented by the Greek letter T, Luc.*Jud.Voc.*12. **b.** *pale for impaling* a corpse, Plu.*Art.*17.

**σταυρό-τῠπος**, ον, *marked with the cross*, in Adv. -πως, Hsch. **-φόρος**, ον, *bearing a cross*, *MAMA*3.632 (Corycus).

**σταυρ-όω**, (σταυρός) *fence with pales*, Th.7.25; σ. τὰ βάθη ξύλοις D.S.24.1:—Pass., Th.6.100. **II.** *crucify*, Plb.1.86.4, *Ev.Matt.*20. 19, Critodem. in *Cat.Cod.Astr.*8(4).200: metaph., σ. τὴν σάρκα *crucify* it, *destroy* its power, *Ep.Gal.*5.24, cf. 6.14: ἧλος ἐσταυρωμένος nail *from a cross*, as amulet, Asclep.Jun.ap.Alex.Trall.1. 15. **-ωμα**, ατος, τό, *palisade* or *stockade*, Th.5.10, 6.64,74, X. *HG*3.2.3, etc. **-ώσιμος**, ον, *deserving crucifixion*, Hsch. s.v. σκολοπώνυμον. **-ωσις**, εως, ἡ, *stockade*, Th.7.25.

® **στᾰφῐδευταῖος**, α, ον, (σταφίς) *of dried grapes*, = στεμφυλίτης, τρύγες Hp.*Morb.*3.17; **σταφίδιοι** οἶνοι *raisin* wines, ibid.; **σταφιδίτης** οἶνος Orib.*Fr.*19, *Gloss.*

**στᾰφῐδοποιία**, ἡ, *making of raisins*, *Gp.*5.52.

**στᾰφῐδόω**, *dry grapes*, *make* them *into raisins*, Dsc.5.19:—Pass., *Gp.*5.45.4.

® **στᾰφίς**, ίδος, ἡ, = ἀσταφίς I (q.v.), Lxx *Nu.*6.3, al., *PCair.Zen.*13. 16 (iii B.C.), *Inscr.Délos* 464.5 (ii B.C.). **II.** a plant, σ. ἀγρία, *stavesacre*, *Delphinium Staphisagria*, Hp.*Nat.Mul.*95, Dsc.4.152; *staphis*, Plin.*HN*23.17.

**στάφος**· σκάφος, λεκάνη, Hsch.

**στᾰφῠλ-άγρα**, ἡ, *forceps for taking hold of the uvula*, Hp.*Medic.*9, Paul.Aeg.6.31. **-επάρτης**, ου, ὁ, (ἐπαίρω) = foreg., Id.3.26. ® **-ή**, ἡ, *bunch of grapes*, σταφυλῇσι μέγα βρίθουσαν ἀλωὴν Il.18.561; ἡμερὶς ἡβώωσα τεθήλει δὲ σταφυλῇσι Od.5.69, cf. 7.121; σταφυλαὶ παντοῖαι 24.343, cf. Pl.*Lg.*844e, *Apoc.*14.18; Πυρναίαις σ. Theoc.1.46; of ripe, fresh grapes, opp. ὄμφαξ on the one hand, and σταφίς on the other, *AP*5.303: collectively in sg., *PPetr.*3 p.60 (iii B.C.), *PCair.Zen.*300.14 (iii B.C.), *POxy.*116.18 (ii A.D.), etc. **2.** σ. ἀγρία, = μήλωθρον I, Thphr.*HP*3.18.11, Plin.*HN*23.21. **II.** *uvula when swollen at the end so as to resemble a grape* on the stalk, Hp. *Prog.*23, Nicopho 28, Arist.*HA*$493^{a}3$; of the *uvula* generally, Archig. ap.Gal.12.969,974; *inflammation of the uvula*, *IG*$4^{2}$(1).126.30 (Epid., ii A.D.), Gal.7.731 (pl.). **III.** parox. σταφύλη, *plummet of a level*, ἵπποι.. σταφύλῃ ἐπὶ νῶτον ἐΐσαι horses equal in height even *by the level*, matched to a nicety, Il.2.765, cf. Call.*Fr.*159, Hsch., *EM*742. 44. **-ηγέω**, *transport grapes*, *PTeb.*585 (ii A.D.).

**στᾰφῠλη-κόμος**, ον, (κομέω) *cultivating grapes*, Nonn.*D.*9.29, 12. 21. **-τομία**, ἡ, *excision of the uvula*, Poll.4.185. ® **-τόμος**, ον, *grape-cutting*, Nonn.*D.*7.165. **-φόρος**, ὁ, *grape-gatherer*, *PLond.* 1821.220.

**στᾰφῠλίζειν**· τὸ συνι(σ)άζειν τὰς ὤας τοῦ ἱματίου, Hsch.

**στᾰφῠλῖνος**, ὁ, and (in Numen.ap.Ath.9.371c) ἡ, *carrot*, Hp.*Steril.* 242, Nic.*Fr.*71; σ. κηπευτός, *cultivated carrot*, *Daucus Carota*, Dsc. 3.52; σ. ἄγριος, *wild carrot*, *Daucus guttatus*, ibid.; σ. χλωρός Aët. 12.42. **2.** = βρυωνία, Crateuas ap.Sch.Nic.*Th.*858. **II.** σ., ὁ, an insect, about the size of the σφονδύλη (perh. *the Meloë*), Arist. *HA*$604^{b}18$, *Hippiatr.*119, Hsch.

**στᾰφῠλιοκαύστης**, ου, ὁ, *instrument for cauterizing the uvula*, Paul.Aeg.6.31 (v.l. σταφυλο-).

**στᾰφύλ-ιον** [ῠ], τό, Dim. of σταφυλή, M.Ant.6.13, *PFay.*127.8 (ii/ iii A.D.). **-ίς**, ίδος, ἡ, *bunch of grapes*, Theoc.27.9. **II.** *swollen uvula*, Hp.*Morb.*2.29 vulg. (-ή Littré with good Mss.); gloss on γαργαρεών, Hsch. **-ίτης** [ῑ], ου, ὁ, *guardian of grapes*, epith. of Dionysus, Ael.*VH*3.41.

**στᾰφῠλο-βολεῖον**, τό, Poll.7.151, 10.129; and **-βόλιον**, Id.1.245, *AB*303, *vat* or *basket in which grapes are put for pressing*. **-δενδρον**, τό, *bladder-nut*, *Staphylea pinnata*, Plin.*HN*16.69. **-δρόμας**, α, ὁ, a religious official at Sparta, *IG*5(1).650,651; **-δρόμος** in *AB*305, Hsch.; expld. as participants in a ceremonial pursuit at the Carneia, *AB* l.c.; as παρορμῶντες τοὺς ἐπὶ τρύγῃ, Hsch. l.c. **-κάτοχον**, τό, = σταφυλάγρα, Aët. ap. J.G.Schneider ad Nic. *Al.*511 p.243 (Halle 1792). **-καύστης**, ου, ὁ, = σταφυλιο- (q.v.), Paul.Aeg.6.79. **-κλοπίδης**, ου, Dor. **-δας**, ὁ, *grape-stealer*, *AP*9. 348 (Leon.Alex.). **-λόγον**, v. σταχυολόγον. **-τομέω**, *cut grapes*, or *excise the uvula*; a play on both meanings in Artem.3.46 (Pass.): the latter sense in Vett.Val.127.20 (Pass.). **-τομία**, ἡ, *excision of the uvula*, Id.110.3. **-τόμον**, τό, *knife for cutting the uvula*, Paul. Aeg.6.31. **-φόρος**, ον, *carrying grapes*, κόφινοι Eust.1625.14. **II.** τὸ σ. μόριον, = σταφυλή II, *the uvula*, Arist.*HA*$493^{a}2$.

**στᾰφύλωμα** [ῠ], ατος, τό, *a defect in the eye inside the cornea*, Cels. 7.7.11, Dsc.1.105, Gal.7.732, 19.435, Aët.7.36,37.

**σταχάνη**, ἡ, (ἵστημι, στήκω) *balance*: prov., δικαιότερος σταχάνης Zen.3.16, Diogenian.4.28, Lib.*Ep.*1363, Suid., etc.

® **στάχι**, τό, a sort of *vermilion*, Theodos.*Can.* p.343 H.

**στᾰχῠη-κομέω**, *to be decked with ears of corn*, of fields, Opp.*C.*2. 150. ® **-κόμος**, ον, *cultivating ears of corn*, Δημήτηρ Nonn.*D.*1. 104. **-λόγος**, ον, *gleaning ears of corn*, Eust.100.14.

**στᾰχῠηρός**, ά, όν, *bearing ears of corn*, σπέρμα Thphr.*HP*9.16.4; τὰ σ. *plants that bear ears*, *cereals*, ib.1.11.4, al.

**στᾰχῠη-τόμος**, ον, *cutting ears of corn*, *reaping*, ὅπλον *AP*6.95 (Antiphil.). ® **-τρόφος**, ον, *nourishing ears of corn*, αὖλαξ ib.7.209 (Antip.). **-φορέω**, *bear ears of corn* (v.l. σταχυοφ-), Ph.2.400, al. **-φόρος**, ον, *bearing ears of corn*, *IG*3.1311, Ph.2.583, Doroth. ap.Heph.Astr.3.30, Man.4.454.

**στᾰχῠ-ῖτις**, ιδος, ἡ, = ποταμογείτων, Ps.-Dsc.4.100 (v.l. -ίτης). **II.** = τριπόλιον, Id.3.106, 4.132 (v.l. -ίτης). **-μήτωρ**, ορος, ἡ, *mother of ears of corn*, of Isis, *APl.*4.264; τύρσις, of Egypt, *Sammelb.*5829.7.

**στᾰχῠο-βολέω**, *put forth ears*, Thphr.*CP*1.20.2. **-ειδής**, ές, *spiked like an ear of wheat*, Dsc.4.15. **-θριξ**, τρῐχος, ὁ, ἡ, = foreg., νάρδος *AP*4.1.43 (Mel.). **-λογέω**, *glean ears of corn*, Sch.Theoc.3.32. **-λόγον**, τό, prob.l. for σταφυλο-, Suid. s.v. ποίην. **-ομαι**, Pass., *grow in a spike* or *as an ear*, σπέρμα ἐσταχυωμένον Dsc.4.1. **-πλόκᾰμος**, ον, *wreathed with ears of corn*, Orph.*L.*242. **-στέφᾰνος**, ον, *crowned with ears of corn*, Δηώ *AP*6.104 (Phil.). **-τομέω**, *reap corn*, Sch. A.R.4.982. **-τόμος**, ὁ, = Lat. *tribulum*, Charis. p.554 K. **-τρόφος**, ον, *nourishing ears of corn*, Orph.*H.*40.3. **-φορέω**, *bear ears of corn*, Ph.2.400.

® **στάχυς** [στᾰχῡς E.*HF*5, but στᾰχῠν Call.*Dian.*130, A.R.1.688], υος, ὁ: pl. στάχυες *IG*$1^{2}$.280.78, $2^{2}$.1424*a*333, etc.; Ep. dat. σταχύεσσιν Il.23.598; acc. στάχῡς Ar.*Eq.*393, *OGI*56.68 (Canopus, iii B.C.), but στάχυας Lxx *Ge.*41.7, etc.:—*ear of corn*, in pl., Il.l.c., Hes.*Op.*473, *Ev. Matt.*12.1, etc.; τοὺς ὑπερέχοντας τῶν σ. Arist.*Pol.*$1284^{a}30$: in sg., A.*Supp.*761, *Fr.*304.7, S.*Fr.*395, and freq. in E., *Hec.*593, al.: metaph., σ. ἄτης A.*Pers.*821; ἐκ καλάμης.. στάχυες, of Bacchylides' poems, *AP*4.1.34 (Mel.):—of the Theban Σπαρτοί, E.*Ph.*939, *HF*5, *Ba.*264; of *the crop reaped* by Cleon in capturing the Spartans at Sphacteria, Ar.*Eq.*393; βίον θερίζειν ὥστε κάρπιμον σ. E.*Fr.*757.6. **2.** generally, *scion*, *progeny*, σ. ἄρσην Id.*Fr.*360.22, cf. Lyc.214; δισσὸν Βορέου σ. Orph.*A.*218; τέκνων Man.6.304; Ἰνδῶν Nonn.*D.*18.267; Ἑλλάδος ἀμώων ἄγαμον σ. *AP*9.362.25. **3.** name of the chief star in the constellation Virgo, *Spica Virginis*, Arat.97, Ptol.*Alm.*7.5: in pl., Man. 2.134. **II.** *lower part of the abdomen*, Heliod.ap.Orib.50.26 tit., Poll.2.168, cf. Eust.194.4, 410.17. **III.** *base horehound*, *Stachys germanica*, Dsc.3.106, Plin.*HN*24.136. **IV.** νάρδου στάχυς, = ναρδόσταχυς, *Gp.*7.13.1; ὁ τῆς νάρδου σ. Gal.6.267. **V.** *surgical bandage*, '*spica*' *bandage*, Heliod.ap.Orib.48.46 tit., Gal.18(1). 814. **VI.** παρὰ τοῖς ναυπηγοῖς τὸ ἐπὶ τῆς φάλαγγος μεριζόμενον, Hsch. **VII.** = Heb. *shibboleth*, Lxx *Jd.*12.6.

**στᾰχῠώδης**, ες, *like ears of corn*: *cereal*, τῶν σιτηρῶν τὰ σ. Thphr. *HP*1.14.2; πᾶν τὸ σ. ib.8.3.3; σ. κούρη *the constellation Virgo* (cf. στάχυς I. 3), Nonn.*D.*2.655.

**στεάζω**, *fatten*, Al.*Ps.*19(20).4.

® **στέαρ**, τό, gen. στέατος [v. sub fin.]; contr. **στῆρ**, *PCair.Zen.*703. 2,6 (iii B.C.), Archig. ap. Gal.12.861, Thd.*Bel* 27, gen. στῆτος *PCair. Zen.*176.183 (iii B.C.); also **στεῖαρ**, gen. στείατος Choerob. *in Theod.* 1.350 H.:—*hard fat*, *suet*, such as ruminating animals have, opp. πιμελή (soft fat), ἐκ δὲ στέατος ἔνεικε μέγαν τροχὸν a large cake of *suet*, Od.21.178; οὔτε πιμελὴν οὔτε στέαρ Arist.*PA*$651^{a}26$; τὸ τῶν ἰχθύων σ. πιμελῶδες Id.*HA*$520^{a}21$, al. **2.** any *animal fat*, σ. τῆς ἄρκτου Thphr.*Od.*63; σ. δελφίνων X.*An.*5.4.28; freq. in Lxx (*Le.*3. 15,16,17, al.); also *PRev.Laws* 50.14 (iii B.C.), *PCair.Zen.* ll. cc.; so σ. χήνειον, ὀρνίθειον, etc., Dsc.2.76. **II.** = σταῖς (q.v.), *dough made from flour of spelt*, Hp.*Nat.Mul.*27 (but σταῖς is prob. l.), Arist.*Pr.*$879^{a}10$, Thphr.*HP*9.20.2, Lxx *Ps.*80(81).17, al., Str.17.2.5 (citing Hdt.2.36, where σταῖς is in our text). [Gen. στέατος disyll., Od. l. c.; στέᾰτι trisyll., Diph.119; cf. στεάτιον.] (Prob. fr. *στᾱγ-αρ, cf. Skt. *styā̆yate* 'congeal, grow hard'.)

**στεάτ-ῖνος** [ᾰ], η, ον, (στέαρ II) = σταίτινος, Aesop.58:—also **-ίτης** [ῑ] (sc. πλακοῦς), ὁ, Hsch. s.v. πίονες. **-ιον**, τό, Dim. of στέαρ, Alex.84. **II.** = ζύμη (cf. Aët.8.51), Paul.Aeg.3.28.8.

**στεᾱτο-κήλη**, ἡ, *sebaceous formation in the scrotum*, Gal.14. 780. **-ομαι**, Pass., *to be fatted*, μόσχοι ἐστεατωμένοι Lxx *Ez.*39. 18. **II.** *have a* στεάτωμα, *Hippiatr.*26.11,27.

**στεᾱτ-ώδης**, ες, *like tallow* or *suet*, φάρμακα Hp.*Ulc.*2, cf. Arist. *PA*$651^{b}30$, al.; ζῷα σ. animals *that have tallow* or *suet*, Id.*HA*$520^{a}14$; -ώδης ἀποφορά Dsc.2.76.12, cf. Antyll.ap.Sch.Orib.45.2.3. **-ωμα**, ατος, τό, *sebaceous tumour*, Dsc.*Eup.*1.148, Antyll.ap.Orib.45.2.1, Gal.10.158, Poll.4.203:—also Dim. **-ωμάτιον**, τό, Heliod.ap.Orib. 45.5.3.

**στεγ-άζω**, = στέγω, *cover*, ἀσπίδες στεγάζουσι τὰ σώματα X.*Cyr.*7.1. 33; τὸ στεγάζον, of the body *which covers* the soul, Epicur.*Ep.*1 p.21 U., cf. pp.8, 20 U. (Pass.); *roof* a building, *IG*$2^{2}$.1046.16 (i B.C.), Lxx 2*Ch.*34.11; [περιστάσεις] σ. γείσεσιν λιθίνοις *OGI*483.126 (Pergam., ii A.D.): metaph., στεγάσαι φρενὸς εἴσω Emp.3; ὕπνος σ. τινά *covers, embraces*, S.*El*.781:—Pass., στεγάζεσθαι τῇ γῇ Thphr.*CP*1.12.3, cf. X.*Oec*.19.13; πλοῖον ἐστεγασμένον a *decked* vessel, Antipho 5.22; ἵνα στεγασθῇ (sc. τὰ χώματα) *be rendered water-tight*, *PSI*5.486.10 (iii B.C.); [οἰκία] ἐστεγασμένη *roofed*, *PCair.Zen*.251.7 (iii B.C.). **-άνη** [ᾰ], ἡ, *a covering*, *AP*6.294 (Phan.): hence **-ανίσαι**· στέγη ὑποδεχθῆναι, Hsch.

**στεγᾰνομ-έομαι**, Med., *provide oneself with rented lodgings*, *PHal*.1.172 (iii B.C.). **-ιον**, τό, *room-rent, rent of lodgings*, Poll.1.75, 10.20, Ath.1.8d, Mitteis *Chr*.96 iii 3 (iv A.D.). 2. = ὁ τόπος ἐν ᾧ ἐστιῶνται, Eust.1761.25. **-ος** (parox.), ον, (στέγη, νέμω A. III) *inhabiting a house*, Lyc.1095; ὁ σ. *the master of a house*, Poll.1.74, 10.20. 2. title of a religious official, *SIG*1021.33 (Olympia, i B.C.).

❋ **στεγᾰνόπους**, ποδος, ὁ, ἡ, *covering oneself with one's feet*, Alcm. 118. II. *web-footed*, opp. σχιζόπους, Arist.*HA*504ᵃ7, 593ᵃ27, al.; τὰ στεγανόποδα Id.*PA*692ᵇ24, al.

❋ **στεγᾰν-ός**, ή, όν, (στέγω) *covering so as to keep out water, water-tight*, τρίχα X.*Cyn*.5.10; πλοῖα Arist.*Fr*.554; of other things, κλῶνες.. κεράμων -ώτεροι *AP*9.71 (Antiphil.); πυκνὸν καὶ σ. Plu.2.692a; προβλημάτων -ώτατον πρὸς οἰστούς Id.*Ant*.45. 2. generally, *enclosing, confining*, δίκτυον A.*Ag*.358 (anap.). II. *closely covered, sheathed*, λευκῆς χιόνος πτέρυγι στεγανός, of Polynices, represented as an eagle, *covered* by his white Argive shield (cf. λεύκασπις), S.*Ant*.114 (anap.); of a building, ἄνωθεν σ. *roofed over*, Th.3.21, cf. *Trag.Adesp*.115, Call.*Cer*.55, D.H.1.26; οὓς [ναοὺς].. δοκὸς στεγανοὺς παρέχει E.*Fr*.472.6 (anap.). 2. *strongly fortified*, πόλις Aristid.*Or*.21(22).12 (Comp.); ἕρκη Lib.*Decl*.23.77 (Sup.). 3. *indoor*, δίαιτα, opp. open-air life, Ph.2.297. 4. metaph., τὸ ἀκόλαστον αὐτοῦ καὶ οὐ σ. its intemperance and *leakiness*, Pl.*Grg*.493b; and of persons, *close, reserved*, prov., Ἀρεοπαγίτου -ώτερος Alciphr.1.13, cf. Them.*Or*.21.263a, *Or*.26.323d, etc. III. Adv. -νῶς *confinedly, through a covered passage* or *tube*, ἡ πνοὴ ἰοῦσα σ. Th.4.100; πωμάσαι σ. cover *tightly*, Dsc.2.76.14: Comp., -ώτερον πρὸς τὰς τῶν ὑετῶν φορὰς ἀντέχειν Ph.2.513; ναῦς -ώτατα ἔχει Aristid.*Or*.34(50).31. 2. metaph., -ώτερον φρονεῖν *AP*5.215 (Agath.); -ώτατα κατεῖχεν ἔνδον τὴν αὐτοῦ γνώμην Memn. 6.—Cf. στεγνός. **-ότης**, ητος, ἡ, *imperviousness*, Eust. ad D.P. 1166. **-όω**, = στέγω, Alex.Trall.3.2:—Pass., *to be covered over, silted up*, Ephor.65(b) J.; *to be blocked*, of pores, *Hippiatr*.44. **-ωμα**, ατος, τό, *roofing-timber*, *EM*725.43, Hsch.

**στέγ-αρχος**, ὁ, *master of the house*, Hdt.1.133, Antiph.171. ❋ **-άσιμος** [ᾰ], ον, *for roofing*, πάπυροι στεγάσιμοι εἰς τὴν θαλαμηγόν *PLond. ined*.2093 (iii B.C.). 2. *shady*, Hsch. s.v. ἐρέψιμον. ❋ **-ᾰσις**, εως, ἡ, *covering*: *roofing*, *IG*4²(1).102.214, al. (Epid., iv B.C.), *Inscr.Délos* 459.9 (ii B.C.); also written **-ασσις**, *IG*4²(1).103.60 (Epid., iv B.C.); **-αξις**, ib.286. **-ασμα**, ατος, τό, *anything which covers* or *shelters, covering*, X.*An*.1.5.10 (pl.); ἐν τεύτλου κρύπτεται στεγάσμασιν Antiph. 181; σ. ᾠὰς ἢ διφθέρας *SIG*1259.5 (Athens, iv B.C.); τὰ σ. τοῖς πλοίοις *awnings*, *PCair.Zen*.53.7 (iii B.C.). 2. *roof*, opp. σκέπασμα, Pl.*Plt*.279d, cf. *Criti*.111c. **-αστέον**, *one must cover*, τί τινι X.*Eq*. 12.7. **-αστήρ**, ῆρος, ὁ, *coverer*: hence, *tile*, Hsch. s.v. σωλῆνες; κέραμος σ. Poll.7.124, 10.182; ὁ σ. ὄροφος ib.172. II. = τὸ θριωτὸν (θρίωπον cod.) ἔψημα, Hsch. **-αστής**, οῦ, ὁ, *one who covers*, *Gloss*. **-αστός**, ή, όν, *covered, sheltered*, Str.16.4.13, Poll.10.52. **-αστρίς**, ίδος, ἡ, *serving for waterproof covering*, διφθέραι Hdt. 1.194. II. as Subst., prob. *roof*, *OGI*109.4 (Antaeopolis, ii A.D.). ❋ **-αστρον**, τό, *covering, cover, wrapper*, esp. of leather (Poll. 10.180), A.*Ch*.992(984), *Fr*.367, Plu.*Crass*.3, *POxy*.109.20 (iii/iv A.D.); = *segestrum*, *Gloss*.; cf. Varro *LL*5.166. 2. *place in which to hide* or *keep* anything, *receptacle*, Antiph.52.9. ❋ **-η**, Dor. and Aeol. **στέγα**, ἡ, *roof*, A.*Ag*.897, Hdt.6.27, X.*Mem*.3.8.9, *Ev.Marc*.2.4, etc.; παρέχειν τινὶ σ. give one *shelter*, Arist.*Fr*.631; στέγῃ δέχεσθαί τινας *OGI*665.25 (Egypt, i A.D.). 2. *ceiling*, Alc.15, Call.*Iamb*.1.115 (*Hermes* 69.169). II. *roofed place, chamber, room*, Hdt.2.2, 148, 175, Eup.347, X.*Oec*.8.13, etc.; *covered vestibule*, *IG*2².1046.13; ἑρκεῖος σ., of *a tent*, S.*Aj*.108; a hare's *seat* or *form*, Id.*Fr*.174; ἐκ κατώρυχος σ., of the grave, Id.*Ant*.1100, cf. 888. 2. *storey* of a house, *PStrassb*.110.6 (iii B.C.), *PCair.Zen*.766.4 (iii B.C.), etc.; ἡ ἀνωτάτη σ. Str.15.3.7; αἱ στέγαι the upper *storeys*, *PPetr*.2 p.28 (iii B.C.), cf. *SIG*344.16 (Teos, iv B.C.), *IG*4²(1).102.293 (Epid., iv B.C.), *PLond*.3.1164*f* 28 (iii A.D.). 3. freq. in pl., *house, dwelling*, A.*Ag*.3, 518, al.; κατὰ στέγας at *home*, S.*OT*637, al.; ἐπελεῦσαι τῷ ἀνδρὶ ἐπὶ στέγαν to the man's *house*, *Leg.Gort*.3.46, cf. *Schwyzer* 177.3 (Crete, v B.C.). III. *deck of a ship*, in Lat. *stega*, Plaut.*Bacch*.278, *Stich*.413. **-ήρης**, ες, *roofed*, οἶκος Moschio Trag.6.7. **-ῖτις**, ιδος, ἡ, (στέγος IV) *prostitute*, Poll.7.201, Hsch.

**στεγνο-πᾰθέω**, *suffer from constriction*, Sor.1.29, 65, Cass.*Pr*. 70. ❋ **-ποιέω**, (στεγνός I. 2) *build barracks* or *dwellings*, in Med., *Inscr.Perg*.158.

**στεγν-ός**, ή, όν, = στεγανός, *watertight, waterproof*, πῖλος Hdt.4.23; οἰκήματα σ. πρὸς ὕδωρ καὶ πρὸς χιόνα Hp.*Aër*.18, cf. Thphr. *CP*6.19.3; βοῶνες *PSI*5.497.5 (iii B.C.); τέγη *IG*12(7).62.25 (Amorgos, iv B.C.); στέγν' ἔχων σκηνώματα, of a cave, E.*Cyc*.324; of a boat, *PPetr*.3 p.136 (iii B.C.); of embankments, *PSI*5.486.8 (iii B.C.); of cisterns, etc., *OGI*483.194, al. (Pergam., ii A.D.). 2. Subst. στεγνόν, τό, *covered dwelling*, X.*An*.7.4.12, D.S.18.25, etc.; ἐν στεγνῷ ποιεῖσθαι τὰς νεοττιάς *under cover*, Arist.*HA*618ᵃ35; ἐν τῷ σ. φυλάττειν Id.*Mir*.844ᵇ13. II. *costive*, Hp.*Mul*.1.36, Dsc.5.9; τὰ σ. περὶ κύστιν καὶ νεφροὺς πάθη Id.1.3. III. στεγνὰ πτερά wings *joined by a membrane*, like those of the bat, Nic.*Th*.762. **-ότης**, ητος, ἡ, *closeness, costiveness*, Hp.*Acut*.(*Sp*.)46; ἡ τῶν σωμάτων σ. *density, imperviousness*, Id.*de Arte* 11.

**στεγνοφυής**, ές, *of thick nature*, *AP*11.354.15 (Agath.).

**στεγν-όω**, *close*, πώματι τὸ ἀγγεῖον Gal.17(2).160, cf. 161:—Pass., Hero *Spir*.1 *Praef*., al.; of the pores, Gal.18(1).145. 2. *make* a building *watertight*, *IG*11(2).154*A* 36, cf. 161*A* 114 (Delos, iii B.C.):—Pass., of embankments, χώματα ἐστεγνωμένα *PSI*4.315.25 (ii A.D.). II. *make costive*, Alex.Aphr.*Pr*.1 *Praef*. (Pass.); *check discharge*, μήτρα ἐστεγνωμένη Dsc.1.23; ὦτα πυορροοῦντα στεγνοῖ Id.2.81. 2. *compress*, πάπυρος στεγνουμένη Id.1.86; ἔριον μαλακὸν ἐστενωμένον (fort. ἐστεγνωμένον) Heliod.ap.Orib.46.19.2. **-ωσις**, εως, ἡ, *making watertight*, τοῦ ἱεροποιοῦ *IG*11(2).165.7 (Delos, iii B.C.): pl., *BGU*1116.12 (i B.C.). II. *making close* or *costive, checking of natural evacuations*, κοιλίας Dsc.1.115; *stoppage of the pores*, Gal.6.218, Orib.*Syn*.5.16; opp. χαύνωσις, S.E.*P*.1.238; cf. στένωσις. **-ωτικός**, ή, όν, *making costive, astringent*, Dsc.1.115; σ. κοιλίας ibid., cf. Meges ap.Orib.44.24.9.

❋ **στεγο-νόμια**, τά, = στεγανόμιον, *rent*, Just.*Nov*.88.2. **-ποιέομαι**, Med., *build oneself a house*, Procl. ad Hes.*Op*.569.

**στέγος**, εος, τό, = τέγος, prop. *roof*, Lxx *Ep.Je*.10 (v. l. τέγους), D.S. 19.45, *IG*5(1).1114.14 (Geronthrae), Poll.1.81, Lib.*Or*.11.162, and so perh. in E.*IT*48; ἐπὶ τὸ αὐτὸ σ. ἐλθεῖν 'under the same *roof*', *SIG* 1179.20 (Cnidus). II. mostly, like στέγη, *house, mansion*, A.*Pers*. 141 (anap.), *Ag*.310, S.*Aj*.307, etc.; prob. in *OGI*619.5 (Syria, iv A.D.). III. δέξαι μ' ἐς τὸ σὸν σ., i.e. into *the urn* containing his ashes, S.*El*.1165; *grave*, Lyc.1098. IV. *brothel*, στεγέεσσι Man. 2.430, cf. 6.533.

**στεγύλλιον**, τό, *workshop*, Herod.7.83.

**στέγω**, used by early writers mainly in pres. and impf.: fut. στέξω dub. cj. in D.S.11.29: aor. ἔστεξα Plb.8.12.5, Plu.*Alex*.35, etc.:—Med., aor. ἐστέξατο cj. for ἐδέξατο in *AP*13.27 (Phal.):—Pass., aor. ἐστέχθην Simp. in *Epict*.p.117 D.:—*cover closely, so as to keep* a fluid either *out* or *in*, Pl.*Ti*.78a (of fire): **A.** *keep out* water, δόμος ἅλα στέγων a house *that keeps out* the sea, i.e. a good ship, A.*Supp*.135 (lyr.): abs., νῆες οὐδὲν στέγουσαι not *water-tight*, Th.2.94; εὐνὰς τοιαύτας οἵας.. στέγειν.. ἱκανὰς εἶναι Pl.*R*.415e, cf. *Ti*. 45c, *Cra*.412d; τῇ.. στεγούσῃ γῇ in the *impervious* earth, Id.*Criti*. 111d; συμμύει καὶ στέγει, of timber, Thphr.*HP*5.7.4, cf. 5.4.5; οἰκία στέγουσα *IG*2².2498.23, cf. 12(5).568.12 (Ceos, v/iv B.C.):—so in Med., στέγετο.. ὄμβρους *kept off* the rain *from himself*, Pi.*P*.4.81; νεῦς οὐκ ἐστέξατο κῦμα *AP*l. c. (v. supr.); ταῦτα δὲ παρέξοντι οἰκοδομημένα καὶ στεγόμενα καὶ τεθυρωμένα *Tab.Heracl*.1.142. 2. of other things, *fend off, repel*, οὔτε οἱ πῖλοι ἔστεγον τὰ τοξεύματα Th.4.34; δόρυ πολέμιον στέγειν A.*Th*.216; στέγων γὰρ ἐχθροὺς θάνατον εἵλετ' ib.1014; σ. τὰς πληγάς Ar.*V*.1295; στέγει ἡ σὰρξ τὸ προσπῖπτον θερμὸν Arist. *Pr*.889ᵃ11. 3. later, *bear up, sustain, support*, ἡ θάλαττα.. σ. τὰ βάρη Id.*Fr*.217; σ. τὸν ὄροφον J.*AJ*5.8.12; τοῦ κρυστάλλου στέγοντος τὰς διαβάσεις στρατοπέδων D.S.3.34; *bear up against, endure, resist*, τὴν ἐπιφοράν, ἔφοδον, Plb.3.53.2, 18.25.4, cf. *SIG*700.23 (Lete, ii B.C.); σ. νόσον *AP*11.340 (Pall.); τὸ δυσῶδες Memn.2.4; τὰς ἐνδείας Ph.2.526; ἡ ἀγάπη.. πάντα σ. 1*Ep.Cor*.13.7, cf. 9.12: abs., *contain oneself, hold out*, στέγειν, καρτερεῖν *Lyr.Alex.Adesp*.1.30, cf. 1*Ep.Thess*.3.1, 5; ἔστεξα ἕως ἔλθῃς *POxy*.1775.10 (iv A.D.) (in S.*OT* 11 στέξαντες is f.l. for στέρξαντες).

**B.** *keep in, hold* water, etc., δάκρυον ὄμματ' οὐκέτι στέγει prob. f.l. in E.*IA*888 (troch.); οὐκ ἂν δυναίμην μὴ στέγοντα πιμπλάναι I could not fill *leaky vessels*, Id.*Fr*.899; ὕδωρ σ., of a vessel, Pl.*R*.621a: metaph., τὴν ψυχὴν κοσκίνῳ ἀπῄκασε.. τετρημένην, ἅτε οὐ δυναμένην στέγειν δι' ἀπιστίαν καὶ λήθην Pl.*Grg*.493c; [ψυχὴν] στέγουσαν οὐδὲν Id.*Lg*.714a; in Id.*R*.586b, τὸ στέγον ἑαυτῶν prob. means the *continent part* of each man, cf. στεγανός II. 4. II. generally, *contain, hold*, ἄγγος σῶμα τοὐκείνου σ. S.*El*.1118, cf. E.*Ion* 1412; ὄχλον σ. δῶμα Id.*Hipp*. 843. III. *shelter, protect*, πύργοι πόλιν στέγουσιν S.*OC*15 codd., cf. A.*Th*.797: metaph., ὅρκος σ. τὴν ὁμόνοιαν αὐτῶν D.S.11.29 (cj.); τὸ ξύλον ἔστεξεν ἡ γῆ *retained and cherished* it, so that it struck root, Plu. *Rom*.20, cf. *Alex*.35. 2. *conceal, keep hidden*, κακόν τι κεύθεις καὶ στέγεις ὑπὸ σκότῳ E.*Ph*.1214; ἥξει.., κἂν ἐγὼ σιγῇ στέγω S.*OT*341; τί χρὴ στέγειν ἢ τί λέγειν; Id.*Ph*.136 (lyr.); τὸ γὰρ γυναιξὶν αἰσχρὸν σὺν γυναῖκα χρὴ στέγειν Id.*Fr*.679; σ. τἀμὰ καὶ σ' ἔπη E.*El*.273; στέξαι τὸ κριθέν Plb.4.8.2:—Pass., *to be kept secret*, Th.6.72; παρ' ὑμῶν εὖ στεγοίμεθ' *let my counsel be kept secret* by you, S.*Tr*.596. IV. *close up*, in Pass., τὰ τῶν ἀγγείων στόματα στεγόμενα Paul.Aeg.6.7. (Cf. Skt. *sthagati* 'cover, hide', Lat. *tego*, Engl. *thatch*.)

**στέγωσις**, εως, ἡ, = στέγασις, *roofing in*, *POxy*.1450.9 (iii A.D., pl.).

**στέθματα**· τὰ στέμματα, Hsch.; cf. στέφω.

**στειβεύς**· ὁδευτής, Hsch.

**στείβω**, Il.11.534, E.*Ion* 495 (anap.): Ep. impf. στεῖβον Od.6.92, Iterat. στείβεσκον Q.S.1.352: aor. ἔστειψα (κατ-) S.*OC*467:—*tread* or *stamp on, tread underfoot*, of horses, στείβοντες νέκυάς τε καὶ ἀσπίδας Il.11.534, cf. 20.499; εἵματα.. στεῖβον ἐν βόθροισι *trod* the clothes in pits, in order to wash and clean them, Od.6.92; ποσὶν σ. δόμον *AP* 9.327 (Hermocr.):—Pass., κονία στειβομένα Theoc.17.122; αἱ στειβόμεναι ὁδοί the *beaten* tracks, X.*An*.1.9.13. 2. c. acc. cogn., *tread* or *walk on* a path, κέλευθον ποδὶ E.*Hel*.869; πέδον A.R.3.836; χοροὺς στείβουσι ποδοῖν *tread* measures, E.*Ion* 495 (anap.); νομὸν σ. Nic.*Th*. 609. 3. abs., *tread*, κατ' αἰγίλιπος πέτρης σ. κάρηνα *h.Hom*.19.4; ἵνα στείβουσι κύνες E.*Hipp*.217 (anap.), cf. Opp.*C*.1.456.

**στειλέα**, v. στελεά. **στειλειάριον**, v. στελεός. **στειλειή**, v. στελεά. **στειλειόν**, v. στελεόν. **στειλεός**, v. στελεός.

**στειναύχην**, ενος, ὁ, ἡ, *narrow-necked*, Ion. for στεν-, λάγυνος *AP* 6.248 (Marc. Arg.).

**στεινόπορος, στεινός, στεινότης**, Ion. for στεν-.

**στεῖνος**, εος, τό, a *narrow, close*, or *confined space*, ἐν σ. Od.22.460; στεῖνος ὁδοῦ κοίλης Il.23.419; of the Isthmus of Corinth, Call.*Sos.* vi 5. **II.** generally, *straits, distress*, στείνει ἐν αἰνοτάτῳ Il.8.476; μάχης ἐν σ. τῷδε 15.426; πόνοι καὶ στείνεα *h.Ap.*533; στένος in A., σωφρονεῖν ὑπὸ στένει to learn wisdom *by suffering, Eu.*521 (lyr.).

**στείνω**, *make strait, straiten, confine, crowd*, στείνοντες Nonn.*D.*23.5: Ep. impf. στεῖνον Orph.*A.*114. **II.** used by Hom. and Hes. only in pres. and impf. Pass., *to become strait, be narrowed*, θύρετρα φεύγοντι στείνοιτο Od.18.386; of persons, *to be straitened for room*, στείνοντο δὲ λαοί Il.14.34; of sheep, A.R.2.128. **2.** *to be* or *become full, be thronged*, γαῖα στεινομένη Hes.*Th.*160: c. gen., στείνοντο δὲ σηκοὶ ἀρνῶν ἠδ' ἐρίφων Od.9.219; νεκρῶν ἐστείνετο γαῖα Q.S.7.100: c. dat., [ποταμὸς] στεινόμενος νεκύεσσι *crowded with..*, Il.21.220; νῆσοι στεινόμεναι Κόλχοισι A.R.4.335; πώεσι.. αὐλὴ σ. Opp.*H.*4.398; στείνοντο.. ἀγροὶ μυκηθμῷ *were filled with..*, Theoc.25.97. **3.** metaph., *to be straitened, distressed*, ἀρνειὸς λάχνῳ στεινόμενος *burdened* with its wool, Od.9.445. (στέν-yω, cf. στενός.)

**στείνων**· ὡραϊστής, καὶ ἐπ' αὐτῷ ἀρέσκων, Hsch. **στεινωπός**, v. στενωπός. **στειπτός**, v. στιπτός.

**στεῖρα** (A), ἡ, (στερεός) *forepart of a ship's keel*, continued into the *stem* or *cutwater*, ἀμφὶ δὲ κῦμα στείρῃ πορφύρεον μεγάλ' ἴαχε Il.1.482, Od.2.428: cf. στείρωμα, στερέωμα 3, στήριγμα (στείρη only in *An.Ox.* 3.396). **2.** a kind of *bandage*, Heliod.ap.Orib.48.20.12. **II.** f.l. for σπεῖρα in Poll.2.31.

* **στεῖρα** (B), ἡ, a cow or other animal *that has not brought forth young*, στεῖραν βοῦν.. ῥέξειν Od.10.522; αἶγα στεῖραν *PCair.Zen.*429.15 (iii B.C.). **II.** of women, *barren*, Diocl.*Fr.*29, Lxx *Ge.*11.30, 25.21, *Ev.Luc.*1.7,36; Μοῖρα σ. *AP*7.468 (Mel.); στείρησι γυναιξί Orph.*L.*459; of women past childbearing, Hp.*Mul.*2.127: metaph., στεῖρα διάνοια, φύσις, ψυχή, Ph.1.441,636,478. **2.** *not having had offspring, virgin*, Lyc.670, Luc.*Tim.*17. (Cf. Skt. *staris* 'barren cow, heifer', Lat. *sterilis.*)

**στειρεύω**, *to be barren*, Gal.7.943: metaph., c. gen., Eust.113.27.

**στεῖρος**, ον E.*Andr.*711, *barren*, of females, ἣ στεῖρος (v.l. for στερρὸς (B)) οὖσα μόσχος E. l. c.; εὐνούχους στείρους Man.1.125.

**στειρότης**, ητος, ἡ, *sterility*, cj. Wytt. in Plu.2.366c, for στερρ-.

**στειρ-όω**, *make barren*, Ph.1.598:—Pass. -όομαι Lxx *Si.*42.10 (cod. A), Ph.1.564, al.; χώρας διά τινας αὐχμοὺς στειρωθείσης Phld. *Acad.Ind.* p.24 M.: metaph., οἱ -ωμένοι σοφίαν Ph.1.409. **-ώδης**, ες, *as it were barren*, Hp.*Mul.*2.158, Iamb.*VP*17.73. **II.** = στεῖρος, Vett.Val.7.26, al., Man.1.49; ζῴδια Ptol.*Tetr.*190. **-ωμα**· τρόπις, Hsch. **-ωσις**, εως, ἡ, *barrenness, unfruitfulness*, Ph.2.310, Heph. Astr.1.22. **-ωτικός**, ή, όν, *making barren*, Vett.Val.17.25.

**στείχω**, Il.2.287, Alc.19, A.*Th.*467, etc.; also **στίχω**, Hdt.3.14, Hsch.; subj. στίχῃ Hdt.1.9 (v.l. στείχῃ): Ep. impf. στεῖχον Il.9.86, etc.: aor. 1 ἔστειξα (only in compd. περίστειξας Od.4.277): aor. 2 ἔστιχον Il.16.258, Call.*Del.*153, Theoc.25.223, etc., but never in Trag.:—Poet. Verb, used by Ep., Lyr., Trag. (also Aeol., Sapph. *Supp.*16, Alc.19, and in Aeol. Prose, *IG*12(2).6.6 (Mytil., iv B.C.), *Inscr.Perg.*5.25 (Temnos, iii B.C.); used by Cic.*Att.*6.5.2 in a mock-heroic phrase, ἐξ ἄστεος ἑπταλόφου στείχων): *walk, march, go* or *come*, the direction being given by a Prep. or by the context, **a.** of motion *to* or *towards*, πρὸς οὐρανόν Od.11.17; ποτὶ πύργους A.*Th.* 297 (lyr.); πρὸς δόμους Id.*Ag.*1657 (troch.); πρὸς φίλων τάφον E.*Or.* 97; στεῖχ' εἰς ἀγορὰν πρὸς τοὺς Ἑρμᾶς Mnesim.4.2 (anap.); ἐπὶ τὴν εὐνήν Hdt.1.9; σ. ἀνά, κατὰ ὁδόν, Od.23.136, 17.204; ἀνὰ ἄστυ 7.72; δι' ἄστεως A.*Supp.*496; εἰς Ἄργος Id.*Ch.*675; ἐς Ἅιδην κατ' ἄκρας E. *Hipp.*1366 (anap.); θύραζε Od.9.418; ἔσω A.*Ch.*554; δεῦρο S.*OC* 1151: c. acc. loci, *go to, approach*, γύας, πόλιν, δόμους, A.*Pr.*708, *Supp.* 955, S.*OC*643: abs., Id.*Tr.*179, E.*Rh.*992 (anap.). **b.** of motion *from*, ἀπ' Ἄργεος σ. Il.2.287; ἀπ' Ὀλύμπου Hes.*Th.*690; ἐκ δόμων S.*OT*632; οἴκοθεν Pi.*N.*9.20: abs., *go, depart*, στείχωμεν A.*Pr.*81, cf. *Ch.*98, S.*Ant.*98, *Fr.*257. **2.** *march in line* or *order* (whence στίχος, στίχες, στοῖχος), ἐς πόλεμον σ. *march* to war, Il.2.833; οἱ δ' ἅμα Πατρόκλῳ ἔστιχον 16.258; σ. ἐπὶ τοὺς ξείνους against them, Hdt. 9.11; ἐν εὐθείαις ὁδοῖς σ. Pi.*N.*1.25. **3.** c. acc. cogn., ὁδοὺς A.*Ag.* 81 (anap.); τὰν νεάταν ὁδόν S.*Ant.*808 (lyr.); ἀνὴρ ὁπλίτης κλίμακος προσαμβάσεις στείχει πρὸς πύργον A.*Th.*467. **4.** metaph., ἀοιδὰ σ. ἀπ' Αἰγίνας Pi.*N.*5.3; ἐπ' ἐμοὶ ῥιπὴ A.*Pr.*1090 (anap.); ἴουλος ἄρτι διὰ παρηΐδων Id.*Th.*534; πρὸς τοὺς φίλους στείχοντα.. κακά S.*Ant.*10; τὴν ἄτην.. στείχουσαν ἀστοῖς ib.186. (Cf. Skt. *stighnoti* 'step up, mount', Goth. *steigan* 'climb'.)

**στεκτέον**, *one must support*, [βρέφος] περιβολαῖς ἱματίων (when it sits up) Sor.1.114.

**στεκτικός**, ή, όν, (στέγω) *of* or *for keeping out water*, c. gen., τέχναι ῥευμάτων στεκτικαί, i. e. house-building, Pl.*Plt.*280c. Adv. -κῶς, metaph., *guardedly*, Poll.5.147.

**στελγιδοποιός, στελγίς, στέλγισμα, στέλγιστρον**, v. στλεγγ-.

**στελεά**, ἡ, *haft, shaft*, ⌊στυρακίου⌋ Aen.Tact.18.10 (unless = *socket*); Ep. στελεή, τυπίδος A.R.4.957: also **στειλειή**, *haft* of an axe, Od.21.422, v.l. in Nic.*Th.*387. **II.** metaph., στειλέαν, = τὴν μακρὰν ῥάφανον, Antiph. (*Fr.*121?) ap. Hsch. (cf. στελεός). (The statement of Hsch., *EM*726.52, Eust.1531.37, that στειλειή = *hole* in the axe-head, may be due to a misunderstanding of Od. l. c.) (With στελεά, στελεόν, στελεός, cf. OE. *stela* 'stem, stalk', Engl. (dial.) *steal* 'handle of a hammer, axe, rake, etc., shaft of an arrow or javelin'.)

**στελεόν**, τό, = στελεά 1, [φορμορραφίδος] Aen.Tact.18.11; of an axe, Hsch., *EM*726.52; = *manubrium*, *Gloss.*: pl. στελεά Babr.143: Ep. **στειλειόν** Od.5.236, Ps.-Babr.ap.Suid. s. v. στειλειόν.

**στελεός**, ὁ, = στελεά 1, of an axe, *EM*339.57, 725.49; nom. pl. στελεοί *IG*2².1673.29,30; = σκυταλίδες 1.3, J.*AJ*3.6.6; acc. pl. written στελειούς *IG*2².1673.55: gender uncertain in acc. sg. στελεόν (perh. = *rolling-pin*) Anaxipp.6.3, cf. Antiph.121 (*Rh.Mus.*81.381), and in gen. sg. στελεοῦ Ph.*Bel.*67.13, *AP*6.297 (Phan.): dat. sg. στελεῷ Alciphr.3.55 codd. (στελέχῳ cj. Mein.); στελεοῖς ἐχρῶντο (to punish adulterers) μὴ παρουσῶν τούτων (sc. τῶν ῥαφανίδων) *App.Prov.* 5.43 (cf. στελεά II): also nom. **στειλειός**, Aesop.122, gen. στειλειοῦ (gender uncertain) Nic.*Th.*387 (v. l. στειλειῆς): also **στειλεός**, οἱ σ. τῶν σκαφίων Hp.*Fract.*8, cf. *Mul.*1.90 (with vv. ll. in both places, as also in the citations by Paul.Aeg.6.99, 115, 118):—hence Dim. **στειλειάριον**, Eust.1531.38.

**στελεόω**, *furnish with a handle*, in pf. Pass., *AP*6.205 (Leon.).

**στελέφουρος**, ὁ, *haresfoot plantain, Plantago Lagopus*, also called ἀρνόγλωσσον, ὄρτυξ, Thphr.*HP*7.11.2, Plin.*HN*21.101.

**στελεχ-ηδόν**, Adv. *stem by stem*, v. l. for στοιχηδόν, A.R.1.1004. **-ητόμος**, ον, *cutting trunks*, πέλεκυς *AP*6.103 (Phil.). **-ιαῖος**, α, ον, *forming a trunk*: φλὲψ σ. *the vena portae*, from which all the others were supposed by the ancients to branch, Gal.2.574, 8.413. **-ιον**, τό, Dim. of στέλεχος, Hsch. (pl.).

**στελεχόκαρπος**, ον, *bearing fruit on the stem*, Thphr.*HP*4.2.4.

**στέλεχ-ος**, εος, τό, also ὁ Luc.*VH*1.8, Poll.10.166, cj. in Alciphr. 3.55:—*crown of the root*, whence the stem or trunk springs, δρυὸς ἐν στελέχει Pi.*N.*10.61, cf. Hdt.8.55, Arist.*Ath.*60.2; αἴγειρος.. διεδιχασμένη ἑνὸς ἐκ στελέχους Lyr. in *Philol.*80.334. **2.** *trunk, log*, στελέχη φέρειν Ar.*Lys.*336 (lyr.); ἐκπρεμνίζειν στελέχη D.43.69; εἰσδυόμενος εἰς τὰ σ., of *hollow trunks*, Arist.*HA*559ᵃ10; κύων σ. ἔτεκε Hecat.15 J. **3.** metaph., *blockhead*, Lysipp.7. **-όω**, *form a stem*:—Pass., *grow into one*, Str.15.1.21, Ph.1.9. **II.** metaph., *bring to full growth*, ἀρετάς Id.2.456:—Pass., ib.348. **-ώδης**, ες, *with a stem* or *trunk*, Thphr.*HP*3.15.1, 3.17.1; κλάδοι -ώδεις Dsc.4.72.

**στελήν**, sine expl., dub. in Hdn.Gr.2.923.

**στελιον** (unaccented), τό, = *manubrium*, *Gloss.* (cf. στελεόν).

**στελίς**, ίδος, ἡ, *mistletoe, Viscum album*, Thphr.*CP*2.17.1; acc. *stelin* Plin.*HN*16.245: pl., prob. in *BGU*1120.17 (i B.C.).

**στέλλα**· ζῶσμα, Hsch. **στελλάνδρα**· ἡ κόρη, Id.

**στελλίδιον**, τό, v.l. for στελεόν in Babr.143.

**στέλλω**, Il.4.294, etc.: fut. στελῶ S.*Ph.*640, Ep. στελέω Od.2.287: aor. ἔστειλα Th.7.20, Ep. στεῖλα Od.14.248: pf. ἔσταλκα Arr.*An.*2.11.9, (ἀπ-, ἐπ-) Isoc.1.2, E.*Ph.*863: plpf. ἐστάλκει Arr.*An.*3.16.6, (ἐπ-) Th.5.37:—**Med.**, Il.23.285, etc.: fut. στελοῦμαι Lyc.604: aor. ἐστειλάμην, Ep. στειλ-, Il.1.433, S.*OT*434, etc.:—**Pass.**, fut. σταλήσομαι (ἀπο-) Aeschin.3.114 (v.l.), D.24.93; simple σταλήσομαι J.*AJ*2.4.2: aor. ἐστάλθην (in compd. ἀποσταλθέντες) *GDI*5186.4 (Crete), cf. Sch. Od.8.21; more freq. ἐστάλην [ᾰ], Pi.*O.*13.49, Hdt.4.159, (ἐπ-) Th.1.91, etc.: pf. ἔσταλμαι Hdt.7.62, Pl.*Lg.*833d, etc.: plpf. ἐστάλμην Philostr. *VA*3.25, 3 pl. ἐστάλατο Hes.*Sc.*288; ἐσταλάδατο and ἐστελάδατο dub.ll. in Hdt.7.89 (leg. ἐστάλατο):—*make ready*, οὓς ἑτάρους στέλλοντα καὶ ὀτρύνοντα μάχεσθαι Il.4.294; οὔτε κέ σε στέλλοιμι μάχην ἐς κυδιάνειραν 12.325; νῆα σ. *rig* or *fit* her *out*, Od.2.287, cf. 14.247; πλοῖον Hdt.3.52; ναῦς τριάκοντα Th.7.20; τὰ ἐκ νεὼς S.*Ph.*1077: also στρατιήν, στόλον, στρατόν, *fit out* an armament, *get* it *ready*, Hdt.3.141, 5.64, A.*Pers.*177, etc.; ᾧ δὴ τόνδε πλοῦν ἐστείλαμεν S.*Aj.*1045: also στέλλειν τινὰ ἐσθῆτι *furnish with, array in*, a garment, Hdt.3.14; χιτῶνι S.*Tr.*612: c. dupl. acc., στολὴν σ. τινά E.*Ba.*827 sq.; σ. τινὰς ὡς δεσποίνας X.*HG*5.4.5; σ. ἕλκος *dress* it, Hp.*VC*14; *bury*, ἐνὶ γαίῃ σ. A.R.3.205:—Med., στεῖλαί νυν ἀμφὶ χρωτὶ.. πέπλους *put on* robes, E.*Ba.*821: c. dat., ἐσθῆτι στειλάμενοι *having dressed themselves in..*, Luc.*Philops.*32: metaph., σ. κιθάρην Hermesian.7.2:—Pass., *fit oneself out, get ready*, ἄλλοι δὲ στέλλεσθε do you others *prepare* (to compete in the games), Il.23.285; στρατὸν κάλλιστα ἐσταλμένον Hdt.7.26, cf. 3.14, 7.93: c. acc. cogn., τὴν αὐτὴν ταύτην ἐστ. ib.62: c. dat., πρεπούσῃ στολῇ ἐστ. Pl.*Lg.*833d: folld. by a Prep., ἐσταλμένος ἐπὶ πόλεμον X.*An.*3.2.7; ἐς ἄγραν, ἐπ' ἄγρην, Lyc 604, *AP* 7.535 (Mel.); περὶ ὄργια E.*Ba.*1000 (lyr.): c. inf., ἐστέλλετο ἀπιέναι he *prepared* to go, Hdt.3.124; κινεῖν κώπας E.*Tr.*181 (lyr.). **II.** *dispatch, send*, ἐς οἶκον πάλιν A.*Pr.*389, cf. E.*IA*119 (lyr.), etc.; ἐξ ἑνὸς στείλαντος S.*OC*737:—Med. and Pass., *set out*, or (esp. in aor. 2 Pass.) *journey*, Hdt.1.165, 3.53, 4.159, 5.92.β': c. acc. cogn., ὁδὸν στέλλεσθαι S.*Ph.*1416 (anap.), cf. A.R.4.296; πρὸς θάλασσαν E.*Hel.*1527; ἐπὶ τὸν χρυσὸν Hdt.3.102; ἐπὶ πλοῖα X.*An.*5.1.5; τούτων γὰρ οὕνεκ' ἐστάλην S.*Aj.*328; ἴδιος ἐν κοινῷ σταλεὶς Pi.*O.*13.49; οἷπερ ἐστάλην ὁδοῦ S.*El.*404; οἴκαδε Τροίας ἄπο E.*Tr.*1264; κατὰ γῆν (v. l. γῆς) X.*An.*5.6.5: abs., στέλλου, κομίζου *begone!* A.*Pr.*394: c. acc. loci, ὀμφαλὸν γῆς σ. E.*Med.*668; μέλαθρα Id.*HF*109 (lyr.); of things, *to be sent*, S.*Tr.*776: metaph. of speech, ἀέρα ἐκπέμπειν στελλόμενον ὑφ' ἑκάστων τῶν παθῶν Epicur.*Ep.*1 p.27 U. **2.** Act. intr. in sense of the Pass. (in Hdt. and Trag.), *prepare to go, start, set forth*, ἔστελλε ἐς ἀποικίην Hdt.4.147, cf. 148, 5.125, S.*Ph.*571,640: c. acc. cogn., κέλευθον τήνδε.. ἔστειλα A.*Pers.*609. **3.** Med., *set out upon* a task, στέλλεσθαι πρός τι Pl.*Phlb.*50e; ἐπί τι Id.*Sph.*230b; ἐπ' αὐτὸ δὴ τοῦτο στελλώμεθα; Id.*Lg.*892e; ἐπὶ θήρας πόθον ἐστέλλου E.*Hipp.*234 (anap.); ἐπὶ τυραννίδ' ἐστάλης Ar.*V.*487. **III.** *summon, fetch, bring* a person to a place, S.*OT*860, cf. *OC*298, *Ph.*623,983; ὑμᾶς ἔστειλ' ἱκέσθαι Id.*Ant.*165, cf. *Ph.*60,495; [ἐμπορίαν] Pl.*Ep.*313e:—Med., σ' ἂν οἴκους τοὺς ἐμοὺς ἐστειλάμην I would have *sent for* thee.., S.*OT*

434:—Pass., Id.*OC*550 (cj.). **b.** ἡ ὁδὸς εἰς Κόρινθον στέλλει *leads* to Corinth, Luc.*Herm.*27. **IV.** *gather up, make compact*, esp. as a nautical term, *furl, take in*, ἱστία.. στεῖλαν Od.3.11, 16.353; στείλασα λαῖφος A.*Supp.*723:—Med., ἱστία μὲν στείλαντο Il.1.433, cf. Call.*Del.* 320, Arist.*Mech.*851ᵇ8: abs., στέλλεσθαι (sc. ἱστία) Teles p.10 H., Plb.6.44.6; so ἐπιστολάδην δὲ χιτῶνας ἐστάλατο they *girded up, tucked up* their clothes to work, Hes.*Sc.*288, cf. A.R.4.45: abs., στειλάμενος σιγᾶς *AP*11.149. **2.** *check*, Epicur.*Ep.*1 p.7 U.; *repress*, Ph.2.274, etc.:—Med., Plb.8.20.4; λόγον στειλώμεθα *draw in, shorten our* words, i.e. not speak out the whole truth, E.*Ba.*669; σ. τὸ συμβεβηκός *hush* it *up*, Plb.3.85.7; πρόσωπον στέλλεσθαι *draw up* one's face, look rueful, Phryn.*PS* p.107 B. **3.** Medic., *bind, make costive*, τὰ στέλλοντα *astringents*, opp. τὰ καθαίροντα, Gal.1.221, cf. Alex.Aphr.*Pr. Praef.*:—Pass., φλέβες στέλλονται *shrink up*, Nic.*Al.*193. **4.** Med., *restrict one's diet*, οὔτ' ἂν ἀπόσχοιντο ὧν ἐπιθυμέουσιν, οὔτε στείλαιντο (v.l. ὑποστ-) Hp.*VM*5; στελλόμενοι τοῦτο *avoiding* this, 2*Ep.Cor.*8.20; στέλλεο Περσεφόνας ζᾶλον *Supp. Epigr.*2.615 (Teos). (Cf. εὔσπολον, κασπολέω, σπολάς, σπόλος, σπελλάμεναι; prob. I.-E. *sqᵘel-*, but not found in cogn. languages; I.-E. *st(h)el-* is prob. found in OSlav. *stĭlati* 'spread out', Lat. *lātus* (fr. **stlātus*) 'broad', with which στέλλω may be cogn.)

⊛ **στέλμα**, ατος, τό, = στέφος, στέμμα, Hsch.; so perh. in *PMag. Lond.*121.785.

**στελμονίαι**, αἱ, *broad belts* put round dogs when used to hunt wild beasts, X.*Cyn.*6.1.

**στελύπην**· ἀσφόδελον, Hsch.

**στεμβ-άζω**, = λοιδορῶ, Hsch.; aor. inf. -άξαι, = ὑβρίσαι, *EM*158.37. **-άσεις**· λοιδορίαι, Hsch.

**στέμβω**, *shake about, agitate*, A.*Fr.*440; *misuse, handle roughly*, Eust.235.8.

⊛ **στέμμα**, ατος, τό, (στέφω) mostly in pl. (sg. in Il.1.28, Ar.*Pax*948), *wreath, garland, chaplet*, esp. of the priest's laurel-wreath, wound round a staff, στέμματ' ἔχων ἐν χερσὶ.. χρυσέῳ ἀνὰ σκήπτρῳ Il.1.14, 373; σκῆπτρον καὶ σ. θεοῖο ib.28, cf. E.*Andr.*894; sts. worn on the head, σ. ἐπὶ τῶν κεφαλῶν ἐχούσας Pl.*R.*617c; Φοῖβος ἔλακεν ἐκ τῶν σ. from *shrine with chaplets decked*, Ar.*Pl.*39, cf. E.*Ion*1310, Th.4.133; used in sacrificial ceremony, στέμμασι πυκασθείς (of victim) Hdt.7.197, cf. *SIG*1025.31 (Cos, iv/iii B.C.); σ. πάλας, as a prize, *Epigr.Gr.* 247 (Mysia); στέμματ' Ὀλυμπιάδων ib.881 (Cyzicus), etc.; ὁ ἐπὶ τῶν στεμμάτων an official connected with the *crowns of office* of magistrates (cf. στεπτικός, στέφανος), *PFay.*87 i 10 (ii A.D.), *POxy.*2130.7 (iii A.D.), cf. *PRyl.*77.28 (ii A.D.). **2.** Sch.S.*OT*3 says the στέμματα were *wreaths of wool* wound round the olive-branch; hence στέμματα ξηνασ' E.*Or.*12. **II.** in pl., στέμματα *pedigrees, family trees*, Plu.*Num.*1; Lat. *stemmata quid faciunt?* Juv.8.1, cf. Plin.*HN*35.6. **2.** *guild*, *CIG*3995b (Iconium); = φυλή, ib.9897 (Smyrna, Jewish); ὑπὲρ φιλοκυνηγῶν τοῦ σ. *guild* of huntsmen, *Supp.Epigr.*3.499 (Philippi).

**στεμμᾰτηφορέω**, *to be decked with a wreath*, Tz.*H.*1.477.

**στεμμᾰτ-ιαῖον**· δίκηλόν τι ἐν ἑορτῇ πομπέων δαίμονος, Hsch.; defined as μίμημα σχεδιῶν, αἷς ἔπλευσαν οἱ Ἡρακλεῖδαι τὸν μεταξὺ τῶν Ῥίων τόπον, *AB*305. **-ίας**, ου, ὁ, *one who wears a wreath*, of Apollo, Paus.3.20.9.

**στεμμᾰτο-φορία**, ἡ, = στεφανηφορία, Vett.Val.3.18, al. **-φόρος**, ον, = στεφανηφόρος II, Ptol.*Tetr.*176.

**στεμμᾰτόω**, *furnish with a wreath* or *chaplet*, E.*Heracl.*529.

**στεμφῠλ-ίας**, with or without οἶνος, = στεμφυλίτης, *PCair.Zen.* 737.2, al. (iii B.C.), Hsch. s.v. λάκυρος. **-ίς**, ίδος, ἡ, = στεμφυλῖτις, Philem.Gloss.ap.Ath.2.56c. **-ίτης** [ῑ], ου, ὁ, fem. **-ῖτις**, ιδος, *made from grapes already pressed*, τρύγες στεμφυλίτιδες wine made in this way, Hp.*Vict.*2.52, *Morb.*3.17: -ίτης, = *vinacium*, Gloss. ⊛ **-ον**, τό, (στέμβω) *mass of olives from which the oil has been pressed, olive-cake*, Ar.*Eq.*806: mostly in pl., Hp.*Acut.*64, Ar.*Nu.*45 (ubi v. Sch.), *Fr.*392; λιπῶσι στεμφύλοις Phryn.Com.38, cf. Androcl.ap.Arist.*Rh.* 1400ᵃ13, Ath.2.56d. **II.** pl., *mass of pressed grapes*, Hp.*Morb.*2.69, *Aff.*27 (where it seems to be a drink), Lyc.678, *PSI*6.554.20 (iii B.C.), *PCair.Zen.*527.8 (iii B.C.); οἶνον ἀπὸ στεμφύλων Lxx *Nu.*6.4; σταφυλῆς στέμφυλα Arist.*Fr.*107: in sg., Gal.6.576.—Signf. I is said to be Att. by Phryn.384. **-ούργιον**, τό, *wine-press*, *BGU*531 ii 12 (ii A.D.). **-ουργός**, ὁ, *worker in a wine-press*, *PCair.Zen.*737.18 (iii B.C., pl.).

**στέναγ-μα**, ατος, τό, *sigh, groan, moan*, S.*OT*5, E.*Or.*1326, *Heracl.* 478, Ar.*Ec.*367 (all in pl.), etc. **-μᾰτώδης**, ες, *like a sigh* or *groan, accompanied therewith*, πνεῦμα Gal.8.331. **-μός**, ὁ, *sighing, groaning*, Pi.*Fr.*168.4, A.*Pers.*896 (lyr., pl.), *Fr.*385 (pl.), S.*OT*30 (pl.), 1284, E.*Or.*959 (pl.), Pl.*R.*578a (pl.). **-μώδης**, ες, = στεναγματώδης, ἀναπνοή Paul.Aeg.3.20.

**στενάζω**, A.*Pr.*696, etc.: fut. -άξω Aeschin.3.259, Lyc.973, (ἀνα-) E.*IT*656 (lyr.): aor. ἐστέναξα Diph.33.6, etc.:—Pass., pf. ἐστέναγμαι Lyc.412:—prop. Frequentat. of στένω, *sigh deeply*: generally, *sigh, groan*, A. l.c., *Pers.*1046 (lyr.), *Eu.*788 (lyr.), S.*Ph.*917; ἐπ' ἄτῃ Id.*El.*1299; σ. κακοῖς E.*Alc.*199; οἴκοις *in* the house, Id.*Ph.* 1035 (lyr.); freq. with a neut. Adj., οἰκτρόν, δεινὸν σ., Id.*Supp.*104, *Med.*1184; μέγα σ. Id.*IT*957, D.27.69; τί ἐστέναξας τοῦτο; why *utteredst thou* this *moan?* E.*IT*550: c. acc. cogn., παιᾶνα σ. Id.*Tr.* 578 (lyr.), cf. *HF*753 (lyr.); ἀρὰς τέκνοις Id.*Ph.*334 (lyr.); πηλίκον τί ποτ' ἂν στενάξειαν; D.23.210. **2.** trans., *bemoan, bewail*, πότμον S.*Ant.*882 (lyr.), cf. *OC*1672 (lyr.), etc.; τινα E.*Ph.*1640, *Ba.* 1027.

**στενακ-τέον**, *one must bewail*, τὰ τούτων E.*Supp.*291. ⊛ **-τικός**, ή, όν, = sq. 2, Hsch. s.v. στενόεσσα. **-τός**, ή, όν, *to be mourned, giving cause for grief*, ἀνήρ S.*OC*1663; ἄτα E.*HF*917 (lyr.). **2.** *mournful*, ἰαχά Id.*Ph.*1302 (lyr.).

**στενάσαι**· τινὲς πλῆξαι καὶ παῖσαι, Hsch. **στεναύχην**, v. στειν-. **στεναχεῖλαι**· δαμάζεσθαι, Id.

**στενᾰχ-έω**⊛ -ή, = στοναχέω, στοναχή, *IG*12(8).441.20 (Thasos), *Epigr.Gr.*707; cf. sq. **-ίζω** or **στονᾰχίζω** (the latter form is a freq. v.l. in Hom.), Ep. lengthd. form of στενάχω (q.v.), only pres. and impf., *groan, sigh, wail*, Il.19.304, Od.9.13, 11.214, Hes. *Th.*858; μεγάλα σ. Il.23.172; ἁδινὰ σ. ib.225, Od.24.317:—Med., μέγα -ίζετο γαῖα Il.2.784, cf. 7.95. **II.** perh. trans. (cf. στενάχω II), *bewail, lament*, c. acc., Od.1.243.

**στενάχω** [ᾰ], poet. lengthd. form of στένω, only pres. and impf., Ep. στενάχεσκον Il.19.132, Q.S.3.549 (aor. is ἐστονάχησα, v. στοναχέω), and mostly in pres. part.:—*groan, sigh, wail*, freq. in Hom., ἁδινὰ σ. Il.24.123, al.; βαρέα σ. 8.334, al.; βαρὺ σ. Od.8.95, 534; μεγάλα (as v.l. for βαρέα) 4.516, 23.317; πυκνὰ μάλα σ. Il.18.318, 21.417; also in Trag. (lyr.), as S.*El.*141; πατρός (dub. l.) ib.1076: metaph. of the roar of torrents, Il.16.391 (Med. of the loud breathing of horses galloping, ib.393); θὴρ.. στενάχων βρέμει A.R.1.1247; στοᾶς στεναχούσης *groaning* from being overcrowded, Ar.*Ach.*548. **2.** Med. in act. sense, Ep. impf. στενάχοντο Il.19.301, 23.1, al. **II.** trans., *bewail, lament*, τὴν αἰεὶ στενάχεσκε 19.132, cf. Callin.1.17; so in Trag. (lyr.), τὸ παρὸν.. πῆμα στενάχω A.*Pr.*99 (anap.), cf. E.*Ph.* 1551 (lyr.), al.:—Med., τοὺς δὲ στενάχοντο Od.9.467. Cf. στεναχίζω, στοναχέω.

**στένιον**· στῆθος, Hsch. (cf. στέρνιον).

**στενο-βρῑθής**, ές, v. στερνοβριθής. **-βρογχος**, ον, *narrow-throated*, κεράμιον Arr.*Epict.*3.9.22. **-επιμήκης**, ες, *of a narrow oblong shape*, Hero *Geom.*14.11, Eust.849.8. **-θώραξ**, ᾱκος, ὁ, ἡ, *narrow-chested*, Gal.17(2).532. **-κοίλιος**, ον, *narrow-bellied*, Ael. ap.Porph. *in Harm.*p.217 W. **-κομῐδή**, ἡ, *straitened circumstances*, *PThead.*17.7 (iv A.D.). **-κορίᾱσις**, εως, ἡ, (κόρη III) *unnatural contraction of the pupil*, Veget.2.16. **-κύμων** [ῡ], ονος, ὁ, ἡ, *surging in a strait*, πορθμός Archestr.*Fr.*16. **-κώκῡτος**, ον, of hair, *so fast set in, that one screams when it is pulled out*, Com. word in Ar.*Lys.*448. ⊛ **-λεσχέω**, *talk subtly, quibble*, περὶ καπνοῦ Id.*Nu.*320. **-λέσχης**, ου, ὁ, *one that talks subtly, quibbler*, Suid. **-λεσχία**, ἡ, *quibbling*, Id. **-λογέω**, gloss on -λεσχέω, Hsch. **-λόγον**, τό, *compression in speech*, τῆς συνεκφωνήσεως (in synizesis) Eust.25.33. **-μακρος**, ον, *narrow and long*, Sch. S.*Tr.*100:—also **-μήκης**, ες, Sch.E.*Hec.*29. **-πᾰθέω**, *to be distressed*, f.l. in Cass.*Pr.*70 (Ideler στεγνοπ-). **-πορθμος**, ον, *at* or *on a strait*, Χαλκίς E.*IA*167 codd. (lyr.):—pecul. fem. **στενοπορθμίς**, ίδος, Μεσσήνη Archestr.*Fr.*56.4. **-πορία**, ἡ, *narrow way, defile*, X.*HG* 3.5.20, D.C.48.41. **-πορος**, Ion. στειν-, ον, *with a narrow pass* or *outlet*, πύλαι A.*Pr.*729; ἔξοδοι E.*Andr.*1143; ὅρμοι Αὐλίδος Id.*IA* 1497 (lyr.); διὰ κυανέας σ. πέτρας Id.*IT*890 (lyr.); ἀκτή Lyc.ap. Arist.*Rh.*1405ᵇ36; ὦτα S.E.*P.*1.126, cf. Gal.6.759. **2.** Subst. στενόπορα, Ion. στειν-, τά, *narrows*, Hdt.7.223; τὰ σ. τῶν χωρίων *defiles*, Th.7.73: sg. στενόπορον, τό, *a strait, narrow*, Hdt.7.211 (στειν-), X.*HG*4.6.9, *Ath.*2.13. **-πους**, ὁ, ἡ, gen. ποδος, *narrow-footed*, Polem.*Phgn.*2.85; f.l. for στεγανό- (q.v.), Arist.*Phgn.*810ᵃ24. **-πρόσωπος**, ον, *narrow-faced*, ib.809ᵇ5 (Comp.). **-πρωκτος**, ον, *narrow-rumped*, Phot. **-ρρύμη** [ῡ], ἡ, (ῥύμη II) *narrow alley*, Hdn.*Epim.*123, Phot. s.v. στενωπός. **-ρρύμιον** [ῡ], τό, Dim. of foreg., *Stud.Pal.*1.7.14 (v A.D.).

⊛ **στενός**, Ion. **στεινός**, ή, όν, Aeol. **στένος** Alc.*Supp.*34 (dub. l.):—*narrow*, opp. εὐρύς, πλατύς, Hdt.2.8 (Sup.), 4.195, al.; ψαλίς S.*Fr.*367; δίαυλος E.*Tr.*435; ἐσβολή Hdt.7.175 (Comp.); πόρος ib.176; ἡ ἔσοδος Th.7.51; οὔτ' εὐρεία οὔτε στενὴ διαφυγή Pl.*Lg.*737a; ἐν στενῷ, Ion. στεινῷ, *in a narrow space*, A.*Pers.*413, Hdt.8.60.β'; ποιεῖν τὸν δῆμον εὐρὺν καὶ σ. Ar.*Eq.*720; σ. ποδεῶν Hdt.8.31; ἔντερον Ar.*Nu.*161; πόροι, φλέβες, Ti.Locr.101a, Pl.*Ti.*66a; κεφαλή, πόδες, X.*Cyn.*5.30. **2.** Subst., τὰ σ. *the narrows, straits*, of a pass, Hdt.7.223; of a sea, Th.2.86, etc.; of the *straits* of Gibraltar, Str.3.5.5; so τὸ σ. the *strait* (Hellespont), Luc.*DMar.*9.1; ἐπὶ σ. τῆς ὁδοῦ X.*HG*7.1.29; ἡ στενή *a narrow strip* of land, Th.2.99; τὰ σ. *passes, defiles*, Phld.*Rh.*1.334 S. **II.** metaph., *close, confined*, ἀπειληθέντες ἐς στεινόν driven into *a corner*, Hdt.9.34; σ. ζῶμεν χρόνον Men.410; εἰς στενὸν κομιδῇ τὰ τῆς τροφῆς τινι καταστήσεται D.1.22; εἰς σ. τοῦ καιροῦ φθείρεσθαι Alciphr.1.24. **2.** *scanty, petty*, Pl.*Grg.*497c; ὑποθέσεις Plb.7.7.6; ἐλπίδες D.H.4.52; ἐρωτήσεις Philostr.*VS*2.30; *small-minded, narrow-minded*, in Adv. Comp., *PGiss.*40 ii 7 (iii A.D.). **3.** of sound and style, *thin, meagre*, Arist.*Aud.*803ᵇ24, *Rh.*1413ᵇ15; *hard* to pronounce, συλλαβὴ σ. καὶ δύστομος Phld.*Po.*2.15.—Choerob. *in Theod.*2.76 H., *EM*275.50 say that στενός, like κενός, forms the Comp. and Sup. στενότερος, στενότατος, and these forms are explainable from *στενϝότερος, *στενϝότατος, which are implied by the Ionic forms στεινότερος, -ότατος (στεινότερος occurs in Hdt.1.181, 7.175, στενότερος in *IG*7.3073.109 (Lebad., ii B.C.), Pl.*Phd.*111d, X.*Cyr.*2.4.3 with v.l.); and στενοτάτου is required by the metre in Scymn.922; the form στενώτερος is however found in Hp.*VM*22, Arist.*PA*675ᵃ35, al. **III.** Adv., στενῶς διακεῖσθαι to be *in difficulties*, *PCair.Zen.*498 (iii B.C.), *PTeb.* 760.19 (iii B.C.), D.L.8.86, cf. Lxx 1*Ki.*13.6.

**στένος**, εος, τό, v. στεῖνος II.

**στενό-σημος**, ον, *with narrow border*: ἡ σ., = Lat. *tunica angusticlavia*, opp. πλατύσ-, Arr.*Epict.*1.24.12. **-στομος**, ον, *narrow* *mouthed*, τεῦχος A.*Fr.*108; ποτήρια Artem.1.66; μῆτραι Hp.*Mul.* 1.2, Sor.2.56; λιμήν Str.7.4.2; ἀγγεῖα Herod.Med.ap.Orib.5.30. 23. ⊛ **-της**, Ion. στειν-, ητος, ἡ, *narrowness*, Ἑλλήσποντον, ἐόντα στεινότητα μὲν ἑπτὰ σταδίους Hdt.4.85 (-ότητι, -ότατα, -ότατον codd.); τῇ τοῦ λιμένος σ. Th.7.62, cf. 4.24; θώρηκος -ότητες Hp.*VM*23; διὰ τὴν σ. τῶν χωρίων, of Thermopylae, Lys.2.30; of the oesophagus, Arist.*HA*495ᵃ20: pl., ῥέουσα κατὰ τὰς σ. through the *narrows*, Id. *Mete.*354ᵃ6. II. metaph., *scantiness*, δαπανημάτων J.*AJ*19.7. 5. **-τράχηλος** [ᾰ], ον, *narrow-necked*, Sch.A.R.2.569. **-φλεβος**, ον, *with narrow, small veins*, Gal.1.339, Paul.Aeg.1.67. **-φλεβοτόμος**, ὁ, *narrow lancet*, Id.6.8, as v.l. for στενοῦ φλεβοτόμου. **-φυής**, ές, *narrow by nature*, Alex.268. **-φυλλία**, ἡ, *narrowness of leaf*, Thphr.*CP*6.18.8. **-φυλλος**, ον, *narrow-leaved*, Id.*HP*8.4.1, Dsc.2.108, Alex.Aphr.*in Top.*118.31. **-φωνος**, ον, *with a weak, thin sound*, ὄργανον Poll.2.111.

⊛ **στενοχωρ-έω**, *to be straitened, confined*, Macho ap.Ath.13.582b: metaph., *to be anxious, in difficulty*, ἐπί τινι Hp.*Praec.*8; εἰς τὴν ἀκρίβειαν τῆς ἑρμηνείας στενοχωρεῖ ὁ λόγος *IPE*I².39.18 (Olbia, not before ii A.D.). II. trans., *crowd, straiten*, τοὺς ἀπαντῶντας Luc.*Nigr.*13; τὰς πύλας, τὰς ὁδούς, Charito 5.3, 4.7; ταλάντοις τοὺς θησαυρούς Lib.*Or.*59.15:—Pass., with fut. Med. (Them.*Or.*25.310d), *to be crowded together*, D.S.20.29, Charito 3.2; ἐν ταὐτῷ σ. Luc. *Tox.*29; χῶραι -οῦνται ποσὶ μιαιφόνων J.*BJ*4.3.10; ἀγορὰ -ουμένη ὄχλῳ D.H.6.67; of stricture, Heliod.ap.Orib.50.9.1; *to be cramped* or *confined*, ὁ Εὐφράτης -ούμενος Isid.Char.1, cf. Sch.Il.*Oxy.*221 xi 8, Porph.*Sent.*27; of a picture, Them. l. c. 2. metaph., *press closely*, τινα Lxx *Jd.*16.16:—Pass., *to be straitened, cramped*, ib.*Is.*28.19(20), Procl.*Inst.*98; ἐν τοῖς σπλάγχνοις 2*Ep.Cor.*6.12; ὑπὸ τῶν κακῶν Sch.E.*Med.*57. **-ημα**, ατος, τό, *a case of straitening, difficulty*, Hsch. s. v. στεῖνος. **-ής**, ές, = στενόχωρος, Arist. *GA*755ᵃ27. **-ησις**, εως, ἡ, = στενοχωρία, *oppression* of breathing, Gal.8.120. **-ία**, Ion. -ίη, ἡ, *narrowness of space, a confined space*, Hp.*Art.*14 (codd., but v. στενυγροχωρίη); σ. τῇ φάρυγγι παρέχειν ib. 41; *want of room*, by sea or land, Th.2.89, 4.26, 30, Pl.*Lg.*708b; ὑπὸ στενοχωρίας Id.*Tht.*195a; opp. εὐρυχωρία and ἄνεσις, Plu.2.679f, cf. 182b; σ. βίου *the short space* of life *remaining*, Ael.*VH*2.41; τὸν λόγον ἀπὸ τῆς ἐκεῖ στενοχωρίας εἰς πεδίον ἐξαγάγῃ Lib.*Or.*64.10. II. metaph., *straits, difficulty*, ἡ σ. τοῦ ποταμοῦ *difficulty of passing* the river, X.*HG*1.3.7, cf. Lxx *De.*28.53, al.; *distress*, *OGI*339.103 (Sestos, ii B.C.); ἡ τῆς πόλεως Plb.1.67.1, etc.; ἡ τοῦ καιροῦ D.C. 39.34: pl. in 2*Ep.Cor.*6.4, *PLond.*5.1677.11 (vi A.D.); also, *narrow limits*, prob. in Phld.*Rh.*2.220 S. **-ος**, ον, *narrow, strait*, Hp. *Mul.*1.2 vulg. (v.l. -στομος codd. opt.); ὁδοὶ σ. (in the lungs) Gal. 18(2).171: metaph., ἐν σ. καιροῖς *BCH*12.86 (Panamara).

**στενόω**, Ion. **στεινόω**, *straiten, confine, contract*, αὐτήν (the trachea) Gal.18(2).949; τὴν γαστέρα Lib.*Decl.*31.20; = *angusto*, Dosith.p.435 K.:—mostly in Pass., ἐς στενώτερον ἐστενωμένα (prob. f. l. for συνηγμένα) Hp.*VM*22; ὄρη τὰς διεξόδους ἐστένωται *have* their outlets *narrow*, Hdn.8.1.6; στεινούμενον αὐλαῖς . . ἄλσος, sc. by comparison, *AP*9.656.13; cf. στεγνόω II. 2: metaph., *to be in difficulty*, τοῖς στιχουργήμασι Sch.Lyc.324.

**Στέντωρ**, ορος, ὁ, *Stentor*, a Greek at Troy, famous for his loud voice, Il.5.785: prov., μεῖζον ἐμβοᾶν τοῦ Σ. Luc.*Luct.*15:—Adj. **Στεντόρειος**, ον, *Stentorian, with a voice like Stentor's*, κῆρυξ Arist. *Pol.*1326ᵇ7; βοᾶν Στεντόρειον Aristid.2.28 J.

**στενυγρός**, ή, όν, Ion. for στενός, ἀτραπός Semon.14, cf. Hp.*Epid.* 5.48; ἰσθμός Max.Tyr.35.7; στενυγρή, ἡ, *a narrow pass* or *strait*, Orac.ap.Oenom.ap.Eus.*PE*5.20, prob. for στενύσταν in Orac.ap. Apollod.2.8.2.

**στενυγροχωρίη**, ἡ, Ion. for στενοχωρία, Hp.(*Art.*14) as cited by Gal.18(1).411; so **στενυγρόω**, Ion. for στενόω, *contract*, Hp.(*Epid.*6. 2.1) as cited by Gal.17(1).896.

⊛ **στένω**, only pres. and impf.: Ep. impf. στένον Hom. (v. infr.):— Poet. Verb, *moan, sigh, groan*, μέγα δ' ἔστενε κυδάλιμον κῆρ Il.10. 16, Od.21.247, cf. Il.18.33; ἐν δέ τέ οἱ κραδίῃ σ. ἄλκιμον ἦτορ 20. 169; of the sea, ὁ δ' ἔστενεν οἴδματι θύων 23.230; στένει βυθός A. *Pr.*432 (lyr.); ἐκοίμισε στένοντα πόντον S.*Aj.*675; of the turtle-dove, Theoc.7.141; in Trag. of persons *groaning aloud*, A.*Pers.*285, *Ag.*445 (lyr.); δμωαῖς προθήσειν πένθος . . στένειν S.*Ant.*1249:— Med., κλαίω, στένομαι A.*Th.*873 (anap.); στενομένα πόλις E.*Ion* 721 (lyr.). 2. after Hom., c. gen., *moan* or *sigh for . .*, Ἑλλάδος E.*IA* 370 (troch.); also ὑπέρ τινων A.*Pr.*68; κακοῖς Id.*Pers.*295; ἐπί τινι E.*Hipp.*903; ἀμφ' ἐμοί S.*El.*1180:—Med., περί τινας A.*Pers.*62 (anap.). 3. c. acc., *bewail, lament*, in Trag., A.*Pr.*435 (lyr.), S.*OT*64, *Ph.*338, al.; παλαιὰ καινοῖς δακρύοις οὐ χρὴ στένειν E.*Fr.*43: rarely in Com., abs., Ar.*Ec.*462, Men.*Her.*5, *Kith.Fr.*1.2: c. acc. et gen., κακῶν σῶν, Οἰδίπου, σ' ὅσον στένω E.*Ph.*1425; στένω σε τᾶς τύχας I *pity* thee *for* thy ill fortune, A.*Pr.*399 (lyr.):—Med., στένεσθαί τινα E.*Ba.*1372 (anap.). (Cf. Skt. *stánati* 'thunder, roar', Lith. *stenëti* 'groan'.)

**στεν-ώδης**, ες, *somewhat narrow*, αὐχήν interpol. in *Peripl.M.Eux.* 58. **-ωμα**, ατος, τό, *narrow place* or *pass*, *Peripl.M.Rubr.*2.

**στενώπ-αρχος**, ὁ, *surveyor of lanes* or *roads*, D.C.55.8. **-εῖον**, τό, = στενωπός, Ach.Tat.8.9, Suid. **-ός**, Ion. and Ep. **στεινωπός**, όν, (στενός, ὀπή) *narrow*, στεινωπὸς ὁδός Il.7.143, 23.416; στενωπότεραι αἱ διέξοδοι τροφῆς Hp.*Vict.*2.40; πόντος στειν. A.R.2.1191; στειν. παλάμαι Emp.2; ἐν οὕτω στενωπῷ in so *narrow a space*, D.S.31.0 codd. Phot. II. mostly as Subst., στενωπός, ὁ (στενωπή, ἡ, Plu.*Prov.*1. 61), *narrow passage, strait*, of the straits of Messina, στεινωπὸν ἀνεπλέομεν Od.12.234; στενωποῦ πλησίον θαλασσίου A.*Pr.*366; σ. ἁλός A.R.2.333, cf. 549 (so, of the Hellespont, σ. ὕδωρ Ἕλλης D.P.515); *mountain-pass, defile*, S.*OT*1399; *lane, alley*, Pherecr.108.4, Nicostr.Com.24, Thphr.*Vent.*29, D.S.12.10, Paus.5.15.2; σ. Ἅιδου *the narrow entrance* to Hades, S.*Fr.*832; of the blood-vessels, Pl.*Ti.*70b.

**στένωσις**, εως, ἡ, *a being straitened*, Lyd.*Ost.*19 (pl.), Sch.Ar. *Ec.*355; σ. γλίσχρων χυμῶν (in the eye) prob. f. l. for στέγνωσις in Alex.Trall.2.

**στεπτήριος**, ον, *of* or *for crowning*, τὰ σ., = στέμματα, Hsch.: Στεπτήριον, τό, a festival at Delphi, Plu.2.293c.

**στεπτικός**, ή, όν, *for crowning*: στεπτικόν, τό, payment by magistrates *for the crown* of office, *POxy.*1413.4, al. (iii A.D.); cf. στέμμα, στέφανος.

**στεπτός**, ή, όν, (στέφω) *crowned*, prob. l. in *APl.*4.306 (Leon.).

**στέπτω**, = στέφω, *SIG*1025.29 (Cos, iv/iii B.C.).

⊛ **στεργάνος**, ὁ, = κοπρών, Lat. *sterquilinium*, Hsch.

⊛ **στέργ-ηθρον**, τό, (στέργω) *love-charm*, applied to various plants; = ἀείζωον μέγα, Dsc.4.88; also, = κοτυληδών, Ps.-Dsc.4.91, *Gloss.* II. *love itself, affection*, in sg., A.*Ch.*241: pl., Id.*Pr.*492; ἑορτῆς στέργηθρ' ἔχουσαι Id.*Eu.*192; στέργηθρα φρενῶν E.*Hipp.*256 (anap.). **-ημα**, ατος, τό, *love-charm*, τινος to influence him, S.*Tr.*1138.

**στεργίς**, v. στλεγγίς.

**στεργοξύνευνος**, ον, *loving one's consort*, Lyc.935.

⊛ **στέργω**, A.*Eu.*911, Ar.*Eq.*769, etc.: impf. ἔστεργον Hdt.9.117, E.*Ion* 817: fut. στέρξω S.*Ph.*458, D.18.112, etc.: aor. ἔστερξα Semon.7.45, S.*OT*1023, etc.: pf. ἔστοργα Hdt.7.104:—**Pass.**, aor. ἐστέρχθην Lyc.1190, Plu.*Ant.*31, etc.: pf. ἐστεργμαι Emp.22.5, *AP* 6.120 (Leon.):—*love, feel affection*, freq. of the mutual *love* of parents and children, S.*OT*1023, *OC*1529, Demetr.Lac.*Herc.*1012.46, etc.; παῖς στέργει τε καὶ στέργεται ὑπὸ τῶν γεννησάντων Pl.*Lg.*754b; σ. τὰ νεογνὰ βρέφη X.*Oec.*7.24; πατέρα, τοὺς γονέας, E.*El.*1102, D. 25.65, cf. Arist.*EN*1161ᵇ18; of the *love* of the ruled people for a ruler, Hdt.9.113, cf. S.*Ant.*292; of the *love* of a tutelary god for the people, A.*Eu.*911; so ἐμὲ γὰρ ἔστερξαν . . Μοῦσαι Ar.*Ra.*229; of a wheedling demagogue, ὦ Δῆμ', εἰ μή σε . . στέργω Id.*Eq.*769; of a city and her colonies, Th.1.38; of the *love* of dogs for their master, X.*Cyn.*7.12. 2. less freq. of the *love* of husband and wife, Hdt.2.181, 7.69, S.*Tr.*577, *Aj.*212 (anap.); ἄλλην τιν' εὐνήν E.*Andr.*907, cf. 468 (lyr.); πόσιν στέργοντ' ἔχειν Id.*Fr.*1062; of brothers and sisters, Id.*IA*502; of friends, Lxx *Si.*27.17, etc. 3. seldom of sexual love, X.*Smp.*8.14, 21, Sosicr.4; of a horse and mare, Hdt.3.85; πρόβατα ἄρνα εἰ μὴ σ. Crateuas ap.Sch.Nic.*Th.* 681:—Med., c. gen., δυοῖν γυναικοῖν εἷς ἀνὴρ οὐ στέργεται *Com. Adesp.*284. II. generally, *to be fond of, show affection for*, μή μ' ἔπεσιν μὲν στέργε Thgn.87; λόγοις ἐγὼ φιλοῦσαν οὐ στέργω φίλην S. *Ant.*543; στέργει γὰρ οὐδεὶς ἄγγελον κακῶν ἐπῶν ib.277, cf. Ar.*V.* 1054, etc.: also of things, οὐκ οἰκός ἐστι . . εὐνοίην . . διωθέεσθαι, ἀλλὰ σ. *accept* it *gladly*, Hdt.7.104; μακράν γε . . ῥῆσιν οὐ σ. πόλις A.*Supp.* 273, cf. *Th.*717; ὕβριν γὰρ οὐ σ. οὐδὲ δαίμονες S.*Tr.*280; ἔστερξε τὴν ἁπλῶς δίκην Id.*Fr.*770; τὴν ἀλήθειαν Pl.*R.*485c, etc.: reversely, στέργοι με σωφροσύνα E.*Med.*635 (lyr.). III. *to be content* or *satisfied, acquiesce* (cf. ἀγαπάω III), S.*OT*11 (unless, *having desired*, cf. infr. IV), *OC*7; στεργέτω Pl.*Lg.*849e; στέρξω καὶ σιωπήσομαι D. 18.112; στέρξον *oblige me, do me the favour*, S.*OC*518 (lyr.). 2. c. acc., ἔστεργον τὰ παρεόντα *were content with, acquiesced in* them, Hdt.9.117; τὴν Διὸς τυραννίδα *bear with* it, A.*Pr.*11; ἐθέλω τάδε μὲν σ. δύστλητά περ ὄντα Id.*Ag.*1570 (anap.), cf. *Eu.*673; ἀνάγκῃ προὔμαθον σ. κακά S.*Ph.*538, cf. E.*Ph.*1685, *PGrenf.*1.53.21 (iv A.D.); σ. τὴν γυναῖκα S.*Tr.*486, cf. E.*Andr.*180; τὴν τύχην D.55.22. 3. c. dat., σ. τοῖσι σοῖς E.*Supp.*257; τοῖς παροῦσιν Isoc.*Ep.*2.23; τῇ ἐμῇ τύχῃ Pl.*Hp.Ma.*295b; ταῖς ὑμετέραις γνώσεσι D.26.5; στέρξαι καὶ ἐμμεῖναι τῇ δίκῃ *Sammelb.*5681.32 (v A.D.); also σ. ἐπὶ τούτῳ D.39. 6; ἐν μικροῖς εἶναι E.*El.*407. 4. c. part., οὐ γὰρ ἔχω πῶς ἂν στέρξαιμι κακὸν τόδε λεύσσων S.*Tr.*992 (anap.); σ. ξυμφορᾷ νικώμενοι E.*Hipp.* 458; Ζεὺς εἴτ' Ἀΐδης ὀνομαζόμενος στέργεις whether *thou likest* to be named Zeus or Hades, Id.*Fr.*912 (anap.). 5. rarely c. inf., οὐκ ἔστεργέ σοι ὅμοιος εἶναι E.*Ion* 817. IV. *desire, entreat*, c. acc. et inf., Ἀπόλλω καὶ κασιγνήταν . . στέργω μολεῖν S.*OC*1094 (lyr.); μειλιχίοις στέρξοι τε παραιφάμενος ἐπέεσσιν Orph.*A.*771 (s. v. l.); for S.*OT*11 v. supr. III. 1.

**στερεῖνος**, ον, *hard*, τόποι *PLond.*1.131ʳ.314 (i A.D.).

**στερεμνι-όομαι**, Pass., *become solid*, Zeno *Stoic.*1.29. **-ος**, α, ον, also ος, ον Aret.*SD*2.10:— = στερεός, *hard, fast, firm*, οὐρανός *Placit.*2.11.2; φύσις Pl.*Epin.*981d; ὠτειλαί Aret. l. c.; σιτίον Ath.1. 10c; τὰ σ. *solid* food, *BKT*3 p.20; also τὰ σ. *solid objects*, Epicur. *Ep.*1 pp.9, al. U. (also sg., Id.*Nat.*2.3, al.); σ. πύκνωμα Phld.*D.*3.11; τὰ -ώτερα D.S.1.7; σ. κίνησις *stable* motion, Bito 60.7. Adv. -ίως *firmly*, κλῖμαξ σ. ἐνδεδεμένη ibid., cf. Hp.*Alim.*5. **-ώδης**, ες, *of solid nature*, Porph.ap.Stob.1.49.50.

**στερεο-βαρής**, ές, v. στερροβ-. **-βάτης** [ᾰ], ου, ὁ, *foundation course of a building*, Vitr.3.4.1. **-βόας**, ου, ὁ, gloss on χαλκοβόας, Sch.S.*OC*1046. **-δερμος**, ον, *with hard skin* or *coat*, Sch.Nic.*Th.* 376. **-ειδής**, ές, *of solid nature*, κόσμος Pl.*Ti.*32b. **-κάρδιος**, ον, *hard-hearted*, Lxx *Ez.*2.4 (v.l.).

**στερεομετρ-έω**, *measure solids*, Onos.10.16 (Pass.). **-ης**, ου, ὁ, *one who measures solids*, Gal.*Thras.*47. **-ία**, ἡ, *measurement of solids, geometry of three dimensions*, Pl.*Epin.*990d, Arist.*APo.*78ᵇ38, Ph.1.23, Theo Sm.p.1 H. **-ικός**, ή, όν, *of* or *for the measurement of solids*, γένος μετρήσεως Hero *Geom.*3.18.

**στερεο-πᾰγής**, *ές*, *hard*, of missiles from slings, Tim.*Pers.* 26. **-ποιέω**, *make hard*, *firm*, or *solid*, Sor.2.9, cf. 1.82 (Pass.). **-ποίησις**, *εως*, *ἡ*, *making firm*, ib.81. **-πους**, *ὁ*, *ἡ*, gen. *ποδος*, *solid-footed*, *Hippiatr.*95; gloss on *χαλκόπους*, Sch.D Il. 8.41.

⊛ **στερεός**, *ά*, *όν*, also **στερρός** (q.v.), *firm*, *solid*, *σ.* *λίθος ἠὲ σίδηρος* Od.19.494; *βοέαι* Il.17.493; *αἰχμὴ σ.* *πᾶσα χρυσέη* all of *solid* gold, Hdt.1.52, cf. 183; *ἕρμα σ. γῆς* E.*Hel.*854, cf. X.*Cyn.*9.16; *γῆ σ. καὶ ἀδιάλυτος* Epicur.*Nat.*14.2; *τὰ -ώτερα τῶν ὀστέων*, opp. *τὰ ἀραιότερα*, Hp.*Fract.*33; *τὸ σ.*, opp. *κενόν*, Democr.ap.Arist.*Ph.*188ᵃ22, *Metaph.*985ᵇ7; opp. *μαλθακός*, Pl.*Phdr.*239c; *κυσὶ σ. καὶ ἰσχνοῖς*, opp. *προβάτοις πίοσι καὶ ἁπαλοῖς*, Id.*R.*422d; *ἀθλητής* D.L.2.132; *βραχίονες* Theoc.22.48; *δέρματα* Pl.*Prt.*321a; *νῆμα* Id.*Plt.*282e; *σ. κέρας solid*, opp. *κοῖλον*, Arist.*HA*500ᵃ6; *σ. κάλαμος* Thphr.*HP*4. 11.10; *στερεὰ τροφή solid* food, D.S.2.4, *Ep.Hebr.*5.12, Arr.*Epict.*2. 16.39 (Comp.); *τὸ σ. σῶμα*, opp. *ὁ χυλός*, Gal.15.463; *σ. κοιλίη costive*, Hp.*Acut.*(*Sp.*)56. Adv. *-ρεῶς firmly*, *fast*, *κατέδησαν* Od.14.346; *ἐντέτατο* Il.10.263; *νῶτα.. ἑλκόμενα σ.*, of wrestlers, 23.715. b. of money, *standard*, *of full value*, *ἀργυρίου στερεὰ τάλαντα* *SIG*826*D* 20 (Delph., ii B.C.); so perh. of sums due in kind, *πυροῦ στερεοῦ* *PRein.*8.5 (ii B.C.), al.; and of linear and square measures, *τῆς προσούσης αὐλῆς πηχῶν σ. ὀκτὼ τὸ ἐπιβάλλον αὐτῷ μέρος ἥμισυ πήχεις σ. τέσσερας* eight (four) *standard* cubits, *PStrassb.*87 (ii B.C.), cf. *PLond.*3.1024.19 (ii B.C.); *πόδες σ. standard* feet, *Milet.*7 p.59 (Didyma); *μέτρημα σ.* *Supp.Epigr.*4.446.11 (ibid, iii/ii B.C.). c. *ὠρύγη ποταμὸς ἐπὶ τὰ τρία σ.* the ditch was restored by digging to its three *normal dimensions*, *OGI*672 (Canopus, i A.D.), cf. 673, where the Latin version has *at tria soldu(m)*. 2. metaph., *stiff*, *stubborn*, *στερεοῖς ἐπέεσσι*, opp. *μειλιχίοις*, Il.12.267; *κραδίη -ωτέρη ἐστὶ λίθοιο* Od.23.103. Adv. *-ρεῶς*, *ἀποειπεῖν* Il.9.510, cf. 23.42. 3. later, *hard*, *stubborn*, *cruel*, *πῦρ* Pi.*O.*10(11).36; *ὀδύναι* Id.*P.*4.221; *ἀπειλαί* A.*Pr.* 174 (anap.); *ἁμαρτήματα* S.*Ant.*1262 (lyr.); *ἦθος* Pl.*Plt.*309b; *οὕτω σ.* ⟨*τι*⟩ *πρᾶγμα θερμόν ἐσθ' ὕδωρ* Antiph.245; *σ. φωνή* Tryph.490; *τοῦτο ἤδη -ώτερον harder*, *more difficult*, Pl.*R.*348e. 4. of language, *τὸ εὔτονον καὶ σ. solidity*, D.H.*Din.*8; *ποιήματα* Phld.*Po.*5.5, cf. 4 (Sup.). 5. *σ. ζῴδια*, i.e. productive of *settled* conditions, Serapio in *Cat.Cod.Astr.*1.100.17, Ptol.*Tetr.*32, *PMag.Lond.*46. 47. II. of bodies and quantities, *solid*, *cubic*, opp. *ἐπίπεδος* (plane), Pl.*Phlb.*51c; *σ. γωνία* a *solid* angle, Id.*Ti.*54e sq., cf. Euc. 11 *Def.*11; *σ. πῆχυς* *POxy.*669.7 (iii A.D.); *σ. ἀριθμός* a *cubic* number, Arist.*Pol.*1316ᵃ8; *τὰ σ. cubic numbers*, *representing bodies of three dimensions*, Pl.*Tht.*148b: dat. sg. *στερεῷ in the third power*, *Theol.Ar.*4. (Cf. Skt. *sthirás* 'firm, hard, solid', OHG. *star* 'rigid', OE. *starian* 'stare fixedly'.)

**στερεόσαρκος**, *ον*, *with hard* or *firm flesh*, Hp.*Mul.*1.1 (Comp.), cf. Sor.1.56.

**στερεόστρᾰκος**, *ον*, *τὰ σ. τῶν μετάλλων solid parts*, *slag*, Zos.Alch. p.107 B.

**στερεό-της**, *ητος*, *ἡ*, *hardness*, *firmness*, *solidity*, Pl.*Ti.*74e, Arist. *PA*664ᵇ2; of atoms, Epicur.*Ep.*1 p.8 U.: metaph. of persons, *σ. καὶ καρτερία* *Cat.Cod.Astr.*5(3).84. **-φρων**, *ονος*, *ὁ*, *ἡ*, (*φρήν*) *stubborn-hearted*, S.*Aj.*926 (lyr.). **-ω**, *make firm* or *solid*, *τοὺς πόδας* X.*Eq.*4.3, cf. 5; *τὴν γῆν ἐπὶ τῶν ὑδάτων* Lxx *Ps.*135(136).6; *τὸν οὐρανόν* ib.*Is.*45.12:—Pass., Hp.*Vict.*1.9, Arist.*GA*735ᵇ2. 2. *strengthen*, *τοῦτον* *Act.Ap.*3.16; *confirm*, *κρίσιν* Lxx *Si.*3.2:—Pass., *to be made strong*, X.*Cyr.*8.8.8, *Act.Ap.*3.7: metaph., *to be firmly established*, *confirmed*, Lxx 1 *Ki.*2.1, al., D.S.15.57.

**στερέσιμος**, *η*, *ον*, *liable to be taken away*, *OGI*515.29 (Mylasa, iii A.D.), Hierocl.*Facet.*246; *-έσιμον*, = *commissum*, *Gloss.*

⊛ **στέρεσις**, *εως*, *ἡ*, = *στέρησις* 2, *PRev.Laws* 54.13 (iii B.C.), *PTeb.* 27.75 (ii B.C.).

**στερέω**, 3 sg. imper. *στερείτω* Pl.*Lg.*958e; otherwise pres. occurs only in form *στερίσκω* and compd. *ἀπο-στερῶ*: fut. *στερήσω* S.*Ant.* 574, *στερῶ* A.*Pr.*862: aor. *ἐστέρησα* E.*Andr.*1213 (lyr.), Pl.*Lg.*873e, *PCair.Zen.*93.13 (iii B.C.); inf. *στερέσαι* Od.13.262; *ἐστέρεσεν* *IG*12 (8).600.15 (Thasos), v.l. in Lxx *Nu.*24.11, al.; *στερέσας* *IG*14.902 (Capri); *ἐστέρισεν* ib.12(9).293 (Eretria, iv/iii B.C.), *AP*11.335.4, prob. for *ἐστέρησεν* ib.124.2 (Nicarch.): pf. *ἐστέρηκα* (*ἀπ-*) Th.7.6, Plb.31.19.7, etc.:—**Pass.**, pres. (apart from *ἀπο-στερέομαι*) found in early writers only in forms *στέρομαι*, *στερίσκομαι* (*στεροῖτο* X.*Cyr.*7. 3.14, *στερουμένους* *An.*1.9.13, *στερεῖσθαι* E.*Supp.*793 (lyr.), perh. ff. ll.); part. *στερούμενος* Ph.*Fr.*29 H., J.*AJ*2.7.3, Gal.18(2).19; imper. *στερείσθω* *OGI*483.173 (Pergam., prob. ii B.C., but inscribed in ii A.D.); *στερέσθω* ib.176, 179; 3 pl. *στερείσθων* *IG*12(9).207.44 (Eretria, iii B.C.): fut. *στερηθήσομαι* D.C.41.7, etc., v.l. in Isoc.6. 28, cf. 7.34, but in the best codd. *στερήσομαι*, as in S.*El.*1210, Th. 3.2, X.*An.*1.4.8, 4.5.28, *Mem.*1.1.8: aor. *ἐστερήθην* (v. infr.): poet. aor. 2 part. *στερείς* E.*Alc.*622, *Hec.*623, *Hel.*95, *El.*736 (lyr.): pf. *ἐστέρημαι* (v. infr.); *ἐστέρεσμαι* *An.Ox.*1.394: plpf. *ἐστέρητο* Th.2.65:— *deprive*, *bereave*, *rob* of anything, c. acc. pers. et gen. rei, *οὕνεκά με στερέσαι τῆς ληΐδος ἤθελε* Od.13.262; *ἄνδρ' ἕκαστον αἰῶνος στερεῖ* A. *Pr.*862, cf. S.*Ant* 574, E.*Heracl.*807, etc.; *σ. τινὰ τῆς σωτηρίας*, *ψυχῆς*, etc., Th.7.71, Pl.*Lg.*873e, etc.; *ὅσα τροφὴν ἡ γῆ πέφυκεν βούλεσθαι φέρειν*, *μὴ στερείτω τὸν ζῶνθ' ἡμῶν* ib.958e:—Pass., *to be deprived* or *robbed* of anything, c. gen., *στερηθεὶς ὅπλων* Pi.*N.*8.27; *τῶν ὀμμάτων*, *τῆς ὄψιος στερηθῆναι*, Hdt.6.117, 9.93; *φροντίδος στερηθεὶς* A.*Ag.*1530 (lyr.); *τῆς βασιληΐης ἐστέρημαι* Hdt.3.65, cf. 5.84; *τοῦ παιδὸς ἐστερημένος* Id.1.46; *γαίας πατρῴας* A.*Eu.*755; *μετοικίας τῆς ἄνω* S.*Ant.*890; *φίλων* Id.*Fr.*863; *τῆς πόλεως* Antipho 2.2.9 (as v.l.), X.*Mem.*1.1.8; *ἀγαθῶν* And.3.8, cf. Isoc.5.133, Pl.*Phlb.*66e, etc.: abs., *τὸ ἐστερῆσθαι state of negation* or *privation*, Arist.*Cat.*12ᵃ 35. II. rarely c. acc. rei, *take away*, *μισθόν* *AP*9.174.12 (Pall.): —Pass., *to have taken from one*, *πλούτου.. κτῆσιν ἐστερημένη* S.*El.* 960 (though the acc. may be construed with *στένειν*); *φασγάνῳ βίον στερείς* E.*Hel.*95.

**στερέ-ωμα**, *ατος*, *τό*, *solid body*, Hp.*Flat.*8, Anaxag.ap.*Placit.*2.25. 9. b. *ἄϋλα σ.* immaterial *solids*, Dam.*Pr.*425, cf. 205. 2. *foundation* or *framework*, e.g. the skeleton, on which the body is, as it were, built, Arist.*PA*655ᵃ22; *στερεώματος ἕνεκα τοῦ περιτρήτου* to *strengthen* it, Hero *Bel.*95.8: metaph., *solid part*, *strength* of an army, Lxx 1 *Ma.*9.14; also, *ratification*, *ἐπιστολῆς* ib.*Es.*9.29; *steadfastness*, *τῆς πίστεως* *Ep.Col.*2.5. 3. = *στεῖρα* (of a ship), Thphr. *HP*5.7.3. 4. *firmament*, i.e. the sky, the heaven above, Lxx *Ge.* 1.6, *Ez.*1.22, al.; *τὸν τῶν οὐρανίων σ. δεσπότην* *Tab.Defix.Aud.*242. 8 (Carthage, iii A.D.). **-ωμᾰτίζω**, *stamp*, *trample out*, Aq.2 *Ki.* 22.43. **-ωπός**, *ή*, *όν*, *solid*, Emp.21.6. **-ωσις**, *εως*, *ἡ*, *making firm*, Lxx *Jb.*37.18 (v.l. *-θείς*); *making solid*, *Theol.Ar.*47; *solid union* of broken bones, Cass.*Pr.*38. 2. *ἡ σ. τῆς μάχης obstinacy* of conflict, Lxx *Si.*28.10. **-ωτής**, *οῦ*, *ὁ*, *one who strengthens*, Sch. Opp.*H.*4.421. 2. title of a grade in the mysteries of Mithras, *Röm.Mitt.*49.206 (Dura). **-ωτικός**, *ή*, *όν*, *strengthening*, *consolidating*, *σαρκός* Antyll.ap.Orib.6.32.3.

**στέρ-ημα**, *ατος*, *τό*, *that which is taken away*, *ναὸς σ.* f.l. (variously emended) in S.*Fr.*241. II. = *στέρησις*, Ps.-Callisth.2.43. **-ήσιμος**, *ον*, *liable to confiscation*, *τὸ πλοῖον σ. ἔστω* *POxy.*36 ii 11 (ii/iii A.D.); also **στερέσιμος** (q.v.). **-ησις**, also **-εσις** (q.v.), *εως*, *ἡ*, *deprivation*, *loss*, of a thing, *ἀρχῆς* Th.2.63; *πνεύματος* Pl.*Lg.*865b; *σ. αἰσθήσεως ὁ θάνατος* Epicur.*Ep.*3 p.60 U.; *σ. τῆς ἀναπνοῆς* Gal.15.795; *σ. τοῦ ὀφθαλμοῦ*, *ὀφθαλμῶν*, i.e. blindness, Hp.*Judic.*42, Gal.17(1). 401. 2. *confiscation*, *πλοίου* *OGI*572.22 (Myra, ii/iii A.D., dub. l., fort. *στέρεσις*). 3. *negation*, *privation*, Arist.*Rh.*1408ᵃ7, *Cat.*12ᵃ 26, *Metaph.*1004ᵇ27, Thphr.*HP*1.2.5; *περὶ τῶν κατὰ στέρησιν λεγομένων on negatives*, title of work by Chrysipp., *Stoic.*2.5. **-ητέος**, *α*, *ον*, *to be deprived*, *τινος* Hp.*Acut.*39. **-ητικός**, *ή*, *όν*, *having a negative quality*, *τὰ σ.* Plu.2.947c. II. = *ἀποφατικός*, *expressing privation*, i.e. *negative*, of propositions, opp. *κατηγορικός*, *καταφατικός*, Arist.*APr.*25ᵃ6, al., cf. Thphr.*CP*6.6.3, Chrysipp.*Stoic.*2.52; *σ. φωνή* Gal.8.34. Adv. *-κῶς negatively*, Arist.*APr.*26ᵇ22; *privatively*, Id. *Metaph.*1056ᵃ29.

**στερίζω**, only in aor. *ἐστέρισεν*, v. *στερέω*.

**στέριπο**, for *στέριφος*, barbarism in Ar.*Th.*1185.

**στερίσκω**, collat. pres. of *στερέω*, *τινά τινος* Th.2.43, Teles p.22 H., D.S.1.60, Gal.8.54; *τὴν ψυχὴν ἀπό τινος* Lxx *Ec.*4.8:—Pass., c. gen., Hdt.4.159, [7.162], Th.1.73, 2.49, E.*Supp.*1093, Agatho 5, Pl.*R.* 413a, X.*Cyr.*7.5.62, *Eq.Mag.*8.8, *Ages.*11.5, Arist.*HA*487ᵃ18, al., *BGU*446.18 (ii A.D.), Gal.8.53.

**στερῐφεύομαι**, Med., *to be unmarried*, Hsch.

**στεριφνός**, *ή*, *όν*, cited by Erot. (s. v.l., *στριφνούς*, *-νοί* cj. Klein) from Hp.*Salubr.*2 (where our text has *στρυφνούς*), and Ar.*Ach.*180 (where *στιπτοί*).

**στερῐφόομαι**, Pass., *become hard* or *solid*, Ph.2.117.

**στερῐφό-πεπλος**, = *ὁ μικρὸς πέπλος*, Suid. **-ποιέω**, *make firm* or *hard*, Id.

**στέρῐφ-ος**, *η*, *ον*, = *στερεός*, *firm*, *solid*, of ground, *διὰ τοῦ ἕλους*, *ᾗ ἦν.. -ώτατον* Th.6.101, cf. Anon.ap.Suid. s. h. v.; *τὰς πρῴρας -ωτέρας ἐποίησαν* Th.7.36; *στερίφοις.. τοῖς ἐμβόλοις* with their rams *made solid*, ibid. 2. Subst. *στέριφον*, *τό*, *rock-bottom*, *IG*2².1668.8, 1682.5. II. = *στεῖρα* (B), *barren*, *unfruitful*, of women, Ar.*Th.* 641, Pl.*Tht.*149b; of animals, Arist.*HA*611ᵃ12; of fruit, Thphr.*CP* 2.11.1. **-ότης**, *ητος*, *ἡ*, *stoutness*, *solidity*, Sch.Il.11.256. **-ωμα**, *ατος*, *τό*, *solid foundation*, App.*BC*4.109 (pl.).

**στερκ-τέον**, (*στέργω*) *one must acquiesce*, *τινι* in a thing, Din.1.91; *id σ. putabo* Atticus ap.Cic.*Att.*9.10.7: c. acc., Zen.1.84 (c. dat. as cited by Suid. s.v. *ἀνάγκη*). **-τικός**, *ή*, *όν*, *disposed to love*, *affectionate*, *πρὸς τὰ συνήθη* Arist.*HA*629ᵇ11; *τέκνων* Plu.2.7e; *τὸ σ.*, = *στοργή*, ib.769c, cf. *Alex.*8; *ἔχομεν φύσει τι σ.* Arr.*Epict.*2.10. 23. **-τός**, *ή*, *όν*, *amiable*, *lovable*, S.*OT*1338 (lyr.).

**στερνίδιον**, *τό*, = *προστερνίδιον*, Iamb. post Polem. p.50 Hinck (pl.).

**στέρνιξ**, *ικος*, *ἡ*, = *ἐντεριώνη*, Hsch.

**στέρνιον**, *τό*, some kind of meat difficult to digest, perh. *breast* of an animal, or = Lat. *sterilicula*, Alex.Trall.2, al.; *τῶν κρεῶν βούλβιον* (= Lat. *vulva*) *καὶ σ. καὶ πόδες.. τῶν βοῶν ἢ ῥύγχη* Id.11.6; *στέρνιον* and *στέρνιν*, = Lat. *sterile* (in a list of eatables, betw. *ypogastrion* and *vulva*), *Gloss.*

**στερνίτης** [ῑ], *ου*, *ὁ*, only fem. **-ῖτις**, *ιδος*, *of the breast*, *πλευραί*, i.e. the *5th and 6th* ribs, Poll.2.182.

**στερνο-βρῐθής**, *ές*, *with a strong chest*, *ἵπποι* Polyaen.4.7.12 (v.l. *στενο-*). **-κοπέομαι**, *beat one's breast for grief*, Sch.Arat. 195, Aesop.351. **-κτύπος** [ῠ], *ον*, *beating the breast*, Tim.*Pers.* 112. **-μαντις**, *εως*, *ὁ*, *ἡ*, [ῠ], = *ἐγγαστρίμυθος*, S.*Fr.*59; cf. *θυμόμαντις*.

⊛ **στέρνον**, *τό*, *breast*, *chest*, in Hom. both in sg. and pl., always of males (*στῆθος* being used of both sexes), *βάλε δουρὶ σ. ὑπὲρ μαζοῖο* Il.4. 528, cf. 2.479, etc.; *κρήδεμνον ὑπὸ στέρνοιο τάνυσσαι* Od.5.346, cf. Pi. *N.*10.68, X.*An.*1.8.26: pl., *εὐρύτερος δ' ὤμοισιν ἰδὲ στέρνοισιν* Il.3.194; *ἐν δέ τέ οἱ κραδίη.. στέρνοισι πατάσσει* 13.282; *σ. λαχνάεντα* Pi.*P.*1. 19; so in X., *Cyr.*1.2.13; *παίσας εἰς τὰ σ... παῖδα* ib.4.6.4; of horses,

Il.23.365 (sg. in 508); of sheep, Od.9.443; in Trag. also of women, in sg., E.*Hec.*563: pl., μαστούς τ' ἔδειξε στέρνα θ' ib.560; στέρνων πλαγαί beating of the *breast*, S.*El.*90 (anap.); ἐν στέρνοισι πεσοῦνται δοῦποι Id.*Aj.*633 (lyr.); στέρν' ἄρασσε A.*Pers.*1054. **2.** Poet., esp. Trag., also, the *breast* as the seat of the affections, *heart*, ἀνδρῶν γὰρ ἐσθλῶν σ. οὐ μαλάσσεται S.*Fr.*195; τὸ σὸν μὴ σ. ἀλγύνοιμι Id.*Tr.*482: mostly in pl., ἤλγυνεν ἐν στέρνοις φρένα A.*Ch.*746, cf. S.*Ph.*792; οὕτω χρὴ διὰ στέρνων ἔχειν one ought to feel thus, Id.*Ant.*639; στέρνοις ἐγκαταθέσθαι τι Simon.(?)85; Ἄρη ἐν στέρνοις ἔχειν E.*Ph.*134; ἐξ εὐμενῶν σ. δέχεσθαί τινα S.*OC*487; οἷς πολιοῦχος ὑπὸ στέρνοις ἀρετά τε καὶ αἰδώς Isyll.16. **II.** metaph., στέρνα χθονός Suid., cf. Sch. S.*OC*691. **2.** ὑπὸ στέρνοισι καμίνου in the *heart* of the fire, Nic. *Th.*924.—Rare in early Prose (v. supr.); found also in Medic., in signf. I. 1, Hp.*Flat.*10 (pl.), Sor.1.103, al., Gal.16.608, 18(2).65, al. (all sg.); τὰ σ. μαχαίρᾳ ἀνσχίσσαντα *IG*4$^2$(1).121.99 (Epid., iv B.C.); never in Arist. (f.l. for στενῶν in *Pr.*905$^b$40). **III.** *breastbone*, Gal.2.592, *UP*6.8.

**στερνο-σχῐδής**, ές, dub. sens. in *PCair.Zen.*534.36 (iii A.D.). **-σώματος**, ον, v. στερροσώματος. **-τῠπέομαι**, = στερνοκοπέομαι, Hippias Erythr.1, J.*AJ*4.8.48, Plu.2.114f. **-τῠπής**, ές, *of* or *from beaten breasts*, κτύπος E.*Supp.*604 (lyr.); σ. πάταγος *AP*7.711 (Antip.); cf. στέρνον I. 1. **-τῠπία**, ἡ, *beating of the breast* for grief, Ph.2.579, Luc.*Luct.*19. **-τύπτης**, ου, ὁ, = ὁ τὸ στῆθος τύπτων, Hsch., Phot., Suid.

**στερν-οῦχος**, ον, *broad-swelling*, χθὼν σ., of the plain of Athens, S.*OC*691 (lyr.); cf. στέρνον II. 1. **-όφθαλμος**, ον, *with eyes in the breast*, A.*Fr.*441.

**στερνοφορέω**, *obtain breast of victim as perquisite*, prob. in *IG*1$^2$.190.20.

**στέρομαι**, Dor. imper. 3sg. **σταρέστω** *BCH*50.15 (Delph., iv B.C.); only used in pres. and impf., the other tenses being derived from στερέομαι (v. στερέω):—*to be without*, *lack*, *lose*, νίκης τε στέρεται Hes. *Op.*211; στέρεσθαι τῆς χώρης Hdt.8.140.α', cf. Th.1.70, al.; στερομέναν φίλων A.*Ag.*1429 (lyr.), cf. E.*IA*889 (troch.); στέρεσθαι κρατός A. *Pers.*371; στέρομαι δ' οἴκων, σ. παίδων E.*Ion*865 (anap.); φίλτρων στέρομαι Id.*El.*1309 (anap.); στερόμενος ὧν ὁ θεὸς ἔδωκεν Antipho 4.1.3; στερέσθω τῆς ἀρχῆς Pl.*Lg.*948a; ὅπως ἂν..τῶν αὐτῶν στέρωνται Id. *R.*433e; στερέσθω τοῦ βοσκήματος *IG*12(9).90.12 (Eretria, iv B.C.), cf. *PHib.*1.29.20 (iii B.C.), *PRev.Laws* 49.22, al. (iii B.C.); τῶν ὑπαρχόντων στέρεσθαι *BGU*1812.6 (i B.C.), cf. στερέω: abs., χαίρειν τε καὶ στέρεσθαι S.*Tr.*136 (lyr.); ὑπὸ Ἀγησιλάου στέρεσθαι οὐδεὶς οὐδὲν πώποτε ἐνεκάλεσε X.*Ages* 4.1.

**στεροπ-ή**, ἡ, poet. word, like ἀστεροπή, ἀστραπή, *flash of lightning*, σ. πατρὸς Διός Il.11.66, cf. Hes.*Th.*845; ἀκτῖνες στεροπᾶς ἀπορηγνύμεναι Pi.*P.*4.198; στεροπᾶν κεραυνῶν τε πρύτανις, i.e. Zeus, ib.6.24; ἕλικες..στεροπῆς ζάπυροι A.*Pr.*1084 (anap.); βροντῇ στεροπῇ τε Id.*Supp.*34 (anap.), etc. **2.** generally of *dazzling light*, *gleam*, χαλκοῦ στεροπή Il.11.83, Od.4.72; of the sun, ὦ λαμπρᾷ στεροπᾷ φλεγέθων S.*Tr.*99 (lyr.). **-ηγερέτα**, ὁ, Ep. for *στεροπηγερέτης, either (from ἀγείρω, so Hsch., cf. ἀστεροπαγερέτας, νεφεληγερέτα), *he who gathers the lightning*, or (from ἐγείρω), *who rouses the lightning*, Ζεύς Il.16.298, Nonn.*D.*8.370; Διὸς -έταο Q.S.2.164. [ᾰ in nom., except by position.] ⊛ **-ης**, ου, ὁ, *Lightner*, name of one of the three Cyclopes, Hes.*Th.*140, Call.*Dian.*68.

**στέροψ**, οπος, ὁ, ἡ, *flashing*, σ. λιγνύς S.*Ant.*1127 (lyr.).

**στερρο-βᾰρής**, ές, *hard and heavy*, prob. in Hsch. s.v. κορύνη, for στερεοβαρής. **-γυιος**, ον, *with strong limbs*, *APl.*4.52 (Phil.). **-νους**, ουν, *hard-*, *stern-minded*, Tz. ad Hes.*Op.*129 (Comp.). **-ομαι**, Pass., in aor. opt. στερρωθείη Hp.ap.Erot., glossed ὀρθωθείη by Bacchius ibid. **-ποιέω**, *harden*, *strengthen*, Dsc.5.121 (Pass.), *PLeid.X.*2, Sch.Od.9.393; τίς ὁ τὰ ὀστέα -ήσας; *Corp.Herm.*5.6: metaph., φίλον App.*Pun.*61:—Med., οὐραγίαν Plb.5.24.9.

**στερρός** (A), ά, όν, also ός, όν E.*Hec.*296:—collat. form of στερεός, *stiff*, *firm*, *solid*, πόροι Ti.Locr.101a (Comp.); of earth, opp. χαῦνος, v.l. in Arist.*Pr.*934$^b$11; of water, *frozen*, ῥεῖθρον Hdn.6.7.7; also, *hard*, Plu.2.725d (Comp.); *stiff*, *strong*, δόρυ E.*Supp.*711; σ. ἀντικνήμιον *stiff*, *numb* with age, Ar.*Ach.*218: Comp. -ότερος, δέρμα Gal.6.32. **b.** *concrete*, σῶμα (viz. the uvula), opp. πάθος, Aret.*SA*1.8. **2.** *hard*, *rugged*, *uneasy*, λέκτρα E.*Tr.*114 (anap.); σ. τροφή *hard* fare, Luc.*Lex.* 23. Adv., στερρότατα βιῶσαι Id.*Macr.*8. **3.** metaph., *stubborn*, *hard*, *cruel*, ἀνάγκης σ. δῖναι A.*Pr.*1052 (anap.), cf. E.*Hec.*1295 (anap.); σ. δαίμων, ἀλγηδόνες, Id.*Andr.*98, *Med.*1031; ψυχή Ar.*Nu.*420. Adv. στερρῶς *stiffly*, *obstinately*, X.*An.*3.1.22; στερρῶς φέρειν χρὴ συμφοράς Men.*Mon.*480; *tightly*, ἐμφραττέτω τὰ ὦτα Paul.Aeg.3.24.

**στερρός** (B), όν, *barren*, στερρὸς οὖσα μόσχος E.*Andr.*711; [ζῷα] σ. Arist.*GA*773$^b$30,33; cf. στεῖρα (B), στεῖρος.

**στερρο-σώμᾰτος**, ον, *with strong body* or *frame*, Xenarch.1.10 (Lob. for στερνοσώματος). ⊛ **-της**, ητος, ἡ, (στερρός (A)) *hardness*, *firmness*, τοῦ πάγου, of ice that will bear, Plu.2.969a; [τῶν ἀτόμων] Epicur.*Fr.*282: metaph., *firmness*, Ph.1.276. **II.** (στερρός (B)) *barrenness*, Arist.*GA*773$^b$27.

**στερρῶνυξ**, ῠχος, ὁ, ἡ, *with strong claws*, Hdn.*Epim.*204.

**στερφίνα**· δερματίνη, οἱ δὲ δέρματα ὄνεια· οἱ δὲ στεῖρα ἢ σκληρά, Hsch. **στέρφνιον**· σκληρόν, στερεόν, Id.

**στερφόπεπλος**, ον, *clad in hide* or *skin*, Lyc.652.

⊛ **στέρφ-ος**, εος, τό, *hide*, *skin*, στέρφεσιν αἰγείοις A.R.4.1348, cf. *AP* 6.298 (Leon.); σ. ἐγχλαινούμενον Lyc.1347; Ion. word acc. to Sch. Nic.*Al.*248; dub. in *IPE*1$^2$.76.15 (Olbia, perh. iv B.C.); cf. τέρφος, ἔρφος. **II.** = κεράμιον, Sch.A.R. l.c. **-όω**, *cover with hide*, Sch. A.R.4.1348, Sch.Nic.*Al.*248, etc. **-ωσις**, εως, ἡ, *covering with hide*, dub. cj. for στρέφωσις in Hsch. **-ωτήρ**, ῆρος, ὁ, *clad in hides*, σ. στρατός Ibyc.59.

**στερχανά**· περίδειπνον, Ἠλεῖοι, Hsch. ⊛ **στέρψανον**· ἀξίνη, πέλεκυς, Id.

**στέρωμα**, ατος, τό, misspelling of στερέωμα or *στέρρωμα, *Gloss.*

**στεῦμαι**, Epic Verb, used by Hom. only in 3 sg. pres. and impf., στεῦται, στεῦτο, once by A. in 3 sg. στεῦται; 1 sg. στεῦμαι cj. for ὑπισχνοῦμαι in Orph.*L.*82, 3 pl. impf. στεῦντο Maiist.60:—In Il. always with inf. fut., *make as if one would..*, *promise* or *threaten that one will..*, στεῦται γάρ τι ἔπος ἐρέειν Il.3.83; στεῦτο γὰρ εὐχόμενος νικησέμεν 2.597; στεῦται γὰρ νηῶν ἀποκόψειν ἄκρα κόρυμβα 9.241; στεῦτο γὰρ..οἰσέμεν ἔντεα καλά 18.191; στεῦτο..ἀπολεψέμεν οὔατα χαλκῷ 21.455; ἐμοί τε καὶ Ἥρῃ στεῦτ' ἀγορεύων Τρωσὶ μαχήσεσθαι 5.832; once with inf. aor., στεῦται δ' Ὀδυσῆος ἀκοῦσαι *declares* he has heard of O., Od.17.525; στεῦται..ζυγὸν ἀμφιβαλεῖν δούλιον Ἑλλάδι A.*Pers.*49 (anap.); with inf. pres., στεῦται δ' Ἠελίου γόνος ἔμμεναι *boasts* that he is.., A.R.2.1204; with acc. and inf. pres., στεῦντο θεοπλήγεσσιν ἐοικότας εἰδώλοισιν ἔμμεναι ἢ λάεσσιν *declared* that they were.., Maiist. l.c.: abs. once in Od., στεῦτο δὲ διψάων, πιέειν δ' οὐκ εἶχεν ἑλέσθαι he *made eager efforts* in his thirst, 11.584. (Aristarch. seems to have connected it with ἵστημι: τὸ στεῦτο κατὰ διάνοιαν ὡρίζετο, οὐκ ἐπὶ τῆς τῶν ποδῶν στάσεως, Sch.Il.2.597, cf. Apollon. *Lex.*, Hsch.: but more prob. στεῦτο (from *στεῦστο with dissimilation) corresponds to Ved. *astoṣṭa* 'solemnly proclaimed concerning himself', 3 sg. sigmatic aor. middle of *stu-*.)

**στεφᾰλίβᾰνος** [ῐ], ὁ, a kind of *unguent*, *PGrenf.*1.39$^v$ ii 2 (ii/i B.C.).

⊛ **στεφάν-η** [ᾰ], ἡ, (στέφω) *anything that surrounds* or *encircles* the head, etc., for defence or ornament: **I.** *brim* of the helmet, βάλ' ἔγχεϊ ὀξυόεντι αὐχέν' ὑπὸ στεφάνης εὐχάλκου Il.7.12; σ. χαλκοβάρεια 11.96; the *helmet* itself, ἐπὶ στεφάνην κεφαλῆφιν ἀείρας θήκατο χαλκείην 10.30, cf. Plu.2.726f. **2.** as a woman's head-dress, *diadem*, *coronal*, Il.18.597, *h.Hom.*6.7, Hes.*Th.*578, Ar.*Ec.*1034; found on statues, *IG*2$^2$.1126.31 (Amphict. Delph., iv B.C.); distd. fr. στέφανος, in list of offerings, ib.1$^2$.264.62, al.; of men, δωρήσασθαι χρυσέῃ στεφάνῃ τὸν κυβερνήτην *crown of honour*, Hdt.8.118 (v.l. for χρυσέῳ στεφάνῳ); as a piece of outlandish luxury, Ar.*Eq.*968: metaph., of a city, ἀπὸ στεφάναν κέκαρσαι πύργων thou hast been shorn of thy *coronal* of towers, E.*Hec.*910 (lyr.), cf. *Tr.*784 (anap.), *AP*9.97 (Alph.). **b.** σ. τριχῶν the *outer fringe* of hair round bald or shaven crowns, as represented on comic masks, Poll.4.144, cf. 2.40. **3.** Medic., *sutura coronalis*, Aret.*CD*1.2, Poll.2.39. **b.** in the eye, *rim of the cornea* where it joins the sclerotic, Gal.18(2).47, *UP*10.2, Ruf.*Onom.*26, Hsch.; *rim of the eyelids*, Ruf.*Onom.*20, Gal.14.767; *eyeball*, Hp.*Vid.Ac.*4. **c.** a *circular muscle*, such as the *sphincter ani*, Poll.2.211; = *corona glandis*, Antyll.ap.Orib.50.3.6, Ruf.*Sat.Gon.*5. **d.** of animals, *upper rim of the hoof*, *coronet*, Opp.*C.*1.232. **e.** in pl., *stripes* of the wild ass, ib.3.188. **4.** a kind of *laurel*, of which crowns were made, v.l. for στέφανος II. 10 in Dsc.4.145. **5.** Geom., *plane figure contained between two concentric circles*, Hero *Deff.*37. **b.** *external periphery of a vault*, Id.*Mens.* 16. **6.** pl., *rings* composing the universe, Parm.ap.*Placit.*2.7.1. **II.** *brim* or *edge* of anything, *brow of a hill*, *edge of a cliff*, Il. 13.138, *Inscr.Prien.*361 (iv B.C.), 42.55 (ii/i B.C.), *SIG*685.60 (Crete, ii B.C.), Plb.1.56.4, Conon 35; τοῦ θεάτρου Plb.7.16.6; Τείθρωνος *IG*9$^2$(1).51.2 (Thermum, iii B.C.): generally, *edge*, *border*, *moulding*, Thphr.*HP*5.6.2, Lxx *Ex.*25.23, al.; ταλάροιο Mosch.2.55; τύμβου A.R.2.918; *parapet*, Lxx *De.*22.8: pl., = αἱ τῶν βωμῶν ὠλέναι, Hsch. **2.** *part of the* ποδοστράβη, X.*Cyn.*9.12, cf. Poll.5.32. **-ηδόν**, Adv. *like a crown*, Man.4.429.

**στεφᾰνηπλοκ-έω**, Aeol. **στεφανᾱ-**, *plait wreaths*, Sapph.73, Ar. *Th.*448. **-ια**, τά, *place where wreaths are plaited* or *sold*, *AP*12.8 (Strat.): sg. **στεφανοπλόκιον**, = *coronarium*, *Gloss.* **-ος** (parox.), ὁ, ἡ, Dor. **στεφᾰνᾱπλ-** *Rev.Arch.*22 (1925).63 (Callatis):—*plaiter of wreaths*, Thphr.*HP*6.8.1, *BGU*1528.1 (Ptolemaic), Plu.2.645f; also **στεφανοπλόκος**, Parmenio ap.Ath.13.608a, Dsc.3.75, 4.71, *PLond.* 1.125.35 (iv A.D.).

**στεφᾰνηφορ-έω**, Dor. **στεφανᾱφ-**, *wear a wreath*, E.*HF*781 (lyr.), D.21.51, *SIG*352.4 (Ephesus, iv/iii B.C.); -φοροῦντες καὶ πανηγυρίζοντες Gauthier et Sottas *Décret trilingue en l'honneur de Ptolémée IV* p.66 (iii B.C.), cf. Anon.Hist. (*FGr.H* 160) p.886 J., *OGI*90.50 (Rosetta, ii B.C.), al.: c. acc., σ. κιττοῦ στέφανον *IG*12(9).192 (Eretria, iv B.C.): metaph. of virtue, -οῦσα πομπεύει Lxx *Wi.*4.2. **II.** *to be a* στεφανηφόρος (signf. II), *SIG*695.1 (Magn. Mae., ii B.C.), al.—Also **στεφανοφορέω**, Hp.*Ep.*17 (v.l. for στεφανηφ-); τοῦ Ἀπόλλωνος *Supp.Epigr.*4.263.6 (Panamara, i A.D.). ⊛ **-ία**, Dor. **στεφανᾱφ-**, ἡ, *wearing of a wreath*, esp. of victory, Pi.*O.*8.10; νίκας σ. E.*El.*862 (lyr.); πανήγυριν..συντελεῖν μετὰ -ίας καὶ θυσιῶν *OGI* 56.40 (Canopus, iii B.C.), cf. 6.23 (Scepsis, iv B.C.); -ίαν ἄγειν *PGiss.* 27.8 (ii A.D.). **II.** *the right of wearing a crown*, which belonged to certain magistrates (v. στεφανηφόρος II), D.21.33; ταῖς κοιναῖς σ. Lex ap.Aeschin.1.21; πολλὰς..σ. πεποιηκώς *CIG*2771 i 4 (Aphrodisias), cf. 2814 (ibid.), al. **-ια**, τά, festival at Alexandria, *PSI*5.514.2 (iii B.C.). **-ικός**, ή, όν, *pertaining to the* στεφανηφορία, νόμος *Milet.*7.28 (ii B.C.); φιέλη prob. rest. in *Inscr.Prien.*113.93 (i B.C.). **2.** of one who has enjoyed the right of στεφανηφορία, ἀνήρ *IGRom.*4.1644 (Philadelphia). ⊛ **-ος** (parox.), ον, *wearing a crown* or *wreath*, θίασοι E.*Ba.*531 (lyr.); χοροί prob. in B.18.51; ἵπποι Theoc.

16.47; σ. ἀγών, = στεφανίτης, a contest *in which the prize was a crown*, Hdt.5.102, And.4.2; hence Ἀλφειέ, Διὸς σ. ὕδωρ *AP*9.362; σ. ὧραι *Scol.*3; νίκη *APl.*4.62. II. στεφανηφόρος, ὁ, title of certain magistrates in Greek states *who had the right of wearing crowns* when in office, as the Archons at Athens, σ. ἀρχή Aeschin.1.19; compared with the Roman *flamen* by D.H.2.64, cf. Ath.5.215b, 12.533e; freq. in Inscrr., Φοίβου σ. ἱρεύς *IG*14.1020 (Rome), cf. *CIG* 2671, al. (Iasus), *SIG*169.2, al. (ibid., iv B.C.), *OGI*213.35 (Milet., iv/iii B.C.), al.; and of women, *IG*12(8).526.7 (Thasos); ὁ ἄρχων τὴν σ. ἀρχήν ib.12(5).821.6 (Tenos, ii B.C.); στεφανηφόρος Κλεοπάτρας θεᾶς *PRein.*10.6 (ii B.C.); σ. ἐξηγητεία *PRyl.*77.34 (ii A.D.). III. δραχμαὶ Στεφανηφόρου, i.e. officially minted, the Athenian mint being attached to a temple of the hero Σ., *IG*2$^2$.1013.31, 1028.30 (ii B.C.), cf. Antipho *Frr.*36, 44: also δραχμὰς στεφανηφόρους *with a wreath on the reverse*, *JHS*54.142 (Delos, ii B.C.).

**στεφᾰν-ιαῖος**, α, ον, *of* or *like a crown*, κάλαμοι σ. τὸ πάχος D.S.2.59 (s.v.l.); σ. ῥαφή *sutura coronalis*, Gal.*UP*9.7, al., Antyll.ap.Orib.7.14.1; of the ἐπινέμησις (direction) of a bandage, *like a* στέφος I, Gal.18(1).786; of the eyelashes, (sc. τρίχες) Id.14.771. **-ίας**, ου, ὁ, = στεφανηφόρος, Arg.E.*Hipp.* **-ίζω**, Dor. aor. I ἐστεφάνιξα, *crown*, Ar.*Eq.*1225; Att. aor. inf. -ίσαι Hsch. **-ικός**, ή, όν, *of* or *for a crown*, σ. τέλεσμα, = Lat. *aurum coronarium*, at Rhodes and Ancyra, Suid.; so στεφανικὸν χρῆμα *Theb.Ostr.*95 (ii A.D.), 96 (iii A.D.); πράκτωρ στεφανικῶν collector of the στέφανος tax (cf. στέφανος II. 5,6), *POxy.*1441.4 (ii A.D.), *BGU*452 i 3 (iii A.D.), *PSI* 7.733.5 (iii A.D.). **-ιον**, τό, Dim. of στέφανος, *IG*11(2).223 *B* 13 (Delos, iii B.C.); στεφάνια τῷ Ἀδώνει *PPetr.*3 p.332 (iii B.C.), cf. *PFay.*103.4 (iii A.D.), Alciphr.1.36. 2. *gratuity, official reward*, *UPZ*64.12 (ii B.C.), *Ostr.*1530 (ii B.C.). 3. *cake in the form of a crown*, *BGU* 1668.3 (i A.D.), *POxy.*936.12 (iii A.D.). **-ίς**, ίδος, ἡ, = στεφάνη II, *parapet*, Sch.Ar.*Ach.*922. **-ίσκος**, ὁ, Dim. of στέφανος, Anacr.54, *Anacreont.*42.15, *SIG*1106.122 (Cos, iv/iii B.C.), Dsc.1.30.4, Longus 1.9, al.: also **-ίσκη**, ἡ, Theognost.*Can.*110. **-ίτης** [ῑ], ου, ὁ, *of* or *consisting of a crown*: σ. ἀγών a contest *in which the prize was a crown*, X.*Mem.*3.7.1, Isoc.15.301 (pl.), D.20.141 (pl.), Lycurg.51 (pl.), Ister 60b, Lync.ap.Ath.13.584c, *SIG*577.55 (Milet., iii/ii B.C.), *OGI*231.14 (Magn. Mae., iii/ii B.C.), Plu.2.820d, etc.; written **-είτης**, *IG*12(8).190.41 (Samothrace, i B.C.). 2. later, of persons, *wearing a wreath*, as magistrates or as victorious athletes, *Supp.Epigr.*7.3 (Susa, i B.C.), *Sammelb.*4224.9 (i B.C.), *CIG*2931 (Tralles), *IG*14.1054 (Rome, ii A.D.), *BSA*26.166 (Sparta, ii A.D.). 3. σ. φόρος, v.l. for στεφανιτικός, J.*AJ*12.3.3. II. fem. **στεφανῖτις**, ιδος, *for wreaths*, μυρσίνη Sch.Il.17.51. 2. ἡ σ. (sc. ῥαφή) *sutura coronalis*, Poll.2.37. 3. a kind of *vine*, Plin.*HN*14.42. **-ῑτικός**, ή, όν, = στεφανικός, φόρος J.*AJ*12.3.3. **-ίων**· εἶδος κολοιοῦ (fort. κλοιοῦ), Hsch.

**στεφᾰνο-πλόκιον, -πλόκος**, v. στεφανηπλ-. **-ποϊκή**, ἡ (sc. τέχνη), *art of making crowns*, Phld.*Mus.* p.88 K. **-ποιός**, ὁ, *chaplet-maker*, Arist.*MM*1206$^a$27, A.D.*Adv.*189.9. **-πώλης**, ου, ὁ, *dealer in crowns* or *chaplets*, *PRyl.*224.9 (i A.D., dub. rest.), Poll.7.199, Suid.:— fem. ⊛**-πωλις**, ιδος, *Sammelb.*1080, Plu.2.646e, 972d, Ael.ap.Ar.Byz. *Epit.*64.15; Στεφανοπώλιδες, name of a comedy by Eubulus; also **-πωλήτρια**, ἡ, Poll.7.199.

⊛**στέφᾰνος**, ὁ, (στέφω) *that which surrounds* or *encompasses*, πάντη γάρ σε περὶ σ. πολέμοιο δέδηεν the *circling* fight, Il.13.736; of the *wall round* a town, Pi.*O.*8.32; σ. πόλεος Anacr.72, cf. Orph.*A.*761,897; cf. στεφάνη I. 2; καλλίπαις σ. *circle* of fair children, E.*HF*839. II. *crown, wreath, chaplet*, *h.Hom.*7.42; χρύσεος ib.32.6; στεφάνους ..ἄνθεα ποίης Hes.*Th.*576, cf. Pi.*P.*4.240; κισσίνους σ. δρυός τε E.*Ba.*703; δάφνας σ. Isyll.19; ῥόδινος, ῥοδόεις, Anacr.83, Theoc.7.64; ἀνθεμεῦντες Anacr.62; πλεκτὸν σ. ἐκ λειμῶνος φέρω E.*Hipp.*73, cf. Xenoph.1.2; μύρτων Ar.*Ra.*330 (lyr.); κιττοῦ καὶ ἴων Pl.*Smp.*212e; φιλύρας Xenarch.13, etc.; στεφάνωσεν δρακόντων στεφάνοις E.*Ba.*102 (lyr.); σ. εἴρειν, πλέκειν, ἀνείρειν, Pi.*N.*7.77, *I.*8(7).74, Ar.*Ach.*1006; ὑφαίνειν Plu.2.646e; πέρθεσθαι φόβαισι Sapph.78, cf. E.*Med.*984 (lyr.); θεῖσα ἀμφὶ βοστρύχοις ib.1160; σ. ἐλαίας ἀμφέθηκά σοι Id.*Ion* 1433; περιθεῖναι σ. τινί Ar.*Eq.*1227; χρυσῷ σ. ἀναδῆσαί τινα Th.4.121; χρυσῷ στεφάνῳ στεφανωθῆναι Pl.*Ion* 530d; μύρα, στεφάνους ἑτοίμασον for a feast, Men.273, cf. Amphis 9.4, Alex.250, etc.; hung at the door on festive occasions, Ephipp.3.2. b. in pl., οἱ σ. the *garland-market*, Antiph.83. 2. *crown of victory* at the public games, Pi.*O.*8.76; τῆς ἐλαίης τὸν διδόμενον σ. Hdt.8.26; νικᾶν παγκρατίου στέφανον Pi.*N.*5.5, cf. *I.*1.21; σ. ἔλαχεν Id.*O.*10(11).61; ὁ ἐπὶ τοῦ σ., title of an officer who had charge of these matters in Roman times, *IGRom.*4.1435.15 (Smyrna). b. *honorary wreath* or *crown*, freq. worked in gold, awarded for public services in war or peace, *IG*1$^2$.110.10, 2$^2$.212.24, 338.19, al., Pl.*Lg.*943c, Aeschin.2.46, *OGI*49.7 (Egypt, iii B.C.), al., Callix.2: such crowns were freq. dedicated in temples, *IG*2$^2$.1386.33, cf. 11(2).199 *B* 60, al. (Delos, iii B.C.); περὶ τοῦ σ., title of D.18, cf. Aeschin.3.187, al.: metaph., *prize, reward*, αὐτῷ μὲν σ. περιθείς, Σαμίοισι δὲ κῦδος Epigr. ap.Hdt.4.88; τοὺς παῖδας..δημοσίᾳ ἡ πόλις θρέψει, ὠφέλιμον σ...τῶν ..ἀγώνων προτιθεῖσα Th.2.46; τοῦδε γὰρ ὁ σ. his is the *prize* (or perh. for (bringing) him the *prize* is offered), S.*Ph.*841 (hex.). c. σ. πυργωτὸς καὶ οὐαλλάριος, = Lat. *corona muralis et vallaris*, a Roman military decoration, *OGI*560.10 (Tlos, i A.D.); σ. τειχικός ib.540.19 (Pessinus, i A.D.). 3. *crown of glory, honour*, οὐκ ἂν αἰσχυνθείην εἰπὼν στέφανον τῆς πατρίδος εἶναι τὰς ἐκείνων ψυχάς Lycurg.50; ἐλευθερίας ἀμφέθετο σ. Simon.98; σ. εὐκλείας μέγας S.*Aj.*465, cf. Pi.*P.*1.100, E.*Supp.*315; μέγας γάρ σοι ὁ σ. ἐστιν ὑπὸ πάντων εὐλογεῖσθαι *PSI* 4.405.4 (iii B.C.); σ. ζωῆς, δόξης, *Ep.Jac.*1.12, 1*Ep.Pet.*5.4; ὁ τῆς δικαιοσύνης σ. 2*Ep.Ti.*4.8· ἀνδρὸς στέφανος παῖδες Hom.*Epigr.*13, cf. E.*IA*194 (lyr.), 1*Ep.Thess.*2.19. 4. *crown as a badge of office*, D.21.32; πέπαυνται ἄρχοντες καὶ τοὺς σ. περιῄρηνται Id.26.5; ὁ βασιλεὺς ὅταν δικάζῃ περιαιρεῖται τὸν σ. Arist.*Ath.*57.4; ὁ σ. οὗτος, of the office of ἀρχιερεὺς Ἀσίας, Philostr.*VS*1.21.2, cf. *OGI*470.21 (Asia Minor), Lib.*Or.*53.4; ἔχειν τὸν σ. *to be in office*, *SIG*1007.22 (Pergam., ii B.C.); ἡ ἀπόθεσις τῶν σ. ib.900.16 (Panamara, iv A.D.); ἀναδήσασθαι τὸν σ. τοῦτον *POxy.*1252$^v$.20 (iii A.D.): v. στεφανηφόρος II, στεφανόω II. 5. 5. in Egypt, *money gift to the sovereign, levied by the state*, *PTeb.*746.24 (iii B.C.), *PSI*4.388.5 (iii B.C.), *PCair.Zen.*36.27 (iii B.C.), etc.; likewise in Syria, Lxx 1*Ma.*10.29; also of similar gifts to a court favourite, *PFay.*14 (ii B.C.), cf. *Ostr.Bodl.* i 202 (ii B.C.). 6. τὰς εἰς τὸν σ. ἐπαγγελίας οὐκ ἔλαβον, = *aurum coronarium non accepi*, *Mon.Anc.*11.22, cf. *PFay.*20.7 (iii/iv A.D.). 7. *donation*, euphemism for a bribe, διεθέντος μου ὑπάρξει σοι εἰς σ. τάλαντα δεκαπέντε *PGrenf.*1.41.2 (ii B.C.), cf. *OGI*221.6 (Ilium, iii B.C.), *PGoodsp.Cair.*5.5 (ii B.C.); *gratuity, bonus*, *PFlor.*74.14 (ii A.D.). 8. the constellation *Corona*, Epimenid.25, Arist.*Mete.*362$^b$10, Arat.71, *PHib.*1.27.58,187 (iii B.C.); σ. τόν τε κλείουσ' Ἀριάδνης A.R.3.1003. 9. name of a πηγή in the Chaldaean system, Dam.*Pr.*96. 10. = δάφνη Ἀλεξανδρεία, Dsc.4.145; Ἡλίου σ., = ἅλιμος, Ps.-Dsc.1.91.

**στεφᾰνοσταύριον**, τό, *cross in a wreath*, *Palestine Exploration Fund Quarterly Statement* 1931.67 (Beth Shan).

**στεφᾰνοῦχος**, ον, *wearing a crown*, *AP*7.88 (D.L.).

**στεφᾰνοφορέω**, v. στεφανηφ-.

**στεφᾰν-όω**, Med., Syracusan 2 sg. imper. στεφάνουσο Sch.Theoc.11.42:—Pass., fut. -ώσομαι Aristid.1.496 J.; -ωθήσομαι Aeschin.3.20, al., *PCair.Zen.*60.7 (iii B.C.): I. used by Hom. and Hes. only in Pass., *to be put round in a circle* or *as a rim* or *border*, and hence *to be put round*, ἣν περὶ μὲν πάντῃ Φόβος ἐστεφάνωται *round about* the aegis *is* Terror *wreathed*, Il.5.739; τῇ δ' ἐπὶ μὲν Γοργὼ ἐστεφάνωτο 11.36; ἀμφὶ δέ μιν θυόεν νέφος ἐστεφάνωτο *all round about* him *was* a cloud, 15.153; νῆσον, τὴν πέρι πόντος ἐστεφάνωται the sea *lies round about* the island, Od.10.195: rarely c. acc., τείρεα, τά τ' οὐρανὸς ἐστεφάνωται constellations which heaven *has all round it*, Il.18.485, cf. Hes.*Th.*382, *IG*4$^2$(1).129.9 (Epid.); of a crowd of spectators *surrounding* a dancing-floor, ἀμφὶ δ' ὅμιλος ἀπείριτος ἐστεφάνωτο *h.Ven.*120; περὶ δ' ὄλβος ἀπείριτος ἐστεφάνωτο around *were*..riches *in a circle placed*, Hes.*Sc.*204: so in later Ep., A.R.3.1214, Q.S.5.99, Orph.*A.*45, etc.: also in Act., περίτροχον ἐστεφάνωσαν αἱμασιήν *made* a fence *round*, Opp.*C.*4.90. 2. *to be surrounded*, ἐστεφανωμένος τιάραν μυρσίνῃ *having his* tiara *wreathed* with myrtle, Hdt.1.132; πεδία ἐστεφάνωται ὄρεσιν *are surrounded by*.., Hp.*Aër.*19; ὅπλοισιν πόλις Epigr.ap.Paus.9.15.6; χθὼν ἅτε νῆσος -ωται D.P.4: so in Act., [Βαβυλῶνα] τείχεσιν ἐστεφάνωσεν Id.1006. II. after Hom. in Act., *crown, wreathe*, χαίταν Pi.*O.*14.24; Ὀρέστην σ. E.*Or.*924; κρᾶτα κισσίνοις βλαστήμασιν Id.*Ba.*177; στεφάνοις ib.101 (lyr.); c. gen., πίτυος Longus 2.31; σ. τινὰ ὡς σωτῆρα And.1.45; τὸν νικῶντα θαλλῷ Pl.*Lg.*946b; νῖκαι σ. τινά Pi.*N.*11.21; of crowning a corpse, Ar.*Ec.*538; a tomb, *IG*1$^2$.1037, *Sammelb.*7457.10 (iii/ii B.C.), Luc.*Cont.*22, *PLips.*30.2 (iii A.D.); ships, Plu.2.981e; of the nuptial crown, Lxx *Ca.*3.11; κατηρῶντο τοῖς ἐστεφανωμένοις *newly wedded couples*, Lib.*Or.*33.29; στεφανοῦν εὐαγγέλια *crown* one *for* good tidings, Ar.*Eq.*647; στεφανοῦσα, title of a statue by Praxiteles (v. στέφω III), cf. Ath.12.534d:—Pass., *to be crowned* or *rewarded with a crown*, Hdt.7.55, 8.59, *PCair.Zen.* l.c., 2*Ep.Ti.*2.5; ἐλαίᾳ Pi.*O.*4.13; ποίᾳ Id.*P.*8.19; φυτὸν στεφανούμενος Ach.Tat.1.5; σ. καὶ ἀνακηρύττεσθαι And.2.18:—Med., *crown oneself*, στεφανωσαμένη δρυῒ καὶ.. σπείραισι δρακόντων S.*Fr.*535 (anap.); στεφανοῦσθε κισσῷ E.*Ba.*106 (lyr.); στεφανωσάμενος καλάμῳ Ar.*Nu.*1006; στεφανωσάμενος αὐτόν (sc. τὸν στέφανον) Phalar.*Ep.*40; στεφανοῦνται τῶν ἀνθέων Philostr.*Her.*12$^a$.2; τῆς πίτυος D.Chr.9.10: also abs., of one going to sacrifice, Th.4.80; τῷ θεῷ X.*HG*4.3.21; at a festival, Ar.*Ach.*1145, Men.518.15, etc.; *win a crown*, of the victor at the games, Pi.*O.*7.15, 81, 12.17, *N.*6.19:—Pass., c. dupl. acc., ἐστεφανώθη Ἐλεύθερος..Ἀδριάνεια πάλην *IG*2$^2$.2087.64 (ii A.D.). 2. *crown* as an honour or reward (cf. στέφανος II. 2b), D.19.193, Theopomp.Hist.239, Men.84, *IG*2$^2$.212.30 (iv B.C.), etc.; *reward* by a gift of money, etc. (cf. στέφανος II. 5), Καλλισθένην ἑκατὸν μναῖς Lycurg.*Fr.*19, cf. D.S.14.53, Plu.*Tim.*16; σ. τινὰ πεντακοσίοις ἀργυρίου ταλάντοις, χιλίοις δὲ λιβανωτοῦ Plb.13.9.5: also ἐστεφανωκότος..τὰς δυνάμεις χρυσῶν μυριάδων τριάκοντα Gauthier et Sottas *Décret trilingue en l'honneur de Ptolémée IV* p.67 (iii B.C.). 3. metaph., *confer glory upon, decorate, honour*, τινὰ μολπᾷ Pi.*O.*1.100; τοὺς πρεσβυτέρους ἤθεσι χρηστοῖς Ar.*Nu.*959; ἀπὸ τῶν ὑπαρχόντων τὴν πόλιν (by a victory in the games) And.4.26; Ἑλλάδα E.*Tr.*1030, cf. Critias 4 D.; ἔργοις γένος *TAM*1.44 (Xanthus); [τὸ ῥόδον] ἐγκωμίῳ Philostr.*Ep.*51; ἀριστείοις D.S.4.32; πανοπλίᾳ Id.20.84:—Pass., σοφίας ἀριστεῖα ἐστεφανοῦτο Philostr.*Her.*10.4. 4. *crown* or *honour* with libations, σ. τύμβον αἵματι E.*Hec.*126 (anap.). 5. *crown* with the badge of office, esp. of persons sacrificing, Lys.26.8:—Pass., X.*An.*7.1.40; of magistrates in office, ὁ ἐστεφανωμένος ἄρχων D.21.17; βούλεται -ωθῆναι ἐξηγητείαν *PRyl.*77.37 (ii A.D.). **-ώδης**, ες, *like a wreath, wreathed*, χλόα E.*IA*1058 (lyr.). ⊛ **-ωμα**, ατος, τό, *that which surrounds, crown, wreath*, Thgn.1001; βωμῶν Pi.*I.*4(3).62(80); μεγάλαιν θεοῖν ἀρχαῖον σ. S.*OC*684 (lyr.); σ. πύργων [the city's] *coronal* of towers, the *encircling* towers, Id.*Ant.*122

(lyr.). **2.** a *crown* as the prize of victory, Pi.*P.*12.5; σελίνων Id.*I.*2.15. **3.** pl., *the place where crowns or garlands were sold,* Ar.*Ec.*303 (lyr.), Pherecr.2. **4.** *plants used for making garlands,* Cratin. 150, Thphr.*HP*6.6.1, cf. Ath.15.672f, Hsch. **II.** *reward, honour, glory,* πλούτου, Κυράνας, Pi.*P.*1.50, 9.4; παγκρατίου Id.*I.*4(3).44(62); παῖδα Διὸς ὑμνῆσαι, σ. μόχθων *as a reward* for.., E.*HF*355 (lyr.). **-ωμᾰτικός,** ή, όν, *used for making garlands,* Thphr.*HP*1.12.4, 6.6.1, al.; λυχνὶς σ. Dsc.3.100; ἕρπυλλος ib.38. ❀ **-ωσις,** εως, ἡ, *crowning,* *IG*12(1).155*d*67 (Rhodes), Ath.15.673a sq.; μετὰ τὴν σ. τῶν δήμων *after being crowned* by the peoples, *CIG*3067.24 (Teos, ii B.C.), cf. 3068a.19 (ibid., pl.); ἀναγράψαι.. τὰς γενομένας σ. *Inscr.Prien.*99.18 (ii/i B.C.). **-ωτής,** οῦ, ὁ, *one who crowns,* Hdn.*Epim.*211. **-ωτικός,** ή, όν, = στεφανωματικός, Thphr.*HP*1.13.3, al. **2.** *concerning a crown,* λόγος Men.Rh. p.422 S. **II.** ❀στεφανωτικόν, τό, *money for crowning a tomb,* Judeich *Altertümer von Hierapolis* Nos.133, 195. **III.** -κά, τά, dub. sens. in *POxy.*1652 (iii A.D.). **-ωτρίς,** ίδος, ἡ, *of* or *fit for a crown* or *wreath,* Apolloph.5; βύβλος Theopomp.Hist.22(c), cf. Thphr.*Fr.*142: also **-ωτίς,** μυρρίναι Id.*HP*5.8.3.

**στεφέτην·** ἱκέτην, Hsch.

**στεφη-πλόκος,** ον, v.l. for στεφανηπλόκος, Plu.2.41e. **-φορέω,** = στεφανηφορέω, D.H.3.21 codd., *Sardis* 7(1).8.15 (i B.C., perh. an error of the engraver). **-φόρος,** ον, = στεφανηφόρος, Lyc.327, Vett. Val.45.32, al.

❀ **στέφος,** εος, τό, (στέφω) poet. for στέφανος, *crown, wreath, garland,* Emp.112.6, Simon.158, E.*IA*1512 (lyr.), etc.: pl. στέφη, = στέμματα, A.*Ag.*1265, *Th.*101 (lyr.), S.*OT*913: also in late Prose, Gal.18(1).786, Vett.Val.248.28; τὸ σ. τῶν φιλοσόφων, sc. Zosimus, Olymp. Alch. p.83 B. **2.** of libations, A.*Ch.*95; cf. στέφω II.3.

❀ **στέφω,** Od.8.170, S.*Ant.*431, Hyp.*Fr.*103: impf. ἔστεφον Il.18.205, A.*Th.*50; στέφον Hes.*Op.*75: fut. στέψω S.*Aj.*93, E.*Tr.*576 (anap.): aor. ἔστεψα Pl.*Phd.*58c:—Med., fut. στέψομαι Ath.15.676d: aor. ἐστεψάμην *AP*9.363.3 (Mel.), D.H.*Rh.*1.6, etc., (ἐπ-) Il.1.470:—Pass., fut. στεφθήσομαι Gal.*Protr.*13: aor. ἐστέφθην E.*Hel.*1360 (lyr.): pf. ἔστεμμαι A.*Supp.*345, Pl.*Phd.*58a, etc.; Ion. pf. part. ἐστεθμένος *Schwyzer* 725 (Milet., vi B.C.), cf. στέθματα.—στεφανόω is more freq., esp. in Prose:—*put round,* ἀμφὶ δέ οἱ κεφαλῇ νέφος ἔστεφε δῖα θεάων Il.18.205; ἀλλὰ θεὸς μορφὴν ἔπεσι στέφει Od.8.170; μνημεῖα πρὸς ἅρμ' Ἀδράστου χερσὶν ἔστεφον *hung* them *round* it, A.*Th.*50; λάφυρα δαΐων.. ἁγνοῖς δόμοις στέψω πρὸ ναῶν ib.279:—Med., *put round one's head,* ποίην *AP*9.363 (Mel.); σκόροδα prob. in Ath.15.676d; κύκλους ἐλαίης Orph.*A.*325; ἰούλους *Anacreont.*42.10. **II.** *encircle, crown, wreath,* τινὰ ἄνθεσι Hes.*Op.*75; σε παγχρύσοις λαφύροις S.*Aj.*93; κρᾶτα μυρσίνης κλάδοις E.*Alc.*759; ἐρίῳ Pl.*R.*398a; κάρα κισσῷ E.*Ba.*341; σ. τὴν πρύμναν τοῦ πλοίου Pl.*Phd.*58c; νεκρόν Lyc.799; στήλην Call.*Epigr.*8, cf. *AP*7.657 (Leon.); ὁ στρατηγὸς ἔστεψέν [τινα] εἰς γυμνασίαρχ[ον] Wilcken *Chr.*41 ii 8 (iii A.D.):—Med., στέφου κάρα *crown thy* head, E.*Ba.*313; ἀμφὶ δὲ φύλλοις στεψάμενοι A.R.1.1124; βάκχοισιν κεφαλὰς περιανθέσιν ἐστέψαντο Nic.*Fr.*130:—Pass., *to be crowned,* A.*Supp.*345; τινι *with* a thing, Id.*Eu.*44; τινος Nonn.*D.*5.282: with acc. of the games in which the prize is won, στεφθεὶς παγκράτιον *CIG*4380*m* 10 (Oenoanda); ἔστεψαι τὰ Ὀλύμπια Luc.*Merc.Cond.*13; ποσσάκις ἐστέφθης δρόμον; *IG*14.1603 (Rome); στεφθεὶς στάδιν (= στάδιον) ib.1108 (ibid.); of a magistracy, στεφέσθω Ἀχιλλεὺς κοσμητείαν *PRyl.*77.34 (ii A.D.):—Med., Ἴσθμια καλλικόμοις στεψάμενον πίτυσιν Orph.*Fr.*290; στεψάμενοι σταδίοις *APl.*5.371. **2.** *wreathe* a bowl or cup with leaves, Alex.119.6, cf. Ar.*Fr.*380; γυλλὸς ἐστεμμένος *SIG*57.26 (Milet., v B.C.); γυλλοὶ ἐστεθμένοι *Schwyzer* l.c. **3.** *crown* or *honour* with libations, χοαῖσι τρισπόνδοισι τὸν νέκυν σ. S.*Ant.*431; τύμβον λοιβαῖσι.. στέψαντες Id.*El.*53; ὅπως.. αὐτὸν ἀφνεωτέραις χερσὶ στέφωμεν ib.458, cf. E.*Or.*1322. **III.** Pass., στέφανον τὸν ἐκ τῆς βύβλου στεφόμενον *twined* of papyrus, Ath.15.676d codd.:—Act., στέφουσα, title of a statue by Praxiteles, v.l. for στεφανοῦσα in Plin. *HN*34.70. (τὸ στέφειν πλήρωσιν τινα σημαίνει Arist.*Fr.*101 (arguing from Hom.); cf. ἐπιστέφω, ἐπιστεφής; the orig. sense and etym. are doubtful.)

❀ **στεφών·** ὑψηλός, ἀπόκρημνος, Hsch.: as Subst., *summit* of range of hills, ὡς ὁ σ. περιφέρει κύκλῳ *Schwyzer* 709.8 (Ephesus, iii B.C.).

**στέψις,** εως, ἡ, *wreathing, crowning,* *BGU*362 iii 26 (iii A.D.), *POxy.*2147 (iii A.D.), Sch.A.R.2.159.

**στέωμεν,** v. ἵστημι. **στηβύσσειν·** ἀδολεσχεῖν, Hsch. **στήγανον,** *segestrum, Gloss.* **στήγω,** v. στήκω.

**στήδην,** Adv. = στάδην, *by weight,* Nic.*Al.*327.

**στηδόν·** γλαυκόν, Hsch. **στήης, στήῃ,** v. ἵστημι.

**στηθαῖον,** τό, (στῆθος) *breastwork, parapet,* Sch.E.*Ph.*1180.

**στηθάριον,** τό, *bust,* σ. ἐπὶ βάσεως Hermes Trism. in *Rev.Phil.*32.260.

**στήθ-ειος,** ον, *of the breast,* ἱμάντες Eust.1189.54. **-ιαῖος,** α, ον, *of the breast,* λῶροι Sch.Ar.*Eq.*765. **2.** = *pectorosus, Gloss.* **II.** ἀνδριάντες, perh. = *clupei, thoraces,* *IG*14.956*B*6 (Rome, iv A.D.). **-ίας,** ου, ὁ, a kind of *bird,* Hsch. **-ίδιον,** τό, = στηθίον, Phryn.361, Suid. **-ικός,** ή, όν, *of the breast,* τοῦ σ. τόπου Arist.*PA*666ᵇ7. **-ίν,** τό, prob. = sq., but in sense *breast-ornament,* *PAmh.*2.125.8 (i A.D.). **-ίον,** τό, Dim. of στῆθος, Alex.98.13, Arist.*Phgn.*810ᵇ23. **-ιστήρ,** ῆρος, ὁ, *poitrel* of a war-horse, *Gloss.*

**στηθο-δέσμη,** ἡ, woman's *breast-band,* *EM*749.44; also **-δεσμία,** ἡ, Sor.1.55; **-δεσμίς,** ίδος, ἡ, *PCair.Zen.*456.1 (iii B.C.), Lxx *Je.*2.32, Phleg.*Fr.*36.1 J., Gal.18(1).823; **-δεσμος,** ὁ, Poll.7.66: a bandage, Heliod. ap. Orib.48.49 tit.:—Dim. **-δέσμιον,** τό, *EM*749.40. **-ειδής,** ές, *rounded like the breast,* μαχαιρίς Hp.*Morb.*2.47.

❀ **στῆθος,** εος, τό, *breast,* of both sexes, being the front part of the θώραξ, divided into two μαστοί (Arist.*HA*493ᵃ12, *PA*688ᵃ13, al.), Hom. and later (cf. στέρνον), esp. in Prose, rare (and usu. metaph.) in post-Homeric verse; found once in Pi., twice in B., twice in A., never in S. or E. (v. infr. I, II); βάλε σ. παρὰ μαζόν Il.4.480; ἔβαλε σ. μεταμάζιον 5.19; κληῒς ἀποέργει αὐχένα τε στῆθός τε 8.326, cf. Pl.*Ti.*69e, 79c (pl.), *Prt.*352a (pl.): in pl., διὰ στήθεσφιν (Ep. gen.) ἔλασσε Il.5.41; στήθεά τ' ἠδ' ἁπαλὴν δειρήν (of Briseis) 19.285; of animals, 11.282, 16.163, al., cf. X.*Cyn.*4.1, Arist.*HA*496ᵃ9, 15, al., *PCair.Zen.*532.7, 18 (iii B.C.), *BGU*469.7 (ii A.D.); σ. φάσσης ἑψημένης Sor.2.41, cf. 1.51: as the seat of the voice and breath, Il.3.221, 9.610, B.5.15, A.*Th.*563 (lyr.), 865 (anap.); more freq. as the seat of the heart, Il.1.189, Od.1.341, Sapph.2.6, etc.; *chest,* Hp.*Prorrh.*1.70, Ar.*Nu.*1012, 1017 (both anap.), Th.2.49 (pl.), Diocl.*Fr.*142, *IG*4²(1).121.100 (pl., Epid., iv B.C.), freq. in Arist. (v. supr.), *PEnteux.*79.7 (iii B.C.), *PTeb.*316.19 (i A.D.), Sor.1.70ᵇ, al.; τὰ σ. *breasts* of a woman, Hp.*Mul.*2.133. **II.** metaph., *the breast as the seat of feeling and thought,* as we use *heart,* freq. in Hom., but always in pl., θυμὸν ἐνὶ στήθεσσιν ὄρινε Il.2.142, al.; θάρσος ἐνὶ σ. ἐνῆκεν 17.570; ἔχει κότον.. ἐν σ. ἑοῖσι 1.83; ἐν γάρ τοι σ. μένος πατρώϊον ἧκα 5.125; νόον καὶ θυμὸν ἐνὶ σ. ἔχοντες 4.309; μῆτιν ἐνὶ σ. κέκευθε Od.3.18, cf. Pi.*Fr.*218, B.10.54: in Prose, εἰπεῖν ἃ ἔφησθα ἐν τῷ σ. ἔχειν Pl.*Phdr.*236c; πλῆρες τὸ σ. ἔχειν ib.235c. **III.** = στέρνον III, *breastbone,* Hp.*Art.*14. **2.** *ball of the foot,* ib.55, 58, cf. *Epid.*4.1, Ruf.*Onom.*125; τὸ σαρκῶδες [τοῦ ποδὸς] κάτωθεν στήθος Arist.*HA*494ᵃ13; *ball of the hand* (below the thumb), Ruf.*Onom.*86; (below the fingers), Gal.14.704; *palm,* dub. in Hp.*Oss.*9: cf. προστηθίς. **3.** *swelling, tumour,* ἐν τῷ ἥπατι Aret.*CA*2.6 (pl.). **IV.** *breast-shaped hill* or *bank,* Plb.4.41.3, *PMasp.*169*b*47 (vi A.D.), cf. Hsch. (στῆθος has pan-Hellenic η, Sapph., Pi. ll.cc., *IG*4²(1) l.c., Call. *Lav.Pall.*88, Theoc.2.79, 15.108, 135.)

**στηθύνιον** [ῠ], τό, Dim. of στῆθος, Ephipp.3.7 = Eub.150.4, Lxx *Ex.*29.26, al., Poll.2.162, *IG*2².1365, 1366; condemned by Phryn.361.

**στήκω,** late pres. formed from ἕστηκα (pf. of ἵστημι), *stand,* Lxx 3*Ki.*8.11, *Ep.Rom.*14.4, 1*Ep.Cor.*16.13, *Hippiatr.*69; imper. στῆκε *PMag.Par.*1.923; part., παρὼν καὶ **στήγων** (sic) *PLips.*40 ii 4 (iv/v A.D.); so **ἐστήκω,** Posidipp. ap. Ath.10.412e.

❀ **στήλη,** Dor. **στάλα,** Aeol. **στάλλα** (q.v.), ἡ, *block of stone* used as a *prop* or *buttress* to a wall, στήλας τε προβλῆτας ἐμόχλεον Il.12.259; *block* of rock-crystal, in which the Ethiopian mummies were cased, Hdt.3.24: generally, *block* or *base,* κόρη χρυσῆ ἐπὶ στήλης *IG*1².256.5; μεταξὺ τοῦ κίονος καὶ τῆς σ. ἐφ' ᾗ ἔστιν ὁ στρατηγὸς ὁ χαλκοῦς And.1.38, cf. Thphr.*Lap.*25; σ. ξύλιναι, λέβητε ἀπὸ στηλῶν, *IG*1².314.130, 133. **II.** *block* or *slab* used as a memorial, *monument*: **1.** *gravestone,* Il.11.371, 16.457, Od.12.14, Hippon.15, Simon.183; ὥς τε σ. μένει ἔμπεδον, ἥ τ' ἐπὶ τύμβῳ ἑστήκῃ Il.17.434; ὥς τε στήλην ἀτρέμας ἑσταότα 13.437; στῆλαι ἀπὸ σημάτων Th.1.93; οὐ στηλῶν μόνον.. ἐπιγραφή Id.2.43; μήτε στήλαις μήτε ὀνόμασι δηλοῦντας τοὺς τάφους Pl.*Lg.*873d; στάλαν θέμεν Παρίου λίθου λευκοτέραν (metaph. of a poet) Pi.*N.*4.81. **2.** *monument* inscribed with record of victories, dedications, votes of thanks, treaties, laws, decrees, etc., Hdt.2.102, 106, 4.87, Ar.*Ach.*727, Th.5.56; στήλη λιθίνη, χαλκῆ, ib.47, *IG*1².13.18; τί βεβούλευται περὶ τῶν σπονδῶν ἐν τῇ σ. παραγράψαι; Ar.*Lys.*513; τὰς θυσίας τὰς ἐκ τῶν κύρβεων καὶ τῶν σ. Lys.30.17, cf. And.1.96, 3.34; ἐν στήλῃ ἀναγραφῆναι, whether for honour, as in Hdt.6.14; or for infamy, as in And.1.51, cf. D.9.41, etc. (cf. στηλίτης, στηλιτεύω):—also the *record* itself, *contract, agreement,* στήλας ἀναγράψαι Lys.30.21; κατὰ τὴν σ. according to the *agreement,* Ar.*Av.*1051; σ. αἱ πρὸς Θηβαίους D.16.27; μάτην ἐν ταῖς σ. ἐστίν Isoc.4.176; τῆς σ. τὰ ἀντίγραφα D.20.127; παραβῆναι τὰς σ. Plb.24.8.4. **3.** *post placed on mortgaged ground,* as a record of the fact, Poll.3.85; cf. στίζω 3. **4.** *boundary-post,* στήλας ὁρίσασθαι X.*An.*7.5.13; στήλαις διαλαβεῖν τοὺς ὅρους Decr. ap. D.18.154; *turning-post* at the end of the racecourse, *IG*1².817, S.*El.*720, 744, X.*Smp.*4.6: hence περὶ στήλην διαφθείρεσθαι Lys.*Fr.*1.4. **5.** for Στῆλαι Ἡρακλήϊαι, v. Ἡράκλειος, and cf. Str.3.5.5; so σ. Διονύσου mountains in India marking the limits of the progress of Dionysus, D.P.623, cf. 1164. (Written στήλλη in some late Inscrr., *CIG*3627.1 (Ilium), 3982.18 (Philomelium), al.)

**στήληκα·** τὴν νύσσαν, Hsch.

❀ **στηλ-ίδιον,** τό, Dim. of στήλη, *little monument,* Thphr.*Char.*21.9; *boundary-stone,* Hsch. ❀ **-ίον,** τό, = foreg., *Supp.Epigr.*2.432.5 (Macedonia, iii A.D.). ❀ **-ίς,** ίδος, ἡ, = foreg., gen. sg. στηλεῖδος *IG*14.1703 (Rome); acc. pl. στηλῖδας *Epigr.Gr.*425.7 (Phrygia): f.l. for στυλίδα, Str.3.5.5, 6.1.5. **II.** a kind of number, = δοκίς, Iamb. *in Nic.* p.95 P.

❀ **στηλίτ-ευμα** [ῐ], ατος, τό, *invective,* Poll.6.181. **-εύω,** *inscribe on a* στήλη, τὴν κατάραν Plu.2.354b; *record,* τὰς ἀρετὰς ἐν ταῖς γραφαῖς Ph.2.2 (Pass.), cf. 2.24, al.:—Pass., τὰ ὀνόματα αὐτῶν ἐστηλιτεύθη Philoch.111. **2.** = στηλοκοπέω, ἐστηλίτευσαν, ἐστηλιτευμένος cited among forms of punishment by Poll.8.73; οἱ ἀπογνωσθέντες ὑπ' αὐτῶν καὶ -ευθέντες *held up to public scorn,* Iamb.*VP*35.252. **-ης,** ου, ὁ, fem. **-ῖτις,** ιδος, *of* or *like a* στήλη, λίθος Luc. *Philops.*11; ἐπὶ σταλίτιδι πέτρᾳ (Dor.) *AP*7.424 (Antip. Sid.). **II.** *inscribed on a* στήλη, *posted* or *placarded as infamous,* στηλίτην τινὰ ἀναγράφειν, -ίτας ποιεῖν, Isoc.16.9, D.9.45; σ. γεγονὼς ἐν τῇ ἀκροπόλει Thrasyb. ap. Arist.*Rh.*1400ᵃ32; cf. foreg.

**στηλο-βάτης** [ᾰ], ου, ὁ, = foreg. II, Tz.*H.*9.330. ⊛ **-γρᾰφέω**, *inscribe on* or *as on a tablet*, Ph.1.477, J.*AJ*16.6.2 (Pass.), *OGI*335.151 (Pergam., ii B.C., Pass.), Ἀρχ.Δελτ.2.145, 147 (Beroea, iii A.D.). ⊛ **-γρᾰφία**, ἡ, title of various psalms, = Hebr. *mikhtām* (a kind of psalm or song, cf. Arab. *kitmu*), Lxx *Ps.*55(56), etc. **-ειδής**, ές, v.l. for στυλ-. **-κόπας**, ου, ὁ, *tablet-glutton* (formed like ματτυοκόπας (-ης ?)), epith. of Polemo, who went about copying the inscriptions on public monuments (στῆλαι), Herodic.ap.Ath.6.234d. ⊛ **-κοπέω**, *inscribe on a* στήλη, as a form of punishment, Hyp.*Fr.*239 (Pass.): metaph., αὐτὸς ἑαυτὸν τῇ συγγραφῇ -κόπησε D.C.43.9.

**στηλοῦχος**, dub. l. in *Epigr.Gr.*214.7 (Rhenea): v. σταλ-.

⊛ **στηλ-όω**, Dor. **σταλόω**, *set up as a* στήλη or *monument*, πέτρον στάλωσε ἐπ' ἠρίῳ *AP*7.394 (Phil.); τάφον Epigr. in *POxy.*662.28 (Amyntas); σωρὸν λίθων ἐπί τινα Lxx 2*Ki.*18.17:—Pass., *to be so set up, stand firm*, ib.*Jd.*18.16, etc.:—Med., στηλοῦσθαί τινι *devote oneself to* another, Suid. 2. *inscribe on a* στήλη, *OGI*221.15 (Ilium, iii B.C.):—Pass., *Milet.*6.36 (Didyma). 3. *mark out with boundary pillars*, τὴν χώραν *OGI*225.30 (Didyma, iii B.C.), cf. 335.74 (Pergam., ii B.C.). **-ύδριον**, τό, Dim. of στήλη, *BCH*2.323, 35.286 (Delos). **-ωμα**, ατος, τό, *pillar*, Aq.*Jd.*9.6, Thd.*Is.*6.13. **-ωσις**, εως, ἡ, *recording on a tablet*, τοῦ ψηφίσματος *CIG*3600.20 (Ilium): practically = στήλη, Lxx 2*Ki.*18.18 (cod. A).

**στῆμα**, ατος, τό, *the exterior part of the membrum virile*, Ruf.*Onom.* 101, *Sat.Gon.*5, Poll.2.171. II. *stamen* of a flower, Hsch. III. as nautical term, prob. = σταμίν, Id. IV. *shaft* or *bearing* in which axle of slip-hook works, Hero *Bel.*76.6.

**στημαγορίς**, v. σταμ-.

⊛ **στημάτιον**, τό, *trunnion* or *gudgeon*, Hero *Dioptr.*3, al. II. Dim. of στῆμα IV, Id.*Bel.*78.2.

**στήμεναι**, Ep. inf. aor. 2 of ἵστημι (q. v.).

**στημίον**, τό, = sq., *PTeb.*413.12 (ii/iii A.D.), *POxy.*1142.7 (iii A.D.), 1740.5 (iii/iv A.D.).

**στημνίον**, τό, *yarn*, *IG*11(2).159*A* 16 (Delos, iii B.C.): pl., *PMich. Zen.*16.1 (iii B.C.), cf. Hsch.

**στημον-ίας**, ου, ὁ, (στήμων II) σ. κίκιννος a *thread-like* curl, Cratin. 353. **-ίζομαι**, of the spider, *lay down the spokes of a circular web*, Arist.*HA*623ᵃ9.—Act. στημονίζω is expld. by λεπτύνω in Zonar.; but Eust.1770.64 has στημονίζων = τρίβων, *threadbare garment*. **-ικός**, ή, όν, *for the warp*, λίνον *POxy.*1414.8, 10 (iii A.D.). **-ιον**, τό, Dim. of στήμων I, Arist.*Pol.*1265ᵇ20, Max.Tyr.21. 3: στημόνια is v.l. for στήμονα in Apollod.*Poliorc.*169.7. **-ιος**, ον, *of* or *like the threads of the warp*, διαλήψεις φύλλου Thphr.*HP*3.18. 11.

**στημονο-νητικός**, ή, όν, (στήμων, νέω B) τέχνη σ. the art *of spinning*, Pl.*Plt.*282e, cf. Poll.7.30, 209. **-φυής**, ές, *of the same kind with the threads of the warp*, Pl.*Plt.*309b.

**στημονώδης**, ες, *having too much warp*, τῆς ὑφῆς τὸ μὴ διεχὲς μηδὲ σ., of a spider's web, Plu.2.966f.

**στημορραγέω**, (ῥήγνυμι) intr., *to be torn to shreds*, λακίδες σ. ἐσθημάτων A.*Pers.*836.

⊛ **στήμων**, Dor. **στάμων** [ᾱ] *AP*6.160.6 (Antip. Sid.), ονος, ὁ: (ἵστημι, cf. στῆσαι τὸν σ. Poll.7.32):—the *warp* in the upright loom, στήμονι δ' ἐν παύρῳ κρόκα πολλὴν μηρύσασθαι Hes.*Op.*538; ἅπτεσθαι Hermipp.2; ἀκλώστους σ. Pl.Com.221; κρόκη καὶ σ. *PLille* 6.12 (iii B.C.); ξύλων.. στήμονα ἐχόντων τοὺς κάλους laths with the cords as their *warp* (so as to form mats), Apollod.*Poliorc.*169.7; cf. Pl.*Plt.*281a, 282d, *Cra.*388b, Orph.*Fr.*33. 2. pl., in woodwork, dub. sens., of parts of a ceiling, *Inscr.Délos* 504 *A*6, 9, 10 (iii B.C.). II. *thread*, σ. ἔνησα Batr.183, cf. Ar.*Lys.*519, Men.892; προσεμβαλόντες σ. καινόν *PCair.Zen.*423.10 (iii B.C.), cf. 484.14 (dub. sens.); στήμονος ἡμιμναῖον *PEnteux.*31.4 (iii B.C.); φαντασίαι.. οἷον τριχῶν ἢ κρόκης ἢ στήμονος Gal.18(2).73; οἱ σ. οἱ ἑψόμενοι Thphr.*Ign.*43; σ. ἐξεσμένος, nickname of a very thin person, '*threadpaper*', Ar.*Fr.* 728; *strand* in torsion engine, Ph.*Bel.*58.19: metaph., ἐκ σαπροῦ κρεμάμενοι σ. Plu.*Phoc.*30.

**Στήνια**, τά, *a festival in which the* ἄνοδος *of Demeter was celebrated* by women by night, with mutual abuse and low language, Ar. *Th.*834, Eub.148, *IG*2².674.7:—hence the Verb **στηνιῶσαι** *to be scurrilous*, Hsch.

**στήνιον**· στῆθος, Hsch.

**στῆνος**, τό, late spelling of στεῖνος, διὰ τὴν (sic) τῶν χρημάτων σ. financial *straits*, *PGoodsp.Cair.*15.24 (iv A.D.).

**στήρ**, v. στέαρ. **στῆρα**· τὰ λίθινα πρόθυρα, Hsch.

⊛ **στήριγ-μα**, ατος, τό, *support, foundation*, χερὸς.. στηρίγματα *the support of* one's hand, E.*IA*617; στηρίγματ' οἴκου, of children, *Trag. Adesp.*427; θνητῶν σ. κραταιόν Orph.*H.*18.7; περιπλοκῆς δεῖται καὶ στηρίγματος Plu.2.649c, cf. Ph.1.644: in pl., of a tower, J.*BJ*2.17. 8. 2. = στῆριγξ 2, Nicostr.Com.39 (στήριγγα z. Kock), Plu.*Cor.* 24. 3. = στεῖρα (A), στερέωμα 3, Nonn.*D.*40.451. 4. = στερέωμα 4, *PMag.Lond.*121.509. 5. τὸ λοιπὸν τοῦ σ. the rest of the *multitude*, Lxx 4*Ki.*25.11. 6. pl., *surgical supports*, = ἀποστηρίγματα, distd. fr. ἑρμάσματα, Gal.18(2).917. **-μοθέτης**, ου, ὁ, in pl., *foundation-layers*, epith. of δαίμονες, *PMag.Par.*1. 1356. **-μός**, ὁ, *being fixed, standing still*, τῶν πλανήτων ἀστέρων D.S.1.81, cf. Gem.1.20, Plu.2.76d, Theo Sm.p.148 H., Ptol.*Tetr.*22, Vett.Val.34.28, al., *PPar.*19*bis* 11, 13 (iii A.D.), Paul.Al.*G.*1, *Theol. Ar.*15, *Cat.Cod.Astr.*8(4).241. 2. *fixedness*, of steady light, opp. flashing, Arist.*Mu.*395ᵇ7. 3. metaph., ἐκπεσεῖν τοῦ ἰδίου σ. from your proper *firmness*, 2*Ep.Pet.*3.17. 4. Rhet., *sustaining* of the voice on certain words or syllables, so as to give them force, αἱ μακραὶ συλλαβαί, στηριγμούς τινας ἔχουσαι καὶ ἐγκαθίσματα D.H. *Comp.*20; στηριγμοὺς ἔχειν πρὸς ἄλληλα τὰ ὀνόματα mutual *support, buttressing*, Longin.40.4; cf. ἀντιστηριγμός.

**στῆριγξ**, ιγγος, ἡ, *support, prop, stay*, σ. τοῦ σώματος, of the κνήμη or large bone of the leg, X.*Eq.*1.5; αἱ σ. [τῶν πύργων] D.S. 18.70. b. = παρακερκίς 1, Poll.2.191 (pl.). 2. *fork with which the shaft* or *pole of a two-wheeled chariot was propped*, until the beasts were yoked to it, Lys.*Fr.*330 S., Plu.2.280f: acc. στήριγγαν Maiuri *Nuova Silloge* 48 (Rhodes).

⊛ **στηρίζω**, E.*Hipp.*1207, etc.: fut. -ίξω Hp.*Morb.*4.52 (v.l.), 1*Ep. Pet.*5.10, -ίσω Lxx *Si.*38.34, *Je.*17.5, -ιῶ ib.*Si.*6.37, *Je.*24.6: aor. ἐστήριξα Il.4.443, Ep. στήριξα Hes.*Th.*498; inf. στηρίξαι Od.12.434, Gal.19.192, *PSI*5.452.3 (iv A.D.); part. στηρίξας Sor.2.57; opt. στηρίξειεν Th.2.49; ἐστήρισα Lxx *Ge.*27.37, App.*BC*1.98; imper. στηρισάτω *AP*14.72:—Med., aor. ἐστηριξάμην Il.21.242, Hp.*Fract.* 11, etc. (v. infr.); later -ισάμην Lxx *Is.*59.16, Plu.*Eum.*11: fut. στηρίξομαι Philostr.*VA*5.35:—Pass., fut. στηριχθήσομαι Gal.*UP*9. 16: aor. ἐστηρίχθην Tyrt.11.22, Hp.*VC*3, Gal.15.126: pf. ἐστήριγμαι Hes.*Th.*779, Hp.*Morb.*3.3, etc.; inf. ἐστηρίσθαι Lxx 1*Ki.* 26.19: plpf. ἐστήρικτο Il.16.111, Hes.*Sc.*218, etc. (Cf. στῆριγξ, σκηρίπτομαι):—*make fast, prop, fix*, [ἴριδας] ἐν νέφεϊ στήριξε *sets* rainbows in the cloud, Il.11.28; οὐρανῷ ἐστήριξε κάρη, of Eris, 4. 443; στηρίζειν αὐτὸ αὐτό φησι τὸ ἄπειρον (sc. Anaxagoras) Arist.*Ph.* 205ᵇ2, cf. Sor.2.61; σ. σήματ' ἐν οὐρανῷ Arat.10; so prob., [λίθον] Ζεὺς στήριξε κατὰ χθονὸς he *set* the stone *fast* in the ground, Hes. *Th.*498; βάσιν ἐστήριξαν Nic.*Fr.*74.49; λίθον διορίζοντα ὅρους.. στηριχθῆναι ἐκέλευσαν *OGI*769 (Palestine, iii/iv A.D.). 2. *support*, σίτῳ τινά Lxx *Ge.*27.37; *feed up* a patient, Gal.19.192; σ. τὴν δύναμιν εὐστομάχοις τροφαῖς Id.18(2).34, cf. Aret.*CA*1.1: metaph., *confirm, establish*, τὴν ἀρχήν App.*BC*1.98; τοὺς ἀδελφοὺς *Ev.Luc.*22. 32, cf. 2*Ep.Thess.*2.17, 1*Ep.Pet.*5.10; *corroborate*, Sor.2.57. 3. Med., *ground, establish for oneself*, κόσμον ἑαῖς στηρίξατο βουλαῖς Orph. *Fr.*299; πόδα ἐπὶ γαίης *AP*14.72; πόντος στηρίξατο κῦμα νήνεμον *settled its* wave into a calm, ib.9.271 (Apollonid.).

B. Pass. and Med., *to be firmly set* or *fixed, stand fast*, οὐδὲ πόδεσσιν εἶχε στηρίξασθαι he could not *get a firm footing*, Il.21.242, cf. Plu.*Eum.*11; οὐδαμῇ ἐστήρικτο Hes.*Sc.*218; [δώματα] κίοσιν ἀργυρέοισι πρὸς οὐρανὸν ἐστήρικται the house *is lifted up* to heaven on pillars, Id.*Th.*779; ὀρθῇ δ' ἐς ὀρθὸν αἰθέρ' ἐστηρίζετο E.*Ba.*1073; στηριχθεὶς ἐπὶ γῆς Tyrt.11.22; πρὸς τῇ γῇ Arist.*Mete.*376ᵇ23 (s.v.l.); ὅσοι ἐστηρίξαντο τῇ πτέρνῃ ἰσχυρῶς πηδήσαντες *light heavily on* it, Hp. *Fract.*11, cf. *Art.*86; ὕβον, ἐφ' οὗ ἐστήρικται τὸ ἄλλο σῶμα *is steadied*, Arist.*HA*499ᵃ17; ἐστηριγμένα [ἔχειν] τὰ σπλάγχνα *supported*, opp. κρεμάμενα, Gal.15.570; ἄμπελος κάμακι σ. *AP*7.731 (Leon.); Ἀσκληπιὸν -ιζόμενον βάκτρῳ *IG*4²(1).88.9 (Epid., ii A.D.); of the fixed stars, Arat.230, 274, etc.; opp. ἀκοντίζεσθαι, Arist.*Mu.*395ᵇ4; λίθος ἐστήρικται Call.*Ap.*23; χάσμα μέγα ἐστ. *Ev.Luc.*16.26; of places, merely *to be situated*, D.P.204. 2. metaph., κακὸν κακῷ ἐστήρικτο evil *was set upon* evil, Il.16.111; τί τοι χόλος ἐστήρικται; A.R.4. 816; δέκατος μεὶς οὐρανῷ ἐστήρικτο the tenth month *was set* in heaven, *h.Merc.*11; of a person, ὅπου.. στηρίζει ποτέ wheresoever *thou art tarrying, art settled*, S.*Aj.*194 (lyr.); ὅροι ἐστηριγμένοι *fixed* principles, Hero *Geom.*3.25; ἀνάγκη στηριχθῆναι τὸ ν̄ must *be firmly pronounced*, D.H.*Comp.*22. 3. of diseases, = infr. II. 2, μέχρις ἂν [οἱ νοσοποιοὶ χυμοὶ] ἔν τινι τῶν ἀσθενεστέρων στηριχθῶσιν Gal.15.126, cf. 789, 855, Aret.*SA*1.5. II. Act. intr. in same sense, οὐδέ πῃ εἶχον.. στηρίξαι ποσὶν ἔμπεδον.. Od.12.434; κῦμ' οὐρανῷ στηρίζον a wave *rising up* to heaven, E.*Hipp.*1207: metaph., οὐρανῷ στηρίζον.. κλέος Id.*Ba.*972; πρὸς οὐρανὸν καὶ γαῖαν ἐστήριξε φῶς ib.1083, cf. Plu.*Sull.*6. 2. of diseases, *fix, settle, determine* to a particular part, ὁπότε εἰς τὴν καρδίαν στηρίξειεν (sc. ἡ νόσος) Th.2.49; ἐνταῦθα σ. ἡ νοῦσος Hp.*Aph.*4.33; εἰ.. ἐς τὸ ὀστέον στηρίξειε τὸ βέλος Id.*VC*12; cf. στήριξις 2. 3. of planetary phases, *pause, stand still*, Gem.12.23, Plu.2.76d, Theo Sm.p.147 H., Ptol. *Tetr.*75, Vett.Val.183.1, Paul.Al.*G.*2. 4. metaph., ἐπὶ δόγματος σ. *hold fast* to an opinion, D.L.2.136.

**στηρ-ικτέον**, *one must fix, make firm*, Poll.1.213. **-ικτής**, οῦ, ὁ, gloss on λίθον εὐναστῆρα, Sch.Opp.*H.*3.373. **-ικτικός**, ή, όν, *stationary*, of planetary phases, Procl.*Hyp.*5.87. **-ικτός**, ή, όν, *solid, firmly based*, *Hymn.Is.*163. 2. = foreg., *Cat.Cod.Astr.*1. 100. **-ιξις**, εως, ἡ, *fixed position*, Sch.Ar.*Nu.*1509. 2. *determination of a disorder to a particular part*, ἐς ὀφθαλμόν Hp.*Epid.* 4.35; cf. στηρίζω B. II. 2.

⊛ **στήριον**· ἱεράκιον, Seleuc.ap.Hsch.

**Στησίλειος**, α, ον, *founded* or *dedicated by* Στησίλεως, σκάφιον *Inscr.Délos* 369 *A* 9 (iii B.C.), etc.: also **Στησίλειον**, τό (sc. ποτήριον), *IG*11(2).132.18 (ii B.C.), etc.; neut. pl. **Στησίλεια**, τά, *games founded by S.*, *Inscr.Délos* 366 *A* 133 (iii B.C.).

**στήσιος**, ὁ, (ἵστημι) Ζεὺς Σ., = Lat. Jupiter *Stator*, Plu.*Cic.*16; cf. Ἐπιστάσιος.

**στησί-φυλλον** [ῐ], τό, = τηλέφιλον, Hsch. ⊛ **-χορος**, ον, *establishing* or *leading* χοροί:—hence as pr. n., **Στησίχορος**, Dor. **Στᾱσ-**, ὁ, the Lyric poet *Stesichorus*, Simon.53, Pl.*Phdr.*243a: prov., οὐδὲ τὰ τρία Στησιχόρου (i.e. strophe, antistrophos, epode) γνῶναι, of illiterate persons, Diogenian.7.14:—Adj. **Στησιχόρειος**, ον, Plu.2.1135c, etc. 2. *a throw of the dice which showed eight pips*, said to be named from the eight-sided monument of the poet at Himera, Poll. 9.100.

**στήτα,** ἁ, pseudo-Doric, = γυνή, Theoc.*Syrinx* 14, Dosiad.*Ara* 1. (The form arose from a false reading of Il.1.6, διὰ στήτην ἐρίσαντε having quarrelled about a *woman*, cf. Eust.21.43, Sch.D.T. p.11 H.)

**στητώδης,** ες, contr. for στεατώδης, Hp.ap.Gal.19.140.

⊛ **στία** [ῑ], ἡ, *small stone, pebble,* ἐσχάρη..στιάων an altar made of *pebbles,* A.R.2.1172 (Sicyonian acc. to Sch.): also **στῖον, τό,** Hp.ap. Gal.19.140. [ῑ: written στηά and στηάς in Hsch., who adds the senses στενοχωρία and λιθοκονία: pl. στεῖαι acc. to Sch.Cyrill. in Reitzenstein *Ind.Lect.Rost.*1890/91.8: perh. cogn. with στέαρ.]

**στῑάζω,** *pelt with pebbles,* Hsch.

**στῐβάδ-ειον** [ᾰ], τό, = στιβάδιον, prob. in *Inscr.Perg.*222. **-εύω,** *use as litter* for animals, Dsc.3.24 (Pass.). **-ιον, τό,** Dim. of στιβάς, Plu.*Phil.*4, Luc.*Tox.*31, App.*BC*1.61.

**στῐβᾰδο-κοιτέω,** *sleep on litter,* Plb.2.17.10; ἐν σάγοις Str.3.3. 7. **-ποιέομαι,** *make oneself a bed of straw and leaves,* Arist.*HA* $607^{b}20$, $612^{b}25$, but prob. f.l. for στιβάδα ποιούμενος in S.*Fr.*1097.

**στῐβάζω,** *tread upon,* ἐστίβακα· πεπάτηκα, Hsch. **2.** *spread as bedding,* Sch.Theoc.7.67 (Pass.). **3.** Med., *follow the track, track out,* Aesar.ap.Stob.1.49.27. **4.** ἐστιβασμένος *over-dressed,* opp. ῥυπαροφόρος, Steph.*in Hp.*2.251 D.

**στῐβᾰρ-ηδόν,** *by concentration,* opp. σποράδην, *Orac.Chald.*ap.Dam. *Pr.*70. **-ός,** ά, όν, *strong, stout, sturdy,* freq. in Hom. and Hes., of men's limbs, ὦμος, αὐχήν, βραχίονες, Il.5.400, 18.415, Od.18. 69; χείρ 8.189; μέλεα Hes.*Sc.*76; πλευραί Pi.*Fr.*111; of weapons, ἔγχος, σάκος, Il.5.746, 3.335, etc.; δίσκος -ώτερος *more massy,* Od. 8.187; later, of persons, σ. τις καὶ καρτερά Ar.*Th.*639; σ. τὸ σῶμα J.*BJ*6.2.8; σ. τῇ γλώσσῃ Lxx *Ez.*3.6; μοῖρα σ. Epigr.ap.Paus.10.12. 6; εὐεπίη (of Aeschylus) *AP*7.39 (Antip.Thess.); ἀπειλά *Hymn.Is.* 170; λέξις D.H.*Th.*24, cf. *Comp.*22; -ώτερος λόγος a *bulkier* book, Sor.1.2; γυμνάσια -ώτερα, -ώτατα, *more (most) violent,* Antyll.ap. Orib.6.21.4, 6.35.2. Adv., πύλαι..πύκα -ρῶς ἀραρυῖαι gates *close* shut, Il.12.454; βαρύνων τὸν κλοιὸν σ. Lxx *Hb.*2.6; φρόντιζε σ. M.Ant.2. 5. (Prob. cogn. with στείβω.)

⊛ **στῐβάς,** άδος, ἡ, (στείβω) *bed of straw, rushes,* or *leaves,* whether strewn loose (cf. *Ev.Marc.*11.8), or stuffed into a mattress, E.*Hel.* 798; χαμαιπετής Id.*Tr.*507; σχοίνων Ar.*Pl.*541; ἐπὶ στιβάδων ἐστρωμένων μίλακι καὶ μυρρίναις Pl.*R.*372b; χἁ σ. ἐσσεῖται πεπυκασμένα..κνύζᾳ τ' ἀσφοδέλῳ τε Theoc.7.67, cf. 13.34. **b.** *straw strewn at a sacrifice,* hence as name of the ceremony, *IG*$2^{2}$.1368.48, al. (ii A.D.). **2.** *mattress,* Hdt.4.71, Ar.*Pl.*663; ἐπὶ στιβάδος κατακείμενος Epicur.*Fr.*207; esp. one used by soldiers, Eup.254, Ar. *Pax* 348, X.*HG*7.1.16, Plb.5.48.4. **3.** generally, *bed,* Theopomp. Hist.166. **4.** *nest* or *lair* of mice, Arat.1140; of the fish φυκίς, Arist.*HA*$607^{b}21$. **5.** *grave, BCH*13.37 (Iasus), 22.373 (Caria), *Ath.Mitt.*15.277 (ibid.).

**στίβᾰσις,** εως, ἡ, perh. written for στοίβ-, *building up, laying,* of bricks, *PKlein.Form.*1023 (iv/v A.D.).

**στιβδός·** μαστιγίας, δραπέτης, Hsch. (fort. στικτός).

**στῐβ-εία,** ἡ, (στίβος) *treading, walking*: hence, = ὁδός, Hdn.*Epim.* 128. **II.** *tracking* with hounds, D.S.4.13; cf. στιβίη. **-εῖον, τό,** *fuller's workshop, PTeb.*417.23 (iii A.D.). **-εύς,** έως, ὁ, *walker, traveller,* Hsch. (στιδεύς cod.); cf. στειβεύς. **2.** *fuller,* who cleans clothes by treading them, *PPetr.*3 p.173 (iii B.C.), *BGU*1087.7 (iii A.D.), Sch.A.R.2.30, Sch.Nic.*Th.*376. **II.** *one who tracks out,* σ. κύων Opp.*C.*1.463. **-ευτής,** οῦ, ὁ, = foreg. II, σ. κύων Sostrat. ap.Stob.4.20.70; = *vestigator, Gloss.* **-εύω,** *track out,* D.S.5.3, Plu.2.966c; *explore,* διὰ τῶν εὐλόγων τὸ μέλλον ib.399a:—Pass., στιβευόμενος τόπος ib.918b. **II.** intr., *walk, travel,* Hsch. **-έω,** *tread, traverse,* once in Pass., πᾶν ἐστίβηται πλευρόν every side *has been traversed, searched,* S.*Aj.*874.

**στίβη** [ῐ?], ἡ, = στίμμι, Phryn.*PS* p.118 B., *AB*114. **II.** στιβή, ἡ, = *stipa, Gloss.* (fort. στοιβή, = *stuppa*).

**στίβ-η** [ῑ], ἡ, *rime, hoar frost,* Od.5.467, 17.25, Call.*Epigr.*33. (Perh. cogn. with στέαρ.) **II.** = ἀνδράχνη, Hsch. ⊛ **-ήεις,** εσσα, εν, *frosty, rimy,* ἀγχοῦρος Call.*Hec.*1.4.10, cf. Suid.

**στίβι** [στῐ], τό, Lat. *stibium,* = στίμμι (q.v.).

**στῑβῐάω,** (στίβη) *freeze,* Hsch.

**στῐβίζομαι,** Med. or Pass., *paint one's* eyelids and eyebrows *with black paint* (στίβι), Lxx *Ez.*23.40, Str.16.4.17, Cyran.64.

**στῐβίη,** ἡ, Ep. for στιβεία II, Opp.*C.*1.37, al.

⊛ **στῐβική,** ἡ, *tax on* στίβι, *PCair.Zen.*136.247 (iii B.C.).

**στιβιλίς,** ίδος, ἡ, in pl., = φῷδες, Sch.Ar.*Pl.*535.

**στίβος** [ῐ], ὁ, (στείβω) *trodden way, track, path, h.Merc.*352; ἔρημος ἔνθ' ἂν ᾖ βροτῶν σ. S.*Ant.*773, cf. *Ph.*157 (lyr.), E.*IT*67, *Or.*1274 (lyr.); ὀγμεύειν σ. S.*Ph.*163 (anap.); ξύμβλητο κατὰ στίβον Ἡρακλῆϊ A.R.1.1253. **II.** *track, footstep, h.Merc.*353, Hdt.4.140, A.*Ch.*210, 227, S.*Ph.*48, *Ichn.*109, E.*Ion* 743, etc.; ἕπεσθαι κατὰ στίβον on the *track* or *trail,* Hdt.5.102, cf. 4.122, 9.59; στίβοι ποδῶν A.*Ch.*205; ἵππων X.*An.*1.6.1; λέχος καὶ στίβοι φιλάνορες *traces* of one who had lain there, A.*Ag.*411 (lyr.); στίβου οὐδεὶς κτύπος (v.l. τύπος) S.*Ph.* 29, cf. 206 (lyr.); ῥινῶν ὀξὺς σ., of hounds on *the track, AP*9.516 (Crin.). **III.** *fuller's workshop, PHib.*1.114.3, al. (iii B.C.).

**στῐγ-εύς,** έως, ὁ, (στίζω) *tattooer,* Hdt.7.35 (pl.). **II.** glossed κεντητήριον, prob. *awl* or *needle for puncturing,* Suid. **-μα,** ατος, τό, *tattoo-mark,* Hdt.5.35, Arist.*HA*$585^{b}33$, *GA*$721^{b}32$, *IG*$4^{2}$(1).121. 48, al. (Epid., iv B.C.), Polyaen.1.24; σ. ἱρά, showing that the persons so marked were devoted to the service of the temple, Hdt. 2.113; esp. of a slave, Pl.Com.187, Ps.-Phoc.225, *Cod.Theod.*10. 22.4; or a soldier, ibid., Aët.8.12; στίγματα ἐξαίρει βατράχειον καταπλασθέν Dsc.*Eup.*1.110: so metaph., σ. Ἰησοῦ *Ep.Gal.*6.17 (pl.); ἀνωφελῆ σ., of inscribed laws, D.Chr.80.5. **2.** generally, *mark, spot,* as on the dragon's skin, Hes.*Sc.*166, cf. Paus.8.2.7, 8.4. 7. **3.** *stud,* Lxx *Ca.*1.11. **4.** σ. χρυσοῦν *colour* of gold, Ps.-Democr.ap.Zos.Alch.p.119 B., cf. p.126 B. **5.** = *cicatricis signum, Gloss.*

**στιγ-μᾰτηφορέω,** *bear tattoo-marks,* Luc.*Syr.D.*59; cf. στιγματοφόρος. **-μᾰτίας,** ου, Ion. **-ίης,** εω, ὁ, *one who bears tattoo-marks,* Hp.*Epid.*4.2; esp. *branded culprit* or *runaway slave,* Asius 1, Eup.159. 14, 276.2, Ar.*Lys.*331 (lyr.), Hermipp.63.19, X.*HG*5.3.24, D.C.47.10; σ. οἰκέτης Ath.13.612c. **2.** in Com., *one whose property is marked* as mortgaged, Cratin.333. **II.** jocular nickname of Nicanor, the student of punctuation, Eust.20.12, interpol. in Suid. s.v. Νικάνωρ. **-μᾰτοφόρος,** ον, *bearing tattoo-marks,* Polyaen.1.24; cf. στιγματηφορέω. ⊛ **-μή,** ἡ, *spot* on a bird's plumage, Alex.Mynd. ap.Ath.9.398d (pl.); *brand-mark,* D.S.34/5.2.1 (pl.). **2.** *mathematical point,* Arist.*Top.*$108^{b}26$, *EN*$1174^{b}12$, *de An.*$427^{a}10$, al., Apollod.*Stoic.*3.259; ὅσον σ. αἱματίνη 'a *speck* of blood', Arist.*HA* $561^{a}11$. **3.** metaph. of anything very small, *jot, tittle,* εἴ γ' εἶχε στιγμὴν ἢ σκιὰν τούτων D.21.115, cf. Men.1067; of time, Simon. 196, Lxx *Is.*29.5; ἐν σ. χρόνου in a *moment, Ev.Luc.*4.5; σ. χρόνου ὁ βίος Plu.2.13a, cf. *AP*7.472 (Leon.); ἐν σ. without χρόνου, Vett.Val.131.4; στιγμῇ καιροῦ, = *puncto temporis, Gloss.* **II.** Gramm., σ. or τελεία σ. *full stop, period,* μέση σ. *colon,* D.T.630.6, cf. ὑποστιγμή: Nicanor made 8 στιγμαί, Sch.ibid.p.24 H., cf. Suid. s.v. Νικάνωρ; σ. πᾶσα σημεῖον αὐτοτελείας A.D.*Adv.*182.17, cf. *Pron.*53. 16, al. ⊛ **-μιαῖος,** α, ον, *no bigger than a point,* χρόνος Gem.2.33, cf. Plu.2.117e, 1084b, Gal.19.187, Cleom.1.8, Vett.Val.257.10; στιγμαῖος is f.l. in Plu.2.117e. **-μικός,** ή, όν, μονάδες, i.e. geometrical points, Sophon.*in de An.*31.17. Adv. -κῶς *coincidently with the end of a word,* καταπεραιοῦν Eust.399.44. **-μός,** ὁ, *pricking,* A.*Supp.* 839 (lyr., pl.); στιγμόν, = *distinctum, Gloss.*

**στίγος,** ὁ, or **στίγον,** τό, *point,* Archim.*Aren.*1.16 (s.v.l.).

**στίγων,** ωνος, ὁ, = στιγματίας I.1, Ar.*Fr.*97.

**στίζω,** Simon.78: fut. στίξω Hdt.7.35, Eup.259, Men.*Sam.*108: aor. ἔστιξα Hdt.5.35:—Med., Luc.*Syr.D.*59, etc.: aor. ἐστιξάμην Nonn.*D.*43.232:—Pass., aor. part. στιχθείς Porph.*VP*15: pf. ἔστιγμαι Hdt.5.35, Ar.*Av.*760:—*tattoo,* τὸ ἐστίχθαι εὐγενὲς κέκριται (among the Thracians) Hdt.5.6, cf. Phanocl.1.25; ἀποξυρήσας τὴν κεφαλὴν ἔστιξε Hdt.5.35; ἐστιγμένους ἀνθέμια X.*An.*5.4.32; of the Britons, τὰ σώματα στίζονται γραφαῖς ποικίλαις καὶ ζῴων εἰκόσιν Hdn.3.14.7; of a Syrian, to indicate dedication to gods (cf. στιγματηφορέω), *UPZ* 121.8 (ii B.C.). **2.** esp. *tattoo* as a mark of disgrace, Hdt.7.35, Ar.*Ra.* 1511 (anap.); στίξω σε βελόναισιν τρισίν Eup. l.c., cf. Men. l.c., Call. *Iamb.*1.235 (*Hermes* 69.177), Hermog.*Stat.*11; στιξάτω τὸ μέτωπον *PLille* 29 ii 36, cf. i 14 (iii B.C.); δραπέτης ἐστιγμένος Ar.*Av.*760, cf. And.*Fr.*5; ἐστ. αὐτόμολος Aeschin.2.79; αἰχμαλώτους Σαμίων στίζειν κατὰ τοῦ προσώπου καὶ εἶναι τὸ στίγμα γλαῦκα Ael.*VH*2.9, cf. Diph. 66.7. **3.** *mark* as one's property, στίξαι ἵππον (glossed ἐγκαῦσαι) Phot.; σ. χωρίον *mark* a piece of land as mortgaged, by a notice set up upon it, Poll.3.85 (Pass.). **4.** rarely c. dupl. acc., τοὺς δὲ ἔστιζον (codd., ἔστιξαν Plu., Hude) στίγματα βασιλήϊα *tattooed* them with the royal tattoo-marks, Hdt.7.233; σ. ἵππον εἰς τὸ μέτωπον *tattoo* the figure of a horse on one's forehead, Plu.*Nic.*29; σ. εἰς τὸ μέτωπον γλαῦκας Id.*Per.*26, cf. X. l.c. **5.** metaph., εἶσ' ἅλα στίζοισα πνοά Simon.78; στιζόμενος βακτηρίᾳ beaten black and blue, Ar.*V.* 1296. **6.** σ. τοὺς ὑμένας *cause stabbing pains in,* Gal.17(1).400. **II.** Gramm., *put a punctuation mark,* Steph.*in Hp.*2.496 D., *AP*15.38 (Cometas); τελείαν δεῖ στίξαι Herm.*in Phdr.*p.84 A. (Cf. OE. *stician* 'to stab', Germ. *sticken* 'to stitch, embroider'.)

**στικτέον,** *one must put a punctuation mark* (στιγμή), Sch.Il.2.173, al.

**στίκτης,** ου, ὁ, *tattooer,* Herod.5.65.

**στικτόπους,** ουν, gen. ποδος, *with spotted feet,* ἔλαφοι Opp.*C.*1.307.

**στικτός,** ή, όν, (στίζω) *pricked, tattooed,* βραχίονες *AP*7.10; γράμματα σ. Lxx *Le.*19.28. **2.** *spotted, dappled,* of fallow-deer, S.*Ph.* 184 (lyr.), *El.*568; νεβρίδες E.*Ba.*111 (lyr.), cf. 835; ἔλαφος *IG*14. 1293c; ὕαιναι Opp.*C.*3.288; βασιλεὺς..σ. οἷον ταῶς Philostr.*Im.*2. 31; σ. πτέρυξ, of the ἔποψ, A.*Fr.*304.8; στικτοῖς ὄμμασιν δεδορκότα, i.e. with eyes all over the body, E.*Ph.*1115.

**στῖλα,** ἡ, unknown utensil mentioned in a marriage-contract, *PMasp.*6 ii 48 (vi A.D.).

**στιλβ-αῖος,** *coloratus, Gloss.* **-άς** (sc. γῆ), άδος, ἡ, *shining* earth, perh. *antimony* or *mica,* Zos.Alch.p.226 B., *PHolm.*1.41, 2.9. **-η,** ἡ, *lamp,* Ar.*Fr.*561, Hermipp.28, Pl.Com.190. **II.** Att. for *mirror,* Hsch. **-ηδόν,** Adv. *shining, glittering,* Suid. **-ηδών,** όνος, ἡ, *brilliance, brightness, polish,* σ. δέχεται Thphr.*HP*5.4.2. **2.** *flashing,* [ὀφθαλμῶν] Phld.*Ir.*p.5 W. (pl.); of stars, *twinkling,* Simp.*in Cael.* 453.21; τῶν δρώντων ὀφθαλμῶν σ., as expl. of St. Elmo's Fire, *Placit.*2. 18.2. **-όντως,** Adv. *brilliantly,* Sch.Arat.330. **-οποιέω,** *make to shine,* Dsc.1.70. **-ός,** ή, όν, = στιλπνός, Id.5.84 (Sup., v.l.), Gal.6. 804, *Gloss.* **-ότης,** ητος, ἡ, v.l. for στιλπνότης, Plu.*Alex.*57. **-όω,** = στιλπνόω, Lxx *Ps.*7.13, Dsc.1.84, 5.154. **-ω,** chiefly pres. and impf.: aor. ἔστιλψα Charito 2.2, Aristaenet.1.25:—*glitter, gleam,* of polished or bright surfaces, χιτῶνας..ἧκα στίλβοντας ἐλαίῳ Il.18. 596; κάλλεϊ τε στίλβων καὶ εἵμασιν 3.392; κάλλεϊ καὶ χάρισι στίλβων Od.6.237; λαμπραὶ δ' ἀκτῖνες ἀπ' αὐτοῦ αἰγλῆεν στίλβουσι *beam* from him, *h.Hom.*31.11; ὀμμάτων στίλβειν ἄπο..φλόγα B.17.55; σ. ὅπλοις

E.*Andr.*1146; ἰδὼν στίλβοντα τὰ λάβδα, i.e. the λ upon the Spartan shields, Eup.359; σ. νῶτον πτερύγοιν χρυσαῖν Ar.*Av.*697; σ. ἄνθει.. ἐπωμίδας Achae.4.3; σ. ἐν χρωμάτων ποικιλίᾳ Pl.*Phd.*110d, cf. Thphr. *Sens.*77; ἱμάτια στίλβοντα *Ev.Marc.*9.3: abs., of gold, Pl.*Ti.*59b; of sleek horses, σ. ὥστε κύκνου πτερόν E.*Rh.*618; of brilliant complexion, Theoc.2.79, etc.; of water in motion, Arist.*Mete.*370ᵃ18; of the white *gleam* on the eye, Id.*HA*561ᵃ32, Gal.16.610; ὁρᾶν τῷ στίλβοντι Thphr.*Sens.*26; of fixed stars, opp. planets (exc. Mercury, v. στίλβων), *twinkle*, Arist.*APo.*78ᵃ30, *Cael.*290ᵃ18: c. acc. cogn., σ. ἀστραπάς *flash* lightning, E.*Or.*480: metaph., σ. ὁμηλικίην ἐρατεινήν Orph.*A.*1115. 2. metaph., *shine, be bright*, E.*Hipp.*194 (anap.). II. trans., = στιλπνόω, στίλβει πρόσωπον Dsc.1.84 (v.l. for στιλβοῖ); στίλψασα τὰς παρειὰς ἐντρίμματι Aristaenet. l.c. **-ωθρον,** τό, *cosmetic*, Dsc.1.30. **-ωμα,** ατος, τό, = στίλβωθρον, ib.47, Aët. 8.6, al. **-ων,** οντος, ὁ, name of the planet Mercury, Arist.*Mu.* 392ᵃ26, Eudox.*Ars* 5.10, Cic.*ND*2.20.53; gen. -ωνος (v.l. -οντος) Plu.2.430a; acc. -ωνα *Placit.*2.15.4 (στίλβοντα codd.Plu.2.889b), 2.16.7. **-ωσις,** εως, ἡ, *making to shine*, γενέσθαι εἰς σ. to be made bright, Lxx *Ez.*21.10(15), cf. Dsc.2.80. **-ωτής,** οῦ, ὁ, = *colorator*, *Gloss.*

**στίλη** [ῐ], ἡ, *drop*: metaph., like στιγμή, *little bit, moment*, ἀπεκοιμήθημεν ὅσον ὅσον στίλην Ar.*V.*213.

**στίλος·** ὁ προηγούμενος τῆς ποίμνης κριός, Hsch. (Fort. κτίλος.)

⊕ **στιλπν-ός,** ή, όν, *glittering, glistening*, ἕερσαι Il.14.351; ὀφθαλμοί Arist.*Phgn.*812ᵇ11; of cosmetics, Dsc.5.84 (Sup., v.l.): αὐγὰς -οτέρας τοῦ χρυσίου Jul.*Or.*4.150c: Sup., D.Chr.35.23; μαργαρῖται Luc.*Im.* 9. **-ότης,** ητος, ἡ, *brightness*, Plu.2.921a, Gal.7.245, Aq.*Dt.*7. 13, *Za.*4.14, Plot.2.1.7. **-όω,** *make to shine, polish*, Arr.*Epict.*2. 8.25 (Pass.), Gal.12.198. **-ωτής,** οῦ, ὁ, *polisher*, Lyd.*Mag.*1.46.

**στίλπων,** ωνος, ὁ, Sybar. name for a *dwarf*, Ath.12.518f.

**στίλψις,** εως, ἡ, (στίλβω) *shining, glittering*, Tz.*H.*10.330, al.

**στίμμι** or ⊕**στῖμι,** ιος or εως, or ιδος, τό, *powdered antimony*, used for eye-paint, *kohl*, Erot., *POxy.*1088.10 (i A.D.), Plin.*HN*33.101, Aq., Sm., Thd.*Is.*54.11:—also **στίμμις** or **στῖμις,** ἡ, acc. στίμμιν Ion Trag.25, Antiph.189: also **στιμία,** ἡ, Cyran.64: also **στίβι,** Lxx *Je.*4.30 (v.l. στιμη), Dsc.5.84 (v.l. στίμμι): acc. pl. στίβεις dub. l. in 1*Enoch* 8.1. (Copt. *stēm*.)

**στιμμίζω** (also written **στιμίζω**), *tinge* the eyelids *black with* στίμμι, Ps.-Democr.*Symp.Ant.* p.5 G.:—Med., *tinge* one's eyelids *with black*, Gal.6.439; σ. τοὺς ὀφθαλμούς Lxx 4*Ki.*9.30, *Ez.*23. 40. 2. later, *apply any eye-salve*, Aët.7.41 (Pass.); cf. στιβίζομαι.

**στίμμις,** ἡ, v. στίμμι.

**στίμμισμα,** ατος, τό, in pl., *blackening with* στίμμι, τῶν ὀφθαλμῶν Crito ap.Gal.12.447, Hsch. s.v. ὑπογράμματα (στημί- cod.).

⊕***στίξ,** ἡ, gen. στιχός Il.16.173, 20.362, acc. στίχα Epigr.ap.D.S. 11.14, *AP*7.56; nom. and acc. pl. στίχες, στίχας (v. infr.):—*row, line, rank* or *file*, esp. of soldiers, τῆς μὲν ἰῆς στιχὸς ἦρχε Μενέσθιος Il.16. 173; στιχὸς εἶμι διαμπερές 20.362, cf. Epigr.ap.D.S. l.c.: elsewhere in pl., στίχες ἀνδρῶν, Τρώων, Κεφαλλήνων, etc., Il.4.231,221,330, al.; ἀσπιστάων ib.90; mostly of foot, but also πολλὰς σ. ἡρώων πολλὰς δὲ καὶ ἵππων 20.326; κατὰ στίχας *in ranks* or *lines*, ἵζοντο κατὰ σ. 3.326; but ἦλθε κατὰ σ. *through the ranks*, 16.820, cf. 5.590, 11.91; of dancers, θρέξασκον ἐπὶ στίχας ἀλλήλοισι 18.602:—also in Trag. and Com., ξένων στίχες A.*Th.*924 (lyr.); πολεμίων, Καδμείων, E.*Heracl.* 676, *Supp.*669; τῶν λαῶν Ar.*Eq.*163; συῶν ἠδὲ λεόντων Hes.*Sc.*170; γεράνων Arat.1031, cf. Q.S.11.114. 2. metaph., ἀνέμων στίχες Pi. *P.*4.210; ἐπέων στίχες *verses, lays*, ib.57; later, στίχα νήσων D.P. 514; βίβλων *AP*7.56.—Cf. στίχος, στοῖχος.

**στίξις,** εως, ἡ, (στίζω) *marking*, e.g. of musical notes, Anon. Bellerm.p.79. 2. *spot* or *mark*, Sch.A.R.1.221 (pl.).

**στίον,** v. στία.

**στιπεουργός,** ὁ, = στιππυουργός, *PSI*6.573 (iii B.C.).

**στιπουργός,** ὁ, = foreg. (cf. στιππουργός), *Stud.Pal.*20.193 (vi A.D.).

**στιππεῖον,** τό, = στυππεῖον, *PRyl.*245.14 (iii A.D.); also **στιππῖον,** *PSI*5.469.12,19 (iv A.D.).

**στιππόϊνος,** η, ον, = στιππύϊνος, *PLond.*3.928.2 (iii A.D.).

⊕ **στιπποκογχιστής,** οῦ, ὁ, *purple-dyer of tow*, *POxy.*1943.3 (v A.D.).

**στίππον,** τό, = στιππύον, in gen. sg. στίππου, *PGoodsp.Cair.*30 xxxvii 11 (ii A.D.).

**στιππο-πραγμᾰτευτής,** οῦ, ὁ, *tow-merchant*, *POxy.*893.3 (vi/vii A.D.). **-τῑμητής,** οῦ, ὁ, *tow-valuer*, ib.103.28 (iv A.D.).

⊕ **στιππουργός,** ὁ, = στιππυουργός, *PLond.*2.387.20 (vi/vii A.D.).

**στιπποχειριστής,** οῦ, ὁ, *agent of the tow-merchants*, *POxy.*1889.6 (v A.D.), 1980 (vi A.D.).

**στιππύϊνος,** η, ον, (cf. sq.) *made of tow*, Lxx *Le.*13.47,59.

**στιππύον,** τό, = στυππεῖον, Lxx *Jd.*15.14, al., *PSI*4.404.2,9 (iii B.C.), *PCair.Zen.*176.43, 472.9, 779, al. (iii B.C.); στίππυον Ph.*Bel.* 90.11 codd.; dat. -ύῳ ib.94.10.

**στιππῠουργός,** ὁ, *worker in tow*, *PCair.Zen.*479.2, al. (iii B.C.).

**στιπτός,** ή, όν, prop., *trodden down*, στιπτὴ φυλλάς, = στιβάς, S.*Ph.*33: metaph., σ. γέροντες *tough, sturdy* old fellows, Ar. *Ach.*180 (perh. with allusion to στιπτοὶ ἄνθρακες, *hard* charcoal, Thphr.*Ign.*37). (In some codd. of S. written στειπτός, as also ἄ-στειπτος for ἄ-στιπτος.)

**στιπύϊνος,** η, ον, = στιππύϊνος, *BGU*1515.2 (Ptolemaic).

**στιτθόν·** εἶδος ἀκρίδος, Hsch.

**στῖφος,** εος, τό, *body of men in close array*, A.*Pers.*20 (anap.), Hdt. 9.57; νεῶν στῖφος the *close array* of ships, A.*Pers.*366; σ. ποιήσασθαι Hdt.9.70; νεανιῶν σ. Ar.*Eq.*852, cf. *Pax* 564, Th.8.92, X.*Cyr.*1.4.19, etc.: pl., *masses, groups*, Plb.2.68.4, Ph.1.445: metaph., ἁμαρτημάτων ib.322. 2. = two ἐπιξεναγίαι of light-armed, or 4096 men, Ascl.*Tact.*6.3, Ael.*Tact.*16.3, Arr.*Tact.*14.5.

**στιφράω,** *harden*, Ath.7.323f, Eust.1913.45.

⊕ **στιφρός,** ά, όν, *firm, solid*, Men. in *POxy.*1803.1, al.; of olives, Ar. *Fr.*141; σκέλη X.*Cyn.*4.1, cf. 5.30; πλεκτάνη Crobyl.7; καυλὸς σαρκώδης καὶ σ. Arist.*HA*510ᵇ28; of wood, Thphr.*HP*3.11.4, 5.1.11 (Comp.); opp. μαδαρός, of flesh, Arist.*HA*531ᵇ13; opp. ὑγρός, Id. *GA*735ᵇ18; opp. σομφός, ib.732ᵇ35; τὸ τῶν βατράχων ᾠὸν στερεὸν καὶ σ. ib.754ᵃ34; of persons, *stout, sturdy*, νεανίας Philostr.Jun.*Im.* 15, cf. 1,3.—στρυφνός is a freq. v.l.

⊕ **στιφρότης,** ητος, ἡ, *solidity, stoutness*, Timocl.22.3.

**στῐχ-ἀοιδός,** ὁ, *one who sings verses, poet*, *APl.*4.316 (Michaelius).

**στῐχάομαι,** Ep., used by Hom. only in Ep. 3 pl. impf. ἐστιχόωντο: (*στίξ, στείχω):—*march in rows* or *ranks*, esp. of soldiers, Il.2.92, 4.432, etc.; of ships in line, 2.516,602, etc.; of herdsmen with their herds, 18.577; of cattle, Theoc.25.126; κῆρας, ὅσαι στιχόωνται ἐπ' ἀγρούς Orph.*L.*272: of two persons *marching*, Il.3.266,341.— Act. στιχάει is prob. in Il.15.635 (cf. ὁμοστιχάω); later Ep. στιχόωσι *stand in rows*, Arat.191, A.R.1.30, Mosch.2.142; part. neut. στιχόωντα Arat.372.

⊕ **στῐχάριον** [ᾰ], τό, Dim. of στίχη, *variegated tunic*, σ. λινοῦν *Sammelb.*6222.27 (iii A.D.), cf. *PGen.*80.3 (iv A.D.), etc.; perh. to be read in *Dura*⁴ 100 (iii A.D.); also **στιχαρο** (sic) **μαφόριον,** *Sammelb.* 7033.39 (v A.D.), *Stud.Pal.*20.275.6 (vi A.D.).

**στῐχάς,** άδος, ἡ, poet. for στίχος, in dat. pl. στιχάδεσσι, *Epigr.Gr.* 1035.16 (Pergam.).

**στιχάω,** v. στιχάομαι.

**στῐχελεγεῖον,** τό, *elegiac verse*, Choerob. *in Heph.* p.211 C.

**στίχες,** αἱ, v. *στίξ.

⊕ **στίχη,** ἡ, a kind of *tunic* (cf. στιχάριον), prob. in *Edict.Diocl.*7.56.

**στῐχ-ηδόν,** Adv. *in rows*, Hdn.4.9.5, Sch.D.T.p.192 H. **-ήρης,** ες, *in rows* or *ranks*, Hld.3.2. **-ηρός,** ά, όν, *of a verse*, λαγάρωσις Eust.1103.18. **-ίαμβος,** ὁ, *iambic verse*, Choerob. *in Heph.*p.211 C. **-ίδιον,** τό, Dim. of στίχος, Plu.2.60a,668a, etc. **-ίζω,** in Pass., ἐξέδραι ἐστιχισμέναι (v.l. ἐστοιχ-) *arranged in a row*, Lxx *Ez.*42.3. **-ικός,** ή, όν, *of lines* or *verses*, περίοδοι Sch.Ar.*Ach.* 970, cf. Tz. in *An.Ox.*3.317. **-ῖνος,** η, ον, *of lines* or *verses*, σ. θάνατος of one *who was rhymed to death*, *AP*11.135 (Lucill.).

**στίχιον,** = *stignum* (*genus vestimenti*), dub. in *Gloss.*; also *strigium*.

**στῐχ-ισμός,** ὁ, *numbering of the lines* of a book, Tz.*H.*9.291 (pl.). **-ιστής,** οῦ, ὁ, *writer of verse*, Id. ad Lyc.425; condemned by Thom.Mag.p.189 R.

**στῐχο-γράφος** [ᾰ], ὁ, *verse-writer*, *App.Anth.*5.12. **-λογέω,** *recite verses*, dub. l. in *PLips.*97 x 7 (iv A.D.). **-λογία,** ἡ, *recitation of verses*, dub. ib. xiii 10 (iv A.D.). ⊕ **-λόγος,** ὁ, = *palleatus*, *Gloss.* **-μῡθέω,** *answer one another line by line*, Poll.4.113. **-μῡθία,** ἡ, *conversation in alternate lines*, ibid. ⊕ **-πλᾰνήτης,** ου, ὁ, corrupt word in Dicaearch.1.9. **-πλόκος,** ὁ, (πλέκω) *versifier*, condemned by Thom.Mag.p.189 R. **-ποιέω,** *make verses*, *Gloss.* **-ποιία,** ἡ, *versification*, Plu.2.45a, *Gloss.*

⊕ **στίχος** [ῐ], ὁ, *row* or *file* of soldiers, X.*Lac.*11.5,8, *Eq.Mag.*3.9, v.l. for στοιχ- in *Cyr.*8.3.9; of trees, Id.*Oec.*4.21, *PFay.*111.24 (i A.D.); of numbers, Pl.*Phd.*104b; of the cells in a honey-comb, Arist.*HA* 624ᵃ11; *course* of masonry, *SIG* 247 ii 72 (Delph., iv B.C.). 2. old name for λόχος, Ascl.*Tact.*2.2, cf. Ael.*Tact.*5.2, Arr.*Tact.*6.1. II. *line* of poetry, *verse*, Ar.*Ra.*1239, Arr.*Epict.* 2.23.42, *BGU*1026 xxii 18 (iv A.D.), etc.; ἡρωϊκοὶ σ. Pl.*Lg.*959a; τὸν βίον ἔθηκας εἰς στίχον, i.e. have described life in one *line*, Nicostr. Com.28; but used of a couplet, *BMus.Inscr.*1074 (Coptos); defined by Heph.*Poëm.*1, cf. Sch.Heph.p.262 C. b. *line* of prose, of about the same length as the average hexameter verse, viz., about 15 or 16 syllables, used in reckoning the compass of a passage or work, D.H.*Th.*10,13,19,33, Gal.2.227, 5.656 (cf. 655), 10.781, 15.9, al., Anon. in *Tht.*3.32, Ath.13.585b, Men.Rh.p.434 S., *PLond.* in *Zentralblatt für Bibliothekswesen Beiheft* 61.88 (iii A.D.), *PFlor.*371.19, 23 (iv A.D.), Simp. *in Cat.*18.20; rarely used in citations, κατὰ τοὺς διακοσίους σ. D.L.7.33, cf. 187,188; ὡς πρὸ σ' στίχων τοῦ τέλους Sch. Orib.4 p.532, cf. p.534, al. 2. *chapter* of a book, Zos.Alch. p.213 B. III. ἐκτὸς τοῦ σ., = Lat. *extra ordinem*, *OGI*441.64 (Lagina, i B.C.). IV. Philos., = συστοιχία II, *series, order*, Plot.5. 3.14 (v.l. στοῖχος); *causal chain*, Id.6.7.6 (στοῖχος Volkmann).

**στῐχουργ-έω,** *make verses*, Eust.32.22. **-ημα,** ατος, τό, and **-ία,** ἡ, *versification*, Sch.Lyc.324,817. **-ός,** ὁ, *versifier*, Thom. Mag. p.189 R. (who censures the word).

**στῐχῳδός,** ὁ, contr. for στιχαοιδός, Menaechm.9.

**στῐώδης,** ες, (στῖον) *stony, hard*, Gal.19.140.

**στλεγγίδιον,** τό, Dim. of στλεγγίς II, Theopomp.Hist.240, *IG*11 (2).287 *B* 17 (Delos, iii B.C.), al.

**στλεγγῐδο-λήκῠθος,** ὁ, *the slave who carried his master's* στλεγγίς *and* λήκυθος to the bath, Poll.3.154 (who censures the word). **-ποιός,** όν, *making* στλεγγίδες, Str.15.1.67; also **στελγιδο-,** *EM*730.36.

**στλεγγ-ίζω,** *scrape* or *dress with the* στλεγγίς, Suid. (Pass.). **-ίον,** v. στλεγγίς. ⊕ **-ίς,** ίδος, ἡ, older word for ξύστρα (Erot.), *scraper*, to remove the oil and dirt from the skin in the bath or after the exercises of the Palaestra, Hp.*Acut.*65 (v. sub fin.), *Epid.*4.32, Ar. *Fr.*139, Pl.*Hp.Mi.*368c, Gal.6.406, al.; σ. and λήκυθος are freq.

coupled as typical articles of everyday use, οὐδ' ἔστιν αὕτη στλεγγὶς οὐδὲ λήκυθος Ar.*Fr.*207, cf. Cic.*Fin.*4.12.30, Plu.2.59f, 461e:—at Sparta reeds were used, but generally the σ. was of metal, ib.239b, cf. D.S.13.82. **II.** a sort of *tiara* overlaid with metal (ἐπίτηκτος), *IG*2².1638.45, 1640.6,7, 5(1).1390.14 (Andania, i B.C.), cf. Poll.7.179; of gold, *IG*11(2).161*B*34, al. (Delos, iii B.C.), Plb.25.4.10 (where στελγ-), Hippoloch.ap.Ath.4.128e; offered as a prize, X.*An.*1.2.10; worn by the θεωροί sent to an oracle or at a solemn festival, Heraclid.Tar.ap.Erot., Sosib.4:—in Ar.*Th.*556, the women are said to draw wine with their στλεγγίδες; so τῇ σ. κἂν ἀρύσαιτό τις Arist.*Top.*145ª23.—Many forms occur, **στελγίς** Plb. l. c., Hsch., Suid., *EM*725.47, v.l. in Gal.6.250; also dat. sg. στέλγει, = ξύστρα (i.e. -ᾳ), Hsch.; **στελγγίς** (sic) *IG*2².1541.15; **στεγγίς** Hp.*Acut.* l.c. (cod. A, λ add. A² post τ), Erot. l.c. (in lemmate); **στελεγγίς** v.l. in Gal.15.713; **στλέγγος,** ὁ, Sch.D.T.p.195 H.; **στεργίς** Artem. 1.64 codd.; **στρεγγίς** Heraclid. l.c.; Dim. **στλεγγίον,** Sch.D.T. p.195 H. **-ισμα,** ατος, τό, like γλοιός, *the oil and dirt scraped off by the* στλεγγίς, Arist.*Mir.*839ᵇ25; in form στέλγισμα, Lyc. 874. **-ιστρον,** τό, = στλεγγίς, *EM*725.48 in marg., in forms στέλγ- and στέργ-. **-ος,** v. στλεγγίς.

**στλεγγύς,** a kind of *wheat*, Thphr.*HP*8.4.3.

**στλίξ,** v. στρίξ.

**στοά,** ᾶς, ἡ, *SIG*29 (Attic, found at Delphi, vi/v B.C.), al., *IG*1².115.7, al.; also **στοιά** (in anapaest. verse) Ar.*Ec.*676,684,686, and in some dialect Inscrr., *IG*12(3).170.22 (Astypalaea), 4²(1).115.20 (prob., Epid., iv/iii B.C.), Ἀρχ. Ἐφ.1913.227 (Lesbos); **στωΐά** *Inscr.Magn.* 67.6 (Cnossian decree, iii/ii B.C.), *IG*12(2).14.2, al. (Mytil.):—*roofed colonnade, cloister*, Hdt.3.52, Th.4.90,8.90, X.*HG*5.2.29,7.4.31, *Ev. Jo.*10.23, *CPHerm.*94.3 (iii A.D.), etc. **II.** at Athens, **1.** *storehouse, magazine*, esp. for corn, Ar.*Ach.*548; στοιὰ ἀλφιτόπωλις Id.*Ec.* 686, cf. 14. **2.** ἡ στοιὰ ἡ βασίλειος the *court* where the βασιλεύς sat, ib.684; ἡ τοῦ βασιλέως σ. Pl.*Tht.*210d, cf. *Euthphr.*2a, Paus.1.3.1, 14.6, Poll.8.86; σ. βασιλική at Thera, *IG*12(3).326.19. **3.** ἡ στοὰ ἡ ποικίλη, v. ποικίλος II.3: also ἡ σ. alone, And.1.85; so οἱ ἀπὸ τῆς σ., of the Stoics (since Zeno taught there), *Placit.*1.5.1, S.E.*M.*9.11, Gal.10.15, etc.; οἱ ἐκ τῆς σ. Id.18(1).259: also ἡ Σ. alone, the *Stoic school*, Phld.*Rh.*2.68 S. **4.** of other porticoes, ἡ σ. ἡ τῶν Ἑρμῶν Aeschin.3.183; ἡ μακρὰ σ. D.34.37; ἡ τοῦ Διὸς τοῦ Ἐλευθερίου σ. Pl.*Thg.*121a. **III.** *long roof* or *shed* used in sieges, *SIG*569.36 (Halasarna, iii B.C.), Plb.1.48.2:—*gallery, communication trench*, whether above ground or excavated, Ph.*Bel.*83.32, 85.10, 91.31.

**στοαοροφή,** ἡ, *portico-roof*, *BCH*28.78 (Tralles).

**στοβ-άζω,** *scold, abuse*; and **-ασμα,** ατος, τό, *scolding*, Hsch. **-έω,** *scold*, *EM*385.19, cf. Epic. in *Arch.Pap.*7 p.9 (dub. sens.). **-ος,** ὁ, *abuse, bad language, insolence*, κόκκυγα κομπάζοντα μαψαύρας στόβους Lyc.395, cf. Hsch.

**Στοδμηνός,** epith. of Zeus at Acmonia, *IGRom.*4.661.23 (i A.D.).

**στοιά,** v. στοά.

**στοιβ-άζω,** *pile* or *heap up, pack together*, Lxx *Le.*1.7, al., Luc.*Cat.* 5:—Pass., of a wall, *to be packed, filled up*, κεράμοις *CPR*232.16 (ii/iii A.D.); cf. διαστοιβάζω. ⊛ **-άς,** άδος, ἡ, = ἡ στρωμνή, Zonar.; v. στιβάς. **-ασία,** ἡ, *stuffing, heaping up*, *EM*727.37. **-άσιμος,** ον, = *stipabilis*, *Gloss.* **-ασις,** εως, ἡ, = στοιβασία, Al.*Le.*24.6. **-αστής,** οῦ, ὁ, *packer, stevedore*, *PCair.Zen.*754.8 (iii B.C.); = *stipator*, *Gloss.* **-αστός,** ή, όν, *packed, pressed together*, *PLond.*3.856.20 (i A.D.). **-ή,** ἡ, (στείβω) *thorny burnet*, *Poterium spinosum*, Hp. *Mul.*2.186, Thphr.*HP*6.1.3, Lxx *Is.*55.13, Dsc.4.12; its branches were used to make brooms, τὴν στέγην ὀφέλλοντα. . πυθμένι στοιβῆς Hippon.51; also to pack wine-jars, Trypho ap.A.D.*Conj.*247.27. **2.** *cushion, pad*, Arist.*PA*654ᵇ26. **3.** *padding*, Eup.*Fr.inc.*132 M. (om. Kock, v. *Fr.*409 K.); καθάπερ σ. like *stuffing*, Gal.*UP*7.2,8, cf. 12.3: metaph., '*padding*', *an expletive*, Ar.*Ra.*1178, cf. Phld.*Rh.*2.40 S. **4.** *foundation-course* below stylobate, *IG*4²(1).102.3, al. (Epid., iv B.C.), 5(2).33 (Tegea, iii B.C.). **5.** *heap of corn*, Lxx *Ru.* 3.7; *sheaf, shock* of corn, ib.*Jd.*15.5 cod. A (στυβ-). **-ηδόν,** Adv. *crammed in*, Simp.*in Cat.*18.25. **-ίον,** τό, = στοιβή I, Ps.-Dsc.4.12.

**στοιβοειδής,** ές, *loose, porous*, σάρξ Alex.Aphr.*Pr.*2.72.

**στοΐδιον,** τό, Dim. of στοά, *IG*11(2).146*A*69 (Delos, iv B.C.), Str. 9.1.15: cf. στῴδιον.

**Στοϊκός,** v. Στωϊκός.

**Στοιχᾰδεύς,** έως, ὁ, title of Zeus at Sicyon, Sch.D.T.p.192 H.

**στοιχᾰδίτης** [ῑ], ου, ὁ, *flavoured with* στοιχάς II, οἶνος Dsc.5.42.

**Στοιχαῖος,** = Στοιχαδεύς (sc. Ζεύς), *IG*12(3).376 (Thera).

⊛ **στοιχάς,** άδος, ὁ, ἡ, (στοῖχος) *in a row one behind another*, esp. αἱ Στοιχάδες (sc. νῆσοι), name of the islands which lie *in a row* east of Toulon, now *les Îles d'Hyères*, A.R.4.554, Str.4.1.10. **2.** ἐλᾶαι σ. olive-trees (prob. because planted *in rows*) which were not sacred, like the μορίαι, Sol.ap.Poll.5.36, Philoch.62. **II.** στοιχάς, ἡ, an aromatic plant, *cassidony*, *Lavandula Stoechas*, Orph.*A.*918, Dsc. 3.26.

**Στοιχεία,** ἡ, epith. of Athena at Epidaurus, *IG*4²(1).487.

**στοιχειᾰκός,** ή, όν, *connected with the elements*, ὄλεθρος, of destruction by water, Eust.35.24. Adv. **-κῶς** Id.83.39.

**στοιχειο-γρᾰφέω,** in Pass., *to be written in the order of the Zodiac*, Vett.Val.162.34, 335.30. **-κράτωρ** [ᾰ], ορος, ὁ, pl. σ. θεοί gods *who presided over the elements*, Simp. *in Cael.*107.15.

**στοιχεῖον,** τό: **I.** in a form of sun-dial, *the shadow of the gnomon, the length of which in feet indicated the time of day*, ὅταν ᾖ δεκάπουν τὸ σ. when the *shadow* is ten feet long, Ar.*Ec.*652, v. Sch.; δειπνεῖν ἂν εἴκοσι ποδῶν. . τὸ σ. ᾖ Eub.119.7, cf. Philem.83. **II.** *element*, **1.** a *simple sound* of speech, as the *first component* of the syllable, Pl.*Cra.*424d; τὸ ῥῶ τὸ σ. ib.426d; γραμμάτων σ. καὶ συλλαβάς Id.*Tht.*202e; σ. ἐστι φωνὴ ἀδιαίρετος Arist.*Po.*1456ᵇ22; φωνῆς σ. καὶ ἀρχαὶ δοκοῦσιν εἶναι ταῦτ' ἐξ ὧν σύγκειται αἱ φωναὶ πρώτων Id. *Metaph.*998ª23, cf. Gal.15.6:—στοιχεῖα therefore, strictly, were different from *letters* (γράμματα), Diog.Bab.*Stoic.*3.213, Sch.D.T.p.32, al., but are freq. not clearly distd. from them, as by Pl.*Tht.* l.c., *Cra.*426d; τὰ σ. τῶν γραμμάτων τὰ τέτταρα καὶ εἴκοσι Aen.Tact.31.21; σ. ε̅ *letter* ε (in a filing-system), *BGU*959.2 (ii A.D.); ἀκουόμενα σ. *letters* which are pronounced, A.D.*Adv.*165.17; γράμματα and σ. are expressly identified by D.T.630.32; the σ. and its name are confused by A.D. *Synt.*29.1, but distd. by Hdn.Gr.ap.Choerob.*in Theod.*1.340, Sch.D.T. l.c.:—κατὰ στοιχεῖον *in the order of the letters, alphabetically*, *AP*11.15 (Ammian.); dub. sens. in Plu.2.422e. **2.** in Physics, στοιχεῖα were the *components into which matter is ultimately divisible, elements*, reduced to four by Empedocles, who called them ῥιζώματα, the word στοιχεῖα being first used (acc. to Eudem.ap.Simp.*in Ph.*7.13) by Pl., τὰ πρῶτα οἱονπερεὶ σ., ἐξ ὧν ἡμεῖς τε συγκείμεθα καὶ τἆλλα *Tht.*201e; τὰ τῶν πάντων σ. *Plt.*278d; αὐτὰ τιθέμενοι σ. τοῦ παντός *Ti.*48b, cf. Arist.*GC*314ª29, *Metaph.*998ª28, Thphr.*Sens.*3, al., D.L.3.24; σ. σωματικά Arist.*Mete.*338ᵇ22, Thphr.*Fr.*46; ἄτομα σ. Epicur.*Ep.*2 p.36 U.; equivalent to ἀρχαί, Thales ap.Plu.2.875c, Anaximand.ap. D.L.2.1, Anon.ap.Arist.*Ph.*188ᵇ28, *Metaph.*1059ᵇ23, al.; but Arist. also distinguishes σ. from ἀρχή as less comprehensive, ib.1070ᵇ23; τὰ σ. ὕλη τῆς οὐσίας ib.1088ᵇ27; τρία τὰ σ. Id.*Ph.*189ᵇ16; distd. from ἀρχή on other grounds by *Stoic.*2.111; σ. used in three senses by Chrysipp., ib.136, cf. Zeno ib.1.24, al.; in Medicine, Gal.6.3, 420, al., 15.7, al.; Αἰθέρ, κόσμου σ. ἄριστον Orph.*H.*5.4; ἀνηλεὲς σ., of the sea, Babr.71.4; τὸ σ., of the sea, Polem.*Cyn.*44; ἄμφω τὰ σ., i.e. land and sea, ib.11, cf. Hdn.3.1.5, Him.*Ecl.*2.18. **3.** the *elements of proof*, e.g. in general reasoning the πρῶτοι συλλογισμοί, Arist.*Metaph.*1014ᵇ1; in Geometry, the propositions whose proof is involved in the proof of other propositions, ib.998ª26, 1014ª36; title of geometrical works by Hippocrates of Chios, Leon, Theudios, and Euclid, Procl. *in Euc.*pp.66,67,68 F.: hence applied to whatever is one, small, and capable of many uses, Arist.*Metaph.*1014ᵇ3; to whatever is most universal, e.g. the unit and the point, ib.6; the line and the circle, Id.*Top.*158ᵇ35; the τόπος (argument applicable to a variety of subjects), ib.120ᵇ13, al., *Rh.*1358ª35, al.; στοιχεῖα τὰ γένη λέγουσί τινες Id.*Metaph.*1014ᵇ10; τὸ νόμισμα σ. καὶ πέρας τῆς ἀλλαγῆς coin is the *unit*. . of exchange, Id.*Pol.*1257ᵇ23; in Grammar, σ. τῆς λέξεως *parts* of speech, D.H.*Comp.*2; but also, the *letters* composing a word, A.D.*Synt.*313.7; *letters* of the alphabet, Diog. Bab.*Stoic.*3.213; σ. τοῦ λόγου the *elements* of speech, viz. *words*, or the *kinds of words, parts* of speech, Thphr.ap.Simp. *in Cat.*10.24, Chrysipp.*Stoic.*2.45, A.D.*Synt.*7.1, 313.6. **4.** generally, *elementary* or *fundamental principle*, ἀρξάμενοι ἀπὸ τῶν σ. X.*Mem.*2.1.1; σ. χρηστῆς πολιτείας Isoc.2.16; τὸ πολλάκις εἰρημένον μέγιστον σ. Arist.*Pol.*1309ᵇ16; σ. τῆς ὅλης τέχνης Nicol.Com.1.30, cf. Epicur. *Ep.*1 p.10 U., *Ep.*3 p.59 U., Phld.*Rh.*1.127 S., Gal.6.306. **5.** ἄστρων στοιχεῖα the *stars*, Man.4.624; σ. καυσούμενα λυθήσεται 2*Ep.Pet.*3.10, cf. 12; esp. *planets*, στοιχείῳ Διός *PLond.*1.130.60 (i/ii A.D.); so perh. in *Ep.Gal.*4.3, *Ep.Col.*2.8; esp. a *sign of the Zodiac*, D.L.6.102; of the Great Bear, *PMag.Par.*1.1303. **6.** σ. = ἀριθμός, as etym. of Στοιχαδεύς, Sch.D.T.p.192 H.

**στοιχει-όω,** *instruct in the basic principles* (στοιχεῖα), Chrysipp. *Stoic.*2.39, Phot.:—Pass., **-ωθήσεται** *will be instructed*, Ael.*Tact. Prooem.*5, cf. Ath.Mech.5.5. **-ώδης,** ες, *elementary, of the nature of an element*, Arist.*GC*315ª24 (Comp.), Phld.*Rh.*1.69 S., al., Plu.2. 1004a (Comp.), Gal.1.506, 6.384, al.: Sup. **-έστατος** Arist.*Metaph.* 988ᵇ35, Hierocl. *in CA*20 p.465 M.: esp. of Grammar, τὰ σ. μόρια D.H.*Th.*22; of the numbers from 1 to 9, *Theol.Ar.*57. Adv. **-δῶς** Demetr.Lac.*Herc.*1647.24, D.L.7.131, 10.34. **2.** v. στοιχώδης. **-ωμα,** ατος, τό, *elementary* or *basic principle*, Epicur.*Ep.*1 p.4 U., Phld.*Rh.*1.140 S. **-ωμᾰτικοί,** οἱ, *persons who cast nativities from the signs of the Zodiac* (cf. στοιχεῖον II. 5), Ps.-Ptol.*Centil.* 9. **-ωσις,** εως, ἡ, *teaching*, ἀρετῆς Hierocl. *in CA*11 p.445 M.; *elementary exposition*, τῶν ὅλων δοξῶν Epicur.*Ep.*1 p.4 U.; αἱ δώδεκα σ., a work by Epicurus, Id.*Fr.*56; ἡ ἠθικὴ σ., work by Eudromus, *Stoic.*3.268; σ. καθολικαί Phld.*Rh.*1.104 S.; τὰ ἁπλᾶ πρὸς στοιχείωσίν ἐστιν ἐπιτήδεια *elementary teaching*, Simp.*in Cat.*13.29. **2.** *doctrine of the elements*, Gal.7.678, 15.175, 19.356. **-ωτής,** οῦ, ὁ, *teacher of elements*, of Grammarians, regarded as creators of language, A.D.*Synt.*309.5, Sch.Hermog. in Rh.7(2).903 W.; ὁ σ. the *arranger of the letters* of the alphabet, Sch.D.T.p.492 H.; of Euclid, the *author of the Elements*, Elias *in Cat.*251.18. **-ωτικός,** ή, όν, *elementary*, Epicur.*Fr.*242. **2.** *serial*, ὁ τῆς ἑπταζώνου σ. λόγος Paul.Al.*I.*3. **-ωτός,** ή, όν, *composed of elements*, Olymp.*in Phlb.*p.246 S., Dam.*Pr.*58, al.

**στοιχ-ευτής,** οῦ, ὁ, = *elementarius*, *Gloss.* ⊛ **-έω,** *to be drawn up in a line* or *row*, οὐδ' ἐγκαταλείψω τὸν παραστάτην, ὅτῳ ἂν στοιχήσω *beside* whom *I stand* in battle,—from the oath of Athenian citizens, ap.Stob.4.1.48, cf. Poll.8.105; *move in line*, X.*Cyr.*6. 3.34, *Eq.Mag.*5.7; *to be in rows*, of leaves or joints, Thphr.*HP*3. 18.5, 3.5.3; κατὰ τὸ στοιχοῦν *in sequence*, Arist.*Int.*19ᵇ24. **2.** *correspond*, ὅπως ἀεὶ ἡ ἡμέρα στοιχῇ καθ' ἑκάστην πόλιν *OGI*458.52 (i B.C.). **3.** *to be satisfactory* to one, στοιχεῖ μοι πάντα τὰ προγεγραμμένα *BGU*317.14 (vi A.D.), cf. *Sammelb.*6258 (v/vi A.D.), etc. II. c. dat., *fit*, [καταστρωτῆρα] στοιχοῦντα τοῖς κειμένοις *IG*7.3073.153 (Lebad., ii B.C.): metaph., *to be in line with, walk by, agree with, submit to*, τῇ τῆς συγκλήτου προθέσει Plb.28.5.6; διὰ τῶν ἔργων στοιχεῖν αὐτοσαυτῷ *SIG*734.6 (Delph., i B.C.); τῇ πρός τινα εὐνοίᾳ *BCH*55.44 (Odessus, i B.C.); ταῖς πλείοσι γνώμαις D.H.6.65; τῷ νομίσματι S.E.*M*.1.178; τοῖς προειρημένοις φιλοσόφοις ib.11.59; Πνεύματι *Ep.Gal*.5.25, cf. *Ep.Phil*.3.16; τοῖς ἴχνεσι τῆς πίστεως *Ep.Rom*.4.12; στοίχεις (Aeol. pres. part.) τοῖς προϋπαργμένοισι *IGRom*.4.1302 (Cyme, i B.C./i A.D.); ἠθέλησεν στοιχοῦσαν τοῖς προπεπραγμένοις παρέχεσθαι τοῖς πολίταις τὴν αὐτοῦ διάληψιν *OGI*764.45 (Pergam., ii B.C.); μιᾷ σ. *to be contented* with one wife, Sch.Ar.*Pl*.773; στοιχῶν πᾶσιν ὑπέγραψα *CPR*30 ii 41 (vi A.D.): abs., στοιχεῖν βουλόμενος καὶ τοῖς ἐκείνων ἴχνεσιν ἐπιβαίνειν *SIG*708.5 (Istropolis, ii B.C.); στοιχεῖς τὸν νόμον φυλάσσων *observest it regularly*, *Act.Ap*.21.24. **-ηγορέω**, *tell in regular order*, A.*Pers*.430. **-ηδίς**, Adv. = sq., Theognost.*Can*.163. **-ηδόν**, Adv. *in a row*, Arist.*GA*770ᵃ26, Thphr.*HP*3.12.7, A.R.1.1004. 2. *line by line, following the lines*, Puchstein *Epigr.Gr*.p.7. **-ημα**, ατος, τό, *deposit*, Eust.1312.21. **-ητέον**, *one must agree with*, τινι Theognost.*Can*.98. **-ητής**, οῦ, ὁ, dub. cj. for στυχιτης, = *stabilis*, in *Gloss*. (fort. στυλίτης). **-αῖος**, α, ον, *equal to one row* or *course*, in masonry, ὑπερτόναια..πάχος στοιχαῖα μῆκος ὀκτώποδα *IG*2².463.57. **-ίζω**, *set in a row*, esp. *set a row of poles with nets* to drive the game into, X.*Cyn*.6.8; cf. στοῖχος II, περιστοιχίζω:—Pass., *to be set in rows*, v.l. for ἐστιχ- in Lxx*Ez*.42.3. II. *order* or *arrange in system*, τρόπους μαντικῆς A.*Pr*.484. **-ικός**, ή, όν, *serial*, ὁ τῆς ἑπταζώνου σ. λόγος *Cat.Cod.Astr*.7.113. **-ισμός**, ὁ, *surrounding with hunting-nets*, Poll.5.36.

✱ **στοιχομυθέω**, = στοιχηγορέω, Sch.A.*Pers*.430, Phot.

**στοῖχος**, ὁ, (στείχω, cf. στίχος) *row in an ascending series*, ὁ πρῶτος σ. τῶν ἀναβαθμῶν the first *course* of (masonry composing) the steps, Hdt.2.125; *course* of bricks, etc., in building, *IG*2².463.58, 1682.10; esp. *file* of persons marching one behind another, as in a procession, ἐπὶ στοίχου, = στοιχηδόν, Ar.*Ec*.756; νῆσοι κατὰ στοῖχον κείμεναι Th.2.102; κατὰ στοίχους Ar.*Fr*.79; of ships, *column*, ἐν στοίχοις τρισί A.*Pers*.366; of soldiers, *file*, Th.4.47; διὰ στοίχων ὁπλῖται παρατεταγμένοι D.C.63.4; of deer swimming, Opp.*C*.2.226; of the *files* (opp. ζυγόν VIII) of the chorus in plays, Poll.4.108,109; *row* of columns, *IG*2².1668.12; of factors, Arist.*Metaph*.1092ᵇ34; of verses, ἔπη..ἀλλότρια τοῦ σ. τῆς ποιήσεως Afric.*Cest.Oxy*.412.51. II. *a line of poles supporting hunting-nets*, into which the game were driven, X.*Cyn*.6.10,21. III. τοῦ σ. καταλαβόντος τὴν ἡμετέραν βουλήν since the *turn* has come to our senate, *POxy*.1119.12 (iii A.D.).

**στοιχούντως**, Adv. *conformably*, *OGI*532.27 (Neoclaudiopolis, Aug.).

**στοιχώδης**, ες, *in vertical rows*, κριθὴ σ. barley *which has its grains one directly under another*, cj. in Thphr.*HP*8.4.2 (στοιχειώδης codd.).

**στολᾰγωγ-έω**, *lead an expedition*, οἱ τὴν ἀποικίαν -ήσαντες Dion.Byz.8. **-ός**, ὁ, = στολάρχης, Polem.*Cyn*.35 codd. (στολαγοῦ Hinck).

**στολ-άζομαι**, Med., *array oneself in*, πάντες ἐστολάδαντο.. φάρεα *BCH*50.529 (Marathon, ii A.D.). ✱ **-άρχης**, ου, ὁ, *commander of a fleet*, *PCair.Zen*.48.2 (iii B.C.), *Epigr.Gr*.337 (Cyzic.), *PSI*4.298.15 (iv A.D., gen. -ου), Hsch.; fem. **-αρχίς**, ίδος, ἡ, epith. of Isis, *POxy*.1380.8 (ii A.D.). **-αρχος**, ὁ, = στολάρχης, Poll.1.119 cod. B. **-άς**, άδος, ἡ, (στόλος I. 3) *moving in close array*, Λίβυες οἰωνοὶ στολάδες E.*Hel*.1480 (lyr.), as v.l. for στοχάδες *in a row*. II. *leathern jerkin*, Ael.*Tact*.2.8. **-ή**, ἡ, Aeol. **στολά** (q.v.): (στέλλω):—*equipment, fitting out*, στρατοῦ A.*Supp*.764. 2. *armament*, Id.*Pers*.1018 (lyr.). II. *equipment in clothes, raiment*, ib.192; σχῆμα Ἑλλάδος σ. S.*Ph*.224, cf. E.*Heracl*.130; ἱππάδα στολὴν ἐνεσταλμένοι Hdt.1.80; σ. ἱππική Ar.*Ec*.846; Σκυθική Hdt.4.78; Θρῃκία E.*Rh*.313; Μηδική X.*Cyr*.8.1.40; γυναικεία Ar.*Th*.851, cf. 92; τοξική Pl.*Lg*.833b; στολὴν ἔχειν ἣν ἂμ βούληται *SIG*1003.14 (Priene, ii B.C.): metaph. of birds, σ. πτερῶν Ach.Tat.1.15. 2. *garment, robe*, S.*OC*1357,1597, *PCair.Zen*.54.32 (pl.), 263.4,8 (iii B.C.), *BGU*1860.4 (i B.C.), etc.; σ. θηρός, of the lion's skin which Heracles wore, E.*HF*465; ἐν σ. περιπατεῖν in *full dress*, M.Ant.1.7 (v.l. -λίῳ ap.Suid.), cf. *Ev.Marc*.12.38. 3. *act of dressing*, μετὰ τὴν σ. Orib.*Syn*.5.21. III. (στέλλω IV) *check to motion, pressure*, τοῦ ἀέρος Epicur.*Nat*.11.11, cf. 14.4. 2. *reduction, diminution*, τῶν σιτίων Herod.Med.ap.Aët.5.129.

**στολίδ-ιον** [ῐδ], τό, Dim. of στολίς, *leather jerkin*, Aen.Tact.29.4. **-όομαι**, Med., *dress oneself in*, νεβρίδα στολιδωσαμένα E.*Ph*.1755 (lyr.). 2. Pass., *become wrinkled*, of a bandage, Sor.*Fasc*.42. **-ώδης**, ες, *full of* or *like folds, wrinkled*, Hp.*Art*.59 (Comp.), Sor.1.18, Paul.Aeg.4.26, 6.71. **-ωμα**, ατος, τό, *fold*, περισφίγγει -ώμασι πέπλος *AP*5.103 (Marc. Arg.). **-ωτός**, ή, όν, (στολίς II) σ. χιτών a long tunic *hanging in many folds*, X.*Cyr*.6.4.2, cf. Poll.7.54.

**στολ-ίζω**, (στολίς) *put in trim*, στολίσας νηὸς πτερά *drawing in* the sail, Hes.*Op*.628. 2. *equip, dress*, τινὰ πέπλοις *Anacreont*.15.29; ἀγαλμάτιον Plu.2.366f; τοὺς θεούς *Stud.Pal*.22.183.90 (ii A.D.):—Pass., ἐστολισμένος δορὶ *armed* with spear, E.*Supp*.659; νῆες σημείοισιν ἐστ. Id.*IA*255 (lyr.); νυμφικῶς ἐστ. Ach.Tat.3.7; ἐστ. τὴν βασιλικὴν στολήν Lxx*Es*.8.15: abs., ἐστ. *in full dress*, ib.1*Es*.1.2, al. 3. metaph., *deck, adorn*, τὰς φρένας τινὶ *AP*9.214 (Leo Phil.). II. *to be a* στολιστής, *IG*3.162.9. ✱ **-ιον**, τό, Dim. of στολή II, *scanty garment*, of the dress of philosophers, *AP*11.157 (Ammian.), Arr.*Epict*.3.23.35; v. στολή II. 2. **-ίς**, ίδος, ἡ, = στολή II, *garment, robe*, E.*Ph*.1491 (lyr.), *AP*7.27 (Antip. Sid.), *Sammelb*.6178 (Egypt, metr.), etc.; νεβρῶν στολίδες, i.e. fawnskins *worn as garments*, E.*Hel*.1359 (lyr.). 2. *sails*, *AP*10.6 (Satyr.). II. pl., *folds* in a woman's robe, πέπλων E.*Ba*.936; τῶν ἀνδριάντων Arist.*Aud*.802ᵃ38; cf. στολιδωτός: of *wrinkles* or *folds* in the womb or other parts, Sor.1.14, Heliod.ap.Orib.44.8.14; of rugose ulcers, Gal.12.231, al.; also *wrinkles* on the forehead, Poll.2.46, cf. Plu.2.64a. **-ισις**, εως, ἡ, *a clothing, dressing*, Ph.2.157. **-ισμα**, ατος, τό, *equipment, garment*, E.*Hec*.1156, *Stud.Pal*.22.183.45 (ii A.D.), etc., prob. in *PTeb*.598 (ii A.D.). **-ισμός**, ὁ, *equipping, dressing*, θεῶν *OGI*56.4 (Canopus, iii B.C.), 90.6 (Rosetta, ii B.C.). 2. *equipment, dress*, Lxx 2*Ch*.9.4, al., Aristeas 96, *BGU*1.3 (iii A.D.), Pap. in *Sitzb.Heidelb. Akad*.1923(2).18; = *pectorale*, *Gloss*. **-ιστεία**, ἡ, *office of* στολιστής, Wilcken *Chr*.81.10 (ii A.D.), etc. **-ιστήριον**, τό, *place where the priests attired themselves* or *the statues of the gods, vestry*, Plu.2.359a, *BGU*338.1, al. (ii/iii A.D.). **-ιστής**, οῦ, ὁ, = ἱερόστολος, Lxx 4*Ki*.10.22, Plu.2.366f, Wilcken *Chr*.77 ii 8 (ii A.D.), *IG*3.140, Jul.Laod. in *Cat.Cod.Astr*.5(1).189, cj. in Luc.*Sacr*.14 (for σοφιστῶν). **-μός**, ὁ, = στολή, *equipment, raiment*, E.*Supp*.1055; but mostly with a word added, πρόστερνοι σ. πέπλων A.*Ch*.29 (lyr.); μέλανα σ. πέπλων E.*Alc*.216 (lyr.), cf. 923 (anap.); στολμοὺς μελαμπέπλους ib.818; also σ. τε χρωτὸς τῶνδε..πέπλων over the body, Id.*Andr*.148; also of chaplets, στεφέων ἱεροὺς σ. Id.*Tr*.258 (lyr.), cf. *HF*526; also of sails, στολμοί τε λαίφους A.*Supp*.715.

**στολοδρομέω**, *sail in line*, Hero *Aut*.22.5.

**στολοκρατές**· τὸ τῆς Ἰοῦς μέτωπον, διὰ τὰ κέρατα, Hsch. (= *Trag. Adesp*.598, fort. στολόκρου κρατός).

✱ **στόλοκρος**, ον, of a kid, *with knobs instead of horns*, Hsch. s.v. κόλον: τὸ σ. the *knob* or *young horn*, = κορδύλη, Phot. 2. of men, *bald*, Hsch.: metaph., *ugly, rude*, Id.

✱ **στόλος**, ὁ, (στέλλω) *equipment*, esp. for warlike purposes, *expedition* by land or (more frequently) sea, freq. in Hdt.; στόλον..οὐκέτι κατὰ θάλασσαν στείλαντες ἀλλὰ κατ' ἤπειρον 5.64; freq. folld. by ἐπί c. acc., ὁ ἐπ' Αἰθίοπας σ. 3.25; ἐπὶ Λιβύην στρατιῆς μέγας σ. 4.145; ἐλέγετο ὁ σ. εἶναι εἰς Πισίδας X.*An*.3.1.9; ὁ πρὸς Ἴλιον σ. S.*Ph*.247; οὔτε τοῦ πρώτου σ. ib.73; λεκτὸν ἀροῦμεν στόλον A.*Pers*.795, cf. E.*Hec*.1141; τεθριπποβάμων σ. *an equipage* with four horses, Id.*Or*.989 (lyr.). 2. generally, *journey* or (oftener) *voyage*, ὁ οἴκαδε σ. S.*Ph*.499; οὐ μοι μακρὸς εἰς Οἴτην σ. ib.490; σ. ποιεῖσθαι X.*An*.1.3.16; πλεῦσαι S.*Ph*.1037; ἰδίῳ σ. *in a journey* privately undertaken, on one's own account, opp. δημοσίῳ σ., Hdt.5.63, cf. Th.8.9; κοινῷ σ. Hdt.6.39; ἐλευθέρῳ σ. with free *course*, Pi.*P*.8.98; πατρῷον στόλον (acc. cogn.) ἑσπόμην by my father's *sending*, S.*Tr*.562. b. *the purpose* or *cause of a journey, mission, errand*, Id.*OC*358; τίνι σ. προσέσχες..; πόθεν πλέων; where Neoptolemus answers ἐξ Ἰλίου..ναυστολῶ, Id.*Ph*.244; ὁ δὲ σ. νῷν ἐστι παρὰ τὸν Τηρέα Ar.*Av*.46: metaph., τρίτος ἡμῖν σ. ἐστὶ τοῦ λόγου ἐπὶ τὴν τέχνην D.H.*Rh*.11.9. c. *equipment* in concrete sense, πραθέντος τοῦ στόλου εἰς βασίλεια *IPE*1².32*A* 45 (Olbia, iii B.C.); ἱερὸς σ. sacred *vestments*, *Milet*.1(7).209 (iii A.D.). 3. *armament, army*, τὸν ἑπτάλογχον σ., of the Seven against Thebes, S.*OC*1305, cf. *Tr*.226,496, etc.; *sea-force, fleet*, Hdt.5.43; σ. χιλιοναύτης, of the expedition against Troy, A.*Ag*.45 (anap.), cf. 577; ναυβάτῃ στόλῳ S.*Ph*.270; οὐ πολλῷ στόλῳ, i.e. in one ship, ib.547, cf. 561; νεῶν σ. Th.1.31; σ. ἀγείρειν ib.9; συναγείρειν Hdt.1.4; καταλύειν Id.7.16.β′: generally, *party, band, troop*, freq. in A.*Supp*., 28 (anap.), 187, al.; παίδων, γυναικῶν, καὶ σ. πρεσβυτίδων Id.*Eu*.1027, cf. 856 (pl.); νοσεῖ δέ μοι πρόπας σ. all the *people*, S.*OT*170 (lyr.); *guild*, ὁ σ. τῶν σωληνοκεντῶν *OGI*756.5 (Milet.). 4. παγκρατίου σ., periphr. for παγκράτιον, Pi.*N*.3.17; λόγου σ. a set narrative, Emp.17.26. II. *appendage, excrescence*, σ. ὀμφαλώδης Arist.*GA*752ᵇ6; *stump of the tail*, in animals, Id.*PA*658ᵃ33; σμικροῦ γ' ἕνεκεν [κέρκου] ἔχουσί τινα στόλον ib.689ᵇ5. 2. *a ship's prow*, Pi.*P*.2.62; plated with brass, χαλκήρης σ. A.*Pers*.408, cf. E.*IT*1135 (lyr.), *Trag.Adesp*.272 (pl.); δώδεκα σ. ναῶν f.l. for δωδεκάστολοι νᾶες, Ps.-E.*IA*277 (lyr.); δρυοπαγὴς σ., = πάσσαλος, S.*Fr*.702.

**στολυξώδης**· μικρολόγος, Hsch.

✱ **στόμα**, τό, Aeol. **στύμα** Theoc.29.25; gen. στόματος, but στομάτοιο *Hymn.Mag*.2(2).10,28:—*mouth*, Il.14.467, etc.; σύν τε στόμ' ἐρεῖσαι Od.11.426; ἱμείρων γλυκεροῦ σ. Sol.25; of animals, Hes.*Sc*.146,389, S.*Ph*.1156 (lyr.), etc.:—pl. is sts. used for sg., ἀμφιπίπτων στόμασιν, of kissing, Id.*Tr*.938, cf. E.*Alc*.403 (lyr.), and freq. in later Poets, A.R.4.1607, Nic.*Al*.210,240, etc.: metaph., πτολέμοιο, ὑσμίνης στόμα, *the very jaws* of the battle, as of a devouring monster, Il.10.8, 20.359 (but cf. infr. III. 1). 2. esp. *the mouth as the organ of speech*, δέκα μὲν γλῶσσαι, δέκα δὲ στόματ' 2.489, cf. Thgn.18; βραχύ μοι σ. πάντ' ἀναγήσασθαι Pi.*N*.10.19; freq. in Trag., σ. τὸ Δῖον the *mouth* of Zeus, A.*Pr*.1032; τὸ Φοίβου θεῖον ἀψευδὲς σ. Id.*Fr*.350.5, cf. S.*OC*603; τοῦ στόματος τὸ στρογγύλον Ar.*Fr*.471; Μοισᾶν καπυρὸν σ. their *mouthpiece, organ*, Theoc.7.37, cf. Mosch.3.72; Πιερίδων τὸ σοφὸν σ., of Homer, *AP*7.4 (Paul. Sil.), cf. 7.6 (Antip. Sid.), 7.75 (Antip.), 9.184; τὸ μισόχρηστον σ. τῆς κωμῳδίας Phld.*Piet*.p.93G.; *speech, utterance*, S.*OT*426,706, *OC*132 (lyr.), etc.; εἰς τόδ' ἐξελθόντος ἀνόσιον σ. ib.981; κἂν καλὸν φορῇ σ. Id.*Fr*.930; τὸ σὸν..σ. ἐλεινόν Id.*OT*671; διδόναι σ. καὶ σοφίαν *Ev.Luc*.21.15: in pl. of a single speaker, S.*OT*1220 (lyr.):—special phrases: οἴγειν σ. A.*Pr*.611; τοὐμὸν οὐ λύω σ. E.*Hipp*.1060, cf. Isoc.12.96; διᾶραι τὸ σ. D.19.112; κοίμησον σ. keep silence, A.*Ag*.1247; δάκνειν σ., i.e. to keep a stern silence (cf. ὀδάξ), Id.Fr.397; ἴσχε δακὼν σ. σὸν S.Tr.977 (anap.); ὀδόντι πρῖε τὸ σ. Id.Fr.897; so κλῄσας σ. E.Ph.865; οὐκ ἐφέξετε σ.; Id.Hec.1283; σῖγ' ἕξομεν σ. Id.Hipp.660; εὖ ἔχειν σ., = εὐφημεῖν, Eup. 381; συγκλῄειν σ. Ar.Th.40 (anap.):—of style, τὸ Λυσιακὸν σ. D.H.Lys. 12. 3. with Preps., a. ἀνὰ στόμα ἔχειν have always in one's mouth, whether for good or ill, E.El.80; ἀνὰ σ. καὶ διὰ γλώσσης ἔχειν Id.Andr.95. b. ἀπὸ στόματος εἰπεῖν speak from memory (cf. ἀπὸ γλώσσης), Pl.Tht.142d, X.Mem.3.6.9, Philem.48, Plu.Sol.8, etc. c. διὰ στόμα λέγειν A.Th.579, cf. E.Or.103 (so κατὰ τὸ σ. ᾄδειν Ar.Nu.158); διὰ στόμα ἔχειν Id.Lys.855; οἶκτος οὔτις ἦν διὰ στόμα A.Th.51; πᾶσι διὰ στόματος 'tis the common talk, Theoc.12. 21. d. ἐν στόμασι εἶχον Hdt.3.157, 6.136; πολλῶν κείμενος ἐν στόμασιν Thgn.240; ἐν τῷ σ. λέγειν Ar.Ach.198. e. ἐξ ἑνὸς σ. with one voice, Id.Eq.670. Pl.R.364a, PGiss.36.13 (ii B.C.), Gal.15. 763; so ὡς ἀφ' ἑνὸς σ. AP11.159 (Lucill.). f. ἐπὶ στόμα on one's face, face-foremost, ἐξεκυλίσθη πρηνὴς.. ἐπὶ σ. Il.6.43, cf. 16.410; ὡς κύων ἐπὶ σ. κείμενος Archil.Supp.2.9; ὗς ἔκειτ' ἐπὶ σ. Men.21; ἐπὶ σ. κεῖται lies prone, of the right ventricle, Hp.Cord.4; ἐπὶ σ., = pronus, Gloss.; ἐπὶ σ. πεσόντα Plu.Art.29; ἐπὶ σ. φερόμενον ἐν πᾶσι Timae. ap.Plb.12.8.4; also ὅ τι νῦν ἦλθ' ἐπὶ σ. whatever came uppermost, A.Fr.351; ἐπὶ στόματος Φαραὼ by the command of P., Lxx 4Ki.23. 35. g. κατὰ στόμα face to face, Hdt.8.11, E.Heracl.801, Rh.409, X.An.5.2.26; οἱ κατὰ σ. θεοί (cf. ἀντήλιοι) E.Fr.781.33; κατὰ σ. τινὸς confronted with him, Pl.Lg.855d; στόμα κατὰ στόμα λαλήσω αὐτῷ Lxx Nu.12.8; στόμα πρὸς στόμα 2Ep.Jo.12, 3Ep.Jo.14, PMag. Berol.1.39. II. mouth of a river, Il.12.24, Od.5.441, A.Pr.847, Hdt.2.17, etc.; so ἠϊόνος σ. μακρόν the wide mouth of the bay, Il.14. 36, cf. Od.10.90; σ. τοῦ Πόντου Th.4.75; κόλπου ib.49; τὸ σ. τῆς ἐσβολῆς Ar.Ec.1107; τὸ ἄνω σ. [τῆς διώρυχος] the width of the trench at top, Hdt.7.23 (but τὰ σ. τ. δ. mouths, ib.37). 2. any outlet or entrance, ἀργαλέον σ. λαύρης Od.22.137; σ. τῆς ἀγυιᾶς X.Cyr.2. 4.4; σ. φρέατος Id.An.4.5.25; καδίσκου Ar.Fr.581, cf. AP6.251 (Phil.); χθόνιον Ἀΐδα σ. Pi.P.4.44; τὰ τῶν διεξόδων σ. Pl.Phdr. 251d; ἑπτάπυλον σ. the seven gates of Thebes, S.Ant.119 (lyr.): Medic., τῶν μητρέων, τῶν ὑστερέων, = os uteri (not distinguished from the cervix), Hp.Mul.1.36, Aph.5.46; τῆς κοιλίας Arist.APo. 94$^{b}$15, Sor.1.50; γαστρός Nic.Al.20, Gal.5.274; [ἕλκους] Arist.Pr. 863$^{a}$11. III. foremost part, face, front: 1. of weapons, point, κατὰ στόμα εἱμένα χαλκῷ Il.15.389; [ὁ κριὸς] ἔχει σ. σιδηροῦν Ath. Mech.24.2; τὸ σ. τῆς αἰχμῆς Philostr.Her.19.4; edge of a sword, μαχαίρας Ascl.Tact.3.5, Ev.Luc.21.24, etc.: metaph., ἐθηλύνθην σ. S.Aj.651. b. the front ranks of the battle, the front, ἀπὸ στόματος (opp. ἀπὸ τῆς οὐρᾶς) X.An.3.4.42, cf. HG4.3.4; τὸ σ. τοῦ πλαισίου Id.An.3.4.43, cf. 5.4.22, Plb.10.12.7 (so perh. σ. πολέμοιο, ὑσμίνης in Hom., v. supr. I. 1). c. τὸ τῶν λοχαγῶν τάγμα σ. καλεῖται Ascl.Tact.2.5. 2. ἄκρον σ. πύργων the edge or top of the towers, E.Ph.1166; πρὸς τῷ σ. τοῦ βίου at the very verge of life, X.Ages.11. 15. 3. = ὀμφαλός III. 3, Ael.Tact.7.3. (Cf. Avest. staman-, m. 'mouth (of dog)', Welsh safn 'mouth'.)

**στομᾰκάκη** [κᾰ], ἡ, a disease in which all the teeth fall out, scurvy of the gums, Str.16.4.24 (-κάκκη codd.), Plin.HN25.20.

**στομαλγ-έω**, have a sore mouth, Poll.4.185. -ία, ἡ, soreness of the mouth, ibid.: metaph., mouth-plague, i.e. incessant chattering, Id.2.101.

**στομᾰ-λίμνη**, ἡ, like λιμνοθάλαττα, salt-water lake, lagoon, Str.4. 1.8, 13.1.31; μεσσηγὺς ποταμοῖο Σκαμάνδρου καὶ στομαλίμνης v.l. (ap. Sch.) in Il.6.4. -λίμνιον, τό, = foreg., Theoc.4.23.

**στομαργ-ία**, ἡ, endless talking, Ph.2.219. ❀ -ος, ον, noisily prating, loud-tongued, A.Th.447, S.El.607; σ. γλωσσαλγία wearisome talkativeness, E.Med.525:—the forms στομάργου, also στυμ- and στρυμ- are cited as vv. ll. for Στομάργεω or Στυμάργεω (gen. sg. of pr. n. Στομάργης or Στυμάργης Hp.Epid.2.2.4, 2.4.5) by Diosc. Gloss. and others ap.Gal.19.141,142. (-αργος perh. taken from γλώσσ-αργος.)

**στομᾰτεύω**, gloss on λεσβιάζω, Hsch.

**στομᾰ-τικός**, ή, όν, good for the mouth, (sc. φάρμακον) Dsc.3.5, cf. Antyll.ap.Orib.10.36.2, Gal.10.357, 12.14; σ. πτερά for inducing emesis or applying remedies, Herod.Med.in Rh.Mus.58.87; τὰ σ. (sc. πάθη) affections of the mouth, Dsc.1.87; αἱ σ. (sc. φλεγμοναί) Id. 4.37. -άτιον [ᾰ], τό, Dim. of στόμα, Sor.1.108, Gloss.

**στομᾰτοδιαστολεύς**, έως, ὁ, surgical instrument used to keep the mouth open, Heliod.ap.Orib.44.14.13.

**στομᾰτουργός**, όν, word-making, γλῶσσα Ar.Ra.826.

❀ **στομαυλέω**, mimic a flute with the lips, Pl.Cra.417e, cf. Poll.2.101.

**στομᾰχ-έω**, = Lat. stomachor, Dosith.p.432 K. -ῐκεύομαι, to be disordered in the stomach, Aët.3.109. ❀ -ῐκός, ή, όν, of the stomach, πάθος Aret.SD2.6; συγκοπή Gal.7.128. 2. disordered in the stomach, Dsc.4.38, Arr.Epict.3.21.1, Aret.CD2.6, etc.; οἱ σ. ἢ οἱ μελαγχολικοί Plu.2.732a. Adv. -κῶς Gal.8.368. 3. good for the stomach, Ruf.ap.Orib.8.47.11, Gal.6.451. -ιον, τό, dub. sens., title of a work by Archimedes. -ος, ὁ, (στόμα) throat, gullet, ἀπὸ στομάχους ἀρνῶν τάμε νηλέϊ χαλκῷ Il.3.292, cf. 19.266; κατὰ στομάχοιο θέμεθλα νύξε 17.47; = οἰσοφάγος, Arist.HA495$^{b}$19 sq., 493$^{a}$8, Nic.Al.22. 2. neck of the bladder, τῆς κύστιος Hp. Aër.9; or of the uterus, Id.Mul.1.18, Steril.217; τοῦ αἰδοίου Id. Mul.1.36. 3. later, orifice of the stomach, = στόμα τῆς γαστρός, τῆς κοιλίας, Plu.2.687d, Gal.6.431, 7.127; the stomach itself, 1Ep. Ti.5.23, Dsc.5.6, Plu.2.698b, Sor.1.15, al., Gal.6.227, 15.460, M.Ant.10.31, Ath.3.79f; ἀμφοτέρας (sc. τὰς χεῖρας) ἐπὶ τοῦ σ. PMag.Leid.W.18.36; cf. Lat. stomachus. 4. anger, γέγονε σ. πρὸς δουλικὸν πρόσωπον Vett.Val.216.3; ἵνα μὴ ἔχωμεν στομάχους μηδὲ φθόνον POxy.533.14 (ii/iii A.D.).

**στόμβος**, η, ον, = βαρύηχος, βαρύφθογγος, Hp.(Morb.2.33) ap.Gal. 19.141 (φθέγγεται σομφὸν codd.Hp.).

**στομήρης**, ες, v. στομώδης.

**στομίας**, ου, ὁ (sc. ἵππος), = στόμις (q.v.), hard-mouthed horse, Afric.Cest.p.21 V., Suid.

**στομίζομαι**, take with the mouth, Aq.Jb.39.30.

**στόμιον**, τό, Dim. of στόμα: generally, mouth, Posidipp.26.16 codd. Ath.; στομίοισι δυσαλθές Nic.Al.12; of a venomous beast, ib. 524, Th.233. II. mouth of a vessel, κέρασι χρυσᾶ σ. προσβεβλημένοις A.Fr.185; [sc. συρίγγων] Emp.100.3; mouth of a cave used as a grave, S.Ant.1217: hence cave, vault, as if it were the entrance of the lower world, A.Ch.807 (lyr., of Delphi), cf. Pl.R.615d, e: of any aperture or opening, Ti.Locr.101d, Arist.HA623$^{a}$4; cavity from which winds issue, Id.Mu.395$^{b}$27; σ. γαστρός Nic.Al.509; σ. τῆς ὑστέρας os uteri, Sor.1.9, al.; [τῆς κύστεως] Gal.6.65, cf. 18(2).265, Aret. SD2.1, al.; socket of a bolt, στομίοις κλεῖθρα δέχοισθε AP7.391 (Bass.); mouth of a canal, CPR42.13 (iii A.D.), etc. III. bridle-bit, bit, χαλινοὺς καὶ στόμια ἐμβαλεῖν Hdt.4.72, cf. 1.215; χάλυβος.. στόμιον παρέχουσα S.Tr.1261 (anap.); γνώμῃ στομίων ἅτερ εὐθύνων A.Pr.289 (anap.); δακὼν δὲ σ. ὡς νεοζυγὴς πῶλος ib.1009; στόμια δέχεσθαι S.El.1462; ἐνδακοῦσαι στόμια E.Hipp.1223; συνδάκνειν X.Eq.6.9; σ. Τροίας a bit or curb for Troy, of the Greek army, A.Ag.132 (lyr.). 2. = φορβειά, Eust.539.16. 3. female ornament for the neck, Poll.5.98.

**στόμις**, ὁ, hard-mouthed horse, A.Fr.442 (v.l. στομίας).

❀ **στομίς**, ίδος, ἡ, = στόμιον III. 2, Poll.10.56. II. f.l. for τομίς in Lxx Pr.24.37 (30.14).

**στομο-δόκος**, ον, = στωμύλος, Pherecr.234. -κοπέω, = maxillo (perh. strike on the jaw), Gloss. -ποιέω, (as if from στομοποιός) = στομόω III, Sch.Od.9.393.

**στομόω**, (στόμα) muzzle or gag, Hdt.4.69:—Pass., πώλους.. φιμοῖσιν.. ἐστομωμένας having their mouths muzzled, A.Fr.326. II. (στόμα II) furnish with a mouth or opening, λιμένα Poll.2.100. 2. Medic., = ἀναστομόω, open, either by the knife, or by plasters, Hp. Art.40, cf. Heliod.ap.Orib.44.8.21; dilate, of the womb, Hp.Mul.1. 25 (Pass.). 3. metaph., provide with a mouth, i.e. with eloquence, prob. in E.Cret.44 (Pass.). III. (στόμα III. 1) of iron, harden, make into steel, in Pass., Ph.Bel.102.20, Plu.2.943e; [ἔγχος] ἐστομωμένον Epigr.Gr.790.5 (Achaea); Chrysippus compared the creation of the soul to the hardening of πνεῦμα in the cold air, Stoic.2.134, 222. 2. metaph., steel, harden, train for anything, Ar.Nu.1108, 1110; σ. στομάχους Muson.Fr.18A p.97 H. (Pass.):—Pass., στομοῦσθαι καὶ κρατύνεσθαι [τὰ βρέφη] Plu.Lyc.16. IV. ἀκοντισταῖς τὴν οὐραγίαν καὶ τὰς πλευρὰς σ. edge, fringe, fence with javelin-men, Id.Ant.42; so perh., in Pass., [δράκαινα] ἐχίδναις ἐστομωμένη E.IT287.

**στομφ-άζω**, (στόμφος) mouth, rant, vaunt, Ar.V.721 (anap.), Com. Adesp.1011. 2. speak a broad dialect, Hermog.Id.1.6. 3. = αἱμωδιάω, Jo.Sic. in Rh.6.225 W. -αξ, ᾰκος, ὁ, ἡ, ranter, as Aeschylus is called by Pheidippides in Ar.Nu.1367. -ασμός, ὁ, creation of a mouth-filling word, as ἀμφασία, γνάμπτω for ἀφασία, γνάπτω, Eust. 1123.41, 1350.24. -αστικός, ή, όν, mouth filling, ὄγκος Id.12.4.

**στομφολογέω**, gloss on στομφάζω, Hsch.

**στόμφος**, ὁ, lofty phrases, Longin.3.1: also bombast, Id.32.7.

**στομφ-ός**, όν, high-sounding, bombastic, bragging, Sch.Hermog. in Rh.7(2).963 W. -όω, brag, Phld.Herc.1232 p.66 V. -ώδης, ες, = στομφός, Sch.Hermog. in Rh.7(2).963 W., Herm. in Phdr.p.63 A.

**στομώδης**, ες, = εὔστομος, εὔφημος, clear-voiced, S.Fr.1098 (v.l. στομήρη). 2. pleasant to the taste, of milk, γλυκὺ καὶ σ. Sor.1.91.

**στόμ-ωμα**, ατος, τό, (στομόω II) = στόμα II, mouth, Πόντου A.Pers.878 (lyr.). II. (στομόω III) hardened iron, steel, Χαλυβδικὸν σ. Cratin. 247, Daimach.4 J., cf. Lxx Si.34(31).26; τὰ -ώματα ποιοῦσιν οὕτως Arist.Mete.383$^{a}$33, cf. Plu.2.510f, 625b, 693a; ὀξεῖ διαπύρου σιδήρου σ. κατασβέσας Id.Lyc.9; hard edge or point welded into a blade or shaft, or steel for this purpose, PCair.Zen.782(a).6, 64, al. (iii B.C.), PPetr.2 pp.6,7 (iii B.C.), Arr.Tact.12.2, Ael.Tact.13.2, BGU1028.14 (ii A.D.), PSI10.1125.4 (iv A.D.); steel plates for repair of gates, ταῖς πύλαις.. στομώματα K. Kourouniotes Ἐλευσινιακά 1.190.25, cf. 29 (Eleusis). 2. λεπὶς στομώματος a scale which flies from hammered iron, Dsc.5.78, Gal.12.416; στόμωμα alone, Dsc.4.48 (dub. l.), Cels. 6.6.5, Plin.HN34.108. 3. metaph. of an army (cf. στόμα III. 1b), τῆς Ἰταλίας τὴν ἐν Ῥώμῃ δύναμιν ὥσπερ σ. προτεταγμένην Plu.2.326b; οἱονεὶ σ. τῆς δυνάμεως D.S.19.30: hence σ. εἰς μάχην ἢ ἀρχὴ Plu.Flam. 2, cf. 3: also σ. τοῦ οἴνου Id.2.692d; τῆς ἀνδρείας ib.988d. -ωμάτιον, τό, = denticulum aciarium, Gloss. -ωσις, εως, ἡ, hardening of iron, making it into steel, PCair.Zen.782(a).54 (iii B.C.), Supp. Epigr.4.447.42 (Didyma, ii B.C.); πελέκεως Plu.2.156b; δεῖσθαι στομώσεως Muson.Fr.18A p.97 H.; ὁ σίδηρος δέχεται τὴν στόμωσιν Plu.2.73c; metaph., στόμα πολλὴν ἔχον στόμωσιν a mouth that hath much hardness of tongue, S.OC795; of the formation of the soul, καθάπερ στομώσει τῇ περιψύξει τοῦ πνεύματος μεταβαλόντος Chrysipp. Stoic.2.222; strengthening, Dam.Pr.414. 2. surgical opening, τοῦ ἀποστήματος, τοῦ σπλάγχνου, Heliod.ap.Orib.44.10.4, 13.4. -ωτής, οῦ, ὁ, = Lat. indurator, Gloss. -ωτός, όν, hardened, cj. Herm. in A.Fr.252.

**στονᾰχ-έω**, 3 pl. -εῦντι Mosch.3.28: aor. ἐστονάχησα, the only tense used by Hom., (ἐπ-) Il.24.79, inf. στοναχῆσαι 18.124, cf.

Q.S.1.573:—Ep. form of στενάχω, *groan, sigh*, Il.l.c.; σ. πόντος Orph.*H*.38.17. II. trans., *sigh, groan over* or *for*, τινα S.*El*.133 (prob. f.l., στενάχειν cj. Elmsl., lyr.), cf. Mosch.3.28. **-ή**, ἡ, (στενάχω) *groaning, wailing*, Il.24.512,696, Od.16.144; σ. ἀγκαλέσωμαι E.*Ph*.1499 (lyr.): pl., *groans, sighs*, Il.2.39, al., Pi.*N*.10.75, S.*Aj*.203 (anap.), etc.; στοναχὰς μέλποντο τεκέων E.*Andr*.1037 (lyr.); so στοναχῇσι θαλάσσης *AP*7.142. **-ίζω**, v. στεναχίζω. **-ος**, ὁ, = στοναχή, Suid. (dub. l.).

**στονόεις**, εσσα, εν, (στόνος) *causing groans* or *sighs*, βέλεα Il.8.159; στονόεσσαν ἀϋτήν (war-cry) Od.11.383; στονόϝεσσαν ἀϝυτάν *IG*9(1).868 (Corc., vi B.C.); ὅμαδος Pi.*I*.8(7).25; ὀϊστοί Od.21.60; κήδεα 9.12; εὐνή 17.102; ἄεθλοι Hes.*Sc*.127; πλαγά A.*Pers*.1053 (lyr.); σίδαρος S.*Tr*.886 (lyr.); ἄλγη Tim.*Pers*.199; τύμβος *IG*3.1354. 2. *full of moaning*, ἀοιδή Il.24.721; γῆρυς S.*OT*187 (lyr.); ἁ σ. ὄρνις, of the nightingale, Id.*El*.147 (lyr.); στονόεντα πορθμόν the *moaning* sea, Id.*Ant*.1145 (lyr.): neut. as Adv., στονόεν λέλακε χώρα A.*Pr*.407 (lyr.), cf. Opp.*C*.3.213.

**στόνος**, ὁ, (στένω) *sighing* or *groaning*, Ἔρις ὀφέλλουσα στόνον ἀνδρῶν Il.4.445; αἷμα καὶ ἀργαλέος σ. ἀνδρῶν 19.214; τῶν δὲ στόνος ὤρνυτ' ἀεικής 10.483, Od.22.308; στόνον.. ἄκουσα κτεινομένων 23.40; διήκει δὲ καὶ πόλιν σ. A.*Th*.900 (lyr.); στόνον σαυτοῦ ποεῖ; S.*Ph*.752; in pl., A.*Th*.146 (lyr.); of the sea, στόνῳ βρέμουσιν.. ἀκταί S.*Ant*.592 (lyr.): rare in Prose, Th.7.71.

⊛ **στόνυξ**, ὕχος, ὁ, *sharp point* (prop. spear-*point* acc. to Sch.A.R.4.1679), as of a rock, πρὸς ὀξὺν στόνυχα πετραίου λίθου E.*Cyc*.401 (restd. for γ' ὄνυχα); πετραίῳ στόνυχι A.R.4.1679; νησιωτικὸς σ., Πάχυνος Lyc.1181; Οἰταῖος σ., of the boar's *tusk*, Id.486; λοίγιος σ., of the *barb* of the fish τρυγών, Id.795; στονύχεσσι λεόντων *fangs*, Opp.*C*.3.232; συλόνυχας στόνυχας nail-removing *prongs*, i.e. nail-scissors, *AP*6.307 (Phan.).

**στόποδες**, οἱ, = ἱστόποδες, *Gloss.*

**στορβάζειν**· κακολογεῖν, Hsch. (cf. στοβ-).

**στοργ-έω**, = στέργω, Hsch. ⊛ **-ή**, ἡ, *love, affection*, Emp.109.3, Antipho *Fr*.73; γνησίων πολιτῶν *BMus.Inscr*.4.481*.9 (Ephesus), cf. *CIG*2802 (Aphrodisias); ἐχόμενος τῆς εἰς σὲ ἀεὶ στοργῆς *POxy*.1766.3 (iii A.D.); esp. of parents and children, ἡδύ γε πατὴρ τέκνοισιν, εἰ στοργὴν ἔχοι Philem.200; γονέων πρὸς ἔκγονα σ. Plu.2.1100d, cf. Cic.*Att*.10.8.9; σ. φυσικὴ πρὸς τὰ τέκνα Demetr.Lac.*Herc*.1012.44: pl., Man.4.378, etc. 2. rarely *sexual love*, *AP*5.165 (Mel.), 190 (Id.), 7.476 (Id.). ⊛ **-ικός**, ή, όν, v.l. for στερκτικός in Gal.*Nat.Fac*.1.12.

**στορέννυμι**, v. στόρνυμι.

**στορεύς**, έως, ὁ, *one who spreads smooth*, metaph. *a calmer*, Hsch. II. *the undermost of two substances by which fire is produced* (cf. πυρεῖον), Sch.A.R.1.1184.

**στόρθη**· τὸ ὀξὺ τοῦ δόρατος, καὶ ἐπιδορατίς, Hsch. (cf. sq.).

**στόρθυγξ**, υγγος, ὁ or ἡ (both in Lyc.), *point, spike*, esp. *tyne* of a deer's horn, S.*Fr*.89.4; δικέραιος σ. *AP*6.111 (Antip.); *tusk* of a boar, Lyc.492; *point* or *tongue of land*, Id.761,865,1406; *tag* of hair, *Com.Adesp*.1152; = σαυρωτήρ, Sch.Il.13.443 (v.l. στρόφιγξ). (Cf. foreg.)

**στόρνη**, ἡ, = ζώνη, Call.*Hec*.1.1.15 (cf. Suid.), Lyc.1330.

⊛ **στόρνῡμι**, E.*Heracl*.702 (anap.); imper. στόρνυ Ar.*Pax*844; part. στορνύντες, στορνύντα, Hdt.7.54, S.*Tr*.902; compd. καστορνῦσα (= καταστ-) Od.17.32; also **στορνύω** (v.l. στρωννύω), A.D.*Synt*.295.4; **στρώννῡμι**, A.*Ag*.909, *Com.Adesp*.1211 (written with one ν in *SIG*589.44 (Magn. Mae., ii B.C.), but with two, ib.9); also **στρωννύω**, Aristid.1.216J., (ὑπο-) Ath.2.48d: impf. ἐστρώννυον *Ev.Matt*.21.8: later **στορεννύω, στορέννυμι**, Eust.748.31,32; pres. part. στορεννύς (v.l. στρωννύς) Sch.Ar.*Ach*.877: fut. στορῶ (παρα-) Ar.*Eq*.481, (ὑπο-) Eub.90.1; also στρώσω Lxx *Is*.14.11, (ὑπο-) E.*Hel*.59, Amphis 46; and στρωννύσω (ἐπι-) Ps.-Luc.*Philopatr*.24; Dor. inf. στορεσεῖν Theoc.6.33: aor. ἐστόρεσα, Ep. and Lyr. στόρεσα, Il.9.621,660, al., B.12.129, A.*Pr*.192 (anap.), Hdt.8.99; also ἔστρωσα Id.6.139, A.*Ag*.921: pf. ἔστρωκα Lxx *Pr*.7.16: plpf. ἐστρώκειν Hld.4.16, (ὑπ-) Babr.34.2:—**Med.**, στόρνῠμαι (ὑπο-) X.*Cyr*.8.8.16: impf. ἐστόρνυντο Theoc.22.33, Call.*Aet*.3.1.16: fut. στρώσομαι Lxx *Ez*.27.30: aor. ἐστορεσάμην, Ep. στ-, Theoc.13.33, A.R.1.375, (ὑπ-) Ar.*Ec*.1030; also ἐστρωσάμην Theoc.21.7:—Pass., στρώννῠμαι (v.l. στορέννυμαι) Sch.Theoc.7.57d; ὑποστορέννυσθαι is f.l. in Thphr.*Char*.22.5: aor. ἐστορέσθην Plu.2.787e, D.C.67.14, (κατ-) Hp.*VM*19; ἐστορήθην Hsch.; ἐστρώθην (κατ-) D.S.14.114: pf. ἐστόρεσμαι (ὑπ-) Philostr.*VA*6.10; ἔστρωμαι *h.Ven*.158, E.*Med*.380, Th.2.34, etc.: plpf. ἐστόρεστο D.C.74.13, Him.*Ecl*.13.2; also ἔστρωτο Il.10.155, Hdt.7.193:—*spread* the clothes over a bed, λέχος στορέσαι *spread* or *make up* a bed, Il.9.621,660; so δέμνια, ῥῆγος σ., Od.4.301, 13.73; δέμνια S.*Tr*.902; κλίνην στρώσαντες Hdt.6.139; σ. τισὶ λέχος Ar.*Pax*844; λέκτρα σοι ἀντὶ γάμων ἐπιτύμβια *AP*7.604 (Paul. Sil.) (also in Med., ἐστόρνυντο τὰ κλισμία Call. l.c.): abs., *make a bed*, χαμάδις στορέσας Od.19.599; στρῶσον ἡμῖν ἔνδον Macho ap.Ath.13.581b, cf. *Act.Ap*.9.34. b. generally, *spread, strew*, ἀνθρακιὴν σ. Il.9.213; φιτροὺς σ. καθύπερθεν ἐλαίης A.R.1.405; [στιβάδας] εἰς ὁδόν *Ev.Marc*.11.8: also in Med., freq. in Theoc., as 13.33, al. 2. *spread smooth, level*, πόντον σ. Od.3.158, cf. *h.Hom*.33.15, Theoc.7.57, etc.; τὸ κῦμα ἔστρωτο Hdt.7.193; στόρεσεν πόντον οὐρία B.12.129; αἰθὴρ νήνεμος ἐστόρεσεν δίνας A.R.1.1155; χρηστὴν ἡμῖν ἡ θάλαττα τὴν γαλήνην ἐστ. Alciphr.1.1; metaph., *calm, soothe*, ἀτέραμνον στορέσας ὀργήν A.*Pr*.192 (anap.); [φθόνου] στορεσθέντος Plu.2.787e. b. *level, lay low*, πλάτανον δαπέδοις *AP*9.247 (Phil.): metaph., Μήδων δύναμιν Simon.90; λῆμα μὲν οὔπω στόρνυσι χρόνος τὸ σόν E.*Heracl*.702 (anap.); ἵνα Πελοποννησίων στορέσωμεν τὸ φρόνημα Th.6.18. 3. ὁδὸν σ. *pave* a road, *IGRom*.4.1431.5, al. (Smyrna), dub. in *IG*12(5).229.7 (Paros):—Pass., ἐστρωμένη ὁδός Hdt.2.138; ἔδαφος λίθων πλαξὶ λείαις ἐστρ. Luc.*Am*.12, cf. D.C.67.14. II. *strew* or *spread with* a thing, μυρσίνῃσι τὴν ὁδόν Hdt.7.54, cf. 8.99; πέδον πετάσμασιν A.*Ag*.909, cf. 921; *saddle a horse, provide a mount*, τινι *POxy*.138.22 (vii A.D.):—Pass., Pl.*R*.372b; of a room, *to be furnished with* στρώματα, *Ev.Marc*.14.15; πλοῖον.. ἐστρωμένον καὶ σεσανιδωμένον dub. sens. in *PLond*.3.1164(*h*)7 (iii A.D.). (Cf. Skt. *stṛṇómi, stṛṇā́mi* 'strew', Lat. *sterno*, Engl. *strew*.)

**στορνυτέος**, α, ον, = καταστρωτέος, Hsch.

**στορπάν** (στορτίαν cod.)· τὴν ἀστραπήν, Hsch.: hence **Στορπᾶος**, epith. of Zeus at Tegea, *IG*5(2).64 (v B.C.): cf. στροπά.

**στορύνη** [ῡ], ἡ, = κατιάδιον, Aret.*CD*1.2.

**στορχάζω**, *pen, shut up* cattle, Hsch. **στουμνά**· αὐστηρά, Id. **στοῦπος**· ἡ τοῖς τετελευτηκόσιν ἐπὶ τῶν φορείων σκηνή, Id.

⊛ **στοχ-άζομαι**, Pl.*Grg*.465a, etc.: impf. ἐστοχαζόμην Id.*Euthd*.277b: fut. -άσομαι Isoc.*Ep*.6.10, M.Ant.10.6: aor. ἐστοχασάμην Pl.*Grg*.464c, Hp.*VM*9: pf. ἐστόχασμαι Pl.*Lg*.635a, Arist.*HA*$571^a$27:—Gal. uses this pf., as also aor. ἐστοχάσθην, in pass. sense, pf. in 10.885, 11.35, aor. in 13.713, cf. Ruf.ap.Orib.7.26.40; ἐστοχάσθην in act. sense, Ps.-Callisth.1.3 (cod. L): (στόχος):—*aim* or *shoot at*, c. gen., [σκοποῦ] Pl.*R*.519c, Isoc.l.c.; δίκην τοξότου σ. τινός Pl.*Lg*.706a; ἄλλου στοχαζόμενος ἔτυχε τούτου *aiming at* another man hit the deceased, Antipho 2.1.4; σ. ἀνθρώπων X.*Cyr*.1.6.29. 2. metaph., *aim at, endeavour after*, μέτρου Hp.*VM*9; τοῦ ἡδέος Pl.*Grg*.465a; τοῦ μεγίστου ἀγαθοῦ Id.*R*.462a; τῆς σωτηρίας Id.*Lg*.962a; ἡ φύσις ἐστόχασται ἑκάστου οὐδέν τι ἔλασσον τῆς ἀπολήξεως ἢ τῆς ἀρχῆς M.Ant.8.20; τοῦ γέλωτα ποιῆσαι Arist.*EN*$1128^a$6; τοῦ ὡς ἐπὶ τὸ πολὺ γινομένου Id.*HA* l.c.; σ. τῶν μάλιστα φίλων κριτῶν *aim at having* them as judges, X.*Cyr*.8.2.27; so τῆς τοῦ δήμου βουλήσεως Plb.6.16.5; τῶν πολιτῶν Lxx 2*Ma*.14.8; also πρός τι Pl.*Lg*.693c, cf. 962d; οὕτω σ. ὅπως.. Hp.*Art*.4, cf. Diocl.*Fr*.138, *SIG*609.7 (Delph., ii B.C.), *PTeb*.27.70 (ii B.C.). II. *endeavour to make out, guess at* a thing, c. gen., τῆς τότε διανοίας τοῦ τιθέντος αὐτὰ ἐστοχάσθαι Pl.*Lg*.635a; τῆς τῶν θεῶν σ. διανοίας Isoc.1.50; σ. τοῦ συμβουλευομένου *guessing at the mind of* their consultant, Pl.*La*.178b: abs., *make guesses, feel one's way*, εὖ γε στοχάζει S.*Ant*.241 codd.; στοχαζομένη τὰ συμφέροντα ἐκπληροῦν *by guessing*, X.*Mem*.2.2.5; οὐ γνοῦσα, ἀλλὰ στοχασαμένη Pl.*Grg*.464c, cf. *Phlb*.56a; *calculate*, Cleom.2.1; *infer*, ἔκ τινος *SIG*601.13 (Teos, ii B.C.), Plb.1.14.2, al.; διά τινος Id.3.68.10; ἀπό τινος Ocell.1.1: c. acc. et inf., στοχαζόμεθα τὸν Δημήτριον μὴ κατειληφέναι Ζηνόδωρον ἐν πόλει *PCair.Zen*.367.13 (iii B.C.), cf. *POxy*.931.9 (ii A.D.): c. acc., *survey, explore*, ὁδόν Lxx *De*.19.3; αἰῶνα ib.*Wi*.13.9; *guess at*, τοὺς πλησίον ib.*Si*.9.14; τοιοῦτον τὸν κόσμιον στοχάζου *expect* the κόσμιος *to be* like that, Polem.*Phgn*.2.60. 2. *have regard to*, c. gen., Hero *Bel*.102.8. III. = φείδομαι, condemned by Luc.*Sol*.7. **-ανδόν**, Adv. *by conjecture*, Theognost.*Can*.162 (but prob. ὡς τὸ [στο]χανδόν). **-άς**, άδος, ἡ, *an erection of stone or wood for fixing net poles* (στοῖχοι II) *on uneven ground*, Poll.5.36. 2. Adj., *in a row*, Λίβυες οἰωνοὶ στοχάδες (v.l. στολάδες) E.*Hel*.1480 (lyr.). **-ᾰσις**, εως, ἡ, = στοχασμός, Pl.*Phlb*.62c. **-ασμα**, ατος, τό, *missile*, ἀγκυλωτοῖς Θεσσαλῶν -άσμασιν E.*Ba*.1205. ⊛ **-ασμός**, ὁ, *guessing*, μελέτης σ. the *power of guessing* which comes from practice, Pl.*Phlb*.56a; στοχασμῷ λαμβάνων, σ. πινομένη, '*quantum sufficit*', Dsc.1.48, *Eup*.2.21; τὸν σ. ἀεὶ καὶ μᾶλλον ἐξακριβοῦν Gal.6.129; as a technical term in Rhet., Phld.*Rh*.1.167S., al.; esp. *use of circumstantial evidence*, Hermog.*Stat*.2,3. 2. *regard for*, τινος Plu.2.981b; τοῦ πρέποντος ib.616b; *attention to*, τῶν εἰρημένων ἀστέρων Ph.1.28. II. *fixing* of a hunting-net, Poll.5.36. **-αστέον**, *one must aim at*, τοῦ μέσου Arist.*Pol*.$1266^b$28; *one must make a point of*, ὡς μή.. Gal.16.143. II. *one must form a conjecture*, ἔκ τινος Plb.9.15.13. ⊛ **-αστής**, οῦ, ὁ, *diviner*, Lxx *Is*.3.2; τῶν μελλόντων J.*BJ*4.4.6. 2. *one who aims at*, τῶν πιθανῶν καὶ εἰκότων, ἀλλ' οὐχὶ τῆς ἀκραιφνοῦς ἀληθείας Ph.1.10. ⊛ **-αστικός**, ή, όν, *skilful in aiming at, able to hit*, c. gen., τοῦ ἀρίστου Arist.*EN*$1141^b$13; ἀρετὴ τοῦ μέσου σ. ib.$1106^b$15. b. τὸ σ. τῶν φίλων *consideration for the wishes of*.., M.Ant.1.9. 2. *proceeding by guesswork*, ἡ -κή (sc. τέχνη) Pl.*Phlb*.55e; σ. τέχναι *Stoic*.3.6, Gal.14.685; σ. ἐπιστῆμαι, opp. πάγιοι, Phld.*Rh*.1.26,59S.; σ. διάγνωσις Gal.6.365; ζητήματα Syrian. *in Hermog*.2.34R.; *sagacious*, Pl.*Grg*.463a. Adv., πρὸς τὰ ἔνδοξα -κῶς ἔχειν Arist.*Rh*.$1355^a$17; -κῶς τὸ μέτρον λαμβάνεται Gal.6.360; -κῶς ἐξετάσομεν Hermog.*Stat*.4.

**στόχος**, ὁ, *pillar* of brick, *IG*$2^2$.463.59, al. 2. = στοχάς, Poll.5.36. 3. *butt, target*, X.*Ages*.1.25 (Wyttenbach for στοίχων). 4. *aim, aiming*, E.*Ba*.1100 (Reiske for τ' ὄχον). 5. *guess, conjecture*, A.*Supp*.243.

**στρᾰβᾰλοκόμας**, α, ὁ, *curly-headed*, S.(*Fr*.1099) ap.Poll.2.23 (who blames the word), Hsch.

**στραβαλός**· ὁ στρογγυλίας καὶ τετράγωνος ἄνθρωπος (Achaean), Hsch.

**στραβέλαφος**, dub. sens., as pr. n., in *BMus.Inscr*.574 (Ephesus).

**στραβεύς**· κωπεύς, Hsch.

**στράβηλος** [ᾰ], ὁ and ἡ, *snail* or *shell-fish*, ἁλία σ. S.*Fr*.324, cf. Arist.*Fr*.304, Speus.ap.Ath.3.86c. II. *wild olive*, Pherecr.13 (lyr.).

**στρᾰβ-ίζω**, (στραβός) *squint*, Hsch. s.v. ἰλλώπτω, *EM*713.13. **-ισμός**, ὁ, *squinting*, Gal.19.436: pl., Id.7.150, Alex.Aphr.*Pr*.2.11.

**στρᾰβοπόδης**, ου, ὁ, *with twisted feet*, Hdn.*Epim*.5,212.

**στρᾰβ-ός**, ή, όν, *squinting*, Sor.1.31, Gal.19.141, Alex.Aphr.*Pr.* 1.124, *Ostr.*93 (ii A.D.), *Stud.Pal.*10.207 (vi A.D.); = *luscus*, *Gloss.*; rejected by Poll.2.51, Phryn.*PS* p.108 B. **-ότης**, ητος, ἡ, *distortion*, ὀφθαλμῶν Eust.915.31: pl., Orib.*Syn.*8.51.1. **-ων**, ωνος, ὁ, = στραβός, *Com.Adesp.*334.

**στραγγᾰλ-άω**, = στραγγαλίζω, Men.1069:—Pass., Lxx *To.*2.3, D.S.1.68 codd. **-η**, ἡ, *halter*, S.E.*P.*3.15; ἐπὶ τὴν σ. πορεύεσθαι *death by strangling*, Plu.*Agis* 20; -η διαφθείρειν J.*AJ*9.4.6: pl., ib. 6.8.2. **2.** *ligature*, Dem.Ophth.ap.Aët.7.50. **-ιά**, ἡ, *induration in the limbs*, esp. caused by humours, *Hippiatr.*51. **II.** = στραγγαλίς, Ptol.*Tetr.*200, Hsch., *Gloss.*: metaph., Lxx *Is.*58. 6. **-ιάω**, *tie knots, start difficulties*, Plu.2.618f. **-ίζω**, *strangle*, Str.6.1.8 (as v. l.), Plu.2.530d; τὸν τράχηλον Alciphr.3.49. **-ίς**, ίδος, ἡ, *intricate knot*, Stratt.48; ὑμεῖς.. ἀεὶ στραγγαλίδας ἐσφίγγετε tied *knots* fast (cf. στραγγαλιάω), Pherecr.21: hence Aristocreon called Chrysippus τῶν Ἀκαδημιακῶν στραγγαλίδων κοπίδα, a knife to cut Academic *knots*, ap.Plu.2.1033e. **2.** *knot* or *induration* in the breast or other parts, Arist.*HA*587ᵇ22; cf. στραγγαλιά. **3.** some kind of ornament, Lxx *Jd.*8.26; σ. ἀργυρᾶ, σ. χρυσᾶ κεκολλημένη, *POxy.*1449.18,23 (iii A.D.). **-ισμός**, ὁ, = *strangulatus*, *Gloss.* **-ιώδης**, ες, metaph., *knotted, tortuous*, οὐδὲν σκολιὸν οὐδὲ σ. Lxx *Pr.*8.8, cf. *Com.Adesp.*904. **-όομαι**, Pass., *to be twisted* or *knotted up*, Ph.*Bel.*57.42; ἡ οὐρὰ σ. *is curled tight*, Alex.Aphr.*Pr.*1.76.

**στραγγεία**, ἡ, *hesitation, loitering*, rejected by Poll.9.137; restd. for στρατεία in M.Ant.4.51, and for στρατηγία in Hsch. s. v. τευτασμός.

**στραγγεῖον**, τό, *medicine-dropper*, Alex.Aphr.*Pr.*2.59.

**στράγγ-ευμα**, ατος, τό, *act of hesitation* or *delay*, dub.cj. in Plu.*Alex.* 68 for στράτευμα codd. (τραῦμα Reiske). **-εύομαι**, Med., *loiter, delay*, ἐγὼ δῆτ' ἐνθαδὶ στραγγεύομαι; Ar.*Ach.*126 (cj. Kuster; στραγεύγομαι cod. R, στρατεύομαι cett.); τί ταῦτ' ἔχων σ.; why do I keep *loitering* thus? Id.*Nu.*131 (στραγεύομαι codd. RV, στρατεύομαι codd. opt. Suid. s. v. ἰτητέον, στραγγεύομαι codd. deteriores Ar. et Suid. l. c.); σ. περὶ τὰς συμβολάς Macho ap. Ath.13.580e; = τριψημερεῖν, Hsch.; restd. for στρατεύομαι in Pl.*R.*472a, Zen.4.19, Ptol.Asc.p.401 H., Hsch. s. v. μαρηγηλλᾶ, Id. s. v. στρεύγει, Phot., Suid. s. v. ἣ δεῖ χελώνης, *EM*755.39; written **στραγεύομαι**, Ar. (v.l., v. supr.), *PTeb.* 713.5 (ii B.C.), Sm.*Pr.*24.10 (v.l.), Hsch., Sch.Ar.*Nu.* l. c. (cod. V), Suid. (codd. AV), Id. s. v. τευτάζειν, Eust.1441.59; στρατεύομαι (s. v. l.) has this sense in Lxx *Jd.*19.8, *BGU*1127.28 (i B.C.), 1131.20 (i B.C.); στρατεύεσθαι (s. v. l.), = *aginare*, *Gloss.* **2.** στραγγευομένη κάθαρσις *coming slowly*, Orib.*Fr.*138. **II.** Act. in med. sense, Sch.Ar.*Lys.*17 (restd. for ἐστράγευσεν, ἐστράτευσεν), Suid. s. v. κυπτάζειν, *EM*330.56 (restd. for στρατεύειν); = *agino*, *Gloss.* (στρατ-).

**στραγγίας** πυρός, ὁ, a kind of *wheat*, Thphr.*CP*3.21.2.

**στραγγίζω**, (στράγξ) *squeeze out*, ὕδωρ Dsc.1.30; στραγγιεῖ τὸ αἷμα Lxx *Le.*1.15; *press, squeeze the water out of* crushed olives which have been immersed, *Gp.*9.32.1:—Pass., Dsc.2.76; ἐρεβίνθους στραγγιζομένους *Hippiatr.*38; ἐστραγγισμένου τοῦ ὕδατος ibid. **II.** Med., = στρεύγομαι, Sch.Il.15.511, *EM*729.50: Act. in same sense, Sch.Od.12.351.

**στραγγίς**, ίδος, ἡ, = στράγξ, dub. in Phot.

**στραγγός**, ή, όν, *twisted, crooked*, Hsch., Phot., Suid. **II.** *complicated, irregular*, πυρετοί Ruf.ap.Orib.8.24.30: Comp., αἱ μονοπάθειαι τῶν ὀφθαλμῶν -ότεραί εἰσιν *more violent* or *serious*, Cass.*Pr.* 14. **2.** *shameless*, Phot., Suid. **III.** (στράγξ) *flowing drop by drop*, κάθαρσις Sor.1.2, al.: Comp., Antyll.ap.Orib.8.6.6, Sor.1.27. Adv. -γῶς, καθαίρεσθαι ib.31.—In Hsch., Phot., Suid. written στραγός; in cod. Sor. στραγκός: Comp. στραγώτερος Antyll.ap.Orib. l. c., Phot. (-ότερος Suid.).

**στραγγουρ-έω**, (στράγξ, οὖρον) *suffer from strangury*, Poet.*de herb.* 38. **-ία**, Ion. -ίη, ἡ, *strangury*, Hp.*Aph.*3.16 (pl.), al., Ar.*V.*810, Pl.*Ep.*358e, Thphr.*HP*7.6.3, Aret.*CA*2.9. **-ιάω**, = στραγγουρέω, Ar.*Th.*616, Pl.*Lg.*916a, Dsc.4.4. **-ικός**, ή, όν, *liable to, suffering from strangury*, Hp.*Morb.*4.55: τὰ σ.. = στραγγουρία, Id.*Coac.*444; πάθη Epicur.*Fr.*138. **-ιώδης**, ες, *of the nature of strangury*, Hp. *Epid.*1.5,10; *suffering from it*, ib.2.2.17.

**στραγεύομαι**, v. στραγγεύομαι.

**στράγξ**, ἡ, gen. στραγγός, *trickle, drop* (ὁ διὰ λεπτοτάτης ὀπῆς σχολῇ κατιὼν σταλαγμός, Sch.Ar.*Nu.*131), ἄσιτος ἑπτὰ μῆνας, ὕδατος στράγγ' ἔχων Men.238; μικρὰς στράγγας ἀπ' ὠκεανοῦ *AP*4.1.38 (Mel.); κατὰ στράγγα *drop by drop*, Thphr.*HP*9.18.9, D.H.*Dem.*28, Gal.16.750, *UP*5.16. (στράγξ (στράιγξ) is a monosyll. of seven letters acc. to Trypho ap.Sch.D.T. p.346 H., but the word is στράγξ with ᾰ acc. to *An.Ox.*3.243.)

**στραγός**, v. στραγγός. **στράνθανα**· ὀξέα, Hsch.

**στράπή**, ἡ, = ἀστραπή, *EM*514.32.

**στράπτω**, rarer and later for ἀστράπτω, *lighten, flash*, S.*OC*1515, A.R.1.544; metaph., νοεραῖς σ. τομαῖς Dam.*Pr.*122. **2.** c. acc. cogn., αἴγλην Orph.*H.*19.2; μαρμαρυγήν Opp.*C.*3.349.

**στρατᾱγέω, στρατᾱγός**, v. στρατηγέω, στρατηγός.

**στρᾰτ-αρχέω**, *command an army*, τινι for one, v. l. for τετραρχέω in J.*BJ*4.1.10; metaph., θεοῦ -οῦντος ἀοράτως Ph.2.383. **-άρχης**, ου, ὁ, *general of an army*, = στρατηγός, A.*Fr.*182 (but f. l.), Hdt.3. 157, 8.44, Ph.2.533; gen. στρατά[ρχου] restd. in *OGI*519.16 (Asia Minor, iii A.D.). **-αρχία**, ἡ, *office* or *dignity of general*, Ph.2.90, Vett.Val.194.19. ✱**-αρχικός**, ή, όν, *fit for command*, Id.45. 2. **-αρχος**, ὁ, = στρατάρχης, Pi.*P.*6.31, *I.*5(4).40.

✱ **στρᾰτεία**, Ion. -ηΐη, ἡ, (στρατεύω) *expedition, campaign*, στρατηΐην ποιεῖσθαι ἐς..., ἐπί.., Hdt.1.71,171, etc.; πολλὰς σ. ἐποιήσαντο Th.2.11; σ. ἐστράτευσ' ὀλεθρίαν E.*Supp.*116; σ. ἡμῖν εἰς Ποτείδαιαν ἐγένετο Pl.*Smp.*219e, cf. *IG*12(2).645.15 (Nesus), etc.; ἀπὸ στρατείας coming from *war*, after *service done*, A.*Ag.*603, *Eu.*631; κατὰ τὴν Σιτάλκου σ. about the time of his *expedition*, Th.2.101; εἰς δὲ σ. πάντας Ἀργείους ἄγων E.*Supp.*229; ἐπὶ στρατείας εἶναι to be on *foreign service*, Pl.*Smp.*220c (codd., στρατιᾶς Cobet, Burnet); so ἐν στρατείᾳ ὄντας X.*Cyr.*5.2.19; ἐν τῇ σ. *PEnteux.*48.3 (iii B.C.); παραγγέλλειν τινὶ σ. κατὰ γῆν X.*HG*7.1.13; ἐκδήμους σ. οὐκ ἐξῆσαν Th.1.15; στρατείαν ξυνεξελθεῖν ib.3; σ. δ' οὐ φέρει περιουσίαν Men.382, cf. *OGI*5.44 (Scepsis, iv B.C.); τῆς σ. γιγνομένης ἐκ καταλόγου Arist.*Ath.*26.1; freq. in pl., *military service, warfare*, Pl.*R.* 404a; πρὸς ταῖς αὑτοῦ σ. in addition to the *campaigns* which he is bound to serve, Id.*Lg.*878d; ἐν ταῖς σ. μισθοφορεῖν Arist.*Ath.*27.2; ἀπὸ σ. ἱππικῶν *IGRom.*3.58 (Bithynia); στρατείας στρατεύεσθαι *IG*2². 505.54; ἀφειμένος στρατείας, = Lat. *exauctoratus*, Plu.2.274a. **2.** σ. ἐν τοῖς ἐπωνύμοις *levy of those liable to serve* in the year of such and such archons, Harp. s. v., cf. Arist.*Ath.*53.7. **3.** σ. ἡ ἐν τοῖς μέρεσιν *expedition* for special service, to train the young soldiers next after serving as περίπολοι, Aeschin.2.168, cf. Suid. s. v. τερθρεία. **4.** *military discipline*, ἡ ἀκριβὴς σ. D.C.78.36. **5.** *military appointment*, ἐπώλησε στρατείας Id.72.12.—στρατιά is a constant v. l., and is sts. undoubtedly used = στρατεία (*campaign*), v. στρατιά II and cf. Sch.Ar.*Th.*835 (= Eup.369); but στρατεία = *army, expeditionary force* is very rare, E.*IA*495 (restd. in *Rh.*263 (lyr.)): in Inscrr. στρατεία never = *army*, but both -εία (*IG*2².1132.14, *SIG*398.2 (Cos, iii B.C.), al.) and -ιά (q. v.) = *campaign*.

✱ **στράτειος** [ᾰ], ὁ, as a name of Zeus, *warrior*, *Michel* 725.6 (Mylasa, ii B.C.); so **στρατεία**, ἡ, of Aphrodite, *CIG*2693*f* (ibid., i B.C.).

**στράτ-ευμα** [ᾰ], ατος, τό, *expedition, campaign*, ἐφ' Ἑλλάδα A.*Pers.* 758 (troch.); τὸ σ. τὸ ἐπὶ Σάμον Hdt.3.49; διέφυγον τὸ σ. escaped the threatened *invasion*, Id.8.112, cf. Ar.*Lys.*1133. **II.** *armament, army, host*, Hdt.7.48; ὑγιαίνω.. μετὰ τοῦ σ. *OGI*453.10 (Epist. Antonii, i B.C.), cf. Lxx 1*Ma.*9.34, al.; ὑπὲρ τιμῆς ἐλαίου τῶν ἐνταῦθα σ. *Ostr.*1595 (iii A.D.), cf. *Ev.Luc.*23.11, *BGU*1564.5 (ii A.D.); πεζὸν σ. A.*Pers.*469; διαπόντιον σ., i.e. composed of Asiatic mercenaries, Hermipp.58; ἱππικόν X.*Cyr.*3.3.26; πολιτικόν Id.*HG*5.4.41; ἱερὰ σ. *SIG*880.7 (Pizus, iii A.D.): also, a *naval armament*, Th.6.74; τὸ ναυτικὸν σ. Ἀχαιῶν S.*Ph.*59. **2.** = στρατός 2, *the people*, σ. Παλλάδος E.*Supp.*601 (lyr.); φῦλα τρία τριῶν στρατευμάτων dub. l. in 653. **-ευσείω**, Desiderat. *to be anxious for war*, D.C.53.25, *Fr.*40.33. **-εύσιμος**, ον, *fit for military service, serviceable*, ἡλικία X.*HG*6.5.12, J.*AJ*2.15.1; σ. ἔτη X.*Cyr.*1.2.4; οἱ σ. Plb.6.19. 6: Subst. -εύσιμον, τό, *payment in lieu of military service*, *PMonac.* 1.54 (vi A.D.). **-ευσις**, εως, ἡ, *expedition*, like στρατεία, Hdt. 1.189, D.H.*Th.*38, Sm.*Ps.*59(60).12. **-ευτικός**, ή, όν, *inclined to war, warlike*, Alex.234 (Sup.). ✱ **-εύω**, (στρατός) *advance with an army* or *fleet, wage war*, of rulers, officers, or men, Κροῖσος ἐνένωτο -εύειν ἐπὶ τοὺς Πέρσας Hdt.1.77; Θηβαῖοι.. ἐστράτευον ἐπὶ τοὺς Πλαταιέας Id.6.108, cf. 7 (v.l.), Th.3.7, *OGI*327.2 (Pergam., ii B.C.), etc.; οἱ Ἀθηναῖοι -εύσαντες ἐς Πλάταιαν Th.2.6; Καρχηδόνιοι -εύσαντες ἐπὶ Σικελίαν X.*HG*1.1.37; εἰς Σικελίαν -εύσαντες ib.1.5.21; ἐστράτευσαν πρὸς Ἄβυδον ib.1.2.16; σ. ὅποι Κῦρος ἐπαγγέλλοι Id.*Cyr.*7.4.9: c. acc. cogn., οἶσθ' ἣν στρατείαν ἐστράτευσ' ὀλεθρίαν (sc. ἐγὼ Ἄδραστος) E.*Supp.*116; Λακεδαιμόνιοι.. τὸν ἱερὸν καλούμενον πόλεμον ἐστράτευσαν Th.1.112; metaph., ἑνὸς δ' ἐπ' ἀνδρὸς δώματα στρατεύομεν (Iris et Lyssa loq.) E.*HF*825 (nisi leg. σῶμα συστρατεύομεν):—so in Med., στρατεύομαι Hdt.7.61, etc.: fut. -εύσομαι ib.11, D.8.23: aor. ἐστρατευσάμην Hdt.1.204, S.*Aj.* 1111, Isoc.5.144, etc.; also ἐστρατεύθην Pi.*P.*1.51, Apollod.1.9.13: pf. ἐστράτευμαι Is.4.29, etc.; Boeot. 3 pl. pf. Med. ἐστροτεύαθη *IG*7. 3174.27 (Orchom. Boeot.), al.: εἰ μὴ στρατεύοισθ' ἐς τὸν Ἑλλήνων τόπον A.*Pers.*790; -εύσονται ἐπὶ τὴν ἡμετέρην [Ἀθηναῖοι] Hdt.7.11; οἱ δὲ -ευόμενοι οἵδε ἦσαν, Πέρσαι μέν.. ib.61, cf. 64,66, al.; ἐστρατευμένοι γάρ εἰσι *they have been soldiers, have seen war-service*, Ar.*Ra.* 1113, cf. *IG*1².1.3, 18.9, Lys.9.4; ψιλὸς αὖ στρατεύσομαι Ar.*Th.* 232, cf. Eup.117.8; ὁπλίτης σ. X.*Mem.*3.4.1; ἐκ καταλόγου σ. ibid.; ὅταν ἡλικίαν ἐκπέμπωσι προγράφουσιν ἀπὸ τίνος ἄρχοντος καὶ ἐπωνύμου μέχρι τίνων δεῖ στρατεύεσθαι Arist.*Ath.*53.7; σφι ἐδόκεε -εύεσθαι ἐπὶ τὰς Θήβας Hdt.9.86; ἐπὶ τοῦ κρυστάλλου -εύονται.. πέρην ἐς τοὺς Σίνδους Id.4.28; σ. μετά τινων E.*IA*967; ὑπὲρ τῆς πόλεως Pl.*R.*429b; τῆς σῆς οὕνεκ'.. γυναικός S.*Aj.*1111; ὑπό τινι Plu.*Cam.*2; ἐπ' Αἴγυπτον Hdt.3.139; ἐς τὴν Ἀσίην Id.1.4, cf. And.3.30, etc.; κατὰ Ἐφεσίων *OGI*437.70 (Pergam., i B.C.); πρὸς τὴν τῶν Ὀλυνθίων πόλιν X. *HG*5.3.3; μισθοῦ σ. Id.*Cyr.*3.2.7; πανδημεὶ ἔξω σ. Pl.*Lg.*814a; opp. ἐπιδημεῖν, Lys.20.21; opp. δημηγορεῖν, And.4.22; στρατευσάμενος, = *a militiis*, *IG*14.716 (Naples): c. acc. cogn., τὰς στρατείας -ευόμενος Is.10.25. **2.** Med., *serve in the army*, τυὶ πρᾶτον ἐστροτεύαθη the following *have joined the army* for the first time, *IG*7 l. c.; μηδεὶς ἐαθῇ -εύσασθαι *to join the army*, *UPZ*110.162 (ii B.C.), cf. *Sammelb.* 7354.6 (ii A.D.), *BGU*1680.9 (iii A.D.); οἱ -ευόμενοι Ἕλληνες the Greeks *who are in the army*, *PTeb.*5.168 (ii B.C.).—In Hdt. codd. vary between Act. and Med., as in 6.7,108; in Att. and later Gr. (*PGrenf.*1.21.3 (ii B.C.), *PTeb.*5.168 (ii B.C.), etc.) the Med. is much the more freq. **II.** later, in Act., *take* or *receive into the army, enroll, enlist*, D.S.25.12, App.*BC*1.42, 2.141, 5.137, Hdn.2.14.6:—Pass., τῶν νεολέκτων τῶν -ευθέντων ὑφ' ἡμῶν *POxy.*1103.5 (iv A.D.); ὁ νῦν -ευθεὶς τίρων *PLond.*2.237.31 (iv A.D.). **III.** v. στραγγεύομαι.

⟨σ⟩τ⟨ρ⟩ατή· πόρνη, Hsch.; cf. στατή.

**στρᾰτηγ-εῖον**, v. στρατήγιον. ✱ **-έτης**, ου, ὁ, = στρατηγός, *SIG*

588.60 (Milet., ii B.C.), Ps.-Luc.*Philopatr.*9; Cret. σταρταγέτας (q.v.): fem. -έτις, ιδος, Tz.*H.*12.967. ❀ -έω, Dor. **στρᾰτᾱγέω** *SIG* 421.16 (Thermum, iii B.C.), etc.; Aeol. **στροτᾱγέω** *IGRom.*4.1243 (Thyatira), but **στρατ-** in the duplicate, *IG*12(2).243.3 (Mytil.):—*to be general*, Hdt.5.28, E.*Heracl.*391; esp. at Athens (v. στρατηγός II), Ar.*Eq* 288, *Nu.*586, Th.1.57, etc.; προγόνων εἶναι τῶν ἐστρατηγηκότων Aeschin.1.27, cf. D.34.50; καὶ πολιτεύεσθαι καὶ σ. Isoc.5.140; σ. ἀπὸ μεγάλων (sc. τιμημάτων) they *are eligible as general* beginning from a high property-qualification, Arist.*Pol.*1282ᵃ31: in Egypt, *hold the office of* στρατηγός, *BGU*1297.4 (iii B.C.), *PEnteux.*8.10 (iii B.C.), etc.: at Rome, *to be consul*, Plb.2.21.7, 3.114.6; more freq., *to be praetor*, Plu.*Ant.*6; στρατηγῶν καὶ ὑπατεύων Id.*Cat.Ma.*4, cf. Arr.*Epict.*4.1.149. b. c. gen., *to be general of* an army, τῶν Λυδῶν, Ἐρετριέων, etc., Hdt.1.34, 5.102, etc.; freq. in Att., Th.1.29, D.20.82, etc.; also σ. τῆς Σάμου Plu.*Per.*26; πολέμου D.H.3.22 (v.l. -ον); τοῦ σὺ στρατηγεῖς τοῦδε; S.*Aj.*1100. c. c. dat., ἐστράτηγησε Λακεδαιμονίοισι ἐς Θεσσαλίην Hdt.6.72, cf. A.*Eu.*25, E.*Tr.*926, *Andr.*324, Lys.13.62; but σ. Ξέρξῃ *to be general* of his army, Paus.9.1.3. d. folld. by a Prep., σ. ἐπὶ Δηλίῳ And.4.13; ἐν Τροίᾳ S.*El.*1; ἐς Θεσσαλίην Hdt. (v. supr. c); σ. ὑπὲρ τῆς Ἀσίας *serve as general* on the side of Asia, Isoc.4.154. e. c. inf., *manoeuvre so as..*, μάχην θέσθαι Plu.*Pyrrh.*21, cf. *Crass.*25, etc. f. c. acc. cogn., σ. στρατηγίας And.1.147, Dinsmoor *Archons of Athens* 7; ναυμαχίαν, πόλεμον, D.13.21, 49.25: with neut. Adj., *do a thing as general*, τοῦτο X.*An.*7.6.40; πάντα ὑπὲρ Φιλίππου *carry on the* whole *war* in Philip's favour, D.3.6; τοιαῦτα σ. *manage* matters so *in his command*, Hdt.9.107; εἰ μὲν ἄλλο τι καλῶς ἐστρ. X.*HG*6.5.51:—Pass., τὰ στρατηγούμενα D.4.25,47. g. Pass., *to be commanded by a general*, ἡ πόλις.. ὑπὸ ὑμῶν.. στρατηγεῖται Pl.*Ion* 541c; στρατιὰ ὑπό τινων στρατηγουμένη Isoc.4.185; δυοῖν.. στρατηγεῖται φυγή E.*Heracl.*39; στρατηγηθῆναι *serve under a* στρατηγός, Arist.*Pol.*1277ᵇ11; *to be governed as a province*, App.*Mith.*105. 2. metaph., ἡ τύχη ἐστρ. X.*An.*2.2.13, cf. 3.2.27; ἐστρ. ἡ σιωπὴ τὸν ἀγῶνα Plu.2.506e. II. c. acc. pers., *out-general*, D.4.41 (Pass.), Plb.3.71.1, 9.25.6, Lxx 2*Ma.*14.31 (Pass.), cf. D.H.5.29 codd.: metaph. of Homer, δημαγωγῶν καὶ στρατηγῶν τὰ πλήθη Str.1.2.9; in Med., of Pythagoras, Socr.*Ep.*28 (τερατευσαμένῳ Hercher). 2. c. acc. rei, τῷ σχήματι τοῦ προσώπου στρατηγεῖν τὴν τοῦ πλήθους εὐθυμίαν (of a general) Onos.13.3. -ημα, ατος, τό, *act of a general*, esp. *piece of generalship, stratagem*, X.*Mem.*3.5.22 (pl.), Isoc.12.78, Plb.3.18.9, Onos.*Praef.*7, etc.:—στρατηγήματα was the title of works by Polyaenus and Frontinus; cf. also *BMus.Inscr.*1020 (Smyrna, i A.D.). 2. *trick, device*, Cic.*Att.*5.2.2, Plu.2.755d; σ. τῶν λόγων *trick* of speech, D.H.*Rh.*9.8. -ητέον, *one must be a general, one must command*, Pl.*Sis.*389d. -ία, Ion. -ίη, ἡ, *office of general, command*, Hdt.1.59, 5.26, E.*Andr.*678,704, Eup.100, Phryn.Com.22, etc.; παραλύειν τινὰ τῆς σ. Hdt.6.94; ἀνάσσων Ἑλλάδος στρατηγίας being chief general of Greece, E.*IT*17; τυραννίδος μᾶλλον.. μίμησις ἢ σ. Th.1.95; of a naval command, Id.5.26, X.*HG*6.2.13. 2. at Athens, *office of* στρατηγός, Ar.*Pl.*192, Aeschin.2.41: in pl., Pl.*Ap.*36b, *R.*599c, etc.; ἐν ταῖς ἐνιαυσίοις σ. Plu.*Per.*16: *presidency* of the Achaean league, Plb.4.37.1, etc.; in Egypt, *office of* στρατηγός, πρὸς τῇ σ. deputy-στρατηγός, *PEnteux.*63.10 (iii B.C.), *UPZ*108.28 (ii B.C.); πρὸς τῇ σ. also, = στρατηγός, *BGU*12.6 (ii A.D.); at Rome, *praetorship*, Plu.*Cat.Mi.*39, *Sull.*5, etc.; cf. στρατηγός II. 3,4. 3. *period of command, campaign*, X.*HG*6.2.39. 4. *troops commanded by one general, command*, prob. in *OGI* 266.54 (Pergam., iii B.C.). II. *generalship*, X.*Cyr.*1.6.14, *Mem.*3.1.5, Pl.*Euthd.*307a, etc.; *piece of strategy*, D.S.17.23. III. *province governed by a* στρατηγός, Str.12.1.4, al., Plin.*HN*6.27, App.*Mith.*105. IV. = φαλαγγαρχία, a force of 4096 men, Arr.*Tact.*10.7, Ael.*Tact.*9.8. 2. = στρατιά (which is found in codd. AB), Lxx *Ju.*5.3. -ιάω, Desiderat. of στρατηγέω, *wish to be a general*, Pherecr.250, X.*An.*7.1.33, D.19.295, Plu.*Eum.*14; *wish to make war*, Str.4.6.7; *to be going to war*, ἐπί τινας Id.7.4.3. -ικός, ή, όν, *of* or *for a general*, πρᾶξις Pl.*Plt.*304e; [ἐπιστήμη] Arist.*EN*1096ᵃ32; [τέχνη] ib.1094ᵃ9; ἔργα X.*Oec.*20.6; οἴκησις *PPetr.*3 p.343 (iii B.C.); κατάλυσις *BGU*1767.6 (i B.C.); σκηνή Plu.*Luc.*16; μαχαιροφόρος *PGen.*31.14 (ii A.D.): ἡ -κή (sc. τέχνη), = στρατηγία II, Pl.*Euthd.*290d, etc.: so τὰ σ. X.*Cyr.*1.6.12; also a *treatise on strategy*, D.L.5.80; σ. βιβλία Ael.*Tact.*1.2. II. of persons, *suited* or *fitted for command, general-like, versed in generalship*, Pl.*Grg.*455c, X.*Mem.*1.1.8, etc.: Sup., Id.*Cyr.*8.4.7, Phld.*Mus.* p.76K. Adv. -κῶς, εὖ καὶ σ. Ar.*Av.*362: Comp. -ώτερον Plb.10.32.7. 2. at Rome, *praetorian*, ἐπαρχία Str.14.6.6; οἱ σ., = *milites praetoriani*, Plu.*Oth.*9; σ. βῆμα *tribunal praetorium*, D.H.5.28. b. = *praetorius, ex-praetor*, *SIG*840 (Olympia, ii A.D.). -ιον (in codd. sts. -εῖον, as D.L.1.50), τό, *general's tent*, S.*Aj.*721. 2. at Athens, *the place where the* στρατηγοί *held their sittings*, Aeschin.2.85, 3.146, D.42.14, *IG*2².500.39, prob. in 1².77.19, 2².1479.66, cf. Plu.*Per.*37, Id.2.519b, D.L.1.50. 3. in Egypt, *business-office of the* στρατηγός, *PPetr.*2 p.26 (iii B.C.). 4. = Lat. *praetorium*, Ph.*Bel.*102.5, Plb.6.31.1, D.H.5.28, 9.6, Plu.2.813e, D.C.53.16. 5. *camp*, Suid. (citing S. l.c.).

**Στρατήγιος**, Dor. -άγιος, epith. of Apollo, *IG*12(1).161 (Rhodes, Στρατιαγίου lapis).

❀ **στρᾰτηγ-ίς**, ίδος, ἡ, fem. Adj. *of the general*, σκηνή Paus.4.19.1; πύλαι the door or entrance *of the general's tent*, S.*Aj.*49; ναῦς σ. *flag-ship*, Th.2.84 (pl.), cf. And.1.11; so ἡ σ. alone, Hdt.8.92; at Rome, σ. σπεῖραι *cohortes praetoriae*, Plu.*Ant.*39, cf. App.*BC*3.45; τάξεις ib.5.3. II. as Subst., fem. of στρατηγός, *female commander*, Ar.*Ec.*835,870, Pherecr.235. ❀ -ός, ὁ (the fem. in Ar.*Ec.*491,500 is merely comic), Arc. and Dor. **στρᾰτᾱγός** *IG*5(2).6.9 (Tegea, iv B.C.), *SIG*597 *B* (Thermum, iii B.C.), etc.; Aeol. **στρότᾱγος** *IG*12(2).6.7 (Mytil.), 11(2).1064 *b* 27 (Delos):—*leader* or *commander of an army, general*, Archil.58.1, A.*Th.*816, Arist.*Ath.*22.3, etc.; ἀνὴρ σ. A.*Ag.*1627, Pl.*Ion* 540d; opp. ναύαρχος (admiral), S.*Aj* 1232 (v. infr. II. 1). 2. generally, *commander, governor*, πόλει κήρυγμα θεῖναι τὸν σ. Id.*Ant.*8, cf. Arist.*Mu.*398ᵃ29. 3. c. gen., στρατηγοὶ τοῦ πεζοῦ Hdt.7.83; τῶν παραθαλασσίων Id.5.25, etc.; Ἀχαιῶν S.*Aj.* l.c.; στρατεύματος X.*An.*1.7.12. 4. metaph., παραλαβὼν.. οἶνον σ. Antiph.18; στρατηγοὶ κυνηγεσίων *masters* of hounds, Arist.*Mu.*398ᵃ24; so *strategum te facio huic convivio*, Plaut.*Stich.*702. II. at Athens, the title of 10 *officers elected by yearly vote to command the army and navy, and conduct the war-department at home, commanders in chief and ministers of war*, Hdt.6.109, Th.1.61, 4.2, Arist.*Ath.*26.1, 44.4, 61.1, D.4.25; οἱ σ. οἱ εἰς Σικελίαν And.1.11, cf. *IG*1².302.46, al.; σ. εἵλοντο δέκα X.*HG*1.5.16, cf. Eup.117.4, Pl.Com.185, etc.; τῷ σ. τῷ ἐπὶ τὰς συμμορίας ᾑρημένῳ *IG*2².1629.209; when distd. from ναύαρχος and ἵππαρχος, the στρατηγός is *commander of the infantry*, Decr.ap.D.18.184, Arist.*Ath.*4.2; χειροτονηθεὶς σ. ἐπὶ τὸ ναυτικόν, ἐπὶ τὰ ὅπλα, *IG*2².682.5,31; ἐπὶ τὴν παρασκευήν ib.22; ἐπὶ τὴν χώραν ib.24. 2. also of *chief magistrates* of the cities of Asia Minor, Hdt.5.38; of many other Greek states, *IG*5(2) l.c. (Tegea, iv B.C.), 12(9).191 *A* 44 (Eretria, iv B.C.), *OGI*329.42 (Aegina, ii B.C.), Timae.114, Plb.2.43.1, etc. 3. in Ptolemaic and Roman Egypt, *military and civil governor of a nome*, *PEnteux.*1.12, al. (iii B.C.), *PCair.Zen.*351.4 (iii B.C.), *BGU*1730.11 (i B.C.), *OGI*184.3 (Philae, i B.C.), Wilcken *Chr.*41 ii 6 (iii A.D.), 43.1 (iv A.D.); also in other parts of the Ptolemaic empire, e.g. at Calynda in Caria, *PCair.Zen.* 341(*a*).20 (iii B.C.); in Cyprus, *OGI*84 (iii B.C.); ὁ σ. τῆς Ἰνδικῆς καὶ Ἐρυθρᾶς θαλάσσης ib.186 (Philae, i B.C.); in the Attalid empire, ib.267.13 (Pergam., iii B.C.), al.; σ. τῆς πόλεως at Alexandria, *BGU*729.1 (ii A.D.); at Ptolemais, *OGI*743 = *Raccolta Lumbroso* 299 (i B.C.), *Sammelb.*7027 (ii A.D.). 4. σ. ὕπατος *consul*, *IG*5(1).1165 (Gythium, ii B.C.), 9(2).338 (Cyretiae, ii B.C.), 4²(1).306*D* (Epid., ii B.C.), Plb.1.52.5; also σ. alone, Id.1.7.12, al., *SIG*685.20 (Crete, ii B.C.), and ὕπατος alone, v. ὕπατος; σ. ἀνθύπατος *proconsul*, ib.826 *I* 1 (Delph., ii B.C.), 745.2 (Rhodes, i B.C.); ἑξαπέλεκυς σ. *praetor*, Plb.3.106.6; used of the *praetor urbanus*, Id.33.1.5; called σ. κατὰ πόλιν *IG*14.951 (i B.C.), etc.; σ. alone, = *praetor*, D.H.2.6, Arr.*Epict.*2.1.26: also of the *duumviri* or *chief magistrates of Roman colonies*, as of Philippi, *Act.Ap.*16.20: later of the *Comes Orientis*, Lib.*Or.*56.21. 5. *an officer who had the custody of the Temple at Jerusalem*, ὁ σ. τοῦ ἱεροῦ *Ev.Luc.*22.52, *Act.Ap.*4.1, J.*BJ*6.5.3. 6. νυκτερινὸς σ. *superintendent of police* at Alexandria, Str.17.1.12. 7. = φαλαγγάρχης (q.v.), Arr.*Tact.*10.7, Ael.*Tact.*9.8.

**στρατηΐη**, v. στρατεία.

**στρᾰτηλ-ᾰσία**, Ion. -ίη, ἡ, *expedition, campaign*, Hdt.4.105, 7.14, al.; ἐπὶ Αἴγυπτον ἐποιέετο σ. Id.2.1; *campaigning*, Plu.2.326b. II. *army*, Hdt.8.140.α'. III. *office of magister militum*, Just.*Nov.*38 *Prooem.*3 (pl.). IV. generally, *military command*, Ptol.*Tetr.*177 (pl.). -ᾰτέω, *lead an army into the field*, ἐπί τινας, ἐπὶ χώρην, Hdt.1.124, 5.31, cf. 7.5; ἐκεῖσε A.*Pers.*717 (troch.); δεῦρο E.*Heracl.*465: abs., Hdt.7.10.θ', A.*Eu.*687, E.*IA*1195. II. c. gen., *to be commander of, command*, Id.*HF*61, *Rh.*276: c. dat., Id.*Ba.*52, *El.*321, 917. -άτης [ᾰ], ου, ὁ, *leader of an army, general, commander*, Pratin.Lyr.1.9, S.*Aj.*1223, E.*Ph.*1241, and in late Prose, *OGI*648 (Palmyra, iii A.D.), *PLips.*48.23 (iv A.D.), etc.; = *magister militum*, Zos.2.33, *Gloss.*, *POxy.*1983.2 (vi A.D.), etc.; Ἑλλάδος E.*Or.*970 (lyr.); also of an admiral, σ. νεῶν A.*Eu.*637. -ᾰτικός, ή, όν, *of* or *for a commander*, Procl.*Par.Ptol.*247. -ᾰτις, ιδος, ἡ, fem. of στρατηλάτης, voc. -ᾰτι, addressed to the Moon, *PMag.Par.*1.2275.

❀ **στρᾰτιά**, Ion. -ιή, ἡ, = στρατός, *army*, Pi.*O.*6.16, A.*Pers.*534 (anap.), *Ag.*799 (anap.), etc.; σ. ναυτική, πεζή, Th.6.33, 7.15; ναύφρακτος σ. *IG*1².296.30; ἔς τε τὴν σ. καὶ τὴν πόλιν τὴν Ἀθηναίων ib.108.40; τῆς σ. κάκιστος ἦν ἀνήρ Eup.31: abs., *a land force*, as distd. from seamen, Hdt.6.12. 2. generally, *host, company, band*, Pi.*P.*11.50, *N.*11.35; ἡ σ. τοῦ οὐρανοῦ Lxx 2*Ch.*33.3; αἱ σ. τῶν οὐρανῶν ib.*Ne.*9.6; = *cohors ministrorum*, Lib.*Or.*54.7. II. sts. = στρατεία, *expedition*, Hdt.5.77 (v.l. -είην), Ar.*Eq.*587 (lyr.), *Th.*828, 1169, *Lys.*592, Th.8.108, *IG*2².351.31; ἐπὶ στρατιᾶς Ar.*V.*354, 557, Pl.*Phdr.*260b, And.2.14; ἴτε.. ἐπὶ στρατιάν go.. on *service*, Ar.*Ach.*1143; κατὰ στρατιὴν Hp.*Medic.*14; πολιτικαὶ στρατιαί, ξενικαὶ σ., ibid.; v. στρατεία.

**στρᾰτί-αρχος**, ὁ, = στράταρχος, X.*Lac.*13.4, *Supp.Epigr.*7.12.7 (Susa, i B.C.); = *praefectus*, D.C.42.4, al.: also -άρχης, ου, ὁ, Id.55.28, al.

**στράτιος** [ᾰ], α, ον, *of an army* or *war, warlike*, Ἄρευος στρατιωτέροις Alc.29 (leg. στροτ-); epith. of Zeus, Hdt.5.119, Arist.*Mu.*401ᵃ22; of Ares, Plu.2.757d; στρατία, of Athena, Luc.*DMeretr.*9.1; of Isis, *POxy.*1380.102 (ii A.D.): στράτιον as Adv. *valiantly*, μέγα καὶ σ. κατέπαρδεν Ar.*V.*618.

**στρᾰτῐωτ-άριον**, τό, *sack* or *chest of military stores*, *POxy.*1657 (iii A.D.). ❀ -ης, ου, ὁ: voc. στρατιῶτα Philem.155: (στρατιά):—*soldier*, Hdt.4.134, al., Cratin.143, *IG*1².60.12, etc.; στρατιώτας καταλέγειν Ar.*Ach.*1065; σ. μισθωσάμενος, of Pisistratus, Arist.*Ath.*15.2; ἄνδρες σ., in a speech, Th.7.61; collectively, in sg., ὁ πολὺς ὅμιλος καὶ σ. Id.6.24; also of soldiers serving on ship-board, Id.2.88. 2. later, *professional soldier*, = μισθοφόρος, Arist.*EN*1116$^{b}$15, cf. Archestr.*Fr.*61; *soldier* in Ptolemaic and Roman Egypt, *PEnteux.* 54.8 (iii B.C.), *OGI*86.12 (iii B.C.), *PLond.*1.142.4 (i A.D.), etc.; Κάσσανδρος τῶν Ἀπολλωνίου στρατιωτῶν *PCair.Zen.*301.1 (iii B.C.). II. *water-lettuce* (σ. ἔνυδρος Gal.12.131), *Pistia Stratiotes*, Meno *Iatr.*6.22, Dsc.4.101; σ. χιλιόφυλλος, *Achillea Millefolium, yarrow* or *milfoil*, ib.102. ⊛ **-ικός**, ή, όν, *of* or *for soldiers*, ἔκπωμα Critias 34; οἰκήσεις Pl.*R.*415e; σκηνή X.*Cyr.*4.5.39; ὅρκος D.H.6.23; [χρήματα] D.19.291; διδαχή *BGU*140.15 (ii A.D.); βίος Gal.6.810; βαλλάντιον *PSI*10.1128 (iii A.D.): τὸ σ. (sc. ἀργύριον) *the pay of the forces*, D.13.4; but τὸ σ. (sc. πλῆθος) *the soldiery*, Th.8.83, *UPZ*110.103 (ii B.C.), Hdn.1.5.8; τὰ στρατιωτικά (sc. ἔργα, πράγματα) *military affairs*, Pl.*Ion* 540e, X.*Cyr.*2.1.22; *military funds*, ὁ ταμίας τῶν σ. Arist.*Ath.*47.2, *IG*2².1009.19, *OGI*771.44 (Delos, ii B.C.); ταμιεῖον ὃ καὶ -κὸν ἐπωνόμασε, = Lat. *aerarium militare*, D.C.55.25. II. *fit for a soldier, military*, like στρατεύσιμος, σ. ἡλικία the *military* age, X.*Cyr.*6.2.37; φίλον εἶχόν τινα στρατιωτικόν a *military* friend, Phoenicid.4.5; νεανίσκος σ. *serving in the army*, Gal.6.376. Adv. -κῶς, ζῆν Isoc.12.79: Comp., of ships, -κώτερον παρεσκευασμένοι equipped *rather as troop-ships*, Th.2.83. III. *warlike, soldierlike*, γένη Arist.*Pol.*1269$^{b}$25, cf. Plb.22.22.3; -κώτερος ἢ πολιτικώτερος Id.22.10.4; -ωτικὴ προπέτεια, opp. στρατηγικὴ πρόνοια, Id.3.105.9. Adv. -κῶς *like a rude soldier, brutally*, Id.21.38.2. IV. σ. φάρμακα, κολλύριον, name of certain *eye-salves*, Aët.7.79; *stratioticum*, *CIL*13.10021.199 (Gaul); στρατι⟨ωτι⟩κωτέραις ὕλαις dub. cj. in Sever.*Clyst.*31. ⊛ **-ις** (properisp.), ιδος, fem. of στρατιώτης; as Adj., σ. ἀρωγή *martial* aid, A.*Ag.*47 (anap.); τέχναι Plu.*Marc.*14; λεχὼ σ. *a soldier's* wife, Eup.256. 2. σ. ναῦς *troop-ship, transport*, *IG*1².22.10, Th.1.116, 6.43, 8.62, X.*HG*1.1.36. 3. (sc. μυῖα) the *soldier-fly*, Luc.*Musc.Enc.*12. 4. = στρατιώτης II, *Gp.*2.5.4. 5. pl., *stratiotides*, = στρατιωτικός IV, *CIL*13.10021.10 (Gaul).

**στρᾰτο-κῆρυξ**, ῡκος, ὁ, *herald of a camp* or *army*, Lxx 3*Ki.*22.36, *BGU*992 ii 4 (ii B.C.). 2. *one of* 5 ἔκτακτοι *attached to a* τάξις or σύνταγμα, Arr.*Tact.*10.4, Ael.*Tact.*9.4, Ascl.*Tact.*2.9; or *to a* ἑκατονταρχία, Arr.*Tact.*14.4, Ael.*Tact.*16.2, Ascl.*Tact.*6.3. **-λογέω**, (λέγω (B)) *levy an army, enlist soldiers*, D.H.11.24, J.*AJ*5.1.28, al.:—Pass., ἐκ συμμάχων στρατολογηθέντων D.S.12.67, cf. Plu.*Caes.*35. ⊛ **-λογία**, ἡ, *raising, levying an army*, D.H.6.44, Hermog.*Prog.*10, *PLips.*54.10,13 (iv A.D.). **-μαντις**, εως, ὁ, *prophet to the army*, A.*Ag.*122 (lyr.).

**Στρᾰτονίκ-εια** [ῐ], τά, *festival in honour of Stratonice*, *Inscr.Délos* 320*B*58 (iii B.C.). **-ίς**, ίδος, ἡ, epith. of Aphrodite at Smyrna, *SIG*990 (iii B.C.), *OGI*229.12 (iii B.C.).

⊛ **στρᾰτοπεδ-άρχης**, ου, ὁ, *military commander*, *BGU*1822.13 (i B.C., prob.), D.H.10.36, J.*BJ*6.4.3, Mitteis *Chr.*87.5 (ii A.D.), Procl.*Par. Ptol.*245; = *praefectus castrorum*, *CIL*3.13648, 14187$^{5}$ (Pontus), Luc.*Hist.Conscr.*22, *Gloss.* **-αρχικός**, ή, όν, *of a* στρατοπεδάρχης, ἀξιώματα Ptol.*Tetr.*176. **-εία**, ἡ, *encampment*, X.*HG*4.1.24, Aen.Tact.16.15, Lxx *Jo.*4.3, Plb.1.48.10, al., D.H.10.23, Ael.*Tact.*3.3. **-ευμα**, ατος, τό, *army*, D.S.15.83 codd. (στράτευμα Dind.). **-ευσις**, εως, ἡ, *encamping*, X.*Cyr.*8.5.6, Pl.*R.*526d. 2. *encampment, position of an army*, X.*HG*4.1.25 (pl.). **-ευτικός**, ή, όν, *of an encampment*, σχήματα Plb.6.30.3; *concerning encampments*, βίβλος Aen.Tact.21.2. **-εύω**, *encamp, bivouac, take up a position*, X.*An.*7.6.24 (v.l. in *Cyr.*4.2.6), Lxx *Ge.*12.9, al.: more freq. in Med., Hdt.1.62,76, 2.141, Th.1.30, X.*An.*2.2.15, etc.; of a fleet, *to be stationed*, Hdt.7.124. ⊛ **-ον**, τό, *camp, encampment*, Id.5.63, A.*Th.*79 (lyr.), S.*Ph.*10, Gal.15.709; Στρατόπεδα, name of a part of Egypt, Hdt.2.154, cf. 112: hence, *encamped army*, Id.4.114, Gal.15.119, etc.; in both senses, Th.2.81. 2. at Rome, the *Castra Praetoriana*, D.C.60.1, al. II. generally, *army*, Hdt.1.77, 9.51,53; also, *squadron* of ships, Id.8.94, Th.1.117, Lys.21.6, *IG*1².105.29; σ. ναυτικὰ καὶ πεζικά X.*HG*6.3.18. 2. the Roman *legion*, Plb.1.16.2, *BGU*362 xi 15 (iii A.D.), D.C.55.23, etc. III. *the court* or *suite* of the emperor or his representative, Jul.*Ep.*46.

**στρᾰτόπλωτος**, ον, (πλέω) *transporting an army*, ῥῆτραι σ. orders *for sailing*, Lyc.1037.

**στρᾰτός**, ὁ, Aeol. **στρότος** Sapph.*Supp.*5.1:—*army, host*. ἀνὰ στρατὸν Il.1.53,384, al.; κατὰ σ. ib.318, al.; ἐπὶ δεξιόφιν παντὸς στρατοῦ 13.308, cf. 326; κατὰ σ. εὐρὺν Ἀχαιῶν 1.229, al.; ἐνὶ στρατῷ 14.371; πόλιν ἀμφὶ δύω στρατοὶ ἥατο λαῶν 18.509; Ep. gen. στρατόφι 10.347; σ. ἀνδρῶν a military force, Hdt.1.53; without ἀ., *SIG*1 (Abu Simbel, vi B.C.); of a naval force, σ. ναυβάτας A.*Ag.*987 (lyr.); χιλιόναυς E.*Or.*352 (anap.); νηΐτης Th.4.85; ναυτικός Id.7.71, A.*Ag.*634; σ. ἱππήων, πέσδων, νάων, Sapph. l.c.; in Prose it is to be supplied with ὁ πεζός, ὁ ναυτικός, Hdt.8.130, etc., cf. 7.124 and πεζὸς στρατός A.*Pers.*728 (troch.). 2. *the commons, people*, = λαός, δῆμος, opp. οἱ σοφοί, Pi.*P.*2.87, cf. *O.*9.95, A.*Eu.*683,762, S.*El.*749. 3. *band* or *body* of men, as of the Amphictyons, Pi.*P.*10.8; of the Centaurs, ib.2.46; of the Amazons and Arimaspi, A.*Pr.*723,804: metaph., ἐριβρόμου νεφέλας σ. ἀμείλιχος Pi.*P.*6.12.

**στρᾰτο-ϋπηρέτης**, ου, ὁ, *army servant*, prob. in *Sammelb.*4293.8. **-φύλαξ** [ῠ], ᾰκος, ὁ, *commanding officer*, Str.12.5.1, 15.1.46.

**στρᾰτόω**, in Med. and Pass., *to be on a campaign, in the field*, ἐστρατόωντο Il.3.187, 4.378; στρατόωντο A.R.2.387; στρατωθὲν *assembled as a host*, A.*Ag.*133 (lyr.): contr. στρατῶ, glossed στρατοπεδεύομαι, Hdn.Gr.1.442.

**στρᾰτύλλαξ**, ὁ, perh. Comic Dim. of στρατηγός, *toy captain*, Cic.*Att.*16.15.3.

**Στρᾰτωνίδης**, ου, ὁ, Comic patronymic, as we might say *Son of a Gun*, Ar.*Ach.*596.

⊛ **στράτωρ**, ὁ, = Lat. *strator, groom* on the staff of a Roman officer, *OGI*628 (Arabia, i A.D.).

**στράφω**, v. στρέφω. **στραχύ**· τραχύ, Hsch. post στράβωνες. **στρέβλα**, ἡ, gloss on βέμβιξ, Id.

**στρέβλευμα**, ατος, τό, as if from στρεβλεύω, *perversity, frowardness*, Sm.*Pr.*6.12.

**στρέβλη**, ἡ, (στρεβλός) *winch* used in ship-building, A.*Supp.*441 (pl. = τὰ ξύλα τῶν νεῶν ἐν οἷς διασφηνοῦνται γομφούμενα (sic, fort. -μεναι), Hsch.). 2. in pl., the *twisted cords* in a mechanical toy, the untwisting of which releases the motive power, Arist.*MA*701$^{b}$3,9. 3. *clothes-press*, prob. worked by a screw, Plu.2.950a. 4. part of a filter, τὸν τρυγώδη διὰ σάκκου καὶ στρέβλης ἠθεῖν οἶνον Phot. s. v. σακίζειν. II. *an instrument of torture*, Plb.18.54.7, Lxx 4*Ma.*7.4, J.*AJ*19.1.6, Luc.*Nec.*14, etc. 2. *torture*, λύπας, μερίμνας, ἁρπαγάς, στρέβλας, νόσους Diph.88, cf. *PTeb.*789.15 (ii B.C.), D.S.13.86 (pl.), Phld.*Rh.*1.234S.; ζημίαι καὶ σ. ib.2.152S. (pl.).

**στρεβλο-κάρδιος**, ον, *perverse* or *froward of heart*, Aq., Sm., Thd. *Pr.*11.20. **-κέρᾰτος**, ον, *with crumpled horns*, Hsch. s. v. ῥαικακερεῖς. **-κερως**, ων, = foreg., Eust.1394.39. **-πους**, πουν, gen. ποδος, *crook-footed*, Tz.*H.*10.623; = *scaurus*, *Gloss.*

**στρεβλ-ός**, ή, όν, *twisted, crooked*, πόσθιον.., σ. ὥσπερ κύτταρον Ar.*Th.*516; στρεβλὸν ὀρθῶσαι κλάδον Men.711; λοξοβάται, στρεβλοί, of crabs, Batr.295; μυκτήρ Nic.*Al.*442; κανών Arist.*Rh.*1354$^{a}$26; *squint-eyed*, like στραβός, Hp.*Aër.*14, Eup.182, Phryn.*PS*p.108B., Hsch. s. v. ἰλλός; of the brows, *knit, wrinkled*, *AP*7.440 (Leon.). II. metaph., *crooked, cunning*, στρεβλοῖσι παλαίσμασι by *cunning* dodges in wrestling, Ar.*Ra.*878 (mock heroic); *perverse, froward*, Lxx *Ps.*17(18).27, *Si.*36.(22)25, Aesop.66. **-ότης**, ητος, ἡ, *being twisted, crookedness*, τῆς αἰχμῆς Plu.*Mar.*25; καμπαῖς καὶ στρεβλότησι, of roads in an ant-heap, Id.2.968b. II. *frowardness, perversity*, Aq., Thd.*Pr.*4.24, Aq., Al.ib.6.14. **-όω**, fut. -ώσω Plu.*Phoc.*35: aor. ἐστρέβλωσα Din.1.63:—*twist* or *strain tight*, ὄνοισι ξυλίνοισι τὰ ὅπλα *drawing* the cables *taut* with windlasses (cf. στρέβλη I), Hdt.7.36; *screw up* the strings of an instrument, τὰς χορδὰς ἐπὶ τῶν κολλόπων στρεβλοῦν Pl.*R.*531b. II. *twist* or *wrench* a dislocated limb, with a view to setting it, σ. τὸν πόδα Hdt.3.129; also of wrestlers, Philostr.*Im.*2.6, cf. 1.6 (Pass.):—Med., ἐς τοὐπίσω τὰς χεῖρας σ. Alciphr.3.43:—Pass., στρεβλωθῆναι *acquire a squint*, Herod.Med. in *Rh.Mus.*58.78; ἐσχηκότες στρεβλουμένους τοὺς ὀφθαλμούς ibid. 2. *stretch on the wheel* or *rack, to rack, torture*, applied to slaves for the purpose of extracting evidence, Ar.*Nu.*620, *Ra.*620, Antipho 5.32, Herod.2.89; στρεβλοῦν..τοῦτον ὡς κατάσκοπον Antiph.277:—Pass., ἐπὶ τροχοῦ στρεβλούμενος Ar.*Lys.*846, *Pl.*875; ἀπέθανε στρεβλωθεὶς Lys.13.54, cf. And.1.44, Gal.6.312: fut. Med. στρεβλώσομαι in pass. sense, Pl.*R.*361e. 3. metaph., *pervert* or *distort* words, 2*Ep.Pet.*3.16:—Pass., Lxx 2*Ki.*22.27. **-ωμα**, ατος, τό, *wrench, twist*, Erot. s.v. σχάσματα. ⊛ **-ωσις**, εως, ἡ, *putting to the torture*, J.*AJ*19.1.5, Plu.2.1070b. ⊛ **-ωτήριος**, α, ον, *racking, torturing*, Hsch. s. v. λυγῶδες: στρεβλωτήριον, τό, *rack*, Lxx 4*Ma.*8.13. **-ωτής**, οῦ, ὁ, = στρεβλωτήριον, Lat. *eculeus*, *Gloss.*

**στρέμμα**, ατος, τό, *that which is twisted, thread*, στυππίου Lxx *Jd.*16.9. 2. *twist, roll*, = στρεπτός II. 2, Hsch. II. *wrench, strain, sprain*, Hp.*Off.*23; κἂν ῥῆγμα κἂν στρέμμα D.2.21, 11.14, cf. Dsc.1.85, Gal.10.890. III. *conspiracy, band of conspirators*, συνέστρεψε στρέμματα Lxx 4*Ki.*15.30 (cod. B).

**στρέπτ-αιγλος**, α, ον, (στρέφω, αἴγλη) *whirling-bright*, Νεφελᾶν στρεπταίγλαν (or -ᾶν)..δρμάν Ar.*Nu.*335, cf. Philox.18. **-άριον**, τό, a *twist* of lint (cf. στρεπτός II. 3), Paul.Aeg.6.50. **-ήρ**, ῆρος, ὁ, = στροφεύς, *AP*5.293.7 (Agath.). **-ίκιος ἄρτος**, = στρεπτός II. 2, Ath.3.113d. **-ικός**, ή, όν, *of* or *for twisting*: τὸ σ., as a part of ὑφαντική, Pl.*Plt.*282d, cf. Poll.7.209. **-ίνδα**, Adv., a game in which a piece of money, shell, or the like, being laid down, was to be struck by another *so as to be made to turn over*, Id.9.110,117. **-όλῡτον**, τό, (λύω) a grammatical figure, in which the *clauses are as it were intertwined*, Sch.Aristid.ap Phot.*Bibl.* p.401B. **-ός**, ή, όν, *easily twisted, pliant*: σ. χιτών was (acc. to Aristarch.) a shirt *of chain-armour* or *mail*, Il.5.113, 21.31; σ. λύγοι *pliant* withes, E.*Cyc.*225; σ. κάλωες *twisted*, Orph.*A.*623; ἀρπεδόνα *AP*6.160 (Antip. Sid.); φλοιὸς σ. ἑλιττόμενος *twisted, gnarled*, Thphr.*HP*3.13.2; σ. κεκρύφαλοι *twined, wreathed*, *AP*6.219.4 (Antip.); θύσανοι ib.225 (Nicaen.); ῥυτίδες ib.5.203 (Mel.); ἐσθῆτες Diog.Oen.10; κυμάτιον, of a moulding, Lxx *Ex.*25.10(11), al.; τὰ σ. τῶν στύλων, τῶν γλυφῶν, ib.3*Ki.*7.41. II. Subst. στρεπτός, ὁ (in D.S.5.45, σ. κύκλος), *collar of twisted* or *linked metal*, χρύσεος σ. περιαυχένιος Hdt.3.20, cf. 9.80, Pl.*R.*553c, X.*Cyr.*1.3.2, J.*AJ*11.6.10:—also **στρεπτόν**, τό, *IG*2².1388.28, Men.*Epit.*187: pl., Plu.*Art.*15. 2. of pastry, *twist, roll*, D.18.260, cf. Hippoloch.ap.Ath.4.130d, Poll.6.77: also στρεπτόν, τό, Jul.*Ep.*180. 3. σ. μοτός or τιλτός a *twist* of lint, Gal.14.795, Paul.Aeg.6.6. III. metaph., *to be bent* or *turned*, στρεπτοὶ καὶ θεοὶ αὐτοί the gods themselves *may be turned* (by prayer), Il.9.497; σ. φρένες ἐσθλῶν 15.203; also σ. γλῶσσα *glib, pliant* tongue, 20.248. IV. *bent, curved*, σ. σίδηρος, of a pick-axe, E.*HF*946; κορώνη, of a bow, Theoc.25.212; ἄγκιστρα *AP*6.27 (Theaet.).

⊛ **στρεπτοφόρος**, ον, (στρεπτὸς II. 1) *wearing a collar* or *necklace*, Hdt.8.113.

**στρευγεδών**, όνος, ἡ, *distress, suffering*, Nic.*Al.*313.

**στρεύγω**, *distress, pain*, Hsch.; but in Ep. used in Pass., *to be exhausted* or *worn out, weary oneself*, δηθὰ στρεύγεσθαι ἐν αἰνῇ δηϊοτῆτι Il.15.512, cf. A.R.4.1058; δηθὰ σ. ἐὼν ἐν νήσῳ ἐρήμῃ Od.12.351; ἄσθματι σ. Tim.*Pers.*93; σ. καμάτοισι A.R.4.384; νούσῳ Call.*Cer.* 68: abs., *to be distressed, suffer distress* or *pain*, A.R.4.621, Nic.*Al.* 291.

* **στρέφανον**· ἀξίνη, καὶ πέλεκυς, Hsch.

**στρεφεδῑνέω**, *spin, whirl round*:—Pass., *spin round and round*, στρεφεδίνηθεν δέ οἱ ὄσσε, of one stunned by a blow, Il.16.792. II. intr. in Act., *spin, whirl round*, Q.S.13.7. Cf. στροφοδινέομαι.

**στρέφος**· στρέμμα, δέρμα, βύρσα, Δωριεῖς, Hsch. (cf. στέρφος, στρέφωσις).

**στρέφω**, Il.23.323, etc.; Dor. **στράφω** [ᾰ] *IG*12(3).92.6 (Nisyrus, dub.); Aeol. **στροφῶ** (leg. στρόφω) *EM*728.44: Ep. impf. στρέψασκον Il.18.546: fut. στρέψω E.*Med.*1152, etc.: aor. 1 ἔστρεψα Id.*Tr.*1243, etc., Ep. στρέψα Od.4.520: pf. ἔστροφα (ἀν-) Cerc.17.30, (ἀντ-, v.l. ἀν-) Theognet.1.8, (ἐπ-) Plb.5.110.6, (μετ-) Aristid.1.435 J.; also ἔστρᾰφα (κατ-) Plb.23.11.2 codd.:—**Med.**, Il.18.488, etc.: fut. στρέψομαι 6.516, etc.: aor. ἐστρεψάμην S.*OC*1416, (κατ-) Th.1.94, etc.: pf. Pass. (in med. sense) ἔστραμμαι (κατ-) Isoc.5.21:—**Pass.**, fut. στρᾰφήσομαι Lxx 1*Ki.*10.6, (ἀνα-) Isoc.5.64, (δια-) Ar.*Eq.*175, *Av.*177, (μετα-) Pl.*R.*518d; fut. Med. (in pass. sense) στρέψομαι (ἀπο-) X.*Cyr.*5.5.36: aor. 1 ἐστρέφθην freq. in Hom., Il.5.40, al., rare in Att., Ar.*Th.*1128, Pl.*Plt.*273e; Dor. ἐστράφθην Sophr. 88, Theoc.7.132, also v.l. (for κατεστράφησαν) in Hdt.1.130 (but στραφῆναι Id.3.129): aor. 2 ἐστράφην [ᾰ] Sol.37.6, always in Trag., S.*Ant.*315, etc., freq. in Att., Ar.*Ach.*537 (μετα-), Th.5.97 (κατα-), Pl.*Ti.*77b: pf. ἔστραμμαι *h.Merc.*411, Hp.*Aër.*5, X.*An.*4.7.15, etc.; ἔστρεμμαι Eudox.*Ars* 12.10 (Pap.), cf. ἀποστρέφω, καταστρέφω:—*turn about* or *aside*, ἂψ δὲ θεοὶ οὖρον στρέψαν Od.4.520; ἵππους σ. *turn* horses, Il.8.168, Od.15.205, etc.; σ. πηδάλιον Pi.*Fr.*40; τὸν οἴακα Anaxandr.4.5, cf. Men.482.4; σάκος S.*Aj.*575; of persons, ἡλίου πρὸς ἀντολὰς στρέψασα σαυτήν A.*Pr.*708; πρόσωπον πρὸς κασίγνητον στρέφε E.*Ph.*457, cf. *Hec.*344; πάλιν στρέψεις κάρα Id.*Med.*1152; ὄμμα πανταχῇ στρέφων Id.*IT*68; σ. ἀνταυγεῖς κόρας Ar.*Th.*902; σεαυτὸν εἰς πονηρὰ πράγματα Id.*Nu.*1455; πόλιν πρὸς κέρδος ἴδιον E. *Supp.*413; στρατὸν πρὸς ἀλκήν Id.*Andr.*1149; *wheel* soldiers *round*, X.*Lac.*11.9; v. infr. D. 2. *cause to rotate* as on an axis, κεραμικὴν γαῖαν σ., i.e. on the potter's wheel, Sannyr.4; τὸν ἄτρακτον Hdt.5.12; τὸν κόσμον μήτε αὐτὸν στρέφειν ἑαυτόν, μήτε.. ὑπὸ θεοῦ στρέφεσθαι διττὰς περιαγωγάς Pl.*Plt.*269e, cf. *Epin.*977b. II. πάντ' ἄνω τε καὶ κάτω σ. *turn* upside down, A.*Eu.*651; κάτω σ. S.*Ant.* 717, Ar.*Ec.*733; σ. λόγους ἄνω καὶ κάτω Pl.*Grg.*511a, cf. *Euthd.*276d; ἄνω κάτω τοὺς νόμους σ. D.21.91; so δίκα καὶ πάντα πάλιν στρέφεται E.*Med.*411 (lyr.); στρέφειν alone, *overturn, upset*, Id.*IT*1166, *Fr.*536 (troch.); γῆν σ. *turn* it *over* by digging or ploughing, X.*Oec.*16.15: c. acc. cogn., πάσας σ. στροφάς Pl.*Ti.*43e; γράμματα πανταχῇ σ. Id. *Cra.*414c: c. inf., *change* a thing *so as to*.., εὔκλειαν ἔχειν βιοτὰν στρέψουσι φᾶμαι E.*Med.*416 (lyr.). III. σ. σφυρόν *sprain* or *dislocate* it, Epict.*Ench.*29.2, Arr.*Epict.*3.15.4 (so στραφῆναι τὸν πόδα Hdt.3.129, cf. Pl.*Lg.*789e). 2. metaph. of pain, *twist, torture*, κακὸν στρέφει με περὶ τὴν γαστέρα Antiph.177, cf. Ar.*Pl.*1131, *Fr.*462, Ael. *NA*2.44 (Pass.), Gal.19.141; βρέμει ἡ κοιλίη καὶ στρέφει καὶ βορβορύζει Hp.*Int.*6: so σ. τὴν ψυχήν *torment*, Pl.*R.*330e. 3. of corruptions in Music, κάμπτων καὶ στρέφων Pherecr.145.15. IV. *twist, plait*, σπάρτα ἐστραμμένα X.*An.*4.7.15; ἐμβολάδην ἐστραμμέναι ἀλλήλῃσι *h.Merc.*411; *spin*, ὑπὸ μακρῷ λίνῳ στρεφομένη Luc.*JConf.*7, cf. 1; ἔστρεψεν Μοιρῶν μία νήματα *IG*14.607*i* (Caralis); κρόκην σ. Luc.*Fug.* 12: metaph., μεγάλας σ. περιόδους Plu.2.235e. V. t.t. of wrestlers, *twist* the adversary *back*, Poll.3.155: metaph., ἔριδα σ. Pi.*N.*4. 93. VI. metaph., *turn* a thing *over* in one's mind, τί στρέφω τάδε; E.*Hec.*750; πρὸς ἀλλήλους Luc.*Alex.*8; βουλὴν ἐν ἑαυτῷ Ael. *NA*10.48; τὸ πρᾶγμα πανταχῇ στρέφων ἀγαγεῖν ἐπ' ἐμέ D.21. 116. VII. *return, give back*, ἀργύριά τισι *Ev.Matt.*27.3. VIII. *convert*, τὴν πέτραν εἰς λίμνας ὑδάτων Lxx *Ps.*113(114).8, cf. 29(30). 12, *Ex.*4.17; στραφήσῃ εἰς ἄνδρα ἄλλον ib.1*Ki.*10.6; *transmute* metals, Zos.Alch. p.195 B. IX. f.l. for τρέπω in Lys.32.20.

B. Pass. and Med., *twist* or *turn oneself*, στρεφθεὶς *having turned face upward*, Od.9.435; *turn round* or *about, turn to and fro*, Il.5.40, 575, etc.; ἔν τε κύνεσσι κάπριος ἠὲ λέων στρέφεται 12.42; ἐστρέφετ' ἔνθα καὶ ἔνθα, of one *tossing* in bed, 24.5; τί δυσκολαίνεις καὶ στρέφει τὴν νύχθ' ὅλην; Ar.*Nu.*36, cf. Amphis 20.4; of patients, Gal.7. 664. 2. *turn to* or *from* an object, ἔμελλε στρέψεσθ' ἐκ χώρης Il. 6.516, cf. Od.16.352; στρεφθεὶς μετόπισθεν *turning* back, Il.15.645; *return*, S.*OC*1648, *Ant.*315, etc.; στραφέντες ἔφευγον X.*Cyr.*3.3.63, *An.*3.5.1; ποῖ στρέφει; *whither away?* Ar.*Th.*230,610. 3. of the heavenly bodies, *revolve, circle*, Od.5.274, Pl.*Ti.*40b; of the distaff, Id.*R.*617a; of a joint, ἐν ἄρθροις σ. κοτυληδών Ar.*V.*1495. II. *turn* or *twist about*, like a wrestler trying to elude his adversary: hence, in argument, *twist and turn, shuffle*, τί ταῦτα στρέφει; Id.*Ach.* 385; τί δῆτα ἔχων στρέφει; Pl.*Phdr.*236e, etc.; πάσας στροφὰς στρέφεσθαι *twist* every way, Id.*R.*405c, cf. *Euthd.*302b. 2. *turn and change*, κἂν σοῦ στραφείη θυμός S.*Tr.*1134; στρεφόμενα λέγων *things that tell both ways*, D.H.*Rh.*8.15: c. gen. causae, τοῦ δὲ σοῦ ψόφου οὐκ ἂν στραφείην *I would* not *turn for* any noise of thine, S.*Aj.* 1117. III. *to be always engaged in* or *about*, ἐν τούτοις στρέφεται καὶ ἑλίττεται ἡ δόξα Pl.*Tht.*194b; περὶ τὸ αὐτὸ γένος στρέφεται ἡ σοφιστικὴ Arist.*Metaph.*1004b22, cf. Phld.*Rh.*2 p.124 S. 2. generally, *to be at large, go about*, ἀνειμένη στρέφει S.*El.*516; ἐν κυσὶν.. ἐστράφην λύκος Sol.37.6; στρέφεσθαι περὶ τὰ δικαστήρια Phld.*Rh.*2.139 S.; of things, *to be rife*, ταῦτα μὲν ἐν δήμῳ στρέφεται κακά Sol.4.23. 3. of places, τόποι ἐπὶ.. τὰς ἄρκτους ἐστραμμένοι *turned, lying* towards.., Plb.2.15.8, etc.

C. in strict med. sense, *turn about with oneself, take back*, στράτευμ' ἐς Ἄργος S.*OC*1416.

D. intr. in Act., like Pass., *turn about*, Il.18.544,546, where, however, ζεύγεα may be supplied from 543, as may ὗς in Od.10.528, and ἵππους in X.*Eq.*7.18; of soldiers, *wheel about*, Id.*An.*4.3.26 and 32; στρέψαντες ἀπεχώρουν Id.*Ages.*2.3; ποῖ στροφαί.. μανιῶν στρέφουσι; S.*Ichn.*224; τὸν στρέφοντα κύκλον ἡλίου *revolving*, Id.*Fr.*738, cf. E.*Ion* 1154; στρέψαι δεῦρ', of the Comic Chorus, Pl.Com.92; στρέψον τι, δούλη *withdraw* a little, Herod.1.8; ἔστρεψεν ὁ θεός *Act.Ap.*7.42.

**στρέφωσις**· κάλυψις ἀγγείων δέρματι γινομένη, Hsch. (cf. στέρφος).

**στρεψαῖος**, = στροφαῖος, Ar.*Fr.*123 (perh. a pr. n.).

**στρεψαύχην**, ενος, ὁ, ἡ, *neck-twisting*, Theopomp.Com.54.

**στρεψηλάκᾰτος** [ᾰκ], ον, *turning the spindle*, epith. of δαίμονες, *PMag.Par.*1.1358.

**στρεψί-κερως** [ῐ], ωτος, ὁ, ἡ, an African *antelope with twisted horns*, the *addax*, Plin.*HN*11.124. * **-μαλλος**, ον, *with tangled fleece*: σ. τὴν τέχνην, metaph. of Euripides, in reference to his *complex phrases*, Ar.*Fr.*638.

**στρέψις**, εως, ἡ, *a turning round*, Arist.*PA*696b28. 2. metaph., *deceit*, Hsch.

**στρεψο-δῐκέω**, *twist* or *pervert the right*, Ar.*Nu.*434. **-δῐκοπᾰνουργία**, ἡ, *cunning in the perversion of justice*, Id.*Av.*1468.

**στρήνα**, ἡ, = Lat. *strena*, Ath.3.97d, Lyd.*Mens.*4.4.

**στρηνής**, ές, *rough, harsh*, esp. of sounds: hence neut. as Adv., [ὕδωρ] στρηνὲς περὶ στυφελῇ βρέμει ἀκτῇ A.R.2.323; στρηνὲς φωνεῦσα [θάλασσα] *AP*7.287 (Antip.); σάλπιγξ στρηνὲς φθεγξαμένη *piercing*, ib.6.350 (Crin.): cf. στρηνός, στρηνύζω. (Perh. connected with στερεός, Lat. *strenuus*.)

**στρηνιάω**, *run riot, wax wanton*, Antiph.82, Sophil.6, Diph.132, Lyc.*Fr.*1.2, *Apoc.*18.7,9, *PMeyer* 20.23 (iii A.D.); = *gerrio, gestio*, *Gloss.*; cf. Phryn.357.

**στρῆνος**, ὁ, Lyc.438; but in *AP*7.686 (Pall.), Lxx and *NT* (v. infr.) εος, τό:—*insolence, arrogance*, Lxx 4*Ki.*19.28. 2. *wantonness*, *Apoc.*18.3, *AP*l.c. II. c. gen., *eager desire*, μόρου Lyc.l.c.

**στρηνός**, ή, όν, = στρηνής, Nicostr.Com.42.

**στρηνόφωνος**, ον, *rough-* or *loud-voiced*, Call.Com.30.

**στρηνύεται**· στρηνιᾷ, Hsch.

**στρηνύζω**, (στρηνής) *trumpet*, of elephants, Juba 37 (corr. Schneider for στρυνύζω).

**στρῆξις**, prob. f.l. for στήριξις in Al.*Le.*26.9.

**στρῐβῐλίκιγξ**, Comic word, οὐδ' ἂν σ. not *the least*, not *a fraction*, Ar.*Ach.*1035: Sch. cites also * **στρίβος**, *a weak fine voice*; comparing also λίκιγξ, *a bird's voice*.

**στρίγλος**, ὁ, = νυκτικόραξ, Hsch. **στριγχός**, ὁ, = θριγκός, Id. **στρικτόριον**, τό, = foreg., Id. **στρικτός**, ή, όν, = *strigosus*, *Gloss.* 2. **στρικτόν**, τό, a narrow kind of *shoe*, Sch.Luc.*Rh.Pr.* 15; Latin word acc. to Suid.

**στρίξ**, ἡ, gen. στριγός (not found), acc. στρίγγα *Carm.Pop.*26:—*owl*, Theognost.*Can.*41,132 (where also a form **στλίξ** is cited).

**στριφνός**, ή, όν, *firm, hard, solid*, Hp.*VM*15 cod. M (στρυφν- cett.); γυναῖκες -ότεραι Id.*Mul.*2.111 (codd. boni, v.l. στρυφν-), *Nat.Mul.* 1 (v.l. στριφρ-, στρυφν-); ὁ ἐγκέφαλος συνέστηκε καί ἐστι στριφνός (v.l. στιφρός, στρυφνός) Id.*Morb.Sacr.*10; δέρμα σ. Plu.2.642e codd.; ὀστέα στριφνότατα Hp.*Carn.*3 (v.l. στρυφν-); ἀλεκτρυὼν μάλα σ. Men. *Epit.*168; οὐρὴ σ. τ' ἐκτάδιός τε, v.l. for στρυφνή in Opp.*C.*1.411: στριφνός is Hellenistic for Att. στιφρός acc. to Moer. p.342 P., cf. *Gloss. Oxy.*1803.1: στριφνός = *acerbus* (leg. στρυφνός), *Gloss.*; also = *rigidus* and *strigosus*, ib.; στριφνοὶ γέροντες Ar.*Ach.*180 (as cited by Erot. s.v. στριφνούς (στεριφνοί codd.); στιπτοί codd. Ar.).

**στρίφνος**, ὁ, *tough* or *gristly meat*, σ. ἀμάσητος ἀκατάποτος Lxx *Jb.* 20.18.

**στριφνότης**, ητος, ἡ, metaph., *close texture*, of style, D.H.*Dem.*34 codd.; cf. στρυφνότης.

**στρίφος**, η, ον, dub. sens., of ἀστράγαλοι, Suid. s.v. λίσπη (στρυφνούς Sch.Ar.*Ra.*848). 2. τὰ στρίφη dub. sens. in *Sammelb.*6264. 23.

**στριφοῦ**· λαμπόδικε, ἀπόκνισον, Hsch. **στροβάζων**· συνεχῶς στρεφόμενος, Id. **στροβανῖκος**· ἡ τῷ στροβεῖν νικῶσα, Id. **στροβανίσκος**, ὁ, *tripod*, Id.

**στροβεία**, ἡ, perh. *fuller's workshop*, *SIG*546*A* 12 (Delph., iii B.C.).

**στροβελόν**· σκολιόν, καμπύλον, Hsch. **στροβελός**· σοβαρός, τρυφερός, Id.

**στροβεύς**, έως, ὁ, an instrument (perh. a *screw-press*) used by fullers, Sch.Ar.*Eq.*385.

**στροβ-έω**, A.*Ch.*1052, etc.: fut. στροβήσω Lyc.756: aor. ἐστρόβησα Plu.*Num.*13:—**Pass.** and **Med.**, v. infr.: pf. ἐστρόβημαι Lyc.172: (στρόβος, cf. στρόμβος):—*twirl* or *whirl about*, πάντα τρόπον σαυτὸν στρόβει Ar.*Nu.*700, cf. *Com.Adesp.*219; στρόβει (sc. σεαυτόν) Ar.*Eq.* 386, *V.*1528: metaph., τίνες σε δόξαι.. στροβοῦσι; A.*Ch.*1052 (for *Ag.*1215 v. ὑποστροβέω); *distract, distress*, ὁ φόβος αὐτοῦ μή με στροβείτω Lxx *Jb.*9.34, cf. 13.11, al.; νόσος ἐστρόβησε τὴν Ῥώμην Plu. *Num.*13, cf. Jul.*Or.*2.85c:—Med., μανίας ὑπὸ δεινῆς ὄμματα στροβήσεται Ar.*Ra.*817 :—Pass., *whirl about*, οἵοισιν ἐν χειμῶσι στροβούμεθα A.*Ch.*203 ; *to be distracted*, νύκτωρ καὶ μεθ' ἡμέραν Plb.23.10.13, cf. Polystr. p.22 W. **-ητός,** ή, όν, *wheeled round* or *about*, Luc.*Trag.* 12. Adv. -τῶς Hsch.

⊛ **στροβῑλ-ᾶς,** ᾶ, ὁ, *dealer in pine-cones*, *POxy.*1446.58 (ii/iii A.D.). **-έα,** ἡ, = στρόβιλος 7, *fir-tree*, 1*Enoch* 32.4 ; = *nux pinea*, *Gloss.* **-εϊνόν,** = *pinetum* (fort. *pineum*), ib. **-έω,** = συστρέφω, dub. l. in Phryn.374. **-εών,** ῶνος, ὁ, (στρόβιλος 7), Lat. *pinetum*, *Gloss.* **-η,** ἡ, *plug of lint twisted into an oval shape like a pine-cone*, Hp.*Fist.*3. **-ίζω,** *twist about*, αὐχένα *AP*6.94 (Phil.). **-ινος,** η, ον, *of a pine-cone*, ῥητίνη Dsc.1.71, Gal.6.288 ; cf. στροβιλεϊνόν. **-ιον,** τό, Dim. of στρόβιλος 6, *small pine-cone*, Dsc.*Eup.*2.112, Sor.1.123, *PLit.Lond.*171 (iii A.D.) ; σ. μεγάλα *POxy.*1142.6 (iii A.D.). **2.** *cone-shaped ear-ring*, *Com.Adesp.*1154. **-ίτης** [ῑτ], *flavoured with pine-cones*, οἶνος Dsc.5.35. **-οειδής,** ές, *like a* στρόβιλος, *conical*, σχῆμα Thphr.*HP*3.12.9, cf. Ruf.*Anat.*32 ; ὕψος Str.17.1.10. Adv. -δῶς Ruf.*Oss.*21.

⊛ **στρόβῑλ-ος,** ὁ, (στρόβος) *round ball*, στρόβιλος ἀμφάκανθον εἱλίξας δέμας rolling its prickly body *into a ball*, of the hedgehog (ἐχῖνος), Ion Trag.38.4 ; ὀστράκου σ. the *ball* of an egg-shell, i.e. a round egg-shell, Lyc.506, cf. 89. **2.** *spinning-top*, Pl.*R.*436d, Plu.*Lys.* 12. **3.** *cyclone*, *whirlwind*, Arist.*Mu.*395$^a$7, Epicur.*Ep.*2 p.47 U., Men.536.4 (metaph., Id.*Sam.*210) ; τρικυμίαι καὶ σ. Luc.*Tox.*19, cf. Aristid.1.164 J., Poll.4.159. **4.** *twist* or *turn in music*, Pherecr.145.14, Pl.Com.254. **5.** *whirling dance*, *pirouette*, Καρκίνου στρόβιλοι Ar.*Pax* 864, cf Ath.14.630a. **6.** later (Phryn.374, Gal.6.591, 15.848), = κῶνος, *pine-cone*, Thphr.*HP*3.9.1, *POxy.*1088.55 (i A.D.), 1211.6 (ii A.D.), etc. ; κόκκοι στροβίλου *IG*14.966.12 (Rome). **7.** *fir*, *pine*, *PCair.Zen.*157 (iii B.C.), Plu.2.648d. **8.** *stone pine*, *Pinus Cembra*, Dsc.1.69, *Gp.*11.11.1. **9.** *winch*, or perh. *rotating shaft*, *POxy.* 1704.11 (iii A.D.) ; τὸ μυλαῖον σὺν τῷ στροβίλλῳ (sic) *PMerton* 39.9 (v/vi A.D.). **10.** = κοχλίας ἢ θαλάττιος κῆρυξ, Sch.Ar.*Pax* 864. **11.** dub. sens. in *PMag.Osl.*1.339, *BCH*51.395. [ῑ regularly, as in ll. cc. ; but ῐ in signf. 6, *AP*6.232 (Crin.(?), dub.).] **-ός,** ή, όν, *whirling*, λιγνύς cj. in *AP*15.25 (Besant.*Ara*). **-όω,** *turn about*, *keep going*, τὴν γλῶσσαν Plu.2.235e. **-ώδης,** ες, = στροβιλοειδής, ὄρος Id.*Sull.* 17 ; τόποι Ath.Mech.37.4.

**στροβόομαι,** = ἰλιγγιάω, Moer. p.196 P.

**στρόβος,** ὁ, *whirling round*, ποιμένος κακοῦ στρόβῳ, of a *whirlwind*, A.*Ag.*657 : pl. in Hsch.

**στροβύλος,** prob. misspelling of στρόβιλος, *Gloss.* **II.** = *stropylus*, *Aegyptia avis per os coiens*, ib.

**στρογγῠλ-αίνω,** *make round* or *globular*, *Hippiatr.*104 :—Pass., *Placit.*3.4.5. **-ευμα,** ατος, τό, = γογγύλωμα, Hsch. (pl.). **-ίζω,** *round off*, τὰ νοήματα D.H.*Lys.*13 :—Pass., Id.*Comp.*14. **-ιον,** τό, *round pot*, *flask*, *POxy.*155.8 (vi A.D.). **-ισμα,** ατος, τό, *pithy*, *terse expression*, Anon.*Fig.* p.111 S.

⊛ **στρογγύλλω,** (στρογγύλος) *round off*, *make round*, Aret.*SA*1.8 (Pass.). **II.** *twirl*, *spin*, χειρὶ σ. κρόκην *AP*7.726 (Leon.) : dub. sens. in Archig.ap.Gal.8.90.

**στρόγγυλμα,** ατος, τό, *globular morsel*, *grain*, Aglaïas 11.

**στρογγῠλό-γλῠφος,** ον, *with carved mouldings*, Hero *Aut.*25.7. **-δίνητος** [ῑ], ον, *turned into a round shape*, *rounded*, Archestr. *Fr.*4.11. **-ειδής,** ές, *of round form*, τύπωμα Plu.2.1121c, cf. Dsc.3.54 (interpol.). Adv. -δῶς Alex.Aphr.*Pr.*1.107, Alex.Trall. 2. **-καυλος,** ον, *with a round stalk*, Thphr.*HP*7.4.5. **-λοβος,** ον, *with round pods*, ib.8.5.2. **-ναύτης,** ου, ὁ, *merchant-seaman*, Ar.*Fr.*861. **-πλευρος,** ον, *round-sided*, of an eel, Stratt. 44. **-πους** δίφρος, chair *with round legs*, *IG*2$^2$.1414.13 (-πος lapis). **-πρόσωπος,** ον, *round-faced*, Arist.*HA*495$^a$2, *Phgn.*807$^b$33, *PPetr.*3 p.4 (iii B.C.), *PCair.Zen.*76.9 (iii B.C., τρ-), *PGrenf.*1.25 (2).12 (ii B.C.), etc.

⊛ **στρογγύλος** [ῠ], η, ον, *round*, *spherical*, opp. πλατύς, Hp.*VM*22, *Art.*61, Hdt.2.92, Ar.*Nu.*676, 751, 1127, Pl.*Phd.*97e, etc. ; ἄτομοι -ώταται Epicur.*Ep.*1 p.21 U. ; λίθοι σ. *pebbles*, X.*Eq.*4.4 ; ξύλα σ. *unsquared* logs of timber, opp. σχιστά and πελεκητά, Thphr.*HP*5.5.6 ; of the sphere, σ. τὴν ὄψιν Hermipp.4 ; of gourds, Epicr.11.25 (anap.). **2.** *curved*, τὸ σ., opp. τὸ εὐθύ, Pl.*Men.*74d, cf. 75a ; σ. καὶ προμήκη σχήματα Id.*Ti.*73d ; δίφροι σ. *IG*5(1).1390.23 (Andania, i B.C.) ; πόλοι, of dowel-pins, ib.2$^2$.1675.11 ; σ. ἀνάτριψις, = ἐγκάρσιος ἀ., Gal.6.93. **3.** of persons, *round*, *compactly formed*, Xenarch. 4.8, cf. Pl.*Smp.*189e ; so of lions, opp. μακρός, Arist.*HA*629$^b$34 (Comp.) ; of dogs, σκέλη X.*Cyn.*4.1. **4.** of ships, σ. νῆες *round*, i.e. *merchant-ships*, as opp. to the long narrow warships (μακραὶ νῆες), Hdt.1.163, cf. Th.2.97 ; πλοῖον X.*HG*5.1.21, D.20.162. **b.** of cups and vessels, Alex.270, Men.30. **5.** of sail, *rounded*, *full*, App.*BC*4.86. **II.** metaph. of words and expressions, *well-rounded*, *compact*, *terse*, σ. ῥήματα Ar.*Ach.*686 ; σ. ὀνόματα ἀποτετόρνευται Pl.*Phdr.*234e, cf. Plu.2.45a ; λέξις D.H.*Comp.*7 fin., *Is.*3 ; αὐτοῦ τοῦ στόματος τὸ σ. his *compactness*, *terseness* of expression (of Euripides), Ar.*Fr.*471. Adv. -λως, συστρέφειν τὰ νοήματα καὶ σ. ἐκφέρειν express *neatly and tersely*, D.H.*Isoc.*11 ; προστιθεὶς τὸ διότι -ώτατα *as tersely as possible*, Arist.*Rh.*1394$^b$33. **2.** Adv., -λως καὶ Λακωνικῶς βιωσομένους wishing to live *closely*, i.e. *simply*, *economically*, Plu.2.157b.

**στρογγῠλό-της,** ητος, ἡ, *roundness*, Pl.*Men.*73e, 74b, Arist. *Metaph.*1035$^a$14, Thphr.*HP*4.12.2. **-τομία,** ἡ, *operation for abscess*, Cass.Fel.18. **-ω,** *to be round*, Al. 3*Ki.*7.31. **II.** Pass. **στρογγυλόομαι,** *to be* or *become round*, *globular*, *Placit.*3.4.2, Erot. s. v. αἰθόλικες. **2.** σ. τὴν ὄψιν *to have the semblance of roundness*, opp. to being really round, Plu.2.1121b.

⊛ **στρογγύλ-ωμα** [ῠ], ατος, τό, *pillow* or *mosquito-net*, τριχῶν Al. 1*Ki.* 19.16. ⊛ **-ωσις,** εως, ἡ, *a rounding*, Hp.*Art.*61. **II.** *trench*(?), Lxx 1*Ki.*17.20 cod. A, cf. Aq., Sm., Thd. 1*Ki.*26.5. **-ώψ,** ῶπος, *round-eyed*, synon. of Κύκλωψ, Serv.Dan.ad Verg.*A.*8.649.

**στροιβᾶν·** ἀντιστρέφειν, Hsch. **στροίβηλος·** ἔπαρμα πληγῆς ἐν κεφαλῇ, Id. **στροιβός·** δεινός, Id. (fort. δῖνος).

⊛ **στρομβ-εῖον,** τό, Dim. of στρόμβος 5, θύμβρης Nic.*Th.*629. **-έω,** = στροβέω, συστρέφω, Phot. **-η,** ἡ, = στρόμβος 1, Sch. rec. A *Pr.* 887. **-ηδόν,** Adv. *like a top*, *whirling*, *APl.*4.300. **-ιλον·** περιδεδινημένον, Hsch.

**στρομβοειδής,** ές, and **-ώδης,** ες, *like a* στρόμβος 3 : τὰ στρομβώδη *spiral shells and the creatures in them*, *snails*, etc., freq. in Arist., as *HA*528$^b$8, *PA*684$^b$34, al., also Xenocr.ap.Orib.2.58.91 ; τὰ στρομβοειδῆ Arist.*HA*528$^b$17, cf. Xenocr.ap.Orib.2.58.79.

**στρόμβ-ος,** ὁ, *a body rounded* or *spun round* : hence, **1.** *top*, Il. 14.413 ; ὥσπερ σ. στρέφεσθαι Luc.*Asin.*42. **2.** = στροφάλιγξ, *whirlwind*, A.*Pr.*1084 (anap.), prob. in Id.*Fr.*195.3. **3.** *trumpet-shell*, Arist. *HA*492$^a$17, al. ; *sea-snail*, Artem.2.14 ; of a *shell used as a trumpet*, *conch*, Lyc.250, Theoc.9.25, Plu.2.713b. **4.** *snail*, Arist.*HA*548$^a$18, cf. 530$^a$6, *PA*661$^a$23. **5.** = στρόβιλος 6, Nic.*Th.*884. **6.** *spindle*, Lyc.585. **-όω,** 3 sg. στρομβοῖ· συστρέφει καὶ τὰ ὅμοια, Hsch. **-ώδης,** v. στρομβοειδής.

**στροπά·** ἀστραπή, Πάφιοι, Hsch.

**στροταγέω, στρόταγος, στρότος,** v. στρατηγέω, στρατηγός, στρατός.

**στρουθ-άριον** [ᾰ], τό, Dim. of στρουθός 1, Eub.123, M.Ant.5.1. **-ειος,** α, ον, *of an ostrich*, ᾠόν *PMich.Zen.*9$^r$.2 (iii B.C.) ; ὀειὸν (= ᾠόν) τρούθ[ιον] *Sammelb.*7243.21 (iv A.D.) ; cf. στρουθός fin. **2.** (sc. κρέας), = *passerina caro*, *Gloss.* (written *stroiton*). **II.** -ειον μῆλον, τό, a kind of *quince*, *Pyrus Cydonia*, *AP*6.252 (Antiphil.) ; so without μῆλον, Nic.*Al.*234 ; also written στρούθιον, Thphr.*HP*2.2.5, Dsc.1.115, cf. Philem.1, Gal.6.450 (parox.), 602. **III.** -ειον, = στρουθός III. *soap-wort*, *Saponaria officinalis*, Orph.*A.*960, Hp.*Nat Mul.* 32, Thphr.*HP*6.4.3, Eub.104 (lyr.), *PCair.Zen.*430.15 (iii B.C.), Dsc.2.163, *POxy.*1088.26 (i A.D.), Aret.*CA*1.2 ; usu. written **στρούθιον** in codd., but **στρούθειον** in Orph. l. c., corroborated by the metre and by **στρούθεον** in *PCair.Zen.* l. c. ; the metre is doubtful in Eub. l. c. ; both στρούθιον and -ειον are found in *PHolm.*, 15.2, al., 25.22. **-ίας,** ου, ὁ, = στρουθός IV, *Com.Adesp.*592. **-ιασμός,** ὁ, = Lat. *petigo*, *scab*, *Gloss.* **-ίζω,** *chirp like a* στρουθός, *twitter*, Ar.*Fr.*947 = *Com.Adesp.* 1155, Thd.*Is.*10.14, 38.14. **II.** *cleanse with the herb* στρούθειον, *PSI*4.429.16 (iii B.C.), Dsc.2.74, *PHolm.*15.2. **-ινος,** η, ον, *of* στρούθειον, στέφανος Ath.15.679b. **-ίον,** τό, Dim. of στρουθός 1, Anaxandr.7, Arist.*HA*539$^b$33, 613$^a$29, Lxx *To.*2.10, *Ps.*10(11).1, al., *Ev.Matt.*10.29, Gal.6.435 ; τὸ σ. ἡ συκαλίς Id.15.882 ; **στρουθίν,** *Gloss.* **II.** στρούθιον, v. στρούθειος III. **-ίς,** ίδος, ἡ, Dim. of στρουθός 1, Alex.144. **-ισμός,** ὁ, *cleansing with* στρούθειον, *PHolm.*15.1, 25.21. **-ίων,** ωνος, ὁ, = sq., *Gloss.*

**στρουθο-κάμηλος** [ᾰ], ὁ, also ἡ, *ostrich*, from its camel-like neck, D.S.2.50, Str.16.4.11, Sor.1.84, Gal.6.702, 705 ; *struthiocamelus*, Plin.*HN*10.143. **II.** = στρούθειον III, Ps.-Dsc.2.163. **-κέφᾰλος,** ον, *with the head of a* στρουθός, Plu.2.520c, Gal.19.454. **-πῐαστής,** οῦ, ὁ, (πιάζω) *birdcatcher*, *fowler*, Hsch. s. v. ἰξευτής, Aët.2.231. **-πους,** πουν, gen. ποδος, *with sparrow's* or *ostrich's feet* (for authorities differ, Sch.Ar.*Av.*877 explaining it of *large*, Plin.*HN*7.24 of *small* feet).

**στρουθός,** ὁ, also ἡ (v. infr.), (στροῦθος acc. to Chares ap.Hdn.Gr. 1 p. xix L.) *sparrow*, *Fringilla domestica*, Il.2.311 (fem.), Sapph.1.10, Hdt.1.159, Ar.*V.*207, *Av.*578, Epich.45, Ael.*NA*17.41, *Edict. Diocl.*4.35, etc. ; οἱ μικροὶ σ. Gal.6.700 ; interpol. in κατάμομφα δὲ φάσματα στρουθῶν A.*Ag.*145 (lyr.). **2.** σ. αἱ μεγάλαι *ostriches*, X. *An.*1.5.2, cf. Gal.6.702, *POxy.*920.8 (ii/iii A.D.) ; οἱ μεγάλοι σ. Gal.6.788 : also σ. κατάγαιος (i.e. the bird that runs, does not fly), Hdt.4.175, 192 ; χερσαῖος Ael.*NA*14.13 ; ὁ σ. ὁ Λιβυκός Arist.*PA*695$^a$17, 697$^b$14, etc. ; ὁ ἐν Λιβύῃ Id.*HA*616$^b$5 ; ὁ Ἀράβιος Heraclid.Cum.2 : simply στρουθός, ἡ, Ar.*Ach.*1105, *Av.*875 ; ὁ, Luc.*Dips.*6. **3.** of the mythic birds of Lake Stymphalus, *IG*14.1293C. **4.** σ. κατοικάς *hen*, Nic.*Al.*60, 535. **II.** a flat fish, *flounder*, *Pleuronectes flesus*, Ael.*NA*14.3. **III.** σ., ὁ, a plant, = στρούθειον, Thphr.*HP*9.12.5. **IV.** σ., ὁ, *lewd fellow*, *lecher*, Hsch. (Hsch. cites a form **στροῦς** : a form ***τρουθός** may perh. be inferred from the pr. name Τρούθων *IG*12(9).249*B*75 (Eretria, iii B.C.), compared with **Στρούθιππος** ib.241.83 (ibid., iv B.C.) ; cf. στρούθειος I. 1.)

**Στρουθοφάγοι** [ᾰ], οἱ, *Ostrich-eaters*, name of a tribe of Ethiopians, Agatharch.57, Str.16.4.11.

**στρουθ-ώδης,** ες, *like an ostrich*, Sch.Ar.*Av.*877. **-ωτός,** ή, όν, *painted* or *embroidered with birds*, Sophr.100.

**στρουκτώριον,** τό, prob. *dining-room* (Lat. *structor* = τραπεζοκόμος, παραθέτης), *SIG*823*C*4 (Delph., i/ii A.D.).

**στροφαῖος,** α, ον, (στροφεύς II) epith. of Hermes, *standing as porter at the door-hinges*, Ar.*Pl.*1153, with a play on the etymol. meaning, *twisty*, *shifty*, v. Sch. ad loc.

**στροφάλ-ιγξ** [ᾰ], ιγγος, ἡ, (στρέφω, στροφαλίζω) *whirl*, *eddy*, ἐν στροφάλιγγι κονίης Il.16.775, Od.24.39 ; μετὰ σ. κ. Il.21.503 ; ἀελλάων Opp.*H.*1.446 ; καπνοῖο A.R.4.140 ; of water in a bucket, Id.3.759 ; of an earthquake, Q.S.3.64 : metaph., σ. μάχης *AP*7.226 (= Anacr. 100) ; ἄοκνος σ., of existence, Dam.*Pr.*148. **II.** *curve*, *bend*, D.P. 162, 584, Q.S.8.236 ; *orbit* of a heavenly body, Arat.43, Orph.*Fr.*

236; of the bowels, Androm.ap.Gal.14.34. III. *anything of a round shape*, e.g. *a cheese*, Nic.*Th.*697. IV. = στρόφιγξ, *pivot, hinge*, Epigr. in *An.Par.*4.385. ⊛**-ίζω**, lengthd. form of στρέφω, ἠλάκατα σ. *twist* the wool, i.e. spin, Od.18.315; φόβην *AP*6.218. 8 (Alc.). **-ος**, ὁ, = ῥόμβος A. I or 2a, used in magic, Marin.*Procl.*28.

**στροφ-άς**, άδος, ὁ, ἡ, (στρέφω) *turning round, revolving, circling*, of the constellations, ἄρκτου στροφάδες κέλευθοι the Bear's *circling* paths, S.*Tr.*131 (lyr.), cf. D.P.594; στροφάδεσσιν ἀέλλαις *whirlwinds*, Orph.*A.*677; of cranes *on their return*, Arat.1032; of fish, στροφάδες παρὰ πέτρην Numen.ap.Ath.7.319b; of worms, Hsch. II. Στροφάδες (sc. νῆσοι), αἱ, *the Drifting Isles*, a group not far from Zacynthus, supposed to have been once floating, Apollod.1.9.21, Str. 8.4.2, St.Byz. **-άω**, *turn hither and thither*, δαίμων.. βίου στροφόωσα πορείην v.l. for στρωφῶσα in Nonn.*D.*48.381. **-εῖον**, τό, *twisted noose, cord*, X.*Cyn.*2.6, Poll.5.29 (gen. pl. στροφίων). II. *machine* used in the theatre in representing heroes translated to heaven or dying at sea or in war, Id.4.127,132. 2. *windlass, capstan*, Luc. *Nav.*5: hence, b. στροφεῖα, τά, perh. *dues payable by ships for the use of a windlass*, i.e. *harbour-dues*, *IG*11(2).138*B*8 (Delos, iv/iii B.C.), 203*A*30 (iii B.C.). 3. = στροφεύς II, Kourouniotes Ἐλευσινιακά I. 190 (Eleusis, iv B.C., pl.). III. = στρόφιον II, *POxy.*33 iii 5 (ii A.D.). **-εύς**, έως, ὁ, *vertebra*, Poll.2.130. II. *socket* in which the pivot of a door (cf. στρόφιγξ) moved, Ar.*Th.*487, *Fr.*255, Hermipp. 47.9 (anap.), Thphr.*HP*5.6.4, Kourouniotes Ἐλευσινιακά I.190 (Eleusis, iv B.C.), *IG*11(2).287*B*148 (Delos, iii B.C.), Plb.7.16.5. 2. *the pivot itself*, = στρόφιγξ, ὁ κατὰ τοῦ ὀλμίσκου βεβηκὼς σ. S.E.*M.*10. 54, cf. *BGU*1201.17 (i B.C./i A.D.), *PMag.Osl.*1.136, Luc.*DMeretr.* 12.3. 3. part of a weasel-trap, *Gloss.* ⊛**-έω**, *cause the colic* (cf. στρόφος II), Ar.*Pax* 175. **-ή**, ἡ, *turning*, e.g. of a horse, X.*Eq.*7. 15,17, 10.15; *revolving, circling*, ἄρκτου στροφαί S.*Fr.*432.11; τοῦ σώματος (sc. τῆς σελήνης) Epicur.*Ep.*2 p.41 U.; ὡρῶν Pl.*Lg.*782a; of a snake, Arist.*PA*692ᵃ6; ἐν στροφαῖσιν ὀμμάτων with *rolling* of the eyes, E.*HF*932. 2. *twist*, such as wrestlers make to elude their adversary, πάσας στροφὰς στρέφεσθαι Pl.*R.*405c: metaph., *slippery trick, dodge*, οὐκ ἔργον ἔστ' οὐδὲν στροφῶν Ar.*Pl.*1154, cf. *Ec.*1026, *Ra.*775; δημηγόρους εὐπιθεῖς σ. A.*Supp.*623. 3. in Music, *twist* or *turn*, κατακάμπτειν τὰς σ. Ar.*Th.*68. 4. *winding up* of a winch, *CPHerm.* p.79 (iii A.D.). 5. *turning of a road*, τὸν νεκρὸν.. ἐν ταῖς σ. μὴ καττιθέντων μηδαμεῖ *Schwyzer* 323 *C*33 (Delph., iv B.C.). 6. metaph., (στρέφω B. III) *occupation, concern*, περί τι Herm. *in Phdr.* p.67 A. II. *turning* of the Chorus: hence, *the strain sung during this evolution, strophe* (cf. ἀντίστροφος IV, ἀντιστροφή I), Pherecr.145. 9, Phld.*Po.Herc.*994 *Fr.*19, D.H.*Comp.*19, Ph.2.484, etc. III. στροφαί· ἀστραπαί, Hsch. (v. στροπά). IV. *transmutation* of metals, Zos.Alch. p.195 B. **-ίγγιον**, τό, Dim. of sq., θύρας Zonar. ⊛**-ιγξ**, ιγγος, ὁ (ἡ, *EM*446.31): (στρέφω):—*pivot, axle* or *pin on which a body turns*, E.*Ph.*1126. 2. pl., *pivots working in sockets*, at top and bottom of a door, Thphr.*HP*5.5.4, al., *PCair.Zen.* 782(*a*).7 (iii B.C.), Plu.*Rom.*23, Gal.*UP*1.15. 3. metaph., γλώττης σ., of a *well-hung* tongue, Ar.*Ra.*892; of the vertebrae, Pherecr. 236, Pl.*Ti.*74a,b. 4. νύμφη ἡ ἐν τῷ σ., dub. sens. in *AJA*30.249 (Cyprus). **-ικός**, ή, όν, *fit for turning, turned*, v. λίσχροι. **-ίολος**, ὁ, *fringe, border*, ἐν ταῖς σκουτλώσεσι Hero *Geom.*23.3. **-ιον**, τό, Dim. of στρόφος, *band worn by women* round the breast, Pherecr. 100, Ar.*Lys.*931, *Th.*139,255, *Fr.*647, *IG*2².1388.19. II. *headband worn by priests*, etc., Philoch.141 B, *IG*5(1).1390.179 (Andania, i B.C.), Plu.*Arat.*53, Arr.*Epict.*3.21.16, *SIG*869.21 (Eleusis, ii A.D.); cf. στροφεῖον III. III. = ἱμάς, *boxing-glove*, Philostr.*Gym.*10 (14). **-ιος**, ὁ, = *Vertumnus*, *Gloss.* **-ιοῦχος**, ὁ, epith. of Hermes, *wearing the* στρόφιον, cj. for τροφ- in Orph.*H.*28.5. ⊛ **-ις**, ιος, ἡ, *slippery fellow, twister*, Ar.*Nu.*450 (anap.), Poll.6.130; cf. στρέφω B. II. ⊛ **-ίς**, ίδος, ἡ, = στρόφιον I, E.*Andr.*718. **-ίσκος**, ὁ, Dim. of στρόφιον II, *Inscr.Prien.*202.13 (ii B.C.?).

**στροφοδῑνέομαι**, Pass., *wheel eddying round*, of vultures wheeling round their nest, A.*Ag.*51 (anap.): cf. στρεφεδινέω.

**στροφόομαι**, Pass., (στρόφος II) *have the colic*, Dsc.1.30, Arr.*Epict.* 4.9.4, Gal.6.462; εἰλεωδῶς στροφουμένης τῆς μήτρας prob. in Sor.2. 29.

**στροφοποιός**, ὁ, = *ressor*, i.e. *restio, ropemaker*, *Gloss.*

**στρόφ-ος**, ὁ, (στρέφω) *twisted band* or *cord*, ἐν δὲ σ. ἦεν ἀορτήρ on it (the wallet) was *a cord* to hang it by, Od.13.438: generally, *cord, rope*, Hdt.4.60, *IG*2².1631.336. 2. *women's girdle*, A.*Th.* 872 (anap.); prob. for στρόβους, Id.*Supp.*457. 3. *swaddling-band*, *h.Ap.*122,128. II. *twisting of the bowels, colic*, σ. μ' ἔχει τὴν γαστέρα Ar.*Th.*484, cf. Hp.*VM*10, *Aph.*4.11, Damox.2.25, Sor.2.85, Gal.6.263; κοιλίης Hp.*Acut.*37. **-ώδης**, ες, *of the nature of colic*, dub. l. in Hp.*Prorrh.*1.156; περιωδυνία Bacch.ap.Erot. s.v. τρύζειν; *causing colic*, Hp.*Vict.*2.56. Adv. -δῶς Archig.ap.Gal.8.110. **-ωμα**, ατος, τό, *hinge, joint*, Hero *Bel.*89.2, Orib.49.4.19. II. = στρόφιγξ, στροφεύς, τῶν θυρῶν *IG*11(2).287*A*102 (Delos, iii B.C.). III. = *vertebra*, *Gloss.* **-ωμάτιον**, τό, Dim. of foreg. I, Hero *Spir.*1. 11. ⊛ **-ωτήρ**, ῆρος, ὁ, μεθ' οὗ δεσμοῦνται αἱ κῶπαι, *Gloss.* (sine alio interpr.). **-ωτός**, ή, όν, *made with pivots, turning on them*, θυρώματα Lxx *Ez.*41.23(24).

**στρύζω**, = τρύζω, Erot. s.v. τρύζειν, Gal.18(2).134.

**Στρῡμονίας**, Ion. -ίης ἄνεμος, ὁ, *a wind blowing from the Strymon* towards Greece, i.e. *a NNE. wind*, Hdt.8.118.

**στρύμοξ**· ξύλον μεμηχανημένον ἐν ταῖς ληνοῖς πρὸς τὴν τῶν σταφυλῶν ἔκθλιψιν, Hsch.

**Στρῡμών**, όνος, ὁ, *the Strymon*, a river of Thrace, Hes.*Th.*339, A. *Ag.*192 (lyr.), Hdt.1.64, etc.:—Adj. **Στρῡμόνιος**, α, ον, *of the Strymon*, A.*Pers.*867 (lyr.), E.*Rh.*386 (anap.), etc.; pecul. fem. **Στρῡμονίς**, ίδος, St.Byz.: also **Στρυμονικός**, ή, όν, Str.7 *Fr.*32, Ptol.*Geog.*3.12.7.

**στρυννύζω**, v. στρηνύζω.

⊛ **στρυπτηρία**, ἡ, = στυπτ-, *Inscr.Prien.*364.15 (Thebes on Mycale, iii/ii B.C.).

**στρῡφαλίς**, ίδος, ἡ, = τροφαλίς, *cheese*, Lxx 1*Ki.*17.18 cod. A.

**στρυφνός**, ή, όν, of taste, *sour, harsh, astringent*, Pl.*Ti.*65d, X. *Hier.*1.22, Thphr.*HP*3.12.4, Gal.6.68,450; τὸ σ. συνάγειν τὰν γεῦσιν πέφυκε Ti.Locr.101c; σ. μῆλα Antiph.188; βόλβα (because served with vinegar, etc.) Luc.*Epigr.*46; οἶνος Dsc.5.6; γάλα Sor.1.91; μᾶζα Hsch.; στρυφνοῦ καὶ αὐστηροῦ τὸ κοινὸν γένος ὀνομάζεται στῦφον Gal.6.475; τὸ σ. defined as more στῦφον than τὸ αὐστηρόν, ib.778, 15.641. II. metaph. of temper or manner, *harsh, austere*, σ. ἦθος Ar.*V.*877, Arist.*HA*491ᵇ16; ἄνθρωποι X.*Cyr.*2.2.11 (Comp.); οἱ σ. Arist.*EN*1157ᵇ14; ἐν τοῖς σ. καὶ πρεσβυτικοῖς ib.1158ᵃ2; οἴνου πολίτης ὢν κρατίστου στρυφνὸς εἶ Amphis 36. Adv. -νῶς, ἐχθροῖς προσφερόμεθα Eust.931.45. 2. of style, *harsh, austere*, D.H.*Amm.* 2.2; τὸ τραχὺ καὶ σ. (v.l. στριφνόν) Id.*Comp.*22. III. *stiff, rigid*, dub. in Hp.*VM*14,15 (στριφν- cod. M); οὐρή dub. in Opp.*C.*1.411 (v.l. στριφνή).

⊛ **στρύφνος**, f.l. for στρύχνος, *Gp.*2.5.4 codd.

**στρυφνότης**, ητος, ἡ, *rough, harsh taste, sourness*, Arist.*Cat.*9ᵃ30, *Pr.*864ᵇ5: pl., Diocl.*Fr.*138, Gal.6.465. II. metaph., *harshness* of style, prob. in D.H.*Dem.*34 (στριφνότης (q.v.) codd.); περὶ τὸ ἦθος Plu.*Mar.*2.

**στρυφνόω**, *act as an astringent*, τοῦ στρυφνοῦντος πικροῦ v.l. in Plu.2.624e. II. metaph. of style, *make harsh*, Eust.1181.27.

**στρύχνον**, τό (also στρύχνος, ὁ, v. infr.), name of various plants: 1. σ. ἁλικάκκαβον, *winter cherry, Physalis Alkekengi*, Dsc. 4.71, Plin.*HN*21.177. 2. σ. κηπαῖον, *hound's berry, Solanum nigrum*, Dsc.4.70; v.l. στρύχνος, ὁ, and so Thphr.*HP*7.15.4. 3. σ. μανικόν (στρύχνος μανικός ib.9.11.6), *thorn-apple, Datura Stramonium*, Dsc.4.73. 4. σ. ὑπνωτικόν (στρύχνος ὑπνώδης Thphr.*HP*9. 11.5), *sleepy nightshade, Withania somnifera*, Dsc.4.72 (στρύχνος is f.l. for στρίφνος in Lxx *Jb.*20.18, and στρύχνον for τρύχνον in Nic.*Th.* 878).

**στρῶμα**, ατος, τό, (στρώννυμι) *anything spread* or *laid out for lying* or *sitting upon, mattress, bed*, ἀσπάλαθοι δὲ τάπησιν ὁμοῖον στρῶμα θανόντι Thgn.1193, cf. *PEleph.*5.5 (iii B.C.), etc.; used on the funeral bier, *IG*12(5).593.3 (Ceos, v B.C.), *Schwyzer* 323 *C*29 (Delph., iv B.C.): pl., *bedclothes, coverings of a dinner-couch*, Ar.*Ach.*1090, *Nu.* 37,1069, al.; of a bird's nest, Arist.*HA*616ᵃ2; σ. πορφυρόβαπτα Pl. Com.208; coupled with ἱμάτια, ἔπιπλα, Lys.32.16; αἴρεσθαι τὰ σ. Ar.*Ra.*596 (lyr.); σ. ὑποσπᾶν to pull the *bed* from under one, D.24. 197: cf. στρωματεύς I. 2. *horsecloth, horse-trappings*, X.*Cyr.*8.8.19, Antiph.109, cf. Poll.1.183; *trappings* of an ass, Luc.*Asin.*38. II. *pavement*, *IG*1².313.71, 2².1666*B*37, 7.4255.6 (Oropus, iv B.C.), *Inscr.Délos* 502*A*24 (iii B.C.), *IG*12(8).380 (Thasos), etc.

**στρωμᾰτ-εύς**, έως, ὁ, *coverlet, bedspread*, Antiph.38, Alex.115, Thphr.*HP*4.2.7; also, = στρωματόδεσμον, Poll.7.79, condemned in this sense by Phryn.379. 2. in pl. στρωματεῖς, *patchwork*, as title of literary *Miscellanies*, Gell.*Praef.*7; the στρωματεῖς of Plu. is cited by Eus.*PE*1.7. II. *a flat fish marked with divers colours*, Philo ap.Ath.7.322a. **-ίζω**, *load* a beast of burden with a pack-saddle, Poll.10.14 (Pass.), Hsch. II. *pave*, *IG*2².1668.9. **-ιον**, τό, Dim. of στρῶμα, *mattress* or *cushion*, *PCair.Zen.*60.9, 241.3 (iii B.C.), al.: pl., *bedclothes*, M.Ant.5.1, *POxy.*1645.9 (iv A.D.). **-ίτης** ἔρανος [ῑ], ὁ, a picnic *at which the guests found their own* στρώματα, Cratin. 445, cf. Hsch. s.v.

**στρωμᾰτό-δεσμον**, τό, *a leathern* or *linen sack in which slaves had to tie up the bedclothes* (στρώματα), Ar.*Fr.*253, Pherecr.185, X.*An.*5. 4.13, Aeschin.2.99; σ. συσκευάσασθαι Pl.*Tht.*175e; δῆσαι Arist. *Mu.*398ᵃ8: also **-δεσμος**, ὁ, Amips.38, Plu.*Caes.*49, cf. Phryn. 379. **-φθορέω**, *spoil carpets*, v. σωματοφθ-. **-φύλαξ** [ῠ], ἄκος, ὁ, ἡ, *one who has the care of the bedding, tablecloths*, etc., Plu.*Alex.*57.

**στρωμνάομαι**, in pf. part. ἐστρωμνημένος· ὁ ἐν τῇ στρωμνῇ μένων, Phot.

**στρωμνή**, Aeol. -α, Dor. -ά, ἡ, *bed spread* or *prepared*: generally, *bed, couch*, Sapph.*Supp.*23.21, Pi.*P.*1.28, A.*Ch.*671, E.*Ph.*421, Th.8. 81, X.*Smp.*4.38, etc.; *mattress, bedding*, Id.*Mem.*2.1.30, Pl.*Prt.* 321a, Sor.1.85, Gal.6.44, 16.568; σ. ἄφθιτος, of the golden fleece, Pi.*P.*4.230; στρωννύτω στρωμνάς, of the *lectisternium*, *SIG*589.44 (Magn. Mae., ii B.C.), cf. 1106.95 (Cos, iv/iii B.C.).

**στρωμνηφόρος**, ον, *carrying the bedding*, Theognost.*Can.*96.

**στρώννυμι** and -ύω, v. στόρνυμι.

**στρῶσις**, εως, ἡ, *spreading, covering*, Heraclid.Cum.5; τοῦ χοῦ *POxy.*1631.27 (iii A.D.); esp. of the *lectisternium*, *IG*2².1329.15 (ii B.C., pl.). II. *paving*, ib.4²(1).102.52 (Epid., iv B.C.), *Ephes.* 3 p.100 No.8 (i A.D.); ὁδῶν D.H.3.67, Str.5.3.8; τῆς πόλεως Fitzler *Steinbrüche* p.109 (i A.D.); λίθου στρώσει πεποικιλμένα J.*BJ*7.8.3, cf. *IG*14.317 (Thermae Himer.).

**στρω-τήρ**, ῆρος, ὁ, *rafter laid upon* the bearing beam; mostly in pl., Ar.*Fr.*72; of a drunken man, ὅταν μὴ δύνηται τις τοὺς στρωτῆρας ἢ τὰς δοκοὺς ἀριθμεῖν Thphr.*Vert.*12, cf. *IG*2².1672.63, al., 4²(1).102. 179,235 (Epid., iv B.C.), Ph.*Bel.*87.25, Plb.5.89.6, *IG*12(3).324.11 (Thera, ii A.D.): generally, *cross-beam*, Hp.*Art.*7,78; expld. by σανίδες εἰς ὀροφὴν ἐπιτήδειοι, *AB*302; opp. δοκοί, Str.16.4.13; difft.

from δοκοί and ἀπότομα, *BGU*1546.8 (iii B.C.). **-τηρίδιον,** τό, Dim. of foreg., Hsch., Suid. s.v. γερράδια. **-τήριον,** τό, = foreg., *EM* 228.49. ❀ **-της,** ου, ὁ, *one that spreads*, esp. *one that gets ready the beds and dinner couches*, Heraclid.Cum.5, Plu.*Pel*.30. **-τός,** ή, όν, *spread, laid, covered*, λέχος Hes.*Th*.798, E.*Or*.313; λέκτρα Id. *Hel*.1261; στρωτὰ φάρη, = στρώματα, S.*Tr*.916.

❀ **στρωφάω,** poet. and Ion. Frequentat. of στρέφω, *turn constantly*, ἠλάκατα σ. *keep turning* the wool, i.e. spin, Od.6.53, al.; πηδάλιον παλάμῃ *steer*, *AP*9.242 (Antiphil.): metaph., βουλὴν ἀμφὶ πολὺν στρώφα χρόνον A.R.3.424; δαίμων.. βίου στρωφῶσα πορείην Nonn.*D*.48.381:—Pass., *turn oneself about, keep turning*, κατ' αὐτοὺς στρωφᾶτ' Il.13.557; *roam about, wander*, δηρὸν ἑκὰς σ. 20.422; ἐπὶ δῆμόν τε πόλιν τε *visit* cities, Hes.*Op*.528; καθ' Ἑλλάδα.., ἀνὰ νήσους Thgn.247; ἀνὰ τὴν πόλιν Hdt.2.85; ἄλλῃ κἄλλῃ δωμάτων S.*Tr*.907: hence, *move freely in* a place, *abide* there, κατὰ μέγαρα Il.9.463, cf. Hp.*Art*.60; ἐν λέχει στρωφώμενος, i.e. claiming a husband's rights, A.*Ag*.1224; ἐν νέοις στρωφωμένη E.*Alc*.1052; ἐν Διδύμοις στρωφωμένου ἠελίοιο Orph.*Fr*.285.16; of the heavenly bodies, *revolve*, Man.2.34. II. intr., στρωφᾶν for στρωφᾶσθαι, ἐπὶ γαῖαν A.R.3.893, cf. Orph.*Fr*.285.46.

**στρωφέομαι,** *keep turning round*, ἐν κύκλῳ Aret.*CD*1.4.

**στυαγόν·** τὸ στόμα, παραγώγως, Hsch.

**στύβη,** ἡ, = *stuppa*, *Gloss.* (fort. στοιβή).

**στῠγάνωρ** [ᾱ], ορος, ὁ, ἡ, (στυγέω, ἀνήρ) *hating the male sex*, στρατός, of the Amazons, A.*Pr*.724.

**στύγαξ,** ὁ, f.l. for στύπαξ or στύππαξ in Eust.1650.60.

**στύγει** (post στυπάζει)· στρέφεται, Hsch.

**στῠγερ-ός,** ά, όν, poet. Adj. *hated, abominated, loathed*, or *hateful, abominable, loathsome*, freq. in Ep. and Trag., both of persons and things; σ. Ἀΐδης Il.8.368; Ἐρινῦς Od.2.135; δαίμων, πόλεμος, γάμος, πένθος, etc., 5.396, Il.4.240, Od.1.249, Il.22.483, etc.; μοῖρα, μοῦσα, A.*Pers*.909 (anap.), *Eu*.308 (anap.); γᾶ S.*Ph*.1175 (lyr.); μάτηρ E.*Med*.113 (anap.); τυραννίη Xenoph.3.2: c. dat., *hateful* to one, Il.14.158; λάθα Πιερίσι σ. S.*Fr*.568 (lyr.). 2. *hateful, wretched*, βίος Id.*Tr*.1017 (s. v. l., lyr.); σ. πάθεα, σ. ἐγώ, Ar.*Ach*.1191, 1208 (paratrag.); πλοῦτος.. θνάσκοντι -ώτατος Pi.*O*.10(11).90. II. Adv. -ρῶς *to one's sorrow, miserably*, Il.16.723, Od.23.23, S.*Ph*.166 (lyr., nisi leg. σμυγερῶς). **-ώπης,** ες, (ὤψ) *horrible*, ζῆλος Hes.*Op*.196: **-ωπός,** όν, χῶρος σ. ἰδέσθαι *AP*9.662 (Agath.): and **-ώψ,** acc. -ῶπα, dub.l. in Orph.*Fr*.126.

**στῠγ-έω,** Il.7.112, Hdt.7.236, E.*El*.1017, etc.: aor. 1 ἔστυξα, opt. στύξαιμι Od.11.502 (v. infr. II): aor. 2 ἔστῠγον (κατ-) 10.113, Il.17.694: later aor. 1 ἐστύγησα A.*Supp*.528 (lyr.), E.*Tr*.710: pf. ἐστύγηκα J.*Ap*.2.24, (ἀπ-) Hdt.2.47:—Pass., fut. στυγήσομαι in pass. sense, S.*OT*672: aor. ἐστυγήθην A.*Th*.691, E.*Alc*.465 (lyr.): pf. ἐστύγημαι Lyc.421; ἔστυγμαι Hsch.:—poet. Verb (also in Hdt. and later Prose, Phld.*Lib*. p.13 O., J. l.c.), *hate, abhor*, c. acc., Il.20.65, al., Hes. (*Th*. 739, al.), and Trag. (v. infr.); also in Thgn.278, Pi.*Fr*.203.2, Emp.115.12, 116, Hdt.7.236; Com. only in paratragoedic and lyric passages, Ar.*Ach*.33 (cf. Sch. ad loc.), 472, *Th*.1144 (lyr.), Diph.73.5, *Com.Adesp*.1278; never in Att. Prose: stronger than μισέω, for it means *to show hatred*, not merely to feel it, τὸ πρᾶγμα.., ἣν μὲν ἀξίως μισεῖν ἔχῃ, στυγεῖν δίκαιον E.*El*.1017: c. inf., *hate* or *fear* to do a thing, Il.1.186, 8.515, S.*Ph*.87, A.R.2.628:—Pass., *to be abhorred, detested*, τὸν μέγα στυγούμενον A.*Pr*.1004; Φοίβῳ στυγηθέν Id.*Th*. 691; τί δ' ἐστὶν.. πρός γ' ἐμοῦ στυγούμενον; what is *the horrid thing that I have done?* S.*Tr*.738. II. in aor. 1, *make hateful*, τῷ κέ τεῳ στύξαιμι μένος καὶ χεῖρας then *would I make* my courage and my hands *a hate and fear* to many a one, Od.11.502: but this aor. is used in the common sense by A.R.4.512, *AP*7.430 (Diosc.). **-ημα,** ατος, τό, *an abomination*, E.*Or*.480; ὦ σ., in addressing a person, Babr.95.62. **-ηρός,** ά, όν, = στυγητός, Hsch. **-ητός,** όν, *hated, abominated, hateful*, Ἥρα σ. A.*Pr*.592: abs., Ph.2.202, *Ep.Tit*.3.3, *POxy*.433.28; σ. ἔρως Hld.5.29.

**Στύγιος** [ῠ], α, ον, A.*Pers*.668 (lyr.); also ος, ον E.*Med*.195 (anap.), *Hel*.1339 (lyr.), Plu. (v. infr.): (Στύξ):—*Stygian, of the nether world*, ἀχλύς A. l.c.; δόμος S.*OC*1564 (lyr.); ποταμός Pl.*Phd*.113c. II. = στυγητός, *hateful, abominable*, λῦπαι, ὀργαί, E. ll.cc.; ἡμέρα Plu.2.828a.

**στυγν-άζω,** (στυγνός) *to have a gloomy, lowering look*, ἐπὶ τῷ λόγῳ *Ev.Marc*.10.22: abs., *PMag.Leid.W*.5.5, Steph. *in Hp*.2.514 D.; of threatening weather, *Ev.Matt*.16.3. **-ᾰσις,** εως, ἡ, = στυγνότης, Apollod.ap.Stob.1.49.50. **-ία,** ἡ, *sadness, gloom*, Sch.Il.24.253.

**στυγνοποι-έω,** *sadden, make gloomy*, *Gloss.* **-ός,** όν, *making sad* or *gloomy*, Sch.D Il.14.158, Sch.S.*Tr*.1049.

**στυγν-ός,** ή, όν, *hated, abhorred*, of persons and things, Archil.80; ἄτη A.*Pr*.886 (anap.); ὦ στυγνὲ δαῖμον Id.*Pers*.472; ὦ στυγνὸς αἰών S.*Ph*.1348; λῷβαι Id.*Aj*.561, etc.: c. dat., *hateful* or *hostile* to one, A.*Pers*.286 (lyr.), S.*El*.918. Adv. Comp. -οτέρως, ἔχειν πρός τινα *BGU*1301.8 (ii/i B.C.). II. *gloomy, sullen*, πρόσωπον A.*Ag*.639, E.*Alc*.777; ὀφρύων νέφος Id.*Hipp*.172 (anap.), cf. 290; στυγνοὶ κλαίουσιν Ἔρωτες Mosch.3.67; ὁρᾶν στυγνός, opp. φαιδρός, X.*An*.2.6.9, cf. 11, Hp.*Mul*.2.182, Lxx *Is*.57.17, Arr.*Epict*.3.5.9 (Comp.), Aret.*SD*1.5; νύξ Lxx *Wi*.17.5; οἱονεὶ πυρὸς εἰσπεσόντος εἰς ὕδωρ στυγνὸν σέλας ἐκπέμπουσα [λιγνύς] Adam.*Vent*.34; σ. διαγωγαὶ καὶ ἀναγνώσεις καὶ διηγήματα, opp. ἐρεθιστικὰ τῶν ἀφροδισίων, Sor.2.46; στυγνὸς μὲν εἴκων δῆλος εἶ *sullenly, with an ill grace*, S.*OT*673: neut. as Adv., στυγνὸν οἰμώξας Id.*Ant*.1226. **-ότης,** ητος, ἡ, *gloominess, sullenness*, Alex.197, Plb.3.20.3; βλέμματος Plu.*Mar*.43; of the sky, Plb.4.21.1. **-όω,** v. sq. (dub. sens.):—Pass., *to be gloomy*, κλαίοντι καὶ ἐστυγνωμένῳ ὄμμα *AP*9.573 (Ammian.).

**στύγνωσον·** χώρισον, Hsch.

**στῠγόδεμνος,** ον, *hating marriage*, νόος *AP*10.68 (Agath.).

**στύγος** [ῠ], εος, τό, *hatred*, A.*Ch*.392 (lyr.); esp. as expressed in looks, *sullenness, gloom*, τὸ δύσφρον σ. Id.*Ag*.547; φρενῶν σ. ib.1308, *Ch*.81 (lyr.). II. *object of hatred, abomination*, Id.*Ag*.558, A.R.4.445, *AP*7.405 (Phil.); of persons, δεσπότου σ. thy *hated* lord, A.*Ch*. 770; στύγη θεῶν, of the Erinyes, Id.*Eu*.644, cf. *Th*.653, *Ch*.1028; τοῦτ' ἐμήσατο σ. this *deed of horror*, ib.999(991). Rare, exc. in A.

**στῦλ-άριον,** τό, Dim. of στῦλος (prob. 4), *PIand*.11.8 (iii A.D.). **-ίδιον,** τό, Dim. of στῦλος, *small pillar*, Str.1.3.4. **-ίζω,** dub. sens. in *Ostr.Strassb*.669.8 (ii A.D.). **-ίον,** τό, Dim. of στῦλος, dub. in *Sammelb*.2025b. ❀ **-ίς,** ίδος, ἡ, Dim. of στῦλος I, *IG*1².313.95, *OGI*332.9 (Elaea, ii B.C.), Ph.*Bel*.74.8, D.H.3.21: pecul. acc. στυλλεῖδαν *CIG* 3293 (Smyrna). II. *mast to carry a flag at the stern*, Eratosth. *Cat*.35, Plu.*Pomp*.24, cf. Poll.1.90. III. *cartilage which separates the nostrils*, Id.2.79. **-ίσκος,** ὁ, Dim. of στῦλος, *peg*, Hp.*Mochl*. 38, Str.3.4.17, Orib.49.4.69. II. = στυλίς II, Eust.1039.38. III. *small stanchion*, Hero *Bel*.88.1; also, *small pillar* on which to mount an astronomical instrument, Procl.*Hyp*.3.19: dub. sens. in *IG*11(2).161 *B* 101 (Delos, iii B.C.). **-ίτης** [ῑ], ου, ὁ, *standing* or *dwelling on a pillar*, Suid.: fem. -ῖτισσα *Stud.Pont*.3.134 (Amasia).

❀ **στῦλο-βάτης** [ᾰ], ου, Dor. **-βάτας,** ὁ, *base of a column, stylobate*, Pl.Com.42, *Delph*.3(5).88 *C* 2 (iv B.C.), *IG*2².1668.40, 4²(1).102.8, al. (Epid., iv B.C.), *Inscr.Délos* 365.30 (iii B.C.), Hero *Aut*.16.1, Vitr. 3.4.2, 4.8.2. **-γλύφος** [ῠ], some sort of *pillar*, dub.l. in Ph.Byz. *Mir*.1.1. **-ειδής,** ές, *like a stilus, styloid*, ἀποφύσεις Ruf.*Onom*.142 (στηλ- codd.); ἀπόφυσις Gal.2.252, 271; ἐκφύσεις Id.*UP*7.19. (βαρβαρίζοντες -ειδεῖς προσαγορεύουσι (cf. στῦλος 4) Gal.*UP* l.c., who glosses it by γραφιοειδής: but Lat. *stilus* has ĭ, not ȳ.) II. Adv. -δῶς *in pillar form*, cj. in Epicur.*Ep*.2 p.47 U. ❀ **-πῐνάκιον** [ᾰ], τό, *pillar with figures on it*, *AP*3 tit. (Cyzicus).

❀ **στῦλος,** ὁ (fem. at Epidaurus, *IG*4²(1).102.66, al. (iv B.C.), but also masc. there, ib.109 iii 92 (iii B.C.)), *pillar* (= κίων acc. to Gal.6.544), esp. as *a support* or *bearing*, Hdt.2.169, *IG* ll. cc.; στέγης A.*Ag*.898; δόμων E.*IT*50; σ. μονόλιθοι *BGU*1713 (ii/iii A.D.): metaph., σ... οἴκων εἰσὶ παῖδες ἄρσενες E.*IT*57, cf. *Ep.Gal*.2.9, 1*Ep.Ti*.3.15. 2. σ. πυρός Lxx *Ex*.13.21, *Apoc*.10.1. 3. *wooden pole*, E.*Fr*.203, Plb.1.22.4; [σκηνῆς] tent-*poles, uprights*, opp. διατόναια, *PCair.Zen*. 353.9 (iii B.C.); *plank*, Hp.*Art*.47. 4. *stile* for writing on waxed tablets; wrongly used in this sense by Greek speakers at Alexandria and in the East acc. to Herophil.ap.Gal.*Anat.Ad* xiv (Arabic version, ii p.183 ed. M. Simon, Leipzig 1906); cf. στυλοειδής.

❀ **στῦλ-όω,** *prop* or *stay with pillars*, Apollod.*Poliorc*.145.10 (Pass.); ἀχυρὼν ἐστυλωμένος *Inscr.Délos* 445.22 (ii B.C.): metaph., ζωὴν στυλώσασθαι *give stay to one's* life (by means of children), *AP*7.648 (Leon.). **-ωμα,** ατος, τό, *prop, support*, Apollod.*Poliorc*.145. 7. **-ωσις,** εως, ἡ, *colonnade*, *PTeb*.781.15 (ii B.C.). **-ωτός,** ή, όν, *having pillars*, Sch.Il.20.11.

**στύμα,** v. στόμα. II. dub. sens. in *PTeb*.815 *Fr*.6 iii 58 (iii B.C.), and in Hsch. s.v. στυαγόν.

**στῦμα,** ατος, τό, (στύω) *priapism*, Pl.Com.173.20.

**στύμεον,** τό, dub. sens. in *Schwyzer* 664.21 (Orchom. Arc., iv B.C.).

**στῦμμα,** ατος, τό, (στύφω) *astringent*, Aret.*SA*2.2; esp. used for thickening oil, that it may retain scent better, Dsc.1.63, Gal.6.424, 12.605.

**στυμνός,** ή, όν, *solid*, στυπτηρία *PHolm*.18.4 (στημ- Pap.); glossed by σκληρός in Hdn.Gr.1.174, Hsch. **στύμος·** στέλεχος, κορμός, Id.

**Στύμφᾱλος,** Ion. **-ηλος,** ἡ, Paus.8.22.2 (also ὁ, Plb.4.68.6, Str.8.8.4):—*Stymphalus*, a city and mountain of Arcadia, Il.2.608, *IG*5(2). 357.74 (Stymphalus, iii B.C.), etc.:—Adj. **Στυμφάλιος** [ᾰ], α, ον, ib.94, Pi.*O*.6.99, etc.; fem. ❀ **Στυμφαλίς,** ίδος, A.R.2.1053, Str.8.6.8, 8.8.4; Ion. **-ηλίς** Hdt.6.76.

**Στύξ,** ἡ, gen. Στυγός, (στυγέω) *the Styx*, i.e. *the Hateful*, Il.8.369: also the nymph of this river, Hes.*Th*.361. 2. *a well of fatal coldness in Arcadia*, Hdt.6.74, Str.8.8.4, Paus.8.18.5. II. as Appellat., *monster, reptile*, ἄπρωτον.. ὑπὸ στυγός (στύγος cod.M) A.*Ch*. 532 (sed leg. στύγους). 2. *piercing chill, as of frost*, in pl., αἱ στύγες εἰσδύονται εἰς τὰ σώματα Thphr.*CP*5.14.4. 3. *hatred, abhorrence*, esp. of mankind, Alciphr.3.34. 4. = σκώψ, Ant.Lib.21.5, Hygin. *Fab*.28.4 Rose, Hsch.: cf. στρίξ.

**στῠπάζει·** βροντᾷ, ψοφεῖ, ὠθεῖ, Hsch. **στύπαξ,** v. στύππαξ. **στύπεα,** = στέλεχος, Id. **στύπη,** = στύπος, Id. **στῠπογλύφος,** ον, *cutting, working trunks* or *stems*, Id.

**στύπος** [ῠ], εος, τό, *stem, stump, block*, στιβαρὸν σ. ἀμπέλου A.R.1.1117; pl., Plb.1.48.9, 21.27.4; also = κύτος, σ. ὅλμου Nic.*Th*.951, *Al*.70.

**στύπος,** = στύππη, κάλοι ἀπὸ στύπου Gal.19.126.

**στύππαξ,** ὁ, = στυππειοπώλης, nickname of Eucrates, Ar.*Fr*.696 (vv. ll. στύπαξ, στύγαξ).

**στυππεῖνος,** η, ον, *of tow*, *PRev.Laws* 103.2 (iii B.C.), condemned by Phryn.233; also **στυππύϊνος,** *PMich.Zen*.120.3 (iii B.C.); and **στιππόϊνος, στιππύϊνος, στιπύϊνος** (qq.v.); **στύππινος,** *IG*2². 1414.26, 1527.34, *PCair.Zen*.755.6 (iii B.C.), Ph.*Bel*.102.15, D.S.1. 35, cf. 11. II. metaph., *like tow, feeble*, γέρων στύππινος *Com. Adesp*.855.

⊛ **στυππεῖον**, τό, *the coarse fibre of flax* or *hemp, tow, oakum*, Hdt. 8.52, X.*Cyr*.7.5.23, D.47.20, Aen.Tact.33,35, Plb.1.45.12, 5.89.2, D.S.14.51, Plu.*Cic*.18, Gal.16.622, App.*Hann*.33, *Ill*.11, Luc.*Asin*. 31. (In Papyri and codd. written also στιππύον, στιππεῖον (qq. v.), στυπεῖον, στυπίον, στυππίον (cf. στυππίον· τὸ λίνον, Hsch.); **στυπεῖον** is confirmed by *IG*2$^2$.1631.336, **στυππεῖον** by *PCair.Zen.* 177.6, 514.7 (iii B.C.), and by στυππειοπλόκος, στυππειουργός (qq. v.); cf. [στυπ]πέον *IG*2$^2$.1629.1150.)
⊛ [**στυπ**]**πειο-πλόκος**, ὁ, = sq., *IG*2$^2$.1673.15,41. **-ποιός**, ὁ, *tow-maker*, *EM*339.56 (στυππιο-). **-πώλης**, ου, ὁ, *dealer in oakum*, Ar.*Eq*.129, Critias 70 D., *IG*2$^2$.1570.24, 1572.8.

**στυππειουργός**, ὁ, written **στυππεουργός**, *tow-worker*, *PCair.Zen.* 489.12 (iii B.C.); also written στιππυουργός, στιπεουργός, στιππουργός, στιπουργός (qq. v.).

**στύππη**, ἡ, = στυππεῖον, J.ap.Suid. s. v.

⊛ **στυπτηρ-ία**, Ion. -ίη (sc. γῆ), ἡ, name of any of a group of *astringent substances* containing (a) alum or (b) ferrous sulphate (χαλκῖτις (q. v.)), Hdt.2.180, freq. in Hp. (e.g. *Ulc*.14), Arist.*HA* 547a20, *Mir*. 842b22, *PCair.Zen*.326bis26 (iii B.C.), Ti.Locr.99d, Sor.1.50, Aret.*CA* 1.9, *POxy*.1429.4 (iii/iv A.D.), *PHolm*.1.4,7, al. II. in Egypt, *the alum monopoly*, *POxy*.2116 (iii A.D.). **-ιᾰκὸν δέρμα**, = *aluta*, *Gloss*. **-ίζουσα**, = *aqua qua alumen lavatur*, ib. **-ιος**, α, ον, *treated with alum*, φῦκος *PHolm*.16.32. **-ιώδης**, ες, *like* στυπτηρία, *containing it*, ὕδατα Hp.*Aër*.9, Thphr.*CP*2.5.1; γῆ Arist.*Pr*. 937b23, Str.3.2.8; λουτρόν Antyll.ap.Orib.10.3.1; τὰ σ. Gal.6.35, al.

**στυπτικός**, ή, όν, (στύφω) *astringent*, Diocl.*Fr*.130, Thphr.*Od*.21, Dsc.1.30.3 (Comp.), Ath.Med.ap.Orib.*inc*.23.27, Plu.2.624e, Sor.1. 61, Gal.6.426, Antyll.ap.Orib.10.24.6; τὰ σ. *astringents*, Hp.*Aph*.7. 37, Theo Sm. p.14 H. Adv. -κῶς Paul.Aeg.3.18.

**στῠρᾰκ-ᾶτον**, τό, *styrax-wine*, interpol. in Orib.5.33.12. **-ίζω**, (στύραξ (B)) *thrust with the butt end of a lance*, Hsch., *EM*732.6. II. (στύραξ (A)) *to be like the gum of the storax*, esp. in smell, Dsc.2. 84. **-ῐνος**, η, ον, (στύραξ (A)) *made of storax*, χρῖσμα Id.1.66; ἔλαιον *Edict.Diocl.Delph*.8. 2. *made of the wood of the tree* στύραξ, ἀκοντίσματα Str.12.7.3; ῥάβδος Lxx *Ge*.30.37. **-ιον**, τό, Dim. of στύραξ (B), ἀκοντίου Th.2.4, Aen.Tact.18.10, prob. cj. in Luc.*Tox*. 55. II. Dim. of στύραξ (A) I, *POxy*.1142.5.

**στύραξ** [ῠ] (A), ᾰκος, ὁ, *storax*, Mnesim.4.62 (anap.), Arist.*HA* 534b25, Thphr.*HP*9.7.3, Dsc.1.66, Sor.2.29, Aret.*CD*1.2, *PSI*4.297. 12 (V A.D.). II. στύραξ, ὁ or ἡ, *the tree producing this gum*, *Styrax officinalis*, fem. in Hdt.3.107, masc. in Str.12.7.3, Plu.*Lys*.28.

⊛ **στύραξ** [ῠ] (B), ᾰκος, ὁ, *spike at the lower end of a spear-shaft*, X. *HG*6.2.19, Pl.*La*.184a; *shaft*, ἀκοντίων Onos.10.4 (pl.).

**στυρβάζω**, = τυρβάζω, *AB*303.

**στυριόω**, dub. sens., perh. *guarantee* by promise of oath, συγγραφὴ ..μὴ ἐστυριωμένη Mitteis *Chr*.31 iv 18 (ii B.C.): hence **στυρίωσις**, εως, ἡ, ib. vii 2.

**στῠτικός**, ή, όν, (στύω) *causing priapism*, σ. δυνάμεις *aphrodisiacs*, Phylarch.35(b) J. (στυπτ- codd.Ath.).

**στυφαλμεῖν**· σκυβαλίζειν, Hsch. **στυφᾶν**· βροντᾶν, Id. **στυφεδανός**, ὁ, v. τυφεδανός.

**στῠφελ-ιγμός**, ὁ, *ill-usage, abuse*, Ar.*Eq*.537 (pl.). **-ίζω**, *strike hard*, τρὶς δέ οἱ ἐστυφέλιξε..ἀσπίδ' Ἀπόλλων Il.5.437; πολλὰ δὲ χερμάδια μεγάλ' ἀσπίδας ἐστυφέλιξαν 16.774; στυφέλιξε δέ μιν (sc. ἐγχείη) 7.261; ὡς ὁπότε νέφεα Ζέφυρος στυφελίξῃ *drives away* the clouds, 11. 305; εἰ..κ' ἐθέλῃσιν Ὀλύμπιος..ἐξ ἑδέων στυφελίξαι *thrust* us from our seats, 1.581; τὸν δ'..ἐκ δαιτύος ἐστυφέλιξε 22.496; οὐδέ μιν ἐκτὸς ἀταρπιτοῦ ἐστ. Od.17.234; τινὰ κορύνῃ A.R.2.115; κῦμα..νaύτας ἐς κοίλην ἐστυφέλιξεν ἅλα *AP*7.665 (Leon.); ἐκ θεμέθλων ἄνακτας ib.15. 22 (Simm.); Ποσείδαν..ἐστυφέλιξε πόντον Alc.26. 2. generally, *treat roughly, maltreat*, Il.21.380,512, Od.18.416; τινὰ ὀνείδεσι A.R. 1.273.—Ep. word, used by Pi.*Fr*.225, S.*Ant*.139 (lyr., abs.); also σ. τρώματα Hp.*Fract*.31: in late Prose, Plu.*Nob*.9. **-ός**, ή, όν, A.R.2.323, also ός, όν A.*Pers*.965 (lyr.), Parth.*Fr*.29.4, etc.:—*hard, rough*, στυφελοῦ..ἐπ' ἀκτᾶς A. l. c. (lyr.); in later Poets, ἀκτὴ σ. A.R. l. c., etc.; σκόπελος *AP*11.31 (Antip.); ὀδούς Opp.*C*.3.442. II. of flavour, *astringent, sour, acid*, μέλι *AP*4.1.22 (Mel.); σταγών ib.9. 561 (Phil.). III. metaph., *harsh, severe, cruel*, ἐφέται A.*Pers*.79 (lyr.); Κόλχοι Orph.*A*.1012. (στυφελός was a Clitorian word for *hard, rough*, and used at Cyrene for χέρσος, acc. to Zenod.ap.Sch. A.R.2.1005.) **-ώδης**, ες, = στυφελός, Q.S.12.449.

**στυφλάριος**, α, ον, *rough, rocky*, *IG*7.2808.8 (Hyettus, iii A.D.): but perh. a pr. n.

**στύφλος**, ον, = στυφελός I, στύφλους παρ' ἀκτάς A.*Pers*.303; τῆσδ' ἀπὸ στύφλου πέτρας Id.*Pr*.748; στύφλος δὲ γῆ καὶ χέρσος S.*Ant*.250; ὑπὸ στύφλοις πέτραις E.*Ba*.1137, cf. *IT*1429, Lyc.737.

**στῠφόεις**, εσσα, εν, = στυπτικός, v.l. in Nic.*Al*.375 (v. Sch. l. c.); cf. στύφω.

**στῠφοκόπος**, ὁ, = ὀρτυγοκόπος, player of the game described by Phot., Suid. s. h. v., Ar.*Av*.1299 (στυφοκόμπου codd. and Sch., but cf. Poll.7.136, 9.107: Dionysius ap.Sch.Ar. read (or conjectured) ὀρτυγοκόμπου: στυφοκόμπος = ὁ μάχιμος ἀλεκτρυών acc. to Hsch.).

**στύφος**· κέρδος, Hsch.

**στῠφ-ός**, ή, όν, *astringent*, οἶνος *Gp*.6.11.2 (Comp.), but σ. οἶνος, = *viscidus*, *Gloss*., and so perh. *Gp*. l. c.: metaph., Νεμέσεως ἀστὴρ.. τῇ γενέσει σ. Vett.Val.2.23. **-ότης**, ητος, ἡ, *thickness, denseness*, opp. μανότης, Plu.2.96f. **-ω**, Hp.*Int*.14, etc.: aor. inf. στῦψαι Hsch.:—Pass. (v. infr.):—*contract, draw together*, τὴν κοιλίην στύφεσθαι *becomes costive*, Hp.*Aër*.7; στῦψαι πλάδον Aret.*CA*1.1; esp. of an astringent taste, χείλεα στυφθεὶς *having* his lips *drawn up* by the taste, *AP*9.375; δέρμα ἐστυμμένον, i.e. made water-tight, Gal.12.846; *mix with* στυπτηρία, *PMag.Leid.V*.6.18; aor. 2 part. Pass. στυφέντα in this last sense, *PHolm*.24.13 (στυφόεντα cj. Lagercrantz): metaph. of sounds, φωναὶ στύφουσαι τὴν ἀκοήν, opp. διαχέουσαι, D.H.*Comp*.15. 2. in dyeing, *treat* fabrics, etc., *with a mordant*, Lysis ap.Iamb.*VP*17.76; στῦψον τῇ ἰσάτι *prepare* it *by a preliminary dyeing* with woad, *PHolm*.21.42; στύφει [τὴν ἄγχουσαν] *fixes* alkanet, ib.15.18. 3. intr. in Act., στύφει κατ' ὀλίγον τὸ οὖρον gradually *diminishes*, Hp.*Int*.14. II. intr., *to be astringent*, Arist.*Pr*.863b17, Philonid.ap.Ath.15.675e, Dsc.1.116,118, Sor. 1.81, Gal.6.68, Hices.ap.Ath.7.321a. 2. metaph., *to be harsh, austere, gloomy*, Them.*Or*.27.339a, cf. Hsch. s. v. στύψαι. [ῡ, Nic.*Al*. 278, cf. 375 (ἐν-); ῠ to be assumed in στυφέντα (s. v. l.).] **-ώδης**, ες, *rather sour-tempered*, *Cat.Cod.Astr*.8(1).184.

**στυφωνία**, ἡ, = στοιχάς, Ps.-Dsc.3.26; but τυφωνία is prob., v. Apul. *Herb*.42.

**στῦψις**, εως, ἡ, *contraction, astringency*, Thphr.*Od*.32, Diph.Siph. ap.Ath.3.80f, Dsc.1.39, Sor.1.81, Phylotim.ap.Orib.4.10.2, Aret.*SA* 2.2; of food which has a *costive* effect, Hp.*Acut*.10, cf. Aen.Gaz.*Ep*. 20; *contraction of the skin*, Sch.Il.14.216. II. in dyeing, *steeping of the fabric in an astringent solution*, to prepare it for taking the dye, Arist.*Col*.794a29 (pl.). III. in perfumery, *thickening of oil with certain drugs* to make it retain the scent longer, Dsc.1.6 (pl.).

**στύω**, fut. στύσω [ῡ] *AP*10.100 (Antiphan.): aor. 1 inf. στῦσαι Ar. *Lys*.598:—*make stiff* or *erect*: sens. obsc., *penem erigere*, Ar. l. c.:— Pass. (with intr. pf. Act. ἔστυκα Id.*Av*.557, *Lys*.989, Lacon. 3 pl. -αντι ib.996), Id.*Av*.1256; ἐπί τινα Luc.*Alex*.11: aor. Pass. ἐστύθην Diog.*Ep*.35.3.

**στωά**, v. στοά.

**Στώαξ**, ἄκος, ὁ, (στοά) *one of the Porch*, i.e. *a Stoic*, Herm.Iamb.1.

**στωΐδιον** (or **στῴδιον**, as *EM*486.20, 550.6), τό, Dim. of στοά, *IG* 11(2).203 *B* 4, *C* 15 (Delos, iii B.C.), D.L.5.51; *shed* as protection for besiegers, Ath.Mech.31.6; cf. στοΐδιον.

**στωϊκ-εύομαι**, *play the Stoic*, πρός τινα Numen.ap.Eus.*PE*14. 7. ⊛ **-ός**, ή, όν, (στοά) *of a colonnade* or *porch*: hence, *Stoic* (because Zeno taught in the στοὰ Ποικίλη), οἱ τῆς Σ. αἱρέσεως ἡγεμόνες D.H. *Comp*.2, cf. Str.13.1.57, 14.6.3; ἡ Σ. Phld.*Rh*.2.227 S., D.L.6.14; οἱ Σ. *the Stoics*, Phld.*Rh*.2.296 S., cf. *IG*3.1359, D.L.7.5; οἱ Σ. φιλόσοφοι *Act.Ap*.17.18. (**Στοϊκός** in *AP*9.496 (Athenaeus).)

**στώμιξ**, ικος, ἡ, *wooden beam*, Hsch.

**στωμοδόκον**· στωμύλον, Hsch.

**στωμῠλ-εύομαι**, Med., = στωμύλλομαι, Alciphr.2.2; τι περί τινος Phot.*Bibl*. p.415 B. **-ήθρα**, ἡ, = στωμυλία, Numen.ap.Eus.*PE*14. 7; **στωμυλλήθρα**, Phryn.*PS* p.5 B. **-ηθρος**, ον, *talkative, fluent*, Aristaenet.1.1; ὦ στωμυλῆθραι δαιταλεῖς, as if from στωμυλήθρας, ὁ, unless it be abstract for concrete, *Com.Adesp*.30 D. **-ία**, ἡ, *wordiness*, Ar.*Ra*.1069, Plb.9.20.6; *persiflage, small talk*, *AP*7.222 (Phld.); σ. Ἀττική Stesimbr.4 J.

**στωμῠλιοσυλλεκτάδης**, ου, ὁ, *gossip-gleaner*, Ar.*Ra*.841.

⊛ **στωμ-ύλλω**, (στωμύλος) *to be talkative, chatter, babble*, τριβολεκτράπελα Ar.*Nu*.1003; Com. of birds, Id.*Ra*.1310. II. more freq. in Med. στωμύλλομαι, Id.*Th*.1073, *Ra*.1071: fut. στωμῠλοῦμαι Id.*Eq*. 1376: aor. ἐστωμυλάμην Id.*Ach*.579, *Th*.461 (cj. Dind.): also in good sense, *talk, chat*, εἰς ἀλλήλους Id.*Pax* 995. **-υλμα**, ατος, τό, = στωμυλία, Id.*Ra*.943. II. of persons, *chatterbox*, ib.92, quoted by D.H.*Rh*.10.18. **-ύλος** [ῠ], ον, also η, ον Luc.*Musc.Enc*.10, *Im*.15: (στόμα):—*wordy, talkative*, Ar.*Ach*.429, Pl.*Erx*.397d, Theoc.5.79, etc.; τὰ σ. ταῦτα *this nonsense*, *AP*9.39 (Music.): in good sense, *fluent, suave*, σ. εὐτυχίη, of Menander, ib.187; = *lepidus*, *Gloss*.: c. inf., ὁμιλῆσαι σ. Luc.*Im*.15; λαλῆσαι σ. Alciphr.3.65: so ἔχουσί τι σ. have a *gossipy* flavour, Demetr.*Eloc*.151. Adv. -λως Poll.5.161: Comp. -ωτέρως Lyd.*Mag*.3.73.

**στωνευμέναν**· διαστρέφουσαν συντόνως, Hsch.

⊛ **σύ** [ῠ], *thou*: Pron. of the second pers.:—Ep. nom. **τύνη** [ῡ] Il.5. 485, al. (Lacon. **τούνη** Hsch.); Aeol. **σύ** Sapph.*Supp*.16.6, 21.9; Dor. **τύ** [ῠ] Pi.*O*.1.85, Epich.34, al., Theoc.3.33, etc.; Boeot. **τού** [short syll.] Corinn.*Supp*.2.83, A.D.*Pron*.55.6 (also **τούν** ib. 50.27, 55.6): Nom. σύ, Od.18.31, A.*Ag*.1035, Ar.*Nu*.29, etc.; voc., Od.21.193, Ar.*Ach*.165, *Pl*.1069.—Gen. **σοῦ**, *h.Hom*.29.4, elsewh. only Att., Ar.*Ach*.302, etc.; enclit. σου, S.*Ph*.761, *OT*538, etc.; never in Hom., who uses σεῦ, Il.3.206, al., σέο ib.446, al. (also in Lyr., Archil.(?) in *PLit.Lond*.54 B.3.65), σεῖο Il.3.137, al.; also σέθεν 1.180, al. (which also occurs in Lyr., Sapph.33, B.10.9, and Trag., A.*Th*.264, al.), and as enclit. σευ, Il.5.811, al., σεο 1.396: Hdt. has only σέο 1.124, σεο (enclit.) ib.9, σεῦ ibid., 3.42,85,7.38, σευ (enclit.) 3.36,134,7.49:—Dor. τεῦ, τευ, Theoc.5.19, 10.36, etc.; rarely τέο, Alcm.17; lengthd. **τεοῦ** Epich.145, Sophr.84, and **τεοῖο** Il.8.37, 468; Boeot. **τεῦς** Corinn.24; Dor. **τεοῦς** Sophr.59; also **τιοῦς** A.D. *Pron*.74.27; **τεῦς** Theoc.2.126; τοι v.l. in Id.7.25; enclit. τεος Sophr.83; Cret. **τέορ** Hsch.; other Dor. forms are τίω, τίως, both Rhinth.13, **τίος** A.D.*Pron*.75.24.—Dat. **σοί**, Il.1.158,167, Archil.88, Mimn.8, Sapph.7,99, A.*Pr*.3, Hdt.3.42,6.86.α',7.52, etc.; Dor. **τοί** Alcm.86 (oxyt.); Dor., Lesb., and Ion. enclit. τοι Alcm.33, Sapph. *Frr*.2.2,8, Archil.79, Hippon.20, Anacr.44, 75.3, Pi.*N*.3.76, B.10. 101, Hdt.1.115, 3.35,63,85; in Hom., Lesbian Lyr., and Ion. Lyr. and Prose τοι is always enclit., σοί never enclit. (τοί and σοι are not found exc. σοι Od.3.359, 11.381, σ(οί) Il.1.170, and in codd. of Pi.*P*.

4.270, 9.55; rarer than τοι in Hdt., 3.69, al.); in Att. both σοί and σοι (enclit.) are used (σοί Ar.*Nu.*361, etc., σοι ib.87, etc.), τοί and τοι are not used; σοι is never elided exc. in Il.1.170, τοι is elided in Od. 1.60, 347, Alc.55, Id.*Oxy.*1788 *Fr.*15 ii 9, Sapph.28.2; Ep. and Lyr. also **τεΐν**, Il.11.201, Od.4.619, Epigr.ap.Hdt.5.60, 61, Ar.*Av.*930; also **τίν** [ῐ], Alcm.16, Pi.*P.*1.29, 8.68 (dub. l.); **τίν** [ῑ], Id.*I.*6(5).4, Theoc.2.20 (τίν before a consonant, Pi.*O.*10(11).93); also **τεί** Alcm.53; τίνη Rhinth.13.—Acc. **σέ**, Il.6.256, al.; enclit. σε, 1.26, Sapph.1.2, *Supp.*23.9, Hdt.3.42, etc.; in late Gr. σέν, *Anatolian Studies* p.76; Dor. **τέ** Alcm.52, Pi.*O.*1.48, Theoc.1.5, Call.*Fr.*114; τ' v.l. (cod. R) in Ar.*Ach.*779 (on the accent v. A.D.*Pron.*54.14, 83.4); τρέ (leg. τFέ) Hsch.; or (enclit.) τυ *IG*4²(1).121.69 (Epid., iv B.C.), Ar.*Eq.*1225, *Ach.*730 (dub. in *Ach.*779), Theoc.1.56, 78, etc.:—also τίν Corinn.4, Cerc.7.6, Theoc.11.39, 55, 68. 2. in combination with γε, **σύ γε, σέ γε**, etc. (cf. ἔγωγε), *thou at least, for thy part*, freq. in Hom. and Att.; Dor. τύγε Epich.[272], Timocr.1 (v.l. τύ γα); τύγᾰ Theoc.5.69, 71; Boeot. **τούγα** A.D.*Pron.*55.6: dat. **σοί γε** Il.1.557: acc. **σέ γε** 10.96, etc.:—also **σύ περ** 24.398. 3. σύ c. inf. (as imper.), Hdt.3.134, 4.163. II. Dual nom. and acc. **σφῶϊ**, Il.1.336, 4.286, al., *you two, both of you*; **σφώ** (not σφῴ, cf. A.D. *Pron.*85.17), Il.1.574, 11.782, 13.47, S.*OC*344, 1543, etc.—Gen. and Dat. **σφῶϊν**, Il.4.341, al.; contr. σφῷν once in Hom., Od.4.62, and always in Att. (Hdn.Gr.1.475) and Trag., e.g. A.*Pr.*12, S.*OC*342, *OT*1495, Pl.*Lg.*892e (codd. Pl. have σφῶϊν in *Tht.*193c, al., σφῶν *Euthd.*273e, al.). None of these forms are enclit., A.D.*Pron.*38.9, 85.12; cod. A of Pl.*Lg.*658c, 673e, 689a wrongly makes σφῳν enclit.; Ζεὺς σφὼ is prescribed in Il.15.146 by Hdn.Gr.2.93.—σφῶϊ is never dat.; in Il.4.286 it is the acc. depending on κελεύω; σφῶϊν is never acc.; in Od.23.52 it is dat. commodi. III. Plur. nom. **ὑμεῖς**, Il.2.75, al. (before a vowel, 4.246, 7.194, al.), Pherecyd.Syr. 11, Democr.29ᵃ, Hdt.3.72, etc., *ye, you*; Aeol. and Ep. ὔμμες Il.1.274, al., Sapph.24.25; Dor. ὑμές Sophr.60, Ar.*Ach.*760, 761, 862; ὑμέν *SIG*685.118 (Crete, ii B.C.), *GDI*5155.6 (ibid., ii B.C.); Boeot. οὑμές Corinn.6; a resolved form ὑμέες, Parth.*Fr.*14, is a poetic licence (so A.D.*Pron.*93.3) rather than genuine Ionic (v.l. in Hdt.8.22).—Gen. **ὑμῶν**, Ar.*Ach.*143, etc.; ὑμέων (disyll.) Il.7.159, Od.13.7, al., Archil.74.6 (ὑμῶν codd.), Sol.11.5 (v.l. ὑμῶν); ὑμέων also Hdt.3.73, 6.130, al.; as trisyll., Herod.2.27; ὑμείων Il.4.348, 7.195, al.; Dor. ὑμέων Sophr.46; also ὑμῶν, A.D.*Pron.*95.23; Aeol. ὐμμέων Alc. 96; Boeot. οὑμίων Corinn.22.—Dat. **ὑμῖν**, Od.2.46, Hdt.1.126, etc.; Ion. enclit. ὗμιν A.D.*Pron.*97.28, also Dor., Sophr.91; Dor. (not enclit.) ὑμίν [ῐ] Id.92; ὑμίν [ῐ] also in S.*Aj.*864, 1242, *OT*991, 1402, *Ant.*308, *El.*804, al. (but ὗμιν shd. perh. be restd. where the sense needs an enclitic on the principle stated by A.D.*Pron.*35.6, 36.5, *Synt.*130.23); ὕμιν (as enclit.) is prescribed by Hdn.Gr. (2.124) in Il.24.33, by *EM*432.34 in Od.1.376, 2.141, etc.:—Aeol. and Ep. **ὔμμι, ὔμμιν**, Od.2.316, 11.336, al., Hes.*Sc.*328, Sapph.14, Alc.*Supp.* 26.9, Pi.*O.*11(10).17.—Acc. **ὑμᾶς**, Ar.*Ach.*325, etc. (-ῠ Orph.*A.*820, v.l. in S.*Ph.*222; ὗμας or (more prob.) ὕμας is required by the metre in Babr.9.9, 47.11); Ion. ὑμέας (disyll.) Od.21.198, al.; enclit. ὕμεας (disyll.) Herod.2.60 (Pap.); ὑμέας also Hdt.1.126, al.; Aeol. and Ep. ὔμμε Il.23.412, al., Pi.*I.*6(5).19; also in A.*Eu.*620 (trim.), and S.*Ant.*846 (lyr.); Dor. ὑμέ Alcm.3, Sophr.52, Ar.*Ach.*737, *Lys.*1076, *SIG*528.3 (Cretan dial., iii B.C.), 622 *B* 8 (Cretan, ii B.C.).—The pl. is sts. used in addressing *one* person, when others are included in the speaker's thought, as Od.12.81, Archil.89. (With σύ cf. Lat. *tu*, Goth. *þu*; with τοι Skt. gen. and dat. *te*; the origin of σφῶϊ is doubtful; with ὑμεῖς cf. Skt. acc. pl. *yuṣmān.*)

⊛ **σῠάγρ-ειος**, ον, (σύαγρος II) *of the wild boar*, πέλματα *PCair.Zen.* 692.18 (iii B.C.); κρέα ib.311.15 (iii B.C.), and without κρέα Lync.ap. Ath.9.402a; στέαρ Dsc.2.76.8. **-εσία**, ἡ, *boar-hunt*, *AP*6.34 (Rhian.). **-ευτής**, οῦ, ὁ, *boar-hunter*, Tz.*H.*7.69. **-ιόμορφος**, ον, *like a wild boar*, prob. in Orph.*A.*979. **-ιος**, v. σύαγρος III. **-ίς**, = συναγρίς (nisi hoc legend.), Epich.28, 69. **-ος**, ὁ, name of a dog, S.*Fr.*154. II. = σῦς ἄγριος or ἀγρία, *wild boar* or *sow*, *wild swine*, Antiph.42, Dionys.Trag.1.2, *PRyl.*238.3 (iii A.D.), etc.; σ. ἄρρην Gal.12.633; un-Attic acc. to Phryn.358. III. name of a kind of *frankincense*, Dsc.1.68 codd. (Συάγριος cj. Wellmann, i.e. *obtained from Σύαγρος in Arabia*). 2. a kind of *date*, Plin.*HN*13.42. **-ώδης**, ες, *like a wild boar*, Plb.34.3.8.

**σύαγχος** [ῠ]· ῥίζα, ἐν ᾗ οἱ σῦς θηρεύονται, Hsch. **συαγών**, v. σιαγών.

**σύαινα** [ῠ], ἡ, (σῦς) properly, *sow*: name of *a sea-fish*, Opp.*H.*1.129.

**συάκιν** (-ιον Suid.), τό, Dim. of σύαξ II, *Gloss.*

**συᾶνία**, v. συηνία.

**σῦαξ**, ἄκος, ὁ, a kind of *pulse*, Choerob. *in Theod.*1.288 H.: cf. σαῦσαξ. II. a kind of *fish*, = ῥόμβος B. 2, *Gloss.*

**σύαρον**· τὸν κλῶνα, Hsch. ⊛ **σύαρτον**· βούγλωσσον, Id. **συάς**, άδος, ἡ, *sow*, in pl., Id. **σύβαξ**, ἄκος, ὁ, ἡ, (σῦς) *hoglike, swinish*, Id.: also **σῠβάλλας, σύβας**, *ruttish, lustful*, Id.

**Σῠβάρ-ειος** [ᾰ], α, ον, = Συβαριτικός, Epich.215. **-ίζω**, *live like a Sybarite* or *voluptuary*, Archyt.ap.Stob.4.1.138.

**σῠβᾰρ-ίζω, -ισμός**, v. συβριάζω, -ασμός.

**Σύβᾰρ-ις** [ῠ], ἡ, gen. εως D.S.8 *Fr.*19, Ath.12.521a; dat. ει Ar.*V.* 1435; Ion. gen. ιος Hdt.6.21; also ιδος Str.8.7.5, Philostr.*VA*4.27:—*Sybaris*, Hdt.5.44, etc. II. as Appellat., *luxury, voluptuousness*, συβάριδος μεστοί Philostr. l.c., cf. Plu.*Crass.*32. **-ίτης** [ῑ], ου, ὁ, *Sybarite*, Hdt.5.44, Ar.*V.*1427: fem. -ῖτις, ιδος, ib.1438: as Adj., Συβαρίτιδες εὐωχίαι *Sybaritic* feastings, Id.*Fr.*216; Σ. λίμνα Theoc.5.146. **-ῑτικός**, ή, όν, *of Sybaris*: λόγοι Σ., a class of fables among the Greeks, Ar.*V.*1259, ubi v. Sch. and cf. Mnesim.6, Ael. *VH*14.20. Adv. -κῶς Malch.p.397 D.

**συβαρνίς**· περίκομμα, Hsch. **σύβας**, v. σύβαξ. **συβαύβαλος**, ὁ, cf. συοβ–. **σύββολον**, v. σύμβολον.

⊛ **σῠβήνη**, ἡ, *flute-case*, *IG*1².280.86, Ar.*Th.*1197, 1215 (where a barbarian is speaking), Poll.7.153, 10.153, *EM*732.25, Hsch.

**συβίνη**, v. σιβύνη.

⊛ **σῠβόσιον**, τό, (σῦς, βόσκω) *a herd of swine*, Il.11.679 = Od.14.101 (pl. -ια, with ῑ metri gr., written συβόσεια as v.l. in Il. l.c.), Plb.12.4.8, Lib.*Decl.*31.16. II. *pigsty*, Suid.

**Σύβοτα**, τά, the name of some islets near Corcyra, with part of the opposite coast, originally, no doubt, *swine-pastures*, Th.1.47, 50, 52, 54.

**σῠβότης**, ου, ὁ, = συβώτης, Arist.*Po.*1454ᵇ28, Hsch., *Gloss.*

**σῦβρι-άζω**, = συβαρεύομαι, τρυφάω, Hsch.; expld. as put by metathesis for συβαρίζω, *EM*732.26; hence restd. for σῠβᾰρίζειν in Ar. *Pax* 344. **-ακός**, ή, όν, = πολυτελής, Hsch. ⊛ **-ασμός**, ὁ, = ἡ ἐν εὐωχίᾳ θόρυβος, Id.; hence restd. for σῠβᾰρισμός (v.l. συβαριασμός) in Phryn.Com.64.

**συβροί**· ἰσχνοί, λαγαροί, τάφροι (i.e. ταῦροι?), Hsch.: also **σύβρα**· ἐπὶ βοῶν, σημαίνει δὲ τὰ πρὸς ῥυπαρόν τι ἐχούσας, Id.: **σύ[μ]βρος**· κάπρος, Id.

**σῠβωτ-έω**, *to be a swineherd*, Att. for ὑοβοσκέω, Moer. p.355 P. (v.l. συβοτεῖν). ⊛ **-ης**, ου, ὁ, (σῦς, βόσκω) *swineherd*, Od.4.640, 14.420, Hdt.2.47, 48, Pl.*R.*373c, etc. **-ικός**, ή, όν, *of* or *for a swineherd*, μέλος *swineherd's* song, Pl.Com.211, cf. Plu.2.776e. **-ρια**, ἡ, fem. of συβώτης, Pl.Com.211.

**συγγάλακτος** [γᾰ], ον, = *collactaneus*, *Gloss.*

**συγγᾰλακτοτροφέω**, *bring up as a foster-child with* one's own, *PCair.Preis.*31.79 (ii A.D.).

**συγγᾰληνιάω**, *to be calm* or *smooth together with*, Eust.1233.64.

**σύγγαμβροι**, οἱ, *the husbands of two sisters*, Poll.3.32, etc.: sg., *brother-in-law*, *PCair.Zen.*475.11 (iii B.C.), *MAMA*3.493 (Corycus); = *congener*, *Gloss.*

⊛ **συγγᾰμέτης**, ου, Dor. **-τας**, ὁ, *husband*, *IG*12(5).307 (Paros).

**συγγᾰμ-έω**, *marry together* or *at the same time*, S.E.*M.*10.99, Ps.-Democr.Alch.p.51 B., Zos.Alch.p.153 B. **-ος**, ον, *united in wedlock, married*, ἄλλῳ to another, E.*El.*212 (lyr.); σ. δάμαρ Lyc.1220: as Subst. σύγγαμος, ὁ or ἡ, *husband* or *wife*, Orph.*A.*595, *IG*12(3).1188 (Melos). 2. generally, *connected by marriage*, E.*Ph.*[428]. 3. σύγγαμός σοι Ζεύς *sharing* your *marriage-bed*, of Amphitryon, Id.*HF*149: in pl., *the rival wives of one man*, Id.*Andr.* 182.

**συγγᾰνύσκομαι**, Med., = συγχαίρω, τινι Them.*Or.*4.57d.

**συγγείτνιος**, ον, *neighbouring*, *CPR*206.9 (ii A.D.).

**συγγείτων**, ονος, ὁ, ἡ, *bordering, neighbouring*, γαῖα E.*Supp.*386, cf. Epigr. in *POxy.*662.43 (Leon.): as Subst., *PLond.*5.1708.188.

**συγγελάω**, *laugh with, join in laughter*, E.*Fr.*362.22, Hegesand.6, Lxx *Si.*30.10; οἴνῳ καίρια σ. Call.*Epigr.*23.8.

⊛ **συγγέν-εια**, ἡ, *kinship*, E.*IA*492, Th.3.65, etc.; πρὸς συγγενείας καὶ κηδεστίας X.*HG*2.4.21; ἡ πρώτη σ. primary *kinship*, Epicur. *Sent.Vat.*61: c. gen., *kin, relationship, with* or *to* another, ἡ τοῦ θεοῦ σ. Pl.*Prt.*322a; διὰ τὴν τοῦ Ἡρακλέους σ. Id.*Ly.*205c: c. dat., κατὰ τὴν αὐτῶν ἑκατέροις σ. *with* either of them, Id.*Plt.*307d; σ. ἔχειν τινί ib.257d; ἡ πρὸς τοὺς παῖδας σ. Isoc.6.18; ἡ πρὸς ἀλλήλους σ. Id.4.43, etc.: not properly applied to the relation of parents and children (v. συγγενής II. 1 b), γένος γάρ, ἀλλ' οὐχὶ συγγένεια, τοῦτ' ἔστιν Is.8.33 (but cf. D.S.13.20). 2. *ties of kindred, family connexion, family influence*, Pl.*R.*491c, *Smp.*178c; of the relation between Athens and Thebes, Decr.ap.D.18.186. 3. metaph., κατὰ σ. τῆς μορφῆς Arist.*HA*539ᵃ22; ἡ πρὸς τὸ.. ἱερὸν πῦρ σ. [παντὸς πυρός] Plu.2.702f; ὤτων καὶ γλώττης Luc.*Herc.*5; of metals, Zos.Alch. p.197 B. 4. *congenital character* of disease, Hp.*Mul.*2.125. II. *kinsfolk, family*, E.*Or.*733 (troch.), Men.923.1; of a single *kinsman*, E.*Or.*1233: collectively, *kinsfolk, kinsmen*, Id.*Tr.*754; ἡ Περικλέους ὅλη οἰκία ἢ ἄλλη σ. Pl.*Grg.*472b, cf. *Lg.*627c, *Ev.Luc.*1.61: pl., *families*, D.25.87; ἡ σ. ἡ Ἀγανιτέων *clan*, *BCH*46.397 (Mylasa), cf. *Michel* 476.9 (Olymus). 2. of animals, *kind, species*, παρὰ τὰς σ. συνδυάζεσθαι Arist.*HA*566ᵃ26: generally, *kind, class*, Id.*APo.*76ᵃ9, Chrysipp.*Stoic.*2.39. ⊛ **-ειος**, ον, *akin, kindred*, Ζεὺς σ. *presiding over kindred*, E.*Fr.*1000. **-έτειρα**, ἡ, (cf. γενέτης) *parent, mother*, Id. *El.*746 (lyr.). ⊛ **-εύς**, έως, ὁ, = συγγενής, only in dat. pl., *JHS*22.358 (Pisidia), Lxx 1 *Ma.*10.89 cod. A, *Ev.Marc.*6.4, *Ev.Luc.*2.44. **-ημα**, ατος, τό, *birth-mark*, Vett.Val.111.1 (pl.), *Gloss.* (prob.). ⊛ **-ής**, ές, *congenital, inborn*, ἦθος Pi.*O.*13.13; εὐδοξία Id.*N.*3.40; σ. εἶδος, = φύσις, *character*, Hp.*Hum.*1; νόσημα σ. ἐστί τινι Id.*Prorrh.*2.2; φόβος A.*Eu.*691; ταύροις.. ἐστὶ συγγενὲς τόδε *natural* to them, Id.*Ag.*832; ἡ τύχη προσγίγνεθ' ἡμῖν σ. τῷ σώματι Philem.10; πότμος σ. Pi.*N.*5.40; προϊδεῖν σ. οἷς ἕπεται who have the *natural* gift to foresee, ib.1.28; συγγενεῖς μῆνες my *connate* months, the months *of my natural life*, S.*OT*1082; σ. τρίχες the hair *born with one*, i.e. the hair of the head as opp. to the beard, Arist.*HA*518ᵃ18, 584ᵃ24; σημεῖα σ. *birth*-marks, ib.585ᵇ31; δυνάμεις αἱ σ., opp. αἱ ἔθει and αἱ μαθήσει, Id.*Metaph.*1047ᵇ31; αὔξει τὸ σ. increases *its natural force*, Id.*EN*1119ᵇ9. Adv. **-νῶς** δύστηνος miserable *from his birth*, E.*HF*1293; v. σύμφυτος. II. *of the same kin, descent*, or *family, akin to*, τινι Hdt.1.109, 3.2, E.*Heracl.*229: abs., *akin, cognate*, θεός A.*Pr*.14; γυνή E.*Andr*.887; χείρ S.*OC*1387; συγγενέστατον φύσει πάντων *most nearly akin*, Is.11.17; σ. γάμος ἀνεψιῶν A.*Pr*.855; of animals, Arist.*HA*539$^{a}$23, *GA*747$^{a}$31, al.: hence, b. Subst., *kinsman, relative*, οὖσα σ. ἐκείνου Ar.*Pax* 618 (troch.); τῆς ἐμῆς γυναικὸς ξυγγενεῖ (dual) Id.*Av*.368 (troch.); πρὸς σ. τε καὶ οἰκείους αὐτῶν Pl.*R*.378c; ἔργον εὑρεῖν συγγενῆ πένητός ἐστιν Men.4; γάμει τὴν συγγενῆ Id.929: freq. in pl., οἱ σ. *kinsfolk, kinsmen*, Pi.*P*.4.133, Hdt.2.91, etc.; not properly applied to children (ἔκγονοι) in relation to their parents, and so opp. ἔκγονοι in Is.8.30, v. συγγένεια I (but cf. And.1.17); τοῖς συγγενέσι τὰ τοῦ συγγενοῦς ψηφίζεσθαι Is.4.23. c. τὸ σ., = συγγένεια, *kindred, relationship*, A.*Pr*.291 (anap.), S.*El*.1469, Th.3.82, etc.; also, *the spirit of one's race*, Pi.*P*.10.12, *N*.6.8; εἰ τούτῳ προσήκει Λαΐῳ τι σ. if he had any *connexion* with him, S.*OT*814; of tribes, κατὰ τὸ ξ. Th.1.95. 2. metaph., *akin, cognate, of like kind*, τοὺς τρόπους οὐ συγγενής Ar.*Eq*.1280 (troch.), cf. *Th*.574; ξυγγενὴς ὁ κύσθος αὐτῆς θητέρᾳ (for τῷ τῆς ἑτέρας) Id.*Ach*.789; freq. in Pl., [ἡ ψυχὴ] σ. οὖσα τῷ θείῳ *R*.611e; τῇ πολεμικῇ σ. ἡ πάλη *Lg*.814d; τοῖς..λόγοις τὴν αἰτίαν συγγενῆ δεῖ νομίζειν Arist.*GA*788$^{b}$9, cf. *Rh*.1398$^{a}$21 (Comp.): rarely c. gen., νοῦς αἰτίας σ. Pl.*Phlb*.31a, cf. *Phd*.79d, *R*.403a, 487a: abs., σ. τιμωρίαι *fitting, proper* punishments, Lycurg.122 (but prob. f.l. for εὐγ–); συγγενῆ *things of the same kind, homogeneous*, Arist.*APo*.76$^{a}$1; τὰ σ. καὶ τὰ ὁμοειδῆ Id.*Rh*.1405$^{a}$35; σ. τέχναι *Stoic*.2.30; ἐν γαίῃ μὲν σῶμα τὸ σ. its *congener*, *IG*9(1).882.7 (Corcyra). Adv., συγγενῶς ἔρχεσθαι Pl.*Lg*.897c; σ. τρέχων Πλάτωνι Alex.1 (codd. D.L.); τὰ σ. εἰρημένα *to similar effect*, Phld.*Mus*.p.92K. III. συγγενής represented a title bestowed at the Persian court by the king as a mark of honour, 'cousin', X.*Cyr*.1.4.27, 2.2.31, D.S.16.50; also at the Ptolemaic and Seleucid courts, *OGI*104.2 (Delos, ii B.C.), al., *BGU*1741.12 (i B.C.), Lxx 1*Ma*.10.89; οἱ σ. τῶν κατοίκων ἱππέων prob. a category of *nobles* among the κάτοικοι, *PTeb*.61(*b*).79 (ii B.C.); συγγενεῖς κάτοικοι *UPZ*14.8 (ii B.C.). **–ησις**, εως, ἡ, *meeting*, Pl.*Lg*.948e (pl.). ⊛ **–ικός**, ή, όν, *congenital* or *hereditary*, of a predisposition to disease, Hp.*Epid*.3.1.ς', cf. Plu.*Per*.22; σ. τρίχες Arist.*Pr*.878$^{b}$27 (cf. συγγενής I); τὸ σ. τέλος our *congenital* end, Nausiph.2, Polystr.*Herc*.346 p.86V., cf. Epicur.*Ep*.3 p.63U. Adv. –κῶς Id.*Ep*.1 p.24U. II. *of* or *for kinsmen*, σ. φιλία *between kinsfolk*, opp. ἑταιρική, Arist.*EN*1161$^{b}$12; σ. ἱερωσύναι D.H.2.21; σ. ἀρχιερατικοὶ στέφανοι *OGI*470.20 (Odemish, i A.D.); τὰ ἀρχῆθεν ὑπάρχοντα ταῖς πόλεσιν πρὸς ἀλλήλας σ. δίκαια *IG*12(9).4.7 (Carystus, ca. i B.C.); κατὰ τὸ σ. *Sammelb*.4638.6 (ii B.C.); συγγενικῆς θεᾶς Ἴσιδος *Bull.Soc.Arch.Alex*.5.273 (ii A.D.). Adv. –κῶς *like kinsfolk*, D.25.89, Polyaen.5.2.8. 2. metaph., *kindred, of a common kind*, ἔχειν τὴν μορφὴν σ. Arist.*HA*623$^{b}$6; τὰ κοινὰ καὶ σ. things common and *of our own nature*, Alex.30.7; εἴδη πρὸς ἄλληλα σ. Arist.*HA*531$^{b}$22. 3. *of, belonging to the* συγγενεῖς (III), Phan.Hist.11, *Arch.Pap*.1.220 (Ptolemaic). **–ίς**, ίδος, pecul. fem. of συγγενής, *Ev.Luc*.1.36, Plu.2.265d, *CIG*2995 (Ephesus), *IG*14.829 (Puteoli), 3.479, *PAmh*.2.78.9 (ii A.D.); acc. to Poll.3.30, ἐσχάτως βάρβαρον.

**συγγενν-άω**, *assist in procreating*, Arist.*HA*632$^{a}$20 (s.v.l.): metaph., σ. τὸ χρῶμα *assist in generating* it, Pl.*Tht*.156e; *create together with..*, θεοὺς σ. τῷ κόσμῳ, of the Stoics, Plu.2.426b:—Pass., *come into existence at the same time*, Plb.6.10.4, Ph.2.346, Plu.2.574b: c. dat., Ruf.*Syn.Puls*.2.3. **–ημα**, ατος, τό, *birth-mark*, *Gloss*. (fort. συγγένημα). **–ήτωρ**, opos, ὁ, ἡ, *one who assists in generating, common parent*, τέκνων Pl.*Lg*.874c (where it refers to the wife).

**συγγενοκτόνος**, ον, (κτείνω) *slaying one's kindred*, Tz *H*.9.391.

**συγγεοῦχος**, ὁ, *fellow*-γεοῦχος, *Arch.Pap*.1.209 (Ptolemaic).

**συγγέρων**, οντος, ὁ, *co-mate in old age*, Babr.22.7.

**συγγεύομαι**, *taste also*, τῶν σπλάγχνων Sch.Ar.*Pax* 1115: aor. inf. Act. συγγεῦσαι, = *degunere*, dub. in *Gloss*.

**συγγεωργ-έω**, *to be a fellow-labourer*. Is.9.18. 2. trans., *help to till*, χωρίον Eun.*VS* p.467B., cf. *PAmh*.2.94.17 (iii A.D.), etc.; μετὰ τῶν συγγεωργουμένων αὐτῇ (sc. τῇ μηχανῇ) ἀρουρῶν *PSI*1.77.20 (vi A.D.). ⊛ **–ος**, ὁ, *fellow-labourer*, Ar.*Pl*.223 (proparox., v. Sch.), *Sammelb*.7457.3 (Egypt, ii B.C.), *PSI*9.1043.20 (ii A.D.).

**συγγηθέω**, pf. –γέγηθα, *rejoice with*, τινι E.*Hel*.727.

**συγγηρ-άσκω**, fut. –γηράσομαι E.*Fr*.1058: aor. –εγήρᾱσα Alciphr.2.3:—*grow old together with*, γηράσκοντι [τῷ σώματι] συγγηράσκουσι [αἱ φρένες] Hdt.3.134; ἐγώ σ' ἔθρεψα σὺν δὲ γηράναι θέλω (cf. γηράσκω) A.*Ch*.908, cf. E. l. c., Isoc.1.7:—pres. **συγγηράω** Aret.*CA*1.5. **–ος**, ον, *growing old with* another, *AP*7.260 (Carph.), 635 (Antiphil.).

⊛ **συγγίγνομαι**, Ion. and later Gr. **συγγίν–** [ῑ]: fut. –γενήσομαι, aor. –εγενόμην, pf. –γέγονα (also συγγεγένημαι Ar.*Eq*.1293 (lyr.)):—*to be born with*, ἅμα σ. γινομένοις Arist.*HA*547$^{b}$31, cf. D.S.2.56, Man.1.200. II. *associate, keep company with, hold converse with*, τινι Hdt.3.55, E.*El*.603, *Ba*.237, Ar.*Nu*.1317 (lyr.), *V*.1468 (lyr.), Th.2.12, etc.; χαλεποὶ συγγενέσθαι Pl.*R*.330c; πᾶσαν τὴν συνουσίαν σ. Id.*Lg*.672a; also ξ. ταῖς Νεφέλαισιν ἐς λόγους Ar.*Nu*.252: abs., *coexist, cohere*, ἀήθεα Emp.22.8. 2. of disciples or pupils, *hold converse with* a master, *consult* him, περί τινος, τίνος πέρι; Pl.*Phd*.61d, Ar.*Av*.113, cf. Pl.*Men*.91e, X.*Mem*.1.2.27; φροντίσι Ar.*Eq*.1293 (lyr.); of the master, Plu.*Per*.4. 3. σ. γυναικί *have sexual intercourse with* her, X.*An*.1.2.12, Pl.*R*.329c; παιδὶ καλῷ *IG*4$^{2}$(1).121.105 (Epid., iv B.C.); of the woman, Hdt.2.121.ε', Pl.*Lg*.930d, Plu.*Sol*.23. 4. *come to assist*, τινι A.*Ch*.245, 456 (lyr.): abs., S.*El*.411; ξὺν δὲ γενοῦ πρὸς ἐχθρούς A.*Ch*.460 (lyr.). 5. abs., *come together, meet*, Th.4.83, 5.37; σ. ἐς πόσιν Hdt.1.172; οἱ συγγιγνόμενοι *comrades*, X.*Mem*.1.2.16; ἀριθμὸς συγγ. *coming to our aid*, Pl.*Epin*.978a. III. *become acquainted* or *conversant with*, σπλάγχνοισι Eup.108, cf. 38; ἐνδείᾳ Pl.*Phlb*.45b; ὑδροποσίαις Id.*Lg*.674a; λόγῳ Arist.*Rh.Al*.1420$^{b}$28.

**συγγιγνώσκω**, Ion. and later Gr. **συγγῑν–**: fut. συγγνώσομαι E.*Ion* 1440, etc.: aor. 2 συνέγνων A.*Supp*.215, etc.: pf. συνέγνωκα:—*think with, agree with*, τινι X.*Cyr*.7.2.27; μοι ταῦτα Is.8.38; μετὰ πολλῶν τὴν ἁμαρτίαν ξυνέγνωσαν *shared* the error *with* them, Th.8.24: abs., *consent, agree*, Hdt.4.5, Th.2.60:—Med., Hdt.3.99. b. *come to agreement* legally, ἀμφὶ τὰν δαῖσιν *Leg.Gort*.5.46, cf. *PGnom*.169 (ii A.D.); of the parties to a treaty, *SIG*56.33 (Argos, v B.C.). 2. later, *to be privy* to a thing, *join in a plot with*, τινι App.*BC*2.6: c. acc., τὴν ἐπιβουλήν D.C.44.13; τὴν φυγήν *Cat.Cod.Astr*.1.98; οἱ συνεγνωκότες *conspirators*, App.*BC*2.5. II. σ. ἑαυτῷ *to be conscious*, with part. in nom., σ. καὶ αὐτοὶ σφίσιν ὡς ἠδικηκότες Lys.9.11; παθόντες ἂν ξυγγνοῖμεν ἡμαρτηκότες S.*Ant*.926; σ. ἑαυτοῖς κακῶς βουλευόμενοι (as v.l. for –οις) D.H.2.55: with part. in dat., σ. αὐτοῖσι ἡμῖν οὐ ποιήσασι ὀρθῶς Hdt.5.91, cf. D.H.3.60:—Med., συνεγινώσκετο ἑωυτῷ οὐκέτι εἶναι δυνατός Hdt.3.53. 2. *acknowledge, own, confess*, τι Id.4.3; οὐχ ἧσσον ταῦτα ἐκείνου Th.7.73: c. acc. et inf., συγγνόντες ποιέειν σε δίκαια Hdt.1.89, cf. 91: c. dat. et inf., οὔ οἱ σ. λέγειν ἀληθέα Id.4.43; also σ. ὡς.. Pl.*Lg*.717d: abs., *confess one's error*, νῦν συγγνοὺς χρήσομαι τῇ ἐκείνου γνώμῃ Hdt.7.13, cf. 9.122:—Med., οὔτε συγγινωσκόμενοι (sc. τοῦτο) Id.5.94, cf. 6.92: c. inf., οὐ συνεγινώσκετο αὐτὸς..εἶναι αἴτιος ib.61, cf. 1.45, 4.126, 5.86: c. acc. et inf., Id.6.140. 3. ἡ συνεγνωσμένη ζωή life *as generally understood*, opp. οὐσιώδης, Dam.*Pr*.139; so θάνατος ὁ –σμένος Porph.*Sent*.9; τὰ κατ' αἴσθησιν –σμένα ib.38; τῶν –σμένων τοῖς πολλοῖς Syrian.*in Metaph*.26.14. 4. *recognize*, τινα *Arch.Pap*.1.219 (Ptolemaic). III. *collect* or *conclude from premisses*, εὖ γε ξυνέβαλεν αὔτ'· ἀτὰρ δῆλόν γ' ἀφ' οὗ ξυνέγνω Ar.*Eq*.427; ἐκ θεσφάτων ὅτι.. D.H.4.4. IV. *have a fellow-feeling with another*: hence, *make allowance for* him, *excuse, pardon*, S.*El*.257, E.*Ion* 1440, X.*Cyr*.5.1.13; τινι S.*Tr*.279, E.*El*.1105, etc.; σ. τινὶ τὴν ἁμαρτίαν Id.*Andr*.840, cf. A.*Supp*.215 (where εὐγνώῃ codd.); δημοκρατίαν αὐτῷ τῷ δήμῳ συγγιγνώσκω X.*Ath*.2.20; αὐτοῖς τῆς ἐπιθυμίας Pl.*Euthd*.306c; βαρβάροις ὅτι.. Id.*Mx*.244b; ξ. εἰ.. Ar.*V*.959; also σ. τοῖς εἰρημένοις E.*El*.348, cf. Pl.*Smp*.218b; κλοπαῖς E.*IT*1400, cf. Ar.*Eq*.1299 (lyr.); σ. ἡμῖν τοῖς λελεγμένοις E.*Hel*.82:—Med., A.*Supp*.216, Hdt.7.12, Democr.253.

**συγγλοιόομαι**, *coagulate*, Lyd.*Mens*.4.26.

**σύγγνοια**, ἡ, = συγγνώμη, only in S.*Ant*.66.

**συγγνώμη**, *fellow-feeling, forbearance, lenient judgement, allowance*, Ar.*Pax* 997, Pl.*Criti*.107a, Arist.*EN*1143$^{a}$23, 1*Ep.Cor*.7.6. Phrases: a. συγγνώμην ἔχειν *judge kindly, excuse, pardon*, E.*Or*.661, Ar.*Pax* 668, etc.; τινι Hdt.1.116, 155, S.*Ph*.1319, Lys.12.29, Pl.*Phd*.88c, X.*HG*6.2.13, etc.; ἑαυτῷ κακῷ ὄντι Pl.*R*.391e; τινος for a thing, Hdt.6.86.γ', S.*El*.400, Ar.*V*.368, Lys.10.2, Pl.*Phdr*.233c, etc.; περί τι Arist.*EN*1143$^{a}$22; folld. by ὅτι, Hdt.7.13, Pl.*R*.472a; by εἰ.., E.*Hipp*.117, etc.; by inf., S.*Aj*.1322; c. gen. abs., σ. ἔχε ἐμοῦ παρανοήσαντος Ar.*Nu*.1479; so σ. ποιήσασθαι Hdt.2.110; διδόναι Plb.8.35.2; νέμειν Paus.2.27.4, Jul.*Or*.2.50c; ἀπονέμειν Luc.*Nigr*.14: opp. b. συγγνώμης τυγχάνειν X.*Mem*.1.7.4, And.1.141, Lys.1.3; παρά τινος from a person, Id.24.17, Isoc.12.38, etc.; συγγνώμης τινός, ὑπέρ τινος τυχεῖν, for a thing, E.*Hipp*.1326, Isoc.12.271; ξυγγνώμην ἁμαρτεῖν..λήψονται will be *pardoned for* offending, Th.3.40; συγγνώμην αἰτεῖσθαι Pl.*Criti*.106b; σ. ἔχει calls for *forbearance*, S.*Tr*.328; ἔχοντάς τι ξυγγνώμης Th.3.44; ἐχέτω σ. *let it pass*, Plu.2.1118e. c. πολλὴ ἔκ γε ἐμεῦ ἐγίνετο σ. Hdt.9.58; συγγνώμη τοι I *excuse* you, Id.1.39, cf. Th.8.50 (both c. inf.): συγγνώμη [ἐστί], c. acc. et inf., it is *excusable* that.., Id.4.61, 5.88, cf. D.19.238; τὸ πεπεῖσθαι..σ. Id.*Prooem*.34: also with a part., σ. [ἐστί τινι] πλοῦτον ἀγειρομένῳ *AP*11.389 (Lucill.); σ. [ἐστὶ] εἰ.., ἐὰν.., Th.1.32, 4.114, Pl.*Hp.Mi*.372a. 2. Rhet., *confession and avoidance*, Hermog.*Stat*.2, al.

**συγγνωμον-έω**, later form for συγγιγνώσκω IV, Apollod.2.7.6, J.*AJ*11.5.3, *PGnom*.161 (ii A.D., Pass.), S.E.*M*.1.126, etc. **–ητέον**, *one must make allowance*, Anon.*in Rh*.77.23. **–ικός**, ή, όν, *inclined to make allowance, indulgent*, Arist.*Rh*.1384$^{b}$3, *EN*1143$^{a}$21. Adv. –κῶς Hierocl. *in CA*12 p.447M. II. of things, *pardonable*, Arist.*EN*1136$^{a}$5; οὐ θαυμαστόν, ἀλλὰ σ. ib.1150$^{b}$8. 2. *pertaining to* συγγνώμη 2, Hermog.*Stat*.5. Adv. –κῶς ib.3.

**συγγνωμοσύνη**, ἡ, = συγγνώμη, θέσθαι σ. S.*Tr*.1265 (anap.).

**συγγνώμων**, ον, gen. ονος: (συγγιγνώσκω I):—*agreeing with*, Pl.*Lg*.770c; σφίσι App.*BC*2.122; τῆς ἀνάγκης *about*.., Plu.*Cleom*.10; *sharing knowledge with*, ἀλλήλοισι cj. in Hp.*Vict*.1.6 (*Vorsokr*. i p.106). II. (συγγιγνώσκω IV) *disposed to pardon* or *forgive, indulgent*, E.*Fr*.645, cf. Pl.*Lg*.921a, Arist.*EN*1143$^{a}$19; σ. εἶναί τινι to be *indulgent*, show favour to a person, X.*Mem*.2.2.14; σ. εἶναί τινος to be *disposed to forgive* a thing, E.*Med*.870, cf. X.*Cyr*.6.1.37; σ. τινί τινος D.H.1.58; ξυγγνώμονες ἔστε [τισι] κολάζεσθαι, τῆς τιμωρίας τυγχάνειν, *allow* them to.., Th.2.74; τὸ σύγγνωμον *indulgence*, Pl.*Lg*.757e; Ἀπόλλωνι καὶ Ἀσκληπιῷ συγγνώμοσιν *IG*4$^{2}$(1).432 (Epid., iv A.D.). 2. Pass., *pardoned, deserving pardon* or *indulgence*, ξ. ἐστὶ τὸ ἀκούσιον Th.3.40; ξ. τι γίγνεσθαι πρὸς τοῦ θεοῦ Id.4.98.

**συγγνωρίζω**, *share in knowledge*, Arist.*EE*1244$^{b}$26:—Pass., οἱ –όμενοι persons *acquainted*, Polem.*Phgn*.1.1.

**σύγ-γνωσις**, εως, ἡ, = συνείδησις, *consciousness*, Phld.*Mort*.34. **-γνωστέα**, *one must pardon, indulge*, τινι Pl.*Phdr*.236a: also -γνωστέον, Vett.Val.157.33. **-γνωστός**, όν, also ή, όν Sch.S.*Tr*.727:—*pardonable, allowable*, E.*Heracl*.435,981, Ar.*Th*.418, Phld.*Mort*.20, etc.; συγγνωστόν or συγγνωστά ἐστι, c. inf., S.*Fr*.352, E.*Alc*.139, *Med*.491,703, cf. *Ba*.1039: c. part., αὐτοῖς συγγνωστὰ πλάττουσιν.. *they may be forgiven for*.., v.l. in Plu.2.1083f. 2. of persons, σ. τῆς φιλοτιμίας Philostr.*VS*1.8.3, cf. Max.Tyr.4.3: c. part., σ. ἐπικλασθεὶς *for* being.., Plu.*Cor*.36, cf. Luc.*Anach*.34; σ. εἰ.. Id.*DDeor*.6.3.

**συγγογγύλλω**, *twist round*, Ar.*Th*.61 (anap., γογγυλίσας cod.), *Lys*.975 (anap., -υλίσας codd.).

**συγγομφόω**, *fasten together with nails*, *IG*2[2].463.77, D.S.14.72, Aret.*SD*1.6, Plu.*Num*.9: metaph., ὥσπερ ἐν σῶμα συγγεγομφωμένον ἑαυτῷ Id.*Pyrrh*.33.

* **συγγονή**, ἡ, = σύστασις, Democr.137.

**σύγγονος**, ον, poet. Adj. = συγγενής, *congenital, inborn, natural*, ἀτρεμία Pi.*N*.11.12; σύγγονόν [ἐστι] βροτοῖσι τὸν πεσόντα λακτίσαι A.*Ag*.884. II. *connected by blood, akin*, Pi.*P*.9.108, E.*Hipp*.1379 (lyr.), etc.; σ. ἑστία Pi.*O*.12.14: σ. τέχναι the arts *proper to his race*, Id.*P*.8.60; συγγόνῳ φρενί A.*Th*.1039; συγγόνων Ἐρινύων Id.*Ag*.1190: as Subst., *brother, sister*, E.*IT*805,795; σ. Διοσκόροιν Ἑλένη Id.*Hec*.441, etc.; σύγγονοι *kinsfolk*, Pi.*O*.8.80, *P*.3.39, E.*IA*1153. III. *native, of one's country*, ὕδωρ S.*Fr*.911.

**σύγ-γραμμα**, ατος, τό, *writing, written paper*, Hdt.1.48, X.*Cyr*.8.4.25 (cf. 16); *written composition, book, work*, Id.*Mem*.2.1.21, 4.2.10, Pl.*Grg*.462b, *Tht*.166c, Arist.*EN*1181b[2], Gal.15.424, etc.; *systematic work*, opp. ὑπόμνημα, Id.16.532; esp. *prose work, treatise*, τὰ κατὰ λόγον or καταλογάδην σ., opp. ποιήματα, Pl.*Lg*.810b, Isoc.2.7, cf. 42; *written speech*, Id.*Ep*.1.5. II. *written form, regulation, ordinance*, Pl.*Plt*.299d sq.; σ. πολιτικόν Id.*Phdr*.258d; *clause* of a law, Aeschin.3.127 (s.v.l.); οὐκ ἄξιον συγγράμματος not worth a *note*, Gal.15.909. **-γραμμᾰτεύς**, έως, ὁ, *fellow*-γραμματεύς, *BGU*451.14 (i/ii A.D.). **-γραμμᾰτεύω**, *to be* γραμματεύς *along with another*, *IG*1[2].202.36, 203.2, *POxy*.1427.2 (iii A.D.). **-γραμμάτιον**, τό, Dim. of σύγγραμμα, Luc.*Herod*.1, Longin.1.1. **-γραμμᾰτοφύλαξ** [ῠ], ᾰκος, ὁ, *keeper of books*, Sch.Luc.*Apol*.2, Suid. s.v. ῥῆτραι.

**συγγραπτέον**, *one must compose*, Hp.*Vict*.1.1.

* **συγγρᾰφ-εύς**, έως, ὁ, *one who collects and writes down historic facts, historian*, X.*HG*7.2.1, D.H.*Th*.5: then, generally, *prose-writer*, opp. poet, Pl.*Phdr*.235c; λόγων ib.278e, Isoc.15.35; and, simply, *writer, author*, Ar.*Ach*.1150, Pl.*Phdr*.272b, Phld.*Mus*. p.68 K., Gal.15.593, al. II. συγγραφῆς, οἱ, *commissioners appointed to draw up measures*, Th.8.67, *IG*1[2].22.3, al., Philoch.122, Isoc.7.58. III. *party to a contract*, *BGU*636.23 (i A.D.). **-ή**, ἡ, *writing* or *noting down*, Hdt.1.93; ἔχει συγγραφήν affords *material for writing*, Aristid.*Or*.47(23).3. II. *that which is written, writing, book*, esp. *in prose*: *history, narrative*, ἡ Ἀττικὴ ξ. Th.1.97, cf. Arr.*An*.6.16.5, Paus.10.19.5, etc. 2. *draft decree* drawn up by the συγγραφῆς (cf. συγγραφεύς II), *IG*1[2].76.47; also *written contract, covenant, bond*, Hp.*Jusj*., Th.5.35, Pl.*Lg*.953e, *IG*12(7).67*B*76, al. (Amorgos, iv/iii B.C.), *PCair.Zen*.265.5, 666.6 (iii B.C.), etc.; σ. ναυτικαί *bond to secure money* lent on bottomry, D.35.27, cf. 32.1,5; so in sg., Id.34.6, 35.1; κατὰ τὰς σ. according to the *bond* or *covenant*, Lys.30.17; ἀνδριάντ' ἐκδεδωκὼς κατὰ σ. having *contracted* for its execution, D.18.122; an architect's *specifications*, *IG*2[2].1665.2, 1668.2 (both pl.), 1678.16 (sg.); μὴ κατὰ συγγραφάς Aeschin.1.160; ἐπειδὰν δοκιμασθῇ [τὸ ἔργον] κατὰ τὴν σ. ταύτην *Inscr.Délos* 502*A* 15 (iii B.C.); συγγραφὰς ἔχειν παρ' ἑτέρων to have entered into *contracts* with others for the execution of paintings, And.4.17; σ. γαμική, μισθώσεως, etc., *POxy*.1034.6 (ii A.D.), *PEnteux*.54.3 (iii B.C.), etc. III. a *mark* in the eye, σ. ὕφαιμος, as definition of αἰμάλωψ, Erot. s.v. οὔρει αἱμαλῶδες. **-ία**, Ion. -ίη, ἡ, = συγγραφή, Aret.*CA*2.11 (s.v.l.). **-ικός**, ή, όν, *given to writing*, esp. *prose works*, ποιητικὸς ἢ ξ. Luc.*Merc.Cond*.35, cf. Jul.*Or*.7.205b; *of* or *in prose composition*, δεινότης Luc.*Pisc*.23; ἀρετὴ καὶ κακία Id.*Hist.Conscr*.42; -ώτερον εἶδος *more suited to prose*, Men.Rh. p.411 S. Adv., -κῶς ἐρεῖν speak *like a book*, i.e. with great precision, Pl.*Phd*.102d; opp. ὑπομνηματικῶς, Gal.18(1).529. **-ιον**, τό, *receipt*, *PSI*4.356.6 (iii B.C.).

* **συγγρᾰφοδιαθήκη**, ἡ, *contract with marriage settlement*, *BGU*252.1 (i A.D.).

**σύγγρᾰφος**, ἡ, Boeot. σούγ-, = συγγραφή, *IG*7.3171.4, al. (Orchom. Boeot., iii B.C.), 5(1).1421.14 (Cyparissia, iv/iii B.C.), etc.: also Dor. **σύγγροφος**, ib.4[2](1).103.159 (Epid., iv B.C.), 4.823.49 (Troezen), *SIG*246 i 51 (Delph., iv B.C.):—also **σύγγραφα**, τά, = συγγραφή II. 2, *IG*12(9).188 (Eretria, v/iv B.C.): sg., *inscribed list*, dub. in *Supp.Epigr*.6.262 (Phrygia). II. Adj., *given in writing*, ἀσφάλεια *Stud.Pal*.1.7 ii 5 (v A.D.).

**συγγρᾰφοφύλαξ** [ῠ], ᾰκος, ὁ, *keeper of bonds* or *contracts*, *PHib*.1.84(*a*).14, al. (iv/iii B.C.), *PCair.Zen*.265.7 (iii B.C.), *OGI*120 (Naukratis, ii B.C.), etc.

* **συγγράφω** [ᾰ], *write* or *note down*, X.*Cyr*.8.4.16 (Pass.):—Med., *have* a thing *written down*, Hdt.1.47,48, 7.142. 2. *describe*, εἶδος ὁκοῖόν τι ἔχει ὁ κάμηλος οὐ συγγράφω Id.3.103, cf. 6.14. II. *compose a writing* or *a work in writing*, περί τινος X.*Eq*.1.1, Pl.*Min*.316d: c. acc., τὰς Κνιδίας γνώμας Hp.*Acut*.1; πόλεμον ξ. *write the history of* the war, Th.1.1, cf. 6.7; ὁ τὴν ὀψοποιίαν συγγεγραφὼς the *author of the book on* cookery, Pl.*Grg*.518b; συμβουλὴν περὶ βίου σ. Id.*Lg*.858c; *describe*, Theoc.*Ep*.22.4 (where it is used of poetry, cf. *AP*9.165 (Pall.)): esp., *write in prose*, opp. poetry (ποιεῖν), Pl.*Ly*.205a, Isoc.9.8; σ. ἐπαίνους καταλογάδην Pl.*Smp*.177b; σ. τέχνας *compose* manuals, D.H.*Comp*.1. 2. esp., *compose* a speech, Isoc.1.3:—Med., σ. λόγους οἵους εἰς τὰ δικαστήρια *get* speeches *composed*, Pl.*Euthd*.272a:—Pass., λόγος συγγεγραμμένος Id.*Phdr*.258a. III. Med., συγγράφεσθαί τι *draw up a contract* or *bond* (συγγραφή II. 2), συγγραψάμενος ἃ δεήσει ἀποδοῦναι X.*Eq*.2.2; συγγράφεσθαι εἰρήνην πρός τινα *make a treaty of* peace *with* another, Isoc.12.158; σ. περί τινος Id.4.177; τοιαῦτα -όμενοι *promising*, Phld.*Rh*.1.343 S.; σ. συγγραφὴν *PHal*.1.258 (iii B.C.), etc.: abs., *sign a treaty*, Th.5.41; *make a contract*, *PCair.Zen*.199.5 (iii B.C.), *POxy*.729.17 (ii A.D.); συγγέγραμμαι τῇ Ἑσπέρου θυγατρί I *have signed a contract* (of marriage) *with* the daughter of H., *UPZ*66.2 (ii B.C.); σ. γάμον *make a contract of* marriage, Plu.2.1034b: c. inf., Thphr.*HP*5.5.5; συνεγράψατο πρὸς Διόδωρον Εὐτέληαν γαμήσειν *Supp.Epigr*.2.294.6 (Delph., i A.D.); and elliptically, συγγράφεσθαι ἐς ἐμπόριον *make a contract* [to carry a ship] to a port, D.56.11,47; [δραχμαί] ἃς συνεγραψάμην Διονυσοδώρῳ *for* which I *gave a bill* (or *I.O.U.*) to.., *PCair.Zen*.7 (iii B.C.), cf. *PEnteux*.49.5 (iii B.C.); ὁ συγγεγραμμένος *the signatory to a contract*, Hp.*Jusj*.; pl., *PCair.Zen*.666.5 (iii B.C.). IV. *draw up a form of motion* to be submitted to vote, τάδε οἱ ξυγγραφῆς ξυνέγραψαν *IG*1[2].76.3; τάδε Δημόφαντος συνέγραψεν Lex ap. And.1.96; νόμους καθ' οὓς πολιτεύσουσι X.*HG*2.3.2, cf. Arist.*Ath*.29.2, 30.1; παράνομα συγγεγραφέναι X.*HG*1.7.12:—elsewh. in Med., μετὰ τῆς γραμματέως συγγράψομαι Ar.*Th*.432; οἱ ἐν τῷ δήμῳ συγγραφόμενοι Pl.*Grg*.451b. V. *represent in a painting, paint*, τὸν Ῥωξάνης καὶ Ἀλεξάνδρου γάμον Luc.*Herod*.4:—Pass., Ar.*Av*.805 (s.v.l., σύ γε γεγραμμένῳ cj. Mein.). 2. *paint together*, τινὰς ἐν γραφαῖς D.C.58.4, cf. 50.5 (Pass.). VI. of an architect, *draw up specifications*, *IG*1[2].24.8, 44.6, 81.16. VII. *enrol*, in Pass., πατέρες συγγεγραμμένοι, = Lat. *patres conscripti*, Plu.*Rom*.13.

**συγγυμν-άζω**, *train*, ἐπὶ ταὐτὸ τὴν φάλαγγα καὶ τοὺς μισθοφόρους Ἕλληνας Plb.5.65.3; ἑαυτὸν πρὸς βλασφημίας D.L.6.90; πρὸς θέσιν τοὺς μαθητάς Id.5.3:—Med., *exercise oneself with* or *together*, Pl.*Smp*.217b,c, Arist.*EN*1172a4, Phld.*Sto.Herc*.339.9, etc.: in aor. Pass., συγγυμνάσθητι ἐμπείροις *BGU*615.25 (ii A.D.) (but aor. Med. συνεγυμνάσατο Phot.*Bibl*. p.173 B.).—Pass., *to be organized*, καταλήψεις -γεγυμνασμέναι Zeno *Stoic*.1.21. 2. Pass., τοῖς ἔργοις συγγεγυμνασμένος *experienced*, dub.l. in Gal.19.217; συγγυμνασθῆναι ποικιλώτερον *gain* more varied *experience*, Sor.*Vit.Hippocr*.4. II. Pass. aor. -εγυμνάσθην *struggle, contend*, πρός τινας *PSI*1.93.6 (iii A.D.). **-ᾰσία**, ἡ, *common exercise*, τῶν αἰσθήσεων *Placit*.4.2.8, cf. Lxx *Wi*.8.18; *strain of copulation*, Zeno *Stoic*.1.36. 2. *experience, training*, Dsc.1.42, Sor.1.3, Marcellin.*Puls*.164. **-αστής**, οῦ, ὁ, *companion in bodily exercises*, Pl.*Sph*.218b, *Lg*.830b, Charito 8.6, etc.; ἐν παλαίσματι X.*Lac*.9.4. **-όομαι**, Pass., *to be laid bare also*, -ωθέντος ὀστοῦ Gal.18(1).119.

**συγγῡναικονόμος**, ὁ, *fellow*-γυναικονόμος, *BSA*27.226 (Sparta, ii A.D.).

* **συγγώνιον**, τό, dub. sens., perh. *corner-room*, *BCH*54.98 (Delos, ii B.C., pl.).

**σύγε**, v. σύ.

**συγκαθᾰγίζω**, *burn up together*, Plu.*Aem*.24; *burn along with*, χολὴν τοῖς ἄλλοις ἱεροῖς Id.2.141e. 2. metaph., *help to sanctify*, Phld.*Herc*.1232 p.70 V.

**συγκαθαιρέω**, Ion. συγκατ-, *put down together, join in putting down*, τὸν βάρβαρον Th.1.132; τὴν ἐκείνων δύναμιν Id.6.6; τοὺς κρατοῦντας Id.8.46. 2. *take down with* others, ἐκείνην τοῖς ὑπηρέταις συγκαθεῖλε *with* their *help took down* her body, Plu.*Agis* 20; φορτίον σ. *help to take* it *off*, opp. συνανατιθέναι, Pythag.ap.Porph.*VP* 42, cf. D.L.8.17. II. *win with* any one, πέντε σφι ἀγῶνας τοὺς μεγίστους σ. Hdt.9.35.

**συγκαθαίρω**, *purify together, at the same time*, in Pass., Ph.1.647.

**συγκᾰθᾰρεύω**, *to be pure* (καθαρός I. 5b) *along with*, Eust.143.6.

**συγκαθ-αρμόζω**, *join in composing the limbs* of a dead man, *join in preparing for burial*, S.*Aj*.922. **-εδρος**, ὁ, *assessor, colleague*, Ulp. ad D.21.178, Hsch. s.v. συνθάκων; condemned by Thom.Mag. p.292 R. **-έζομαι**, *sit down together*, Pl.*Tht*.162d, *Prt*.317e, Isoc.12.18; of a body of people, γερουσία Plu.*Marc*.23; τοῖς ἄρχουσιν συγκαθεσθεὶς their *assessor*, *TAM*2(1).186 (Sidyma). II. *crouch down, cower*, Plu.2.970e (συνεκαθεζόμην and its part. are aor. exc. in Plu.*Marc*. l.c.). **-είμαρμαι**, pf. Pass., *to have been decided also by fate*, Chrysipp.*Stoic*.2.292: in pres. sense, *to be joined together by fate*, ἀλλήλοις Hierocl. p.54 A. **-είργω**, Att. for συγκατείργω, *shut up with* others, τινὰ ἁμάξῃ πράγματι X.*Cyr*.6.1.36, etc.:—Pass., *to be shut up with*, Aeschin.1.182; τινι Luc.*Cal*.18: also -είργνυμι, in Pass., Plu.*Sol*.20, *Cat.Mi*.63. **-έλκω**, *drag down with* or *together*, fut. Pass. ξυγκαθελκυσθήσεται A.*Th*.614. **-εύδησις**, εως, ἡ, *sexual intercourse*, Sch.D*Od*.23.346. **-εύδω**, fut. -ευδήσω, *sleep with*, τούτῳ θανοῦσα ξ. A.*Ch*.906; esp. of sexual intercourse, σ. τινί Cratin.279, Ar.*Ec*.1009, Pl.*Lg*.838b. **-έψω**, *boil down with*, τί τινι Dsc.2.107:—Pass., Id.1.128, *Eup*.2.69. **-ημαι**, Ion. **-κάτημαι**, used as pf. of συγκαθέζομαι, *sit as assessor with*, [τῷ Καίσαρι] Wilcken *Chr*.14 ii 5 (i A.D.); *live in the same quarters*, Hdt.3.68; of a number of persons, *sit together*, E.*Ba*.811, X.*An*.5.7.21; esp. of persons sitting to deliberate, *sit in conclave, meet in assembly*, ἐν τῇ Πυκνὶ.. πρόβατα -ήμενα Ar.*V*.32; ἐν συνεδρίῳ X.*HG*2.4.23; περὶ εἰρήνης Th.5.55: abs., Aeschin.3.115. II. *sink* or *subside together, settle down*, Str.16.4.

16; ἐς γόνυ συγκαθήμενος Luc.Pseudol.20. -ιδρύω, set up or dedicate with, τὸν Ἑρμῆν ταῖς Χάρισιν Plu.2.44d, cf. IG7.2713.50 (Acraeph., i A.D., -καθειδρ-), Jul.Or.4.150d:—Pass., POxy.1256.14 (iii A.D.); οἱ συγκαθιδρυμένοι θεοὶ IG5(1).497.17 (Sparta), cf. Str.9.2.29. -ιερόω, join in dedicating, Sardis 7(1).8.13 (i B.C.), Plu.Cam.8, CIG (add.) 3827q (Cotiaeum); dedicate together, Ph.1.451, 2.240 (Pass.), Plu.2.612d. ※-ίζω, make to sit together or in a body, τὰ συνέδρια Hell.Oxy.11.4; τὸν λαόν Lxx Ex.18.13:—Med. or Pass., sit in conclave, meet for deliberation, σ. τὸ δικαστήριον X.HG5.2.35, cf. D.Prooem.23 (v.l. -καθεζ-). II. intr. in Act., sit together, Lib.Or.11.216. 2. settle down in a boiling pot, PHolm.19.8. III. sit or settle down, of quadrupeds that lie down by doubling their legs under them, Arist.HA498a9; σ. ἐπὶ τὰ ὄπισθεν ib.578a21, cf. Lxx Nu.22.27; σῶμα συγκεκαθικός a bent, stooping figure, Arist.Phgn.807b5; of men, crouch down, Plu.Arat.21; of women, Thessalus in Cat.Cod.Astr. 8(3).147; also τὰ νέφη εἰς τὰ κοῖλα σ. Thphr.Sign.3. -ίημι, fut. -καθήσω E.Hel.1068:—let down with or together, deposit together, κόσμον l.c.; αὑτὴν σ. let oneself down, lower oneself, εἴς τι Pl.Tht.174a; ὁμοῦ σ. ἑαυτὸν εἰς τὴν θάλατταν threw himself into it along with her, Plu.2.163c; insert together with, ἄγκιστρον τῷ δακτύλῳ Heliod.ap. Orib.44.14.3, cf. Dsc.2.76, 5.40; σ. Μούσας τοῖς Βατράχοις bring them upon the stage at the same time with.., Arg.2 S.OC:—Pass., stoop down and enter, εἰς τόπον, of an ambush, Plb.8.24.4. II. (sc. ἑαυτόν) settle down, crouch, squat, Arist.Pr.869b11, D.S.20.51; συγκαθείσης τῆς θηλείας ἐπιβαίνει τὸ ἄρρεν Arist.HA539b29. 2. stoop, condescend, accommodate oneself, οἱ..γέροντες συγκαθιέντες τοῖς νέοις Pl.R.563a; εἰς.. D.H.6.56, etc.: abs., Pl.Prt.336a, Tht.168b; εἰς τὰ ἀναγκαῖα cj. in Epicur.Sent.Vat.44. 3. of a seller, σ. τῇ τιμῇ come down in price, Lync.ap.Ath.7.313f. ※-ίστημι, join in bringing back, τὸν στόλον μετὰ τῶν ἄλλων τριηράρχων Test.ap.D. 21.168, cf. PSI6.602.8 (iii B.C.). 2. join in setting up or establishing, esp. of setting up kings, τὴν τυραννίδα A.Pr.307; τὰς μοναρχίας Isoc. 4.125, cf. Lex ap.And.1.97, Th.8.68, Pl.R.567b, X.Ages.2.31; help to set in order, ταῦτα Th.4.107. 3. help in treating, curing, νόσον E.Hipp.294. 4. help to effect, κυνὸς κόμιστρ' ἐς Ἄργος σ. Id.HF 1387. II. in Pass., and intr. tenses of Act., go down (into the arena) with another, take one's ground for a contest with any one, σ. τοῖς πολεμίοις εἰς τὴν μάχην, τοῖς ὑπεναντίοις κατὰ πρόσωπον, Plb.11. 23.4, 9.3.6; πρός τινα Id.31.12.8; οἱ συγκαθεστῶτες the contending parties. Id.4.12.6, cf. PTeb.25.10 (ii B.C.); σ. μετὰ συνηγόρων PAmh. 2.33.16 (ii B.C.). -οράω, see at once or together, συγκατοφθήσεται αὐτῷ ὁ λόγος Gal.11.553. -ορμίζομαι, Pass., to be at anchor along with one, Plb.5.95.3. -οσιόω, consecrate together with, in Pass., J. AJ16.2.4, Plu.2.636e. -ῠφαίνω, interweave with, in Pass., Lxx Is.3.23.

※σύγκαιρος, ον, of the season, ἄνθη Alciphr.3.16; seasonable, suitable, τῇ ὥρᾳ Anon.ap.Suid.

συγκαίω, Att. -κάω [ᾱ], set on fire with or at once, burn up, Pl.Ti. 22c:—Pass., to be burnt up, calcined, ib.49c, PCair.Zen.129.17 (iii B.C.), etc.; also of the effect of intense cold, D.L.2.118. 2. overheat, inflame, [ὁ οἶνος] σ. τὰς φλέβας Hp.Aër.9; ταῦτα σ. τὴν κοιλίην Id.VM10, cf. Gal.15.559:—Pass., τὸ συγκεκαυμένον Prodic.4; κοιλίη συνεκαύθη Hp.Epid.1.26.δ':—intr. in Act., κοιλίαι συγκαίειν ἀγαθαί liable to inflame, Id.Aër.7.

συγκᾰκοπᾰθέω, partake in sufferings, 2Ep.Ti.1.8.

συγκᾰκ-ουργέω, to be party with another in injuring, τῇ κόρῃ τοὺς γονεῖς D.H.1.78, cf. 6.41, BGU15 ii 11 (ii A.D.): abs., join in the injury, Arg.D.32. -ουχέομαι, Pass., endure adversity with, τῷ λαῷ Ep.Hebr.11.25. -όω, injure, harm, or corrupt conjointly, Ptol. Tetr.201, Vett.Val.117.13:—Pass., to be injured also, together, Hp. Mochl.23. -ύνω, = foreg., Thphr.Od.56.

※συγκᾰλέω, fut. -καλέω Hom.Epigr.14.8, Att. -καλῶ X.An.3.1. 46: 1. call to council, convoke, convene, Il.2.55, A.Supp.517, Hdt.1. 206, Ar.Av.201, X. l.c., etc.; τὰς γυναῖκας ἐπί τι Ar.Lys.22; σ. τινὰς παρεῖναι Luc.Vit.Auct.1:—Med., Hdt.2.160, Ev.Luc.9.1, etc. 2. invite with others to a feast, σ. αὐτοῖς καὶ Ἀρτάβαζον X.Cyr.8.4.1.

συγκᾰλινδέομαι, Pass., roll about with, c. dat., Placit.4.19.3, v.l. for συγκυλ- in X.Smp.8.32.

συγκαλλύνω, sweep up together, Arist.Pr.936b27.

συγ-κάλυμμα [κᾰ], ατος, τό, a covering, Lxx De.22.30(23.1), 27. 20: -κᾰλυμμός, ὁ, found in Ar.Av.1496 (σύγκ- Dawes). -κᾰλυπτέος, α, ον, to be veiled, concealed, λόγος A.Pr.523. -κᾰλυπτός, ή, όν, wrapped up, κνίσῃ κῶλα σ. ib.496. -κᾰλύπτω, cover or veil completely, σὺν δὲ νεφέεσσι κάλυψε γαῖαν Od.5.293; σ. τι χρόνῳ E.Ph. 872, cf. Pl.R.452d; τὴν ἀλήθειαν Olymp.Alch. p.70B.; συγκαλύψαντές μου τὴν κεφαλήν BGU1816.19 (i B.C.); ὁ συγκεκαλυμμένος πατήρ, with reference to a well-known fallacy (cf. ἐγκαλύπτω I), Epicur.Nat.9; ἐξάγει συγκεκαλυμμένην muffled up, Plu.Num.10, cf. Lxx Su.39:—Med., aor. συγκαλύψασθαι, wrap oneself up, cover one's face, X.Cyr.8.7.28, Smp.1.14; -ψασθαι τὴν κεφαλήν IG4$^2$(1).126.6 (Epid., ii A.D.). 2. intr. in Act., λόγος συγκαλύψας ἀχλύϊ Them. Or.4.59b.

σύγκαμμα, ατος, τό, dat. pl. συγκάμμασι (-κλάσμασι cod.), gloss on λυγίσμασι, Hsch. (fr. συγκάμπτω).

συγκάμνω, labour or suffer with, sympathize with, σοῖς πήμασι A. Pr.414 (lyr.), cf. 1059 (anap.); κακοῖσι σοῖσι E.Alc.614; συγκαμνούσης [τῇ γαστρὶ] τῆς ζωτικῆς δυνάμεως Gal.15.599; [ἡ ψυχὴ] συννοσεῖ [τῷ σώματι] καὶ συγκάμνει Plu.2.137d. 2. work with, τινι S.El.987, PSI9.1075.6 (v A.D.); τῇδε χθονὶ E.Rh.396; ἔν μοι.. σύγκαμε Id. HF1386; τὰ πολλά Paus.8.14.9: abs., S.Aj.988; συγκαμὼν δορί with the spear, E.Rh.326.

συγ-καμπή, ἡ, bight, joint, of the elbow joints, Hp.Nat.Hom.11 (pl.); αὐχὴν λαγαρὸς τὰ κατὰ τὴν σ. X.Eq.1.8; αἱ σ., of the fingers, Arist.HA513a3; αἱ τῶν ἄρθρων σ. Poll.2.234. -καμπτός, ή, όν, flexed, Arist.IA709b7. -κάμπτω, bend, τὸ σκέλος Hp.Art.14, Pl. Phd.60b; συγκάμψας τὰν χῆρα καθ' ἕνα ἐκτείνειν τῶν δακτύλων IG4$^2$(1). 121.28 (Epid., iv B.C.); of legs, arms, spine, etc., Diocl.Fr.141; τὸν νῶτόν τινων Lxx Ps.68(69).24: intr., bend down, ib.4Ki.4.35:—Pass., opp. ἐκτείνεσθαι, X.Eq.12.5; συγκεκαμμένῳ τῷ σκέλει, of a person mounting a horse, ib.7.2; συγκεκαμμένος τοῖς δακτύλοις with the fingers doubled up, D.L.6.29; esp. of the action of sitting down, συγκαμφθεὶς κάθημαι Pl.Phd.98d, cf. Hp.Off.9, Arist.Pr.885b34; of the foetus in the womb, Id.HA586b1, Sor.2.60; of the chest in phthisis, Hp.Loc.Hom.14; of animals lying down with their knees bent under them, σ. ἡ βοῦς Arist.HA575a14:—in Pass. also, bend together with, ἐπιφανείας -εσθαι τοῖς σώμασιν Plu.2.63c. -καμψις, εως, ἡ, a bending together, Hp.Off.15; ἐν τῇ συγκάμψει at the bend of the arm, Id.Fract.3; ἡ σ. τοῦ σκέλους Arist.IA711b2; τοῦ σώματος Id. Pr.870b1; τῶν κώλων Poll.2.234 (as v.l. for κάμψεις).

συγκᾰνηφορέω, help as κανηφόρος, v.l. in Scol.22, as cited by Eust. 1574.20.

συγκαρβαλώσας· συστρέψας, Hsch.

συγκαρκῐνόομαι, Pass., entwine or interlace its roots, of wheat, Pherecr.20, cf. Poll.7.150.

συγκᾰσιγνήτη, ἡ, own sister, E.IT800.

σύγκᾰσις, εως, ἡ, = foreg., κούρα E.Alc.410 (lyr.).

※συγκατα-βαίνω, fut. -βήσομαι: aor. -έβην:—go or come down with, σᾷ πτέρυγι E.Andr.505 (lyr.); ἅμα τοῖς ᾠοῖς Arist.GA756a25; of curls, σ. ταῖς παρειαῖς Philostr.Ep.58. 2. go down together, opp. ἀνέρχομαι, Arist.Mete.358b32; esp. to the sea-side, Th.6.30; εἰς ὁμαλοὺς τόπους Plb.1.39.12; ἀπὸ τοῦ λόφου Plu.Crass.31: metaph., σ. ταῖς ἡλικίαις ἐπὶ τὸν αὐτὸν καιρόν Arist.Pol.1334b34, cf. 1335a 31. 3. come down to one's aid, Ζεὺς..Μοῖρά τε συγκατέβα A.Eu. 1046 (lyr.), cf. Ch.727 (anap.). 4. like Lat. descendere in arenam, σ. εἰς κίνδυνον, εἰς πόλεμον, etc., Plb.3.89.8, 5.66.7, D.S.12.30, etc.; εἰς παράταξιν Id.17.98. 5. come down to, agree to, εἰς κρίσιν Plb. 3.90.5. 6. metaph., let oneself down, submit to, εἰς φόρους καὶ συνθήκας Id.4.45.4; σ. εἰς πᾶν agree to all conditions, Id.3.10.1: generally, stoop, condescend, Id.26.1.3; εἰς λοιδορίαν Phld.Rh.1. 383S. 7. come down in one's price or demands, Plb.21.26.12. Cf. συγκαθίημι. -βάλλω, throw down along with, τισὶ ἑαυτόν Plu. Luc.23; τὰ χρήματα σ. contribute, D.C.48.53; πλέον AP4.3a.24 (Agath.). 2. lay as a foundation, metaph. in Pass., of the solid parts of the foetus, Gal.6.4. -βᾰσις, εως, ἡ, condescension to the level of an audience, Phld.Rh.2.25S.; also of the gods, esp. Attis, Jul.Or.5.171b. ※-βῐβάζω, decoy or draw into action, Plb.5.70. 8. II. transfer accent to final syllable, A.D.Adv.173.11. -βιόω, live with or together, μετ' εὐνοίας Plu.2.754a, cf. Alciphr.1.32; ἡ κακία τοῖς πολλοῖς σ. Plu.2.500f.

συγκατᾰγᾰπάω, put up, be content with, Phld.Rh.1.135S.

συγκατα-γήρᾱσις, εως, ἡ, growing old together, Pl.Lg.930b. -γηράσκω, pf. -γεγήρακα Epicur.Fr.217:—grow old with or together, τινι Is.2.7, Epicur. l.c., Lxx To.8.7; λύπη ἀπόρῳ σ. βίῳ lasts to the end of it, Men.Kith.Fr.1; of fast colours, σ. τῷ εἰρίῳ Hdt.1.203; of a morbid growth, Arist.GA776a5: abs., σ. οἱ ὀδόντες Hp.Carn.12, cf. Mul.2.116. ※-γιγνώσκω, later -γῑνώσκω, condemn along with or at once, σ. ὑμῶν παθεῖν τι Aristid.1.495J.:—Pass., App.BC1. 62.

συγκατ-άγνυμι, crush, Sm.Ps.28(29).5, al.; break, Jul.Or.2.60a.

συγκατα-γομφόω, nail together, join together, Plu.2.426b. -γράφω [ᾰ], inscribe together, εἴς τι f.l. in Gem.5.14 codd. II. join in executing a conveyance, PLond.2.251.20 (iv A.D.).

συγκατ-άγω [ᾰγ], bring down along with or together, Arist.HA 620b18, Mete.371a12; bring with one to port, PHib.1.49.5 (iii B.C.). 2. join in bringing back, τὸν τύραννον Ar.Th.339, cf. Isoc. 16.13; τὸν Διόνυσον (at the Καταγώγια, q.v.); τὸν δῆμον Aeschin.2. 78; from exile, Pl.Ep.333e. -ᾰγωγή, ἡ, f.l. for οὖν κ., Ph.Bel.74. 50.

συγκατα-δαρθάνω, in aor. 2 -έδαρθον, as aor. of συγκαθεύδω, sleep with one, Ar.Ec.613, 622 (anap.). -δεσμέω, bind together, Paul.Aeg.6.114. -διώκω, pursue with or together, Th.8.28 (Pass.). -δουλόω, join in enslaving, τινί τινας ib.46, cf. Aristid. 1.411J.:—Med., Th.3.64, Hyp.Fr.272. -δύνω [ῡ] and -δύω: aor. -κατέδυν:—sink or set together with, Πλειάδι AP7.534 ((Alex.) Aet. or Autom.), cf. Hipparch.1.5.17, al., Procop.Gaz. p.140B.; sink, be drowned together, Phld.Ir. p.89 W., Plu.2.599b:—Med., dive together, Luc.Tox.18. II. trans., σ. τὸν ἥλιον Eust.182.28. -δῠσις, εως, ἡ, a setting together, Hipparch.1.1.10, al., Str.1.1.21 (pl.), Ptol. Alm.8.4 (pl.). -ζεύγνῡμι, yoke together, join in marriage, τινά τινι Plu.Cam.2, cf. Sor.1.34:—Pass., ἄτῃ συγκατέζευκται κακῇ has become a yoke-fellow with misery, S.Aj.123; cf. συγκεράννυμι. -ζῶ, spend one's life with, τινι Plu.2.749e, 1129b. -θάπτω, bury along with, Hdt.2.81, 5.92.η', Lys.2.60. ※-θεσις, εως, ἡ, approval, assent, Plb.2.58.11, Phld.Rh.1.210S., Andronic.Rhod.p.577M., OGI484.32 (Pergam., ii A.D.), etc.; opp. ἀντίφασις, Diog.Oen.18 (pl.); agreement, concord, 2Ep.Cor.6.16; in legal sense, BGU194. 11 (ii A.D.), etc.; flattering assent, Plu.Ant.24. 2. in Stoic philos., assent given by the mind to its perceptions, Zeno Stoic.1.39, al., cf. Plot.1.8.14, etc.; a term introduced into Latin by Cicero, Plu.*Cic.*40: cf. συγκατατίθημι. 3. Gramm., *affirmative*, A.D.*Conj.*226.17, D.T.642.5; αἱ δύο ἀρνήσεις μίαν σ. ποιοῦσι Sch.S.*OT* 1053. **-θετέον**, *one must agree with*, τοῖς νέοις οὐ σ. Dsc.*Praef.*2, cf. A.D.*Pron.*4.5, Sor.1.98. **-θετικός**, ή, όν, *assenting, approving*, Chrysipp.*Stoic.*2.40, Plu.2.1122b, Arr.*Epict.*1.17.22. 2. *affirmative*, Suid. s. v. ἀππαπαῖ. Adv. -κῶς Arr.*Epict.*1.14.7. **-θετός**, marg. gloss on συγκάταινος in D.S.4.40. **-θέω**, *make an inroad with* another, X.*Cyr.*5.3.1. **-θλάω**, *break all to pieces*, ποτήριον Macho ap.Ath.8.348f. **-θνήσκω**, poet. aor. -κάτθανον, *die along with*, τινι Mosch.3.65, *AP*7.139. **-θύω**, *sacrifice together*, Ph.2.398, Eust.1875.10.

**συγκατ-αίθω**, *burn together*, S.*Ant.*1202. **-αινέω**, *agree with, favour*, τινι X.*Cyr.*3.3.20, Plb.36.9.3: abs., Phld.*Rh.*2.13S. II. c. acc. rei, *sanction, approve*, Hp.*Praec.*1, Plb.24.11.6: abs., Id.15.8.9, Plu.*Cam.*6. 2. *yield, grant*, τί τινι Lyc.1223. **-αινος**, ον, *agreeing with, assenting*, τινι Philipp.ap.D.18.167, cf. *PTeb.*22.5 (ii B.C.), D.S.15.92; πρός τι J.*AJ*4.8.23. **-αιρέω**, v. συγκαθαιρέω. **-αίρω**, *come to land together*, Plu.*Crass.*20, Lib.*Or.*61.4: metaph., αἱ νῖκαι σ. τινὶ εἰς μητρόπολιν Them.*Or.*3.42b. **αιτιάομαι**, in aor. 1 συγκαταιτιαθῆναι as Pass., *to be jointly accused*, J.*AJ*15.7.10.

**συγκατα-καίνω**, = συγκατακτείνω, App.*BC*4.42. **-καίω**, Att. **-κάω** [ᾱ], *burn along with* a thing, τὰς σκηνάς X.*An.*3.2.27, cf. *IG*12(2).526*a*.13 (Eresus, iv B.C.), *AP*11.133 (Lucill.):—Pass., *to be burnt with*, τισι Hdt.4.69, D.S.2.28, 19.33. **-κᾰλύπτω**, *wrap up with* or *in*, σῶμα τρίβωνι Id.18.46. **-κειμαι**, Pass., *lie with*, of sexual intercourse, ἀνδράσι Ar.*Ec.*614 (anap.): abs., Pl.*Smp.*191e, *Phdr.*255e. 2. *recline with at meals*, δεσπότῃ, of a dog, Gal.18(1).291: abs., οἱ συγκατακείμενοι *the guests*, Plu.2.660a. **-κεράννυμι**, *commingle, mix up with*, Aesar.ap.Stob.1.49.27 (Pass.). **-κλειστέον**, *one must shut up together*, *Gp.*6.2.7. ⊛ **-κλείω**, Ion. -κληΐω, *shut in* or *enclose with* or *together*, Hdt.1.182, Arist.*HA*557ᵇ4 (both Pass.), Alc.Com.23 (dub. l.); ἄνδρας λέουσι Luc.*DMort.*14.4: metaph., σ. τινὰ ἀπορίᾳ Id.*Vit.Auct.*9:—Dor. **συγκατακλαΐζω**, aor. part. -κλαιχθείς *Chron.Lind.* D62. **-κληρονομέομαι**, *inherit along with*, Lxx *Nu.*32.30. **-κλίνω** [ῑ], *represent as lying with*, τινὰ γαμετῇ Plu.2.655a, cf. Lib.*Or.*59.24:—Pass., *lie with*, Ar.*Nu.*49; συγκατακλιθέντες πλησιάζειν Arist.*HA*546ᵃ26; τινι *with* one, Clearch.6, Plu.2.138d. 2. *make to lie with* at table, νέῳ νέον ib.618e:—Pass., ᾄσεται ξυγκατακλινείς Ar.*Ach.*981 (lyr.). **-κλῐσις**, εως, ἡ, *lying together with* another, ἀνδρὸς ἀλλοτρίου σ. Plu.2.768b. **-κοιμίζω**, *cause to sleep with* another, J.*AJ*12.4.6 (v. l. -κοίμησεν).

**συγκατᾰκολουθέω**, *follow together*, τινι Str.17.1.34.

**συγκατα-κομίζω**, *bring down together*, Plu.2.846b. **-κόπτω**, *cut up* or *in pieces along with* or *together*, Mnesith.Cyz.ap.Orib.4.4.1:—Pass., Plu.*Sull.*32, *Caes.*18, al. **-κοσμέω**, *order* or *arrange together*, Id.2.938f. **-κόσμησις**, εως, ἡ, *ordering* or *settling together*, Phld.*Mus.*p.111 K. **-κρημνίζω**, *throw down a precipice along with* or *together*, J.*BJ*4.1.9 (Pass.), cf. Ph.1.408 (metaph.). **-κτάομαι**, *join with* another *in acquiring*, σ. Φιλίππῳ τὴν ἀρχήν D.18.63, cf. D.S.14.98. II. *acquire at the same time*, τούτους ἅμα σ. Str.6.4.2. **-κτείνω**, *slay together*, aor. 2 part., συγκατακτὰς .. βοτὰ καὶ βοτῆρας S.*Aj.*230 (lyr.); but -έκτᾰνον E.*Or.*1089. **-κῠλίνδομαι**, Pass., pf. -κεκύλισμαι, *to be rolled down together with*, D.H.*Comp.*20 (v. l. συγκυλίεται). **-λαγχάνω**, *occupy, have assigned in common*, τί τισι Dam.*Pr.*58. **-λαμβάνω**, *seize, take possession of together*, X.*Cyr.*4.2.42; *occupy at the same time*, in a military sense, τὸ χωρίον Th.7.26; τὴν πόλιν Isoc.19.19. 2. *comprehend together with*, τινι D.L.9.97 (Pass.). 3. *take in with*, τὰ συγκαταλαμβανόμενα τῶν πνευμάτων αὐτοῖς the air *which they have taken in with* their food, Diocl.*Fr.*141. **-λέγω** (A), *lay down with*, pres. wrongly inferred from συγκατέλεκτο, etc., v. συγκαταλέχω. **-λέγω** (B), *repeat* or *quote along with*, [γνώμας τοῖς λόγοις] Arist.*Rh.Al.*1434ᵃ38. 2. *appoint in addition*, πολλοὺς [πρεσβευτὰς] τῶν ἀνεπιτηδείως ἐχόντων Plu.2.819a; ταῖς ἐντιμοτάταις ἀρχαῖς σ. παρασίτους Clearch.1. 3. *include in* or *add to a list* or *catalogue*, Str.8.4.1, 13.3.1 (Act. and Pass.), Gal.15.454: c. gen., τοῦδε ἢ τοῦδε τοῦ κλίματος -λεχθέντα Str.11.12.1; τινάς τισι Apollod.3.6.3, cf. J.*AJ*2.7.4 (Pass.). **-λείπω**, *leave together*, σ. φρουράν *leave a joint* garrison in a place, Th.5.75. **-λέχω**, *lay down with*, in aor. 1 Act., συγκατέλεξε κόρῃ Epigr. in *Philol.*88.139 (Crete):—Med., *lie down with*, in non-thematic aor., συγκατέλεκτο ἡμῖν Luc.*Charid.*4. **-λήγω**, *leave off together*, Demetr.*Eloc.*2. **-λογίζομαι**, *take into account together*, J.*AJ*15.7.4, 16.4.1. **-λύω**, *help in undoing* or *putting down*, τὸν δῆμον Th.8.68, And.1.101, Lys.16.5; *put down also*, κἀκεῖνον Plu.*Pomp.*67; σ. βίον ἅμα τινί D.H.*Isoc.*1; *help to reduce*, πληθώραν Gal.18(1).725; σ. τὴν δύναμιν ἑαυτῷ Id.15.607, cf. 16.598 (Pass.). II. intr., *halt* or *stop for the night together*, Plu.2.94a. 2. *cease together with*, Lib.*Or.*64.118. **-μείγνυμι**, *mix in with, mingle, blend with*, Χάριτας Μούσαις συγκαταμειγνύς E.*HF*674 (lyr.); ᾠδαῖς καὶ θαλίαις τὴν ψυχὴν συγκαταμειγνύναι X.*Hier.*6.2:—Pass., σ. εἰς τὸ σῶμα *to be absorbed into*.., Pl.*Plt.*288e; τῷ ὑγρῷ Arist.*Mete.*357ᵇ7. **-μύω**, *to be quite closed up*, *AP*9.311 (Phil.).

**συγκατᾰναγκάζω**, v. l. for συναναγκ-, Hp.*Art.*71.

**συγκατα-ναυμᾰχέω**, *assist in conquering by sea*, Χείλωνα τὸν.. ναύαρχον Aeschin.2.78, cf. D.S.5.52. **-νέμω**, *count among*, τινά τισι Longin.ap.Porph.*Plot.*20. II. Med., *divide jointly among themselves*, τὴν γῆν Th.6.4, cf. Str.10.3.4. **-νευσῐφάγος** [φᾰ], ον, *living by saying* '*yes*', Comic epith. of κόλακες, Crates Theb. 11 D. **-νεύω**, *agree, consent to*, τοῖς λεγομένοις Plb.3.52.6, etc.; ἐκείνῳ ἅπαντα -ένευον *agreed with* him at every point, Id.7.4.9, cf. 30.1.9: abs., *AP*5.286.8 (Agath.). **-παίζω**, *jest* on a thing *at the same time*, τι Eust.1653.26. **-παύω**, *bring at the same time to an end*, τὸ βιβλίον Id.1393.57:—Pass., Olymp. *in Mete.*34.6. **-πέμπω**, *send along with*, c. dat., Jul.*Or.*4.153b:—Pass., J.*AJ*18.1.1. **-πίμπλημι**, *infect likewise* (cf. ἀναπίμπλημι II. 2), τοὺς ἀναιτίους Antipho 2.1.10. **-πίμπρημι**, *burn together with*, Ael.*NA*7.40:—Pass. -πίμπραμαι, aor. -επρήσθην Paus.2.35.4, D.C.44.50, *to be burnt with* or *together*, Ph.2.21, Paus., D.C. ll. cc. **-πίνω** [ῑ], *swallow together with*, τί τινι Gal.6.695:—Pass., *to be swallowed together*, Ph.1.311, 2.178 (with v. l.), Gal.*Nat.Fac.*3.8. **-πίπτω**, *fall down along with*, σ. ταῖς τύχαις *let one's spirits fall with* one's fortunes, D.H.*Isoc.*9; ταῖς διανοίαις *become despondent too*, Onos.13.2; *fall together* in battle, J.*AJ*7.7.1; in wrestling, Gal.*Nat.Fac.*3.3. **-πλαστέον**, *one must plaster also*, Herod.Med. in *Rh.Mus.*58.92. **-πλέκω**, *intertwine* or *intermix with*, τοῖς κάρφεσι πηλόν Arist.*HA*612ᵇ23; ψόγους τοῖς ἐπαίνοις D.H.*Pomp.*1, cf. Plu.*Sol.*3:—Pass., Id.2.648b, Ph.2.151 (with v. l.), Herod.Med. in *Rh.Mus.*58.98, Philum.ap.Orib.45.29.31. **-πλέω**, *sail into port with*, of a pilot, *PHib.*1.38.4 (iii B.C.); *sail down* the Nile *with*, *PCair.Zen.*299.4 (iii B.C.), *PMich.Zen.*46.9 (iii B.C.). **-πολεμέω**, *join in subduing*, τοὺς Ἀθηναίους D.S.16.22; Ἀλεξάνδρῳ τὴν Ἀσίαν Id.19.15, cf. Str.13.4.2, J.*AJ*13.5.11. **-ποντόω**, *sink in the sea together*, S.E.*M.*5.92 (Pass.). **-πράσσω**, Att. -ττω, *join in accomplishing* or *acquiring*, D.5.23, D.C.59.10:—Med., D.8.27 (as v. l. for κατα-).

**συγκατᾰριθμέω**, *reckon in, include*, Phld.*Lib.*p.47 O., *BGU*1208.34 (i B.C.); τινί τι Ael.*VH*2.41, Str.4.1.8, Gal.6.728, etc.:—Med., *reckon in, take into account*, Arist.*Cat.*11ᵃ22:—Pass., *to be included in*, Demetr.Lac.*Herc.*1012.43, Ph.1.83, Plu.2.120b Gal.6.78.

**συγκατα-ρράπτω**, *sew in with*, in Pass., prob. in Cyran. 27. **-ρρέω**, fut. -ρυήσομαι, *flow down* or *fall off together*, Onos. 4.4, v. l. in Dsc.5.88. **-ρρίπτω**, *throw down together*, D.S.29.32, Luc.*Cont.*5.

**συγκατάρχω**, in Med., *begin the sacrifice together*, Din.*Fr.*89.34.

**συγκατα-σβέννῡμι**, *help to extinguish*, τὸν ἄκρατον Plu.2.648b:—Pass., *to be extinguished with*, c. dat., ib.973d. **-σῑτέομαι**, *feed together*, Phld.*Sto.Herc.*339.9. **-σκάπτης**, ου, ὁ, *joint-destroyer*, Lyc.222. **-σκάπτω**, *demolish with another* or *altogether*, E.*Or.*735 (troch.), *Ph.*884, *Rh.*391, And.1.101. **-σκεδάννῡμι**, *pour over at the same time*, in Med., X.*An.*7.3.32, with vv. ll. ⊛ **-σκευάζω**, *help in establishing* or *organizing*, τὴν ἀρχήν Th.1.93, cf. X.*Lac.*8.3; πάνθ' ὁπόσα τὸν ἀνθρώπινον βίον σ. Pl.*Plt.*274d, cf. Isoc.3.6, etc.; [δημιουργοὶ] τὸν βίον ἡμῖν σ. τέχναις Pl.*Lg.*920e; τὸ ἐπιτήδειον X.*Vect.*4.38; σ. τὸν ἐν Ἀμφίσσῃ πόλεμον *join in promoting* it, D.18.143; πάντα σ. τινί *assist* him *in promoting*, Id.3.17: abs., Id.17.15:—Med., *BCH*55.43 (Odessus, i B.C.):—Pass., Phld.*Lib.*p.25 O.; -αζόμενος στοχασμός, of mutually confirmatory or cumulative evidence, Hermog.*Stat.*3, cf. Arg.D.19.14, Gal.8.566. ⊛ **-σκηνόω**, *establish in the same quarters*, X.*Cyr.*5.4.17. **-σκήπτω**, *swoop down together*, ἀετοὶ δύο σ. Plu.*Brut.*37. **-σπασις**, v. συγκατάστασις. **-σπάω**, *pull down with oneself*, τὸν ἥρωα Luc.*Nigr.*11:—Pass., *to be dragged down along with* another, ἐπὶ τὴν ὁμοίαν διαβολήν Id.*Pisc.*32; τινι Plu.2.914e; of the collar-bone, Gal.8.361; τὰ φρούρια τὰ εἰς τὴν Σύρων ἐπικράτειαν συγκατασπασθέντα *which were at the same time brought* under their dominion, X.*Cyr.*5.5.24 (v. l.). II. *gulp down, swallow together*, ἄγκιστρον δελέατι Luc.*DMort.*8. **-σπείρω**, *sow* or *plant together*, Gal.19.168, Eun.*Hist.*p.251 D.:—Pass., Hld.3.12. **-στᾰσιάζω**, *help in ruining by faction*, τὴν πόλιν Plu.*Phil.*13,15. **-στάσις**, εως, ἡ, *a falling in with so as to fight*, Plb.4.12.8; pl., Id.38.11.5; σ. τῶν θηρίων *a conflict with* animals, Id.4.8.9 (where Suid. συγκατάσπασις). **-στρέφω**, *bring to an end together*, τῇ ἐλευθερίᾳ τὸν βίον Plu.*Dem.*3. II. Med., *help to conquer*, Th.6.69, Isoc.5.126, *IG*2².127.44 (iv B.C.), Jul.*Ep.*9; σ. τὴν ἀρχὴν X.*Cyr.*8.1.8. **-σύρομαι** [ῡ], *to be dragged down with*, τινι Ph.*Fr.*101 H. **-σχημᾰτίζομαι**, Pass., *to be in conformity with*, τινι Plu.2.442d, cf. Ptol.*Tetr.*63. ⊛ **-σχίζω**, *divide at the same place as*, τῇ ἀρτηρίᾳ, of a vein, Gal.15.532 (Pass.). **-τάσσω**, Att. -ττω, *arrange* or *draw up together*, τινὰς εἰς τὴν φάλαγγα X.*Cyr.*6.3.32: metaph., σ. τινὰ εἰς τὴν ἑαυτῶν φιλίαν Polyaen.5.2.22; *take into account*, τὴν πρώτην ἡμέραν.. Ph.1.692; *classify with*, Paul.Aeg.2.11:—Pass., *range oneself beside*, μετὰ Ἀθηναίων *IG*2².237.12 (iv B.C.): metaph., *to be arranged harmoniously*, M.Ant.7.9. **-τεθειμένως**, Adv. pf. part. Pass. of -τίθημι, *in an orderly way*, Hsch. s. v. ἀθέτως. **-τείνω**, *extend with* or *together*, τὸ σκέλος Hp.*Art.*71. **-τήκομαι**, Pass., *melt away together with*, συγκατατήκεσθαι τοῖς ἔργοις *pine away over*, M.Ant.5.1. ⊛ **-τίθημι**, *deposit together* or *at the same time*, ἐμαυτὴν συγκατέθηκα τάφῳ *Epigr.Gr.*367 (Cotiaeum), cf. Poll.8.157:—Med., Is.6.32. 2. Med., σ. τινὶ τὴν αὐτὴν δόξαν περί τινος (where δόξαν represents ψῆφον) *put down* the same vote or opinion *with* another, *agree entirely with* him, Pl.*Grg.*501c: with dat. only, *agree with, assent* or *conform to*, ταῖς δόξαις Epicur.*Sent. Vat.*29; τοῖς παρακαλουμένοις Philipp.ap.D.18.166; ταῖς ἐπιβολαῖς σ. τινί Plb.3.71.5, etc.: σ. ὅτι.. *agree* that.., Arist.*Top.*116ᵃ11: abs., *assent*, Sphaer.*Stoic.*1.141, Phld.*Sign.*38, A.D.*Pron.*49.12, *BSA*18.140 (Beroea, ii A.D.), etc.: later in Act., -θεῖναί εἴς τι *agree to*, Porph.*VP*61, Iamb.*VP*33.236: cf. συγκατάθεσις. **-τρέχω**, *to be in motion together with*, ἀλλήλοις Leucipp.ap.D.L.9.31. **-τρίβω** [ῑ], *waste completely*, Plu.*Cleom.*26. **-τρώγω**, aor. -έτρᾰγον, *eat at the same time*, Id.*Sol.*20, prob. f. l. for κατα-. **-φᾰγεῖν**, aor. inf. of συγκατεσθίω. ❋ **-φέρω**, *carry down with* other things, Id.2.994d:—Pass., *to be carried down together*, Arist.*Pr.*931ᵇ21, *Mete.*357ᵃ17, Lxx *Is.*30.30, Hld.8.16; σ. τῷ βάρει τῆς πληγῆς *sink down with*.., D.S.16.12; of arteries, etc., *take the same course as*, c. dat., Gal.2.376, 18(1).653; σ. δόξῃ περί τινος *to be carried away by* an opinion, Plb.10.5.9, cf. 33.18.11. **-φεύγω**, *flee to for safety together*, εἰς τὸ ἱερόν Ath.13.593b; πρὸς τὰς ἁμάξας D.C.38.33. **-φθείρω**, *lose together*, Plb.9.26.6. **-φλέγω**, *burn with* or *together*, Ph.2.527; τὸν κόσμον Luc.*Luct.*14:—Pass., τῷ ἀνδρὶ σ. Plu.2.499c, cf. *SIG* 768.14 (Mylasa, i B.C.), Ph.2.27, Luc.*Nigr.*30; αὐτὸς καὶ πόλις ὁμοῦ συγκατεφλέγησαν Polyaen.7.24. **-φονεύω**, *put to death with* or *together*, Id.8.69. **-φυρτος**, ον, (φύρω) *mixed* or *kneaded in together*, Philox.3.17. **-χώννῡμι**, *bury with*, *Gp.*1.6.3, in Pass. ❋ **-χωρίζω**, *treat as identical*, opp. διαζευγνύναι, Phld.*Po.*5.30. II. *deposit* or *register* a deed *together with* others, *BGU*578.19 (ii A.D.), etc. **-ψεύδομαι**, *join in a lie against*, τινος Aeschin.2.158. **-ψηφίζομαι**, *condemn with* or *together*, Plu.*Them.*21. II. Pass., *to be reckoned along with*, μετά τινων *Act.Ap.*1.26. **-ψύχω** [ῡ], *make cool*, Gal.1.674:—aor. inf. Pass. -ψῠγῆναι *PHolm.*23.40.

**συγκατ-έδομαι**, fut. of συγκατεσθίω. **-ειμι**, (εἶμι *ibo*) *go down with*, τινι Luc.*DMort.*27.7; of hair on the side of the face, σ. τῷ ἰούλῳ παρὰ τὸ οὖς Philostr.*Im.*1.10: abs., *descend together*, Arist.*Pr.*907ᵇ11. **-είργω**, v. συγκαθείργω. **-εξανίσταμαι**, dub. l. in Plu.*Caes.*8. **-επείγω**, *hasten together*, Eust.682.61 (Pass.). **-εργάζομαι**, *help* or *assist* any one *in achieving*, τῷ Κύρῳ τὴν βασιληΐην Hdt.1.162, cf. E.*Or.*33; τὸ πᾶν ξ. Th.1.132: c. dat. only, *aid, assist*, Hdt.2.154, 8.142. 2. *help to conquer* a country, Plu.*Pyrrh.*18. 3. *join in murdering*, E.*HF*1024 (lyr.). **-έρχομαι**, *sink downwards together*, Arist.*Insomn.*461ᵇ12; τὸ -ερχόμενον αὐτῷ χολῶδες περίττωμα Gal.15.686. II. *come back, return from exile together*, Lys.31.9, Arist.*Pol.*1300ᵃ18, etc.; τινι *with* one, Lys.31.13; μετά τινος Plu.*Dio* 29. **-εσθίω**, fut. -έδομαι Ath.9.386e; also -φάγομαι Lxx *Is.*9.18(17): pf. -εδήδοκα Plu.2.94a: aor. -έφᾰγον Jul.*Mis.*338c:—*eat up, devour with* or *together*, Plu. l. c., *Thes.*22, Mnesith. ap.Ath.8.357e, etc.; τοῖς ἄρτοις τὰς τρίχας Jul. l. c. **-ευθύνω**, *help to direct*, γνώμην ἐφ' ὃ δεῖ Plu.2.778f, cf. 446b. **-εύχομαι**, *join in praying for*, ταῦτα S.*Ant.*1336. II. *pray to together with* another deity, Plu.2.492c. **-έχω**, *keep together with*, αὐτῷ Pl.*Cra.*404a. II. *help in seizing*, τῷ Κύλωνι τὴν ἀκρόπολιν Lib.*Decl.*22.33; *help in holding down*, *Tab.Defix.Aud.*156.44 (Rome, iv/v A.D.).

**συγκατηγορ-έω**, *join in accusing*, τινὸς μετά τινος D.19.291, cf. 51.16; τινι *with* one, Id.18.223: abs., Hyp.*Eux.*12, *Lyc.Fr.*3. II. in Logic, *predicate jointly*, A.D.*Synt.*201.5 (Pass.). **-ησις**, εως, ἡ, *joint accusation*, Sch.Ar.*Eq.*826 (v.l. -ήσας). **-ος**, ὁ, *joint accuser, counsel for the prosecution*, Hyp.*Eux.*13.

**συγκατηρεφής**, ές, *quite covered*, Lyc.1280.

**συγκατοικ-έω**, *dwell with* one, τινι Plu.*Per.*20: metaph., γέρων γέροντι συγκατῴκηκεν πίνος S.*OC*1259. **-ία**, ἡ, *joint settlement*, Μουσ. Σμυρν.1878.97 (Lydia). **-ίζω**, *colonize jointly, join in colonizing*, τὴν Σάμον Hdt.3.149, cf. Th.6.4; *restore jointly*, Λεοντίνους ib.79. II. σ. τινά τινι *settle* or *plant* in a place *along with*, αὐταῖς σ. δάκη E.*Hipp.*646. III. metaph., *establish jointly*, μνημεῖα κακῶν τε κἀγαθῶν ἀΐδια Th.2.41; τοῖς λογισμοῖς ἔρωτα Max.Tyr.7.5.

**συγκατ-οικτίζομαι**, Med., fut. -ιοῦμαι, *lament with* or *together*, S.*Tr.*535. **-ολισθάνω**, *slip and fall together*, D.S.1.30. **-ορθόω**, *help in righting*, αὐτά Isoc.5.151; πάσας αὐτῷ τὰς πράξεις Str.13.2.3, cf. D.H.6.86. ❋ **-ορύσσω**, Att. -ττω, *bury with*, τί τινι Plu.*Lys.*30, cf. Luc.*Luct.*14; ἐφεξῆς τῷ Δημοκρίτῳ τὸν Παρμενίδην Plu.2.1113e:—Pass., σ. τινί Satyr.3.

**συγκαττ-υτής**, οῦ, ὁ, = *concinnator*, *Gloss.* **-ύω**, *patch up, cobble*, of shoemakers, saddlers, etc., θώραξ ἐκ δερμάτων συγκεκαττυμένος Luc.*Hist.Conscr.*23, cf. *Sat.*28.

**σύγκαυσις**, εως, ἡ, (συγκαίω) *burning*, Pl.*Ti.*83a; *baking* of horn and pottery, Arist.*Aud.*802ᵇ4; *parched state* of body, Gal.15.895, *Nat.Fac.*2.9.

**συγκαχρύω**, aor. inf. συγκαχρῦσαι, prob. cj. in Hsch. for συγκαγχρῆσαι· συγχέαι, συμφῦραι, συφρύξαι, and in Phot. for συγκαρύγαι· συνταράξαι.

**συγκέας**, v. συγκαίω.

❋ **σύγκειμαι**, Pass., *lie together*, τρεῖς ὁμοῦ σ. S.*Aj.*1309, cf. Thphr. *HP*1.2.1; νεκρὸς μόνα τὰ ὀστᾶ κατὰ σχῆμα συγκείμενος *having* only the bones *lying together* in their places, Luc.*Philops.*31. II. as Pass. of συντίθημι, *to be composed* or *compounded*, σύγκειται τὸ σῶμα ἐξ ὀστῶν καὶ νεύρων Pl.*Phd.*98c; ἐκ στοιχείων Id.*Tht.*201e, cf. X.*Cyn.*5.29; τὴν φύσιν ἡμῶν ἔκ τε τοῦ σώματος συγκεῖσθαι καὶ τῆς ψυχῆς Isoc.15.180; χορὸς ἐξ ἀνθρώπων σ. X.*Oec.*8.3; μέλος ἐκ τριῶν σ., λόγου, ἁρμονίας, ῥυθμοῦ Pl.*R.*398d, cf. *Phd.*92a; δέον συγκεῖσθαι τὴν ἀρίστην πολιτείαν ἐκ δημοκρατίας καὶ τυραννίδος Arist.*Pol.*1266ᵃ1; of quack-doctors, οἱ ἐξ [ἀδοξίης] συγκείμενοι Hp.*Lex* 1; ἐξ ὀνομάτων σ. ἄνθρωπος Aeschin.3.229; ἐξ ἀσελγείας καὶ ὠμότητος ἔχων συγκειμένην τὴν ψυχήν Plu.*Sull.*13; c. gen. only, ἅρμα ἵππων σ. τεττάρων Philostr.*Im.*1.17; εἰς ἓν σ. *compounded* into one body, Pl.*Phlb.*29d: in later Gr. c. gen., *belong to*, πολιτείας *PMasp.*20.15 (vi A.D.). 2. of written compositions, *to be composed*, κτῆμα ἐς αἰεὶ.. ξύγκειται [ὁ λόγος] Th.1.22, cf. Pl.*Hp.Ma.*286a; ποίημα σ. Id.*Ly.*221d; λόγοι πρὸς Δημοσθένην αὐτῷ συγκείμενοι Aeschin.2.47; συμφοραὶ ὑπὸ ποιητῶν συγκείμεναι misfortunes *composed* or *invented* by poets, Isoc.4.168; οὔπω σ. τέχνη περὶ αὐτῶν no art of Rhetoric *has* yet *been put together*, Arist.*Rh.*1403ᵇ35, cf. 1402ᵃ17; ὁ μῦθος σ. ἐκ θαυμασίων Id.*Metaph.*982ᵇ19; also λόγος λαμπρὸς καὶ συγκείμενος Suid. s. v. Μεθόδιος; of persons, τὴν γλῶτταν ξ. Philostr.*VA*4.36. 3. *to be contrived, concocted*, τῇδε σ. δόλος E.*Rh.*215; πιστότερον ἢ ἀληθέστερον σ. Antipho 3.3.4; πάντα αὐτῷ σύγκειται καὶ μεμηχάνηται Lys.3.26; τὰ ὑπὸ τῶν τριάκοντα πλασθέντα.., συγκείμενα ἐπὶ τῇ τῶν πολιτῶν βλάβῃ *concocted*, Id.12.48. 4. τὴν οὐσίαν τὴν συγκειμένην *composed* of matter and form, Arist.*Metaph.*1054ᵇ5; τὸ σ. *complex*, ib.1051ᵇ4, 1076ᵇ18, cf. σύνθετος I.2. 5. Math., *to be the sum of*.., ὁ κῶνος, ἐξ ἴσων συγκείμενος κύκλων Democr.155; οἱ κύλινδροι ἐξ ὧν σύγκειται τὸ ἐγγραφὲν σχῆμα Archim.*Con.Sph.*21, cf. *Sph.Cyl.*1.11, etc.; ὁσάκις σύγκειται ἁ ΓΔ γραμμὰ ἐν τᾷ ΑΔ as many times as the straight line ΓΔ *is contained in* ΑΔ, Id.*Spir.*1; also, *to be* a ratio *compounded of two others*, Euc.6.23, Apollon.Perg.*Con.*1.11, etc. III. *to be agreed on* by two parties, σημεῖον ὃ ξυνέκειτο Th.4.111; ταῦτα ἡμῖν οὕτω συγκείσθω Pl.*Lg.*822c; also τὰς σπονδὰς οὐδετέρας ἔφη καλῶς ξυγκεῖσθαι Th.8.43: freq. in part., *agreed on, arranged*, ἡμέραι αἱ συγκείμεναι Hdt.3.157; ὑστέρησαν ἡμέρῃ μιῇ τῆς σ. Id.6.89; φλογὸς σημεῖα τὰ ξ. Ar.*Ec.*6; ὁ σ. [χρόνος] the time *agreed upon*, Hdt.4.152; σ. χωρίον Id.8.128, cf. 5.50; κατὰ τὰ σ. according to *the terms of the agreement*, Id.3.158, etc.; κατὰ τὰ σ. πρός τινα according to *what had been agreed on* with him, Id.6.14, cf. Arist.*Pol.*1308ᵃ1; ἐκ τῶν ξ. Th.5.25; παρὰ τὰ σ. Luc.*JTr.*37; ἀπὸ ξ. λόγου Th.8.94. 2. impers. σύγκειται, *it has been* or *is agreed on*, τῆς ὥρης ἐς τὴν συνέκειτό σφι ἀπαλλάσσεσθαι Hdt.9.52: abs., καθάπερ ξυνέκειτο Th.4.23; ὥσπερ σ. X.*HG*5.1.10, cf. Pl.*Cra.*433e, etc.; καθάπερ ἦν ξυγκείμενον Ar.*Ec.*61; συγκειμένου σφι, c. inf., *although* they *had agreed to*.., Hdt.5.62.

**συγκειμένως**, Adv. *continuously, without interval*, Eust.1634.54.

**συγκεκομμένως**, Adv. of συγκόπτω, *concisely*, *AB*751.

**συγκεκρᾰμένως**, = Lat. *attemperate*, *Gloss.*

**συγκεκροτημένως**, Adv. of συγκροτέω, *in a finished way*, Luc.*Merc. Cond.*35.

**συγκελεύω**, *join in ordering, bidding*, E.*IA*892 (troch.), Th.8.31.

**συγκελλάριος**, ὁ, *contubernalis*, of gladiators, *IGRom.*3.541 (Telmessus).

❋ **συγκέλλω**, *push together*, Opp.*H.*5.602.

**συγκενόω**, *empty out together*, Ruf.*Fr.*80.5 (Pass.), Gal.4.712, Porph. *in Ptol.*183, Alex.Trall.1.17.

**συγκεντέω**, *pierce together, stab at once*, Hdt.3.77, Plb.4.22.11, Lxx 2*Ma.*12.23:—Pass., ἔμελλε συγκεντηθήσεσθαι Hdt.6.29; cf. συνακοντίζω.

**συγκεντρογρᾰφέω**, dub. sens. in aor. Pass., ἐὰν -γραφηθῇ *Cat. Cod.Astr.*8(1).174 (συνκετρο- codd.).

**συγκέντρωσις**, εως, ἡ, Astron., *a simultaneous relation of centres*, i.e. when the sun's centre is at that point of the ecliptic which rises, sets, or culminates coincidently with the rising, etc., of a given star, Ptol.*Alm.*8.5 (pl.).

**συγκερ-άννῡμι** or **-νύω**, poet. **συγκεράω** Nic.*Al.*321:—Pass., fut. συγκρᾱθήσομαι E.*Ion* 406: aor. 1 συνεκράθην [ᾱ], Ion. -εκρήθην Hp.*Vict.*1.32; also -εκεράσθην Pl.*Lg.*889c: pf. συγκέκρᾱμαι (v. infr.):—*mix, blend with*, πολλὰ [ἐνὶ] or εἰς ἕν, Id.*Cra.*424d, *Ti.*68d; λύπῃ τὴν ἡδονὴν σ. *temper* pleasure *by a mixture* of pain, Id.*Phlb.*50a; τὸ πικρὸν μέλιτι *AP*12.154 (Mel.). 2. *mix together, commingle*, πολλά Pl.*Cra.*424e; τὸν πέμπτον [κύαθον] *AP*12.168 (Posidipp.); μέλος συγκεράσας τις ἐγχέοι *Anacreont.*20.4; ἐξ ἀμφοτέρων σ. *make a mixture* of both, Pl.*R.*397c. 3. *attemper, compose*, ὁ θεὸς -κέρασε τὸ σῶμα 1*Ep.Cor.*12.24. II. more freq. in Pass., *to be mixed* or *blended with, coalesce*, τινι Pl.*Ti.*68c; πρὸς ἄλληλα Id.*R.*618d. 2. *to be commingled, blended*, τὰ παλαιὰ συγκερ. ἄλγη the old *commingled* woes, A.*Ch.*744: c. dat., Call.*Aet.*3.1.75; παίδων ὅπως νῷν σπέρμα σ. E. l. c.; ὁμοῦ τό τε φαῦλον καὶ τὸ μέσον καὶ τὸ πάνυ ἀκριβῶς.. ξυγκραθέν Th.6.18; τῇ τῶν ἐναντίων κράσει σ. Pl.*Lg.*889c; ἔκ τινων Id.*Ti.*37a; ἀπό τινων Id.*Phd.*59a; παιδεία εὐκαίρως συγκεκραμένη D.61.43; συγκέκραται αὐτῶν ἡ φύσις, of the dog and fox, X.*Cyn.*3.1. 3. of friendships, *to be formed by close union*, φιλίαι μεγάλαι συνεκρήθησαν Hdt.4.152:—Med., πρός τινα φιλίην συγκεράσασθαι *form a close* friendship with any one, Id.7.151, cf. D.H.6.7; so τὸ ἔχθος τὸ ἐς Λακεδαιμονίους συγκεκρημένον (cj. Reiske for συγκεκυρημένον) Hdt.9.37. 4. of persons, *to be closely attached to, be close friends with*, τοῖς ἡλικιώταις X.*Cyr.*1.4.1. b. *to become closely acquainted with, become deeply involved in*, συγκέκραμαι δύᾳ S.*Ant.*1311 (lyr.); πολυφόρῳ συγκέκραμαι δαίμονι Ar.*Pl.*853; πενία δὲ συγκραθεῖσα δυσσεβεῖ τρόπῳ S.*Fr.*944; οἴκτῳ τῷδε συγκεκραμένη *deeply affected* by.., Id.*Aj.*895; for *Tr.*662 (lyr.), v. πάγχριστος. 5. of a wife, ἀξίοις γάμοις -κερασθεῖσα *IG*5(2).268.32 (Mantinea, i B.C.), cf. Plu.2.768b. III. Med., *mix with* or *for oneself*, εἰς μίαν πάντα ἰδέαν Pl.*Ti.*35a, cf. 69d; σ. αἰσθήσεις νῷ Id.*Lg.*961e. **-ασμός**, ὁ, *mixing, tempering*, *Gloss.* ❋ **-αστός**, ή, όν, *tempered by mixing*; τὸ σ. *a mixed drink, aqua calda*, ib.

**συγκερᾰτίζομαι**, *fight with the horns*, Lxx *Da.*11.40.

**συγκεραυνόω**, *strike with* or *as with a thunderbolt*, Cratin.187, E.*Ba.*1103, Lxx 2*Ma.*1.16:—Pass., συγκεραυνωθεὶς *thunder-stricken*, οἴνῳ σ. φρένας Archil.77.

**συγκεράω**, v. συγκεράννυμι.

**συγκερκίζω**, *weave together*, Pl.*Plt.*310e.

**συγκεφᾰλαι-όω**, *bring together under one head, sum up, make a summary of*, τὰ λεχθέντα Arist. *de An.*431ᵇ20: more freq. in Med., βούλει συγκεφαλαιωσώμεθα ἑκάτερον; Pl.*Phlb.*11b, cf. *Sph.*219b; τὰς πράξεις X.*Cyr.*8.1.15; εἰπεῖν συγκεφαλαιωσαμένους Arist.*Pol.*1322$^{b}$30:—Pass., *to be brought under one head, summed up*, Aeschin.3.59, Arist.*Metaph.*1052$^{a}$17; σ. πᾶσαι πράξεις εἰς ὀλίγους ἐπιστάτας all business *is summarily done* by few officers, X.*Cyr.*8.6.14; ἐκ πολλοῦ ὀλίγον σ. a small quantity *is distilled* from a large, Arist.*Pr.*877$^{b}$31. **-ωμα**, ατος, τό, *sum total*, Nicom.*Ar.*1.16, Iamb. *in Nic.* p.64 P. **-ωσις**, εως, ἡ, *summing up, summary*, Pl.*Def.*415b, Plb.9.32.6; τῶν εἰρημένων Phld.*Rh.*1.79 S.; σ. τῶν ἐπὶ μέρους εἰς τὸ καθόλου S.E.*M.*7.224; *sum* of numbers, Nicom.*Ar.*1.8, cf. Gal.18(2).652; *entry* in a register, *PLond.*2.259.56 (i A.D.), etc. **-ωτέον**, *one must sum up*, *Theol.Ar.*28. **-ωτικός**, ή, όν, *summing up*, ἐπιστήμη *Stoic.*3.64, Andronic.Rhod.p.578 M., cf. Eust.1521.19.

**συγκεχῠμένως**, Adv. of συγχέω, *indiscriminately*, Arist.*EN*1145$^{b}$16, Plu.2.168a, S.E.*M.*7.171, etc.; φεύγειν J.*AJ*13.4.4; εἰπεῖν (opp. σαφῶς) Hermog.*Id.*1.11.

**συγκηδεστής**, οῦ, ὁ, *brother-in-law, wife's sister's husband*, D.36.15, *Com.Adesp.*1157. 2. *father-in-law*, D.S.33.7.

**συγκηδεύω**, *join in burying*, Phylarch.26 J.; *bury along with*, πλοῦτόν τινι πολύν J.*AJ*7.15.3, cf. Suid. s. v. δανάκη: metaph., κακὰ συγκηδευόμενά τινι Plu.2.114e.

**συγκηρέω**, inf. -εῖν, f.l. for συγκυρεῖν or for συγκηροῦν (*destroy*) in *Cat.Cod.Astr.*8(3).119.

**συγκινδῡν-ευτέον**, *one must face danger along with*, τινι Cic.*Att.*9.4.2, Epict.*Ench.*32.3. **-εύω**, *incur danger along with* others, τινι Th.8.22, Plu.*Art.*8, etc.; τῷ φράζειν σ. τινί by saying, Pl.*Lg.*969a; μετά τινος Plb.2.3.5: abs., *share in the danger, be partners in danger*, X.*Ages.*11.13, Pl.*Phlb.*29a, D.15.19, etc.; πρὸς τοὺς βαρβάρους *OGI* 765.21 (Priene): c. dat. modi, τῷ ναυτικῷ with their navy, Isoc.8.97.

❋**συγκῑν-έω**, *stir up* or *excite*, Plb.15.17.1, *Act.Ap.*6.12; *stir up* a mixture, Gal.13.1041:—Pass., *move along with* or *together*, Arist.*Top.*113$^{a}$30, *Pr.*921$^{b}$28, Gal.16.520, etc.; σ. κινήσεις ἀνελευθέρους Plu.2.704d; τὸ συγκεκινημένον *sympathetic emotion*, Longin.15.2; συγκεκ. λόγοι Id.29.2. II. apparently intr., Arist.*Pr.*949$^{a}$19 (dub. l.). **-ημα**, ατος, τό, *commotion*, S.E.*M.*9.170 (but f.l. for κίνημα). **-ησις**, εως, ἡ, *commotion*, τοῦ θερμοῦ Arist.*Pr.*945$^{b}$9; πάθος ψυχῆς σ. ἐστίν Longin.20.2; περὶ τὰ μόρια Sor.1.31, cf. Apollon.ap.Orib.7.19.5. 2. *movement in the same direction*, opp. ἀντικίνησις, *Corp. Herm.*2.6. **-ητικός**, ή, όν, *stimulative*, Herod.Med. in *Rh.Mus.*58.86, Ptol.*Tetr.*87, Cass.*Pr.*16 (ed. Sylburg, συγκριτικήν Ideler).

**συγκίρνημι**, = συγκεράννυμι, Ath.2.38f:—Pass., Ti.Locr.96a, Iamb.*Comm.Math.*10; also **συγκιρνάω**, Tz. ad Lyc.p.2 S.:—Med., Ath.11.476a, D.L.7.158:—Pass., Porph.*Sent.*4, Sch.S.*OC*159.

**συγκλάζω**, *sound together with*, in aor. 2 σύριγγι συνέκλαγον αὐλοί Nonn.*D.*5.286.

**συγκλαίω**, *weep with*, τινι Luc.*Asin.*22, *AP*9.573 (Ammian.).

**σύγ-κλᾰσις**, εως, ἡ, *breaking*, Thd.*Pr.*19.29. **-κλασμός**, ὁ, *breaking*, ἔθετο..τὰς συκᾶς μου εἰς σ. Lxx *Jl.*1.7. ❋**-κλάω**, *break, break off*, κλήματα Ar.*Ec.*1031, cf. Chaerem.14.13, Thphr.*HP*4.7.3; ὅπλον Lxx *Ps.*45(46).10; of a bad carver, *mangle*, τὰ μέρη Herm. *in Phdr.* p.189 A.; dub. sens. in Phld.*Mus.*p.23 K.:—Pass., of persons engaged in servile occupations, *to be cramped* or *stunted*, τὰς ψυχὰς συγκεκλασμένοι τε καὶ ἀποτεθρυμμένοι διὰ τὰς βαναυσίας Pl.*R.*495e; οἱ δοῦλοι..κάμπτονται καὶ συγκλῶνται Id.*Tht.*173a; of lines, Arist.*Pr.*892$^{a}$15.

**συγκλείς**, κλεῖτος, ἡ (i.e. συγκλής, κλῆτος), Thess. for σύγκλητος, ἡ, *IG*9(2).517.10 (Larissa, iii B.C.).

**σύγ-κλεισις**, old Att. **ξύγκλῃσις**, εως, ἡ: (συγκλείω):—*shutting up, closing up* (of a line of battle), Th.5.71; τῆς φάλαγγος ἡ σ. Arr.*An.*1.4.3; συγκλείσει κωλύειν τὴν δίοδον Thphr.*Od.*36. 2. *locking up, safe storage*, σίτου *PLond.*2.237.21 (iv A.D.). II. *a being closed*, ἰσχυρὰν..τὴν σ. αὐτῶν πρὸς ἄλληλα κέκτηται has them closely locked together, Pl.*Ti.*81b, cf. Hp.*Loc.Hom.*6; ἐπὶ συναφῆς καὶ συγκλείσεως χάριν Arist.*Spir.*484$^{b}$22; *locking* of shields in χελώνη, Arr.*Tact.*11.6. 2. συγκλείσεις *narrow passes, defiles*, Plb.5.44.7, v.l. for συγκλίσεις in Plu.*Cam.*41. ❋**-κλεισμα**, ατος, τό, *border*, Lxx 3*Ki.*7.29; cf. συγκλειστός 3. ❋**-κλεισμός**, ὁ, *a being shut up, confinement*, ib.*Ez.*4.3,7, *BGU*1786.7 (i B.C.), Sm.*Is.*24.22: metaph., σ. καρδίας *closeness, hardness* of heart, Lxx *Ho.*13.8. II. *conclusion*, τοῦ ὅλου χρόνου *POxy.*275.20 (i A.D.); ἔτους *PFlor.*50.114 (iii A.D.). **-κλειστός**, ή, όν, *shut up*, ζόφῳ Luc.*Trag.*64. 2. *with the power of closing*, ὄστρακα Arist.*HA* 528$^{b}$15. 3. ἔργον συγκλειστόν, = σύγκλεισμα, Lxx 3*Ki.*7.28. **-κλείω**, fut. -κλείσω: Ion. **-κληΐω**, fut -κληΐσω: old Att. **ξυγκλῄω**, fut. -κλῄσω: Ep. aor. συνεκλήϊσσα Nonn.*D.*48.309:—Pass., aor. συνεκλείσθην, old Att. ξυνεκλῄσθην: pf. συγκέκλειμαι Isoc.15.68, but -εισμαι Men.670, D.S.15.63, v.l. in E.*Hec.*487; old Att. ξυγκέκλῃμαι, Ion. συγκεκλήϊμαι (v. infr.):—*shut* or *coop up, hem in, enclose*, Hdt.4.157, 7.41; ξ. τὴν ἐκκλησίαν ἐς τὸν Κολωνόν Th.8.67; πρὶν συγκλεῖσαι (sc. τοὺς ἰχθῦς τοῖς δικτύοις) Arist.*HA*533$^{b}$26; αἱ συγκλείουσαι πλευραὶ τὸ στῆθος Id.*PA*654$^{b}$35; σ. τινὰς ἐντὸς τειχῶν Plb.1.17.8; εἰς πολιορκίαν Id.1.8.2 (Pass.); σ. [θεοὺς] τῇ ὕλῃ *include* them in matter, Plu.2.426b; [ἡ πολεμία] ξυνέκληε διὰ μέσου *shut off and intercepted* them, Th.5.64:—Pass., λίμνη συγκεκληιμένη πάντοθεν ὄρεσι Hdt.7.129; τὸ στόμα τῶν μητρέων ὑπὸ πιμελῆς -είεται Hp.*Aër.*21; σ. εἰς στενὴν ἐντομήν D.S.1.32; ξυγκεκλῃμένη πέπλοις *close muffled*, E.*Hec.*487. 2. generally, of straits or difficulties, τινὰ εἰς ἀγῶνα Plb.3.63.3; εἰς τὸν ἔσχατον καιρόν Id.11.2.10:—Pass., συγκλείεσθαι ὑπὸ τῶν καιρῶν, τῶν πραγμάτων, Id.2.60.4, 11.20.7; εἰς χαλεπὸν..συγκεκλεισμένος βίον '*cabin'd, cribb'd, confined*', Men. l. c. 3. *pit against one another, set to fight as in the lists*, οἵ σε καὶ Ἑρμιόναν ἔριδι..ξυνέκλῃσαν E.*Andr.*122 (lyr.). 4. ὁ συγκλείων, = *smith*, Lxx 4*Ki.*24.14:—Pass., χρυσίον συγκεκλεισμένον ib.3*Ki.*6.20. II. *shut close, close*, στόμα E.*Hipp.*498; ὄμμα Id.*Hec.*430, *Ion* 241; [τὰ βλέφαρα] X.*Mem.*1.4.6 (Pass.); ξ. τὰς πύλας Th.4.67; τὰς θύρας Aeschin.1.74; τὰς θυρίδας Gal.16.578: abs., σύγκλῃε *shut the doors*, Ar.*Ach.*1096; σ. τὰ δικαστήρια *close* the courts, Id.*Eq.*1317; τὰ καπηλεῖα Lys.*Fr.*1.3; σ. τοὺς ὀφθαλμούς *close* them *up* by blows, D.54.8:—Pass., τὸ δεσμωτήριον συνεκέκλειστο And.1.48 codd. (συνεκέκλῃτο Sauppe); of bivalve fish, Arist.*HA*528$^{a}$16; of eyebrows, *come together*, Hp.*Loc.Hom.*3; of wounds, Dsc.*Ther.*2. 2. intr. in Act., ὥρας ἤδη συγκλειούσης as the season *was* now *closing in*, i.e. the days becoming shorter, Plb.18.7.3, cf. D.S.10.4; τοῦ καιροῦ συγκλείοντος εἰς χειμῶνα *GDI*3087.19 (Chersonesus). III. *close jointly*, συνανοιγόντων καὶ συγκλειόντων *IG*1$^{2}$.91.17. IV. σ. τὰς ἀσπίδας *lock* their shields, X.*Cyr.*7.1.33: hence, abs., *close up* the ranks, Th.4.35; τὸ διάκενον καὶ οὐ ξυγκλῃσθέν *the part that was* not *closed up*, of a gap in the line, Id.5.72. 2. *connect closely together*, τὰ ἀνόμοια ἁρμονίᾳ συγκεκλεῖσθαι Philol.6; ἐν ἄρθροις συγκεκλῃμένον καλῶς well *linked* or *compacted*, E.*Ba.*1300; σ. (sc. τὴν πόλιν) εἰς ταὐτόν Pl.*Criti.*117e, cf. *Ti.*76a, etc.; σ. τὴν ἀρχὴν τῶν ῥηθήσεσθαι μελλόντων τῇ τελευτῇ τῶν προειρημένων Isoc.12.24, cf. 15.68 (Pass.):—Pass., συγκλεισθήσονται ταῖς τε ἐπιγαμίαις καὶ ἐγκτήσεσι παρ' ἀλλήλοις X.*HG*5.2.19. V. *conclude, complete*, λόγον, διάνοιαν, A.D.*Adv.*121.1, *Synt.*66.8:—Pass., ib.11.9.

**συγκλέπτης**, ου, ὁ, *fellow-thief*, Poll.6.158.

**συγκλέπτω**, *steal along with*, μετά τινος Antipho 6.35; τὰς ψήφους S.E.*M.*2.39. II. *deceive, elude*, σ. τὴν γνώμην καὶ τὴν ὄψιν αἱ ῥαφαί Hp.*VC*12.

**συγκληρία**, ἡ, in pl., *connexions*, παθημάτων Hp.*Epid.*6.7.1.

❋**συγκληρονομ-έω**, *to be joint-heir*, Lxx *Si.*22.23(29). ❋**-ος** (parox.), ον, *joint-heir*, Χριστοῦ *Ep.Rom.*8.17, cf. *Ep.Eph.*3.6.

❋**σύγκληρ-ος**, ον, *having lots or portions that join, bordering, neighbouring*, χθών E.*Heracl.*32; τείχεα Nic.*Al.*1; *sharing a* κλῆρος, *PCair.Zen.*1.19 (iii B.C.). II. *joined by lot to, allotted to*, θνητῷ βίῳ Plu.2.103f, cf. Luc.*Am.*24: c. gen., *belonging to as portion*, Lyc.995. **-όω**, Dor. **-κλᾱρόω** *IG*12(1).3.10 (Rhodes, i A.D.):—*join* or *embrace in one lot*, δύο τμήματα Pl.*Lg.*745c. 2. *choose by lot*, δικαστήριον v.l. in Plu.*Alc.*19. 3. Med., *draw a lot with others*, J.*BJ*3.8.7; Astrol., *acquire* κλῆρος *jointly with*, Vett.Val.68.5. II. *join by lot*, τινί τι D.14.18; τινά τινι Aeschin.2.183; αὐτόματος φορὰ καὶ τύχη τὰς ἀρχὰς συνεκλήρωσεν Jul.*Or.*5.162a:—Pass., τὰ ἄλογα πολλὰ τῶν ἀνθρωπίνων..ἔχει συγκεκληρωμένα *assigned to them along with* men, Ael.*NA Praef.*; συγκεκληρῶσθαι σιωπῇ *to be all doomed* to silence, ib.15.28, cf. Dam.*Pr.*257. **-ωσις**, εως, ἡ, = *consortium*, *Gloss.*

**σύγκλῃσις, συγκλῄω**, v. σύγκλεισις, συγκλείω.

**συγ-κλητικός**, ή, όν, *of senatorial rank*, Lat. *senatorius*, D.S.20.36, Plu.*Galb.*9, Luc.*Alex.*25, freq. in Inscrr., *IG*3.677, etc.; of a woman, *IGRom.*3.95 (Pontus); σ. οἰκίαι ib.4.1404.16 (Smyrna, iii A.D.). II. σ. μέλος *summoning*, Ael.*VH*8.7. **-κλητος**, ον, *called together, summoned*, στράτευμα E.*IA*301 (lyr.); σύγκλητον τήνδε γερόντων..λέσχην S.*Ant.*160 (anap.); οἱ σ. *invited guests*, Poll.6.12. II. σ. ἐκκλησία at Athens, an assembly *specially summoned*, opp. κυρία, Decr.ap.D.18.37, cf. 73, *IG*2$^{2}$.945.5 (ii B.C.). 2. generally, σύγκλητος (sc. βουλή), ἡ, *summoned council*, opp. ἐκκλησία, Arist.*Pol.*1275$^{b}$8; at Carthage, Plb.10.18.1; in the Achaean League, Id.29.24.6, *IG*7.411.13 (Oropus, ii B.C.); freq. of the Roman *Senate*, Plb.21.1.3, al., Str.3.4.20, D.S.4.83, etc., and in Inscrr., as *SIG*591.68 (Lampsacus, ii B.C.), 785.12 (Chios, i A.D.), etc.; personified, θεὸς Σ. *OGI*479.4 (Dorylaeum, ii A.D.): cf. συγκλείς. 3. πρὸς τὴν σ. dub. sens. in *PTeb.*5.197 (ii B.C.).

**συγκλῑνής**, ές, (κλίνω) *inclining together*, τὸ σ. ἐπ' Αἴαντι, perhaps, *the united force* directed against Ajax, A.*Fr.*84.

**συγκλῑνίαι**, αἱ, *slopes*, αἱ σ. τῶν τόπων the *slopes* or *configuration* of the ground, Plu.*Pomp.*32, cf. *Pyrrh.*28, *Phil.*4.

❋**σύγκλῑνος**, ον, *sharing one's couch*, = συγκλίτης, Men.1070.

**συγκλίνω** [ῑ], *lay together*:—Pass., *lie with*, [γυναικί] Hdt.2.181; of the woman, οὐκ ἔστιν ἥτις τῷδε -κλιθήσεται E.*Alc.*1090. 2. intr. in Act., *lean, incline*, ταῖς εὐνοίαις Plb.7.11.4. II. *inflect similarly*, A.D.*Synt.*102.11. III. συγκεκλιμένου τοῦ σκέλεος, = συγκεκαμμένου (which is v.l.), Hp.*Art.*60.

**σύγκλῐσις**, v. σύγκλεισις II. 2.

❋**συγκλίτης** [ῐ], ου, ὁ, *one who lies with* one, *companion at table*, Plu.2.149b, 503a, Ἀρχ.Ἐφ.1931.177 (Thessaly).

**συγκλονέω**, *dash together, confound utterly*, συνεκλόνεον γὰρ ὀϊστοὶ [τοὺς Τρῶας] Il.13.722; νέας *AP*9.755; ἀκολασίῃ ψυχήν, ὥσπερ νῆα ἄνεμοι.., σ. Eus.Mynd.12; τοὺς καρπούς *EM*378.48; of *concussion* of joints, Gal.7.185.

**συγκλῠδάζομαι**, = sq.: metaph., Iamb.*VP*15.65.

❋**συγκλύζω**, *wash over*, ποταμοὶ οὐ συγκλύσουσί σε Lxx *Is.*43.2, cf. *Ca.*8.7:—Pass., *to be washed over by the waves*, of a ship, Plu.2.206d, 467d. 2. *shake up together*, κονία συγκλυζομένη Dsc.*Eup.*1.57. II. metaph. in Pass., *to be overwhelmed*, Phld.*Rh.*2.303 S.; *to be plunged in debt*, Plu.2.831e. 2. *to be in agitation, confusion*, τὰ τῆς Ἀσίας συγκεκλυσμένα πράγματα Philostr.*VS*1.18.2.

**σύγκλῠς**, ῠδος, ὁ, ἡ, *washed together* by the waves; but only metaph., ξύγκλυδες ἄνθρωποι *promiscuous crowd, mob, rabble*, Th.7.5;

σύγκλυδες alone, Pl.*R.*569a, Str.4.2.1, etc.; σ. ὅμιλος Plu.*Mar.*45: with neut. Subst., συγκλύδων καὶ μιγάδων ἠθῶν ἀνάπλεοι Ph.2.312: Hsch. cites a neut. pl. σύγκλυδα.

**συγκλυσμός**, ὁ, *meeting of waves*, Men.536.6, Arist.*Mir.*843$^{a}$14.

**συγκλώθω**, *connect by spinning*, M.Ant.10.5, Dam.*Pr.*251:—Pass., *to be interwoven*, Chrysipp.*Stoic.*2.265, Plot.2.3.15; συγκεκλωσμένον ἦν αὐτῷ, c. inf., Sch.Pi.*O.*1.38.

**σύγκλωσις**, εως, ἡ, *a spinning together*, of the thread of destiny, M.Ant.2.3, 3.11.

**συγκνισόομαι**, Pass., *to be stewed together with*, συγκεκνισωμένων ζωμῷ κρεῶν Ath.9.395f.

**σύγκοιλον**, τό, *hollow, combe*, *Inscr.Prien.*42.49 (ii B.C.).

**συγκοιμ-άομαι**, Pass., *sleep with, lie with*, of the man, τινι Hdt.3.69, Lys.*Fr.*4; of the woman, A.*Ag.*1258, S.*El.*274, E.*Ph.*54; of an infant, συγκοιμάσθω τὸ βρέφος αὐτῇ Sor.1.106: abs., *to be bedfellows*, of children, Arr.*Epict.*2.22.13. II. metaph., σ. τοῖς πράγμασι, of an historian, Plb.12.26$^{D}$.3; τῷ Ὀρέστῃ συγκεκοίμημαι D.C.60.28. **-ημα**, ατος, τό, *partner of one's bed*, in pl., E.*Andr.*1273. **-ησις**, εως, ἡ, *a sleeping together, lying with*, ἡ τῶν γυναικῶν σ. Pl.*R.*460b, cf. *Phdr.*255e; μετὰ τῶν ἐραστῶν D.C.79.13. **-ητής**, οῦ, ὁ, *bedfellow*, Hsch. s.v. ἐπευνακταί. **-ίζω**, *put to bed together, join in wedlock*, τινά τινι Ar.*Av.*1734.

**συγκοινόομαι**, Med., *communicate, impart*, τινί τι Th.8.75 (v.l. -νωνήσαντο). 2. in Pass., *to be fastened firmly to*, c. dat., Hero *Aut.*13.9:—Pass. also, -ωμένα *let in, sunk*, Id.*Bel.*76.6.

**σύγκοινος**, ον, = κοινός, *Schwyzer* 197.70 (Crete, iii B.C.): v. σύγκωμος.

**συγκοινων-έω**, *have a joint share of*, τῆς δόξης ταύτης D.57.2; *to be connected with*, τῆς κνήμης Hp.*Art.*85; σ. τινί τινος *go shares with* one *in* a thing, Alex.162.5. 2. in *NT* c. dat., *take part in, have fellowship with*, ταῖς ἁμαρτίαις *Apoc.*18.4; τοῖς ἔργοις *Ep.Eph.*5.11; σ. μου τῇ θλίψει *Ep.Phil.*4.14. **-ός**, όν, *partaking jointly of*, τῆς ῥίζης *Ep.Rom.*11.17, cf. 1*Ep.Cor.*9.23; ἐν τῇ θλίψει *Apoc.*1.9; τῆς βασιλείας μου Steph. *in Hp.*1.76 D.: Subst., *partner*, *PMasp.*158.11 (vi A.D.).

**συγκοιτ-άδιος**, ον, = σύγκοιτος, Hsch. (-τάλιος cod.). **-άζω**, *make to lie with*, [εἴδωλον] αὐτῇ Tz.*H.*2.773:—Pass., *lie (down) with*, Id. ad Lyc.848, Aq.*De.*28.30, Cyran.63. **-ιον** (sc. ἀργύριον), τό, *harlot's hire*, Hsch. **-ις**, ιδος, pecul. fem. of sq., *Gloss.* **-ος**, ὁ, ἡ, *bedfellow*, *Com.Adesp.*1203.7, Lxx *Mi.*7.5, *AP*5.151, 190 (both Mel.), *MAMA*1.301 (Phrygia): metaph., σ. γλυκὺν ὕπνον Pi.*P.*9.23; ἡ κακία σ. ὀδυνηρά Plu.2.100f. II. as Adj., *of* or *for sexual intercourse*, φίλτρα *AP*5.195 (Mel.).

**συγκολάζω**, *help in chastising*, τινί τινας Pl.*Lg.*730d. II. *chastise as well*, τινάς.. τῷ εἰργασμένῳ J.*AJ*2.6.8, cf. Ph.2.326 (Pass.).

**συγκολάπτω**, *hew in pieces*, Aq.*Le.*22.24.

⊕ **συγκολλ-άω**, *glue* or *cement together*, *IG*2$^{2}$.1668.82 (iv B.C.), Luc.*Alex.*14: metaph., Pl.*Mx.*236b, Ar.*V.*1041 (anap.); τινὰ εἰς ταὐτόν Pl.*Ti.*43a:—Pass., *unite*, of a wound, Sor.1.36. **-ημα**, ατος, τό, *connecting-rod*, Thd.*Ex.*38.11, 12 (37.9, 10). **-ήσιμος**, ον, *glued together*, τόμος σ. *PGrenf.*2.41.18 (i A.D.); βιβλείδια *POxy.*2131.4 (iii A.D.): Subst. -ήσιμα, τά, ib.34 i 13 (ii A.D.), etc. ⊕**-ησις**, εως, ἡ, *gluing together*, Clearch.44; *adhesion*, σπέρματος Sor.1.43: metaph., *attachment*, Them.*Or.*22.268a. **-ητής**, οῦ, ὁ, *one who glues together, fabricator*, ψευδῶν Ar.*Nu.*446 (anap.). **-ος**, ον, (κόλλα) *glued together*, βάρη Nic.*Fr.*78:—mostly in Adv. συγκόλλως, *in accordance with*, ἐμοί A.*Supp.*310; σ. ἔχειν to agree, Id.*Ch.*542; σ. κολλᾶν τι ἐπί τινι *App.Anth.*7.6: also neut. pl. as Adv., λόγος σύγκολλα.. τεκταίνεται S.*Fr.*867.

**συγκολυμβάω**, *swim with* or *together*, Antisth.ap.D.L.6.6 (= Aristipp.ap.Gal.*Protr.*5, where συνεκκ-), Anticl.7.

**συγκομ-ιδή**, ἡ, of harvest, *gathering in*, ἐν καρποῦ ξυγκομιδῇ ἦσαν Th.3.15; σ. τῶν ἐκ γῆς καρπῶν Pl.*Tht.*149e, etc.; τῶν ὡραίων Id.*Lg.*845e; σίτου X.*HG*7.5.14: abs., *ingathering, harvest*, *PCair.Zen.*225.9 (iii B.C.), *IG*2$^{2}$.1100.28 (ii A.D.), *PFlor.*175.25 (iii A.D.), etc.: cf. συγκομίζω I. 2. 2. in pass. sense, *being gathered together, crowding*, ἐκ τῶν ἀγρῶν ἐς τὸ ἄστυ Th.2.52. 3. σ. ἱστορίας *compiling* of history, Hdn.1.1.1. ⊕**-ίζω**, *carry* or *bring together, collect*, Hdt.1.21, 2.121.δ', 9.80, Th.7.85:—Med., Hdt.2.94; *bring together to oneself, collect round one*, ἰατροὺς ἀρίστους πρὸς αὑτόν X.*Cyr.*8.2.24; συγκεκόμισθε κάλλιστον κτῆμα εἰς τὰς ψυχάς *you have stored up* in your souls, ib.1.5.12; ὀλίγα τῇ μνήμῃ Luc.*Nigr.*10; σ. πρὸς ἐμαυτόν *concentrate* in myself, X.*Cyr.*4.3.17:—Pass., ἐκέατο ἁλέες συγκεκομισμένοι *heaped together*, Hdt.8.25: metaph., ἐνταῦθα γάρ μοι κεῖνα συγκομίζεται *are gained both at once*, S.*OC*585. 2. of the harvest, *gather in*, X.*Mem.*2.8.3, D.S.5.68, etc.: freq. in Med., X.*An.*6.6.37, etc.:—Pass., of the harvest, ὀργᾷ συγκομίζεσθαι it is ripe *for carrying*, Hdt.4.199, cf. *PCair.Zen.*225.9 (iii B.C.), *PRev.Laws* 43.5 (iii B.C.); ἐλαχίστοις πόνοις συγκομίζεται *is got in*.., D.S.1.36. II. *help in burying* or *cremating*, τόνδε τὸν νεκρὸν.. μὴ συγκομίζειν S.*Aj.*1048; ἔφθη τὸ σῶμα συγκομισθέν the body was already *cremated*, Plu.*Sull.*38, cf. *Ages.*19. **-ιστέον**, *one must gather, collect*, Hsch. **-ιστήρια** (sc. ἱερά), τά, *the feast of harvest-home*, Id., Eust.772.22. **-ιστής**, οῦ, ὁ, *gatherer*, καρποῦ Id.1488.59. **-ιστός**, ή, όν, *brought together*, ἄρτος σ. bread *of unbolted meal*, Hp.*VM*14, cf. *Acut.*37, Diocl.ap.Hsch., Trypho and Diph.Siph.ap.Ath.3.109c, 115d, Dsc.2.85; σ. διαιτήματα *rough, coarse* food, Hp.*Vict.*3.68, cf. 2.56.

**συγκομμάτιον**, τό, = σκευασία τις παρὰ τοῖς ὀψαρτυταῖς, Hsch.

**συγκονίομαι** [ῑ], Pass., *roll in the dust with another*, i.e. *wrestle* or *struggle with*, τινι Plu.2.5 b, 97a, Max.Tyr.7.6 (-ιόομαι codd.).

**συγκοπ-ή**, ἡ, *cutting up into small pieces*, Plu.2.912e, *POxy.*1654.6 (ii A.D.), Sch.Luc.*Vit.Auct.*19; *cutting of metal into pieces* for coinage, *Peripl.M.Rubr.*6: metaph., *extreme conciseness*, opp. συντομία, ἡ ἄγαν τῆς φράσεως σ. Longin.42. 2. Gramm., *syncope*, i.e. *cutting* a word *short by striking out one* or *more letters*, A.D.*Adv.*169.15, al., Plu.2.1011e; κατὰ συγκοπὴν καλεῖσθαι Id.*Rom.*11. b. = ἀποκοπή v, Longin.39.4. II. *stoppage, cutting short*, ἡ τοῦ πνεύματος σ. D.H.*Comp.*15; αἱ σ. τῶν ἤχων ib.22. III. *sudden loss of strength, syncope*, Aret.*SA*2.3, Gal.9.290, 10.837, Philagr.ap.Orib.5.21.7; cf. σύγκοπος, συγκόπτω III. **-ιάτης** [ᾱ], ου, ὁ, *fellow-labourer*, *Sammelb.*343, 1990 (Alexandria). ⊕**-ιάω**, *to be a fellow-labourer*, prob. in *Supp.Epigr.*6.473 (Lycaonia, iv A.D.). **-ος**, ον, (συγκοπή III) *falling down in a swoon*, D.S.3.57. **-τικός**, ή, όν, *of syncope*, σύμπτωμα Gal.15.462; *apt to cause syncope*, Id.7.467, Alex.Trall.*Verm.* Adv. -κῶς *like a sufferer from syncope*, νοτίζεσθαι Gal.18(2).6. **-τός**, ή, όν, *chopped up*, λάχανα Ath.9.373a. **-τω**, pf. -κέκοφα Pl.*Tht.*169b, etc.:—*chop up*, X.*Cyr.*6.4.3; χειμὼν.. συνέκοψε πάντα καὶ διέλυσε Hdt.7.34:—Pass., *to be broken up*, *IG*7.303.53 (Oropus); συγκεκομμένα μέρη τοῦ σώματος *BGU*1857.10 (i B.C.): metaph., πολλαὶ φιλίαι συνεκόπησαν Luc.*Cal.*1. 2. *thrash soundly*, τινας Lys.3.16, cf. Pl. l.c., X.*Smp.*8.6, Metag.9, D.21.57; ξύλοις τὰς κεφαλάς Duris 67 J.; of cocks fighting, v.l. in Aesop.22 (i p.68 Chambry):—Pass., συγκεκομμένος E.*Cyc.*228, cf. X.*Cyr.*2.3.20; συγκεκόφθαι Ar.*Nu.*1426, etc.; συγκοπῆναι Hyp.*Fr.*272a Jensen. 3. Med., *beat oneself, lament*, Sch.A.*Ch.*23. II. *cut short* a sound or word (v. συγκοπή I. 2, II), D.H.*Comp.*16, *EM*299.28, etc.:—Pass., τὸ -κεκόφθαι Phld.*Po.Herc.*1676.9. III. *wear out*, τὸν μὲν ἀποπνίξας τάχιστα, τοῦ δὲ συγκόψας τὴν δύναμιν Gal.15.504:—Pass., esp. in pf., *to be worn out, suffer from* συγκοπή (III), Thphr.*Lass.*2; συγκεκομμένοι τὰ πνεύματα D.H.5.44; συγκεκ. ὑπὸ τῶν ἀγώνων Plu.*Comp.Cim.Luc.*3, cf. Gal.9.291, 10.846, al. **-ώδης**, ες, *accompanied by syncope*, Id.7.688; σ. μαρασμός Id.10.542.

**συγκορδυλέομαι**, Pass., *to be wrapped close up*, συγκεκορδυλημένος Phot. (-δημένα cod.), cf. Hsch. (-λιμένα cod.).

**συγκορυβαντιάω**, *join in Corybantic revels, share in inspiration* or *frenzy*, Pl.*Phdr.*228b, Numen.ap.Eus.*PE*14.8, Anon.ap.Suid. s.v. κορυβαντιᾷ; πρὸς τὴν ἐπιθυμίαν Eun.*VS* p.503 B.

**συγκόρυφ-ος**, ον, *with the vertices joined*, κῶνοι Arist.*Pr.*912$^{b}$18. **-όω**, *bring together to one point*, Longin.24; *bring to a head, complete*, D.H.*Th.*9:—Pass., Phld.*Rh.*2.229 S., Dam.*Pr.*54, *Theol.Ar.*16. **-ωσις**, εως, ἡ, = συγκεφαλαίωσις, ib.25.

**συγκοσμ-έω**, *arrange together, adjust*, Arist.*Cael.*293$^{a}$27; ἀγῶνα *SIG*1073.43 (Olympia, ii A.D.):—Pass., τὸ ἐκ τῶν ἐναντίων συγκοσμούμενον M.Ant.7.48. II. *confer honour on, to be an ornament to*, X.*Cyr.*2.2.26:—Pass., Vett.Val.46.28, al. 2. *join in honouring*, Polem.*Cyn.*49. **-ησις**, εως, ἡ, *adornment*, *BCH*5.479 (Samos). **-ος**, ὁ, *fellow-κόσμος*, at Praesus, *SIG*524.3 (iii B.C.), *Historia* 5.226.

**συγκοτταβίζω**, *play at the cottabos together*, *Com.Adesp.*586.

**συγκουφίζω**, *help to lift* or *lighten*, τὸ βάρος S.E.*P.*3.15; *help to keep above water*, τινα Luc.*Tox.*20, cf. *DDeor.*20.6.

**συγκραδαίνω**, *shake together*, Arist.*Mu.*395$^{b}$33:—Pass., Hypsae.ap.Stob.4.31.45.

**σύγ-κρᾱμα**, ατος, τό, *mixture*, Arist.*Mir.*832$^{b}$26, Plu.2.943e. **-κρᾱμᾰτικός**, ή, όν, *mixed together*, dub.l. in *Placit.*5.2.3. ⊕**-κρᾱσις**, εως, Ion. -κρησις, ἡ, *mixing together, commixture, blending, tempering*, Hp.*VM*24, E.*Fr.*21.4, Pl.*Phlb.*64d, etc.; ἡ σ. τῶν χρωμάτων Id.*Plt.*277c; τῶν στοιχείων (heat and cold) Asclep.ap.*Placit.*5.21.2; ἥ τε ἐς τοὺς ὀλίγους καὶ τοὺς πολλοὺς ξ. *blending* of oligarchy with democracy, Th.8.97; ἡ.. ὑγρότης μὴ φέρουσα τὴν πρὸς τὸ φῶς σ. Plu.*Arat.*10; of friendship, Id.*Ant.*31, *BCH*49.483 (Delph.); of bodily *constitution* or *temperament*, Ptol.*Tetr.*8, 10. b. Astrol., *combination of influence* of heavenly bodies, Herm.ap.Stob.1.49.3, Ptol.*Tetr.*83, 121, Man.2.400. c. ἡ σ. τοῦ ἔτους the *temperature* or *climate*, Dsc.1 *Praef.*7. II. *mixture, compound*, οὐ θνητὸς οὐδ' ἀθάνατος, ἀλλ' ἔχων τινὰ σ. but *compounded* so to say *of both*, Alex.240.2; τὸν καιρὸν.. τῆς σ., i.e. the moment when the dish is neither too hot nor too cold, Id.173.10; τὴν τοῦ βίου σ. Men.685.

**συγκρᾱτέον**, (συγκεράννυμι) *one must mingle*, Pl.*Phlb.*62b.

**συγκρᾰτ-έω**, *hold together*, ἡ ψυχὴ σ. ἡμᾶς Anaximen.2; *keep* troops *together*, Plu.*Phoc.*12. 2. *strengthen*, τὰ μέλεα Aret.*SD*1.5. 3. *hold in, keep under control*, τὸ πνεῦμα D.L.6.76; ἀπορρήτους λόγους Plu.2.508d. **-ησις**, εως, ἡ, *retention*, τοῦ σπέρματος, = σύλληψις, Sor.1.43; τοῦ πνεύματος D.L.6.77.

**συγκρᾱτικός**, ή, όν, = συγκραματικός, Ptol.*Tetr.*82, Vett.Val.55.5, 359.14. Adv. -κῶς *in combination*, *Cat.Cod.Astr.*2.168.

**σύγκρᾱτος**, ον, *mixed together*, Luc.*Am.*12, Hld.3.15; *closely united*, σ. ζεῦγος E.*Andr.*495 (lyr.).

⊕ **συγκρᾰτύνω**, *strengthen, make firm*, τὸ πῦρ σ. τὸν κέραμον Plu.2.656e:—Pass., *become so*, Hp.*Epid.*2.1.8.

**συγκρέκω**, *accompany by playing on the* κιθάρα, τῷ χορῷ μέλος Ael.*NA*11.1.

**συγκρημνίζω**, *throw down a precipice together*, Plb.8.32.7.

**συγκρητ-ίζω**, (Κρής) of two parties, *combine against a common enemy*, *EM*732.55. **-ισμός**, ὁ, *union, federation of Cretan communities*, Plu.2.490b.

**σύγκρῐμ-α**, ατος, τό, *body formed by combination, compound*, Epicur.*Fr.*76 p.345 U. (pl.), *Placit.*1.15.8, al., Plb.34.5.3, S.E.*P.*2.24, Sor.1.22, Gal.8.928; anatomical *structure*, Id.2.899, Philum.*Ven.*18.2; of the *union* of body and soul, Zeno *Stoic.*1.40; σ. νοητόν Phld.*D.*3.11. 2. σ. μουσικῶν *concert*, Lxx *Si.*35(32).(7)5. II. *judgement, decree*, ib.1*Ma.*1.57, *PAmh.*2.68.34 (i A.D.), Thd.*Da.*4.21. III. = σύγκρισις III, Lxx *Da.*5.26. **-ατικός**, ή, όν, = συγκραματικός, Gal. *Phil.Hist.*106: Comp. -ώτερος Sch.E.*Rh.*346 (-κρεμ- codd.). **-άτιον**, τό, Dim. of σύγκριμα I. 1, M.Ant.8.25, Philum.ap.Aët.16.105(115).

⊛ **συγκρίνω** [ῑ], *bring into combination* or *aggregation*, opp. διακρίνω, Emp.ap.Arist.*Metaph.*985$^a$24, cf. 984$^a$10, Epich.[245]; σ. [τὴν ὄψιν] Pl.*Ti.*67d, cf. Ti.Locr.101c; τὰ συγκρινόμενα *bodies which are formed by combination*, Anaxag.4, cf. Pl.*Phd.*72c, *Prm.*157a; συνεκρίθη, συνέστη Hp.*Epid.*6.2.25; συγκρίνεσθαι εἰς ὕδωρ, of vapour, Arist.*Mete.*370$^a$30, cf. 350$^a$13; ἐξ οὗ συνεκρίθη of which it *was formed*, *Placit.*5.3.1 (nisi leg. ἀπεκρίθη). 2. *combine*, συγκρινόμενος τούτοις καὶ ὁ Ἑρμῆς *Cat.Cod. Astr.*2.164. II. *compare*, τι πρός τι Arist.*Rh.*1368$^a$21, *Pol.*1295$^a$27, cf. Thphr.*CP*1.8.2, Philem.109; κάλυκας βάτῳ *AP*12.204 (Strat.); ἑαυτόν τινι Plu.*CG*4, cf. 2*Ep.Cor.*10.12; σ. τι ἐκ παραθέσεως Plb.12.9.1; σ. τὰ λεγόμενα *compare and examine* them, Id.14.3.7, cf. Arist. *EN*1165$^a$32; μή με τάφῳ σύγκρινε do not *measure, estimate* me by my tomb, *AP*7.137:—Pass., ὁ Ἐπικούρου βίος τοῖς τῶν ἄλλων -όμενος Epicur.*Sent.Vat.*36:—Med., *measure oneself with another, strive* or *contend*, τινι D.S.4.14; εἰς ἅμιλλαν Id.1.58; a usage censured by Luc.*Sol.*5, Thom.Mag. p.345 R. III. *interpret*, τὰ λεγόμενα Plb.14.3.7, cf. 1*Ep.Cor.*2.13; esp. σ. ἐνύπνια *interpret* dreams, Lxx *Ge.*40.8, al. IV. *decree*, ζημίας, ἧς ἂν ὁ στρατηγὸς συγκρίνῃ *PPetr.*3 p.69 (iii B.C.), cf. *PCair.Zen.*355.102, al. (iii B.C.); *decide*, ib.371.14 (iii B.C.); τί ποιήσωσιν Lxx *Nu.*15.34; ἐν τόπῳ ὃν ἂν -κρίνῃ ὁ ἀρχιτέκτων *Inscr.Prien.*119.25 (i B.C.); also εἰς ὃν ἂν σ. τ. ὁ ἀ. ib.107.44 (ii B.C.); *give judgement*, c. inf., *PEnteux.*62.11 (iii B.C.), *PFay.*12.30 (ii B.C.):—Pass., ἐπιτελέσαι καθότι συγκέκριται *BGU*1827.13 (i B.C.); τῶν συγκεκριμένων ἀπαιτεῖν α (ἔτους) ἐκφόριον *the lands for which it has been decided* to demand one year's rent, *PTeb.*61(*b*).1 (ii B.C.); ἡ συγκριθησομένη τροφή *which shall be adjudged*, *OGI*56.71 (Canopus, iii B.C.); ὅσον ἂν συγκριθῇ ἱκανὸν εἶναι δίδοσθαι *Sammelb.* 7450.11 (iii B.C.).

**συγκρῐσία**, ἡ, prob. f. l. for σύγκρισις or ἰδιοσυγκρισία in Sor.2.56.

⊛ **σύγκρῐσις**, εως, ἡ, *aggregation, combination, condensation*, opp. διάκρισις, Ti.Locr.100e, Pl.*Ti.*64e, 65c, Arist.*Ph.*260$^b$11 sq., *Metaph.*984$^a$15, Thphr.*Sens.*84, Epicur.*Ep.*1 p.19 U., etc.; of *formation and birth*, opp. dissolution (διάκρισις), D.H.2.56; διὰ τῆς ποιᾶς σ. τῶν ἀγγείων Sor.2.4; γεώδους ἀντεχόμενα σ. *of an* earthy *consistency*, D.S.1.7. 2. in a concrete sense, *compound substance*, Arist.*Mete.*346$^a$16, al., *GA*728$^b$2, Thphr.*Sens.*75, Epicur.*Ep.*1 p.6 U., al., Metrod.*Fr.*9. 3. *physique, constitution*, Sor.1.22, 86, al.; ῥέουσαν σ. στῆσαι a collapsing *constitution*, Herod.Med.ap.Orib.5.27.1; τὴν ὅλην ἐξενεγκεῖν σ. the whole *mass* or *structure* (viz. foetus), Sor.2.63. 4. σ. δείπνου, = *collatio*, *Gloss.* 5. = *cerniculum*, ib. II. *comparison*, Philem.109, *Lyr.Alex.Adesp.*32; πρὸς ἄλληλα Arist. *Top.*102$^b$15; τῶν ἀψύχων τοῖς ἀψύχοις Plb.6.47.10; οὐκ ἔχων σ. πρός τι admitting of no *comparison* with.., i.e. beyond all *comparison* better, Demetr.Sceps.ap.Ath.14.658b; συγκρίσεις τῆς ῥητορικῆς τῇ φιλοσοφίᾳ Phld.*Rh.*2.146 S.; συγκρίσει *by comparison*, Babr.101.8; κατὰ σύγκρισιν Phryn.*PS* p.1 B., Suid. s. v. συγκριτικῶς; πρὸς σύγκρισιν *IG*5(2).268.53 (Mantinea, i B.C.), *OGI*669.56 (Egypt, i A.D.); freq. in late Prose, as Plu.*Flam.*21, al., Luc.*Asin.*56. III. σ. ἐνυπνίου *interpretation* of a dream, Lxx *Ge.*40.12, al.; τῆς γραφῆς Thd.*Da.*5.7, 17. 2. *decision*, *PEnteux.*8.6 (iii B.C.), *BGU*1185.27 (i B.C.), *PLond.*2.359.3 (ii A.D.); ἐν συγκρίσει of land *awaiting the decision* of the dioecetes whether it shall be assessed for rent, *PTeb.*61(*b*).220, cf. 72.149, al. (ii B.C.).

**συγκρῐτ-έον**, (συγκρίνω) *one must compare*, Arist.*Pol.*1296$^b$24. **-ής**, οῦ, ὁ, *judge's assessor*, *EM*779.17; Dor. **συγκρίτας** *Schwyzer* 197.56, 65 (Crete, iii B.C.). **-ικός**, ή, όν, *of* or *for compounding*, opp. διακριτικός, τμῆμα Pl.*Plt.*282c, cf. Arist.*Top.*107$^b$30; λευκὸν μὲν τὸ διακριτικὸν μέλαν δὲ τὸ σ. Thphr.*Sens.*86: ἡ -κή (sc. τέχνη) Pl. l. c. b, c. II. *comparative*, ὑπόθεσις Plu.2.616d; τὰ σ. (sc. ὀνόματα) *comparative degree* of adjectives, D.T.635.9, Plu.2.677d, A.D.*Synt.*58.28. Adv. -κῶς D.L.9.75. III. = μετασυγκριτικός, φάρμακα, opp. χαλαστικά, Gal.2.343: τὰ σ., title of work by Thessalus, Id.10.7. **-ος**, ον, *compact, firm*, Xenocr.ap.Orib.2.58.44. II. *comparable*, τοῖς ἐπιφανεστάτοις τῶν ἡρώων Plb.12.23.7, cf. Phld.*D.*1.21, Ph.2.440, prob. l. in D.H.*Th.*51.

⊛ **συγκροτ-έω**, *strike together*, σ. τὼ χεῖρε *clap* the hands for joy, X.*Cyr.*2.2.5, Ath.10.420c; ταῖς χερσίν Lxx *Nu.*24.10; *smite* them *together* in grief or anger, Luc.*Somn.*14; σ. τοὺς ὀδόντας ὑπὸ τρόμου, ὑπὸ τοῦ κρύους, Id.*JTr.*45, *Cat.*20. 2. abs., *clap, applaud*, Polem.*Call.*62; *join in applauding*, Eun.*VS* p.484 B.:—Pass., *to be applauded*, X.*Smp.*8.1. II. *hammer* or *weld together*, Ar.*Eq.*471; ἀσπὶς συγκεκροτημένη Plu.*Nic.*28. 2. metaph., σ. ὀνόματα *weld* words *together* into unities, Pl.*Cra.*409c, 415d, 416b; of style, λέξις συγκεκροτημένη *pithy, terse*, D.H.*Dem.*18, *Isoc.*2, etc. b. *knock together, compose*, ἀνάπαιστα Luc.*Symp.*18; κατηγορίαν Id. *Eun.*13. c. *weld* a number of men into one body, i.e. *organize* them, τὸν χορόν D.21.17; σύνδειπνον Plu.2.528b (Pass.); πότον Luc. *Gall.*12 (Pass.); ξυνωμοσίαν Id.*Phal.*1.4; γάμους Ach.Tat.2.11; esp. of military or naval forces, *collect, levy*, σ. δύναμιν, στράτευμα, Hdn.1.9.1, 2.14.6, cf. Aristid.2.157 J.; μίαν Λάκαινάν τις ὑβρίζων κοινὸν πόλεμον ἐφ' ἑαυτὸν συγκροτεῖ Chor.29.80 F.-R.:—Pass., ἐκεῖνό μοι φράσον, εἰ πάλαι ξυγκροτεῖται αὐτοῖς ἡ ἔρις Luc.*JTr.*33; πόλεμος.. ἐπὶ ὑπηκόους συνεκροτεῖτο *was being waged* against subjects, Chor.3.11 F.-R. d. *train*, D.L.7.185:—Pass., ib.31: freq. in pf. part. Pass. συγκεκροτημένος, *well-trained, disciplined*, ναῦς συγκεκρ. X.*HG*6.2.12; συγκεκροτημένοι τὰ τοῦ πολέμου D.2.17; εἰς πολεμικὴν ἄσκησιν Hdn.7.2.2; συγκεκρ. πληρώματα Plb.1.61.3; ἑταιρεῖαι Plu.*Lys.*13. e. ἐπιτήρει δὲ καὶ ἡμέραν καὶ ὥραν ἐν ᾗ συγκροτεῖται μάλιστα ὁ χρησμός on which the oracle *works* best, Astramps.*Orac.* p.3. f. *assist, help*, συγκρότησε (i.e. -ῆσαι) τὸν εὐγενῆ Παῦλον *POxy.*1872.2 (v/vi A.D.); συγκροτεῖ.. συμπράττει, Suid. **-ημα**, ατος, τό, *organization*, μετὰ σ. τινός Sch.Ar.*Pl.*325. II. *artifice, crafty conduct*, Ulp. ad D.21.139 (pl.); *contrivance*, gloss on κρότημα, Sch.E.*Rh.*499. ⊛ **-ησις**, εως, ἡ, *welding*, χαλκοῦ Eust. ad D.P.558. II. *approval, favour, support*, *PFlor.*378.9 (v A.D.), *Gloss.* **-ούσιος**, v. συγκρούσιος.

**σύγ-κρουμα**, ατος, τό, *borrowed money*, or *a compound dish*, Hsch. **-κρούσιος** γέλως, ὁ, laughter *accompanied by clapping of the hands, immoderate mirth*, Zen.2.100, Diogenian.3.76; γέλως **συγκροτούσιος**, Suid. **-κρουσις**, εως, ἡ, *collision*, ἀνέμων Thphr. *Vent.*53; ὅπλων Onos.26.1; [ἀτόμων], νεφῶν, Epicur.*Ep.*1 p.8 U., 2 p.45 U., cf. Diog.Oen.33; of ships, D.C.49.1; *hiatus* or *concurrence*, φωνηέντων Chrysipp.*Stoic.*2.96, Demetr.*Eloc.*68, D.H.*Comp.*22 (pl.), Hermog.*Id.*1.3, al. 2. metaph., *collision, conflict*, Plu.*Num.*17; πρός τινα Arg. iii Ar.*Nu.* II. in Music, *rapid alternation of two notes, trill*, Ptol.*Harm.*2.12. III. Rhet., *collision of contradictory statements*, Aps. p.270 H. ⊛ **-κρουσμός**, ὁ, = foreg., νεῶν Plu. *Marc.*16; νεφῶν *Placit.*3.3.12, cf. Simp. *in Cael.*470.3; ὅπλων Lxx 1*Ma.*6.41; πόλεμος καὶ συγκρουσμοί Nech. in *Cat.Cod.Astr.*7.148. **-κρουστέον**, *one must admit concurrence of*, βραχέα σ. βραχέσιν Demetr. *Eloc.*207. **-κρουστικός**, ή, όν, *of* or *for* σύγκρουσις III, Arg.D.19.14. **-κρουστός**, ή, όν, *struck together*, ἱμάτιον σ. a cloth *with a close shaggy pile*, like velvet or plush, Hsch. II. σύγκρουστον, τό, *tomb-chamber, vault*, *IGRom.*4.737, 738, 746 (Eumeneia). **-κρούω**, *strike together*, σ. τὼ χεῖρε *clap* the hands, Ar.*Ra.*1029; ἀλλήλοις τὰ πλοῖα Plu.*Luc.*12; τοῖς δόρασι τὰς ἀσπίδας Apollod.1.1.5; τὰ σύμφωνα τῶν στοιχείων Philostr.*VS*2.13. 2. metaph., *bring into collision*, ὁ Φίλιππος.. πάντας συνέκρουε D.18.19, cf. 163; σ. τινὰς ἀλλήλοις *wear out by collision*, Th.1.44; σ. φίλους φίλοις καὶ τὸν δῆμον τοῖς γνωρίμοις Arist.*Pol.*1313$^b$17; διάλυε, μὴ σύγκρουε μαχομένους φίλους Men.*Mon.*122; σ. τινὰ πρός τινα Luc.*Icar.*20, etc., cf. Babr.44.4; τὰ δοξάσματα πρὸς ἄλληλα Iamb.ap.Stob.2.2.7; σ. πόλεμον D.S.12.3; σ. τι τῶν ἐκείνου πραγμάτων *throw* them *into confusion*, Isoc.4.134:—Pass., σ. εἰς μάχην Dosith. p.433 K. 3. intr., *clash, come into collision*, τὸ ἀντίπρῳρον ξυγκροῦσαι Th.7.36; of troops, Wilcken *Chr.*11.25, 38 (ii B.C.); of a horse's front and hind hoofs, Arist.*HA*604$^b$2; νῆες ἀλλήλαις συγκρούουσαι Plb.1.50.3, cf. D.S.3.51, etc.: metaph., Thphr.*Char.*12.14, Epicur.*Nat.*114 G., Phld.*Sign.*38, Plu.*Alex.*47. II. = συγκροτέω, *weld together*: metaph., *try to reconcile* discrepancies, Str.11.7.4.

**συγκρύπτω**, *cover up* or *completely*, [ὅπλοις] δέμας E.*Heracl.*721; *conceal*, Hp.*Fract.*20, E.*IT*1052, *Fr.*683, X.*Cyr.*8.1.40, D.2.20; πενίαν Amphis 17; τῷ λόγῳ σ. τι D.*Prooem.*37 (συγκρύψεται Schäfer); δυσμένειαν Plu.*Galb.*18. II. *join* or *help in concealing*, σ. τινὶ τὴν ἁμαρτίαν And.1.67, cf. Antipho 2.3.4, Isoc.3.53, 17.18, Men.*Sam.*93, *SIG*360.16 (Chersonesus, iii B.C.).

**συγκτάομαι**, *win* or *gain along with*, ἐκείνοις ἐφ' ἃ ἦλθον Th.6.69, cf. 7.57; τὴν χώραν ὅλην συγκτήσασθαι *to have gained joint possession of* it, Arist.*Pol.*1307$^a$30. II. *get together*, γῆν πολλήν Aristid.*Or.*26(14).24. III. *get at the same time*, τὰς ἄλλας ἀρετάς Ph.2.442.

**συγκτερεΐζω**, *join in paying the last honours to a corpse*, A.R.2.838.

**συγκτησείδιον** or -ίδιον, τό, Dim. of sq., Jul.*Ep.*4.

⊛ **σύγ-κτησις**, εως, ἡ, *joint possession*, Keil-Premerstein *Dritter Bericht* No.84 (Hypaepa). **-κτήτωρ**, ορος, ὁ, *joint-possessor*, *Gloss.*

**συγ-κτίζω**, *join with* another *in founding* or *colonizing*, σ. Βάττῳ Κυρήνην Hdt.4.156, cf. Th.7.57; τῶν συνεκτικότων τὴν πατρίδα *CIG*2771 i 6 (Aphrodisias), cf. 2814 (ibid.), *Jahresh.*28.57 (ibid.). 2. αὐλῶνες εὖ συνεκτισμένοι well *cultivated*, Str.4.6.9. II. Pass., *to be created along with*, μετά.. Lxx *Si.*1.14. **-κτίσις**, εως, ἡ, *joint-founding*, πόλεων καὶ ἱερῶν Nicom.*Ar.*1.3. **-κτίστης**, ου, ὁ, *joint-founder* or *colonizer*, Hdt.5.46 (pl.).

**συγκτῠπέω**, *clang together*, κύμβαλα Nonn.*D.*3.240.

**συγκῠβ-ευτής**, οῦ, ὁ, *person with whom one plays at dice, fellow-gamester*, Aeschin.1.57, 60, D.C.45.47. **-εύω**, *play at dice with*, τινι Hdt.2.122, cf. Arist.*EN*1172$^a$4.

**συγκῠέομαι**, Pass., *to be generated together*, τινι Porph.*Antr.*28: also **-κῠΐσκομαι**, Id.*Gaur.*9.3.

**συγκῠκάω**, *throw into a ferment, confound utterly*, τὴν Ἑλλάδα Ar. *Ach.*531; *mix confusedly*, ἐς ταὐτὸν ὑμᾶς τρύβλιον Id.*Pl.*1108; τοιαῦτα σ. *make* such *confusion*, Pl.*Lg.*669d; *make a* κυκεών, Hp.*Int.*12:—Pass., *to be thrown into confusion*, Sabin.ap.Orib.9.20.6.

**συγκυκλ-έω**, *help in rolling* or *revolving*, Pl.*Plt.*269c. **-ίζομαι**, *revolve along with*, Phlp. *in Mete.*31.32. ⊛ **-όομαι**, Med., *encircle completely*, Arist.*HA*533$^b$22.

**συγκύκλωψ**, ωπος, ὁ, *fellow-Cyclops*, Eust.1622.49 (pl.).

**συγκῠλινδέομαι**, Pass., *roll about* or *wallow together*, ἀκρασίᾳ X. *Smp.*8.32 codd.; so **συγκῠλίνδομαι** S.E.*M.*1.291.

**συγκῠλίομαι** [ῐ], Pass., = foreg., D.S.5.33; Διογένει *with* him, Aristipp.ap.Ath.13.588e, cf. Ptol.Euerg.3 J. 2. of an eagle, *swoop*, ἐπὶ γῆν D.S.16.27.

**συγκῡμαίνομαι**, Pass., *to be swollen with a* (tidal) *wave*, of the Atlantic Ocean, Seleuc.ap.Stob.1.38.9.

**συγκῡνηγ-ετέω**, *hunt together*, Plu.2.97a, 173d, *Alex.*41. **-έτης**, ου, ὁ, = συγκυνηγός, X.*Cyn.*10.3, Aeschin.3.255. **-έω**, = συγκυνηγετέω, Arist.*EN*1172ᵃ4, D.S.4.34, Parth.36.2. **-ός**, Dor. and Trag. **συγκῡνᾱγός**, ὁ, ἡ, *fellow-hunter*, E.*IT*709, *Ba.*1146, Plu.2.749e; fem., *fellow-huntress*, E.*Hipp.*1093.

**συγκῠνίζω**, *play the dog* (i.e. *the cynic*) *together*, Crates *Ep.*28, 29.

**συγκύπτης**, ου, ὁ, in pl., *rafters* or *sloping beams* of roof of engine, Ath.Mech.18.10, al.

**συγκύπτω**, *bend forwards, stoop and lay heads together*, παιδάρια συγκύψανθ' ἅμα βληχᾶται Ar.*V.*570; σ. πρὸς ἀλλήλας, of mares, Arist.*HA*572ᵃ23: metaph., οἱ κακοῦντες τὰ κοινὰ συγκύψαντες ποιεῦσι they do it *in concert*, Hdt.3.82, cf. 7.145; καὶ συγκύψαντες ἅπαντες γελῶσιν Phryn.Com.3.6; τοῦτο δ' εἰς ἕν ἐστι συγκεκυφός Ar.*Eq.*854. 2. *draw together*, ἣν συγκύπτῃ τὰ κέρατα τοῦ πλαισίου X.*An.*3.4.19, cf. 21. II. *to be bowed down, bent double*, as under a burden, *Ev.Luc.*13.11, Philostr.*Im.*2.20; συγκεκῡφώς Them.*Or.*7.90b; σ. τῷ προσώπῳ LXX *Jb.*9.27; μελανίᾳ ib.*Si.*19.26.

**συγκῠρ-έω**, aor. -εκύρησα and -έκυρσα (v. infr.):—*come together by chance*, μή πως συγκύρσειαν ὁδῷ ἔνι μώνυχες ἵπποι Il.23.435; of ships, Hdt.8.92; *meet with* an accident, τῇδε συγκῦρσαι τύχῃ S.*OC* 1404; κήτεσι πολλοῖς συγκεκυρηκέναι D.S.17.106; τραγικοῖς πάθεσι Id.20.21; εὐτυχίᾳ Phld.*Mort.*38; εἰς ἓν μοίρας συνέκυρσας *art involved* in one and the same fate, E.*Andr.*1172 (anap.). 2. c. part., like τυγχάνω, συνέκυρσε θέων *happened* to be running, Emp.53; εἰ συνεκύρησε.. παραπεσοῦσα νηῦς whether it fell in the way *by chance*, Hdt. 8.87. II. of events and accidents, *happen, occur*, ἤν δέ τι δεινὸν συγκύρσῃ Thgn.698; τάδε οἶδα.. τοῖσι ἐν Ἰταλίῃ συγκυρήσαντα Hdt.4.15; σ. μοι ἡδονά E.*Ion* 1448 (lyr.); τίς τύχα μοι συγκυρήσει; Id.*IT*874 (lyr.); τὰ συγκυρήσαντα *what had occurred*, Hdt.1.119, cf. D.S.1.1; ὁ καὶ συνεκύρησε Plb.2.65.7, cf. Phld.*Rh.*1.132 S.; τὰ παρὰ τοῦ δαιμονίου -ήσαντα D.H.5.56: impers., c. inf., συνεκύρησε γενέσθαι *it came to pass* that.., Hdt.9.90, cf. Hp.*Oct.*10:—Pass., τὸ ἔχθος τὸ ἐς Λακεδαιμονίους συγκεκυρημένον Hdt.9.37 (nisi leg. συγκεκρημένον). III. of places, *to be contiguous to*, χώραις -οῦσαν θάλατταν Plb.3.59.7, etc.; πρὸς τόπον Plu.*Arist.*11; Ἐσεβὼν καὶ ταῖς -ούσαις αὐτῇ LXX *Nu.*21.25. IV. v. συγκύρω. **-ημα**, ατος, τό, *occurrence*, Plb.4.86.2, D.H.9.38, Porph.*Marc.*5, etc.; *coincidence*, καιροῦ Epicur.*Ep.*2 p.54 U., cf. Cic.*Att.*2.12.2; *combination*, Eust.1363.15. **-ησις**, εως, ἡ, *concurrence, coincidence*, κατὰ συγκυρήσεις καιρῶν Epicur.*Ep.*2 p.43 U.; *conjuncture*, Plb.9.12.6. **-ία**, ἡ, = foreg., τὰ ἀπὸ συγκυρίης λυπήματα γνώμης *chance* annoyances, Hp.*Hum.*9; διὰ συγκυρίην Id.*VM*10; κατὰ συγκυρίαν *Ev.Luc.*10.31, Eust.376.12.

**συγκυρκᾱνάω**, = συγκυκάω, Epin.1.8.

**συγκῡρόω**, *sanction along with*, Men.Rh.p.404 S.

**σύγκυρσις**, εως, ἡ, = συγκύρησις, dub. in Phld.*Po.Herc.*994.24.

**συγκύρω** [ῠ], *appertain*, τὸ ἱερὸν καὶ τὰ -κύροντα *appurtenances*, *OGI* 52.1 (Ptolemais, iii B.C.), cf. *PCair.Zen.*460 (iii B.C.), *POxy.*247.29 (i A.D.); τῇ σιτηρᾷ ἀπομοίρᾳ *OGI*55.20 (Telmessus, iii B.C.): also -κῡρέω, πᾶν τὸ συγκυροῦν Phld.*Rh.*2.264 S.; τὰ -κυροῦντα *POxy.*907.9 (iii A.D.).

**συγκωθωνίζομαι**, *tipple together*, Ath.1.19d: aor. part. -ισθέντων Wilcken *Chr.*11.56 (ii B.C.).

**σύγκωλος**, ον, *with limbs set close together*, σκέλη X.*Cyn.*5.30.

**συγκωλύω**, *prevent at the same time*, τὸ ἀδικεῖν Aristid.2.62 J.

**συγκωμάζω**, Dor. fut. -άξω, *march together in a* κῶμος, Pi.*O.*11(10).16; τινὶ πρός τινα Antig.Caryst.ap.Ath.13.603e: generally, *join in revelling*, τινι Posidipp.ap.Ath.10.414e, J.*AJ*17.3.1, Luc.*Salt.*11.

**σύγκωμος**, ὁ, ἡ, *partner in a* κῶμος, *fellow-reveller*, E.*Ba.*1172 (lyr.), Ar.*Ach.*264 (lyr.): c. dat., σ. Διονύσῳ A.*Fr.*355 (lyr.) (as Tyrwhitt for σύγκοινος): also ⊛**συγκωμαστής**, οῦ, ὁ, Tz.*H.*6.895.

**συγκωμῳδέω**, *join in satirizing*, Luc.*Pisc.*26.

**συγξαίνω**, *card wool with* or *together*, Crates Theb.*Fr.*3 D.

**συγξενῑτεύω**, *live abroad along with* another, *IG*14.1413 (Rome).

**συγξέω**, *smooth by scraping* or *planing*:—Pass., metaph. of style, *to be polished*, Alcid.*Soph.*20, D.H.*Comp.*22, *Dem.*40, Plu.2.853d.

**συγξηραίνω**, *dry up together*, Gal.11.585, 15.487 (both Pass.).

⊛ συγξύω, *shred* or *grate up*, φάρμακον Hp.*Haem.*3: metaph., πάντα συγξύσας *having scraped together every penny*, D.L.4.47.

**συγχάζω**, = συγχωρέω, Hsch.

**συγχαίρω**, aor. -εχάρην [ᾰ] Plb.15.5.13, 30.18.1, imper. -χάρηθι *Anacreont.*31.30:—*rejoice with*, A.*Ag.*793 (anap.), Ar.*Pax* 1317 (anap.); χαῖρε.. καὶ σοὶ ξυγχαίρομεν ἡμεῖς Id.*Eq.*1333 (anap.); σ. ἐπὶ τοῖς σοῖς ἀγαθοῖς X.*Hier.*11.12; σ. ἀγαθῷ γενομένῳ Pl.*Epin.*988b: c. dat. pers., τὸν συναλγοῦντα καὶ σ. τῷ φίλῳ Arist.*EN*1166ᵃ8; οὐ σ. οὐδὲ συναλγεῖν ἑαυτοῖς ib.1166ᵇ18: later in Med., *IG*14.966.5 (Rome, ii A.D.). II. *wish* one *joy of*.., D.15.15; σ. συγκλήτῳ ἐπὶ τοῖς γεγονόσιν Plb.30.18.1, cf. *SIG*700.41 (Lete, ii B.C.); σ. τῇ πόλει ὅτι.. Aeschin.2.45.

**συγχᾰλάω**, *relax with* or *at the same time*, Archyt.1.

**συγχᾰλεπαίνω**, *to be angry as well*, Memn.51.

**συγχαλκεύω**, *weld together*, Ath.11.488f (Pass.).

**συγχᾰράσσω**, *lacerate at the same time*, Aret.*CD*1.2 (Pass.). 2. *mark*, συγκεχάρακται στιγμαῖς Philum.*Ven.*22.1.

**συγχᾱρητικός**, ή, όν, = sq., q. v.

**συγχαρτικός**, ή, όν, *congratulatory*, J.*BJ*4.10.6 (v.l. συγχαρητικός, which occurs in Zonar. and in Ph.1.81 (ubi συγχαριτικόν cod. M)).

**συγχαυνόομαι**, Pass., *to be swollen, puffed up*, τινι Tz.*H.*10.932.

**συγχειλίαι**, αἱ, *points of junction of the lips*, Arist.*Phgn.*811ᵃ18.

⊛ **συγχειμάζω**, *winter along with*, τινι App.*BC*5.77:—Med., *go through the winters with* one, Ar.*Pl.*847.

**συγχειρίζω**, *administer along with*, τινί τι Plb.6.11ᴬ.7. 2. Pass., of diseases, *to be treated in the same way*, Gal.14.787.

**συγχειρο-γρᾰφέω**, *execute a deed jointly*, *BGU*1032.13 (ii A.D.), *POxy.*1451.28 (ii A.D.). **-πονέω**, *do also by manual labour*, ὀλίγα Luc.*Lex.*2. **-τονέω**, in Pass., *to be elected together with, at the same time*, *Inscr.Prien.*111.144 (i B.C.).

**συγχειρουργέω**, *put hand to* a thing *together, accomplish*, τὰ ἱερά Is.8.16; ἀδίκημα Ph.2.15; φόνον τινί J.*AJ*17.3.2.

**συγχερσεύω**, *become waste land*, *PAmh.*2.68.7 (i A.D.).

⊛ **συγχέω**: Hom. uses pres. and impf. Act. and 2 sg. aor. σύγχεας Il.15.366, but more freq. Ep. aor. συνέχευα, inf. συγχεῦαι, aor. Pass. σύγχῠτο:—aor. Pass. -εχύθην [ῠ], for which -εχέθην is f.l. in Apollod. 1.7.2, Luc.*DMar.*9.2:—*pour together, commingle, confound*, συνέχευε ποσὶν καὶ χερσὶν [τὰ ἀθύρματα] Il.15.364; τὰ διακεκριμένα Pl. *Phlb.*46e; ἄνω κάτω τὰ πάντα σ. ὁμοῦ E.*Ba.*349; σ. τὰς ψήφους *mix* them *up*, Is.5.18; τὰ σύμβολα D.21.173; τὰς τάξεις Plb.1.40.13; τὰς ὄψεις, of lightning, Poll.1.118:—Pass., ἡνία δέ σφι σύγχυτο Il. 16.471; μεταλλεία συγκεχυμένα *in confusion*, Pl.*Lg.*678d; τὴν κρόκην καὶ τοὺς στήμονας συγκεχυμένους διακρίνομεν Id.*Cra.* 388b. 2. *obliterate, demolish*, σ. τοὺς τάφους Hdt.4.127; τὴν ὁδόν Id.7.115; δῶμα E.*Ion* 615. 3. *confuse, blur*, τὰ γράμματα Id.*IA*37 (anap.), cf. Arist.*GA*721ᵇ34 (Pass.), *Aud.*801ᵇ18 (Pass.); συγκεχυμένον μέλαν an *indistinct* black mark, Id.*HA*585ᵇ34; φωνὴ σ. D.S.1.8; πλαδαρὰ καὶ σ. σάρξ flabby and *ill-defined* flesh, Theon ap.Gal.6.96; συνεκέχυτο δ' ἔτι τοῦτο *was* still *confused*, not yet distinguished, Gal.15.30, cf. 713. II. of the mind, *confound, trouble*, μή μοι σύγχει θυμὸν Il.9.612, cf. 13.808; σὺν δὲ γέροντι νόος χύτο 24.358; συνεχέοντο αἱ γνῶμαι τῶν φαμένων Hdt.7.142; ὁ βίος δι' ἀπιστίαν συγχυθήσεται Epicur.*Sent.Vat.*57: with the person as object, ἄνδρα γε συγχεῦαι Od.8.139, cf. Hdt.8.99:—Pass., τί συγχυθεῖσ' ἕστηκας; E.*Med.*1005; μὴ ἀθυμείτω τις, ἐὰν συγχέηται Gal.15.584. 2. *confound, make of none effect*, πολὺν κάματον καὶ ὀϊζὺν σύγχεας Ἀργείων Il.15.366, cf. 473; τὴν πάρος σ. χάριν S.*Tr.* 1229; esp. of contracts, engagements, etc., *make of none effect, frustrate, violate*, ἐπεὶ σύν γ' ὅρκι' ἔχευαν Τρῶες Il.4.269, cf. Pl.*R.*379e, Hp.*Jusj.*, E.*Hipp.*1063; τὰ πάντων ἀνθρώπων νόμιμα Hdt.7.136, cf. Antipho 4.1.2, *SIG*45.33 (Halic., v B.C.); τὴν πολιτείαν D.4.91; ἄλιαν *Schwyzer* 323 *D* 28 (Delph., iv B.C.); συγκέχυκε νῦν τὴν πίστιν ὁ καθ' ἡμᾶς βίος Men.781, cf. *OGI*669.18 (Egypt, i A.D.); ξυνουσίαν Luc.*Bis Acc.*17:—Pass., λέλυται πάντα, συγκέχυται D.25.25. III. πόλεμον σ. *stir up* a war, Plb.4.10.3, 15.2.4, 28.17.6.

**συγχῑλίαρχος**, ὁ, *fellow-tribune*, J.*AJ*19.1.5.

⊛ **συγχίς**, ίδος, ἡ, a kind of *shoe* or *sock*, *AP*6.294 (Phan.), Suid.: also **συκχάς**, άδος, Poll.7.86, Hsch.; also **σύκχοι**, ων (Phrygian), Id.

**συγχόνδρωσις**, εως, ἡ, *junction* of two bones *by cartilage*, Gal.2.738.

**συγ-χορδία**, ἡ, *harmony*, S.*Fr.*412. **-χορδος**, ον, *in harmony*, of musical strings, Hsch. s.v. ἀντίχορδα.

**συγχορ-εία**, ἡ, = συνῳδία, Hsch. **-ευτής**, οῦ, ὁ, *companion in the dance*, Pl.*Lg.*654a, 665a, X.*HG*2.4.20. **-εύτρια**, fem. of foreg., *partner in the dance*, Ar.*Fr.*863. **-εύω**, *join in the dance*, Id.*Av.* 1761, Ph.2.135, Corn.*ND*14: c. dat., ψυχῇ σ. ἡλίῳ Ph.2.242. II. *to be of the same chorus*, Arist.*Pol.*1284ᵇ12, v.l. in Plu.2.94b.

**συγχορηγ-έω**, *assist with supplies*, σφίσι εἰς τοὺς περιεστῶτας καιρούς Plb.4.46.5; τισι Id.5.55.1, etc.: c. acc. rei, σ. τροφάς τισι Plu.*Rom.* 6: abs., σ. ἀφειδῶς Id.*Cleom.*6. II. *contribute towards*, τοῖς γάμοις Id.*Phoc.*30. **-ός**, όν, *sharing with a partner in the expense*, D.29.28.

**σύγχορος**, ον, *partner in the chorus*, Νυμφῶν Orph.*H.*11.9; Ἑλικωνιάσιν *BCH*26.153 (Thespiae).

**σύγχορτος**, ον, *with the grass joining*, i.e. *bordering upon, marching with*, χθόνα σύγχορτον Συρίᾳ A.*Supp.*5 (anap.); Οἰνόη σύγχορτα.. πεδία E.*Fr.*179; c. gen., σύγχορτοι Ὁμόλας Id.*HF*371 (lyr.); Φθίας.. καὶ πόλεως Φαρσαλίας σύγχορτα.. πεδία, i.e. *the marches* or *boundaries* of.., Id.*Andr.*17.

**συγχοῦν**, v. συγχώννυμι.

**συγχράομαι**, *make use of, avail oneself of*, τῇ συμμαχίᾳ, τοῖς καιροῖς, etc., Plb.1.8.1, 18.51.6, etc.; πρὸς τὴν ἀδικίαν ταῖς ναυσί Id.4.6.2; συναγωνιστῇ τῷ ποταμῷ as a coadjutor, Id.3.14.5; τῇ ἀπὸ τῶν φίλων εὐνοίᾳ *SIG*685.45 (Crete, ii B.C.); πόρῳ *OGI*544.23 (Ancyra, ii A.D.); of commercial dealings, σ. τῇ νήσῳ *Peripl.M.Rubr.*31: generally, *have dealings, associate with*, Σαμαρείταις *Ev.Jo.*4.9, cf. Diog.Oen.*Fr.*64. II. *borrow jointly*, τινῶν τριήρεις Plb.1.20.14:—Pass., σιτικὰ τὰ συγχρησθέντα *PPetr.*2 p.64 (iii B.C., cf. *Arch.Pap.*3.518).

**συγχρημᾰτ-ίζω**, *to be associated with*, συγχρηματίζειν τῇ Ῥωμαϊκῇ καὶ τὴν Ἑλληνικὴν ἡμέραν the Greek date *shall be used along with* the Roman, *OGI*458.53 (i B.C.), cf. Ptol.*Tetr.*79, Vett.Val.278.11; *act together with*, τινὶ ἐν τοῖς τῆς πόλεως λόγοις *POxy.*2135.3 (ii A.D.), cf. *Ath.Mitt.*37.277 (Pergam.), *PTeb.*397.26 (ii A.D.), *PSI*10.1104.14 (ii A.D.): abs., *PPetr.*3 p.221 (iii B.C., cf. *Arch.Pap.*7.79), *PLille* 49.3 (iii B.C., cf. *Arch.Pap.*7.297); ἐπιγράφεσθαι ἐπὶ τῶν συγχρηματιζομένων shall have his name inscribed at the head of *contracts*, *IGRom.*4.292.38 (Pergam., ii B.C.). **-ισμός**, ὁ, *agreement*, *POxy.*237 iv 26 (ii A.D.).

⊕ **σύγχρησις**, εως, ἡ, *common* or *joint use*, τῶν ἐμπορίων *Peripl.M. Rubr.*27. II. σ. ὀνομάτων *use* of words *as synonymous*, Ath.11. 477c.

**συγχρηστηρι-άζομαι**, *consult an oracle together*, Sch.Ar.*Eq.*1089, Eust. ad D.P.369. **-ον**, τό, prob. an error for χρηστήριον, *PSI*6. 698.6 (iv A. D.).

**συγχρίμπτω**, = συγκρούω, Hsch. (Pass.).

**σύγ-χρισμα**, ατος, τό, *ointment, salve*, Dsc.1.99 (pl.), Philum. ap. Orib.45.29.46. ⊕ **-χρισμός**, ὁ, = foreg., Paul.Aeg.3.18 (pl.). **-χριστέον**, *one must anoint*, Herod.Med. in *Rh.Mus.*58. 92, Archig.ap.Aët.6.39, Alex.Trall.1.15. **-χριστός**, όν, *to be applied as ointment*, λιπάσματα Paul.Aeg.3.18. **-χρίω** [ῑ], *anoint at the same time*, τὼ χεῖρε Aret.*CA*1.2; τὴν κεφαλὴν μύρῳ Ath.2.46a (Med.):—Pass., *to be rubbed in*, Dsc.1.19.

**συγχροΐζω**, = συγχρῴζω 1 (q. v.):—συ]γχροΐσθεις dub. rest. in Sapph.*Supp.*3.9.

⊕ **συγχρον-έω**, *to be contemporary with*, τινι Erot. p.5 N., Iamb.*Protr.* 21, *Theol.Ar.*40, Suid. s. v. Φερεκύδης; of several persons, *to be contemporaries*, Ath.13.599c. 2. Astron., *take the same time* in rising *with*, Ptol.*Alm.*1.16; cf. sq. II. 3. II. abs., *to be contemporaneous*, Diog.Oen.26:—Med., *to be in the same tense*, A.D.*Synt.*205.1. **-ίζω**, = foreg. I. 1, τινι S.E.*P.*2.245, cf. Sch.Ar.*Ach.*850, v. l. in *Vit. Aesch.* 2. = foreg. I. 2, Ptol.*Alm.*1.16. II. *spend some time in* a place, Lxx *Si.Prol.* 2. Pass., *to be of long standing*, Iamb.*Protr.* 20. 3. *take the same time*, of compounding a mixture, συγχρονισάτω (nisi leg. -ησάτω) Gal.13.1044. **-ισμός**, ὁ, *agreement of time*, Gell.17.21.1 (pl.). **-ος**, ον, *contemporaneous*, Max.Tyr.15.1, Nonn. *D.*3.385, 41.364.

⊕ **σύγχροος**, ον, contr. **-χρους**, ουν, (χρόα) *of like colour* or *look*, Plb. 3.46.6. II. *skin to skin, touching*, Posidipp.ap.Ath.13.596d, Nic. *Fr.*32.

**συγχρῴζω**, *give the same colour to*, [τοῖς σώμασι] τὸν μεταξὺ ἀέρα *give* to the .. air *the same colour* as the bodies, *Placit.*4.13.7 (-χροΐζ- codd.):—Pass., *take the same* or *a like colour*, Ar.Byz.*Epit.* 17.5, D.S.2.52, Plu.2.934d. II. Pass. also, *to be closely joined*, *Com.Adesp.*285, D.H.*Comp.*23.

**συγχρωμᾰτ-ίζομαι**, f.l. for συγχρωτίζομαι in *Corp.Herm.*10.17:—Act., f.l. ib.12.10. **-ισμός**, ὁ, = ὁμόχροια 1, Hsch. s. v. ἀχροίην.

**συγχρῶτα** or **σύγχρωτα**, Adv. as if from σύγχρως, *body to body*, Artem.1.79.

**συγχρωτίζομαι**, Pass., *to be in* (*defiling*) *contact with*, τοῖς νεκροῖς Hecato ap.D.L.7.2, cf. *Corp.Herm.*10.17 (codd. Stob.), 12.10 (Act., as cj.); of sexual intercourse, Eust.1069.1.

**συγχῡλόομαι**, Pass., *to be converted into chyle*, Dsc.*Eup.*2.141.

**σύγχῡμος**, ον, *easily converted into nutriment*, *Et.Gud.*571.34.

**συγ-χύνω**, *confound*, by reasoning, *Act.Ap.*9.22:—Pass., A.D. *Pron.*104.12. **-χῠσις**, εως, ἡ, (συγχέω) *mixture, confusion, confounding*, ἡ τῶν ἄλλων (v.l. ὅλων) σ. Hp.*Epid.*6.3.1; of Babel, Lxx *Ge.* 11.9; σ. ποιήσασθαι Plb.30.22.7; σ. λαβεῖν *to be commingled*, Plu.2. 990a; σ. ὅρων ib.122c; σ. *litterularum*, Cic.*Att.*6 9.1; *political confusion*, σ. τῆς πολιτείας ib.7.8.4, cf. Plb.14.5.8. b. *formation of a compound*, Chrysipp.*Stoic.*2.153, al. 2. *confusion, ruin*, βίου, δόμων, E.*Andr.* 291 (lyr.), 959; σ. τοῦ κατὰ φύσιν ἡ νόσος Thphr.*CP*5.8.1; σ. θανάτου μεγάλη 'indiscriminate mortality' Lxx 1*Ki.*5.6; σ. λήψεται Epicur. *Fr.*300. 3. Gramm., of composition, *confusion, indistinctness*, A.D.*Pron.*12.15, *Synt.*24.18; opp. εὐκρίνεια, Hermog.*Id.*1.4. 4. *an injury to the eye, synchysis*, Dsc.4.12, *Eup.*1.33, Gal.14.776, Aët. 7.58. II. of persons, *confusion*, Luc.*Nigr.*35; σ. ἔχοντες *confounded*, E.*IA*1128; σ. ὀμματίων *AP*5.129 (Maec.). III. of contracts and the like, *violation*, τῶν σπονδῶν Th.1.146, 5.26; νόμων Isoc.4.114 (pl.); σ. ὁρκίων Plu.*Alc.*14; τὴν τῶν ὅρκων καὶ σπονδῶν σ. Pl.*R.*379e. 2. *confusion*, *SIG*684.7 (Dyme, ii B. C.), *Act.Ap.*19. 29. ⊕ **-χυσμός**, ὁ, *pouring* of oil into lamps, *Stud.Pal.*22.183.105 (ii A. D.). **-χῠτικός**, ή, όν, *confounding*, τὸ ψυχρὸν ἁφῆς σ. Plu.2. 948d; prob. l. for συντυχ- in 611a; τί γὰρ ἀναρχίας -κώτερον; Ph.1. 696.

**συγχυτρόω**, in Pass., *become dilapidated*, of an oil-mill, Wilcken *Chr.*176.14 (i A. D.).

**συγχωλαίνω**, *halt along with*, Ὁμηρικῷ μέτρῳ Eust. ad D.P.742.

**συγχωνεύω**, *melt down*, Lycurg.117, D.22.70, *Inscr.Délos* 443 *Bb*42 (ii B. C.). b. *melt down also*, *PHolm.*1.17,23, *PLeid.X.* 19. 2. *join in making pottery*, *PSI*4.420.11 (iii B. C.).

**συγχώννῡμι** and **-ύω**, in earlier writers pres. inf. συγχοῦν Hdt. 4.120, X.*HG*3.1.18:—pf. Pass. -κέχωσμαι Hdt.8.144:—*heap with earth, cover with a mound, bank up*, [τὴν σορόν] Id.1.68; σ. τὰς κρήνας, τὰ ὕδατα, *fill* them *up with earth*, Id.4.120,140, cf. X.*HG*3.1.18, etc.; also of persons, σ. τοὺς ἀποσφαγέντας εἰς τάφρους *bury* them, D.S.19.107, cf. Plu.*Alex.*77. II. *demolish*, τὸ ἔρυμα Hdt.7.225; [τὰ τείχεα καὶ τὰ οἰκήματα] Id.9.13; τὴν ὁδόν Id.8.71:—Pass., οἰκήματα συγκεχωσμένα ib.144; τὰ συγχωσθέντα τῶν εὐρείπων *SIG*799.7 (Cyzicus, i A. D.). 2. generally, *confound*, κῦμα..τῶν τ' ἄστρων διόδους A.*Pr.*1049 (anap.).

⊕ **συγχωρ-έω**, fut. -ήσω X.*HG*3.2.12 (codd., f.l. for -ήσαι), Isoc.6.13, -ήσομαι E.*IT*741, Pl.*Tht.*191c, Men.*Her.Fr.*6, etc.:—*come together, meet*, πέτραι συγχωροῦσαι the Symplegades, E.*IT*124 (lyr.); *combine*, opp. ἐκχωρέω, Anaxag.15; σ. ἕτερον ἑτέρῳ Arist.*Cael.*297$^a$11; also συγχωρεῖν λόγοις *meet* in argument, bandy words with one, E.*Hipp.* 703; but in Antipho 5.27, σ. τῷ τινων λόγῳ = *assent*. II. *get out of the way, make way*, τινι Ar.*V.*1516 (anap.) *give way, yield, defer to*, τινι Id.*Lys.*1111 (anap.), Th.1.140, Pl. l.c., etc.; ταῖσι κατὰ τὸν βίον ἀνάγκαις Democr.289, cf. E.*Fr.*965; Συρηκοσίοισι σ. τῆς ἡγεμονίης *withdraw* in their favour from the command, Hdt.7.161; ξ. ἀλλήλοις *make a compromise*, c. inf., Th.3.75; *to be in collusion with, connive at*, τοῖς πονηροῖς D.34.52; ξ. πρός τινας *come to terms* with them, Th.2.59, 3.27; οὐ ξυγχωρεῖν refuse *to come to terms*, Id.2. 66, cf. 3.96, X.*HG*7.1.27. 2. *accede, assent to, acquiesce in*, τῇ γνώμῃ Hdt.4.148, Th.7.72; γνώμῃ μιᾷ συνεχωρεῖτην, c. inf., *agreed* to do, E.*Hec.*125 (anap.); c. acc. et inf., *allow* that.., Hdt. 2.2, Pl.*Phd.*100a; τοῖσιν εὖ λεχθεῖσι σ. λόγοις E.*Hipp.*299; opp. ἐναντιοῦσθαι, And.3.1; σ. πάθεσιν ἢ ἐναντιουμένην Pl.*Phd.*94b: abs., *agree, acquiesce, assent*, συγχώρει θέλων S.*Ph.*1343, cf. Hdt. 3.83, 4.43, 5.40, Pl.*Lg.*794c, D.18.227; τὸ συγκεχωρηκὸς τῆς εὐσεβείας *yielding, unexacting temper* of piety, Id.21.59:—later in Pass., *to be allowed*, τέως οὐ συνεχωρήθην ἐξελθεῖν *POxy.*1842.8 (vi A. D.). 3. c. acc. rei, *concede, give up*, συγχωρησάντων ταῦτα τῶν Σπαρτιητέων Hdt.9.35; ταῦτα συγχωρήσεται; E.*IT*741; σ. τούτοισι τἀπισικῇ Ar.*Nu.*1438, cf. *Av.*1685; σ. τινὶ τὴν εἰρήνην X.*HG*7. 4.10; σ. τι περὶ τῆς χώρας Isoc.6.70; σ. θάνατον ἑαυτῷ τὴν ζημίαν *acquiesce* in death being his punishment, Din.1.8:—Med., σ. τόπου τισί *IGRom.*4.921 (Cibyra, ii A. D.):—Pass., τὰ συγχωρηθέντα χρήματα D.38.4; εἰρήνη, ἡμέρα συγχωρηθεῖσα, Id.18.20, 42.13; τὰ δ' ἄλλα ὡς συγκεχωρημένα τῇ φύσει τίθεται Thphr.*CP*2.3.5, cf. 5.3.3; συγχωρηθείσης τῆς..γραφῆς the reading *being admitted*, Gal.16.712; ἡ -χωρηθεῖσα τιμή the *agreed* price, *PGrenf.*2.15 ii 9 (ii B. C.), etc. 4. *concede* or *grant* in argument, τί τινι Pl.*Lg.*811b, cf. *R.* 383c, al.: c. acc. et inf., *grant that*.., ib.489d, *Tht.*169d, 183b, al.; σ. ὅτι.. Id.*Lg.*705e; σ. τάδε, ὡς.. Id.*R.*543b; σ. τοῦτο, ὡς.. Id. *Euthphr.*13c, al.; σ. τοὺς τόκους *agree to accept*, D.56.22:—Pass., τὰ συγκεχωρημένα ὑπὸ πάντων Pl.*Phlb.*14d. 5. *forgive* a debt, D.L. 1.45. 6. *allow*, c. acc. et inf., οἱ παχεῖς [κυκλίσκοι] τὰς..σάρκας σήπεσθαι συγχωροῦσι Gal.14.47. 7. impers. συγχωρεῖ, *it is agreed, it may be done*, ὅπῃ ἂν ξυγχωρῇ as *may be agreed*, Th.5. 40. 8. εἰ συγχωροίη if *it were possible*, v.l. in X.*Eq.*9.11. **-ημα**, ατος, τό, *concession*, Plb.5.67.8, al.; σ. λαβεῖν παρά τινος Id.4.73.10; περί τινος Id.1.85.3; σ. γίγνεταί τινι Id.6.13.3; σ. τιμῆς Plu.*Publ.* 20. 2. *agreement*, *PSI*2.189.18 (ii A. D.), etc. ⊕ **-ησις**, εως, ἡ, *agreement, consent*, Pl.*Lg.*770c, *OGI*508.9 (Ephesus, ii A. D.); τὴν σιγὴν σ. θήσω take silence for *consent*, Pl.*Cra.*435b; τὴν τῷ λόγῳ σ. your *agreement* to my argument, Id.*Lg.*837e; *assent*, Aristid.Quint. 2.10 (pl.); coupled with συνδρομή, Hermog.*Id.*2.1. 2. *agreement submitted to a court* in conformity with a verdict, *settlement* of an action, Mitteis *Chr.*31 ii 11 (ii B. C.). b. *any legal agreement in the form of a memorial presented to the* καταλογεῖον *of the chief justice* at Alexandria, *BGU*1053 ii 17, al. (i B. C.), 1574.13 (ii A. D.), *CPR*188. 24 (ii A. D.), etc.; *cession, conveyance* of property in this form, *BGU* 1772.23 (i B. C.), *Arch.Pap.*5.390 (i A. D.), *Sammelb.*6016.24 (ii A. D.), etc. 3. *forgiveness*, Eustr. *in EN*374.4. **-ητέος**, α, ον, *to be conceded*, Luc.*Herm.*74. 2. neut. **συγχωρητέον**, *one must concede*, Pl.*Phdr.*234e, etc.: so in pl. συγχωρητέα, S.*OC*1426, Pl.*Lg.* 895a, etc. **-ητικός**, ή, όν, *assigning a place to*.., νοῦς σ. πάντων Herm.ap.Stob.1.18.3. **-ία**, Ion. **-ίη**, ἡ, *indulgence* in diet, Hp. *Praec.*14. **-ίζω**, *separate*, *BGU*1208.30 (i B. C.). 2. c. dat., *remove along with*, Alex.Aphr. *in Sens.*33.17. **-ος**, ον, = *confinis*, *Gloss.*

**σύγ-χωσις**, εως, ἡ, *filling up* of trenches, Ath.Mech.16.2 (pl.); prob. for σύγχυσιν in Plu.2.434c. **-χωσμα**, ατος, τό, = foreg., *PLond.*3.1177.315 (ii A. D.).

**σύδην** [ῡ], Adv., (σεύω) *impetuously, hurriedly*, σ... αἴρονται φυγήν A.*Pers.*480.

**σύειος** [ῡ], α, ον, (σῦς) *of swine*, χρῖμα σ. *hogs'*-lard, X.*An.*4.4.13; τὰ σ. (sc. κρέα) Luc.*Hist.Conscr.*20; σ. δίκτυα hunting nets, Aen. Tact.11.6.

**συϝοικία**, v. συνοικία. **συζάω**, only in form συζῶ (q. v.).

⊕ **συ-ζεύγνῡμι**, *yoke together, couple*, ἵππους Hdt.4.189, X.*Cyr.*2.2. 26 (Pass.); esp. in marriage, τῷ μὲν φίλην σύζευξον ἄλοχον E.*Alc.* 166, cf. X.*Oec.*7.30; σ. νέους καὶ νέας Arist.*Pol.*1335$^a$16 sq.; τὸν Ἄρη πρὸς τὴν Ἀφροδίτην ib.1269$^b$28:—Med., *yoke for oneself*, ἅρμα X.*Cyr.* 6.1.51:—Pass., *to be yoked with, coupled with, paired*, μετ' ἀλλήλων Arist.*HA*585$^b$9; πρὸς ἀλλήλας Plb.8.4.2: metaph., τῷ συνέζευξαι πλάνῳ; v.l. for προσ- in E.*Alc.*482; τὸν ἐμὸν δαίμον', ᾧ συνεζύγην Id.*Andr.*98; τίνι πότμῳ συνεζύγην; Id.*Hel.*255; οἵᾳ ξυμφορᾷ συνεζύγης Id.*Hipp.*1389 (conversely, συνέζευκται τὸ πάθος τινί Phld. *Ir.* p.57 W.); συζυγέντες ὁμιλοῦσι they live *in close familiarity*, X. *Lac.*2.12. 2. less freq., also in Pass., of things, *to be closely united*, ἃ ψυχὰ τῷ σώματι συνέζευκται Philol.14; πεμπάδι συζυγείς Pl.*R.*546c; συνέζευκται ἡ φρόνησις τῇ τοῦ ἤθους ἀρετῇ Arist.*EN* 1178$^a$16, cf. 1175$^a$19; διορίζεται τοῖς συνεζευγμένοις συμπτώμασι Gal.16.535. **-ζευκτέον**, *one must pair*, ἀριθμοὺς εὐτάκτως Nicom.*Ar.*1.19. **-ζευκτικός**, όν, *conjunctive*, ἔγκλισις Dosith. p.406 K. **-ζευξις**, εως, ἡ, *a being yoked together*, esp. of *wedded union*, Pl.*Lg.*930b, Arist.*Pol.*1253$^b$10, 1335$^a$10. 2. of things, *close union, combination*, Hp.*Art.*14, Pl.*R.*508a, Thphr.*Sens.*73; ὁ τῆς σ. τῆς τούτων ἀριθμός the number of their *combinations*, Arist.*Pol.*1290$^b$32; τοσαῦτ' εἴδη .. ὅσαιπερ αἱ σ. τῶν μορίων ib.36; αἱ μέχρι πλείονος τῶν ἄρθρων σ. the *confinement* of the joints in swaddling clothes, Sor.1.84. b. κατὰ σύζευξιν, of an army marching *in parallel columns*, Ascl.Tact.11.2.

**συζέω**, *boil together*, σύζεσον τρίς Dsc.2.76.9.

**σύζησις**, εως, ἡ, *a living together*, Syrian. *in Metaph.*156.7.

**συζητ-έω**, *search* or *examine together with*, τινι Pl.*Cra.*384c, etc.; τινὶ περί τινος Id.*Men.*90b :—Pass., *to be discussed*, Demetr.Lac. *Herc.*1006 tit. II. σ. τινί or πρός τινα *dispute* with.., *Act. Ap.*6.9, 9.29, cf. *POxy.*1673.20 (ii A.D.); σ. πρὸς αὐτοὺς *Ev.Marc.* 1.27, *Ev.Luc.*22.23. **-ησις**, εως, ἡ, *joint inquiry, discussion*, Epicur.*Sent.Vat.*74, Cic.*Fam.*16.21.4, Phld.*Ir.* p.44 W. II. *disputation*, Ph.1.191, cf. 113 (pl.), Phld.*Rh.*2 p.240 S. (pl.), *Act.Ap.*15.7 (v.l.), etc. **-ητής**, οῦ, ὁ, *joint inquirer*: *disputant*, 1*Ep.Cor.*1.20. **-ητικὸς** τρόπος, the mode *of joint inquiry* or *discussion*, Phld.*Rh.*1.241 S.

**συζοφόω**, *darken*, in Pass., *AP*9.290 (Phil.).

**συζῠγ-έω**, *draw together in a yoke, to be yoke-fellows*, of beasts of draught: hence metaph., ὅπου γὰρ ἰσχὺς συζυγοῦσι καὶ δίκη A.*Fr.* 381: c. dat., Ζεὺς συζυγεῖ τῇ Ἥρᾳ Procl. *in Ti.*1.450 D. 2. of soldiers, *stand in one rank*, Plb.10.23.7; *stand next in rank*, Arr. *Tact.*7.2, 8.2. 3. *to be correlative, correspond*, ἀντιθέτως Plu.2. 1022e; ἀλλήλοις S.E.*M.*7.151. 4. Gramm., of forms, *correspond*, c. dat., A.D.*Synt.*193.8: abs., ib.100.22, *EM*416.6. **-ή**, ἡ, = συζυγία, transl. of Χεβρών, Ph.1.194.236. **-ής**, ὁ, ἡ, *consort*, Lxx 3*Ma.*4.8. II. Adj. = σύζυγος 1. 1, Plot.6.6.5, Procl.*Inst.*42. 2. Geom., σ. διάμετροι *conjugate* diameters, defined in Apollon. Perg.*Con.*1 *Def.*6; σ. ἄξονες ib.*Def.*8, cf. Papp.590.21. **-ία**, ἡ, = σύζευξις, *union*, E.*HF*675 (lyr.); *union of branches with the trunk*, σ. τῶν φλεβῶν Arist.*HA*586$^{b}$21. II. *yoke of animals, pair*, σ. πώλων E.*Hipp.*1131 (lyr.); of persons, Plu.*Demetr.*1: generally, *pair*, Pl. *Phd.*71c, *Prm.*143d, Arist.*IA*704$^{b}$20; σ. πτερύγων, μήλων, δονάκων, *AP*5.267.6, 289 (both Paul. Sil.), 6.27 (Theaet.); ἄρσενα σ., of two sons, *IG*12(8).442.6 (Thasos); κατὰ συζυγίας in *pairs*, esp. of animals, κατὰ συζυγίας φωλοῦσιν.. οἱ ἄρρενες θήλεσιν Arist.*HA*599$^{b}$6, cf. 631$^{b}$1; in plants, Thphr.*HP*3.11.3, al.: hence, 2. *coupling, copulation*, *AP*5.220 (Paul.Sil.), 10.68 (Agath.). 3. in war, *squadron of four war-chariots*, = two ζυγαρχίαι, Ascl.*Tact.*8, Ael. *Tact.*22.2. III. *conjunction* of words or things in pairs, *syzygy*, Arist.*Top.*113$^{a}$12, *GC*332$^{b}$3 (pl.), *Mete.*378$^{b}$11 (pl.), *Stoic.*2.132, Gal. 6.95, al.: more generally, *combination* of words, οὐκ ἐν τῷ κάλλει τῶν ὀνομάτων ἡ πειθώ, ἀλλ' ἐν τῇ σ. D.H.*Comp.*3, cf. 6; of letters, ib.22; *coupling* of terms in a syllogism, Chrysipp.*Stoic.*2.50. 2. Gramm., *conjugation*, D.T.638.6 (pl.), A.D.*Adv.*161.28, *POxy.*469.13 (iii A.D.); or *declension*, A.D.*Adv.*198.6, *Synt.*271.16, Ath.9.392b; any *group of related words*, e.g. *sapiens, sapienter, sapientia*, Cic.*Top.* 3.12, cf. 9.38. 3. in Prosody, *syzygy, dipodia*, Heph.7.8, Aristid. Quint.1.14, Syrian. *in Hermog.*1 p.31 R. b. *syncope*, Anon.Rhythm. 3.19. IV. Astron., *syzygy*, of two stars one of which rises and sets as the other sets and rises, Autol.1.4; of zodiacal signs rising and setting between the same points of the horizon, Gem.2.27; of the moon's conjunctions and oppositions with the sun, Ptol.*Alm.* 5.1, *Cat.Cod.Astr.*1.131; so of planets, Ptol.*Alm.*5.10. V. Math., αἱ κατὰ συζυγίαν ἀντικείμεναι [τομαί] *conjugate* opposite sections, i.e. *conjugate* hyperbolas, each with two branches, Apollon.Perg.*Con.* 2.17, al. **-ιος**, α, ον, poet. for σύζυγος, *joined, united*, Χάριτες E. *Hipp.*1148 (lyr.). II. Act., *joining, uniting*, epith. of Hera, as *patroness of marriage*. Stob.2.7.3$^{a}$, cf. Poll.3.38. ❋ **-ος**, ον, *yoked together, paired, united*, esp. by marriage, σ. ὁμαυλίαι *wedded* union, A.*Ch.*599 (lyr.); of fish, *swimming in pairs*, Arist.*HA*610$^{b}$8. 2. as Subst., fem., *wife*, E.*Alc.*314,342; masc., *yoke-fellow, comrade*, Id.*IT*250, Ar.*Pl.*945, *Ep.Phil.*4.3 (unless pr. n.); *brother*, E.*Tr.* 1001; a gladiator's *adversary*, Herzog *Koische Forschungen* No.133, *JHS*34.19 (Lycia), *Epigr.Gr.*318 (Smyrna); of things, ἀδελφὰ τούτοις καὶ σ. πεποιηκότες Plu.2.1cd. II. *common*, σ. πᾶσι πατρίς *App.Anth.*2.26. Adv. **-γως** *conjointly with*, τινι A.D.*Pron.*51.9, etc.

**συζῡμόω**, *leaven, make to ferment*, v.l. for ζυμόω in Sch Lyc.640.

❋ **σύζυξ**, ῠγος, ὁ, ἡ, = σύζυγος, [ἵππος] Pl.*Phdr.*254a; of wedded pairs, E.*Alc.*921 (anap.), cf. *CIG*4175 (Aezani). II. *united*, ἐπιμέλειαι Isoc.15.182.

**συζῶ**, imper. σύζηθι Philem. p.69 Demiańczuk :—*live with*, σ. τινί Ar.*Fr.*580, D.19.69; μετ' ἀλλήλων Arist.*EN*1156$^{a}$27: c. dat. rei, σ. φιλοπραγμοσύνῃ *pass one's life in..*, D.1.14; βίῳ αὐχμηρῷ σ. Luc. *Salt.*1; θηρίον ὕδατι συζῶν a creature *living in* water, Phryn.*PS* p.6 B. 2. abs., *live together*, [πολιτεία] χαλεπὴ συζῆν Pl.*Plt.*302b, cf. Arist.*EN*1126$^{b}$11, 1170$^{b}$11, al., *Pol.*1278$^{b}$21, 1280$^{b}$38; οἱ συζῶντες Id.*EN*1157$^{b}$7.

**σύζωμα**, ατος, τό, *girdle*, A.*Supp.*462 (pl.).

**συζώννῡμι**, *gird together, gird up*, [κροκωτόν] Ar.*Th.*255 :—Med., *gird up one's loins*, ib.656 (anap.), *Lys.*536 (lyr.). 2. Med. also, *gird on one's* armour, Lxx 1*Ma.*3.3.

**συζωοποιέω**, *quicken together with*, τινὰς τῷ Χριστῷ *Ep.Eph.*2.5, cf. *Ep.Col.*2.13.

**σύηβόλος**, ον, *striking* or *killing swine*, Opp.*C.*2.27.

**συῆλαι**· τόποι βορβορώδεις, Hsch.

**συηνέω, συηνία**, v. ὑηνέω, ὑηνία. **σύθην, σύθι**, v. σεύω.

❋ **συΐδιον** [ῠῐ], τό, Dim. of σῦς, *porker*, Arr.*Epict.*4.11.11, M.Ant.10.10.

**σύϊνος**, η, ον, v.l. in X.*An.*4.4.13 for σύειον.

❋ **σῡκάζω**, (συκῆ) *gather* or *pluck ripe figs*, Ar.*Av.*1699 (lyr., with a play on συκοφαντέω, cf. συκαστής), Poll.1.242, etc.; τὰ σῦκα σ. X.*Oec.*19. 19; σ. ἀπὸ δένδρων D.C.56.30; σ. τὰς συκᾶς *gather figs from* the fig-trees, Poll.1.226. II. *scrutinize*, Aristaenet.1.22, Hsch.: hence sens. obsc., Stratt.3. Cf. συκοφαντέω II.

**σῡκᾰλίς**, ίδος, ἡ, (σῦκον) *beccafico*, including the blackcap and other warblers, Arist.*HA*592$^{b}$21, Alex.Mynd. ap. Ath.2.65b, Dsc.2.56 (v.l.), Gal.15.882, Poll.6.77, Ael.*NA*13.25: also **συκαλλίς**, Epich. 46, Dsc. l. c., Hdn.Gr.1.91, Orib.*inc.* 4.22 cod.; ❋**συκαλλός**, *Gloss.* (s. v.l.): cf. μελαγκόρυφος.

**συκαλόβον**· ῥάβδον ποιμενικήν (Mysian), Hsch. s. v. καράμβας.

**συκαμήδωρος**· μωρός, Id.

❋ **σῡκᾰμῑνέα**, ἡ, = συκάμινος, Aesop.71, Dsc.1.126 (v.l.), Gal.6.589: also in form **συκαμενέα**, *PGrenf.*2.98.2 (vi A.D.).

❋ **συκαμινεών**, = *moretum*, *Gloss.*. *PFlor.*50.32 (iii A.D.).

**σῡκᾰμίν-ῐνος** [μῐ], η, ον, *of* or *belonging to the* συκάμινος, σ. τρῖμμα Sotad.Com.1.4; [ξύλα] *PCair.Zen.*270.1,6 (iii B.C.); *made of* συκαμίνος, πλοῖον ib.188.6. **-οακάνθινος**, ον, *growing* συκάμινος II *and acanthus*, *PHib.*1.70$^{a}$.5 (iii B.C.). ❋ **-ον**, τό, *fruit of the* συκάμινος, *mulberry*, Amphis 38, Arist.*Rh.*1413$^{a}$21, Diocl.*Fr.*140, Lxx *Am.*7. 14; its juice was used by women as a wash, Eub.98.2, Philippid. 19.1. II. = συκόμορον, Dsc.1.127. III. = σῦκον II, Sch.Ar.*Ra.* 1278. IV. a disease of horses, *Hippiatr.*127. ❋ **-ος**, ἡ, more rarely ὁ, = μορέα, *mulberry-tree*, ὁ σ. συκάμιν', ὁρᾷς, φορεῖ Amphis 38, cf. Menestor ap.Thphr.*HP*5.3.4, *Com.Adesp.*1269, etc.; there were two kinds, red (or black) and white, Thphr.*CP*6.6.4, *HP*1.6.1, al. II. σ. ἡ Αἰγυπτία, = συκόμορος, ib.1.1.7, cf. *PCair.Zen.* 83.3 (iii B.C.), Str.17.2.4, D.S.1.34, *Ev.Luc.*17.6. III. σ. ἀγρία, = βάτος (A), Phan.Hist.33. **-ώδης**, ες, *like a mulberry*, σφαῖρα, διαγοναί, ibid.; of a kind of oak, Thphr.*HP*3.7.4.

❋ **σῡκ-άριον** [ᾰ], τό, Dim. of σῦκον, *small fig*, Eup.179, *Gloss.* **-άς**, άδος, ἡ, = συκίς I, Poll.1.242, *Gloss.* **-άσιος**, ον, *of* or *belonging to figs*, Ζεὺς συκάσιος, = καθάρσιος (because figs were used in lustration), Eust.1572.56; or (from some Com. Poet) *the god of sycophants*, Hsch. s. v. Δὶ Συκασίῳ. **-αστής**, οῦ, ὁ, = συκοφάντης, *EM*733.55: fem. **-άστρια**, Hsch.

❋ **σῡκέα**, ἡ, only Dor. (v. συκία), Ep. nom. pl. συκέαι Od.7.116, acc. συκέας 24.341 (both disyll.); Ion. acc. sg. συκέην Hdt.1.193, 4.23, gen. pl. συκέων 1.193; elsewh. only in contr. or analogical forms from συκῆ (Ep. and Ion. nom. συκῆ Od.24.246, Archil.19, acc. συκῆν Hippon.34), *IG*1$^{2}$.313.163, Ar.*Ec.*708, etc. :—*fig-tree, Ficus Carica*, Hom. only in Od.; σ. γλυκεραί 7.116; for various kinds, v. Thphr.*HP* 1.3.1, 3.9.3, 4.2.3, 4.4.4, Ath.3.74c sq.; ἱερὰ σ. a suburb of Eleusis, where Demeter first produced the fig-tree, *IG* l. c., Paus.1.37.2, Ath.3.74d, Philostr.*VS*2.20.3. 2. σ. Αἰγυπτία, = κερωνία, Thphr. *HP*1.11.2. 3. σ. περὶ τὴν Ἴδην, *Amelanchier, Amelanchias vulgaris*, ib.3.17.4. 4. = χαμαισύκη, Dsc.4.169. 5. *banyan, Ficus bengalensis*, Thphr *HP*4.4.4. II. = σῦκον I, *fig*, Ar.*Av.*590. III. a *tar* or *resin* in Aleppo pine, Thphr.*HP*3.9.3, Plin.*HN*16.44. IV. a kind of *spurge*, = πέπλιον, Ps.-Dsc.4.168, Plin.*HN*27.119. V. = σῦκον II, *excrescence* on the body, Dsc.2.170, Poll.4.203, *Hippiatr.* 82. VI. a *seaweed*, Thphr.*HP*4.6.2.

**σύκ-ειον** ξύλον, = σύκινον, *Gloss.* (s. v.l.). **-εών**, ῶνος, ὁ, *fig-yard*, Lxx *Am.*4.9.

**σῡκηγορία**, ἡ, (σῦκον, ἀγορεύω) = συκοφαντία I. 2, Hsch.

**σῡκία**, ἡ, Heraclean Dor. for συκῆ, *Tab.Heracl.*1.172; also Aeol., *IG*12(2).74.7 (Mytil.): but Dor. **συκέα** in an Inscr. of Halaesa, ib.14.352 i 66 (i B.C.).

**συκιδαφόρος**· ἐνίοτε ὁ συκοφάντης· ποτὲ δὲ ὁ συκόπρωκτος, Hsch.

❋ **σῡκ-ίδιον** [κῐ], τό, Dim. of σῦκον, Ar.*Pax* 598. **-ίζω**, *fatten with figs*, in Pass., *AP*9.487 (Pall.); cf. συκόομαι. ❋**-ῐνος**, η, ον, *of the fig-tree*, σ. ξύλον *fig*-wood, Hp.*Ulc.*12, Ar.*V.*145 (where reference is made to the pungent smoke produced by burning it, cf. Arist.*Fr.*227, Thphr. *Ign.*72); κλῳὸς σ. Ar.*V.*807; τορύνη Pl.*Hp.Ma.*290d sq.; σύκινα Χῖα Chian *fig-trees*, *PCair.Zen.*33.12 (iii B.C.): the wood of the fig was proverbially cheap and useless, Zen.3.44, Sch.Ar.*Pl.*947: hence, 2. metaph., σ. ἄνδρες *worthless, good-for-nothing fellows*, Theoc.10.45; σ. σοφιστής Antiph.122.4; prov., σ. ἐπικουρία, of *feeble, useless* help, Hsch. (v. σκύτινος); σ. γνώμη Luc.*Ind.*6; σ. σύζυγος a *false, treacherous* comrade, with a play on συκοφαντικός, Ar.*Pl.*946. II. *of figs*, πῶμα σ. *fig*-wine, Plu.2.752b; ὁ σ. καρπός the *fig*-harvest, *PCair.Zen.*354.20 (iii B.C.).

**σῡκινόφυλλον**, τό, *fig-leaf*, *Gloss.*

**σῡκ-ίον**, τό, *decoction of figs*, Hp.*Morb.*2.28,31. **-ίς**, ίδος, ἡ, *slip* or *cutting from a fig-tree*, Ar.*Ach.*996, *Fr.*374. II. *one suffering from* σῦκον II, Hsch. **-ίτης** [ῑ], ου, ὁ, fem. **-ῖτις**, ιδος, *of figs*, οἶνος *fig*-wine, Dsc.5.32. 2. *sycitis, a fig-coloured gem*, Plin.*HN*37. 191. II. a Spartan name of Dionysus, Sosib.13.

**σῡκο-βᾰσίλεια**, τά, *royal figs*, a very fine kind, Ath.3.78a. **-βῐος**, ον, *living on figs*: *living by slander* (cf. συκοφάντης), Sch.Ar.*Pl.*874, *EM*733.56. **-λογέω**, *gather figs*, Ar.*Pax* 1346 (lyr.). II. *speak about figs*, Ath.3.79a. **-λόγος**, ον, *gathering figs*: *picking up slander* (cf. συκόβιος), Sch.Ar.*Pl.*874, *EM*733.57. **-μάμμας**, ου, ὁ, *poltroon*, Sch.Pl.*Alc.*1.118e; cf. βλιτομάμμας.

❋ **σῡκομορ-έα** or **-αία**, ἡ, = συκόμορος, *Ev.Luc.*19.4. **-ον**, τό, *fruit of the* συκόμορος, Str.17.2.4, Dsc.1.127, Gal.6.617, Ath.2.51b: also the tree, Dsc. l. c. ❋ **-ος**, ἡ, (μόρον) *sycamore-fig, Ficus Sycomorus*, Cels.5.18.7; cf. συκάμινος II. (Heb. *shikemah.*)

**σῦκον**, Boeot. τῦκον (Stratt. 47.5), τό, *fruit of the* συκῆ, *fig*, Od.7. 121, Hdt.2.40, etc.; βασίλεια σ. were a large kind, Philem. 241; to eat figs in the heat of the day was thought to cause fever, Pherecr. 80, Ar.*Fr.*463, Nicopho 12; ξηρὰ σ. Pl.*Lg.*845b: prov., ὅσῳ διαφέρει σῦκα καρδάμων 'as different as chalk from cheese', Henioch.4.2; σύκῳ.. σ. οὐδὲ ἓν οὕτως ὅμοιον γέγονεν Poet.ap.Cic.*Att.*4.8b.2, cf. Herod.6.60; τὰ σῦκα σῦκα.. ὀνομάζων Luc.*Hist Conscr.*41 (cf. σκάφη); σῦκα αἰτεῖν, prov. for τρυφᾶν, Ar.*V.*302 (lyr.); σῦκον χειμῶνος ζητεῖν, of a foolish enterprise, M.Ant.11.33. 2. σ. Αἰγύπτιον, *fruit of κερωνία*, Thphr.*HP*4.2.4, *Od*.5. II. from its shape, *a large wart* on the eyelids, Ar.*Ra*.1247, cf. Hp.*Epid*.3.7 ; *of tumours* in other places, Poll.4.200, Orib.*Syn*.7.40. III. *pudenda muliebria*, Ar.*Pax* 1350.

**σῡκό-ομαι**, Pass., *to be fattened with figs*, *AP*9.487 (Pall.). **-πέδῑλος**, ὁ, *fig-sandaled*, a parody on Homer's χρυσοπέδιλος, with a play on συκοφάντης, Cratin.69. **-πρωκτος**, ον, dub. sens. in Hsch. s. v. συκιδαφόρος. **-πώλης**, ου, ὁ, *fig-vendor*, *PLille* 58 ii 6 (iii B. C.). **-σκόπος**, = συκωρός, Zenodor. ap. Miller *Mélanges* 412. **-σπᾰδίας**, ου, ὁ, (σπάω) expld. as = συκοφάντης, Sch.Ar.*Pl*. 874. **-τρᾰγέω**, *eat figs*, Thphr.*Char*.10.8, Poll.6.40. **-τρᾰγίδης** [ῐ], ου, ὁ, *fig-nibbler*, comic nickname for a miser, Archil.194, Hippon.134. **-τράγος**, ον, (τρᾰγεῖν) *fig-eating*, Ael.*NA*17. 31. **-φάγος** [ᾰ], ον, = συκοτράγος, Hsch. s. v. κραδοφάγος, Sch.Pl. *Alc*.1.118e.

⊕ **σῡκοφαντ-έω**, *to be a* συκοφάντης I, παππῷος ὁ βίος συκοφαντεῖν ἐστί μοι Ar.*Av*.1452, cf. *Ach*.828, *Ec*.562, al., Lys.22.1, Isoc.15.23, 21.5, al., D.53.1, 55.1, al., Men.*Epit*.1, al. ; σ κατ' ἀγοράν Diph.32.16 : c. acc. pers., *prosecute vexatiously*, *blackmail*, συκοφαντεῖς τοὺς ξένους ; Ar. *Av*.1431, cf. *V*.1096 (lyr.) ; τοὺς συμμάχους Isoc.15.318 ; ἑτέρους ἔσειε καὶ ἐσυκοφάντει Antipho 6.43 ; σ. τοὺς τὰς οὐσίας ἔχοντας Arist.*Pol*. $1304^b22$, cf. Lys.19.9 (Pass.) ; συκοφαντοῦμαι νῦν ὑπ' αὐτῶν ἀδίκως Id. *Fr*.43, cf. X.*Oec*.11.21, Thphr.*Char*.23.4 ; ἰδόντες.. σε ὑπὸ Δημέου συκοφαντούμενον *PMich.Zen*.57.2 (iii B. C.), cf. *PCair.Zen*.212.4, 628.3 (iii B. C.), *CPR*232.3 (ii/iii A. D.) ; freq. of blackmail by officials, *PTeb*. 43.26, 789.21 (ii B. C.), *UPZ*112 i 4, 113.10,16 (ii B. C.) ; συκοφαντῆσαι ἡμᾶς καὶ διασεῖσαι *BGU*1756.11 (i B. C.) ; μηδένα διασείσητε μηδὲ συκοφαντήσητε *Ev.Luc*.3.14, cf. *CPR*238.6 (ii A. D.), *PFlor*.382.57 (iii A. D.) ; τοῦ συκοφαντῆσαι ἡμᾶς *to seek occasion against* us, *oppress* us, Lxx *Ge*.43.18 ; ὁ συκοφαντῶν πένητα ib.*Pr*.14.31 ; *accuse falsely*, ταυτὶ γὰρ συκοφαντεῖσθαι τὸν Ἕκτορα ὑπὸ τοῦ Ὁμήρου that is *a false charge brought against* Hector by Homer, Philostr.*Her*.$12^b$ ; κύριε Γάϊε, συκοφαντούμεθα Ph.2.598, cf. 1.145, D.C.38.28, al. : c. acc. et gen., τὸν θεὸν ὀλιγωρίας Ael.*Fr*.40 : c. acc. rei, *denounce as contraband*, Μεγαρέων τὰ χλανίσκια Ar.*Ach*.519 ; *extort by false charges* or *threats*, τριάκοντα μνᾶς Lys.26.24 ; εἴ τινός τι ἐσυκοφάντησα, ἀποδίδωμι τετραπλοῦν *Ev.Luc*.19.8 : abs., Isoc.18.10. 2. *criticize in a pettifogging way*, τοὺς ποιητάς Arist.*Po*.$1456^a5$, cf. D.H.*Th*.52, *Dem*.34, D.S.26.1 ; *lay verbal traps for* one, τὸν ῥήτορα βουλόμενος δικαίως ἐξετάζειν καὶ μὴ σ. D.18.232 ; σ. Θρασύμαχον Pl.*R*.341c ; ὑποσκελίζειν καὶ σ. D.18.138 : c. acc. rei, *quibble about*, μὴ τὰ συμβάντα συκοφάντει ib.192 ; σ. τὸ πρᾶγμα Id.23.61, D.H.*Dem*.25 ; *carp at*, *stint*, τὸν ἐπὶ τοῖς καλλίστοις ἔργοις ἔπαινον D.S.4.8 : abs., *quibble*, Pl.*R*.341b, Arist.*Top*.$139^b26$, $157^a32$, D.20.62. II. = κνίζω ἐρωτικῶς, Pl.Com. 255, Men.1071. **-ημα**, ατος, τό, *vexatious prosecution* or *accusation*, Aeschin.2.39, *OGI*669.40 (Egypt, i A. D., pl.), J.*AJ*16.10.8, Plu.*Per*.37, *CPR*232.14 (ii/iii A. D.). II. *quibble*, Arist.*SE*$174^b$ 9. **-ης**, ου, ὁ, *common informer*, *voluntary denouncer* (there being no Public Prosecutor), e.g. of contraband imports, καὶ σ. εἴ τις ἦν ὠνείδισας ; did you dare to reproach a σ.? Ar.*Ach*.559, cf. 725,825 ; of unlawful possession, Id.*Pl*.873,879,885 ; of disaffection to Athens, Isoc.15.313 (cf. 316–18) ; κλητὴρ εἰμὶ νησιωτικὸς καὶ σ. Ar.*Av*.1423 ; the σ. became notorious as pettifoggers, Lycurg.31 (cf. Ar.*Ach*.920 –4), D.20.62, vexatious prosecutors of innocent persons esp. if rich, Lys.25.3, D.57.34, and blackmailers, Antipho 5.78,80, Lys.7.20, And.1.105, D.21.103, 58.27, Aeschin.2.5, 3.256, Hyp.*Lyc*.2, Theopomp.Hist.107,267, Luc.*Tim*.36 ; having thus abused their legal powers, they were treated as criminals, [οἱ τριάκοντα] τοὺς σ... ἀνῄρουν Arist.*Ath*.35.3, cf. X.*HG*2.3.38, Isoc.15.313, 18.3 ; συκοφαντῶν προβολαί Arist.*Ath*.43.5, cf. Aeschin.2.145 ; they were numerous in democracies, Thphr.*Char*.26.5 ; χρῆν.. ἐγγίγνεσθαι.. πάσῃ δημοκρατίᾳ σ. Plu.*Tim*.37 ; δημαγωγῶν πλῆθος καὶ σ. at Syracuse, D.S.11.87 ; rarer in oligarchies, e.g. Boeotia, Ar.*Ach*.904 ; βασιλεὺς ἐνδεὴς προσόδων μέγας σ. a great *extortioner*, Lxx *Pr*.28. 16. 2. in New Com., *professional swindler* or *confidential agent*, πράττει δ' ὁ κόλαξ ἄριστα πάντων, δεύτερα δ' ὁ σ. Men.223.17, cf. *Georg*. *Fr*.1, Philippid.29 : so in Lat. *sycophanta*, Plaut.*Poen*.1032, *Trin*. 815, Ter.*Andr*.815 ; *humbug*, Favorin.ap.Gell.14.1.32. 3. = Lat. *delator*, ὁ πικρὸς σ. Ἰσίδωρος Ph.2.597, cf. *OGI*669.41 (Egypt, i A. D.), *Cod.Just*.1.4.34.17, al. (From σῦκον φαίνειν, orig. used of denouncers of the attempted export of figs from Athens, acc. to Ister 35, Plu. *Sol*.24, 2.523b ; orig. of citizens entrusted with the collection of figs as part of the public revenues of Athens and the denouncing of tax-evaders, acc. to Philomnest.1 ; of denouncers of figs which had been stolen from the sacred fig-trees during a famine and had become cheap, the famine having passed, Sch.Ar.*Pl*.31, cf. Fest. p.393 L. ; these and modern explanations are mere guesses ; the word first in Ar. but implied by συκοπέδιλος.) **-ητέον**, *one must quibble*, Phld.*Herc*.1251.14. **-ητός**, ή, όν, *to be quibbled about*, οὐ σ. ἦν τὰ τοιαῦτα after all, such points *need not be unduly pressed*, Sch.Ar.*Ra*.53. **-ία**, ἡ, *vexatious* or *dishonest prosecution*, *chicane*, *barratry*, *blackmail*, Lys.4.14, 28.6 (pl.), X.*HG*2.3. 12, D.18.249, Charondas ap. D.S.12.12 ; σ. τοῖς πράγμασι προσάγειν employ *chicane* in the case, D.19.98 ; τοῖς οἰκείοις σ. δέδωκεν has given them an *opportunity for chicane*, Id.23.67, cf. *POxy*. 472.33 (ii A. D.) ; contrasted with φήμη, Aeschin.2.145 ; [γραφὴ] συκοφαντίας Arist.*Ath*.59.3 ; συκοφαντίας αὐτοῦ κατέγνωτε Lys.13. 65. 2. *oppression*, σ. πένητος Lxx *Ec*.5.7, cf. *Ps*.118(119). 134 ; *extortion*, *PTeb*.43.36 (ii B. C.) ; τὸ τακτὸν εἰς τὸ πρόστιμον τῆς σ. *PFlor*.6.6 (iii A. D.). II. *quibble*, *sophism*, Arist.*Rh*. $1402^a15$, cf. *EE*$1221^b7$. **-ίας**, ου, ὁ (sc. ἄνεμος), Com. word in Ar.*Eq*.437, καικίας καὶ συκοφαντίας πνεῖ. **-ικός**, ή, όν, *typical of a* συκοφάντης, *blackmailing*, δίκη D.37.3 (Comp.) ; *skilled as an 'agent provocateur'*, Philostr.*VA*7.27 : metaph., σ. πνεύματα, = συκοφαντίας, Lib.*Or*.13.16. Adv. -κῶς Isoc.15.308, Luc.*Hist.Conscr*.10. II. *sophistical*, λόγοι Phld.*Oec*. p.65 J., cf. *Rh*.1.119 S. **-ις**, ιδος, ἡ, = sq., Suid. s. v. συκίνη μάχαιρα (dub.). **-ρια**, ἡ, fem. of συκοφάντης, Ar.*Pl*.970, *PMasp*.97 ii 39 (vi A. D.). **-ώδης**, ες, = συκοφαντικός, δίκη Lys.*Fr*.1.1 (Comp.) ; κρίσεις D.S.15.40 ; κατηγορία Mitteis *Chr*. 68.19 (i A. D.) ; οἱ Ἀττικοὶ σ. Dicaearch.1.4.

**σῡκόφᾰσις**, εως, ἡ, = συκοφαντία, *AP*7.107 (D. L., pl.).

**σῡκοφορ-εῖον**, τό, *basket for carrying figs*, *Gloss*. : also **-φόρον**, ib. **-έω**, *carry figs*, *AP*9.563 (Leon.). **-ος** (parox.), ον, *fig-bearing*, γῆ Str.4.1.2.

**σῡκόφυλλον**, τό, *fig-leaf*, Apul.*Herb*.38, Hsch. s. v. ἀποτεθρίακεν.

**συκχάς, σύκχος**, v. συγχίς.

**σῡκ-ώδης**, ες, *fig-like*, γλυκύτης Arist.*HA*$623^b24$ ; ὄγκος Gal.12.822 ; ἐπαναστάσεις σ., of warts or piles, Orib.*Syn*.8.37 tit., cf. Dsc.1.128.5 ; cf σῦκον II. II. = συκοφαντώδης, Sch.Ar.*Pl*.874, *EM*733.56. **-ωμα**, ατος, τό, = σύκωσις, Gal.14.778 (nisi leg. σάρκωμα), Sch.Ar.*Ra*. 1278. **-ών**, ῶνος, ὁ, *fig-yard*, Lxx *Je*.5.17, *BGU*563 ii 3 (i A. D.), *Gloss*. **-ωρέω**, *watch figs*, Poll.7.143. **-ωρός**, ὁ, *fig-watcher*, ib.140,143, Phot. II. = συκοφάντης, Sch.Ar.*Pl*.874. **-ωσις**, εως, ἡ, *ulcer resembling a fig ripe to bursting*, with projecting edges, esp. on the eyelids, Cels.6.3, Gal.12.348,716, *UP*10.11, Sever.ap. Aët.7.45 ; τοῦ γενείου Archig.ap.eund.8.14. **-ωτικός**, ή, όν, *for piles*, *medicamentum*, Cass.Fel.74. **-ωτός**, ή, όν, *fed on figs*, τῶν σύκοις σιτευθέντων χοίρων καὶ διὰ τοῦτο συκωτῶν καλουμένων Aët.2.127 ; ἧπαρ σ. the liver *of an animal so fatted*, Gal.6.679,704, Orib.2.39.2 ; τὰ καλούμενα σ. Gal.15.657 ; cf. ζυγωγόν.

**σῦλα**, v. σύλη.

**σῡλᾰγωγέω**, (σῦλον) *carry off as booty*, *lead captive*, τινα *Ep.Col*. 2.8, Hld.10.35. II. *rob*, *despoil*, τὸν οἶκον Aristaenet.2.22.

**σῡλ-άω**, impf. contr. in Ep. ἐσύλα, σύλα, Il.6.28, 4.116 ; Ion. Iterat. σύλασκε Hes.*Sc*.480 :—Pass., fut. συληθήσομαι A.*Pr*.761, συλήσομαι Paus.4.7.10 :—*strip off*, esp. *strip off* the arms of a slain enemy, Hom. (only in Il.), Lyr., etc. Construction : 1. in full, c. acc. pers. et rei, *strip off from* another, *strip* him *of* his arms (cf. σκυλεύω), μή μιν Ἀχαιοὶ τεύχεα συλήσωσι Il.15.428, cf. 16.500 ; ἔπειτα δὲ καὶ τὰ (sc. ἔναρα).. νεκροὺς ἂμ πεδίον συλήσετε 6.71 ; με κασίγνητον συλᾷς E.*IT*157 (anap.) ; τὴν θεὸν τοὺς στεφάνους σεσυλήκασιν D.24.182 :—Pass., c. acc. rei, *to be stripped*, *robbed*, *deprived of* a thing, σκῆπτρα συληθήσεται A.*Pr*.761 ; ταῦτ' (sc. τὰ τόξα) ἐσυλήθην ἐγώ S.*Ph*.413 ; λέκτρα συλᾶσθαι βίᾳ E.*IA*1275 ; συληθεὶς τὰς βοῦς Isoc.6.19 ; σεσυλήμεθα τὰ ἡμέτερα ὑπὸ τούτων D.35.26. 2. c. acc., *strip* a person of his arms, ἤ τινα συλήσων νεκύων Il.10.343 : generally, *pillage*, *plunder*, τὰ ἱρά, τοὺς θεούς, etc., Hdt.6.101, Pl.*Lg*.864d, etc. ; τοὺς νεώς Isoc.4.155 ; θεῶν βρέτη A.*Pers*.810 ; νεκρόν Pl.*R*.469d :—Pass., βαρβάρων συλᾶσθ' ὕπο E.*Hel*.600. 3. c. acc. rei, *strip off*, ὄφρα τάχιστα τεύχεα συλήσειε Il.4.466, etc. ; freq. with additions, ἀπ' ὤμων τεύχε' ἐσύλα 6.28, etc. ; τὰ μὲν ἔντε' ἀπὸ χροὸς.. συλήσας 13.641. b. *take off* or *out*, ἐσύλα τόξον *took out* the bow [from its case], 4.105 ; σύλα πῶμα φαρέτρης *took* the lid *off* the quiver, ib.116 ; with a notion of violence or suddenness, κρᾶτα σ. Μεδοίσας Pi.*P*.12.16. c. *carry off*, τοὺς πολεμίους οὐ συλήσειν αὐτά (sc. τὰ χρήματα) *will* not *seize* them *as booty*, Hdt.5.36, cf. 9.116 ; θεῶν γέρα σ. A.*Pr*.83, cf. S.*OC* 922, *Ph*.1365 ; λόγοις τὰ τῶν προγόνων ἔργα συλήσας καὶ διασύρας D. 19.313 ; σ. κατὰ βραχὺ τὴν τῶν πυρετῶν διάθεσιν Steph. *in Gal*.1. 295 D. :—Pass. *to be carried off as spoil*, ἄγαλμα σεσυλημένον Hdt.6. 118 ; *to be taken away*, E.*Hipp*.799 : metaph., συλᾶται ὕπνος ἀπὸ γλεφάρων B.*Fr*.3.10. d. *exercise right of* σῦλαι, *IG*9(1).333.3 (Locr., v B. C.) :—Pass., πανταχοῦ συλωμένων ἡμῶν *the right of reprisals was exercised* against us everywhere, Isoc.3.33. 4. after Hom., c. acc. pers. et gen. rei, τίς σε δαίμων συλᾷ πάτρας ; *carries* thee *away from*.., E.*Hel*.669 :—Pass., συλαθεὶς ἀγενείων *stealing from among* the boys, and enlisting among the men, Pi.*O*.9.89. **-εύς**, έως, ὁ, *privateer*, *GDI*2516 (Delph., iii B. C.). **-εύω**, Ep. form of συλάω, only pres. and impf., *despoil of arms*, τὸν μὲν ἄρ'.. ἐσύλευον Il.5.48 : also, *despoil secretly*, *trick*, *cheat*, 24.436. 2. *steal away*, σ. βλεφάρων φάος *AP*5.230 (Maced.). ⊕ **-έω**, = συλάω, Q.S.1.717 ; ῥήματα σ. ἀλλήλους dub. in Xanth.1 :—Med., *steal for oneself*, κηρίον ἐκ σίμβλων συλεύμενον Theoc.19.2. II. *rescue*, συλέων τινὰ ἐλεύθερον ἐόντα, a formula in the manumission of slaves at Delphi, *GDI*1686.11, etc. ⊕ **-η**, ἡ, or **σῦλον**, τό, *the right of seizing the ship* or *cargo* of a foreign merchant, to cover losses received through him : generally, *right of seizure*, *right of reprisal*, prop. of goods (opp. ἀνδροληψία), σῦλον ἔχειν κατά τινος Arist.*Oec*.$1347^b23$ ; ἐν σύλῳ *when engaged in privateering*, *IG*12(5).24.11 (Sicinos) : but mostly in pl. σῦλαι or σῦλα, διὰ τὰς σύλας D.51.13 ; ὅπου ἂν σῦλαι μὴ ὦσιν Ἀθηναίοις where the Athenians have [to fear] no *right of seizure*, Syngr.ap.D.35.13 ; δεδομένων συλῶν Φασηλίταις κατὰ Ἀθηναίων Id.35.26 ; [ὁρῶν] Βοιωτοὺς σῦλα ποιουμένους [seeing] the B. exercising *this right*, Lys.30.22 (v.l.) ; μήνυτρα σύλων ὧν ὁ θεὸς ἐσυλήθη Babr.2.12. II. σῦλον is *the cargo seized* in *IG*9(1).333.5 (Locr., v B. C.) : σῦλα, τά, = *booty*, Str.17.1.8 ; σύλη, ἡ, *booty*, *SIG*10 (Samos, vi B. C.). ⊕ **-ησις**, εως, ἡ, *spoiling*, *plundering*, S.*Ichn*.75, Pl.*Lg*.853d (pl.), Max.583 (unless συλήσιος is an Adj. *stolen*). **-ήτειρα**, ἡ, *plunderer*, δόρκα σ. ἀγρωσσᾶν E.*HF* 377 (lyr.). **-ητής**, οῦ, ὁ, = sq., *Gloss*. **-ήτωρ**, ορος, ὁ, *plunderer*,

A.*Supp.*927, Nonn.*D.*24.306. **-ικός**, ή, όν, *relating to booty*, δίκη *IG*5(2).443.23 (Megalopolis, ii/i B.C.).

⊕ **συλλᾰβ-ή**, ἡ, (συλλαμβάνω IV) *conception, pregnancy*, only in Men. 1085. 2. *grip, hold*, in wrestling, metaph., Simp. *in Cael.*354.5; so perh. mental *grasp, participation*, Phld.*Mus.*p.103 K. (pl.). II. Act., *that which holds together*, συλλαβαὶ πέπλων, i.e. a girdle, A. *Supp.*457. 2. Pass., *that which is held together*, esp. of *several letters taken together* so as to form one sound, *syllable*, βοᾷ.. γραμμάτων ἐν συλλαβαῖς Id.*Th.*468; ἄφωνα καὶ φωνοῦντα (sic codd.) συλλαβάς τε θείς E.*Fr.*578.2, cf. Pl.*Tht.*202b, Gal.15.6, etc.; γράψαντος τὰς αὐτὰς σ. ἅσπερ Κτησιφῶν νῦν γέγραφε *verbatim et literatim*, D.18.83; σ. βραχεῖα καὶ μακρά Arist.*Cat.*4ᵇ33, cf. Zeno *Stoic.*1.70, Phld.*Po.*2. 15, etc. 3. συλλαβαί, = Lat. *literae, a letter*, *Cod.Just.*1.1.7 *Prooem.*, Men.Prot. p.41 D., *Sammelb.*7438.5 (vi A.D.). 4. pl., *letters* of the alphabet, Luc.*Jud.Voc.*2,8. 5. pl., = *apices*, *Gloss.* III. in Music, the *perfect fourth*, Philol.6, *PTeb.*694.25 (iii B.C.), Nicom. *Harm.*9, Aristid.Quint.1.8. IV. Arith., *sum* of two or more numbers, *Theol.Ar.*54. **-ίζω**, *join letters into syllables, pronounce letters together*, Plu.2.496f, Luc.*Gall.*23. **-ικός**, ή, όν, *syllabic*, χώρα A.D.*Pron.*86.20, cf. *Synt.*7.25; τόνος, of the grave accent, D.T.674.31, Sch.D.T. p.139 H. Adv. -κῶς *EM*820.17.

**συλλᾰβο-μᾰχέω**, *fight for syllables*, Ph.1.526, cf. *Fr.*73 H. **-πευσῐλᾰλητής**, οῦ, ὁ, (συλλαβή, πεύθομαι, λαλέω) *examining each syllable before pronouncing it*, Epigr.ap.Hegesand.2.

**συλλαγνεύω**, = συμπορνεύω, Hsch.

⊕ **συλλαγχάνω**, *to be joined by lot with*, τινι Pl.*Plt.*266c,e, *Ti.*18e; ὁ ταῖς ὥραις ἐκείναις συνειληχὼς μεσοβασιλεύς *who was chosen by lot to be* interrex at that time, Plu.*Num.*7.

**συλλᾰλ-έω**, *talk with* or *together*, τινι *PCair.Zen.*315.2 (iii B.C.), *PHib.*1.66.4 (iii B.C.), Lxx *Ex.*34.35, Plb.4.22.8; μετά τινος *Ev.Matt.*17.3, etc.; πρός τινα *Ev.Luc.*4.36; ἐπαχθέντες ἐπὶ τὸν δῆμον ὑπὲρ ἁπάντων *OGI*229.23 (Smyrna, iii B.C.); ὑπὲρ τοῦ ἐνδοῦναι Plb.1.43. 1. **-ημα**, ατος, τό, *conversation*, Hsch. s.v. συναιρήματα. **-ησις**, εως, ἡ, = foreg., Phld.*Ir.*p.47 W. **-ιά**, ἡ, = foreg., *Gloss.*

⊕ **συλλαμβάνω**, fut. -λήψομαι: pf. -είληφα, Pass. -είλημμαι: aor. συνέλᾰβον, inf. συλλᾰβεῖν:—Med., pres. in Philem.53.4: aor. συνελαβόμην Hdt.3.49, etc.:—Pass. (v. infr.; in X.*An.*7.2.14 συλληφθήσεται has been restored for συλλήψεται):—*collect, gather together*, esp. *rally* scattered troops, τῆς στρατιῆς τοὺς περιγενομένους Hdt.5.46; τὸ στράτευμα X.*Cyr.*3.3.1; τὰς δυνάμεις Pl.*Grg.*456a; σ. θοινάτορας E.*Ion* 1217. 2. *take with one, carry off*, S.*Tr.*1153; ξυλλαβὼν κατέκλινεν αὐτὸν εἰς Ἀσκληπιοῦ Ar.*V.*122, cf. *AP*5.52 (tm., Diosc.); συλλαβὼν θεσπίσματα κεῖται παρ' Ἅιδῃ *with all* his prophecies, S.*OT*971; ἔρρε, τάσδε συλλαβὼν ἀράς Id.*OC*1384; ἔκπλει σεαυτὸν συλλαβὼν ἐκ τῆσδε γῆς *pack yourself off*, Id.*Ph.*577. 3. *put together, close*, τὸ στόμα καὶ τοὺς ὀφθαλμούς (of a corpse) Pl.*Phd.*118a; ξ. αὐτοῦ τὸ στόμα *shut* his mouth, Ar.*Ach.*926, cf. Arist.*HA*623ᵇ2; *enclose*, τῇ ἐπιδέσει συλλαμβάνοντα συνάγειν τοὺς μηρούς Sor.2.86; ξ. καὶ τοὺς τένοντας τοῖσι ἐρίοισι Aret.*CA*1.6. b. *combine in pronunciation*, λέγε δὴ μόλωμεν ξυνεχὲς ὡδὶ ξυλλαβών *say* αὐτὸ μόλωμεν *as one word*, Ar.*Eq.*21. 4. in speaking, *comprehend, comprise*, ἑνὶ ἔπεϊ πάντα συλλαβόντα εἰπεῖν Hdt.3.82; πᾶν.. συλλαβὼν εἴρηκας Id.7. 16.γ'; εἰς ἓν πάντα σ. Pl.*Sph.*234b, cf. *Tht.*147d; τὰ ἄλλα εἰς ταὐτὸ Id.*Plt.*263d:—Pass., *to be comprehended* (logically), μετὰ τοῦ γένους αἱ συλλαμβανόμεναι διαφοραί Arist.*Metaph.*1037ᵇ31, cf. 998ᵇ28; σὺν τῇ ὕλῃ συνειλημμένος, i.e. *concrete*, opp. *abstract*, ib.1039ᵇ21, cf. 1035ᵃ25, al. II. *lay hands on, seize*, ὁλκάδας Hdt.6.26; κόμην ἀπρὶξ ὄνυξι συλλαβὼν χερί S.*Aj.*310; τέττιγα τοῦ πτεροῦ Archil. 143 (loosely paraphrased, cf. *Hermes* 23.279); τὰ ποτήμενα συλλαβῆν Theoc.29.30; ξ. τῶν σχοινίων *lay hold* of them, *help* to pull, Ar.*Pax* 437:—Med., τίς ξυλλάβοιτ' ἂν τοῦ ξύλου; Id.*Lys.*313, cf. *Pax* 465 (lyr.). b. *buy up*, τὰ τρύβλια Id.*Eq.*650. 2. *seize the person of*.., *apprehend, arrest*, *IG*1².39.7, Hdt.2.121.ε', Ar.*Ach.*206, Antipho 5.29, And.1.45, *PCair.Zen.*15ᵛ.44, 202.2 (iii B.C.); συνέλαβον αὐτὸν καὶ ἀπήχθη εἰς τὸ δεσμωτήριον ib.484.21 (iii B.C.); σ. ζῶντα, ὅμηρον, E.*Rh.*513, *Or.*1189; τινὰ ἐπὶ θανάτῳ Isoc.4.154; συλλαβόντας αὐτὸν ἴσχειν *seize* and hold him, *IG*4²(1).122.40 (Epid., iv B.C.):—Pass., πρὶν ξυλληφθῆναι before *they were arrested*, Th.1.20, cf. Hdt. 1.80, al., And.1.101, *PCair.Zen.*15ᵛ.7 (iii B.C.). 3. of the mind, *grasp the meaning of, comprehend*, τὸ χρηστήριον, τὸ ῥηθέν, τὸν λόγον, τὴν φωνήν, Hdt.1.63,91, 2.49, 4.114; παρκείμενον συλλαβὼν τέρας Pi.*O.*13.73, cf. Pl.*Sph.*218c, etc. III. *receive at the same time, enjoy together*, Hdt.1.32. IV. of females, *conceive*, Arist.*HA*582ᵃ19, *GA*727ᵇ8, Sor.1.28, etc.; ἐν γαστρί Hp.*Aph.*5.46; ξυλλαβοῦσα τὴν γονήν Id.*Steril.*220; of the womb, σ. τὸ σπέρμα Arist.*HA*583ᵇ29, al., cf. Luc.*VH*1.22: but συνειληφυῖα τοῦ τεκεῖν *near to* be delivered, Lxx 1*Ki.*4.19. V. *take with* or *besides, take as an assistant*, τὴν δίκην σ. E.*Fr.*584; ἄτεγκτον σ. καρδίαν Id.*HF* 833. VI. c. dat. pers., *take part with* another, *assist* him, οὐ τοῖς ἀθύμοις ἡ τύχη ξ. S.*Fr.*927, cf. E.*Med.*813, Hdt.6.125, etc.; τὰ δυνατὰ τῇ πόλει ξ. Ar.*Ec.*861; σ. τισί τι *take part with* or *assist* them in a thing, Id.*Lys.*540 (lyr.), X.*Cyr.*7.5.49, etc.; σ. τινί τινος E.*Med.*946, Ar.*V.*734 (lyr.); σ. τινί τινι D.18.20: with a Prep., συνέλαβε γὰρ ἄλλα.. ἐς τὸ πείθεσθαι *contributed* towards persuading, Hdt.7.6, cf. X.*Mem.*2.6.28: abs., *assist*, A.*Ch.*812 (lyr.), S.*Tr.*1019 (lyr.), Ar.*Eq.* 229, Th.1.118; δεῖ δὲ ξυλλαμβάνοντα τοὺς θεοὺς ἐπικαλέεσθαι while invoking the gods one must *help oneself*, Hp.*Insomn.*87. 2. Med., c. gen. rei, *take part in*, συνελάβοντο τοῦ στρατεύματος Hdt.3.49; ὅστις νόσου κάμνοντι συλλάβοιτο S.*Ph.*282; ξυνελάβοντο τοῦ τοιοῦτου οὐχ ἥκιστα, ὥστε.. especially *contributed* to this, Th.4.47: c. dat., καιρῷ χειμῶνος συλλαβέσθαι κυβερνητικὴν *intervene* in a storm *together with* circumstance, Pl.*Lg.*709c: sts. in tmesi, ξύμ μοι λάβεσθε τοῦ μύθου Id.*Phdr.*237a, cf. *AP*9.559 (Crin.).

**σύλλαμψις**, εως, ἡ, *union of light*, Plu.2.625f.

**συλλανθάνω**, *escape at the same time*, τὴν Ἥραν καὶ τὸν ἔλεγχον *Gp.*11.22.1, cf. Afric.*Cest.*p.23 V.

**συλλατρεύω**, *serve with* or *together*, Plu.2.941e.

**συλλᾰφύσσω**, *devour* or *carry off together*, Lyc.1267.

**σύλλαψις**, v. σύλληψις.

**συλλεαίνω**, Ion. **συλλειαίνω**, *pound up with*, τί τινι Aret.*CA*1.1, Orib.*Fr.*85; ὁμοῦ πάντα Androm.ap.Gal.13.133; simply, *grind up*, *PLeid.X.*19,69. 2. metaph., *combine*, in Pass., τὸ μὴ -εσθαι ⟨τὸ ν⟩ τῷ ἑξῆς (in ἀνθρώπων πράγματα) D.H.*Dem.*43. II. Pass., *subside*, of swellings, Hp.*Epid.*2.2.6.

**σύλλεγμα**, ατος, τό, *collection, heap*, Hsch. s.v. ἀμόργμα; = *caterva*, *Gloss.*; *gleaning*, Al.*Le.*23.22.

⊕ **συλλέγω**, aor. -έλεξα Ar.*Ra.*1297, etc.: pf. -είλοχα D.18.308, 21.23, prob. in Dsc.*Eup.*2.168:—Med., fut. -λέξομαι Od.2.292: aor. -ελεξάμην, Ep. 3 sg. συλλέξατο Il.18.413: pf., v. infr.:—Pass., fut. -λεγήσομαι Aeschin.3.100: aor. -ελέχθην Hdt.1.97, etc., rare in Att., Ar.*Lys.*526 (anap.), Pl.*Lg.*784a; aor. 2 -ελέγην being preferred, Ar.*V.*1107, *Ec.*116, Th.4.25, etc., and sts. in Hdt., 7. 173, 9.27: pf. -είλεγμαι Ar.*Av.*294, Th.3.94, etc. (also in med. sense, X.*Mem.*4.2.1, Hyp.*Eux.*32, D.59.18); 3 pl. συνειλέχατο J. *AJ*17.10.2; part. rarely -λελεγμένος, Hdt.7.26, 9.41, Ar.*Ec.*58, *PTeb.* 700.27 (ii B.C.):—*bring together, collect, gather*, [κτέατα] Il.18. 301; χρ]ήματα Alc.*Supp.*5.12; ἀργύριον.. τοῦ ἐπετείου οὗ αὐτοὶ ξυνελέξαμεν *IG*1².301.32; χαλκία συνλέξαντες ib.393; ξύλα S.*Fr.*225; τὰ ὀστέα, τὸν λιβανωτόν, Hdt.1.68, 3.107; σ. σφίσι φερνάς Id.1.93; φρύγανα X.*An.*4.3.11; βίον ἄνευ πόνου E.*El.*81; ἐράνους D.21.184; παρὰ τῶν φίλων ἔρανον Antipho 2.2.9; ἀμμώδη ἐν τῇ κύστει Dsc.5. 118, cf. Aët.15.12; σ. μονῳδίας, μέλη, *compose*, or rather *compile, scrape together*, Ar.*Ra.*849,1297, cf. *Ach.*398; ῥήματα καὶ λόγους D. 18.308; σ. ὕβρεις αὐτοῦ *compile a list of* them, Id.21.23: abs., ὁ μὲν γὰρ αὐτῷ συλλέγει *collects* for himself, Men.*Kol.*43; περιιόντα συλλέγειν to go about *picking up information*, D.21.36:—Med., *collect for oneself, for one's own use*, ὅπλα τε πάντα λάρνακ' ἐς ἀργυρέην συλλέξατο Il.18.413, cf. Ar.*Pax* 1327 (anap.), Pl.*R.*553c, *Lg.*936c, etc.; ξυλλέγεται βίοτον Sol.13.50:—Pass., αἷμα συλλέγεταί τινι ἐπὶ τοὺς τιτθούς *gathers* there, Hp.*Epid.*2.6.32, cf. Sor.1.55; ἁμαρτήματα.. συνειλεγμένα D.10.1, etc. 2. ἐκ τῆς ἀσθενείας σ. ἐμαυτόν *rally* myself, Pl. *Ax.*370e:—Med., σύλλεξαι σθένος E.*Ph.*850:—Pass., ψυχὴν αὐτὴν εἰς αὐτὴν συλλέγεσθαι Pl.*Phd.*83a. 3. Pass., *come together, become customary*, ἡ πολυλογία σ. αὐτῷ X.*Cyr.*1.4.3. II. of persons, *collect, get together*, στασιώτας Hdt.1.59; ἐγχωρίους E.*IT*303; χορόν Antipho 6.11; ἐκκλησίαν X.*HG*3.3.8; στρατὸν *raise* or *levy* an army, Th.4.77, etc.:—Med., ἑταίρους.. συλλέξομαι Od.2.292; λόχον -ελέξατο X.*An.*7.4.8:—Pass., *come together, assemble*, Hdt.1.81, 7.8, Lys. 24.19, etc.; ἐκεῖσε σ. And.1.133; εἰς ταὐτὸ σ. Pl.*Lg.*961a.

**Συλλεῖα**, τά, *sacrifice in honour of Sulla*, *IG*2².1039.57.

**συλλείβω**, *collect by streams*, τὸ ὕδωρ Arist.*Mete.*350ᵃ9:—Pass., [τὸ καταμηνιῶδες περίττωμα] συλλείβεται εἰς αὐτὴν τὴν ὑστέραν Id.*GA* 751ᵃ5; of blood, *a flow takes place*, Hp.*Oss.*15, cf. *Virg.*1; of rivers, ἐκ πλειόνων πηγῶν συλλείβεσθαι Demetr.Sceps.ap.Str.13.1.43.

**συλλειοτρῖβέω**, *pound up*, Gal.13.800:—Pass., Sor.2.13, Orib. *Syn.*9.48.5.

**συλλειόω**, *pound up together*, τῷ ὄξει *PMag.Leid.V.*6.19, cf. *PMag. Lond.*46.376, *Gp.*17.5.3, Orib.*Syn.*8.3.10 (Pass.).

**συλλειτουργέω**, *to be a joint* λειτουργός, *IG*2².1329.15, 5(1).1390. 115 (Andania, i B.C.): metaph., Ph.2.227.

**σύλλεκτος**, ον, *gathered* or *brought together*, Str.7.7.2, Hsch. s.v. συγκλύδων; λίθοι Hecat.Abd.ap.J.*Ap.*1.22.

**σύλλεκτρος**, ον, *partner of the bed, husband* or *wife*, E.*HF*1268, cf. *Supp.Epigr.*2.874 (Egypt); σ. ἄνασσα *AP*9.657 (Marian.); σ. Διός *sharing* [Alcmena's] *bed with* Zeus, of Amphitryon, E.*HF*1; so, of Ixion, σ. τῷ Διί Luc.*DDeor.*6.5.

**σύλλεξις**, εως, ἡ, *contribution*, Antiph.210, cf. Poll.6.179.

**συλλεπτύνω**, *make thin*, Gal.18(2).912.

**συλλεσχηνεύω**, *converse with*, τοῖς παροῦσι App.*BC*2.98.

**συλλήβδην**, Adv. *collectively, in sum, in short*, Thgn.147 (= Phoc. 17); βραχεῖ δὲ μύθῳ πάντα σ. μάθε A.*Pr.*505; ταῦτα ἐπράθη σ. ἅπαντα *IG*1².325.21; ἀγαθὰ σ. ἅπαντά σοι φέρω Ar.*Pl.*646; τὸν φόρον.. σ. τὸν προσιόντα Id.*V.*657 (anap.); ἡ ἀδικία καὶ ἡ ἀσέβεια καὶ σ. πᾶν τὸ ἐναντίον τῆς.. ἀρετῆς Pl.*Prt.*324a, cf. 325c; σ. διδάσκειν Isoc.4.29; opp. κατὰ σμικρόν (little by little), Pl.*R.*344b; opp. καθ' ἓν ἕκαστον, X.*Oec.*19.14.

**συλλήγω**, *come to an end together*, σ. ὁλκάδι καιομένῃ *AP*7.585 (Jul.), cf. Chor.23.9 F.-R. II. *have the same termination*, A.D. *Synt.*168.13.

**συλληΐζομαι**, *join in plundering*, J.*BJ*2.22.2.

**σύλλημμα**, ατος, τό, *foetus*, Gal.14.154, Ps.-Callisth.1.4,10 (ed. Meusel), Sch.Orib.3 p.681 D.

**σύλληξις**, εως, ἡ, (λαγχάνω) *joining together by lot* or *fate*, Pl.*Ti.* 18e, M.Ant.3.11, etc.; σ. πυκτῶν *pairing* of boxers *by lot*, Pl.*Lg.* 819b.

**συλληπ-τέον**, *one must seize together*, τι E.*Cyc.*472. 2. συλληπτέος, α, ον, *to be seized*, Luc.*DMar.*6.3. **-τικός**, ή, όν, *collective, comprehensive*, ὀνόματα Eust.219.45; τὸ πάντες συλληπτικόν Sch.Il.1.

424; σ. σχῆμα, = σύλληψις 1.2, Anon.*Fig*.p.158S. Adv. -κῶς Eustr. *in EN*74.34: Comp. -ώτερον Eust.5.7. II. *apt* or *able to conceive*, τὰ θήλεα Arist.*GA*748ᵃ18. b. *promoting conception*, Aët.ap.Phot. *Bibl*.p.180B. III. *helpful, assisting*, Nicom.*Ar*.2.19; τὸ σ. Plu.2. 486a. IV. *punctual*, in Adv. -κῶς, opp. καθυστερικῶς, Ptol.*Phas*. p.11H. -τρια, ἡ, fem. of sq., Ar.*Fr*.864 (cf. συλλήστρια), X.*Mem*. 2.1.32, Iamb.*Comm.Math*.7. -τωρ, ορος, ὁ, *accomplice, assistant*, A.*Ag*.1507; τινος in a thing, E.*Or*.1230, Antipho 3.3.10, X.*Mem*.2. 2.12, Pl.*Smp*.218d, etc.

**συλληστ-εύω**, *join in robbing*, Eun.*Hist*.p.218D.; σ. τινί Eust.ad D.P.680. -ής, οῦ, ὁ, *fellow-robber*, X.Eph.1.15, Charito 3.3:—fem. -ρια, v.l. for συλλήπτρια in Ar.*Fr*.864.

**σύλληψις**, εως, ἡ, Ion. **σύλλαψις** v.l. in Heraclit.10:—*taking together, conjunction*, of sounds, Nicom.*Harm*.9; of two consonants, Sch.Heph.p.104C., al.; *inclusion, comprehension*, A.D.*Pron*.19.20, *Synt*.216.17, Dam.*Pr*.427; συλλήψεως ἐπιρρήματα (e.g. ἅμα) D.T. 642.14; *summing up*, τῶν ἀποδείξεων Id.643.9; *compendious statement*, σ. διὰ βραχέων τῆς ὅλης θεωρίας Gal.18(2).848. 2. Rhet., *a figure by which a predicate belonging to one subject is attributed to several*, Hdn.*Fig*.p.100S., etc. b. ὁ κατὰ -ψιν ὅρος, i.e. embracing the adversary's counterplan as well as the original plan, Hermog. *Stat*.4, cf. Arg.D.21.12. II. *seizing, laying hold of, arresting, apprehending*, λῃστῶν ξ. *IG*1².42.24; τὴν ξύλληψιν ποιεῖσθαι *arrest*, Th.1.134; τήν τινος σ. κατασκευάσαι Aeschin.3.223, cf. Lys.19.7; σ. νεώς Plb.1.46.9. III. *conception, pregnancy*, Arist.*HA*582ᵇ11, al., Sor.1.23, al.; ἡ ἐν τῇ μητρὶ Ῥωμύλου σ. Plu.*Rom*.12; ἀκόλαστοι σ. Plot.4.4.30. IV. *taking part with another, assistance*, Plu.2. 808f (pl.).

⊕ **συλλιθηγία**, ἡ, *assistance in transport of stone*, *Supp.Epigr*.2.569. 23, 4.447.50 (Didyma, ii B.C.). [Written συνλ-.]

**σύλλιθος**, ον, *paved*, τόπος Hippiatr.52.

**συλλιπαίνομαι**, *to be melted together*, Str.5.2.6, Plu.2.1011b.

**συλλίρ**· θύλακος, Hsch. (Prob. Lacon. for θυλλίς.)

⊕ **συλλογ-εύς**, έως, ὁ, *collector*, Polyaen.2.34, *IG*7.3498.33 (Oropus); at Athens, *one who called in confiscated property*, ib.1².129. 3 (prob.), 2².1257 *A* 7, *B*1, 1496.83,114, Is.*Fr*.103. -ευτικός, ή, όν, *of* or *for collection*, τὸ σ. (sc. ἀργύριον) *Test.Epict*.5.9, 7. 10. -ή, ἡ, *gathering, collecting*, φρυγάνων Th.3.111; of herbs, Dsc.1 *Prooem*.6; [ἀρωμάτων] Thphr.*Od*.37; τῶν καρπῶν Arist.*PA* 662ᵇ8 (pl.); and so abs., *IG*2².411.17; σ. τοῦ βίου *scraping together* of the means of life, Antipho Soph.49, Philem.92.4 (pl.): metaph., ἐν γενείου ξυλλογῇ τριχώματος *in the first harvest* of a beard, i.e. in early manhood, A.*Th*.666: generally, *acquisition*, πλούτου Metrod. *Herc*.831.7; τῇ σ. χαίροντες Lib.*Or*.9.6. 2. *raising, levying* of soldiers, συλλογὴν ποιεῖσθαι X.*An*.1.1.6. 3. *summary, collection of instances*, [ὕβρεων] D.21.23. II. (from Pass.) *assembly, meeting*, Hdt.5.105; *summoning* of βουλή and δῆμος, *IG*2².890; ποιεῖν σ. hold *an assembly*, Lys.20.26 codd. (leg. σύλλογον); *aggregation*, αἵματος Arist.*PA*688ᵇ26; ῥευμάτων, πνευμάτων, Epicur.*Ep*.2 p.44U., p.46U. (pl.); of morbid *accumulations*, Aret.*SD*2.1, Aët.15.12. -ίζομαι, Med., aor. -ελογισάμην Pl.*R*.618d, al.; rarely -ελογίσθην ib.531d: pf. -λελόγισμαι (v. infr.):—*compute, reckon up*, τὰ ἐξ Ἑλλήνων τείχεα Hdt.2.148; ἕτερα σ. πρὸς τὸ κεφάλαιον Lys.32.22; τὰς ἑορτὰς εἰς τὸν ἐνιαυτόν Pl.*Lg*.799a; ταῦτα πάντα σ. Id.*Chrm*.160d; τὰ κατηγορημένα ἀπ' ἀρχῆς σ. *recapitulate*, D.19.177; τοὺς καιρούς, τὰς ὑποσχέσεις, ib.47; ἐκ τῶν εἰρημένων σ. καὶ συναγαγόντας τὸ κεφάλαιον Arist.*Metaph*.1042ᵃ3; μανθάνειν καὶ σ. τί ἕκαστον Id.*Po*.1448ᵇ 16; τὰς χρείας Plb.1.44.1; τὸ μέγεθος τοῦ τολμήματος Plu.*Pomp*. 60; σ. ὅτι.. Pl.*Lg*.670c. II. *conclude from premisses, infer*, τὰ συμβαίνοντα ἐκ τοῦ λόγου Id.*Grg*.479c, al.; σ. τί συμβαίνει ἐκ τῶν ὡμολογημένων ib.498e; σ. περί τινος, ὅτι.. Id.*R*.516b; σ. περὶ [τῆς μήτρας], ὡς..διαστελλομένης Gal.15.694; σ. ἐξ αὐτῶν ποῖός τις.. Pl. *R*.365a; σ. ὀρθῶς τίνος εἵνεκα ἔπραττε D.18.172; τἀφανὲς διὰ τοῦ φαινομένου Epicur.*Nat*.14.4, cf. Phld.*Rh*.2.40S.: c. acc. et inf., -σάμενος τὸ ἄλειμμα οὐκ ἄξιον ἔσεσθαι *Inscr.Prien*.112.57 (i B.C.); τὴν νόσον ἐπὶ τὴν Ἀττικὴν ἥξειν Sor.*Vit.Hippocr*.7; τὸ..αἷμα μὴ σεσῆφθαι Gal. 18(2).108. 2. in the Logic of Aristotle, *infer by way of syllogism, infer syllogistically*, σ. τὸ Α κατὰ τοῦ Β, A of B, *APr*.40ᵇ30; τὸ.. ἄκρον τῷ μέσῳ σ. ib.68ᵇ16; τινὰ ἔκ τινων *Rh*.1357ᵃ8; σ. ὑπάρχειν τὸ Α τῷ Β *APo*.79ᵇ30: pf. in pass. sense, οὗτος ὁ λόγος οὐ συλλελόγισται is not *syllogistic*, *APr*.42ᵃ39; συλλελογισμένα *syllogistically concluded*, opp. ἀσυλλόγιστα, *Rh*.1357ᵃ8. 3. συλλελογισμένον ἦν αὐτῷ μὴ πρότερον ἐγχειρεῖν ἕως.. *he had planned* not to.., Plb.14. 4.4. -ιμαῖος, α, ον, *collected from divers places*, ὕδατα (opp. πηγαῖα) Arist.*Mete*.353ᵇ23; ἄνθρωποι Luc.*Tox*.19; σ. φορυτός, of a man, *Com.Adesp*.906. ⊕ -ισμός, ὁ, *computation, calculation*, κατὰ τοὺς τῶν πατέρων σ. according to the (military) *ratings* of their fathers, D.S.17.94; κατὰ τὸν σ. τοῦ κοινοῦ πολέμου ἔχειν τὰ κτήματα shall have the property according to the *assessment* of.., *SIG*364. 38 (Ephesus, iii B.C.). 2. generally, *ratiocination, reasoning*, Hp.*Decent*.11, Pl.*Tht*.186d, Arist.*PA*656ᵃ27, etc. 3. *plan, scheme*, συνελογίσατο..συλλογισμὸν Ἰβηρικὸν καὶ βαρβαρικόν Plb.3. 98.3; οὐ τῇ τύχῃ πιστεύων ἀλλὰ τοῖς σ. Id.10.7.3. II. *putting together of observed facts*, Pl.*Cra*.412a; σ. ἐστιν ὅτι τοῦτο ἐκεῖνο Arist.*Rh*.1371ᵇ9: generally, *inference*, Phld.*Sign*.14, al. 2. in the Logic of Arist., *a syllogism* or *deductive argument*, defined provisionally as an argument in which, certain things being posited, something different from them necessarily follows, *APr*.24ᵇ18, cf. 47ᵃ34, al.; of several kinds, e.g. ὁ ἀποδεικτικὸς σ. *APo*.74ᵇ11; ὁ διαλεκτικὸς σ. *Top*.100ᵃ22; ἐριστικὸς σ. ib.ᵇ24; sts. opposed to ἐπαγωγή (q.v.); ὁ ἐξ ἐπαγωγῆς σ. the *syllogism* which springs out of induction, *APr*.68ᵇ15; τὸ ἐνθύμημα σ. τις *Rh*.1355ᵃ8. III. Rhet., *inference from written to unwritten law*, Hermog.*Stat*.2, al. (cf. Syrian. *in Hermog*.2.198R., al.): pl., ib.11. -ιστέος, α, ον, *to be concluded*, Pl.*R*.517c. II. neut. συλλογιστέον *one must infer*, Arist.*Top*.161ᵃ26; *one must compute*, Id.*EN*1101ᵃ34. -ιστικός, ή, όν, *inferential*, Pl.*Def*.414e; σύνδεσμοι D.T.642.26, cf. A.D.*Conj*. 252.5; σημεῖον Gal.15.419. 2. *syllogistic*, Arist.*APr*.42ᵃ36, al. Adv. -κῶς Id.*Rh*.1401ᵃ8. 3. οἱ -κοί *dialecticians*, Ph.1.346. -ος, ὁ, *assembly, concourse, meeting* of persons, whether legal or riotous, σ. ἐγίνετο Hdt.8.74; Ἀχαιῶν σ., name of a play by Sophocles; ξ. γυναικοπληθεῖς E.*Alc*.951; σ. στρατεύματος Id.*IA*514, cf. 825; ἐν θεοῖς σ. σοῦ πέρι ἔσται Id.*Hel*.878; σ. ποιῆσαι Th.1.67, 4.114 (cf. ἐκκλησία); σ. ποιέεσθαι Hdt.7.8 init., 8.24, cf. E.*Heracl*.335; σ. διαλύειν Hdt.7.10.δ'; of the people, διαλύεσθαι ἐκ τοῦ σ. Id.3.73; σ. σχολαστικοί Arist.*Pol*.1313ᵇ3; συμπόσια καὶ ἄλλοι σ. Phld.*Mus*. p.110K.; ὁ σ. ὁ Ἁλικαρνασσέων *SIG*45.1 (Halic., v B.C.), cf. 278. 3 (Priene, iv B.C.), al.; at Athens, of *any special public meeting* or *assembly*, opp. the common ἐκκλησία, Th.2.22, Pl.*Lg*.764a; ἐκκλησίᾳ καὶ ἄλλῳ σ. παντί, ὅστις ἂν πολιτικὸς σ. γένηται Id.*Grg*.452e, cf. X.*An*.5.7.2, D.19.122; freq. of *a muster* of forces, X.*Cyr*.6.2.11, al.; so σ. νεῶν And.3.38; σ. θεραπευτής a medical *consultation*, Hp. *Praec*.13. II. metaph., *collectedness, presence of mind*, σύλλογον ψυχῆς λαβέ E.*HF*626.

**συλλοιδορέω**, *join in reviling*, Lxx *Je*.36(29).27, Jul.*Mis*.353b.

**συλλού-ομαι**, Med. or Pass., *bathe with*, c. dat., Plu.*Cat.Ma*.20; μετά τινων *Inscr.Prien*.112.78 (i B.C.); *bathe with* a plaster on, Gal. 13.249. -τρον τὸ Ἀπολλιναρίου, name of eye-salve, Orib.*Syn*. 3.118.

**συλλοχ-άω**, aor. συνελόχησε f.l. for συνελόχισε (so Suid.) in Lxx 1 *Ma*.4.28; part. συλλοχήσας prob. f.l. for συλλοχίσας in Plu.*Galb*. 15. -ία, ἡ, *place where soldiers were collected into* λόχοι, metaph., κατὰ τὰς σ. Hp.*Oct*.12 (expld. by ἀθροίσματα by Gal.19. 143). -ίζω, *embody* or *incorporate* soldiers, εἰς ἓν τάγμα Plu.*Galb*. 15 (cj. for -ήσας); εἰς ἑκατοστύας Id.*Rom*.8, cf. App.*BC*5.3; κατὰ φῦλα Plu.2.761b; cf. συλλοχάω. II. *arrange* λόχοι *in order* (cf. sq.), Ael.*Tact*.3.2,4, Arr.*Tact*.5.2. -ισμός, ὁ, *parallel arrangement of* λόχοι, Ascl.*Tact*.2.4, Ael.*Tact*.6.1,2, Arr.*Tact*.7.1,2. II. *muster-roll, census*, Lxx 1 *Ch*.9.1. -ίτης [ῑ], ου, ὁ, *soldier of the same* λόχος, Hdt.1.82.

**συλλυπέω**, *hurt* or *mortify together*, σ. τινὰς αὐτοῖς *make* them *share* their *grief*, Arist.*EN*1171ᵇ7. II. Pass., with fut. -λυπηθήσομαι Hdt.6.39, also -λυπήσομαι Pl.*R*.462e:—*share in grief, sympathize* or *condole*, Hdt.l.c., Antipho 3.2.8; τῷ πάθει Hdt.9.94: c. dat. pers., Thphr.*Char*.1.2; τίς σοι -ηθήσεται; Lxx *Is*.51.19.

⊕ **σύλλυσις**, εως, ἡ, *settlement, agreement, treaty*, *SIG*588.35 (Milet., ii B.C.), 665.13 (Olympia, ii B.C.), 685.35 (Crete, ii B.C.), *IG*11 (4).1065.17 (Delos, ii B.C.), 4²(1).75.11 (Epid., ii B.C.), D.S.12.4, 25.

**συλλυσσάομαι**, Pass., *go mad with*, τινι *APl*.4.83.

**συλλύται** (συνλ-) [ῠ], οἱ, *conciliators*, *IG*5(2).357 (Stymphalos).

**συλλύω**, *help in loosing*, ξύλλυε μητρὸς δεσμόν E.*Andr*.723:—Med., τῷ Πριάμῳ συλλυσόμενοι τὸν παῖδ' *assist* him *in redeeming*.., Ar.*Fr*.678. II. *solve difficulties, settle, put an end to*, τὰ νείκη, τὸν πόλεμον, D.S.3.64, 29.22; σ. τινάς *reconcile* them, *IG*7.21.8 (Megara, ii B.C.), cf. *SIG*599.13 (Priene, ii B.C.), *Klio* 18.281 (Delph., ii B.C.), Phld.*Rh*.1.268S.; and so prob. S.*Aj*.1317, εἰ μὴ ξυνάψων, ἀλλὰ συλλύσων πάρει not to stir conflict, but *to reconcile*:—Med. and Pass., *come to a settlement*, πρός τινα D.S.12.4; τισι Lxx 1 *Ma*.13.47; ἐπὶ πᾶσι τοῖς δικαίοις ib.2 *Ma*.11.14. III. in A.*Ch*. 294, δέχεσθαι δ' οὔτε συλλύειν τινά, Sch. expl. συλλύειν by συγκλύειν (leg. συγκαταλύειν), συνοικεῖν, *rest under the same roof*.

**σῦλον**, v. σύλη.

⊕ **σῡλόνυξ**, ῠχος, ὁ, ἡ, (συλάω) *paring the nails*, *AP*6.307 (Phan.).

**σῦμα**, Lacon. for θῦμα, Foed.ap.Th.5.77.

**συμβαδίζω**, *go with*, τινι J.*AJ*1.20.3, D.C.77.13, Ael.*NA*7.41.

⊕ **συμβαίνω**, fut. -βήσομαι Hdt.2.3, etc.: pf. -βέβηκα, 3 pl. -βεβᾶσι E.*Hel*.622, Ion. inf. -βεβάναι Hdt.3.146: pf. inf. Pass. -βεβάσθαι Th. 8.98: aor. 2 συνέβην (v. infr.): aor. 1 subj. Pass. ξυμβαθῇ Id.4.30:—*stand with the feet together*, Hp.*Off*.3; διαβαίνοντες μᾶλλον ἢ συμβεβηκότες X.*Eq*.1.14; συμβεβηκὼς τὼ πόδε Poll.3.91; συμβᾶσα τὼ πόδε, opp. περιβάδην, Ach.Tat.1.1; Παλλάδιον τοῖς ποσὶ συμβεβηκός a statue *with closed feet*, as in early Greek art, Apollod.3.12.3. 2. σ. κακοῖς *to be joined to* them, i.e. *increase* them, E.*Hel*.37. 3. *meet*, σὺν δ' ἔβη ἐν Φιλότητι Emp.21.8; τὸν συμβαίνοντά σοι Eup.136 (dub.); σ. αὐτοὶ αὐτοῖς X.*HG*1.2.17; ξυμβέβηκε δ' οὐδαμοῦ has never *come in my way, has had* naught *to do with me*, E.*Hel*.1007. 4. *attack jointly*, ἐπὶ Ναξίους Parth.9.1. II. most freq. metaph., *come to an agreement, come to terms*, E.*Ph*.71, etc.; ἐπ' ἐλάττονι σ. *agree* on (i.e. to accept) less, *POxy*.237 viii 11 (ii A.D.): c. dat., Th.3.52, 4. 128, etc.; πρὸς ἀλλήλους ib.61, etc.: with neut. Adj., ἐὰν ξυμβῶ τί σοι Ar.*Ra*.175; ἥν τι ξυμβαίνωσι Th.2.5; ξ. τὰ πλείω, οὐδέν, Id.4.117, 5.36; τἄλλα τοῖς Λακεδαιμονίοις Id.8.98: c. inf., συνέβησαν ἐς τὠυτὸ.., τὸν δὲ βασιλεύειν Hdt.1.13; ξ. ὑπήκοοι εἶναι Th.1.117; ξ. ἥν τις ἁλίσκηται,..δοῦλον εἶναι ib.103; ξ. τοῖς Πλαταιεῦσι παραδοῦναι σφᾶς αὐτούς Id.2.4; ξ. πρὸς Νικίαν..ἐπιτρέψαι Id.4.54; also συνέβησαν.. ὥστε τριηκοσίους μαχέσασθαι Hdt.1.82; σ. εἰς τὸ μέσον *agree* to a compromise, Pl.*Prt*.337e; λόγοις σ., of a verbal agreement, E.*Med*.

737, *Andr.*233: generally, *make friends with*, ἐκ πολέμου ξ. Ar.*V.* 867; ἀπὸ τοῦ ἴσου Th.4.19; ἐπὶ τοῖς εἰρημένοις E.*Ph.*590(troch.): in pf. συμβεβάναι and Pass., of the agreement, δοκέοντες πάντα συμβεβάναι that everything *had been settled*, or that they *had settled* everything, Hdt.3.146; ἐπὶ τούτοις ξυμβεβάσθαι Th.8.98; ἕως ἄν τι περὶ τοῦ πλέονος ξυμβαθῇ Id.4.30. 2. *agree with, be on good terms with*, οὐ..'Αθηναίοισι συνέβαιν' Αἰσχύλος Ar.*Ra.*807; σ. ἑκατέρᾳ τῶν στάσεων *hold with* one and other of them, D.H.2.62. 3. of things, *tally, correspond with*, ὁ χρόνος ἐδόκεε τῇ ἡλικίῃ συμβαίνειν Hdt.1.116; ἐθέλων εἰδέναι εἰ [οἱ ἐκείνων λόγοι] συμβήσονται τοῖσι λόγοισι τοῖσι ἐν Μέμφι Id.2.3; ξυμβαίνει ταῦτα τοῖς πρὸ τοῦ Lys.8.9; εἰς ταὐτὸ σ. τοῖς ἐμοῖς στίβοις A.*Ch.*210: abs., ὅπως ἂν ἀρτίκολλα συμβαίνῃ τάδε ib.580; χρησμοί τε συμβαίνουσι *are in harmony* therewith, Ar.*Eq.*220, cf. S. *Tr.*1164; αὐτὸ σ. εἰς ταύτην εἶναι πέμπτην five days later exactly *tallies*, D.19.60; τοῦτο σ. οὐ πλέον ἢ εἰς δώδεκα *comes* to no more than 12, X.*HG*6.4.12; αἱ πεντακόσιαι μάλιστά πως συνέβαινον δραχμαί Aristid.*Or.*50(26).94; τὸ φαρμακεύεσθαι τῷ καθαίρεσθαι εἰς ταὐτὸν σ. *comes* to the same thing as.., Gal.15.901; of ashlar-work, *fit* or *range exactly*, M.Ant.5.8. 4. *fall to one's lot*, c. dat. pers., μοι σ. ἆται E.*IT*148 (lyr.), etc.; ἡδοναί τινι Isoc.15.222; τριηραρχία μοι D. 47.49; ἀτυχία Id.57.65; εὐεργεσιῶν συμβαίνειν καιρόν Id.20.121. 5. *to be an attribute* or *characteristic of*, ξυνεβεβήκει..'Αθηναίοις τοῦτο Th. 2.15; τὰ ὀφείλοντα ταῖς ἀρίσταις συμβεβηκέναι τιτθαῖς Sor.1.87, cf.91, 2.6. III. of events, *come to pass, fall out, happen*, συμβαίνει δ' οὐ τὰ μέν, τὰ δ' οὔ A.*Pers.*802; τῶνδε ναμέρτεια σ. S.*Tr.*173; ἐὰν μὴ θεία τις σ. τύχη Pl.*R.*592a; αἱ ἀεὶ συμβαίνουσαι τύχαι Id.*Criti.*120e; εἰ καιρὸς σ. X.*Eq.Mag.*2.5; χρηστόν τι σ. παρὰ θεῶν D.1.11; τοὐναντίον συμβαίνειν πέφυκε Gal.15.460: c. dat., ib.67, 16.724: also euphem., ἄν τι ξυμβῇ if anything *happen* (i.e. any evil), D.21.112, cf. *Riv.Fil.*60.59 (ii B.C.): generally, *occur, be found, exist*, ἐν τῇ ἀρχαίᾳ ἡμετέρᾳ φωνῇ σ. τὸ ὄνομα Pl.*Cra.*398b, cf. A.D.*Pron.*29.15: but, b. mostly impers., sts. c. dat. et inf., αὐτῷ 'Ολυμπιάδα ἀνελέσθαι συνέβη Hdt.6.103, cf. 3.50, Th.1.1; συμβαίνει τῷ πλοίῳ ἀργεῖν *PCair.Zen.*650.2 (iii B.C.), cf. *PMich.Zen.*21.3, al. (iii B.C.): sts. c. acc. et inf., συνέβη Γέλωνα νικᾶν Hdt.7.166, cf. Th.8.25; συμβαίνει διὰ παντὸς ἡμᾶς περιφόβους εἶναι *PCair.Zen.*160.6, cf. 132.5 (iii B.C.), *PEnteux.*6.2, al. (iii B.C.), Gal.15.476; σ. τῷ οἰκοδόμῳ μουσικῷ εἶναι Arist.*Metaph.*1017$^a$11; folld. by ὥστε, S.*Tr.*1152, Th.4.79, Arist.*Pol.*1261$^a$34: c. part., σ. ὄν, γιγνόμενον, λεγόμενον, Pl. *Sph.*244d, *Phlb.*42d, *Cra.*412a. c. τὸ συμβεβηκός *chance event, contingency*, Id.*Prm.*128c; τὰ συμβαίνοντα X.*Cyr.*1.6.43; τὰ συμβάντα Id.*An.*3.1.13; ἀπὸ τοῦ συμβαίνοντος ὁ τόπος εἴληφε τὴν προσηγορίαν Plb.10.28.7: hence κατὰ συμβεβηκός *by accident, contingently* (v. infr. IV. 1); τοῦ συμβαίνοντός ἐστι it *depends upon accident*, easily happens, Is.4.13. 2. joined with Adverbs or Adjectives, *turn out* in a certain way, ὀρθῶς σφι ἡ φήμη συνέβαινε ἐλθοῦσα Hdt. 9.101; κακῶς, καλῶς συμβῆναι, X.*Mem.*1.2.63, *Cyr.*5.4.14, E.*IT*1055; τὰ μητρὸς..ἔχθιστα συμβέβηκεν S.*El.*262; ταῦτα..λαμπρὰ σ. Id.*Tr.* 1174; ξυμβεβᾶσιν οἱ λόγοι..ἀληθεῖς E.*Hel.*622; ἄπιστ' ἀληθῆ πολλὰ σ. βροτοῖς Id.*Fr.*396; σ. μέγιστον κακὸν ἡ ἀδικία Pl.*Grg.*479c, cf. *Alc.* 1.130c, *Cra.*398e; δοκεῖ τὸ μαντεῖον τοὐναντίον ξυμβῆναι ἢ.. Th.2.17; τοιούτου τούτου συμβάντος Id.1.74; συμβαίνει καὶ σοί (sc. ἄριστον) Pl. *Lg.*903d: abs., *turn out well*, ἢν ξυμβῇ ἡ πεῖρα Th.3.3; εἴ μοι σ. τοῦτο Pl.*Lg.*744a. 3. of consequences, *come out, result, follow*, δαπανῶντες ἐς τοιαῦτα ἀφ' ὧν ἡ ἀσθένεια ξυμβαίνει Th.8.45; κάλλιστον δὴ ἔργων ὑμῖν ξυμβήσεται Id.6.33; τὰ συμβάντα, opp. ἡ προαίρεσις, D.18.192; δηλοῦται ἐκ τοῦ συμβάντος Gal.16.583; ἐὰν μὴ ὅτι τάχος ἀποσταλῇ τὰ ὑποζύγια, συμβήσεται τὰ μελίσσεια ἀπολέσθαι *PCair.Zen.* 467.8, cf. 481.2, al. (iii B.C.). b. of logical conclusions, *result, follow*, freq. in Pl. and Arist., Pl.*Grg.*459b, etc.; σ. ἐκ τῶν κειμένων Arist.*Top.*156$^b$38, al., cf. D.25.73: impers., *it follows*, c. inf., Pl.*Tht.*170c, *Phd.*74a, Arist.*EN*1152$^b$25, al.; also σ. μήτε κουφότητ' ἔχειν μήτε βάρος, ἔπειθ' ὅτι ἀδύνατον κινηθῆναι Arist.*Cael.*270$^a$ 5: also pers., συμβαίνει εἶναι or γίγνεσθαι *turns out* to be, i.e. *consequently* or *inevitably is* or *happens*, κάθαρσις εἶναι τοῦτο σ. Pl.*Phd.*67c, cf. 80b, *Cra.*396a, *Phlb.*55a,64e, *Prm.*134b, *R.*438e; ὅσα συμβαίνει γίγνεσθαι κακὰ καὶ ὅσα συμβήσεται Id.*Plt.*301e: hence συμβεβηκός (v. infr. IV. 2). IV. in Philos., τὸ συμβεβηκός has two senses: 1. *a contingent attribute* or '*accident*' (in the modern sense), Arist. *APo.*73$^b$4, *Top.*102$^b$4, al.; κατὰ συμβεβηκός '*accidentally*', opp. καθ' αὑτό, Id.*Ph.*192$^b$22, cf. *Metaph.*1052$^a$18, Thphr.*Sens.*22; opp. ἁπλῶς, Arist.*APo.*71$^b$10, al.; opp. φύσει, Id. *de An.*406$^a$14; opp. κυρίως, πρώτως, Gal.15.629, cf. 16.575, al.; opp. ἄντικρυς, Id.18(2).180. 2. *an attribute necessarily resulting from* the notion of a thing, but not entering into the definition thereof, οἷον τῷ τριγώνῳ τὸ δύο ὀρθὰς ἔχειν Arist.*Metaph.*1025$^a$31; distd. by the addition of καθ' αὑτό, Id. *APo.*83$^b$19, al.; in Epicurus, *essential attribute, property*, opp. σύμπτωμα '*accident*', τὰ τούτων συμπτώματα ἢ σ. *Ep.*1 p.6U., cf. *Nat.*4 G., al.; σ. ἀνθρώπου τὸ θνητὸν εἶναι Phld.*Sign.*3, al.; in the Stoics, *consequence*, opp. αἴτιον, Zeno *Stoic.*1.25.

**συμβακχ-εύω**, *join in Dionysiac revelry*, abs., πᾶν συνεβάκχευ' ὄρος E.*Ba.*726; μετά τινος Pl.*Phdr.*234d; ἡ γῆ σ. τῷ Διονύσῳ Philostr. *Im.*1.14, cf. 2.17. ❀ **-ος**, ὁ and ἡ, *joining in Dionysiac revelry*, Philomnest.2; ὦ σύμβακχε Κασάνδρα θεοῖς E.*Tr.*500.

**συμβᾰλᾰνεύομαι**, Med., *bathe together with*, τισι Lyd.*Mag.*3.62.

**συμβαλλο-μᾰχέω**, = *concinno*, *Gloss.* **-μᾰχία**, ἡ, = *concinnatio*, ib. **-μάχος** [μᾰ], ον, *joining in the fight*, ib., *Et.Gud.*

❀ **συμβάλλω**, fut. -βᾰλῶ: aor. -έβᾰλον, inf. -βᾰλεῖν: pf. -βέβληκα: aor. 1 Pass. -εβλήθην:—of these tenses Hom. uses only pres. Act., aor. Act. and Med., but most commonly Ep. intr. aor. forms συμβλήτην, -βλήμεναι, Med. σύμβλητο, -βληντο, -βλήμενος, subj. 2 sg. -βλήεαι prob. cj. for -βλήσεαι in Il.20.335, 3 sg. contr. -βληται Od.7.204:—*throw together, dash together*, σύν ῥ' ἔβαλον ῥινούς, of men in close combat, Il.4.447, 8.61; ἀσπίδας E.*Ph.*1405, Ar. *Pax* 1274 (hex.), X.*HG*4.3.19, etc.; *bring together, unite*, e.g. of rivers that fall into one another, ἐς μισγάγκειαν συμβάλλετον ὄβριμον ὕδωρ Il.4.453; ῥοὰς Σιμόεις συμβάλλετον ἠδὲ Σκάμανδρος 5.774:—Med., πολλοὶ ποταμοὶ σ. τὸ σφέτερον ὕδωρ Hdt.4.50 (cf. δάκρυα δάκρυσι σ. E.*Or.*336 (lyr., Act.)); ὁ 'Ακεσίνης τῷ 'Ινδῷ τὸ ὕδωρ σ. Arr.*An.*6. 1.5; σ. τὰ ὦτα πρὸς τὴν γῆν *have* their ears *reaching* to.., Arist.*HA* 606$^a$15:—Pass., κατὰ τὰς ῥάγας συμβεβλημένων [τῶν δακτύλων] Sor. 2.60. 2. *collect*, X.*Cyr.*2.1.5; *store up, accumulate*, κριθὰς ἵπποις συμβεβλημένας πολλὰς Id.*An.*3.4.31. 3. *jumble up together*, διαφέροντα σ. εἰς ταὐτὸν Pl.*Plt.*285a. 4. intr. in Act., *fit* (cf. σύμβολον I. 1), Arist.*EE*1239$^b$14; *to be suitable*, τὰ χεδροπὰ σ. εἰς τὰς νέας Thphr.*CP*3.20.7 (unless = *sow, set*). b. *to be profitable*, σ. τῷ πολιτικῷ ..δικαίῳ εἶναι Phld.*Rh.*2.285 S.; σ. ἀναμένειν ἡμέραν μίαν Gal.16. 496. 5. intr., *come together*, ἔνθα δίστομοι..σ. ὁδοί where two roads *join*, S.*OC*901, cf. Str.6.3.7; τὰ συμβάλλοντα the *watersmeet*, *IG*9(2) p.xi (Delph., iii/ii B.C.); [φλέψ] σ. τῇ ἀποσχίσει Arist.*HA*514$^a$12; *collide*, τοὺς τύπους ἀνάγκη συμβάλλειν ἑαυτοῖς Thphr.*Sens.*52: Geom., *meet*, τὸ σημεῖον, καθ' ὃ συμβάλλουσιν the point in which (the straight lines) *meet*, Archim.*Sph.Cyl.*1.23, etc. 6. βλέφαρα σ. ὕπνῳ *close* the eyes in sleep, A.*Ag.*15; σ. ὄμμα, in death, ib.1294 (but ποῖον ὄμμα συμβαλῶ; how shall I *meet her eyes with mine?* E.*IA*455). 7. generally, *join, unite*, σ. σχοινία *twist* ropes (cf. συμβολεύς), Ar.*Pax* 37; so τοπεῖα *IG*2$^2$.1672.311 (iv B.C.); ὠμόλινον σ. πεντάπλουν Hp.*Fist.*4; στέφανον Philostr.*Her.Prooem.*; [αἱ φλέβες] σ. [τὸ σῶμα] εἰς ἓν Arist.*PA*668$^b$24; *fit together*, ἁρμοὺς *IG*7.4255.23 (Oropus, iv B.C.); σ. καὶ κολλῆσαι ib. 2$^2$.1668.73(iv B.C.); κεραῖαι συμβεβλημέναι *PCair.Zen.*566.10(iii B.C.); δεξιὰς σ. ἀλλήλοισι *join* hands, E.*IA*58. 8. σ. συμβόλαιά τινι or πρός τινα *make a contract with* a person, esp. *lend* him money *on bond*, D. 34.1, Pl.*R.*425c, cf. Th.5.77 (Med.); συμβόλαιον εἰς τἀνδράποδα συμβεβλημένον money *lent* on the security of the slaves, D.27.27: abs., in same sense, Isoc.21.13; *make a contract*, Pl.*Alc.*1.125d, *OGI*669.21 (Egypt, i A.D.), *Cod.Just.*1.3.55.4; of a marriage contract, Mitteis *Chr.*372 vi 22, cf. 8 (ii A.D.); *advance, lend*, πέρα μεδίμνου κριθῶν Is.10.10; ἱμάτια, χρυσία, etc., Ar.*Ec.*446; ἐπὶ τισι on certain terms, D.H.6.29; σ. δανεισμῷ Pl.*Lg.*921d; ὁ συμβαλών the *lender, creditor*, D.56.2, cf. D.H.5.63 (but οἱ συμβ. the *borrowers, debtors*, Id.4.9):—Med., with pf. Pass., *pay a share, contribute*, ὁλκάδα οἱ συμβαλέεσθαι *give* him a merchant-vessel, Hdt.3.135, cf. Lys.32.24, X.*Ages.* 2.27; σ. χρήματά τινι εἰς τροφὴν τῶν στρατιωτῶν *advance* it, Id.*An.* 1.1.9, cf. *IG*7.2418 (Thebes, iv B.C.); τριήρεις εἰς κίνδυνον Isoc.4. 98; ἐφόδιον *PSI*4.407.12 (iii B.C.). 9. generally, *contribute*:—Pass., συμβάλλεταί τις..μερίς Alex.149.4:—in this sense mostly in Med., τέμενος συμβάλλεσθαι *add thereto*, Pi.*I.*1.59; ἡ τύχη οὐδὲν ἔλασσον ξυμβάλλεται ἐς τὸ ἐπαίρειν Th.3.45, cf. Hp.*Aër.*2, Sosip.1. 37, Damox.2.11; τὸ μὴ ἀγανακτεῖν..ἄλλα τέ μοι πολλὰ συμβάλλεται, καὶ.. many circumstances *contribute* to my feeling no vexation, and especially.., Pl.*Ap.*36a; σ. βοήθειαν οὐ σμικρὰν πρός τι Id.*Lg.*836b; τιμὴν καὶ δόξαν τῇ πόλει σ. Isoc.*Ep.*8.6; οὐ δεῖ λογίζεσθαι, πότερος πλείω συμβέβληται X.*Oec.*7.13; freq. with μέρος as obj., ἔργων οὐκ ἐλάχιστον μέρος σ. And.1.143; μέρος σ. πρὸς ἀρετήν Pl.*Lg.*836d, cf. *R.*331b, D.41.11; οὐκ ἐλάχιστον μέρος πρὸς εὐδαιμονίαν Isoc.7.79; συμβαλλέσθω τὸ μέρος ἕκαστος εἰς τὸ ἀνάλωμα *PHal.*1.108, cf. 113 (iii B.C.); τὴν μεγίστην εἰς αὐτὰ μοῖραν Pl.*Ti.*47c, cf. X.*Cyr.*6.1. 28: also abs., οὔτε ποταμὸς οὔτε κρήνη οὐδεμία ἐσδιδοῦσα ἐς πλῆθός οἱ συμβάλλεται *contributes to* its volume, Hdt.4.50; σ. πρὸς τὸ λανθάνειν X.*Cyr.*2.4.21, cf. Isoc.7.21; συμβαλλόμενα *contributory causes*, Thphr.*Sud.*6: abs., *to be helpful*, πολλά ἐστι τὰ συμβαλλόμενα τοῖς βουλομένοις Antipho 5.79, cf. Pl.*Lg.*905b, D.21.133; φόνου κηκὶς ξ. *contributes* to the proof, A.*Ch.*1012: rarely c. gen. partit., ξυμβάλλεται πολλὰ τοῦδε δείματος many things *contribute* [*their share*] *of* this fear, i.e. join in causing it, E.*Med.*284. 10. συμβάλλεσθαι γνώμας *contribute one's* opinion to a discussion, Hdt.8.61; περί τινος Pl.*Plt.* 298c; συμβαλέσθαι περί τινος λόγους X.*Cyr.*2.2.21; λόγον σ. περὶ βίου *contribute* an opinion about life, Pl.*Lg.*905c; also συμβαλέσθαι τι to *have* something *to say*, Id.*Ion* 532c, cf. 533a; ταὐτά σοι περὶ Ἔρωτος σ. Id.*Smp.*185c; συμβαλοῦ γνώμην *contribute* your opinion, help in judging, S.*OC*1151; σ. τὴν γνώμην τῆς βουλῆς, with or without εἰς τὸν δῆμον, *communicate* it, *IG*2$^2$.79.6, 103.17, al.; *cast* votes, *Schwyzer* 84.15 (Tylisus, v B.C.). 11. συμβάλλειν (sc. λόγους) *converse*, σ. τινί or πρός τινα, Plu.2.222c, *Act.Ap.*4.15:—Med., ἀτὰρ τί ἐγὼ περὶ κλοπῆς σ.; X.*An.*4.6.14. II. *bring* men *together* in hostile sense, *pit* them against each other, *match* them, ἀμφοτέρους θεοὶ σύμβαλον Il.20.55; ἐμὲ..καὶ Μενέλαον συμβάλετε..μάχεσθαι 3.70; σ. σκύμνον λέοντος σκύλακι κυνὸς *set* one *to fight with* the other, Hdt.3.32; ἄνδρα ἀνδρὶ καὶ ἵππον ἵππῳ σ. Id.5.1; τοὺς ἡβῶντας σ. εἰς ἔριν περὶ ἀρχῆς X.*Lac.*4.2; ἀλεκτρυόνας σ. Id.*Smp.*4.9; ἄνδρας φίλους Id.*Cyr.*6.1.32; εἰς χεῖρα δοῦλον δεσπότῃ μὴ συμβάλῃς Philem. 206: metaph., ἀναισχυντίᾳ σ. τινὰ καὶ προσγυμνάζειν *make* him *contend with*.., Pl.*Lg.*647c. b. Med., *join in fight*, σὺν δ' ἐβάλοντο μάχεσθαι ἐναντίον Il.12.377. c. intr., *come together*, σύμβαλον μάχεσθαι 16.565; also σ. alone, *come to blows, engage*, πρίν γ' ἠὲ ξυμβλήμεναι ἠὲ δαμῆναι 21.578; freq. in Hdt., either abs., as 1.77,82, or c. dat. pers., ib.80,104; Ἄρης Ἄρει ξυμβαλεῖ, Δίκα Δίκᾳ A.*Ch.*461 (lyr.), Ἕλληνες Μήδοις σ. Simon.136; also σ. πρός τινα X.*Cyr.*7.1.20,

Isoc.4.69; εἰς μονομαχίαν πρός τινα Str.14.5.16; συμβάλλων *coming into collision*, Pl.*Plt.*273a, cf. Wilcken *Chr.*16.6 (ii A.D.). 2. σ. πόλεμον καὶ δηϊοτῆτα *engage in* war, Il.12.181 (prob. interpol.); so in Trag., σ. βάκχαις μάχην E.*Ba.*837; ἔχθραν τινί Id.*Med.*44; ἔριν φίλοις ib.521: metaph., συμβαλεῖν ἔπη κακά *bandy* reproaches, S.*Aj.*1323; αἰσχρὸν δέ μοι γυναιξὶ συμβάλλειν λόγους E.*IA*830. 3. Med., *fall in with* one, *meet* him, c. dat., freq. in Hom., who uses Ep. aor. forms beginning ξυμβλη- or συμβλη- solely in this sense, Νέστορι δὲ ξύμβληντο Il.14.27, cf. 39; εἰ δ' ἄρα τις..ξύμβληται ὁδίτης Od.7.204; ξυμβλήμενος ἄλλος ὁδίτης 11.127; ὅτε κεν συμβλήσεαι (leg. -βλήεαι) αὐτῷ Il.20.335; ξυμβλήτην ἀλλήλοιιν Od.21.15. 4. so in Act., συμβαλών *having met*, A.*Ch.*677; οἱ συμβάλλοντες those *who come in contact with one*, Plu.*Marc.*20; φιλοσόφῳ σ. Arr.*Epict.*3.9.13, cf. 12, *POxy.*1063 (ii/iii A.D.), *PFay.*129.2 (iii A.D.). III. *compare*, σμικρὰ μεγάλοισι Hdt.2.10; ἑωυτόν τινι Id.3.160; ἓν πρὸς ἓν Id.4.50; τι πρός τι Lycurg.68; πρὸς ἄλληλα Pl.*Tht.*186b; οὐδὲν ἦν τούτων..πρὸς ἀτταγῆνα συμβαλεῖν Phoenicid.2.5:—Pass., Hdt.2.10, 3.125; τὸ ἀργύριον τὸ Βαβυλώνιον πρὸς τὸ Εὐβοϊκὸν συμβαλλόμενον τάλαντον the Babyl. talent *being compared with, reduced to*, the Euboic, ib.95. b. *compare* for the purpose of checking, μέτρῳ συμβεβλημένῳ πρὸς τὸ χαλκοῦν Wilcken *Chr.*410.11 (iii B.C.), etc. 2. Med., *reckon, compute*, Hdt.2.31, 4.15, 6.63, 65:—Pass., ἡ ὁδὸς ἡ ἡμερησίη ἀνὰ διηκόσια στάδια συμβέβληταί μοι Id.4.101. 3. *conclude, infer, conjecture, interpret*, συμβαλεῖν τι Pi.*N.*11.33; σ. ὅτι.. Pl.*Cra.*412c; τοῦτο σ. S.*OC*1474; τοῦτο σ., ὅτι.. Ar.*V.*50; τὰ πρὶν οὐκ εὔγνωστα σ. E.*Or.*[1394]; εὖ ξυνέβαλεν αὐτά Ar.*Eq.*427; ἣν [νόσον] οὐδ' ἂν εἷς γνοίη ποτ' οὐδ' ἂν ξυμβάλοι Id.*V.*72; σ. ἔπη E.*Med.*675; τοὔναρ Id.*IT*55; τὴν μαντείαν Pl.*Cra.*384a; τὸν χρησμόν Arist.*Fr.*532, cf. 76; σήματα σ., εἰ..ἤ.. Arat.1146: abs., καθὼς συμβάλλομεν ἐκ τοῦ.. Sor.2.63:—Med., abs., Heraclit.47, freq. in Hdt., as 2.33, 4.87; c. acc., *make out, understand*, τὸ πρῆγμα ib.111; τι ἔκ τινος 6.107; τῇδε, ὅτι.. from the fact that.., 3.68: c. acc. et inf., 1.68, 2.33, 112, al.; folld. by indirect question, 4.45. IV. *agree, arrange*, καθάπερ ξυνέβαλον ἢ διέθεντο *IG*1$^2$.46.14; πρὸς ἐμὲ πάντες συμβάλλετε X.*Cyr.*6.2.41:—Med., *make a treaty*, Foed.ap.Th.5.77; *agree upon, fix, settle*, λόφον εἰς ὃν δέοι ἁλίζεσθαι X.*An.*6.3.3; ἔδει σε, καθότι συνεβάλου ἡμῖν, Ἡρακλείδην..ἀπεσταλκέναι *PCair.Zen.*314.1 (iii B.C.).

**σύμβᾰμα**, ατος, τό, (συμβαίνω III) *chance, casualty*, Luc.*Vit.Auct.*21 (but as a parody on signf. II), M.Ant.7.58, Palaeph.2(5). 2. *misfortune*, Procop.*Goth.*1.12 (dub. in *Aed.*4.3). II. in Stoic Philos., = κατηγόρημα, *complete predicate*, such as an intrans. Verb, e.g. Σωκράτης περιπατεῖ, opp. παρασύμβαμα, παρακατηγόρημα, e.g. Σωκράτει μεταμέλει, *Stoic.*2.59.

※ **συμβᾰμᾰτικός**, ή, όν, *fortuitous*, Ptol.*Tetr.*203, Petos.ap.Vett.Val.112.19.

**συμβαπτίζομαι**, Pass., *to be plunged along with* others *in*, τῷ πάθει Hld.4.20.

**συμβᾰρέω**, *weigh down, oppress together*, in Pass., Heph.Astr.3.10 in *Cat.Cod.Astr.*8(1).152.

**συμβᾰρύνω**, *use the grave accent with*, A.D.*Adv.*170.9 (Pass.).

**συμβᾰσείω**, Desiderat. of συμβαίνω II, *wish to make a league* or *covenant*, Th.8.56.

**συμβᾰσῐλ-εύω**, *rule, reign together with*, τινι Plb.30.2.4, Plu.*Lyc.*5, Luc.*DDeor.*16.2, etc.: metaph., 1*Ep.Cor.*4.8: abs., 2*Ep.Ti.*2.12. ※ **-ιστής**, οῦ, ὁ, *fellow-member of guild of* βασιλισταί (q.v.), *Arch.Pap.*5.158.6 (iii B.C.).

**σύμβᾰσις**, εως, Ion. ιος, ἡ, (συμβαίνω I) *bringing one foot up to the other*, in walking, Hp.*Art.*58. 2. *juncture* of ribs, Ruf.*Oss.*25. II. (συμβαίνω II) *agreement, arrangement, treaty*, συμβάσιες ..οὐκ ἐθέλουσι συμμένειν Hdt.1.74; σ. ποιεῖσθαι E.*Supp.*739; δὸς σύμβασιν τέκνοις make them friends, Id.*Ph.*85; εἰς ξ. παῖδα ἄγειν Id.*Andr.*423; ἡ ξ. ἐγένετο Th.3.28; ἀπὸ ξυμβάσεως by *agreement*, Id.4.130. III. (συμβαίνω III) *conjunction*, Pl.*Ep.*359b; *concurrence, coincidence*, συμβάσεως ἔξω πάσης καὶ συνθέσεως, said of τὸ ἕν, Plot.5.4.1, cf. 6.1.26, 6.8.14; κατὰ σύμβασιν, technical term of the Empirics, expld. by Gal.10.164.

**συμβαστάζω**, *carry together with*, τινί τι App.*BC*4.27. II. Pass., *to be compared with*, χρυσίῳ Lxx *Jb.*28.16,19.

**συμβᾰτ-έος**, α, ον, *to be agreed*, Sch.S.*OC*1426. **-εύω**, *couple, mate with* a female, Lat. *coire*, f.l. in Palaeph.39(40). **-ήριος**, ον, = sq., λόγοι Th.5.76, D.H.2.45, al.; σπονδαί Ph.1.390, al. **-ικός**, ή, όν, (συμβαίνω II) *tending* or *leading to agreement, disposed thereto*, λόγοι Th.6.103; οὐδὲν πράξαντες ξ. having effected nothing *towards an agreement*, Id.8.91, cf. 71. Adv., -κῶς ἔχειν to be *disposed for agreement*, Plu.*Flam.*5, etc. 2. *convenient*, ἔφοδοι Ptol.*Tetr.*117. **-ός**, ή, όν, *liable to happen*, οὐδ' ἡ τῶν μελλόντων ἀδηλότης αὐτῷ συμβατή Ph.1.277; συμβατόν ἐστι, = συμβαίνει, Plb.9.2.4.

**συμβεβαι-όω**, *confirm*, τὰς δυνάμεις Vett.Val.213.22; *give joint guarantee*, *SIG*46.5 (Halic., v B.C.), *POxy.*1208.28 (iii A.D.). **-ωτής**, οῦ, ὁ, *joint-guarantor*, ib.6 (iii A.D.), etc.

**συμβεβηκότως**, Adv. pf. part. Act. of συμβαίνω, *per accidens*, Nicom.*Ar.*1.1, Syrian. *in Metaph.*169.24.

**συμβελής**, ές, (βέλος) *hit by several arrows at once*, Plb.1.40.13.

**συμβελτιόομαι**, Pass., *to be improved together*, Phot.*Bibl.* p.94B.

**συμβεννίων**, v. σεβένιον.

**συμβημᾰτίζω**, *keep pace with*, Dam.ap.Simp. *in Ph.*797.4.

**συμβία** [ῐ], ἡ, late word for σύμβιος (ἡ), *wife*, *PLond.*3.978.19 (iv A.D.), etc.

**συμβῐάζομαι**, Med., *force into union*, εἰς ἀλλήλας Longin.10.6, cf. Eun.*Hist.*p.259D.: pf. in pass. sense, πάντα τὰ νῦν συμβεβιασμένα which *have been forced into union*, D.8.41.

**συμβῐβ-άζω**, Causal of συμβαίνω, *bring together*: Pass., *to be put together, to be knit together, framed*, ἔκ τινος *Ep.Eph.*4.16, *Ep.Col.*2.19. 2. metaph., *bring to terms, reconcile*, Hdt.1.74; σ. τινά τινι *reconcile* one to another, Th.2.29; σ. [τινὰς] εἰς τὸ μέσον, as mediator, Pl.*Prt.*337e: abs., *bring about an agreement*, *IG*1$^2$.57.24. II. *put together, compare, examine*, τὰ λεγόμενα Pl.*Hp.Mi.*369d; [τὰς μεταφοράς] Phld.*Rh.*1.174S.; σ. περί τινων ὃ ἕκαστον εἴη Pl.*R.*504a (though Timaeus here expld. it intr. *agree*). III. *elicit a logical consequence, infer* (cf. συμβαίνω III. 3 b), Arist.*Top.*155$^a$25, *SE*181$^a$22; ἔκ τινων Id.*Top.*161$^b$37; σ. ὅτι.. ib.154$^a$36; σ. ὡς.. Id.*Rh.Al.*1426$^a$37, 1441$^a$6; σ. πότερον.. Id.*Top.*158$^b$27; πῶς.. Phld.*Rh.*1.172S. (Pass.); ὅτι.. *Act.Ap.*9.22; c. acc. et inf., Ocell.3.3:—Pass., συμβιβασθέντος *when the conclusion has been drawn*, v.l. in Arist.*SE*179$^a$30. 2. *teach, instruct*, συμβιβάσω ὑμᾶς ἃ ποιήσετε Lxx *Ex.*4.15; συμβιβάσεις τοὺς υἱούς σου ib.*De.*4.9, cf. *Is.*40.14, 1*Ep.Cor.*2.16. ※ **-ᾰσις**, εως, ἡ, *a bringing together, reconciliation*, Hsch., Suid.; *an agreement, union*, Ptol.*Tetr.*182; φιλίαι καὶ σ. Artem.1.67. II. *teaching, instruction*, Hsch. **-ασμός**, ὁ, *conciliation*, Iamb.*VP*16.69, cf. 33.229, prob. in *MAMA*1.10 (*Supp.Epigr.*6.332, Laodicea Combusta); = *transactio*, *Gloss.* **-αστής**, οῦ, ὁ, *reconciler*, ib. **-αστικός**, ή, όν, *leading to reconciliation*, Plu.*Alc.*14; *proving*, Iamb. *in Nic.*p.15P. Adv. -κῶς Olymp. *in Alc.*p.22C.

※ **σύμβῐ-ος**, ον, *living together*, of plants, v.l. in Thphr.*CP*2.17.5: as Subst., ὁ and ἡ, *companion, partner*, Arist.*EN*1171$^a$23, *SIG*763.3 (Cyzicus, i B.C.); *husband*, *Epigr.Gr.*399 (Ancyra); *wife*, ib.815.8 (Crete), *PGiss.*12.8 (ii A.D.), *IG*12(7).53.23 (Arcesine, iii A.D.), D.S.4.46, etc.; cf. συμβία. **-οτεύω**, = συμβιόω, *App.Anth.*3.146 (Theon), etc. **-ότη**, ἡ, *wife*, *JHS*19.296 (Galatia), *BCH*21.94 (Paphlagonia). ※ **-όω**, fut. -βιώσομαι: pf. -βεβίωκα: aor. -εβίων, inf. -βιῶναι, but also aor. 1 -βιῶσαι Thphr.*HP*2.1.2, D.S.4.54, Sor.2.89:—*live with*, τινι Isoc.15.97; μετά τινος Arist.*MM*1212$^b$31; πρός τινα (v. συμβιωτέον); ἥδιστος συμβιῶναι Isoc.*Ep.*4.4; χείρους πρὸς τὸ συμβιοῦν Arist.*EN*1126$^a$31; ὡς κοινῇ συμβιωσόμενοι Pl.*Smp.*181d; of a husband, Wilcken *Chr.*122.3 (i A.D.); of a concubine, *BGU*614.3 (iii A.D.); of a wedded pair, as opp. to mere cohabitation (συνοικεῖν), Plu.2.142f, cf. *BGU*251.4 (i A.D.), etc. 2. of plants, [ἐλάαν φασὶ] πρὸς κιττὸν σ. Thphr. l.c. 3. metaph., σ. τῷ φρονεῖν Clearch.15; ἀγαθῇ τύχῃ D.18.266; χαρὰ σ. τινί Plu.2.1099f; σ. μέσφι θανάτου, of a disease, Aret.*SD*1.4. ※ **-ωσις**, εως, ἡ, *living with, companionship*, Plb.5.81.2, etc.; μετά τινος Id.31.25.10; μετὰ φίλων Phld.*Ir.*p.78W.; σ. θεοῦ ἔχειν Lxx *Wi.*8.3; of *wedded life*, D.S.4.54, *IG*5(1).578.12 (Sparta), 1390.8 (Andania, i B.C.), *BGU*1102.10 (i B.C.), Vett.Val.1.17, etc.; περὶ γυναικὸς συμβιώσεως, title of work by Antipater of Tarsus, *Stoic.*3.254. 2. *good fellowship, camaraderie*, Cic.*Att.*13.23.1. II. *club, society*, *JHS*54.75 (Smyrna), *IG*5(1).813 (loc. incert.).

**συμβῐωτάριον**, τό, *elixir*, Ruf.ap.Orib.8.47.19.

**συμβῐ-ωτέον**, *one must live with*, ἀνδρὶ πρὸς γυναῖκα Arist.*EN*1162$^a$29 (v.l. βιωτέον). ※ **-ωτής**, οῦ, ὁ, *one who lives with, companion, partner*, prob. l. in Eup.448, cf. Plb.8.10.3, Cic.*Fam.*9.10.2. II. esp. of the *confidants* of the Roman Emperors, etc., Plu.2.207c, Jul.*Caes.*326b; σ. τοῦ βασιλέως Βαβυλῶνος Lxx *Bel* 2.

**συμβλάπτω**, *hurt also*, Gem.2.6,12:—Pass., Arist.*PA*690$^b$6, Eust.1946.32.

**συμβλαστάνω**, *sprout together*, M.Ant.11.8, Gal.19.169.

**συμβλέπω**, *observe at the same time*, Phld.*Sign.*36.

**συμ-βλήδην**, Adv., = συλλήβδην, Aret.*CD*1.2. **-βλημα**, ατος, τό, *joint, seam*, Lxx *Is.*41.7. II. *assault-at-arms, gymnastic contest*, *POxy.*42.2 (iv A.D.). **-βλής**, ῆτος, ὁ, ἡ, *thrown together*, Orph.*A.*686. **-βλησις**, εως, ἡ, *union*: *a joint*, Lxx *Ex.*26.24. II. *comparison*, Phld.*Rh.*1.217S. (pl.); κατὰ σύμβλησιν S.E.*M.*7.375, etc.; ἡ πρὸς ἄλλα σ. *reference to..*, D.L.9.87. 2. *interpretation*, τοῦ σημείου Arr.*An.*1.18.7. III. *assistance*, πρὸς βίον D.L.7.105. **-βλητέον**, *one must compare*, *Gloss.* **-βλητικός**, ή, όν, *contributory*, πρός τι Arist.*Pr.*957$^a$29. Adv. -κῶς, either *cooperatively* or *by comparison*, Phld.*D.*1.22. **-βλητός**, ή, όν, *comparable, capable of being compared*, abs. or c. dat., Arist.*Top.*107$^b$17, *Ph.*248$^a$11, *Metaph.*1080$^a$20, 1081$^a$5, *EN*1133$^a$19; πᾶν ἀγαθὸν πρὸς πᾶν σ. Id.*Pol.*1283$^a$4, cf. Theoc.5.92; τὸ πλῆθος Thphr.*CP*6.3.4; οὐ σ. κατὰ τοῦτο, πότερον.. Arist.*Ph.*249$^a$6; κατὰ τὸ μᾶλλον Id.*Top.*107$^b$13. II. *intelligible*, ἀνθρωπίνῃ γνώμῃ οὐ σ. Ael.*Fr.*326, cf. *NA*6.60. III. *capable of combination*, Dam.*Pr.*191. IV. *fitted together, made of two or more pieces*, πηδάλιον, κεραῖαι, etc., *PCair.Zen.*755.2, al. (iii B.C.); τὸ σ. τῶν χειλῶν *line of juncture*, Ruf.*Onom.*41.

**συμβλύω**, *spurt out together*, Nonn.*D.*4.330.

**συμβοάω**, *cry aloud* or *shout together with*, τινι X.*Cyr.*7.5.26; σ. τισὶ τὸ πολέμιον D.C.41.58. II. σ. ἀλλήλους *shout to, call on at once*, X.*An.*6.3.6; so prob., *Cyr.*3.2.6.

**συμβοήθ-εια**, ἡ, *joint aid* or *assistance*, Th.2.82. **-έω**, *render joint aid, join in assisting*, τῇ Λακεδαίμονι X.*Ages.*1.38; ἐφ' ἡμᾶς Ar.*Lys.*247; ἐς Ἄργος Th.3.105: abs., Id.2.80,81, *Sammelb.*159.6, etc. **-ητικὸν** ἐντάγιον, *confirmatory* receipt, *PGrenf.*2.97.7 (vi A.D.). **-ός**, όν, *assisting*, Lxx 3*Ki.*21(20).16.

**συμβολαιογράφος** [ᾰ], ὁ, *notary*, *MAMA*3.460 (Corycus), *PThead.*10.22 (iv A.D.), Hsch., *Cod.Just.*4.21.16.1.

® **συμβόλ-αιον**, τό, = σύμβολον, *mark, sign, token*, Hdt.5.92.η', Parth.3.2: pl., *symptoms*, S.*Ph*.884. **II.** in Law, *contract, covenant, bond*, in acknowledgement of a loan (v. συμβάλλω I. 6), συμβολαίου λαχεῖν (sc. δίκην) obtain leave to bring an action *for enforcing a contract*, Lys.17.3; οὐ τὸ παράπαν σ. ἐξαρνοῦνται μὴ γενέσθαι D.34.3; συμβολαίου οὐκ ὄντος..οὔτε ναυτικοῦ οὔτε ἐγγείου no *bond* with security either on bottomry or on land, Id.33.3, cf. *SIG*742.50 (Ephesus, i B.C.); ἀπώλλυτο καὶ τῷ πατρὶ τὸ σ. his *loan* would have been lost, D.49.2; ποιεῖσθαι τὸ σ. Arist.*Rh.Al*.1431$^{a}$17, etc.; of a *receipt*, *BGU* 1047 ii 3: mostly in pl., τὰ πρὸς ἀλλήλους σ. Pl.*Plt*.295a; σ. ἃ πρὸς ἀλλήλους συμβάλλουσιν Id.*R*.425c; ἀνδρὶ.. συμμείξαντι σ. μετρίως Id.*Lg*.958c; τὰ Ἀθήναζε καὶ τὰ Ἀθήνηθεν σ. *bonds for money lent* on freights to and from Athens, D.32.1; τὰ σ. διαλύειν Arist.*Pol*.1276$^{a}$10, cf. *IG*1$^{2}$.16.7, 116.18, al.; τὰ σ. καὶ τὰ ἄλλα νομίσματα Phld.*Rh*.1.233 S.; δικαστήριον τὸ διαλῦσον τὰ μετέωρα σ. pending *suits for enforcing contracts*, *Supp.Epigr*.1.363.9, al. (Samos, iii B.C.), cf. *SIG*344.24 (Teos, iv B.C.); τὰς δίκας εἶναι τῶν συμβολαίων D.32.1, cf. Arist.*Pol*.1275$^{b}$9; ἀντίδικος ἐκ συμβολαίων the opposite party in such a suit, Is.5.33; συμβόλαια ἀποστερεῖν fail in payment of *money lent on such bond*, Isoc.12.243, D.32.7; πράξεις συμβολαίων exaction *of such moneys*, And.1.88; μικρῶν ἕνεκα σ. for paltry *sums so lent*, Lys.12.98: more generally, τὰ τοῦ καθ' ἡμέραν βίου σ., i.e. the *engagements* of life, common civil rights, D.18.210; τὰ περὶ τὴν ἀγορὰν σ. Arist.*Pol*.1300$^{b}$12; ἀναγραφὴ τῶν σ. Thphr.*Fr*.97.2; ἐὰν μή τις ἄγῃ πρὸς ἴδιον σ. ἐγκαλῶν τι αὐτῷ *SIG*494.8 (Delph., iii B.C.). **2.** generally, *engagement*, E.*Ion* 411; τὰ ἄλλα σ. other *transactions* (than wills), Is.4.12, cf. Isoc.20.16, Pl.*Lg*.913a; of the relation between ward and guardian, ib.922a; τὰ ἑκούσια σ. Id.*R*.556b, Arist.*EN*1164$^{b}$13. **III.** *intercourse*, ἀνδρὸς πρὸς γυναῖκα Plu.*Alex*.30, cf. *Ant*.25. **-αιόομαι,** Med., *interpret symbolically*, Phlp. *in de An*.450.28. **-αιος,** α, ον, *of* or *concerning contracts*, αἱ ξ. δίκαι Th.1.77 (Hsch. has both ξυμβολιμαίας δίκας and συμβολαίας δίκας); otherwise expld. as δίκαι αἱ ἀπὸ συμβόλων, cf. σύμβολον II. **-ᾱτεύω,** = συναλλακτεύω, Epich.100. **-εύς,** έως, ὁ, *twister*, σχοίνων Greg. Cor.p.551 S. **2.** *forked pole* with which fishermen stretch their nets, Hsch. **II.** σ. φίλων *one who sets* friends *at enmity*, Phryn.*PS*p.107 B. **III.** γλώττης σ. *interpreter*, Poll.5.154. **-εύω,** *contribute to a common meal*, σῖτον X.*Lac*.2.5. **-έω,** = συμβάλλομαι, *meet* or *fall in with*, τινι A.*Th*.352 (lyr., cf. σύμβολος), *IG*4$^{2}$(1).122.29 (Epid., iv B.C.), App.*BC*4.65,85. **-ή,** ἡ, *coming together, meeting, joining*, συμβολὰς τριῶν κελεύθων A.*Fr*.173, cf. X.*HG*7.1.29; *confluence* of two rivers, *IG*9(2).205.12 (Melitea, iii B.C.), D.S.17.97, Arr.*An*.6.4.4, *IG*14.352 i 17, ii 49 (Halaesa), etc.; συμβολὴ τῶν ὀπτικῶν νεύρων Gal.*UP*10.13; *putting together*, τῶν κώλων Sor.1.103 (prob.); τῶν χειλῶν συμβολαί, opp. τῆς γλώσσης προσβολαί, of the pronunciation of labial and lingual letters, Arist.*PA*660$^{a}$6; σ. φωνηέντων *meeting* of vowels in compound words, D.H.*Dem*.40, cf. Phld.*Po.Herc*.994.28; εἰς φωνήεντα τελευτᾶν ταῖς σ. Arist.*Rh.Al*.1434$^{b}$35. **2.** in concrete sense, *joint, juncture*, [τοῦ ζωστῆρος] Hdt.4.10; [τῶν ἀξόνων] X.*Eq*.10.10; of an alchemical apparatus, Zos.Alch.p.139 B.; τῶν ὀστέων, of the joints, Hp.*Art*.79, cf. Pl.*Phd*.98d, Gal.2.683, *UP*3.16, 16.10; πρὸς τοῦ ἰσχίου Hp.*Epid*.5.7; *suture* of the skull, Poll.2.36. **3.** *twisting, plaiting*, τοπείων *IG*2$^{2}$.1672.311; νεύρων Arist.*Aud*.802$^{b}$16. **4.** *point of contact*, Arched.*Stoic*.3.263; *bond of union*, τοῦ χωρίου καὶ τῆς γνώμης Aret.*SD*1.6. **II.** in hostile sense, *encounter, engagement*, συμβολῆς γενομένης Hdt.1.74, cf. 7.210; συμβολὴν ποιέεσθαι Id.6.110; τῇ σ. νικῆσαι, ἑσσωθῆναι, Id.4.159, 1.66; of ships, A.*Pers*.350; ἀλεκτρυόνων σ. Hdn.3.10.3 (pl.); τάλας ἐγὼ ξυμβολῆς βαρείας Ar.*Ach*.1210. **III.** = σύμβολον II. 3, *IG*5(2).419.12 (Phigaleia), etc.; τῶν ἄλλοθι (sc. συμβολαίων) ἀπὸ ξυμβολῶν κατὰ τὰς οὔσας ξυμβολὰς πρὸς Φασηλίτας τὰς δίκας εἶναι ib.1$^{2}$.16.13, cf. 60.9, al.; δικάζεσθαι κὰ (i.e. κατὰ) τᾶς συμβολᾶς ib.9(1).333.15 (Locr., v B.C.); συνθῆκαι καὶ σ. πρός τινας Arist.*Rh*.1360$^{a}$15. **2.** *marriage-contract*, Vett.Val.40.10 (pl.). **IV.** pl., *contributions* made to provide a common meal, συμβολὰς πράττεσθαι make people pay *their share of the reckoning*, Ar.*Ach*.1211, Eub.72; τὰς ξ. κατατιθέναι, καταβάλλειν, pay *one's shot*, Antiph.26.8, Diod. Com.2.13; σ. φέρειν, εἰσφέρειν, Alex.143, Hegesand.31 (sg.); πίνειν ἀπὸ συμβολῶν Alex.97, cf. Diph.43.28. **b.** *the meal* or *entertainment* itself, *picnic*, X.*Smp*.1.16. **c.** [τὸν δακτύλιον] εἰς συμβολὰς ὑπόθημ' ἔδωκε as a pledge into the *pool* (in dicing), Men.*Epit*.287; συμβολὰς or συμβολὴν καταθεῖναι, Luc.*Herm*.81, *DMeretr*.7.1. **2.** *contribution, subscription* to the expenses of a festival, etc., *IG*12(7).22.28 (Arcesine, iii B.C.), *PTeb*.112.26 (ii B.C.), etc.; διὰ τὸ μὴ πεσεῖν πάσας τὰς σ. because the *subscriptions* had not all been paid, *PCair.Zen*.341 (*a*).19 (iii B.C.), cf. *PPetr*.3 p.325 (iii B.C.), *UPZ*98.139 (ii B.C.): metaph., συμβολὰς διδόναι τῇ πολιτείᾳ Plu.*Agis* 9, cf. *Arat*.11; εἰς τὸν πόλεμον σ. παρασχέσθαι Id.*Comp.Dion.Brut*.1. **V.** metaph., *cooperation*, dub. in Phld.*D*.1.22. **-ησις,** εως, ἡ, = foreg. I.2, v.l. in Poll.2.37. **-ήτρα,** ἡ, perh. *a kind of gymnasium*, or *exchange where contracts were made*, *Supp.Epigr*.2.509.6 (Crete, v B.C.). ® **-ικός,** ή, όν, *of* or *belonging to a* συμβολή or *a* σύμβολον, esp., **1.** *symbolical, figurative, riddling*, ἀπόκρισις Ph.1.617, cf. Plu.2.354f; τρόπος τῆς διδασκαλίας Iamb.*VP*5.20: Comp., Ph.2.295. Adv., -κῶς φράζειν *by signs*, Plu.2.511b, cf. Ph.2.242, al., Gal.13.272: Comp., Luc.*Salt*.59; also, *by way of correspondence* (cf. σύμβολον III. 5), τῷ ἐρωτήματι ἕπεται -κῶς ἡ ἀπόκρισις *Stoic*.2.62. **2.** *paid for by subscription*, πρόποσις *AP*5.133 (Posidipp.); κώθων Antig.Caryst.ap.Ath.12.547d. **3.** *conventional*, μετάθεσις A.D.*Synt*.187.7, cf. *Conj*.226.20; τὸ ἐπικείμενον ἑκάστῳ ὄνομα σ. ἐστιν Syrian. *in Hermog*.1.106 R. Adv. -κῶς ibid., A.D.*Synt*.314.6: Comp., ib.8. **4.** -κά, τά, *charge for making out a receipt*, *POxy*.1650$^{a}$5 (ii A.D.), etc. **5.** -ική, ἡ, mantic art which employs σύμβολα III. 2, Gal.14.615. **-ικτρον,** τό, prob., *confluence* of two streams, *Schwyzer* 664.26 (Orchom. Arc., iv B.C.). **-ῐμαῖος,** α, ον, = συμβόλαιος (q.v.), Hsch. **-ιον,** τό, *machine which twists cords together*, στοιχείων (σχοινίων cj. Wescher) Hero *Bel*.81.13.

**συμβολοκοπ-έω,** (συμβολή IV) *to be given to feasting*, Lxx *De*.21.20, *Si*.18.33. **-ος** (parox.), ον, (κόπτω) *given to feasting*, Aq., Sm., Thd.*Pr*.23.21.

® **σύμβολον,** τό, *tally*, i.e. *each of two halves* or *corresponding pieces* of an ἀστράγαλος or other object, which two ξένοι, or any two contracting parties, broke between them, each party keeping one piece, in order to have proof of the identity of the presenter of the other, ἀποδεικνύντες τὰ σ. ἀπαίτεον τὰ χρήματα Hdt.6.86.β'; ξένοις τε πέμψω σύμβολ', οἳ δράσουσί σ' εὖ E.*Med*.613 (cf. Sch.); διαπεπρισμένα ἡμίσε' ἀκριβῶς ὥσπερεὶ τὰ σ. Eub.70; ὡς σ. ὀρέγεται ἀλλήλων [τὰ ἐναντία] Arist.*EE*1239$^{b}$31; ζητεῖ..τὸ αὑτοῦ ἕκαστος σ. Pl.*Smp*.191d; καθάπερ ἐκ συμβόλων Arist.*Mete*.360$^{a}$26, cf. *GA*722$^{b}$11, *Pol*.1294$^{a}$35; ἔχειν σύμβολα πρὸς ἄλληλα *complementary factors*, Id.*GC*331$^{a}$24; ποιησάσθω σύμβολα ἡ βουλὴ πρὸς τὸν βασιλέα τὸν Σιδωνίων, ὅπως ἂν ὁ δῆμος ὁ Ἀθηναίων εἰδῇ, ἐάν τι πέμπῃ κτλ. *IG*2$^{2}$.141.19. **b.** of other devices having the same purpose, e.g. a seal-impression on wax, Plaut.*Pseud*.55 (hence σ. = *signet-ring*, Plin.*HN*33.10); an extant bronze hand is inscribed σ. πρὸς Οὐελαυνίους *IG*14.2432 (Gaul), cf. 279 (Lilybaeum, ii B.C., where the word does not occur). **2.** any *token serving as proof of identity*, ἔλαβε σ. παρὰ βασιλέως τοῦ μεγάλου φιάλην χρυσῆν Lys.19.25; πολλῶν ἀγαθῶν..εὐπορήσειν διὰ τὸ σ. ibid.; ὡς ἔγνω..τὰ παρὰ τῆς γυναικὸς σ. X.*Cyr*.6.1.46; τὰ μητρὸς σ. E.*Ion* 1386, cf. *Hel*.291, *El*.577, *Com.Adesp*.17.16 D., D.S.4.59, Plu.*Thes*.6; ἰδοὺ τὰ σ. here are my *credentials*, Arr.*Epict*.1.16.11, cf. 3.22.99, 4.8.20; ἔχοντες σ. σαφὲς λύπης bearing clear *credentials* (consisting) of (a common) grief, S.*Ph*.403, cf. Aristid.1.416 J. **3.** *guarantee*, σ. τῆς παιδεύσεως πιστότατον Isoc.4.49; σ. ὅτι παρ' ἐμοῦ [ἡ ἐπιστολή] ἐστι Pl.*Ep*.360a, cf. 363b; σ. τῆς σωτηρίας D.15.4; σ. τοῦ συμφέροντος εἰς τὸ μὴ βλάπτειν ἀλλήλους Epicur.*Sent*.31. **4.** *token*, esp. of goodwill, χρυσίον σ. φιλίας καὶ ξενίας Plu.*Pyrrh*.20, cf. *Art*.18; χρυσοῦν στέφανον ἔλαβον σ. περιέχοντα τῆς ὑμετέρας πρός με εὐσεβείας *PLond*.3.1178.13 (ii A.D.). **5.** identity-*token* given to Athenian dicasts on entering the courts, entitling them to vote, and on presenting which they received another σ., in exchange for which they received their fee, Ar.*Pl*.278, D.18.210, Arist.*Ath*.65.2, 68.2, Poll.8.16; also in the ecclesia, Ar.*Ec*.297 (lyr.); διάδοσις τῶν σ. *IG*2$^{2}$.1749.76: extant *theatre-tokens* (without the word σ.) in *IG*5(2).323 (Mantinea, iv B.C.). **6.** at Rome, = *tessera, token* entitling the bearer to a donation of corn or money, D.C.49.43. **II.** of written documents, **1.** *passport* or the *seal* thereon, Ar.*Av*.1214 (cf. Sch.); ἐκπλεῖν μηδένα ἀστῶν μηδὲ μέτοικον ἄνευ σ. Aen.Tact.10.8: metaph., Arr.*Epict*.3.12.15. **2.** *passenger-list*, ἐμοῦ [τοῦ Ἑρμοῦ] τοὺς νεκροὺς ἀπαριθμοῦντος τῷ Αἰακῷ κἀκείνου λογιζομένου αὐτοὺς πρὸς τὸ..πεμφθὲν αὐτῷ σ. Luc.*Cat*.4. **3.** pl., *treaty* between two states providing for the security of one another's citizens and sts. for the settlement of commercial and other disputes (usu. in the law-courts of the defendant's city (cf. Harp. s.v.)); εἰσὶ.. αὐτοῖς συνθῆκαι περὶ τῶν εἰσαγωγίμων καὶ σ. περὶ τοῦ μὴ ἀδικεῖν Arist.*Pol*.1280$^{a}$39; σ. ποιήσασθαι πρὸς πόλιν D.7.11, cf. And.4.18; τὰ σ. συγχέων D.21.173; ἀπὸ συμβόλων δικάζεσθαι, κοινωνεῖν, Antipho 5.78, Arist.*Pol*.1275$^{a}$10; αἱ ἀπὸ συμβόλων δίκαι Id.*Ath*.59.6; cf. συμβολή III: sg. in same sense, *Foed.Delph.Pell*.1 *A* 7 (also written συββ- ib. 1 *B* 10, al.); ἡ κατὰ τὸ σ. δικαιοδοσία πρός τινα Plb.23.1.2, cf. 32.7.3; κατὰ τὸ σ. *IG*12(7).67.48 (Arcesine, iv/iii B.C.), 9(1).331.5 (Chaleion, ii B.C.); κατὰ τὸ δοχθὲν κοινᾷ σ. *GDI*5040.70 (Crete). **4.** *contract* between individuals, *PCair.Zen*.724.7,13, 790.2 (iii B.C.), *PTeb*.5.212 (ii B.C.), 52.10 (ii B.C.); αἰσχρὰ κακοῖς ἔργοις σ. θηκάμενοι forming disgraceful *compacts* (sealed) by evil deeds, Thgn.1150; τὰ τῷ Καίσαρι πεπραγμένα κυροῦν συμβόλῳ App.*BC*2.132. **5.** *receipt*, sts. made out in duplicate, σ. διπλᾶ ἐσφραγισμένα *PSI*4.324.4 (iii B.C.), cf. *PRev.Laws* 52.19 (iii B.C.), *UPZ*25.25, 26.16 (ii B.C.); τὸ σ. τῆς ἀποχῆς *PCair.Zen*.144.2 (iii B.C.); σ. ἀποχῆς *PEnteux*.73.4 (iii B.C.); σύμβολον ποιήσασθαι πρὸς αὐτόν *PLille* 4.18 (iii B.C.), cf. *PHib*.1.67.16 (iii B.C.); σ. καὶ ἀντισύμβολα *BGU*1741.10 (i B.C.); *receipt for a pledged article*, *PCair.Zen*.120.3 (iii B.C.). **b.** *fee for making out a receipt*, *PRyl*.192.10 (ii A.D.), *BGU*1605.13 (ii A.D.), etc. **6.** *unilateral undertaking* in writing, *guarantee*, *PPetr*.3 p.164 (iii B.C.), *PMich.Zen*.57.4 (iii B.C.), *UPZ*112 ii 1 (ii B.C.). **7.** *warrant* entitling the holder to draw allowances over a period, τοῦ κθ' ἔτους τὸ σ. τοῦ ὀψωνίου καὶ τῆς ἀγορᾶς σύνταξον γράψαι *PSI*5.504.8 (iii B.C.); σ. σιτικὰ καὶ ἀργυρικά (bequeathed) *PGrenf*.1.21.16 (ii B.C.); σφράγισαι τὸ σ. *PCair.Zen*.375.11 (iii B.C.), cf. *PSI*4.349.2,7 (iii B.C.), *UPZ*14.89 (ii B.C.); τὰ σ. τῶν σιταρχιῶν *BGU*1755.5 (i B.C.). **8.** *warrant* or *commission* from the Emperor, by which officers held their posts, *Cod.Just*.1.5.12.1, 11; σ. τριβούνου ib.12.33.8 *Intr*. **III.** more generally, *token*, φυλάσσω λαμπάδος τὸ σ. the beacon-*token*, A.*Ag*.8; τέκμαρ τοιοῦτο σ. τέ σοι λέγω ib.315; μανθάνω τὸ σ. E.*Or*.1130, cf. *Rh*.220; *clue*, S.*OT*221; χειμῶνος σ. a *sign* of an approaching storm, Anaxag.19, Sch.Arat.832; νόμισμα σ. τῆς ἀλλαγῆς ἕνεκα γενήσεται Pl.*R*.371b; ἔστι τὰ ἐν τῇ φωνῇ τῶν ἐν τῇ ψυχῇ παθημάτων σ., καὶ τὰ γραφόμενα τῶν ἐν τῇ φωνῇ Arist.*Int*.16$^{a}$4, cf. 24$^{b}$2, *Sens*.437$^{a}$15; τὰ τεχνητὰ τῶν σ. Plu.*Per*.6; νίκης σ. Ἰσθμιάδος, of the celery-wreath,

Call.*Fr.*103; τὰ τῶν στρατοπέδων σ. legionary *standards*, Hdn.4.7.7; *insignia* of deities, D.H.8.38; τῆς βασιλείας Plu.*Comp.Cim. Luc.*3; εἰράνας σ. καὶ πολέμου, of a trumpet, *AP*6.151 (Tymn.). 2. *omen, portent*, Archil.44, A.*Ag.*144 (lyr.); σ. δ' οὔ πώ τις ἐπιχθονίων πιστὸν ἀμφὶ πράξιος ἐσσομένας εὗρεν θεόθεν Pi.*O.*12.7 (cf. Sch.); οἱ διὰ συμβόλων . . προλέγοντες distd. from other kinds of μάντεις, Gal. 15.442; περὶ οἰωνῶν καὶ σ. καὶ διοσημιῶν Iamb.*VP*13.62; = *auspicium*, *Gloss.*; ἐν τοῖς λικμητηρίοις γεννώμενα τὰ βρέφη ἐτίθεσαν εἰς σ. εὐτροφίας Sch.Arat.268. 3. Medic., *symptom*, Gal.19.217, Aret.*CD*1.4, al. 4. *prearranged signal*, ἐπιχειρήσεως Plu.*Rom.*14; *watchword*, E.*Rh.*573. 5. *secret code*, τὰ μυστικὰ σ. τῶν περὶ τὸν Διόνυσον ὀργιασμῶν, ἃ σύνισμεν ἀλλήλοις οἱ κοινωνοῦντες Plu.2.611d, cf. Orph.*Fr.*31.23; consisting of a *signum* and a *responsum*, Firm. *De Errore* 18; τὰ σ. [Πυθαγόρου] Arist.*Fr.*197, Plu.2.727c; περὶ Πυθαγορικῶν σ., title of a work by Androcydes, Iamb.*VP*28.145; *secret sign*, γράψαι τι σ. ἐν πίνακι, . . μαθεῖν τὸν θέντα τὸ σ. ib.33.238, cf. 23.103, 32.227, Luc.*Laps.*5; *allegory*, Chrysipp.*Stoic.*2.256,257, Demetr. *Eloc.*243; διὰ συμβόλων μηνύειν Ph.2.559, cf. 1.681, al., Dam.*Pr.* 210. 6. *religious creed*, τὸ ἅγιον μάθημα ἤτοι σ. *Cod.Just.*1.1.7.11, cf. 13. IV. pl., *standard weights*, *IG*2².1013.8. V. a *small coin*, perh. a half-obol, shaped D, Hermipp.61, Ar.*Fr.*44, Archipp. 8: hence σύμβολον κεκαρμένος *with half the head shaved*, Hermipp.14.

**σύμβολος**, ον, *meeting by chance* (ξυμβολοῦσιν cj. Valckenaer for -οισιν), A.*Supp.*502. II. σύμβολος (sc. οἰωνός), ὁ, = σύμβολον III. 2, *augury, omen*, ἐνόδιοι σ. Id.*Pr.*487; ξ. ὄρνις Ar.*Av.*721 (anap.); cf. S.*Fr.*148, X.*Ap.*13, Marin.*Procl.*10; dub. sens. in A. in *PSI*11.1210. 4, *IG*4²(1).123.34 (Epid., iv B.C.).

**συμβολοφύλαξ** [ῠ], ἄκος, ὁ, *keeper of receipts*, *PRev.Laws* 10.2, al. (iii B.C.).

**συμβόσκομαι**, Pass., *feed together*, Lxx *Is.*11.6.

**σύμβοτος**, ον, *pastured in common*, Hsch. **συμβουάδ(δ)ει**· ὑπερμαχεῖ, Λάκωνες, Id. **συμβοῦαι**· συνωμόται, Id.

**συμβουλ-εία**, ἡ, written for -βουλία, *PSI*1.41.15 (pl., iv A.D.). **-ευμα**, ατος, τό, *advice given*, X.*Ap.*13, *Eq.*9.12; σ. Περιάνδρου πρὸς Θρασύβουλον Arist.*Pol.*1311ᵃ20; *official instruction*, *PFay.*20.18 (iii/iv A.D.). **-ευσις**, εως, ἡ, *advice*, Pl.*Def.*413c. **-ευτέος**, α, ον, *to be given as advice*, Th.1.140. II. συμβουλευτέον, *one must advise*, τισι Isoc.15.175. **-ευτής**, οῦ, ὁ, *adviser, counsellor*, Pl.*Lg.* 921a, Lxx 1*Es.*8.11. II. (βουλευτής) *fellow-councillor* or *-senator*, Din.*Fr.*89.33; at Rome, D.C.59.26; in Roman Egypt, *PGiss.*34.7 (iii A.D.). **-ευτικός**, ή, όν, *of* or *for advising, hortatory*, opp. βιαστικός, Pl.*Lg.*921e; of oratory, *deliberative*, opp. δικανικός and ἐπιδεικτικός, Arist.*Rh.*1358ᵇ7; ἡ -κή (sc. τέχνη) S.E.*M.*2.90; so τὸ -κόν and τὰ -κά, Arist.*Rh.*1391ᵇ21, Plu.2.744e, Philostr.*Her.*19.3; τὸ σ. μέρος Phld.*Rh.*2.214S., cf. *Stoic.*2.96. Adv. -κῶς Hermog.*Stat.* 1, Poll.4.26. **-εύω**, *advise, counsel*, c. dat. pers. et inf., *advise* one to do a thing, Hdt.1.53,59, 2.107, Th.1.65, etc.; οὐ συμβουλεύων Ξέρξῃ στρατεύεσθαι *advising* him not . ., Hdt.7.46: rarely c. acc. et inf., συμβουλεύω . . συμβῆναι ὑμᾶς I *advise* that you should . ., Pl.*Prt.* 337e, cf. Gal.16.501. 2. without inf., σ. τινί τι Hdt.1.71, etc.; ὅτι ἂν δύνωνται ἀγαθὸν Ἀθηναίοις *IG*1².106.19; τοῖς ὀλίγον διαπνεομένοις ἀσιτίαν Gal.15.508; τινὶ περί τινος Pl.*Prt.*319d, etc.; εὖ σ. τινί Thgn.38; σ. τι *recommend* a measure, τὰ ἄριστα Hdt.7.237; χρηστόν τι Ar.*Nu.*793; πορείαν X.*An.*5.6.12, etc.: but c. acc. cogn., σ. συμβουλάς *give* advice, Pl.*Grg.*520d:—Pass., συμβουλεύεταί τι *advice is given*, Id.*Ep.*330d; τὰ παρὰ τῶν θεῶν συμβουλευόμενα X.*Cyr.* 1.6.2; τὰ συμβουλευθέντα Isoc.3.13; τὰ -βεβουλευμένα *res de consilii sententia actae*, *IG*7.413.58 (Oropus, i B.C., Senatus consultum); of persons, *to be advised*, ὑπό τινος *POxy.*118.3 (iii A.D.). 3. folld. by a relat., σ. περί τινος ὡς . . X.*Vect.*4.30; σύμ μοι βούλευσον, ποτέρην ἄγω Call.*Epigr.*1.5. 4. abs., *advise, give advice*, S.*OT*1370, etc.; ὁ συμβουλεύων or -εύσας *adviser*, Arist.*Rh.*1354ᵇ31, Lex ap.And.1. 96; τὰ συμβουλεύοντα τῶν ποιημάτων *didactic* poems, Isoc.2.42. II. Med., *consult with* a person, i. e. *ask* his *advice*, τινι Hdt.2.107, Pl. *Ep.*331a, *Thg.*122a, etc.; τι in a matter, Th.8.68; σ. τι μετά τινος *debate* a matter with another, Ar.*Nu.*475: abs., *consult, deliberate*, X.*Cyr.*2.1.7, etc.—Act. and Med. opposed, συμβουλευομένου ἂν συμβουλεύσειε τὰ ἄριστα *if one asked his advice he would give* him the best, Hdt.7.237; [τοῖς Ἕλλησι] συμβουλευομένοις συνεβούλευσε τάδε X.*An.*2.1.17. 2. = Act., Sch.Hes.*Sc.*338, f. l. in X.*HG*6.5. 34. 3. *agree, make a contract*, θύρας λιθίνης ἧς συνεβουλεύσατο κόψαι *PMich.Zen.*37.3 (iii B.C.). **-ή**, ἡ, = συμβουλία, Hdt.1.157, 3.1, Pl.*Phdr.*260d, Call. in Διηγήσεις vii 19, etc.: prov., ἱερὸν συμβουλή *counsel* is a sacred thing, Ar.*Fr.*33 (v. ἱερός IV. 11): pl., συμβουλὰς συμβουλεύειν Pl.*Grg.*520d, cf. Din.1.47. II. *deliberation, debate*, εἰς σ. τοὺς φίλους παρακαλεῖν Pl.*Prt.*313a; σ. πολιτικῆς ἀρετῆς *a debate on* it, ib.322e; ὅταν περί τινος σ. ᾖ Id.*Grg.*455c; ἕνεκά τινος Id.*Lg.* 942a. **-ησις**, εως, ἡ, *goodwill, help*, θεῶν Hld.8.11. **-ία**, Ion. -ίη, ἡ, *advice* or *counsel given*, esp. in public affairs, Hdt.3.125, 4.97, al., X.*Mem.*1.3.4, *Cyr.*1.6.2; ἡ Περιάνδρου Θρασυβούλῳ σ. Arist.*Pol.*1284ᵃ 27; *advice* of an oracle, ἡ τοῦ Ἀπόλλωνος σ. *SIG*633.19 (Milet., ii B.C.), cf. 590.14 (ibid., ii B.C): pl., *counsels*, X.*Cyr.*1.6.2, D.19.5, etc. II. *counsel, consultation*, λαβεῖν τινα εἰς σ. Men.*Mon.*355. III. *prescription, recipe* for a charm, Cyran.16. ⊕ **-ιον**, τό, *advice, counsel*, esp. with purposes of evil, *Ev.Matt.*12.14, *Ev.Marc.*3.6. II. *a council* of advisors or assessors, *PTeb.*286.15 (ii A.D.), Plu.*Luc.*26; esp. freq. of the *consilium* of a Roman magistrate, governor, etc., *SIG*684.11 (Dyme, ii B.C.), al., *Supp.Epigr.*2.265 (Delph., ii B.C.), *Act.Ap.*25.12, Plu.*Rom.*14, 2.196e, etc. **-ομαι**, *will* or *wish together with*, συμβούλου μοι θανεῖν E.*Hec.*373; ταὐτὰ X.*HG*6.5.34 (v.l.): c. inf., *agree with in a wish*, τινι Pl.*Cra.*414e, *La.*189a: abs., *consent*, Id.*Lg.*718b, *Euthd.*298b, *SIG*364.50 (Ephesus, iii B.C.); *agree together*, c. acc. et inf., D.15.22 (cj.). **-ος**, ὁ, *adviser, counsellor*, in public or private affairs, Hdt.5.24, 7.50, S.*Ph.* 1321, Th.3.42, *IG*2².832.16 (iii B.C.), *PMich.Zen.*57.6 (iii B.C.), *Ep. Rom.*11.34, etc.; σ. πονηρός Antipho 5.71: as fem., X.*HG*3.1.13: c. gen. pers., one's *adviser*, A.*Pers.*175 (troch.), Ar.*Th.*921, etc.: c. dat., καί μοι γενοῦ ξ. Id.*Nu.*1481, cf. X.*Smp.*8.39; μωρίᾳ ξ. τοῦ κασιγνήτου E.*Hel.*1019, cf. Isoc.2.43: also c. gen. rei, σ. λόγου τοῦδέ μοι γένεσθε A.*Pers.*170 (troch.); τῆς ἀρχῆς . . ξυμβούλοισιν . . ὑμῖν χρήσωμαι Ar.*Ec.*518 (anap.); τῶνδε σύμβουλοι πέρι A.*Ch.*86, cf. Pl.*Prt.* 319b; ὑπέρ τινος Isoc.1.35: ξύμβουλός εἰμι, = συμβουλεύω, *advise*, c. inf., A.*Eu.*712, cf. Pl.*Lg.*930e: opp. συκοφάντης, D.18.189. II. as a title, 1. at Athens, the θεσμοθέται were empowered to appoint σύμβουλοι (perh. in a private capacity), Id.58.27. 2. at Sparta, *a board of advisers* sent with the general, Th.5.63. 3. *officers* at Thurii, Arist.*Pol.*1307ᵇ14. 4. = Lat. *legatus*, Plb.6. 35.4; also used to expl. Lat. *con-sul*, D.H.4.76.

**συμβρᾰβεύω**, *to be assessor with*, τινι Lxx 1*Es.*9.14.

**συμβρέμω**, *roar along with* or *together*, D.C.66.22.

**συμβρέχω**, *wet* or *moisten together*, *Gp.*13.3.1.

**σύμβρος**, ὁ, = κάπρος, Hsch. (leg. σύβρος).

⊕ **συμβροχ-έω**, = συμβρέχω, *BGU*938.8 (iv A.D.). **-ος**, ον, *irrigated*, *PSI*2.188.9 (v A.D.); opp. ἄβροχος, *PLond.*5.1771.6 (vi A.D.).

**συμβρύκω** [ῡ], *gnash*, ἐπὶ τῆς γλώσσης τοὺς ὀδόντας Iamb.*VP*31. 194.

**συμβύω**, *cram* or *huddle together*, in Pass., Ar.*V.*1110.

**σύμβωμος**, ον, *sharing the altar, worshipped on a common altar*, θεοί *Sammelb.*7470.7 (iii/ii B.C.), *SIG*1126.5 (Delos, ii/i B.C.), *CIG* 2230 (Chios), Str.11.8.4, etc., cf. σύνναος; σ. τινί *Trag.Adesp.*143, Plu.2.492c.

**σύμμαγμα**, ατος, τό, *mass of rubble*, Hsch. s. v. εὐθυντηρία.

**συμμᾰθητής**, οῦ, ὁ, *fellow-disciple, schoolfellow*, Pl.*Euthd.*272c, Gal. 12.835, Ps.-Callisth.1.13; ἐγένονθ' ἑαυτῶν συμμαθηταὶ τῆς τέχνης *fellow-pupils* in the art, Anaxipp.1.2.

**συμμαίνομαι**, pf. 2 συμμέμηνα: aor. συνεμάνην [ᾰ]:—*to be mad together, join in madness*, τινι with one, Luc.*Salt.*83, v.l. in Lxx 4*Ma.* 10.13; ὁ μαινομένοις μὴ συμμαινόμενος οὗτος μαίνεται prov. ap. Suid. s. v. μετὰ γάρ, cf. Gal.*Nat.Fac.*1.15: abs., Men.421.

**συμμᾰλάσσω**, *soften together*, τινί τι Dsc.1.66 (v.l.), cf. Chrysipp. Tyan.ap.Ath.14.647e:—Pass., Dsc.2.63, Lyc.ap.Orib.9.25.2.

**συμμανθάνω**, *learn along with, share in the knowledge*, τινι X.*Smp.* 2.20; ὁ συμμαθών *one that is accustomed to* a thing, Id.*An.*4.5.27; οὐδεὶς ἐπίσταταί με συμμαθεῖν τόπος no place knows that I *have shared its secret*, S.*Aj.*869 (lyr., s. v.l.; διδάξαι Sch.).

**συμμᾰραίνομαι**, *wither together*, Phleg.*Fr.*36.15 J.

**συμμάρπτω**, *seize* or *grasp together*, συμμάρψας δόνακας μυρίκης τ' . . ὄζους Il.10.467; πᾶσαν γενεὴν Orac.ap.Hdt.6.86.γ'; σὺν δὲ δύω μάρψας Od.9.289, cf. E.*Cyc.*397.

**συμμαρτυρέω**, *bear witness with* or *in support of* another, ξυμμαρτυρῶ σοι S.*Ph.*438, E.*Fr.*319 (συμ-), cf. Th.8.51; ἐδείκνυε . . βίβλους αὐτῷ συμμαρτυρούσας Gal.15.444; τι *to* a fact, Sol.36, cf. X.*HG*3.3. 2; σ. τὰ ῥηθέντα τοῖς ἔργοις Isoc.4.31; folld. by a relat., ὡς . . σύ μοι ξυμμαρτυρῇς οἷα πέφυκα E.*Hipp.*286; σ. ὡς . . Id.*IA*1158; σ. τινὶ πάντα ὡς ἀληθῆ λέγοι X.*HG*7.1.35; σ. τινὶ ὅτι . . Pl.*Hp.Ma.*282b: abs., S.*El.*1224, *BGU*86.40 (ii A.D.). 2. Astrol., *to be in aspect with, configurate with*, Ptol.*Tetr.*124.

**συμμαρτυρία**, ἡ, *configuration* of planets, Vett.Val.49.26.

**συμμαρτύρομαι** [ῡ], Med., = συμμαρτυρέω, v.l. in *Apoc.*22.18.

**συμμάρτῠρος**, ον, *configurate*, of planets, Man.6.393,441.

**σύμμαρτῠς**, ῠρος, ὁ, ἡ, *fellow-witness, joint-witness*, S.*Ant.*846 (lyr., pl.), Pl.*Ep.*311e; τινος *of* or *to* a thing, Id.*Phlb.*12b, cf. *CIG*3194 (Smyrna).

**συμμαστάζω**, aor. -εμάσταξα, *chew as well*, *Hippiatr.*119.

**συμμαστῑγόω**, *whip* or *lash along with*, αὐτῷ Luc.*Ind.*9.

**συμμᾰχ-έω**, aor. συνεμάχησα *IG*2².10 A 7 (v B.C.): pf. συμμεμάχηκα *SIG*588.61 (Milet., ii B.C.)—*to be an ally, to be in alliance*, A.*Pers.* 793, Th.1.35, 7.50, etc.: c. acc. cogn., σ. τὴν μάχην *IG* l. c.: c. dat., *SIG*366.8 (Delph., iii B.C.), etc.; οὐ ξ., ἀλλὰ ξυναδικεῖν *join* not *in war* but in doing wrong, Th.1.39: generally, *help, succour*, σ. τινί S.*Ant.*740, *Ph.*1368, Pl.*R.*440c, *Phlb.*14b, etc.; τοῖσιν εὖ φρονοῦσι συμμαχεῖ τύχη Critias 21; σ. ὥστε . . *assist* towards . ., Hdt.1.98:—Med., pf. part. συμμεμαχημένος in act. sense, Luc.*Tyr.*7:—Pass., συμμαχοῦμαι ὑπό τινος Id.*Cal.*22. Cf. συμμάχομαι. **-ία**, Ion. -ίη, ἡ, *alliance, offensive and defensive* (opp. an ἐπιμαχία or *defensive* one, Th.1.44), *IG*1².52.16, al., Hdt.2.181, 4.120, etc.; σ. ποιέεσθαι πρός τινα Id.5.73, cf. 63, X.*HG*3.2.21, *IG*2².43.26, etc.; τινι Th.1.44,57; ἡ ἔξω ξ. Id.3.65; σ. παρέχεσθαι Pl.*R.*474b. 2. generally, *the duty of an ally*, ξυμμαχίας ἁμαρτὼν A.*Ag.*213 (lyr.) (which others take in signf. II). 3. συμμαχίαν φρουρεῖν, i. e. συμμάχων χώραν, Th.5. 33. II. = τὸ συμμαχικόν, the *body of allies*, Hdt.1.77,82, E.*Rh.*994 (anap.), Th.1.118,119, etc.; συμμαχίας συνελθούσης Aeschin.2.32. 2. *allied* or *auxiliary force*, Th.6.73; σ. πέμπειν X.*HG*4.8.24, cf. *SIG* 763.5 (Cyzicus, i B.C.); ἔξωθεν ἐπάγεσθαι σ. Pl.*R.*556e: generally, *body of friends*, Pi.*O.*10(11).72. **-ικός**, ή, όν, *of* or *for alliance*, θεοὶ ξ. the gods *invoked at the making of an alliance*, Th.3.58; σ. αἵρεσις, νόμος, etc., Plb.9.23.7, Plu.*CG*5, etc.; Σ. [λόγος] of Isoc., = *de Pace*, Arist.*Rh.*1418ᵃ32. II. τὸ συμμαχικόν the *allies, allied forces*,

Hdt.6.9, 9.106, Ar.*Ec.*193, Th.3.91, 4.77; τὰ σ. *the forces of the alliance*, X.*Cyr.*3.3.12. 2. -κόν, τό, *treaty of alliance*, Th.5.6; *funds of the alliance*, συντελεῖν εἰς τὸ σ. Arist.*Ath.*39.2. 3. *of a standard authorized by a league*, ἀργυρίου συμμαχικὰ τάλαντα πεντήκοντα *SIG*826*D* passim (Delph., ii B.C.). III. Adv. -κῶς *like an ally*, Isoc.4.104, 8.134, Plb.15.24.4. -ίς, ίδος, pecul. fem. of σύμμαχος, *allied*, νῆες Th.8.23, X.*HG*1.6.29; ξ. πόλις an *allied* state, Th.1.98, Isoc.6.52 (pl.), *IG*2$^2$.43.70 (pl.), etc.; also without πόλις, Th.2.2, X.*HG*7.3.11. II. = τὸ ξυμμαχικόν, *body of allies*, Th.5.36,110; φευγέτω ἅπασαν τὴν Ἀθηναίων ξ. prob. in *IG*1$^2$.10.30. ※ -ομαι, fut. -οῦμαι X.*An.*5.4.10: aor. συνεμαχεσάμην Aeschin.2.169:—*fight along with* others, *to be an ally, auxiliary*, Th.4.44, 8.26, Pl.*Lg.*699a, X.*HG* 3.2.13: c. dat., Id.*An.*5.4.10, 6.1.13; τὸ οἰκὸς ἐμοὶ συμμάχεται probability *is on* my *side*, Hdt.7.239; σ. πρὸς τὸν δῆμον against.., Arist.*Pol.*1300$^a$18; σ. τὴν μάχην Aeschin. l. c.—Prose word, συμμαχέω being used by Poets. ※ -ος, ον, *fighting along with, leagued* or *allied with*, τινι A.*Ch.*2,19, Hdt.1.22, etc.: freq. abs. as Subst., *ally*, Sapph.1.28 (fem.), etc.; and in pl. *allies*, Hdt.1.102, al., *IG*1$^2$.76.14, etc.; σ. ἐπί τινα X.*An.*5.5.22. 2. as a real Adj., of things, places, circumstances, συμμάχῳ δορί A.*Eu.*773; αὐτὴ γὰρ ἡ γῆ ξ. κείνοις πέλει Id.*Pers.*792; συντυχίη ἐπεγένετό τινι σ. Hdt.5.65; νόμον σ. τῷ θέλοντι Id.3.31; τὸ εἰκὸς σ. μοί ἐστιν Antipho 5.43; τοῦ χωρίου τὸ δυσέμβατον ξύμμαχον γίγνεται Th.4.10, cf. Hdt.4.129; πολλά ἐστι τὰ σύμμαχα X.*An.*2.4.7; σ. ἔχειν τὸ δίκαιον Lys.2.10; ὅρκοι καὶ ξυνθῆκαι ib.62; τάχος σ. εἰς τὸ πραχθῆναι X.*Cyr.*3.2.4: c. gen. rei, ἀρετὴ τῶν ἐν πολέμῳ σ. ἔργων Id.*Mem.*2.1.32. 3. *assistant* (esp. messenger), *POxy.*1223.10 (iv A.D.), 904.4 (pl., v A.D.), etc.

**συμμεθ-αρμόζομαι**, Med., *adapt*, D.H.*Dem.*45. **-εξις**, εως, ἡ, *participation in*, τῶν χαλεπῶν Arist.*EE*1245$^b$34. **-έπω**, *sway jointly*, σκῆπτρα interpol. in *AP*15.15 (Constantin. Rhod.). **-ίστημι**, *change at the same time*, Arist.*Pr.*940$^b$5; 3 sg. συμμεθιστᾷ (from -ιστάω) Str.1.3.13. II. Pass., with aor. 2 and pf. Act., *change places simultaneously with* another, Plu.*Pyrrh.*16, etc.

**συμμεθύσκομαι**, Pass., = sq., Plu.2.97a,124c.

**συμμεθύω**, *get drunk together with*, τινι Phan.Hist.13, Heraclit.*Ep.*7.3.

**συμμείγνῡμι** (freq. written -μιγ- in codd.), Ar.*Av.*701 (Pass.), E.*Supp.*224, etc.; more rarely -ύω, X.*Mem.*3.14.5, impf. Id.*Cyr.*7.1.26, etc.; imper. συμμείγνυ Pl.*Phlb.*25d; Ep. and Ion. pres. **συμμίσγω**, as always in Hom., Thgn., Hdt., sts. in Att. (Th.7.6, Pl.*Lg.*678c, *Phlb.*23d) and later Prose, *SIG*1025.8 (Cos, iv/iii B.C.) (συμμείσγω *PTeb.*716.3 (ii B.C.), 12.7 (ii B.C.)): fut. -μ(ε)ίξω X.*Cyr.*2.1.11, etc. (v. μείγνυμι): aor. συνέμειξα until iii B.C., *PCair.Zen.*545.13, 596.4 (other passages s.v. μείγνυμι), and sts. later, *OGI*751.3 (Attalus II, ii B.C.), 763.3 (Eumenes II, ii B.C.), *BGU*1784.2 (i B.C.), etc.; -μιξ- first in late iii B.C. (v. μείγνυμι) and freq. f.l. in codd., as of *h.Ven.*50,251, Pi.*O.*3.9, etc.: pf. -μέμῖχα Plb.16.10.1, 38.13.5, Apollon.Perg.*Con.Praef.*:—Med., fut. -μ(ε)ίξομαι, in pass. sense, Thgn.1245, Bacis ap.Hdt.8.77:—*mix together, commingle*; the Act. first in *h.Merc.*81, *h.Ven.*50,250, though the Pass. occurs in Il. (v. infr.); of two things, both in acc., συμμίσγων μυρίκας καὶ μυρσινοειδέας ὄζους *h.Merc.* l. c.; βοὰν αὐλῶν ἐπέων τε θέσιν συμμ(ε)ῖξαι Pi.*O.*3.9, etc.: c. acc. et dat. rei, τοῦτο.. γάλακτι συμμίσγοντες Hdt.4.23; πῶς κεδνὰ τοῖς κακοῖσι συμμ(ε)ίξω; A.*Ag.*648, cf. Pl.*R.*415a, etc.; or c. acc. only, ὀργὴν συμμίσγων *mixing in, adding*, Thgn.214; συμμ(ε)ίξαντες τὰ στρατόπεδα *having combined* them, Hdt.4.114; ἐς τὠυτὸ ῥέεθρον τὸ ὕδωρ συμμίσγοντες Id.7.127:—rarely in Med., χρώματα συμμ(ε)ίξασθαι Poll.7.128:—Pass., with fut. Med. (v. supr.), *to be commingled*, ὅ γε Πηνειῷ συμμίσγεται Il.2.753; συμμίσγεται τῷ Ἴστρῳ Hdt.4.48; οὔποθ' ὕδωρ καὶ πῦρ συμμείξεται Thgn.1245; σ. θαλίαισι νέκταρ Sapph.5; οὐρανὸς σ. τῇ γῇ E.*Cyc.*578; ἀπὸ πλείστων Hp.*Aër.*8; τινι or πρὸς ἄλληλα, Pl.*Ti.*83c,57d; *join forces*, of two armies, Th.2.31; *to be formed by combination*, opp. διακρίνομαι, Anaxag.17; ἐξ ἀμφοῖν συμμ(ε)ιχθεὶς Pl.*Phlb.*22a, cf. 23d: metaph., εἶναι οὐδένα τῷ κακὸν οὐ συνεμ(ε)ίχθη there is none who *has* not misery *as an ingredient in his fate*, Hdt.7.203; cf. συγκεράννυμι; συμμεμ(ε)ιγμένος Ἑλληνικὸς καὶ βαρβαρικὸς παιών Lys.2.38; συμμιγέντων τούτων πάντων when all these things *happened together*, Hdt.8.38. 2. *unite sexually, couple*, θεοὺς γυναιξὶ *h.Ven.*50, cf. 250; λέχος τινὶ σ. Ar.*Th.*891, cf. E.*Supp.*222,224:—Pass., συμμ(ε)ιχθῆναι γυναικί Hdt.4.114; πάλιν ξυμμι(σ)γέσθω Hp.*Superf.*26; συμμιγῆναι ἀλλήλοις Pl.*Smp.*207b; ὅταν.. συμμ(ε)ιχθῆτον εἰς ταὐτὸν δύο E.*Fr.*898.11; Ἔρως ξυνέμ(ε)ιξεν ἅπαντα· ξυμμ(ε)ιγνυμένων δ' ἑτέρων ἑτέροις γένετ' οὐρανός Ar.*Av.*700. 3. Med. and Pass., *associate with* persons, Hdt.6.138; ἀνοσίοισι συμμιγεὶς.. ἀνδράσιν *mixed up, connected with* ungodly men, A.*Th.*611. 4. metaph., τινὰ εὐθαλεῖ τύχᾳ *introduce* him *to, make* him *acquainted with* high fortune, Pi.*P.*9.72; χρῆμα δὲ συμμ(ε)ίξῃς μηδενὶ *communicate* it not to any one, Thgn.64; κοινόν τι πρῆγμα συμμ(ε)ῖξαί τινι *communicate* to one a subject of common interest, Hdt.8.58; σ. συμβόλαια *form mutual* contracts, Pl.*Lg.*958c. II. intr. in Act., in sense like the Pass., *have dealings* or *intercourse with, associate* or *communicate with*, κακοῖσι, ἀγαθοῖς, Thgn.36,1165, cf. Hdt.4.151, etc.; πονηροῖς ἀνθρώποις D.32.11; Διονυσίῳ Phld.*Acad.Ind.*p.7 M.; σ. πρός τινα *join* him, X.*HG*1.3.7; generally, *meet for conversation* or *traffic*, Hdt.2.63, 6.23, etc.; σ. τινὶ *talk* or *converse with*, Id.1.123, E.*Hel.*324, Ar.*Ec.*516 (anap.), X.*Cyr.*8.1.46; διὰ λόγων σ. τινὶ Pl.*Plt.*258a; πρός τινα X.*Cyr.*7.4.11; Ἱέραξ ὁ παρὰ σοῦ συμμείξας *BGU* l. c.; of ambassadors interviewing kings, *OGI* ll. cc. 2. of sexual intercourse, Pl.*Lg.*930d. 3. in hostile sense, *meet in close fight, come to blows, engage*, τινι with one, Hdt.1.127, 6.14, Th.7.6, etc.: abs., Id.1.49, 8.104, X.*An.*4.6.24; also σ. τῇ ναυμαχίῃ Hdt.1.166; σ. τινὶ ἐς μάχην Id.4.127, etc.; σ. ὁμόσε τισί X.*Cyr.*7.1.26; σ. εἰς χεῖράς τινι ib.2.1.11; of ships, Th.2.84: c. acc., νείκεα συνμείσχιν (= συμμεῖξειν) πόλεμόν θ' ἅμα *IG*1$^2$.920. 4. generally, *meet*, τοῖς ἄλλοις εἰς λιμένα X.*An.*6.3.24, cf. *PEleph.*29.11 (iii B.C.), etc.; θάλατται πρὸς ἀλλήλας σ. Arist.*Mete.*354$^a$1; ποταμοὶ σ. ἀλλήλοις D.S.2.37.

**συμμ(ε)ικτέον**, *one must commingle*, Pl.*Phlb.*62e, *Lg.*828c.

**σύμμεικτος** (on the spelling v. μείγνυμι), ον, also η, ον Stob.3.17.28 (v.l.):—*commingled, promiscuous*, καρπὸς Hes.*Op.*563; σύμμεικτα ..βουκόλων φρουρήματα S.*Aj.*53; θηρώμενοι ξύμμικτα μὴ δίκαια καὶ δίκαι' ὁμοῦ E.*Fr.*419; σ. εἶδος, of the Minotaur, ib.996; esp. of irregular troops, σ. στρατός Hdt.7.55; ἄνθρωποι, ὄχλοι, Th.6.4,17; opp. true citizens, Id.4.106; ξενικὸν ἀργύριον σ. *miscellaneous*, *IG*1$^2$.310.302; σ. χαλκώματα Lys.19.27; χρυσία σ. διάλιθα *IG*2$^2$.1388.63; πρόβατα *PTeb.*53.19 (ii B.C.), etc. Adv. -τως Str.1.2.27 (v.l.). 2. c. dat., θυσίαι τελεταῖς σ. Pl.*Lg.*738c. 3. *compounded*, ἐκ γῆς τε καὶ ὕδατος Id.*Ti.*61a, cf. *Lg.*692a; σ. [λόγος] *consolidated* account, *PLond.*3.1157.1 (iii A.D.).

**σύμμειξις**, v. σύμμιξις.

**συμμειόομαι**, Pass., *become less along with*, Gal.2.532, 15.726, Ptol.*Tetr.*3 (where also Act.), Eust.834.59.

※ **συμμειρᾰκιώδης**, ες, *altogether childish*, Lucil.*Fr.*187 Marx (dub.).

**συμμεῖραξ**, ᾰκος, ὁ, ἡ, *partner in youth*, Tz.*H.*4.673.

**συμμελαίνομαι**, Pass., *become quite black*, καπνῷ Plu.2.587c; *become black together with*, τῷ δέρματι Phleg.*Fr.*36.34 J.

**συμμελετάω**, *exercise* or *practise with* or *together*, Antipho 3.4.6, *AP*12.206 (Strat.).

**συμμελής**, ές, *in time*, κρότος ἐμμελὴς καὶ σ. Ael.*NA*5.13; τῷ ποδὶ κρούων συμμελές Philostr.*Im.*1.10: metaph., σ. λόγοις Ael.*NA*9.29. Adv. Sup. -έστατα *accurately*, διαγνῶναι Gal.18(1).297.

**συμμέμᾱα**, *to be eager together with*, Διὶ συμμεμαῶτες v.l. for συμμογέοντες in Q.S.5.105.

**συμμεμετρημένως**, Adv. pf. part. Pass., (συμμετρέω) *in due proportion*, Hp.*Mochl.*38, Poll.4.167.

**συμμεμιγμένως**, Adv. *confusedly*, Sch.Nic.*Th.*677.

**συμμένω**, *hold together, keep together*, αἴτιον τοῦ ἓν εἶναι καὶ συμμένειν Arist.*Metaph.*1077$^a$24; of an army, Th.7.80, Isoc.4.148, D.8.46; of two states, οὕτω.. μάλιστα συμμένοιμεν ἂν X.*HG*7.1.2; of persons, *PAmh.*2.124.1 (ii A.D.). 2. of treaties or agreements, *hold, stand fast, continue*, συμβάσιες ἰσχυραὶ οὐκ ἐθέλουσι συμμένειν Hdt.1.74; ξυνέμεινεν ἡ ὁμαιχμία Th.1.18; ἡ ἀρχὴ ἐς τοῦτο ξυνέμεινεν Id.8.73; χαλεπὸν φιλίαν συμμένειν Pl.*Phdr.*232b, cf. Arist.*EN*1133$^a$12; τῷ ἀντιποιεῖν.. σ. ἡ πόλις ib.1132$^b$34: cf. μένω I. 5.

**συμμερ-ίζω**, *distribute in shares*, in Med., πολύπουν κυσὶ D.L.6.77; *parcel out*, Judeich *Altertümer von Hierapolis* 336.11:—Pass., τὸ πλῆθος ἦν ἑκατέροις -όμενον ταῖς γνώμαις D.S.37.2.12. 2. Med., *take share in* or *with*, κλέπτῃ v.l. in Lxx *Pr.*29.24; τῷ θυσιαστηρίῳ 1*Ep.Cor.*9.13: so in fut. Act. συμμεριοῦσι (v.l. -μετριοῦσι) Vett.Val.264.20. 3. Pass., *to be divided together with*, c. dat., Procl.*Inst.*190, Dam.*Pr.*271. **-ιστής**, οῦ, ὁ, *sharer*, esp. under a will, *BGU*600.6 (ii/iii A.D.), cf. Suid. s.v. μερίτην: also **-ίτης** [ῑ], Sch.rec.A.*Th.*508: fem. **-ίστρια**, Sch.rec.A.*Pers.*703. **-ῐτεύω**, *share with*, c. dat., *BGU* 993 iii 2 (ii B.C.).

**συμμεσουρᾰν-έω**, *culminate together*, Ptol.*Tetr.*79, *Alm.*8.4, al. **-ημα**, ατος, τό, *culmination of a star*, ἑῷον, as the sun is rising, ἑσπερινόν, as the sun is setting, Ptol.*Alm.*8.4. **-ησις**, εως, ἡ, *simultaneous culmination*, Str.1.1.21, Ptol.*Alm.*8.4.

**συμμετα-βαίνω**, *pass over together*, J.*AJ*15.6.6, S.E.*M.*10.26, Luc.*Nigr.*38: c. dat., τὰ ῥήματα -βαίνει τοῖς προσώποις A.D.*Synt.*236.4. **-βάλλω**, *change along with*, τύχας χρώμασι καὶ πέπλοις *AP*15.46.4; ταῖς ὥραις τὰς διαίτας Plu.*Luc.*39, cf. Gal.15.734; σ. τοὺς τόπους *exchange* places *simultaneously*, Arist.*Mete.*358$^b$33 (Ald.); σ. τὰς χώρας *change* their places of abode, Plu.2.424e, cf. Jul.*Or.*1.13d; τὸ γένος *change its* gender, A.D.*Adv.*184.3:—Med., *change sides and take part with*, τινι Aeschin.3.165, cf. Luc.*Epigr.*14.4. II. intr. in Act., *change with* or *together*, Arist.*GA*716$^b$4, *MA*702$^b$23, *EN*1100$^a$28, Str.10.2.12, Ph.1.276.

**συμμετ-άγω** [ᾰ], *carry away together*, τὸν ἀκροατὴν ἑαυτῷ Eust. ad D.P.p.75.32 B.

**συμμεταδίδωμι**, *impart information about* a matter, σ. τινὶ τινος or περί τινος, Plb.5.36.2, 22.14.7.

**συμμετ-αίτιος**, ον, *contributing jointly*, πρός τι Pl.*Ti.*46e.

**συμμετα-κῑνέω**, *transfer at the same time*, Gal.18(2).888:—Pass., Plot.4.4.29. **-κοσμέω**, *revise* a manuscript, Gal.17(1).854:—Pass., *change one's habits along with*, τινι Plu.*Alex.*47. **-λαμβάνω**, *partake in* a thing *with* another, τινί τινος J.*AJ*5.9.1: c. gen., κινήσεων M.Ant.9.41; πάθους A.D.*Adv.*162.7.

**συμμετ-αλλάσσω**, *change at the same time*, τὸ ἦθος Tim.Gaz. ap. Ar.Byz.*Epit.*89.16, cf. Phld.*D.*1.24.

**συμμετα-πίπτω**, *change along with*, τοῖς αὐτομολοῦσιν Aeschin.3.75; τῷ συμφέροντι Arist.*MM*1209$^b$16, cf. Gal.17(2).569, 18(2).203; τῷ μεταβαλλομένῳ συμμετέπιπτε θρόῳ *AP*9.584.14. **-ποιέω**, *alter along with* or *together*, Philum.*Ven.*4.8. **-ρρέω**, *flow away together*, Simp.*in Epict.*p.112 D. **-ρρυθμίζω**, *bring into harmony with*, τῷ πρέποντι τὰ πράγματα Men.Prot.p.14 D. **-σχημᾰτίζω**, *make a corresponding change in* a thing, τὰς ψυχὰς Onos.13.2:—Pass., *change form along with*, τὰ πτωτικὰ -ίζεται τοῖς ἀριθμοῖς A.D.*Adv.*

143.13 : metaph., οἱ τοῖς καιροῖς -όμενοι Aesop.307. **-τίθημι,** *transfer at the same time*, in Med., τὸν θυρεὸν συμμετατίθεσθαι πρὸς τὸν τῆς πληγῆς καιρόν *shift one's* shield *at the same time* to meet the blow, Plb.18.30.7 :—Pass., *change along with*, ταῖς τῶν πραγμάτων μεταβολαῖς Id.9.23.4, cf. A.D.*Synt.*239.9: abs., ib.162.19. **-τρέπω,** *change along with*, Sch.Ptol.*Tetr.*8. **-φέρω,** *transfer at the same time*, *Placit.*4.14.1 ; σ. τὴν ἀτοπίαν τῷ λόγῳ *carry over together with*, Plu.2.1071b :—Pass., *to be borne away together*, Id.*Ant.* 66. **-χειρίζομαι,** Med , *take charge of along with*, μεθ' ἡμῶν τὸ σῶμα Is.8.22. **-χωρέω,** *change position with*, c. dat., Alex.Aphr. *in Mete.*152.1.

**συμμετέχω,** *partake of with*, *take part in with*, c. dat. pers. et gen. rei, Βάκχαις συμμετασχήσω χορῶν E.*Ba.*63 ; τινὶ τῆς μάχης, τῆς ἀριστείας, Plu.*Pyrrh.*4, *TG*4 : c. dat. pers., *PLond.*5.1660.19 (vi A.D.): c. gen. rei, δορός E.*Supp.*648 ; τοῦ ἔργου X.*An.*7.8.17 (v.l.) ; βουλῆς Arist.*Pol.*1330$^a$21 : abs., Pl.*Tht.*181c : cf. συμμετίσχω.

**συμμετεωρίζομαι,** Pass., *to be raised together with*, Str.1.3.15 : metaph., *to be excited together with*, Phld.*Rh.*1.352 S. 2. of the breathing, *become shallow at the same time*, Hp.*Epid.*6.7.1.

**συμμετεωροπολέω,** *walk on air together with*, τῷ θεῷ Philostr.*VA* 6.11.

**συμμετ-ίσχω,** = συμμετέχω, τῆς αἰτίας S.*Ant.*537. **-οικέω,** *emigrate* or *move along with*, εἰς Ῥώμην τινί Plu.*Num.*21, cf. Sotion *Parad.* p.189 W. **-οικίζομαι,** Pass., *migrate*, *change abodes together with*, τινι Ael.*NA*12.35 ; τῷ Αἰακῷ..εἰς Φθίαν Eust.77.4. ⊛ **-οχος,** ον, *partaking with* another *in* a thing, τινί τινος J.*BJ*1.24.6, cf. *Ep. Eph.*5.7 : as Subst., *joint owner*, *PLond.*5.1733.52 (vi A.D.).

**συμμετρ-έω,** *measure jointly* or *in company*, *Tab.Heracl.*1.11, 2. 10. 2. *include in the reckoning*, κόλπος, λίμνη, Agathem.5.24, 3.10 (both Pass.). II. *measure* or *calculate by comparison*, τὸ αἱρετώτερον Phld.*Rh.*2.11 S. :—Pass., *to be so measured*, Arist.*Mech.*853$^b$39; ἦμαρ ξυμμετρούμενον χρόνῳ this day *measured by comparison with* or *calculated by* the time of his absence, S.*OT*73 ; [ἔφθιτο]..μακρῷ συμμετρούμενος χρόνῳ he died *in right measure with* (i.e. *having reached to*) length of days, ib.963 : abs., οἷς ἐνευδαιμονῆσαί τε ὁ βίος καὶ ἐντελευτῆσαι ξυνεμετρήθη who *had* their life *measured out*.., Th. 2.44 ; πρὸς εὐωδίαν σ. αἱ τροφαί *are calculated* to produce, Thphr.*CP* 6.18.3 ; σ. πρὸς ἀνδρὸς πνεῦμα *is calculated to suit* it, D.H.*Dem.*43 ; σ. τινί Luc.*Gall.*27 ; εἴς τι Philostr.*Im.*1.28. III. Med., *measure for oneself*, συμμετρήσασθαι τὴν ὥρην τῆς ἡμέρης *compute* the *exact* time of day, Hdt.4.158 ; ξυνεμετρήσαντο [τὸ τεῖχος] ταῖς ἐπιβολαῖς τῶν πλίνθων *calculated* its height *by counting* the courses of bricks, Th.3.20 ; σ. πρὸς ἄλληλα Pl.*Ti.*39c ; σ. τὴν δαπάνην, τὰς ἐφόδους, D.H.4.19, 7.10 ; τὰ διανύσματα Plb.9.15.3 ; *check* measured quantities, *PAmh.*2.59.10 (ii B.C.). IV. *limit*, φιλοχρηματίαν Poll.4. 39 :—Med., σ. τὸν δρόμον ἐς τὸ ἀνεκτόν τινι Philostr.*Im.*2.2 :—Pass., συμμεμετρημένον *of limited size*, Poll.3.88, cf. 9.24 ; τῇ τῶν λεπτῶν ἐδωδῇ -ηθείς *limited to*.., Iamb.*VP*3.13. **-ησις,** εως, ἡ, *measuring by comparison*, ἡ ξ. τῶν κλιμάκων *computation* of their length, Th.3. 20 ; τῇ σ. καὶ συμφερόντων καὶ ἀσυμφόρων Epicur.*Ep.*3 p.63 U., cf. Phld.*Ir.* p.76 W. ; τοῦ χρόνου D.H.*Lys.*5, cf. Herod.Med.ap.Orib.10. 5.4. **-ία,** ἡ, *commensurability*, opp. ἀσυμμετρία, Arist.*Metaph.*1061$^b$ 1, cf. 1004$^b$11, *EN*1133$^b$18 ; πρὸς τὴν σ. τῶν καθ' ἡμᾶς ἀνθρώπων *in comparison* with, measured by the *standard* of.., *PMonac.*6.39 (vi A.D.). II. *symmetry*, *due proportion*, one of the characteristics of beauty and goodness, βίου συμμετρίῃ by *harmony* of life, Democr. 191, cf. Pl.*Phlb.*64e sq. ; ἡ νυκτὸς πρὸς ἡμέραν σ. Id.*R.*530a ; ἡ πρὸς ἄλληλα σ. Id.*Sph.*228c ; of exercise to food, Hp.*Vict.*1.2 ; τροφῆς καὶ ἀέρος Thphr.*CP*2.9.13 ; σ. τῶν λαμβανομένων Sor.1.94 ; σιτίων τε καὶ πομάτων Gal.6.7 ; τῶν φαρμάκων Id.13.988 ; κατὰ μίαν σ. in a fixed *proportion*, Id.6.272 ; παρὰ τὴν σ. out of *proportion*, Arist.*Pol.*1308$^b$12; but σ. πρός τι, also, *proportion calculated to produce*.., Pl.*Ti.*66d ; ἡ τῶν καλῶν σ. Id.*Sph.*235e ; ὑγίειαν ἐν..σ. θερμῶν καὶ ψυχρῶν τίθεμεν Arist.*Ph.*246$^b$5, cf. Gal.6.13,15, al. ; ἡ τοῦ τῶν γάμων χρόνου σ. *suitability*, Pl.*Lg.*925a : pl., αἱ σ. the *proportions*, Id.*Ti.*87d, *Sph.* 235d, 236a. b. *suitable relation*, *convenient size*, πόρων Epicur. *Ep.*2 p.49 U. : pl., σ. καὶ ἁρμονίαι τῶν..πόρων Id.*Fr.*250. 2. *a woman's robe without a train*, *PSI*4.341.7 (iii B.C.), Poll.7.54, Hsch. **-ικός,** ή, όν, *of moderate size*, Poll.9.24. **-ιος,** ον, *of the same class* or *standard*, *PMasp.*310.10 (vi A.D.), *PLond.*5.1711.28 (vi A.D.). ⊛ **-ος,** ον, (μέτρον) *commensurate with*, *of like measure* or *size with*, σύμμετρος σῷ ποδί (sc. ἡ βάσις) E.*El.*533 ; χαμεύνῃ Id.*Fr.* 676 ; βόστρυχον..σύμμετρον τῷ σῷ κάρᾳ *exactly like* it, A.*Ch.*230: esp. of Time, *commensurate with*, *keeping even with*, δαλὸν ἅλικα ξύμμετρόν τε διαὶ βίου ib.610 (lyr.); τῷδε τἀνδρὶ σ. *being of like age with* him, S. *OT*1113 ; ποίᾳ ξύμμετρος προὔβην τύχῃ ; *coincident with* what chance have I come ? i.e. in the very nick of time, Id.*Ant.*387, cf. E.*Alc.*26 (infr. III). 2. in Mathematics, *having a common measure*, σύμμετροι αἱ τῷ αὐτῷ μέτρῳ μετρούμεναι (sc. γραμμαί) Arist.*LI*968$^b$6 ; freq. denied of the relation between the diagonal of a square and its side, Id.*APo.*71$^b$27, *APr.*41$^a$26, *Ph.*221$^b$25, *Rh.*1392$^a$18 ; [τὸ νόμισμα] πάντα ποιεῖ σύμμετρα *commensurable*, Id.*EN*1133$^b$22 ; μήκει οὐ σύμμετροι τῇ ποδιαίᾳ not lineally *commensurate* with the one-foot side, Pl.*Tht.*147d, cf. 148b : Comp., of musical intervals, ταῖς αἰσθήσεσιν εὐληπτότερα τὰ -ότερα Ptol.*Harm.*1.10. 3. *in accord with the metre*, S.*Eleg.*1 ; σύμμετροι ἐπεκτύπεον ποδῶν χορείαις *in time*, Tim. *Pers.*213. II. *in measure with*, *proportionable*, *exactly suitable*, λόγοι ἀνδράσι σ. Isoc.4.83, cf. 5.110, 12.135 ; γῆ θηρίοις μᾶλλον ἢ ἀνθρώποις σ. Str.15.1.26 ; σ. πρός τι Pl.*Lg.*625d, Metrod.*Fr.*1, etc. ; c. dat., Pl.*Men.*76d, *Ti.*67c, Epicur.*Fr.*81 (Comp.). 2. abs., *in right measure*, *in due proportion*, *symmetrical*, opp. ὑπερβάλλων and ἐλλείπων, Arist.*EN*1104$^a$18, al. ; τὸ σ. καὶ καλόν Pl.*Phlb.*66b ; τῶν φύσει ξηροτέρων..ὡς πρὸς τὸν σ. παραβάλλειν Gal.6.360, cf. 27, al. 3. generally, *fitting*, *meet*, *due*, ξύμμετρον δ' ἔπος λέγω A.*Eu.*532 (lyr.) ; δένδρον πολυκαρπότερον τοῦ συμμέτρου Pl.*Ti.*86c, cf. Phld.*Rh.*1.288 S., al. ; ξύμμετρος ὡς κλύειν *within fit distance* for hearing, S.*OT*84. 4. *moderate*, πόνοι Isoc.1.12 ; ὥστε σύμμετρον..τὸ πνεῦμα..ποιεῖν Antiph.202.16 ; σ. τροφαί Sor.1.26, cf. 49, al. ; σ. στέγη *moderate in size*, X.*Oec.*8.13 ; *of suitable size*, σκῆπτρον *OGI*56.62 (Canopus, iii B.C.). III. Adv. -τρως *in moderation*, Isoc.1.32, etc. ; *in due time*, ἀφίκετο E.*Alc.*26 ; σ. πρὸς ἑωυτόν *conveniently*, Hp.*Off.*3 ; σ. ἔχειν πρός τι to be *in proportion* to.., X.*Eq.*1.16 ; εἴς τι Arist.*Mir.* 834$^a$15 ; σ. ἴσχειν λεπτότητος καὶ πάχους Pl.*Ti.*85c ; τὸ μετὰ νοῦ καὶ τὸ σ. Nicom.Com.1.36 ; = μετρίως, φέρειν *IG*12(7).396.31 (Amorgos, ii B.C.), cf. Aristid.Quint.2.5. Comp. -ότερον *more fittingly*, D.61. 27 (v.l. -ώτερον). **-ότης,** ητος, ἡ, = συμμετρία, Gal.19.491.

**συμμην-ία,** ἡ, (μήνη) *period when the moon does not shine*, *Peripl. M.Rubr.*46 codd. (νεομηνία cj. Müller) : pl., Theo Sm. p.194 H. **-ιακός,** ή, όν, *monthly*, σύνοδος ibid. **-ος,** ὁ, *colleague on the monthly committee* of ναοποιοί *Supp.Epigr.*4.535.16, 536 (Ephesus).

**συμμηρία,** ἡ, *meeting of the thighs*, Sor.1.103 (pl.).

**σύμμηρος,** ον, *with the thighs closed*, μηροὶ σ. Hp.*Art.*77, *Hippiatr.* 14 ; = *compernis*, *Gloss.*

**συμμηρ-ύομαι,** *wind together*, *connect*, M.Ant.8.23 (Pass.). **-ῦσις,** εως, ἡ, *winding together*, *connexion*, Id.4.40.

**συμμήστωρ,** ορος, ὁ, *fellow-counsellor*, A.R.1.228 ; συμμήστορα Μοίρην Orph.*Fr.*47 adn.14.

**συμμητῐάομαι,** *take counsel with* or *together*, Il.10.197.

**συμμηχᾰνάομαι,** *help to provide* or *procure*, τὰ ἐπιτήδειά τισι X. *Cyr.*1.6.11 ; τὰ πρὸς τὸν βίον Muson.*Fr.*14 p.72 H. 2. *form plans with*, τινι Plu.*Alex.*72. II. Pass., *to be mechanically adapted*, Arist.*PA*687$^b$6.

**συμμῐαίνω,** *defile together with*, τινι Lxx *Ba.*3.10, J.*BJ*4.6.3.

**συμμῐαιφονέω,** *to be a murderer with*, τινι Heraclit.*Ep.*7.3.

**σύμμῐγᾰ,** Adv. *promiscuously with*, c. dat., Hdt.6.58.

**συμμίγδην,** Adv. = foreg., Nic.*Th.*677, Man.4.266, etc.

**συμμῐγής,** ές, *mixed up together*, *commingled*, *promiscuous*, βοσκήματα S.*Tr.*762 ; φόνος E.*Rh.*431 ; τεύχη Id.*Cyc.*226 ; βοή Tim.*Pers.* 35, Ar.*Av.*771 (lyr.) ; ἠχὴ ἄκριτος καὶ σ. Plu.*Tim.*27 ; ὑπὸ συμμιγεῖ σκιᾷ in a *dense* shade, opp. ἐν ἡλίῳ καθαρῷ, Pl.*Phdr.*239c ; σ. δρυμοί Plu.*Caes.*20 ; of water, σ. καὶ θολερός Id.2.725e. 2. c. dat., *commingled with*, μελίσσης νάμασιν..συμμιγῆ..θρόμβον milk *mixed with* honey, Antiph.52.7, cf. Gal.6.45,160 ; πόνοι..νέοι παλαιοῖσι συμμιγεῖς κακοῖς A.*Th.*741 (lyr.), cf. S.*Fr.*398 ; ἀνδρὶ καὶ γυναικὶ σ. κακά *common* to both, Id.*OT*1281. 3. name of a bandage, Sor.*Fasc.*19.

⊛ **σύμμιγμα,** ατος, τό, *commixture*, Plu.2.922a, 955a.

**σύμμικτος,** v. σύμμεικτος.

**σύμμιλτος,** ον, *coated with vermilion*, *IG*7.3073.117, al. (Lebadea).

**συμμῑμ-έομαι,** *join in imitating*, Pl.*Plt.*274d. **-ητής,** οῦ, ὁ, *joint imitator*, *Ep.Phil.*3.17.

**συμμιμνήσκομαι,** Pass., *bear in mind along with*, ταῦτα συμμέμνησθέ μοι D.46.2.

**συμμῐνύθω** [ῠ], *decrease together with*, σελήνῃ Philostr.*VA*5.2.

**σύμμιξ,** ιγος, ὁ, ἡ, = συμμιγής, Hdn.Gr.1.525.

**συμμιξία,** ἡ, = sq., as gloss on συνουσιασμός, Phot.

⊛ **σύμμιξις** (or **σύμμειξις**), εως, ἡ, *commingling*, *commixture*, πάντων χρημάτων Anaxag.4 ; τινῶν πρὸς ἄλληλα Pl.*Phlb.*23d, cf. *Plt.*309b ; αἰσθήσεως καὶ δόξης Id.*Sph.*264b ; ἡ τῶν γάμων σ. καὶ κοινωνία Id. *Lg.*721a ; ἐκ συμμίξεως by *commixture*, Arist.*GA*785$^b$5, cf. Pl.*Ti.* 60d. II. *sexual intercourse*, Id.*Lg.*839a, Plu.*Num.*4. III. οἱ υἱοὶ τῶν σ. mistranslation of Hebr. *b$^e$nē hatta'ărūbôth* 'sons of pledges', i.e. 'hostages', through confusion of root with '*ēreb* 'mixed horde', Lxx 4*Ki.*14.14.

**συμμίσγω,** v. συμμείγνυμι.

**συμμῑσέω,** *join with in hating*, τοῖς φίλοις τοὺς ἐχθρούς Plb.1.14.4.

**συμμισθόω,** *lease along with*, *PSI*10.1143.31 (ii A.D.) :—Pass., *POxy.*1637.30 (iii A.D.) :—Med. in act. sense, ib.499.37 (ii A.D.).

**συμμῑσοπονηρέω,** *feel common hatred of what is bad*, Lxx 2*Ma.*4.36.

**συμμνημόν-ευσις,** εως, ἡ, *concurrent recollection*, S.E.*M.*7.279, *P.*3. 108. **-εύω,** *remember at the same time*, τῶν ὁμοίων Plu.2.460a ; ἵνα -σῃς τίνος μέρος εἶ M.Ant.9.22 :—Pass., Gal.18(2).327.

**συμμνήμων,** Dor. **-μνᾱ-,** ονος, ὁ, *fellow-magistrate* at Chersonesus, *SIG*709.49 (ii B.C.).

**συμμνηστέον,** *one must mention at the same time*, Eust.728.51.

**συμμογέω,** *share suffering with*, τινι Opp.*H.*5.567 ; *toil with*, Διὶ Q.S.5.105 (v.l. συμμεμαῶτες).

**συμμοιράω,** *impart at the same time* : τὰ συμμεμοιραμένα *things allotted*, *destiny*, M.Ant.2.5.

**σύμμολπος,** ον, = συνῳδός, E.*Ion* 165 (lyr.), dub. in *Ath.Mitt.*24.93 (Tire, Asia Minor).

**συμμολύνω** [ῡ], *defile* or *disgrace together*, ἑαυτὸν καὶ τὴν αἵρεσιν Phld.*Herc.*1289 p.60 V. :—Pass., Lxx *Da.*1.8, Iamb.*Comm.Math.*4.

**συμμοναρχέω,** *reign along with*, τινι App.*BC*5.54.

**συμμονή,** ἡ, *holding together*, *coherence*, *permanence*, [τοῦ κόσμου] Chrysipp.*Stoic.*2.173 ; [αἱ ψυχαὶ] τῷ σώματι συμμονῆς ἦσαν αἴτιαι ib. 321 ; *holding together* of the divine order, M.Ant.5.8 ; σ. τῶν σπερμάτων *preservation*, Dsc.*Prooem.*9 ; *living together*, Muson.*Fr.*13$^A$ p.68 H. ; in Gramm., *close connexion*, τῶν πτώσεων A.D.*Adv.*202.5.

**συμμονόομαι**, Pass., *to be alone with*, ἀλλήλοις J.*AJ*17.2.4: abs., ib.3.4.1.

❋ **συμμορ-ία**, ἡ, (μόρα) *taxation-group* of citizens at Athens, formed for the levy of εἰσφορά in 378/7 B.C., and later for the discharge of the τριηραρχία, in 357/6 B.C.; see D.14 (περὶ τῶν σ.) passim, and cf. Clidem.8, Philoch.126, Ulp. ad D.2.29; στρατηγὸς ὁ ἐπὶ τὰς σ. ᾑρημένος *IG*2².1629.209 (325/4 B.C.), cf. Arist.*Ath.*61.1; ἡγεμὼν συμμορίας, = συμμοριάρχης, D.21.157, 28.4, Hyp.*Fr.*147; ἐπιμελητὴς τῆς σ. D.47.22; μετοικικαὶ σ. *IG*2².244.26 (337/6 B.C.). **2.** *a division* of the Athenian fleet, X.*HG*1.7.30. **3.** *a division* of the people at Teos, *CIG*3065–6 (ii B.C.); *class* of ἔφηβοι, *PTeb.*316.4, al. (i A.D.). **4.** *a company* in general, δειπνεῖν κατὰ σ. J.*AJ*5.7.3; αἱ Ἀσκληπιοῦ σ., of the medical profession, Aristid.2.20J., cf. Lib. *Or.*1.44, 17.26, 20.3; a *class* at school, ἔστι τῆς σ. ὁ κράτιστος he is top of the *class*, Id.*Ep.*139.2. **5.** of the Roman *classes* in the Servian constitution, D.H.4.18. **-ιάρχης** and **-ιαρχος**, ὁ, *president of a* συμμορία, Hyp.*Fr.*148, *PTeb.*316.6, al. (i A.D.), *PSI*5.464.4 (iii A.D.). **-ιάω**, *to be in the same* συμμορία, Hsch. **-ίτης** [ῑ], ου, ὁ, *member of a* συμμορία, Hyp.*Fr.*146, Poll.3.53, Harp. s.v. συμμορία.

**σύμμορος**, ον, *united in the same* μόρα, Θηβαῖοι καὶ οἱ ξύμμοροι αὐτοῖς Th.4.93.

**συμμορφ-ή**, ἡ, *common* or *general aspect* of disease, ἡ αὐτὴ ξ. Aret. *SA*2.6; ἴκελον τῇδε ⟨τῇ⟩ ξυμμορφῇ ib.11, cf. 9. ❋ **-ίζομαι**, Pass., *to be conformed to*, τινι *Ep.Phil.*3.10. **-όομαι**, Pass., = foreg., Lib. *Descr.*30.5, Men.Prot. p.67 D., v.l. in *Ep.Phil.*3.10. **-ος**, ον, *of the same shape as*, τινι Nic.*Th.*321, cf. *Ep.Phil.*3.21; τινος *Ep.Rom.*8.29: abs., *similar*, Luc.*Am.*39.

**συμμοχθέω**, *share in toil with*, τινι E.*IT*690.

**συμμοχθηρεύομαι**, *contribute to suffering* of patient, Ruf.*Fr.*69.9, Philum.ap.Aët.5.119.

**συμμῡέω**, *initiate together*, Plu.*Alex.*2 (Pass.).

**συμμῠολόγος**, ον, *one that shuts up his words*, Hsch.

**σύμμῠσις**, εως, ἡ, *closing up*, as of the womb, Hp.*Superf.*29; σ. καὶ δίοιξις, of flowers, Thphr.*CP*2.19.3.

**συμμύστης**, ου, ὁ, *one who is initiated with* others, *IG*12(8).173.13 (Samothrace, i B.C.), *IGRom.*3.225 (Galatia), *Arch.Anz.*30.88 (Bulgaria), Phot.*Bibl.* p.97 B.: fem. **σύμμυστις**, ιδος, ἡ, acc. *synmistin*, v.l. for *synmysten* in Serv. ad Verg.*Ecl.*8.78.

**συμμύω**, *shut up, close*, of wounds, σὺν δ' ἕλκεα πάντα μέμυκεν Il.24.420; of the eyelids, Pl.*Ti.*45e; ἄνω κεχηνὼς ἢ κάτω συμμεμυκώς looking up with open lips or down *with closed lips*, Id.*R.*529b (hence, *to be silent*, ἵνα συμμύσαντες πειθαρχῶσιν prob. in Plb.30.32.8); also of other openings, as of the *os uteri*, Hp.*Aph.*5.51, Arist. *HA*582ᵇ19, al.; of pores, Pl.*Phdr.*251b; of bivalve shell-fish, Epich.42, Arist.*HA*535ᵃ18; of the 'sleep' of plants, Thphr.*CP*2.19.1, al., *Gp.*11.20.3; of shields which 'give' under a blow, Thphr. *HP*5.3.4; of the double reed of a musical instrument, ib.4.11.4; of green wood, ib.5.6.3.

**συμμωραίνω**, *to be foolish together*, Sch.E.*Ph.*394.

**σῡμός**, Lacon. for θυμός, *An.Ox.*1.197.

**συμπᾰγ-ής**, ές, *joined together, compacted*, Pl.*Ti.*45c,46b,56e, Gal. 18(2).72. **-ία**, ἡ, = σύμπηξις, Stob.1.49.69; *fitting together*, τῶν γραμμάτων prob. in Phld.*Po.Herc.*994.25 (pl.); cf. συμπηγία.

**συμπάθ-εια** [πᾰ], ἡ, *fellow-feeling, sympathy*, Arist.*Pr.*7 tit., etc.; τῆς ἐλαίας πρὸς τὴν ἄμπελον *Gp.*9.14.1; *pity*, οὐδεμίαν σ. λαμβάνειν D.S.13.57; *mea σ.* my *self-pity*, Cic.*Att.*10.8.10. **2.** in the Philosophy of Epicurus, *corresponding 'affection'* or *quality, affinity*, *Ep.*1 p.11 U. (pl.), al.; ὁμούρησις καὶ σ. of body and soul, ib. p.20 U.; also in Stoic. Philos., *affinity*, τῶν μερῶν πρὸς ἄλληλα κοινωνία καὶ σ. *Stoic.*2.170, cf. 145; in Music, used of chords *which vibrate together*, Theo Sm. p.51 H.; *sympathetic vibration* of bronze vessels, Plb.21.28.9. **3.** *affinity, concord* of heavenly bodies, Vett.Val.5.13. **4.** Gramm., *analogy*, A.D.*Adv.*173.26, *Synt.*168.18. **5.** Medic., *sympathetic affection* of the body, opp. ἰδιοπάθεια, Sor.1.63, 2.22, Gal.8.30; ἔστι τις [τῇ μήτρᾳ] πρὸς τοὺς μαστοὺς φυσικὴ σ. Sor.1.15. **-έω**, *to be sympathetically affected*, δοκεῖ ἡ ψυχὴ καὶ τὸ σῶμα συμπαθεῖν ἀλλήλοις Arist.*Phgn.*808ᵇ11; ξ. κεφαλῇ τὰ μέσα Aret.*CD*1.4, cf. Gal.8.33:—Pass., J.*AJ*16.11.8. **2.** c. dat. pers., *sympathize with*, τοῖς φίλοις Epicur.*Sent.Vat.*66. **3.** c. dat. rei, *sympathize in, feel for*, ἀτυχίαις Isoc.4.112 (dub.), cf. *Ep. Hebr.*4.15, Plu.*Cleom.*1, etc. **4.** abs., *feel sympathy*, Id.*Tim.*14, *IG*14.760 (Naples, i A.D.); ἐκ τοῦ παθεῖν γίγνωσκε καὶ τὸ συμπαθεῖν· καὶ σοὶ γὰρ ἄλλος συμπαθήσεται παθών (fut. Med. in act. sense) Philem.230, cf. Phld.*Po.*5.33. **-ής**, ές, *affected by like feelings, sympathetic*, οὐδεὶς δαίμων -έστερος φίλος Pl.Com.192; σ. ἐστιν ὁ ἀκροατὴς τῷ ᾄδοντι Arist.*Pr.*921ᵃ36, cf. *Pol.*1340ᵃ13; πρὸς τὰ γεννηθέντα συμπαθέστεραι μᾶλλον αἱ μητέρες γίνονται [τῶν τιτθῶν] Sor.1.87, cf. 88. **2.** *exerting mutual influence, interacting*, ἡ ψυχὴ καὶ τὸ σῶμα συμπαθῆ Arist.*Phgn.*808ᵇ19, cf. Epicur.*Ep.*1 p.20 U.; νεῦρα ἀλλήλοις σ. *AP*11.352 (Agath.); *sensitive to influence*, τὸ ἐν τῇ καρδίᾳ θερμόν..-έστατον Arist.*PA*653ᵇ6, cf. Thphr.*CP*1.7.4; of the members of an organism, Hp.*Alim.*23, Plot.4.5.8; ὁ κόσμος σύμπνους καὶ σ. αὐτὸς αὑτῷ Chrysipp.*Stoic.*2.264; *exciting sympathy*, χερῶν σ. ὑπτιασμός Phld.*Rh.*1.52 S., cf. D.H.2.45: Sup., *PHerc.*176 p.39 V. **3.** of planets, *in concord*, Vett.Val.37.14; defined by Serapio in *Cat.Cod.Astr.*8(4).226. **II.** Adv. **-θῶς** *sympathetically*, Phld. *Lib.* p.37 O., Cic.*Att.*12.44.1; τῇ σελήνῃ Str.3.5.8; σ. ἔχειν πρός τινα J.*AJ*7.10.5; -έστερον ἐρᾶσθαι Arist.*Mir.*846ᵇ9, cf. Plu.2.3c; -έστατα *IG*12(2).58b33 (Mytil., i B.C.). **-ησις**, εως, ἡ, *sympathy*, Hp.*Praec.*14. **-ία**, Ion. -ίη, ἡ, = συμπάθεια, Phld.*Mort.*8, Aret.*SA*1.8 (v.l.), *APl.*4.143 (Antip.Thess.), *IGRom.*4.503.19 (Pergam.).

**συμπαιᾱνίζω**, v. συμπαιωνίζω.

**συμπαιγμός**, ὁ, *collusion*, Mitteis *Chr.*31 vi 15 (ii B.C.), *Gloss.*

**συμπαιγνία**, ἡ, = συμπαιγμός, *Gloss.*

**συμπαιδᾰγωγέω**, *bring up along with*, Them.*Or.*9.124a, *Or.*18.225a.

**συμπαιδεύω**, *teach together*, τοὺς υἱούς J.*AJ*16.8.3:—Pass., *to be educated with* others, Isoc.9.22; μετά τινος Is.9.28; τινι ib.37, cf. Plb.6.44.9. **2.** *educate at the same time*, εἴς τι X.*Oec.*5.13.

**συμ-παίζω**, fut. -ξομαι Luc.*DDeor.*4.3:—*play* or *sport with*, ἄναξ, ᾧ..Ἔρως καὶ Νύμφαι..συμπαίζουσι, of Dionysus, Anacr.2.4, cf. 14.4, S.*OT*1109 (lyr.), Men.*Epit.*261, *POxy.*471.82 (ii A.D.): abs., Hdt.1.114, Theoc.11.77: c. acc. cogn., μετ' ἐμοῦ ξύμπαιζε τὴν ἑορτήν *keep* the feast *together* with me, Ar.*Pax* 817 (lyr.): but c. acc. pers., *make sport of*, *PCair.Preis.*2.11 (iv A.D.): so c. dat., *BGU*1027.20 (iv A.D.). **-παίκτης**, ου, Dor. -τας, ὁ, = συμπαιστής, *AP*5.213 (Mel.):—fem. **συμπαίκτρια**, ἡ, Ant.Lib.21.1; **συμπαίκτειρα**, Orph. *H.*29.9. **2.** in Lat. form *senpectas* (acc. pl.), = *consolers*, *Benedicti Regula Monachorum* 27, *Gloss.* **-παίκτωρ**, ορος, ὁ, v.l. for -παίστωρ (q.v.). **-παίσδεν**, Dor. for συμπαίζειν, Theoc.11.77. **-παιστής**, οῦ, ὁ, *playmate, playfellow*, Pl.*Min.*319e, Ael.*NA*14.28:—fem. **-παίστρια**, ἡ, Ar.*Ra.*413, Hld.2.24, 7.14. **-παίστωρ**, ορος, ὁ, = foreg., X.*Cyr.*1.3.14 (v.l. -παίκτ-), *AP*6.154 (Leon. or Gaet.), 162 (Mel.).

**συμπαίω**, *dash together* or *against*, πῶλοι..μέτωπα συμπαίουσι.. ὄχοις S.*El.*727. **II.** intr., ἔριδος συνέπαισε κλύδων E.*Hec.*116 (anap.) (-πεσε codd., Sch.).

**συμπαιωνίζω**, *sing the paean with* another, D.19.128 (-παιᾱν- cod. A), Lib.*Or.*24.23 (v.l. -παιᾱν-): generally, *shout out together*, Plb.2.29.6 (-παιᾱν-).

**συμπᾰλαίω**, *wrestle in company with*, Plu.*Alc.*4; abs., metaph., Plb.24.13.2; *assist in wrestling*, τινι Philostr.*Im.*2.21; *wrestle with* an opponent, Gal.6.316, Longus 2.2.

**Συμπᾰνέλληνες**, οἱ, *all the Hellenes together*, *CIG*3833 (Aezani).

**συμπᾰνηγῠρ-ίζω**, *attend a solemn assembly together*, D.H.4.25, *Rh.*2.5, *POxy.*1025.11 (iii A.D.): c. dat. pers., J.*AJ*9.13.2, Plu. *Demetr.*25, Arr.*Epict.*3.5.10, Hdn.4.9.4. **-ισταί**, οἱ, *persons who join in keeping festival*, Poll.1.34.

**συμπᾰνουργέω**, *play the knave along with*, τινι Plu.2.64c.

**σύμπαντι**, Adv. *in all, amounting to a total of*, *POxy.*513.20 (ii A.D.).

**συμπαρά**, Adv. *in association*, τῶν σ. αὐτῶν, = τῶν μετόχων, *Ostr. Mich.*235,236 (iii A.D.).

**συμπαρα-βᾰδίζω**, *go along together*, Them.*Or.*22.272b. **-βύω**, *cram in along with*, τινά τινι Luc.*Merc.Cond.*32:—Pass., Id.*Pisc.*12.

**συμπαρ-αγγέλλω**, *help in canvassing for* an office (v. παραγγέλλω IV. 2), D.H.10.58, Plu.*Crass.*7.

**συμπαραγίγνομαι**, *to be ready at the same time*, of crops ripening, Hdt.4.199. **2.** *arrive* or *be present at the same time*, *PSI*5.502.24 (iii B.C.); *come together*, *Ev.Luc.*23.48. **3.** *come together with*, of planets, Vett.Val.64.22. **II.** *stand by* another, τινι D.59.72, v.l. in 2*Ep.Ti.*4.16; *come in to assist*, Th.2.82, 6.92.

**συμπαρ-άγω** [ᾰγ], *help to move sideways*, τὴν γνάθον Hp.*Art.*30. **II.** *lead alongside*, τὴν πεζὴν στρατιὰν σ. παραπλεούσαις ταῖς ναυσίν D.S.14.59. **III.** Pass., *to be a parallel derivative*, A.D.*Pron.*33.1.

**συμπαρα-δηλόω**, *show at the same time, incidentally*, Str.2.5.13. ❋ **-δίδωμι**, *give up along with*, Procl. *in Cra.* p.3 P. **-θέω**, *run along together*, ἄνω κάτω D.4.41; πεζῇ Luc.*Hist.Conscr.*45, cf. Plu.*Them.*10, etc.

**συμπαρ-αινέω**, *join in recommending*, χρηστὰ τῇ πόλει ξ. Ar.*Ra.*687; καλῶς κακῶς πράσσοντι συμπαραινέσαι S.*Fr.*576. **2.** *join in approving*, Ar.*Av.*852 (lyr.). **-αιτέομαι**, *deprecate at the same time*, A.D.*Synt.*296.19.

❋ **συμπαρα-καθέζομαι**, *sit down beside also*, aor. συμπαρεκαθέζετο Pl. *Ly.*207b; *sit down beside*, Them.*Or.*22.272b. **-καθίζω**, *sit close beside*, ἐν θρόνῳ ib.15.189c:—Med., *make to sit beside one also*, D.28.15. **-κᾰλέω**, *call upon* or *exhort together*, ἐπὶ συμμαχίαν Pl.*R.*555a; *invite at the same time*, εἰς τὴν θήραν X.*Cyr.*8.1.38; ἥρωας σ. οἰκήτορας *invite* them as.., ib.3.3.21; c. inf., σῶσαι Din.1.65; *summon at the same time*, ἀπὸ τῶν συμμάχων πρέσβεις X.*HG*4.8.13. **-κατακλίνω** [ῑ], *make to lie beside*, τινά τινι D.C.60.18. **-κειμαι**, *to be adjacent*, Epicur.*Ep.*2 p.49 U., Plb.6.53.8, Judeich *Altertümer von Hierapolis* 348:—Gramm., -κειμένη θέσις ῥημάτων καὶ ὀνομάτων of verbs and substantives, as ἵδρωθ' ὃν ἵδρωσα, Eust.477.42. **-κελεύομαι**, Med., *help in inciting*, Isoc.13.21.

**συμπαρ-ακμάζω**, *decay simultaneously with*, τινι Dsc.2.180. **-ἀκολουθέω**, *follow along* or *in a parallel line with, keep up with*, τινι Pl.*Plt.*308d, etc.; ἡ τύχη σ. τῷ ἀνθρώπῳ Aeschin.3.157; ἡ μνήμη σ. τῷ χρόνῳ Isoc.5.134; σ. τῷ λόγῳ Pl.*Plt.*271c: abs., φόβος -ῶν X.*Hier.*6.6, cf. Aeschin.3.233.

**συμπαρα-κομίζω**, *bring along the coast with* one, τὰς ναῦς, of a naval commander, Th.8.41:—Pass., of the ships, ib.39. **II.** Med., *assist in convoying*, D.S.3.21. **-κύπτω**, *bend oneself along with*, Luc.*Icar.*25. **-λαμβάνω**, *take along with* one, *take in as an adjunct* or *assistant*, κοινωνόν τι σ. Pl.*Phd.*65b, cf. 84d, *La.*179e, *Act. Ap.*15.37; τινὰ ἑαυτῷ *BGU*226.12 (i A.D.); σ. τὴν ἐκτὸς εὐετηρίαν *include in their account*, Arist.*EN*1098ᵇ26; τὰς τῶν προτέρων δόξας Id.

*de An.*403b22; τὰ ὁμολογούμενα Thphr.*CP*5.3.7; σ. τοὺς ἐκτὸς τῆς πολιτείας *adopt as partisans*, Arist.*Pol.*1304a16; *call in for advice*, φίλους Phld.*Oec.* p.72 J.; in receipts, aor. συνπαρέλαβα *received also by me*, *PRyl.*189.8 (ii A.D.):—Pass., *to be invited*, Anticl.ap. Ath.4.157f, Ph.1.328, J.*AJ*15.2.7; σ. ἐπὶ τὰ πράγματα *to be called into counsel*, D.H.7.55; *to be incidentally involved*, Phld.*Lib.* p.29 O.; *to be called in to help*, Sor.2.15. **-ληπτέον**, *one must bring in also*, Arist.*Rh.Al.*1442a15, Ptol.*Tetr.*79. II. **-τέος**, α, ον, *to be included also*, Arist.*MM*1208b6. **-ληπτικός**, ή, όν, *disposed to take into counsel*, ἑτέρων Phld.*Vit.* p.24 J. **-ληψις**, εως, ἡ, *calling in, enlistment*, ἑτέρων ὡς συνεργῶν Ph.1.17, cf. 134. **-λύομαι**, Pass., *to be paralysed together*, Gal.8.210. **-μείγνυμι**, *mix in together*, Thphr. *HP*9.11.6; also **-μειγνύω**, Ar.*Pl.*719 (-μιγ- codd. in both). **-μένω**, fut. -μενῶ *PSI*1.64.3 (i B.C.):—*stay along with* or *among*, Hp.*Prorrh.* 2.15, *Int.*6: c. dat., Th.6.89, *SIG*567 *A* 12 (Calymna, iii B.C.); [γυνὴ] ἀτυχοῦντι συμπαρέμεινεν Men.325.11, cf. *PSI* l.c.; *endure as long as*, τῷ βίῳ Jul.*Caes.*324d.

**συμπαρ-ᾰνᾱλίσκω**, aor. -ανάλωσα, *destroy at the same time*, D.C. 47.39.

**συμπαρα-νεύω**, *express assent also*, Arist.*Rh.*1407a37; τοῖς λεγομένοις Aristid.*Or.*51(27).33. **-νέω**, *swim beside together*, τοῖς ἰχθύσι ib.33(51).29; so **-νήχομαι**, Luc.*Tox.*20. **-νομέω**, *transgress the laws along with*, J.*BJ*4.5.5 (in Pass.). **-πέμπω**, *escort along with* others, τὴν παραπομπὴν Aeschin.2.168; τοὺς πρέσβεις J.*Vit.*52, cf. *SIG*$^2$848.5 (Delph.); τὰν Πυθαΐδα *SIG*$^3$697 *G* (ibid., ii B.C.); τὸν κῶμον Plu.*Alex.*67; τὴν ὄψιν σ. τινί *follow* him with one's eyes, Id.*Ages.* 32. **-πίπτω**, *occur to*, θεωρήματα οὔπω ἡμῖν συμπαραπεπτωκότα prob. in Archim.*Eratosth.* p. 430 H. **-πλέω**, *sail along with also*, Plb.5.68.9, D.S.4.18, Plu.*Demetr.*19, Arr.*Fr.*127 J., etc. **-πληρωματικός**, ή, όν, *expletive*, Sch.Ar.*Ach.*1.

**συμπαρ-απόλλῡμι**, *destroy along with*: Med., *perish along with* or *besides*, D.19.175.

**συμπαρα-πομπός**, ὁ, *escort*, *Schwyzer* 369.25 (Amphissa, ii B.C., pl.), prob. in *IG*5(1).1428.14 (Messene, ii/i B.C.). **-σκευάζω**, *assist in getting ready* or *bringing about*, ὁ δαίμων ἡμῖν ταῦτα συμπαρεσκεύακεν X.*Cyr.*7.5.81, cf. D.18.158; σ. τὰ ἔνδον X.*Cyr.*5.3.14; πλοῖα Id.*An.*5.1.10; σ. τὸν ἀγῶνα *help in providing for* it, And.1.132; καιρὸν σ. κατά τινων D.23.183; ὁπλίτας σ. ὅπως αἰχμάλωτοι γένωνται Id.19.230:—Med., συμπαρασκευασάμενος δύναμιν f.l. in Isoc.5.101.

**συμπαρ-ασπίζω**, *assist in battle together*, Tz.*H.*5.227.

**συμπαρα-σπονδέω**, *join in breaking a truce*, Eust.479.32. **-στᾰτέω**, *stand by so as to assist*, ἑκόνθ' ἑκόντι Ζηνὶ σ. A.*Pr.*220, cf. Ar. *Ec.*15, Gal.19.172: abs., Ar.*Ra.*387 (lyr.). **-στάτης** [στᾰ], ου, ὁ, *one who stands by to aid, joint helper* or *assistant*, S.*Ph.*675, Ar.*Pl.* 326. **-σύρω** [ῡ], '*throw in' incidentally*, φατικῶς Phld.*Mus.* p.79 K., cf. p.54 K. **-ταξις**, εως, ἡ, *meeting in battle*, Sch.rec.A. *Th.*633. ✻**-τάσσομαι**, Att. **-ττομαι**, Pass., *to be set in array with* others, *fight along with*, X.*HG*3.5.22; μετά τινων v.l. in D.18.229, cf. ib.216; τισι Isoc.12.180, Lycurg.144. **-τείνω**, *stretch out alongside of*, τινί τι Gal.*UP*16.10:—Pass., *to be so stretched out*, Id. 18(1).298, Zos.3.25, Mich. *in EN*553.30:—intr. in Act., Plot.3.7.13, Simp. *in Cat.*244.22. **-τηρέω**, *take care at the same time*, ὅπως... D.16.10; *observe carefully at the same time with*, c. dat., Gal.1.137, Aristid.2.44 J.:—Pass., c. dat., Gal.*Phil.Hist.*9, S.E.*P.*2.100. **-τήρησις**, εως, ἡ, *observation at the same time*, Id.*M.*8.154; of indirect observation, Gal.1.109,127. **-τίθημι**, *place alongside*, πεζοὺς Plb.2.66. 7:—Med., *deposit* a document *at the same time*, *BGU*324.18 (ii A.D.): —Pass., *POxy.*1649.10 (iii A.D.). **-τρέφω**, *bring up* or *keep at the same time*, of wild animals kept for hunting, X.*Oec.*5.5. **-τρέχω**, *run alongside with*, Plu.*Cat.Ma.*5, *Arat.*7. **-τροχάζω**, = foreg., Id.2. 970b. ✻**-τυγχάνω**, *happen to be present together*, of planets, *Cat.Cod. Astr.*6.70. **-φέρω**, *bring with one*, hence, *exhibit, exemplify*, Phld. *Rh.*2.27 S. 2. *carry along together with*, Ptol.*Geog.*1.22.5:—Pass., Plu.*Caes.*34; *rush along together*, X.*Cyn.*3.10 (v.l. συμπερι-); *follow the same course*, of blood-vessels, etc., Gal.2.391,822. **-φύομαι**, Pass., *grow together*, Gal.*UP*16.9, Them.*Or.*4.56a. **-χωρέω**, *give way together with*, τῷ ἡλίῳ Thphr.*Vent.*61, cf. Ph.ap.Eus.*PE*8. 7.

**συμπαρ-εδρεύω**, *sit beside*, τοῖς ἀθανάτοις Sch.Luc.*DMort.*1.1. 2. of planets, *to be situated together*, τῷ δεσπόζοντι τῶν χρόνων Nech.ap. Vett.Val.291.20. ✻**-ειμι**, (εἰμί *sum*) *to be present also* or *at the same time*, Hp.*VM*17, And.1.12, X.*Lac.*2.2, 12.3, etc.; freq. in Pap., *PSI*5.509.8 (iii B.C.), etc.; of a desire, Sor.1.38; of planets, *occupy a position together*, Vett.Val.60.21. 2. *stand by, come to help*, τινι X.*HG*4.6.1; ἐν ἔργοις Phld.*Piet.*37; of an advocate, D.24.158; *act as* one's *representative*, *PRyl.*120.3 (ii A.D.), etc. **-ειμι**, (εἶμι *ibo*) *march beside together*, impf. συμπαρῄει, X.*HG*2.1.28, Aeschin.2. 111. **-εισέρχομαι**, *go in along with*, μετά τινος Luc.*Tim.* 28. **-εκτείνω**, *stretch out side by side, apply*, τὴν νόησιν τοῖς λεγομένοις M.Ant.7.30, cf. Iamb.*Comm.Math.*14:—Pass., *to be coextensive with*, Ascl.*Tact.*6.2, Gal.*UP*12.15, al., Cleom.2.1, al., Alex. Trall.*Verm.* p.587 P.:—Med., *come into competition with*, τινι Suid. s.v. τὴν κατὰ σαυτόν. **-εμφαίνομαι**, Pass., *to be expressed as well*, i.e. *appear by implication*, Chrysipp.*Stoic.*2.107. **-ενεκτέον**, *one must carry along with*, Them.*Or.*22.275a. **-έπομαι**, *go along with, accompany*, X.*Cyr.*7.1.8, *Eq.*11.12: metaph., ὕλη τῇ ἡμέρῃ Hp. *Epid.*5.89; τιμαὶ.. ἑκάστοις -είποντο X.*Cyr.*2.1.23, cf. *Hier.*8.5, Phld. *Oec.*p.53 J.; ὅσοις σ. τις χάρις Pl.*Lg.*667b; αἱ -όμεναι ὀσμαί Arist.*Pr.* 907a1. **-έρχομαι**, *pass by together*, Ph.2.513. **-έχω**, *assist in causing*, φόβον τοῖς πολεμίοις X.*An.*7.4.19; *assist in procuring*, ἀσφάλειάν τινι ib.7.6.30:—Med., εὔκλειαν Id.*Smp.*8.43. **-ήκω**, *to be present together with, accompany*, τῷ αἰσθητῷ τὸ αἰσθανόμενον σ. Plu. 2.1024c = 1032b.

**συμπαρθένος**, ἡ, *fellow-maiden*, Ael.*VH*12.1.

**συμπαρ-ιππεύω**, *ride along with*, τινι D.C.63.2. **-ίπταμαι**, *fly along with*, Luc.*DDeor.*20.6. **-ίστημι**, *place by one's side together*, τᾷ μὲν (sc. Εὐάδνᾳ).. Ἐλευθὼ συμπαρέστασέν τε Μοίρας f.l. in Pi.*O.*6. 42; *express at the same time*, A.D.*Synt.*235.11, al.:—Med., *set by one's side*, τὴν φιλοσοφίαν Them.*Or.*7.99d, cf. *Or.*34 p.450 Dind. II. Pass., with fut. Med., aor. and pf. Act., *stand beside so as to assist*, τῆμῇ φρενί S.*OC*1340, cf. Lxx *Ps.*93(94).16, *CIG*2056.8 (Varna), *PSI*4.392.13 (iii B.C.), etc.; ἅπαντι δαίμων ἀνδρὶ συμπαρίσταται εὐθὺς γενομένῳ Men.550; 2 pl. aor. 2 imper. συμπαράστατε *Sammelb.*7452. 6 (perh. iii A.D.). **-οδεύω**, *accompany*, ψῦξις σ. τῇ ἀπεψίᾳ Herod. Med.ap.Aët.4.45. **-οικος**, ον, *dwelling beside together*, Eup. 177. **-οίχομαι**, *to have passed by together*, S.E.*M.*10.201, 202. **-ολισθάνω**, *slip past together with*, τοῖς ὑγροῖς Plu.2. 699a. **-ομαρτέω**, = συμπαρέπομαι, X.*Cyr.*1.6.24, App.*Ill.*27; of things, *accompany*, σ. πάσῃ ἡλικίᾳ τὸ κάλλος X.*Smp.*4.17; φόβος σ. τινί Id.*Cyr.*8.7.7; ὀσμαί Id.*Oec.*4.21, Ael.*VH*3.1; of symptoms, Aret.*SD*2.1, Steph. *in Gal.*1.237 D. **-οξύνω**, *provoke along with* or *together*, τινα Plu.2.859f, etc.; εἴς τι X.*Oec.*6.10:—Pass., *to be exacerbated at the same time as*, λυγμὸν -όμενον τοῖς πυρετοῖς Gal.15. 847. **-ορμάω**, *urge on in addition*, Thphr.*Vent.*15: metaph., *hearten together*, τοὺς φιλίους Phld.*Mus.* p.27 K., cf. Nic.Dam.*Fr.* 130.18 J., Plu.*Cic.*3; πρός τι Arist.*MM*1208a16: c. inf., Ath.12. 519f. **-οτρύνω**, = foreg., Sch.rec.S.*El.*299. **-ουσία**, ἡ, *presence together*, of planets, Petos.ap.Vett.Val.80.4, Paul.Al.*H.*1: generally, *presence alongside*, Phlp. *in Mete.*48.29.

✻**σύμπᾱς**, σύμπᾱσα, σύμπᾰν, Att. **ξύμπας** (ξύμπαντα in Od.7.214, 14. 198, though the metre does not require it):—*all together, all at once*, mostly (in Hom. always) in pl.; υἷας Ἀχαιῶν σύμπαντας Il.1.241, etc.; σύμπασιν δ' ὑμῖν, opp. εἷς ἕκαστος, Sol.11.6; ξύμπαντά τ' εἰπών A.*Fr.* 350.3; αἱ σ. ἡμέραι Antipho 6.44; σ. τε θεῶν καὶ ἀνθρώπων Pl.*Smp.* 197e; συμπάντων κεφάλαιον *IG*1$^2$.91.23; in Att. the Art. is usually added in the case of Numerals, πέντ' ἦσαν οἱ ξ. S.*OT*752, cf. X.*An.*1.2. 9, Pl.*Prt.*317c; but also without Art., ξ. ἐγένοντο τετρακισχίλιοι Th.1. 107. II. in sg. with collective Nouns, *the whole*, ὁ σ. στρατός Hdt.7. 82; στρατὸς σ. S.*Ph.*387; στρατῷ ξ. Id.*Aj.*1055; τῷ σ. στρατῷ Id.*Ph.* 1257; ξ. λαός ib.1243; πόλις ξύμπασα the state *as a whole*, Th.2.60, 3.62; ὁ σ. δᾶμος *IG*12(1).847.15 (Lindus); τὴν σ. Ἑλλάδα Sor.*Vit. Hippocr.*5; σ. ὁ φόρος *IG*1$^2$.64.8; σ. ἡ πόλις Pl.*R.*423d, al.; also with some other Nouns, χρόνῳ σύμπαντι Pi.*O.*6.56; αἰῶνα τὸν σύμπαντα E. *Hec.*757; ἡ σ. (sc. γῆ) S.*Fr.*411, cf. Ar.*Nu.*204; ξ. γνώμη the *general* scope (of a speech), Th.1.22; σ. ἡ ὁδός X.*An.*7.8.26; σ. ἀρετή, σ. πονηρία, Pl.*Lg.*630b, *Grg.*477c; σ. ἀριθμός Id.*R.*525a; σ. κεφάλαιον *IG*1$^2$.313.148; κεφάλαιον τόκου ξύμπαντος ib.324.101; τὸ σ. πλάτος Sor.1.68, cf. 2.89; but, in Arithm., ὁ σύμπας the *sum*, Dioph.*Polyg.* 4 (c. gen., ibid.).—For the Att. position of the Art., v. πᾶς B. 2. τὸ σ. the *whole together*, the *sum* of the matter, τὸ σ. εἶπαι Hdt.7.143, cf. Th.7.49; the *universe*, Isoc.11.12; the *whole*, opp. τὸ μέρος, Pl. *Phdr.*246c, Arist.*Top.*135a22. b. τὸ σύμπαν as Adv., *altogether, on the whole, in general*, Th.4.63, Isoc.2.17, etc.; so σύμπαντα Pl.*Lg.* 679e; σύμπαν *in all*, with numerals, *POxy.*289.3 (i A.D.), etc. Cf. συνάπας.

**σύμπασμα**, ατος, τό, *powder for sprinkling*, Sor.2.15,28, Cael.Aur. *TP*3.5.

**συμπάσσω**, *besprinkle, bespatter, bestrew*, Plu.2.89d, 638e; βρέφος [ἅλατι] Sor.1.82, cf. Orib.*Fr.*78: also σ. τοὺς ἅλας Sor. l.c.

**συμπάσχω**, *have the same thing happen to one*, οἱ τοὺς χασμωμένους ..δρῶντες ταὐτὸν τοῦτο σ. Pl.*Chrm.*169c, cf. *Ep.Rom.*8.17; θαυμαστὸν..τὸ συμπάσχειν τὰς τραγέας Thphr.*Od.*62. II. c. dat., *to be affected in common with*, ἀλλήλοις Arist.*APr.*70b16; *commotiunculis*, Cic.*Att.*12.11; προσώποις, of a mimic dancer, *IG*14.2124.3 (Rome, ii/iii A.D.); τοῖς τῆς ψυχῆς παθήμασι τὸ σῶμα σ. Arist.*Phgn.*805a6; εἰ [ὅλον τὸ σῶμα] σ. τι τῇ ἀκοῇ Thphr.*Sens.*57; τοῖς ἀναπνευστικοῖς ὀργάνοις τὸ ἧπαρ σ. Gal.18(1).25, cf. 16.555, Sor.2.20, al. III. *have a fellow-feeling, sympathize, feel sympathy*, Pl.*R.*605d, Antiph. 84, Sor.1.4. Cf. συμπαθέω.

**συμπᾰτᾰγέω**, *strike together, clap*, χειρῶν -ουσῶν (v.l. συμπλατ-) S.E.*M.*6.20, cf. Hsch.; v. συμπλαταγέω.

**συμπᾰτάσσω**, *strike along with* or *together*, E.*Supp.*699.

**συμπᾰτέω**, *tread together*, as clothes in washing, Cratin.275; *trample under foot*, γέννημα φρύνου Babr.28.1; σταφυλάς *Gp.*8.23.1: metaph., κόσμον Clearch.3; τινας *OGI*519.30 (Aragueni, iii A.D.):—Pass., *to be trampled under foot*, as by horses, etc., Aeschin.3.164, Thphr.*HP*8.7.5, Plb.1.34.7, J.*AJ*9.6.4, etc.

**συμπατριώτης**, ου, ὁ, *fellow-countryman*, Archipp.54.

**συμπατρονόμος**, ὁ, *fellow*-πατρονόμος, τῷ θεῷ Λυκούργῳ *BSA*27.226 (Sparta, ii A.D.): c. gen., ib.239.

**συμπαύομαι**, Pass., *cease together with*, τινι Gal.*UP*12.15.

**συμπᾰχύνω**, *make thick together*, Hp.*Morb.*4.52:—Pass., τῇ σελήνῃ ὁ αἴλουρος σ. Demetr.*Eloc.*158.

**συμπεδάω**, pf. -πεπέδηκα Phld.*Po.Herc.*994.33:—*bind together, bind hand and foot*, Onos.11.3, etc.:—Pass., Plu.2.924f. 2. metaph. of frost, *benumb*, v.l. for συνεποδίσεν, X.*An.*4.4.11.

**συμπέδιος**, ον, *adjacent to a plain*, [sc. γᾶ] *IG*12(2).74 *B* 6 (Mytil., iii B.C.).

**συμπειθήνιος**, ον, *obedient also*, σ. ἔχειν τὸν κάμνοντα Pall. *in Hp.* 2.109 D.

**συμπείθω**, pf. part. -πεπεικυῖα Hyp.*Ath.*4 (aor. part. συμπείσας is f.l. for συμπιέσας in Plu.2.580d):—*win by persuasion, persuade*, abs., Pl.*Lg.*720d: c. acc. pers., Lycurg.102, *UPZ*114 i 22 (ii B.C.), Plu. *Cam.*23: c. acc. rei, τὰ μὲν συμπείθων, τὰ δὲ βιαζόμενος X.*Mem.*2. 4.6; σ. τἀναντία D.H.6.49; ταῦτα συμπείθεις με σύ; Men.*Epit.*527: c. acc. pers. et inf., σ. πολλοὺς ὁμογνωμονεῖν X.*Cyr.*2.2.24, cf. Aeschin. 3.142, D.18.147, *IG*12(7).386.15 (Amorgos, iii B.C.):—Pass., *join in a view*, Arist.*Pol.*1307$^{b}$15; *allow oneself to be persuaded*, c. inf., ib. 1296$^{a}$38; τι *to* a thing, Aeschin.3.71, *SIG*364.96 (Ephesus, iii B.C.): c. dat., *to be convinced* of.., Phld.*Mus.* p.89 K.: abs., Demetr.Com. Vet.4; συμπεπεισμένοι καθ' ἡμῶν Luc.*JTr.*45; τὸ -πεπεισμένον the sum *agreed*, *BGU*1163.8 (i B.C.); συνεπείσθησαν πρὸς ἀλλήλας μὴ ἐγκαλεῖν *Sammelb.*7338.10 (iii/iv A.D.).

**σύμπειρος**, ον, *acquainted with*, ἀγωνίᾳ Pi.*N.*7.10.

**συμπείρω**, *pierce through together*, Plu.*Cam.*41, Q.S.1.612.

**συμπέμπω**, *send* or *dispatch along with* or *at the same time*, ὕμνον Pi.*I.*5(4).63; ὀπάονας A.*Supp.*493; πρεσβείαν *IG*2$^{2}$.1.24 (v B.C.): c. dat. pers., νεηνίας καὶ κύνας σ. ἡμῖν Hdt.1.36; τοῖσι παισὶ φύλακον Id.8.104, cf. 5.80, *PCair.Zen.*230.4 (iii B.C.), 2*Ep.Cor.*8.22; ἀγωγούς τινι Th.2.12; φύλακας X.*Cyr.*1.4.7, cf. *HG*1.4.21 (Pass.). 2. *help in conducting*, τὴν πομπήν Is.6.50, Lys.13.80; συμπέμψοντες τὴν Πυθαΐδα *SIG*697 B (Delph., ii B.C.).

**συμπενθέω**, trans., *join in mourning for*, τοὺς τεθνεῶτας Isoc.8.87, cf. Lycurg.43. II. intr., *mourn together*, τινι *with* one, A.*Ch.* 199: abs., E.*HF*1390, D.60.33.

**συμπένομαι**, Med., *to be poor along with* another *in* a thing, τινί τινος Pl.*Men.*71b.

**σύμπεντε**, *five together, by fives*, v.l. in Hyp.*Fr.*134.

**συμπεπαίνομαι**, Pass., *come to a head*, Hp.*Epid.*6.1.10, Ruf.ap. Orib.45.30.27:—Act., *bring to a head*, Ruf.*Ren.Ves.*2.8.

**συμπεπλεγμένως**, Adv., (συμπλέκω) *complicatedly*, Gal.19.489: c. dat., *in conjunction with*, Hermog.*Stat.*4.

**συμπεπτικός**, ή, όν, *promoting digestion, digestive*, Gal.14.694, 764. 2. *dissolving*, οἰδημάτων Dsc.2.86.

**συμπέπτω**, = συμπέσσω, Gal.12.101, v.l. for συμπέττω in Dsc.1.54.

⊛ **συμπεραίνω**, *accomplish jointly*, τι Isoc.4.171, v.l. in E.*Med.*887:—Med., συμπεραναμένων τῶν...συνεργῶν αὐτῷ τὴν πρὸς Θηβαίους ἔχθραν had *effectually helped* him *to create* the ill-feeling, D.18.163; ἀπέραντα ξυμπεραίνῃ Luc.*Philops.*9:—Pass., *to be accomplished simultaneously*, τὰ συμπερανθέντα τάχη Pl.*Ti.*39d. 2. *finish, work out*, ἐπειδὰν συμπεράνωμεν (-αίνωμεν codd.) τὸν...λόγον Gal.6.214:—Pass., ib.15. II. *decide* or *conclude absolutely*, ξ. φροντίδα make up one's mind, E.*Med.*341; σ. καὶ κλώθειν ἑκάστῳ τὰ οἰκεῖα Arist.*Mu.*401$^{b}$21; κλῇθρα μοχλοῖς *make* the doors *doubly sure* by bars, E.*Or.*1551 (troch.); ὁ συμπεραίνων (sc. ἀριθμός) the *last* counted, in a series, Speus.ap.*Theol.Ar.*62:—Pass., *to be quite finished*, X.*Cyr.*6.1. 31. 2. in Logic, Med. συμπεραίνεσθαι *conclude syllogistically, draw conclusions*, Arist.*APr.*57$^{b}$20, *EN*1094$^{b}$22:—Pass., *to be so concluded*, Id.*Ph.*186$^{a}$24; τὸ συμπερανθέν the *conclusion drawn*, Id. *EN*1146$^{a}$26; ἔστω συμπεπερασμένον Id.*APr.*42$^{a}$8; σ. τι κατά τινος ib.66$^{a}$38. III. intr. in Act., *extend equally far*, Id.*HA*541$^{a}$2.

**συμπεραι-όω**, *conclude along with* or *together*, διάνοιαν Demetr.*Eloc.* 2, cf. Stob.4.44.74:—Pass., *to be concluded together*, Ph.2.374, Nech. ap.Vett.Val.279.7, etc.; ἔν τινι Phot.*Bibl.* p.21 B. **-ωσις**, εως, ἡ, *conclusion, sum*, τῶν ἐτῶν Vett.Val.137.24.

**συμπεραν-τέον**, *one must conclude*, Gal.*Nat.Fac.*3.11. ⊛ **-τικός**, ή, όν, *tending to a conclusion*, only in Adv. -κῶς *in the form of a conclusion*, εἰπεῖν Arist.*SE*174$^{b}$11.

**συμπέρασ-μα**, ατος, τό, *finishing, end*, Ocell.1.3, Hierocl. *in CA* 20 p.463 M., Eust.73.27, etc.; τοῦ ἐνιαυτοῦ, τῶν ἑορτῶν, Ph.2.298, 278; of a letter, Jul.*Ep.*183. II. in Logic, *conclusion* in a syllogism, Arist.*APr.*30$^{a}$5, 42$^{a}$5 sq., *Top.*155$^{b}$23, al., *Stoic.*2.78, Gal.15. 550,633. 2. *subject of the conclusion*, Arist.*APr.*53$^{a}$17. III. Math., *conclusion* of a proposition, Procl. *in Euc.* p.75 F., al., Hero *Deff.*136.13. **-ματικός**, ή, όν, *indicating the conclusion*, of the particle ἄρα, Sch.E.*Hec.*511; of ὥστε, Simp. *in Ph.*335.31; σ. ὅρος definition *embodying conclusion* of syllogism, Asp. *in EN*49.3. Adv. -κῶς Arist.*Rh.*1401$^{a}$3. **-μός**, ὁ, f.l. for συμπέρασμα, Artem. 3.58.

**συμπερᾰτόω**, = συμπεραίνω, Phlp. *in de An.*588.4.

**συμπεράω**, *cross* a river *together*, Lex.ap.Plot. *de Pulchr.* p.134 Creuzer.

**συμπέρθω**, *destroy with* or *together*, E.*Hel.*106 (tm.).

**συμπερι-ᾰγής**, ές, *curved so as to coincide with*, τινι Ph.*Bel.*63. 27. **-άγνῡμαι**, Pass., *to be curved all round*, -νύμενος κόλπος Sch. D.P.121. **-άγω** [ᾰ], *carry about along with* or *together*, X.*Oec.*8. 12, Theo Sm.p.151 H.:—Pass., *to be so carried, go round with* or *together*, X.*Cyr.*4.3.1, Arist.*Mete.*344$^{a}$12; τῇ στρατιᾷ Arr.*An.*4.14.3:—Med., *lead about with oneself*, X.*Hier.*2.8, D.C.77.7, etc. **-ᾰγωγή**, ἡ, *revolution in the same sense with*, Simp. *in Cael.*500.19, Phlp. *in Mete.*90.25. **-ᾰγωγός**, ὁ, ἡ, *assistant in converting others*, Pl.*R.* 533d. **-αιρετέον**, *one must strip off*, Theon *Prog.* p.84 S. **-βάλλω**, *cover all round together*, Dsc.*Eup.*2.20, Gal.18(2).896. **-βομβέω**, *buzz about together*, Them.*Or.*2.36a. **-γίγνομαι**, aor. part. -γενόμενον glossed by συμπεριλαμβανόμενον, Hsch. **-γράφω** [ᾰ], *circumscribe* or *cancel together with*, τοῖς ἄλλοις ἑαυτήν S.E.*P.*1.14, cf. Plot.6.5.11. **-δῑνέομαι**, Pass., *to be whirled round with* or *together*, Ti.Locr.96d, Ach.Tat.*Intr.Arat.*39:—also **-δονέομαι**, Cass.*Pr.* 60. **-ειλέω**, *wrap round also*, Orib.49.28.10. **-ειμι**, (εἶμι *ibo*) *go round with*, κυνί X.*Cyn.*10.4, cf. Them.*Or.*25.310c: c. acc., τὸ τεῖχος Aen.Tact.38.2. **-έλκω**, *drag about together*, in Pass., c. dat., *PSI*5.495.16 (iii B.C.), *Placit.*2.20.13. **-ενεκτέον**, *one must accommodate oneself to*, ἀγνώμονι πατρί Socr.ap.Stob.4.25. 42. **-έρχομαι**, *go round together*, τὰς Ἄλπεις App.*BC*5.20 codd. (dub. l.); σ. τινί *go round with*.., Cleom.1.11. **-έχω**, *embrace in the same circuit*, D.H.3.43, in Pass. **-ζώννῠμαι**, Med., *gird round oneself, gird oneself with*, Ath.12.551d. **-θέω**, *revolve with*, M.Ant.7.47, Jul.*Or.*4.150b; *run about with*, ἄνω καὶ κάτω Luc.*Merc. Cond.*24; τινι App.*BC*4.18. **-ίπταμαι**, *fly about with*, ταῖς ἀκρίσιν Zos.1.57. **-ίσταμαι**, Pass., *close in, draw together*, Thphr.*HP*5. 5.2. **-κῑνέω**, *move round together*, Cass.*Pr.*27. **-κλείω**, *include together*, Sch.Luc.*Anach.*17, Tz.*H.*6.399. **-κομίζω**, *convey round with*, *IG*11(2).165.6 (Delos, iii B.C.). **-λαμβάνω**, *gather together*, τὸ τοῦ ἱματίου περικεχυμένον Sor.*Vit.Hippocr.*12; *enclose* or *include together*, [τοῖς νεύροις] ὀστᾶ καὶ μυελόν Pl.*Ti.*74d, cf. Hp.*Fist.*4; τὰ ᾠά Arist.*HA*549$^{a}$33; πολλὴν ἀναθυμίασιν Id.*Mete.* 358$^{a}$33:—Pass., Pl.*Ti.*83d. 2. *embrace, include*, τὰ γένη ib.58a; *comprehend* in a treaty *with* others, ἐν ταῖς συνθήκαις Philipp.ap.D. 18.77 (Pass.), cf. Decr.ap.eund.18.29, Epicur.*Nat.*28.9; *embrace in the same* history, Plb.8.11.4, cf. D.S.16.94, etc.:—Pass., ἐν τῷ λόγῳ συμπεριειλῆφθαι Arist.*Top.*142$^{a}$31, cf. Thphr.*HP*6.1.1, al.; ὅπως -ληφθῶμεν ἐν ταῖς συνθήκαις *SIG*591.64 (Lampsacus, ii B.C.). 3. in literal sense, *embrace*, *Act.Ap.*20.10. II. Med., *take part in together*, τινος Luc.*Dom.*4 codd. **-ληπτέον**, *one must include*, Thphr. *HP*6.6.1. **-λύω**, *release*, dub.l. in *POxy.*259.25 (i A.D.). **-νοέω**, *consider well with* or *together*, M.Ant.8.36. **-νοστέω**, *go round together with, follow along with*, τινι Luc.*Tox.*56, cf. Them.*Or.*11. 146a, etc.; σ. τῇ σκιᾷ τῆς γῆς Cleom.1.11; σ. ἡμῖν ὁ λόγος Paus.5. 14.10. **-οδεύω**, *come round together with*, ἀμπώτεις σ. τῇ σελήνῃ Arist.*Mu.*396$^{a}$26; *travel together with*, *PSI*5.502.15 (iii B.C.). II. Pass., *to be described at the same time*, c. dat., Str.17.1.1, 17.2. 1. **-πᾰτέω**, *walk round* or *about with*, τινι Pl.*Prt.*314e, Men.117: abs., τοὺς συμπεριπατοῦντας *their companions in walking round*, Arist. *Rh.*1409$^{b}$24, cf. J.*Vit.*63, Them.*Or.*22.269b. **-πέτομαι**, *fly about with*, ib.19.233a (with vv.ll.). **-πίπτω**, *fall about together*, Hypsaeus ap.Stob.4.31.45. **-πλᾰνάομαι**, Pass., *wander about together*, v.l. in Ph.1.16. **-πλέκω**, in Pass., *embrace*, ἐν ἀγάπαις Thd. *Pr.*7.18. **-πλέω**, *sail about with*, c. dat., App.*BC*5.96, Ps.-Hdt. *Vit.Hom.*8. **-πλοκή**, ἡ, *inter-connexion*, τῶν πραγμάτων Luc.*Hist. Conscr.*55. ⊛ **-ποιέω**, *help in procuring*, τὴν ἀρχήν τινι Plb.3.49.9, cf. D.S.11.81. **-πολέω**, *go round together with*, τοῖς ἄστροις Phld. *D.*3.9; τῷ ἡλίῳ *Cat.Cod.Astr.*1.136; *accompany*, Ph.1.16 (-πολη θείς, v.l. -πλανηθείς), Plu.2.745e, etc.:—hence **-πόλησις**, εως, ἡ, Procl. *in Alc.* p.138 C., Herm. *in Phdr.* p.92 A., Dam.*Pr.*370. ⊛ **-πολος**, ὁ, *fellow*-περίπολος, *Philol.*71.92 (Phocis, pl.), cf. Them.*Or.*13. 165b. **-σπάω**, *to circumflex also*, A.D.*Adv.*170.10:—Pass., c. dat., Id.*Synt.*335.18, *EM*171.39. **-σπωμένως**, Adv. *by reason of sharing the circumflex accent*, A.D.*Adv.*175. 23. **-στέλλω**, *help in cloaking*, ἁμαρτίας Plb.10.22.9. **-στρέφομαι**, Pass., *revolve along with*, τῷ οὐρανῷ, of the fixed stars, Arist. *Mu.*392$^{a}$10, cf. Gem.5.62; τὸ πῦρ τῇ δίνῃ Plu.2.927c; of pain in colic, Gal.8.384. **-τειχίζω**, *help in walling round*, Plu.*Tim.* 9. **-τίθημι**, *put round together*, σ. ὄγκον αὐτῷ καὶ δόξαν *take part in getting* honour for another, Id.*Nic.*5:—Pass., -τιθεμένων τῶν στεμφύλων τῷ ἀγγείῳ Dsc.1.57:—the Act. is dub. l. in Nech.ap.Vett. Val.290.21. **-τρέπω**, *overthrow together with*, ἑαυτήν τισι S.E.*P.* 2.188, cf. 193 (Pass.):—Pass. also, of leaves of heliotrope, τῇ τοῦ ἡλίου κλίσει Dsc.4.190 (v.l. -φερ-). **-τρέχω**, *run round together*, Luc.*Dem.Enc.*37, *Cat.Cod.Astr.*11(2).178. **-τρίβομαι** [τρῐ], *to be rubbed up together*, Gal.13.1041 (citing Dsc.1.57, where συμπεριτιθεμένων). **-τυγχάνω**, *fall in with at the same time*, τινι v.l. in X.*An.* 7.8.22. **-φαντάζομαι**, Med., *form conceptions of also*, M.Ant.10. 38. **-φερής**, ές, *circular*, χρῶμα, of the ἅλως, Olymp. *in Mete.*226. 20. ⊛ **-φέρω**, *carry round along with* or *together*, Pl.*R.*404c, Arist. *HA*548$^{a}$19, Thphr.*HP*7.5.2; οἱ συμπεριφέροντες τὴν ὄψιν ταχὺ σκοτοῦνται Id.*Vert.*7. II. Pass., *to be carried round together*, Pl.*R.* 617b; συμπεριφέρεσθαι περιφοράν Id.*Phdr.*248a; τὸν αὐτὸν κύκλον Epicur.*Ep.*2 p.53 U.; τοῖς φανεροῖς ἄστροις *with*.., *Placit.*2.13.9; τὰ ἀπλανῆ συμπεριφέρεται τῷ οὐρανῷ *Stoic.*2.195, cf. Theo Sm. p.134 H.; σ. [τοῦ ἡλιοσκοπίου] ἡ κόμη τῇ τοῦ ἡλίου κλίσει Dsc.4.164, cf. 190 (v.l. for -τρεπ-); τοῦ ὄμματος περιφερομένου συμπεριφέρεσθαι καὶ τὰς ὄψεις Hero *Deff.*135.10. 2. συμπεριφέρεσθαί τινι *go about with* one, *have intercourse with* one, *live in* his *society*, Plb.2.17.12, 4. 35.7, 5.15.2, Ath.12.548a, Hierocl. *in CA*9 p.432 M.; of a king's intercourse with a queen, D.S.17.77; of a queen's intercourse with her husband and her son, *OGI*308.13 (Hierapolis, ii B.C.); συμπεριενεχθῆναι εἴς τινα εὐχρώμως prob. in *PRyl.*237.8 (iii A.D.). 3. of circumstances, *accommodate* or *adapt oneself to*, τοῖς καιροῖς σ. πρὸς τὸ κράτιστον Aeschin.2.164, cf. *PEnteux.*45.6 (iii B.C.), *SIG*707.10 (Olbia, ii B.C.), *Inscr.Prien.*135 (i B.C.); ταῖς ἐνισχυούσαις δόξαις Phld.*Piet.*27; τοῖς πράγμασιν ἐλαφρῶς καὶ μετρίως Plu.2.468e; καλῶς -οισθησόμεθα τοῖς τῆς φύσεως Polystr.*Herc.*346 p.89 V.: abs., *show indulgence*, *IPE*1$^{2}$.32 *A* 31 (Olbia, iii B.C.), *Musée Belge* 11.99 (Ceos, iii B.C.), *OGI*244.16 (Daphne, ii B.C.): c. dat. pers., *PCair.Zen.* 367.10 (iii B.C.). 4. of things, *understand and follow, be conversant with*, τοῖς πολιτικοῖς πράγμασιν Phld.*Rh.*2.49 S.; τοῖς λεγομένοις, τοῖς παραγγελλομένοις, Plb.3.10.2, 10.23.9. **-φθείρομαι**, Pass., *go about with* any one *to one's own ruin*, Luc.*Pseudol.*18, Ath.7.289c; cf. φθείρω II. ⊛ **-φορά**, ἡ, *intercourse, companionship, society*, Plb.5.26.15, Phld.*Hom.* p.21 O., D.S.3.64: pl., *social intercourse*, Phld.*Ind.Sto.*3, *Cat.Cod.Astr.*8(4).178. 2. *accommodating temper, indulgence, complaisance*, *UPZ*110.44 (ii B.C.), Plb.1.72.2, 23.2.10, Plu.2.124b, *POxy.*1590.5 (iv A.D.); ἡ τῶν νόμων σ. Epicur.(?) *Oxy.*215 ii 7; κατὰ -ὰν λέγειν Phld.*Piet.*115; ἡ πρὸς τὰ τέκνα σ. καὶ ὁμόνοια *OGI*308.17 (Hierapolis, ii B.C.); ὄχλων Jul.*Or.*6.200c; σ. ποιεῖσθαι χρημάτων to be indulgent in demanding repayment, *IG*12(5).860.14 (Tenos, i B.C.). **-φορητός**, ή, όν, *accommodating, complaisant*, Apollon.*Lex.* s.v. συμφερτή. **-φράσσω**, *fence all round* or *together*, Arist.*Phgn.*$811^{a}8$ (v.l.).

**συμπερονάω**, *pin together*, χεῖρας θυρεοῖς συμπεπερονημένας Plu.*Crass.*25, cf. Apollod.*Poliorc.*168.6, Them.*Or.*21.253a.

**συμπέσσω**, Att. **-ττω**, *mature by heating, cooking*, ὁμαλῦναι καὶ συμπέψαι Arist.*Mete.*$381^{a}20$, cf. *HA*$625^{a}6$, Thphr.*HP*8.7.7; *concoct, bring to a head*, etc., Dsc.2.86, Gal.6.247,825, 15.889; *hatch* eggs, Arist.*HA*$549^{b}7$, cf. $560^{b}17$ (Pass.), *GA*$752^{b}17$; ἡ γῆ σ. τῇ θερμότητι ib.$753^{a}19$, cf. $752^{b}33$ (Pass.); *promote digestion*, Thphr.*HP*6.3.6, *Od.*49:—Pass., Arist.*PA*$677^{b}27$, *HA*$590^{a}21$; of food, *to be digested*, Id.*Mete.*$379^{b}23$.

**συμπετάννῡμι**, *spread out with* or *together*, Aen.Tact.37.9.

**συμπέτομαι**, *fly with* or *together*, Luc.*Musc.Enc.*6, Ael.*NA*2.48; νεβροῖς Philostr.*Im.*2.2.

**συμπεφορημένος**, *closely pressed together*, *Gloss.* Adv. -ως *eclectically*, σ. γέγραφε Thphr.*Fr.*41.

**σύμπεψις**, εως, ἡ, *concoction* of crude humours, Gal.17(2).712, 18(2).273, Alex.Trall.4.1.

**συμπηγ-ία**, ἡ, = συμπαγία, Heliod.ap.Orib.49.4.39, al., Gal.8.849. **-μα**, ατος, τό, *framework, superstructure*, Apollod.*Poliorc.*166.6, dub. l. in Ar.Byz.*Epit.*16.2. **-νῡμι** and **-ύω** (Arist.*Resp.*$472^{a}34$, Epicur.*Nat.*14.5):—*put together, construct, frame*, τάφον E.*Supp.*938; ψεύσταν λόγον Pi.*N.*5.29; στέγασμα Pl.*Ti.*73d; σύριγγα Theoc.8.23, etc.; τινὰ ἐξ ἄλλων Epicur. l.c.; τὴν οὐσίαν ἐκ.. Plu.2.1118e:—Med., *construct for oneself*, δίφρον Critias 2.11, cf. Luc.*DDeor.*25.3, *Am.*53; μηχανάς App.*Mith.*30. 2. Pass., with pf. 2 συμπέπηγα, *to be compounded*, Anaxag.4, Pl.*Ti.*46b; of the human frame, Hp.*VM*20, Them.*Or.*21.249c. II. *make solid, congeal, condense*, Il.5.902 (v. sub ἐπείγω III. 2); σ. τὸ σῶμα Arist. l.c., cf. Pl.*Ti.*85d:—Pass., with pf. 2, *become solid, to be condensed*, ib.59e,81b,91b, etc.; of calculi in the bladder, Hp.*Aër.*9.

**συμπήδημα**, ατος, τό, *a leap taken with* or *together*, Hsch. s.v. συνάλματα.

**σύμ-πηκτος**, ον, *put together, constructed, framed*, οἰκήματα σ. ἐξ ἀνθερίκων Hdt.4.190; πλαίσια ξ. *compact*, f.l. for ξύμπτυκτα in Ar.*Ra.*800. 2. *curdled*, σ. γάλα Philox.2.36. **-πηλόω**, *close up with clay*, Zos.Alch. p.226 B. **-πήξ**, ῆγος, ὁ, ἡ, = σύμπηκτος, Theognost.*Can.*40. **-πηξις**, εως, ἡ, *putting together, constructing, framing*, ξύλων Hdn.4.2.6; σύγκρασις καὶ σ. Plu.2.433d, cf. 95b; τοῦ σώματος Aristeas 155; τῆς λέξεως Phld.*Po.Herc.*994.34; of astrological tables, κανονικαὶ σ. Vett.Val.141.14. 2. *condensation, coagulation*, γόνου Hp.*Aër.*19; τοῦ ὑγροῦ Arist.*Mu.*$394^{a}35$. **-πήσσω**, later form for -πήγνυμι, Str.7.3.18 (Pass.), Dsc.4.9, Gal.*Thras.*27. **-πιαίνω**, v. συμπιέζω.

**συμπῐ-έζω** (for -πιάζω v. infr.), *press* or *squeeze together, grasp closely*, τὰς τρίχας Pl.*Phd.*89b; τι ταῖς χερσί Id.*Sph.*247c; σ. τὸ στόμα Ephipp.6.3, cf. Plu.2.580d (prob.); σ. χείλεα χείλεσι *AP*5.127 (Marc. Arg.); τὸ ἔλαττον σ. τὸ πλέον Arist.*Pr.*$929^{b}39$:—Pass., *to be squeezed up*, opp. διέλκεσθαι, X.*Mem.*3.10.7; σ. τὰς ἀκοάς Arist.*Pr.*$904^{a}21$; ἡ κοιλία σ. ταῖς πλευραῖς ib.$964^{b}3$; συμπιασθῆναι, of the body, *to be pinched in, grow lean*, Hp.*Epid.*7.68 (but, *to be fattened up*, from συμπιαίνω, acc. to Littré): aor. Pass. subj. 3 pl. συμπιεχθῶσιν αἱ δίοδοι Id.*Loc.Hom.*9; of an army, συνεπιέζετο τὰ μέσα D.C.36.49. **-εσις**, εως, ἡ, *compression*, Pl.*Cra.*427a, Gal.17(1).434. **-εσμα**, ατος, τό, *gathering, binding*, τὸ ὑπ' ἀγκάλῃ σ. τῶν δραγμάτων Eust.1162.26. **-εσμός**, ὁ, = συμπίεσις, S.E.*M.*9.82.

**συμπῑλ-έω**, *force together like felt*: generally, *compress*, Pl.*Ti.*45b:—more freq. in Pass., ib.49c, *Plt.*281a, Arist.*Ph.*$216^{a}31$, Hero *Spir.*1 *Prooem.*, etc.; τὰ λεῖα, κἂν..βίᾳ συμπιληθῇ, ῥᾳδίως ἀπολύεται Diocl.*Fr.*26; συμπεπιλημένος *of felted texture*, Thphr.*HP*3.7.5; θρὶξ συνεπιλήθη *was matted together*, Pl.*Ti.*76c; κόμη αὐχμηρὰ καὶ συμπεπιλημένη Luc.*Tox.*30; τὸ αὐτὸ μέγεθος οὐ δοκεῖ συμπιληθὲν γίνεσθαι βαρύτερον Arist.*Cael.*$305^{b}7$; ἀναπνοαὶ συμπεπιλημέναι, of Vesuvius, D.C.66.21; πορφύρα ἄκρατος συμπεπ. Plu.*Demetr.*41; of the intestines, *to be obstructed*, Hp.*Loc.Hom.*10, *Morb.*3.14. **-ησις**, εως, ἡ, *compression*, Poll.7.171. **-ητικός**, ή, όν, *apt to compress* or *close*, πόρων Ti.Locr.100e. **-όω**, = συμπιλέω, Sch.Od.21.122:—Pass., Dsc.1.7.

**συμπίνω** [ῑ], Aeol. imper. σύμπωθι Alc.54:—*drink together*, μετά τινος Hdt.2.121.δ', Ar.*Ach.*277; παρά τινι X.*Cyr.*5.2.28; σ. ἀλλήλοις εἰς μέθην Pl.*Min.*320a: abs., κᾆτά τις εἶπεν τῶν ξυμπινόντων Pherecr.153.5 (hexam.); συμπιεῖν καὶ συμφαγεῖν *SIG*1179.18 (Cnidus, Tab. Defix.); συμπίεσθε, ἢ οὔ; *will you..?* Pl.*Smp.*213a; συμπιεῖν δεινός Aeschin.2.52. 2. pf. part. Pass. συμπεπομένον *absorbed*, Ph.*Bel.*61.40. 3. *soak*, ἔασον συμπιεῖν ἡμέραν μίαν Dsc.1.25, cf. Bilabel 'Οψαρτ.p.10, *PHolm.*5.9, Cleopatra (?) ap.Paul.Aeg.3.2.6.

**συμπῑπίσκω**, *give to drink together*, ἀμεῖ τοὺς Λαβυάδας *Schwyzer* 323*D*48 (Delph., iv B.C.).

**συμπιπράσκω**, pf. -πέπρᾱκα *PGen.*23.8 (i A.D.):—*sell with* or *together*, in Pass., J.*AJ*12.4.4, App.*BC*4.24.

**συμπίπρημι**, *set fire to* or *burn at the same time*, πάντα J.*BJ*6.5.2: c. dat., Str.17.3.14:—Pass., Ph.2.565.

**συμπίπτω**, Ion. Iterat. συμπίπτεσκον Emp.59:—*f ll together, meet violently*, of winds, σὺν δ' Εὖρός τε Νότος τ' ἔπεσον Od.5.295; of two champions beginning to fight, *fall to, fight hand to hand*, σύν ῥ' ἔπεσον Il.7.256, 21.387; opp. distant fighting, συμπεσόντας αἰχμῇσι καὶ ἐγχειριδίοισι συνέχεσθαι Hdt.1.214, cf. 5.112, Pi.*I.*4(3).51(69), Luc.*Tox.*36; ἐς νείκεα σ. Hdt.3.120, 9.55; of a hound, σὺν δὲ πεσών *PCair.Zen.*532.7 (iii B.C.): c. dat. pers., ξυμπεσὼν μόνος μόνοις S.*Aj.*467; εἰς ἀγῶνα τῷδε συμπεσών Id.*Tr.*20; σ. πολεμίοις X.*Cyr.*2.1.11; εἰς μάχην θηρίῳ D.S.3.35; ἀντίοι σ. τοῖς ὑποζυγίοις Plb.3.51.5; of ships, λάβρῳ κλύδωνι σ. E.*IT*1393; ξυμπεσούσης νηῒ νεώς Th.7.63; ξ. πρὸς ἀλλήλας τὰς ναῦς Id.2.84. 2. generally, *fall in with, meet with*, esp. with accidents or misfortunes, c. dat. rei, ἀσιτίῃσι Hdt.3.52; φόνῳ S.*OT*113; κακοῖς τοιοῖσδε Id.*Aj.*429; but simply, *fall in with, meet*, τινι *UPZ*62.10 (ii B.C.), *PTeb.*58.56 (ii B.C.). II. of accidents, ailments, symptoms, events, *fall upon, happen to*, τοῖσιν αὐτουργίαι ξυμπέσωσιν μάταιοι A.*Eu.*337 (lyr.); ἐάν ποτέ σοι σ. καιρός Isoc.1.32; εὐπαιδίας τυχεῖν ἅμα καὶ πολυπαιδίας..καὶ τοῦτ' αὐτῷ συνέπεσεν Id.9.72; ἀσθένεια, νοσήματα σ. τινί, Pl.*Ti.*17a, 82c; συμπίπτει τοῖσι πλείστοισι τοιάδε· ἐρυθήματα προσώπου κτλ. Hp.*Acut.*(*Sp.*)6; πάθη D.26.18; ἡμῖν σ. πρὸς ἡμᾶς αὐτοὺς φιλία Pl.*Lg.*698c; σ. τι ἔς τινας Hdt.7.137. 2. abs., *happen, occur*, τῆς αὐτῆς ἡμέρης συμπιπτούσης τοῦ τε ἐν Πλαταιῇσι καὶ τοῦ ἐν Μυκάλῃ..τρώματος Id.9.100; τοιούτων καιρῶν συμπεσόντων Lys.19.24; τῶν κακῶν τῶν σ. Philem.101.[4]; of heavenly bodies, *coincide*, Vett.Val.190.9 (sed leg. συνεμπέσῃ). 3. c. part., like τυγχάνω, καὶ τόδε ἕτερον συνέπεσε γενόμενον Hdt.9.101; συνεπεπτώκεε ἔρις ἐοῦσα Id.1.82; 'Αρισταγόρῃ συνέπιπτε τοῦ αὐτοῦ χρόνου πάντα ταῦτα συνελθόντα Id.5.36; but part. is sts. omitted, ἐὰν ἴσοι συμπέσωσιν (sc. ὄντες) Arist.*Pol.*$1318^{a}39$. 4. freq. impers. or with neut. pron., *it happens, comes to pass*, folld. by inf., τόδε σφι ὧδε συμπέπτωκε γίνεσθαι Hdt.1.139; by ὥστε c. inf., Id.8.15,132,141; ξυνέπεσεν ἐς τοῦτο ἀνάγκης ὥστε.. matters *came to such a pass* that.., Th.1.49: or c. acc. et inf., συνέπιπτε [αὐτὸν] ἀπῖχθαι Hdt.5.35, cf. Th.4.68, etc.; πρὸ ρκ' ἐτῶν συνέπεσε κατ' αὐτὰς τὰς χειμερινὰς τροπὰς ἄγεσθαι τὰ Ἴσια Gem.8.21: c. dat. et inf., ὅσαις ἂν .. συμπέσῃ ἐμέσαι Arist.*HA*$588^{a}1$; ὅταν ἀτυχεῖν σοι συμπέσῃ τι Philippid.18; εἴ τινι συνέπεσε τὸν ἀδελφεὸν ἀπολέσθαι *SIG*306.7 (Tegea, iv B.C.): abs., ἀπὸ ταὐτομάτου, ἀπὸ τύχης, διὰ τύχην σ., Arist.*Cael.*$289^{b}22$, *Rh.*$1385^{b}2$, *Pol.*$1270^{b}20$; τὰ συμπίπτοντα one's *lot* or *fortune*, E.*Fr.*572, cf. Isoc.2.35; πρὸς τὸ συμπῖπτον ἀεὶ διατάττων X.*Cyr.*8.5.16; τὸ συμπεσόν the *incident*, Arist.*Pol.*$1284^{a}32$; καθάπερ ἐν κατάρροις ἐνίοτε συμπίπτει Gal.16.527, cf. 18(2).185, al. III. *coincide, agree* or *be in accordance with*, σ. τούτοισι τόνδε τὸν λόγον Hdt.7.151; ὥστε σ. τὸ πάθος τῷ χρηστηρίῳ *turned out in accordance with* it, Id.6.18: abs., *agree by chance*, Id.2.49; εἰς ταὐτὸν σ. *agree* in one, Pl.*Tht.*160d, *R.*473d, etc.; ἐμοὶ σὺ συμπέπτωκας ἐς ταὐτὸν λόγου *have come to exactly* the same point with me, E.*Tr.*1036. IV. *fall together*, i.e. *fall in*, esp. of a house, συμπίπτει στέγη Id.*HF*905; πόλις ὑπὸ σεισμοῦ ξυμπεπτωκυῖα Th.8.41; οἰκία σ. X.*An.*5.2.24; φοβουμένη μὴ συμπέσῃ [τὸ ἰσιεῖον] *PEnteux.*6.3 (iii B.C.); esp. of the vessels of the body, *fall in, collapse*, Hp.*Off.*13, Sor.1.16, al.; οἱ κρόταφοι συμπίπτουσι Gal.18(2).29; μυκτῆρες συμπεπτωκότες, opp. ἀναπεπταμένοι, X.*Eq.*1.10; σῶμα συμπεσόν a frame *fallen in* or *emaciated*, Pl.*Phd.*80c; ὀφθαλμοὶ σ. Arist.*HA*$561^{a}21$; αἱ κοιλίαι σ. τοῦ νέφους Id.*Pr.*$940^{b}31$, al.; of plant-structures, Thphr.*CP*1.4.4; *collapse*, of animals, *PSI*6.584.25 (iii B.C.); of the heart, *contract*, Ruf.*Syn.Puls.*3.6; συνέπεσε τῷ προσώπῳ his face *fell*, Lxx *Ge.*4.5; τὸ πρόσωπον συνέπεσεν ib.1*Ki.*1.18; -πέπτωκα τῇ καρδίᾳ ἀπὸ μερίμνης ib.1*Ma.*6.10. 2. σταφυλὴ λευκὴ συμπεπτωκυῖα *dried* grapes, Aët.9.30; πάντα δεδομένα κρέα συμπεπτωκότα ἔστω μέχρι δυοῖν ἡμερῶν *hung*, ibid. V. *fall together, fall into the same line*, σ. ἐπ' ἀλλήλων ὑπὸ στενοχωρίας *impinge* one on another, Pl.*Tht.*195a; *converge, meet*, τὸ τὰς παραλλήλους σ. οἴεσθαι Arist.*APo.*$77^{b}23$, cf. Euc.1*Def.*23, Archim.*Spir.*20, al.; οἱ πόροι παρ' ἀλλήλους εἰσὶ καὶ οὐ σ. Arist.*HA*$495^{a}15$; of the sides of a triangle, Plb.2.14.5; of a river, σ. τῷ Κηφισῷ Plu.*Sull.*16.

**συμπιστεύω**, *believe* or *trust along with*, J.*BJ*1.26.5.

**συμπιστόομαι**, Med., *confirm*, τὸ δόγμα S.E.*M.*1.271.

**συμπίτνω**, poet. for συμπίπτω, *fall* or *dash together*, of waves, A.*Pr.*432 (lyr.). II. *concur*, πολλοὶ γὰρ εἰς ἓν συμπίτνουσιν ἵμεροι Id.*Ch.*299; δίκᾳ..οὐ σ. κακόν E.*Hec.*1029 (lyr., dub. l.); δεινόν γε, θνητοῖς ὡς ἅπαντα σ. ib.846; μοι ἐς ταὐτὸν..σ. *meets* me *exactly here*, ib.966.

**συμπλάζομαι**, f.l. in S.*Fr.*373.5 for συνοπάζεται.

**συμπλᾰνάομαι**, *wander about with*, τινι D.S.3.59, Plu.*Ant.*29, Philostr.*Ep.*56: metaph., ταῖς ἀγνοίαις..τῶν συγγραφέων Plb.3.21.10.

**σύμπλᾰνος**, ον, *wandering about together*, κώμων σ. Νύξ Night *the fellow-roamer* of revelry, *AP*5.164 (Mel.), cf. 190 (Id.), 6.248 (Marc. Arg.).

**συμπλᾰσις**, εως, ἡ, = *confictio*, *Gloss.*

**συμπλάσσω**, Att. **-ττω**, pf. -πέπλᾰκα prob. cj. in J.*Ap.*2.2:—*moula* or *fashion together*, γαίης of clay, Hes.*Th.*571, cf. Hermipp.41; of bees, Arist.*HA*$628^{a}34$, *GA*$761^{a}7$; of Prometheus, τὸν ἄνθρωπον Aristid.*Or.*42(6).7:—Pass., σησαμῆ ξυμπλάττεται Ar.*Pax* 869; τῶν ἐντὸς [τῆς κνήκου]..μέλιτι συμπλασθέντων Diocl.*Fr.*140. 2. of speakers and writers, συνομολογοῦντες καὶ σ. *by agreeing on* an hypothesis and *a fiction*, Pl.*Chrm.*175d:—Med., συγγράφεσθαι καὶ συμπλάττεσθαι D.C.50.5. **3.** metaph., *feign* or *fabricate together*, αἰτίας καὶ ἐγκλήματα D.36.16; σ. ἑαυτῷ ἐνύπνιον Aeschin.3.77.

**συμπλαστεύω**, *fashion, mould*, or *construct with*, c. dat. et acc., *PSI*2.171.19 (ii B.C.).

**συμπλᾰτᾰγέω**, *sound by striking together*, χερσί *clap* with the hands, Il.23.102 (v.l. συμπατάγησεν); ῥαδινὰς συμπλαταγεῖτε χέρας *Ath.Mitt.*17.272 (Athens, ii A.D.); χεῖρας Tz.*H.*9.631: intr., χειρῶν συμπλαταγουσῶν v.l. for συμπατ- in S.E.*M.*6.20. **2.** *sound together with*, ἱππείῳ χρεμετισμῷ κελάδημα σ. λεόντων Nonn.*D.*43.202.

**συμπλέγδην**, Adv. *by plaiting together*, Nonn.*D.*10.158.

❀ **σύμπλεγμα**, ατος, τό, *entanglement*, name of a sculptured group representing a pair of wrestlers *with their limbs entwined*, *OGI*481.5 (Ephesus, ii A.D.); of an erotic subject, Plin.*HN*36.24,35.

**συμπλείονες**, neut. -ονα, *several together*, Arist.*Pol.*1286$^b$36; σύντρεις καὶ σ. Aristid.*Or.*23(42).32; συμπλέονες πόλιες *SIG*56.31 (Argos, v B.C.).

**συμπλεκ-ής**, ές, *entwined, entangled*, Nonn.*D.*3.27, al. **-τειρα**, ἡ, f.l. for συμπαίκτειρα (q.v.). **-τέον**, *one must mix*, μέλιτι γάλα Sor.1.87. **-τῐκός**, ή, όν, *twining* or *plaiting together*, Pl.*Plt.*282d; ἡ σ. τέχνη Poll.7.207. **2.** Gramm., σ. σύνδεσμος a *copulative* conjunction, Chrysipp.*Stoic.*2.68, D.T.642.24, A.D.*Adv.*218.14, al. Adv. -κῶς Id.*Synt.*9.22. **-τος**, ον, *plaited*, Lxx*Ex.*36.31 (39.23); *twined together*, ἔρνεσι *AP*4.1.18 (Mel.). **-ω**, 2 aor. Pass. συνεπλάκην [ᾰ] and συνεπλέκην (v. infr. II. 1 and 2):—*twine* or *plait together*, συνδεῖν καὶ σ. Pl.*Plt.*309b; στέφανον Plu.*Eum.*6; σὺν δ' ἀναμὶξ πλέξας ἶριν *having twined* the iris therewith, *AP*4.1.9 (Mel.); ἄτριον κερκίδι Theoc.18.34; τὼ χεῖρε ἐς τοὐπίσω ξυμπλέκοντες *joining* their hands behind them, Th.4.4; σ. τινὶ τὰς χεῖρας *join hands, become intimate* with one, Plb.2.45.2, cf. 47.6; so σ. σπέρμα καὶ γάμους τέκνων E.*Fr.*326.5: abs., πλάταισιν ἐσχάταισι σ. perh. *binding* the whole *together*, Id.*IA*292 (lyr.):—Pass., *to be twined together, plaited*, ἐκ τῶν θαλλῶν Din.1.18; ἡ ψυχὴ διὰ τὸ συμπεπλέχθαι πρὸς τὸ σῶμα Arist. *de An.*406$^b$28, cf. *Placit.*1.7.31; πρὸς ἄλληλα Pl.*Ti.*80c; λύγοισι σῶμα συμπεπλεγμένοι E.*Cyc.*225; ὅταν συμπλακῇ [τὰ στελέχη] when they *are twisted together*, Thphr.*CP*5.5.4; ἴχνη συμπεπλεγμένα tracks *entangled, crossing in different directions*, opp. ὀρθά, X.*Cyn.*5.6. **2.** *combine* notions logically under one term, σ. εἰς τὸ αὐτὸ κίνησιν καὶ ἀριθμόν Arist. *de An.*409$^b$11, cf. *EN*1119$^b$30; *join* words so as to form a proposition, σ. τὰ ῥήματα τοῖς ὀνόμασι Pl.*Sph.*262d, cf. *Tht.*202b:—Pass., ἔκ τινος Id.*R.*533c; of words, opp. ἁπλῶς λέγεσθαι (to be used singly), Arist.*Ph.*195$^b$15, cf. *Metaph.*1014$^a$13; κατηγορίαι συμπεπλεγμέναι *complex*, opp. ἁπλαῖ, Id.*APr.*49$^a$8, cf. *Int.*16$^a$23, *PA*643$^b$30; περὶ τοῦ -πεπλεγμένου on the *compound sentence*, title of work by Chrysipp., *Stoic.*2.68. **3.** more generally, εὖ τοῖς ὀνόμασι σ. τοὺς νόμους *mix up* or *interweave* the laws with rhetorical ornament, D.58.41; σ. τὰς πίστεις τῶν ἀσθενῶν τοῖς προτεινομένοις *combines* the proof of the weak points with.., D.H.*Rh.*8.5; cf. συμπλοκή; σ. πράξεις *connect, involve* them *in mutual relations*, Plb.5.105.4, D.S.16.42; [συμπτώματα] Gal.18(2).157; but σ. ἀλλήλαις τὰς πράξεις *mix* them *up, confuse* them in a narrative, Plb.5.31.4, cf. Vett.Val.352.27; ἑτερογενῆ σημεῖα συμπλέκων Gal.16.747. **4.** *mix* ingredients, Sor.1.77, Gal.12.647:—Pass., Arist.*Ph.*189$^b$5, Philum.ap.Orib.45.29.59. **II.** Pass., of persons wrestling, *to be intertwined, locked together* (cf. σύμπλεγμα), συμπλεκέντος Γωβρύεω τῷ Μάγῳ Hdt.3.78, cf. Gal.15.124: generally of combatants, *to be engaged in close fight*, συμπλακέντες διαγωνίζεσθαι D.9.51, cf. Plb.1.28.2, Luc.*Symp.*44; σ. τοῖς πολεμίοις Plb.3.69.13; πρὸς τὴν οὐραγίαν Id.4.11.7; of a ship, *to be entangled* with her opponent, Hdt.8.84, Plb.1.23.6: metaph., *to be at grips with*, συμπλακέντα τῇ Σκυθῶν ἐρημίᾳ (i.e. Euathlus) Ar.*Ach.*704; συμπεπλέγμεθα ξένῳ *we are entangled* or *engaged with* him, E.*Ba.*800, cf. Aeschin.2.153; περὶ τὸ βῆμα τῷ Περικλεῖ Plu.*Per.*11; of war, ἐπειδὰν ὅμορος πόλεμος συμπλακῇ D.2.21; of disputes, etc., *to be involved in*, λοιδορίαις σ. Pl.*Lg.*935c; ταῖς μάχαις, τοῖς πολιτικοῖς πράγμασιν, Phld.*Mus.*p.27 K., *Rh.*1.11 S., cf. *BGU*1011 iii 7 (iii B.C.); σ. τοῖς Στωικοῖς Luc.*Symp.*30; σ. καὶ μεμψιμοιρεῖν Plb.18.8.3. **2.** of sexual intercourse, Θέτιδι συμπλακείς S.*Fr.*618; συμπλέκεσθαι ἀλλήλοις *to be locked together*, Pl.*Smp.*191a, cf. e; in Arist. of animals, *HA*541$^b$3, 542$^a$16. **3.** Astrol., *enter into combination*, τῇ Σελήνῃ ὁ τοῦ Διὸς σ. Vett.Val.120.2.

**σύμπλεξις**, εως, ἡ, *an inclusive term*, Arist.*PA*644$^a$4; cf. foreg. I. 2. **2.** *complexity* of the pulse, Gal.9.50.

**σύμπλεος**, α, ον, *quite full*, τινος of a thing, Hp.*Flat.*3 cod.M; Att. **σύμπλεως** X.*An.*1.2.22.

**σύμπλευρος**, ον, *side by side*, λίθοι *Milet.*7.57 (Didyma), *Rev.Phil.*43.199,202 (ibid.).

**συμπλέω**, *sail in company with*, τινι Hdt.4.149, 5.46, E.*IA*102; ἐν τῇ Ἀργοῖ Hdt.4.179; μετὰ τῶν ὁλκάδων Th.6.44: abs., Id.1.27, Antipho 5.20, prob. in *IG*1$^2$.99.10; τῶν συμπλεόντων Pl.*Grg.*511e; συμπλέοντες ναῦται *IG*3.236: metaph., σ. τοῖς φίλοισι δυστυχοῦσι E.*HF*1225.

**συμπληγάς**, άδος, ἡ, *striking* or *dashing together*, πέτραι Συμπληγάδες the *clashing* rocks, i.e. the Κυάνεαι νῆσοι, which were supposed to close in on all who sailed between them (also called συνδρομάδες), E.*IT*355, cf. Str.1.2.10, 3.2.12; Κυάνεαι σ. π. E.*Med.*1263 (lyr.); Συμπληγάδες (sc. πέτραι) ib.2, *IT*260,1389: sg., κυανέαν Συμπληγάδα ib.241; Ἄξενον .. ἐκπερᾶσαι ποντίαν Ξυμπληγάδα, of the passage out of the Euxine (ποντιᾶν Ξυμπληγάδων Herm.), Id.*Andr.*794 (lyr.). **II.** as Subst., *collision, conflict*, Arist.*Mu.*392$^b$13, Him.*Or.*19 tit.

❀ **συμπλήγδην**, Adv. *with clapping of hands*, Theoc.24.56.

**συμπληθ-ύνω** [ῡ], *help to increase*, X.*Oec.*18.2. **2.** Pass., *to be multiplied as well as*, c. dat., Procl. *in Prm.*p.546 S. **II.** *give plural form to as well*, σ. τῷ ὀνόματι τὸ ἄρθρον A.D.*Synt.*54.17:—Pass., *take plural forms*, ib.205.1. **-ύω**, *help to fill* or *increase*, ποταμόν Hdt.4.48, cf. 50; *multiply*, τὰς ἀτυχίας Longin.23.3; τὸ γένος, τὴν πατρίδα, D.C.52.42, 56.2.

**συμπλημμελέω**, *sin together with*, τινι Aq., Sm., Thd., Quint.*Ho.*4.15.

**σύμπληξις**, εως, ἡ, *collision*, Demetr.*Eloc.*207; *concurrence*, τῶν δύο [ὀνομάτων] ib.105.

**συμπλήρ-ης**, ες, = σύμπλεος, Pl.*Epin.*985b; *solid*, Thphr.*HP*4.11.10. **-όω**, *help to fill*, σ. τοῖσι Ἀθηναίοισι τὰς νέας *help* them *in manning*.., Hdt.8.1. **II.** *fill up* or *completely*, ἑξήκοντα ναῦς *man* them *fully*, Th.6.50, cf. *Hell.Oxy.*14.1; σ. τὸ περιηγηθέν Pl.*Lg.*770b; τὸν μεταξὺ τόπον, τὸ μ., Arist.*Mete.*340$^a$18, *PA*694$^b$1, cf. Pl.*Smp.*202e, *IG*2$^2$.1668.71; τοὺς πόρους Thphr.*Od.*45, Diocl.*Fr.*147; ἔρανον Plu.2.694b:—Med., σ. τὰ διαστήματα Pl.*Ti.*35c, cf. 36b; τριήρεις *Hell.Oxy.*2.4:—Pass., τὸ δὲ [τῆς σύριγγος] πάλιν ξυμπληρωθείη Hp.*Fist.*4; πάντα συμπεπλήρωται σαρξίν Pl.*Ti.*75a; εὐδαιμονία Phld.*D.*1.2; σ. ἔκ τινων Ti.Locr.105a, D.S.1.2; ὑπό τινων Archim.*Eratosth.*3. **b.** Medic., *cause congestion of*, τὰ ὑποθυμιάματα σ. τὴν κεφαλήν Sor.1.72:—Pass., *suffer from congestion of the brain*, *IG*4$^2$(1).126.28 (Epid., ii A.D.), Gal.15.902. **2.** *complete*, τὸ ὅλον Arist.*GC*336$^b$31; ἔν τι τῶν συμπληρούντων τοῦτο Plot.1.8.3, cf. 2.6.1; τὰ συμπληροῦντα τὴν ἀρίστην μαῖαν the qualities *which make up the complete* good midwife, Sor.1.4, cf. Gal.6.166, *UP*1.9:—Pass., [δένδρα] συμπεπληρωμένα πᾶσι τοῖς οἰκείοις μορίοις, opp. ἀρχόμενα φύεσθαι, Id.16.492, cf. 526,685, Ath.15.671a. **3.** *fulfil, attain*, τὸ τῆς φύσεως τέλος Polystr.*Herc.*346 p.86 V.:—Med., τὸ τῆς ψυχῆς καὶ τοῦ σώματος ἀγαθόν Epicur.*Ep.*3 p.62 U.:—Pass., Polystr.p.31 W. **4.** *finish*, περὶ τοῦ λίαν ὀξέος ὀξυμέλιτος συμπληρώσας τὸν λόγον Gal.15.683, cf. 572. **-ωμα**, ατος, τό, *blocking* or *filling up* of a body, Arist.*Pr.*901$^a$4, Epicur.*Ep.*1 p.11 U. **-ωματικῶς**, Adv. *by way of supplement*, Sch.Od.8.567 ap.*An.Par.*3.457, Eust. ad D.P.41. **-ωσις**, εως, ἡ, *completion*, τῆς εὐδαιμονίας Plb.5.90.4; ἐτῶν Lxx 2*Ch.*36.21; *filling up*, φρέατος Str.3.5.7; *blocking* of blood-vessels, Heliod.ap.Orib.47.14.4; σ. ἀπὸ πάντων *aggregation* of all.., Longin.12.2. ❀ **-ωτικός**, ή, όν, *able to complete, forming an essential part of*, ὑγιείας Epicur.*Ep.*3 p.64 U.; εὐδαιμονίας, τελειότητος, *Stoic.*3.18,35; τῆς ἐννοίας ἢ τῆς οὐσίας Gal.6.200, cf. Plot.2.6.1, 6.2.15. **2.** *causing congestion*, τῆς κεφαλῆς Antyll.ap.Orib.6.1.8, Sor.1.119: abs., σ. τὸ καστόριον Id.2.85.

**συμπλήσσομαι**, Med., ἡ ζωτικὴ δύναμις πρὸς ἐλάχιστον συμπληξαμένη *reduced*, Marcellin.*Puls.*407.

**συμπλοϊκός**, ή, όν, *sailing with* or *together*, φιλία friendship *of shipmates*, Arist.*EN*1161$^b$13.

❀ **συμπλοκή**, ἡ, *intertwining, complication, combination*, τῇ [τῶν ἀτόμων] συμπλοκῇ.. πάντα γεννᾶσθαι Democr.ap.Arist.*Cael.*303$^a$7, cf. Thphr.*Sens.*66, Sor.2.4; used by Pl. as a generic term for *weaving* and its kindred arts, *Plt.*281a, cf. 306a, al.; ἡ ἁπάντων πρὸς ἄλληλα σ. Plb.1.4.11, cf. Phld.*Sign.*37, *D.*3.8 (pl.); συνέχεια καὶ σ. Plot.3.1.4; εἱμαρμένη defined as σ. αἰτιῶν, *Stoic.*2.284. **2.** *struggle*, esp. of wrestlers, ἡ ἐν ταῖς σ. μάχη a close struggle, Pl.*Lg.*833a, cf. Plb.1.15.3, Gal.15.126,197; of ships, *close engagement*, Plb.1.27.12, 1.28.11, *SIG*567.11 (Calymna, iii B.C.); of cavalry, Onos.10.6. **3.** *embrace, sexual intercourse*, Pl.*Smp.*191c, Arist.*HA*540$^b$21, Corn.*ND*24, Sor.1.31, al. **4.** *combination* of letters to form a word or of words to form a proposition, Pl.*Plt.*278b sq.; λόγος ἐγένετο.. ἡ πρώτη σ. Id.*Sph.*262c, cf. *Tht.*202b, D.H.*Pomp.*6; σ. τῶν ὀνομάτων Demetr.Lac.*Herc.*1113.2, cf. Phld.*Po.*2.33, al.; also *combination* of mental acts so as to form one entity, οὐδὲ σ. δόξης καὶ αἰσθήσεως φαντασία ἂν εἴη Arist. *de An.*428$^a$25, cf. *PA*643$^b$16; *combination* of subject and predicate, σ. γὰρ νοημάτων ἐστὶ τὸ ἀληθὲς ἢ ψεῦδος Id. *de An.*432$^a$11, cf. *Top.*113$^a$1; κατὰ συμπλοκὴν λέγεσθαι, opp. ἄνευ συμπλοκῆς, Id.*Cat.*1$^a$16, cf. *Stoic.*2.69, etc. **5.** Gramm., the *copula*, D.H.*Dem.*9. **6.** Rhet., *interweaving* of various styles, Id.*Rh.*8.8: but also name of a rhet. figure, Alex.*Fig.*p.30 S. **7.** Medic., of ingredients, μετὰ τῆς πρὸς τοὺς φοίνικας σ. *in combination with*.., Sor.1.50, cf. 115.

**σύμπλοκος**, ον, *entwined, interwoven, involved*, Nonn.*D.*12.339, *AP*5.254.13 (Paul. Sil.), 289 (Id.).

**σύμπλοος**, ον, contr. **-πλους**, ουν, (πλέω) *sailing with* one in a ship, *shipmate*, Hdt.2.115, 3.41, Ephor.27 J., Plu.2.148a; τινι E.*Hel.*1207, Antipho 5.21, etc.; σύμπλοι ἢ συστρατιῶται Pl.*R.*556c; poet. of ships, ναῦς σ. εἰς ἄγρην *AP*7.381 (Etrusc.), cf. 585 (Jul.). **2.** metaph., *partner* or *comrade* in a thing, πάθους S.*Ant.*541.

**σύμπνευσις**, εως, ἡ, = *conspiratio*, *Gloss.*

**συμπνευσμός**, ὁ, = σύμπνοια, Hsch.; *conspiracy*, ἐπὶ ψευδολογίᾳ τινός J.*AJ*17.12.2.

**συμπνέω**, poet. **-πνείω** *Supp.Epigr.*7.12.11 (Susa, i B.C.):—*breathe together with*, τινι M.Ant.8.54, *AP*7.595 (Jul.): metaph., ἐμπαίοις τύχαισι συμπνέων *going along with* the sudden blasts of fortune, *yielding* or *bowing* to them, A.*Ag.*187 (lyr.); συμπνέον τῇ ὀργῇ, gloss on ἔγχεος ζακότοιο, Sch.Pi.*N.*6.90. **2.** abs., *coalesce, achieve unity*, Pl.*Lg.*708d, Arist.*Pol.*1303$^a$26, Plu.*Comp.Lyc.Num.*4; συμπνευσάντων ἡμῶν καὶ Θηβαίων D.18.168; οἱονεὶ σ. ἐς γάμον Ael.*NA*3.44.

**συμπνῑγής**, ές, *choking by pressure*, περίστασις D.S.3.51.

**συμπνίγω** [ῑ], *press closely*, of crowds, τινα *Ev.Luc.*8.42; σ. τὸ σπέρμα *choke* it, *Ev.Marc.*4.7: metaph., σ. τὸν λόγον *Ev.Matt.*13.22, cf. *Ev.Luc.*8.14:—Pass., δένδρα συμπνιγόμενα Thphr.*CP*6.11.6; οἱ ἄνθρακες συμπνίγονται *are damped down*, Sch.Ar.*Nu.*96. 2. in Pass., *to be drowned*, of the Gadarene swine, Porph.*Chr.*49.

**συμπνοή**, ἡ, = *conspiratio*, *Gloss.*

**σύμπνοια**, ἡ, *breathing together*, τῶν φυσῶν Artem.2.37: metaph., *agreement, union*, D.L.2.137, Hdn.7.6.3, Jul.*Or.*6.189a, Iamb.*Myst.* 5.26; of the body, joined with σύρροια, Hp.*Alim.*23; ἡ τῶν οὐρανίων πρὸς τὰ ἐπίγεια σ. Chrysipp.*Stoic.*2.172; ἡ ἁπάντων σ. Aret.*CD*2.5, cf. Plot.2.3.7, Dam.*Pr.*88, Aen.Gaz.*Thphr.* p.49 B.

**σύμπνοος**, ον, contr. **-πνους**, ουν, (πνοή) *concordant*, Plu.2.574e; *agreeing with, in accord with*, τινι *AP*6.227 (Crin.), 11.372 (Agath.); *accordant*, Plu.2.618d, Aret.*SA*1.10, etc.; *animated by one spirit*, σ. καὶ σύρρουν ἐστὶ τὸ σῶμα Gal.*Nat.Fac.*1.12; *animated by a common* πνεῦμα, κόσμος σ. αὑτῷ Chrysipp.*Stoic.*2.264.

**συμποδηγ-ετέω**, *join in guiding*, S.*Ichn.*163. **-έω**, *conduct* or *lead together*, Pl.*Plt.*269c, 270a.

**συμποδ-ίζω**, *tie the feet together, bind hand and foot*, τινα Ar.*Ra.* 1512; σ. τινὰ χεῖράς τε καὶ πόδας καὶ κεφαλήν Pl.*R.*615e; cf. συμπεδάω:—Pass., ἀμφοῖν ποδοῖν σ. Luc.*Ocyp.*149; *to be entangled in a net*, of dogs, X.*Mem.*3.11.8. II. metaph., *entangle, enchain*, μέθη τινὰ Pl.*R.*488c:—Pass., ὑπό τινος σ. ἐν τοῖς λόγοις Id.*Grg.*482e, cf. *Tht.*165e. ⊛ **-ισμός**, ὁ, gloss on ὑφεσμός, Hsch. (pl.).

**συμποιέω**, *help* or *assist in doing*, τι And.1.62, Is.8.16; συμποιοῦντος αὐτοῖς καὶ Φίλωνος *PEnteux.*55.9, cf. 83.6 (iii B.C.); v. σύν C. II. *compose jointly with*, τοὺς Ἱππέας ξυνεποίησα τῷ φαλακρῷ τούτῳ (i.e. Eupolis *in partnership with* Aristophanes) Eup.78 (troch.); Εὐριπίδῃ ..συνεποίεις..τὴν τραγῳδίαν Ar.*Fr.*580, cf. *Th.*158; of a sculptor, συμποιεῖσθαι ἄγαλμα μετά τινος Sch.Ar.*Nu.*857.

**συμποικίλλομαι**, Pass., *to be wrought in with*, J.*AJ*3.7.5. 2. *vary with*, τοῖς μερικοῖς πράγμασι Sch.Ptol.*Tetr.*19.

**συμποιμαίνω**, *to be a shepherd with*, τισι J.*AJ*1.19.3:—Pass., *feed together, herd together*, E.*Alc.*579 (lyr., tm.).

**συμπολεμέω**, *join in war*, Th.1.18, 8.46, And.3.24, X.*HG*6.5.28, etc.; Κύρῳ πρὸς αὐτόν Id.*An.*1.4.2; μεθ' ἡμῶν Pl.*R.*422d; σ. τὸν πόλεμον D.18.87, *SIG*529.7 (Dyme, iii B.C.).

**συμπολίζω**, *unite into one city*, Pass., τῶν ἑπτὰ λόφων συμπεπολισμένων τῇ Ῥώμῃ D.H.1.71, cf. 32, Corn.*ND*20; Αἴγιον ἐξ ἑπτὰ δήμων συνεπολίσθη Str.8.3.2. 2. *cover with buildings*, τὰ προσάρκτια J.*BJ*5.4.2. 3. *join in building*, Id.*AJ*15.8.5. 4. *rebuild*, Id.*BJ*1. 8.4 (Pass.).

**συμπολιορκέω**, *join in besieging, besiege jointly*, Hdt.1.161, *IG*1$^2$. 108.40 (prob.), Th.8.15, D.23.131, *IG*2$^2$.666.14, etc.:—Pass., Th.3. 20,68, Plb.2.7.8.

**συμπολῑτ-εία**, ἡ, *federal union* of several states, *with interchange of civic rights, confederacy*, τῶν Ἀχαιῶν Plb.3.5.6, cf. 2.41.12, 44.5, D.S.29.18. 2. *sharing of political life*, Phld.*Mus.* p.93 K. (pl.). **-ευσις**, εως, ἡ, *fellow-citizenship*, *IG*4$^2$(1).59.12 (Epid., iii B.C.). ⊛ **-εύω**, *live as fellow-citizens* or *members of one state*, τισι with others, Th.6.4, 8.47,73; νόμοις τοῖς αὐτοῖς χρῆσθαι καὶ σ. X.*HG* 5.2.12, cf. *IG*9(1).32.6 (Stiris, ii B.C.):—Med. συμπολιτεύομαι, Lys. 9.21, *IG*4$^2$(1).59.12 (Epid., iii B.C., prob.), Epicur.*Sent.*38, etc.; θεοῖς καὶ ἀνθρώποις Phld.*Piet.*14; μηδενί *with* no one, D.*Prooem.*21; μετὰ τῶν Ἀχαιῶν Plb.22.8.9; οἱ συμπολιτευόμενοι *one's fellow-citizens*, Isoc.3.4, 12.29; ὁ δῆμος καὶ οἱ -πολιτευόμενοι Ῥωμαῖοι *Supp. Epigr.*6.646 (Adalia, i B.C.), cf. *OGI*143.6 (Cyprus, ii B.C.); σ. καὶ κοινωνεῖν πόλεως Arist.*Pol.*1324$^a$15: metaph., τὰ σύντροφα καὶ συμπολιτευόμενα ἀδικήματα Plu.*Cat.Mi.*47. 2. *hold public office jointly with*, *IG*4$^2$(1).642 (Epid.):—Med., c. dat., ib.(5)1.551.6 (Sparta, iii A.D.). **-ης**, ου, ὁ, *fellow-citizen*, E.*Heracl.*826, J.*AJ*19.2.2, *IG* 14.1878 (Rome); condemned by Phryn.150: fem. **-ῖτις**, D.S.34/5. 2.16, Eust.119.6.

**συμπολλαπλᾰσιάζω**, *multiply at the same time*, Papp.24.19 (Pass.).

**σύμπολλοι**, αι, α, *many together*, Pl.*Alc.*1.114c, *Plt.*261e, al.

**συμπομπ-εύω**, *accompany in a procession*, Aeschin.1.43, Arist.*Rh. Al.*1423$^b$3, 1424$^a$5, Polyaen.1.23.2, Plu.*Arat.*53, Arr.*Epict.*4.1.104, *IG*4.679 (Hermione), *SIG*577.76 (Milet., ii B.C.), etc. ⊛ **-ή**, ἡ, *joint procession*, *OGI*309.11 (Teos, ii B.C., pl.).

⊛ **συμπονέω**, *toil* or *suffer with* or *together*, τινι *with* one, συμπονήσατε τῷ νῦν μογοῦντι A.*Pr.*276; συμπόνει πατρί S.*El.*986, etc.; σ. καὶ συγκινδυνεύειν τισί X.*Cyr.*7.5.55; τοῖς κακοπαθοῦσι Plu.*Ant.*43; σ. τινὶ πόνους E.*Or.*[1224]; σ. κακοῖσι *take part in* them, ib.683: abs., *labour together*, S.*Ant.*41, etc.; σ. πολλά Ar.*Ach.*695 (lyr.); ἐάν τι πονήσῃ μέρος, συμπονεῖ τὸ ὅλον Arist.*Pr.*883$^a$14, cf. Thphr.*Sud.*34.

**συμπονηρεύομαι**, *join others in villainy, play the knave together with*, τισι Ar.*Lys.*404, cf. Isoc.15.224.

**συμπονία**, ἡ, *cooperation*, Mich. *in EN*507.28.

⊛ **σύμπονος**, = *assessor*, *Gloss.*

**συμπορεύομαι**, *come, go*, or *proceed together*, Th.8.87, E.*IT*1488, X.*An.*1.3.5, etc.; συμπεπορευμένοι τῇ βασιλίσσῃ ἕως τῶν ὁρίων *PCair. Zen.*251.2 (iii B.C.); ἡ ψυχὴ -ευθεῖσα θεῷ Pl.*Phdr.*249c; σ. ταῖς ἑταιρίαις *Abh.Berl.Akad.*1925(5).7 (Cyrene, iii B.C.); τῷ χρόνῳ Procl.*Inst.* 50; ἐπί τινι συμφέροντι for some advantage, Arist.*EN*1160$^a$9. II. *assemble*, of the Senate, Plb.6.16.4; of a workers' guild, *SIG*460. 3 (Delph., iii B.C.): metaph., *consort together, hold intercourse*, ἀλλήλοις Plu.*Lyc.*15.

**συμπορθ-έω**, *help to destroy* or *sack*, ὃς σῷ πατρὶ συνεπόρθει Φρύγας E.*Or.*888, cf. *BCH*21.599 (Delph., iv B.C.); οἱ συμπεπορθημένοι *involved in like ruin*, Str.8.3.29. **-ητής**, οῦ, ὁ, *one who helps to destroy*, Sch.Lyc.222.

**συμπορ-ίζω**, *help in procuring*, ἐκ τῶν ξυμμάχων τι Th.7.20; πολλὰ αὐτῷ Jul.*Or.*3.125c:—Med., *do so for oneself*, Th.8.1, Isoc.4.32:—Pass., *to be got together*, Plu.*Mar.*40. **-ισμός**, ὁ, *assistance in procuring*, J.*BJ*2.20.8.

**συμπορνεύω**, gloss on συλλαγνεύω, Hsch.

⊛ **σύμπορος**, ον, *accompanying*, Procl. *in Alc.* p.165 C.

**συμπορπάομαι**, Pass., *to be fastened together*, Lxx *Ex.*36.13(39.6), Anon. (Arr.*Parth.Fr.*20 Roos) ap.Suid. s. v. θώραξ.

**σύμπορπον**· τὸν μὴ ῥαφαῖς συνειλημμένον..χιτῶνα, Hsch.

**συμπορσύνω** [ῠ], *help to arrange, promote*, τὴν κατόρθωσιν Hp.*Art.* 16; κέλευθόν τινι A.R.4.549 (tm.).

**συμποσί-α**, ἡ, *drinking together*, Alc.46, Pi.*P.*4.294, Lxx 3*Ma.*5. 15, al. **-άζω**, *drink together*, Hld.5.28, Aen.Gaz.*Thphr.* p.48 B. **-αῖος**, α, ον, = sq., Eust.770.14. **-ακός**, ή, όν, *of* or *fit for a drinking-party, convivial*, λόγοι Id.89.46; τὰ σ. distinguished from τὰ συμποτικά by Plu.2.629e. **-αρχέω**, *to be a* συμποσίαρχος, Arist.*Pol.*1274$^b$12, Plu.2.620c. **-αρχία**, ἡ, *office of* συμποσίαρχος, ib.620a. ⊛ **-αρχος**, ὁ, *president of a drinking-party, toastmaster*, X.*An.*6.1.30, Alex.21, Plu.2.208b, 620f, *OGI*646.14 (Palmyra, iii A.D.), etc.; also **-άρχης**, ου, ὁ, *Supp.Epigr.*7.151,168 (ibid., ii A.D.). Cf. συμποτικός. **-ον**, τό, *drinking-party, symposium*, Thgn. 298,496, Phoc.11, Alc.*Supp.*23.3, Pi.*N.*9.48, al., Hdt.2.78, X.*Cyr.*8. 8.10, etc.; σ. κατασκευάσαι, φίλοις παρασχεῖν, συνάγειν, Pl.*R.*363c, Plu.2.198b, Ath.5.186c, etc.; παιδαγωγεῖν Pl.*Lg.*641b.—Pl., X., and Plu. wrote dialogues under this name. II. *the party itself, the guests*, Lxx 3*Ma.*5.36, Plu.2.157d,704d; ἀνακλιθῆναι..συμπόσια συμπόσια *in groups*, *Ev.Marc.*6.39. III. *the room in which such parties were given*, τοῦ σ. στέγη Callix.2, cf. *BGU*1793.11 (i B.C.); σαίρειν τὸ σ. Luc.*DDeor.*24.1, etc. ⊛ **-ος**, α, ον, = συμποτικός, *EM* 139.49.

**συμποσόω**, *reckon together*, Heph.Astr.2.27, Eustr. *in EN*37.34, Tz.*H.*13.447.

**συμπότης**, ου, ὁ, *fellow-drinker, boon-companion*, Pi.*O.*1.61, Hdt. 2.78,173, E.*Alc.*343, Ar.*Ach.*1135, Antipho 2.1.4, Pl.*Prt.*347d, etc.

**συμποτιγίνομαι**, v. συμπροσγίγνομαι.

**συμποτικός**, ή, όν, *convivial*, σ. πράγματα Ar.*Ach.*1142; νόμοι σ. the laws *of drinking-parties*, enforced by the συμποσίαρχος, Pl.*Lg.* 671c; σ. ἁρμονίαι modes *suited for drinking-songs*, Id.*R.*398e; σ. [μουσική] Phld.*Mus.* p.82 K.; [ἀρετή] Id.*D.*3 *Fr.*76; σ. διάλογοι, work by Persaeus, Ath.4.162b; σ. προβλήματα, title of a work by Plu. (v. συμποσιακός); ὑπομνήματα σ., of a work by Persaeus, D.L.7.1; συμποτικός *a jolly fellow*, Ar.*V.*1209, Plb.31.13.8: Comp. **-ώτερος** Luc.*Ep.Sat.*32: Sup. **-ώτατος** Id.*Tim.*46, Philostr.*Im.*1.25. Adv. **-κῶς** Poll.6.20.

**συμπότρια**, fem. of συμπότης, *Gloss.*

⊛ **σύμπους**, ποδος, ὁ, ἡ, *with the feet together* or *closed*, Ar.*Fr.*865, Herm.Trism. in *Rev.Phil.*32.254; *with feet tied together*, Herod.3.96; σύμποδα [ἐλέφαντα] δεσμεῖν Str.15.1.42.

**συμπραγμᾰτεύομαι**, aor. -επραγματεύθην *IG*11(4).1055.10 (Delos, iii B.C.), Lycon ap. D.L.5.71:—*assist in transacting* business, τισι Plu.*Cat.Ma.*21; σ. τὰ περὶ τοὺς νόμους Id.*Lyc.*5; μετά τινων περί τινος *IG*2$^2$.844.17 (iii B.C.), cf. *PTeb.*812.13 (ii B.C.): abs., Plu.2. 417a, *CIG* (add.) 1997*d* (Edessa).

**συμπρακτικός**, ή, όν, *cooperating*, Ptol.*Tetr.*51.

**συμπρακτορεύω**, *to be assistant tax-collector*, *PLond.*2.306.23 (ii A.D.).

**συμπράκτρια**, ἡ, fem. of sq., Sch.A.R.3.942.

**συμπράκτωρ**, Ion. **-πρήκτωρ**, ορος, ὁ, *helper, assistant*, Hdt.6.125, cf. X.*Cyr.*3.2.29: c. gen. rei, σ. ὁδοῦ *a companion* in travel, S.*OT* 116; συμπράκτορες τῆς αἰτίας *involved as accomplices* in the charge, Antipho 3.4.6.

**συμπραξία**, ἡ, = sq., Sch.Pi.*N.*10.6.

**σύμπραξις**, εως, ἡ, *assistance*, J.*AJ*9.7.2; τῶν βουλευμάτων *taking joint counsel*, ib.18.1.1; σ. κοινή Plu.2.478d.

⊛ **συμπράσσω**, Att. **-ττω**, Ion. **-πρήσσω**:—*join* or *help in doing*, τινί τι A.*Pr.*297 (anap.); σωτηρίαν E.*IT*980; σ. τινὶ τἀγαθά *assist* one *in procuring* what is good, Arist.*Rh.*1381$^b$23, cf. *EN*1167$^a$1, *IG*1$^2$.106.18: c. acc. rei, σ. τὰ ἄλλα S.*Aj.*1396; ξ. τὰ πρὸς τοὺς Ἀθηναίους Th.4.74; εἰρήνην *help in negotiating*, X.*Ages.*7.7: c. dat. pers. only, *act with, cooperate with*, Th.3.101, Isoc.18.7, etc.; τινὶ περί τινος X.*An.*5.4.9; ὑπέρ τινος Plb.28.7.2; σ. ὥστε γενέσθαι τι X.*Cyr.*3.2.28, etc.; σ. τινὶ ὅπως ἕξει Isoc.4.126. 2. abs., *lend aid, cooperate*, δεῖ σ'..αὐτὸν εἰκαθόντα σ. S.*Tr.*1177, cf. Lys.12.85, etc.; οἱ ξυμπράσσοντες *the confederates*, Th.4.67, 8.14, X.*HG*3.3.10. II. intr., σὺν κακῶς πράσσουσι σ. κακῶς *share in* others' woe, E.*Heracl.* 27. III. Med., *assist in avenging*, συνεπρήξαντο Μενέλεῳ τὰς Ἑλένης ἁρπαγάς Hdt.5.94.

**συμπράτης** [ᾱ], ου, ὁ, in pl., = οἱ σὺν ἄλλοις πιπράσκοντες, Lys.*Fr.* 329 S. Also **συμπρᾱτήρ**, ῆρος, ὁ, *warrantor*, *AB*193.

**συμπρᾱΰνομαι**, *to be mitigated at the same time*, of fever, Gal.18 (1).70.

**συμπρεπής**, ές, *befitting*, A.*Supp.*458, *Th.*13.

**συμπρέπω**, *befit, beseem*, βοὰ σὺν Ἀριστοκλείδᾳ πρέπει Pi.*N.*3.67, cf. Plu.*Phil.*11, Aristaenet.1.12.

**συμπρεσβευτής**, οῦ, ὁ, *fellow-ambassador*, Lys.27.1, Aeschin.1. 168, *IG*2$^2$.786.11, *OGI*339.11 (Sestos, ii B.C.).

**συμπρεσβεύω**, *to be a fellow-ambassador, be joined* or *associated with on an embassy*, D.19.189, Aeschin.2.169, *IG*2$^{2}$.844.15, *OGI*333.12 (ii B.C.) :—Med., *join in sending an embassy*, Th.3.92, 5.44.

**σύμπρεσβυς**, εως, ὁ, = συμπρεσβευτής, only in pl. (cf. πρέσβυς II), Th.1.90sq., X.*An*.5.5.24, D.19.188.

⊛ **συμπρεσβύτερος** [ῠ], ὁ, *fellow-presbyter*, 1*Ep.Pet*.5.1, *Supp.Epigr.* 6.347 (Lycaonia).

**συμπρήκτωρ, συμπρήσσω**, v. συμπράκτωρ, συμπράσσω.

**συμπρίασθαι**, aor. 2 inf. (no pres. in use, cf. *πρίαμαι), *buy up*, σῖτον Lys.22.5 ; πάντα τὸν σίδηρον Arist.*Pol*.1259$^{a}$24.

**συμπρο-άγω** [ᾰ], *lead forward together*, τάξιν Hierocl. *in CA*1 p.417 M. ; *contribute*, τισὶν εἰς αὔξησιν D.H.*Dem*.48. II. intr., *move forward with* or *together*, Plu.*Phil*.21, *Agis* 19. **–αύξομαι**, Pass., *increase with* or *together*, Hp.*Epid*.2.1.8. ⊛ **–βαίνω**, 3 sg. pres. –ει, = *concrescit*, *Gloss.* **–βάλλω**, *project together with itself*, Dam.*Pr*.13. **–βουλος**, ον, *fellow*-πρόβουλος, *IG*9(1).485 (Acarnania, iii B.C.), Arg.Ar.*Lys.* **–γιγνώσκω**, *foreknow* or *foresee along with*, Iamb.*Myst*.6.4. **–δίδωμι**, *join in betraying*, Aen.Tact.11.3. **–δότης**, ου, ὁ, *fellow-traitor*, Jo.Sic. in Rh.6.198 W. **–εδρος**, ὁ, *joint-president*, *IG*2$^{2}$.450.8 (iv B.C.), al., Aeschin.2.85, Decr.Att.ap.J.*AJ* 14.8.5, *IG*4$^{2}$(1).84.25 (Epid., i B.C.). **–ειμι**, (εἶμι *ibo*) *go forth along with* or *together*, Arist.*Mech*.850$^{b}$22, J.*AJ*12.9.4, Hdn.1.16.3, Ath.6.272e. **–έρχομαι**, = foreg., Satyr.3, *OGI*248.15 (Pergam., ii B.C.), J.*Vit*.56, Gal.2.558, Dam.*Pr*.74. **–θῡμέομαι**, *have equal desire with, share in eagerness with*, τινι Th.2.80 ; τινὶ περί τι D.Chr. 59.10 : abs., X.*HG*5.1.14, 5.4.5, Orib.8.6.13. 2. c. acc. rei, *join zealously in promoting*, τὸν ἔκπλουν Th.8.1, cf. X.*Cyr*.6.1.19. 3. c. dat. rei, *zealously help*, τῇ προαιρέσει, τῇ ἁλώσει, D.S.14.41, Luc.*Cal*.21. 4. c. inf. fut. or aor., *have a joint zeal, share in the desire that*. ., Th.8.2, Pl.*Euthphr*.11e, *La*.200e, X.*An*.3.1.9, etc. ; σ. ὅπως. . ib.7.1.5. **–ίημι**, in Med., *join in paying*, of a bank official, *BGU* 1748.4 (i B.C.), al.

**συμπροικίζω**, *furnish with a dower together*, gloss on συνεκδίδωμι, Sch.D.18.268.

**συμπροκόπτω**, *increase with*, τινι Nicom.*Ar*.1.19.

**συμπρομηθέομαι**, *have providence over together with*, Jul.*Or*.5.167b.

**συμπρο-μνάμων** [ᾱ], ονος, ὁ, *joint*-προμνάμων (q.v.), *IG*9(1).513 (Acarnania, ii B.C.), 5(1).29 (ibid., ii B.C.). ⊛ **–νοέω**, *join in providing*, *CIG*4051 (Ancyra, dub.). **–νομεύω**, *join in plundering*, τινι J.*BJ* 4.9.3. **–ξενέω**, *help in furnishing with means*, E.*Hel*.146 codd. LP, but σὺ πρ. is prob. **–πέμπω**, *join in escorting*, τινα Hdt.9.1, Ar.*Ra*.404,410, X.*Cyr*.1.6.1, etc. ; σ. τινὰ ναυσίν Th.1.27 ; τὸ σῶμά τινος, in funeral procession, D.H.8.59. **–πίπτω**, *rush forth with*, τινι f.l. in Plb.31.14.1. **–πορεύομαι**, *travel forward with*, Lxx *De*. 31.8 cod. A (συμπορ– cod. B).

**συμπροσ-άγω** [ᾰ], *bring along with* or *together*, Aen.Tact.10.23 (Pass.), Gal.7.617 (Act.). ⊛ **–γίγνομαι**, Dor. **συμποτιγίν–**, *help, assist*, c. dat., *Delph*.3(3).118.9 (ii B.C.), *IG*5(1).961.4 (Laconia, ii B.C.), *BCH*55.43 (Odessus, i B.C.). 2. *to be further added*, of planetary combination, Ptol.*Tetr*.186, Vett.Val.60.28, al. ⊛ **–ειμι**, (εἰμί *sum*) *to be present together*, Lxx *Ps*.93(94).20, *Ec*.8.15, *PRev.Laws* 27.18 (iii B.C.), Nech.ap.Vett.Val.280.4. **–έρχομαι**, = συμπροσγίγνομαι 2, Procl.*Par.Ptol*.260. **–ίσχομαι**, Pass., *attach oneself to*, τινος Plu.2.322f. **–λαμβάνω**, *take besides*, Nic.Dam.*Fr*.130.29 J. **–μείγνῡμι**, intr., *to be in company with*, συμπροσέμειξα τῷ ἀνδρί Pl.*Tht*.183e. **–πίπτω**, *happen at the same time*, Gal.1.124, Theon ap.eund.6.210. 2. *occur to* one *at the same time*, τινι M.Ant.7.22. **–πλέκομαι**, Pass., *contend* or *struggle hard*, Thd.*Da*.11.10.

**συμπροστάτης** [ᾰ], ου, ὁ, *joint*-προστάτης, *PTeb*.64(*a*).110 (ii B.C.), *IGRom*.3.95.12 (Sinope).

**συμπροστίθημι**, *make up deficiency of* εἰσφοραί, *SIG*1215.10 (Myconus).

**συμπροτερέω**, *precede*, τῆς πρώτης Ὀλυμπιάδος Suid. s.v. Ἡσίοδος.

**συμπρο-τίθημι**, *cause to be placed first at the same time*, A.D.*Synt*. 128.20. ⊛ **–τρέπω**, *urge on* or *exhort at the same time*, D.H.*Rh*.7.6.

**σύμπρουρος**, v. σύμφρουρος.

**συμπρο-φαίνω**, *bring forth to light together*, Plot.5.8.4. **–φέρω**, *pronounce at the same time*, Sch.Pi.*O*.3.81. 2. *involve*, Simp. *in Ph*.904.21.

**συμπροφητεύω**, *prophesy along with* or *together*, Plu.2.860d, cf. Him.*Or*.21.8.

**συμπρο-χέω**, *pour out together*, Orph.*A*.575. **–χωρέω**, *go forward together*, Poll.1.215.

**συμπρῠτᾰνεύω**, *administer together*, Sch.Pi.*N*.11.1.

⊛ **συμπρύτᾰνις** [ῠ], εως, ὁ, *joint-prytanis*, *IG*2$^{2}$.1.7 (v B.C.), Din.*Fr*.89. 33, *IG*14.617,618 (Rhegium).

**συμπτερόομαι**, Pass., *get wings together*, Longin.15.4.

**συμπτερύσσομαι**, *fly with*, Eust. ad D.P. p.75.33 B.

**σύμπτυκτος**, ον, *folded together, trussed up*, ἄρνα σ. Diph.90 ; σ. ἀνάπαιστοι *folded* anapaestics, dub. sens. in Pherecr.79 (*spondaic* acc. to Sch.Metr.Pi.*O*.4) ; πλαίσια ξύμπτυκτα (perh. *dovetailed*) is the best reading (Poll.10.148, Suid.) in Ar.*Ra*.800 (συμπηκτά is v. l.).

**σύμπτυξις**, εως, ἡ, *folding up* or *together, closing*, Procl.*Hyp*.5.116 ; *embrace, enfolding*, ἡ τοῦ κύκλου πρὸς τὸ μέσον σ. Dam.*Pr*.29 ; ἡ νοητὴ σ. ib.155.

**συμπτύσσω**, *fold* or *pack together*, S.*Tr*.691 :—Pass., βλέφαρα συμπτυσσόμενα eyelids *which close*, Gal.*UP*10.6. 2. Pass., συμπτύσσεσθαι τὰ ἐπίπεδα *are folded together* fan-wise, Procl.*Hyp*.5.115 : metaph., *to be implicit, not yet unfolded*, ἀριθμὸς ἔτι συνεπτυγμένος Dam.*Pr*.1 ; ἐν τῷ κέντρῳ –έπτυκται ὁ κύκλος ib.32, cf. Procl.*Inst.* 171. 3. *knock in, dent*, συνεπτυγμένον ἄργυρον, = *collisum argentum*, *Gloss.*

**συμπτῠχή**, ἡ, *coat* of stomach, Gal.2.568.

**σύμ-πτωμα**, ατος, τό, (συμπίπτω) *anything that happens, a chance, occurrence*, τὰ σ. καὶ τὰ ἀπὸ τύχης Arist.*Rh*.1367$^{b}$24 ; ἀπὸ συμπτώματος, coupled with ἀπὸ τύχης, Id.*Ph*.199$^{a}$1, cf. *Pol*.1274$^{a}$12 ; opp. αἴτια, Id.*Div.Somn*.462$^{b}$27, cf. *de An*.434$^{a}$32 ; κατὰ σύμπτωμα Thphr.*Vent*.17, cf. 31. 2. *mishap, mischance*, Th.4.36, Arist.*Pol*.1304$^{a}$1, Chrysipp.*Stoic*.2.339, *IG*7.411.4 (Oropus, ii B.C.) ; ἀκούσιον σ. D.56. 43 ; ὅταν τις . . ἀδίκοις περιπέσῃ σ. Men.590 ; τὰ κοινὰ κοινῶς δεῖ φέρειν σ. Id.817. II. *property, attribute*, Epicur.*Ep*.1 p.20 U., al. : pl., distd. fr. συμβεβηκότα, ib. p.6 U., p.24 U. ; τὸν χρόνον σ. συμπτωμάτων λέγει Id.*Fr*.294 ; πνεύματος σ. Gal.4.706 ; Νουμήνιος σ. αὐτῆς (sc. τῆς συγκαταθετικῆς δυνάμεως) φησιν εἶναι τὸ φανταστικόν Porph.ap. Stob.1.49.25 ; σ. φυσικόν Iamb.*Comm.Math*.24. 2. Geom., *property*, of curve, etc., Archim.*Con.Sph*.12, Papp.54.21, al. III. in diseases, *symptom*, Phld.*Ir*. p.29 W., Sor.1.48, al., Gal.7.50, 10.70, al. ; σ. κεφαλῆς Aret.*SD*1.3 ; *symptomata* is expld. by *sudor nequissimus*, *Gloss.* IV. *falling in, collapse*, in Medical sense, Pl.*Ax*. 364c ; of a horse, *PEnteux*.14.9 (iii B.C.) ; σ. τῆς δυνάμεως, τῆς διανοίας, Diocl.*Fr*.192 ; of the *lacus Fucinus*, D.C.60.33. **–πτωματικός**, ή, όν, *accidental*, Thphr.*HP*7.15.1 ; *casual*, Gal.9.418. Adv. –κῶς, ἔχειν *to be of the nature of coincidences*, Thphr.*Metaph*.28, cf. Ptol.*Tetr*.105. ⊛ **–πτωσις**, εως, ἡ, *falling together, collapsing*, Hp.*Aph*.1.3, *Epid*.6.3.1 ; τῆς οἰκίας Str.14.5.4, cf. 5.3.7, S.E.*M*.5.91, *CIG*3293 (Smyrna). II. *falling together, meeting*, [ποταμῶν] Plb. 3.49.6 ; ὀρῶν Id.2.14.8 ; *point of meeting* or *intersection*, Archim.*Sph.Cyl*.1.10, al., Str.2.1.10,37, Ptol.*Geog*.1.3.1, Dam.*Pr*.29. 2. in hostile sense, *attack, onset*, Plb.1.57.7, etc. 3. = συνέμπτωσις, Sch.Ar.*Th*.21, A.D.*Adv*.151.5, *Synt*.52.8 (v.l. συνέμ–). 4. σ. φωνηέντων *collision* of vowels, Phld.*Rh*.1.163 S. III. *incident, accident*, Arist.*HA*585$^{b}$25 ; *circumstance*, Plb.3.49.5. IV. a disease of the eye, prob. *contraction of the pupil*, Gal.14.777 ; also, *contraction of the throat*, Aret.*CA*1.4. **–πτωτός**, ή, όν, *secant, ultimately self-intersecting*, of a curve, Procl. *in Euc*.1 p.177 F. II. *collapsing easily*, Anon.Lond.27.18.

**συμπῠκάζω**, *cover quite up*, D.S.17.116.

**σύμπυκνος**, ον, *pressed together, compressed, tight*, X.*Eq*.10.10.

**συμπυκνόω**, *press close together, make compact*, Hp.*Oss*.16, Thphr.*CP*5.4.2 ; λόχους Tz.*H*.5.332 :—Pass., *to be condensed*, Hp.*Oss*.14.

**συμπυνθάνομαι**, *inquire about with*, τινί τι E.*Hel*.328 : simply, *learn*, Eun.*Hist*. p.259 D.

**συμπῠριάω**, *apply heat*, Hp.*Mul*.2.145, Gal.12.863.

**συμπῠρόω**, *burn up, consume along with* or *together*, E.*Cyc*.308, *Rh*.960 :—Pass., Id.*Supp*.1071.

**συμπυρπολέω**, = foreg., Tz.*H*.11.83 (Pass.).

**συμπωλέω**, *sell with* or *together*, D.C.59.21 ; *confirm the sale*, *IG*12 (5).872.114 (Tenos), *SIG*169.41 (Iasos, iv B.C.), *PGrenf*.1.25 ii 12 (ii B.C.).

**συμπωρόομαι**, Pass., *solidify*, of stones in the kidneys, Hp.*Int*.14 : —later in Act., c. dat., Gal.13.536.

**συμφάγῃ**, 3 sg. aor. subj. of συνεσθίω, Pl.*Lg*.881d.

**συμφαίνομαι**, Pass., *appear along with* or *together*, Eun.*VS* p.460 B.

**συμφάνεια** [φᾰ], ἡ, *appearance, aspect*, Aristeas 99.

⊛ **συμφᾰνής**, ές, *manifest, evident*, σ. ποιεῖν τι Arist.*Pr*.922$^{a}$17, cf. *SIG*559.24 (Megalop., iii B.C., found at Magn. Mae.), al. ; σ. ἐστιν ἐκ τοῦ λόγου Arist.*EN*1099$^{b}$25, cf. *de An*.405$^{b}$22 ; σ. γενέσθαι or γεγονέναι, Plb.2.25.5, Ezek.*Exag*.54, *SIG*601.16 (Teos, ii B.C.), Aristeas 91, *BGU*1785.14 (i B.C.), Gal.18(2).532 ; μὴ σ. ᾖ τοῖς πολεμίοις Ph.*Bel.* 82.27 ; συμφανεῖς εἰσι παρηγμέναι *are evidently* derived, A.D.*Pron.* 103.18 : Comp. –έστερος Thphr.*CP*3.18.2.

⊛ **σύμφανσις**, εως, ἡ, *shining together*, πολλῶν ἀστέρων Eust.1060.55.

**συμφαντάζομαι**, Pass., *to be imagined along with*, τινι Plu.2. 392e. 2. Med., *entertain fancies along with*, σ. τῇ μητρὶ τὰ ἔμβρυα Porph.*Gaur*.5.4.

**συμφαντικός**, v. συμφατικός.

**σύμφᾰσις**, εως, ἡ, *appearance of meeting, conjunction*, φασὶν εἶναι τοὺς κομήτας σ. τῶν πλανήτων ἀστέρων Arist.*Mete*.342$^{b}$28.

**συμφάσκω**, = σύμφημι, τῇ μητρί J.*AJ*20.2.4 : abs., Aristid.1.430, 2.306 J.

**συμφᾰτικός**, ή, όν, *agreeing*, Eun.*VS* p.502 B. ; v. l. συμφαντικός.

**συμφερόντως**, Adv. pres. part. (συμφέρω), *profitably*, τινι Antipho Soph.*Oxy*.1364.15 (ξυμ–), Pl.*Lg*.662a, Isoc.2.25, cf. X.*Mem*.1.2.50, *IG*12(8).640.8 (Peparethus, ii B.C.), etc. ; οὔτε δικαίως οὔτε σ. *on* no *plea* either *of* justice or *expediency*, Antipho 2.1.9 ; σ. ἔχει Isoc.8.137, cf. Demetr.Lac.*Herc*.1012.45.

**συμφερτός**, ή, όν, *united, in conjunction*, συμφερτὴ ἀρετή Il.13.237 ; ἠχώ, θάλασσα, λιβάδες, Nonn.*D*.5.387, 41.298, 47.88.

⊛ **συμφέρω**, fut. συνοίσω A.*Th*.510 : aor. 1 συνήνεγκα E.*HF*488, Ion. –ήνεικα Hdt.7.152 : aor. 2 συνήνεγκον Th.2.51 : pf. συνενήνοχα D.18. 198. A. Act. I. *bring together, gather, collect*, τὰ κακὰ ἐς μέσον Hdt. 7.152 ; τάλαντα ἐς τὠυτό Id.3.92, cf. D.24.74 ; δαπάνην σ. Th.1.99 ; esp. of dead bodies, X.*An*.6.4.9, Lycurg.45 codd. 2. *bring together, contribute*, βουλεύματα A.*Pers*.528 ; ἐκ πάντων γόους E. l. c. ; πολλοὶ πολλὰ συνενηνόχασι μέρη Arist.*SE*183ᵇ33:—Med., of a river, Φάσιδι σ. ῥόον A.R.4.134. **3.** *bring into conflict*, πολεμίους θεούς A.*Th.*510; *give* battle, συνοίσομεν ὀξὺν Ἄρηα Tyrt.1.40 Diehl: v. infr. B. I. 2. **4.** *bear along with* or *together*, ὁ ἵππος ὅπλον σ. X.*Cyr.*4.3.13; ἐγώ σοι ξυμφέρω (sc. τὴν παμπησίαν) Ar.*Ec.*869; *bring with*, λύχνον..παῖς μοι συμφέρει Epich.35.8; of sufferings, labours, and the like, *bear jointly, help to bear*, ξυνοίσω πᾶν ὅσονπερ ἂν σθένω S.*El.*946; σ. κακά E.*HF*1366; πένθος τινί Id.*Alc.*370; τὰς τούτων ἁμαρτίας Antipho 3.2.11: hence, *suffer, bear with, indulge*, ὀργὰς ξυνοίσω σοι A.*Eu.* 848. **II.** intr., *confer a benefit, be useful* or *profitable*, οὔ οἱ συνήνεικε τὸ ἔχθος *did* not *do* him any *good*, Hdt.9.37; τὸ καὶ συνήνεικε ποιησάσῃ Id.8.87; καλῶς ἂν ἡμῖν ξυμφέροι ταῦτα A.*Supp.*753, cf. Ar. *Ach.*252; τοῦτο σ. τῷ βίῳ Id.*Pl.*38; ἅπαντ' ἐπὶ τὸ βέλτιον ξ. *turn out* for the best, Id.*Ec.*475; σῖτον..καὶ οἶνον..καὶ εἴ τι ἄλλο βρῶμα, οἵ' ἂν ἐς πολιορκίαν ξυμφέρῃ Th.4.26; πάντα ὅσα ἂν οἴηται συνοίσειν αὐτοῖς πρὸς τὸν βίον X.*Mem.*2.2.5; ὃ σ. πρὸς τὴν πολιτείαν Arist.*Pol.* 1272ᵃ30, etc. **2.** impers., *it is of use, expedient*, mostly c. inf., ξυμφέρει σωφρονεῖν ὑπὸ στένει A.*Eu.*520 (lyr.), cf. S.*El.*1440, Th.2.63, etc.; with Art. prefixed to inf., τὸ περιγενέσθαι..ἀμφοτέροις σ. X. *Mem.*3.4.10; the inf. is freq. to be supplied, Th.1.123, X.*Ath.*3.11; also ὡς νομίζω συμφέρειν ἡμῖν γενομένων τούτων Pl.*Phdr.*230e; folld. by a clause, σ. τῷ κοινῷ, ἦν.. Id.*Lg.*875a, cf. *PCair.Zen.*21.41 (iii B.C.); σ. ἐπὶ τὸ βέλτιον, ἐπὶ τὸ ἄμεινον, X.*An.*7.8.4, Decr.ap. And.1.77. **3.** part. συμφέρων, ουσα, ον, *useful, expedient, fitting*, S.*OT*875 (lyr.), etc.; βίος..ἐκεῖσε συμφέρων *profitable* even beyond the grave, Pl.*Grg.*527b; ἔστιν ἡσυχία..συμφέρουσα τῇ πόλει D.18.308. **b.** in neut. as Subst., συμφέρον, οντος, τό, *use, profit, advantage*, S.*Ph.*926, Antipho 5.50, etc.; ἐς τὸ ξ. καθίστασθαί τι Th.4.60; ἥδιω τοῦ συμφέροντος more pleasant *than is good for one*, X.*Smp.*4.39; περαιτέρω τοῦ ὑμετέρου σ. Aeschin.3.80; τὸ σ. τινός Pl.*R.*338c, 340c, al.; τὸ σ. τινί ib.341d, 342b, D.18.139; πρὸς τὸ σ. αὐτῷ *PCair. Zen.*451.15 (iii B.C.): freq. also in pl., τὰ σ. S.*Ph.*131, etc.; τὰ μικρὰ σ., opp. τὰ ὅλα, the petty *interests*, D.18.28; τὰ συμφέροντα ἀνθρώποις Pl.*Lg.*875a, cf. *IG*4²(1).68.84 (Epid., iv B.C.); but also τὰ τῆς πατρίδος σ. Din.1.99, cf. Pl.*Plt.*297a, D.18.120, etc.; also in aor. part., τό τῳ ξυνενεγκόν Th.2.51; συμφέρον ἐστί, = συμφέρει, Heraclit.8, Ar.*Pl.* 49, X.*An.*6.1.26, etc.; εἰ μὴ ξυμφέρον (sc. ἐστί) Th.3.44. **III.** intr., also, **1.** *work with, assist*, σφῷν ὅπως ἄριστα συμφέροι θεός S.*Ph.*627; πάντα συμφέρουσ' Ἰάσονι E.*Med.*13; συμφέροντι (or Συμφέροντι as pr. n.) Ἡρακλεῖ *IG*2².2114. **2.** *agree with*, τοὐμὸν ξυνοίσειν ὄνομα τοῖς ἐμοῖς κακοῖς S.*Aj.*431; εἴ τι ξυνοίσεις..τοῖς θεσφάτοις Ar.*Eq.* 1233; ἐὰν μὴ τῇ γυναικὶ συμφέρῃ Id.*Lys.*166; *come to terms with, give way to*, τοῖς κρείσσοσι S.*El.*1465; v. infr. B. II. **3.** *fit, suit*, ᾗ μήτε χλαῖνα μήτε σισύρα συμφέρει (v. χλαῖνα) Ar.*Ra.*1459; [γυνὴ] σιμὴ ἄν σοι ἰσχυρῶς συμφέροι X.*Cyr.*8.4.21. **4.** of events, *happen, take place, turn out*, c. acc. et inf., Hdt.1.73, 3.129, 6.23, 117, etc.; with ὥστε.., Id.1.74; τὰ ἄλλα..αὐτῇ συνήνεικε ἐς εὐτυχίην γενόμενα *turned out* for her advantage, Id.8.88; v. infr. B. III. 2.

**B.** Pass. συμφέρομαι: fut. συνοίσομαι: aor. Pass. ξυνηνέχθην Th. 7.44, Ion. συνηνείχθην Hdt.1.19, 2.111, 3.10: pf. συνενήνεγμαι (Hes. *Sc.*440), v. συνενείκομαι:—*come together*, opp. διαφέρεσθαι, Heraclit. 10, cf. Pl.*Sph.*242e, etc.; *meet, associate with*, Theoc.*Ep.*8.2; of sexual intercourse, Luc.*Herm.*34, *Tox.*15. **2.** in hostile sense, *meet in battle, engage*, πτόλεμόνδε Il.8.400; μάχῃ 11.736; τινι with one, A. *Th.*636: abs., Th.7.36; so συνοισόμεθα πτολεμίζειν Hes.*Sc.*358; σ. κακῷ *encounter* it, Hdt.6.50. **II.** *agree with*, οὐδαμοῖσι ἄλλοισι σ. ἀνθρώπων, in custom, Id.1.173, cf. 2.80, etc.; in statement, ib.44, al.; περί τινος Id.4.13; opp. διαφέρεσθαι, Antipho 5.42; *live on friendly terms with*, τισι Hdt.4.114, Opp.*H.*5.34: abs., *agree together, be of one mind*, εἰ δὲ μὴ συμφεροίατο if *they could* not *agree*, Hdt.1.196; ἐὰν δὲ ἀνὴρ καὶ γυνὴ μηδαμῇ συμφέρωνται Pl.*Lg.*929e; also ξ. γνώμῃ ὥστε ἀπαλλάσσεσθαι τοῦ πολέμου Th.4.65; καθ' αὑτοὺς ξ. *settle their affairs* by themselves, Id.6.13; *concur*, τῇδε γὰρ ξυνοίσομαι S.*OC*641; ἐγὼ δὲ τούτοις κατὰ τοῦτο εἶναι οὐ συμφέρομαι Pl.*Prt.* 317a. **2.** *to be in harmony with*, εὖ τοῖς πράγμασι σ. Id.*Cra.*419d; *adapt oneself to*, τοῖς παροῦσιν Plu.*Tim.*15; σ. τὰ πολλὰ πολλοῖς *correspond with*, E.*Heracl.*919 (lyr.); χαίτης πῶς συνοίσεται πλόκος; *correspond, be like*, Id.*El.*527; συμφέρεται ὧυτὸς εἶναι Hdt.2.79; ἔργῳ τοὔνομα συμφέρεται Call.*Epigr.*6.6. **III.** of events, *happen, turn out, occur, come to pass*, ἔμελλε τοιοῦτό σφι συνοίσεσθαι Hdt.8.86; οὐδὲν γάρ σφι χρηστὸν συνεφέρετο Id.4.157; οὐδέν οἱ μέγα ἀνάρσιον πρῆγμα συνηνείχθη Id.3.10; ἐπὶ τὸ βέλτιον τὸ πρᾶγμα..συνοίσεται Ar.*Nu.*594; οὐδὲ πυθέσθαι ῥᾴδιον ἦν.., ὅτῳ τρόπῳ ἕκαστα ξυνηνέχθη Th.7.44; ξ. θόρυβος Id.8.84; μεταβολαί Pl.*Plt.*270c, etc. **2.** impers., συμφέρεται ἐπὶ τὸ ἄμεινον *it happens, falls out* for the better, Hdt.7.8.α'; ἄμεινον συνοίσεσθαι Id.4.15; αὐτῷ συνεφέρετο παλιγκότως it *turned out* ill to him, ib.156; so συνηνείχθη τοιόνδε γενέσθαι πρῆγμα Id.1.19, cf. 6.86.α', Th.1.23, al.; σ. οἱ τυφλὸν γενέσθαι Hdt.2.111; v. supr. A. III. 4. **IV.** literally, *to be carried along with*, ἄστρασι μήνη σ. Man.6. 319; κύδεα..ψυχαῖς οὐ μάλα σ. do not *follow* them (beyond the grave), *AP*4.4.4 (Agath.). **V.** Gramm., *to be constructed with*, αἰτιατικῇ, etc., A.D.*Synt.*285.1, al.: also, *agree in form with*, σ. φωνῇ [τῇ] πρὸς τὰς δοτικάς Id.*Adv.*209.28.

**συμφερώτερος**, α, ον, *more expedient*, Arist.*Top.*118ᵇ32 codd. (leg. συμφορώτερος).

**συμφεύγω**, fut. -φεύξομαι E.*Ph.*1679:—*flee along with*, τινι Hdt.4. 11; σὺν φεύγουσι συμφεύγω E.*Heracl.*26: abs., D.S.14.91. **2.** *to be banished along with*, Lycurg.25; συνέφυγε τὴν φυγὴν ταύτην *shared in* this banishment, Pl.*Ap.*21a. **II.** *take refuge*, ὠνομάσθαι Δίκτυνναν ἀπὸ τοῦ συμφυγεῖν εἰς ἁλιευτικὰ δίκτυα D.S.5.76; συμφευξόμεθα ἐπί.., c. acc., we *will have recourse* to.., Herod.Med. in *Rh. Mus.*58.72.

**σύμφημι**, fut. -φήσω Pl.*Prt.*357b, al.: aor. 1 συνέφησα Id.*R.*342e, *Sph.*236d, al.: aor. 2 συνέφην freq. in Pl. (v. infr.), Elean συνέφα *Schwyzer*416.5:—*assent, approve*, or *agree fully*, A.*Pr.*40, S.*Ph.* 1310, etc.; ξύμφημι κἀγώ Id.*El.*1257; ξ. δή σοι Id.*Aj.*278, cf. E. *Hipp.*266 (anap.), Pl.*Ti.*72d, etc. **2.** c. acc. rei, *concede, agree to, grant*, ταῦτα..πάντες ἄρα συνέφασαν Id.*Smp.*177e, cf. *Sph.*247a, *Prt.* 330d, X.*An.*5.8.8, etc.: hence abs., σύμφημι (σοι) *I grant* you, Pl.*R.* 403c, 608b; freq. in Platonic dialogue, σύμφαθι ἢ ἄπειπε *say yes* or no, ib.523a, cf. *Grg.*500e; συνέφη Id.*Phd.*102d, al. **3.** c. acc. et inf., *agree* that.., S.*OT*553, Pl.*Lg.*831b, etc.; σ. τῷ νόμῳ ὅτι καλός, = σ. τὸν νόμον καλὸν εἶναι, *Ep.Rom.*7.16. **4.** c. inf. fut., *promise*, X.*HG*5.2.5.

**συμφήτωρ**· μάντις, μάρτυς, Hsch.

**συμφθάνω** [ᾰ], *keep pace with*, τῇ ῥύμῃ τοῦ λόγου Suid. s. v. Σίβυλλα.

*** σύμφθαρσις**, εως, ἡ, *simultaneous destruction*, τῶν μιγνυμένων ἄλλου τινὸς γεννωμένου σώματος Alex.Aphr.*Mixt.*216.24, cf. Meno *Iatr.* 14.16. **2.** *melting into one another*, (sc. τῶν ἰδεῶν) Hermog.*Id.*1. 12, cf. Iamb. *in Nic.* p.80 P.

**συμφθέγγομαι**, *sound with*, ἡ λύρα τῷ χρωμένῳ σ. Plu.*Alc.*2, etc.; ἐμοὶ ὁ νόμος συμφθέγγεται Chor.p.55 B.: abs., D.C.74.3, restored for -φθειρ- in D.Chr.78.20. **II.** *converse with*, Plu.2.580d.

*** συμφθείρω**, *destroy together* or *altogether*, E.*Andr.*947, Luc.*Prom. Es*5, S.E.8.480:—Pass., *perish along with*, τινι Arist.*Top.*150ᵃ33: abs., *perish together*, Plb.6.5.6. **2.** Pass., *to be with a person to his* or *one's own hurt*, τίνι συμφθείρομαι; *whose partner in crime am I?* Heraclit.*Ep.*7.3; εἰς ταὐτὸ συμφθαρέντες *having unfortunately met* at one place, Plu.2.708e; of illegitimate sexual intercourse, Ps.-Luc. *Philopatr.*9, Steph. *in Hp.*1.76 D., Suid. s. v. Ἱλάριος. **II.** Pass., of colours, *melt* or *die away into each other*, Plu.2.436b; of sounds, D.H.*Dem.*48; -εφθαρμένα ἀλλήλοις, of π and σ in ψ, Id.*Comp.*14; of qualities, Iamb. *in Nic.* p.81 P.

**συμφθίνω** [ῑ], *decay along with*, τὰ ὀστᾶ σ. τῷ σώματι Arist.*GA* 745ᵃ16, cf. Ael.*NA*12.13; of stones which *wane along with* the moon, Sch.Ptol.*Tetr.*3.

**σύμφθογγος**, ον, *sounding together*, χορὸς σύμφθογγος, οὐκ εὔφωνος *in concert*, but not in harmony, of the Furies, A.*Ag.*1187; σ. λύρης ἀοιδή Epigr. in *BCH*26.134 (Honestus).

**συμφιβλόομαι**, gloss on συμπερονάομαι, Hsch.

**συμφῐλέω**, *love mutually*, opp. συνέχθω, S.*Ant.*523.

**συμφῐλία**, ἡ, *mutual friendship*, f.l. for συμφυλία (q. v.).

**συμφῐλο-δοξέω**, *agree in promoting* one's honour, σ. *gloriae meae*, Cic.*Att.*5.17.2; *share* one's *public spirit*, σ. τῷ ἀνδρὶ *Rev.Ét.Gr.*19. 115 (Aphrodisias), cf. *BCH*28.46 (Panamara), *Supp.Epigr.*4.275, 281 (ibid.). *** -κᾰλέω**, *join in love of the beautiful*, Plu.2.53c, *Sert.* 14; τινι *with* one, J.*AJ Prooem.*2; εἴς τι D.S.3.59. **-λογέω**, *join in literary studies*, Cic.*Fam.*16.21.8, Iamb. *in Nic.* p.125 P. **-μᾰθέω**, *join in love of knowledge*, Dion.Calliph.23. **-νῑκέω**, *take part with, side with*, τινι And.4.20, Pl.*Prt.*336e, Str.8.6.23, D.H.6.57, etc. **2.** abs., *join in a disputation*, Plu.*Arat.*3: hence **-νῑκία**, ἡ, dub. in Phld.*Rh.*1.161 S. **-σοφέω**, *join in the love and pursuit of wisdom*, Arist.*EN*1172ᵃ5, Plu.*Cic.*24, Luc.*DMort.*18.2, etc.; σ. τινὶ τὰ Ἀριστοτέλεια *study* Aristotle's *philosophy with*.., Str.16.2.24, cf. Epicur. *Fr.*217 (Testamentum Epicuri). **-τῑμέομαι**, *join in zealous efforts*, abs. or c. dat., D.S.2.18, Plu.2.813c, *Luc.*6, *Supp.Epigr.*4. 319.2 (Panamara, ii A.D.), etc.; τινὶ εἴς τι *IG*2².1225.6 (Salamis, iii B.C.), D.S.19.52:—also Act., -τιμῶν τῇ τοῦ πατρὸς προαιρέσει *Supp. Epigr.*4.442 (Milet., ii B.C.).

**συμφλάω**, *crush in pieces*, Hp.*Foet.Exsect.*1, *Epid.*5.74, *Mul.*1.70, *IG*11(2).199*B*16, 203*B*46 (Delos, iii B.C.).

**συμφλεγμαίνω**, *to be inflamed at the same time*, Gal.10.909, 16.539, al., Aret.*CA*2.8.

**συμφλέγω**, *burn up, burn to cinders*, E.*Ba.*595 (lyr.); σ. κεραυνῷ Theoc.22.211; σ. αὐτοὺς κύκλῳ Lxx *Is.*42.25; with love, *AP*5.110 (Antiphil.):—Pass., συμφλέγεσθαι ὑπὸ τῶν κεραυνῶν Plu.*Alex.*60.

**συμφλογίζω**, = foreg., Lxx *2Ma.*6.11, Thd.*Is.*42.25.

**συμφλῠᾱρέω**, *chatter* or *trifle along with*, τινι M.Ant.9.41.

**συμφοβέω**, *frighten at the same time*, D.C.51.26:—Pass., *to be afraid at the same time*, Th.6.101.

**συμφοιτ-άω**, Ion. -έω, *go regularly to* a place *together*, Hdt.2.60, 4.180; esp., *go to school together*, Ar.*Eq.*988 (lyr.), Pl.*Euthd.*272d, D.39.24, Gal.6.756; τινι *with* one, Luc.*Ind.*3; παρά τινα Pl.*Euthd.* 304b, etc.; εἰς ταὐτὸ διδασκαλεῖόν τινι X.*Smp.*4.23; εἰς Ἀσκληπιοῦ Aristid.*Or.*23(42).16. (Cf. φοιτάω I. 5, φοιτητής.) **-ησις**, εως, ἡ, *going to school together*, Aeschin.1.10; to the Senate, D.C.55. 3. **2.** *coming together*, of the coupling of beasts, πρὸς ἀλλήλους Ael.*NA*6.60. **-ητής**, οῦ, ὁ, *schoolfellow*, Pl.*Euthd.*272c, *Phdr.* 255a, X.*HG*2.4.20, Arist.*EN*1162ᵃ33, Gal.16.684. **II.** *fellow-pilgrim* to the temple of Asclepius, Aristid.*Or.*50(26).42 (pl.), 48(24). 27, 28(49).133. (Cf. φοιτητής.)

**συμφονεύω**, *kill along with, join in killing*, τινά τινι E.*Hec.*391, cf. *Ion*851, 1044.

*** συμφορ-ά**, Ion. -ρή, ἡ, (συμφέρω) *bringing together, collecting*, βελῶν Polem.*Cyn.*24; *conjunction*, νούσων μυρίων τε καὶ κακῶν Aret. *SD*2.11; *comparison*, τὰς ξ. τῶν βουλευμάτων S.*OT*44 (but in signf. II. 1, = τὰς συντυχίας καὶ ἀποβάσεις, acc. to Sch.):—pedantically for συμβολή, *a contribution*, Luc.*Lex*.6. II. commonly (from συμφέρω A. III. 4, and B. III), *event, circumstance, chance, hap*, πᾶν ἐστι ἄνθρωπος συμφορή Hdt.1.32; αἱ σ. τῶν ἀνθρώπων ἄρχουσι, καὶ οὐκὶ ὥνθρωποι τῶν σ. Id.7.49; συμφορὰς βίου A.*Eu*.1020 (lyr.), cf. 897, *Fr*.96A; ἔν τε συμφοραῖς βίου S.*OT*33; ξυμφορᾶς ἵν' ἕσταμεν in what a *plight* I am, Id.*Tr*.1145; ὦ ξ. τάλαινα τῶν ἐμῶν κακῶν Ar.*Ach*.1204; ξυμφορᾶς τίνος κυρῆσαι; E.*Ion* 536 (troch.); πρὸς τὰς ξ. καὶ τὰς γνώμας τρέπεσθαι Th.1.140; αἱ ξ. τῶν πραγμάτων ibid. 2. *mishap, misfortune*, Hippon.49.4, etc.; early writers freq. add an epith., σ. ἄχαρις Hdt.1.41, 7.190; οἰκτρά Pi.*O*.7.77; κακή A.*Pers*.445; τάλαινα S.*El*.1179: c. gen., σ. πάθους A.*Pers*.436; κακοῦ ib.1030 (lyr.): but the word came to be used alone in a bad sense, συμφορᾷ δεδαιγμένοι (or δεδαγμ-) Pi.*P*.8.87; ὑπὸ τῆς σ. ἐκπεπληγμένος Hdt.3.64; συμφορῇ τοιῇδε κεχρημένος Id.1.42, cf. Antipho 3.2.8; αἱ παροῦσαι σ. S.*Ph*.885; ἐς (ἐπὶ codd.) συμφορὴν ἐμπεσεῖν, of a hurt or a disease, Hdt.7.88; of *defects* of character, τριῶν τῶν μεγίστων ξ., ἀξυνεσίας ἢ μαλακίας ἢ ἀμελείας Th.1.122; of overpowering passion, X.*Cyr*.6.1.37: euphem. for ἄγος, S.*OT*99; for ἀτιμία, And.1.86; for banishment, X.*HG*1.1.27, Isoc.5.58; *offence, trespass*, Pl.*Lg*.854d, 934b; συμφορήν or μεγάλην σ. ποιεῖσθαί (τι) look upon or consider a thing as a great *misfortune*, Hdt.1.83, 4.79, 5.35, etc.; folld. by ὅτι, Id.1.216, etc.; σ. νομίζειν, κρίνειν, ἡγεῖσθαι, X.*Ages*.7.4, 11.9, Pl.*Phd*.84e: prov., πῖνε, πῖν' ἐπὶ συμφοραῖς Simon.(14) ap.Ar.*Eq*.406; of a person, μηδὲ συμφορὰν δέχου τὸν ἄνδρα, i.e. ὡς ὄντα σ., S.*Aj*.68; τὸν ἄνθρωπον ..κοινὴν τῶν Ἑλλήνων σ. Aeschin.3.253; σ. τῆς πόλεως Din.1.65. 3. rarely in good sense, *good luck, happy issue*, A.*Ag*.24, S.*El*.1230 (pl.); σ. καίριοι A.*Ch*.1064; εὔανδροι Id.*Eu*.1031; σ. ἐσθλαί, εὐδαίμονες, E.*Alc*.1155, *Hel*.457; σ. ἀγαθαί Ar.*Eq*.655. **-άζω**, *bewail*, Lxx *Is*.13.8, Orph.*Fr*.49.52, Sch.S.*Ant*.528; τὰς ἰδίας κακοπαθείας Phld.*Mort*.25, cf. Crates *Ep*.26, Diog.*Ep*.29.1:—Med., Ps.-Callisth.2.15. **-αίνω**, = foreg., Ps.-Hdt.*Vit.Hom*.14. **-εύς**, έως, ὁ, a Spartan staff-officer, *aide-de-camp*, X.*HG*6.4.14. **-έω**, = συμφέρω, in the primary sense, *bring together, collect, heap up*, Hdt.5.92.η′; τὰ ὀστέα ἐς ἕνα χῶρον Id.9.83; τὰ χρήματα ib.81; τὰ γέρρα ib.99; λίθους καὶ ξύλα Th.6.99; εἰς μίαν οἴκησιν πάντα χρήματα Pl.*Lg*.805e; πνεῦμα σ. τὴν χιόνα X.*Cyn*.8.1; αἰτίας καὶ σκώμματα καὶ λοιδορίας σ. D.18.15; συμπτωμάτων πλῆθος οὐχ ὁμογενῶν Gal.16.811; [λόγους] Luc.*Pisc*.22:—Med., *collect for oneself*, Arist.*Mir*.832$^{a}$24 (perh. Pass.); of birds building nests, Id.*HA*559$^{a}$10:—Pass., *to be collected*, opp. διαφορεῖσθαι, Pl.*Lg*.693a, cf. Epicur.*Ep*.1 p.23 U.; ἵππος εἰκῇ συμπεφορημένος *put together* anyhow, Pl.*Phdr*.253e; καλιὰν ἐκ δένδρων συμπεφορημένην Luc.*VH*2.40; συμπεφορημένη *jumbled together* (with a play on συμφορά), Pl.*Phlb*.64e; *join streams*, of rivers, A.R.1.39. 2. metaph., συμπεφορημένος, of a person whose philosophy is a *jumble* of opinions, Epicur.*Nat*.14.7; cf. συμπεφορημένως. **-ημα**, ατος, τό, *that which is brought together, compound*, Ph.1.184, Plu.2.955a; τέφρας καὶ ὕδατος Ph.1.654. **-ησις**, εως, ἡ, *bringing together*, Plu.*Per*.34, *Oth*.14; of the *concourse* of atoms, Epicur.*Ep*.1 p.18 U. II. *collection*, προτάσεων Plot.5.8.4. **-ητός**, ή, όν, (ος, ον Arist.*Pol*.1286$^{a}$29) *brought together, collected*, πόλις ἐκ πολλῶν σ. ἐθνῶν D.H.3.10; χρησμοὶ ἐκ πολλῶν τόπων Id.4.62; σ. ὄχλος Id.*Dem*.36; σ. ἐκ ποικίλων πτερῶν Luc.*Pseudol*.5; ἐκ σ. ῥακίων ἠπημένος *BCH*51.326 (Athens). 2. σ. δεῖπνα, σ. ἑστίασις, a meal *towards which each guest contributes, picnic*, Arist.*Pol*.1281$^{b}$3, 1286$^{a}$29. **-ία**, ἡ, = *calamitas*, *Gloss*. (s.v.l.). **-ίας**· συμπεφορημένης, συμμίκτου, Hsch. **-ος**, ον, *accompanying*, λιμὸς ἀεργῷ σύμφορος ἀνδρί hunger is the sluggard's *companion*, Hes.*Op*.302: c. gen., πενίης οὐ σύμφοροι, ἀλλὰ κόροιο Id.*Th*.593. II. *suitable, useful, profitable*, c. dat., ἕκτη..κούρῃ οὐ σύμφορός ἐστιν the sixth day is not *good* for a girl, Id.*Op*.783; οὐ.. σύμφορόν ἐστι γυνὴ νέα ἀνδρὶ γέροντι Thgn.457; ἡ πενίη κακῷ σύμφορος ἀνδρὶ φέρειν Id.526; πολλῷ ξυμφορώτερον ἐς.. Th.3.47; πρὸς.. Pl.*Lg*.766e, Isoc.6.74 (Sup.); σύμφορόν ἐστι, = συμφέρει, Hdt.8.60.α′, S.*OC*592; Πλούτῳ..τοῦτο -ώτατον Ar.*Pl*.1162, cf. Th.2.36: τὰ σ. *what is expedient*, S.*OC*464, etc.; τῶν ἀναγκαίων ξυμφόρων διαναστάς departing from his necessary (i.e. natural) *interests*, Th.4.128; δρᾶν τὰ -ώτατά τινι E.*Med*.876; τὸ ὑμέτερον ξ. your *plea of expediency*, opp. τὸ δίκαιον, Th.5.98, cf. 3.47. Adv., -ρως ἔχειν to be *expedient*, Isoc.5.102; χρῆσθαι X.*Cyr*.4.2.45: Comp. -ώτερον Id.*HG*6.5.39: Sup. -ώτατα Th.8.43, X.*Cyr*.5.3.22, *PCair.Zen*.637.14 (iii B.C.), etc. 2. rarely of persons, ξυμφορώτατοι προσπολεμῆσαι *most convenient* to make war upon, Th.8.96. III. τὸ σύμφορον ὄνομα is f.l. for τὸ σῦφαρ ὄνομα (cj. Schöne, *Berl.Sitzb*.1924.100) in Gal.6.379.

**συμφράδμων**, ονος, ὁ, ἡ, *one who joins in considering, counsellor*, αἲ γὰρ..τοιοῦτοι δέκα μοι συμφράδμονες εἶεν Il.2.372; σ. θέσθαι τινά Call.*Aet*.3.1.28, Naumach.ap.Stob.4.23.7, cf. Posidon.ap.Gal.5.400, Tryph.112. II. *harmonious, in accord*, κανόνες σ. αὐλῶν *AP*9.365 (Jul.); θυμός A.R.*Fr*.8.

**συμφράζομαι**, Med., Ep. fut. -άσσομαι Il.9.374: pf. ξυμπέφρασμαι S.*Ant*.364 (lyr.):—poet. Verb, *join in considering, take counsel with*, c. dat., ἑῷ συμφράσσατο θυμῷ, ὅππως.. Od.15.202; also τίς νύ τοι θεῶν συμφράσσατο βουλάς; who *imparted* his counsels to thee? 4.462, cf. Il.1.537, 9.374: but μῆτιν συμφράσσασθαι (sc. ἑαυτῷ) *contrive* a plan, Hes.*Th*.471; νόσων φυγὰς ξυμπέφρασται S. l.c. II. in later Prose Act. **συμφράζω**, *mention at the same time*, Str.8.6.17:—Pass., *to be used in the same context with*, c. dat., Gal.16.706; τὰ συμφραζόμενα *the context*, Plu.2.22a, Gal.16.707, 18(1).437. 2. Pass., *to be synonymous with*, c. dat., Aret.*SD*1.5.

**συμφράκτωρ**, ορος, ὁ, *coactor*, *Gloss*. (fort. συμπρ-).

⊛ **σύμφραξις**, εως, ἡ, *closing up, obstruction*, Thphr.*CP*5.11.3.

**σύμφρᾰσις**, εως, ἡ, *continuous speech*, Hdn.Gr.1.10, Phot.*Bibl*. p.107 B.; v.l. for συμφρόνησις, Philol.10.

**συμφράσσω**, Att. **-ττω**, fut. -ξω:—*press* or *pack closely together*, τὰς ναῦς X.*HG*1.1.7; τὰς σαρίσας Plb.2.69.9. 2. abs., of troops, *close their ranks, form in close order*, Id.4.64.7, 10.14.12, Plu.*Ages*.18:—Med., D.C.62.12. 3. Med., *conspire*, Agath.4.28. II. *fence all round*, λιθοειδεῖ περιβόλῳ Pl.*Ti*.74a, cf. e; *make air-tight*, [πίλους] Hdt.4.73. 2. *block up, close*, τὰ παράδρομα X.*Cyn*.6.9; τοὺς πόρους Thphr.*Fr*.10.6:—Pass., of passages in the body, Hp.*Aër*.9, *Mul*.1.40; ἔλυσε τὰ συμπεφραγμένα *the obstructed pores*, Pl.*Phdr*.251e, cf. Thphr.*CP*6.11.7. III. Act. intr. in signf. II, ἡ ἀναπνοὴ συμφράττει Arist.*Pr*.964$^{a}$31.

**συμφρονέω**, *to be of one mind with* any one, *agree* or *conspire with*, σ. ἀλλήλοις εἴς τι Plb.4.60.4, cf. Lxx 3*Ma*.3.2; ἐπί τινι Plb.3.2.8; περί τινων πρὸς τοὺς φίλους Id.4.81.3, cf. 7.16.3; σ. ταὐτά Id.6.46.8: abs., *agree together*, Id.2.22.1, etc. 2. *think with, be in harmony with*, τῷ νοερῷ M.Ant.8.54. II. *become aware of, think of, notice, understand*, ὃ δέον εἴη ποιεῖν Plb.18.26.2, cf. D.H.5.9, Plu.*Nic*.19, 23, *Them*.28, *Brut*.10, *Pyrrh*.11, *Eum*.19, *Cam*.29, 36, etc. 2. *collect oneself, become conscious*, Id.*Cat.Mi*.70, *Alex*.73. III. *bring together in thought*, τὰ πλεῖστον ἀλλήλων ἀφεστῶτα τοῖς τόποις Arist.*Mu*.391$^{a}$14 (v.l. τῇ διανοίᾳ συνεφόρησε, which may be a gloss).

**συμφρόνησις**, εως, ἡ, *agreement, union*, Philol.10, Plb.2.37.8, J.*AJ*19.8.1, App.*BC*4.17, etc.

**συμφροντίζω**, *have a joint care for*, τινος Luc.*Dem.Enc*.25: abs., *IG*2$^{2}$.1329.18.

**συμφροσύνη**, ἡ, = συμφρόνησις, App.*BC*2.9.

⊛ **σύμφρουρος**, ον, *watching with*, μέλαθρον ξύμφρουρον ἐμοί the chamber *that keeps watch with* me, i.e. *in which I lie sleepless*, S.*Ph*.1453 (anap.). II. Thess. σύμφρουρος, ὁ, *joint-φρουρός*, Ἀρχ.Ἐφ.1911.124 (Gonni); also **σύμπρουρος**, *IG*9(2).1058 (pl., Mopsium).

**συμφρυγμός**, ὁ, *burning ague*, Al.*Le*.26.16.

**συμφρύγω** [ῡ], *burn* or *parch quite up*, Thphr.*Ign*.62; ἐπιθυμία ὕδατος σ. τινά Lxx 4*Ma*.3.11:—Pass., aor. συνεφρύγην [ῠ] ib.*Jb*.30.30, al.

**σύμφρων**, ονος, ὁ, ἡ, (φρήν) *of one mind, brotherly*, A.*Ag*.110 (lyr.): c. dat., *agreeing*, Pl.*Ep*.324b. 2. *favouring, propitious*, θεοί A.*Ch*.802 (lyr.).

**συμφῠάς**, άδος, ἡ, (συμφύω) *a growing together, connexion by natural growth*, δύο ὀστέων Hp.*Fract*.44; σ. δένδρων Sch.Il.22.191.

**συμφῠγᾰδεύω**, *banish at the same time*, Iamb.*VP*35.262, Phot.

⊛ **συμφῠγάς**, άδος, ὁ, ἡ, *fellow-exile*, E.*Ba*.1382 (anap.), Th.6.88, X.*HG*1.2.13.

**συμφύγιον**, *confugium*, *Gloss*.

**συμφῠή**, ἡ, = σύμφυσις, Ael.*NA*14.16.

⊛ **συμφῠής**, ές, *born with one, congenital, natural*, ὕδωρ..εἴτ' ἐπακτὸν εἴτε συμφυές Arist.*Mete*.382$^{b}$11; συμφυέστερον ἀνελευθερία..τῆς ἀσωτίας Id.*EN*1121$^{b}$14; σ. κακά Plb.6.4.8. Adv., συμφυῶς ἔχειν πρὸς ἄλληλα to be *naturally* related, Arist.*Phgn*.805$^{a}$10, cf. Ael.*NA*12.27. 2. *adapted by nature*, ἀκοῇ σ. ἀήρ Arist.*de An*.420$^{a}$4; τοῖς σώμασιν Epicur.*Fr*.30, cf. *Ep*.1 p.14 U. II. *grown together, naturally united*, of the embryo in the womb, Arist.*GA*737$^{b}$17; of the shells of bivalves, opp. μονοφυής, Id.*HA*525$^{a}$22, *Fr*.304; of roots or branches, Thphr.*HP*5.2.4, al.; also σ. λίθος *compact, solid*, Id.*CP*3.6.5; τοῖχος D.S.2.49. 2. c. dat., *attached, adhering*, ἡ γλῶττα τῇ κάτω σιαγόνι σ., of the crocodile, Arist.*PA*660$^{b}$28; συμφυεῖς οἱ τένοντες ὑπάρχουσι τοῖς ὀστοῖς Gal.6.194; μῆλον..σ. ἀκρεμόσιν *AP*6.252 (Antiphil.): abs., *forming one body, coalescing*, of the tongue of the τέττιξ, Arist.*HA*532$^{b}$12; of vision and the organ of vision, Pl.*Ti*.45d, cf. *Sph*.247d; of matter, *cohesive, compact*, Arist.*GC*327$^{a}$1, *Ph*.255$^{a}$12; τὰ συμφυέα the *undivided* (*median*) organs, viz. tongue and nose, opp. διεστῶτα (eyes, arms, legs), Aret.*SD*1.7; τῷ κοινῷ συμφυεῖς *organic parts of* the commonwealth, Plu.*Lyc*.25. III. rarely c. gen., γένος ἀνθρώπων σ. τοῦ παντὸς χρόνου *congenital* or *bound up with*.., Pl.*Lg*.721c; σ. ἡμῶν *combined with* us, Id.*Ti*.64d.—Cf. σύμφυτος.

**συμφῠΐα**, ἡ, = σύμφυσις, Ph.2.319, Plu.2.1080f, 1112a, S.E.*M*.7.129, etc.

**συμφῠλᾰκίτης** [ῑ], ου, ὁ, *fellow-φυλακίτης*, *PRein*.17.1 (pl., ii B.C.).

⊛ **συμφύλαξ** [ῠ], ᾰκος, ὁ, *fellow-watchman* or *guard*, Th.5.80, Pl.*R*.463b,c; σ. τινὶ τῆς ἀρχῆς, τῆς εὐδαιμονίας, X.*Cyr*.8.6.11, 8.1.10.

**συμφῠλάσσω**, *keep guard along with* others, Hdt.7.172; τὴν οὐσίαν X.*Mem*.2.8.3, cf. Pl.*R*.451d; τὴν πρὸς Ῥωμαίους εὔνοιαν *SIG*742.10 (Ephesus, i B.C.), etc.

**συμφῡλ-έτης**, ου, ὁ, *of the same φυλή*, *IG*12(2).505.18 (Methymna): generally, *fellow-countryman*, 1*Ep.Thess*.2.14. **-ία**, ἡ, *kindred material*, Epicur.*Ep*.2 p.54 U. (v.l. συμφιλία); *kinship*, Phld.*D*.3.*Fr*.87. **-ος**, ον, *of the same stock* or *race with*, αἱ μέλιτται καὶ τὰ σ. ζῷα ταύταις Arist.*PA*682$^{b}$10; οἱ σύμφυλοι *his congeners*, Babr.101.3. II. metaph., *of the same class with*, βρονταί τε καὶ ἀστραπαὶ.. καὶ τἆλλα ἃ δὴ τούτοις ἐστὶ σ. Arist.*Mu*.394$^{a}$19; *cognate, suitable*, νομή, τροφή, Plu.2.729c, 991b; τὸ σ. ib.661e; of digested food, συμφυλοτέραν τῷ ζῴῳ γενομένην Gal.6.303; τὰ σ. τῷ σώματι Plu.2.137b; τὸ -ότατον [τῷ ἀνθρώπῳ] Phld.*Vit*.p.28 J.; τῶν σ. ἡμῖν οἶνος Orib.*Fr*.124; σ. ἡ νόησις τῷ μερισμῷ Dam.*Pr*.146. 2. συμφύλων (-φίλων cod.) χειρῶν προσαφῇ (πρὸς ἀφὴν cod.) θάλποντα (translated *cum quodam calidarum manuum amplexu*, Cael.Aur.*TP*3.22) Sor.2.28 (dub.).

**συμφύνω**, v. συμφύω.

**συμφῡράω**, = συμφύρω, Hp.*Int.*23:—Pass., Dsc.2.24 (v.l. -ρμένον), J.*AJ*3.9.4, Plu.2.94d (v.l. -ρμένον), Ath.11.464b. 2. *mix up with*, λίθῳ καὶ χαλκῷ [θεόν] Plu.2.398a; τρωθεὶς συνεφυρήθη ἑτέροις πτώμασι Vett.Val.275.19.

**συμφύρ-δην**, Adv. *mixedly*, Nic.*Th.*110. **-σις**, εως, ἡ, *confusion*, τῶν θείων εἰδῶν Procl.*inPrm.*p.598 S. **-τος**, ον, *commingled, confounded*, E.*Hipp.*1234.

**συμφύρω** [ῡ], aor. 2 Pass. συνεφύρην [ῠ] J.*BJ*2.8.10: fut. Pass. συμφῠρήσομαι Sch.Pi.*N.*1.100: most freq. in pf. part. Pass.:—*knead together*, σ. εἰς ἕν Pl.*Phlb.*15e: mostly Pass., σ. κόμμι αἵματι Dsc.2.24 (as v.l. for -αμένον); αἷμα συμπεφυρμένον πυρί E.*Med.*1199; πλούτῳ..πάντα συμπεφ. Pherecr.108.1; ἡδοναὶ συμπεφ. λύπαις Pl.*Phlb.* 51a; ψυχὴ συμπεφ. μετὰ κακοῦ Id.*Phd.*66b; βιοτὴ..πολλῇσι κηρσὶ συμπεφυρμένη Democr.285. 2. *mess up, disfigure*, πληγαῖς συνέφυρε πρόσωπον Theoc.22.111; αἵματι συνεπέφυρτο τὴν κεφαλήν Plu.*Fab.*16: metaph., *confuse, confound*, Phld.*Vit.*p.27 J.; τὴν πόλιν συμπεφ. ταῖς οἰκήσεσιν *built without plan*, Plu.*Cam.*32.

**συμφῡσάω**, *blow together*, metaph., εἰς ταὐτὸν (τὸ λεγόμενον) συμφυσῆσαι *blow* (as the saying is) *together*, i.e. *work together*, Pl.*Lg.* 708d:—Pass., of the wind, *blow at the same time*, Plu.*Sert.* 17. II. *weld together*, συντῆξαι καὶ συμφυσῆσαι εἰς τὸ αὐτό Pl.*Smp.*192d:—Pass., Arist.*Cael.*304$^{a}$21: metaph., *contrive*, ταῦτ' ἐφ' οἷσίν ἐστι συμφυσώμενα Ar.*Eq.*468 (cf. Sch.).

**σύμφῠσις**, εως, ἡ, (συμφύω) *growing together, natural junction*, esp. of the bones, Hp.*Fract.*37, cf. *Art.*34; opp. ἁφή, as being not *mere contact*, but *continuity of substance*, Arist.*Metaph.*1014$^{b}$22, cf. 1069$^{a}$12, *Ph.*227$^{a}$23; σ. ὀστῶν Id.*HA*518$^{b}$8; so of bones united, κατὰ σύμφυσιν, opp. articulation (κατ' ἄρθρον), Gal.2.734, *PLit.Lond.*167.19 (ii/iii A.D.); of attachment of muscles to bones, Gal.2.445,484; ἡ σ. τοῦ δέρματος καὶ τῆς σαρκός Pl.*Ti.*77d, cf. Arist.*HA*547$^{a}$16, *PA* 693$^{b}$25; ἡ πρὸς τὴν μήτραν σ. [τοῦ χορίου] Sor.1.73; *closing* or *healing up* of an injured tree, Thphr.*HP*9.2.6; ἡ σ. καὶ ἡ τάξις *structure* and arrangement of a physical body, Id.*Sens.*79, cf. *Lap.*11; ἔντερον συμφύσεις ἔχον, of intestines divided into chambers by constriction, Arist.*HA*507$^{b}$35; ἡ σ. τοῦ πνεύμονος κατὰ ῥάχιν Aret.*SD*1.9; of the tongue, ib.7. 2. metaph. of the mystic's union with the Supreme Being, Porph.*Abst.*1.29.

**συμφῠτ-εύω**, *plant along with* or *together*, *Gp.*12.7.2:—Pass., c. dat., Dsc.4.162, 5.67. 2. metaph., σύν τέ οἱ δαίμων φυτεύει δόξαν *helps* him *to achieve* glory, Pi.*I.*6(5).12; δοκῶν ξυμφυτεῦσαι τοὔργον *to have had a hand in contriving*, S.*OT*347:—Pass., *to be implanted also*, ἐν τῷ αὐτῷ σώματι συμπεφ. τῇ ψυχῇ αἱ ἡδοναί X.*Mem.*1.2.23. **-ικός**, ή, όν, *causing to unite*, c. gen., Olymp.*in Mete.*275.2; φάρμακον Gal.10.347. 2. *tending to close up*, of a wound, Arist.*Pr.*863$^{a}$15. **-ον**, τό, *comfrey*, *Symphytum bulbosum*, Arist.*HA*616$^{a}$1, Dsc.4.10, Ael.*NA*4.47. 2. σ. πετραῖον, *low pine*, *Coris monspeliensis*, Dsc.4.9. 3. = ἑλένιον, Id.1.28. 4. = γλυκύρριζα, Id.3.5 (versio Latina). **-ος**, ον, *born with one, congenital, innate*, ἀρετά Pi.*I.*3.14; κακόν, ἐπιθυμία, Pl.*R.*609a, *Plt.*272e; of diseases, Hp.*Coac.*502; βλάβαι καὶ διαφθοραὶ τοῦ σώματος Gal.6.3; *natural*, τῶν σιτίων ἔνια ἔχει γλυκύτητα σ. ib.475, cf. 731; σ. ἐχούσης ὑγρότητα τῆς γλώττης Id.16.508; σ. αἰών our *natural* age, i.e. our old age (acc. to the Sch.), A.*Ag.*107 (lyr.); νεικέων τέκτονα σ. the *natural* author of strife, i.e. a cause of strife *natural to the race*, ib.152 (lyr.); εἰς τὸ σ. according to *one's nature*, E.*Andr.*954; ὕδωρ σ. ἐν γάλακτι, opp. ἐπακτόν, Arist.*Mete.*382$^{b}$12; τὸ μιμεῖσθαι σ. τοῖς ἀνθρώποις Id.*Po.*1448$^{b}$5; σ. [πνεῦμα], i.e. the vital spirit, Id.*Spir.* 482$^{a}$8; σ. ὑγρὸν καὶ θερμόν (in a seed) Thphr.*HP*1.11.1; πρῶτον ἀγαθὸν καὶ σύμφυτον ἡδονή Epicur.*Ep.*3 p.63 U.; τὰ σ. *natural functions* or *parts*, Arist.*GA*753$^{a}$17, *Ph.*253$^{a}$12. 2. c. dat., *natural to*, σ. αὐτοῖς δειλία Lys.10.28; ἀΰδρία τισὶ τόποις σ. Pl.*Lg.*844b; τὰ ὑγρὰ σ. τοῖς ζῴοις, opp. τὰ ὑστερογενῆ (such as milk), Arist.*HA*521$^{b}$17, cf. Thphr.*Sens.*1,16. 3. c. gen., [τῶν φθόγγων] σ. ἡδοναί Pl.*Phlb.* 51d; εὐβουλία ἀρετὴ λογισμοῦ σ. Id.*Def.*413c: cf. συγγενής, σύγγονος. 4. *like by nature, cognate, kindred*, Id.*Phlb.*16c. II. *grown together*, διάστασις τῶν σ. μερῶν Arist.*Top.*145$^{b}$3; σ. τῷ χιτῶνι Id.*HA*557$^{b}$18; ἐγκεφάλου σκέπασμα σ. μὲν οὐκέτι, πολλαχόθι μέντοι συμφυές Gal.*UP*8.9; σ. ἐμποιεῖν τινί τι Pl.*Phd.*81c; *united*, Id.*Phdr.* 246a, *Ep.Rom.*6.5; of qualities in relation to matter, ὕλη..λαβοῦσα ποιότητας..καὶ οἷον συμφύτους αὐτὰς ἔχουσα καὶ συγκεκραμένας ἀλλήλαις Plot.3.6.8, cf. 3.6.11. III. *thickly wooded*, Plb.1.74.6, D.C.40.29. 2. *fully cultivated*, ἀμπελὼν σ. *PGrenf.*2.28.7 (ii B.C.), *PLips.*1.5 (ii B.C.).

**συμφύω**, later **-φύνω** *CR*33.5 (near Antioch):—*make to grow together, unite* a wound, D.S.32.11 (cj.), Dsc.1.128; σ. τὰ ὁμογενῆ Arist.*Mete.*378$^{b}$15; σ. τοὺς ἄνωθεν ὀδόντας imagine them *unite into one*, Id.*PA*659$^{b}$24; σ. τινὰς εἰς φιλότητα *unite* them, Pl.*Ep.*323b: but συμφῦσαι in Id.*Smp.*192e is f.l. for συμφυσῆσαι. II. Pass., with pf. Act. συμπέφῡκα, aor. 2 συνέφῡν (3 sg. opt. συμφύη Sor.2.89); also συνεφύην Arist.*Pol.*1262$^{b}$13, Thphr.*CP*5.5.3, Sor.1.36, etc.: fut. συμφυήσομαι *Gp.*4.12.9:—*grow together*, Emp.26.7,95 (tm.), Pl.*Smp.*191a, *Ti.*76e, X.*Cyr.*4.3.18, etc.; [ψυχὴ καὶ σῶμα] Pl.*Phdr.* 246d; of a political constitution, Plb.4.32.9. 2. *grow together, unite*, as a wound, Hp.*Aph.*6.24, al.; of bones, Id.*Art.*14, Sor.2.57; of the mouth of the womb and other passages, Arist.*GA*773$^{a}$16, cf. 747$^{a}$12; τὰ χείλη καὶ τὰ βλέφαρα καὶ τῶν δακτύλων τὰ μεταξὺ πολλάκις ἑλκωθέντα συνέφυ, κατὰ φύσιν δὲ ἔχοντα..οὐ συμφύεται διὰ λειότητα Diocl.*Fr.*26; διὰ τί οἱ αἰδούμενοι τοὺς ὀφθαλμοὺς συμπεφύκασι; Alex.Aphr.*Pr.*1.70. 3. *unite with*, οὐ τῷ τυχόντι συμφύεται τὸ τυχόν Arist.*Sens.*438$^{b}$1; συμπεφυκυῖαι ἰδέαι εἰς ἕν, e.g. Chimaera, etc., Pl.*R.*588c; εἰς ταὐτὸν συμφύεσθαι ib.503b; σ. πρός τι Plu.2.924e. 4. *become assimilated, become natural*, Arist.*EN*1147$^{a}$22.

**συμφων-έω**, *sound together, be in harmony* or *unison* (cf. συμφωνία), ἐκ πασῶν μία ἁρμονία συμφωνεῖ Pl.*R.*617b, cf. Thphr.*Sens.*85, Arist.*Pr.*919$^{b}$2, Ion Eleg.3; of reed-tongues, *to be of the same quality*, Thphr.*HP*4.11.7; κιθαρισταὶ σ. Callix.2; cf. συμφωνία III:—Pass., τὰ συμφωνούμενα *consonants* (lit. things *which are sounded with* vowels), D.H.*Dem.*43. II. metaph., *harmonize with*, ποῖα ποίοις σ. τῶν γενῶν Pl.*Sph.*253b, cf. *Phd.*101d, Arist.*EN*1107$^{a}$32; σ. τοῖς εἰρημένοις Pl.*R.*398c; τὰ ἔργα οὐ σ. τοῖς λόγοις Id.*La.*193e; συμφωνοῦντα τοῖς ἔργοις *in harmony with* practical experience, Gal.19.217; ἐπιθυμίαι οὐ σ. ἀλλήλαις Isoc.5.87; οὐ συμφωνοῦσι..φροντίδες μακαριότητι Epicur.*Ep.*1 p.28 U.; also ταῦτα πρὸς ἄλληλα σ. συμφωνίαν τὴν ἀρίστην Arist.*Pol.*1334$^{b}$10; *hold* or *express the same opinions*, ταῦτα συμφωνοῦσι πάντες Thphr.*CP*6.9.2; ἔν τισι Pl.*Phdr.*263b; περί τινος or τινων, Democr.107, D.H.2.47:—Med., Thphr.*CP*1.1.1:—Pass., *to be agreed to*, παρὰ πᾶσι D.S.1.20; εἰ συνεφωνεῖτο πάντα τοῖς γράψασι περὶ τροφῆς Gal.6.454, cf. 15.107: c. inf., ἡ ἔφοδος σ. γενέσθαι D.H.1.74: impers., τὴν ἁρπαγὴν γεγονέναι συμπεφώνηται D.S.5.69, cf. Gal.6.391; σ. ὅτι.. D.S.1.26. 2. *make an agreement* or *bargain with* any one, ἰδίᾳ σ. πρὸς αὐτούς *PCair.Zen.*302.13 (iii B.C.); συμφωνήσας Ἡρακλείδης μετὰ Θοτέως ib.330.2 (iii B.C.); περί τινος Plb.2.15.5; σ. τινὶ δηναρίου *for* a denarius, *Ev.Matt.*20.13:—Pass., συνεφωνήθη ὑμῖν πειράσαι *Act.Ap.*5.9; ὥστε.. D.S.14.26; τὸ συμφωνηθέν *the agreement*, Id.30.19; τὰ συμφωνηθέντα *IG*4$^{2}$(1).77.20 (Epid., ii B.C.); τὰ εἴκοσι τάλαντα τὰ συμφωνηθέντα ib.2$^{2}$.844.9 (iii B.C.); ἀπέχω τὴν συμπεφωνημένην αὐτοῦ τιμήν *BGU*1643.20 (ii A.D.). 3. *unite for a bad purpose, conspire*, τοῖς πένησι ἐπὶ τοὺς μέσους Arist.*Pol.*1297$^{a}$1. III. *agree in saying*, ὡς πάντα καλῶς κεῖται Pl.*Lg.*634e; ὅτι οὐκ ἀσφαλές ἐστι Arist.*Mir.*838$^{b}$34. IV. *to be satisfactory*, συμφωνεῖ μοι πάντα, ὡς πρόκειται *PAmh.*2.149.22 (vi A.D.), cf. *PLips.* 26.13 (iv A.D.), etc. 2. of remedies, *to be suitable*, Archig.ap.Aët.9.35, Gal.11.806. **-ημα**, ατος, τό, *agreement*, *PFlor.*379.7 (ii A.D.), Sch.Th.7.33; *watchword, token*, Sch.E.*Or.*1130. **-ησις**, εως, ἡ, *agreement*, 2*Ep.Cor.*6.15. II. = συνίζησις, *An.Ox.*4.326. **-ία**, ἡ, *concord* or *unison of sound*, τὴν ἐν τῇ ᾠδῇ ἁρμονίαν, ἣ δὴ σ. καλεῖται Pl.*Cra.*405d; ἡ γὰρ ἁρμονία σ. ἐστί, σ. δὲ ὁμολογία τις Id.*Smp.*187b, cf. *R.*430e; λόγος ἀριθμῶν ἐν ὀξεῖ ἢ βαρεῖ Arist.*APo.*90$^{a}$18, cf. *de An.*426$^{a}$29; κρᾶσίς ἐστι λόγον ἐχόντων ἐναντίων πρὸς ἄλληλα Id.*Pr.*921$^{a}$2. 2. of two sounds only, *musical concord, accord*, such as the fourth, fifth, and octave, Pl.*R.*531a,c; ἡ διὰ πασῶν σ. Arist.*Pr.*921$^{a}$13, cf. Hp.*Vict.*1.8; distd. from mere ὁμοφωνία, Arist.*Pol.*1263$^{b}$35. 3. *harmonious union of many voices or sounds, concert*, οἱ τῶν σ. λόγοι, the Pythag. doctrine *of the music of the spheres*, Id.*Cael.*290$^{b}$22, cf. *IG*14.793 (Naples). II. metaph., *harmony, agreement*, Pl.*Lg.*689d, Arist.*Pol.*1334$^{b}$10; σ. τις καὶ ἰσότης Thphr.*Fr.*89.8; σ. τῷ λόγῳ Pl.*R.*401d; σ. [τῆς ψυχῆς] ἑαυτῇ Id.*Ti.*47d; μείξας πάντα κατὰ συμφωνίαν, of a cook, Damox.2.54; *unanimity*, σ. τῶν ἱστορησάντων Gal.15.134; opp. διαφωνία, ib. 440; *concordance*, of theory with observed fact, ἔχειν τοῖς φαινομένοις σ. Epicur.*Ep.*2 p.36 U., cf. Phld.*Mort.*10; also ἡ πρὸς τὰ πάθη σ. Polystr.p.15 W.: in concrete sense, ἡ σ., = τὸ συμπεφωνημένον (cf. συμφωνέω II. 2), the *amount agreed upon*, *Ostr.*364 (i A.D.). III. *band, orchestra*, Ἑλληνικά 1.19 (Gytheum, i A.D.), *PFlor.*74.5 (ii A.D.), *POxy.*1275.9 (iii A.D.), and so perh. in Plb.26.1.4, 30.26.8, but used of a musical instrument in Lxx *Da.*3.5; so Lat. *symphonia*, of a kind of drum, Isid.*Etym.*3.22.14, but of a wind instrument, Plin.*HN*8.157; *symphoniae et cymbala strepitusque*, Cels.3.18.10; ἤκουσε συμφωνίας καὶ χορῶν *Ev.Luc.*15.25. **-ιᾰκός**, ή, όν, *of* or *for a choir*: *pueri symphoniaci*, *singing* boys, Cic.*Mil.*21.55. II. ἡ -κή, a variety of ὑοσκύαμος, Pall.*Agr.*11.12.8, Apul.*Herb.*4; ὑοσκύαμος -κή *Hippiatr.*22; cf. σύμφωνος III. **-ικός**, ή, όν, *specified in an agreement*, *PLond.*5.1676.41 (vi A.D.). ❀ **-ος**, ον, *agreeing in sound, harmonious*, Ar.*Av.*221 (anap.), 659 (anap.); χορδαί *h.Merc.* 51; μέλος S.*Ichn.*319; *echoing to* cries, Id.*OT*421; of a musical *accompanist*, *AP*9.584. 2. as musical term, *in concord* or *unison with*, Pl.*Ti.*80a, *Lg.*812d; σ. φθόγγοι Thphr.*Fr.*89.7; distd. from ἀντίφωνος and ὁμόφωνος, Arist.*Pr.*918$^{b}$30, 921$^{a}$7; distd. (as epith. of fifths, fourths, etc.) from ὁμόφωνος (of octaves, double octaves, etc.) and ἐμμελής (of smaller intervals), Ptol.*Harm.*1.7; τὸ σ., = συμφωνία, Pl.*Phlb.*56a. 3. τὰ σ. *consonants*, D.T.631.12, A.D.*Pron.*11.2, al., Heph.1.1, etc. 4. *having the same speech*, Philostr.*VA*5.36. II. metaph., *harmonious, in harmony* or *proportion*, τίνες σ. ἀριθμοί, καὶ τίνες οὔ Pl.*R.*531c; σ. φοραί Arist. *de An.*406$^{b}$31; ὁ βίος σ. τοῖς λόγοις πρὸς τὰ ἔργα Pl.*La.*188d; of a person, σ. ἑαυτὸν κατασκευάσαι κατὰ τὸν βίον Plb.31.25.8; τὸ σ. *harmonious order*, Arist.*Mu.*396$^{b}$8. 2. *harmonious, agreeing, friendly*, ἡσυχία Pi.*P.*1.70; δεξιώματα S.*OC*619; σ. τινί *in harmony* or *agreement with*, σ. αὐτὰ αὑτοῖς Pl.*R.*380c; σύμφωνα οἷς ἔλεγες Id.*Grg.*457e; σ. τῷ ὀνόματι Id.*Cra.*395e, cf. 436c, Gal.16.790 (Comp.); ἡδοναὶ..σ. τοῖς ὀρθοῖς λόγοις Pl.*Lg.*696c, cf. Thphr.*CP*6.11.14; esp. *concordant*, of theory with observed fact, Id.*Ign.*61; σ. τοῖς φαινομένοις Epicur.*Ep.*2 p.52 U., *Nat.*11.10 (Comp.), al. (and so Adv., -νως τοῖς φ. Id.*Ep.*2 p.36 U.); rarely with πρός, as πρὸς ἀρετήν, Pl.*Ep.*332d; σταθμοῖς καὶ μέτροις συμφώνοις ποτὶ τὰ δαμόσια *IG*5(1).1390.100 (Andania, i B.C.): c. gen., ὅσα τοῦ γένους ἐστὶ τούτου σύμφωνα Pl.*Phlb.*11b; ἐγένετο πᾶσι σύμφωνον περί τινος they *were agreed*, Plb.23.4.8; σ. ἐστί τινι πρός τινα

Id.6.36.5: rarely of persons, σ. γενέσθαι περί τινων Id.18.9.5; σ. εἶναί τισι Id.30.8.7; of planets, *in harmony*, Vett.Val.37.25. Adv. -νως Pl.*Epin*.974c, D.S.15.18, Herod.Med. in *Rh.Mus*.49.555, 58. 86; τινι D.S.1.98, cf. Lxx 4*Ma*.14.6; σ. ἔχειν τινί Ptol.*Geog*.1.17. 2. 3. Pass., *agreed upon*, σ. ὅροι D.S.5.6; σύμφωνον καὶ ὁμόλογον ταῖς πόλεσιν ὑπὲρ τῆς πανηγύρεως *OGI*444.1 (Ilium, i B.C.); ἐκ συμφώνου *BGU*917.8 (iv A.D.), *Cod.Just*.8.10.12; κατὰ τὸ γεγονὸς σύμφωνον πρὸς Διογένην *TAM*2.119 (Lycia). III. σύμφωνος, ἡ, = συμφωνιακή II, Aret.*CD*2.5; name of a cough-mixture used by Antonius Musa, Gal.13.61. -ούντως, Adv. *in harmony with*, σ. ἑαυτῷ λέγειν Pl.*Lg*.662e.

**συμφωτίζομαι**, Med., *give light together with*, ἀλλήλοις *Placit*.3.1. 6:—Pass., Gal.18(2).72.

**σύμψαλμα**, ατος, τό, *a sounding in concert*, Sch.Pi.*O*.3.11, *Gloss*.

**σύμψαυσις**, εως, ἡ, *contact*, Arist.*PA*660$^b$24. 2. *touching* of two notes *together*, Ptol.*Harm*.1.7.

**συμψαύω**, *touch one another*, Hp.*Off*.11, Arist.*HA*562$^a$27, *Fr*.208, Thphr.*HP*8.5.2, *IG*7.3073.107 (Lebad., ii B.C.); τοῖς σώμασι X.*Smp*. 4.26; ἀλλήλοις Plb.6.29.3: c. gen., Str.11.8.8, Iamb.*VP*27.130.

**συμψάω**, *rake together*, συμψήσασα τἀργυρίδιον Eup.113; εὗρεν.. συμψῶντας τὸν ψυγμόν (the corn in the drying place) *PPetr*.2 p.110 (iii B.C.); συμψῆσαι *obliterate* the traces left by anything in sand, Ar.*Nu*.975 (anap.); of a rapid river, *sweep away*, ὁ ποταμὸς τὸν ἵππον συμψήσας ὑποβρύχιον οἰχώκεε φέρων Hdt.1.189, cf. Iamb.ap.Suid. s.v., Eus.Mynd.63; *carry off, arrest* a man, *PTeb*.13.15, 48.31 (both ii B.C.):—Pass., *to be swept up* or *away*, εὗρον τὸν ψυγμὸν συνεψημένον *PRyl*.139.11 (i A.D.): aor. -εψήσθην, Lxx *Je*.22.19, 31(48).33.

**συμψέλια**, τά, = Lat. *subsellia*, *IGRom*.4.1316 (Lydia), *POxy*.921 *Intr*. (iii A.D.); written **συψέλια**, *App.Anth*.5.31; **σεμψέλλια**, *PGrenf*.2.111.37 (v/vi A.D.): in sg. **συνψέλιον**, *TAM*2.210 (Sidyma); *sympselion*, *Gloss*.; **συνψέλειν**, *Sammelb*.4292 (ostracon); **σεμσέλλιον**, *PMasp*.6$^v$.89 (vi A.D.).

**συμψελλίζω**, *stammer with* or *together*, Arr.*Epict*.2.24.18, Max. Tyr.7.8.

**συμψεύδομαι**, Med., *tell a lie together*, Plb.6.3.10; τινι with one, Plu.2.508e.

**συμψηφ-ίζω**, *reckon together, count up*, *Act.Ap*.19.19, *PMag.Leid. W*.9.4; *reckon in, add*, *PMag.Leid.V*.11.2. II. Med., *vote with*, τινι Ar.*Lys*.142, cf. Poll.8.15:—Pass., App.*BC*3.22, *Sammelb*.7378. 9 (ii A.D.), v.l. in Lxx *Je*.29(49).21. -ιστής, *computator*, *Gloss*.

**συμψηφο-θετέω**, = συμψηφίζω I, Nech.ap.Vett.Val.279.5 (Pass.). -λογέω, *apply mosaic to a surface*, in Pass., κόγχη συνεψηφολογημένη Hero *Stereom*.2.35.

⊛ **σύμψηφος**, ον, *voting with*, τινι Pl.*Grg*.500a, cf. *La*.184d, etc.; σ. τινί τινος *voting with* one *for* a thing, Id.*R*.380c, *Cra*.398c: c. dat. rei, σ. τῷ ἐπαίνῳ, τοῖς λόγοις, Id.*Lg*.811e, 907b; ὁ λόγος..σ. ὤν (sc. τοῖς πάθεσιν) Arist.*MM*1206$^b$25, cf. 1203$^b$27: abs., *voting together, of the same opinion*, λαβεῖν τινα σ. Pl.*Lg*.929b, D.16.17, cf. Phld.*Sto. Herc*.339.16. 2. = *computator*, *Gloss*.

**συμψῐθυρίζω**, *whisper with*, τισι Plu.2.519f.

**συμψῑλόω**, *pronounce with the spiritus lenis also*, in Pass., *An.Ox*. 1.132, *EM*317.46.

**συμψοφέω**, *make a noise together*, τοῖς ὅπλοις Plb.1.34.2; σ. ταῖς μαχαίραις τοὺς θυρεούς *rattle upon* the shields with the swords, Id. 11.30.1, cf. 15.12.8.

**συμψύχομαι** [ῡ], Pass., *grow cold together*, Hp.*Nat.Puer*.25, Gal. 11.584, Olymp.Alch.p.76B.

**σύμψῡχος**, ον, *of one mind, at unity*, *Ep.Phil*.2.2; *united in soul*, τῇ γῇ Polem.*Call*.54.

⊛ **σύν** [ῠ], old Att. ξύν; Boeot. σούν *IG*7.3171.39 (Orchom. Boeot., iii B.C.): Prep. with dat. (rarely c. gen., σ. τῶν ἐν αὐτῷ νεκρῶν Mitteis *Chr*.129.23 (ii B.C.); σ. ἡρώων *IPE*2.383 (Phanagoria); σ. γυναικός ib.301 (Panticapaeum), cf. *Ostr*.240.5 (ii A.D.), *PLond*.1.113 iv 19 (vi A.D.)):—*with*. The form ξύν rarely occurs in Hom., though it is not rare in compds. even when not required by the metre, as in ξυνέαξα, ξυνοχῇσιν, ξύμβλητο, ξύμπαντα; Hes. also uses ξύμπας, ξυνιέναι; in Ion. verse we find ξύν Thgn.1063 (but σύν Id.50), Sol. 19.3 (perh. old Attic), but σύν Archil.4, cf. συνωνίη, συνίημι; in early Ion. Prose (including Inscrr., cf. *SIG*1.2 (Abu Simbel, vi B.C.), 167.37 (Mylasa, iv B.C.), etc.) ξύν is only found in ξυνίημι Heraclit.51, Democr.95 (cf. ἀξύνετος, ἀξυνεσίη, ξύνεσις), and in the phrase ξὺν νῷ (νόῳ codd.) Heraclit.114, Democr.35; Hdt. has only σύν, and in codd. Hp. ξύν has weaker authority than σύν (i p.cxxv Kuehlewein); in the late Ionic of Aret., ξύν prevails over σύν; in Aeol. and Dor. it is rare, ξυνοίκην Sapph.75; ξυναλίαξε Ar.*Lys*.93; elsewh. Dor. σύν, *Leg.Gort*. 5.6, *IG*9(1).334.47 (Locr., v B.C.), etc.; but in old Att. Inscrr. ξύν is the only form up to 500 B.C.; σύν appears in v B.C. and becomes usual towards the end; after 378 B.C. ξύν survives only in the formula γνώμην δὲ ξυμβάλλεσθαι κτλ.; the phrase ξὺν νῷ is found in Ar.*Nu*. 580, Pl.*Cri*.48c, *Men*.88b, *R*.619b (σὺν E.*Or*.909); otherwise, of Att. Prose writers Th. alone uses the preposition ξύν, Antipho and Lysias have ξυν- a few times in compds.; codd. Pl. have both ξυν- (*Lg*.930a, al.) and συν-; in Antipho Soph.*Oxy*.1364, Aristox., Arr., Ael., and Anon.Rhythm. ξυν- is very freq.; in Trag. both forms occur. The Prep. σύν gradually gave way to μετά with gen., so that whereas A. has 67 examples of σύν to 8 of μετά with gen., the proportions in Th. are 400 of μετά to 37 of σύν, in D. 346 of μετά to 15 of σύν, and in Arist. 300 of μετά to 8 of σύν: for these and other statistics see C. J. T. Mommsen, *Beiträge zur Lehre von den griechischen Präpositionen* (Frankfurt 1886–95): in Att. Prose and Com. σύν is restricted for the most part to signf. 8, 9 and a few phrases, such as σὺν θεῷ, σὺν (τοῖς) ὅπλοις; Xenophon uses it freely, having 556 examples to 275 of μετά; in Pap., *NT*, and later Prose its use is much less restricted (v. infr.). 1. *in company with, together with*, δεῦρό ποτ' ἤλυθε..σ. Μενελάῳ Il.3.206; ξ. παιδὶ..πύργῳ ἐφεστήκει 6.372; σ. τοῖσδε ὑπέκφυγον Od.9.286; καταφθίσθαι σ. ἐκείνῳ 2.183; ἀπελαύνειν σ. τῷ στρατῷ Hdt.8.101; ἐπαιδεύετο σ. τῷ ἀδελφῷ X.*An*.1.9.2; σ. αὐτῷ σταυροῦσι δύο λῃστάς *Ev.Marc*.15.27; οὐδένα ἔχω σ. ἐμοί *PSI*10. 1161.12 (iv A.D.). 2. with collat. notion of help or aid, σ. θεῷ *with* God's *help* or *blessing*, as God wills, Il.9.49; σ. σοί, πότνα θεά Od.13. 391; πέμψον δέ με σ. γε θεοῖσιν Il.24.430, cf. 15.26; σ. θεῷ φυτευθεὶς ὄλβος Pi.*N*.8.17; σ. θεῷ εἰρημένον spoken as by inspiration, Hdt.1. 86; σ. θεῷ δ' εἰρήσεται Ar.*Pl*.114; σ. θεῷ εἰπεῖν Pl.*Tht*.151b, *Prt*. 317b; ξ. θεοῖς Th.1.86; so σ. δαίμονι, σ. Ἀθήνῃ καὶ Διί, Il.11.792, 20. 192; σ. Χαρίτεσσιν Pi.*N*.9.54, cf. *P*.9.2; ξ. τῷ θεῷ πᾶς καὶ γελᾷ κὠδύρεται S.*Aj*.383; also θεοῦ σ. παλάμᾳ, σ. θεοῦ τύχᾳ, Pi.*O*.10(11).21, *N*.6.24: generally, of personal cooperation, σ. σοὶ φραζέσθω let him consult *with* you, Il.9.346; λοχησάμενος σ. ἑταίρῳ Od.13.268; ξ. τῇ βουλῇ *in consultation with* the Council, *IG*1$^2$.63.17; σ. τινὶ μάχεσθαι fight *at* his *side*, X.*Cyr*.5.3.5, cf. *HG*4.1.34; σ. τινὶ εἶναι or γίγνεσθαι to be *with* another, i.e. *on* his *side, of* his *party*, Id.*An*.3.1.21, *Smp*.5.10; οἱ σ. αὐτῷ his friends, followers, Id.*An*.1.2.15, cf. *Act.Ap*.14.4, etc. 3. *furnished with, endued with*, σ. μεγάλῃ ἀρετῇ ἐκτήσω ἄκοιτιν Od.24. 193; πόλιν θεοδμάτῳ σ. ἐλευθερίᾳ ἔκτισσε Pi.*P*.1.61. 4. of things that belong, or are attached, to a person, σ. νηΐ or σ. νηυσί, i.e. on board ship, Il.1.389, 179, etc.; σ. νηυσὶν ἀλαπάξαι, opp. πεζός, 9.328 (so in Prose, σ. ναυσὶ προσπλεῖν X.*HG*2.2.7, etc.); σ. ἵπποισιν καὶ ὄχεσφιν Il.5.219; esp. of arms, μιν κατέκηε σ. ἔντεσι 6.418; στῆ δ' εὐρὰξ σ. δουρί 15.541; ἀντιβίην or ἀντίβιον σ. ἔντεσι or σ. τεύχεσι πειρηθῆναι, 5. 220, 11.386; σ. ἔντεσι μάρνασθαι 13.719; σκῆπτρον, σ. τῷ ἔβη 2.47; ἄγγελος ἦλθε..σ. ἀγγελίῃ ib.787; σ. (or ξ.) ὅπλοις Th.2.2, al., Pl.*Lg*. 947c, Aen.Tact.17.1; σ. (or ξ.) τοῖς ὅπλοις Th.2.90, 4.14, *Hell.Oxy*. 10.1, Pl.*Lg*.763a, Aen.Tact.11.8; σ. ἐγχειριδίοις *Hell.Oxy*.10.2; ξ. ξιφιδίῳ καὶ θώρακι Th.3.22; ξ. ἑνὶ ἱματίῳ Id.2.70; in some such cases σ. is little more than expletive, as σ. τεύχεσι θωρηχθέντες Il.8.530, etc.: with αὐτός (cf. αὐτός I. 5), chiefly in Hom., ἀνόρουσεν αὐτῇ σ. φόρμιγγι Il.9.194, cf. 14.498; αὐτῷ σ. τε λίνῳ καὶ ῥήγεϊ Od.13. 118. 5. of things accompanying, or of concurrent circumstances, ἄνεμος σ. λαίλαπι Il.17.57, cf. Od.12.408; of coincidence in time, ἄκρᾳ σ. ἑσπέρᾳ Pi.*P*.11.10; καιρῷ σ. ἀτρεκεῖ ib.8.7; σ. τῷ χρόνῳ προϊόντι X.*Cyr*.8.7.6; *in the course of*, κείνῳ σ. ἄματι B.10.23, cf. 125, Pi.*Fr*.123. 6. of necessary connexion or consequence, σὺν μεγάλῳ ἀποτεῖσαι to pay *with* a great loss, i.e. suffer greatly, Il.4.161; δημοσίῳ σ. κακῷ *with* loss to the public, Thgn.50; σ. τῷ σῷ ἀγαθῷ *to* your advantage, X.*Cyr*.3.1.15; ὤλοντο... σὺν μιάσματι *with* pollution, S.*Ant*.172; to denote agreement, *in accordance with*, σ. τῷ δικαίῳ καὶ καλῷ X.*An*.2.6.18; σ. δίκᾳ Pi.*P*.9.96; σ. κόσμῳ Hdt.8.86, Arist.*Mu*.398$^b$23; σ. τάχει S.*El*.872, etc. 7. of the instrument or means, *with the help of, by means of*, σ. ἐλαίῳ φαρμακώσαισα Pi.*P*.4.221; διήλλαχθε σ. σιδάρῳ A.*Th*.885 (lyr.); πλοῦτον ἐκτήσω ξ. αἰχμῇ Id.*Pers*.755 (troch.); ἡ [τῶν φίλων] κτῆσίς ἐστιν οὐδαμῶς σ. τῇ βίᾳ X.*Cyr*.8.7.13; ξ. ἐπαίνῳ Th.1.84. 8. *including*, κεφάλαιον σ. ἐπωνίοις *IG*1$^2$.329.5, cf. 2$^2$.1388.85, 1407.12, al.; τοῦ Πειραιῶς ξ. Μουνυχίᾳ Th.2.13, cf. 4.124, 5.26, 74, 7.42, 8.90, 95; δισχίλιαι γάρ εἰσι (sc. δραχμαί) σ. ταῖς Νικίου Ar.*Fr*.100; ἀνήλωσα σ. τῇ τῆς σκευῆς ἀναθέσει ἑκκαίδεκα μνᾶς Lys.21.4, cf. 2; αἶγας ἀπέδοτο σ. τῷ αἰπόλῳ τριῶν καὶ δέκα μνῶν Is.6.33, cf. 8.8, 35, 11.42, 46, Aeschin. 2.162, D.19.155, 27.23, al., Arist.*HA*525$^b$15, 17, *Ath*.19.6, Hipparch. 1.1.9, al., *PSI*10.1124.14 (ii A.D.). 9. *excluding, apart from, plus*, ἓξ ἐμοὶ σ. ἑβδόμῳ six *with* (but not including) me the seventh, A. *Th*.283; αἱ γὰρ καμπαὶ τέτταρες, ἢ δύο σ. τοῖς πτερυγίοις Arist.*HA* 490$^a$32; σ. τοῖς ἀρχαίοις τὸν οἶκον ἐκ τῶν προσόδων μείζω ποιῆσαι D. 27.61; τὴν ἐφαπτίδα σ. τῇ σακκοπήρᾳ ἐν ᾗ ἐνῆν *together with*.., *PEnteux*.32.7, cf. 89.9 (iii B.C.); οἱ γραμματεῖς σ. τοῖς πρεσβυτέροις *Ev.Luc*.20.1, cf. *Ep.Gal*.5.24.

B. Position:—σύν sts. follows its case, Il.10.19, Od.9.332, 15. 410. It freq. stands between Adj. and Subst., as Od.11.359, Il.9. 194, etc.; more rarely between Subst. and Adj., Od.13.258, Pi.*P*. 8.7. 2. freq. in tmesis in Hom., as Il.23.687, Od.14.296, etc. 3. in late Gr. σὺν καί c. dat., στεφανηφορήσας σ. καὶ Αὐρ. Ἰάσονι *IG*12(7). 259 (Amorgos, iii A.D.), cf. *Supp.Epigr*.4.535 (Ephesus, ii/iii A.D.), *Rev.Phil*.50.11 (Sardis, i/iii A.D.), *CPR*26.16 (ii A.D.); cf. infr. C. 2.

C. σύν as Adv., *together, at once*, κενεὰς σ. χεῖρας ἔχοντες Od.10. 42; mostly folld. by δέ or τε, σ. δὲ πτερὰ πυκνὰ λίασθεν Il.23.879; σ. τε δύ' ἐρχομένω 10.224 (cf. σύνδυο); ξ. τε διπλοῖ βασιλῆς S.*Aj*.960 (lyr.). It is sts. hard to distinguish this from tmesis, e.g. in Il.23. 879; so ξὺν κακῶς ποιεῖν is = *ξυγκακοποιεῖν in Th.3.13. In Old Testament Gr. it is sts. used to translate the Hebr. *'ēth* (particle prefixed to the definite accus.) through confusion with the Prep. *'ēth* 'with', ἐμίσησα σὺν τὴν ζωήν Lxx *Ec*.2.17; οὐκ ἐμνήσθη σ. τοῦ ἀνδρός ib.9.15; ἔκτισεν ὁ θεὸς σὺν τὸν οὐρανὸν καὶ σὺν τὴν γῆν Aq.*Ge*.1.1, etc. 2. *besides, also*, σ. δὲ πλουτίζειν ἐμέ A.*Ag*.586; σ. δ' αὕτως ἐγώ S.*Ant*. 85, etc.; σ. δ' ἐγὼ παρών Id.*Aj*.1288, cf. *El*.299; Δίρκα τε..σ. τ' Ἀσωπιάδες κόραι E.*HF*785 (lyr.); in later Poetry σ. καί A.R.1.74, Herod.4.3, Nic.*Th*.8, D.P.843 (also in late Prose, Ath.2.49a; cf. supr. B. 3).

D. In Compos. I. *with, along with, together, at the same time*, hence of any kind of union, connexion, or participation in a thing, and metaph. of agreement or unity. In Compos. with a trans. Verb σύν may refer to the Object as well as the Subject, as συγκατακτείνειν may mean *kill one person as well as another*, or, *join with another in killing*. **2.** of the completion of an action, *altogether, completely*, as in συνάγνυμι, συνασκέω 2, συνθρύπτω, συγκόπτω, συμπατέω, συμπληρόω, συντελέω, συντέμνω; sts., therefore, it seems only to strengthen the force of the simple word. **3.** joined with numerals, σύνδυο *two together*, which sense often becomes distributive, *by twos, two and two*; so σύντρεις, σύμπεντε, etc., like Lat. *bini, terni*, etc. **II.** σύν in Compos., before β μ π φ ψ, becomes συμ-; before γ κ ξ χ, συγ-; before λ συλ-; before σ usu. συσ-; but becomes συ- before σ followed by a conson. (e.g. συστῆναι), before ζ, and perh. sts. before ξ. In a poet. passage, ap.Pl.*Phdr.*237a, we have ξύμ alone in tmesi, ξύμ μοι λάβεσθε for συλλάβεσθέ μοι; cf. ὅτε ξὺμ πρῶτ' ἐφύοντο Emp.95: in Inscrr. and Papyri these assimilations are freq. not found.

**συνᾰβολέω**, aor. συνηβόλησα, *meet*, ἀλλήλοις Babr.61.3.

**συναγάλλομαι** [ᾰγ], *rejoice with*, c. dat., *Historia* 6.597 (Crete, iv/v A.D.), Eustr.*in EN*106.22.

**συνᾰγᾰνακτ-έω**, *to be vexed along with*, τινι Plb.4.7.3, Phld.*Rh.*2.140S., D.H.10.6, Str.4.4.2; τινὶ ἐφ' οἷς ἔπαθεν Plb.2.59.5: abs., Men.543, D.S.19.61, Plu.*Rom.*7. **-ησις**, εως, ἡ, *common anger* or *vexation*, Arist.*HA*612ᵇ35, D.H.7.45.

**συνᾰγᾰπάω**, *love along with*, [τοῖς φίλοις] τοὺς φίλους Plb.1.14.4.

**συναγγέλλω**, *announce together*, v.l. in D.H.10.26; simply, *announce*, Zos.4.55, 5.14.

**συνάγγελος**, ὁ, *fellow messenger*, Hdt.7.230.

**συναγγία**, ἡ, *confined space*, Babr.27.2, but f.l. for συναγκίη.

⊛ **συνᾰγείρω**, aor. συνήγειρα, Ep. ξυνάγειρα Il.20.21: Ep. 3pl. aor. 1 Pass. συνάγερθεν Theoc.22.76:—*gather together, assemble*, ὧν ἕνεκα ξυνάγειρα (sc. τοὺς θεούς) Il. l.c., cf. Pl.*Criti.*121c; ἐκκλησίην Hdt.3.142, cf. 1.206; τὸν Ὀλυμπικὸν.. ἀγῶνα, ἵνα τοὺς Ἕλληνας ἅπαντας.. ξυναγείρει Ar.*Pl.*584; also σ. ἀγῶνα Lys.33.1; σ. κύκλους Antiph.190.9; esp., *collect* armies, soldiers, etc., Hdt.1.4, 4.4, Plb.2.18.7, etc.; σ. στρατιὰν εἰς Βαβυλῶνα X.*Cyr.*8.6.19; τοὺς ἀριστέας ἐπὶ τὸν σῦν Ant.Lib.2:—Pass., *gather together, come together, assemble*, συναγειρόμενοι Il.24.802; but συναγρόμενοι, Ep. part. aor. 2 Pass., 11.687. **2.** *collect* the means of living, βίοτον Od.4.90:—Med., *collect for oneself*, ὅσα [κτήματα] ξυναγείρατ' Ὀδυσσεύς 14.323, 19.293; for Il.15.680, v. συναείρω. **3.** metaph., σ. ἐμαυτόν *collect* myself, Pl.*Prt.*328d:—Pass., of the soul, πανταχόθεν ἐκ τοῦ σώματος σ. Id.*Phd.*67c; μοι ἡ θρασύτης συνηγείρετο Id.*Chrm.*156d, cf. Theoc.15.57:—Med., συναγείρατο θυμόν A.R.1.1233.

**συνᾰγελ-άζομαι**, Pass., *herd together*, Democr.164; of gregarious fish, μετ' ἀλλήλων Arist.*HA*610ᵇ1, cf. *Frr.*308,316,339; σ. εἰς τὸ ὁμόφυλον, of men, Plb.6.5.7, cf. Plu.*Cam.*10; σ. τοῖς ἄρρεσι, of sows, Id.2.917c: metaph., ἡ διάνοια σ. τοῖς ψέγουσι *takes part with*.., ib. 40a. **-ασμός**, ὁ, *herding together*, ib.980a, *Gp.*16.1.10; of men, Porph.*Sent.*32: in pl., *forming of* ἀγέλαι, παίδων Plu.*Comp.Lyc.Num.*4. **-αστικός**, ή, όν, *gregarious*, of fish, Arist.*Fr.*321, cf. Xenocr.ap.Orib.2.58.13, Porph.*Abst.*3.11; of men, Hierocl.p.52A.: τὸ -κόν *gregariousness*, Artem.2.20. **-ισμός**, ὁ, = -ασμός, Hippod.ap.Stob.4.1.94.

**συναγερμός**, ὁ, *gathering together, assembling*, Poll.3.129, 9.142, Dam.*Pr.*108,401; ὁ λογισμὸς σ. μνήμης Porph.ap.Stob.1.49.54.

⊛ **συναγέσκεο**· ἰσχνοπρεπεῖς, Hsch.

**συνᾰγιάζω**, *share in holiness*, τινι *Corp.Herm.*1.32.

**συνᾰγῑνέω**, *collect*, Arr.*Ind.*8.

**συνάγκεια**, ἡ, = μισγάγκεια, Thphr.*CP*2.4.8, *AP*6.188 (Leon., pl.), Plb.18.31.5, D.S.3.68, Str.12.2.3 (pl.), Plu.*Tim.*28, Arr.*Fr.*155J.: συναγκίη is prob. in Babr.27.2.

**σύναγκος**, εος, τό, = συνάγκεια, Them.*Or.*11.151d (pl.).

**συναγλαΐζω**, *deck out, adorn at the same time*, Eust.1053.45.

**σύναγμα**, ατος, τό, (συνάγω) *collection, concretion*, such as *stone* or *gravel in the kidneys*, Hp.*Epid.*6.3.7. **2.** v.l. for σύνθεμα in Lxx *Ec.*12.11 cod.A.

**συναγνεύω**, *to be pure* or *chaste together*, πρός τι Porph.*Abst.*4.6.

**συναγνοέω**, *to be ignorant with* or *together*, Hierocl. *in CA*13 p.448M.

**συνάγνῡμι**, aor. συνέαξα (the only tense in use):—*break to pieces, shiver*, ἔγχεος, ὃ ξυνέαξε Il.13.166; νῆας.., τάς οἱ ξυνέαξαν ἄελλαι Od.14.383; ἐλάφοιο τέκνα.. συνέαξε *breaks* their *necks*, Il.11.114.

**συνᾰγορ-άζω**, pf. συνηγόρᾰκα *IG*2².903.6:—*buy up*, τὸν σῖτον πάντα Arist.*Oec.*1347ᵇ5, cf. *PCair.Zen.*106.3 (iii B.C.), *PEnteux.*2.3,11 (iii B.C.), *PMich.Zen.*42.3 (iii B.C., Pass.), *SIG*976.52 (Samos, ii B.C., Pass.), Posidon.36J., Ath.1.6a (Pass.). **II.** *frequent the market-place with*, τισι Plu.2.796d. **-ασμός**, ὁ, *buying up*, τῶν ὑποζυγίων καὶ σάκκων *PSI*4.370.4 (iii B.C.); πυροῦ *PCair.Zen.*787.7 (iii B.C.), *PMich.Zen.*42.10 (iii B.C.). **-αστικὸς πυρός**, = *frumentum emptum*, *PLond.*2.301.2 (ii A.D.); -κὴ κριθή *BGU*381.2 (ii/iii A.D.). **-ευσις**, εως, ἡ, *advocacy*, Poll.4.26. **-εύω** (the fut. in use being συνερῶ (v. συνερέω), aor. συνεῖπον (q.v.), pf. συνείρηκα):—*advocate* a course of action *jointly with*, ὁ Εὐρυμέδων αὐτῷ ταὖτα ξ. Th.7.49, cf. 6.6, 8.84, Lys.12.25, X.*Cyr.*2.2.21, 2.3.16, Plu.*Fab.*18, etc.: c. inf., σ. στρατιὰν ποιεῖν X.*HG*5.2.20; folld. by ὡς χρεὼν εἴη.., Id.*Cyr.*6.2.24:—Pass., τὸ συναγορευόμενον the course *advocated*, Plu.2.841f; ἡ συναγορευομένη is dub.l. in *PStrassb.*41.23 (iii A.D.). **2.** c. dat. rei, Ῥοδίων σ. τῇ σωτηρίᾳ D.15.15; σ. νόμῳ Arist.*Rh.Al.*1424ᵇ16; τῇ συμμαχίᾳ ib.35; ταῖς ἐπιθυμίαις Isoc.5.3; σ. τοῖς λεγομένοις *agree* or *assent to*, Id.4.139; τοῖς κακῶς εἰρημένοις Gal.16.516, cf. 589, al.

**συνᾰγορέω**, **-άγορος**, Dor. for συνηγορέω, -ήγορος (qq. v.).

**συναγραυλέω**, *live in the country along with*, τινι D.H.1.39.

**συναγρεύω**, *join in the chase*, *AP*9.337 (Leon.):—Pass., -ευθεῖσα Λυαίῳ Nonn.*D.*20.387.

**συναγρῐαίνω**, *to be fierce along with*, τινι Them.*Or.*15.191c.

⊛ **συναγρίς**, ίδος, ἡ, *a sea-fish*, Epich.69 (v.l. σναγρ-), Arist.*HA*505ᵃ15, 506ᵇ16.

**συναγρυπνέω**, *keep awake with*, Aristaenet.2.22, Philostr.*Ep.*7.

**συναγρώσσω**, = συναγρεύω, Nonn.*D.*11.75,303.

**συνᾰγυρ-μός**, ὁ, *bringing together, collecting*, φρονήσεως Pl.*Plt.*272c; τροφῆς D.H.12.1 (pl.). **-τός**, όν, *collected*, ὕδωρ σ., opp. πηγαῖον, Pl.*Lg.*845e.

**συνάγχ-η**, ἡ, (ἄγχω) a kind of *sore throat*, Demad.ap.Poll.7.104, Plu.*Dem.*25, Aret.*CA*1.7, Favorin. in *PVat.*11.5.39, etc.; cf. κυνάγχη. **-ίαι**, αἱ, written *sinanciae* and expld. as *folia gulae*, dub. in *Gloss.* ⊛ **-ικός**, ή, όν, *affected with* συνάγχη, Dsc.1.56, Ruf.ap.Orib.8.24.30, Aret.*CA*1.7; *of the nature of* συνάγχη, πάθη Gal.15.790. Adv. -κῶς Id.11.192. ⊛**-ος**, ὁ, = συνάγχη, Hp.*Acut.*(*Sp.*)9.

⊛ **συνάγω** [ᾰ], impf. συνῆγον, Dor. -ᾶγον A.*Th.*756 (lyr.), prob. in E.*IA*290 (lyr.), Ep. σύνᾰγον Il.14.448: fut. συνάξω: aor. 1 συνῆξα, Dor. -ᾶξα *GDI*1772,1791 (Delph., ii B.C.); inf. συνάξαι v.l. in *Ev.Luc.*3.17; part. συνάξας f.l. for συννάξας in Hdt.7.60: but the regul. aor. is συνήγαγον: Att. pf. συνῆχα X.*Mem.*4.2.8; συναγήοχα Arist.*Oec.*1346ᵃ28 (v.l. -γιοχ-, -γιωχ-, γειοχ-), Dsc.1.68, Iamb.*VP*35.254, etc.; Dor. συναγάγοχα *Test.Epict.*3.12: pf. Pass. συνῆγμαι, Dor. -ᾶγμαι Ti.Locr.101b.—Old Att. ξυνάγω, which Hom. also uses metri gr.:—*bring together, gather together*: **I.** of persons, animals, etc., ἡ δὲ ξυνάγουσα γεραιὰς νηόν.. *to* the temple, Il.6.87, cf. Hdt.2.111, 3.150, etc.; ἐς ἕνα χῶρον σ. μυριάδα ἀνθρώπων Id.7.60; ἔνθα ποτ' Ὀρφεὺς σύναγεν δένδρεα μούσαις, σύναγεν θῆρας E.*Ba.*563 (lyr.); ποίμνας Ὀλύμπου σ. S.*Fr.*522; Ἕλληνας εἰς ἓν καὶ Φρύγας σ. E.*Or.*1640, cf. Ar.*Lys.*585 (anap.); σ. ἐς ὀλίγον *crowd* them into a narrow compass, Th.2.84; σ. εἰς ταὐτόν Pl.*Phdr.*256c, cf. *Tht.*194b; εἰς ἕν, εἰς μίαν ἀρχήν, Arist.*Pol.*1280ᵇ13, 1299ᵇ13; much like συνοικίζω, ib. 1285ᵇ7. **2.** *bring together* for deliberation or festivity, βουλήν Batr.134; δικαστήριον Hdt.6.85; τοὺς στρατηγοὺς Id.8.59; ἐκκλησίαν τινὸς ἕνεκα Th.2.60; ἔς τι, περί τινος, Id.1.120, X.*HG*7.1.27; οἱ νόμοι σ. ὑμᾶς, ἵνα.. D.19.1; τὴν βουλὴν καὶ τὸν δῆμον Arist.*Ath.*43.3; σ. πανηγύρεις, ἑταιρείας, συσσίτια, etc., Isoc.4.1,79, Pl.*R.*365d, *Lg.*625e, etc.; σ. ἔρανον Μηνὶ Τυράννῳ *IG*3.74.21, cf. *GDI*1772,1791 (Delph., ii B.C.):—Pass., πανήγυρις.. συναγομένη *SIG*888.129 (Scaptopara, iii A.D.): abs., *hold a club dinner* or *meeting*, Thphr.*Char.*30.18, and so perh. *OGI*130.5 (Egypt, ii B.C.); σ. ἀπὸ συμβολῶν Diph.43.28; ἔλεγον "συνάγειν" τὸ μετ' ἀλλήλων πίνειν Ath.8.365c, cf. Sophil.4.2, Men.158, Hsch.; νυνὶ.. συνάγουσι they *are at dinner*, Men.*Epit.*195. **3.** in hostile sense, ξ. Ἄρηα, ἔριδα Ἄρηος, ὑσμίνην, *join* battle, *begin* the battle-strife, etc., Il.2.381, 5.861, 14.448, al.; πόλεμον σ. Isoc.4.84. **b.** *match, pit* two warriors *one against the other*, A.*Th.*508: hence intr., ἐς μέσσον σ. *engage* in fight, Theoc.22.82; σ. τινί Plb.11.18.4; εἰς χεῖρας Plu.*Publ.*9. **c.** *collect* or *levy* soldiers, X.*HG*3.1.5, etc.; *collect* slaves for work, *PMich.Zen.*62.15 (iii B.C.). **4.** *bring together, join in one, unite*, ἄμφω ἐς φιλότητα *h.Merc.*507; παράνοια σ. νυμφίους φρενώλεις A.*Th.*756 (lyr.); τὸ κακὸν σέ τε κἀμὲ σ. E.*Hel.*644 (lyr.), cf. Ar.*Ach.*991 (lyr.); ἀνθρώπους εἰς κηδείαν X.*Mem.*2.6.36; γυναῖκα καὶ ἄνδρα, of Isis, *IG*12(5).14.20 (Ios, iii A.D.): hence γάμους σ. *contract* marriages, X.*Smp.*4.64. **5.** *bring together, make friends of, reconcile*, Emp.ap.Arist.*Metaph.*1000ᵇ11, D.58.42, 59.45; *bring* persons *together* in works of fiction, Κρέοντα καὶ Τειρεσίαν Pl.*Ep.*311b. **6.** σ. ἑαυτόν *collect* oneself, Plu.*Phil.*20. **7.** *lead with one, receive*, σ. εἰς τὸν οἶκον Lxx 2*Ki.*11.27, cf. *Jd.*19.15; ξένος ἤμην καὶ συνηγάγετέ με *gave hospitality to*.., *Ev.Matt.*25.35:—Pass., *Act.Ap.*11.26. **II.** of things, σύναγεν νεφέλας Od.5.291, cf. Thphr.*Vent.*42; ἵνα οἱ σὺν φόρτον ἄγοιμι Od.14.296; κήρυκες ὅρκια πιστὰ θεῶν σύναγον Il.3.269; τὰ χρήματα ἐκ τῶν ἀγρῶν X.*An.*6.2.8; τὸ ἔλαιον ἐν ἀγγείοις interpol. in Hdt.6.119; τὰς εἰσφορὰς Arist.*Pol.*1314ᵇ15, cf. *PHib.*1.157 (iii B.C.), *PCair.Zen.*315.1 (iii B.C.), etc.; καρπόν Plb.12.2.5; κόγχον καὶ κύαμον Crates Theb.7; τρυγᾶν καὶ σ. *PRev.Laws* 24.14 (iii B.C.); τὴν μήκωνα σ. *Sammelb.*4305 (iii B.C.); σ. εἰς μίαν γωνίαν τὸ ἀποκτένισμα τοῦ στιππύου *PCair.Zen.*176.41 (iii B.C.); συναγαγεῖν καὶ συναθροῖσαι τὸ θερμόν Thphr.*Ign.*17; εἰς ἀποθήκας *Ev.Matt.*6.26; κοινὸν σ. τὸν βίον Pl.*Plt.*311c; σ. ἐκ δικαίων τὸν βίον Men.*Mon.*196; of an artist, σ. τὰ κάλλιστα ἐκ πολλῶν X.*Mem.*3.10.2, cf. Pl.*R.*488a. **b.** of a historical writer, σ. τὰς πράξεις Isoc.12.252, 15.45; συνηγμένος *concise* in speech, D.L.4.33; of an anthologist, ὅλας ῥήσεις εἰς ταὐτὸν σ. Pl.*Lg.*811a; σ. εἰς ταὐτὸν τὰ κάλλιστα τοῖς αἰσχίστοις *jumble together, identify*, Aeschin.2.145, cf. Pl.*Sph.*251d; Σειληνὸν καὶ Μαρσύαν.. εἰς ἓν Str.10.3.14. **2.** *draw together*, so as to make the extremities meet, τὰ κέρεα (of an army) Hdt.6.113; Αἴας δὲ.. δεξιὸν κέρας πρὸς τὸ λαιὸν (dub. l.) ξυνᾶγε E.*IA*290 (lyr.); σ. ἐς τετράγωνον τάξιν τοὺς ὁπλίτας Th.4.125, cf. 1.63, etc.; σ. τὰ τέρματα, of two rivers which gradually approach one another, Hdt.4.52; σ. ἑαυτόν, of a snake, Arist.*HA*594ᵃ19; σ. τοὺς πόρους, of a styptic, Thphr.*Od.*36; σ. τὰν ἀφάν, τὰν γεῦσιν, Ti.Locr.101c; συναγμένα [φωνά] ib.101b. **b.** *draw together, narrow, contract*, [τὴν διώρυχα] Hdt.7.23; πρῴρην σ. *bring* it *to a point*, Id.1.194; τόν.. χρόνον ὡς εἰς μικρότατον σ. D.*Prooem.*36; τὴν πόλιν Plb.5.93.5, etc.; ἐκ μεγάλας δαπάνας εἰς μικρὸν *IG*12(2).645a.16 (Nesos, iv

B.C.):—Pass., *συνάγεται καὶ διοίγεται ὁ φάρυγξ* Arist.*PA*664$^{b}$25; *εἰς ὀξὺ συνῆχθαι* Id.*HA*496$^{a}$19; *εἰς μικρόν* Id.*Mete.*354$^{a}$7, Democr.ap. Thphr.*Ign.*52; *εἰς στενόν* Didym.ap.Ath.11.477f; *ποτήριον συνηγμένον εἰς μέσον* Callix.3; *συνῆκται ἡ κοιλία* *is pinched in, drawn in,* Archig.ap.Aët.6.3; *ἐπὶ στενὸν συνάγεται τὸ στόμιον* Sor.1.9. c. σ. *τὰς ὀφρῦς* S.*Fr.*1121, Ar.*Nu.*582 (troch.), Antiph.218.2; *ἐπισκύνιον* Ar.*Ra.*823 (lyr.); *τὰ ὄμματα* Arist.*Pr.*958$^{a}$21; *σ. τὰ βλέφαρα* *close* the eyelids, ib.38, Gal.18(2).62; but *σ. τὰ ὦτα* *prick* the ears, of dogs, X.*Cyn.*3.5, cf. Ar.*Eq.*1348; *τὰ σκέλη πρὸς ἄλληλα* Sor.1.101, cf. 2.61 (Pass.), Diocl.*Fr.*141. d. metaph., *σ. τινὰς ἐς κίνδυνον ἔσχατον* App.*Hann.*60; *συνάγεσθαι* *to be straitened, afflicted,* *λιμῷ, σιτοδείᾳ,* Plb.1.18.7,10; *συνάγεσθαι τοῖς χαρακτῆρσι* *to become pinched* in its features, Sor.1.108; but *πεφυκότος τοῦ θερμοῦ συνάγειν καὶ τονοῦν τὴν γαστέρα* *pull* the stomach *together,* Gal.15.195; *τὰ στύφοντα ἐδέσματα σ. καὶ σφίγγει τὰ σώματα* ib.462, cf. 6.90, al. 3. *conclude* from premisses, *infer, prove,* Arist.*Rh.*1357$^{a}$8, 1395$^{b}$25, *Metaph.*1042$^{a}$3, *Pol.*1299$^{b}$12, Phld.*Sign.*12, al.; *σ. ὅτι..* Arist.*Rh.*1377$^{b}$6, cf. A.D. *Conj.*249.7: c. inf., Luc.*Hist.Conscr.*16: c. gen. abs., *σ. ὥς τινος γενομένου* *form a conclusion of* his having been.., Arist.*Pol.*1274$^{a}$25; *συνάγοντες λόγοι* *cogent* arguments, *Stoic.*2.77, Arr.*Epict.*1.7.12: also, *sum up* numbers, D.H.4.6, Ptol.*Alm.*9.10, Dioph.3.6, al.; also, *obtain* them by multiplication, *ὁ συνηγμένος [ἀριθμὸς] ἐκ τῶν κβ καὶ πθ* the *product*.., Aristarch.Sam.13, cf. Papp.22.7, Paul.Al.*K.*1; of division, *give* a quotient, Dioph.2.9; of an integer, *yield* a fraction ($9 = \frac{72}{8}$), ib.12; of any calculation, *yield* a result, Id.1.25, al. (Pass.). 4. Pass., *συνάγεται τᾷ περιφορᾷ* *is carried along with* it, Ti.Locr.98e. 5. *bring about,* *τὸ τέλος τῆς νίκης* App.*BC*1.101; also *σ. τι εἰς τέλος* ib.5.145.

**συνᾰγωγ-εύς,** *έως, ὁ,* *one who brings together, assembler,* *τῶν πολιτῶν* Lys.12.43, cf. Luc.*Peregr.*11; *convener* of a *σύνοδος,* Durrbach *Choix d'inscr. de Délos* 162 (i B.C.), *OGI*573.10 (Cilicia, i A.D.), *Supp.Epigr.* 1.330*B*3 (Istros, ii A.D.); *λόγος σ. τῆς τῶν ἀνθρώπων ἀγέλης* Max.Tyr. 7.3. II. *one who unites,* *ἔρως τῆς ἀρχαίας φύσεως σ.* Pl.*Smp.*191d; *matchmaker,* *ὁ τοῦ γάμου σ.* Lib.*Ep.*1488.1. III. *οἱ συναγωγέες* the *sphincter ani muscles,* Hp.*Oss.*14. **–ή,** *ἡ,* *a bringing together*: I. of persons, *ἀνδρὸς καὶ γυναικός* Pl.*Tht.*150a; *collecting,* *ὄχλων, ἀνδρῶν,* etc., Plb.4.7.6, D.L.2.129, etc.; *συμποσίου* Ath.5.192b; *assembling, meeting,* *τῶν λογιστῶν* *IG*1$^{2}$.91.9, cf. *Test.Epict.*4.7. 2. *assembly,* Lxx *Ex.*12.3, *OGI*737.1 (Egypt, ii B.C.), etc.; *τῶν συνέδρων* *IG*5(1).1390.49 (Andania, i B.C.), cf. *Test.Epict.*4.25; *place of assembly,* esp. of the Jewish *synagogue,* *Ev.Luc.*8.41, *Act.Ap.*9.2, *BCH* 56.293 (Stobi), etc.; *meeting-house,* *Μαρκιωνιστῶν* *OGI*608.1 (Syria, iv A.D.); *conventicle,* *Cod.Just.*1.5.18.3. II. of things, *σ. [τῶν ἐκπεπταμένων]* Hp.*Off.*11, cf. Epicur.*Nat.*14.4, etc.; opp. *διαιρέσεις,* Pl.*Phdr.*266b; *σ. πολέμου* *levying* of war, Th.2.18; *gathering in* of harvest, *τοῦ σίτου* *PCair.Zen.*433.5 (iii B.C.), Plb.1.17.9, etc.; *χρημάτων* Democr.222, *SIG*410.14 (Erythrae, iii B.C.), Plb.27.12.2, cf. Phld.*Oec.*p.51 J.; *ὑδάτων* Lxx *Ge.*1.9 (pl.), cf. *Le.*11.36; *πύου* Heras ap.Gal.13.815 (pl.); *ξύλων* *PMich.Zen.*84.15 (iii B.C.); *harvest,* *ἑορτὴ συναγωγῆς* Lxx *Ex.*34.22. 2. *drawing together, contracting,* *συναγωγὰς καὶ ἐκτάσεις στρατιᾶς* *forming* an army *in column* or in line, Pl.*R.*526d; *contraction* of ranks either in front or depth, Arr.*Tact.*11.3; *αἱ τοῦ προσώπου σ.* *pursing up* or *wrinkling* of the face, Isoc.9.44; *μετώπου* Hp.*Coac.*210; *bringing together, closing up* of a wound, Gal.10.191; *σ. τῶν μηρῶν* Sor.2.41; *τῶν ὀφθαλμῶν* Arist.*Pr.*876$^{b}$10; opp. *διαστολή,* Id.*Ph.*217$^{b}$15; *σ. ἔχειν, σ. λαμβάνειν,* = *συνάγεσθαι,* Thphr.*HP*3.10.5, *PCair.Zen.*54.6 (iii B.C.), Str.8.2.3, cf. 12.2.4. 3. *collection,* *τῶν νόμων καὶ τῶν πολιτειῶν* Arist.*EN*1181$^{b}$7 (pl.); of writings, D.H.2.27, Cic.*Att.*9.13.3, 16.5.5, Herod.Med. in *Rh.Mus.* 58.114, Gal.12.836, Orib.1 *Prooem.*2. 4. *combination,* *[πολιτειῶν]* Arist.*Pol.*1316$^{b}$40. 5. *conclusion, inference,* Id.*Rh.*1400$^{b}$26, 1410$^{a}$22, Gal.16.676, S.E.*P.*2.143,170; *cogent reasoning,* Chrysipp.*Stoic.* 2.89; *demonstration,* Phld.*Rh.*1.91 S. **–ία,** *ἡ,* = *προαγωγεία,* prob. interpol. in Plu.2.632e. **–ιμον δεῖπνον,** *τό,* = sq., Alex.251, cf. Ephipp.4. **–ιον,** *τό,* (*συνάγω* I.2) *picnic,* Men.159: also, *the place of a picnic,* Poll.6.7. II. *synagogue,* Ph.1.675. **–ός,** *όν,* *bringing together, uniting,* Democr.164; *ἀμφοῖν* Pl.*Ti.*31c; *δεσμοὶ φιλίας σ.* Id.*Prt.*322c; *τὸ σ. ἀνθρώπων εἰς εὔνοιαν* Plu.2.632e; *comprehensive,* of the general, David *Proll.*165.11: abs., S.E.*M.*9.10, etc. 2. *collecting,* *ἡ σ. [μέλιτος] μέλιττα* Ph.2.255. 3. Subst., = *συναγωγεύς* I, *convener* of a *σύνοδος,* *Sammelb.*12 (i A.D.), al. II. *living together,* Hsch. s.v. *συνέστιοι.*

**συνᾰγωνιάω,** *share in anxiety,* Plb.3.43.8, Plu.2.95e, etc.: c. dat., with one, Cic.*Att.*5.12.2, D.S.17.100; *ὑπέρ τινος* Plu.2.486b.

**συνᾰγων-ίζομαι,** Dor. aor. *συναγωνιξάμην* *Delph.*3(3).126, etc.:—*contend along with, share in a contest,* *τινι* *with* one, Ar.*Th.*1061, cf. Antipho 5.93, Th.1.143, etc.; *τινὶ πρὸς τοὺς πολεμίους* Pl.*Alc.*1.119e; *ἀλλήλοις ἐφ' ἡμᾶς* D.43.10; *τινὶ ἐν ταῖς προσευχαῖς* *Ep.Rom.*15.30; *σ. ἐν μάχῃ* *Marm.Par.*63: c. acc. cogn., *ἀγῶνα* *SIG*711 *L*29 (Delph., ii B.C.); *μάχας* *OGI*280.3 (Pergam., iii B.C.). b. generally, *ξ. τινί* *share in the fortunes of* another, Th.3.64. 2. *aid, succour,* *τινι* D.21.190; *τινί τι* one in a thing, Id.18.25, 30.31; *τινὶ πρός τι* one towards a thing, Id.18.20; *εἴς τι* D.H.4.4, *Michel* 452 (iv/iii B.C.): generally, *assist,* *τῇ διατροπῇ* Metrod.*Herc.*831.19; *μετὰ σοῦ κοινῇ* D.48.43. 3. abs., *fight on the same side,* *οἱ ξυναγωνιούμενοι* Th.5.109, cf. 1.123, X.*Cyr.*4.5.49, etc.; of the Tragic chorus, *join in the action,* Arist.*Po.*1456$^{a}$26:—Act. *–ίζω,* dub. l. in Nic.Dam.*Fr.*130.18 J. **–ισμα,** *ατος, τό,* *succour in a contest*: generally, *succour, support,* *πρός τι* Plb.10.43.2. **–ιστής,** *οῦ,* Dor. **–τάς,** *ὁ,* *one who shares with* another *in a contest, fellow-combatant,* Pl.*Alc.*1.119d, Isoc.4.142, etc.; *τινος* for a thing, Aeschin.2.183, 3.89, D.18.41; *accomplice, confederate,* Hyp.*Ath.*3; *πρός τι* Plb.10.34.2. 2. *οἱ σ.* *those who take part in contending for the prize,* *Michel* 1016 (Teos, ii B.C.); *τραγικοὶ σ.* *OGI*51.56 (Ptolemais, iii B.C.); of *a company* of Dionysiac artists, *CIG*3082 (Teos). 3. generally, *fellow-worker,* *POxy.*1676.36 (iii A.D.).

* **συνάδελφος** [ᾰ], *ον,* *one that has a brother* or *sister,* opp. *ἀνάδελφος,* X.*Mem.*2.3.4. II. *member of an association,* *PMasp.*2.11 (vi A.D.).

**συνᾰδηλέομαι,** Pass., *to be obscure together,* *τὸ ἀληθές* S.E.*M.*8.2.

**συνᾰδῐκέω,** *join in wrong* or *injury,* *τινι* *with* another, Th.1.37, X.*An.*2.6.27: abs., Th.1.39, Pl.*R.*496d, *SIG*167.42 (Mylasa, iv B.C.), etc.; *wrong* or *injure in addition,* *πάντα τὸν κόσμον* Iamb.*VP*9.46; *τὸ κατὰ γαστρός* (the foetus) Sor.1.79:—Pass., *to be wronged alike,* D.56.44, etc.; *ἐπί τινι* Id.21.126.

**συνᾱδολεσχ-έω,** *chatter with,* Gal.18(1).259. **–ος,** *ὁ,* *companion,* *Sammelb.*343, cf. 1990 (where *συναδελ–*).

**συνᾰδοξέω,** *share in disgrace,* Plu.2.96a, Agath.5.24.

* **συνᾴδω,** = *συναείδω* (q.v.), *sing with* or *together, accompany in a song,* *μετά τινων τὸν παιᾶνα* Aeschin.2.163; *σ. παιᾶνά τινι* ib.162; *σ. ᾠδάν* Ar.*Av.*858 (lyr.); also of an instrument, Plu.*Alc.*2: metaph., Id.2.55d. 2. generally, *to be in accord with, agree with,* *τινι* Ar.*Lys.*1088, Pl.*Phd.*92c, etc.; *ταὐτόν* Id.*R.*432a; *ἐν μακρῷ γήρᾳ ξ. τινί* S.*OT*1113: abs., *to be in unison,* opp. *διᾴδειν,* Heraclit.10, cf. Pl. *Prt.*333a. II. trans., *sing of* or *celebrate together,* *τινα* Theoc. 10.24.

**συνάεθλος,** *ὁ,* *fellow-toiler,* Opp.*C.*1.195, Nonn.*D.*2.338, al.

**συνᾰείδω,** poet. for *συνᾴδω,* Arat.752, Theoc.10.24, Hymn. in *IG*4$^{2}$(1).131.3 (Epid.).

**συνᾰείρω,** = *συναίρω,* *raise up together,* *σὺν δ' ἕταροι ἤειραν [αὐτὸν] ἐπ' ἀπήνην* Il.24.590. II. *bind* or *yoke together* (cf. *συνήορος, συνωρίς*), *σὺν δ' ἤειρεν ἱμᾶσι* 10.499:—Med., *ἐκ πολέων πίσυρας συναείρεται ἵππους* 15.680 (v.l. in Sch., Eust., *συναγείρεται* codd.).

**συνᾰηδίζομαι,** Pass., *to be displeased together,* Ph.1.405.

**συνᾰθετέω,** *declare spurious as well,* Sch.Ar.*Ra.*1500, Phot.*Bibl.* p.512 B.

**συναθλέω,** = *συναγωνίζομαι,* *τινι* *with* one, *Ep.Phil.*4.3; *struggle together,* *τινι* for a thing, ib.1.27. II. *impress by practice upon,* *μεταφορᾶς μνήμῃ συνηθλημένης* D.S.3.4.

**συναθρ-οίζω,** pf. *–ήθροικα* (*–υκα* Pap.) *POxy.*1253.5 (iv A.D.):—*gather together, assemble,* esp. of soldiers, X.*An.*7.2.8, etc.; *τὸ ναυτικόν* Lys.2.34; *ἀγέλην* Babr.124.8; *σ. ἐπὶ τὴν πόλιν..Ἕλληνάς τε καὶ βαρβάρους* Pl.*Mx.*243b:—Pass., X.*An.*6.5.30, *Act.Ap.*12.12. 2. of things, *gather into one mass,* *τὸ κάταγμα εἰς ἕν* Ar.*Lys.*585 (anap.); *τὸ σῶμα σ.* *bring* the body *together,* Pl.*Ti.*44d:—Pass., *ἐὰν εἰς μίαν..πόλιν..συναθροισθῇ τὰ..χρήματα* Id.*R.*422d; *τούτων συνηθροισμένων* *to sum up,* therefore, ib.563d; *σ. εἰς ἕν* Id.*Ti.*25b; *εἰς ταὐτό* Arist.*HA*546$^{b}$18; *συνηθροισμένη τῇ πόλει δόξα* Lycurg.110; *συνηθροισμένον πᾶν ἰσχυρόν* Thphr.*Ign.*12, cf. *Vent.*26; *χρόνῳ τὸ μῖσος –ηθροίσθη* Phld.*Piet.*30. 3. of a single person, *οὐ συνήθροισται στρατῷ* *has* not *joined* the main army, E.*Rh.*613. **–οισις,** *εως, ἡ,* *collecting,* Arist.*GA*739$^{b}$10; of persons, *gathering,* Sch.S *OC* 537 (pl.). * **–οισμα,** *ατος, τό,* *assemblage,* Apollon.*Lex.* s.v. *ἀγορά.* **–οισμός,** *ὁ,* *collection, union,* *τῶν λεπτομερῶν σωμάτων* *Placit.*1.24.2; *ὑγρῶν* Cass.*Pr.*80; opp. *μερισμός,* Dam.*Pr.*412; *assembly,* *πάντων τῶν ζῴων* Aesop.242. II. a rhetor. figure, by which dissimilar things *were associated,* Alex.*Fig.*p.17 S., Quint. *Inst.*8.4.27. **–οιστής,** *οῦ, ὁ,* *collector,* prob. in Hsch. s.v. *ἀγρετᾷ.* **–οιστ⟨ικ⟩ός,** *ή, όν,* *of* or *for collecting,* Id. s.v. *ἀγυρτούς.*

**συνᾰθύρω** [ῡ], *play with,* *τισι* Mosch.2.30.

**συνᾱΐγδην,** Adv. *pressing violently* or *boisterously together,* Hes. *Sc.*189.

**συναιγλία,** v. *συναικλία.* * **συναΐδιος·** *συνυπάρχων,* Hsch.

**συναιθριάζω,** *clear at the same time,* v.l. in X.*An.*4.4.10.

**συναιθύσσω,** *stream* or *wave with,* *λιγυρῷ ἀήτῃ* Nonn.*D.*10.183: trans., *πλοκάμους θυέλλαις* ib.43.346.

**συναικλία,** *ἡ,* (*αἶκλον*) Lacon. for *σύνδειπνον,* Alcm.70 (pl.): written **[συν]αιγλία** in *SIG*1106.90 (Cos, iv/iii B.C.).

**σύναιμος,** *ον,* (*αἷμα*) *of common blood, kindred,* *γονᾷ ξ.* S.*El.*156 (lyr.); *ξ. ὄμμα* Id.*Ai.*977: c. dat., *μητρὶ..σύναιμος* Philicus in *Stud. Ital.*9.44. 2. as Subst., *kinsman, kinswoman,* esp. *brother, sister,* S.*Ant.*198,488: pl., *kinsmen,* Id.*OC*943. 3. *Ζεὺς ξ.* as *presiding over kindred,* Id.*Ant.*659; *νεῖκος ξ.* strife *between kinsmen,* ib.794 (lyr.).—Poet. word.

**συναίμων,** *ον,* gen. *ονος,* = foreg., Ps.-Phoc.206, *IG*12(8).441.15 (Thasos), *Supp.Epigr.*1.464.9 (Galatia, iii A.D.), prob. in E.*Ph.*817 (lyr.).

**συναίν-εσις,** *εως, ἡ,* *approval, consent, assent,* Ph.1.382, al., Plu. 2.258b; *τοῦ βουλευτηρίου* *POxy.*2110.8 (iv A.D.), cf. 506.54 (ii A.D.), etc. **–ετέον,** *one must assent to,* *τινι* Ph.2.344. **–ετικόν,** *τό,* = *ἐπερώτησις ἀμοιβαία,* *compromiss⟨i⟩o,* *Gloss.* **–έω,** fut. *–αινέσω* S.*El.*402: aor. *–ήνεσα* A.*Ag.*484 (lyr.):—*consent,* abs., ib.1208, S. *Ph.*122, *El.*1280 (lyr.), Pl.*R.*393e, etc.; *σ. τισί* *agree with,* Hdt. 5.92.η', cf. S.*El.*402, Sor.1.58, al.:—Med., *Inscr.Prien.*85 (ii B.C.). 2. c. acc., *concede, give,* *χάριν* A.*Ag.*484; *agree upon,* *πόλιν* *SIG*633.83 (Milet., ii B.C.): but most freq. c. Adj. neut., *agree to,* *ἅπερ ξυνήνεσα* S.*OC*1508; *σ. ταῦτα* Id.*Fr.*368 (Med.), X. *Cyr.*4.2.47, etc.; *σ. τινί τι* *grant,* *δῶρά μοι –αίνεσον* E.*Rh.*172, cf. X.*Cyr.*8.5.20, *An.*7.7.31. 3. c. inf., *agree* or *consent* to do, Id.*Cyr.*4.4.8, 7.2.14.

**συναινίττομαι,** *allude to,* Eun.*Hist.*p.263 D.

**σύναινος,** ον, *agreeing with,* τινι Hsch.

**συναίνυμαι,** *gather up,* Λητὼ δὲ συναίνυτο τόξα Il.21.502.

⊕ **συναίρ-εμα,** ατος, τό, *aggregate, sum,* μονάδων Olymp. *in Phlb.* p.284 S., cf. Dam.*Pr.*4; *total,* πυροῦ, σιτικῶν, *PTeb.*340.5 (iii A.D.), Wessely *Karanis* p.11, cf. *BGU*1626 (iii A.D.), *PFlor.*35.12 (prob. l., v. *Arch.Pap.*4.430 (ii A.D.)); also **συναίρη(μα)** θησαυροῦ *Ostr.Bodl.* iii 157 (ii A.D.). II. = sq. 4, Eust.1447.52. **-εσις,** εως, ἡ, *taking* or *drawing together,* ἡ τῶν ἄκρων εἰς ταὐτὸ σ. Longin.10.3; σ. (sc. καρπῶν) Ath.11.489f; *contraction, closing,* τῶν διοδευθησομένων χωρίων Sor.2.59. 2. *contraction* of front, opp. αὔξησις, Ascl.*Tact.* 11.7; *shortening, reduction* of an estimated distance, Ptol.*Geog.*1. 8.3; τοῦ μήκους (of a fractured limb) Sor.*Fract.*19 (συνερεισις cod.). 3. *aggregation,* Dam.*Pr.*96; *synthesis,* ib.277,280; *concentration,* τῆς νοερᾶς οὐσίας Simp. *in Ph.*635.32; *generalization,* opp. διαίρεσις, Elias *in Porph.*76.19. 4. in Gramm., *synaeresis,* whereby two vowels are not changed, but coalesce into a diphthong, as ὀϊστός, οἰστός, opp. διαίρεσις, Quint.*Inst.*1.5.17, A.D.*Adv.*132. 25; but also *contraction,* as of κύημα to κῦμα, Gal.6.642. **-εσιώτης,** ου, ὁ, *partisan,* Serapio in *Cat.Cod.Astr.*8(4).230, Phot.*Bibl.*p. 97 B. **-ετέον,** *one must bring together,* Plot.3.7.5; *one must withhold,* Ath.Med.ap.Orib. *inc.*21.9. **-ετικός,** ή, όν, *coaggregative,* οἱ ἄζωνοι -κοὶ βούλονται εἶναι τῶν ζωνῶν Dam.*Pr.*132. 2. *tending to suppress,* ib.106. **-ετίστης,** ου, ὁ, *member of the same faction,* of planets, Vett.Val.55.24, al., *Cat.Cod.Astr.*7.215, al.; misspelt **συναιρέτης** in *Cat.Cod.Astr.*8(4).256, Sch.Ptol.*Tetr.*96, and **συναιρέτις** ib.99.

⊕ **συναιρέω,** in Hom. only 3 sg. aor. σύνελεν, and part. συνελών:— *grasp* or *seize together,* χλαῖναν μὲν συνελὼν καὶ κώεα Od.20.95; *seize at once,* πάντα ξυνῄρει ἡ νόσος Th.2.51; of the mind, λογισμῷ τὸ πρᾶγμα σ. Plu.*Lys.*22:—Med., συνελόμενος σκαφεῖον *seizing* a mattock, *PPetr.*2 p.59 (cf. 3 p.xiii, iii B.C.):—Pass., *to be brought together,* Arist.*SE*181$^b$33; so εἰς ἓν λογισμῷ συναιρούμενον to a unity *brought together* by reasoning, Pl.*Phdr.*249c; τὸ φιλεῖν καὶ τὸ μισεῖν.. συνῄρηται *are taken into account,* Arist.*Rh.*1354$^b$9 (nisi leg. συνήρτηται): hence δεῖ συναιρεῖν ἐκ πάντων τούτων ὅτι.. from all this we should *collect, infer* that.., Procl. *in Prm.*p.492 S. 2. *bring into small compass, shorten,* τὸν χρόνον D.S.17.116:—Pass., συναιρεῖσθαι εἰς ἥμισυ *to be halved,* Ascl.*Tact.*2.1; *to be contracted,* τὰ τῶν Ἀθηναίων ταχὺ ξυναιρεθήσεσθαι (v.l. ξυναναιρ-) Th.8.24; ὁ περίβολος τῆς πόλεως ..νῦν..καὶ μᾶλλον ἔτι συνῄρηται Plb.10.11.4. b. esp. of speaking, ξυνελὼν λέγω *concisely, briefly, in a word,* Th.2.41, cf. 1.70; ὡς συνελόντι εἰπεῖν X.*An.*3.1.38, *Mem.*3.8.10, etc.; συνελόντι φάναι Gal.16.502; so συνελόντι alone, Is.4.22; συνελόντι ἁπλῶς D.4.7; συνελόντες τὰ ἐν μέσῳ Luc.*Phal.*1.6; συνελεῖν [λόγον] εἰς βραχὺ κεφάλαιον Gal.15.754. c. Gramm., *contract,* τὸ ε καὶ τὸ α A.D. *Pron.*99.24; of the accent of compounds, Id.*Synt.*304.8. II. *make away with, destroy all trace of, annihilate,* ἀμφοτέρας δ' ὀφρῦς σύνελεν λίθος Il.16.740 (but perh. = συνέχεε καὶ εἰς ἓν συνήγαγεν, as Sch. ad loc.): metaph., *make an end of,* σ. τὰς ἀσπίδας *abolished* them, D.S.15.44; τὸ καῦμα καὶ τὸ δίψος δεινῶς τοὺς λοιποὺς συνῄρει D.C.40. 23, cf. 37.13, 50.35; συνῃρηκὼς ὥρᾳ μιᾷ χρόνου μήκιστον..πόλεμον Plu.*Lys.*11; ὡς ἡμέραις δυσὶ συναιρήσων τὴν πολιορκίαν Id.*Sert.*13; *diminish* a measurement, τινὶ μέτρῳ προσλιπεῖν ἢ συνελεῖν *IG*7.3073.24 (Lebad., ii B.C.):—Pass., τοῦ πρώτου τῶν Καρχηδονίων πολέμων ἔτει δευτέρῳ καὶ εἰκοστῷ συναιρεθέντος Plu.*Marc.*3; τοῦ πλήθους ἤδη συνῃρημένου the congestion having been *reduced* or *ended,* Gal.16.499. b. *annihilate, make short work of* a distance, ταχὺ σ. πολλὴν ὁδὸν Plu. 2.759d:—Pass., τὸ διάστημα ταχέως ὑπὸ προθυμίας τῶν ἐλαυνόντων συνῄρητο Id.*Lys.*11. 2. *help to take* or *conquer,* τὴν Σύβαριν Hdt. 5.44; βουλόμενοι σφίσι..ξυνελεῖν (v.l. for ξυνεξ-) αὐτόν wishing that he *should help* them *to conquer,* Th.2.29.

**συναίρω,** poet. **συναείρω** (q.v.):—Med. aor. συνηράμην E.*Or.*767, etc.; poet. aor. inf. συνᾰρέσθαι prob. cj. in Bion *Fr.*8.8 (συνερᾶσθαι codd.): v. αἴρω, ἄρνυμαι: pf. inf. written συνῆρσθαι, *BGU*975.15 (i A.D.), *PLips.*27.15 (ii A.D.):—*take up together,* Arist.*Pr.*945$^a$39, Plu.2.659a; σ. λόγον μετά τινος *cast up* accounts.., *Ev.Matt.*18.23, *PLond.*1.131$^r$.194 (i A.D.), cf. *PSI*7.801.3 (ii A.D., Pass.), *Ostr.Bodl.* iii 336 (ii/iii A.D., Pass.): abs., συναίρειν *Ev.Matt.*18.24. 2. = συνάγω, *gather in* a harvest, τὰ γενήματα *TAM*2.245.9 (Lycia):— Pass., ὁ ἐπὶ τοῖς βαλανείοις συναιρόμενος ῥύπος *collected,* Dsc.1.30 (v.l. -αγόμενος). 3. ὅπως συνάρωμεν διπλῆν εἰλαπίνην that we *may celebrate together* a double festival, *BGU*1080.9 (iii A.D.). 4. τῷ Καίσαρι συναίρει *espouses* Caesar's *cause,* D.C.46.3 codd. (fort. -εται). II. Med., *take part in* a thing, c. gen. rei, συνάρασθαι τοῦ πολέμου, τοῦ κινδύνου, Th.5.28, 4.10; σ. τισὶ τοῦ πολέμου D.H.6.3: c. acc. rei, *help in bearing* or *undertaking,* ξυναίρεσθαι κίνδυνον Th.2. 71; τὰ πράγματα D.1.24; also σ. Κύπριν *engage in* love *with* another, A.*Pr.*650; φόνον τινὶ E.*Or.*767 (troch.); σ. τὴν χάριν τινός *espoused his cause,* D.C.45.15; συνάρασθαι εἰς τὸ αὐτὸ *co-operate,* X.*Ath.*2.2; μηδενὸς ὑμῶν μηδὲν συναραμένου D.*Prooem.*41, cf. 33; σ. τινί *with* one, Plu.*Galb.*18, etc.; τινὶ ἐς ἀποικίαν Paus.3.1.7; πρὸς οὐδὲν αὐτῷ συνήρατο D.C.37.49; ἐπί τινα in attacking him, Plu.*Comp.Dion. Brut.*3; *help, assist,* ταῖς ἀναγωγαῖς τοῦ πύου Gal.11.683, cf. 6.265; εἰς εὐτροφίαν τοῖς νεύροις ib.209. 2. *raise* or *use in helping,* οὐ συναίρεται δόρυ E.*Rh.*495; πᾶν ὅ τι ἔχομεν σ. τῷ κάλλει *enlist* all we have *in the service of* beauty, Luc.*Charid.*12. 3. τῶν σκελῶν σ. *catch by both* legs, trip up, Plu.*Lys.*15. III. Med. in signf. 1.1, σ. λογάριον *PFay.*109.6 (i A.D.), cf. *POxy.*113.27 (ii A.D.). IV. Med., *annul jointly with* another, ἐφ' ᾧ συναρεῖταί μοι ἣν ἔχει ἡμῶν συνοικεσίου συγγραφὴν *PTeb.*809.4 (ii B.C.), cf. *PRein.*31.8 (ii B.C.), *BGU* l.c. (i A.D.), *PLips.* l.c. (ii A.D.), *CPR*23.17 (ii A.D.):— Pass., *PRein.*8.7 (ii B.C.).

**συναισθ-άνομαι,** *perceive simultaneously,* Arist.*HA*534$^b$18 codd. (leg. πόρρωθεν αἰσθάνεται): c. gen., Id.*EN*1170$^b$4, cf. Plot.4.4.24, Hierocl. *in CA*11 p.444 M.: c. acc., Arist.*Aud.*803$^b$36; διὰ τί οὐ συναισθάνεται ἡ ἑτέρα (sc. αἴσθησις) τὸ τῆς ἑτέρας κρίμα; Plot.6.4. 6. II. *share in perception* or *sense,* συζῆν καὶ σ. Arist.*EE*1245$^b$ 22; σ. ἀλλήλοις Plu.*Sol.*18. III. *to be aware of in oneself,* τὰς ἁμαρτίας Phld.*Lib.*p.30 O.: c. part., Id.*Vit.*p.17 J.: c. gen., τινὲς τῶν ἤδη συνῃσθημένων τοῦ ὑδροφόβα *conscious victims of* hydrophobia, Philum.*Ven.*4.11. **-ημα,** ατος, τό, *joint-perception,* *IG*2$^2$.1099.32 (Epist. Plotinae, ii A.D.). **-ησις,** εως, ἡ, *joint-sensation, joint-perception,* Arist.*EE*1245$^b$24, Sor.1.125, Alex.Aphr. *in Sens.*36.12. 2. *awareness,* τινος Plu.2.75b,76b, Arr.*Epict.*1.2.30, Procl.*Inst.*39, Herm. *in Phdr.*p.94 A., Dam.*Pr.*3; *self-consciousness,* Plot.3.8.4; *conscious perception,* σ. ἀμυδρά Phld.*Rh.*2.6 S.; τῆς αὐτοῦ ἀσθενείας Arr.*Epict.*2.11.1; [τῆς κίσσης] Sor.1.49; τῆς ἐκμυζήσεως ib.77; κοπώδης σ. a tired *feeling,* ib.26, cf. 44, al.; ὀσφύος τε καὶ ἤτρου σ. ib.27; *accompanying sensation,* in disease, Aret.*SA*2.9, *SD*2.2, Cass. *Pr.*23,65. ⊕ **-ητικός,** ή, όν, only Adv. -κῶς, *by way of* συναίσθησις, Sch.Ptol.*Tetr.*88.

**συναΐσσω,** *hasten together,* A.R.4.1112, Q.S.2.456.

**συναισχύνω,** *begrime, soil at the same time,* Max.Tyr.18.9 (Pass.).

**συναιτέω,** *demand together with,* δούλῳ σ. = *servo competere, Gloss.*: —Med., *join in demanding for oneself,* *POxy.*54.31 (iii A.D.).

**συναιτιάομαι,** Med., *accuse along with,* Plu.*Fab.*8.

**συναίτιος,** ον, also α, ον (v. infr. 2): 1. c. gen. rei et dat. pers., *being the joint* or *contributory cause of* a thing which benefits another, σ. τινὶ ἀθανασίας *helping* him *towards*.., Isoc.5.33, cf. ib.44; εἰ τῶν πεπραγμένων ἐκείνοις μηδὲν σ. ἐγενόμην if I *had contributed* nothing to their success, Id.15.96; πᾶσιν ἀγαθοῦ σ. ὢν X.*Cyr.*1.4.15, etc. 2. c. gen. rei only, *being joint-cause of, accessory to, contributing to,* Pl. *Plt.*281c, *Grg.*519b, D.18.64, Thphr.*Sens.*27, etc.; σ. τούτου συνειπὼν Φιλοκράτει *by* acting as his advocate, D.19.97: as Subst., ἡ ξυναιτία φόνου *accomplice* in murder, A.*Ag.*1116 (lyr.); δοξάζεται..οὐ συναίτια, ἀλλ' αἴτια εἶναι τῶν πάντων Pl.*Ti.*46d. 3. abs., *being a joint* or *concurrent cause, contributory,* Id.*Plt.*287b, Arist. *de An.*416$^a$ 14, Gal.15.303, 19.393; ἀναγκαῖον λέγεται, οὗ ἄνευ οὐκ ἐνδέχεται ζῆν ὡς συναιτίου Arist.*Metaph.*1015$^a$21.

**συναιχμάζω,** *fight along with* or *together,* *AP*15.50: c. dat., Nonn. *D.*2.201, al.

**συναιχμᾰλωτ-ίζω,** *take captive along with,* τισι S.E.*M.*1.295, cf. *Theol.Ar.*40 (both Pass.). **-ος,** ὁ, *fellow-prisoner,* *Ep.Rom.*16.7, Luc.*Asin.*27:—fem. ⊕ **-ωτις,** ιδος, Conon 13 (pl.).

**σύναιχμος,** ον, *allied with, an ally,* Hsch., Phot., Suid.

**συναιωρ-έομαι,** Pass., *to be swayed with,* συναιωρούμενον τῷ ὑγρῷ τὸ πνεῦμα Pl.*Phd.*112b, cf. Plu.2.564d. **-ησις,** εως, ἡ, *oscillation,* Pl.*Ti.*80d.

**συνακαταληπτέομαι,** Pass., *to be incomprehensible together,* S.E. *M.*1.243, 11.38.

⊕ **συνακμάζω,** *blossom* or *flourish at the same time,* of plants, *AP* 11.417; of persons, Ἰφίτῳ σ. *with* Iphitus, Arist.*Fr.*533, cf. Plb.6. 43.6, 31.26.3, Gal.15.455: abs., *flourish together,* Plu.*TG*3. II. συνακμάσαι ταῖς ὁρμαῖς πρὸς τὴν τῶν πραγμάτων αὔξησιν *rise to a great occasion,* Plb.16.28.1.

**συνᾰκολασταίνω,** *live dissolutely with,* τισι Plu.*Demetr.*24; μετά τινων Id.*Sull.*2, cf. 2.140b.

**συνᾰκολουθ-έω,** *follow along with* or *closely, accompany,* τῇ στρατιᾷ Th.6.44, cf. Hyp.*Lyc.*6, *BGU*1755.3 (i B.C.), *Ev.Marc.*14.51, etc.; σ. τινὶ οἴκαδε Ar.*Pl.*43; πρὸς τὴν θεόν Id.*Ra.*400; μετὰ τοῦ στρατηγοῦ Isoc.4.146. 2. *follow* with the mind, *attend to,* σ. ταῖς τύχαις Arist.*EN*1100$^b$4; *follow* an argument *completely,* λόγῳ Pl.*Phlb.*25c, *Lg.*629a; σ. τινί τι *follow* him *in* a matter, ib.792c; τισι Arist. *Ph.*188$^b$26, Thphr.*Sens.*72. 3. *to be correlated,* ἀλλήλοις Arist. *GA*764$^b$24, cf. Thphr.*HP*7.2.9. 4. *follow* with the sense of *obeying,* c. dat., Pl.*Lg.*711c,716b. 5. *accrue, enure,* τινι *BGU*906. 22 (i A.D.). II. of effects, *follow closely upon* the cause, πάντα σ. τῷ τοῦ παντὸς παθήματι Pl.*Plt.*274a; μετὰ τοῦ ῥήματος..σ. τὰς ἡδονάς Id.*R.*464a; σ. τοῖς πλούτοις ἄνοια καὶ μετὰ ταύτης ἀκολασία Isoc.7.4, cf. Arist.*Mete.*370$^b$10, Gal.18(2).135. III. in the Logic of Arist., *follow necessarily with* a term, *be involved in it,* *APr.*52$^b$11; *to be mutually implied,* σ. αἱ ἀρχαί *Metaph.*1085$^a$16. **-ία,** ἡ, *imitation,* Ps.-Philol.ap.Stob.1.20.2. **-ος,** ον, *coupled with,* Arist. *Rh.Al.*1435$^b$2.

⊕ **συνᾰκοντίζω,** *throw a javelin along with* or *at once,* Antipho 3.4. 5. II. *strike with many javelins,* Plb.1.43.6:—Pass., Id.1.34.7, 11.1.9, al.

**συνάκοος** [ᾰ], ὁ, *fellow-hearer,* Them.*Or.*33.366b (pl.).

**συνᾰκούω,** *hear along with* or *at the same time,* τι X.*HG*2.4.36; τινος Arist.*Cael.*290$^b$24; but ἀλλήλων *hear each the other,* X.*An.*5.4. 31; σ. σφίσι τὰ ἐπεσταλμένα D.C.46.41: abs., Plu.*Pyrrh.*5, etc. II. *understand* so as to complete, τῷ ὅρῳ τι S.E.*M.*7.239.

**συνακρᾱτίζομαι,** *breakfast with,* μετά τινος Antiph.285.

**συνακρῑβόω,** *give an accurate, systematic account of,* τι Phld.*Rh.*2. 188 S., Vett.Val.18.13.

❋ **συνακροάομαι**, *listen together, be a fellow-hearer*, Pl.*Mx*.235b; σ. ἡμῖν ἀνδρός *to be his hearer with* us, Id.*Sis*.387b.

**συνακτέον**, (συνάγω) *one must bring together* or *collect*, μαθήματα εἰς σύνοψιν Pl.*R*.537c; τὴν λιγνύν Dsc.1.77; *one must reduce*, εἰς ὀλίγα καὶ κοινά Arist.*Pol*.1319b24; *one must unite* a wound, ῥαφῇ Antyll.ap.Aët.7.74. II. *one must conclude*, ὅτι.. Arist.*Rh*.1377b6, cf. Hp.*Hum*.18.

**συνακ-τήρ**, ῆρος, ὁ, *that which draws together, pair of drawers*, J.*AJ*3.7.1. ❋ **-τήριον**, τό, *assembly*, Hsch. **-τικός**, ή, όν, *able to bring together*, τὸ σ. καὶ κρουστικόν *power of accumulation* in oratory, of Demosthenes, Luc.*Dem.Enc*.32: c. gen., ἃ δικαιότας κοινωνίας συνεκτικὰ καὶ συνακτικά Diotog.ap.Stob.4.7.62; σ. τοῦ καταρτίζεσθαι μηρὸν ἐξαρθρήσαντα Apollon.Cit.3. 2. of drugs, *constrictive*, Gal.11.710. II. *conclusive*, λόγοι Epict.*Ench*.44, cf. *Stoic*.2.78, Phld.*Rh*.2.98 S., S.E.*P*.2.137, al. Adv. **-κῶς** ib.170. **-τός**, ή, όν, *collected*, ὕδωρ Porph.*Abst*.1.42.

**συνᾰλᾰλάζω**, *cry aloud together*, Plb.1.34.2, Plu.*Sull*.28, etc. 2. c. acc., ἣν..ὑμεναίοισι..σ. whom *they greeted with loud* wedding-songs, E.*HF*11.

**συνᾰλάομαι**, *roam together*, Man.4.290; σ. τινί *partake in exile with* any one, D.L.6.20.

**συναλγ-έω**, *share in suffering*, S.*Aj*.253 (lyr.): c. dat. pers., with a person, Arist.*EN*1166a7, etc. 2. abs., δήλωσον ἡμῖν τοῖς ξυναλγοῦσιν τύχας reveal them to us *who are partners in his sorrow*, S.*Aj*.283, cf. E.*Alc*.633, *HF*1202, Antipho 3.2.8, Pl.*R*.462d; τῇ ψυχῇ *in* one's soul, D.18.287; τῇ διανοίᾳ Arist.*Pr*.887a16. 3. c. dat. rei, *sympathize, show sympathy at* or *in*, ταῖς σαῖς τύχαις A.*Pr*.290 (anap.); σοῖς κακοῖς E.*Rh*.807; τοῖς λυπηροῖς Arist.*Rh*.1381a5; τῇ δυστυχίᾳ αὐτῶν Gal.6.754. II. *ache* or *be painful as well*, ἔτι δὲ καὶ ψύαι καὶ ἰσχία σ. τισί Sor.2.31. **-ηδών**, όνος, ἡ, *joint grief*: in pl., = αἱ συναλγοῦσαι, *fellows* or *partners in pain*, E.*Supp*.74 (lyr.). **-ύνω**, *fill with compassion*, Opp.*H*.1.726.

**συναλδής**, ές, *growing together*, καρπός Nic.*Al*.623.

**συνᾰλεαίνω**, *help to warm*, Plu.2.691e.

**συνάλ-ειμμα** [ᾰλ], ατος, τό, *salve*, Dsc.3.137, Herod.Med.ap.Orib. 10.18.5, Id. in *Rh.Mus*.58.78, al., Sor.2.32 (perh. also 1.49). **-ειπτικός**, ή, όν, *coalescing by* συναλιφή, τὸ -κόν Eust.25.33. Adv. **-κῶς** *with* or *by* συναλιφή, S.E.*M*.1.165, Eust.834.5. **-ειπτός**, όν, f.l. for ἀσυνάλειπτος in *An.Ox*.2.412. **-είφω**, *clog up*, γῆ ὑγρά.., ἐὰν ξηρανθῇ, σ. τὸ σπέρμα Thphr.*CP*3.23.1:—Pass., τὰ μὲν ἄνω [τῆς γῆς] συναληλίφθαι διὰ τοὺς ὄμβρους *have been clogged up, turned into impermeable clay*, Arist.*Mete*.365a21; *coalesce*, -ομένων ἀλλήλοις τῶν περάτων Simp. *in Ph*.892.9, cf. 931.17. b. *anoint thoroughly*, Sor.1.46, 64, al.; *rub in thoroughly*, Dsc.*Eup*.1.233. c. metaph., *gloss over, whitewash, minimize*, τἀγαθὰ μὲν ὑπερεπαινεῖν, τὰ δὲ φαῦλα συναλείφειν Arist.*Rh*.1383b33. 2. Gramm., *unite two syllables into one*, D.H.*Comp*.22, etc.:—Pass., *coalesce*, of two syllables, Id.*Dem*. 38; cf. συναλιφή. II. *assist in anointing*, τινα Plu.*Pomp*.73, cf. Phld.*Vit*.p.29 J.

**συνᾰλέω**, *grind together*, *Gp*.15.2.23.

**συναληθεύω**, *to be true together*, Arist.*Int*.19b36, cf. Gal.7.838. II. *join in seeking* or *speaking the truth*, Plu.2.53b.

**συνᾰλήθω**, = συναλέω, *Gloss*.

**συνᾰλητεύω**, *wander about with*, Hld.6.7.

**συνάλθομαι**, aor. inf. -αλθεσθῆναι, Pass., *heal up*, of a wound or fracture, Hp.*Art*.14; also in the form **συναλθάσσομαι**, Id.*Fract*.9 (v.l. -αλθέεται).

**συνᾰλιάζω**, Dor. 3 sg. aor. ξυναλίαξε, (ἁλία) = sq., Ar.*Lys*.93.

**συνᾰλίζω** (A), aor. συνήλισα Hdt.1.176, -άλισα ib.125:—*bring together, collect, assemble*, τινας Hdt.1.125; σ. ἐς τὴν ἀκρόπολιν τὰς γυναῖκας ib.176, cf. 2.111; τοὺς ἐπιεικεστάτους..πρὸς τὴν σκηνήν X.*HG*1.1.30:—Pass., *come together, assemble*, Hdt.1.62, 5.15,102, X.*An*.7.3.48, etc.; σ. εἰς τοὺς τελείους ἄνδρας Id.*Cyr*.1.2.15; of things, τὸ πλεῖστον ἐκ τοῦ μυελοῦ σ. Hp.*Oss*.15; βορβόρου περὶ αὐτὰ συναλισθέντος Arist.*GA*763a33.

**συνᾰλίζω** (B), in Pass., *eat salt with, eat at the same table with*, *Act.Ap*.1.4, Man.5.339; συναλίζεται = *convescitur*, *Gloss*. (Cf. ἅλς, σύναλος; συναυλιζόμενος is v.l. in *Act.Ap*. l.c.)

❋ **συνᾰλίσγομαι**, *to be sullied with*, c. dat., Aristeas 142 (cod. L and ap.Eus.*PE*8.9).

**συνᾰλίσκομαι**, Pass., *to be taken captive together*, Plu.*Comp.Dion. Brut*.3, Ael.*NA*11.12; τινι *with* one, D.L.2.105.

**συνᾰλῐφή**, ἡ, *stopping of a hiatus, coalescing* of two syllables into one, either by synaeresis, crasis, or elision, D.H.*Comp*.6, 22, al., S.E.*M*.1.161; κατὰ συναλιφὴν τοῦ ἄρθρου (in ὦλλοι) A.D.*Synt*.5.28; τῆς σ. Ἰωνικωτέρας γενομένης (in ὑπόδρα for ὑφ–) Id.*Adv*.139.14, cf. 152.20; Eust.1561.6 speaks only of crasis and synaeresis; κατὰ τὴν σ. Str.8.6.7; = *coeuntes litterae*, Quint.*Inst*.9.4.35: generally, *running together* of words, Demetr.*Eloc*.70. 2. = νουμηνία, Gem.8.11. [In codd. freq. written συναλειφή (e.g. Sch.A *Il*.24.12) or συναλοιφή, but -αλιφ-, which is mentioned by Eust.1561.6, is found in the best codd. of D.H.*Comp*. ll.cc., A.D.*Synt*.140.14 (v. Uhlig ad loc.), al., Heph.2.4, Suid. s.v. ἔνθους, ἔνωσις, Sch.A *Il*. passim, *EM*116.23, al. (v. p.2464 Gaisf.), Sch.S.*OC*504,1588, Sch. E.*Hec*.336; cf. ἀλιφή, ἀπαλοιφή, καταλιφή, περιαλιφή.]

**συναλλ-ᾰγή**, ἡ, *interchange*, esp. for purposes of *conciliation*, ἐν ξυναλλαγῇ λόγου by *reconciling* words, S.*Aj*.732; λόγων ξυναλλαγαῖς E.*Supp*.602 (lyr.): abs., *reconciliation, making of peace*, Th.4.20; ὅρκοι ξυναλλαγῆς Id.3.82: in pl. συναλλαγαί, *treaty of peace*, X.*HG* 6.5.8. 2. *commerce, dealings*, λέκτρων ἦλθες ἐς συναλλαγάς (of a procuress) E.*Hipp*.652; ἔν τε δαιμόνων συναλλαγαῖς in the *dealings* of men with the immortals, S.*OT*34; ἐπὶ συναλλαγαῖς γάμου D.H. 1.60; *covenant, contract*, Id.6.22, *POxy*.70.4 (iii A.D.); αἱ πρὸς ἀλλήλους σ. *OGI*669.18 (Egypt, i A.D.). 3. *rate of exchange, agio*, *PMasp*. 131.1, al. (vi A.D.). II. *that which is brought about by the intervention* or *agency of* another, *visitation*, νόσου ξυναλλαγῇ S.*OT*960; *conjuncture*, Id.*OC*410; μολόντ' ὀλεθρίαισι σ. Id.*Tr*.845 (lyr., unless = *meeting, converse*). **-αγμα**, ατος, τό, *covenant, contract*, D.24.213, Arist.*Rh*.1354b25, *PEleph*.1.14 (iv B.C.), *PEnteux* 55.6 (iii B.C.), etc.; σ. ποιεῖσθαι D.30.21; διαλύειν D.H.6.22; *commitments*, διὰ -μάτων ἀνάγκην Aen.Tact.5.1. 2. generally, in pl., *dealings, transactions*, Archyt.3, Hp.*Medic*.1; ἑκούσια σ., i.e. sales, loans, etc., distd. from ἀκούσια σ., i.e. crimes of force or fraud, Arist.*EN*1131a2, cf. *Rh*.1376b12; βίαια σ. Lxx *Is*.58.6; σ. καὶ ἐγκλήματα *OGI*229.54 (Smyrna, iii B.C.). **-αγμᾰτικός**, ή, όν, *of* or *for contracts*, Sch.Th.1.77. **-αγμᾰτογρᾰφία**, ἡ, *writing of contracts*, *PTeb*.140 (i B.C.). **-αγμᾰτογράφος** [γρᾰ], ὁ, *notary, recorder of contracts*, ib.42.6 (ii B.C.), *POxy*.237 viii 36 (ii A.D.). **-ακτέομαι**, *to be negotiated*, *Inscr.Prien*.19.13 (iii B.C.). **-ακτεύω**, gloss on συμβολατεύω, *barter*, Hsch. ❋ **-ακτής**, οῦ, ὁ, *mediator, negotiator*, Id. II. an official concerned with the tax on sales (?), *POxy*.43v ii 4, al. (iii A.D.). **-ακτικός**, ή, όν, *of* or *for contracts*, οἱ νόμοι οἱ σ. D.H.4.13; γράμματα σ. Vett.Val.16.19; of persons, *versed in business*, Ptol.*Tetr*.66. ❋ **-αξις**, εως, ἡ, *exchange*, Pl.*Lg*.850a (pl.). 2. *contract*, *PFay*.11.22 (pl.). *PTeb*.6.32, 61(*b*). 22 (all ii B.C.). 3. *right of disposal by contract*, *BGU*1120.52 (i B.C.). ❋ **-άσσω**, Att. -ττω, pf. συνήλλαχα *SIG*742.55 (Ephesus, i B.C.), etc.: 2 aor. Pass. συνηλλάγην *PTeb*.329.10:—*bring into intercourse with, associate with*, δίκαιον ἄνδρα τοῖσι δυσσεβεστέροις A.*Th*.597:—Pass., *have intercourse with*, Ἑλένῳ συναλλαχθεῖσαν εὐναίοις γάμοις E.*Andr*.1245; ἡ [εὐνὴ] ξυνηλλάχθης ἐμοί S.*Aj*.493. 2. *reconcile*, τινάς τισι Th.1.24; τινας, opp. διαλλάττειν, X.*Vect*.5.8; τινὰς εἰς εἰρήνην *Act.Ap*.7.26: abs., Pl.*Lg*.930a:—Pass. and Med., *to be reconciled* or *come to terms with, make a league* or *alliance with*, πρός τινας Th.8.90, X.*An*.1.2.1: abs., *make peace*, Th.5.5, X.*HG*2.4.43, etc.; μετρίως on fair terms, Th.4.19. II. intr., *have dealings with* another, S.*OT*1110, E.*Heracl*.4; ἦ ξυνήλλαξάς τί που; *hast thou had* any *dealings with* him, S.*OT*1130. 2. *enter into engagements* or *contracts* (cf. συνάλλαγμα II), *Leg.Gort*.9.44, al., Arist.*EN*1162b24, 1178b11, D.24.192, Din.ap.Gramm. in Reitzenstein *Ind.Lect.Rost*. 1892/3 p.7, *PCair.Zen*.359.6,12 (iii B.C.), *SIG* l.c.; οἱ συνηλλαχότες the *parties to a contract*, *PTeb*.5.212 (ii B.C.), cf. *POxy*.34 i 10, al. (ii A.D.): c. acc. cogn., τοιοῦτον πρᾶγμα συναλλάττων D.30.12, cf. D.H.6.22, *BGU*1062.10:—Pass., *to be the subject of a contract*, *PTeb*.329.10 (ii A.D.).

**συναλλοι-όω**, *alter at the same time*, Arist.*Phgn*.808b12, Thphr.*CP*2.14.3, Gal.1.403, Dam.*Pr*.280. **-ωσις**, εως, ἡ, *concurrent modification*, ib.440.

**συνάλλομαι**, *leap together*, Luc.*Anach*.4; of a horse, f.l. in Plu. 2.970e. II. *start back with terror*, Artem.1.57.

**συναλλύω**, v. συναναλύω.

**σύναλμα**, ατος, τό, *leap taken together*, Hsch.

**σύνᾰλμος**, ον, (ἅλμη) *salted*, Macho ap.Ath.13.580d.

❋ **συνᾰλοάω**, Ep. aor. -ηλοίησα:—*thresh out together, trample in pieces* (by oxen), Heraclid.ap.Ath.12.524a. 2. *grind to powder, crush*, Hippon. in *PSI*9.1089.4, Theoc.22.128, Plu.*Marc*.15, Opp.*C*. 1.268, Q.S.11.472, etc.

**συνᾰλοιφή**, v. συναλιφή.

**σύνᾰλος**, ον, *eating salt with* one, *Gloss*.

❋ **συνᾰλύω**, *wander about with*, τινι Plu.*Ant*.29.

**συνᾰλωνιάζω**, (ἅλων) *keep the threshing festival together*, Suid.

**συνᾰμᾶ**, Adv. for σὺν ἅμα, *together*, *AP*7.9 (Damag.), Luc.*Pisc*.51, *Bis Acc*.11, etc.; τισι *with* them, Theoc.25.126; freq. in tmesi: συνάμα is dub.l. in S.*Ichn*.70 (lyr.).

**συνᾰμᾰθύνω**, *annihilate together*, σὺν κάρφεα πάντ' ἀμ. A.R.3.295.

**συνᾰμάομαι**, Med., *gather together*, A.R.3.154, *EM*83.3.

**συνᾰμαρτάνω**, *sin along with* or *together*, Plu.2.53c, App.*Ill*.8, Chor.23.60 F.-R.

**συνᾰμείβω**, *interchange*, A.D.*Synt*.63.10 (Pass.); *change along with*, Steph. *in Gal*.1.252 D. (Pass.).

**συνᾰμιλλάομαι**, Med., *contend* or *struggle together*, E.*HF*1206 (lyr., συναμιλλαταί 'rivals' Murray), Plu.2.786f.

**συνάμιλλος** [ᾰ], ον, *rival*, of a wine, Gal.14.15.

**σύναμμα**, ατος, τό, (συνάπτω) *clamp*, Arist.*PA*687b15; *ganglion, knot*, Id.*GA*788a10. II. περὶ συναμμάτων dub. sens. in title of work by Chrysipp., D.L.7.191.

**συναμμᾰτίζομαι**, Pass., *to be tied*, Sch.Nic.*Al*.382.

**συναμοργός**· δεξαμενή, Hsch. (ξυν- cod.).

**συναμπέχω** and **-ίσχω**, *cover up together* or *closely, wrap up*, ἦ πού τι σεμνόν ἐστιν ὃ ξυναμπέχεις A.*Pr*.521:—Med., τί συναμπίσχῃ κόρας; why *dost veil thine* eyes? E.*HF*1111.

**συναμπρεύω**, *help in drawing*, Arist.*HA*577b31.

**συνᾰμύνω** [ῡ], fut. ξυναμυνῶ E.*IA*62:—*join in assisting*, τινι l.c.:—Med., Eratosth.*Cat*.33, Ael.*NA*3.46.

**συναμφιάζω**, *envelop closely*, τοὺς πόδας ληδίῳ Clearch.25.

**συναμφιβάλλομαι**, Pass., *to be matter of doubt together*, Eust.316. 26.

**συναμφότεροι**, αι, α, *both together*, Thgn.820, Hdt.1.147, 3.97, al., *SIG*56.5 (Argos, v B.C.); τὰ σ. Pl.*Phlb*.46c, etc. 2. sg. in collective sense, ὁ σ. [βίος] ib.22a: τὸ σ. the *complex* of both, Id.*Smp.*209b, *Ti.*87e, Epicur.*Sent.*3, Gal.6.237, Plot.4.3.26, 6.9.2; or without the Art., Pl.*R.*400c, *Sph.*250c, Gal.16.743; τοῦτο σ. this *united power*, D.2.14. 3. Math., of the sum of two things, συναμφότερα τὰ Δ, Μ,.. Euc.5.8: more freq. in sg., συναμφότερος ὁ Α, Δ, *the sum of* Α, Δ, Id.7.5; συναμφότερος ὁ ΑΓ *the sum* ΑΓ (sc. of ΑΒ, ΒΓ), ib.28, cf. Papp.94.7: neut. as Subst., τὸ σ. ὅ τε κύκλος καὶ τὸ Β χωρίον Archim.*Sph.Cyl.*1.6, cf. 2.9, *Spir.*27.

**συνάμφω**, οἱ, αἱ, *both together*, Pl.*Plt.*278c, *IG*4$^2$(1).109 iii 115 (Epid., iii B.C.), *Supp.Epigr.*2.479 (Olbia), etc.; οἱ σ. Plb.1.63.5, etc.: c. gen., Ἰαπύγων καὶ Μεσσαπίων συνάμφω Id.2.24.11, cf. 65.9. 2. with the Art. in sg., ὅροι τοῦ συνάμφω Arist.*Metaph.*1043$^a$22, cf. *Int.*20$^b$37; τοῦ σ., τῆς τε Λιβύης καὶ τῆς Ἀσίας Str.2.4.5, cf. 2.1.29; κατὰ τὸν σ. χρόνον Id.1.2.36.

**συνανα-βαίνω**, *go up with* or *together*, freq. of going into central Asia, Hdt.7.6, X.*An.*5.4.16, Isoc.4.146; τινι *with* one, ib.145, X.*An.*1.3.18; τινὶ εἰς Ἱεροσόλυμα *Ev.Marc.*15.41; μετά τινος *OGI*632.2 (Palmyra, ii A.D.); σ. μέχρι Συήνης Str.2.5.12, cf. 11.5.2; *pass upwards also*, διὰ τῶν ὀστῶν Gal.2.711; *ascend the sky with*, τῷ πόλῳ Vett.Val.8.14. 2. σ. ἅρμα *mount* it *together*, Luc.*Charid.*19. **-βακχεύω**, *break into Bacchic frenzy together*, Lib.*Or.*18.75. **-βῐβάζω**, causal of συναναβαίνω, Al.*Ge.*50.25, Orib.49.23.22, 49.24.24:—Pass., of the accent, *to be thrown back together*, A.D.*Adv.*135.2. **-βλαστάνω**, *shoot forth together*, Thphr.*HP*3.4.2, Ph.1.344,444. **-βοάω**, *cry out together*, X.*Cyr.*5.1.6. **-βόσκομαι**, Pass., *grow up together with*, c. dat., Plu.2.409a (s.v.l.). **-γιγνώσκω**, *read together*, ib.180d; τισι ib.97a, cf. Gal.18(2).321:—Pass., Phot.*Bibl.*p.145 B., al.

**συνᾰναγκ-άζω**, *press together, compress*, Hp.*Art.*37; τὰς προθέσεις Longin.10.6. II. *join* or *assist in compelling*, ἡ χρεία σ. Arist.*Pol.*1256$^b$7; σ. τινὰ ποιεῖν τι D.58.7, *Prooem.*10, cf. *PCair.Zen.*149 (iii B.C.), *PPetr.*3 p.69 (iii B.C.):—Pass., *to be compelled at the same time*, c. inf., X.*Hier.*3.9, D.26.10, Arist.*Ath.*40.1. III. *achieve by force also*, Isoc.4.89:—Pass., ὅρκοι συνηναγκασμένοι *extorted* (κατην- Stob., prob. rightly), E.*IA*395 (troch.). **-ασμός**, ὁ, *constraining proof*, Iamb.*Protr.*21.κε'.

**συνανά-γνωσις**, εως, ἡ, *reading together*, Plu.2.700c, Phot.*Bibl.*p.99 B., etc. **-γράφω** [γρᾰ], *register* or *record at the same time*, D.S.17.1:—Pass., συναναγραφῆναι ἐν τοῖς συμμάχοις Aeschin.2.83. **-γυμνόω**, *expose together*, Plu.*Comp.Lyc.Num.*3:—Pass., S.E.*M.*8.274.

**συνανάγω** [ᾰγ], *carry back together*, in Pass., *retire together*, Plb.1.66.10, Ael.*NA*10.34. II. Pass. also, *go to sea together*, D.34.10, Lib.*Or.*11.54, Procop.Gaz.*Ep.*31. 2. τὸ -αχθὲν ὕδωρ *shipped at the start*, Aristid.2.362 J.

**συνανα-δείκνῡμι**, *proclaim together with*, τέμενος ἑαυτῷ ἄσυλον *SIG*630.12 (Delph., ii B.C.); ἑαυτῷ τὸν παῖδα βασιλέα Zos.1.24. **-δεύω**, *mix into a paste with*, αὐτοῖς ἄλευρον *Hippiatr.*34. **-δέχομαι**, *undertake together*, τὸν κίνδυνον Plb.16.5.6. **-δίδωμι**, *give back along with*, τι μετά τινος Luc.*Symp.*15; *distribute together*, Gal.18(2).152, Alex.Aphr.*Pr.*1.5:—Pass., prob. in Sor.1.88. **-δίπλωσις**, εως, ἡ, *reduplication*, *Gloss.* ⊛**-ζεύγνῡμι**, *set out along with*, Plu.*Eum.*3. **-ζέω**, *make to boil together*, τινι Dsc.1.30, *Hippiatr.*34, Aët.9.31: intr., Dsc.1.55. **-ζητέω**, *search out with*, Hld.6.7. **-ζωπῠρέω**, *kindle together*, Men.Prot.p.27 D. **-θεμᾰτίζω**, *pronounce a curse together*, Phot.*Bibl.*p.286 B.

**συναναθλέω**, *join in accomplishing a task*, τινί τι Eun.*VS*p.500 B.

**συνανα-θρηνέω**, *mourn over along with*, X.Eph.3.3. **-θῡμιάομαι**, Pass., *to be burnt together*, Arist.*Pr.*907$^a$38.

**συναναίρ-εσις**, εως, ἡ, *simultaneous abolition*, S.E.*M.*10.267. **-έω**, *take up together with*, τινά τινι Antipho 5.42. II. *destroy together with*, τινά τινι Isoc.*Ep.*2.3, Plb.5.11.5, etc.; τι ἅμα τινί Id.6.46.7; simply, *destroy at the same time*, Phld.*Mus.*p.37 K.:—Pass., *to be destroyed together with*, τινι Lycurg.60: abs., Diog.Oen.58. 2. *destroy altogether* or *utterly*, in Pass., τὰ τῶν Ἀθηναίων ταχὺ ξυναναιρεθήσεσθαι v.l. for ξυναιρ- in Th.8.24. 3. in the Logic of Arist., σ. τὸ γένος καὶ ἡ διαφορὰ τὸ εἶδος the genus and difference (being abolished) *abolish also* the species, *Top.*141$^b$28, cf. 123$^a$15, *Metaph.*1059$^b$30; τὸ ..αἰσθητὸν ἀναιρεθὲν συναναιρεῖ τὴν αἴσθησιν· ἡ δὲ αἴσθησις τὸ αἰσθητὸν οὐ σ. *Cat.*7$^b$38, cf. Ammon. *in Cat.*74.6,19. III. *give the same answer*, ἐὰν καὶ ἡ Πυθία συναναιρῇ Pl.*R.*540c; cf. ἀναιρέω A.III. IV. παρακληθεὶς.. συνανίρηται (= -ῄρηται) αὐτοῖς ὀνόματα δύο *has taken up in conjunction with* them two loans, *BGU*1133.4 (i B.C.); cf. ἀναιρέω B.I.6.

**συνανα-κᾰθαίρω**, aor. -ᾶρα, *assist in cleaning up*, *IG*11(2).163*A*56, 287*A*49 (Delos, iii B.C.). **-κάμπτω**, intr., *return along with*, Plb.8.27.6; *walk backwards and forwards with*, τινι D.L.2.127, cf. 139. ⊛**-κειμαι**, Pass., *recline together* at table, *Ev.Matt.*9.10, etc. **-κεράννῠμαι**, aor. -εκράθην [ᾱ] and -εκεράσθην, Pass., *to be mixed up with*, τινι Luc.*Gall.*26: abs., ὕδατος -κραθέντος Dsc.2.70: metaph., Plu.*Them.*29 (v.l. for ἀν-); δύναμις δυνάμει -κερασθεῖσα Vett.Val.350.16:—Med., Ph.2.315. II. Gramm., *suffer synecphonesis*, Eust.11.32. **-κεφᾰλαιόω**, *sum up briefly*, τοὺς χρόνους f.l. for συγκ- in D.H.*Th.*12. **-κηρύσσω**, *proclaim together*, Phot.*Bibl.*p.255 B. **-κινδῡνεύω**, *run risk together with*, Nic.Dam.*Fr.*66.15 J. **-κῑνέω**, *stir up together*, *Gp.*8.41.2. **-κίρνημι**, *mix up with*, τινί τι S.E.*P.*3.59 (Pass.), cf. Hero *Spir.*1 *Praef.*p.14 S.:—also Pass. συνανακιρνάομαι, Alex.Aphr. *in Metaph.*35.21. **-κλίνομαι** [ῑ], Pass., *lie down along with*, esp. *in bed* or *at table*, μετά τινος Luc.*Asin.*3; = *concubo*, *Gloss.* **-κομίζω**, in Med., *help* one *to recover*, τοῖς Ἀμφικτύοσι τοὺς νόμους Plb.4.25.8. **-κόπτω**, *beat up together*, Heliod.ap.Orib.44.14.11, Gal.13.31. **-κράω**, late form for συνανακίρνημι, in Pass. -κρᾶται, Phot. s.v. συμφύρεται. **-κρίνω** [ῑ], *examine together with*, Arist.*Fr.*447. **-κυκλέομαι**, Pass., *come round together*, Pl.*Plt.*271b. **-κῠλίομαι** [ῑ], Pass., *roll along with*, Diog.*Ep.*35.3. **-κύπτω**, *raise up the head along with*, Them.*Or.*18.223c. **-λαμβάνω**, *take up along with*, τινι Plu.2.214f, Aq.*Ex.*9.24, Ath.3.113d; *incorporate* a drug in an ointment, Dsc.*Eup.*1.161, Antyll. ap. Orib.9.24.15:—Pass., *to be included*, *CPR*19 a 5 (iv A.D.). 2. *receive*, *BGU*918.9 (ii A.D.). **-λάμπω**, *shine forth together*, Ph.2.141: c. acc., *shed lustre on at the same time*, *SIG*798.3 (Cyzicus, i A.D.). **-ληψία**, ἡ, *restoration to a healthy state*, Sor.1.29.

**συνᾰνᾱλίσκω**, *consume together* or *likewise*, τοὺς λεγομένους ἅλας σ. *consume in company* the proverbial salt, i.e. live in close companionship, Arist.*EN*1156$^b$27; ὅσα ἐδεῖτο εἰς τὴν ναῦν σ. D.50.42: metaph., σ. τὸ μεμνῆσθαι τὴν χάριν Id.1.11. II. *help by spending money*, X.*Mem.*2.4.6.

**συνανα-λογέομαι**, v. συναπολογέομαι. **-λύω**, Elean συναλλύω, in Med., *remit* a debt, *Schwyzer* 418.7 (v B.C.). **-μᾰλάσσω**, *soften along with* or *together*, Dsc.*Eup.*2.25, Orib.*Fr.*75, Aët.7.84. **-μείγνῡμι**, *mix up together*, Hp.*Nat.Mul.*97, Ath.5.177b:—Pass., c. dat., Thphr.*HP*8.8.3, Phld.*D.*3.9; *associate with*, τισι Clearch.25; πόρνοις 1*Ep.Cor.*5.9; of two bodies of men *meeting*, Plu.*Phil.*21; ἡ ἄνοια ξ. αὐτοῖς *is part of* their *nature*, Luc.*Cont.*15. **-μέλπω**, *sound with, sing with*, Ael.*NA*11.1. **-μῐγος**, ον, *mixed up with, included among*, *POxy.*718.16, al. (ii A.D.). **-μιμνήσκω**, *remind together*, τινων of things, Plu.2.397e; *bring to mind together with*, σ. αὐτοῖς καὶ τὰ λοιπά Gal.15.510:—Pass., *recall together with*, ὑμῖν Pl.*Lg.*897e. **-μιξις**, εως, ἡ, *combination with another*, Thd.*Da.*11.23. **-μίσγω**, = συναναμείγνυμι, Steph. *in Hp.*1.170 D. **-νεόομαι**, Med., *join in renewing*, ξενίας Plb.12.6$^A$.3; ἐπιχωρεῖ ἡμῖν ὁ δανείσας Ἱππόνικος συνανανεώσασθαι *to renew the term* (at the end of which the mortgagee can claim the property as his), *PEnteux.*15.5 (iii B.C.). **-ξηραίνω**, *dry up at the same time*, Ath.Med.ap.Orib.9.12.11. **-πάλλομαι**, Pass., *fly forth along with*, Philostr.*Im.*1.24. **-παύομαι**, Pass., *sleep with*, γυναικί D.H.*Rh.*9.4, cf. Plu.2.125a, Hld.6.8; *to be refreshed, receive comfort along with*, ὑμῖν *Ep.Rom.*15.32. **-πείθω**, *assist in persuading*, τινὰς ποιεῖν τι Th.6.88, Isoc.4.46; τινα Plu.*Publ.*21. ⊛**-πέμπω**, *send up together*, Id.*Rom.*28. **-πηδάω**, *spring up along with*, App.*Hisp.*88. **-πίμπλημι**, *infect* with, ταραχῆς σ. τὸν δῆμον Plu.2.324e:—Pass., J.*BJ*7.8.7. ⊛**-πίπτω**, *concubo*, *Gloss.* **-πλάσσω**, *help in refashioning*, Max.Tyr.24.5. 2. *make up into pills*, Dsc.4.164. **-πλέκω**, *entwine also*, Aq.*Jb.*39.13:—Pass., Luc.*Gall.*13, *Anach.*15: metaph., Longin.20.1; *combine*, Vett.Val.99.19. 2. *mix up together*, Alex.Trall.*Febr.*4. **-πληρόω**, *fill up at the same time*, Thphr.*HP*4.13.4 (Pass.); τὰς μεταξύτητας Nicom.*Harm.*6; *make up* or *compensate*, τινί τι Plb.22.20.7; μετ' εὐφημίας τὸ ἐλλεῖπον Plu.2.795b.

**συναν-απλόω**, *unfold* or *expand together*, Dam.*Pr.*71.

**συνανα-πράσσω**, Att. -ττω, *join in exacting payment*, μισθὸν παρά τινος X.*An.*7.7.14. **-πτύω**, *spit up at the same time*, aor. Pass. -επτύσθη Gal.8.262.

**συνανάπτω**, fut. Pass. -αναφθήσομαι, *attach oneself to* a thing, Phld.*Lib.*p.7 O.

**συναναρῐθμέω**, *reckon in*, *PLond.*3.1293.2 (iv A.D.).

**συναναρριπτέω**, *throw up together*, v.l. for ἀν-, Luc.*Zeux.*10.

⊛**συναναρτάομαι**, Pass., *to be closely connected*, D.C.38.24 codd. (συνανήρηται Reiske).

**συνανα-σκάπτω**, *dig up besides*, τοὺς τάφους Str.8.6.23. ⊛**-σκευάζω**, *refute along with*, S.E.*M.*7.214, Gal.*Opt.Doctr.*6:—Pass., c. dat., Phld.*Sign.*12, al. **-σκευή**, ἡ, *joint refutation*, S.E.*M.*7.214. **-σπάω**, *draw up together*, Ph.*Bel.*95.1, Ph.1.643, 2.513, Gal.*UP*8.14, Luc.*Cat.*18.

**συναναστομ-όω**, *join by a mouth* or *opening*, Gal.*UP*15.4:—Pass., *to be joined by a mouth or opening, open into*, τὸ ἔξω [πέλαγος] συνανεστόμωται τῇ Προποντίδι Arist.*Mu.*393$^b$1, cf. Gal.2.375, al.: so in Act., λίμνη Μαιῶτις εἰς τὸν Ὠκεανὸν συναναστομοῦσα *Peripl.M.Rubr.*64. **-ωσις**, εως, ἡ, in pl., of supposed *communications* between arteries and veins, Erasistr.ap.Gal.4.709, cf. 8.352, 11.152.

⊛**συνανα-στρέφω**, *turn back together*, intr., J.*BJ*5.2.2, Plu.*Galb.*10, 25. II. Pass. and Med., *live together, associate with*, τινι D.S.3.58, Plu.*Lyc.*17, Hierocl.p.58 A.; τοῖς πολίταις καλῶς *SIG*534.8 (Delph., iii B.C.); μοχθηρῶς φίλοις Carneisc.*Herc.*1027.13, cf. Phld.*Rh.*1.377 S.:—so in Act., Agatharch.42. 2. *wrestle with*, τινι Lxx *Ge.*30.8. **-στροφή**, ἡ, *living with, intercourse*, Epicur.*Sent.Vat.*18, Lxx *Wi.*8.16, Phld.*D.*3 *Fr.*87, J.*AJ*18.6.9; πρός τινας *Supp.Epigr.*7.825.7 (Jerash, ii A.D.): pl., D.S.4.4, Arr.*Epict.*1.9.5, Hierocl. p.58 A. **-σῴζω**, *restore along with*, τινί τι Plb.4.25.6, cf. 3.77.6:—Pass., Str.10.4.15. **-τᾰράσσω**, *stir up*, τῇ χειρί Dsc.5.78. **-τείνω**, *extend at the same time*, Gal.18(2).369:—Pass., Id.2.583. **-τέλλω**, *rise* or *grow up with* or *together with*, τινι Ael.*VH*13.1; of stars, etc., Hipparch.2.4.1, Gem.17.39, al., *PGiss.*3.2 (ii A.D.), Ptol.*Tetr.*79, Nonn.*D.*1.175, 3.431. **-τήκω**, *melt with* or *together*, Plu.*Pomp.*8. **-τίθημι**, *help in putting on*, φορτίον τοῖς βαστάζουσιν Porph.*VP*42, cf. Iamb.*VP*18.84. II. *join in dedicating*, *IG*2$^2$.1299.93, Luc.*Phal.*2.7. **-τολή**, ἡ, *rising together*, Hipparch.2.4.4, Str.1.1.21, etc. **-τρέπω**, *overturn* or *defeat together*, Ph.1.696. II. *confuse* (οὐσία with ἔννοια), Gal.10.

141. -τρέφω, *rear along with*, Inscr.*Prien.*107.20 (ii B.C.), Conon 19 (Pass.), etc. -τρέχω, *run up along with*, Plu.*Alex.*15. -τρίβω [ῑ], *rub up together*, Dsc.1.25:—Pass., *to be rubbed against*, τοῖς ῥάκεσιν [τῶν πτωχῶν] D.L.7.22; *wrestle with*, Epict.*Ench.*33.6, Diog. *Ep.*35.2. -τροφος, gloss on σύντροφος, Hsch. -φαίνω, *display at the same time*, Dam.*Pr.*27,246:—Pass., *appear together with*, τινι Demetr.*Eloc.*6, Luc.*Salt.*7, etc. -φέρω, fut. -ανοίσω prob. in Hsch.: —*carry up together*, Lxx *Ge.*50.25; ἑαυτῷ τοὺς παχεῖς χυμοὺς Gal.15.634:—Pass., *to be carried up* or *ascend together with*, [ὁ ἀὴρ] σ. τῷ.. πυρί Arist.*Mete.*341ᵃ7; *to be carried along with*, τῷ αἵματι Gal.*Nat. Fac.*2.2, cf. Id.2.819; *to be imparted* (to milk), Sor.1.95; *to be brought up to the surface*, of heat, Herod.Med.ap.Orib.5.30.9. 2. Astron., *rise with*, in Pass., Hipparch.2.3.30, Vett.Val.6.10. II. metaph., *bring up together with itself*, Plu.2.451a; τὴν ἀρχὴν *refer to* its origin *at the same time*, Plb.5.32.4, cf. Dam.*Pr.*64. 2. *certify at the same time*, συνανενηνοχέναι τινὶ συγχώρησιν Mitteis *Chr.*31 iii 28 (ii B.C.); *report*, τὸ καθ' ἓν σ. *PSI*4.386.32 (iii B.C.). -φθέγγομαι, *cry out at the same time*, Plu.*Mar.*19. -φλέγω, *set fire to along with* or *together*, Ph.1.345, v.l. for συγκατα- in 2.27. -φορά, ἡ, *referring at the same time*, ἡ ἐπὶ τὰ θεῖα σ. M.Ant.3.13. II. *rising together*, Ptol.*Alm.*2.7 tit., Heph.Astr.2.10, *Cat.Cod.Astr.*1.138. -φῡράω, = sq., τι μετά τινος Dsc.1.55. -φύρω [ῡ], *knead* or *mix up together*, τινὰ μετά τινος *PHolm.*26.39:—Pass., Gal.15.577: also, *wallow together*, ἐν τῷ πηλῷ Luc.*Anach.*1; σ. ἐν καπηλείοις μεθ' ἑταίρων Ath.13.567a; παισὶν ἢ γυναιξὶν συναναφῠρέντες Luc.*Sat.*28. -χᾰλάω, *relax at the same time*, Sor.1.31. -χέω, *pour upon together with*, τινί τι Hld.5.16. -χορεύω, *dance in chorus with*, τοῖς ἄστροις Arist.*Mu.*391ᵇ18. -χρέμπτομαι, *cough up together*, τι μετά τινος Luc.*Gall.*10. -χρώννῡμι (also -χρώζω *Gp.*6.2.9), *impart by mixture* or *contact*: metaph., *impart*, τῆς ἀπ' αὐτῶν ὀσμῆς *Gp.* l.c.:—Pass., τούτου -χρωσθέντος τὸ πᾶν γίνεται χρῆμα κολλῶδες D.S.3.16: metaph., *to be imbued and infected*, βαρβάροις καὶ μοχθηροῖς Plu.2.4a; τοῖς ἀνθρωπίνοις ἤθεσιν ib.975f:—Med., -χρωννύμενοι τοῖς πολίταις *infecting* the citizens, Id.*Agis* 10. -χρωσις, εως, ἡ, *infecting contact*, Id.2.680e. -χρωτίζω, = συναναχρώννυμι, Gem.2.14 (Pass.). -χωρέω, *retire together*, μετά τινος Pl.*La.*181b.

**συνανδάνω**, v. συνεύαδον.

**συνανδρᾰγᾰθέω**, *behave bravely together*, D.S.1.55.

**συνανδρόομαι**, Pass., *grow up along with*, δικόσοισι ἂν συνανδρωθῇ τὸ νόσημα Hp.*Prorrh.*2.9; ἡ διάθεσις σ. ταῖς ἡλικίαις J.*BJ*1.23.1.

**συνάν-ειμι**, (εἶμι *ibo*) *go up together*, Ph.1.461; σ. τὴν ἡλικίαν *grow up with*, Ael.*NA*6.63. -είργω, *assist in repelling*, Arist. *de An.*404ᵃ15. -έλκω, *draw up together*, Thphr.*CP*5.6.3, Ph.2.513, Sch.Ar.*Pax* 706. -έρχομαι, *come* or *rise up with*, τινι A.R.2.913, Arat.561, prob. l. in Ph.1.311; εἰς τὴν μητρόπολιν *BGU*638.10 (ii A.D.). -έχω, intr., *rise together*, Arist.*Mete.*372ᵃ15; τινι *with* one, Them.*Or.*3.42b. II. *abstain as well*, Aret.*CA*2.3 (s.v.l.). -ηβάω, *grow young again with* or *together*, Them.*Or.*18.223c. -ήκω, *have reference also to* a thing, Phot.*Bibl.*p.162 B.

**συνανθέλκω**, *draw back at the same time*, Herod.Med. in *Rh.Mus.* 58.90 (Pass.).

**συνανθέω**, *blossom together*, metaph., τῇ Θεμιστοκλέους ἀρετῇ Plb. 6.44.2. 2. of wine, '*bloom*' (i.e. form a crust) *at the same time* as, Thphr.*Od.*63. II. *to be wrought with divers colours also*, J.*AJ* 3.6.2.

**συνανθομολογέομαι**, *assent*, τινι Aristeas 252.

**συνανθρωπ-εύομαι**, *live with* or *among men*, ἐν ταῖς οἰκήσεσι Arist. *HA*599ᵃ21; ζῷα -ευόμενα *domesticated* animals, ib.542ᵃ27, Thphr.*HP* 3.2.2, etc.:—later in Act., Porph.*Abst.*1.36, 4.22. -έω, = foreg., Plu.2.823b; τὰ -ωποῦντα [θηρία] Porph.*Abst.*1.14.20, 3.9. -ίζω, = συνανθρωπεύομαι, Arist.*HA*488ᵇ3; τὸ -ίζον καὶ οἰκουρόν Ath.13. 611c. -ισις, εως, ἡ, *common humanity*, Eustr. *in EN*63.22.

**συνανῑάομαι**, Pass., *suffer affliction together*, Poll.5.129.

**συναν-ίημι**, *relax along with* or *together*, Ph.2.23:—Pass., *to be soluble in*, Dsc.5.112. -ίστημι, *make to stand up* or *rise together*, μεθ' ἑαυτοῦ τινα X.*Smp.*9.5; *assist in restoring*, τὰ μακρὰ τείχη Id. *HG*4.8.9. II. Pass. with aor. 2 Act., *rise at the same time*, Id.*An.* 7.3.35; τινι *with* one, Id.*Cyr.*5.1.5. -ίσχω, = συνανέχω, *rise* or *spring forth together*, of rivers, Ael.*NA*14.23, cf. 10.45; πῶλος σ., out of the sea, Philostr.*Im.*2.14. -ιχνεύω, *track along with*, Ael. *NA*10.45.

**συνανοηταίνω**, *join in foolish conduct*, Sch.E.*Ph.*394.

**συναν-οίγω**, *open in company with*, συνανοιγόντων καὶ συγκλειόντων τὰς θύρας τοῖς.. ταμίαις *IG*1².91.16; συνανοίγνουσα (sic) τὰ συγχωσθέντα *SIG*799.8 (Cyzicus, i A.D.):—Pass. συνανοίγνῠμαι Them.*Or.* 20.235c. -οιμώζω, *bewail together with*, τινι App.*Pun.*91. -ορθόω, *help in correcting* a text, Tz.*Proll.Com.*p.24 K.

**Συνᾰνουβιασταί**, οἱ, *fellow-worshippers of Anubis*, *Michel* 1223 (Smyrna, iii B.C.).

**συνανταίρω**, *rise against together*, Eulogius ap.Phot.*Bibl.*p.282 B.

⊛ **συναντ-άω** (cf. συνάντομαι): Ep. impf. -ήντεον A.R.4.1486, Ep. 3 dual συναντήτην Od.16.333: fut. -ήσω Lxx *Is.*34.14, *Act.Ap.*20.22: aor. -ήντησα X.*An.*1.8.15: pf. -ήντηκα Plb.1.52.6, Ps.-Luc.*Philopatr.* 1:—Med., once in Il., elsewh. only in late Prose (v. infr.): fut., Lxx *Ec.*2.15, etc.:—*meet face to face*, of two persons, Od. l.c.; of many persons, *meet together*, *assemble*, εἰς Φωκίδα Philipp.ap.D.18. 157, cf. *OGI*56.5 (Canopus, iii B.C.); *meet in battle*, Plb.3.93.9: c. dat., Isyll.68. II. *meet with*, *encounter*, c. dat., E.*Ion* 787, Ar.*Ach.* 1187, *Pl.*41,44, etc.: abs., τὰ συνηντηκότα τῶν πλοίων Plb.1.52.6; σ. συνάντησιν E.*Ion* 534 (troch.); of heavenly bodies, *Cat.Cod.Astr.* 7.204; *present oneself*, *PCair.Zen.*300.6 (iii B.C.); φυγοδικοῦντας μὴ συναντῆσαί μοι *PEnteux.*65.4 (iii B.C.), cf. *PCair.Zen.*179.9 (iii B.C.); εἰς.. *go to meet at* a place, ib.56.3, 247.2 (iii B.C.):—Med., φ.. -αντήσωνται ἐν ὕλῃ ἄνδρες Il.17.134; πρός τινα *PHamb.*25.11 (iii B.C.). b. *fall in with*, *meet* a person's needs or wishes, *SIG*528.14 (Cos, iii B.C.), 590.43 (Milet., found at Cos, ii B.C.). 2. c. dat. rei, *come in contact with*, φόνῳ E.*IT*1210 (troch.). 3. c. acc., *meet*, only among Asiatic Greeks, Iamb.*Bab.*12, Lesb.Gramm.10. III. *befall*, *happen to* a person, τινι Plu.*Sull.*2, *Act.Ap.*20.22, D.L.6.38: abs., μετρίως τὸ -τῆσαν οἴσει Phld.*Lib.*p.34 O., cf. *Mort.*37; of conception, Sor.1.44; εἰ ἔρρωσαι καὶ τἆλλά σοι κατὰ τρόπον σ. *PSI*4.392.1 (iii B.C.):—Med., σ. τι παρά τινος Plb.21.24.14, *SIG*601.14 (Teos, ii B.C.). -ή, ἡ, = συνάντησις (which is v.l.), Lxx 3*Ki.*18.16, 4*Ki.*5.26. -ημα, ατος, τό, *incident*, *occurrence*, ib.*Ec.*9.2,3. 2. *visitation*, of plague, etc., ib.*Ex.*9.14, *PMag.Leid.W.*18.5, Anon. in Rh.1.646 W.; σ. νυκτερινόν nightmare, Cyran.31. 3. *confirmation*, in pl., Phld. *Sign.*19. ⊛ -ησις, εως, ἡ, *meeting*, E.*Ion* 535 (troch.), Lxx *Ge.*18.2, al., v.l. in *Ev.Matt.*8.34; περὶ συναντήσεως εἰς Μέμφιν *PCair.Zen.* 541.8 (iii B.C.); κατὰ τὰς σ. in *chance-meetings*, D.H.4.66; *encounter*, *controversy*, πικροὶ πρὸς τὰς σ. Hp.*Decent.*3; of heavenly bodies, Vett.Val.147.29, Paul.Al.*R.*3. -ιάζω, = συναντάω, τινι S.*OT*804.

**συναντιβάλλω**, *confer*, μετ' ἐμπείρων *IG*12(5).132.5 (Paros, iii A.D.).

**συναντίζω**, in 1 sg. fut. -ιῶ, = συναντάω, Aq.*Mi.*2.8.

**συναντί-θεσις**, εως, ἡ, *conjoined opposition*, Elias *in Cat.*158. 2. -λαμβάνομαι, Med., *help in gaining* a thing, τῆς ἐλευθερίας D.S.14.8; τῶν τῇ πόλει συμφερόντων *SIG*412.7 (Delph., iii B.C.); τῆς θεραπείας Phld.*Lib.*p.19 O.; *assist in supporting*, τὴν ὁρμὴν τοῦ λαοῦ Lxx *Nu.*11.17: abs., *render assistance*, περί τινων *PHib.*1.82.18 (iii B.C.); εἴς τι *OGI*267.26 (Pergam., iii B.C.). II. c. dat., *take part with*, *help*, Lxx *Ex.*18.22, *Ps.*88(89).22, *Ev.Luc.*10.40. -μεσουρᾰνέω, *to be in the opposite meridian at the same time*, *Cat.Cod.Astr.* 8(1).230.

**συνάντισμα**, ατος, τό, *occurrence*, Aq.*De.*23.10.

**συναντλέω**, *drain along with*, σ. πόνους τινί *join* him *in bearing all* his sufferings, E.*Ion* 200 (lyr.).

**συνάντομαι**, only pres. and impf., poet. for συναντάω, *fall in with*, *meet*, abs., Od.15.538; τινι 4.367, 21.31, Archil.89.5; ἀλλήλοισι δὲ τώ γε συναντέσθην παρὰ φηγῷ Il.7.22, cf. Hes.*Th.*877; in hostile sense, *meet* in battle, Il.21.34, cf. Pi.*O.*2.39; κόρος οὐ δίκᾳ συναντόμενος satiety *that accompanies* not justice, ib.96: metaph., φόρμιγγι σ. *approach* (i.e. *use*) the lyre, Id.*I.*2.2.—Also in late Prose, Ant. Lib.35.2, Hdn.1.17.4 (v.l.).

**συνᾰνύτω** [ῠ], = sq. (in intr. sense), *come to an end together with*, ξυνανύτει βίου δύντος αὐγαῖς A.*Ag.*1123 (lyr.).

**συνᾰνύω**, *accomplish together*, δρόμον App.*Pun.*47. 2. intr., *arrive together*, Arist.*Phgn.*813ᵇ19, Plu.*Alc.*27, etc.—Hsch. also cites **ξυνάνεσθαι**.

**συνάξῐμος**, ον, = συνακτός, Eust.929.32.

**συναξῐόω**, *join in thinking fit*, c. acc. et inf., X.*Cyr.*7.1.15; *join in demanding*, *BGU*1011.15 (ii B.C.).

**σύναξις**, εως, ἡ, (συνάγω) *gathering*, καρποφορηθέντων Procl.*Par. Ptol.*118; *assembly*, λαοῦ Eust.1335.55; = *cenaculum*, *collectum*, *conventiculum*, etc., *Gloss.*, cf. *POxy.*1357.1 (vi A.D.), *Cod.Just.*1.5. 20.1.

**συναοιδία, συναοιδός**, v. συνῳδία, συνῳδός.

**συνᾰορέω**, *accompany*, γλυκεῖά οἱ συναορεῖ ἐλπίς Pi.*Fr.*214.

**συνᾰοριστέομαι**, *acquire indefiniteness at the same time*, A.D.*Synt.* 306.22.

**συνάορος**, v. συνήορος.

**συναπάγω** [ᾰγ], *lead away with* or *together*, τινι X.*Cyr.*8.3.23: abs., Id.*HG*5.1.23. 2. *carry off with*, οἱ γλυκεῖς οἶνοι.. οὐ συναπάγουσιν ἑαυτοῖς τοὺς χολώδεις χυμούς Gal.15.638. II. Pass., τοὺς συναπαχθέντας ἡμῖν γεωργοὺς *arrested with* us, *PCair.Zen.*640.14 (iii B.C.). 2. metaph., *to be led away likewise*, *Ep.Gal.*2.13, 2*Ep.Pet.* 3.17. 3. = συμπεριφέρομαι (συμπεριφέρω II. 3), *Ep.Rom.*12.16.

**συναπαιδευτέω**, *deal foolishly together*, Sch.E.*Ph.*394.

**συναπ-αίρω**, plpf. 3 sg. συναπήρκει prob. in Men.*Kith.*14:—intr., *sail* or *march away together*, D.S.5.49,59, Str.4.1.4, al., Luc.*Tox.*18; μετά τινων Phld.*Sto.Herc.*339.9; τινι *with* one, Luc.*Bis Acc.*27, Ael. *VH*3.26; τινὶ ἐκ τοῦ βίου J.*AJ*9.8.6. 2. *depart at the same time*, Arist.*HA*597ᵇ16. -αιτέω, *demand at the same time*, Men.*Epit.* 89. -αντάω, *come to* a place *at the same time*, Arist.*Mir.*834ᵇ6, *PSI*6.689.9 (v A.D.). -αρτίζω, *bring to an end together with*, [λόγῳ] λόγον Sor.1.126:—Pass., *come to an end together with*, Alex. Aphr. *in Sens.*115.22. II. intr., *to be commensurate with*, *vary with*, ἡ τῶν σκελῶν κίνησις (in walking) σ. τι τῇ ὁρμῇ Chrysipp.*Stoic.* 3.114. 2. *come to an end simultaneously with*, [κῶλα] μὴ συναπαρτίζοντα τοῖς στίχοις D.H.*Comp.*26, cf. 22, Hermog.*Inv.*4.4, prob. cj. in D.H.*Dem.*39. 3. of a place, *to be of the same length as*, τῇ νήσῳ Str.13.2.2; similarly, τῷ μὴ συναπαρτίζειν τὸ ζῴδιον τῷ δωδεκάτῳ μέρει τοῦ ζῳδιακοῦ Sch.Arat.545. -αρτισμός, ὁ, = *consummatio*, *Gloss.*

**συνάπᾱς** [ᾰπ], ᾶσα, ᾰν, = σύμπας, strengthd. for πᾶς, πᾶσα, πᾶν, *all together*, mostly in pl., with or without Art., Hdt.1.98,134,178, 5.49, 9.29; αἱ συνάπασαι ἐπιστῆμαι Pl.*Phlb.*13e, etc. II. in sg., with collective Nouns, τὸ σ. στράτευμα Hdt.7.187; especially of countries, Αἰγύπτῳ τῇ σ. Id.2.39, cf. 9.45; ὁ χῶρος ὁ σ. Id.2.112; μουσικὴ σ. *the whole range of*.., Pl.*Sph.*224a.

**συνᾰπᾰτάω**, in Pass., *to be deceived along with* others, Plu.*Comp. Nic.Crass.*4; -ωμένη ἀκοή Procop.Gaz.*Ep.*125.

**συναπαυξίφως** [ῐ], ωτος, ἡ, *decreasing in light together with*, c. dat., Arg.Man. post Max.p.99 L.

**συνᾰπειλέω**, *threaten at the same time*, Luc.*Demon.*15; ὡς.. J.*AJ* 20.2.4.

**συνάπ-ειμι**, (εἶμι *ibo*) *go away, depart together*, X.*An.*2.2.1, Lys. 13.52. 2. *depart* or *die simultaneously*, Arist.*Pr.*862$^b$23. **-ελαύνω**, *drive away together*, Aret.*CD*1.5. **-ελευθερική**, ἡ, *colliberta*, and ⊛**-ελεύθερος**, ὁ, *collibertus*, *Gloss.* **-εμπολάω**, *sell with* or *together*, Eust.772.37. **-εργάζομαι**, *help in finishing* or *completing*, Pl.*R.*443e, *Ti.*38e. II. σ. τοὺς μύθους τῇ λέξει, τοῖς σχήμασι, *elaborate* the plots by language and gestures, Arist.*Po.*1455$^a$22,30; of an orator, σ. σχήμασι καὶ φωναῖς καὶ ἐσθῆτι καὶ ὅλως τῇ ὑποκρίσει *help the effect* by the use of gestures, etc., Id.*Rh.*1386$^a$31. **-ερείδω**, v. συνεπερείδω. **-έρχομαι**, *depart together with*, τινι Id.*GA*725$^b$14; μετά τινος Id.*Mete.*383$^a$19: abs., πωριδίων συναπελθόντων *being passed with* the urine, Ruf.*Ren.Ves.*3.5; φλὲψ συναπιοῦσα *branching off together*, Gal.19.522. **-ευθύνω**, *make straight together, help to guide*, Plu.2.426c,1027a, Heliod.ap.Orib.48.33.7. **-εχθάνομαι**, *become an enemy together*, Plu.2.96b. **-έχω**, *to be remote from at the same time*, Dam.*Pr.*73. II. trans., *receive also*, *PFay.*14.7 (ii B.C.), *PGen.*23.7 (i A.D.), etc.

**συναπίσταμαι**, Ion. for συναφίσταμαι (q.v.).

**συναπλόω**, *unfold together*, metaph., τοῖς πραττομένοις Hdn.*Fig.* p.104 S.; *simplify at the same time*, Dam.*Pr.*71:—Pass., of metal, *to be beaten out together*, Callistr.*Stat.*11.

**συναπο-βαίνω**, *disembark together with*, τινι Hdt.6.92; σ. τῆς γῆς *go away* from it *together*, Philostr.*VA*3.15; *dismount together with*, συναποβῶμεν τῷ Πριάμῳ τοῦ ζεύγους Procop.Gaz.p.170B. **-βάλλω**, *lose at the same time*, D.S.3.7, Plu.*Phil.*21:—Pass., Gal.14.588. **-βῐάζομαι**, Med., *assist in checking* or *repressing by force*, Arist.*HA*581$^a$24, *Pr.*962$^a$7. **-βλέπω**, *fix one's gaze on as well*, Aristid.*Or.*19(41).3. **-βρέχω**, *macerate along with*, Dsc.1.47. **-γεννάω**, *generate together*, Plot.6.6.2, 6.8.14, Procl.*Inst.* 70. **-γίγνομαι**, *to be absent together*, Anon.in Rh.1.607 W. **-γραπτέον**, *one must enrol oneself with*, τοῖς ἀρίστοις Cic.*Att.*9.4.2. ⊛**-γράφομαι** [γρᾰ], Med., *enter one's name together with* others, as a candidate, Plu.*Aem.*3. b. *register at the same time*, τὴν γυναῖκα *PGrenf.* 2.49.9 (ii A.D.), etc.:—Pass., *Sammelb.*7440.35 (ii A.D.). 2. σ. τινι *enter one's name with* his, as a supporter, *support* him, *be* his *follower*, Posidon.36 J., cf. S.E.*M.*10.45, Ath.9.385c. II. *receive the impression of*, τῶν οὐκ ἀστείων τὰ πταίσματα Porph.*Chr.*27; *copy, represent exactly*, πάντα Ptol.*Geog.*1.1.1:—later in Act., Eust.ad D.P. p.78.30 B. **-γυμνόομαι**, Pass., *to be stripped naked along with*, Sch. Hes.*Op.*753. **-δείκνυμι**, *demonstrate together*, Euc.*Phaen.*p.98 M., Ptol.*Alm.*1.16, al., Alex.Aphr.*in Sens.*149.1:—Pass., S.E.*M.*11.216, Gal.15.619. II. *appoint at the same time*, in Pass., *Inscr.Prien.* 82.18, al. (ii B.C.). **-δεικτέον**, *one must demonstrate also*, A.D.*Adv.*170.3. **-δειξις**, εως, ἡ, *joint demonstration*, Plu.*Fr.* 7.26. **-δέρω**, *skin together*, Gal.2.364, 8.103. **-δέχομαι**, *join in admitting*, -δεδέχθαι [τὸ τέμενος] ἄσυλον εἶμεν *SIG*629.18 (Aetolia, ii B.C.). **-δημέω**, *go abroad* or *travel with*, Arist.*Pol.*1314$^b$13; τινι with one, D.S.4.4, Plu.*Crass.*3, *Brut.*3, al., *POxy.*1122.10 (v A.D.); μετά τινων *IG*2$^2$.641.15, cf. Luc.*DMeretr.*9.1. **-δημοι**, οἱ, *those who go abroad together*, Arist.*Pol.*1263$^a$17, *OGI*196.5 (Philae): sg. of *one who accompanies* an Emperor, Lat. *comes*, σ. τοῦ.. αὐτοκράτορος *Ephes.*3 No.29. **-διδράσκω**, *run away along with*, ξυναποδρᾶναί τινι (aor. 2) Ar.*Ra.*81, cf. J.*BJ*1.8.6; aor. 1 part. συναποδράσαντος Luc.*Asin.*27. **-δίδωμι**, *repay at the same time*, *BGU*853.13 (ii A.D.), etc. 2. *render* or *recount together*, Ptol. *Geog.*1.2.4 (Pass.), Sor.1.1; *administer at the same time*, τισι Ruf. ap.Aët.11.29, S.E.*M.*8.1, etc.; τῇ ἐννοίᾳ συναποδέδοται *is rendered* or *represented with* the idea, Id.*P.*1.11. II. Med., *sell together, be a joint vendor*, D.C.59.21, *PLeid.N.*ii 8. **-δοκῐμάζω**, *join in reprobating*, τι X.*Oec.*6.5. **-δοκῐμαστέον**, *one must include in one's reprobation*, Eust.185.46. **-δύομαι**, Med., *strip off from oneself* or *put off together*, τὸ Αἰθίοπες εἶναι Philostr.*VA*6.11; τῇ φαινόλῃ τὸ νουνεχές Men.Prot.p.1 D.: abs., συναποδύεσθαί [τινι] εἰς ἀγῶνα *strip oneself* for a contest *along with* another, Plu.2.94c, cf. Ath.1.15c.

**συναπ-οδύρομαι** [ῡ], *lament together*, J.*Ap.*2.26.

**συναπο-θέλγομαι**, *bewitch*, *IG*12(7)p.1 (Arcesine, dub.l.). **-θεόω**, *deify together*, ὥσπερ τῇ ψυχῇ καὶ τὸ σῶμα Lyd.*Mens.*4.40. **-θλάω**, *pound up together*, Cleopatra ap.Gal.12.404. **-θλίβω** [ῑ], *crush together*, Dsc.4.153. **-θνῄσκω**, *die together with*, τινι Hdt.3.16, 5.47; αἱ δυνάμεις σ. τοῖς σώμασι Isoc.*Ep.*8.5: abs., opp. συζῆν, *2Ep. Cor.*7.3, Ath.6.249b; συναποθνῄσκοντες, title of comedy by Diphilus, Ter.*Adelph.Prol.*6; ὧν τὰ συγγράμματα τοῖς μὲν ἤδη συναπέθανε, τοῖς δὲ συντεθνήξεται Gal.15.68; τοῦ ἀποθανόντος οὐ σ. ἡ ψυχή Pl.*Phd.* 88d; σ. νοσήματα, i.e. *cling* to one *until death*, Hp.*Aph.*2.39, cf. Arist.*GA*775$^b$34.

**συναπ-οικίζω**, in Pass., *go as colonists together*, Luc.*Nav.*3. **-οίχομαι**, *to have gone away together*, τῷ πρόσθεν ἠδεῖ Aret.*CD*1.4.

**συναπο-κᾰθαίρομαι**, Pass., *to be washed off together with*, c. dat., Dsc.1.8. **-καθίστημι**, *accompany* a person *on the return journey*, *Schwyzer*631 A8 (Lesbian, found at Miletus, ii B.C.):—Pass., *return to the same point together*, Vett.Val.235.6, Procl.*Hyp.*4.45, Dam.*Pr.* 305, Phlp.*in Mete.*40.35. 2. Pass., *subside together with*, Gal. 8.166, 9.525, Procl.*Inst.*209, Aët.5.121. **-κᾰλέω**, *call by a name also*, Plu.*Fr.*2.2. **-κᾰλύπτω**, *disclose at the same time*, Iamb. *Comm.Math.*34. **-κάμνω**, *cease from weariness together*, E.*IT* 1371. **-κατάστᾰσις**, εως, ἡ, *joint return*, πάντων ἐν τῷ οὐρανῷ μετὰ τῆς γῆς Ptol.*Tetr.*7, cf. *Alm.*9.3, Vett.Val.233.25, *Cat.Cod. Astr.*8(1).238. **-κειμαι**, f.l. in S.*OC*1752; cf. ξυνός. **-κινδῡνεύω**, *encounter danger along with*, Longin.22.4, Hld.6.7. **-κλείω**, *shut up altogether*, Lxx 1*Ki.*1.5,6 cod. A. **-κληρόω**, *choose, assign*, Porph.*Chr.*35. ⊛**-κλίνω** [ῑ], *turn aside together with*, pf. Pass. -κέκλῐμαι Lib.*Descr.*22.5. II. intr., *turn aside together*, ἐπ' ἀμφότερα Plu.2.790e: abs., J.*BJ*1.24.2; ἡ δειρὴ τῷ παντὶ σ. προσώπῳ Lib.*Descr.*18.3. **-κλύζω**, *wash away with* or *at once*, Philum.*Ven.*1. **-κομίζω**, *carry away together*, D.S.1.20, 3.15:—Pass., J.*AJ*14.4.5. **-κόπτω**, *cut off together*, Plu.2.529c:—Pass., Gal.14.247; of a final letter or syllable, A.D.*Conj.*255. 6. **-κρίνομαι** [ῐ], Pass., *to be secreted and carried off together*, Arist.*HA*581$^b$30; *to be extruded*, of the afterbirth, Sor.1. 70. **-κρύπτω**, *join in concealing*, Ael.*NA*7.25; *conceal together*, Lxx *Ep.Je.*48, Lib.*Descr.*13.4, etc. **-κτείνω**, *kill together*, Antipho 5.39, Aeschin.2.148; τινι *with* one, D.C.*Fr.*11.18. **-κτίννῡμι**, = foreg., Arist.*EE*1246$^a$23, D.H.8.80. **-κῠλίνδω**, aor. -εκύλῑσα, *roll away together with*, ἑαυτῷ τὸν ἀντίπαλον Sch.B *Il.*23. 730. **-λαμβάνω**, *receive in common* or *at once*, esp. that which one has a right to, τὰ ἑαυτῶν X.*An.*7.7.40. II. Pass., *to be entirely suppressed*, Hp.*Prorrh.*2.24. **-λάμπω**, *shine forth together*, τινι Luc.*Dom.*7; μετά τινος Id.*Gall.*13. **-λαυσις**, εως, ἡ, *joint enjoyment*, Porph.ap.Eus.*PE*4.23. **-λαύω**, *share in the enjoyment*, Arist.*HA*623$^a$24, *EE*1244$^b$18; τινος *of* a thing, D.S. 9.20, Luc.*Musc.Enc.*8, Diog.Oen.1, *Supp.Epigr.*4.259 (Panamara); τινι *with* a person, Them.*Or.*4.57d, etc. 2. *share in the good* or *evil of*.., τὸ ἀσύμμετρον..οὐ σ. τῶν μερῶν Arist.*Pr.*883$^a$15; in bad sense, αἱ στάσεις συναπολαύειν ποιοῦσι τὴν ὅλην πόλιν make it *suffer with them*, Id.*Pol.*1303$^b$32; σ. νόσου, τοῦ κακοῦ, Them.*Or.*1.7b, Max. Tyr.18.9; τῆς ἀναθυμιάσεως Gal.18(2).74; cf. ἀπολαύω II. 1. 3. simply, *share in, have somewhat of*, τινος Thphr.*CP*6.8.3. **-λείπω**, *leave behind along with*, τινά τινι D.S.19.69:—Pass., *BGU*1761.10 (i B.C.), Dsc.1.43. II. intr., *fail* or *cease together*, Thphr.*CP*2.19. 3. **-λήγω**, *cease along with*, σ. τοὺς πόδας τῷ ἀκρωτηρίῳ *to have* the feet *ending with* (i.e. *reaching to*) it, Philostr.*Her.*1.3; χάρις σ. τινί Id.*Im.*2.18, cf. Them.*Or.*3.47a. **-λῐθόω**, *petrify at the same time*, Pass., c. dat., Sch.Lyc.843.

**συναπόλλῡμι**, *destroy together*, μετά τινος Antipho 5.82; σ. τοὺς φίλους *destroy* one's friends *as well as oneself*, Th.6.12; συνηγόρους καλεῖν τοὺς συναπολοῦντάς τινα Hyp.*Lyc.*19; σ. τὰ χρήματα *lose* the money *also*, D.34.2; τινί τι one thing *with* another, Plu.*Cat.Mi.* 38:—Pass., *perish together*, Th.2.60, Lys.12.88: c. dat., Hdt.7.221, Pl.*Criti.*121a, *Ep.Hebr.*11.31.

**συναπο-λογέομαι**, *join in defending*, D.24.157,159, Hyp.*Lyc.Fr.* 3, etc.; σ. τοῖς νόμοις Lex ap.D.24.23; μισθοῦ *for* hire, Lycurg.138; συναπελογεῖτο is prob. cj. for συνανελογεῖτο in Din.1.28. **-λύω**, *release together*, τινά τινι J.*AJ*10.9.1:—Pass., Plu.2.406e, S.E.*M.*11. 66. **-μᾰλάσσω**, *soften together*, Aristaenet.1.1. **-μᾰραίνομαι**, Pass., *fade away and die together*, X.*Smp.*8.14; ταῖς τῶν σωμάτων ῥώμαις Plu.*Phil.*18; of the pulse, Gal.8.479, Paul.Aeg.2.11. 23. **-μειόω**, *diminish at the same time*, Just.*Nov.*163. **-νεύω**, *sway together*, τοῖς σώμασιν αὐτοῖς ἴσα τῇ δόξῃ..ξυναπονεύοντες *swerving* with their bodies *in sympathy* with their thought, of the spectators of the sea-fight at Syracuse, Th.7.71; *swerve from the upright position together*, Plu.2.780a; *bend away so as to meet*, ταῖς τοῦ ἰούλου ἀρχαῖς Philostr.Jun.*Im.*14, cf. Poll.4.95.

**συναπ-ονίνᾰμαι**, *derive benefit from together*, Them.*Or.*4.58a.

**συναπο-νοέομαι**, Med., *share in folly with*, τινι D.S.34/35.2. 26, Ph.2.160, etc.: aor. Pass. in med. sense, ib.118, J.*AJ*5. 2.9. **-ξύω**, *scrape* or *strip off together*, τὸ γῆρας Them.*Or.*18. 223c. **-παύομαι**, Med., *leave off together*, Herod.Med.ap.Orib. 6.20.12, Gal.7.408, Ach.Tat.*Intr.Arat.*28. **-πέμπω**, *send off together*, X.*Cyr.*3.1.2 (v.l. συνέπεμπε); *send out as well*, ὑμένα Gal.2. 523. **-πίπτω**, *fall off at the same time*, Id.17(1).672. **-πλέω**, *float out, be washed out together*, Sor.1.73; *sail away with*, c. dat., Zos.4.43. **-πτύω**, *spit out together*, Gal.8.262, Philum.ap.Orib. 45.29.47.

**συναπορέω**, *call in question together with*, τοῖς ἀδήλοις τὰ γινωσκόμενα Gal.4.721:—Pass., S.E.*P.*2.21, *M.*10.5. II. *suffer poverty together*, τὸ -ῆσαι E.*Fr.*953.26.

**συναπο-ρρέω**, *run off together*, Thphr.*CP*6.17.1, Agatharch.27, Plu. 2.1005e. **-ρρήγνῡμι**, *break* or *tear off together*, Id.*Mar.*12, J.*BJ*5.6. 4. **-ρρίπτω**, *throw away along with*, Alex.Trall.5.6. **-ρρύπτομαι**, Med., *wash together with*, τὸ τραῦμα τῷ σώματι Philostr.*Her.*2.2, cf. Ph. 1.115 (nisi -ρριπτ- leg.). **-σβέννῡμι**, *put out, extinguish with* or *together*, ὄμμασι (sight) πνοιήν (breath) *AP*7.367 (Antip.Thess.); τῇ περιγραφῇ τῆς χρείας [ἡ φύσις] συναπέσβεσε τὸ ἔργον (sc. τὴν κάθαρσιν) Sor. 1.28; σ. τὰς ψυχάς Them.*Or.*4.59d:—Pass., with aor. -έσβην, pf. -έσβηκα, *to be put out together*, D.S.37.2.14, Plu.*Marc.*24, etc.; πυρσὸς συναπέσβετο λύχνῳ *AP*5.278 (Paul.Sil.). **-σεμνύνω**, *exalt* or *extol highly together*, D.S.1.92. **-σπάω**, *tear* or *drag off together* or *with*, τὰς αἶγας αὐτῷ *PRyl.*114.11 (iii A.D.), cf. Jul.*Ep.*14, v.l. in Gal.*UP*8.14:—Pass., Apollod.2.7.7. **-στάζω**, *let drop along with*, τινι Him.*Or.*1.19. **-στάτης** [ᾰ], ου, ὁ, *fellow-rebel*, D.S.15. 66. ⊛**-στέλλω**, *dispatch together with*, τινι Th.6.88; Στράτωνι νεανίσκον *PCair.Zen.*18.5 (iii B.C.); τινὰ μετ' ἐμοῦ ib.439.3 (iii B.C.);

*join in dispatching*, Is.6.27, X.*HG*5.2.37, etc. **-στενόω**, *diminish in number*, τοὺς τυραννοκτονήσαντας Lib.*Decl*.43.29. **-στερέω**, *help to strip* or *cheat*, τινά τινος one *of* a thing, D.30.31, cf. ib.3, J.*AJ*15.2.7. II. *help in abstracting*, πολλὰ χρήματα Pl.*Lg*.948c. **-σύρω** [ῡ], *clean off also*, Aët.5.118. **-σφίγγω**, *include in the ligature*, Paul.Aeg.6.51 (Pass.). **-τείνω**, *make equal in length*, τινί τι Him.*Or*.2.22. **-τελέω**, *help to complete*, Pl.*Plt*.258e, *Epin*.986c. **-τέμνω**, *cut off together*, Gal.2.531 :—Pass., Ruf.*Sat. Gon*.10. **-τερμᾰτίζομαι**, Pass., *to be conterminous with*, τῷ σώματι Sch.Od.19.242. **-τεφρόω**, *reduce to ashes together*, Lyd.*Mag*.3.70 (Pass.). **-τίθεμαι**, Med., *put off at the same time*, τὸ αἰδεῖσθαι Plu.2.37d; τὰς ἐπιμελείας τοῖς σώμασι Jul.*Or*.1.46b. II. abs., *abdicate together with*, Πομπηΐῳ App.*BC*2.32. **-τίκτω**, *join in producing*, Pl.*Tht*.156e. II. *produce at the same time*, τοῖς χρηστοῖς φαῦλα Plu.*Cor*.1. **-τίλλω**, *pluck off along with* or *together*, τινί τι Dsc.1.8 (Pass.). **-τίνω**, *join in paying*, τὰ δάνεια *SIG*546 *B*18 (Delph., iii B.C.); τὰ χρέα *PEleph*.2.11 (iii B.C.). **-τρέπω**, *turn away together*, Socr.*Ep*.1.9; [ἀδικίαν] Zaleuc.ap.Stob.4.2.19. **-τροχάζω**, *run off together*, *AB*427. **-φαίνω**, *prove together*, Phot.*Bibl*.p.172 B. II. in earlier writers only Med., *assert likewise* or *together*, σ. τι τοιοῦτον, ὡς.. Aeschin.2.42; *agree in asserting*, Isoc.12.264; σ. τῷ λόγῳ Str.15.1.6; περί τινος σ. τοῖς εἰποῦσιν Id.2.1.20; σ. τινί, c. inf., Plb.4.31.5, etc.; σ. οὕτως (sc. εἶναι) Str.15.1.11. **-φᾰσις**, εως, ἡ, *a combined denial*, Arist.*Metaph*.1056ᵃ35. **-φάσκω**, *deny at the same time*, Ps.-Alex.Aphr. *in Metaph*.627.38, Dam.*Pr*.445. **-φέρω**, *help to carry off*, πάντας κοιλίη συναπήνεγκεν Hp.*Epid*.3.8. 2. *carry off with*, ἵππος σ. αὐτῷ τὸν ἀναβάτην Gal.5.303; τὰς λύπας ἐμαυτῷ Alciphr.2.3 :—Pass., *to be borne along with*, τῷ ῥεύματι Demad.15, cf. Plu.2.626b, Gal. *UP*1.19; τῷ παντί Theo Sm.p.176 H. :—Med., *take away with one*, Gal.6.178, Ath.6.273f. **-φθίνω** [ῐ], aor. 1 -απέφθισα, *destroy together*, Opp.*H*.5.576 :—Pass., *perish together*, συναπέφθιτο ib.587. **-φύω**, *cause to branch off with*, of blood-vessels, Gal. *UP*4.11 :—Pass., ib.10.2, al. **-χέω**, *decant*, Olymp.Alch.p.75 B. **-χράομαι**, *exploit together*, Plb.(?)*Fr*.119. 2. *join in peculation*, *PAmh*.2.79.26 (ii A.D.). ⊛ **-χωρέω**, *go away together*, Plb.13.8.3, 20.10.5.

**συναπ-τέον**, *one must unite*, τι πρός τι Arist.*Ph*.254ᵃ16, cf. Philum.ap.Orib.45.29.13; *one must add* an account of.., Aët.8.16, Paul.Aeg.2.11.20. **-τικός**, ή, όν, *capable of adjusting*, τῶν μερῶν πρὸς ἄλληλα Phld.*Piet*.8. II. Gramm., σ. σύνδεσμος or ὁ σ. alone, *hypothetical* conjunction (εἰ, εἴπερ, etc.), Chrysipp.*Stoic*.2.68, D.T.642.32, Plu.2.386f, A.D.*Conj*.218.11. Adv. **-κῶς**, gloss on αὐτοσχεδόν, Sch.Hes.*Sc*.189; on ἄφαρ, Sch.D Od.2.169. III. = συστρεπτικός, of cold, Gal.17(2).37. **-τός**, όν, or ή, όν (v. infr.), *joined together, linked together*, χάλα συναπτοὺς ἡνίας Ar.*Ec*.508; συναπτὰς ποιεῖν τὰς πράξεις Arist.*Rh.Al*.1438ᵇ18. Adv. **-τῶς**, gloss on ἄφαρ, Eust.158.39; = *continuatim*, *Gloss*.

⊛ **συνάπτω**, *join together*, I. in physical sense, χειρὶ χεῖρα, of dancers, Ar.*Th*.955 (lyr.); ξ. καὶ ξυνωρίζου χέρα, in sign of friendship, E.*Ba*.198, cf. *IA*832, Pl.*Lg*.698d; ἰδού, ξύναψον (sc. τὴν χεῖρα) E.*Ph*.106; but σ. χεῖρέ τινος ἐν βρόχοις *bind* them *fast*, Id.*Ba*.615 (troch.), cf. 546 (lyr.); ξ. πόδα, σ. ἴχνος τινί, meet him, Id.*Ion* 538 (troch.), 663; πόδα ἐς ταὐτὸν ὁδοῦ Id.*Ph*.37; δρόμῳ σ. *meet* in full career, ib.1101; ξ. κῶλον τάφῳ approach the grave, Id.*Hel*.544; φόνος ξ. τινὰ γᾷ Id.*Ph*.673 (lyr.); ξ. βλέφαρα κόραις *close* the eyes, Id.*Ba*.747; στόμα σ. *kiss* one, Id.*IT*375; κακὰ κακοῖς σ. *link* misery with misery, Id.*HF*1213 (lyr.); κακὰ ξ...τινί *link* him *with* misery, Id.*Med*.1232; prov., σ. λίνον λίνῳ *join* thread to thread, i.e. compare things of the same sort, Stratt.38, Pl.*Euthd*.298c, Arist.*Ph*.207ᵃ17, cf. Sch.Pl. l.c.; also δύ' ἐξ ἑνὸς κακὼ σ. E.*IT*488, cf. *Hipp*.515; κοινὴν ξ. δαῖτα παιδί *share with* him a common meal, Id.*Ion* 807 (troch.). 2. metaph. of *combination in thought*, σ. αὐτὰ εἰς ἓν τρία ὄντα Pl.*R*.588d; σ. ἐν τοῖς λόγοις Id.*Sph*.252c; ἔχουσί τι κοινὸν [αἱ ἀρχαὶ] τὸ συνάπτον αὐτάς Arist.*Fr*.17; εἴ τι σ. ἢ ἀφαιρεῖ ἡ διάνοια Id.*Metaph*.1027ᵇ32 (διαιρεῖ Alex.Aphr.); ἀδύνατα σ. Id.*Po*.1458ᵃ27, cf. Phld.*Sto.Herc*.339.13; σ. τὸ γίγνεσθαί θ' ἅμα καὶ τὴν τελευτὴν τοῦ βίου Alex.149.18; σ. μηχανὴν *frame* a plan, A.*Ag*.1609, cf. E.*Hel*.1034; σ. ὄναρ εἴς τινα *connect* it *with* him, *refer* it *to* him, Id.*IT*[59]; σ. λόγον πρός τι D.60.12; πρὸς τὸ ἄκρον οὐ σ. τὸν συλλογισμόν Arist.*APr*.69ᵃ18; σ. ἀλλήλοις τό τ' "ἐκστάντες" καὶ τὸ "ὀξέως" *take together*, Gal.16.547; συνῆψε τὸν λόγον he *continues* as follows, Id.15.148; but σ. τὸν λόγον *abridge*, Theopomp.Com.22: c. acc. et dat., *associate with* or *attribute to*, τί τινι Epicur.*Nat*.11.9, *Sent.Vat*.39, Demetr.Lac.*Herc*.1055.15, cf. Phld.*Sign*.20 :—Pass., συνάπτεται ἕτερον ἐξ ἄλλου Pl.*Sph*.245e, cf. *Phd*.60b (v.l.), Epicur.*Ep*.2 p.37 U., *Nat*.28.11; of the words of a sentence, συνάπτεσθαι ἀλλήλοις Gal.16.546. II. with regard to persons, 1. in hostile sense, σ. τὰ στρατόπεδα εἰς μάχην *bring* them *into action*, Hdt.5.75; ἐλπὶς.. ἢ πολλὰς πόλεις συνῆψε *has engaged* them *in conflict*, E.*Supp*.480; so συνῆψε πάντας ἐς μίαν βλάβην *involved* them in.., Id.*Ba*.1303; for S.*Aj*.1317, v. συλλύω II. b. σ. μάχην *join* battle, Hdt.6.108; στρατεύματι A.*Pers*.336, cf. E.*Heracl*.808; σ. πόλεμον πρός τινας Th.6.13; συνάψαι πόλεμον Ἕλλησιν μέγαν E.*Hel*.55, cf. Hdt.1.18; τοῖς σοφοῖς εὐκτὸν σοφῷ ἔχθραν συνάπτειν Id.*Heracl*.459; σ. ἀλκήν Id.*Supp*.683; also (without μάχην), *engage*, Hdt.4.80, cf. Ar.*Ach*.686 (troch.); σ. συνάψεις Lxx 4*Ki*.10.34; σ. φασγάνων ἀκμάς E.*Or*.1482 (lyr.); ἔγχη Id.*Ph*.1192; οὐκ εὐθὺς συνῆψε τὰς ἀπορίας has not immediately *rejoined by stating* the difficulties, Procl. *in Prm*.p.533 S.: abs., *approach, make contact*, Plu.*Tim*.25 :—Pass., μοι πρός τινας νεῖκος συνῆπτο Hdt.7.158, cf. 6.94. 2. in friendly sense, σ. ἑαυτὸν εἰς λόγους τινί enter into conversation with him, Ar.*Lys*.468 (cf. infr. B. II. 1); φιλία σ. τοὺς καλούς τε κἀγαθούς X.*Mem*.2.6.22 :—Pass., παλλακαῖς συνημμένος, of Aristotle, *App.Anth*.5.11. b. c. acc. rei, σ. μῦθον E.*Supp*.566; σ. ὅρκους Id.*Ph*.1241; κοινωνίαν X.*Lac*.6.3; φιλίαν πρός τινα D.H.19.13, cf. 2.30; freq. in E., σ. τινὶ γάμους, λέκτρα, κῆδος, *form an alliance by* marriage, *Ph*.1049 (lyr.), 49, *Andr*.620, etc.; γέννην Id.*Fr*.558; τὸν ἔρωτα τῇ κούρῃ Aret.*SD*1.5 :—in Med., κῆδος ξυνάψασθαι τῆς θυγατρός *get one's daughter married*, Th.2.29 :—Pass., οἱ γάμοι συνήφθησαν *PLips*.41.7 (iv A.D.); ᾧ συνήφθην ἐκ παρθενίας *PSI*1.41.5 (iv A.D.); συναφθεῖσά μοι ὡς γαμετή,.. συνήφθην σοι πρὸς γάμου καὶ βίου κοινωνίαν, *PMasp*.153.5,8 (vi A.D.); μὴ πρὸς γάμον ἡ παῖς καὶ ἑτέρῳ τινὶ συναφθείη Chor. p.227 B. III. Math., esp. in pf. Pass., ὁ λόγος συνῆπται ἔκ τε τοῦ..καὶ τοῦ..the ratio *is compounded of*.., Archim.*Sph.Cyl*.2.4, al.; ἀναλογία συνημμένη *continued* proportion (cf. συνεχής I. 3), Nicom.*Ar*.2.21; συνημμένη μεσότης *geometric* mean, ibid. 2. in Music, συνημμένα τετράχορδα *conjunct* tetrachords, Plu.2.1029a; ἡ συνημμένων νήτη ib.1137c. 3. in Logic, συνημμένον ἀξίωμα or τὸ σ., *hypothetical proposition* as premiss in a syllogism, Chrysipp.*Stoic*.2.68, Phld.*Sign*.32, S.E.*M*.8.109, Gell.16.8.9: pl., Plu.2.43c, Procl. *in Prm*. p.533 S.; κοῖα συνῆπται; what *conclusion follows?* Call.*Fr*.70.3 :—cf. συνάρτησις II.

B. intr.: I. in local sense, *border on, lie next to*, τὸ πεδίον τοῦτο συνάπτει τῷ Αἰγυπτίῳ πεδίῳ Hdt.2.75; Τήνῳ συνάπτουσ' Ἄνδρος A.*Pers*.885 (lyr.); γεώλοφοι συνάπτοντες [τῷ ποταμῷ] *reaching to*.., Plb.3.67.9; ἐὰν διώρυγες συνάπτωσι τοῖς χώμασι *PLille* 1ᵛ.7 (iii B.C.); [τῆς τραχείας ἀρτηρίας] τὸ συνάπτον τῷ στόματι πέρας Gal.6.421; ποταμοῦ στόμα συνάπτον θαλάττῃ ib.712; αὗται μὲν σ., αἱ δ' ἄλλαι ἀσύναπτοι Arist.*HA*516ᵃ30; δύο πόροι εἰς ἓν σ. ib.508ᵃ13; τὰ βράγχια σ. ἀλλήλοις ib.507ᵃ5; ἡ κοιλία σ. πρὸς τὸ στόμα ib.507ᵃ28; of the sides of a cone, πρὸς μίαν κορυφὴν συνάπτειν Thphr.*Vert*.4. 2. of Time, *to be nigh at hand*, ὥρα συνάπτει Pi.*P*.4.247; σ. πρὸς τὸν χειμῶνα Hp.*Aph*.2.25; συνάψαντος τοῦ χρόνου Plb.2.2.8; συνάψαντος τοῦ καιροῦ Id.6.36.1, etc. 3. metaph., σ. ἐν αὐτῇ πάνθ' ὅσα δεῖ τοῖς φίλοις ὑπάρχειν *meet together*, Arist.*EN*1156ᵇ18; οὐ σ. [αὗται αἱ φιλίαι] do not *combine*, ib.1157ᵃ34; *to be connected with*, τῷ γένει αἱ ἰδέαι σ. Id.*Metaph*.1042ᵃ15; σ. πρός τι Id.*Pol*.1276ᵃ7, *Cat*.4ᵇ26, *APr*.41ᵃ1; *attach*, Id.*HA*580ᵃ15; λύπη σ. [τῷ θεραπεύειν] E.*Hipp*.187 (anap.), cf. Chrysipp.*Stoic*.2.174; ὁ πόνος ὁ ὑπερβάλλων συνάψει θανάτῳ *will border upon* death, Epicur.*Fr*.448; σ. εἴς τι *have reference to*, Thphr.*CP*6.1.2. II. of persons, ξ. λόγοισιν *enter into* conversation, S.*El*.21; ἐς λόγους σ. τινί E.*Ph*.702; σ. εἰς χορεύματα *join* the dance, Id.*Ba*.133 (lyr.); ἐς χεῖρα γῇ *come close* to land, Id.*Heracl*.429; σ. εἰς τὸν καιρόν *come in* just at the right time, Plb.3.19.2; σ. τοῖς ἄκροις *reach* them, Id.3.93.5, etc.; σ. εἰς Σελεύκειαν Id.5.66.4; πρὸς τὴν παρεμβολήν Id.3.53.10, etc. 2. τύχα ποδὸς ξυνάπτει (s.v.l., -πτοι Murray) μοι, i.e. I have come fortunately, E.*Supp*.1014 (lyr.). 3. Astrol., of a heavenly body, *to be in conjunction* (συναφή) with another, Nech.ap.Vett.Val.280.2, Ptol.*Tetr*.52, *PMag.Leid.W*.24.15, Man.2.452, Paul.Al.*H*.1.

C. Med., *unite for oneself* and so *form*, φιλίαν D.S.13.32; κῆδος D.C.41.57; v. supr. A. II. 2b. 2. *to be next to, connected with*, τινι X.*Oec*.5.3. 3. *lay hold of*, τοῦ καιροῦ Plb.15.28.8. 4. *take part with* one, *assist*, τινι E.*Hel*.1444: abs., A.*Pers*.742 (troch.); τινος in a thing, ib.724 (troch.), S.*Fr*.874. 5. *bring upon oneself*, πληγάς D.40.32.

**συναπωθέω**, *help to push off* or *back*, Luc.*Tox*.19, Orib.47.5.13 :—Pass., Arist.*Pr*.963ᵃ20, Gal.6.197 (v.l. συνεπ-).

**συνᾰρᾰρίσκω**, aor. συνῆρσα, Ep. σύναρσα, *join together*, γάμον.. Πηλῆϊ συνάρσαμεν Q.S.3.100. II. intr. in pf., συνάρηρεν ἀοιδή the song *hangs well together*, *h.Ap*.164; φάλαγξ συναρυρυῖα, for συντεταγμένη, Luc.*Zeux*.8; θοοῖς συναρηρότα γόμφοις A.R.2.1112, cf. 1.497.

**συνᾰράσσω**, Att. -ττω, *dash together, dash in pieces, crush*, Hom. only in tmesi, σύν κεν ἄραξ' ἡμέων κεφαλάς Od.9.498; σὺν δ' ὀστέ' ἄραξεν πάντ' ἀμυδις Il.12.384; σ. οἶκον E.*HF*1142; σ. τινὰ λίθοις, ὀδοῦσι, D.H.8.59, Luc.*VH*1.30; σ. τοὺς ἵππους D.H.5.15 :—Pass., *to be dashed in pieces*, σύν τ' ὀστέ' ἀράχθη Od.5.426; συναραχθέντων τῶν πλοίων, by the storm, Hdt.7.170; συναράσσονται κεφαλὰς *have their* heads *broken*, Id.2.63; -ομένων ὀδόντων Pancrat.*Oxy*.1085.19; νῆσοι σ. ἀλλήλαις Luc.*VH*1.41. 2. intr., *dash together*, of winds, Arist.*Mu*.397ᵃ20: of enemies, σφίσιν αὐτοῖς D.C.73.15. II. *beat* or *hammer together, make fast*, A.R.2.614, 3.1318; συνάρηρε is v.l., v. *EM*237.58.

**συνᾰραχνόομαι**, *to be covered as with a spider's web*, v. συναρθμόομαι.

⊛ **συνᾰρέσκω**, *please* or *satisfy together*, συνήρεσκε ταὐτά μοι *pleased* me *too*, D.19.202; οὐδέ γε τὸ φρουροὺς μισθοῦσθαι συνήρεσκέ μοι X.*HG*2.3.42; ὅππα κε Θερσίππω συναρέσκῃ *IG*12(2).645*a*48 (Nesos); ἂν συναρέσῃ σοι τοὐμὸν ἐνθύμημ' Men.*Epit*.295; διδόναι τοὺς συναρέσαντας μισθοὺς *agreed on* by both parties, *Sardis* 7(1).18.23 (v A.D.), cf. *PFlor*.384.38 (v A.D.), etc. :—Pass., *agree with* a proposition, Phld.*Sign*.31; τῷ μὴ..εἶναι S.E.*M*.10.60; *approve of*, c. dat., Heliod.ap.Orib.49.9.39. II. *concede, grant*, τινί τι A.R.3.901, cf. 4.373. 2. Med., *agree with*, τινι Id.3.1100.

⊛ **συναρθμ-έω**, *to be fitted together*, σ. ἐπέεσσι *to agree*.., A.R.4.418. **-ιος**, ον, stronger form of ἄρθμιος, Opp.*H*.5.424. **-όομαι**, Pass., *to be closed*, of the cervix uteri, Hp.*Mul*.2.169 as cited by Gal.(19.143) and Erot. (συναραχνοῦται codd.Hp.).

**συναρθρ-όομαι**, Pass., *to be joined by articulation*, Hp.*Mochl.*1, Gal.2.653. II. later in Act., *attach the article*, *An.Ox.*1.49. **-ος**, v. σύνορθρος. II. *accompanied by the article*, ἀντωνυμίαι D.T.641.10, A.D.*Pron.*13.6; dub. sens. in Gal.18(2).784. 2. σ. ἀντωνυμία *possessive pronoun*, A.D.*Pron.*95.16. **-ωσις**, εως, ἡ, *an immovable articulation*, opp. διάρθρωσις, Gal.2.481. 2. *joining together of the members* of an organism, metaph., *Corp.Herm.*13.8.

⊛ **συνᾰριθμ-έω**, *reckon in, take into account, enumerate*, τὰς ψήφους Is.5.18; αὐτὸ τοῖς φρενιτικοῖς σ. σημείοις Gal.16.521:—Med., Pl.*Phlb.*23d, Aeschin.2.101,130:—Pass., *to be counted with*, ἑκατέροις Arist.*Pol.*1318$^{a}$38; *to be reckoned in, taken into account*, Id.*Rh.*1363$^{b}$19, *SE*167$^{a}$25, *EN*1105$^{b}$1; *to be included in enumeration*, ib.1097$^{b}$17, *MM*1184$^{a}$16, Thphr.*Lap.*29. 2. Med., *join in receiving payment*, *POxy.*1208.17 (iii A.D.). **-ησις**, εως, ἡ, *counting up, enumeration*, Sor.1.21, Gal.10.738, 18(2).233, Ath.11.490c. II. *sum of the letters of a word taken as arithmetical signs* (v. ἀριθμός x), ἡ σ. τοῦ κόσμου ὀνόματος ἑξακόσιά ἐστι Anatolius ap.*Theol.Ar.*37. **-ητέον**, *one must count in*, Herod.Med.ap.Orib.10.37.15.

**συναρίθμ[ιος]**, [ον], = sq. 1, ὀνομασία prob. in *PMasp.*151.166 (vi A.D.).

**συνάριθμος**, ον, *counted with, included in a number with*, τινος Phalar.*Ep.*128. II. *of like* or *equal number*, *AP*7.431 (Simon. (?)); in form **συνήριθμος**, ib.389.3 (Apollonid.).

**συνᾰριστάω**, *take breakfast* or *luncheon with*, τοῖς ἥρωσιν Ar.*Av.*1486, cf. Aeschin.1.43, Alex.47, Luc.*Asin.*50: abs., Phld.*Lib.*p.56 O.: Συναριστῶσαι, name of a play by Menander.

**συνᾰριστεύω**, *do brave deeds together*, ἅμα τινί E.*Tr.*804 (lyr.).

**συνάριστος** [ᾰ], ον, (ἄριστον) *breakfasting with*, Luc.*Asin.*21.

**συναρκέομαι**, *acquiesce in, put up with*, τινι Thphr.*Char.*3.6.

**συναρμογή**, Dor. **-γά**, ἡ, *combination*, Ti.Locr.95b, Diotog.ap. Stob.4.7.62, Plu.*Aem.*32, etc. 2. *wedlock*, Ptol.*Tetr.*182, Vett. Val.38.1, al. 3. *musical combination*, Iamb.*VP*25.114.

⊛ **συναρμόζω**, Att. **-όττω** Pl.*Ti.*32b, etc.: Dor. aor. **-οξα** Pi.*N.*10.12:—pf. Pass. -ήρμοσμαι, aor. -ηρμόσθην (v. infr.): I. in physical sense, *fit together*, κεραίαν δίχα πρίσαντες ξ. πάλιν ὥσπερ αὐλόν Th.4.100; ξυνάρμοσον βλέφαρα.. χερί *close* them, E.*Ph.*1451, cf. *IT* 1167; σ. τοὺς πόρους Thphr.*Sens.*9; τι πρός τι Hp.*Aër.*9, Arist.*HA* 541$^{b}$4:—Pass., λίθοι εὖ συνηρμοσμένοι Hdt.1.163; ἀλλήλοιν συναρμοσθῆναι Pl.*R.*412a; *to be joined in wedlock*, Arist.*Mir.*840$^{b}$14, *PSI*2.166.17 (ii B.C.), *IG*5(2).268.30 (Mantinea, i B.C.), *BGU*1103.23 (i B.C.). b. *put together*, so as to make a whole, σκάφος, ἵππον, E.*Hel.*233 (lyr.), *Tr.*11; πόλιν σ. Pl.*Lg.*628a; σ. τοὺς πολίτας πειθοῖ τε καὶ ἀνάγκῃ Id.*R.*519e; τὰ τῆς ἀρχῆς οὐ συνηρμοσμένα καλῶς D.11.8:—Pass., συναρμοσθέντ' Ἀφροδίτῃ Emp.71.4. 2. of combination *in act* or *thought*, ὁμοῦ βίην τε καὶ δίκην σ. Sol.36.14; καρπὸν δίκᾳ Pi.*N.*10.12; σ. εἰς ταὐτόν Pl.*Ti.*35a; τρία ὄντα σ. Id.*R.*443d; ἰδέας ἀλλήλων ἀφεστώσας Isoc.15.11; *compound* a word, ἀπὸ τοῦ θεῖν καὶ ἄλλεσθαι Pl.*Cra.*414b:—Pass., ἡ συνηρμοσμένη λέξις Phld.*Po.Herc.*994.26; πρὸς ἄλληλα σ. ib.35. 3. metaph., *adapt* or *conform* one thing to another, εὐχερείᾳ σ. βροτούς, i.e. make them indifferent to crime, A.*Eu.*495 (lyr.); σ. τοῖς παροῦσι τὸν τρόπον Ephipp.7; ταῖς ποιότησι τὰς ποσότητας Theon ap.Gal.6.96:—Pass., πρὸς παρόντα συνηρμοσμένος X.*Ap.*16; esp. of Music, λύρα συνηρμοσμένη πρὸς τὸν αὐλόν Id.*Smp.*3.1. II. intr., *fit together*, Pl.*Tht.*204a, Arist.*GA*747$^{b}$1, *PA*654$^{b}$19. 2. metaph., *agree together*, ἀλλήλοις Pl.*Prt.*333a, Phld.*Po.Herc.*994.27; τοσαύτῃ φιλίᾳ Lys.*Fr.*261 S.; σ. εἰς φιλίαν X.*Mem.*2.6.20: abs., Id.*Cyr.*7.5.60, etc.; σ. εἰς ἅπαντα Pl.*Lg.*729a. III. Med. much like Act., *join together, unite*, Id.*Ti.*53e, *Plt.*309c; δεῖ γάμον -εσθαι πρὸς τὸν ἴδιον τόνον τᾶς ψυχᾶς Callicrat. ap.Stob.4.28.18, cf. Plu.*Sol.*15; *join in wedlock*, νέαν καὶ ὡραίαν Ocell.4.6. 2. *adapt oneself*, ἅπαντι καιρῷ D.L.4.37, cf. Socr.ap.Stob.3.4.58.

**συναρμολογέω**, *compagino*, *Gloss.*:—Pass., *to be fitted* or *framed together*, *Ep.Eph.*2.21, 4.16.

**συναρμονιάω**, *fit together*, Sch.Ar.*Eq.*463.

**σύναρμ-ος**, ον, *joined* or *framed together*, Ph.*Bel.*64.14; of pyramids, σ. καὶ κατεξεσμένον τὸ πᾶν ἔργον Ph.Byz.*Mir.*2.3. **-οσις**, εως, ἡ, *fitting together*, of musical notes, Porph. in *Harm.*p.264 W.; = *compaginatus*, *Gloss.* **-οστέον**, *one must fit together*, Pl.*Ti.*18c. **-οστής**, οῦ, ὁ, *one who fits together*, λίθων Luc.*Somn.*2; σ. ὁ θεός Theo Sm.p.12 H. **-οστικός**, ή, όν, *of* or *for uniting*, τινος Diotog.ap.Stob.4.7.62, Iamb.*Myst.*4.12, Dam.*Pr.*342. **-οττόντως**, Adv. pres. part. of sq., *fittingly*, Pl.*Lg.*967e. **-όττω**, Att. for συναρμόζω (q. v.).

**συναροτριάω**, *bring under the plough*, in Pass., συνηροτριαμένη prob. in *Milet.*6.36 (iii B.C.).

⊛ **συναρπᾰγή**, ἡ, *robbery, plundering*, ἐκτὸς συναρπαγῆς καὶ κλοπῆς *Stud.Pal.*22.177.30 (ii A.D.), cf. Sm.*Ps.*34(35).20, *Cod.Just.*12.60 (61).7, Wilcken *Chr.*6.13 (v A.D.), *Cat.Cod.Astr.*8(4).168; = *obreptio*, *Gloss.* 2. συναρπαγῇ in my *haste*, *Cat.Cod.Astr.*1.104.

**συναρπάζω**, fut. -άσω E.*IA*535, Luc.*DDeor.*8.1, -άσομαι Ar.*Lys.*437, Xenarch.8:—*snatch and carry away with* one, *carry clean away*, S.*OC*819, E.*Or.*1493 (lyr.), X.*Mem.*1.4.8, *PSI*4.353.12 (iii B.C.), Gal.6.301, etc.; ξ. [τινὰ] βίᾳ A.*Pers.*195; βίᾳ ἐκ τῆς ὁδοῦ σ. τινάς Lys.3.46, cf. 12.96; πάντα σ. ὥσπερ θύελλα S.*El.*1150; ὁ κρατῶν ἅμα πάντα σ. X.*Cyr.*4.2.26; ἀετὸς τὸν λαγὼ σ. ib.2.4.19; *seize and retain*, οὐ δύνανται συναρπάζειν αἱ μῆτραι τὸν γόνον Hp.*Aër.*21: metaph., *carry away with* one (by persuasive arguments), ξυναρπάσας στρατόν E.*IA*531, cf. Call.*Epigr.*32.5, Longin.16.2, Gal.*UP*3.10; οὐδένα ὑμῶν συναρπάζω I am not '*rushing*' you, Diog.Oen.24; σ. ἑαυτὸν εἰς τὸ ἄνω, of mystical union with the One, Plot.5.3.4:—Pass., *to be seized and carried off*, βίᾳ ξυναρπασθεῖσαν S.*Aj.*498; σ. βουκόλων ὕπο Id.*Fr.*659; by death, Phld.*Mort.*37. 2. ξ. χεῖρας *seize and pin* them *together*, E.*Hec.*1163, cf. Lys.*Fr.*75.4:—Med., ξ. τινὰ μέσον, of a wrestler, Ar.*Lys.*437. 3. metaph., ξ. φρενί *seize* with the mind, *grasp*, S.*Aj.*16, cf. Ar.*Nu.*775; τὸ ῥηθέν Simyl.ap.Stob.4.18.4; σ. τὸ ζητούμενον, in arguing, *to be guilty of a petitio principii*, Luc.*JTr.*38, S.E.*P.*2.35, etc.; so συνήρπασται εἰς κτητικὴν σύνταξιν *is hastily concluded* to have a possessive force, A.D.*Synt.*165.9. 4. *carry away, destroy all traces of*, τι Luc.*Dom.*16. 5. Pass., of persons, συνηρπασμένοι *having been robbed*, *PRyl.*119.28 (i A.D.).

**συναρρωστέω**, *to be sick with* or *together*, Gal.15.241, 17(2).423.

**σύναρσις**, εως, ἡ, *balancing* of books, λόγου, λόγων, *Ostr.*1135 (iii A.D.), *POxy.*2143.3 (iii A.D.), *PAmh.*2.101.4 (iii A.D.). II. *union, support*, Olymp. in *Mete.*297.18; *assistance*, Porph.*Chr.*31, Simp. in *Cael.*703.1.

**συναρτ-άω**, *knit* or *join together*, σ. γένος E.*Med.*564; τὴν γῆν ἅμα καὶ τὴν θάλασσαν Luc.*DDeor.*21.1:—Pass., *to be closely engaged*, δύο περὶ μίαν καὶ ἔστιν ᾗ καὶ πλείους ναῦς.. ξυνηρτῆσθαι Th.7.70; ἡ ἄνω γνάθος.. συνήρτηται τῇ κεφαλῇ καὶ οὐ διήρθρωται Hp.*Art.*30, cf. Arist.*HA*495$^{b}$6, Sor.2.85; πρός τι Arist.*HA*496$^{b}$12, Thphr.*Sens.*26; σ. εἰς ἕν Arist.*PA*670$^{a}$7; ἀφ' ἑνός, ἐξ ἑνός, Id.*HA*516$^{a}$8, *Pr.*957$^{b}$40; πολλαχόθι μὲν συμφύονται [οἱ ὑμένες], πολλαχόθι δὲ συναρτῶνται Gal.*UP*15.5. 2. metaph., ὁ μηθὲν ἀκόλουθον -αρτῶν Epicur.*Nat.*14.9: mostly in Pass., συνηρτημέναι [ἀρεταί] τοῖς πάθεσι Arist.*EN*1178$^{a}$19; τῷ ἀθανάτῳ τὸ ἀθάνατον σ. Id.*Cael.*270$^{b}$9; *to be implicated in*, c. dat., τόδε σ. τῷδε ἐξ ἀνάγκης Phld.*Sign.*35; συνηρτῆσθαι πολέμῳ *to be involved in*.., Plu.*Num.*20; σ. διώξεσι καὶ φυγαῖς *to be always engaged in*.., Id.*Sert.*12; συνηρτῆσθαί τινι *to be engaged with* him, Id.*Marc.*24, cf. *Pomp.*51. 3. Gramm., in Pass., *to be construed with*, πρὸς τὰς εὐθείας A.D.*Synt.*12.11. **-ησις**, εως, ἡ, *junction, union*, τῶν φλεβῶν καὶ νεύρων Arist.*Pr.*883$^{b}$22; *joint* of machine, Ph.*Bel.*91.8; *combination* of words, A.D.*Synt.*17.8. II. *connexion, cohesion* of premisses with one another and with the conclusion in a syllogism, *Stoic.*2.79; of the clauses in a conditional sentence, Plu.2.387a, S.E.*P.*2.111. **-ίζω**, *accommodate*, ὑποτακτικὴ ἔγκλισις συνηρτισμένη οἷς ὑποτέτακται subjunctive mood being *accommodated* to the conjunction which governs it, A.D.*Synt.*246.16; f.l. for συναπαρτίζω in D.H.*Comp.*22. II. συνηρτίζοντο· συνηθροίζοντο, Hsch. **-ύνω** [ῡ], *fit out, furnish with*, ἀσπίσι νῆα A.R.2.1076:—Med., *join in accomplishing*, τι Id.4.355. ⊛ **-ύω**, *season* food *as well*, Xenocr.ap.Orib.2.58.89. II. *to be joint-ἄρτυνος*, *IG*4.554 (Argos). III. συνήρτυες· συνήρμοττες, Hsch.

**συναρχαιρεσιάζω**, *help in canvassing for election*, Plu.2.97a, 200c.

⊛ **συναρχία**, ἡ, *joint administration* or *government*, τινων D.C.53.2; πρός τινα Id.47.7; περὶ τὰ στρατιωτικά Str.15.1.52. II. in pl., αἱ σ. the *collective magistracy*, Arist.*Pol.*1298$^{a}$14, Aen.Tact.4.11, Anon. Hist. (*FGrH*160) p.887 J., *IG*7.15 (Megara, ii B.C.), 4$^{2}$(1).79 (Arcadian, found at Epid., ii B.C.), Decr.Aetol.ap.Eust.279.40, Plb.27.2.11, etc.: so in sg., *SIG*426.32 (Bargylia, found at Teos, iii B.C.), al., Str.5.3.2.

⊛ **συναρχιεράομαι**, *to be a colleague in the high-priesthood*, τινι *with* one, *CIG*4385.12 (Isauria).

**συναρχ-ίνη** [ῑ], ἡ, *joint-ἀρχ(ε)ίνη*, dub. in *IG*12(5).659.9 (Syros). **-ίς**, ίδος, ἡ, title of Aphrodite at Samos, *Ath.Mitt.*37.216 (ii/i B.C.). **-ομένως**, Adv. *with the same beginning*, *EM*306.48, *An.Ox.*2.412. **-ος**, ὁ, *partner in office, colleague*, Arist.*Pol.*1287$^{b}$31, *IG*5(1).124 (Laconia), 9(1).706 (Corc., iv B.C.), al., v.l. in D.C.67.15. **-οστατέομαι**, Med., *take part in elections*, *IG*9(1).32.13 (Stiris, ii B.C.). ⊛ **-ω**, *rule jointly with*, τινι Hdt.8.130. 2. *to be a colleague* or *partner in office*, c. dat., Th.7.31: ὁ συνάρχων *colleague in office*, Id.6.25, 8.27, Lys.12.52, Pl.*R.*463b, freq. in Inscrr., *IG*1$^{2}$.304.6, al.; στεφανοῦσθαι ὑπὸ τῶν συναρχόντων Hyp.*Lyc.*16; τῶν τούτου συναρχόντων Lys.12.79. II. Med. συνάρχομαι, *begin in like manner*, A.D.*Synt.*168.12: c. dat., Id.*Pron.*56.29. 2. *begin at the same time as*, c. dat., Phlp. in *de An.*588.4.

**συνάρωγός**, όν, *helper*, *h.Mart.*4, *AP*6.259 (Phil.).

**συνασβολόω**, *blacken with soot*, πάντα *Epic.Alex.Adesp.inc.*6.

⊛ **συνᾰσεβέω**, *join in impiety*, Antipho 4.1.3, D.S.16.61.

**συνᾰσελγαίνω**, *to be a companion in debauchery*, D.C.79.19.

**συνασθενέω**, *to be ill together with*, συνασθενούσης τῷ σώματι τῆς διανοίας Chor.*Milt.*68.

**συνασκ-έω**, *help* one *to practise*, σωφροσύνην καὶ δικαιοσύνην Isoc.13.21; δεινότητ' ἢ εὐφωνίαν D.19.339. 2. *train, educate*, or *discipline fully*, D.L.4.67, 6.23; σ. τὴν αἴσθησιν D.H.*Lys.*11; ἡμᾶς εἰς τοὺς πολέμους Id.*Rh.*7.4; ἔν τινι S.E.*M.*1.190; ἑαυτὸν περὶ τοὺς λόγους Eun.*VS* p.487 B.; σ. [τὴν θυγατέρα] ὑπεροπτικὴν τοῦ πλέονος εἶναι D.L.2.72:—Pass., φάλαγξ συνησκημένη Plu.*Cleom.*20; τὴν ψυχὴν ἀγύμναστον ἐᾶς,..ἣν ἐχρῆν πρώτην ἐπὶ τὰ τοιαῦτα συνησκῆσθαι καὶ μόνην Phalar.*Ep.*67.1; συνασκηθεὶς ἐν τῇ ἰατρικῇ Sor.*Vit.Hippocr.*4; μειρακίου ἀστρολογεῖν συνασκουμένου D.L.3.29; -ησκημένη ἕξις, παρατήρησις, Phld.*Rh.*1.58, 77 S. 3. *work up together*, πευκῆεν λίπασμα σὺν ἐλαίῳ Man.4.345. 4. συνησκημένος, = *agitatus*, *Gloss.* 5. *co-operate*, Aret.*SD*2.9. **-ησις**, εως, ἡ, *training*, opp. φύσις, Phld.*Rh.*1.1, cf. D.H.2.74, S.E.*M.*7.146, 11.248; *military training*, Ael.Tact.3.1; σ. ὅπλων Lyd.*Mag.*3.33.

**συνασμεν-ίζω**, *rejoice* or *be glad with*, *EM*655.25; *take pleasure in the same things as*, τοῖς πολλοῖς Ph.2.259: hence **-ισμός**, ὁ, Id.*Fr.* 75 H.

**συνᾰσοφέω**, *to be unwise* or *foolish along with*, τοῖς μὴ σοφοῖς E. *Ph.*394.

**συνασπάζομαι**, *greet at the same time*, τινα *PUniv.Giss.*20.40 (ii A.D., written σειν-).

**συνασπ-ῐδόω**, *keep the shields close together, stand in close order*, X.*HG*7.4.23; *fight side by side*, ib.3.5.11. ❋ **-ίζω**, fut. **-ιῶ** Hsch.:— *to be a shield-fellow* or *comrade*, E.*Cyc.*39; *second* or *support*, τινι Sch. Hermog. in Rh.7.353 W.:—Med., S.E.*M.*7.328 (metaph.). II. = συνασπιδόω, Plb.4.64.6, Phld.*Ir.* p.52 W., Plu.*Rom.*18, Ascl.*Tact.* 4.1, etc.; *fight side by side*, ἐπί τινα Luc.*Pisc.*1; σ. τισί *stand in line with* them, D.S.17.84, cf. 4.16. III. trans., σ. τοὺς μετ' αὐτοῦ *forms* them *in close order*, J.*BJ*4.1.5. **-ισμός**, ὁ, *holding of the shields together, fighting in close order*, D.S.16.3, Arr.*Tact.*11.4, Plu. *Tim.*27, etc. **-ιστής**, οῦ, ὁ, *shield-fellow, comrade*, S.*OC*379 (pl.); σ. τινί *APl.*4.184 (Antip.). **-ιστική** ἄμυνα, *consisting of shields held together*, Eust.864.24.

**συνασταχύω**, *to be full of ears of corn*, Arat.1050.

**συναστρᾰγᾰλίζω**, *play at* ἀστράγαλοι *with*, Max.Tyr.9.6.

**συναστράπτω**, *flash like lightning together*, Nonn.*D.*1.457, etc.

**συναστρ-έω**, *to be born under the same star*, Ps.-Callisth.1.4. **-ία**, ἡ, *favourable conjunction of the stars*, Ps.-Plaut.*Querol.*2.3.168, *Cat. Cod.Astr.*5(1).180; κοινὴν σ. ἔχων ἐκείνῳ Pap. in *Arch.f.Religionswiss.* 18.258 (ii/iii A.D.). 2. *friendship*, Ptol.*Tetr.*193, Procl.*Par.Ptol.* 267; ἰατρῶν σ. *Cat.Cod.Astr.*5(1).210.

**συνασφᾰλίζομαι**, Pass., *to be fortified*, Sch.D Od.7.45 (gloss on ἀρηρότα).

**συνασχᾰλάω**, *sympathize indignantly with*, τίς οὐ ξυνασχαλᾷ κακοῖς τεοῖσι; A.*Pr.*162 (lyr.), cf. 245; but in 305, θεωρήσων τύχας ἐμὰς.., καὶ ξυνασχαλῶν κακοῖς, ξυνασχαλῶν must be fut. of **συνασχάλλω**.

**συνασχημονέω**, *join in unseemly conduct*, Plu.2.64d, D.C.79.13.

**συνασχολέομαι**, Pass., *share in business* or *occupation with*, τινι Plu.*Phil.*4, cf. Id.2.95d,e.

**συνᾰτενίζω**, = Lat. *contueor*, Dosith. p.433 K., *Gloss.*

**συνᾰτῑμ-άζω**, *insult* or *dishonour at the same time*, Ph.2.201:— Pass., Manetho ap.J.*Ap.*1.26; τινι Plu.*Agis* 17. **-όομαι**, = foreg., Id.*Flam.*19; and **-άομαι**, Eust.67.21.

**συνατμίζομαι**, Pass., *to be joined in vaporous form*, D.L.6.73.

**συνᾰτονέω**, *to be relaxed* or *languid together* (*with*), Sor.1.38,46, Gal.13.194.

**συνᾰτροφέω**, *waste away together*, Gal.18(1).401.

**συνᾰτῠχέω**, *to be unlucky with* or *together*, μετά τινος Lycurg.131; τινι D.S.13.52, Plu.2.64c, etc.

**συναυαίνω**, *dry quite up*, τι Hp.*Aër.*9, E.*Cyc.*463:—Pass., *to be dried up also*, Hp.*Loc.Hom.*40, Pl.*Phdr.*251d.

**συναυγ-άζω**, *illuminate*, ἀκτίνας –ούσας πάντα τὸν τόπον Damian. *Opt.*5. **-ασμός**, ὁ, *meeting of rays*, *Placit.*3.1.6. **-εια**, ἡ, = foreg.; esp. *meeting of the rays of sight from the eye* (ὄψις) *with the rays of light from the object seen*, ib.4.13.11.

**συναυδάω**, *speak together*: hence, like σύμφημι, *agree, confess, allow*, S.*Aj.*943, cf. Thphr.*Metaph.*16.

❋ **συναυλ-έω**, (αὐλός) *play on the flute at the same time*, Luc.*Dom.*16, Ath.14.617b, Longus 2.35. ❋ **-ία** (A), ἡ, (αὐλός) *concert of lyre and flute*, S.*Fr.*60, Ath.14.617f (prob. from Ephipp.7); *symphony of flutes*, Poll.4.83, Sch.Ar.*Eq.*9, Hsch.: generally, *instrumental music, concert*, opp. μονῳδία, Pl.*Lg.*765b; σ. ᾄδειν Antiph.47.1; ξυναυλίαν κλαύσωμεν Οὐλύμπου νόμον to sob or whimper one of Olympus' pieces *in concert*, Ar.*Eq.*9. 2. metaph., δύσορνις ἅδε ξ. δορός this ill-omened *concert* of battle, of the single combat of the brothers, A.*Th.*839 (lyr.); σ. θρήνου Philostr.*Im.*1.11; πένθους Lib.*Or.*61.20. **-ία** (B), ἡ, (αὐλή, cf. συναυλίζομαι, μοναυλία (B), ὁμαυλία) *dwelling together* as man and wife, σ. ποιεῖσθαι Arist.*Pol.* 1335$^a$38. **-ίζομαι**, (αὐλή) Pass., *have dealings with*, *Cat.Cod. Astr.*7.110; *congregate*, θηρῶν ὅμιλος συνηυλίσθη Babr.106.6: also aor. Med., μᾶλλον λέουσι συναυλισαίμην ἄν Phalar.*Ep.*34: freq. v.l. for συναλίζομαι, as in X.*Cyr.*1.2.15, *Act.Ap.*1.4. **-ος** (A), ον, (αὐλός) *in concert with the flute*; then generally, *sounding in concord* or *unison, harmonious*, ξ. ὕμνων βοά Ar.*Ra.*212 (lyr.): generally, *in harmony with*, ξ. βοὰ χαρᾷ E.*El.*879 (lyr.); ὅτε τις κύκνος.. ἀνέμου σύναυλος ἠχῇ *Anacreont.*60.10. **-ος** (B), ον, (αὐλή) *dwelling with, living in the folds with* (sc. ταῖς ποίμναις), S.*OT*1126: metaph., θείᾳ μανίᾳ ξ., i.e. afflicted with madness, Id.*Aj.*611 (lyr.).

**συναυξ-άνω**, impf. συνηύξανε Suid. s.v. συνήκμαζε (also Pass. -αυξάνομαι X.*Cyr.*8.7.6, D.8.72), but usu. **-αύξω**, aor. -ηύξησα Plb.6. 15.7, Plu.*Sert.*9, also -ηῦξα, Dor. -αῦξα, Plb.32.1.7 (corr. Reiske), *Supp.Epigr.* (v. infr.):—*increase* or *enlarge along with* or *together*, συναύξειν τῇ γῇ τὰ χρήσιμα X.*Mem.*4.3.6 (in *h.Cer.*267, Ignarra restored συνάξουσι):—Pass., *increase with* or *together, wax larger together with*, αὐξομένῳ τῷ σώματι συναύξονται καὶ αἱ φρένες Hdt.3. 134, cf. Hp.*Art.*12,53; εἰ μὴ ξυναύξοινθ' οἱ πέπλοι τῷ σώματι E. *El.*544; ἀνδρὶ γενομένῳ ταῦτα πάντα συνηυξήθη Isoc.9.23, cf. 1.7; πρός τι συμμέτρως συναυξάνεσθαι in proportion to, X.*Eq.*1.16; σπουδὴν..προσφερόμενος εἰς τὸ συναύξεσθαι τὸν δῆμον *BCH*48.3 (Prusa, ii(?) B.C.). 2. *join* or *assist in increasing*, ἕξιν κακίης συναύξει Democr.184; συναύξειν οἴκους X.*Oec.*3.10; συναύξει τὴν ἐνέργειαν ἡ ἡδονή Arist.*EN*1175$^a$30, cf. Thphr.*Sens.*18, *Ign.*27, Sor.1.29; τὰν ὑπάρχουσαν ὁμόνοιαν...ἐπὶ πλεῖον συναύξησε *Klio* 15.41 (Delph., iii B.C.); τὰν φιλίαν συναῦξε *Supp.Epigr.*2.270.6 (ibid., ii B.C.); συναύξοντες τὴν ἀρχὴν τῷ Κύρῳ X.*Cyr.*8.3.21; τὰς τῶν θεῶν τιμάς *Supp.Epigr.*4.720.15 (Chalcedon, iii B.C.); *join in exaggerating*, τι Plb.6.15.7, cf. Thphr.*HP*9.19.3. **-ημα**, ατος, τό, *increase*, *IG* 2$^2$.1097.18. **-ησις**, εως, ἡ, *growing together, common growth*, τῶν ὀστέων Hp.*Art.*53; τοῦ ὀστράκου Arist.*HA*622$^b$15; simply, *enlargement, growth*, of the breasts, Sor.1.76; τοῦ ἐμβρύου ib.10; *increase*, ἀποκρίσεως, opp. μείωσις, ib.20; *aggravation*, νόσων Herod. Med.ap.Orib.5.30.6: abs., Plb.1.6.3.

**συναυξομειόομαι**, Pass., *increase and decrease together with*, τῷ Νείλῳ Str.*Chr.*17.38.

**συναυχμέω**, *to be squalid together*, Lib.*Descr.*19.8.

**συναφαιρέω**, *take away at the same time*, A.D.*Conj.*255.4 (Pass.); in surgery, Sor.*Fract.*7 (Pass.), Gal.2.263, Aët.7.64; τί τινος Max. Tyr.2.1:—Med., *assist in rescuing*, Th.8.92.

**συνᾰφᾰνίζομαι**, Pass., *disappear* or *perish together with*, τοῖς σώμασιν D.H.1.1, cf. Str.6.1.6, 12.8.17, etc.: abs., S.E.*M.*5.51.

**συνάφεια** [ᾰ], Ion. **ξυναφίη** (Aret.*SA*1.10), ἡ, *combination, connexion, union, junction*, πραγμάτων καὶ τόπων Plu.*Demetr.*5; γένους Phalar.*Ep.*25; πρὸς γένος Sopater in Rh.8.126 W.; of marriage, Hld. 4.10; γάμου *PFlor.*93.17 (vi A.D.); of rivers, Sch.Pi.*Oxy.*841 *Fr.* 129; of connexion in grammar, A.D.*Conj.*217.24; of polysyndeton, Demetr.*Eloc.*63; σ. τῆς ἁρμονίας, of a building, J.*BJ*5.4.4. 2. in Prosody, *the continuous repetition of the same foot an indefinite number of times in an anapaestic or Ionic system*, Mar.Vict.2.8.11, 3.17.10, Ter. Maur.1516,2071. 3. Astrol. and Astron., *conjunction*, Ptol.*Tetr.*52, Procl.*Hyp.*5.6; σ. γαμική *Cat.Cod.Astr.*4.153. 4. Medic., *crisis, emergency*, *Hippiatr.*129. 5. ἀρίθμησις κατὰ συνάφειαν enumeration with *conjunction*, so that the last of one series is the first of the next, Gal.18(2).233.

**συνάφεσις**, εως, ἡ, *letting loose together*, ἁρμάτων Hsch. s.v. ἁματροχεῖν. II. *running out together*, as of rivers meeting, Sch.Od.10.515.

**συναφέψω**, *boil off* or *down together*, Dsc.5.8, Gal.6.538, Orib.*Fr.* 60: pf. part. Pass. συναφεψημένος Herod.Med. in *Rh.Mus.*58.75.

❋ **συνᾰφή**, ἡ, *connexion, union*, Arist.*Spir.*484$^b$22, Thphr.*Ign.*33, Plu.2.1080f (pl.), etc.; κατὰ συναφήν in *connexion* with other things, opp. αὐτοτελῶς, Epicur.*Ep.*2 p.36 U.; *conjunction* of heavenly bodies, *PMag.Leid.W.*24.21, Nech.ap.Vett.Val.279.23, Man.1.74, al.; *application*, opp. ἀπόρροια I. 3, Gal.19.543, Paul.Al.*H.*1; generally, *combination*, Epicur.*Nat.*11.13, 28.9; opp. ἀφαίρεσις, Phld. *D.*3.12, etc.; ἡ πρὸς ἀλλήλους σ. Thphr.*CP*4.12.8, cf. *Metaph.*2; *confluence*, τινὸς πρός τι Ptol.*Geog.*3.16.8, etc.; *junction* of branches of the Milky Way, Id.*Alm.*8.2. II. *point* or *line of junction*, as in bivalve shells, Arist.*PA*680$^a$24; *tangential point* of a circle and straight line, Id.*LI*971$^b$17; ἡ τοῦ βέλους πρὸς τὸ ξύλον σ. Plb. 6.23.11; τῶν μισθοφόρων καὶ τῶν ἱππέων Id.12.18.10; κατὰ τὴν σ. ἐγκεκλιμέναι Plu.2.1079d; Astron., = σύνδεσμος VI. 1, *node*, Cleom. 2.5. III. in Music, *conjunction of two tetrachords*, opp. διάζευξις 2, Plu.2.491a, Cleonid.*Harm.*10, Bacch.38,81, Gaud.6, *POxy.*667. 11 (Aristox.(?)); cf. συνάπτω A. III. 2.

**συναφηβάω**, *decrease in vigour with*, γυμνάσματα –ῶντα τῇ τοῦ σώματος ἀκμῇ Ph.ap.Eus.*PE*8.11.

❋ **συνᾰφής**, ές, *united, connected*, Arist.*PA*667$^a$7; κόλποι σ. ἀλλήλοις Id.*Mu.*393$^a$21; ὑμὴν σ. αὐτῷ καὶ ἀστόμωτος Sor.1.57; τὸ ἄλειφα, ἅτε σ. ἐὸν *cohering*, Hp.*Morb.*4.49; τὰ σ. *connected matters*, Phld.*Oec.* p.32 J.; but τὰ συναφέα *the adjoining parts*, Aret.*SD*1.7; ὁ σ. τόπος the *next* place, Dion.Byz.35; Gramm., τὸ συναφές A.D.*Conj.*217.18: c. dat., *constructed with*, Id.*Synt.*157.20.

**συναφ-ιδρύομαι**, Pass., *to be dedicated together*, Sch.Pi.*N.*1. 3. ❋ **-ίημι**, *send forth together*, μετὰ τοῦ ὕδατος καὶ γῆν Arist.*Pr.* 935$^b$24, cf. 925$^b$9; ἐκπώματα ταῖς σπονδαῖς *drop* into the sea *together with*.., D.S.17.104. 2. *let loose also* upon the enemy, Plb.11.12. 7. **-ικνέομαι**, *arrive together*, Epicur.*Ep.*1 p.10 U. **-ίστημι**, Ion. συναπ–, *draw into revolt together*, Th.1.56; *cause to desert*, J.*BJ* 1.24.2:—Pass., Ion. συναπίσταμαι, with aor. 2 and pf. Act., *fall off* or *revolt along with*, τινι Hdt.5.37,104; ὁ δῆμος οὐ ξυναφίσταται τοῖς ὀλίγοις Th.3.47; οἱ ξυναποστάντες Id.1.104; τὰ ξυναφεστῶτα χωρία ib.59, cf. Jul.*Or.*1.26c. 2. *retire together with*, Dam.*Pr.* 305. **-ομοιόω**, *make quite like*, ἑαυτὸν ἅπασιν Plu.2.52e, cf. 51d, Antig.*Mir.*25. **-ορίζω**, *mark off together*, ἅμα τοῖς ὅλοις τὰ μέρη Plu.2.425b.

**συνάχθομαι**, fut. -αχθεσθήσομαι Aeschin.3.242, Thphr.*Char.*29.5: aor. opt. -αχθεσθείην D.20.113, etc.:—*to be troubled* or *grieved along with* or *together, condole with*, c. dat. pers., πιεζευμένοισι ὑμῖν συναχθόμεθα Hdt.8.142, cf. Isoc.4.112, 6.103, D.20.113, etc.: c. dat. rei, *at* a thing, X.*Cyr.*4.6.5, D.58.59; ἐπί τινι X.*Cyr.*8.2.2, D.53.7; περί or ὑπέρ τινος Phalar.*Ep.*85, Thphr.*Char.* l.c.: also c. gen. rei, *because of* a thing, Alciphr.1.31; σ. ἦν.. X.*Cyr.*1.6.24, *Smp.*8.18.

**συνάχνῠμαι**, Pass., *to be grieved along with*, τινι Q.S.2.625, Nonn. *D.*11.213.

**συνᾰχῠρηγέω**, *assist in transporting chaff*, *PCair.Zen.*176.212 (iii B.C.).

**σύναψις**, εως, ἡ, = συναφή, *contact*, Arist.*Ph.*227$^a$15, *Metaph.*1069$^a$ 9, *LI*971$^b$22, Thphr.*Sens.*73; ἡ σ. αἰσθήσεως πρὸς διάνοιαν Pl.*Tht.* 195d: pl., Id.*Ti.*40c, Plu.2.558f, etc.; dub. in Heraclit.10. II. *point* or *line of junction*, τῶν πλευρῶν Arist.*Mech.*854$^b$39; τῆς θερμαστρίδος ib.854$^a$23; τοῦ ἥπατος τῇ μεγάλῃ φλεβί Id.*PA*667$^b$8; τῆς ἀορτῆς (sc. τῷ πλεύμονι) Id.*HA*513$^b$13. III. in concrete sense, *union, cluster* (of stars), Id.*Mete.*343$^b$8. 2. *enumeration* of misdeeds, *PFlor.*295.7 (vi A.D.). IV. *league*, Lxx 3*Ki.*16.20, 4*Ki.* 10.34.

**συνάωρ**, v. συνήωρ.

**συνβετρανός**, ὁ, = *conveteranus*, *Rev.Arch.*18(1911).443 (Thrace).

**συνδᾶΐζω**, fut. -ξω, *kill with the rest, kill also*, S.*Aj.*361 (lyr.).

**συνδαίνῦμι**, aor. part. -δαίσας E.*Hel.*1439 :—*entertain together*, γάμους τινί *share* a marriage *feast with* one, l. c. :—Med., *feast together*, Satyr.3.

**συνδαιτ-ᾶλεύς**, έως, ὁ, *fellow-guest*, Ath.8.354d, Suid. s. v. δαιταλεύς. **-ης**, ου, ὁ, = συνδαίτωρ, Luc.*Ep.Sat.*36 ; fem. voc. σύνδαιτι, Orph.*H.*55.10. **-ωρ**, ορος, ὁ, *companion at table*, οὐδέ τις ξ. A.*Eu.* 351 (lyr.).

**συνδάκνω**, *bite together*, τὸ στόμιον, of a horse, *take* the bit *in his teeth* and run away, X *Eq.*6.9 ; *crush by closing the teeth*, Arist.*HA* 612$^{a}$24, 621$^{b}$2 ; σ. τὸ πνεῦμα *hold* the breath, Cerc.1 :—Pass., *smart exceedingly*, Lxx *To.*11.12.

**συνδακρύω**, *weep with* or *together*, E.*IA*1242 ; τῷ πάθει Clearch. 37 : abs., J.*AJ*16.4.3. II. c. acc., *lament together*, Plu.*Luc.*29.

**συνδᾱμιοργός**, v. συνδημιουργός.

**συνδάμνᾰμαι**, Pass., *to be subdued together*, Nic.*Al.*173.

**συνδᾰνείζομαι**, Med., *get together by borrowing*, Plu.*Eum.*13. 2. *to be a joint borrower*, *PGrenf.*2.18.8 (ii B.C.), *PRein.*26.12 (ii B.C.).

* **συνδᾰπᾰνάω**, *join in defraying expenditure*, *MAMA* 4.208 (Apollonia).

**συνδᾰσύνω**, *aspirate also*, *EM*317.47 (Pass.).

* **συνδαυχνᾱφόρος**, ὁ, *fellow-*δαυχναφόρος, *IG*9(2).1027 (Thess.).

**συνδεαίνω**, v. συνδυαίνω.

**συνδεδεμένως**, Adv. *conjunctively*, opp. ἀσυνδέτως, Sch.S.*OT*344.

**συνδέδια**, pf. with pres. sense, *have a common fear*, App.*BC*2. 141.

**συνδείκνυμι**, in Med., *demonstrate also*, τῷ λόγῳ τῷδε περὶ τῆς κράσεως Gal.15.651 ; ὁδὸς ἡ συνδειχθεῖσα the road *which has been pointed out jointly*, *OGI*225.42 (Didyma, iii B.C.).

**συνδεινόω**, *make terrible along with*, φράσις τῇ τῶν πραγμάτων -ουμένη σκυθρωπότητι Eust.1711.51.

**συνδειπν-έω**, *dine* or *sup with*, συνδειπνέω τῷ λῶντι Epich.35, cf. X.*HG*4.1.6 ; μετά τινων Is.3.14, Test.ap.D.21.121 : abs., *dine* or *sup with others* or *together*, Pl.*Smp.*174e, 217c, X.*Cyr.*4.5.9, Lys.1.22, *PTeb.*43.18 (ii B.C.), etc. ; οἱ συνδειπνοῦντες *the members of a picnic party*, X.*Mem.*3.14.2. **-ιον**, τό, *dining-room*, *PCair.Zen.*764.45 (iii B.C.). II. = sq., Call.*Cer.*73, D.S.14.42, Ath.4.140c. **-ον**, τό, *common meal* or *banquet*, Ar.*Fr.*153, Pl.*Smp.*172b, Lys.*Fr.*66, Cic.*Fam.*9.24.3, etc. **-ος**, ὁ, ἡ, *companion at table*, E.*Ion* 1172, X.*Cyr.*3.2.25, 8.2.3, Lxx *Si.*9.16 ; σ. τινὰ ποιεῖσθαι X.*An.*2.5.27, *Cyr.*2.2.28 ; σ. τῇ γαστρί, οὐ τῇ ψυχῇ Plu.2.660b ; Σύνδειπνοι, title of a satyric drama by S., Cic.*QF*2.16.3, etc. ; *members of a dining-club*, opp. ξένοι, *PTeb.*118.4,10 (ii B.C.).

**συνδεκᾰδίζω**, *celebrate the tenth day together with*, c. dat., cj. in D. 58.40.

**συνδεκάζω**, *bribe all together*, τοὺς δικαστάς X.*Ath.*3.7 ; τὴν ἡλιαίαν Lex ap.D.46.26 ; τὰ δικαστήρια Aeschin.1.86, etc. ; συνδικάζω is a freq. f.l.

**συνδενδρ-ία**, ἡ, *thickly-wooded place*, Eust.1652.16. **-όομαι**, Pass., *become a tree together*, Lib.*Eth.*11.4. **-ος**, ον, *thickly-wooded*, Dicaearch.1.8, Plb.12.4.2, Sch.Il.*Oxy.*1086.10 ; τόποι Arr.*Tact.*27. 4 ; ὕλη Babr.43.1 ; ἔν τινι συνδένδρῳ in a *thickly-wooded place*, Plu. 2.310e.

**συνδέομαι**, *join in entreating*, c. dat., Plu.*Caes.*66 ; σ. τινὶ ἵνα.. Pl.*Prm.*136e ; σ. τινὸς μὴ ποιεῖν τι *beg* of him *also*.., Id.*Ep.*318c ; τί τινος something *of* a person, D.36.57.

**σύνδερμον**, τό, *a common hide*, Tz. ad Lyc.88.

**σύνδεσις**, εως, ἡ, *binding together*, of milk by fig-juice, Plu.2.697b ; πρὸς τὴν τῆς κονίας σ. so as to *bind* the mortar or stucco, D.S.13. 113 ; *continuation of a text*, *POxy.*1737.23 (ii/iii A.D.) : metaph., τῆς ψυχῆς πρὸς [τὸ σῶμα] Porph.*Antr.*14 ; κοινωνία καὶ σ. Procl.*Inst.* 32 ; *connecting link*, Pl.*Ti.*43d. II. (from Pass.) *constriction*, τοῦ δέρματος Hp.*Epid.*6.3.1, cf. *Oss.*11, Gal.17(2).2. III. Gramm., *conjunctive construction*, A.D.*Conj.*216.11.

**συνδεσμ-εύω**, *bind together*, Plb.3.42.8 ; later **-δεσμέω**, Gal.2. 268, Charito 2.2, Sch.D.T.p.61 H. **-ικός**, ή, όν, *conjunctive*, A.D. *Conj.*235.5, al. **-ιος**, ον, *convinctus*, Gloss.

**συνδεσμοειδής**, ές, *of the form of conjunctions*, μόρια, interpol. post A.D.*Conj.*214.3.

* **σύνδεσμ-ος**, ὁ, heterocl. pl. σύνδεσμα E. (v. infr.) :—*that which binds together, bond of union, fastening*, ξ. ἦν.. τὰ ξύλα, τοῦ μὴ ἀσθενὲς εἶναι τὸ οἰκοδόμημα Th.2.75 ; ἀραρότως σύνδεσμα χρυσὸς εἶχε the golden headband kept its *bonds* firmly fixed, E.*Med.*1193 ; ἀμμάτων σύνδεσμα *fastenings* of garments, Id.*Ba.*697 ; οἱ περὶ [τὸ θύρωμα] σ. Aristeas 85 ; μελέων σύνδεσμα, of *sinews* or *ligaments*, E.*Hipp.*199 (anap.), cf. Ti.Locr.100b, Arist.*PA*652$^{a}$16, *IA*712$^{a}$2, *Ep.Col.*2.19, Sor.2.57, Gal.18(1).734. 2. metaph., *bond of union* ; ὁ σ. τῆς πόλεως *the bond that keeps* the state *together*, of good citizens, Pl.*R.* 520a, cf. *Plt.*310a ; νόμος ὁ βοηθῶν.. τῷ τῆς πόλεως συνδέσμῳ Id.*Lg.* 921c ; σ. τοῦ οὐρανοῦ Id.*R.*616c ; σ. τὰ τέκνα δοκεῖ εἶναι Arist.*EN* 1162$^{a}$27 ; τὴν ἀγάπην, ὅ ἐστι σ. τῆς τελειότητος *Ep.Col.*3.14. 3. Gramm., *conjunction*, Arist.*Rh.*1407$^{a}$20 ; σ. ἓν ποιεῖ τὰ πολλά ib. 1413$^{b}$32, cf. *Rh.Al.*1434$^{b}$13, *Po.*1456$^{b}$38, Chrysipp.*Stoic.*2.45, D.T. 634.6, A.D.*Conj.* passim, Hermog.*Id.*2.7. II. = σύνδεσις 1, Pl. *Epin.*984c ; συνδέσμῳ ἕν Arist.*APo.*93$^{b}$36, *Metaph.*1045$^{a}$13, cf. *Int.* 17$^{a}$9. III. *that which is bound together, bundle*, ἐπιστολῶν Hdn. 4.12.6. IV. *conspiracy*, Lxx 4*Ki.*11.14, al. V. *sodomy*, ib. 3*Ki.*14.24. VI. Astron., *node*, Eudox.*Ars* 18.13, Theo Sm. p.194 H., Cleom.2.5, Ptol.*Alm.*6.5. 2. Σ. *the Knot*, i. e. the star α Piscium, Hipparch.1.11.20, Gem.3.7, Id.*Calend.*10, Ptol.*Alm.*8. 1. 3. Astrol., *connexion* of heavenly bodies, Vett.Val.163.13, al. ; of the moon, Paul.Al.*S.*3. **-ώτης**, ου, ὁ, *fellow-prisoner*, Th. 6.60, Pl.*R.*516c.

**συνδεσποτεύω**, Astrol., *rule at the same time*, Sch.Ptol.*Tetr.*38.

**συνδετ-έος**, α, ον, *to be tied* or *bound together*, Ar.*Ec.*785 ; πρός τι Hp.*Art.*77. II. **συνδετέον**, *one must bind together*, Paul.Aeg.6. 101. **-ης**, ου, ὁ, (συνδέω) *one bound hand and foot*, ἀλύσει μακρᾷ Posidon.36 J., cf. Suid. s. v. (pl.). II. Act., *one who binds together*, ξύλων ἢ φακέλων Phld.*Rh.*1.74 S. **-ικός**, ή, όν, *binding together, conjunctive, connective*, *Placit.*5.18.6, etc. ; τὸ σ. *a bond of union*, Plu. *Comp.Lyc.Num.*4 ; τὸ ἴσον -κὸν εἰς ὠφέλειαν Ph.*Fr.*101 H. ; νεῦρα σ. Gal.13.161. Adv. -κῶς Procl. *in Alc.*p.52 C. 2. Gramm., *conjunctive*, A.D.*Synt.*18.13. **-ος**, ον, *bound hand and foot*, S.*Aj.*65, 296. 2. *united with*, αὐτὰ αὑτοῖς Pl.*Plt.*279e ; τὰ σ. *compounds*, concrete things, Procl.*Inst.*157. 3. *well knit together*, Arist.*Phgn.* 807$^{b}$15. II. Subst. σύνδετον, τό, *band*, E.*Ion* 1390.

**συνδεύω**, *moisten*, εἴρια Q.S.4.213 codd.

**συνδέχομαι**, *receive as a guest*, *POxy.*1162.8 (iv A.D.).

**συνδέω**, *bind* or *tie together*, of two or more things, συνέδησα πόδας δεινοῖο πελώρου Od.10.168 ; σὺν δὲ πόδας χεῖράς τε δέον 22.189 ; οἶνος σ. πόδας χεῖράς τε γλῶσσάν τε νόον τε Hes.*Fr.*121 ; τοὺς πόδας καὶ τὰς χεῖρας Pl.*Euthphr.*4c ; σ. γαύλους *bind* them *together, side by side*, Hdt.8.97, cf. Plb.1.22.9 ; δέλτον λύειν καὶ σ. *fasten* it *up*, E.*IA*110 ; *act as binding material*, ὁ συνδέων πηλός *CPR*232.17 (ii/iii A.D.) :—Pass., τὰς χεῖρας συνεδέθησαν *had* their hands *tied together*, Demad.13 ; ἰσχία μὴ συνδεδεμένα flanks not *well-knit*, of dogs, X.*Cyn.*4.1, cf. Arist.*Pr.*873$^{a}$33. 2. of persons, *bind hand and foot*, ὁππότε μιν ξυνδῆσαι Ὀλύμπιοι ἤθελον ἄλλοι Il.1.399, cf. Hdt 9.119, S.*Aj.*62, *Ph.* 1016, E.*Cyc.*238, etc. ; λαγὼς αὐτὸς σ. ἑαυτόν *entangles* itself, X *Cyr.* 1.6.40 :—Pass., συνδεδεμένος *constrained, cramped*, Philostr.*Im.*2. 21. b. *bind up* a wound, σφενδόνῃ *with*.., Il.13.599. 3. *bind up with, combine closely*, σάρκας ὀστοῖς Pl.*Ti.*84a, cf. 73b, *Smp.*202e, *Tht.*160b ; also τι ἀπό τινος Luc.*Syr.D.*29 ; of parts growing together, Hp.*Mul.*1.40. 4. generally, *bind together, unite*, [ἰσότης] φίλους φίλοις πόλεις τε πόλεσι συμμάχους τε συμμάχοις σ. E.*Ph.*538 ; τὸ κοινὸν συνδεῖ τὰς πόλεις Pl.*Lg.*875a ; ἡδονῆς καὶ λύπης κοινωνία συνδεῖ Id.*R.*462b ; σ. καὶ συνέχειν Id.*Phd.*99c ; σ. τινὰ πενίᾳ *bind* him *to*.., Alciphr.3.49. 5. *connect*, opp. διαζευγνύω, A.D.*Conj.* 214.6, al. II. Med., σύνδησαι πέπλους *gird up thy* robes, E.*Andr.* 832 (lyr., Reiske for πέπλοις). 2. *have* things *bound together*, Ti. Locr.99a, Them.*Or.*4.59a. 3. *unite themselves, form a union*, πρὸς παίδων γέννησιν Pl.*Plt.*310b, cf. Betion ap.D.L.4.54.

**σύνδηλ-ος**, ον, *quite clear* or *manifest*, Arist.*Po.*1451$^{a}$10, Hp.*Ep.* 27. * **-όω**, *make altogether clear*, Arist.*Rh.*1395$^{a}$27 :—Pass., Thphr. *HP*1.1.8 ; *to be signified*, A.D.*Synt.*312.21 ; συνεδηλοῦτο [τὸ ἄχροον] τῷ μέλασι Gal.16.513.

**συνδημᾰγωγέω**, *help in captivating the populace*, Plu.*Pomp.*2 ; συνεδημαγώγησε τῷ πάθει τοὺς πολλούς *joined with* his calamity *in persuading* the mob, Id.*Caes.*5 :—Pass., App.*BC*3.24.

* **συνδημιουργ-έω**, *create together*, Jul.*Or.*5.167b, Iamb.ap.Stob.1. 49.67, Hierocl. *in CA*26 p.478 M. **-ός**, ὁ, *fellow-workman*, Pl. *Lg.*671d. II. Dor. συνδᾱμιοργοί, τοί, *fellow-*δαμιοργοί, of magistrates in Locris, *IG*9(1).335 (v B.C.).

**συνδημότης**, ου, ὁ, = δημότης, Sch.Ar.*Pax*909 ; rejected by Thom. Mag. pp.96, 292 R.

**συνδηόω**, *join in ravaging*, τινὶ τὴν Ἰουδαίαν J.*BJ*5.1.6.

**συνδια-βαίνω**, *go through* or *cross over together*, Th.6.101, X.*An.* 7.1.4 ; τινι *with* one, Plu.*Sert.*12, Lib.*Or.*18.67. **-βάλλω**, *cross together*, πάντα [τὰ πλοῖα] ξυνδιέβαλλε τὸν κόλπον Th.6.44. II. *accuse along with*, D.61.12 :—Pass., *to be accused together*, Th.6.61, Lys.12.93, D.39.19. **-βαπτίζομαι**, Med., *infuse itself into*, φύσις σ. τοῖς σώμασι Procl. *in Prm.* p.617, cf. p.690 S. : also as v.l. for διαin D.25.41. **-βαστάζω**, *carry through together with*, Eust.1603. 62. **-βῐβάζω**, causal of συνδιαβαίνω, *carry through* or *over together*, Pl.*Lg.*892e, X.*HG*6.2.10 ; *help to convey across*, τὴν στρατιάν Plu.*Luc.* 4. **-βρέχω**, *wet through together*, Gal.6.421 (Pass.). **-γίγνομαι**, *to be contemporary with*, Πλάτωνος δόγμασιν Id.*Phil.Hist.* 3. **-γιγνώσκω**, *join with* one *in determining* or *decreeing*, ἐμὲ.., ᾧ ξυνδιέγνωτε πολεμεῖν Th.2.64, cf. D.C.43.25 ; *distinguish at the same time*, Gal.5.625, *UP*2.6. **-γνωμονέω**, *decide in the same sense*, τινι Eust.341.7.

**συνδι-άγω** [ᾰ], *go through together*, τὴν ἡμέραν Hsch. : abs. (sc. τὸν βίον), *live together*, Arist.*Rh.*1381$^{a}$30 ; σ. τινί Id.*EN*1166$^{a}$7, Dsc. *Prooem.*4 ; μετ' ἀλλήλων Arist.*EN*1157$^{b}$22 ; ἐπιθυμίαις ἀνόμοις σ. Plu.2.993c. **-ᾰγωγή**, ἡ, *living together, association*, D.L.10.6, *Cod. Just.*1.3.43(44).1.

**συνδια-δέχομαι**, *receive together*, Aristid.*Or.*36(48).84. **-δίδωμι**, *absorb*, ἔλαιον Diocl.*Fr.*147. **-ζώννυμι**, in Pass., *to be linked by aspect* with a planet, of the moon, *Cat.Cod.Astr.*8(3).103.3. **-θερμαίνω**, *warm thoroughly together*, Hp.*Morb.*1.24. **-θέω**, *keep running together*, μετά τινος Pl.*Plt.*266c.

**συνδι-αιρέω**, *divide together*, Plu.2.425b, Procl.*Inst.*123 :—Pass., Iamb. *in Nic.*p.3 P., Dam.*Pr.*205 ; *to be incised together*, Heliod.ap. Orib.45.7.5. II. Med., *divide the proceeds* of a robbery, *PCair.*

*Zen.*491 (iii B.C.); but, *divide, share* a property, *PTeb.*383.48 (i A.D.). 2. *divide in addition, include in a division,* γῆν *PEnteux.* 65.15 (iii B.C.). -αίρω, *help to lift upwards,* ἵππος..τῷ ὁμοζύγῳ σ. τὸ ὄχημα Them.*Or.*20.234c.

**συνδῐαιτ-άομαι,** Pass., *live with* or *together,* Th.2.50, Isoc.15.87, Pl.*Lg.*929d; μετὰ ἀλλήλων Id.*Ti.*18b; τινι Plu.*Num.*4, etc.: abs., *keep house together, PMasp.*153.14 (vi A.D.): metaph., λόγῳ θεωρητοῖς πράγμασιν Ph.1.470; συνδιαιτᾶται ὑπὸ τοῦ περιφύντος πώρου *is held together,* Gal.18(2).412 (s.v.l.). II. Act. **συνδῐαιτάω,** *decide as* διαιτητής *together,* Poll.8.129, Them.*Or.*11.146b. **-ημα,** ατος, τό, = sq., Agath.3.13 (pl.). **-ησις,** εως, ἡ, *living together, intercourse,* Metrod.*Herc.*831.13, Ph.2.591, J.*AJ*1.1.2, Plu.*Aem.*1, Dio 16, etc.; σ. εἰς τοὺς ὑπηκόους *ordinary behaviour* towards them, Arr. *An.*4.7.4. **-ητής,** οῦ, ὁ, *joint arbitrator,* D.33.19,31. II. *one who lives with another, companion,* Luc.*Ep.Sat.*36 (v.l. for -δαίτης), Sch.Ar.*Pl.*602. **-ος,** ὁ, = συνδιαιτητής II, Ant.Lib.30.4; θεῶν Tz. *H.*5.464; τινι Hierocl. p.54 A.

**συνδιαιωνίζω,** *pass all one's life with,* Hsch. II. *co-exist perpetually with,* τῷ κόσμῳ σ. γράμματα Ph.2.216, cf. 419, al.

**συνδια-καίω,** *burn* or *heat through at the same time,* Plu.2.752d (Pass.). **-κειμαι,** Pass., *take part with,* τινι Them.*Or.*22.270b. II. Medic., = συμπάσχω, Herod.Med. in *Rh.Mus.*58.105. **-κινδῡνεύω,** *share in danger,* Hdt.7.220; μετά τινος, τινων, Pl.*La.*189b, *IG*2$^2$.505. 32. **-κομίζω,** fut. -κομιῶ, *assist in bringing over,* πλοῖον *PHib.* 1.54.31 (iii B.C.):—Pass., *cross over together,* Plb.3.43.4, Plu.*Brut.* 37.

**συνδιᾱκονέω,** v. συνδιακτορέω.

**συνδιάκονος** [ᾱ], ὁ, *fellow-servant,* Posidipp.26.1.

**συνδια-κόπτω,** *cut through together,* in Pass., Heliod.ap.Orib.46. 7.2, Aët.7.62. **-κοσμέω,** *set in order together,* τὴν πόλιν καὶ τοὺς νόμους Pl.*Lg.*712b, cf. Plu.*Num.*1, *Sol.*26. **-κρίνω** [ῑ], *determine together,* Ti.Locr.104e; τῇ γλώττῃ τὰ γευστά Gal.*UP*16.2. II. Pass., *to be separated,* ἀλλήλοις Arist.*Xen.*977$^a$4.

**συνδῐακτορ-έω,** *join in conducting,* Ἑρμῆς ταῦτα σ. Timocl.1 D. (-κτονεῖ Pap., -κονεῖ Koerte). **-ος,** ὁ, *fellow-*διάκτορος, of Hermes, Luc.*Cont.*1.

**συνδια-κῠβερνάω,** *guide* or *govern jointly,* Pl.*Plt.*304a, Jul.*Or.*5. 18b. **-λαμβάνω,** *examine together,* Ptol.*Tetr.*8; περί τινων Plb. 16.25.1:—Pass., *to be distributed together with,* τοῖς μέρεσι Plot.6.4. 4; τὸ συνδιειλημμένον φλέγμα Herod.Med. in *Rh.Mus.*58.89. ⊛**-λέγομαι,** *converse with* or *together,* Ath.3.97d, Ach.Tat.6.18, *Gloss.* **-ληψις,** εως, ἡ, *joint consideration,* M.Ant.1.10.

**συνδιαλλάσσω,** Att. -ττω, *help in reconciling,* ἵνα συνδιαλλάττωσιν αὐτῷ τοὺς Ἀλεῖς πρὸς τοὺς Φαρσαλίους D.19.36, cf. Plu.*Lys.*8, etc.:— fut. Pass. συνδιαλλαχθήσομαι Men.*Pk.*428. II. *alter together,* A.D.*Adv.*162.1 (Pass.).

**συνδια-λῡμαίνομαι,** *help to ruin,* D.H.1.23. **-λύω,** *help in putting an end to,* τὰς ταραχάς Isoc.4.134. 2. Med., *help to pay,* Luc.*Dem.Enc.*45, Aristid.2.456 J. II. Pass., *to be dissipated, melt away with,* δόξα τισὶν ὁμοῦ -ομένη Plu.2.823e; *to be abolished at the same time,* ἡ τυραννὶς -εται Aen.Gaz.*Thphr.* p.58 B. **-μάχομαι** [μᾰ], *fight to the end together,* ὑπὲρ τῶν δευτερείων νῷ πρὸς ἡδονὴν Pl. *Phlb.*66e. **-μένω,** *stand one's ground with* others, X.*Cyr.*4.5.53, Arist.*EE*1235$^b$9; *to be fixed also,* Gal.18(2).767. **-μνημονεύω,** *call to remembrance along with,* Aeschin.1.18, D.19.19. **-νέμω,** *distribute together with,* ἑαυτοὺς..τοῖς καλοῖς Lib.*Decl.*45.27:—Pass., c. dat., Plu.2.1024c,1082b, cf. Gal.2.391. **-νεύω,** *slew* or *turn together,* of war-engines, Plb.1.23.10: c. dat. instr., τῷ προσώπῳ Plu. 2.63b: metaph., σ. τῇ διανοίᾳ ἐπί τι Plb.3.38.5. **-νήχομαι,** *swim through together with,* τοῖς κολυμβῶσι Sotion ap.Stob.3.14.10. **-νοέομαι,** *deliberate along with,* τινὶ περί τινος Plb.2.54.14; σ., πῶς ἄν.. Id. 31.12.7. **-περαίνω,** *assist in bringing to an end,* τὸν λόγον Pl.*Grg.* 506b. **-πέτομαι,** *fly about together,* Id.*Tht.*199e. **-πήγνῡμαι,** Pass., f.l. in Sor.1.115 (ἂν οὖν παγῇ restd. fr. Aët.). **-πίπτω,** *fall upon together, descend to* an heir *from many ancestors,* εἰς ὃν ἁ τᾶς Ἑλλάδος εὐγένεια ἐν τοῖς μάλιστα συνδιαπείπτει *IG*4$^2$(1).86.10 (Epid.). **-πλάσσω,** *set* a fracture, Pall. *in Hp.Fract* 12. 278 C. **-πλέκω,** *interweave,* πάντα ἐν τάξει Herm. *in Phdr.* p.110 A.:—Pass., Iamb. ap. Stob.1.49.31, Phot. **-πλέω,** *sail across with,* τινι Luc.*Bis Acc.*27. ⊛**-πνέω,** *blow through together,* f.l. in Ps.-Philol.*Fr.*21. 2. *discharge with the perspiration,* [ἡ φύσις] σ. τούτῳ τὸ ζέσαν Gal.18(2).279. **-πολεμέω,** *carry on a war along with,* τὸν πόλεμον *IG*1$^2$.108.50: abs., ib.2$^2$.732 (iii B.C.); νῆες αἱ μετὰ Γυλίππου ξυνδιαπολεμήσασαι *which remained with* him *throughout the war,* Th.8.13. **-πονέω,** *continue to work together,* μετά τινος Pl. *Sph.*218b; περί τι Id.*Lg.*842e.

**συνδι-ᾰπορέω,** *start doubts* or *questions together,* Plu.*Arist.*11; περί τινος Id.*Pomp.*75; ὑπέρ τινος D.H.11.25; τοῖς φίλοις Phld.*Rh.* 1.91 S., cf. *BGU*1770.4 (i B.C.), Plu.*Caes.*32.

**συνδια-πορθμεύομαι,** *cross over by ferry together,* Procop.*Goth.*4. 20. **-πράσσω,** Att. -ττω, *accomplish together* or *besides,* Isoc.4. 38, Luc.*DDeor.*24.1, etc. II. Med., *negotiate at the same time,* ὑπὲρ τῶν Κόλχων X.*An.*4.8.24.

**συνδι-αρθρόω,** *express distinctly at the same time,* Arist.*Metaph.* 989$^b$5. **-αρκέω,** *last as long as,* c. dat., Them.*Or.*5.68b.

**συνδια-ρράπτω,** *sew together,* μυσὶ τοὺς τένοντας Gal.13.601. **-ρρέω,** *flow through along with,* τοῖς ὑγροῖς D.S.3.22. **-σείω,** *concutio, Gloss.* **-σήπω,** *make putrid together,* Gal.7.297:—Pass., *to be* or *become so,* ib.388 **-σκέπτομαι,** = sq., Hierocl. p.54 A. **-σκοπέω,** fut. -σκέψομαι J.*AJ*6.6.2: aor. 1 inf. -σκέψασθαι Pl. *Prt.*349a:—*look through* or *examine along with,* Pl.*Prt.* l. c., 361d:— so in pres. Med., Id.*R.*458b. **-σπάω,** *part forcibly at the same time,* Gal.8.55. **-στέλλω,** *distinguish at the same time,* τὸ γένος A.D. *Synt.*103.26. 2. Pass., *to be expanded together,* of lungs and chest, Gal.8.325. **-στρέφω,** *distort together,* Id.18(2).833: metaph., ψυχήν Plu.2.521b:—Pass., Id.*Lys.*17, Gal. l. c., etc. **-σύρω** [ῡ], *join in depreciating,* prob. cj. in Plu.2.631e. **-σῴζω,** *assist in preserving,* Th.4.62, 7.57; πόλιν *SIG*529.9 (Dyme, iii B.C.); σ. τινὶ τὴν οὐσίαν D.28.15, cf. Epicur.*Fr.*217 (Test. Epicuri); σ. καὶ τὰ ὅπλα καὶ αὐτὸν ἐμέ *save* both my arms and myself *together,* Pl.*Smp.* 220e. **-τᾰλαιπωρέω,** *endure hardship with* or *together,* Pl.*Cri.* 45d. **-τᾰράσσω,** *alarm all at once,* Plu.*Demetr.*28. **-τείνω,** *help to stretch,* Gal.8.288:—Pass., *extend all together with,* τοῖς σώμασι Plu.2.63c. ⊛**-τελέω,** *continue with to the end,* Pl.*Phd* 91b, D.61.38, Arist.*Phgn.*808$^b$19, Iamb.*Protr.*20. **-τηρέω,** *assist in maintaining,* Thphr.*CP*6.10.6, Plb.2.58.3, *SIG*569.23 (Cos, iii/ii B.C.), *OGI*229.65 (Smyrna, iii B.C.), etc. ⊛**-τίθημι,** *help in arranging,* Ἰφίτῳ σ. τὴν Ὀλυμπιακὴν ἐκεχειρίαν Arist.*Fr.*533, cf. Plu.*Tim.*24:—Med., Hierocl. *Prov.* p.171 B. 2. *compose, put together,* ἐν τῇ ψυχῇ Porph.*Plot.* 8. II. *help in disposing,* τὴν ψυχὴν πρός τι Longin.7.3, cf. 39.3; *cause a sympathetic affection of,* τὴν καρδίαν Diocl.*Fr.*59:—Pass., *to be sympathetically affected together,* Plu.2.443b, D.L.4.18, Jul.*Ep.*89b, Chor.29.75 F.-R., *Cod.Just.*1.4.34.3; Medic., = συμπάσχω, Diocl.*Fr.* 38, Sor.1.50, Gal.15.88,793. 2. Gramm., of the verb, *to be affected in voice,* A.D.*Synt.*205.2. **-τρέπομαι,** Pass., *turn away* or *be ashamed along with,* τὸ πρόσωπον σ. τῇ ψυχῇ Plu.2.528e. **-τρέφω,** *bring up together with,* τινά τινι Ael.*NA*3.45 codd. **-τρῐβή,** ἡ, *passing time together, intercourse, discussion,* τεχνίταις Phld.*Hom.* p.28 O., cf. Ph.2.671, etc. **-τρίβω** [ῑ], *pass* or *spend* time *with* or *together,* σὺν.. Κίμωνι αἰῶνα πάντα σ. Cratin.1.5; τὸν ἄλλον σ. χρόνον (sc. τοῖς τεθνηκόσι) Antiph.53.6. 2. more freq. without acc., *live constantly with,* μετά τινος, Pl.*Smp.*172c, Isoc.2.27, cf. *Vit.Philonid.* p.12 C.; οἱ τῷ Σωκράτει συνδιατρίβοντες his disciples, X.*Mem.*1.2.3, 4. 1.1. II. of things, *occupy oneself with,* μύθοις Isoc.4.158, cf. 2.43, 9.76. **-ττάω,** *pass through the sieve as well,* in Pass., οὐ -ᾶται Gal. 18(1).471. **-τῡπόω,** *form together with,* τινί τι *Placit.*4.13. 8. **-φαίνομαι,** Pass., *to be manifest together with,* τούτοις Steph. *in Hp.*1.107 D. **-φέρω,** *bear along with one,* ἄνεμος σ. τὴν ναῦν Luc.*Hist.Conscr.*45. II. *bear to the end along with, help in maintaining,* οἱ Μιλήσιοι τοῖσι Χίοισι τὸν..πόλεμον συνδιήνεικαν Hdt.1.18, cf. 5.79,99; ξυνδιήνεγκαν μεθ' ἡμῶν ἐσβολάς τε καὶ μάχας Ar.*Eq.*597 (troch.); σ. πάθος Plu.*Brut.*13, cf. Jul.*Or.*8.241c:—Med., τὰ τοῦ πολέμου Ph.1.323. **-φεύγω,** *escape along with,* D.C.48.44. **-φθείρω,** *destroy at the same time,* Arist.*HA*585$^a$10, Jul.*Or.*1.24d; *corrupt at the same time,* ἑαυτῷ σ. καὶ τἄλλα Gal.15.874:—Pass., *to be corrupted along with,* ἡμῖν Isoc.8.41, cf. Din.3.19, Gal.15.697; συνδιαφθαρεὶς τῷ σώματι τὰς φρένας *having* his mind *destroyed with..,* D.H.3.36: pf. συνδιέφθορα in pass. sense, D.S.38.15. **-φθορά,** ἡ, *mutual corruption, Cod.Just.*1.3.44(45). **-φορέω,** *disperse together,* Longin. 40.1:—Pass., Steph. *in Hp.*2.336 D. **-φόρως,** Adv. *together with a difference,* Iamb. *in Nic.* p.13 P. **-φῠλάσσω,** *assist in preserving,* Lycurg.143, *CIG*3048.31, 3058 (Teos), *AJP*48.18 (Rome); *assist in guarding,* φρούριον *SIG*363.5 (Ephesus, iii B.C.); σ. τινὶ τὴν ἀρχήν, τὰ πράγματα, Plb.7.3.7, Plu.*Comp.Dion.Brut.*3; ἀλλήλοις τὴν ἐλευθερίαν *OGI*5.54 (Scepsis, iv B.C.). 2. *preserve as well,* τὴν εὐσχημοσύνην τῷ πλήθει the elegance as well as the numbers, Lib.*Or.*11. 199. **-χειμάζω,** *spend the winter along with* or *together,* μετά τινος Plu.*Ages.*40; τινι Id.*Ant.*37. **-χειρίζω,** *assist in accomplishing,* τὰ λοιπά Hdt.9.103. **-χέω,** *dissolve* a thing *into* a liquid, Plu.2.953d (Pass.).

**συνδῐδάσκω,** *produce together with,* of a drama, Sch.Ar.*Th.*1021, cf. Demetr.Lac.*Herc.*1012.31.

**συνδίδωμι,** *contribute,* τινί τι Plu.2.660c; ξηρὸν ἐς τὰ ἕλκεα Aret. *CD*1.8. 2. *grant,* τινὶ προθεσμίαν *POxy.*1130.22 (v A.D.):—Pass., *to be allowed also,* A.D.*Adv.*175.14. II. intr., *cooperate,* Hp.*Art.* 30. 2. *abate, slacken,* of symptoms, Id.*Epid.*3.1.ιβ', Aret.*SD*1. 13; *relax,* opp. συντείνω, Hp.*Off.*23; of the eyes, *sink in,* Arist.*Pr.* 876$^a$37. 3. *extend, spread,* ξυνδιδοῖ τὸ κακὸν ἐς τὸ πᾶν Aret.*SA*1. 6. 4. τοῦ συνδοθέντος εἰς τὴν γαστέρα ὑγροῦ *collected in* the stomach, Herod.Med.ap.Aët.9.2.

**συνδιεγείρομαι,** *arise together,* of prayers, τῷ Σεβαστῷ *Sardis* 7(1). 8.9 (i B.C.).

**συνδιεκ-βάλλω,** *make to pass through with,* Gal.*UP*9.8. **-κύπτω,** *slip out and through together with,* τῇ κεφαλῇ Eust.1114.24. **-πίπτω,** *escape together,* Plu.*Publ.*19, Gal.8.227.

**συνδι-ελαύνω,** intr., *pass,* ἐκ παίδων εἰς ἐφήβους Them.*Or.*34 p.456 Dind. **-έξειμι,** *go through together with,* πάντα τοῖς συνοῦσι X. *Mem.*4.7.8: so **-εξέρχομαι,** Gal.18(1).471, Aët.7.1, Hsch. **-έπω,** *manage together,* βασιλεῖ τὴν Αἴγυπτον J.*AJ*2.7.1, cf. Ph.2. 452. **-ερευνάομαι,** *search through together,* τὰ τοῦ Πλάτωνός τισι Lib.*Or.*17.26, cf. Poll.5.85. **-έρχομαι,** *go together with, belong to* a thing, Gal.8.705; gloss on παραγγέλλων, Suid. **-ηθέομαι,** Pass., *to be filtered through together,* Pl.*Ti.*66e, Gal.17(1).836.

**συνδιημέρ-ευσις,** εως, ἡ, *passing one's days together,* Plu.*Demetr.* 32, *Nic.*5 (both pl.). **-εύω,** *spend one's days with,* τινι X.*Smp.*4. 44, Arist.*Rh.*1381$^a$30, *EN*1162$^b$16 (v. l. for συνημ-); ἐπισφαλὲς τοῖς ὑπὸ φθόης συνεχομένοις συνδιημερεύειν Gal.7.279; μετά τινων Arist.*EN* 1166$^b$14 (v. l. for συνημ-).

**συνδιίσταμαι**, aor. -έστην, *become separate together with*, τοῖς σώμασι Procl.*Inst.*190; *differ at the same time*, τοις ὀνόμασιν Dam.*Pr.*143.

**συνδῐκ-άζω**, Dor. fut. -δικαξῶ *IG*9(1).32.28 (Stiris, ii B.C.):—*have a share in judging*, Pl.*Lg.*768b; of the βουλή, Lys.30.11,14; τὰς δίκας *IG* l. c.; σ. τοῖς ζῶσιν ὁ τεθνεώς Lib.*Or.*12.15. **-ᾰσία**, ἡ, sine expl., prob. *common lawsuit*, Poll.8.24. ⊛ **-αστής**, οῦ, ὁ, *fellow-juryman*, Ar.*V.*197,215, al., *IG*9(1).689.11 (Corcyra, ii B.C.). **-έω**, *act as one's advocate*, A.*Eu.*579, X.*Mem.*1.2.51, etc.; σ. τινί Pl.*Lg.* 937e, D.32.12, al.; Ζεύς σοι τόδε συνδικήσει Zeus *will be* thy *advocate* herein, E.*Med.*158 (lyr.). 2. *to be one of the public advocates* (σύνδικος I. 2), οἱ φυλέται οἱ ᾑρημένοι μοι συνδικεῖν And.1.150, cf. D. 20.153; σ. τῷ δήμῳ Lex ap.Aeschin.1.47; τῷ βασιλικῷ συνδεδικηκώς, = Lat. *advocatus fisci*, D.C.78.13. **-ία**, ἡ, *advocacy*, σ. κακή Pl.*Lg.* 938b; εἰς συνδικίας δημοσίων πραγμάτων *CIG*2768 (Aphrodisias); συνδικίαι καὶ ἱερατεῖαι *IG*5(2).516.11 (Lycosura, i A.D.). ⊛ **-ος**, ὁ, ἡ, (δίκη) *one who helps in a court of justice, advocate*, ἀρωγοὺς ξυνδίκους θ' ἥξω λαβών A.*Supp.*726; μητρὸς τάσδε σ. δρῶν Id.*Eu.*761; μάρτυρες καὶ σύνδικοι Pl.*Lg.*929e; τὸν νόμον σ. ἔχων having the law *on one's side*, Isoc.19.14; σ. ὑπέρ τινος D.18.134: metaph., σ. αὐτῷ Ἰολάου τύμβος Pi.*O.*9.98. 2. after the 30 Tyrants, *judges appointed to determine disputes respecting confiscated property*, Lys.16.7, cf. Harp. s. v. 3. *public advocate, appointed to represent the state* in matters concerning its interests or dignity, at Athens, *IG*2$^2$.1100.55 (ii A.D.), etc.; ᾕρηνται δὲ τῷ νόμῳ σ. καὶ μάλισθ' οἱ δεινοὶ λέγειν ἄνδρες D.20.146, cf. 152; at Sparta, *IG*5(1).65; at Delphi, σ. τοῦ Πυθίου *SIG*825 C5 (ii A.D.); at Palmyra, *OGI*629.14 (ii A.D.); also *advocates chosen by the tribes to defend their interests*, D.23.206, cf. *IG*2$^2$.1196. 17; of certain officials of an ἔρανος, ib.1369.36; of *public advocates* under Valentinian and later, Lib.*Or.*56.20, *Cod.Just.*12.35.18.2a; σ. Ὀξυρυγχίτου (sc. νομοῦ) *PFreib.*11.3 (iv A.D.), etc. 4. *accomplice*, *Tab.Defix.*66. II. *belonging jointly to*, σ. Ἀπόλλωνος καὶ Μοισᾶν κτέανον their *joint* possession, Pi.*P.*1.2. Adv. ξυνδίκως *with joint sentence, jointly*, A.*Ag.*1601.

**συνδι-ογκόομαι**, Pass., *swell up together*, Sor.1.15. ⊛ **-οικέω**, *administer together*, Is.7.9, Plb.6.11$^a$.7; ἀγῶνα *Milet.*1(7).203 a 17 (ii B.C.); τινι *with* one, D.24.160; *bring about together with*, μετὰ τῆς πρεσβείας, ὅπως.. *SIG*353.5 (Ephesus, iv B.C.):—Med., παρὰ τῶν πρυτάνεων, ὅπως.. Thphr.*Char.*21.11 (s. v. l.):—Pass., *share the advantage of*, τὰ φυτὰ τῇ [τῶν μεγάλων δενδρῶν] -ούμενα στερεότητι Sor.1.96. **-όλλῡμι**, *kill together*, E.*Fr.*551:—Pass., *perish together*, Procop.*Arc.*19. **-οράω**, *examine together*, folld. by a relat., Isoc. 4.187. **-ορθόω**, *straighten at the same time, set* a dislocated joint, Hp.*Fract.*4. 2. *correct* or *improve at the same time*, τι Arist.*Top.* 151$^b$7; τί τινι prob. in Men.*Pk.*161; τινα Iamb.*VP*19.92; ἴχνος εἰς ὁμοιότητα Porph.*Plot.*1. **-ορίζομαι**, Pass., *to be determined also*, Str.2.3.1 (where Kramer restores τοῖς περισκίοις καὶ τοῖς ἀμφισκίοις for τοὺς κτλ.): c. dat., Dam.*Pr.*36.

**συνδιπλόω**, *double at the same time*, Gal.19.143.

**συνδισκεύω**, *play at quoits with*, τινι Luc.*DDeor.*14.2.

**σύνδιφρα**, τά, = *bisellia*, *IGRom.*4.210 (Ilium).

**συνδιψάω**, *thirst along with*, διψῶντι Arist.*EE*1240$^a$38.

**συνδῐώκω**, *chase away together, join in the chase*, Th.1.135, 8.17, *PEnteux.*70.5 (iii B.C.), Plb.1.17.13, etc.:—Pass., *to be constrained*, ὑπὸ τῆς ἀνάγκης Longin.43.5; τοῦ πάθους τὸ συνδεδιωγμένον *hurry, vehemence*, Id.21.1; so τόνοι καὶ ῥυθμοὶ συνδεδ. Phld.*Mus.* p.22 K.; συνδεδ. σφυγμός Herod.Med. in *Rh.Mus.*58.99; πόνοι συνδεδ. ὑπὸ τῆς πνιγὸς ἀμαυροῦνται Aret.*SA*1.7. II. as law-term, *join in the prosecution*, Lex ap.D.43.57, etc.

**συνδίωξις** [δῐ], εως, ἡ, *joint pursuit*, Sch.D *Il.*17.597.

**συνδοκέω**, *seem to one as to another, seem good also*, ταῦτα κἀμοὶ συνδοκεῖ Ar.*Av.*811; εἴ τοι δοκεῖ σφῷν ταῦτα, κἀμοὶ ξυνδοκεῖ ib.1630, cf. *Lys.*167; ξυνεδόκει τοῖς ἄλλοις ξυμμάχοις ταῦτα Th.8.84; ὅ τι ἂν καὶ τοῖς ἄλλοις.. ξυνδοκῇ Id.6.44; εἴ σοι συνδοκεῖ ὅπερ ἐμοί Pl.*Prt.* 340b; πᾶσι συνέδοξε ταῦτα X.*Cyr.*2.2.28; ἆρ' οὖν σοι συνδοκεῖ μέτριος χρόνος; Pl.*R.*460e; διάνοιαν ἣ σ. τοῖς πολλοῖς Arist.*Pol.*1273$^a$23; κἀμοὶ τοῦτο οὕτω περὶ αὐτοῦ σ. Pl.*Sph.*235b; συνεδόκει ἡμῖν.. ταῦτα Id.*Euthd.*289b: abs., συνεδόκει ib.c. 2. more freq. impers., *it seems good also*, σοὶ δὲ συνδοκεῖν χρεών E.*IT*71; εἰ ξυνδοκοίη τοῖσιν ἄλλοις ὀρνέοις Ar.*Av.*197; ἦ καὶ σοὶ συνδοκεῖ οὕτως; Pl.*Prt.* 331b; σ. ὅτι.. Id.*Hp.Ma.*283b: folld. by inf., X.*Cyr.*1.6.8; συνέδοξε.. τὸν ἐλάττονα αἱρετέον (sc. εἶναι) Pl.*Ti.*75c. 3. part., οὐκ ἐμοὶ -οῦντα πεπόνθατε *not with my approval*, D.H.6.44; but the part. is mostly used abs. like ἐξόν, παρόν, etc., συνδοκοῦν ἅπασιν ἡμῖν *since* we all *agree*, X.*HG*2.3.51; συνδόξαν τῷ πατρὶ καὶ τῇ μητρὶ *since* the father and mother *approved*, Id.*Cyr.*8.5.28, cf. 8.1.8. b. Plato has also part. pf. Pass., λόγος τοῖς ἐπιεικεστάτοις συνδεδογμένος *in which* they *also agree*, *Lg.*659d, cf. 719c, *Phdr.*267d; also of persons, συνδεδογμένοι τινί *of like opinion with* him, Numen.ap.Eus.*PE* 14.5. II. apparently = δοκέω, οὕτω μοι συνέδοξεν *BCH*56.293 (Stobi, ii/iii A.D.).

⊛ **συνδοκῐμάζω**, *examine along with* or *together*, Pl.*Tht.*197b, Isoc. 2.29; εἴτε.., εἴτε.. Pl.*Ti.*20d. 2. *approve*, γνώμην J.*AJ*20.2.2; τὰ τοπικὰ τῶν βοηθημάτων Sor.2.15.

**συνδοκτικόν**· συνδεδογμένον, Hsch.; gloss on ἡδικτόν, Id.

**συνδονέω**, *shake together*, Hp.*Ep.*23, Androm.ap.Gal.14.39; ἀὴρ καὶ δένδρα -εῖτο τοῖς πνεύμασι Procop.Gaz. p.135 B. [In Hp. l.c. the sense points rather to συνδινέω, in Gal.18(1).542 to συνδουμένης fr. συνδέω.]

**συνδοξάζω**, *join in approving*, νόμοι συνδεδοξασμένοι ὑπὸ πάντων Arist.*Pol.*1310$^a$15. 2. *agree with*, τῷ σώματι Plot.1.2.3, Porph. ap.Stob.3.1.123, Marin.*Procl.*21. II. *glorify* or *extol jointly*, in Pass., *Ep.Rom.*8.17.

**σύνδορπος**, ον, = σύνδειπνος, Lyc.135.

**συνδορῠφορέω**, *constipo*, Gloss.

**σύνδοσις**, εως, ἡ, *effusion*, ὑγρῶν κατὰ κοιλίην Hp.*Aph.*4.62. 2. *transference* of disease, ἐς πνεύμονα Aret.*SA*1.7, cf. *CD*2.2. 3. *remission*, Id.*CA*2.11. 4. *influx* of population, ἡ ἔξωθεν σ. Lyd.*Mens.*4.73.

**συνδοτικός**, ή, όν, *apt to give way*, Hp.*Art.*47.

**συνδουλ-εύω**, *to be a fellow-slave*, Din.*Fr.*89.32; τινι *with* one, E. *Hec.*204 (lyr.). ⊛ **-ος**, ὁ, ἡ, *fellow-slave*, masc., Id.*Ion* 1109, Ar.*Pax* 745 (anap.), Theopomp.Com.32.8, Lys.*Fr.*331 S., Herod.5.56, *Ev.Matt.* 18.29, etc.; fem., Hdt.2.134, E.*Med.*65, etc.; also fem. συνδούλη, Hdt.1.110, Babr.3.6. 2. metaph. in *NT*, *Ep.Col.*1.7, *Apoc.*6.11, al. (The statement of Moeris p.273 P., ὁμόδουλος Ἀττικῶς, σύνδουλος Ἑλληνικῶς, is incorrect: Poll.3.82 distinguishes σ. 'slave of the same master' fr. ὁμόδουλος 'companion in slavery'.)

**συνδράσσω**, *clutch*, ἄορ συνέδραξε Q.S.13.185:—Med., c. gen., Sch.Aristid.3.325.

**συνδράω**, *do along with* or *together, help in doing*, τοῖς δρῶσι καὶ συνδρῶσιν S.*El.*498 (lyr.), cf. 1025, Th.6.64; σ. τινί τι E.*Andr.*40; σ. αἷμα καὶ φόνον *help in* bloodshed and murder, Id.*Or.*406; τὸ συνδρῶν.. χρέος the *joint* necessity, Id.*Andr.*337.

**συνδρήστειρα**, ἡ, Ion. for *συνδράστειρα, *joint-agent, assistant*, σύν τε δρήστειρα πέλεσθαι A.R.3.700.

⊛ **συνδρομ-άς**, άδος, pecul. fem. of σύνδρομος, πέτραι αἱ σ., = συμπληγάδες, E.*IT*421 (lyr.); Κυάνεαι σ. Theoc.13.22; μέσας τέρμασιν ἄκροις συνδρομάδας (two) mean *proportionals* to extremes, Eratosth. 35.6. ⊛ **-ή**, ἡ, *tumultuous concourse* of people, Cephisod.ap.Arist. *Rh.*1411$^a$29, Plb.1.67.2 (pl.), Lxx *Ju.*10.18, *Act.Ap.*21.30; ἐπί τινα, κατά τινων, D.S.3.71, 15.90; σ. τῶν ὄχλων εἰς τὴν ἐκκλησίαν Posidon. 36 J.; ἀπὸ συνδρομῆς *tumultuously*, D.S.13.87. 2. of things, στενὴ πορθμοῦ σ. (cf. foreg.) Lyc.649; σ. αἵματος εἰς τὸν πληγέντα τόπον *a determination* of blood, Arist.*Pr.*889$^b$30; σ. θερμοῦ Plu.2. 695a; *combination*, κέκληται ἡ σ. τούτων καυλός Sor.1.9; σ. ἀγαθῶν Str.5.3.7; ἡ σ. τοῦ λόγου its *conclusion, moral*, *AP*9.203 (Phot. or Leo Phil.); esp. Medic., *concurrence* of symptoms, 'clinical picture', Gal. 11.59, Aret.*CA*1.10. b. *contraction* of a muscle, Antyll.ap.Orib. 45.15.5, *Cat.Cod.Astr.*8(3).147 (pl.); of the prepuce, Paul.Aeg.6. 55. 3. in Rhet., *provisional concession* of an adversary's standpoint, Hermog.*Id.*2.1,7, Aristid.*Rh.*1 p.491 S. **-ος**, ον, *running together, meeting*, σ. πέτραι, = συνδρομάδες, Pi.*P.*4.208; σύνδρομα πετράων A.R.2.346; of Time, τὴν ὥραν τὴν τοῦ τρυγᾶν Ἀρκτούρῳ σ. *coincident with*, Pl.*Lg.*844e, cf. *APl.*4.276 (Bianor). 2. Subst., *a place where several roads meet*, Nearch.ap.Str.15.1.43. II. *running along with, following close*, ἀήτην οὔριον.. σ. ἐς λιμένας *AP*6.251 (Phil.), etc.; σ. Ἀρτέμιδος Call.*Lav.Pall.*110. Adv., ἴχνος -μως ῥινηλατεῖν A.*Ag.*1184; so σύνδρομά τινι πορεύεσθαι to keep *up with* in *running*, Pl.*Plt.*266c. 2. metaph., *in agreement with*, λογίοις Nic. Dam.*Fr.*52 J.

**συνδρωπᾰκίζω**, = Lat. *compilo*, Dosith. p.435 K.

⊛ **συνδῠ-άζω**:—Pass., aor. -εδυάσθην Arist.*GA*724$^b$15: pf. συνδεδύασμαι ib.729$^b$30:—*join one and one, couple*, Id.*EN*1131$^b$8; τι πρός τι Id.*Pol.*1321$^a$18:—Pass., *to be taken two at a time*, ib.1300$^a$19, 1317$^a$ 1, Gal.6.214; *to be coupled with* another person or thing, Arist. *Top.*118$^b$15: abs., *to be coupled with something else*, Id.*Rh.*1377$^a$ 30. 2. Pass., freq. of marriage or sexual intercourse, *pair, copulate*, Id.*Pol.*1252$^a$26, etc.; σ. τῷ τυχόντι Id.*EE*1242$^a$24; esp. of animals, X.*Cyn.*5.6, Arist.*HA*539$^b$9, al.: c. dat., συνδυασθέντες ἄρρην θηλείᾳ καὶ θήλεια ἄρρενι Pl.*Lg.*840d, cf. Arist.*HA*612$^b$33, *GA*746$^b$12, al. II. intr. in Act., *join oneself with, combine with*, of persons and things, τινι Plb.4.38.6, S.E.*M.*9.254: abs., *combine*, Plb.30.5. 8. III. as law-term, συνδυάζεσθαί τινι *to be in collusion with* any one, Just.*Nov.*130.7; cf. συνδυασμός II. **-αίνω**, *double*, Hp.ap. Gal.19.143 (written συνδεαίν-). **-άς**, άδος, ἡ, *paired*, σ. [ἄλοχος] one's *wedded wife*, E.*Alc.*473 (lyr.). **-ασμός**, ὁ, *a being taken two together*, πάντες οἱ ἐνδεχόμενοι σ. all possible *combinations of one and one* (i.e. of *n* things two at a time), Arist.*Pol.*1290$^b$35, cf. 1294$^b$ 2. 2. *mating, copulation*, Hp.*Mul.*2.146 vulg. (om. Littré), Arist. *Pol.*1335$^a$11; esp. of animals, Id.*HA*539$^b$26, al.; ἐκ συνδυασμοῦ γίνεσθαι ib.539$^a$27; σ. πρὸς τὴν θήλειαν Id.*GA*720$^b$29; τὸ ὄργανον τὸ πρὸς τὸν σ. ib.717$^b$14. II. in Law, *collusion*, *PTeb.*703.274 (iii B.C.), *Gloss.* **-αστικός**, ή, όν, *disposed to live in pairs*, ἄνθρωπος γὰρ τῇ φύσει συνδυαστικὸν μᾶλλον ἢ πολιτικόν Arist.*EN*1162$^a$17, cf. Hierocl. p.52 A.

**συνδῠναστεύω**, *rule* or *have chief power along with*, αὐτῷ Nic.Dam. *Fr.*80 J.

**συνδύνω**, v. συνδύομαι.

⊛ **σύνδυο**, οἱ, αἱ, τά, *two together, two and two, in pairs*, *h.Ven.*74, Pi. *P.*3.81, Hdt.4.66, Hyp.*Eux.*16, Pl.*Lg.*962e, *IG*2$^2$.1671.21 (iv B.C.), etc.; ἀνὰ σύνδυο Gal.6.216; κατὰ σύνδυο ib.214, *UP*15.4; σύνδυο unaltered in dat., Plb.8.4.2.—For Il.10.224, v. συνέρχομαι I.

**συνδύομαι**, *sink together*, metaph., M.Ant.8.45: Act. in form -δύνω, *set together with*, τῷ ἡλίῳ Thphr.*Sign.*2, Autol.1.6: fut. συνδύσεται ibid.: aor. 2 inf. συνδῦναι ib.8. II. μετὰ τῶν.. μηλονόμων συνδεδυμένων τούτοις (sc. τοῖς λῃσταῖς) *in league* with them, *PMasp.* 2 iii 13 (vi A.D.); unless = συνδεδεμένων, *constrained, forced* by them.

**συνδυστῠχέω**, *share in misfortune*, E.*Or.*1099, Is.6.1.

**συνδώδεκα**, οἱ, αἱ, τά, *twelve in all*, E.*Tr.*1076 (lyr.).

**συνδωρέομαι**, *present at the same time*, Polyaen.8.16.6 (v.l. συνεχαρίσατο).

**συνεᾰρίζω**, *pass the spring with*, τισι Plu.2.959c.

**συνεγγ-ίζω**, *draw near*, Plb.1.23.8; τινι *to* a person or thing, Id.3.69.13, D.S.3.72, 17.41; –ιζούσης τῆς ἀποτέξεως Sor.1.56; –ίζοντος τοῦ ἡλίου Gem.17.28; *approximate*, τῇ τῶν ἀγαθῶν φύσει *Stoic.* 1.48; τῇ ἀληθείᾳ Hipparch.1.10.8, cf. Phld.*Rh.*1.362 S.; τῇ μανίᾳ Id.*Mus.* p.99 K.; abs. (sc. τῇ σοφίᾳ), Id.*Ir.* p.74 W.; θέρους τοῦ –ίζοντος τῷ φθινοπώρῳ in the part of summer *verging on* autumn, Dsc.2.77; σ. τῇ ἀκμῇ *nearing* the prime of life, Marcellin.*Puls.*339. ※ **–ισμός**, ὁ, *approach, nearness*, of constellations, Str.3.5.9, Ptol.*Geog.*1.13.1, etc.; τῆς ἀποτέξεως Sor.1.66; πρὸς τὴν ἀρετήν Arr.*Epict.*1.4.8.

**συνεγγράφω** [ᾰ], *register* or *enter along with*, εἰς θεούς Plu.2.763e; τῷ ψηφίσματι συνεγγραφήσονται D.H.6.84; τοῖς κατ' ἔτος ἐφήβοις συνεγγραφόμενοι *PSI*10.1160.4 (i B.C.).

**συνεγγῠ-άω**, *join in betrothing*, Plu.*Cat.Mi.*25:—Med., *join in warranting*, τι Ph.2.60: abs., *PHib.*1.94.16 (iii B.C.). **–η**, ἡ, Arc. **συνιγγύα**, *pledge, mortgage*, *SIG*306.41 (Tegea, iv B.C.).

**σύνεγγυς**, Adv. (freq. used like an Adj.): 1. of Place, *near*, Hp.*Art.*41, Th.4.24, X.*HG*6.5.17, etc.; *near at hand*, *PEnteux.*27.5 (iii B.C.); σ. ἀλλήλων *quite close* one to another, Arist.*HA*541$^a$8, etc.; τὸ μὴ σ. non-*proximity*, Id.*Pol.*1280$^b$24; πάντα τὰ σ. πράγματα all his *local* interests, *OGI*229.94 (Smyrna, iii B.C.): Sup. συνέγγιστα Plu.2.619d, Vett.Val.341.23. 2. of Time, Arist.*Rh.* 1382$^a$25. 3. of relationship, descent, Id.*EN*1162$^a$3, al. 4. of Quality, οἱ σ. persons *of similar rank*, Id.*Pol.*1296$^a$5; τὰ σ. τοῖς ὑπάρχουσιν *closely allied* to the real qualities, Id.*Rh.*1367$^a$33, cf. 1386$^b$17; σ. εἰσὶ τοῖς ὀστοῖς..ὄνυχές τε καὶ ὅπλαι κτλ. Id.*PA*655$^b$2, cf. 681$^a$15, *Pol.*1272$^b$27; τὰ σ., opp. τὰ πολὺ διεστῶτα, Id.*Top.*116$^a$7, cf. *APr.*66$^a$37; καὶ τούτοις ἄλλα ὀνόματα σ. (= ὅμοια) Id.*Pol.*1321$^b$40, cf. *EN*1111$^b$20.

**συνεγείρω**, *help in raising*, κτῆνος Ps.-Phoc.140; *raise also*, νεκρούς *Ep.Eph.*2.6; *help in stirring up*, θρήνους Plu.2.117c:—Pass., *rise together*, Lxx *Is.*14.9, *Ep.Col.*2.12, etc.; of an invalid, *revive*, Aristid. *Or.*48(24).43.

**συνεγ-καίω**, aor. –έκαυσα, *help to brand*, κτήνη *IG*11(2).287 *A* 58 (Delos, iii B.C.). **–κηδεύω**, *bury as well*, prob. rest. in *CIG* (add.) 4303$h^8$ (Lycia). **–κλίνω** [ῑ], in Pass., *collapse completely*, D.S.3.26. II. Act., *write as an enclitic*, Sch.Th.1.11: hence **συνεγκλῐτικός**, ή, όν, *enclitic*, Hdn.Gr.1.551, cf. *AB*1142. **–κωμιάζω**, *collaudo*, *Gloss.*

**συνέδρ-α**, ἡ, = συνεδρεία, *IG*9(1).694.95 (Corc., ii B.C.); = Lat. *statio*, Hsch. **–εία**, ἡ, *sitting as* σύνεδροι or *in conference, session, meeting*, Aeschin.3.93,94, *SIG*330.34 (Ilium, iv B.C.), *PFrankf.*7$^v$.14 (iii B.C.), *PTeb.*43.30, 61(*b*).223, 72.155,171 (ii B.C.); ἀποχωροῦντα ἀπὸ τῆς σ. withdrawing from the *circle of friends*, X.*Mem.*4.2.3; ἡ μετὰ τῶν φίλων σ. his *conference* with his friends, Plb.18.54.2; παρακληθεὶς ἐπὶ συνεδρείαν Phld.*Vit.* p.31 J.; coupled with συμβουλή, *Vit. Philonid.* p.10 C.; *sitting* of the Roman Senate, D.C.55.3. II. *tenure of office of* σύνεδρος, *OGI*504.7, 507.11 (Aezani, ii A.D.). III. v. συνεδρία. (Written –ία in X. and Aeschin. ll. cc., *SIG* l. c. (gen. pl. –ιων), Phld.*Rh.*1.378 S., but –εία in other Pap. from iii B.C., also *OGI* ll. cc. and codd. of Plb. and D.C. ll. cc.) ※ **–εύω**, (σύνεδρος) *sit in council*, Ἀθήνησι Aeschin.3.91, cf. 98; οἱ συνεδρεύοντες *members of council*, D.17.15, cf. Aeschin.3.74, *PPetr.*3 p.30 (iii B.C.), *PTeb.*701.274 (iii B.C.), *OGI*56.6 (Canopus, iii B.C.), *UPZ*110.140 (ii B.C.), etc. 2. *hold a council, consult, deliberate*, D.10.6, Plb. 2.26.4, Onos.3.1; σ. τινί *consult with, sit in council with*, Plb.3.68.15; σκεψάμενος μετὰ τῶν –όντων Ἀρποκρατίωνι στρατηγῷ *PSI*10.1100.2 (ii A.D.); τὸν Ἀπόλλω –οντα τῷ θεῷ τῷδε Jul.*Or.*4.135d; σ. τῷ λόγῳ *to be present at, take part in* a discussion, Arist.*Metaph.*987$^a$2. 3. τὰ –όμενα *orders in council, decrees of the senate*, D.H.10.13. II. *lie in ambush together*, Hsch. s. v. συνελόχισε. 2. of troops, *close up, draw together*, Ascl.*Tact.*3.6. III. metaph., *attend, accompany, be present together*, of symptoms, Sor.2.10, Gal.7.627, 15.740, Aët.15.10: generally, *inhere in, be a constituent of*, Phld.*Sign.*20, Longin.10.1. 2. Gramm., τὰ συνεδρεύοντα αὐτοῖς their *accompanying relations*, D.H.*Comp.*5, cf. 16. **–ία**, ἡ, *sitting together*, of birds from whose position favourable omens were drawn, A.*Pr.*492 (pl.); τὰς διεδρείας (v.l. διέδρας, διεδρίας) καὶ τὰς συνεδρείας (v.l. συνεδρίας) οἱ μάντεις λαμβάνουσι· δίεδρα μὲν τὰ πολέμια τιθέντες, σύνεδρα δὲ τὰ εἰρηνεύοντα πρὸς ἄλληλα Arist.*HA*608$^b$28, cf. *EE*1236$^b$10. (The form συνεδρία [ῐ] is corroborated by the metre in A. l. c., and should perh. be restd. in Arist. ll. cc.; but cf. συνεδρεία.) **–ιάζω**, = συνεδρεύω, Lxx *Pr.*3.32. **–ιακός**, ή, όν, *governed by a* συνέδριον, πολιτεία Plb. 31.2.12. **–ιάομαι**, poet. for συνεδρεύω, A.R.1.328. ※ **–ιον**, τό, *council*, σ. κατασκευάζειν, συνάγειν, Pl.*Prt.*317d, Aeschin.3.89; ὁμογνώμονες τοῦ σ. πάντες *IG*14.952.28 (Acragas, iii B.C.); *meeting*, μεταπεμφθέντων εἰς κοινὸν σ. τῶν .. δεκανῶν *PTeb.*27.31 (ii B.C.); of a *council of war*, X.*HG*1.1.31, etc.; of the Areopagus, Aeschin.1.91, Din.1.54; τὰ σ., of the 600 together with the Areopagus, *IG*2$^2$. 3640; of a *board of trade*, D.58.8; of the Roman *Senate*, Plb.1.11.1, etc.; the Carthaginian *Senate*, Id.1.31.8; the Jewish *Sanhedrin*, *Ev.Matt.*5.22, etc. (also of local *Councils* attached to synagogues, ib.10.17, *Ev.Marc.*13.9, *Cod.Just.*1.9.17); the *Senate* at Constantinople, Lib.*Or.*20.37; τὸ σεμνότατον σ. τῆς γερουσίας, at Thasos, *IG*12(8).388; τὸ σ. σ. τῶν γερόντων *IGRom.*4.782 (Apamea); τὸ χωρίον ἐν ᾧ σ. ἦν αὐτῷ τῶν πολιτῶν Gal.6.332; freq. of a *congress* of Allies or Confederates, Hdt.8.56,75, X.*HG*7.1.39, D.18.22, Aeschin. 2.70, 3.58, D.S.16.89, etc.; τὸ σ. τῶν Ἑλλάνων *IG*12(3).1259.4 (Smyrna, iv B.C.); ἁμῶν (sc. τῶν Ἀμφικτιόνων) *OGI*234.17 (Delph., iii B.C.), cf. *SIG*613.10 (ibid., ii B.C.); τὸ Ἑλληνικὸν σ. Plu.*Arist.* 19. 2. *place of meeting, council-chamber*, Hdt.8.79, X.*HG*2.4.23, *POxy.*717.8 (i B.C.); ἐν σ. *in court*, Lys.9.6; ἐνεπρήσθη τὰ σ. τῶν Πυθαγορείων Plb.2.39.1. **–ίτης** [ῑ], ου, ὁ, *fellow-officer of the Guard*, σ. ὢν αὐτῷ πρὸ τῶν βασιλείων θυρῶν Nic.Dam.*Fr.*3 J. ※ **–ος**, ον, (ἕδρα) *sitting with in council*, of persons, Hdt.3.34, Ps.-E.*IA*192 (lyr.); ἐκ.. συνέδρου καὶ τυραννικοῦ κύκλου, = ἐκ κύκλου τῶν συνεδρευόντων τυράννων, S.*Aj.*749. 2. of birds, *sitting together, friendly*, Arist.*HA*608$^b$29. II. as Subst., σ., ὁ, ἡ, *one who sits with others, assessor, coadjutor*, Δίκη ξ. Ζηνὸς..νόμοις S.*OC*1382; ξύνεδροι *select commissioners*, Th.4.22, cf. 5.86, *SIG*273.2 (Milet., iv B.C.), *IG*2$^2$. 686.5 (iii B.C.); *delegates to the assembly* of the second Athenian league, ib.43.44 (iv B.C.), al., Isoc.8.29, Jusj.ap.D.24.150. 2. in pl., = βουλή, *IG*12(9).234.40 (Eretria, ii B.C.); γνώμη συνέδρων *OGI*213.1 (Didyma, iv/iii B.C.); οἱ σ. τῶν νησιωτῶν ib.40.1 (iii B.C.).

**συνεέργᾰθον**, **συνεέργω**, v. συνέργω.

**συνεζευγμένως**, Adv. part. pf. Pass., *by pairs*, Sch.Ar.*Av.*305.

**συνέζομαι**, Med., *sit together*, in fut. inf. συνεδεῖσθαι, Hsch., Phot. II. *to be assessor*, βήματι *Epigr.Gr.*395.4 (Amasia).

**συνεθέλω**, *have the same wish, consent*, Antipho 3.2.8, X.*Eq.Mag.* 9.7; τινι to a thing, Aen.Tact.11.13; poet. **συνθέλω**, S.*OC*1344, *Fr.*489, E.*HF*832, also in Arist.*EN*1167$^a$1: fut. συνθελήσω E.*Tr.* 62.

**συνεθ-ίζω**, *accustom*, ἕτερον ἑτέρῳ Pl.*R.*589a; σ. τινὰ ποιεῖν τι *accustom* him to do.., D.13.13, Aeschin.1.24, etc.; σ. [τὰ τέκνα] πρὸς τὰ ψύχη *accustom* them to bear cold, Arist.*Pol.*1336$^a$13, cf. *HA*567$^a$6; *make customary*, Phld.*Mus.* p.107 K.:—Pass., *become used* or *habituated*, and in aor. 1 and pf. *to have become so*, Th.4.34, Pl.*Tht.*146b, *Plt.*285a, Arist.*Pol.*1340$^a$16, Sor.1.89: c. inf., συνειθίσθην ποιεῖν τι Isoc.2.38, X.*Mem.*3.14.6; τινι to a thing, Arist.*Pr.* 917$^a$15, Phld.*Mus.* p.102 K.: impers., συνειθισμένον ἦν *it had become the custom*, Lys.1.10. II. intr. in Act., *grow accustomed*, ἐν ταῖς ἁπλαῖς..διαίταις Epicur.*Ep.*3 p.64 U., cf. p.60 U. **–ισμός**, ὁ, *habituation*, Plot.1.3.3, Jul.*Or.*8.248a. **–ιστέον**, *one must accustom oneself*, c. inf., Pl.*R.*520c. II. *one must accustom*, πρὸς ταῦτα σ. αὐτούς, folld. by infs., Plu.2.522d.

**συνειδέναι**, v. σύνοιδα.

**συνείδησις**, εως, ἡ, *knowledge shared with another*, τῶν ἀλγημάτων (in a midwife) Sor.1.4. 2. *communication, information*, εὑρήσεις σ. *PPar.* p.422 (ii A.D.); σ. εἰσήνεγκαν τοῖς κολλήγαις αὐτῶν *POxy.* 123.13 (iii/iv A.D.). 3. *knowledge*, λῦε ταῦτα πάντα μὴ διαλείψας ἀγαθῇ σ. (v.l. ἀγαθῇ τύχῃ) Hp.*Ep.*1. 4. *consciousness, awareness*, [τῆς αὐτοῦ συστάσεως] Chrysipp.*Stoic.*3.43, cf. Phld.*Rh.*2.140 S., 2*Ep.Cor.*4.2, 5.11, 1*Ep.Pet.*2.19; τῆς κακοπραγμοσύνης Democr.297, cf. D.S.4.65, *Ep.Hebr.*10.2; κατὰ συνείδησιν ἀτάραχοι διαμενοῦσι Hero *Bel.*73; *inner consciousness*, ἐν σ. σου βασιλέα μὴ καταράσῃ Lxx *Ec.*10.20; in 1*Ep.Cor.*8.7 συνειδήσει is f.l. for συνηθείᾳ. 5. *consciousness of right* or *wrong doing, conscience*, Periander and Bias ap. Stob.3.24.11,12, Luc.*Am.*49; ἐὰν ἐγκλήματός τινος ἔχῃ σ. Anon. *Oxy.*218(*a*) ii 19; βροτοῖς ἅπασιν ἡ σ. θεός Men.*Mon.*654, cf. Lxx *Wi.*17.11, D.H.*Th.*8 (but perh. interpol.); σ. ἀγαθή *Act.Ap.*23.1; ἀπρόσκοπος πρὸς τὸν θεόν ib.24.16; καθαρά 1*Ep.Ti.*3.9, *POsl.*17.10 (ii A.D.); κολαζομένους κατὰ συνείδησιν Vett.Val.210.1; θλειβομένη τῇ σ. περὶ ὧν ἐνοσφίσατο *PRyl.*116.9 (ii A.D.); τὸν..θεὸν κεχολωμένον ἔχοιτο καὶ τὴν ἰδίαν σ. *Ath.Mitt.*24.237 (Thyatira); *conscientiousness*, *Arch.Pap.*3.418.13 (vi A.D.).—Senses 4 and 5 sts. run one into the other, v. 1*Ep.Cor.*8.7, 10.27 sq. 6. *complicity, guilt, crime*, περὶ τοῦ πεφημίσθαι αὐτὴν ἐν σ. τοιαύτῃ *Supp.Epigr.*4.648.13 (Lydia, ii A.D.).

**συνεῖδον**, inf. –ιδεῖν, aor. 2 of συνοράω.

**συνειδοποιέομαι**, Pass., *to be specified together with*, Dam.*Pr.*102.

**συνεικάζω**, *bring into the estimate*, Ptol.*Tetr.*120. II. *copy, mimic*, Ath.9.391b.

**συνεικανα**· σύνοδος, Hsch. (fort. Dor. συνσκανία, v. συσκ–).

**συνείκοσι**, only in form ξυνεείκοσι (q. v.).

**συνείκω** (A), *give way, yield*, τῷ καιρῷ Plb.32.13.3, cf. 5.71.10; of things, σ. τὸ ξύλον Anon.ap.Suid., cf. D.S.2.8, Dsc.5.74, Sor.2.63 (συνήκει cod.), *Fract.*6.

**συνείκω** (B), 3 sg. συνείκει (–κη cod.)· συμφέρει, Hsch.: οὐ μὴ συνείκῃ *IG*4.156.2 (Aegina, iv B.C.): but the latter form may be from συνενείκῃ aor. of συμφέρω.

**συνείκω** (C), late spelling (s.v.l.) of Dor. συνίκω = συνήκω, ὅσα ποτὶ τὸ κοινὸν συν[ε]ίκει the moneys which *accrue to*.., *IG*9(1).694. 121 (Corc., ii B.C.).

**συνειλᾰπινάζω**, *feast with* or *together*, Nonn.*D.*11.76.

※ **συνειλ-έω**, *crowd together*, τὰ τέκνα καὶ τὰς γυναῖκας ἐς τοὺς νεωσοίκους συνειλήσας Hdt.3.45; also of things, *bind together*, ῥάβδους Id.4.67:—Pass., *to be crowded* or *pressed together*, εἰς ἔλαττον into less compass, X.*HG*7.2.8; περὶ τὸν ναόν J.*BJ*5.3.1: abs., Plu. *Alex.*60 (so ἑαυτὸν συνειλήσας, of the hedgehog, Ael.*NA*6.64); τροφὴ συνειληθεῖσα *compressed*, Thphr.*CP*3.14.8; κύστις σ. εἰς ἑωυτήν Aret.*SD*1.7; ἐς κυκεῶνα πάντα συνειλέονται Luc.*Vit.Auct.* 14: metaph., σ. ἀπορίᾳ S.E.*M.*7.304. **–ησις**, εως, ἡ, *rolling oneself up*, of a hedgehog, Ael.*NA*6.64; *rolling up*, Sch.Arat.156; *synthesis*, ἀνάπλωσις καὶ σ. Iamb.*Comm.Math.*12.

**συνειλίσσω**, v. συνελίσσω. **συνείλλω**, v. συνίλλω.

**συνειλύω**, *roll together*, *EM*333.42.

⊛ **συνείμαρται**, (μείρομαι) *has been determined by fate*, Aristid.*Or.*24 (44).56; συνειμαρμένα *jointly determined by fate*, Plu.2.569f, cf. Lyd.*Mens.*4.81.

⊛ **σύνειμι** (εἰμί *sum*), fut. -έσομαι, Dor. fut. -εσσέομαι *SIG*526.19 (Itanos, iii B.C.): Elean 3 pl. pres. opt. συνέαν ib.9 (Olympia, vi B.C.):—*to be with*, *be joined with*, ἔμελλον ἔτι ξυνέσεσθαι ὀϊζυῖ Od.7.270; ξ. ὀνείρασιν *to be haunted by* dreams, A.*Pers.*177; σ. νόσῳ, = νοσεῖν, S.*OT*303; κακοῖς πολλοῖς ξυνοῦσα *acquainted with*.., Id.*El.*600; τῷ κόπῳ ξ. Ar.*Pl.*321 (lyr.); γνώμαις καὶ μερίμναις Id.*Nu.*1404; [πράγμασι] *to be engaged in* business, Id.*Ra.*959; ξ. ᾧπερ ἥδεσθον βίῳ Id.*Fr.*583; [μέρει πολέμου] Th.4.18; τρυφερῷ βίῳ σ. Men.*Kith.Fr.*1.9; γεωργίᾳ σ. X.*Oec.*15.12; εὐωχίαις, ἡδοναῖς, δείμασι, Pl.*R.*586a,b, *Lg.*791b; ἀπορίᾳ, εὐδαιμονίᾳ, Luc.*Sat.*11, *Bis Acc.*3: reversely, ὅτῳ τὸ μὴ καλὸν ξύνεστι S.*Ant.*372 (lyr.); ὅτῳ γάμοι ξυνόντες ηὑρέθησαν ἀνόσιοι Id.*OC*946; ἐμοὶ ξύνεστιν ἐλπίς E.*Tr.*682; εἴ μοι ξυνείη.. μοῖρα S.*OT*863 (lyr.): abs., ἆται ἀεὶ ξυνοῦσαι Id.*OC*1244 (lyr.); τὰ πάλαι νοσήματα ξυνόντα Id.*Aj.*338; ὁ χρόνος ξυνὼν μακρὸς Id.*OC*7. II. *have intercourse with*, *live with*, τοῖς φονεῦσι τοῦ πατρός Id.*El.*264, cf. E.*Fr.*897.7 (anap.), etc.; μετά τινος Ar.*Pl.*504, Pl.*Smp.*195b, etc.; σ. ἐμαυτῷ *live alone*, X.*Hier.*6.2; φιλικῶς, οἰκείως ξ. τινί, Id.*An.*6.6.35, *HG*7.3.5; σ. ἀλλήλοις ἐν τῷ πότῳ Pl.*Prt.*347c: also ξυνῆμεν.. ἐγώ τε καὶ σύ Ar.*V.*236; οἱ συνόντες τινί, of fellow-travellers, *Act.Ap.*22.11: abs., τὸν νεανίσκον συνὼν διέφθορεν Eup.337. 2. of a woman, *live with* a husband, = συνοικέω, Hdt.4.9, S.*El.*276,611, etc.; and then, merely, *have sexual intercourse*, Ar.*Ec.*619 (anap.), Arist.*Pol.*1262$^a$33, *PSI*1.64.19 (i B.C.), etc.; of animals, *copulate*, Arist.*HA*540$^a$13. 3. *attend*, *associate with*, a teacher, X.*Mem.*1.2.8,24, etc.; also of the teacher, Id.*Cyr.*3.1.14, Pl.*Tht.*151a, etc.; of a fellow-pupil, ἐμοὶ συνών περὶ μαθήματα Gal.16.684; also of a *follower* in war, ξ. Βρασίδᾳ Ar.*V.*475 (lyr.); οἱ συνόντες *followers*, *partisans*, *associates*, *disciples*, Antipho 5.68, Pl.*Ap.*25e, *Tht.*168a, al.; *guests*, Ar.*V.*1300, X.*Smp.*1.15, etc.; *comrades* in war, Id.*Cyr.*8.2.2; Δίκη ξυνοῦσα φωτί *attending on*, *favouring*, A.*Th.*671, cf. S.*OT*275, etc.; *accompany*, οὐδὲ τῷ ὀρέγεσθαι τὸ εὔκαιρον σύνεστι Sor.1.38, cf. 26. 4. *have dealings with*, τινι Th.4.83; σ. ἵπποις *have to do with* them, Pl.*Ap.*25b. 5. *take part in*, *attend*, συνόδοις *Rev.Arch.*22(1925).62 (Callatis); ὑπογραψάντων πάντων τῶν συνόντων all the *members* of the σύνοδος, *Sammelb.*7457.48 (ii B.C.). 6. abs., αἴ κα.. μὴ συννῇ (= συνῇ) γνήσια τέκνα if there *are* not *in addition* children of the blood, *Leg.Gort.*10.41; ὅπου κεφαλαλγία σύνεστι Gal.16.662. III. of heavenly bodies, *to be in conjunction*, Man.1.78, al., Gal.19.552.

⊛ **σύνειμι**, (εἶμι *ibo*) *go* or *come together*, *assemble*, ἐς χῶρον ἕνα ξυνιόντες ἵκοντο Il.4.446; ἐς τὠυτό Hdt.1.62; ἐς τὸν Ἰσθμόν Th.2.10, cf. *SIG*835*A* 4 (Delph., ii A.D.); συνιόντος ὄχλου πολλοῦ *Ev.Luc.*8.4. 2. in hostile sense, *meet in battle*, Il.14.393, Hes.*Th.*686; ἐς μέσον.. συνίτην μεμαῶτε μάχεσθαι Il.6.120; ἔριδι ξυνιόντες 20.66, Hes.*Th.*705; ἔριδος πέρι θυμοβόροιο Il.16.476; σ. ἐς τὴν μάχην Hdt.1.80; of states, *engage in war*, Th.2.8. 3. in peaceable sense, *come together*, *meet to consult* or *deliberate*, ib.15, Lycurg.126, etc.; σ. περὶ νόμων θέσεως Arist.*Pol.*1298$^a$17; of a conspirator, σ. τοῖς φυγάσιν ἐπὶ καταλύσει τοῦ δήμου Din.1.94, cf. D.24.144; also of festive meetings, συνόδους συνιέναι Pl.*Smp.*197d. b. of the council, σύλλογον ὃν εἴπες συνιέναι Id.*Lg.*962c. 4. σ. εἰς τὴν κοινωνίαν, of marriage, ib.773a; of copulation of animals, Arist.*HA*540$^a$10. II. of things, *gather*, σ. ἀήρ Pl.*Ti.*49c; τὸ ὑγρόν Thphr.*CP*2.19.3; of clouds, Arist.*Mete.*364$^b$33; opp. χωρίζεσθαι, Id.*GC*327$^b$28; σ. πρὸς αὑτήν *recur*, Pl.*Ti.*58a, cf. 76a. 2. of money, *come together*, *come in*, of revenue, Hdt.1.64, 4.1. 3. *to be contracted*, σ. καὶ ψύχεσθαι Arist.*Mete.*342$^a$19. 4. of stars, *come into conjunction*, Man.2.423, al.; of the moon, συνιούσης, opp. αὐξομένης, Lyd.*Mens.*3.11.

**σύνειξις**, εως, ἡ, *giving way*, Sor.*Fract.*16.

**συνεῖπον**, imper. συνειπε Hyp.*Lyc.*20, aor. of συναγορεύω or σύμφημι:—*speak with* any one, *confirm* what another says, τί τινι Isoc.20.22, cf. X.*Cyr.*4.2.46, etc.; opp. ἀντειπεῖν, Lys.12.34. 2. σ. τισί *advocate* their cause, Is.4.1, cf. D.21.206: generally, *help*, *further*, σ. ταῖς ἐπιθυμίαις τινός Isoc.*Ep.*3.3. 3. *tell along with*, *help to tell*, E.*Hipp.*557 (lyr.). 4. 1 aor. Med. συνειπάμην, *agree*, *conspire*, c. inf., Lxx *Da.*2.9, D.H.5.51: abs., συνειπάμεναι ἐπένθησαν ib.48; καθάπερ σοι συνειπάμην as I *arranged* with you, *PCair.Zen.*229.6 (iii B.C.).

**συνείργνῡμι**, = συνέργω, Plu.*Rom.*5.—Pass., ἐς θάλαμον Id.*Alex.*2; ἐν δεσμῷ Id.2.493d, cf. *Crass.*8.

**συνείργω**, v. συνέργω.

**συνειρμός**, ὁ, *connexion*, τῶν λόγων Demetr.*Eloc.*180.

**συνείρω**, Aeol. aor. part. fem. συνέρραισ(α) dub. in Sapph.78:—*string together*, Ar.*Av.*1079; ᾠδαῖς τε καὶ ὀρχήσεσιν ἀλλήλοις Pl.*Lg.*654a; σ. [ὀνόματα] *connect* them with their roots, Id.*Cra.*425b; σ. ἐπανελθόντες ἐπὶ τὴν ἀρχὴν μέχρι τῆς τελευτῆς τὸν λόγον *trace its connexion*, Id.*Plt.*267a; σ. [τοὺς κύνας] ἀπό τινος *lead* them on *connectedly* from a point, X.*Cyn.*6.21; σ. στεφάνους Aristid.1.143J.; ὄρπακας ἀνήτοιο (-τω codd.) Sapph. l. c.:—Pass., συνείρεται τὸ ἐφεξῆς *is closely connected*, *follows of itself*, Arist.*GA*741$^b$9, cf. *GC*336$^b$33; συνειρομένη πραγματεία a *connected* system, Id.*Metaph.*986$^a$7. II. in speaking, freq. in a disparaging sense, σ. λόγους ἀπνευστεί D.18.308; συνείρουσι μὲν τοὺς λόγους, ἴσασι δ' οὔπω Arist.*EN*1147$^a$21, cf. Phld.*Rh.*1.247 S.; ὑπὸ τὴν ἀναπνοὴν ἑπτὰ καὶ πέντε στίχους σ., in a breath, Plb.10.47.9; σ. λήρους Luc.*Tim.*9, cf. *Nigr.*8, *Bacch.*7; also simply of a continuous speech, σ. καθ' ἓν ἕκαστον Isoc.15.184; σ. τὰς ἑξῆς πράξεις D.S.16.76; τὴν κατηγορίαν Luc.*Pisc.*22; τὸ γνῶθι σαυτὸν πολλάκις Id.*DMort.*2.2. 2. seemingly intr. (sc. λόγους), *discourse*, περὶ τῆς κλοπῆς Id.*Prom.*5; *connect one's reasoning*, *continue* the subject, Arist.*Top.*158$^a$37, *Metaph.*995$^a$10, 1093$^b$27; σ. εἰς τὸ πρόσω Id.*Div.Somn.*464$^b$4; ἀπὸ τῶν εἰρημένων Id.*GA*716$^a$4: and then, more generally, *continue*, c. part., συνεῖρον ἀπιόντες, i.e. they went off *without pausing*, X.*Cyr.*7.5.6; σ. κινούμενος *continue* moving, Arist.*Ph.*262$^a$16, cf. Diocl.*Fr.*142: abs., *to be continuous* or *connected*, Arist.*SE*175$^a$30, *Mete.*362$^b$29, *GC*318$^a$13, al., Epicur.*Ep.*3 p.64 U.

**συνεισ-άγω** [ᾰ], *bring in together*, τὰ ἐπιτήδεια X.*Cyr.*3.2.24; τὰ ἱερὰ ὀφειλήματα *PEleph.*26.6 (iii B.C.); ἡ ἔχθρα σ. τῷ μίσει φθόνον Plu.2.91b, cf. *Placit.*1.27.3, Hierocl. *in CA*6 p.428 M., 22 p.468 M.:—Med., πυροῦ [ἀρτάβας] σ. τῇ ἐφετείᾳ φορολογίᾳ *BGU*1760.28 (i B.C.):—Pass., ᾧ συνεισάγεται *in* which *is included*.., S.E.*P.*2.86, cf. Steph. *in Hp.*1.107 D. ⊛ **-ακτος**, ον, *introduced together*: Lat. *synisactas*, expld. by *sociatrices*, *pudicas vel abstinentes* (i.e. a priest's *house-keeper*), *Gloss.* 2. θυγατέρες σ. *illegitimate*, Eust.1954.8. **-βαίνω**, *embark in together with*, ξυνεισβὰς πλοῖον.. ναύταισι A.*Th.*602; ταὐτὸν Ἀργῷον σκάφος E.*Med.*477; εἰς τὸ πλοῖον Antipho 5.82. **-βάλλω**, intr., *make an inroad into* a country *together*, *join in an inroad*, ἐς Ἀθήνας Hdt.9.17; μετά τινων *with* others, X.*HG*6.5.22: abs., Th.2.31, 4.94; *join in a charge*, X.*Cyr.*7.1.30. II. *enter together*, σύν τισι J.*BJ*3.7.31; *appear together with*, of symptoms, τῷ νοσήματι Gal.17(2).390, cf. 17(1).503; of bodily constitution, Id.10.234; of states of the weather, Id.17(1).24. **-βολή**, ἡ, *clash* of fighters, Eust.76.10. **-δίδωμι**, *submit* to a court *together with* another, μοι συγχώρησιν Mitteis *Chr.*31 ii 11 (ii B.C.). **-δύω**, *slip into together*, Arist.*Mir.*838$^b$5. **-ειμι**, (εἶμι *ibo*) *go in* or *enter together*, Id.*Resp.*472$^a$9, *Col.*794$^a$26; δεῦρο σὺ ξυνείσιθι ἐμοί Athenio 1.45. **-ελαύνω**, intr., *enter along with*, Plu.*Art.*13, 2.814d. **-ένεξις**, εως, ἡ, *collatio*, *Gloss.* **-έρχομαι**, *enter along with* or *together*, σοὶ δόμους E.*Hel.*327; ἐς οἴκους τινί ib.1083; ἐς τὸ τεῖχος Th.4.57; οἴκαδε And.4.17; εἰς τὴν οἰκίαν Mitteis *Chr.*91 ii 26 (ii A.D., prob.); of things, S.E.*P.*1.10, Gal.*UP*8.7, Lib.*Or.*64.12, etc. **-ευπορέω**, *furnish besides*, σοι ταῦτα Ath.9.367b. **-ηγέομαι**, *help in introducing*, λόγους Plu.2.795b. **-θρῴσκω**, in form -θορεῖ, sine expl., Hsch. **-κατοικέω**, *settle in together*, dub. l. in Hp.*Ep.*23. **-κρίνομαι** [ῑ], Pass., *to be introduced* (as into the body) *with* or *together*, ταῖς ἀναπνοαῖς τὴν ὀδμήν *Placit.*4.17.2; of chemical reactions, Ps.-Democr.*Alch.*p.43 B.

**συνείσομαι**, v. σύνοιδα.

**συνεισ-πέμπω**, *send into along with*, Ael.*VH*12.43 codd. **-πηδάω**, *leap into with*, c. dat., App.*Mith.*98. **-πίπτω**, *rush in along with* or *together*, εἰς τὴν θάλατταν X.*An.*5.7.25; esp. of soldiers pursuing the besieged to their own gates and getting in with them, σ. φεύγουσι ἐς τὸ τεῖχος Hdt.3.55, cf. 78, 9.102, Th.6.100, X.*HG*7.2.7, etc.; μετὰ σοῦ Ar.*Ec.*1095; σ. εἴσω τῶν πυλῶν σὺν τῷ ὄχλῳ X.*An.*7.1.18; κατὰ τὰς πύλας Id.*HG*4.7.6: abs., Lys.3.15; of fevers, Paul.Aeg.4.22. **-πλέω**, *sail into together*, εἰς λιμένα X.*HG*1.6.16: abs., Eun.*VS* p.485 B. **-ποιέω**, *admit to a share in*, χάρισι, φιλίαις, Plu.2.482e,484d. **-πορεύομαι**, *enter together*, ἅμα τινί D.H.9.52; ὁ λογισμὸς σ. ταῖς γνώμαις Ph.1.112. **-πράσσω**, Att. -ττω, *help* one (τινι) *in exacting* money *from* another (τινα), D.49.69, cf. *IG*2$^2$.111.14, *SIG*1215.9 (Myconus, iii/ii B.C.); τιμωρίας παρά τινων D.H.10.11. **-ρέω**, *flow in together*, J.*BJ*2.17.6, Ael.*NA*1.2. **-τρέχω**, *run into together*, Aen.Tact.39.1,2, App.*Pun.*113. **-φέρω**, *join in paying war-tax* (εἰσφορά), X.*HG*2.1.5 (with v.l.), D.H.4.11, etc.: generally, *join in payments*, *PGrenf.*1.13.3 (ii B.C.), *OGI*455.16 (Aphrodisias, i B.C., Senatus consultum), 483.33 (Pergam., ii A.D.): metaph., σ. τι ἐπί τι, πρός τι, Ptol.*Geog.*1.6.2, Them.*Or.*7.88a; εἴς τι Sor.1.33, Jul.*Or.*1.4d (Med.):—Med., σ. κριόν Alciphr.3.35. 2. metaph., ὃς ἂν μὴ συνεισενέγκῃ τὰ σχήματα τοῖς λόγοις *make* gestures *appropriate to* his words, Lib.*Or.*64.74. II. in literal sense, *insert* or *administer at the same time*, Sor.2.62, Philum.ap.Orib.45.29.23. III. Pass., of property, *to be brought into the common stock* by one or other party to a marriage, *PMasp.*151.181 (vi A.D.), *PFlor.*93.18 (vi A.D.), etc. ⊛ **-φορά**, ἡ, *joint contribution*, Poll.8.157, *Arch.Pap.*6.219 (Elephantine, ii A.D.), *OGI*609.17 (Syria, iii A.D.), *CIG*4422 (Trajanopolis), Asp. *in EN*73.22. **-φορος**, ον, *liable for payment of contributions* or *taxes*, τοῖς.. στεφάνοις *Sammelb.*7337.26 (i B.C.); τῇ γινομένῃ δαπάνῃ *PFlor.*18.25 (ii A.D.), cf. *Sammelb.*4284.11 (iii A.D.). **-φρέω**, *let into together*, Hsch.

**συνεκ-βαίνω**, *go out together*, ἐπὶ τὸ ὄρος X.*An.*4.3.22, cf. Str.15.2.13. **-βάλλω**, *cast out along with*, τῷ τέκνῳ τὰς μήτρας Hdt.3.108; τὸ πνεῦμα μετὰ τῶν φθόγγων Arist.*Aud.*804$^b$9; of the effects of sneezing, Gal.2.883, Aët.6.97. 2. *assist in casting out* or *expelling*, X.*HG*3.2.13, 6.5.33; Περίανδρον τοῖς ἐπιθεμένοις Periander *with the help of* the other assailants, Arist.*Pol.*1304$^a$32. II. intr. of a river, *discharge itself together*, Ael.*NA*14.23. **-βῐβάζω**, causal of συνεκβαίνω, *help in bringing out*, τὰς ἁμάξας, sc. from the mud, X.*An.*1.5.7. **-βιόω**, *live to the end along with*, τῷ -βεβιωκέναι τῇ λύπῃ, i.e. their not ceasing to grieve before they died, Lib.*Or.*2.62. **-βλύζω**, *spirt out together*, Sor.1.36. **-βοάω**, *shout out together*, Hdn.2.2.10; ὅτι.. D.C.39.19. **-βοηθέω**, *join in going out to aid* one, D.S.25.10. **-βόσκομαι**, *absorb*, *suck up as well*, Gal.12.29. **-βράσσω**, of the sea, *throw on shore along with*, στρατηλάτην ναύταις Lyc.898:—Pass., *to be ejected*, Hsch. **-δᾱ-**

πᾰνάω, *use up together*, Gal.10.1016. **-δέχομαι**, *take on oneself a share of*, [ὀργήν] Plu.2.482e; [ἡδονὴ] σ. τὸν κάμνοντα *takes* him *over along with* (the remedies), ib.662b. II. *supply in thought a word or phrase in connexion*, Corn.*ND*17,30, S.E.*P*.1.200,202.

**συνεκδημ-έω**, Dor. **συνεσδᾱμέω** *IG*12(5).868*A*7 (Cretan, found at Tenos):—*go* or *be abroad with another*, Ephor.96J., *PCair.Zen.* 396.2 (iii B.C.), Plu.*Cat.Mi.*5. **-ητικός**, ή, όν, *fond of going abroad together*, name of a play by Ion, Poll.2.88. **-ία**, ἡ, *being* or *going abroad together*, Gloss. **-ος**, ὁ, *fellow-traveller*, *Act.Ap.*19.29, J.*Vit.* 14, Plu.*Oth.*5, Palaeph.45; = Lat. *comes*, συνέγδημος Μεσσάλλα τοῦ ἀνθυπάτου *OGI*494.13 (Milet., ii A.D.): Dor. nom. pl. **συνέγδᾱμοι**, of private persons *accompanying* a public mission, *IG*12(8).186.9 (Samothrace, i B.C.). 2. σ. συντάγματα *portable* handbooks, *vade-mecums*, Paul.Aeg.*Prooem.*; σ. κολλούριον Aët.7.103.

**συνεκ-διαφορέομαι**, Pass., *to be dispersed also*, Olymp. *in Mete.* 281.15. **-δῐδάσκω**, *teach together*, Dexipp.*in Cat.*42.11. **-δίδωμι**, *join in giving out*, τὴν ἀποχὴν *PFlor.*95.15 (iv A.D.); *yield up together*, αὐτούς Plu.*Dem.*23; *give out also*, Id.2.699b:—Pass., Philostr. *VA*3.39. 2. *help* a poor man *in portioning out* his daughter (cf. ἐκδίδωμι I. 2), σ. τισὶ θυγατέρας Lys.19.59, D.18.268:—Med., *PEnteux.*91.2 (iii B.C., but dub. sens.), D.H.2.10. 3. Pass., *to be lent as well*, of money, Lys.*Oxy.*1606.323. II. intr., *end in like manner*, *EM*812.51:—Pass., ib.800.21. **-δῐκος**, ὁ, *fellow*-ἔκδικος, *Inscr.Prien.*111.129(i B.C.), *Supp.Epigr.*4.230(Mylasa). **-δοτος**, ον, *co-responsible* (?), *PAvrom.*1*B*29 (i B.C.). **-δοχή**, ἡ, *understanding one thing with another*: hence in Rhet., *synecdoche*, an indirect mode of expression, *when the whole is put for a part* or *vice versa*, Quint.*Inst.*8.6.19, Aristid.Quint.2.9, Ps.-Plu.*Vit.Hom.*22. **-δοχικός**, ή, όν, *making use of* συνεκδοχή. Adv. **-κῶς** *by way of synecdoche*, D.S.5.31 (prob. a gloss). **-δρομή**, ἡ, *running out together*: metaph., *following the same rule*, *analogy*, A.D.*Adv.*142.9, *Synt.* 49.14, Simp. *in Ph.*274.25, Eust.341.22, *EM*66.52. **-δρομικῶς**, Adv. *approximately*, λέγειν Sch.Iamb. *in Nic.*p.131 P., Sch.Th. 1.10. **-δύομαι**, Med., *put off together*, ἅμα κιθῶνι ἐκδυομένῳ συνεκδύεται καὶ τὴν αἰδῶ γυνή Hdt.1.8, imitated by Chor.14.6 p.182 F.-R. II. Pass., *go out together*, Polyaen.2.31.2. **-ζέω**, *boil up together*, Damocr.ap.Gal.13.42. **-θειάζω**, *join in placing among the gods*, Plu.2.492d. **-θερμαίνω**, *make hot like oneself*, Id.*Pomp.* 8, Gal.7.387:—Pass., Hp.*Vict.*2.66. **-θέω**, *run out along with*, τινὶ ἐκ τῶν τάξεων App.*Mith.*49: metaph., σ. τῷ πάθει ὁ λογισμός Gal.5.375: abs., *run out of bounds also*, εἰ καὶ τὸ τοῦ λόγου συνεκθέοι μῆκος Jul.*Or.*2.54b. **-θηλύνω**, *help to make womanish*, Clearch. 4, J.*BJ*7.8.7. **-θλίβω** [ῑ], *squeeze out together*, Arist.*Pr.*876$^b$1 (Pass.): Gramm. (cf. ἔκθλιψις), Sch.Heph.p.106C. **-θνήσκω**, *faint along with* or *together*, -θανεῖν τῷ πώματι, i.e. drink till wine and drinker fail together, E.*Cyc.*571.

**συνεκκαίδεκα**, *sixteen together*, *by sixteens*, D.18.104.

**συνεκ-καίω**, *set on fire together*, τὰ δένδρα Ael.*VH*13.1; τὸν ἀέρα Plu.*Alex.*35; αὐτῷ τὸ πᾶν σῶμα Gal.11.406: abs., *help to flare up*, Thphr.*Ign.*27,37: metaph., *help to inflame*, τινα Plb.3.14.3; τὸν θυμόν Plu.*Pel.*19, *Caes.*44. **-κᾰλέομαι**, Med., *call out* or *excite together*, τινὰς πρός τι Plb.18.19.11, cf. 11.1$^a$.2; τὴν ὄρεξιν Plu.2. 917c; τὴν ὁρμήν Thphr.*Sud.*16. **-κάμνω**, *work out together*, τι Them.*Or.*3.42d. **-κειμαι**, Pass., *to be exposed with* a child, Men. *Epit.*136,233, Hld.2.31, Longus 4.18. **-κενόω**, *empty out together*, τοὺς χολώδεις χυμούς Gal.15.638:—Pass., Id.4.713, 15.78. **-κεντέω**, *pierce* or *stab at once*, Lxx 2*Ma.*5.26. **-κλέπτω**, *help to steal away*, E.*Tr.*1018, *Hel.*1370; σ. γάμους *help in concealing* it, Id.*El.*364.

**συνεκκλησι-άζω**, *share in membership of the* ἐκκλησία, *IG*9(1).32. 13 (Stiris, ii B.C.), Plu.*Sol.*18: hence **-αστής**, οῦ, ὁ, Poll.6.157.

**συνεκ-κλίνω** [ῑ], *decline* (morally) *together*, Posidon.ap.Gal.5. 469. **-κλῐτικός**, ή, όν, *conjugable*, λέξεις, i.e. verbs, Dosith. p.406K. **-κλύζω**, *wash out together*, Arist.*Col.*795$^b$6:—Pass., Id. *GA*727$^b$16, Dsc.2.101. **-κολυμβάω**, *swim out from together*, Gal. *Protr.*5,14. **-κομίζω**, *help to carry away*, αὐτῷ τὴν μητέρα Isoc. 19.20. 2. *attend the funeral of*, Phylarch.26J., Plu.*CG*14:—Pass., *Mitt.Ver.Klass.Philol.in Wien* 10.122 (Ephesus, i A.D.). II. σ. τινὶ κακά, πόνους, Κύπριν, *help* one *in bearing* them, E.*Or.*685, *El.*73, *Hipp.* 465. **-κόπτω**, *help to cut away*, X.*An.*4.8.8. 2. *excise also*, Antyll.ap.Aët.7.74; τὴν πίστιν Plu.2.1101c. 3. *cut off also*, κλῆμα τὸ τοὺς βότρυας ἔχον συνεκκοπέντας Gloss. **-κρίνω** [ῑ], *help in clearing out by secretion*, Arist.*GA*737$^b$35:—Pass., *to be got rid of by secretion also*, σ. ἡ περίττωσις ib.727$^a$17; ἱδρῶτι *with the* perspiration, Id.*Mete.*357$^b$4, cf. 370$^b$15 (v.l. συγκρ-), Plu.*Crass.*33, Gal.18(1).40, al. **-κρούομαι**, *to be driven from one's purpose with*, τῇ πάντων φορᾷ Plu.*Caes.*33; τῇ διανοίᾳ Vett.Val.238.33 cod. V (συννεκροῦται cod. S). **-λᾰλέω**, *utter along with*, Eust.728. 55. **-λαμβάνω**, *take out together with*, τινί τι Ptol.*Harm.*2. 3 (Pass.). II. *farm* taxes *with*, σ. ἄλλοις τὴν αὐτὴν ἔγληψιν εἰς τὸ αὐτὸ ἔτος *UPZ*114.16 (ii B.C., συνεγ-). **-λάμπω**, *shine forth together*, Plu.2.627c, Longin.44.3. **-λεαίνω**, *pound together*, Dsc. *Alex.*4, Damocr.ap.Gal.13.1056, Philum.ap.Orib.45.29.71. **-λέγομαι**, Med., *choose*, *select*, Gal.11.362. 2. *contract* an illness, Luc.*Ep.Sat.*28 (v.l. συνελέξαντο). **-λειόω**, = συνεκλεαίνω, Apollon.ap.Gal.12.528, Dsc.3.23 (v.l. -λεαιν-), Alex.Trall.7.5. **-λείπω**, *vanish with* or *also*, Str.10.2.12, Plu.2.415f,777a, al., Gal.12.412; Νομᾶ.. ἐν εἰρήνῃ τὴν Ῥώμην ὑπάρχειν συνεξέλιπε *ended with* his life, Plu.*Comp.Lyc.Num.*4. **-λεκτός**, ή, όν, *chosen along with* or *together*, 1*Ep.Pet.*5.13. **-λέπω**, *help to hatch out*, Porph.*Abst.* 3.10. **-λύω**, *help to relax*, *enfeeble*, Onos.10.11; τὴν τρυφερίαν τοῦ σπέρματος Sor.1.46:—Pass., *to be relaxed along with*, c. dat., ib.25; συνεκλελυμένοι τοῖς σώμασι τὰς ψυχάς Plu.2.596a; πάντα συνεκλέλυται *AP*6.56 (Maced.); of language, *lose its force with*, τῷ μήκει τῶν χρόνων Longin.39.4. **-μᾰλάσσω**, *soften completely*, Damocr.ap.Gal.14. 200, Dsc.1.66. ✱ **-μαρτῠρέω**, *bear favourable testimony to*, ὁ θεὸς τῷ βασιλεῖ *OGI*237.6 (Iasus, ii B.C.). **-μᾰχέω**, *march out to fight together*, Ar.*Lys.*1154. **-μοχλεύω**, *join in forcing open*, ib.430. **-πέμπω**, *send out* or *forth together*, τοὺς ἀχρείους εἰς Πελλήνην X.*HG*7.2.18; τοὺς οἰκέτας Id.*Oec.*7.35; τῶν ἅμ' αὐτοῖς -θέντων ἐπὶ Θερμοπύλας D.S. 11.4; *help to get away*, Plu.*Brut.*45:—Pass., Id.*Mar.*40. 2. of things, *send forth* or *eject together*, τὸ πῶμα Pl.*Ti.*91a; φωνήν Anon. ap.Suid. s.v. φιμοῖ. **-πεπαίνω**, *help to ripen*, Plu.2.700f. **-περάω**, *come out together*, Aret.*SD*2.11; μετά τινος X.*Cyn.*4.5. ✱ **-πέσσω**, Att. -ττω, *digest*, *get rid of by digestion*, Arist.*Pr.*868$^a$30, Plu.2.647e, Ael.*VH*12.37; *help to digest*, Plu.2.648f. II. *assist in ripening*, Thphr.*CP*4.9.5; *make mild*, *mellow*, οἶνον Plu.2.676b, al. **-πηδάω**, *run out together*, *PTeb.*15.4 (ii B.C.); *spring out along with*, ὁ θυμὸς τῇ γνώμῃ Philostr.*Her.*10.5. **-πῐαστέον**, *one must press out together*, *Gp.*3.7. **-πιέζω**, *premo*, Gloss. **-πικραίνομαι**, Pass., *to be much provoked also*, Plu.2.468b. **-πίμπρημι**, *inflame also*, τὸν ἀέρα Arist.*Mete.*371$^a$17. **-πίνω** [ῑ], *drink off together*, τὸ κέρας X.*An.*7.3.32. ✱ **-πίπτω**, *fall out* or *be ejected together*, Hp.*Vict.*1. 27 (v.l. συνεμ-), Arist.*HA*587$^a$13; αἴσθησις -ουσα μετὰ τοῦ αἰσθητοῦ Pl.*Tht.*156b; δεῖ.. συνεκπίπτειν τὴν ὅρασιν τῷ ὁρατῷ Plot.5.3.10, cf. 6.2.9. II. c. dat., *rush out together with*, Plu.*Pel.*32, *Lys.*28; *to be carried away by*, ταῖς ὁρμαῖς τῶν πολιτῶν Id.*Per.*20, cf. Plb.27.9. 9. 2. *to be driven out* or *banished together with*, Plu.*Ant.*32. 3. *disappear together with*, ἀτμὸς σ. ἀπιόντι τῷ θερμῷ Id.2.946a, cf. Luc. *Hist.Conscr.*62. III. (from voting tablets *coming out of* the urn in which they were collected) *come out in agreement*, *happen to agree*, κατὰ τὠυτὸ αἱ γνῶμαι συνεξέπιπτον Hdt.1.206; αἱ γνῶμαι αἱ πλεῖσται σ. ναυμαχέειν *agreed in advising* to fight, Id.8.49; οἱ πολλοὶ σ. Θεμιστοκλέα κρίνοντες *agreed in* choosing, ib.123. 2. c. dat., *come out equal* to another, *run a dead heat with* him, ἀγωνιζόμενος στάδιον συνεξέπιπτε τῷ πρώτῳ Id.5.22, cf. Plu.2.1045d. IV. *fail together*, ἔν τινι Demad.8 (s.v.l.); of a play, *to be rejected together with* the actor, Luc.*Nigr.*8. V. of flesh, *fall away together*, Pl. *Ti.*84b. VI. *degenerate together*, εἴς τι Longin.41.1. **-πλέω**, Ion. **-πλώω**: fut. inf. -πλευσεῖσθαι Lys.13.25:—*sail out along with*, c. dat., Hdt.1.5, etc.; μετά τινος Lys.13.27: abs., ib.25, Th.4.3: Συνεκπλέουσα or -αι, name of a Comedy by Philippides. **-πληρόω**, *fill up the measure of*, *complete*, τὸ ἐλλιπές Plb.16.28.2; τὰς ἐπιβολάς Id.14.4.3; *indulge to the full*, τὰς ὁρμάς Id.3.78.5. **-πλήσσω**, Att. -ττω, *combine to carry away* (metaph.), τὸν ἀκροατήν Plu.2. 41c. **-πνέω**, *breathe one's last along with*, τινι E.*IT*684, cf. *PHerc.* 1041.3; σ. τῷ χαίρειν Luc.*Laps.*3. **-ποιέω**, *suffice*, *IG*2$^2$.968.43 (ii B.C.):—Pass., *to be sufficiently supplied by*, χορηγίαις Plb.6.49.7; cf. ἐκποιέω III. **-πολεμέω**, *vanquish together*, Lxx *De.*1.30, al., D.S. 15.25, 16.43. **-πολεμόω**, *excite to war together*, αὐτὸν (sc. Ἰουστινιανὸν) Πέρσαις Anon.ap.Suid. s.v. πολεμῶσαι:—Pass., *become hostile together*, πρὸς ἀλλήλους Plu.2.380b. **-πονέω**, *help in working out*, τῷ θανόντι χάριτα E.*Hel.*1378; *help in achieving* or *effecting*, φυγάς Id.*IT*1063; τάδε Id.*Hel.*1406. 2. without acc., σ. τινί *join in labour with*, *assist to the utmost*, Id.*Ion* 850, *Fr.*136; συνεκπονοῦσα κῶλον perh. *sharing the* leg-*work*, i.e. helping me to walk, Id.*Ion* 740. **-πορεύομαι**, Pass., *go forth together with*, τινι Lxx *Jd.*13. 25: abs., Plb.6.32.5. **-πορέω**, *help to provide*, Ecphant.ap.Stob. 4.7.64. **-πορίζω**, *help in procuring* or *supplying*, τινί τι X.*An.* 5.8.25; προφάσεις Plu.2.73e; τὰ ἀναγκαῖα Hierocl. *in CA*11 p.444M. **-ποτέα**, (συνεκπίνω) *one must drink off at the same time*, καὶ τὴν τρύγα Ar.*Pl.*1085. **-πράσσομαι**, Ion. **-πρήσσομαι**, Med., *assist in avenging*, συνεξεπρήξαντο αὐτῷ τὸν.. θάνατον Hdt.7.169; cf. συμπράσσω III. **-πτωμα**, ατος, τό, *concomitant feature*, Phld.*Mort.* 36. ✱ **-πῠρόω**, *inflame together*, in Pass., Pl.*Ti.*65e, Diocl.*Fr.* 147, Gal.7.278. **-ραίνω**, *distil at the same time*, ὑγρότητα Thphr. *HP*3.13.2. **-ρέω**, *flow* or *run out along with* or *together*, Aret.*SD* 2.11: metaph., *vanish together*, Epict.*Gnom.*19. **-ροφέω**, *gulp down together*, Max.Tyr.20.4. **-σάττω**, v. συνεσσάδδω. **-στρᾰτεύω**, *march out together*, J.*AJ*7.10.1. ✱ **-σῴζω**, *help in preserving* or *delivering*, ξένον S.*OC*566; τὸ σῶμα ἡ ψυχὴ σ. *with itself*, Antipho 5. 93. **-τᾰνύω**, = συνεκτείνω, Hp.*Art.*57. **-τᾰπεινόω**, *join in making submissive*, τισὶ ἑαυτόν Plu.2.529e. **-τάσσω**, Att. -ττω, *arrange in line with*, X.*Cyr.*6.3.18. **-τείνω**, *prostrate beside*, Ἄρει τὴν Ἀφροδίτην Heraclit.*All.*54:—Pass., *to be extended together*, Gal.*UP*2.15. 2. trans., *extend together with*, τῇ διανοίᾳ ἑαυτήν (sc. ὄψις) Ph.2.23, cf. Zos.4.33; μακρῷ βίῳ.. πόλεμον Lib. *Or.*38.18. II. intr., *extend along with*, *be equal*, τινι *Placit.*4.13. 11 codd.Plu. (συνεντεινομένου Stob.):—Pass., Gal.*UP*10.9. **-τελέω**, *help in completing*, τὰ πράγματα Aristid.1.442J.; *help in ripening*, Thphr.*CP*1.13.9. **-τέμνω**, *excise together with*, ἀδικίᾳ κοιλίαν Plu. 2.159c:—Pass., *to be excised also*, Heliod.ap.Orib.45.5.2.

**συνεκτέον**, (συνέχω) *one must keep together*, τοὺς ἀγαθοὺς ἄνδρας X.*Cyr.*7.5.70.

**συνεκ-τήκω**, *dissolve off as well*, τὸ σαρκίον Gal.*UP*10.11. **-τίθημι**, *put on shore along with*, c. dat., Plu.2.27c; τὰ καθαρτικὰ αὐτὰ σ. *carry* themselves *off also*, S.E.*M.*8.480:—Med., *expose together with*, Hld.4.8, al.:—Pass. in same sense, Men.*Epit.*59. **-τῐθηνέομαι**, *assist in fostering*, Plu.2.321d,662b.

⊕ **συνεκτικός**, ή, όν, (συνέχω) *fit for holding together*, ἡ τῶν ὅλων σ. αἰτία Arist.*Mu.*397b9; τὸ σ. Plu.2.735f; τὸ ἐν ἑνὶ πάντων σ. Jul.*Or.*4.135c; σ. τόνος Plu.2.946c; σ. αἴτιον, in Stoic Philos., οὗ παρόντος μένει τὸ ἀποτέλεσμα καὶ αἰρομένου αἴρεται, *Stoic.*2.121, cf. 273; σ. αἰτία ib.144; σ. αἴτιον νοσήματος Gal.15.111; σ. δύναμις Id.7.525, cf. 1.85, 9.2, Sor.2.3; τὰ σ. τῶν λόγων the *essence* of the argument, A.D.*Adv.*141.21; τὸ -κώτατον δόγμα the *most essential*.., Ph.1.283; -κώτατα *the most essential* doctrines, Iamb.*VP*32.226; -κώτατον κεφάλαιον Vett.Val.172.28; σ. τᾶς σωφροσύνας Phintys ap.Stob.4.23.61 (Sup.); of the soul, σ. ἑαυτῆς self-*maintaining*, Hierocl.p.20A.; v. συνακτικός I. 1. 2. *firmly gripping*, of wrestlers, Philostr.*Gym.* 38. II. Adv. -κῶς *summarily*, Procl.*in Alc.*p.52C., Zonar.

**συνεκ-τίκτω**, *bring forth together*, τροφὴν σ. τοῖς τέκνοις *produce* food *simultaneously with* the young, as oviparous animals do, Arist.*GA*774b30, cf. *Pol.*1256b10, cj. in Pl.*Tht.*156b. **-τίνω** [ῐ], fut. -τείσω, *pay along with* or *together*, *help in paying*, Id.*Lg.*855b, D.53.26, Plu.*Rom.*13. **-τοκίζω**, *help in parturition*, Sm.*Is.*66.9. **-τομή**, ἡ, f.l. for οὖν ἐκτ. in Ph.*Bel.*64.27 codd. (pl.). **-τρᾰχηλίζομαι**, Pass., *to be thrown as by a horse*, Plu.2.802d. **-τρᾱχύνομαι**, Pass., *to be furious together*, of torrents, Id.*Sull.*16. **-τρέπομαι**, Pass., *vary with*, c. dat., Ptol.*Tetr.*3 (as cited by Sch.p.4): abs., *vary together*, Gal.6.384. **-τρέφω**, *rear up along with* or *together*, τὸ γεννηθὲν κοινῇ μετ' ἐκείνου Pl.*Smp.*209c; σ. τοὺς παῖδας *assist in bringing* them *up*, Id.*Mx.*249a: metaph., πῦρ Plu.*Brut.*31:—Pass., *grow up with*, συνεκτραφεὶς ἐμοί E.*IT*709, cf. And.1.48, Luc.*Am.*32. **-τρέχω**, aor. -έδρᾰμον, *run out along with* or *together*, *sally out together*, X.*HG*4.3.17, *Ages.*2.11; σ. ἅμα τῷ λόγῳ *rushed together to the rescue of* the argument, Plu.2.933f; *to be an accomplice*, ἰδὼν ποτ' αἰσχρὸν πρᾶγμα μὴ συνεκδράμῃς Men.*Mon.* 272. b. Astrol., of the moon in conjunction, μηδέπω τὰς τοῦ Ἡλίου συνεκδραμούσης αὐγάς not yet having *abetted* (sc. by reflection) the sun's rays, Heph.Astr. in *Cat.Cod.Astr.*8(1).158. 2. of plants, *shoot up together*, Thphr.*CP*5.6.11 (v.l.). II. *fall to the lot of*, Plb.5.33.7, 10.40.6, 12.13.5, 38.5.3. 2. *coincide*, τῶν οἰωνισμάτων οἷς συνεξέδραμεν ὁ τόκος Lib.*Or.*59.26; τῇ ἀκολουθίᾳ πως τοῦ λόγου συνεξέδραμεν the digression *suited* in a way the sequence of the argument, Gal.10.238. III. *to be of the same length*, D.H.*Comp.* 26, Plu.2.723b; *have the same ending by analogy*, A.D.*Pron.*55.5, al., Eust.769.28. **-τρίβω** [ῑ], *destroy utterly together*, Lxx *Wi.*11.19. **-τροφος**, ον, *reared up together*, ib.1*Ma.*1.6 (cod. B συντρόφους). **-τροχάζω**, *compete*, πρὸς τὸν ὅμοιον ζῆλον τῆς ἀρετῆς *Ath. Mitt.*31.431 (Galata, ii B.C.). **-φαίνω**, *show forth* or *display together*, τὴν παρασκευήν App.*BC*1.39; *signify together*, τινί τι Plu.2.33d, cf. Gal.16.725:—Pass., Ar.Did.*Epit.*28. **-φαντικός**, ή, όν, *connotative*, *EM*30.8, *An.Ox.*1.436. ⊕ **-φέρω**, *carry out together*, esp. to burial, τινα Phylarch.26J., prob. in Lycurg.45 (ξυνενεγκεῖν cod.); *attend a funeral*, Th.2.34, D.C.56.42. 2. *disgorge together*, τῷ νοσήματι τὸν λόγον Plu.2.453d. 3. in Surgery, *remove together*, Antyll. ap.Aët.7.74. II. *bear to the end along with*, τινὶ ἔρωτας E.*Fr.* 339: metaph., Plot.6.8.16. III. *express with* or *together*, of an artist, τῇ μορφῇ τὴν ἀρετήν Plu.2.335b, cf. 25c; ἔργα ὕψος τι διανοίας σ. Id.*Demetr.*20. IV. Pass., *to be carried away* by emotion, etc., Phld.*Lib.*p.42O.; τῇ δυνάμει τῶν συνηγορούντων D.S.1.76; τοῖς θυμοῖς Id.17.70; τῇ νίκῃ, φιλοτιμίᾳ, Plu.*Aem.*22, *Ages.*23; τισι Philostr.*VA*5.33. **-φεύγω**, *escape with*, Id.*Im.*2.2 codd. (ὑπ- Kayser). **-φλεγμαίνω**, *become inflamed together*, Thphr. *Lass.*12. **-φλογόομαι**, Pass., *to be burnt together*, Olymp.*in Mete.* 333.13. **-φοιτάω**, *go constantly together*, εἰς τὰ θέατρα Them.*Or.* 24.304b. **-φορά**, ἡ, *public funeral*, Aen.Tact.17.1. II. *uttering together*, D.H.*Comp.*22. **-φορέω**, *remove* furniture *together with*, Hld.4.17. **-φρύγω** [ῡ], *parch at the same time*, Damocr.ap. Gal.13.1003. **-φύομαι**, Pass. with aor. 2 Act., *to be born together*, Philostr.*Im.*2.27; *have its origin with*, Gal.18(2).941, Ruf.*Anat.* 38. **-φωνέω**, *exclaim at the same time*, Ach.Tat.1.12:—Pass., *to be uttered together*, D.T.639.14, Longin.38.3, S.E.*M.*1.102. **-φώνησις**, εως, ἡ, Gramm., = συνίζησις 2, Heph.2.1, Aristid.Quint.1.23, cf. Eust.25.33. **-φωτίζω**, *join in illuminating*, Plu.2.806a. **-χέω**, *pour out together*, [ἰὸν] τῷ γλεύκεϊ Aret.*SD*2.13; πνεῦμα κωκυτῷ *AP* 7.608 (Eutolm.):—Pass., *stream out together*, D.S.3.29: metaph. of men, Plb.9.9.7, 11.14.7; τὸ μείλιχον -εχεῖτο Eun.*VS* p.465 B. **-χῡλίζω**, in Pass., *have the juice squeezed out with*, κάρυα.. -ιζόμενα μετὰ τῆς κέγχρου ῥόφημα γένοιτο ἂν τοῖς πυρέσσουσι Dieuch. ap.Orib.4.7.17. **-χυμόω**, *assist nature in emptying* the vessels of the body, Hp.*Epid.*6.2.1, cf. Gal.19.143.

**συνέλᾰσις**, εως, ἡ, *driving together*, *Gloss.*

⊕ **συνελαύνω**, fut. -ελάσω [ᾰ]: Ep. aor. συνέλασσα: pf. part. συνεληλάμενος Arat.176 (on the accent, v. A.D.*Adv.*135.5, al.), but συνεληλαμένος Plb.4.48.2, Aret.*SA*2.1: plpf. -ηλάμην Lxx 2*Ma.*4.26: aor. Pass. -ηλάσθην Plb.18.22.6, Lxx 2*Ma.*5.5, Plu.*Caes.*17, *BGU* 1568.7 (iii A.D.). Used by Hom. only in pres. and Ep. aor. (exc. σὺν δ' ἤλασε in tmesi); he uses the form ξυν- where required by the metre:—*drive together*, ληΐδα δ' ἐκ πεδίου συνελάσσαμεν Il.11.677; τὰς μὲν [βοῦς] συνέλασσεν ἐς αὔλιον *h.Merc.*106, cf. X.*Cyr.*1.4.14; σὺν δ' ἤλασ' ὀδόντας *drove* his teeth *together*, Od.18.98; *hammer together*, Plu.2.567e; *weld* iron, Hp.*Vict.*1.13; *draw together*, συνέλασσε κάρη χεῖράς τε *h.Merc.*240; *drive*, *force*, τινὰ εἰς ὀλίγην κῆρα *AP*7.614.10 (Agath.), cf. Jul.*Ep.*89b; σ. εἰς στενόν Luc.*Herm.*63:—Pass., *to be driven* or *forced* into a contracted space, *compressed*, Epicur.*Ep.*2 p.50U., Plb.4.48.2, *Placit.*4.1.4; εἰς βραχὺ διάζωμα σ. *to be contracted* into.., Plu.*Phoc.*13: metaph., εἰς ἀπορίαν ἐσχάτην ἡ σωτηρία συνηλάθη Chor. p.226B.; συνεληλαμένοι σφυγμοί Aret. *SA*2.1. 2. *constrain*, *force*, τινὰ ἀποστῆναι τῶν οὐ δικαίως αὐτῷ προσηκόντων *Sammelb.*5357.11 (v A.D.); σ. τινὰ πρὸς εὐγνωμοσύνην *bring* him to reason, ib.13 (Pass.), cf. *PLond.*5.1711.60 (vi A.D.); εἰς τέλος σ. *bring* to an end, *PMonac.*13.70 (vi A.D.). II. *match in combat*, *set to fight*, θεοὺς ἔριδι ξυνελάσσαι Il.20.134; θεοὺς ἔριδι ξυνελαύνεις 21.394: abs., ξυνελάσσομεν ὦκα Od.18.39. 2. intr., ἔριδι ξυνελαυνέμεν *meet* in quarrel, Il.22.129.

**συνελέγχω**, *convict together*, dub. l. in Arr.*An.*6.29.11 (Pass.); *convict*, Luc.*Ocyp.Prooem.* II. *confute besides*, A.D.*Synt.*92.17 (Pass.); *help to prove*, ib.207.5.

⊕ **συνελεουρέω** (pres. inf. written -ορεν), *to be joint-curator of marsh-pastures*, *Rev.Phil.*60 (1934).294 (Erythrae, iv B.C.).

⊕ **συνελευθερόω**, *join in freeing from*, τινὰς τοῦ μουνάρχου Hdt.5.46; τὴν πόλιν ἀπ' Ἀθηνάων *IG*12(9).187.8 (Eretria, v B.C.). 2. abs., *join in freeing*, τὴν Ἑλλάδα Hdt.7.157, cf. 51, Th.2.72, 6.56.

**συνέλευσις**, εως, ἡ, *coming together*, *meeting*, Aq.*Ps.*1.1; *co-operation*, *PMasp.*20 ii 7 (vi A.D.); *co-operative community* of monks, ib. 96.32 (vi A.D.); *sexual intercourse*, Vett.Val.47.8; τῶν ἀφροδισίων Ptol.*Tetr.*205; τῶν ῥινοκερώτων Id.*Geog.*1.9.4; τινι Arg.5 E.*Ph.*(p.8 Dind.); *marriage*, Vett.Val.120.22, *PSI*5.450.10 (ii/iii A.D.). 2. of things, *coming together*, *combination*, *union*, Plu.2.1112c, S.E.*P.* 3.40,90, *M.*9.370; [συμπτωμάτων] Gal.14.691; *group*, κιόνων J.*AJ* 3.6.3. 3. Gramm., *contraction*, A.D.*Pron.*97.15; *crasis*, Id.*Conj.* 228.27. 4. *stronghold*, Lxx *Jd.*9.46,49.

**συνελευστικός**, ή, όν, *disposed for society*, τὸ σ. Plu.2.757c.

**συνεληλῠθότως**, Adv., (συνέρχομαι) *in company*, dub. l. in Hsch. s. v. συνάγουσι.

**συνελίσσω**, Ion. **συνειλ-** (as also in E.*Ion* 1164 codd.), Att. -ττω, aor. imper. συνειλιξάτω *IG*2².204.31:—*roll together*, *roll up*, εἴριον Hp.*Art.*9, cf. Thphr.*HP*4.7.5:—Pass., σὺν δ' ἑλίσσεται τμητοῖς ἱμᾶσι S.*El.*746; of certain insects, *roll themselves up into a ball*, Arist.*PA* 682b22; of the chamaeleon's tail, Id.*HA*503a20. 2. *roll up with*, συνήλιξα τὴν ἐπιστολὴν Ἀπολλωνᾶτος τῇ Ἑρμοφίλου *PGiss.*25.7 (ii A.D.); συνήλλιξα τῇ ἐπιστολῇ δεῖγμα *POxy.*113.5 (ii A.D.). 3. intr., *coil itself up*, of a serpent, σπείραις σ. dub. l. in E. l.c.

**συνελκυστέον**, *one must draw together*, X.*Ages.*9.4.

**συνέλκω**, aor. -είλκῠσα, *draw together*, σ. πανταχόθεν τὸ δέρμα ἐπὶ τὴν γαστέρα νῦν καλουμένην Pl.*Smp.*190e; σ. τὰς ὀφρῦς, of frowning, Antiph.307; *draw in*, *retract*, τὴν θρυαλλίδ' εἰς ἑαυτὸν ξυνελκύσας Ar.*Nu.*585 (troch.); τὸν αὐχένα J.*BJ*6.1.8:—Pass., [τὰ ὕδατα] σ. πρὸς τὸ βάθος Str.3.5.7; of cramp, Sor.2.28, Antyll.ap.Orib.8.6.32; ὅτε εἰς αὐτὴν ἡ μήτρα συνέλκεται Sor.1.70b. b. metaph., συνειλκυσμένος ὑπὸ τοῦ ἀνθρώπου ⟨τῇ⟩ πρὸς σὲ.. αἱρέσει *drawn into association* with the man by his friendship with you, *UPZ*146.4, cf. 31 (ii B.C.); dub. sens. in *POxy.*1188.9 (i A.D.). II. *pull along with*, *help to pull*, Ar.*Pax* 417; σ. μετ' αὐτῶν ἡμᾶς αὐτούς *help* them *in dragging* us *over* (in the game διελκυστίνδα), Pl.*Tht.*181a; τοὺς νεκροὺς εἴσω φάλαγγος X.*Ages.*2.15.

**συνελπίζω**, *join in hope*, Phot. and Suid. s. v. λύκος ἔχανεν.

**συνεμ-βαίνω**, fut. -βήσομαι *PTeb.*729.3 (ii B.C.):—*embark together*, τινι *with* one, Luc.*Nav.*15; συνεμβήσητε (sic) ἅμα ἡμῖν εἰς ῥῶμσιν Pap. in *Glotta* 2.150; συνεμβὰς μοι εἰς πλοῖον *BGU*1817.12 (i B.C.): metaph., σ. τινὶ εἰς τὴν θάλατταν *embark with* one *upon* naval power, Plb.1.20.7; εἰς πόλεμον (sc. τινι) Id.29.3.8; εἰς ἀπέχθειαν ἅμα τινί Id.16.26.6; ἐν πλείοσιν τῶν τῇ πόλει συμφερόντων καὶ κοινῇ τοῖς πολίταις καὶ ἰδίᾳ ἑκάστῳ σ. *Supp.Epigr.*7.62.9 (Seleucia Pieria, ii B.C.); ἐς τὰ παρακαλούμενα ὑφ' ὑμίων συνεμβάντες *GDI*5183.18 (Crete, found at Teos, ii B.C.); σ. εἰς ἡρωϊκὰ μεγέθη *engage in* them, of a poet, Longin.9.10, cf. 13.4. **-βάλλω**, *help in applying*, τοὺς μοχλοὺς Ar.*Lys.*246. 2. *put in together with*, αὐτῷ λωτομήτρας σπέρμα *PMag.Par.*1.754, cf. Dsc.1.52, Plu.2.380e, *PHolm.*7.40:—Pass., Agatharch.28, Herod.Med.ap.Orib.6.20.5. II. intr., *fall upon also*, *join in attacking*, X.*HG*7.4.22; σ. εἰς τὴν Ἀττικήν *make a joint inroad*.., D.18.213, cf. 229. **-βῐβάζω**, causal of συνεμβαίνω, *put on board together*, prob. in D.S.20.68. **-βλητέον**, *one must throw in together*, Gal.12.565, Orib.*Fr.*58. **-βλητέος**, α, ον, *to be thrown in together*, Herod.Med.ap.Aët.9.37. **-βολή**, ἡ, *throwing in together*, κώπης ῥοθιάδος ξ. *the regular dip of all* the oars *together*, to the sound of the κέλευσμα, A.*Pers.*396:—in Id.*Ag.*984 (lyr.), πρυμνησίων ξυνεμβολάς (Headlam) may be read for ξυνεμβόλοις, in concrete sense the cables *cast out* from the stern.

**συνέμεν**, Dor. aor. 2 inf. of συνίημι (q.v.).

**συνεμέω**, *vomit up together*, ἕλμινθας Hp.*Prorrh.*2.28.

**συνεμ-πάσσω**, *strew upon along with* or *together*, Dsc.5.75. **-πίπρημι**, *burn together*, E.*Rh.*469, Nic.Dam.*Fr.*68J.:—Pass., συνεμπεπρῆσθαι τῷ ναῷ Str.14.1.22, cf. 15.1.68, Ar.Did.*Epit.*12. **-πίπτω**, *fall* or *be put in also*, ἐς τὸ πῦρ Luc.*Peregr.*24, cf. *DMort.*10.4. 2. *fall on* or *attack together*, Plu.*Brut.*42 (s.v.l.); of diseases, σ. τινί Hp. *Acut.*42, Gal.16.493, Aret.*SA*2.6 codd. (leg. συμπ-). 3. *befall also*, εἴ τι τοιοῦτον συνεμπέσοι αὐτῷ *might befall* him *too*, Arist.*Rh.Al.* 1444a14. 4. *to be thrown together*, κατὰ τωὐτό Hp.*Vict.*1.27 (v.l. συνεκ-), cf. Plu.2.399e; *coincide in form*, -ουσαι λέξεις A.D.*Pron.*52.4, al.; τοῖς παλαιοῖς, i.e. by repeating their words, Artem.2.1; of metrical phrases, Sch.Ar.*Nu.*651; Astrol., *come together*, Vett.Val.90.27, 333.23. 5. *fall to be included in*, σὺν τοῖς καὶ εἰς τούτους συνεμπεσουμένοις φορτίοις πᾶσι *POxy.*243.33 (i A.D.), cf. 503.14 (ii A.D.). **-πλέκω**, *implicate also*, αἰτίαις σ. τινά J.*BJ*7.11.2; τῷ ἐγκλήματί τινα

Plu.2.71f:—Pass., *συνεμπέπλεκται τῷ ἀναγνωσθέντι ὑπομνήματι is also involved in..*, Mitteis *Chr.*89.32 (ii A.D.). **-πνέω,** *inspire along with*, μετὰ τῶν λόγων μένος καὶ θυμόν Phld.*Ind.Sto.*35. II. *blow favourably on*, τοῖς ἀγῶσι Longin.9.11. **-πορος,** ὁ, ἡ, *fellow-traveller, companion*, A.*Ch.*208,713, S.*Tr.*318, *Ph.*542: c. gen. pers., οἱ ξ. σέθεν A.*Supp.*939; opp. ἡγεμών (a guide), Pl.*Phd.*108b: c. dat., ξυνεμπόρους ἐμοί E.*Ba.*57, cf. *Hel.*1538. 2. metaph., λύπη δ' ἄμισθός ἐστί σοι ξ. A.*Ch.*733: c. gen. rei, χορείας *partner in..*, Ar.*Ra.*398 (lyr.); σ. ἀνέρι κέρδους *partner with* him *for* gain, *AP*9.415 (Antiphil.). **-πτωσις,** εως, ἡ, *formal coincidence*, [μέτρων] Sch.Heph. p.154 C.; σ. Σοφοκλεῖ καὶ Εὐριπίδῃ *a coincidence* (of language) *between..*, Sch.Ar.*Th.*21; σ. ἱστορική Ptol.Heph.ap.Phot.*Bibl.*p.148 B. II. in Gramm., *similarity* of form, A.D.*Pron.*52.5,al.; τόνου Id.*Adv.*155.13. **-πῠρίζω,** *burn, consume at the same time*, *Supp.Epigr.*6.184 (Phrygia, iii A.D.). **-φαίνω,** *indicate at the same time* or *incidentally*, Thphr. *HP*3.8.1, Demetr.Lac.*Herc.*1012.37, Gal.15.795, Ath.14.663c, Iamb. *Comm.Math.*8; σ. ὅτι.. D.S.3.3:—Pass., *appear together*, Thphr. *HP*1.12.2; *to be indicated at the same time*, Chrysipp.*Stoic.*2.51, Gal.6.93, 7.319, Hermog.*Id.*2.6. **-φᾰνίζω,** = foreg., Aristid. Quint.2.9. ⊛ **-φᾰσις,** εως, ἡ, *joint* or *secondary indication*, τινος of a thing, S.E.*M.*7.239, Ath.7.325b. **-φέρω,** *bring in with*, M.Ant. 3.4:—Pass., *to be imported with*, Aët.7.40. **-φύρομαι** [ῡ], Pass., *to be plunged in*, πόνοις -φῠρείς Vett.Val.330.16. **-φύω,** in Pass., *grow together, unite*, Gal.2.376, 18(2).977.

**συνεν-δείκνυμι,** *indicate together*, Gal.10.626:—Med. and Pass., c. dat., Id.6.647,648, 15.464, al. **-δεκᾰτίζω,** f.l. for ἐνδεκάζω in D.58.40, according to Harp.; cf. συνδεκαδίζω. **-δησις,** εως, ἡ, *binding in together*, τινὸς πρός τι Sch.Il.4.133. **-δίδωμι,** *give way also*, Str.1.3.5, Plu.*Caes.*31; *give way*, D.S.17.43; ἐπιθυμίαις Plu.*Per.*15. **-δοσις,** εως, ἡ, *giving in, giving way*, Id.2.680a. **-δύομαι,** Med. with aor. 2 -ενέδυν, *put on*, θώρακα Arr.*An.*1.25.2.

**συνενείκομαι,** Ep. for συμφέρομαι, *strike* or *dash against*, τῷ δὴ συνενείκεται Hes.*Sc.*440.

**συνένειμι,** *to be all in together*, *POxy.*929.12 (ii/iii A.D.).

⊛ **συνενεργ-έω,** *to be active at the same time*, Plot.3.4.6, Ascl. *in Metaph.*282.5. **-ής,** ές, *active at the same time*, ib.286.22.

**συνενεχῠράζω,** = βεβαιόω I. 3, *IG* $2^{2}$.1183.35.

**συνεν-θάπτω,** in Pass., *to be buried together*, *TAM* 2.599.4 (Tlos). **-θουσιάζω,** *to be inspired and rave together*, of the Bacchae, D.S.4.3. **-θουσιάω,** = foreg., Plb.38.12.7; ταῖς ὑπερβολαῖς Str. 3.2.9, etc.; τινι *with* a person, Plu.*Cor.*17; or *at* a thing, Longin. 13.2; *to be inspired with admiration for*, c. dat., Eun.*Hist.*p.215 D.

**συνενίζω,** = συνενόω, in Pass., πρός τι Procl. *in Prm.* p.530 S.

**συνεννέπω,** *agree with*, τινι A.R.4.1277 (tm.).

**συνεννο-έω,** *join in thought*, Ph.2.331:—Med., *remind oneself also*, Eust.71.28. **-ητέον,** *one must supply in thought*, Id.262.4, al.

**συνενοχλέω,** *trouble as well*, Aët.9.42.

**συνενόω,** *unite*, Ar.Byz.*Epit.*38.12, Damocr.ap.Gal.13.800, Zos. Alch.p.142 B., Phlp. *in GA*20.33:—Pass., pf. συνένωμαι or -ήνωμαι, *to be united*, c. dat., J.*BJ*5.4.3, S.E.*M.*9.130, *PStrassb.*31.11 (iii A.D.), etc.; Gramm., *form a compound with*, ὀνόματι A.D.*Synt.*314.1.

**συνέν-τᾰσις,** εως, ἡ, *a putting on the stretch*, Chrysipp.*Stoic.* 2.233, Plu.2.589a, *Placit.*4.15.3, Antyll.ap.Orib.6.27.11, Gal.6. 171. **-τᾰφή,** ἡ, *right of joint burial*, *TAM*2.601,604 (Tlos). **-τείνω,** *put on the stretch together*, τὸ πνεῦμα Sor.1.$70^{b}$; τοὺς κατ' ἐπιγάστριον μῦς Gal.6.173:—Med., *exert oneself also*, -ομένης ἅμα τῆς κυούσης Sor. 1.73:—Pass., *to be on the stretch together*, ψυχὴ σ. σώματι Muson. *Fr.*11 p.58 H., cf. *Stoic.*2.234, Gal.6.177, v.l. for συνεκ- in *Placit.*4. 13.11. **-τευξις,** εως, ἡ, = συντυχία, Hsch.

**συνέντης,** ὁ, = συνεργός, Hsch.; cf. αὐθέντης.

**συνεξ-άγω** [ᾰ], *lead out together*, στρατιήν Hdt.5.75; σ. τι εἰς φῶς *assist in bringing* it *out*, Pl.*Tht.*157d. II. *carry off together, assist in removing*, οἱ ἔμετοι σ. τὸ γλίσχρον Arist.*Pr.*$868^{b}$7; ἥλιος σ. τὴν ὑγρότητα Thphr.*CP*4.13.5; τοὺς συναγωνιστάς Plu.2.787e; σ. ἑαυτήν, of suicide, App.*BC*4.23. 2. Pass., *to be carried away at the same time*, οἴκτῳ καὶ μανίῃ *APl.*4.128. **-αιθερόω,** *change into air together*, v.l. in Lyd.*Mens.*4.40. **-αιθριάζω,** *put into the open air together*, Dsc.3.146 (Pass.). **-αιμᾰτόω,** *make bloody together*, Ph.2. 96. **-αιρέω,** *take out together, help in removing*, συνεξελεῖν ὑμῖν τὸ θηρίον ἐκ τῆς χώρης Hdt.1.36; συμφόνευε καὶ συνεξαίρει δόμων E.*Ion* 1044:—Med., σ. τὸ προνοεῖσθαι *take* it *away also*, X.*Cyn.*5.28. 2. Act., *help in taking*, σ. τισὶ Σελλασίαν Id.*HG*7.4.12, cf. Th.2.29 (v.l. ξυνελεῖν); μετά τινος Ἀμφίπολιν Aeschin.2.32, cf. *IG* $2^{2}$.127.45; σ. δορὶ E.*Ion*61; Φρύγας Id.*Tr.*24; Τροίαν Isoc.9.18. II. Med., *help in rescuing*, Plb.5.11.5. **-αίρω,** *assist in raising*, τὴν θάλατταν Str.3.5.7; *raise together*, εἰς ὄγκον τοὺς μῦς Gal.6.296:—Pass., *to be raised together*, τῷ διαφράγματι ib.173; *to be swollen at the same time*, Id.18(2).268; συνεξαρθεὶς ὑπό τινων *being lifted up by the joint effort of..*, Plu.*Ant.* 12. 2. metaph., σ. τὴν ἠχώ *help in calling forth* the echo, Philostr. *Im.*1.18; σ. θρῆνον Hld.7.15; σ. τὴν φιλοτιμίαν Plu.2.819f; *help to excite*, Luc.*Dom.*4; συνεξαρθεὶς τοῖς λόγοις *excited with the rest* by.., D.S.17.72. II. intr., *rise together*, of the sea, Str.1.3.5; *go out along with*, τινι Id.16.2.35; of colonists, Plb.12.5.8. III. *remove as well*, in dissection, Gal.2.699. **-ᾰκολουθέω,** *follow constantly, attend everywhere*, συνεξακολουθεῖ τισι ὄνειδος Plb.2.7.3, cf. 58.11; τὸ νικᾶν σφίσι σ. Id.3.63.11, etc.; συνεξηκολούθει αὐτῷ ἀσέλγεια *was habitual* to him, Id.36.15.4. 2. of events, *turn out in accordance with*, τῇ βουλήσει τινός *OGI*763.48 (Milet., ii B.C.); ταῖς Ῥωμαίων προθέσεσι Plb.18.32.12; τὸ σ. τούτοις their *consequences*, Id.3.55.3. 3. in Gramm., = συνεκτρέχω III, Eust.630.20, *An.Ox.*1.97: hence Subst. **-ησις,** εως, ἡ, Eust.630.21. **-ᾰκοντίζομαι,** Pass., *spurt out along with*, τῇ ῥύσει τοῦ αἵματος Id.1108.3. **-ᾰκούω,** *hear all together at the same time*, S.*Tr.*372; τινων Plu.2.720d. II. *understand as implied in* a thing, S.E.*M.*7.241, Eust.769.58, etc. **-ᾰλᾰπάζω,** *help to sack*, *BCH*21.599 (Delph., iv B.C.). **-ᾰλείφω,** *abolish also*, in Pass., Plu.*Cat.Mi.*17, Gal.11.10. **-αλλάσσω,** *permute*, Dam.*Pr.*36. **-αλλοιόω,** in Pass., *change at the same time*, Gal.17 (1).42, Simp. *in Ph.*320.22. **-άλλομαι,** *leap out along with*, τινι Eust.837.26. **-ᾰμαρτάνω,** *err along with, share in a fault*, Th.3. 43, Lys.3.12, etc.; τισι with them, Isoc.6.19, D.61.19, Chrysipp. *Stoic.*2.38, etc.; μετά τινος Antipho 5.76; σ. τοῖς Αἰτωλῶν ἀσεβήμασιν Plb.5.11.1. **-ᾰμείβω,** *exchange at the same time*, τόπους ἄλλους δεσπόταισιν ἐκδήμοις Babr.59.15. **-ᾰμιλλάομαι,** *struggle jointly with*, c. dat., Plu.2.137d. **-ᾰνᾱλίσκομαι,** Pass., *to be exhausted together with*, τοῖς χρήμασι D.H.4.23. **-αναπληρόω,** *fill up again with* or *together*, Hp.*Anat.*1. **-ανθέω,** *blossom* or *break out together*, Plu.2.434b. **-ανίεμαι,** Pass., *to be relaxed together with*, συνεξανίεται [τῇ ψυχῇ] τὸ σῶμα Sor.1.25. **-ανίστημι,** *stir up* or *excite together*, Plu.2.44c. II. Pass., with aor. 2 and pf. Act., *rise and come forth with*, Id.*Ages.*12; *to be roused to action* or *ready for action with* or *together*, ἅμα τισί Id.*Pyrrh.*11; πρός τι Id.*Dem.*18, *Cat. Mi.*59; σ. τοῖς καιροῖς Plb.16.9.4. 2. *rise in rebellion, revolt along with* or *together*, Id.5.39.4, etc.; τινι D.C.71.27. 3. *to be in enthusiastic sympathy with*, τούτῳ ταῖς ὁρμαῖς, of the crowd at a wrestling-match, Plb.27.9.3. **-ανοίγω,** *help one to open a way*, c. dat., v.l. in J. *BJ*5.2.2. **-ᾰνύω,** D.Chr.12.43, also **-ᾰνύτω** [ῠ], J.*BJ*5.2.2, Plu. 2.137d,298a:—*accomplish together*, D.Chr. l.c.; *join in achievement*, Plu.2.137d. II. *equal in running*, ib.298a; *reach safety together with*, c. dat., J. l.c. (v.l. -ανοίγειν). **-ᾰπᾰτάω,** *deceive together* or *also*, D.23.159:—Pass., Id.16.2, Str.14.1.24; ὁ Συνεξαπατῶν, name of a play by Bato. **-αποστέλλω,** *send forth together*, Plb.8.19.6, D.S.14.20:—Pass., fut. -στᾰλήσομαι, *go out with*, ἅμα τινί Plb.22. 14.11. **-άπτω,** *set on fire*, Plu.2.433d,929c; τὸν ἔρωτα Hld.7.9; ψυχὴν τῷ νῷ Procl.*Inst.*129:—Pass., M.Ant.9.9. **-ᾰριθμέω,** *reckon in* or *besides*, *Inscr.Délos* 372 *A* 107 (iii/ii B.C.):—Pass., ἔν τισι D.S. 15.53, J.*BJ*3.4.2. **-αρκέω,** *suffice*, Str.14.1.41. **-άρχω,** *join in leading*, δήμῳ Pl.*Ax.*368d. **-ατμίζω,** *cause to evaporate together*, τὸ ὑγρόν Arist.*Mete.*$382^{b}$20. 2. intr., *evaporate*, Id.*GA*$752^{a}$35, $783^{a}$17, *PA*$650^{b}$18. **-ᾰτονέω,** *lose tension* or *vigour together with*, τὸ πρόσωπον τῇ ψυχῇ σ. Plu.2.528e. **-εγείρομαι,** Pass., *to be roused together*, Plb.4.47.3. **-ειμι,** (εἶμι *ibo*) *go out along with* or *together*, μετά τινων Th.3.113; τινι X.*Cyr.*1.4.15, Arist.*Mete.*$388^{b}$14, etc.; ἅμα τισί J.*BJ*2.2.1. II. *pass away together*, [νοῦσος] τῷ κάλλεϊ σ. τῆς ὥρης Aret.*SD*1.4. ⊛ **-ελαύνω,** *drive out along with* or *together*, τινὰ πατρί A.*Ag.*1606; βοΐδιον βουσί *AP*9.715 (Anacr.). **-ελεύθερος,** ὁ, *fellow-freedman*, *BGU*1141.20 (i B.C.), *PSI*5.473.2 (ii A.D.), *IG*3. 1434, D.C.60.15: fem. **-έρα,** Perdrizet *Mélanges d'arch. et d'hist.*25. 82 (Salonica, i A.D.). **-ελίττομαι,** Pass., *to be unrolled together*, χαλκὸς..πλοκαῖς σ. *follows all* the curls, Callistr.*Stat.*11. **-έλκομαι,** Pass., *to be formed by derivation*, παραγωγαῖς A.D.*Pron.*92.2. **-εμέω,** *vomit out also*, Arist.*HA*$547^{a}$27:—Pass., Antyll.ap.Orib.8.5. 1. **-εργάζομαι,** *destroy together*, τινάς τισι Aristid.1.412 J. **-ερεύθω,** *inflame together*, only in 3 sg. aor. opt. Pass. -ερευθείη, Hp.*Prog.*23 (with many vv.ll.), *Coac.*359. **-ερευνάω,** *examine thoroughly with*, in aor. Med., Pl.*Tht.*155e. **-ερύω,** *draw off along with*, *AP*6. 57 (Paul. Sil.). ⊛ **-έρχομαι,** *go* or *come out with*, c. dat., Hdt.5.74, E.*Hec.*1012, Th.8.61, X.*HG*3.4.2. 2. of things, Hp.*Nat.Hom.* 14, Arist.*HA*$587^{a}$17, *GA*$783^{a}$36, Gal.18(1).135. 3. *come out* or *result in identity with*, τινι S.E.*M.*7.421. **-ετάζω,** *search out and examine along with* or *together*, Pl.*Lg.*900d, Ph.2.197, Iamb.*Comm. Math.*14:—Pass., *to be reckoned with* or *among*, οἱ συνεξεταζόμενοι μετά τινος or τινι his *party* or *adherents*, D.21.127,190, cf. Luc.*Pr. Im.*15; but also συνεξετάζεσθαί τινι *measure oneself with* one, *rival* him, Alciphr.3.54. **-εταστής,** οῦ, ὁ, *fellow-investigator*, Procl. *in Prm.* p.529 S. **-ευπορέω** or **-ίζω,** f.l. for συνεκπορίζω in X.*An.*5. 8.25: fut. inf. -ήσειν Iamb.*Comm.Math.*34: aor. inf. -ῆσαι Procl. *in R.*2.96 K. **-ευρίσκω,** *assist in finding out*, τινα Ar.*Th.*601; πάντα Isoc.4.47; τινὶ τὰς ὗς *join* him *in finding out*, D.H.3.70; σ. ὅπως..σωθήσεσθε E.*Heracl.*420; σ. ὅ τι πρακτέον εἴη Jul.*Or.*3.114b. **-ηγέομαι,** *indicate, explain at the same time*, A.D.*Pron.*37.18, *Synt.*73.19, Gal. 17(1).596. **-ημερόομαι,** Pass., *to be civilized together*, ὁ δῆμος ἅμα τῇ χώρᾳ σ. Plu.*Num.*16. **-ιάομαι,** *heal together*, τὰς ὀδύνας Gal. 10.820. **-ιδρόω,** *sweat out together*, συνεξιδρῶσαι δυσώδη evil-smelling *when exuded with the perspiration*, Arist.*Pr.*$908^{b}$34. **-ικμάζω,** *exude* or *throw off together*, ἄλλα περιττώματα μετὰ τοῦ ἱδρῶτος ib.$883^{b}$28, cf. Thphr.*Sud.*13. **-ικνέομαι,** *coincide*, κατὰ τὸ εὖρος τῷ μήκει Procop.*Aed.*5.5, cf. 1.1. **-ιππάζομαι,** Pass., *ride away together*, Memn.34 (v.l. συνεπισπασαμένοις). **-ῑσάζω,** = sq., Dexipp. *in Cat.*6.7, Simp. *in Cat.*213.4. **-ῑσόω,** *equalize*, τοῖς μεγέθεσι τοὺς λόγους D.H. *Pomp.*5:—Pass., Id.10.16, D.S.2.10, *IG*12(2).58 *b* 7 (Mytil.). **-ίσταμαι,** Pass., *make common cause with*, Plb.3.34.9, 3.68.8, 5.39. 4. **-ισχύω,** *to be strong enough to*, c. inf., Olymp. *in Mete.*31. 21. **-ιχνεύω,** *trace out along with*, τινί τι Plu.*Cic.*18. **-οδεύω,** *go out along with*, τινι Satyr.3. II. *to be carried in a procession* (ἐξοδεία), *OGI*90.42 (Rosetta, ii B.C.). **-όζω,** *smell of* a thing *besides*, Thphr.*Od.*60. **-οιδέω,** *swell up together*, Gal.18(1). 44. **-οικονομέω,** *alienate jointly*, *PRyl.*118.15 (i B.C.). **-οκέλλω,**

intr., *run aground together*, c. dat., App.*BC*5.121: metaph., Plu.2.985c. **-ολισθαίνω**, = sq., Herod.Med.ap.Aët.9.37. **-ολισθάνω**, *slip out along with*, Man.5.43, in aor. -ώλισθεν. **-όμνυμι**, in Med., *swear jointly in the negative*, *GDI*4986.18 (Crete).

**συνεξομοι-όω**, *assimilate*, *make similar*, τί τινι Plu.2.1054b; τὰ ἤθη ib.97a; ἑαυτῇ τὸ σπέρμα Gal.*UP*14.7; *suit*, *accommodate*, τὸ.. σχῆμα τοῖς λόγοις Herm. *in Phdr.* p.76 A.:—Pass., *to become* or *be like*, Thphr.*CP*1.9.3, *Fr.*173, Plb.31.18.4, *Placit.*1.6.1; κακίᾳ καὶ φθόνῳ Vett.Val.304.27; συνεξομοιοῦνται τὰ τρεφόμενα ταῖς τρεφούσαις Sor.1.88; τῷ περιέχοντι συνεξομοιοῦσθαι *become assimilated*, Plb.4.21.1. **-ωσις**, εως, ἡ, *complete assimilation*, πρὸς τοὺς τόπους Eust.1541.39.

**συνεξ-ορθιάζω**, *excite together*, φόβῳ (s.v.l.) Plu.2.998e. **-ορίζω**, *banish together*, Sch.E.*Ph.*1679 (Pass.). **-ορμάω**, *help to urge on*, Isoc.10.52; τὰ ζῷα πρὸς τοὺς συνδυασμούς Plu.2.685e; ὁ ἥλιος σ. τὰ πνεύματα *assists in raising* them, Arist.*Mete.*361b14. II. intr., *rush forth* or *sally out together*, X.*Cyr.*1.4.20 (v.l. ἐξορμᾷ), 7.1.29, *Hell. Oxy.*15.3, Plb.10.37.6; ὕλη συνεξορμᾷ τῷ σίτῳ *shoots up along with* the corn, X.*Oec.*17.12,14:—Pass., D.C.41.9. 2. *set out together*, ἅμα ἡμῖν *Arch.Pap.*2.515.8 (i B.C.), cf. *PTeb.*18.8 (ii B.C.). **-ορούω**, *rush out with*, τῷ κύματι Clearch.73. **-οτρύνω**, = συνοτρύνω, Nic.Dam.*Fr.*66.16 J., Them.*Or.*21.256a. **-ουρέω**, *discharge with the urine*, Hp.*Aph.*4.77, Gal.8.84 (both Pass.). **-ούσιος**, ὁ, perh. *fellow-magistrate*, *Sammelb.*343. **-υγραίνω**, *moisten with* or *together*, Plu.2.752d. **-υμνέω**, *praise loudly together*, Them.*Or.*8.102b. **-ωθέω**, *drive out together*, ἱδρῶτα Hp.*Vict.*2.66; *puff out*, [τὴν φιλοτιμίαν] Plu.2.820a; σ. αὐτὸς ἑαυτὸν ἐπὶ τὴν γῆν ib.984f; τινὰ ἐκ τοῦ ζῆν ib.1110e; συνοδίαν εἰς τὰς φάραγγας Str.4.6.6; *dismiss at the same time*, Lib.*Or.*18.131. **-ωραΐζω**, *beautify together*, Eust.1598.49.

**συνέορσις**, ἡ, f.l. in Plu.2.449a (pl.); prob. συνθροήσεις.

**συνεορτ-άζω**, *join in keeping festival*, D.S.4.4, *CIG*2820.19 (Aphrodisias), *POxy.*1025.12 (iii A.D.); ἡμῖν *with* us, Plu.2.666d, cf. Arr.*Epict.*4.1.104; τῇ μητρὶ ἐπιτελούσῃ τοὺς ἀγῶνας *SIG*798.12 (Cyzic., i A.D.); σ. γάμους τινί D.C.59.8; τὰ προοίμια τῆς παλιρροίας Them.*Or.*14.181a. **-αστής**, οῦ, ὁ, *sharer in a festival*, Pl.*Lg.*653d.

**συνεοχμός**, ὁ, poet. for *συνοχμός, = συνοχή, *joining*, *joint*, κεφαλῆς τε καὶ αὐχένος ἐν συνεοχμῷ Il.14.465.

⊛ **συνεπ-άγω** [ᾰ], *lead together against*, ἐπί τινας Th.3.11. 2. *join in bringing in against* another, of those who *call in a foreign force to aid* them, Id.4.1,79,84:—Med., *bring* or *take with one*, τὸν ἀδελφόν *IG*12(3).174.16 (Cnidus, Epist. Aug.), cf. *BGU*1780.6 (i B.C.), J.*AJ*18.9.5, Plu.*Cat.Ma.*17, D.C.41.7; *draw* a net *along with* one, Ael.*NA*14.29, cf. Gal.11.508: metaph., τὰ ἐπιρρήματα σ. τὴν πρόθεσιν ἐπὶ τὰ ῥήματα A.D.*Synt.*338.4. **-αγωνίζομαι**, *join in stirring up a contest besides*, τοῖς γεγονόσι *besides* all that had happened, Plb.3.118.6. **-ᾴδω**, poet. -αείδω, *join in celebrating*, συνεπαείδετ' Ἄρτεμιν E.*IA*1492 (lyr.). II. *sing* spells or charms *at the same time*, συνεπᾴδειν ἐπῳδήν Thphr.*HP*9.10.4. **-αινέω**, *approve together*, *give joint assent*, *consent*, *approve*, πόλις καὶ τὸ δίκαιον ξ. A.*Th.*1079 (anap.), cf. X.*Cyr.*4.3.23 (v.l.), D.18.179: c. inf., ξ. μάχεσθαι *join in the recommendation* to fight, Th.4.91, cf. X.*Cyr.*5.3.34; σ. τι *approve*, *consent* or *agree to*, Id.*An.*7.3.36, Pl.*Hp.Mi.*363a; σ. τινὶ ὅ τι ἂν πράττῃ *agree with* one in all that he does, D.*Prooem.*28. II. *join in praising*, τινα X.*Eq.Mag.*5.14 codd., Pl.*Mx.*246a:—Pass., Arist.*Rh.*1415b28. **-αινος**, ον, *joining in approbation of* a thing, σ. εἶναι or γίνεσθαι *give one's consent to* a thing, τινι Hdt.3.119, 5.31: abs., ib.20, Nic.Dam.*Fr.*130.18 J.: c. acc. et inf., *consent that*.., Hdt.7.15: c. dat. pers., D.C.57.15. **-αίρω**, *raise* or *lift at the same time*, ἑαυτόν X.*Eq.*7.2; τὰ πρόσθια σκέλη Arist.*HA*576b27:—Pass., *swell at the same time*, Gal.18(2).266; *to be elevated together*, ἡ λέξις τῷ μεγέθει τῶν λεγομένων σ. Luc.*Hist.Conscr.*45, cf. Procl.*Inst.*209. II. *urge on together* or *also*, c. inf., X.*Smp.*8.24, *Oec.*5.5:—Pass., *rise together with*, τοῖς δημαγωγοῖς, of the rabble, Plu.*Cor.*12, cf. J.*BJ Prooem.*2. III. συνεπαιρομένου σὺν τῷ αἵματι καὶ τοῦ μοχθηροῦ χυμοῦ *being carried to* (the foetus) with the blood, Aët.9.22.

**συνεπαισθ-άνομαι**, *feel together*, Gal.*UP*9.11. **-ησις**, εως, ἡ, *consciousness*, *apperception*, Epicur.*Nat.*20 G.

**συνεπ-αιτιάομαι**, *accuse also of* a thing, Μηδισμοῦ ξ. καὶ τὸν Θεμιστοκλέα Th.1.135; Λακωνισμοῦ σ. τινάς Plu.*Per.*10: abs., Id.*Them.*23. **-αιωρέομαι**, Pass., *continue soaring over*, Id.*Alex.*33. **-ᾰκολουθέω**, *follow closely*, *accompany*, Pl.*Phd.*81e, Plu.*Alex.*41; τινι Str.8.6.22; Νεῖλος συνεπηκολούθηκα I Nilus *have been present too* (at the transaction), *PFay.*43.4 (i B.C.), cf. *PLond.*2.256(e).3 (i A.D.); of things, Hp.*Oss.*4, Ocell.2.22, Sor.1.31, etc. **-ακτήρ**, ῆρος, ὁ, *fellow-huntsman*, Eust.1688.24. **-ᾰλαλάζω**, *join in raising the war-cry*, τινι J.*BJ*4.5.1. **-ᾰμύνω** [ῡ], *join in repelling*, Th.6.56. II. *join in assisting*, τινι App.*BC*3.32. **-ανήκω**, *return at the same time*, c. dat., Them.*Or.*15.197c. **-ανίσταμαι**, Pass., with aor. 2 Act., *join in a revolt* or *rebellion*, Hdt.3.84, Th.1.132, *OGI*218.118 (Ilium, iii B.C.); τινι *with* one, Hdt.3.61; ἅμα τινί Id.1.59; αὐτοῖς μεθ' ὑμῶν *against* them *with* you, D.H.6.74. **-ανορθόω**, aor. συνεπηνώρθωσα (cf. ἀνορθόω) D.10.34:—*join in re-establishing*, l. c., Plb.30.20.4. **-άπτομαι**, Ion. for συνεφάπτομαι. **-ᾰρήγω**, *succour together*, Eust.40.25. **-αρτιμένος** (sic)· συνημμένος, Hsch. **-ασκέω**, *join in training*, *making efficient*, Aristid.1.452 J. (dub.l.). **-αύξω**, *help to increase*, τοῖς θεοῖς τὴν πανήγυριν *IG*12(5).129.58 (Paros, ii B.C.), cf. *SIG*695.75 (Magn. Mae., ii B.C.), 601.23 (Teos, ii B.C.), Gal.*UP*4.7, al., D.C.39.25. **-αφίημι**, *throw upon together*, J.*BJ*3.7.28.

**συνέπεια**, ἡ, (ἔπος) *connexion of words* or *verses*, D.H.*Comp.*23 (v.l. συνέχεια), A.D.*Synt.*41.25; acc. sg. συνεπ[ει]αν is dub. l. in Phld.*Po.*2.28.

**συνεπείγω**, *help to urge on*, ἐπὶ τὸ κάκιον Hp.*Epid.*1.8; ἐς τὸν κίνδυνον Aret.*CA*1.4: abs., ib.10, etc.: intr., *hasten on*, ib.2.2:—Pass., in same sense, ib.1.10. II. συνεπείγεσθαί τινι *increase* or *grow with*, Ael.*NA*14.23.

**συνέπειμι**, (εἶμι *ibo*) *join in attacking*, μετ' αὐτῶν ἄλλοις Th.3.63.

**συνέπειξις**, εως, ἡ, *great haste*, Nicom.*Harm.*1.

**συνεπείσ-ειμι**, (εἶμι *ibo*) *go upon together*, τὴν σκηνήν Plb.30.22.9. **-κυκλέω**, *introduce besides*, Phot.*Bibl.*p.145 B. **-πίπτω**, *rush in upon together*, εἰς πόλιν ἅμα τινί Plu.*Fab.*17. **-ρέω**, *flow in upon together*, *Corp.Herm.*9.2. **-φέρω**, *bring in as well*, Vett.Val.359.14, Syrian. *in Metaph.*90.36:—Med., *help to bring in*, τὸν βάρβαρον τῇ Ἑλλάδι X.*HG*6.5.43 (v.l. ἐπεισφέρεσθαι).

**συνεπεκ-πίνω** [ῐ], *drink off together*, ἅμα τινί *AP*6.292 (Hedyl., dub.l.). **-τείνω**, *extend* or *spread over together*, τινί τι Aristaenet.2.15:—Pass., Arist.*Ph.*216b29, Gal.*UP*14.14; *expand with*, Id.2.562; *extend* or *project against* the enemy *as well*, Ael.*Tact.*13.3.

**συνεπελαφρ-ίζω**, in Pass., *to be made light with* something, Ph.2.513: metaph., *to be relieved with*, Orib.8.30.1. **-ύνω**, *help to make light*, i.e. *assist in bearing*, σ. τισὶ τὸν πόλεμον Hdt.1.18.

**συνεπ-εμβαίνω**, *mount upon together*, σ. τοῖς καιροῖς, ταῖς ἀτυχίαις, *pounce upon* opportunities, etc., Plb.20.11.7, 30.9.21. II. σ. τινί *join in trampling on* him, Aristid.1.471 J. **-εξεργάζομαι**, *help in performing*, Id.2.175 J. **-ερείδω**, *help in driving against*, c. acc. rei, Plu.2.939b; *help in inflicting*, πληγήν Id.*Brut.*52; σ. ὑπόνοιάν τινι *help to fix* a suspicion on him, Id.*Caes.*8, cf. *Cic.*21 (cj. for συναπ-); *drive home* a weapon, Id.*Phil.*10; συνεπερείσας τῇ ῥύμῃ τοῦ ἵππου *charging* him with all the force of his horse, Id.*Marc.*7; *give additional force*, Arr.*Tact.*12.2,10. II. Med., = Lat. *conitor*, Dosith. p.433 K., *Gloss.* **-ερίζω**, *contend also with*, ποταμῷ *AP*9.709 (Phil.). ⊛ **-έρχομαι**, *attack together*, *SIG*700.22 (Macedonia, ii B.C.), *PLips.*40 ii 5,17 (iv A.D.). **-εσπόμην**, Ion. aor. of συνεφέπομαι. **-ευδοκέω**, *consent*, *GDI*1785.2 (Delph., ii B.C.). **-ευθύνω**, *help to direct* or *guide*, ἀρχὰς πραγμάτων Plu.*Rom.*7. **-ευφημέω**, *join in cheering* or *applauding*, D.S.1.72, 17.72. **-εύχομαι**, *join in prayer*, Th.6.32; *pray also to*, [θεοῖς] συννάοις σ. Plu.2.708c: c. acc. et inf., *profess also that*.., Ar.*Th.*951: c. inf. fut., *make a vow also to*.., σ. τοῖς θεοῖς θύσειν X.*An.*3.2.9. **-έχω**, *refer together to* a thing, Iamb. *in Nic.* p.8 P. **-ηχέω**, *join in singing*, *join in a chorus*, ἐξῆρχε παιᾶνα, οἱ δὲ πάντες συνεπήχησαν X.*Cyr.*3.3.58, cf. 7.1.25; κορυφαίου κατάρξαντος σ. πᾶς ὁ χορός Arist.*Mu.*399a15; συνεπήχουν πρὸς τὸ ἐνδόσιμον Max.Tyr.7.7: metaph., *chime in with*, Ph.1.321, Plu.2.44c, Them.*Or.*18.218a. II. *re-echo*, οἶκος Luc.*Dom.*3, cf. J.*AJ*12.9.4, D.C.66.22. III. Pass., *to be sounded at the same time*, τῶν ἡμιφώνων τι -εφηχεῖται (sic) Phld.*Po.*2.16.

⊛ **συνεπι-βαίνω**, *mount together*, Arist.*HA*591b21; τοῦ τείχους *on* the wall, Plu.*TG*4; *mount a ladder together*, Plb.10.13.8. II. *enter upon* or *undertake along with*, τινι Antipho 2.2.13. III. *trample on as well*, σ. ἐν ταῖς συμφοραῖς τινι J.*BJ*1.24.8. IV. trans., aor. 1 part. -βήσας, *cause to mount*, πύργοις ἀκοντιστάς ib.3.7.30. ⊛ **-βάλλω**, (ἐπιβάλλω II. 3) *apply one's mind also*, *consider* a thing *together* or *also*, Arist.*Fr.*29, Plb.3.38.4, S.E.*M.*7.348: folld. by indirect question, M.Ant.3.11. II. *coincide with*, καιροῖς Plb.2.56.4. **-βλάπτομαι**, Pass., *to be damaged together with*, τινι Arist.*Pol.*1270b15. **-βλέπω**, *regard at the same time*, Antip.*Stoic.*3.256; *consider as well*, Gal.9.498. **-βοηθέω**, *come to aid together*, Plb.4.69.4, Gal.8.16, Pall. *in Hp.*2.116,128 D. **-βουλεύω**, *join in plotting*, X.*HG*5.4.22, D.S.5.50, etc.; τινὶ μετά τινος Is.6.55, D.H.3.29, etc. **-βουλος**, ὁ, *fellow-plotter*, J.*AJ*18.6.6. **-γαυρόω**, *encourage*, *hearten*, τὸ φιλότιμον, τὸ γενναῖον, Plu.2.746d, 796a. **-γελάω**, *laugh at together*, Ammon.*Diff.* p.56 codd. (ἐπιγελᾶν Valck.). **-γίγνομαι**, *come on together*, of troops, Plb.10.38.10; of fevers, D.S.32.10; *occur as well*, αἴτια κακῶν Vett.Val.222.34.

**συνεπιγρᾰφ-εύς**, έως, ὁ, *fellow-registrar*, *fellow-clerk*, Isoc.17.41. **-ή**, ἡ, *written consent*, *POxy.*273.23 (i A.D.), 2134.26 (ii A.D.). **-ω**, *inscribe together with* other writing, *PMag.Lond.*121.421; *indicate as joint author*, τύχην κατορθώμασι Plu.2.816e; ἑαυτὸν σ. τοῖς πραχθεῖσι Gal.11.202:—Pass., *to be named jointly as auctor* of a decree of the Senate, *Notiz.Arch.*4.21.75 (Cyrene, Aug.); οἱ -γραφέντες μοι μάρτυρες *named jointly with* me as witnesses, Mitteis *Chr.*28.24 (iii B.C.), cf. *PStrassb.*87.14 (ii B.C.), *POxy.*265.16 (i A.D.):—Med., *subscribe*, *assent*, c. dat., Hipparch.1.3.1, Phld.*Rh.*1.374 S., Ph.1.464: abs., Id.2.311.

⊛ **συνεπι-δείκνυμι**, *display at the same time*, Plb.33.5.1, Iamb.*Myst.*2.7:—Pass., *to be indicated together*, Plb.3.38.5, Gal.9.420, 18(2).100. **-δεσμέω**, *bind up together*, Sor.1.84. **-δέω**, *bandage as well*, Hp.*Off.*24, Gal.18(1).806. **-δημέω**, *travel* to a place *together*, Str.15.1.2; -ησάντων τῇ κιβωτῷ τῶν δεινῶν the plagues *having visited* them *with* the ark, J.*AJ*6.1.2. ⊛ **-δίδωμι**, *give up wholly* or *willingly*, ἑαυτόν τινι or εἴς τι Plb.31.24.5, 32.5.10; ἐς πάντα τὰ καλῶς ἔχοντα ἑαυτὸν *Supp.Epigr.*4.601.8 (Teos, ii B.C.), cf. 3.468.16 (Thess., i B.C.); τῇ Κλωθοῖ σεαυτὸν M.Ant.4.34; simply, συνεπέδωκε αὐτοσαυτὰν ἁ σύνοδος *SIG*698.6 (Delph., ii B.C.); τὰ σώματα προκινδυνεῦσαι D.H.3.15, cf. *Inscr.Prien.*109.156 (ii B.C.). 2. *join in presenting* an application, *PAmh.*2.85.24 (i A.D.), *Sammelb.*7363.25 (ii A.D.), etc. 3. *offer together*, τὴν χεῖρά τινι Them.*Or.*7.90a. II. intr., *increase along with* or *together*, Plu.2.448d. **-ζεύγνυμαι**, Pass., *to* *be closely connected with*, συνεπεζεῦχθαί τινι Phld.*Ir.*p.66 W. -ζητέω, *examine along with*, τινί τι Aristaenet.2.3. -θειάζω, *ascribe to divine interposition*, Plu.*Sull.*6; σ. τὸ χρηστήριον *recognize* it *as divine*, Id.2.409c. -θεσις, εως, ἡ, *joint assault*, Aq.*Ps.*118(119).118. -θέτης, ου, ὁ, *abettor*, *BGU*984.23 (iv A.D.). -θεωρέω, *contemplate at the same time*, S.E.*M.*7.46. -θήγω, *help to sharpen* or *stimulate*, Plu.2.433d. -θλίβω [ῑ], *exert pressure at the same time*, Gal.8.15. -θορυβέω, *join in applauding loudly*, Plu.2.531c. -θρηνέω, *join in bewailing*, ib.56a, M.Ant.7.43; τοῖς ἀβουλήτοις Plu.2.541a. -θρήνησις, εως, ἡ, *joint bewailing*, ib.610b (pl.). -θρυψις, εως, ἡ, *participation in luxury*, ib.1092d (pl.). -θυμέω, *desire along with*, σοι τῶν καλῶν X.*Eq.Mag.*1.8. -θυμητής, οῦ, ὁ, *one of the same desires*, Pl.*Clit.*408c. -θωΰσσω, *halloo so as to cheer on together*, Plu.2.757d. -καίω, *set on fire together*, ἅμα Thphr.*CP*5.17.6. -κᾰλέομαι, Med., *invoke together with*, τινά τινι Arr.*An.*6.3.1. -κειμαι, Pass., *join in attacking*, Ar.*Eq.*266. 2. *weigh upon*, -κειμένων μου τῇ ψυχῇ κακῶν Phld.*Rh.*2.139 S. -κελεύω, *encourage by consent*, *PLond.*3.1204.17 (ii B.C.), *PStrassb.*84.19 (ii B.C.), *PGrenf.*2.26.24 (ii B.C.). ® -κιρνάω, *mix with besides*, Procl.*Par.Ptol.*207:—Pass. -κίρνασθαι Vett.Val.5.4. -κλάω, *break* or *bow down at once*, metaph., τῆς αἰσθήσεως συνεπικλώσης τὴν διάνοιαν Plu.*Phil.*9. -κλίνω [ῑ], *incline at the same time*, Gal.6.151 (Pass.), Dam.*Pr.*168. -κοσμέω, *help to adorn*, X.*Hier.*8.6; τὸν λόγον Arist.*Top.*157ᵃ11; τὸν βίον Id.*EN* 1100ᵇ26, cf. Phld.*Mus.*p.39 K.:—Pass., prob. in *OGI*470.23 (Lydia, i A.D.). -κούρειος, ὁ, *fellow-Epicurean*, Arr.*Epict.*2.20.13. -κουρέω, *help to succour*, X.*Hier.*3.2; ταῖς ἀπορίαις τινός Id.*Cyr.*1.6.24; Astrol., *join as ally*, τῷ ἡλίῳ S.E.*M.*5.32. -κουφίζω, *lighten at the same time*, Plu.*Cam.*25, Gal.19.245. II. *help in relieving*, Ph.2.364; *raise aloft*, metaph., τοῖς φρονήμασιν Plu.*Eum.*9. -κρᾰδαίνω, *move backwards and forwards together with*, σὺν ταῖς οὐραῖς τὰ σώματα, of dogs near game, X.*Cyn.*6.16. -κρᾰτέω, Astrol., *dominate together*, Vett.Val.293.15. -κρίνω [ῑ], *help to judge between*, ἡμᾶς Pl.*Lg.*792c. 2. *help to decide* a matter, Plu.2.53b, Longin.1.2, Plot.2.1.6. -κροτέω, *join in applauding*, Plu.2.56b,63a. -κρύπτω, *help to conceal*, Id.*Alc.*28, *Tim.*10:—Med., Iamb.*VP*34.245. -κυρόω, *join in ratifying*, δόγμα Plb.4.30.2; τῷ δήμῳ τοὺς νόμους Plu.*Caes.*14. -κωμάζω, *join in a κῶμος*, Satyr.1, S.E.*M.*6.8. -λαμβάνω, *take part with* a person, λόγῳ καὶ ἔργῳ σ. τινί Th.2.8; τοῦ βίου Max. Tyr.14.7; πρὸς ἀσφάλειαν ἑκατέρῳ ἑκάτερος Id.16.8: c. dat. rei, τῇ σωτηρίᾳ τῆς νεώς.. Id.21.4: abs., *assist*, *PPetr.*3 p.57 (iii B.C.), Arr.*An.*6.3.3, Gal.6.212. 2. *envelop also*, τι τοῦ περὶ τὴν διάρθρωσιν συνδέσμου Id.2.301, cf. 18(2).937. II. Med., *take part in together*, *partake in*, c. gen. rei, τοῦ στρατεύματος, τοῦ πολέμου, Hdt.3.48, 5.45, cf. Th.8.26: abs., Id.1.115, *OGI*244.36 (Daphne, iii/ii B.C.). 2. σ. τινί τινος *take part with* or *assist* one *in* a thing, σ. τινὶ τοῦ ἔργου Luc.*Prom.*13, cf. *Im.*8; σ. τισὶ σωτηρίας *help* them *towards* it, Plb.11.24.8, etc.; σ. τισὶ τοῦ φόβου *contribute towards increasing* their fear, Th.6.70: c. dat. pers. only, *take part with*, *support*, Id.3.74, Plb.5.90.2, etc.; συνεπιλαβοῦ (sc. αὐτῷ) ἵνα κομίσηται *help* him to recover (the money), *PCair.Zen.*553.9 (iii B.C.); συνεπιλαβόμενος τοῦ ἐντυχεῖν αὐτὸν Ἀπολλωνίῳ τὴν ταχίστην *PMich.Zen.*23.7 (iii B.C.). 3. c. gen. pers., τῶν Ἑλλήνων σ. *help in* (the persuasion of) the Greeks, Plu.*Them.*12. 4. c. gen. rei, *take also into consideration*, Ptol.*Phas.*p.11 H. -λαμπρύνω, *help to brighten*, τὸ φρόνημα Plu.2.795c. -λάμπω, *illumine at the same time*, Thphr.*CP*4.4.13, Plot.4.3.17. -λέγω, *utter in addition*, τὸν λόγον τοῦτον *PMag.Par.*1.1037. 2. Med., *read over together*, Hld.10.13. -λείπω, *fail together with*, Plot.6.5.12, Iamb.*VP*35.252. -λεκτέον, *one must further add*, Eust.1406.50. -λογίζομαι, *calculate also*, Ptol.*Alm.*2.4, Procl.*Par.Ptol.*121:—Pass., Ptol.*Alm.*13.4. -λογιστέον, *one must also calculate* or *must reckon in*, ibid., Eust.366.34. -λύομαι, perh. *join in cancelling a mortgage*, *Delph.*3(2).233 (ii B.C.).

**συνεπιμαρτῠρ-έω**, *join in attesting*, Arist.*Mu.*400ᵃ15, Thphr.*CP*6.16.6, *Ep.Hebr.*2.4; τινι *with* one, Plb.25.6.4, Aristeas 191, Plu.2.542c, Gal.15.583, Ath.13.595e; *add one's evidence*, Plu.2.486c,539d. II. Astrol., *to be also configurate*, of planets, Nech.ap.Vett.Val.279.3, *Cat.Cod.Astr.*2.187. -ησις, εως, ἡ, *joint testimony* or *approval*, M.Ant.1.10.

**συνεπι-μείγνῡμι**, *join, unite*, μόλιβδον ἀργύρῳ Aristaenet.1.10:—Pass., of veins, muscles, etc., Gal.2.816, *UP*7.11. -μειδιάω, *smile at together*, τοῖς πάθεσι Plu.2.672e. -μελέομαι or -μέλομαι, *join in taking care of* or *attending to*, τινος Th.8.39, X.*Eq.Mag.*1.8, etc.; τῆς στρατιᾶς *have joint charge of*, Id.*An.*6.1.22; σ. μεθ' ἡμῶν ὧν προσήκει D.48.5, cf. Arist.*Ath.*49.3; συνεπιμέλεσθαι δὲ αὐτῷ καὶ τοὺς στρατηγοὺς *IG*1².59.14, cf. 88.19; τοῦ ἀναθήματος.. τῇ βουλῇ -ήθησαν Ἀρχ.Ἐφ.1917.41 (Attic decree, iv B.C.): abs., X.*Mem.*2.8.3; συνεπιμεληθῆναι ὅπως καταστῶσιν Pl.*Lg.*754c; ὅπως ἂν τάχιστα τυθῇ *IG*1².39.68; ὅπως τι λημφθῇ *PCair.Zen.*217.6 (iii B.C.), cf. *IG*2².678.14; σ. ἵνα.. *OGI* 214.24 (Milet., iii B.C.). -μελητής, οῦ, ὁ, *fellow-curator, coadjutor*, X.*Cyr.*5.4.17, *IG*2².1317.2 (both pl.). -μερίζω, *assign at once, at the same time*, Eust.100.4, 828.12 (both Pass.). II. *contribute also* (stellar influence), Vett.Val.178.25. -μεριστέον, *one must construe also*, τὸ.. μάλα εἰς.. Eust.1769.64. -νεύω, *join in assenting*, Arist.*SE*169ᵃ33, *IPE*2.52 (Panticapaeum, i A.D.), Wilcken *Chr.*14 ii 13 (i A.D.), Plu.2.53b; ἐξ ὅλης τῆς ψυχῆς ταῖς ἡδοναῖς σ. ib.446a. 2. c. acc., *join in granting*, τιμαῖς (Aeol. acc. pl.) *IGRom.*4.1302.20 (Cyme, i B.C./i A.D.). II. literally, of an orator's *gestures in accordance with* his speech, Phld.*Rh.*1.73 S. -νήχομαι, *float on the surface together*, Aristaenet.1.3. ® -νοέω, *join in contriving*, S.E.*M.*8.161; σ. πῶς.. Plb.8.15.2; *devise as well*, A.D.*Synt.*103.27 (Pass.). II. Pass., *to be included in the idea of* a thing, c. dat., Phld.*Vit.*p.38 J., Dam.*Pr.*57: abs., *to be taken into consideration* or *understood as well*, Gal.6.105, 11.5, 17(2).707. -νοητέον, *one must understand also*, Eust.821.1. -ορκέω, *join in swearing falsely*, Plu.2.808a. -πάσχω, *feel emotion together*, μετὰ πάθους τινός ib.1037b. -πλέκω, *plait in with the rest*, *AP*4.2.13 (Phil.). II. Pass., metaph., τῇ ἀλόγῳ ψυχῇ τοῦ θηρίου -πλέκεται ἡ λογικὴ ἡ τοῦ ἀνθρώπου Herm. in *Phdr.*p.153 A. ® -πλέω, *join in a naval expedition*, D.50.59. -πλοκή, ἡ, *association*, φίλων Ptol. *Tetr.*111,181; of planets, Nech.ap.Vett.Val.279.6. -πονέω, *help in extra work*, X.*Cyr.*5.4.17 (as v.l. for ἐπιπονεῖν). -πορεύομαι, *march through together*, *OGI*12.15 (Priene, iii B.C.). -ρρέπω, *incline towards together*, Plu.*Phoc.*2. -ρρέω, *flow to together*, Gal.13.668, *PGrenf.*2.69.19 (iii A.D.); σ. ὁ ὄχλος D.H.10.16; *extend in flow*, ἔλαιον σ. πορρωτάτω Plu.2.696d. -ρρώννῡμι, *help to strengthen* or *support*, τοὺς Ἕλληνας Plu.*Alex.*33, cf. *Brut.*49:—Pass., of language, *to be based firmly at the same time on*, τοῖς ὕψεσι Longin.11.2. -σημαίνω, *help to indicate*, τῇ τοῦ θεοῦ προνοίᾳ Plu.2.398a, cf. Gal.19.188: mostly in Med., *join in expressing a judgement of* a thing (c. acc.), whether in disapproval, Plb.4.24.4; or in approval, D.S.17.25. 2. Med., *explain* or *interpret in addition*, Gal.17(1).600. -σκεπτέον, *one must examine together*, Ph.2.335, Gal.6.250. -σκέπω, *protect at the same time*, Ascl.*Tact.*1.3 (Pass.). -σκευάζω, *join in repairing*, *OGI*483.33 (Pergam., ii A.D.). 2. Med., *work up in addition*, Procl.*Par.Ptol.*14. -σκοπέω, fut. -σκέψομαι Pl.*Cra.*422c: aor. -εσκεψάμην (v. infr.): non-Att. pres. -σκέπτομαι, Gal.6.827, 10.215, Ptol.*Phas.Prooem.*8, Alex.Aphr. in *Sens.*5.16: pres. Med. and Pass. -σκοποῦμαι Gal.6.256, 10.662, 2.681:—*join in examining*, *examine* or *consider together with*, ἀλλά μοι τόδε συνεπίσκεψαι Pl.*Hp.Ma.*296b; συνεπίσκεψαι μετ' ἐμοῦ Id.*Cra.*422c; ἐκ τῶν ἀπορουμένων λόγων συνεπισκεψάμενοι Arist.*MM*1200ᵇ22; συνεπισκοπεῖν καὶ τὰ ὑπ' ἐκείνου λεχθέντα Str.8.3.23; ταῦτα συνεπισκόπει καὶ αὐτός Plu.2.83e, cf. 714c; συνεπισκέψασθε ἦ.. Pl.*Ap.*27a. -σκυθρωπάζω, *look sternly at with* or *together*, Plu.2.672e. -σπάω, *draw on together*, βίᾳ σ. τὸν ἡνίοχον εἰς τὸ ῥεῖθρον Id.*Crass.*19. II. mostly in Med., *draw on along with one*, esp. to ruin, τοὺς φίλους Pl.*R.*451a, cf. D.19.224, *IPE*1².352.23 (Chersonesus, ii B.C.); of things, *involve, bring on*, κακά Phld.*Ir.*p.23 W., cf. p.77 W.; also without any bad sense, Pl. *Ti.*44a, X.*Cyr.*2.2.24: literally, of the magnet, σ. τὸν σίδηρον Epicur. *Fr.*293; of ligaments, ἑαυτοῖς σ. τοὺς σπονδύλους Gal.18(1).506. 2. *draw on along with one*, i.e. *to one's own views*, τινὰ πρὸς τὸ συμφῆσαι Pl.*Sph.*236d; πρὸς τὴν αὐτῶν γνώμην Plb.30.6.7:—Pass., Epicur. *Nat.*121 G. 3. σ. τὸν ἀέρα *inhale at the same time*, Arist.*Pr.*906ᵃ6. -σπεύδω, *join in forcing onward*, τὰς ἁμάξας X.*An.*1.5.8.

**συνεπίσταμαι**, *to be privy to*, τὴν ἐπανάστασιν X.*HG*5.4.19; ἀπιστότατον ἔργον σ. μοι πεποιηκότι Gorg.*Pal.*21; σ. τινὶ πονηρὰ δράσαντι Luc.*Cat.*23, cf. 27; οὐδὲν ἐμαυτῷ ψεῦδος εἰπόντι σ. Id.*VH*2.31, cf. *Cal.*9; ἃ ἐμαυτῷ συνεπίσταμαι Lxx *Jb.*19.27. 2. *know perfectly well* or *fully*, πολλάκις ἑώρακα.. τὸν ἥλιον καὶ σελήνην δρῶντας ταῦθ' ἃ ἀεὶ πάντες συνεπιστάμεθα Pl.*Lg.*821c; οὐκ ἄρα συνεπίστανται ὅτι ἐπίστανται; Arist.*SE*177ᵃ27.

**συνεπι-στᾰσις**, εως, ἡ, *joint attention*, Iamb.*VP*31.188. -στᾰτέω, *act as a joint supervisor*, Pl.*R.*528c; -ούντων τῷ ἔργῳ οἱ ταμίαι *IG*1².92.39 (dub.); -ήσω ἐγὼ πᾶσι τούτοις *will jointly supervise* all these works, *PCair.Zen.*34.22, cf. 574.5 (iii B.C.). -στέλλω, *authorize at the same time*, *BGU*1741.8 (i B.C.), *POxy.*1024.6 (ii A.D.); *send with* or *together*, Luc.*Sat.*15. -στενάζω, *groan at* or *over together*, Epict.*Ench.*16; ταῖς ἀλγηδόσιν Diog.Oen.61. -στένω, = foreg., Plu.*Galb.*23. -στήμων, ονος, ὁ, ἡ, *sharing in knowledge*, Zonar. s.v. συνίστωρ. -στρᾰτεύω, *join in making war*, τινι Th.5.48, D.5.16, etc. -στρέφω, *turn at the same time*, τοῦ ἀτράκτου τὴν περιφορὰν Pl.*R.*617c:—Pass., -ομένου τοῦ ἄξονος Heliod.ap.Orib.49.9.27; of one being massaged, Gal.6.177. 2. *help to make attentive*, Plu.*Num.*14; πρὸς ἑαυτοὺς τὸν ἀκροατὴν *turn towards them also*, Id.2.542c, etc. II. *twist together* like strands, Pl.*Ti.*84d:—Pass., πρὸς ἓν τέλος συνεπιστρέφεσθαι τοῖς ἤθεσιν *to be intertwined* in their characters with a view to.., Id. *Comp.Lyc.Num.*4. III. intr., *turn jointly towards*, πρὸς ἀλλήλας Id.*Num.*13. -σῡκοφαντέω, *join in misrepresenting, cavilling at*, τινας dub. l. in Id.2.1096e. -σύρομαι [ῡ], Med., *draw to oneself together*, Archig.ap.Aët.12.1; *draw with oneself*, Gal.*UP*8.7. -σφάζω, *kill besides*, Parth.6.6 (s.v.l.). -σφρᾱγίζω, *seal* or *approve together*, in Med., *PRev.Laws* 42.19, 84.2 (iii B.C.).

**συνεπ-ισχύω**, *join in supporting, assist*, X.*Mem.*2.4.6; τισι Lxx 2*Ch.*32.3, Plb.6.6.10, etc.; κατά τινων Id.6.8.1; ταῖς πλεονεξίαις αὐτῶν Id.28.5.5; σ. μοι ἀπαιτοῦντι *BGU*1189.14 (i B.C./i A.D.); αὐτοῖς ἀντεχομένοις ib.1795.9 (i B.C.), cf. *PSI*10.1160.9 (i B.C.); τοὺς ἄρχοντας συνεπισχύειν τοῖς ἀγορανόμοις, ὅπως.. *SIG*799.19 (Cyzicus, i A.D.), cf. *IG*2².1013.6. 2. Astrol., *combine energy*, of planetary influence, Vett.Val.107.14. 3. Medic., of symptoms, σ. πρὸς ⟨τὸν ?⟩ τοῦ κάμνοντος κίνδυνον *contribute to*.., Gal.17(1).628.

**συνεπι-τᾰσις**, εως, ἡ, *joint exertion*, Iamb.*VP*16.69. -τᾰχύνω, *join in hastening*, Plu.*Agis* 7; τὴν κίνησιν Id.2.1005a. -τείνω, *help to strain* or *intensify*, αὐτῶν τὴν ὀργὴν Plb.3.13.1; τὴν ψυχρότητα Plu.2.691c, etc.:—Pass., *to be increased along with*, τινι ib.1020c: abs., Herod.Med.ap.Aët.9.37. 2. intr., *agree in intensity with*, τινι Arist.*Insomn.*460ᵇ13, v.l. in Plu.2.451d. -τελέω, fut. -τελέσω *BGU*

237.14 (ii A. D.):—*help to accomplish*, Arist.*Mete.*379$^b$23 (Pass.), Plu. *Per.*13. 2. *join in performing*, παιᾶνα θεῷ X.*Ages.*2.17. **-τέλλω**, *rise together with*, Autol.2.11, Gem.17.26, Adam.*Vent.*42. **-τέμνω**, *abridge in accordance with*, Eust.1167.61 (Pass.). **-τίθημι**, *help in putting on, put on still more*, βάρος Plu.2.728c. II. Med., *join in attacking*, τῷ Μήδῳ Th.3.54, cf. 6.17; τῷ τῆς τύχης πταίσματι Phld.*Vit.* p.21 J.; μετά τινος Th.1.23, 6.10, Pl.*Phlb.*16a: abs., X.*Cyr.* 4.2.3, Is.6.29, Arist.*Pol.*1311$^b$17, Lxx *De.*32.27, *Act.Ap.*24.9. 2. σ. τῷ ἔργῳ *fall to* the work *together*, Th.6.56. 3. *set upon and use to one's own advantage*, σ. τῇ ἀγνοίᾳ, τῷ μίσει τινός, Plb.6.43.4; τοῖς καιροῖς Id.3.15.10, 5.87.2. 4. σ. τισὶ ἁμαρτίαν *lay* a sin *to their charge*, Lxx *Nu.*12.11. **-τιμάω**, *join in chiding*, Plu.*Lys.* 15. **-τρέπω**, *join in permitting*, τινὶ ποιεῖν τι Epist.ap.J.*AJ*16.6.7. **-τρέχω**, *to be correspondingly cursory*, Sch.Il.7.256 (in *An. Par.*3.10). **-τρίβω** [ῐ], *destroy at once* or *utterly*, πάντα X.*An.*5.8.20. **-τροπεύω**, *act as joint guardian over*, τὰ τῇδε τῷ θεῷ Olymp. *in Alc.* p.60C., cf. *IPE*2.52,53 (Panticapaeum, i A. D.), *POxy.*265.29 (i A. D.). ❋ **-τροπος**, ὁ, *joint guardian*, D.27.14,16. **-τροχάζομαι**, Pass., *to be hurried along with*, τῇ σπουδῇ τινος Eust.1719.14. **-τυφόω**, *help to make vain*, Plu.2.56b. **-φαίνω**, *make perceptible at the same time*, τὸν αὐτοῦ χυλόν (taste) Thphr.*Od.*10:—Pass., *appear together*, Plu.2.767c, Gal.10.693, al.: c. dat., Plu.2.353c, Gal.16.839. **-φάσκω**, *assent also*, Plu.2.63c. **-φέρω**, *carry with one*, πίστιν D.H.*Lys.*18; *help to induce*, τὰς τοιαύτας διαθέσεις Phld.*Mus.* p.6 K.; ὀλιγημέρους θανάτους Gal.15.490; *join in applying*, ὄνομα Plu.*Pomp.*2:—Med. in act. sense, Phld.*Ir.* p.80 W.:—Pass., συνεπενηνέχθαι τινί *to be dragged in together with*, Id.*Po.*5.18; *to be borne along with*, ναῦς -φερομένας ταῖς τῶν πολεμίων τριήρεσι D.S.13.45. II. of a term, *carry along with it*, i.e. *imply, involve*, τὸ πεζὸν καὶ τὸ δίπουν τὸ ζῷον Arist.*Top.*144$^b$17, cf. 157$^b$23, *APr.*52$^b$7. **-φημι**, *assent, acquiesce*, Plu.2.511f. **-φθέγγομαι**, *reinforce* one's *utterance*, Id.*Tim.*27; ὁ αὐλὸς σ. τῷ παιᾶνι τὸ θεῖον *sounds* it *with*.., Id.2.713a. **-φορτίζω**, *help to load still more*, ib. 728c. **-φύομαι**, *to be attached together with*, Gal.2.446, 18(2). 975. **-φωνέω**, *raise a shout of approval together*, Aristeas 235, 294. **-χειρέω**, *make an attempt together upon*, πανταχόθεν ἅμα τοῖς πολεμίοις Plb.3.84.1. **-χειρονομέω**, *second by fresh violence*, τοῖς παρανομήμασι D.S.33.5 (prob. ἐπιχειρ-). **-χωρέω**, *concur in*, c. dat., *IG*12(7).58.6 (Arcesine, iii B. C.), *Inscr.Délos* 396*A* 50, al. (ii B. C.). **-ψεύδομαι**, *join in lying*, Call.*Dian.*223, Luc.*DMeretr.* 13.5: c. acc., κλοπὴν οὐ γενομένην Ph.2.341. **-ψηφίζω**, *join in ratifying* a law, σ. τὰ δόξαντα τοῖς γέρουσι Arist.*Pol.*1272$^a$11: abs., Plb.21.32.1, *SIG*893*A*11 (Olympia, iii A. D., Med.).

**συνεποικοδομέω**, *help in rebuilding*, *IG*2$^2$.505.34 (iv B. C.).

**συνεποκέλλω**, *put on land together*, Plu.2.161a.

**συνέπομαι**, fut. -έψομαι Pl.*Ti.*53c: aor. -εσπόμην (v. infr.):—*follow along with, accompany*, σὺν δ' ὁ θρασὺς εἵπετ' Ὀδυσσεύς (where however σύν may be an Adv.) Od.10.436, cf. Hdt.7.39, Th.1.60, X.*An.*3.1.2, etc.; σ. τινὶ A.*Ag.*955, Hdt.5.47, Thphr.*Vent.*47, etc.; ποίμναις ..συνειπόμην *used to follow* the flocks, i.e. *tend* them, S.*OT*1125; οὔ σοι τῷ βίῳ ξυνέσπετο (thy fortunes) *remained* not *constant* to thy life, ib.1523 (troch.); ταῦρος ἄντυγι ξ. *kept pace with* it, E.*Hipp.* 1231; τῷ χρόνῳ σ. Pl.*Lg.*721c. 2. *comply* or *be in accordance with*, τῷ νόμῳ συνεπόμενος ib.916d; τοῖς ἀποβαίνουσιν Arist.*EN*1127$^a$4; μετὰ δεδοκιμασμένου μὴ ξυνέπεσθαι ἐθέλειν Th.3.38; τῇ τῶν μελιττῶν ἡδονῇ σ. *ministering* to the taste of the bees, Pl.*Lg.*843d. 3. of things, μουσικῇ συνεπόμεναι τέχναι the arts *attendant on* music, Id.*Phlb.*56c; τὰ τούτοις συνεπόμενα *the consequences* of these, Id.*Lg.* 679e, cf. 706a, *Ti.*52d: also c. gen., ὁπόσα τούτων συνεπόμενα εἴπομεν Id.*Lg.*899c. 4. σ. τῷ λόγῳ *follow* the argument *to its consequences*, ib.695c: abs., συνέπομαι *I follow*, i.e. understand, you, Id.*Sph.* 238e; συνέψεσθε Id.*Ti.*53c.

**συνεπ-όμνῡμι**, *swear to in addition* or *besides*, τι Ar.*Lys.*237: c. inf., X.*An.*7.6.19:—Med., J.*AJ*16.7.3. **-οπτεύω**, *view as an* ἐπόπτης *together*, Them.*Or.*20.235c. 2. *consider, take into account also*, Sor.1.38. **-οτρύνω**, *join in urging on*, S.*El.*299 (tm.). **-ουλόομαι**, *to be scarred quite over*, Gal.18(1).13. **-ούλωσις**, εως, ἡ, *scarring quite over*, Arist.*Pr.*865$^a$31. **-ουρίζω**, *help onwards in one's own course*, metaph. from a fair wind, τὴν κίνησιν Id.*Cael.* 301$^b$29, cf. *HA*598$^b$9:—Pass., Id.*Mech.*855$^a$20.

**συνεπτυγμένως**, Adv., (συμπτύσσω) *folded* or *taken together*, Ps.-Alex.Aphr. *in Metaph.*467.3.

**συνεπῳάζω**, *sit on eggs together with*, τῇ θηλείᾳ Arist.*HA*555$^b$14.

**συνεπωθέω**, *help to push on*, τὸ σιτίον Plu.2.1005a, cf. Gal.*Nat.Fac.* 3.8; τὸ πορθμεῖον Plu.2.1128c; σ. ἡμᾶς ἐπί τι Arr.*Epict.*3.7.23:—Med., Ph.2.99.

**συνερᾰν-ίζω**, fut. -ίσω Plu.2.963b: pf. -ηράνικα Phld.*Vit.* p.24 J.:—*join in contributing, contribute jointly*, τὰς χρείας ἀλλήλοις App.*BC* 2.9, cf. D.L.4.38:—Med., *receive contributions*, Plu.*Ages.*35. II. *collect, gather*, τινας Phld. l. c., Luc.*Lex.*17; παραδείγματα Plu.2.963b:—Med., ὀλίγα ἐκ τῆς γραφῆς ῥήματα Them.*Or.*21.252d:—Pass., αἱ.. ἐκ πλειόνων -ισμέναι δυνάμεις Ph.1.386; συνηρανισμένον ἐκ συγκλύδων (v. l. σύγκλυδος) ὄχλου *collected by chance contributions* from.., Pl.*Ax.* 369a, cf. D.H.*Isoc.*3, S.E.*M.*7.295, Gal.14.676, 18(1).193. **-ισμός**, ὁ, *gathering in, collecting*, Plu.2.992a. ❋ **-ιστής**, οῦ, ὁ, *member of a club*, *IG*12(1).155.46 (Rhodes), 2$^2$.2721. **-ιστός**, όν, *one who is contributed* (but does not contribute) to a picnic, of a parasite, Crobyl. 1 (Pors. for συνερανιστής).

**συνεραστής**, οῦ, ὁ, *joint lover*, Timocl.8.6; σ. τινῶν τῇ πόλει *loving* them *jointly with*.., X.*Smp.*8.41, cf. Plot.5.8.10.

**συνεράω** (A), *pour together, gather together*, πολλὰ συνεράσας ᾠὰ εἰς κύστιν Arist.*GA*752$^a$4; συνερᾶν καὶ συμφέρειν, to explain ἔρανος, Ath. 8.362e: συνερασαι (sine accentu) is v. l. for συγκεράσαι in Isoc.5. 138.

**συνεράω** (B), *love jointly* or *together with*, σοὶ καὶ ξυνήρων E.*Andr.* 223; χρή σε..μοι τὠραμένῳ συνεράν ἀδόλως σέθεν Theoc.29.32; σύν μοι πῖνε, συνήβα, συνέρα *Scol.*22, cf. Plu.*Ages.*20, *Alex.*41, Procop. Gaz. p.164 B.; ἡ Συνερῶσα, play by Menander. II. Med. and Pass., καλὸν δέ τ' ἐρασσαμένῳ συνερᾶσθαι Bion *Fr.*8.8 codd. (συναρέσθαι is prob. cj.); ὅσα συνηράσθησαν what *loves they had enjoyed together*, D.C.51.8.

**συνεργ-άζομαι**, fut. -άσομαι S.*Ant.*41:—*work with, co-operate*, l. c., Arist.*GA*753$^a$18, Thphr.*Vent.*21; σ. πρός τι *contribute* towards or to a thing, X.*Cyr.*7.1.33, Arist.*Pr.*880$^b$23, Thphr.*Lass.*15; *take part in a work* of construction, *IG*7.3073.21 (Lebad., ii B. C.); εἰς ἐργάτην τὸν -αζόμενον αὐτῷ *PCair.Zen.*176.23 (iii B. C.); σ. μετά τινος *POxy.* 527.3 (iii/ii A. D.); with neut. Adj., πολλά τισι ξυνειργασμένη Luc.*Dem. Enc.*38, cf. *Prom.Es*3; ὁ Συνεργαζόμενος, title of mime by Herodas. II. in pass. sense, ἀεὶ συνεργαζομένης [γῆς]..ἐξαναχωρεῖν retires from land as it *is brought under cultivation*, Thphr.*HP*6.3.3; γῆ συνεργασθεῖσα Id.*CP*3.12.1; λίθοι ξυνειργασμένοι stones *wrought so as to fit together*, i.e. *wrought for building, ashlar*, Th.1.93; ἐκ χρυσίου ξυνειργασμένος *wrought of*.., Luc.*Gall.*24; τοῦτο συνειργάσθη ἔργον *was wrought*, *AP*9.807; συνεργασθεὶς ῥοδίνῳ ὁ ἄρτος (bread poultice) ἐπιπλάττεται Lycusap.Orib.9.26.1. ❋**-ασία**, ἡ, *company* or *guild of fellow-workmen*, ἡ σ. τῶν ἀργυροκόπων *SIG*1263 (Smyrna), cf. *JHS*54.75 (ibid.), *SIG*704*H*26 (Delph., ii B. C.), *OGI*495.6 (Cibyra); ἡ τῶν γναφέων σ. *IGRom.*4.643 (Acmonia). II. *a place where many slaves are lodged, as workers' barracks*, Lat. *ergastulum*, εἰς σ. ἐμβαλεῖν D.S.20.13, 34/5.2.36. **-άτης** [ᾰ], ου, ὁ, *fellow-workman, helpmate*, πεμφθεὶς..σοὶ ξ. S.*Ph.*93; σκότος ξ. E.*Hipp.*417: c. gen. rei, *an accomplice* or *assistant in*, ἄγρας Id.*Ba.*1146; fem., **-άτις** φόνου Id. *El.*100. **-ατίνης** [ῑ], ου, ὁ, *composed of* συνεργάται, σ. ἰχθυβόλων θίασος *AP*7.295.10 (Leon.). **-εια**, v. συνεργία. **-ειον**, v. συνέργιον. **-επιστατέω**, *to be joint-foreman*, *BCH*18.23 (Western Asia Minor). **-έω**, pf. -ήργηκα Epicur.*Nat.*43 G.:—*work together with, help in work, co-operate*, E.*Hel.*1427, etc.; ἀλλήλοιν X.*Mem.*2.3.18, cf. 2.9. 8; μετ' ἀλλήλων Arist.*MM*1200$^a$10: generally, *co-operate with, assist*, c. dat., D.25.97, Thphr.*Ign.*30, *Od.*7, al., *PSI*4.376.4 (iii B. C.), Sor.1. 27; σ. τῇ πράξει ὁ λόγος Muson.*Fr.*5 p.21 H.; [τὸ γυμνάσιον] ἀναδόσεσι σ. Gal.6.88, cf. 463, 15.727; σ. ἑαυτοῖς τὰ συμφέροντα *do* one another fitting *service*, X.*Mem.*3.5.16; εἰς τὰς εὐτυχίας Arist.*EN*1171$^b$23; εἰς τὴν ἐλευθερίαν τῇ πόλει *IG*2$^2$.654.15, cf. Epicur. l. c., *IPE*1$^2$.352.45 (Chersonesus, ii B. C.), Sor.1.56, M.Ant.6.42; σφίσι πρὸς τοὺς καιρούς Plb.3.97.5; σ. πρός τι *contribute* to or towards.., Arist.*MM*1185$^a$35, Thphr.*CP*4.8.3, Phld.*Oec.* p.43 J., Gal.15.419; σ. ὅπως.. Sor.1.25; *facilitate*, τὸν δρασμὸν τοῖς Πέρσαις Hld.9.11:—Pass., *to be helped*, c. dat. rei, D.H.9.23; ὑπό τινος Phld.*Rh.*1.224 S., *Vit.* p.24 J., Plu.2. 840c. 2. *to be conspired against*, *PMich.Zen.*57.3 (iii B. C.). **-ημα**, ατος, τό, *assistance, support*, Plb.22.4.3: pl., Id.2.42.4, 30.4.13; πρός τι Id.3.99.9, cf. Phld.*Mus.* p.70 K., *Rh.*2.83 S.; τὸ ἑκάστου ἀριθμοῦ σ., of the One, i.e. *a factor in* every number, *Theol.Ar.*7. **-ής**, ές, *working with, co-operating*, Aristeas 242. Adv., -γῶς ἔχειν εἴς τι Phld.*Oec.* p.19 J. **-ητέον**, *one must assist*, τῇ ἐκβολῇ Sor.2.48, cf. Archig. ap.Gal.12.676. **-ήτης**, ου, ὁ, = συνεργατίνης, λαός *AP*7.693 (Apollonid.). **-ητικός**, ή, όν, *co-operative*, M.Ant.6.42, Arr.*Epict.* 2.22.20: τὸ -κόν ib.4.4.18. **-ία**, ἡ, *co-operation*, Arist.*Pr.*876$^b$15, Plb.8.33.10; εἰς τὸν βίον, πρὸς τοὺς πολέμους, Phld.*Rh.*1.270 S., *Mus.* p.69 K.: also **συνέργεια**, *UPZ*36.14 (ii B. C.), Gal.19.472: pl., Arist. *Oec.*1343$^b$17 (-ίαι, v. l. -ειαι). II. *conspiracy, collusion*, D.56.8; περί τι Din.1.112. ❋ **-ιον**, τό, = συνεργασία I, *PMich.Zen.*57.2 (iii B. C.), *IGRom.*3.810.9 (Side), *JHS*11.236 (Cilicia), *Gloss.*; also **-ειον** and **-ιν**, ib.

**συνεργολάβος** [ᾰ], ον, *contracting for work in partnership with* others, Str.8.3.30.

**σύνεργον**, τό, *implement, tool*, Artem.3.36, *POxy.*1069.8 (iii A. D.), 1159.20 (iii A. D.). II. pl., *trimmings*, κιθωνίου *Sammelb.*7250. 11, cf. 7248.21 (iii/iv A. D.).

**συνεργοπονέω**, *help in work* or *labour*, ἡμῖν S.E.*M.*9.41.

**συνεργός**, όν, *working together, joining* or *helping in work*, and as Subst., ὁ, ἡ, *helper*, E.*Or.*1446 (lyr.), *Med.*396, Pl.*Chrm.*173d, *IPE* 1$^2$.352.37 (Chersonesus, ii B. C.); in bad sense, *accomplice*, Th.8.92, *PFay.*12.10 (ii B. C.), *BGU*1761.8 (i B. C., pl.): c. dat. pers., E.*Hipp.* 523, Th.3.63, X.*Cyr.*8.4.17, Pl.*Smp.*180e, Men.*Epit.*83; so metaph., σ. πλοῦτος..κακίᾳ Teles p.46 H.; distd. from συναίτιον, Gal. 19.393: rarely c. gen. pers., ἡμῶν τι σ. (unless ἡμῶν is partit.) Epicur.*Nat.*98 G.; θεοῦ 1*Ep.Cor.*3.9: c. gen. rei, *taking part in* a thing, σ. τείχεος *helping to make* it, Pi.*O.*8.32; σ. τῶν ἐν τῷ κόσμῳ γινομένων Heraclit.75; ξ. ἀδίκων ἔργων, ἀρετᾶς, *helping towards* them, E.*Hipp.*676, *Med.*845 (both lyr.); σ. τινί τινος *helping* a person *in* a thing, θρήνων ἐμοί (prob. for θρήνοις ἐμῶν) ξ. Id.*Hel.*1112 (lyr.), cf. X.*An.*1.9.21; σ. εἴς τι Id.*Mem.*4.3.10, *Smp.*8.38, *Ep.Col.*4.11; πρός τι X.*Mem.*4.3.7; πρὸς κακοδίαν Thphr.*Sud.*8; πρὸς τὴν τῆς πόλεως σωτηρίαν Zeno *Stoic.*1.61; ἐν μάχαις Ar.*Eq.*588 (lyr.): c. inf., σ. τῷ παιδὶ μὴ 'κπεσεῖν E.*Ion* 48. 2. Astrol., *in co-operation*, of planetary influence, Vett.Val.55.15; distd. from ὑπουργός, Serapio in *Cat.Cod. Astr.*8(4).226. II. *person of the same trade as another, fellow-*

*workman, colleague*, c. gen. pers., D.19.144, cf. *IG*1$^2$.374.87, *PCair. Zen.*758.8 (iii B.C.), Plu.*Per.*31:—in this sense some write *σύνεργος*, Ammon.*Diff.* p.126 V., Thom.Mag. p.339 R.

**συνέργω**, = συνείργω, pres. first in Sor.1.117: fut. συνέρξω (v. infr.): Ep. **συνεέργω**, impf. συνέεργον or συνεέργαθον: in later Att. **συνείργνυμι** (q. v.): Att. aor. part. συνείρξας Gal.4.495; 3 sg. aor. opt. συνείρξειε Plu.2.398b:—*shut up* or *enclose together*, ὅσον συνεέργαθον ἄκραι *enclosed between them*, Il.14.36; οὐ ξυνέρξεθ' ὡς τάχος; i.e. *shut the doors*, S.*Aj.*593; οὐδὲ τὰς hoδὼς . . συνhέρξοντι *Tab.Heracl.*1.133; *wrap up closely*, αὐτοὺς ἱματίοις Gal. l. c. 2. *restrict, limit*, τὸ πλῆθος τῆς σαρκός (obesity) Sor. l. c. II. *fasten together*, [ὄϊας] συνέεργον . . λύγοισι Od.9.427; συνέεργον ὁμοῦ τρόπιν ἠδὲ καὶ ἱστόν 12.424; ζωστῆρι . . συνέεργε χιτῶνα 14.72; *unite*, (sc. τινας) Pl.*Ti.* 34c; esp. as man and wife, Id.*R.*461b.

**συνέρδω**, fut. -έρξω (v. infr.), *co-operate, help*, S.*El.*350; κειμένῳ οὐκ εἶ ξυνέρξων; Id.*Tr.*83.

* **συνερείδω**, *press together, close*, χερσὶ κατ' ὀφθαλμοὺς ἐλέειν σύν τε στόμ' ἐρεῖσαι Od.11.426; σ. ὀδόντας *set* the teeth, *lock* them *fast*, Hp.*Coac.*230 (where συνερίζειν is f.l.), *Mul.*2.201; *bind together, bind fast*, τινὰ περόναις E.*Ba.*97 (lyr.):—Pass., αἱ γνάθοι συνερειδόμεναι *being set* or *locked*, Hp.*Epid.*5.74; χέρας δεσμοῖς -ερεισθέντες *with their* hands *tight bound*, E.*IT*457 (anap.), cf. Theoc.22.68; διὰ τὸ μὴ σ. τὴν ἀρτηρίαν Arist.*Aud.*801$^a$2; χεῖρες ξυνηρεισμέναι arms *flexed*, Aret.*SA*1.6. 2. σ. τὸν λογισμόν reason *closely*, Plu.2.600e codd. II. intr., *to be firmly set*, οἱ ὀδόντες συνηρείκασι Hp.*Morb. Sacr.*7, cf. Sor.2.27, *Fract.*4 (prob.); ξυνερείσουσιν οἱ ὀδόντες Aret. *SA*1.5; γένυς ξ. τῇ ἄνω *is locked with* . ., ib.6; also of soldiers, σ. πρὸς ἀλλήλους Plb.12.21.3, cf. Arr.*Tact.*16.14. 2. *meet in close conflict*, τοῖς ἐναντίοις Plb.5.84.2; *dash together*, of ships, D.S.13.46, Plu.*Them.*14; *press on*, τοὺς ὠθισμοὺς τοῖς προτεταγμένοις Arr.*Tact.* 12.3.

**συνερείπω**, *overthrow, destroy*, τὴν τῶν ὀνομάτων οἰκοδομίαν Alcid. *Soph.*25.

**συνέρ-εισις**, εως, ἡ, *setting firmly together*, ὀδόντων Hp.*Epid.*7.18, cf. Sor.2.17. **-ειστικός**, ή, όν, *making a firm foundation*, τόνος *Stoic.*2.134, cf. Plu.2.954e, Hierocl. p.23 A.

**συνερέω**, Att. -ερῶ, pf. -είρηκα, fut. and pf. without pres. in use (v. συναγορεύω):—*speak with* or *together, advocate, support in a speech*, X.*Cyr.*2.2.22, 8.1.6: c. dat., Lys.12.86, D.16.1, 22.40, Hyp.*Lyc.*19; σ. νόμῳ D.20.153. Cf. συνεῖπον.

**συνέρημα**, ατος, τό, late spelling of συναίρημα, *Stud.Pal.*22.168.1 (ii A.D.).

**συνερίζω**, *contend together*, ὑπέρ τινος Lxx 2*Ma.*8.30: aor. Pass. in act. sense, ὁ Ἑρμῆς συνηρίσθη αὐτῇ (sc. τῇ Μοίρᾳ) *PMag.Leid.W.*5. 13. II. v. συνερείδω I. 1.

* **συνέρῑθος**, ἡ, *fellow-worker, helpmate*, esp. *one who is hired to assist in domestic work*, as spinning or sewing, Od.6.32, *PEnteux.*30.3 (iii B.C.), *AP*9.89 (Phil.), etc.; Μοῦσα . . μήτ' ἔλθῃς σ. αὐτοῖς Ar.*Pax* 786 (lyr.); Κύπρις σ. ἀέθλων A.R.3.942; σ. τέχναι *assistant* arts, Pl. *R.*533d; ὅσαι ταύταις εἰσὶ σ. τέχναι Id.*Lg.*889d: less freq. as masc. Adj., σ. ἄτρακτος *AP*7.726 (Leon.); λύχνος συνέριθος ὀδυνάων Musae. 11.

**συνερκτικός**, ή, όν, (συνέργω) of a speaker, *driving* his opponent *into a corner, cogent*, Ar.*Eq.*1378 codd.: Sch., συνείρων τοὺς λόγους, points to **συνερτικός** (συνείρω II).

**συνερμαϊσταί**, οἱ, *fellow-members of a guild of worshippers of Hermes*, *BCH*32.430 (Delos).

**σύνερξις**, εως, ἡ, (συνέργω) *forcing together, junction*, ἐν τῇ σ. in *close order* of battle, D.C.50.32; ἡ τῶν γάμων σ. *wedlock*, Pl.*Ti.*18d: abs., Id.*R.*460a. 2. *confinement*, ἡ εἰς σῶμα σ. Porph.*Sent.*28, cf. Plu.*Fr.*6.2; ζῴων Porph.*Abst.*1.40.

**συνέρομαι**, only in aor. inf. συνερέσθαι, *ask with* or *together*, Hsch., Phot., and part. -ερόμενος· συμβαλλόμενος, Hsch. (dub. l.).

**συνερπύζω**, *creep* or *go together*, Opp.*H.*1.328: also **συνέρπω**, Arr. *Epict.*2.24.18, *AP*4.4.5 (Agath.), *Gloss.*

**συνέρραισα**, v. συνείρω.

**συνέρρωγα**, pf. 2 of συρρήγνυμι (II):—συνέρρωσε, in Heraclit.*All.* 52, is f.l. for συνέρρωγε.

**συνερτικός**, v. συνερκτικός.

**συνερύω**, Ion. συνειρύω, *draw together*, in aor. Pass., ὁκόταν . . συνειρυσθῇ ὑπὸ τοῦ ῥίγεος Hp.*Morb.*1.26: pf. Pass. συνείρ(υ)ται· συνέσπασται, Hsch. 2. metaph. in Act., τίς σε δαιμόνων κακῇ ἀθυμίῃ ξυνείρυσεν; Epigr.ap.D.L.2.112.

* **συνέρχομαι**, fut. -ελεύσομαι Plu.2.306e, Phintys ap.Stob.4.23.61; but the Att. fut. is σύνειμι (εἶμι *ibo*), q. v., with aor. 2 συνῆλθον (Dor. part. συνενθόντες *Abh.Berl.Akad.*1925(5).21 (Cyrene)) and pf. συνελήλυθα:—*go together* or *in company*, σύν τε δύ' ἐρχομένω Il.10. 224. II. *come together, assemble, meet*, Hdt.1.152, 3.159, 7. 97, E.*Ba.*714, Th.1.3, etc.; συνέρχεσθαι τοὺς συνέδρους *IG*4$^2$(1).68. 66 (Epid., iv B.C.); σ. ἐς τὠυτό Hdt.1.202; εἰς ταὐτὸ εἰς μίαν νῆσον X.*Ath.*2.2; εἰς τὸ κοινόν Pl.*Lg.*680e; εἰς ἓν ἱερόν ib.767c; ἐνθάδε Ar.*Lys.*39; δεῦρο ἐς Κλεισθένους ib.621 (lyr.); ἐκ τῶν ἀγρῶν Id.*Pax* 632 (troch.); ἀπὸ τῶν πόλεων Th.5.55; ἐς λόγους σ. Hdt.1. 82, cf. Ar.*Eq.*1300 (troch.): c. dat., without ἐς λόγους, *BGU*1778.2 (i B.C.); σύνελθε πρὸς Θέωνα *PSI*9.1079.3 (i B.C.); ἐπὶ τὸν ἀγῶνα, i.e. the Dramatic ἀγών, D.21.55; and simply, ξ. τινί *have dealings with*, S.*OT*572; σ. χοροῖς *take part in* . ., E.*Hel.*1468 (lyr.). 2. in hostile sense, *meet in battle*, σ. ἐς πεδίον Hdt.1.80; εἰς μάχην Pl.*Tht.* 154e; κάπρῳ γὰρ ὡς συνῆλθεν ἀντίαν ἔριν *PCair.Zen.*532.16 (iii B.C.); also of the battle, μάχῃ ὑπό τινων ξυνελθοῦσα *engaged in, contested* by them, Th.5.74. 3. *come together, be united* or *banded together*, ἐς τὠυτό Hdt.4.120; φίλος φίλῳ ἐς ἓν σ. E.*Ph.*462; δύο οἰκίαι σ. εἰς ταὐτόν Pl.*Chrm.*157e; σ. τοῦ ζῆν ἕνεκεν Arist.*Pol.*1278$^b$24; σ. ἐπὶ κοινωνίᾳ βίῳ Phintys l. c.; *form a league*, of states, D.18.19; *come together*, after quarrelling, ἀδελφοὶ . . οὔτε ῥᾳδίως σ. Plu.2.481c. b. of sexual intercourse, σ. τῷ ἀνδρί Hp.*Mul.*2.143; σ. γυναικί X.*Mem.*2. 2.4, cf. Pl.*Smp.*192e, Str.15.3.20; σ. εἰς ὁμιλίαν τινί, of a woman, D.S.3.58; freq. of marriage-contracts, *BGU*970.13 (ii A.D.), *PGnom.* 71, al. (ii A.D.), etc.: abs., of animals, *couple*, Arist.*HA*541$^b$34. 4. c. acc. cogn., ταύτην τὴν στρατείαν ξ. *joined in* this expedition, Th.1. 3 (ξυνεξ- is prob. cj.); τὸ σὸν λέχος ξυνῆλθον *shared* thy bed, S.*Aj.* 491. III. of things, *to be joined in one*, συνερχόμεν' εἰς ἕν Emp.17. 7; χάρις κείνου τέ σοι κἀμοῦ ξ. S.*Tr.*619; τἀπ' ἐμοῦ τε κἀπὸ σοῦ ἐς ἓν ξ. E.*Tr.*1155; σ. εἰς ἕν Arist.*Cael.*288$^a$16; of one river *joining* another, Ar.*Fr.*150 (dub. l.); of heavenly bodies, *to be in conjunction*, Arist.*Mete.*343$^b$31, 344$^a$1; of a chasm, *close*, Plu.2.306e; so of a fistula, Meges ap.Orib.44.24.10. 2. of events, *concur, happen together*, Hdt.6.77; τῆς τύχης οὕτω σ. Plu.*Cam.*13.

**συνέρωμα**, ατος, τό, = συναίρημα, *Stud.Pal.*22.182.1 (ii/iii A.D.).

**συνερωτ-άω**, *ask a series of questions* (*about*), Luc.*Bis Acc.*22, Eun.*VS* p.466 B. II. λόγον σ. *propound* an argument *by means of a series of questions*, in Pass., S.E.*P.*2.131, cf. Luc.*Hist.Conscr.* 17. **-ησις**, εως, ἡ, *method of argument by a series of questions*, S.E.*P.*2.253 (sg. and pl.). **-ητέον**, *one must employ the method of successive questions*, ib.251.

**συνεσθίω**, aor. συνέφᾰγον, *eat together*, Charon 10, Arist.*EE*1245$^a$ 13; συμπιεῖν καὶ συμφαγεῖν *SIG*1179.19 (Cnidus, Tab. Defix.): c. dat., Pl.*Lg.*881d, *Ev.Luc.*15.2; μετά τινων Lxx *Ge.*43.32, *Ep.Gal.*2.12.

**σύνεσις**, Att. **ξύνεσις**, εως, ἡ, (συνίημι) *uniting, union*, πέτρη τε ξύνεσίς τε δύω ποταμῶν Od.10.515 (with ξυν- metri gr.). 2. metaph., with allusion to foreg. signf. and signf. II, χωρὶς ἕκαστος εἰς τὸ φρονεῖν ἀσθενής, συμβάλλων δὲ εἰς ἓν πᾶς ἐν τῇ συνόδῳ καὶ τῇ ὡς ἀληθῶς συνέσει τὸ φρονεῖν ἐγέννησε καὶ εὗρε Plot.6.5.10. II. *faculty of quick comprehension, mother-wit, sagacity*, Democr.77, Th.2.62, 3.82, etc.; οἰκείᾳ ξυνέσει Id.1.138, cf. Pl.*Cra.*412a, *Phlb.* 19d, Arist.*EN*1143$^a$17, D.18.127, *Ev.Luc.*2.47, Gal.6.457, etc.; hence of animals, ὃ [ζῷον] συνέσει . . ὑπερέχει τῶν ἄλλων Pl.*Mx.* 237d:—Phrases, ὅστις γε σύνεσιν ἔχει Hdt.2.5, 7.49; ἀρκεῖν ξυνέσει E.*Tr.*674; ξ. καὶ σοφία Id.*HF*655 (lyr.); φρόνησίς τε καὶ ξ. Pl. *Cra.*411a; σ. λαβεῖν, of children, Arist.*EN*1161$^b$26; μοῖραν ἔχειν συνέσεως (= αἰσθήσεως) Democr.ap.Thphr.*Sens.*71; also with qualifying words added, σ. φρενῶν Pi.*N.*7.60; γνώμης ξ. Th.1.75; σ. πολιτική Arist.*Pol.*1291$^a$28; ἡ περὶ τὴν διάνοιαν σ. Id.*HA*588$^a$23; ἡ ὑμετέρα σ. as form of address, *Sammelb.*7433.6 (V A.D.). 2. c. gen. objecti, *intelligence in* a thing, *sagacity in respect to* it, Pl.*Cra.* 412c, D.S.1.1; περὶ τῶν παρόντων Th.2.97. III. *conscience*, = συνείδησις, ἡ σ. (sc. μ' ἀπόλλυσι)· ὅτι σύνοιδα δείν' εἰργασμένος E.*Or.* 396, cf. Men.632, Plb.18.43.13. IV. *a branch of art or science*, οἱ περὶ τὴν σ. ταύτην, i.e. music, Arist.*Pol.*1342$^b$8. b. *knowledge*, opp. ἄγνοια, Id. *de An.*410$^b$3. V. *decision, decree*, *IG*5(1).1390.112 (Andania, i B.C.). (Plato (*Cra.*412a) derives σύνεσις II from συνιέναι (σύνειμι) *come together*, neglecting the unwritten aspiration (συνιέναι); but the form and signfs. point to συνίημι II, *perceive, apprehend*, cf. Arist.*EN*1143$^a$17.)

**συνεσκευασμένως**, Adv. *by joint preparation*, v.l. in X.*Oec.*11. 19.

**συνεσπειρᾱμένως**, Adv. *in a concentrated form*, Procl. *in Prm.* p.533 S., Id. *in Ti.*1.149 D.; opp. ἀνειλιγμένως, Herm. *in Phdr.* p.137 A.; σ. καὶ ἡνωμένως ib. p.114 A.

**συνεσπουδασμένως**, Adv. *with earnest zeal*, Eun.*VS* p.468 B.

**συνεσσάδδω**, aor. inf. συνεσσάξαι, Cretan for *συν-εκ-σάττω, *help to remove* property, *Leg.Gort.*3.13, 16.

**συνεσταλμένως**, Adv., (συστέλλω) *contractedly*: I. Gramm., *with a short vowel*, Ath.3.106b, 9.393c. II. of a mode of life, *simply, frugally*, σ. ζῆν Plu.2.216e, etc.; *humbly*, Poll.3.137.

**συνεστέον**, (σύνειμι) *one must associate with*, Πρωταγόρᾳ Pl.*Prt.* 313b.

**συνεστηκότως**, Adv., (συνίστημι) *in a constrained way*, σ. ἔχειν Arist.*Pol.*1340$^b$1.

**συνεστῐ-άζω**, = συνεστιάω, *BSA*23.73 (Macedonia, ii A.D., Pass.). **-ᾱσις**, εως, ἡ, *banqueting together*, D.H.4.49, *Gloss.* **-άτωρ** [ᾰ], ορος, ὁ, *boon-companion*, ib.: metaph., Vett.Val.345.10. **-άω**, *help to entertain*, *AP*4.3.24 (Agath.):—Pass., *live* or *feast along with* or *together*, Lys.*Fr.*53.2, Is.3.70, D.19.190, etc.; [θεοῖς] Plu.2. 121f; μετά τινων *IG*2$^2$.1214.14. * **-ος**, ον, *sharing one's hearth* or *house*, S.*OT*249, E.*Alc.*1151; σύσσιτος καὶ σ. Pl.*Ep.*350c; ξυνέστιοι πόλεος his fellow-citizens, A.*Th.*773 (lyr.); σ. δαιτός, of a bottle, *AP*6.248 (Marc. Arg.): c. dat. pers., σ. σοι καὶ ὁμοτράπεζος Pl.*Euthphr.*4b, cf. *Lg.*868e; ἀθανάτοισι σ. A.R.1.1319; ἀμβροσίῃσι σ. *AP*7.41; ὄρνις σ. ἀνθρώποισι Opp.*C.*3.118: c. dat. pers. et gen. rei, χρὴ συνεστίους ἐμοὶ θοίνης γενέσθαι *associates with* me in the feast, E.*El.*784. 2. epith. of Zeus, *guardian of the hearth*, A.*Ag.* 703 (lyr.); σ. θεοί *sharing the same hearth*, i.e. temple, *PGiss.*99.26 (ii A.D.).

**συνεστραμμένως**, Adv., (συστρέφω) *as if twisted up*, σ. εἰπεῖν speak *tersely*, Arist.*Rh.*1401$^a$5 (v.l.).

**συνεστώ**, οῦς, ἡ, (σύνειμι) = συνουσία II, *living together*, ἐν τῇ συνεστοῖ Hdt.6.128; cf. ἀπεστώ, εὐεστώ.

**συνεταιρ-έω**, f.l. for ἑταιρέω in Aeschin.*Ep*.7.3. **-ίζω**, *make* another *one's companion*, Aq.*Ps*.107(108).10 (Pass.). **-ος**, ὁ, *companion, partner, comrade*, Sapph.*Supp*.20*a*5, Hdt.7.193, Lxx *Jd*.15.2, *Da*.2.17, *Supp.Epigr*.1.572.7 (Egypt): fem. **-ίς**, ίδος, Erinn. 5.7, Lxx *Jd*.11.37, Ph.1.194.

**συνετίζω**, *cause to understand*, Lxx *Ps*.118(119).27,34, *Ne*.8.7.

**συνετόβουλος**, gloss on ποικιλόφρων, Sch.E.*Hec*.133.

**συνετός**, ή, όν, (συνίημι) *intelligent, sagacious, wise*, Democr.98, Pi.*P*.5.107, Hdt.1.185 (Comp.), etc.; φωνᾶεντα συνετοῖσιν Pi.*O*.2.85; of Zeus and Apollo, ξυνετοὶ καὶ τὰ βροτῶν εἰδότες S.*OT*498 (lyr.); ξ. φρένες Ar.*Ra*.876 (lyr.); of animals, Arist.*HA*589ᵃ1 (Comp.); σ. ἡλικίη the age *of wisdom*, *AP*5.111 (Phld.), etc.; ἡ συνετή alone, ib. 11.25 (Apollonid.); also τὸ σ., = σύνεσις, E.*Or*.1180, Th.2.15; τὸ πρὸς ἅπαν ξ. Id.3.82: c. gen. rei, *intelligent in* a thing, ξ. πολέμου E.*Or*. 1406 (anap.): c. acc., τά τ' οἰκτρὰ σ. εἰμὶ καὶ τὰ μή Id.*IA*1255; τὰ ἀχρεῖα Th.1.84; τὰ πολιτικά D.H.4.45. II. Pass., *intelligible*, εὔμαρες σύνετον πόησαι πάντι τοῦτ' Sapph.*Supp*.5.5; οὐ ξ. θνητοῖς πείρατα Thgn.1078; φρονέοντι συνετὰ γαρύω B.3.85; συνετὰ αὐδᾶν, λέγειν, Hdt.2.57, E.*Ph*.498, etc.; esp. in oxymora, ἀναβοήσεται οὐ συνετὰ συνετῶς Id.*IA*466; δυσξυνέτου ξυνετὸν μέλος Id.*Ph*.1506 (lyr.): act. and pass. senses conjoined, εὐξύνετον ξυνετοῖς βοάν Id.*IT*1092 (lyr.); φωνὴ σ. *significant*, Arist.*Po*.1456ᵇ23. III. Adv. **-τῶς** *intelligently*, E.*IA*466, Ar.*V*.633 (lyr.). 2. *intelligibly*, διαλέγεσθαι Arist.*Pr*.902ᵃ17; φθεγξαμένου.. οὐδὲν σ. Plu.*Sull*.27; συνετὰ ὁμιλεῖν to discourse *intelligibly*, Babr.*Prooem*.11.

**συνετῠμολογέω**, *join in deriving a word*, Tz. ad Hes.*Op*.54.

**συνεύᾰδον**, Ep. aor. of *συνανδάνω, *please likewise*, συνεύαδε A.R.3. 30, cf. Ps.-Phoc.191.

⊛ **συνευᾰρεστέω**, *give one's consent*, *IG*7.3325 (Chaeronea), *Test. Epict*.1.4, 4.4, *Supp.Epigr*.2.299 (Delph., i B.C., written συναυαρ-):— Med., D.S.40.8.

**συνευαστήρ**, ῆρος, ὁ, *fellow-bacchanal*, Orph.Εὐχή 34.

**συνευδαιμονέω**, *share in happiness*, X.*HG*5.1.16; τινι *with* one, Luc.*Herm*.10.

**συνευδοκ-έω**, *join in approving, give one's consent*, Demad.17, Plb. 7.1.3, *SIG*712.46 (Crete, ii B.C., Dor. -ιόντων), *PGrenf*.2.26.25 (ii B.C.), D.S.4.24, *Act.Ap*.22.20, etc.; συνευδοκέοντος τοῦ δεῖνα, in forms of sale, *GDI*1532*a*4, 1555*a*5 (Delph.), etc. 2. c. dat. rei, *consent* or *agree to* a thing, Lxx 1*Ma*.1.57, *POxy*.1644.27 (i B.C.), *BGU*1731.12 (i B.C.), *Ev.Luc*.11.48, etc. 3. c. dat. pers., *agree* or *sympathize with*.., *Ep.Rom*.1.32. II. Pass., aor. συνευδοκήθην in signf. 1. 3, D.S.18.49; so ὄκκα [τὰ μέρεα].. συνευδοκῆται ἀλλάλοις Theag.ap.Stob.3.1.117. **-ησις**, εως, ἡ, *formal consent*, *POxy*. 1276.19, 1638.31 (both iii A.D.).

**συνεύδω**, *sleep* or *lie with*, c. dat., Hdt.3.69; τῷ παλαμναίῳ S.*El*. 587, cf. E.*El*.1145; τοῦ ξυνεύδοντος χρόνου the time *coincident with sleep*, A.*Ag*.894.

**συνευεργετέω**, *join in doing good to*, prob. cj. in J.*AJ*18.8.9 (Pass.).

**συνευημερέω**, *enjoy the day* or *be happy together*, Plu.*Cor*.4.

**συνευθῡμέομαι**, *acquiesce in, approve*, τοῖς δρωμένοις Them.*Or*.8. 102d.

**συνευθύνω**, *straighten as well*, Them.*Or*.27.338b, Paul.Aeg.6.120 (v.l. εὐθυνέτω).

**συνευκαιρέω**, *share delight in*, τερατείαις Sch.Luc.*Icar*.p.98 R.

**συνευκοσμέω**, *assist in regulating*, γυμνικοὺς ἀγῶνας *Arch.Pap*.3. 134 (Thera, iii/ii B.C.): c. dat. pers., *IG*5(2).265.7 (Mantinea, i B.C.).

**συνευν-άζω**, *cause to lie with*, τινά τινι Apollod.2.4.10, etc.:— Pass., *lie with*, Pi.*P*.4.254, S.*OT*982, Hp.*Nat.Mul*.17. **-άομαι**, Pass., = συνευνάζομαι, Hdt.6.69,107, Luc.*VH*2.46. **-ετέω**, *to be a consort, sleep with*, τινι Tz.*H*.9.536 (συνευνητεῖ codd.). **-έτης**, ου, ὁ, *bed-fellow, consort*, E.*Med*.240, *Hipp*.416 (pl.), etc.; Dor. **ξυνευνέτας** *Supp.Epigr*.7.69 (near Antioch on Orontes, i A.D.): fem. **-έτις**, ιδος, ἡ, *wife* or *concubine*, E.*Andr*.908, *APl*.4.182.8 (Leon.). **-ιος**, ον, = σύνευνος, Hsch., Phot., Suid. **-ίς**, ίδος, ἡ, *wife*, *Supp.Epigr*. 6.796.24 (Cappadocia, iii A.D.).

**συνευνοέομαι**, *to be well disposed towards*, τινι *PStrassb*.40.39 (vi A.D.).

**συνευνομιῶται**, οἱ, *colleagues in the* εὐνομία (q.v. in Addendis), *GDI*5119a (p.422, Crete).

**σύνευνος**, ὁ, ἡ, (εὐνή) *bed-fellow, consort*, mostly of the *wife*, Pi.*O*. 1.88, A.*Ag*.1116 (lyr.), 1442, S.*Aj*.1301, E.*Med*.1001 (lyr.), *BGU* 1080.23 (iii A.D.), etc.; but of the *husband*, A.*Pr*.866, Ar.*Ec*.953 (lyr.), *AP*7.599 (Jul.), 600 (Id.): fem. **συνεύνα** ib.5.194 (dub. l., Mel.), *IG*12(3).238 (Astypalaea).

**συνευπαίδευτος**, ον, *scientific*, ἀνείλησις, of gymnastic exercises, Aret.*CD*1.2.

**συνευπάσχω**, *receive favours* or *derive profit together*, D.8.64,65, but better written σὺν εὖ πεπονθότων, cf. ἀντευπάσχω.

**συνευπορέω**, *contribute*, c. acc., τριάκοντα μνᾶς ἐδεῖτό μου.. συνευπορῆσαι D.33.6: abs., σ. ἐκ τῶν ἰδίων πρὸς τὴν κοινὴν σωτηρίαν Lycurg. 139. 2. c. dat. pers. et gen. rei, *contribute towards*, σ. τινὶ προικὸς Is.11.37; σ. ἐκείνῳ χρημάτων, αὐτῷ ἀναλωμάτων, D.8.19, 59.72. 3. generally, *assist, help*, τινι Din.1.58; *help in contriving*, σ. ὅπως ἄν.. Plu.*Lyc*.15.

**συνευρίσκω**, *find also*, Men.*Epit*.84; *help to find*, Luc.*JTr*.5:— Pass., *to be found with*, c. dat., Sch.D.T.p.204 H.; dub. sens. in *PSI*1.98.1 (vi A.D.), *PLond*.5.1708.88 (vi A.D.).

**συνευρύνω**, *widen* or *extend together*, Ph.1.209 (Pass.).

**συνευσεβέω**, *join in worship*, Benndorf-Niemann *Reisen in Lykien* p.156 No.134 (Lagina, Caria), *BCH*11.376 (Panamara), *Supp.Epigr*. 4.302,390 (ibid.).

**συνευσχημονέω**, *observe decency with*, τῇ κρίσει Plu.2.442e.

**συνευτονέω**, *to be vigorous at the same time*, Sor.1.88.

**συνευτροφέω**, *to be well-nourished also*, Sor.1.97.

**συνευτῠχέω**, *to be fortunate together*, βίον during life, E.*Hipp*.1117 (lyr.); τισι Str.10.4.10, 13.4.1.

**συνευφημέω**, *use words of good omen, shout applause* or *blessings*, Ph.2.58, Plu.2.272a, v.l. in D.S.5.49.

**συνευφράζομαι**, Med., *counsel well with*, A.R.3.918; better written divisim, σὺν εὖ φρ., with some codd.

**συνευφραίνομαι**, Pass., *rejoice together*, D.H.*Rh*.2.5, Ph.1.405; μετὰ γυναικός Lxx *Pr*.5.18; τινι *with* one, D.18.217, Hdn.2.8.9.

**συνευχή**, ἡ, *united prayer*, in pl., Charito 6.2, 8.6.

**συνεύχομαι**, *join in prayer*, E.*IT*1221 (troch.); ταὐτὰ δὴ ξ. Id.*Hel*. 646; παῖς πατρὶ σ. Pl.*Lg*.687e, cf. *JRS*17.51 (Phrygia, iv A.D.), etc.: c. acc. rei et inf., ξ. τέλεα πόλει.. γενέσθαι Ar.*Th*.352 (lyr.); σ. σοι ταῦτα γενέσθαι Pl.*Phdr*.257b, cf. X.*Oec*.7.8; μετά τινος Pl.*Lg*.909e; also τοῖς φίλοις ταῦτα *for* one's friends *too*, ib.687d, cf. *Phdr*.279c, D.C.52.4.

**συνευωχ-έομαι**, Pass., *feast together*, Arist.*EE*1245ᵇ5, Posidon. 15 J., Ph.2.355; ὑμῖν 2*Ep.Pet*.2.13, cf. J.*AJ*1.3.5, *BGU*596.10 (i A.D.), Luc.*VH*2.15, etc.; [ἀνδριάντι] *PMag Par*.1.3150. **-ητής**, οῦ, ὁ, *fellow-banqueter*, Sch.D Il.17.577, Hsch. s.v. εἰλαπιναστής.

**συνεφ-αιρέομαι**, *choose in addition by consent*, *GDI*1832.13 (Delph.). **-άπτομαι**, Ion. συνεπ-: 1. c. gen. rei, *lay hold of jointly*, ξίφους τινί Plu.*Brut*.52; so without gen., συνεφάπτεσθαι.. ταῖς χερσί (with the hands) καὶ αὐτόν Gal.10.430: metaph., *put hand to along with* another, *take part*, Pi.*O*.10(11).97; οὐκ ἔφη.. γιγνώσκειν τῶν συμμάχων τοὺς ὥσπερ συνεφαπτομένους τοῖς σπένδουσι τῶν ἱερῶν said he did not acknowledge *those* allies *who* as it were *lay hands along with* the offerers of libations *upon* the victims, i.e. who wish to share the profits, without the expenses and dangers of the war, Aeschin.2.84; σ. τῆς στρατείας Plu.*Tim*.8, Luc.*Am*.6; τῆς διακονίας Plu.*Phil*.2; τοῦ φόνου Id.*Brut*.17; τῆς δημιουργίας τῷ θεῷ Jul.*Or*.4.150b; *to be connected with*, [τοῦτο] σ. ἑτέρου γένους νοσήματος Gal.10.233; of a muscle, -όμενος καὶ τοῦ πήχεως Id.18(2). 986. 2. c. gen. pers., *join one in attacking*, Hdt.7.158. **-αρμόζω**, *fit along with* or *together*, τινί τι Sch.Ar.*Av*.424, cf. Procl.*Par.Ptol*. 284. **-εδρεύω**, *wait in reserve*, of troops, τισι Plb.1.27.9, cf. 7. 16.5. II. *watch closely*, τῷ τῶν Ἀρδιαίων ἔθνει Id.2.12.2; σ. τοῖς καιροῖς Id.31.8.6. **-ειάζω**, v. συνεφίαζεν. **-έλκω**, aor. -είλκῠσα (cf. ἕλκω):—*draw after* or *along with one*, Pl.*Phd*.80e, *Ep*.335b, Arist. *de An*.406ᵇ21:—Pass., *to be drawn on together*, Id.*Ph*.244ᵃ11; τῇ τοῦ ὅλου περιφορᾷ Id.*Mete*.341ᵃ2; *to be drawn up also*, Id.*Pr*.949ᵃ 16, Thphr.*CP*4.13.5:—Med., much like Act., Hp.*Mul*.1.68, Phld. *Mus*.p.62 K., Ph.2.61, al., Plu.2.529c, Aret.*SD*1.13, Eun.*VS* p.498 B. **-έπομαι**, aor. -εφεσπόμην, Ion. -επεσπόμην, poet. imper. συνεπίσπεο *Lyr.Alex.Adesp*.20.2:—*follow together*, Hdt.9.102, X.*Cyr*. 6.4.10, Pl.*Lg*.701a, etc.; τινι with one, X.*An*.4.8.18, etc.: metaph., σ. τῷ λόγῳ Pl.*Sph*.254c.

**συνεφηβ-εύω**, *serve as* ἔφηβοι *together*, Plu.2.816b. **-ία**, ἡ, *group of* συνέφηβοι, *Supp.Epigr*.4.301.15 (Panamara, ii A.D., pl.). **-ος**, ὁ, *fellow-*ἔφηβος, Aeschin.1.49, 2.167, *IG*2².1043.70, 2127.5, *OGI*188. 7 (Philae), Plu.2.482a, Charito 8.6, Luc.*Tim*.48; at Sparta, *member of the same* ἀγέλη, *IG*5(1).38, al.; Συνέφηβοι, a name of comedies by Menander and others.

**συνεφίαζεν** (leg. -φεί-)· "εἶα" (leg. εἶα) ἐκάλει, Hsch.

**συνεφ-ίημι**, *join in granting*, συνεφίοντος κατὰ τὸ δάνειον καὶ συνομολογοῦντος Πυθοκρίτου *IG*12(5).872.75 (Tenos, iii B.C.). **-ίστημι** and **-ιστάνω** (Plb.7.13.2): aor. 1 -επέστησα Demad.57:—*set as watchers* or *guards*, τοὺς ἱππεῖς D.S.17.84: metaph., *set on the watch, make attentive*, τοὺς ἀναγινώσκοντας Plb.10.41.6; τινὰ ἐπὶ τὰς μάχας Id.11.19.2; τοὺς φιλοπευστοῦντας περί τινων Id.3.59.6. 2. seemingly intr. (sc. τὸν νοῦν), *attend to, observe along with*, ἐπὶ τὰ λεγόμενα Id.3.9.4; τοῖς ὑπομνήμασι Id.9.2.7, cf. 4.40.10, etc.; dub. l. in Vett.Val.241.15. II. Pass. συνεφίστᾰμαι, with aor. 2 Act., *stand over, superintend along with* or *together*, Th.2.75. 2. *rise together*, κατά τινων *against* them, *Act.Ap*.16.22. 3. *occur together*, τινι *with*.., Dsc.*Ther.Praef*., v.l. for συνυφ- in Porph.*Sent*.27. **-οδιάζω**, *help in equipping* or *assisting*, Ptol.*Tetr*.47. **-οράω**, *inspect* or *superintend together*, ib.146, Them.*Or*.9.122c. **-ορεύω**, *to be joint-ephor*, *IG*5(1).1317 (Thalamae, iv/iii B.C.). **-ορμάω**, *urge on together*, Hsch. **-ορος**, ὁ, *joint-ephor*, *CIG*4157 (Sinope).

**συνέχεια**, ἡ, *continuity*, τῆς κινήσεως Arist.*Metaph*.1050ᵇ26; [τῶν νεύρων] Id.*HA*515ᵇ6; [ἡ ῥάχις] μία μὲν διὰ τὴν σ., πολυμερὴς δὲ τῇ διαιρέσει τῶν σπονδύλων Id.*PA*654ᵇ15, cf. *HA*559ᵃ7; σ. ἔχειν πρός τι Id.*PA*652ᵇ3; ὁ ὅλος ὄγκος ὥσπερ κατὰ συνέχειαν τρέφεται καὶ ἐπιδίδωσι Thphr.*CP*1.12.4; σ. γίνεται there is a *continuous succession* (of flowering), Id.*HP*6.8.4, cf. 7.10.3; σ. τῶν ἀκροβολισμῶν, τῆς μάχης, Plb.5.100.2, Hdn.8.5.2. b. *coherence*, πρὸς τὰ οἰκεῖα μέρη *Stoic*.2.145; νόσος.. τῆς σ. [τοῦ σώματος] τῶν μερῶν διαίρεσις Gal.7. 2; ὀδύνη γίνεται.. τῆς σ. λυομένης Id.15.515. c. κατὰ συνέχειαν ἀριθμεῖσθαι to be reckoned *by conjunction* (e.g. 1, 2, 3, 4; 4, 5, 6, 7), Steph. in *Hp*.1.198 D. 2. mere *sequence* of words, Pl.*Sph*.261e, 262c; *connexion* in a sentence, τῶν ὀνομάτων D.H.*Vett.Cens*.5.2, cf. *Comp*.23; γραμμάτων Demetr.*Eloc*.68; also of argument, αἱ κατὰ συνέχειαν [προτάσεις], = συνημμένα ἀξιώματα (cf. συνάπτω A. III. 3), *Stoic*.2. 71, cf. 85; σ. ἀποδείξεων Luc.*Dem.Enc*.32; ἡ ἐν τῷ λογίζεσθαι σ. Plu.

2.792d; πυκνότης καὶ συνέχεια Hermog.Id.2.10. 3. of Time, *link*, Arist.Ph.222$^{a}$10. 4. *sequence, chain* of cause and effect, ἐπισύνδεσις καὶ σ. τῶν αἰτίων Alex.Aphr.Fat.195.3; τῶν ἐφεξῆς σ. καὶ συμπλοκή Plot.3.1.4. 5. *continuity of substance, viscosity*, (sc. ἐλαίου) Thphr.Od.18; of dripping honey, μὴ..ὑγρόν, ὡς ἀποσπᾶσθαι τῆς σ. Gal.6.270; ἡ πρὸς τὸν ὀμφαλὸν τοῦ ἐμβρύου σ. Sor.1.71; of broken bones, Id.Fract.5, al.; σ. τῶν φυτῶν Hdn.7.2.5. 6. *compactness, close order*, of military formation, Arr.Tact.11.4, Ael.Tact.11.4. II. *continued attention, perseverance*, D.18.218; *continuance* of an action, τῇ σ. τῆς μελέτης Hierocl. in CA27 p.484M.; *practice*, Plot.4.6.3; συνεχείας δηλωτική, = *frequentativa*, Gloss.

⊛ **συνεχής**, ές, *holding together*: I. of Space, *continuous*, Parm.8.6,25, Arist.Metaph.1069$^{a}$5, Ph.200$^{b}$18, al.; of quantity, opp. διωρισμένος, Id.Cat.4$^{b}$20; σ. νῶτον Pl.R.616e; συνεχὲς ποικίλον *a continuity* of variety, Id.Phd.110d; σ. οἰκήματα Th.3.21. b. c. dat., *continuous with* or *contiguous to, in a line with*, Hdt.4.22, E.Hipp.226 (anap.), Arist.Mete.339$^{a}$22, Mu.392$^{a}$23, etc.: less freq. c. gen., ib.393$^{a}$29 (s.v.l.); τομαὶ σ. ἀπὸ μιᾶς μέχρι τῶν δέκα Pl.Lg.738a: abs., σ. ἦσαν Κίλικες Plb.30.25.4, cf. Str.11.6.2. 2. of words, etc., ξ. ῥῆσις Th.5.85; πᾶς ὁ σ. λόγος Plb.1.5.5; τούτῳ συνάπτοντες τὸ σ. Id.3.3.2; τὸ σ. *connexion* of letters, Plu.Lys.19: c. dat., λόγος σ. τῷ νυνδὴ γενόμενος Pl.Ep.318e; σκέψις σ. τοῖς πρότερον Thphr.CP 6.3.3. 3. Math., of proportions, σ. ἀναλογία *continued* proportion (opp. διῃρημένη), i.e. three terms in geometrical progression, Arist.EN1131$^{a}$33, Archim.Aequil.2.9; κατὰ τὸ σ. ἀνάλογον Id.Sph.Cyl.2.5, etc. b. *successive*, of integers as terms in a series, Theol.Ar.54; of middle terms in argument, Arist.APo.87$^{b}$6. 4. of things, *continuous, conjoined*, Id.HA509$^{b}$13, etc.; folld. by a Prep., σ. πρός τι ib.495$^{b}$20; of substance, *clinging, dense*, τὸ γλίσχρασμα [τῆς πτισάνης] λεῖον καὶ σ...ἐστι Hp.Acut.10, cf. Gal.6.822; ἀήρ, ἔλαιον, Plu.2.396a,696b; τὸ πυκνὸν καὶ σ. ib.701f; [γάλα] λεῖον καὶ ὁμαλὸν καὶ σ. ἑαυτῷ Sor.1.91. II. of Time, *continuous, unintermitting*, σ. πυρετός, opp. διαλείπων, Hp.Aph.3.21; sts. distd. from σύνοχος πυρετός, Anon.ap.Gal.17(1).220; σ. καύματα καὶ πυρετούς Pl.Ti.86a; [θερμότης] Thphr.Ign.33; κίνησις Id.Lass.15; πόνος -έστερος Th.7.81; πόλεμος διὰ βίου σ. Pl.Lg.625e; συνουσία, βασιλεία, X.Smp.8.18 (Comp.), Ages.1.4; πότοι Men.914, cf. Sophil.3; σ. κακοπαθίαι OGI244.12 (Daphne, ii B.C.); σ. γίνεσθαι, πνεῖν, of winds, Arist.Mete.362$^{a}$11,26, Thphr.Vent.1; τὸ ἀκρίτως ξ. τῆς ἁμίλλης Th.7.71; τὸ σ. ἔργου (prob. for ἔργον) Anaxandr.63; τοῦ δήμου τὸ σ. *continuous intercourse with*.., Plu.Per.7; κατὰ τὸ σ. *continuously*, Plb.2.2.7; *consecutively, in what follows*, Gal.15.116; ἐκ τούτου κατὰ τὸ σ. *immediately* after that, ib.902. 2. *frequent*, τῶν ὀρνίθων ἥκιστα σ. καὶ συνήθης [ὁ γύψ] Plu.2.286a; λουτροῖς συνεχέσι χρῆσθαι Sor.1.65; χάσμη σ. ib.24; -εστέρα ἔστω ἡ ἐκμύζησις ib.97. III. of persons, *constant, persevering*, X.Oec.21.9; ἐν ταῖς..πρὸς τὰ πάθη διαμάχαις Plu.2.74c; cf. Poll.4.20, 6.147.

B. Adv. συνεχῶς, Ep. and Ion. -έως (v. sub fin.): I. mostly of Time, *continually, continuously, unremittingly*, Hes.Th.636, Hdt.7.16.γ', E.IA1008, IG1$^{2}$.57.54, etc.; ξ. πολεμεῖν Th.2.1, cf. 1.11, 5.24, Antipho 6.44; συνεχέως αἰεί Hdt.1.67, cf. Pl.Lg.706a; ἀεὶ σ. ib.807e; οἱ σ. ἐτῶν οὐκ ὀλίγων ἐφεξῆς γενόμενοι (v.l. γιν-) λιμοί Gal.6.749: Comp. -έστερον A.D.Pron.65.17: Sup. -έστατα X.Mem.4.2.6. b. *without leaving an interval, immediately*, ἐπίθυε.., καὶ λέγε τὸν λόγον συνεχῶς τὸν τῆς ἐπικλήσεως PMag.Par.1.1865, cf. BGU451.15 (i/ii A.D.), PFlor.332.18 (ii A.D.); δίδοται πρὸς τὰ θανάσιμα σ. πινόμενον καὶ ἐξεμούμενον Dsc.1.30; βδέλλας καύσας καὶ λεάνας χρῶ σ. προεκτίλας (sc. superfluous eyelashes) Aët.7.69. c. *at frequent intervals*, ἵνα μὴ σ. λούηται τὸ βρέφος Sor.1.99; μελίκρατον σ. ἐνστάζομεν ib.123; τὰ βρέφη -έστερον ἐξερᾷ [τὸ γάλα]..ναυτιῶντα ib.109; ποτίζων -έστερον ἐκ διαστημάτων Gp.10.18.5; -έστερον, = *saepius*, Gloss.; -έστατα, = *saepissime*, ib. 2. freq. with Numbers, *in succession, consecutively*, ὁρμαθοὺς μελῶν ἐφεξῆς τέτταρας ξ. Ar.Ra.915; ἡμέρας ἑβδομήκοντα ξ. Th.2.75; μῆνας ὀκτὼ σ. Ephipp.5.15 (anap.); similarly, οὐ σ. ἐφεξῆς ἐν τάξει πεποιημένος [τὸν λόγον] Gal.15.496. 3. rarely of Space, σ. εἶναι πᾶσαν οἰκουμένην Arist.Mete.362$^{b}$29; σ. μέχρι.. Plb.2.14.6. II. συνεχές as Adv. freq. in Ep., as Il.12.26; strengthd., σ. αἰεί *unceasing* ever, Od.9.74; also in Pi.I.4(3).65(83), Ar.Eq.21, and freq. in later Ep., Arat.20, Call.Ap.60, etc.; also in later Prose, Luc.Somn.4, D.L.2.32, al. [σῡνεχές Hom. ll. cc. and σῡνεχέως Hes. l. c., B.5.113, metri gr.; also Theoc.20.12, A.R.1.1271.]

**συνεχθ-αίρω**, *hate together, join in hating*, Phld.Hom. p.41 O., AP 6.20 (Jul.). **-ραίνω**, = foreg., Plu.2.490f. **-ω**, poet. for συνεχθαίρω, S.Ant.523.

**συνεχ-ίζω**, (συνεχής) *persist*, ἔν τινι Metrod.Herc.831.8: c. part., Phld.Mus. p.23 K.: abs., Id.Oec. p.70 J., Rh.1.150 S.; *make continuous*, Dam.Pr.112; ἀναπνοὴ -ίζουσα respiration *which leaves no intervals, rapid*, Herod.Med. in Rh.Mus.58.70. **-ισμός**, ὁ, = συνέχεια, Phld.Mus. p.23 K., Agathin.ap.Orib.10.7.5. **-όντως**, Adv. = συνεχῶς, Phld.Rh.1.47 S.

⊛ **συνέχω**, aor. συνέσχον:—Med., fut. συνέξομαι in pass. sense, D.Ep.3.40: so συσχόμενος (v. infr.), Pl.Sph.250d:—Pass., aor. συνεσχέθην Epicur.Ep.2 p.35 U.: fut. inf. συσχεθήσεσθαι Phld.Ir. p.97 W.:—*hold* or *keep together, confine, secure*, ὅθι ζωστῆρος ὀχῆες χρύσειοι σύνεχον [θώρηκα] Il.4.133, 20.415; ἵνα τε ξυνέχουσι τένοντες ἀγκῶνος where the sinews of the elbow *hold* [it] *together*, ib.478 (but perh. *meet*, v. infr. II); Ὠκεανὸς..συνεῖχε σάκος *enclosed, compassed* it, Hes.Sc.315; Αἴτνα σ. [Τυφῶνα] Pi.P.1.19; τὼ μηρὼ σ. *hold* them *together*, Ar.Nu.966; τὰ σκέλη [τοῦ βρέφους] συνεχέτω Sor.1.101; τοὺς τρεῖς ξυνέχων τῶν δακτύλων Ar.V.95; συνέσχον τὰ ὦτα αὐτῶν *closed* or *stopped* their ears, Act.Ap.7.57; μηδὲ συσχέτω ἐπ' ἐμὲ φρέαρ τὸ στόμα αὐτοῦ let not the pit *close* its mouth upon me, Lxx Ps.68(69).15, cf. Is.52.16; τὸ δέρμα σ. [τὰ ὀστᾶ] Pl.Phd.98d; Ἄτλας ἅπαντα σ. ib.99c; λάκκους συντετριμμένους, οἳ οὐ δυνήσονται ὕδωρ συνέχειν Lxx Je.2.13:—Pass., τὸ λεγόμενον "ἐν φρέατι συσχόμενος" *trapped* in a well, Pl.Tht.165b; ὁ καρπὸς..ἂν μὴ πλυθῇ..συνέχεται *sticks together*, Thphr.HP3.15.4; τὸ στόμα οὐ συνεσχέθη ἔτι my mouth *was* no longer *closed*, Lxx Ez.33.22. 2. *keep together, keep from dispersing*, στράτευμα, δύναμιν, X.An.7.2.8, D.8.76; σ. ἐν τῷ χάρακι Plb.10.39.1; ὥπλισε..καὶ συνεῖχε τοῦ τείχους ἐντός Plu.Cam.23; περὶ Κύπρον σ. τὸ ναυτικόν Id.Cim.18; *continue, keep on*, μὴ πλείους πέντε ἡμερῶν σύσχῃς τὸ ὕδωρ (the flooding) PCair.Zen.155.5 (iii B.C.); *keep*, τοὺς πολίτας σ. ἐν τοῖς ὅπλοις Plu.Sol.22, cf. 2.193e; προστάξαντος αὐτοῦ ἐν τοῖς ὅπλοις συνέχειν ἑαυτόν, ὁ δὲ ἀπεδύσατο Ael.VH14.48; *preserve*, οἱ ἅλες ἐπὶ πλεῖστον [τὰ σώματα] συνέχοντες Ph.2.255; *maintain*, σ. τοὺς στρατιώτας ἐκ τῶν ἱεροσυληθέντων λειψάνων D.S.16.61:—Pass., *to be continuous*, Parm.8.23; *to be maintained*, πᾶσα ἕξις..ὑπὸ τῶν καταλλήλων ἔργων συνέχεται καὶ αὔξεται Arr.Epict.2.18.1. b. of social and political order, σ. πόλεις *keep* states *together, keep* them *from falling to pieces, maintain* them, E.Supp.312, cf. And.1.9; τὸ φρονεῖν σ. δώματα E.Ba.392 (lyr.), cf. 1308; καὶ θεοὺς καὶ ἀνθρώπους ἡ κοινωνία σ. Pl.Grg.508a; ἡ τὰ πάντα πολιτεύματα συνέχουσα εἰς ἓν δίκη Id.Lg.945d, cf. Plt.311c; σ. τὴν πολιτείαν D.24.2; τὴν πολιτικὴν κοινωνίαν Arist.Pol.1278$^{b}$25, cf. 1270$^{b}$17; ὀρθῶς ἐν τῇ Ἑλλάδι τὴν δύναμιν τῶν Ἀθηναίων συνεῖχεν Plu.Per.22; ἐν οἴνῳ τὰς ἀρχὰς συνεῖχε *conducted* the government over wine, Id.2.714b; also ὁ τὸν ὅλον κόσμον συντάττων καὶ συνέχων X.Mem.4.3.13, cf. Lxx Wi.1.7; ξ. τὴν εἰρεσίαν *keep* the rowers *together, make* them *pull in time*, Th.7.14:—Pass., μετ' ἀλλήλων συνέχεσθαι Pl.Ti.43e. c. *keep together in friendship*, ἁμέ Ar.Lys.1265 (lyr.); τοὺς ἐρωμένους Ath.13.563e:—Pass., τὸ ὂν συνέχεται.. φιλίᾳ Pl.Sph.242e; τὰ πράγματα ὑπ' εὐνοίας D.11.7. d. Pass. also, *engage in close combat*, ἐγχειριδίοισι Hdt.1.214; of sexual intercourse, Arist.HA540$^{a}$24, GA731$^{a}$19, Thphr.Char.28.3. e. *occupy* or *engage*, ἑαυτὸν ἐν γυναιξὶ καὶ θιάσοις Plu.Cleom.34; [γυναῖκα] συνέχειν ἐπὶ καπηλείου Id.2.785d. 3. *contain, comprise, embrace*, εἷς λόγος πάσας τὰς αἰσθήσεις σ. Pl.Hp.Mi.374d; τὸ συνέχον *the chief matter*, Plb.2.12.3, Cic.Att.9.7.1, Gal.16.516; τὸ σ. καὶ κυριώτατον Phld.Lib. p.22 O.; τὰ συνέχοντα Plb.6.46.6, Gal.15.2; τὰ σ. ἀγαθά Phld.D.1.25: c. gen., τὸ σ. τῆς ἐκκλησίας *the chief reason for*.., Plb.28.4.2, cf. 4.51.1, 18.39.3; τῆς σωτηρίας *the chief means of*.., Id.10.47.11; τὰ σ. τῶν ἐγγράπτων the *chief* clauses, Id.3.27.1; τὸ σ. τῆς ἐννοίας Id.3.29.9, cf. 4.5.5, 18.44.2:—Pass., τὸν πρὸς τῇ ὑπεκλύσει πυρετὸν ὑπ' ἄλλης αἰτίας συνέχεσθαι *is chiefly caused* (cf. συνεκτικός) by.., Sor.2.4. 4. *detain*, τὰς καμήλους ἐν τῇ Νεχθενίβιος (sc. κώμῃ) PMich.Zen.103.3 (iii B.C.); *sequestrate*, PEnteux.3.7, 85.3 (iii B.C.); *keep under arrest*, PMich.Zen.36.6 (iii B.C.), BGU1824.27 (i B.C.), Ev.Luc.22.63; προσαπήγαγέν με εἰς τὴν φυλακὴν καὶ συνέσχεν ἐφ' ἡμέρας δ̄ PEnteux.83.7 (iii B.C.), cf. 84.11 (iii B.C.):—Pass., συνέχομαι ἐμ φυλακῇ PPetr.2 p.50 (iii B.C.), cf. PCair.Zen.347.3 (iii B.C.), PRyl.65.11 (i B.C.), etc.; of things *held* as security, PCair.Zen.373.3 (iii B.C.). 5. *constrain* or *force* one to a thing, ἡ ἀγάπη τοῦ Χριστοῦ σ. ἡμᾶς 2Ep.Cor.5.14; *oppress*, Ev.Luc.8.45, 19.43; ἡ σκληροκοιτία λυπεῖ καὶ σ. τὸ σῶμα Gal.15.196:—used by early writers only in Pass., συνέχεσθαί τινι *to be constrained, distressed, afflicted*, and, generally, *to be affected by* anything whether in mind or body, πατρὶ συνείχετο..χαλεπῷ Hdt.3.131; ξ. τοῖσι Λυκούργου πατριώταις Pherecr.11; σ. πολέμῳ, δουλητίῃ, Hdt.5.23, 6.12; ὀνείρασι A.Pr.656; φροντίδι E.Heracl.634; δίψῃ, πόνῳ, Th.2.49, 3.98; πυρετῷ Ev.Luc.4.38; κακῷ Ar.Ec.1096; μεγάλοις καὶ ἀνιάτοις νοσήμασιν Pl.Grg.512a; πάσῃ ἀπορίᾳ Id.Sph.250d; ἀγρυπνίαις IG4$^{2}$(1).122.50 (Epid., iv B.C.); τῷ λόγῳ (v.l. πνεύματι) Act.Ap.18.5; γέλωτι συσχεθέντα τελευτῆσαι D.L.7.185; ἔρωτι συσχεθείς Conon 40.3; ἄνθρωπος συνεχόμενος ἀπὸ οἴνου Lxx Je.23.9; συνεχομένη τῇ συνειδήσει ib.Wi.17.11. 6. *constrain, hinder, hold back*, E.Rh.59; σύσχῃ τὸν οὐρανόν *shut up* the heaven, Lxx De.11.17; συνεσχέθη ὁ ὑετὸς ἀπὸ τοῦ οὐρανοῦ ib.Ge.8.2; συνεσχέθη ἡ θραῦσις ἐπάνωθεν Ἰσραήλ the plague *was stayed* from Israel, ib.2Ki.24.25: metaph., ὑπὸ τοῦ γένους A.D.Adv.122.22, cf. Synt.342.18. 7. *hold at the same time*, δύο σχολάς Str.14.1.48. 8. *buy up and withhold, make a corner in*, σῖτον Lxx Pr.11.26. 9. Gramm., σ. τὸ ἄρθρον *to be accompanied by* the article, A.D.Synt.35.2, al. 10. συνέσχον I *also received*.., BGU577.16 (iii A.D.), etc. II. intr., *meet*, v. supr. I.1; εἰς ἕν Arist.HA530$^{b}$27; πρός τι *to be connected with*, S.E.P.1.145.

**συνέψημα**, ατος, τό, *boiling together*, f.l. in Gal.6.531.

**συνεψητέον**, *one must boil together with*, Gp.14.24.2.

**συνεψιάω**, *play together*, AP5.287 (Paul. Sil.).

**συνέψω**, aor. -έψησα SIG1171.16 (Lebena):—*boil together*, [κράμβῃ] τὰ λιπαρὰ τῶν κρεῶν Dsc.2.122, cf. PHolm.21.33, etc.; of the *coction* of humours, Hp.VM19 (Pass.); of *digestion*, Id.Vict.3.79; of urine retained and *heating* in the bladder, Id.Aër.9; of heat, *cause to ferment*, Thphr.CP1.21.2 (Pass.), etc.:—Pass., *to be boiled together*, Arist.Fr.110, Luc.JTr.30, Sor.2.13, Gal.13.39; *to be boiled* or *smelted with*, χαλκῷ Arist.Mir.835$^{a}$11; κρέασι Thphr.HP9.18.2.—The pres. **συνεψέω** occurs in late writers, Gal.Vict.Att.115, Id.15.692, Aret.CA1.2 (Pass.), Alex.Trall.Febr.3, Gp.8.36.2; cf. ἕψω: aor. συνῆψας is corrupt in Timocl.21.4 (leg. αἶσιν ἧψες).

® **συνηβάω**, *pass youth together with, join in youthful sport*, οὐ γὰρ ἐμοὶ παῖς ἐθέλει συνηβᾶν Anacr.24, cf. *Scol.*22, Opp.*H.*5.471; τοῖς Δελφοῖς ἡ Πυλαία σ. Plu.2.409a.

**συνηβολ-έω**, *fall in with, meet*, ἀλλήλοις Babr.61.3. ® **-ίη**, ἡ, *occurrence*, A.R.2.1157.

**σύνηβος**, ὁ, ἡ, (ἥβη) *young comrade*, E.*HF*438 (lyr.).

**συνηγέομαι**, *command together*, D.S.14.81. II. Pass., *to be treated as equivalent*, *PTeb.*340.16,40 (iii A.D.).

**συνηγμένως**, Adv., (συνάγω) *collectively*, Hsch. s.v. ἀθρόως, *An.Ox.* 4.407, Tz.*H.*11.123, etc.

**συνηγορ-έω**, Aeol. **συνᾱγορέω** *IG*12(2).526*b*31 (Eresus, iv B.C.): aor. inf. misspelt -ᾶσαι *PAmh.*2.33.20,32, part. written correctly -ήσας, -ήσαντες, ib.34,31 (ii B.C.):—*plead in court*, Pl.*Lg.*937a, *PAmh.* ll. cc., etc.; ἐπὶ μισθῷ τινι σ. Arist.*Rh.Al.*1444$^{a}$20; σ. τινί *to be* his *advocate, plead* his *cause*, Ar.*Ach.*685, Aeschin.2.15, etc.; [τᾷ πόλι] *IG* l.c.: c. dat. rei, πονηρῷ πράγματι Isoc.1.37; ὑπὲρ τοῦ δικαίου D.51.18; ὑπὲρ Εὐκτήμονος Arist.*Rh.*1374$^{b}$36; σ. περὶ τῶν ἀριστείων τῇ ἡδονῇ *advocate* its claims to the first place, Id.*EN*1101$^{b}$28; σ. εἰς τὸ πάντα πραχθῆναι τὰ συμφέροντα τῷ δήμῳ *IG*2$^{2}$.844.14:—Pass., οἱ -γορούμενοι ὑπ' ἐμοῦ my *clients*, *PHamb.*29.11 (i A.D.); ἐνδέχεται..τὴν δόξαν οὐκ ὀρθῶς συνηγορεῖσθαι Gal.15.36. 2. σ. τῷ κατηγόρῳ *second* the accuser, S.*Tr.*814. **-ημα**, ατος, τό, = συνηγορία, D.C.37.33 (pl.), 47.11. **-ητέον**, *one must act as advocate*, τινι S.E.*M.*2.11. ® **-ία**, ἡ, *advocacy of* another's *cause*, Aeschin.3.7 (pl.); μετὰ -ίας ἐπιρρωννύντες Phld.*Ir.*p.65 W.; εἰς τὴν -ίαν τοῦ ἴδια πάθη γίνεσθαι γυναικῶν Sor.2.3, cf. Gal.15.578; *right to practise as an advocate*, *PGiss.*40 ii 4 (iii A.D.): pl., περὶ τῶν συμμάχων Arist.*Rh. Al.*1425$^{a}$7, cf. *OGI*567.19 (Attalia, ii A.D.), *CIG*2795 (Aphrodisias). 2. ἡ συνηγορία τοῦ τι εἶναι the *affirmative*, A.D.*Synt.* 235.13. 3. ἀπὸ -ῶν ταμείου *sometime advocatus fisci*, *IG*3. 712a. **-ικός**, ή, όν, *of* or *for a* συνήγορος, Poll.4.25, etc. Adv. -κῶς ib.26. II. τὸ σ. *advocate's fee*, paid to public συνήγοροι, Ar. *V.*691, cf. Sch. ad loc.: in Egypt, *Ostr.*1537 (ii B.C.), *PLeid.F.*ap. Wilcken *Ostr.* i p.302. **-ος** (Aeol., etc. **συνάγορος** [ᾱ] *IG*12(2). 526*b*28 (Eresus, iv B.C.), etc.), ον, (ἀγορά) *speaking with, of the same tenor with*, μαντεῖα καινὰ τοῖς πάλαι ξ. S.*Tr.*1165:—as Subst., *one who agrees with* another, συνήγορόν μ' ἔχεις A.*Ag.*831. II. *advocate*, ἐάν τις..σ. ὢν λαμβάνῃ χρήματα ἐπὶ ταῖς δίκαις ταῖς ἰδίαις ἢ δημοσίαις Lex ap.D.46.26: 1. *public advocate*, chosen by the state, e.g. at Athens, to defend laws against proposed changes before the νομοθέται, D.24.36; or to conduct public prosecutions, Ar.*Ach.*715 (troch.), *Eq.*1358, *V.*482 (troch.), Decr.ap.Plu.2.833f; also ten appointed by lot annually to represent the state at the εὔθυναι of magistrates, Arist.*Ath.*54.2; two appointed by εἰσαγωγεῖς in connexion with assessments of tribute, *IG*1$^{2}$.63.8 (dub.); in Boeotia the magistrates in charge of the εὔθυναι were called συνήγοροι, ib.7. 303.26 (Oropus), cf. Arist.*Pol.*1322$^{b}$11. b. σ. τοῦ ἱερωτάτου ταμιείου, = Lat. *advocatus fisci*, *Ath.Mitt.*25.124 (Lydia, ii/iii A.D.); σ. τοῦ ἐν Φρυγίᾳ ταμιείου καὶ τοῦ ἐν Ἀσίᾳ *IGRom.*4.819 (Hierapolis). 2. *private advocate*, D.21.127, 59.14.

**συνηδέατε**, v. σύνοιδα.

**συνήδομαι**, fut. -ησθήσομαι X.*An.*5.5.8, Pl.*R.*462e, etc.: aor. -ήσθην E.*Ion* 728, Isoc.5.8:—*rejoice together*, Pl. l.c., X.*Mem.*3.11. 10, etc.; σ. τινί *rejoice with, sympathize with*, E. l.c., D.21.202, etc.; σ. τινὶ περιεόντι Hdt.3.36; opp. συλλυπεῖσθαι, Antipho 3.2.8, Pl. l.c.; opp. συνάχθεσθαι, X.*Cyr.*1.6.24, Arist.*EN*1171$^{a}$8; opp. συναλγεῖν, ib.1166$^{a}$27; σ. ὅτι.. X.*An.*5.5.8, etc. 2. c. dat. rei, *rejoice at* a thing, σ. τοῖς ἀγαθοῖς Arist.*Rh.*1381$^{a}$4; τῷ νόμῳ τοῦ θεοῦ *Ep.Rom.*7.22; ἐπὶ τοῖς ἀγαθοῖς X.*Cyr.*8.2.2, etc.; τινος *because of*.., App.*Mac.*17, *OGI*504.5 (Aezani, ii A.D.), Lib.*Or.*53.2. 3. c. dat. pers. et rei, S.*OC*1398. II. sts. used like ἐφήδομαι of *malicious joy at misfortune*, οὐδὲ συνήδομαι..ἄλγεσιν δώματος E.*Med.*136 (lyr.); τί τάλας τοῖσδε συνήδῃ..; Id.*Hipp.*1286 (anap.); θανόντι γ' οὐδαμῶς σ. Id.*Rh.*958; συνηδόμενοι ταῖς συμφοραῖς restd. from Poll.3.101 for συνησθησόμενοι (v.l. ἐφησθ-) in Isoc.8.87.

**συνηδύνω**, *sweeten* or *make pleasant to the taste*, τὸν ἄρτον Plu.2. 668f; -ηδυσμένη τροφή ib.661b, cf. Herod.Med.ap.Orib.*Syn.*6.32 (v.l. συνοδευέσθω), Paul.Aeg.2.41. 2. generally, *help in cheering*, Arist.*EN*1126$^{b}$30.

® **συνήθεια**, ἡ, *habitual intercourse, acquaintance, intimacy*, αἱ πρὸς ἀλλήλους σ. Isoc.1.1; διατριβαὶ καὶ -θειαι μετά τινων Aeschin.2.23; ἡ τῶν φίλων σ. ib.152; σ. καὶ φιλία Arist.*GA*753$^{a}$12; ἡ πολιτικὴ σ. Id.*EN*1181$^{a}$11; τὰς τῶν φαύλων σ. ὀλίγος χρόνος διέλυσε Isoc.1.1; ὅπως ἂν αἱ σ. διαζευχθῶσιν Arist.*Pol.*1319$^{b}$26; καὶ αὐτῷ δέ μοί εἰσι σ. *PCair.Zen.*42.2 (iii B.C.); ὧν ἡμῖν ἐν συνηθείᾳ *PMich.Zen.*82.3 (iii B.C.). b. *sexual intercourse*, X.*Cyr.*6.1.31 (v.l.); σ. ἔχειν μετὰ γυναικός Plu.2.310e; πρὸς γυναῖκα Vett.Val.288.23. 2. of animals, *herding together*, Arist.*HA*575$^{b}$19; νέμεσθαι κατὰ συνηθείας in *herds*, ib.611$^{a}$7, cf. Ael.*NA*2.31; so of soldiers, κατὰ συνηθείας in *messes*, Plb.35.4.14. II. *habit, custom*, *h.Merc.*485 (pl.), Hp.*VM*3, Pl.*R.* 516a, etc.; pl., φαῦλαι σ. bad *habits*, Epicur.*Sent.Vat.*46; κατὰ συνήθειαν τοῦ προτέρου βίου Pl.*R.*620a; ἐν τοῖς ἤθεσι τοῖς τῆς ἑαυτοῦ συνηθείας in his own *accustomed* haunts, Id.*Lg.*865e; ἡ σ. τοῦ ἔργου *habituation* to it, X.*Cyn.*12.4; λήθην ἢ συνήθειαν τῶν ἀδικημάτων D. 19.3, cf. 60.27; πολλῆς..σ. ἡ ῥητορικὴ Epicur.*Fr.*46; τῇ σ. τοῦ εἰδώλου *by being used* to it, 1*Ep.Cor.*8.7; *practice*, Plb.1.42.7, cf. Pl. *Lg.*656d: with Preps., διὰ συνήθειαν Id.*Sph.*248b; διὰ τὴν σ. Arist. *HA*494$^{b}$21; ἐκ συνηθείας *OGI*629.12,79 (Palmyra, ii A.D.); κατὰ σ. Pl.*R.* l.c.; παρὰ συνήθειαν Id.*Lg.*655e; ἠναγκάσμεθα ὑπὸ συνηθείας Id.*Tht.*157b; σ. ἔχειν τῇ πολιτείᾳ to be *used* to it, *practised* in it, Plb.39.5.2; σ. κτᾶσθαι πρὸς τὰ κοινά Plu.2.791a. 2. *the customary usage* of language, ἐκ σ. ῥημάτων καὶ ὀνομάτων Pl.*Tht.*168b, cf. Chrysipp.*Stoic.*3.33; εἰς συνήθειαν ἐποίησε τοῦ λόγου τούτου τὴν πόλιν καταστῆναι brought the city to *habitual use* of this phrase, Aeschin. 1.165; ἡ σ. τῶν Ἑλλήνων, αἱ κατὰ τὰς διαλέκτους σ., Phld.*Rh.*1.59 S., Gal.18(2).237, Phld.*Po.*5.2; ἐν τῇ τεχνικῇ καὶ μὴ εἰκαίᾳ σ. Diocl. Magn.*Stoic.*3.214: abs., *ordinary language*, ἐν τῇ σ. Plu.2.22f, cf. ib.c, 1113a; κατὰ τὴν σ. A.D.*Synt.*323.22, cf. Demetr.*Eloc.*69, al., D.H. *Amm.*2.11, Herod.Med. in *Rh.Mus.*49.549. III. *customary gratuity*, *Sammelb.*7336.13 (iii A.D.), 7369.25 (vi A.D.), *PLond.*1.113 (3).11, 3.1036.8 (both vi A.D.): pl., *perquisites*, *Cod.Just.*3.2.4, Just. *Nov.*134.1, al.

**συνηθέομαι**, Pass., *to be filtered together*, Gal.19.649.

® **συνήθης**, ες, gen. εος, contr. ους, gen. pl. συνηθέων, contr. συνηθῶν (or συνήθων, Hdn.Gr.1.428):—*dwelling* or *living together, accustomed* or *used to each other*, συνήθεες ἀλλήλῃσιν Hes.*Th.*230; *like each other in habits*, Th.1.71; συνήθεις καὶ γνώριμοι *acquaintances*, Pl.*R.* 375e, cf. Arist.*EN*1126$^{b}$25; φίλοι καὶ σ. Philem.213.13; σ. τινί *well-acquainted* or *intimate with* one, Pl.*Cri.*43a, *La.*188a, Men.*Pk.* 258: less freq. as Subst., *friend, intimate*, Phld.*Rh.*1.332 S., etc.: c. gen., D.S.19.47, Plu.*Num.*1. II. *habituated, accustomed*, τῷ σκότῳ Pl.*R.*517d; σώματα πᾶσι ποτοῖς καὶ πόνοις σ. γιγνόμενα Id.*Lg.* 797e; of animals, χειρὶ σ., = χειροήθης, *AP*9.287 (Apollonid.): abs., τὰ σύντροφα καὶ σ. those reared and *bred with* him, Arist.*HA*629$^{b}$11; οἱ σ. τόποι their *wonted* haunts, ib.596$^{b}$29: c. inf., σ. ᾄδειν γενόμενοι Pl.*Lg.*666d. 2. of things, *habitual, customary, usual*, ἔθος, πότμος, S.*Ph.*894, *Tr.*88; σ. ὄμμα a *customary* vision, Id.*El.*903, cf. Hp.*Aph.* 2.49; δίαιτα Th.1.6; σημεῖα τῷ γένει -έστερα And.2.26; τὸ ξ. ἥσυχον your *habitual* quietness, Th.6.34; τὸ ξ. φοβερόν ib.55; σύνηθες αἰεὶ ταῦτα βαστάζειν ἐμοί E.*Alc.*40, cf. Arist.*Pol.*1295$^{b}$17; διὰ τὸ μὴ σ. νομοθέτῃ Pl.*Lg.*739a: τὸ σ. the *customary*, X.*Mem.*3.14.6; *custom*, Arist.*Rh.*1369$^{b}$16, al.; τὸ τῆς ἑορτῆς σ. Pl.*Ti.*21b; of language, *in common use*, A.D.*Pron.*45.1, al.; τὸ σ. *usage*, Id.*Adv.*178.28. III. Adv. -θως, ἔχειν τινί to be *acquainted, friendly with*, D.37.26. 2. *habitually, as is usual*, σ. παρακολουθεῖν Aeschin.2.132; ἐξαπατᾶσθαι Plu.*Galb.*15. 3. *according to common usage*, opp. τοπικῶς, Sch. Th.*Oxy.*853 xiii 4; ἡ σ. νοουμένη οἰκονομία as *commonly* conceived, Phld.*Oec.*p.29 J.

**συνηθία**, ἡ, = συνήθεια, Hdn.Gr.1.292.

**συνηκολουθηκότως**, Adv. *by way of consequence, consistently*, Chrysipp.*Stoic.*2.257.

**συνήκοος**, ον, (ἀκοή) *hearing together*, οἱ σ. τῶν λόγων Pl.*Lg.*711e; τῷ κορυφαίῳ σ. *as able to hear* as the first, Plu.2.678e.

® **συνήκω**, *to have come together, be assembled, meet*, Th.5.87. II. σ. εἰς ἕν, of walls, *meet* in a point, X.*Vect.*4.44; σ. εἰς στενόν to narrow down, Arist.*IA*710$^{b}$2; so εἰς ὀξύ Id.*HA*495$^{b}$10, Thphr.*HP* 3.11.1.

**συνηλῐκί-α**, poet. -ίη, ἡ, *body of comrades* or *playmates*, *Supp. Epigr.*6.140.22 (Phrygia, iv A.D.). **-ώτης**, ου, ὁ, later Gr. for ἡλικιώτης, *Ep.Gal.*1.14, *CIG*4929 (Philae), Alciphr.1.12.

**συνῆλιξ**, ῐκος, ὁ, ἡ, *of like* or *equal age, playmate, comrade*, ἐμοὶ ξυνήλικες A.*Pers.*784; ἠκούσατ', ὦ σ.; Eup.181.5; συνήλικα (acc. sg.) Anaxil.7; as fem., συνάλικες *AP*7.711 (Antip.): neut. pl., παιδάρια συνήλικα Thd.*Da.*1.10.

**συνηλόω**, *nail* or *pin together*, Ph.*Bel.*57.34, Polyaen.7.21.3:—Pass., Ph.*Bel.*57.26; βραχίονος θώρακι -ουμένου Paul.Aeg.6.88.

**σύνηλῠς**, ῠδος, ὁ, ἡ, in pl., *convenae*, *Gloss.*

**συνηλῠσίη**, ἡ, *meeting, assembly*, *AP*9.665 (Agath.).

**συνήλωσις**, εως, ἡ, (συνηλόω) *a being pinned together*, by an arrow or lance, Paul.Aeg.6.88; = *conclavatio*, *Gloss.*

**συνημέρ-ευσις**, εως, ἡ, *daily intercourse*, Arist.*EE*1239$^{b}$19 (pl.). **-ευτής**, οῦ, ὁ, *daily companion*, Id.*Pol.*1314$^{a}$10. **-εύω**, *pass one's days together*, Pl.*Smp.*217b, *Phdr.*240b; σ. καὶ συζῆν Arist.*EN*1156$^{b}$4; τινι X.*Mem.*1.4.1, Arist.*EN*1157$^{b}$15, al.; μετά τινων ib.1166$^{b}$14; ἔν τινι in a practice, ib.1172$^{a}$5.

**συνημερόομαι**, Pass., *to be brought into cultivation, reclaimed*, of land, Thphr.*HP*6.3.3.

**συνημμένως**, Adv. of συνάπτω, *connectedly*, Gal.19.84, Alex.Aphr. *in Metaph.*467.2, *Gloss.*

® **συνημοσύνη**, ἡ, in pl., *agreements, covenants*, Il.22.261. II. *ties of friendship* or *relationship*, A.R.1.300, 3.1105: sg., Thgn.284, as v.l. for φιλημοσύνῃ.

**συνήμων**, ον, gen. ονος, *united*, ἡ δὲ σ. λάθα my *comrade* oblivion, of one dead, dub. l. in *IG*12(3).1064 (Pholegandros): pl., *friends, comrades*, A.R.4.1210.

**συνήνεμος**, ον, *exposed to the wind*, Poll.5.110; σ. ἐλπίδες *all unstable*, Heraclit.*All.*33 cod. (dub. l.).

**συνηνῐοχέω**, *drive a chariot together*, Sch.Ar.*Nu.*25.

**συνηνωμένως**, Adv., (συνενόω) *unitedly*, Tz.*H.*12.60.

® **συνήορος**, Dor. and Trag. **συνάορος**, ον: (συναείρω II):—poet. Adj. *linked with, wedded to*, ἣ [φόρμιγξ] δαιτὶ συνήορός ἐστι θαλείῃ Od.8. 99; εὐλογία φόρμιγγι σ. Pi.*N.*4.5; *in communion with*, ξυνάορον ξυναῖς γυναιξί Id.*Fr.*122.12. 2. abs., *joined in wedlock*, and as Subst., *consort*, whether *husband*, E.*Or.*1136 (pl.); or (as more usual) *wife*, ib.654, 1556, 1566, *Alc.*824, etc.

**συνηπειρώτης**, ου, ὁ, *fellow-Epirote*, Varro *RR*2.5.

**συνηπεροπεύω**, *join in cheating* or *tricking*, Ar.*Lys.*843.

**συνηρεμέω**, *remain stationary also*, of water, Hero *Spir.*1.2.

**συνηρετ-έω**, *work with, assist, befriend*, τινι S.*Aj*.1329 (as Lob. from Hsch. (ξυνηρετίσεις· συνήσεις, συζυγήσεις) for ξυνηρετμεῖν); ἆρ' ὄλβος αὐτοῖς .. ξυνηρετεῖ; E.*Fr*.776 (prob. cj. for συνηρεφεῖ codd. Stob.); ξ. τύχαις *adapt oneself* to.., ib.282.7 (but κἀξυπηρετεῖν (codd. Gal.) may be right). **–ης**, ου, ὁ, = σύμφωνος, *colleague*, Phot.

**συνηρέφ-εια**, ἡ, *thick tangled shade of trees*, wrongly written συνηρεφία in App.*BC*4.103 codd. **–έω**, *throw a thick shade over*, Thphr.*HP*3.1.5; cf. συνηρετέω. **–ής**, ές, (ἐρέφω) *thickly shaded* or *covered*, χώρη .. ἴδησι σ. Hdt.1.110; ὄρεα .. ἴδησι καὶ χιόνι σ. Id.7.111, cf. Thphr.*HP*5.1.12, Str.5.4.5; σᾶμα .. πτελέησι σ. *AP*7.141 (Antiphil.); σ. χώρα, λόφος, Plu.*Luc*.32, *Marc*.29; ἐν τῷ σ. Luc. *Anach*.18: metaph., ξυνηρεφὲς πρόσωπον εἰς γῆν βαλοῦσα E.*Or*. [957]. 2. *close-covering*, ἐπικάλυμμα Arist.*HA*527$^{b}$33 (Comp.), 541$^{b}$31 (Comp.); ὄστρακον Id.*PA*679$^{b}$29; ὕλη Plu.*Demetr*.49.

**συνῃρημένως**, Adv., (συναιρέω) *in general*, Ammon.*Diff*.p.63 V., etc. 2. *by contraction*, Hsch. s.v. ἅλιον.

**συνήρης**, ες, *joined together, added*, δαῖτα συνήρεα χιονόεσσαν a feast of snow *mixed with* (sc. the vinegar already mentioned), Nic.*Al*. 512.

**συνήριθμος**, v. συνάριθμος.

**συνηρμοσμένως**, Adv., (συναρμόζω) *conformably*, M.Ant.4.45.

**συνηρτημένως**, Adv., (συναρτάω) *in a trained manner, expertly*, σ. καὶ τεχνικῶς Phld.*Rh*.2.91 S.

**συνήσθησις**, εως, ἡ, *sympathetic joy*, App.*BC*5.69 (dub. l.).

**συνησκημένως**, Adv., (συνασκέω) *neatly*, Lat. *polite*, *Gloss*.

**συνησσάομαι**, Att. **–ττάομαι**, Pass., *to be conquered together*, X. *Cyr*.6.4.14.

**συνησῠχάζω**, *rest together*, Ph.2.168.

**συνηχ-έω**, *sound together* or *in accord*, τὰ χαλκεῖα καὶ τὰ κέρατα Arist.*Aud*.801$^{b}$9, cf. Plu.*CG*3, *Ant*.18; τοὺς σαλπικτὰς σ. κελεύσας D.C.51.9. II. *ring with, echo to*, ὡς συνηχεῖν αὐτοῖς τὴν ἀγοράν Thphr.*Char*.6.10, cf. Plb.2.29.6, Ph.2.153, al.:—Pass., πόλεις κελάδοις –εῖσθαι Posidon.10 J. III. trans., γυναῖκες –ηχοῦσι κωκυτόν J.*BJ* 3.7.26. **–ησις**, εως, ἡ, *sounding in accord*, Thphr.*Fr*.89.8, Ph.2. 226, Plu.2.1021b.

**συνήωρ**, ἡ, = συνήορος, acc. συνήορα Orac.ap.Eun.*VS* p.465 B.; ξυνάωρ· εὐναία δάμαρ..., Hsch.; gen. συνάορος, Suid.

**συνθᾰκ-έω**, *sit with*, νυκτὶ *take counsel with* the night, E.*Heracl*. 994. **–ος**, ον, *sitting with* or *together*, ἔστι γὰρ Ζηνὶ σ. θρόνων Αἰδώς *partner* of his throne, S.*OC*1267. 2. generally, *partner*, E.*Or*.1637, *Hipp*.1093.

**συνθαλπ-τέον**, *one must warm thoroughly, foment*, *Gp*.16.4. 3. **–ω**, *warm thoroughly*, ἑαυτούς Plu.2.974c, cf. Hp.*Salubr*.7:— Pass., Id.*Aff*.15. 2. metaph., *warm* or *soothe* by cheering words, μηδέ μ'.. ξύνθαλπε μύθοις ψευδέσιν A.*Pr*.685.

**συνθαμβέω**, *to be astounded in keeping with*, τοῖς λεγομένοις Pl.*Ion* 535e.

**συνθάπτω**, *bury together, join in burying*, τινα A.*Th*.1032, S.*Aj*. 1378, E.*Hel*.1545, Pl.*Lg*.909c, etc.; τινά τινι one *with* another, E. *Alc*.149, Demad.13, *IG*14.943 (Ostia):—Pass., *to be buried with*, τῷ ἀνδρί Hdt.5.5, cf. Th.1.8; συνετάφη τοῖς σώμασιν ἡ ἐλευθερία Lycurg. 50; συνετάφημεν [τῷ Χριστῷ] διὰ τοῦ βαπτίσματος *Ep.Rom*.6.4.

**συνθαυμάζω**, *join in wondering*, εἰ.. v.l. in Pl.*Tht*.162c; *join in admiring*, τὴν ἀκρίβειαν Eun.*VS* p.469 B.

**συνθεάζω**, *join in divine frenzy*, D.S.4.51 codd. (but συνενθ– is prob. cj.).

**συνθε-άομαι**, *view* or *see together*, of spectators at games, Pl.*La*. 178a, X.*Oec*.3.7; οἱ συνθεώμενοι the *other spectators*, Antipho 3.4. 5. 2. *examine together*, τὰ ἱερά X.*An*.6.4.15; σ. τὰ κατὰ τὴν μοῦσαν Pl.*Lg*.967e. 3. *take in at a glance*, Plb.1.25.1, 1.40. 7. **–ᾱτής**, οῦ, ὁ, *fellow-spectator*, Pl.*R*.523a, *La*.179e: fem. **–ᾱτρια**, Ar.*Fr*.472: but, *fellow-actress*, Procop.*Arc*.9.

**συνθέλω**, poet. form of συνεθέλω (q.v.): also in Prose, Arist.*EN* 1167$^{a}$1, *Inscr.Prien*.109.163 (ii B.C.), J.*AJ*14.8.1.

**σύνθεμα**, ατος, τό, later Gr. for σύνθημα, Hedyl.ap.Ath.11.497d (where both forms occur), *PLips*.33 ii 26 (iv A.D.). 2. *compound word*, Eust.340.35. 3. *sum*, Dioph.1.27, al. 4. *collection*, Lxx *Ec*.12.11. 5. *ointment made of several ingredients, mixture*, *PMag.Berol*.1.256, al.; medicinal *mixture*, *Hippiatr*.22; chemical *compound*, Ps.-Democr.Alch.p.55 B. 6. *whole* of parts, Apollod. *Poliorc*.180.9, al.

**συνθερᾰπεύω**, *treat medically as well*, καὶ τὴν κεφαλήν Steph. *in Gal*. 1.338 D.:—Pass., ταῦτα –εται τῷ παντὶ σώματι Herod.Med.ap.Aët. 5.129. 2. *pay court to* one *along with* or *together*, Philostr.*VA*6. 30 (Pass.).

**συνθερίζω**, *reap together*, Ar.*Ach*.948 codd.

**συνθερμαίνω**, *warm together* or *thoroughly*, Arist.*HA*562$^{b}$21, J.*AJ* 7.14.3:—Pass., Thphr.*CP*1.3.4, Arist.*Pr*.888$^{b}$23, Dsc.1.52, Gal.15. 487.

*συν-θεσία, ἡ, = σύνθεσις III, mostly in pl., *covenant, treaty*, πῇ δὴ συνθεσίαι..; Il.2.339, cf. A.R.1.340, etc.: also in sg., Id.4.340, al., Epic.*Oxy*.214$^{r}$.13; περὶ συνθεσίης for a *wager*, Posidipp.ap.Ath.10. 412e (καίπερ σ. codd.). 2. οὐδ' .. ἐλήθετο συνθεσιάων nor did he forget the *instructions*, Il.5.319. II. Medic., = *continuatio*, *Gloss*. **–θεσίδιον**, τά, Dim. of sq. IV, *gown*, *PGiss*.21.8 (ii A.D.), *Stud.Pal*.20.41.5 (iii A.D.). * **–θεσις**, εως, ἡ, *putting together, composition, combination*, Pl.*Phd*.93a, *R*.611b; τῶν λίθων Arist.*EN*1174$^{a}$23, cf. *IG*4$^{2}$(1).103.56 (Epid., iv B.C.), 7.3073.92 (Lebad., ii B.C.); τῶν σπονδύλων Sor.1.102; *storage*, τῶν μήλων (quinces in a βίσκος) Phylarch.10 J.; but ἐλαιῶν σ. a *preserve* of olives, *Gp*.9.28.2. b. in concrete sense, *junction*, ὀστῶν Arist.*PA*658$^{b}$19; συνθέσεις (λέγω τὰς γωνίας) Id.*Pr*.910$^{b}$14. 2. in various technical senses: a. in Grammar, *composition*, γραμμάτων τε συνθέσεις, i.e. syllables and words, A.*Pr*.460, cf. Arist.*Metaph*.1092$^{a}$26; σ. ἔκ τε ῥημάτων γιγνομένη καὶ ὀνομάτων, i.e. sentences, Pl.*Sph*.263d, cf. *Cra*.431c, Arist. *Po*.1458$^{a}$28, Gal.15.487; περὶ συνθέσεως ὀνομάτων, title of work by D.H.; also, *the juxtaposition* of letters in a word, Arist.*Rh.Al*.1434$^{b}$34; of an author's *composition*, Isoc.10.11; so ἡ τῶν μέτρων σ. metrical *composition*, Arist.*Po*.1449$^{b}$35; ἡ τῶν ἐπῶν σ. D.S.5.74; ἡ τοῦ παίωνος ξ. *the way* the paeon *is made up*, Plu.2.1143d; *the constitution* of things, Hp.*Virg*.1. b. Math., *synthesis* of a problem (opp. ἀνάλυσις), Archim.*Sph.Cyl*.2.7, explained in Papp.634; ἡ κατὰ σ. ἀγωγή *synthetic* procedure, Id.412.2. c. Math., σ. λόγου transformation of a ratio known as *componendo*, Euc.5 *Def*.14; κατὰ –σιν, = *componendo*, Archim.*Aequil*.2.9. d. Math., *addition*, Ph.1.11, Plu.2. 1018c, Dioph.1 *Intr*.; καθ' ἀντινοῦν –σιν *however many times added*, i.e. whatever number of times taken (multiplied), Archim.*Spir*.1:—also as Pythag. name for 2, Anatol.ap.*Theol.Ar*.8. e. in Logic, *union* of noun and verb or of two objects of thought in a statement, Arist. *Int*.16$^{a}$12, *de An*.430$^{a}$27; also ὁ παρὰ τὴν σ. [λόγος] the fallacy of *composition*, opp. διαίρεσις, Id.*SE*177$^{a}$33. f. in Physics, *composition* of substances, parts of organisms, from their elementary constituents, Id.*PA*646$^{a}$12, *Top*.151$^{a}$23; opp. μίξις (combination), Id.*GC*328$^{a}$6. g. in Medicine, *compounding* of essences and drugs, τῶν μύρων Thphr. *Od*.14, al., cf. D.S.4.45, Aglaïas 8. II. *combination of parts so as to form a whole*, γενέσεις καὶ σ. Pl.*R*.533b; ἡ τῶν στρωμάτων σ. Id. *Plt*.280b, cf. Arist.*PA*645$^{a}$35, *Metaph*.1014$^{b}$37; in plants, Thphr.*HP* 5.5.2. b. in concrete sense, *a social* or *political combination*, Arist. *Pol*.1276$^{b}$7; *a military formation*, Ael.*Tact*.18.5. III. *agreement, treaty*, Pi.*P*.4.168, *Fr*.205; πὸς τὰς συνθέσις in accordance with the *agreements*, *IG*5(2).343.41,60 (Orchom. Arc., iv B.C.); ἐκ συνθέσεως by *arrangement*, D.S.13.112, etc.; συνθέσεις περὶ γάμων Plu. *Sull*.35. 2. σ. λόγων *making up* accounts, *Stud.Pal*.4.70.391 (i A.D.); so σ. alone, εἰς σύνθεσιν τῷ βασιλεῖ *PTeb*.714.6 (ii B.C.). IV. *set, service* (most freq. in Lat. *synthesis*): 1. *collection of clothes, wardrobe*, *Dig*.34.2.38.1; also, *dress, gown, costume, suit*, σ. τελείας λευκὰς δεκατρεῖς, γυναικείας σ., *PHamb*.10.13,21 (ii A.D.), cf. *POxy*. 1153.23 (i A.D.), 496.4 (ii A.D.), *PSI*10.1117.11,13 (ii A.D.), Mart.2. 46.4, 5.79.2; *synthesinam indutus*, Suet.*Ner*.51. 2. *service* of plate, σ. πινακίων *BGU*781 i 5 (i A.D.), cf. Mart.4.46.15, Stat.*Silv*.4. 9.44. **–θετέον**, *one must compound*, Pl.*Cra*.434b, Arist.*Pol*.1294$^{a}$35. **–θέτης**, ου, ὁ, *composer, writer*, Pl.*Lg*.722e, Gal.18(2).778; καλῶν ποιημάτων Phld.*Po*.5.35; σ. ὀνομάτων, etc., D.H.*Dem*.36; σ. λόγων a prose-*writer*, like συγγραφεύς, opp. ποιητής, Paus.10.26. 1. **–θετίζομαι**, *arrange*, J.*BJ*4.9.10. **–θετικός**, ή, όν, *skilled in putting together*, τινος Luc.*Hist.Conscr*.47; σ. ἐπιστῆμαι *constructive* sciences or arts, Pl.*Plt*.308c; ἡ σ. ἐπιστήμη the art *of composition*, D.H.*Comp*.6, al.; φαντασία σ. *Stoic*.2.43. 2. *component*, Erot. s.v. ἶνες; αἱ σ. τῆς γραμμῆς στιγμαί S.E.*M*.9.291; τὸ σ. [τοῦ ἀνθρώπου] στοιχεῖον Gal.15.38; σ. μόρια Id.1.237. **–θετισμός**, ὁ, *setting*, of bones, Id.14.781. * **–θετος**, ον, also fem. συνθέτη (or συνθετή as in Lys.*Fr*.34, Arist.*Ph*.265$^{a}$21, *Metaph*.1051$^{b}$27, al.): (συντίθημι):—*put together, compounded, composite*, Pl.*Phd*.78c, al.; of a centaur, διαιρετὸς .. καὶ πάλιν σ. X.*Cyr*.4.3.20, cf. Lys. l.c.; τὸ σ. the *composite* part of man, Arist.*EN*1178$^{a}$20; σ. ἐκ πολλῶν Pl.*R*. 611b; ἐκ τῶν αὐτῶν Id.*Phlb*.29e; σ. ἀναγνώρισις *complex*, Arist.*Po*. 1455$^{a}$12. 2. σύνθετον, τό, *compound*, Id.*Ph*.187$^{b}$12; τὰ σ., opp. τὰ στοιχεῖα, Id.*Cael*.306$^{b}$20, cf. *Metaph*.1070$^{b}$8; so ἡ σύνθετος οὐσία ib.1043$^{a}$30; ἡ συνθέτη οὐσία ib.1023$^{b}$2, cf. *de An*.412$^{a}$16; αἱ μὴ σ. οὐσίαι Id.*Metaph*.1051$^{b}$27; cf. σύγκειμαι II. 4. 3. in various technical senses, a. in Grammar, φωνὴ σ. a *compound* sound, i.e. a syllable, Id.*Po*.1456$^{b}$35; or a word, ib.1457$^{a}$11; φωνῶν αἱ μὲν ἁπλαῖ (e.g. Δίων), αἱ δὲ σ. (e.g. Δίων περιπατεῖ) S.E.*M*.8.135; σ. ὀνόματα *compound* nouns, Arist.*Rh.Al*.1434$^{b}$34, Demetr.*Eloc*.91, Philomnest. 2; σ. σχῆμα D.T.635.21; σ. προσηγορία (e.g. ὑπνώδης καταφορά) Gal.7.643. Adv. –τως Str.13.2.5, Sor.2.26, Gal.6.549. b. in Metre and Music, σ. ῥυθμός a *compound* foot, Pl.*R*.400b; [διαστήματα] σ. Aristid.Quint.1.7, cf. Plu.2.1135b; ἁρμονίαν εἶναι σ. πρᾶγμα Pl.*Phd*. 92a. c. in Arithmetic, σ. ἀριθμός a number *composed* of several factors, Arist.*Metaph*.1020$^{b}$4, Euc.7 *Def*.14. d. in Medicine, σύνθετα *solid excrements*, Hp.*Coac*.109: also φάρμακον σ. *compound* drug, τὸ ξ. [φάρμακον] τὸ διὰ τῆς λιμνήστιδος καὶ εὐφορβίου καὶ πυρέθρου Aret.*CD*1.2, cf. Hsch. s.v. φαρικόν. II. *put together, got up, fictitious*, λόγοι A.*Pr*.686. III. metaph., *agreed upon, covenanted*, ὥσπερ ἐκ συνθέτου *by agreement*, Hdt.3.86.

**συνθέω**, fut. –θεύσομαι Od.20.245:—*run together with*, τοῖς ἀνέμοις Poll.1.196: metaph. of things, *go along with, go smoothly with*, οὐχ ἡμῖν συνθεύσεται ἥδε γε βουλή Od. l.c. II. *run together*, i.e. to the same place, εἰς ταὐτό Arist.*HA*533$^{b}$24; πρὸς τὸ μέσον Id.*Cael*. 297$^{a}$26: abs., Id.*HA*611$^{a}$1. 2. of lines and the like, *run together, meet in one point*, X.*Eq*.10.11. 3. metaph., *agree*, τῷ Ἐφόρου λόγῳ Aristid.*Or*.36(48).71. 4. *shrink up, retract*, μύες Hp.*Fract*. 35.

**συνθεωρ-έω**, *contemplate* or *observe at the same time*, Arist.*PA*645$^{a}$12, *APr*.67$^{a}$37, Thphr.*HP*1.14.4, *BGU*1855.4 (i B.C.); *take a comprehensive survey of*, Epicur.*Ep*.2 p.55 U., *Nat*.11.10:—Pass., Phld. *Po.Herc*.994.38; συνθεωρεῖσθαι.. τὴν γῆν ἀσπορήσειν it was observed *also* that.., *PTeb*.61(*b*).33 (ii B.C.). II. *act as* θεωρός or *go to a* *festival together*, Ἐλευσῖνάδε Lys.8.5; τινι *with* one, Ar.*V.*1187; σ. καὶ συνευωχεῖσθαι Arist.*EE*1245$^b$4. **-ημα**, ατος, τό, *agreed theoretical principle*, Phld.*Rh.*1.140 S. **-ητέον**, *one must observe together*, τι D.L.10.96. **-ητος**, ον, *fully established by theory*, διάπτωσις Phld.*Rh.*1.11 S. **-ος** (proparox.), ὁ, *colleague in a mission* (θεωρία), *OGI*42.9 (Cos, iii B.C., pl.), *Inscr.Délos* 421.63 (ii B.C., pl.), Poll.2.55.

**συνθήγω**, *sharpen*, ὀργῇ συντεθηγμένος φρένας E.*Hipp.*689.

⊛ **συνθήκη**, ἡ, (συντίθημι) *compounding*, esp. of words and sentences, Luc.*Hist.Conscr.*46, Hermog.*Id.*1.1,3, Philostr.*VS*1.17.4, Herm. *in Phdr.* p.175 A.: in concrete sense, *a compound*, Luc.*Prom.Es* 5:—but in early writers, II. *convention, compact*, σ. καὶ ὁμολογία Pl.*Cra.*384d, cf. 433e; ὁ νόμος σ. καὶ ἐγγυητὴς ἀλλήλοις τῶν δικαίων Arist.*Pol.*1280$^b$10, cf. *Rh.*1376$^a$33; ἐκ συνθήκης *by agreement*, Pl.*Lg.*879a; διὰ συνθήκης Arist.*APr.*50$^a$18; κατὰ συνθήκην *conventionally*, opp. φύσει, Id.*EN*1133$^a$29; so συνθήκῃ ib.1134$^b$32: pl., συνθήκας ποιεῖσθαι τὰς ὑπὲρ τοῦ μὴ βλάπτειν ἄλληλα Epicur.*Sent.*32. 2. *article of a compact* or *treaty*, τὴν ξ. προφέροντες ἐν ᾗ εἴρητο Th.5.31, cf. 1.78: also, *treaty*, σ. καὶ συμμαχία *SIG*421.1 (Thermon, iii B.C.): but in this signf. mostly in pl., *articles of agreement*, and hence, *covenant, treaty*, between individuals or states, A.*Ch.*555, Ar.*Lys.*1267, Isoc.4.176, etc.; συνθῆκαι περὶ εἰρήνης X.*Mem.*4.4.17; γάμων σ. Plu.*Luc.*18; σ. κύριαι, ἄκυροι, Lys.18.15; ἐπ' ἄλλους στρατεύειν οὐκ εἶναι ἐν ταῖς σ. X.*HG*7.5.4, cf. *SIG*135.1 (Olynthus, iv B.C.), al.; ξυνθῆκαι Λακεδαιμονίων πρὸς βασιλέα.., σπονδὰς εἶναι καὶ φιλίαν κατὰ τάδε Foed.ap.Th.8.37, cf. *IG*1$^2$.90.21, Pl.*Cri.*54c, D.15.29; συνθήκας ποιεῖσθαι Hdt.6.42, Ar.*Pax* 1065, X.*HG*7.1.2; ὑπὲρ τῶν βαρβάρων Isoc.4.177; ποιεῖν τινι πρός τινα *between* them, X.*Lac.*15.1; σ. συνεθέμεθα Lys.13.88; γράψαι, γράψασθαι, D.48.10, D.S.1.66; ἀναιρεῖν, λύειν, Isoc.17.31, 18.24; παραβῆναι Pl.*Cri.* l.c.; ὑπερβαίνειν Aeschin.1.164; παρ' οὐδὲν ἡγεῖσθαι Decr.ap.D.18.164; συνθήκαις ἐμμένειν Isoc.4.81; ἐκ τῶν σ. according to the *covenant*, ib.179; κατὰ τὰς ξ. Th.1.144, cf. Pl.*Tht.*183c; opp. παρὰ τὰς σ. Id.*Cri.*52d. III. = θήκη, *coffin*, v.l. in Lib.*Or.*8.11.

**συνθηκο-γράφος** [ᾰ], ὁ, *notary*, *SIG*344.31 (pl., Teos, iv B.C., Epist. Antig.). **-ποιέομαι**, = συνθήκας ποιέομαι, *EM*663.51, Hsch. s.v. σύνθεο:—Act. in Sch.Ar.*Pl.*1060. ⊛ **-φύλαξ** [ῠ], ἄκος, ὁ, *guarantor of a covenant*, Sch.Il.23.486, Sch.A.R.4.1558; = *sequester*, *Gloss.*

**σύνθημα**, ατος, τό, *anything agreed upon, preconcerted signal*, Hdt.8.7; given by means of a beacon-fire, Th.4.112; συνθήματα εἶναι τὰ ὀνόματα that names are *conventional signs*, Pl.*Cra.*433e; τὰ παρὰ φύσιν σ. Id.*Grg.*492c; so δέλτοι ἐγγεγραμμένην ξυνθήμαθ' having *ciphers* inscribed upon it, S.*Tr.*158; *dispatches* or *letters in cipher*, Plb.8.15.9; *military signal-code*, Ph.*Bel.*90.45, al.; cf. συνθηματικός. 2. *password*, Hdt.9.98, Th.7.44, etc.; σ. παρέρχεται *the word* is passed round, X.*An.*1.8.16, cf. 6.5.25; σ. παραδιδόναι to pass *it*, ib.7.3.34; σ. παρφέροντι E.*Ph.*1140; παραγγέλλειν, παρεγγυῆσαι, X.*An.*1.8.16, *Cyr.*7.1.10; *signal* for battle, τοῦ σ. δοθέντος Plu.*Sull.*28; ἐνδιδόναι Luc.*Salt.*10. 3. *any token* or *sign*, ξυμφορᾶς ξ. ἐμῆς S.*OC* 46; τὰ Θησέως Πειρίθου τε.. ξυνθήματα the *tokens* or *pledges of* their *compact*, ib.1594; = Lat. *tessera*, Plb.6.34.8; *passport*, Jul.*Ep.*13; *symbol*, Dam.*Pr.*210,213; τῆς τελετῆς τὸ σ. *IG*3.173 (iv A.D.). b. *military standard*, D.S.1.86. 4. = συνθήκη, *agreement, covenant*, σ. ποιήσασθαι X.*An.*4.6.20; σ. ἦν.. παίειν Id.*HG*5.4.6; ἀπὸ συνθήματος *by agreement*, Hdt.5.74, Th.4.67, 6.61, etc.; so ἐκ σ. Hdt.6.121; ἀφ' ἑνὸς σ. Plu.*Aem.*19; ὑφ' ἑνὶ σ. Hdn.2.13.4. II. *communion, connexion*, τί σ. ἀσπίδι καὶ βακτηρίᾳ; Ath.5.215e.

**συνθημᾰτ-ιαῖος**, α, ον, *agreed on, bespoken*, στέφανοι Ar.*Th.*458. **-ίζω**, *give signal for*, μάχην Eust.700.12. **-ικός**, ή, όν, *by preconcerted signs*, σ. γράμματα writings *in cipher*, Plb.8.16.9. Adv. **-κῶς** *in cipher*, Id.8.17.4. II. *symbolical*, Dam.*Pr.*210. **-ώδης**, ες, *symbolical*, ibid.

⊛ **συνθηρ-ᾱτής**, οῦ, ὁ, *one who joins in quest of*, τῶν φίλων X.*Mem.*3.11.15. **-άω**, *hunt together, join in the chase*, Id.*An.*5.3.10; τινι or τισι *with* one, Id.*Cyr.*3.1.14,38. 2. *catch* or *find together*, in Med., σὺν δέ νιν θηρώμεθα S.*Ant.*433:—Pass., χεῖρες.. συνθηρώμεναι hands *caught and bound together*, Id.*Ph.*1005. **-ευτής**, οῦ, ὁ, = συνθηρατής, X.*Cyr.*2.4.15, Them.*Or.*21.254d. **-εύω**, = συνθηράω, Pl.*R.*451d; σ. ὥσπερ κύνες ib.466d. 2. *catch* or *win together*, E.*Fr.*981.5:—Med., *quest after, reach by efforts*, ἃ δ' οὐ κεκτήμεθα, μίμησις.. ταῦτα συνθηρεύεται Ar.*Th.*156. 3. *catch hold of, gather up*, φαίνεται τὸ λιπαρὸν.. τὰ κάρφη καὶ τὰ τοιαῦτα συνθηρεύειν Diocl.*Fr.*147. **-ος**, ον, *hunting with*, τῷ Κύρῳ X.*Cyr.*3.1.7; σ. κύνες *hunting with* (Artemis), *AP*9.303 (Adaeus): as Subst., σ. Ἀρτέμιδος her *fellow-huntress*, Apollod.3.8.2: c. gen. object., *joining in quest of*, τῶν ἀγαθῶν φίλων X.*Mem.*2.6.35.

**συνθητεύω**, *to be a hireling together*, μετά τινός τινι Eust.1338.62.

**συνθῐᾰσ-εύω**, *join in leading the* θίασος, Str.10.3.18. **-ῑτεύω**, *to be a fellow-member of a* θίασος, *PEnteux.*20.2, 21.3 (iii B.C.). **-ίτης** [ῑ], ου, ὁ, = -ώτης, *PGrenf.*1.31.5 (ii B.C.), Demitsas Μακεδ. p.319 (Ressova): fem. **-ῖτις**, ιδος, ἡ, *PEnteux.*21.2 (iii B.C.), *Inscr.Délos* 1403 *Bb* ii 94 (ii B.C.). **-ώτης**, ου, ὁ, *partner in the* θίασος, Ath.8.362e codd., Them.*Or.*4.53d: generally, *fellow, comrade*, c. gen., ἡλικίας τῆς αὐτῆς Ar.*V.*728; ξ. τοῦ ληρεῖν *fellow*-gossip, Id.*Pl.*508.

**συνθιγγάνω**, *touch together*, τινος Them.*Or.*20.235b.

**συν-θλασμός**, ὁ, *gnashing*, Hsch. s.v. γομφιασμόν. **-θλέσσω**, = συνθλάω, Sch.rec.A.*Pers.*412. **-θλαστέον**, *one must crush, squeeze*, Sor.2.63. **-θλάω**, *crush together*, Eratosth.*Cat.*11, D.S.2.57, Arr.*An.*6.29.9:—Pass., [ποτήριον] ὦτα συντεθλασμένον Alex.270, cf. *IG*2$^2$.1544.21; συνεθλάσθη τὴν κεφαλήν Aen.Gaz.*Thphr.* p.32 B.; βίῃ συνθλώμενος ὀστᾶ Man.5.201: abs., *to be crushed*, Arist.*Pr.*863$^b$13, *Ev.Matt.*21.44, *Gp.*9.29.

**συνθλίβω** [ῑ], *press together, compress*, Arist.*Rh.*1361$^b$17, *Cael.*307$^b$12, Thphr.*Ign.*58,74; of a crowd, *Ev.Marc.*5.24:—Pass., Pl.*Ti.*92a, Arist.*HA*555$^b$26; σ. εἰς τὴν κοιλίαν Id.*Pr.*895$^b$2; πρὸς ἄλληλα ib.929$^a$15; συντεθλιμμένον ἤτοι συνεπτυγμένον ἄργυρον, = *collisum argentum*, *Gloss.*: aor. 2 συνεθλίβην [ῐ] Plu.2.408e,430c.

**σύνθλιψις**, εως, ἡ, *compression*, Arist.*Resp.*472$^b$1: metaph., ἔπους (e.g. ὑπέκ) Longin.10.6.

**συνθνήσκω**, fut. -θᾰνοῦμαι A.*Ag.*1139, *Ch.*979:—*die with* or *together*, A. ll. cc., S.*Tr.*720, etc.: c. dat., θανόντι συνθανεῖν ib.798, *Fr.*953. 2. of things, συνθνήσκουσα δὲ σποδὸς *expiring with* (the flames), A.*Ag.*819; οὐ γὰρ ηὐσέβεια (cj. for ἡ γὰρ εὐσέβεια) σ. βροτοῖς S.*Ph.*1443; ἡ ποίησις οὐχὶ συντέθνηκέ μοι Ar.*Ra.*868; cf. συναποθνήσκω.

**συνθοιν-άτωρ** [ᾱ], ορος, ὁ, *partaker in a feast*, E.*El.*638. **-ος**, ον, = σύνδειπνος, Polem.Hist.78, D.S.10.22.

**συνθολ-όω**, *make muddy*, metaph., τὴν γνώμην Lib.*Or.*18.286:—Pass., ψυχὴ μὴ ξυντεθολωμένη ὑπὸ τοῦ οἴνου Philostr.*VA*2.37; ἐν ταῖς μέθαις καὶ ταῖς ἀπεψίαις πᾶς ἀτμὸς.. συντεθόλωται Sor.1.38. **-ωσις**, εως, ἡ, *making turbid*, metaph., λογισμοῦ Tz.*H.*8.875, cf. Sophon.*in de An.*139.19.

**συνθορῠβέω**, *join in putting down by clamour*, D.S.13.101.

**συνθρᾰνόομαι**, Pass., *to be broken in pieces, shivered*, E.*Ba.*633 (troch.).

**σύνθραυσις**, εως, ἡ, *breaking*, μελῶν Vett.Val.127.16: pl., *Cat.Cod.Astr.*8(1).248.

⊛ **συνθραύω**, *break in pieces, shiver*, E.*Or.*1569, Plu.*Arist.*18; *crumble*, ἄρτον *Gp.*9.23.5:—Pass., X.*Ages.*2.14, Plb.8.5.11, etc.

**συνθρην-ήτρια**, ἡ, *fellow-mourner*, Sch.E.*Ph.*1518. **-ος**, ον, *mourning with*, Ἀφροδίτη *AP*7.407 (Diosc.): *partner in mourning*, Arist.*EN*1171$^b$9.

**συνθρησκ-ευτής**, οῦ, ὁ, *fellow-worshipper*, *BCH*37.95 (Thessalonica), *Cod.Just.*1.5.20.6. **-εύω**, *assist in worshipping*, *BCH*12.253, 15.204 (both Panamara).

**συνθρῐαμβεύω**, *share in a triumph*, Plu.*Mar.*44, *Luc.*36.

**συνθρίζω**, = συντέμνω, in aor. συνέθρ[ο]ισε· συνέτεμε, Hsch.

**συνθρόησις**, εως, ἡ, (θροέω) *perplexity*, S.E.*M.*9.169: pl. is prob. cj. for συνεόρσεις in Plu.2.449a.

**συνθρονίζω**, *enthrone beside*, τῷ Διί Ps.-Callisth.2.22 (Pass.).

⊛ **σύνθρονος**, ον, *enthroned with*, σύνθρονος Ἡφαίστῳ Orac.ap.Luc.*Peregr.*29, cf. *OGI*383.60 (Nemrud Dagh, i B.C.), D.S.16.92, etc.; σ. τέρμασιν εὐμαθίας *AP*12.257.8 (Mel.): c. gen., σ. τῶν ἐν Αἰγύπτῳ θεῶν *IG*14.961 (Rome), cf. Ph.1.136; σ. Δίκης, of a Roman proconsul, *Supp.Epigr.*4.467.6 (Didyma, iii A.D.): abs., σ. Δίκη *AP*9.445 (Jul. Aeg.).

**σύνθροος**, ον, *sounding together*, ἠχώ Nonn.*D.*16.335; [Ἀρίων] σ. κιθάρῃ *AP*9.308 (Bianor).

**συνθρυλλέω**, *bruit abroad together with*, τισὶν αἰτίαν Procop.*Vand.*1.12.

**συνθρύπτω**, *break in pieces*: *crush*, τὴν καρδίαν *Act.Ap.*21.13.

**συνθρῴσκω**, *spring, rush together*, Ael.*NA*5.7, in aor. 2 συνέθορον.

**συνθῡμ-έω**, *to be of one mind*, Epich.208. **-όομαι**, Pass., *to be angry with* or *together*, τῷ δεσπότῃ Procop.Gaz. p.165 B.

⊛ **συνθύξω**· συναντήσω, Hsch.

⊛ **συνθῠσί-α**, ἡ, *common festival*, *SIG*849.11 (Ephesus, ii A.D.); σ. οἰκουμένης *Anatolian Studies* p.222 (coins of Anazarbus). II. *office of* συνθύτης, *IG*2$^2$.1368.134 (ii A.D.). **-άζω**, *sacrifice together*, Eulogius ap.Phot.*Bibl.* p.536 B. **-αστής**, οῦ, ὁ, *member of a* συνθυσία, τὸ κοινὸν τὸ Συνθυσιαστᾶν *Annuario* 2.148 (Rhodes).

**συνθύτης** [ῠ], ου, ὁ, *fellow-sacrificer*, E.*Fr.*852, *IG*4.679.16 (Hermione, ii B.C.), 12(1).157 (Rhodes), 7.1785 (Thespiae), *BSA*27.226 (Sparta, ii A.D.), Apollod.2.7.2.

**συνθύω**, *offer sacrifice together, join in sacrifice*, Is.8.15, Aeschin.3.52, Men.*Pk.*446; οἱ συνθύσοντες Plb.4.49.3; τινι *with* one, X.*Oec.*7.8; τῷ δάμῳ *Delph.*3(2).50.5 (ii B.C.); εἰ δὲ ξένους ἀστοῖσι συνθύειν χρεών strangers and countrymen together, E.*El.*795; μετά τινος D.57.47.

**συνθωκ-έω**, = συνθακέω, J.*AJ*15.3.8. ⊛ **-ος**, ον, = σύνθακος, Jul.*Or.*5.166b. II. Subst. σύνθωκος, ὁ, *public seat*, Sophr.153.

⊛ **συνῐαίνω**, *cheer together*, θυμόν τινος Opp.*C.*3.167.

**συνιατρεύω**, *to be an assistant-doctor*, *Klio* 15.337 (Delph., ii B.C.); τοὺς -εύοντας ἡμῖν Gal.12.944.

**συνῐδῐάζω**, *give a special signification to together*, τινί τι A.D.*Synt.*42.10. II. intr., *to be used specially with*, [ταῖς πτώσεσι] ib.49.15.

**συνιδρόω**, *perspire much*, D.S.3.28, Dsc.5.36, Archig.ap.Paul.Aeg.4.5, *Gp.*18.8.5.

**συνιδρύω**, *dedicate together with*, Καίσαρα τοῖς θεοῖς App.*BC*5.132:—Pass., συνιδρῦσθαι Ἑρμῇ Ath.13.561d:—Med., Sch.Pi.*P.*3.137.

**συνίδρωσις**, εως, ἡ, *excessive perspiration*, Crito ap.Gal.12.447 (pl.), Paul.Aeg.4.1.

**συνιερ-άομαι**, *join in performing holy rites*, ἡ γυνὴ τῷ ἀνδρὶ Plu.2.276d. **-ᾱτεύω**, = foreg., *BCH*44.77 (Lagina, Caria), 5.186 (ibid.). **-εύς**, έως, ὁ, *fellow-priest*, *Clara Rhodos* 2.211 (Lindus, i B.C., pl.), J.*Ap.*2.23, Plu.*Aem.*3, *IG*2$^2$.1368.18 (pl., ii A.D.), D.C.40.62: fem. συνιέρεια, Procl.*Chrest.*ap.Phot.*Bibl.* p.322 B. **-ῑτεύω**, = συνιερατεύω, *CIG*5130 (Cyrene), *Africa Italiana* 1.331 (ibid.).

**συνιερο-μνάμων** [ᾱ], ονος, ὁ, *joint-*ἱερομνάμων, *SIG*506.8 (Decr.

Amphict., iii B.C., pl.), *Inscr.Magn.*91*a*6, *d*6. **-ποιέω,** *join in sacrifice with,* τινι Is.8.20. **-ποιός,** ὁ, *joint-sacrificer,* Din.*Fr.*89.33, *IG*2$^{2}$.1672.299,303, 11(2).162*A*37 (Delos, iii B.C.).

**συνίερ-ος,** ον, *having joint sacrifices,* Plu.2.753f. **-ουργέω,** = συνιεροποιέω, D.H.4.14, *SIG*798.11 (Cyzicus, i A.D.), Ph.1.653, Plu.2.292d.

**συνιζ-άνω,** *sink* or *settle down, collapse,* Arist.*Somn.Vig.*456$^{a}$13, Gal.8.325,500, 15.570; σάρκες δ' ἱδρῶτι συνίζανον Theoc.22.112; πηλὸν ἐν πυρὶ..συνιζάνειν Plu.*Publ.*13. 2. *sink,* εἰς βυθόν Thphr.*Od.*29; of the blood, Id.*Sens.*43; of the wind, Luc.*VH*1.29. II. causal, *cause to collapse* or *sink,* Arist.*Resp.*474$^{a}$14. **-ησις,** εως, ἡ, *subsidence, collapse,* of the earth, ἐς τὰ κοῖλα Id.*Mu.*396$^{a}$3 (but γῆ [ἐγένετο] κατὰ συνίζησιν (sc. τοῦ ὕδατος) Sch.Hes.*Th.*115); οἰκοδομημάτων Plu.*Crass.*2: metaph., Plot.2.2.1. 2. *synizesis, melting of two vowels into one,* without alteration of letters, as in πόλεως, μὴ οὐ, etc., *EM*735.36, Sch.Heph.2.1; but = συγκοπή, *EM*279.8. 3. *compression* of air, Hero *Spir.Praef.* **-ω,** *sit together, hold a sitting* (for the discharge of business), of a court of magistrates, Hdt.6.58. 2. *fall together, collapse,* Hp.*Oct.*11, Arist.*Pr.*868$^{a}$18, 927$^{b}$34, *Resp.*479$^{b}$14, Thphr.*Sud.*25; so εἰς ταὐτὸν σ. Pl.*Ti.*72d; τὸν ἄργυρον συνιζῆσαι τακέντα Plu.2.665b; τὸ συνιζηκὸς τῶν πόρων Gal.10.472. II. causal, *make to sink,* τὸν πνεύμονα αἴρειν καὶ σ. Arist.*Resp.*479$^{a}$27, cf. 475$^{a}$8.

**συνίημι,** also **ξυν-,** 2 sg. ξυνίης [ῑ] S.*El.*1347, Ar.*Pl.*45, (συν-) Pl.*Sph.*238e; 3 sg. and pl. συνίει, συνίουσι, Lxx 1*Ki.*18.15; imper. ξυνίει Od.1.271, etc. (ξύνιε Thgn.1240 is prob. corrupt); 3 sg. subj. συνιῇ Pl.*Prt.*325c; inf. συνιέναι, Ep. -ῑέμεν Hes.*Th.*831; also συνιεῖν Thgn.565, later συνίειν Lxx 1*Ki.*2.10, al.; part. ξυνῑείς Ar.*Lys.*1016 (lyr.), (συν-) Pl.*Sph.*253b, etc.; later συνίων Lxx 1*Ki.*18.14: impf. συνίην Ach.Tat.1.9; συνίειν (s.v.l.) Luc.*DDeor.*6.2, *Philops.*39; 3 sg. ξυνίει X.*An.*7.6.9; 3 pl. ξυνίεσαν Th.1.3, Ep. ξύνιεν Il.1.273: fut. συνήσω Hdt.9.98, Pl.*Prt.*325e: aor. 1 συνῆκα A.*Ag.*1112,1243, Hdt.5.92.γ', Ar.*Ach.*101, etc.; Ep. ξυνέηκα Il.1.8, al.; ἐξυνῆκα Anacr.146; ἐσύνηκα Alc.131; but aor. 2 imper. ξύνες, S.*Tr.*868; pl. σύνετε v.l. in *Ev.Marc.*7.14; part. συνείς A.*Pers.*361, Hdt.1.24, 5.92.γ' and η'; Aeol. σύνεις Alc.*Supp.*4.10; Dor. inf. συνέμεν Pi.*P.*3.80: pf. συνεῖκα Plb.5.101.2 (συνηκέναι codd., corr. Schweigh.), etc.; Dor. 1 pl. συνείκαμες Plu.2.232d; pf. part. συνεικώς prob. l. in J.*Vit.*45.—In Hom. we find of pres., only imper. ξυνίει Od. l.c.; of impf., 3 pl. ξύνιεν for ξυνίεσαν, Il.1.273; of aor. 1, Ep. 3 sg. ξυνέηκε; of aor. 2, imper. ξύνες 2.26, al.; of aor. 2 Med., 3 sg. ξύνετο Od.4.76; subj. 1 pl. συνώμεθα Il.13.381; all except the last form with ξυν-, though seldom required by the verse. [As in ἵημι, the 1st syll. is short in Ep., long in Trag. and Com.: Hes. however has συνῑέμεν (l.c., metri gr.); S. ξυνῑημι in a dactylic verse, *El.*131; and Ar. ξυνῑημ' in an iamb. trim., *Av.*946, cf. Philem.123.3.]

I. *bring* or *set together,* in hostile sense, τίς τ' ἄρ σφωε..ἔριδι ξυνέηκε μάχεσθαι; Il.1.8; οὓς ἔριδος μένεϊ ξυνέηκε μάχεσθαι 7.210; but ἀμφοτέρης..ἕνα ξυνέηκεν ὀϊστόν *shot* one arrow at both *together,* Musae.18. 2. Med., *come together, come to an agreement,* ὄφρα..συνώμεθα..ἀμφὶ γάμῳ Il.13.381. 3. *send herewith, PSI*6.665.7 (iii B.C.). II. metaph., *perceive, hear,* freq. in Hom. (who also has Med. in this sense, ἀγορεύοντος ξύνετο Od.4.76); ὣς φάθ', ὁ δὲ ξυνέηκε Il.15.442; εἰ δ' ἄγε νῦν ξυνίει Od.1.271:—Constr., c. acc. rei, ξυνέηκε θεᾶς ὄπα φωνησάσης Il.2.182; ἐμέθεν ξυνίει ἔπος Od.6.289, cf. S.*Ant.*1218, Ar.*Pax* 603: c. gen. pers., νῦν δ' ἐμέθεν ξύνες ὦκα Il.2.26; καὶ κωφοῦ συνίημι Orac ap.Hdt.1.47: rarely c. gen. rei, μευ βουλέων ξύνιεν Il.1.273. 2. *to be aware of, take notice of, observe,* τοῖιν Od.18.34; τῶν δὲ σὺ μὴ ξύνιε Thgn.1240 (sed leg. ξυνίει): c. acc., Hdt.1.24; folld. by a relat., ξύνες δὲ τήνδ', ὡς..χωρεῖ S.*Tr.*868 (lyr.): abs., πολλά με καὶ συνιέντα παρέρχεται Thgn.419. 3. *understand,* ξ. ἀλλήλων *understand* one another's language, Hdt.4.114, Th.1.3; εὖ λέγοντος..τοῦ Δελφικοῦ γράμματος οὐ σ. Pl.*Alc.*1.132c, cf. *Lg.*791e: freq. c. acc. rei only, Pi.*P.*3.80, A.*Pers.*361, Hdt.3.46, Ar.*Pl.*45, etc.; ξυνῆκα τοὔπος ἐξ αἰνιγμάτων A.*Ch.*887, cf. *Ag.*1243, S.*El.*1479; ξ. δὲ αὐτὸς Ἑλληνιστὶ τὰ πλεῖστα X.*An.*7.6.9; δι' ἑρμηνέων ξ. τι Id.*Cyr.*1.6.2; συνιέντες τὰ ναυτικά Id.*HG*1.6.4: abs., τοῖς ξυνιεῖσιν *to the intelligent,* Thgn.904; in Com. dialogue, parenthetically, συνίης; like μανθάνεις; Lat. *tenes?* Alex.124.6, Diph.32.13; οὐχὶ ξυνίης; S.*El.*1347; οὔπω ξυνῆκα A.*Ag.*1112: also folld. by a clause, οὐ ξυνιᾶσιν ὅκως.. Heraclit.51; ξυνίημ' ὅτι βούλει Ar.*Av.*946 (ξυνῆχ' cj. Brunck); σ. τὸ γράμμα ὃ βούλεται Pl.*Prm.*128a, cf. Hdt.9.110: also, like other Verbs of perception, c. part., ξυνιᾶσι τιμώμενοι Democr.95; οὐ συνίης καταναλίσκων; Plu.2.231d; συνῆκα ἡδὺς γεγενημένος Luc.*DDeor.*2.1, cf. *Tim.*8.

**συνῐκετεύω,** *supplicate together with,* τινι Plu.*Arist.*4, Hegesias 2: abs., Charito 2.7.

**συνικμάζομαι,** Pass., *get wetted,* Thphr.*CP*4.13.6, *Lap.*11.

**συνικνέομαι,** *reach quite,* πρός τι Thphr.*CP*2.4.4 codd. (Schneid. μὴ διικνεῖσθαι). 2. *pertain to, interest,* Arist.*EN*1101$^{a}$25.

**συνίκω** [ῑ], *coincide,* κατὰ τὸν χρόνον τὸν συνίκοντα *Inscr.Magn.*44.29 (Corc., iii/ii B.C.).

**συνίλλω** (perh. rather **συνείλλω**), *press together, contract,* Aristid.Quint.2.13:—Pass., Eub.104.3 (lyr.), Hp.*Mul.*2.163.

**συνῑπόω,** *comprimo, Gloss.*

**συνιππ-άζομαι,** *ride with,* τινι J.*BJ*1.20.3, Plu.2.1043c. **-αρχος,** ὁ, *joint commander of horse,* Hdt.7.88. **-εύς,** έως, ὁ, *comrade in cavalry service,* D.21.134. **-ευσις,** εως, ἡ, *close formation* of cavalry, Ael.*Tact.*18.5. ⊛ **-εύω,** = συνιππάζομαι, D.C.50.5, 76.14: metaph., θυέλλαις Nonn.*D.*47.358. **-ία,** ἡ, *troop of horse, Gloss.* **-ος,** ον, *together with a horse,* Tz.*H.*3.868.

**συνίπταμαι,** *fly with* or *together,* Ph.Bybl.ap.Eus.*PE*1.10.

**συνίρνα·** συνέχεις, Hsch.

**σύνῐσαν,** Ep. 3 pl. impf. of σύνειμι (εἶμι *ibo*), *went together,* Il.14.393.

**συνισθμίζω,** *form an isthmus,* πρὸς τὴν Ποντικήν Scymn.371.

⊛ **συνῐσόομαι,** Pass., *to be* or *be made identical,* c. dat., A.D.*Adv.*174.22, cf. Quint.*Ps.*93(94).20.

**συνίσσεις·** ἀντὶ τοῦ συγκλείεις, Hsch. (fort. συνίλλεις).

⊛ **συνίστημι,** also **συνιστάνω** (Plb.4.82.5, J.*BJ Prooem.*5, Sor.1.126 (Pass.)); **συνιστάω** (Arist.*GA*777$^{a}$6, *Pr.*928$^{a}$9, Conon 48, 2*Ep.Cor.*6.4; impf. συνίστα Plb.3.43.11, dub. in D.H.8.18): impf. συνίστην, fut. συστήσω, aor. 1 συνέστησα: trans. pf. συνέστᾰκα, found only in later texts, *PSI*9.1035.14 (ii A.D.), S.E.*M.*7.109, *AP*11.139 (Lucill.), Iamb.*VP*35.261:—*set together, combine,* τὰς χορδὰς ἀλλήλαις Pl.*R.*412a; τὰς ἄρκυς καὶ τὰ δίκτυα f.l. in X.*Cyn.*6.12. II. *combine, associate, unite,* σ. τοὺς Ἀρκάδας ἐπὶ τῇ Σπάρτῃ Hdt.6.74, cf. 3.84; Πελοποννήσου τὰ δυνατώτατα Th.6.16; ταύτας (sc. τὰς πόλεις) Isoc.5.30; πόλεις πρὸς ἀλλήλας X.*HG*3.5.2; τοὺς ἐπιτηδείους ἐς ξυνωμοσίαν Th.8.48; τὰ πάντα ἀριθμοῖς S.E.*M.*7.109. b. σ. Ἀσίην ἑωυτῷ *unite* Asia in dependence on himself, Hdt.1.103; μαντικὴν ἑωυτῷ συστῆσαι *bring* prophetic art *into union with* himself, i.e. *win, acquire* it, Id.2.49; σ. τινὰ ἀντίπαλον ἑαυτῷ X.*Cyr.*6.1.26; σ. τισὶν ἡγεμόνα Plb.2.24.6, cf. 3.42.6, 15.5.5. III. *put together, organize, frame,* ζῷον ἔμψυχον Pl.*Ti.*91a; τέχνην Id.*Smp.*186e; πρᾶγμα ὁτιοῦν ἐκ μοχθηρῶν καὶ χρηστῶν σ. Id.*Plt.*308c; σ. τὴν ὀλιγαρχίαν Th.8.48; ἐκ δημοκρατίας καὶ μοναρχίας τὴν πολιτείαν Arist.*Pol.*1266$^{a}$23, cf. 1284$^{b}$18; ἑταιρείαν Lex ap.D.46.26:—Med., τοῖς ἑτέραν αἵρεσιν (school) συστησαμένοις Gal.15.505; οἱ συνιστάμενοι τὰς τέχνας ib.449; θεωρήματα συνίστασθαι Id.16.725. 2. *contrive,* σ. θάνατον ἐπί τινι Hdt.3.71; ἐφ' ἡμᾶς πόλεμον D.15.3; ἐπίθεσιν ἐπὶ τοὺς Σπαρτιάτας Arist.*Pol.*1306$^{b}$35; σ. τιμάς *settle* prices, D.56.7. 3. Med. in these senses, τὸ ὅλον συνίστασθαι Pl.*Phdr.*269c; τὸ δεῖπνον Diph.43.5: mostly aor. 1, μὴ ἐκ χρηστῶν καὶ κακῶν ἀνθρώπων συστήσηται πόλιν Pl.*Plt.*308d; οὐρανόν Id.*Ti.*32b; πᾶν τόδε ib.69c, cf. *R.*530a; πόλεμον Isoc.10.49, Plb.2.1.1; σ. μοι μάχην *PTeb.*44.14 (ii B.C.); πολιορκίαν Plb.1.30.5; κίνδυνον Id.3.106.4; παρατάξεις D.S.1.18; ἀντιλογίαν πρός με *PGrenf.*1.38.8 (ii/i B.C.), cf. *PSI*3.167.14 (ii B.C.), Mitteis *Chr.*31 iv 21 (ii B.C.); ἀηδίαν *PLond.*2.342.6 (ii A.D.), *BGU*22.15 (ii A.D.); οὐδένα λόγον συνισταμένη πρὸς ἡμᾶς *rendering* no account to us, *PAmh.*2.31.17 (ii B.C.), cf. *PRein.*18.33 (ii B.C.); σ. ἀγῶνας Plu.*Fab.*19; ἑορτήν Apollod.3.14.6; ναυτικὰς δυνάμεις, μισθοφόρους, Plb.1.25.5, 4.60.5; also, *arrange in order of battle, rally,* Id.3.43.11, dub. in D.H.8.18. 4. Math., *erect* two straight lines from points on a given straight line *so as to meet* and form a triangle, in Pass., Arist.*Mete.*376$^{a}$2, $^{b}$2, cf. Euc.1.7, Papp.106.12; of two arcs of great circles on a sphere, Id.476.19,22. 5. of an author, *compose,* μύθους, τὴν Ὀδύσσειαν, etc., Arist.*Po.*1455$^{a}$22, 1451$^{a}$29, etc. IV. *bring together as friends, introduce* or *recommend one to another,* τινάς τινι Pl.*La.*200d, cf. X.*Smp.*4.63; ἵνα τῳ τῶν..σοφιστῶν..συστήσω τουτονί, as a pupil, Pl.*Thg.*122a; τινὰ ἰατρῷ σ. περὶ τῆς ἀσθενείας Id.*Chrm.*155b; σύστησον αὐτοὺς..ὅπως πλέωσι *PCair.Zen.*2.2 (iii B.C.), cf. 195.6 (iii B.C.), *PMich.Zen.*6.2,3 (iii B.C., Act. and Pass.):—Pass., συνεστάθη Κύρῳ X.*An.*3.1.8; Κύρῳ συσταθησόμενος ib.6.1.23, cf. *PCair.Zen.*447.1,11 (iii B.C.), Phld.*Acad.Ind.* p.49 M.; ἔχειν τινὰ συνεσταμένον, συνιστάμενον, regard him as *introduced* or *recommended, POxy.*787 (i A.D.), *PHolm.* p.42. b. *recommend, secure approval of* a course of action, *SIG*679.90 (Magn. Mae., ii B.C.):—Med., *recommend* persons for appointment, *PLond.*3.1249.7 (iv A.D.). c. τὸ οἰκεῖον συνιστάναι *bring about* intimacy, Men.602. d. *place in the charge of,* συνέστησεν ὁ ἀρχιδεσμώτης τῷ Ἰωσὴφ αὐτούς Lxx *Ge.*40.4; συνέστησά σοι Χαιράμμωνα δοῦλον πρὸς μάθησιν σημείων *POxy.*724.2 (ii A.D.). e. *appoint* to a charge, Lxx *Nu.*27.23; *appoint* a representative, σ. ἀντ' ἐμαυτῆς τὸν ἕτερον ἐμοῦ ἀδελφόν *PTeb.*317.10 (ii A.D.); συνέστησά σε φροντιοῦντά μου τῶν ὑπαρχόντων *BGU*300.3, cf. 20 (ii A.D.):—Pass., *Sammelb.*4512.39 (ii B.C.); ἐπίτροπος συσταθείς *CPHerm.*55.5 (iii A.D.); συσταθεὶς συνήγορος Plu.2.840e. 2. of a debtor, *offer* another *as a guarantee,* τινί τινα Isoc.17.37: c. inf., συστήσαντος ἀποδοῦναι *introduce the party* who was to pay, D.41.16, cf. ib.6: c. acc. rei, *guarantee* a loan, ἃς (sc. δραχμὰς) συνέστησεν Ἀρτεμίδωρος ἀργυ(ρίου) ρ' *PCair.Zen.*326.167 (iii B.C.); ἃς (sc. δραχμὰς) παρὰ Ἱέρωνος συνεστήσαμεν *PMich.Zen.*61.28 (iii B.C.); Σέλευκός μου αὐτοὺς (sc. τοὺς τρεῖς στατῆρας) ἐκκέκρουκε λέγων ὅτι συνέστακας ἑαυτῷ *PFay.*109.9 (i A.D.). V. *make solid* or *firm, brace up,* τὸ σῶμα Hp.*Aph.*3.17, cf. Thphr.*CP*1.8.3; σ. [τὰ ἴχνη] *sets* them, X.*Cyn.*5.3; ὑπὲρ τοῦ συνεστῶτος [τοῦ τείχους], i.e. the unbroken part, Jul.*Or.*2.64c; *contract, condense,* opp. διακρίνω or διαλύω, Arist.*GC*336$^{a}$4, *Cael.*280$^{a}$12; of liquids, *make* them *congeal, curdle,* γάλα Poll.1.251; φλέγμα Hp.*Vict.*2.54 (v.l.): metaph., συστήσας τὸ πρόσωπον *with a frown,* Plu.2.152b. VI. *exhibit, give proof of,* εὔνοιαν Plb.4.5.6; σ. ὅτι.. Id.3.108.4: c. acc. et inf., D.S.14.45: c. part., σ. τινὰς ὄντας Id.13.91. 2. *prove, establish,* Phld.*Sign.*4, *Rh.*1.112 S.

B. Pass., with aor. 2 Act. συνέστην: pf. συνέστηκα, part. συνεστηκώς, contr. συνεστώς, ῶσα, ώς or ός (Pl.*Ti.*56b), Ion. συνεστεώς, εῶσα (neut. not found), Hdt.1.74, 6.108: fut. συσταθήσομαι X.*An.*6.1.23, Arist.*Mete.*376$^{a}$2; fut. Med. ξυστήσομαι A.*Th.*435,509,672, Pl.*Ti.*54c: aor. Pass. συνεστάθην [ᾰ] X.*An.*3.1.8, al., *PCair.Zen.*447.1,11 (iii

B.C.), *PTeb.*27.35 (ii B.C.), etc. :—*stand together*, περὶ τὸν τρίποδα (of statues) Hdt.8.27; opp. διίστασθαι, X.*Cyn.*6.16; of soldiers, *form in order of battle*, Id.*An.*5.7.16, 6.5.28, al.; συστάντες ἀθρόοι ib.7.3.47. II. in hostile sense, *to be joined*, of battle, once in Hom., πολέμοιο συνεσταότος Il.14.96; τῆς μάχης συνεστεώσης Hdt.1.74; πόλεμος ξυνέστη Th.1.15, cf. Hdt.7.144, 8.142; περὶ ταῦτα μάχη τις συνέστηκεν Pl.*Sph.*246c; τοῦτο συνεστήκεε this combat *continued*, Hdt.7.225. 2. of persons, συνίστασθαί τινι *meet in fight, be engaged with*, A.*Th.*509, Hdt.6.108, Ar.*V.*1031; θνατὸς δ' ἀθανάτῳ συστήσομαι *AP*5.92 (Rufin.); τινὶ ξ... ἐν μάχῃ E.*Supp.*847; ξυσταθέντα διὰ μάχης Id.*Ph.*755; συνεστάναι μαχομένους Hdt.1.214; συνέστασαν χρόνον ἐπὶ πολλόν Id.6.29: metaph., συνεστήκεε δὲ ταύτῃ τῇ γνώμῃ ἡ Γωβρύεω *was at odds with*.., Id.4.132: abs., συνεστηκότων τῶν στρατηγῶν when the generals *were at issue*, Id.8.79; γνῶμαι μὲν αὗται συνέστασαν Id.1.208, cf. 7.142; συνίσταται ἐπ' ἐμέ *makes a dead set at* me, Men.*Sam.*211. 3. *to be involved* or *implicated* in a thing, λιμῷ, πόνῳ, λιμῷ καὶ καμάτῳ, Hdt.7.170, 8.74, 9.89; ἀλγηδόνος ᾇ ξυνέστας S.*OC*514 (lyr.); συνεστῶτες ἀγῶνι ναυτικῷ Th.4.55; καρτερᾷ μάχῃ ib.96. III. of friends, *form a league* or *union, band together*, Id.6.21,33, etc.; κατὰ σφᾶς αὐτοὺς ξ. Id.2.88; ἀλλήλοις X.*HG*2.1.1; ξυνίστασθαι πρὸς ἑκατέρους *league themselves* with one side or the other, Th.1.1, cf. 15; μετά τινος D.34.34, etc.; ἐπί τινας against them, Lys.22.17, cf. 30.10 (abs.); καί μ' οὐ λέληθεν οὐδὲν ἐν τῇ πόλει ξυνιστάμενον no *conspiracy*, Ar.*Eq.*863, cf. X.*Cyr.*1.1.2; οἱ συνιστάμενοι the *conspirators*, Ar.*Lys.*577 (anap.); τὸ ξυνεστηκός Th.8.66. 2. generally, *to be connected* or *allied*, as by marriage, c. acc. cogn., λέχος Ἡρακλεῖ ξυστᾶσα S.*Tr.*28: in magic, συνιστάνου..τοῖς..θεοῖς *put yourself into connexion with*.., *PMag. Leid.W.*1.29; συσταθεὶς πρὸ(ς) τὸν ἥλιον *PMag.Par.*1.168: in law, Αὐρηλία Βησοῦς μετὰ συνεστῶτος Αὐρηλίου Θέωνος A. B. *acting with* A. T., *POxy.*912.4 (iii A.D.), cf. *Sammelb.*7338.5 (iii/iv A.D.). 3. of an assembly, *to be in session*, ἔτι τῆς ἐκκλησίας συνεστώσης Plu. *Nic.*28; τῆς τῶν Νεμείων πανηγύρεως σ. Id.*Phil.*11; οἱ τὴν σύνοδον συνεσταμένοι εἰς τὸ ἐν Σήτει ἱερόν *OGI*111.25 (Egypt, ii B.C.). IV. *to come* or *be put together*, of parts, συνιστάμεν' ἄλλοθεν ἄλλα Emp.35.6, cf. E.*Fr.*910.6 (anap.), Pl.*R.*530a; ἐπειδὴ πάντα συνειστήκει X.*Cyr.*6.1.54; σ. ἐξ ὀλιγίστων μερῶν Pl.*Ti.*56b, cf. 54c; ἡ πόλις ἐξ οἰκιῶν σ. X.*Mem.*3.6.14; ἐξ ὧν ὁ κόσμος σ. Arist.*EN*1141$^b$2; esp. in military sense, ξυνεστὼς στρατός an *organized* army, E.*IA* 87; ἱππικὸν συνεστηκός an *organized* force of cavalry, X.*An.*7.6.26; τὸ συνεστηκὸς στράτευμα the *organized* force, D.8.17,46. b. of a play, *to be composed*, Arist.*Po.*1453$^b$4; ἡ πολιτεία (compared to a tragedy) συνέστηκε μίμησις τοῦ καλλίστου βίου Pl.*Lg.*817b. c. *arise, take shape* or *body*, τὸ συνιστάμενον κακόν D.18.62, cf. 6.35; πόλις οὕτω συστᾶσα Pl.*R.*546a; ἐνταῦθα συνίστανται [ψύλλαι] Arist. *HA*556$^b$26, cf. Thphr.*CP*4.4.10, Sor.2.37, al., Gal.*Vict.Att.*9; σ. ἀπό τινος *arise* from.., Phld.*Ir.* p.76 W. d. in aor. 2 and pf., *come into existence, exist*, μεγάλη συνέστη δύναμις βασιλέων Pl.*Ti.*25a; συμμαχία ἡ περὶ Κόρινθον συστᾶσα Isoc.4.142; τοῦ καιροῦ τῆς τῶν γενημάτων συναγωγῆς συνεστηκότος *PSI*3.173.12 (ii B.C.); κεχωρίσθαι ἀπ' ἀλλήλων τῆς συστάσης αὐτοῖς συμβιώσεως *BGU*1102.9 (i B.C.); οἰκία..σὺν τοῖς συνεστῶσι μέτροις καὶ πηχισμοῖς καὶ συνεστῶσι θεμελίοις *Sammelb.*5247.6,11 (i A.D.). V. *to be compact, solid, firm*, οὔτε σκιδνάμενον οὔτε συνιστάμενον Parm.2.4; συνεστῶτα σώματα, of animals in good condition, X.*Cyn.*7.8, cf. Pl.*Ti.*83a; *acquire substance* or *consistency*, of eggs, Arist.*HA*567$^a$28; of blood, honey, milk, ib.516$^a$5, 554$^a$6, Hp.*Vict.*2.51; of the embryo, συνίσταται καὶ λαμβάνει τὴν οἰκείαν μορφήν Arist.*GA*733$^b$20; of the brain, ib.744$^a$22; of the bowels, Hp.*Epid.*3.17.α', *Coac.*589; ῥεῦμα συνεστηκός *concentrated*, Id.*Medic.*7; συνεστηκυῖα χιών *congealed, frozen*, Plb.3.55.2. VI. *to be contracted*, συνεστῶτι τῷ προσώπῳ *frowning*, Plu. *Demetr.*17; τοῦ ξυνεστῶτος φρενῶν (cf. σύστασις B. II. 3) E.*Alc.*797; συνεστηκώς *absorbed in thought*, Men.*Pk.*291. VII. συνέστηκε c. acc. et inf., *it is well known* that.., = Lat. *constat*, Marcian.*Peripl.*1 *Prooem.* VIII. *to be weighed together*, συνεστάθη *Inscr.Délos* 1423*A a i* 17, 1429*B i* 3 (ii B.C.).

**συνιστορέω**, *know together*, σ. αὐτῷ τι *to be conscious of* a thing, Men.632; ἑαυτῷ ὅτι.. Aristeas 215; ἑαυτῷ κακὸν πεπραχότι Id.260, cf. *PSI*1.64.22 (i B.C.), Phld.*Mus.* p.84 K.: c. inf., Aristeas 243 (dub. l.). 2. σ. κακοῖς *consort with*.., Vett.Val.126.22; οἱ συνιστοροῦντες *accomplices*, Heph.Astr.3.37 in *Cat.Cod.Astr.*8(1).156. 3. c. acc., *connive at*, φόνον *SIG*985.22 (Philadelphia), cf. *PSI*8.901.12 (i A.D.). II. *record as well*, Cleanth.*Stoic.*1.133, Ptol.*Geog.*1.17.4, Eust.265.34. 2. *reckon up*, τὰ πλήθη τῶν ὑποστελλομένων *PTeb.* 24.51 (ii B.C.).

❀ **συνίστωρ**, ορος, ὁ, ἡ, *knowing along with* another, ὡς θεοὶ ξυνίστορες as the gods are *witnesses*, S.*Ph.*1293, cf. *Ant.*542, E.*Supp.*1174, Th. 2.74, *PCair.Zen.*625.2 (iii B.C.). 2. *privy* to a crime or other secret, c. gen., Plb.30.8.1, *AP*5.3.1 (Phld.), 5.4.1 (Stat.Flacc.), Vett. Val.11.1, *Cat.Cod.Astr.*2.175; σώματα συνίστορα τῆς πράξεως Aen. Tact.23.10: c. acc. (with the verbal constr.), πολλὰ συνίστορα..κακά (sc. τὴν στέγην) A.*Ag.*1090 (lyr.).

❀ **συνισχναίνω**, in Pass., *shrivel up*, Hp.*Morb.Sacr.*5, al.; *to be contracted* or *made slim*, Antyll.ap.Orib.6.10.6. 2. metaph., *join with in reducing*, ὁ νόμος αὐτὰ τῷ χρόνῳ ξυνισχνᾶνεῖ E.*IA*694 (v. ἰσχναίνω).

**συνισχῡρίζω**, *help to strengthen*, τινα X.*Cyr.*2.2.26:—Med., -ίζεται *confortiat*, Gloss.

**συνίσχω**, = συνέχω, *retain*, *PTeb.*746.10 (iii B.C.):—Pass., *to be retained* or *detained*, *PGrenf.*2.14.13 (iii B.C.); *to be afflicted*, νοσήμασιν Pl.*Grg.*479a.

**συνῑτικός**, ή, όν, *disposed to come together* or *to be condensed*, σ. εἰς αὐτό, opp. διιτικός, Arist.*Pr.*905$^b$14 (Comp.).

**συνιχνεύω**, *track out with*, παρθένον Διονύσῳ Nonn.*D.*16.193.

**σύνναιος**, ον, *dwelling with*, θεοῖς, of the dead, *Riv.Fil.*57.379 (Crete, iii/iv A.D.).

**συνναίω**, *dwell* or *live with*, γυναιξί A.*Th.*195; τοῖσιν ἐχθίστοισι σ. ὁμοῦ S.*Tr.*1237, cf. *El.*241 (lyr.).

**σύνναος**, ον, *having the same temple*, θεοῖς σ. καὶ συμβώμοις *CIG* 2230 (Chios), al., *SIG*1126.5 (Delos, ii/i B.C.), cf. *PTeb.*281.5 (ii B.C.), Plu.2.708c: c. gen., σ. καὶ συνίερος τοῦ Ἔρωτος ib.753f, cf. Cic.*Att.*12.45.3, D.C.55.1: c. dat., *OGI*332.9 (Elaea, ii B.C.), Str.7.7.12.

**συννάσσω**, *pack tight together*, συννάξαντες Hdt.7.60 (Reiske for συνάξ-, v.l. συνάψ-):—Pass., παγαῖς συνεναγμένον (sic)..ὕδωρ prob. in *Supp.Epigr.*7.13.7 (Susa, i A.D.).

**συνναυᾱγέω**, *suffer shipwreck together*, Aesop.300.

**συνναυβάτης** [ᾰ], ου, ὁ, *shipmate*, S.*Ph.*565.

**συνναύκληρος**, ὁ, f.l. for σύγκληρος in Luc.*Trag.*328.

**συνναυμᾰχέω**, *engage in a sea-fight along with*, τισι Hdt.8.44, cf. Ar.*Ra.*702 (troch.), Th.1.73, *IG*1$^2$.108.41.

**συνναυσθλόομαι**, Pass., *cross by ship together*, Hsch. (συναυθλοῦμαι cod.).

**συνναυστολέω**, *to be a shipmate*, σοὶ..συννεναυστοληκότες (Dobree for οἱ νεναυστ-) S.*Ph.*550.

❀ **συνναύτης**, ου, Dor. -τας, ὁ, *shipmate*, S.*Aj.*902 (lyr.), E.*Cyc.*425, 705,708, Pl.*R.*389c. II. pl., members of a guild of worshippers of Isis, *IGRom.*1.817.21 (Callipolis).

**συννεάζω**, *to be young with* another, συννεάζων ἡδὺ παῖς νέῳ πατρί E.*Fr.*317.6: abs., σ. καὶ συγγηράσκειν Alciphr.2.3; *join in youthful wantonness*, Philostr.*VS*2.21.2.

**συννεᾱνιεύομαι**, *wanton youthfully together*, ἀλλήλοις D.C.51.8, cf. 72.4.

**συννεκρόω**, *make dead together*, in Pass., τῇ διανοίᾳ συννεκροῦται (sic cod. S, συνεκκρούεται cod. V) Vett.Val.238.33.

**συννέμησις**, εως, ἡ, *relation*, πρὸς τὸν χρόνον Plu.2.393a.

❀ **συννέμω**, *feed* or *tend together*, of the shepherd:—Pass., *feed with*, τοῖς θήλεσι, of the males, Arist.*HA*572$^b$21. 2. generally, *make one's partner* or *associate*, εἰσαγαγεῖν τὴν δοκιμασίαν συννείμαντας *IG* 2$^2$.850.20; Ῥώμη προσποιοῦσα ἑαυτῇ καὶ συννέμουσά τινας Plu.*Rom.* 16:—Pass., *to be associated*, Id.2.424a; ποιητικὴν μουσικῇ -ομένην ib.744f; ἀχθόμενος ἐπὶ τῷ -νέμεσθαι πολλάκις Ἀκέστορι Satyr.*Vit.Eur.* *Fr.*39 xv 29; cf. συννομέομαι.

**συννενέαται**, v. συννέω (B).

**σύννευμα**, ατος, τό, *sign of consent*, Antiph.47.7.

**συννεύρωσις**, εως, ἡ, *union by sinews*, Gal.2.738.

**σύν-νευσις**, εως, ἡ, *convergence*, πρός τι Str.4.5.1, Plu.2.428a: abs., Procl.*Inst.*146: metaph., *agreement, union*, πρὸς ἀλλήλας Plb. 2.40.5. II. *bending*, Antyll.ap.Orib.6.34.2, Sor.1.85 (prob.), 2.19, Gal.7.624 (pl.); *obliquity*, Sor.*Fract.*12. 2. *beckoning*, so as to invite, Thom.Mag.p.277 R. **-νεύω**, *contract*, τὰς ὀφρῦς Ps.-Luc.*Philopatr.*1. II. intr., *incline to a point, converge*, εἰς ὀξύ Thphr.*Ign.*51; εἰς ἓν κέντρον Plu.*Num.*9; εἰς ταὐτό Id.2.666c; πρὸς τὴν αὐτὴν ὑπόθεσιν Plb.3.32.7; διαστρέφεται συννεύουσα ἢ παραλλάσσουσα ἄνω ἢ κάτω, of a broken jaw, Sor.*Fract.*12; σ. ἔνδον *tending* inwards, Aret.*SA*1.7; τῶν πραγμάτων συννενευκότων *converged* (to a favourable issue), J.*BJ*4.10.7. 2. *bow down together*, Arr.*An.* 1.1.9, 6.10.2; κάτω σ. Luc.*Anach.*24. 3. *consent, agree*, ξύννευσον S.*OT*1510; πρὸς ἓν ἔργον Muson.*Fr.*14 p.73 H., cf. Plu.*Num.* 6. III. *invite by beckoning*, Thom.Mag.p.276 R.

**συννέφ-εια** or -ία, ἡ, *clouded sky*, Arist.*Pr.*[944$^b$26] (as gloss on ἐπίνεψιν), Ptol.*Tetr.*84, Thd.*Jb.*3.5, Olymp.Hist.p.463 D., *Cat.Cod. Astr.*2.161, Sch.Ar.*Nu.*583, *EM*236.29. **-ελος**, ον, = συννεφής, Th.8.42, Alciphr.1.10. **-ής**, ές, *clouded over, cloudy*, ἀήρ Thphr. *Vent.*2 (Sup.); νύκτες, ἀήρ, Plb.9.15.12, 9.16.3; ἡμέραι D.S.5.25, cf. Q.S.2.347; καιρός Str.10.2.12; οὐρανός Lxx *De.*33.28; of persons, *gloomy*, E.*Ph.*1307 (troch.); σ. μέτωπον ἔχειν Arist.*Phgn.*811$^b$34; ὄμμα *AP*12.159 (Mel.); ὀφρύς Philostr.Jun.*Im.*17. **-ος**, ον, = συννεφής, J.*AJ*18.8.6. **-ω**, pf. συννένοφα:—*collect clouds*, Ζεὺς ξυννέφει Ar.*Av.*1502; σ. τὸ περιέχον Plu.2.641d: impers. συννέφει, *it is cloudy*, εἰ συννέφει, εἰκὸς ὕσαι Arist.*Rh.*1393$^a$6; ξυννένοφε Ar.*Fr.* 46. 2. trans., συννεφεῖν (leg. -νέφειν) νεφέλας ἐπὶ τὴν γῆν Lxx *Ge.*9.14. II. metaph. of persons, συννέφουσαν ὄμματα *wearing a dark and gloomy* look, E.*El.*1078; κύψασα κάτω καὶ ξυννενοφυῖα βαδίζει Ar.*Fr.*395 (anap.), cf. Philostr.*VS*1.18.1; ἐπερωτηθεὶς διὰ τί συννένοφε D.C.55.11. 2. *to be under a cloud, in adversity*, opp. εὐτυχεῖν, E.*Fr.*330.7. (συννεφεῖ, etc., codd., corr. Cobet.)

**συννέω** (A), (νέω A) *swim together*, Luc.*Tox.*20, Ael.*NA*1.17; τινι Luc.*Philops.*34.

**συννέω** (B), (νέω C) *pile* or *heap together, heap up*, [τὰ ἀκόντια] ἐς τοὺς θαλάμους συννένησε Hdt.1.34; συννήσας πυρήν ib.86, 7.107:—Ion. 3 pl. pf. Pass. συννενέαται Id.2.135, 4.62; τῶν νεκρῶν ὁμοῦ ἐπ' ἀλλήλοις ξυννενημένων Th.7.87.

**συννεωτερίζω**, *join in innovation* or *sedition*, τισι Str.6.4.2; τῷ τινος νεωτερισμῷ Id.14.5.2.

**συννήθω**, aor. -ένησα, *spin along with* or *together*, of fate, σεαυτὸν πράγμασι M.Ant.4.34.

**σύννησις**, εως, ἡ, *spinning together*: *connexion*, M.Ant.4.40.

**συννήχομαι**, *swim* or *float together with*, τινι Plu.2.984e, Luc.*VH* 1.33, X.Eph.3.2.

**συννῑκάω**, *have part in a victory*, τινι *with* another, E.*Alc.*1103; χορῷ *IG*$2^2$.3101 (tm.); μετ' ἀλλήλων X.*Cyr.*6.4.14: abs., And.3.27:—Pass., *to be conquered together*. D.C.49.10.

**συννο-έω**, *meditate, reflect upon* a thing, τὰξ ἐμοῦ παλαίφατα S.*OC* 453, cf. Pl.*Smp.*220c, *Phdr.*241c, *Lg.*712d, *PTeb.*24.30 (ii B.C.); σ. τί τις χρήσεται *think* what one can do with it, Pl.*Lg.*835d:—Med., ἐν ἐμαυτῷ τι συννοούμενος E.*Or.*634, cf. *Ion*644. 2. *make plans*, πάντα -οῦμεν ἐκπράξειν χερί Patrocl.1.5. II. *comprehend, understand*, Pl.*Tht.*164a, al.: c. part., σ. τινὰ μανθάνοντα Id.*Epin.*976b, cf. Plu.*Pomp.*74: folld. by a relat., σ. ὅτι.. *understand* that.., Pl. *Plt.*280b, Arist.*Pol.*1284$^a$32; σ. ὡς.. Pl.*Sph.*238c, etc.:—Med., Ar. *Ra.*598 (lyr.). 2. *know at the same time*, Mich. *in EN*518. 34. —**ητέος**, α, ον, *to be reflected on*, *Cat.Cod.Astr.*2.120, Vett. Val.91.21. —**ητικός**, ή, όν, *reasoning within itself*, Plot.2.2.1.

**σύννοια**, ἡ, (σύννοος) *meditation*, συννοίῃ (Ion.) ἐχόμενος wrapped in *thought*, Hdt.1.88; ἐμοὶ..ἡ ξ. βουλεύει πάλαι S.*Ant.*279; εἰς σ. αὐτὸς αὑτῷ ἀφικέσθαι Pl.*R.*571d, cf. *Lg.*790b; ἐπὶ συννοίᾳ or -ας βαδίζειν Luc.*Pisc.*13, *Sat.*11; ἐπὶ συννοίας γενέσθαι Alciphr.3.67; μετὰ συννοίας [ποιεῖν τι] Arist.*Pr.*917$^b$39. 2. *anxious thought, anxiety*, συννοίᾳ δάπτομαι κέαρ A.*Pr.*437; πόδ' ἐπὶ συννοίᾳ κυκλεῖς E. *Or.*632; σύννοιαν ὄμμασιν φέρων Id.*Heracl.*381, cf. Phld.*Ir.*p.72 W. II. συννοίᾳ..οἷον δέδρακεν ἔργον *remorse* for the deed, E. *Andr.*805; expld. in Pl.*Def.*415e, by διάνοια μετὰ λύπης.

**συννοισία**· τὸ εἰς τὸ αὐτὸ συμφέρειν, Hsch.

**συννομ-έομαι**, *live together*, Plu.2.1065e; συννεμησομένων cj. Madvig. —**εύς**, έως, ὁ, *fellow-shepherd*, Sch.Theoc.9.28, *Gloss.* ⊛ —**ή**, ἡ, *a feeding together, joint pasture*, Pl.*Plt.*268c. II. γενόμενα ἀνὴρ καὶ κλῆρος συννομή the man and his allotment being *a joint affair*, Id.*Lg.*737e. III. Dor. **συννομά**, a division of the people at Camirus, *Clara Rhodos* 6/7.428.

**συννομίζω**, *agree in thinking*, ταὐτὰ αὐτοὺς αὑτοῖς σ. Pl.*Min.* 316d.

**συννομοθετέω**, *to be a joint-lawgiver*, Pl.*Lg.*833e, Decr.ap.D.24. 27.

⊛ **σύννομος** (A), ον, (νέμω, νομή) *feeding in herds* or *together*, ταῦροι, κριοί, τράγοι, Arist.*HA*571$^b$22; ἵπποι ib.611$^a$10; μᾶλα Theoc.8.56 codd. (dub. l.): ἀγέλη (metaph., of mankind) Zeno *Stoic.*1.61 (also σύννομον ἡ φιλία ζῷον, οὐκ ἀγελαῖον Plu.2.93e); φῦλα πάντα συννόμων *of birds that flock together*, Ar.*Av.*1756 (lyr.), cf. 209 (anap.); πάνθ' ὅσα σύννομα ζῷα all animals that *herd together*, Pl.*Criti.*110b, cf. *Lg.*666e: c. dat., *living with*, τινι Luc.*Syr.D.*54: metaph., ἔρωτες ἄταισι σ. *associated with*.., A.*Ch.*598 (lyr.); πνεύματα πόλει σ. Hp.*Aër.*3. 2. c. gen. rei, *sharing* or *partaking in* a thing, σ. τινί τινος *partner with* one *in*.., Pi.*I.*3.17; τῶν ἐμῶν λέκτρων γεραιὰ ξύννομε *partner of*.., A. *Pers.*704 (troch.); τῶν ἐμῶν ὕμνων Ar.*Av.*678 (lyr.): metaph., θαλάσσῃ (v.l. -ης) σύννομοι Σκιρωνίδες πέτραι, of the Scironides which *lie between* two seas, E.*Hipp.*979; πταναὶ σύννομοι νεφέων δρόμου winged *partners with* the racing clouds, i.e. swift as the clouds, Id.*Hel.*1488 (lyr.). 3. abs. as Subst., σύννομος, ὁ, ἡ, *partner, consort, mate*, of soldiers, A.*Th.*354 (lyr.); ὡς λέοντε συννόμω S.*Ph.*1436; of wives, αἱ δὲ σ. τἄξω..τροφεῖα πορσύνουσ' ἀεί Id.*OC*340; of a paramour, Id.*El.* 600; of a lioness, A.R.4.1339; θήλεια καὶ ἔρρην οἷον σύννομοι ἴτωσαν εἰς τὸν οἶκον Pl.*Lg.*925c, cf. 943b; of certain tunnies, ἐστὸν κατὰ τοὺς λύκους συννόμω prob. in Ael.*NA*15.3 (εἰς τὸν..σύννομον codd.). II. of things, *kindred, correspondent*, [τέχναι] ὅσαι σύννομοι Pl.*Plt.*287b, cf. 289b; ἤθη Id.*Lg.*930a; ἄστρον Id.*Ti.*42b; φωνή, ὀσμή, D.H.1.39; λίθοι σ. stones *cut so as to fit, ashlar*, Plb.8. 37.1, Str.5.3.8, 17.1.48.

**σύννομος** (B), ον, (νόμος) *lawful, regular*, συναγωγὰ τῶν συνέδρων *IG* 5(1).1390.48 (Andania, i B.C.). Adv. -μως *as required by law*, *Sardis* 7(1).20.28 (vi A.D.).

⊛ **σύννοος**, ον, Att. contr. -**νους**, ουν, *in deep thought, thoughtful*, Isoc.1.15, Plu.2.206b, etc.; σ. πρὸς ἑαυτῷ Id.*Them.*3. 2. *anxious, gloomy*, βλέμμα Arist.*Pr.*958$^a$18, cf. Hp.*Ep.*15, D.H.4.66, etc.; *grave*, Hp.*Medic.*1. 3. *thoughtful, circumspect*, σ. γενέσθαι Arist. *Pol.*1267$^a$36; τὸ σ. Phld.*Vit.*p.13 J.

**συννοσέω**, *to be sick* or *ill together*, Hp.*Aph.*2.15, E.*IA*407; νενοσηκότος τοῦ δέρματος καὶ ἡ θρὶξ σ. Arist.*GA*784$^a$30; τινι *with* one, E.*Andr.*948. Cic.*Att.*2.2.1, Luc.*Am.*46, etc.; νοσοῦντι συννοσοῦσ' ἀνέξομαι E.*Fr.*909.11 (troch.); σ. νοσούσῃ τῇ πατρίδι Alex.Aphr. *in Top.*139.33, cf. Sor.1.35.

**συννυκτερεύω**, *pass the night with*, Plu.*Dio*55, Ach.Tat.6.21.

**συννυμφοκόμος**, ον, *helping to deck a bride*, E.*IA*48 (anap.).

⊛ **σύννυμφος**, ἡ, *husband's brother's wife*, Lxx *Ru.*1.15, Keil-Premerstein *Zweiter Bericht* No.128 (Attaleia, ii A.D.), Eust.648. 43.

**συνογκάομαι**, *bray along with*, ὄνῳ Arr.*Epict.*2.24.18.

**συνογκόομαι**, *to be swollen together*, Sor.1.66; τῷ πνεύματι interpol. in Lib.*Descr.*23.6.

**συνόδ-ευσις**, εως, ἡ, *travelling in company*, Eust.1789.35. —**ευτής**, οῦ, ὁ, = συνοδοιπόρος, Sch.Ar.*Ra.*400. —**εύω**, *travel in company*, Plu.*Pomp.*40, Charito 2.3, etc.; τινι *with* one, *Act.Ap.*9.7, Plu.2. 609d, Ach.Tat.7.3. II. Astron., *to be in conjunction*, σ. τῷ ἡλίῳ *Placit.*2.29.6, Cleom.1.3, cf. Vett.Val.297.28, etc. III. metaph., *have fellowship with*, Lxx *Wi.*6.23(25); *accompany*, "ὦ" σ. τῇ κλητικῇ Trypho ap.A.D.*Synt.*48.19, cf. 89.21; συνοδεῦσαι δεῖ πρὸς ταῦτα αἴσθησίν τε καὶ νοῦν Marcellin.*Puls.*11. 2. as Pass. or Med., *go with*, τοῖς λαχάνοις -ενέσθω φύλλα μήκωνος Herod.Med.ap. Orib.*Syn.*6.32 (v.l.). —**ηγός**, ὁ, *guide*, *Lyr.Alex.Adesp.*1.15. ⊛ —**ία**, ἡ, *journey in company, companionship on a journey*, Cic.*Att.*10.7.2, J.*AJ*6.12.1, Plu.2.48b, *Galb.*20, Charito 6.2; ἀνδρὸς πονηροῦ φεῦγε συνοδίαν ἀεί Men.*Mon.*24. II. in concrete sense, *party of travellers, caravan*, Str.4.6.6, 11.14.4, *Ev.Luc.*2.44, *OGI*633.2 (Palmyra, ii A.D.); ἀνακομίσαι συνοδίας ib.646.6 (ibid., iii A.D.); σ. πρεσβευτοῦ ἢ ἀνθυπάτου Arr.*Epict.*4.1.91. III. *family*, Lxx *Ne.*7.5 (pl.), al.:—in Suid. also **συνοδεία**. —**ιάρχης**, ου, ὁ, *leader of a caravan*, *OGI*632.2, 633.5 (Palmyra, ii A.D.): hence —**ιαρχία**, ἡ, *office of συνοδιάρχης*, *Supp.Epigr.*7.139.6 (ibid., ii A.D.). —**ικός**, ή, όν, Astron., *of* or *from a conjunction* of sun and moon, συζυγίαι σ. Ptol.*Tetr.*92, cf. Vett.Val.21.20, al., *POxy.*470$^r$.18 (iii A.D.); *in astral conjunction with*, Procl.*Hyp.*1.17. 2. *of* or *for a σύνοδος* (B) I. 2, οἶνος *PGrenf.*1.51.5 (iii A.D.). —**ίτης** [ῑ], ου, ὁ, *member of a σύνοδος* (B) I, *IG*$2^2$.1348.19, 14.2000 (Rome, ii A.D.), *Sammelb.*4549. 10 (iii A.D.). II. = Latin *Comes*, Καίσαρος σ. *BGU*1137.9 (i B.C.). III. *relating to the σύνοδος* (B. II. 2) *of sun and moon*, λίθοι Dam.*Isid.*233. (Freq. written -είτης.)

**συνοδοιπορ-έω**, *travel together*, τινι *with* one, Nic.Dam.*Fr.*66.19 J., Luc.*Herm.*13, *PGiss.*27.4 (ii A.D.). —**ία**, ἡ, *travelling together*, Babr.110. —**ος** (parox.), ὁ, *fellow-traveller*, X.*Mem.*2.2.12, Luc. *DMort.*27.7, prob. in *Supp.Epigr.*3.781 (Crete); as epith. of Ὑγίεια, *SIG*1147 (Lebena, ii/iii A.D.).

**συνοδοντίς**, ίδος, ἡ, (συνόδους) a large kind of *tunny*, Ath.7. 312b. b. a fish of the Nile, Diph.Siph.ib.8.356f: hence **συνοδοντῖτις** (sc. λίθος), ιδος, ἡ, *a stone found in its head*, Plin.*HN*37. 182.

**συνοδοπανσέληνος**, ἡ, *conjunction*, Rhetor. in *Cat.Cod.Astr.*8(4). 199 (v.l. συζυγία).

**σύνοδος** (A), ὁ, ἡ, = συνοδοιπόρος, *AP*7.635 (Antiphil.), Arr.*Epict.* 2.14.8, 3.21.5, Certamen 245, Man.5.58.

⊛ **σύνοδος** (B), ἡ, *assembly, meeting*, esp. for deliberation, Orac.ap. Hdt.9.43, And.1.47, Th.1.96,119, *IG*$4^2$(1).68.93 (Epid., iv B.C.), etc.; ξ. Ἀχαιῶν E.*Hec.*107 (anap.); σ. κώμης *BGU*1648.6 (ii A.D.); σ. συλλεγῆναι Hdt.9.27; ποιῆσαι Ar.*Th.*301 (prose decree); ἀπὸ κοινῶν ξ. βουλεύειν Th.1.97; ἐκ τῶν ξ. Id.5.17; σ. πρὸς τῷ διαιτητῇ *meeting* of parties in court, D.54.29: pl., of *political clubs* or *conspiracies*, Sol.4.22, Ar.*Eq.*477, Th.3.82, Pl.*Tht.*173d; ἑταιρείας μὴ ποιεῖσθε μηδὲ σ. Isoc.3.54; also of private *meetings* or *gatherings* for discussion, διαλεκτικαὶ σ. Arist.*Top.*159$^a$32; of *synods* of the church, *Cod.Just.*1.1.7.12. 2. *national gathering*, Th.3.104, Pl.*Smp.*197d; αἱ ἀρχαῖαι θυσίαι καὶ σ. Arist.*EN*1160$^a$26: hence, *society for festal purposes*, τῶν ἐρανιστῶν *IG*$2^2$.1369.32; τῶν μυστῶν *SIG*851.25 (Smyrna, ii A.D.); τῶν Ἀσκλαπιαστᾶν *IG*$4^2$(1).679 (Epid.). 3. *company, guild*, τεχνιτᾶν *SIG*698.1 (Delph., ii B.C.); [συγγεωργῶν] *Sammelb.*7457.5,9 (ii B.C.); athletic *club*, *OGI*486. 17 (Pergam., ii A.D.), 713.9 (Alexandria, iii A.D.); ἡ ἱερὰ ξυστικὴ περιπολιστικὴ..σ. *PLond.*3.1178.38 (ii A.D.), cf. *POxy.*908.9 (ii A.D.), *IG*$2^2$.1350. 4. in hostile sense, *meeting* of two armies, Ar.*Ra.*1532, Th.3.107, 5.70, X.*An.*1.10.7, etc. 5. = συνουσία, *sexual intercourse*, Arist.*HA*541$^a$31, Clearch.49, Ph.1.148, Plu.*Lyc.* 15, Gal.15.47. II. of things, *coming together, constriction*, κυάνεαι σύνοδοι θαλάσσας, of the *straits* of the Bosporus, E.*IT*393 (lyr.); ἡ σ. τοῦ πλησίον ἀλλήλων τεθῆναι the *coming together* resulting from juxtaposition, Pl.*Phd.*97a; ἡ τῆς πιλήσεως σ. Id.*Ti.* 58b; ἡ τοῦ ὕδατος σ., viz. ice, ib.61a; ὅσον διαχυτικὸν..τῶν περὶ τὸ στόμα σ. whatever relaxes..*constriction* in the organ of taste, ib. 60b; ἀναγκαῖον τῶν τοιούτων γίνεσθαι σύνοδον, ἀλλ' οὐ διὰ ψύξιν Arist. *GA*764$^b$7; ἡ εἰς αὑτὸν σ. *contraction* of a muscle, Gal.*UP*12.8, cf. Id.4. 391; ἡ σ. ἡ κατὰ [τὴν οὐσίαν] λεγομένη the *union* of matter and form, viz. the concrete object, Arist.*Metaph.*1033$^b$17; *concourse, assemblage*, παθῶν Longin.10.3; of the parts of the foetus, Sor.2.64; *combination* of numbers, *Theol.Ar.*8; σημείων Gal.16.505. 2. Astron., *conjunction*, τῶν πλανήτων καὶ πρὸς αὐτοὺς καὶ πρὸς τοὺς ἀπλανεῖς Arist. *Mete.*343$^b$30; of the sun and moon, Plu.2.269c, *IG*14.2126 (Rome); ἡλίου καὶ σελήνης Gal.18(2).240; σ. ἐκλειπτικὴ σελήνης πρὸς ἥλιον Plu. *Rom.*12; αἱ σ., of the times of new moon, Zeno *Stoic.*1.34; αἱ τῶν μηνῶν σ. ψυχραὶ διὰ τὴν τῆς σελήνης ἀπόλειψιν Arist.*GA*738$^a$20, cf. Thphr.*Sign.*5, Lxx *De.*33.14. 3. Gramm., *construction*, A.D.*Synt.* 28.11, al. III. *incoming* of revenue, χρημάτων σύνοδοι Hdt.1. 64; *revenues*, ἀπὸ τῶν σ. *IG*11(4).1217 (Delos); τῶν φερόντων τὴν σ. τοῦ Διὸς τοῦ ξενίου ib.$2^2$.1012.15 (ii B.C.); οἱ τὴν σ. φέροντες τῷ θεῷ ib.$2^2$.1326.6. (Written *sunhod-*, i.e. συνοδ-, in a Latin inscr., *CIL*$1^2$.2519.2,3,4 (i B.C.(?)); also *synhod-*, ib.6, *IG*14.2495 (Nemausus), *CIL*12.3183 (ibid.), 6.10117 (Rome).)

⊛ **συνόδους**, οντος, ὁ, ἡ, *with teeth opposing, rather than notching into, one another*, opp. καρχαρόδους (q.v.), τὰ συνόδοντα *animals with such teeth*, Arist.*HA*595$^a$9. II. Subst. συνόδοντες, οἱ (sg. ἡ, Numen.ap.Ath.7.322b), a kind of *sea-bream*, prob. *Dentex vulgaris*, Epich.69, Anaxandr.41.51 (anap.), Archestr.*Fr.*17, Opp.*H.*1.170: sg. nom. **συνόδων** Antiph.132.3 (anap.), Philox.2.15; but **συνόδους** Sch.Opp.*H.*3.186, Artem.2.14. Cf. σινόδους, συνώδοντα.

**συνοδυνάομαι**, Pass., *suffer pain with* another, Lxx *Si.*30.10.

**συνοδύρομαι** [ῡ], *lament together*, Pl.*Mx.*247c, Plu.2.56a.

**συνόζω**, *smell* (intr.) or *be smelt together with*, τινι Arist.*Pr.*907$^a$3.

**σύνοιδα**, pf. with pres. sense, 1 pl. σύνισμεν Pl.*Sph.*232c, Ion. συνοίδαμεν Hdt.9.60, 3 pl. συνίσασι S.*El.*93 (anap.), Isoc.8.113, X. *Cyr.*3.1.9, etc. (rarely συνοίδασι Lys.11.1, Plb.27.9.11); imper.

σύνισθι E.*Hec.*870; inf. ξυνειδέναι S.*Ant.*266: plpf. with impf. sense, συνῄδειν, Att. συνῄδη, dual συνῄστην, pl. -ῇσμεν, -ῇστε, -ῇσαν, Ion. 2 pl. συνηδέᾰτε Hdt.9.58: fut. συν(ξυν-)είσομαι Ar.*Ec.*17, *V.*999, X.*HG*2.4.17 (rarely συνειδήσω Isoc.1.16, and aor. part. -ειδήσας Phld.*Lib.* p.32 O.):—*know* something *about* a person, esp. *as a potential witness for* or *against* him, ἣ (sc. Δίκη) σιγῶσα σύνοιδε τὰ γιγνόμενα πρό τ' ἐόντα Sol.4.15; τά τοι ἐγὼ καὶ ἀμφότερα συνειδὼς ἔχω μαρτυρέειν to both of which I, *knowing them true of* you, can testify, Hdt.5.24; εἰ τέοισί τι χρηστὸν συνῄδεε πεποιημένον Id.8.113; ἐπαινεόντων τούτους τοῖσί τι καὶ συνηδέατε Id.9.58; τὰ Μηδικὰ καὶ ὅσα αὐτοὶ σύνιστε our other services *to* which *you can testify*, Th.1.73; ἃ ξύνισμεν τοῖσιν ἵπποις βουλόμεσθ' ἐπαινέσαι Ar.*Eq.*595 (troch.); συνοίδαμεν ὑμῖν ὑπὸ τὸν παρεόντα τόνδε πόλεμον ἐοῦσι πολλὸν προθυμοτάτοισι Hdt.9.60; ὑπολαμβάνων παρ' ὑμῶν ἑκάστῳ τὸ συνειδὸς ὑπάρχειν μοι believing that I can rely on your *acknowledgement* of my services, D.18.110; τί μοι σύνοισθα τοιοῦτον εἰργασμένῳ; X.*Smp.*4.62; σύνοιδα τῷ μειρακίῳ κοσμίῳ τὸν πρότερον ὄντι χρόνον ἀεί Men.*Sam.*57; πότερον οὐ συνοίδασιν αὐτῷ ποιοῦντι τὰ δίκαια Plb.27.9.11; ξυνειδὼς οὐ φράσεις; S.*OT* 330; ἵνα τούτῳ ταῦτα συνειδῶμεν Pl.*Prt.*348b; ἐρῶ..ἃ σύνοιδα αὐτῷ X.*Mem.*2.7.1; οὐκ αἰσχυνοῦμαι..εἰπεῖν (v.l.) ἅπασιν ὅσα σύνοιδ' αὐτῷ κακά Ar.*Fr.*200; ξύνοιδ' ἄντροισιν αἰσχύνην τινά E.*Ion* 288; θνῄσκοντι συνείσῃ (cj. Reiske for συνοίσῃ) *thou wilt witness* my death, S.*Ph.* 1085 (lyr.); διὰ δικαιοσύνην, τήν οἱ ἄλλην συνῄδεε ἐοῦσαν Hdt.7.164; τοιοῦτον αὐτοῖς Ἄρεος εὔβουλον πάγον ἐγὼ ξυνῄδη χθόνιον ὄνθ' S.*OC* 948; δύ' ἡμῶν ἢ τρία κακὰ ξυνειδὼς εἶπε δρώσας μυρία (sc. Εὐριπίδης) Ar.*Th.*475, cf. 553; ἀφανίζει τὸν παῖδα, ὃς συνῄδει περὶ τῶν χρημάτων Isoc.17.11, cf. Men.*Epit.*210; τῆς ἁρπαγῆς τοῦ παιδὸς εἰ ξύνοισθά τι, ταχέως λέγειν χρή Antiph.74.3; καὶ τίνα σύνοισθά μοι καλουμένη βροτῶν; A.*Ch.*216; σύνοιδ' Ὀρέστην πολλά σ' ἐκπαγλουμένην ib.217; σύνοιδα τοῖς πλείστοις αὐτῶν ἥκιστα χαίρουσι I *can bear witness* that most of them are far from pleased.., Isoc.7.50; with a mixture of dat. and acc. constr., συνίσασι γὰρ αὐτῷ..καθιστάμενον, ἐκ δὲ τούτων..δυνάμενον Id.15.120; ἐγώ σοι σ...ἀνιστάμενον καὶ..βαδίζοντα καὶ ἀναπείθοντα X.*Oec.*3.7; freq. with reflex. Pron. in dat., ἔμ' αὔτᾳ τοῦτο σύνοιδα Sapph.15; ἐξ ὧν αὐτὸς σύνοισθα σαυτῷ ἐν τῇ τῶν γραμμάτων μαθήσει from your *experience of* yourself.., Pl.*Tht.*206a; σύνοιδ' ἐμαυτῇ πολλὰ ⟨δείν'⟩ Ar.*Th.*477, cf. X.*Mem.*2.9.6, Pl.*R.*331a; ξυνειδέναι τί μοι δοκεῖς σαυτῷ καλόν Ar.*Eq.*184; πολλὴν ἑαυτοῖς συνειδέναι ἀσέβειαν X.*Ap.*24; συνειδὼς ἐμαυτῷ ἀμαθίαν Pl.*Phdr.*235c; τὴν πατρίδα, εἰς ἣν τοσαύτην εὔνοιαν ἐμαυτῷ σύνοιδα D.*Ep.*2.20; σ. ἑαυτοῖς ἄγνοιαν Arist.*EN*1095$^{a}$25; σ. αὑτῷ τὴν δειλίαν Id.*HA*618$^{a}$26; μηδὲν ἑαυτοῖς ἄτοπον συνειδέναι Socr.ap.Stob.3.24.13, cf. Isoc.3.59, Lxx *Jb.*27.6, 1*Ep.Cor.*4.4; συνειδότες αὑτοῖς *with full consciousness*, Polystr. p.15 W.:—with part. **a.** in nom., πῶς οὖν ἐμαυτῷ τοῦτ' ἐγὼ ξυνείσομαι, φεύγοντ' ἀπολύσας ἄνδρα; Ar.*V.*999; ἡνίκ' ἄν τις ἐσθλὸς ὢν αὑτῷ συνειδῇ S.*Fr.*931; ὅστις τούτων σύνοιδεν αὑτῷ παρημεληκώς X.*An.*2.5.7; σύνισμεν ἡμῖν αὐτοῖς ἀπὸ παίδων ἀρξάμενοι ἀσκηταὶ ὄντες τῶν καλῶν κἀγαθῶν ἔργων Id.*Cyr.* 1.5.11; συνειδέναι σαυτῷ δοκεῖς οὐπώποτ' ἀμελήσας αὐτῶν ib.1.6.4, cf. 3.3.38, *HG*2.3.12; οὔτε μέγα οὔτε σμικρὸν σύνοιδα ἐμαυτῷ σοφὸς ὤν Pl.*Ap.*21b; ὅταν καὶ μηδὲν σαυτῷ συνειδῇς ἐξαμαρτάνων Isoc.5.79. **b.** in dat., σύνοιδα ἐμαυτῷ ἀντιλέγειν οὐ δυναμένῳ Pl.*Smp.*216b; σύνισμεν ἡμῖν αὐτοῖς κηλουμένοις ὑπ' αὐτῆς Id.*R.*607c; τὸ συνειδέναι πεπρακόσιν αὑτοῖς τὰ πράγματα D.19.208; συνειδόθ' αὑτῷ φαῦλα διαπεπραγμένῳ Philem.229. **2.** c. dat. rei, *know* something *about* a thing, τοῖς διὰ τῶν εἰκότων τὰς ἀποδείξεις ποιουμένοις λόγοις σύνοιδα οὖσιν ἀλαζόσιν Pl.*Phd.*92d; διὰ τὸ συνειδέναι τοῖς σφετέροις πράγμασι τετρυ[μ]μένοις καὶ κάμνουσιν ἤδη τῷ πολέμῳ Plb.1.62.7; σε..συνειδότα τοῖς πρὸς ἐμὲ σοὶ πεπολιτευμένοις Phalar.*Ep.*109; καιρὸς..σὲ εἰπεῖν ἃ σύνοισθα τῷ βίῳ ἑκάστῳ what *you know about* each life, Luc.*Gall.*15. **II.** *share the knowledge of* something *with* somebody, *to be implicated in* or *privy to* it, οὐδὲ ξυνῄδει σοί τις ἔκθεσιν τέκνου; E.*Ion* 956; δουλοῖ γὰρ ἄνδρα,..ὅταν ξυνειδῇ μητρὸς ἢ πατρὸς κακά Id.*Hipp.*425; ξύνοιδε δ' οὔτις οἰκετῶν νόσον ib. 40; συνίσασί σοι πάντα ὅσα ἔπραξας X.*Cyr.*3.1.9; ξυνίσασ' εὐναὶ..ὅσα θρηνῶ S.*El.*93 (anap.); πλῆθος ὃ ξυνῄδει Th.4.68; ξυνειδώς τις ibid.; ὁ συνειδὼς καὶ μὴ φράζων Pl.*Lg.*742b; οἱ ξυνειδότες σφίσι Th. 1.20; οἱ συνειδότες πεποιηκότι τι δεινόν Arist.*Rh.*1382$^{b}$6; σύνοισθά που καὶ αὐτὸς ὅτι.. Pl.*Phdr.*257d; σύνισμεν ὡς.. Id.*Sph.*232c; σύνοιδέ μοι εἰ ἐπιορκῶ X.*An.*7.6.18; συνειδέναι δὲ (sc. τὰς μαντηΐας) καὶ τοὺς Πυθίους Hdt.6.57; συνειδυίας καὶ τῆς γυναικός *Act.Ap.*5.2:—with part. **a.** in dat., μήτε τῳ ξυνειδέναι τὸ πρᾶγμα βουλεύσαντι S.*Ant.*266; εἰ μὴ συνῄδη Σωκράτει τε καὶ Ἀγάθωνι δεινοῖς οὖσι περὶ τὰ ἐρωτικά Pl.*Smp.*193e. **b.** in acc., ἀνδράποδα, ἃ συνῄδει τὴν γυναῖκα..θάνατον μηχανωμένην Antipho 1.9, cf. Pl.*Lg.*773b, 870d, D.49.58, 59.67, 61.23. **III.** *know well*, αὐτὸς ξυνειδώς, ἢ μαθὼν ἄλλου πάρα; as *from his* own *knowledge*, or..? S.*OT*704; so also (unless there is ellipse of reflex. Pron.) σύνοιδα δείν' εἰργασμένος E.*Or.*396; σύνοισθά γ' εἰς ἔμ' οὐκ εὔορκος ὤν Id.*Med.*495. **IV.** c. dat. rei, *to be privy to*, *BGU*1141.50 (i B.C.); τῷ φόνῳ Sch.Hermog. in Rh.4.355 W. **V.** τὸ συνειδός *complicity*, τὸ σ. τοῦ πράγματος Plu.*Publ.*4; *consciousness*, τοῦ ἐνδεοῦς Id.2.84d. **2.** *conscience*, ὑπὸ συνειδότος ἐπαρρησιάζετο ἀγαθοῦ Paus.7.10.10, cf. Hld.6.7, Alciphr.1.10.5, Chor. p.38 B. **VI.** ὡς ἂν συνειδῇς as you may *think proper*, Aët.13.2.

**συνοιδ-έω**, *swell up together*, Hp.*Loc.Hom.*9, al., Mnesith.ap.Orib. 8.38.9, D.S.1.7, Ph.2.101 (συνοικ- cod.). **-ησις**, εως, ἡ, *swelling up together*, Mnesith.ap.Orib.8.38.2, Sor.2.31.

⊛ **συνοικει-όω**, *bind together as friends* or *kinsmen*, *associate*, *bring into connexion*, τινί τινα Plu.*Num.*8, *Ant.*75, cf. 2.355b; *adapt exactly*, τὰ σώματα ταῖς ὥραις Luc.*Anach.*24, cf. S.E.*M.*5.95; *bring into relation with*, τοὺς ἀγνοουμένους τῶν τόπων τοῖς γνωριζομένοις Plb.5.21.5; of allegorical identifications, τοὺς θεοὺς ἀψύχοις σ. Phld.*Piet.*13, al.:—Pass., *to be bound by ties of kindred*, *to be closely united*, Arist.*EN* 1162$^{a}$2; τῷ γεννηθέντι ib.1161$^{b}$21; ἡδονὴ συνῳκείωται τῷ γένει ἡμῶν ib.1172$^{a}$20, cf. 1175$^{a}$29, 1178$^{a}$15, Plu.*Lyc.*4: generally, *to be associated with*, τῷ μὴ ψευδεῖ Phld.*Mus.* p.29 K. **2.** Astrol., in Pass., *to be situated together in the domicile*, ὁ -ούμενος τῇ Σελήνῃ Vett.Val. 101.5. **-ωσις**, εως, ἡ, *binding together*, *bringing into combination*, in Astrol. sense, Ptol.*Tetr.*50, *Cat.Cod.Astr.*1.114. **2.** a figure in Rhetoric, *whereby heterogeneous things were combined* or *attributed to one person*. Arist.*Rh.Al.*1425$^{b}$38, Rutil.2.9, Quint.*Inst.*9.3.64. **3.** *allegorical identification*, in pl., Phld.*Piet.*14, 15.

**συνοικ-έσιον**, τό, = συνοίκησις, esp. *marriage*, -ίου συγγραφή *PTeb.* 809.5 (ii B.C.), *POxy.*250 (i A.D.), cf. *Cat.Cod.Astr.*7.110, Lyd.*Mens.* 4.89, etc. **II.** συνοικέσια, τά, = συνοίκια, Sch.Ar.*Pax* 1019. **-έτης**, ου, ὁ, = συνοικητήρ, Hsch. ⊛ **-έω**, *dwell* or *live together*, Hom.*Epigr.* 15.15, Pl.*R.*577a, etc.; ξ. τινί *live with*, A.*Ch.*909, Ar.*Av.*414 (lyr.), Th.6.63, etc.; ξ. τῇδ' ὁμοῦ S.*Tr.*545; σ. μετά τινων Plu.*Rom.*9; of peoples, *live together*, *form a community*, συνοικήσων τούτοισι Hdt.4. 148: abs., S.*OT*57, Th.2.68. **2.** *live with in wedlock*, of the man, Hdt.1.91, 196, E.*Med.*242, Ar.*Pax* 708, Pl.*Criti.*113d, *PEnteux.* 91.2 (iii B.C.), etc.; of the woman, ἔοισα (fort. νέοισι) γεραιτέρα Sapph. 75, cf. Hdt.1.37, 108, E.*Andr.*18, etc.: abs., *live in wedlock*, Hdt.1.93, 4.168, 1*Ep.Pet.*3.7, etc.; τούτων συνοικησάντων γίνεται Κλεισθένης from their *marriage* sprang Cleisthenes, Hdt.6.131. **3.** metaph. of feelings, circumstances, etc., μυρίον ἄχθος ᾧ ξυνοικεῖ with which *he dwells*, S.*Ph.*1168 (lyr.); σ. φόβῳ E.*Heracl.*996; ἡδοναῖς, ἀμαθίᾳ, Pl.*R.*587c, *Alc.*1.118b; φόβοις Phld.*Ir.* p.56 W.; βαρυτάτη συνοικῆσαι (sc. ἄνομος μοναρχία) Pl.*Plt.*302e; also ἱππικοῖς ἐν ἤθεσιν πολὺς ξ. *being* much *versed* in their ways, E.*Hipp.*1220 codd. (sed leg. ἱππικοῖσιν ἤθεσιν). **b.** reversely, with the thing as subject, γῆρας ἵνα πρόπαντα κακὰ κακῶν ξυνοικεῖ S.*OC*1238 (lyr.); ᾗ ἂν συνοικίᾳ μήτε πλοῦτος συνοικῇ μήτε πενία Pl.*Lg.*679b; ὅπου σ. ἐρημία Lyc.957; of the poisoned robe of Heracles, *cling closely*, S.*Tr.*1055. **c.** Astrol., *share the same domicile*, ὅταν ἡ Παφίη Ἑρμῇ στείχουσα συνοικῇ Man. 5.165. **II.** c. acc. loci, *people* or *colonize jointly with*, σ. Κυρηναίοισι Λιβύην Hdt.4.159; Τροιζηνίοις Ἀχαιοὶ συνῴκησαν Σύβαριν Arist. *Pol.*1303$^{a}$29:—Pass., of a place, *to be thickly peopled*, X.*Oec.*4.8, Pl.*Criti.*117e, Str.6.2.4, Plu.*Num.*15, etc. **-ημα**, ατος, τό, *that with which one lives*, νομίσας δῆμον εἶναι σ. ἀχαριτώτατον a most unpleasant *house-fellow*, Hdt.7.156. ⊛ **-ησις**, εως, ἡ, *cohabitation*, esp. of *marriage*, ἐπωλέοντο ἐπὶ συνοικήσι (Ion. for -ήσει) Hdt.1. 196; σ. ποιεῖσθαι Pl.*Lg.*930b. **II.** πόλεων συνοικήσεις *collections* of people into cities, ib.713b; *settlement*, *community*, ib.735b, 739b, 752e; μετέσχε τῆς ξυνοικήσεως Arr.*An.*4.4.1. **-ητήρ**, ῆρος, ὁ, *house-fellow*, λιμός, ἐχθρὸς σ. Semon.7.102. **-ήτωρ**, ορος, ὁ, = foreg., ξ. ἐμοί A.*Eu.*833. **-ία**, ἡ, = συνοίκησις, δέξομαι Παλλάδος ξυνοικίαν will accept her offer of *living with her*, ib.916 (lyr.). **II.** *a body of people living together*, *settlement*, *community*, Id.*Supp.*267; ταύτῃ τῇ συνοικίᾳ ἐθέμεθα πόλιν ὄνομα Pl.*R.*369c, cf. *Lg.*679b; φίλοι, βοηθοί, μάρτυρες, συνοικίαι Philem.65.5; ἀψευδήων ἂν τὰν συϝοικίαν τοῖς Ἐρχομινίοις *IG*5(2).343.39, cf. 58 (Orchom. Arc., iv B.C.). **III.** *house in which several families live*, *tenement-house*, Th.3.74, Ar.*Th.* 273, X.*Ath.*1.17, Is.5.27, 6.21, D.36.6, 45.28, *OGI*326.21 (Teos); ὅπου πολλοὶ μισθωσάμενοι μίαν οἴκησιν διελόμενοι ἔχουσι, συνοικίαν καλοῦμεν Aeschin.1.124; ἓν στόμ' ἐστὶ τῆς συνοικίης πάσης Herod.3.47; *lodging-house*, *PPetr.*3 p.186 (iii B.C.), *BGU*1573.25 (ii A.D.). **2.** *store-room*, Ar.*Eq.*1001 (cf. Sch. ad loc.). **3.** perh. *village*, *hamlet*, Plb.16.11.1 (pl.), Plu.2.280e.

**συνοίκ-ια** (sc. ἱερά), τά, at Athens, *a public feast in memory of Theseus' uniting all the towns of Attica into a single city-state*, celebrated on the 17th Boëdromion, Th.2.15, *IG*1$^{2}$.188.60 (prob.), St.Byz. s.v. Ἀθῆναι. **II.** sg. συνοίκιον, τό, *a joint lodging*, Petron.93 (in Lat. form *synoecium*). ⊛ **-ιάζω**, *enlarge a house*, or perh. *turn* a house *into a tenement-house*, *PLond.*5.1735.11 (vi A.D.). **-ίδιον**, τό, Dim. of συνοικία III, Gorg.ap.Stob.4. 51.28, *Inscr.Délos* 1416 *B* i 80, 106, ii 32 (ii B.C.), *BGU*1573.12 (ii A.D.). ⊛ **-ίζω**, fut. Att. -ιῶ D.S.2.6: pf. -ῴκικα Str.12.3.10:—*make to live with*, Isoc.19.34, dub. l. in Ps.-Epich.298; σ. τινὶ τὴν θυγατέρα *to give* him one's daughter *in marriage*, Hdt.2.121.ζ', cf. *PEnteux.*22.8 (iii B.C.), D.S.2.6; σ. νύμφας νυμφίοις Pl.*R.*546d, cf. *Sph.*242d; ἐμὲ..εὐνὴν Ἡρακλεῖ συνοικίσας E.*HF*68; rarely with the reverse constr., τοὺς δούλους ταῖς τῶν δεσποτῶν γυναιξὶ σ. Plb. 16.13.1. **II.** *combine* or *join in one city*, μὴ Τροίαν ἀθροίσῃ καὶ ξυνοικίσῃ πάλιν E.*Hec.*1139; *unite into a city-state*, ἐς τὴν νῦν πόλιν οὖσαν ξ. πάντας Th.2.15; Θησεὺς..τὰς δώδεκα πόλεις εἰς τὸ αὐτὸ συνῴκισεν *Marm.Par.*35 (cf. συνοίκια); ξ. τὴν Λέσβον ἐς τὴν Μυτιλήνην Th.3.2; Ἐρέτρια συνῴκισε τὰς περὶ Παλλήνην πόλεις Arist. *Fr.*603:—Pass., ξυνοικισθείσης πόλεως a city *having been regularly formed*, opp. κατὰ κώμας οἰκίζεσθαι, Th.1.10, cf. 2.16, 3.93; ἐκ μικρῶν πόλεων συνοικισθέντες X.*Ath.*2.2; Χαλκιδέων εἰς ἓν συνῳκισμένων D. 19.263; σ. κατὰ πόλεις Isoc.15.82; ἐκ τῶν τυχόντων ἀνθρώπων σ. Lycurg.62. **2.** *unite in one building*, *PMich.Zen.*84.9 (Pass., iii B.C.). **III.** *join in peopling* or *colonizing* a country, Th.1.24; τισι Id.6.5. **IV.** generally, *unite*, *associate*, οἵῳ με δαίμων φιλοσόφῳ συνῴκισεν Theognet.1.6; λιμὸν σ. τινί Alciphr.1.20; ἀλλοτρίῳ δαίμονι συνοικιζομένους Plu.*Cor.*13. ⊛ **-ισία**, ἡ, = -ισμός, τῆς τετραπόλεως *Athenaeum (Pavia) nuova serie* 12 (1934).3 (Apollonia on the Pontus, iii B.C., found at Chios). 2. *marriage*, συγγραφὴ -ισίας *PEleph.*1.2 (iv B.C.). -ίσιον, τό, = foreg. 2, συγγραφὴ -ισίου *PEnteux.*91.3 (iii B.C.), Mitteis *Chr.*284ᵛ (ii B.C. (?)), cf. *UPZ*123.10 (ii B.C.), *PTeb.*822.11 (ii B.C.). -ῐσις, εως, ἡ, *combination* or *union into one city-state*, Th.3.3. ® -ισμός, ὁ, *living together, wedlock*, D.S.18.23; ἀνδρὸς καὶ γυναικός Plu.*Sol.*20. II. = foreg., Plb.4.33.7: pl., πόλεων Str.10.4.8; *founding a city*, Plu.*Rom.*9. ® -ιστήρ, ῆρος, ὁ, *one who joins in peopling, fellow-colonist*, Pi.*O.*6.6, *Fr.*186. ® -ιστής, οῦ, ὁ, *co-founder of a colony*, St.Byz. s.v. Αἱμονία.

**συνοικο-δεσπότης**, ου, ὁ, *joint lord of the house*, of a planet, Ptol. *Tetr.*63, Vett.Val.77.20: hence -δεσποτέω, Ptol.*Tetr.*61,66, Vett.Val.71.10: -δεσποτία, ἡ, *joint predominance*, Ptol.*Tetr.*39, Vett.Val.164.28. -δομέω, *build together*, ἐκ πολλῶν ἓν οἰκητήριον Plu.*Comp.Thes.Rom.*4:—Pass., *IG*2².1180.16; οἰκίαι ἐκ πλίνθων συνῳκοδομημέναι *entirely built*, D.C.39.61, cf. *POxy.*1648.60 (ii A.D.): metaph. in Pass. of believers, *Ep.Eph.*2.22. 2. Pass., *to be built in with other materials*, λίθοι ξυνῳκοδομημένοι Th.1.93; σ. οἱ κίονες τοῖς τοίχοις D.S.13.82. 3. *build up, block up*, Id.3.37. -νομέω, *administer jointly*, of executors, Thphr.ap.D.L.5.56; ὤνησιν καὶ πρᾶσιν *CIG* 3597*b* (Assus); -νομοῦσα γαμετή Phld.*Oec.*p.28 J. II. *treat* chemically *together*, Zos.Alch. p.154 B.

® **σύνοικος**, ον, Delph. σύνϝοικος (v. infr. 1c), *dwelling in the same house with*, τῷ γυναικείῳ γένει A.*Th.*188, cf. *Ch.*1005; ξ. εἴσειμ' enter the house *as an inmate*, S.*El.*818; of animals, Plu.2.974d, Hdn.1.12.2. b. of persons *living in the same city* or *country, fellow-inhabitant* (prop. of those *who join in colonizing* a place, opp. ἔποικοι, Arist.*Pol.*1303ᵃ28), σ. ἐγένοντο Ἀθηναίοισι (sc. οἱ Πελασγοί) Hdt.1.57, cf. 2.51, 7.73; ξ. ἐπαγαγέσθαι τινάς Th.2.68; ξ. δέξασθαι or προσδέξασθαι, Ar.*Pl.*1147, Pl.*Lg.*708a; σ. ἔχειν ἐν τῇ πόλει Isoc.12.178; σ. ἡμῖν ἐν τῇ πόλει Pl.*Lg.*920a; ἐν τῇ χώρᾳ σ. ὑμῶν γίγνεται Lycurg.145; of gods worshipped in the country, τὸν θεὸν βαρὺν ξ. θησόμεσθα A.*Supp.*415, cf. Isoc.10.62; ἡ σ. τῶν κάτω θεῶν Δίκη S.*Ant.*451. c. = μέτοικος or πάροικος, *SIG*480.2 (Delph., iii B.C.): in form σύνϝοικος, *Schwyzer* 324.12 (Delph., iv. B.C.). 2. metaph., *associated with, wedded to, tied to*, of persons, τίς ἄταις ἀγρίαις, τίς ἐν πόνοις ξ.; S.*OT*1206 (lyr.); σ. ἐνδείᾳ, κακῷ, Pl.*Smp.*203d, *R.*367a. b. of things, *associated with*, ὁ δυσφιλεῖ σκότῳ λιμὸς ξύνοικος A.*Ag.*1642; ᾧ τίς οὐκ ἔνι κηλὶς κακῶν ξ.; S.*OC*1134; ὑμῖν τὰς μεγίστας ἡδονὰς σ. εἶναι Pl.*Phlb.*63d; ὁ ἀεὶ σ. ἐμοὶ ἔρως X.*Smp.*8.24; τοῦ [τῇ καρδίᾳ] συνοίκου αἵματος Diocl.*Fr.*44.

**συνοικουρ-έω**, *live at home together*, D.H.8.46; ὅπως [Ἔρως] συνοικουρῇ τῷ γάμῳ Plu.2.769d. II. metaph. of rust, *adhere throughout*, Ph.*Bel.*60.25. -ία, ἡ, Astrol., *partnership of domicile*, Paul.Al.*E.*3. -ος, ον, *living at home together*: c. gen., σ. κακῶν *a partner in* mischief, E.*Hipp.*1069 (vv. ll. -ουρούς, -ουργούς).

**συνοικτίζω**, *have compassion on*, τινα X.*Cyr.*4.6.5.

**συνοίμιος**, ον, (οἴμη) *harmonizing with*, c. dat., φόρμιγγι σ. ὕμνος A.R.2.161: neut. **συνοίμιον**, τό, glossed by προοίμιον, Suid.

**συνοιμώζω**, *lament together*, Sch.Il.23.14.

**συνοίομαι**, aor. -ῳήθην, *hold the same opinion, assent*, ἐγὼ..σ. Pl.*R.*500a; εἰ..αὐτὸς μὲν ᾤετο, τὸ δὲ πλῆθος μὴ σ. Id.*Tht.*171a: with neut. pron., αὐτὸ τοῦτο σ. *assent to*.., Id.*R.*500b; καὶ τόδε συνοιήθητι ib.517c.

**συνοίσειν**· εἰς ταὐτὸ συμφέρειν (Tarentine), *AB*300; = *confore, expedire*, *Gloss.*; συνοῖσον, gloss on συμφέρον, Hsch.

**συνοιστός**, ή, όν, (συμφέρω) *accordant*, A.D.*Adv.*123.2, 131.25.

**συνοίσω**, v. συμφέρω, συνοίσειν.

**συνοίχομαι**, *disappear at the same time*, A.D.*Synt.*292.24.

**συνοκλάζω**, *cower and sink down*, πρός τι so as to avoid.., J.*BJ*3.7.25.

**συνόκτω**, οἱ, αἱ, τά, *eight together, by eights*, Sopat.20 (divisim, dub. l.).

® **συνοκωχή**, ἡ, = συνοχή, *joining*, στήθεος Hp.*Oss.*7.

**συνοκωχότε**, v. συνόχωκα.

**συνολισθάνω** (-αίνω Dsc.*Eup.*2.168), *slip and fall together*, Str.4.1.7, Plu.*Per.*6, *Alex.*60, al. 2. *slip with*, Dsc. l.c.: metaph., σ. [τοῖς φίλοις] παραβαίνουσιν Plu.2.807d; συνώλισθεν ἅμ' ἀδελφῇ.. θανάτῳ *Supp.Epigr.*2.479 (Olbia).

**συνολκή**, ἡ, *contraction*, of circles, Hierocl. p.62 A.; *retraction*, Antyll.ap.Orib.45.15.2. 2. *spasm*, Id.ib.8.5.1; in tetanus, Aret.*SA*1.6; hysteric *convulsions*, Sor.2.26; *cramp*, Gal.14.736. 3. *gulp*, Aesop.223.

**συνολκόομαι**, *to be displaced at the same time*, of the uterus, Sor.2.29.

**σύνολκος**, ον, *drawn together*, Arist.*Pr.*923ᵇ13.

**συνόλλῡμι**, *destroy together*, Bion 1.29 (divisim):—Med., *perish along with*, αὐτῷ γ' οὐ ξυνωλόμην ὁμοῦ E.*Hel.*104.

**συνολμοκοπέω**, *bray in a mortar together*, Orib.*Fr.*76 (Pass.).

**συνολολύζω**, *raise a loud cry together*, of women, X.*An.*4.3.19.

**σύνολος**, ον, Arist.*Metaph.*1037ᵃ32; also η, ον ib.26, Pl.*Plt.*299d:—*all together*, ll. cc., *POxy.*1420.11 (ii A.D.); συνόλη ἡ κώμη *PGen.*54.23 (iv A.D.); τὸ σῶμα τὸ σ. Arist.*HA*491ᵃ28, etc.; ἡ σ. οὐσία the *complete* substance, i.e. the εἶδος with the ὕλη, Id.*Metaph.*1037ᵃ32; τὸ σ. in this sense, ib.995ᵇ35, 1060ᵇ24; but τὸ σ. τὸ ἐκ τούτων (viz. σῶμα and εὐκινητότατον εἰς τὸν ἄνω τόπον) συντιθέμενον the *whole* composed of these (here genus and differentia), Id.*Top.*130ᵃ12. II. τὸ σ. as Adv., *on the whole, in general*, Pl.*Sph.*220b, *Lg.*654b, D.61.21, Philem.2, Sor.2.16, etc.; ὡς τὸ σ. εἰπεῖν Thphr.*CP*2.3.3; after a neg., *at all, whatsoever*, μὴ εἶναι χρῆσθαι τὸ ξ. *IG*1².6.43; οὐδὲν τὸ σ. *PFlor.*32*b* 15 (iii A.D.), cf. *PGrenf.*2.76.18 (iv A.D.), etc. 2. regul. Adv. -λως Isoc.12.217, Ph.1.228, Ath.1.31b.

**συνολοφύρομαι** [ῠ], *wail with* or *together*, Theon *Prog.*10: abs., J.*BJ*5.13.1; *bewail together with*, τινά τινι Id.*AJ*17.11.2.

® **συνόμαιμος**, ον, = sq., *Pae.Delph.*3, *JRS*18.30 (Tembris, written -μημ-), Orph.*A.*1193.

**συνομαίμων**, ον, gen. ονος, *of the same blood, kindred*, Ps.-Phoc.206:—as Subst., *brother* or *sister*, A.*Pr.*410 (lyr.), E.*Hel.*640 (lyr.), *IT*848 (lyr.).

**συνομᾰλ-ίζω**, = sq., *IG*7.4255.15 (Oropus, iv B.C.). -ύνω, *make quite level*, Plu.*Tim.*22, *Sull.*14.

**συνομαρτέω**, *follow along with, attend on*, τινι Sol.13.55, Perict.ap. Stob.4.28.19, Aret.*SD*1.9, Jul.*Or.*7.210a: abs., σὺν δ' ὁμαρτοῦσιν φίλοι E.*Or.*950.

**συνομβρ-ίζω**, *deluge with rain*, Plu.*Daed.*7. -ος, ον, *joined* or *mixed with rain*, *EM*407.31.

**συνομέστιος**, ον, *sharing the hearth*, θνατοῖς σ. Lyr.*Alex.Adesp.*34.2.

® **συνόμευνος**, ὁ, ἡ, *bedfellow*, *AP*3.3 (Inscr. Cyzic.), *IG*14.2117 (Rome), 12(5).310 (Paros): fem. -ομευνίς, ίδος, ἡ, *Supp.Epigr.*6.796 (Cappadocia, iii A.D.).

**συνομήθης**, ες, = συνήθης, *AP*6.206 (Antip. Sid.).

**συνομῆλιξ**, Dor. -ᾱλιξ, ικος, ὁ, ἡ, *fellow, comrade*, Theoc.18.22, *AP*7.203 (Simm.), Epigr. in *Inscr.Prien.*268*b* (ii B.C.).

**συνομηρεύω**, *to be a joint hostage*, ἅμα τινί Plb.21.11.9.

**συνομήρης**, ες, *assembled*, Nic.*Al.*449.

**συνομῑλ-έω**, *converse with*, μετά τινος Ceb.13; τινι *Act.Ap.*10.27. -ητής, οῦ, ὁ, *companion*, Elias in *Porph.*15.27: metaph. of books, Ath.Med.ap.Orib.*inc.*21.20: fem. -ήτρια, Hsch. s.v. συνεψία. -ία, ἡ, *intercourse*, Ph.2.653. ®-ος, ον, *living with, an associate*, Hsch.: as Adj., ἐπιστήμη Vett.Val.109.4.

**συνόμνῡμι** or -ύω (D.57.64, *SIG*527.71 (Dreros, iii B.C.)), fut. συνομοῦμαι *IPE*4.79.37 (Chersonesus, iv/iii B.C.): pf. -ομώμοκα Hyp. *Lyc.*7, etc.:—*swear together*, ἦ μὴν τὸν παῖδα..φιλεῖσθαι X.*Smp.*9.6; ἀποκτείνειν (ἀποκτενεῖν Cobet) Lycurg.126; ὅρκους Hdt.1.176; ὅρκον Plu.*Brut.*12. 2. c. acc. rei, *pledge one's oath to* a thing, *promise by oath*, ἅ μοι ξυνώμοσας S.*Ph.*1367 codd.; ξυνώμοσαν μὲν θάνατον..πατρὶ *joined in swearing* death against him, A.*Ch.*978:—Pass., τὸ πρᾶγμα πανταχόθεν ξυνομώμοται Ar.*Lys.*1007. II. *join in a league* or *confederacy*, Th.5.48, 6.18; ξυνώμοσαν γάρ, ὄντες ἔχθιστοι τὸ πρίν, πῦρ καὶ θάλασσα A.*Ag.*650. 2. σ. τισί *form a confederacy with*.., Th.1.71, 2.72; of an individual, συνομωμοκυῖα πρὸς ἐμέ Hyp. l. c.:—Med., *form a league with*, Βοιωτοῖς Plu.*Alc.*14. 3. esp. in bad sense, *conspire* with others, τοῖς τριάκοντα Arist.*Rh.*1400ᵃ18; ἐπί τινι against one, Hdt.7.235; ἐπὶ τῷ δήμῳ Ar.*Eq.*236; ἐπί τινα D.57.64; συνωμοσίαν σ. *IPE* l.c.: so in Med., οἱ τῷ Περπέννᾳ συνομοσάμενοι his *fellow-conspirators*, Plu.*Sert.*27.

**συνομοζωνία**, ἡ, *joint equidistance from solstice*, Paul.Al.*E.*3.

**συνομοιόομαι**, Pass., *to become quite like*, D.H.4.3 (v.l. συνεξομ-), Plu.2.1003a; *become like also*, Vett.Val.107.21.

**συνομοιοπᾰθέω**, *to be similarly affected with* another, τινι Arist.*Rh.*1408ᵃ23 (v.l. συνομοπ-).

**συνομοίωμα**, ατος, τό, *similar occurrence*, *PMasp.*4.10 (vi A.D.).

**συνομολογ-έω**, *say the same thing with, agree with*, σφι Hdt.2.55, cf. X.*Oec.*1.13, 21.2, etc.; *confess the whole, concede*, αὐτὰ ταῦτα Th.1.133; freq. of disputants, *concede, agree upon*, ὅσα ἂν συνομολογῶμεν X.*Smp.*4.56, cf. Pl.*R.*342d, *Grg.*504b, etc.: c. acc. et inf., περὶ δικαιοσύνης σ. πάντα εἶναι ταῦτα καλά Id.*Lg.*859d, cf. *Phd.*91d:—Med., Id.*Euthd.*280b, *Lg.*660d:—Pass., τὰ ἄλλα συνωμολόγηται X.*HG*7.1.2; οὐκοῦν καὶ τόδε συνομολογοῖτο; Pl.*Phlb.*60b; συνωμολογημένον τοῦτο κεῖται ib.41d; τοῦτο ἡμῖν..μενέτω συνομολογηθέν Id.*Sph.*248a, cf. *Plt.*284c; τὸ -ούμενον, opp. τὰ ἀμφισβητούμενα, Isoc.2.52; ἔστω συνωμολογημένον ἡμῖν Arist.*Pol.*1323ᵇ23. 2. Med., *correlate*, ἅμα ταῦτα πρὸς ἄλληλα -ήσασθαι χαλεπόν Hp.*Epid.*6.8.26. II. *agree to do, promise*, ταῦτα X.*An.*4.2.19, etc.: c. inf. fut., Id.*Cyr.*3.1.10. III. *come to terms, make a covenant*, ib.5.3.15, etc.:—Med., Pl.*Ep.*356b. -ητέον, *one must concede*, Phld.*Rh.*1.128 S. -ία, ἡ, *concession, agreement*, Pl.*Sph.*252a, *Lg.*966a.

**συνομο-νοέω**, *to be of one mind with*, *PMasp.*159.22 (vi A.D.). -νοια, ἡ, *agreement*, ib.4.11 (vi A.D.).

**συνομοπᾰθέω**, = συνομοιοπαθέω, v.l. in Arist.*Rh.*1408ᵃ23, cf. Plu.2.96e, *Alc.*23.

**συνομόπλοος**, ὁ, *fellow-voyager*, *IG*12(5).305.7 (Paros).

**συνομορέω**, *border on, abut upon*, τῇ συναγωγῇ *Act.Ap.*18.7.

**συνομοτᾰγέω**, *correspond*, ταῖς θηλείαις ὑγιεινὴν -εῖν τὴν παρθενίαν *is correspondingly* healthy for females, Sor.1.30.

**συνομόψηφος**, ον, *entitled to vote as well*, *BCH*51.220 (Thasos).

**συνομωνῠμ-έω**, *to be synonymous*, Sch.Ar.*Ra.*497. -ος, ον, *having the same name with*, τινος Achae.13.2, *AP*6.206 (Antip. Sid.), Orac.ap.D.S.8.23; τινι *Supp.Epigr.*2.615 (Teos).

**συνοξ-ύνω**, *bring to a point*, *PCair.Zen.*54.7 (iii B.C.), Plb.6.22.4 (Pass.). II. *pronounce with the acute accent together with*, in Pass., c. dat., prob. in A.D.*Adv.*149.4, cf. Jo.Alex.p.38.1. -υς, υ, *pointed*, ῥίζα Thphr.*HP*1.6.8.

® **συνοπᾱδός**, όν, Ion. -ηδός, *following along with, accompanying*, τοῖς ἀνθρώποις Pl.*Sph.*216b; ψυχὴ θεῷ σ. γενομένη Id.*Phdr.*248c;

ξείνῳ σ. A.R.4.745; ὄνειαρ σ. ἀοιδῆς Panyas.12.13; ἐν αὐλοῖς σ. Telest.5.

**συνοπάζομαι**, *accompany*, S.*Fr.*373.5 (v.l. συμπλάζεται), dub. in *Rev.Ét.Anc.*31.311 (Thrace).

**συνοπάων** [ᾱ], ονος, ὁ, ἡ, *companion*, Ἑρμῆς..Ναϊάδων σ. *IG*2².4728, cf. Orph.*H.*31.5.

**συνοπλ-ίζομαι**, Pass., *to be a companion in arms*, Poll.1.152. **-ος**, ον, *under arms together, allied*, δόρατα E.*HF*127 (lyr.).

**συνοπλοφορέω**, *bear arms together*, Them.*Or.*4.59a.

**συνοπτάω**, *roast together*, in Pass., Hippoloch.ap.Ath.4.129b, Heraclid.Lemb.3, Dsc.2.144.

**συνοπ-τέον**, *one must consider, attend to*, Hp.*Medic.*2. **-τικός**, ή, όν, *seeing the whole together, taking a comprehensive view*, Pl.*R.*537c. Adv. -κῶς Marin.*Procl.*13, Sch.Ptol.*Tetr.*9. **-τος**, ον, *that can be seen, visible*, τάφος σ. πρὸς τὴν τῶν Κορινθίων χώραν *visible* from Corinthian territory, Arist.*Pol.*1274ᵃ38; τοῖς μακρὰν ἀπέχουσι σ. Id.*Mir.*843ᵃ9; ἀντίγραφα εἰς τὸ δημόσιον μάλιστα ἑστάναι σ. τοῖς ἀναγιγνώσκουσιν *PFay.*20.23 (iii A.D.); ὅρος, ἐξ οὗ σ. ἐστιν ἡ Ῥώμη D.H.9.24; κίνδυνος ἅπασι σ. Plb.2.28.9; σ. οὐδὲν ἦν ἀπὸ τῶν πολεμίων Plu.*Tim.*27; ἐν συνόπτῳ εἶναι to be within *sight of land*, v.l. for ἀπόπτῳ in Aeschin.*Ep.*1.4. II. *intelligible*, Hsch. **-τρον**, τό, *orrery*, Id.

**συνορ-ᾱτέον**, *one must consider together*, Heph.Astr.1.23. II. -έος, α, ον, *to be considered together*, Nech.ap.Vett.Val.291.17. **-ᾱτικός**, ή, όν, = συνοπτικός, Arr.*Epict.*1.6.1, Ptol.*Tetr.*10, Asp. *in EN*140.30. **-άω**, fut. συνόψομαι: aor. συνεῖδον, inf. -ιδεῖν:—*to be able to see, have within the range of one's vision*, πυρὰ ἔκαιον καὶ συνεώρων ἀλλήλους X.*An.*4.1.11, cf. 5.2.13, Arr.*An.*5.11.2; θυρεὸν.. οὗ τὴν ἐπιγραφὴν οὐκ ἦν συνιδεῖν the inscription on which it was impossible to *make out*, *Inscr.Délos* 1417 *A* i 23 (ii B.C.); εἴ τις μὴ συνορῴη τὸ γινόμενον ἀλλὰ διὰ τῆς ἀκοῆς μόνον κρίνοι Artemo ap.Ath.14.637e; συνιδόντες [τὸν στόλον].. ἀνήγοντο Plb.1.23.3, cf. 1.28.7, 3.66.3, *PRein.*18.17 (ii B.C.), Lxx 2*Ma.*15.21, al., Plu.2.940d:—Pass., δύνασθαι δεῖ συνορᾶσθαι τὴν ἀρχὴν καὶ τὸ τέλος Arist.*Po.*1459ᵇ19. II. *see, comprehend*, ταῦτα πάντα Pl.*Lg.*904b, D.1.28; τὰ πολλαχῇ διεσπαρμένα Pl.*Phdr.*265d, cf. *Lg.*965b; πράγματα συνιδεῖν ἱκανός Memn.3.2; δεινὴ φύσιν μικρῶν παιδίων συνιδεῖν εὐπρεπῆ clever at *picking out* or *detecting*.., D.59.18; νόμοι.. ῥᾴδιοι συνιδεῖν Isoc.12.144; ἡ τῶν δημοσίων γραμμάτων φυλακὴ.. ἀπέδωκε τῷ δήμῳ, ὁπόταν βούληται, συνιδεῖν τοὺς πάλαι μὲν πονηρούς, ἐκ μεταβολῆς δ' ἀξιοῦντας εἶναι χρηστούς Aeschin.3.75; οὐδεὶς ἐφ' αὑτοῦ τὰ κακὰ συνορᾷ, ..ἑτέρου δ' ἀσχημονοῦντος ὄψεται Men.631; ὀρθῶς συνεώρακε τὸ ἀγνόημα Hipparch.2.3.20; τὸ πλῆθος τῶν τόνων συνιδεῖν Ptol.*Harm.*2.9; συνιδεῖν ἦν τῷ προσέχοντι τὸν νοῦν [ἡ ἀρχὴ] ἰσχυρὰ οὖσα, i.e. one might *see* that it was .., X.*An.*1.5.9; εἰ μέλλοι τις τὰ διαφέροντα καθαρίως ἐν [τῇ Ῥωμαίων πολιτείᾳ] συνόψεσθαι Plb.6.3.4; συνιδὼν.. ἰσχυρὸν ὑπάρχοντα.. τὸν ἀέρα Ph.*Bel.*77.17; ταχεῖαν καὶ ἄχρονον θεοῦ δύναμιν μὴ συνεωρακότας Ph.1.177, cf. 635; μάχην οὗτος οὐ συνορᾷ he doesn't *see* any contradiction, Arr.*Epict.*1.5.8, cf. 2.19.1; τὴν κοινότητα συνορᾶν Plu.2.34c, cf. 950d,977e, *Cam.*40; ὁ Κάλχας οὐ συνεῖδε τὸν καιρόν Id.2.29c; τὸ αἴτιον ἐκ τῶν νῦν λεχθέντων σ. Arist.*GA*772ᵇ11, cf. Plb.1.4.7; freq. in Epicur., *Nat.*28.11, al.; σ. περὶ τῶν ἀδήλων *Ep.*1 p.5 U.; ἐκ τῶν λέξεων *Nat.*28.6; ἐν τοῖς τοιούτοις ἀκροαταῖς οἳ οὐ δύνανται διὰ πολλῶν συνορᾶν οὐδὲ λογίζεσθαι πόρρωθεν cannot *see* an argument built up from many particulars, Arist.*Rh.*1357ᵃ4; συνεωρακέναι καὶ λελογίσθαι ὅτι.. D.45.68; συνορᾶν ὅτι.. Isoc.5.56, Epicur.*Fr.*53, Sor.1.46, Plu.2.698e; ὡς.. Thphr.*Sens.*36, Luc.*JTr.*42; χαλεπὸν συνιδεῖν εἰ.. Isoc.2.7; σ. ποία πολιτεία ἀρίστη Arist.*EN*1181ᵇ21; πότερον.. Id.*Ph.*241ᵇ32:—Pass., οὔπω συνῶπται ἱκανῶς *has not yet been* sufficiently *observed*, Id.*GA*762ᵃ34, cf. *HA*580ᵃ20; ἐκ τούτου πρῶτον συνοφθῆναι τὴν δύναμιν Thphr.*HP*9.10.2. 2. *pay attention to, see to* a thing, τὰ προσφερόμενα ἅπαντα χρὴ συνορῆν ὅπως συνοίσει Hp.*Medic.*3; πρὸς τοὺς χρόνους τῆς ὥρης.. συνορῆν, ὅκως.. ib.4. 3. aor. part. συνιδών, *having become aware of*, *Act.Ap.*12.12; συνιδόντες κατέφυγον ib.14.6. III. *resolve*, c. inf., Lyd.*Mag.*3.26, *Cod.Just.*1.4.29.8; συνορῶ τέως ἐν ταυτότητι μεῖναι τὰς βύσεις I *desire* that.., *POxy.*940.2 (v A.D.); *decide* judicially, *PMonac.*1.20, 6.55, al. (vi A.D.); ἐὰν συνίδῃ δεόμενον τὸ πρᾶγμα ζητήσεως *Cod.Just.*4.20.15.2.

**συνοργιάζω**, *celebrate mysteries together*, Plu.2.944d, Them.*Or.*20.236c.

**συνοργίζομαι**, fut. -ισθήσομαι D.21.100, -ιοῦμαι Lib.*Or.*42.29: aor. συνωργίσθην D.21.6:—*to be angry together*, τοῖς ἀδικηθεῖσιν Isoc.4.181, cf. Plu.2.490c: abs., D.21.6, Plu.2.63c, Marin.*Procl.*20; *meet anger with anger*, Phld.*Ir.*p.34 W.

**συνορέγομαι**, Med., *desire along with*, τινι Arr.*Epict.*2.17.23, 4.7.20.

**συνορέω**, *to be conterminous*, Plb.1.8.1, 5.55.1; τινι *with*.., Str.8.7.5, cf. Plu.*Demetr.*7.

**συνορθιάζω**, *rise up together*, Ph.1.319.

**συνορθόω**, *restore* a ruined building *along with*, *IG*12(3).325.39 (Thera, ii A.D.):—Pass., *to be successful together with*, τινι Arr.*An.*3.9.8.

**σύνορθρος**, ον, *dawning along with*, ἥξει σύνορθρον αὐγαῖς *dawning with* the first beams of day, A.*Ag.*254 (lyr.), as restored by Wellauer and Herm. for σύνορθον αὐταῖς: two codd. give συνάρθρον.

**συνορία**, Ion. -ίη, ἡ, *border-land*, Αἰγύπτου καὶ Αἰθιόπων Ruppel *Der Tempel von Dakke* 3 p.52 No.67, cf. *Peripl.M.Rubr.*65, *POxy.*918 v 17 (ii A.D.), *BGU*831.9 (iii A.D.).

**συνοριγνάομαι**, *desire together*, τοῦ πλείονος Anon.ap.Suid.

**συνορίζω**, *bring together*, opp. διακρίνω, Arist.*Cael.*307ᵃ33, ᵇ2:—Pass., v.l. in Ptol.*Harm.*1.9. 2. Med., *give one's consent to a boundary*, *Sammelb.*5240.15 (i A.D.). 3. Med., *bet* (cf. συντίθημι B. II. 2), συνορισάμενος ψευδὲς ἐπιδείξειν τὸ ἐν Δελφοῖς μαντεῖον Aesop.55. II. intr., = συνορέω, *to be conterminous with*, c. dat., *OGI*221.69 (Ilium, iii B.C.), Antig.*Mir.*78, D.S.1.30, *Peripl.M.Rubr.*64: with πρός c. acc., Scymn.839: abs., D.S.14.44, 17.4.

**συνορίνω** [ῑ], *rouse* or *stir up*, ἵνα οἱ σὺν θυμὸν ὀρίνῃς Il.24.467:—Pass., συνορινόμεναι κίνυντο φάλαγγες 4.332; κέαρ συνορίνεται ἄτῃ *is stirred up, agitated*, A.R.3.56.

® **συνόριον**, τό, = συνορία, Hdn.*Epim.*173.

**συνορκ-έω**, *to be a sworn ally of*, c. dat., prob. l. in *OGI*5.40 (Scepsis, Epist. Antig.). **-ος**, ον, *bound together by oath*, X.*Vect.*5.9.

**συνορμάς**, άδος, ἡ, = συνδρομάς, συμπληγάς, Simon.22 (pl.).

**συνορμάω**, *set in motion together*, τῷ φωτὶ τὰς πράξεις Plu.2.1129e. II. intr., *move on together*, Phalar.*Ep.*72: c. dat., Porph. *Gaur.*5.3, Steph. *in Gal.*1.322 D.

**συνόρμενος**, v. συνόρνυμαι.

**συνορμ-έω**, *lie at anchor with*, c. dat., Plb.5.68.6, 110.2. **-ίζω**, *bring to anchor together*, τὰς ναῦς X.*HG*1.1.17; τὸν στόλον Plb.2.96.14, etc.:—Pass., γυναῖκας ἀνδράσι -ορμισθῆναι θέλεις, of Isis, *POxy.*1380.147 (ii A.D.).

**συνόρνυμαι**, Pass., *start* or *set forth together*, ἀφ' Ἑλλάδος αἴας συνορμένοις (aor. 2 part.) A.*Ag.*429 (lyr.).

**σύνορος**, Trag. **ξύνουρος**, ον, *marching with, conterminous*, τῇ Ἀττικῇ or τῆς Ἀττικῆς, Plu.*Lys.*29, *Dem.*17; *neighbouring*, χώρα Thphr.*HP*3.3.6: metaph., κόνις πηλοῦ κάσις ξύνουρος dust *twin-sister* of mud, A.*Ag.*495; σύνοροι πολιτεῖαι Arist.*EN*1160ᵇ17; σ. ἡ πραγματεία τοῦ ἰατροῦ καὶ τοῦ φυσικοῦ Id.*Resp.*480ᵇ25; προτάσεις σύνοροι defined in Gal.*Inst.Log.*6.3.

**συνορούω**, *rush on together*, συνόρουσαν ἐναντίοι A.R.2.88.

**συνοροφόω**, *roof over*, τὸν πέριξ ἀέρα Luc.*Am.*12.

**συνορφᾰνιστής**, οῦ, ὁ, *fellow guardian of orphans*, prob. in *SIG*364.28 (Ephesus, iii B.C.).

**συνορχέομαι**, Med., *dance together*, Plu.2.52b, Philostr.*VA*4.21; παλλακίσι Plu.2.612a, cf. Luc.*Salt.*11.

**συνόσα**· ὁμοῦ, Hsch.

**συνοσφραίνω**, *give to smell together*, Archig.ap.Gal.13.175.

**συνοτρύνω**, *urge on together*, Them.*Or.*23.295b codd. (fort. συνεξοτρ-).

**συνουετρανός**, ὁ, *fellow-veteran*, *BGU*327.5 (ii A.D.); cf. συνβετρανός.

**συνουλ-όω**, *cause to cicatrize completely*, Gal.13.503, *Gp.*12.12.2. **-ωσις**, εως, ἡ, *complete cicatrization, soundness*, Lxx *Je.*40(33).6, Orib.44.13.3; of plants, *Gp.*4.13.4. **-ωτικός**, ή, όν, *promoting cicatrization*, Gal.10.199, Hsch.

**σύνουρος** (**ξύνουρος**), v. σύνορος.

**συνουσί-α**, Ion. -ίη, ἡ: (συνών, συνοῦσα part. of σύνειμι):—*being with* or *together*, esp. for purposes of feasting or conversing, *social intercourse, society*, Hdt.6.128, A.*Eu.*285, S.*OC*647, etc.; κομψὸς ἐν συνουσίᾳ Ar.*Nu.*649; σ. τινός *intercourse with* one, σοφοὶ τύραννοι τῶν σοφῶν ξυνουσίᾳ S.*Fr.*14; γυναικῶν σ. (with a play on signf. 4) Ar.*Ec.*110 = *Trag.Adesp.*51; ἡ τοῦ θείου σ. *communion with*.., Pl.*Phd.*83e; τῆς νόσου ξυνουσίᾳ *by long intercourse with* it, S.*Ph.*520; προϊούσης τῆς σ. as the *conversation* goes on, Pl.*Tht.*150d; σ. ποιεῖσθαι hold *conversation together*, Id.*Sph.*217e, *Smp.*176e, al.; τὴν σ. διαλῦσαι Id.*La.*201c: pl., Isoc.4.45, Pl.*Phd.*111b, al.; ξυνουσίαι θηρῶν, = οἱ ξυνόντες θῆρες, S.*Ph.*936. 2. οὐ λόγοις.., ἀλλὰ τῇ ξυνουσίᾳ but by *habitual association, constant resort*, Id.*OC* 63. 3. *intercourse with a teacher, attendance at his teaching*, μισθὸς τῆς σ. X.*Mem.*1.2.60, cf. 6.11; ἡ πρὸς Σωκράτην σ. αὐτοῖν their *intercourse with* him, ib.1.2.13; ἡ περὶ γράμματα σ. τῶν μανθανόντων Pl.*Plt.*285c; ἡ σὴ σ. *intercourse with* you, Id.*Prt.*318a. 4. *sexual intercourse*, Democr.32, Pl.*Lg.*838a, X.*Cyr.*6.1.31 (v.l.), Epicur.*Fr.*62, etc.; ἡ ἀνδρὸς καὶ γυναικὸς σ. Pl.*Smp.*206c (interpol.); ἀνδρῶν X.*Oec.*9.11; ἡ πρὸς τοὺς ἄρρενας σ. Arist.*Pol.*1269ᵇ27; ἡ τῶν ἀφροδισίων σ. Pl.*Smp.*192c; ἡ τῆς παιδογονίας Id.*Lg.*838e; of animals, *copulation*, Arist.*HA*630ᵇ35, al.; cf. σύνειμι (εἰμί *sum*) II. 2. II. in concrete sense, *a society, company, party*, Hdt.2.78 (pl.), Pl.*Smp.*173a, *Lg.*672a; ἡ ἐν οἴνῳ σ., = συμπόσιον, Id.*Lg.*652a; αἱ ἐν τοῖς πότοις σ. Isoc.1.32; πότοι καὶ σ. Id.15.286; αἱ σοφαὶ ξυνουσίαι literary *parties, conversazioni*, Ar.*Th.*21; εἰς τὰς σ.. παραλαμβάνουσι τὴν μουσικήν Arist.*Pol.*1339ᵇ22. **-άζω**, *keep company with*: esp., *have sexual intercourse*, Theopomp.Hist.65, Phld.*Mort.*4, Plu.*Alex.*22, Sor.1.31. II. trans., *bring into such intercourse*, τινά τινι X.Eph.2.9, Sch.Ar.*Pl.*1068. ® **-ασμα**, ατος, = sq., *Berl.Sitzb.*1934.1041 (Boeotia, Tab. Defix., pl.). **-ασμός**, ὁ, = συνουσία I.4, Lxx *Si.*23.6, Plu.2.1d, Sor.1.61. ® **-αστής**, οῦ, ὁ, *companion*, Pl.*Min.*319e; *disciple*, X.*Mem.*1.6.1, Plu.2.8b. **-αστικός**, ή, όν, *sociable*, ξυμποτικὸς καὶ ξ. Ar.*V.*1209. 2. *capable of holding intercourse with*, ὁ ἄνθρωπος.. τῷ θεῷ -κός *Corp.Herm.*12.19. II. *promoting sexual intercourse, aphrodisiac*, Chrysipp.*Stoic.*3.199, Paul.Aeg.1.79; σ. τόπος, μόρια, Heph.Astr.1.1, *Cat.Cod.Astr.*2.177. 2. *lewd, salacious*, Ph.2.22 (Sup.). **-όομαι**, Pass., *to be joined essentially with*, Alex.Aphr.*Pr.*1.121, Jul.*Or.*5.170d, Dexipp. *in Cat.*57.7, Ascl. *in Metaph.*110.7, Herm. *in Phdr.* p.131 A.; τὸ φῶς -οῦται τῷ ἡλίῳ Steph. *in Hp.*1.89 D.; of chemical combination, Ps.-Democr.Alch. p.43 B. **-ωσις**, εως, ἡ, *essential connexion*, Hsch., Simp. *in Ph.*35.20.

**συνουτάομαι**, Pass., *to be wounded together with*, τινι Nonn.*D*.29. 150.

**συνοφείλω**, in Pass., *to be owed jointly*, *PSI*4.391.17 (iii B.C.).

**συνοφρ-ύόομαι**, Pass., *to have the brow knitted*, ἀήθης καὶ συνωφρυωμένη S.*Tr*.869, cf. Dam.*Isid*.138; προσώπῳ συνωφρυωμένῳ with *frowning* countenance, E.*Alc*.777, cf. 800. **-υς**, υ, gen. υος, *with meeting eyebrows*, Arist.*Phgn*.812$^{b}$25, *PPetr*.3 p.25 (iii B.C.), Teucer in *Cat. Cod.Astr*.7.199, Anatolius ib.8(3).188; of girls, Theoc.8.72, *PPetr*. 3 p.19; σύνοφρυν βλεφάρων ἴτυν κελαινήν *Anacreont*.15.16; cf. Poll.2. 49. II. *with knitted brow*, Hsch. **-ύωμα**, ατος, τό, *meeting of the eyebrows*, Sch.Il.17.136, *EM*364.8.

**συνοχ-εύς**, έως, ὁ, *one that holds together*, ὁ τῶν ἐνύλων εἰδῶν σ. θεός Jul.*Or*.5.165d, cf. Procl. *in R*.2.307K., al.: pl., *maintainers*, a certain order of gods in Neo-Platonism, Id. *in Prm*.p.494S., Dam. *Pr*.96. 2. generally, *one who holds the loyalty* of others, ἄνθρωπος σ. καὶ ἑνωτικός Horap.2.116. **-έω**, only in Pass., *travel together in a chariot*, Plu.*Galb*.20; μετά τινος Id.*Ant*.11. ❋**-ή**, ἡ, (συνέχω) *holding together*, μηχανημάτων Orib.49.4.75; *grasping in the hand*, ῥόας Philostr.*VA*4.28. 2. *maintenance, control*, σ. ἡ ἑαυτοῦ self-*maintenance*, Chrysipp.*Stoic*.2.173; προνοίᾳ καὶ σ. θεοῦ *Placit*.2.4.2; σ. τῆς ἰδίας εὐδαιμονίας Epicur.*Fr*.361. II. (συνέχομαι) *a being held together*, 1. *contraction*, ἐν ξυνοχῇσιν ὁδοῦ where the road *contracts*, at *a narrow part* of the road, Il.23.330; ἁλὸς ἐν ξυνοχῇσιν in the *narrows* or *straits*, A.R.2.318; ἐνὶ ξυνοχῇ λιμένος Id.1. 1006. 2. *conflict* in battle, ἐνὶ ξυνοχῇσιν ἀγῶνος Q.S.4.342; ἐνὶ ξυνοχῇ πολέμοιο A.R.1.160; στυγερῶν ἐγ ξυνοχαῖς πολέμων *IG*9(1). 1064 (Anticyra, iii B.C.). 3. *continuity*, Arist.*Top*.122$^{b}$26, cf. Alex.Aphr. ad loc.; σ. κατὰ τόπον Apollod.*Stoic*.3.260; *coherence*, σ. καὶ ἕνωσις τῶν μερῶν Dam.*Pr*.112, al.; *combination* of elements, Plot.2.9.5. b. *intension* or *connotation*, Dam.*Pr*.263. 4. *line of union, meeting-place*, βλεφάρων Coluth.74; ξ. χιτῶνος the *joining* of the tunic on the shoulder, A.R.1.744; ἡ κατὰ τὴν ἐσθῆτα σ. the *clinging* of the garment to the body, Arr.*Epict*.4.11.12. 5. metaph., *distress, affliction*, *Ev.Luc*.21.25, 2*Ep.Cor*.2.4; *oppression*, Vett.Val.2.8(pl.), *PMag.Lond*.122.35; *detention, imprisonment*, *BGU* 1821.21 (i B.C.), *PLond*.2.354.24 (i B.C.), Vett.Val.74.23, Man.1. 313 (pl.), al.: but of *going to bed* in disease, ἀκίνδυνος ἔσται ἡ σ. Serapio in *Cat.Cod.Astr*.1.102. 6. *trap, gin, snare*, Lxx *Jd*.2.3 (pl.). **-ηδόν**, Adv. *in confinement*, *AP*9.343 (Arch.). **-ῆτς**, ῖδος, ἡ, *a holder-together*, Hero *Deff*.136.24, Procl. *in Euc*. p.129 F. **-ικός**, ή, όν, *concerning* or *creating continuity*, ibid., Id. *in Cra*. p.48 P., Dam.*Pr*.112,244, Simp. *in Ph*.1355.6. **-ίτης** [ῑ], ὁ, or **-ῖτις**, ἡ, a precious stone, Plin.*HN*37.192.

**συνοχμάζω**, *bind together*, δεσμῷ πόδα Luc.*Trag*.216.

**συνοχμός**, v. συνεοχμός.

**σύνοχος**, ον, (συνέχω) *joined together*: metaph., *in accord with*, παίγματα.. σύνοχα φοιτάσιν E.*Ba*.164 (lyr.); κακοῖς.. ξ. δάκρυα Id. *Hel*.172 (lyr.). 2. *unintermittent*, of fevers, Hp.*Nat.Hom*.15, Alex.Aphr.*Pr*.2.10, Gal.10.603, 19.218 (who censures its use); distd. fr. συνεχής (q.v.).

**συνοχῠρόομαι**, *to be firmly bound together*, Heraclit.*All*.40.

❋**συνόχωκα**, old Ep. intr. pf. of *συνοχόω, *to be* σύνοχος, ὤμω ἐπὶ στῆθος συνοχωκότε shoulders *bent in* or *contracted* upon the chest, Il.2.218 (συνοκωχότε in Hsch. is prob. an ancient cj., as if pf. of συνέχω). II. *collapse*, τείχεος ὡς ἤδη συνοχωκότος ἐν κονίῃσιν Q.S. 7.502.

**συνοψ-ίζω**, *bring into a general view, sum up*, Herm. *in Phdr*. p.156A., Simp. *in Ph*.918.13. 2. *estimate*, *PFay*.26.13 (ii A.D.):—Pass., *to be estimated*, πρὸς τὰ ἐγνωσμένα *PTeb*.82.2 (ii B.C.), cf. *Stud.Pal*.4 p.70 (i A.D.); [τὸ χῶμα] συνωψίσθη δεῖσθαι ναυβίων ν' *POxy*.1469.7 (iii A.D.). **-ις**, εως, ἡ, *a seeing all together, general view*, whether with the eyes or mind, ἡ σ. τῶν νόμων Pl.*Lg*.858c; συνακτέον εἰς σ. one must bring under *one view*, Id.*R*.537c; ὑπὸ μίαν σ. ἀγαγεῖν Plb.1.4.1; εἰς σ. ἀγαγεῖν Gal.6.77; τόπος ἐπιτηδειότατος εἰς σ. Plb.6.27.1; ἐν σ. ἀλλήλων in *sight* of one another, Id. 38.18.6; ἐς σ. ἐλθεῖν (sc. ἀλλήλων) D.S.24.1; πεσεῖν εἰς σ. λογισμοῦ D.H.*Th*.6. 2. *epitome*, Plu.2.1057c tit.; *recapitulation*, Herm. *in Phdr*. p.158A. 3. *estimate*, ἡ λεγομένη κατὰ σύνοψιν ἀπαίτησις the collection of taxes according to the *estimate*, *OGI* 669.55, cf. 58 (Egypt, i A.D.), *Sammelb*.5230.50 (i A.D.), *PRyl*.221. 24 (iii A.D.); τὴν σ. τῶν δεομένων τόπων ζωγραφίας τοῦ.. βαλανίου *POxy*.896.6 (iv A.D.), cf. 1450.12 (iii A.D.); ὁ τὴν σ. εἰληφώς the official who accepted the *tender*, ib.1117.7 (ii A.D.); = *aestimatum, opinio, taxatio*, *Gloss*. 4. *expense*, ἄνευ δημοσίας σ. *Sammelb*.7475. 14 (vi/vii A.D.).

**συνοψοφᾰγέω**, *to be gluttonous with others*, Plu.2.124c.

**συνρ-, συνσ-, συνσκ-, συνστ-**:—for words so written v. συρρ-, συσσ-, συσκ-, συστ-.

**συντᾱγεύω**, *to be a fellow*-ταγός, Ἀρχ.Ἐφ.1917.2 (Perrhaebia).

**συντᾰγή**, ἡ, *order, command*, κατὰ συνταγὴν *IG*9(1).717 (Corcyra); of an oracle, κατὰ σ. σωθεὶς χαριστήριον *Abh.Berl.Akad*.1932(5).35 (Pergam.); *preconcerted signal* in war, v.l. in Lxx *Jd*.20.38; ἀπὸ συνταγῶν *at appointed times*, ib.2*Es*.10.14; *physician's prescription*, Artem.2.44. II. pl., *covenant*, Iamb.*VP*31.185.

**σύνταγμα**, ατος, τό, *that which is put together in order*: 1. *body* of troops *drawn up in order*, τὸ σ. τῶν συμμάχων their *contingent*, X. *HG*3.4.2, cf. 5.2.20; σ. ἱππέων *corps* of cavalry, Plb.9.3.9; τὸ σ. τῶν πεζῶν, = Lat. *cohors*, Id.11.23.1: metaph., τὸ σ. τῶν οἰμωζομένων the *whole army* of them, Luc.*Tim*.58. b. *double* τάξις or *battalion*, Ascl.*Tact*.2.8. 2. *the constitution of a state*, σ. πολιτείας *a form* of constitution, Isoc.7.28, 12.151; τὸ Λακωνικὸν κατάστημα καὶ σ. Plb. 6.50.2; σ. τῆς πολιτείας τρία three *classes* or *orders* of men in the state, D.S.1.74. 3. *arrangement of musical notes, scale* or *mode*, συντάγματα τὰ μὲν Δώρια τὰ δὲ Φρύγια καλοῦσιν Arist.*Pol*.1290$^{a}$22; μουσικῷ σ. *CIG*2722 (Stratonicea). 4. *treatise, work, book*, D.S. 1.3, Plu.2.1036c, Gal.15.490, etc.; *body of doctrine*, Plu.*Num*.22 (pl.). 5. = σύνταξις II. 3, Aeschin.3.95,97. 6. = σύνταξις II. 2, μάχαι αἱ κατὰ σ. battles by *arrangement*, i.e. matches, Ephor. 149 J. 7. *a word in a grammatical construction, syntactical element*, A.D.*Adv*.122.17.

**συνταγμᾰτ-άρχης**, ου, ὁ, *leader of a* σύνταγμα I, *SIG*1225 (Rhodes, iii B.C.), Luc.*Bacch*.2, *Pseudol*.18: hence **-αρχέω**, Ph.2.66: **-αρχία**, ἡ, in pl., Arr.*Tact*.10.9, Ael.*Tact*.9.10. **-ικός**, ή, όν, *of* or *like a* σύνταγμα 4; συνταγματικά *regular treatises*, opp. ὑπομνηματικά, Ammon. *in Cat*.4.4, cf. Phlp. *in Cat*.3.12, Simp. *in Cat*.4.20. **-ιον**, τό, Dim. of σύνταγμα 4, Eust. ad D.P.1. **-ογράφος** [γρᾰ], ὁ, *compiler of treatises*, Vett.Val.150.6.

**συντᾰκής**, ές, *consumptive*, Philostr.*VS*2.1.15.

**συντακ-τέον**, *one must arrange*, S.E.*M*.9.367; *one must prescribe*, Sor.1.26. 2. *one must construe with*, c. dat., Gal.17(1).908, Eust. 1391.48. **-τήρ**, ῆρος, ὁ, *one who arranges*, *EM*421.24. ❋**-τικός**, ή, όν, *putting together, composing*, Theo Sm. p.12 H., Suid. II. (συντάσσω IV) *of* or *for departure*, ὁ σ. (sc. λόγος) or ἡ σ. (sc. ῥῆσις) *a farewell speech*, Men.Rh.pp.430,432 S., cf. Him.*Ecl*.11 tit. III. **-κός**, ὁ, official in Egypt, *classifier* of soldiers, cleruchs, etc., into categories, *PTeb*.120.50 (i B.C.), cf. 191 (i B.C.), *BGU*1565.3 (ii A.D.). **-τήριος**, ον, *arranging*, *EM*421.24. **-τός**, ή, όν, *constructed with* (cf. συντάσσω II. 5), ὀρθῇ πτώσει *Stoic*.2.59: also abs., πρᾶγμα συντακτὸν περί τινος, as a definition of κατηγόρημα, Apollod. ibid., cf. Diog.Bab. ib.3.213.

**συντᾰλαιπωρ-έω**, *endure hardships together, share in misery*, τάδε S.*OC*1136; ξ. μετά τινος Ar.*Lys*.1221; ξ. ἡ ἀρτηρίη τῷ στομάχῳ *suffers* or *sympathizes* with it, Aret.*SA*2.2. II. Med., *collaborate with*, c. dat., Ruf.*Fr*.72. **-ία**, ἡ, *joint sufferings*, Plb.28.6.7 (pl.).

**συντᾰλᾰσιουργέω**, *work wool together*, Clearch.6.

❋**συντᾰμίας**, ου, ὁ, *colleague in the quaestorship*, D.C.48.21.

**συντάμνω**, v. συντέμνω.

**συντᾰνύω**, = συντείνω, *stretch together*, πολλῶν πείρατα συντανύσαις ἐν βραχεῖ *bringing together* the strands of many matters in small compass, Pi.*P*.1.81.

**συνταξιαρχία**, ἡ, *battalion*, = σύνταγμα 1b, Ascl.*Tact*.2.9.

**συντάξῐμον**, τό, prob. = λαογραφία, with the addition of certain minor taxes, *PSI*10.1133.3, *Aegyptus* 13.573, *PFay*.45.3, *PGiss*. 94.4, *BGU*1590 a 3 (all i A.D.), etc.

**σύνταξις**, εως, ἡ, *putting together in order, arranging*, esp. of soldiers, τοῦ στρατεύματος σ. ποιήσασθαι *array in battle-order*, Th.6. 42, cf. X.*Cyr*.2.4.1, Arist.*Pol*.1322$^{a}$36; ἡ στρατιωτικὴ σ. X.*Cyr*.8.1. 14; ἄνευ συντάξεως ἄχρηστον τὸ ὁπλιτικόν Arist.*Pol*.1297$^{b}$19. 2. generally, *system, arrangement, organization*, Pl.*R*.462c, 591d, *Ti*. 24c; ἡ συσταθεῖσα σ. its *organization*, of the Assyrian empire, Id. *Lg*.685c; τῆς πολιτείας Arist.*Pol*.1325$^{a}$3; ὅλον τὸν τρόπον τῆς σ. (of the symmories) D.14.17; σ. μίαν εἶναι τὴν αὐτὴν τοῦ τε λαμβάνειν καὶ τοῦ ποιεῖν τὰ δέοντα one and the same *system* or *rule* for.., Id.1. 20, cf. 13.9; ἡ σ. τοῦ βίου Alex.162.10; *the order* or *system of the world*, Sosip.1.31; τῶν ὅλων, as a definition of εἱμαρμένη, Chrysipp. *Stoic*.2.293; σ. βιβλιοθήκης Str.13.1.54: also concrete, εἰς τὰς σάρκας καὶ τὴν ἄλλην σ. τῶν μερῶν Arist.*Mete*.355$^{b}$10; συντάξεις [ἁρμονίης] musical *modes*, Hp.*Vict*.1.18, cf. Artemo ap.Ath.14.636e; ἡ σ. τοῦ ἐνιαυτοῦ the *composition* or *system* of the year, the calendar year, *OGI* 56.43 (Canopus, iii B.C.); ἡ σ. τοῦ περιθύρου the *framework, structure*, *Ephes*.4(1) No.28 (v A.D.). b. ἐκτὸς κοινῆς συντάξεως, = *extra ordinem*, of admission of envoys to the Senate, *Supp.Epigr*.3.378 B 18 (Delph., Roman law, ii/i B.C.). 3. *composition*, but more freq. concrete, *systematic treatise*, Arist.*Rh.Al*.1446$^{a}$34, Plb.1.3.2, 1.4.2, al., Hipparch.1.1.8, Phld.*Rh*.1.130 S., D.H.*Comp*.4, Str.1.1.23; *collection* of treatises, *composite volume*, D.L.7.190 sqq.: pl., Ptol.*Tetr*. 16, Gal.19.200; *rules for construction*, Ph.*Bel*.55.18: but ἡ τοῦ μεγέθους σ. the *scale*, ib.57.10. 4. *grammatical putting together* of words, *syntax*, περὶ τῆς σ. τῶν λεγομένων, title of work by Chrysipp., *Stoic*.2.6, cf. Plu.2.731f (pl.); τὴν σ. τῶν ὀνομάτων Gal.16. 736, cf. 720; περὶ συντάξεως, title of work by A.D.; but also, *compound forms*, Id.*Conj*.214.7; ποιεῖσθαι μετά τινος τὴν σ. ib.221. 19; also, *rule for combination of sounds* or *letters*, τὸ χ (in δέγμενος) εἰς γ μετεβλήθη, τῆς σ. οὕτως ἀπαιτούσης *EM*252.45, cf. Luc.*Jud. Voc*.3; also, *connected speech*, ἐν τῇ σ. ἐγκλιτέον Sch.Il.16.85. II. = σύνταγμα, *body of troops*, ἡ εἰς τοὺς μυρίους σ. their *contingent* towards.., X.*HG*5.2.37; σ. Ἑλληνική the *combined forces* of Greece, Plu.*Arist*.21. b. *company, troupe* of entertainers, *PColumbia* 441 (*Journ.Eg.Arch*.18.16). 2. *covenant, previous arrangement*, ἐκ τῶν Πατρῶν κατὰ τὴν σ. ἔπλει Plb.5.3.3; κατὰ τὴν τοῦ Ἀριανοῦ σ. at the *time and place arranged* by A., Id.8.16.5; ὥσπερ ἀπὸ συντάξεως ἥκοντας τὴν αὐτὴν λέγειν γνώμην Plu.2.813b; *ordinance* or *resolution*, *SIG*577.8 (Milet., iii/ii B.C.). 3. *assigned impost, tribute, levy*, D.5.13; χρημάτων σ. Id.18.234; κοινωνεῖν τῆς σ. Aeschin.3.96; σ. ὑποτελεῖν Isoc.7.2; διδόναι Id.8.29, D.58.37, cf. Theopomp.Hist. 92, *OGI*1.14 (Epist. Alex. Magni); κατ' ἄνδρα τελούντων σύνταξιν *PTeb*.103.1 (i B.C.), cf. 189 (i B.C.); ὑφίσταται τοῦ ζυτοπωλίου.. σ. δώσειν εἰς τὸ βασιλικὸν τὴν ἡμέραν κριθῶν (ἀρταβῶν) ιβ', i.e. undertakes to deliver the product (in beer) of 12 artabae of barley per day, *PCair. Zen.*199.4 (iii B.C.), cf. *PPetr.*3 pp.219,221 (iii B.C.), *PRev.Laws* 47.1, 48.13 (iii B.C.), *PLille* 9.7 (iii B.C.); λαϊκὴ σ., = λαογραφία, *PMich. Teb.*121r II viii 2 (i A.D.). 4. *subvention, pension*, D.8.21,23 (pl.), Plu.*Alex.*21, *Luc.*2; συντάξεις τῶν ἀναγκαίων D.S.1.75; εἰς τὰς συντάξ(ε)ις ἱερῶν *PTeb.*5.54 (ii B.C.), cf. *UPZ*40.6 (ii B.C.), *PSI* 10.1151.9 (ii A.D.); *pay* of soldiers and officers, *PStrassb.*105.2 (iii B.C.), D.S.5.46, Luc.*DMeretr.*15.3; *salary* of a barber, *PEnteux.* 47.3 (iii B.C.); of the librarian of the Museum, σ. βασιλική Ath.11.493f. 5. ὅσοι.. ἐν συντάξει ἔχουσιν κώμας καὶ γῆν, i.e. those who hold land in *assignment*, i.e. are in receipt of revenue from land (without themselves administering it), *PRev.Laws*43.12 (iii B.C.), cf. *PTeb.*705.6 (iii B.C., restd.); ὁ ἐπὶ τῆς σ. the official administrator of land so granted, *PCair.Zen.*73.11 (iii B.C.); ὁ ἐπὶ συντάξεως *PLille* 4.24 (iii B.C.); ἀπαιτούμεθα τὸν τῆς σ. στέφανον *BGU*1851.3 (i B.C.); τῶν φερομένων ἐν τῇ τῶν μαχίμων σ. reckoned in the *assignment* to the μάχιμοι, *PTeb.*60.27 (ii B.C.); ὁ πρὸς τῇ σ. τῶν κατοίκων ἱππέων ib.31.6 (ii B.C.); ὁ πρὸς ταῖς σ. *PRein.*7.29 (ii B.C.).

**συντᾰπεινόομαι**, Pass., *to be lowered* or *depressed together with*, τινι Str.17.1.48, Arr.*Epict.*3.24.1, Iamb.*Protr.*21.κϛʹ.

**συντάρᾰξις** [τᾰρ], εως, ἡ, *total disturbance*, in medic. sense, Hp. *VM*21 (pl.), Arist.*Pr.*859a26: generally, τῶν στρωμάτων Plu.2.728b.

**συντᾰράσσω**, Att. -ττω, *throw into confusion* or *disorder*, σὺν δ' ἵππους ἐτάραξε Il.8.86; σὺν δ' ἡμῖν δαῖτα ταρ. 1.579; τὴν κρήνην σ. καὶ συνέχωσαν Hdt.9.49, cf. Arist.*HA*596a1; σ. τὴν Ἑλλάδα Hdt.3.138; τιμὰς τὰς ἐούσας σ. *alter* them, Id.1.59; σ. πόλιν E.*Heracl.*378 (lyr.), And.1.68; πρὸς ἀλλήλας τὰς πόλεις Aeschin.2.106; τὸ στρατόπεδον Isoc.4.147; σ. ἅπαντα *confound* all arguments, Ar.*Nu.*1037; τὰ πράγματα D.24.44; τὴν εὐπρέπειαν Id.61.12; ἑαυτούς Epicur.*Sent.* 37; τὰς αἰσθήσεις ib.24:—Pass., ξυντετάρακται αἰθὴρ πόντῳ air *is confounded with* sea, A.*Pr.*1088 (anap.); *to be thrown into confusion*, of soldiers, Th.7.81; of social order, συνταράσσονται πόλεις S.*Ant.* 1080, cf. E.*IT*557, X.*HG*3.4.7, etc.; ξυνταραχθέντος τοῦ βίου τῇ πόλει Th.3.84; νόμοι πάντες ξυνεταράχθησαν all established customs *were disturbed*, Id.2.52; ὁ τῆς πόλεως καὶ τῶν νόμων κόσμος D.25.19; of plans, *to be upset*, Hdt.5.65: metaph. of persons, *to be confounded, troubled*, τῷ θανάτῳ τοῦ παιδὸς συντεταραγμένος Id.1.44; συνταραχθεὶς ὑπὸ νόσων Pl.*Lg.*798a; τί συντετάραξαι; Ar.*Lys.*7. II. c. acc. rei, σ. πόλεμον *stir up* war, Plb.4.14.4, Plu.*Arist.*20.

**συνταργᾰνόομαι**, Pass., *to be wrapped up, entangled in*, Lyc.1101.

**συνταρρ-όομαι**, Pass., *to be full of interlacing roots*, ὥστε συνταρροῦσθαι τὰ χωρία Thphr.*CP*3.7.7. **-ος**, ον, (ταρρός, ταρσός) *interwoven, entangled*, δένδρον σ. a tree *with interlacing roots*, ib.3.7.2, cf. 10.7.

**σύντᾰσις**, εως, ἡ, *tension, rigidity*, ὑποχονδρίου Hp.*Epid.*1.12, cf. 1.26.βʹ, 2.3.6, Arist.*Pr.*879b17, Sor.2.17, Gal.6.198, 15.609. 2. *vehement effort, exertion*, Pl.*Smp.*206b, *Phlb.*46d.

**συντάσσω**, Att. -ττω, *put in order together*, esp. as a military term, *draw up, put in array*, Hdt.7.78, Th.8.28, X.*HG*4.8.28, etc.; σ. πεζοὺς αὐτοῖς (sc. τῷ ἱππικῷ) *draw up* the foot *with* the horse, ib. 7.5.24:—Pass., *to be drawn up in order of battle*, E.*HF*191, X.*Cyr.* 1.4.18, etc.; μάλιστα ξυντεταγμένοι παντὸς τοῦ στρατοῦ in the best *order* of all the army, Th.3.108; μεθ' ὅπλων συντεταγμένοι D.21.223; τισι or μετά τινων *with* others, X.*HG*1.2.15, *Vect.*2.3, cf. *Cyr.* 6.4.14, etc.:—Med., *form in order of battle*, ὁμόσε χωρῶμεν ξυνταξάμενοι Ar.*Lys.*452: Med. also trans., συνταξάμενος βαθεῖαν τὴν φάλαγγα *having drawn up his* phalanx in deep order, X.*HG*2.4.34. b. *place under command of*, τινὶ τάξιν Arr.*An.*4.24.10:—Pass., metaph., τὰ πάθη τῇ τοῦ λογισμοῦ ἡγεμονίᾳ Hierocl. *in CA*19 p.461M. c. *place in the same class*, c. dat., Plot.6.1.25, Dam. *Pr.*1, al. 2. Pass., of single persons, *to be collected, resolute*, συντεταγμένος στρατηγός X.*HG*4.8.22; περὶ παίδων ἀγωγὴν ἄκρως σ. D.L.5.65; so of the mind, πρὶν ξυνταχθῆναι.. τὴν δόξαν before *they have time to get* their thoughts *collected*, Th.5.9 (ξυνταθῆναι is prob. cj.); ἡ ἐπὶ τοῦ συντετάχθαι.. φρόνησις οὖσα Amphis 33.4; ἔφοδος ἐνεργὸς καὶ σ. Plb.3.19.5. II. *arrange, organize*, τὸ σῶμα Pl.*Grg.* 504a; τὰ συσσίτια συντέταχεν ὁ νόμος Id.*Lg.*625c; ἐνιαυτούς τε καὶ ὥρας καὶ μῆνας Id.*Phlb.*30c; σύνοδον Plu.*Ant.*71: in bad sense, *concoct*, ψευδῆ κατηγορίαν Aeschin.2.183:—Pass., ψυχὴ συντεταγμένη σώματι *organically united with*, Pl.*Lg.*903d; ὀλιγαρχικῶς συντετ. Arist.*Pol.*1317a6; σημεῖον πολιτείας συντεταγμένης of an *organized* state, ib.1272b30; Τροιζήνιοι σ. εἰς τοὺς Ἀχαιούς *joined* the Achaean League, Plu.*Arat.*24; οἱ συντεταγμένοι *the conspirators*, X.*HG*3.3.7:—Med., *arrange for oneself*, i.e. *make one's own plans* of life, Hp. *VM*10: also, *get* matters *organized* or *arranged*, or simply *ordain, settle*, τὰ νόμιμα ἡμῖν συνετάξατο [ὁ νομοθέτης] Pl.*Lg.*626a, cf. 625e, 781b; τὴν περὶ τοὺς νέους ἐπιμέλειαν Lycurg.106; καταστήσαντες.. εἰς τὴν προγεγραμμένην κώμην Τεβτῦνειν οὗ ἐὰν Ἀρίστων συντάσσηται wherever A. may *arrange* to accept delivery, *PSI*10.1098.24 (i B.C.). 2. of taxation, *assess*, *IG*1².63.17; σύνταγμα συντάξας εἰς ἑκατὸν ταλάντων πρόσοδον Aeschin.3.95:—Pass., *to be organized for paying contributions*, ib.97, D.13.3,9; but τὸ συντεταγμένον the *assessed sum*, Arist.*Pol.*1330a7:—Med., *agree to such assessment*, D.27.7, cf. 28.8; τι εἰς τροφὴν συνταξάμενος ἐδίδου gave *an allowance* for food, Aeschin.1.102: cf. σύνταξις II. 3. 3. *compose* or *compile* a narrative or book, Plb.2.40.4, Plu.*Brut.*4:—Med., Pl.*Phdr.*263e, Plb.1.3.8, Gal.19.221: abs., *write a book*, Plb.9.2.2; οἱ τὰ Ῥωμαϊκὰ συνταξάμενοι D.H.4.7; σ. ὑπόθεσιν *treat of*.., Id.*Comp.*4:—Pass., προοίμιον συντεταγμένον εἴς τι Pl.*Lg.*930e, cf. Aeschin.3.201. 4. c. inf., *ordain, prescribe, order*, δασμοὺς ἀποφέρειν τινάς X.*Cyr.*8.6.8, cf. Aeschin.2.22, *PEnteux.*27.13, 84.10,16 (iii B.C.), *PCair.Zen.*28.1, al. (iii B.C.), Plb.3.50.9, *PStrassb.*100.21 (ii B.C.): without inf., συντάξαντος ἡμῖν Ἀμύντου *PCair.Zen.*27.1 (iii B.C.); καθὼς συνέταξεν αὐτοῖς ὁ Ἰησοῦς v.l. for προσέταξεν in *Ev.Matt.*21.6. b. c. acc. rei, *prescribe*, of a physician, θεραπείαν Plu.*Per.*13, cf. D.S.1.70, Sor.1.60; also σ. τί πρῶτον οἰστέον Alex.186.3:—Pass., τοιαύτης ἐπιμελείας συνταχθείσης Sor.2.48: generally, *to be prescribed* or *ordained*, ταὐτὸν περὶ τὰς ἡδονὰς συντεταγμένον ἐν τοῖς νόμοις Pl.*Lg.*634b, cf. 817e; ταῦτα τῷ ναυάρχῳ συνετάχθη Epist.ap.D.18.78; ἄν τις πόλις μὴ ἀποστείλῃ τὴν δύναμιν τὴν συντεταγμένην *IG*4²(1).68.95 (Epid., iv B.C.). 5. Gramm., *combine* in interpretation, τοῖς προειρημένοις συντάττουσι ταῦτα Gal.15.897, cf. 16.533 (Pass.); *construct* or *construe* a word, τὰ ἀρρενικὰ τοῖς θηλυκοῖς D.H.*Amm.*2.11, cf. A.D.*Conj.*218.10; τὴν ἐν πρόθεσιν μετὰ γενικῆς Greg.Cor. p.44S.:—Pass., A.D.*Pron.*69.15, D.L.7.64; συντάσσεται ἀπὸ γενικῆς εἰς αἰτιατικήν (e.g. ἀφαιρῶ σοῦ τόδε) Thom.Mag.p.33R.; cf. συντακτός, σύνταξις I.4. b. Pass., *to be added to*, c. dat., A.D.*Pron.*38.1; of syllables, τὸ σκλα καὶ στρα συντετάξεται Id.*Synt.*313.16. III. Med., *agree together*, πάντα συνταξάμενοι καὶ οὐδὲν ἀπὸ ταὐτομάτου τούτων ἔπραττον D.24.27; συνταξάσθω πρὸς αὐτοὺς.. πόσον δεῖ ἔλαιον.. πωλεῖν *PRev.Laws* 47.13 (iii B.C.); σ. πρὸς ἀλλήλους Plb.3.67.1: c. inf., συνετάττετο κοινῇ πρεσβεύειν D.19.13:—Pass., κατὰ τὸ συντεταγμένον in accordance with *what had been arranged*, Plb.3.42.9, 3.43.6; πραξάντων τὸ συνταχθὲν Id.8.28.10; κελεῦσαι προελθόντα στῆναι πρὸ τῆς πόλεως ἐπὶ τὸν συνταχθέντα τάφον the *pre-arranged* tomb, Id.9.17.2; cf. σύνταξις II. 2. IV. Med., *take leave of* one, *bid* him *farewell*, τινι Charito 8.4, Men.Rh. p.430S., *AP*9.171 (Pall.); cf. ἀποτάσσω IV.

**συντᾰτ-έον**, (συντείνω) *one must strive earnestly*, Pl.*Ep.*340c. **-ικός**, ή, όν, *astringent*, Gal.10.303; τὸ σ. Id.18(1).702.

**συνταυροτάφος** [ᾰ], ὁ, *fellow-burier of bulls*, *POxy.*395 (i A.D.).

**σύντᾰφος**, ον, *buried in the same grave*, Pl.*Lg.*873d.

**συντᾰχύνω**, *hurry on*, τὴν ἐπιχείρησιν Hdt.3.71; τὸν βίον Id.2.133: abs., Id.3.72, Orib.46.24.2. 2. intr., *correspond in rapidity of its course*, of a disease, Ruf.*Ren.Ves.Praef.*2.

**συντείνω**, *strain, draw tight, brace up*, σ. [τὰ ὀστᾶ], opp. χαλάω, Pl.*Phd.*98d: metaph. of the mind, E.*Hipp.*257 (anap.); ἁρμονίαις σ. τὰς ψυχάς Pl.*Lg.*800d:—Pass., *to be in a state of tension*, Hp. *Art.*8, *Epid.*3.1.δʹ, Sor.2.18, Gal.6.170. 2. *strain to the uttermost, urge on, exert*, ποδὸς ὁρμάν E.*El.*112 (lyr.); δράμημα κυνῶν Id.*Ba.*872 (lyr.); λόχιαι στερρὰν παιδείαν Μοῖραι συντείνουσι, of the pains of childbirth, Id.*IT*207 (lyr.); σαυτόν Pl.*Euthphr.*12a:—Pass., *strain all one's powers*, πᾶν ποιεῖν συντεινομένους Id.*R.*504e; συντεταμένον καὶ σπουδάζοντα Id.*Euthd.*288d; γνώμῃ συντεταμένῃ with *earnest, serious* purpose, X.*Oec.*2.18. 3. intr. in Act., *exert oneself, strive*, Pl.*Sph.*239b; τοῖς τόξοις Hp.*Aër.*20; τῷ πνεύματι Arist.*APr.*893a2; *hasten*, δρόμῳ εἰς τὸ ἄστυ Plu.*Nic.*30; of things, *become intense*, συντείνοντος τοῦ κακοῦ Id.*Dio* 45. II. *direct earnestly* to one point, πάντα τὰ αὑτοῦ εἰς τοῦτο Pl.*R.*591c, cf. *Grg.* 507d; ἐπὶ πόλεμον τὰς αὑτῶν σ. πόλεις Id.*Plt.*308a:—Pass., συντετάσθαι πρὸς τὸ μέλλον ταῖς φροντίσι, of mental *tension* or *anxiety*, Plu.2.473c. 2. intr., *direct all one's powers to* one object, *to be bent upon*, ἐπὶ τὸ μαθεῖν.. τὸν λόγον Pl.*Lg.*641e; and of things, *tend* or *contribute towards*.., c. inf., σφάξαι σ' Ἀργείων.. συντείνει.. γνώμα E.*Hec.*189 (lyr.); τὸ δ' ἐμοὶ δοκεῖ πάντα εἰς ταὐτόν τι συντείνειν Pl.*Cra.*403b; τὰ συντείνοντα πρὸς τὸ ζῆν καλῶς Athenio 1.43, cf. Ael.*Tact.*2.1; πάντα τὰ συντείνοντα εἰς τὴν λειτουργίαν *POxy.*904.5 (v A.D.); ἕν, εἰς ὃ πάντα σ. D.10.54 vulg. (τείνει codd. opt., ἕν om. S); εἰς ἀδικίαν ἢ δικαιοσύνην, etc., Arist.*EN*1127a34, cf. Epicur.*Ep.*2 p.35 U.; εἰς ταὐτὸν κεφάλαιον Gal.15.613; ἐπὶ τὴν ἀνδρείαν Pl.*Plt.*309b; πρὸς ἀρετήν Id. *Lg.*731a, Isoc.15.67, cf. Epicur.*Ep.*1 p.29U.; πρὸς τὸν σκοπόν, etc., Arist.*EN*1144a25, al. III. in physical sense, *lead to*, εἰς μίαν τινὰ ἰδέαν σ. Pl.*Tht.*184d; σ. πρὸς τὸν ἄνω τόπον, πρὸς τὴν καρδίαν, Arist.*Juv.*469a16,20; σ. αἱ ἀδένες ἐπὶ σφᾶς τὸ ἄλλο σῶμα Hp.*Gland.* 2. IV. Pass., *to be exasperated* against, πρός τινα *Com.Adesp.* 22.56D.

**συντειχίζω**, *help to build a wall* or *fortification*, Th.4.57, X.*Cyr.*3.2.24. 2. *enclose within the same wall*, τὴν παλαιὰν πόλιν πρὸς τὴν ὑπάρχουσαν *AJP*56.361 (Colophon, iv B.C.).

**συντεκμαίρομαι**, *conjecture from signs* or *symptoms*, Hp.*Prog.*2; *examine carefully*, Id.*Aph.*1.9; συντεκμηράμενοι ἡνίκ' ἂν φοντο.. *calculating the time* when.., X.*HG*7.1.15; ξυντεκμηράμενοι *having calculated the distance*, Th.2.76, cf. X.*Smp.*2.8. 2. *take into account also*, τὴν δύναμιν τοῦ φαρμάκου Sever.*Clyst.*42.

**συντεκμηριόομαι**, = foreg., Eun.*VS* p.455B.

**συντεκνοποιέω**, *breed children with*, τινι X.*Mem.*2.2.5.

**σύντεκν-ος**, ὁ, ἡ, *foster-brother* or *-sister*, *BMus.Inscr.*1010 (Cyzicus). **-όω**, *breed*, ζῷα Ar.*Th.*15. II. *produce* or *rear children with* another, *Stud.Pont.*38 (Phazimonitis), 85 (ibid.), 159 (Amasia).

**συντεκταίνομαι**, *help in constructing* or *making*, τὸ πᾶν Pl.*Ti.*30b, cf. 45b. 2. metaph., *help in devising*, εἴ τινά οἱ σὺν μῆτιν ἀμύμονα τεκτήναιτο Il.10.19; σ. δόλον A.R.1.1295.

**συντελέθω**, = συντελέω III, *belong to*, Pi.*P.*9.57.

❊ **συντέλεια**, ἡ, (συντελέω II) *joint contribution for the public burdens*, χρημάτων σ. ποιῆσαι D.18.237; σ. φόρου D.C.42.6; εἰς σ. ἄγειν τὰς χορηγίας, i.e. to leave the choregia to be *defrayed by subscription*, not by a single person, D.20.23; μικρᾶς σ. ἑκάστῳ γιγνομένης ibid.; πρὸς σ. χρημάτων Arist.*Rh.Al.*1423b1. 2. metaph., Pl.*Lg.*905b; ἡ παρὰ τοῦ διδασκάλου σ., i.e. *instruction*, Aristid.2.226 J. 3. = *collatio*, (*compulsory*) *provision* of recruits, εἰς τὴν τῶν τειρώνων σ. Keil-

Premerstein *Dritter Bericht* p.87 (inc. loc.); συντελείας βουργαρίων.. ἄνεσιν prob. in *SIG*880.52 (Pizus, iii A.D., cf. *JRS*8.26 sqq.). II. at Athens, *a body of citizens who contributed jointly* to bear public burdens (cf. συντελής 1), Antipho *Fr.*56; αἱ σ. τῶν τριηράρχων Decr. ap.D.18.105, cf. 106. 2. generally, *company*, ὦ ξυντέλεια (sc. θεῶν), of the gods, who separately were called τέλειοι, A.*Th.*251, cf. Sch. ad loc. 3. *union of communities* grouped together or united to a larger state, Plb.5.94.1, D.S.5.80, Plu.*Comp.Phil.Flam.* 1, Paus.7.15.2, *OGI*565.13 (Oenoanda). III. *the consummation* of a scheme, opp. ἐπιβολή, Plb.1.3.3, cf. 3.1.5; σ. ἐπιτεθεικὼς τοῖς ἔργοις Id.11.33.7; σ. σχεῖν, λαμβάνειν, Id.1.4.3, 4.28.3, cf. *SIG*695.13 (Magn. Mae., ii B.C.), Plu.*Per.*13; εἰς σ. ἐλθεῖν Plb.2.40.6; ἡ σ. τῆς ἐπιβολῆς Id.5.32.3; ἡ σ. τοῦ ἀγῶνος *IG*7.2712.78, 82 (Acraephia); τοῦ πολέμου *OGI*327.6 (Pergam., ii B.C.), Plb.4.28.5; τῶν ἔργων *PPetr.*3 p.109 (iii B.C.); τὰν τῶν μυστηρίων καὶ τᾶν θυσιᾶν σ. *IG*5(1).1390.184 (Andania, i B.C.); καταθύμιος λογισμῶν συντέλεια Vett.Val.173.11; *completion, end*, τοῦ ἐνιαυτοῦ Lxx *De.*11.12; τοῦ διεληλυθότος ἔτους *POxy.*1270.42 (ii A.D.); αἰῶνος *Ev.Matt.* 13.39; ποιῆσαι εἰς σ. make *an end of*, Lxx *Ez.*20.17; ἀνέβη σ. τῆς πόλεως εἰς οὐρανόν ib.*Jd.*20.40; *full realization*, τῶν τελῶν Phld.*Rh.*2.86 S. IV. *unjust gain*, Lxx 1*Ki.*8.3; = κακία, Hsch. V. in Grammar, *completed action*, Demetr.*Eloc.*214, A.D.*Synt.*205.14, *EM* 472.23. VI. = ἐντελέχεια, *reality*, Ocell.2.3.

**συντελει-όω**, *complete*, τὰ ἔργα *TAM*2.396 (Patara, i A.D.):— Pass., *to be completed*, Ptol.*Tetr.*209, Vett.Val.243.14, 266.35; **συντελεόομαι** f.l. in Polyaen.8 *Prooem.* **-ωσις**, εως, ἡ, *discharge of obligation in full*, *PFlor.*6.17 (iii A.D.). II. *a completed action*, opp. παράτασις, A.D.*Synt.*71.1.

**συντελεσιουργία**, ἡ, *completion*, Poll.9.157.

**συντέλεσ-ις**, εως, ἡ, = foreg., τοῦ ναοῦ *SIG*282 II 7 (Priene, iv B.C.); τῶν τειχῶν v.l. in Plb.22.7.6. **-μα**, ατος, τό, *joint contribution*, Al.*Esdr.*4.13, *PLips.*64.39 (iv A.D.). II. *completion*, Brut.*Ep. Praef.* III. *solution* of a problem, ἡ τετρακτὺς πρὸς πολλὰ διατείνει φυσικὰ σ. Porph.*VP*20. **-τής**, οῦ, ὁ, *member of a land-owners' union which is responsible for the collection and payment of its taxes*, *Cod.Just.*1.4.18, Just.*Nov.*163.1, *PSI*4.283.7 (vi A.D.). **-τικός**, ή, όν, *capable of causing* or *effecting*, τινος Epicur.*Nat.*14.4, Phld.*Rh.*2.49 S., Ptol.*Harm.*1.15. II. Gramm., ὁ σ. (sc. χρόνος) the tense *of completion*, viz. pf. and aor., opp. παρατατικός, S.E.*M.*10.91, 92, 101. Adv. **-κῶς** ib.101. **-τρια**, ἡ, fem. of συντελεστής, *PMasp.* 325 iv *A* 12 (vi A.D.), Priscian.*Inst.*5.7.40.

**συντελευτάω**, *die along with*, τοῖς βασιλεῦσι D.S.3.7, cf. Chor.35.51, 87 F.-R.

⊛ **συντελ-έω**, fut. -έσω *SIG*1044.27 (Halic., iv/iii B.C.), Att. συντελῶ *BCH*54.270 (Rhamnus, iii B.C.):—*bring to an end, complete*, σ. τὴν δαπάνην *make up the whole* expense, D.14.20; σ. εἰς τὰ ἑκατὸν ἅρματα *make up the number* of the chariots to one hundred, X.*Cyr.*6.1.50; of a workman, σ. γεῖσον *finish* it *off*, Lys.*Fr.*185 S. (Pass.), cf. *IG*1².372 *E* 14; στέφανον Test.ap.D.21.22; ναῦς Plb.1.21.3 (Pass.); σ. ταχὺ *finish* it in a hurry, Alex.149.12; σ. τὴν ἐπίνοιαν *accomplish* it, Plb.4.81.3; λόγον Lxx *Is.*10.22, Gal.15.59:—Med., Plb.1.9.6, *PFay.*12.8 (ii B.C.), D.S.1.59; ἵνα περὶ ὧν καταπέπλευκας συντετελεσμένος.. ἀναπλεύσῃς *PSI*6.614.9 (iii B.C.), cf. Plb.5.100.9:— Pass., *Inscr.Délos* 502 *A* 15 (iii B.C.), *PCair.Zen.*124.7 (iii B.C.), D.S.12.26, *Ev.Marc.*13.4, etc.; λιθάρια συντετελεσμένα *PHolm.*5.4. b. Act., c. inf., σ. καταφαγεῖν *finish* eating, Lxx *Ge.*43.2, cf. *Si.*24.28: c. part., ib.*Nu.*4.15, 3*Ki.*8.54. c. *perpetrate*, βίαιόν τι *BGU*1818.21 (i B.C.):—Med., περὶ ὧν συντετέλεσται, τυχεῖν αὐτὸν.. τιμωρίας *PEnteux.*50.7 (iii B.C.), cf. *Klio* 16.150 (Delph., ii B.C.):— Pass., *SIG*684.5 (Dyme, ii B.C.), *BGU*1762.7, al. (i B.C.). 2. Pass., *to be caused, brought about*, freq. in Epicur., πλεοναχῶς σ., of a plurality of causes, *Ep.*2 p.37 U., cf. p.50 U.; simply, *occur, happen*, τὰς συντελουμένας.. φάσεις Ptol.*Phas.* p.10 H. 3. *celebrate* or *hold* sacred rites, ἁγιστείας Pl.*Ax.*371d; θυσίας *SIG*1044.27, al., *Supp. Epigr.*1.366.29 (Samos, iii B.C.); τὴν ἡμέραν Epicur.*Fr.*217; τὸν ἀγῶνα, τὴν πανήγυριν, D.S.11.29, 17.16; τὰ Ἴσθμια Plu.*Ages.*21; τοὺς κόσμους παρὰ τῇ Μητρί *Michel* 537 (Cyzicus, i B.C.):—Pass., θυσία τῷ Διὶ σ. Arist.*Mir.*844ᵃ35, cf. *PEnteux.*6.6 (iii B.C.). 4. *make an end of, destroy*, Lxx 2*Ch.*20.23. II. *pay towards common expenses, contribute*, σ. ἑξήκοντα τάλαντα Aeschin.3.95; but mostly without the sum expressed, ἐν ταῖς εἰσφοραῖς σ. εἰς τὸν πόλεμον *contribute* by payment of the εἰσφοραί towards the war, D.20.28. 2. generally, *contribute*, πρὸς or εἰς τὴν γένεσιν, Arist.*GA*715ᵃ12, *HA* 509ᵃ29; πρὸς μίαν ἀρχὴν Id.*PA*669ᵇ19; πρὸς ἓν ἅπαντα σ. Id.*EN*1096ᵇ 28; εἰς ἀνάδοσιν τροφῆς Gal.15.196: also c. dat., *to be of service, be profitable, help*, τῷ βίῳ Alex.271; τῇ λεπτυνούσῃ διαίτῃ Gal.*Vict.Att.* 6; τινὶ πρός τι Luc.*Alex.*36:—Pass., *to be contributed*, εἴς τι Arist. *GA*725ᵃ5, al. 3. ὧν οὐδὲν εἰς τὴν ἐξαλλαγὴν σ. τῆς ἐπιμελείας none of which *make for (require)* a change of treatment, Sor.2.17. III. since at Athens all citizens were classed acc. to their rateable property, and the *contributions* to which they were liable, σ. εἰς.. meant *to belong to* a class, *be counted* in it (cf. τελέω II. 3), σ. εἰς ἄνδρας Isoc.12.212; εἰς τοὺς νόθους D.23.213; ἐς τὸ μετοικικόν, ἐς τὸ συνέδριον, Luc.*Bis Acc.*9, *Deor.Conc.*15: c. dat., σ. τῷ χορῷ Alciphr.3.71. 2. σ. ἐς Ἀθήνας, ἐς Ὀρχομενόν, εἰς τὸ Ἀρκαδικόν, used of communities united in or to a state, Th.2.15, 4.76, X.*HG*7.4.12: c. dat., σ. Θηβαίοις Isoc.14.8, cf. Plu.*Arat.*34: abs., Μακεδονίας καὶ τῶν συντελούντων *the tributaries*, ib.54: cf. sq. III. **-ής**, ὁ, ἡ, and **-ής**, ές, *joining in the payment of taxes*, etc., *contributor*, Antipho *Fr.*56; ἕκτος καὶ δέκατος σ. D.18.104; οὐδὲ τριηράρχους ἔτ' ὠνόμαζον ἑαυτούς, ἀλλὰ συντελεῖς ibid.; διακοσίους καὶ χιλίους πεποιήκατε σ. Id.21.155, cf. Poll.8.156; σ. τινός *with* another, *IG*2².1631.525, al.: c. dat., αἵδε τῶν πόλεων Χερρονησίοις συντελεῖς οὖσαι ἀπέδοσαν ib.1².214.24: metaph., Πάρις.., οὔτε σ. πόλις neither Paris nor *his associate* city, A.*Ag.*532; θεοὺς τοὺς συμβώμους καὶ σ. *Sammelb.*7470.7 (iii/ii B.C.). II. generally, *contributory*, ἡ κοιλία καὶ τὰ σ. μόρια Arist. *PA*674ᵃ22: cf. συντελέω II. 2. III. *united to a state*, Σηλυμβρίαν ὡς αὐτοὺς συντελῆ ποιεῖν D.15.26; οἱ συντελεῖς Aristid.1.141 J. IV. τὸ παρῳχημένον καὶ σ. τοῦ χρόνου past and *completed* time, opp. παράτασις, A.D.*Synt.*252.9. **-ικός**, ή, όν, *belonging to* (cf. συντέλεια II. 3, συντελέω III. 2), Πατρεῖς καὶ τὸ μετὰ τούτων συντελικόν Plb.38.16.4; συντελικὰ χρυσία gold *paid by a body of persons paying tax jointly*, *PMasp.*4.15 (vi A.D.); *contributory*, Simp. *in Cat.*373.1; ὅσα σ. τῆς τροπῆς the *effectively completing* parts of the metaphor, Hermog.*Inv.*4.10. II. Gramm., τὸ σ. the *aorist*, Phryn.315, Id.(?) in *PLit.Lond.* 183, Sch.A Il.21.33; διάθεσις σ. prob. in A.D.*Synt.*70.9; περὶ σ. ἀξιωμάτων, title (dub. sens.) of work by Chrysippus, *Stoic.*2.5. Adv. **-κῶς** Sch.A Il.9.578, Sch.T Il.1.600, Apollon.*Lex.* s. v. ἰών. 2. ὁ παρακείμενος καλεῖται ἐνεστὼς σ. the perfect is called the *completed* present, Sch.D.T. p.251 H., cf. Choerob. *in Theod.*2.12 H. 3. στάσις σ., = *conjectura*, Athenaeus ap.Quint.*Inst.*3.6.47. **-ίσκω**, = *transcribo*, Dosith. p.434 K.

**συντέλλω**, = συντελέω, prob. in *SIG*56.4 (Argos, v B.C.).

**συντέλομαι**, pres. with fut. sense, = συνέσομαι, *SIG*527.69 (Drerus, iii B.C.).

⊛ **συντέμνω**, Ion. **-τάμνω** Hdt.7.123: fut. **-τεμῶ**: aor. **-έτεμον**:—*cut down, cut short*, ξ. τὰς πρῴρας ἐς ἔλασσον Th.7.36; σ. χιτῶνας *cut out, shape* them, X.*Cyr.*8.2.5; συντέμνει δ' ὅρος ὑγρᾶς θαλάσσης the sea *cuts short, terminates* (my realm), A.*Supp.*258; σ. τὰς πλεκτάνας *cut* them *off*, Alex.187, cf. 84. 2. metaph., εἰς ἕν.. πάντα τὰ μέλη ξυντεμῶ Ar.*Ra.*1262; τὸν ἐνιαυτὸν σ. εἰς μῆν' ἕνα Philippid.25.1; τιμὰς ξ. *abridge* them, A.*Eu.*227; πόνους E.*Rh.*450:—Med., πάντα τοι ξυντέμνεται Κύπρις.. βουλεύματα S.*Fr.*941.16. 3. esp. of expenses, σ. τὴν μισθοφοράν Th.8.45; σ. τὰς δαπάνας εἰς τὰ καθ' ἡμέραν *cut down* one's expenses to one's daily wants, X.*Hier.*4.9:—Pass., εἰ.. ἐς εὐτέλειάν τι ξυντέτμηται (v. εὐτέλεια II) Th.8.86; συντμηθῆναι τὴν σύνταξιν that my allowance *has been cut down*, *PCair.Zen.*577.11 (iii B.C.). 4. of persons, *cut* them *off*, συντέμνουσι γὰρ θεῶν.. τοὺς κακόφρονας Βλάβαι S.*Ant.*1103. 5. *divide logically*, Pl.*Sph.* 227d, *Plt.*261a. II. of speech, ἐν βραχεῖ πολλοὺς λόγους Ar. *Th.*178, cf. Aeschin.2.31; σύντεμνέ μοι τὰς ἀποκρίσεις καὶ βραχυτέρας ποίει Pl.*Prt.*334d: then (λόγον being omitted), *cut the matter short, speak briefly*, ὡς δὲ συντέμω E.*Tr.*441; ἅπαντα συντεμὼν φράσω Id. *Hec.*1180; σύντεμνε *cut short, make an end*, Mnesim.3.4; οἶνον εἰπὲ συντεμών Antiph.52.12; συντεμόντι, like συνελόντι εἰπεῖν, *in brief*, Anaxil.22.30: also σ. (sc. τὴν ὁδόν) *cut the way short, cut across*, σ. ἀπ' Ἀμπέλου ἄκρης ἐπὶ Καναστραῖον ἄκρην Hdt.7.123. III. intr., τοῦ χρόνου συντάμνοντος as the time *became short*, Id.5.41. IV. *hew out*, καινὴν.. καὶ ἐρήμην ἀνοδίαν Porph.*Chr.*1. V. *cut together, join by an incision*, ἵνα συντμηθῇ πάντα καὶ γένηται μία ἕλκωσις Heliod.ap.Orib.44.23.69.

**συντερᾰτεύομαι**, *tell marvels together*, Eust.ad D.P.525.

**συντερετίζω**, *whistle an accompaniment*, Thphr.*Char.*19.10.

**συντερμονέω**, *march with, border on*, χώρᾳ Plb.1.6.4, 2.21.9.

**συντέρμων**, ον, gen. ονος, *bordering on, close together*, *APl.*4.185.

**συντέρπομαι**, Pass., *join in feeling delight*, Sch.Ar.*Lys.*227: metaph. of metals, Zos.Alch. p.153 B.

**συντεταγμένως**, Adv., (συντάσσω) *in set terms*: v. sq.

**συντετᾰμένως**, Adv., (συντείνω) *earnestly, eagerly, vigorously*, Ar. *Pl.*325, Pl.*Ap.*23e, *R.*499a, *Phlb.*59a (in Pl. always with v. l. συντεταγμένως).

**συντετελεσμένως**, Adv. *completely*, Phld.*Ir.* p.72 W.

**συντετηρημένως**, Adv. *with utmost care*, *UPZ*20.30 (ii B.C.).

**συντετμημένως**, Adv., (συντέμνω) *concisely*, Sch.Th.8.53, Tz.*H.*2.489.

**συντετραίνω**, A.*Ch.*451 (lyr.), Hdt.2.11, later **συντίτρημι**, pres. inf. **-τιτράναι** Gal.5.238, 3 sg. pres. imper. Pass. **-τιτράσθω** Heliod. ap.Orib.44.23.59: fut. **-τρήσω**: aor. **-έτρησα**: pf. Pass. **-τέτρημαι**:— *unite by a boring, channel*, or *passage*, ἀλλήλοισι σ. τοὺς μυχοὺς Hdt. 2.11 (cf. παραλλάσσω II. 1); τὴν τοῦ ποτοῦ διέξοδον συνέτρησαν εἰς τὸν μυελὸν *they carried* the passage *through* into the marrow, Pl.*Ti.* 91a, cf. *Criti.*115d; τοῖς συντρήσασιν εἰς τὰ τῶν πλησίον who *have run a gallery* into their neighbours' mines, D.37.38:—Pass., [οἱ οὐρητῆρες] ἐς τὰ αἰδοῖα συντέτρηνται *open directly into*.., Hp.*Aër.*9 (interpol.); εἰς ἀλλήλους -τετρῆσθαι Pl.*Phd.*111d; [φάραγγες] συντετρημέναι πρὸς ἀλλήλας D.S.3.44; εἰς ὃν ἡ θάλαττα συντέτρητο Pl. *Criti.*115e; συντετρῆσθαι τὰ πελάγη Str.7.5.9; συντέτρηνται [αἱ κοιλίαι] πρὸς τὸν πλεύμονα Arist.*HA*513ᵃ35; συντετρῆσθαι τὴν ὄσφρησιν τῷ στόματι Id.*Pr.*907ᵇ28, cf. 963ᵇ7; οὐκ εἰς τὴν ψυχήν, ἀλλ' εἰς τὴν γλῶτταν ἡ ἀκοὴ συντέτρηται Plu.2.502d; συντετρημένων τῶν μυκτήρων *connected by a passage*, Arist.*Resp.*474ᵃ21. II. metaph., δι' ὤτων δὲ συντέτραινε μῦθον *let* the words *pierce in* through thy ears, A. l. c.

**σύντευξις**, εως, ἡ, (συντυγχάνω) *coincidence*, M.Ant.3.11, Phot.

**συντεχν-άζω**, *help in contriving*, ἀπάτην Plu.*Tim.*10: abs., *join in plots with*, τινι Id.*Marc.*20. **-άομαι**, Med., *assist in the art* of shipbuilding, Id.*Demetr.*43. **-ία**, ἡ, *guild*, λινουργῶν, ἡλοκόπων, *IGRom.*3.896 (Anazarbus, ii A.D.), Judeich *Altertümer von*

Hierapolis 133. **-ῑτεύω**, *help to elaborate*, σοι τοὺς νόμους Heraclit. *Ep.*7. ® **-ίτης** [ῑ], ου, ὁ, = sq., *Gloss.*, v.l. in *Act.Ap.*19.25. **-ος**, ὁ, ἡ, *fellow-craftsman*, Ar.*Fr.*183: c. gen., Id.*Ra.*763; Athena is the σύντεχνος of Hephaestus, Pl.*Plt.*274c:—as Adj. **σύντεχνος**, ον, πῦρ Ael.*Fr.*101.

**σύντηγμα**, ατος, τό, *waste product*, used by Arist. (and Thphr.*Lass.* 6, Gal.6.184) to express the humours that permeate the body, but are not regularly either secreted or excreted, difft. from τὰ περιττώματα (v. περίσσωμα), Arist.*GA*724b27, *Somn.Vig.*456b35, *Pr.*864a18; apparently of a morbid or abnormal kind, τὸ ἀποκριθὲν.. ὑπὸ τῆς παρὰ φύσιν ἀναλύσεως Id.*GA* l.c.

**συντηκ-τικός**, ή, όν, *able to liquefy*, τὸ ἁλμυρὸν σ. γλώττης Arist. *de An.*422a19, cf. *Somn.Vig.*456b35, *Resp.*479b21; *liquefactive*, φάρμακα Gal.11.757. II. (from Pass.) *easily liquefied*, Arist.*HA* 622a15. 2. *wasting*, of sick persons, Aret.*SD*1.13, Plin.*HN*28. 125; πυρετὸς σ. Gal.18(2).42. **-τός**, όν, τὰ σ., = τὰ συντήγματα (which is v.l.), Arist.*Mete.*389b8. **-ω**, *fuse into one mass*, [πῦρ] συντῆκον τὴν γῆν Antipho Soph.30; *weld together*, ὑμᾶς σ. καὶ συμφυσῆσαι εἰς τὸ αὐτό Pl.*Smp.*192d; τὰ μόρια γόμφοις σ. Id.*Ti.*43a; συμμιγνύειν καὶ σ. τὰς ψυχάς Plu.2.156c. 2. *dissolve, liquefy*, σ. καὶ διακρίνειν Thphr.*CP*6.13.2; *melt down*, στέαρ *PRev.Laws* 50.17 (iii B.C.); *consume*, αὐτὰ ἑαυτά Arist.*Long.*466b29. 3. metaph., *cause to waste* or *pine away*, ἐμὲ συντήξουσι νύκτες ἡμέραι τε δακρύοις E.*IA*398 (troch.); τὸν πάντα συντήκουσα δακρύοις χρόνον Id.*Med.*25. II. Pass. συντήκομαι, aor. 1 συνετήχθην, aor. 2 συνετάκην [ᾰ]: intr. pf. Act. συντέτηκα:—*to be fused into one mass*, συγχυθέντων καὶ συντακέντων Plu.2.395c; ᾠοῦ λέκιθος τούτοις.. διὰ μέλιτος.. συντακεῖσα Sor.2.13; ἄλειμμα τὸ δι' ἐλαίου.., συντακέντος ὀλίγου κηροῦ Id.1.121: metaph., c. dat., *become absolutely one with*, .. γαμέτας συντηχθεὶς αὔραις.. ἀλόχοιο E.*Supp.*1029 (lyr., dub.l.); κακὸς κακῷ συντέτηκε Id.*Fr.*296; ἀγαθὴ γυνὴ ἀνδρὶ συντέτηκε Id.*Fr.* 909.3; συντακεὶς τῷ ἐρωμένῳ Pl.*Smp.*192e, cf. 183e. 2. *melt away, dissolve, disappear*, [ἴχνη] οὐ ταχὺ συντήκεται X.*Cyn.*8.1; σ. ὑπὸ τοῦ πυρός Pl.*Ti.*83b. 3. metaph., *waste away*, συντήκεσθαι ὑπὸ λιμοῦ Hp.*VM*11, cf. Thphr.*Od.*61(59), Sor.2.45, Gal.6.76; λύπαις, νόσῳ, E.*El.*240, *Or.*34, cf. 283, *Med.*689; πυρετοῖσι Aret.*SD*1.8.

**σύντηξις**, εως, ἡ, *colliquescence*, opp. περίττωμα (cf. σύντηγμα), Arist.*PA*677a13, *GA*726a21, 726b24, Thphr.*CP*1.22.6, *Lass.*1, al.; esp. as a disease, Hp.*Epid.*1.8, *Prog.*12, al., Sor.2.7; τῆς κύστεως (diabetes) Cael.Aur.*TP*3.7: pl., Aret.*SD*1.13. 2. metaph., *sympathy*, Cic.*Att.*10.8.9.

**συντηρ-έω**, *keep* or *preserve closely*, ἑαυτὸν ἀδωροδόκητον Aristeas 209; τὴν ψυχήν μου μὴ φαγεῖν Lxx *To.*1.11; σ. [τὴν γνώμην] παρ' ἑαυτῇ *keep* it *close*, Plb.30.30.5, cf. Lxx *Si.*39.2, *Ev.Luc.*2.19. 2. *preserve, maintain*, of grants or privileges, *SIG*705.48 (Delph., ii B.C.), al., *BGU*1074.2 (i A.D.):—Pass., *IG*12(5).860.44 (Tenos); ἀμφότεροι -οῦνται (sc. ὅ τε οἶνος καὶ οἱ ἀσκοί) *Ev.Matt.*9.17. 3. *observe strictly*, τὸ τῆς φύσεως τέλος Epicur.*Fr.*554; τὰ νόμιμα Aristeas 127; τὰς ὁδοὺς αὐτοῦ Lxx *Si.*2.15; τὴν εὐταξίαν *Arch. Pap.*3.134 (Thera, iii/ii B.C.); τήν τε φιλίαν καὶ τὴν συμμαχίαν *Riv.Fil.*60.60 (Cyrene, ii B.C.); σ. τὸ διάστημα *keep* distance, Ascl. *Tact.*12.11, Ael.*Tact.*42.1. 4. *watch one's opportunity*, συντηροῦντα παίειν Plu.*Marc.*12. 5. *watch over, protect*, τοῖς φυλακίταις (sc. συντάξαι) συντηρῆσαι τὰ.. γενήματα *BGU*1851.8 (i B.C.). **-ησις**, εως, ἡ, *preservation*, *PTeb.*725.9 (ii B.C.), *BGU* 1835.16 (i B.C.), 1*Enoch* 1.8, Gal.1.115; ἡ ἑαυτοῦ σ. Hierocl. p.33 A. **-ητέον**, *one must preserve*, ἐν ὑγιείᾳ τὸν ἄνθρωπον Gal.14. 728. **-ητικός**, ή, όν, *preservative*, Id.1.115; δύναμις Porph. *Antr.*15; *good at keeping things*, Vett.Val.7.12.

**συντίθημι**, used by Hom. only in Med., v. infr.:—Pass. (v. infr.), but σύγκειμαι is more freq. as Pass.:—*place* or *put together*, τὴν οὐρὴν καὶ τὸν σπλῆνα.. συνθεὶς ὁμοῦ Hdt.2.47, cf. 4.67; ὅπλα ἐν τῷ ναῷ X.*HG*2.3.20; ἅπαντα εἰς ἕν E.*IT*1016; ἐν ὀλίγῳ πάντα Id.*Supp.*1126 (lyr.); ὁ πρῶτος συνθεὶς εἰς ταὐτὸν τὰ δύο ταῦτα βιβλίδια Gal.15.109; σ. ἱμάτια, opp. ἀνασείειν, *fold* them *together*, X. *Oec.*10.11; σ. σκέλη, opp. ἐκτείνειν, Id.*Cyn.*5.10; opp. διαιρεῖσθαι, Pl.*Sph.*252b; σ. ἄρθρα στόματος *close* the lips, E.*Cyc.*625; εἰς τὸ οὐλον (αυλον cod.) σ. τὴν κόμην, = *calamistrat*, *Gloss.*:—Pass., τὸ συντίθεσθαι καθ' ὀντινοῦν τρόπον ῥῖγος οὐκ ἀγαθόν ἐστι any sort of *combination* of shivering (with other symptoms), Gal.16.746. 2. technical uses, a. Math., *add together*, of numbers, Hdt.3.95 (Pass.); τό τε ἀρχαῖον καὶ τὸ ἔργον principal and interest, D.27.17, cf. 29.30: Geom., of lines and figures, Archim.*Spir.Praef.*, Papp.70. 4. b. Math. also, of the transformation of a ratio *componendo*, Arist. *EN*1131b8 (Pass.), Euc.5.18, 24 (Pass.). c. Logic, *combine* the terms of a proposition, Arist.*Metaph.*1012a4, 1024b19 (Pass.); also, *use the fallacy of composition* (cf. σύνθεσις I. 2e), Id.*Rh.*1401a24. d. Rhet., *accumulate*, joined with ἐποικοδομεῖν (to form a *climax*), ib.1365a16. e. σ. λόγον *make up* an account, *PHib.*1.48.15 (iii B.C.). II. *put together constructively*, so as to make a whole, πεντηκοντέρους καὶ τριήρεας (as a bridge) Hdt.7.36; λίθους, of builders, Th.4.4, *IG*4²(1).103.59 (Epid., iv B.C.); πλίνθους, ξύλα, X.*Mem.*3.1.7, etc.; τὰ ὄστρακα *IG*4²(1).121.82 (Epid., iv B.C.); τὰ κομισθέντα Sor. 2.64; ἐκ τούτων τὰ μέγιστα.. συνθεὶς τούτον.. τὸν λόγον ποιήσομαι Hippias Eleus 6 D.; συλλαβάς Pl.*Cra.*424e. 2. *construct, frame*, τὸ θνητὸν γένος Pl.*Ti.*69d; ὁ συνθεὶς the *creator*, ib.33d:—Pass., *to be constructed*, of the material universe, opp. διαλύεσθαι, Arist.*Cael.* 304b30. b. σ. τι ἀπό τινος *compose* or *make* one thing *of* or *from* another, Hdt.4.23; τὸ ἐκ τῶν νεῶν καὶ τοῦ πεζοῦ πλῆθος συντιθέμενον Id.7.184; ἐξ ὧν [συλλαβῶν] τὰ ὀνόματα συντίθενται Pl.*Cra.*425a, cf. 434a; συνθεὶς πρᾶγμα πράξει δι' ὀνόματος καὶ ῥήματος Id.*Sph.*262e; εἴδωλον οὐρανοῦ ξυνθεῖσ' ἄπο (Reiske for ὕπο) E.*Hel.*34: metaph., συντιθεὶς γέλων πολύν S.*Aj.*303; δυοῖν ἅμιλλαν ξ. *strive* for two things *at once*, E.*El.*95. 3. *construct* or *frame* a story, συνθέντες λόγον Id.*Ba.*297, cf. Ar.*Ra.*1052 (anap.), Pl.*Phdr.*260b; οἱ τὰς τέχνας τῶν λόγων συντιθέντες Arist.*Rh.*1354a12; *narrate in writing*, τὰ Ἑλληνικά Th.1.97, cf. 21; *compose*, σ. μύθους, ποίησιν, μελῳδίαν, ὀρχησιν, Pl.*R.*377d, *Phdr.*278c, *Lg.*812d, 816c; αἴνιγμα Id.*Ap.*27a; ὁ τὴν ἐνθάδε συνθεὶς ἀνατομήν Gal.15.147:—Pass., pf. συντέθειται ib.797; περὶ ὀλίγας οἰκίας αἱ.. τραγῳδίαι συντίθενται Arist.*Po.*1453a19. 4. Math., of the *synthesis* of a geometrical problem, opp. ἀναλύω, Id. *SE*175a28, Papp.648.13; συντεθήσεται τὸ πρόβλημα οὕτως *the synthesis* of the problem *will proceed* thus, Archim.*Sph.Cyl.*2.1, cf. Apollon. Perg.*Con.*1 *Praef.*, 2.44, al. 5. *frame, devise, contrive*, ὁ συνθεὶς τάδε the *framer* of this plot, S.*OT*401, cf. Th.8.68; ἐξ ἐπιβουλῆς σ. ταῦτα Antipho 5.25; σ. λόγους ψευδεῖς Id.6.9; ψευδεῖς αἰτίας D.25.28; τὴν κατηγορίαν And.1.6, etc.; rarely in good sense, εὖ πρᾶγμα συντεθὲν ὄψεσθε D.18.144. 6. *put together, take in, comprehend*, παιδὸς μόρον A.*Supp.*65 (lyr.); ὕμνυ.. θεῶν συντιθεὶς ἅπαν γένος E.*Med.*747; πάσας συντιθεὶς ψέγει γυναῖκας Id.*Fr.*657, cf. *Hec.* 1184; ἐν βραχεῖ ξυνθεὶς λέγω *putting* things shortly *together*, speaking briefly, S.*El.*673. III. *commit* to a person's *care, deliver* to him for his own use or that of others, *PMich.Zen.*2.3, 14 (iii B.C.), *PCair. Zen.*4.23, 6.11, 64, 299.9, al. (iii B.C.); γνώριζε οὐχ ὑπάρχον παρ' ἡμῖν ἀργύριον τοσοῦτο ὥστε ἱκανὸν συνθεῖναι Πυρρίχῳ *PMich.Zen.*28.18, cf. 32.7, *PSI*4.392.7, 5.524.3, 6.613.8, 7.862.1, *PLille* 15.3 (all iii B.C.); τινὶ ὀστᾶ, ἐπιστολάς, πλῆθος χρυσίου, etc., Plb.5.10.4, 8.17.4, 15. 25.16, cf. 27.7.1, 28.22.3, *IG*12(5).590.12 (Ceos, ii B.C.), 11(4).1056. 4 (Delos, ii B.C., cf. *Jahresh.*24.171), *OGI*345.11 (Delph., i B.C.). 2. αὐτοὶ δ' ἔνοχοι εἴημεν τῷ ὅρκῳ ὁπηνίκ' ἂν εὖ συνθῶμεν perh. as soon as we have duly *delivered* (or *executed*) this declaration, *BGU*1738.32 (i B.C.); συνθεὶς τούτους μου τοὺς λιβέλλους ἐπιδίδωμι τῇ σῇ λαμπρότητι *PLond.*3.1000.7 (vi A.D.). IV. *collect, conclude, infer*, Plb. 28.17.14, Arr.*Ind.*34.

B. Med. συντίθεμαι, used by Hom. only in aor. 2 and in signf. I: I. *put together for oneself*, i.e. *observe, give heed to*, σύνθετο θυμῷ βουλήν Il.7.44; φρεσὶ σύνθετο θέσπιν ἀοιδήν Od.1.328; ἐμεῖο δὲ σύνθεο μῦθον 17.153; συνθέμενος ῥῆμα Pi.*P.*4.277; and, simply, *perceive, hear*, κλαιούσης ὄπα σύνθετο Od.20.92: in Hom. mostly abs., σὺ δὲ σύνθεο do thou *take heed*, Il.1.76, Od.15.318, etc.; σὺ δὲ σύνθεο θυμῷ ib.27. 2. *set in order, organize*, δύναμιν X.*HG*4.8.20; τὰ τῆς πόλεως ib.6.1.17. II. *agree on, conclude* (cf. συνθήκη), ἄνδρεσσι κακοῖς συνθέμενοι φιλίην Thgn.306; συντίθεσθαι συμμαχίην, ὁμαιχμίην τισί, Hdt.2.181, 8.140.α'; τὰς ξυνθήκας ἃς ξυνέθεντο *IG*1².117.4, cf. 116.27, al.; εἰρήνην Isoc.15.109; σ. ναῦλον *agree upon* the fare, X. *An.*5.1.12; ταῦτα συνθέμενοι *having agreed on* these points, Th.3. 114, cf. Ar.*Lys.*178, Plu.*Alc.*31; ξυνέθεσθε κοινῇ τάδε E.*Ba.*807, cf. 808; so τάπερ τῷ Δαρείῳ συνεθήκατο *with* D., Hdt.3.157; σ. Ἴωσι ξεινίην Id.1.27; μισθόν τινι Pl.*Grg.*520c; σ. τι πρός τινα Hdt.7.145, etc.:—Pass., τοῦ συντεθέντος χρόνου *agreed upon*, Pl.*Phdr.*254d. 2. c. inf., *covenant, agree* to do, συνέθευ παρέχειν φωνάν Pi.*P.*11.41 (dub. l.); σ. ἀλλήλοις μήτ' ἀδικεῖν μήτ' ἀδικεῖσθαι Pl.*R.*359a, cf. And. 4.18, Arist.*Pol.*1257a35: c. inf. fut., ξυνέθεντο ἥξειν Th.6.65; σ. τινὶ folld. by inf. fut., συνθέμενοι ἡμῖν.. ἀντιώσεσθαι Hdt.9.7.β', cf. And.1.42: an inf. must be supplied in the phrases, κατὰ (i.e. καθ' ἃ) συνεθήκαντο, καθ' ὅτι ἂν συνθῶνται, etc., Hdt.3.86, Foed.ap.Th.5.18: also σ. ὡς.. Hdt.6.84; ὡς δεῖ ἕκαστα γίγνεσθαι X.*HG*5.4.2. 3. abs., *make a covenant*, ἔβαν συνθέμενοι Pi.*N.*4.75 (constr. uncertain in Alc.*Supp.*5.11): c. dat., Hdt.6.115, X.*An.*1.9.7, *POxy.*1668.12 (iii A.D.); αὐτὸς σαυτῷ συνέθου Pl.*Cra.*435a; συνθέσθαι πρός τινα *come to terms* with him, Decr.ap.D.18.187, *POxy.*908.18 (ii/iii A.D.); περί τινος πρὸς ἀλλήλους D.S.1.98; also, *bet, wager*, Thphr. *HP*9.17.2, Men.*Epit.*288; πρός τινας Plu.*Alc.*8. 4. *vote with, support*, τούτοις Lys.*Fr.*68, cf. Call.*Epigr.*1.14, D.H.*Isoc.*18, Paus. 4.15.2; τοῖς ἀπὸ Ἡροφίλου Sor.2.53; *assent to*, πᾶσι τοῖς προκειμένοις *PFay.*34.20 (ii A.D.); ἵνα μὴ δόξω συνθέσθαι τῇ τοῦ πραγματικοῦ ἀγνοίᾳ *POxy.*78.23 (iii A.D.). 5. *conclude, infer* (cf. A. IV), *Stoic.*2.63, Phld.*Sign.*2, al.:—Pass., τὰ ὕστερον -τεθησόμενα ib.28.

**συντίκτω**, *procreate together*, ἡ φύσις ἑκάστῃ ἡλικίῃ τὰ οἰκεῖα ξ. Aret.*CD*1.4; ἐκ γενετῆς συντίκτεται αὐτοῖς τὰ σίνη Sch.Ptol.*Tetr.* p.139bis.

**συντίλλω**, *pluck as well*, *AP*12.27 (Stat. Flacc., Pass.).

**συντῑμ-άω**, *honour together* or *alike*, Lys.31.31 (Pass.); τινι *with* another, Apollod.Hist.147 J. (Pass.). II. Med., *value* or *estimate*, συνετιμήσανθ' ὑπὲρ ἐμοῦ ταύτην τὴν εἰσφορὰν *they fixed* this *as the estimate of* my contribution, D.27.8, cf. 28.11, *PPetr.*2 p.83, al. (iii B.C.), etc.:—Pass., ὅθεν περ.. συνετιμήθη τὰ περὶ τὸν σῖτον and that is how *prices were rigged*, D.56.8. ® **-ησις**, εως, ἡ, *valuation*, *PRev.Laws* 24.11 (iii B.C.), *PCair.Zen.*300.3 (iii B.C.), Lxx *Le.*27.18, 4*Ki.*12.4, *PGnom.*70 (ii A.D.), *POxy.*1764.7 (iii A.D.), etc.

**συντῑμωρέω**, *contribute to help* or *cure*, Hp.*Art.*48; τῷ πνεύμονι Aret.*SA*2.7; *conspire together*, σ. ἀλλήλοισι δίψος καὶ ποτόν Id.*SD*2. 2, cf. 2.1, Hp.*Acut.*17.

**συντῐνάσσω**, *shake to the foundations*, Arist.*Mu.*395b35; σὺν δὲ μάχην ἐτίναξε, i.e. closed with him, Theoc.22.90 (v.l. for ἐτάραξε):—Pass., τινασσομένου τινὸς συντ. *to be shaken also*, Plu.2.1089e, cf. Sor.1.46; συντιναγεῖσαν gloss on *concussam*, *POxy.*1099.8 (v A.D.).

**συντίνω** [ῐ], *pay together*, χρέος τινί Them.*Or.*34 p.461 Dind.

**συντῐταίνω**, = συντείνω, Hp.*Mul.*2.110, Aret.*SD*2.11.

**συντίτρημι**, v. συντετραίνω.

**συντιτρώσκω**, *wound*, X.*HG*3.1.18, Plu.*Alex.*63; of ships, *disable*, Id.*Alc.*27. II. *wound at the same time*, τὰ συντιτρωσκόμενα (sc. τοῖς ὀστέοις) νεῦρα Hp.*Fract.*35.

**συντλάω**, = sq., Dor. aor. 2 sg. συνέτλας E.*Alc.*411 (lyr.).

**συντολμάω**, *venture together*, ἕτερά τινα Eun.*VS* p.496 B., cf. *Hist.* p.240 D. (Pass.), Anon.ap.Suid. s. v. φαιάν.

**συντομ-εύω**, *cut short*, Suid. and Zonar. s. v. ἀποσχεδιάσας:—also συντόμησον, for -ευσον or -ισον, Suid. s. v. κεφαλαίωσον. **-ή**, ἡ, *gallery* in a mine, *IG*2².1587.15 (pl.). II. *cutting*, καλάμου *POxy.* 1692.15 (ii A. D.). 2. *cutting down, reduction*, τῆς μισθοφορᾶς D.C. 78.28. III. *edict*, Aq.*Is.*28.22. ❋ **-ία**, ἡ, *conciseness*, λόγων Pl. *Phdr.*267b, cf. Lycurg.102, Arist.*Rh.*1407ᵇ28, Phld.*Rh.*1.176 S., Gal.6.458. II. *simplicity*, in Music, Philoch.66. **-ίζω**, = συντέμνω, Suid. **-ιον**, τό, in pl., = *tessera*, *Gloss.* ❋ **-ος**, ον, *cut short, abridged*, esp. of a road, ἀτραπὸς ξ. a *short* cut, Ar.*Ra.*123; ἡ κατάβασις -ωτέρη Hdt.7.223; τὰ σύντομα τῆς ὁδοῦ Id.1.185, 4.136; -ώτατον *the shortest cut*, Id.2.158, 4.183; τὰ -ώτατα Th.2.97; σύντομος (sc. ὁδός) Hdt.5.17, X.*HG*7.2.13, etc.; -ωτάτη ὁδός Heraclit.(?) 135; τὴν -ωτάτην..ἦγε X.*HG*7.5.21; cf. συντέμνω II, III. 2. of language, *concise, brief*, μῦθος A.*Pers.*698 (troch.), cf. E.*Heracl.*784 (Sup.), etc.; -ώτερος ὁ λόγος Isoc.3.27; σ. λέξις Arist.*Rh.*1414ᵃ25; ἐπεισόδια Id.*Po.*1455ᵇ 16; σ. ἀνάμνησις a *concise* summary, Id.*Rh.Al.*1433ᵇ29; διαλογισμός Epicur.*Ep.*2 p.35 U.; φανῶ..σημεῖα τῶνδε σ. S.*OT*710; τὸ σ. *conciseness*, D.H.*Vett.Cens.*3.1. 3. of other things, -ωτάτη διαπολέμησις Th.7.42; σ. ἐμβολή, παρουσία, etc., Plb.3.78.6, 11.1.1, etc. 4. of stature, *short*, Call.*Epigr.*13. II. Adv. -μως *concisely, briefly*, σ. φημίσασθαι, λέξειν, etc., A.*Ag.*629, *Eu.*585, etc.; πεύσει τὰ πάντα σ. ib.415; ὡς σ. εἰπεῖν Pl.*Ti.*25e: also neut. pl., εἰπέ μοι μὴ μῆκος, ἀλλὰ σύντομα S.*Ant.*446 (v. l. συντόμως): Comp. -ώτερον Isoc.4.64, etc.: Sup. -ώτατα Id.10.30; συντομώτατον εἰπεῖν Alex.245.4: but also -ωτέρως, Is.11.3 (cj.), Epicur.*Ep.*1 p.27 U.; -ωτάτως S.*OC*1579. 2. of Time, *shortly, quickly, immediately*, ἀπολλύναι Hp.*Aph.*3.12, cf. S.*OT*810, *PCair.Zen.*412.9 (iii B. C.), Plb.8.16.7, J.*AJ*7.9.7, Sor.1. 91, etc.: Sup. -ώτατα *Rev.Arch.*22(1925).62 (Callatis, iii B. C.), *PCair.Zen.*28.8 (iii B. C.).

❋ **συντον-άριος**, *pedicularius*, *Gloss.* **-ία**, ἡ, *tension*, of the body or its organs, Hp.*Acut.*(*Sp.*)29, Pl.*Ti.*84e, Arist.*HA*540ᵃ6, al., Thphr.*Lass.*7, Gal.6.174, 7.789; ῥώμη ἢ σ. Id.6.154. 2. *tension of mind, intense application* or *exertion*, opp. ἄνεσις, Arist.*Pol.*1341ᵇ 41, *Rh.*1370ᵃ12; σ. ψυχῆς πρὸς τὸ καταμαθεῖν Pl.*Def.*413d. II. *intensity*, φλεγμονῆς Hp.*Prog.*6 (interpol. in 2 codd., om. Kühl.); φορᾶς Epicur.*Ep.*2 p.45 U. III. *agreement*, τῶν οὐρανίων πρὸς τὰ ἐπίγεια Chrysipp.*Stoic.*2.172.

**συντονολῡδιστὶ** ἁρμονία, ἡ, a musical mode, Pl.*R.*398e, dub. cj. in Poll.4.78 for σύντονος λυδιστί (λ. om. cod. B; σ. καὶ λ. codd. FS).

**σύντονος**, ον, *strained tight*, ἔχειν τὸ σ. to be *strained tight*, X. *Cyn.*6.7; χορδὴν κατατείνας σ. Arist.*GA*787ᵇ23. II. *intense*, κεφαλῆς πόνος Hp.*Coac.*156; ἐπιθυμίαι τε καὶ ἔρωτες Pl.*Lg.*734a; σπουδή, ὄρεξις, Epicur.*Sent.*30, *Fr.*483; ὀργαί, δείματα, Ti.Locr.102e, 104d; βήξ Aret.*SA*2.2. 2. of actions and the like, *impetuous, eager*, συντόνῳ χερὶ λύει τὸν αὑτῆς πέπλον S.*Tr.*923; συντόνῳ..αὐλῶν πνεύματι E.*Ba.*126 (lyr.); σ. δραμήματα ib.1091; τάχος -ώτερον Epicur.*Ep.*2 p.46 U.; οἱ ἀπὸ κραιπάλης γέμοντες συντόνοις κινήσεσιν ἐλέγχονται *jerking* or *violent* movements, Sor.1.26, cf. Gal.6.153, 413 (Comp.); τοῦ χειμῶνος τοὺς περιπάτους καὶ τὰ λοιπὰ γυμνάσια συντονώτερα δεῖ ποιεῖσθαι Diocl.*Fr.*141; σ. πῦρ Arist.*HA*560ᵇ2; σ. πορεία *forced* march, Plb.5.47.4. 3. of persons, *earnest, eager, vehement*, ἀνδρεῖος ὢν..καὶ σ. Pl.*Smp.*203d, cf. Arist.*EN*1125ᵃ15; τὰ περὶ τὴν δίαιταν ἀκριβὴς καὶ σ. Plu.*Cat.Mi.*3. 4. of Music, Μοῦσα σ. *severe*, opp. ἀνειμένη, Pratin.Lyr.5; τῶν Μουσῶν αἱ συντονώτεραι (sc. Heraclitus), opp. μαλακώτεραι, Pl.*Sph.*242e; σ. ἁρμονίαι, opp. ἀνειμέναι καὶ μαλακαί, Arist.*Pol.*1342ᵇ21, cf. ᵃ24, 1290ᵃ27: metaph., συντονωτέραν ποιεῖν τὴν πολιτείαν ib.1304ᵃ21. 5. of sound, also, *high-pitched, acute*, opp. βαρύς, ὀξύς, Id.*GA*787ᵃ1, *Pr.*904ᵇ23; οἰμωγά Tim.*Pers.*181. III. *in harmony, accordant with*, only Ps.-E.*IA*118 (anap.). IV. Adv. -νως *intensely, earnestly*, βλέπειν, μένειν, Pl.*Phdr.*253a, *R.*539d; σ. ἰέναι *eagerly, rapidly*, Id.*Ti.*88a; κτείνοντα συντόνως, of poisons, Diocl. *Fr.*145; τρέχειν, βαδίζειν, Arist.*Pr.*882ᵇ1, *MM*1188ᵇ22 (Comp.), al.; πορεύεσθαι Diocl.*Fr.*142; ὁδοιπορεῖν Gal.16.496; διογκούμενοι σ. οἱ μαστοί Sor.1.76; σ. ζῆν *strictly*, Pl.*R.*619b; ὀργίζεσθαι Phld.*Ir.* p.95 W.: also neut. pl. σύντονα *intently, carefully*, E.*Hipp.*1361 (lyr.): Comp. -ώτερον Arist.*Pol.*1312ᵇ28, etc.; also -ωτέρως Thphr. *Vent.*58: Sup. -ώτατα, τὸ θεῖον θεραπεύων Eun.*VS* p.502 B.

**συντονόω**, *pronounce with the same accent*, in Pass., A.D.*Adv.* 149.3, *Synt.*342.16, al.

**συντοξεύω**, *shoot together*, Eun.*VS* p.465 B.

**σύντοπ-ος**, ὁ, *fellow-resident*, τινος Ps.-Callisth.2.33 (cod. Leid.). **-ωσις**, εως, ἡ, = σύμπτωσις, Simp. *in Ph.*626.28.

**συντορεύω**, *make round*, in Pass., ἁψῖδες -μέναι J.*AJ*8.3.6.

**συντορέω**, *pierce, transfix*, Opp.*H.*4.546 (tm.).

**συντορμόω**, *fasten with tenons*, Ph.*Bel.*75.49 (Pass.).

**συντορῡνάω**, *stir with a spoon*, Archig.ap.Orib.8.46.16.

**συντρᾰγῳδέω**, *help*, or *join in, a solemn piece of acting*, Luc.*Alex.* 12: c. acc. cogn., σ. τὴν ἱκεσίαν Plu.*Them.*24, cf. *Nic.*5. II. *play in accordance with*, τινι Id.2.771a (Pass.).

**συντρᾱνόομαι**, Pass., *to be made dear together*, v.l. in Ph.2.271.

**συντράπεζος** [ᾰ], ον, *messmate*, X.*An.*1.9.31; βίον σ. ἔχειν *live* with one, E.*Andr.*658; of a dog, Babr.74.7.

**συντράχηλος** [ᾰ], ον, *with head sunk between shoulders*, Philostr. *Gym.*35.

**σύντρεις**, οἱ, αἱ, -τρια, τά, *three together, by threes*, σύντρεις αἰνύμενος Od.9.429; κατὰ σύντρεις γωνίας Pl.*Ti.*54e; cf. σύνδυο.

**συντρέπω**, *turn with*, of the tides, θαλασσῶν συντρεπουσῶν ταῖς ἀνατολαῖς καὶ ταῖς δύσεσι (sc. τῆς σελήνης) τὰς ἰδίας ὁρμάς Ptol.*Tetr.* 3:—Pass., ibid., Porph. *in Ptol.*183; *to be turned also*, Aret.*SD*1.5: c. dat., τῷ σαρκιδίῳ M.Ant.10.24; τῷ ἡλίῳ, of plants, Iamb.*Protr.* 21.λη´; συνετέτρεπτο is f. l. for συνετέτριπτο (corr. Reiske) in D.S. 15.17.

**συντρέφω**, *feed together* or *besides*, ἵππον X.*Oec.*5.5, cf. *Mem.*4.3. 6. II. Pass., *to be brought up together*, Pl.*Lg.*752c; ἐν τῷ αὐτῷ X.*Cyr.*6.4.14; συντέθραψαι προσπόλοισι βασιλέως *with* them, E.*Hel.* 1036; τινὶ ἐκ παιδίου Is.9.30: abs., τὰ συντρεφόμενα ζῷα, such as dogs, Arist.*GA*744ᵇ20. 2. of feelings, etc., *to be bred up with, grow up with, become customary* or *familiar*, [τὸ ἡδὺ] ἐκ νηπίου ἡμῖν συντέθραπται Id.*EN*1105ᵃ2; ἐμπεφυκὼς καὶ συντεθραμμένος αὐτῷ ζῆλος Plu. *Alex.*8, cf. *Mar.*14, *AP*12.42 (Diosc.); of diseases, Hp.*Morb.Sacr.* 8, 11. 3. *to be educated in*, ταῖς γεωργικαῖς ἐπιμελείαις, τοῖς μαθήμασι, πονηροῖς ἐθισμοῖς, D.S.1.74, 2.29, 60. 4. *grow by composition* of different substances, *to be organized*, of bodies, Pl.*Phd.*96b, *Ti.*75b; πυρὸς ἐν τόποις τισὶ -τρεφομένου Epicur.*Ep.*2 p.52 U.

**συντρέχεια**, ἡ, *agreement*, *PFlor.*288.2 (vi A. D.).

❋ **συντρέχω**, fut. -δρᾱμοῦμαι X.*An.*7.6.6: aor. 2 συνέδρᾰμον (v. infr.): pf. -δεδράμηκα *PTeb.*48.26 (ii B. C.):—*run together so as to meet* in battle, *encounter*, Πηνέλεως δὲ Λύκων τε συνέδραμον Il.16.335; ξιφέεσσι σ. ib.337; εἰς τὰς χεῖρας σ. Plb.2.33.5; σ. εἰς χεῖράς τινι Plu.*Art.*7: metaph., εἰπὲ τῷ μόρῳ ξυντρέχει say with what death *she has met*, S.*Tr.*880 (lyr.). 2. *assemble, gather together*, Hdt.8.71; ἐς τὴν ὁδόν Id.2.121.δ´; εἰς τὴν ἐκκλησίαν Lycurg.16; *run up to the rescue*, Plu. *Cam.*27; συνδράμετε, Ῥωμαῖοι, Lat. *concurrite*, *POxy.*33 iii 8 (ii A. D.); συνδραμόντων πλειόνων καὶ ἐπιτιμώντων αὐτῷ *PLond.*1.106.19 (ii B. C.); ἐξέπεσον ἐκ τῆς ἰδίας, συνδραμόντων ἐπ' αὐτοὺς τῶν ὁμοεθνῶν, διὰ τὸ παρασπονδῆσαι τοὺς αὑτῶν οἰκείους Plb.2.7.6; of clouds, *gather*, Hdt. 1.87; of liquids, κάθυδρος οὗ κρατὴρ μειλιχίων ποτῶν ῥεύματι συντρέχει *is mingled with*.., S.*OC*160 (lyr.); πρὸς τὴν τῆς ἐκμυζήσεως συναίσθησιν πλεῖον ἐπὶ τοὺς τόπους συντρέχει [τὸ γάλα] Sor.1.77, cf. Gal.15. 512; ὑπερθοῦ..ἵνα καὶ τὰ κουφά σοι συνδράμῃ wait..till your jars *come in* (*accumulate*), *PFlor.*134*.7 (iii A. D.); τῶν ἀργυρίων ὀφλόντων συνδραμεῖν *PLips.*64.13 (iv A. D.); ἔλεγεν..συντρέχειν ἔτη πρὸς τὰ πη´ said the total *amounted to* 88 years, *UPZ*162 v 32 (ii B. C.). 3. *concur, agree*, ἀμφοτέρων ἐς τὠυτὸ αἱ γνῶμαι συνέδραμον Hdt.1.53; συντρέχειν τοῖς κριταῖς *concur in the choice of* judges, X.*Cyr.*8.2.27; μηκέτι τῆς βουλήσεως συνδραμούσης Alex.Aphr. *de An.*73.2. 4. of lines, *run together, meet*, εἰς μίαν βάσιν E.*Fr.*382.12: metaph., δεῖ τινα τέσσαρα συνδραμεῖν εἰς οἴκου σύστασιν Arist.*Fr.*182; κατὰ τὴν πρόθεσιν αὐτῷ συντρεχόντων τῶν πραγμάτων Plb.3.43.11. 5. *concur, coincide*, of points of time, εἰ μὴ τέρμα συντρέχοι βίου A.*Fr.* 362; τοῦ..χρόνου τὸ μῆκος αὐτὸ σ. exactly *coincides*, E.*Or.*1215; εἰς ταὐτὸν τὸ δίκαιον ἅμα καὶ ὁ καιρὸς καὶ τὸ συμφέρον συνδεδράμηκεν D.17. 9, cf. Isoc.6.68; of symptoms, Sor.2.8; impers., συντρέχει εἰς ἓν τόδε *there is a concurrence* in this one point, E.*Fr.*580; σ. τινί *concur* or *coincide with*, S.*Tr.*295; συντρέχει τῇ γνώσει τὸ τερπνόν Epicur. *Sent.Vat.*27 (= Metrod.*Fr.*47); σ. τῇ διαβολῇ *concur in*, *second*, Luc. *DMeretr.*10.4, cf. Mitteis *Chr.*96.11 (iv A. D.); σ. βασιλῆϊ *vie with*, *AP* 7.420 (Diotim.). 6. *run together, shrink up*, μύες Hp.*Fract.*35; τρίχες X.*Cyn.*10.17, cf. Arist.*GA*782ᵇ27; πλεκτάνη σ. εἰς ἑαυτήν Plu. 2.978d; χιτῶνος ἐπανισταμένου καὶ..εἰς ἑαυτὸν σ. (with the respiration) Gal.8.744; εἰς ἑαυτό, of a tumour, *disappear* on pressure, Aët.7.86; συντρέχοντος τοῦ δέρματος διὰ τὴν ἰδίαν μαλακότητα *yielding*, Antyll. or Heliod.ap.Orib.45.18.33. II. *run a race with*, τινι Pl.*Plt.*266c. 2. *run alongside*, X.*Cyr.*2.2.9; συμπαίζωμεν, συνδράμωμεν Philostr.*Ep.*55. 3. *run away together*, σὺν τοῖς λοιποῖς γεωργοῖς *PTeb.* l. c. (unless in signf. I. 2).

**σύντρησις**, εως, ἡ, (συντετραίνω) *connexion by a passage* or *channel*, ἡ ἐκ τῶν μυκτήρων σ. εἰς τὸ στόμα Arist.*HA*495ᵃ25, cf. 507ᵇ27, Heliod.ap.Orib.44.23.59, 76, Gal.16.527; ἡ καρδία τὴν σ. ἔχει πρὸς τὸν πλεύμονα Arist.*Resp.*478ᵃ26; *junction of bore-holes*, Apollod.*Poliorc.* 151.7.

**σύντρητος**, sine expl., Suid.

**συντρῐαινόω**, *shatter with a trident*, Pl.Com.24: generally, *shatter*, στρεπτῷ σιδήρῳ συντριαινώσω πόλιν E.*HF*946.

**συντρῑβή**, ἡ, *crushing*, τινος Hld.10.28. II. = συντριμμός, Lxx *Pr.*16.18, al.; *ruin*, Vett.Val.74.4.

**συντρῑβής**, ές, *living together*, Hsch. 2. *crushed by, worn out by*, καμάτῳ Procop.*Goth.*4.23, cf. *Aed.*1.7.

**συντρίβω** [ῑ], *rub together*, σ. τὰ πυρεῖα *rub* dry sticks *together* to procure a light, Luc.*VH*1.32; *grind*, φάρμακα (for paints) Plu.2.436b (Pass.); κολλύριον *IG*14.966 (Rome). II. *shatter, shiver to atoms*, τοὺς χόας Cratin.187; τὴν χύτραν Ar.*Ach.*284 (troch.), Pl.*Hp.Ma.*290e; τὰ σκευάρια Aeschin.1.59; σ. [τὰς ναῦς] *stave* them *in*, by running them aground, Th.4.11 (v. infr. 2b); τὰ δόρατα, τὴν ἀσπίδα, X.*HG*3.4.14, Men.78 (Pass.); τὰ ποτήρια Eub.62; τὰ ᾠά Arist.*HA*613ᵇ27; θύραν *PTeb.*47.13 (ii B. C.), *BGU*1855.9 (i B. C.):—Pass., συντριβέντων τῶν σκευῶν, of a ship, D.18.194; τὰ συντετριμμένα σκεύη *IG*4²(1).121.81 (Epid., iv B. C.); στοὰ συντετριμμένη ib.12(9).906.9 (Chalcis, iii A. D.); [νῆες] συντετριμμέναι, opp. τελέως διεφθαρμέναι, D.S.13.16,

17. 2. of persons, *beat to a jelly*, E.*Cyc.*705, etc.; of parts of the body, *crush, shiver*, λίθῳ σ. τὸ μέτωπον, etc., Lys.3.8, etc.:—Pass., τὰ . . τοῦ σώματος μέρη συντετρῖφθαι Pl.*R.*611d; συντετριμμένοι σκέλη καὶ πλευράς X.*An.*4.7.4; τὴν κλεῖν συνετρίβην And.1.61; συντριβόμεθα τὰς κεφαλὰς Lys.3.18. b. c. gen. partis, συντρῖψαι τῆς κεφαλῆς Isoc.18.52:—Pass., ξυντριβῆναι τῆς κεφαλῆς *to have* one's head *broken* (cf. κατάγνυμι fin.), Ar.*Pax*71:—in Th.4.11, φυλασσόμενοι τῶν νεῶν μὴ ξυντρίψωσιν, some take the gen. as partit., v. supr. II. 1. 3. metaph., *shatter, crush*, τὴν ἐπίνοιαν Ar.*V.*1050 (anap.); τὴν ἐλπίδα Demad.12, cf. D.10.44 (Pass.); ὅταν πέσῃ . ., πλεῖστα συντρίβει καλά Men.531.15; ὁ τρόπος συντρίβει σε Id.*Epit.*561; σ. τοὺς διαβεβηκότας Plb.5.47.1; δέος σ. τὸν ἄνθρωπον Plu.2.165b:—Pass., *PPetr.*2 p.8 (iii B.C.); κινδυνεύσει συντριβῆναι τὰ πράγματα *Hell.Oxy.*14.3; συντριβεὶς τῇ διανοίᾳ Plb.21.13.2; ταῖς ἐλπίσιν D.S.4.66; τὴν καρδίαν Lxx*Ps.*146(147).3, *Is.*61.1; συνετρίβη ἡ καρδία ib.*Je.*23.9, cf. *Ps.*50(51).19.

**συντρῐηραρχ-έω**, *to be a* συντριήραρχος, c. dat., Lys.6.47, *IG*2².1629.503: abs., Isoc.18.60. **-ημα**, ατος, τό, *contribution made by a* συντριήραρχος, *IG*2².1629.567. **-ος**, ὁ, *partner in the equipment of a trireme*, D.21.161, 47.22, *IG*2².1623.80 (pl.).

**συντρίκλῑνος**, ον, *reclining at the same table*, *IG*2².2030.13 (ii A.D., -κλειν-).

**σύν-τριμμα**, ατος, τό, *fracture*, Arist.*Aud.*802ᵃ34, Lxx*Le.*21.19, Gal.18(2).850; *abrasion*, Asclep.Jun.ap.eund.13.346. II. *affliction, ruin*, Lxx*Is.*59.7, *Je.*3.22. III. *collection*, ἁμαρτωλῶν ἀνθρώπων (v.l. σύστρεμμα, q.v.) ib.*Nu.*32.14. **-τριμμός**, ὁ, = σύντριμμα II, *ruin*, ib.*Ze.*1.10, al. II. συντριμμοὶ θανάτου *afflictions, miseries*, ib.2*Ki.*22.5.

**σύντρῐχος**, ον, *covered with hair*, δέρματα Sch.Philostr.*Her.* p.404 B.

⊕ **Σύντριψ**, ῐβος, ὁ, *the Smasher*, a lubber-fiend that breaks all the pots in the kitchen, Hom.*Epigr.*14.9.

**σύντριψις**, εως, ἡ, *ruin, destruction*, Lxx*Jo.*10.10. II. *crushing*, τοῦ ὀστέου Cass.*Pr.*38.

**σύντροπος**, dub. sens. in *PMag.Lond.*121.766 (σύντροφος (signf. I. 3) cj. Preisendanz).

**συντροφ-έω**, *to be reared together*, dub. in Thphr.*CP*3.5.2. **-η**, ἡ, *foster-sister*, *CIG*(add.)3857i (Phrygia). **-ία**, ἡ, *common nurture*, Ph.2.11, Plu.*Cat.Ma.*20, *PTeb.*407.6 (ii A.D.). 2. generally, *living together, society*, σ. καὶ συνήθεια Plb.6.5.10, cf. D.H.6.74; τινος *with* one, D.S.30.17; ἡ πρὸς ἡμᾶς σ. Str.8.3.3. 3. *familiarity*, κρημνοβατεῖν ἐπιστάμενοι διὰ τὴν τοῦ τόπου σ. Lyd.*Mens.*4.14. II. *brood*, *AP*7.216 (Antip. Thess.). ⊕ **-ος**, ον, *brought up together with*, τινι Hdt.1.99; ὦ Κύπριδι . . καὶ Χάρισι . . ξύντροφε Διαλλαγή Ar.*Ach.*989 (lyr.); also c. gen., *foster-brother*, οἱ μόθακες σ. Λακεδαιμονίων Phylarch.43 J.; σ. τοῦ βασιλέως Σελεύκου, etc., *OGI*247.2 (Delos, ii B.C.), al., Plb.5.9.4, 32.15.10; and in Com. phrase, τηγάνων σ. μειρακύλλια Eub.75.2; freq. of domestic animals, σ. τοῖσι ἀνθρώποισι Hdt.2.65; τοῖς θηρίοις πόθος τῶν σ. X.*Mem.*2.3.4; ἔστι [λέων] πρὸς τὰ σ. καὶ συνήθη σφόδρα φιλοπαίγμων Arist.*HA*629ᵇ11; κυνίδιον σ. Plu.*Aem.*10; ὄρνις Luc.*Lex.*6: abs., τὸ σ. γένος *bred up with* me, says Ajax of the Athenians, S.*Aj.*861; *of like habits with oneself*, Pl.*Lg.*949c:—freq. in Inscrr. and Pap., *SIG*798.6 (Cyzicus, i A.D.), etc.; Ζωτίκῳ συντρόφῳ *his foster-brother*, *CIG*3109 (Teos), cf. 3142.3 (Smyrna), 3268 (ibid.), *BGU*1058.50 (i B.C.); cf. συντρόφη:—τὸ σ., = συντροφία I. 1, Arist.*EN*1161ᵇ34. 2. generally, *living with*, τοῖς φονεῦσι S.*El.*1190; ξ. ὄμμα the eye or presence *of a companion*, Id.*Ph.*171 (lyr.); *used to* a thing, σ. ὧν (sc. ἀνάγκαις) E.*IT*1119 (lyr.); γυμνασίῳ Plu.2.130c; φιλοσοφίᾳ, πενίᾳ, κολακείᾳ, Luc.*Nigr.*12, 15: c. gen., σ. τῆς τόλμης Plb.1.74.9; ἁρμονίης, μέθας, *AP*7.26, 423 (both Antip. Sid.). 3. of things, *habitual*, νόσημα Hp.*Aër.*7; ἦν μὴ ἐκ παιδίου σύντροφος ᾖ [ἡ νοῦσος] Id.*Morb.Sacr.*10; οὐκέτι συντρόφοις ὀργαῖς ἔμπεδος S.*Aj.*639 (lyr.); τὰ ξ. *everyday* evils, Th.2.50; τὸ τῆς πάλαι ποτὲ φύσεως σ. the *congenital property* of nature, Pl.*Plt.*273b; πῦρ τὸ σ. *innate* heat, Hp.*de Arte*12; σ. τινὶ *natural to*, χυμῷ Id.*Off.*11; φάρμακον σ. ἐπιτέγξει Id.*Fract.*29; ἡ σ. τισὶ φιλοπρωτία Phld.*Rh.*2.158 S.; τὸ ἐναντιώτατον [πρόσωπον] οὐδὲ σ. ἡμῖν ὑπάρχον the opposite face (that of the dying patient) not being *familiar* to us, Gal.18(2).25; τῇ Ἑλλάδι πενίη αἰεί σ. Hdt.7.102: c. gen., κτύπος φωτὸς σύντροφος his *habitual* cry, S.*Ph.*203 (lyr.), cf. σύντροπος. Adv., -φως ἔχειν c. dat., to be *suitable*, Hp.*Fract.*32. II. Act., *joint-herd, fellow-herdsman*, τῆς ἀγέλης Pl.*Plt.*267e. 2. τοῖς ὕδασι σ. τῶν ἀναβλαστανόντων *assisting in nourishing* . ., Pl.*Lg.*845d.

**συντροχάζω**, *run together* or *with*, Lxx*Ec.*12.6, *AP*7.417 (Mel.), *Anacreont.*29.3, Plu.*Ages.*36, Plot.2.4.8:—also **συντροχάω**, Man.2.492.

**σύντροχος**, ον, *agreeing with*, σύντροχα λέγειν τινί Tz.*H.*12.187.

**συντρῡγάω**, *gather* grapes *together with*, τινί τι *Gp.*5.17.3.

**συντρῡφάω**, *share in luxury with*, τινι D.C.48.27.

**συντρώγω**, *eat together*, Tz.*H.*10.637.

**συντυγχάνω**, fut. -τεύξομαι Hsch., Phot., Suid.: aor. 2 συνέτῠχον: pf. -τέτευχα Chrysipp.*Stoic.*2.174, *PTeb.*22.3 (ii B.C.): I. of persons, *meet with, fall in with*, τινι Hdt.4.14, Ar.*Nu.*608 (troch.), *PTeb.* l.c., etc.; so μοίρᾳ τοὐδ' ἐχθίονι σ. S.*Ph.*682 (lyr.); σ. νεκροῖς ἀσπαίρουσι Antipho 2.4.5; ξυνέτυχεν ἐξιόντι μοι ἄνθρωπος ἀποφράς Eup.309: abs., S.*OT*122; but οἱ συντυγχάνοντες, of two persons *meeting*, Hdt.1.134, cf. Pl.*Ti.*56d. 2. rarely c. gen., like the simple verb, συντυχὼν κακῶν ἀνδρῶν perh. *having like others met with* evil men, S.*Ph.* 320 (σὺν τυχὼν Paley), cf. *OC*1482 codd. (lyr., σοῦ τύχοιμι Cobet). 3. ὁ συντυχών *the first that meets one*, ὁ αἰεὶ ξυντυχών E.*Hec.*1182 (also without ὁ, Id.*Rh.*864): rarely in pres., ὁ συντυγχάνων Pl.*Lg.*762c: also of things, τὸ συντυχόν *the first that comes to hand, average*, οὐ τὸ σ. ἔργον Hdt.1.51; πᾶν τὸ σ. ἡδέως ἤσθιεν X.*Ages.*9.3. II. of accidents and chances, *happen to, befall*, τὰ συντυχόντα σφι Hdt.8.136; ὅσα δεῖ χώρᾳ συντυχεῖν Pl.*Lg.*709c: abs., *happen, fall out*, εὖ ξυντυχόντων *if things go* well, A.*Th.*274; πᾶν τὸ συντυχὸν πάθος S.*Aj.*313; ὁ ξ. κίνδυνος Th.3.59; πρὸς τὰ σ. according to *circumstances*, Plu.*Oth.*13, cf. 9: impers. συνετύγχανε, συνέτυχε, *it happened that* . ., c. inf., Th.7.70, Plb.15.4.5, Plu.*Lys.*12, *Pel.*18; συνέτυχε οὕτως, ὥστε . . Aristeas 307: c. part., ἡ οὐσία συντέτευχε τὸν μέσον κατειληφυῖα τόπον Chrysipp. l.c.

**συντῠλόω**, in Pass., *to be covered with a callus*, Aët.13.133 (*Hermes* 42.539).

**συντυμβωρῠχέω**, *help in grave-digging*, pedantic word in Luc.*Lex.*2.

**συντῠπόω**, *help to form*, τὸ κατὰ τὴν φάρυγγα Gal.5.237:—Pass., συντυποῦσθαι τὰς ψυχὰς τοῖς παροῦσι *allow* the soul *to be moulded* by circumstances, Simp. *in Epict.* p.69 D.

**συντῠρανν-έω**, *share in absolute power with*, τῷ δεσπότῃ Str.13.1.57. **-οκτονέω**, *join in slaying tyrants*, Luc.*Tyr.*7. **-ος**, ὁ, *fellow-tyrant*, Plu.2.105b.

**συντῡρόω**, *make into cheese together*: hence, comically, τὰκ Βοιωτῶν . . συντυρούμενα *the troubles that are being concocted* on their part, Ar.*Eq.*479.

**συντυφλόω**, *blind at the same time*, Tz.*H.*3.221 (Pass.).

**συντύχημα** [ῠ], ατος, τό, = συντυχία, Apollod.Com.23.

**συντῠχ-ία**, Ion. -ίη, ἡ, *occurrence, happening, incident*, freq. with a qualifying epithet, ἀγαθή Thgn.590 = Sol.13.70; σ. κρυόεσσα Pi.*I.*1.38; δεινὴ καὶ μεγάλη Hdt.3.43; κατὰ σ. ἀγαθὴν Ar.*Av.*544 (lyr.); καλὴ ἡ ξ. the *conjuncture* is fair, Th.1.33; ἐρωτικὴ ξ. an *incident* of a love-affair, Id.6.54: without any qualifying word, μεταλλαγαὶ συντυχίας changes *of fortune*, E.*HF*766 (lyr.); σ. τις τοιαύτη ἐπεγένετο Hdt.3.121; συντυχίῃ ταύτῃ χρησαμένη Id.5.41; θυμοῦμαι τῇ ξ. Ar.*Ra.*1006 (anap.); ὡς ἑκάστοις τῆς ξυντυχίας . . ἔσχεν according to *the circumstances* of each party, Th.7.57; ἅμα τοῦ ἔργου τῇ ξ. at *the very moment* of action, Id.3.112; ἀπὸ τοιαύτης ξ. Id.5.11; κατὰ συντυχίην by *chance*, Hdt.3.74, 9.21; κατά τινα σ. Plb.10.32.3, Gal.16.837; κατὰ σ. also, *as it happens, as a matter of fact*, *OGI*331.19 (Pergam., ii B.C.): pl., *the chances* or *incidents of life, circumstances*, Th.3.45. 2. abs. also, acc. to the context, of *good* or *evil chances*, a. *happy event, success*, Pi.*P.*1.36 (pl.); συντυχίῃ χρησάμενος καὶ σοφίῃ Hdt.1.68; θεῶν ἐπὶ συντυχίαις *the happy issues* due to them, S.*Ant.*157 (anap.). b. *mishap, mischance*, ξυντυχίᾳ βαρυνόμενοι Cratin.166, cf. E.*Tr.*1119 (anap.), *El.*1358 (anap.), Pl.*Phdr.*248c, etc. c. μειράκιον . . ἀποσκορακίσαν τὴν τοῦ Πυθαγόρου σ. the *intervention* of P., Iamb.*VP*25.112. **-ίζειν**· συνσωρεύειν, Hsch. **-ικός**, ή, όν, *accidental*, ὀλισθήσεις Plu.2.611a (συγχυτικαὶ Reiske).

**συνυβρίζω**, *join in violence* or *insolence*, Plu.2.631f, Lib.*Or.*1.230:—Pass., *to be insulted as well*, Agath.1.4.

**συνῠγιαίνω**, *to be well along with*, c. dat., Meno *Iatr.*17.9.

**συνυγραίνομαι**, Pass., *to be wet along with* or *together*, Gal.11.585.

**συνυθλέω**, *chat together*, Luc.*Lex.*14.

**συνῠλακτέω**, *bark together*, Nonn.*D.*3.176, etc.

**συνῠμεναιόω**, *join in the bridal hymn*, Plu.2.138b.

⊕ **συνυμνέω**, *sing hymns together*, Sch.rec.Theoc.10.24.

⊕ **συνυμνῳδός**, ὁ, *fellow-singer of hymns*, *CIG*3170.16 (Smyrna).

⊕ **συνυπ-άγω** [ᾰ], *remove, withdraw together with*, ἑαυτῷ ὑγρότητα Olymp. *in Mete.*276.29, al., cf. Gal.17(2).191. II. *make dependent together*, τῷ ἄρθρῳ τὸν λόγον Sch.E.*Or.*854:—Pass., *to be brought under the power of*, Eustr. *in EN*26.25. **-ᾰκουστέον**, *one must understand, supply* a word, Str.9.5.5, v.l. in Sch.E.*Or.*234. **-ᾰκούω**, *obey together*, τινι Plb.5.56.9, cf. D.S.18.9; πρός τι *in* a thing, Plb.1.66.7. II. *comprehend under the meaning of terms*, Stob.2.7.5ᵇ, Ptol.*Phas.*p.12 H. (both Pass.); *understand* [a word] *together*, A.D.*Synt.*339.18 (Pass.), Gal.16.776 (Pass.). **-αλλάσσομαι**, *vary also*, prob. for νῦν ὑπ- in Gal.17(1).31. **-αρκτικός**, ή, όν, *capable of coexistence*, ἀντίθεσις Simp. *in Cat.*384.22. **-αρξις**, εως, ἡ, *coexistence*, S.E.*P.*2.199, *M.*10.267, A.D.*Adv.*194.1, Gal.1.116. **-άρχω**, *exist together, coexist*, Arist.*EE*1241ᵇ27, Thphr.*Vent.*21, Plb.6.39.2, Ph.2.507, Gal.6.441, Arr.*Epict.*2.1.2; ἀλλήλοις with one another, S.E.*P.*2.144; ἀναγκαῖον ἀνθρώποις συνυπάρξαι τὰς τέχνας Ph.2.512, cf. Gal.16.555, al.

**συνύπᾰτος**, ὁ, *colleague in the consulship*, D.H.6.22, D.C.78.14:—hence **συνυπᾰτεύω**, Str.5.1.11, Plu.*Publ.*1, *Fab.*25, etc.

**συνύπειμι**, (εἰμί *sum*) *to be in* or *under together*, Ocell.2.22, 3.1.

**συνυπεξάγω** [ᾰ], *remove together with*, τὸ φάρμακον σ. ἑαυτῷ τι Archig.ap.Aët.9.28.

**συνυπερβάλλω**, *pass over together*, τὸν Ταῦρον Plb.4.48.6.

**συνῠπηρετέω**, *concur in helping*, τῷ νομοθέτῃ Pl.*Lg.*934b, cf. Arist.*PA*685ᵃ21.

**συνυπο-βάλλω**, *subject at the same time*, τῷ λόγῳ τὰ πάθη prob. in Plu.*Lib.*1. **-γράφω** [ᾰ], *subscribe together*, *PAmh.*2.31.13 (ii B.C.), *PGrenf.*2.23.4 (ii B.C.):—Pass., *agree with*, Ph.2.600. **-δείκνῡμι** and -ύω (Plb.18.15.2), *help to indicate*, τὰς ὁδοὺς αὐτοῖς Id.3.48.7, cf. D.S.11.6 (interpol.); σ. αὐτοῖς ὅτι . ., πῶς . ., Plb.

1.27.1, 5.98.11: and so verb. Adj. **-δεικτέον**, Id.5.21.4. ⊛ **-δέχομαι**, *receive, entertain together*, τινί τινα Sch.Theoc.7.149. **-δίδωμι**, *deposit also*, prob. in *PGrenf.*1.14.21 (ii B.C.). **-δύομαι**, Pass. and Med., *insinuate oneself along with*, τινι Plu.2.542b. II. c. acc., *undergo together*, κίνδυνον Id.*Brut.*18. **-ζεύγνυμι**, *put under the yoke together*, Ath.12.533d. **-κειμαι**, *to be appended also*, of a document, τὸ -κείμενον ἄκυρον εἶναι *Inscr.Perg.*163 *D* 12 (ii B.C.); συνυποκείσθω *let it be assumed also*, Gal.15.503; *underlie at the same time*, Jul. *Or.*4.133d:—f. l. in Lib.*Decl.*4.61. **-κορίζω**, *call by a diminutive name in accordance with*, Eust.1283.40. **-κρίνομαι** [ῑ], *accommodate oneself by pretending*, Plb.3.31.7; συνυπεκρίθη τίθεσθαι φιλίαν πρὸς αὐτούς Id.3.52.6; σ. τὸ προσποίημα τῷ Μαρίῳ *helping* M. *to maintain his pretence*, Plu.*Mar.*14; συνυπεκρίνετο τοῖς προθύμως..διακειμένοις *pretended to agree with* the eager spirits, Plb.3.92.5, cf. *Ep.Gal.*2.13, Plu.*Mar.*17. **-λαμβάνω**, *help in supporting*, *Gp.*15.3.8. **-λείπομαι**, *to be left behind together with*, τοῖς συμμένουσι Epict.*Gnom.*34 (prob. l.). **-ληψις**, late Dor. **-λᾶμψις**, εως, ἡ, *support, relief*, τᾶς πόλεως *IG*5(1).1146.21 (Gytheum, i B.C.). **-νοέω**, *supply in thought*, Arist.*SE*176$^{a}$39; διότι.. Plb.4.24.2. **-πίπτω**, *to be presented to the senses together with*, ἀλλήλοις S.E.*M.*8.174.

**συνυποπτεύω**, *suspect*, Plb.14.4.8.

**συνυπό-πτωσις**, εως, ἡ, *simultaneous presentation to the senses*, S.E. *M.*8.174. **-στᾰσις**, εως, ἡ, *coexistence*, Plot.6.7.2,40, Dam.*Pr.* 292. **-στέλλομαι**, Pass., *crouch together under* (a wall), Max.Tyr. 21.10. II. *to be shortened* or *contracted together*, S.E.*M.*9. 262. **-σύρω** [ῡ], *draw down together*, [αἱ ἕλμινθες] συνυποσύρονται τοῖς ῥοφήμασι Herod.Med.ap.Aët.9.37. **-τάσσομαι**, Pass., *to be subject* or *obedient together*, Hsch. s.v. ἀτιμαγέλας. **-τίθεμαι**, Med., *assume also*, in arguing, Pl.*Ax.*370a. II. *help in devising*, σ. τινὶ λόγον Plu.*Cat.Mi.*66. III. *suggest* or *advise as well*, Gal. 8.118.

⊛ **συνυπουργέω**, *join in serving, co-operate with*, τινι Hp.*Art.*58, cf. 2*Ep.Cor.*1.11, Luc.*Bis Acc.*17.

**συνυπο-φέρω**, *sustain along with*, τῷ ἀδελφῷ τὴν τύχην Sch.E. *Or.*1. **-φύομαι**, Pass., *grow up together*, ἐκ τῆς αὐτῆς χώρας Plu. 2.554a. **-χωρέω**, *retire together*, ib.248b.

**συνῠφαίνω**, pf. συνύφαγκα D.H.*Comp.*18, Ruf.*Anat.*9:—*weave together*, of the spider, Arist.*HA*623$^{a}$11; ἡ τῶν χιτώνων τῶν τὸν ὀφθαλμὸν συνυφαγκότων πλοκή Ruf. l. c.:—Med., πλέγμα ἐξ ἀέρος καὶ πυρὸς συνυφηνάμενος Pl.*Ti.*78b:—Pass., of the horns of certain oxen, *to be entangled*, Arist.*Fr.*363. 2. metaph., *weave together, frame with art*, ἵνα τοι σὺν μῆτιν ὑφήνω Od.13.303; ἡ πάντα συνυφαίνουσα [πολιτική] *which weaves* all *into one web*, Pl.*Plt.*305e; σ. τὸν λόγον Arist.*Rh.Al.*1439$^{a}$31; [τοὺς ῥυθμούς] D.H. l. c.; ὑπόμνημά τι Luc.*Hist.Conscr.*48; ἐκέρασε τᾷ πολυτεκνίᾳ τοὺς..οἴκους εἰς τὸ αὐτὸ συνυφήνας *IG*4$^{2}$(1).86.15 (Epid., i A.D.):—Pass., ὥστε ταῦτα συνυφανθῆναι so that this *web was woven*, i.e. this business contrived, Hdt.5.105; of the parts of a sentence, D.H.*Comp.*23; θύννοι ἀλλήλοις συνυφασμένοι *quite close together*, Ael.*NA*15.3. II. *weave in company*, Men.142, *PSI*3.167.9 (ii B.C.).

**συνύφαν-σις** [ῠ], εως, ἡ, *weaving together*, metaph., Pl.*Plt.* 310e. **-τέον**, *one must weave together*, Ph.1.528. **-της**, ου, ὁ, *one who weaves together*, metaph., opp. ἀναλύτης, Dam.*Pr.*161.

**συνύφασμα** [ῠ], ατος, τό, *contextus*, *Gloss.*

**συνύφειαι** [ῠ], αἱ, *bees' cells* (from their *net-like* appearance), *honeycomb*, Arist.*HA*624$^{a}$11.

**συνυφέλκω**, f. l. for συνεφ- in Ph.2.232.

⊛ **συνῠφή**, ἡ, = συνύφασμα, *web*, Pl.*Lg.*734e. 2. metaph., *construction*, οἰκήσεων Id.*Epin.*975b; ἐρωτικὴ ξ. amorous *embrace*, Max. Tyr.26.5 (ξυμφυήν Reiske).

**συνῠφής**, ές, *woven together*; ἱστοί, of honeycombs, Arist.*HA*624$^{a}$ 6; τι συνυφές a kind *of web*, ib.622$^{b}$10.

**συνυφίστημι**, *call into existence together with*, τινι Plot.5.6.5, Jul.*Or.*4.142a, Procl.*Inst.*57:—Pass., with pf. and aor. 2 Act., *coexist*, Ph.1.175, Plu.2.572d, S.E.*P.*3.26, *M.*8.273, Alex.Aphr.*Mixt.* 228.21. II. Med., *undertake along with*, αὐτοῖς πάντα -στησομένους Plb.4.32.7.

**συνῳδέω**, = συνᾴδω, for which it is v.l. in Ecphant.ap.Stob.4.7. 64.

**συνῳδία**, ἡ, *concord*, and metaph., *agreement, assent*, Pl.*Lg.*837e, etc.: lit., συνῳδίαι χορῶν Aristid.*Or.*18(20).7; of the Spheres, Iamb. *VP*15.65: also **συνᾰοιδία**, Onatas ap. Stob.1.1.39; **συνῳδή**, *concentus*, *Gloss.*, cf. Charis.p.552K.

**συνῳδικός**, ή, όν, *making for harmony*, ἀγαθὸν χρῆμα καὶ ξ. Call. Com.2(*b*)D.

**συνωδίνω** [ῑ], *to be in travail together*, σ. κακοῖς *share in the agony of* woes, E.*Hel.*727; οἱ συνωδίνοντες ὄρνιθες Arist.*EE*1240$^{a}$36; οἱ ἄρρενες ταῖς θηλείαις σ. Ael.*NA*3.45:—Pass., στεροπῇσι συνωδίνοντο κεραυνοί Nonn.*D.*2.507.

**συνῳδός** (also **συνᾰοιδός** E.*HF*787 (lyr.)), όν, (ᾠδή) *singing* or *sounding in unison with, echoing* or *responsive to*, ὄρνις..ἄχεσι σ. E. *Ph.*1518 (lyr.); θρηνήμασι φίλαι ξυνῳδοί Id.*Or.*133, cf. *Hel.*174 (lyr.). 2. abs., *in harmony, accordant*, λόγος Pl.*Phd.*92c; ἦχος D.H.*Comp.*22; ῥῆμα *APl.*4.226 (Alc.); ὦ ξυνῳδοὶ κτύποι cj. in E. *Supp.*73 (lyr.). II. metaph., *according with, in harmony with*, c. dat., Hdt.5.92.γ′, E.*Med.*1008, etc.; ἐμοὶ φρονῶν ξυνῳδά Ar.*Av.* 635 (lyr.); λόγοι σ. τοῖς ἔργοις Arist.*EN*1172$^{b}$5, cf. 1098$^{b}$30; σ. εἰσὶν οἱ ἀστέρες τοῖς ἀποτελέσμασι *PMich.* in *Class.Phil.*22.16; ὁκόσα πεπέρει ξυνῳδά pepper and *cognate* substances, Aret.*CA*1.10: c. gen., τὴν ὁμοείδειαν σ. τοῦ τόνου A.D.*Adv.*165.23: abs., ἴσως ξυνῳδὸς τῷ χρόνῳ γενήσεται Call.Com.2(*a*)D.

⊛ **συνωθ-έω**, *force together, compress forcibly*, τὰ σμικρὰ εἰς τὰ τῶν μεγάλων διάκενα Pl.*Ti.*58b; τὰ ὁμοιότατα μάλιστ' εἰς ταὐτόν ib.53a; πρὸς τὸν πόλον ὡς εἰς στενότατον X.*Oec.*18.8; τὸ πνεῦμα κατέχειν καὶ πρὸς τὴν λαγόνα συνωθεῖν Sor.2.59; ἡ φύσις.. σ. τὸ πῦον εἰς τὰς παρακειμένας χώρας Gal.18(2).103:—Pass., συνέωσται εἰς αὐτό Pl.*Ti.*59e; συνωσθεῖσα ib.85e; εἰς μικρόν Arist.*Resp.*479$^{b}$24; διὰ τὸ συνωθεῖσθαι πλεῖστον ἀέρα πρὸς ἄρκτον Thphr.*Vent.*2, cf. 53. 2. *help to propel*, βολήν App.*Hann.*22. II. intr., *force one's way in* or *rush in*, Arist.*Mir.*838$^{b}$8; ἐπὶ τὸ στρατεύεσθαι Epicur.*Fr.*171 (nisi leg. ὁρμῆσαι). **-ησις**, εως, ἡ, *compulsio*, *Gloss.* **-ισμός**, ὁ, *jostling*, Eun.*Hist.* p.246 D.

**συνώμεθα**, v. συνίημι.

**συνωμ-ία**, ἡ, (ὦμος) *space between the shoulder-blades, withers*, in the bull of Phalaris, Plb.12.25.3 (pl.); in a horse, *Hippiatr.*128 (pl.); τῶν ἐν τῇ ῥάχει καὶ τῇ σ. γενομένων ἑλκῶν ib.26; in a human being, ἀλγοῦσιν, οἱ μὲν τὴν κεφαλήν, οἱ δὲ συνωμίας καὶ ὀσφύν Paul.Aeg.3.20; καθ' ὅλων τῶν κατὰ τὴν σ. μερῶν Id.6.88. **-ίασις**, εως, ἡ, *pain in the* συνωμία, *Hippiatr.*26. **-ίς**, ίδος, ἡ, *shoulder-blade*, in pl., Orib.*Fr.*52, *Gloss.*

**συνωμ-οσία** (sts. wrongly written συνομ-), ἡ: (συνόμνυμι):—*being leagued by oath, conspiracy*, Ar.*Eq.*476 (pl.), Th.6.60, etc.; ξ. δήμου καταλύσεως *for* putting down the democracy, Id.6.27, cf. *IPE*I$^{2}$.401. 36 (Chersonesus Taurica, iii B.C.); οἱ ἐν τῇ ξ. Th.8.49; οἱ ἐκ τῆς σ. Plu.*Ant.*13; ἡ ἐπί τινα, ἡ κατά τινος σ., Id.*Sert.*26, *Cat.Mi.*29. 2. *confederacy*, ἡ πρὸς Ἀργείους γενομένη ξ. Th.5.83. II. *body of men leagued by oath, political union* or *club*, Id.8.54,81, Pl.*Ap.*36b, *R.* 365d. **-όσιον**, τό, *joint oath*, D.H.10.31; simply *oath*, Longus 4. 31. ⊛ **-όσιος**, ὁ, = sq., Sch.Ar.*Av.*1075. **-ότης**, ου, ὁ, *one who is leagued by oath, fellow-conspirator, confederate*, S.*OC*1302, Ar.*Eq.*452 (lyr.), *V.*507 (troch.), And.4.4, Lys.12.43, etc.; ἄνδρες..ξ. Ar.*Eq.* 257 (troch.); οἱ σ. ἐπὶ τῷ Πέρσῃ Hdt.7.148; οἱ Κατιλίνα σ. his *fellow-conspirators*, Plu.*Ant.*2; σ. τῆς ἐπιβουλῆς *confederate in* the plot, Hdn.4.14.2: metaph., ὕπνος πόνος τε, κύριοι ξ. A.*Eu.*126. **-οτία**, ἡ, *band of sworn soldiers, file*, Ascl.*Tact.*2.2. **-οτικός**, ή, όν, *of or for a conspiracy*, only in Adv. -κῶς, Plu.2.813a. **-οτος**, ον, *leagued by oath*: ξυνώμοτον, τό, *league, confederacy*, Th.2.74; *conspiracy*, D.C. 37.39. II. of things, *agreed to under oath*, Thom.Mag. p.346R. (fem. η).

**συνων-έομαι**, *buy together, collect by purchase*, νησιῶται ἵππον συνωνέονται μυρίην Hdt.1.27. II. *buy up*, σῖτον Lys.22.6, X.*HG* 5.4.56; μαθήματα Pl.*Sph.*224b; θηρία Plu.*Brut.*21:—Pass., προσέταξεν [χρυσὸν] συνωνηθῆναι *POxy.*2106.4 (iv A.D.):—the pf συνεώνημαι is used as Pass., ὁ συνεωνημένος [σῖτος] corn *bought up*, Lys.22. 12; but with act. sense in D.13.30, 23.208. III. *assist one to buy*, Thphr.*Char.*2.7. **-ή**, ἡ, *buying up*, Lyd.*Mag.*3.70, Procop.*Arc.* 22, *Cod.Just.*10.27.2.5, al.; simply, *purchase*, χόρτου, πυροῦ, *POxy.* 507.24 (ii A.D.), 909.21 (iii A.D.). **-ητής**, οῦ, ὁ, *one who buys up*, *Gloss.* **-ητος**, ον, *bought up*, *Cod.Theod.*11.15.1.

**συνωνῠμ-έω**, *to be synonymous with*, τινι Ph.1.304, Sor.1.60, Ath.1. 11e; τὸ -εῖν συνδέσμους ἐπιρρήμασιν *same words serve* as conjunction and adverb, A.D.*Synt.*335.27. 2. *to have the same name and nature as*, c. dat., Dam.*Pr.*96. **-ία**, ἡ, *synonym*, Arist.*Rh.*1404$^{b}$ 39, Quint.8.3.16; ἡ -ία τοῦ δῶμα, i.e. οἶκος, A.D.*Pron.*84.19; cf. Demetr.Lac.*Herc.*1012.22. **-ος**, ον, *having the same name as*, c. gen., ἡ..συνώνυμος τῆς ἔνδον οὔσης ἔγχελυς Antiph.217.1, cf. E. *Hel.*495; ὁ σ. τῇ πόλει [ποταμός] Plb.9.27.5. II. in the Logic of Arist. συνώνυμα are *things having the same name and the same nature and definition*, *Cat.*1$^{a}$6, cf. *Top.*123$^{a}$28, 148$^{a}$24, Thphr.*HP*9.11.5; ἔστι τις ἀδικία παρὰ τὴν ὅλην ἄλλη ἐν μέρει, συνώνυμος, ὅτι ὁ ὁρισμὸς ἐν τῷ αὐτῷ γένει Arist.*EN*1130$^{a}$33; τὰ πολλὰ τῶν σ. τοῖς εἴδεσι the many particulars *which have the same name as* the forms, i.e. *things denoted by the same univocal or unambiguous word*, e.g. man and ox, both called ζῷον in the same sense of ζῷον, opp. ὁμώνυμος (v. ὁμώνυμος IV), Id.*Metaph.*987$^{b}$10. Adv. -μως Id.*Cat.*3$^{a}$34, Plb.3.33.11, Phld. *Rh.*1.148S. 2. of pairs of the form 'A : non-A', opp. ἑτερώνυμα (q.v.), Procl. *in Prm.* p.955S. III. in Rhet. τὰ σ. are *synonyms, words having different forms but the same sense*, as πορεύεσθαι and βαδίζειν, Arist.*Rh.*1405$^{a}$1; τὸ σ. τοῦ νέφους, i.e. νεφέλη, A.D.*Synt.* 199.27.

**συνωρ-ιαστής**, οῦ, ὁ, *one who drives a* συνωρίς, Luc.*Zeux.*9. **-ίζω**, *yoke together*, Ael.*NA*15.24:—Med., ξυνωρίζου χέρα *join* thy hand *with mine*, E.*Ba.*198. II. intr., *to be yoked together*, Nic.*Fr.*74. 23, Man.4.453. **-ικεύομαι**, *drive a pair*, Ar.*Nu.*15.

⊛ **συνώριος**, α, ον, *in season*, ὄφρα κεν ἀλκήτωρ τελέθων τὰ συν[ώρ]ια τεύχω dub. in Ramsay *Studies in the Eastern Provinces* p.128 (Phrygia); doubtful also in *Supp.Epigr.*2.666 = 4.726 (Bithynia).

**συνωρ-ίς**, ίδος, ἡ, *pair of horses* (with or without a chariot or carriage, σ. χωρὶς δίφρου Pl.*Criti.*119b), E.*Rh.*987, Ar.*Nu.*1302, Pl. *Phdr.*246b, *IG*5(2).550.27 (Megalopolis, iv B.C.), etc.; τέθριππα καὶ ξυνωρίδες *Com.Adesp.*1281; εἰς τοὺς τροχοὺς τῆς [συνω]ρίδος *PCair. Zen.*782(*a*).21 (iii B.C.); εἰς ἵππους θηλείας τῆς σ. τῆς ἀγαγούσης ἐγ Μέμφεως εἰς Φιλαδέλφειαν Ζήνωνα ib.292.66 (iii B.C.); εἰς τὰ παραγενόμενα τῇ γ′ ἅρματα ε′ (ἵππων) β′ συνωρίδας γ′ (ἵππων) γ′ τοῖς πᾶσιν ἵπποις ιθ′ *PPetr.*2 p.74 (iii B.C.); σ. πωλικὴ *IG*4$^{2}$(1).101.46 (Epid., i A.D.), cf. Paus.10.7.8; ἵππων τελείων Id.5.8.10; of mules, Id.5.9.2; ἐλεφάντων ἅρμα καὶ σ. Plb.30.25.11 (dub.): *a coin stamped with a biga* (cf. πῶλος II), E.*Fr.*675. 2. generally, *a pair* or *couple of* anything, A.*Ag.*643; τέκνων E.*Med.*1145, cf. S.*OC*895, *Com.Adesp.*834 (= *Trag.Adesp.*

198). II. of things, πέδας τε χειροῖν καὶ ποδοῖν ξυνωρίδα manacles for the hands and for the feet, *a coupling fetter*, A.*Ch.*982; ὅπου γὰρ ἰσχὺς συζυγοῦσι καὶ δίκη, ποία ξ. τῶνδε καρτερωτέρα; what *pair* is stronger than this? Id.*Fr.*381. **-ιστής**, οῦ, ὁ, *driver of a* συνωρίς, *PLond.ined.*2087, 2358 (iii B. C.), *PSI* 4.406.3 (iii B. C.). 2. *driven in a* συνωρίς, ἡμίονοι *PCair.Zen.*8.11 (iii B. C.); so perh. ib.673 (iii B. C.).

**σύνωρον**· σύμφωνον, ὁμολογούμενον, ἢ συγγενῆ, Hsch.

**συνωροσκοπέω**, *occupy the horoscope jointly*, of planets, Vett.Val. 60.11.

**σύνωσις**, εως, ἡ, (συνωθέω) *forcing together, compression*, Pl.*Ti.*62b, Epicur.*Ep.*2 p.49 U., al., Paul.Aeg.6.73; διώσεις ἢ σ. Arist.*Ph.*243$^b$9.

**συνωφελέω**, *join in aiding*, αὐτούς X.*Mem.*3.5.16; τὴν γῆν Id.*Oec.* 18.2, etc.; τινὰ εἴς τι ib.2.14; rarely τινι, S.*Ph.*871: abs., *to be of use* or *assist together*, ἔν τισι Hp.*Art.*18, cf. *Supp.Epigr.*3.583.13 (Olbia, ii/iii A. D.); εἴς τι X.*An.*3.2.27:—Pass., *derive profit together*, Lys.12.93.

**συνωχᾰδόν**, Adv., (συνέχω) poet. for συνοχηδόν, of Time, *perpetually, continually*, Hes.*Th.*690, Q.S.14.517.—On the form, v. A.D. *Adv.*196.14.

**σῠο-βαύβᾰλος**, *of* or *from a pig-sty*, σ. λόγος *a swineherd's* song, Cratin.312:—as Subst. (sc. σταθμός) *pig-sty*, Hsch., Phot. **-βοιωτοί**, οἱ, *Hog-Boeotians*, Cratin.310 (corr. Porson). **-βόσκης**, ου, ὁ, *swineherd*, Hsch. s. v. ὑοβότης. **-βόσκιον**, τό, *herd of swine*, Charis. p.551 K. **-βοσκός**, ὁ, *swineherd*, Gloss. **-βρωτος**, ον, *bitten by a wild boar*, Aët.13.4 tit. **-δήλητος**, ον, *hurt* or *slain by a boar*, Aglaïas 10. **-θήρας**, ου, ὁ, *boar-hunter*, Philostr.*Im.*2.17:—Συοθῆραι, οἱ, title of poem by Stesich., Ath.3.95d. **-κτᾰσία**, ἡ, = sq., *AP*7.421.12 (Mel.). **-κτονία**, ἡ, *slaughter of swine*, D.P.853 (pl.). **-κτόνος**, ον, *slaying swine* or *boars*, Call.*Dian.*216, Nonn. *D.*1.27.

**σῠόομαι**, Pass., *become swine*, Elias *in Porph.*119.22.

**σῠο-πλουτοσύνη**, Dor. **-νᾱ**, ἁ, *swine-wealth*, Cerc.4.14. **-ρόγχαι**· βλαπτικοί, Hsch. **-τρόφος**, ον, *feeding swine*, χώρα J.*BJ*1.21.13:—as Subst. *swineherd*, Sch.D Od.13.404. **-φόνος**, ον, *boar-slaying*, λόγχη E.*Fr.*495.29. **-φόντης**, ου, ὁ, *swine-slayer*, only in fem. **-φόντις**, *AP*11.194 (Lucill.).

**σῠοφορβ-έομαι**, Pass., *to be fed like swine*, Longin.9.14. **-ιον**, τό, *herd of swine*, Arist.*HA*571$^b$19, D.H.1.79, Hsch.:—on the form, v. *An.Ox.*2.309. **-ός**, όν, later form of συφορβός, Plb.12.4.6, D.H. 1.84 codd., Hsch.

* **συππῖνᾶς**, ᾶδος, ὁ, prob. = στιππυουργός, *JHS*54.75 (Smyrna, pl.).

**συπύη**, ἡ, = σιπύη, *PCair.Zen.*14(*b*).14 (iii B. C.).

**σῦρ**, σῠρός, τό, = φορτίον, Theognost.*Can.*133; but Hdn.Gr. has only Σῦρ, an old name for Φοινίκη, 2.910,919.

**σύρα**, ἡ, = συρία, interpol. in Poll.10.64.

**Σῠραιγύπτιος**, α, ον, *Syro-Egyptian*, *PTeb.*814.42 (iii B. C.).

**Σῠράκουσαι** [ᾱ], αἱ, *Syracuse*, Th.5.4, Scymn.282, *IGRom.*1.495 (Sicily, i A. D.); Ion. **Σῠρήκουσαι** Hdt.7.154; Dor. **Σῠράκοσαι** Pi. *P.*2.1, D.S.22.8; also **Σῠράκοσσαι**, Pi.*O.*6.6 (with vv. ll.), cj. in B. 5.184 (-κουσσ- Pap., as also *Marm.Par.*52,71): **Σῠράκουσα**, ἡ, D.S.13.75, 14.14, St.Byz., **Συράκουσσα** Hdn.Gr.1.270 codd. Arc.; **Σῠράκοσα**, D.S.21.4; also **Σῠρακώ**, οῦς, ἡ, Epich.185 (name of a marsh, St.Byz.; called *Tyraco*, Vibius Sequester p.154 Riese).—Adj. **Σῠρᾱκόσιος**, α, ον, *Syracusan*, and as Subst. *a Syracusan*, *BMus.Cat.Coins Sicily* p.145, Th. l. c., *IG*12(9).1187.15 (Euboea, iii B. C.), etc.; Ion. and poet. **Σῠρηκόσιος** Hdt.7.154, *AP*5.191 (Mel.), Nonn.*D.*6.354; a form **Σῠρακόσσιος** Hdn.Gr.1.120; **Σῠρακούσιος** Pl.*Ep.*326b (s. v. l.); **Συρρακούσιος** v. l. in Lib.*Or.*12.36, cf. Choerob. *in Theod.*2.242, al.; fem. **Σῠρᾱκοσσίς**, γλῶσσα Nonn.*D.*9.22:—ἡ **Σῠρακοσία** [χώρα] *the territory of S.*, Th.6.52 (and so L. Dind. reads for ἡ Συράκουσα or Συράκοσα in D.S. (v. supr.)): Συρακοσίων τράπεζα, prov. of luxurious living, Ar.*Fr.*216:—**Σῠρᾱκοσεύς**, έως, ὁ, St.Byz.

**Σῠραττικός**, ὁ, *Syro-Attic*, nickname in Ath.9.368c.

**σύρβᾰ**, v. τύρβα. * **συρβάβυττα**, *topsy-turvy*, Ar.*Fr.*866. **σύρβη**, ἡ, v. τύρβη. II. = αὐλοθήκη, Hsch. s. v. συρβηνεύς.

**συρβηνεύς**, ὁ, *noisy*, χορός Cratin.84; ὁ τῶν -έων χορός Ath.15. 669b, 671c, 697f, cf. Zen.6.1 (where Leutsch -νός).

**σύργαστρος**, ὁ, (σύρω, γαστήρ) *trailing the belly*, as a snake, *AP*15. 26.14 (Dosiad.*Ara*). II. metaph., *day-labourer*, Alciphr.3.19,63; also **συργάστωρ**, ορος, ὁ, v. l. ibid. (in 63).—Both words are expld. by συοφορβός or ὑ(ο)φορβός in Hsch., Phot., *EM*736.25 (Συργάστωρ is also an ὄνομα βαρβαρικόν acc. to Hsch.).

**σύρδην**, Adv., (σύρω) *dragging, in a long line*, Βαβυλὼν .. πάμμικτον ὄχλον πέμπει σ. A.*Pers.*54 (anap.). II. *as if dragged along, violently*, σ. ἅπαντα .. ἀναλῶσαι δορί E *Rh.*58; τοῦ κονιορτοῦ σ. ἁπανταχόθεν ἐμπίπτοντος Aristid.*Or.*51(27).9.

**σύρεον**, = τορδύλιον, Plin.*HN*24.177.

* **συρία**, ἡ, a kind of *garment*, *PHib.*1.38.7, 51.3 (iii B. C.), *Ostr. Bodl.* i 143 (iii B. C.), *PEnteux.*1.8 (iii B. C.), *PCair.Zen.*10.25 (iii B. C.), *BGU*1564.6 (ii A. D.), *PLips.*57.29 (iii A. D.): = αὐτόποκον ἱμάτιον acc. to Poll.7.61; so called because made by Cappadocian Syrians, acc. to Hsch.

**Σῠρι-άρχης**, ου, ὁ, *president of the provincial council of Syria*, *Cod. Theod.*15.9.2, Just.*Nov.*89.15. **-αρχία**, ἡ, *office of* Συριάρχης, *Cod.Theod.*6.3.1, *Cod.Just.*1.36, 5.27.1.

**σῡριγγ-έμβολος**, ὁ, *pipe-line* for conveying water, Eust.1189. 47. **-ιᾰκός**, ή, όν, *for fistulae* or *ulcers*, κολλύριον Orib.*Fr.*102, cf. Paul.Aeg.3.80. **-ίας κάλαμος**, ὁ, reed *used for making pipes*, Thphr.*HP*4.11.10 (corr. Schneider), Dsc.1.85. **-ιάω**, *suffer from fistula*, *Hippiatr.*128. * **-ιον**, τό, Dim. of σῦριγξ, *little reed* or *pipe*, Plu.2.456a, Artem.4.72: also **-ίδιον**, Hero *Spir.*1.16. 2. *hole in a wheel*, Hsch. 3. *small fistula* or *ulcer*, Hp.*Epid.*6.8.27. 4. = σῦριγξ I. 4, Dsc.1.13. 5. *groove, channel*, Ath.Mech.14. 10. **-ίς**, ίδος, ἡ, *like a pipe*, κασία, i. e. *quill-cassia*, Androm.ap.Gal. 14.73. **-ίτης** [ῑ], ου, ὁ, fem. **-ῖτις**, ιδος, a precious stone, Plin. *HN*37.182.

**σῡριγγό-ποδες στίχοι**, prob. cj. for συρόποδες (= *fistulares versus*) in Diom. p.498 K. **-ποιός**, ὁ, *pipe-maker*, prob. rest. in *Tab.Defix.* 55.2. **-τόμον**, τό, *a knife for cutting fistulae*, Heliod.ap.Orib. 44.23.57, Gal.10.415, Paul.Aeg.6.72; *syringotomium* in Veget.*Mul.* 2.27.2.

**σῡριγγ-όω**, *make into a pipe, carry along like a pipe*, σ. φλέβα Hp. *Oss.*13,16:—Pass., *grow hollow, end in a fistula*, Id.*Prog.*18, *Fist.* 1, Gal.18(2).209; σεσυριγγωμένος τόπος D.S.32.11. * **-ώδης**, ες, *like a pipe* or *tube*, hence *perforated, carious*, ὀστέα Hp.*Epid.*5.41, cf. 7.5. **-ωμα**, ατος, τό, *fistula*, Vett.Val.110.37 (pl.). **-ωσις**, εως, ἡ, *formation of a fistula*, Antyll.ap.Orib.44.23.4.

**σῡριγκτής**, v. συριστής.

**σύριγ-μα** [ῡ], ατος, τό, *sound of a pipe*, in pl., E.*Ba.*952, Ar.*Ach.* 554; *whistling*, κυνορτικὸν σ. S.*Ichn.*167; ἀνέμων Orph.*H.*34.25; *hissing* of the serpent Pytho, *Pae.Delph.*20 (pl.). **-μᾰτώδης**, ες, *like the sound of a pipe, whistling*, ἦχος Cass.*Pr.*82. **-μός**, ὁ, *shrill piping sound, hissing*, as of serpents, Arist.*HA*536$^a$6, Str.9.3. 10 (pl.); in sign of derision, X.*Smp.*6.5; as a military signal, Aen. Tact.24.17; σ. καὶ χλευασμοί Plb.30.29.6; σ. κάλων the *whistling* of rigging, D.H.*Comp.*16; of the sound of sibilants, ib.14; *hissing* in the theatre, Plu.*Cic.*13; of the cry of elephants, Arr.*An.*5.17.7; *singing in the ears*, Dsc.2.78.

* **σῦριγξ**, ιγγος, ἡ, *shepherd's pipe, Panspipe*, αὐλῶν συρίγγων τ' ἐνοπή Il.10.13; νομῆες τερπόμενοι σύριγξι 18.526; συρίγγων ἐνοπή *h.Merc.*512; ὑπὸ λιγυρῶν συρίγγων ἵεσαν αὐδήν Hes.*Sc.*278; οὐ μολπὰν σύριγγος ἔχων S.*Ph.*213 (lyr.); καλαμίνη σ. Ar.*Fr.*719; κατ' ἀγροὺς τοῖς νομεῦσι σῦριγξ ἄν τις εἴη Pl.*R.*399d. 2. *cat-call, whistle, hiss*, as in theatres, Id.*Lg.*700c; cf. συρίζω II. 2, συριγμός:—the last part of the νόμος Πυθικός was called σύριγγες, prob. because it imitated the dying *hisses* of the serpent Pytho, Str.9.3.10. 3. *mouthpiece of the* αὐλός, Plu.2.1138a, 1096b. 4. *quill* of the cassia, Androm.ap.Gal.14.73, Dsc.1.13; cf. συριγγίς. II. *anything like a pipe*: 1. *spear-case*, = δορατοθήκη, Il.19.387. 2. *hole in the nave of a wheel*, A.*Th.*205 (lyr.), *Supp.*181, S.*El.*721, E.*Hipp.* 1234, Theoc.24.120, etc.; cf. Suid. 3. *hollow part of a hinge*, Parm. 1.19. 4. Medic., in pl., *pores* or *bronchial passages* of the lungs, Arist.*Resp.*478$^a$13, 480$^b$7, *HA*496$^b$3, 513$^b$5; δι' οὗ μερίζεται τὸ πνεῦμα κατὰ τὰς ἀρτηρίας εἰς τὰς σ. Id.*PA*664$^a$28; of other *ducts* or *channels* in the body, λίφαιμοι σαρκῶν σύριγγες Emp.100.2, cf. Max.169; σύριγγες ἄνω φυσῶσι μέλαν μένος S.*Aj.*1412 (anap.); of the trachea, Hp. *Cord.*2; the liver-*duct*, ἡ σ. τοῦ ἥπατος Id.*Mul.*1.78 (cf. θρίξ III); σ. αἱματόεσσα, of a *vein*, A.R.4.1647; ἱερὰ σ. *cavity* of the spine, Poll. 2.180; *passage* through the elephant's trunk, Aret.*SD*2.13. 5. *fistulous sore* or *abscess*, Hp.*Coac.*501, Plu.2.60a, Gal.6.244; ἐν τῷ γόνατι Artem.1.47. 6. σ. πτεροῦ, v. πτερόν I. 1. 7. *groove* or *barrel* of a catapult, Ph.*Bel.*61.46, 62.40, Hero *Bel.*100.5, Vitr.10.10. 3. 8. *subterranean passage, gallery, mine*, Plb.9.41.9, 21.28.6, Str.3.2.9, al.; of *the burial vaults* of the Egyptian kings at Thebes, Ael.*NA*6.43, Paus.1.42.3, Baillet *Inscr. des tombeaux des rois à Thèbes* Nos.13,245, al. 9. *covered gallery* or *cloister*, Callix.1, Plb.15.31. 3; σύριγγας τῶν ὑσπλήγων δύο *BCH*35.286 (Delos). 10. *channel* for counterweight in automaton, Hero *Aut.*2.8. 11. perh. *loop*, J.*AJ*3.7.5.

**σύριγξις**, εως, ἡ, *playing on the syrinx*, Sch.E.*Or.*145.

* **σῡρίζω**, A.*Pr.*357, *Th.*463, Hp.*Int.*10, E.*Ion* 501 (lyr.), Apollod. 3.10.2; Att. **συρίττω** Pl.*Tht.*203b, Arist.*HA*611$^b$26; Dor. **συρίσδω** Theoc.1.3, etc.: fut. συρίξομαι Luc.*Bis Acc.*12, etc.; συρίσω Hero *Spir.*1.41, Longus 2.23; συριῶ Lxx *Is.*5.26, al.: aor. ἐσύριξα Ar. *Pl.*689; later ἐσύρισα Babr.114.4, Luc.*Harm.*2: (*συριγγ-yω, cf. σῦριγξ):—*play the* σῦριγξ, *pipe*, ὅτε .. συρίζεις, ὦ Πάν E. l. c.; ἁδὺ δὲ καὶ τὺ συρίσδες Theoc.1.3; συρίζων ὁ κηροδέτας κάλαμος E.*IT*1125 (lyr.): c. acc. cogn., συρίζων ποιμνίτας ὑμεναίους Id.*Alc* 576 (lyr.). II. *make any whistling* or *hissing sound, hiss* like a serpent, συρίξας ἐγώ Ar.*Pl.*689; ψόφος .. οἷον συριττούσης τῆς γλώττης, of the tongue sounding σ, Pl.*Tht.*203b; συριζόντων κατὰ πρύμναν .. πηδαλίων E.*IT* 431 (lyr.); of the wind, *whistle*, Babr. l. c.: c. acc. cogn., συρίζων φόβον A.*Pr.*357; φιμοὶ δὲ συρίζουσι βάρβαρον βρόμον Id.*Th.*463. 2. *hiss* an actor (cf. σῦριγξ I. 2), ἐξέπιπτες ἐγὼ δ' ἐσύριττον D.18.265, cf. Timocl.2 D., Luc.*Nigr.*10, etc. b. c. acc. pers., *hiss* him, D.21. 226:—Pass., Aeschin.3.76,231, Pl.*Ax.*368d, Aristid.*Or.*34(50).7.

**Σῠρίζω**, *speak like a Syrian*, S.E.*M.*1.314, Luc.*Merc.Cond.*10, Porph.*Abst.*3.5.

**Σῠρίη**, ἡ, v. Σῦρος, Σύρος.

**Σῠριηγενής**, ές, *Syrian-born*, Orac.ap.Hdt.7.140, Orph.*L.*262.

**Σῠρικός**, ή, όν, *from Syria, Syrian*, St.Byz.:—**Συρικόν**, τό, = σάνδυξ, *lead oxide*, Alex.Trall.3.7, Aët.2.70, Paul.Aeg.7.3: cf. σηρικός 3.

**συρικτής**, v. συριστής.

* **Σύριος** [ῠ], α, ον, *of* or *from Syria*, A.*Pers.*84 (lyr.), etc.: cf. Σῦρος.

**συρίσδω**, v. συρίζω. * **συρίσκος**, * **συρισσος**, ὁ, v. ὑρισός.

* **σύρ-ισμα** [ῡ], ατος, τό, and **-ισμός**, ὁ, later forms of σύριγμα, -μός; the former in Hsch. s. v. ἄσθμα, the latter in Lxx *Jd.*5.16, al., Luc. *Anach.*32. **-ιστηρίδιον**, τό, Dim. of συριστήρ (v. sq.), but perh. =

*small Panspipe*, *BGU* 1125.3,23 (i B.C.). ※ **-ιστής**, οῦ, ὁ, also **-ικτής**, Arist.*Pr.* 917ᵃ8, Corn.*ND* 27; **-ίγκτης** (s.v.l.) Phot. s.v. λαπήττειν; Dor. **-ικτάς** Theoc.7.28, *AP* 6.73 (Maced.), 237 (Antist.); and **-ιστήρ**, ῆρος, ib.5.205 (Leon.):—*player on the Panspipe, piper*, *SIG* 589.45 (Magn. Mae., ii B.C.), 1257 (Ephesus, i A.D.), *PGnom.* 187 (ii A.D.), Luc.*Syr.D.* 43; *whistling*, of the pipe, *AP* 5 l.c.; of branches, ib.6.237 (Antist.). II. *the male crane*, so called from his note, Hsch.

**Σῠριστί**, Adv. *in the Syrian language*, Σ. ἐπίστασθαι to understand *Syrian*, X.*Cyr.* 7.5.31, cf. *PPetr.* 3 p.14 (iii B.C.), Plu.*Ant.* 46, Luc.*Alex.* 51.

**σῡριστική** (sc. τέχνη), ἡ, *the art of piping*, Sch.D.T.p.111 H.

**συρίτης** [ῑ], ου, ὁ, stone found in wolf's bladder, Plin.*HN* 11.208.

**σῡρίττω**, v. συρίζω. ※ **σύρῖχος**, ὁ, v. ὑριχός. **συρκίζω**, Aeol. for σαρκάζω, Hsch.

**σύρμα**, ατος, τό, (σύρω) *anything trailed* or *dragged*: I. *a theatric robe with a long train*, Arr.*Epict.* 1.29.41, Poll.7.67, *An.Par.* 1.19; σ. ἱματίου *train*, Ptol.*Tetr.* 24; without ἱματίου, Heph.Astr.1.1; Lat. *syrma*, Juv.8.229, Mart.4.49.8, al.; cf. σύρω I, συρτός II: periphr., σύρμα πλοκάμων *long flowing* hair, *AP* 5.12 (Phld.); σ. τερηδόνος *a long* woodworm, ib.12.190 (Strat.). 2. *sweepings, refuse, litter*, ὄνους σύρματ' ἂν ἑλέσθαι μᾶλλον ἢ χρυσόν Heraclit.9; cf. συρφετός. 3. Medic., perh. *abrasion, scaly skin-disease*, Hp.*Epid.* 4.30; ἀπὸ..συρμάτων ἀποθνήσκοντες Ptol.*Tetr.* 201 (but κλασμάτων Procl. ad loc.); cf. ἀπόσυρμα I. 1. II. *dragging, trailing motion*, μόσχων Mesom.*Sol.* 23; *trail* left by a serpent, D.Chr.5.19, Ael.*NA* 9.61:—σ. Ἀντιγόνης a place at Thebes, where Antigone was said *to have dragged* the body of Polynices to his brother's pyre, Paus.9.25.2. 2. Music, *drawing out* or *prolonging the tones*, Ptol.*Harm.* 2.12. 3. *syrma*, = *dictio longa*, *Gloss.*

**συρμ-αία**, Ion. **-αίη**, ἡ, (συρμός II) *purge-plant*, a name given to *the radish*, as used by the Egyptians (cf. μελανοσυρμαῖος), Hdt.2.88, 125, Ar.*Pax* 1254, *PPetr.* 3 p.327 (iii B.C.), D.S.1.64, cf. Erot. s.v. ἀπὸ συρμαϊσμοῦ, Did.ap.Sch.Ar. l.c.:—its juice mixed with salt water they used as *a purgative and emetic*, Hp.*Mul.* 1.78, cf. Hsch. II. *a mixture of honey and suet*, given as a prize at Sparta, in a contest of the same name, *IG* 5(1).222.7 (v B.C.?), Hsch. **-αΐζω**, *take an emetic* or *purge*, of the Egyptians, συρμαΐζουσι τρεῖς ἡμέρας ἐπεξῆς μηνὸς ἑκάστου, ἐμέτοισι θηρώμενοι τὴν ὑγιείην καὶ κλύσμασι Hdt.2.77, cf. Ael.*NA* 5.46, Ps.-Diocl.ap.Paul.Aeg.1.100. **-αιοπώλης**, ου, ὁ, *one who sells emetics* or *purges*, Ar.*Fr.* 265, Critias 70 D. **-αϊσμός**, ὁ, *use of an emetic*, ἐμεῖν ἀπὸ σ. Hp.*Art.* 40, cf. Gal.18(1).484, Ruf.*Interrog.* 70, Ps.-Diocl.ap.Paul.Aeg.1.100.

**συρμάς**, άδος, ἡ, (σύρω) *snowdrift*, in pl., Anon. in Rh.3.579 W.

**συρμᾰτική φωνή**, *long drawn-out* accent (cf. σύρμα II. 2), Steph. *in Rh.* 309.24. II. *syrmaticum* jumentum, a mule *suffering from string-halt*, Veget.*Mul.* 2.86.1.

**συρμᾰτὶς στρατιά**, *one which sweeps up, carries away*, Hsch.

**συρμᾰτῖτις κόπρος**, ἡ, manure *mixed with litter* (cf. σύρμα I. 2), Thphr.*HP* 2.7.4, 7.5.1.

**συρμή**, ἡ, *trail* of a snake, Sch.Luc.*Herm.* 79.

**συρμίον**· λαχανόν τι σελίνῳ ἐοικός, Hsch. (cf. σίον).

**συρμιστήρ**, ῆρος, ὁ, *one who sells shavings*, etc., *for firing*, Hsch.

**συρμός**, ὁ, (σύρω) *any sweeping motion*, γινέσθω μὴ κατὰ πληγὴν ἢ ἐγχάραξις, ἀλλὰ κατὰ σ. Antyll.ap.Orib.7.18.6; *track* of meteors, πρηστήρων Pl.*Ax.* 370c, cf. Arist.*Mir.* 843ᵃ11; *sweep* of waves, Ph.1.298; νιφετῶν, ἀνέμων, *AP* 7.8 (Antip. Sid., pl.), 498 (Antip.); χαλαζήεις ib.6.221 (Leon.); *trail* of a serpent, Plu.*Ant.* 86. II. *vomiting* or *purging* (cf. συρμαία), Nic.*Al.* 256.

**σύρξ**, v. σάρξ.

**σύρον**, τό, name of a plant, Plin.*HN* 26.33.

**συροπέρδιξ**, ῑκος, ὁ, = Σύρος πέρδιξ, *Damascus* or *desert partridge*, *Ammoperdix heyi*, Ael.*NA* 16.7.

**συρόποδες**, v. συριγγόποδες.

**σῡροποιός**, ὁ, *maker* of σύραι (= συρίαι), *IGRom.* 1.1482 (Philippopolis).

**σύρος** [ῠ], ὁ, *broom, brushwood*, Varro *Sat.Men.* 271.

**Σῦρος**, ὁ, *Syros*, one of the Cyclades, Str.10.5.8; called **Συρίη** in Od.15.403 (acc. to Str. l.c.: but more probably Συρίη is Sicily and the name is connected with Συράκουσαι); later **Σύρα**, Suid. s.v. Φερεκύδης, f.l. in D.L.1.119:—**Σύριος**, ὁ, *a Syran*, *IG* 1².193.32 (pl.), D.L.1.116. ※ **Σύρος** [ῠ], ὁ, *Syrian*, *IG* 1².329.18, Hdt.3.91 codd. (v.l. in 2.30, 104, 159, 3.5), *Trag.Adesp.* 162; of the Λευκόσυροι, S.*Fr.* 638, Hdt.1.6 codd., 7.72 codd. (but Σύριοι of the Λ., v. infr.); freq. used as a slave's name, Anaxandr.51, Eriph.6, Hegesipp.Com.1.4, D.45.86, *IG* 2².2937.12, etc.:—fem. **Σύρα**, Ar.*Pax* 1146 (troch.), Philem.125.—Syria was called **Συρία**, Ion. **-ίη**, ἡ, Hdt.1.105, etc.; Σ. ἡ Παλαιστίνη Id.3.91, 4.39; Σ. Παλαιστίνη *IGRom.* 3.172.22 (Ancyra, ii A.D.), *OGI* 601.6 (Amastris, ii A.D.); ἡ Φοινίκη Σ. D.S.19.93; Κοίλη Σ. between Lebanon and Anti-Lebanon, v. κοῖλος; ἡ ἄνω Σ. (dub.l.) Str.2.5.38.—The Syrians were also called **Σύριοι**, a name which in early times was given to the Assyrians, Hdt.7.63, cf. A.*Pers.* 84 (lyr.), Luc.*Syr.D.* 1; and to the Cappadocians or Λευκόσυροι (Str.12.3.5, al.), Hdt.1.72, 2.104, 3.90, 5.49; Σ. Καππαδόκαι (v.l. Σ. καὶ Κ.) Id.1.72; Σ. οἱ ἐν τῇ Παλαιστίνῃ Id.2.104.—Adj. **Σύριος** [ῠ], α, ον, *Syrian*, A.*Ag.* 1312, E.*Ba.* 144 (lyr.), etc.; Σ. πόα Arist.*HA* 627ᵇ17; Σ. πύλαι (v. πύλη II. 2):—also **Συριᾰκός**, ή, όν, Thphr.*CP* 2.17.3, Str.2.1.31, etc.—Adv. **Συρίηθεν** *from Syria*, D.P.895.

**Σῡρο-φοῖνιξ**, ῑκος, ὁ, *Syro-Phoenician*, Luc.*Deor.Conc.* 4, cf. Juv.8.159:—fem. **-φοίνισσα**, *Ev.Marc.* 7.26.

※ **σύρρα**, = σὺν ῥα, Ζηνὸς δ' ἐνὶ γαστέρι σ. πεφύκει Orph.*Fr.* 167: σύρρα· ὁμόσε, εἰς τὸ αὐτό, Hsch.

**συρρᾰγή**, ἡ, = sq., Tz.*H.* 3.721, al.

**σύρραγμα**, ατος, τό, *conflict*, μάχης cj. for σύγγραμμα in Plu.2.346e; cf. σύρρηγμα.

**συρράδιος**, ον, = νόθος, μικτός, εἰκαῖος, Hsch.; cf. ὑρράδιος.

**συρραδιουργέω**, *commit a crime with*, τινι Ph.2.196, Plu.2.53c.

**συρρᾰθᾰγέω**, *crunch*, Nic.*Th.* 194.

**συρρᾰΐζω**, *recover health with*, ῥαΐζοντι Pall. *in Hp.* 2.108 D.

**σύρραξις**, εως, ἡ, *dashing together*, [τῶν κλυδώνων] πρὸς ἀλλήλους Arist.*Mir.* 843ᵃ16; ὅπλων Plu.2.339b, cf. Id.*Caes.* 44; cf. σύρρηξις.

**συρραπτός**, όν, *sewn together*, Arr.*Tact.* 35.3, Gal.18(1).773.

**συρράπτω**, *sew* or *stitch together*, δέρματα νεύρῳ βοὸς Hes.*Op.* 544, cf. Hdt.2.86, 4.64, Sor.*Fasc.* 46; τὴν ῥῖνα Hp.*Morb.* 2.36; ῥῆγμα Archipp.38; [κοιλίαν], γαστέρα, *IG* 4²(1).122.18, 33 (Epid., iv B.C.); σ. τὰ στόματα τῶν ἀνθρώπων *sew* men's mouths *up*, i.e. *stop* their mouths, *muzzle* them, Pl.*Euthd.* 303e; τὰς ἐπιθυμίας σ. ταῖς ἀπολαύσεσι *bring* appetites *into connexion with* enjoyment, i.e. gratify them immediately, Plu.2.565d; σ. ῥήματα πρὸς ἕκαστα Them.*Or.* 21.252d; σ. Βάκχον μηρῷ *sew* him *up* in.., Nonn.*D.* 7.152. II. metaph., *put together, compose*, of a treatise, Phld.*Ind.Sto.* 4 (Pass.); σ. τοιαῦτα *form* such *machinations*, dub. cj. for συνέγραψε in D.C.38.14.

**συρράσσω**, Att. **-ττω**, *dash together, fight with*, ἄδηλον ὂν ὁπότε σφίσιν αὐτοῖς ξυρράξουσι Th.8.96; ἀντιμέτωπος συνέρραξε τοῖς Θηβαίοις X.*HG* 4.3.19, cf. 7.5.16; σ. εἰς τὴν μάχην D.S.16.4; of ships, Id.20.51; of rivers, *meet with a roar*, Id.17.97; τοῦ κουφοτάτου καὶ βαρυτάτου..συρραξάντων διαμάχη Ph.2.513.

**συρραστωνέω**, *subside together*, of symptoms, Gal.17(2).128.

**συρρᾰφ-εύς**, έως, ὁ, *one who stitches together*, Sch.Ar.*Nu.* 445. **-ή**, ἡ, *sewing together, seam*, Hp.*Off.* 9, Heliod.ap.Orib.48.50.1, 48.58.4, Sor.*Fasc.* 47. **-ής**, ές, = συρραπτός, κώεα συνραφέ' ἀλλήλοισι *Epic.Alex.Adesp.* 2.31.

**συρρέζω**, *celebrate together*, ὄργια *IG* 14.1020.

**συρρέμβομαι**, *roam together*, v.l. in Lxx *Pr.* 13.20, D.L.9.63, Hsch.Mil.7.54.

**συρρέπω**, *incline together*, τῇ διανοίᾳ ἐπί τι Plb.3.38.5.

**σύρρευσις**, εως, ἡ, *flowing together, conflux*, Arist.*HA* 551ᵇ28, Corn.*ND* 30; the form **σύρρῠσις** in Plb.9.43.5, D.S.1.39, D.H.*Comp.* 16, etc.

**συρρέω**, fut. -ρῠήσομαι Theo Sm.p.124 H.: pf. -ερρύηκα Isoc.8.44: aor. Pass. -ερρύην X.*HG* 2.3.18, Arist.*Pr.* 876ᵃ17, 888ᵇ11 (later aor. -έρρευσα, Alex.Trall.5.4: pf. -έρευκα (v. infr. III)):—*flow together* or *into one stream*, εἰς τοῦτο τὸ χάσμα συρρέουσι..πάντες οἱ ποταμοί Pl.*Phd.* 112a, cf. 109b,c; ὁ ὀπὸς συρρεῖ εἰς.. Dsc.4.170, cf. Sor.1.36, al., Gal.6.66, al.: metaph. of men, *flow* or *stream together*, συνέρρεον ἐς τὴν ἀγορήν Hdt.5.101, cf. 8.42, X.*An.* 5.2.3, *HG* l.c., Isoc. l.c., Pl.*Lg.* 708d; and of money, Is.2.28; of evils, Plu.*Sull.* 13; εἰς [τὸ γῆρας] πάντα τὰ χαλεπὰ σ. X.*Ap.* 8; of pathological conditions, ἡνίκα συρρεῖ ὀπῶρος Cass.*Pr.* 57; διασκορπίζειν τὸ συρρυέν Sever.ap.Aët.7.87. II. *float along together with*, κατὰ ῥοῦν σ. τῷ ὕδατι Luc.*Herm.* 86. III. *fall into ruin*, λάκκος συνερευκὼς καὶ ὁ τροχὸς ὁμοίως συνερευκὼς ἐκ μέρους *POxy.* 1475.16 (iii A.D.).

**σύρρηγμα**, ατος, τό, *clash, collision*, φάλαγγος Plu.2.350e codd. (fort. σύρραγμα).

**συρρήγνῡμι**, fut. -ρήξω: pf. Pass. -έρρηγμαι: aor. Pass. -ερράγην [ᾰ]: intr. pf. 2 -έρρωγα: I. trans., *break in pieces*, τὴν κεφαλήν Plu.*Tim.* 34:—Pass., κακοῖσι συνέρρηκται *he is broken down* by sufferings, Od.8.137. 2. *unite by breaking* partitions, τὸ γὰρ ἄστυ μίαν οἴκησίν φημι ποιήσειν συρρήξασ' εἰς ἓν ἅπαντα Ar.*Ec.* 674 (anap.): intr., of rivers, ποταμοὶ καὶ ἄλλοι καὶ Ὕλλος συρρηγνῦσι ἐς τὸν Ἕρμον *break into* the Hermus, *join* it, Hdt.1.80:—Pass., of sores, *run together, pass into one another*, κίνδυνος ἂν εἴη συρραγῆναι τὰς ὠτειλάς Hp.*Art.* 11; so, of ducts in the body, τὸ ἐξωτάτω τρῆμα συνερρωγὸς εἰς ταὐτό Arist.*HA* 497ᵃ25; of internal ruptures, Diocl.*Fr.* 79, Erasistr.ap.Gal.8.318. II. *dash together*: metaph., σ. πόλεμον *cause* war *to break out*, Plu.2.1049d:—Pass., ὁ πόλεμος ξυνερρώγει Th.1.66, cf. J.*BJ* 1.19.1, D.C.38.47; πολέμου συρραγέντος Plu.2.322b; κραυγὴ συνερρήγνυτο Id.*Arat.* 21; πότου νεανικοῦ συρραγέντος Id.*Alex.* 50; also συνερρωγότων..αὐτῶν εἰς τὸν πόλεμον D.C.48.28. 2. Pass., *meet in battle, engage*, αἱ δυνάμεις συνερράγησαν Plu.*Sull.* 18, cf. *Caes.* 45; τινι or πρός τινα, Id.*Mar.* 26 (where συρράξεως follows), D.C.40.17; generally, *clash together*, δύο σωμάτων συρραγέντων Plot.4.5.5; *collide*, of ships, J.*BJ* 3.9.3: metaph., ἐθνῶν ἔθνεσι συρραγέντων ib.*Prooem.* 1.

**σύρρηξις**, εως, ἡ, *internal rupture* (into another part) of abscess, Heliod.ap.Orib.44.9.1, Archig.ap.Aët.8.73, Ruf.ap.eund.11.18, Aret.*CD* 1.13. 2. *clashing together*, Plot.4.5.5 (nisi σύρραξιν legend.).

**συρρήσσω**, *confligo*, *Gloss.*; συρρήσσοντα[ς], *singultantem*, ib.

**συρρητορεύω**, *to be a rhetorician with*, τινι Nic.Dam.*Fr.* 135 J.

**συρριζόομαι**, Pass., *to have the roots united*, Arist.*de An.* 415ᵇ29, Luc.*VH* 1.8. II. *to be rooted* or *founded with*, τινι Them.*Or.* 14.183d.

**σύρριζος**, ον, *joined to the root, root and all*, Sch.rec.S.*El.* 512, Eust.93.5. 2. *well supplied with roots*, ποιῆσαι τὸν ἵππον..χλωροφαγῆσαι ἐπὶ πεδίον σ. *Hippiatr.* 10.

**συρρίπτω**, *throw together*, κώμας εἴκοσι εἰς πόλιν D.S.15.72.

**συρρίφη**· συνσκέπη, Hsch.

**συρροή**, ἡ, = σύρρευσις, *conflux*, Thphr.*Lap.* 1, *Ign.* 50, al.; ἰχώρων

Plu.*Cleom.*39; συνροὰ (Dor.) ὑδάτων *Mnemos.*42.332 (Argos, iv B.C.); *exudation* which forms a bulbil, σ. δακρυώδης Thphr.*HP*6.6.8; *accumulation* of earth, ib.7.15.2: also **σύρροια**, Hp.*Alim.*23, Plb.2.32.2, Str.1.3.12, Aret.*CD*1.13 (ξύρρ–); σύνροια *IG*5(1).1431.20 (Messene).

⊛ **σύρροος**, ον, contr. **σύρρους**, ουν, *flowing together, confluent*, Ti. Locr.101e, 104a; λίμνη τῇ θαλάττῃ σ. Plb.10.10.12, cf. 4.40.9: abs., Str.4.1.2, al.; of an isthmus, σύρρουν ποτὲ ὑπάρξαντα, i.e. once covered by the seas, Id.1.2.32. II. σύρρους, ὁ, *compluvium*, *Gloss.*

⊛ **σύρροπον**, τό, dub. sens. (perh. *casting-weight*) in *Supp.Epigr.*7.808 (Syria).

**σύρρῠσις**, v. σύρρευσις.

**συρρώννῠμαι**, Pass., *to be strengthened together* or *at once*, Ph.1.223.

**συρρώομαι**, impf. συνερρώοντο *rushed also*, Nonn.*D.*39.74.

**σύρσις**, εως, ἡ, *drawing* of a plough by oxen, *PStrassb.*32.5 (iii A.D.); = *tractio, tractus*, *Gloss.* II. place-name (?) in *Sammelb.*5677.15 (iii A.D.).

⊛ **σύρτης**, ου, ὁ, (σύρω) *cord for drawing with, rein*, Man.5.172, Hsch. II. σύρτης or συρτός, v. συρτός, ὁ.

**Σύρτις**, gen. εως, Ion. ιος, also ιδος D.P.477, ἡ: (σύρω):—*the Syrtis*, name of two large shallow gulfs on the coast of Libya, Hdt.2.32, 150, etc. II. metaph., *destruction*, ἄλλα δ' ἄλλαν θραύει σ. Tim. *Pers.*99, cf. Cic.*Orat.*3.41.163, Hsch.

**συρτῖτις**, ιδος, ἡ, name of a gem, Plin.*HN*37.182, Isid.*Etym.*16.14.10.

**συρτός**, ή, όν, *swept* or *washed down by a river*, of gold-dust, etc., Plb.34.9.10, Str.3.2.10, 5.4.6. II. *trailing*, χιτὼν σ., = σύρμα 1.1, Sch.Ar.*Lys.*45, cf. Poll.4.118; ζῷον, of the ἔχιδνα, Cyran.58.

⊛ **συρτός**, ὁ (or **σύρτης**, ου, ὁ), the name of a dance, ἡ τῶν συρτῶν πάτριος ὄρχησις *IG*7.2712.66 (Acraephia, i A.D.).

**σύρφαξ**, ᾱκος, ὁ, = συρφετός 2a, Ar.*V.*673 (anap.), Luc.*Lex.*4, etc. II. as Adj., = συρφετώδης, δῆμος Anon.ap.Suid.

**συρφετ-ός**, ὁ, *anything dragged* or *swept together, sweepings, refuse, litter*, χόρτος καὶ σ. Hes.*Op.*606, cf. Call.*Ap.*109, Plu.2.97f; συρφετὸν ἡγεῖσθαί τι ib.811e; σ. ῥημάτων Jul.*Or.*7.218c; cf. σύρμα 1.2. 2. metaph., *mixed crowd, mob, rabble*, σ. δούλων Pl.*Grg.*489c; τῷ πολλῷ σ. to the many-headed *mob*, Id.*Tht.*152c; ἐλθεῖν εἰς τοιοῦτον σ. Euphro 10.6, cf. Jul.*Or.*5.173a. b. of a single person, *one of the mob*, οὐ κομψός, ἀλλὰ σ. Pl.*Hp.Ma.*288d:—hence as Adj., *of* or *like the mob, vulgar*, Simp. *in Epict.* p.86 D., Sch.Hermog. in Rh.4.40 W. **-ώδης**, ες, *promiscuous, vulgar*, σ. ὄχλος Plb.4.75.5, cf. Luc.*Salt.*83, etc.; βωμολοχία σ. Plu.2.454e; πράγματα Jul.*Or.*6.202b.

**σύρφη**· φρύγανα, Hsch.

**σύρφος**· θηρίδιον μικρόν, ὁποῖον ἐμπίς (cf. σέρφος?), Hsch.

⊛ **σύρω** [ῡ], Batr.75, etc.: fut. σῠρῶ Lxx 2*Ki.*17.13: aor. ἔσῡρα (κατ–) Hdt.5.81, (παρ–) A.*Pr.*1065 (anap.), (δι–) D.19.313: pf. σέσυρκα (δια–) Diph.75, (ἐπι–) D.H.1.7:—**Med.**, aor. ἐσῡράμην (περι–) Hyp. *Fr.*264, (ἀν–) D.S.1.85:—**Pass.**, aor. ἐσύρην [ῠ] Paus.2.32.1: pf. σέσυρμαι (ἐπι–) Plb.12.4c.3, Luc.*Nav.*2:—*draw, drag, trail along*, χιτῶνα Theoc.2.73; μέχρι τῶν σφυρῶν τὴν ἐσθῆτα σ. D.C.46.18; βλαύτας σύρων *trailing* his torn slippers, Anaxil.18.2 (anap.); cf. σύρμα 1.1; *drag* a net, *Ev.Jo.*21.8, Plu.2.977f; σ. πηκτίδα, v. πηκτίς 1.2; of oxen, ἵνα σύρῃ τὰ ξύλα *PFlor.*158.7 (iii A.D.); *drag about*, τι Luc.*Asin.*56, Orph.*H.*81.4:—Pass., *hang trailing, trail along*, οὐρή, νηδύς, Tryph. 82, *AP*9.310 (Antiphil.); of a person, *crawl*, σύρεσθαι γαστέρι ib.5.293.12 (Agath.):—also intr. in Act., of a column of ships compared to a serpent, Lyc.217; *crawl*, συρόντων ἐπὶ γῆν Lxx *De.*32.24. 2. *drag by force, hale*, αἰχμάλωτον Theoc.*Adon.*12; Πριαμίδην *AP*7.152 (Pass.); ἄνδρας καὶ γυναῖκας *Act.Ap.*8.3; of waves or rivers, *sweep, sweep away*, κλύδων ἐπὶ χέρσον ἔσυρεν δελφῖνα *AP*7.216 (Antip. Thess.), cf. 9.84 (Antiphan., Pass.); πόλεμος χειμάρρου δίκην πάντα σ. Plu.2.5f: metaph., φάραγγα σ. the dough *has* a cleft *made in it*, Eub.75.12:—Pass., σύρεσθαι κατὰ ῥοῦν Plu.*Mar.*23; χρυσὸς οὐ μεταλλεύεται μόνον, ἀλλὰ καὶ σύρεται, of gold-dust (cf. συρτός), Str.3.2.8: abs. in Pass., of a stream, *flow* or *run down*, D.P.46, cf. Orac.Chald.ap.Dam.*Pr.*262: metaph. in *AP*10.62 (Pall.). 3. metaph. in Pass., *to be dragged, drawn*, εἰς οὐκ ἀναγκαῖα πράγματα Diog.Oen.1, cf. Iamb.*VP*3.16. 4. Pass., of taxes, *to be attached* to land, pf. part. σεσυρομένης (sic) *PLond.*5.1686.33 (vi A.D.), cf. ἐπισεσυρομένα in *PFlor.*294.41 (vi A.D.), and ἐπισύρεσθαι in *PMasp.*151.135 (vi A.D.).

**σῦς**, v. ὗς.

**συσβέννῡμι** or **-ύω**, *help to extinguish*, Sch.Ar.*Lys.*349:—aor. Med. in pass. sense, συνέσβετο Opp.*H.*2.477.

**συσῑνᾱπιστέον**, *one must plaster* head *as well* as chest *with mustard*, Paul.Aeg.7.19 (v.l. συσσ–).

**συσκανία, σύσκανος**, v. συσκηνία, σύσκηνος.

**συσκάπτω**, *trench and fill in*, Thphr.*CP*3.12.1.

**συσκεδάννῡμι**, *scatter to the winds*, Ar.*Ra.*903 (lyr.).

**συσκέλλω**, *dry up*: pf. –έσκληκα, *to be dried up*, *AB*304, Agath.2.14.

**σύσκεμμα**, ατος, τό, *joint consideration*, Eust.1404.52.

**συσκεπάζω**, *cover entirely*, Apollod.2.5.12, Sor.1.83, *Fasc.*54 (all Pass.).

**συσκεπτ-έον**, *one must consider*, μετά τινος Pl.*Sph.*218b. ⊛ **-ομαι**, = συσκοπέω, Sm.*Ps.*2.2, *Gloss.*

**συσκέπω**, *cooperio*, *Gloss.*

**συσκευ-άζω**, *make ready by putting together, pack up* baggage for another, X.*Cyr.*1.4.25. 2. *help in preparing*, τὸ δεῖπνον νῷν Ar. *V.*1251:—Pass., συνεσκευασμένα παρασκευάσματα X.*Oec.*11.19. b. in bad sense, *contrive, concert, get up*, D.24.206:—Pass., Id.18.144, 19.76; ἅπαντα εἰς ἓν ψήφισμα ib.54; σ. λοιδορίας ψευδεῖς κατά τινων Hyp.*Lyc.*9; τοιαῦτα κατά τινος Hdn.3.12.4. II. Med., with pf. συνεσκεύασμαι, *pack up one's own baggage, pack up*, Th.7.74, X.*Cyr.*5.3.16, etc.; σ. ὡς εἰς στρατείαν Id.*HG*3.4.11; εἰς τὸ ἀπιέναι ib.5.2.28; πρὸς τὴν φυγήν Luc.*Tim.*4: esp. in aor. part. or pf. Med., *all packed up, in marching order, ready for a start*, παρεῖναι συνεσκευασμένος X.*Cyr.*3.2.3; πορεύεσθαι συσκευασάμενοι ib.6.2.3, cf. *PTeb.*765.11 (ii B.C.), etc. 2. c. acc., οἷον στρωματόδεσμον συσκευάσασθαι Pl.*Tht.*175e; συσκευασάμενος τὰ ἑαυτοῦ ἐνθένδε *with all* his goods *packed up and brought* thence, Lys.31.9, cf. Lycurg.17, Din.1.80, X.*Smp.*1.11, etc.; *prepare, make ready*, τὴν πορείαν Id.*Cyr.*8.5.1; τὸν ὄνον *PSI*4.359.6 (iii B.C.). b. in bad sense, like Act. (1.2b), *contrive, organize*, τόλμαν καὶ κραυγὴν καὶ ψευδεῖς αἰτίας καὶ συκοφαντίαν καὶ ἀναισχυντίαν .. συνεσκευασμένοι D.25.9; φαρμακείαν κατά τινος Plu.*Art.*18; ἐπί τινα Luc.*Pisc.*25; εἰς ἡδονὴν σ. τὸν βίον Plu.*Cat.Ma.*11. 3. *arrange* or *organize for one's own interests, seize control of*, τὴν Ἑλλάδα D.19.303; σ. πάντας ἀνθρώπους ἐφ' ἡμᾶς Id.8.5; Ἔρως πέφυκε συσκευάζεσθαι ἄνθρωπον X.*Cyr.*5.1.16. **-ᾰσία**, ἡ, *packing up, getting ready*, for a journey or march, ib.4.2.35. **-αστής**, οῦ, ὁ, *factionarius*, *Gloss.* **-ή**, ἡ, *intrigue, plot*, *CPHerm.*25 ii 1 (iii A.D.), Hdn.3.12.3, *PLond.*5.1674.65 (vi A.D.), *EM*286.24.

**συσκευοφορέω**, *carry baggage together*, v.l. in X.*Cyr.*8.3.7.

**συσκευωρ-έομαι**, *contrive, organize*, τὰ ἄλλα D.18.259. **-ημα**, ατος, τό, *intrigue*, prob. l. in *PAmh.*2.79.37 (ii A.D.).

**σύσκεψις**, εως, ἡ, *much consideration*, Sm.*Ps.*63(64).3.

**συσκην-έω**, *live in the same tent with* another, *lodge together*, X.*HG*3.2.8; ἐν τῷ αὐτῷ ib.5.3.20; τινι *with* one, Id.*Lac.*13.1; *mess together*, ib.5.4, *Cyr.*2.2.1, 3.2.25. 2. *share the same berth* on board ship, [μοι] *BGU*1817.13 (i B.C.). **-ήτρια**, ἡ, *female messmate*, Ar.*Th.*624. **-ία**, ἡ, of soldiers, *messing together*, X.*HG*5.3.20, v.l. in *Cyr.*2.1.26:—Dor. **συσκᾱνία**, Hippod. ap. Stob.4.1.94. **-ια**, τά, *messes*, of the Spartan φιδίτια, X.*Lac.*5.2: sg., = *contubernium*, *Gloss.* **-ιος**, = sq., Lxx *Ex.*16.16 cod. B. **-ος**, ὁ, *one who lives in the same tent, messmate, comrade*, Th.7.75, Lys.13.79, X.*An.*5.8.6, Plu.2.27f, *BGU*984.24 (iv A.D.), etc.; σ. φίλοι *BMus.Inscr.*1077 (Sudan); Dor., οἱ **σύνσκᾱνοι** *IG*12(2).640 (Tenedos), cf. 9²(1).117 (Aetolia, iii B.C.); *fellow-actor*, ib.14.2342 (Aquileia), dub. in *Supp.Epigr.*2.60 (Laconia, ii/i B.C.). **-όω**, = συσκηνέω, Aristid.*Or.*24(44).10, Ael.*VH*4.9, etc.; συσκηνοῦν τινι X.*HG*7.1.38. **-ωσις**, εως, ἡ, *lodging together*, dub. in *CIG*3069.30 (Teos).

**συσκῐ-άζω**, *shade quite over*, Hes.*Op.*613; σκηναὶ σ. τοὺς περιπάτους Moschio ap.Ath.5.207e; σ. γένυν, i.e. to get a beard, E.*Supp.*1219:—Pass., συσκιασθεῖσα κεφαλή, opp. ψιλή, Pl.*Ti.*75e. 2. metaph., *throw into obscurity*, συγκρύψαι καὶ σ. τὰς ἁμαρτίας D.11.13, cf. 2.20 (v.l.); τὰ τῆς φύσεως ἀπόρρητα Ph.1.635; of events, *overshadow*, ὁ.. πόλεμος σ. τὸ περὶ τὴν γυναῖκα πάθος Eun.*Hist.*p.254 D.:—Pass., φράσις συνεσκιασμένη *obscure*, Porph. *in Ptol.*181 *Prooem.*; εἰ μὴ ἀπάτῃ συσκιάζεσθε *are* not *under the shadow* of a delusion, Hp.*Ep.*11. II. intr., ἄγκος .. πεύκαισι συσκιάζον a vale with pines *thick-shading*, E.*Ba.*1052; [ἡ σελήνη] συνεσκίασε καὶ ἀπέκρυψε νεφῶν συνελθόντων Plu.*Arat.*22. **-ᾰσις**, εως, ἡ, *obumbratio*, *Gloss.* **-ασμα**, ατος, τό, *shadow*, *Cat.Cod.Astr.*7.188. **-ασμός**, ὁ, = συσκίασις, Aq.*Ps.*26(27).5, al. **-ος**, ον, *closely shaded, thickly shaded*, X.*Cyn.*8.4, Arist.*HA*556a25; τὸ σ. *the thick shade* of a tree, Pl.*Phdr.*230b; the *closely-shaded place*, Luc.*Anach.*16.

**συσκῑρόομαι**, Pass., *become indurated together*, Gal.4.564.

**συσκιρτάω**, *leap together*, Ael.*NA*2.6, Nonn.*D.*8.28.

**συσκολύπτομαι**, Pass., = συγκαλύπτομαι, Hsch. (in pf. Pass.).

**συσκοπέω**, *contemplate along with* or *together*, τὸν λόγον Pl.*Phd.*89a; τὰ λεγόμενα Id.*La.*197e: fut. συσκέψομαι Hdn.1.17.7: pf. part. Pass. συνεσκεμμένα Iamb.*Protr.*21.λα'.

**συσκοτ-άζω**, *make dark*, τὰ ἄστρα Lxx *Ez.*32.7; ἡμέραν εἰς νύκτα σ. ib.*Am.*5.8. II. intr., *grow quite dark*, ὁ οὐρανὸς σ. νεφέλαις ib.3*Ki.*18.45, cf. *Jl.*3.15, al.:—but, 2. in early writers, always impers., ξυσκοτάζει (sc. ὁ θεός) *it grows dark*, Th.1.51, 7.73, cf. X.*Cyr.*7.5.15, etc.; ἤδη συσκοτάζοντος (sc. τοῦ θεοῦ) *when it was* now *getting dark*, Lys.*Fr.*75.4, cf. Diocl.*Fr.*141; συσκοτάζοντος ἄρτι τοῦ θεοῦ Plb.31.13.9. **-όομαι**, Pass., *become quite dark*, Porph. *ad Il.* p.295 S.

**συσκυθρωπάζω**, *look sad* or *gloomy together*, τινι *with* one, E.*Fr.*909.9 (troch.): abs., X.*Cyr.*6.2.21.

⊛ **συσκύλλομαι**, in aor. Pass., συνσκύληθι αὐτῷ *give* him *your best attention*, *POxy.*63.12 (ii/iii A.D.).

**συσμᾰρᾰγέω**, *roar in unison*, τελετῇ Βρομίοιο σ. Ἐνυώ Nonn.*D.*28.41.

**συσμηρίζω**, *fit together* two tubes one inside the other so as to make their contact air-tight, Hero *Spir.*1.28 (Pass.).

**συσμῑκρύνω**, in Pass., *become smaller together with*, Gal.17(2).55.

**συσπᾰράσσω**, Att. **-ττω**, *tear in pieces*, *Ev.Luc.*9.42, Max.Tyr.13.5.

**σύσπᾰσις**, εως, ἡ, *contraction*, Arist.*GA*782b28.

**σύσπαστος**, ον, or **συσπαστός**, όν, *capable of being drawn together, closed by drawing together*, βαλλάντια Pl.*Smp.*190e, Gal.2.424, Ath.11.783f; σ. ἐγχειρίδιον a stage-dagger, the blade of which *runs back into the hilt*, such as was used in the Ajax (815 sq.), Polem.Hist.95.

⊛ **συσπάω**, *draw together, contract*, Pl.*Ti.*71c; opp. ἀνίημι, Arist.*Pr.*949a9, al.; τὸ δέρμα ib.888a39, cf. Thphr.*Sens.*65; συνεσπακὼς τοὺς δακτύλους Luc.*Tim.*13; τὰς ὀφρῦς Id.*Vit.Auct.*7:—Med., σ. τὰς κοχώνας Ar.*Fr.*482 (s.v.l.):—Pass., *to be drawn up, retracted*, Arist.*HA*508a21, etc.; but also, *to be shrivelled up* by fire, Lxx *La.*5.10; συνεσπασμένους ὑπὸ νόσου D.L.6.92; συνεσπασμένοι καὶ κακοπινεῖς *shrivelled* and dirty, Ath.13.565d: metaph., λόγοι ἰσχνοὶ καὶ συνεσπ. dry and *shrunken*, D.H.*Dem*.15. II. *draw together* by stitching, *sew together*, διφθέρας X.*An*.1.5.10. III. in Med., *draw along with one*, Plu.*Publ*.16.

**συσπειράω**, *contract*, ἡ γαστὴρ συναγαγοῦσα..ἑαυτὴν καὶ συσπειράσασα Gal.*UP*4.7:—Med. and Pass., *shrink up, contract*, Pl.*Smp*.206d; of skin and flesh, Antyll.ap.Orib.45.15.3. b. metaph., ἡ ἀμέρεια σφίγγουσα καὶ -ῶσα Procl.*Inst*.86; ἐν ἑαυτῷ συνεσπειραμένον Dam.*Pr*.138; εἰς αὐτὰ τὰ χρήσιμα συσταλέντας καὶ -αθέντας Plu.2.828c. 2. Med. and Pass., of soldiers, *to be formed in close order* (v. σπεῖρα II), X.*Cyr*.7.5.6, *An*.1.8.21, etc.; σ. ἐπὶ τὴν Μουνιχίαν *march in close order* to.., Id.*HG*2.4.11; οἱ ἐχθροὶ -σάμενοι Eun.*VS* p.488 B.; of bees, περὶ τὸν βασιλέα συνεσπειραμέναι Arist.*HA*625$^{b}$8. 3. Med. and Pass., *coil* or *be coiled up*, σ. ὡς καθευδήσων Plu.2.77e; σ. εἰς ἑαυτό, of the wood-louse, Thphr.*HP*4.3.6; πλόκαμος συνεσπειραμένος Luc.*Nav*.2. II. *wrap up*, (ὁ σκύλαξ) γᾷ συνεσπείρασεν (τὸν σῦν) *wrapped* him in earth, i.e. laid him low, *PCair.Zen*.532.21 (iii B.C.). 2. *tie up together, bunch together*, βελόναις συνεσπειραμέναις κατακεντήσας with *a bunch of* needles, Paul.Aeg.4.5.

**συσπειρόω**, *coil up*, in Pass., of serpents, Thphr.*HP*4.4.13.

**συσπείρω**, *sow* or *scatter together with*, *Gp*.11.5.2, 12.7.2:—Pass., Luc.*Dom*.8, Porph.*VP*44; ἐν ἑαυτῷ συνεσπαρμένον Dam.*Pr*.107.

**συσπένδω**, *join in making a libation*, D.19.190, Aeschin.3.52, Herm.Hist.2.

**συσπεύδω**, *assist zealously*, φιλεῖ δὲ τῷ κάμνοντι συσπεύδειν θεός A.*Fr*.395; σ. Πανταλέοντι γενέσθαι τὴν ἀρχήν Hdt.1.92; σ. ἡμῖν τοῦ μὴ ἀνοιχθῆναι τὴν παλαίστραν *PSI*4.340.15 (iii B.C.); σ. Πολυνείκει τὴν κάθοδον Paus.2.19.8; *help in promoting*, τὰ λοιπά *PCair.Zen*.62(*b*).7 (iii B.C.); προῖκα πάντα Phld.*Rh*.2.140 S.

**συσπῑλόω**, *defile utterly*, Gloss.

**συσπλαγχνεύω**, *join in eating the sacrificial meat*, Ar.*Pax* 1115.

**συσποδόω**, *mince up*, Hsch. (in pf. part. Pass.).

**σύσπονδος**, ον, = ὁμόσπονδος, Aeschin.2.163 (pl., v.l.).

**σύσπορος**, ον, *sown together*, *Epic.Alex.Adesp*.9 vi 2 (συσσπ-).

**συσπουδ-άζω**, *make haste together, join in zealous exertion*, X.*An*.2.3.11; περὶ τῆς νίκης Ar.*Pax* 768 (anap.); ὅπως μὴ διαφύγωσιν *PCair.Zen*.15$^{v}$.35 (iii B.C.): also c. acc. rei, *pursue* or *execute zealously together with*, πᾶν ὅτι δέοι φίλοις X.*Ages*.8.2. 2. *take part eagerly with*, ἀθλητῇ τινι D.C.63.26, cf. 59.5, *CIG*4006 (Iconium). **-αστικός**, ή, όν, *zealous in supporting*, M.Ant.1.16.

**συσσαίνομαι**, Pass., *feel flattered* by a thing, διαλέκτῳ Plb.1.80.6.

® **συσσᾰρᾱπιαστής**, οῦ, ὁ, *fellow-worshipper of Sarapis*, *BCH*51.220 (Thasos, συνσ-).

**συσσαρκ-όομαι**, Pass., *to be grown over with flesh also*, Heliod.ap.Orib.44.13.3. **-ωσις**, εως, ἡ, *a being overgrown with flesh*, Antyll.ap.Orib.44.23.47, Archig.ap.Gal.12.577, Gal.2.738, *PMed.* in *Arch.Pap*.4.269 (iii A.D., συνσ-). **-ωτικός**, ή, όν, *depending on συσσάρκωσις*, ἀποθεραπείας τρόπος οὐκ ἔναιμος ἀλλὰ σ. Antyll.ap.Orib.45.15.9.

**συσσάττω**, *stop* or *fill quite up*, Arist.*Pr*.938$^{b}$28, and prob. for συντάττῃ ib.889$^{b}$1.

**συσσεισμός**, ὁ, *commotion of earth* or *air, earthquake* or *hurricane*, Lxx 3*Ki*.19.12, 4*Ki*.2.1, Lyd.*Ost*.44.

**συσσείω**, *shake together*, τὰ τείχη Polyaen.6.3; τῷ πτερῷ τοῦ κρατῆρος τὴν βάσιν *Gp*.11.17.4:—Pass., Arist.*Pr*.966$^{b}$12, Him.*Or*.2.23. 2. *make to tremble*, Lxx *Ps*.28(29).8. 3. metaph. of intoxication, συνέσεισέ μ' ἐκποθεῖσα φιάλη Xenarch.2.2.

**συσσεύω**, *urge on together*, βοῶν κάρηνα *h.Merc*.94; συνεσσεύοντο Ποιναί Orph.*A*.982.

**συσσημ-αίνω**, *signify* one thing *along with* another, S.E.*P*.1.199: abs., *acquire a meaning through its context*, A.D.*Synt*.9.16:—Pass., -αίνεται ἐν τῷ λοιπῷ ἔργῳ Gal.7.47. II. Med., *seal with* others, τὰς θύρας *IG*1$^{2}$.91.17; *seal* or *sign with* others, *join in signing*, D.35.15, 41.22, Lycurg.*Fr*.51, *PPetr*.1 p.67 (iii B.C.). **-αντικός**, ή, όν, *co-significative*, Plot.6.1.5, Dexipp. *in Cat*.11.10, Simp. *in Cat*.131.9, *EM*649.19. **-ειόομαι**, Med., *sign also*, of an official, *PTeb*.383.61 (i A.D.). **-ον**, τό, = σύμβολον, *signal*, Aen.Tact.4.1, al.; δεδώκει σ. *Ev.Marc*.14.44; τὸ σ. ἀνέβη Lxx *Jd*.20.40; αἴρειν τὸ σ. Str.6.3.3, D.S.11.22; ἦρε τὸ συγκείμενον πρὸς μάχην σ. Id.20.51. 2. *stamp* on weights and measures, ἀπὸ συσσήμου πωλεῖν Str.15.1.51. 3. *badge, ensign*, τὰ τῆς ἀρχῆς σ. *insignia, regalia*, D.S.1.70; *token, means of recognition*, Men.*Pk*.362 (censured by Phryn.393): metaph. of a patronymic, Ps.-Plu.*Vit.Hom*.24. 4. *pledge, pawn*, Hedyl.ap.Ath.8.345b.

**συσσήπω**, *macerate* food *completely*, for digestion, Arist.*PA*675$^{a}$13:—Pass., with pf. Act., *grow putrid together*, Hp.*Loc.Hom*.29, Ael.*NA*10.13, Porph.*VP*44.

**σύσσηψις**, εως, ἡ, *putrefaction*, Arist.*HA*546$^{b}$24, *Gp*.2.22.3.

**συσσιναπιστέον**, v. συσιναπιστέον.

**συσσῑτ-έω**, *mess with*, τινι Ar.*Eq*.1325 (anap.), Lys.13.79, Thphr.*Char*.10.3, etc.; μετ' ἀλλήλων Arist.*Pol*.1317$^{b}$38:—Med., σ. ἀλλήλοις Philostr.*Her*.2.3: abs. in pl., *mess together*, συσσιτοῦμεν..ἐγώ τε καὶ Μελησίας Pl.*La*.179b, cf. *Smp*.219e, D.19.191. **-ησις**, εως, ἡ, = sq., Plu.*Lyc*.12 (pl.). **-ία**, ἡ, *messing together* or *in common*, Pl.*Lg*.781a, Aen.Tact.10.5, Dosiad.Hist.1; *a mess*, X.*Oec*.8.12. **-ικός**, ή, όν, *of* or *for a mess*, οἶκος Dosiad.Hist.1; σ. νόμος Ath.13.585b. ® **-ιον**, τό, only in pl. (exc. in E.*Ion* 1165), *common meal, public mess*, such as were used in Crete and Sparta, Hdt.1.65, Ar.*Ec*.715, Pl.*Lg*.625e, etc.; cf. Arist.*Pol*.1271$^{a}$33, 1272$^{a}$1, 1330$^{a}$3. 2. *mess, company*, Anaxil.19. II. *mess-room, common-hall*, ἐν μέσῳ συσσιτίῳ κρατῆρας ἕστησ' E. l.c.; συσσίτια ἐν οἷς..τὴν δίαιταν ποιητέον Pl.*Lg*.762c; σ. χειμερινά Id.*Criti*.112b; γυμνάσια σ. τε ibid.c; *common-room* of the Museum at Alexandria, Str.17.1.8. **-οποιέω**, *knead up with*, ἄρτῳ Dsc.4.148 (Pass.). ® **-ος**, ὁ, *messmate*, Thgn.309, Hdt.5.24, Ar.*V*.557 (anap.), *Ra*.1075 (anap.), *Pl*.602 (anap.), Pl.*Lg*.806e (ξυσσιτίων codd.), X.*Cyr*.8.7.14, Arist.*Pol*.1314$^{a}$10; *member of common-room* of the Museum at Alexandria, *OGI*712 (ii A.D.).

**συσσῑωπάω**, *keep silence together with*, ὁ δῆμος τῇ βουλῇ σ. App.*Pun*.91.

**συσσοίη**· ἡ ἀνεμπόδιστος φορά, Hsch. **συσσοῦμαι**, pres. inf. συνσοῦσθαι· ἐπὶ τὸ αὐτὸ συμφέρεσθαι, Id.

**συσσῡκοφαντέω**, *join in laying false informations*, D.59.41.

**συσσύρω** [ῡ], *pull about*, Lxx 2*Ma*.5.16; *sweep together*, ὀνομάτων συρφετόν Phryn.400. 2. *sweep along with one*, τοὺς ἀκούοντας, of Carneades compared to a torrent, Numen.ap.Eus.*PE*14.8.

**συσσῴζω**, *help to save* or *preserve*, E.*IA*1209, *Hel*.1389, Ar.*Th*.270; ὑμᾶς τε καὶ ἡμᾶς αὐτούς Th.1.74; τινὰ μεθ' ὑμῶν Is.*Fr*.66; τοὺς πολίτας *Supp.Epigr*.7.62.18 (Seleucia Pieria, ii B.C.); also σ. τινάς τισι *save* them *together with, as well as* others, Plb.5.11.5. II. *observe completely*, Id.2.14.1, 10.47.10.

**συσσωμ-ᾰτοποιέω**, *incorporate, amalgamate*, Arist.*Mu*.396$^{a}$14 (Pass.). **-ᾰτος**, ὁ, *fellow-slave*, *Supp.Epigr*.6.721 (Pamphylia, συνσ-). **-ος**, ον, *united in one body*, *Ep.Eph*.3.6.

**συσσωρεύω**, *heap up together*, Heraclid.Lemb.3, D.S.3.40, Dsc.2.181, Vett.Val.131.3.

**συσσωφρονέω**, *to be of sound mind with* another, συνσωφρονεῖν σοι βούλομ', ἀλλ' οὐ συννοσεῖν E.*IA*407.

**συστάδην** [ᾰ], Adv. = sq., Plb.3.73.8, 13.3.7, Str.10.1.13, Hdn.4.15.2.

**συστᾰδόν**, Adv., (συνίσταμαι) *standing close together*, ξ. μάχαις χρῆσθαι fight in *close* combat, Th.7.81; σ. ἀγωνίζεσθαι D.C.41.60; v.l. for -δην in Hdn.4.7.2, 6.7.8.

**συστᾰθεύω**, *help to roast*: metaph., *help to cajole*, Ar.*Lys*.844.

® **σνσταθμ-ία**, ἡ, *adjustment of weights*, Dsc.1.54, Gal.12.483, *Theol.Ar*.59. **-ίζω**, *weigh relatively*, Ps.-Democr.ap.Zos.Alch.pp.178, 217 B.:—Med., = συμμετρέω, Iamb. *in Nic*. p.121 P. **-ισις**, εως, ἡ, *relative weighing*, Zos.Alch.p.178 B. **-ος**, ον, (σταθμός III) *of equal weight*, Hp.ap.Gal.19.143.

**συστᾰλάσσω**, *fuse together*, Vett.Val.248.24 (dub. l.).

**συσταλτέον**, *one must pronounce short*, Sch.Il.4.151. 2. *one must diminish, restrict*, Ath.Med.ap.Orib. *inc*.21.14, Paul.Aeg.1.14.

® **συσταλτικός**, ή, όν, *depressing*, [μελοποιία], ἦθος, Aristid.Quint.1.12, Cleonid.*Harm*.13.

**σύστᾱμα**, τό, Dor. for σύστημα.

**συσταμνίζω**, *put into the same vessel with*, Nic.*Fr*.70.13.

® **συστάς**, άδος [ᾰ], ἡ, *standing together*, τῶν ἀμπέλων συστάδες vines *planted closely* (not in exact rows, στοιχάδες), Arist.*Pol*.1330$^{b}$29; = εἰκῇ πεφυτευμένη, Hsch. s.v. ξυστάδες, cf. eund. s.v. παστάδες, Eust.1524.33; ξυστὰς ἡ ἀμπελόφυτος γῆ Poll.7.146. 2. συστάδες θαλάσσης, ὀμβρίων ὑδάτων, *cisterns, reservoirs*, Str.16.4.13, 14.

**συστᾰσ-ία**, ἡ, = σύστασις, opp. ἀφάνισις, Plot.6.7.20 (s.v.l.). **-ιάζω**, *join in faction* or *sedition*, Th.4.86, Lys.30.11, etc.; τοῖς κληρικοῖς Jul.*Ep*.114. II. trans., *band together for seditious purposes*, τινας D.C.36.16. **-ιαστής**, οῦ, ὁ, *fellow-rioter*, *Ev.Marc*.15.7 (v.l.), J.*AJ*14.2.1.

® **σύστᾰσις**, εως, ἡ, (συνίστημι) *bringing together, introduction, recommendation*, πατρικὴν ἔχων σ. Plb.1.78.1; ἡ πρός τινα σ. Id.4.82.3, cf. *SIG*591.62 (Lampsacus, ii B.C.), D.H.*Rh*.5.2, Plu.*Them*.27; σ. τῆς πρός τινα εὐνοίας J.*AJ*15.6.7; *care, guardianship*. ἔτι νηπίας οὔσας (ἀπέδωκεν[?]) εἰς σύστασιν Πτολεμαίῳ Γλαυκίου *UPZ*20.23 (ii B.C.); *power of attorney*, *PTeb*.317.14 (ii A.D.), etc. 2. *communication* between a man and a god, ταῦτα σοῦ εἰπόντος τρίς, σημεῖον ἔσται τῆς συστάσεως τόδε *PMag.Par*.1.209, cf. 220, 260, al., *PMag.Lond*.47.1, 121.505. 3. *protection*, ἵνα διὰ τῆς σῆς δεξιᾶς ᾖ μοι σ. *PSI*6.717.12 (ii A.D.). II. *proof*, Alex.Aphr. *in Metaph*.12.3, 409.16; *confirmation*, εἰς σύστασιν [τῶν ἀξιωμάτων] καὶ πίστιν ib.271.14; σ. καὶ πίστεις τινός Hermog.*Id*.1.10; πρὸς σύστασιν καὶ ἀσφάλειαν ἐπωμοσάμην *PLond*.1.77.62 (vi A.D.), cf *BGU*1187.31 (i B.C.).

B. (συνίσταμαι) *standing together, close combat, conflict*, ἐν τῇ σ. μάχεσθαι Hdt.6.117, cf. 7.167; ἡ ἐν ταῖς συμπλοκαῖς μάχη καὶ σ. Pl.*Lg*.833a; ἡ ἐκ σ. μάχη Hdn.4.15.3; ὅταν..σύστασιν ὁ ἀγὼν ἔχῃ Plu.*Demetr*.16, cf. *Aem*.20: metaph., *disturbance* in the human body, καθάρσεων καὶ συστάσεων τοῦ σώματος ἀρίστη ἡ διὰ τῶν γυμνασίων Pl.*Ti*.89a; καταστεῖλαι τὴν σ. τὴν ἀπὸ τοῦ γυμνασίου Antyll.ap.Orib.6.26.5; σ. ὅλου τοῦ σώματος (as a plague-symptom) Ruf.ap.eund.44.17.2; ξ. τῆς γνώμης *conflict* of mind, intense anxiety, Th.7.71; μένος μὲν ξ. τε σῶν φρενῶν δεινή E.*Hipp*.983; so ἥν τις πόνος ἢ σ. γίνηται τῷ ἀνθρώπῳ Hp.*Morb.Sacr*.17 vulg. (f.l. for τάσις). 2. *meeting, accumulation*, e.g. of humours, σ. ὑγροῦ περὶ τὴν ὑπερῴην Id.*Coac*.233; of water, Thphr.*CP*5.14.5 (pl.), cf. D.S.3.36; of winds, ib.51, *POxy*.1768.9 (iii A.D., dub.): metaph., λόγων Pl.*R*.457e; *combination*, τραγῳδίαν..εἶναι τὴν τούτων σ. πρέπουσαν ἀλλήλοις Id.*Phdr*.268d. 3. *knot of men assembled*, E.*Andr*.1088 (pl.), *Heracl*.415 (pl.); κατὰ ξυστάσεις γιγνόμενοι forming into *knots*, Th.2.21, cf. X.*Eq*.7.19. b. *political union*, more general than ἑταιρεία or σύνοδος, Isoc.3.54, cf. D.45.67; ἐθνικαὶ σ. national *unions*, Plb.23.1.3; κατὰ συστάσεις κωμάζειν D.C.*Fr*.39.7. c. *contingent of four light-armed* λόχοι (32 men), Ascl.*Tact.*6.3, Arr.*Tact.*14.3, Ael.*Tact.*16.1. 4. *friendship* or *alliance*, Plb.1.78.2; πρός τινας Id.3.78.2; *conspiracy*, ἐπί τινα Plu.*Pyrrh.*23. II. *composition, structure, constitution* of a person or a thing, τῷ κόσμῳ Ti.Locr.99d, cf. Pl.*Ti.*32c; τῶν ὡρῶν, τῆς ψυχῆς, Id.*Smp.*188a, *Ti.*36d; of the parts of an animal, Arist.*PA*646ᵃ20, *GA*744ᵇ28, al.; σώματος Sor.1.111; τῶν ἀτόμων Epicur.*Nat.*35 G.; ἡ περὶ τὴν κεφαλὴν σ. Pl.*Ti.*75b; φυσικὴ σ. Arist. *Cat.*9ᵇ18; ἡ σ. τῆς πόλεως Id.*Pol.*1295ᵇ28, cf. 1332ᵃ30; τῶν πραγμάτων Id.*Po.*1450ᵃ15; τοῦ μύθου ib.1452ᵃ18; abs., *plot* of a drama, ib. 1453ᵃ31; τὴν σ. ἔχειν ἐκ τοῦ ψεύδους Phld.*Rh.*1.361 S.; περὶ τρόπων συστάσεως, title of work by Chrysipp.; προσώπου σ. *expression* of face, Plu.*Per.*5. b. abs., *political constitution*, Pl.*R.*546a, *Lg.* 702d, etc. c. χωρίον ἀμπελικὸν ἐν συστάσει ἀρουρῶν ὅσων ἐστίν *consisting* of.., *PGiss.*56.7 (vi A.D.). 2. *coming into existence, formation*, νόσων Pl.*Ti.*89b, cf. c; πόλεων σ. καὶ φθορᾶς Id.*Lg.*782a; ἡ ἐξ ἀρχῆς τῶν ὅλων σ. D.S.1.7, cf. Plu.2.427b; τὴν σ. λαμβάνειν Arist.*HA*547ᵇ14, Plb.6.4.13, etc.; of a river, τὴν ἀρχὴν τῆς σ. λαμβάνειν Id.9.43.1; σ. ἐπιβουλῆς Id.6.7.8. 3. of bodies, *density* or *consistency*, πυκνότης καὶ σ., opp. ὑγρότης καὶ διάχυσις, Thphr.*Vent.* 58; σ. καὶ πῆξις Plu.2.130b; *degree of solidity, consistency*, σπέρμα.. τρυφερὰν ἔτι καὶ νεοπαγῆ τὴν σ. ἔχον Sor.1.46, cf. 58; *solid knot* or *lump*, [μαστοὶ] θρομβώδεις συστάσεις ἔχοντες ib.88; μέχρι συστάσεως ἐμπλαστρώδους ἑψηθέν Gal.11.134, cf. 6.249, Dsc.3.7; τὰ ὑδατώδη ὑγρὰ πάχος καὶ σ. μηδεμίαν ἔχοντα Gal.16.761; λεαίνεται μέχρι σ. Orib.*Fr.*55. 4. *a substance*, πλάττειν ἐκ πηλοῦ ζῷον ἤ τινος ἄλλης ὑγρᾶς σ. Arist.*PA*654ᵇ30, cf. Plu.2.696a; ξηραὶ σ. Arist.*HA*519ᵇ19.

**συστᾰσιώτης**, ου, ὁ, *member of the same faction, partisan*, in pl., Hdt.5.70,124, Str.14.5.14.

**συστᾰτ-έω**, *to be consistent, coherent*, πρὸς αὐτά Epicur.*Nat.*28. 4. ⊛ **-ης**, ου, ὁ, *organizer, creator*, τῶν κατὰ φιλοσοφίαν τεχνῶν, of Protagoras, Gal.*Phil.Hist.*3. II. *delegate of appointments*, σ. τῆς μελλούσης λειτουργεῖν φυλῆς *PFlor.*39.4 (iv A.D.), cf. *POxy.*1116 (iv A.D.), *PSI*10.1108 (iv A.D.). III. pl., *pairs* of young men *matched* for wrestling and other games, φίλοι καὶ σ. *IG*2².2023, cf. 2024. IV. pl., *rafters of the roof which meet at the top*, Ath.Mech. 17.10, al., Sch.Il.23.711: sg., *Gloss.* **-ικός**, ή, όν, *of* or *for putting together, component*, μόρια S.E.*M.*8.84, cf. 1.104; opp. διαιρετικός, Ammon.*in Porph.*118.13. 2. *drawing together, consolidating*, opp. διαχυτικός, Thphr.*Sens.*84. 3. *probatory, confirmatory*, Hermog. *Id.*2.9; λόγοι σ. τινός Phld.*Rh.*1.12 S.; σ. δημόσιος χρηματισμός a publicly deposited deed *confirmatory* (of a gift), *PGrenf.*2.69.20, al. (iii A.D.). II. *of* or *for bringing together, introductory, commendatory*, τὸ κάλλος παντὸς ἐπιστολίου -ώτερον personal appearance is *better introduction* than any letter, Arist.ap.D.L.5.18, cf. Plb.31.16.3; σ. ἐπιστολαί letters *of introduction*, 2*Ep.Cor.*3.1; ἡ σ. alone, D.L.8.87; also σ. γράμματα Arr.*Epict.*2.3.1, *POxy.*1587.20 (iii A.D.). III. **-κόν**, τό, *deed of representation, power of attorney*, ib.505.2 (ii A.D.); *agreement to appoint a representative*, *PFay.*35.11 (ii A.D.). 2. = *minervalicium* (prob. *teacher's fee*), *Gloss.* IV. *productive*, ὑπὸ τῆς φλεγμονῆς ταρασσομένην τὴν καρδίαν τοῦδε τοῦ πάθους συστατικὴν γίνεσθαι Herod.Med. in *Rh.Mus.*58.70. ⊛ **-ός**, ή, όν, *capable of being formed*, A.D.*Pron.*113.18, *Synt.*174.1, al. 2. *constructed*, ἐξ ἑτέρων S.E.*M.*1.104; *well-made, consistent*, μάθημα ib.57. 3. = εὐσύστατος II (quod fort. legend.), Vett.Val. in *Cat. Cod.Astr.*2.170.

**συσταυρόομαι**, Pass., *to be crucified together with*, τινι *Ev.Marc.* 15.32, *Ep.Gal.*2.20.

**συστεγάζω**, *cover entirely*, τινι *with* a thing, Pl.*Ti.*75c:—Pass., X.*Cyr.*6.2.17.

**συστεγνόω**, *solder together*, Hero *Spir.*1.37, al.

**σύστειπτος**, ον, *pressed together*, prob. in Hsch. (συνστείητον cod.).

**συστείχω**, aor. συνέστιχον, *walk together with*, c. dat., Nonn.*D.*4. 312, al.: abs., ib.14.190.

⊛ **συστέλλω**, *draw together*: *shorten sail*, συστείλας ἄκροισι χρώμενος τοῖς ἱστίοις Ar.*Ra.*999 (lyr.): Com. metaph., συστείλας γε τοὺς ἀλλᾶντας εἶτ' ἀφήσω κατὰ κῦμ' ἐμαυτὸν οὔριον Id.*Eq.*432; *draw in, contract*, of the mouth, Hp.*VM*22; σ. ἑαυτόν, of a snake, Arist.*HA* 594ᵃ19; σ. καὶ προβάλλειν τὴν γλῶτταν Id.*PA*660ᵃ23; σ. τὸ πρόσωπον, so as to express disgust, Luc.*DMeretr.*13.5; of soldiers, σ. τινὰς εἰς τὸ τεῖχος, εἴσω τοῦ χάρακος ἑαυτούς, Plu.*Sull.*9, *Cam.*34:—Pass., *contract oneself, draw in*, Arist.*MA*701ᵇ15, *Pr.*949ᵃ17, Sor. 1.7; τὸν ἀέρα .. τυποῦσθαι συστελλόμενον ὑπὸ τοῦ δρωμένου καὶ τοῦ δρῶντος Thphr.*Sens.*50; συνέσταλται .. τὸ θερμόν Id.*Ign.*13; σ. εἰς ὀλίγον Plu.*Arist.*14; εἰς μεῖόν τι X.*Vect.*4.3; εἰς τρίβωνα ῥᾳδίως συστέλλομαι (cf. infr. II) Crates Theb.16; ἐς βραχὺ Luc.*Icar.*12; τοῖς ὄγκοις συνεσταλμένοι D.S.4.20; βραχίονας καὶ καρποὺς.. ἐν τοῖς συνεσταλμένοις ἀποδεσμεύειν at the *narrow parts*, Gal.12.693; **-όμεναι** ὥσπερ ὄρνιθες *gathering together*, Plu.2.565e; cf. συνεσταλμένως. 2. *contract, reduce*, τὴν τῶν βασιλέων γένεσιν εἰς τὸ μέτριον Pl.*Lg.*691e; ἁμαρτήματα ὡς εἰς ἐλάχιστα σ. D.18.246; σ. ἐπὶ τὸ ταπεινότερον Arist.*Rh.Al.*1423ᵇ24; τὰς φυσικὰς λύπας εἰς μικρόν Diog.Oen.2; τὴν ῥύσιν Sor.2.41; τὰ συσσίτια πρὸς τὸ σωφρονέστερον D.C.54.2:—Pass., *draw cowering together*, συσταλέντες .. σιγῇ καθήμεθ' E.*IT*295; τῇ διαίτῃ συνεστάλθαι *to be moderate*, Hp.*Art.*50, cf. Phld.*Vit.*p.22 J.; ξ. ἐς εὐτέλειαν *retrench* expenses, Th.8.4; ἵνα συνσταλῶσιν αἱ λίαν ἄκαιροι δαπάναι *IG*2².1329.11, cf. *PAmh.*2.70.3 (ii A.D.). b. *deprive of all food and drink*, συστέλλειν, εἰ δὲ μὴ ἀντέχοι τις, ἐπ' ὀλιγοσιτίας καὶ ὑδροποσίας τηρεῖν Sor.2.15, cf. 86. 3. *humble, abase*, τά τοι μέγιστα πολλάκις θεὸς.. συνέστειλεν E.*Fr.*716; ταπεινοῦντα καὶ σ. Pl.*Ly.*210e; αἱ συμφοραὶ σ. τινάς Isoc.8.85; opp. ἐξαίρω, Phld.*Vit.* p.20 J.; *depress* (opp. διαχέω, ἀνίημι), διάνοιαν Aristid.Quint.2.9,10:—Pass., *to be lowered* or *cast down*, συνέσταλμαι κακοῖς E.*HF*1417, cf. *Tr.* 108 (anap.); [δοῦλοι] σ. τὰς φύσεις Heraclid.Pont.ap.Ath.12.512b. 4. σ. λέξιν *lower* it, *make* it *mean*, Hermog.*Id.*1.6; *pronounce* a syllable *short*, opp. ἐκτείνω, D.H.*Comp.*14 (Pass.); δίχρονα συνεσταλμένα doubtful vowels *when shortened*, A.D.*Pron.*11.19. 5. [ὀνόματα] συστέλλεται ἐκ τῆς πολλῆς ποιότητος τῇ παραθέσει τοῦ ἄρθρου *are reduced* or *restricted* out of their generality, Id.*Synt.*69.4. II. *wrap closely up, shroud*, οὐ δάμαρτος ἐν χεροῖν πέπλοις συνεστάλησαν E.*Tr.*378, cf. Luc.*Im.*7:—Med., ξυστειλάμεναι θαἰμάτια *wrapping our* cloaks *close round us*, Ar.*Ec.*99; συστέλλου σεαυτήν *gird up your* loins, *get ready for action*, ib.486 (lyr.); ξυσταλείς *tucked up, ready for action*, Id.*V.*424 (troch.), cf. *Lys.*1042 (troch.). 2. *cloak*, συνέστελλε καὶ συνέκρυπτεν.. τὴν δυσμένειαν Plu.*Galb.*18 (unless in signf. I. 2).

**σύστεμα**, ατος, τό, = σύστημα 5, *Inscr.Prien.*55.16 (ii B.C.), 113.21 (i B.C.), 114.18 (i B.C.), *SIG*742.38 (Ephesus, i B.C.); τὰ σ. τῶν φαλαγγιτῶν v.l. in Plb.11.12.1; cf. σύστημα 8.

**συστενάζω**, *lament with*, φίλοις E.*Ion* 935: abs., *Ep.Rom.*8.22.

**συστενάχομαι** [ᾰ], = foreg., Nonn.*D.*40.158.

**συστενοχωρέω**, *drive into a narrow place, trammel*, Plu.2.601d.

**συστένω**, = συστενάζω, Arist.*EN*1171ᵇ10.

**συστερέομαι**, Pass., *to be deprived together*, τιμῆς Sch.Il.1.505: also **συστέρομαι**, impf. συνεστέρετο, παραγωγῆς A.D.*Synt.*100.14.

**συστεφᾰνηφορέω**, *wear a crown with*, *Scol.*22.

**συστέφᾰν-ος**, ὁ, *fellow wearer of a crown*, *IG*2².2025 (ii A.D.). **-όω**, *crown at once, together*, *AP*5.35 (Rufin.):—Pass., *wear a crown with*, συνεστεφανοῦτο καὶ συνεπαιώνιζεν Φιλίππῳ D.19.128; *to be crowned together*, *BSA*16.113 (Pisidia), *CIG*3200 (Smyrna), 4353 (Side).

⊛ **συστέφομαι**, Pass., *to be crowned together*, *TAM*2.586 (Tlos), *CIG* 4380g (Cibyratis), *IG*5(1).258 (Laconia).

⊛ **σύστημ-α**, ατος, τό, *whole compounded of several parts* or *members, system*, Pl.*Epin.*991e, Arist.*GA*740ᵃ20; of *the composite whole* of soul and body, Epicur.*Ep.*1 p.21 U.; τὸ ὅλον σ. τοῦ σώματος D.H. *Rh.*10.6. b. in literary sense, *composition*, ἐποποιικὸν σ. [πραγμάτων] Arist.*Po.*1456ᵃ11; λυρικὰ σ. *SIG*660.3 (Delph., ii B.C.); τέχνη ἐστὶ σ. ἐκ καταλήψεων συγγεγυμνασμένων Zeno *Stoic.*1.21, cf. Arr.*Epict.*1.20.5; of the syllogism, S.E.*P.*2.173. c. = σύστασις B.II. 2, Arist.*GA*758ᵇ3. 2. *organized government, constitution*, Pl.*Lg.* 686b, Arist.*EN*1168ᵇ32; σ. δημοκρατίας Plb.2.38.6, cf. 6.10.14; τὸ ἐκ θεῶν καὶ σοφῶν σ. Diog.Bab.*Stoic.*3.241; *confederacy*, σ. τῶν Ἀχαιῶν Plb 2.41.15, cf. 9.28.2; τὸ Ἀμφικτιονικὸν σ. *SIG*761 *A* 16 (Delph., i B.C.), *Delph.*3(1).480.16; *band* of partisans, J.*AJ*20.9.4; σ. τοῦ γένους ἡμῶν, of a Jewish *community*, Id.*Ap.*1.7:—it seems to have meant also *a company* or *guild*, *CIG*2508 (Cos, Dor. **σύστᾱμα**), 2562 (Hierapytna), 2699 (Mylasa); or *a committee*, τῆς γερουσίας ib.2930 (Tralles). 3. *body of soldiers, corps*, usu. of a definite number, like τάγμα, σύνταγμα, σ. μισθοφόρων, ἱππέων, etc., Plb.1.81.11, 30.25.8, etc.; but τὸ τῆς φάλαγγος σ. the phalanx itself, Id.5.53.3. b. a boat's *crew*, Alciphr.1.8. 4. generally, *flock, herd*, Plb.12.4.10; τὰ βασιλικὰ σ. τῶν ἱπποτροφιῶν Id.10.27.2. 5. *college* of priests or magistrates, Id.21.13.11, Str.17.1.29, etc.; of the Roman Senate, Plu. *Rom.*13, cf. Lib.*Or.*11.146. 6. in Music, *system* of intervals, *scale*, Pl.*Phlb.*17d; σ. ἐναρμόνια, ὀκτάχορδα, Aristox.*Harm.*p.2 M., cf. Ph.1.10, Plu.2.1142f, Cleonid.*Harm.*1. b. *strain*, Jul.*Caes.* 315c. 7. in Metre, *metrical system*, as in Anapaestics, Heph. *Poëm.*3. 8. Medic., *accumulation of sediment*, Hp.*Epid.*7.83; τὰ τῶν ὑδάτων σ. LXX *Ge.*1.10 (v.l. συστέματα), cf. Ezek.*Exag.*134, Sotion p.183 W. 9. Medic., *the pulse-beats taken collectively*, Gal.9. 279. 10. *machine, apparatus*, Apollod.*Poliorc.*138.13.—The word first occurs in Hp. and Pl., but is chiefly used in later Prose. **-ᾰτικός**, ή, όν, *of* or *like an organized whole, systematic*, Plu.2.1142f, S.E. *M.*7.41, Anon. in *Tht.*15.6; σ. μέτρα *forming a complete system*, Heph.*Poëm.*3, etc.; cf. σύστημα 7. 2. *constitutive*, μονάς Anatol. ap.*Theol.Ar.*8. II. σ. ἀνωμαλία, of the pulse, opp. κατὰ μίαν πληγήν, Gal.8.502, 9.279; of the breathing, Id.7.800.

**σύστηνον**· ἐστενοχωρημένον, τρίχινος χιτών, ἢ ῥυπαρός, Antim.96 (ap.Hsch.).

**συστηρίζω**, *establish together*, Ph.1.644, Ptol.*Alm.*3.1 (Pass.).

**συστῑχάομαι**, *accompany*, Ep. impf. -εστιχόωντο Nonn.*D.*34.255.

**συστοιβάζω**, *stop up*, Lat. *constipo*, *Gloss.*

**συστοιχ-έω**, *stand in the same rank* or *line*, of soldiers, Plb.10.23. 7. 2. *correspond to*, τὸ Σινᾶ ὄρος.. σ. τῇ νῦν Ἰερουσαλήμ *Ep.Gal.* 4.25. **-ία**, ἡ, *column* or *series* of things or ideas, Arist.*APr.*66ᵇ 27, *Metaph.*1004ᵇ27, 1066ᵃ15, 1072ᵃ31, Thphr.*CP*6.5.6; ἐκ τῶν σ. ὅσαι μὴ ἐπαλλάττουσιν ἀλλήλαις from *series* which are mutually exclusive, Arist.*APo.*79ᵇ7; ἐν τῇ αὐτῇ σ. τῆς κατηγορίας in the same *line* of predication, Id.*Metaph.*1054ᵇ35, 1058ᵃ13; esp. in Pythag. philosophy, *pair of co-ordinate* or *parallel columns*, αἱ ἀρχαὶ αἱ κατὰ συστοιχίαν λεγόμεναι in *a series of co-ordinate pairs*, as *odd* and *even, one* and *many, right* and *left*, ib.986ᵃ23; also, *either of such parallel columns*, ib.1093ᵇ12, *PA*670ᵇ21, *EN*1096ᵇ6, al., Thphr.*Vent.* 58, Gal.18(2).167.

**σύστοιχος**, ον, *belonging to the same column* or *series, co-ordinate, correspondent*, πῦρ καὶ γῆν καὶ τὰ σ. τούτων (viz. air and water) Arist. *GC*315ᵃ21, cf. *Mete.*340ᵃ5; λέγεται σύστοιχα τὰ τοιάδε· οἷον τὰ δίκαια καὶ ὁ δίκαιος τῇ δικαιοσύνῃ Id.*Top.*114ᵃ27, cf. *Rh.*1364ᵇ34; σύστοιχα ἀλλήλοις Id.*PA*670$^{b}$22; τὰς..σ. τῶν ἐν τοῖς μέρεσι [κινήσεων] ἀρχάς Id.*IA*707$^{a}$11; τὸ γλυκὺ καὶ τὸ λευκὸν καλῶ σύστοιχα, γένει δ' ἕτερα Id.*Sens.*448$^{a}$16; ὁ γλυκὺς καὶ λιπαρὸς καὶ ὅσοι σ. τούτοις Thphr.*CP*6.4.2, cf. Epicur.*Ep.*1 p.27 U.; of the *concomitant circumstances* of disease, Diocl.*Fr.*34. Adv., τὰ -χως λεγόμενα Arist.*Sens.*448$^{a}$14. **2.** Gramm., = ἀντίστοιχος II, Eust.468.31. **3.** generally, *consonant, congruous*, τὰ λοιπὰ δ' ἦν τούτοις ὅμοια καὶ σ. Plb.13.8.1, cf. Antioch. Astr. in *Cat.Cod.Astr.*8(3).117; οὐδὲ γὰρ σύνστοιχοι ἑατῶν γίνεσθε γεγραφηκότες..you are not even *consistent with* one another, *BGU* 1205.9 (i B.C.); ὁ μὲν νοῦς σ. ἔστω καὶ πυκνός, ἡ λέξις δὲ.. Luc.*Hist. Conscr.*43.

**συστολ-ή**, ἡ, (συστέλλω) *drawing together, drawing up, contraction*, σ. εἰς αὑτάς (of souls in pain) Plu.2.564b; [τὴν ψυχὴν] ποτὲ μὲν εἰς ἡδονὰς καὶ διαχύσεις ἄγεσθαι, ποτὲ δὲ εἰς οἴκτους καὶ συστολάς Ptol. *Harm.*3.7; λύπη ἐστὶν ἄλογος σ. *Stoic.*3.95, cf. Thphr.*Fr.*77, Zeno *Stoic.*1.51, Epicur.*Fr.*410; esp. in Medic., a *contraction* of the heart or lungs, opp. διαστολή, Herophil.ap.*Placit.*4.22.3; σφυγμός ἐστι διαστολὴ καὶ σ. καρδίας καὶ ἀρτηριῶν Gal.8.700; of other organs, [τῆς μήτρας] Sor.1.70$^{b}$; συστολαί τινες ἀνειδεῖς εἰς ἄρθρα Alex.Trall. *Verm.* p.589 P., cf. Gal.18(2).128. **2.** *contraction, limitation*, συστολῆς μᾶλλον ἢ προσθέσεως τὰς τιμὰς δεῖσθαι Plu.*Caes.*60, cf. 2.135a. **3.** *abasing, taking down*, ib.544e. **4.** Gramm., *change of a long vowel into a short*, e.g. ξερόν for ξηρόν, A.D.*Synt.*281.7; σ. Ἰωνικὴ ἢ ποιητική *EM*735.51; also *pronouncing as short* a syllable that is strictly long, D.H.*Comp.*25, D.T.633.12, S.E.*M.*1.108. **5.** *lessening* of expenses, *retrenchment*, Plb.27.13.4, Phld.*Oec.* p.71 J. (pl.). **6.** *spareness, tenuity*, τῶν ἀγαλμάτων Demetr.*Eloc.*14. **7.** *pusillanimity*, Poll.5.122. **8.** *fasting*, Sor.1.49, 2.15, al. **9.** in fevers, *remission*, Alex.Trall.*Febr.*4; but also a *chill*, the *cold stage* of ague, Gal.7.428. **-ίζω**, *draw* or *put together, fabricate*, ἀγάλματα λίνῳ *with* or *out of* yarn, E.*Or.*1435 (lyr.). **II.** *unite*, Μούσας σ. Χάρισιν *AP*7.419 (Mel.).

**συστομ-όομαι**, Pass., *to be joined by a mouth*, στόματι μεγάλῳ [τῇ Μαιώτιδι λίμνῃ] Str.7.4.1. **-ος**, ον, *with a narrow mouth*, opp. μεγαλόστομος, Arist.*PA*662$^{a}$24 (Comp.); of a μέτοικος (called σκάφη), -ώτερος σκάφης, prov. of one whose low birth makes him keep silence, Men.191, Thphr.*Fr.*103; τὰ σ. τῶν τευχέων Archyt.1; πίθος μέγας καὶ σ. Moer.p.392 P., cf. Hero *Spir.*1 *Praef.* **2.** *mouth to mouth*, of a kiss, Telecl.12.

**συστονᾰχέω**, = συστενάζω, Q.S.1.296.

**συστορνύω**, *smooth out*, στρωμάτων ἐξαναστὰς συνέλισσε αὐτὰ καὶ τὸν τύπον συνστόρνυε Iamb.*Protr.*21.κθʹ; ἐξανίσταμαι τὸν ἀμφιτάπητα συστορέσας Diph.51: cf. συστρώννυμι.

**συστοχάζομαι**, *aim at together*, τοῦ κατ' ἀξίαν M.Ant.3.11.

**συστρᾰτ-άομαι**, = συστρατεύω, Ep. impf. -όωντο Nonn.*D.*17.138. **-εία**, ἡ, *common campaign*, X.*HG*3.1.6, D.C.40.7, al.: pl., *alliances*, Aeschin.*Ep.*11.12 (v.l.). **-εύω**, more freq. in Med. **-εύομαι**:—*join* or *share in an expedition*, abs., Hdt.5.44, 6.9, 9.11, Th.1.99, 2.56, X.*HG*3.5.16 (Act.), etc.; τινι *with* another, Hdt.7.11, 9.106, Th.2.12, X.*HG*3.5.5 (Act.), etc.; μετά τινων Th.2.29,80, etc.; σὺν βασιλεῖ X.*HG*2.4.36 (Med.).—Hdt. always uses it in Med., as also Pl. (*R.* 468b,471d); Th. prefers Act., but also uses Med., cf. 1.99, 2.12, al., with 2.56,80, al.; X. has both, but more freq. Med., as also Lys. 20.29, etc.

**συστρᾰτηγ-έω**, *to be a fellow-general*, D.19.191, Plu.*Per.*8. **II.** trans., *help in procuring*, τῷ πατρὶ τὴν κάθοδον Str.6.1.8. **-ος** (proparox.), ὁ, *fellow-general*, E.*Ph.*745, Th.2.58, X.*An.*2.6.29, Μουσ. Σμυρν.1878 p.54 (Erythrae), etc.

**συστρᾰτιώτης**, ου, ὁ, *fellow-soldier*, X.*An.*1.2.26, Pl.*R.*556c, Arist. *EN*1159$^{b}$28, *OGI*218.45 (pl., Ilium, iii B.C., συσστ-), *PTeb.*793 iv 22 (pl., ii B.C., συνστ-), *Ep.Phil.*2.25: c. gen., τὸν ἑαυτῶν σ. *Sammelb.* 7456 (Ptolemaic, συνστ-), cf. *Ostr.*1535 (ii B.C., συνστ-):—fem. **-ῶτις**, ιδος, metaph., Them.*Or.*15.197c; τύχῃ σ. χρῆσθαι J.*BJ*6.9.1.

**συστρᾰτοπεδεύομαι**, *encamp along with*, σύν τινι X.*An.*2.4.9.

**σύστρεμμα**, ατος, τό, *anything twisted up together*: hence, **1.** *globe, ball*, ἐξ ἐρίου Sor.2.87; ἐρίου ibid., Orib.*Syn.*9.55.1; ἐκ σχοινίου Hsch. s.v. σπεῖον; συστρέμματα *round drops* of water, Arist.*Mu.* 394$^{a}$32. **2.** *body of men, crowd, concourse*, Plb.1.45.10, 35.4.14; *band, company*, Id.4.58.4, Lxx 2*Ki.*4.2, al.; esp. *corps of* 1024 *light-armed* (= 2 ξεναγίαι), Ascl.*Tact.*6.3, Ael.*Tact.*16.3, Arr.*Tact.*14.5; of ἔφηβοι, *IG*2$^{2}$.2047 (συνστ-), al.: whence **συστρεμμᾰτάρχης**, ου, ὁ, title of 4 ἔκτακτοι attached to an ἐπίταγμα τῶν ψιλῶν (cf. ἐπιξεναγός), Ascl.*Tact.*6.3, Arr.*Tact.*14.6, Ael.*Tact.*16.4, *IG*2$^{2}$.3749; and **-αρχέω**, *IG*2$^{2}$.2127 (συνστ-), 2197, al. **3.** *tumour*, Hp.*Prorrh.* 2.41, *Epid.*2.3.12, Gal.*UP*8.8, etc. **b.** *concretion* in the motions, Hp.*Epid.*4.52, Antyll.ap.Orib.8.6.21, Gal.16.762.

**συστρεμμάτιον**, τό, Dim. of foreg., σ. ὕδατος *whirlpool*, Arist.*Mir.* 832$^{b}$4. **2.** *little knot* or *coil*, Poll.4.116.

**συστρεπτ-έον**, *one must stiffen, check*, τὴν κοιλίαν (in diarrhoea) Aët.4.6. **-ικός**, ή, όν, *coagulative*, of cold, Hp.*Epid.*6.3.6, *Vict.*2.54.

* **συστρέφω**, *twist up, roll up*, of a whirlwind, μή σ' ἀναρπάσῃ.. συστρέψας ἄφνω A.*Fr.*195, cf. Ar.*Lys.*975, *Th.*61; φρυγάνων πλῆθος *Act.Ap.*28.3; ἔριον περὶ μηλωτρίδα *POxy.*234 ii 12 (ii/iii A.D.); of animals, *gather* themselves *together*, in preparing to spring, σ. ἑαυτὸν ὥσπερ θηρίον Pl.*R.*336b; σ. τὸν αὐχένα, of one struggling to get loose, Eup.339; τὰ ὄμματα διὰ κενῆς, ὡς εἴ τι βλέπων, ξυνέστρεφε *screwed up* his eyes, Hp.*Epid.*7.83; συστρέψαι ἑαυτούς, of dolphins, Arist.*HA*631$^{a}$27; [τὸ χόριον] σ. περὶ αὑτὸ τὴν ὑστέραν Sor.1.71:—Pass., εἰ τὸ χόριον εἰς αὑτὸ συνεστραμμένον εἴη ib.73; συνεστραμμένη χείρ *clenched* fist, ib.102; of a whirlwind, Men.536.4; of the moon, dub. sens. in Palchus in *Cat.Cod.Astr.*8(1).250. **II.** of soldiers, σ. ἑωυτούς *form in a compact body*, for attack or defence, *collect* themselves, *rally*, Hdt.9.18; σ. εἰς ταὐτό (sc. τὰς ἵππους) Arist.*HA*572$^{b}$14: freq. in Pass., συστραφέντες *in a body*, Hdt.4.136, 6.6, cf. 40; συστρεφόμενοι Id.9.62, Th.7.30; ξυνεστρέφοντο ἐν σφίσιν αὐτοῖς Id.2.4; ὅσον..ἦν ξυνεστραμμένον ibid.; ἐπὶ πεντήκοντα ἀσπίδων συνεστραμμένοι ἦσαν *they were formed in a mass* 50 deep, X.*HG*6.4.12; so of bees, fishes, Arist. *HA*629$^{a}$19, 621$^{a}$16. **2.** of soldiers, also, συστρέφειν ἐπὶ δόρυ *wheel* them to the right, v.l. in X.*Lac.*13.6; so prob. σ. τὸν ἵππον *turn* him *sharply*, Plu.*Pyrrh.*16; σ. τὴν ὄψιν Satyr.3. **III.** *form into an organized whole, unite*, τὸ Μηδικὸν ἔθνος Hdt.1.101; τοὺς τὰς οὐσίας ἔχοντας Arist.*Pol.*1304$^{b}$23:—Pass., *club together, conspire*, Th.4.68, 8.54; ἐπ' ἐμὲ συστραφέντες ἥκουσι Aeschin.2.178, cf. Lxx 4*Ki.*10.9:—in Act., ib.3*Ki.*16.9. **IV.** Pass., *collect, gather*, σ. αἷμα ἐς.. Hp.*Aph.*5.40; νιφετοῦ συστραφέντος Arist.*Mu.*394$^{b}$2; of humours, *gather, come to a head*, φύματος συστραφέντος Hp.*Prog.*23; of gravel *collecting* in the bladder, Id.*Aër.*9. **V.** *make* the hair *curl*, Theodect.17.3:—Pass., συνεστραμμένα ξύλα *knotted, gnarled*, Thphr.*HP*3.11.2; σ. ῥίζα Id.*CP*1.3.3; κιττὸς συνεστραμμένος ταῖς ῥίζαις Id.*HP*3.18.9. **VI.** *condense, congeal, harden*, τὸ ψυχρὸν συστρέφον καὶ συσφίγγον Ath.2.41b; of condensing fluids by heat, ἐν ἡλίῳ Dsc.3.7 (Act. and Pass.), cf. Gal.12.834, Aët.7.91; τὰ γυμνάσια τὰς σάρκας σ. Antyll.ap.Orib.6.10.15:—Pass., *to be condensed, acquire substance* or *consistency*, ἀφρὸς σ. Arist.*HA*569$^{b}$18; esp. in pf. part. Pass., σπέρμα ξηρὸν καὶ συνεστραμμένον ib.523$^{a}$24; νέφος ἐστὶ πάχος ἀτμῶδες σ. Id.*Mu.*394$^{a}$27; πῦρ σ. *concentrated*, Epicur.*Ep.*1 p.28 U.; *compact*, σ. τὸ εὐπαγές Phld.*Po.Herc.*994.34; σωμάτιον σ. Arr.*Epict.* 1.24.8; συστρέφεσθαι καὶ ἀπεψῦχθαι, of an infant, Sor.1.108; γάλα μελιτοειδῶς συστραφέν ib.91. **VII.** of sentences, narratives, and the like, *bring into a close form, compress*, ἐὰν μὴ συστρέφῃ τὰ πράγματα Cratin.85; ἐνθυμήματα σ. Arist.*Rh.*1419$^{a}$19; σ. τὰ νοήματα, τὸν νοῦν ἐν ὀλίγοις ὀνόμασι, D.H.*Isoc.*11, *Pomp.*2.5: abs., συστρέψας γράφει writes *briefly, curtly*, Aeschin.3.100; σ. εἰπεῖν τὸ πρᾶγμα D.H. *Lys.*24:—freq. in Pass., ῥῆμα βραχὺ καὶ συνεστραμμένον a short and *pithy* saying, of the Spartans, Pl.*Prt.*342e; λέξις συνεστραμμένη, opp. διῃρημένη, D.H.*Rh.*5.7; ἡ Ἀττικὴ γλῶσσα σ. τι ἔχει Demetr. *Eloc.*177; συνέστραπται τοῖς νοήμασι D.H.*Lys.*5, cf. *Dem.*19. **b.** also, *speak* or *write in an involved style, twist* one's words, Antiph.52.17, 217.17.

**συστροβῑλέω**, = foreg. I, v.l. in Phryn.374.

**συστρογγύλλω**, *roll up into a ball*, οὐσίαν συνεστρόγγῡλεν *played at ball with* it, i.e. *squandered* it (*made ducks and drakes of it* is our phrase), Alex.246.4; οὐσίδιον.. συνεστρόγγῡλα κἀξεκόκκισα (συνεστρογγύλικα codd.Ath.) Nicom.Com.3.

* **συστροφ-ή**, ἡ, *twisting together*, σ. χαύνην λαμβάνειν *to be* loosely *twisted*, of yarn, Pl.*Plt.*282e. **2.** *turning round*, v.l. (ap.Plu.2.891e) in *Placit.*2.29.3, for συντροφή. **3.** *condensation, density*, Arist.*Pr.*964$^{a}$18. **4.** pl., *dealings, converse* between men, Epicur. *Sent.*33. **5.** metaph. of style, *terseness, concentration*, D.H.*Dem.* 18, *Th.*53, Demetr.*Eloc.*8; ἐν συστροφῇ *concisely*, *PMag.Lond.*46.25. **II.** *that which is rolled into one mass*: hence, **1.** *collection, gathering*, πλήθεος σ. Hdt.7.9.αʹ; *seditious meeting, concourse*, Plb. 4.34.6, *Act.Ap.*19.40; κατὰ συστροφάς in *knots*, D.H.5.31, etc.; μετὰ συστροφῆς in *close array*, D.S.11.8; also, *swarm* of bees, Lxx *Jd.* 14.8 (v.l.); *flock* of birds, Artem.2.20; of other things, σ. δρυῶν D.Chr.1.52. **2.** *physical mass, aggregate*, in pl., Epicur.*Ep.*1 pp. 25,28 U.; esp. *morbid collection* or *deposit*, of tubercles, Hp.*Art.*41; αἱ περὶ τοὺς κονδύλους σ. chalk-stones, Dsc.1.30; σ. νεύρων a *complication* of nerves or sinews, Id.5.117, *Eup.*1.229; χάριν τοῦ..τὰ νεῦρα καθάπερ ἐκ σ. τινος ἁπλοῦσθαι Sor.1.101; συστροφαὶ νοσημάτων Hp.*Acut.*(*Sp.*)4; *tumour*, Plu.2.664f, Gal.15.773, Hp.ap.eund.19.143. **3.** *twisted grain* in wood, Thphr.*HP*5.2.3, 5.5.1. **4.** συστροφή, with or without ὄμβρου, a *sudden storm* of rain, Plb.3.74.5, 11.24.9; σ. ἀνέμου, πνεύματος, *whirl*wind, Phryn.374, Thphr.*Vent.* 34, Lxx *Ho.*4.19; νέφη καὶ σ. Antig.*Mir.*40. **5.** of stars, νεφελοειδὴς σ., = *nebula*, Heph.Astr.1.3, cf. Ptol.*Tetr.*149 (pl.), *Alm.*7.5, al. **-ία**, ἡ, *versatility*, Plb.23.2.2 codd. (εὐστροφίας Reiske, συστροφῆς B.-W.). **II.** *familiarity* with an author, f.l. for συντρ-, D.H.*Din.* 7; also f.l. for συντρ- in D.S.30.17, Lxx 3*Ma.*5.32. **-όομαι**, Pass., *to become dizzy*, Hsch. s.v. ἰλιγγιᾶν. **-ως**, Adv. *briefly*, prob. in Men.*Kith.*92.

**σύστρωμα**, ατος, τό, *pavement*, *Ephes.*3 No.9, Judeich *Altertümer von Hierapolis* No.152 (συνστρ-).

**συστρώννῡμι**, *pave*, συνστρώσει τὸ ἔδαφος λίθοις, πίναξιν ἅπαν τὸ χωρίον, *IG*2$^{2}$.1668.61,72, prob. l. in 7.4255.24 (Oropus); συνστρώσας σχοινίοις *PPetr.*3 p.121 (iii B.C.). **II.** *spread out together*, συνέστρωσε πάντα Aristeas 183:—Pass., ἐς ὁμαλότητα ἅπαντα συνέστρωντο Eun.*VS* p.501 B.; cf. συστορνύω.

**συστυγνάζω**, *mourn with* one, Simp. *in Epict.* p.90 D.

**σύστῡλος**, ον, *with columns standing close*, Vitr.3.3.1.

* **συστύφω** [ῡ], *draw together, contract*, τὰ στόματα τῶν φλεβῶν Hp. *Vict.*3.70 (v.l.):—Pass., *to be gloomy, morose*, Sch.Ar.*Ra.*1545, dub. in Hsch.

**συσφάζω**, *slay along with*, οὐ χρὴ.. σοι.. συσφᾰγῆναι E.*IT*685 (nisi leg. σὺν σφαγῆναι).

**συσφαιρ-ίζω**, *play at ball together*, Plu.2.94a, Antyll.ap.Orib.6.32.3. * **-ιστής**, οῦ, ὁ, *one who plays at ball with another*, Pl.*Ep.*363d,

Ath.1.19a (as cited by Suid. s. v. σφαῖρα), Antyll.ap.Orib.6.32.3; dat. pl. συνφαιρονταῖς dub. in *IG*2².4794.

**συσφάλλομαι**, Pass., *fall with*, τινι Max.Tyr.13.4.

**συσφηκόω**, *join closely together*, Timo 24.

⊛ **συσφίγγω**, *bind close together*, τοὺς ἀγκῶνας Herod.5.25; συσφιγχθεὶς χεροῖν τένοντας *APl*.4.199 (Crin.); τὸ λόγιον Lxx *Ex*.36.29 (39.21); *gird up*, τὴν ὀσφὺν ib.3*Ki*.18.46; *grasp*, ἄκροις δακτύλοις τὸ προβόλιον Procop.Gaz. p.167 B.; cf. σύσφιγμα.

**συσφιγκ-τήρ**, ῆρος, ὁ, = σφιγκτήρ III, Sm.*Ps*.44(45).14. **-τος**, ον, *laced close together*, Aq., Sm.*Ex*.28.4,14 (v.l. σύσφιγμα in Aq.), Thd.*Ex*.28.2.

**σύσφιγμα**, ατος, τό, *chain*, v. foreg.; so **συσφίγξεις**, αἱ, Aq.*Ex*.28.39 (sed leg. καὶ συσφίγξεις (fut.)).

**συσφρᾱγίζω**, *seal jointly with* others, εἰς τὸ προστῆναι τοῖς δημοσίοις θησαυροῖς καὶ συνσφραγίζειν *PRyl*.90.9,44 (iii A. D.); συνμαρτυρῶ καὶ συσφραγιῶ (a document) *BGU*86.40 (ii A. D.):—Med., *join in sealing and signing*, τὰς ὁμολογίας *OGI*229.86 (Smyrna, iii B. C., συνσ-), cf. *PHib*.1.29.35 (iii B. C., συνσ-). II. Med., *enclose under the same seal*, *BGU*1204.3 (i B. C.):—Pass., τὴν συνεσφραγισμένην ἐπιστολὴν *PTeb*.712.18 (ii B. C.); ἀντίγραφον συνεσφράγισται *UPZ*108.6 (ii B. C.), *Sammelb*.6236.7 (i B. C.), cf. *OGI*629.153 (Palmyra, ii A. D.).

**σύσχεσις**, εως, ἡ, *detention, imprisonment*, Vett.Val.292.9.

**συσχετήριον**, τό, *repository, place of confinement*, Herm.ap.Stob.1.49.68.

**συσχημᾰτ-ίζω**, *correct, remodel*, σ. [τοὺς ὁρισμοὺς] πρὸς τὸ.. ἔχειν ἐπιχείρημα Arist.*Top*.151ᵇ8; τὰ φαντάσματα Plu.2.83c:—Pass., *form oneself after* another, *to be conformed* to his example, πρός τινας ib. 100f; τῷ αἰῶνι τούτῳ *Ep.Rom*.12.2, cf. 1*Ep Pet*.1.14. II. Astron., in Pass., *to be similarly situated*, Ptol.*Phas*.p.12 H., *Tetr*.34, S.E. *M*.5.33, Vett.Val.42.22, al. **-ισις**, εως, ἡ, *similar situation*, τῶν ἀστέρων Sch.Ptol.*Tetr*.15,18. **-ισμός**, ὁ, = foreg., S.E.*M*.5.30, Ptol.*Phas*. p.5 H., Procl.*Par.Ptol*.142; *configuration*, Paul.Al. *E*.4. 2. Gramm., *correspondence of formation*, Ammon. *in Int*. 65.8 (pl.).

**συσχίζω**, *conscindo*, *Gloss*. (συνσχ-).

**συσχολ-άζω**, *spend one's leisure with* others: *to be a fellow-pupil in philosophy, study together* or *with*, οἱ -άζοντες *fellow-students*, Phld.*Lib*.p.35 O., al., cf. Plu.*Lyc*.16, *Alc*.24; Ἀριστάρχῳ -εσχολᾰκώς Phld.*Acad.Ind*.p.101 M.; τοῖς φιλοσόφοις Ath.4.168a, cf. Plu. *Alex*.65, Luc.*Jud.Voc*.8, etc.; Χρυσίππῳ παρὰ Κλεάνθει Ath.8.354e. **-αστής**, οῦ, ὁ, *school-fellow, fellow-student*, Phld.*Acad.Ind*. p.91 M., D.H.*Rh*.9.12, Plu.2.47e, *BCH*32.430 (Delos); σ. τινός Zeno ap.D.L.7.9; τινὸς παρά τινι Str.13.1.67.—The word is noted as not Att. by Phryn.378 and prob. by Thom.Mag.p.337 R. (where codd. have σχολαστάς).

**σύτο**, v. σεύω.

**σύφαξ**, ὁ, = γλεῦκος I, Hsch.: hence **συφακίζω**, = ὀπωρίζω, Id.

**σῦφαρ**, τό, *a piece of old* or *wrinkled skin*, Sophr.55, Call.*Fr*.49; *slough* of a serpent, Luc.*Herm*.79, cf. Phryn.*PS* p.114 B. 2. *skim* of milk, = γραῦς II, Sch.Nic.*Al*.91, Hsch. 3. *wrinkled fig*, Id. II. as Adj., σῦφαρ, ὁ, ἡ, *wrinkled, decrepit*, Lyc.793; between ὠμογέρων and πέμπελος, prob. in Gal.6.379 (cf. *Berl.Sitzb*.1924.100).

**σῠφεός**, ὁ, *hog-sty*, Od.10.238, 14.13,73, Parth.12.2; συφεόνδε *to the sty*, Od.10.320:—Ep. form **συφειός**, ib.389. (Prob. from σῦς.)

**σῠφεών**, ῶνος, ὁ, later form for συφεός, Agath.5.13.

**σῡφορβ-έω**, *to be a swineherd*, Sch.Od.17.219. **-ιον**, τό, = συοφόρβιον, *AP*11.363 (Diosc.), Polyaen.4.19. **-ός**, ὁ, (σῦς, φέρβω) *swineherd*, Il.21.282, Od.14.504, Theoc.16.54 (as v.l.), Plu.*Rom*.6; in Prose **συοφορβός** (q. v.):—Hom. also uses **ὑφορβός**, δῖος ὑφορβὸς Od.14.413, cf. 3, al.—Noted as not Att. by Thom.Mag.p.328 R.

**σῠφός**, ὁ, = συφεός, Lyc.676, Poll.7.187.

**σῠχν-άζω**, *to be frequent, do* or *come frequently*, = θαμίζω, *EM*299.31. **-άκῐς** [ᾰ], Adv. *frequently, often*, Luc.*Scyth*.2. **-ασμα**, ατος, τό, *that which is done frequently*, Poll.6.183. **-εών**, ῶνος, ὁ, *thicket*, Aq.*Ge*.22.13.

**σῠχνός**, ή, όν: I. in sg., 1. of Time, *long*, χρόνος σ. Hdt. 8.52, Pl.*Phd*.57a, Gal.15.152, etc.; χρόνῳ σ. ὕστερον, σ. ὕστερον χρόνῳ, X.*An*.1.8.8, Pl.*Grg*.518d: c. gen., συχνὸν τοῦ βίου *a great part* of life, Id.*Ep*.322e. 2. *long* in point of time, σ. λόγος *a long* speech, Id.*Grg*.465e, etc.; μάλα σ. λόγος Id.*Tht*.185e; σ. πραγματεία *long, wearisome*, D.52.21. II. of Number, *many*, ἔθνεα Hdt.1.58; πόλιες Id.6.33; πόνοι ib.108; [πρόλογοι] Ar.*Ra*.1237; πληγαί, κακά, Id.*Av*.1014, Pl.*R*.544c, etc.; ἡμέρας συχνὰς for *many* days *together*, Id.*Prt*.313a, cf. D.35.30; τεκεῖν πέντε συχνὰ ταῖς αὐταῖς ὠδῖσι five *at once*, Plu.2.429f (s.v.l., τέκνα is cj.): c. gen., συχναὶ τῶν νήσων Hdt.3.39; σ. τῶν λόγων Pl.*Grg*.519e; τῶν ληφθέντων σ. Th.4.106, cf. X.*An*.5.4.16, etc.: abs., συχνοί *many people together*, Th.2.52, etc.; ἄλλοι σ. *many* others, Ar.*Ec*.388. 2. with sg. nouns, *great, large*, λεπαστή Theopomp.Com.41; σφύραινα Antiph. 97; [τὸ πολίχνιον] σ. ποιεῖν make the small town *populous*, Pl.*R*. 370d; σ. χώρα Str.15.1.28; οἰκία Anon.ap.Suid.; σ. θεραπεία εὐνούχων Iamb.ap.eund. b. *much, great*, οὐσία Ar.*Pl*.754; πειθώ Pl. *R*.414c; σ. ἔργον *great, difficult*, ib.511c; σ. εὐλάβεια, σκέψις, μελέτη, *great, constant*, ib.539b, *Lg*.968b, Thphr.*Fr*.175; σ. τὸ ὑπεραῖρον τὸ ὕδωρ *large part* (of the plant), Id.*HP*4.8.10; σ. ἐλεὸς *often-recurring*, Pl.*Plt*.287e; ἡ διοίκησις σ. the expense was *great*, D.59.42; σ. αἷμα ἐρρύη Hp.*Epid*.7.77; διέρχεται φλέγμα σ. Gal.16.584; δεῖπνον σ. *plentiful*, *AP*6.303 (Aristo); σ. θεραπεία, πληθύς, ἀργύριον, etc., Plu.*Publ*.5, *Pomp*.39, *Lys*.16, etc.: c. gen., τῆς μαρίλης συχνήν Ar. *Ach*.350. III. of Space, προσεπιδεῖν καὶ ἔνθεν καὶ ἔνθεν ἐπὶ συχνόν Hp.*Fract*.14; συχνοτέρας κινήσιας ἔχει *more extensive* movements, Id.*Mochl*.1.

B. the Adv. συχνῶς (Antipho 3.3.3, *PGiss*.20.25 (ii A. D.), Gal. 16.684) is rare, the neut. συχνόν, συχνά being used instead, I. *often, much*, συχνὸν διαμαρτάνεις Pl.*Phdr*.257d; συχνὰ χαίρειν ἐᾶν Id.*Phlb*.59b; ἐπὶ συχνὸν Hp.*Fract*.14. 2. *far*, διαλείποντα συχνὸν ἀπ' ἀλλήλων X.*An*.1.8.10; προελαύνουσι Id.*Cyr*.6.3.12; ἀποπτὰς Arist.*HA*619ᵃ32. II. dat. συχνῷ is freq. joined with a Comp. Adj., like πολλῷ, σ. βελτίων *far* better, Pl.*Lg*.761d, cf. Hp.*Mul*.1. 69, Gal.6.471; νεώτερος ἐμοῦ καὶ συχνῷ younger *by a good deal*, D.39. 27. III. Adv. Comp. -οτέρως *EM*665.20; -ότερον Aristaenet.1.17.

**συχνοσύνθετος**, ον, *consisting of a long compound word*, χωρίον Eust.1277.48.

⊛ **συψειρικόν**, τό, = Lat. *subsēricum*, *Edict.Diocl*.20.9, al. (variously written).

**συψέλιον**, v. συμψ-.

⊛ **σῠώδης**, ες, *swinish, gluttonous*, Plu.2.716e; σ. ['Αρκάδες] Philostr.*VA*8.7; *brutish, stupid*, Eun.*VS* p.480 B.

**σφᾰγ-εῖον**, τό, (σφάζω) *bowl for catching the blood of the victim* in sacrifices, E.*El*.800, *IT*335, *Cyc*.395 (dub. l.), Ar.*Th*.754, *IG* 2².1543: pl., ib.1424a145:—in A.*Ag*.1092, for ἀνδρὸς σφάγιον Dobree restored ἀνδροσφαγεῖον. **-εύς**, έως, ὁ, *slayer, butcher*, E.*Rh*.254 (lyr.), *IT*623, *HF*451, etc.; at a sacrifice, *SIG*1025.44 (Cos, iv/iii B. C.); *murderer, cut-throat*, Decr.ap.And.1.78, D.13.32; ὁ σφαγεὺς ἕστηκε, of the sword on which Ajax is about to throw himself, S.*Aj*.815; *sacrificial knife, spit*, E.*Andr*.1134. **-ή**, ἡ, *slaughter*; the sg. is freq. in E., as *Hec*.571,1037, al.; in pl., A.*Eu*. 187,450, S.*El*.37, E.*Hec*.522, al.; ἕστηκε.. μῆλα πρὸς σφαγὰς πυρός ready for the sacrificial fire, A.*Ag*.1057; πολυθύτους τεύχειν σ. to offer many sacrifices, S.*Tr*.756: also in Prose, ὑπὸ σφαγῆς Pl.*R*. 610b; θανάτους τε καὶ σφαγάς Id.*Lg*.682e; σφαγὰς ποιεῖσθαι X.*HG* 4.4.2; σφαγὰς τῶν γνωρίμων ποιήσαντες ib.2.2.6, cf. Isoc.8.96, D.19. 260; ἐν ταῖς πόλεσι σφαγὰς ἐμποιοῦντες Isoc.5.107. 2. with collat. sense of *a wound*, αἷμα τῶν ἐμῶν σ. S.*Tr*.573, cf. 717; ἐκφυσιῶν.. αἵματος σφαγήν the blood gushing from the wound, A.*Ag*.1389; καθάρμοσον σφαγάς close *the gaping wound*, E.*El*.1228 (lyr.); ἐσφάγη.. σφαγὴν βραχεῖαν Ath.9.381a. II. *the throat*, the spot where the victim is struck (κοινὸν μέρος αὐχένος καὶ στήθους σφαγή Arist. *HA*493ᵇ7), Antipho 5.69: pl., ἐν σφαγαῖσι βάψασα ξίφος A.*Pr*.863; ἐς σφαγὰς ὦσαι ξίφος E.*Or*.291; so in Prose, οἰστοὺς.. ἐς τὰς σ. καθιέντες Th.4.48, cf. Sor.2.63; εἰς τὴν κεφαλὴν.. διὰ τῶν σ. Arist. *HA*511ᵇ35. **-ιάζομαι**, *slay a victim, sacrifice*, Hdt.9.61,72: abs., ἐσφαγιάζετο αὐτῷ [τῷ ποταμῷ] Id.6.76 (but just below, σφαγιασάμενος τῇ θαλάσσῃ ταῦρον); σ. τῇ Ἀγροτέρᾳ X.*HG*4.2.20, cf. *An*.4. 5.4; σ. εἰς τὸν ποταμόν ib.4.3.18. II. Act. **σφαγιάζω**, Ar.*Av*. 569 (anap.), D.S.13.86, Parth.35.2, Plu.2.221a: also pres. Pass., ὅταν χίμαιρα σφαγιάζηται X.*Lac*.13.8; pres. part. Pass., Ar.*Av*.570 (anap.): aor. part. Pass. σφαγιασθείς Hdt.7.180, *SIG*685.27 (Crete, ii B. C.), *BMus.Inscr*.1036 (Caria, ii/i B. C.). **-ιασμός**, ὁ, *slaying, sacrificing*, E.*El*.200 (lyr., pl.), Plu.*Ages*.6, Corn.*ND*34. **-ίδιον**, τό, Dim. of σφαγίς, Suid. **-ιον**, τό, *victim, offering*, σφάγιον ἔθετο ματέρα E.*Or*.842 (lyr.); σὴν παῖδ' Ἀχιλεῖ σ. θέσθαι Id.*Hec*.109 (anap.); διδόναι τύμβῳ σ. ib.119 (anap.); ἑαυτὰς ἔδοσαν σφάγιον τοῖς πολίταις ὑπὲρ τῆς χώρας D.60.29: mostly in pl., σφάγια παρθένους κτανεῖν E.*Ion* 278; τὰ σ. ἐγίνετο καλά Hdt.6.112, cf. A.*Th*.379, X. *An*.1.8.15; οὐ γάρ σφι ἐγίνετο τὰ σ. χρηστά Hdt.9.61, cf. 62; τὰ σ. οὐ δύναται καταθύμια γενέσθαι ib.45; τῶν σ. οὐ γινομένων (without any Adj.) not proving favourable, ib.61; σ. ἔρδειν, τέμνειν, A.*Th*. 230, E.*Supp*.1196; προφέρειν Th.6.69; ἅπτεσθαι τῶν σ. Antipho 5. 12; τὰ σ. δέξαι, addressed to a goddess, Ar.*Lys*.204. 2. in E. also, *slaughter, sacrifice*, δοῦλα σφάγια *Hec*.135 (anap.); σφάγια τέκνων *Or*.815 (lyr.), cf. 658. **-ιος**, α, ον, *slaying, slaughtering*, σ. μόρος *slaughter*, S.*Ant*.1291 (lyr.); *fatal, deadly*, Hp.*Fract*.35; σ. ξίφεα Man.1.316. II. σφαγία· ἡ τῆς ἱερουργίας ἡμέρα, Hsch. III. *of the throat*, σύριγγες Max.169. ⊛ **-ίς**, ίδος, ἡ, *sacrificial knife*, E.*El*.811,1142, D.H.7.72, Polyaen.3.9.40. **-ιστήριον**, τό, = σφαγεῖον, Sch.Lyc.194. ⊛ **-ῖτις**, ιδος, ἡ, (σφαγή II) *of the throat*, φλέβες σφαγίτιδες Arist.*HA*514ᵃ4, Gal.2.801, 14. 718: sg., Id.2.798, Orib.45.17.6. **-μα**, ατος, τό, *slaughter*, Sch. E.*Hec*.137 (pl.).

**σφάγνος**, ὁ, = ἐλελίσφακον, Diocl.*Fr*.139, Dsc.3.33. II. = ἀσπάλαθος, Id.1.20.

**σφᾰδ-άζω**, *toss the body about, struggle*, of unbroken horses, A. *Pers*.194; εἰκὸς σφαδᾴζειν ἦν ἄν, ὡς νεόζυγα πῶλον E.*Fr*.821.3, cf. 1020; σὺ δὲ σ., πῶλος ὣς εὐφορβίᾳ S.*Fr*.848; of a woman, *to be restless*, Hp.*Mul*.1.38, cf. Philostr.Jun.*Im*.16; ἐσφάδαζον· διηπόρουν, ἐφρόντιζον, Hsch.; of young children, κλαίει τε καὶ κινεῖται πλημμελῶς, ὥσπερ σφαδάζοντα Gal.6.43; *struggle* in death, Plu.*Ant*.76; of wounded horses, X.*Cyr*.7.1.37; of a dying fish, Plb.34.3.5, Ath.7. 283c. 2. *chafe, be strongly moved* or *excited*, Plu.2.10c,550e; ἐπὶ τὴν μάχην Id.*Caes*.42; πρὸς τὸν ἀγῶνα Id.*Phil*.6; πρὸς δόξαν Id.2. 1100a; ὑπὲρ κτημάτων Id.*Ages*.35; ὡς ἐπὶ.. συμφορᾷ Ph.2.37, cf. 396,451; ἀλόγως σφαδάζεις Id.1.145, cf. 460 (dub. l.).—Hdn.Gr.2. 929 prescribes the form σφαδᾴζω (σφαδάζω), cf. σφαδασμός, and v. ματάζω, τεράζω; σφαδιάζω is written in *POxy*.1381.99. **-ασμός**, ὁ, *spasm, convulsion*, Pl.*R*.579e. **-αστικῶς**, Adv. *convulsively*, Eust.1693.5.

⊛ **σφάζω**, Od.4.320, Hdt.2.39, E.*Tr*.134 (lyr.); in Com. (Cratin.

361) and Prose, from Pl. (*Grg.*468c) downwards, **σφάττω**, cf. Σφαττόμενος title of play by Diph., *IG*2².2363.34, and σ[φά]ττετ[αι] *SIG* 1024.36 (Myconus, iii/ii B.C.); Boeot. **σφάδδω** *An.Ox.*4.325: fut. σφάξω E.*Heracl.*493: aor. ἔσφαξα Il.2.422: pf. ἔσφᾰκα, known from plpf. ἐσφάκειν D.C.73.6, (ἀπο-) 78.7:—Pass., fut. σφᾰγήσομαι E.*Andr.* 315, *Heracl.*583, (ἀπο-) X.*HG*3.1.27: aor. ἐσφάγην [ᾰ] Trag. (A.*Eu.* 305, etc.) and late Prose, Plu.*Publ.*4, etc.; less freq. ἐσφάχθην, Pi.*P.* 11.23, Hdt.5.5, E.*IT*177 (lyr., nowhere else in Trag.): pf. ἔσφαγμαι Od.10.532, D.23.68:—*slay, slaughter*, properly *by cutting the throat* (v. σφαγή II), in Hom. always of cattle, μῆλ' ἀδινὰ σφάζουσι καὶ εἰλίποδας ἕλικας βοῦς Od.1.92, cf. 9.46, 23.305, Il.9.467. **II.** esp. *slaughter* victims for sacrifice, 1.459, etc.; ἔσφαζ' ἐπ' ὤμων μόσχον *cut its throat*, as it hung from the servant's shoulders, E.*El.*813; σ. παρθένου δέρην Id.*Or.*1199:—Pass., Od.10.532; ἀρνίον ἐσφαγμένον *Apoc.* 5.6. **2.** generally, *slay, kill*, of human victims, as Iphigeneia, Menoeceus, Pi.*P.*11.23, E.*Ph.*913, cf. A.*Ag.*1433, *Ch.*904; σ. τινὰ ἐς τὸν κρητῆρα so that the blood ran into the bowl, Hdt.3.11:—Pass., σφάζεται ἐς τὸν τάφον Id.5.5; πρὸς βωμῷ σφαγείς A.*Eu.* 305. **3.** of any slaughter by knife or sword, Hdt.5.25, 7.107; σ. ἑαυτόν Th.2.92; σ. καὶ ἐκδέρειν Pl.*Euthd.*301c; τὸν ἴδιον ἀδελφόν *PMag.Osl.*1.5, cf. 1*Ep.Jo.*3.12. **4.** of animals, *tear by the throat*, σ. ὥσπερ οἱ λύκοι τὰ πρόβατα Arist.*HA*612b2. **5.** of any killing, *BGU*388 ii 21 (ii A.D.), *OGI*697 (Egypt), *Sammelb.*7436.7 (vi A.D.), *Gloss.* **6.** metaph., *torment*, τινα *POxy.*259.33 (i A.D.).

® **σφαῖρᾰ**, ας, ἡ, *ball*, σφαίρῃ παίζειν play *at ball*, Od.6.100; σφαῖραν ἔρριψε ib.115; σ. καλὴν μετὰ χερσὶν ἕλοντο 8.372; σφαίρῃ ἂν' ἰθὺν πειρήσαντο ib.377; ὥσπερ σφαῖραν ἐκδεξάμενος τὸν λόγον Pl.*Euthd.* 277b; ῥαπτὴ σ. *AP*12.44 (Glauc.), cf. Nicom.Com.1.25, Antiph.234; διὰ σφαίρας.. ἐκπονῆσαι τὸ σῶμα Gal.6.134, cf. Sor.1.49,93; ἡ διὰ τῆς σ. ὄρχησις Ath.1.14d: metaph., σφαῖραν ἐποίησε τὴν οὐσίαν (cf. συστρογγύλλω) Alex.246.3: prov., σ. κατὰ πρανοῦς, of accelerating motion, Eust.249.1. **2.** *any globe*, Parm.8.43; *sphere*, as a geom. figure, Ti.Locr.95d, etc.; esp. *the terrestrial globe, earth*, Str.2.3.1; *an artificial globe*, Hermesian.7.88, Str.12.3.11. **3.** *hollow sphere* or *globe*: in the Ancient Physics, from the time of Anaximander (cf. *Placit.*2.16.5), of the *spheres* believed to revolve round the earth carrying the heavenly bodies, and according to the Pythagoreans arranged after the intervals of the musical scale (cf. Alex.Eph.ap. Theon.Sm.p.139 H., Cic. *de Rep.*6.18), Arist.*Metaph.*1073b18, *Cael.* 286b24, *Mete.*341b20, 354b24, Thphr.*Ign.*4; σ. ἀπλανής, = ἡ τῶν ἀπλανῶν σ. the *sphere* of the fixed stars, Procl.*Hyp.*5.1; so ἡ ἀπλανής, without σ., ib.7.25; αἱ πλανώμεναι σ. planetary *spheres*, Plu.2.1028a; Astrol., ἡ ὀρθὴ σ. right *sphere*, i.e. the celestial sphere as viewed from the equator, Rhetorius in *Cat.Cod.Astr.*8(1).231. **4.** *a weapon of boxers*, prob. *iron ball*, worn with padded covers (ἐπίσφαιρα) instead of boxing-gloves (ἱμάντες) in the σφαιρομαχίαι, Pl.*Lg.*830b, cf. Plu. 2.80b. **5.** αἱ σ. τῶν ὀμμάτων eye-*balls*, Arist.*Pr.*958a7. **6.** σ. θαλάττιαι sea-*balls*, Id.*HA*616a20, Crito ap.Gal.12.437. **7.** *pill*, Archig.ap.Orib.8.2.18. **8.** πλατάνου σφαῖραι, i.e. globular catkins, Dsc.4.73. **9.** as a quantitative measure, ἐπίβαλε.. φύκους στυπτηρίου ὡς σφαῖραν *PHolm.*16.32.

**σφαιρ-άρχης**, ου, ὁ, *president of the σφαιρομαχία*, Baillet *Inscr. des tombeaux des rois à Thèbes* 1495, cf. 1661. **-ειος**, α, ον, = σφαιρικός, Ps.-Alex.Aphr. *in Metaph.*486.28. **-εύς**, έως, ὁ, a Spartan youth, between ἐφηβεία and manhood, Paus.3.14.6, *IG*5(1).566, 674, al.; prob. from his then beginning to use the boxing-gloves (σφαῖρα 4). **-ηδόν**, Adv. *like a sphere, globe*, or *ball*, ἧκε δέ μιν σφαιρηδὸν ἑλιξάμενος Il.13.204, cf. *AP*6.45, Arat.531, Herod.Med. ap.Orib.8.7.3, Vett.Val.270.24. **-ίζω**, Lacon. **φαιρίδδω** Hsch:—*play at ball*, Pl.*Tht.*146a, Damox.3.1, Cleanth.*Stoic.*1.135, Plu.*Alex.* 39, etc. **II.** Pass., gloss on τυμπανίζομαι, Hsch. s. v. ἐτυμπανίσθησαν. **-ικός**, ή, όν, *globular, spherical*, *Placit.*1.14.2, al., Cleom.1. 1, al., Arist.*PA*680b14 (v.l.), Ptol.*Geog.*1.20.2. Adv. **-κῶς** *like a globe, spherically*, Arist.*Mu.*393a1, Plu.2.404f. **2.** σ. ἀριθμός, = ἀποκαταστατικὸς (q. v.) ἀριθμός, Nicom.*Ar.*2.17, *Theol.Ar.*48, cf. σφαιροειδής 1. 2. **II.** *of a sphere*, ἐπιφάνεια Euc.*Opt.*23 (recens.Theonis); προὐφέστηκεν ἡ γεωμετρία τῆς σφαιρικῆς (sc. ἐπιστήμης) Procl. *in Euc.* p.37 F.: Dor. fem. σφαιρικά, ᾶ, Archyt.1. **2.** *concerning the celestial spheres*, σφαιρικὰ..[τέχνα] Ἀράτου *IG*12(5).891.4 (Tenos); ὁ σ. λόγος the doctrine *of the spheres*, D.S.4.27; so τὰ σ. *AP*11. 318 (Phld.), Porph.ap. Eus.*PE*3.7, Jul.*Or.*4.148b; ἡ τῶν Θεοδοσίου σφαιρικῶν ἀστρονομία, a work cited by Olymp. *in Phlb.* p.280 S.; called τὰ Θεοδοσίου σ. by Sch.Autol. p.4 H., and still extant with the latter title (ed. J. L. Heiberg, *Abh. d. Gesellsch. d. Wiss. zu Göttingen*, Phil.-Hist. Kl., N. F. xix 3, Berlin 1927). **III.** ἡ -κή (sc. τέχνη), = ἡ σφαιριστική, Ath.1.14e,15c. **IV.** -κόν, τό, name of an eye-salve, Gal.12.784. ® **-ίον**, τό, Dim. of σφαῖρα, Pl.*Ep.*312d; oak-*gall*, Thphr.*HP*3.7.4; ivy-*berry*, Dsc.2. 179; *globular catkin* of the πλάτανος, Id.1.79, Cleom.1.10 fin.; but, *cylindrical catkin* of λεύκη, Dsc.1.81. **II.** *molecule, atom*, Democr. ap.Arist. *de An.*409a12. **III.** *round ball* or *token*, entitling the bearer to a present specified upon it, D.C.61.18. **IV.** *the end of the nose*, Poll.2.80, Heliod.ap.Orib.45.26.1, 48.32.3, Ruf.*Onom.*38, Sor. *Fasc.*11. **V.** *pill*, Lycus ap.Orib.8.43.1, Archig.ib.8.46.16, *Gp.*7. 13.2. **VI.** *sugar-plum, sweetmeat*, *POxy.*920.9,11 (ii/iii A.D.). **VII.** name of a plaster, Aët.15.36, Paul.Aeg.7.17. **VIII.** dub. sens. in *Inscr.Délos* 1432 *Ba* i 14 (ii B.C.). **-ισις**, εως, ἡ, *a playing at ball*, Arist.*Rh.*1371a2. **-ισμα**, ατος, τό, = σφαίρισις, Eust.1601.61: **σφαιρισμός**, ὁ, Artem.4.69. **-ιστήριον**, τό, *ball-court*, Thphr. *Char.*5.9, *IG*11(2).199 *A* 110 (Delos, iii B.C.), *BCH*23.566 (Delph., iii B.C.), Phld.*Herc.*1457.7, *POxy.*1450.5 (iii A.D.). **-ιστής**, οῦ, ὁ, *ball-player*, Antig.Car.ap.Ath.12.548b, *AP*5.213 (Mel.). **-ιστικός**, ή, όν, *of* or *for playing at ball*, ἐπιμέλεια -ωτάτη Arr.*Epict.*2.5.20; σφαιριστικός, ὁ, *a clever player*, Gal.6.154, Poll.9.107; περὶ -κῆς (sc. τέχνης), title of a work by Timocrates, ap.Ath.1.15c. **-ίστρα**, ἡ, = σφαιριστήριον, *Inscr.Délos* 1417 *A* i 140 (ii B.C.), Plu.2.839c. **-ῖτις κυπάρισσος**, ἡ, a kind of *cypress*, so called from its globular fruit, Gal.12.418.

**σφαιρο-γρᾰφία**, ἡ, *celestial globe*, Sch.Arat.248. **-ειδής**, ές, *globular, spherical*, Hp.*Aër.*14, Pl.*Ti.*33b,63a, Euc.*Phaen.* p.4 M., Chrysipp.*Stoic.*2.224, etc.; of the *rounded end* of a lance, X.*An.*5. 4.12. Adv. **-δῶς** D.L.7.158, etc. **2.** = σφαιρικός 1. 2, Theo Sm.p.38 H. **II.** τὸ σ. *spheroid*, Archim.*Con.Sph.Praef.*p.252 H., al. **-θεσία**, ἡ, *position on the celestial sphere*, Sch.Arat. 147. **-θήκη**, ἡ, *sphere-holder*, Gem.5.63. ® **-μᾰχέω**, *spar with the* σφαῖραι (σφαῖρα 4), Pl.*Lg.*830e. **2.** *play at ball*, Plb. 16.21.6. ® **-μᾰχία**, ἡ, *sparring-match with the* σφαῖραι (σφαῖρα 4), Aristomen.13, Seneca *Ep.*80.1, Stat.*Silv.*4 *Praef.*, Poll.3.150, Aristid.2.322 J.; and **-μάχια**, τά, a Spartan game, Eust.1601.25, Pius ap.Sch.Od.8.372. **-μάχος** [ᾰ], ὁ, *one who spars with the* σφαῖρα 4, A.D.*Adv.*188.26, *POxy.*1050.13 (ii/iii A.D.). **-παικτέω**, *play at ball*, Suid. **-παίκτης**, ου, ὁ, *ball-player, juggler*, *Gloss.* **-παικτικός**, ή, όν, *given to ball-playing*, Sopat. in Rh.5.22 W. **-ποιέω**, *make spherical*, Str.1.3.12, Plu.2.355a. **2.** *make globes*, Ptol.*Hyp.* 1.1. **-ποιία**, ἡ, *artificial sphere*, Gem.12.23, Theo Sm.pp.146, 151 H.; *making of* the heavenly *spheres*, Phld.*Po.Herc.*1676 *Fr.* 2. **-ποιός**, = *pilarius*, *Gloss.*

**σφαῖρος**, ὁ, = σφαῖρα, the condition of the Universe (ὁ Κόσμος), when brought together by Eros, Emp.27.4, al. **II.** cf. σφῆρος. **III.** dub. sens. in *POxy.*1727.15 (ii/iii A.D.).

**σφαιρ-όω**, *make into a globule*, πάπυρον Alex.Aphr.*Pr.*1.93:—Pass., *to be rounded*, Dsc.2.35, Antyll.ap.Orib.7.9.2, Aret.*SA*1.6, etc.; στήθεα δ' ἐσφαίρωτο his chest *was round and arched*, Theoc.22. 46. **2.** Pass., *to be curled up in a ball*, ψυχὴ -ωθεῖσα Ael.*VH*3. 11. **3.** Pass., metaph., *to be concentrated*, Dam.*Pr.*400. **II.** in Pass. also of blunted weapons, ἐσφαιρωμένα ἀκόντια spears *with buttons* at the point, X.*Eq.*8.10; γρόσφοι -ωμένοι Plb.10.20.3; σιδήρια D.C.71.29; opp. λελογχωμένον δόρυ, Arist.*EN*1111a12. **-ωμα**, ατος, τό, *anything made round* or *globular*: **1.** *round weight*, in steelyards, Arist.*Mech.*853b32. **2.** pl., *buttocks*, S.E.*P.*2.211, Gal. 14.707; sg. in Paul.Aeg.3.77. **3.** generally, *curve*, ζῳδιακοῦ κύκλου Man.5.32. **4.** dub. sens. in *PCair.Zen.*659.12 (iii B.C.). **-ών**, ῶνος, ὁ, *round fishing-net*, Opp.*H.*3.83. **-ωσις**, εως, ἡ, *spherical shape, rotundity*, Paul.Aeg.6.62; *formation of a sphere*, Simp. *in Cael.*543.28, *Theol.Ar.*19, Olymp. *in Phd.*p.196 N. ® **-ωτήρ**, ῆρος, ὁ, *thong, latchet*, *PLond.*2.402v.22 (ii B.C.), Hsch.; cf. σφυρωτήρ. **II.** *a ball* to ornament pillars, *knop*, Lxx *Ex.*25.30(31): pl., as heraldic device, *Tab Heracl.*1.184. **-ωτός**, ή, όν, *rounded*, Opp.*C.*2. 92. **II.** *with a ball* or *button at the end*, X.*Eq.*8.10.

**σφάκελ-ίζω**, *suffer from* σφάκελος, *to be gangrened, mortify*, ἐσφακέλισέ τε τὸ ὀστέον καὶ ὁ μηρὸς ἐσάπη Hdt.3.66; σφακελίσαντος τοῦ μηροῦ καὶ σαπέντος Id.6.136, cf. Pl.*Ti.*74b,84b, Arist.*HA*519b6; of the eyes, Lxx *Le.*26.16, *De.*28.32: also in Pass., ὁκόσοισιν ἂν σφακελισθῇ ὁ ἐγκέφαλος Hp.*Aph.*7.50, cf. *Morb.*2.5 (v.l.). **2.** of the effect of severe cold on single limbs, *to be frost-bitten*, D.H.12.8. **3.** of plants and trees, *to be blighted*, Arist.*Juv.*470a31, Thphr.*HP*4.14.4, etc. **II.** *to have spasms* or *convulsions*, ἀπορεῖν καὶ σ. τῷ δεινῷ Cratin.342, cf. Pherecr.80. **-ισμός**, ὁ, = sq., ὀστέων Hp.*Art.* 33 (pl.); τοῦ ἐγκεφάλου Id.*Morb.*2.5, cf. Arist.*PA*672a33; of plants, *rot*, Thphr.*HP*4.14.2,4, 8.10.1; of the effect of cold on the foetus, Arist.*Pr.*860a19, cf. Erot.*Fr.*18. **2.** = λύπη σφοδρά, *Stoic.*3. 100. **3.** *epilepsy* in horses, *Hippiatr.*108. **-ος**, ὁ, *gangrene, mortification*, or, of bones, *caries*, Hp.*Aph.*7.78; τοῦ ἐγκεφάλου Id. *Aër.*10 (pl.); so called when farther advanced than γάγγραινα, cf. Gal.2.632, 18(1).687. **2.** generally, *spasm, convulsion*, A.*Pr.*878 (anap.); κατὰ δ' ἐγκέφαλον πηδᾷ σ. E.*Hipp.*1352 (anap.): metaph., σ. ἀνέμων *the convulsive fury* of winds, A.*Pr.*1045 (anap.). **3.** *the middle finger*, Suid. s. v. σφακελισμός: so **σφάκηλος** (or **φάκηλος**) *PLond.*1821.297. **-ώδης**, ες, *like gangrene*, ἑτεροκρανίαι, of migraine (as though the brain were rotting), Archig.ap.Gal.8.92; νοῦσος (dub. sens.) Hp.*Morb.*2.75.

**σφάκηλος**, v. σφάκελος 3. **σ(φ)άκια**· τῆς ἀμπέλου τὰ κλήματα, Hsch.

® **σφάκος** [ᾰ], ὁ, *sage-apple, Salvia calycina*, Cratin.325, Eup.14.3, Ar. *Th.*486, Thphr.*HP*6.1.4. **II.** a kind of *lichen* or *tree-moss*, found on oaks, Plin.*HN*24.27; also written *sphagnos*, ibid. and 12.108; found on rocks, Hsch. s. v. βρύα (where σκάφος cod.); **φάσκον** in Thphr.*HP*3.8.6; **φάσκος** in Hsch.

**σφάκ-της** (al. -τής), ου, ὁ, *slayer, murderer*, Zen.3.94, Aq.*Da.*2. 14. **-τικός**, ή, όν, *of* or *for slaughtering*, μάχαιρα Zonar. s. v. πανδούριον. **-τός**, ή, όν, *slain, slaughtered*, δαίς E.*Hec.*1078 (lyr.); θηρία *Rev.Arch.*30(1929).29 (Gortyn, iv A.D.). **-τρια**, fem. of σφάκτης, *priestess*, Ael.*Fr.*44. **-τρον**, τό, *tax paid for victims*, *OGI*629.153 (Palmyra, ii A.D.), Poll.10.97.

**σφᾰκώδης**, ες, *abounding in sage*, κλ(ε)ιτύς Hsch. **σφάλαξ**, v. σπάλαξ.

**σφαλάσσειν**· τέμνειν, κεντεῖν, Id.

**σφᾰλερόνηκτος**, ον, *dangerous to swim*, ποταμοί Poll.3.103.

**σφᾰλερός**, ά, όν, (σφάλλω) *likely to make one stumble* or *trip*: metaph., *slippery, perilous*, τυραννὶς χρῆμα σ. Hdt.3.53; γνωμέων

..τὴν -ωτέρην σεωυτῷ Id.7.16.α′; σφαλερὸν ἡγεμὼν θρασύς E.*Supp.*508; τοῦτο δέ γ' ἐστὶν τὸ καλὸν σ. Id.*IA*21 (anap.); ὦ βιοτή..ἐπὶ παντὶ σφαλερὰ κεῖσαι Id.*Fr.*916 (lyr.); πάντων -ώτατον, of future events, Th.4.62, cf. Hp.*Aph.*1.1; -ώτατοι καιροί Phld.*Oec.*p.48J., *SIG*796*B*10 (Epid., i A.D.); of poems, Pl.*Lg.*810b; σ. τρόπος (v.l. τόπος) Hp.*Prog.*22; σφαλερόν [ἐστι], c. inf., Pl.*R.*451a, *Lg.*688b; τὸ ἐπιχειρῆσαι σ. X.*HG*2.1.2. Adv. Comp. -ώτερον, νοσεῖν to be *more dangerously* ill, Gal.15.724. II. (σφάλλομαι) *ready to fall, tottering, reeling,* κῶλα A.*Eu.*371 (lyr.); ῥῦμα S.*Aj.*159 (anap.); σῶμα σ. ἐν ταῖς κινήσεσι, of revellers and sufferers from coma, Gal.7.645; ἕξις σ. πρὸς ὑγίειαν *uncertain* in point of health, Pl.*R.*404a. Adv. -ρῶς, ὑγιαίνειν enjoy health *precariously*, Gal.6.810. III. of persons, where the sense often fluctuates between I and II, ἴχνεσι σφαλεροῖ Nic.*Al.*189, cf. 400; σ. σύμμαχοι *uncertain*, D.1.7; προστάτης σ. E.*Fr.*774.3. Adv. -ρῶς Id.*IA*600 (anap.), Isoc.7.1.

**σφᾰλίζω**, *fetter* (cf. σφαλλός 2), Hsch. s.v. ἐσφάλιξεν, Phot. s.v. ἐσφάλιζεν. ⊛ **σφάλλον·** κολάκευσον, Hsch.

**σφαλλός** or **σφᾰλός**, ὁ, *a round leaden plate*, which was thrown by a strap attached to a ring, a variety of the δίσκος, Poll.8.72, Hsch. II. *a round block of wood* with two holes for the feet, *pair of stocks*, Epich.148 (σφάκελλος codd. Ath.), Poll. l. c., Hsch.; cf. σφέλας.

**σφάλλω**, S.*Fr.*192, Hdt.7.16.α′, etc.: fut. σφᾰλῶ Th.7.67: aor. 1 ἔσφηλα, Ep. σφῆλα Od.17.464, Dor. ἔσφᾶλα Pi.*P.*8.15: but the intrans. ἔσφαλεν Lxx *Jb.*21.10, *Si.*13.22, *Am.*5.2, opt. σφάλαι ib.*Jb.*18.7, are prob. forms of a Hellenistic aor. 1 *ἔσφᾰλα (presupposing *ἔσφᾰλον as ἦλθα presupposes ἦλθον, etc.): pf. ἔσφαλκα Plb.8.9.2:— **Pass.**, fut. σφᾰλήσομαι S.*Tr.*719,1113, Th.3.14, etc.; freq. in med. form σφᾰλοῦμαι, S.*Fr.*588, X.*Smp.*2.26: aor. ἐσφάλην [ᾰ] Alc.*Supp.*27.13 (prob.), Hdt.4.140, Th.8.24, etc.; ἐσφάλθην only in Gal.5.62: pf. ἔσφαλμαι E.*Andr.*896, Pl.*Cra.*436c: plpf. ἔσφαλτο Th.7.47:— *make to fall, overthrow*, properly *by tripping up, trip up in wrestling*, οὔτ' Ὀδυσεὺς δύνατο σφῆλαι οὔδει τε πελάσσαι Il.23.719; οὐδ' ἄρα μιν σφῆλεν βέλος Od.17.464; Ἕκτορα Pi *O.*2.81; ἀλλάλους σφάλλοντι παλαίμασι Theoc.24.112; [πώλους] E.*Hipp.*1232; γόνυ τινός Id.*Heracl.*128; τινὰ γνύξ A.R.3.1310; τινὰ ἐπὶ τὴν γῆν D.S.14.23; τὸ μὴ ὑπερπίνειν ἧττον ἂν καὶ σώματα καὶ γνώμας σ. X.*Cyr.*8.8.10, cf. 1.3.10 (Pass.); σ. ναῦς *throw them on* their *beam-ends*, Plu.*Them.*14, cf. Polyaen.3.11.13; [ἵπποι] ἔσφηλαν (gnomic aor.) τὸν ἀναβάτην *throw* him, X.*Eq.*3.9:—Pass., *to be tripped up*, Φρυνίχου παλαίσμασιν Ar.*Ra.*689 (troch.); of a drunken man, σφαλλόμενος προσέρχεται *reeling, staggering*, Id.*V.*1324, cf. Heraclit.117; σ. ὑπὸ οἴνου X.*Lac.*5.7, cf. *AP*11.26 (Marc. Arg.); σ. ἵππος Plu.*Phil.*18; σ. [ἱππεύς] *is thrown*, X.*Eq.*7.7. II. generally, *cause to fall, overthrow*, βίᾳ καὶ μεγάλαυχον ἔσφαλεν Pi.*P.*8.15; ἀνθρώπων κακῶν ὁμιλίαι σ. τινά Hdt.7.16.α′; σμικροὶ λόγοι ἔσφηλαν ἤδη καὶ κατώρθωσαν βροτούς S.*El.*416; σφάλλω ..ὅσοι φρονοῦσιν εἰς ἡμᾶς μέγα E.*Hipp.*6; [ὀργὴ] πλεῖστα..σ. βροτούς Id.*Fr.*31; ἡ καταφρόνησις, ἡ ἀπειρία σ. τινά, Th.1.122, 2.87: abs., ἀτρεκεῖς ἐπιτηδεύσεις φασὶ σφάλλειν πλέον ἢ τέρπειν E.*Hipp.*262 (anap.): also of things, ἁμαρτίαι σ. τὴν σωτηρίαν S.*Fr.*192; δειναὶ τύχαι σ. δόμους E.*Med.*198 (anap.); σ. τὰς πόλεις Th.3.37, etc.; σ. δίκαν E.*Andr.*780 (lyr.); σφάλλων, name of a throw of the dice, Eub.57.5 (s. v. l.):—Pass., *to be overthrown, fall*, esp. of persons falling from high fortunes, σφαλεὶς γὰρ οὐδεὶς εὖ βεβουλεῦσθαι δοκεῖ Chaerem.26, cf. S.*Tr.*297,719, E.*Fr.*262.2, etc.; ἦν σφαλῇ [ἡ Ἑλλάς] Hdt.7.168; ἦν ἄρα τι σφαλλώμεθα, opp. κατορθοῦν, Th.1.140, cf. Ar.*Ra.*736 (troch.), *Pl.*351; σφαλλομένους ἐπανορθῶν X.*Mem.*2.4.6; ταῖς τύχαις σφάλλεσθαι Th.2.87, cf. 43; ὑπὸ νόσων, ἐρώτων, μέθης ἐσφαλμένος, Pl.*R.*396d; ὑπὸ χρόνων τι σ. *suffer* from length of time, Id.*Lg.*769c: c. dat. modi, σφάλλεσθαι ἀξιόχρεῳ δυνάμει Th.6.10; τοῖς ἀγῶσι Id.7.61; τοῖς ὅλοις Plb.1.43.8: with a Prep., ἐν τῇ μάχῃ X.*HG*7.2.2, cf. Hdt.7.50; τι ἐν τοῖς λόγοις Pl.*Grg.*461d; περί τι Id.*R.*451a; περί τινος Plu.2.164c: with neut. Adj., σφάλλεσθαι ἐν μέγα Pl *Lg.*648e; ἐν τοῖς δικασταῖς, κοὐκ ἐμοί, τόδ' ἐσφάλη this *mishap took place* by means of.., S.*Aj.*1136; οὔ τι μὴ σφαλῶ γ' ἐν σοί *I shall* not *fail* in thy business, Id.*Tr.*621. III. *baffle, balk, frustrate*, of an oracle, Hdt.7.142; θεὰ ἤδη μ'..ἔσφηλεν S.*Aj.*452, cf. E.*Alc.*34 (anap.), *Andr.*223; ἐκ τοῦ φανεροῦ τὴν πόλιν σ. Aeschin.3.125:— Pass., *err, go wrong, be mistaken*, κατὰ γνώμην Hdt.7.52: abs., S.*El.*1481, E.*IA*1541, etc.; μῶν ἐσφάλμεθ'; *am I mistaken?* Id.*Andr.*896; ἡ ψυχὴ πολλὰ σφάλλεται Isoc.1.32; γνώμῃ σφαλέντες Th.4.18; διανοίᾳ σ. Pl.*Sph.*229c; so σ. τὴν γνώμην, τὸν λογισμόν, Clearch.23, Plu.*Sull.*15: c. inf., οὐκ ἂν σφαλείη..ἑλέσθαι *be led astray* into choosing, Id.2.711b. 2. Pass. also, c. gen. rei, *to be balked of* or *foiled in* a thing, ἢ καὶ πατήρ τι σφάλλεται βουλευμάτων; A.*Eu.*717; γάμων, δόξης, τύχης, E.*Or.*1078, *Med.*1010, *Ph.*758; τῆς δόξης Th.4.85; τοῦ αὐχήματος Id.7.66, cf. 5.110; οὐκ ἔσφαλται τῆς ἀληθείας Pl.*Cra.*436c; τῶν πραγμάτων ἢ ἔχει Id.*Hp.Mi* 372b; ἀνδρὸς *lose* him, S.*Tr.*1113; τοῦ παντός Plu.*Brut.*20:—σφάλλειν τινὰ ἀπ' ἐλπίδος *cast* him *down* from his hope, Luc.*Dem.Enc.*29.

**σφάλ-μα**, ατος, τό, *trip, stumble, false step*, *AP*7.634 (Antiphil.), Man.4.289. 2. *a glide*, in a surgical operation, Heliod.ap.Orib.49.8.38, Ruf. ib.49.28.13. II. metaph., 1. *fall, failure, defeat*, Hdt 7.6, 9.9, Th.5.14 (pl.), etc.; σφάλματα ποιοῦντες causing *losses*, Pl.*Plt.*298b. 2. *fault, error*, Hdt.1.207, 7.10.ζ′; τὰ πρόσθε σ. E.*Andr.*54, *Supp.*416, cf. Pl.*Tht.*168a, *R.*487b, Phld.*Rh.*1.348S., Gal.6.68. **-μάω**, or **-μέω**, = σφάλλομαι, of a horse, Plb.35.5.2:— Hsch. explains σφαλμάω by σκιρτάω, σφαδάζω. **-μός**, ὁ, *error, failure*, Aq.*Ps.*120(121).3, *Is.*58.3.

**σφάλος**, τό, = σφάλμα, dub. in Trag.*Oxy.*676.16.

**σφᾰλός**, v. σφαλλός.

**σφάλ-σις**, εως, ἡ, = σφάλμα, Vett.Val.285.35. **-της**, ου, ὁ, *one who trips up* or *throws down*, Lyc.207.

**σφάνιον·** κλινίδιον, Hsch.; cf. ἐν σφανίῳ· ἐν κλιναρίῳ, Id. (Perh. σφάνιον, Dor. etc. for *σφήνιον, abbrev. for σφηνόπους, q. v.)

**σφάξ**, σφαγός, = σφαγή II, Sch.E.*Hec.*571; elsewh. only in compds., διασφάξ, etc. II. **σφάξ**, σφᾱκός, Dor. for σφήξ, Theoc.5.29.

**σφᾰρᾰγ-έομαι**, *burst with a noise, crackle, sputter*, as liquids when thrown upon the fire, σφαραγεῦντο δέ οἱ πυρὶ ῥίζαι the roots of his eye *crackled* or *hissed* (when Odysseus burnt them with the hot stake), Od.9.390. II. *groan with fulness, to be full to bursting*, οὔθατα γὰρ σφαραγεῦντο ib.440. **-ίζω**, *stir up with noise and bustle*, σὺν δ' ἄνεμοι ἐνοσίν τε κονίην τ' ἐσφαράγιζον Hes.*Th.*706. **-ος·** βρόγχος, τράχηλος, λαιμός, ψόφος, Hsch.: = φάρυγξ, Apion ap.Phot.

**σφᾶς** and **σφάς**, acc. of σφεῖς (q. v.): but σφάς [ᾰ], acc. fem. of σφός. **σφάττω**, v. σφάζω. **σφε**, v. σφεῖς. **σφεᾶ, σφέᾶς**, v. σφεῖς.

⊛ **σφεδᾰνός**, ή, όν, = σφοδρός, *vehement, violent*, στάσιες Xenoph.1.23; γέννες (sc. λέοντος) *AP*6.219.12 (Antip.); τόξον Euph.9.10; κάρηαρ Nic.*Th.*642; ῥοιζός Epic. in *Arch.Pap.*7 p.4. II. Hom. only neut. sg. as Adv., *eagerly*, σφεδανὸν Δαναοῖσι κελεύων Il.11.165, 16.372; σφεδανὸν ἔφεπ' ἔγχεϊ 21.542 (Aristarch. and several codd. σφεδανῶν, from **σφεδανάω**, *raging*, cf. Theognost.*Can.*12, Hsch.).

⊛ **σφειδρόν·** καθαρόν, εὐῶδες, Hsch. (**σφεδρόν** Theognost.*Can.*12).

**σφειλόν·** λοξόν, πυκνόν, εὐκίνητον, προσφυές, δριμύ, Hsch.: cf. σφηλόν.

⊛ **σφεῖς**, A. Forms: nom. σφεῖς Hdt.7.168, Th.5.46,65, X.*An.*7.5.9, *HG*5.2.8, Pl.*R.*487c:—the uncontr. form σφέες is never found, cf. A.D.*Pron.*93.1, though recognized by Greg.Cor.p.479S.:—the obl. cases only are used by Hom. 2. Gen. σφέων, in Hom. a monosyll., and sts. enclitic, Il.18.311, Od.3.134; poet. σφείων only in Il., and always in phrase ὦσαν ἀπὸ σφείων, 4.535, 5.626, 13.148; σφέων also in Hdt.2.4, 4.35, al.; Att. σφῶν *IG*1².39.67, al., Th.1.120, al., Antipho 6.23, etc., also in Hom. in the phrase σφῶν αὐτῶν, Il.12.155, 19.302. 3. Dat. σφίσι(ν) or σφισι(ν) 4.2, 17.453, 22.288,474, A.*Pr.*481, Hdt.1.4, al., Th.1.19, al., X.*HG*1.7.5, etc.; more freq. in the forms σφι, σφιν, Il.2.612,614, al., A.*Pr.*254, al., Hdt.1.31, al. (not in Att. Prose); in Trag. never σφι; sts. elided σφ', Il.3.300, 8.4, etc.; σφιν also in Dor. Prose, *SIG*56.48 (Argos, v B.C.), *IG*2².1126.25 (Delph Amphict., iv B.C.), *Schwyzer* 92.5 (Argos, iii B.C.), Anon. in *PSI*9.1091.21:—σφίσι(ν) is not enclitic acc. to A.D.*Pron.*98.12, sts. enclitic acc. to Hdn.Gr.2.42 (who says elsewh. (2.57) that pronouns beginning with σφ- are always enclitic); σφι(ν) is enclitic, exc. at the beginning of a phrase, as σφὶν δ' αὐτοῖς Hes.*Fr.*49 (cited by A.D.*Pron.*98.11). 4. Acc., Ep. and Ion. σφέας (enclit. σφεας) Hom. (v. infr.), Archil.27.2, Hdt.1.4,5, al.; freq. to be pronounced as one long syllable, as in οὐ μέν σφεας ἔτ' ἔολπα Od.8.315, cf. 480, 13.213,276; but also as a disyll., Il.12.43, Od.12.225, al.; σφᾶς enclit. in Il.5.567, Parm.1.12, Theoc.21.16, not enclit. in Opp.*C.*1.471, *H.*2.231; Att. σφᾶς *IG*1².101.3, Th.1.24, E.*Med.*1378, *Or.*1127, etc.; enclit. σφας [ᾰ, cf. S.*Ant.*128 (anap.)] S.*OT*1470,1508, *OC*486; also σφε Il.19.265, Simon.99, Pi.*P.*5.86, A.*Th.*630 (lyr.), 788 (lyr.), 864 (anap.), S.*OT*1505, *OC*605,1669, E.*Med.*394, etc.; never in Com. (for Ar.*Eq.*1020 is a burlesque oracle), nor in Att. Prose; once in Hdt. (7.170, sed leg. σφέας): neut. σφεα (v. infr. III). II. Rare dialectic forms:—Lacon. dat. φιν, *EM*702.41; used also by Emp.22.3, Call.*Dian.*125,213, *Fr.*183, Nic.*Th.*725: Aeol. dat. and acc. ἄσφι, ἄσφε, Sapph.43, Alc.73: Syrac. dat. and acc. ψιν, ψε, Sophr.93,94, Theoc.4.3; ψε and ψεαυτόνς also Cretan, *Rendic.Pont. Accad.Rom. di Arch.*7.106, *Riv.Fil.*58(1930).473; Cret. dat. ψιναυτοῖς *Riv.Ist.Arch.*2.19: Arc. dat. σφεις *IG*5(2).6.10,18 (Tegea).— For the dual v. σφωέ: like other pl. forms σφε can be used with reference to two persons, Il.11.111, Od.8.271, 21.192,206; so σφεας, Il.11.128. III. Gender:—in Hom. this Pron. has no neut.; in Od.9.70, 10.355, it refers to things, denoted by feminine nouns: but in Ion. Prose occurs the neut. pl. σφεα, Hdt.1.46,89, 2.119, 3.53 (σφε codd.), 7.50, Abyd.9; σφε is acc. pl. neut. in Theoc.15.80.

B. Meanings: I. *they, them*, pl. of οὗ B. I, ἐκ γάρ σφεων φρένας εἵλετο Παλλὰς Ἀθήνη Il.18.311; τῶ σφεων πολέες κακὸν οἶτον ἐπέσπον Od.3.134; μετὰ δέ σφισι πότνια Ἥβη νέκταρ ἐῳνοχόει Il.4.2; οὔ σφι θαλάσσια ἔργα μεμήλει 2.614; ἐγὼ σφισιν ἔδειξα κράσεις ἠπίων ἀκεσμάτων A.*Pr.*481, cf. 443,457, S.*OT*1470, al., E.*Med.*1378; this use is not found in Prose, exc. in dialects, *SIG*56.48 (Argos, v B.C.), *IG*2².1126.25 (Delph. Amphict., iv B.C.), Hdt.1.3, 2.15, al. b. παρὰ δέ σφιν ἑκάστῳ δίζυγες ἵπποι ἑστᾶσι beside each of *them*, Il.5.195. 2. reflexively, as pl. of οὗ B. II. 1, ὦσαν ἀπὸ σφείων 4.535, al.; αἳ ἑ μετὰ σφίσιν εἶχον 22.474, cf. Th.2.76; later with the same restriction as for οὗ B. II. 1, e.g. φράζοντες ὡς οὔ σφι περιοπτέη ἐστὶ ἡ Ἑλλὰς ἀπολλυμένη· ἦν γὰρ σφαλῇ, σφεῖς γε οὐδὲν ἄλλο ἢ δουλεύσουσι τῇ πρώτῃ τῶν ἡμερέων Hdt.7.168, cf. Th.5.46,65, X.*An.*7.5.9, *HG*5.2.8, Pl.*R.*487c. 3. oblique cases in combination with αὐτῶν, αὐτούς, etc., forming a reflex. Pron. used without the foreg. restriction, ἐντὸς δὲ πυκάζοιεν σφέας αὐτοὺς Od.12.225; σφῶν δ' αὐτῶν κήδε' ἑκάστη Il.19.302, cf. 12.155; σφᾶς δ' αὐτάς Hes.*Th.*34; Κερκυραῖοι σφῶν αὐτῶν τοὺς ἐχθροὺς δοκοῦντας εἶναι ἐφόνευον Th.3.81, cf. 1.139, al.; it sts. = ἀλλήλοις (-ων), ἀλλήλοις κοτέοντες ἐπὶ σφέας ὁρμήσωσι Hes.*Sc.*403; ποθεινοτέρως σφῶν αὐτῶν ἔχειν X.*Lac.*1.5; σφᾶς (σφὰς cod. L) αὐτοὺς . . ἐπέφραδον *informed one another*, A.R.2.959; but σφᾶς ἑωυτάς is prob. f.l. in Hp.*Epid*.2.1.3: cf. Thom.Mag.p.329R. II. as sg., = *him, her*, in the dat. and acc. forms σφι(ν), σφε; σφιν is so used in *h.Pan*.19, *h.Hom*.30.9, A.*Pers*.759, S.*OC*1490 (in Od.15.524 σφιν refers to all the suitors, and in Hes.*Sc*.113 to Ares and Cycnus); σφι in Lyc.1242; σφε = *him, her*, in Pi.*I*.6(5).74, A.*Pr*.9, *Th*.469, al., S.*OT*761, *Ant*.44, *Ph*.200 (anap.), al., E.*Alc*.107 (lyr.), 149, 200, *Med*.33, al.; = *it* (of a masc. noun) in S.*OC*40: f.l. for σφεα in Hdt.3.52,53, and for σφεας Id.1.71, al. III. once as 2 pers. pl. reflex., ἠνώγει δέ μ' ἰόντα . . πυθέσθαι ἠὲ . . ἦ . . φύξιν βουλεύοιτε μετὰ σφίσιν Il.10.398 (reported from φύξιν βουλεύουσι μετὰ σφίσιν ib.311); σφέας for ὑμᾶς in Hdt.3.71 (but with v.l. σφεα). IV. later as 1 pers. pl. (cf. σφέτερος, σφωΐτερος, ἑός), ἧμιν ἐνὶ σφίσι A.R.2.1278; σφᾶς = ἡμᾶς, Men.Prot.p.119D.; censured by Luc.*Sol*.8,9.

® **σφεκλαράριος**, v. σπεκλάριον.

**σφέκλη**, ἡ, = *faecula*, Alex.Trall.12, Paul.Aeg.7.13, interpol. in Dsc.*Eup*.2.141.

® **σφέκλον**, τό, = Lat. *speculum*, Phlp. *in Ph*.642.17 (v.l. ὕελον).

® **σφέλας**, τό, *footstool*, Od.18.394: Ep. pl. σφέλα 17.231; dat. σφέλαϊ A.R.3.1159. II. *pedestal* of a statue, *Schwyzer* 760 (Delos, vi B.C.). III. *hollow block of wood*, for putting anything into, Nic.*Th*.644.

**σφελίσκον**, τό, Dim. of foreg., *Michel* 832.50 (Samos, iv B.C.).

**σφέλμα**, ατος, τό, *blossom of the holm-oak* (πρῖνος), Hsch.

® **σφενδάμνινος**, η, ον, *of maple wood*, τράπεζαι Cratin.301: metaph. for *tough, stout*, '*hearts of oak*', Ar.*Ach*.181.

**σφένδαμνος**, ἡ, *Olympian maple, Acer monspessulanum*, Thphr.*HP*3.3.1 (cj.), 3.11.1, Dicaearch.2.2.

**σφενδικίζω**, = σφενδονάω, Luc.*Pseudol*.24 (dub. l.).

**σφενδον-αίαν**· σφενδόνην, ἡ τὴν σφραγῖδα, Hsch. ® **-άω**, *use the sling*, Th.2.81, X.*An*.3.3.7,15, etc.; τοῖς λίθοις σ. ib.17; ἐν τῷ σφενδονᾶν ἡ χεὶρ γίνεται κέντρον Arist.*Mech*.852b7. 2. *strike by slinging*, τὰς αὔρας Babr.26.5: metaph., ἔντερ' ἁλὶ καὶ σιλφίῳ σ. Axionic.8.4. II. *throw as from a sling*, Lxx 1*Ki*.25.29:—Pass., ἐκ κλιμάκων ἐσφενδονᾶτο χωρὶς ἀλλήλων μέλη E.*Ph*.1183, cf. Hld.10.30. 2. *move like a swing, swing to and fro*, ὅπλισμα . . διαφέρων ἐσφενδόνα E.*Supp*.715. **-έω**, later form of σφενδονάω, Str.15.3.18. **-η**, ἡ, *sling*, Il.13.600 (where it is used as a *bandage*), Archil.3, E.*Ph*.1142, Ar.*Av*.1185, Th.4.32; σφενδόνῃ οὐκ ἂν ἐφικοίμην αὐτόσ' could not reach it *with a sling*, Antiph.55.19. 2. *a sling* as part of a crane used in unloading ships, *SIG*241*A*46 (Delph., iv B.C.): so perh. metaph., σφενδόνας ἀπ' εὐμέτρου A.*Ag*.1010 (lyr.). II. *anything of like shape*: 1. *sling for a disabled arm*, Hp.*Art*.16 (cf. Il. l.c.); *suspensory abdominal bandage*, Hp.*Mul*.2.144, Sor.*Fasc*.48. 2. *headband* worn by women, *broad in front*, Poll.5.96, Eust. ad D.P.7. 3. *hoop of a ring in which the stone was set* as in a sling, esp. *the outer or broader part round the stone, collet*, E.*Hipp*.862, Pl.*R*.359e, Arist.*Ph*.207a3. 4. *white of the eye*, Poll.2.70. III. *stone* or *bullet of the sling*, X.*An*.3.4.4, 5.2.14, etc.; τοιαύταις σ., of hailstones, Ar.*Nu*.1125 (troch.). **-ηδόν**, Adv. *like a sling*, Sch.Il.11.165, *EM*738.25. **-ησις**, εως, ἡ, *slinging*, Hp.*Fract*.2, Pl.*Lg*.794c, Apollod.*Poliorc*.141.8. ® **-ήτης**, ου, ὁ, *slinger*, Hdt.7.158, Th.6.22, Pl.*Criti*.119b, Lxx *Jd*.20.16: Boeot. σφενδονάτας Ἀρχ.Δελτ.14 Pl. iv 26 (Thespiae, iii B.C.). **-ητικός**, ή, όν, *of* or *for slinging*, εὐστοχία Sch.Lyc.633: ἡ -κή (sc. τέχνη) *the art of slinging*, Pl.*La*.193b. **-ίζω**, = σφενδονάω, βολίδας Ps.-Callisth.2.16. **-ιστής**, οῦ, ὁ, = -ήτης, Them.*Or*.11.152c.

**σφενδονοειδής**, ές, *sling-shaped*, i.e. broad and tapering at the ends, Posidon.98J.

**σφεός**, -εή, Dor. -εά, -εόν, = σφός, σφέτερος, *their* (*own*), σφεὰ δώματα A.R.1.849; ἴομεν αὖτις ἕκαστοι ἐπὶ σφεά each to *his own*, ib.872. 2. = σφωΐτερος, *your* (in addressing a pair), Alcm.30. 3. *his, her*, σφεᾶς ἔειξε χώρας Id.31; σφ(ε)ὸς ἔσκε πατήρ prob. in *Sammelb*.7289.

**σφερία**, ἡ, dub. sens. in *PFay*.347 (ii A.D.).

**σφέρτα**· τὰ ἄφορα δένδρα, Hsch.

**σφετερ-ίζω**, *make one's own, appropriate, usurp*, ἐὰν ἐσμοὺς ἀλλοτρίους σφετερίζῃ τις Pl.*Lg*.843d; τὰ πράγματα κατὰ τὴν πόλιν ἐσφετέρισαν ib.715a; τὸν χόρτον -ίσαντες *PGen*.49.15 (iv A.D.):—Pass., τῆς ἐσφετερισμένης ἀρχῆς App.*Hann*.45. II. more freq. in Med. σφετερίζομαι, σφετεριξάμενοι (Dor. aor.) παραδέλφειαν A.*Supp*.38 (anap.), cf. X.*HG*5.1.36, D.32.2; σ. τι τῶν ἀλλοτρίων Arist.*Pr*.952a29; τι τῶν πέλας Plb.2.19.4; χρήματα *SIG*833.7 (Epist. Hadriani); ὄνομα Gal.6.543; ὅλον τὸν ἀκροατὴν σφετεριζόμενος Luc.*Cal*.8: pf. Pass. in same sense, D.H.10.32; plpf. ἐσφετέριστο D.C.50.1: also c. gen., -ομένους τῶν κοινῶν Phld.*Rh*.2.174S.; τῶν κτημάτων -ονται *BGU* 195.17 (ii A.D.). **-ισμός**, ὁ, *appropriation*, ἐπὶ σφετερισμῷ ἑαυτοῦ *for one's own use and advantage*, Arist.*Rh*.1374a16. **-ιστής**, οῦ, ὁ, *appropriator*, opp. ἐπίτροπος, Id.*Pol*.1315b2. **-ος**, α, ον, possessive Adj. of the 3rd pers. pl. σφεῖς, *their own, their*, Il.17.287, Od.1.274, al., Hes.*Th*.155, Pi.*P*.10.38; strengthd., αὐτῶν σφετέρῃσιν ἀτασθαλίῃσιν Od.1.7; rare in Com., Ar.*Ra*.1464, *Fr*.350; in Prose the gen. ἑαυτῶν is commonly used, but σφέτερος also occurs, Th.3.95, 7.1, *IG*1$^2$.29.6, 57.46, Pl.*Euthd*.304c; τὰ σ. *their own property*, Th.2.20, X.*HG*5.3.12; ὅσοι τὰ σ. φρονοῦντες . . περιῆσαν Th.3.68, cf. X.*HG*7.5.5; τὸν σ. (sc. φόβον) *their own* (fear), Th.6.36; τὸ σ. αὐτῶν *their own* business, Pl.*Sph*.243b; τὸ σ. αὐτῶν συμφέρον *their own* interest, Arist.*Pol*.1296a36; ἀπὸ τῆς σ. αὐτῶν (sc. χώρας) X.*Ath*.2.5, cf. *IG*12(1).977.16 (Carpathos, iv B.C.); νόμοις χρῆσθαι τοῖς σ. αὐτῶν ib.2$^2$.1.15; οἱ σ. *their own people*, Th.6.71, X.*HG*2.4.18. 2. also of the 3rd pers. sg., *his or her own, his, her*, for ἑός, ὅς, Hes.*Sc*.90, Pi.*O*.13.61, *P*.4.83, A.*Ag*.760 (lyr.), *Pers*.900 (lyr.), and in later Prose, Plb.7.14.3, etc. II. sts. also used of other persons: 1. of 2nd pl., = ὑμέτερος, *your own, your*, Il.9.327 (sed leg. μαρναμένοις), Hes.*Op*.2, A.R.4.1327, *AP*9.134; cf. σφεῖς B. III. b. of 2nd dual, Alcm.3. 2. of 2nd sg., = σός, *thine own*, only in Theoc.22.67. 3. of 1st sg., = ἐμός, *mine own*, Id.25.163. 4. of 1st pl., = ἡμέτερος, *our own*, X.*Cyr*.6.1.10 codd., A.R.4.1353, Plb.11.4.3, 11.31.6, App.*Mith*.5, etc. —Cf. σφός.

**σφετρίδες**· ἐπιβλήματα, Hsch. (Fort. ἐφεστρίδες.)

**σφέων**, Ep. and Ion. gen. of σφεῖς. **σφῇ**, dat. fem. of σφός.

**σφηκαλέων**, οντος, ὁ, '*lion-wasp*', a kind of insect, σ. τοὺς ἐν τῇ ἀράχνῃ *PMag.Leid.W*.8.8 (σφυν-, but υ erased).

**Σφήκεια**, ἡ, *Wasp-land*, old name of Cyprus, Lyc.447, Hsch.

**σφήκ-ειον**, τό, *an insect that stings like a wasp*, Nic.*Th*.738. ® **-ιά**, ἡ, *wasps' nest*, S.*Fr*.778, E.*Cyc*.475, Ar.*V*.224, Lxx *Ex*.23.28; σφηκιαὶ ἐχθρῶν, opp. ἑσμὸς φίλων, Plu.2.96b. **-ίας**, ου, ὁ, = σφηκίσκος II, Pherecr.238. II. a verse divided by caesura into parts containing an equal number of syllables, Ps.-Plu.*Metr*.2. **-ικός**, ή, όν, = σφηκώδης II, κατὰ τροχαῖον -ική, i.e. with a trochee instead of a spondee, Eust.641.35. **-ίον**, τό, *comb in a wasps' nest*, as κηρίον in that of bees, Arist.*HA*628a17, al., Thphr.*HP*4.8.7, Ael.*NA*4.39. **-ίσκος**, ὁ, *piece of wood pointed like a wasp's tail, pointed stick* or *stake*, Ar.*Pl*.301. II. *roof-timber, rafter*, *IG*1$^2$.372.81, 2$^2$.1668.53, Plb.5.89.6. III. *lintel*, *IG*1$^2$.313.108, Arist.*Ath*.65.2. IV. v.l. for σφηνίσκος III (q.v.). ® **-ισμός**, ὁ, *an imitation of the buzzing of a wasp on the flute*, Hsch. **-ίωσις**· κηρία σφηκῶν, Id.

**σφηκοειδής**, ές, = σφηκώδης I, Sch.Nic.*Th*.805.

**σφηκός**, ή, όν, = σφηκώδης I, S.*Fr*.29. II. = σφήκωμα I, Hsch.

**σφῆκος**, εος, τό, acc. pl. σφήκη, perh. *strings* (of figs), *PCair.Zen*.99.3, 544.3 (iii B.C.).

**σφηκ-όω**, (σφήξ) *make like a wasp*, i.e. *pinch in at the waist, bind tightly*, Phryn.Com.91; σ. τὸ ὅλον σῶμα Hld.10.31; χεῖρας *APl*.4.195 (Satyr.); ἀγγεῖον *close* the vessel, Dsc.5.54; τοὺς κορακίνους Ael.*NA*13.17: aor. Med. σφηκώσατο Nonn.*D*.1.192, 15.147. II. Pass., πλοχμοί θ', οἳ χρυσῷ τε καὶ ἀργύρῳ ἐσφήκωντο *were bound tightly*, Il.17.52; ἐσφήκωντο κορύμβαις prob. in Antim. in *PMilan*.17.4; κόμη ἐσφηκωμένη Poll.2.25; σφηκούμενος *one binding up his hair*, Ph.2.479; δειρὴν ἐσφήκωται *he is narrow* in the neck, Nic.*Th*.289; ὁ δὲ τέτρατος (sc. κύκλος) ἐσφήκωται λοξὸς ἐν ἀμφοτέροις *is fixed*, Arat.526, cf. 441; θυρίδες εὖ καὶ καλῶς ἐσφηκωμέναι *well-closed* window-shutters, Aristid.*Or*.51(27).8 (-σφην- is prob. cj.); so καλύμματ' ἐσφήκ. Anacr.21.3: metaph., coupled with πλεκτόν in Phld.*Po*.2.45. **-ώδης**, ες, *wasp-like*, Sch.Nic.*Al*.183; *pinched in at the waist like a wasp*, Ar.*Pl*.561 sq. II. στίχος σ. *a wasp-like verse, with a time wanting in the middle*, Sch.Heph.p.168W., Sch.Od.10.60; so σφηκῶδές τε καὶ σφηκοειδές Eust.641.31. **-ωμα**, ατος, τό, *the point of a helmet* where the plume is fixed in, εὐλόφῳ σ. S.*Fr*.341, cf. Ar.*Pax* 1216. II. *cord*, *PCair.Zen*.518 (iii B.C.), Phryn.*PS* p.110B., Philum.*Ven*.7.7, *Hippiatr*.24, Hsch., Paul.Aeg.6.25; dub. sens. in *IG*11(2).144*A*37 (Delos, iv B.C.). **-ών**, ῶνος, ὁ, *wasps' nest*, cj. for sq., Arist.*HA*628a13. **-ωνεύς**, έως, ὁ, = σφηκίον I, Arist. l.c. (s.v.l.).

**σφῆλαι, σφῆλεν**, v. σφάλλω. **σφηλόν**· λοξόν, πυκνόν, εὐκίνητον, Hsch.; but, σφηλόν· τὸ ἰσχυρόν, Id. s.v. ἄσφηλοι (cf. also σφειλόν); cf. ἐρίσφηλος.

**σφήν**, σφηνός, ὁ, *wedge*, Ar.*Ra*.801, A.R.1.1204, Arist.*Mech*.853a19, *PCair.Zen*.759.2 (iii B.C.), etc.; used as *an instrument of torture*, A.*Pr*.64, Plu.2.498d, Lxx 4*Ma*.8.13, al. [σφην- prob. from σφαν-, cf. σφάνιον and v. sub σφηνόπους.]

**σφην-άριον**, τό, Dim. of σφήν, *small wedge*, Heliod.ap.Orib.44.14.13, Hsch. s.v. γόμφοισι, Suid. s.v. σφήν: so σφηνίδα (cod. Par.) and σφηνίδιον (vulg.), both dub. in Hero *Bel*.82.2. **-εύς**, έως, ὁ, *a sea-fish*, a kind of *mullet*, prob. from its wedge-like shape, Euthyd.ap.Ath.7.307b, *PSI*4.428.67 (iii B.C.), *PCair.Zen*.12.43 (iii B.C.). **-ίσκος**, ὁ, Dim. of σφήν, Hp.*Mochl*.38, prob. in Sch.Hes.*Op*.425. II. *wedge-shaped plug, pledget* for the nose, Paul.Aeg.2.58. III. Math., *an irregular truncated pyramid*, with v.l. σφηκίσκος, Hero *Deff*.114, cf. *Stereom*.1.25: cf. βωμίσκος. 2. *a number with 3 unequal factors*, Anon. *in Tht*.43.14, Nicom.*Ar*.2.6. IV. *wedge-shaped ornament* on shoe, Herod.7.22 (prob. rest.).

**σφηνο-ειδής**, ές, *wedge-shaped*, Thphr.*CP*1.6.8, Ascl.*Tact*.7.2, Heliod.ap.Orib.49.4.35, Gal.2.752. **-κέφαλος**, ον, *with wedge-shaped* or *peaked head*, Str.2.1.9. **-πους**, πουν, gen. ποδος, *with wedge-shaped legs*, of a bier, κλίνη *IG*12(5).593*A*6 (Ceos, v B.C.). [The spelling with -η- shows that σφήν has Att.-Ion. η from ᾱ: cf. σφάνιον.] **-πώγων**, ωνος, ὁ, *with wedge-shaped* or *peaked beard*, as Hermes is represented, Artem.2.37; in Comedy old men were thus represented, Luc.*Ep.Sat*.24.

**σφην-όω**, *shape like a wedge*, *Gp*.17.19.4:—Pass., *to be cloven with a wedge*, Arist.*Mech*.853a27; κλίνη χρυσῷ ἐσφηνωμένη *inlaid*, Luc.*Asin*.53 codd. 2. *fix by means of a wedge*, Hero *Bel*.107.14:—Pass., *to be wedged in*, εἰς τὸ μέσον Plb.27.11.4; *to become fixed like a wedge*, Sor.2.55, Gal.6.179. 3. *plug up, close up*, τρήματα σπόγγοις Sch.Ar.*Ach*.462; τοῖς μότοις Orib.*Fr*.134:—Med., τὸ πρόθυρον σφήνου *close* the vestibule, *AP*5.40 (Rufin.):—Pass., f.l. in Dsc.5.31; ὅταν σφηνωθῇ ἡ ὀπὴ *Gp*.9.10.4; σφηνοῦνται τὰς κεφαλάς *they catch a cold* in the head, Cass.*Pr*.25; σφηνωθεὶς ἀπέθανεν, *of obstruction*, Anon.ap.Suid. II. *torture, rack* (v. σφήν), Plu.2.498d. ® **-ωσις**, εως, ἡ, *the use of the wedge*, Hp.*Fract.*31, Orib.49.8.13. **2.** *closing up, obstruction*, τοῦ πνεύματος Plu.2.127d, cf. 654a, *Placit.*3.15.5; *difficult passage*, of calculi, Aret.*SD*2.3 (pl.); *obstruction*, Alex.Aphr. *Pr.*1.107, cf. Gal.1.284 (pl.); τῶν πόρων Alex.Trall.1.2; [τῆς κεφαλῆς] *plugging up, cold* in the head, Cass.*Pr.*25; *impaction* of foetus, Sor.2.60, Paul.Aeg.3.76.

**σφήξ**, σφηκός, Dor. **σφάξ**, σφᾱκός (Theoc.5.29), ὁ (fem. only in *An.Par.*1.168 and as f.l. in Antisth.ap.Stob.3.13.38):—*wasp*, σφῆκες μέσον αἰόλοι Il.12.167, cf. Hdt.2.92, Ar.*Ach.*864, etc.; called εἰνόδιοι, from their making their nests in the road, Il.16.259; σφῆκες ἐκ γῆς Call.*Iamb.*1.98; on the different species, v. Arist.*HA*627$^{b}$23, cf. 554$^{b}$22: prov., μή πως ἐγείρῃς σ. τὸν κοιμώμενον *AP*7.405 (Phil.), cf. 408 (Leon.). **II.** = σφηκίσκος II, Pherecr.238, *IG*11(2).156 *A* 56, al. (Delos, iii B. C.).

**σφῆρος**, ὁ, *horoscope*, *Supp.Epigr.*7.370 (Dura-Europus, iii A. D.). (Later spelling of σφαῖρος.)

**σφηρός·** τὸ τοῦ ἱματίου σημεῖον, Hsch. (between σφραγίς and σφριαί: perh. for σφρηγίς, cf. σφραγίς II. 2).

**Σφηττός**, ὁ, a deme of the Acamantian φυλή in Attica, Str.9.1.20; **Σφηττοῖ** *in* or *at Sphettos*, Lys.17.5, Aeschin.1.97; **Σφηττόθεν** *from S.*, *IG*1$^{2}$.591, Plu.*Thes.*13; **Σφηττόνδε** *to S.*, St.Byz.:—**Σφήττιος**, ὁ, *a Sphettian*, *IG*1$^{2}$.304.20, Ar.*Nu.*156, Aeschin.1.100; also as Adj., ὄξος Σ., proverbial, Ar.*Pl.*720, cf. Did.ap.Ath.2.67d.

**σφι, σφιν**, v. σφεῖς.

**σφιγγία**, ἡ, *greed*, LXX *Si.*11.18, perh. f.l. for σκνιφία.

**σφιγγίδιον**, τό, Dim. of σφίγξ, *small sphinx* (as an ornament), *IG* 2$^{2}$.1467.21 (pl.).

**σφιγγίον**, τό, *bracelet* or *necklace*, Luc.*Apol.*1. **II.** a kind of *ape*, *IG*14.1302 (Praeneste, -ια perh. fem. sg.), Plin.*HN*6.173, 10.199.

**σφιγγο-κᾱρίων**, ωνος, ὁ, title of play by Eubulus, Ath.3.80a. **-πους**, ποδος, ὁ, ἡ, *with sphinxes' feet*, κλῖναι Callix.2; λιβανωτίς *Inscr.Délos* 1409 *Aa* 100 (ii B. C.).

⊛ **σφίγγω**, Emp.38.4, etc.: fut. σφίγξω *AP*12.208 (Strat.): aor. ἔσφιγξα Alex.31, *AP*10.75 (Pall.), etc.:—**Med.**, aor. ἐσφιγξάμην Hermesian.7.81, Nonn.*D.*15.247, al.:—**Pass.**, aor. ἐσφίγχθην *AP*6.331 (Gaet.), (ἀπ-) Hp.*Mochl.*35: pf. ἔσφιγμαι D.H.7.72, Luc.*Musc. Enc.*3; inf. ἐσφίγχθαι Demetr.*Eloc.*244, Philostr.*VA*2.13: plpf. συνέσφικτο Procop.Gaz. p.168 B.:—*bind tight, bind fast*: **I.** of the person or thing bound, ἄρασσε μᾶλλον, σφίγγε A.*Pr.*58; σφίγγετ', ἀμαλλοδέται, τὰ δράγματα Theoc.10.44; κεκρύφαλοι σ. τεὴν τρίχα; *AP*5.259 (Paul. Sil.); κρημνᾷ ἑαυτὴν σφίγξασα ἐκ τοῦ τραχήλου Luc.*Asin.*24; σ. πύλας *shut close*, *AP*5.293.5 (Agath.); τόκους *clutch*, ib. 11.289 (Pall.); σ. τὴν φράσιν *straiten, abridge*, Plu.2.1011e, cf. Demetr.*Eloc.*244; πολλῷ χρόνῳ τὸν λόγον σφίγξαντες *having severely restrained* their utterance, Plu.2.6e:—Pass., ἐσφίγγετο πέπλος ζωστῆρι Theoc.7.17; σ. ὑπὸ τοῦ βρόχου D.S.12.17; σφιγχθεὶς χέρας *APl.*4.198 (Maec.); σ. δράκοντι *AP*6.331 (Gaet.); οὐ κατὰ τοὺς σφῆκας πάνυ ἐσφιγμένοι Luc.*Musc.Enc.*3:—also Med. (in act. sense), Hermesian.7.81, Nonn.*D.*13.11, al. **2.** of the thing used in binding, στραγγαλίδας ἐσφίγγετε *you tied* knots *fast*, i.e. raised all sorts of difficulties, Pherecr.21; σ. τὴν ἀγκύλην τῆς ἐμβάδος Alex.31; σφίγξω σοῖς περὶ ποσσὶ πέδην *AP*5.178 (Mel.); σφίγγουσα τὰ πρὸς τοῖς γόνασι (sc. σπάργανα) Sor.1.84; νεβρίδα στέρνοισι Nonn.*D.*1.36; πέπλα.. ἐῷ καρήνῳ Musae.252; σφιγχθεὶς στέφανος *AP*12.135 (Asclep.). **II.** *bind* or *hold together*, αἰθὴρ σ. περὶ κύκλον ἅπαντα Emp.38.4; σ. πάντα Pl.*Ti.*58a; ὁ ὠκεανὸς σ. τὴν οἰκουμένην Arist.*Mu.*393$^{b}$9, cf. Melinno ap.Stob.3.7.12, *AP*5.293.20 (Agath.). **2.** *tie up in a bundle*, ἀργύριον LXX 4*Ki.*12.10. **3.** *tighten up*, τὴν ἐκ τῆς μαλακῆς τρίψεως ἀραιότητα σ. Gal.6.91; of astringents, ib.477; σύες.. τοῖς ἄρρεσιν ἐμφερῶς ἐσφιγμέναι sows *with firm flesh* like boars, Sor.1.30; ὑπὸ τῆς ἐμφύτου θερμασίας ἀναχαλᾶται τῶν ἐσφιγμένων ἕκαστον Id.2.10. **4.** *press together*, πόδας.. κατὰ γαστέρος Batr.71; χεῖρας ib.88.

**σφιγκ-τήρ**, ῆρος, ὁ, *that which binds tight, lace, band*, etc., κόμας σφιγκτῆρα.. κεκρύφαλον *AP*6.206 (Antip. Sid.); σ. δεσμός Nonn.*D.*16.391. **II.** *muscle closing an aperture* which naturally remains in the state of contraction, *AP*12.7 (Strat.), Heliod.ap.Orib.44.23.55, Sor.1.16, Gal.*UP*4.19, Paul.Aeg.6.78. **III.** *a Tarentine* χιτών, prob. because *laced tight to the body*, Hsch. **-της**, ου, ὁ, = κίναιδος, Cratin.446, Hsch. **-τός**, ή, όν, *tight-bound*: **1.** of the person bound, *AP*5.229 (Paul. Sil.), 9.641 (Agath.). **2.** of the thing that binds, σ. στεφάνων ἀμφὶ κόμαισι μίτος ib.5.174 (Mel.); σ. μόρος death *by strangling*, Opp.*H.*3.590; σ. ἐπίδεσμοι Paul.Aeg.6.99 (Comp.). Adv. **-τῶς** Eust.1424.49: neut. pl. σφιγκτά as Adv., *AP*6.272 (Pers.). **-τωρ**, ορος, ὁ, poet. for σφιγκτήρ I, ib.233 (Maec.).

**σφίγμα**, ατος, τό, *jamming* in a machine, Hero *Aut.*2.4.

⊛ **Σφίγξ**, ἡ, gen. Σφιγγός, Boeot. **Φίξ**, Φικός:—*Sphinx*, Φῖκ' ὀλοὴν Hes.*Th.*326 (where the Boeot. form Φίξ is given by Sch., cf. Pl.*Cra.*414d), cf. Apollod.3.5.8; on the riddle of the S. guessed by Oedipus, Ath.10.456b, Arg.S.*OT*, A.*Frr.*235–7, E.*Ph.*1507 (anap.), cf. Sch.E.*Ph.*45, Str.17.1.28,32; cf. ἀνδρόσφιγξ; σφίγγες καὶ γρῦπες as ornaments of a precinct of Dionysus, Hdt.4.79; Sphinxes on a shield, E.*El.*471 (lyr.). **2.** metaph. of *rapacious* persons, Anaxil.22, *Carm.Pop.*46.24,33; Μεγαρικαὶ σ., = πόρναι, Call. Com.23: also of those *who speak riddles*, Σφίγγ' ἄρρεν', οὐ μάγειρον Strato Com.1.1; ἡ ἀφροσύνη.. σ. ἐστιν Cebes 3. **II.** a kind of *ape*, found in Ethiopia, Agatharch.73, Artem.ap.Str.16.4.16, Plin.*HN* 8.72, Ael.*NA*16.15, and v. σφιγγίον II. (The form Φίξ connects the name with Mount Φίκιον in Boeotia, cf. Sch.Hes. l. c., and is found in Plaut.*Aul.*701, *Picis divitiis qui aureos montis colunt ego solus supero*; cf. Non. p.222 L.; Βῖκας = Σφίγγας, Hsch. (Σφίγξ may be a later form); **Σφίξ**, gen. Σφικός, Choerob. (Sophronius) *in Theod.* p. 400 H.)

**σφίγξις**, εως, ἡ, *binding tight, constriction*, Hp.*Fract.*26, Aret.*CD* 2.3, Antyll.ap.Orib.7.12.1, Ael.*NA*8.18; τὸ κατὰ σφίγξιν operation by *ligature*, Aët.7.37. **2.** *constipation*, Sor.1.125.

**σφίδες·** χορδαὶ μαγειρικαί, Hsch. **σφίδη·** χορδή, Id. (Hence Lat. *fides* is perh. borrowed.)

**σφικάω**, *hum, buzz*, of gnats, Anon. ap. Valck. *Animadv. ad Ammon.* p.175 V.

**σφιν, σφισι, σφισιν**, v. σφεῖς. **σφισίμολος·** διαφορὰ τῆς κινήσεως, Hsch. **σφογγιά, σφογγίον, σφόγγος**, v. σπογγιά, σπογγίον, σπόγγος.

**σφοδελός**, ὁ, = ἀσφόδελος, Ar.*Fr.*674, cf. Hdn.Gr.2.152; proparox. in Hsch. (σφοδελός and σποδελός were read by some in Hom., v. Hdn.Gr. l. c.)

**σφοδελοφόρους·** τοὺς μετοίκους, Hsch.

⊛ **σφόδρ-ᾰ**, Adv., properly neut. pl. of σφοδρός, *very much, exceedingly*: **I.** with Verbs, ἐμήδιζον γὰρ σ. Hdt.9.17; σ. ἱμείρουσα S.*El.*1053; καὶ σ. πείθει persuades them *too well*, Id.*Aj.*150 (anap.); σ. λέγειν *with vehemence*, Antipho 6.15; σ. κολάζειν *severely*, Th.3.46; σ. ὁρίσασθαι *exactly*, Pl.*Phdr.*263d, cf. *Phlb.*58d, *Phd.*68a, 73a; σ. χαίρω I am *exceedingly* glad, *POxy.*41.17 (iii/iv A. D.). **2.** with Adjs., σ. ὑπέρτεροι *far* superior, Pi.*N.*4.37; μισόδημον σ. Ar.*Fr.*108; σ. ἄδικος Pl.*R.*361a; ἁλμυρὸν σ. Arist.*Mete.*359$^{a}$13; κακοδαίμων σ. Antiph.56; σ. γενναῖος Men.223.14; πολλοῦ σ. at a *very* high price, *very* dear, Id.197; πολλοὶ σ. Bato 7.1; ἐνιαυτοὺς σ. ὀλίγους Men.481.6; χαρὰ μεγάλη σ. *Ev.Matt.*2.10:—with Adjs. it most freq. follows, and in Com. Poets it usu. stands at the end of the verse. **3.** with a Subst., τὴν σ. φιλίαν Pl.*Lg.*731e; τινῶν σ. γυναικῶν *very womanish* women, ib.639b; τῆς σ. προθυμίας ib.952c; τῆς σ. μανίας Id.*Phdr.*251a; ἐν τοῖς σ. ψύχεσιν Arist.*HA*599$^{a}$19. **4.** with other Advbs., ἐπάταξε πῶς οἴει σ. Ar.*Ra.*54; θαυμαστῶς ὡς σ., ἀμηχάνως ὡς σ., Pl.*R.*331a, *Phdr.*263d; μάλα σ. Id.*Alc.*1.124d; πάνυ σ. Ar.*Pl.*25, 745; σ. πάνυ Aeschin.2.36; πάνυ καὶ σ. Pl.*Lg.*627a; οὐ σ. not *very much*, Hp.*Aër.*15, Antiph.204.11, Pl.*Phd.*100a; οὕτω σ. ἦν ἀρχαῖος Antiph.273; οὕτω σ. ἐστὶ.. Βοιώτιος Eub.39. **5.** τὸ σ., = σφοδρότης, Pl.*Smp.*210b, al. **6.** σφόδρα, σφοδρῶς LXX *Ge.*7.19. **II.** σ. γε or καὶ σ. γε, in answers, strongly affirmative, freq. in Pl., πάνυ γε σ. *Men.*82b; πάνυ σ. ταῦτα λέγω *Ap.*25a. **-όομαι**, Pass., *to be violent*, of a wind, Ph.2.99 (v.l. for σφοδρυν-); of diseases, Gal.17(2).509. ⊛ **-ός**, ά, όν, also ός, όν Pl.*R.*586c:—*vehement, violent, excessive* (used by Hom. once in Adv., v. infr.), πόνος Hp.*Aph.*2.46; καῦμα, γυμνάσιον, Gal.15.39,153; ἀγρυπνία Id.18(2) 33; σφυγμός Sor.2.27; μῖσος Th.1.103; λόγοι *Com.Adesp.*28 D.; ἐπιθυμία Pl.*Plt.* 308a (Comp.); αἱ σ. ἡδοναί Id.*Phlb.*52c; ἀλγήματα τοῦ σώματος πάνυ σ. D.54.11; δίψος σ. *PTeb.*272.7 (ii A. D.); δίψα σ. Gal.16.564; -οτέρα ὁμοιότης Arist.*Top.*103$^{a}$22; ταραχὴ -οτέρα Phld.*D.*1.12; -ότερος κίνδυνος Gal.16.686; τὸ σ. *vehemence, excess*, Pl.*Phlb.*52c. **2.** of men, *violent, impetuous*, νέος καὶ σ., σ. καὶ νέος, Id.*Lg.*698e, 839b; φιλότιμοι καὶ σ. Id.*Ap.*23e; σ. ἐφ' ὅτι ὁρμήσειεν ib.21a; πρὸς τὸ πλεονεκτεῖν X.*Cyr.*2.2.25; also, *active, zealous*, ὑπηρέται ib.2.1.31; *strong, robust*, ἡ γεωργία σ. τὸ σῶμα παρέχει Id.*Oec.*5.5. **II.** Adv. **-ῶς** *vehemently*, etc., μάλα σ. ἔλααν Od.12.124; πάνυ σ. X.*Oec.*1.21; alone, ib.5.4,13, Pl.*Ap.*23e, *Ti.*43d, Arist.*Cat.*8$^{b}$22; σ. χειμαζομένων *Act.Ap.*27.18; θερμαίνοντες ἢ ψύχοντες σ. Gal.15.63; but in Att. σφόδρα (q. v.) is the common Adv.: Comp. **-ότερον** LXX 4*Ma.*5.32, Gal.15.126; **-οτέρως** Thphr.*CP*5.9.13, 5.10.1, Phld.*Piet.*76: Sup. **-ότατον** X.*Eq.*12.13. **-ότης**, ητος, ἡ, *vehemence, violence*, Id.*HG*7.2.23, Pl.*Plt.*306e; ἡ σ. δὲ θηρός is the quality of a beast, Alex.245.12; ἡ τοῦ πυρετοῦ σ. Gal.16.534: in pl., Pl.*Lg.*733b; πάγων σφοδρότητες Thphr.*CP*5.12.2. **-ύνω**, *make vehement, intensify*, Ph.1.355, Porph. *in Harm.* p.238 W.:—Pass., *to be* or *become so*, σφοδρύνει γ' ἀσθενεῖ σοφίσματι *thou puttest overweening trust in..*, A.*Pr.*1011; ποιότητες σφοδρυνόμεναι, opp. μαραινόμεναι, Plu.2.732c; νόσοι οὐκ ἄγαν σφοδρυνθεῖσαι Gal.19.563, cf. 17(1).207; πόνος (pain) σφοδρυνόμενος Sor.2.21: also in aor. Med., Poll.4.25. **II.** intr. in Act., ἄνεμος -ύνει Alex.Aphr.*Pr.*1.73.

**σφονδύλ-η** [ῠ], ἡ, *an insect which lives on the roots of plants*, prob. a kind of *beetle*, which has a strong smell when attacked, Ar.*Pax* 1078 (hex.), cf. Arist.*HA*542$^{a}$10 (v.l. σπονδύλη), 604$^{b}$19, Thphr.*HP*9.14.3. **II.** **σπονδύλη·** ἡ γαλῆ παρ' Ἀττικοῖς, Hsch. **-ιον** [ῠ], τό, Dim. (in form only) of σφόνδυλος, Il.20.483 (pl.), Antim.65. **II.** *cow-parsnip, Heracleum sphondylium*, Dsc.3.76; **σφονδύλειον** [ῠ], Nic.*Th.*948; **σπονδύλιον**, Sor.1.63, Gal.14.180; *spondylium*, Plin.*HN*12.128. **III.** = κόκκυξ IV, Poll.2.182. **-ίς**, ίδος, ἡ, = σφονδύλιον II, Ps.-Dsc.3.76. **-ίων** μυελός, ὁ, *spinal* marrow (suggested by a misunderstanding of Il.20.483), Poll.2.130.

**σφονδῠλο-δίνητος** [ῑ], ον, *twirled by the spindle's whorl*, νῆμα *AP* 6.247 (Phil.). **-εις**, εσσα, εν, *composed of vertebrae*, τράχηλος Man.1.319. **-μαντις**, εως, ὁ, ἡ, *prophesying from the spindle*, Poll.7.188.

⊛ **σφόνδῠλ-ος**, ὁ (ἡ, v. infr. 1b), Ion. and later Greek **σπόνδῠλος** (as in Hp. (v. infr.), Str.2.5.6, also in Pherecr.23 (codd.Clem.Al.), and some passages of Arist., as *PA*654$^{b}$16):—*vertebra*, Ar.*V.*1489 (anap.), Pl.*Ti.*74a; σύγκειται ἡ ῥάχις ἐκ σφονδύλων Arist.*HA*516$^{a}$11, cf. *PA* 651$^{b}$34; esp. *one of the cervical vertebrae*, Hp.*Aph.*3.26, cf. Arist.

*PA*686a21, 692a3: pl., *backbone, spine*, E.*Ph.*1413 (so in sg., Pherecr.23); or *neck*, E.*El.*841 (so in sg., Lxx *Le.*5.8). b. generally, *joint*, esp. in the scorpion's tail, Nic.*Th.*798 (where it is fem.), 781, Hipparch.3.4.2. c. *prickly ridge* on the head of the κεστρεύς, Dorio ap.Ath.7.306f. d. a kind of *mussel* or *oyster*, Sor. 1.51, Gal.6.734; σ. θαλάσσιοι *Edict.Diocl.*5.10; Lat. *spondylus*, Plin. *HN*32.60,154. II. from resemblance to vertebrae, 1. *one of the tambours* in a column, Callix.1 (σπ–), *Milet.*7.59, al. (Didyma), *IG*2².1668.43, 1672.310; not necessarily round, ib.11(2). 161 *A* 70 (Delos, iii B.C.); σ. μεγάλοι perh. *drums of columns* used as missiles, Ath.Mech.37.7. 2. *circular whorl* which balances and twirls a spindle, Pl.*R.*616c sq., Thphr.*HP*3.16.4, Plu.2.745f, Sor. 1.110, Poll.7.31, *Edict.Diocl.*13.5; σπόνδυλος Poll.10.125 (v.l. σφ–), Them.*Or.*32.356c. b. *the shape of that part of the terrestrial sphere which lies between the Equator and the Arctic Circle*, Str.2.5.6. c. *voting pebble*, Poll.8.17 (v.l. σπ–), Hsch., Eust.1669.62. 3. *head of* a kind of *artichoke* (κινάρα), Gal.6.637, *Gp.*18.19.2, *Edict. Diocl.*6.2. 4. *roller for closing* or *opening a trap-door*, σπονδύλου προϋποτιθεμένου Aen.Tact.36.2. **–ώδης, ες,** *like vertebrae*, in form σπονδ–, Sch.Il.5.586.

**σφορτάν·** λιμόν, Hsch.

**σφός,** σφή, σφόν, *their, their own, belonging to them*, Il.1.534, Sapph. 10, Pi.*P.*5.102, etc. (never in Att.). 2. in post-Hom. Poets also, *his* or *her, his own* or *her own*, Hes.*Th.*398, Alcm.56A, Thgn. 712, Call.*Aet.Oxy.*2080.75. II. = σός, Orph.*L.*168. 2. = ἐμός, *CR*11.136 (Phrygia, metr.). 3. = σφωΐτερος, *your* (in addressing a pair), v.l. in Il.11.142. (σφός is to σφε, σφέτερος as *ἡμός (ἀμός) to ἀμέ, ἡμέτερος.)

**σφρᾱγίδιον** [ῐδ], τό, Dim. of σφραγίς, *signet*, Ar.*Th.*427, Thphr. *Lap.*18, *IG*2².1544.25, 11(2).161 *B*43, al. (Delos, iii B.C.), *POsl.*46. 18 (iii A.D.).

**σφρᾱγῑδ-ονῠχ-αργο-κομήτης,** ου, ὁ, Comic name for a coxcomb, *lazy long-haired fop with his rings and natty nails*, Ar.*Nu.*332.

**σφρᾱγῑδο-φῠλάκιον** [ᾰκ], τό, *ring-* or *jewel-box*, Harp., Phot. s. v. πυελίδα: so also **–φύλαξ,** ἄκος, ὁ, *AB*295, Hsch. and Phot. s. v. πυελίς.

**σφρᾱγ-ίζω,** Ion. **σφρηγίζω,** *close* or *enclose with a seal*, σφραγίζεις λύεις τ' ὀπίσω..πεύκην ( = δέλτον) E.*IA*38 (anap.); ταβέλλας *PHamb.* 29.23 (i A.D.); τὸ σιτάριον *BGU*249.21 (i A.D.):—Med., τὸν θησαυρόν *PAmh.*2.41.7 (ii B.C.); μόνη δὲ κλῆθρ' ἐγὼ σφραγίζομαι E.*Fr.*781.10; –ισάμενος τὸν ναὸν ἐκέλευσε σφραγίσαι τῷ τοῦ βασιλέως δακτυλίῳ Lxx *Bel* 14; [τὸ ταμιεῖον] –ισάμενος εἴσω τὸν δακτύλιον διὰ τῆς ὀπῆς ἐρρίπτει D.L.4.59; δεῖγμα σφραγισάσθω let him *seal up with his seal* a sample (of the corn), *PHib.*1.39.15 (iii B.C.):—Pass., ἐν ᾧ [δώματι] κεραυνός ἐστιν ἐσφραγισμένος A.*Eu.*828; ἐσφράγισται ἐν τοῖς θησαυροῖς μου Lxx *De.*32.34; οὐ δύναμαι ἀναγνῶναι [τὸ βιβλίον]· ἐσφράγισται γάρ ib.*Is.*29.11; θυλάκιον ἐσφραγισμένον *PCair.Zen.*69.6 (iii B.C.); ἐσφραγίσθη γῇ λευκῇ *POxy.*929.13 (ii/iii A.D.). 2. *authenticate* a document *with a seal*, *IG*9(1).61.78,95 (Daulis, ii B.C.):—Med., ib. 61.41; ἵνα μὴ κυριεύσας (sc. τῆς σφραγῖδος) κοινὴν ἐπιστολὴν κατὰ πάντων γράψας σφραγίσηται αὐτῇ τῇ σφραγῖδι *PHib.*1.72.19 (iii B.C.); ἐξαποστεῖλαι εἰς Ῥόδον τοῦδε τοῦ ψηφίσματος ἀντίγραφον, σφραγισαμένους τῇ δημοσίᾳ σφραγῖδι *IG*12(5).833.14 (Tenos, ii B.C.), cf. 835. 31, al., 11(4).1065b28 (Delos(?), ii B.C.); τὸ βιβλίον τῆς κτήσεως τὸ ἐσφραγισμένον Lxx *Je.*39(32).11; τὴν παρὰ τοῦ βασιλέως διὰ τῆς θυρίδος ἐσφραγισμένην..⟨ἔντευξιν⟩ *UPZ*53.5 (ii B.C.). 3. *certify* an object *after examination by attaching a seal* (cf. Hdt.2.38), μέτροις ..ἐξητασμένοις καὶ ἐσφραγισμένοις ὑπὸ τοῦ οἰκονόμου *PRev.Laws* 25. 10 (iii B.C.); ἐπεθεώρησα μόσχον ἕνα..καὶ δοκιμάσας ἐσφράγισα ὡς ἔστιν καθαρός Wilcken *Chr.*89.5 (ii A.D.); cf. σφραγίς II. 1. 4. Med., *seal* an article to show that it is pledged, ἐγγύην σ. Plu.*Pomp.* 5, Arr.*Epict.*2.13.7: abs., *make an impression with a seal* for any purpose, καθάπερ οἱ σφραγιζόμενοι τοῖς δακτυλίοις Arist.*Mem.*450a 32. II metaph. senses: 1. *close up as if with a seal*, in Pass., ἐσφραγισμένην ἀκριβῶς οὐλήν a fully *closed* cicatrix, Gal.12.215:—Med., οὓς..ἀφθόγγων στομάτων σφρηγίσσατο δεσμῷ, i. e. made them mute, Nonn.*D.*26.261. 2. *accredit* as an envoy, etc., τινα *Ev.Jo.* 6.27:—Med., ὁ χρίσας ἡμᾶς θεός, καὶ –ισάμενος ἡμᾶς 2*Ep.Cor.*1. 22. 3. *set a seal of approval upon, confirm*, *AP*9.236 (Loll.); σ. ὅτι.. *Ev.Jo.*3.33:—freq. in Med., σ. ποιητικαῖς φωναῖς S.E.*M.*1. 271; σ. αὐτοῖς τὸν καρπόν *assure* them *of* it, *Ep.Rom.*15.28. 4. generally, *mark*, ψάμμος..νῶτον οὐκ ἐσφράγισεν the sand never *marked* his back, i. e. he never fell in the sand, *APl.*3.25 (Phil.); δεινοῖς..σημάντροισιν ἐσφραγισμένοι, of wounded persons, E.*IT*1372; σφραγιζομένη γελασίνοις *marked* with dimples, *AP*5.34 (Rufin.); καμήλους ἐσφραγισμένας εἰς τὸν δεξιὸν μηρὸν νῦ καὶ ἦτα *BGU*87.12,26 (ii A.D.). 5. *set an end* or *limit to, complete*, σφραγίσαι ἁμαρτίας Thd.*Da.* 9.24 (σπανίσαι Lxx):—Med., Ῥώμην ἀνερχομένῳ σφράγισαι ἠελίῳ *AP* 9.297 (Antip.); πάντα δι' ἀλλήλων ὁ πολὺς σφραγίζεται αἰών, i. e. the death of one creature is the birth of another, Archelaus ap.Antig. *Mir.*89. ❋ **–ίς,** Ion. **σφρηγίς,** ῖδος, ἡ: Aeol. acc. σφρᾶγιν Choerob. *in Theod.*1.327 H. (v.l. σφράγιν), Eust.265.18:—*seal, signet*, Hdt.1. 195, 3.41, *PHib.*1.72.19 (iii B.C.), Numen.ap.Eus.*PE*14.7, etc.; distd. from δακτύλιος, Ar.*Fr.*320.12, Pl.*Hp.Mi.*368c; σ. ἐπιβάλλειν Ar.*Av.*560 (anap.), *Th.*415; τῶν σφραγῖδας ἐχόντων, i.e. *fops*, Id.*Ec.* 632 (anap.); ἔχων..σφραγῖδα καὶ μεμυρισμένος Antiph.190.2; of the public *seal* of a state, [ὁ ἐπιστάτης] τηρεῖ τὴν δημοσίαν σ. Arist.*Ath.* 44.1, cf. *IG*2².204.40, Str.9.3.1; τὸν στρατηγὸν καὶ ἐπὶ τῆς σ. keeper of the privy *seal*, *IGRom.*4.1712 (Samos, ii B.C.). 2. *gem* or *stone for a ring*, Hdt.7.69, cf. Arist.*Mete.*387b17, Thphr.*Lap.*44; τὰς τῶν δακτυλίων σ. Arist.*Aud.*801b4; σ. ἴασπις χρυσοῦν δακτύλιον ἔχουσα *IG*2².1388.87; σ. ὑάλιναι ib.90. 3. generally, *gem*, κιθάραν ..σφραγῖσι..κατακεκοσμημένην Luc.*Ind.*8. II. *impression of a signet-ring, seal*, σ. δακτυλίου Lex Solonis ap.D.L.1.57; σφραγῖδος ἕρκος S.*Tr.*615, cf. *El.*1223, E.*IA*155 (anap.), Th.1.129; παρασημήνασθαι σ. to counterfeit *it*, ib.132; *warrant* attached to a camel, οἴσομεν ὑμῖν τὴν σ. καὶ οὐδὲν ζητηθήσεται πρὸς ἡμᾶς *PBasel* 2.11 (ii A.D.): metaph., σφρηγὶς ἐπικείσθω τοῖσδ' ἔπεσιν, as a warrant, Thgn.19; but ἀρρήτων ἐπέων γλώσσῃ σ. ἐπικείσθω (for secrecy) Luc.*Epigr.*11; σ. δ' ἡμετέρης γλώττης ἐπὶ τοῖσδεσι κεῖται Critias 5; διάτορον σφραγῖδα θραύων στόματος Tim.*Pers.*160; ἔχεις κόσμου σφρηγῖδα τυπῶτιν, of the Creator, Orph.*H.*34.26, cf. 64.2; ὁρκίζω σφραγῖδα (σφρακ– pap.) θεοῦ, ὅπερ ἐστὶν ὅρασις *PMag.Berol.*1.306; *drawing*, γράφε χαλκῷ γραφίῳ τὴν ὑποκειμένην σ. τοῦ ζῳδίου *PMag. Osl.*1.39. 2. *any mark*, as the spots on a leopard, Opp.*C.*2. 299: v. σφηρός. 3. *wound, blow*, Lyc.780. III. *tablet of Lemnian medicinal earth* certified as such by bearing the impression of the seal of the Lemnian priestess of Artemis, Dsc.5.97; σ. Λημνία Id.*Alex.Prooem.*, Gal.12.169, Aret.*CA*2.2, so prob. in Archig.ap. Orib.44.26.11, 51.42.5. IV. *governmentally defined and numbered area of land* (including plots belonging to different owners) in Egypt, *POxy.*918 ii 8 (ii A.D.), *PFay.*339 (ii A.D.), *BGU*831.6 (iii A.D.), *PHamb.*12.2 (iii A.D.), *Sammelb.*4325 ii 4 (iii A.D.). 2. *registered holding of land*, *PTeb.*105.13, al. (ii B.C.), *PLond.*3.880.20 (ii B.C.), *PAmh.*2.87,90 (ii A.D.), etc. 3. *numbered area* on a world-map, Eratosth.ap.Str.2.1.22, al.: pl., 11.12.5. V. Medic., *pastille*, ἡ Πολυείδου σ. Gal.13.834, Paul.Aeg.7.12, cf. Cels.5.20.2, al. b. Πακκίου σ., Paccius's *brand*, name of an eye-salve, Gal.12.751; eye-salves were certified by their makers by a seal-impression, e.g. *D. Galli Sesti sfragis ad aspritudines*, *CIL*13.10021.76 (Gaul). **–ισμα,** ατος, τό, *impression of a signet-ring, seal*, E.*Hipp.*864, X.*HG*1.4.3; μοχλοῖς καὶ διὰ σφραγισμάτων σῴζειν δάμαρτα with bars and *seals affixed to the door*, E.*Fr.*1063.9. **–ισμός,** ὁ, *sealing*, *PAmh.*2.41.13 (ii B.C.); μόσχου Wilcken *Chr.*88.7 (iii A.D.); πιττακίου *OGI*674.22 (Coptos, i A.D.). 2. *seal*, ἀκολούθως τῷ ἐπισταλέντι ἐπὶ σφραγισμῶν χρηματισμῷ Mitteis *Chr.*217.7 (ii A.D.). **–ιστήρ,** ῆρος, ὁ, *sealer*, i. e. *seal-ring, signet*, Nicom.*Ar.*1.23, D.L.7.50. **–ιστήριον,** τό, *seal, stamp*, *PLond.*5.1657.13 (iv/v A.D.); = *signaculum, signatorium*, *Gloss.* **–ιστής,** οῦ, ὁ, *sealer*, title of Egyptian priests who *sealed* the victim before sacrifice, Plu.2.363b (cf. μοσχοσφραγιστής): also, *witness who seals* a will, *BGU*361 iii 13 (ii A.D., pl.). **–ιστός,** ή, όν, *stamped with the public seal*, μέτρον *IG*2².1013.67. 2. *marked*, καμήλους πέντε σφραγιστούς *BGU*869.11 (cf. iii p.7, ii A.D.).

**σφραγμός,** ὁ, = φραγμός, τοὺς σ. *PGiss.*56.12 (vi A.D.).

**σφρηγίζω, σφρηγίς,** Ion. for σφραγ–. **σφριαί·** ἀπειλαί, ὀργαί, Hsch.

**σφρῑγ-ανός,** ή, όν, *plump, fresh*, Hp.ap.Tim.*Lex.*; σφριγανώτερα ὄμφακος ὤμας v.l. in Theoc.11.21; = ἰσχυρὸς καὶ στερεός, Sch.A.R. 3.1258; *puffy*, ὁ ὠχρὸς σ. ἐστι ταῖς σαρξὶ καὶ περίκομος Poll.4. 137. **–άω** [v. fin.], *to be full to bursting, to be plump*, esp. of a woman's breasts, Hp.*Mul.*1.71; οὔθατα σ. Poll.1.250: then, 2. generally, of young persons, high-fed horses, etc., *to be fresh, vigorous, in full health and strength*, νέῳ τε καὶ σφριγῶντι σώματι E.*Andr.*196; εὐσωματεῖ καὶ σφριγᾷ Ar.*Nu.*799; σφριγᾷ τὸ σῶμά σου Id.*Lys.*80; τὰ σώματα σφριγῶντες Pl.*Lg.*840b; ἥβῃ σφριγῶντες Achae.4; οἱ μύες (muscles) σφριγῶντες, ὡς ἂν εἴποι τις Archig.ap.Gal. 8.91; of animals, σφριγῶσα ἡμίονος Eust.1322.34; βόες τὸν αὐχένα σφριγῶντες Hld.3.1; of trees, δένδρα σφριγῶντα νέοις κλωσίν *luxuriant*, Luc.*Am.*12; βότρυες σφριγῶντες D.Chr.7.75; εὐδίᾳ καὶ γαλήνῃ σ. Ph.1.14. 3. metaph., *full-blooded, swollen* with passion or pride, σφριγῶντα θυμόν A.*Pr.*382; μῦθον E.*Supp.*478. 4. *swell with desire, be at heat*, Opp.*C.*3.368; τῶν σφριγώντων ἐν λόγοις *Com.Adesp.* 276: c. inf., Ael.*NA*14.5. Chiefly used in the pres. part. [In Opp. l. c., for σφρῖγᾷ Lobeck conjectured σφρῖγάᾳ.] **–ος,** εος, τό, *full strength*, σφρίγει βραχιόνων Hermipp.58. **–ώδης,** ες, *swollen*, μαστοί Orib.9.51.2.

**σφυγ-μᾰτώδης,** ες, *throbbing*, Hp.*Art.*40 (as v.l. for σφυγμώδεs), Pl.*Ax.*368d, Plu.2.1088d, Sor.2.10. Adv. –δῶς Gal.5.157. **–μικός,** ή, όν, *of the pulse*, Id.9.4, al. Adv. –κῶς Ruf.*Anat.*4.

**σφυγμολογέω,** *infer from the pulse*, Steph. *in Hp.*1.74 D., Pall. *in Hp.*2.112, 113 D.

**σφυγ-μός,** ὁ, *throbbing of inflamed parts*, Hp.*Aph.*7.21, Plu.2. 581f. 2. *beating of the heart*, and, generally, of an artery or vein, *pulsation*, Hp.*Loc.Hom.*3, al., Arist.*Spir.*482b15, *Resp.*479b19, al., Gal.6.149, 8.453–765; τῶν σ. ἅψασθαι Id.19.207: metaph. of a *vibration* of the earth, οἷον σ. Arist.*Mete.*366b15, cf. Plu.*Alex.*35. 3. metaph., οἷον ἐν σ. γενομένης τῆς ψυχῆς Id.*Cor.*21; *unhealthy excitement*, Diog.Oen.57: pl., Plu.2.565d. **–μώδης,** ες, *like the pulse*, Arist.*Spir.*483a11, v. l. in Hp.*Art.*40. Adv. –δῶς Anon.Lond.29.6, Gal.10.334.

**σφῡδόω,** *to be in full health* or *vigour*, σφυδῶν· εὔρωστος, ἰσχυρός, σκληρός, Hsch., cf. διασφυδόω:—Pass., δειπνοῦσιν ἐσφυδωμένοι τἀλλότρια they sup *even to bursting*, Timocl.29; cf. σφυρόομαι.

**σφυδρόν,** τό, = σφυρόν, *Act.Ap.*3.7 (v. l. σφυρά), *PFlor.*391.53,56 (iii A.D.): = *circumtallum*, *Gloss.*: σφυδρά· ἡ περιφέρεια τῶν ποδῶν, Hsch.

**σφύζω,** Dor. **σφύσδω,** only pres. and impf.:—*throb, beat violently* (cf. σφυγμός), Hp.*Epid.*2.5.16, 2.6.5, *Judic.*33, Theoc.11.71. 2. *beat*, of the pulse, σ. τὸ αἷμα ἐν ταῖς φλεψί Arist.*HA*521a6; πηδῶσα οἷον τὰ σφύζοντα like *the veins* or *arteries*, Pl.*Phdr.*251d ; μέρος [ἐμβρύου] μήτε θερμὸν μήτε σφύζον Sor.2.63. 3. metaph. of any violent motion, σφύζοντος καὶ σφαδάζοντος καὶ πηδῶντος Longin.*Rh.* p.201 H., cf. Dam.*Pr.*221 ; σ. ἐπὶ ταῦτα *to be very eager* after.., Anon. ap.Suid. 4. prob. f.l. in Thphr.*Char.*19.6.

**σφύξ**, sine expl., Theognost.*Can.*132 : σφ]ύγα φυσαλέαν inflated *pulse*, dub. in Cerc.6.15.

**σφύξις**, εως, ἡ, = σφυγμός 2, Arist.*Resp.*480$^a$14, *GA*781$^a$25.

**σφῦρα**, ἡ, *hammer*, Od.3.434, A.*Fr.*307, Hdt.1.68, Cratin.87(hex.), Arist.*GA*789$^b$11. 2. *beetle, mallet*, for breaking clods of earth, Hes.*Op.*425, Ar.*Pax* 566. II. *balk between the furrows of ploughed land*, Poll.7.145. 2. *a land measure*, *IG*9(1).61.39 (Daulis, ii A.D.), Hsch. s.v. δμόσφυρος. III. a fish, = κέστρα, Id.

**σφυραθία**, v. σπύραθος.

**σφύραινα**, ἡ, a sea-fish, of two sorts acc. to Opp.*H.*1.172 : a. the *bicuda, Sphyraena spet* ; b. = Att. κέστρα, Stratt.28, Antiph.97, Arist.*HA*610$^b$5. [ῠ, Opp. l. c., but Stratt. l. c. has σφῦρ-.]

**σφῦράς**, Att. for σπυράς.

**σφῠρ-ηδόν**, Adv. *like a hammer*, σ. τῇ δεξιᾷ πλήξας Philostr.*Gym.* 20. **-ηλᾰτέω**, *work with the hammer*, Ph.1.247. **-ήλᾰτος**, ον, (σφῦρα, ἐλαύνω) *wrought with the hammer*, σίδηρος, πέδαι, A.*Th.*816, *Pers.*747 (troch.). 2. of statues, opp. to those of cast metal (χωνευτά), εἰκὼ χρυσέην σ. ἐποιήσατο Hdt.7.69 ; Παλλὰς χρυσῇ σ. *AP*14.2, cf. Str.8.6.20, D.S.18.26, etc. ; σ. οἷα κολοσσός Theoc.22. 47, cf. Epigr.ap.Phot. s.v. Κυψελιδῶν ἀνάθημα ; σ. ἐν Ὀλυμπίᾳ σταθῆτι Pl.*Phdr.*236b. II. metaph., *wrought as of iron*, σ. ἀνάγκαι Pi.*Fr.*207 ; σ. φιλία Plu.2.65b ; σ. νοῦς, like Homer's πυκινὸς νόος, ib.408e,511b ; σ. λόγος Luc.*Dem.Enc.*14. **-ήματα**· τὰ σιδήρια, ὅτι οὐ χεῖται, Hsch.

**σφυρίδιον** [ῐδ], τό, = σπυρίδιον (q.v.): written -ίδιν, *POxy.*529.5 (ii A.D.), etc. ; -ίδον, *PRyl.*382 (ii A.D.).

**σφῠρῐδοφόρος**, ον, *basket-carrying*, παιδάρια *BGU*1518 (iii B.C.).

**σφῠρίον**, τό, = σφυρίδιον, *POxy.*1658.6 (iv A.D.), etc.

**σφῠρίον**, τό, also proparox. σφύριον, Dim. of σφῦρα, *small hammer, mallet*, Thphr.*HP*5.7.8, *PCair.Zen.*759 (iii B.C.), Ph.*Bel.*65. 40, Heliod.ap.Orib.46.11.28.

⊛**σφυρίς**, ίδος, ἡ, = σπυρίς (q.v.) ; *nose-bag* or *-basket*, *PSI*5.543.54 (iii B.C.).

**σφῠρόβολος**, ὁ (or -ον, τό), instrument of unknown use, *IG*4$^2$(1). 110.40 (Epid., iv B.C.), 11(2).165.8 (Delos, iii B.C.).

**σφῠροδέται**· ἡ λέξις παρὰ τοῖς τὰ ἱπποτροφικά, Hsch. (Prob. = *ankle-band.*)

**σφῠροκόπ-ᾰνον**, τό, *hammer, Gloss.* **-εῖον**, τό, sine expl., Zonar. **-έω**, *beat with a hammer*, Lxx *Jd.*5.26, Phld.*Sign.*2. **-ία**, ἡ, *beating with the hammer*, Sm.*Pr.*19.29. **-ος** (parox.), ον, *one who beats with the hammer*, Lxx *Ge.*4.22, Ph.1.247 : name of a play by S., also called Πανδώρα.

**σφῠροκτῠπέω**, *beat with the hammer*, Sch.Par.A.R.2.84.

⊛**σφῠρ-όν**, τό, *ankle*, κνῆμαί τε ἰδὲ σφυρά Il.4.147, cf. 518, Hp.*Loc. Hom.*6 ; ποδῶν τέτρηνε τένοντε ἐς σφυρὸν ἐκ πτέρνης Il.22.397 ; ὀρθῷ ἕστασας ἐπὶ σφυρῷ (metaph.) Pi.*I.*7(6).13 ; βαίνουσα..σ. κούφῳ E. *Alc.*586 (lyr.) ; μονόχαλα σ., of a horse, Id.*IA*225 (lyr.) ; τὸ σ. ἐξεκόκκισε *put out* his ankle, Ar.*Ach.*1179 ; τὸ ἔσχατον ἀντικνημίου σ. Arist.*HA*494$^a$10 ; σ. Ἰφίκλειον the *ankle* of Iphiclus (the runner), Call.*Aet.*3.1.46. II. metaph., *the lower part* or *edge, foothills*, of a mountain, ἐν Παλίου σφυροῖς Pi.*P.*2.46, cf. *AP*6.114 (Simm.), 7.501 (Pers.), Nonn.*D.*1.165, etc. ; Λιβύας ἄκρον σφυρόν the very *furthest part* of Libya, Theoc.16.77 ; σ. νήσων Musae.45 ; ὕλης Nonn.*D.*2. 1. **-όομαι**, Pass., *to have buskins on*, ἐθέλει γὰρ ὁ θεὸς ὀρθὸς ἐσφυρωμένος διὰ μέσου βαδίζειν *Carm.Pop.*7 (ἐσφυδωμένος cj. Meineke).

**σφῠροπέλεκυς**, εως, ὁ, *hammer-axe*, *IG*1$^2$.313.132.

**σφῠρο-πρησῐπύρα** [ῠ], ἡ, (πρήθω, πῦρ) *firing the ankle*, epith. of the gout, Luc.*Trag.*199. **-τομέω**, *bleed* a person from a vessel *near the ankle*, Aët.8.50.

**σφύρωσις** [ῠ], εως, ἡ, *hammering*, *Supp.Epigr.*4.447.10 (Didyma, ii B.C.) ; = διάροσις, Hsch. (cf. σφῦρα I. 2).

⊛ **σφῠρωτήρ**, ῆρος, ὁ, *leather thong, shoe-latchet*, Lxx *Ge.*14.23 cod. Vat. (σφαιρ- cett.) : ἀπὸ τοῦ σφυρὰ τηρεῖν acc. to Jo.Chr.ap.Phot. *Bibl.*p.510B.

**σφύσδω**, Dor. for σφύζω.

**σφύττω**, (= σφύζω), *to be eager*, c. inf., D.Chr.4.116.

**σφώ**, v. σύ II, σφωέ.

**σφωέ**, dual nom. and acc. of the Pron. of 3rd pers., of which the gen. sg. and nom. pl. are οὗ, σφεῖς (qq. v.) ; dat. σφωΐν :—*they two, both of them*, only masc. and fem., and always enclit., Il.1.8, al. ; strengthd., σφωῒν ἀμφοτέροιιν Od.20.327 :—the form σφώ is only found in post-Homeric Ep., as Antim.9,11 (in Il.17.531 σφω' Αἴαντε is the best reading, cf. A.D.*Pron.*88.24, Hdn.Gr.2.72).

**σφῶϊ, σφῶϊν**, v. σύ II. **σφωΐν**, v. σφωέ.

⊛ **σφωΐτερος** [ῐ], α, ον, possess. Adj. of σφῶϊ, Pron. of 2nd pers. dual, *of you two*, σ. ἔπος the word *of you two*, Hera and Athena, Il.1. 216. 2. of σφωέ, Pron. of 3rd pers. dual, *of them two* or *both of them*, Antim.10,13. II. = σφέτερος in A.R. : 1. for 2nd pers. pl., *your own, your*, 4.454. 2. for 2nd pers. sg., *thine own, thine, thy*, 3.395. 3. for 3rd pers. sg., *his* or *her own*, 2.465,544, al. (so Theoc.25.55) ; *his* or *her*, 1.643, 3.600. 4. for 3rd pers. pl., *their own*, 1.1286, Man.2.190.

**σφῶν**, v. σύ II. **σχαδίζω**, v. σχαλίζω. ⊛ **σχάδιον** [ᾰ], τό, = ἰσχάδιον, *Gloss.* ⊛ **σχαδοκάρυνα**, v. ἰσχ- in Addendis.

**σχᾰδών** or **σχάδων** (as in Arist.), όνος, ἡ, *larva of the bee* or *wasp*, Arist.*HA*554$^a$29, 555$^a$8, 624$^a$8. II. *breeding-cell* of the larva, Theaet.ap.Sch.Theoc.1.147. III. *honey-cell*, and in pl. *honeycomb*, Ar.*Fr.*318.6, 569.3, Antiph.275, Anaxandr.41.53, Theoc. l. c., *PCair.Zen.*354.8 (iii B.C.) ; so also in sg., σχαδόνα δεῖ πάντως φαγεῖν Euthycl.1. IV. a throw of the dice, Hsch.

**σχάζω**, Hp.*Epid.*6.5.15, *Aff.*4, X.*HG*5.4.58 ; also **σχάω**, inf. σχᾶν Pl.Com.127, κατα-σχᾶν Hp.*Epid.*7.76 ; so impf. ἔσχων, Ar. *Nu.*409 ; 3 pl. ἔσχαζον Anon.ap.Phryn.194 ; also ἐσχάζοσαν Lyc. 21 : fut. σχάσω (ἀπο-) Crates Com.41 : aor. ἔσχᾰσα Pi.*P.*10.51, E.*Tr.*811 (lyr.), Ar.*Nu.*740 :—Med., aor. ἐσχασάμην ib.107, Pl. Com.32 :—Pass., 3 sg. pres. σχᾶται Hp.*Art.*30 : fut. σχασθήσομαι Lxx *Am.*3.5 : aor. ἐσχάσθην Hp.*Ulc.*24, Antisth.ap.Stob.3. 18.26, etc. : pf. ἔσχασμαι in plant-name ἐσχασμένη, = ὀνοβρυχίς, Ps.-Dsc.3.153. 1. *slit open so as to let something escape*, οὐκ ἔσχων ἀμελήσας [τὴν γαστέρα] I carelessly forgot to *slit* the haggis, Ar.*Nu.*409 (anap.) ; σ. φλέβα *open* a vein, Hp.*Epid.*6.5.15, X.*HG* 5.4.58, Plu.*Ages.*27, etc. ; ἐκ βραχιόνων τὰς φλέβας Arr.*Fr.*168 J. (so σ. τὸ φλεγμαῖνον μόριον *lance* the boil, Gal.11.119) ; freq. also without φλέβα, Aret.*CA*2.7, etc. ; σ. ὑπὸ τὴν γλῶτταν *bleed* it under the tongue, Arist.*HA*603$^b$15 ; σ. τὸν ἀγκῶνα, i.e. *bleed in* the arm, Hp.*Int.*37 ; τὴν κεφαλὴν Id.*Aff.*2 : c. acc. cogn., σ. τομήν make an incision, Aret.*CA*1.7 ; αἷμα σ. Poll.2.215 ; τὸ πρωτόσφακτον ὅρκιον σχάσας *slaying* the.. victim, Lyc.329 : metaph. in Pass., *to be purged by bleeding*, Antisth.ap.Stob.3.18. 26. 2. *open*, ἐσχάσαμεν κάλυκας we (roses) *have opened* our buds, *AP*6.345 (Crin.) ; στόμα Lyc.28. 3. *let go*, σχάσας τὴν φροντίδα *letting* your mind *go, relaxing* your thought, Ar.*Nu.*740 ; σχάσαντες τὴν ἀγκύλην τοῦ βρόχου *slackening*, Paul.Aeg.6.51 ; σ. τὰς μηχανάς *let off* the engines, Plu.*Marc.*15 ; σχάσει τὴν χεῖρα, ὥστε ἀφεθῆναι τὸ βέλος Hero *Spir.*1.41 :—Pass., ἐσχάζετο αὐτόματον [τὸ βέλος] Ph. *Bel.*73.51, cf. 70.45, 78.31 ; -όμενον παττάλιον (in a mousetrap) Poll.7.114 ; εἰ σχασθήσεται παγὶς ἄνευ τοῦ συλλαβεῖν τι ; Lxx *Am.*3. 5 ; ἐσχαστο ἡ ὕσπληξ the ὕσπληξ (= σχαστηρία I) *had been let off*, Hld.4.3 ; βαλβῖδα μηρίνθου σχάσας, i.e. starting the race, Lyc.13 (= βαλβῖδος μήρινθον acc. to Sch.) ; κἀπὸ γῆς ἐσχάζοσαν ὑσπλήγγας *were starting off* from shore, Id.21 ; of the jaw, ἐκπίπτει μὲν γνάθος ὀλιγάκις, σχᾶται μέντοι πολλάκις ἐν χάσμησι *slips*, Hp.*Art.*30 (= χαλᾶται acc. to Paul.Aeg.6.112) :—also Act., of the surgeon, ἐξαπίνης σχάσαι *let* the jaw *slip back into position, let it go*, ibid. ; καὶ κατὰ παλαίστραν δὲ τὸ σχάσαι σημαίνει τὴν χεῖρα ταχέως ἄγειν πρὸς αὐτὴν (leg. αὑτὴν ?) ἐκ τῆς ἔμπροσθεν θέσεως Gal.18(1).438. 4. *relax effort, cease* an action, esp. rowing, κώπαν σχάσον *easy !*, i.e. cease rowing, Pi.*P.*10.51, cf. E.*Tr.*811 (lyr.), Call.*Fr.*104 ; τί σιγᾷς γῆρυν ἄφθογγον σχάσας ; E.*Ph.*960 ; σχάσον δὲ δεινὸν ὄμμα καὶ θυμοῦ πνοάς ib.454 : abs., φοβοῦμαι μὴ σχάσῃ, νεναυσίακε γάρ I fear he *may give up*, *BGU*1097.4 (i A.D.) :—Med., σχασάμενος τὴν ἱππικὴν *giving up* horses, Ar.*Nu.*107 ; τὰς ὀφρῦς σχάσασθε καὶ τὰς ὄμφακας Pl.Com.32 (cf. ὄμφαξ II. 3). 5. *let fall, drop*, τὴν οὐράν X.*Cyn.*3.5 ; πεύκης ὀδόντας, i.e. the anchor, Lyc.99 ; λάθρᾳ κατὰ μηχανὰς σχασθέντων τῶν φραγμάτων Hippoloch.ap.Ath.4.130a. 6. *cause to collapse*, θάλαμον σχάσε μῆνις *AP*9.422 (Apollonid.) ; σχάσας..ἐν πέδῳ γόνυ, i.e. kneel down, *Sammelb.*5629.3 (iii B.C.) :—Pass., μήπω σχασθῇ lest the dyke *collapse*, *PLond.*1.131.243 (i A.D., abbrev.). 7. metaph., *cause to collapse* or *fail, foil*, πῦρ.., λεόντων..ὄνυχας, ἀκμὰν καὶ δεινοτάτων σχάσαις ὀδόντων, of Peleus subduing the metamorphosed Thetis, Pi.*N.*4.64 ; φεῦ, οἵαισιν ἐν φροντίσι Κνώσιον ἔσχασεν στραταγέταν B.16.121.

**σχᾰλίδωμα** [ῐ], ατος, τό, *forked prop* or *stay*, Poll.5.19,31.

**σχαλίζω**, *suckle*, Hsch., Phot., Suid. ; σχαδίσαι in *EM*739.42 ; cf. ἰσχαλεῦσαι.

**σχᾰλίς**, ίδος, ἡ, *forked stick used as a prop* for nets, etc., X.*Cyn.*2. 8 (σταλ- codd.), 6.7, Poll.5.19,31 sq. ; θέντες ἀμίστυλλον ταῦρον ἐπὶ σχαλίδων cj. in Call.*Aet.Fr.*7.35 P. ; cf. στάλιξ.

**σχάρα** [ᾰ], ἡ, = ἐσχάρα, *Gloss.* **σχάς** [ᾰ], σχάδος, ἡ, = ἰσχάς (*dried fig*), ib.

**σχάσις** [ᾰ], εως, ἡ, *slitting* of a tree, [τὸ κόμμι] ῥέει καὶ πληγείσης καὶ αὐτόματον ἄνευ σχάσεως (cj. for σχίσεως) Thphr.*HP*4.2.8. 2. *venesection*, Aret.*CA*1.10 (pl.), 2.3. 3. *release, letting off*, of an engine, Ph.*Bel.*77.1.

**σχάσμα**, ατος, τό, *incision*, Hp.*Ulc.*24,27. II. *release, letting off*, of an engine, Ph.*Bel.*69.1.

**σχαστήρ**, ῆρος, ὁ, *clothes-hanger* or *-stretcher*, Lat. *tendicula*, *Gloss.*

**σχαστηρία**, ἡ, *trigger, release-mechanism*, Arist.*Mu.*398$^b$15, Ph. *Bel.*74.27, Hero *Aut.*13.9, *Bel.*78.3, Plb.8.5.10, 8.6.3, Apollod.*Poliorc.* 188.7 ; *trigger* (worked by the foot) of a mechanism (cf. ὕσπληξ) for starting a race, Gal.18(1).438. II. perh. *curtain-releasing mechanism*, or *curtain-rod*, κατασκευάσαντι σ. χαλκᾶς εἰς τὸν νεὼ τοῦ Ἀσκληπιοῦ.. καὶ τῷ ἐνέντι τὰς σ. εἰς τὸν νεὼ *Inscr.Délos* 372 *A* 110 (iii B.C.) ; κίρκων καὶ σχαστηριῶν ib.320 *B* 67 (iii B.C.). III. pl., *attachments for relaxing* the pressure of a surgical noose, Heraclas ap. Orib.48.7.3. IV. place-name in *IG*2$^2$.2776.17,203.

**σχαστήριον**, τό, *lancet*, Hippiatr.24.

**σχάστης**, ου, ὁ, sine expl. (grouped with ἀφρός, ἐπαφᾶται, πομφόλυξ, σχίζεται), Milne *Greek Shorthand Manuals* p.42.

**σχαῦδαι**· ἰσχνόφωνοι, Hsch. **σχάω**, v. σχάζω.

**σχεδ-άριον**, τό, *sketch*, Leont.*in Arat.*4 ; *rough draft*, Eust.961.21 ; = Lat. *recitatum*, Lyd.*Mag.*3.11. **-εκδότης**, ου, ὁ, *editor*, dub. cj.

in *Lex. de Spir.* p.197 V. (σχεδεκτοτῶν codd.). -η, ἡ, *leaf, page*, dub. cj. in *Lex. de Spir.* p.214 V.; Lat. *scheda* is a Greek word acc. to Isid. *Etym.* 6.14.8; cf. σχίδα.

**σχέδην**, Adv., (ἔχω, σχεῖν) *gently, slowly*, X.*Eq.Mag.* 3.4, Macho ap.Ath.8.349b, Semus 20, freq. in Plu., *Crass.* 23, al.; σ. ἐκρέειν *trickle out*, Aret.*SD* 1.9; πότερον ἠπειγμένως ἢ σ. (σχεδὸν codd.) prob. in Gal.19.201. II. *at close quarters*, Anon.ap.Suid.

**σχεδί-α**, Ion. -ίη, ἡ, *raft, float*, ἐπὶ σχεδίης πολυδέσμου Od.5.33, cf. 174, *PLille* 25.4 (iii B.C.), *PTeb.* 701.152,318 (iii B.C.); ὥσπερ ἐπὶ σχεδίας Pl.*Phd.* 85d; ἐπὶ σχεδιῶν Th.6.2; σ. διφθέριναι *rafts* of hides, X.*An.* 2.4.28: poet., *boat, ship*, E.*Hec.* 111 (anap.), Theoc.16.41. 2. *bridge of boats* or *pontoons*, of the bridge of Darius, Epigr.ap.Hdt. 4.88, cf. 97, al.; so λινοδέσμῳ σ. πορθμὸν ἀμείψας A.*Pers.* 68 (lyr.), cf. *Marm.Par.* 66. 3. *frame*, σ. ὑπότροχος a frame on wheels for moving anything upon, Ath.Mech.10.1. II. *cramp, holdfast*, Ph.Byz.*Mir.* 4.2. (In signf. 1 the word is prob. fem. of σχέδιος (sc. ναῦς or γέφυρα), *something knocked up off-hand*: signf. II must be connected with σχεῖν, cf. σχεδόν.) ⊛ **-άζω**, *do a thing off-hand* or *on the spur of the moment*, σχεδιάζοντα λέγειν ὅ τι ἂν τύχῃ Pl.*Sis.* 387e: abs., *play off-hand*, λαβὼν τὸ μελετητήριον, εἶτ' ἐσχεδίασε δριμέως Anaxandr.15.3, cf. Cic.*Att.* 6.1.11; *invent stories*, Plb.12.4.4, D.H.1.7, D.S.1.23; *improvise*, Phld.*Rh.* 1.100 S. (Pass.); *give free play to the imagination*, Sor.2.65. 2. *act with insufficient care*, τοῖς κοινοῖς πράγμασι in public affairs, Plb.22.9.12; ἔν τινι D.S.13.31; πρός τι LXX *Ba.* 1.19.

**σχεδιακῶς**, v. σχεδικός.

**σχεδιάς**, άδος, ἡ, acc. to Gal.19.144 = ἄγχουσα, Hp.*Mul.* 1.75.

**σχεδίασ-μα**, ατος, τό, *freak, whim, caprice*, Cic.*Att.* 15.19.2. -**μός**, ὁ, *doing, speaking*, or *writing off-hand*, Pl.*Sis.* 390c, Agatharch.4, Str.12.3.22, Eust.146.19. -**τικῶς**, Adv. *off-hand, hastily*, Id. 836.38.

**σχεδίην**, Ep. Adv. formed from the fem. of σχέδιος, of Place, *at close quarters*, τύψον δὲ σχεδίην Il.5.830: cf. αὐτοσχεδόν. II. of Time, *soon*, Nic.*Al.* 88; *straightway, at once*, Babr.57.4 (s.v.l.).

⊛ **σχεδικός**, ἡ, όν, *riddling*, νόμῳ σχεδικῷ Eust.241.8; ἡ σ. τόλμα the daring *of riddle-composers*, Id.714.51; οἱ τὰ σ. λαλοῦντες Id.1634.16. Adv. -κῶς, perh. to be restd. for σχεδιακῶς in Id.1545.7.

**σχέδιος**, α, ον (ος, ον in Aret.*SD* 1.16, al.), (σχεδόν): I. of Place, *near*, σ. ξίφη weapons *for close combat*, A.*Ch.* 163 (lyr.); σ. δόρυ Arist. *Fr.* 498; ἐν σ. μάχῃ *Epigr.Gr.* 333.3 (Pergamon). 2. (cf. σχέδην) *gentle, slow*, ἱππασία Poll.1.214. II. of Time, *casual, temporary*, αἰτίη, πρόφασις, πόνος, Aret.*SD* 2.7, 2.13, 2.12, etc.; ἐπὶ σχεδίου as Adv., ib.1.6; *on the spur of the moment, off-hand*, ποτόν *AP* 11.64 (Agath.); λόγος D.H.*Comp.* 18, etc.; ὥσπερ ἐν σχεδίῳ πόλις ἀποδείκνυται *in a moment*, J.*BJ* 3.5.2; σχέδιον, τό, *extemporaneous speech, impromptu*, Hermog.*Meth.* 17 fin. 2. *done* or *made off-hand, ordinary, common* (= εὐτελής, Hsch., Phot.), οἴνη Nic.*Th.* 622. Adv. -ίως *temporarily*, Aret.*SD* 1.2; *sketchily*, ἄρτος σ. ὠπτημένος Sch.Luc.*Pisc.* 45; *at random*, Arat.1154.

**σχεδιουργός**, ὁ, *raft-builder*, Them.*Or.* 26.316b.

**σχεδισμός**, ὁ, *an effeminate kind of dance*, Sch.T Il.22.391.

⊛ **σχεδογρᾰφία**, ἡ, *the art of parsing*, Tz. ad Hes.*Op.* 285. II. v.l. for σφαιρογραφία in Sch.Arat.248.

⊛ **σχεδ-όθεν**, Adv., prop. *from nigh at hand*; but used much like sq., *nigh at hand, near*, ὤμων μεσσηγὺς σ. βάλε Il.16.807, cf. A.R.4.662; σ. δέ οἱ ἦλθεν Ἀθήνη Od.2.267, 13.221, etc.; στῆ ῥ' αὐτῶν σ. 19.447. -**όν**, Adv., (ἔχω, σχεῖν): I. of Place, *near, hard by*, Ep. and Lyr., δυσμενέες δ' ἄνδρες σ. εἵαται Il.10.100; σ. εἴσιδε γαῖαν Od.5.392, cf. 24.493; σ. οὔτασε *at close quarters*, Il.5.458; μή πώς σ' ἠὲ βάλῃ ἠὲ σ. ἄορι τύψῃ 20.378, cf. 13.576, 16.828: sts. c. dat., οὐ γάρ σφιν παῖδες σ. εἵαται 10.422; νῆσοι ναιετάουσι σ. ἀλλήλῃσι Od.9.23; οἵ δή σφι σ. εἰσι Hes.*Sc.* 113; so στάθεν τύμβῳ σ. Pi.*N.* 10.66 (also πὰρ ποδὶ σ. Id.*O.* 1.74; ἀμφ' ἀνδριάντι σ. Id.*P.* 5.40): more freq. c. gen., Φαιήκων γαίης σ. Od.5.288, cf. 475, 6.125, 9.117, 10.156, etc.; σ. αἵματος 11.142. 2. with Verbs of motion, σ. ἐλθεῖν τινι Il.9.304, cf. Hes.*Sc.* 435; τινος Od.4.439; Ἀχαιΐδος 11.481; ὅστις σ. ἔγχεος ἔλθῃ Il.20.363. II. metaph. of relationship, καὶ πηῷ περ ἐόντι μάλα σ. Od.10.441. 2. *similar to*, c. dat., σ. τούτοις.. αἱ παραλλαγαί.. εἰσίν Iamb.*Comm.Math.* 27. III. of Time, [θάνατος] δή τοι σ. εἰσι Il.17.202, cf. Od.2.284; σοὶ δὲ γάμος σ. ἐστιν 6.27; σοὶ.. φημὶ σ. ἔμμεναι, ὁππότε.. [the time] is *near*, when.., Il.13.817. IV. after Hom., *about, approximately, more or less, roughly speaking*, σ. κατὰ ταὐτά Hdt.6.42; σ. τι ταὐτά Pl.*Prm.* 128b; σ. τι τοιαῦτα Id.*Smp.* 201e; σ. τι ταῦτα Id.*Grg.* 472c; σ. πάντες Hdt.1.65, 2.48, X.*HG* 6.5.33, cf. *Act. Ap.* 13.44, *PRyl.* 81.7 (ii A.D.); πάντα σ. Arist.*Mete.* 350b21; σ. ἅπαντας Ar.*Ec.* 1157; πάντες σ. ἢ οἵ γε πλεῖστοι Arr.*Epict.* 1.11.7; σ. ἐκ κρηνῶν οἱ πλεῖστοι ῥέουσιν Arist.*Mete.* 350b34; σ. περὶ τριακόσια στάδια ib.351a14; σ. τι πρόσθεν ἤ.. *not long* before, S.*OT* 736; σ. ἤδη τῆς κοίτης ὥρη προσέρχεται ὑμῖν Hdt.5.20; σὺν τοῖς θεοῖς σ. ἔσται ὁ διάλογος (audit) ἕως τῆς λ' τοῦ Παχών *PTeb.* 58.58 (ii B.C.); σ.... τὸν αὐτὸν.. καιρόν *Inscr.Prien.* 105.13 (i B.C.); also σ. ἴσως Pl.*Sph.* 253c, Arist.*Top.* 118a13; σ. που D.S.36.10; σ. ὡς εἰπεῖν Arist.*APo.* 79a20, *Rh.* 1382b28, Gem.16.28; σ. εἰπεῖν one might *almost* say, Pl.*Sph.* 237c, Ath.Mech.3.4, *POxy.* 1033.11 (iv A.D.), *PLips.* 34.16 (iv A.D.). 2. with Verbs (freq. in pf.), esp. of saying or knowing, σ. εἴρηχ' ἃ νομίζω συμφέρειν D.3.36; εἴρηται σ. ἱκανῶς Arist.*APr.* 32a16; διώρισται σ. Id.*Pol.* 1328a19; τὸν ἐμὸν.. σ. ἤδη νομίζων ἐκτετοξεῦσθαι βίον Ar.*Pl.* 33; σ. ἐπίσταμαι S.*Tr.* 43; σ. οἶδα E.*Tr.* 898; ἐγὼ σ. τὸ πρᾶγμα γιγνώσκειν δοκῶ Ar.*Pl.* 860; freq. used to soften a positive assertion with a sense of modesty, sts. of irony, σ. γὰρ.. συνίημι Hdt.5.19; σ. τι τὴν σὴν οὐ καταισχύνω φύσιν *I dare say* I do not.., S.*El.* 609; σ. τι μώρῳ μωρίαν ὀφλισκάνω *I dare say* it is a fool who thinks me foolish, Id.*Ant.* 470; σ. δέ τι καὶ τὸ ξύμπαν *generally speaking* in every respect, Th.3.68; σ. οὐδ' ὁπωστιοῦν σοι πείσεται *probably* not at all, Pl.*Phd.* 61c; σ. γὰρ ἔχω ὃ εἰπὼν ἀναγκάσω σε *I think* I have an argument, Id.*Phdr.* 236d. 3. used in affirmative answers, *I suppose so, I dare say*, Id.*Sph.* 250c, 255c, al. V. *perhaps*, ὑποδραμὼν σ. φασεῖ (φάσει codd.) Dius ap.Stob.4.21.17. VI. = σχέδην, ἠκολούθει σ. J.*BJ* 1.17.2 (unless = followed *at no long distance*).

⊛ **σχέδος**, εος, τό, *riddle*, Eust.1634.13.

⊛ **σχεδουργός**, ὁ, *riddle-maker*, Tz.*H.* 11.575 (pl.): also **σχεδουργικοὶ** λαβύρινθοι Prov. ib. § 379 tit.

**σχεδρός**· τλήμων, καρτερικός, Hsch.

**σχέδῠνος**, η, ον, (ἔχω, σχεῖν) *tenacious*, φιλότης Emp.19.

⊛ * **σχέθω**, assumed as a collat. form of ἔχω by Gramm. (Hdn.Gr.1.440, *EM* 739.51), but all forms in use may be referred to aor. ἔσχεθον, a poet. lengthd. form of ἔσχον, the accents σχέθειν, σχέθων being errors for σχεθεῖν, σχεθών:—*hold*, πάροιθεν ἀσπίδας.. σχέθον αὐτοῦ Il.14.428, cf. 4.113; ἀσπίδα.. σχέθ' ἀπὸ ἕο 13.163; ἐπ' ἀγκῶνος κεφαλὴν σχέθεν Od.14.494; σχέθον ἔξω νῆα 10.95. 2. *have, get*, νόον σχέθε τόνδ' ἐνὶ θυμῷ 14.490; Ἄργει τ' ἔσχεθε κῦδος Pi.*O.* 9.88; τόλμαν σχεθεῖν A.*Pr.* 16; ἐν φρεσὶν καρδίαν σχεθών Id.*Ch.* 832 (lyr.) codd.; τεύχει.., ὅσων παρ' ἄλλων οὔποτ' ἂν σχέθοις βροτῶν Id.*Eu.* 857, cf. Pi.*O.* 1.71; ἐκ μὲν Ἐριχθονίου.. ἔσχεθε κοῦρον *had* a child, S.*Fr.* 242 (hexam., prob an Epic fragment); ἐν φυλακᾷ σχεθέμεν τινά Pi.*P.* 4.75. II. *hold back, keep away* or *off*, στεφάνη δόρυ οἱ σχέθε Il. 11.96, cf. 12.184; ἔσχεθεν ἱεμένους περ Od.16.430; σχέθον ἵππους Il.16.506; ἔσχεθον αὐδήν 19.418; σχεθέτω φόρμιγγα Od.8.537; νύκτα σχέθεν 23.243; αἷμα ἔσχεθον *staunched* it, 19.458: c. gen.. σχέθε δ' ὅσσε γόοιο 4.758; ὅπως ἂν αὐτὰς ὕβρεως σχέθω Ar.*Lys.* 425, cf. Theoc. 22.96: c. part., ἐρέφοντα σχέθοι *might stop* him from wreathing, Pi. *I.* 4(3).54(72): c. inf., οὔτ' ἂν Αἴαντος δόρυ μὴ πάντα πέρσαι.. σχέθοι E.*Rh.* 602. III. abs., οὐδ' ἄρ' ὀχῆες ἐσχεθέτην *did* not *hold*, Il.12.461.—Rare in Prose, Aret.*CA* 2.4.

**σχεῖται**· ἐμεῖ, Hsch.

**σχέλινος**· ἀγρία κυπάρισσος, οἱ δὲ ἄρκευθος, Hsch.

⊛ **σχελίς**, ίδος, ἡ, mostly in pl. σχελίδες, *ribs of beef*, A.*Fr.* 443, Ar. *Eq.* 362 (cf. Sch.ad loc., Hsch.), *Fr.* 253; σ. ὀλόκνημοι Pherecr.108.13, cf. Luc.*Lex.* 6; also κάπρου σχελίδες cj. Mein. in Archipp.11.3 (lyr.); σ. λαγωῶν Poll.6.33:—later written **σκελίδες**, ὑῶν *sides* of bacon, D.Chr.7.44, cf. *PSI* 4.428.5 (iii B.C.), and so prob. in Poll.2.193.

**σχελυνάζει**· φλυαρεῖ, Hsch. (aor. ἐσχελύνασεν Id.). ⊛ **σχέμα**· σχῆμα, Ἀχαιοί, Id. (Implied also by the Lat. loan-word *schĕma*.) II. σχέμα· τὸ ὄχημα, Theognost.*Can.* 12 (sed leg. τὸ σχῆμα). **σχέμεν**, v. ἔχω.

**σχενδῦλα**, ἡ, *a ship-carpenter's and blacksmith's tool*, perhaps *a pair of pincers* or *tongs*, ναυπηγοῖς σ. *AP* 11.203 (κένδυλα cod.): also **σχενδύλη**, *IG* 2².1672.102, Hsch. s.v. σχενδυλόληπτοι. Hsch. also cites **σχενδῦλάω** (ibid.); the Dim. **σκενδύλιον** (q.v.) implies a form ***σκενδύλη** which is not found.

**σχενδυλόληπτοι**· ἐσχενδυλῆσθαι ἔλεγον τοὺς ἐν τοῖς ταύροις (sic) ἀπὸ τοῦ χαλκευτικοῦ ὀργάνου, ὃ σχενδύλη λέγεται, Hsch.

**σχέο**, v. ἔχω.

**σχεράς**, άδος, ἡ, *shingle*, v.l. in Il.21.319: cf. πολυσχεράς.

**σχέρᾰφος**, v. σκέραφος.

**Σχερία**, Ep. -ίη, ἡ, *Scheria*, the country of the Phaeacians, Od.5.34, al.: identified with the island later called Κέρκυρα by Str.7.3.6.

⊛ **σχερός**, ὁ, found only in dat., ἐν σχερῷ *in a line, one after another, uninterruptedly, successively*, Pi.*N.* 1.69, 11.39, *I.* 6(5).22: written ἐνσχερώ in A.R.1.912; cf. ἐπισχερώ, ἰσχερώ (perh. for Cypr. ἰν σχερῷ). II. σχερός· ἀκτή, αἰγιαλός, Hsch., cf. Theognost.*Can.* 12: also σχερόν, = κῦμα ἕτοιμον, Amerias ap.Hsch.

**σχές, σχέσθαι**, v. ἔχω.

**σχέσις**, εως, ἡ, (ἔχω, σχεῖν) *state, condition*, σ. τοῦ σώματος *habit* of body, much like διάθεσις, which is alterable, opp. ἕξις (constitution or temperament, which is permanent), Hp.*Art.* 8; hence ἐν σχέσει, of *temporary, passing conditions*, opp. those which have become constitutional (ἐν ἕξει), Gal.10.533; τί διαφέρει σ. ἕξεως; Luc.*Symp.* 23, cf. *Herm.* 81; σ. ἀθλητική *the habit* of an athlete, D.L.5.67. b. *stationary condition*, whether stable or not, opp. κίνησις, *Stoic.* 3.19, 2.115 (pl.), Apollod.ib.3.260, Plot.3.1.7; ἐν σχέσει, opp. ἐν κινήσει, but inclusive of ἐν ἕξει, *Stoic.* 3.26. 2. generally, *nature, quality*, οὔτ' εἶδος, .. οὐθ' ὅπλων σ. A.*Th.* 507; ἡ τῆς ὁπλίσεως αὐτῶν σ. Pl.*Ti.* 24b; τριχῶν καὶ ἐσθῆτος X.*Smp.* 4.57; ἐν ταύτῃ τῇ σ. διάγει τὸν βίον D.45.68, cf. Epicur.*Nat.* 2.2; κρεάδια.. δροσώδη τὴν σχέσιν Alex.124.12. 3. *expression, attitude*, Phld.*Acad.Ind.* pp.50,53 M.; *position, posture*, as in dancing, Plu.2.747c. 4. *relation*, Arist.*Fr.* 182, Zeno *Stoic.* 1.49, etc.; ἡ πρός τι σ. D.L.9.87: abs., Sch.Ar.*Pl.* 2: also, *relationship*, Arr.*Epict.* 4.6.26 (but σχέσιν ἀδελφικὴν ἔχειν πρός τινα to be fraternally *disposed* towards.., *POsl.* 55.6 (ii/iii A.D.); φιλικὴ σ. *POxy.* 1588.3 (iv A.D.)). b. Gramm., *relation*, A.D.*Adv.* 183.3, al.: also in Metric, κατὰ σχέσιν εἶναι or γεγράφθαι to be *relative*, i.e. composed *with strophic correspondence*, Aristid.Quint.1.29, Heph.*Poëm.* 3, Sch.Ar.*Nu.* 518. 5. αἱ δέκα σ., = the ten *categories* or σχήματα τῆς κατηγορίας, *Theol.Ar.* 59, Iamb.*in Nic.* p.11 P. 6. αὗται αἱ σ., ἑπτὰ οὖσαι the seven *positions* (sc. ἄνω, κάτω κτλ.), Cleom. 1.1; 'up' and 'down' were not relative (οὐ κατὰ σχέσιν) according to the Stoics, *Stoic.* 2.176. II. *checking, retention*, τῆς καθάρσιος (pus or phlegm) Hp *Aph.*7.80; τοῦ οὔρου Id.*Epid.*5.79; opp. ῥοή, Pl.*Cra.*424a. III. *possession*, Aristaenet.1.19; ὅπλων *bearing*, Pl.*R.*452c.

**σχετ-έος**, α, ον, *what ought to be stopped*, σχετέα δρᾶν, v.l. for σχέτλια, Hp.*Mul.*2.133. **-ήριον**, τό, *check, remedy*, λιμοῦ *against* hunger, E.*Cyc.*135; *astringent*, Orib.9.43.11. **-ικός**, ή, όν, *of* or *for holding firm, retentive*, τινος Plu.2.428d,725b: abs., ib.952b; *stable, permanent*, σ. τυπώσεις *Stoic.*2.229. II. *relative*, Iamb. *in Nic.*p.11 P. Adv. -κῶς, Dam.*Pr.*131. III. *depending on a* σχέσις I. 1, *temporary*, πυρετός, opp. ἑκτικός, Gal.10.533. Adv. -κῶς *as the result of precarious conditions*, opp. ἀπὸ ἕξεως καὶ διαθέσεως, Ph.1.129, cf. Sor.1.43.

**σχετλι-άζω**, *complain of hardship, utter indignant complaints*, Ar. *Pl.*477, Aeschin.3.146, D.40.53, Thphr.*Char.*8.9, etc.; σ. φάσκων.. Antipho 3.4.4; σ. ὡς δεινὰ πάσχουσι Pl.*Grg.*519b; σ. καὶ λέγειν ὡς.. Aeschin.2.154; σ. ἐπὶ τῇ τόλμῃ D.34.19; πρὸς τὴν τύχην Aristaenet. 2.7: c. neut. Adj., σ. τὸ συμβάν Id.1.6; τοιαῦτα σ. Plu.*Cam.* 31. ❋ **-ασμός**, ὁ, *indignant* or *passionate complaint*, Th.8.53, Arist. *Rh.*1395$^a$9, Posidon.ap.Gal.5.401, D.H.*Rh.*9.5. ❋ **-αστικός**, ή, όν, *expressive of anger*, A.D.*Pron.*34.30, al.; ἔννοια Hermog.*Id.*2.7; σχήματα Aps.*Rh.*p.333 H.; ἐπίρρημα Sch.Ar.*Nu.*1.

**σχετλιοποιός**, όν, *doing terrible things*, Sch.E.*Hec.*69.

**σχέτλιος**, α, ον, fem. σχετλίη Il.3.414, Od.23.150; σχέτλιαι 4.729; rarely **σχέτλιος**, ον E.*IT*651 (lyr.): (σχεθ-εῖν, v. *σχέθω). I. of persons, *able to hold out, unwearying, unflinching*, σ. ἐσσι, γεραιέ· σὺ μὲν πόνου οὔ ποτε λήγεις Il.10.164; σ. εἰς, Ὀδυσεῦ· περί τοι μένος οὐδέ τι γυῖα κάμνεις Od.12.279. 2. mostly in bad sense, *flinching from no cruelty* or *wickedness, merciless, headstrong*, in Hom. mostly of heroes, as Achilles, Il.9.630, 16.203; Hector, 17.150, 22.86; Patroclus, 18. 13; Odysseus, Od.11.474, al.; Heracles, Il.5.403; σ., οὐδὲ θεῶν ὄπιν αἰδέσατ' Od.21.28; of the Cyclops, 9.351,478; of Zeus, Il.2.112, Od. 3.161; of the gods generally, σχέτλιοί ἐστε, θεοί Il.24.33, Od.5.118; of Cronos, Hes.*Th.*488; of Odysseus and his companions, σχέτλιοι, οἳ.. Od.12.21; of women, 4.729, al.: so also in Att. of men, *wicked*, πῶς ἂν ἄνθρωποι -ώτεροι ἢ ἀνομώτεροι γένοιντο; Antipho 6.47, cf. D.30. 36; -ώτατος And.1.124, Isoc.5.103, etc.; σ. καὶ ἀναιδής D.19.16, etc.; of wild beasts, ὅσα σ. καὶ ἀνιηρά *savage*, Hdt.3.108. 3. *miserable, wretched*, A.*Pr.*644; freq. with a notion of contempt, ὦ σχετλιώτατε ἀνδρῶν *O most wretched fool!* Hdt.3.155; ὦ σχέτλιε S.*Ph.*369,930, E. *Alc.*824; ὦ σχετλία S.*Ant.*47: sts. c. gen., ὦ σχετλία..τῶν πόνων *because of sufferings*, E.*Hec.*783, cf. *Alc.*741 (anap.), *Andr.*1179 (lyr.). —This sense of *miserable* never occurs in Hom.; in Il.3.414, 18.13, the sense of *headstrong* should be retained. II. of things, first in Od., ὕπνος σ. *cruel* sleep, during which Odysseus was betrayed by his companions, 10.69; and in the phrase σ. ἔργα, *cruel, shocking, abominable* doings, 9.295, 22.413 (= ἀτασθαλίαι v. 416); opp. δίκη and αἴσιμα ἔργα, 14.83, cf. Hes.*Op.*238, Thgn.733, Hdt.6.138, etc.; σ. πέπονθα πράγματα Ar.*Pl.*856; τοῦτο δὴ τὸ σ. πάθημα X.*An.*7.6.30; also σχέτλια alone, σχέτλια παθεῖν E.*Supp.* 1074 (lyr.), *IA*932, etc.; σ. λέγεις καὶ ὑπερφυῆ Pl.*Grg.*467b; σ. καὶ δεινά Ar.*Ra.*612; δεινὰ καὶ σ. πείσεται Isoc.18.35, cf. E.*Cyc.*587; σχέτλιον *shocking*, *h.Ven.*254; σ. γε Ar.*Lys.*498 (anap.); ὃ δὲ πάντων -ώτατον Isoc.6.56; also σχέτλια [ἐστί], c. acc. et inf., *hard*, S.*Aj.* 887 (lyr.). III. Adv. -ίως Isoc.19.31: Sup. -ιώτατα f.l. in S.*Tr.* 879. [Hom. always puts σχέτλιος emphatically at the beginning of a line, exc. once in fem., Il.3.414; and twice in neut., Od.14.83, 22.413. He always uses the 1st syll. long, exc. in Il.3.414, where σχετλίη has the first syll. short, as in E.*Andr.*1179 (lyr.), *Cyc.*587, al., and Ar. ll.cc.]

**σχέτο**, v. ἔχω.

❋ **σχῆμα**, ατος, τό, (ἔχω, σχεῖν) *form, shape, figure*, E.*Ion* 238, Ar.*V.* 1170, Pl.*R.*601a, Thphr.*Ign.*52, etc.; καθ' Ἡρακλέα τὸ σ. καὶ τὸ λῆμ' ἔχων Ar.*Ra.*463; διερεισαμένη τὸ σ. τῇ βακτηρίᾳ Id.*Ec.*150; Ἱππομέδοντος σ. καὶ μέγας τύπος A.*Th.*488: in Trag. freq. in periphr., ὦ σ. πέτρας, = πέτρα, S.*Ph.*952; σ. καὶ πρόσωπον εὐγενὲς τέκνων E.*Med.* 1072; σ. δόμων Id.*Alc.*911 (anap.), cf. *Hec.*619; Ἀσιάτιδος γῆς σ. Id. *Andr.*1: in pl., of one person, φωτὸς κακούργου σχήματ' Id.*Fr.*210; μορφῆς σχῆμα or σχήματα, Id.*Ion* 992, *IT*292, cf. *IG*3.1417.14; τὴν αὐτὴν τοῦ σ. μορφήν Arist.*PA*640$^b$34 (but ἐν μορφῇ θεοῦ ὑπάρχων, opp. σχήματι εὑρεθεὶς ὡς ἄνθρωπος, *Ep.Phil.*2.6 and 8); τὰ σ. καὶ χρώματα Pl.*R.*373b; σχήμασι καὶ χρώμασι μιμεῖσθαι Arist.*Po.*1447$^a$19; κατὰ χρόαν ἢ ὄγκον ἢ σ. [τοῦ προσώπου] Gal.18(2).309; ὅσα παθήματα γίνεται ἀπὸ σχημάτων caused by *peculiar conformations*, Hp.*VM*22. b. *atom*, imagined as differing from other atoms mainly in shape, ἐκ περιφερῶν συγκεῖσθαι σχημάτων Democr.ap.Thphr.*Sens.*65; ἐκ μεγάλων σ. καὶ πολυγωνίων ib.66, cf. 67, al., *Od.*64. 2. *appearance*, opp. the reality, οὐδὲν ἄλλο πλὴν..σ. a mere *outside*, E.*Fr.*25, cf. 360.27, Pl.*R.*365c; *show, pretence*, ἦν δὲ τοῦτο..σ. πολιτικὸν τοῦ λόγου Th.8.89; οὐ σχήμασι, ἀλλὰ ἀληθείᾳ Pl.*Epin.*989c; σχήματι ξενίας *under the show* of.., Plu.*Dio* 16, etc. 3. *bearing, air, mien*, Hdt.1.60; τύραννον σ. ἔχειν S.*Ant.*1169; ἄφοβον δεικνὺς σ. X.*Cyr.*6.4.20; ταπεινὸν σ. ib.5.1.5; ὑπηρέτου σ. D.23.210; τῷ σχήματι, τῷ βλέμματι, τῇ φωνῇ Id.21.72; ὄμμασι καὶ σχήμασι καὶ βαδίσματι φαιδρός *gestures*, X.*Ap.*27, cf. *Mem.* 3.10.5; esp. *outside show, pomp*, τὸ τῆς ἀρχῆς σ. Pl.*Lg.*685c; *dignity, rank*, οὐ κατὰ σ. φέρειν τι in a manner not *dignified* or *seemly*, Plb.3.85.9, cf. 5.56.1, Plu.2.44a,631c, Luc.*Peregr.*25; πρεσβείας, ἱερείας σ., Aristid.1.490 J., *Inscr.Olymp.*941; ἔχει τι σ., c. inf., there's something to be said for.., E.*Tr.*470, cf. *IA*983; of the *stately air* of a horse, X.*Eq.*1.8, 7.10. 4. *fashion, manner*, ἑτέρῳ σ. ζητεῖν Hp.*VM*2; σ. μὲν γὰρ Ἑλλάδος στολῆς ὑπάρχει *fashion* of dress, S.*Ph.* 223; σ. τοῦ κόσμου E.*Ba.*832, 1*Ep.Cor.*7.31; σ. βίου, μάχης, E.*Med.* 1039, *Ph.*252 (lyr.); τούτῳ..κατῴκουν τῷ σ. Pl.*Criti.*112d. b. *dress, equipment*, ἀρχαίῳ σ. λαμπρός Ar.*Eq.*1331; βαβαιὰξ τοῦ σ. Id. *Ach.*64, cf. X.*Oec.*2.4, Theoc.10.35, App.*BC*1.16; τὸ τῆς πορφύρας σ., = Lat. *latus clavus*, *IGRom.*3.1422 (Prusias); ἐν τῷ σ. ἱερέ[ως] ib. 69.17 (ibid., cf. *Glotta* 14.80), cf. *Sammelb.*7449.10 (v A. D.), *PLond.*5. 1729.25 (vi A. D.). 5. *character, role*, μεταβαλεῖν τὸ σ. Pl.*Alc.*1.135d; πάντα σ. ποιεῖν Id.*R.*576a; ἐν μητρὸς σχήματι Id.*Lg.*918e, cf. 859a; ἀπολαβεῖν τὸ ἑαυτῶν σ. to recover their proper *character*, X.*Cyr.*7.1. 49. 6. *character, characteristic property* of a thing, [πόλεως] Th.6. 89; πολιτείας Pl.*Plt.*291d; βασιλείας σ. ἔχει *the form* of monarchy, Arist.*EN*1160$^b$25; τὸ σ. τῆς λέξεως δεῖ μήτε ἔμμετρον εἶναι μήτε ἄρρυθμον Id.*Rh.*1408$^b$21 (but τὰ σ. τῆς λέξεως the *forms* (*modes*) used in poetry, such as entreaty, threat, command, Id.*Po.*1456$^b$9); τὰ τῆς κωμῳδίας σ. its *characteristic forms*, ib.1448$^b$36; ἐν σχήματι νόμου in *form* of law, Pl.*Lg.*718b; ἐν ἀπολογίας σ. Isoc.15.8; ἐν μύθου σ. Arist.*Metaph.*1074$^b$2, cf. Pl.*Ti.*22c; τὸ τῆς διαίτης σ. Gal.15.582; αἱ κατὰ σχήματα πυρετῶν διαφοραί Id.19.183. 7. a *figure* in Dancing, Ar.*V.*1485: mostly in pl., *figures, gestures* (cf. σχημάτιον), E.*Cyc.* 221, Ar.*Pax* 323, Pl.*Lg.*669d, Epigr.ap.Plu.2.732f, etc.; σχήματα πρὸς τὸν αὐλὸν ὀρχεῖσθαι X.*Smp.*7.5; ἐν..μουσικῇ καὶ σχήματα..καὶ μέλη ἔνεστι *figures* and tunes, Pl.*Lg.*655a; also of *the postures* of an athlete, Isoc.15.183: generally, *posture, position*, Hp.*Off.*11, al., Ar. *Ra.*538 (lyr.), Thphr.*Lass.*3,14; of the foetus, Sor.2.55; τὸ τῆς κατακλίσεως σ. the patient's *attitude* as he lies in bed, Gal.16.578, cf. 665; cf. σχηματίζω II. 3. b. Rhet., *figure* of speech, Pl.*Ion* 536c, Cic.*Brut.* 37.141, etc.; [ἡ τοῦ Θουκυδίδου φράσις] πλήρης σχημάτων D.H.*Pomp.* 5, cf. *Amm.*2.2; for σ. Πινδαρικόν, etc., v. Hdn.*Fig.*p.100 S. c. in Logic, *figure* of a syllogism, Arist.*APr.*26$^b$33, al., Thphr.*Fr.*59. d. τὸ σ. τῆς λέξεως, both the *grammatical form* of a sentence, Arist.*SE* 166$^b$10, cf. Gal.16.709, etc.; and its *rhythmical form*, Arist.*Rh.* l.c. supr.6, etc. e. grammatical *form* of a word, Hp.*Vict.*1.23, D.T.635. 21, A.D.*Pron.*17.25, al. 8. *geometrical figure*, Arist.*de An.*414$^b$20, al., Onos.10.28; μονωτάτη πάντων ἀριθμῶν δυὰς σχήματος οὐκ ἔστιν ἐπιδεκτική *Theol.Ar.*7. b. *phase* of the moon, Ptol.*Tetr.*21, Vett.Val. 106.28. c. Astrol., *aspect*, Plot.2.3.1, Man.3.5,212, al. d. *configuration* of birds in augury, τοῖς τῶν γυναικῶν σχήμασι σῴζεσθαι to be saved by the *configurations* (of birds) appropriate to women, Gal.15. 445. 9. in Tactics, military *formation*, X.*An.*1.10.10. 10. = τὸ αἰδοῖον, Lxx *Is.*3.17.

**σχημᾰτ-ιαῖος**, α, ον, *adorned with insignia*, [ἀνδριάντας] *Supp. Epigr.*1.318 (Thrace, ii (?) A. D.). **-ίζω**, pf. Pass. ἐσχημάτισμαι, v. infr. II. 1; but in sense of Med., v. infr. I. 2. I. intr., *assume a certain form, figure, posture*, or *position*, ὅσα σχηματίζουσι τὰ στρατόπεδα ..ἐν ταῖς μάχαις Pl.*R.*526d, cf. Polyaen.5.16.1, Ascl.*Tact.*12.1; τὰ αἰσχρὰ καὶ πονηρὰ σχήματα σ. Pl.*Hp.Mi.*374b: abs., *gesticulate, dance figures*, Ar.*Pax* 324, *Fr.*678:—Med., Poll.4.95 (also σ. ἑαυτόν *put* oneself *in posture*, Luc.*Salt.*17), v. infr. II. 3; προστάσεως, ἣν πρὸς τοὺς ἔξω σχηματίζονται the pompous appearance, which *they assume*, Pl.*R.*577a. 2. Med., *demean oneself* in a certain way, *make a show of* being or doing, ἀγνοεῖ ταῦτα ἃ πρὸς τοὺς ἄλλους ὡς εἰδὼς ἐσχημάτισται Id.*Sph.*268a; σεμνύνεται ἐσχηματισμένη ὡς.. gives itself airs *under the pretence* that.., Id.*Grg.*511d: c. inf., σχηματίζονται ἀμαθεῖς εἶναι Id.*Prt.*342b; σχηματιζόμενος, opp. ἀληθῶς τι πεπονθώς, Id.*Phdr.* 255a. 3. Astrol., of a heavenly body, *to be in configuration*, Man.4.500:—Pass., Heph.Astr.1.9 (printed ἐσχατ.), Tz.*H.* 1.471. II. trans., *give* a certain *form to* a thing, *shape, fashion*, σ. τὸ ἁρμόσσον σχῆμα (sc. τὸ ὀθόνιον) *give* such *a form to* the cloth as will fit.., Hp.*Art.*37; τὰ ἁπλᾶ σώματα σ. Arist.*Cael.* 306$^b$3, cf. Phld.*Rh.*1.196 S.; τὸν ὄγκον Arist.*GC*327$^b$15; παρθένον ἀκέφαλον σ. Eratosth.*Cat.*9; ἕκαστον μέρος πρὸς τὸ βέλτιον D.S. 5.73; τὸ πρόσωπον εἰς ἡδονήν Ach.Tat.6.11; τὸν βραχίονα γυμνὸν οἷον ἐφ' ὕβρει Plu.*CG*13:—Med., σχηματίζεσθαι κόμην *arrange one's* hair, E.*Med.*1161:—Pass., τὰ κατὰ φύσιν ἐσχηματισμένα Arist.*Cael.* 302$^b$26; τῶν ἐσχ. τι [γίνεται] ἐξ ἀσχημοσύνης Id.*Ph.*188$^b$19, etc.; ἐσχημάτισται δ' ἀσπίς A.*Th.*465; τῶν -ιζομένων θεῶν the gods *who possess figure*, Dam.*Pr.*261; τὸ πρόσωπον τὸ -ισθέν Phld.*Mus.*p.73 K. 2. *deck out, dress up*, ἑαυτὸν ὡς κοσμιώτατα Luc.*Merc.Cond.*14, cf. *Fug.* 13, *JTr.*16, Jul.*ad Ath.*274c: Rhet., σ. λόγον Philostr.*VS*1.21.5, cf. 2.1.11; opp. εὐθέως εἰπεῖν, Aristid.*Rh.*1 p.462 S.:—Pass., ἐσχηματισμένοι περιέρχονται Lys.*Fr.*73; θεοὶ κατὰ τέχνην ἐσχηματισμένοι Luc. *JTr.*8; τὸ ἐσχηματισμένον *figurative style*, Demetr.*Eloc.*294, cf. D.H. *Rh.*8,9, Philostr.*VS*2.17; ἐσχηματισμένα ζητήματα Hermog.*Id.*1. 4. 3. *arrange in* certain *figures*, χορούς Chamael.ap.Ath.1.21f; σ. αὑτόν *pose* oneself, for being painted, ib.12.543f:—Pass. and Med., *put oneself in certain forms* or *postures, assume various shapes*, Hp.*Fract.*2; εἴθισται ἐσχηματίσθαι *to assume a position*, ib.15 (om. codd. MV, Gal.); ἐς σχήματα σχηματίζεσθαι Id.*Art.*10; of sick persons, Id.*Coac.*463; of the foetus, Sor.2.60; of actors, *gesticulate*, X.*Smp.*1.9; σχηματιζόμενοι ῥυθμοί *accompanied with gestures*, Arist.*Po.*1447$^a$27. 4. *adapt*, τι πρός τι *Gp.*10.4.1, cf. 10.75.9. 5. *form* a word, D.T.635.2, A.D. *Pron.*58.7, al., Sch.Od.17.134. 6. *use* σχήματα (v. σχῆμα 7d), σ. φορτικῶς D.H.*Isoc.*3; *construct*, περίοδοι ὁμοίως -ιζόμεναι Id.*Pomp.* 5, cf. Hermog.*Inv.*3.10. **-ικός**, ή, όν, *pertaining to phases*, αἱ ζ' -καὶ μορφαὶ τῆς σελήνης *Theol.Ar.*45. **-ιον**, τό, Dim. of σχῆμα: in pl., *the figures of a dance*, Λακωνικὰ σχημάτια Hdt.6.129; *figures* of speech, Longin.17.1. **-ισις**, εως, ἡ, *configuration*, Arist.*HA*537$^a$ 26, Epicur.*Ep.*1 p.7 U., Plot.4.4.34, Iamb.*in Nic.*p.61 P., Procl.*Par.*

*Ptol.*4. **-ισμός,** ὁ, *configuration,* οἱ κατὰ μῆνα σ. [τῆς σελήνης] Arist.*Cael.*297ᵇ26, cf. Gem.9.11, Ptol.*Tetr.*1, Porph.ap. Eus.*PE*3.11; τοῦ στόματος Arist.*Aud.*800ᵃ23, cf. Phld.*Mus.*p.73 K.; τῆς φλογός Thphr.*Ign.*54. **2.** *bearing, attitude,* ὅλον τὸν τοῦ σώματος σ. Pl.*R.*425b, cf. Zeno *Stoic.*1.58 (pl.), Hipparch.1.4.10, Plu.*Dem.*9, *Num.*8, *Dio* 13; σχηματισμοὶ προσώπου *expressions assumed by* .., D.H.*Dem.*54; τοῦ τε προσώπου καὶ τῶν χειρῶν Plu.2.1047a. **3.** in bad sense, *assumption of manner,* σχηματισμοῦ καὶ φρονήματος κενοῦ.. ἐμπιπλάμενος Pl.*R.*494d: generally, *assumption* of what does not belong to one, *pretence,* Plu.*Nic.*3, *Arat.*49. **II.** = σχῆμα, *shape,* even of something immutable, as an atom, Epicur.*Ep.*1 p.15 U. (pl.), al. **2.** the *atom* itself, ὁ πυρὸς ἀποτελεστικὸς σ. ἐξολισθαίνων ἀστραπὴν γεννᾷ Id.*Ep.*2 p.45, cf. p.46 U. **3.** in Tactics, *formation,* Ascl.*Tact.*12.1 (pl.). **III.** in language, ὁ ποιητικὸς σ. the poetical *formation* (πελειάς = Πλειάς), Ath.11.490d; πληθυντικὸς σ. a plural *form,* Dam.*Pr.*337. **2.** *figure* in a dance, Plot.4.4.33. **-ιστέον,** Medic., *one must place* the patient, ἐπὶ τὰ γόνατα Sor.2.59, cf. Paul. Aeg.3.76.

**σχημᾰτο-γρᾰφέω,** *describe figures,* Nicom.*Ar.*2.8, al.; *illustrate by a plan* or *figure,* Ph.*Bel.*62.25, Ath.Mech.39.7, Simp. *in Ph.*457.17. **-γρᾰφία,** ἡ, *figure described,* Nicom.*Ar.*2.8, Ptol.*Tetr.*142, Paul.Al.*L.*2, Simp. *in Cael.*428.3, *in Ph.*457.14. **2.** *plan* or *map* of land, *PMeyer* 1.20 (ii B.C.), *PSI*10.1118.10 (i A.D.). **-δεσμος,** ὁ, a kind of *bandage,* Orib.45.18.5. **-θήκη,** ἡ, *magazine of gestures,* of a parasite, Clearch.25. **-ποιέω,** *bring into a certain form* or *shape,* σ. τι οἷον ἂν θέλωσι Thphr.*HP*9.4.10; -ποιοῦσα γραμμή a line *forming a figure,* Procl. *in Euc.*p.111 F.:—Pass., *take a certain shape* or *posture,* X.*Eq.*10.5: Rhet., *to have a particular character* or *air,* Aristid.*Rh.*2 p.535 S. **2.** Med., *represent in pantomime,* Poll.4.95. **-ποιία,** ἡ, *configuration, grouping,* of a constellation, Eratosth.*Cat.*3. **2.** in writings, *mannerism,* Aristid.*Rh.*2 p.535 S. (pl.). **3.** *pantomimic gesticulation,* Ath.14.628e.

**σχημᾰτότης,** ητος, ἡ, late form for σχῆμα, Gal.19.473,475, Herm. ap.Stob.1.4.8.

**σχημᾰτουργ-έομαι,** *to be fashioned,* of the foetus, Gal.19.177. **-ία,** ἡ, *configuration,* of the planets, *Cat.Cod.Astr.*1.148 (pl.).

**σχῆσις·** ἕξις, ὁρμή, Hsch. **σχητηρίαν·** ἄγκυραν, Id. **σχίδα·** σχίδος σινδόνος, πῆγμα, Id.

**σχῐδᾰκ-ηδόν,** Adv. *splinter-wise,* Dsc.5.106; esp. of fractures of the bones, Erot. s. v. ἀτρεκέως, Sor.*Fract.*10, Gal.10.424. **-ώδης,** ες, *like a splinter,* implied by ὑποσχιδακώδης (q.v.).

**σχῐδᾰνόπους,** = σχιζόπους (q.v.), Arist.*Frr.*345, al.

**σχίδαξ** [ῐ], ἄκος, ὁ, = σχίζα, Lxx 3*Ki.*18.33, D.S.13.84, *AP*6.231 (Phil.), Dsc.1.98, Apollod.*Poliorc.*145.11; of the *bars* of a cancellum, Lyd.*Mag.*3.37; *poles* of a chair, ib.1.32.

**σχίδιον** [ῐ], τό, Dim. of σχίζα, in Lat. form *schidium,* Vitr.2.1.4. **II.** = βάθρον 6, Ruf.ap.Orib.49.26.1. **III.** σχίδια· ὠμόλινα, Hsch.

**σχίδος·** τὴν ἀπόσχισιν, Hsch., cf. eund. s. v. σχίδα.

**σχίζ-α,** ης, ἡ, (σχίζω) *piece of wood cut off, lath, splinter,* σχίζῃ δρυός Od.14.425, cf. Ar.*Pax* 1032: pl., *wood cleft small,* esp. *firewood,* καῖε δ' ἐπὶ σχίζῃς [τοὺς μηρούς] Il.1.462, cf. *PCair.Zen.*191.5 (iii B.C.), *IG* 2².1366.11; τὰ μὲν.. σχίζῃσιν ἀφύλλοισιν κατέκαιον Il.2.425. **2.** *shaft, dart,* Lxx 1*Ki.*20.20 sq., 1*Ma.*10.80, *AP*6.282 (Theod.); so σχίζαι εἰς βέλη καταπαλτῶν *IG*2².1629.996. **-ίας,** ου, ὁ, *long, lathy,* Cratin.447, Dicaearch.Hist.10, *PPetr.*3 p.27 (iii B.C.), *PCair. Zen.*374.5 (iii B.C.); of athletes, Philostr.*Gym.*37, 38. **-ίον,** τό, Dim. of σχίζα, Poll.10.111, Alciphr.*Fr.*6.

**σχιζογυάνδρους·** τοὺς συκοφάντας, Hsch. (= *Com.Adesp.*1378).

**σχιζο-ποδία,** ἡ, *possession of parted toes,* Arist.*PA*643ᵇ31, *Metaph.* 1038ᵃ15. **-πους,** -πουν, gen. -ποδος, *with parted toes,* opp. στεγανόποους (web-footed), Id.*HA*593ᵃ28, *PA*643ᵇ32. **-πτερος,** ον, *with cloven,* i. e. *feathered, wings,* of birds, opp. bats and winged insects (ὁλόπτερα), Id.*IA*710ᵃ5, *PA*697ᵇ11.

❀ **σχίζω,** Hdt.2.17, S.*El.*99 (anap.), etc.: poet. impf. σχίζον Pi.*P.* 4.228: fut. σχίσω Lxx *Su.*55: aor. ἔσχισα Od.4.507 (ἀπο-), *h.Merc.* 128, etc., Ep. σχίσσα Hes.*Sc.*428:—Pass., fut. σχισθήσομαι Lxx *Za.* 14.4: pf. ἔσχισμαι (v. infr.):—*split, cleave,* ῥινὸν ὀνύχεσσι Hes. l. c.; ἔσχισε δώδεκα μοίρας, i. e. *divided* them *into* twelve parts, *h.Merc.* l. c.; σ. νῶτον γᾶς, of the plough, Pi. l. c.; σχίσσαις κεραυνῷ Ζεὺς χθόνα Id. *N.*9.24; ποδὶ γᾶν Id.*Fr.*167; κάρα πελέκει S. l. c.; esp. of wood, X.*An.* 1.5.12, etc.; of the wind, σ. περὶ πρῴραν τὰ κύματα Simon.25 (dub.); but πρῷρα σ. τὸ κῦμα Luc.*Am.*6; [θάλασσα] σχιζομένη ταῖς κώπαις *Placit.*3.3.2; ἔσχισε νῆα θάλασσα *shattered* it, *AP*9.40 (Zos.); σ. ὑποδήματα *cut out,* opp. νευρορραφεῖν, X.*Cyr.*8.2.5 (cf. πρόσχισμα); *tear,* ἱμάτιον *Gloss.*; τριβώνιον ἐσχισμένον *BGU*928.20,22 (iii A.D.); οἱ ἀποθανόντες ἐσχισμένοις ἐνειλοῦνται ῥάκεσιν ὡς καὶ τὰ βρέφη Artem.1.13. **2.** generally, *part, separate, divide,* Νεῖλος μέσην Αἴγυπτον σχίζων Hdt. l. c., cf. 4.49; σ. διχῇ τὸ γένος Pl.*Sph.*264d; κατὰ μῆκος Id.*Ti.*36b; σ. τὰς φλέβας *divide* them, ib.77d:—Pass., σχισθέντα A.*Ag.*623; φλὲψ σχιζομένη Hp.*Art.*20; ἐσχίσθη ὁ ποταμός Hdt.1.75; Νεῖλος σχίζεται τριφασίας ὁδοὺς *branches* into three channels, Id.2.17, cf. 15 (so ὁ λύχνος ἔσχισται διδύμην φλόγα *AP*12.199 (Strat.)); περὶ ὃ σχίζεται τὸ τοῦ Νείλου ῥεῦμα Pl.*Ti.*21e; σχιζομένης τῆς ὁδοῦ Hdt.7.31; ἡ στρατιὴ ἐσχίζετο the army *divided,* Id.8.34; of a bird's wings (cf. σχιζόπτερος), Arist.*PA*642ᵇ28; of feet divided into toes (cf. σχιζόπους), Id.*HA*494ᵃ12; and of various parts of the body, ib.495ᵇ4, 507ᵃ13; *branch off,* ἀπὸ [τοῦ στελέχους] Thphr.*HP*1.1.9; φύλλα ἐσχισμένα εἰς ε' μοίρας Dsc.4.41. **3.** σχίζειν γάλα *make* milk *curdle,* i. e. *separate* the whey from the curds, Id.2.70; cf. σχίσις 2. **II.** metaph. of *divided* opinions, σφεων ἐσχίζοντο αἱ γνῶμαι Hdt.7.219, cf. X.*Smp.*4.59; ἐσχίσθησαν ταῖς γνώμαις Gal.16.728. (Cf. Lat. *scindo,* Goth. *skaidan* 'separate', etc.)

**σχινδάλᾰμος, -αλμός,** ὁ, Att. for σκινδάλαμος (q.v.).

**σχίνδαν·** θερμάστριον, Hsch.

**σχινδύλησις** [ῠ], εως, ἡ, *cleaving into small pieces,* Hp.ap.Gal.19.145.

**σχίν-ειος** [ῐ], α, ον, = σχίνινος, Theognost.*Can.*55. **-έλαιον,** τό, *mastich oil,* made from the berries of the σχῖνος 1, Dsc.1.41 (in lemmate), Suid. **-ίζω,** *clean by chewing mastich-wood,* τοὺς ὀδόντας Iamb.*VP*28.154:—abs. in Med., *EM*740.49, Phot. **II.** Med., of certain movements in a dance, Ath.14.621c. **-ῐνος,** η, ον, *made from mastich,* Hp.*Nat.Mul.*109, Dsc.1.41,70, Sor.1.121, etc. **-ίς,** ίδος, ἡ, *berry of the mastich,* Thphr.*HP*9.4.7.

**σχῑνοκέφᾰλος,** ον, (σχῖνος II) *with a squill-shaped,* i. e. *peaked, head,* epith. of Pericles, Cratin.71, cf. Plu.*Per.*3, 13, Poll.2.43 (with v.l. ἐχιν-).

❀ **σχῖνος,** ἡ, *mastich, Pistacia Lentiscus,* Hdt.4.177, Thphr *HP*9.1.2, Lxx *Su.*54, Sor.1.121, al., Gal.6.644; trodden on by goats, Theoc.5.129, Babr.3.4. **II.** = σκίλλα, Epich.160, Hp.*Mul.*2.201 (cf. Gal. 19.145), Cratin.232, Ar.*Pl.*720, *Fr.*255, Anaxandr.50, Thphr.*CP*5.6.10, *Sign.*55.

**σχῖνο-τρώκτης,** ου, Dor. **-τας,** ὁ, *one who chews mastich-wood* to make his teeth white, Luc.*Lex.*12, Zen.5.96:—also **-τρώξ,** ὁ, Suid.

**σχίσ-ις** [ῐ], εως, ἡ, (σχίζω) *cleavage, parting,* Pl.*Phd.*97a, 101c; of roads, ib.108a; of the wings of birds (cf. σχιζόπτερος), Arist.*HA* 532ᵃ26; of the feet of animals (cf. σχιζόπους), Id.*PA*663ᵃ31; of a plant, Dsc.4.187; of rivers, Plu.2.93f; κατὰ τὴν σχίσιν at the *cleavage* (of the gullet into oesophagus and trachea), cj. for κατὰ σχέσιν (v.l. κατάσχεσιν) in Archig.ap.Orib.8.1.18; ἀδένες.. σχίσεις ἀγγείων στηρίζοντες Gal.6.674, cf. 15.532. **2.** *curdling,* τοῦ γάλακτος (v. σχίζω 1.3) Id.6.694, Philum.ap.Orib.45.29.10. ❀ **-μα,** ατος, τό, *cleft, division,* as of hoofs, Arist.*HA*499ᵃ27 (pl.); of leaves, Thphr.*HP*3.11.1; *rent* in a garment, *Ev.Matt.*9.16. **II.** *division* of opinion, *Ev.Jo.*9.16. **III.** *the vulva,* Ruf.*Onom.*110. **IV.** name of an ὀρχηστικὸν σχῆμα, Hsch. **V.** *ploughing, PLond.*5.1796.7 (vi A.D.). **-μᾰτώδης,** ες, *of the nature of a* σχίσμα, Hsch. (σχιμ- cod.). ❀ **-μή,** ἡ, *cleft,* Lxx *Is.*2.21, al., Hsch. **-μός,** ὁ, *cleaving,* A.*Ag.*1149, *Placit.*3.3.3. **-τός,** ή, όν, (σχίζω) *cloven, divided,* κέλευθος A.*Fr.*173; ὁδὸς S.*OT*733, E.*Ph.*38; ἄντυξ Id.*Rh.*373 (lyr.); λίνον σ. *lint,* Hp.*Nat.Mul.*53 (but cf. 4 infr.); πέρκη σ. a *split* perch, Antiph.132; 'Αργεῖαι σ. a kind of women's shoes, Eup.266; σ. χιτωνίσκος a tunic *open at the side,* Apollod.Com.12; without χιτωνίσκος, *PSI*4.341.7 (iii B.C.), *Schwyzer* 462 *B* 30 (Tanagra, iii B.C.); σχιστὰς ἕλκειν, of a certain dance (cf. σχίσμα IV), Poll.4.105. **2.** *cloven-hoofed,* opp. μῶνυξ, Pl.*Plt.*265d; similarly of wings, etc., Arist *PA* 692ᵇ12, etc. **3.** σ. γάλα *curdled* milk (v. σχίζω 1.3), Dsc.2.70, Gal. 12.292. **4.** λίνον σ. *fine* flax, Lxx *Is.*19.9. **II.** *that may be split* or *cleft, divisible,* σ. κατὰ μῆκος Arist.*HA*515ᵇ15, cf. *Mete.*386ᵇ26, etc.; σ. λίθος, prob. *talc,* Dsc.5.127, cf. 106, etc.; σ. κρόμμυα (v. κρόμμυον II) Thphr.*HP*7.4.7.

**σχοίᾰτο** (Il.2.98), **σχοίην,** v. ἔχω.

**σχοινανθ-ᾶτον,** τό, *wine made with* σχοινάνθη, Orib.5.33.11. **-η,** ἡ, *flower of* σχοῖνος, *Hippiatr.*129.54. **-ιον,** τό, Dim. of foreg., Alex.Trall.9.3.

**σχοινᾶς,** ᾶ, ὁ, *rope-maker, PSI*7.780.5 (iv A.D.), *Gloss.*

**Σχοινάτας,** ὁ, epith. of Asclepius ἐν τῷ Ἕλει, *IG*5(1).602.10 (Sparta, iii A.D.).

**σχοινεύς,** έως, ὁ, an unknown bird, Ant.Lib.7.

**Σχοινηΐς,** ΐδος, ἡ, epith. of Aphrodite, Lyc.832.

❀ **σχοιν-ιά,** ἡ, (σχοῖνος) *clump* or *bunch of rushes,* Thphr.*HP*4.12.2; βοτρύων σχοινιαί *clusters* of grapes, J *AJ*12.2.10, prob. cj. in Aristeas 75. **II.** (σχοῖνος III) *the wall of a city* or *part thereof,* Str.8.6.21, dub. l. in *CIG*(add.)2056*g* (Odessus). **-ιαία,** ἡ, = foreg. II, *IPE*1².32 *B* 58 (Olbia, iii B.C.), 180.4 (Odessus, iii B.C.).

**σχοινίκλος** or **σχοινίλος,** ὁ, a bird, prob. a *wagtail, motacilla,* Arist.*HA*593ᵇ4; cf. σχοινίων.

**σχοιν-ῐκός,** ή, όν, *of the* σχοῖνος (q.v.), ἄνθος *Gp.*20.15; σχοινικά, τά, *goods made of it, BGU*1121.21 (i B.C.). **-ῐνος,** η, ον, (σχοῖνος) *of rushes, made of rushes,* τεύχη E.*Cyc.*208; ἡνίαι Id.*Fr.* 284; ἠθμός Cratin.132; φορμός Ar.*Fr.*172; πιαγίς *IG*11(2).287 *B* 50 (Delos, iii B.C.); κύκλος Str.12.5.4. ❀ **-ίον,** τό, Dim. of σχοῖνος II, *small rope, cord* or *thread,* Hdt.1.26, 5.85,86, Ar.*Ach.*22, etc.; simply, *rope,* e. g. for mooring a ship, *IG*2².1611.254 (pl.); ὅστις ἀναρριχᾶται διὰ σχοινίου Gal.6.140; ἐπὶ σχοινίου περιπατεῖν Arr.*Epict.*3.12.2: prov., τὸ ἐκ τῆς ψάμμου σχοινίον πλέκειν Aristid.2.309 J.; πλεῖς τὴν θάλατταν σχοινίων πωλουμένων; when there are *ropes* for sale? Antiph. 100, cf. *Com.Adesp.*296. **2.** *measuring-line,* Arist.*Mech.*853ᵇ5, Lxx 2*Ki.*8.2, *OGI*669.60 (Egypt, i A.D.): hence, **b.** *measure, portion,* Lxx *Ps.*15.6. **c.** 100 *cubits, the side of an* ἄρουρα, *PTeb.*13.13 (ii B.C.). **3.** *girdle,* Lxx *Je.*45(38).11, *Ep.Je.*43. **4.** σ. βοτρύων, = σχοινιά 1, Aristeas 75 codd. (but σχοινιαί is prob. cj.). **II.** metaph., λύειν σχοινίον μεριμνᾶν the *cord* of cares (which binds one), Pi.*Fr.*248. **III.** Com., *membrum virile,* Ar.*V.*1342.

**σχοινιο-πλόκος,** ὁ, *rope-maker, PGoodsp.Cair.*30 ii 1, al. (ii A.D.), *POxy.*934.4 (iii A.D.), etc. **-στρόφος,** ὁ, *rope-maker,* Poll.7.160; cf. σχοινοστρόφος. **2.** *water-drawer,* Sch.Ar.*Ra.*1332. **II.** σχοινιόστροφον, τό, = ἵππουρις, Ps.-Dsc.4.46. **2.** = κάνναβις ἥμερος,

Id.3.148. **-συμβολεύς**, έως, ὁ, = σχοινιοστρόφος I. 1, Poll.7.160, *AB*302:—also **-σύμβολος**, ὁ, Sch.Ar.*Pax* 37 (cod. Ven. σχοινιοσυνδέταις).

⊛ **σχοιν-ίς** (A), ίδος, ἡ, = σχοινίον, *rope, cord*, Theoc.23.51. 2. *wall-decoration* in form of a rope, *Supp.Epigr.*4.453.17 (Didyma, ii B.C.); similar decoration of a silver cup, *OGI*214.55 (ibid., iii B.C.). II. v.l. for Σχοινῆς (q.v.), Lyc.832. **-ίς** (B), ίδος [ῐ], poet. fem. of σχοίνινος, σχοινίδι κύρτῃ Nic.*Al.*625. **-ισμα**, ατος, τό, *piece of land measured out by the* σχοῖνος, *portion, allotment*, Lxx *De.*32.9, *Jo.*17.14, al. 2. generally, *division, portion* of a people, ib.2*Ki.*8.2. **-ισμός**, ὁ, *measurement* of land, *PTeb.*12.7, 61 (b). 333 (ii B.C.), *Sammelb.*7422.13 (i B.C.), *PAmh.*2.68.4 (i A.D., pl.); as a form of hard labour, Plu.*Luc.*20. II. = foreg. I, *allotment*, Lxx *Jo.*17.5. **-ῖτις**, ιδος, ἡ, *made of rushes*, καλύβη *AP*7.295 (Leon.). ⊛ **-ίων**, ωνος, ὁ, a bird, perh. = σχοινί(κ)λος, Arist.*HA*610$^{a}$8. II. *an effeminate air on the flute*, Plu.2.1132d, 1133a, Poll.4.65,79.

**σχοινο-βάτης** [ᾰ], ου, ὁ, (βαίνω) *rope-dancer*, *Cat.Cod.Astr.*8(4). 213, Man.4.287, *Gloss.*; Lat. *schoenobates*, Juv.3.77:—hence **-βατία**, Ion. **-ίη**, ἡ, *rope-dancing*, interpol. in Hp.*Vict.*3.68; **-βατική** (sc. τέχνη), Sch.D.T.p.110 H. **-δρομία**, Ion. **-ίη**, ἡ, *rope-dancing*, f.l. in Hp.*Vict.*3.68. **-δρόμος**, ὁ, *rope-climber*, ὁ ἐν τῇ νηῒ σ. Hsch. s.v. σχοινίον. ⊛ **-ειδής**, ές, *like a rope* or *cord*, πλέγμα J.*AJ* 12.2.9; ῥαβδία Dsc.4.164. **-μέτρησις**, εως, ἡ, *land-survey*, τῆς Συρίας Alex.Polyh.22. **-πλεκτος**, ον, *plaited of rushes*, ἄγγος Arar.8. **-πλοκικός**, ή, όν, *of* or *for rope-making*, σπάρτον Str.3. 4.9. **-πλόκος**, ὁ, *maker of rush-ropes* or *mats*, Hp.*Epid.*4.2, Sch. Ar.*Pax* 36, Suid. **-πώλης**, ου, ὁ, *rope-seller*, *Gloss.*, prob. l. in *CIG*(add.)4812*d* (Egypt). **-ρραφέω**, *stitch with cord*, Sch.D *Il.*10. 262 (Pass.).

⊛ **σχοῖνος**, ὁ, also ἡ (Ar.*Fr.*34, *Pl.*541 (anap.), Theoc.7.133, Call.*Fr.* 481, Dsc.4.52, etc.):—*rush*, Hdt.4.190, etc.; πλεκτὴ σ. Ar.*Fr.* l. c.; στιβὰς σχοίνων Id.*Pl.* l. c. (anap.); σχοῖνοι ἐπὶ τὰς ὀροφάς *IG*2$^{2}$.1672. 101; esp. *camel-hay*, *Cymbopogon Schoenanthus*, Thphr.*HP*9.7.1, *CP*6.18.1, *Od.*25, 33, D.S.2.49, Dsc.1.17; σ. εὔοσμος Thphr.*CP*6.18. 1; σ. εὐώδης Hp.*Mul.*1.78, cf. 2.192, *Nat.Mul.*33, Aret.*CA*2.8. b. σ. ὀξύς, σ. ἑλεία, σ. λεία, = ὀξύσχοινος, Thphr.*HP*4.12.1, Dsc.4.52, Gal.12.136; σ. κάρπιμος, = μελαγκρανίς, Thphr.*HP*4.12.1; σ. Εὐριπική, = ὁλόσχοινος, Dsc.4.52, cf. Plin.*HN*21.119 (its flower was called σχοίνου ἄνθος, Arist.*Fr.*110). 2. *reed*, used as an *arrow* or *javelin*, Batr.253 (as v.l.); as a 'thorn in the side', Ar.*Ach* 230; as a spit, Pl.Com.201; as a pen, Lxx *Je.*8.8; as a means of exploring a narrow and crooked passage in the skull, καθιέντας ἢ σ. ἢ ὑέλαν τρίχα Gal.*UP* 9.10. 3. *rush-bed*, Od.5.463, Pi.*O.*6.54, Arist.*Mete.*359$^{b}$1. II. *anything twisted* or *plaited of rushes*, esp. *rope, cord*, Orac.ap.Hdt.1. 66, 5.16, Pl.*Ti.*78b, etc. 2. *fence* round a garden, *APl.*4.255. 3. *strap* of a bed, *AP*5.293.12 (Agath., pl.). III. a *land-measure*, used esp. in Egypt, δύναται ὁ σ., μέτρον ἐὸν Αἰγύπτιον, ἑξήκοντα στάδια Hdt.2.6; but varying in length acc. to Artemid.ap.Str.17. 1.24, cf. ib.41, Plin.*HN*6.124; = 40 στάδια acc. to Eratosth.ap.Plin. *HN*12.53; 30 or 48 acc. to Hero *Geom.*23.20,43; τῷ μεγάλῳ (corrected to δικαίῳ) σ. *PCair.Zen.*132.7 (iii B.C.), cf. 172.4, al.; also τέχνῃ κρίνετε, μὴ σχοίνῳ Περσίδι τὴν σοφίην Call.*Aet.Oxy.*2079.18 (cf. *Fr.*481).

**σχοινο-στρόφος**, ον, = σχοινιοστρόφος I. 1, Plu.2.473c. **-τένεια**, ἡ, poet. fem. of sq., formed like ἡδυέπεια, μουνογένεια, of doubtful meaning, σ. ἀοιδὰ διθυράμβων Pi.*Fr.*79A (= *Dith.Oxy.*1604 ii 1); perh. *moving straight forward*, rather than *prolix*. **-τενής**, ές, (τείνω) *stretched out like a measuring line*: hence, I. *drawn in a straight line*, διώρυχες, διέξοδοι, Hdt.1.189,199; σχοινοτενὲς ποιήσασθαι to draw *a straight line*, Id.7.23. 2. metaph., *stretched out, prolix*, ᾄσματα Philostr.*Her.*19.17; ἔννοιαι Eust.946.8; of rhetorical κῶλα exceeding a certain length, Hermog.*Inv.*1.5, 4.4. Adv. **-τενῶς** ib. 4.3. II. *twisted* or *plaited of rushes*, σπυρίδες *AP*6.5 (Phil.). **-τονος**, ον, *stretched with rushes* or *cords*, δίφρος Hp.*Steril.*230.

**σχοινουργ-ία**, ἡ, = σχοινισμός I, *PRyl.*171.18 (i A.D.), *PFlor.*20.17 (ii A.D.). **-ός**, ὁ, *land surveyor*, *PLond.*3.1171.64 (i A.D.).

**σχοινοῦς**, οῦσσα, οῦν, contr. for *σχοινόεις, *grown over with rushes*, Str.3.4.9; as place-name, *Schwyzer* 157.23 (Megara), *IG*2$^{2}$.2498.12, etc.

**σχοινο-φῐλίνδᾰ**, Adv. *a game somewhat like our hunt-the-slipper*, Poll.9.115. **-φόρος**, ον, *carrying rushes, cords*, or *mats*, *EM*740. 38. **-χάλῑνος** [ᾰ], ον, *with rein of twisted rushes*, ἵπποι Str.17. 3.7.

**σχοινώδης**, ες, *full of rushes*, ὄχθαι Nic.*Al.*152. 2. *stringy*, ῥάβδοι, φύλλα, Dsc.3.109, 4.46, cf. 148,175.

⊛ **σχολ-άζω**, Boeot. **-άδδω** *IG*7.2849.6 (Haliartus):—*to have leisure* or *spare time, to be at leisure, have nothing to do*, σὺ δ' ἢν σχολάσῃς Ar. *Lys.*412, cf. Th.4.4, etc.; διὰ τὸ μὴ σχολάζειν ὑπὸ πολέμων because *they have no leisure left* by the wars, Pl.*Lg.*694e; ἀσχολούμεθα ἵνα σχολάζωμεν Arist.*EN*1177$^{b}$5; σ. καλῶς *spend one's leisure* well, Id. *Pol.*1337$^{b}$31; σ. ἐλευθερίως καὶ σωφρόνως ib.1326$^{b}$31: c. inf., *have leisure* or *time to do* a thing, X.*Cyr.*2.1.9, 8.1.18, Pl.*Lg.*763d, etc. 2. *loiter, linger*, A.*Supp.*207, 883, E.*Hec.*730, D.3.35. II. σ. ἀπό τινος *have rest* or *respite* from a thing, *cease* from doing, X.*Cyr.* 7.5.52; ἀπὸ τοῦ Κρώμνου *were set free* from the operations at K., Id. *HG*7.4.28; also σ. ἔργων Plu.*Nic.*28. III. c. dat., *have leisure, time*, or *opportunity for* a thing, *devote one's time to* a thing, πάντα τὸν βίον ἐσχόλακεν [ἐν] τούτῳ D.22.4; σ. φιλοσοφίᾳ, μουσικῇ, etc., Luc.*Macr.*4, *VH*2.15; μόνῃ σ. ὑγιείᾳ Gal.6.168; τῇ γῇ, i.e. agriculture, *Sammelb.* 4284.15 (iii A.D.); so πρὸς ταῦτα X.*Mem.*3.6.6; πρὸς τοῖς ἰδίοις Arist. *Pol.*1308$^{b}$36; ἐπί τινος Id.*PA*682$^{a}$34; περὶ λόγους Plu.*Brut.*22; πρὸς ἐννοίᾳ..πρὸς αὐτόν Id.*Num.*14. 2. c. dat. pers., *devote oneself to*.., τοῖς φίλοις X.*Cyr.*7.5.39; ἑαυτοῖς Gal.6.810; ὁ στρατηγὸς..τοῖς διαφέρουσιν ἐσχόλασεν Wilcken *Chr.*41 i 18 (iii A.D.); esp. of students, *study, attend lectures*, ἐπὶ Παλλαδίῳ Phld.*Acad.Ind.*p.88 M.; σ. τινί *devote oneself* to a master, *attend his lectures*, σ. Καρνεάδῃ, Ἰσοκράτει, ib.p.89 M., Plu.2.844b; τοῖς φιλοσόφοις *IG*2$^{2}$.1028.34 (ii/i B.C.); μετ' Ἐπικούρου Phylarch.24 J.; παρά τισι Alciphr.1.34. 3. abs., *devote oneself to learning*: hence, *give lectures* (cf. σχολή II), Apollon.Perg. *Con.* 1 *Praef.*; σ. Ἀθήνησιν Phld.*Rh.*1.95 S.; ἐν Λυκείῳ D.H.*Amm.*1.5, cf. Plu.*Dem.*5: c. acc. neut., ἅπερ ἐσχολάσαμεν Demetr.Lac.*Herc.*1013. 18; τὰ περὶ τοῦ τέλους σχολασθέντα *lectures* upon.., S.E.*M.*11.167; of a gladiator, *to be master of a school* (*ludus*), εἰς Ἔφεσον *Rev.Arch.*30 (1929).24 (Gortyn). IV. of a place, *to be vacant, unoccupied*, Plu.*CG* 12, Jul.*Caes.*316c: c. dat., *to be reserved for*, τὸ ἀπ' οὐρανοῦ κορυφῆς μέχρι σελήνης θεοῖς καὶ ἄστροις..σχολάζει Herm.ap.Stob.1.49.68. **-αῖος**, α, ον, *leisurely, tardy*, σ. κομισθῆναι to go *leisurely*, Th.3.29; σ. ποιεῖν τὴν πορείαν X.*An.*4.1.13; σχολαῖται ἀπαλλαγαί Hp.*Dieb.Judic.*10; βίος Plu.2.603e. Adv. **-αίως** X.*An.*1.5.8, Arist.*EN*1171$^{b}$24, etc.: Comp. σχολαίτερα Hdt.9.6; **-αίτερον** Th.4.47, Pl.*R.*610d: Sup. **-αίτατα** X.*HG*6.3.6; but also σχολαιότερον, **-ότατα**, Id.*An.*1.5.9, *Lac.*11.3, Gal.6.391 (Adj.); **-οτέρως** Dsc.*Ther.Praef.* **-αιότης**, ητος, ἡ, *leisureliness, laziness*, Th.2.18, Chor.15.7 F.-R.

⊛ **σχολάριος** [ᾰ], ὁ, *one of the Imperial guards*, Procop.*Arc.*24, Just. *Nov.*117.11, Agath.5.15.

**σχολαρχ-έω**, *to be the head of a school*, D.L.4.1, al. **-ης**, ου, ὁ, *head of a school*, Id.5.2, *PRyl.*397.3 (iii A.D.). **-ικός**, ή, όν, *professorial*, prob. for σχολαργικός in Vett.Val.15.27.

**σχολασ-τήριον**, τό, *place for passing leisure in*, Plu.*Luc.*42, Moschio ap.Ath.5.207e. **-τής**, οῦ, ὁ, *one who lives at ease, man of leisure*, *Com.Adesp.*119, Lxx *Ex.*5.17, Plu.*Brut.*3. II. as Adj., *leisurely, idle*, βίος Id.*Cic.*3, 2.135b; ἀργὸς καὶ σ. ὄχλος Id.*Sol.*22. **-τικός**, ή, όν, *inclined to ease, enjoying leisure*, αἱ **-κώτεραι** πόλεις Arist.*Pol.* 1322$^{b}$37, cf. 1341$^{a}$28; σύλλογοι σ. *lounging* parties, ib.1313$^{b}$4; τὸ σ. *leisure*, Id.*EN*1177$^{b}$22. 2. Astrol., σ. τόπος = ἀργός II. 4, Vett.Val. 186.3. II. *devoting one's leisure to learning, learned man, scholar*, Thphr.ap.D.L.5.37, Posidon.36 J., *CIG*2746 (Aphrodisias), al., *Sammelb.*1921, Plu.*Cic.*5. 2. *academic, theoretical*, ῥήτορες, opp. ἔμπρακτοι, Phld.*Rh.*2.265 S. 3. freq. in bad sense, *pedant, learned simpleton*, Arr.*Epict.*1.11.39, M.Ant.1.16, Hierocl.*Facet.*263, al. III. *advocate*, Phoeb.*Fig.*3; as an officially recognized *legal adviser*, *OGI* 693 (iii A.D.), *PSI*1.45.2 (v A.D.), *PMasp.*2 ii 2, al. (vi A.D.), etc.; ἀπὸ σχολαστικῶν, = *ex-σχολαστικός*, *PLond.*5.1701.14 (vi A.D.); esp. *public advocate*, Lat. *defensor civitatis*, *IGRom.*4.765 (Phrygia); σ. καὶ ἔκδικος *BGU*1094.1 (vi A.D.).

**σχολεαῖον**, gloss on ἀσπερχές, Hsch.

⊛ **σχολεῖον**, τό, *school*, Arr.*Epict.*3.23.30. II. perh. *burial-place*, (last) *resting-place*, *BCH*10.414 (Thyatira), *Supp.Epigr.*4.543 (Ephesus).

**σχολερός**, ά, όν, *idle*, σχολερὸν προσθεῖναι τὰς αἰτίας τῷ γράμματι *a waste of time*, Sever.*Clyst.*5.

⊛ **σχολή**, ἡ, *leisure, rest, ease*, Pi.*N.*10.46, Hdt.3.134, etc.; opp. ἀσχολία, Arist.*Pol.*1334$^{a}$15, etc.; σχολὴν ἄγειν to *be at leisure, enjoy ease, keep quiet*, Hdt. l.c., E.*Med.*1238, Th.5.29; ἐπί τινι *for* a thing, Pl.*Ap.*36d; περί τι Antip.*Stoic.*3.256; πρός τι Pl.*Phdr.*229e, Arr.*Epict.*1.27.15; τινι Luc.*Cal.*15; σ. ἀγαγεῖν ἐπί τινα to *give up one's time* to him, Id.*DDeor.*12.2, etc.; σ. ἔχειν to *have leisure*, E.*Andr.* 732, Pl.*Lg.*813c, etc.; ἀμφὶ ἑαυτόν for one's own business, X.*Cyr.*7. 5.42; σ. ποιεῖσθαι to find leisure, πρός τι Id.*Mem.*2.6.4: c. inf., Pl. *Ion* 530d; μὴ σχολὴν τίθει, i.e. make haste, A.*Ag.*1059; ἡνίκ' ἂν σχολὴν λάβω E.*IT*1432; σχολὴ [ἐστί] μοι I have *time*, οὐ σχολὴ αὐτῷ Pl.*Prt.*314d; οὐκ οὔσης σ. Ar.*Pl.*281; also παρούσης πολλῆς σ...πρός τι Pl.*Plt.*272b: prov., οὐ σ. δούλοις Arist.*Pol.*1334$^{a}$21: c. inf., οὔτοι ..τῇδ' ἐμοὶ σ. πάρα τρίβειν A.*Ag.*1055, etc.; εἴ τῳ καὶ λογίζεσθαι σ. S. *Aj.*816; εἴ σοι σ. προϊόντι ἀκούειν Pl.*Phdr.*227b; καταβαίνειν οὐ σ. Ar. *Ach.*409, al.; σ. πλείων ἢ θέλω πάρεστί μοι A.*Pr.*818; σχολὴ ἐδόκει γίγνεσθαι he thought he had *plenty of time*, Th.5.10; σ. διδόναι, παρέχειν τινί, X.*Cyr.*4.2.22, *Hier.*10.5; σ. καταναλίσκειν εἴς τι Isoc.1. 18; τὴν τοῦ πράττοντος σ. περιμένειν to wait his *leisure*, Pl.*R.*370b; σχολῆς τόδ' ἔργον a work for *leisure*, i.e. requiring attention, E. *Andr.*552: freq. with Preps., ἐπὶ σχολῆς at *leisure*, Pl.*Tht.*172d; κατὰ σχολήν Ar.*Ec.*48, Pl.*Phdr.*228a; μετὰ σχολῆς Id.*Criti.*110a; ὑπὸ σχολῆς Plu.2.667d; v. infr. B. 2. c. gen., *leisure, rest from* a thing, ἔν τινι σχολῇ κακοῦ S.*OT*1286; ὡς ἂν σχολὴν λύσωμεν.. πόνων E.*HF* 725; σ. ἐστί τινι τῶν πράξεων Pl.*Lg.*961b, cf. *R.*370c; also σ. γίγνεταί τινι ἀπό τινος Id.*Phd.*66d; σ. ἄγειν ἀπό τινος to keep *clear of*.., X.*Cyr.*8.3.47; ἡ τῶν ἀναγκαίων σ. Arist.*Pol.*1269$^{a}$35. 3. *idleness*, τίκτει γὰρ οὐδὲν ἐσθλὸν εἰκαία σ. S.*Fr.*308; σ. τερπνὸν κακόν E.*Hipp.* 384. II. *that in which leisure is employed*, οὐ κάμνω σχολῇ I am not weary of *talk*, Id.*Ion* 276; esp. *learned discussion, disputation, lecture*, Pl.*Lg.*820c (pl.), Arist.*Pol.*1323$^{b}$39; παρεκαθίζανον..σχολαῖς φιλομαθεῖν προαιρούμενοι *IG*2$^{2}$.1011.22; ταῦτ' οὐ σχολὴ Πλάτωνος; Alex.158; σχολὰς ἀναγράψαι Phld.*Acad.Ind.*p.74 M., cf. Plu.2.37c, etc.; σ. περὶ πολιτείας γράψασθαι ib.790e; σ. ἀναγνῶναι, λέγειν, Phld. *Acad.Ind.*p.82 M., Arr.*Epict.*4.11.35; ἠθικαὶ σ., title of work by Persaeus, *Stoic.*1.102, cf. Cic.*Tusc.*1.4.7,8. 2. *a group to whom lectures were given, school*, Arist.*Pol.*1313$^{b}$3, Phld.*Ind.Sto.*10, D.H.*Isoc.*1, *Dem.*44, Plu.*Per.*35, *Alex.*7, etc.; σ. ἔχειν to keep *a school*, Arr.*Epict.*

3.21.11; σχολῆς ἡγεῖσθαι to be master of *it*, Phld.*Acad.Ind.*p.92 M., D.H.*Amm.*1.7. **3.** Lat. *schola*, = σχολαστήριον, Vitr.5.10.4, *CIL* 10.831, etc. **III.** σχολαί, αἱ, *regiments of the Imperial guard*, Procop.*Goth.*4.27, Suid. s.v. διέδριον; Lat. *scholae*, *Cod.Theod.*14.17.9 (iv A.D.), etc. **b.** *section* of an office, *PMasp.*57 ii 18 (vi A.D.); of the 15 'schools' of shorthand writers, Lyd.*Mag.*3.6.

**B.** σχολῇ as Adv., *in a leisurely way, tardily*, ἤνυτον σ. βραδύς S.*Ant.*231, cf. Th.1.142, 3.46, And.2.19, etc.; ἀτρεμά τε καὶ σ. Alex. 135.4; σ. καὶ βάδην Plb.8.28.11. **2.** *at one's leisure*, i.e. *scarcely, hardly, not at all*, S.*OT*434, *Ant.*390, Pl.*Sph.*233b, etc.; παραινῶ πᾶσι.. σ. τεκνοῦσθαι παῖδας E.*Fr.*317; σ. γε And.1.102, X.*Mem.*3.14. 3; σ. που Pl.*Sph.*261b: freq. in apodosi, to introduce an *a fortiori* argument, εἰ δὲ μὴ.., ἦ που σχολῇ.. γε if not so.., *hardly* or *much less* so.., And.1.90; εἰ αὗται.. μὴ ἀκριβεῖς εἰσι, σχολῇ αἵ γε ἄλλαι Pl.*Phd.*65b; εἰ μὴ τούτων.., σ. τῶν γε ἄλλων Arist.*Metaph.*999ᵃ10; ὁπότε γὰρ.., answered by σ. γε, Pl.*R.*610e; μὴ γιγνώσκων τὴν οὐσίαν σ. τήν γε ὀρθότητα διαγνώσεται Id.*Lg.*668c.

**σχολι-άζω**, *write scholia* or *commentaries on*, τὰ Λυκόφρονος Tz. ad Lyc.1446. **-αστής**, οῦ, ὁ, *scholiast, commentator*, Eust.194.31.

***σχολικός**, ή, όν, (σχολή II) *scholastic*, ὑπομνήματα Ath.3.83b; παράδοσις Heliod.ap.Orib.49.8.1; *academic*, σ. συγγυμνασία A.D.*Conj.* 213.2; σ. πλάσματα *school* compositions, D.Chr.18.18; σ. ἀγνόημα an error *of the* (Aristarchean) *school*, Sch.Il.2.111; σχολικὸν μᾶλλον ἢ παραγγελματικόν, more *like lectures* than a handbook, D.H. *Comp.*22. Adv. -κῶς *after the manner of the schools*, S.E.*M.*8.13. **2.** *long-winded, tedious*, Longin.3.5, 10.7. **3.** *scholarly*, Philostr.*VS* 2.9.2 (Sup.). **II.** σχολικά, τά, = *causae summatim excerptae*, *Gloss.*

**σχολιογράφος** [ᾰ], ὁ, *writer of scholia, commentator*, Sch.Par.A.R. 3.376.

**σχόλιον**, τό, (σχολή II) *interpretation, comment*, Cic.*Att.*16.7.3; σχόλια λέγειν Arr.*Epict.*3.21.6; esp. *short note, scholium*, Gal.18(2). 847, etc.; σχόλια συναγείρων Luc.*Vit.Auct.*23, cf. Porph.*Plot.*3; σ. εἴς τι *on* a book, Marin.*Procl.*27. **II.** *tedious speech, lecture*, Hsch., Phot.

**σχολύδριον**, τό, Dim. of σχόλιον, Tz. ad Lyc.1414 (-ίδρια codd. plerique).

**σχόμενος**, v. ἔχω. **σχονθύλλω**, = τονθορύζω, Hsch. **σχῦρ**, ὁ, = χήρ, *hedgehog*, Id. **σχῶ, σχῶμεν, σχών**, v. ἔχω. **σῶ**, v. σάω, σήθω. **σῷ**, Att. contr. for σῶοι. **σωάδδει**, v. σῴζω.

**σωδάριον**, τό, = σουδάριον, Hermipp.96 (s.v.l.).

**σῶδες**, αἱ, a kind of *singing-bird*, Dionys *Av.*3.2.

**σωζόπολις**, εως, ὁ, ἡ, gloss on ὀρθόπολις, Sch.Pi.*O.*2.14.

***σῴζω**, with ι wherever ζ follows ω, as σῴζω, *EM*741.27, and so (written σωιζ-) in Inscrr. and Papyri down to iii B.C., e.g. *IG*1².625. 4, 2².687.35, 1611.378, Isyll.75 (lapis), *PCair.Zen.*482.17, 532.23 (iii B.C.), *Test.Epict.*1.6 (iii/ii B.C.), (ἀνα-) *IG*2².492.13, also in cod. Laur. of S.*El.*993, al., but otherwise without it, e.g. ἔσωσε *IG*9(2).257.11 (Thess., v B.C.); but Didym. (and many Hellenistic and later Inscrr. and Papyri) rejected the ι everywhere, v. *EM* l.c., and on the other hand Inscrr. show σῳσ- (always written σωισ-) from v B.C., ἔσῳσεν *IG*1².1085.5, 2².1236.6, συνδιασῴσαντες *GDI*1612.9 (Dyme, iii B.C.), σῷσαι (3 sg. opt.) *IG*5(2).357.152 (Stymphalus, iii B.C.), διέσῳσαν *OGI*56.18 (Canopus, iii B.C.), cf. *PPetr.*3 p.72 (iii B.C.); σοζ[, i.e. σωζ[, occurs in *IG*1².590: fut. σώσω S.*Ph.*1391, Th.1.137, etc.; early Att. σωῶ *IG*1².188.30: pf. σέσωκα, also σέσῳκα, v. ἀνασῴζω:—Med., fut. σώσομαι E.*Ba.*793, (ἐκ-) A.*Pers.*360, (δια-) X.*Cyr.*4.2. 28: aor. ἐσωσάμην Ar.*Ec.*402:—Pass., fut. σωθήσομαι Th.5.111, Ar.*Nu.*77, Hp.*Prog.*1, etc.: aor. ἐσώθην Th.1.110, al., *SIG*167.37 (Mylasa, iv B.C.) (ἐσώσθην only in Hsch.): pf. σέσωσμαι A.*Th.*[821 (820)], σέσωσται E.*IT*607, D.56.33, σεσώσμεθα S.*Tr.*83, etc.; but σέσωται Pl.*Criti.*109d, cf. 110a, σεσωμένος *PCair.Zen.*331.8 (iii B.C.); said to be Att. by Phot.; διασεσῳμένους is found in *IG*2².435.11 (after 336 B.C.) and διασεσῳμένοι in *PCair.Zen.*240.11 (iii B.C.); later σέσῳσται *IG*12(7).386.25 (Amorgos, iii B.C.).—The foll. forms are found in Hom. and dialects, **1.** pres. part. σώζων Od.5.490; 3 sg. ind. or opt. σώζει (-οι) Hes.*Op.*376 (v.l. for εἴη): pres. part. Pass. σωζόμενοι (-ομένοισι) Thgn.68, 235 (s.v.l.). **2.** from σαόω, 3 sg. σαοῖ Thgn. 868, Call.*Del.*22, etc.; 3 pl. σαοῦσι Tyrt.11.13; 2 sg. imper. σάου *h.Hom.*13.3, Call.*Epigr.*35 (as v.l.), etc.: fut. σαώσω Il.10.44: aor. ἐσάωσα 21.611, Pi.*Fr.*231: aor. inf. Pass. σαωθῆναι Il.15.503, Od.10. 473; imper. σαωθήτω Il.17.228; Ep. 3 pl. ἐσάωθεν Od.3.185: fut. Med. σαώσομαι 21.309. **3.** from σάωμι, Aeol. 2 sg. σάως Alc.73 (fort. σάῳς); 2 sg. imper. σάω Od.13.230, 17.595, Call. l.c., etc.: σάω as 3 sg. impf., Il.16.363, 21.238. **4.** from σώω, part. σώοντες Od.9.430; Ion. impf. σώεσκον Il.8.363; σώετε, σώεσθαι, A.R.4.197, 2.610. **5.** from σόω, subj. σόῃς, -ῃ, -ωσι, Il.9.681, 424, 393 vulg., where Tyrannio ap.Hdn.Gr.2.66 reads σοῷς, σοῷ, σοῶσι; in 9.681 Aristarch. read both σαῷς and σοῷς; the forms σοῷς, σοῷ perh. arise from σαόω, by contraction and 'distraction': but σόωσι from σώωσι acc. to Hdn.Gr. l.c.; Hsch. cites also σόεις, σοῦται as = σώζεις, σώζεται. **6.** Lacon. **σωάδδει**· παρατηρεῖ, Hsch.: but also **-σοΐδδω**, aor. ἀπέσοιξεν· ἀπέσωσεν, Λάκωνες, Id. **7. σωννύω**, Dinol.5:—*save, keep*, **1.** of persons, *save from death, keep alive*, σώοντες ἑταίρους Od.9.430; ζωοὺς σάω Il.21. 238; ὅτ' ἄσφ' ἀπολλυμένοις σάως Alc.73, cf. Th.1.91, X.*An.*3.1.38; πόδες καὶ γοῦνα σ. τινά Il.21.611; νὺξ στρατὸν σ. 9.78; *spare*, Od.22. 357:—Pass., *to be saved, kept alive, preserved*, opp. ἀπολέσθαι, Il.15. 503, Od.3.185, etc.; ἀγαπητῶς σεσωσμένους Lys.16.16; *keep a whole skin, escape destruction*, οἱ σωθησόμενοι Pl.*Tht.*176d; so in pres. σωζόμενος, Thgn.68, 235 (s.v.l.); *to be healed, recover from sickness*, Hp.*Coac.*136, Is.1.10 (dub. l.); ὑγιαίνοντες καὶ σωζόμενοι *IG*2².1028. 89 (i B.C.); σώζεο, as a wish, *God bless you, farewell*, Call.*Del.*150, *AP*5.240 (Paul. Sil.), 9.372; σώζοισθε ib.171 (Pall.); also, *save oneself, escape*, σώθητι Pl.*Cri.*44b; μόγις or μόλις σῴζεσθαι *escape* with difficulty, Id.*Ep.*332c, D.S.2.48, etc.; χαλεπῶς σ. Thgn.675. **b.** esp. in *NT*, of God or Christ, 1*Ep.Cor.*1.21, etc.; σ. τὸ ἀπολωλός *Ev.Luc.*19.10; σ. τὸν κόσμον *Ev.Jo.*12.47:—freq. in Pass., *to be saved* or *in a state of salvation*, *Ev.Matt.*19.25, etc.; οἱ σῳζόμενοι *Ev. Luc.*13.23, *Act.Ap.*2.47. **2.** of things, *keep safe, preserve*, rare in Hom., σάω μὲν ταῦτα, σάω δ' ἐμέ Od.13.230; σπέρμα πυρὸς σώζων 5. 490; πόλιν καὶ ἄστυ σ. Il.17.144; σαώσει Ἀργείους καὶ νῆας 10.44, cf. 9.230: freq. in Trag. and Att., σ. φάρμακον S.*Tr.*686; τὰ τόξα Id. *Ph.*766; τὰ σκεύη, παῖδας οἶκον χρήματα, καρπούς, Ar.*Pax*730 (anap.), *Av.*380 (troch.), 1062 (lyr.); τὰ πατρῷα, τὰ ὑπάρχοντα, Id.*Th.*820 (lyr.), Th.1.70; σ. πόλιν *preserve* the city or the state, Hdt.8.34, A. *Th.*749 (lyr.), S.*Ant.*1058, Pl.*R.*417a, cf. *Grg.*512b, etc.; τὰ πράγματα Th.1.74; τὴν Ἑλλάδα Ar.*Lys.*525 (lyr.); τὰς πολιτείας, τὴν δημοκρατίαν, etc., Arist.*Pol.*1309ᵇ15, 36; τόνδε γὰρ [λόγον] σῴζων *keeping* it *secret*, A.*Pr.*524, cf. S.*OC*1530; σ. καιρόν *save* or *recover* an opportunity, D.19.6, cf. 23.4:—Med., *keep* or *preserve for oneself*, τὴν εὐλάβειαν S.*El.*993, cf. E.*Alc.*146, etc.; αὐτὸς αὑτῷ σ. τι Ar.*Ec.*402, cf. *Eq.*1017 (hex.):—Pass., τὸ ἄπραγμον οὐ σῴζεται is not *secure*, Th.2. 63; ἡ.. πόλις οὐκ ἂν ἐσῴζετο; Ar.*Ec.*219; *to be preserved* or *extant*, of books, Longin.ap.Porph.*Plot.*20, Gal.15.705, D.C.70.2. **3.** *keep, observe, maintain* laws, etc., σ. ἐφετμάς A.*Eu.*241; τὸν παρόντα νοῦν Id.*Pr.*394; τοὺς καθεστῶτας νόμους S.*Ant.*1114, cf. Arist.*VV*1250ᵇ 17; τοὺς σοὺς λόγους E.*Hel.*1552; τὸ μόρσιμον ib.613; τὰ πρὸς τοὺς κατοίκους δίκαια *BGU*562.19 (ii A.D.); *confirm*, τὸ τοῦ ποιήσαντος Arist.*Mu.*400ᵇ24, cf. Antig.*Mir.*45 (Pass.); πρὸς τὸ τὰ φαινόμενα σῴζειν *to retain* the observed facts, Procl.*Hyp.*5.10; κατὰ ποσὸν σῴζει τὴν πρὸς τὸ μῶλυ ἐμφέρειαν *retains*, i.e. *does not lack*, a certain resemblance to.., Dsc.3.46, cf. 98. Sor.*Fasc.*8:—Pass., *to be maintained*, τοῦ μήκους σῳζομένου Arist.*Mete.*386ᵃ2; ἐφ' ᾧ τοῖς θεοῖς τὰ ἱερὰ σωθήσεσθαι *PHib.*1.77.7 (iii B.C.). **4.** *keep in mind, remember*, E.*Hel.*266, Pl. *R.*486c: more freq. in Med., παρῆκα θεσμῶν οὐδέν, ἀλλ' ἐσῳζόμην.. ὅπως δύσνιπτον ἐκ δέλτου γραφήν S.*Tr.*682, cf. *El.*1257; μηδ' ἃ ἔμαθε σῴζοιτο Pl.*R.*455b; in full, μνήμην σῴζομαι στρατεύματος E.*IA*302 (lyr.), cf. Pl.*Grg.*501a, *Tht.*163d. **II.** Constr.: **1.** simply c. acc., v. supr. **2.** with a sense of motion to a place, *bring* one *safe* to, τὸν δ' ἐσάωσεν ἐς ποταμοῦ προχοάς Od.5.452; ἐς ὅμιλον Il.19. 401; πόλινδε 5.224, etc.; ἐς οἴκους S.*Ph.*311; εἰς τὴν βασιλείαν τὴν ἐπουράνιον 2*Ep.Ti.*4.18:—Pass., *come safe to* a place, σωθέντος ἐμεῦ ὀπίσω ἐς οἶκον Hdt.4.97, cf. 9.104; πρὸς ἤπειρον σεσῶσθαι A.*Pers.*737; δεῦρο E.*Ph.*725; οἴκαδε X.*HG*1.6.7; σῴζεσθαι ἐπὶ τὴν ὑμετέρην [χώρην] Hdt.5.98; ἐς δόμους σωθέντ' S.*Tr.*611; σωθῶμεν ἐπὶ θάλατταν X.*An.* 6.5.20: c. dat. pers., μόλις ὔμμιν ἐσώθην Theoc.15.4. **3.** σ. τινὰ ἐκ φλοίσβοιο, ἐκ πολέμου, *carry off safe, rescue from*.., Il.5.469, 11.752; ἐκ ποταμοῖο 21.274; ἐκ θανάτοιο Od.4.753; ἐκ πολλῶν πόνων S.*El.* 1356; ἀπὸ στρατείας A.*Ag.*603; διὰ δεινῶν πραγμάτων σεσωσμένοι X. *An.*5.5.8: c. gen., σώσας ἐχθρῶν χθόνα *having rescued* it *from* them, S.*Ant.*1162; σῶσαί τινα κακοῦ Id.*Ph.*919; σεαυτὸν νούσου *Ath.Mitt.* 56.124 (Smyrna); σωθῆναι κακῶν E.*Or.*779.—Both constructions may be combined, σ. τινὰ ἐκ πολέμοιο νῆας ἔπι Il.17.452; ἐκ π. μετὰ νῆας 12.123; ἐξ Αἰγίνης δεῦρο Pl.*Grg.*511d. **4.** c. acc. et dat. pers., *save for* another, υἱᾶ τινι Od.4.765; ἡμῖν τὸν βίον Pl.*Prt.*356e, etc.:—Pass., σῴζεταί τί τινι Ar.*Pax*1022, X.*An.*7.7.56. **5.** c. inf., [σπονδαί] αἵ σε σῴζουσιν θανεῖν which *save* thee *from* dying, E.*Ph.*600 (troch.). **6.** c. part., σῴζεσθαι φεύγοντες by flight, X.*Cyr.*3.3. 51. **7.** abs., τὰ σώσοντα *what is likely to save*, D.6.5; ἡ σῴζουσα [ψῆφος] Luc.*Harm.*3. **b.** σώζων, ὁ, *Saviour*, of a god, *JRS*14.28 (Iconium); epith. of Apollo, *CR*19.368 (Sizma). **c.** σῴζουσα, ἡ, = ἀρτεμισία, Ps.-Dsc.3.113.

**σωκάριον**, τό, = σχοινίον, Hero *Geom.*4.11, dub. l. in *Gp.*20.42.

***σωκέω**, *have power* or *strength*, A.*Eu.*36. **2.** c. inf., *to be in a condition* or *state to* do, S.*El.*119 (anap.).

**σῶκος**, ὁ, *the stout, strong one*, epith. of Hermes, Il.20.72, cf. Corn. *ND*16, Zonar.; of the planet Mercury, *Cat.Cod.Astr.*1.173: as pr. n. in Il.11.427.

**Σωκρᾰτ-εῖον**, τό, *monument to Socrates*, Marin.*Procl.*10. **II.** pl. -εια, τά, *festival in memory of S.*, ib.23. **-έω**, *do like Socrates*, '*Socratize*', Ar.*Av.*1282 (ἐσωκράτων cod. R). **-ης**, ὁ, *Socrates*: gen. Σωκράτους; acc. sg. in Pl. Σωκράτη (as also in Ar.*Nu.*182, etc.), in X.*Mem.*1.2.33 Σωκράτην; voc. Σώκρατες:—Dim. **Σωκρᾰτίδιον**, *dear little Socrates!* Ar.*Nu.*222, al. **-ίζω**, = Σωκρατέω, Alciphr.2.2, Poet. in Arg.4 Ar.*Nu.* **-ικός**, ή, όν, *Socratic, of Socrates*, λόγοι Arist. *Po.*1447ᵇ11; μνημονεύματα Phld.*Vit.*p.41 J.; ἐπιστολαί Wilcken *Chr.* 155 (iii A.D.); οἱ Σ. the *philosophers of his school*, Luc.*Am.*23. Adv. -κῶς *more Socratico*, Cic.*Att.*2.3.3. **-ιστής**, οῦ, ὁ, *imitator of Socrates*, Arg.3 Ar.*Nu.*

**Σωκρᾰτόγομφος**, ον, *patched up by Socrates*, of the plays of Euripides, Mnesilochus ap.D.L.2.18 (v. Telecl.*Fr.*39 K.).

***σωλάριον**, τό, = Lat. *solarium*, *CIG*3281, 3386 (Smyrna), *BMus. Inscr.*645 (Ephesus), *Cod.Just.*8.10.12.5.

***σωλήν**, ῆνος, ὁ (also **σωλῆνος**, ὁ, Anan.*Oxy.*1087.57), *channel, gutter*, Archil.5, Aen.Tact.18.6, *PPetr.*2 p.119 (iii B.C.), Ph.*Bel.*91. 26, 28. **2.** *pipe*, Hdt.3.60, Hero *Spir.*1.1, al., Arr.*Epict.*4.11.9; κεραμεοῖ σ. Plu.2.526b; σκύτινος Str.16.2.13; μολίβδινος *Gp.*10.18.6; *ventilation-pipe*, ib.2.27.2; ἀργυροῦς καὶ χρυσοῦς (for unguents) Plu.

*Galb.*19 (pl.). 3. *cylindrical box* for keeping a broken limb straight, Hp.*Off.*14, *Fract.*16,22. 4. *grooved tile, IG*4$^2$(1).109 iv 116,117 (Epid., iv B.C.), 11(2).203*B*97 (Delos, iii B.C.), Hsch., etc. 5. a shell-fish, perh. the *razor-fish*, Epich.42, Sophr.24, Philyll.13, Arist. *HA*528$^a$18, 548$^a$5, al., Gal.6.734. 6. *membrum virile*, Hsch. 7. *the cavity of the spine*, Poll.2.180. 8. *grooved rails* in which wheels run, Hero *Aut.*2.2; σωλῆνες καταπαλτῶν, σκορπίων σωλῆνες, *IG*2$^2$. 1628.512,515, 1629.986,990. 9. vulgar name for *lienteria*, Steph. *in Gal.*1.314 D.

**σωλην-άριον**, τό, Dim. of σωλήν, Hero *Spir.*1.10, al., Heliod.ap. Orib.50.9.8, Gal.10.1001, Alex.Trall.8.2. **-ένομαι**, Pass., *to be carried round as in a pipe*, *EM*385.27, Hsch. **-ίδιον**, τό, *small groove*, Ph.*Bel.*75.41. 2. *small pipe*, Bito 46.5, Gal.14.787. **-ίζω**, *hollow out like a pipe*, Ruf.ap.Orib.49.27.5; cf. σωληνόομαι. **-ικός**, ή, όν, *tubular*, λέβης cj. in *POxy.*1002 (vi A.D.). **-ιον**, τό, Dim. of σωλήν, Bito 46.4, Ph.*Bel.*75.46, Dsc.*Eup.*1.61, Antyll.ap.Orib.10. 19.4. **-ίσκος**, ὁ, = foreg., Hero *Spir.*2.22, Sch.D Il.18.401. **-ισμός**, ὁ, *hollowing out like a pipe*, Ruf.ap.Orib.49.26.5. **-ιστής**, οῦ, ὁ, *one who fishes for the* σωλήν 5, Phaenias ap.Ath.3.90e.

**σωληνο-ειδής**, ές, *pipe-shaped, grooved*, Aen.Tact.16.6, Ph.2.244, D.C.49.30. Adv. -ειδῶς *like a pipe*, Ruf.*Oss.*24; *groove-wise*, Sor. 1.85. **-θήρας**, ου, ὁ, *one who fishes for the* σωλήν 5, Phaenias ap. Ath.3.90f. **-κέντης**, ου, ὁ, *fisher of* σωλῆνες, *OGI*756.5 (Milet.). **-ομαι**, Pass., *serve as a groove* or *pipe*, v.l. for -ίζομαι in Paul.Aeg.6.106.

**σωληνος**, ὁ, v. σωλήν.

**σωληνώδης**, ες, = σωληνοειδής, Aristid.Quint.2.17.

**σωληνωτός**, ή, όν, *like a* σωλήν, ὑφάσματα Lyd.*Mag.*2.4 (= Lat. *tubulamenta*).

**σωλίγξαι**· δραμεῖν, Hsch.

⊛ **σῶμα**, ατος, τό (Arc. dat. pl. σωμάτεσι *IG*5(2).357.156 (Stymphalus, iii B.C.)), *body* of man or beast, but in Hom., as Aristarch. remarks (v. Apollon.*Lex.*), always *dead body, corpse* (whereas the living body is δέμας), ὥς τε λέων ἐχάρη μεγάλῳ ἐπὶ σώματι κύρσας Il.3.23, cf. 18.161; σ. δὲ οἴκαδ' ἐμὸν δόμεναι πάλιν 7.79; σ. κατελείπομεν ἄκλαυτον Od.11.53; ὧν.. σώματ' ἀκηδέα κεῖται 24.187; so also in Hes.*Sc.*426, Simon.119, Pi.*O.*9.34, Hdt.7.167, Posidon.14 J., *Ev.Marc.*15.43, etc.; τὸ σ. τοῦ τεθνεῶτος Pl.*R.*469d, cf. *Grg.*524c, D.43.65; σ. νεκρόν *POxy.*51.7 (ii A.D.); νεκρὸν σ. Gal.18(2).93, cf. νεκρός II. 1; μέγιστον σ... σποδοῦ, = σ. μέγιστον ὃ νῦν σποδός ἐστι, S.*El.*758; also later, Wilcken *Chr.*499 (ii/iii A.D.). 2. the *living body*, Hes.*Op.*540, Batr.44, Thgn.650, Pi.*O.*6.56, *P.*8.82, Hdt.1.139, etc.; δόμοι καὶ σώματα A.*Th.*896 (lyr.); γενναῖος τῷ σ. S.*Ph.*51; εὔρωστος τὸ σ. X.*HG*6.1.6; τὸ σ. σῴζειν or -εσθαι save one's *life*, D.22.55, Th.1.136; διασῴζειν or -εσθαι Isoc.6.46, X.*An.*5.5.13; περὶ πολλῶν σ. καὶ χρημάτων βουλεύειν Th.1.85; περὶ τοῦ σ. ἀγωνίζεσθαι for one's *life*, Lys.5.1; ἔχειν τὸ σ. κακῶς, ὡς βέλτιστα, etc., to be in a bad, a good state of bodily health, X.*Mem.*3.12.1, 3.12.5. 3. *body*, opp. *spirit* (εἴδωλον), Pi.*Fr.*131; opp. *soul* (ψυχή), Pl.*Grg.*493a, *Phd.*91d; τὰ τοῦ σ. ἔργα *bodily* labours, X.*Mem.* 2.8.2; αἱ τοῦ σ. ἡδοναί, αἱ κατὰ τὸ σ. ἡδ., ib.1.5.6, Pl.*R.*328d; τὰ εἰς τὸ σ. τιμήματα *bodily* punishments, Aeschin.2.139; τὰ εἰς τὸ σ. ἀδικήματα *PHal.*1.193 (iii B.C.). 4. *animal body*, opp. plants, Pl.*R.* 564a (pl.); but of plants, 1*Ep.Cor.*15.38. 5. *civic rights* (like Lat. *caput*), Lys.23.12; ἄτιμοι τὰ σ. And.1.74; μέρος ἠτιμῶσθαι τοῦ σ. D.51.12. 6. in *NT*, of the sacramental *body* of Christ, τοῦτό ἐστι τὸ σ. μου *Ev.Matt.*26.26, cf. 1*Ep.Cor.*10.16. b. of the *body* of Christ's church, οἱ πολλοὶ ἓν σ. ἐσμεν ἐν Χριστῷ *Ep. Rom.*12.5; ἡ ἐκκλησία ἥτις ἐστὶ τὸ σ. [τοῦ Χριστοῦ] *Ep.Eph.*1. 23. II. periphr., ἀνθρώπου σ. ἐν οὐδέν, = ἄνθρωπος οὐδὲ εἷς, Hdt.1. 32; esp. in Trag., σῶμα θηρός, = θήρ, S.*OC*1568 (lyr.); τεκέων σώματα, = τέκνα, E.*Tr.*201 (lyr.); τὸ σὸν σ., = σύ, Id.*Hec.*301; rarely in sg. of many persons, σῶμα τέκνων Id.*Med.*1108 (anap.). 2. *a person, human being*, τὰ πολλὰ σ., = οἱ πολλοί, S.*Ant.*676; λευκὰ γήρα σ. E.*HF*909 (lyr.); σ. ἄδικα Id.*Supp.*223, cf. Pl.*Lg.*908a, *PSI* 4.359.9 366.7 (iii B.C.), etc.; ἑκάστου τοῦ σώματος *IG*1$^2$.22.14; κατὰ σῶμα *per person*, *PRev.Laws*50.9 (iii B.C.); καταστήσαντες τὸ σ. ἀφείσθωσαν τῆς ἐγγύης *PMich.Zen.*70.12 (iii B.C.); ἐργαζομένη αὐτῇ τῷ ἰδίῳ σ. working for her*self*, earning her own living, *PEnteux.*26.7 (iii B.C.); τὰ φίλτατα σ., of children, Aeschin.3.78; freq. of slaves, αἰχμάλωτα σ. D.20.77, *IG*12(7).386.25 (Amorgos, iii B.C.), *SIG*588.64 (Milet., ii B.C.), etc.; οἰκετικὰ σ. Lex ap.Aeschin.1.16, cf. *SIG*633.88 (Milet., ii B.C.); δοῦλα Poll.3.78; ἐλεύθερα σ. X.*HG*2.1.19, Plb.2.6. 6, etc.; later, σῶμα is used abs. for a *slave*, *PHib.*1.54.20 (iii B.C.), Plb.12.16.5, *Apoc.*18.13, etc.; σ. γυναικεῖον, ᾇ ὄνομα.. *GDI*2154.6 (Delph., ii B.C.); a usage censured by Poll. l. c. and Phryn.355; also of troops, τὴν τῶν σ. σύνταξιν Aen.Tact.1.1; μηχανήμασιν ἢ σώμασιν ἐναντιοῦσθαι ὧδε Id.32.1. III. generally, *a body*, i.e. *any corporeal substance*, δεῖ αὐτὸ (sc. τὸ ὄν) σ. μὴ ἔχειν Meliss.9; ἡ μέγεθός ἐστιν ἡ σ. ἐστιν Gorg.3; σ. ἄψυχον, ἔμψυχον, Pl.*Phdr.*245e, cf. *Plt.*288e, Arist.*Ph.*265$^b$29, al.; ὁ λίθος σ. ἐστι Luc.*Vit.Auct.*25; φασὶν οἱ μὲν σ. εἶναι τὸν χρόνον, οἱ δὲ ἀσώματον S.E.*M.*10.215; κυκλικὸν σ., of one of the spheres, Jul.*Or.*5.162b, al.; τὸ πέμπτον σ. the fifth *element*, Philol.12, *Placit.*1.3.22, Jul.*Or.*4.132c; *metallic substance*, Olymp. Alch.p.71 B. 2. Math., *figure of three dimensions, solid*, opp. a surface, etc., Arist.*Top.*142$^b$24, *Metaph.*1020$^a$14, al. IV. *the body* or *whole* of a thing, esp. of complete parts of the body, τὸ σ. τῶν νεφρῶν Id.*HA*497$^a$9; τὰ σ. τῶν αἰσθητηρίων Id.*GA*744$^b$24; τὸ σ. τῆς γαστρός, τῆς κοιλίας, Gal.15.667,806; σ. παιδοποιόν Ael.*NA*17.42: generally, *the whole body* or *frame* of a thing, ὑπὸ σώματι γᾶς A.*Th.* 947 (lyr.); τὸ σ. τοῦ παντός, τοῦ κόσμου, Pl.*Ti.*31b, 32c; ὕδωρ, ποταμοῦ σ. Chaerem.17; τὸ σ. τῆς πίστεως the *body* of the proof, i.e. arguments, Arist.*Rh.*1354$^a$15; τῆς λέξεως Longin.*Rh.*p.188 H.; of *a body* of writings, Cic.*Att.*2.1.4; *text* of a document, opp. ὑπογραφή, *BGU*187.12 (ii A.D.), cf. *PFay.*34.20 (ii A.D.); of a will, *POxy.*494. 30 (ii A.D.). 2. ξύλα σώματα *logs*, opp. κλάδοι, *POxy.*1738.3 (iii A.D.); σ. μέγα περαίας *CPHerm.*7 ii 27, cf. iii 8 (iii A.D.).

**σῶμαι**, Dor. for σοῦμαι, v. σεύω.

⊛ **σωμάλοιφος**· ὁ κατειλημμένος σώματι τὰ σκύτινα αἰδοῖα, Hsch.

**σωμάριστρον**, = ζωμ-, *soup-ladle*, *PLond.*4.1657.10 (iv/v A.D.).

**σωμασκ-έω**, *exercise the body, practise wrestling*, etc., X.*Cyr.*1.6.17, 3.1.20, Plb.6.47.8, etc.; σ. αὐτόν D.L.8.12: metaph., σ. τὸν πόλεμον *train* War (personified) for action, Plu.*Aem.*8. **-ητής**, οῦ, ὁ, *one that practises bodily exercises*, D.L.8.46. **-ία**, ἡ, *bodily exercise, athletic training of the body*, Pl.*Phlb.*30b, *Lg.*646d, 674b, X.*Mem.*3.9. 11, Ph.2.8 (pl.). **-ίας**, ου, ὁ, *one who takes bodily exercise*, Poll.3. 154; glossed by κατάσαρκος, Hdn.*Epim.*130.

⊛ **σωμᾰτ-εῖον**, τό, *corporate body*, *Cod.Just.*6.48.1.10, al. **-εκμᾰγεῖον**, τό, *body-towel, bath-towel*, Meyer *Ostr.*62.4 (ii B.C.). **-εμπορέω**, *trade in slaves*, Str.14.5.2. **-έμπορος**, ον, *slave-dealer*, Dsc.*Eup.* 1.233, *OGI*524.5 (Thyatira), Artem.3.17, *Cat.Cod.Astr.*8(4).213, Eust.1416.26, *Gloss.* **-ηγέω**, *carry a body*, of saddle-mules, Hsch. s.v. ἀστράβη, Eust.1625.40. **-ηγός**, όν, (ἄγω) *carrying a body*, i.e. *used for riding*, σ. ἡμίονος Suid. s.v. ἀστράβη. **-ίδιον**, τό, Dim. of σῶμα IV. 1, *text* of a document, *PLips.*11.14 (iii A.D.). ⊛ **-ίζω**, *embody*, Herm.ap.Stob.1.49.45. II. *put into documentary form, execute*, *PThead.*5.19 (iv A.D.), *PMasp.*133.6 (vi A.D.). 2. *register, book*, σωματίσαντός μοι..πόρον *POxy.*2131.12 (iii A.D.):—Pass., c. dat., -ίσθησαν τοῖς δεῖνα ἄρουραι ib.1044.26 (ii/iii A.D.). **-ικός**, ή, όν, *of* or *for the body, bodily*, opp. ψυχικός, ἔργα Arist.*EN*1101$^b$33; πάθη ib.1173$^b$9; ἡδοναί ib.1104$^b$5; τὰ σ. ἡδέα ib.1152$^a$5; πόνοι *SIG*708.11 (Istropolis, ii B.C.); ἐργασίαι *PFay.*21.10 (ii A.D.); ἀσθένεια *BGU* 1773.13 (i B.C.), *PFlor.*51.5 (ii A.D.). 2. *bodily, corporeal*, opp. ἀσώματος, Arist. *de An.*404$^b$31, cf. *Metaph.*987$^a$4, *Ph.*214$^a$12, Ti. Locr.96a; σ. ἐποίησαν τὰ δώδεκα ζῴδια κατὰ τὰ μέλη τοῦ ἀνθρώπου *gave somatic application* (cf. μελοθεσία I. 1) *to*.., Rhetor. in *Cat. Cod.Astr.*1.143: Comp. -ώτερος Thphr.*CP*1.14.3: Sup. -ώτατος Id.*Sens.*37. Adv. -κῶς *corporeally*, Ph.1.484, *Ep.Col.*2.9, Plu.2. 424e; ἀργυρικῶς ἢ σ. κολασθήσεται *OGI*664.17 (Egypt, iii A.D.): Astrol. -κῶς, opp. 'in aspect', Ptol.*Tetr.*52, 132, 147: Comp. -ώτερον S.E.*P.*1.7. 3. *forming a corpus*, αἱ σποράδην καὶ οὐ σ. ζητήσεις D.L.7.198. **-ῖνος**, η, ον, = foreg., *Gloss.* **-ιον**, τό, Dim. of σῶμα, *small body, poor body*, Isoc.*Ep.*4.11, Epicur.*Fr.*181, Gnathaena ap.Ath.13.584b, etc.; ἀσθένεια τοῦ σ. *PHerc.*1041.1; of a sick man's body, *PCair.Zen.*254 (iii B.C.), Gal.13.1025, cf. Agathin.ap.Orib.10. 7.4; of an animal, Arist.*Fr.*339; of an infant, Sor.1.117. 2. *corpse*, Plu.2.119b, Pap. in *Stud.Ital.*12(1935).99 (ii A.D.), *PLips.*30. 13 (iii A.D.), Hdn.2.1.1. 3. *slave*, *PSI*6.602.2 (iii B.C.), *PCair. Zen.*93.11 (iii B.C.), *PUniv.Giss.*20.14 (ii A.D.), etc. II. of things, 1. *small body, corpuscle*, Arist. *de An.*409$^a$11, *HA*525$^a$ 2. 2. pl., *padding*, used by actors to improve their figure, Pl. Com.256, Luc.*JTr.*41, Poll.2.235, 4.115. 3. *book, volume*, Heraclit.*All.*1, Porph.*Plot.*26; *structure* of a poem, Longin.9. 13. 4. *text*, opp. signature, *PGen.*11.18, 68.18 (iv A.D.). 5. *instalment* of a sum due, *PEleph.*14.21 (iii B.C.).—σωμάτειον is freq. v.l., cf. *CIG*2829.9, 2835.5 (Aphrodisias). **-ισμός**, ὁ, *embodiment in a legal instrument*, *POxy.*268.18 (i A.D.), 1726.4 (iii A.D.). 2. *registration* of liability to taxation, *PFay.*33.18 (ii A.D.), *PHamb.* 11.11 (iii A.D.): generally, *registration, listing*, *PLond.*3.604.3 (i A.D.); σ. κατ' ἄνδρα *BGU*141 *A* 4 (iii A.D.).

**σωμᾰτο-βλάβεια** [βλᾰ], ἡ, *bodily harm* or *injury*, Procl.*Par.Ptol.* 209. **-ειδής**, ές, *bodily, corporeal*, Pl.*Phd.*83d, 86a; τὸ σ. *corporeal nature*, ib.81b, c. 2. *incarnate*, of a god, Ephor.31(*b*) J., *Rev. Phil.*1930.250 (Egypt, Tab. Defix.). 3. *substantial, solid*, Thphr. *HP*5.9.3, *Ign.*48, al. II. metaph., *organic, systematic*, ἀπαγγελίαι Arist.*Rh.Al.*1442$^b$31; ἱστορία Plb.1.3.4. Adv. -δῶς Arist.*Rh.Al.* 1436$^a$29. **-θήκη**, ἡ, *sarcophagus*, *TAM*2(1).122 (Levissi), 222.1 (Sidyma), *CIG*4224c (near Telmissus), *JHS*34.28 (Lycia), 12.268 (Cilicia). **-θήκιον**, τό, Dim. of foreg., written -θήκιν, *MAMA* 3.753 (Corycus). **-μᾰχέω**, *practise gymnastic exercises with an opponent*, Gal.15.197. **-πλαστέω**, *model a body*, interpol. in Jul. *Ep.*89 (p.138 B.-C.). **-πλαστικός**, ή, όν, *forming bodies*, Lyd. *Mens.*39.

**σωμᾰτοποι-έω**, *give bodily existence to*, ἐνέργειαν Herm.ap.Stob.1. 41.6. 2. *represent in art*, τὸν Ἔρωτα Alex.Aphr.*Pr.*1.87. 3. *personify*, Men.Rh.p.333 S., Sch.Ar.*Ach.*976,989. 4. Pass., *become more solid* or *bulky*, Dsc.5.75, Sor.1.17. II. *organize as a body*, τὸ ἔθνος Plb.2.45.6, cf. D.S.11.86, D.L.2.138; *make into a whole*, σ. τὰ κεχωρισμένα Artem.4 *Prooem.*; σ. τὴν διαίρεσιν, τὴν φράσιν, Sch.Hermog. in Rh.7.60,791 W.:—Pass., Longin.40.1. III. *provide with bodily strength, recruit*, τοὺς ἵππους Plb.3.87.3; τὸν Φίλιππον Id.16.1.9; *subsidize*, τινὰ τῶν πολιτικῶν χορηγίων σωματοποιῶν παρ' ἑαυτοῦ *SIG*762. 40 (Dionysopolis, i B.C.); *provide with refreshment*, Phld.*Acad.Ind.* p.66 M.: metaph., *revive, refresh*, τὰς ψυχάς, πᾶσαν ἐλπίδα, Plb.3.90.4, 33.17.3, cf. *Frr.*229–31; τὰς ὁρμάς D.S.18.10; τοὺς πυρετούς Antyll. ap.Orib.4.11.1. 2. *exalt, magnify*, πράξεις Plb.*Fr.*47:—Pass., ὑπὸ γυναικῶν -ουμένους *Cat.Cod.Astr.*8(4).154. **-ησις**, εως, ἡ, *the giving of bodily existence*, Ptol.*Tetr.*105, Herm.ap.Stob.1.41.6. **-ία**, ἡ, = foreg., Ps.-Ocell.2.10. **-ός**, όν, *giving bodily existence*, Iamb. *Myst.*8.1 (v.l. σώματα ποιά).

**σωμᾰτότης**, ητος, ἡ, *corporeality*, S.E.*M.*3.85, Gal.19.482, Plot.2.4.12, *Theol.Ar.*5, Iamb.*Protr.*21.

**σωμᾰτοτροφεῖον**, τό, *a place where slaves are kept, slave-depot*, D.S.34.2.

**σωμᾰτουργ-έω**, = σωματοποιέω: metaph., *form into a whole*, Procl. *in Ti.*2.71 D., al. **-ία**, ἡ, = σωματοποιία, Herm.ap.Stob.1.49.69, Porph.*Antr.*14. **-ικός**, όν, = σωματοποιός, Procl. *in Ti.*1.358 D., al. **-ός**, όν, *creative of bodies*, Id. *in Prm.*p.638 S., *in Ti.*1.311 D.

**σωμᾰτο-φθορέω**, *pollute with the body*, A.*Ag.*948 (s. v. l.). **-φόρβος**, ον, *nourishing the body*, Man.4.232. **-φόρος**, ον, *bearing a metallic substance*, γῆ Olymp.Alch.p.71 B. **-φρουρητήρ**, ῆρος, ὁ, = σωματοφύλαξ, Man.4.232. **-φυής**, ές, *corporeal*, Gal.*Phil.Hist.*13.

**σωμᾰτοφῠλᾰκ-έω**, *to be a bodyguard*, D.S.14.43: c. acc., J.*AJ*6.6.1, 11.3.1. **-ία**, ἡ, *guarding the body* or *person*, D.S.16.93, 17.65. **-ιον**, τό, *place where a body is guarded* or *kept, sepulchre*, Luc. *Cont.*22.

⊛ **σωμᾰτοφύλαξ** [ῠ], ᾰκος, ὁ, *bodyguard*, *Sammelb.*3941.5 (ii B. C.), Plb.15.32.6, J.*Vit.*18, Gal.14.624: in pl., Plb.8.20.8, al., Lxx *Ju.*12.7, D.S.34.2, Arr.*An.*1.6.5, Hdn.4.13.1: as Adj., *protecting the body*, φυλακτήριον σωματοφύλαξ πρὸς δαίμονας *PMag.Lond.*121.597.

**σωμᾰτ-όω**, *make corporeal*, prob. in Philol.11:—Pass., *become corporeal* or *substantial*, Arist.*GA*739ᵃ12, 744ᵃ17, *Sens.*445ᵃ23, Thphr. *CP*6.11.14. 2. Pass., *to be embodied, associated with a body*, ψυχὴ . . σωματωθεῖσα Plot.1.6.5; -θεῖσα αἴσθησις Dam.*Pr.*16. **-ώδης**, ες, = σωματοειδής 1, Arist.*HA*521ᵇ27; τὰ σ. Id.*GA*737ᵃ35, al.: Comp. and Sup. -έστερος, -έστατος, Id.*Pr.*863ᵇ9, *PA*647ᵃ20. **-ωσις**, εως, ἡ, *embodying, making of bodies*, Herm.ap.Stob.1.41.6; *formation of the body*, *Theol.Ar.*31. 2. *thickening, consolidation*, Thphr. *CP*6.11.14. 3. Math., *becoming solid, acquiring a third dimension*, *Theol.Ar.*16, 36. 4. *the stuff of which bodies are made*, ἐκ τῆς γειναμένης -ώσεως ἐποίησεν ἡμᾶς Herm.ap.Stob.1.41.8.

**σωμελής**, ές, *sound of limb*, *Schwyzer* 181 iv 4 (Crete).

**σωννύω**, = σῴζω (q. v.).

**σώομαι**, = σοῦμαι, σεύομαι, A.R.2.1010, 3.307. II. v. σῴζω.

**σῶος**, v. σῶς.

**Σωπάτρειος**, α, ον, *of Sopatros*, *Inscr.Délos* 438.2 (ii B. C.): neut. -εια, τά, *festival in his honour*, ib.320 B 58 (iii B. C.).

**σωπάω**, Dor. and poet. for σιωπάω, Pi.*I.*1.63; cf. διασιωπάω.

**Σωπή**, = Σιωπή, prob. cj. in Emp.123; σωπὴ γενέσθω Call.*Iamb.*1.102, cf. 255.

**σωπιαίνουσιν**· οἱ κύνες παρὰ Ξενοφῶντι, Hsch.

**σωπομπία**, ἡ, *guaranteed manumission*, *Schwyzer* 336.11 (Delph.).

**σωρά**, ἡ, *scopa*, *Gloss.* (dub.).

**σωρακίς**, ίδος, ἡ, *a sleeve for rubbing down horses*, *PSI*4.430.5 (iii B. C.), Poll.1.185, 10.55. II. = sq., *IG*2².1488.7 (or σωρακί[ον]).

**σώρᾰκος**, ὁ, *basket* or *box*, Ar.*Fr.*248, Aen.Tact.30.2, Babr.108.18, *BGU*14 iv 10 (iii A. D.); καταπαλτῶν, τοξευμάτων, *IG*2².120.37, 1649.14.

**σωράνθεμις** and **σωρανθίς**, ἡ, = ἀνθυλλίς, ff. ll. in Ps.-Dsc.3.136.

**σωρ-εία**, ἡ, *heaping up*, ἡ ἐπὶ τοσοῦτο σ. Plu.*Oth.*14. 2. *summation*, Porph.*Sent.*36, Iamb. *in Nic.*p.81 P., al. 3. *arithmetical progression*, *Theol.Ar.*21. **-είτης**, **-ειτικός**, v. σωρίτης, -ιτικός. **-εός**, ὁ, = σωρός, Sch.Il.23.160, *EM*742.21, Theognost.*Can.*50, Suid. **-ευμα**, ατος, τό, *heap, pile*, X.*Cyr.*7.1.32, Eub.47. **-ευσις**, εως, ἡ, *accumulation*, Arist.*Metaph.*1076ᵇ29, *Gloss.* **-ευτής**, οῦ, ὁ, *one who heaps up wealth*, σ. ἄνθρωποι Phld. *Oec.*p.50 J. (pl.); σ. χρυσοῦ, χρημάτων, *Cat.Cod.Astr.*8(4).174, 149 (both pl.). **-ευτικός**, ή, όν, *addicted to heaping up*, = φιλοκτήματος, Sch.Ptol.*Tetr.*61. **-ευτός**, ή, όν, *heaped up*, Alex.83. **-εύω**, *heap* one thing on another, τι πρός τι Arist.*Rh.*1390ᵇ18; ἐπὶ τοῦ κοσκίνου τὰ τεθλιμμένα Dsc.4.150; ἄλλον ἐπ' ἄλλῳ πλοῦτον Luc. *Epigr.*12.6; ἄνθρακας ἐπὶ τὴν κεφαλήν τινος Lxx *Pr.*25.22, *Ep.Rom.*12.20; περὶ τὸ σῶμα λάφυρα Plu.*Pel.*33; νεκροὺς D.S.12.62; πλοῦτον Id.1.62, cf. 5.46, Phld.*Oec.*p.45 J.:—Pass., Arist.*GC*325ᵇ22, Plb.16.11.4; οὐσίας πλῆθος -εύεται Epicur.*Fr.*480. II. *heap with* something, c. gen., αἰγιαλοὶ σεσωρευμένοι τινῶν Plb.16.8.9: c. dat., σ. βωμοὺς λιβάνῳ Hdn.4.8.9; αὐχένας στέμμασι *AP*7.233 (Apollonid.): metaph., γυναικάρια σεσωρευμένα ἁμαρτίαις 2*Ep.Ti.*3.6. **-ηδόν**, Adv. *by heaps, in heaps*, Plb.1.34.5, *AP*7.713 (Antip.), Lxx *Wi.*18.23. 2. *in arithmetical progression*, *Theol.Ar.*9. **-ι**, v. σῶρυ. **-ικός**, v. σωριτικός. **-ίτης** [ῑ], ου, ὁ, *the fallacy of the heap*, invented by Eubulides of Miletus, D.L.2.108, Cic.*Acad.*2.16.49, S.E.*M.*9.182, Asp. *in EN*56.34, Luc.*Symp.*23, Gal.8.25; περὶ τῶν πρὸς τὰς φωνὰς σωριτῶν λόγων, title of work by Chrysipp., *Stoic.*2.6. (σωρείτης, -ειτικός are freq. vv. ll.) **-ῑτικός**, ή, όν, *of the nature of the* σωρίτης, σ. ἀπορία S.E.*P.*3.80 (**σωρικὴ ἀπορία** in *M.*1.68, 80 may be f. l.), Gal.18(2).254. Adv. -κῶς S.E.*M.*9.182. **-ῖτις**, ιδος, ἡ, of Demeter, *Giver of heaps of corn*, Orph.*H.*40.5.

⊛ **σωρο-βόλιον**, τό, *place for depositing heaps* (of corn or of refuse), *LW*424, 427 (Mylasa). **-ειδής**, ές, *like heaps*, Hsch. s. v. θίς.

**σωρός**, ὁ, *heap*, esp. *heap of corn*, Hes.*Op.*778, Theoc.7.155; σ. σίτου Hdt.1.22; πυρῶν Plu.2.697b (but σιρῷ is prob. cj.); of other things, σ. ψήγματος Hdt.6.125; ἀκανθέων Id.2.75; ξύλων, λίθων, νεκρῶν, X.*HG*4.4.12; λίθινος σ. *APl.*4.254: abs., *heap* or *mound* of earth, X.*Vect.*4.2 (pl.), Diph.100. 2. generally, *heap, quantity*, χρημάτων, κακῶν, ἀγαθῶν, Ar.*Pl.*269, 270, 804: opp. a definite number or quantity, Arist.*Metaph.*1044ᵃ4, 1084ᵇ22; σ. ἢ ὁρμαθὸν ψάμμου Id. *de An.*419ᵇ24: prov., κόγχην προπάροιθεν ἔχειν σωρῶν, of contentment. *Epigr.Gr.*446 (Palestine). 3. as Adj., πυροῦ σωροῦ, of a quality of corn, *PGiss.*63.7 (ii A. D.), *Ostr.*774 (cf. p.437), al.

**σωρότερος**, ὁ, *large cup*, *PLond.*1821.360; also fem., σωροτέρην ἀτάνυσσον ἐμοὶ παλάμηφιν ἑάων Dioscorus in *PLit.Lond.*98 ii 14 (dub.).

**σῶρυ**, τό, a kind of ore, perh. *ferrous sulphate, melanterite*: nom. σῶρι Dsc.5.102 (but σῶρυ as cited by Gal. and Orib.); the gen. is σώρεως in Dsc. l. c., *Hippiatr.*70, 96; *soreos* in Cels.6.9.5; *soreos* (v. l. *sorios, soryos*) in Plin.*HN*34.117.

⊛ **σῶς** (A), ὁ, ἡ, σῶν, τό, defect. Adj. of which the foll. forms occur: Att. and later Gr. nom. σῶς, σῶν, Th.8.81, D.21.126; acc. σῶν Th.3.34, D.20.142; nom. pl. σῷ (written σῶ, but cf. *EM*742.1) cited by Ael.Dion. *Fr.*302 from Th.1.74 (where σῶοι codd.); also σοί Ael.Dion. l. c.; acc. pl. masc. σῶς D.5.17, 8.16, 19.75, Luc.*Phal.*2.4; fem. sg. σᾶ Ar.*Fr.*631, *IG*14.644.15 (Bruttium), prob. in ib.2².123.8, but σῶς as fem., E.*Cyc.*294, Ar.*Fr.*658, Pl.*Phd.*106a, Call.*Aet.*3.1.40; neut. pl. σᾶ E.*Fr.*762, Pl.*Criti.*111c, *Ath.Mitt.*49.3 (Attica, iv B. C.): Ep. nom. sg. masc. σῶς Il.22.332 (here guaranteed by the metre), 13.773, Od.5.305, 15.42, 16.131, 22.28; σόος 19.300; acc. σῶν Il.1.117 (v. l. σόον, σάον), 17.367 (v. l. σόον); σόον 7.310, 8.246, 16.252 (v. l. σάον); nom. sg. fem. σόη 15.497; nom. pl. masc. σόοι 1.344, 5.531, 15.563, Od.4.98; nom. pl. neut. σόα Il.24.382, Od.13.364: Hdt. has nom. sg. σῶς 1.24, al.; neut. σόον (v. l. σῶον) 2.181; pl. σόοι (v. l. σῶοι) 8.39; fem. σόαι (σῶαι codd.) 1.66; neut. σόα (v. l. σῶα) 4.124, 6.86.α'; gen. pl. neut. σόων (v. l. σώων) 2.121.β': Hp. has σῶον *Art.*53: the stem σωο- never appears in Hom. or early poets, but is found in later poetry (nom. σῶος Max.386; Comp. σωότερος A.R.1.918), and in an Att. prose Inscr., neut. σῶον *IG*1².59.13, along with σῶν ib.128.6, 2².1172.14; the foll. forms from σωο- are found in Att. and later texts: σῶος X.*An.*2.1.32, Luc.*Abd.*5; σῶον Lys.7.17, 20.24, Arist.*Oec.*1347ᵃ24, Plu.2.786f, Sor.2.60, Aristid.1.425 J., Lib.*Or.*48.3; σῶοι X.*An.*2.2.21, al., D.19.57, 153, 326; σώους Luc.*Laps.*8, Aristid.1.426 J.; σῶα X.*Cyr.*7.4.13, *HG*1.1.24, Arist. *Ath.*30.4; fem. σώα X.*HG*7.4.4, D.56.37, Aristid.2.78 J.; acc. σώαν D.21.177, Aristid.2.428 J.; gen. σώας D.19.78, *OGI*214.20 (Didyma, iii B. C.): the Papyri have acc. sg. masc. σῶον *PLond.*2.301.13 (ii A. D.), etc., acc. pl. neut. σῶα *BGU*1106.31 (i B. C.), etc.: the word is rare in Lxx, acc. sg. masc. σῶον 2*Ma.*12.24; nom. pl. fem. σῶαι (v. l. σῶοι) Thd.*Bel*17; acc. pl. masc. σώους 3*Ma.*2.7; neut. σῶα 2*Ma.*3.15; not found in *NT*: acc. to Thom.Mag.p.328 R. σῶς is Att. for σῶος, σῶν for σῶον (masc. and neut.), σῶς for σώους and σώας, but all other Att. forms are uncontr. (σῶοι, σῶα): the form σῷος is recommended by Did.ap.*EM*741.43, but rejected by Hdn.Gr.ib.46 (cf. Hdn.Gr.2.53), and is found in cod. Σ of D.18.49, al.; σῴην Babr.94.8; σῷον *AP*6.349.6 (Phld.): the form σάος is preserved as v. l. in Il.1.117 (ap.A.D.*Conj.*223.10), 16.252, and in the Comp. σαώτερος, v. σάος:—*safe and sound, alive and well*, of persons, ἔφης . . σῶς ἔσσεσθ' Il.22.332; οὕνεκά οἱ σῶς ἔσσι Od.15.42; ὅτι οἱ σῶς εἰμι 16.131; βούλομ' ἐγὼ λαὸν σῶν (v. l. σόον, σάον) ἔμμεναι Il.1.117, cf. 8.246; σόοι ἔμμεναι Od.4.98; ἄλοχός τε σόη καὶ παῖδες Il.15.497; σόοι εἶναι Hdt.5.96; σῶς καὶ ὑγιής Id.4.76, Th.3.34, Pl.*Ti.*82b. II. of things, *safe, whole*, ἵνα περ τάδε τοι σόα μίμνῃ (sc. τὰ κειμήλια) Il.24.382, cf. Od.13.364, Hdt.6.86.α'; οὐδέ κε φαίης ἠέλιον σῶν ἔμμεναι (v. l. σόον) Il.17.367; so ἄγαλμα . . , τὸ ἔτι καὶ ἐς ἐμὲ ἦν σόον was *preserved, extant*, Hdt.2.181; αἱ πέδαι ἔτι καὶ ἐς ἐμὲ ἦσαν σόαι Id.1.66, cf. 8.39; ποτὸν . . , εἴπερ ἐστὶ σῶν S.*Ph.*21; ἔστι σῶν [θοἰμάτιον] καὶ οὐκ ἀπόλωλεν Pl.*Phd.*87b; ἡ χιὼν οὖσα σῶς καὶ ἄτηκτος ib.106a; τὸ ἀθάνατον σῶν καὶ ἀδιάφθορον ib.e; ἔχειν τι σῶν X.*An.*7.6.32; τῶν σημάντρων ἐόντων σόων *intact*, Hdt.2.121.β'; σῶαι αἱ σφραγῖδες; Lxx *Bel*17; παραδώσω τὸν γόμον σῶον καὶ ἀκακούργητον *PLond.*2.301.13 (ii A. D.); ἅ τε ἐὰν λάβῃ, σῶα συντηρήσειν καὶ ἀποδώσειν *BGU*1106.31 (i B. C.); of money, *intact, undiminished*, E.*Hec.*994; τἀργύριον σῶν παρέχειν Ar.*Lys.*488, *IG*2².1172.14, cf. Pl.*R.*333c; σῶα ἀποδιδόναι τὰ χρήματα X.*Cyr.*7.4.13. 2. of events, *safe, sure, certain*, νῦν τοι (μοι) σῶς αἰπὺς ὄλεθρος Il.13.773, Od.5.305, 22.28. (σάϝος, cf. Cypr. pr. n. Σαϝοκλέϝης.)

**σῶς** (B), contr. for σόος, σοῦς, ὁ, = βλάστησις, dub. in Hsch. s. v. σῶν.

**σώσανδρον**, τό, = δελφίνιον, Ps.-Dsc.3.73.

**σωσάνιον**, τό, *shoulder-piece of a coat of mail*, Sch.Ar.*Nu.*70.

**σωσίβιοι**· οἱ κωβιοί, Hsch. **σώσικες**· οἱ ἑφθοὶ κύαμοι, Id.

**σωσί-οικος** [ῐ], ον, *saving the house*, Apollon.*Lex.* s. v. σῶκος, Hsch. ⊛ **-πολις**, ιδος and ιος, ὁ, ἡ, *saving the city*, λεώς Ar.*Ach.*163; Ζεύς Str.14.1.41, cf. *SIG*589.48 (Magn. Mae., ii B. C.).

**σωσ-τέος**, α, ον, *to be saved*, Aristid.*Or.*24(44).37. II. σωστέον *one must save*, E.*HF*1385; *you must be saved*, Ar.*Lys.*501.—The form σωτέος is cited by Hsch., Phot., Suid. **-τικός**, ή, όν, *able to save, maintain*, or *preserve*, c. gen., ἡ δικαιοσύνη νόμων σ. Arist.*Top.*149ᵇ33; σ. ἢ ποιητικὸν ἀγαθοῦ Id.*MM*1183ᵇ36; τοῦ θερμοῦ Id.*Pr.*932ᵇ3 (Comp.); τὸ ἴσον σ. ὁμονοίας Id.*Mu.*397ᵃ3: also in later Prose, Dsc.4.81, Max.Tyr.6.2, Alex.Aphr. *in Top.*455.11, Porph. *Abst.*3.26, Procl. *in Alc.*p.55 C., etc. **-τός**, ή, όν, *safe*, πλοῖον Apollon.*Mir.*6.

**σῶστρα**, τά, (σῴζω, cf. σαοστρέω) *reward for saving one's life, thank-offering for deliverance from a danger*, σῶστρα τοῦ παιδὸς θύειν [θεοῖς] Hdt.1.118, cf. *AP*9.378.7 (Pall.); σ. ὀφείλειν τισί Luc.*Salt.*8; ἐκτίνειν τισί Id.*DMar.*14.1. 2. *reward for bringing back* lost cattle or runaway slaves, σ. παρέχειν Hdt.4.9; σῶστρα τούτου ἀνακηρύσσειν X.*Mem.*2.10.2; σῶστρα δὲ μὴ ἐξεῖμ[εν ἐσπρᾶξαι] *Foed.Delph. Pell.*2 A 25. 3. *physician's fee*, Poll.6.186; *thank-offering* to

Asclepios, *IG*14.967*a* 1, *b* 1 (Rome), $4^2$(1).483 (Epid.).—The sg. only in App.*BC*4.62.

**σώτειρα**, ἡ, fem. of σωτήρ, Pi.*O.*13.54, Hdt.2.156, E.*Med.*528, *Heracl.*588, Pl.*Lg.*960c. 2. freq. as epith. of protecting goddesses, of Τύχα, Pi.*O.*12.2 (cf. σωτήρ I. 2); of Θέμις, ib.8.21; of Εὐνομία, ib.9.16; of Athena, Lycurg.17, *IG*2².676.12; of Artemis, *AP* 6.267 (Diotim.), *IG*2².4695; of Hecate, *CIG*(add.) 3827*q* (Cotiaeum); of Rhea, ib.4695 (Egypt), etc.; ἡ Σ. abs., of Demeter, Ar.*Ra.*379 (lyr.), Arist.*Rh.*1419ᵃ3; of Kore, *SIG*1158.5 (Cyzicus, iii B.C.); of Artemis, *IG*2².1343.24,40, etc.; of Cleopatra II or III, *PTheb.Bank* 11.2, *OGI*739.8 (ii B.C.). II. *an antidote*, Gal.ap.Hsch., Paul. Aeg.3.45, 7.11.23.

**σωτέος**, v. σωστέος. **σωτεύματα**· σωτρεύματα, Hsch.

**❋σωτήρ**, ῆρος, ὁ, voc. σῶτερ (v. infr. I. 2): poet. **σαώτηρ** Simon. 129, Call.*Del.*166: (σῴζω):—*saviour, deliverer*, c. gen. of person etc. saved, σ. ἀνθρώπων, νηῶν, *h.Hom.*22.5, 33.6; τῆς Ἑλλάδος Hdt. 7.139; ἑστίας πατρός A.*Ch.*264; but also c. gen. rei, [νόσου], κακῶν, βλάβης, *a preserver from* disease, ills, hurt, S.*OT*304, E. *Med.*360 (anap.), *Heracl.*640; c. dat., σ. τῇ πόλει καὶ νῷν φανείς Ar.*Eq.*149; σ. δόμοις Id.*Nu.*1161; of a philosopher or guide, ὁδηγόν.. ὅν φησι σωτῆρα μόνον Phld.*Lib.*p.20O.; esp. of Epicurus, ὁ σ. ὁ ἡμέτερος Polystr.*Herc.*346 p.80V. 2. epith. of Ζεύς, Pi.*O.* 5.17, *Fr.*30.5, *IG*2².410.18 (iv B.C.), etc.; to whom persons after a safe voyage offered sacrifice, Diph.43.24; there was often a temple of Ζεὺς Σ. at harbours, e.g. the Piraeus, Str.9.1.15; to Ζεὺς Σωτήρ the third cup of wine was dedicated, τρίτον Σωτῆρι σπένδειν Pi.*I.*6(5). 8; τρίτην Διὸς Σωτῆρος εὐκταίαν λίβα A.*Fr.*55; Ζεῦ σῶτερ Ar.*Th.* 1009, Din.1.36; ὦ Ζεῦ σῶτερ Philem.79.21, Men.532.2; to drink this cup became a symbol of good luck, and the third time came to mean the lucky time, τρίτος ἦλθέ ποθεν—σωτῆρ' ἢ μόρον εἴπω; A.*Ch.* 1073 (anap.); whence the proverb τὸ τρίτον τῷ σωτῆρι the third (i.e. the lucky) time, Pl.*R.*583b, *Phlb.*66d, *Chrm.*167a; and Zeus was himself called τρίτος σ., Παλλάδος καὶ Λοξίου ἕκατι καὶ τοῦ πάντα κραίνοντος τρίτου σωτῆρος A.*Eu.*760, cf. *Supp.*26 (anap.). b. epith. of other gods, as of Apollo, Id.*Ag.*512, etc.; of Hermes, Id.*Ch.*2; of Asclepios, *IG*4.718 (Hermione), 7.2808 (Hyettus, iii A.D.), *BMus. Cat.Coins Pontus* p.156 (Nicaea); σ. εὐρυχόρου Λακεδαίμονος Isyll. 82; τὸν σ. τῶν ὅλων Ἀσκληπιόν Jul.*Or.*4.153b; Ζεὺς Ἀσκληπιὸς σ. τῶν ὅλων Aristid.*Or.*42(6).4; of the Dioscuri, *IG*12(3).422 (Thera, iii B.C.), 14.2406.108 (Tarentum), etc.; even with fem. deities, Τύχη σωτήρ, for σώτειρα, A.*Ag.*664, S.*OT*81: generally, of *guardian* or *tutelary gods*, Hdt.8.138, A.*Supp.*982, S.*Ph.*738; τοῖς ἀποτροπαίοις καὶ σωτῆρσι X.*HG*3.3.4. 3. applied to rulers, διὰ σέ, βασιλεῦ (viz. Ptolemy IV Philopator), τὸν πάντων κοινὸν σ. *PEnteux.* 11.6 (iii B.C.); Πτολεμαῖος Σ. *OGI*19.1, al.; Ἀντίοχος Σ. ib.233.3, al.; of Roman Emperors or governors, ib.668.3 (Egypt, i A.D.), *PLond.*1.177.24 (i A.D.), etc. 4. in Lxx and *NT*, applied to God, Lxx *De.*32.15, al., 1*Ep.Ti.*1.1, al.; to Christ, *Ev.Luc.*2.11, al. II. in Poets, as Adj., σ. ναὸς πρόνονος A.*Ag.*897, cf. Pi.*Fr.* 159; with a fem. noun, γονῆς σωτῆρος (as Herm. for γυνή) A.*Th.* 225; τιμαὶ σωτῆρες the office or prerogative *of saving*, of the Dioscuri, E.*El.*993 (anap.). III. name of a month created by Caligula, *BGU*1078 (38 A.D.), *PRyl.*2.149 (39/40 A.D.), etc.

**❋σωτηρ-ία**, Ion. -ίη, ἡ, *deliverance, preservation*, σωτηρίην ὑποθησόμενον ὑμῖν Hdt.5.98; σ. μηχανᾶσθαι Id.7.172; σ. Ἕλλησι δώσουσ' ἔρχομαι E.*IA*1472; σ. κατεργάσασθαι Id.*Heracl.*1045; φέρειν Id.*Tr.* 753; ἀπεργάζεσθαι, πορίζειν, ἐκπορίζεσθαι, Pl.*Lg.*647b, *Prt.*321b, Th.6.83; σωτηρίαν ἔχειν S.*Aj.*1080, E.*Or.*1178, etc.; ζητεῖν Isoc.4. 95; εὑρίσκεσθαι Aeschin.3.134; also σωτηρίας τυχεῖν A.*Pers.*508, *Ch.*203, X.*Cyr.*4.1.2, etc.; ἐνεύχομαί σοι τὴν Ἀπολλωνίου σ. *PCair. Zen.*482.4 (iii B.C.); ὀμνύω σοι (or σοι) τὴν σαυτοῦ σ. ib.324.2 (iii B.C.); ὑπὲρ σωτηρίας.. Αὐτοκράτορος, = Lat. *pro salute Imperatoris*, *OGI*678.1 (Egypt, ii A.D.). 2. *a way* or *means of safety* (= μηχανὴ σωτηρίας A.*Th.*209), ἔστι τις σ.; Id.*Pers.*735 (troch.); ἔχεις τιν'.. σ.; E.*Or.*778 (troch.), cf. Ar.*Eq.*12; εἰς σ. ἄλλην καταφυγεῖν Antipho 2.4. 1, cf. Th.3.20. 3. *safe return*, ἡ ἐς τὴν πατρίδα σ. Id.7.70; ἡ οἴκαδε σ. D.50.16, cf. Plu.2.241e; ἡ σ. ἣν συνέβη τῷ πατρὶ δεῦρο D.57.20; νόστιμος σ. A.*Pers.*797, *Ag.*343, 1238. 4. in Lxx and *NT*, *salvation*, ὁ θεὸς τῆς σ. μου Lxx *Ps.*50(51).14, al.; σ. ψυχῶν 1*Ep.Pet.* 1.9; εὐαγγέλιον τῆς σ. *Ep.Eph.*1.13, etc. II. of things, *keeping safe, preservation*, Hdt.4.98; c. gen., A.*Eu.*909, Pl.*R.*433c, etc.; *maintenance*, τῶν οἰκοδομημάτων καὶ ὁδῶν Arist.*Pol.*1321ᵇ21; τῶν νόμων Pl.*R.*425e; τοῦ οὐρανοῦ, τῶν ἄστρων, Arist.*Cael.*284ᵃ20, *Mete.*355ᵃ 20. 2. *security, guarantee for safety*, σ. ἔστω τῶν ὑποκειμένων *guarantee for the safe keeping* of.., Syngr.ap.D.35.13; σωτηρίας ἕνεκα τοῖς πολλοῖς τῶν σωμάτων for their *safe custody*, Pl.*Lg.*908a; ἐπὶ τῇ τῆς ψυχῆς σωτηρίᾳ ib.909a; σωτηρίαι τῆς πολιτείας *ways of preserving* it, Arist.*Pol.*1301ᵃ23, cf. 1289ᵇ24, Pl.*Prt.*354b. 3. *security, safety*, τοῦ κοινοῦ Th.2.60; τοῦ βίου Pl.*Prt.*356d. 4. c. gen. obj., *security against*, ἀπορίας Philem.213.12. 5. *bodily health, well-being*, *BGU*423.13 (ii A.D.), *POxy.*939.20 (iii A.D.), etc. **-ιακόν**· τὸ εἰς ἐκφορὰν νεκροῦ διδόμενον, Hsch. **-ιασταί**, οἱ, *worshippers of Artemis* Σώτειρα, *IG* 2².1343.9, 12(1).35, al. (Rhodes). **-ικά**, τά, name of a festival, *SIG*539*A* 28 (Delph., iii B.C.). **❋-ιος**, ον, *saving, delivering*, αὐγαὶ ἡλίου A.*Supp.*213, cf. Th.3.53, Pl.*Plt.*311a, etc.; θεοὶ *BGU* 362 v 1 (iii A.D.); of symptoms, *betokening recovery*, Hp.*Aph.*7.37; ὀλιγοχρόνιόν τε καὶ σωτήριον δηλοῖ τὸ νόσημα Gal.9.574; ἐλπὶς σπέρματος σωτηρίου hope of seed *to preserve* or *perpetuate* the race, A.*Ch.* 236; δέχεσθαι τὸν ἱκέτην σωτήριον *who brings safety* to our state, S.*OC* 487 codd. b. c. dat., *bringing safety* or *deliverance to..*, ὕδωρ ἰχθύσι σ. Heraclit.61; ἄριστα καὶ πόλει σ. A.*Th.*183, cf. *Ch.*505, E.*Heracl.*402, *Ph.*918; νησιῶται καὶ ναύτῃσιν *IG*12(8) p.x (Thasos, vi/v B.C.): also c. gen., τῆς βασιλικῆς ἀρχῆς σ. Pl.*Ep.*354b, cf. Arist.*Pol.*1314ᵃ13: Comp. and Sup., τὸ πείθεσθαι σωτηριώτερον αὐτοῖς X.*Mem.*3.3.10; ἵππος -ώτατος τῷ ἀναβάτῃ Id.*Eq.*3.12. 2. of persons, much like σωτήρ, E. *Or.*657, *Ba.*965, etc.; θεοί, Ζεὺς σ., S.*El.*281, *Fr.*425; c. dat., Th.7. 64; [Ἑλένη] ναυτίλοις σ. E.*Or.*1637; c. gen. pers., τάχ' ἂν γενοίμεθ' αὐτοῦ.. σωτήριοι S.*Aj.*779. II. as Subst., σωτήρια, τά, *deliverance, safety*, τἀκείνου σωτήρια Id.*El.*925 (so σ. πράγματα A.*Ag.*646); ἡ ἐλπὶς τῶν σ. Arist.*Rh.*1383ᵃ17: also in sg., ἔρυμα τῆς χώρας καὶ πόλεως σ. A.*Eu.*701; ἐπινοεῖν τι σ. τοῖς παροῦσι Luc.*JTr.*18, cf. *DMeretr.*9. 3. 2. σωτήρια (sc. ἱερά), τά, *a thank-offering for deliverance*, σ. θύειν θεοῖς X.*An.*3.2.9, 5.1.1, cf. *Marm.Par.*7, etc.; σ. ἄγειν Luc.*Herm.* 86; σ. τοῦ βασιλέως πανηγυρίζειν *for his escape*, Hdn.1.10.7; of a festival at Delphi, commemorating the retreat of the Gauls, *SIG*402. 5 (iii B.C.), etc. 3. *physician's fee*, Poll.6.186. 4. *public privy*, at Smyrna, *AP*9.642 (in lemmate), Suid. III. Σωτήριος (sc. μήν), ὁ, also written Σωτήρειος, name of a month, *PLond.*2.141 (i A.D.), *PFlor.* 55 (i A.D.), etc. IV. Adv. -ίως Antip.*Stoic.*3.256, Ph.2.12, al., Plu.*Luc.*5, S.E.*M.*9.113, etc.; σ. ἔχειν to be *capable of recovery*, Plu. 2.918d. **-ιώδης**, ες, *wholesome*, φάρμακον Gal.14.248 (Sup.); *giving safety*, Hld.10.16: Comp., D.C.53.19: Sup., *IGRom.*4.915*c*9 (Cibyra). Adv. -δῶς, ἔχειν to be *on the way to recovery*, Aët.5.51; = *salubriter, salutabiliter*, Gloss.

**σῶτρον**, τό, *wooden felloe of the wheel* (the iron hoop or tire being ἐπίσωτρον), Poll.1.144, 10.53; cf. σωτεύματα.

**σωφρον-έω**, poet. **σαοφ-** Opp.*H.*3.446, *AP*5.301.11 (Agath.):—*to be sound of mind*, Hdt.3.35, *Ev.Marc.*5.15, Gal.15.449; ὃς ἦν φορητὸς οὐδὲ σωφρονῶν Babr.90.4. 2. *to be temperate, moderate, show self-control*, Heraclit.112,116 (v.l.), A.*Pr.*982, *Pers.*829, *IG*1².22.69, Antipho 2.2.5, Th.8.24, Pl.*Phdr.*244a, X.*Cyr.*8.1.30; τὸ σωφρονεῖν, = σωφροσύνη, A.*Ag.*1425, cf. 181, Ar.*Nu.*1061, 1071; ἐς Ἀφροδίτην σ. E.*IA*1159, cf. *Ba.*314 (s. v.l.); περὶ τοὺς θεούς X.*Mem.*1.1.20; of soldiers, σ. καὶ εὐτακτεῖν ib.3.5.21, cf. Lys.12.47; σ. καὶ ὁμονοεῖν And.1.109; opp. ὑπερφρονέω, *Ep.Rom.*12.3: with a part., πέμποντες σωφρονοῖμεν ἄν Pl.*Men.*90d. 3. *come to one's senses, learn moderation*, Hdt.3.64; σ. ὑπὸ στένει A.*Eu.*521 (lyr.); σωφρονοῦντες ἐν χρόνῳ ib.1000 (lyr.); οὐ σωφρονήσεις; S.*Aj.*1259; ἐσωφρόνησας Id.*Ph.*1259; σεσωφρονηκώς *when he had recovered his senses*, Pl. *Phdr.*241b. 4. Pass., τὰ σεσωφρονημένα ἐν τῷ βίῳ μοι *things I had done with discretion*, Aeschin.2.4. **-ημα**, ατος, τό, *an example of self-control*, X.*Ages.*5.4, *Stoic.*3.136; cf. σωφρόνισμα. **-ητέον**, *one must be temperate*, Luc.*Hist.Conscr.*45. **-ίζω**, *recall* a person *to his senses, chasten*, E.*Fr.*209, Pl.*Grg.*478d, X.*Cyr.* 8.6.16, etc.; ἡ τοιαύτη ἧττα σωφρονίζειν ἱκανή ib.3.1.20; τοὺς πονηροτάτους αἱ συμφοραὶ σ. D.25.93: folld. by inf., ἵνα σωφρονίζωσιν τὰς νέας φιλάνδρους εἶναι κτλ. *Ep.Tit.*2.4:—Pass., *to be chastened, learn self-control*, Th.6.78, X.*Cyr.*3.1.19, etc. 2. of passions, things, etc., σ. τὸ θυμούμενον τῆς γνώμης Antipho 2.3.3; οὐ τὴν λαγνείαν λιμῷ σ. X.*Mem.*2.1.16; ἄμπνοὰς σ. to pant less violently, E.*HF*869 (troch.); τῶν κατὰ τὴν πόλιν τι ἐς εὐτέλειαν σ. to reduce the expenses of government at home, Th.8.1. **-ικός**, ή, όν, *naturally temperate, self-controlled*, of persons, X.*Mem.*1.3.9, Arist.*Rh.*1390ᵃ14, *EN*1144ᵇ5, etc.; οἱ βουλόμενοι σ. εἶναι (ironically) *Stoic.*1.100; σ. τὴν ἀναβολὴν Luc.*Tim.*54. Adv. -κῶς Ar.*Eq.*545, Sor.1.33: Comp. -ώτερον Ath.10.426c. 2. of things, Pl.*Plt.*307a; σεμνότης Plb. 22.20.2, etc.; σωφρονικωτέρα τροφή Muson.*Fr.*18ᴮ p.104 H.; τὸ σ. X.*Mem.*3.10.5, cf. Metrod.*Herc.*831.15; τὰ σ. καὶ ἀνδρεῖα Phld.*Mus.* p.50 K. **-ισμα**, ατος, τό, *chastisement, lesson*, A.*Supp.*992, Aristarch. Trag.3 (v.l. -ημα), App.*Pun.*78. **❋-ισμός**, ὁ, *teaching of morality* or *moderation*, Str.1.2.3, J.*BJ*2.1.3, Plu.2.653d, etc.; *self-control*, *Ep. Ti.*1.7. **-ιστήρ**, ῆρος, ὁ, = σωφρονιστής, Plu.*Cat.Ma.*27. II. pl., *wisdom-teeth* (= κραντῆρες), Hp.*Carn.*13, Cleanth.*Stoic.*1.118, Ruf.*Onom.*51, Hsch., etc. III. σωφρονιστὴρ λίθος at Thebes, which *restored reason* to Heracles, Paus.9.11.2. **-ιστήριον**, τό, *house of correction*, Pl.*Lg.*908a, Ph.2.54. **-ιστής**, οῦ, ὁ, *one that chastens* or *chastises*, Th.6.87, Pl.*R.*471a, D.19.285, etc.; ὁ δῆμος.. ἐκείνων σ. Th.8.48; τῆς γνώμης Id.3.65; ὁ σ. λόγος Lyc.*Fr.*3; νόμους σ. ἐπί τισι τιθέναι D.H.2.24. II. at Athens, *superintendents of the youth in the gymnasia*, 10 in number, *IG*2².1156, al., Arist.*Ath.* 42.2, Pl.*Ax.*367a. **-ιστικός**, ή, όν, *making temperate, teaching morality*, δύναμις S.E.*M.*6.21; λόγοι Poll.3.100; [ᾠδή] Eust.137. 37. **-ιστύς**, ύος, ἡ, = σωφρονισμός, σωφρονιστύος ἕνεκα for the sake of *correction*, Pl.*Lg.*934a.

**❋σωφροσύνη** [ῠ], Dor. -ύνα, Ep. and poet. **σαοφροσύνη** (as in Hom. and in later poetry, *IG*2².3632.11, 3753), ἡ, *soundness of mind, prudence, discretion*, Od.23.13; in pl., ib.30; the common form first in Thgn.379, 701, 1138, Epich.101; αἰδὼς σωφροσύνης πλεῖστον μετέχει Th.1.84; σ. λαβεῖν Id.8.64; *sanity*, opp. μανία, X.*Mem.* 1.1.16, cf. *Act.Ap.*26.25. 2. *moderation in sensual desires, self-control, temperance*, Democr.210, Ar.*Nu.*962 (anap.), *Pl.*563 (anap.), And.1.131, Pl.*Phdr.*237e, etc.; σ. τὸ κρατεῖν ἡδονῶν καὶ ἐπιθυμιῶν Id. *Smp.*196c; σ. τὸ περὶ τὰς γυναῖκας (sc. ἔργον) Arist.*Pol.*1263ᵇ9, cf. *EN*1117ᵇ23, Pl.*Phd.*68c, *R.*430e sq., 1*Ep.Ti.*2.9. 3. in a political sense, *a moderate form of government*, Th.8.64.

**σωφρόσῠνος**, η, ον, = σώφρων, Porph.*in Cat.*135.23.

**σώφρων**, Ep. and poet. **σαόφρων** (as in Hom., v. infr., Pi.*Pae.*9. 46), ονος, ὁ, ἡ: neut. σῶφρον:—prop. *of sound mind* (from σῶς, φρήν, cf. Pl.*Cra.*411e, Arist.*EN*1140b11): hence, *discreet, prudent,* οὐκ ἄν με σαόφρονα μυθήσαιο ἔμμεναι Il.21.462, cf. Od.4.158; opp. ἄφρων, Thgn.431, 454, 497; opp. νήπιος, Id.483; opp. ἀνόητος, Hdt.1.4; σώφρονες περὶ θεούς X.*Mem.*4.3.2; σωφρονέστατος ἐν τῇ τέχνῃ Hp.*Prorrh.*2.2. 2. of things, τοῖσι λόγοις σῶφρον ἔπεστιν ἄνθος Ar.*Nu.*1025 (lyr.); σ. οἶκτος *reasonable* compassion, Th.3.59; -έστατον κήρυγμα Aeschin.3.4; σώφρον' εἶπας E.*IA*1024; ἄλλο τι -έστερον γνώσεσθε Th.5.111; σῶφρόν ἐστι c. inf., Id.1.42. II. in Att., esp. *having control over the sensual desires, temperate, self-controlled, chaste* (σώφρων ὁ μετρίας ἐπιθυμίας ἔχων Pl.*Def.*415d, cf. σωφροσύνη I), μοι δὸς -εστέραν πολὺ μητρὸς γενέσθαι A.*Ch.*140, cf. S.*Aj.*132; γυνὴ σ. And. 4.14, cf. S.*Fr.*682; σ. καὶ ἐγκρατὴς ἑαυτοῦ Pl.*Grg.*491d, cf. 1*Ep.Ti.* 3.2, etc. 2. of things, σ. γνώμη A.*Ag.*1664 (troch.); εὐχαί Id. *Supp.*710; σ. ὑμέναιοι, λέχη, E.*Or.*558, *El.*1099; τράπεζα, δίαιτα, Id. *Fr.*893 (lyr.), Pl.*Ep.*336c; ἀριστοκρατία *moderate,* Th.3.82; χάρις ib. 58; βίος Pl.*Lg.*733e; φρονεῖν σώφρονα S.*Fr.*64. 3. τὸ σῶφρον, = σωφροσύνη, Id.*Fr.*786, E.*Hipp.*431, Th.1.37, 3.82; σοῦ τὸ σ. E.*Andr.*365, cf. 346, etc.; ἐπὶ τὸ -έστερον λαμβάνειν τι Hdt.3.71; τὸ -έστατον Th.3. 62; τὰ σώφρονα λάγδην πατεῖται S.*Fr.*683. III. Adv. -όνως A.*Th.* 645, *Eu.*44, Hdt.4.77; σ. τραφῆναι Ar.*Eq.*334 (lyr.); σ. τε καὶ μετρίως Pl.*R.*399b; δικαίως πράττοντες καὶ σ. Id.*Alc.*1.134d; σ. ἐφέπεσθαι *cautiously,* X.*Ages.*2.3: Comp., -έστερον πολιτεύειν adopt a *more moderate* constitution, Th.8.53, cf. 1.84, X.*Eq.Mag.*1.14, etc.; but -εστέρως E.*IA*379 (troch.): Sup. -έστατα Isoc.7.13, Pl.*Lg.*728e.

**σώχω**, Ion. for ψώχω, *rub to pieces, grind,* Nic.*Th.*590, 696, Hsch.; cf. κατασώχω.

**σώω**, Ep. for σῴζω (q. v.).

# T

**T τ, ταῦ, τό,** indecl., twenty-second letter of the Formello abecedaria, *IG*14.2420, but nineteenth of the Ion. alphabet, cf. Pl. *Cra.*394b: as numeral τ' = 300, but ͵τ = 300,000.

**τ',** apostroph. for τε, *and.* 2. τοι is elided in Od.1.60, 347, also in Aeolic verse, θέλω τί τ' εἴπην Sapph.28, cf. Alc.*Oxy.*1788.15 ii 9, but is joined with ἄν, ἄρα by crasis. 3. Attic τό, τά are never elided, but may suffer crasis. 4. τὶ or τί can suffer neither elision nor crasis.

**τά,** v. ὁ, ὅ, and ὅς. II. v. τίς.

**ταβαίτας,** ου, ὁ, *wooden bowl,* a Persian word, Amynt.ap.Ath.14. 500d.

**ταβάλα·** ταβῆλα, Parthian word for a *drum,* Hsch.; cf. *tabulas* (acc. pl.) in codd. of Seneca *Ep.*6.4.4.

**ταβάσιος,** ὁ, perh. = τοπάζιος, *PHolm.*11.38; λίθον τὸν καλούμενον ταβάσι(ν) ib.4.12; ὁ λεγόμενος ταβάσις ἐκ τῆς Αἰγύπτου καταφερόμενος ib.8.7.

**τᾰβέλλ-α,** ἡ, *writing tablet, note, PHamb.*29.23 (i A.D.), *POxy.*273. 7 (i A.D.); τ. ἐλευθερώσεως manumission-*letter, Sammelb.*5217.16 (ii A.D.), cf. *BGU*388 i 11, 16 (ii/iii A.D.). ⊕ **-άριος,** ὁ, = Lat. *tabellarius,* τοῦ κυρίου Καίσαρος *IG*5(2).525.3 (Lycosura), cf. *PCair.Preis.* 11.10 (ii/iii A.D.). **-ίων,** ωνος, ὁ, = Lat. *tabellio, PStrassb.*1.15 (v A.D.), *PMasp.*121.30 (vi A.D.).

**τᾰβερνοδύτης** [ῠ], ου, ὁ, = *ganeo, sabinario, Gloss.*

**τάβλ-α** (so *BGU*1079.29 (i A.D.)) or **τάβλη,** ἡ, = Lat. *tabula,* ἀπὸ χαλκῆς τάβλης Wilcken *Chr.*460.15 (ii A.D.), cf. *BGU*780.15 (ii A.D.); *dice-table,* acc. τάβλην *AP*9.482.27 (Agath.), but τάβλαν ib. 767 lemma; acc. τάβλαν, of a mummy-label, Wilcken *Chr.*499.5 (ii/iii A.D.); acc. pl. τάβλας, of corn-distribution *tokens, Sammelb.*4514 (iii A.D.). ⊕ **-άριος,** ὁ, = Lat. *tabularius, PSI*3.281.39 (ii A.D.), *IGRom.*4.679 (Eulandra), etc. **-ίζω,** *play at dice,* Hsch. s. v. κυβεῦσαι, Suid. s. v. πεττεύουσι, Zonar. s. v. πεττοί; written ταυλ- in Thom.Mag.p.212 R. **-ίον,** τό, *tray,* τ. μαγειρικά *PFay.*104.4 (iii A.D.), cf. *PLond.*1.191.14 (ii A.D.), 3.964.10 (iii A.D.). II. τ. χελώνης the *shell* of a tortoise, *Gp.*12.7.5. III. = *latus clavus,* Suid. s. v. χλαμύς. **-ιόπη,** ἡ, comic word, formed after Καλλιόπη, *a game at dice, AP*11.373 (Pall.). **-ιστήριον,** τό, = κυβεῖον, Sch. Aeschin.1.53. **-ιστής,** οῦ, ὁ, *dice-player, Gloss.*

**τάβλον,** τό, perh. = ταβλίον I, τάβλα γ' *BGU*338.8 (ii/iii A.D.).

**ταβλοπάροχος,** ὁ, sine interpr., *Gloss.*

**τάβλ-ωμα,** ατος, τό, = δρύφακτος, Sch.Ar.*Eq.*672. **-ωτός,** όν, *boarded,* δρύφακτοι Sch.Ar.*V.*348, 385.

⊕ **τᾱγά,** ἁ, *time during which a ταγός holds office,* i. e. war-time, opp. ἀταγία, *SIG*55 (Thessaly, v B.C.).

**τᾱγαῖος,** α, ον, *acting by command,* Hsch. **τάγανα·** ταῦτα, Κρῆτες, Id.

**ταγαρίζα,** τά, perh. = *ταγαρίδια, pl. of Dim. of ταγή 5, *supplies,* or = τὰ γαρίζα, = *γαρίδια, Dim. of γάρος, *POxy.*1158.12 (iii A.D.).

**ταγατίζων·** κιχλίζων, Hsch.

**ταγγ-ή,** ἡ, (ταγγός) *rancidity,* Alex.Aphr.*Pr.*2.70. II. a kind of *scrofulous tumour,* Hp.*Epid.*2.1.7. **-ίασις,** εως, ἡ, = foreg. II, *Gloss.* **-ίζω,** *to be* or *become rancid,* Crito ap.Aët.8.2, *Gp.*9.22. 3. **-ός,** ή, όν, *rancid,* ibid.

**τᾱγεία,** ἡ, *office* or *rank of* ταγός, X.*HG*6.4.34.

**τᾱγείς,** v. τάσσω.

**τάγευμα,** ατος, τό, dub. l. in A.*Myrm.* in *PSI*11.1211.14.

⊕ **τᾱγ-εύω,** *to be* ταγός or *chief* of Thessaly, X.*HG*6.1.19:—Pass., *to be united under one* ταγός, ib.6.1.8. 2. *to be chief of a phratria, Schwyzer*323 *A* 1, *B* 31, 33 (Delph., iv B.C.). 3. *to be magistrate* of a Thessalian town, *IG*9(2).517.24 (Larissa, iii B.C.), 531.2 (Thess., i B.C.). II. Med., *let* soldiers *be posted* or *stationed,* ἄνδρας ἀρίστους . . πυλῶν ἐπ' ἐξόδοισι τάγευσαι A.*Th.*58. **-έω,** *to be ruler,* ἁπάσης Ἀσίδος Id.*Pers.*764.

⊕ **τᾱγή,** ἡ, *line of battle, front,* κἠν ἐκ τᾶς ταγᾶς ἕλσῃ ποκά Ar.*Lys.* 105. 2. *command, province,* Arist.*Oec.*1345b25. 3. *command, order, Supp.Epigr.*4.467.3 (Branchidae, iii A.D.). 4. *pension, alimony, PEnteux.*25.12 (iii B.C.). 5. *ration, PCair.Zen.*333.12, 569. 22, al., *Sammelb.*6796.54 (all iii B.C.), *BGU*1118.16 (i B.C.), *POxy.* 1139.3 (iv A.D.), Hsch.; for a horse, *Hippiatr.*97. 6. *stipulated amount to be delivered,* λίθων *PPetr.*2 p.7 (iii B.C.), cf. *PFlor.*119.6 (iii A.D.), *Sammelb.*7441.7 (iii A.D.). 7. *penalty, fine, TAM*2.40 (Telmessus).

**τᾰγήν·** ὄνομα ὀρνέου, Suid.

**τᾰγην-άριον** [ᾰρ], τό, Dim. of ἀτταγήν, Suid. s. v. ἀτταγᾶς, *Lex. de Spir.*p.192. **-ίας,** ου, ὁ, *pancake,* Magn.1, Cratin.125, Metag.6, Nicopho15. **-ίζω,** = τηγανίζω, *fry, broil,* Eup.351, Gal.6.637, al.:—Pass., Ph.2.250, Gal.6.768. **-ισις,** εως, ἡ, *frying,* ib.787, Alex.Aphr.*in Mete.*196.11. **-ισταί,** οἱ, *the Broilers,* name of a play by Ar. **-ιστός,** ή, όν, *fried,* ἰχθύες Alex.50, cf. Gal.6.812; [ᾰ] ib.706. **-ίτης** [ῑ], ου, ὁ, Att. for τηγανίτης, ib.490, Ath.14.646d.

**τᾰγηνο-κνῖσο-θήρας,** ου, ὁ, *frying-pan-sniffer,* Eup.172.

**τάγηνον** [ᾰ], τό, *frying-pan, saucepan,* Eup.346, Ar.*Eq.*929, Pl. Com.173.12, Anaxandr.33.4, Luc.*Symp.*38:—more freq. in form **τήγᾰνον,** Pherecr.104, 127, Eup.144, Lxx *Le.*2.5, al., Maria ap.Zos. Alch.p.236 B. (codd. vary in Gal.6.490, al.); cf. Ath.6.228f sq., who also cites ἤγανον from Anacr.26.

**τᾰγηνοστρόφιον,** τό, *slice for turning things over in a frying-pan,* Poll.6.89, 10.98:—written τηγανόστροφον in Hsch. s. v. λί(σ)τριον.

**τάγιλος·** φειδωλός, Hsch. **τάγιος·** κῆρυξ, πρεσβευτής, ὀξύς, ταχύς, βάσιμος, Id.

⊕ **τάγμα,** ατος, τό, (τάσσω) *ordinance, command,* νόμου τ. Pl.*Def.*414e; ἐκ δυοῖν τ. from a combination of two *ordinances,* Arist.*Pol.*1294b 6. II. *fixed assessment* or *payment,* Id.*Oec.*1349a24, *CIG*2562.14 (Crete). III. *body of soldiers, division, brigade,* X.*Mem.*3.1.11, *PFrankf.*7.5 (iii B.C.), Ph.*Bel.*96.48, 103.28, *PRein.*14.31 (ii B.C.), Plb.3.85.3, etc. b. = Lat. *manipulus,* Id.6.24.5. c. = Lat. *legio, legion,* D.H.6.42, Str.3.3.8, Plu.*Oth.*12, D.C.71.9, *CIG*4693 (Abukir). IV. *order, rank, IG*14.757 (Naples); βουλευτικὸν τ. *CIG* 4411 *b* 5 (Cilicia); ἱππικὸν τ. ib.2803 (Aphrodisias); τὸ τ. τῶν γυμνασιάρχων *POxy.*1252v.24 (iii A.D.); τοῦ πρώτου τ. *IG*4²(1).81 (Epid., i A.D.): acc. τάγμα as Adv., *CIG*3765 (dub.), cf. *IG*14.748 (Naples). V. generally, *arrangement,* of footprints, τίς ὁ τρόπος τοῦ τ.; S.*Ichn.*114; *row* of bricks, dub. in Alc.153. 2. *status,* φύσεως τάγμα ἔχειν Epicur.*Ep.*1 p.24 U.; *function,* Phld.*Po.*5 *Fr.*1; ἐν τ. γενόμενοι c. inf., being in a *position* to . ., *PLond.*2.358.7 (ii A.D.).

**ταγμᾰτ-άρχης,** ου, ὁ, *leader of a* τάγμα, D.H.20.4, Onos.42.8:—hence **ταγμᾰταρχέω,** Ph.1.368. **-ικός,** ή, όν, *of* or *for a* τάγμα III, ἐπιφοραί D.S.17.94; ὑπηρέτης *PTheb.Bank*8.2 (ii B.C.): ταγματικόν, τό, = τάγμα III, ib.5. II. ταγματικός, ὁ, = *legionarius, Gloss.* **-ιον,** = *legiunculus,* ib.

⊕ **τᾱγός,** ὁ, (τάσσω) *commander, ruler, chief,* ταγὸς μακάρων, of Zeus, A.*Pr.*96 (anap.); ταγοὶ Περσῶν Id.*Pers.*23 (anap.); ξύμφρονε ταγώ prob. in Id.*Ag.*110 (lyr.); νεῶν, ναῶν, Id.*Pers.*324, 480, cf. S.*Ant.* 1057, E.*IA*269 (lyr.); τῶν Ἀθηνῶν Ar.*Eq.*159. II. specially, *federal commander* of Thessalian league, X.*HG*6.1.6, 6.4.28, etc. 2. pl., *college of magistrates* in Thessaly, *IG*9(2).517.3 (Larissa, iii B.C.): sg., *one such magistrate, SIG*55 (v B.C.), *Inscr.Cypr.*116, 170 H. 3. *president* of a phratria, *Schwyzer*323 *A* 11, al. (Delph.). [ᾱ, but ταγοί was read by Aristarch. and others in Il.23.160; if οἵ τ' ἀγοί is read οἵ τ' is relat. (sc. εἰσίν).]

**τᾱγοῦχος,** ὁ, (ταγή, ἔχω) *having command, commander,* A.*Eu.*296.

**τάγῡρι** [ᾰ], τό, indecl., *little bit, morsel,* μαθόντι μηδὲ τάγυρι μουσικῆς Eup.3.—Theognost.*Can.*120 cites it as a noun ending in ι; ταγύρια is perh. corrupt in Hsch.

**τάγχαρας,** foreign word for *gold,* Cosmas ad *OGI*199: the gen. τάγχρου should perh. be read in *AP*15.25.7 (Besant.*Ara,* ταγχούρου cod. A); τάγχουρος γὰρ ὁ χρυσός, ἡ λέξις Περσική Sch. ad loc. (Sch. Theoc.p.351 W.).

**ταγώνιον,** sine expl., Theognost.*Can.*124.

**τᾷδε,** Dor. for τῇδε, *here, Schwyzer*167a (Selinus, v B.C.).

**τάδην** [ᾰ], Adv. of τείνω, *on the stretch, EM*184.49.

**ταθείς, τάθη,** v. τείνω.

⊕ **ταθρίσιον,** τό, or **-ιος,** ὁ, a kind of fish, *PLond.ined.*2143.

**Ταινᾰρεύς,** έως, ὁ, *native of Taenarus,* Orph.*A.*205.

**Ταίνᾰρος,** ἡ, *Taenarus,* a promontory at the southern end of Laconia, Pi.*P.*4.44, 174; also masc. or neut., Th.1.128, 133, 7.19; Ταίναρον ἠνεμόεντα Orph.*A.*1370: neut. **Ταίναρον,** τό, Str.8.5.1: in most passages the word occurs in an obl. case without an Adj., so that the gender is undetermined, as in *h.Ap.*412, Hdt.1.23, 24, Th. 1.133, Ar.*Ra.*187, etc.; Ποσειδῶν οὑπὶ Ταινάρῳ θεός Id.*Ach.*510; πύλη τις ἐστί (sc. of the infernal regions) Ταινάρου πρὸς ἐσχάτοις Men.842, cf. Str. l. c.:—Adj. **Ταινάριος,** α, ον, Ταιναρίην ὑπὸ χθόνα A.R.1.102; epith. of Artemis, Euph.9.11; Τ. λίθος, v. λίθος II. 1: neut. pl. **Ταινάρια,** τά, festival of Poseidon at Taenarus, Hsch. (-ίας cod.): hence **Ταινάριοι,** οἱ, *celebrants of this festival, IG*5(1).211.1:—also Ταιναρίζω, *celebrate this festival*, St.Byz. s.v. Ταίναρος, and **Ταιναρισταί**, οἱ, = Ταινάριοι, Hsch.

**ταινί**, v. ὀνί.

**ταινία**, ἡ, *band, fillet*, esp. *headband*, worn in sign of victory, θήσω δὲ νικητήριον τρεῖς ταινίας Eub.3, cf. Emp.112.6, X.*Smp.*5.9, Pl. *Smp.*212e, Paus.6.20.19, etc.; ταινίας πωλεῖν D.57.31; also, the *breastband* of young girls, etc., *Anacreont.*22.13, cf. Paus.9.39.8, Poll.7.65; *abdominal band*, Diocl.*Fr.*142; *bandage*, Hp.*Art.*50 (pl.), *IG*4²(1).121.49,61 (Epid., iv B.C.), Sor.*Fasc.*25, al.; *ribbon*, distd. fr. λημνίσκος, *PCair.Zen.*696 (iii B.C.). 2. *stripe in fur*, Opp.*C.*1.322. 3. *pennon* of a ship, D.Chr.74.8, Poll.1.90; of a spear, D.S.15.52. 4. = ταινίδιον III or IV, τ. χρυσῆ, ἐφ' ἧς ἐπιγραφὴ Βασίλισσα Στρατονίκη.. *Inscr.Délos* 442 *B* 33 (ii B.C.); τ. περιηργυρωμένη ib. 29. II. *strip* or *tongue of land*, D.S.1.31, App.*Pun.*121, Plu. *Alex.*26; *sandbank*, *PTeb.*5.30, *PStrassb.*85.20 (both ii B.C.), Plb. 4.41.1, Str.1.3.4. 2. name of a strip of land near lake Mareotis, Ath.1.33e. III. in joiner's work, *fillet, fascia*, τὴν τ. ἐπὶ τὸν θρᾶνον τοῦ νεὼ ἐπιθέντι *IG*11(2).161 *A* 50 (Delos, iii B.C.), cf. Lxx *Ez.*27.5, *EM*749.38; περιθήσει ταινίαν μέλαιναν a black *band* (round a mosaic floor), *PCair.Zen.*665.8 (iii B.C.). IV. *tape-worm*, Gal.14.755, *Gp.*12.27.2 (pl.). V. *a long, thin fish*, Epich.56, Arist.*HA* 504ᵇ33. [ῐ, but ῑ metri gr., Emp. l.c., Opp. l.c.]

**ταινιάζω**, = ταινιόω, Anon.(Iamb.*Bab.*(?))ap.Suid. s.v. ἀνέδουν, but perh. f.l. for παιανίζω, cf. Luc.*Zeux.*11.

**ταινίδιον**, τό, Dim. of ταινία, *strip of linen*, Hp.*Acut.*(*Sp.*)15, Sor. *Fasc.*36, al.; *strip of skin*, Heliod.ap.Orib.45.5.3, Antyll.ib.45.26.1. II. Dim. of ταινία III, *PMich.Zen.*38.8 (iii B.C.). III. perh. *small jewel-case*, δακτύλιος χρυσοῦς ἐν -ίῳ ἐνδεδεμένος ξυλίνῳ *IG*11(2).161 *B* 51, cf. 119, 203 *B* 68 (Delos, iii B.C.); στλεγγίδιον χρυσοῦν ἐπὶ ταινιδίῳ ib.82, cf. 91; ὅρμος χρυσοῦς ἐπὶ ταινιδίου *Inscr.Délos* 442 *B* 202 (ii B.C.). IV. *small ribbon*, στέφανον ἐλάας μετὰ -ου φοινικιοῦ *SIG* 1018 (Pergam., iii B.C.); τ. χρυσοῦν *IG*11(2).203 *B* 48; ὁλκὴ.. σὺν ταινιδίοις καὶ λίνῳ ib.81.

**ταινίν**, v. ὀνί.

**ταινιοειδής**, ές, *ribbon-like*, ἱμὰς Hp.*Art.*47, cf. Thphr.*HP*4.6.2.

**ταινίον**, τό, Dim. of ταινία, *small band*, *EM*749.44; ταινίον χρυσοῦν *Inscr.Prien.*112.93 (i B.C.).

**ταινιόπωλις**, ιδος, ἡ, *dealer in* ταινίαι, Eup.243, D.57.34.

* **ταινι-όω**, *bind with a headband*, esp. as a conqueror, Th.4.121, X. *HG*5.1.3:—Pass., *to be crowned*, Ar.*Ra.*395, D.S.17.101: metaph., D.C.39.25; ὀμφαλὸς τεταινιωμένος Str.9.3.6:—Med., *wear a headband*, Ar.*Ec.*1032. -**ώδης**, ες, = ταινιοειδής, Thphr.*Ign.*72. -**ωτικός**, ή, όν, οἶνος, perh. wine *from the* Ταινία (v. ταινία II. 2), Ath.1.33e; cf. *Taeneotica papyrus*, Plin.*HN*13.76.

**ταιννί**, v. ὀνί. **ταῖννυ**, v. ὄνυ.

**τᾰΐτης**, ου, ὁ, (ταῶς) *peacock stone*, = πάγχρους, Cyran.38.

**τᾰκερός**, ά, όν, (τᾰκῆναι, τήκω) *melting in the mouth, tender*, ἀκροκώλια Ar.*Fr.*4, Hp.*Mul.*2.169; σχελίδες τακερώταται Pherecr.108.13; τακεροὺς ποιῆσαι τοὺς ἐρεβίνθους Id.84, cf. Hp.*Aff.*56, Gal.6.498, al.; τακερὰ μηκάδων μέλη Antiph.1.4; τ. ποιεῖν τὰ κρέα Dionys.Com.3.7; τ. πόδες as food for invalids, Herod.Med. in *Rh.Mus.*58.95,98, 100. 2. metaph., *melting, languishing*, Ἔρως Anacr.169; τακέρ' ὄμμασι δερκόμενος Ibyc.2; ὡς τακερὸν.. καὶ μαλακὸν τὸ βλέμμ' ἔχει Philetaer.5; τακεραῖς λεύσσουσα κόραις *AP*9.567 (Antip.); τακερὸν βλέπεις βλέμμα Alciphr.1.28; τ. τι ἐν τοῖς ὄμμασιν πάθος ἀνυγραίνων Luc.*Am.*14. Adv. -ρῶς *meltingly*, of the nightingale's song, ἑλίττειν τὸ μέλος Ael.*NA*5.38. II. Act., *serving to dissolve, soft*, ὕδατα ἕψειν ἄριστα καὶ -ώτατα Hp.*Aër.*7.

**τᾰκερόχρως**, ὁ, ἡ, gen. χρωτος, *with tender flesh*, Antiph.52.5.

**τᾰκερ-όω**, *boil soft*, ἐρίφιον ἐτακέρωσε Athenio 1.30:—Pass., Agathin.ap.Orib.10.7.10, Dsc.4.182. -**ωσις**, εως, ἡ, *boiling to softness*, ἕψε μέχρι -ώσεως Archig.(?)ap.Aët.12.1.

**τᾱκηρός**, ά, όν, = τακερός, Dsc.1.106.

**τάκιστα**, for τάχιστα, barbarism in Ar.*Th.*1214.

**τακ-τέον**, *one must arrange in order*, Pl.*Lg.*631d, Str.9.3.9, Gal. 18(1).780, etc. -**της**, ου, ὁ, *assessor of tribute*, *IG*1².63.41, 218 iii 45. * -**τικός**, ή, όν, *fit for ordering* or *arranging*, esp. in war, τ. ἀνὴρ *tactician*, X.*Cyr.*8.5.15; τακτικὸν ἡγεῖσθαί τι to think it *a good piece of tactics*, ibid.; οἱ τ. ἀριθμοί the *regular* battalions, ib.3.3.11: ἡ τακτική (sc. τέχνη) *the art of tactics*, Nicom.Com.1.37; τὰ τ. X.*Cyr.*1.6.14, etc.; τ. ὑπόμνημα Aen.Tact.tit. (interpol.); τακτικόν, title of work by Democr.(*Fr.*28ᵇ). Adv. Comp. -ώτερον v.l. for τακτικ- in Sch.E.*Ph.*1141. 2. generally, *regulating*, δογμάτων M.Ant. 1.9. II. *ordinal*, of numbers, D.T.636.14.

* **τακτόμισθος**, ὁ, a rank in the army of the Ptolemies. *PPetr.*3 p.26, al. (iii B.C.), *PLond.ined.*2243 (iii B.C.), *PGiss.*2 ii 9 (ii B.C.), *UPZ* 31.3 (ii B.C.), etc.

* **τακτός**, ή, όν, (τάσσω) *ordered, prescribed*, τακτόν τι παρὰ τοῦ Κύρου παραγγέλλων X.*Cyr.*8.3.28; τ. ἀργύριον a *fixed* or *stated* sum, Th.4.65; τ. χρήματα Pl.*Lg.*746a; σῖτος τ. *a fixed quantity of* corn, Th.4.16; τ. τροφὴν λαμβάνειν Pl.*Lg.*909c, cf. Alex.141.6; δίκαι τ. *fixed* penalties, Pl.*Lg.*632b; ἐκφόριον τ. a *fixed* rent, *PPetr.*3 p.250 (iii B.C.); τ. ὁδός a *prescribed* way, D.23.72; ἐν τ. ἡμέραις βουλεύεσθαι Aeschin.2.109; ἐπὶ τὰ τ. ἔτη πέντε *POxy.*101.10 (ii A.D.); κατά τινας χρόνους τ. Arist.*HA*599ᵇ4. Adv. τακτῶς v.l. in Plot.3.1.2.

**τάκω** [ᾰ], Dor. for τήκω.

**τάκων** [ᾰ], ωνος, ὁ, a kind of *sausage* or *rissole*, Crates Com.17, cf. Poll.6.53.

**τάλα**, obscure word in *IG*12(2).74.1 (Mytil., iii B.C.). II. *Palmyra palm, Bonassus flabellifer*, Megasth. ap.Arr.*Ind.*7. III. τάλα· μέγα, Hsch.

* **τᾰλαεργός**, όν, (*τλάω, ϝέργον, cf. ταλαύρινος) *bearing* or *enduring labour*, of mules, Il.23.654,662, Od.4.636, Hes.*Op.*46, al.; of Heracles, Theoc.13.19; *laborious*, πόνος Opp.*H.*5.50.

**τᾰλαίμοχθος**, ον, = ταλαίπωρος, Eust.1735.48.

**τάλαινα** [ᾰ], fem. of τάλας; whence Theognost.*Can.*66 invents a masc. τάλαινος.

**Τᾰλᾰϊονίδης** [ῐονῐ], ου, ὁ, Patron. formed irreg. metri gr. for *Ταλαΐδης, *son of Talaus*, Il.2.566, 23.678.

**τᾰλαιπωρ-έω**, pf. τεταλαιπώρηκα Isoc.8.19, etc.:—Pass., with fut. Med. -ήσομαι Aristid.1.438 J.: aor. ἐταλαιπωρήθην Isoc.3.64, etc.: pf. τεταλαιπώρημαι Gal.6.560:—*do hard work, endure hardship* or *distress*, E.*Or.*672, Th.1.99, 5.74; ὑπὸ χειμῶνος Id.2.101; ἑωυτοῖσι for their own benefit, Hp.*Aër.*16; ἐθέλουσα ταλαιπωρεῖν Antipho 5.93; τῷ σώματι ἀδύνατος ταλαιπωρεῖν Lys.31.12; λυποῦνται καὶ συνεχῶς ταλαιπωροῦσι D.2.16: c. dat., *suffer by reason of*, ἐλπίσι κεναῖς Polystr.p.31 W. II. rarely trans., *distress, trouble*, ὁ πόλεμος πάντας τρόπους τεταλαιπώρηκεν ἡμᾶς Isoc.8.19, cf. D.C.38.20; ἀνδρὸς ..ὑμᾶς μηδ' ὅσον προπέμψαι ποι αὐτὸν ἀπιόντα..-ήσαντος who *did* not *trouble* you even to.., Id.56.41:—freq. in Pass., *to be distressed, suffer hardship*, Hp.*Aër.*19, Th.3.78 (s.v.l.), Pl.*Phd.*95d, *R.*372d; ἐν τοῖς ἀγροῖς..ταλαιπωρουμένους Ar.*Pl.*224; ἵνα μὴ ταλαιπωροῖτο μηδ' ἄχθος φέροι Id.*Ra.*24, cf. *V.*967; τεταλαιπωρημένοι ὑπὸ τῆς νόσου *worn out* by.., Th.3.3; τῷ μήκει τοῦ πολέμου D.18.19; διὰ τὸν πόλεμον Isoc.5.38; τὸ σῶμα ταλαιπωρούμενον *being distressed*, Plu.*Brut.*37; σμικρὰ παιδία..κρύει ταλαιπωρούμενα Gal.6.43; ἐν ταῖς ὁσημέραι πράξεσι πολλὰ -ούμενος ib.471. -**ημα**, ατος, τό, *hardship, distress*, Phalar.*Ep.*135.2 (pl.), Secund.*Sent.*9. -**ησις**, εως, ἡ, = ταλαιπωρία, Arr.*An.*6.26.1. -**ία**, Ion. -ίη, ἡ, *hard labour*, Hp.*Aër.*21, Gal.15.620,741; also simply, *regular use, exercise*, τῆς χειρός Hp.*Art.*53. 2. *hardship, distress*, Th.4.117; τῇ τοῦ σώματος τ. And.2.17; ἡ ἐν τοῖς ἔργοις τ. Plb.3.17.8; ἡ περὶ τὸ πρᾶγμα τ. Phld.*Oec.*p.53 J.: pl., ταλαιπωρίας ἐνδέκεσθαι Hdt.6.11; τετρυμένοι..ταλαιπωρίῃσί τε καὶ ἡλίῳ ib.12. 3. *bodily suffering* or *pain*, caused by disease, Th.2.49. -**ίζω**, = ταλαιπωρέω, Sm.*Is.*21.2. II. *pronounce unhappy, commiserate*, Phld.*Mort.*32. -**ικός**, ή, όν, *full of hardship*, βίος Gal.15.158. -**ισμός**, ὁ, = ταλαιπωρία, *hard conditions*, τοῦ βίου (sc. τῶν ζῴων) Phld.*D.*1.15.

**τᾰλαίπωρος**, ον, *suffering, distressed, miserable*, Θῆβαι Pi.*Fr.*197; βροτοί A.*Pr.*233; ὦ ταλαίπωρ' ib.317, cf.595 (lyr.), 623, S.*OC*14, etc.; ἀνδρῶν γένος Id.*Fr.*945; τ. ἄρα τις σύ γε Pl.*Euthd.*302b; τὸ τ. *hardihood*, Ar.*Nu.*414; *a hard life*, Hp.*Aër.*19. Adv. -ρως Ar.*Ec.*54, Th.3.4. 2. of things, τ. βίος S.*OC*91; πράγματα Ar.*Av.*135; πάθος Alex.144; ταλαιπωρότερον οὐδέν ἐστι..τῆς γαστρός Diph.60.3.

**τᾰλαίφρων**, ονος, ὁ, ἡ, *much-enduring, wretched*, S.*Ant.*866 (lyr.), E.*Hel.*524 (lyr.); voc. ταλαῖφρον S.*Ant.*39, *Aj.*903 (lyr.).

**τᾰλᾰκάρδιος**, ον, (*τλάω) *stout-hearted*, of Heracles, Hes.*Sc.*424; of Oedipus, *much-enduring, miserable*, S.*OC*540 (lyr.), cf. Epigr.ap. Aeschin.3.184: prob. in *Lyr.Adesp.Oxy.*860(a)3.

**τᾰλᾰν-ίζω**, *call* or *deem* one *unhappy*, Aesop.113, 328, Jo Sic. in Rh.6.451 W.:—Pass., Ptol.*Tetr.*208, Heliod. *in EN*19.18:—hence -**ισμός**, ὁ, Jo.Sic. l.c.

**τᾰλαντ-άω**, = ταλαντεύω, *EM*744.15. -**εία**, ἡ, *the swaying motion* of anything suspended, prob. cj. in Pl.*Cra.*395e (ταντᾰλεία codd. BT). -**εύω**, (τάλαντον) *balance, sway to and fro*, τ. τι ἐν ὀφθαλμοῖς *let it hover* before them, Hld.8.17; τ. τὰ καθ' ἡμᾶς ἡ μοῖρα Id.10.9:—Pass., *sway backwards and forwards, ebb and flow*, διὰ τὸ ταλαντεύεσθαι [τὴν θάλατταν] δεῦρο κἀκεῖσε Arist.*Mete.*354ᵃ8; τῆς μάχης δεῦρο κἀκεῖσε ταλαντευομένης D.S.11.22, cf. 16.4; ῥέπει καὶ τ. πρὸς τοὐναντίον Plu.2.682e. 2. *weigh out, measure out*, ὕδασι (i.e. by the κλεψύδρα) ἠελίοιο ταλαντεύουσι κελεύθους *AP*9.782 (Paul. Sil.); Τιτὰν νύκτα ταλαντεύει καὶ φάος *App.Anth.*4.74 (Synesius); τούτων σὺ τὴν αἵρεσιν τ. Alciphr.1.8:—Pass., τὸ ζῆν οὐδ' ὑπὸ τούτοις ταλαντεύεται ib.25. II. intr., *oscillate*, ἐπὶ θάτερα Arist.*IA*708ᵇ14. 2. intr., *weigh down the balance*, τῇ μὲν ἐταλάντευε τὸ ἔλεος, τῇ δ' ἀντέβριθεν ὁ νόμος Ph.2.170. * -**ιαῖος**, α, ον, *worth a talent*, οἶκος D.27.64; κτῆσις Plb.23.4.3; νοσήματα τ. *costing a talent*, prob. in fee to the physician, Alc.Com.12. 2. of persons, *worth a talent*, i.e. *possessed of one*, Crates Com.32; ἔγγυοι τ. giving surety *to the amount of a talent*, Arist.*Oec.*1350ᵃ19. II. *weighing a talent*, ξύλον Id.*Cael.*311ᵇ3; λιθοβόλος τ. an engine throwing stones *of a talent weight*, Plb.9.41.8 codd.; πετροβόλος τ. Ph.*Bel.*85.2. 2. *in which the prize is a talent*, ἀγών *CIG*2810.18 (Aphrodisias). -**ιεῖος**, α, ον, = foreg. II, στρῶμα *PMich.Zen.*13.3 (iii B.C.). -**ισμός**, ὁ, name of a tax, dub. in *BGU*1850.14 (i B.C.). -**ον**, τό, *balance*, Ζεὺς..τὸ τ. ἐπιρρέπει ἄλλοτε ἄλλως Thgn.157; ζυγὸν ταλάντου A.*Supp.*823 (lyr.); ταλάντῳ μουσικὴ σταθμήσεται Ar.*Ra.*797: in this sense used by Hom. only in pl., *pair of scales*, ἔχον ὥς τε τάλαντα γυνή.., ἥ τε σταθμὸν ἔχουσα καὶ εἴριον ἀμφὶς ἀνέλκει ἰσάζουσα Il.12.433; esp. of the *scales* in which Zeus weighed the fortunes of men, χρύσεια πατὴρ ἐτίταινε τ. 8.69, 22.209; γνῶ γὰρ Διὸς ἱρὰ τ. 16.658; ἐπὴν κλίνῃσι τ. Ζεύς, i.e. when he decides the issue of battle, 19.223; τ. βρίσας οὐκ ἰσορρόπῳ τύχῃ A.*Pers.*346; of the *scales of justice*, δίκης κατέκειτο τάλαντα *h.Merc.*324, cf. *AP*6.267.4 (Diotim.): so in sg., δίκας ῥέπει τάλαντον B.17.25. 2. *tax paid for the use of the public scales*, *SIG* 4.7 (Cyzicus, vi B.C.). II. *anything weighed*, 1. *a definite weight, talent*, in Hom. always of gold, δέκα χρυσοῖο τάλαντα Il.9.122; δύω χρ. τ. 18.507; δέκα πάντα τ. ten in all, 19.247, 24.232;

χρυσοῦ.. εὐεργέος ἑπτὰ τ. Od.9.202; χρυσοῖο τάλαντον.. τιμήεντος 8.393: from the order of the prizes in Il.23.262 sq. and other passages its weight was probably not great, cf. Arist.*Fr.*164. 2. in post-Hom. writers, the τάλαντον was both a *commercial weight* (differing in different systems), and also the *sum of money* represented by the corresponding weight of gold or silver; τοῖσι μὲν (of the subjects of Darius) ἀργύριον ἀπαγινέουσι εἴρητο Βαβυλώνιον σταθμὸν τ. ἀπαγινέειν, τοῖσι δὲ χρυσίον ἀπαγινέουσι Εὐβοϊκόν· τὸ δὲ Βαβυλώνιον τ. δύναται Εὐβοΐδας (ὀκτὼ καὶ add. Reiz) ἑβδομήκοντα μνέας Hdt.3.89; τ. Ἀττικόν, Αἰγιναῖον, etc., Poll.9.86; ἐποίησε [ὁ Σόλων] σταθμὰ πρὸς τὸ νόμισμα τρεῖς καὶ ἑξήκοντα μνᾶς τὸ τ. ἀγούσας Arist.*Ath.*10.2. a. of money, τ. ἀργυρίου Hdt.7.28, cf. X.*HG*3.5.1, etc.; χίλια τ. νομίσματος Aeschin.2.174; μνᾶ ἀπὸ τοῦ τ. *IG*1².220.7, cf. 92.37, al. b. of weight, τὸ τ. τὸ ἐμπορικόν ib.2².1013.35; used in weighing lead, ib.1².374.287, 4²(1).103.131 (Epid., iv B.C.), *PMich. Zen.*9.4 (iii B.C.): iron, *PCair.Zen.*144.6 (iii B.C.), *CPHerm.*p.77 (iii A.D.); cloth, *PMich.Zen.*120.8 (iii B.C.), etc. ❋-όομαι, Pass., *to be balanced, sway, oscillate*, ἀνωμάλως πάντη, opp. ἰσορροπέω, Pl.*Ti.* 52e. -οῦχος, ον, (ἔχω) *holding the balance*: metaph., Ἄρης τ. ἐν μάχῃ *he who holds the scale* in battle, A.*Ag.*439 (lyr.). -ωσις, εως, ἡ, *weighing*, Antipho Soph.42. 2. (from Pass.) *ebb and flow, tidal motion*, Arist.*Mete.*354ᵃ11.

ταλᾰ-ός, ή, όν, (*τλάω) = τλήμων, Ar.*Av.*687 (anap.), Q.S.1.759. -πᾰθής, ές, = τληπαθής, Suid. ❋-πείριος, ον, (*τλάω, πεῖρα) *one who has suffered much, much-suffering*, not in Il., ξεῖνος τ. ἐνθάδ' ἱκάνω Od.7.24, cf. 17.84; ἱκέτης τ. 6.193, 14.511; πτωχὸς τ. *AP*10.66 (Agath.). 2. *vagrant, vagabond*, Aen.Tact.10.10. -πενθής, ές, *bearing great griefs, patient in woe*, θυμός Od.5.222; of persons, φωτός B.5.157. 2. of things, *toilsome*, ὑσμῖναι Panyas.12.5; *woeful*, ἀγγελία B.15.26.

ταλάπης, ου, ὁ, a plant similar to the κεντρῖτις, *PMag.Par.*1.812.

τᾰλάρ-ιον [λᾰ], τό, Dim. of τάλαρος, *small basket*, Poll.10.125, *POxy.*936 (iii A.D.). -ίσκος, ὁ, = foreg., Arist.*Pr.*924ᵇ11, Theoc.15.113, *AP*6.174 (Antip. ⟨Sid.⟩). ❋-ος, ὁ, *basket*, ἀργύρεος τ., of a work-basket, Od.4.125; ὑπόκυκλος ib.131; πλεκτοὶ τ. *baskets* of wicker-work, in which new-made cheeses were placed so as to let the whey run off, Od.9.247, cf. Ar.*Ra.*560, *AP*9.567 (Antip.), *IG*3.1309, Gal.6.491; *basket* for fruit, Il.18.568, Hes.*Sc.*293; for flowers, Mosch.2.34, 61, Paus.8.31.2. 2. *wicker cage* for fowls: hence metaph., Μουσέων τ., of the Museum, Timo 12.

❋τάλας (v. sub fin.), τάλαινα, τάλαν (fem. τάλας Ar.*Th.*1038): gen. ᾰνος, αίνης, ανος, also dat. τάλαντι Hippon.12: voc. τάλαν, masc. in Od.18.327, 19.68, Thgn.512, etc., fem. in Ar.*Ra.*559, al. (Adv. acc. to A.D.*Adv.*160.11, Hdn.Gr.2.12, al.): Aeol. nom. τάλαις Choerob. *in Theod.*1.126 H.: (*τλάω):—*suffering, wretched*, ξεῖνε τάλαν Od.18.327, etc.; ὦ τάλας ἐγώ S.*OC*1338, 1401, *Aj.*981; ὦ τάλαιν' ἐγώ A.*Ch.*743; ὦ τάλαν S.*Ph.*1196 (lyr.): c. gen. causae, οἱ 'γὼ τάλαινα συμφορᾶς κακῆς A.*Pers.*445, cf. 517; τάλαιν' ἐγὼ τῆς ὕβρεος Ar.*Pl.*1044: sts. in bad sense, τάλαν *wretch!* Od.19.68: but in Com., τάλαν *poor dear!* as a sort of coaxing address, Ar.*Lys.*910, 914; so ὦ τάλαινα Id.*Ec.*242. 2. in Trag. also of things, *sorry, wretched*, μόχθοι A.*Ch.*1069 (anap.); παρακοπά Id.*Ag.*223 (lyr.); πάθος Id.*Th.*988 (lyr.); νηδύς S.*OC*1263; αὔλιον Id.*Ph.*1088 (lyr.); συμφορά, νόσος, Id.*El.*1179, *Tr.*1084; ἔρις, φυγά, E.*Hel.*248 (lyr.), *Ph.*1710 (lyr.): Sup. ταλάντατος, η, ον, Ar. *Pl.*684, 1046, 1060, Pl.*Cra.*395e.—Poet. word, used by X.*Cyr.*4.6.5, Ph.2.239, Arr.*Epict.*2.16.20, Plu.*Ant.*79, al., Luc.*DMeretr.*10.3. II. Τάλας, ὁ, a constellation (θεός τις κατακέφαλα κείμενος) rising with Sagittarius, *Cat.Cod.Astr.*7.207. [τᾰλᾱς A.*Pr.*158 (anap.), S. (v. supr.), Ar.*Ach.*163, 1192, *Pax* 79, *Av.*1494, *Pl.*930; Dor. also τᾰλᾰς Theoc.2.4, *AP*9.378 (Pall.): voc. τάλᾰν Thgn.512, S.*Ph.*1196 (lyr.), Ar.*Ec.*658, 1005 (both anap.).]

❋τᾰλᾰσ-ήϊος, η, ον, Ep. word, *of wool-spinning*, τ. ἔργα, = ταλασία, A.R.3.292; ταλασήϊος ἱδρὼς *caused by spinning*, Nonn.*D.*6.142. ❋-ία, ἡ, *wool-spinning*, = ταλασιουργία, Pl.*Lg.*805e, X.*Mem.*3.9.11, *Oec.*7.41, Ph.2.328 (pl.), Plu.*Rom.*15, etc. -ιος, ον, = ταλασήϊος, ἔργα X.*Oec.*7.6.

❋τᾰλᾰσιουργ-έω, *spin wool*, X.*Mem.*3.9.11, D.S.2.23, Luc.*VH*2.36. -ία, ἡ, = ταλασία, Pl.*Plt.*282c, 283a, Corn.*ND*20, Ath.Med.ap. Orib.*inc.*5.4. ❋-ικός, ή, όν, *of* or *for wool-spinning*, ὄργανα X.*Oec.* 9.7, cf. Pl.*Plt.*282c; ἡ -κή (sc. τέχνη), = foreg., ib.a. ❋-ός, ὁ, ἡ, *wool-spinner*, Id.*Ion* 540c, Trypho ap.Ath.14.618d.

τᾰλᾰσίφρων, ονος, ὁ, ἡ, (*τλάω) *patient of mind, stout-hearted*, ὑπό κεν ταλασίφρονά περ δέος εἷλεν Il.4.421; mostly as epith. of Odysseus, 11.466, Od.1.87, 129, al., Hes.*Th.*1012; δμῶες τ. Theoc.24.50.

ταλάσσῃς, -σῃ, v. *τλάω.

τᾰλαύρῑνος, ον, (*τλάω, ϝρινός) *bearing a shield of bull's-hide*, epith. of Ares, τ. πολεμιστής Il.5.289, 20.78, etc.; so of Πόλεμος, Ar. *Pax* 241; and, jokingly, of Lamachus, Id.*Ach.*964; τ. χρώς a *thick tough* hide, *AP*7.208 (Anyte): neut. as Adv., ταλαύρινον πολεμίζειν to fight *toughly, stoutly*, Il.7.239 (or masc., to fight *as a bearer of a bull's-hide shield*).

τᾰλάφρων, ονος, ὁ, ἡ, = ταλασίφρων, Il.13.300, Opp.*H.*3.40.

τᾰλάωρ [λᾰ], ωρος, ὁ, *bow*, Euph.9.12, Choerob. *in Theod.*1.301 H.; ταλαώρεα· τοξεύματα, Hsch.

τᾱλίκος, ον, Dor. for τηλίκος.

❋τᾶλις, ιδος, ἡ, *marriageable maiden*, S.*Ant.*629 (anap.), Call.*Aet.* 3.1.3. (Aeol. word acc. to Sch.S.l.c.: also, *betrothed maiden, married woman*, and *bride*, acc. to Hsch.)

ταλῶς· ὁ ἥλιος, Hsch. τάμε, τᾰμέειν, v. τέμνω.

❋τᾱμεία, ἡ, = ταμιεία I, [ὕδατος] J.*AJ*7.7.5.

τᾰμεῖον, v. ταμιεῖον. τᾰμέσθαι, v. τέμνω.

τᾰμεσίχρως, οος, ὁ, ἡ, (τάμνω) *cutting the skin, wounding*, χαλκός, ἐγχεῖαι, Il.4.511, 13.340.

❋τᾰμία, Ep. and Ion. -ίη, ἡ, *housekeeper, housewife*, γυνὴ τ. ἣ πάντ' ἐφύλασσε Od.2.345, cf. Il.6.390, Alcm.31; ἀμφίπολος τ. Il.24.302: also in Prose, X.*Oec.*9.11, 10.10, Lib.*Or.*16.47; as cult-title, παρὰ τὰν Ἱστίαν τὰν Ταμίαν *SIG*1025.29 (Cos, iv/iii B.C.).

τᾱμία, = ζημία, Hsch.

❋τᾰμῐ-ᾰκός, ή, όν, *of* or *for the treasury*, *CIG* (add.) 3641*b*47 (Lampsacus); = Lat. *fiscalis*, ταμιακοὶ λόγοι *PLips.*64.22 (iv A.D.); -καὶ ψῆφοι ib.37: ταμιακόν, τό, the *Fiscus*, *IG*2².1121.35. II. *tamiaca, woman of the* Empress's *bedchamber*, *Gloss.* ❋-ας, Ep. and Ion. -ίης, ου (rarely ταμία *IG*11(2).287*B*100 (Delos, iii B.C.), 4²(1).77.14 (Epid., ii B.C.)), ὁ: old Att. dat. pl. ταμίασιν ib.1².232.2, 237.56: Aeol. τομίαις dub. in Alc.87 (ταμίαις acc. to Gramm. in *PBouriant* 8.16):—prop. *one who carves and distributes, dispenser, steward*, ταμίαι παρὰ νηυσὶν ἔσαν, σίτοιο δοτῆρες Il.19.44, cf. Ar.*V.*613 (anap.), *Ostr. Bodl.*i 324 (ii B.C.); τ. ἀνδράσι πλούτου Pi.*O.*13.7 (pl.). 2. of Zeus, as *the dispenser* of all things to men, Ζεύς, ὅς τ' ἀνθρώπων τ. πολέμοιο τέτυκται Il.4.84; τ. ἀγαθῶν τε κακῶν τε Poet.ap.Pl.*R.*379e; οὐκ ἔστιν πλὴν Διὸς οὐδεὶς τῶν μελλόντων τ. S.*Fr.*590.4 (anap.); Ζῆνα, ὃς ὅρκων θνατοῖς τ. νενόμισται *controller*, E.*Med.*170 (anap.); τῶν ὄμβρων καὶ τῶν αὐχμῶν τοῖς ἄλλοις ὁ Ζεὺς τ. ἐστίν Isoc.11.13; also τ. ἀνέμων, of Aeolus, Od.10.21 (hence of the lungs, τῶν πνευμάτων τῷ σώματι τ. Pl.*Ti.*84d): freq. in Pi., of kings or persons in authority, *controller, director*, τ. Κυράνας, Σπάρτας, *P.*5.62, *N.*10.52; τ. κώμων *master* of the revels, *I.*6(5).57; τ. Διὸς *steward* or *priest* of Zeus, *O.*6.5; ταμίαι Μοισᾶν, i.e. poets, *Fr.*1; οἶκος τ. στεφάνων *that hath store* of crowns, *N.*6.26; also ἐν δ' αὐτῷ θανάτου τ. Hes.*Fr.*11; γνώμης τ. (fort. γλώσσης) *one that is master* of his judgement, Thgn.504; ἀμφοτέρων (sc. νοῦ καὶ γλώσσης) Id.1186; [φιλότητος] Id.1242; ἅμα τῆς τε ἐπιθυμίας καὶ τῆς τύχης.. τ. γενέσθαι *controller* both of his desire and of fortune, Th.6.78; τ. τριαίνης, of Poseidon, Ar.*Nu.*566 (lyr.); ἁλὸς ταμίαι *lords* of the sea, Critias 2.12: abs., τὸν τ. Ἴακχον S.*Ant.*1154 (lyr.). II. in Prose, *controller* of receipts and expenditure, *treasurer, paymaster*, τ. τῶν βασιλέος χρημάτων Hdt.2.121.α', cf. X.*HG*3.1.27; τ. τοῦ ἱροῦ *controller* of the sacred treasure in the citadel of Athens, Hdt.8.51; τ. τῆς θεοῦ Pl.*Lg.*774b, Decr.ap.And.1.77; τ. τῶν τῆς θεοῦ Lex ap.D.43.71: abs., Lys.9.6, Arist.*Pol.*1321ᵇ33; οἱ τῶν τῆς Ἀθηναίας τ. *IG*1².91.18; ταμίαι ἱερῶν χρημάτων τῆς Ἀθηναίας ib.304.2; ὁ τ. τοῦ δήμου ib.2².102.12, etc.; βουλῆς ταμίαι ib.223*C*7: freq. in other Greek states, *SIG*249.9 (Delph., iv B.C.), etc.; παρὰ ταμιῶν Ἁλικαρνασσέων *PCair.Zen.*36.25 (iii B.C.), cf. 317(*a*).17 (iii B.C.); τὸν ἐκ τοῦ ζυτοπωλίου τ. ib.202.2 (iii B.C.). 2. = Lat. *quaestor*, *SIG*700.4 (Lete, ii B.C.), D.H.5.34, Plu.*Publ.*12, etc. -εία, ἡ, *stewardship, management*, Pl.*Lg.*806a, X.*Oec.*7.41, *IPE*1².32*B*64 (Olbia, iii B.C.), *IG*2².1326.37; ἡ τῆς τροφῆς τ. the *storing* of food, by ants, Arist.*HA*622ᵇ26; τ. ψυχροῦ καὶ θερμοῦ Hp.*Nat.Puer.*26. II. *office of treasurer*, Arist.*Pol.*1309ᵇ7. 2. = Lat. *quaestura*, Str.4.1.12, Plu.*Cat.Mi.*17. III. ταμιείᾳ (corr. Daremberg for ταμιεῖαν) is dat. of ταμίας, *housekeeper*, Ath.Med ap.Orib.*inc.*5.6; so ταμιείᾳ πολιτικῶν λημμάτων is written (hypercorrectly) for ταμίᾳ π. λ. in *BGU*934 (iii A.D.). -είδιον, τό, Dim. of sq., Suid., prob. in Men. *Sam.*18. ❋-εῖον, τό, *treasury*, Th.1.96, Pl.*R.*416d, 55cd, Plu.*Cat.Mi.* 18; of the Roman *aerarium*, Plb.6.31.5, *IG*4²(1).63.7 (Epid., ii B.C.); the Imperial *fiscus*, *PRyl.*84.7 (ii A.D.), etc. 2. *magazine, storehouse*, Th.7.24, X.*Eq.*4.1, Arist.*Oec.*1344ᵇ33, *PCair.Zen.*299.7, 472.10 (iii B.C.); *store-room*, *IG*1².4.14, Pl.*Prt.*315d, Men.*Sam.*14, Str. 6.2.7, Babr.108.2, Sor.1.51, Plu.2.9e; *reservoir*, Hp.*Vict.*1.10. 3. *chamber, closet*, Lxx *Ge.*43.30, al., *Ev.Matt.*6.6. (Freq. contr. to ταμεῖον in Papyri, Inscrr., and codd. from i B.C., Phld.*Oec.*p.3 J. (citing Arist. l.c.), Babr. l.c., *CPR*1.83 (i A.D.), *SIG*1242.6 (Ephesus, iii A.D.), etc.; also written ταμῖον *PLond.*2.216.22 (i A.D.), etc.) -ευμα, ατος, τό, in pl., *stores, supplies*, D.S.3.16. II. = sq. I, X.*Oec.*3.15. -ευσις, εως, ἡ, = ταμιεία: metaph., *economy*, χρόνου Ael.*VH*2.5. II. = *fiscatio, proscriptio*, *Gloss.* -ευτήριον, τό, = ταμιεῖον, Sch.Ar.*Th.*426. -ευτής, οῦ, ὁ, = ταμίας, v.l. in Poll. 3.115. ❋-ευτικός, ή, όν, *of* or *for housekeeping, thrifty*, Poll.3.115: τὸ -κόν *economy, thrift*, M.Ant.1.16. II. at Rome, *belonging to the quaestor* or *quaestorship*, Lat. *quaestorius*, ἡ τ. ἐξουσία D.H.8.77; τ. ἀρχὴ *Supp.Epigr.*7.1.3 (Susa, i A.D., Epist. Artabani), Plu.*Cat.Mi.*16; οἱ νόμοι οἱ τ. ibid.; ὁ τ. νόμος the law *concerning the treasury*, Id.*Publ.* 12. -εύτωρ, ορος, ὁ, = ταμίας, Man.4.580. -εύω, fut. -εύσω Ar.*Eq.*948, Is.6.61, etc.: pf. τεταμίευκα D.S.37.8:—Med., fut. -εύσομαι D.H.1.82: aor. ἐταμιευσάμην D.S.4.12, Luc.*Im.*21:—Pass., aor. ἐταμιεύθην Ph.2.539: pf. τεταμίευμαι Lys.30.3 codd., Plu.2.157a; in med. sense, Hyp.*Dem.Fr.*4:—*to be treasurer, paymaster, controller*, *IG*1².467; οὐκέτι ἐμοὶ ταμιεύσεις Ar.*Eq.*948, cf. 959, D.24.129; σὺ γὰρ ταμιεύουσ' ἔτυχες Ar.*V.*964; τ. καὶ τὰς μεγίστας ἀρχὰς ἄρχειν Arist.*Pol.*1282ᵃ31: c. gen., τῆς Παράλου τ. *to be paymaster* of.., D. 21.173; προσόδων *Inscr.Délos* 439*a*18 (ii B.C.); τ. στρατιωτικῶν Plu. 2.842f:—Med., αὐταῖς ταμιεύεσθαι Ar.*Th.*419 (cod. R, ταμιεῦσαι καὶ Reiske), cf. *Ec.*600 (anap.). 2. at Rome, *to be quaestor*, D.S.37.8, *IG*14.751 (Naples), Plu.*Num.*9, App.*BC*1.77, etc. II. trans., *deal out, dispense*, Pl.*R.*465c:—Med., τὰ τίμια ἐκ τῆς ψυχῆς ταμιεύομαι X.*Smp.*4.41; τ. μικρὰς τὰς ψωμίδας, of a bird feeding, Arist.*Fr.*348:—Pass., τὴν δύναμιν ἐκ τούτου -ομένην Pl.*R.*508b; τοὺς νόμους τεταμιεύμεθα *we have* the laws *dealt out*, Lys.30.3 (nisi leg. ἐταμιευόμεθα);

[ὕδωρ] ἐξ ἀγγείου ταμιευόμενον Arist.*Mete.*353$^{b}$21, cf. *GA*770$^{a}$21; of a patient's drinks, ὕστερον -έσθω Aët.9.30. 2. *manage, control,* [ταμίαι] ταμιευόντων ἐμ πόλει ἐν τῷ ὀπισθοδόμῳ τὰ τῶν θεῶν χρήματα *IG*1$^{2}$.91.15; τὰ τῆς πόλεως Lys.21.14; of keeping house, *regulate, manage,* Ar.*Av.*1538, *Lys.*493:—Med., τὸ ἀργύριον..τοὺς ἱεροποιοὺς ἐμ πόλει ταμιεύεσθαι *IG*1$^{2}$.6.121. 3. *store up,* Ζηνὸς ταμιεύεσκε γονάς *she was the depository of* it, S.*Ant.*949 (lyr.):—Med., Arist.*HA*615$^{b}$23:—Pass., c. dat., *to be held in trust for,* Δωριεῖ λαῷ Pi.*O.*8.30; *to be stored* or *saved up for,* ταμιεύεταί σοι Ῥοδιακοῦ (sc. μέλιτος ἡμικάδιον) α' *PCair.Zen.*680.14 (iii B.C.). 4. metaph., *husband,* ἰσχύν Hp.*Art.*47:—Med., οὐκ ἔστιν ἡμῖν ταμιεύεσθαι ἐς ὅσον βουλόμεθα ἄρχειν *control* the limits to which we mean to extend our sway, Th.6.18; ἔξεστιν ἡμῖν ταμιεύεσθαι ὁπόσοις ἂν βουλοίμεθα μάχεσθαι X.*An.*2.5.18, cf. *Eq.Mag.*7.11, *Cyr.*3.3.47, 4.1.18; ταμιεύεσθαι τὴν τύχην, τὸν καιρόν, *make the best use of* fortune or the time, D.H.1.65,82; ἐς τὴν αὔριον ταμιεύεσθαι τὸ μῖσος *lay* it *by..,* Luc.*Prom.*8; ταμιεύεσθαί τινα τῶν ῥητῶν εἰς τὸ Περὶ ἔθους γραφησόμενον ἡμῖν *save up..,* Gal.19.219; τῶν θεῶν ταμιευσαμένων εἰς τοῦτον τὸν ἱερώτατον καιρὸν τὴν τῆς οἰκουμένης ἀσφάλειαν *having preserved..,* *OGI*669.9 = *BGU*1563.26 (i A.D.). b. Med., c. gen., *regulate in amount, exercise control over,* τοῦ πνεύματος Arist.*GA*788$^{a}$32, cf. Plu.2.131d. c. abs., Arist.*GA*788$^{a}$30, *PA*675$^{b}$21. III. = Lat. *fisco, proscribo, Gloss.* **-η, -ης,** Ep. and Ion. for ταμία, ταμίας.

**τᾰμικός,** ή, όν, *belonging to a treasurer,* ὁ πόρος ὁ τ. *treasurer's funds,* *BCH*53.340 (Thasos, i B.C.). 2. **-κόν,** τό, the *office of the fiscus,* ἐτέθη ἐν τῷ τ. *PFlor.*382.94 (iii A.D.).

**τᾰμι-οῦχος,** ὁ, ἡ, (ἔχω) *having charge of the store-room,* Aesop.ap. *Gloss.* iii p.47, Hsch. **-όω,** 3 sg. -οῖ, = *confiscat, Gloss.*

**Ταμιράδαι·** ἱερεῖς τινες ἐν Κύπρῳ, Hsch.; cf. Tacit.*Hist.*2.3.

**τᾰμῐσ-ίνης** τυρός, ὁ, cheese *made with rennet,* Diocl.*Fr.*138. **-ιον,** τό, = *coagulum, Gloss.* **-ος,** ἡ, *rennet,* Hp.*Mul.*2.192; δέρμα νέας ταμίσοιο ποτόσδον Theoc.7.16, cf. 11.66, Nic.*Th.*577, al.

**τάμνω,** v. τέμνω.

**τᾶμον,** Thess. Adv. *to-day,* τὰ ψαφίσματα τό τε ὑππρὸ τᾶς γενόμενον καὶ τὸ τᾶμον yesterday's decree and *to-day's,* *IG*9(2).517.44 (Larissa, iii B.C.). (Perh. neut. of an Adj. *τᾶμος, cf. τῆμος II.)

**τᾶν,** Att. crasis for τοι ἄν: but **τἀν,** for τὰ ἐν.

⊛ **τᾶν,** indecl., only Att. and in phrase ὦ τᾶν, as a form of address, *sir, my good friend,* S.*OT*1145, *Ph.*1387, E.*Ba.*802, Pl.*Ap.*25c, *Ep.*319e, D.1.26: freq. in Com. (not in Ar.), Pl.Com.17 D., Men.*Sam.*202, *Com.Adesp.*21.11 D.: with a pr. n., ὦ τ. Φαίδιμε ib.22.66 D.; used in addressing several persons, τί δρῶμεν, ὦ τᾶν; S.*Ichn.*98; ἆρά γε, ὦ τᾶν, ἐθελήσετε; Cratin.360, cf. Nicopho 29. (A.D.*Adv.*159.11 says ωταν has a long final syllable and two accents: after criticizing earlier theories he derives it from ὦ *ἐτᾶν, in which *ἐτᾶν is a form of ἔτης, comparing μεγιστᾶν, ξυνᾶν: accented ὦ τᾶν in S.*Ichn.* l.c.)

**Τάν,** Cret. for Ζεύς (q.v.).

**τανάγρ-α,** ἡ, *copper, cauldron,* Hsch.:—Dim. **-ίς,** ίδος, ἡ, v.l. for παναγρίς in Poll.10.165.

**Τάναγρα,** ἡ, a town of Boeotia, Hdt.9.15, Th.1.108, etc. (on the accent, v. Hdn.Gr.1.265):—Adj. **Ταναγρ-ικός,** ή, όν, *of Tanagra,* Hdt.5.57, etc.:—⊛ **-αῖος,** ὁ, *a man of Tanagra,* X.*HG*5.4.49, etc.; Ταναγραίων φυή, prov. of enormous bulk, from a native of T., Ephor. 225 J.; fem. **-ίς,** ίδος, *a woman of T.,* Corinn.20 (in poet. dat. Ταναγρίδεσσι); also **-ική,** Sophil.4.4:—ἡ **-αϊκή** the *district of T.,* v.l. in Plu.*Per.*10. [Tᾰ-, Sophil. l.c., Orph.*A.*147.]

⊛ **τᾰνᾰ-ήκης,** ες, (ἀκή) *with long point* or *edge,* ταναήκεϊ χαλκῷ, of a sword or spear, Il.7.77, 24.754; of an axe, 23.118. II. *tall,* σχοῖνος Opp.*H.*4.53; Ἄλπεις Orph.*A.*1126. (τανυήκης is freq. v.l.) **-ηχέτης,** ου, ὁ, *far-sounding,* poet. -ηχέτα, Opp.*C.*2.144.

**τάναι,** αἱ, *emanations of decans,* prob. corrupt in Herm.ap.Stob.1.21.9.

**τᾰναίμῡκος,** ον, *far-bellowing,* βοῦς *AP*6.116 (Samus).

**ταναίχαλκος,** v. τανάχαλκος.

**τᾰνᾰόδειρος,** ον, *long-necked,* οἰωνοί Ar.*Av.*254,1394. [ταν- short by nature, but lengthd. in Ar. ll. cc. in dactylic verses.]

⊛ **τᾰνᾰός,** ή, όν, also ός, όν Il.16.589, E.*Ba.*831: (τείνω: prop. ταναϝός, cf. sq.):—*outstretched, tall, taper,* αἰγανέη Il. l.c.; ἀστάχυες *h.Cer.*454; πῦρ.., ὅσον -ώτερον ἦεν Emp.84.11, cf. ib.5; πλόκαμος τ. *long flowing* locks, E.*Ba.*455, cf. 831; τ. αἰθήρ *outspread* ether, Id.*Or.*322 (lyr.), Men.*Sam.*111; ἀήρ Q.S.1.681; τ. γῆρας *long* old age, *AP*5.281 (Agath.), cf. 11.389 (Lucill.); ὄρνις Opp.*C.*1.51; ταναῇ ὀπί with *loud* voice, Q.S.12.58; τ. χείλεα, of a gadfly, Id.11.209.

**τᾰναύπους** (i.e. ταναϝπους, cf. τανaός), ποδος, ὁ, ἡ, Ep. form for τανύπους (q.v.), *stretching the feet, long-striding, long-shanked,* μῆλα ταναύποδα Od.9.464, *h.Ap.*304, *h.Merc.*232.

**τᾰνᾰ-ϋφής** [ῠ], ές, (ὑφή) *woven long and finely,* Hsch. (τανοϋφῆ cod.), Suid., hence restd. in S.*Tr.*602 for γ' εὐϋφῆ. **-χαλκος,** ον, *of stretched* (i.e. hammer-wrought) *bronze,* f.l. (prob. for ταναίχαλκον) in *AP*6.306 (Aristo). **-ῶπις,** ιδος, ἡ, (ὤψ) *far-sighted,* Emp.122.

**τᾰνεῖαι,** αἱ, *beams,* Thphr.*HP*4.1.2.

**τᾰνηλεγής,** ές, perh. *bringing long woe,* epith. of death, μοῖρα τανηλεγέος θανάτοιο Od.2.100, etc.; δύο κῆρε τ. θ. Il.8.70; κὴρ..τ. θ. Od.11.171, Tyrt.12.35. Adv. τανηλεγέως *Supp.Epigr.*1.450 (Phrygia). (Apparently a compd. of ἄλγος (ἀλέγω) like δυσηλεγής.)

**τᾰνήλοφος,** ον, *long-necked, with a long dome* or *top,* Hsch.

**τανθᾰρύζω** or **τανθᾰλύζω,** *quiver, shake,* found in the following forms: καθαρίζειν (κανθαρίζειν Ammon.*Diff.* p.79 V., τανθαρύζειν cj. Valckenaer) μὲν λέγουσιν οἱ Ἀττικοὶ τὸ τρέμειν, τονθορύζειν (-ίζειν Ammon.) δὲ τὸ ψιθυρίζειν καὶ γογγύζειν Ptol.Asc.p.410 H.; τανθαλύζει (ταντ- cod.)· τρέμει, Δωριεῖς, οἱ δὲ σπαίρει, Hsch.; ἐτανθόριζον· ἔτρεμον, Id.; ταονθορύζειν· τρέμειν, Phot., Suid. (cf. ἐκτανθαρύζω, ταντaλίζω, παμφαλύζω, τοιθορύσσω): hence **τανθαρύκτρια,** cj. Valckenaer for τοιθορύκτρια (q.v.): **τανθαρυστὸς** ὅρμος a necklace *quivering* with suspended gems, Theopomp.Com.95.

**τανί,** v. ὁνί. **τᾱνίκα,** Dor. for τηνίκα.

**Τάνις,** εως or ιος, ἡ, a town in lower Egypt, the Hebrew *Zoan,* Str.17.1.20: hence ὁ **Τανίτης** νομός the *Tanite* nome, Hdt.2.166, *PRev.Laws* 31.10 (iii B.C.), etc.; and τὸ **Τανῑτικὸν** στόμα, of the Nile, Str. l.c.

**τανισια,** = *epinia, Gloss.* (dub.).

**τᾰνίσφῡρος,** ον, *slender-ankled,* Hes.*Fr.*94.23, Ibyc.*Oxy.*1790 *Fr.*1.11, B.3.60, 5.59. (Prob. dissim. fr. τανύσφυρος, q.v.)

**τᾰνίφυλλος** [ῐ], ον, *with long foliage,* ὄρος B.10.55. (Dissim. fr. τανύφυλλος (q.v.), cf. foreg.)

**ταννί,** v. ὁνί. **τάννυν,** v. ὅνυ(ν).

**ταντaλάσσεται** δάκρυα· στάζει δάκρυα, Hsch.

**ταντᾰλ-εία,** ἡ, v. ταλαντεία. **-ειος, -εος, -ίδης, -ικός, -ίς,** v. Τάνταλος. **-ίζω,** *wave about,* Anacr.78; ἐταντάλιζεν· ἔτρεμεν, ἐταντaλίχθη· ἐσείσθη, and ταντaλίζεται· σαλεύεται, Hsch.:—prov., in Med., τὰ Ταντάλου τάλαντα ταντaλίζεται *he weighs* in purse as much as Tantalus, v. Τάνταλος sub fin., Zen.6.4. **-όομαι,** Pass., *to be balanced* or *swung,* ἐπὶ γᾷ πέσε ταντaλωθείς fell *hurtling* to earth, S.*Ant.*134 (lyr.):—the Sch. expl. by διατιναχθείς, διασεισθείς.

**Τάντᾰλος,** ὁ, *Tantalus,* ancestor of the Pelopidae, Od.11.582, etc.; ξυνῆκα γὰρ τοὺς Ταντάλου κήπους τρυγῶν *Com.Adesp.*530:—Adj. **Ταντάλ-ειος,** α, ον, also ος, ον (v. infr.), *of* or *belonging to T.,* οἱ T. ἔκγονοι the descendants *of T.,* E.*El.*1176; Πέλοψ ὁ T. Id.*IT*1, cf. 988, etc.; τιμωρία Ταντάλειος Poet.ap.Plb.4.45.6, cf. Ph.1.512; T. δίκας ὑποφέρειν Luc.*Am.*53; also **-εος,** α, ον, *AP*5.235 (Paul. Sil.); **-ικός,** ή, όν, Man.5.187: **-ίδης,** ου, ὁ, *descendant of Tantalus,* A.*Ag.*1469 (pl., lyr.): **-ίς,** ίδος, *daughter of T.,* i.e. Niobe, *APl.*4.134 (Mel.), cf. 131 (Antip.). (Derived by Pl. from ταλάντατος in reference to his *endurance* of torment, or from ταλαντεία (ταντaλεία codd.) in reference to the story of the rock *balanced and tottering* over his head, *Cra.*395e; by others from his proverbial wealth, τὰ Ταντάλου τάλαντ' ἐκεῖνα Men.301.6; cf. ταντaλίζω.)

**τάνυ,** v. ὅνυ.

**τᾰνύ-γληνος,** ον, *large-eyed, full-eyed,* Nonn.*D.*43.42. **-γλωσσος,** ον, *long-tongued, chattering,* κορῶναι Od.5.66. **-γλώχῑς,** ῖνος, ὁ, ἡ, *with long point,* ὀϊστοί Il.8.297, Simon.106, Q.S.6.463. **-δρομος,** ον, *running at full stretch,* A.*Eu.*371 (lyr.). **-έθειρα,** ἡ, *long-haired, with flowing hair,* Σεμέλα Pi.*O.*2.26. ⊛ **-ήκης,** ες, (ἀκή) = ταναήκης, *with long point* or *edge,* ἄορ Il.14.385, Od.10.439, al. II. *tapering,* ὄζοι Il.16.768. **-ῆλιξ,** ῐκος, ὁ, ἡ, *of advanced age,* *AP*5.205 (Leon.). **-ηχέτᾰ,** ὁ, v.l. for ταναηχέτα, Opp.*C.*2.144. **-ηχής,** ές, Dor. **-αχής,** *far-sounding,* χορδῶν κτύπος prob. in Lyr. in *Aegyptus* 15.295. **-θριξ,** τρῐχος, ὁ, ἡ, *long-haired, shaggy,* αἶξ Hes.*Op.*516; ὗς a *bristly* swine, Semon.7.2. ⊛ **-κνήμῑς,** ῖδος, ὁ, ἡ, *long-legged,* Nonn.*D.*14.370. **-κνημος,** ον, = foreg., ib.28.17, 36.188. **-κραιρος,** ον, *long-horned,* ἔλαφος Opp.*C.*1.191; ταῦροι *AP*6.74 (Agath.). **-κρήπῑς,** ῖδος, ὁ, ἡ, *with long, high base* or *foundation,* Nonn.*D.*28.206. On the accent v. Hdn.Gr.2.621.

**τάνῠμαι,** Pass., = τανύομαι, *to be stretched,* τάνυται Il.17.393.

**τᾰνῠμήκης,** ες, *long-stretched, tall,* ἰτέαι *AP*6.170.

**τανῦν,** better **τὰ νῦν,** *now,* v. νῦν I.

**τᾰνύ-πεπλος** [ῠ], ον, *with flowing robe,* freq. in Ep. as epith. of high-born ladies or goddesses, Ἑλένη Il.3.228, Od.4.305; Θέτις Il.18.385; Ἡνιόχη, Εὐδώρη, Hes.*Sc.*83, *Fr.*180; Ἀλκμήνη *IG*12(8).356 (Thasos, vi B.C.); Φερσεφόνη ib.1$^{2}$.817, cf. B.*Scol.Oxy.*2081(*e*) (= 1361 *Fr.*5):—πλακοῦς τ., comically, Batr.36. **-πλεκτος,** ον, *in long plaits,* μίτραι *AP*7.473 (Aristodic.); ἕρκος Opp.*H.*1.33. **-πλευρος,** ον, *long-sided, enormous,* πέτροι *AP*9.656. **-πλόκᾰμος,** ον, *with long locks of hair,* Nonn.*D.*35.328. **-πους,** ὁ, ἡ, gen. ποδος, = ταναύπους, Ἐρινύες S.*Aj.*837. **-πρεμνος,** ον, *with long stem,* φηγός Nonn.*D.*5.303; λόχμη ib.541; *with tall trees,* Ἴδη v.l. in Coluth.195. **-πρῳρος,** ον, *with long prow,* Q.S.5.348, 9.437. II. τανυπρῴρους· τὰς καλύπτρας, διὰ τὸ περὶ τὸ πρόσωπον περιτετάσθαι, Hsch. **-πτερος,** ον, = τανυσίπτερος, *with extended wings, long-winged,* οἰωνοί *h.Cer.*89; αἰετός Hes.*Th.*523, cf. Ibyc.4, Pi.*P.*5.112; of arrows, Tim.*Pers.*30. ⊛ **-πτέρυξ,** ῠγος, ὁ, ἡ, = foreg., οἰωνοί Il.12.237; ἅρπη 19.350:—also **-πτέρῠγος,** ον, μυῖα Simon.32 (cf. *POxy.*1087.32); gen. pl. -πτερύγων may belong to either, Ἐρώτων *Sammelb.*6699.1 (Ptolemaic). **-πτορθος,** ον, *branching,* κέρατα Nonn.*D.*17.149; δένδρον ib.48.611. **-ρριζος,** ον, (ῥίζα) *with outstretching roots,* αἴγειροι Hes.*Sc.*377. **-ρρῖνος,** ον, (ῥίς) *long-nosed,* prob. cj. in Nonn.*D.*5.10 for τανυρρήνοιο. **-ρροιζος,** ον, *whizzing along,* ἀκωκή Opp.*C.*4.195.

**τᾰνῠσί-δρομος,** ον, *running swiftly,* Sapph.71 (dub. cj. for ἀνυοδρόμον). **-πτερος,** ον, = τανύπτερος, ὄρνιθες Od.5.65, cf. Hes.*Op.*212, Alc.84; κίχλαι Od.22.468; ἀλκυόνες Ibyc.8; οἰωνός *h.Merc.*213; χελιδών Ar.*Av.*1411 (lyr.). **-πτέρῠγος,** ον, = foreg., Man.2.78.

**τάνῠσις,** εως, ἡ, = τάσις, Hp.*Art.*71, Aret.*CA*2.2.

**τᾰνῠσίσκοπος,** ον, *far-seeing*, Φοιβείη ἀκτίς Poet.ap.Jul.*Ep*.89.

**τᾰνύσκῐος,** ον, *with long-stretching shadow*, Opp.*C*.4.356.

**τανύσκομαι,** *to be 'on the stretch'*, τὴν ψυχήν Dam.*Isid*.211 (s.v.l.).

**τᾰνύστροφος,** ον, *long-whirling*, σφενδόνη Orac. in *App.Anth*.6.138.

**τᾰνυστύς,** ύος, ἡ, *stretching*, *stringing*, τόξου Od.21.112.

⊛**τᾰνύ-σφῠρος,** ον, *with long taper ankles* or *feet*, θυγάτηρ *h.Cer*.2, cf. 77; Ὠκεανῖναι Hes.*Th*.364, cf. *Sc*.35. **-τρῖχος,** ον, = τανύθριξ, Opp.*C*.1.187.

**τανῠφάντης,** ου, ὁ, a kind of *weaver*, distd. fr. ποκύφος, *PTeb*.5.171 (ii B.C.).

**τᾰνύ-φθογγος,** ον, *far-sounding*, γέρανοι Q.S.11.110; κῆρυξ Tryph. 111; λαιμοί Nonn.*D*.22.61. **-φλοιος,** ον, of trees, *with long-stretched bark*, i.e. *of tall* or *slender growth*, κράνεια Il.16.767; αἴγειρος S.*Fr*.593.2 (lyr.); ἔρινος Theoc.25.250; ἐλάτη Orph.*A*.607. ⊛**-φυλλος** [νῠ], ον, *with long-pointed leaves*, of the olive, Od.13.102,346, prob. in Pi.(?) *Oxy*.426.7. II. *with thick foliage*, *leafy*, ὄρος Theoc.25.221. **-χειλής** [ῠ], ές, *long-nebbed*, μέλισσαι, ὄρνιθες, Q.S.3.221, 5.12.

⊛**τᾰνύω,** Il.17.391, etc.: fut. -ύσω *AP*5.261 (Paul. Sil.); Ep. -ύω Od.21.152,174, τανύσσω Orph.*L*.181: aor. ἐτάνῠσα, Ep. ἐτάνυσσα Od.24.177; τάνυσσα Il.14.389; part. τανύσας Hp.*Steril*.244:—**Med.**, Ep. fut. τανύσσομαι in pass. sense, Archil.3: Ep. aor. part. τανυσσάμενος Il.4.112:—**Pass.**, 3 sg. pf. τετάνυσται Od.9.116; part. τετανυμένος Gal.13.991, τετανυμμένος (sic) Dioscorus in *PLit.Lond*.98 ii 10: 3 fut. τετανύσσεται Orph.*L*.324: aor. ἐτανύσθην Hes.*Th*.177, etc., Ep. 3 pl. τάνυσθεν Il.16.475, Od.16.175. [ῠ always, exc. ἐκτανῡειν (s.v.l.) in *Anacreont*.35.5.] Ep. Verb (used twice by Pi., never by Trag.):—*stretch*, *strain*, βοείην Il.17.390,391; ἶριν ib.547; τ. βιόν *string* a bow, Od.24.177; οὐ μὲν ἐγὼ τανύω I cannot *string* it, 21.152, cf. 171,174 (so in Med., τὸ μὲν [τόξον].. τανυσσάμενος *having strung his* bow, Il.4.112, cf. Archil.3); of putting the strings to a harp, ῥηϊδίως ἐτάνυσσε νέῳ περὶ κόλλοπι χορδήν Od.21.407 (also in Med., ὀΐων ἐτανύσσατο χορδάς *h.Merc*.51); τ. κανόνα *pull* the weaving-bar *in*, in weaving, Il.23.761; ὅππως .. τανύσῃ βοέοισιν ἱμᾶσιν how to *urge on* [the horses], ib.324; ἐπὶ Ἀκράγαντι τανύσσαις (sc. ὀϊστούς) *having aimed* them, Pi.*O*.2.91; ἐπ' Ἰσθμῷ ἅρμα τάνυεν *was driving* it to the Isthmus, ib.8.49; τ. ὦτα λόγοις *lend attentive* ear, *AP*7.562 (Jul.); τ. ὄμμα ἐπί τινος, ἐς οὐρανόν, ib.5.261 (Paul. Sil.), 9.188:—**Pass.**, *to be stretched* or *strained*, γναθμοὶ τάνυσθεν (for ἐτανύσθησαν) the hollow cheeks *filled out*, Od.16.175; τετάνυστο λαίφεα A.R.1.606. **2.** metaph., *strain*, *make more intense*, μάχην Il.11.336; ἔριδα 14.389; κακὸν πόνον 17.401: more fully, ὁμοιίου πτολέμοιο πεῖραρ ἐπαλλάξαντες ἐπ' ἀμφοτέροισι τάνυσσαν (cf. ἐπαλλάσσω I) 13.359:—Pass., *strain* or *exert oneself*, *run at full stretch*, of horses galloping, τανύοντο δὲ μώνυχες ἵπποι ἄψορρον προτὶ ἄστυ 16.375; ἐν ῥυτῆρσι τάνυσθεν ib.475; of mules, ἄμοτον τανύοντο Od.6.83. II. *stretch out in length*, *lay out*, *lay*, ἀνθρακιὴν στορέσας ὀβελοὺς ἐφύπερθε τάνυσσε Il.9.213; ἔγχος ἐπ' ἰκριόφιν τ. νεός Od.15.283; ἐτάνυσσε τράπεζαν *set out* a *long* table, 4.54, 15.137; τ. τινὰ ἐν κονίῃς, ἐπὶ γαίῃ, *lay* one in the dust, *stretch* him *at his length*, Il.23.25, Od.18.92; ἕνα δρόμον τ. *form* one *long* flight, of cranes, Arat.1011:—Pass., *lie stretched out*, τάπης τετάνυστο *was spread*, Il.10.156; σύες .. εὑόμενοι τανύοντο διὰ φλογός 9.468; ἐπ' αὐτῷ ἠλακάτη τετάνυστο Od.4.135; *extend*, νῆσος παρὲκ λιμένος τετάνυσται 9.116; τετάνυστο περὶ σπείους ἡμερίς 5.68; ἐτανύσθη πάντῃ he *stretched himself* every way, Hes.*Th*.177; ἐπὶ χθονὶ κεῖτο τανυσθείς Il.20.483, cf. 13.392, etc. (so in Med., κεῖτο τανυσσάμενος Od.9.298); also τρίβος τετάνυστο the path *stretched away*, Theoc.25.157; νὺξ τετάνυσται Arat.557; πλόος τ. A.R.4.1583 (dub. l.).

**ταξᾶτος,** η, ον, = Lat. *taxatus*, *PIand*.9.33 (ii A.D.).

⊛**ταξείδιον,** τό, *purpose*, εἴς τινα ταξείδια Ps.-Democr.Alch.p.54 B.

**ταξεώτης,** ου, ὁ, *officer of a magistrate*, *sergeant*, *commissary*, etc., *member of the militia palatina*, *Cod.Just*.1.3.53, *PMasp*.31.13 (vi A.D.), *PSI*8.939 (vi A.D.); written **ταξιώτης,** *An.Ox*.2.307, *Gloss.*: hence Adj. **-ωτικός,** ή, όν, ῥαβδοῦχος *Cod.Just*.1.3.53, Eust.104.24.

**ταξῐαρχ-έω,** *to be a taxiarch*, *command the contingent* (τάξις) supplied by an Athenian φυλή, ταξιαρχῶν καὶ τὴν ἑαυτοῦ φυλὴν ἔχων Th.8.92, cf. Ar.*Pax*444, Lys.13.7, D.39.17, Arist.*Pol*.$1277^{b}$11, *IG*$2^{2}$.956.49; ἐὰν ἡμῶν τις -αρχῇ ἢ λοχαγῇ σοι X.*Mem*.3.1.5. **-ης,** ου, ὁ, less common form of ταξίαρχος, A.*Fr*.182.1 (acc. pl. -ας), Hippod.ap. Stob.4.1.94 (nom. pl. -αι); gen. pl. -έων is v.l. in Hdt.7.99, 9.53, but he uses nom. pl. ταξίαρχοι (v. ταξίαρχος); ταξιαρχῶν is so accented in Pl.*Lg*.755e, but acc. ταξιάρχους occurs ibid.; τ. used as a nickname, Cic.*Att*.16.11.3; cf. ταξίαρχος I. 2 and 3b,c. **-ία,** ἡ, *office of taxiarch*, Arist.*Pol*.$1322^{b}$3, Polyaen.3.9.10. II. = τάξις I. 4b, Ascl.*Tact*.3.4, Arr.*Tact*.10.9, Ael.*Tact*.9.10. **-ικός,** ή, όν, *of a* ταξίαρχος, ἐξουσία *PLond*.5.1708.87 (vi A.D.). **-ος,** ὁ, *commander of a corps* or *squadron*, ταξίαρχοι ἀπὸ τῶν νεῶν Hdt.8.67; ταξίαρχοι τῶν τελέων Id.9.42; τ. καὶ πεζῶν καὶ ἱππέων X.*Cyr*.8.1.10; in the army of Alexander, Arr.*An*.3.9.6; in Ptolemaic Egypt, *PMich.Zen*.70.5 (iii B.C.); cf. ταξιάρχης. **2.** *commander of a* τάξις (128 men), Ascl.*Tact*.2.8, Ael.*Tact*.9.3 (-άρχης Arr.*Tact*.10.2). **3.** = Lat. *centurio*, Plb.6.24.1, al., Zos.3.11. **b.** = *tribunus militum*, D.H.5.41, J.*BJ*3.5.2, Plu.*Cam*.37, App.*BC*5.61, Agath.2.20 (-άρχης Plu.*Pomp*.32, App.*BC*3.39). **c.** = *legatus legionis*, anachronism in App.*Sam*.4.6 (-άρχαι codd.). **d.** = *ordinarius*, Lyd.*Mag*.1.46, *Gloss.*; also glossed by *manipularis* and *evocatus*, ib. II. at Athens, *commander of a* τάξις, or *quota of infantry* furnished by a φυλή, Ar.*Ach*.569 (lyr.), *Pax* 1172 (troch.), *Av*.353 (troch.), Th.4.4, 7.60, Arist.*Ath*.30.2, D.4.26, 54.5, Aeschin.3.169, *IG*$2^{2}$.334.13; [ὁ τ.] ἡγεῖται τῶν φυλετῶν καὶ λοχαγοὺς καθίστησιν Arist.*Ath*.61.3; applied to naval officers, X.*HG*1.6.29,35.

⊛**ταξί-λοχος** [ῐ], ον, *commanding a* λόχος or *division*, τ. λαῶν Arist. *Pepl*.9. **-όζωτος,** ον, *with branches at regular intervals*, Thphr. *HP*1.8.3 (prob. cj. for ἀξιολογώτατα). ⊛**-όομαι,** Pass., *engage in battle*, Pi.*O*.9.78.

⊛**τάξις,** εως, Ion. ιος, ἡ, (τάσσω) *arranging*, *arrangement*: I. in military sense: **1.** *drawing up in rank and file*, *order* or *disposition of an army*, Th.5.68 (init.), 7.5, etc.; τὰ ἀμφὶ τάξεις rules for it, *tactics*, X.*An*.2.1.7; τ. καὶ ἀντίταξις Phld.*Piet*.12. **2.** *battle array*, *order of battle*, κατὰ τάξιν Hdt.8.86; ἐν τάξει Th.4.72, etc.; ἐς τάξιν καθίστασθαι, ἀνάγειν, ib.93, Ar.*Av*.400 (anap.); ἵνα μὴ διασπασθείη ἡ τ. Th.5.70; of ships, ἀποπλῶσαι ἐκ τῆς τάξιος Hdt.6.14. **3.** *a single rank* or *line* of soldiers, ἐπὶ τάξιας ὀλίγας γίγνεσθαι to be drawn up a few *lines* deep, ib.111, cf. 9.31; ἐλύθησαν αἱ τ. τῶν Περσῶν Pl.*La*.191c. **4.** *body of soldiers*, A.*Pers*.298, S.*OC*1311; esp. at Athens, *the quota of infantry furnished by each* φυλή (cf. ταξίαρχος II), Lys.16.16; but freq. of smaller bodies, *company*, X.*An*.1.2.16, 6.5.11, etc.; ἱππέων τ. ib.1.8.21; so of ships, *squadron*, A.*Pers*.380: generally, *band*, *company*, φιλία γὰρ ἥδε τ., of the chorus, Id.*Pr*.128 (lyr.); ἐμφανίσας μοι ἐν ᾗ ἔσομαι τάξει *PCair.Zen*.409.6 (iii B.C.). **b.** esp. *a contingent of* 128 *men*, Ascl.*Tact*.2.8, Arr.*Tact*.10.2, Ael.*Tact*.9.3. **c.** in late Gr., *membership of the militia palatina* (cf. ταξεώτης), Lib.*Or*.27.17. **5.** *post* or *place in the line* of battle, ἀξιεύμεθα ταύτης τῆς τ. Hdt.9.26, cf. 27; ἐν τῇ τ. εἶχε ἑωυτόν Id.1.82; μένειν ἐν τῇ ἑωυτοῦ τ. Id.3.158; τ. φυλάξων E.*Rh*.664; ἡ τ. φυλακτέα X.*Cyr*.5.3.43; ᾗ ἕκαστος τὴν τ. εἶχεν Id.*An*.4.3.29; τῆς πρώτης τ. τεταγμένος Lys.14.11, cf. Th.5.68 (fin.); ἐκλιπόντας τὴν τ. Hdt.5.75, cf. 9.21; λείπειν τὴν τ. And.1.74, Pl.*Ap*.29a, D.13.34, 15.32, Aeschin.3.159, etc.; παραχωρεῖν τῆς τάξεως D.3.36, etc.; but ἡγεμὼν ἔξω τάξεων officer *on the unattached list*, *Arch.Pap*.3.188, cf. *Sammelb*.599, *OGI*69 (Coptos); so οἱ ἔξω τάξεως staff-officers, aides-de-camp, D.S.19.22. II. generally, *arrangement*, *order*, ἡμερῶν τ. εἰς μηνῶν περιόδους Pl.*Lg*.809d; ἡ τῶν ὅλων τ. X.*Cyr*.8.7.22; *disposition*, τῆς ψυχῆς Gorg.*Hel*.14: Rhet., *disposition*, opp. λέξις, Arist.*Rh*.$1414^{a}$29; ἡ τ. τοῦ λόγου Aeschin.3.205, cf. D.18.2, Sor.1.18, Gal.*Libr.Ord*.1; ὕστερον τῇ τ. D.3.15, cf. Gal.6.68, 16.533; ἐν τ. εἶναι, = μένειν, Pl.*Tht*.153e; τ. καὶ ἠρεμία Arist.*EE*$1218^{a}$23; εἰ τὰ γυμνάσια ἔχοι τὴν τ. ἐνταῦθα Id.*Pol*.$1331^{a}$37; difft. from θέσις or mere position, Id.*Ph*.$188^{a}$24, Thphr.*Sens*.60 (θέσεως τ. Gal.6.194; τ. θέσεως is dub. l. in 16.709); ἡ κατὰ τ. τινὰ βασιλεία, opp. ἀόριστος τυραννίς, Arist.*Rh*.$1366^{a}$2; καὶ τοῦτο κατὰ τ., ἕως .. and so *on*, until .., Sor.2.62. **2.** *order*, *regularity*, εἰς τ. ἄγειν ἐκ τῆς ἀταξίας Pl.*Ti*.30a; τ. καὶ κόσμος Id.*Grg*.504a; οὔτε νόμος οὔτε τ. Id.*Lg*.875c, cf. *R*.587a; τ. περιόδου Epicur.*Ep*.2 p.42 U.; διὰ τάξεως γίγνεσθαι Pl.*Lg*.780a; τάξιν ἔχειν *to be regular*, Thphr. *HP*3.9.6; ἐν τάξει *in an orderly manner*, Pl.*Lg*.637e; so τάξει *SIG*741.12 (Nysa, i B.C., rendering of Lat. *ordine*). **3.** *ordinance*, κατὰ τὴν τ. τοῦ νόμου Pl.*Lg*.925b; παρὰ τὴν τοῦ νομοθέτου τ. Id.*Plt*.305c, etc. **b.** *prescription*, τὴν τοῦ λυσιτελοῦντος τοῖς σώμασι ποιεῖσθαι τ. Id.*Plt*.294e; *recipe*, cj. in *PHolm*.2.2. **4.** τ. τοῦ φόρου *assessment* of tribute, X.*Ath*.3.5, cf. *IG*$1^{2}$.63.2, al.; τῶν ὀφειλημάτων περὶ τῆς πράξεως ib.57.13, cf. Lex ap.D.24.45; τ. τῆς ὑδρείας a *ration* of water, Pl.*Lg*.844b. **5.** *political order*, *constitution*, τ. Κρητική, Λακωνική, etc., Arist.*Pol*.$1271^{b}$40, cf. *Ath*.3.1, al. III. metaph. from I. 5, *post*, *rank*, *position*, *station*, ὑπὸ χθόνα τάξιν ἔχουσα A.*Eu*.396 (lyr.); ἡ τῶν ἀκοντιζόντων τ. Antipho 3.2.7; ἰδίᾳ τοῦ βίου τ. Isoc.6.2; ἀνὴρ τῆς πρώτης τ. *CIG*2767.4 (Aphrodisias); οἰκέτου τ. D.18.258, cf. *PGnom*.43,196 (ii A.D.), Mitteis *Chr*.372 v 18 (ii A.D.); τ. ἔχοντος ἐν τῷ Μουσείῳ *Sammelb*.6674.10 (ii A.D.); ἐν τῇ Θετταλῶν τάξει *ranging herself with* the T., D.18.63; ἐν ἐχθροῦ τ. *as* an enemy, Id.20.81, etc.; ἐν ἐπηρείας τάξει by *way* of insult, Id.18.13; ἀδύνατον εἶχεν τ. occupied an impossible *position*, i.e. was unthinkable, Hyp.(?) *Oxy*.1607.60; τὴν ὑπὲρ ὑμῶν ἑλόμενον τάξιν πολιτεύεσθαι *championship* of your cause, D.18.138, cf. *Ep*.3.15; ἐγὼ τὴν τῆς εὐνοίας τ. .. οὐκ ἔλιπον *post* of patriotism, Id.18.173. IV. *order*, *class* of men, X.*Mem*.2.1.7; *function*, D.13.19. **2.** *list*, *register*, ὅπως ταγῇ αὐτοῦ τὸ ὄνομα ἐν τῇ τῶν τετελευτηκότων τ. *Sammelb*.7359.15, cf. 7404.6, *PSI*9.1064.38, 10.1141.10 (all ii A.D.); ἡ τ. τῶν κατοχίμων *PTeb*.318.21 (ii A.D.); τ. λαογράφων *PLond*.2.182 *b* 2 (ii A.D.). **3.** *account*, ἰδίας τάξεως *POxy*.61.8 (iii A.D.), cf. *PLond*.3.1107.26,30 (iii A.D.). **4.** *payment*, ib.966.3 (iv A.D., cf. *Arch.Pap*.4.533). **5.** *category* of land, κατοικικὴ τ. *BGU*379.12 (i A.D.), cf. Wilcken *Chr*.341.15 (ii A.D.), etc. V. *reduction* of hernia by manipulation, Gal.14.781. VI. *degree* of heating power in drugs, Id.11.571,787, cf. Gorg.*Pal*.14. VII. *treatise*, ἐν τῇ ὑστέρᾳ τ. Ps.-Democr.ap.Zos.Alch.p.153 B. VIII. *fixed point of time*, *term*, κατ' ἐνιαυτὸν ἢ κατά τινα ἄλλην τ. ἢ χρόνον Arist.*Pol*.$1261^{a}$34; *end* (or perh. *date fixed for the end*), μέχρι τάξεως αὐτῆς τῆς τρύγης *Sammelb*.5810.15 (iv A.D.).

**ταξίφυλλος** [ῐ], ον, *with leaves set in rows*, Thphr.*HP*1.10.8, prob. in 3.18.8.

**ταξιώτης,** ὁ, v. ταξεώτης.

**τάξος,** ἡ, *yew*, *Taxus baccata*, Sabin.ap.Orib.9.16.3, Gal.12.127 (cited as a Latin word by Dsc.4.79).

**τᾰπεινολογία,** ἡ, *low*, *humble speech*, Poll.2.124.

⊛**τᾰπεινός,** ή, όν, *low*: **1.** of Place, *low-lying*, χώρη Hdt.4.191, cf. Arist.*Mete.*352ᵇ32 (Comp.); νῆσος D.S.3.21; ταπεινὰ νέμεσθαι to live in *low regions*, Pi.*N.*3.82; τ. ἕζεσθαι E.*Or.*1411 (lyr.); ἡ μαῖα καθεζέσθω -οτέρα Sor.1.70ᵃ, cf. 2.61; of stature or size, *low*, ὅστα X. *Eq.*1.4; τροχοί ib.10.6; of position in the body, τὰ τ. τοῦ θώρακος Gal.15.531; of a river, *low*, opp. μέγας, Plb.9.43.3; of stars, *low*, i.e. near the horizon, Cleom.1.5, al.; but also, *near the earth*, Id.2.5; of the sun, opp. ὑψηλός, Diog.Oen.8; λοξὸς καὶ τ. Gal.15.87. 2. of persons, *humbled, abased in power, pride*, etc., Hdt.7.14; σὺ δ' οὐδέπω τ. A.*Pr.*322, cf. 908; τ. παρέχειν τινά X.*An.*2.5.13; τά τοι μέγιστα πολλάκις θεὸς ταπείν' ἔθηκε E.*Fr.*716, cf. *Hec.*245, *Andr.*979; *submissive*, X.*Hier.*5.4 (Comp.), etc.; αἱ τ. τῶν πόλεων *small, poor, weak*, Isoc.4.95, cf. 7.7, X.*Cyr.*7.5.69 (Sup.); τ. δύναμις D.4.23; *of low intelligence*, αἱ τῶν ἀσυνέτων καὶ τ. ἀνθρώπων ψυχαί Gal.19.220; τὴν μικρὰν καὶ τ. [ἰατρικὴν θεωρίαν] ὁ Ἱπποκράτης ηὔξησεν Id.16.550. Adv., ταπεινῶς (or ταπεινὰ) πράττειν to be *in low estate* or *obscurity*, Isoc.5.64, Plu.*Thes.*6; -νῶς ζῆν Philem.227; ὁμιλεῖν Arist.*Pol.*1313ᵇ41. 3. of the spirits, *downcast, dejected*, διάνοια Th.2.61; τ. καὶ ἔρημοι συνεκάθηντο X.*HG*2.4.23, cf. 6.4.16. 4. in moral sense, either bad, *mean, base, abject*, τ. καὶ ἀνελεύθερος Pl.*Lg.*791d, cf. X.*Mem.*3.10.5, Isoc.2.34, etc.; or good, *lowly, humble*, Pl.*Lg.*716a, X.*Cyr.*5.1.5, freq. in *NT*, *Ev.Matt.*11.29, 2*Ep.Cor.*7.6, al. 5. of things, *mean, low, base*, τ. καὶ ἄπορος δίαιτα Pl.*Lg.*762e, cf. Phld. *Oec.*p.48 J.: Sup., -οτάτη περίστασις Id.*Vit.*p.26 J.; θεωρία -οτέρα, opp. τιμιωτέρα, Arist.*PA*639ᵃ1; of style, *low, poor*, τ. λέξις, opp. κεκοσμημένη, Id.*Rh.*1404ᵇ6. Adv., -νῶς λέγειν *in a submissive manner*, ib.1408ᵃ19.

**ταπεινότης**, ητος, ἡ, *lowness* of position, etc., ταπεινότητος εἵνεκα Hdt.4.22; τ. τῆς χώρας D.S.1.31; τῆς μήτρας *Placit.*5.14.2. 2. of condition, *low estate, abasement*, Th.7.75; εἰς τοσαύτην τ. καταστῆσαι Isoc.4.118, cf. D.10.74, Men.531.12, Lxx*Si.*13.20, Phld.*D.*1.11. 3. *lowness of spirits, dejection*, σιωπήν τε καὶ τ. X.*HG*3.5.21. 4. in moral sense, *baseness, vileness*, Pl.*Plt.*309a; joined with μικροψυχία, Arist.*Rh.*1384ᵃ4. 5. of style, *meanness*, Quint. *Inst.*8.3.48.

**ταπεινο-φρονέω**, *to be lowly in mind, humble*, Lxx*Ps.*130(131).2; *to be mean-spirited*, Arr.*Epict.*1.9.10. **-φροσύνη**, ἡ, *humility*, *Ep.Eph.*4.2, al.; *mean-spiritedness*, J.*BJ*4.9.2, Arr.*Epict.*3.24.56. **-φρων**, ονος, ὁ, ἡ, *mean-spirited, base*, Plu.2.336e. 2. in good sense, *lowly in mind, humble*, Lxx*Pr.*29.23, 1*Ep.Pet.*3.8. **-ψῡχος**, ον, *humble-spirited*, Vett.Val.76.17.

**ταπειν-όω**, *lower*, in point of height, *reduce*, σπλῆνα (swollen spleen) Dsc.2.155:—Pass., πᾶν ὄρος ταπεινωθήσεται Lxx*Is.*40.4; πρόσωπον ἐκ μετεώρου ταπεινούμενον Hp.*Coac.*208; of a plant, *decrease in size*, Thphr.*HP*7.13.9; of rivers, D.S.1.36; Astrol., of a planet, *suffer dejection*, Vett.Val.119.15. II. metaph., *lessen*, τὸν φθόνον Plu.*Per.*32; τὸ ἐν μέλιτι χολῶδες Gal.15.683 (to expl. κολάζεται in Hp.*Acut.*59); *disparage, minimize*, Plb.6.15.7, cf. 3.85.7:—Pass., *to be lowered* or *lessened*, Pl.*Ti.*72d. 2. *humble, abase*, X.*An.*6.3.18; τ. καὶ συστέλλων Pl.*Ly.*210e; ταπεινώσαντες..τοὺς νῦν ἐπηρμένους Aeschin.3.235:—Pass., ταπεινωθεὶς ἕπεται Pl.*Phdr.*254e; ὑπὸ πενίας Id.*R.*553c, Phld.*Rh.*1.225 S.; τεταπείνωται ἡ τῶν Ἀθηναίων δόξα X.*Mem.*3.5.4; ἐταπεινοῦντο ταῖς ἐλπίσι D.S.13.11; τεταπεινωμένων τῶν ἄλλων διὰ τὴν τῶν πραγμάτων κατάστασιν Anon.*Oxy.*664.22. b. *violate* a woman, Lxx*Ge.*34.2, 2*Ki.*13.12,14, *Ez.*22.10,11. 3. in moral sense, *make lowly, humble*, ἑαυτόν Phld.*Vit.*p.38 J., *Ev.Matt.*23.12, al.:—Pass., *humble oneself*, τὴν θεὸν ἐξιλάσαντο τῷ ταπεινοῦσθαι σφόδρα Men.544, cf. Lxx*Ge.*16.9, *Si.*18.21, 1*Ep.Pet.*5.6. 4. esp. of fasting or abstinence, θεοῦ ᾧ πᾶσα ψυχὴ ἐν τῇ σήμερον ἡμέρᾳ (i.e. on a fast-day) ταπεινοῦται μεθ' ἱκετείας *SIG*1181.11 (Rhenea, Jewish, ii A.D.); ἐὰν ψυχὴν τεταπεινωμένην ἐμπλήσῃς feed *the hungry*, Lxx*Is.*58.10, cf. *Le.*23.27, al.; οἶδα ταπεινοῦσθαι, opp. περισσεύειν, *Ep.Phil.*4.12. **-ωμα**, ατος, τό, Astrol., the *dejection* of a planet (i.e. the sign opposite to that in which it is exalted), opp. ὕψωμα, Plu.2.149a, S.E.*M.*5.35, Ptol.*Tetr.*41, *PPar.*19 *bis* 19, al. (ii A.D.), *PSI*4.312.12 (iv A.D.). **-ωσις**, εως, ἡ, *lowering*, of a movement in dancing, Pl.*Lg.*815a. 2. *lessening*, opp. αὔξησις, Arist.*PA*689ᵃ25; *reduction* of a swelling, Gal.12.816. 3. *humiliation, abasement*, Zeno *Stoic.*1.51 (pl.), Plb.9.33.10; τ. καὶ δουλεία D.S.2.45; δυνάμεώς τινων ποιεῖν -σιν Id.11.87, cf. Plu.*Arist.*7; ἀγέννεια καὶ τ. Phld.*Herc.*1457.4; *low estate, low condition*, Lxx*Ge.*29.32, *Ev.Luc.*1.48, al. 4. *lowness of style*, Plu.2.7a, Quint.*Inst.*8.3.48. 5. *dejection* of a planet (cf. ταπείνωμα), Doroth.86. **-ωτέον**, *one must disparage*, Arist.*Rh.Al.*1443ᵃ10.

**τάπη**, ἡ, = ταφή, *mummification*, *Sammelb.*6029.11 (i B.C.); *mummy*, ib.761 (ii A.D.).

**✻τάπης** [ᾰ], ητος, ὁ, *carpet, rug*, τάπητα φέρεν μαλακοῦ ἐρίοιο Od.4.124; χλαινάων..οὖλων τε ταπήτων Il.16.224; spread on seats and beds, εἷσεν δ' ἐν κλισμοῖσι τάπησι τε πορφυρέοισιν 9.200, cf. 10.156, 24.645, Od.4.298, 10.12, Herod.2.44, *SIG*1106.121 (Cos, iv/iii B.C.); φορμὸν ἔχειν ἀντὶ τάπητος Ar.*Pl.*542; τάπης Αἰγύπτιος, Ἄφρος, etc., *Edict.Diocl.*19.21,24, al.—Later Att. forms are τάπις, δάπις (qq.v.).

**ταπητ-άριος**, ὁ, *carpet-weaver* or *carpet-merchant*, *POxy.*1431.2 (iv A.D.), *PSI*8.973.5 (vi A.D.); cf. ταπιτάριος. **-έμπορος**, ὁ, *carpet-merchant*, *POxy.*1253.13 (iv A.D.).

**ταπήτιον**, τό, Dim. of τάπης, Alciphr.*Fr.*6.7, *PGen.*80.10 (iv A.D., -ητιν), *POxy.*1431.2 (iv A.D.), etc.

**τᾰπίδιον**, τό, = foreg., *PLond.*2.402ᵛ.17 (ii B.C.), *CPR*p.125 (iii A.D.).

**τᾰπῐδῠφ-άντης**, ου, ὁ, *carpet-weaver*, *PHib.*1.112.76 (iii B.C.); written ταπιδοφ-, *PCair.Zen.*484.2,3,17 (iii B.C.): hence **-αντικά**, τά, *proceeds of tax on carpet-weavers*, *Ostr.Bodl.*i 47 (ii B.C., -υφ-).

**τᾰπῐδῠφος** [ῠ], ὁ, *carpet-weaver*, *PPar.*5 xix 1 (ii B.C.), *Ostr.*1213.

**τάπις** [ᾰ], ιδος, ἡ, = δάπις (q.v.), which is quoted as old Att. by Ael.Dion.*Fr.*116), X.*Cyr.*8.8.16, *An.*7.3.18,27, *IG*11(2).147*B*12 (Delos, iv/iii B.C.).

**τᾰπῐτ-άριος**, ὁ, = ταπητάριος, *BGU*1082.2 (iv A.D.). **-ᾶς**, ᾶ, ὁ, = foreg., *POxy.*1517.3 (iii A.D.). **-ιοῦχος**, ον, *caparisoned*, πῶλος ib.155.9 (vi A.D.).

**ταρ**, acc. to Hdn.Gr.2.22 an enclit. Conjunction (παραπληρωματικὸς σύνδεσμος Trypho in Kenyon *Class. Texts* p.116), εἴ ταρ, οὔ ταρ, to be read in place of εἴτ' ἄρ', οὔτ' ἄρ', as in Il.1.65,93; there is Ms. authority for ταρ in 1.8, 2.761; in 18.182 one of the editions of Aristarch. had ταρ, the other γαρ, and codd. are divided: Cobet conjectured ταρ for γαρ, Il.10.61 (where his cj. is now confirmed by two codd.), and in other places, *Misc.Crit.*315:—on the relation between αὐταρ, αὖ, and ταρ, v. A.D.*Conj.*254.2.

**τάραγ-μα** [τᾰ], ατος, τό, *disquietude*, ἐν φρενῶν τ. πέπτωκα E.*HF* 1091, cf. 907 (lyr.); τ. δαιμόνιον D.H.8.52; πάθη καὶ ταράγματα Demetr.Lac.*Herc.*1012.27. **-μός**, ὁ, *disturbance, disquietude*, τ. ἐς φρένας πίτνει A.*Ch.*1056; τ. ἐμπέπτωκέ μοι E.*Hec.*857, cf. Id. *Oen.*p.39 A.; ἐς ταραγμὸν ἥκειν Id.*HF*533; τ. εἰσῆλθεν πόλιν Id. *Ph.*196, cf. *IT*572: pl., παιδοκτόνους φρενῶν τ. Id.*HF*836.

**τᾰρακ-τήριον**, τό, *stirrer*, gloss on τορύνη, Sch.Pl.*Hp.Ma.*290d. **-της**, ου, ὁ, *disturber*, Lyc.43. **-τικός**, ή, όν, *disturbing*, τῆς ψυχῆς Plu.*Crass.*23 (Sup.); τ. καὶ νεωτερισταί, of political *agitators*, D.H.5.75; of food that does not agree with the stomach, τ. τῶν καθ' ὕπνον ὄψεων Plu.2.734f; οἶνος τ. ib.648b, cf. Sor.1.86 (prob.), Mnesith.ap.Gal.6.645; τ. τῆς κοιλίας Id.ap.Ath.3.92b. **-τός**, ή, όν, *disturbed*: *that may be disturbed*, Sch.Ar.*Ra.*1242, cf. *EM*746.50, prob. f.l. for ταράττον, cf. Hsch. s.v. τάργανον. **-τρον**, τό, *tool for stirring with*: metaph. of a person, = ταρακτικός, Ar.*Pax*654 (lyr.). **-τωρ**, ορος, ὁ, poet. for ταράκτης, τὸν πόλεως τ. A.*Th.*572.

**τάρανδος** [ᾰ], ὁ, a horned beast, native of Scythia, *reindeer*, or more prob. *elk*, Arist.*Mir.*832ᵇ8, *Fr.*371, Thphr.*Fr.*172.1, Ael.*NA* 2.16; **τάρανδρος** is better attested in Ph.1.384, and is v.l. in Arist. *Mir.* l.c.; so *tarandrus* in Plin.*HN*8.123,124 (*parandrum* in Solin. 25.30).

**Τᾰραντῖναρχ-έω**, *command a body of* Ταραντῖνοι, *SIG*697*H*4 (Delph., ii B.C.), *IG*2².958.57, Ἀρχ.Ἐφ.1910.334 (Larissa, ii B.C.). **-ία**, ἡ, *a body of* 256 *horsemen, a double* ἐπιλαρχία, Ascl. *Tact.*7.11, Ael.*Tact.*20.2, Arr.*Tact.*18.3. **✻-ος**, ὁ, *squadron-leader of light cavalry* (Ταραντῖνοι), Ἀρχ.Δελτ.14 Pl. iv 19 (Thespiae, iii B.C.), *SIG*711*G*7 (Delph., ii B.C.):—also **-άρχης**, ου, ὁ, ib.697*K* 6,9 (Delph., ii B.C.).

**Τᾰραντῖν-ίζω**, *ride like a Tarentine horseman*, St.Byz. s.v. Τάρας. **-ινος**, η, ον, *made of Tarentine cloth* (v. Ταραντῖνον), *Schwyzer*462*B* 46 (Tanagra, iii B.C.).

**Τᾰραντῖνοι**, οἱ, *cavalry armed with javelins*, *SIG*697*H*16 (Delph., ii B.C.), Ascl.*Tact.*1.3.

**Τᾰραντῖν-ον**, τό, *garment made of a diaphanous material woven from the byssus of the pinna*, Men.*Epit.*272, Semus 20, Nicostr.Com. 40 (v.l. -ίδιον), *IG*7.2421.3 (Thebes), Aristaenet.1.25, Hsch., Phot., Suid., Sch.Ar.*Lys.*45: Dim. **-ίδιον**, τό, *a light wrap*, Luc.*Cal.*16, *DMeretr.*7.2, Alciphr.1.36; apparently = *pillow*, Gal.14.631 (in this sense also **-ίς**, ίδος, ἡ, ib.639).

**✻τᾰραξίας**, ου, ὁ, = ταράκτης, Suid.

**τᾰραξῐ-κάρδιος**, ον, *heart-troubling*, Ar.*Ach.*315 (troch.). **-πολις**, ιδος, ὁ, ἡ, *troubling the city*, Ph.2.520 (pl.).

**τᾰράξ-ιππος**, ον, *troubling* or *frightening horses*, of Poseidon, D.Chr.32.76:—ὁ τ. the name of an altar on the Olympic race-course, described by Paus.6.20.15,19, 10.37.4. **-ιππόστρᾰτος**, ον, *troubling the horse-array*, of Cleon as a sworn foe to the Ἱππεῖς, Ar.*Eq.*247 (troch.).

**τάραξις** [ᾰ], εως, ἡ, = ταραγμός, *confusion*, τοῦ βίου Ar.*Th.*137, cf. Ael.*NA*9.49. II. Medic., *disorder of the bowels*, Hp.*Hum.*1. 2. *irritation of the eye*, Gal.14.768, Aët.7.3, Paul.Aeg.3.22.

**✻Τάρας** [ᾰρ], αντος, ὁ and (acc. to Eust.1390.59) ἡ, *Tarentum*, a town of Magna Graecia, on a river of the same name, Hdt.1.24, Th.6.34, etc.: also pr. n. of the river-hero, Str.6.3.2, Paus.10.10.8; Τάραντος ἀγλαὸν ὕδωρ Orac.ap.D.S.8.21:—hence **Τᾰραντῖνος**, η, ον, *Tarentine*, ὁ Τ. κόλπος Str.6.1.11; ἡ -νη (sc. χώρα) Id.6.1.4; Τ., ὁ, *a Tarentine*, Hdt.3.138, etc.; Ταραντίνων πολιτεία Arist.*Fr.* 590:—cf. Ταραντῖνοι, Ταραντῖνον.

**τᾰράσσω**, Pi.*O.*2.63, etc.; Att. **-ττω** Ar.*Eq.*902; also **θράσσω** (q.v.): fut. ταράξω ib.358, etc.: aor. ἐτάραξα Od.5.291, (συν-) Il.1.579, 8.86: plpf. συν-ετεταράχει D.C.42.36: Ep. pf. in pass. sense τέτρηχα (v. infr. III):—**Pass.**, fut. ταραχθήσομαι Men.858 (prob.), Epict.*Ench.*3, etc.; Med. ταράξομαι in pass. sense, Th.7.36, X. *Cyr.*6.1.43: aor. ἐταράχθην Ar.*Nu.*386 (anap.), etc.: pf. τετάραγμαι ib.388 (anap.), etc.:—*stir, trouble*, in a physical sense, σύναγεν νεφέλας ἐτάραξε δὲ πόντον [Ποσειδῶν] Od.5.291; κύμασιν ταράσσεται πόντος Archil.54, cf. Sol.54; τ. πέλαγος ἁλός E.*Tr.*88, cf. 692; ὁμοῦ τ. τήν τε γῆν καὶ τὴν θάλατταν εἰκῇ Ar.*Eq.*431; τ. καὶ κυκᾶν Id.*Ach.*688 (troch.), *Eq.*251 (troch.); οὐ χθόνα ταράσσοντες *troubling* not the earth (by ploughing), Pi. l.c.; βροντήμασι.. κυκάτω πάντα καὶ ταρασσέτω A.*Pr.*994; τ. φάρμακον perh. *mix*, Luc.*Lex.*4, cf. Amips.18: metaph., φωνὰν ταρασσέμεν *to wag* the tongue, Pi.*P.*11.42; πάντα τ., of a speaker, *jumble up*, D.19.93;

τὴν τῶν πραγμάτων διδασκαλίαν Gal.15.185. **2.** *trouble* the mind, *agitate, disturb,* με δεινὸς ὀρθομαντείας πόνος στροβεῖ ταράσσων A.*Ag.* 1216; δεινὰ (adverbial) τ. [με] S.*OT*483 (lyr.); ὅταν ταράξῃ Κύπρις ἡβῶσαν φρένα E.*Hipp.*969, cf. *Fr.*1079.4; Νικίαν ταράξω Ar.*Eq.*358 (troch.); τ. καρδίαν E.*Ba.*1321; esp. of fear, A.*Ch.*289, Ar.*Eq.*66, etc.; ἄν τις φόβος τ. X.*Mem.*2.4.6; τὸ σῶμα τ. τὴν ψυχήν Pl.*Phd.* 66a, cf. 103c; so τ. γλῶσσαν E.*IA*1542: abs., *cause confusion,* Pl. *R.*564b, *Hp.Mi.*373b:—Pass., Id.*Phd.*100d, etc.; περί τι Id.*Sph.* 242c; διά τι D.4.3; ταράσσομαι φρένας S.*Ant.*1095; ὄμμα σὸν τ. E. *Or.*253. **3.** of an army, etc., *throw into disorder,* Hdt.4.125, 9.51, etc.; ἐτάρασσον τοὺς ταρσοὺς τῶν κωπέων Id.8.12:—Pass., *to be in disorder,* Id.4.125,129, 8.16, Th.4.25, X.*Cyr.*2.1.27, etc.; ἐν σφίσιν αὐτοῖς τ. Th.7.67. **b.** metaph., *rout* or *upset,* κριτήριον τ. Demetr.Lac.*Herc.*1012.38 (perh. variant of Epicur.*Sent.* 24):—Pass., λόγου ταραχθέντος Phld.*Rh.*1.136S.; εἰ τὰ σημεῖα ταραχθείη Gal.6.262. **4.** τ. τὴν γαστέρα *cause relaxation of* the bowels, *of purges,* Hp.*Nat.Mul.*12, cf. *Acut.*56, Arist.*Pr.* 864ᵇ23, Gal.15.667:—Pass., ἐταράχθης τὴν γαστέρα Ar.*Nu.*386 (anap.); τὸ πνεῦμα Gal.15.903; more generally, τεταραγμένον σῶμα Sor.1.105. **5.** freq. of political agitation, τ. τὴν πόλιν Ar.*Eq.* 867; τὰ πράγματα ib.214:—Pass., *to be in a state of disorder* or *anarchy,* ἐν ἀλλήλοις τ. Th.2.65, cf. D.2.14, Ptol.*Tetr.*164. **6.** ταράττεσθαι ἐπὶ τῶν ἵππων *to be shaken in one's seat* on horseback, X. *Cyr.*5.2.17. **7.** Math., τεταραγμένη ἀναλογία *disturbed* proportion, Euc.5 *Def.*18, Archim.*Sph.Cyl.*2.4. **II.** *stir up,* metaph., τ. νεῖκος, πόλεμον, S.*Ant.*794 (lyr.), Pl.*R.*567a; φόνον E.*Ba.* 797; ἡλίκα πράγματα ταράξασα D.18.153, cf. X.*An.*5.10.9; τ. δίκας τινὶ πρός τινας Plu.*Them.*5:—Pass., πόλεμος ἐταράχθη D.18.151; γόος..ταραχθεὶς A.*Ch.*331 (lyr.). **III.** exc. in the places mentioned, Hom. uses only intr. pf. τέτρηχα, *to be in disorder* or *confusion, be in an uproar,* τετρήχει δ' ἀγορή Il.2.95; ἀγορὴ τετρηχυῖα 7.346; so τετρηχυῖα θάλασσα *AP*7.283 (Leon.); τετρηχότος οἴδματος A.R.1.1167; τετρηχότα βῶλον Id.3.1393; τετρηχότι νώτῳ Nic.*Th.*267; but ἐκ σέθεν..ἄλγεα..τετρήχασι *cruel* woes *arise,* A.R. 4.447, cf. 3.276, Philet.7; in Nic.*Th.*72 τετρήχοντα κλήματα is f.l. for δὲ τρήχοντα. (Alexandrine and later Poets seem to have thought erroneously that τέτρηχα = *to be rough* (cf. τραχύς).) (ταράχ-yω from ταραχ-ή, τάραχ-ος and these from *θᾰρᾰχ-: cogn. with θράσσω from θραχ-yω of which the Ion. pf. is τέτρηχα.)

⊛**τᾰρᾰχή,** also **τάρχη** (Hsch.), ἡ, *disorder,* physiological *disturbance* or *upheaval,* Sor.1.105, 2.59; τοῦ πνεύματος Id.1.46; ἡ ἀπὸ τῆς φλεβοτομίας τ. Id.2.11; esp. of the bowels, τῆς κοιλίης Hp.*Coac.* 205; οὐδὲ θόρυβόν τινα ἢ τ. ἐν τῇ κοιλίᾳ ποιεῖ Gal.6.825. **2.** of the mind, αἱ φρενῶν ταραχαί Pi.*O.*7.30; ἀνωμαλία καὶ τ. Isoc.2.6; ἐν πολλῇ τ. καὶ φόβῳ ὄντας Th.3.79; τ. παρέχειν Pl.*Phd.*66d, cf. *R.*602c; ἐν οἵαις ἦν τ. D.18.218; πολλὴν ἔχει τ. Arist.*Pol.*1268ᵇ4; τ. μειρακιώδους μεστός Isoc.12.230; ταραχῆς γέμων Epicur.*Sent.*17, cf. Phld. *Ir.*p.56 W. (pl.); διανοίας ἰσχυρὰ τ. Sor.1.46; τὴν τ. τοῦ ὀφθαλμοῦ Thphr.*Sens.*81. **3.** of an army or fleet, Th.3.77, etc.; ἐν τῇ τ. in the *confusion,* in the *mêlée,* Hdt.3.126. **4.** *political confusion, tumult,* and in pl. *tumults, troubles.* πολλὴ τ. περὶ τῶν τιμέων ἐγένετο Id.4.162, cf. 6.5; ἐν τῇ τ. Id.3.150; αἱ τ. γεγενημέναι ἦσαν Lys.12.53; τ. ἐγγίγνεταί τισι Is.4.5; τ. ποιεῖν τισι Th.7.86; ἐς τ. καθιστάναι τινάς Id.4.75, cf. Isoc.6.107, etc.; εἰς τ. προκαθεῖναι τὴν πόλιν D.14.5; ἐν τ. καθεστηκέναι Isoc.12.233; ἐν ταραχαῖς εἶναι Id. 4.138; ταραχῆς τε καὶ ἀνομίας μεστὴν πολιτείαν Pl.*Alc.*2.146b, cf. Isoc.3.31; τ. καθίστατο τῶν ξυμμάχων πρὸς τὴν Λακεδαίμονα Th.5. 25, cf. D.18.18; τ. ἐμπίπτει Aeschin.3.81; τ. διαλύειν, κατασβεννύναι, Isoc.4.134, X.*Cyr.*5.3.55; of rebellions or civil wars in Egypt, *OGI*90.20 (Rosetta), Wilcken *Chr.*9.11, 167.14, Mitteis *Chr.*31 v 29 (all ii B.C.): = Lat. *tumultus,* Plu.*Caes.*33.

**τᾰρᾰχοποιός,** όν, *causing disorder* or *confusion,* Aesop.76ᵇ.

⊛**τάρᾰχος** [τᾰ], ὁ, = ταραχή, X.*An.*1.8.2, *Cyr.*7.1.32, *Oec.*8.10, Epicur.*Ep.*1 p.28U., al., Lxx *Es.*1.1, al., Plu.*Pomp.*61, *BGU*889.23 (ii A.D.), etc.

**τᾰρᾰχώδης,** ες, *given to troubling, disturbing,* τὸ θεῖον..ἐὸν φθονερόν τε καὶ ταραχῶδες Hdt.1.32; τύχαι Isoc.4.48; ἐλπίδες, ἔρωτες, Epicur.*Fr.*116, Phld.*Mus.*p.82 K.; ἴχνη τ. *uncertain, baffling,* X. *Cyn.*5.4; τ. ἡ κρίσις, ἡ σκέψις, Arist.*Pol.*1268ᵇ11, 1337ᵃ40; πράξεις Isoc.12.74; φάρμακον Luc.*DMar.*2.2. **2.** of political *agitators,* D.H.6.70. **II.** *troubled, disordered,* κοιλίη τ. Hp.*Epid.*1.2, *Coac.* 10; βίος Ph.2.223 (Sup.); *confused,* μεταβολαί Arist.*Mete.*361ᵇ34; ἀπόρροιαι Thphr.*Sens.*74; φύσις, κινήσεις, Epicur.*Nat.*42,46G. **2.** of an army, etc., τ. ναυμαχία Th.1.49; στράτευμα X.*Cyr.*3.3.26, *Oec.*8.4. **3.** of the mind, *disordered, delirious,* γνῶμαι τ. Hp.*Coac.* 302; τ. ἄγρυπνοι Id.*Prorrh.*1.4 (= τ. καὶ ἄ., where τ. = *slightly disordered mentally,* acc. to Gal.16.513). **4.** *turbid,* of a liquid, Alex.Trall.*Febr.*2. **III.** Adv. -δῶς, τ. ζῆν live *in a state of confusion,* Isoc.5.52; τ. ἔχειν πρός τινας to be *rebelliously* disposed, D. *Ep.*3.10; τ. ὑπειληφέναι περί τινος to have *confused* notions, Isoc. 12.15: Sup., -έστατα διακεῖσθαι Id.7.43, 8.9.

**ταρβᾰλέος,** α, ον, (τάρβος) *affrighted, fearful, h.Merc.*165, S.*Tr.*957 (lyr.); τ. δάκρυα tears *of distress,* Max.331. **II.** *fearful, terrible,* λέων Nonn.*D.*25.191; Ζεύς ib.434.

**ταρβάλυξ,** υγος, ὁ, = ταρακτικός, Hdn.Gr.2.743.

**ταρβαρέον·** δεινόν, φοβερόν, Hsch.

⊛**ταρβ-έω,** Boeot. **τάρβειμι** Hdn.Gr.2.930: (τάρβος):—intr., *to be frightened, alarmed,* Il.2.268, al.; θάρσεο..φρεσί, μηδέ τι τάρβει Il.24.171, cf. 21.288, Od.7.51, 18.331; οὐδέ τι θυμῷ ταρβεῖ οὐδὲ φοβεῖται nor *feels fear,* neither turns to flight, Il.21.575, cf. E.*Ph.* 361; τὼ μὲν ταρβήσαντε καὶ αἰδομένω βασιλῆα στήτην Il.1.331; πῶς δ' οὐχὶ ταρβεῖς τοιάδ' ἐκρίπτων ἔπη; A.*Pr.*932, cf. 898 (lyr.), *Pers.*685; τὸ ταρβοῦν *a state of fear,* E.*Or.*312; μή με ταρβήσας προδῷς *from fear,* S.*Ph.*757; ταρβήσασ' ἔχω Id.*Tr.*37; τεταρβηκώς *fear-stricken,* E.*IA*857 (troch.); τ. φόβῳ S.*Tr.*176, E.*HF*971; τ. μή.. Od.16.179, S.*OT*1011, *Tr.*297, etc.; τ. ἀμφ' αὐτῷ μή..A.R.3.459; τ. εἰπεῖν E.*Ba.*775. **II.** c. acc., *fear, dread,* ταρβήσας χαλκόν Il. 6.469; πληθὺν 11.405; τίς κέ σ' ἔτ' ἄλλος Ἀχαιῶν ταρβήσειεν 17. 586, cf. A.*Pr.*960, *Th.*35, S.*Tr.*723, Theoc.21.62, etc. **2.** *stand in awe of, revere,* σέβας, χρησμούς, A.*Eu.*700,714, cf. S.*OC*292.—Poet. word, rare in Prose, as Epicur.*Ep.*3 p.62U., Pl.*Ax.*370a, Plu. *Ant.*39. **-η,** ἡ, = τάρβος, Suid. **-ήεις,** εσσα, εν, *affrighted,* Nonn. *D.*10.56. **-ος,** εος, τό, *alarm, terror,* Il.24.152, S.*OT*296, etc.; περίφοβόν μ' ἔχει τ. A.*Supp.*736 (lyr.); ἐν χρόνῳ ἀποφθίνει τὸ τ. Id. *Ag.*858; ἀμφὶ τάρβει Id.*Ch.*547; ζωπυροῦσι τ. folld. by acc. of persons feared (cf. δέος I), Id.*Th.*290 (lyr.). **2.** *awe, reverence,* τινος *for* one, Id.*Pers.*696 (lyr.). **II.** *an object of alarm, a fear* or *alarm,* ἔχεις τι θάρσος τοῦδε τοῦ τάρβους πέρι; S.*El.*412; πόλει τάρβος ἦσθα E.*Ba.*1310.—Poet. word, rare in Prose, as Aret. *SD*1.6, Plu.2.666b. (Cf. Skt. *tarjati* 'threaten', Lat. *torvus.*) **-οσύνη,** ἡ, = τάρβος, Od.18.342, *BMus.Inscr.*1004 (Troas). **-όσυνος,** η, ον, *affrighted* or *affrighting,* φόβος A.*Th.* 240 (lyr.).

**ταργαίνω,** = ταράσσω, Hsch.

**ταργάνη,** ἡ, = σαργάνη, *plaited work,* Hsch., *EM*753.54.

**τάργᾰνον,** τό, *vinegar,* Phoen.5. **II.** = τράγος V, Dsc.4.51 (v.l. τράγανον).

**ταργᾰνόομαι,** Pass.: **I.** (τάργανον) *to be turned into vinegar,* οἶνος τεταργανωμένος Pl.Com.189. **II.** (ταργάνη) *to be plaited* or *entwined,* Hsch., *EM*753.54: cf. προσταργανόω.

**Ταργηλιών,** v. Θαργηλιών.

**Ταργυηνός,** epith. of Zeus, Keil-Premerstein *Erster Bericht* p.26 (Philadelphia, i A.D.).

**τάρες,** gen. τάρων, shortd. for τέτταρες, Amphis 30.11; cf. ταρτημόριον.

**τᾰρῑχ-ᾶς,** ᾶ, ὁ, *dealer in salt fish, Stud.Pal.*10.113.6 (ii A.D.). **-εία,** Ion. **-ηΐη,** ἡ, *preserving, pickling,* in pl., εἰς ταριχείας φαῦλοι Arist.*HA*607ᵇ28, cf. *Mete.*359ᵃ16: sg., γογγυλίδας εἰς τ. *POxy.* 736.5 (i A.D.), cf. Gal.6.745. **2.** *mummification, PEleph.*8.8 (iii B.C.), *POxy.*40.9 (ii A.D.). **3.** *maceration,* Olymp.Alch.p.69 B., al. **II.** Ταριχεῖαι prob. *factories for salting fish,* Hdt.2.15,113, Str.3.1.8. **-εῖον,** τό, *pickle-factory, PStrassb.*73.2 (iii A.D.). **-έμπορος,** ὁ, *dealer in salt fish,* D.L.4.46. **-ευσις,** εως, ἡ, *embalming,* of mummies, Hdt.2.85,88. **2.** *pickling, salting,* of fish, Id. 4.53, *Gloss.* **-ευτήρ,** ῆρος, ὁ, = sq. I, Man.4.267. **-ευτής,** οῦ, ὁ, *embalmer,* of mummies, Hdt.2.89, *PEleph.*8.5 (iii B.C.), *UPZ* 102.8 (ii B.C.), Phld.*Sign.*2, D.S.1.91. **2.** *pickler, PFay.*13.4 (ii B.C.), etc. **-ευτικός,** ή, όν, = ταριχηρός (which is v.l.), Dsc.2.32. **-ευτός,** ή, όν, *salted, pickled,* κρέα Plu.2.685d, cf. Dsc.3.45; τὰ τ. Plu.2.912c, Sor.1.94. **-εύω,** *preserve the body by artificial means, embalm,* of Egyptian mummies, Hdt.2.86, Pl.*Phd.* 80c. **II.** *preserve* food *by salting, pickling,* or *smoking,* τ. ὅα Id.*Smp.*190d; ἐλᾶν (= ἐλαίαν) *PRyl.*231.5 (i A.D.):—Pass., [ἰχθύας] ἐξ ἅλμης τεταριχευμένους Hdt.2.77, cf. *PGiss.*93.2 (ii A.D.), etc.; τεμάχη τεταριχευμένα *preserved* meat, X.*An.*5.4.28; χλωρὰ [κάππαρις] πρὶν -ευθῆναι Gal.6.615. **2.** *season* wood by soaking it in water, Thphr.*HP*4.2.2, 5.4.8. **3.** *macerate,* Olymp.Alch.p.70 B., al. **III.** metaph. in Pass., *waste away, wither,* κακῶς ταριχευθέντα παμφθάρτῳ μόρῳ A.*Ch.*296, cf. Sophr.54; τεταριχευμένος *stale,* opp. νεαλής καὶ πρόσφατος, D.25.61. **2.** Medic., *reduce* a patient *by starving,* Gal.15.595. **-ηγός,** ὁ, *salt-fish hawker,* Alex. 218. **-ηρός,** ά, όν, *of* or *for pickled food,* τ. κεράμιον a *pickling-jar,* Arist.*HA*534ᵃ21; τ. ὀσμαί *of it,* ib.19; τ. γάρος *salt fish* pickle, S.*Fr.*606; τὰ τ., opp. τὰ πρόσφατα, Gal.6.351; κρέας τ. Chrysipp. *Stoic.*3.199, cf. *PPetr.*3 p.167 (iii B.C.), Arr.*An.*4.21.10, Gal.15.739; φαληρίδες Cleomenes ap.Ath.9.393c. **2.** *stale,* οὖρον *PHolm.*6. 6. **II.** -ηρός, ὁ, *pickler,* τετάρτη -ηρῶν *PPetr.*3 p.300 (iii B.C.); ἡ σύνταξις ἡ τῶν σειτοποιῶν καὶ τῶν τ. *PFay.*15.4 (ii B.C.). ⊛ **-ιον,** τό, Dim. of τάριχος, Ar.*Pax* 563 (troch.), Cephisod.8, Sor.2.15, *Sammelb.*4425 iii 25 (ii A.D.), *Gloss.* **-ον,** τό, v. τάριχος fin.

**τᾰρῑχό-πλεως,** ων, *full of salt fish,* prob. cj. in Ps.-Hes.ap.Ath. 3.116b. **-ποιέω,** *pickle,* Alex.Aphr.*in Top.*46.27. **-πράτισσα** [ᾱτ], ἡ, *female pickle-seller, PMasp.*23.8 (vi A.D.). **-πωλέω,** *sell salt fish,* Pl.*Chrm.*163b, Luc.*Nec.*17. ⊛ **-πώλης,** ου, ὁ, *dealer in salt fish,* Nicostr.Com.5.3, Alex.15.14, Plu.2.631d, *Gloss.* **-πώλιον,** τό, *salt-fish-market, IG*2².1645.14, Thphr.*Char.*6.9, *Inscr.Magn.* 116.35 (ii A.D.), *Gloss.*; also **-πωλεῖον,** ib., Sch.Ar.*Eq.*1244.

⊛**τάρῑχ-ος** [ᾰ], ὁ, **τάριχος,** εος, τό, and ⊛**τάρῑχον,** τό (v. sub fin.):—*dead body preserved by embalming, mummy,* τεθνεὼς καὶ τάριχος ἐών Hdt.9.120. **II.** *meat preserved by salting, pickling, drying,* or *smoking,* esp. *dried* or *smoked fish,* τὸ ἕλκος..φαίνεται ὥσπερ τάριχος Hp.*VC*19; οὗ τὸ τάριχος ὤνιον Ar.*Eq.*1247; τὸ πολὺ τάριχος Id.*Ra.*558; θρῖον ταρίχους Id.*Ach.*1101; τοῦ ταρίχους..ἀξιωτέρα Id.*V.*491; ἐπὶ τῷ ταρίχει Id.*Fr.*630, cf. *Ach.*967: pl. τάριχοι Hdt. l.c.; ταρίχη Hermipp.63.5, Gal.6.747, etc.: dual ταρίχει Hdn.Gr. 2.322. **III.** metaph. of a stupid fellow, *stockfish,* τὸν τ. τουτονί Ar.*Fr.*200.—It is laid down that the masc. is Ion., the neut. τάριχος Att., *AB*309.14: in fact, the masc. alone occurs in Hdt.; Hp.

uses both forms, masc. (acc. τάριχον, v.l. -ος) in *Morb.*2.50, neut. (acc. τάριχος Γαδειρικόν) in *Int.*25; neut. predominates in Att., e.g. Ar. ll. cc., Chionid.6, Hermipp. l. c., but masc. in Cratin.40, Pl.Com.49, *PCair.Zen.*705.44 (iii B.C.), Sor.1.94,98:—also **τάριχον**, τό, Anaxandr.50, Philippid.9; pl. τάριχα Axionic.3.15, *PMich.Zen.*2.11 (iii B.C.), Sor.1.46; ταρίχου (gender undetermined) *PCair.Zen.*12.38, 81, al. (iii B.C.), Sor.1.52, Gal.6.812. **-ος**, ον, = ταριχευτός, Ael. *NA*12.6.

**τᾰρῑχοφᾰγία**, ἡ, *eating of salt fish*, Gal.ap.Orib.*Syn.*9.3.6, Aët. 8.73, Paul.Aeg.3.32.

**τᾰρῑχώτης**, ου, ὁ, = ταριχευτής, *Berl.Sitzb.*1934.1043 (Tab. Defix.).

**ταρμύσσω**, *frighten*, Lyc.1177. (Hence ἀτάρμυκτος.)

**ταρνόν**· κολοβόν, κολοβόουρον, Hsch. **ταρόν**· ταχύ, Id. (cf. τραρόν).

**τάρπη**, ἡ, *large wicker basket*, *IG*2².1628.506, Poll.10.158, *EM*746.53; Syracusan acc. to Hsch.: so **ταρπόνη**, ἡ, *Peripl.M.Rubr.*65; **ταρπός**, ὁ, Poll.7.174: cf. τερπός.

**ταρπῆναι**, Ep. **ταρπήμεναι**, v. τέρπω.

**τάρριον**, τό, Dim. of ταρρός, *small hurdle*, Poll.1.142.

**τάρροθος**, ὁ, = ἐπιτάρροθος, Lyc.360,400, al.

**ταρρός**, **-ρόω**, **-ρώδης**, **-ρωμα**, v. ταρσ-. **ταρσῆται**, *cheese-crates*, Hsch. **ταρσιά**, ἡ, v. τρασιά.

❋ **ταρσικάριος**, ὁ, *weaver of Tarsian fabrics*, *PLips.*26.9, 89.2, al. (iv A.D.); written θαρσ- in *POxy.*1765.21 (iii A.D.), 1146.16 (iv A.D.).

**Ταρσικ-ός**, ή, όν, *of Tarsus*, λίνου Ταρσικοῦ *PLips.*89.5 (iv A.D.), cf. *Edict.Diocl.*26.14, al.; λίνα Θαρσικά *POxy.*109.8 (iii A.D.); Ταρσικὸν ἐλλύχνιον (as application for swellings) Aët.15.1: **-κοί**, οἱ, name of a school of tragic poets, D.L.4.58.

**ταρσικοϋφικός**, ή, όν, *for weaving Tarsian fabrics*, ἱστός *POxy.*1705.6 (iii A.D.).

**Ταρσογενής**, ές, *born at Tarsus*, *IG*14.1437 (Rome).

❋ **ταρσ-ός**, Att. **ταρρός**, ὁ: also with heterocl. pl. ταρσά, τά, Opp. *C.*3.470, *Anacreont.*9, *APl.*4.283 (Leont.), Nonn.*D.*1.270, al.: (τέρσομαι):—*frame of wicker-work, crate, flat basket*, for drying cheeses on, ταρσοὶ μὲν τυρῶν βρῖθον Od.9.219, cf. Theoc.11.37: generally, *basket*, Ar.*Nu.*226. 2. *mat of reeds*, such as were built into brickwork to bind it together, ταρσοὶ καλάμων Hdt.1.179, *SIG*245 *G* 13 (Delph., iv B.C.); τ. καλάμου Th.2.76. 3. *mass of matted roots*, Thphr.*CP* 3.7.2. II. of various broad flat surfaces, resembling a ταρσός I. 1, as, 1. τ. ποδός *flat* of the foot, *the part between the toes and the heel*, Il.11.377,388, cf. Hdt.9.37, Hp.*Fract.*9, Diog.Apoll.6 (but also, *palm* of the hand, ibid.); οὐλὴ ταρσῷ ἀριστερῷ *PMich.Teb.* 121ʳ III i3 (i A.D.): generally, *foot*, *Anacreont.*5, Opp.*C.*3.470, *AP* 5.26 (Rufin.), 9.653 (Agath.). b. *palm* of the hand, Ruf.*Onom.* 81, Sor.*Fract.*22; v. supr. II. 1a. c. *ankle*, Gal.*UP*3.6; but distd. from σφυρόν, Sor.1.84. 2. τοὺς τ. τῶν κωπέων *the rows of oars* on the sides of ships, Hdt.8.12; so τοὺς τ. alone, Th. 7.40: sg., *IG*2².1628.590, Plb.1.50.3; ὁ δεξιὸς τ. τῆς νεώς Id.16.3.12: sg., *oar*, E.*IT*1346. 3. τ. πτερύγων *flat* of the outstretched wing, *AP*12.144 (Mel.), cf. Babr.72.9; ὁ τ. τῶν πτερῶν Ael.*NA*2.1: abs., *wing*, *Anacreont.*9, *AP*9.287 (Apollonid.), etc.; in Prose, D.H.4.63: of a peacock's *tail*, Mosch.2.60; ταρσοὶ *feathers*, D.S.2.50. 4. τ. ὀδόντων the *row* of teeth in a saw, Opp.*H.*5.202. 5. *Pan's pipe*, ταρσῷ Πὰν ὁ μελιζόμενος *Epigr.Gr.*781.10 (Cnidus). 6. *edge of the eyelid and its lashes*, Hp.*Ep.*23, Poll.2.69, Gal.*UP*10.7. **-όω**, *provide with a* ταρσός II. 3, τὸν Ἑρμῆν..ταρσώσαντες πτεροῖς Lyd. *Mens.*4.76:—elsewh. Pass. **-όομαι**, Att. **ταρρόομαι**, *to be like basket-work, to be matted*, of roots, Thphr.*CP*3.23.3; of the reticulation of veins, περὶ τὴν ὅλην κεφαλὴν ἐκτετάρσωται Hp.*Oss.* 12; τεταρσωμέναι μασχάλαι, of plants *with pinnatifid leaves*, Dsc. 3.156, cf. 4.8; τετ. ναῦς *with its oars complete* (v. ταρσός II. 2), Polyaen.3.9.38. **-ώδης**, Att. **ταρρ-**, ες, *like basket-work, matted*, of roots, Thphr.*HP*6.7.4, 8.2.3; τῇ πλοκῇ ταρσώδεις (v.l. ταρσωταί) D.S.3.22. **-ωμα**, Att. **τάρρωμα**, ατος, τό, = ταρσός: pl., = οἱ στίχοι τῶν κωπῶν, Poll.1.93. II. = κωπηλασία, Ar.*Fr.*868. **-ωτός**, v. ταρσώδης.

**Ταρτάρ-ειος** [ᾰ], α, ον, *Tartarean, horrible*, τάραγμα E.*HF*907 (lyr.), cf. Luc.*Philops.*24:—also **Ταρτάρεος**, *Ath.Mitt.*19.369 (Bithynia); **Ταρτάριος**, Pherecyd.Syr.5, *Epic.Alex.Adesp.*7.5, Orph.*H.*18. 2. **-ίζω**, *quake with cold, shiver*, Plu.2.948f, Serv.ad Verg.*A.*6. 577. **-ίτης** [ῑ], ου, ὁ, *dweller in Tartarus*, *Com.Adesp.*1160.

**Ταρτᾰρόπαις**, παιδος, ὁ, ἡ, *child of Tartarus*, Orph.*A.*977.

❋ **Τάρτᾰρ-ος**, ὁ, also ἡ Pi.*P.*1.15, Nic.*Th.*203: heterocl. pl. Τάρταρα, τά, Hes.*Th.*119,841, etc. (sg. Τάρταρον, τό, St.Byz., Sch.Il.1. 312):—*Tartarus*, Il.8.13,481, Hes.*Th.*807, *h.Ap.*336, *h.Merc.*256,374, etc. (never in Od.); later, *the nether world* generally, Hes.*Sc.*255; ἀπέραντος, κελαινός, A.*Pr.*154 (lyr.), 1051 (anap.); Ταρτάρου μελαμβαθὴς κευθμών ib.221; σκότον νέμονται Τάρταρόν θ' ὑπὸ χθονὸς Id.*Eu.* 72, cf. Lxx *Jb.*40.15, 41.23. II. personified as husband of Gaia and father of Typhoeus, Hes.*Th.*822; ὦ Γᾶς παῖ καὶ Ταρτάρου, of Cerberus, S.*OC*1574 (lyr.). **-οῦχος**, ον, *controlling Tartarus*, *PMag.Par.*1.2242, al.

**Ταρτᾰρόφρουρος**, ον, *guarding Tartarus*, *PMag.Par.*1.1368.

**Ταρτᾰρ-όω**, *cast into Tartarus* or *hell*, Acus.8 J., 2*Ep.Pet.*2.4, Lyd.*Mens.*4.158 (Pass.), Sch.T Il.14.296. **-ώδης**, ες, *Tartarus-like*, τιμωρία Anon.ap.Suid. s.v. σοβαρός. **-ωσις**, εως, ἡ, *casting into Tartarus*, Τιτάνων dub. in Phld.*Piet.*60.

**ταρτημόριον**, τό, shortd. for τεταρτ-, Macho ap.Ath.13.582e, *BGU* 1551.4 (iii B.C.), Hsch., Phot.; Dor. **ταρτᾱμόριον** *Delph.*3(5).78, 82 (iv B.C.): also **ταρτήμορον**, τό, *PCair.Zen.*776.12 (iii B.C.), *BGU* 1517.4, 1551.9 (iii B.C.), *IG*11(2).287*A* 43, al. (Delos, iii B.C.), *Inscr. Délos* 444*B* 105 (ii B.C.); ταρτημο[..] *IG*2².1496.207.

**Ταρτησσός**, ὁ, Hdt.1.163, elsewh. ἡ:—a district of Spain at the mouth of the Baetis, the *Tarshish* of Scripture (Θαρσεὶς in Lxx 3 *Ki.*10.22, al.), Hdt. l. c., Arist.*Mir.*844ᵃ17, Str.3.2.11, etc.: also the river Baetis, Stesich.5 (ap.Str. l. c.):—hence **Ταρτήσσιος**, α, ον, *Tartessian*, Hdt.4.192, Ar.*Ra.*475; **Ταρτήσσιοι**, οἱ, Hdt.1.163, etc.

**τάρφθη**, **τάρφθεν**, v. τέρπω.

**τάρφ-ος**, εος, τό, *thicket*, βαθείης τάρφεσιν ὕλης Il.5.555; βαθέης ἐν τ. ὕλης 15.606; μνιόεντα βυθοῖο τάρφεα A.R.4.1238. (From τρέφω *thicken*.) **-ύς**, εῖα, ύ, fem. ταρφύς A.*Th.*535, prob. in *Pers.*926 (lyr.): —*thick, close*, θρίξ A.*Th.* l. c.; ταρφέος ἐχέτλης Orac.ap.Luc.*JTr.* 31: Hom. only uses the pl., ταρφέες ἰοί Il.11.387, Od.22.246; ταρφέας ἰούς Il.15.472; ταρφέες κεραυνοί Hes.*Th.*693; ταρφέα δράγματα Il.11.69: neut. pl. ταρφέα as Adv., *ofttimes, often*, 12. 47, 13.718, 22.142, Od.8.379: regul. Adv. ταρφέως B.12.86:—Hom. also has a fem. nom. ταρφειαί and acc. ταρφειάς, so accented by Aristarch. and found in most codd., ταρφειαὶ νιφάδες, κόρυθες, Il. 19.357,359; ταρφειὰς [νιφάδας] 12.158; ταρφείας was prescribed (prob. wrongly) by D.T.ap.Hdn.Gr.2.81 in Il.12.158. (Cf. τάρφος.)

**ταρχάνιον**· ἐντάφιον, Hsch. **τάρχανον** (τέρχ- cod.)· πένθος, κῆδος, Id. **τάρχη**· τάραξις, Id.

**ταρχύω**, A.R.3.208: fut. -ύσω Il.16.456: Ep. aor. τάρχῡσα Q.S.1. 801, etc.:—Med., aor. ἐταρχῡσάμην Nonn.*D.*37.96, Ep. ταρχ- A.R. 1.83:—Pass., Ep. aor. ταρχύθην [ῡ] *AP*7.176 (Antiphil.); part. -θεῖσαν Lyc.369: pf. τετάρχῡμαι *IG*14.1374:—*bury solemnly*, ὄφρα ἑ ταρχύσωσι Il.7.85; ἑ ταρχύσουσι τύμβῳ τε στήλῃ τε 16.456; θανοῦσαν..τήνδ' ὑπὸ βῶλον ταρχύσας *Supp.Epigr.*2.874.8 (Egypt): metaph., οὔνομα τ. *AP*7.537 (Phan.). (Cf. ταρχάνιον, τάρχανον, τέρχνεα, and perh. τριχῶσαι: prob. not connected with ταριχεύω.) [ῡ in all tenses.]

**τάσις** [ᾰ], εως, ἡ, (τείνω) *stretching, tension*, τῆς κοιλίης f.l. in one cod. for στάσις, Hp.*Acut.*37; τοῦ οἰσοφάγου Arist.*PA*691ᵃ1, cf. 664ᵃ32; τάσιν ἔχειν to be capable of *tension*, Id.*HA*515ᵇ16, al.; ὀφρύων τ. *contraction* of the eyebrows, *AP*12.42 (Diosc.); of tension accompanying inflammation, Sor.2.19, Gal.10.66. 2. *extension*, τ. ἐπὶ μῆκος καὶ ἐπὶ πλάτος Arist.*HA*495ᵇ23. 3. τάσεις τῆς φωνῆς *pitch* of the voice, *Stoic.*2.96; in music, Plu.2.1020e, cf. 1133c; of the accents, τάσεις φωνῆς αἱ καλούμεναι προσῳδίαι D.H.*Comp.*19; ὀξεῖα τ. Ath.2.53a. 4. *intensity, force*, τάσιν λαβεῖν, of darts, Plu.*Sull.*18. 5. *fixing* of the eyes upon an object, Lib.*Or.*61. 9. II. = *tentigo*, *Gloss.* 2. = *menta*, ib. (also written *tarsis*, ib.).

❋ **τάσσω**, A.*Ag.*332, etc.; Att. **-ττω** Pl.*Prt.*262e, etc.: fut. τάξω A. *Th.*285, etc.: aor. ἔταξα Id.*Supp.*986, etc.: pf. τέταχα X.*Oec.*4.5, (συν-) Pl.*Lg.*625c: plpf. ἐτετάχει Plb.5.65.7:—Med., fut. τάξομαι (in pass. sense) Lxx *Ex.*29.43: aor. ἐταξάμην Hdt.3.13, Th.2.83, etc.:—Pass., fut. ταχθήσομαι D.S.11.41, (ἐπι-) Th.1.140, etc.; later τᾰγήσομαι (ἐν-) Orib.8.1, (ὑπο-) 1*Ep.Cor.*15.28; 3 fut. τετάξομαι E.*IT*1046, Th.5.71, Ar.*Av.*637: aor. ἐτάχθην A.*Eu.*279, etc.; later ἐτάγην [ᾰ] *SIG*708.9 (Istropolis, ii B.C.), Plu.2.965e, Perict.ap.Stob.4.25.50, etc.: pf. τέταγμαι Pi.*O.*2.30, etc.; 3 pl. τετάχαται Th.3.13, (ἀντι-) X. *An.*4.8.5: 3 pl. plpf. ἐτετάχατο Th.5.6, 7.4:—*draw up in order of battle, form, array, marshal*, both of troops and ships, τὴν στρατιήν Hdt.1.191; τοὺς ὁπλίτας Th.4.9; νεῶν στῖφος ἐν στίχοις τρισίν A.*Pers.* 366; πολεμίων στίχας E.*Heracl.*676; τ. εἰς μάχην στρατιάν X.*Cyr.*1.6. 43: abs., Isoc.18.47:—Pass., *to be drawn up*, ἐς μάχην Hdt.1.80; οὐδένα κόσμον ταχθέντες Id.9.69; ἐπὶ τεττάρων ταχθῆναι in four lines, X. *An.*1.2.15; ἐπὶ μιᾶς, of ships, Id.*HG*1.6.29; ἐπὶ κέρως Eub.67.4; κατὰ μίαν ναῦν τεταγμένοι in line, Th.2.84; ἐπὶ ὀκτώ, of troops, Id. 6.67: abs., τεταγμένοι *in rank and file*, Id.2.81 (so metaph., τὸ ἐν τῷ τεταγμένῳ ὄν *the rank and file*, opp. Senators and Equites, D.C.49. 12); στράτευμα τεταγμένον, opp. ἄτακτον, X.*Mem.*3.1.7:—Med., *fall in, form in order of battle*, freq. in Th., 1.48, 4.11, etc.; ὡς ἐς μάχην 2. 20; ἐτάξαντο κύκλον τῶν νεῶν *formed* in a circle, ib.83, cf. 3.78; ἐτάξαντο οὐ πάντες ὁμοίως 5.68; εἴκοσι ναυσὶ ἐτάξαντο 3.77 (but in 2.90 trans., ἐπὶ τεσσάρων ταξάμενοι τὰς ναῦς *having drawn up their* ships in four lines, cf. E.*Heracl.*664). 2. *post, station*, τὰς καμήλους ἀντία τῆς ἵππου Hdt.1.80, cf. E.*Ph.*749; τινὰς ἐπί τινας one group against another, X.*Cyr.*2.1.9 (but τ. τινὰ ἐπὶ τοὺς ἱππέας *set* him over them, to command them, Id.*HG*3.4.20); ἑαυτὸν ὑμῖν τάξαι παρέσχεν for enrolment, Lys.31.9, cf. Lycurg.43:—Pass., *to be posted* or *stationed*, τῇ οὐδεὶς ἐτέτακτο Hdt.1.84, cf. A.*Pers.*381; ἐς τὸ ὄρος Hdt.7.212; but ἐς τὸ πεζόν or ἐς π. τετάχθαι to serve among the infantry, ib.21,81; ἐς τὸν ναυτικὸν στρατὸν -θέντες ib.203: c. gen., τῆς πρώτης τάξεως (or simply τῆς πρώτης) τεταγμένος Lys.14.11, 16.15: c. acc. cogn., τάξιν τινὰ ταχθῆναι Pl.*Phdr.*247a, etc.; δεξιὸν τεταγμένους κέρας E.*Supp.* 657: freq. folld. by Preps. (cf. infr. II. 1, etc.), ταχθῆναι or τετάχθαι ἐπί τινα or τινας *against* another, Th.3.78, etc.; ἐπί τινι or τισι A.*Th.* 448, Th.2.70, 3.13, etc.; also, *to be posted* at a place, ἐφ' ἑπτὰ πύλαις ταχθέντες ἴσοι πρὸς ἴσους S.*Ant.*142 (anap.); ἐπ' εὐωνύμῳ κέρατι *on* the left wing, X.*Oec.*4.19; ἐπὶ τοῦ λαιοῦ κέρως Plb.1.34.4; τ. κατά τινα *over against*.., Hdt.8.85, X.*An.*2.3.19; τ. μετά τινα *behind* him.., Id.*HG*7.2.4 (so ἐπί τινι Id.*Lac.*13.7); μετά τινος *with* him, by his side, Plb.2.67.2, etc., cf. Th.2.63; σύν τινι X.*An.*3.2.17, etc.; παρὰ τὸν ποταμόν Hdt.9.15; περὶ τὸ Ἡραιον ib.69; ἀμφὶ τὴν Κέον Id. 8.76. II. *appoint* to any service, military or civil, the latter being metaph. from the former, ἄρχοντας X.*HG*7.1.24; τινὰ ἐπί τινι

Id.*Cyr.*8.6.17, D.17.20, etc.; ἐπὶ τὰς πράξεις Isoc.5.151, cf. Pl.*Ly.* 209b, etc.; ἀξιῶ σε τάξαι με ἐπί τινος *PCair.Zen.*447.3 (iii B. C.): also τ. ἑαυτὸν ἐπί τι *undertake* a task, Pl.*R.*371c, D.8.71, etc.; πρός τι X. *Mem.*2.4.6 :—Pass., οἱ τεταγμένοι βραβῆς S.*El.*709, cf. 759; πρέσβεις ταχθέντες D.19.69; τετάχθαι ἐπί τινι *to be appointed* to a service, Hdt. 1.191, 2.38, A.*Pers.*298, E.*Ion* 1040, X.*Cyr.*4.6.1; ἐπί τι Ar.*Av.*637, X.*Cyr.*1.4.24, etc.; also ἐπί τινος Hdt.5.109 (ἐπ' οὗ, v.l. ὅκου), D.10. 46; τὸν ἐπὶ τῆς σφαγῆς τεταγμένον Plu.*Cleom.*38, cf. Plb.3.12.5; ὁ πρὸς τοῖς γράμμασι τεταγμένος *secretary*, Id.15.27.7; οἱ πρὸς ταῖς φυλακαῖς (tolls) τετ. *PCair.Zen.*31.15 (iii B. C.). **2.** c. acc. et inf., *appoint* or *order* one to do or be, τάττετ' ἐμὲ ἡγεῖσθαι X.*An.*3.1.25, cf. *Cyr.*7.3. 1, Hdt.3.25, S.*OC*639, E.*Hec.*223, etc.:—Pass., μοῖρα ἡ ταχθεῖσα.. φρουρέειν Hdt.4.133, cf. 8.13, A.*Eu.*279,639, etc.; τασσόμενος πορεύεσθαι X.*Cyr.*4.5.11, etc.; τοῦτο τετάγμεθα (sc. ποιεῖν) E.*Alc.*49; also τεταγμένος κίοι A.*Supp.*504; ὁ ἐπ' Αἴγυπτον ταχθείς (sc. κῆρυξ) *ordered* to Egypt, Hdt.3.62, cf. 68, 6.48. **3.** also τ. τινί c. inf., Id.2.124, X.*Cyr.*1.5.5, etc.: impers., ἴωμεν.., ἵν' ἡμῖν τέτακται (sc. ἰέναι) S.*Ph.*1181 (lyr.); οἷς ἐτέτακτο παραβοηθεῖν Th.3.22; τοῖς δὲ ἕπεσθαι τέτακται X.*Lac.*11.6: also with inf. omitted, κόσμον φυλάσσουσ' ὄντιν' ἂν τάξῃ πόλις (sc. φυλάσσειν) E.*Supp.*245, cf. 460, *Hel.* 1390, etc. **4.** *assign to* a duty or class of dutiful persons, ἐν πᾶσιν ἐμαυτὸν ἔταττον D.18.221; εἰς ὑπηρετικὴν αὑτοὺς τ. Pl.*Plt.*289e; πρός τινας τάξαι αὑτόν Din.3.18; σὺν ἐμοὶ τ. σεαυτήν D.H.8.47; τ. ἐμαυτὸν εἰς τάξιν τινά X.*Mem.*2.8; τινὰς εἰς τοὺς ἀρχικούς ib.7; εἰς τὴν δουλείαν ἐμαυτόν ib.11; τ. ἑαυτόν τινων εἶναι *range* oneself with.., D. 19.302 :—Pass., πρὸς τὴν ξυμμαχίαν ταχθῆναι *to join* it, Th.3. 86. **III.** c. acc. rei, *place in a certain order* or *relative position*, χωρὶς ἑκάτερα τ. Hdt.7.36; τίνα μέσον τάξω λόγον; E.*El.*908; πρῶτον καὶ τελευταῖον τὸ κάλλιστον τ. X.*Mem.*3.1.9; τὰ τυφλὰ τοῦ σώματος καὶ ἄοπλα ἐναντία τάττειν τοῖς πολεμίοις Id.*Cyr.*3.3.45; τοὺς πόδας [τοῦ ἐμβρύου] κατ' εὐθὺ τοῦ στομίου τῆς ὑστέρας τάσσειν Sor.2.60; μὴ κατὰ ἄνεμον τῶν οἰκημάτων τάττειν τὴν ἅλω *Gp.*2.26.1; τάξας.. ἀπὸ μὲν δύσεως μίαν θυρίδα φωτὸς ἕνεκεν ib.14.6.6; [κηρίας] τὴν μεσότητα τάσσειν ὑπὸ τὸ γένειον *PMed.Lond.*155 ii 20, cf. Sor.*Fasc.*25. al.; εἰς ταὐτὸ τ. τὴν εὐτυχίαν τῇ εὐδαιμονίᾳ Arist.*EN*1099ᵇ7; Λυδοὺς.. πρὸς ἅπαντας *range* over against, Pl.*Plt.*262e; τὴν σοφιστικὴν περὶ τὸ μὴ ὂν ἔταξεν Arist.*Metaph.*1026ᵇ15, cf. *Top.*125ᵇ21; c. inf., [Ὅμηρον] ἐν τοῖς..σοφωτάτοις εἶναι τάττομεν Aeschin.1.142; οὐκ εὐλόγως τὸ τοιοῦτον σημεῖον ἐν τοῖς φρενιτικοῖς τάττει Gal.16.521, cf. 18(2).238; τ. τι ἐπί τινος *apply* a term to a certain sense, Ath.1.21a :—Pass., τετάχθαι κατά τινος D.H.2.48; ἔμπροσθεν τ. τινός Pl.*Lg.*631d, cf. X. *Mem.*3.1.7, etc. **b.** with an inf. and Adj., *lay down, rule* to be so and so, ἅπερ ἂν..αἰσχρὰ εἶναι καὶ κακὰ τάττῃ Pl.*Lg.*728a; τά τε δίκαια ταχθέντ' εἶναι καὶ ἄδικα Id.*Plt.*305b. **2.** *ordain, prescribe*, τ. τὰ περὶ τὰ τέκνα Arist.*Pol.*1262ᵇ6: abs., ὁ νόμος οὕτω τ. Pl.*La.*199a; οὕτω τ. ὁ λόγος Arist.*EN*1119ᵇ17 :—Pass., τὸ ταττόμενον Ar.*Ec.*766; τὸ ταχθὲν τελεῖν S.*Aj.*528; τὰ τεταγμένα X.*Cyr.*1.2.5, etc.; τὰ τετ. ἄγειν the things *appointed* to them for conveying, ib.8.5.4; τῆς τροφῆς ἡ βελτίστη τέτακται τοῖς ἐλευθέροις Arist.*GA*744ᵇ18; ἐν τῷ τεταγμένῳ εἶναι to be fulfilling *one's obligations*, *IG*1².57.47, 2².116.48, X. *Cyr.*6.2.37. **3.** of taxes or payments, *assess*, τὸν φόρον ταῖς πόλεσι And.4.11, cf. Aeschin.2.23, D.23.209; ταῖσδε ἔταξαν οἱ τάκται *IG*1². 218.45; so τ. τῷ ναύτῃ δραχμὴν X.*HG*1.5.4: with inf. added, χρήματα τοῖς πᾶσι τάξαντες φέρειν Th.1.19, etc. (Pass., φόρον ἐτάχθησαν φέρειν Hdt.3.97); τάσσειν ἀργυρίου πολλοῦ *fix* a high price, Th.4. 26 :—Pass., τὸ ταχθὲν τίμημα Pl.*R.*551b; εἰσφέρειν τὸ τεταγμένον Arist.*Pol.*1272ᵃ14 :—Med., *take a payment on oneself*, i.e. *agree to pay* it, φόρον τάξασθαι Hdt.3.13, 4.35; χρήματα ἀποδοῦναι ταξάμενοι Th.1.101; χρήματα ταξάμενοι κατὰ χρόνους ἀποδοῦναι *agreeing* to pay by instalments, ib.117, cf. 3.70; πόλεις αὐταὶ ταξάμεναι *IG*1².212. 72, cf. 211 vi 6; also τάξασθαι ἐς τὴν δωρεήν Hdt.3.97 (but also, much like Act., ἐτάξατο φόρους οἱ προσιέναι ib.89). **b.** Med., generally, *agree upon, settle*, ταξαμένους..δέχεσθαι μισθὸν τῆς φυλακῆς Pl.*R.*416e; τὰς τιμὰς Id.*Lg.*743e, cf. 844b,c, al.; τέταγμαι ποιμέσιν, οἵ μοι δώσουσιν τιμὴν *PMich.Zen.*56.19 (iii B. C.); *votum* expld. as εὐχή, ὃ τάττεταί τις θεῷ, *Gloss.*: c. inf. fut., *PEnteux.*54.5 (iii B. C.), Plb.18.7. 7, al. **c.** Med., *pay*, τῆς δὲ τιμῆς τάξονται παραχρῆμα τὸ δ' μέρος, τὸ δὲ λοιπὸν ἐν ἔτεσι γ' *PEleph.*14.18 (iii B. C.), cf. *PEnteux.* 60.9, 89.7, *PMich.Zen.*79.9, *PCair.Zen.*649.16 (all iii B. C.), *PAmh.* 2.31.1, 52.1, *Ostr.Bodl.*i 46,96, al., *PLond.*3.1201.1, 1202.1 (all ii B. C.). **4.** *impose* punishments, τ. δίκην Ar.*V.*1420, etc.; τ. ζημίας, τιμωρίας, Pl.*Lg.*876c, D.20.143; τῷ κλέψαντι θάνατον Lycurg.65 :—also in Med., Hdt.2.65. **b.** *impose* laws, οὓς [νόμους] ἔταξε αὐτοῖς ὁ νομοθέτης Pl.*Lg.*772c. **5.** in pf. part. Pass., *fixed, settled, prescribed*, ὁ τεταγμένος χρόνος (like τακτός) Hdt.2.41, etc.; ὥρα E.*Ba.* 723; ἡμέρα X.*Cyr.*1.2.4; ἔτη Pl.*Lg.*810b; ἡ τετ. χώρα X.*Cyr.*5.3.40; αἱ τετ. θυσίαι the *regular* offerings, Id.*HG*3.3.4; οἱ ἐπὶ τούτῳ τετ. [νόμοι] Pl.*Cri.*50d; ἡ τετ. δίαιτα *prescribed*, Id.*R.*404a; τὰ τετ. ὀνόματα *received*, Isoc.9.9; τετ. τέχνη *regular*, Id.13.12; τεταγμένον, opp. ἄτακτον, Arist.*Cael.*280ᵃ8; νὺξ τὰ τεταγμέν' ἀπέχει *Lyr.Alex. Adesp.*37.6; of geom. figures, *regular*, i.e. *equilateral and equiangular*, Papp.306.2,8, al.—cf. τεταγμένως.

**τατᾶ**, voc., *daddy*, *AP*11.67 (Myrin.): dub. cj. for ταῦτα in Thphr. *Char.*7.10.

**τᾱτᾰλίζω**, *call by pet name* (cf. τατί), *coax*, Herod.1.60, 6.77.

**τᾱτάομαι**, Dor. for τητάομαι. **τᾶτες**, v. τῆτες.

* **τᾱτί**, familiar name applied by slave to mistress, Herod.5.69.

* **τᾰτικός**, ή, όν, (τείνω) neut. τατικόν, *territibile* (sic), *Gloss.* **2.** *exerting tension*, Orib.49.2.7.

**τᾰτός**, ή, όν, *that can be stretched*, Arist.*HA*519ᵃ32.

**τατύρας**, ὁ, oriental name of the *pheasant*, Pamphil.ap.Ath.9. 387e; cf. τέταρος, τέτραξ. (Cf. Mod. Pers. *tedzrev* 'pheasant', Lith. *teterva* 'black grouse', etc.: the bird τέταρος was imported from Media acc. to Ath.14.654c.)

**ταῦ**, τό, the letter τ, Hp.*VC*1, Pl.*Cra.*394c, *IG*2².2783.20 (iv B. C.), Sor.*Fasc.*45, etc.

* **Τᾰΰγετον**, Ion. **Τηΰγετον**, τό, *Mount Taygetus*, between Laconia and Messenia, Od.6.103, Hdt.4.145, etc.: later **Ταΰγετος**, ὁ, Plu.2. 601d, Luc.*Icar.*11 (s.v.l.).

**ταυληρόντα**· ἱμάντα, Ἡρακλέων, Hsch. (perh. cf. εὔληρα).

**ταυρ-άριος**, ὁ, perh. = ταυροκαθάπτης, *Gloss.* **-αφέτης**, ου, ὁ, *the one who releases the bull* at a bull-fight, *LW*499 (Caryanda). **-άω** (v.l. ταυριάω), *want the bull*, of cows, Arist.*HA*572ᵃ31.

* **Ταυρεασταί**, οἱ, worshippers of Poseidon at Ephesus, *Ephes.*2. 75 (i B. C.).

* **ταυρ-εία** (sc. δορά), ἡ, *bull's hide, ox-hide*, hence, **1.** *a kind of drum covered with skin*, *Gp.*14.25.3 (unless in sense 2). **2.** *whip of ox-hide*, Artem.1.70, Phot. s.v. μάραγνα. **-ειος**, α, ον, also ος, ον E.*Hel.*1582 :—*of bulls, oxen*, or *cows*, φόνος A.*Th.*44; κέρατα, αἷμα, S.*Tr.*518 (lyr.), *Fr.*178, Ar.*Eq.*83; χολή Sor.1.64, *POxy.*234. 45 (ii/iii A. D.), *PHolm.*6.37, al.; στέαρ Sor.2.14, Gal.10.957; πούς E.*Hel.*1555; ἀγέλαι Theoc.27.71; βρίμας ταυρείους Orph.*Fr.*79. **2.** *of bull's-hide*, κυνέη, ἀσπίς, Il.10.258, 13.161, etc.; ἱμάντες Onos.10.4: cf. foreg. and ταύρεος. **-ειών**, v. Ταυρεών. **-ελάτης** [ᾰ], ου, ὁ, (ἐλαύνω) *ox-driver*, *PGoodsp.Cair.*30 vi 8 (ii A. D.), *PFlor.*134.3 (iii A. D.), etc. **II.** a Thessalian horseman who played a principal part in the bull-fight, *toreador*, τ. χορὸς ἀνδρῶν *AP*9.543 (Phil.), cf. Hld. 10.30. **-έλᾰφος**, ὁ, *tame Indian buffalo*, Cosmas Indicopleustes 11 (ed. E. O. Winstedt, Cambr. 1909); also a wild Ethiopian species, ibid., Ael.*NA*17.45.

**ταυρεόμορφος**, ον, = ταυρόμορφος, *PMag.Par.*1.2548.

**ταύρεος**, α, ον, = ταύρειος, κόλλα *IG*2².1672.161; τὰ τ. τύμπανα *Lyr. Alex.Adesp.*37.16; τ. κέρατα Orph.*Fr.*168.14; ζωστήρια *PLond.*2. 402ᵛ.8 (ii B. C.). **II.** epith. of Poseidon in Boeotia (cf. ταῦρος I. 2), Hes.*Sc.*104, because bulls were offered to him at Onchestus, acc. to Sch.; written **Ταύρειος**, Hsch. s.v. ταῦρος; **Ταύριος**, Suid.

* **Ταυρεών**, ῶνος, ὁ, name of a month at Miletus, Cyzicus, etc., *SIG* 57.23 (Milet.), *CIG*3657.13 (Cyzic.), Herod.7.86, etc.: also **Ταυρειών**, *IG*12(7).62.10 (Amorgos).

**ταυρ-ηδόν**, Adv. *like a bull*, ἔβλεψε γοῦν τ. ἐγκύψας κάτω Ar.*Ra.* 804; τ. ὑποβλέψας πρὸς τὸν ἄνθρωπον Pl.*Phd.*117b. **-ηλάτης** [ᾰ], ου, ὁ, = ταυρελάτης I, *PFlor.*321.19 (ii A. D.), etc. **-ιάω**, v. ταυράω. **-ίδιον** [ῐδ], τό, Dim. of ταῦρος, Suid. **-ίζω**, gloss on τείνω (s.v.l.), *An.Ox.*2.417. **-ικός**, ή, όν, *of oxen*, ζεύγη *PLille* 8.8, *PCair.Zen.*216.5, *PSI*4.429.25 (all iii B. C.). **2.** neut. ταυρικόν, τό, *ox-team* for ploughing, *PStrassb.*32.17 (iii A. D.), *PGen.*76.6 (iii/iv A. D.), *PFay.*131.17 (iii/iv A. D.).

* **ταυρινάδαι**, οἱ, a guild of cobblers, *Ephes.*2.80,81 [ταυρειν- lapis].

**ταυρίνδα**· φαλλικὴ παιδιὰ παρὰ Ταραντίνοις, Hsch.

**ταυρίνη** [ῑ], ἡ, Lat. *taurina*, a kind of shoe, *Edict.Diocl.*9.15.

**Ταύριος**, v. ταύρεος.

**ταυρο-βόας**, ου, ὁ, *bellowing like a bull*, Orph.*H.*6.3. * **-βόλιον**, τό, *sacrificial slaughter of a bull*, *IGRom.*4.494 (Pergam.), 499 (ibid.), *IG*2².4842.4; in Lat. form *taurobolium*, *CIL*10.1596 (Puteoli). **-βόλος**, ον, *striking* or *slaughtering bulls*, τελετὴ τ., = ταυροβόλιον, *IG*2².4841.3,11, 14.1018,1020. **-βόρος**, ον, *devouring bulls*, λέων *APl.*4.94 (Arch.). **-γαστρικός**, ή, όν, *made of bull's hide*, βίρρος *Edict.Diocl.*22.23. **-γάστωρ**, ορος, ὁ, *with bull's paunch*: metaph., *enormous*, *APl.*4.52 (Phil.). **-γενής**, ές, doubtful epith. of Dionysus, Orph.*Fr.*297. **-δέτης**, ου, ὁ, *bull-binder*, in fem. **-δέτις**, ιδος, βύρσα *AP*6.41 (Agath.). **-δετος**, ον, *made from bull's hide*, κόλλα E.*Fr.*472.7 (s.v.l., anap.). **-δῐδαξία**, ἡ, *training of (performing) bulls*, *Milet.*1(7).205a (ii A. D.). **-δράκαινα** [δρᾰ], ἡ, *half-bull half-snake*, prob. in *PMag.Par.*1.2613 (-διακ- Pap.). **-ειδής**, ές, *bull-like*, τ. τὴν μορφήν Str.17.3.5. **-θηρία**, ἡ, *bull-hunt*, = ταυροκαθάψια, *IG*9(2).531 (Larissa). * **-θύσια** [ῠ], τά, *sacrifice of a bull*, *Supp.Epigr.*4.180.6 (Ceramus, i B. C.). **-θυτέω**, *sacrifice a bull* or *bulls*, *IG*7.2712.22 (Acraeph.). **-θύτος**, ον, *at the sacrifice of a bull*, λοιβή Orph.*A.*614. * **-κᾰθάπτης**, ου, ὁ, *bull-fighter*, *CIG* 2759b (add.) (Aphrodisias), *OGI*533.46 (Ancyra, i A. D.). * **-κᾰθάψια**, τά, *bull-fight*, held on occasion of a festival in Thessaly, Sch.Pi.*P.*2.78; at Smyrna, *CIG*3212; at Sinope, ib.4157: also **-κάθαψις**, εως, ἡ, *IGRom.*4.460 (Pergam.), unless -ψιν is for -ψιον. **-κάρηνος** [ᾰ], ον, *bull-headed*, Nonn.*D.*26.317, *PMag. Par.*1.2808. **-κένται**, οἱ, in Lat. form *Taurocentae*, *bull-stabbers* (in bull-fights), *CIL*10.1074 (Pompeii). **-κέρκουρος**, ὁ, *a kind of river-boat*, *PCair.Zen.*242 (iii B. C.), Suid. * **-κερως**, ωτος, ὁ, ἡ, *bull-horned*, E.*Ba.*100 (lyr.), Euph.14, Orph.*H.*52.2. **-κέφᾰλος**, ον, *bull-headed*, of Bootes, Teucer in Boll *Sphaera* 18,49. **-κόλλα**, ἡ, *glue made from bulls' hides*, Plb.6.23.3, Dsc.3.87, Antyll.ap.Orib. 10.23.6, Gal.12.832, Paul.Aeg.7.3. **-κολλον**, τό, = foreg., *Gloss.* **-κολλώδης**, ες, *like bull's-hide glue*, Dsc.1.67, 4. 170. **-κρᾶνος**, ον, *bull-headed*, E.*Or.*1378 (lyr.), *APl.*4. 126. **-κράτης**, ὁ, gloss on Γάνδαρος, Hsch. **-κτονέω**, *slaughter* or *sacrifice bulls*, θεοῖσιν A.*Th.*276; βοῦς τ. S.*Tr.*760. **-κτόνος**, ον, *killing bulls*, λέοντες Id.*Ph.*400 (lyr.). **II.** proparox. ταυρόκτονος, ον, Pass., *killed by a bull*, Ammon.*Diff.*p.129 V. * **-μᾰχία**, ἡ, *bull-fight*, *OGI*533.45 (Ancyra, i A.D.), *IGRom.*3.631.14 (Xanthus). **-μέτωπος**, ον, *bull-faced*, Orph.*H.*45.1. **-μορφος**, ον, *bull-formed*, ὄμμα Κηφισοῦ E.*Ion* 1261, cf. Ph.2.160, Ath.11.476a; κάνθαρος τ. *PMag.Par.*1.65.

**ταυρόομαι**, Pass., *become savage as a bull*, A.*Ch.*275; *take the form of a bull*, E.*Ba.*922; τ. ὄμμα τινί *cast savage glances* on one, Id.*Med.*92. **2.** Act., ταύρωσον· ταῦρον ποίησον, Hsch.

**ταυρο-πάρθενος**, ἡ, *bull-maiden*, i.e. Io, Lyc.1292, cf. Tz. ad loc. **-πάτωρ** [ᾰ], ορος, ὁ, ἡ, *sprung from a bull*, of bees, Theoc. *Syrinx* 3.

❋ **Ταυροπόλια**, τά, *festival of Artemis Tauropolos*, Ἀρχ.Ἐφ.1932 *Supp.*30 (Attica, iv B.C.), Men.*Epit.*234. **II.** sg. **Ταυροπόλιον**, τό, *temple of Artemis* on the island of Icaria, Str.14.1.19.

❋ **ταυροπόλος**, ἡ, E.*IT*1457, Ar.*Lys.*447, *CIG*2699 (Mylasa); also **ταυροπόλα**, S.*Aj.*172 (lyr.):—a name of Artemis (cf. Ταυρώ), variously interpreted as *worshipped at Tauris*, or *drawn by a yoke of bulls*, or *hunting bulls*; cf. Ister 8; applied to Iphigenia, Ant. Lib.27.3.

**ταυρό-πους**, ὁ, ἡ, πουν, τό, gen. ποδος, *bull-footed*, σῆμα, of a river-god, E.*IA*275 (lyr.). **-πρόσωπος**, ον, *bull-faced*, θεός *PMag. Leid.W.*1.30, cf. Hermes Trism. in *Rev.Phil.*32.266; ναῦς Sch.Par. A.R.2.168. **-πρῳρος**, ον, *having a bull on the prow*, as figure-head, πλοῖον Sch.Lyc.1292.

❋ **ταῦρος**, ὁ, *bull*, Il.2.481, etc.; as a sacrifice to Poseidon, 11.728, Od.13.181; also ταῦρος βοῦς Il.17.389; ἄπεχε τῆς βοὸς τὸν τ., oracularly of Agamemnon and his wife, A.*Ag.*1126 (lyr.). **2.** *priest of Poseidon Taureios*, Ath.10.425c. **3.** a kind of Lycian boat with bull as figurehead, postulated to explain Europa's bull, Poll. 1.83. **II.** *the bull as a sign of the Zodiac*, Eudox.ap.Hipparch. 1.2.10, Arat.167, al., *IG*14.1307, *Supp.Epigr.*7.363.8 (Dura-Europus, ii A.D.), etc. **III.** = κοχώνη, Poll.2.173, Gal.14.706: also *the pudenda muliebria*, Phot.: *the male* αἰδοῖον, Suid. (Cf. Lat. *taurus*, Lith. *tauras*, Slav. *turŭ*, etc.)

❋ **ταυρο-σφᾰγέω**, *cut a bull's throat*, τ. ἐς σάκος *cut its throat* (so that the blood runs) into a hollow shield, A.*Th.*43, cf. Sch.Ar.*Lys.* 189. **-σφάγος** [ᾰ], ον, *bull-slaughtering*, esp. in sacrifice, τ. ἡμέρα S.*Tr.*609; τ. λέαινα Lyc.47; of dithyrambic poets, Tz.*Diff. Poet.*17. **-τενής**, ές, dub. sens. in Dain *Inscr. du Louvre* 60.25 (Heraclea ad Latmum). **-φάγος** [ᾰ], ον, *bull-eating*, epith. of Dionysus, S.*Fr.*668; applied to Cratinus by Ar.*Ra.*357 (anap.). **-φᾰνής**, ές, *bull-like*, D.P.642.

**ταυρόφθαλμος**, ον, *bull-eyed*, Heph.Astr.2.2.

**ταυρό-φθογγος**, ον, *bellowing like a bull*, τ. μῖμοι sounds that imitate *the bellowing of bulls*, A.*Fr.*57.8 (anap.). **-φόνος**, ον, = ταυροσφάγος, τριετηρίς Pi.*N.*6.40; δόρπα *AP*11.60 (Paul. Sil.); τ. λέων *BCH*21.599 (Delph., iv B.C.), Orph.*H.*14.2; f.l. in Theoc.17. 20. **-φόρος**, ον, *stamped with the device of a bull*, τετρᾶχμα *Inscr. Délos* 1429*B* ii 41 (ii B.C.). **2.** *having a bull as a figurehead*, ναῦς St.Byz. s.v. Ταυρόεις. **-φυής**, ές, *bull-shaped*, Nonn.*D.*7. 153. ❋ **-χόλια** (sic)· ἑορτὴ ἐν Κυζικῷ, Hsch.

**Ταυρώ**, οῦς, ἡ, a name of Artemis (cf. ταυροπόλος), Hsch.

**ταυρώδης**, ες, = ταυροειδής, ταυρώδεα λεύσσων Nic.*Al.*222.

**Ταυρών**, ῶνος, ὁ, a month at Alexandria, Ptol.*Alm.*9.7.

**ταυρ-ωπός**, όν, (ὤψ) *bull-faced*, Ion Lyr.9, Orph.*H.*29.4, Corn.*ND* 22: neut. as Adv., ταυρωπὸν ἀποβλεψάμενοι Ph.1.602: fem. **-ῶπις**, Nonn.*D.*32.69; epith. of Isis in Samothrace, *POxy.*1380.107 (ii A.D.). **-ωτικός**, ή, όν, *like a bull*, τὸ τ. Sch.Nic.*Al.*31.

**ταύς**, = μέγας, πολύς, and **ταύσας**· μεγαλύνας, πλεονάσας, Hsch.:—hence Madvig restored κεκτημένος ταῦ χρυσίον (for τ' αὖ πολὺ χρ.) in Poet.ap.Pl.*Tht.*175c—πολύ (which is absent in codd. BT, though added by a later hand in T and found (without τ' αὖ or ταῦ) in the citation by Iamb.*Protr.*14) being a gloss.

**ταύσιος**, v. τηΰσιος.

**ταῦτα**, neut. pl. of οὗτος: but **ταὐτά**, crasis for τὰ αὐτά.

❋ **ταυτᾷ**, Dor. Adv. = ταύτῃ, *IG*12(3).248.15 (Anaphe, ii B.C.): written ταυτα (spondee) ib.5(1).213.4 (Sparta, v B.C.).

**ταὐτίζω**, *use as synonymous*, Eust.8.33, etc.; ἕν εἰσι καὶ ταὐτίζονται Procl. *in Prm.* (*Suppl.*) p.1008 S.

**ταὐτο-γρᾰφέω**, *write in the same way*, Eust.45.46. **-δῠνᾰμέω**, of words, *to be equivalent, mean the same*, Sch.E.*Or.*162. **-ειδής**, ές, *having the form of identity*, Dam.*Pr.*340. Adv. -ειδῶς, synonym for ὡσαύτως, ib.349. **-έπεια**, ἡ, = ταὐτολογία, Hsch., Suid. **-επέω**, gloss on ταὐτολογέω, Phot., Suid.

**ταὐτοῖος**, α, ον, *resembling* or *approaching identity*, Dam.*Pr.*350, 439.

**ταὐτοκλῐνής**, ές, *in the same latitude*, Str.2.1.16, 17.3.8.

**ταὐτολογ-έω**, *repeat what has been said*, περί τινος Plb.1.1.3; ὑπέρ τινος Id.1.79.7; τ. τὸν λόγον Str.12.3.27:—abs., Plb.36.12.2, Phld. *Po.Herc.*994.30, Hermog.*Inv.*3.15. **-ημα**, ατος, τό, *tautology*, Eust.948.56. **-ία**, ἡ, = foreg., D.H.*Comp.*23, Ph.1.529, Quint.*Inst.* 8.3.50: pl. in Plu.2.504d. **-ικῶς**, Adv. *tautologically*, Eust.122. 6. **-ος** (parox.), ον, *repeating what has been said, tautologous*, *AP*9.206 (Eupith.).

**ταὐτο-μήκης**, ες, *of the same length*, Nicom.*Ar.*2.18. **-νοια**, ἡ, *identity of meaning*, Eust.1530.21. **-νομος**, ον, *following the same rule*, Tz. in *An.Par.*1.70.

**ταὐτόομαι**, *become identified*, πρός τι Dam.*Pr.*305: abs., opp. ἑτεροιοῦται, Procl. *in Prm.*p.899S.

**ταὐτο-πάθεια** [πᾰ], ἡ, *reflex signification*, Hdn.Gr.ap.*An.Ox.*3. 271, *EM*67.44. **-ποδία**, ἡ, *repetition of the same foot in the same verse*, Sch.Ar.*Ra.*346, Heph.3.3, Mar.Vict.p.47 K., Atil.Fort.p. 280 K. **-ποιέω**, *act as deputy*, *PPetr.*2 p.45 (iii B.C.). **II.** *do the same thing*, Phld.*Po.*2.1. **-ποιός**, όν, *creating identity*, Procl. *in Cra.*p.20 P., Dam.*Pr.*305, al. **-πολῠλογέω**, *keep repeating the same thing*, Tz.*H.*10.851.

**ταὐτός**, ή, όν, *identical*, in nom. pl. masc. ταὐτοί, Syrian. *in Metaph.*137.22,25,26, Sch.Theoc.1.56 codd.; τὸ ταὐτό Arist.*Metaph.* 1054$^b$15; τὸ ταὐτόν Syrian. *in Metaph.*62.32, al.

**ταὐτό-σημος**, ον, *of the same signification*, Eust.103.23: **-σήμαντος**, ον, Sch.E.*Hec.*16, Eust.101.37. **-συλλᾰβέω**, *have the same syllables*, *EM*193.52.

❋ **ταὐτότης**, ητος, ἡ, *identity*, Arist.*EN*1161$^b$31, *Metaph.*995$^b$21, Gal. 6.643, Dam.*Pr.*423, etc. **II.** *monotony*, D.H.*Comp.*12,19, Hermog.*Meth.*37. **III.** *identical condition*, ἐν τ. μεῖναι *POxy.*940. 2 (v A.D.); *maintenance of identity*, Plot.1.2.7.

**ταὐτο-φᾰνής**, ές, *presenting the appearance of identity*, Dam.*Pr.* 241. **-φωνος**, ον, *of the same sound*, Eust.125.5: hence **-φωνία**, ἡ, ib.20.

**ταὐτόω**, *make identical*, Procl. *in Prm.*pp.899,923 S.

**ταὔτωμα**, ατος, τό, *identified substance*, Procl. *in Prm.*p.863 S.

**ταὐτώνῠμος**, ον, (ὄνομα) *of the same name*, Speus.ap.Simp. *in Cat.* 38.20.

**ταφαιών**, v. ταφεών. **τάφε**, v. τέθηπα.

**τάφ-ειμα** [ᾰ], ατος, τό, *tomb*, *IGRom.*3.1381 (Arabia, prob. ii A.D.). **-εῖος**, v. ταφήϊος. **II.** neut. ταφεῖον, τό, *tomb*, *BCH*52. 401 (Priene). **-εύς**, έως, ὁ, *burier, grave-digger*, S.*OC*582, *El.* 1488, Plu.*Comp.Pel.Marc.*3. **-εών**, ῶνος, ὁ, *burial-ground*, *Supp. Epigr.*7.161,167 (Palmyra, ii A.D.), *OGI*642 (ibid., iii A.D.); written **ταφαιών**, *Supp.Epigr.*7.166 (ibid., ii A.D.):—also **ταφών**, *IG* 12(1).656 (Rhodes). ❋ **-ή**, ἡ, (v. θάπτω) *burial*, ταφῆς τυχεῖν, κυρῆσαι, Hdt.1.24,112: in pl., *mode of burial*, Id.2.85,5.8: pl. also of the *burials* of those who had fallen in battle, δημοσίᾳ ταφὰς ἐποιήσαντο Th.2.34; νόμοι.., οἷς ἐχρῶντο περὶ τὰς ταφάς ib.52, cf. *OGI*90. 32 (Rosetta, ii B.C.). **2.** pl. also, *burial-place*, Hdt.4.71, 5.63, S. *Aj.*1090,1109: later in sg., *Sammelb.*6028.2, al. (i B.C.): but σῆς εἰ στερήσομαι ταφῆς, of the *urn* supposed to contain the ashes of Orestes, S.*El.*1210; so in Egypt, *mummy*, *POxy.*736.13 (i A.D.), Wilcken *Chr.* 499 (ii/iii A.D.), etc.; also, *sarcophagus*, δευτέρα τ., of a double sarcophagus, *PGiss.*68.7 (ii A.D.), *Arch.Pap.*4.133 (ii A.D.). **3.** *payment for burial, burial-fee*, τὸν τὴν τ. τοῦ πατρὸς οὐκ ἀπειληφότα D.25. 58; ἐνδεεῖς γενόμενοι εἰς τὴν τ. τὴν Φιλίππου *PEnteux.*32.6 (iii B.C.); ὑπὲρ τέλους ταφῆς μιᾶς *Ostr.Bodl.* ii 45 (ii A.D.). **-ήϊος**, η, ον, Ep. for ταφεῖος (not found), *of* or *for a burial*, φᾶρος τ. a winding-sheet, shroud, Od.2.99; μῆλα, i.e. for sacrifice, A.R.2.840. **-ικόν**, τό, *burial-money*, *PEnteux.*20.5, 21.8 (iii B.C.), *IG*2$^2$.1323.11 (iii/ii B.C.), *Ostr.Bodl.* i 134 (pl., ii B.C.), *BGU*1668.14 (i A.D.). ❋ **-ιος**, α, ον, = ταφήϊος, λίθος *gravestone*, *AP*7.40 (Diod.). **II.** pl. τάφια, τά, *burial-place*, *IG*12(1).736 (Camirus, iii B.C.): but also τᾶν ταφιᾶν (from ταφία or ταφιά) *Supp.Epigr.*3.674*A* 4, al. (Rhodes, ii B.C.).

**τᾰφοειδής**, ές, *like a burial* or *grave*, στήλη D.C.67.9.

**τάφος** [ᾰ] (A), ὁ, (θάπτω) *funeral-rites*, Il.23.619, Od.4.547; δαινύναι τάφον to give a *funeral-feast*, Il.23.29, Od.3.309; τελέσαι τάφον Ἕκτορι δίῳ to perform *the funeral-rites*, Il.24.660; so ὃν πόλις στυγεῖ, σὺ τιμήσεις τάφῳ; A.*Th.*1051; τάφῳ κτερίζειν S.*Ant.*203; τάφον τινὸς θέσθαι Id.*OT*1447; τ. περιστέλλειν νεκροῦ Id.*Aj.*1170; τάφου τυχεῖν obtain *the rites of burial*, E.*Hec.*47; τοιόσδε ὁ τ. ἐγένετο Th.2. 47: pl. of a single funeral, Pl.*R.*414a; so of cremation, Clitarch. 32 J. **2.** *the act of performing the funeral-rites*, τοῦδε τοῦ τ. φήσεις μετασχεῖν S.*Ant.*534. **II.** *grave, tomb*, Hes.*Sc.*477, Pi.*I.*8(7).63, A.*Pers.*686, *Ch.*168, S.*El.*1218 sq., Hdt.2.136, Th.1.26, etc. (never in Hom.): pl. of a single grave, S.*OC*411; ὄντες ἐν τάφοις *dead and buried*, A.*Eu.*767; μέγας γ' ὀφθαλμὸς οἱ πατρὸς τάφοι *his being dead and buried*, S.*OT*987:—γῦπες ἔμψυχοι τάφοι Gorg.5$^a$. **2.** ἔμψυχός τις τ. a 'living skeleton', Luc.*DMort.*6.2. **3.** = βωμός, Duris 34 J. **4.** Cypr. for φόνος, Sch.Il.23.29.

**τάφος** [ᾰ] (B), εος, τό, (τέθηπα) *astonishment, amazement*, τ. δ' ἔλε πάντας Od.21.122, cf. 24.441; τ. δέ οἱ ἦτορ ἵκανεν 23.93; dat. τάφει Ibyc.21.

**ταφρ-εία**, ἡ, *making of ditches* or *trenches*, D.18.299, *Delph.*3(5). 74.44 (iv B.C.), Plb.5.2.5, etc.: collectively, *entrenchments*, Ph.*Bel.* 80.19, 85.46, D.C.36.54, al. **-ευμα**, ατος, τό, *ditch*, Pl.*Lg.*761b, D.C.*Fr.*57.33, *Fr.*98.1. **-ευσις**, εως, ἡ, *digging, method of digging*, Ael.*NA*9.8. **-ευτής**, οῦ, ὁ, *ditcher*, *PCair.Zen.*744.9 (iii B.C.). **-εύω**, *make a ditch*, Pl.*Lg.*760e, 778e, X.*HG*5.2.4; τάφρους τ. Aeschin.3.236: c. acc., τὰ ἔσωθεν Aen.Tact.33.4. ❋ **-η**, ἡ, Ion. for τάφρος (which is v.l.), Hdt.4.28,201: also **τράφη**, *IG*12(7).62. 27 (Amorgos, iv B.C.).

**ταφρο-βολέω**, *fossam duco*, Gloss. **-ειδής**, ές, *ditch-like, trench-like*, Sch.D Il.2.153. **-ποιέω**, *make a trench for besieging*, D.S.23.7.

**τάφρος**, ἡ, *ditch, trench*, freq. in Il. (once in Od., 21.120); τάφρον ὀρύξομεν Il.7.341, cf. *IG*1$^2$.94.21,34, Th.2.78, al.; ἀμφὶ δὲ τάφρον ἤλασαν drew a *trench*, Il.7.449, cf. Hdt.4.3, Alcid.*Od.*5, etc.; τάφρων ὕπερ over the *trenches*, S.*Aj.*1279, cf. Aen.Tact.37.3, al., *OGI*90.24 (Rosetta, ii B.C.); *irrigation-ditch*, *PHal.*1.97, al., *PSI*6. 597.5 (both iii B.C.): it is sts. found as masc. in codd., e.g. Ph.*Bel.* 99.43 (cod. V), D.S.22.10.5; but βαθύν is Ep. for βαθεῖαν in Call.*Del.* 37: Dor. **τράφος** *Tab.Herad.*1.130, 2.51.

**ταφρ-ώδης**, ες, = ταφροειδής, *AB*394. **-ωρύχος** [ῠ], ὁ, (ὀρύσσω) *sapper and miner*, D.L.4.23. **-ωσις**, *vallatus*, *Gloss.*

**τᾰφών**, v. τέθηπα. II. v. ταφεών.

⊛ **τάχᾰ**, Adv., (τᾰχύς) *quickly, presently, forthwith*, freq. in Hom., who, like Pi. (*O*.2.29, 4.83, al.) and B. (5.89), uses it only of time, Il.1.205, 2.193, al.; ἦ τ. *soon* i'faith, Od.18.73,338; of past time, τ. δ' Ἕκτορος ἄγχι γένοντο Il.8.117: also in Trag. and (more rarely) Att. Prose and Com., with fut., τάχ' εἴσομαι A.*Th*.261, cf. *Ag*.489,1649, *Ch*.305, S.*OT*84, Ar.*Ra*.527, Pl.*Sph*.247d, etc.; ἔοικα θεσπιῳδήσειν τ. A.*Ag*.1161; πέμψον πρὸς ἐμὲ τ. *Sammelb*.7356.25 (ii A. D.); in this sense not found in Lxx or in Papyri (exc. l.c.); τάχα ἐπειδάν, = ἐπειδὰν τάχιστα, *as soon as*, Pl.*Phdr*.242a. II. *perhaps*, to express any contingency from a probability to bare possibility, δὶς μὲν γὰρ καὶ τρὶς τ. τεύξεαι Hes.*Op*.401; τ. οὐδὲ τεθέασθε τυραννουμένην πόλιν Pl.*Lg*.711a, cf. *Hp.Ma*.303b, X.*An*.5.2.17, Theoc.27.61, Bion *Fr*.4.8, Gal.16.685,690: more freq. τάχ' ἄν, *probably, perhaps*, Hdt.1.70, al., freq. in Trag. and Att.; mostly with opt., as Hdt. l. c., A.*Pr*.314, *Eu*.512 (lyr.), S.*OT*139, Th.1.81, etc.; rarely with aor. ind., Pl.*Phdr*.256c, Gal.16.596; with impf. ind., D.36.55; with part., S.*OT*523, Th.6.2; with inf., Luc.*Icar*.10; τάχ' ἄν alone, in answers, Pl.*Sph*.255c, *R*.369a, etc.: strengthd., τάχα.. ἴσως Ar.*Th*.718; ἴσως τ. X.*HG*7.1.24; τ. τοίνυν ἴσως D.21.191; τάχ' ἂν ἴσως Pl.*Plt*.264c; τάχ' ἴσως ἂν Id.*Sph*.247d; ἴσως τάχ' ἄν S.*Aj*.691, Th.6.34, Pl.*Ti*.38e; ἀμφισβητοῦντες προστιθέασιν ἀεὶ τὸ ἴσως καὶ τ. Arist.*Rh*.1389b19; in this sense only twice in Lxx (*Wi*.13.6, 14.19). III. Sup. τάχιστα, v. ταχύς C. II. IV. Ar. formed an acc. pl. τάχας, *perhaps-es*, *Fr*.869.

**τᾰχέως**, Adv. of ταχύς (q. v.).

**τᾰχεωστί**, = foreg., Pherecr.239; cf. μεγαλωστί.

**ταχίζω**, *make swift*, Al.*Hb*.3.19.

**τᾰχῑνά**, v. ταχινός.

**τᾰχίνας**, ὁ, Lacon. name of the *hare*, Ael.*NA*7.47; of the *deer*, Hsch.

**τᾰχῑνός**, ή, όν, poet. and late Prose for ταχύς, φρένες, ἴουλοι, Theoc.2.7, Call.*Jov*.56, cf. A.R.2.1044, Lxx *Wi*.13.2, al., 2*Ep.Pet*.2.1, *Cat.Cod.Astr*.1.137, etc.: Sup. -ώτατος Arat.289: neut. pl. ταχινά, = τάχα, Theoc.14.40.

**τᾰχίων, -ιον, τάχιστος, -ιστα**, v. ταχύς C.

**τάχος** [ᾰ], εος, τό, (ταχύς) *swiftness, speed*, ἵπποισι.. οἶσιν Ἀθήνη νῦν ὤρεξε τ. Il.23.406, cf. 515; τ. καὶ βραδυτής Pl.*Tht*.156c, Arist.*Ph*.228b29, etc.: pl., *velocities*, Pl.*Ti*.39d, *Lg*.893d. 2. τ. φρενῶν *quickness* of temper, *hastiness*, E.*Ba*.670; ὁ χρόνος μάθησιν ἀντὶ τοῦ τάχους.. δίδωσι Id.*Supp*.419; f.l. in Pl.*Lg*.944c; τ. τῆς ψυχῆς *quickness* of apprehension, ib.689c. II. τάχος is freq. used in Adverbial phrases for ταχέως, abs. in acc., A.*Th*.58, *Ag*.945, *Eu*.124, E.*Rh*.986, *HF*860 (troch.), etc.; also in dat., τάχει ὁμοίως *with like velocities*, Pl.*Ti*.36d: with Preps., διὰ τάχους S.*Aj*.822, Th.1.63, etc.; ἐν τάχει Pi.*N*.5.35, A.*Pr*.747, S.*OC*500, Th.1.86, *PCair.Zen*.62(*b*).10 (iii B. C.), etc.; εἰς τάχος X.*Eq*.3.5, Ar.*Ach*.686, etc.; κατὰ τάχος Hdt.1.124,152, Th.1.73; κατὰ τὸ τ. *PCair.Zen*.130.11 (iii B. C.); τὸ τ. (without κατὰ) ib.158.2, 166.4, 428.15, *PHib*.1.62.13 (all iii B. C.), etc.; μετὰ τάχους Pl.*Prt*.332b; μετὰ παντὸς τ. with all *speed*, *POxy*.2107.4 (iii A. D.); σὺν τάχει S.*Aj*.853, *OC*885 (lyr.), 904: also with relatives, ὡς τάχος, = ὡς τάχιστα, A.*Ag*.27, *Ch*.889, Hdt.5.106, Ar.*Lys*.1187; so ὅ τι τάχος Hdt.9.7.β', Th.7.42, *PCair.Zen*.60.8 (iii B. C.); ὅσον τάχος S.*El*.1373, etc.; ᾇ (Dor. ᾷ) τάχος Pi.*O*.6.23, Theoc.14.68: also ὡς τάχεος εἶχε ἕκαστος Hdt.8.107, cf. Th.2.90; ὡς εἶχον τάχους Id.7.2; πῶς πρὸς ἄλληλα τάχους ἔχει Pl.*Grg*.451c.

**τᾰχῠ-άλωτος** [ᾰ], ον, *conquered quickly* or *easily*, χώρη Hdt.7.130. **-βάμων** [ᾱ], ονος, ὁ, ἡ, *fast-walking*, Arist.*Phgn*.813a7; also **-βήμων**, as gloss on αὐριβάτας, Hsch. (-βήλων cod.). **-βάτης** [ᾰ], ου, ὁ, = foreg., E.*Rh*.134 (lyr.). **-βλαστία**, ἡ, *quick sprouting*, Thphr.*CP*4.1.3, 4.8.1. **-βλαστος**, ον, *sprouting quickly*, ib.4.1.3 (Comp.). **-βουλος**, ον, *hasty in counsel*, opp. μετάβουλος, perh. with allusion to the votes respecting Mytilene (Th.3.36), Ar.*Ach*.630; cf. Max.76. **-γάμος**, ον, *early-marrying*, *Cat.Cod.Astr*.2.166. **-γηρος**, ον, *soon becoming decrepit*, neut. pl. ταχύγηρα Hp.*Art*.58; περὶ τοῦ μὴ τ. γίνεσθαι τὸ ζῷον Gal.6.9; ταχύγηροι περὶ τὴν κεφαλήν turning grey early, Id.1.328. **-γλωσσος**, ον, *quick of tongue, talking fast*, Hp.*Epid*.2.6.1, Ruf.*Fr*.70, etc. **-γονία**, ἡ, *quick reproduction*, Arist.*HA*580b27. **-γονος**, ον, *yielding fruit quickly* or *soon*, Thphr.*CP*4.3.6. **-γράφος** [γρᾰ], ὁ, *shorthand writer*, Lyd.*Mag*.3.6, *Stud.Pal*.20.247.2 (vi/vii A. D.):—hence **-γρᾰφέω**, *write shorthand*, Tz.*H*.8.267, Eust.1607.10. **-δαής**, ές, *burning quickly*, Agath.1.10. **-δακρυς**, υ, gen. υος, *soon moved to tears*, Luc.*Nav*.2. **-δῑνής**, ές, *whirling quickly*, Nonn.*D*.34.1. **-δρομέω**, *run fast*, Sch.E.*Med*.1; of Venus, *Cat.Cod.Astr*.1.133. **-δρομία**, ἡ, *quickness in running*, Arist.*Pr*.881b7. **-δρόμος**, ον, *fast-running*, Nonn.*D*.29.365, Orph.*H*.27.3, Aesop.157. II. Subst. -δρόμος, ὁ, *courier*, *PMasp*.131.5, al. (vi A. D.); = *cursor*, *Gloss*. [Proparox. in Nonn. and Orph. ll.cc., parox. in Aesop. and *Gloss*. ll. cc.] **-εργής**, ές, = ταχυεργός, App.*BC*3.19. **-εργία**, ἡ, *quickness in working*, X.*Cyr*.7.1.19. II. *hastiness*, App.*Pun*.33. **-εργός**, όν, *doing* or *working quickly*, Nonn.*D*.28.79; ὀπός ib.29.157; epith. of Horus, *Sammelb*.5620.14. II. *hasty*, App.*Pun*.47, *BC*2.120, Adam.1.16. **-ήρης**, ες, *fast-rowing, rapid*, A.*Supp*.32 (anap.), Opp.*H*.4.569. **-θᾰνᾰσία**, ἡ, *early death*, *Cat.Cod.Astr*.2.165. **-θάνᾰτος** [θᾰ], ον, *liable to sudden death*, Hp.*Aph*.2.44; τ. εἶναι, = ταχέως θνήσκειν, Id.*Epid*.1.12; = *decrepitus*, *Gloss*. II. *killing speedily*, Hp.*Acut*.56, *Art*.66 (Sup.). **-ιππος**, ον, *riding fast*, Sch.Ar.*Nu*.729. **-κάρδιος**, ον, *hasty in spirit*, Thd.*Is*.35.4. **-κατάφορος**, ον, *setting rapidly*, ζῴδια Sch.Ptol.*Tetr*.114. **-κίνησις** [κῐ], εως, ἡ, *quick movement*, ib.17. **-κίνητος** [ῑ], ον, *moving quickly*, Gal.19.631, Porph.*in Harm*. p.240 W., Adam.2.45. **-κρίσῐμος** [κρῐ], ον, *coming quickly to a crisis*, Hp.*Epid*.1.24, Gal.15.172, al. **-μᾰθής**, ές, *quick to learn*, Poll.4.11. ⊛ **-μάχης** [μᾰ], ου, *quick to the fray*, Hsch. s. v. ὠκυβόας. **-μετάβολος**, ον, *quickly changing*, Ptol.*Tetr*.162, *Geog*.1.17.5. **-μηνις**, εως, ὁ, ἡ, *swift to anger*, *AP*9.524.20. **-μητις**, = ταχύβουλος, Hsch. s. v. ἀργιμήτας. **-μορος**, ον, *quickly dying, short-lived*, κλέος A.*Ag*.486 (lyr.): also **-μόριος**, Keil-Premerstein *Zweiter Bericht* No.264 (Phrygia, iii A. D.): and **-μοιρος**, *Epigr.Gr*.365 (Cotiaeum), 367 (ibid.), *Supp.Epigr*.6.159.17 (Phrygia, iii A. D.). **-μῦθος**, ον, *speaking fast*, Nonn.*D*.21.276; φωνή ib.37.319. **-ναυτέω**, *sail fast*, Th.6.31,34, Plb.1.23.9, al.; νῆες ταχυναυτοῦσαι Aeschin.3.97; [τριήρεις] -οῦσαι *IG*2².1623.284 (iv B. C.). **-νοια**, ἡ, = ἀγχίνοια, *AB*210.

**τᾰχύνω**, *make quickly*, κοιλὴν κάπετον χερσὶ ταχύνατε S.*Aj*.1404 (anap.); ὡς δύνασαι.. ταχύνας σπεῦσον κοιλὴν κάπετον ib.1164 (anap.); τάδε τοί με σπερχόμενος ταχύνει such are the words by which he urging *hastens* me, i. e. urges me to hasten, E.*Alc*.257 (lyr.):—Pass., σελὶς ταχυνομένη *quickly written*, *AP*6.227 (Crin.). II. intr., *to be quick, make haste, hurry*, A.*Pers*.692, *Ch*.660, S.*OT*861, *OC*219 (lyr.), Ar.*Ec*.582: in Prose, X.*Cyr*.8.5.15: c. gen., τοῦ ποιῆσαι Lxx *Ge*.18.7. 2. *to be early*, ταχύνουσαν ἢ βραδύνουσαν ἀκμὴν προδιαγνῶναι Gal.19.201.

**τᾰχῠ-πᾰθής**, ές, *soon affected*, χυμός Choerob.Rh.p.247 S. **-πειθής**, ές, *soon persuaded, credulous*, Theoc.2.138, 7.38, Nonn.*D*.22.79. II. *obeying quickly* or *easily*, ἀνέμων ῥιπῇ Tryph.528. **-πέτης**, ες, or **-πετής**, ές, (πέτομαι) *flying fast*, Suid. s.v. ὠκύπτερον. **-πλοέω**, *sail fast*, Plb.3.95.6. **-πλοΐα**, ἡ, *swiftness in sailing*, Poll.1.106. ⊛ **-πλοος**, ον, contr. **-πλους**, ουν, *fast-sailing*, E.*Hyps*.*Fr*.1 iii 12, Sch.Od.15.473, Hsch. s. v. ὠκύπλους. **-πνοέω**, *breathe quickly*, Herod.Med. in *Rh.Mus*.58.96. **-πνοια**, ἡ, *quickness of respiration*, Hp.*Oss*.13, Aët.13.23. **-πομπος**, ον, *quick-sailing*, διωγμοί A.*Supp*.1046 (lyr.). **-πορος**, ον, *fast-going, quick of motion*, Id.*Ag*.486, E.*El*.451; τ. κώπη Id.*Hel*.1272 (all lyr.); τ. φυγή Tim.*Pers*.175; τ. σιδήρια Hp.*Art*.11 (Comp.); of foods, *passing rapidly*, Gal.6.535. **-ποτμος**, ον, = ταχύμορος, Pi.*O*.1.66; Ἀνάγκα *Lyr.Alex.Adesp*.34.9, cf. *IG*14.2005, Nonn.*D*.48.11. ⊛ **-πους**, ποδος, ὁ, ἡ, πουν, τό, *swift-footed*, E.*Ba*.782, Ar.*Eq*.1068; ἴχνος E.*Tr*.232 (anap.); κῶλον Id.*Ba*.168 (lyr.). **-πτερνος**, ον, *with swift heels, swift-footed*, ἵπποι Thgn.551. **-πτερορρυέω**, *moult quickly*, Aristaenet.2.1 (better ταχὺ πτ-). **-πτερος**, ον, *swift winged*, πνοαί A.*Pr*.88. **-πωλος**, ον, *with fleet, swift horses*, epithet of the Greeks, Δαναοὶ τ. Il.4.232, al. (never in Od.); Τυνδαρίδη Theoc.22.136. **-ρροθος**, ον, *swift-rushing*, λόγοι A.*Th*.286. **-ρροος**, ον, *swiftly-flowing*, Hsch. s. v. ἀψορρόου, Sch.Il.18.399. **-ρρωστος**, ον, *swift-rushing, swift-flying*, πελειάς S.*OC*1081 (lyr.).

⊛ **τᾰχύς** [ῠ], εῖα, ύ: I. of motion, *swift, fleet*, opp. βραδύς, 1. of persons and animals, either abs., Il.18.69, etc.; or more fully, πόδας ταχύς 13.249,482, 17.709, etc.; ταχὺς ἔσκε θέειν Od.17.308; θέειν τ. Il.16.186, Od.3.112; κύνες, ἔλαφος, πτώξ, ἵππος, Il.3.26, 8.248, 17.676, 23.347, etc.; οἰωνόν, ταχὺν ἄγγελον 24.292, cf. Od.15.526; τ. βαδιστής a *quick* walker, E.*Med*.1182; σφοδροὶ καὶ τ. X.*Cyr*.2.1.31. 2. of things, τ. πόδες Il.6.514, cf. Od.13.261, etc.; τ. ἰός, ὀϊστοί, Il.4.94, Od.22.3, etc.; πτερά Ar.*Av*.1453; -ύτατα ἅρματα Pi.*O*.1.77; νῆες, τριήρεις, Hdt.8.23, Th.6.43, etc.; [ἴχνος] τὸ τοῦ ποδὸς μὲν βραδύ, τὸ τοῦ δὲ νοῦ ταχύ E.*Ion* 742. II. of thought and purpose, *quick, hasty*, φρονεῖν γὰρ οἱ ταχεῖς οὐκ ἀσφαλεῖς S.*OT*617: c. inf., βλάπτειν τ. Ar.*Ra*.1428; τ. βουλεῦσαί τι ἀνήκεστον Th.1.132, cf. 118, Luc.*Dem.Enc*.12; also τ. πρὸς ὀργήν Plu.*Cat.Mi*.1; τὸ ταχύ *speed, haste*, E.*Ph*.452, X.*Eq*.7.18, etc. 2. of actions, events, etc., *rapid, sudden*, πήδημα S.*Aj*.833; ᾅδης, μόρος, E.*Hipp*.1047, Mosch.3.26; πόλεμος Th.4.55, 6.45; φυγή Id.4.44; μεταβολή Pl.*R*.553d; *short*, τ. ἐλπίδες *fleeting* hopes, Pi.*P*.1.83; ἐπαυρέσεις Th.2.53; ἀτραπός Ar.*Ra*.127; ταχεῖ σὺν χρόνῳ S.*OC*1602; τ. διήγησις *short, rapid*, Arist.*Rh*.1416b30.

B. Adv., 1. regul. τᾰχέως, *quickly*, opp. βραδέως, Il.23.365, Hes.*Th*.103, etc.:—rarely in sense *perhaps* (cf. τάχα II), Plb.16.25.8. 2. the Adv. is also expressed by periphr., διὰ ταχέων *in haste*, Th.1.80, 3.13, Pl.*Ap*.32d, X.*An*.1.5.9; ἐκ ταχείας S.*Tr*.395; cf. τάχος II. 3. neut. ταχύ as Adv., Pi.*P*.10.51, *N*.1.51, S.*Ph*.349, E.*HF*885 (lyr.), Ar.*Eq*.109, Gal.16.665, etc.; ἤδη ἤδη τ. τ. *Sammelb*.4321.21, *BGU*956.3 (both iii A. D.); ἄρτι ἄρτι τ. τ. *Arch.Pap*.5.393 (ii A. D.); also τάχα (q. v.). 4. the Adj. ταχύς is freq. construed with Verbs, where we should use the Adv., ταχέες δ' ἱππῆες ἄγερθεν Il.23.287; ταχεῖά γ' ἦλθε χρησμῶν πρᾶξις A.*Pers*.739; δρμάσθω ταχὺς S.*Ph*.526; δεῦρ' ἀφίξεται τ. Id.*OC*307; τ. χάρις διαρρεῖ Id.*Aj*.1266, cf. Th.2.75, 5.66.

C. Degrees of Comparison: I. Comp.: 1. the form **τᾰχύτερος**, α, ον, is used by Hdt., ἐποίησα ταχύτερα ἢ σοφώτερα 3.65, cf. 7.194; also in Arist.*Mu*.394b3, Arr.*Ind*.9.6, Aret.*SD*1.16, but not in good Att.; ταχύτερον as Adv., Hdt.4.127, 9.101, Hp.*Prog*.17. 2. the more usual form is **θάσσων**, neut. θᾶσσον, gen. ονος, Att. **θάττων**, neut. θᾶττον, Il.15.570, 13.819 (elsewh. only neut. in Hom.), etc.:—neut. as Adv., freq. in Hom., Od.2.307, al.; θᾶσσον ἂν .. κλύοιμι *sooner*, i.e. *rather*, would I hear, S.*Ph.* 631; θᾶσσον also often stands for the Positive, Il.2.440, Od.15.201, 16.130, Pi.*P.*4.181, Ar.*Nu.*506, *V.*187, *Ra.*94; οὐ θᾶσσον οἴσεις; i.e. make haste and bring, S.*Tr.*1183, cf. *OT*430; θᾶττον νοήματος *quicker* than thought, X.*Mem.*4.3.13, cf. Ar.*V.*824, etc.; with a Conj., ὅτι θᾶσσον, like ὅτι τάχιστα, Theoc.24.48; ἐπειδὴ θᾶττον συνεσκότασεν *as soon as..*, D.54.5; ἐπειδὰν θ. συνιῇ τις Pl.*Prt.*325c; ὅταν θ. φθέγγηται ὁ κόκκυξ Arist.*HA*563$^{b}$17, cf. 611$^{a}$5; ἐὰν or ἢν θ. *as soon as..*, X.*Cyr.*3.3.20, *An.*6.5.20, Pl.*Alc.*1.105a; ἂν θ. Men. *Pk.*174; εἰ θ. Pl.*Ep.*324b; ὡς θ. Plb.1.66.1, 3.82.1; θ. rarely = *sooner than*, *before*, ἐξήλαυνον μεσημβρίας οὐ πολλῷ τινι θ. Aristid.*Or.*51 (27).13 (cf. τάχιον infr. 3). **3.** the form **ταχίων** [ῑ], neut. ιον, is freq. in late Prose, as Lxx *Wi.*13.9, 1 *Ma.*2.40, Ph.*Bel.*69.14,17, 73.23, Gem.1.20, D.H.6.42, D.S.20.6, J. (v. infr.), Plu.2.240d, *Ev.Jo.* 20.4, Alciphr.3.4; also in Hp.*Mul.*1.1, Men.402.16; but condemned by Phryn.58, Hdn.*Philet.*p.436P.; τὴν ταχίονα τῆς τροφῆς παράθεσιν *earlier*, *sooner*, Gal.19.206:—Adv. τάχιον *earlier*, πλέεται ..περὶ τὸν Σεπτέμβριον μῆνα.., οὐδὲν δὲ κωλύει κἂν τ. *Peripl.M.Rubr.* 24; τ. τῆς ὑποσχέσεως *sooner* than they had promised, *Rev.Ét.Gr.* 6.159 (Iasus); τ. τοῦ παραγγέλματος J.*BJ*4.4.2; εἰς μακρὸν αὐτῶν γῆρας καὶ βίου μῆκος ὅμοιον τοῖς τ. ἐπερχομένων Id.*AJ*1.3.7; ἀποπαύεται οὔτε τ. ἐτῶν τεσσαράκοντα οὔτε βράδιον ἐτῶν πεντήκοντα Sor. 1.20, cf. 48, al.; *formerly*, ἐπεσκεύασαν τὸ παρόχιον,..τ. γενόμενον γυμνάσιον *IGRom.*3.639 (Lycia, ii A.D.), cf. 4.1517 (Sardis), 1632.14 (Philadelphia), 1665.5 (Tira), Keil-Premerstein *Dritter Bericht* p.79 (iii A.D.), *Hermes* 63.229 (Callatis); cf. supr. 2 fin. **II.** Sup.: **1.** the form **ταχύτατος** is rare, ταχύτατα ἅρματα Pi.*O.*1.77; ταχύτατα as Adv., X.*HG*5.1.27 codd., Antiph.87 codd.; but both passages have been corrected. **2.** the usual form is **τάχιστος**, η, ον, used by Hom. only in neut. pl. τάχιστα as Adv., *most quickly*, *most speedily*, ὅττι τάχιστα *as soon as may be*, *as soon as possible*, Il.4.193, 9.659, al.; ὅτι τάχιστα S.*OT*1341 (lyr.), Th.3.31, etc.; so ὅσον τ. A.*Ch.*772, S. *OT*1436, etc.; ᾳ (prob.) τ. Pi.*O.*13.79; ὅπως τ. A.*Ag.*605, S.*OT*1410, Ar.*V*167; ὡς τ. *IG*1$^{2}$.76.23, Hdt.1.210, Th.4.15, E.*Rh.*147, X.*An.*1. 3.14: these are ellipt. phrases, as may be seen from the foll. examples, ὡς δυνατόν ἐστι τάχιστα Pl.*Lg.*710b, X.*Cyr* 5.4.3; ᾗ δυνατὸν τ. Id.*HG*6.3.6; ὡς or ᾗ ἠδύνατο τ. Id.*Cyr.*3.2.14, *An.*1.2.4; ὡς δύναιτο τ. Hdt.1.79; ὡς or ᾗ ἂν δύνωμαι τ. X.*HG*4.1.38, *Cyr.*7.1.9, cf. *IG*1$^{2}$.106.18. **b.** τάχιστα after Particles of Time, *as soon as*, ἐπεὶ (Ion. ἐπεί τε) τάχιστα A.*Pr.*201, Hdt.1.27,75, 7.163, X.*An.*7.2.6, *PCair.Zen.*34.12 (iii B.C.); ἐπειδὴ τ. Pl.*Prt.*310d, Is.9.3, D.27.16, etc.; ἐπεὰν τ. Hdt.4.134, 7.129, 8.144; ἐπὰν τ. X.*An.*4.6.9; ἐπειδὰν τ. Id.*Cyr.*1.3.14, *An.*3.1.9; ὅταν τ. Id.*Cyr.*4.5.33: also ὡς τ. separated by one or more words, ὡς ἡμέρη τ. ἐγεγόνεε Hdt.1.11, cf. 19, 47,65, al., X.*Cyr.*1.3.2, *Mem.*1.2.16, al.; ὡς δὲ τ. ἐξῆλθε..κόρον ἔτεκε *IG*4$^{2}$(1).121.4 (Epid., iv B.C.); ὡς γὰρ τ. εἰσῆλθον Men.*Pk.*287; ὡς ἂν τ. λάβῃς τὴν ἐπιστολήν *PCair.Zen.*241.1 (iii B.C.); but ὡς τ. γὰρ ἀπεδήμησας ib.472.7 (iii B.C.); ὅπως τ. A.*Pr.*230:—the same notion is sometimes expressed by the part., ἀπαλλαγεὶς τάχιστα, = ὡς ἀπηλλάγη τ., Plu.*Dem.*8, cf. 25. **3.** freq. also in Prose, τὴν ταχίστην (in full, τὴν τ. ὁδόν X.*An.*1.2.20, Luc.*Rh.Pr.*4) as Adv., *by the quickest way*, i.e. *most quickly*, Hdt.1.24,73,81,86, Hyp.*Eux.*7, Men. *Pk.*75, Plb.1.33.4, etc. (Cf. Lith. (dial.) *deñgti*, Lett. *diêgt*, both = 'run quickly', Polish *dążyć* 'hurry'.)

**τᾰχυ-στροφάλιγξ** [φᾰ], ιγγος, *quickly turning*, χορείη Nonn.*D.*45. 273, cf. 48.165. **-τεκνος**, ον, *quickly productive of children*, -όταται μίξεις Aët.16.26.

**τᾰχῠτής**, ῆτος, Dor. **-τάς**, ᾶτος, ἡ (on the accent v. Hdn.Gr.1. 83), *quickness*, *swiftness*, of dogs, Od.17.315; ταχυτῆτος ἄεθλα, of the race, Il.23.740; τ. ποδῶν Xenoph.2.1,17, Pi.*O.*1.95; ἥσσων ἐς ταχυτῆτα Hdt.3.102, cf. Anaxag.9, Archyt.1, Pl.*La.*192a, Arist. *Mete.*342$^{a}$5; of persons, *hastiness*, Id.*EN*1150$^{b}$27.

**τᾰχῠ-τόκος**, ον, *quickly bringing forth*, Arist.*Pr.*891$^{b}$25. **-φθίμενος** [ῐ], η, ον, *quickly perishing*, *short-lived*, ἥβη Nonn.*D.*7.31; ἀνεμώνη ib.11.237. **-φῠής**, ές, *healing quickly*, of fractures, Hp. *Mochl.*38, in neut. pl. ταχύφυα (leg. ταχυφυᾶ). **-φωνος**, ον, *fast-speaking*, Adam.2.56, Polem.*Phgn.*2.67. **-χειλής**, ές, *quick-lipped*, αὐλοὶ τ. flutes or pipes *over which the lips run rapidly*, *AP*5.205 (Leon.). **-χειρ**, ὁ, ἡ, gen. χειρος, *quick of hand*, *nimble*, Critias 55. **-χειρία**, ἡ, *quickness of hand*, *dexterity*, Phryn.*PS* p.111 B., Poll.2.148.

**τάων** [ᾱ], Ep. gen. pl. fem. of ὁ, ἡ, τό.

**τᾰωνικός**, ή, όν, *peacock-coloured*, i.e. *shot with various hues*, ἱμάτια Alex.Aphr. *in Mete.*158.33.

**τᾰώνιος** or **-ειος**, ον, *of a peacock*, πτερά Luc.*VH*2.22.

**τάως·** τέως, Κρῆτες, Hsch.: cf. ἄως.

**τᾰώς**, or **τᾰῶς**, ὁ, Ar.*Av.*102,269, Arist.*HA*488$^{b}$24, al.; gen. ταώ or ταῶ Alex.100.14, *Inscr.Délos* 290.4 (iii B.C.); acc. ταών or ταῶν Eup. 36: pl., nom. ταῴ Arist.*HA*564$^{a}$31; ταοί Menodot.ap.Ath.14.655a; gen. ταῶν Antiph.205; acc. ταώς or ταῶς Id.175.5:—but also nom. **ταών** Aesop.397$^{b}$; gen. ταῶνος Arist.*HA*559$^{b}$29, Gal.6.701, *Gp.*14.7. 28; dat. ταῶνι Ar.*Av.*884: pl., nom. ταῶνες v.l. in Arist.*HA*564$^{a}$31; gen. ταώνων Lxx 3*Ki.*10.22; dat. ταῶσι Ar.*Ach.*63; acc. ταῶνας *Com.Adesp.*59, Plu.*Per.*13:—the form ταός is non-existent acc. to Hdn.Gr.ap.Choerob. *in Theod.*1.284 H.:—*peacock*, *Pavo cristatus*, ll. cc.: metaph. of *coxcombs*, Ar.*Ach.* l.c., cf. Stratt.27, Luc.*Nigr.* 13. **II.** name of a gem, Plin.*HN*37.187. **III.** name of a fish, Philostr.*VA*3.1. (Acc. to Trypho ap.Ath.9.397e, the Athenians pronounced it with an aspirate, ταῶς λέγουσιν Ἀθηναῖοι τὴν τελευταίαν συλλαβὴν περισπῶντες καὶ δασύνοντες; the bird was a native of India (ταῶς ἐξ Ἰνδίας Luc.*Nav.*23); hence ταῶς and Lat. *pavus*, *pavo*, perh. also Hebr. *tukkîyîm* 'peacocks', may be borrowed from the same oriental source.)

⊛ **τε**, enclitic Particle, with two main uses (v. infr. A, B).

**A.** as a Conjunction, **I.** τε..τε, *both..and*, joining single words, phrases, clauses, or sentences, the first τε merely pointing forward to the second, ἀνδρῶν τε θεῶν τε Il.1.544; ἀγαθῶν τε κακῶν τε Hes.*Op.*669; δίψῃ τε λιμῷ τε A.*Pers.*491, cf. S.*Aj.*34,35, Ar.*Ach.* 370,375; τήν τε νῆσον τήν τε ἤπειρον Th.4.8, cf. Antipho 2.3.3, Pl. *R.*373b; λυσόμενός τε θύγατρα, φέρων τ' ἀπερείσι' ἄποινα Il.1.13; παῖδά τε σοὶ ἀγέμεν Φοίβῳ θ' ἱερὴν ἑκατόμβην ῥέξαι ib.443; the elements joined by τε..τε are usu. short in Hom., longer in later Gr., e.g. ἐπειδὴ πρόξενοί τέ εἰσιν Ἀθηναίων καὶ εὐεργέται.., ἔν τε τῇ στήλῃ γέγραπται *IG*1$^{2}$.103.7; ἥ τε γὰρ γῆ..εὔυδρός ἐστι, ποταμοί τε δι' αὐτῆς ῥέουσι Hdt.4.47; χρὴ..τούς τε πρεσβυτέρους ὁμοιωθῆναι τοῖς πρὶν ἔργοις, τούς τε νεωτέρους..μὴ αἰσχῦναι κτλ. Th.4.92, cf. Pl.*R.*474c, X.*Cyr.*1.4.25, Is.1.50; τά τε γὰρ ληφθέντα πάντ' ἂν σῴζοιτο οἵ τ' ἀδικήσαντες κατ' ἀξίαν λάβοιεν τὰ ἐπιτίμια Aen.Tact.16.8, cf. *Gp.*2. 49.1, 12.3.2–3; τούτου γὰρ γενομένου..τά τε ἐχφόρια Χρυσέρμῳ δυνήσομαι ἀποδοῦναι, ἐγώ τε ἔσομαι παρὰ σοῦ φιλανθρωπίας τετευχώς *PEnteux.*60.11 (iii B.C.); κλείειν τε τὰ βλέφαρα δεομένων ἐλπιζόντων τε κοιμηθήσεσθαι Gal.16.494, cf. 495,501; this use is common at all times in οὔτε..οὔτε, μήτε..μήτε, εἴτε..εἴτε (qq.v.); τε may be used three or more times, ἔν τ' ἄρα οἱ φῦ χειρί, ἔπος τ' ἔφατ' ἔκ τ' ὀνόμαζεν Od.15.530, cf. Il.1.177, 2.58, A.*Pr.*89 sq., B.17.19 sq., Lys. 19.17, X.*Cyr.*3.3.36:—ἑνδεκάτῃ τε δυωδεκάτῃ τε prob. means *the eleventh or twelfth*, Od.2.374, 4.588:—sts. τε..τε couples alternatives, ἀπόρως εἶχε δοῦναί τε μὴ δοῦναί τε E.*IA*56, cf. *Heracl.*153, *El.*391; hence we find τε..ἤ.., Pl.*Tht.*143c, *Ion* 535d; on ἤ (or ἤ)..τε in Il.2.289 and A.*Eu.*524 (lyr.) v. ἤ I. 3. **2.** the first clause may be negative, the second affirmative, as ἐκκλησίαν τε οὐκ ἐποίει.., τήν τε πόλιν ἐφύλασσε Th.2.22; but οὔτε..τε is more freq., as οὔτε ποσίν εἰμι ταχύς.., γιγνώσκω τε X.*Cyr.*2.3.6 (v. οὔτε II. 4); we also find οὐ.. τε.., as οὐχ ἡσύχαζον.., παρεκάλουν τε τοὺς ξυμμάχους Th.1.67; and μὴ ..τε.., as ἵνα μή τι διαφύγῃ ἡμᾶς, εἴ τέ τι βούλει κτλ. Pl.*Phd.*95e. **3.** τε (*both*) sts. corresponds to a following δέ (*and*), or τε (*and*) to a preceding μέν, e.g. **a.** τε..δὲ.., as κόμισαί τέ με, δὸς δέ μοι ἵππους Il.5. 359, cf. 7.418, S.*OC*367, *Tr.*285, E.*Ph.*1625; ἐσθὰς ἀμφότερόν νιν ἔχεν, ἅ τε..ἐπιχώριος.., ἀμφὶ δὲ παρδαλέᾳ στέγετο Pi.*P.*4.80; διήκουέ τε.., ἔπειτα δὲ καὶ ἐπῄνεσε X.*Cyr.*4.4.3; so with ἅμα δὲ καί.., ὡσαύτως δὲ καί.., Th.1.25, Pl.*Smp.*186e:—so τε.., ἀτὰρ οὖν καί.., Id.*Hp.Ma.* 295e. **b.** μὲν..τε.., ἄνδρα μὲν.., τρεῖς τε κασιγνήτους Il.19.291–3, cf. Od.22.475–6, Pi.*O.*6.88, 7.88, A.*Th.*924, *Ch.*585 (lyr.), S.*Ant.*963 (lyr.), E.*Heracl.*337 codd., *Cyc.*41 (lyr.), Ar.*Nu.*563 (lyr.), Pl.*Phdr.* 266c, *Lg.*927b: v. μέν A. II. 6c. **4.** a single τε (*and*) joins a word, phrase, or (esp. later) clause or sentence to what precedes, τελευτὴν κεφαλήν τε Pl.*Ti.*69a; θνητὰ ἀθάνατά τε ib.c; Ζεῦ ἄλλοι τε θεοί Il.6.476; κύνεσσιν οἰωνοῖσί τε πᾶσι 1.5; ῥίγησέν τ' ἄρ ἔπειτα ἄναξ ἀνδρῶν Ἀγαμέμνων v.l. for δ' ἄρ in 11.254; ἔν τε οὐδὲν κατέστη ἴαμα.., σῶμά τε αὔταρκες ὂν οὐδὲν διεφάνη.., Th.2.51; τά τε ἱερὰ..νεκρῶν πλέα ἦν.. ib.52; νόμοι τε πάντες ξυνεταράχθησαν ibid.; δάκνει σ' ἀδελφὸς ὅ τε θανὼν ἴσως πατήρ E.*El.*242, cf. 253,262, al.; εἴς τε τὰς ἄλλας..ἀθροίζεσθαι Aen.Tact.3.5; τῶν τε ἀρχόντων.. ib.6, cf. 10.8, al.; ὅ τε γραφεὶς κύκλος.. Archim.*Spir.*11 *Def.*7; πρός τε τούτοις φησίν.. *PEnteux.*63.18 (iii B.C.); χωρίς τε τούτων Plb.2.56.13, 61.1, 3.17.7; ταῦτά τ' ἐγίνετο.. Id.2.43.6, cf. 3.70.4; ἀπαιτούμενός τε ὑπ' ἐμοῦ τὰ ἔρια οὐκ ἀποδίδωσί *PEnteux.*2.6, cf. 8.4, al. (iii B.C.); γράψαι Ἀγαθοκλεῖ τῷ ἐπιστάτῃ διασαφῆσαί τε αὐτῷ ib.81.21 (iii B.C.); καθόλου τε.. Arr.*Epict.*1.19.13, cf. 2.2.17; ἀταράχους τήν τε δύναμιν ἀκαθαιρέτους Sor.1.21, cf. 24, al.; ὄξει βαφικῷ στυπτηρίᾳ τε *PHolm.* 1.4, cf. Gem.16.6; χρὴ..λαχάνων ἅπτεσθαι, κοιλίαν τε λύειν *Gp.*1.12. 19, cf. 2.2.2, al.; this τε may be used any number of times, Od.4. 149–150, 14.75,158–9, Men.*Pk.*15,16,20, Hipparch.1.9.8, *Act.Ap.*2. 43,46, 4.13,14, al. **II.** τε..καί.., or τε καί.., *both*..and.., where τε points forward to καί, and usu. need not be translated, e.g. Ἀτρείδης τε ἄναξ ἀνδρῶν καὶ δῖος Ἀχιλλεύς Il.1.7; εἰ δὴ ὁμοῦ πόλεμός τε δαμᾷ καὶ λοιμὸς Ἀχαιούς ib.61; δειλός τε καὶ οὐτιδανὸς καλεοίμην ib. 293; ζωόν τε καὶ ἀρτεμέα 7.308, cf. 327,338, al.; τῆς τε γῆς ἐούσης ἐπιτηδέης καὶ τῶν ποταμῶν ἐόντων σφι συμμάχων Hdt.4.47; βούλεταί τε καὶ ἐπίσταται Th.2.35; ὁ φύς τε καὶ τραφεὶς Pl.*R.*396c; βάσιν τε γὰρ πάλιν τὴν αὐτὴν ἔχουσι τὴν ZB καί.. Euc.1.47; sts. the elements joined by τε..καί.. are joined in order to be compared or contrasted rather than simply joined, κάκιστος νῦν τε καὶ πάλαι δοκεῖ S.*Ant.* 181; μεσαμβρίη τέ ἐστι καὶ τὸ κάρτα γίνεται ψυχρόν Hdt.4.181; ἔτυχόν τε ὕσταται ἐξαναχθεῖσαι καί κως κατεῖδον Id.7.194; ἐπαύσατό τε ὁ ἄνεμος καὶ τὸ κῦμα ἔστρωτο ib.193; ταὐτὰ..νῦν τε καὶ τότε Ar.*Av.* 24; χωρὶς τό τ' εἰπεῖν πολλὰ καὶ τὰ καίρια S.*OC*808; ὅσον τό τ' ἄρχειν καὶ τὸ δουλεύειν δίχα A.*Pr.*927; sts. (like τε..τε) even used of alternatives, διάνδιχα μερμήριξεν, ἵππους τε στρέψαι καὶ ἐναντίβιον μαχέσασθαι Il.8.168; ἐν δίκᾳ τε καὶ παρὰ δίκαν Pi.*O.*2.16; θεοῦ τε.. θέλοντος καὶ μὴ θέλοντος A.*Th.*427; πείσας τε..καὶ μὴ τυχών Th.3. 42:—on οἵ τε ἄλλοι καί.., e.g. τοῖς τε ἄλλοις ἅπασι καὶ Λακεδαιμονίοις Isoc.12.249, and ἄλλως τε καί.., v. ἄλλος II. 6, ἄλλως I. 3. **2.** in this sense τ' ἠδέ is only Ep., σκῆπτρόν τ' ἠδὲ θέμιστας Il.9. 99, cf. 1.400, al.; also τε.., ἰδέ, χαλκόν τε ἰδὲ λόφον 6.469, cf. 8. 162. **3.** καί..τε, *both..and..*, is occasionally found, as καὶ μητέρα πατέρα τ' E.*Alc.*646. **b.** καί..τε perh. means *and..also* in καὶ ναυτικῷ τε ἅμα Th.1.9; καὶ πρός τε τοὺς Ῥηγίνους Id.6.44; καὶ αὐτός τε Id.8.68; v. infr. c. 10. **4.** τε..τε or τε..καὶ.. sts. join elements which are not syntactically parallel, esp. a part. and a finite verb, ἰοῖσίν τε τιτυσκόμενοι λάεσσί τ' ἔβαλλον (for βάλλοντες) Il.3.80; ἄλλα τε ἐπιφραζόμενος καὶ δὴ καὶ ἐπεπόμφεε Hdt.1.85; ἄλλῳ τε τρόπῳ πειράζοντες καὶ μηχανὴν προσήγαγον Th.4.100; τῆς τε ὥρας ..ταύτης οὔσης.., καὶ τὸ χωρίον..χαλεπὸν ἦν Id.7.47, cf. 4.85, 8.81, 95. **5.** the copulative τε becomes rare in later Gr.; it is found about 340 times in Lxx, mostly in the Pentateuch and 1-4 *Ma.*, only 3 times in *Ps.*; in the *NT* it is found about 150 times in *Act. Ap.*, 20 times in *Ep.Hebr.*, and very rarely in the other books.

**B.** In Ep. (more rarely in other dactylic verse, v. infr. II) τε stands in general or frequentative statements or in statements of what is well known; such statements are freq. made as justifications of a preceding particular statement or of a preceding exhortation to a particular person or persons; the sense of τε thus approaches that of τοι (cf. τοι and τε in Od.2.276-7, and cf. Il.13.115 with 15.203); although associated with numerous particles and other words of particular types (v. infr.) its meaning remains independent of these and applies to the whole sentence in which it stands: αἶψά τε φυλόπιδος πέλεται κόρος ἀνθρώποισιν Il.19.221; οὐ γάρ τ' αἶψα θεῶν τρέπεται νόος αἰὲν ἐόντων Od.3.147; θεοὶ δέ τε πάντα ἴσασιν 4.379, cf. 5.79,447, 10.306, 17.485, Il.9.497, 16.688, 17.176, 21.264; ξυνὸς Ἐνυάλιος καί τε κτανέοντα κατέκτα 18.309, cf. Od.11.537, Il.24.526; ἦ τ' ἔβλητ' ἦ τ' ἔβαλ' ἄλλον 11.410; οὐ μὲν γάρ τε κακὸν βασιλευέμεν Od.1.392; οἱ φύλλοισιν ἐοικότες ἄλλοτε μέν τε ζαφλεγέες τελέθουσιν..ἄλλοτε δὲ.. Il.21.464; ἄλλος γάρ τ' ἄλλοισιν ἀνὴρ ἐπιτέρπεται ἔργοις Od.14.228, cf. 8.169,170, 15.400; τοῦ γάρ τε ξεῖνος μιμνήσκεται ἤματα πάντα, ἀνδρὸς ξεινοδόκου, ὅς κεν φιλότητα παράσχῃ ib.54, cf. 17.322; ῥεχθὲν δέ τε νήπιος ἔγνω Il.17.32; παθὼν δέ τε νήπιος ἔγνω Hes.*Op.*218; αἰεὶ γάρ τε νεώτεροι ἀφραδέουσιν Od.7.294; δύσζηλοι γάρ τ' εἰμὲν ἐπὶ χθονὶ φῦλ' ἀνθρώπων ib.307; τοῦ δέ τε πολλοὶ ἐπαυρίσκοντ' ἄνθρωποι, καί τε πολέας ἐσάωσε Il.13.733-4; τοῦ μὲν γάρ τε κακοῦ τρέπεται χρὼς ἄλλυδις ἄλλῃ, ἐν δέ τέ οἱ κραδίη στέρνοισι πατάσσει.., πάταγος δέ τε γίγνετ' ὀδόντων ib.279-83; ὀλίγη δέ τ' ἀνάπνευσις πολέμοιο 18.201; νέῳ δέ τε πάντ' ἐπέοικεν..κεῖσθαι 22.71; κατέλεξεν ἅπαντα κήδε' ὅσ' ἀνθρώποισι πέλει, τῶν ἄστυ ἁλώῃ· ἄνδρας μὲν κτείνουσι, πόλιν δέ τε πῦρ ἀμαθύνει, τέκνα δέ τ' ἄλλοι ἄγουσι, βαθυζώνους τε γυναῖκας 9.592-4, cf. 22.492,495,499; νεμεσσῶμαί γε μὲν οὐδέν· καὶ γάρ τίς τ' ἀλλοῖον ὀδύρεται ἄνδρ' ὀλέσασα..ἢ Ὀδυσῆ' Od.19.265; σχέτλιε, καὶ μέν τίς τε χερείονι πείθεθ' ἑταίρῳ.., αὐτὰρ ἐγὼ θεός εἰμι 20.45, cf. 23.118, Il.2.292, 9.632; νῦν δὲ μνησώμεθα δόρπου· καὶ γάρ τ' ἠΰκομος Νιόβη ἐμνήσατο σίτου κτλ. 24.602 (where a general inference is implied); ὃν Βριάρεων καλέουσι θεοί, ἄνδρες δέ τε πάντες Αἰγαίων' 1.403, cf. 2.814, 5.306, 10.258, 14.290; sts. of repeated action by particular persons, ἄλλοτε μέν τε γόῳ φρένα τέρπομαι Od.4.102; οὐ μὰ γὰρ Ἀπόλλωνα Διὶ φίλον, ᾧ τε σύ, Κάλχαν, εὐχόμενος..θεοπροπίας ἀναφαίνεις Il.1.86; ἡ δὲ..μ' αἰεὶ..νεικεῖ, καί τέ μέ φησι μάχῃ Τρώεσσιν ἀρήγειν ib.521; μήτηρ γάρ τέ μέ φησι θεά, Θέτις ἀργυρόπεζα, διχθαδίας κῆρας φερέμεν θανάτοιο τέλοσδε 9.410. **2.** in exhortations addressed to an individual, a subsidiary sentence or relative clause in which he is reminded of his special or characteristic sphere of activity is marked by τε, e.g. Ἑρμεία, σοὶ γάρ τε μάλιστά γε φίλτατόν ἐστιν ἀνδρὶ ἑταιρίσσαι καί τ' ἔκλυες ᾧ κ' ἐθέλῃσθα, βάσκ' ἴθι.. Il.24.334; Ἀτρεΐδη, σοὶ γάρ τε μάλιστά γε λαὸς Ἀχαιῶν πείσονται μύθοισι.., νῦν δ' ἀπὸ πυρκαϊῆς σκέδασον.. 23.156; δεῦρο δὴ ὄρσο, γρηῦ.., ἥ τε γυναικῶν δμῳάων σκοπός ἐσσι.., ἔρχεο Od.22.395, cf. Il.17.249. **3.** similarly in general and frequentative statements consisting of two clauses (one of which may be a relative clause, freq. containing the subj. or opt.), in which the fulfilment of the condition stated in the subsidiary or subordinate clause is declared to be generally or always followed by the result stated in the principal clause, either or both clauses may contain τε: **a.** the principal clause alone contains τε, ὅς κε θεοῖς ἐπιπείθηται, μάλα τ' ἔκλυον αὐτοῦ Il.1.218; ὃς δ' ἂν ἀμύμων αὐτὸς ἔῃ καὶ ἀμύμονα εἰδῇ, τοῦ μέν τε κλέος εὐρὺ διὰ ξεῖνοι φορέουσι πάντας ἐπ' ἀνθρώπους, πολλοί τέ μιν ἐσθλὸν ἔειπον Od.19.333; εἴ περ γὰρ θυμῷ γε μενοινάᾳ πολεμίζειν, ἀλλά τε λάθρῃ γυῖα βαρύνεται.., βλάβεται δέ τε γούνατ' ἰόντι Il.19.165-6; ᾧ μέν κ' ἀμμείξας δώῃ Ζεὺς τερπικέραυνος, ἄλλοτε μέν τε κακῷ ὅ γε κύρεται ἄλλοτε δ' ἐσθλῷ 24.530. **b.** the subordinate clause alone contains τε, λάζετο δ' ἔγχος..τῷ δάμνησι στίχας ἀνδρῶν ἡρώων οἷσίν τε κοτέσσεται ὀβριμοπάτρη 5.747; ῥεῖα δ' ἀρίγνωτος γόνος ἀνέρος ᾧ τε Κρονίων ὄλβον ἐπικλώσῃ Od.4.207; ἀντί νυ πολλῶν λαῶν ἐστιν ἀνὴρ ὅν τε Ζεὺς κῆρι φιλήσῃ Il.9.117, cf. 7.298, Od.6.287, 7.74, 8.547, 18.276; with opt., ἀλλὰ πολὺ πρώτιστος.. ἕλεσκον ἀνδρῶν δυσμενέων ὅ τέ μοι εἴξειε πόδεσσι 14.221: it is prob. that τε has been replaced by κε in the text of Hom. in Il.1.218, 9.510 (cf. 508), and some other passages in which κε seems to be used, exceptionally, in general relative clauses. **c.** both clauses contain τε, ὃς μέν τ' αἰδέσεται κούρας Διὸς ἇσσον ἰούσας, τὸν δὲ μέγ' ὤνησαν καί τ' ἔκλυον εὐχομένοιο Il.9.508-9; εἴ περ γάρ τε χόλον γε καὶ αὐτῆμαρ καταπέψῃ, ἀλλά τε καὶ μετόπισθεν ἔχει κότον 1.82-3. **4.** in the subordinate clause of a collective sentence, in which the principal clause states something to be true of all those (i.e. each individual) to whom the predicate of the subordinate clause applies, ὑπόσχωμαι..κτήματα..πάντα μάλ' ὅσσα τ' Ἀλέξανδρος ..ἠγάγετο Τροίηνδ'..δωσέμεν Il.22.115; πάντων ὅσσα τε γαῖαν ἔπι πνείει τε καὶ ἕρπει 17.447, cf. Od.18.131, Il.19.105; βάλλειν ἄγρια πάντα τά τε τρέφει οὔρεσιν ὕλη 5.52, cf. 18.485. **5.** in relative clauses (and in parenthetic principal clauses) which indicate what is customary, ἐπεὶ οὐχ ἱερήϊον οὐδὲ βοείην ἀρνύσθην, ἅ τε ποσσὶν ἀέθλια γίγνεται ἀνδρῶν which are the *usual* prizes.., Il.22.160; ἔργ' ἀνδρῶν τε θεῶν τε, τά τε κλείουσιν ἀοιδοί Od.1.338, cf. 3.435, 4.85, 13.410, 14.226, 17.423, Il.5.332; κύματος ἐξαναδύς, τά τ' ἐρεύγεται ἠπειρόνδε Od.5.438; μολπή τ' ὀρχηστύς τε, τὰ γάρ τ' ἀναθήματα δαιτός 1.152: similarly in clauses with οἷά τε (πολλά), κῆτος ἐπισσεύῃ μέγα δαίμων ἐξ ἁλός, οἷά τε πολλὰ τρέφει..Ἀμφιτρίτη 5.422; οὐ γάρ σ' οὐδέ.. δαήμονι φωτὶ ἐΐσκω ἄθλων, οἷά τε πολλὰ μετ' ἀνθρώποισι πέλονται 8.160, cf. 11.364, 14.63, 15.324,379. **6.** in relative clauses indicating what is true of all persons or things denoted by the same word, οὐ γάρ τις νήσων ἱππήλατος οὐδ' εὐλείμων αἵ θ' ἁλὶ κεκλίαται no one of the islands which lie in the sea (as all islands do, i.e. no island at all), Od.4.608; ἡμίονον..ἥ τ' ἀλγίστη δαμάσασθαι Il.23.655; ἐσθλὸς ἐὼν γαμβρὸς ἢ πενθερός, οἵ τε μάλιστα κήδιστοι τελέθουσι Od.8.582; αἰετοῦ οἴματ' ἔχων..ὅς θ' ἅμα κάρτιστός τε καὶ ὤκιστος πετεηνῶν Il.21.252, cf. 24.294; οὐδέ μιν εἰσοιχνεῦσι κυνηγέται, οἵ τε καθ' ὕλην ἄλγεα πάσχουσιν Od.9.120; δικασπόλοι, οἵ τε θέμιστας πρὸς Διὸς εἰρύαται Il.1.238, cf. Od.5.67,101, Il.1.279, 19.31, 24.415; οἶνός σε τρώει.., ὅς τε καὶ ἄλλους βλάπτει Od.21.293, cf. 14.464; πάρφασις, ἥ τ' ἔκλεψε νόον πύκα περ φρονεόντων Il.14.217; οἰκωφελίη, ἥ τε τρέφει ἀγλαὰ τέκνα Od.14.223. **7.** when the antecedent is a definite group of gods or men, the relative clause with τε indicates an essential characteristic of the antecedent, Ἐρινύες, αἵ θ' ὑπὸ γαῖαν ἀνθρώπους τείνυνται Il.19.259; Σειρῆνας.., αἵ ῥά τε πάντας ἀνθρώπους θέλγουσιν Od.12.39; Φαίηκές μ' ἄγαγον ναυσίκλυτοι, οἵ τε καὶ ἄλλους ἀνθρώπους πέμπουσιν 16.227, cf. 20.187; νυμφάων αἵ τ' ἄλσεα καλὰ νέμονται καὶ πηγὰς ποταμῶν Il.20.8; Λωτοφάγων, οἵ τ' ἄνθινον εἶδαρ ἔδουσι Od.9.84: similarly when the antecedent is an individual person (incl. god) or thing, the relative clause with τε indicates one of his or its general or essential characteristics or aspects, οὐ μὰ Ζῆν' ὅς τίς τε θεῶν ὕπατος καὶ ἄριστος Il.23.43, cf. 2.669, Od.5.4; Ἑρμείαο ἕκητι διακτόρου, ὅς ῥά τε πάντων ἀνθρώπων ἔργοισι χάριν καὶ κῦδος ὀπάζει 15.319; Λάμπον καὶ Φαέθονθ', οἵ τ' Ἠῶ πῶλοι ἄγουσι 23.246; Τειρεσίαο μάντιος ἀλαοῦ, τοῦ τε φρένες ἔμπεδοί εἰσι 10.493; τεύχεα δύνεις ἀνδρὸς ἀριστῆος, τόν τε τρομέουσι καὶ ἄλλοι Il.17.203, cf. 7.112; κεῖται ἀνὴρ ὅν τ' (v.l. ὃν) ἶσον ἐτίομεν Ἕκτορι δίῳ, Αἰνείας 5.467; the relative clause sts. indicates what is customary, οὐδέ σε λήθω τιμῆς ἧς τέ μ' ἔοικε τετιμῆσθαι μετ' Ἀχαιοῖς 23.649; ἔνθα δ' ἀνὴρ ἐνίαυε πελώριος, ὅς ῥά τε μῆλα οἶος ποιμαίνεσκε Od.9.187; τῶν πάντων οὐ τόσσον ὀδύρομαι..ὡς ἑνός, ὅς τέ μοι ὕπνον ἀπεχθαίρει καὶ ἐδωδὴν μνωομένῳ 4.105; σῆς ἀλόχου..ἥ τέ τοι αὔτως ἧσται ἐνὶ μεγάροισιν 13.336; καὶ κήρυκα Μέδοντα σαώσομεν, ὅς τέ μευ αἰεὶ..κηδέσκετο 22.357, cf. 346. **8.** τε is used in descriptions of particular places or things when attention is called to their peculiar or characteristic features, or their position, e.g. Λιβύην, ἵνα τ' ἄρνες ἄφαρ κεραοὶ τελέθουσι Od.4.85; ἔνθα δέ τ' ὄρνιθες τανυσίπτεροι εὐνάζοντο 5.65, cf. 9.124, 13.99,100,107,109,244; ἓξ δέ τέ οἱ (sc. Σκύλλῃ) δειραὶ περιμήκεες 12.90, cf. 93,99,105; ἐν δέ τε Γοργείη κεφαλή (in Athena's *αἰγίς*) Il.5.741; χαλεπὸν δέ τ' ὀρύσσειν ἀνδράσι γε θνητοῖσι (sc. μῶλυ) Od.10.305; δοιαὶ γάρ τε πύλαι ἀμενηνῶν εἰσὶν ὀνείρων 19.562; sts. τε draws attention to a well-known custom or permanent feature, ἀρξάμενοι τοῦ χώρου, ὅθεν τέ περ οἰνοχοεύει 21.142; ἦ μένετε Τρῶας σχεδὸν ἐλθέμεν, ἔνθα τε νῆες εἰρύατ' εὔπρυμνοι Il.4.247, cf. Od.6.266; ἐν ποταμῷ, ὅθι τ' ἀρδμὸς ἔην πάντεσσι βοτοῖσιν Il.18.521, cf. Od.14.353. **9.** a part of the anatomy is defined by a clause (containing τε) which indicates a feature which universally belongs to it, κατ' ἰσχίον, ἔνθα τε μηρὸς ἰσχίῳ ἐνστρέφεται Il.5.305, cf. 8.83, 13.547, 16.481, 20.478; similarly a point of time is defined, ὥρῃ ἐν εἰαρινῇ, ὅτε τ' ἤματα μακρὰ πέλονται Od.18.367. **10.** τε is used in relative clauses which define a measurement of a particular thing or action by reference to the measurement (in general) of some thing or action well known in daily life, γεφύρωσεν δὲ κέλευθον μακρὴν ἠδ' εὐρεῖαν, ὅσον τ' ἐπὶ δουρὸς ἐρωὴ γίγνεται Il.15.358; τοῦ δ' ἤτοι κλέος ἔσται ὅσον τ' ἐπικίδναται ἠώς 7.451; ὅτε τόσσον ἀπῆν ὅσσον τε γέγωνε βοήσας Od.9.473, cf. 3.321, al.; more rarely the definition is by reference to the measurement of a particular thing or action, ἤσθιε..ἕως ὅ τ' ἀοιδὸς ἐνὶ μεγάροισιν ἄειδεν (s.v.l.) 17.358; ἦ τις δὴ τέτληκε τόσα φρεσίν, ὅσσα τ' ἐγώ περ 19.347. **11.** the freq. use of τε B in similes is to be explained under one or other of the foregoing heads, e.g. when reference is made to generally known kinds of things or natural phenomena, to human experience in daily life, or to well-known phenomena of the animal world, Il.2.456,459,463,468,470,471,474,481, 3.23-5,33, 11.415-7, al.; or when universal characteristics of gods, men, animals, etc., are indicated by relative clauses introduced by ὅς τε, ὅς ῥά τε, etc., 3.61,151,198, al.; or by ὥς τε, ἠΰτε, ὥς τίς τε, etc., e.g. 5.136, 17.133, Od.4.535, ὡς εἴ τε 9.314, 14.254, etc. **II.** in post-Hom. Gr. this use of τε is more restricted; outside of Ep. and other early dactylic verse (Hes.*Op.*30,214,233, al., Xenoph.13.3, Thgn.148,359, etc.) it is not found except with relatives, and with these it has scarcely any discernible sense, so that ὅς τε in Lyr. and Trag. is for the most part only = ὅς, e.g. (possibly generalizing) Μοῖρ', ἅ τε πατρώϊον τῶνδ' ἔχει τὸν εὔφρονα πότμον Pi.*O.*2.35, cf. 14.2, A.*Eu.*1024, E.*Hec.*445 (lyr.), etc. (v. ὥστε); without generalizing force, Pi.*N.*9.9, A.*Pers.*297, *Ch.*615, etc.; Hdt. has τά πέρ τε 1.74, ὅκως τε 2.108 codd., ὅσον τε (without a verb, as in Od.9.325, al.) 1.126, 2.96, 3.5, al., οἷά τε 1.93 codd. (adverbially 2.175, 5.11): in Att. Prose and Com. even these uses disappear and we find only a few phrases, as ἅτε, ὥστε, ἐφ' ᾧτε, οἷός τε; in later Gr. we find exceptionally ἔνθεν τε Hp.*Ep.*17; ἀφ' οὗ τε *UPZ*62.8 (ii B.C.); ἀπ' οὗ τε *PCair.Zen.*291.3 (iii B.C.); οἵ τε *GDI*215.23 (Erythrae, ii B.C.); ἥ τ' *PMag.Par.*1.2962; ὅσον τε ὀκτὼ στάδια Paus.6.26.1; καὶ ἔστιν ἔτη Μαντικὰ ὁπόσα τε (= *which*) ἐπελεξάμεθα καὶ ἡμεῖς Id.9.31.5; οἷόν τε καὶ ἐπὶ τῆς "κύων" φωνῆς θεωροῦμεν S.E.*M.*11.28.

C. in Hom. τε is also (but less freq.) used in conjunction with other particles in contexts (mainly particular statements) such as the following: 1. in assurances, statements on oath, and threats, σχέτλιος, ἦ τ' ἐκέλευον ἀπωσάμενον δήϊον πῦρ ἂψ ἐπὶ νῆας ἴμεν Il.18.13; ἐξ αὖ νῦν ἔφυγες θάνατον, κύον· ἦ τέ τοι ἄγχι ἦλθε κακόν 11.362; ἦ τε is similarly used in 11.391, 17.171,236, Od.24.28,311, al.; ἦ τ' ἄν in Il.12.69, al.; γάρ τε (s.v.l.) in οὐ γάρ τ' οἶδα 6.367, cf. Od.10.190; νύ τε in 1.60,347 (but τ' more prob. = τοι, v. σύ); δέ τε in ἀγορῇ δέ τ' ἀμείνονές εἰσι καὶ ἄλλοι Il.18.106; σὲ δέ τ' ἐνθάδε γῦπες ἔδονται 16.836; μέν τε in σφῶ μέν τε σαώσετε λαὸν Ἀχαιῶν 13.47, cf. 4.341; εἴ πέρ τε in οὔ τοι ἔτι δηρόν γε φίλης ἀπὸ πατρίδος αἴης ἔσσεται, οὐδ' εἴ πέρ τε σιδήρεα δέσματ' ἔχῃσιν Od.1.204, cf. 188, Il.12.223,245. 2. also in commands, warnings, and admonitions, σίγα, μή τίς τ' ἄλλος Ἀχαιῶν τοῦτον ἀκούσῃ μῦθον Il.14.90, cf. Od.19.486; ὡς ἄγαγ' ὡς μήτ' ἄρ τις ἴδῃ μήτ' ἄρ τε νοήσῃ Il.24.337; τούσδε τ' (v.l. δ') ἐὰν 16.96 (nisi leg. τούσδ' ἔτ'); δὸς δέ τέ μ' ἄνδρα ἑλεῖν 5.118; μηδέ τ' ἐρώει (nisi leg. μηδ' ἔτ') 2.179, 22.185. 3. also in passionate utterances, in clauses which indicate the cause of the speaker's passion or a circumstance which might have caused others to behave more considerately towards him, ὤ μοι ἐγὼ δειλή.. ἥ τ'.. τὸν μὲν.. θρέψασα.. ἐπιπροέηκα Il.18.55; σχέτλιοί ἐστε, θεοί, ζηλήμονες ἔξοχον ἄλλων, οἵ τε θεαῖς ἀγάασθε.. ἤν τίς τε.. Od.5.119,120, cf. 21.87, Il.15.468, 17.174; ἡμεῖς δ' αὖ μαχόμεσθ', οἵ πέρ τ' ἐπίκουροι ἔνειμεν and we, who (*mark you*) are only allies (not γαμβροί and κασίγνητοι), are fighting, 5.477; τρεῖς γάρ τ' ἐκ Κρόνου εἰμὲν ἀδελφεοί for we, *let me tell you*, are three brothers, sons of Cronos (and Zeus has no prior title to power), 15.187; ποῖόν σε ἔπος φύγεν ἕρκος ὀδόντων δεινόν τ' ἀργαλέον τε· νεμεσσῶμαι δέ τ' ἀκούων Od.21.169; οὐ μὴν οἱ τό γε κάλλιον οὐδέ τ' ἄμεινον Il.24.52. 4. in descriptions of particular events and things where there is no general reference, κνίση μὲν ἀνήνοθεν, ἐν δέ τε φόρμιγξ ἠπύει Od.17.270; ὥς (= *so*) τέ μοι ὑβρίζοντες ὑπερφιάλως δοκέουσιν δαίνυσθαι κατὰ δῶμα 1.227; τοὺς μέν τ' ἰητροὶ πολυφάρμακοι ἀμφιπένονται.. σὺ δ' ἀμήχανος ἔπλευ, Ἀχιλλεῦ Il.16.28; πόλιν πέρι δινηθήτην καρπαλίμοισι πόδεσσι, θεοὶ δέ τε πάντες ὁρῶντο dub.l. in 22.166; εὗρε δ' ἐνὶ σπῆϊ γλαφυρῷ Θέτιν, ἀμφὶ δέ τ' ἄλλαι εἵαθ' ὁμηγερέες ἅλιαι θεαί 24.83 (s.v.l.); ἐν δέ τε φάρμακον ἧκε Od.10.317; νῶϊ δέ τ' ἄψορροι κίομεν Il.21.456; πολλὰς γὰρ δὴ νύκτας.. ἄεσα καί τ' ἀνέμεινα.. Ἠῶ Od.19.342; δέελον δ' ἐπὶ σῆμά τ' ἔθηκε Il.10.466; ἐν δέ τε οἶνον κρητῆρσιν κερόωντο Od.20.252; so with οὐδέ τ' (nisi leg. οὐδ' ἔτ'), τὸν καὶ ὑπέδδεισαν μάκαρες θεοὶ οὐδέ τ' ἔδησαν Il.1.406; οὐδέ τ' ἔληγε μέγας θεός, ὦρτο δ' ἐπ' αὐτόν 21.248; οὐδέ τ' ἄειρε 23.730; οὐδέ τ' ἔασεν 11.437, 21.596, cf. 15.709. 5. ὅτε τε (*when*) freq. introduces a temporal clause defining a point of time in the past by means of a well-known event which occurred then, ἦ οὐ μέμνῃ ὅτε τ' ἐκρέμω ὑψόθεν; Il.15.18; ὅτε τε Κρόνον.. Ζεὺς γαίης νέρθε καθεῖσε 14.203; ἤματι τῷ ὅτε τ' ἦλθον Ἀμαζόνες 3.189 (but ἤματι τῷ ὅτε τε is general in 13.335; so also ὅτε πέρ τε.. κέρωνται in 4.259); ὅτε τ' ἤλυθε νόσφιν Ἀχαιῶν ἄγγελος ἐς Θήβας 5.803, cf. 10.286, 22.102, Od.7.323, 18.257. 6. in ὅ τε (*that* or *because*) the τε has no observable meaning, χωόμενος ὅ τ' ἄριστον Ἀχαιῶν οὐδὲν ἔτισας Il.1.244, cf. 412, 4.32, 6.126, Od.5.357, al. 7. ἐπεί τε = ἐπεί (*when*) is rare in Hom., ἐπεί τ' ἐνόησε Il.12.393, cf. ἐπείτε. 8. where τ' ἄρ occurs in questions, e.g. πῇ τ' ἄρ μέμονας καταδῦναι ὅμιλον; Il.13.307, cf. 1.8, 18.188, al., ταρ (q.v.) should prob. be read, since ἄρ(α) usu. precedes a τε which is not copulative; so perh. ταρα should be read for τ' ἄρα in Od.1.346. 9. in ἢ θέμις ἐστίν.. ἤ τ' ἀνδρῶν ἤ τε γυναικῶν Il.9.276, it is not clear whether τε is copulative (τε A) or generalizing (τε B) or neither (τε C); ἤ is prob. = ἤ (accented as in ἤτοι); ἤ τ' ἀλκῆς ἤ τε φόβοιο is dub. l. in 17.42; ἤ τ' = *or* is found in 19.148, = *than* in Od.16.216. 10. Rarer and later uses: a. *also*, esp. with ἄλλος, Ἑρμεία, σὺ γὰρ αὖτε τά τ' ἄλλα περ ἄγγελός ἐσσι Od.5.29, cf. 17.273, Il.23.483; ἐπεὶ τά τε ἄλλα πράττουσιν καλῶς, ἀναθεῖναι αὐτοὺς καὶ στήλην *IG*2².1298.9, cf. Lycurg.100 (s.v.l.); ἐκομισάμην τὸ παρὰ σοῦ ἐπιστόλιον, ἐν ᾧ ὑπέγραψάς μοι τήν τε παρὰ Ζήνωνος πρὸς Ἰεδδοῦν γεγραμμένην *PCair.Zen.*18.1 (iii B.C.); εἰ οὖν περὶ τούτων ἐπιστροφὴν μὴ ποιήσει, οἵ τε λοιποί μοι τὰς χεῖρας προσοίσουσιν (-σωσιν Pap.) *PPetr.*2 p.10 (iii B.C.); τῶν δὲ παρὰ ταῦτα ποιησόντων τά τε κτήνη ὑπὸ στέρεσιν ἀχθήσεσθαι πρὸς τὰ ἐκφόρια *PTeb.*27.74 (ii B.C.); v. supr. A. II. 3b. b. with ὅδε, adding a slight emphasis to the preceding word, εἰ δὴ τήνδε τε γαῖαν ἀνείρεαι Od.13.238, cf. 15.484. c. τε γάρ rarely = καὶ γάρ or γάρ, Arist.*APo.*75ᵇ41, *de An.*405ᵃ4, *PA*661ᵇ28, *Pol.*1318ᵇ33, 1333ᵃ2; ἐάν τε γάρ for *even* if, 2*Ep.Cor.*10.8; τήν τε γὰρ ἐπιθυμίαν οὐκ ᾔδειν for I had not known *even* lust, *Ep.Rom.*7.7.

D. Position of τε: 1. in signf. A, as an enclitic, it stands second word in the sentence, clause, or phrase, regardless of the meaning: ἐγγύθι τε Πριάμοιο καὶ Ἕκτορος near *both* Priam and Hector, Il.6.317; ἡμέτεραί τ' ἄλοχοι καὶ νήπια τέκνα 2.136, cf. 4.505, 7.295; αἰεί τε δὴ νηλὴς σὺ καὶ θράσους πλέως A.*Pr.*42 codd., cf. 291 (anap.); ἄνευ τε δόλου καὶ ἀπάτης Hdt.1.69; ὑπέρ τε σοῦ καὶ τῆς ἀδελφῆς *PEnteux.*6.6 (iii B.C.); τοῖς τε πόνοις καὶ μαθήμασι Pl.*R.*537a, cf. *Ti.*70b; hence in E.*Or.*897 πόλεος must be taken with what precedes (Porson ad loc.): but article + noun, preposition + noun are freq. regarded as forming a unity indivisible by τε, τοῖς κτανοῦσί τε A.*Ch.*41 (lyr.); πρὸς βίαν τε Id.*Pr.*210; also the order is freq. determined by the meaning, τε being placed immediately after the word (or first word of a phrase or clause) which it joins to what precedes or to what follows, πατὴρ ἀνδρῶν τε θεῶν τε Il.1.544; ἔξω δόμων τε καὶ πάτρας A.*Pr.*665; the copulative or preparatory τε precedes many other particles, e.g. τε γάρ, τ' ἄρα, τέ τις. 2. τε is enclitic in signfs. B, C also, and stands early in its sentence, clause, or phrase (v. supr.), but many particles which follow τε in signf. A precede it in signfs. B, C, e.g. in signfs. B, C we have δέ τε, μέν τε, γάρ τε, ἀλλά τε, δ' ἄρα τε, ὅς ῥά τε, οὔτ' ἄρ τε, καὶ γάρ τίς τε, ὅς τίς τε, καί τε.

E. Etymology: signf. A is found also in Skt. *ca*, Lat. *-que*; for signfs. B and C cf. Skt. *ca* in *yáḥ káś ca* 'whosoever (with following verb)', Lat. *-que* in *quisque, ubique, plerique, usque, neque, nec* (= *non* in *necopinans*, etc.), Goth. *ni-h* 'not' (also 'and not'), Lat. *namque* (= *nam*).

**τέ**, Dor. acc. sg. of σύ (q.v.).

**τέ'**, apostroph. for τεά, neut. pl. of τεός, Il.5.237.

**τεαρσιηκις**, obscure word (perh. a pr. n.) in *Ostr.Strassb.*583 i 3, al. (iii B.C.).

**τεαύτα**, v. τοιοῦτος.

**τεβεις**, dub. l. in *PAmh.*2.39.7 (ii B.C.).

**τεγγύρος**· ὄρνεον ποιόν, Hsch.

**τέγγω**, Alc.39, etc.: fut. τέγξω Pi.*O.*4.19, E.*Supp.*979 (lyr.): aor. ἔτεγξα B.5.157, A.*Pr.*402 (lyr.), Hp.*Nat.Mul.*35:— Pass., aor. ἐτέγχθην S.*Ph.*1456 (anap.), Pl.*Lg.*880e:—*wet, moisten*, τέγγε πλεύμονας οἴνῳ Alc.l.c.; ἀκρήτῳ πνεύμονα τεγγόμενος Eratosth.25; οἴνῳ πνεύμονα τέγγε Poet.ap.Suid. s.v. τέγγε; τέγγει γὰρ [τὸ ἔλαιον] τὸν ξηρὸν χρῶτα Gal.6.229, cf. 366,560, 15.714; esp. of internal moistening by liquid food, opp. βρέχω (moisten on the surface), Id.10.808, 12.186 (the word is not freq. in Prose); φάρεα ποταμίᾳ δρόσῳ τ., so as to wash them, E.*Hipp.*127 (lyr.); ἐν θαλάττῃ τ. τοὺς πόδας Pl.*Lg.*866d:—in Trag. and Lyr. freq. of tears, δάκρυσι κόλπους τέγγουσι A.*Pers.*540 (anap.); ἀπ' ὄσσων παρειὰν νοτίοις ἔτεγξα παγαῖς Id.*Pr.*402 (lyr.); ὄμμα δάκρυσιν τ. E.*Supp.*21, cf. *IA*496; and simply, τ. παρειάν, ὄμμα, S.*Ant.*530 (anap.), E.*Alc.*764; τέγξαι βλέφαρον B.5.157:—Pass., *to be moistened*, δρόσοις S.*Aj.*1209 (lyr.); δάκρυσί μου βλέφαρα τ. E.*Hipp.*854 (lyr.): τέγγομαι (sc. ὄσσε), i.e. I weep, A.*Pers.*1065 (lyr.). 2. c. acc. cogn., τ. δάκρυα *shed* tears, Pi.*N.*10.75; ἀδινῶν χλωρὰν τέγγει δακρύων ἄχναν S.*Tr.*848 (lyr.):—Pass., ὄμβρος χάλαζά θ' αἱματοῦσσ' ἐτέγγετο a shower *fell*, Id.*OT*1279. 3. *soak*, in Pass., distd. from τήκεσθαι, Arist.*Mete.*385ᵇ22; τέγγει is prob. f.l. for στέγει in Id.*Pr.*869ᵇ25. II. *soften* (properly, *by soaking* or *bathing*), ἀοιδαὶ θέλξαν νιν ἀπτόμεναι· οὐδὲ θερμὸν ὕδωρ τόσον γε μαλθακὰ τέγξει (sic Plu.2.467d, τεύχει codd. Pi.) γυῖα (i.e. ὥστε μαλθακὰ γενέσθαι) Pi.*N.*4.4:—metaph. in Pass., τέγγει γὰρ οὐδὲν *thou art* no whit *softened*, A.*Pr.*1008; οὔτε γάρ.. λόγοις ἐτέγγεθ' ἥδε νῦν τ' οὐ πείθεται E.*Hipp.*303; χωρεῖτ' ὀργῇ καὶ μὴ τέγγεσθ' Ar.*Lys.*550; ὑπὸ κακοδοξίας τέγγεσθαι Pl.*R.*361c, cf. *Lg.*880e. III. *dye, stain*: metaph., οὐ ψευδεῖ τέγξω λόγον Pi.*O.*4.19. (Cf. Lat. *tingo*.)

**Τεγέα**, ας, Ion. **Τεγέη**, ης, ἡ, *Tegea* in Arcadia, Il.2.607, Pi.*O.*10(11).66, etc.:—**Τεγεάτης** [ᾱ], ου, Ion. -ήτης, ὁ, *of* or *from Tegea*, Hdt.1.65, etc.; then, by a play upon words, *of* or *from a brothel* (v. τέγος III), Diog.Cyn.ap.D.L.6.61: fem. **Τεγεᾶτις**, ιδος, (sc. χώρα) *the Tegeate country*, Th.5.65:—Adj. **Τεγεατικός**, Ion. -ητικός, ή, όν, Hdt.8.124.

**τεγείδιον**, v. τεγίδιον.

**τέγεος**, ον, (τέγος) *at* or *near the roof*, τ. θάλαμοι, of the women's chambers, = ὑπερῷον, Il.6.248. 2. *roofed*, Διὸς τ. δόμοι Emp.142, and so perh. in Il. l.c., though Apollon.*Lex.* glosses by ὑπερῷοι.

**τέγη**, ἡ, = στέγη, τέγος, D.C.39.61 (τέγναις codd.), Hsch. 2. = τέγος III, Vett.Val.121.32.

**τεγίδιον**, τό, name of a woman's garment, *Schwyzer* 462*B*38 (Tanagra, iii B.C.), *PSI*4.341.7 (iii B.C.); τεγείδιον· κοσμάριον ποιὸν γυναικεῖον, Hsch. (this sense is possible in *PSI* l.c.).

**τεγκτός**, ή, όν, (τέγγω) *capable of being softened in water* (opp. metal, which is τηκτόν), Arist.*Mete.*385ᵇ13 sq. 2. τεγκτούς· χρηστούς (leg. χριστούς), Hsch.

**τέγξις**, εως, ἡ, *wetting, moistening*, Hp.*Epid.*6.8.9, Aret.*CA*2.1: pl., Gal.6.592, Aret.*CA*1.1.

**τέγος**, εος, τό, = στέγος, *roof*, Od.1.333, 10.559, 11.64, al. (never in Il.), Ar.*Nu.*1126,1488, Men.*Sam.*246, Herod.3.40; οὗπι τοῦ τέγους you on the *roof!* Ar.*Nu.*1502, cf. *V.*68; θεῶ μ' ἀπὸ τοῦ τέγους Id.*Ach.*262, cf. Lys.3.11; τ. τοῦ οἰκήματος Th.4.48, cf. X.*Cyr.*7.5.22, *HG*4.4.12, etc. II. any *covered hall* or *chamber*, τ. Παρνάσιον the temple at Delphi, Pi.*P.*5.41; λιθίνῳ ἔνδον τέγει, i.e. in a cave, Id.*N.*3.54. III. later, *brothel, stew*, *AP*11.363 (Diosc.), Plb.12.13.2, Man.6.143. (Not found in Trag.) (Cf. Lat. *tego*.)

**τεθᾱλυῖα, τεθηλώς, τεθᾱλώς**, v. θάλλω.

**τεθαρρηκότως**, Adv. pf. part. of θαρρέω, *boldly*, Plb.2.10.7, 9.9.8, Phld.*Piet.*18, D.S.4.17, etc.

**τεθάφαται**, Ion. 3 pl. pf. Pass. of θάπτω, f.l. in Hdt.6.103.

* **τέθηπα**, pf. with pres. sense, Ep. plpf. ἐτεθήπεα as impf., from ταφ- (v. fin.), of which no pres. is found:—poet. Verb, also used in Ion. and late Prose: 1. intr., *to be astonished, astounded, amazed*, θυμός μοι ἐνὶ στήθεσσι τέθηπεν Od.23.105; mostly in part.

τεθηπώς, *amazed, astonied*, Il.4.243, 21.64, Parm.6.7, Emp.17.21, etc.; ἐτεθήπεα Od.6.166: joined with the part., τέθηπα ἀκούων Hdt. 2.156, cf. Luc.*Merc.Cond.*42.—To this belongs also aor. ἔταφον, used by Hom. only in part. ταφών, in the phrases ταφὼν ἀνόρουσε Il.9.193, Od.16.12, al.; στῆ δὲ ταφών Il.11.545, al.; later in indic., 3 sg. τάφε Pi.*P.*4.95, dub. in B.16.86; 3 pl. τάφον ib.48, A.R.2.207; 1 sg. ἔταφον A.*Pers.*999 (lyr.). 2. c. acc., *wonder* or *be amazed at*, Plu.2.24e, Luc.*Tim.*28,56, etc. (in Od.6.168, the acc. σε belongs only to ἄγαμαι). (Prob. cogn. with θάμβος.)

**τέθμιος**, v. θέσμιος. **τεθμός**, v. θεσμός. **τεθμοφούλαξ**, v. θεσμοφύλαξ.

**τέθνᾰθι, τεθναίην, τεθνάκην, τεθνάμεν, τεθνάμεναι, τεθνάναι, τεθνᾶσι, τεθνεώς, τεθνήξομαι, τεθνήξω, τεθνηώς, τεθνώς**, v. θνήσκω.

**τεθνᾰκοχαλκίδας** [ῐ], α, ὁ, perh. *one who would die for a farthing*, i.e. a miser, Cerc.4.11.

**τεθολώς·** ἀνάπλεως, Amerias ap.Hsch.

**τεθορῠβημένως**, Adv., (θορυβέω) *tumultuously, in a disorderly manner*, ἀποχωρεῖν X.*HG*5.3.5.

**τεθραῖος** and **τεθραΐτος**, apparently = *quadrivium*, *PMag.Lond.* 121.203.

**τεθριππεύω**, *drive a four-horse chariot*, dub. l. in E.*Fr.*228.5 (τέθριππ' ἄγοντος Nauck).

**τεθριππο-βάμων** [ᾰ], ονος, ὁ, = sq., τ. στόλος, = τέθριππον, E.*Or.* 989 (lyr.). **-βάτης** [ᾰ], ου, ὁ, *driver of a four-horse chariot*, Hdt. 4.170.

**τέθριππος**, ον, (τέτταρα, ἵππος) *with four horses yoked abreast*, ἅρμα Pi.*I.*1.14; ζεῦγος A.*Fr.*346; ὄχος E.*Hipp.*1212; τ. ἡλίου σέλας Id.*El.*866; τ. ἅμιλλαι chariot-races, Id.*Hel.*386; of the charioteer, οἱ Λυδοὶ ἐπὶ Πέλοπος τέθριπποι.. ἦσαν [καὶ] ἤδη ἁρματῖται Philostr.*Im.*1.17 (καὶ secl. Schenkl). II. τέθριππον (sc. ἅρμα), τό, *four-horse chariot*, Pi.*O.*2.50, Hdt.6.103, E.*Alc.*428, Pl.*Ly.*205c, etc.; τ. ἵππων *a team of four abreast*, Ar.*Nu.*1407: pl., of a single chariot, Pi.*P.*1.59, E.*HF*177.

**τεθριππο-τροφέω**, *keep a team of four horses*, Hdt.6.125. **-τρόφος**, ον, (τρέφω) *keeping a team of four horses*, οἰκίη τ., i.e. a wealthy family that could support this the most expensive contest in the games, ib.35.

**τεθρῡλημένως**, Adv., (θρυλέω) *as is well known*, Poll.6.207.

**τεθρυμμένως**, Adv., (θρύπτω) *wantonly, effeminately*, Plu.2.801a.

**τεΐ** or **τεί**, Dor. acc. sg. of σύ, Alcm.53.

**τεῖδε**, Dor. for *here* (= ἐνθάδε, Hsch.), Epich.99, Axiop.1.1, v.l. in Theoc.5.32; = *hither*, Hes.*Op.*635 (Cretan for ἐνταῦθα acc. to Procl. ad loc. (631)):—also τειδεί, Ἀρχ.Ἐφ.1911.58 (Rhodes, iv B.C.). (Loc. of the masc. or neut. stem το-.)

**τεϊδένυ**, Arc., = foreg., *IG*5(2).113 (Tegea, v B.C.).

**τεΐν** [ῑ], Dor. and Ep. dat. sg. of σύ (q.v.).

**τεῖνδε**, said to be Dor. for *here* (cf. τεῖδε), v.l. in Theoc.5.118, 5.32 (cf. Sch.), 8.40.

**τεινεσμ-ός**, ὁ, (τείνω) *a vain endeavour to evacuate*, Hp.*Aph.*7.27, *Epid.*1.5 (pl.), Sor.2.12, Gal.8.383 (pl.). ❋**-ώδης**, ες, *like a* τεινεσμός, Hp.*Epid.*1.26.γ'; προθυμίαι -ώδεες Aret.*SA*2.5, cf. Sor.2.20. Adv. -δῶς Ruf.ap.Orib.8.24.24.

**τείνυμαι**, v. τίνω.

**τείνω**, Il.16.365, etc.: fut. τενῶ Ar.*Th.*1205, (ἀπο-) Pl.*Grg.*458b, (ἐκ-) E.*Med.*585: aor. ἔτεινα Il.4.124, Ep. τεῖνα 3.261: pf. τέτᾰκα D.H. 19.12, etc., (ἀπο-) Pl.*Grg.*465e:—**Med.**, fut. τενοῦμαι (παρα-) Th.3.46, (προ-) D.14.5: aor. ἐτεινάμην, Ep. τειν-, A.R.2.1043, 4.705, (προ-) Hdt. 9.34, (δι-) Antipho 5.46, Pl.*Ti.*78b:—Pass., fut. τᾰθήσομαι (παρα-) Id.*Ly.*204c: aor. ἐτάθην [ᾰ] S.*Ant.*124 (lyr.), etc., Ep. τάθην Il.23. 375: pf. τέτᾰμαι Hes.*Op.*549, etc.: plpf. 3 sg. and pl. τέτατο, τέταντο, Od.11.11, Il.4.544; 3 dual τετάσθην ib.536:—*stretch* by force, *pull tight*, κυκλοτερὲς μέγα τόξον ἔτεινε Il.4.124; ἐπ' Ἀλεξάνδρῳ τείνοντα πάλαι τόξον A.*Ag.*364 (anap.); ἐξ ἄντυγος ἡνία τείνας *having tied* the reins *tight* to the chariot-rail, Il.5.262; ναὸς πόδα τείνας *keeping* the sheet *taut*, S.*Ant.*716; κάλων τείνας οὔριον εὐφροσυνᾶν *IG*14. 793; οἱ ἀπείρως κατ' εὐθὺ τείνοντες Sor.1.73; τῷ ψιμύθῳ.. παρειὴν *make* it (look) *full*, *AP*11.374 (Maced.):—Med., τείνατο τόξα *stretched his* bow, A.R.2.1043, cf. Orph.*A.*589; of tendons, etc., Gal. 18(2).58, al.:—Pass., [ἱμὰς] ὑπ' ἀνθερεῶνος.. τέτατο [the strap] *was made tight*, Il.3.372; τελαμῶνε περὶ στήθεσσι τετάσθην 14.404; τέταθ' ἱστία *were stretched taut*, Od.11.11. 2. metaph., *stretch* or *strain*, ἴσον τείνειεν πολέμου τέλος *strain* the issue of war even, Il.20. 101:—Pass., τῶν ἐπὶ ἶσα μάχη τέτατο πτόλεμός τε 12.436, 15.413, cf. Hes.*Th.*638; τέτατο κρατερὴ ὑσμίνη the fight *was strained, was intense*, Il.17.543; ἵπποισι τάθη δρόμος their pace *was strained to the utmost*, 23.375; τοῖσι δ' ἀπὸ νύσσης τέτατο δρόμος they *set off at full speed* from the starting-line, ib.758, Od.8.121: τ. αὐδὰν *strain* the voice, *raise* it *high*, A.*Pers.*574 (lyr.):—Pass. also, *exert oneself, be anxious*, Pi.*I.*1.49; ἀμφ' ἀρεταῖς Id.*P.*11.54. 3. *stretch out, spread*, ὅτε τε Ζεὺς λαίλαπα τείνῃ Il.16.365; ἐπὶ νὺξ τέταται βροτοῖσι night *is spread* over them, Od.11.19; ἀὴρ τέταται μακάρων ἐπὶ ἔργοις Hes.*Op.* 549; of light, αἴγλαν ἃ τέταται S.*Ph.*831 (lyr.), cf. Pl.*R.*616b; of sound, ἀμφὶ νῶτ' ἐτάθη πάταγος S.*Ant.*124 (lyr.); δίκτυα τ. X.*Cyn.* 6.9; ψυχὴν διὰ παντός Pl.*Ti.*34b. b. Gramm., *lengthen* a syllable, A.D.*Pron.*55.1:—Pass., ib.27.25, cf. II. 1 fin. 4. *aim at, direct towards* a point, prop. from the bow, ἐπὶ Τροίᾳ τ. τὰ θεῶν ἀμάχητα βέλη S.*Ph.*198 (anap.): metaph., ἔς τινα τ. φόνον *aim, design* death to one, E.*Hec.*263 (but τ. φόνον *prolong* murder, Id.*Supp.*672); τ. λόγον εἴς τινα Pl.*Phd.*63a:—Pass., ἐς σὲ τ. γλῶσσα E.*Rh.*875; ἡ ἅμιλλα τέταται πρὸς τοῦτο Pl.*Phdr.*271a, cf. *Lg.*770d, *R.*581b. II. *stretch out in length, lay*, ζυγὰ ἐπιπολῆς τ. Hdt.2.96:—Pass., *lie out at length, lie stretched*, ἐπὶ γαίῃ κεῖτο ταθείς Il.13.655; ἐν κονίῃσι τετάσθην, τέταντο, 4.536,544; ταθεὶς ἐνὶ δεσμῷ *hanging stretched* in chains, Od.22.200; [φάσγανον] ὑπὸ λαπάρην τέτατο *hung along* or *by* his side, Il.22.307; διὰ.. αἰθέρος.. τέταται *extends*, Emp.135, cf. 100.2; τῶν ἐκ τῆς χώρας λεωφόρων εἰς τὴν πόλιν τεταμένων Pl.*Lg.*763c; φλέψ.. διὰ τοῦ κοίλου τείνεται Arist.*HA*513$^b$3: τεταμένος sts. becomes a mere Adj., *long*, αὐχένα.. τεταμένον τῇ φύσει, of birds, Id.*PA*692$^b$20; in Gramm., of a *long* vowel, *PBouriant*8 i 1,14. 2. *stretch* or *hold out, present*, τινὰ ἐπὶ σφαγάν E.*Or.*1494 (lyr.); ἀσπίδα, δόρυ, *AP*7.147 (Arch.), 720 (Chaerem.); τὴν χεῖρά τινι or ἐπί τι, A.R. 4.107,1049:—Med., τείνεσθαι χέρε, γυῖα, δειρήν, *one's* hands, etc., Theoc.21.48, A.R.1.1009, 4.127, etc.; συὸς τέκος Id.4.705; ἑανούς ib.1155. 3. *extend, lengthen*, of Time, τὸν μακρὸν τ. βίον A. *Pr.*537 (lyr.), cf. E.*Med.*670; αἰῶνα Id.*Ion* 625; τόνδ' ἐτείνατην λόγον A.*Ch.*510; μακροὺς τ. λόγους E.*Hec.*1177; τί μάτην τείνουσι βοήν; (where others interpr. it like τ. αὐδάν, v. supr. 1. 2) Id.*Med.* 201 (anap.); πολλὰ μὲν τάλαινα πολλὰ δ' αὖ σοφῇ.. μακρὰν ἔτεινας A.*Ag.*1296, cf. S.*Aj.*1040.

B. intr., of geographical position, *stretch out* or *extend*, παρ' ἣν (sc. λίμνην) τὸ.. ὄρος τείνει Hdt.2.6; τὸ πρὸς Λιβύης.. ὄρος ἄλλο τείνει ib.8; τ. μέχρι.. Id.4.38; ἐς.. Id.7.113; ἐπί.. X.*Ages.*2.17; of a dress, ὑπὸ σφυροῖσι τ. E.*Ba.*936; of a mountain, ὑψόθι τ. A.R.2.354: of Time, ἡμερολεγδὸν τείνοντα χρόνον *dragging out* time, A.*Pers.*64 (anap.):—rarely so in Pass., ὄρος τεταμένον τὸν αὐτὸν τρόπον Hdt.2. 8. II. *exert oneself, struggle*, ἐναντία τισί Pl.*R.*492d; *press on, hasten*, οἱ δ' ἔτεινον ἐς πύλας E.*Supp.*720; δηλοῖ τοὔργον, οἱ τ. χρεών Id.*Or.*1129; τὸ μὴ τείνειν ἄγαν S.*Ant.*711; τ. ὥς τινα Ar.*Th.*1205; ἔτεινον ἄνω πρὸς τὸ ὄρος X.*An.*4.3.21; εὐθὺ Βαβυλῶνος Luc.*Nec.*6; τὴν ἐπὶ τοῦ οὐρανοῦ Id.*Icar.*22. III. *extend to, reach*, ἐπὶ τὴν ψυχήν Pl.*Tht.*186c; ἐπὶ πᾶν Id.*Smp.*186b; of the veins *stretching* from one point to another, Arist.*HA*492$^a$20, 513$^a$2, al., cf. Pl.*Ti.* 65c, Diog.Apoll.6. 2. *tend, refer, belong to*, τείνει ἐς σέ *it refers to, concerns* you, Hdt.6.109, cf. 7.135, E.*Ph.*435, *Hipp.*707, etc.; ποῖ τείνει καὶ εἰς τί; to what does it *tend*? Pl.*Cri.*47c, cf. *Tht.*163a, D.10.54; μηδαμόσε ἄλλοσε Pl.*R.*499a; πρός τι Id.*Smp.*188d, *Prt.* 345b; ἐς ταὐτόν Id.*Cra.*439c. 3. τείνειν πρός τινα or τι, *come near to, to be like*, Id.*Tht.*169b, *Cra.*402c; ἐγγύς τι τείνειν τοῦ τεθνάναι Id.*Phd.*65a, cf. *R.*548d. (Cf. τανύω, Skt. *tanóti* 'stretch', Lat. *tendo*, etc.)

**τεῖον·** ποῖον, Κρῆτες, Hsch.: cf. ὀτεῖος (q.v.) and τέουτος (v. τοιοῦτος). **τεῖος**, v. τέως sub fin. **τείρεα, τείρεσ(σ)ιν**, v. τέρας.

**τείρω**, impf. ἔτειρον, found only in pres. and impf. Act. and Pass., and in Aeol. pf. inf. Pass. τέτορθαι Hdn.Gr.2.69:—of the effects of pain, sorrow, etc., on body and mind, *oppress, distress, weaken*, τείρουσι (sc. ἡμᾶς or σε) μαρνάμενοι Il.6.255, cf. 8.102, 24.489; ἀλλά σε γῆρας τείρει 4.315; βέλεος δέ σε τείρει ἀκωκή 13.251; τεῖρε γὰρ αὐτὸν ἕλκος 16.510; ὀδυνάων αἵ νῦν μιν τείρουσι κατὰ φρένας 15.61, cf. Od.1.342; ἱδρὼς γάρ μιν ἔτειρεν Il.5.796; τεῖρε γὰρ αἰνῶς φωκάων.. ὀδμή Od.4. 441; μιν ἔτειρεν ἔρος Hes.*Fr.*105; νιν ἔρως ἔτειρεν Telest.1.6; κακαὶ τ. μέριμναι Mimn.1.7; ἐπεί με.. τύχαι τείρουσ' Ἄτλαντος A.*Pr.*350; ὀδύνη με τ. E.*Rh.*799:—Pass., τείροντο δὲ νηλέϊ χαλκῷ Il.17.376; καμάτῳ τε καὶ ἱδρῷ ib.745; ἔνδοθι θυμὸς ἐτείρετο πένθεϊ λυγρῷ 22.242; τείρετο δ' αἰνῶς *she was* sore *distressed*, 5.352; τειρόμενοι, by war, 11.801, cf. 6.387, al.; ἕλκει -όμενον Pi.*P.*1.52; ἄχθεσι τ. Tyrt.6; ἐν.. κακῷ τείρει (2 sg. Pass.) ψυχὴν ἐξαπατηθεὶς Ar.*Lys.*960; Ἑρμιόνας δούλαν ἃς ὕπο τειρομένα.. τάκομαι E.*Andr.*114 (lyr.).—Poet. word, used by Gal.14.632, Ael.*NA*14.11. (The other tenses are supplied by τέτρυμαι etc. from τρύω (not found before Call. in pres. or impf.), which may be cogn.)

**τείρων**, ωνος, ὁ, = Lat. *tiro, recruit*, *BCH*52.392 (Thasos), *PLips.* 34.29 (iv A.D.), Keil-Premerstein *DritterBericht* p.87 (inc. loc.), etc.; cf. τίρων.

**τειχ-άριον**, τό, *wall*, in contemptuous sense, τειχάρια παλαιά *PRyl.*125.7 (i A.D.). ❋**-εσιπλήτης**, ου, ὁ, (πελάζω) only in voc. -πλῆτα, *approacher of walls*, i.e. *stormer of cities*, epith. of Ares, Il.5.31,455 (where -βλῆτα was read by Zenod. etc.): cf. δασπλῆτις. **-έω**, used by Hdt. for τειχίζω (which he also has), *build walls*, Hdt.1.99, al.: c. acc. cogn., τεῖχος τειχέειν Id.9.7. II. trans., *wall, fortify*, τὸν Ἰσθμόν Id.8.40, 9.8, cf. 5.23, al. **-ήεις**, εσσα, εν, = τειχιόεις, Il.2.646 as cited by Str.10.4.11. ❋**-ήρης**, ες, *within walls, enclosed by walls*: hence, 1. *beleaguered, besieged*, τειχήρεας ποιῆσαί τινας Hdt.1.162, cf. Th.2.101, 4.25; τ. γίγνεσθαι And.3.21; τ. εἶναι X.*HG*5.3.2, Plb.21.10.6, etc.; τ. μένοντες καθήμεθα D.H.6.50. 2. *walled, fortified*, LXX *Nu.*13.20 (19), *De.*9.1, al., Str.13.1.7; τ. τὴν φύσιν *firm* by nature, Philostr. *Her.*10.7. 3. τ. στέφανος, = *corona vallaris*, *BCH*28.425 (Argos, ii A.D.). **-ίδιον**, τό, Dim. of τεῖχος, Zonar. ❋**-ίζω**, fut. Att. -ιῶ Th.6.97, D.6.14, 19.112: aor. ἐτείχισα Hdt.1.175: pf. τετείχικα D. 19.112:—**Med.**, fut. τειχιοῦμαι X.*Cyr.*6.1.19 (v.l. -ίσασθαι): aor. ἐτειχισάμην Th.1.11; Ep. ἐτειχίσσαντο Il.7.449: (τεῖχος):—*build a wall*, Ar.*Av.*838, Th.1.64, etc.: c. acc. cogn., τ. μακρὰ τείχη *build* them, Id.5.82:—Med., τεῖχος ἐτειχίσσαντο *they built them* a wall, Il.7.449, cf. Th.3.105, And.3.38 (ἐτειχίσαμεν codd.); ἔρυμα τῷ στρατοπέδῳ ἐτειχίσαντο Th.1.11:—Pass., *to be built*, πύργος τετείχισται Pi.*I.*5(4).44; ὕμνων θησαυρὸς τετείχισται Id.*P.*6.9. 2. *form a* *wall*, τῇ τῶν ἀσπίδων προβολῇ ὥσπερ τειχίσαντες Hdn.6.5.10. II. trans., *wall, fortify*, ὄρος Hdt.1.175, etc.; τὸν Πειραιᾶ And.3.5; τὴν πόλιν, τὸν κρημνόν, Th.1.93, 6.101; στρατόπεδα δύο Id.3.6; λίθοις τ. τὴν πόλιν D.18.299; χαλκοῖς τείχεσι τὴν χώραν Aeschin.3.84; Μαγνησίαν D.1.22:—Med., τειχίζεσθαι τὸ χωρίον Th.4.3:—Pass., Ἀθηναῖοι ἐτειχίσθησαν Id.1.93; τὰ τετειχισμένα the *fortified parts*, Id.4.9; ἐτετείχιστο.. τὰ βασιλήϊα περιβόλῳ *stood enclosed* by a surrounding wall, Hdt.1.181: metaph., [Αἴγυπτον] τῷ Νείλῳ τετειχισμένην Isoc.11.12; ἀσφάλειαν τετειχισμένην ὅπλοις D.19.84. **-ικὸς** στέφανος, = Lat. *corona vallaris*, *Jahresh*.13.201 (Alabanda, ii A.D.), *IGRom*.3.230 (Pessinus). **-ιόεις**, εσσα, εν, *high-walled*, of towns, Il.2.559,646. **-ίον**, τό, *wall*, μέγα τ. αὐλῆς Od.16.165,343: used of walls of buildings, not, like τεῖχος, of city-walls, v. *IG*1².373.258, Ar.*Ec*.497, *V*.1109, Th.6.66, 7.81, Aen.Tact. 2.2, *PHal*.1.88,91 (iii B.C.), etc.; of a wall as the *fence* of a field, X.*Eq*.3.7, *Eq.Mag*.6.5. **-ισις**, εως, ἡ, *the work of walling, wall-building*, Th.7.6, X.*HG*6.5.4. **-ισμα**, ατος, τό, *wall* or *fort*, E.*HF*1096 codd. (τυκ- is prob. cj.), Th.4.8,115, etc.; Τυρσηνῶν τ. Πελασγικόν, of the wall of Athens, Call. in Διηγήσεις 4.1 (cf. Sch.). ❀ **-ισμός**, ὁ, = τείχισις, Th.5.82, 6.44, etc. **-ιστέον**, *one must fortify*, Lib.*Thes*.2 tit. **-ιστής**, οῦ, ὁ, *builder, mason*, Lxx 4*Ki*.12.12(13); τῆς Τροίας Lib.*Thes*.2.2.

❀ **τειχοδομ-έω**, *build a wall*, *APl*.4.279, Str.8.6.15, Poll.7.118. **-ημα**, ατος, τό, *wall*, in pl., *IG*1²(9).906.6 (Chalcis, iii A.D.). **-ία**, ἡ, *building of walls*, *IPE*1².32 *B*63 (Olbia, iii B.C.), Plu.*Nic*.18. **-ος**, ον (parox.), *building walls*, Man.4.291, Poll.1.161.

**τειχο-καταλύτης** [ῠ], ου, ὁ, *demolisher of walls*, Ctes.*Fr*.57.3. **-κρᾰτέω**, *gain possession of a wall*, Polyaen.4.2.18.

**τειχολέτις**, ιδος, ἡ, *destroyer of walls*, Simyl. ap. Plu.*Rom*.17.

❀ **τειχομᾰχ-έω**, *fight the walls*, i.e. *conduct siege operations*, Hdt.9.70, Th.7.79, X.*HG*1.1.14, etc.; τ. τινί Ar.*Nu*.481; πρὸς τοὺς πολεμίους Plu.*Alc*.28; τειχομαχεῖν δυνατοί skilled *in conducting sieges*, i.e. good engineers, Th.1.102: perh. of *defending a wall*, App.*Hann*.92. **-ης**, ου, Dor. **-ας**, ὁ, *storming walls, besieger*, τ. ἀνήρ Ar.*Ach*.570 (lyr.). **-ία**, Ion. **-ίη**, ἡ, *battle with walls*, i.e. *siege*, Hdt.9.70, Jul.*Or*.2.65d: the twelfth book of the Iliad was so called, Pl.*Ion* 539b. **-ικός**, ή, όν, *of* or *for besieging*, Sch.Ar.*Nu*.480, Hdn.*Epim*.148. **-ος** (parox.), ὁ, *defending a wall*, App.*Hisp*.93: but τ. σίδηρος *for demolishing walls*, Id.*BC*5.36: = *vinearius*, Lyd.*Mag*.1.46.

**τειχομελής**, ές, *walling by music*, of Amphion's lyre, *AP*9.216 (Honest.).

**τειχοπόης**, v. τειχοποιός II.

**τειχοποι-έω**, *build walls* or *fortifications*, *IPE*1².418 (Chersonesus, i B.C./i A.D.), Poll.7.118:— **-ητέον**, Ph.*Bel*.84.4. II. *hold the office of* τειχοποιός, Arg.2 D.18. ❀ **-ία**, ἡ, *building of walls* or *forts*, Aen.Tact.8.3, Ph.*Bel*.86.3 (pl.), al., D.S.13.35, *J.BJ*5.2.5, Plu.2.851a. **-ικός** (also **-ποϊκ-**), ή, όν, *for building walls*, τὰ -κά, name of a fund, *IG*2².244.31 (iv B.C.), *SIG*368.39 (Milet., iii B.C.). ❀ **-ός**, ὁ, *builder of walls* or *forts*, Lyc.617, Luc.*Salt*.41, Poll.1.161. II. οἱ τ. at Athens and elsewhere, *officers chosen to repair the city-walls*, *IG*1².343.90 (prob.), 2².1660, al., *BMus.Inscr*.1005 (Cyzicus, iv B.C.), Docum.ap.D.18.55, Aeschin.3.24, Arist.*Pol*.1321ᵇ26, *SIG*577.82 (Milet., iii/ii B.C.):—also **-πόης**, acc. pl. **-πόας**, ib.273.30 (ibid., iv B.C.).

**τεῖχος**, εος, τό, *wall*, esp. *city-wall*, Ἰλιόφι κλυτὰ τείχεα Il.21.295, cf. 446, Od.6.9, al.; of the *embankment* round the ships, τάφρος Δαναῶν καὶ τ. ὕπερθεν Il.12.4, cf. 25 sqq.; τ. ἐς ἀμφίχυτον (of heaped-up earth) 20.145; Κιμμέρια τ. *earthworks*, Hdt.4.12; but τ. λάϊνα E.*Tr*.1087 (lyr.), cf. Th.1.93, etc.; λίθοις οὓς ἔλιπον εἰς τὸ τ. ἀναλίσκοντες *IG*1².81.9; ξύλινον τεῖχος exceptionally, Orac.ap.Hdt.7.141, cf. 8.51, 9.65, Th.2.75, X.*HG*1.3.4, Orac.ap.Ar.*Eq*.1040 (Pi. uses this phrase for *a funeral pile*, *P*.3.38); τ. χάλκεον Od.10.3; τ. σιδηροῦν, τείχη χαλκᾶ καὶ ἀδαμάντινα, Ar.*Eq*.1046, Aeschin.3.84; τειχέων κιθῶνες coats *of walls*, i.e. walls one within the other, Hdt.7.139; τεῖχος ἐλαύνειν, v. ἐλαύνω III.2; τ. ἔδειμαν Il.7.436; οἰκοδομέειν Hdt.1.98, cf. Ar.*Av*.1132, etc. (τ. οἰκοδομήσασθαι to build oneself *walls*, Th.7.11); τ. ἄξειν Id.6.99; τὰ τ. στῆσαι D.20.74; τ. περιβάλλειν ταῖς πόλεσι Arist.*Pol*.1331ᵃ3; τ. περιβαλέσθαι build *walls* round one's city, Hdt.1.141, cf. Th.1.8, etc. (also τ. περιβαλέσθαι τὴν πόλιν Hdt.1.163:—hence Pass., τεῖχος περιβεβλημένος having a *wall* round it, Pl.*Tht*.174e; τείχη περιβεβλημένοι, of citizens, Arist.*Pol*.1331ᵃ8); but also νῆσον περιβάλλεσθαι τείχει surround one's island with *walls*, Pl.*Criti*.116a; τ. ῥήξασθαι breach the *wall*, Il.12.90, cf. 257; τεῖχος ἀναρρήξας 7.461; so in Prose, τ. διαιρεῖν, περιαιρεῖν, κατελεῖν, κατασκάψαι, etc., Th.2.75, Hdt.6.46,48, Th.4.109, etc. 2. τὰ μακρὰ τ., at Athens, lines of wall connecting the city-wall (ὁ περίβολος) and the harbours, Th.2.13; they were called respectively τὸ βόρειον or Peiraic, and τὸ νότιον or Phaleric wall (Pl.*R*.439e, Aeschin.2.173,174), cf. σκέλος II: an intermediate wall (τὸ διὰ μέσου τ. Pl.*Grg*.455e) ran parallel to the northern, which was therefore called also τὸ ἔξωθεν, Th.2.13: the quarter inside the walls is sts. called τὸ μακρὸν τ. *Long Wall*, And.1.45. II. *fortification, castle, fort*, Pi.*Fr*.213, Hdt.3.14,91, etc. III. *walled, fortified town* or *city*, Id.9.41,115, X.*Cyr*.7.5.13, etc. IV. *wall* of a temple, *PEleph*.20.52 (iii B.C.); of a house, *PHamb*.15.8 (iii A.D.), *PStrassb*.9.8 (iv A.D.), etc. (Cf. Skt. *dehmi* 'anoint, smear, plaster', Goth. *digan* 'mould, create (= πλάσσω)', *daigs* 'dough', Lat. *fingo, figura*, Osc. *feihúss* 'walls', etc.)

**τειχο-σκοπία**, ἡ, *looking from the walls*: name given to a scene in the third book of the Iliad, Sch.E.*Ph*.88. **-φῠλᾰκέω**, *watch* or *guard the walls*, D.H.4.16, Plu.*Crass*.27, Polyaen.7.11.5. **-φύλαξ** [ῠ], ἄκος, ὁ, *one that has the guard of the walls*, Hdt.3.157, Plu.2.694c: pl., Polyaen.8.23.6, App.*Mith*.32.

**τειχ-ύδριον**, τό, Dim. of τεῖχος, X.*HG*2.1.28. **-ωμα**, ατος, τό, gloss on φραγμός, *AB*314:—in Plb.4.63.2, τε χώμασιν is now restored. **-ωτός**, ή, όν, = τειχικός, στέφανος *CIL*3 (Supp.).13648 (Amastris), etc.

**τείως**, Adv., Ep. for τέως (q.v.). **τέκε, τεκεῖν**, v. τίκτω.

**τεκεκτόνος**, ον, f.l. for τεκοκτόνος in Orph.*L*.315.

❀ **τεκμαίρομαι**, fut. τεκμᾰροῦμαι X.*Cyr*.4.3.21: aor. ἐτεκμηράμην Antipho 5.81, etc., Ep. τεκμ- Od.10.563: (τέκμαρ):—*assign, ordain*, esp. of the gods, ἐπεὶ τάδε γ' ὧδε θεοὶ κακὰ τεκμήραντο Il.6.349; Κρονίδης.. κακὰ.. τεκμαίρεται ἀμφοτέροισιν 7.70; πόλεμον, δίκην τισὶ τ... [Ζεύς], Hes.*Op*.229,239: generally, of any person in authority, *appoint*, πομπὴν δ' ἐς τόδ' ἐγὼ τεκμαίρομαι, ὄφρ' εὖ εἰδῇς, αὔριον ἐς I *am arranging* your departure for to-morrow, Od.7.317; ἄλλην δ' ἡμιν ὁδὸν τεκμήρατο Κίρκη 10.563; ἐν οἷς ἂν (sc. τόποις) νομοφύλακες.. τεκμηράμενοι ἕδρας πρεπούσας, ὅρους θῶνται τῶν ὠνίων Pl.*Lg*.849e; with a notion of foretelling, τότε τοι τεκμαίρομ' ὄλεθρον Od.11.112: c. inf., *settle with oneself*, i.e. *design, purpose* to do, *h.Ap*.285, A.R.4.559. II. after Hom. almost always, *judge from signs and tokens, estimate*, προσβάσεις πύργων E.*Ph*.180; κύματα, φύλλα, A.R.4.217: abs., *form a judgement* or *conjecture*, ὡς ἀνθρώποις τεκμαίρεσθαι (sc. δέδοται) Alcmaeon 1; τέτταρσιν ὀφθαλμοῖς X.*Cyr*.4.3.21; λέγουσι περὶ αὐτοῦ τεκμαιρόμενοι *by conjecture*, Id.*Mem*.1.4.1. 2. the ground on which the judgement or conjecture is founded is commonly added in the dat., ἐμπύροις τεκμαίρεσθαι *to judge by* the burnt-offering, Pi.*O*.8.3; τεκμαίρομαι ἔργοισιν Ἡρακλέος Id.*Fr*.169.4; τ. τοῖσι νῦν ἔτι ἐοῦσι Πελασγῶν Hdt.1.57; τοῖσι ἐμφανέσι τὰ μὴ γινωσκόμενα τ. *judge of* the unknown *by* the known, Id.2.33, cf. 7.16.γ'; ἔργῳ κοὐ λόγῳ τ. A.*Pr*.338; τὰ καινὰ τοῖς πάλαι S.*OT*916; τοῖς παροῦσι τἀφανῆ E.*Fr*.574; τοὺς.. περιεσομένους τοῖς ξύμπασι σημείοισι *by* all the symptoms, Hp.*Prog*.24, cf. *Acut*.68; τὰ μέλλοντα τοῖς γεγενημένοις Isoc.4.141; κατὰ [τὴν αἴσθησιν].. τὸ ἄδηλον τῷ λογισμῷ τ. Epicur.*Ep*.1 p.6U.; περὶ τῶν μελλόντων τοῖς ἤδη γεγενημένοις Isoc.6.59; also τ. τὰ μέλλοντ' ἐκ τῶν γεγενημένων Din.1.33, cf. X.*Mem*.4.1.2, Pl.*Smp*.204c, Gal.6.470; ἀφ' αὑτοῦ τὴν νόσον τ. Ar.*V*.76, cf. Th.4.123, X.*Mem*.3.5.6, Pl.*Phd*.108a, *R*.409a,501b; τ. ἀπὸ τούτων εἰς τὰ ἄλλα Id.*Tht*.206b; εἴ τι δεῖ τ. πρὸς τὸν ἄλλον αὐτοῦ τρόπον D.27.22; πόθεν τοῦτο τεκμαίρῃ; Pl.*Cri*.44a, cf. *Phdr*.235c, *R*.433b: rarely c. gen., τ. κατηγορίας οὐ προγεγενημένης *from* the fact that.., Th.3.53; τ. τῷ πυρὶ τῆς ὁδοῦ *judge of* the road by the fire, App.*BC*5.87, cf. 45, *Mith*.5, Arat.1129,1154; τ. τοῦ δένδρου πρὸς τὴν ναῦν *estimate* the tree with reference to.., Philostr.*Im*.2.17, cf. *VA*1.22. 3. c. acc. et inf., τ. τοῦτο οὕτως ἔξειν ἐκ τοῦδε X.*Cyr*.8.1.28, cf. Pl.*R*.578c, Gal.6.588, *PRyl*.74.5 (ii A.D.); also folld. by a relat. Particle, τεκμαιρόμενος ὅτι.. *taking as an indication* the fact that.., Th.1.1, cf. X.*Lac*.8.2; ὡς μέγα.. τὴν Αἴτνην ὄρος εἶναί φασι, τεκμαίρου *guess* how great.., Pl.Com.37; τ. εἰ.. *to be uncertain* whether.., *AP*12.177 (Strat.). 4. *recognize*, ὅπα κούρης A.R.4.73; Ἀλέξανδρον *APl*.4.121. III. *put forth, stretch out*, ὁλκόν, οὖρον (= ὅρον), D.P.101,135,178: abs., *project*, of teeth, Nic.*Th*.231.

B. Act. τεκμαίρω only in post-Hom. Poets, *show by a sign* or *token, make proof of*, τεκμαίρει χρῆμ' ἕκαστον circumstance *proves* the man, Pi.*O*.6.73; τεκμαίρει.. ἰδεῖν *gives signs* [for men] to see, Id.*N*.6.8; ἀλλά μοι.. τέκμηρον, ὅ τι μ' ἐπαμμένει παθεῖν A.*Pr*.605 (lyr.); κελεύθους *indicate* them, Nic.*Th*.680; τ. ἀοιδὴν *guide* it.., Arat.18.

**τέκμαρ**, Ep. **τέκμωρ** (so always in Hom., never elsewhere), τό, indecl.:—*fixed mark* or *boundary, goal, end* (= πέρας, κατὰ τὴν ἀρχαίαν γλῶσσαν, Arist.*Rh*.1357ᵇ9), ἵκετο τέκμωρ he reached the *goal*, Il.13.20; τοῖο μὲν.. εὕρετο τέκμωρ for this he found *an end*, i.e. devised *a remedy*, 16.472; εἰς ὅ κε τ. Ἰλίου εὕρωσιν 7.30; οὐδέ τι τέκμωρ εὑρέμεναι δύνασαι Od.4.373, cf. 466: in Pi., either *end, termination*, τέκμαρ αἰῶνος *Fr*.165; or *end, object, purpose*, *P*.2.49. 2. *fixed line* of separation, δειλῶν τε καὶ ἐσθλῶν τ. ἐναργές Hes.*Fr*.164. II. *sure sign* or *token* of some high and solemn kind, as Zeus says that his nod is ἐξ ἐμέθεν μέγιστον τέκμωρ, *the highest, surest pledge* I can give, Il.1.526; σαφὲς τ. Pi.*N*.11.44; of the moon, as *a sign* in the heavens, τ. δὲ βροτοῖς.. τέτυκται *h.Hom*.32.13, cf. A.R.1.499, 3.1002, etc.; ἦν δ' οὐδὲν αὐτοῖς οὔτε χείματος τ. οὔτ'.. ἦρος A.*Pr*.454; ἔστι τῶνδέ σοι τ.; Id.*Ag*.272, cf. 315; τἀνδρὸς ἐκφανὲς τ. Id.*Eu*.244; τῆσδ' ἀφίξεως τ. Id.*Supp*.483; κυνὸς.. σῆμα, ναυτίλοις τ. E.*Hec*.1273.—Poet. word, used also in the Ion. Prose of Hp. and Aret. for *symptom*, esp. *pathognomic symptom*, Hp.*Mul*.2.123, Aret.*SA*2.2, al.

**τέκμαρ-σις**, εως, ἡ, *judging from signs*: esp. Medic., *judging* or *determining from symptoms*, Hp.*Acut*.2: generally, οὐ δικαίαν τέκμαρσιν ἔχει τὸ ἐκφοβῆσαι affords no just *ground for inference* so as to alarm us, Th.2.87; τὴν τ. ποιεῖσθαι ἔκ τινος, = τεκμαίρεσθαι, D.H.7.71; τ. ἔχειν to have its *interpretation*, of a dream, D.C.47.46. II. *skill in determining, insight*, γυναικείᾳ τεκμάρσει D.H.1.78. **-τέος**, α, ον, *to be determined*, πρός τι according to.., Aret.*CA*1.1. II. τεκμαρτέον, *one must determine*, τινί τι Hp.*Off*.15; *one must judge, estimate*, Archig.ap.Orib.46.27.1. **-τικός**, ή, όν, *skilled in determining, sagacious*, condemned by Poll.9.152. **-τός**, ή, όν, *possible to be determined*, πρὸς εἶδος..οὐδὲν προσιδόντι τεκμαρτόν Cratin.260 (hex.).

**τεκμήρι-ον**, τό, (τεκμαίρομαι) = τέκμαρ II (cf. Arist.*Rh.*1357$^b$8,9), *a sure sign* or *token*, Hdt.2.13, 9.100, etc.; τεκμηρίοισιν ἐξ οἰμωγμάτων A.*Ag.*1366; καὶ μὴν στίβοι γε, δεύτερον τ. Id.*Ch.*205; θανόντος πίστ' ἔχων τ. S.*El.*774; ἐμφανῆ τ. ib.1109; ἀσφαλὲς τ. E.*Rh.*94; ταῦτα δὴ πάντα τ. ὅτι.. Hp.*VM*8: Medic., *a sure symptom*, Id.*Prog.*25, Sor.1.33, Gal.18(2).306. 2. simply *sign, symbol*, τοῦ φιλαποδήμου Sor.*Vit.Hippocr.*12. II. *proof* (properly of an argumentative kind, opp. direct evidence, Is.4.12, 8.6), A.*Eu.*485, Pl.*Tht.*158b, al.; opp. τὰ εἰκότα, Antipho 2.4.10; but οὐκ εἰκότα τ. Id.4.4.2; τ. δίκαιον Id.1.10; τ. τινός *proof of* a thing, A.*Eu.*662, Ar.*Av.*482, etc.; τ. δὲ τοῦδε τὸν Ὅμηρον λαβέ (i.e. the case of Homer) Philem.97.5; also τ. περὶ τῶν μελλόντων And.3.2, cf. Pl.*Tht.*185b; τ. τινὸς δοῦναι, παρασχέσθαι, A.*Pr.*826, X.*Ages.*6.1; λέξω A.*Eu.*447; δείξω, ἐπιδεῖξαι, ἀποδεῖξαι, ib.662, *Supp.*53 (lyr.), Pl.*Tht.*158b; τ. ἀποφαίνειν περὶ σοφίας Id.*Hp.Ma.*283a; ἔχειν A.*Supp.*271. 2. τεκμήριον δέ as an independent clause, *now the proof of it is this* (which follows), *take this as a proof*, Th.2.39, D.20.10, etc.; more fully, τ. δέ μοι τούτου τόδε· αἱ μὲν γὰρ φαίνονται κτλ. Hdt.2.58; τ. δὲ τούτου καὶ τόδε· παρὰ μὲν Κύρου κτλ. X.*An.*1.9.29; χρῆσθαι τεκμηρίῳ ὅτι.. (ὅτι introducing the reason, not the fact) And.1.24, cf. Lys.30.15. 3. in the Logic of Aristotle, *demonstrative proof*, opp. to the fallible σημεῖον and εἰκός, *APr.*70$^b$2, *Rh.*1357$^b$4, 1402$^b$19, cf. Phld.*Rh.*1.369S. **-όω**, *prove positively*, Th.1.3, D.H.1.89, etc.; Ὅμηρος..εἴ τῳ ἱκανὸς τεκμηριῶσαι if he seem a sufficient voucher, Th.1.9; τοσαῦτα ἐτεκμηρίωσεν ὅτι.. thus much *evidence he gave* to the fact that.., Id.3.104; of symptoms, *indicate*, Orib.*Syn.*9.43:—Pass., *to be proved*, τισι *by* facts, D.C.75.13. II. later in Med., *draw inferences*, Phld.*D* 3.8, Ph.2.505, A.D.*Pron.*87.7; ἀπό τινων Phld.*Sign.Fr.*2. **-ώδης**, ες, *of the nature of a* τεκμήριον, Arist.*Rh.*1403$^a$11. Adv. **-δῶς** *Placit.*4.9.17. **-ωμα**, ατος, τό, *proof*, f.l. in Gal.*UP*5.3. **-ωσις**, εως, ἡ, *proof*, Arr.*An.*4.7.5, 5.4.2.

**τεκμορ-εῖοι** ξένοι, *an association who pledged their loyalty* to the Emperor, prob. against Christianity, *Papers of Amer. School at Athens* 3 No. 370. **-εύω**, *give the sign* of loyalty, *CR*19.420, *JHS* 32.123, al. (Antioch in Pisidia), *Supp.Epigr.*2.750 (Pisidia).

**τέκμωρ**, v. τέκμαρ.

**τεκν-ίδιον** [νῐ], τό, Dim. of τέκνον, *little child*, Ar.*Lys.*889. **-ίον**, τό, = foreg., *Trag.* (or *Com.*) *Adesp.* in *PLit.Lond.*84, *Ev.Jo.*13.33, 1*Ep.Jo.*4.4, Luc.*Epigr.*50, Hld.7.12, *PFlor.*365.15 (iii A.D.), *POxy.*1766.14 (iii A.D.).

**τεκνογέννητος**, ον, *of childbirth*, πόνοι *Supp.Epigr.*3.400.8 (Delph., iii B.C.).

**τεκνογον-έω**, *bear young, bear children*, *AP*9.22 (Phil.), 1*Ep.Ti.*5.14. **-ία**, ἡ, *child-bearing*, Arist.*HA*582$^a$28 (pl.), 1*Ep.Ti.*2.15, Gal.15.49. **-ος** (parox.), ον, *bearing children*, A.*Th.*928.

**τεκνο-δαίτης**, ου, ὁ, (δαίω (B), δαίνυμι) *devouring his children*, Orac. ap.Paus.8.42.6. **-δότης**, ου, ὁ, *children-giving*, [κλῆρος] Vett.Val.122.23. **-εις**, v. τεκνοῦς. **-θρεπτος**, ὁ, *foster-child*, *TAM*2.431 (Patara).

**τεκνοκτον-έω**, *murder children*, Hld.10.12, Charito 2.9. **-ία**, ἡ, *child-murder*, Ph.2.318 (pl.), J.*BJ*1.27.3, Plu.2.998e, Charito 2.10. **-ος** (parox.), ον, *murdering children*, μύσος (of a person) E.*HF*1155, cf. Ph.2.82, J.*Ap.*2.24, Hld.10.16.

**τεκν-ολέτειρα**, ἡ, *having lost one's young*, of the nightingale, S.*El.*107 (anap.).

**τέκνον**, τό, (τίκτω,—οὐκ ἔστι μήτηρ ἡ κεκλημένου τέκνου τοκεύς, τροφὸς δὲ.. A.*Eu.*658), *child*, ἄλοχοι καὶ νήπια τέκνα Il.2.136, al.; πατρὸς σωφροσύνη μέγιστον τέκνοις παράγγελμα Democr.208, cf. 222; τέκνα καὶ γυναῖκες Hdt.1.164, 2.30, *SIG*569.10 (Cos, iii B.C.), al., Plb.2.58.9, 9.39.3; γυναῖκες καὶ τ. Hdt.6.19, al., Plb.5.78.1 (cf. 10.34.3), *SIG*633.46 (Milet., ii B.C.), *BGU*1811.5 (i B.C.), etc.: the sg. is used by Hom. only in voc., as a form of address from elders to their youngers, *my son, my child*, sts. with masc. Adj., φίλε τέκνον Il.22.84, Od.2.363, al.: the relat. Pron. or Participle sts. follows in masc. or fem., Pi.*Fr.*171, E.*Supp.*12 sq., *Tr.*740:—the word is used in Prose at Cyrene, *Berl.Sitzb.*1927.160, and Epidaurus, *IG*4$^2$(1).122.82 (iv B.C.), al., but is rarer than παῖς in Att. Prose, Lys.2.74, 11.10, 12.96, D.11.9, Din.1.109; freq. in X., *Lac.*1.8, al., also Arist., *Pol.*1253$^b$7, al., and later, *PPetr.*3p.237 (iii B.C.), *PCair.Zen.*620.9 (iii B.C.), Lxx *Ge.*3.16, al., *PAmh.*2.35.55 (ii B.C.), Plb. (v. supr.); rare in Com. exc. in paratragoedic passages, Ar.*Ach.*891, al.; in Trag. it is generally used with espec. reference to the mother, ὦ τέκνον Νηρῆδος, ὦ παῖ Πηλέως E.*IA*896 (troch.); Ἀγαμέμνονος παῖ (sic codd.) καὶ Κλυταιμήστρας τέκνον Id.*IT*238. 2. of animals, *young*, Od.16.217, Il.2.311, 12.170, al., A.*Th.*292 (lyr.), Hdt.2.66, 3.102, 109, X.*Cyr.*4.1.17, Arist.*GA*753$^a$8, etc. 3. metaph., flowers are γαίας τέκνα A.*Pers.*618; birds αἰθέρος τέκνα E.*El.*897; frogs λιμναῖα κρηνῶν τ. Ar.*Ra.*211, etc. [The penult. is long in Hom.; it is occasionally long in Trag. (e.g. S.*Ph.*249, 260, 875, 914), but much more freq. short, as always in old Com., e.g. Ar.*Lys.*7, *Th.*469, al., except in mock Tragic passages, e.g. Ar.*V.*1518 (lyr.); but sts. long in later Com., Antiph.163.6.]

**τεκνοπαράδοτος**, v. τεχνοπαράδοτος.

**τεκνοποι-έω**, in Act., of the woman, *bear children*, in Med., of the man, *beget them*, cf. X.*Mem.*2.2.4 and 5; μὴ τεκνοποιεῖσθαι ἐξ ἄλλης γυναικός *PEleph.*1.9 (iv B.C.) (but D.S. reverses this usage, cf. 1.73, 4.29); Med., of both parents, *breed children*, X.*Mem.*4.4.22 sq., Arist.*HA*585$^b$10; in Med., also, *have children begotten for one*, X.*Lac.*1.7, Lxx *Ge.*16.2, 30.3, *POxy.*465.154 (ii A.D.). II. Med., of birds, Arist.*HA*597$^a$11. III. Med., *adopt* a child, *UPZ*4.5 (ii B.C.). **-ησις**, εως, ἡ, = τεκνοποιία, Sch.Il.11.243. **-ητικός**, ή, όν, *of* or *for the begetting* or *bearing of children*: ἡ -κή (sc. κοινωνία or ἀρχή), as a subdivision of οἰκονομική, Arist.*Pol.*1253$^b$10 (s.v.l.). ✱**-ία**, ἡ, *begetting* or *bearing of children*, X.*Mem.*1.4.7, *Lac.*1.3, Arist.*EN*1162$^a$19, *Pol.*1265$^a$40, 1270$^a$40, Sor.1.87: of animals, Arist.*HA*589$^a$3; of birds, Plu.2.966d. II. *adoption*, *Gloss.*

**τεκνό-ποινος**, ον, *child-avenging*, μῆνις A.*Ag.*155 (lyr.). **-ποιός**, όν, of the wife, *child-bearing*, Hdt.1.59, 5.40; of the husband, *child-begetting*, E.*Tr.*853 (lyr.): τὰ τ. ἀφροδίσια *legitimate* sexual intercourse, opp. to unnatural crimes, X.*Hier.*1.29. **-ραίστης**, ου, ὁ, *child-destroyer*, Lyc.38. **-σπορία**, ἡ, *begetting of children*, *AP*7.568 (Agath.). **-σπορικός**, ή, όν, *favourable to the begetting of children*, *Cat.Cod.Astr.*5(1).179. **-σπόρος**, ον, *begetting children*, Aristid. Quint.3.21, Man.4.597, 6.540. **-σσόος**, ον, *driving forth his sons*, of Agenor, Nonn.*D.*3.322. **-στοργής**, ές, *full of filial affection*, *TAM*2.235 (Sidyma). **-τροφέω**, *rear children*, Epicur.*Fr.*525, *IG*12(5).655.8 (Syros, ii/iii A.D.); of animals, *rear young ones*, Arist.*HA*625$^b$20. **-τροφία**, ἡ, *rearing of children*, Democr.275, v.l. for τεκνώσεις in Plu.*Comp.Lyc.Num.*3 (pl.). 2. of animals, *rearing of young*, Arist.*HA*562$^b$23. **-τρώκτης**, ου, ὁ, *eating his children*, *An. Par.*3.103.

**τεκνουργία**, ἡ, = τεκνοποιία, Tz.*H.*4.346.

**τεκνοῦς**, οῦσσα, οῦν, contr. for τεκνόεις, εσσα, εν, *having children*, ἄνανδρος ἢ τεκνοῦσσα (Brunck for τεκνοῦσα or τεκοῦσα) S.*Tr.*308 (v. παιδοῦς); οἶνον, ὃς..τὰς γυναῖκας τεκνούσσας ποιεῖ Thphr.*HP*9.18.10, as cited by Ath.1.31f (τεκνούσας codd.Ath., ἀτέκνους codd.Thphr.); αἱ τεκνοῦσαι, opp. αἱ ἀειπάρθενοι, D.C.56.10 codd.

**τεκνο-φᾰγία**, ἡ, *devouring of children*, Luc.*Salt.*80. ✱**-φάγος** [ᾰ], ον, *eating his children*, Κρόνος *JHS*30.262 (Pamphyl.), prob. ib. 32.275 (ibid.).

**τεκνο-φονέω**, *murder children*, *APl.*4.141.6 (Phil.), *AP*9.345 (Leon. Alex., nisi leg. ἐτεκνοφόνα 'liberorum caedem meditabatur'), etc. **-φόνος**, ον, *child-murdering*, Lxx *Wi.*14.23.

**τεκν-όω**, *furnish* or *stock with children*, τ. πόλιν παισί E.*HF*7:—Pass., *to be furnished with children*, i.e. *to have them*, ἐξ οὗ 'τεκνώθη Λάϊος Id.*Ph.*868; ἀπελευθέρας ἀστοῦ τετεκνωμένης ἐξ Αἰγυπτίου *PGnom.*134 (ii A.D.). II. *engender, procreate children*; in Act., commonly of the man, *beget them*, Hes.*Fr.*138, E.*Ph.*19, *Hel.*1146 (lyr.); νύμφης *from* a bride, Id.*Med.*805, cf. *Stud.Ital.*2.382 (Itanus): metaph., Ὀρφεὺς χέλυν ἐτέκνωσε Tim.*Pers.*235 (for τεκνοῦσα in S.*Tr.*308, v. τεκνοῦς):—Med., of the female, *bear children*, ἀρχὴ ταῖς γυναιξὶ τοῦ τεκνοῦσθαι καὶ τοῖς ἄρρεσι τοῦ τεκνοῦν Arist.*HA*585$^a$34: metaph., ὄλβος τεκνοῦται *it has offspring*, A.*Ag.*754; μυρίας ὁ μυρίος χρόνος τεκνοῦται νύκτας ἡμέρας τε S.*OC*618; χθὼν ἐτεκνώσατο φάσματ' ὀνείρων E.*IT*1262 (lyr.):—but Med. is used of the man in Id. *Med.*574, *BCH*1.599 (Delph., iv B.C.), Orph.*H.*29.7; of both parents, E.*Supp.*1087; and Act. of both parents, Arist.*GA*715$^b$10, al.; τεκνώσασα μετ' αὐτοῦ *CIG*4179 (Pontus); ἡ τεκνώσασα Sor.1.87:—Pass., *to be born*, Pi.*I.*1.17: metaph., μὴ καὶ τεκνωθῇ δυσφορώτερος γόος A.*Th.*657; νόμοι..δι' αἰθέρα τεκνωθέντες S.*OT*867 (lyr.); γάμον τεκνοῦντα καὶ τεκνούμενον, i.e. a marriage *where husband and son are one*, ib.1215 (lyr.); αὐτὴ δὲ τεκοῦσ' ὑπὸ τῆσδε τεκνοῦται Theodect.4.2 (hex.). III. in Pass. also, *to be adopted*, D.S.4.67. ✱**-ωμα**, ατος, τό, *child*: metaph., τ. τοῦ πόνου κλέος fame *the child* of toil, A.*Fr.*315. **-ωσις**, εως, ἡ, *begetting, bearing*, τέκνωσιν ποιεῖσθαι to have children, Th.2.44; γίγνεται ἡ τ. τινός Agathocl.2; τὴν τ. ποιεῖσθαι, of birds, Arist.*HA*618$^a$26. II. *adoption*, D.S.4.39.

**τεκοκτόνος**, ον, = τεκνοκτόνος, v. τεκεκτόνος.

**τέκος**, εος, τό, Ep. dat. pl. τέκεσσι Il.5.71, al., τεκέεσσι 3.160, al.:—poet. for τέκνον, 18.63, 24.36, al., Hes.*Sc.*216, al.; as a term of endearment from elders to their youngers, φίλον τέκος Il.9.437, 444, etc.: also in Alc.*Supp.*10.7, Pi.*I.*6(5).30, B.6.13, al., A.*Th.*203, 677, E.*HF*439, *Hec.*475 (mostly lyr.). 2. of animals, Il.8.248: esp. in pl. *the young*, 12.222, al., Ar.*Pl.*292. 3. metaph., δυσσεβίας μὲν ὕβρις τέκος A.*Eu.*534 (lyr.).

**τέκταινα**, ἡ, fem. of τέκτων, Hes.*Th.*ap.Chrysipp.*Stoic.*2.257; γείνεό μοι τέκταινα βίου Call.*Fr.anon.*290, cf. Eust.1129.20.

**τεκταίνομαι**, S.*Fr.*867, etc.: fut. τεκτᾰνοῦμαι Ar.*Lys.*674: aor. ἐτεκτηνάμην E.*IT*951, etc., Ep. τεκτήνατο Il.5.62:—prop. of a carpenter, *frame*, νῆας Il. l.c., cf. Ar. l.c.: abs., *do joiners' work*, as opp. to smiths' work, ἕτερος δὲ χαλκεύει τις, ὁ δὲ τ. Id.*Pl.*163; μηδεὶς χαλκεύων ἅμα τεκταινέσθω Pl.*Lg.*846e, cf. X.*Mem.*4.2.22; opp. πλάττω, Arist.*GA*730$^b$30. 2. of other artificers, τ. χέλυν *h.Merc.*25; τάφον Call.*Jov.*9; τέλεον αὐτὸν [τὸν κόσμον] ἐτεκτήνατο Pl.*Ti.*33b; ὁ τεκταινόμενος *the maker*, ib.28c. 3. metaph., *devise, plan, contrive*, esp. by craft or cunningly (cf. συντεκταίνομαι), λόγος σύγκολλα τἀμφοῖν ἐς μέσον τ. *fits and frames together*, S.*Fr.*867; σιγῇ δ' ἐτεκτήναντ' ἀπόφθεγκτόν μ' *they kept* me from speech of them, E.*IT*951; πᾶν ἐπ' ἐμοὶ τεκταινέσθω (sc. Cleon) Ar.*Ach.*660; τ. μαθήματα Pl.*Sph.*224d, cf. *Ti.*91a; ἐπέων κόσμον Democr.21, cf. Phld.*Rh.*2.49S. II. later, Act. τεκταίνω in same senses, τ. κακά, δόλους, Lxx *Pr.*14.22, 26.24; ἀργύριον ib.*Ba.*3.18: abs., ib.*Ps.*128(129).3; cf. A.R.2.381, 3.592, Luc.*Jud.Voc.*12, Hierocl. *in CA*1p.421M., *AP*6.

80 (Agath.); ζῴδια τεκταίνοντα Hero *Aut.*24.1: even Att. writers have the part. τεκταινόμενα in pass. sense, ταυτί μ' οὐκ ἐλάνθανε τ. τὰ πράγματ' Ar.*Eq.*462; τὰ ὕστερον τ. D.34.48.

**Τεκταῖον**, τό, place-name in Delos, *IG*11(2).156*A*57, al. (iii B.C.); cf. the sculptor **Τεκταῖος**, Paus.2.32.4, 9.35.3.

**τεκτόν-αρχος**, ον, of a Muse, *chief of the builders of verse*, S.*Fr.*159. **-εῖον**, τό, *workshop of a carpenter*, Aeschin.1.124, *Inscr. Délos* 1417*B*ii 163 (ii B.C.), *Gloss.* **-εύω**, = τεκταίνομαι, *do joiners' work*, Hero *Aut.*25.1, Artem.1.51, *Gloss.*

**τεκτον-έω**, = foreg., Ph.1.398. **-ία**, ἡ, *carpentry*, Thphr.*HP*5.7.6 (dub.), *AP*15.14 (Theoph.). **-ικός**, ή, όν, *practised* or *skilled in building*, Pl.*Grg.*460b: as Subst., *a good carpenter* or *builder*, Id.*R.*443c, etc.; as opp. to a smith (χαλκευτικός), X.*Mem.*1.1.7: ἡ -κή (sc. τέχνη) *joiners' work, carpentry*, freq. in Pl., *Plt.*280c, al.; as opp. to smiths' work (χαλκεία, ἡ χαλκευτική), Id.*Prt.*324e, X.*Oec.*1.1, cf. D.L.3.100: τὸ -κόν *skill in carpentry*, Pl.*Cra.*416d. 2. *of* or *for a joiner* or *carpenter*, ὄργανα Id.*Epin.*975c; χρεία Thphr.*HP*5.1.12; κόλλα Gal.12.829, *CPHerm.*p.77 (iii A.D.); τὰ τ. *joinery*, *PMich.Zen.*38.55 (iii B.C.); κεφάλαιον τεκτονικοῦ prob. in *IG*1².374.140.

**τεκτονουργός**· ἀρχιτέκτων, Hsch. (prob. f.l. for -αρχος).

**τεκτονόχειρ**, gen. χειρος, ὁ, ἡ, *with the hand of a* τέκτων, Orph.*Fr.*179.

**τεκτοσύνη**, ἡ, *the art of a joiner, carpentry*, ἀνὴρ εὖ εἰδὼς τεκτοσυνάων Od.5.250; ἄτιμον χέρα τεκτοσύνας hand unhonoured *in its art*, E.*Andr.*1015 (lyr.): metaph., τ. ἐπέων *AP*7.159 (Nicarch.).

⊛ **τέκτων**, ονος, ὁ (fem. in A.*Ag.*1406, E.*Med.*409), *worker in wood, carpenter, joiner*, τέκτονες ἄνδρες, οἵ οἱ ἐποίησαν θάλαμον καὶ δῶμα καὶ αὐλήν Il.6.315, cf. Sapph.91; τέκτονος υἱόν, Ἁρμονίδεω.. ὃς καὶ Ἀλεξάνδρῳ τεκτήνατο νῆας ἐΐσας Il.5.59; νηῶν, δούρων τ., Od.9.126, 17.384, cf. 19.56, 21.43; [πίτυν] οὔρεσι τέκτονες ἄνδρες ἐξέταμον πελέκεσσι Il.13.390; τ., ὅς ῥά τε πάσης εὖ εἰδῇ σοφίης 15.411; τ. γὰρ ὢν ἔπρασσες οὐ ξυλουργικά E.*Fr.*988, cf. A.*Fr.*357, S.*Fr.*474, X.*Mem.*1.2.37: it is freq. opp. to a smith (χαλκεύς), Pl.*Prt.*319d, *R.*370d, X.*HG*3.4.17; to a mason (λιθολόγος), Th.6.44, cf. Ar.*Av.*1154: freq. in Inscrr., *IG*1².373.245, etc., and Papyri, *PCair.Zen.*27.3 (iii B.C.), etc.:—but also, 2. generally, any *craftsman* or *workman*, κεραοξόος τ. *a worker* in horn, Il.4.110, cf. S.*Tr.*768; rarely of *metal-workers*, *h.Ven.*12; τ. Δίου πυρὸς Κύκλωπας E.*Alc.*5; *sculptor, statuary*, ib.348. 3. *master in any art*, as in gymnastics, Pi.*N.*5.49; of poets, τέκτονες σοφοί (sc. ἐπέων) Id.*P.*3.113; τέκτονες εὐπαλάμων ὕμνων Cratin.70 (ap.Ar.*Eq.*530); τέκτονες κώμων, i.e. the χορευταί, Pi.*N.*3.4; τ. νωδυνίας, i.e. a physician, Id.*P.*3.6; δεξιᾶς χερὸς ἔργον, δικαίας τέκτονος a true *workman*, A.*Ag.*1406. 4. metaph., *maker, author*, νεικέων ib.152 (lyr.); κακῶν E.*Med.*409; γένους *the author* of a race, A.*Supp.*594 (lyr.), cf. 283; ψευδῶν τ. Heraclit.28; ὁ γὰρ χρόνος μ' ἔκαμψε, τ. μὲν σοφὸς Crates Com.39. (Cf. Skt. *tákṣan-* 'carpenter', *tákṣati*, *táṣṭi* 'form by cutting, plane, chisel, chop', Lett. *test*, *tēst* 'hew, plane', etc.: cf. τέχνη.)

**τεκών**, aor. part. of τίκτω.

⊛ **τελᾰμών**, ῶνος, ὁ, *broad strap* or *band for bearing* or *supporting* anything (from τελᾰ- 'bear' (v. *τλάω, τελάσσαι), whence also the hero Telamon took his name): 1. *leathern strap* or *belt*, freq. in Hom., Il.17.290; δύω τελαμῶνε περὶ στήθεσσι τετάσθην, ἤτοι ὁ μὲν σάκεος, ὁ δὲ φασγάνου, of Ajax, 14.404; for the sword alone, ξίφος σὺν κολεῷ τε καὶ εὐτμήτῳ τελαμῶνι 7.304, cf. 23.825; μαχαίρας εἶχον ..ἐξ ἀργυρέων τελαμώνων 18.598; περὶ στήθεσσι..χρύσεος ἦν τ. Od.11.610; for the shield, Il.2.388, 11.38, 18.480; it passed over the shoulder and bore the chief weight, 5.796, 16.803, cf. Hdt.1.171; τ. φαεινός Il.12.401; χάλκεος Hes.*Sc.*222. 2. *broad linen bandage* for wounds, Hdt.7.181, Antyll.ap.Orib.7.9.1, Herod. Med.ap.eund.10.18.15, Sor.1.28, al.; ἀμφὶ τραύματ'.. τελαμῶνας βαλεῖν E.*Ph.*1669; also, a *long linen bandage* or *roller*, for swathing mummies, Hdt.2.86, cf. *AP*11.125. 3. *band* for the hair, Callistr.*Stat.*11. II. in Architecture, Τελαμῶνες were *colossal male figures used as bearing-pillars*, being the Roman name for Ἄτλαντες, Vitr.6.7.6. 2. *base* of a στήλη, ἁ στάλα καὶ ὁ τελαμὼν (prob. written τελαμὼ, v. *Mnemos.*58.28) ἱαρὰ τᾶς Ἥρας *IG*4.517 (Argos, v B.C.); [ἀναγράψαι εἰς σ]τήλην λευκοῦ λίθου [κα]ὶ ἀναθ[εῖναι αὐτὴν ἐπὶ τελα]μ[ῶ]νος prob. rest. in *CIG*2056d (loc.inc., perh. Odessus); simply = στήλη, ἀναγράψαι..εἰς τελαμῶνα λευκοῦ λίθου καὶ ἀναθεῖναι κτλ. *SIG*731.41 (Tomi, i B.C.), al., cf. *Milet.*3 p.377 No.153.39, *BMus.Inscr.*1007 (Cyzicus, ii A.D.), etc.

**τελᾰμων-ία**, ἡ, f.l. for στελμονία (q.v.) in Poll.5.55, 10.142 (in the latter place codd. AB have τελμονίαι). **-ίδιον**, τό, Dim. of τελαμών (I.2), Heliod.ap.Orib.48.28.3. **-ίζω**, *bind up a wound*, Satyr.3 (Pass.).

**Τελαμώνιοι κόνδυλοι**· μεγάλοι, χαλεποί, Hsch.: cf. κονδύλους πλάττειν Τελαμών Aristopho 4.7.

**τελάρχης**, ου, ὁ, *commander of a* τέλος (signf. I. 10b), Ascl.*Tact.*2.10, Ael.*Tact.*9.7: v.l. τελεάρχης in Ael. l.c.

**τελάσσαι**· τολμῆσαι, τλῆναι, Hsch. (Cf. τελα-μών.)

**τέλβω, τέλβομαι**, = ἀτέμβω, Hsch. (The order requires τεμβ-.)

**τελδαίνειν**· κομιδῆς ἄξιον, Hsch. (Fort. μελεδαίνειν· κ. ἀξιοῦν.)

**τελεάρχης**, v. τελάρχης.

**τελέαρχος**, ὁ, (τέλος I. 3) *police magistrate at Thebes*, originally in charge of street-cleaning, Plu.2.811b: **τελεαρχία**, ἡ, *his office*, ibid.

**τελέεις**, v. τελήεις.

**τελέθω**, 3 sg. Ion. Iterat. τελέθεσκε *h.Cer.*241:—poet. Verb, cogn. with τέλομαι, τέλλω, and πέλω (qq.v.), *come into being*, νὺξ τελέθει Il.7.282, 293; τελέθουσι γυναῖκες Emp.65.1: then simply *to be* so and so, ἀριπρεπέες τελέθουσι, μινυνθάδιοι τ., Il.9.441, Od.19.328; ζαχρηεῖς τ. Il.12.347; ζαφλεγέες τ. 21.465; ἀμείνων τελέθει Od.7.52; παντοῖοι τ. 17.486; ἵνα τ' ἄρνες ἄφαρ κεραοὶ τ. 4.85; so also Hes.*Op.*181, 506, Thgn.770, Orac.ap.Hdt.7.141, Epich.170, Pi.*P.*2.78, and lyr. passages of Trag., as A.*Supp.*1040, E.*Andr.*783 (not in S.); not in Att. Prose, but in X.*An.*3.2.3, 6.6.36; also Ion., Hp.*Morb.*2.5, al.; and Dor., *Tab.Heracl.*1.111, Theoc.5.18, al., f.l. in Diotog.ap. Stob.4.1.133 (codd. SMA). II. Med. τελέθομαι, *become*, ὀπίσω δὲ θεοὶ τελέθονται Ps.-Phoc.104.

***τελειάζω**, v. τελιάζω.

**τελειογον-έω**, *produce fruit in perfection* or *in due season*, Thphr.*CP*3.18.1; καρπόν Ph.2.400:—Pass., *come complete into the world*, Id.1.29, al.:—**τελεογονέω** in Thphr.*CP*1.11.3; τελεογονέομαι in Plu.2.1018b. **-ία**, ἡ, *perfect production*, ἄγονον εἰς τ. Arist.*GA*748b7, cf. 774b34:—**τελεογονία**, Hp.*Steril.*249, is f.l. for ὀστεολογίη, which Littré adopts from cod. C. **-ος** (parox.), ον, *bearing perfect young*, Arist.*GA*770a33. II. proparox. **τελεόγονος**, ον, Pass., *born in due* or *full time*, Id.*HA*585a18.

**τελειο-καρπέω**, *produce perfect fruit*, Thphr.*HP*1.13.4, al.; **τελεοκαρπέω**, ib.4.8.8, *CP*6.4.3. **-ποιέω**, *make perfect*, cj. in Sch.A.R.4.1027.

⊛ **τέλειος** and **τέλεος**, α, ον, in Trag., Att., and Dor. also ος, ον A.*Eu.*382 (lyr.), Pl.*Phlb.*67a, Arist.*EN*1153b16, *SIG*265 (Delph., iv B.C.), etc.: the form τέλειος is alone used by Hom., neither form in Hes.; τέλεος is alone used by Hdt., exc. in 9.110; in Trag. and Att. both forms occur; Att. Inscrr. up to the end of iii B.C. have only τέλεος, *IG*1².76.39, al., and τέλεος, τελέως, τελεῶ are recommended by Thom. Mag.p.358 R.; τέλειος first in *IG*2².2314.51, al. (early ii B.C.), freq. in Papyri (*PCair.Zen.*429.13, al. (iii B.C.), etc.), but the neut. used as Adv. is sts. τέλεον (*BGU*903.12 (ii A.D.), etc., τέλειον *POxy.*707.31 (ii A.D.), etc.): the form **τέλεως**, acc. τέλεων, with pl. τέλεῳ, is found in *SIG*1025.61, 1026.14 (Cos, iv/iii B.C.), dub. in *Schwyzer* 734 (Zeleia) and Herod.7.20: the form **τέληον** in *GDI*4963 (Crete): (τέλος):—*perfect*, of victims, *entire, without spot* or *blemish*, ἀρνῶν αἰγῶν τε τελείων Il.1.66, cf. 24.34; βοτὸν τ. *Riv.Fil.*56.265 (Cyrene); τὸνς ϝεξήκοντα τελέονς ὄϝινς (acc. pl.) *SIG*56.30 (Argos, v B.C.); of sacrifices, ἱερὰ τ. *perfect, of full tale* or *number*, or *performed with all rites*, Th.5.47, Lex ap.And.1.97, D.59.60; τελέους ἀεὶ τελετὰς τελούμενος τέλεος ὄντως..γίγνεται Pl.*Phdr.*249c; in Il.8.247, 24.315, αἰετὸς τελειότατος πετεηνῶν is prob. *the surest bird of augury* (cf. τελήεις). b. in Dialects, = κύριος, *fully constituted, valid*, ἐν ἀγορᾷ τελείᾳ *Schwyzer* 324.1 (Delph., iv B.C.), *SIG*265 (ibid.), etc.; ἁλιαίᾳ ἔδοξε τελείᾳ ib.594.3 (Mycenae, ii B.C.); *authoritative, final*, ἁ δέ κα ϝράτρα ἁ δαμοσία τελεία εἴε δικάδδοσα *Schwyzer* 412 (Elis); τὸ θέθμιον.. τέλεον εἶμεν *IG*9(1).334.47 (Locr., v B.C.); so in Trag., τελεία ψῆφος a *final* decision, A.*Supp.*739, S.*Ant.*632. 2. of animals, *full-grown*, τέλεον νεαροῖς ἐπιθύσας A.*Ag.*1504 (anap., and so perh. αἶγες τ. in Il. ll. cc.); ἐπ' οὗ θύεται τὰ τ. τῶν προβάτων, opp. γαλαθηνά, Hdt.1.183, cf. *SIG*1015.31 (Halic.), Pherecr.44, *PCair.Zen.*429.13, al. (iii B.C.), *Sammelb.*5277.5 (iii A.D.), etc.; τ. ζῷον defined in Gal.7.677; as Subst., τέλειον καὶ δέκα ἄρνες *SIG*1024.35 (Myconus, iii/ii B.C.); τ. ἵππος, opp. πῶλος, Pl.*Lg.*834c; τ. ἅρμα a chariot *drawn by horses*, opp. ἅρμα πωλικόν, *CIG*2758 III.D2 (Aphrodisias), *SIG*840 (Olympia, ii A.D.), Luc.*Tim.*50; τελέᾳ συνωρίδι *IG*5(2).549.2, al. (Arc., iv B.C.); τελέῳ τεθρίππῳ ib.5; κέλητι τελέῳ ib.550.29; κέλητι τελείῳ ib.7.1772.14, cf. 16; of trees, Thphr.*CP*3.7.5, *POxy.*909.18 (iii A.D.); εἰκὼν τελεία *life-sized*, *GDI*4942b7 (Crete, ii B.C.); of a torsion-engine, *full-sized*, opp. to the model of one, Ph.*Bel.*55.30: of human beings, *full-grown, adult*, Pl.*Lg.*929c, X.*Cyr.*1.2.4, 12, 14, *BGU*1100.10 (i B.C.), *POxy.*485.30 (ii A.D.), Sor.1.10, al. b. *married*, τέλειοι οἱ γεγαμηκότες Paus.Gr.*Fr.*306; Ἥρα Τελεία is so expld. at Stymphalus, Paus.8.22.2, cf. Aristocl.Hist.5 (ap.Sch.Theoc.15.64); v. infr. II. 3. of persons, *accomplished, perfect in his kind*, in relation to quality, Isoc.12.32, 242; ἱστοριῶν συγγραφέα τέλειον *Supp.Epigr.*1.400 (Samos, ii A.D.); τ. σοφιστής Pl.*Cra.*403e; τ. εἴς τι Id.*Phdr.*269e (Sup.); κατὰ πάντα Id.*Ti.*30d; πρός τι Id.*Lg.*647d, 678b, Isoc.12.9, etc.; ἔν τινι Id.*Ep.*4.3 (Sup.); οἱ τ. δογματικοί Gal.15.60; but ἡ τελεία μαῖα the *trained* or *qualified* midwife, distd. from ἡ ἀρίστη (the trained and experienced midwife), Sor.1.4. b. of things, φάρμακον τελεώτατον Pl.*Criti.*106b; τ. ἀρετή, φιλία, etc., Arist.*EN*1129b30, 1156b34, al.; of a syllogism in the 1st figure, the other figures being ἀτελεῖς, Id.*APr.*27a1, etc.; τὸ τελεώτατον ἐκεῖνο γυμνάσιον, ὃ δὴ καὶ κατασκευὴν ὀνομάζουσι Gal.6.169, cf. 208: even of evils, τ. νόσημα a *serious, dangerous* illness, Hp.*Prorrh.*2.30; τελειοτάτη κακία Gal.16.500; ἀδικία τελέα, τελεωτάτη, *absolute*, Pl.*R.*348b, 344a; συνθέσεις λευκὰς τελείας δέκα τρεῖς thirteen *complete* white suits, *PHamb.*10.14 (ii A.D.); τ. ἀποζυγή *complete* divorce, *PGrenf.*2.76.19 (iv A.D.); ὗνις τελεία, κράβακτος ξύλινος τ., etc., *PTeb.*406.19, al. (iii A.D.); of land, *fully inundated*, opp. ἀβροχικός, *PMasp.*107.13, al. (vi A.D.), prob. in *PFlor.*286.23 (vi A.D.). 4. of prayers, vows, etc., *fulfilled, accomplished*, εὐχωλαί Pi.*Fr.*122.15; τέλειον ἐπ' εὐχᾷ ἐολὸν Id.*P.*9.89; τελεία γένεος Οἰδίπου τ' ἀρὰ A.*Th.*832 (lyr.); μὰ τὴν τ. τῆς ἐμῆς παιδὸς Δίκην Id.*Ag.*1432; τέλεα εὔγματα Ar.*Th.*353 (lyr.); of omens or predictions, ὄψις ὀνείρου οὐ τελέη a vision *which imported* nothing, Hdt.1.121; τ. σύμβολον *h.Merc.*526 (s.v.l.); τ. τὸ ἐνύπνιον ἀποτετέλεσται Pl.*R.*443b. 5. of numbers, *full, complete*, τελέους ἑπτὰ μῆνας Ar.*Lys.*104; τ. ἐνιαυτός the *great* year, Pl.*Ti.*39d. b. in Arithm., of *perfect* numbers, which are equal to the sum of their divisors, as 6 = 3 + 2 + 1; 28 = 14 + 7 + 4 + 2 + 1, Id.*R*.546b, Euc.7 *Def*.23, Theo Sm.p.45 H., Nicom.*Ar*.1.16:—but 9 is τ. ὅτι ἐκ τελείου τοῦ γ̄ γίνεται, *Theol.Ar*.58 (3 is τ. because it has ἀρχή, μέσον, τέλος, ib.14). **6.** τ. κρατήρ, i. e. the *third* bowl offered to Ζεὺς Σωτήρ, Ar.*Fr*.526, E.*Fr*.148. **II.** of the gods, *having power to fulfil prayer, all-powerful* (as implied in A.*Ag*.973, Ζεῦ Ζεῦ τέλειε, τὰς ἐμὰς εὐχὰς τέλει), Ζεὺς τ. Pi.*O*.13.115, *P*.1.67; τ. ὕψιστον Δία A.*Eu*.28; τελέων τελειότατον κράτος, Ζεῦ Id.*Supp*.526 (lyr.); of Hera ζυγία, the presiding goddess of marriage (v. supr. I. 2 b, τέλος I. 6), Pi.*N*.10.18, A.*Eu*.214, *Fr*.383, Ar.*Th*.973 (lyr.); of Apollo, Theoc.25.22 (Sup.); of the Eumenides, A.*Eu*.382 (lyr.); Μοῖραι *Supp.Epigr*.3.400.9 (Delph., iii B.C.): generally, θεοὶ τέλειοι τέλειαί τε A.*Th*.167 (lyr.); πῦρ τέλεον ἄρρητον *Lyr.Alex.Adesp*.36.14: also ἀνὴρ τ. *the head* or *lord* of the house, A.*Ag*.972. **III.** = τελευταῖος, *last*, S.*Tr*.948 (lyr.). **IV.** τέλειον, τό, *a royal banquet*, as a transl. of the Pers. τυκτά, Hdt.9.110. **V.** ἡ τελεία (sc. στιγμή) the *full point*, D.T.630.6; so τελείαν δεῖ στίξαι Herm. *in Phdr*.p.84 A. **2.** ἡ τελεία (sc. ἀντίδοτος) the *perfect* antidote, effective against all poisons, Scrib. Larg.177. **VI.** Τέλεος (sc. μήν), ὁ, name of a month at Epidaurus, *IG*4$^{2}$(1).109 ii 114. **VII.** Adv. τελέως *finally, absolutely, with full authority*, A.*Eu*.320,953 (both anap.). **2.** *completely, absolutely, thoroughly*, τ. ἐς ἀσθενὲς ἔρχεται Hdt.1.120; τ. ἐκκλησιάσαιμεν *perfectly*, Ar.*Th*.329 (lyr.); τ. ἄφρων Is.12.4; ἔρια τ. ῥυπαρά *PCair.Zen*.287 (iii B.C.); τ. μ' ὑπῆλθε *completely* deceived me, Epicr.9; τ. ἑστιᾶν *perfectly*, X.*Smp*.2.2; τ. κινήσεται *absolutely*, Pl.*Tht*.182c; τ. γὰρ ἡμᾶς ἐνώχλει he was a *perfect* nuisance to us, *PCair.Zen*.637.4 (iii B.C.); τ. γυμνάζειν put a person through the τέλειον γυμνάσιον, Gal. 6.286; μέσα τ. *completely* neutral, Id.18(2).59, cf. 79, al.—This is the only form of the Adv. allowed by Thom.Mag.p.358 R., but τελείως is found in Gorg.*Hel*.18, Isoc.13.18, Pl.*Def*.411d, Arist.*Metaph*. 1021$^{b}$26, *PPetr*.3 p.114 (iii B.C.), Lxx *Ju*.11.6, Gal.16.639, etc. **3.** the neut. τέλεον is also used as Adv. in later Prose, Luc.*Merc.Cond*. 5, App.*BC*1.8, Sor.2.56, etc. **VIII.** Comp. and Sup.: Hom. uses only τελειότατος: in Prose τελεώτερος, -ώτατος prevail, though the other forms occur in Arist.*EN*1097$^{a}$30, 1174$^{b}$22. Comp. Adv. τελεώτερον Pl.*R*.520b (τελειοτέρως Sch.Il.2.350, v.l. in Procl.*Inst*.18); τελεώτατα Pl.*R*.351b.

**τελειότης**, ητος, ἡ, *completeness, perfection*, Pl.*Def*.412b, Arist.*Ph*. 207$^{a}$21, 261$^{a}$36, Lxx *Jd*.9.16, Gal.1.315; ψυχῆς **τελεότης** Democr. 187: pl., Chrysipp.*Stoic*.3.61.

**τελειο-τοκέω**, *bear perfect young*, Arist.*GA*774$^{b}$17. **-τόκος**, ον, = τελεσφόρος, ἐνιαυτοί *IG*9(1).874 (Corc., ii B.C.).

**τελειουργέω**, *perfect, complete*, Thphr.*CP*2.9.6, Ph.1.8, *Gloss*.

⊛ **τελει-όω** and **τελεόω** (the latter always in Hdt., and the prevailing form in Att. Prose, v. infr., and cf. τέλειος init.):—*make perfect, complete*: **I.** of things, acts, works, time, *make perfect, complete, accomplish*, πάντα ἐτελέωσε ποιήσας Hdt.1.120; τελεώσαντες τὰς σπονδάς *having completed* the libations, Th.6.32; τελειοῖ τὴν ἐνέργειαν ἡ ἡδονή Arist.*EN*1174$^{b}$23; τ. βίου ἐνιαυτούς *complete the tale of* years, *App.Anth*.2.281 (Philadelphia); τὸ ἔργον *Ev.Jo*.4.34; τὰς ἡμέρας *Ev.Luc*.2.43; τὸν δρόμον *Act.Ap*.20.24; τὸν περὶ παιδοτροφίας λόγον ἐνθάδε τελειοῦμεν Sor.1.126:—Med., Iamb.*VP*29.158, *Protr*. 20:—Pass., *to be accomplished*, Hdt.1.160, S.*Tr*.1257; ἐπειδὴ χρόνος ἐτελεώθη Pl.*Plt*.272d; τελεωθέντων ἀμφοτέροισι *when* both men *had their wishes accomplished*, Hdt.5.11. **b.** *execute* a legal instrument, *make* it *valid by completing* it, *PCair.Preis*.43.10 (i A.D.), *PAmh*.2.111.16 (ii A.D.), *BGU*578.21 (ii A.D.), 1657.6 (iii A.D.). **2.** in Logic, τ. τὸ εἶδος *complete, make perfect* the form or species, Arist. *EN*1174$^{a}$16:—Pass., of syllogisms, *to be made perfect* (by reduction to the 1st figure, the other figures being ἀτελεῖς), Id.*APr*.29$^{a}$16, 30, al. **3.** Pass., of prophecies, *to be fulfilled*, *Ev.Jo*.19.28. **II.** *bring to perfection* or *consummation*, ἐπιγενόμενα δὲ ταῦτα τῷ Δαρείῳ ἐτελέωσέ μιν *sealed* his *success*, in his claim to the monarchy, Hdt. 3.86; τελειῶσαι λόχον *make* the ambush *successful*, S.*OC*1089 (lyr.):—Pass., *to be made perfect, attain perfection*, Id.*El*.1510 (anap.); esp. *by reaching maturity* in point of age, Pl.*Smp*.192a, *R*.466e, 487a, 498b, etc.; so of the embryo, plants, *come to maturity*, Arist.*GA* 776$^{a}$31, Thphr.*HP*8.2.6, Sor.1.33, al., Gal.6.531; τελειωθέντος [μειρακίου] κατὰ τὸ μέγεθος ib.162. **2.** in Pass. also, τελειωθῆναι, = γῆμαι, Paus.Gr.*Fr*.306, cf. τέλειος I. 2 b, τέλος I. 6. **3.** Pass., *to be made perfect*, of true Christians, *Ep.Hebr*.11.40, 12.23. **4.** Pass., *die*, *IG*14.628 (Rhegium). **III.** intr., *bring fruit to maturity, come to maturity*, Arist.*GA*757$^{b}$24. **-ω**, Ep. for τελέω (q.v.). **-ωμα**, ατος, τό, *completion*, τῆς οἰκίας Arist.*Ph*.246$^{a}$17; τῆς ψυχῆς Aq.*Jb*. 12.2, Eun.*VS*p.500 B. **2.** Thess. **τελείουμα**, *dedication on the occasion of* τελείωσις II, *IG*9(2).1235 (Phalanna, ii B.C.). **-ωσις** or **τελέωσις**, εως, ἡ, *development, completion*, of physical growth, λαμβάνει τελέωσιν τὰ ᾠά Arist.*HA*543$^{a}$19, cf. 561$^{a}$5, Hp.*Septim*.1, Sor. 1.18, al., Gal.15.26; τὴν τ. τῶν μορίων ἀπολαμβάνειν Arist.*HA*583$^{b}$24, etc.; ἡ τῶν καρπῶν τ. Thphr.*HP*3.4.3; ἕως τελειώσεως to *saturation-point*, Epicur.*Ep*.2 p.38 U.; of a building, Arist.*Ph*.246$^{a}$26; of a statue, *Stoic*.3.48; in moral sense, αἱ ἀρεταὶ τελειώσεις Arist.*Ph*.247$^{a}$ 2, cf. 246$^{a}$13, *Metaph*.1021$^{b}$20; εἰς τὴν τ. ἄγεσθαι τῆς φύσεως Id.*EN* 1153$^{a}$12. **b.** *execution* of a legal instrument *by completing* it, *BGU* 1168.3 (i B.C.), *PFlor*.56.7, al. (iii A.D.). **2.** in Logic, ἡ τ. τῶν συλλογισμῶν Arist.*APr*.42$^{a}$35; cf. τελειόω I.2. **II.** *attainment of manhood*, *AJA*18.324 (Sardis, Epist. Augusti). **b.** *marriage*, Lxx *Je*.2.2; cf. τέλειος I. 2 b, II. **III.** of events, *accomplishment, fulfilment*, *Ev.Luc*.1.45; λόγων Lxx *Ju*.10.9. **-ωτής**, οῦ, ὁ, *accomplisher, finisher*, τῆς πίστεως *Ep.Hebr*.12.2. **-ωτικός**, ή, όν, *perfective, effective*, Procl.*Inst*.78. Adv. -κῶς Id. *in Alc*.p.52 C.

**Τελενῑκίζω**, *make empty*, coined by Cratin. (217) from Τελένικος, the name of a poor man otherwise unknown: hence **Τελενίκειος** ἠχώ an *empty* sound, Phot., Suid.

**τελεο-γονέω, -γονία, -γόνος**, v. τελειογ-. **-δρομέω**, *complete the course*, Ps.-Archyt.ap.Iamb.*Protr*.4. **-δρόμος**, ον, *completing the course*, *AP*5.202 (Asclep.). **-καρπέω**, v. τελειοκ-. **-μηνος**, ον, *with full complement of months*, τ. ἄροτος, i.e. *a full twelvemonth*, S.*Tr*.824 (lyr.); τέκνα τ. children *born after the full number of months*, Arist.*HA*585$^{a}$20.

**τέλεος, τελεότης, τελεόω**, v. τέλειος, τελειότης, τελειόω.

**τελεσιάζω**, (τελέσιος) = τελέω, of sacrifice, *AB*306, *EM*751.9.

**τελεσιάς**, άδος, ἡ, a kind of *armed dance*, named after its inventor Telesias, Ath.14.629d, 630a, Hsch.

**τελεσί-δρομος**, ον, = τελεοδρόμος, Anon.ap.Stob.1.9.7. **II.** Τελεσίδρομος, ὁ, name of a hero, *IG*1$^{2}$.5.4.

**τελεσ-ίερος**, ον, *completing a sacrifice*, παιᾶνα Hsch.: prob. a gloss on **τελεσσίε[ρον** παιᾶνα in Pi.*Pae*.7.2.

**τελεσῐ-καρπέω**, *bring to maturity*, καρπόν Str.17.3.11; and **-καρπος**, ον, *bringing its fruit to maturity*, ἄμπελος Id.15.1.8.

**τελέσιος**, ον, *finishing*: τ. ἡμέρα the *last* day, Hsch.

**τελεσῐουργ-έω**, *bring* their young *to perfection*, of viviparous animals, Arist.*GA*718$^{b}$10, 732$^{a}$25, Sor.1.15:—Pass., Arist.*HA*565$^{b}$23, D.S.5.4, *Placit*.5.13.3: metaph. of sciences, Phld.*Rh*.1.1 S. **2.** *create perfection*, Procl.*Inst*.133. **II.** *accomplish fully*, Plb.5.4. 10, Jul.*Or*.7.222a (Pass.), etc.; *give effect to*, τι Luc.*Nav*.25. **III.** *initiate fully* into a philosophical system, Epicur.*Ep*.1 p.4 U. (Pass.). **-ημα**, ατος, τό, *an accomplished purpose*, Plb.3.4. 12. **-ία**, ἡ, *completion of a work*, Heph.Astr.3.4, Procl. *in Alc*. p.72 C.; *efficacy* of ritual, Iamb.*Myst*.2.11, al.; of numbers, *a making* τέλειος (I. 5 b), *Theol.Ar*.44. ⊛ **-ός**, όν, *completing a work, working out its end, effective*, Pl.*Phdr*.270a, Plb.2.40.2, etc. **2.** *creating perfection*, Procl.*Inst*.145. **3.** epith. of Zeus, τελεσθεὶς Διὶ τ. *Milet*.7.16 (i B.C.).

**τέλεσις**, εως, ἡ, *event, fulfilment*, *App.Anth*.3.146.12 (Theon, pl.); ἵνα τέλεσιν τὴν ταχίστην λάβῃ τὰ λειτουργήματα *POxy*.1412.13 (iii A.D.).

**τελεσῐφάντης** (-φάστας cod.), ου, ὁ, = ἱεροφάντης, ὀργιοφάντης, Hsch.

**τελεσίφρων**, v. τελεσσίφρων.

**τελέσκω**, v. τελίσκω:—τέλεσκον, Ion. impf. of τελέω.

**τέλεσ-μα**, ατος, τό, (τελέω) *money paid* or *to be paid, payment*, D.S.29.19, Sch.Ar.*Ach*.615; τ. σιτικὰ καὶ ἀργυρικά *OGI*669.47 (Egypt, i A.D.), cf. *BGU*1067.14 (ii A.D.), *Cod.Just*.10.16.13.6; *tax*, γῆ καθαρὰ ἀπὸ δημοσίων τ. *POxy*.1270.40 (ii A.D.); τελεῖν τὰ εὐσεβῆ τ. *BGU*917.15 (iv A.D.), cf. *POxy*.1647.45 (ii A.D.), etc.; *outlay*, *IG*12 (1).1032.29 (Carpathos, ii (?) B.C.), *Supp.Epigr*.3.674 *A* 16 (Rhodes, ii B.C.), Luc.*JTr*.11, *Sat*.35; τελέσμασι τοῖς αὐτῶν *at* their own *expense*, *SIG*581.55 (Crete, iii/ii B.C.). **II.** *certified copy, certificate*, *Jahresh*.7 *Beibl*.44 (Ephesus, i B.C.). **-μός**, ὁ, *consecration-ceremony*, συντελοῦντες τὸν τ. καὶ τὴν θυσίαν τῷ Ἀσκληπιῷ *IG* 12(5).865.13 (Tenos). **2.** = *transactio*, *Gloss*.

**τελεσσί-γᾰμος** [ῐ], ον, Ep. for *τελεσίγαμος, *perfecting* or *consecrating a marriage*, Nonn.*D*.48.232, 693, al., Musae.279. **-γονος**, ον, Ep. for *τελεσίγονος, *perfecting* or *completing the birth*, Nonn.*D*.48.827, al. **II.** *perfectly grown, full ripe*, καρποί Orph.*H*.53.10. **-δώτειρα**, poet. for *τελεσιδ-, = τέλος δοῦσα, *she that gives completeness* or *accomplishment*, Μοῖρα E.*Heracl*.899 (lyr.).

**τελεσσίερος**, v. τελεσίερος.

**τελεσσί-νοος** [ῐ], ον, = τελεσσίφρων, Orph.*A*.1311. **-τοκος**, ον, Ep. for *τελεσίτ-, *completing the birth*, Nonn.*D*.48.890. **-φρων**, ονος, ὁ, ἡ, (φρήν) poet. for τελεσίφρων, *working its will*, μῆνις τ., of divine vengeance, A.*Ag*.700 (lyr.). **2.** Μνήμης τελεσίφρονος υἱὲ μέγιστε perh. *perfecting man's mental powers*, *PMag.Lond*.46.415, cf. 121.678.

**τελεσ-τήρ**, ῆρος, ὁ, = τελεστής 2 a, τᾶς Μεγάλας Ματρός *IG*4.757 *B* 10 (Troezen). ⊛ **-τήριον**, τό, *place for initiation*, at Phlyae, Plu. *Them*.1: at Eleusis, Id.*Per*.13. **II.** τελεστήρια (sc. ἱερά), τά, *thank-offering for success*, X.*Cyr*.8.7.3, Ael.*VH*12.1. ⊛ **-τής**, οῦ, ὁ, *an official*, Elean nom. sg. τελεστά *SIG*9 (Olympia, vi B.C.). **2.** *initiator, priest*, Max.Tyr.10.5, Cels.ap.Orig.*Cels*.8.48, Procl. *in Ti*. 1.51 D. **b.** = γόης, *Cat.Cod.Astr*.8(4).221. **3.** *initiated person*, Cleanth.*Stoic*.1.123 (cj., v. τελετής). **-τία** (-σθία cod.)· θυσία τις ἐν Λίνδῳ, Hsch. **-τικός**, ή, όν, *fit for finishing* or *accomplishing*, Arist.*Phgn*.813$^{a}$4; τελεστικὸς τῶν ἁπάντων *bringing to fulfilment*, *Theol.Ar*.60. **2.** *connected with mystic rites*, μαντικὸς ἢ τ. βίος Pl.*Phdr*.248d; Διονύσου τ. ἐπίπνοια ib.265b; τ. σοφία Plu.*Sol*.12; θρῆνος Philostr.*Her*.19.14; τ. καὶ μυστικόν Ael.*NA*2.42. **3.** τελεστικόν, τό, *payment for admission to a priesthood*, *OGI*90.16 (Rosetta, ii B.C.). **4.** τελεστικά, τά, name of a ceremony, dub. l. in *Jahresh*.26 *Beibl*.17 (Ephesus). **-τός**, ή, όν, *fulfilled*, ἐπὶ τελεστῶν ἀγαθῶν dub. in *IG*2$^{2}$.4548. ⊛ **-τρα**, τά, *fees for admission to priesthood*, *Milet*.6.22 (iii B.C.), *IG*12(7).237.27 (Amorgos, ii/i B.C.). **-τρια**, ἡ, fem. of τελεστής, Suid. s.v. Αἰσχίνης. **-τωρ**, ορος, ὁ, poet. for τελεστής, as epith. of Apollo, *AP*9.525.20.

**τελεσφορ-έω**, *bring fruit to perfection*, Thphr.*HP*8.7.6, *Ev.Luc*.8. 14:—Pass., τελεσφορουμένων καρπῶν D.S.2.36. **2.** of young women, *bear perfect offspring*, Artem.1.16; τ. καὶ μὴ ἀποβάλλειν τὸ ἔμβρυον

Dsc.*Eup.*2.97 :—Pass., of the offspring, Corn.*ND*34, Sor.1.41, Jul.*Or.*7.220c. 3. generally, *bring to a head,* ἔαρ ἐς κορυφὴν τ. [νοῦσον] Aret.*SD*1.16, cf. Phld.*Lib.*p.31 O. :—Pass., *to be brought to perfection,* Longin.14.3. II. *pay toll* or *custom,* X.*Vect.*3.5. III. *to be a* τελεσφόρος (III. 2), *GDI*4837 (Cyrene), in form -φορέντες, cf. *Africa Italiana* 2.130,153 (ibid.). **-ησις,** εως, ἡ, *mature development,* Max.Tyr.16.4. **-ία,** ἡ, *initiation in the mysteries,* τ. ἐπετήσιος Call.*Ap.*78, cf. *Cer.*130 (pl., s.v.l.), A.R.1.917 (pl.). II. *toll, custom, AB*309. **-ίων,** v. τελεσφόρος III. **-ος** (parox.), ον, *bringing fulfilment*; used by Hom. always in phrase τελεσφόρον εἰς ἐνιαυτόν, for the space of a *fulfilment-bringing* year, for a *complete* year, Il.19.32, Od.4.86, al., Hes.*Th.*740 ; freq. in Trag., *destined to be accomplished,* τελεσφόροι ἀραί A.*Th.*655 ; τ. εὐχαί Id.*Ch.*212, E.*Ph.*69 ; εὔχομαι τοὔνειρον εἶναι τοὖτ' ἐμοὶ τ. A.*Ch.*541 ; φάσματα δὸς τ. grant *accomplishment* to the visions, S.*El.*646 ; τ. χάριν δοῦναι grant the favour *of fulfilment,* Id.*OC*1489 ; τ. διδοῦσα χρησμόν E.*Ph.*641 (lyr.). II. *able to fulfil* or *accomplish, all-powerful,* Ζεύς *h.Hom.*23.2 ; Μοῖρα A.*Pr.*511 ; πρὸς ἐνδίκοις φρεσὶν τελεσφόροις δίναις κυκλούμενον κέαρ Id.*Ag.*996 (lyr.) ; Δίκη S.*Aj.*1390 ; πεσεῖν ἐς τὸ μὴ τ. to fall fruitless, powerless to the ground, A.*Ag.*1000 (lyr.) ; τ. προθυμία, πειθώ, cited as examples of frigidity of style, Arist.*Rh.*1406ᵃ3. 2. *bearing fruit in due season,* χῶραι Thphr.*CP*3.23.5 ; *bringing their fruit to perfection,* δένδρα Plu.2.2e ; *favourable to production,* ὕδωρ Thphr.*CP*2.6.4. b. Pythag. name for 7 and 9, *Theol.Ar.*42 and 58. 3. *having the management* or *ordering,* δωμάτων τ. γυνή A.*Ch.*663 ; cf. τέλειος II. III. as pr. n., a deity worshipped in company with Asclepios and Hygeia, *IG*2².4533.27, al. :—also **Τελεσφορίων,** ωνος, ὁ, *CIG*6753 (loc.inc., dedicated to Ἀσκληπιὸς Περγαμηνός). 2. title of priest at Cyrene, ib.5145 (cf. τελεσφορέω III). 3. *sorceress,* Lxx *De.*23.17(18).

**τελετ-αρχέω,** *to be in charge of the mysteries,* prob. in *IGRom.*1.817 (Callipolis). **-άρχης,** ου, ὁ, *founder of mysteries,* Orph.*H.*54, etc. 2. in pl., an order of divine beings *who bring initial and final terms into relation,* Dam.*Pr.*96, al., cf. 277. **-αρχικός,** ή, όν, *pertaining to* τελετάρχαι 2, διάκοσμος, φύσις, ib.112. II. *of* or *belonging to initiations,* [ὄνομα] Procl. *in Cra.*p.33 P. **-ή,** ἡ, (τελέω) *rite,* esp. *initiation* in the mysteries, ἡ Δήμητρος τ., τὴν οἱ Ἕλληνες Θεσμοφόρια καλέουσι Hdt.2.171, cf. And.1.111, Pl.*Euthd.*277d ; ἐς χεῖρας ἄγεσθαι τὴν τελετήν take in hand *the matter of initiation,* Hdt.4.79 : pl., *mystic rites practised at initiation,* E.*Ba.*22, 73 (lyr.), Ar.*V.*121, *Pax*413,419 ; Ὀρφεὺς . . τελετάς θ' ἡμῖν κατέδειξε Id.*Ra.*1032, cf. D.25.11 ; καθαρμῶν καὶ τελετῶν τυχοῦσα Pl.*Phdr.*244e ; λύσεις τε καὶ καθαρμοὶ ἀδικημάτων διὰ θυσιῶν . . , ἃς δὴ τελετὰς καλοῦσιν Id.*R.*365a, cf. *Prt.*316d, Isoc.4.28. 2. pl., *theological doctrines,* Chrysipp.*Stoic.*2.17. 3. *a making magically potent, PMag.Par.*1.1596, *PMag.Lond.*46.159, 121.872, etc. II. *a festival accompanied by mystic rites,* mostly in pl. (τελετὰς . . καλοῦμεν τὰς ἔτι μείζους καὶ μετά τινος μυστικῆς παραδόσεως ἑορτάς Ath.2.40d), Pi.*O.*3.41, *P.*9.97, *N.*10.34 : in sg., E.*IT*959, Ar.*V.*876, *Ra.*342, Arist.*Rh.*1401ᵃ15 : metaph., πρωτόγονος τ., of a child's *birth,* Pi.*O.*10(11).51 ; πολέμου τ. Batr.303 ; κατ' αὐτὴν (sc. τὴν περὶ χρείας μορίων πραγματείαν) χρὴ τελεῖσθαι τὴν τ. Gal.*UP*17.1. III. *a priesthood* or *sacred office,* Decr.ap.D.59.104. **-ής,** οῦ, ὁ, = τελεστής, ἱεροφάντης, Euphron.1, Demetr.ap.D.H.*Pomp.*2.6, Cleanth.*Stoic.*1.123 codd.Epiphan. (cf. τελεστής) ; in *PLond.*1821.262, τελετάς = 'all the ney that belong to Dionysus'.

**τελευτ-αῖος,** α, ον, (τελευτή) *last,* in Order, οἱ τ. κύκλοι Hdt.1.98 ; τὰ δύο τὰ τ. the *last* two lines, Id.7.142 ; τὰ τ. the *endings* or *terminations,* Id.5.68 ; ἐν τελευταίοις πίπτειν Pl.*R.*619e ; τελευταίους στῆσαι to station *in the rear ranks,* X.*Cyr.*6.3.25 ; οἱ τ. πόδες the *hind* feet, Arist.*PA*684ᵃ12. 2. more freq. of Time, ἡ τ. ἡμέρα the *last* day allowed for payment, D.28.1 ; of a festival, without ἡμέρα, X.*HG*6.4.16, etc. ; *one's last day,* S.*OT*[1528] (troch.). E.*Andr.*101 ; ὁδὸν τὴν τ. one's *last* journey, S.*Tr.*155 ; τὸν τ. βίον the *end* of life, Id.*OC*1551 ; τ. ἐμοῦ φήμη Id.*Tr.*1149 ; τὸ τ. ἐκβάν D.1.11. 3. *uttermost, extremest,* ὕβρις S.*El.*271 ; ἡ ὀλιγαρχία ἡ τ. Arist.*Pol.*1312ᵇ35 ; ἡ τ. δημοκρατία ib.1298ᵃ31. II. τὸ τ. as Adv., *for the last time,* X.*HG*7.5.20, etc. ; or τελευταῖον, Id.*Cyr.*8.7.28, S.*OT*1183 ; τὰ τ. Pl.*Grg.*515d. 2. τὸ τ. *finally, in the last place,* Ar.*Nu.*945 (anap.), Th.8.8, Pl.*R.*532a, D.18.312, etc. ; τὰ τ. Th.1.24, 8.85 ; τελευταῖον Hdt.1.91 : but, 3. the Adj. is freq. used with Verbs, where we should use the Adv., ὁ τελευταῖος δραμὼν A.*Ag.*314 ; παρελθόντες τελευταῖοι Th.1.67, etc. ; cf. τελευτάω II.4. **-άω,** fut. -ήσω E.*Tr.*1029, etc. : pf. τετελεύτηκα Pl.*Men.*75e, al. :—Pass., fut. Med. τελευτήσομαι always in pass. sense, Il.13.100, Od.8.510, 9.511, E.*Hipp.*370 (lyr.) : aor. ἐτελευτήθην Il.15.74 :—*bring to pass, accomplish,* ὄφρα . . τελευτήσω τάδε ἔργα Il.8.9 ; τ. ἃ μενοινᾷς Od.2.275 ; ἐπὴν ταῦτα τελευτήσῃς τε καὶ ἔρξῃς 1.293, cf. 2.306 ; γάμον τ. 24.126 ; *fulfil* an oath or promise, wish or hope, τ. ἐέλδωρ 21.200 ; τ. ὅσ' ὑπέστης Il.13.375 ; οὐ Ζεὺς ἄνδρεσσι νοήματα πάντα τελευτᾷ 18.328, cf. Od.3.56,62 ; ὅρκια Call.*Aet.*3.1.29 ; τελευτᾶν τινι κακὸν ἦμαρ *bring about* an evil day for one, Od.15.524 ; τ. πόνους Δαναοῖς Pi.*P.*1.54, cf. E.*Ph.*1581 (lyr.) ; οἷ τ. λόγον Id.*Tr.*1029 ; τὸ δ' ἔνθεν ποῖ τελευτῆσαί με χρή ; to what *end* must I *bring* it? S.*OC*476 ; Ζεὺς δ' τι νεύσῃ, τοῦτο τελευτᾷ E.*Alc.*979 (lyr.), etc. :—Pass., *to be fulfilled, come to pass, happen,* ll.cc. sub init. ; πρίν γε τὸ Πηλείδαο τελευτηθῆναι ἐέλδωρ Il.15.74 ; πρὶν τελευτηθῇ φόνος E.*Or.*1218. 2. *finish,* σχεδίην . . ἐπηγκενίδεσσι Od.5.253 ; ἐπεὶ ῥ' ὄμοσέν τε, τελεύτησέν τε τὸν ὅρκον had sworn and *completed* (made binding) the oath, 2.378, etc. ; ἡσύχιμον ἁμέραν τ. *close* a peaceful day, Pi.*O.*2.33 ; ἄρξομαι ἐκ βολβοῖο τελευτήσω δ' ἐπὶ θύννον (sc. τὸ δεῖπνον) Pl.Com.173.6 (hex.). 3. esp. τ. τὸν αἰῶνα *finish* life, i.e. *die,* Hdt.1.32, 9.17, etc. ; τ. βίον A.*Ag.*929, S.*Fr.*646 codd. (sed leg. δρόμον), E.*Hec.*419, Pl.*Prt.*351b ; ὑπ' ἄλλου τ. τὸν βίον, i.e. to be killed, Id *Lg.*870e : also (after the analogy of παύομαι) c. gen., τελευτᾶν τοῦ ἀνθρωπίνου βίου *make an end of* life, X.*Cyr.*8.7.17 ; so λόγου τ. Th.3.59 ; ἐπαίνου τ. ἐς τάδε ἔπη ib.104. b. freq. abs.. *end life, die,* Hdt.1.66, 3.38,40, al., Pl.*R.*614b, al. ; πρὶν τελευτήσαντ' ἴδῃς before you see him *dead,* S.*Fr.*662 ; τ. μάχῃ A.*Th.*617 ; νούσῳ Hdt.1.161 ; γήραϊ Id.6.24 ; τ. ὑπό τινος *die* by another's hand or means, ib.92 ; δόλῳ ὑπό τινος Id.4.78 ; ὑπὸ αἰχμῆς σιδηρέης Id.1.39 ; ὑπ' ἀλλαλοφόνοις χερσίν A.*Th.*930 (lyr.) ; ἐκ τῆς πληγῆς Pl.*Lg.*877b ; of animals, Arist.*PA*667ᵇ11, *PMich.Zen.*67.25 (iii B.C.). II. intr. (as always in Prose, except in signf. I. 3a) : 1. *to be accomplished,* λόγων κορυφαί Pi.*O.*7.68 (as v.l. for τελεύταθεν) ; ἐλπίδες E.*Ba.*908 (lyr.). 2. *come to an end,* A.*Ag.*635, etc. : esp. of Time, τελευτῶντος τοῦ μηνός, τοῦ θέρους, Th.2.4,32, etc. : of actions, events, etc., τ. ἡ ναυμαχία ἐς νύκτα Id.1.51, etc. b. with words indicating the kind of end or outcome, ἦν ὁ πόλεμος κατὰ νόον τ. Hdt.9.45, cf. 7.47 ; εὖ τ. A.*Supp.*211 ; πτωχοὶ τ. *end by being* beggars, Pl.*R.*552c ; οὕτως τ. Th.1.110,138 ; τ. ἔς τι *come to a* certain *end, issue in,* αἱ εὐτυχίαι ἐς τοῦτο ἐτελεύτησαν Hdt.3.125 ; τ. ἐς τὠυτὸ γράμμα *end in* the same letter, Id.1.139, cf. Th.2.51, 4.48, Pl.*R.*618a ; εἰς ἄνδρας ἐκ μειρακίων τ. Id.*Tht.*173b ; ποῖ (= ἐς τί) τελευτᾶν (φασί) ; *came to* what *end*? A.*Pers.*735 (troch.), cf. *Ch.*528, Pl.*Lg.*630b ; also τ. ἐπί τι Id.*R.*510d, *Smp.*211c. 3. *die,* v. supr. I.3b. 4. the part. τελευτῶν, ῶσα, ῶν, is used with Verbs like an Adv., *to finish with, at the end, at last,* as τελευτῶν ἔλεγε Hdt.3.75 ; κἂν ἐγίγνετο πληγὴ τελευτῶσα there would have been a fray *to finish with,* S.*Ant.*261 ; τελευτῶν . . ἐξεβλήθη Ar.*Eq.*524 (anap.) ; τὰς ὀλοφύρσεις τελευτῶντες ἐξέκαμνον *at last* they got tired of mourning, Th.2.51, cf. 47 ; ἦν δέῃ τελευτῶντα τὴν στρωμνὴν ἐξαργυρῶσαι Id.8.81 ; sts. with another part., τὴν τυραννίδα χαλεπὴν τελευτῶσαν γενομένην having *at last* become . ., Th.6.53, cf. Pl.*Phdr.*228b ; πόλεις ἐπάγοντες καὶ τελευτῶντες Λακεδαιμονίους Lys.12.60. 5. of local limits and the like, μέχρι Σολόεντος ἄκρης, ἣ τελευτᾷ τῆς Λιβύης Hdt.2.32 ; τελευτῶντος τοῦ Λαβυρίνθου ἔχεται πυραμίς ib.148 ; τῇ ἡ Κνιδίη χώρη ἐς τὴν ἤπειρον τ. Id.1.174, cf. 2.33, 4.39, *IG*1².900, Pl.*Men.*75e. **-ή,** ἡ, (τελέω) *completion, accomplishment,* τελευτὴν ποιῆσαι [γάμου] accomplish, Od.1.249, 16.126 ; κραίνειν τελευτὰν γάμου Pi.*P.*9.66 ; τ. νόστου ib.1.35 ; οὐ γάρ μοι δοκέει μύθοιο τ. τῇδέ γ' ὁδῷ κρανέεσθαι Il.9.625. 2. *event, issue,* δεῖξεν πᾶσαν τ. πράγματος Pi.*O.*13.75, cf. Thgn.1075 ; γάμου πικραὶ τ. A.*Ag.*745 (lyr.) ; τ. πρευμενεῖς κτίσαι Id.*Supp.*138 (lyr.) ; θεσφάτων Id.*Pers.*740 (troch.) ; κακοῦ θυμοῦ τ. . . κακὴ προσγίγνεται S.*OC*1198. 3. *termination, end,* οὐδέ τις ἦν ἔριδος λύσις οὐδὲ τ. Hes.*Th.*637 ; μή μ' ἀποσβεσθὲν λάθῃ πρὸς τῇ τ. τῆς ὁδοῦ Ar.*Lys.*294 (lyr.) ; ἡ τ. τοῦ πολέμου Th.1.13 ; καλλίστην τελευτὴν ἐπιτιθέντες κινδύνοις Lys.2.47 ; τελευτὴν ἔχειν Pl.*Lg.*782a. 4. esp. βιότοιο τ. Il.7.104, 16.787 ; βίου Hdt.1.30,31, cf. And.4.24 ; τ. τοῦ βίου τελεῖν S.*Tr.*79 ; ἐπὶ τελευτῇ τοῦ βίου Pl.*Grg.*516a. b. freq. without βίου, *the end of life, death,* Pi.*O.*5.22, Pl.*Phd.*118, etc. ; τ. ὑστάτη S.*Tr.*1256 ; τελευτῆς λαχεῖν, τυχεῖν, Th.2.44, X.*HG*4.4.6 ; τ. δοῦναι Id.*Cyr.*8.7.3 ; periphr., θανάτοιο τ. the *end* that is death, Hes.*Sc.*357, cf. τέλος I.4 ; τῆς γηραιοῦ τ. προαποθνῄσκειν Antipho4.1.2. 5. with Preps., in adv. sense, ἐς τελευτὴν *at the end, at last,* *h.Hom.*7.29, Hes.*Op.*333, Thgn.201, S.*OC*1223 (lyr.) ; ἐπὶ τελευτῆς Pl.*Phdr.*267d, etc. ; ἐν τελευτᾷ Pi.*O.*7.26, A.*Th.*936 (lyr.). II. *end, extremity* of anything, as of limbs, Arist.*PA*654ᵇ24, cf. 685ᵃ1, *GA*720ᵇ18, Pl.*Ti.*33b, *Men.*75e. 2. *end, close* of a sentence, Arist.*Rh.*1420ᵇ2, etc. ; of a play, Id.*Po.*1450ᵇ29, cf. Demetr.*Eloc.*257 ; of a word, J.*AJ*1.6.1. **-ητέον,** *one must end,* Gal.18(1).780.

**τελέω,** Ep. also **τελείω,** both in Hom. (τελέοντες Od.3.262, cf. 4.776, al., τελείει 6.234, 23.161) : Ep. impf. τέλεον Il.23.373,768 ; ἐτέλειον 9.456, 15.593 ; Ion. τελέσκον Call.*Dian.*123, *Fr.*434 ; τελέεσκον Q.S.8.213 : fut. τελέω Pi.*N.*4.43, X.*Cyr.*8.6.3, (δια-) Pl.*R.*425e codd., D.21.66 codd. (-τελῶ Cobet in both places), *PAvrom.*2A9 (i B.C.) ; Ep. also τελέω, Il.8.415, 12.59, Od.2.256, etc. ; Att. τελῶ S.*El.*1435, Ar.*Ra.*173, Pl.*Prt.*311b : aor. (ἐ)τέλεσα Od.5.390 ; Ep. τέλεσσα and ἐτέλεσσα 11.246, Il.12.222, 23.543,559, al. (inf. τελέσσαι Pi.*P.*3.9) ; Att. ἐτέλεσα Th.4.78, etc. : pf. τετέλεκα Pl.*Ap.*20a, (δια-) D.18.203 :—Med., fut. (v. infr.) : aor. ἐτελεσάμην Id.38.18, etc. : pf. τετέλεσμαι *Inscr.Prien.*11.34 (iii B.C.) :—Pass., Ep. impf. ἐτελείετο Il.1.5 : fut. τελεσθήσομαι Thphr.*Char.*16.12 ; fut. Med. in this sense, τελεῖται A.*Pr.*929, *Ag.*68 (anap.), etc., τελέεσθαι Il.2.36, τελεῖσθαι Od.23.284 ; part. τελεόμενος Hdt.1.206, τελεύμενος Id.3.134 : aor. ἐτελέσθην Od.4.663, etc. ; Aeol. inf. τελέσθην Sapph.*Supp.*1.4 : pf. τετέλεσμαι Il.18.74, etc. : plpf. τετέλεστο 19.242 : Cret. pf. part. τετελημένος *GDI*4963 ; Ion. 3 pl. pf. τετέληνται dub. in *SIG*1024.22 (Myconus, iii/ii B.C.) : (τέλος) :—*fulfil, accomplish, execute, perform,* freq. in Poets from Hom. downwds., less freq. in Prose (except in signfs. II and III) ; τελέσαι ἔργον τε ἔπος τε Od.2.272, cf. Il.1.108,523, etc. ; τ. φιλοτήσια ἔργα Od.11.246 ; μ' ἔφαντο ἄξειν εἰς Ἰθάκην, οὐδ' ἐτέλεσσαν but *did it* not, 13.212 ; τ. ἀέθλους 3.262 ; πόνον 23.250 ; πύματον δρόμον Il.23.373 ; ὁδὸν Od.2.256, Mimn.11 ; sts. without ὁδόν, ἄτερ καμάτοιο τέλεσσαν ἤματι τῷ αὐτῷ καὶ ἀπήνυσαν οἴκαδ' ὀπίσσω Od.7.325 ; ὁδῷ δὲ τὰ ξυντομώτατα ἐξ Ἀβδήρων ἐς Ἴστρον ἀνὴρ εὔζωνος ἑνδεκαταῖος τελεῖ Th.2.97 ; ταύτῃ τῇ ἡμέρᾳ ἐς

Φάρσαλον ἐτέλεσε Id.4.78; κίνδυνον τελέσσαι *perform* a dangerous feat, Epich.99; ἔργον S.*El.*1399; δίδυμα κακά A.*Th.*782 (lyr.); προστάγματα Pl.*Lg.*926a, cf. d:—Pass., Hdt.1.206; καὶ εἰ τετελεσμένον ἐστί, = τελεῖσθαι δύναται, Od.5.90, Il.14.196; τετέλεστο δὲ ἔργον 7.465; αὐτίκ' ἔπειθ' ἅμα μῦθος ἔην, τετέλεστο δὲ ἔργον '*no sooner said than done*', 19.242; ἐάνπερ ἐπὶ λόγῳ ἔργα τελῆται Pl.*R.*389d, cf. *Plt.*288c; γραφὴ τῶν τετελεσμένων ἔργων *PPetr.*3p.340 (iii B.C.); τετέλεσται *Ev.Jo.*19.30 (cf. 28). **2.** *fulfil* one's word, τ. ἔπος, μῦθον, ὑπόσχεσιν, Il.14.44, Od.4.776, 10.483; τελέω τὰ πάροιθεν ὑπέστην Il.23.20; τελέσαι κότον, χόλον, *glut* one's fury, wrath, 1.82, 4.178: also, *grant* one *the fulfilment* or *accomplishment of* anything, τ. νόον τινί *fulfil* his wish, 23.149, cf. Od.22.51; τ. ἐέλδωρ Hes.*Sc.*36; λιτάς A.*Th.*627 (lyr.); κατάρας ib.724 (lyr.): rarely c. inf., οὐδ' ἐτέλεσσε φέρων δόμεναι *he succeeded* not in.., Il.12.222 (cf. ἀνύω I.6):—Pass., *to be fulfilled*, 2.36,330, al.: esp. pf. part., [μῦθος] τετελεσμένος ἐστί Il.1.388, cf. *h.Ven.*26; elsewh. in Hom. only neut., τὸ δὲ καὶ τετελεσμένον ἔσται Il.1.212, cf. 8.286, al.:—Med., τελέσασθαι δίκην *bring* a suit *to issue*, D.38.18, cf. 39.18 (Pass.). **3.** *grant in full, work out*, ἀγαθόν τινι, ὅ τι φρεσὶν ᾗσι μενοινᾷ Od.2.34; νόστον 15.112; μόγις δ' ἐτέλεσσε Κρονίων 3.119; τ. λυγρά 18.134; γῆρας ἀρειον 23.286; κακὰ κήδεα τ. τινί Il.18.8, cf. Od.4.699, 18.389, S.*Ant.*3; θεῶν τελεσάντων (sc. αὐτό) Pi.*P.*10.49; εὖ τελεῖ θεός A.*Th.* 35. **4.** ὅρκια τελεῖν *make* an oath *effective*, Il.7.69: later, *execute* a legal document, δημόσιος χρηματισμὸς τετελεσμένος δι' ἐπιτηρητῶν ἀγορανομίας Mitteis *Chr.*200.10 (iii A.D.), cf. *POxy.*290.22 (i A.D.), etc. **5.** *bring to fulfilment* or *perfection*, ἀρετὰν.. πεπρωμέναν τελέσει Pi.*N.*4.43; τ. τινά *bless* him *with perfect happiness*, Id.*I.*6(5).46 (dub.); so τετελεσμένον ἐσλόν Id.*N.*9.6; τελεσθεὶς ὄλβος A.*Ag.*751 (lyr.): also, *bring* a child *to maturity, bring* it *to the birth*, E.*Ba.*100 (lyr.). **b.** with an Adj. added, ἅπαντας ἡ παίδευσις ἡμέρους τελεῖ *makes perfectly* gentle, Men.*Mon.*41. **6.** *bring to an end, finish, end*, ἐξ ἀγαθοῦ γὰρ ἀρξάμενος τελέω τὸν λόγον εἰς ἀγαθόν *Lyr.Alex. Adesp.*21.2. **7.** of Time, ὅτε δὴ τρίτον ἦμαρ.. τελέσ' Ἠώς Od.5.390; βίον τ. Simon.36, S.*Ant.*1114; πολλοὺς τρόχους ἡλίου ib.1065; τελευτὴν τοῦ βίου Id.*Tr.*79; also τ. νοῦσον *come to the end of* it, Hes. *Th.*799:—Pass., περὶ δ' ἤματα μακρὰ τελέσθη Od.10.470, cf. Hes. *Th.*59; τετελεσμένον εἰς ἐνιαυτόν ib.795; ἐν τοῖς ἔτεσι τοῖς δὶς ἑπτὰ τετελ. Arist.*HA*581ᵃ14, cf. *Metaph.*994ᵃ26; of men, *come to one's end*, οἴμοι.. δεσπότου τελουμένου A.*Ch.*875 (s.v.l.). **8.** sts. intr., like the Pass., *come to an end, be fulfilled, turn out*, οὐ γὰρ οἶδ' ὅπῃ τελεῖ ib.1021, cf. *Pers.*225 (troch.), S.*El.*1417 (lyr.): later = τελέθω, *to be*, φύσει τελῶν μνησίκακος Tz.*H.*2.83, al. **II.** *pay* what one owes, what is due, λιπαρὰς τελέουσι θέμιστας Il.9.156,298 (unless this means '*will administer* good laws'); νῆας.. αἵ κεν τελέοιεν ἕκαστα ἄστε' ἐπ' ἀνθρώπων ἱκνεύμεναι *bring supplies of* everything, Od. 9.127: generally, *pay, present*, δῶρα, δωτίνην, Il.9.598, Od.11.352; μισθόν Il.21.457, Eup.4; ἀργύριον Pl.*Ly.*208b; ἀργύριον.. μισθόν Id. *Prt.*311d; δύο δραχμὰς μισθόν Ar.*Ra.*173: metaph., τ. ὕμνον Pi.*P.* 1.79, 2.13; τ. ψυχὰν Ἀΐδᾳ, i.e. die, Id.*I.*1.68. **b.** esp. *pay* tax, duty, toll, φόρον Pl.*Alc.*1.123a; τὰ τέλη Cratin.Jun.9.5, Arist.*Ath.* 55.3, cf. Pl.*Lg.*847b; τ. μετοίκιον *pay* the tax of a μέτοικος, ib. 850b; ἱππάδα Is.7.39; θητικόν Arist.*Ath.*7.4, Lex ap. D.43.54; ξενικά D.57.34; συντάξεις Aeschin.3.91; freq. in Papyri, οἱ τελοῦντες τὰ καθήκοντα εἰς τὸ βασιλικόν *PTeb.*5.174 (ii B.C.), etc.; τ. σῖτον *pay one's contribution of* corn, X.*HG*5.3.21: abs., *pay tax*, *IG*1².1.2,3, Hdt.2.109:—Pass., of money, etc., *to be paid*, Id.9.93; of persons, *to be in receipt of rent*, χώραν ἀτέλεστον ἔχουσιν αὐτοὶ τετελεσμένοι D. *Prooem.*55. **2.** *lay out, spend*, χρήματα μεγάλα Hdt.3.137, Pl. *Ap.*20a, cf. X.*Cyr.*8.1.13:—Pass., *to be spent* or *expended*, Hdt.2. 125; ἐς τὸ δεῖπνον τετρακόσια τάλαντα τετελεσμένα *laid out* upon the dinner, Id.7.118; ἕνδεκα μυριάδας μεδίμνων τελεομένας ἐπ' ἡμέρῃ ἑκάστῃ ib.187, cf. Pl.*Lg.*955e. **b.** *consume, eat* (cf. ἀναλίσκω I.3), [σιτία] μέτρια τελεύμενα Hp.*Aff.*47, cf. 26,43,44. **3.** since, in many Greek cities, the citizens were distributed into classes acc. to their taxable property, τ. εἴς τινας meant *to belong to* a class, *to be reckoned among*, τ. ἐς Ἕλληνας, ἐς Βοιωτούς, *belong to* the Greeks, the Boeotians, Hdt.2.51, 6.108; εἰς ἀστοὺς τ. *become* a citizen, S.*OT* 222; εἰς ἄνδρας τ. *come to* man's estate, Pl.*Lg.*923e; εἰς γυναῖκας ἐξ ἀνδρὸς τ. *become* a woman instead of a man, E.*Ba.*822; ἕκαστος ἡμῶν ὑπό τινα τελεῖ δαίμονα ὃς πάσης ἡμῶν τῆς ζωῆς ἐπάρχει *belongs*.., Herm. *in Phdr.*p.93 A. **4.** from the last sense perh. may be expld. the phrase, κοῖός τις δοκέοι ἀνὴρ εἶναι πρὸς τὸν πατέρα τελέσαι *to compare* with his father, Hdt.3.34 (τελέσαι om. cod. E, secl. Hude). **III.** *initiate* in the mysteries, τινα Pl.*Euthd.*277d; τῇ μητρὶ τελούσῃ τὰς βίβλους ἀναγιγνώσκειν D.18.259; τυμπανίζειν καὶ τ. Plu.2.60a; τ. τῷ Διονύσῳ *Milet.*6.23:—Pass., *to have oneself initiated*, Ar.*Nu.*258; τετελεσμένος Pl.*Phd.*69c, *Berl.Sitzb.*1927.169 (Cyrene), etc.; ἐτέλεις, ἐγὼ δ' ἐτελούμην D.18.265; Διονύσῳ τελεσθῆναι *to be consecrated* to Dionysus, *initiated in* his *mysteries*, Hdt.4.79; ὀργίοισι Hp.*Lex*5, cf. X.*Smp.*1.10: c. acc., Βακχεῖ' ἐτελέσθη Ar.*Ra.*357 (anap.); τελέους τελετὰς τελούμενος Pl.*Phdr.*249c, cf. 250b; also τ. μεγάλοισι τέλεσι Id.*R.*560e. **b.** in Magic, *endow* a thing *with potency, consecrate* it, *PMag.Par.*1.1744, *PMag.Lond.*46.242, 121.590, Sch.Ar.*Pl.* 884. **c.** *enchant*, Παλλάδιον τετελεσμένον Eust.ad D.P.620. **2.** metaph., τελεσθῆναι στρατηγός *to be formally appointed* general, D. 13.19; τετελεσμένος σωφροσύνῃ *a votary of* temperance, X.*Oec.*21. 12. **3.** also of sacred rites, *perform*, ἱερά E.*Ba.*485, cf. *IT*464 (anap.); θυσίαν τοῖς θεοῖς D.S.4.34, cf. Plu.*Thes.*16; ὄργια *IG*14. 1183 (Rome), Paus.4.14.1; γάμον, γάμους, Call.*Ap.*14, Lyc.1387:—Pass., Pl.*Lg.*775a. **4.** Pass., of women, *to be married*, *GDI*3721. 5,9 (Cos).

**τελέως**, Adv., v. τέλειος VII. **II.** τέλεως nom. sg., v. τέλειος sub init. **τελέωσις**, v. τελείωσις.

**τελήεις**, εσσα, εν, (τελέω) Ep. Adj. = τέλειος, *perfect, complete*, of victims, in Il. and Od. always τεληέσσας ἑκατόμβας, i.e. hecatombs *of full tale* or *number*, or *of full-grown beasts*, or *of beasts without blemish*, Il.1.315, 2.306, Od.4.352, 17.50, al.; τελήεντες οἰωνοί birds *of sure augury*, as if they brought about what they betokened, opp. μαψιλόγοι, *h.Merc.*544 (as perhaps τελειότατος πετεηνῶν, cf. τέλειος I.1a): in this sense Tyrt.4.2 has τελέεντ' ἔπεα *sure* predictions, from the form τελέεις. **II.** Ὠκεανοῖο τελήεντος ποταμοῖο prob. the river *in which all others end*, or *ending in itself, ever-circling*, Hes. *Th.*242,959.

**τέλθει**· ἐν ᾠδῇ τέρπει, Hsch., cf. Phot., Suid.

**τέλθος**, εος, τό, *debt, payment due*, κομίζευ.. τ. ὀφειλόμενον Call. *Lav.Pall.*106; τ. ἀπαιτησῶν ἑκατὸν ϝόας Id.*Cer.*78.

**τελιάζω**, late spelling of *τελειάζω, *perform*, τὰς λοιπὰς φιλοτειμίας τελιάσαντα ἁγνῶς καὶ ἀμέμπτως *OGI*485.13 (Magn. Mae.).

**τελικός**, ή, όν, *pertaining to the supreme end*, ἀγαθὰ τ. (opp. ποιητικά) *Stoic.*3.25, al.; κεφάλαια τ. topics *drawn from these goods*, Hermog. *Prog.*6, al. **2.** more generally, *connected with final* or *intentional causality*, τ. αἴτιον, = Aristotle's οὗ ἕνεκα, Procl. *in Prm.*p.612 S., cf. *in Ti.*3.126 D.; in Medicine, Alex.Aphr.*Febr.*23. **II.** *in the end* or *termination* of a word, Clearch.63, D.T.632.0, Heph.1.2, *EM*289. 33. **III.** *perfect*, εἰς τελικὴν φιλίας ἕξιν prob. in Phld.*Acad.Ind.*p.56 M.

**τελίσκω**, = τελέω, τὸν ὅρκον *GDI*5075.23 (Crete, i B.C.); - Lat. *perago*, Dosith.p.434 K.; ἄγονον σπόρον.. τελίσκει *makes* the seed barren, Nic.*Al.*583 codd. plerique (but **τελέσκων** is prob. cj. for τελέσχων in Id.*Fr.*74.10):—Pass., *to be initiated*, *Berl.Sitzb.*1927.169 (Cyrene); *to be dedicated* or *offered*, εἰς τὰ.. ἱερὰ μετὰ θυσιῶν *OGI*90. 32 (Rosetta, ii B.C.); τελισκόμενος *an initiate*, a ἱερόδουλος, LXX *De.* 23.17(18), Hsch., Phot. (**τελεσκόμενος** Suid.); ταῦτα δὲ πάντα τελίσκεται καὶ γίνεται μεθ' ἡδονῆς *are done*, Vett.Val.241.1; εὐσύνοπτα τὰ θνητῶν τελίσκεται Id.346.10, cf. 354.16 (v.l.).

**τελλίνη** [ῑ], ἡ, *a small bivalve shell-fish*, = ξιφύδριον, Hp.*Vict.*2.48, Sopat.7, Xenocr.ap.Orib.2.58.116, Dsc.2.6.

**τέλλις**, ἡ, = foreg., prob. l. in Epich.43,114.

**τέλλω**, aor. ἔτειλα Pi.*O.*2.70:—**Pass.** τέλλομαι:—poet. Verb, but used in Cretan Prose (v. infr.), *accomplish*, ἔτειλαν ὁδόν Pi.l.c.; *perform* duties, rites, etc., τέλλεμ (inf.) μὲν τὰ θῖνα καὶ τὰ ἀντρώπινα *Leg.Gort.*10.42:—Med., τελλόμεναι χορόν, apparently = στελλόμεναι, *PSI*10.1181.39:—Pass., *come into being*, γένος φυτευθὲν λοιπὸν αἰεὶ τέλλετο Pi.*P.*4.257; ὕμνοι ὑστέρων ἀρχὰ λόγων τέλλεται καὶ ὅρκιον Id.*O.*11(10).6; ἐς χάριν τέλλεται *turns* to good, ib.1.76; ἀπὸ θεσφάτων ἀγαθὰ φάτις.. τέλλεται cj. Emper. for στέλλεται, A.*Ag.* 1133 (lyr.); of the gadfly, οἷόν τε νέαις ἐπὶ φορβάσιν οἶστρος τέλλεται (= γίγνεται) A.R.3.277; ἠοῦς τελλομένης Id.1.1360; πρόκα τελλομένου ἔτεος as soon as a year is *complete*, ib.688. **2.** Pass., of stars, = ἀνατέλλω, *rise*, Arat.285,320,382. **II.** intr. in Act., = ἀνατέλλω, ἡλίου τέλλοντος at *sunrise*, S.*El.*699; ἶρις τέλλει *grows up*, Nic.*Fr.* 74.32. (Cf. πέλω (πέλομαι) fin., with which τέλλομαι (Pass.) is cogn.; the Act. τέλλω (fr. which δικασπόλος, θυηπόλος, ὑμνοπόλος, etc. are derived) may be formed fr. the Pass., with causal meaning ('cause to come into existence or be done'), as πείθω fr. πείθομαι, πεύθω fr. πεύθομαι; the sense *rise* is perh. derived from that of *revolve* as used of stars; ἐντέλλω, ἐπιτέλλω (A) may orig. have meant 'cause to be done (by another)'.)

***τέλμα**, ατος, τό, *standing water, pond, marsh, swamp*, Ar.*Av.* 1593, Pl.*Phd.*109b, X.*Oec.*20.11, Men.*Epit.*532, Thphr.*HP*1.4.2: pl., *low lands subject to inundation, water-meads*, Hdt.2.93, Thphr. *Fr.*174.1, Gal.6.709, 15.121, Jul.*Mis.*358a; *mud at the edge of a river-bank*, Ael.*VH*12.46. **II.** *mud used as mortar*, τέλματι χρεώμενοι ἀσφάλτῳ Hdt.1.179; cf. τελμίς. **2.** *space pointed with mortar*, between the courses of masonry, Procop.*Aed.*2.1.

**τελμᾰτ-ιαῖος**, α, ον, *of a marsh*, [ὕδατα] τ. *stagnant* waters, Arist. *Mete.*353ᵇ24; [ζῷα] Id.*HA*487ᵃ27; βάτραχοι ib.626ᵃ9; ποταμοί Id.*GA* 741ᵇ2. **-όομαι**, Pass., *become marshy*, αἱ λίμναι Str.17.1. 7. **-ώδης**, ες, *marshy, swampy, muddy*, λίμνη Arist.*HA*570ᵃ8; πεδίον D.S.1.30; ὕδωρ Plu.*Mar.*38; χωρία Gal.6.702. **II.** τελματώδεα *parts of the body full of humours*, Hp.*Gland.*4.

**τελμίς**, ῖνος, ὁ, = τέλμα II 1, *mud, slime*, Is.ap.*EM*751.24: pl., Procop.*Goth.*4.26.

**τέλομαι**, = ἔσομαι, *SIG*527.46 (Drerus, iii B.C.); τέλεται, = ἔσται, *GDI*5040.67 (Hierapytna): also 3 sg. τένται *Abh.Berl.Akad.*1925 (5).21, *Berl.Sitzb.*1927.158, 164 (all Cyrene): cf. συντέλομαι. (Dor. form of πέλομαι.)

***τέλος**, εος, τό, (τέλλομαι, τέλλω) *coming to pass, performance, consummation*, εἰ γὰρ ἐπ' ἀρῇσιν τ. ἡμετέρῃσι γένοιτο Od.17.496; ἐν [θεοῖς] τ. ἐστὶν ὁμῶς ἀγαθῶν τε κακῶν τε Hes.*Op.*669; δίκη δ' ὑπὲρ ὕβριος ἴσχει ἐς τ. ἐξελθοῦσα issuing in *fulfilment, execution*, ib.218; καθάπερ ἐκ δίκης κατὰ νόμον τ. ἐχούσης *PEleph.*1.12 (iv B.C.), cf. *IG*12(7).67.48 (Arcesine, iv/iii B.C.); καθήκει νῦν [τὰν γνώμαν] ἐπὶ τέλος ἀχθῆμεν *SIG*793.7 (Halasarna, i A.D.); ἔλπομαι μέν, ἐν θεῷ γε μὰν τ. Pi.*O.*13.105, cf. *N.*8.45, 10.29, D.18.193; ἣν θεὸς ἀγαθὸν τ. διδῷ αὐτῷ X.*Cyr.*3.2.29; ἐν πείρᾳ τ. διαφαίνεται Pi.*N.*3.70; ψευστήσεις, οὐδ' αὖτε τ. μύθῳ ἐπιθήσεις Il.19.107, cf. Isoc.5.71, 6.77; *result*, τ. δ' οὔ πώ τι πέφανται Il.2.122; εἵως κε τ. πολέμοιο κιχείω 3. 291; ἐν γὰρ χερσὶ τ. πολέμου 16.630; ἶσον τείνειεν πολέμου τ. 20.

101, cf. Hes.*Th.*638 (but ἢ πολέμοιο ἢ λοιμοῖο τ. ποτιδέγμενοι the *coming to pass* (*outbreak*) of.., A.R.4.1282); τί μὰν ἀφήσει τ.; S.*OC*1468 (lyr.); τί ἔσται τὸ τ. τῶν γιγνομένων τούτων ἐμοί; Hdt.1.155, cf. Isoc.6.50; ἀποίητον..θέμεν ἔργων τ. undo things done, Pi.*O.*2.17; ὁδοῦ τ. S.*OC*1400; φόνου τ. A.R.1.834; τοῦ δ' ὔμμι τέλος κρηῆναι ἔοικεν Id.3.172; τῷ τ. πίστιν φέρων the *outcome*, S.*El.*735; Ζεὺς πάντων ἐφορᾷ τ. Sol.13.17; ἀκόλουθον τὸ τ. ἐξέβη τοῦ κινδύνου ταῖς ἐπιβολαῖς Plb.4.11.9; ἀμφίδοξα τὰ τ. τῶν κινδύνων αὐτοῖς ἀπέβαινε Id.18.28.11, cf. 18.32.12, 3.5.7; τ. τοιόνδε ἐγένετο τῆς μάχης Hdt.9.22, cf. Plb.1.61.2; μάχης..κεκύρωται τ. A.*Ch.*874; διὰ μάχης ἥξω τέλους, = διὰ μάχης ἥξω, Id.*Supp.*475; ἐπ' ἀμφότερα μαχᾶν τάμνειν τ. to seek to determine the *issue* of the battles in both directions, Pi.*O.*13.57; more generally, *event*, οὐ γὰρ ἔγωγέ τί φημι τ. χαριέστερον εἶναι ἢ ὅτε.. Od.9.5: in concrete sense, *result*, *product*, τ. εὐπεψίας αἱματικῆς πιμελὴ καὶ στέαρ Arist.*PA*672$^a$4, cf. *GA*725$^b$8. **2.** in contexts like Hes.*Op.*669, Il.16.630 (v. supr.), τ. can be understood as *power of deciding*, *supreme power*, and so we have τ. μὲν Ζεὺς ἔχει..πάντων ὅσ' ἐστί Semon.1.1; ἐν δ' ἐμοὶ τ. αὐτοῖν γένοιτο τῆσδε τῆς μάχης πέρι S.*OC*423; [Ἄπολλον]..ὅθεν πολεμόκραντον ἁγνὸν τ. ἐν μάχᾳ A.*Th.*162 (lyr.); τελέων τελειότατον κράτος, ὄλβιε Ζεῦ Id.*Supp.*525 (lyr.); τ. ἔχει δαίμων βροτοῖς, τ. ὅπᾳ θέλει E.*Or.*1545 (lyr.); τ. δ' ἐφ' ἡμῖν, εἴτε..εἴτε.. Id.*Hel.*887; καὶ τοῖσ' (sc. ἰητροῖς) οὐδὲν ἔπεστι τ. they have no *power* or *efficacy*, Sol.13.58: and in the civil sphere, τ. ἔχειν, of persons, to have *the power to ratify*, *IG*1$^2$.57.25, Foed.ap.Th.4.118, Arist.*Pol.*1322$^b$13; ὅ τι ἂν δόξῃ τοῖς πλείοσι τοῦτ' εἶναι τ. the decision of the majority must be *final*, ib.1317$^b$6; κύριος ἔστω ἐπιβάλλειν κατὰ τὸ τ. shall have authority to inflict a fine up to the limit of his *powers*, Lex ap.D.43.75; κατὰ τὸ τ. ζημιοῦσθαι Is.4.11; τοῖς κατ' ἐμπορίαν παραγιγνομένοις μηδὲν ἔστω τ. πλὴν ἐπὶ κήρυκι ἢ γραμματεῖ Foed.ap.Plb.3.22.8; τ. ἔχειν, of things, to have *decisive* or *final authority*, σφῷν μὲν ἐντολὴ Διὸς ἔχει τ. δή A.*Pr.*13; ἡ..τούτου αἰτίασις οὐκ ἔχει τ. has no *validity*, Antipho 5.89; πρὶν τ. τι αὐτῶν ἔχειν before any of the terms had *validity*, i.e. had been ratified, Th.5.41, cf. D.35.27; τοῦ ζῆν καὶ μὴ ζῆν τὸ τ. ἐστὶν ἐν τῷ ἀναπνεῖν the *decisive difference* between.., Arist.*Resp.*480$^b$19. **3.** *magistracy*, *office*, τ. δωδεκάμηνον Pi.*N.*11.9 (δυω- codd.); οἱ ἐν τ. men in *office*, *magistrates*, S.*Aj.*1352, *Ph.*385, Th.3.36; ἔξω τῶν βασιλέων καὶ τῶν μάλιστα ἐν τ. Id.1.10, cf. 6.88; οἱ ἐν τέλεϊ ἐόντες Hdt.3.18, 9.106; poet., οἱ ἐν τέλει βεβῶτες S.*Ant.*67; οἱ τὰ τ. ἔχοντες Foed.ap.Th.5.47; ὀρμέγιστον τ. ἔχοι *Schwyzer* 409.3 (Elis, v B.C.); τοὺς..τὸ ὀροφυλακικὸν τ. ἔχοντας *SIG*633.94 (Milet., ii B.C.); τὸ τ. the *government*, τοιαῦτ' ἔδοξε τῷδε Καδμείων τέλει A.*Th.*1030; τὰ τ. the *magistrates*, Th. (with a masc. part. and pl. (v.l.) verb) 1.58, 4.15, X.*An.*2.6.4. **4.** *decision*, *doom*, Ζεὺς..οἶδε, ὁπποτέρῳ θανάτοιο τ. πεπρωμένον ἐστί Il.3.309; Κῆρες δὲ παρεστήκασι.., ἡ μὲν ἔχουσα τ. γήραος ἀργαλέου, ἡ δ' ἑτέρη θανάτοιο Mimn.2.6; μήτηρ..μέ φησι διχθαδίας Κῆρας φερέμεν θανάτοιο τέλος δέ (or τέλοσδε) Il.9.411, cf. 13.602; ἐξέφυγον θανάτου τ. Archil.6.3; τ. θανάτου ἀλεείνων Od.5.326; τ. θανάτοιο κάλυψεν Il.5.553; οὐδέ κέ μ' ὦκα τ. θανάτοιο κιχείη 9.416, cf. 11.451; ἡμετέρου θανάτοιο κακὸν τ., οἷον ἐτύχθη Od.24.124, cf. A.*Th.*906 (lyr.):—judicial *decision*, ἀμμενῶ τ. δίκης Id.*Eu.*243; κύριον μένει τ. ib.544 (lyr.); οὐκ ἔχουσα τῆς δίκης τ. not having *authority to decide* the case, ib.729; ἦ κἀπ' ἐμοὶ τρέποιτ' ἂν αἰτίας τ.; will you submit the *decision* of this case to me? ib.434; τὸ τ. κρίνειν Pl.*Lg.*768b; τ. ἐπιθέτω τῇ δίκῃ ib.767a, cf. 761e, 957b; *decision* of an assembly, A.*Supp.*603, 624; of a king, Id.*Ag.*934; ἐξαιτράπης ἐὼν Ἰωνίης, τ. ἐποίησε τὴν γῆν εἶναι Μιλησίων prob. in *SIG*134*b*30 (Milet., iv B.C.); ὥς τοι ἐγὼ μύθου τ. ἐν φρεσὶ θείω the *summing up* or *crux* of the matter, Il.16.83. **5.** *something done* or *ordered to be done*, *task*, *service*, *duty*, γνῶ..ὅ οἱ οὔ τι τ. κατὰ καίριον ἦλθεν on no fatal *errand*, Il.11.439 (nisi leg. κατακαίριον); οὐδὲ μακύνων τ. οὐδέν Pi.*P.*4.286; ὅσοις τοῦτ' ἐπέσταλται τ. A.*Eu.*743, cf. *Ag.*908; μ' Ἀπόλλων τῷδ' ἐπέστησεν τέλει ib.1202, cf. *Ch.*760; ἄυπνα ὀμμάτων τέλη the wakeful *duties* (or *services*) of the eyes, E.*Supp.*1137 (lyr.); ἀμφοτερᾶν τοι χαρίτων..ζεύξω τ. the *rendering* of both services, Pi.*I.*1.6; αἰτουμένῳ μοι κοῦφον εἰ δοίης τ. a small *service* or *favour*, A.*Th.*260; ἡξῶ ναὶ τὸν Πᾶνα κακὸν τ. αὐτίκα δωσῶν Theoc.4.47; *obligation to render a service* or *payment*, ὅτε δὴ μισθοῖο τ. πολυγηθέες ὧραι ἐξέφερον the *payment*(*-day*) of the wage, Il.21.450; οἱ δ' ἐλάττω τῶν ἱκανῶν κεκτημένοι, τὴν ἀναγκαίαν ἀτέλειαν ἔχοντες, ἔξω τοῦ τ. εἰσὶ τούτου D.20.19, cf. Poll.8.156; ἐν τέλει μαθεῖν to be taught for a *fee*, Id.4.46. **6.** pl., *services* or *offerings due* to the gods, δαίμοσιν θῦσαι θέλουσα πελανόν, ὧν τέλη τάδε A.*Pers.*204; ἔνθ' ὁρίζεται βωμοὺς τ. τ' ἔγκαρπα Κηναίῳ Διί S.*Tr.*238; ἔλιπον Ζηνὶ τροπαίῳ πάγχαλκα τ. Id.*Ant.*143 (anap.); γῇ δὲ τῇδε Σισύφου σεμνὴν ἑορτὴν καὶ τέλη προσάψομεν E.*Med.*1382; θεοῖσι μικρὰ θύοντες τέλη Id.*Fr.*327.6; of the Eleusinian mysteries, οὗ πότνιαι σεμνὰ τιθηνοῦνται τ. S.*OC*1050 (lyr.), cf. *Fr.*837; σεμνῶν ἐς ὄψιν καὶ τ. μυστηρίων E.*Hipp.*25; called μεγάλα τ., Pl.*R.*560e; rarely in sg., τοῦδε μυστικοῦ τέλους this mystic *rite*, A.*Fr.*387; of the marriage *rite*, τ. γάμοιο Od.20.74, cf. A.R.4.1202, *AP*6.276 (Antip.); γαμήλιον τ. A.*Eu.*835; τὰ νυμφικὰ τ. S.*Ant.*1241; τ. ὁ γάμος ἐκαλεῖτο Poll.3.38, cf. Paus.Gr.*Fr.*306, Sch.Ar.*Th.*982, Stob.2.7.3$^a$. **7.** *service rendered* by a citizen in the Solonian constitution to the state, also his *rating according to this service*, θητικοῦ ἀντὶ τέλους ἱππάδ' ἀμειψάμενος Epigr.ap.Arist.*Ath.*7.4; τιμήματι διεῖλεν εἰς τέτταρα τ. four *ratings* or *classes*, ib.7.3; later, τὸ τῶν ἱππέων τ., Lat. *ordo* equester, D.C.48.45, al. **8.** *dues* exacted by the state, Ar.*V.*658 (pl.), Pl.*R.*425d (pl.); ἀγορᾶς τ. a market-*toll*, Ar.*Ach.*896; πορνικὸν τ. Aeschin.1.119; τ. πρίασθαι, πωλεῖν, farm a *tax* or let *it*, D.24.144, Aeschin. l.c.; ἐκλέγειν, πράττειν, levy *it*, D. l.c., Alex.263.3, Aeschin.3.113; τελεῖν pay a *tax* or *duty*, Pl.*Lg.*847b; εἰ τὰ τ. τελεῖ, ποῖον τ. τελεῖ, questions put to candidates at Athens, Din.2.17, Arist.*Ath.*7.4; τέλη κατατίθησιν Antipho 5.77; καταβαλεῖν And.1.93; freq. in Inscrr., *IG*1$^2$.46.12, al., *SIG*135.14 (Olynthus, iv B.C.), al., and Papyri, τὸ ὡρισμένον τῆς αἰτήσεως τ., etc., *POxy.*1473.30 (iii A.D.), cf. *PCair.Zen.*240.7 (iii B.C.), etc.: metaph., τέλη λύειν, v. λύω v. 2. **9.** *financial means*, *expenditure*, usu. in dat. pl., ὃς ἂν τοῖς ἰδίοις τ. μὴ ἑαυτὸν μόνον, ἀλλὰ καὶ τὴν πόλιν ὠφελῇ by the use of his own *means*, Th.6.16; κακῶς ἡμᾶς αὐτοὺς ποιούντων τέλεσι τοῖς οἰκείοις if we harm ourselves at our own *expense*, Id.4.60; ἀναγραψάτω..τέλεσι τοῖς Λεωνίδου *IG*1$^2$.56.22, cf. 94.14, al.; Χερρόνησον τοῖς αὑτοῦ τ. διορύξει D.6.30; δημοσίοις τέλεσι Plu.*Phoc.*38: in nom. sg., μάτην γὰρ οἴκῳ σὸν τόδ' ἐκβαίη τ. E.*Fr.*639. **10.** a *military station* or *post with defined duties* (cf. signf. 5), ἐλθεῖν εἰς φυλάκων ἱερὸν τ. Il.10.56; αἶψα δ' ἐπὶ Θρηκῶν ἀνδρῶν τ. ἷξον ἰόντες ib.470; δόρπον ἔπειθ' ἑλόμεσθα κατὰ στρατὸν ἐν τελέεσσιν at our *posts*, in the *ranks*, 11.730, cf. 18.298; later, *military unit*, *division*, *squadron*, τέλει ἑνὶ τῶν ἱππέων Th.2.22, cf. 4.96; πελταστῶν τέλη E.*Rh.*311; κατὰ τέλεα Hdt.1.103, 7.87, al.; κατὰ τέλη Th.6.42, Plb.11.11.6, cf. 11.15.2, Polyaen.2.1.17; in the Roman army, *legion*, J.*AJ*14.16.2, *BJ*1.17.9, Plu.*Ant.*18, 56, App.*BC*5.87, al. **b.** *a force of* 2048 *infantry*, = μεραρχία, Ascl.*Tact.*2.10, Arr.*Tact.*10.5, Ael.*Tact.*9.7. **c.** *a force of* 2048 *cavalry*, Ascl.*Tact.*7.11, Arr.*Tact.*18.4, Ael.*Tact.*20.2. **11.** δίρρυμά τε καὶ τρίρρυμα τέλη *troops* or *columns* of..chariots, A.*Pers.*47 (anap.); of ships, τρία τ. ποιήσαντες τῶν νεῶν Th.1.48: also ὀρνίθων τέλεα *flocks* of birds, v.l. for γένεα, Hdt.2.64; τ. ἀθανάτων A.*Fr.*151 (anap.). **12.** a territorial division, Στρατικὸν τ. *SIG*421.44 (Acarnania, iii B.C.); Κορωνείων τὸ τ. *Supp.Epigr.*3.354 (Thebes, iii B.C.); τὸ Λοκρικὸν τ. *GDI*2070 (Delph., ii B.C.).

**II.** *degree of completion* or *attainment*, τόσσον μὲν ἔχον τ., οὔατα δ' οὔ πω..προσέκειτο Il.18.378; *degree of maturity*, *age*, ἐπὴν δὴ τοῦτο τ. παραμείψεται ὥρης Mimn.2.9; ἥβης πρὶν τ. ἄκρον ἰδεῖν Simon.123; ἥβης τ. μολόντας E.*Med.*920; εἰς ἀνδρὸς τ. ἰέναι man's *estate*, Pl.*Mx.*249a; εἰς πρεσβύτου τ. ἀφικομένοις Id.*Epin.*992d; τὸ τῶν παίδων τ. ἄδηλον οἷ τελευτᾷ κακίας καὶ ἀρετῆς ψυχῆς τε πέρι καὶ σώματος Id.*Smp.*181e; οὐδὲ γήρως ἔβας τ. σὺν τᾷδε E.*Alc.*413 (lyr.). **b.** a *length of time* (or *space*), *term*, *course*, ἀρετάς, αἷσι Κλεωνυμίδαι θάλλοντες αἰεὶ σὺν θεῷ θνατὸν διέρχονται βιότου τ. Pi.*I.*4(3).5(23); so perh. in E.*Hipp.*87 (v. infr. 3), and in διὰ τέλους (v. infr. 2 c). **2.** *state of completion* or *maturity*, τ. λαβεῖν, ἔχειν, of plants or animals, to attain *maturity*, Pl.*Phdr.*276b, *Lg.*834c, cf. 899e: hence, *completion*, *end*, *finish*, τ. ἐπιθεῖναι τῷ λόγῳ *complete* it, Id.*Smp.*186a, cf. *Prt.*348a; ὃ πᾶσι τοῖς προτέροις ἐπέθηκε τ. as a *finish* to all his former acts, D.18.140; τὸ τ. τῆς σκηνῆς ἐποιήσαντο X.*Cyr.*2.3.24; ταύτης..τῆς ἡμέρας τοῦτο τὸ τ. ἐγένετο Id.*An.*1.10.18; τ. λαβεῖν to be *completed*, Pl.*R.*501e, Isoc.4.5; τ. ἔχειν Pl.*Lg.*772c; οὐ τ. ἵκεο μύθων didst not reach the *end* of thy speech, Il.9.56; ἐπὶ τέλους τοῦ δρόμου Pl.*R.*613d; μέχρι τοῦ τὸ προκείμενον ἐπὶ τέλος ἀχθῆναι *PTeb.*14.8 (ii B.C.); ἑκάστων πρὸς τέλος ἀχθέντων *UPZ*108.29 (ii B.C.), cf. *BGU*1816.11 (i B.C.); ἡ εἰκοστὴ τοῦ νοσήματος ἡμέρα τ. μὲν τριῶν ἑβδομάδων, ἓξ δὲ τετράδων Gal.18(2).234:—freq. in Adverbial phrases: **a.** τέλος *at last*, ὥστε τ. ἡσυχίαν ἦγον Th.2.100, cf. 5.46; but most freq. at the beginning of the clause, μάχης δὲ καρτερῆς γενομένης, τέλος οὐδέτεροι νικήσαντες διέστησαν Hdt.1.76, cf. 4.131, al.; τέλος δέ Id.1.36, Thgn.1294, etc.; ἀλλὰ τ. Hdt.6.137; τ. μέντοι Id.5.89, X.*HG*5.4.30; τ. γε μέντοι S.*Ant.*233; καὶ τ. Hdt.4.154, Th.1.109; τό γε τ. Pl.*Lg.*740e. **b.** ἐς τ. in the *end*, in the *long run*, πάντως ἐς τ. ἐξεφάνη Sol.13.28, cf. Hdt.9.37; εἰς τ. S.*Ph.*409; θνητῶν δ' εἰς τ. ὄλβιος οὐδείς E.*IA*161 (anap.), cf. Hdt.3.40; ὁρῶντες τὴν Λιβύην εἰς τ. ἀβλαβῆ διαμένουσαν *altogether*, *completely*, Plb.1.20.7, cf. *PTeb.*38.11 (ii B.C.), *OGI*90.12 (Rosetta, ii B.C.), *PSI*10.1120.5 (i B.C./i A.D.); ἐς τ. ἄνυε μοίρας dub. l. in Theoc.1.93. **c.** διὰ τέλους (orig. perh. from signf. I. 1 or 5, or II. 1b, through the (whole) *performance* or *time*), *through to the end*, *completely*, A.*Pr.*275, S.*Aj.*685, E.*Supp.*270, Isoc.5.24, 8.17, 19.4; *throughout*, *all the time*, *always*, Antipho 5.42, Timocl.8.5, Hegesipp.Com.2.3; so διὰ τέλεος Hp.*Acut.*46 (= διὰ παντὸς καὶ ἀεί acc. to Gal.15.618); διὰ τέλους ἀεί Pl.*Phlb.*36e; *permanently*, *for good*, τοῦ ἀφεθῆναί σε διὰ τ. *PPetr.*2p.45 (iii B.C.). **d.** ἐπὶ τέλος at the *end*, opp. ἐν ἀρχῇ, Gal.19.183. **e.** τέλει perh. *in the end*, S.*OT*198 (lyr.). **3.** esp. τ. ἔχειν βίου to have reached the *end* of life, to be dead, Pl.*Lg.*801e; ἐμοὶ μὲν τοῦ βίου τὸ τ. ἤδη πάρεστιν X.*Cyr.*8.7.6; πᾶσίν ἐστιν ἀνθρώποις τ. τοῦ βίου θάνατος D.57.27; εἰς τ. τοῦ ζῆν ἀφικνεῖσθαι S.*OC*1530: less freq. abs., *death*, ἐλπίς ἐστι νύκτερον τ. μολεῖν A.*Th.*367 (lyr.); οἱ νεηνίαι οὐκέτι ἀνέστησαν ἀλλ' ἐν τέλεϊ τούτῳ ἔσχοντο Hdt.1.31; ἔχει τὸ κάλλιστον τ. X.*Cyr.*7.3.11; ἔχει τ., = τετελεύτηκε, Laconian phrase acc. to Hsch.; τῶν ἤδη τ. ἐχόντων Pl.*Lg.*717e, cf. 772c, *BGU*1857.7 (i B.C.); reversely, τ. ἔχει τινά Pl.*Lg.*740c; οἷόν σε βίου τ. εἷλε E.*Rh.*735 (anap.):—but ὀλβίως ἔλυσεν τὸ τ. βίου has paid life's *toll* (cf. supr. I. 8), S.*OC*1720 (lyr.); τὸ τ. ὁ χρόνος ἀπαιτεῖ Poet. in *Mus.Script.* p.452 von Jan; also τ. δὲ κάμψαιμ' ὥσπερ ἠρξάμην βίου E.*Hipp.*87 (cf. supr. II. 1b); πρὶν ἂν πέλας (v.l. τέλος) γραμμῆς ἵκηται καὶ τ. κάμψῃ βίου Id.*El.*955–6. **4.** *end*, *cessation*, ὡς δὲ πρὸς τ. γόων ἀφίκοντ' S.*OC*1621; πῶς τροχηλάτου μανίας ἂν ἔλθοιμ' ἐς τ. πόνων τ' ἐμῶν; E.*IT*83; ὅταν δὴ πημάτων λάβῃ τ. Id.*Hel.*534; τ. δέχει δὴ τῶν ἐμῶν προσφθεγμάτων Id.*Hec.*413; ἡ μὲν οὖν ἐπανάστασις..τοῦτο τὸ τ. ἔσχεν *Hell.Oxy.*10.3; ἐπειδὴ οὐχ οἷόν τε εἰς ἄπειρον, τ. ἔσται πάσης φορᾶς Arist.*Metaph.*

1074$^{a}$30. 5. *end* of a word, A.D.*Pron.*12.25, al.; of a sentence, ἐπὶ τέλει πρόσκειται Sor.1.43, cf. Gal.15.20; of a chapter or book, ἐπὶ τέλει ἀναλυθήσεται Archim.*Sph.Cyl.*2.4, cf. Gal.15.10; πρὸς τῷ τ. ῥηθήσεται Pl.*Lg.*957b; πρὸς τῷ τ. τοῦ ἐντέρου Arist.*PA*675$^{a}$16; ἀπὸ τέλους τοῦ σταδίου, opp. ἀπὸ μέσου, Id.*Ph.*239$^{b}$34 (cf. infr. III. 2). III. *achievement, attainment*, τηλοῦ ἐμοὶ νόστοιο τ. γλυκεροῖο γενέσθαι Od.22.323, cf. Pi.*N.*3.25; τ. δὲ τῆς ἀπαλλαγῆς τοῦ Αἰθίοπος ὧδε ἔλεγον γενέσθαι Hdt.2.139; πῶς ἂν καὶ τοῦτο τοῦ τ. τυγχάνοι, i.e. might be achieved, Gem.8.36. 2. *winning-post, goal* in a race, πρὸς τ. ὀρνύμενον B.5.45; in a contest, ἔστιν δ' ἀφάνεια τύχας καὶ μαρναμένων, πρὶν τ. ἄκρον ἱκέσθαι Pi.*I.*4(3).32(50); εἰς τ. ἐλθεῖν, of runners in a race, Pl.*R.*613c. b. *prize*, ἔφερε πυγμᾶς τ. Pi.*O.*10(11).67; οὐ γὰρ ἦν πενταέθλιον ἀλλ' ἐφ' ἑκάστῳ ἔργματι κεῖτο τ. Id.*I.*1.27; ποτὶ γραμμᾷ μὲν αὐτὰν στᾶσε κοσμήσαις, τ. ἔμμεν ἄκρον Id.*P.*9.118 (perh. 'to be the *winning post and prize*'); κρίνεις τ. ἀρετᾶς B.10.6: metaph., οὐκ ἔχω εἰπεῖν τίνι τοῦτο Μοῖρα τ. ἔμπεδον ὤρεξε Pi.*N.*7.57. 3. Philos., *full realization, highest point, ideal*, ἅπτεσθαι τοῦ τ. Pl.*Smp.*211b; πρὸς τ. ἰὼν τῶν ἐρωτικῶν ib.210e; πρὸς τ. ἀρετῆς ἐλθόντα Id.*Clit.*410e, cf. *R.* 613c. b. the *end* or *purpose* of action, τ. εἶναι ἁπασῶν τῶν πράξεων τὸ ἀγαθόν Id.*Grg.*499e; freq. in Arist., *EN*1094$^{a}$18, al.: hence, the *final cause*, = τὸ οὗ ἕνεκα, Id.*Metaph.*994$^{b}$9, 996$^{a}$26, al.; hence simply = τὸ ἀγαθόν, the *chief good*, Id.*EN*1097$^{a}$21, Zeno *Stoic.*1.45, etc.

**τέλοσδε**, Adv. *towards the doom*, θανάτοιο τ. Il.9.411, 13.602.

**τέλσας**· στροφάς, τέλη, πέρατα, Hsch.

⊛ **τέλσον**, τό, *headland*, i.e. land where the plough turned, τέλσον ἀρούρης Il.13.707, 18.544; νειοῖο..τέλσον ἱκέσθαι ib.547. (Cf. τέλος, πόλος, etc.)

**Τελχίς** (Hdn.Gr.1.17, Choerob. *in Theod.*2.267 H.), later **Τελχίν** (Choerob. l.c., Sch. rec. A.*Pers.*353), ῖνος, ὁ, *one of the Telchines*, described as inhabitants of Crete (hence called **Τελχῖνία**, St.Byz.), Rhodes (**Τελχῖνίς**, Str.14.2.7), Sicyon (St.Byz. s.v.), Ceos (Call.*Fr.* 9.65 P.), or Cyprus (Paus.9.19.1), and the first workers in metal; but of ill report as *spiteful sorcerers* (Τ. γόητες Call. l.c.), D.S.5.55, Str. 10.3.19, 14.2.7:—⊛**Τελχίνιος** [ῑν], α, ον, epith. of Apollo, Hera, and the Nymphs, D.S. l.c.; of Athena at Teumessus, Paus. l.c.:—**Τελχίνια** [ῑν], τά, a festival at Delphi, *Schwyzer* 323 *D* 9 (iv B.C.). II. later, as Appellat. τελχίν, *a spiteful person, backbiter*, Call.*Aet.Oxy.*2079.1 (pl., glossed by βάσκανοι); τελχίν τις ἢ δαίμων Sch.rec.A. l.c.; as Adj., τελχῖνες σῆτες βίβλων, of Grammarians, *AP*11.321 (Phil.); as fem., τ. δεξιά Lib.*Or.*60.9. III. τελχῖνες, αἱ, = αἱ ὑπὸ πληγῆς εἰς θάνατον καταφοραί, Hdn.Gr.1.17. (Connected with θέλγειν by ancient Gramm., cf. Ael.Dion.*Fr.*436, Hsch. s.v. Θελγῖνες; Τ. was a king of Sicyon acc. to Paus.2.5.6.)

**τελχιτένοντες**· σκληροτραχηλοῦντες, Hsch.; but **τελχιταίνει**· ἀντερίζει, σκληροτραχηλεῖ, Phot., Suid.

**τελων-άρχης**, ου, ὁ, *controller of customs*, *PKlein.Form.*82 (vi A.D.). **-εία**, ἡ, = τελωνία, *OGI*669.10 = *BGU*1563.29 (pl., Egypt, i A.D.). **-εῖον**, τό, *custom-house*, Suid. **-έω**, pf. τετελώνηκα Phld. *Rh.*1.344 S.:—*to be a* τελώνης, *PPetr.*2 p.108 (iii B.C.), Plu.2.236b, Luc.*Pseudol.*30; in bad sense, κλέπτει, τελωνεῖ Apollod.Com.13.13, cf. Phld. l.c. II. c. acc., τ. τινὰ πικρῶς *take* heavy *toll of* one, Str.9.3.4:—Med., ἐτελωνήσατο ἐξάγων δούλην *has paid toll*, *BGU* 913.11 (iii A.D.), cf. 882.2 (iii A.D.); freq. in pf., τετελώνηται διὰ πύλης ἐξάγων *PAmh.*2.116, 117 (ii A.D.), *PLips.*81, 82 (iii/iv A.D.), etc.:—Pass., τελωνουμένους σκληρῶς *OGI*55.17 (Telmessus, iii B.C.); *to be demanded* or *paid as toll*, Lxx 1 *Ma.*13.39; καθότι ἂν οἱ Μιλήσιοι -ῶνται *are subject to tax*, *Milet.*3.149.25 (ii B.C.); τὰ μὴ τετελωνημένα *articles on which customs-duty has* not *been paid*, *PTeb.* 5.26 (ii B.C.): metaph., dub. in Erot.*Prooem.* **-ης**, ου, ὁ, (τέλος I. 8, ὠνέομαι) *farmer* or *collector of tolls, customs*, or *taxes*, Ar.*Eq.*248 (troch.), Aeschin.1.119, Herod.6.64, *PCair.Zen.*31.20 (iii B.C.), *UPZ* 113.8 (ii B.C.), Aristocl.ap.Eus.*PE*15.2, etc.: freq. with a sense of reproach, πάντες τελῶναι, πάντες εἰσὶν ἅρπαγες, of the Oropians, Xeno 1; ἐφ' οἷς ἂν καὶ τελώνης σεμνυνθείη βάναυσος Plb.12.13.9, cf. Gal. 8.587, 9.804; = Lat. *publicanus*, *Ev.Matt.*5.46, al.; πορνοβοσκοὶ καὶ τ. Asp. *in EN*102.21. **-ητής**, οῦ, ὁ, = foreg., Man.4.329. **-ία**, ἡ, *office of* τελώνης: *tax-farming*, D.21.166; τελώνας (leg. τελωνίας) καὶ βιαίους πράξεις ἀποτελεῖ Vett.Val.2.11. **-ιάς**, άδος, ἡ, *of tolls* or *customs*, μᾶζα τ. the good fare *of the* τελῶναι, *AP*6.295 (Phan.). **-ικός**, ή, όν, *relating to tax-farming*, νόμοι D.24.101, *PRev.Laws* 21.12 (iii B.C.); πρόσοδοι Plu.2.201b; τὰ τ. the *tolls*, Pl. *Lg.*842d. 2. *of* or *for tax-farmers*, of certain μοῖραι in Cancer, Vett. Val.15.16. **-ιον**, τό, *custom-house*, Posidipp.13, *Ev.Matt.*9.9, *Ev. Marc.*2.14; τὸ τ. τῆς ἰχθυϊκῆς *OGI*496.9 (Ephesus, ii A.D.). II. *customs-duty*, Str.16.1.27, 17.1.16, Harp. s.v. δεκατευτάς. **-ίσιμος**, ον, *liable to pay customs*, *PCair.Zen.*289 (iii B.C.).

⊛ **τέλωρ**· τελώριον, μακρόν, μέγα, Hsch. (Dial. form of πέλωρ, cf. sq.)

**τελώριος**· μέγας, πελώριος, Hsch.; occurs in Puchstein *Epigr.Gr.* p.76 (Memphis, i B.C.).

**τεμᾰχ-ί**, Adv. *in pieces*, Suid. **-ίζω**, *cut up fish for salting*, Xenocr.ap.Orib.2.58.19, Gal.6.728 (Pass.): metaph., *slice up*, τὴν πραγματείαν Plu.2.837e; *cut to ribbons*, μεληδὸν τὸν νόμον Porph.*Chr.* 31; τ. τὴν ἀπόδειξιν Them. *in APo.*14.7; *cut up* fruit, Paul.Aeg.7.11 (Pass.). **-ιον**, τό, Dim. of τέμαχος, Hp.*Aff.*43 (v.l.), Pl.*Smp.*191e, Amphis 35, Crobyl.8. **-ισμός**, ὁ, *cutting up, slicing*, Hdn.*Epim.* 264. **-ιστός**, ή, όν, *sliced and salted*, Macho ap.Ath.6.244c, Ath. Med.ap.Orib.*inc.*23.27. **-ίτης** [ῑ], ου, ὁ, *sliced and salted*, ἰχθῦς Eub.9, Alciphr.3.5, cf. *PFlor.*388.24 (ii A.D.).

⊛ **τεμᾰχοπώλης**, ου, ὁ, *dealer in salt fish*, Antiph.128.

⊛ **τέμᾰχος**, εος, τό, (τεμᾰ-, root of τέμνω, τέτμημαι) *slice of fish* (τόμος being commonly employed of meat, cf. Phryn.13), Hp.*Aff.*41, Ar.*Eq.*283, *Pl.*894, X.*An.*5.4.28, Alex.186.8, *PCair.Zen.*82.10 (iii B.C.), etc.; κεστρᾶν τεμάχη Ar.*Nu.*339; θύννου Ephipp.12 (anap.): later, generally, for *slices of meat*, Luc.*Gall.*14, Philostr.*VA*1.21, 2.6; of fruit, Paul.Aeg.7.11: sg. in collective sense, prob. in *IPE*1$^{2}$.76. 15 (Olbia, cf. *Supp.Epigr.*3.587): metaph., τεμάχη τῶν Ὁμήρου δείπνων Aesch.ap.Ath.8.347e.

**τέμενες**, v. τέμενος.

⊛ **τεμεν-ίζω**, *make a sacred precinct, consecrate*, τεμένη τ. τισί Pl.*Lg.* 738c, cf. *IG*1$^{2}$.45.11, D.H.3.70: abs., Ἡρακλέης τεμένισσε..Φερσεφαάσσῃ Inscr.ap.Arist.*Mir.*843$^{b}$27:—Pass., ἐτεμενίσθη D.C.57.9, al. **-ικός**, ή, όν, *of* or *for a* τέμενος, Anaxandr.12 (dub.); τεμενικόν, τό, *name of the temple of* so-and-so, St.Byz. s.v. Ἰσεῖον, *EM*278. 35. II. τ. πρόσοδοι the rent *of* τεμένη, Did.ap.Harp. s.v. ἀπὸ μισθωμάτων; ὁ τ. λόγος, title of speech by Isaeus, Harp. s.v. ἅμιπποι. ⊛ **-ιος**, α, ον, *of* or *belonging to the* τέμενος, φυλλάς the grove *in the* τέμενος, S.*Tr.*754; οἶκος *SIG*987.3 (Chios, iv B.C.). II. epith. of Hestia, ib.1014.9 (Erythrae, iii B.C.). **-ισμα**, ατος, τό, *the precincts of a temple*, D.C.42.26, 57.9. ⊛ **-ίτης** [ῑ], ου, ὁ, = τεμένιος: at Syracuse, *Apollo of the Temenos* (i.e. the precinct of Demeter and Persephone), Th.6.75, Cic.*Verr.*4.53.119; τεμενίτης also epith. of Poseidon at Myconus, *SIG*1024.5 (iii/ii B.C.); of Zeus at Amorgos, *IG*12(7).62.37 (iv B.C.): fem., ἡ ἄκρα ἡ **Τεμενῖτις** the height *on which was the Temenos*, Th.7.3. ⊛ **-ος**, εος, τό, Arc. nom. and acc. sg. τέμενες *IG*5(2).432.31, 42 (Megalop., ii B.C.); Aeol. gen. sg. τεμένηος Alc.152: (τέμνω):—*a piece of land cut off and assigned as an official domain*, esp. to kings and chiefs, καὶ μέν οἱ [Βελλεροφόντῃ] Λύκιοι τ. τάμον ἔξοχον ἄλλων καλὸν φυταλιῆς καὶ ἀρούρης, ὄφρα νέμοιτο Il.6.194, cf. 20.184, 391; τ. περικαλλὲς..πεντηκοντόγυον 9.578, cf. 12.313; τ. βασιλήϊον 18.550; δμῶες Ὀδυσσῆος τ. μέγα κοπρίσσοντες Od.17.299, cf. 6.293: in pl., τεμένεα 11.185; τεμένη, μέρος τιμῆς Arist.*Rh.*1361$^{a}$35. II. *a piece of land marked off from common uses and dedicated to a god, precinct*, ἔνθα τέ οἱ τ. βωμός τε θυήεις Il.8. 48, cf. 2.696, al., Pi.*N.*10.19, *IG*1$^{2}$.94.29, etc.; τὸ τ. τῶν ἡρῴων *Test. Epict.*2.13; in it stood the temple or shrine, Hdt.2.112, 155, 3.142; Πρωτεσίλεω τάφος τε καὶ τ. περὶ αὐτόν Id.9.116: hence the Pythian race-course is called a τέμενος, Pi.*P.*5.33; Syracuse is the τ. Ἄρεος ib.2.2; the *sacred valley* of the Nile is the Νείλοιο πῖον τ. Κρονίδα ib. 4.56; the lake formed by the Cephisus is the τ. Καφισίδος ib.12.27; the Acropolis is the ἱερὸν τ. (of Pallas), Ar.*Lys.*483 (lyr.): poet. also, τέμενος αἰθέρος A.*Pers.*365; ἀνέμων Philet.13; Μαραθὼν σῆς ἀρετῆς τ. *IG*14.1185 (Rome); τρόπαια στησάμενοι Διὸς..τέμενος to be a *grove* of Zeus, Tim.*Pers.*211; of sacred *groves*, *h.Ven.*267. III. *temple*, ἄγαμαι τοῦ τ. τῆς ὀροφῆς Chor.p.88 B., cf. p.116 B. **-ουρός**, ὁ, *guardian of a* τέμενος, Ἑρμῆς *Epigr.Gr.*781.11 (Cnidus): **τεμενωρός**, Hsch. **-οῦχος**, ον, (ἔχω) *holding a* τέμενος, epith. of Poseidon (?), Epic.ap.A.D.*Synt.*138.13 (v. *Hermes* 51.480), Orac.ap. Kern *Genethliakon für Robert* 100 (Tralles). **-ωρός**, v. τεμενουρός.

**Τεμέση**, ἡ, a place whence (acc. to Od.1.184) the Taphians obtained copper in exchange for iron: some identified it with Temesa in Bruttium; others read Ταμασόν or Τάμασιν, i.e. Tamassos in Cyprus, v. Str.6.1.5, Paus.6.6.8, St.Byz.: ὁ ἐν Τεμέσῃ ἥρως, prov. of misplaced rage, Eust.1409.14.

**τέμμαι**· τείνει, Hsch. (τίνι cj. F. de Saussure, comparing τέμμαι with Avest. *čahmāi*, dat. of *ka-*, interrog.-indef. pron.: τίνει M. Schmidt): **τέμμειν**· πείθειν, τιμᾶν, ἡγεῖσθαι, Id. **τέμματα**· στεφανώματα, Id. (Perh. Lacon. for στέμματα.)

⊛ **τέμνω** (A), Ion., Dor., and Ep. **τάμνω**, Il.3.105, al. (τέμνω once in Hom., Od.3.175), Hdt.2.65, Democr.263, Hp.*Acut.*22, *SIG*1026.20 (Cos, Pass.), cf. ἀποτέμνω, διατέμνω: 3 sg. pres. **τέμει** only in Il. 13.707 (2 sg. τέμεις prob. in Epigr.ap.Suid. s.v. βοῦς ἕβδομος): τέμνω is f.l. in Pi.*P.*3.68 and v.l. in *O.*13.57, cf. τάμνω ib.12.6, B.5.17, 16.4, but is the only Att. pres., Th.3.26, *IG*1$^{2}$.76.56, etc. (v. also τμήγω): Iterat. τέμνεσκον A.R.1.1215, Q.S.6.217: fut. τεμῶ E.*Ba.*493, Th.1.82, etc.; Ion. τεμέω Hp.*Jusj.*: aor. Ion. and Dor. ἔτᾰμον, Ep. τάμον, Il.3.292, al., *SIG*4.10 (Cyzicus, vi B.C.), Pi. *N.*3.33, Hdt.7.132; Ep. inf. ταμέειν Il.19.197; Att. ἔτεμον Th.6.7, *IG*2$^{2}$.1666 *A* 8, etc.: pf. τέτμηκα Arist.*SE*178$^{a}$21, (ἀπο-) Pl.*Men.* 85a; Dor. 3 sg. τετμάκει Archim.*Con.Sph.*22, 26; Ion. and Ep. part. (in pass. sense) τετμηώς A.R.4.156:—Med., fut. τεμοῦμαι (ὑπο-) Ar. *Eq.*291 (lyr.), X.*Cyr.*1.4.19, etc.: aor. ἐταμόμην, inf. ταμέσθαι Il.9. 580; Att. ἐτεμόμην Pl.*Plt.*280d (ἀπ-), Luc.*Pr.Im.*24:—Pass., fut. τμηθήσομαι Arist.*LI*968$^{b}$17; Dor. τμα- Archim.*Aequil.*2.2; also τετμήσομαι Philostr.*VA*4.24, (ἐκ-) Pl.*R.*564c: aor. ἐτμήθην E. *Tr.*480, Th.2.18, etc.; Dor. ἐτμα- Archim.*Con.Sph.*11: pf. τέτμημαι Od.17.195, Th.3.26, etc.; Dor. τετμα- Archim.*Con.Sph.*12 (τετμη- Pi.*I.*6(5).22 codd.):—*cut*, in Hom. and elsewhere usu. of particular kinds of cutting (v. infr.); generally, ὀδόντας οἵους τέμνειν fit for *cutting*, X.*Mem.*1.4.6; τοιοῦτον τμῆμα τέμνεται τὸ τεμνόμενον, οἷον τὸ τέμνον τέμνει; Pl.*Grg.*476d. 2. *cut, wound, maim*, ἀλλήλων ταμέειν χρόα χαλκῷ Il.13.501, 16.761; πρὸς δέρην τ. *wound* her in the neck, A.*Eu.*592; οἱ στενοὶ (sc. τελαμῶνες) τέμνουσι narrow bandages *cut* the patient, Sor.1.83. 3. of a surgeon, *cut*, ἐκ μηροῦ τ. βέλος Il.11.844; τ. τὰν κοιλίαν *IG*4$^{2}$(1). 122.40 (Epid., iv B.C.); τὴν χεῖρα (in blood-letting) Gal.16.810: abs., *use the knife*, as opp. to cautery (κάειν), ἤτοι κέαντες ἢ τεμόντες A.*Ag.*849, cf. X.*An.*5.8.18, Pl.*Grg.*456b, 480c, 521e, etc.:—Pass., *to be operated upon*, Hp.*Aph.*7.44, Pl.*Grg.*479a. 4. *cut*, *castrate*, ἐρίφους, βοῦν, κάπρον, Hes.*Op.*786,791; of men, Luc.*Syr. D.*15. 5. *prune* vines, Lxx *Le.*25.3, cf. *Is.*5.6 (Pass.); *cut*, i.e. gather, herbs, Dsc.3.132 (Pass.). II. *cut up, cut to pieces*, of animals, Il.9.209; τ. μελεϊστί, διὰ μελεϊστί, κατὰ μέλη, 24.409, Od.9.291, Pi.*O.*1.49; τ. ἰχθῦς Hdt.2.65, cf. 3.42, etc.:—Med., ταμνομένους κρέα πολλὰ Od.24.364. b. *slaughter, sacrifice*, ταμέειν Διί τ' Ἠελίῳ τε Il.19.197; σφάγια τ. E.*Supp.*1196:—Pass., σφάγια τέμνεται Id.*Heracl.*400. 2. ὅρκια τάμνειν *sacrifice* in attestation of an oath, and hence, *take solemn* oaths, Il.2.124, Od.24.483, etc. (also in late Prose, as Plb.21.24.3, 21.32.15, al.); φιλότητα καὶ ὅρκια πιστὰ ταμόντες Il.3.73, etc.; θάνατόν νύ τοι ὅρκι' ἔταμνον *I made* a truce which was death to thee, 4.155; ἐπὶ τούτοισι τ. ὅρκιον on these terms, Hdt.7.132; without ὅρκιον, τ. τισὶ μένειν τὸ ὅρκιον *make a covenant that*.., Id.4.201; also σπονδὰς τέμωμεν E.*Hel.*1235; ἆρα φίλιά μοι τεμεῖ; Id.*Supp.*376 (lyr.):—Med., of two parties, ὅρκια τάμνεσθαι Hdt.4.70. 3. φάρμακον τέμνειν *cut* or *chop up* a plant for purposes of medicine or witchcraft, Pl.*Lg.*836b: metaph., ib.919b, *Ep.*353e: hence πόρον or ἄκος τέμνειν *contrive* a means or remedy, A.*Supp.*807 (lyr., dub. l.), E.*Andr.*121 (lyr.). 4. *divide*, of a river, μέσην τ. Λιβύην *cut* it in twain, Hdt.2.33, cf. E.*El.*411; of a mountain-chain, D.P.340,890; τ. δίχα *cleave* in two, Pl.*Smp.*190d:—Med., ἑπτὰ μέρη τεμόμενος *having divided* it into seven parts, Id.*Lg.*695c:—Pass., γραμμὴ δίχα τετμημένη Id.*R.*509d; τετμημένος ἐξ ἑνὸς δύο *cut* from one into two, Id.*Smp.*191d. b. διὰ τῆς δριμυφαγίας εἰ καὶ τὸ πάχος τέμνοιτο τοῦ γάλακτος *were to be diluted, thinned*, Sor.1.98; ἡ τῆς πτισάνης [ὕλη] τ. καὶ ὑγραίνει τὰ τῆς ἀναπτύσεως δεόμενα Gal.15.507, cf. 6.352, 14.742; τέμνειν καὶ λεπτύνειν τὰ παχέα τῶν ὑγρῶν Id.6.760, cf. *Vict.Att.*1, al. 5. *divide* logically, τ. δίχα Pl.*Phlb.*49a, *Plt.*287b; τ. τὸν ἀριθμὸν ἀρτίῳ καὶ περιττῷ into even and odd, ib.262e, cf. 266e, al.; εἰς δύο μέρη τέμνουσι [τὴν πραγματείαν] Sor.1.1:—Pass., διχῇ τέμνεσθαι Pl.*Sph.*223c. III. *cut off, sever*, ἐκ κεφαλέων τρίχας Il.3.273; κεφαλὴν ἀπὸ δειρῆς 18.177; δρακόντοιν κάρα A.*Ch.*1047, cf. S.*Ph.*619; λαιμούς τινος Ar.*Av.*1560; πλόκον, φόβας, βόστρυχον, S.*Aj.*1179, *El.*449,901 (Pass.), etc.; τράχηλον σώματος χωρὶς E.*Ba.*241; Ὕδραν τ. Pl.*R.*426e: with double acc., ἐρινεὸν ὀξέϊ χαλκῷ τάμνε νέους ὅρπηκας *cut the* branches *off* the fig-tree, Il.21.38 (ἐρινεοῦ cj. Agar):—Pass., τρίχας ἐτμήθην *had* them *cut off*, E.*Tr.*480. 2. *part off, mark off*, τέλσον ἀρούρης Il.13.707; τέμενος 6.194; so in Med., 9.580; also τάμνοντ' ἀμφὶ βοῶν ἀγέλας *they cut* them *off, surrounded* them, 18.528. IV. *cut down, fell*, of trees and timber, δένδρεα, δρῦς, φιτρούς, 11.88, 23.119, Od.12.11, etc.; δοῦρα Hes.*Op.*807; τίς.. ἔτεμε τὰν δακρυόεσσαν Ἰλίῳ πεύκαν; E.*Hel.*231 (lyr.); τ. ὕλην Th.2.98; τ. ξύλα ἐκ τοῦ Κιθαιρῶνος ib.75; χάρακας ἐκ τοῦ τεμένους Id.3.70:—Pass., [μελίη] χαλκῷ ταμνομένη Il.13.180; ῥόπαλον τετμημένον Od.17.195; ἡ ὕλη ἡ τετμ. the *felled* timber, D.42.30:—Med., δοῦρα τάμνεσθαι *fell oneself* timber, Od.5.243, cf. Hdt.5.82, E.*Hec.*634 (lyr.). 2. λίθον τ. *hew* or *quarry* it, *IG*1$^2$.76.56, cf. 2$^2$.1666*A*8, 4$^2$(1).102.41, al. (Epid., iv B.C.), Pl.*Criti.*116a, *PPetr.*2p.6 (iii B.C.), D.S.5.13; τ. μέταλλον *open* or *work* a mine, Hyp.*Eux.*35 (Pass.):—Med., λίθους τάμνεσθαι *have* them *wrought* or *hewn*, Hdt.1.186. 3. *cut down* for purposes of destruction, γῆς τ. βλαστήματα E.*Hec.*1204; τ. τὸν σῖτον X.*Mem.*2.1.13; also τ. τὴν γῆν *lay waste* the country *by felling the fruit-trees, cutting the corn*, etc., Hdt.9.86, cf. Th.2.19,55, And.3.8 (Pass.); τῆς γῆς ἔτεμον οὐ πολλὴν Th.6.7: c. partit. gen., τῆς γῆς τ. *waste* part of it, Id.1.30, 2.56:—Pass., ib.18,20. V. *cut into shape*, δέρμα βόειον Od.14.24; ἱμάντας ἐκ τοῦ δέρματος Hdt.5.25:—Med., νομέας ταμόμενοι Id.1.194. VI. *cut lengthwise*, τ. γῆν, ἄρουραν, *plough* it, Sol.13.47, A.*Fr.*196. 2. τ. ὁδόν *cut* or *make* a road, τ. ὁδοὺς εὐθείας Th.2.100; τ. διάπλους ἐκ τῶν διωρύχων Pl.*Criti.*118e; τάφρον τεμέσθαι *PHal.*1.107 (iii B.C.); ὁ τέμνων (sc. τὴν τάφρον) ib.110: metaph., ὀχετοὺς ἐπὶ τὸν πλεύμονα ἔτεμον *carried* channels or ducts to the lungs, Pl.*Ti.*70d, cf. 77c; οὐκ.. ἐγὼ πρῶτος ταύτην ἐτεμόμην τὴν ὁδόν Luc.*Pr.Im.*24:—Pass., μυρίαι τέτμηνται κέλευθοι Pi.*I.*6(5).22; οὐ τετμημένων [τῶν] ὁδῶν Hdt.4.136, etc. b. *make* one's way, *advance*, ὦ τὴν ἐν ἄστροις.. τέμνων ὁδὸν.. Ἥλιε E.*Ph.*1; διὰ μέσου.. αἰθέρος τέμνων κέλευθον Ar.*Th.*1100; τὴν μεσόγαιαν τ. τῆς ὁδοῦ *take* the inland road, *strike through* the interior, Hdt.7.124, 9.89: metaph., μέσον τι τέμνειν *hold* a middle course, Pl.*Prt.*338a; τὴν μέσην τ. Plu.2.7b; μέσον τινὰ [βίον] τ. Pl.*Lg.*793a; βιότοιο τ. τρίβον *AP*9.359 (Posidipp. or Pl.Com.), 360 (Metrod.): abs., *make one's way*, A.R.2.1244, 4.771. 3. of ships, *cut through* the waves, *plough* the sea, τ. πέλαγος μέσον, κύματα θαλάσσης, Od.3.175, 13.88, cf. Pi.*P.*3.68: metaph., ψευδῆ.. τάμνοισαι κυλίνδοντ' ἐλπίδες men's hopes are tossed about *as they cut through* the sea of lies, Id.*O.*12.6: of birds, αἰθέρος αὔλακα τ. *cleave* the air, Ar.*Av.*1400, cf. *h.Cer.*383, E.*Epigr.*2. VII. *cut short, bring to a crisis* or *decision*, μαχᾶν τ. τέλος Pi.*O.*13.57; κίνδυνον τ. σιδάρῳ E.*Heracl.*758 (lyr.); λόγῳ τὰ διάφορα τεμεῖν Lib.*Or.*18.164; τὰς δίκας τ. *Cod.Just.*3.1.12, cf. 2.12.27.2, al. VIII. ταμών metaph. for ἀρύσας, Emp.143. (Cf. Slovenian *tnèm tę́ti* 'to hack', Ir. *tamnaim* 'I mutilate'.)

**τέμνω** (B), only in τέμνοντα· ἀμέλγοντα, Hsch.; ἔτεμεν· ἤμελγεν, Id. (Perh. cf. Skt. *ā-cāmati*, pl. *-camanti*, 'sip', Icel. *hvóma* 'swallow'.)

* **Τέμπ-εα**, contr. **Τέμπη**, τά, *Tempe*, the valley between Mounts Olympus and Ossa, through which the Peneus escapes into the sea, Hdt.7.173, Call.*Del.*105. II. *any sequestered vale*, Cic.*Att.*4.15.5, D.P.219,916,1017; ἢ κατὰ Πηνειῶ καλὰ τέμπεα, ἢ κατὰ Πίνδω Theoc.1.67: also in late Prose, Aristid.*Or.*23(42).20, 36(48).120, Philostr.*Ep.*16. **-είτης**, ου, ὁ, *dweller in the vale of Tempe*, Ἄπλουνι Τεμπείτᾳ *IG*9(2).1034 (Gyrton, iii B.C.). **-ικός**, ή, όν, *in* or *of Tempe*, Plu.2.1136a, Ael.*VH*3.1:—fem. **Τεμπίς**, ίδος, Nic.*Al.*199. **-όθεν**, Adv. *from Tempe*, Call.*Iamb.*1.230.

**τεμποῦροι**· ἀρχὴ ἐπιμελουμένη τῆς τῶν γυναικῶν εὐκοσμίας, Hsch.

**Τεμπώδης**, ες, *like a vale*, Eust. ad D.P.1017.

**τέμω**, v. τέμνω.

**τενᾰγ-ίζω**, *to be covered with shoal-water*, Str.1.3.4; ὁ ῥοῦς τ. *stands in pools*, Plu.*Luc.*24. * **-ῖτις**, ιδος, fem. Adj. *shallow*, *AP*9.551 (Antiphil.). **-όομαι**, Pass., *to be formed by shoal-water*, λίμναι Xenocr.ap.Orib.2.58.35. **-ος**, εος, τό, *shoal-water, shallows, lagoon*, whether in the sea or in rivers, Pi.*N.*3.24; ἕλεά τε καὶ τ. Hdt.1.202, cf. 7.176, 8.129, Th.3.51, *PPetr.*2p.17 (iii B.C.), etc.; φύεται [τὰ ὄστρεα].. ἐν τοῖς τενάγεσι Arist.*HA*548$^a$1. **-ώδης**, ες, *formed of shoal-water, standing in pools*, A.R.4.1264, Plb.1.75.8, 10.8.7, D.S.2.60, Jul.*Or.*1.39a, etc. 2. *living therein*, [σκορπίος] Hices.ap.Ath.7.320d.

**τενάντιον**, τό, *hook to fasten dress*, in gloss on ἐνετή, Eust.976.25.

**τέναρον**, τό, *media manus*, Gloss.; cf. θέναρ.

**τέναρος**· κακοῦργος, συκοφάντης, Hsch., Phot., Suid.: perh. cf. τεωρεῖς.

**τένδω**, *gnaw, gnaw at*, Hes.*Op.*524 (τένθει v.l. ap.Sch.Ar.*Pax* 1009, Suid. s.v. τένθαις), cj. in *AP*9.438.1 (Phil.). (Prob. cf. Lat. *tondeo*.)

* **τένεα**· κόρυζα, Hsch.

**Τένεδος**, ἡ, *Tenedos*, Il.1.38, etc.: hence **Τενέδιος ἄνθρωπος**, prov. ἐπὶ τῶν φοβερῶν τὰς ὄψεις, Men.200; Τ. αὐλητής, prov. of false accusation, St.Byz.; Τ. ξυνήγορος a sharp-tongued advocate, Id.; Τ. πέλεκυς, v. πέλεκυς I. 2.

**τενεκοῦντι**· ἐνοικοῦντι, Αἰολεῖς, Hsch.

**τενθ-εία**, ἡ, *lickerishness, gluttony*, Ar.*Av.*1691, Alciphr.3.24. **-εύω**, *eat greedily*, Poll.6.122, dub. cj. in Lib.*Or.*62.25. **-ης**, ου, ὁ, *gourmand*, Cratin.320 (lyr.), Ar.*Pax*1009,1120, Cephisodorus ap. Eus.*PE*15.2, Ath.1.6c, 3.112b; cf. προτένθης. (Expld. as λωποδύται, μοιχοί, Hsch., but as οἱ λίχνοι, Id. s.v. τένδω; τ. δὲ ὁ λίχνος καὶ τὸ ἀπὸ παντὸς ἥδιστον θηρώμενος μεταφέρων αὐτὸ ἄλλοτ' ἐπ' ἄλλα Anon. in *EN*182.10.)

**τένθινοι**· λίθοι πλατεῖς, Hsch.

**τενθρ-ηδών**, όνος, ἡ, a kind of *wasp* that makes its nest in the earth, Arist.*HA*629$^a$31, Dsc.5.109; cf. sq. **-ήνη**, ἡ, = foreg., Nic.*Al.*547. **-ήνιον**, τό, *the nest of the τενθρηδών*, Arist.*HA*629$^b$1. **-ηνιώδης**, ες, *honeycombed*, Hp.*Anat.*1 (τεθρ- codd.), Democr.ap.Ael.*NA*12.20 (ubi θρηνῶδες), Plu.2.721f (ubi τενθρηνῶδες).

**τένθω**, v. τένδω. **τέννει**· στένει, βρύχεται, Hsch. **τέννος**· στέφανος ἐλάϊνος ἐρίῳ πεπλεγμένος, Id.

**τενοντάγρα**, ἡ, *stiffness of the sinews*, Cael.Aur.*TP*5.2.

**τενοντοκοπέω**, *cut through the neck, behead*, Aq.*Ex.*34.20: also **τενοντόω**, Id.*Ex.*13.13.

**τενοντότρωτος**, ον, *wounded in the tendons*, Gal.13.575.

* **τένων**, οντος, ὁ, (τείνω) *sinew, tendon*, ἀπέκοψε τένοντας αὐχενίους Od.3.449; freq. in dual, ἄμφω ῥῆξε τένοντε Il.5.307, al., cf. 4.521, Hes.*Sc.*419; of the arm, ἵνα τε ξυνέχουσι τένοντες ἀγκῶνος Il.20.478; of the foot, ποδῶν τέτρηνε τένοντε 22.396, cf. E.*Ph.*42; τ. ποδός the outstretched foot, Id.*Cyc.*400; ὁ τ. ὁ ὀπίσθιος the Achilles tendon, Hp.*Fract.*11; ὁ τ. ὁ ἐν τῇ κνήμῃ τοῦ ποδὸς ib.16, cf. Arist.*HA*515$^b$9; τ. defined as a species of νεῦρον, Gal.2.739, cf. 6.772: abs., for the *foot*, πτέρναι τενόντων θ' ὑπογραφαὶ A.*Ch.*209, cf. E.*Med.*1166, *Ba.*938; τένοντα σείων, of a mule, Babr.62.3. II. metaph., *mountain-ridge*, Καυκάσιος τ. *AP*4.3$^b$.12 (Agath.).

* **τέξις**, εως, ἡ, (τίκτω) *child-bearing*, Hp.*Mul.*1.34.

**τέο**, gen. of interrog. τίς, v. τις B init. II. **τεο**, gen. of enclit. τις, v. τις A init. III. **τέο**, Dor. gen. of σύ (τύ), v. σύ; Ep. **τεοῖο**, ibid. **τεοισι, τέοισι**, Ion. for τισι, τίσι, v. τις A and B init. **τέος**, Dor. gen. of σύ (q.v.).

* **τεός**, ή, όν, Ep. for σός, Il.5.234, Hes.*Op.*27, etc.; Dor. **τεός**, ά, όν, Pi.*O.*4.1, *N.*8.44, al., B.9.13, 16.21, and in lyr. passages of Trag., as A.*Pr.*163, *Th.*105, S.*El.*1091 (cj.), E.*Heracl.*911; Aeol. **τέος**, α, ον, Alc.14; Boeot. acc. pl. masc. **τιώς** Corinn.*Supp.*2.58. [**τεός** as one short syll. in Praxill.1 (cited by Heph. for this reason).]

**τέος** and **τεός**, Ion. and Dor. for τίς, τις, rare in nom. and acc., οὔτε γὰρ οὐ τεον ἔστι nor is there a Nothing, Parm.8.46; but some of the oblique cases occur in Hdt., etc., v. τέῳ, τέων, τέοισι; **τεοις** Xenoph.37; cf. also τέο.

**τεοῦ**, Dor. gen. of σύ, Epich.145, Sophr.84, Call.*Cer.*99, cf. A.D. *Pron.*75.16. II. τέου, gen. of τίς, Archil.95.

**τεοῦς**, Dor. and Boeot. gen. of σύ, Sophr.59, Corinn.11.

**τέουτος**, v. τοιοῦτος.

**τεπόριον**, = 'the.. of the well', *PLond.*1821.193: the next lemma, glossed 'ditto', is τροχαρέα, hence perh. *roller* of a windlass.

**τεπτά**· ἑπτά, Hsch. (τ prob. an error for ⊢ = spir. asp.).

**τεράδερμον**, v. τετράδερμα.

**τεράζω** or (acc. to Hdn.Gr.1.443) **τερᾴζω**, *interpret portents* or *prodigies*, A.*Ag.*125 (lyr.).

**τέραμνον** or **τέρεμνον**, τό, a word used esp. by E., but only in pl. and always (except once, τέραμνά τ' οἴκων *Hipp.*418) in lyr. passages, *chamber, house*, like μέλαθρα, τ. ἀπὸ νυμφιδίων *Hipp.*768; παστάδων ὑπὲρ τ. *Or.*1371; Περγάμων.. καταίθεται τ. *Tr.*1296; ἐξ Ἀίδα τεράμνων *Alc.*457; ἐπὶ Πυθίοις τ. *Hipp.*536; ὑπὲρ τέραμνα *Ph.*

333: dat. sg. τεράμνῳ Maiist.12: also in late Prose, τέρεμνα Artem. 2.10. [–εμνα *Or.*1371 codd. ALP, *Ph.*333 codd. VA, *Hipp.*418 codd. exc. L, which has –α–: Maiist. l.c. corroborates the spelling –αμνον.]

**τέραμνον**· ἀπαλόν, ἑψανόν, Phot., Suid.

**τερᾰμότης**, ητος, ἡ, *softness*, Thphr.*CP*4.12.10.

**τεράμων** (A) [ᾰ], ον, gen. ονος, (τείρω, τέρην) *becoming soft by boiling*, of pulse, Thphr.*HP*8.8.6, *CP*4.12.1 sq., cf. Plu.2.701d: Comp. –ονέστερος Thphr.*CP*5.6.12: also of soil fit for such plants, ib.4. 12.3; of water, Phot.

**τεράμων** (B) [ᾰ], ωνος or οντος, ὁ (?), = κάλαμος, Anacr.ap.Hilgard *Excerpta ex libris Herodiani* (Leipzig 1887) p.21, Pl.*Sph.* ibid.: v. *Hermes* 35.544. (Said to be declined as –ντ– stem by Anacr. l.c. (this stem mentioned also by Arc.13), but –ων –ωνος by Pl. l.c.: not found in our text of Pl.*Sph.*, but τεράμωσι (or perh. τεράμουσι) is to be restored in 221a for καλάμοις.)

**τέρας**, τό: gen. Ep. αος (not in Hom. or Hes.), Ion. εος Hdt.8. 37: pl., nom. Ep. τέραα Od.12.394, Ion. τέρεα Hdt. l.c., τεράᾱτᾰ D.P.604, Q.S.5.43; τέρᾱ A.R.4.1410, but τέρᾰ Nic.*Th.*186; τέρα (quantity not stated) Att. acc. to Moer.p.369 P., cf. Ar.*Ra.*1343; gen. Ep. τεράων Il.12.229, τερέων Alc.155; Att. τερῶν acc. to Moer. l.c., Thom.Mag.p.348 R.; dat. Ep. τεράεσσι Il.4.398, al.; later τέρασι Lxx *De.*26.8, al.: the forms τέρατ-ος, –ι, –α, –ων are Hellenistic, Moer. pp.366,369 P., Thom.Mag. p.348 R. (τέρατα Lxx *Ex.*4.21, al., τεράτων ib.*Ps.*104(105).27); gen. sg. τέρως v.l. in Paus.10.26.3: lengthd. metri gr. τείρεα Il.18.485 (= *IG*4²(1).129.9), Arat.692, A.R. 3.1362; τείρεσιν *h.Mart.*7; later τείρεσσι *IG*14.2461.11 (Massilia):— *sign, wonder, marvel, portent*, ἡμῖν μὲν τόδ' ἔφηνε τ. Ζεύς Il.2.324; ἠτέομεν δὲ θεὸν φῆναι τ. Od.3.173; τοῖσιν.. θεοὶ τέραα προὔφαινον 12.394; τέρας ἧκε Κρόνου παῖς 21.415; Ζεὺς δ' Ἔριδα προΐαλλε.., πολέμοιο τ. μετὰ χερσὶν ἔχουσαν *a sign* of coming battle, Il.11.4; esp. of *signs* in heaven, ἀστέρα ἧκε Κρόνου παῖς.., ναύτῃσι τ. 4.76; ἴρισσιν ἐοικότες, ἅς τε Κρονίων ἐν νέφεϊ στήριξε τ. μερόπων ἀνθρώπων 11.28, cf. 17.548; and with pass. Verbs, τ. φανήτω Od.20.101:—so always when the first syll. is lengthd., v. supr.:—also in Prose, ἢν δὲ χειμῶνος βροντὴ γένηται, ὡς τέρας θωμάζεται Hdt.4.28, cf. 6.98; τ. πέμπειν X.*Mem.* 1.4.15; ἐφάνη Hdt.7.57; ἐπιγίνεταί σφι τέρεα Id.8.37, cf. Hes.*Th.* 744, Pi.*O.*13.73, etc.; freq. in *NT*, σημεῖα καὶ τέρατα *Ev.Marc.*13. 22, al. II. in concrete sense, *monster*, Διὸς τ. αἰγιόχοιο, of the Gorgon's head, Il.5.742; of a serpent, 12.209, *h.Ap.*302; δάϊον τ., of Typhoeus, A.*Pr.*354; ἀπρόσμαχον τ., of Cerberus, S.*Tr.*1098; οὔρειον τ., of the Sphinx, E.*Ph.*806 (lyr.); ταῦρον, ἄγριον τ. Id.*Hipp.* 1214, cf. 1247; ὅλον τ. ὀπτήσας.. βασιλεῖ παρέθηκε κάμηλον Antiph. 172.7 (anap.), cf. Epicr.3.13; used by Cicero of Caesar, *Att.*8.9.4. 2. *monstrous birth, monstrosity*, Pl.*Cra.*393b, 394a, Aeschin.3.111, Arist.*GA*769ᵇ30, 773ᵃ3, Vett.Val.341.13; ὡς ἔθρεψεν ἔκπαγλον τ. A. *Ch.*548. III. in colloquial language, τέρας λέγεις καὶ θαυμαστόν Pl.*Hp.Ma.*283c, cf. *Tht.*163d; τέρας λέγεις, εἰ.. Id.*Men.*91d; 'a marvel' of a cup, Theoc.1.56: pl., of incredible statements, Phld. *Mus.*p.74 K.

**τερασκόπος**, ὁ, poet. for τερατοσκόπος, Pi.*P.*4.201, A.*Ch.*551, *Eu.* 62, S.*OT*605: Adj., καρδία τ. '*my prophetic* soul', A.*Ag.*978 (lyr.).

**τέρασμα**, ατος, τό, *marvel, prodigy*, Plu.2.1123b.

**τερασπορία**, ἡ, *sowing of portents*, corrupt in *Corp.Herm.*3.3.

**τεράστιος**, ον, *monstrous, prodigious*, ὡς τ. τι πεποιηκώς (Bernard. rightly ὥσπερ ἀστεῖόν τι) Thphr.*Char.*19.9; τ. τι πάσχεις Luc. *DMort.*17.1; τ. τὸ πρᾶγμα ἐφαίνετο Id.*Alex.*16; τ. σημεῖον Ezek. *Exag.*91, cf. Sm.*Nu.*13.34(33), al.; τ. ἔργον Ph.1.544; τεράστιοι perh. = τερατουργοί in Rhetor. in *Cat.Cod.Astr.*8(4).148: Ζεὺς τ. *the god of portents*, Luc.*Tim.*41, Aristid.2.65 J., *IG*5(1).1154 (Gythium); δαίμονες τ. Hld.2.5: τὸ τ., = τέρας, J.*AJ*10.2.1; *a monstrous birth*, Paul.Aeg.3.76 (pl.). Adv. –ίως Eust. ad D.P.*Proll.* p.79 B.

**τερᾰτ-εία**, ἡ, *talking marvels*, Ar.*Nu.*318, Isoc.12.1, Plb.2.17.6; '*fairy story*', Phld.*Piet.*27 (pl.); ἡ ποιητικὴ τ. Jul.*Or.*2.56d. 2. *the knowledge of* τέρατα, as part of the equipment of Pythagoras, Luc. *Vit.Auct.*2. **–ευμα**, ατος, τό, *juggling trick*, Ar.*Lys.*762, D.H.2. 19, etc. **–εύομαι**, *talk marvels*, Ar.*Eq.*627, *Ra.*834; ἀποθαυμάζων καὶ τ. Aeschin.1.94; τ. τῷ σχήματι *indulge in strange* gesticulation, Id.2.49; ψεύδεται καὶ τ. ib.98, cf. 3.160; ἐν τοῖς ὀνόμασι Gal. 15.787: c. acc., οἱ τερατεύεσθαί τι πρὸς τοὺς πολλοὺς βουλόμενοι Epicur.*Ep.*2 p.53 U.; τὰ τοιαῦτα Agatharch.7; τοὺς γρῦπας Sch.A.*Pr.* 803. **–ίας**, ου, ὁ, = τερατουργός, *worker of marvels*, D.S.34/5.2. 8. **–ικῶς**, Adv. *wonderfully*, τ. εὖ Epicur.*Fr.*161. **–ισμός**, ὁ, = τέρας, Lyd.*Ost.*4 (pl.).

**τερᾰτο-γονία**, ἡ, *monstrous birth*, Poll.7.188. **–γόνος**, ον, *favouring the birth of monsters*, Vett.Val.18.1. **–γρᾰφέω**, *write of* τέρατα, Str.1.2.11. **–εργάτης** [γᾰ], ου, ὁ, *wonder-worker*, Tz.*H.*2. 921.

**τερᾰτολογ-έω**, *tell of marvels* or *strange phenomena*, Arist.*Mete.* 368ᵃ25; τ. ὑπέρ τινος D.S.1.63; τὰ τοιαῦτα τ. Luc.*Philops.*37:— Pass., *to be related as a marvel*, S.E.*P.*2.70, 3.31, Iamb.*Protr.*21. γ'. **–ημα**, ατος, τό, *marvellous tale*, Ant.Diog.14 (pl.). **–ία**, ἡ, *telling of marvels, marvellous tales*, Isoc.15.285 (pl.), Str.6.2.4, Ph.1.505, Procl. *in Cra.*p.55 P., Ps.-Luc.*Philopatr.*2. **–ος** (parox.), ὁ, *marvel-monger*, Poll.9.147 (citing Plato, v. II), Philostr.*VA*3. 32. II. Adj., in pass. sense, *portentous*, φύσεις Pl.*Phdr.*229e.

**τερᾰτό-μορφος**, ον, *of monstrous shape*, Cass.*Pr.*51, Tz.*H.*8. 636. **–ομαι**, Med., *stare at as a wonder*, Timo 34. **–ποιία**, ἡ, *miracle-mongering*, Arist.*Fr.*191. **–ποιός**, όν, *working wonders*, Lxx 2 *Ma.*15.21, Procl.*Par.Ptol.*225. **–πρόσωπος**, ον, *with monstrous face*, Hdn.*Epim.*17. **–σκοπία**, ἡ, *interpretation of* τέρατα, Poll.7.188. **–σκόπος**, ὁ, *observer of* τέρατα, *soothsayer, diviner*, Pl.*Lg.*933c,e, Arist.*Fr.*75, Lxx *De.*18. 11: cf. τερασκόπος. **–τοκέω**, *give birth to a monster*, Arist.*GA* 770ᵇ4.

**τερᾰτουργ-έω**, *work wonders*, ψευδῶς τι Sch.Pi.*I.*7(6).13. **–ημα**, ατος, τό, *miracle*, Suid. s.v. Διονύσιος ὁ Ἀρεωπαγίτης. **–ία**, ἡ, *working of wonders*, Porph.*Abst.*2.42; ἡ περὶ γαστέρα τ. its *wonderful working*, Ph.1.60. II. *use* or *love of the marvellous*, ἡ ἐν τοῖς λόγοις τ. Luc.*Icar.*6, cf. Plu.2.17b (pl.). **–ός**, ὁ, *wonder-worker*, D.S. 34/5.2.5, Ptol.*Tetr.*160, Luc.*Gall.*4: Adj., τ. ἡδονή Ph.2.267.

**τερᾰτ-ώδης**, ες, *portentous, prodigious*, Ar.*Nu.*364; σοφία τ. X. *Ep.*1; also of men, τ. εἰς σοφίαν Pl.*Euthd.*296e; τὸ τερατῶδες Arist. *Po.*1453ᵇ9; τ. ἀναπλασμοί Metrod.*Herc.*831.5, cf. Jul.*Or.*7.206c. II. *monstrous*, of strange births (τέρας II. 2), Arist.*GA*772ᵃ36, al., Sor. 2.55; τὰ τ. Phld.*Sign.*7; τ. ζῴδια, viz. Pisces, Cancer, Scorpio, Capricorn, *Cat.Cod.Astr.*1.166: Sup., –ωδεστάτη ὄψις Ph.2.99, cf. Phld. *Mort.*38. Adv. –δῶς, opp. κατὰ φύσιν, Arist.*HA*496ᵇ18, cf. D.S.1. 26. **–ωπός**, όν, *marvellous-looking*, τ. ἰδέσθαι *h.Pan.*36.

⊕ **Τερβινθεύς**, ὁ, epith. of Apollo at Myus, *SIG*633.79 (Milet., ii B.C.): v. τέρμινθος.

⊕ **τερεβινθ-ίζω**, *to be like turpentine*, Dsc.5.142. **–ῐνος, τερέβινθος**, v. τερμίνθινος, τέρμινθος. **–ώδης**, ες, *full of terebinth-trees*, νησὶς *AP*9.413 (Antiphil.).

**τέρεινος**, collat. form of τέρην, restored by Salmas. in *Anacreont.* 53.2, for τερινόν.

**τερείτης**, ου, ὁ, a term in Music, perh. name of an instrument, Αἰγυπτίοις τερείταις ὑποαυλισμοὺς δύο *BGU*1125.4, cf. 3,23,29 (i B.C.).

**τερεμίνθ-ινος, –ος**, v. τερμίνθινος, τέρμινθος.

**τέρεμνον**, τό, v. τέραμνον. **τέρεμνος**, ον, = στερεός, στερρός, Hsch.

**τερενόχρως**, ωτος, ὁ, ἡ, *with tender skin*, τερενόχρωτες μαζῶν ὄψεις Anaxandr.41.37 (anap.); heterocl. dat. τερενόχροϊ Opp.*H.*2.56; nom. pl. τερενόχροες Orph.*L.*33.

⊕ **τερετ-ίζω**, *hum* a tune, τερετιῶ τι πιστικόν Phryn.Com.14, cf. Teles p.7 H., Arist.*Pr.*918ᵃ30, Babr.9.4, Alciphr.3.55; πρὸς τὸ δίχορδον τ. Euphro 1.34; αὐτὸς αὐτῷ τ. Thphr.*Char.*27.15:—Pass., Phld. *Mus.*p.99 K. 2. *twitter*, of swallows, Hsch. 3. *accompany* with the voice, = τὸ αὐτὸ μέλος ᾄδειν, Phot., Suid. II. *talk idly, prattle*, Zeno *Stoic.*1.23: cf. συντερ–. (Onomatop.) **–ισμα**, ατος, τό, *a humming, twanging*, φορμίγγων Diog.ap.D.L.6.104 (alluding to E.*Fr.*200), Luc.*Nigr.*15, *AP*7.612, cf. 11.352 (both Agath.); *chirruping* of cicadas, Hsch. II. metaph., *a mere sound* or *twittering*, τερετίσματα τὰ εἴδη (the Platonic ideas) Arist.*APo.*83ᵃ33; τὰ συνήθη ταῦτα τ. the ordinary *prattle*, Procop.Gaz.*Ep.*33; τὸ πόημα οὐχ ὡς τ. καὶ κροῦμα νοοῦμεν Phld.*Po.*2 p.228 H. **–ισμός**, ὁ, = foreg., of flutes, *trilling*, Poll.4.83, cf. Anon.Bellerm. p.26.

**τερέτριον**, τό, Dim. of sq., Thphr.*HP*5.7.8.

**τέρετρον**, τό, (τετραίνω) *borer, gimlet*, Od.5.246, 23.198, *IG*1².313. 127, Lxx *Is.*44.12, *AP*6.103 (Phil.), Plu.2.997d; *trepan*, Aret.*CD*1.4.

**τερέω**, fut. –έσω Eust.1532.2:—*bore through, pierce*, l.c. 2. **τέρεσσεν**· ἔτρωσεν, ἐτόρνωσεν, Hsch.

**τερηδον-ίζομαι**, Pass., *to be worm-eaten*, of orris-root, Dsc.1.1; –ίζεται ὁ ὀπός (of συκόμορον, when dried) ib.127; of bones, *to be carious*, Antyll.ap.Orib.44.23.10. **–ισμός**, ὁ, *carious condition*, κρανίου Heliod.ap.Orib.46.22 tit.

**τερηδών**, όνος, ἡ, *wood-worm*, Ar.*Eq.*1308, Thphr.*HP*5.4.4, Plb. 6.10.3. 2. *a grub* which infests beehives, larva of the wax-moth, *Galleria mellonella* (cf. πυραύστης), Arist.*HA*605ᵇ17. 3. *a worm in the bowels*, Id.*Fr.*241. II. *caries*, in the bones, Hp.*Morb.*2. 24, al. (Cf. τετραίνω, Skt. *tṛṇatti* 'bore through', Lith. *trandìs* 'hair-worm, moth'.)

⊕ **τέρην**, ειvᾰ, εν, gen. τέρενος, είνης, ενος; poet. fem. gen. τερένης, Dor. and Aeol. –ας, Alc.61, *AP*9.430 (Crin.):—poet. Adj. *soft, delicate*, in Hom. mostly in neut., τέρεν δάκρυ Il.3.142, al.; τέρενα φύλλα 13.180, Od.12.357; τέρεν' ἄνθεα ποίης 9.449, cf. Sapph. 54; τέρεν αἷμα Emp.100.6; τ. δέμας ib.11: metaph., τέρεν ἄνθος ἥβης Hes.*Th.*988: masc. only in the phrase τέρενα χρόα, Il.4.237, al., Hes.*Op.*522, *Th.*5: fem., γλήχωνι τερείνῃ *h.Cer.*209; παρθένος τέρεινα Hippon.90; παιδὶ τερείνῃ Thgn.261; τέρειναν ματέρ' οἰνάνθας ὀπώραν Pi.*N.*5.6; poet. gen. τερένας ὀπώρας Alc. l.c.; τέρειν' ὀπώρα A.*Supp.*998; μυρσίναις τερείναις *Anacreont.*30.1; τέρεινα δάφνα Ibyc. 6; ὄψιν τέρειναν a *tender* sight, i.e. one *that causes tender feelings*, E.*Med.*905: of sound, τέρεν φθέγγεται (sc. παῖς) Thgn.266; τερένων ὑπ' αὐλῶν Anacr.20: Comp. τερενώτερος *Lyr.Adesp.*76; τερέντερος Antim.97; τερεινότερος *AP*5.120 (Phld.). (Cf. τέρυ, Sabine *tereno–* 'soft', Lat. *tenero–* (prob. influenced by *tenuis*), Skt. *táruṇas* 'young, tender'.)

**τερθρ-εία**, ἡ, *use of extreme subtlety, hair-splitting, formal pedantry*, Isoc.10.4, Phld.*Oec.*p.75 J., Ph.2.191, al.; τ. μυθική in religion, D.H. 2.19; of disputes about words, Gal.8.637, *UP*4.9; εἴ τις εἰς τὴν Στωϊκὴν τ. ἀπάγοι τὸν λόγον Procl. *in Prm.* p.534 S. II. = στρατεία 3, Phot., Suid. **–εύομαι**, *use extreme subtlety*, Arist. *Top.*156ᵇ38, Plu.2.43a, Gal.*UP*6.12, dub. cj. by Bgk. in Ar.*Fr.*198.9, cf. Pherecr.18 (dub.); τ. περί τινος D.61.15. **–εύς**, έως, ὁ, *quibbler*, sarcastically as a pr. n. in Hermipp.42.

**τερθρηδών**, όνος, ὁ, v. τερθρωτήρ.

**τέρθριος**, ὁ, *rope from the end of a sail-yard* (τέρθρον), used for reefing, Ar.*Eq.*440, cf. Sch. ad loc.; τ. κάλοι Erot., Gal.19.145. II.

**τερθρία πνοή**, cited from S. (*Fr.*333) in *EM*753.7, is there expld. by ὀπισθία, a *stern* wind, but perh. rather a *stiff* gale requiring the use of τέρθριοι.

* **τέρθρον**, τό, prop. *the end of the sail-yard*, Erot., Gal.19.145; cf. τέρθριος. II. generally, *end, extremity*, ῥινῶν ἔσχατα τ. Emp. 100.4, cf. Poll.2.134; αἶψα δὲ τέρθρον ἵκοντο.. Οὐλύμποιο its *summit*, *h.Merc.*322 (v.l. ἵκοντο κάρηνα). 2. *extremity, crisis*, in a disease, ἐπὴν τὸ τ. ᾖ τοῦ πάθεος Hp.*Mul.*2.125 (v.l. τὸ στερεόν), cf. Erot. and Gal. l.c.: hence, *the end*, i.e. *death*, E.*Fr.*371. (Cf. τέρμα.)

**τέρθρος**, ὁ, = τέρθριος, Hsch. (dub.).

**τερθρωτήρ**, ῆρος, ὁ, *the part of a ship from which the πρῳρεύς kept a look-out*, Hsch.; who also cites **τερθρηδών** (τεθρηδών cod.)· πρῳρεύς.

**τερίκαρπον**· μεγαλόκαρπον, Hsch. **τερίμη**· τάφρος, Id. (Perh. cf. τέρχνεα.) **τερίνη**· τετριμμένη (cf. τερύνης), οἱ δὲ τερπωλή, Id. **τερῖνος**· τηρῶν διάνοιαν, λυπῶν, Id.

**τέρμα**, ατος, τό, *end, boundary*, chiefly poet.: I. *goal round which horses and chariots had to turn* at races, περὶ τέρμαθ' ἑλισσέμεν Il.23.309; περὶ τ. βαλούσας, εὖ σχεθέειν περὶ τέρμα, ib.462,466; τέρματα θεῖναι or σημῆναι, ib.333,358; ἔστασεν ἐν τέρμασιν ἀγῶνος Pi.*P.* 9.114; τ. δωδεκάγναμπτον, i.e. doubled twelve times, Id.*O.*3.33; δρόμου τέρματα dub. l. in S.*El.*686; ἐξωτέρω ἀποκάμπτειν τοῦ τ. Arist. *Rh.*1409$^b$23. 2. *mark set to show how far a quoit was thrown*, ἔθηκε δὲ τέρματ' Ἀθήνη Od.8.193. 3. metaph., *issue, event*, A. *Ag.*781,1177 (both lyr.). II. generally, *end, limit*, δολιχῆς τ. κελεύθου Id.*Pr.*286 (anap.), cf. 706,823; ποῦ τὸ τ. τῆς φυγῆς; Id.*Eu.* 422: pl., ὁδοῦ τέρματα Thgn.1166; ἐπὶ τέρμασι τοῖσι ἐκείνης (sc. τῆς Εὐρώπης) Hdt.7.54; συνάγουσι τὰ τέρματα (of two rivers) they contract their *bounds*, i.e. draw together and so contract the space between them, Id.4.52: metaph., πλούτου τέρμα *a limit* to wealth, Thgn. 227. 2. *end*, in point of time or distance, ἐπὶ τέρμ' ἀφίκετο reached the *limit*, was at the *end*, S.*Aj.*48; Ἑρμῆς σφ' ἄγει.. πρὸς αὐτὸ τ. Id.*El.*1397 (lyr.); βιότου τ. the *term* or *end* of life, *death*, Simon. 85.13; τ. βίου or τοῦ βίου, A.*Fr.*362, S.*OT*1530 (troch.), E.*Alc.*643; γήρως ἐσχάτοις πρὸς τ. Id.*Andr.*1081; τ. μόχθων, πόνων, ἄθλου, A.*Pr.*100 (anap.), 186 (lyr.), 259; Σισύφου πέτρος ἀνήνυτος, οὗ τὰ τέρματα αὖθις ἄρχει πόνων Pl.*Ax.*371e; ἐπὶ τέρματι *at last*, A.*Eu.*633: also τέρμα abs., like τέλος, Ps.-Phoc.138. 3. *culmination, highest point, goal*, τ. ἀέθλων *prize*, Pi.*I.*4(3).85(67); κακῶν E.*Supp.* 369 (lyr.); πρὸς τέρμασιν ὥρας Ar.*Av.*705; τέρματα νίκης Archestr. *Fr.*34.10; τ. τέχνης Parrhas.2; ὑγιείας ἀκόρεστον τ. the *bounds* of health are insatiable, A.*Ag.*1002 (lyr.); ἀγχόνης τέρματα Id.*Eu.*746; θανάτου τ. E.*Hipp.*140 (lyr.). 4. *highest power, supremacy*, τ. Κορίνθου ἔχειν to be *sovereign* of Corinth, Simon.112; θεοὶ.. πάντων τέρμ' ἔχοντες E.*Supp.*617 (lyr.); σωτηρίας γὰρ τέρμ' ἔχεις ἡμῖν μόνη you are the *arbiter*.., Id.*Or.*1343; τ. τῆς σωτηρίας *final pledge*.., S.*OC*725; δαίμονες οἳ φιλίης τέρματ'.. ἔχετε *AP*12.170 (Diosc.). (Cf. τέρμων, τέρθρον, Skt. *tárati, tiráti* 'cross, win through, overcome', Lat. *terminus, trans, in-trare*.)

**τερμ-άζω**, = τερματίζω, *Tab.Heracl.*1.10, 2.9, *SIG*421.10 (Thermon, iii B.C.). **-αστῆρες**, οἱ, *boundary-commissioners*, *IG*4$^2$(1).71. 85 (Epid., iii B.C.). * **-ατίζω**, *limit, bound*, Str.9.4.2; *make an end of, finish*, τι S.E.*M.*10.102; τρεῖς δεκάδας *Epigr.Gr.*539 (Phanagoria):—Pass., τ. εἰς τὸ ἄδηλον Hippod.ap.Stob.4.34.71, cf. Ruf.*Anat.*38, Gal. 14.794, Vett.Val.245.10:—Med., *have as one's end*, γῆρας τ. βαρύ E. *Fr.*952 cod.Orion. (ἐρμ- Nauck). **-άτιον** [ᾰ], τό, Dim. of τέρμα, Suid. s.v. τήνελλα (s.v.l.). **-ατοῦχος**, gloss on βαλβιδοῦχος, Hsch.

* **Τερμέρειον** or **Τερμέριον κακόν**, τό, prov., *a misfortune one brings on oneself*, said to be derived from one Τέρμερος a highwayman, Philipp. ap.Sch.E.*Rh.*509, Plu.*Thes.*11, Jul.*Or.*7.210d; prob. to be restored for μερμέριον κ. in Luc.*Lex.*11: τερμερίης prob. *portentous* in *Epic.Alex. Adesp.*2.15. 2. τὸ τ., = *membrum virile*, dub. in *AP*11.30 (Phld.).

**τερμιεύς** (sc. Ζεύς), ὁ, *guardian of boundaries*, Lyc.706.

**τερμίνθῐνος**, η, ον, *of the terebinth-tree*, ῥητίνη *turpentine*, Diocl. *Fr.*140, Thphr.*HP*9.2.2, Dsc.4.150 (τερεμ- cod. E, τερεβ- cett., Wellm.), Sor.2.14, al. (τερεβ-), *PHolm.*6.33 (τερεβ-), Gal.6.288 (v.l. τερεβ-), 292,354; οἶνος Dsc.5.30, etc.; prob. to be restored for τερεβίνθινος in X.*An.*4.4.13:—pecul. fem. **τερμινθίς**, ίδος, Nic.*Al.*300.

* **τέρμινθος**, ἡ, *terebinth*, *Pistacia Terebinthus*, Hp.*Mul.*2.192, Arist. *Mir.*837$^a$33, Thphr.*HP*3.2.6, 9.2.2, Theoc.*Ep.*1.6, *AP*4.1.30 (Mel.), Dsc.1.71, Gal.6.351, 616 (v.l. τερεβ-), 624 (v.l. τερεβ-), etc. 2. *a swelling like the fruit of the terebinth-tree*, Hp.*Hum.*20, *Epid.*6.3. 23, Diocl.*Fr.*82, cf. Erot., Gal.16.461. (This is apparently the oldest form, but τερεμινθ- and τερεβινθ- are freq. vv. ll.: τερέμινθος is given freq. by codd. A and B of Lxx, and τερέβινθος by all the uncials in *Is.*1.30, 6.13 and four times elsewhere, cf. *AP*9.282 (Antip. Thess.), *Gp.*9.18.1; in Gal. codd. vary (v. supr.); a fem. τερεβίνθη prob. in *PMag.Par.*1.1312, v.l. in Gal.6.644; τρέμιθος (q.v.) is also found; τεττερέβινθος in *Gloss.* seems to be an error: cf. Τερβινθεύς.) II. a parasitic growth on the olive, Thphr.*CP*2.17. 4. 2. a flax-like plant from which the Athenians made fishing-lines, Hsch., Phot., *EM*753.10. III. = πιστάκη, Thphr.*HP*4.4.7.

**τερμινθοφάγος** [ᾰ], ον, *eating terebinth*, Πέρσαι Nic.Dam.*Fr.*66.34 J.

* **τερμιόεις**, εσσα, εν, (τέρμις, if = πέζα II. 2) prob. *fringed*, ἀσπὶς Il. 16.803 (prob. read by Zenod. in Il.3.334, v. τερσανόεσσα); χιτών Od.19.242, Hes.*Op.*537.

**τέρμιος**, α, ον, (τέρμα) *at the end, last*, always of Time, τ. ἁμέρα the day *of death*, S.*Ant.*1330 (lyr.); χώρα τ. the spot *where one is destined to end life*, Id.*OC*89.

**τέρμις**· πούς, Hsch.

**τερμοδρομέω**, *run to the goal*, Man.4.520.

**τερμον-ίζω**, *fix boundaries of, delimit*, τὰν χώραν *IG*4$^2$(1).71.11 (Epid., iii B.C.): hence **-ισμός**, ὁ, *delimitation*, ib.8.

**τερμόνιος**, α, ον, *at the world's end*, πάγος A.*Pr.*117 (lyr.).

**τερμοσύνη**, ἡ, *ending*, βίου dub. in *Trag.Adesp.*509 (lyr.).

**τέρμων**, ονος, ὁ, = τέρμα, *boundary*, A.*Fr.*191 (anap.), E.*Hipp.*746 (lyr.); pl., ib.3,1159, *Heracl.*37, al.; *edge*, δίσκου Id.*Hel.*1472 (lyr.): chiefly poet., but cf. Str.3.5.5, Plu.*Pyrrh.*12 (pl.), Porph.*Chr.*13: prose word in dialects, *IG*14.352 (Halaesa), *SIG*421.8 (Thermon, iii B.C.). 2. = Lat. *Terminus*, Plu.*Num.*16. II. *end*, A. *Supp.*629 (anap.); βίου E.*Ph.*1352.

**τέρνακα**· τῆς κάκτου τοῦ φυτοῦ καυλός, Hsch.

* **τέρος**, εος, τό, = τέμενος (cf. τέραμνον), dub. in *Inscr.Cypr.*65 H.

**τερπῐκέραυνος**, ον, *delighting in thunder*, epith. of Zeus, Il.1. 419, al., Hes.*Op.*52.

* **τερπνός**, ή, όν, (τέρπω) *delightful, pleasant* (Hom. only as v.l., Od.8.45), Thgn.1019 (= Mimn.5.3), Pi.*O.*6.57, al., A.*Ag.*143 (lyr.), etc.; τερπνὰ παθών Tyrt.12.38; also in Prose, Democr.211; πρὸς τὸ τερπνόν Th.2.53, cf. Pl.*Cra.*419d; τὰ τ. *delights, pleasures*, Isoc.1. 21, X.*Mem.*2.1.23; τὸ τ. *enjoyment*, Metrod.*Fr.*47. 2. rarely of persons, αὐτῷ δὲ τερπνός *to* his own *content*, S.*Aj.*967; γέρων τ. *Anacreont.*37.1. II. regul. Comp. τερπνότερος Phld.*Oec.*p.9 J.: Sup. -ότατος Thgn.256; irreg. τέρπνιστος Call.*Fr.*256; Adv. -ιστα (or -ίστα[τα]) Id. in *PSI*11.1218*c*6. III. Adv. τερπνῶς Thgn. 914, S.*Fr.*583.5.

**τερπνότης**, ητος, ἡ, *pleasantness, delight*, Lxx *Ps.*15(16).11 (pl.), 26(27).4, Aristeas 307, Poll.3.97, Hsch. s.v. τέρψις.

**τέρπος**, εος, τό, = τερπωλή, in pl., *Supp.Epigr.*3.774.8 (Itanus, i B.C./i A.D.).

**τερπός**, ὁ, perh. = ταρπός, *PCair.Zen.*693.9 (iii B.C.).

**τερπότραμις**, = ἡ τῶν ἀφροδισίων τέρψις (Phot.), Telecl.66; expld. by Meineke as ὁ τοῖς ἀφροδισίοις τερπόμενος.

**τέρπω**, Od.1.347, etc.; Ep. subj. τέρπησι 17.385: Ion. impf. τέρπεσκον Q.S.7.378, *AP*9.136 (Cyrus): fut. τέρψω S.*Tr.*1246, etc.: aor. ἔτερψα *h.Pan.*47, E.*Heracl.*433, Pl.*Lg.*658b:—the **Pass.** and **Med.** have a fivefold aor., 1. ἐτέρφθην Od.5.74, 8.131, 17.174, S.*OC*1140, E.*Ion* 541 (troch.); rare in Prose, X.*Mem.*2.1.24. 2. Ep. ἐτάρφθην, τάρφθην, Od.6.99, 19.213,251, 21.57. 3. Ep. ἐτάρπην, τάρπην, 23.300, Il.11.780, al.; inf. ταρπῆναι Od.23.212, and ταρπήμεναι ib.346, Il.24.3; subj. τρἀπείω, Ep. 1 pl. τρἀπείομεν (v. infr. II. 2). 4. Ep. also ἐταρπόμην, only in 1 pl. subj. ταρπώμεθα Od.4.295, al.; also redupl. through all moods, τετάρπετο Il.19.19, 24.513; τεταρπώμεσθα Od.11.212, Il.23.10,98; τεταρπόμενος Od. 1.310, al. 5. aor. 1 ἐτερψάμην, in Ep. subj. τέρψομαι 16.26 (but τέρψομαι is fut. Med. in Il.20.23, S.*Fr.*677); opt. τέρψαιτο *h.Ap.* 153; part. τερψάμενος Od.12.188:—*delight, gladden, cheer*, ὅ κεν τέρπησιν ἀείδων 17.385; τῇ [φόρμιγγι] ὅ γε θυμὸν ἔτερπεν Il.9.189, al.; πεσσοῖσι.. θυμὸν ἔτερπον Od.1.107; καὶ τὸν ἔτερπε λόγοις Il. 15.393; τοὐμὸν.. τ. κέαρ S.*Tr.*1246; θοίνῃ σε τ. Achae.17; ἡ ἀγγελίη.. ἔτερψε [αὐτούς] Hdt.8.99; sts. in Att. Prose, ἔπεσι.. τὸ αὐτίκα τέρψει *will give* momentary *pleasure*, Th.2.41, cf. Pl.*Lg.* 658b,e, etc.; τ. τὴν ἀκοήν, τὰς ἀκοάς, Phld.*Po.*5.26,28; ἧλιξ τέρπει τὸν ἥλικα, prov. in Pl.*Phdr.*240c, etc.: abs., *give delight*, Od.1.347, 8. 45, S.*Aj.*475; τὰ τέρποντα *delights*, Id.*OC*1217 (lyr.); ῥήματα τερψαντά τι ib.1281; οἱ τέρποντες λόγῳ ῥήτορες Th.3.40; τὰ τέρψοντα X.*Ages.*9.4. II. more freq. in Pass. and Med., 1. in Ep. the aor. Pass. is used, c. gen. rei, *have full enjoyment of, enjoy to one's heart's content*, ἐπεὶ τάρπημεν ἐδητύος ἠδὲ ποτῆτος Il.11.780; ἐπεὶ τάρπησαν ἐδωδῆς Od.3.70; σίτου τάρφθεν 6.99; τεταρπόμενοι φίλον ἦτορ σίτου καὶ οἴνοιο Il.9.705; ὕπνου, εὐνῆς ταρπήμεναι, 24.3, Od.23. 346; φιλότητος ἐταρπήτην ib.300; ἥβης ταρπῆναι ib.212: metaph., *take one's fill* of lamentation, τεταρπώμεσθα γόοιο Il.23.10,98, Od. 11.212, cf. 19.213, 21.57. 2. *enjoy* or *delight oneself*, c. dat. instr., φρένα τ. φόρμιγγι Il.9.186; μύθοισι Od.23.301; δαιτί 1.26; γόῳ φρένα 4.102; δίσκοισιν Il.2.774; ἐν θαλίῃς Od.11.603, Hes.*Op.*115; φιλότητι (or ἐν φ.) τραπείομεν εὐνηθέντε Il.3.441, 14.314 (whereas in the phrase λέκτρονδε τραπείομεν εὐνηθέντες (v.l. -θέντε), Od.8.292, the form τραπείομεν seems to be taken by the poet as belonging to τρέπω, though others retain the usu. sense by connecting λέκτρονδε with εὐνηθέντες or by punctuating after λέκτρονδε); so in Trag., λαμπάδι τερπόμεναι A.*Eu.*1042 (lyr.), cf. S.*OC*1140, etc.; *delight in*, τῇ τῶν πυραμίδων μεγαλειότητι *OGI*666.26 (Egypt, i A.D.); τοῖς εὐώδεσι Sor. 2.29; ἐπί τισι E.*Rh.*194: c. part., λόγοις.. οἷς σὺ μὴ τέρψῃ κλύων S.*Ant.*691; τέρπεται τιμώμενος E.*Ba.*321; τί ἂν.. ἀκούσας τερφθείης; X.*Mem.*2.1.24: abs., πῖνε καὶ τέρπευ drink and *be merry*, Hdt.2. 78. 3. with internal acc., οἵην μοῖραν δέκα μοιρέων τέρπεται ἀνήρ *has* only one tenth part *of the enjoyment*, Hes.*Fr.*162; κενὴν ἐτερπόμην .. τέρψιν S.*Fr.*577; τέρπου κενὴν ὄνησιν E.*Or.*1043. 4. freq. with words which limit its sense, θυμῷ Il.19.313, Od.16.26; θυμόν Il.21.45; κατὰ θυμόν Hes.*Op.*58,358; φρένα Il.1.474, Od.4.102, etc.; φρεσὶν ᾗσι τετάρπετο Il.19.19, cf. Od.5.74; ἐνὶ φρεσίν 8.368; τεταρπόμενος φίλον κῆρ 1.310; ἀπάταισι θυμὸν τέρπεται Pi.*P.*2. 74. (Cf. Skt. *tr̥pnoti* 'take one's fill', Causative *tarpáyati* 'delight (trans.)', OPruss. *ka enterpo..?* 'what is the use of..?', Goth. *þaurfts*, OE. *þearf* 'benefit', Goth. *þarf* 'I need'.)

**τερπωλή**, ἡ, poet. and later Prose for τέρψις, Od.18.37, Archil. 13, Thgn.984,1068, Luc.*Icar.*16, Aret.*CA*2.3.

**τερπών**, όνος, ἡ, cited without translation as derivative of τέρπω, *EM*141.17, 812.20.

**τερρατόν**· ἔσχατον, ἡδύ, τερπνόν, Hsch. **τερρητόν**· τριήρης, Id. (Perh. Aeol.)

**τερσαίνω**, *dry up*, αἷμα μέλαν τέρσηνε Il.16.529: pres. in Lyc. 390, Nic.*Al*.551:—Pass., *to be dried up*, μυῖαι τερσαίνοντο A.R.4.1405; *to be dried*, of figs, Jul.*Ep*.180: cf. τέρσομαι.

**τερσᾰνόεσσα**, epith. of ἀσπίς, Il.3.334 as read by Zenod.ap.Sch. A (τερμιόεσσαν corr. Robert).

**τερσιά**, ἡ, = τρασιά, Jul.*Ep*.180.

**τέρσομαι**, Pass., with aor. inf. τερσῆναι, τερσήμεναι (v. infr.), as if from ἐτέρσην:—*to be* or *become dry, dry up*, ἕλκος ἐτέρσετο παύσατο δ' αἷμα the wound *dried up* and the blood was staunched, Il.11.267,848; οὐδέ μοι αἷμα τερσῆναι δύναται 16.519; θειλόπεδον τέρσεται ἠελίῳ *is baked* by the sun, Od.7.124; εἵματα δ' ἠελίοιο μένον τερσήμεναι αὐγῇ 6.98; ὅταν [τὰ ῥάκεα] ἐν ἡλίῳ τέρσηται Hp.*Mul*.1.11; ὄσσε δακρυόφιν τέρσοντο his eyes *became dry* from tears, Od.5.152. II. Act. first in later Ep. (Hom. using only τερσαίνω), aor. subj. τέρσῃ (-σει codd.) Theoc.22.63; inf. τέρσαι Nic.*Th*.96,693 (v.l. τέρσον both times); opt. Med. τέρσαιο ib.709:—Hsch. cites ἐτέρρατο· ἐξηράνθη. (Cf. Lat. *torreo, tostus*, Skt. *tṛ́ṣyati* 'to be thirsty'.)

⊕ **τέρτα**· ἡ τρίτη, Hsch., cf. Choerob. in *An.Ox*.2.275, *EM*665.41. (Prob. Aeol.; cf. Τέρτιος Aeol. pr. n. *IG*12(2).275.1, = Arc. Τρίτιος, and Τέρτυλλος *Act.Ap*.24.1, etc., = Arc. Τρίτυλλος.)

**τερτᾶτος**, α, ον, Aeol. for τρίτατος, cj. Ahrens for τέρπατος in Pi. *O*.8.46.

**τερτιοκήριος**, ὁ, = Lat. *tertiocerius*, *Cod.Just*.4.59.1.1.

**τέρυ**· ἀσθενές, λεπτόν, Hsch. **τέρυνας** ἵππους· οὕτω λέγονται ὅσοι ἀδδηφάγοι εἰσί. ἔνιοι τοὺς ἀσθενεῖς, Id. **τερύνης**· τετριμμένος ὄνος, καὶ γέρων, ἢ δυσανάληπτος γέρων, Id. **τερύσκ-εται**· νοσεῖ, φθίνει, and **-ετο**· ἐτείρετο, Id.

⊕ [**Τε**]**ρφεῖος**, ὁ, a month at Mytilene or Eresus, *Inscr.Magn*.52.38 (restored by Bechtel *Aeol*.62).

**Τερφεύς**, έως, ὁ, a month at Cyme, *Schwyzer*646.18 (ii B.C.).

⊕ **τέρφος**, εος, τό, = ἔρφος, στέρφος, *skin, shell*, Nic.*Al*.268; τάπιδος Id.*Th*.323; τέρφη· λέπυρα, Hsch.

**τέρχανον**, v. τάρχανον.

⊕ **τέρχνος**, εος, τό, *twig, young shoot*, Max.502, Hsch.; also **τρέχνος**, εος, τό, *AP*15.25 (Besant., pl.), Hsch.: τὰ τέρχνιja or τρέχνιja *plants, young trees*, *Inscr.Cypr*.135.9 H. II. **τέρχνεα**·.. ἐντάφια, Hsch. (Cf. ταρχύω.)

**τερψιεπής**, ές, *of sweet utterance*, ἀοιδαί B.12.230.

**τερψίμβροτος**, ον, *gladdening the heart of man*, Ἠέλιος Od.12.269, *h.Ap*.411; αὐλοί B.12.72; ἠώς Orph.*A*.1049.

**τερψίνοος** [ῐ], ον, *heart-gladdening*, φόρμιγξ *AP*9.505(2).

**τέρψις**, εως, ἡ, also ιος Orph.*Fr*.11: (τέρπω):—*enjoyment, delight*, τινος *from* or *in* a thing, τέρψις ἀοιδῆς Hes.*Th*.917, cf. Ar.*Ra*.676 (lyr.); δείπνων τέρψιες Pi.*P*.9.19, cf. Th.2.38; χλιδανῆς ἥβης τ. A.*Pers*.544 (anap.); κυλίκων S.*Aj*.1201 (lyr.); εἰς τέρψιν τινῶν ἐλθεῖν E.*Ph*.195, cf. *IT*797; βραχεῖα τ. ἡδονῆς κακῆς Id.*Fr*.362.23: τ. ἐστί μοι, c. inf., it is my *pleasure* to.., ἥν μοι τ. ἐκπεσεῖν χθονός S.*OC*766, cf. 775: abs., *joy, delight*, Thgn.787, Pi.*O*.12.11, B.1.59, A.*Ag*.611, etc.: pl., αἱ διὰ τῶν αἰσθήσεων τ. Phld.*D*.3.14: distd. from the more general term ἡδονή by Prodic.ap.Arist.*Top*.112$^{b}$23, cf. Pl.*Phlb*.11b.

**τερψίφρων**, ον, gen. ονος, *delighting the mind, delightful*, ὕλη Nonn.*D*.42.44.

**Τερψῐ-χόρη**, ἡ, Dor. and Att. **-χόρα** Pi.*I*.2.7, Pl.*Phdr*.259c, cf. Choerob. *in Theod*.2.42 H.:—*Terpsichore* the Muse of the dance, Hes.*Th*.78, etc. 2. Pythag. name of 9, *Theol.Ar*.58. ⊕ **-χορος**, ον, *enjoying the dance*, esp. the choral dance, of Apollo, *AP*9.525.20.

**τεσσᾰράβοιος** [ρᾰ], ον, *worth four steers*, Il.23.705.

**τεσσᾰρᾰκαίδεκα**, v. τεσσαρεσκαίδεκα.

**τεσσᾰρᾰκαι-δεκάδωρος** [κᾰ], ον, (δῶρον II) *fourteen hand-breadths long*, *AP*6.114 (Simm.). **-δέκᾰτος**, η, ον, *fourteenth*, *Mittheil. aus der Samml.d. Pap. Erzherzog Rainer* ii 4 (ii A.D.), Sch.Ar.*Nu*.1005, Anon. in *GGM* ii 493. ⊕ **-δεκέτης**, ες, or **-ετής**, ές, *fourteen years old*, *BCH* 47.83 (Philippi, metr.): **-δεκαέτης** Gal.11.290: abbreviated in *PRyl*.103.5 (ii A.D.): fem. [τετταρ]ακαιδε[κέ]τις Arist.*Ath*.56.7. ⊕ **-εικοσίπους** [σῐ], πουν, gen. ποδος, in form **τεττ-**, *twenty-four feet long*, *IG*1$^{2}$.373.62.

**τεσσᾰρᾰκονθήμερος**, ον, *after forty days*, ἐκπυήσιες ῥήγνυνται -ήμεροι Hp.*Prog*.15.

⊕ **τεσσᾰράκοντα** [ρᾰ], Att. **τετταράκοντα** *IG*2$^{2}$.334.23; Ion. **τεσσεράκοντα** (q.v.); Sicilian Ionic τετράϙοντα *Supp.Epigr*.4.64 (vi B.C.); Dor. **τετρώκοντα** *Tab.Heracl*.1.20, al., *SIG*241.67 (Delph., iv B.C.), *IG*5(2).357.16 (Stymphalus, iii B.C.), 9(1).880.15 (Corc.), cf. τετρωκοντάλιτρος and v. τεσσαρακοστός; once Dor. **τεταράκοντα** *IG*4.823.63 (Troezen); Boeot. **πετταράκοντα** (q.v.): οἱ, αἱ, τά, indecl.:—*forty*, Il.2.524, etc. II. οἱ τ. *the Forty*, a body of justices who went round the Attic demes to hear all causes up to ten drachmae, Isoc.15.237; also cases of assault, D.37.33: changed from Thirty to Forty after the expulsion of the Thirty Tyrants, Arist.*Ath*.53.1.

**τεσσᾰρᾰκοντᾰ-δραχμιαία**, ἡ, *40-drachma tax*, *Stud.Pal*.4.62.9 (i A.D., abbrev.). **-δύο**, *forty-two*, *PSI*10.1132.6 (i A.D.). **-εννέα**, *forty-nine*, ib.1140.28 (ii A.D.). **-ετής**, ές, *forty years old*, Hes.*Op*.441; τ. χρόνος *Act.Ap*.7.23, 13.18; ἡλικία Sor.1.34:—Att. fem. **τετταρακοντάετις**, ιδος, Pl.*R*.460e: masc. also **τεσσᾰρᾰκοντούτης**, Gal.15.504, M.Ant.11.1, (**τεττ-**) Luc.*Herm*.13. **-ετία**, ἡ, *space of forty years*, Ph.2.175; *age of forty years*, D.H.2.58. **-καιπεντάκις** [τᾰκ], Adv. *forty-five times*, Aristarch.Sam.13 (Wallis, τεσσαρακοντάκις καὶ πεντάκις codd.). **-καιπεντᾰκισχῑλιοστός**, Att. **τεττ-**, ή, όν, *forty-five thousandth*, Pl.*Lg*.877d.

**τεσσᾰρᾰκοντάκις** [τᾰ], Adv. *forty times*, Theo Sm. p.125 H.

**τεσσᾰρᾰκοντα-μναῖος**, ον, *amounting to forty minae* in value, ἔρανος *GDI*1878.11 (Delph., **τεττ-**); in weight, στρώματα (mattresses) *PMich.Zen*.13.2 (iii B.C.). **-πέντε**, *forty-five*, *PCair.Zen*.94.21 (iii B.C.). **-πηχυς**, υ, *forty cubits high*, Callix.2, J.*BJ*5.5.3.

**τεσσᾰρᾰκοντ-άρουρος** [ᾰρ], ον, *tenant of forty* ἄρουραι, *PCair.Zen*.1.6 (iii B.C.), *PTeb*.441 (i A.D.). **-άς**, άδος, ἡ, *period of forty days*, Hp.*Septim*.9.

**τεσσᾰρᾰκοντα-στάδιος** [στᾰ], ον, *forty stades long*, Str.17.1.24, Eust. ad D.P.403. ⊕ **-χοίνῑκος**, ον, *containing forty* χοίνικες, ἀρτάβη *PCair.Zen*.4.15 (iii B.C.).

**τεσσᾰρᾰκοντ-ήρης**, ες, perh. *with forty rowers to each group of four oars*, Callix.1, Plu.*Demetr*.43. **-όργυιος**, ον, *forty fathoms high*, Hdt.2.148, in form **τεσσερ-**. **-ορος**, ἡ (sc. ναῦς), *forty-oared ship*, Sch.Ael.*Tact*.p.234 K.-R. **-ούτης**, ου, ὁ, = τεσσαρακονταετής (q.v.).

⊕ **τεσσᾰρᾰκόσιοι**, αι, α, late form of τετρακόσιοι, Str.6.2.1.

**τεσσᾰρᾰκοστ-αῖος**, α, ον, Att. **τεττ-**, *on the fortieth day*, Hp.*Epid*.6.7.1, Arist.*HA*583$^{b}$14, Thphr.*HP*8.2.6, *IG*2$^{2}$.1365.22. ⊕ **-όγδοος**, η, ον, *forty-eighth*, Tz.*H*.7.183. ⊕ **-ός**, ή, όν, *fortieth*, Th.1.60, etc.; Dor. **τετρωκοστός**, ά, όν, Archim.*Aren*.4.10, al.; also Ion. apparently, *SIG*167.17 (Mylasa, iv B.C.): but Ion. **Τετρηκοστή** (pr. n.) *GDI*5755.5 (ibid.). II. ἡ τεσσαρακοστή (sc. μοῖρα): 1. *tax of one-fortieth*, Ar.*Ec*.825; ἐπίτροπος τεσσαρακοστῆς *MAMA*4.113 (Lysias, i/ii A.D.). 2. *a fortieth*, a coin of Chios, Th.8.101.

**τεσσᾰράμηνον** [ρᾰ], τό, *period of four months*, *BGU*979.11 (ii A.D.).

⊕ **τεσσᾰράριος**, also written **τεσσαραλ-**, **τεσσαλαρ-**, **θεσσαλαρ-**, etc., ὁ, = Lat. *tesserarius*, *non-commissioned officer who communicates the password*, Plu.*Galb*.24, *POxy*.43$^{r}$ ii 21 (iii A.D.), etc.; also a civil official of uncertain functions, *PSI*10.1106.4 (iv A.D.), *I Got*.6.7 (iv A.D.); τ. πλοῖα *dispatch*-boats, *IG*12(5).941 (Tenos, i B.C.).

**τεσσᾰρᾰκαιδέκατος**, v. τεσσαρεσκαιδέκατος.

⊕ **τέσσᾰρες**, οἱ, αἱ, τέσσαρα, τά, gen. ων: dat. τέσσαρσι(ν) Th.2.21, *Act.Ap*.12.4, etc.; poet. τέτρᾰσι Hes.*Fr*.188, Pi.*O*.8.68, al., and in late Prose, as Lxx *Jd*.9.34, Str.13.1.3, Hermog.*Meth*.29, Alex.Aphr. *in Top*.208.12, *in Sens*.54.18, *PSI*10.1126.9 (iii A.D.), v.l. in *Act.Ap*.11.5 (cod. D), and in good codd. of Arist.*IA*704$^{a}$11, al., *Theol.Ar*.19, etc.; also τέταρσι *SIG*729.3 (Delph., i B.C.), *PSI*9.1028.10 (i A.D.):—Att. **τέττᾰρες**, τέττᾰρα, dat. τέτταρσιν Isoc.12.3; also τάρων (v. τάρες) for τεττάρων; Phocian dat. τεττάροις *IG*9(1).32.78 (Stiris, ii B.C.):—Ion. and later Gr. **τέσσερες**, τέσσερα, *SIG*57.25 (Milet., v B.C.), *Schwyzer* 289.120 (Rhodian, ii B.C.), etc. (dat. τέσσερσι Hdt.6.41, τεσσέρασιν *SIG*633.98 (Milet., ii B.C.)), but τέσσαρες in Hom., and *Schwyzer*707*B* 4 (Ephesus, vi B.C.), etc.: codd. of Lxx have τέσσαρες (nom. and acc.), τεσσάρων, τέσσαρσι, but τέσσερα(ς), τεσσεράκοντα; since however τέσσερα(ς) and τεσσεράκοντα, apart from Ion., are not common in Papyri before ii A.D., the Lxx autographs prob. had τέσσαρα(ς) and τεσσαράκοντα; the form τέσσερα(ς) is here due to avoidance by the copyists of the sequence ε-α-α:—Dor. **τέτορες**, τέτορα, Hes.*Op*.698, Phoc.3, Simon.91, Epich.149, *SIG*240*I*8 (Delph., iv B.C.), al., Theoc.14.16:—Ep. (prob. Aeol.) **πίσῠρες** [ῐ] Od.5.70, 16.249, A.R.2.1110, Nic.*Th*.182; acc. πίσυρας Od.22.111, Il.15.680, al., Call.*Dian*.105, *IGRom*.4.360.26 (Pergam., ii A.D.); gen. πισύρων Dam.*Isid*.290 (metrical ?), prob. in Hsch.; dat. πισύρεσσι, πισύροισι, -ρσι, -αις, Nonn.*D*.16.119, 38.176,236, 39.377, *AP*14.7.4: Aeol. also **πέσῠρες**, neut. **πέσυρα** *Epigr.Gr*.988.6 (Balbilla); and **πέσσῠρες**, **πέσσυρα**, Hsch.:—Boeot. **πέττᾰρες**, α (q.v.):—*four*, Od.9.335, etc.; διὰ τεττάρων the musical interval of *the fourth*, Damox.2.55, etc.; τὰ τέσσαρα *the four simple bodies* of Empedocles, Plot.6.2.2; *the four kinds of quality* or four Aristotelian senses of ποιόν, Id.6.1.10; *the four cardinal principles* of Epicurus (cf. τετραφάρμακος), Phld.*Herc*.1251.11. (Cf. Skt. *catvā́ras* (acc. *catúras*), Lat. *quattuor*, Lith. *keturì*, etc.: I.-E. *qʷetuor*-.)

⊕ **τεσσᾰρεσκαίδεκα**, Ion. **τεσσερ-**, οἱ, αἱ, τά, *fourteen*, the first part remaining unaltered even with a neut. Subst., as ἔτεα τεσσερεσκαίδεκα Hdt.1.86; or with a gen., μέχρι τῶν τεσσαρεσκαίδεκα Hp.*Morb*.3.16:—but sts. the first part changed its gender, τέσσαρα καὶ δέκα Simon.12.

**τεσσᾰρεσκαιδεκά-γωνος** [κᾰ], ον, *14-angled*, Hero *Geep*.164. **-εδρον**, τό, *solid with 14 faces*, Id.*Deff*.104, Sch.Papp.ap.Archim.ii p.540 H. **-έτης**, ες, later **-ετής**, ές, = τεσσαρεσκαιδεκέτης, *Sammelb*.7440.28 (ii A.D.); as fem., ἡλικία Ph.1.45: fem. **-έτις**, ιδος, ἡλικία Gal.6.60,165.

**τεσσᾰρεσκαιδεκάκις** [ᾰκ], Adv. *fourteen times*, Theo Sm.p.126 H.

**τεσσᾰρεσκαιδεκά-μηνον** [κᾰ], τό, *period of fourteen months*, *PCair.Zen*.507.25 (iii B.C., abbrev.). **-πηχυς**, υ, *fourteen cubits long*, *IG*11(2).165.45 (Delos, iii B.C.), 199*A* 58, al.; **τεττ-**, *Inscr.Délos* 372*A* 159,161 (200 B.C.). **-σημος**, ον, *of fourteen time-units*, Aristid.Quint.1.14. ⊕ **-σύλλᾰβος**, ον, *of fourteen syllables*, Heph.7.7.

**τεσσᾰρεσκαιδεκᾰταῖος**, α, ον, *on the fourteenth day*, ἀποθανεῖσθαι Hp.*Prog*.15, cf. *Judic*.15, *Morb*.4.48, dub. l. in *Nat.Mul*.15.

⊕ **τεσσᾰρεσκαιδέκᾰτος**, Ion. **τεσσερ-**, η, ον, *fourteenth*, Hdt.1.84, *PEleph*.1.1 (iv B.C.), *SIG*633.27 (Milet., ii B.C.), Sor.1.20, etc.: also **τεσσᾰρασκαιδέκατος**, *JRS*17.34 (Cyrene, i B.C.); **τεττ-**, *Inscr.Délos* 1408*A* ii 12 (ii B.C.); cf. τεσσαρακαιδέκατος.

**τεσσᾰρεσκαιδεκέτης**, ες, *fourteen years old*, Plu.*Aem.*35: fem. in the form -**δεκαέτις** (q.v.); cf. τεσσαρακαιδεκέτης.

**τεσσεδάριος**, ὁ, prob. = τεσσαράριος or ἐσσεδάριος, a kind of gladiator, *Supp.Epigr.*2.555 (Caria).

⊕ **τεσσερᾰκαιεβδο[μη]κοντούτης**, ες, *seventy-four years old*, *IG*12(5).252 (Paros, vi B.C.).

⊕ **τεσσεράκοντα** [ρᾰ], Ion. and Hellenistic for τεσσαράκοντα, Hdt.1.166, al., *BMus.Inscr.*1005 (Cyzicus, iv B.C.), *OGI*214.53 (Didyma, iii B.C.), etc.; similarly **τεσσερακονταεννέα**, etc., *forty-nine*, etc., *PSI* 10.1140.21 (ii A.D.), etc.; but also Ion. τεσσαράϙοντα *Schwyzer* 707 *B* 8 (Ephesus, vi B.C.); in Hdt. some codd. usually have this form.

**τέσσερες**, οἱ, αἱ, -ρα, τά, Ion. and later Gr. for τέσσαρες (q.v.).

**τεσσίχου**· τὸ μικρόν, Hsch. (Fort. τεσσίχον· οὕτω μικρόν: perh. a dial. form of *τοσσίχον, cf. δοσίχος, with τε- as in τέουτος, τεσσοῦτος.)

**τεσσοῦτος** (leg. τέσσουτος), Aeol. for τοσοῦτος, Sch.D.T.p.498 H., *An.Ox.*1.325, R.Schneider *Bodleiana* (1887) 43; but Aeol. **τοσσοῦτος** acc. to Jo.Gramm.*Comp.*2.10.

**τεταγμένως**, Adv. pf. part. Pass. of τάσσω, *in orderly manner, regularly*, ποιεῖν τι X.*Oec.*8.3; ἄρχεσθαι Pl.*Lg.*700d; πολιτεύεσθαι Isoc.8.49; παραθεῖναι κἀφελεῖν Sosip.1.48. 2. Math. in Conics, *ordinate-wise*, κατάγειν, ἀνάγειν, hence ἡ τεταγμένως the *ordinate*, Apollon.Perg.*Con.*1 *Def.*4, al., cf. Archim.*Aequil.*2.

**τετᾰγών**, όντος, ὁ, Ep. redupl. part. aor. 2, with no pres. in use, ῥῖψε ποδὸς τεταγὼν *having seized* him *by* the foot, Il.1.591; also simply, ῥίπτασκον τεταγών 15.23. (Cf. Lat. *tango, tetigi.*)

**τετᾰμένως**, Adv., (τείνω) *energetically*, Sch.S.*OC*499, Eust. ad D.P.14.

**τετᾰμῐευμένως**, Adv., (ταμιεύω) *frugally, sparingly*, τ. χρῆσθαί τινι D.H.*Th.*51; ἐπαινεῖν τὰς ἀρετάς ib.45, cf. D.S.10.9.

**τετᾰνικός**, ή, όν, *suffering from* τέτανος, Dsc.3.80, Cael.Aur.*CP*3.6; *tetanica passio*, ib.3.17. Adv. -κῶς Gal.14.276.

**τετᾰνόθριξ**, ὁ, ἡ, gen. τριχος, *with long straight hair*, Pl.*Euthphr.* 2b, S.E.*M.*5.95; = *prolixus*, *Gloss.*

⊕ **τετᾰνός**, ή, όν, (τείνω, τανύω) *stretched, rigid*, Hp.*Fract.*2 (Sup.); *straightened, smooth*, ἔρφος, ῥινός, Nic.*Al.*343,464; πῆχυς *AP*6.204 (Leon.); φύλλον Thphr.*HP*3.11.1; θρίδαξ Lycus ap.Ath.2.69e; τ. καὶ καθαρὸν πρόσωπον Crito ap.Gal.12.825; f.l. in E.*Fr.*472.6 (anap., codd. Erot.). II. = τετανόθριξ, *PPetr.*3 p.2, al. (iii B.C.), *PCair.Zen.*76.11 (iii B.C.), *PLond.*3.879.17 (ii B.C.), *PAmh.*2.51.22 (i B.C.), etc.

⊕ **τέτᾰνος**, ὁ, *convulsive tension, tetanus*, Hp.*Aph.*7.13, *Acut.*(*Sp.*) 37, Pl.*Ti.*84e, Arist.*HA*604$^b$4. II. *erectio penis*, Ar.*Lys.*553 (anap.), 846. **τέτανος**, ἡ, v. τίτανος.

**τετᾰν-όω**, *stretch, free from wrinkles*, χρῶτα Dsc.4.182. **-ώδης**, ες, *of the nature of* τέτανος, Hp.*Epid.*5.79. **-ωθρον**, τό, *lotion for freeing the skin from wrinkles, cosmetic*, τ. τῶν προσώπων Dsc. 3.88. **-ωμα**, ατος, τό, = τετάνωθρον, Crito ap.Gal.12.446, Aët. 8.4.

**τετᾰραγμένως**, Adv., (ταράσσω) *confusedly*, Pl.*Lg.*668e, Isoc.15.245, Epicur.*Ep.*1 p.14 U., J.*Vit.*17, Plu.*Ant.*37.

**τέτᾰρος**, ὁ, *pheasant*, Ptol.Euerg.2 J.; cf. τατύρας.

**τετάρπετο**, -πόμενος, -πώμεσθα, v. τέρπω.

**τεταρτ-αΐζω**, *have a quartan fever*, Apollon.*Mir.*30, Dsc.2.34, Gal. 14.277; αἱ -ίζουσαι περίοδοι Ph.1.427. **-αϊκός**, ή, όν, *of a quartan fever*, περίοδος Alex.Trall.*Febr.*6; sc. πυρετός, Dsc.*Eup.*2.20; of persons, Gal.13.66. ⊕ **-αῖος**, Aeol. **τετόρταιος** Theoc.30.2, α, ον, *on the fourth day*, τ. γενέσθαι to be *four days* dead, Hdt.2.89; ἀφικνεῖσθαι τεταρταίους Pl.*R.*616b. 2. τ. πυρετός *quartan* fever, Id.*Ti.* 86a; ῥῖγος *POxy.*1151.37 (v A.D.); so without πυρετός, Hp.*Aph.*2.25, *POxy.* 1088.38 (i A.D.), etc.; πυρετῷ καὶ τεταρταίῳ *IG*3.1424; τ. πονεῖσθαι to have fits *every four days*, Hp.*Judic.*36; ἑπτὰ τεταρταίῳ μῆνας ἔκαμνε πυρί Call.*Aet.*3.1.17; λύτρα τεταρταίοιο δυσαλγέος οὕνεκα παῦσαν *Rev.Bibl.*14.295 (Lycia). II. τεταρταίη, = ἡ τετάρτη, *the fourth day*, Arat.806. 2. *quartan fever*, Orph.*L.*635.

**τεταρτεύς**, έως, ὁ, a measure of capacity, *SIG*1027.12 (Cos, iv/iii B.C.), 1003.11 (Priene, ii B.C.).

**τεταρτημορ-ιαῖος**, α, ον, *of* or *about a quarter* or *quadrant*, Ptol. *Alm.*13.1, Theo Sm.p.156 H., Procl.*Hyp.*2.6. **-ιον**, τό, *fourth part*, Hdt.2.180; esp. of an obolus, Arist.*Pol.*1323$^a$31 (= Lat. *quadrans*, Plu.*Publ.*23); $\frac{1}{4}$ *of a* κοτύλη, Hp.*Int.*26. 2. in Music, *quarter-tone*, Cleonid.*Harm.*7, etc.; τεταρτημορίων διέσεων Euc.*Sect.Can.*p.202 H. II. *quadrant*, Ptol.*Tetr.*33, Paul.Al.*D.*2. (Cf. ταρτημόριον.) **-ιος**, ον, = -μοριαῖος, *holding a* τετάρτη (τέταρτος III. 2a), λύχνοι *PMag.Leid.W.*1.9, 3.40. **-ίς**, ίδος, ἡ, *fourth part*, σπλάγχνων *SIG*1015.11, 1044.39 (both Halic., iv/iii B.C.).

**τεταρτηρόν**, τό, a measure of capacity, *PGot.*17.12, al. (vi/vii A.D.).

**τεταρτήχωρον**, τό, a measure of capacity (cf. δίχωρον), *Sammelb.* 4425 ii 5 (ii A.D.).

**τεταρτικός**, ή, όν, *in the fourth place*, -κοῦ ἀφετικοῦ ἀστέρος Vett. Val.159.4:—τὰ τεταρτικά dub. sens. in *PPetr.*3 p.194 (iii B.C.).

**τεταρτο-λογέω**, *confiscate one-fourth* of a person's property, in Pass. of the person, *PGnom.*116, al. (ii A.D.), prob. in *POxy.*513.11 (ii A.D.): -ηθῶμεν, *quartemur*, *Gloss.* **-μερίτης** [ῑ], ου, ὁ, *holder of a fourth share*, *PBaden* 2.37 (ii B.C.), *PRyl.*261 (ii B.C.). **-μοιρία**, ἡ, *fourth share*, *PFlor.*50.111 (iii A.D.), 325.8 (v A.D.): hence -μοι-(ρίταις) *POxy.*1910.24 (vi/vii A.D.).

**τεταρτονεικοστή**, ἡ, *tax of* $\frac{1}{24}$, *PHib.*1.95.7,10 (iii B.C.).

**τεταρτοπώλης**, ου, ὁ, dub. sens. in *PTeb.*180 (i B.C.).

⊕ **τέταρτος**, η, ον, Ep. also **τέτρᾰτος** (q.v.), Boeot. **πέτρᾰτος** (q.v.), *fourth*, Il.23.301, etc. II. τὸ τέταρτον as Adv., *the fourth time*, 5.438, etc.: without Art., *fourthly*, Pl.*Phdr.*266e: regul. Adv. -τως, *fourfold*, Id.*Ti.*86a. 2. (sc. μέρος) *a quarter*, D.S.1.50, *POxy.*1293.25 (ii A.D.). III. ἡ τετάρτη: 1. (sc. ἡμέρα) *the fourth day*, Hes.*Op.*800, X.*An.*4.8.21. 2. (sc. μοῖρα) *a liquid measure*, Hdt.6.57:—also, *a measure of weight*, λαβὼν χρυσοῦ τετάρτας ⟨β′⟩ *PMag.Leid.V.*6.24, cf. 6.22. b. *a fourth part*, ἐπὶ τετάρταις ἐργάζονται τῶν καρπῶν Str.15.1.40. 3. *tax of* 25%, τ. ἐπὶ τοῖς καρποῖς App.*Mith.*83, cf. *SIG*4.8 (Cyzicus, vi B.C.); ὧν τετάρτη goods which pay a *tax of* 25%, *PCair.Zen.*12.59,70, al. (iii B.C.); τ. σιτοποιῶν ib.206.34 (iii B.C.). IV. Τέταρτος, ὁ, a month in Locris, *GDI*1901.2, 2097.5 (Delph., ii B.C.). (Skt. *caturthás*, Lith. *ketviȓtas*, Lat. *quartus*, etc.: I.-E. *q$^u$eturto-* and *q$^u$ctur̥to-*.)

**τετάσθην**, **τετᾰτο**, v. τείνω. **τετάχᾰται**, v. τάσσω. **τετευχᾰται**, **τετεύχετον**, v. τεύχω.

**τετευχῆσθαι**, (τεῦχος) Ep. pf. inf. Pass. without any pres. in use, *to be armed*, Od.22.104.

**τετεχνημένως**, Adv., (τεχνάω) *artificially*, *EM*123.19.

**τετηρημένως**, Adv., (τηρέω) *attentively, observantly*, Sch.A.R.1. 296.

**τετίημαι** [ῐ], an Ep. perf. with no pres. in use, *to be sorrowful*, τετιήσθην Il.8.447; elsewh. Hom. always uses part., in the phrase τετιημένος, τετιημένη ἦτορ, Il.11.556, Od.4.804, al., cf. Hes.*Th.* 163.—We also find the Act. pf. part. τετῑηώς (in same sense) mostly in the phrase τετιηότι θυμῷ, with *sorrowing* heart, Il.11.555, 17.664, 24.283; also ἷζον τετιηότες 9.13; δὴν δ' ἄνεῳ ἦσαν τετιηότες they were long silent *from grief*, ib.30,695. (Perh. cogn. with Lat. *quies.*)

**τέτλᾰ**, shortd. for τέτλαθι, v.l. for τέττα in Il.4.412, Arat.ap.Hellad. ap.Phot.*Bibl.*p.531 B.

**τέτλᾰθι**, **τετλαίην**, **τετλάμεν**, **τετλάμεναι**, **τετληώς**, v. *τλάω.

**τετμηώς**, Ep. pf. part. of τέμνω (with pass. sense), A.R.4.156; late Ep. aor. Pass. ἐτέτμετο *was cut*, ἄλμη..ὑπὸ τρόπιν ἔνθα καὶ ἔνθα Orph.*A.*364.

⊕ **τέτμον**, and **ἔτετμον**, Ep. aor. without any pres. in use, used by Hom. in indic. both with and without augm.:—*overtake, reach, find*, ἔνθ' ὅ γε Νέστορ' ἔτετμε Il.4.293, cf. 6.515, Od.3.256, al.; ὃν..γῆρας ἔτετμεν 1.218; οὐκ ἔνδον ἀμύμονα τέτμεν ἄκοιτιν Il.6.374, cf. Od.5. 58; ὄφρ' ἔτι..μητέρα τέτμῃς 15.15; 3 pl. τέτμον A.R.3.1275; opt. τέτμοιμεν Theoc.25.61. 2. c. gen., *partake of, have allotted one*, ὃς δέ κε τέτμῃ ἀταρτηροῖο γενέθλης Hes.*Th.*610.

**τετολμηκότως**, Adv., (τολμάω) *boldly*, Plb.1.23.5, 9.4.2.

**τέτορες**, οἱ, αἱ, τέτορα, τά, Dor. for τέσσαρες (q.v.).

**τέτορθαι**, v. τείρω. **τετόρταιος**, v. τεταρταῖος.

**τετρᾰ-**, Boeot. **πετρᾰ-**, Thess. **πετρο-** (qq.v.), *four*, in compd. words. (I.-E. *q$^u$etur̥-*.)

**τετράαχμον**, v. τετράδραχμον.

**τετρᾰ-βάμων** [βᾰ], ον, gen. ονος, (βῆμα) *four-footed*, ἵπποι E.*El.*476; τ. ἀπήνα, = τέθριππον, Id.*Tr.*517; τ. χαλαί the hoofs *of horses*, Id. *Ph.*808, cf. 792 (dub.); τετραβάμοσι γυίοις in the shape *of a quadruped*, Id.*Hel.*376. (Dor.; the Att.-Ion. τετραβήμων is not found: used by E. only in lyr.) **-βᾰρής**, ές, *four times as heavy*, Alc. 153, in poet. gen. pl. τετραβαρήων. **-βιβλος**, ον, *consisting of four books*, πραγματεία Gal.7.311; title of work by Ptolemy. **-βόειος**, ον, *of four bull-hides*, Call.*Dian.*53, Q.S.6. 547. ⊕ **-βόλος**, ἡ, *female animal which has given birth to offspring four times*, ὄνοι θήλειαι τ. *PSI* 1.79.10 (iii A.D.). **-βρᾰχυς**, εος, ὁ, a metrical *foot consisting of four short syllables*, = προκελευσματικός, Sch.Ar.*Av.*238. **-βυρσος**, ον, *of four hides*, Sch.Lips.Il.15. 479 (ed. Bekker).

**τετράγγουρον**, τό, *large cucumber*, Suid. s.v. σικυΐα.

**τετρᾰ-γενής**, ές, dub. l. in Orph.*Fr.*55 (epith. of ὕλη). **-γηρυς**, υ, *four-toned*, of the tetrachord, ἀοιδά Terp.5.

**τετράγκων**· ὄργανον πολεμικόν, Hsch.

**τετρά-γλώχῑς**, ῑνος, ὁ, ἡ, *with four angles, square*, καὶ σὺ -γλώχιν.. Μαιάδος Ἑρμᾶ *AP*6.334 (Leon.). **-γνᾰθος**, ον, *with four jaws*, φαλάγγια Str.16.4.12, cf. Agatharch.59, Ael.*NA*17.40. **-γονία**, ἡ, *a fourth generation*, Aristid.*Or.*38(7).5; εὐγενεῖς ἐκ -γονίας Lib. *Or.*42.22. **-γράμμᾰτος**, ον, *of four letters*: τὸ τ. *the word of four letters*, i.e. the sacred Hebr. name YHWH (i.e. *Yahweh*), Ph.2.152, *Gloss.* **-γραμμιαῖος**, ον, (γράμμα II. 5) *weighing four scruples*, of gold coins, *BGU*316.16 (iv A.D.), *PFlor.*95.10 (iv A.D.). ⊕ **-γραμμος**, ον, perh. = τετράγωνος, ὑποβάθμιον *Inscr. gr. et lat. de la Syrie* 1153 (Cyrrhus). **-γῠος**, ον, *containing four* γύαι *of land*, μέγας ὄρχατος..τ. Od.7.113; νειὸς τ. Call.*Dian.*176 (v.l. τετρόγ- in *PAmh.*2.20$^v$.3), A.R.3.412,1344. 2. neut. as Subst., *a measure of land, as much as a man can plough in a day*, Od.18.374; also τ. αὖλαξ Orph.*A.*871.

**τετρᾰγων-έω**, Astrol., *to be in quartile aspect with* another, ὁ Ἄρης τετραγωνήσει τὸν Δία Ps.-Luc.*Philopatr.*24. **-ία**, ἡ, *square-berry, Euonymus latifolius*, so called from its *square* fruit, Thphr.*HP*3.4.2, 6. **-ιαῖος**, α, ον, = τετράγωνος, *Gp.*2.2.4. **-ίας**, ου, ὁ, *square-faced* or *square-built*, of a person, *PPetr.*3 p.23 (iii B.C.), prob. ib.p.16 (iii B.C.), and in *Arch.Pap.*3.513 (iii B.C.), *PCair.Zen.*613 (iii B.C.). **-ίζω**, *make square, square*, of lines or numbers, Pl.*R.*527a, Arist. *Metaph.*996$^b$21; ὅσαι γραμμαὶ τὸν ἰσόπλευρον..ἀριθμὸν τετραγωνίζουσι all lines which *form* an equilateral number *as their square*, Pl. *Tht.*148a; τ. τὸν κύκλον *square* the circle, Arist.*SE*171$^b$16:—Pass.,

Id.*APr.*69ᵃ31. 2. Astrol., *to be in quartile aspect*, Ptol.*Tetr.* 34. ⊛**-ικός**, ή, όν, *of a square, square*, Iamb. *in Nic.* p.59 P., al., Procl.*Hyp.*3.6, Simp. *in Ph.*59.19. Adv. **-κῶς** Iamb. *in Nic.* p.27 P. **-ισμα**, ατος, τό, *rectangle*, Antyll.ap.Orib.45.25.3, 45.26. 3. **-ισμός**, ὁ, *squaring, quadrature*, Arist. *de An.*413ᵃ17; of the circle, Id.*Cat.*7ᵇ31, *SE*171ᵇ15; ἐν τ. τὰ αὐτοῦ ἔχει in the *form of a square plot* of land, *PEnteux.*66.6 (iii B.C.).

**τετρᾰγωνο-ειδής**, ές, *square-shaped*, of military formations, Eust. 892.12, *EM*674.47. Adv. -ειδῶς Eust.469.9. **-πρόσωπος**, ον, *square-faced*, of certain animals, Hdt.4.109.

⊛ **τετράγων-ος** [ᾰ], ον, *with four angles*, but usu. *square*, Hdt.1.178, 181, 2.124, Hp.*Fract.*13; δοκοὶ τ. *squared*, Th.4.112; ξύλα τ. *IG*1².313.101, 4²(1).108.162, al. (Epid., iv/iii B.C.); τ. ἐργασία, of the Hermes-statues, Th.6.27; πρόσωπον -ότερον Arist.*Phgn.*809ᵇ16; κύκλος τετράγωνος ταῖς ἐπιφανείαις a ring *with four surfaces*, the breadth of the outer and inner equal to the depth of the two sides, Ptol.*Alm.*5.1 (with the commentary of Procl.*Hyp.*6.3). 2. τὸ τ. *a square*, Pl.*R.*510d, and freq. in Geom., but sts. of any *quadrilateral*, Arist.*Metaph.*1054ᵇ2, cf. Hero *Deff.*100, Procl. *in Euc.* p.166 F. b. in Tactics, *a body of men drawn up in square*, X.*Lac.*12.1; τ. τάξις Th.4.125. 3. τ. ἀριθμός *a square* number, i.e. a number *made up of two equal factors*, Pl.*Tht.*147e, Phld.*Sign.*1,15. 4. *in quartile aspect*, Gem.2.16, Max.446, Procl.*Hyp.*1.16. II. metaph., *square*, i.e. *perfect as a square*, χερσί τε καὶ ποσὶ καὶ νόῳ τετράγωνος τετυγμένος Simon.5.2; τὸν ἀγαθὸν ἄνδρα φάναι τετράγωνον Arist.*Rh.*1411ᵇ27, cf. *EN*1100ᵇ21. III. ἱμάτιον τ., of the χλαῖνα *which hung square*, while the χλαμύς took a circular form, Id.*Fr.*500; contrasted with the ἡμικύκλιον formed by the Roman toga, Posidon.36 J., App.*BC* 5.11. 2. οἱ ἔμποροι καὶ οἱ τὴν τ. ἐργαζόμενοι perh. *those who trade in the* ἀγορὰ τετράγωνος, Durrbach *Choix d'Inscrr. de Délos* 138. IV. Adv. -νως Philostr.*VA*7.42. **-ότης**, ητος, ἡ, *rectangular shape*, Antyll.ap.Orib.45.25.3. **-ώδης**, ες, = τετραγωνοειδής, v.l. in Sch.D.T. p.18 H. **-ῳδία**, ἡ, etym. of τραγῳδία, ibid.

**τετρᾰδακτῠλ-ιαῖος**, α, ον, *four fingers long* or *broad*, Dsc.1.68, S.E.*M.*10.156. **-ος**, ον, *four-toed*, πόδες Arist.*PA*688ᵃ5; of birds, Id.*HA*504ᵃ9. 2. *four fingers long, broad*, etc., Hp.*Art.*7, *PLond.* 3.1177.236 (ii A.D.); δόχμη τὸ τ. Ael.Dion.*Fr.*136.

**τετρᾰδαρχ-έομαι**, *to be governed in tetrarchies*, Hermog.*Id.*1.10. **-ία**, ἡ, = τετραρχία, App.*Syr.*50, f.l. in D.9.26.

**τετράδειον** [ᾰ], τό, *square*, ἐν τῷ τετραδείῳ τῆς πόλεος *Supp.Epigr.* 7.135.18 (Palmyra, ii A.D.). (Choerob. in *An.Ox.*2.269 distinguishes τετράδειον (sine expl.) from τετράδιον the ὑποκοριστικόν.)

**τετράδερμα**, ατος, τό, *leather mattress, ground sheet* (cf. *CR*47.211), *POxy.*1294.4 (ii/iii A.D.), *Dura*⁴155 (iii A.D.), restored in *PSI*6.678 (iii B.C.); τε(τ)ράδερμον, = *segestrum, Gloss.*

**τετρᾰδ-ικός**, ή, όν, *consisting of four*, ἀριθμός Syrian. *in Metaph.* 145.28; περίοδος Gal.17(1).247; ἐπιπλοκὴ ἑξάσημος τετραδική expld. in Sch.Heph.p.257 C. Adv. **-κῶς**, ἀριθμοῦνται Steph. *in Hp.*1.198 D. **-ιον**, τό, a *guard* of soldiers (normally consisting of four men), Ph.2.533, *Act.Ap.*12.4. II. *quaternion* of parchment, *POxy.*2156.10 (iv/v A.D.), Tz.*H.*9.290; cf. τετράδειον. **-ιος** πυρετός, *quartan* fever, *BGU*956 (iii A.D.). **-ίσκιον**, τό, *small quaternion*, Tz.*H.*9.283. ⊛ **-ισταί**, οἱ, *young people who met to make merry on the fourth of the month*, Alex.258. II. *men born to a life of toil*, like Heracles, who was born *on the fourth of the month* (τετράς I. 2a, q.v.), *AB*309, *EM*754.15, Suid.

**τετραδραχμιαῖος**, ον, *of 4 drachmas per mina per month*, τόκος *IG* 5(1).1146.36 (Gythium, i B.C.).

**τετράδραχμος**, ον, *worth four drachmas*, Arist.*Oec.*1347ᵃ33. II. ⊛**τετράδραχμον**, τό, *silver coin of four drachmas, tetradrachm*, *IG*1².280. 91, Pl.*Ax.*366c, Plu.*Sull.*25, etc.: later **τετράαχμον**, *IG*11(2).219 *B* 55, 287 *B* 54 (Delos, iii B.C.); also **τετρᾶχμον** (on the accent, v. *EM* 754.40), Zeno *Stoic.*1.23 (v.l.), *IG*2².1534.252, 7.303.79 (Oropus), 3498.62 (ibid.), 11(2).203 *B* 40 (Delos, iii B.C.), 287 *B* 47 (ibid.), *Inscr. Délos* 298 *A* 35 (iii B.C.), *SIG*729.3 (Delph., i B.C.), Phld.*Ir.*p.37 W.

**τετράδῠμος** [ᾰ], ον, *fourfold*, Opp.*C.*2.181; τ. τίκτειν to bear *four at a birth*, Str.15.1.22. (Cf. δίδυμος, τρίδυμος, ἑπτάδυμος.)

**τετράδων**, ὁ, prob. = τετράων, Alc.154.

⊛ **τετρά-δωρος** [ᾰ], ον, (δῶρον II) *four palms long*, Anon.ap.Plin.*HN* 35.171, = Vitr.2.3.3. **-εδρος**, ον, *having four faces*, πυραμίδες Iamb. *in Nic.*p.93 P.: Subst. -εδρον, τό, Hero *Deff.*99, Papp.352.12, *Theol.Ar.* 24. **-ειδος**, ον, *compound of four ingredients* (εἴδη), Aët.8.61, Phlp. *in GC*269.34; written **τετράϊδον** in Cyran.22: cf. ἑξάειδος, ἑπτάειδος, τρίειδος. **-έλικτος**, ον, = *four times coiled round*, ὄφις *AP*7.210 (Antip.); τετραέλικτον ἅλμαν, ἦχον τρικυμίαν, Hsch. **-ελίκωπες**· τέσσαρας ὀφθαλμοὺς ἔχουσαι ναῦς, Id. **-έλιξ**, ῐκος, ὁ, ἡ, *four times wound round*: τετραέλιξ, ἡ, a plant of the thistle kind, Id.; τετράλιξ in codd. of Thphr.*HP*6.4.4. **-ένης**, ες, *of four years, four years old*, Theoc.7.147: also **-ενος**, ον, Call.*Fr.*13ᵃ. **-εντον**, τό, *the four points of the compass*, ἐκ τετραέντου κυκλόθεν *PMasp.*151.114 (vi A.D.). **-εξηκοστόν**, τό, *sixty-fourth part*, *PCornell* 20.15 (iv A.D.). **-ερμῆς**, ὁ, *four-sided herm*, ib.33.6 (iii A.D.).

**τετράετα** [ᾰ], τά, (ἀετός IV) a form of vaulting, consisting of four triangular surfaces, *Arch.Anz.*19.8 (Milet.).

**τετραέτ[ει]α**, ἡ, v. τετραετία.

**τετρᾰέτηρ-ία**, ἡ, *term of four years*, *Gloss.* ⊛ **-ικός**, ή, όν, *of a* τετραετηρίς, Jul.*Or.*4.155b. ⊛**-ίς** (sc. ἑορτή), ίδος, ἡ, *a quadrennial festival*, *CIG*2741.22, 2812 (Aphrodisias); cf. πετροετηρίς. II. *period of four years*, Eudox.*Ars*3.31, Vett.Val.189.2, Horap.1.5, Censorin.*Nat.*18 (*tetraheterida* codd. DV). **-ος**, ον, = sq., Hsch.

⊛ **τετρᾰέτ-ής**, ές, or **τετραέτης**, ες, *four years old*, ἐπεὰν τ. γένηται (sc. τὰ παιδία) Hdt.4.187; τ. ἦθος ψυχῆς Pl.*Lg.*793e. II. *of four years*, χρόνος Hdt.1.199, D.H.3.69; διάστημα Plb.9.1.1. **-ία**, ἡ, *term of four years*, Thphr.*CP*3.7.7, Plu.*Pomp.*55, *IG*2².333c17 (iv B.C.), 9(1).12.10 (Ambryssus, iii A.D., where τετραετ[εί]ᾳ). **-ικός**, ή, όν, epith. of βδέλλα II in *Edict.Diocl.*32.55 (perh. an error for πετρατικός, cf. Plin.*HN*12.35).

**τετρά-ζευκτος**, ον, gloss on τέτρωρον, Eust.573.27. **-ζῠγής**, ές, = sq., ὄχοι Trag. (Satyr.) *Oxy.*1083 *Fr.*13. **-ζῠγος**, ον, *four-yoked*, ὄχοι E.*Hel.*1039. 2. generally, *fourfold*, ὀμφή Nonn.*D.*12. 107. **-ζυξ**, ῠγος, ὁ, ἡ, = foreg., ib.7.6, 12.169.

**τετράζω**, *cackle like the* τέτραξ, on laying an egg, Alex.Mynd.ap. Ath.9.398d. II. (τετράς) *observe a four-day cycle*, Philostr.*Gym.*47.

**τετρᾰ-ήμερος**, ον, *of* or *lasting four days*, κατὰ τετραήμερον *in four days*, Arist.*HA*553ᵃ10; cf. τετρήμερος. **-θέλυμνος**, ον, (θέλυμνον) *of four layers*, σάκος τ. a shield *of four ox-hides*, Il.15.479 = Od.22. 122. **-θῠρος**, ον, *with four doors* or *openings*, Arist.*HA*628ᵃ13, Callix.1; κιβωτός prob. l. in *IG*1².330.2.

**τετραΐζω**, *suffer from quartan fever*, Cyran.45.

**τετραίνω** (pres. in compd. συν- A.*Ch.*451 (lyr.), Hdt.2.11); fut. τετρᾰνῶ Kourouniotes Ἐλευσινιακά i 190 (iv B.C.); Ion. fut. τετρᾰνέω (δια-) Hdt.3.12: Ep. aor. τέτρηνα, the only tense used by Hom.; Att. inf. τετρᾶναι *IG*1².372 *E*8, 2².1678 *aA* 5; part. ἐν-τετράνας ib. 1665.18, 1672.176:—Med., aor. ἐτετρηνάμην Gal.*UP*15.6, (δι-) Ar. *Th.*18:—Pass., aor. ἐτετράνθην Lyc.781, *AP* (v. infr.). Other tenses are formed from stem τρη- (never τρᾱ-), fut. τρήσω Lyc.665: aor. ἔτρησα Hp.*Morb.*2.28, Lxx 4 *Ki.*12.9, *IG*7.3073.71 (Lebad., ii B.C.), etc., (συν-) Pl.*Ti.*91a, etc.:—Med., aor. ἐτρησάμην (δι-) Gal.4.708:— Pass., aor. ἐτρήθην *Gp.*5.33.7, (ἀν-) Trypho ap.Ath.4.182e: pf. τέτρημαι (v. infr.): plpf. 3 pl. τετρήατο Emp.84.9. A pres. **τιτραίνω** occurs in Thphr.*HP*5.4.5 (Pass.), with an aor. ἐτίτρᾶνα ib.2.7. 6, 5.4.5: 3 pl. impf. Pass. τετρήνοντο in Call.*Dian.*244 is f.l. for τετρήνατο or τετραίνοντο, and τετρήνεται in Hp.*Nat.Puer.*17 f.l. for τετραίν-. The pres. **τιτράω** first in Pass. τιτρᾶται Hero *Spir.*2. 35, Dsc.5.75, Hsch.; 2 sg. pres. imper. Act. τίτρα *PHolm.*4.40: the pres. **τίτρημι** first in 3 sg. pres. κατα-τίτρησι Gal.13.937; pres. part. nom. sg. fem. τιτρᾶσα Id.*UP*16.6; nom. pl. δια-τιτράντες D.C.69. 12. The compds. with διά and σύν are more used than the simple Verb; cf. also those with κατά, ἀνά, ἐν, and ἐκ:—*bore through, pierce, perforate*, ποδῶν τέτρηνε τένοντε Il.22.396; τέτρηνα δὲ πάντα τερέτρῳ Od.23.198, cf. 5.247:—Pass., πυκιναῖς τέτρηνται ἄλοξιν Emp.100.3; λίθος τετρημένος Hdt.2.96; ὁ οὐρανὸς τέτρηται *has holes in it*, Id.4.158; τέτρηται δικτύου πλέον (Ahrens for τέτρωται) A.*Ag.*868; τέτρηνται, of the urinary passage, v.l. in Hp.*Aër.*9; ὥσπερ κόσκινον τέτρηται Ar.*Fr.*480; ὁ τετρημένος πίθος, v. πίθος 1.2; [χάσμα] δι' ὅλης τῆς γῆς τετρημένον Pl.*Phd.*112a; κοιλίαι εἰς τὸν πλεύμονα τετρ. Arist.*HA* 496ᵃ22; τετρανθεὶς αὐλός *AP*6.296 (Leon.). (Cf. τέρετρον, τερηδών.)

**τετραῖον**· ὀρνιθάριόν τι, Λάκωνες, Hsch.

**τετρά-ϊππον** [ᾰ], τό, written *tetraipon*, = *quadriga* (i.e. τέθριππον), *Gloss.*; cf. τέτραλον. **-ίστορον**, τό, *group of four* ἱστορίαι, Tz.*H.*2. 868.

**τετρᾰκαιδεκά-εδρον** [κᾰ], τό, *solid with fourteen faces*, Papp.ap. Archim.ii p.538 H. **-έτης**, ες, *of fourteen years*, D.H.6.21 (v.l. τετρακαιδεκέτης). II. fem. **τετρᾰκαιδεκέτις**, ιδος, *fourteen years old*, κόρη Isoc.19.22. **-πεδος**, ον, *fourteen feet long*, ξύλα *IG*4²(1). 109 ii 139 (Epid., iii B.C.).

**τετρᾰκαιδέκ-ᾰτος**, ον, *fourteenth*, v.l. in Il.10.561 (ap.Sch.A), Tz. *H.*6.260. **-έτης**, v. τετρακαιδεκαέτης.

⊛ **τετρᾰκαι-εικοστός**, ή, όν, *twenty-fourth*, *PFay.*82.12 (ii A.D.), *Ostr.Bodl.* ii 55 (ii A.D.): fem. -εικοστή, ἡ, name of a tax, *PHib.* 1.80 (iii B.C.), *PTeb.*36.9 (ii B.C.), etc. ⊛ **-εξηκοστόν**, τό, *sixty-fourth part*, *PCornell*20.113 (iv A.D.).

**τετρᾰκάμᾰρος** [κᾰ], ον, *with four vaults*, Hero *Stereom.*2.1.

**τετρακάτιοι**, v. τετρακόσιοι.

**τετρᾰ-κέρᾰτος**, ον, *four-horned*, Orph.*Fr.*77. **-κερως**, ων, = foreg., ἔλαφος *App.Anth.*1.95; ὗς Opp.*C.*2.378. **-κέφᾰλος**, ον, *four-headed*, Epigr.ap.Eust.1353.8, Phleg.36.20 J., Lyd.*Mens.*3.8, Sch.Ar.*Ach.*1081 [with penult. long, as if -κέφαλλος, Epigr. l.c., cf. κυνοκέφαλος].

**τετρᾰκίνη**, ἡ, = θρίδαξ, Hippon.135.

**τετρᾰκῑόνιον**, τό, *shrine with four pillars*, Paus.Dam. p.158 D.

**τετράκις** [ᾰ], Adv. *four times*, Od.5.306, Hdt.2.142, *IG*1².606, Ar. *Pl.*851, etc.:—post-Hom. also ⊛**τετράκι**, *IG*4.561.5 (Argos), Pi.*N.*7. 104 (prob.), Call.*Epigr.*53.2, *MAMA*4.157 (Apollonia); and **τετράκιν**, *IG*5(1).213.9 (Sparta, v B.C.).

**τετρᾰκισ-επίπεμπτος** (sc. λόγος), ὁ, *superquintipartient*, Nicom. *Ar.*1.23. **-εφέβδομος** (sc. λόγος), ὁ, *ratio of* 11 : 7, ibid. **-μύριοι** [ῡ], αι, α, *four times ten thousand, forty thousand*, X.*Cyr.*2.1.5, Arist. *Mu.*393ᵇ20. **-χίλιοι** [ῐλ], αι, α, *four thousand*, Hdt.2.9, al.; by tmesis, τετράκις γὰρ χίλιοι Th.6.31: Lacon. **τετρᾰκινχήλιοι** *IG* 5(1).1 (Sparta, v B.C.); Cyrenaic **τετρᾰκιχήλιοι** *Abh.Berl.Akad.* 1925(5).25; Boeot. **πετρᾰκισχείλιη** (fem., q.v.).

**τετρᾰ-κίων** [ῑ], ον, gen. ονος, *with four pillars*, Orph.Εὐχή 39. **-κλαστος**, ον, *broken fourfold, in four*, Procl.ad Hes.*Op.*440. **-κληρος**, ον, f.l. for τετράπλευρος (cf. *CQ*17.54) in *Cat.Cod.Astr.*8(4). 223. **-κλῖνος**, ον, *with four seats* or *couches*, ἅμαξα Luc.*Tox.*46; οἶκοι Ath.2.47f; σκηνή *PSI*5.533.3 (iii B.C.). **-κνημος**, ον, *four-*

*spoked*, Pherecyd.51(b) J.; Dor. **-κνᾱμος**, δεσμός, of Ixion's wheel, Pi.*P.*2.40; ἴυγξ the wryneck *tied on the four-spoked wheel*, ib.4.214. **-κόλουρος**, ον, *quadruply truncated*, Nicom.*Ar.*2.14, Iamb. *in Nic.* p.97 P. **-κοντα** (-Ϙοντα), v. τεσσαράκοντα. **-κόρη**, ἡ, a name of Persephone (Κόρη), *Epigr.Gr.*406.11 (Iconium). **-κόρυμβος**, ον, *thick-clustering*, κισσός *AP*7.23 (Antip. Sid.). **-κόρωνος**, ον, *four times a crow's age*, Hes.*Fr.*171.2.

⊛ **τετρᾰκόσι-οι**, αι, α, Dor. **-κάτιοι** [κᾰ] *Tab.Herad.*1.52, etc.; poet. (once) **τετρηκόσιοι** *AP*11.67 (Myrin.):—*four hundred*, Hdt.1.178, etc.: in sg., τ. ἀσπίς X.*An.*1.7.10. II. οἱ τ., at Athens, 1. the oligarchy established in 411 B.C., Th.8.69, Lys.30.7, Decr.ap.And.1.78, etc. 2. a more ancient Council, Ael.*VH*5.13. **-οστός**, ή, όν, *four hundredth*, ἔτος Din.1.73, Lxx 3*Ki.*6.1. II. τετρακοσιοστή, ἡ, tax of $\frac{1}{400}$, *PCair.Zen.*12.78 (iii B.C., spelt -αστή).

**τετρᾰκοστά**, τά, *celebration of the fortieth day after birth*, *PFay.*113.14 (i/ii A.D.); but τετρακοστός, ή, όν, = τετρακοσιοστός, Tz.*H.*13.99.

**τετρᾰκότῠλ-ος**, ον, *holding four* κοτύλαι, κύλιξ Hp.*Int.*28, Theophil.2, cf. Alex.176, *PSI*5.535.7 (iii B.C.), *Inscr.Délos* 1429 *B*i 54 (ii B.C.), 1432 *Ab* ii 28 (ii B.C.):—also **-ιαῖος**, α, ον, πλῆθος S.E.*P.*3.94.

⊛ **τετρακτύς**, ύος, ἡ, (τετράς) Pythagorean name for *the sum of the first four numbers*, i.e. 10 (= 1+2+3+4), ναὶ μὰ τὸν ἁμετέρᾳ ψυχᾷ παραδόντα τετρακτύν, παγὰν ἀενάου φύσεως *Carm.Aur.*48, cf. S.E.*M.*7.94, TheoSm.p.94 H., Hierocl.*in CA*20 p.465 M. II. *the four terms* (6 : 8 : 9 : 12) *of the proportion corresponding to the chief musical intervals*, Nicom.*Exc.*7.10; also *their sum* + 1 (= 36), ibid.; *the sum of the first* 8 *numbers*, Plu.2.381f.

**τετρά-κυκλος** [ᾰ], ον, *four-wheeled*, ἕλκον τ. ἀπήνην Il.24.324; ἅμαξαι ἐσθλαὶ τετράκυκλοι Od.9.242, cf. Hdt.1.188, 2.63, Hp.*Aër.*18: as Subst., *four-wheeled wagon*, τροχοὶ τετρακύκλου *IG*1².313.116. [ᾰ only in Od. l. c., where Bentley conjectured τεσσαράκυκλοι.] **-κῡμία**, ἡ, *quadruple wave*, produced by four winds, Eust.1537.33. **-κωλος**, ον, *with four limbs*, μηχανή *Rev.Phil.*44.251 (Didyma, ii B.C.). 2. *in four sections*, [σύριγγες] Nicom.*Harm.*10. 3. *of four members*, περίοδος Sch.D.2.3; τετράκωλον, = *quadrimembris sententia*, *Gloss.* ⊛ **-κωμία**, ἡ, *a union of four villages*, Str.9.2.14. **-κωμος**, ὁ, *a triumphal song and dance* sacred to Heracles and also called τέσσαρες κῶμοι, Trypho ap.Ath.14.618c, Hsch.; ὁ δὲ τ., τὸ τῆς ὀρχήσεως εἶδος, οὐκ οἶδα εἴ τι προσῆκον ἦν τοῖς Ἀθήνησι τ., οἳ ἦσαν Πειραιεῖς Φαληρεῖς Ξυπεταίονες Θυμοιτάδαι (leg. Θυμαιτ-, cf. *IG*2².1598, 3102) Poll.4.105; τοῦ τετρακώμου Ἡρακλείου, ἐν ᾧ τοὺς γυμνικοὺς ἀγῶνας ἐτίθεσαν τοῖς Παναθηναίοις St.Byz. s.v. Ἐχελίδαι. **-λασσον**, dub. sens. (of flax) in *Edict.Diocl.*28.61; τετράλασον (sic) λέντιν *PSI*8.971.17 (iii/iv A.D.); cf. δίλασσον. **-λῖνον**, τό, prob. *a four-fold lace* or *string*, *Gloss.* **-λιξ**, v. τετραέλιξ. **-λογία**, ἡ, (λόγος) *a group of four* Platonic *dialogues*, Thrasyll.ap.D.L.3.57, cf. 9.45. II. *a group* or *series of four dramas*, three Tragedies and one Satyric play (or sts. four Tragedies), Arist.*Fr.*619, D.L.3.56.

**τέτραλον**· (post τετρυχωμένος) τετράϊππον, Hsch.

⊛ **τετρᾰμαίνω**, = τρέμω, Hp.*Mul.*2.171, Ar.*Nu.*294,374, Xenarch.4.19 (prob.), Hp.ap.Gal.19.146 cod. opt. (cf. *Eranos* 17.99), Hsch.; τετρεμαίνω (q.v.) is v.l. in Ar. ll. cc., Gal. l. c.

**τετρᾰ-μερής**, ές, *quadripartite*, Arist.*Fr.*47, Lxx 2*Ma.*8.21, S.E.*P.*1.23, Sor.*Fasc.*40. Adv. -ρῶς Sm.*Ez.*1.8, Eust.1572.24: hence **-μέρεια**, ἡ, = sq., Tz.*H.*3.341. **-μερία**, ἡ, *formation in four divisions*, -ίᾳ πορεύεσθαι Ascl.*Tact.*11.6. **-μέτρητος**, ον, *containing four* μετρηταί, Callix.2. **-μετρος**, ον, *consisting of four metres*, i.e. in iambic and trochaic verse, *consisting of four double feet* or *syzygies*: τὸ τετράμετρον is generally *the trochaic tetrameter*, Ar.*Nu.*642,645, X.*Smp.*6.3, Arist.*Rh.*1404$^{a}$31, 1409$^{a}$1, *Po.*1459$^{b}$37: also *the anapaestic tetrameter*, called τὸ Ἀριστοφάνειον (as in *Nu.*957 sq.), D.H.*Comp.*25; cf. τρίμετρος. 2. γωνίαι τ. *square*, i.e. *right*, angles, Callix.2 (dub. l.). ⊛ **-μηνιαῖος**, α, ον, = sq., σπονδαί D.S.11.80; of the foetus, Gal.14.154. **-μήνιος**, ον, *lasting four months*, γυμνασιαρχία *POxy.*1418.18 (iii A.D.). ⊛ **-μηνος**, ον, (μήν) *of four months, lasting four months*, σπονδαί Th.5.63; τετράμηνοι ὀχεύουσι *at four months old*, Arist.*HA*545$^{b}$1; τετράμηνον *for a space of four months*, ib.573$^{a}$13, cf. *PCair.Zen.*291,498 (iii B.C.), etc.; ἡ πρώτη τ. *SIG*410.4 (Erythrae, iii B.C.); so τετράμηνα Hp.*Aph.*4.1: Boeot. πετράμεινος (q.v.). **-μναῖος**, α, ον, = sq., D.S.3.16. **-μνους**, ουν, (μνᾶ) *worth* or *weighing four minae*, Posidon.13 J. **-μοιρία**, ἡ, *a fourfold portion*, X.*An.*7.2.36, 7.6.1. **-μοιρος**, ον, *fourfold*, τ. νυκτὸς φυλακή E.*Rh.*5 (anap.). ⊛ **-μορος**, ον, in neut. -μορον, τό, *four parts*, κηροῖο Nic.*Th.*106, cf. Aglaïas 25. **-μορφος**, ον, *four-shaped, fourfold*, ὧραι τ. the *four changing* seasons, E.*Fr.*943; of Janus, Lyd.*Mens.*4.1.

**τέτρᾰμος**, ὁ, = τρόμος, Hp.*Morb.*1.24 (cod. θ), Erot.; cf. τέτρομος.

**τετράμῠρον** [ᾰ], τό, *an ointment compounded of four ingredients*, Asclep.ap.Gal.13.1013.

**τετράμφοδον**, = *quadrivium*, *Gloss.*

**τετράμφορος**, ον, *holding four amphorae*, *Sardis* 7(1).17 (abbrev.).

**τετράνομον** [ᾰ], τό, *coin of value of* 4 νόμοι (v. νόμος III), *Inscr. Délos* 407.21, 442 *B*215 (both ii B.C.), cf. p.348.

**τετραντίας**· τετράγωνος καὶ ἰσχυρός, Hsch.

**τέτραξ**, ᾶγος (so *Stud.Ital.*N.S.2.394 (Phalasarna, iv B.C., amulet)), and **ᾶκος** (dat. τέτρακι Ar.*Av.*884), ὁ, name of two kinds of *wild birds*, 1. ὁ μείζων, prob. *hazel-grouse* or *ryper*, Ath.9.398f, Eust.1205.27, *Poet.Lat.Min.* iii p.203 Baehrens; coupled with the peafowl by Ar. l. c. 2. a small bird, like the σπερμολόγος, Epich.45,46, Alex.Mynd.ap.Ath.9.398c. (Cf. τέτριξ, τετράων, τετράδων, τατύρας, τέταρος, τετράζω; Skt. *tittir-is* or *-as* (the francolin or Indian partridge); Lith. *teterva* (black-cock); prob. onomatop.)

**τετράξοος**, ον, (ξέω) *split four times*, ἐλάται καὶ πεῦκαι τ. trees *of which the wood has four lines of fissure*, Thphr.*HP*5.1.9: cf. δίξοος, μονόξοος.

**τετραξός**, ή, όν, *fourfold*, γραμμαὶ τετραξαί *four sets of* lines, Arist. *Metaph.*1076$^{b}$32.

**τετράζων**· εἶδος χαλινοῦ, Hsch. (-άζων cod. invito ordine).

**τετρᾰ-οδία**, ἡ, and **-όδιον**, τό, (ὁδός) *a place where four roads meet*, *Gloss.* **-οδῖτις**, ἡ, *haunting crossroads*, epith. of the Moon-goddess, *PMag.Par.*1.2561,2818. **-οδος**, ἡ, = τετραοδία, Orac.ap. Paus.8.9.4; cf. τρίοδος.

**τετρ-αοίδιος**, ον, *of four notes*, in Music, name of a Νόμος of Terpander, Plu.2.1132d.

**τετρᾰ-ονία**, ἡ, *team of four donkeys*, *PRyl.*236.3 (iii A.D.), *PFlor.*175.28 (iii A.D.). **-όργυιος**, ον, *four fathoms long* or *broad*, D.C.70.4 (-οργοι codd.); cf. τετρόργυιος.

**τετρᾱ-ορία**, ἡ, *four-horsed chariot*, Pi.*O.*2.5, *P.*2.4, al. **-ορος**, contr. **τέτρωρος**, ον, (ἀείρω) *yoked four together*, τ. ἄρσενες ἵπποι Od.13.81, cf. E.*Hel.*723, Tim.*Pers.*204; τ. ἅρμα *a four-horsed* chariot, Pi.*P.*10.65, etc.; δίφρος S.*Fr.*958 (cj.); ὄχοι E.*Supp.*675; also contr., τέτρωρος ὄχος Id.*Hipp.*1229; τέτρωρον ἅρμα Id.*Alc.*483, *Heracl.*860; τέτρωρον *a team of four*, Ael.*NA*1.36, Philostr.*Im.*2.18. II. *four-legged*, τετραόρου φάσμα ταύρου S.*Tr.*508 (lyr.). III. τέτρωρον, τό, *upper surface of astragalus*, Ruf.*Oss.*38, Gal.2.775.

⊛ **τετρᾰ-ούγκιον**, = *triens* (i.e. *coin of four unciae*), *Cod.Just.*6.4.4.16, al., *Gloss.*; cf. τετρούγκιον. **-πᾰλαι**, Adv. *four times long ago*, i.e. *long long ago*, Call.*Epigr.*2.4. **-πᾰλαιστιαῖος**, α, ον, = sq., Orib.49.23.3, *Gp.*5.44.2. ⊛ **-πάλαστος** [πᾰ], ον, *four spans long* or *broad*, -παλαιστ- in codd. of Hdt.2.149, Callix.2. 2. *tetrapaleston* (i.e. τετραπάλαιστον), = *laterculus*, *Gloss.* **-πεδικόν**, τό, *rectangle*, Hero *Mens.*42. **-πέδιον**, τό, = foreg., Id.*Stereom.*1.33. ⊛ **-πεδος**, ον, *with four surfaces* or *sides, squared*, λίθοι D.S.20.95, cf. *IG*4²(1).119.14, al. (Epid.), Arr.*An.*6.29.5 (v.l. τετραπόδου), Hdn.8.4.2. II. *of four feet*, κλίμακα τῷ πλάτει τετράπεδον Plb.8.4.4, cf. Orac.ap.Plu.*Aem.*15. **-πεζος**, ον, (πέζα) *four-footed*, Orph.*L.*747. **-πελεθρία**, v. τετραπλεθρία. **-πηχυαῖος**, α, ον, = sq., Apollod.2.4.9. **-πηχυς**, υ, gen. ους *Ath.Mitt.*33.377 (Pergam.); nom. and acc. pl. -πήχεις Ar.*V.*553, *Ra.*1014; acc. pl. neut. -πήχη *PCair.Zen.*353.9 (iii B.C.):—*four cubits* (six feet) *long*, Hdt.7.69; of men, *six feet high, tall fellows*, Ar. ll. cc., cf. Pl.*R.*426d, Philostr.*Im.*1.25; nom. **-πήχης**, ες, Hdn.Gr.1.82.

**τετρᾰπλάσι-άζω**, *make fourfold*, Nicom.*Ar.*1.21 (Pass.), Hdn.3.13.4 (Pass.). **-αῖος**, α, ον, = τετραπλάσιος, Gal.(2.710, where -πλάσιος) as cited by Orib.24.1.5. **-επιδῐμερής**, ές, $4\frac{2}{3}$ *times as great* (14 : 3): so **τετρᾰπλᾰσιεπίπεμπτος**, ον, $4\frac{1}{5}$ *times as great* (21 : 5); **τετρᾰπλᾰσιεπιτέταρτος**, ον, $4\frac{1}{4}$ *times as great* (17 : 4); **τετρᾰπλᾰσιεπιτετρᾰμερής**, ές, $4\frac{4}{5}$ *times as great* (24 : 5); **τετρᾰπλᾰσιεπιτρῐμερής**, ές, $4\frac{3}{4}$ *times as great* (19 : 4); **τετρᾰπλᾰσιεπίτρῐτος**, ον, $4\frac{1}{3}$ *times as great* (13 : 3); **τετρᾰπλᾰσιεφημίσυς**, υ, $4\frac{1}{2}$ *times as great* (9 : 2):—all found in, or implied by, Nicom.*Ar.*1.22, 23. ⊛ **-ος**, α, ον, *fourfold, four times as much*, Pl.*R.*369e, al.; τὸ τ. μέρος *OGI*665.30 (Egypt, i A.D.): c. gen., *four times as large as*, ἧπαρ τ. τοῦ βοείου Arist.*HA*508$^{a}$1: τὴν τ. (sc. ζημίαν) τίνειν pay a *fourfold* penalty, Pl.*Lg.*878c (τριπλασίαν Orelli), cf. 756e. Adv. -ίως Sm.2*Ki.*12.6. **-ότης**, ητος, ἡ, *fourfoldness*, Nicom.*Ar.*2.5. **-ων**, ον, gen. ονος, = τετραπλάσιος, Dsc.1.61.

⊛ **τετρᾰ-πλεθρία**, ἡ, *area of four plethra*, *IG*9(1).693.7 (Corcyra); written **-πελεθρία**, ib.6. **-πλεθρος**, ον, *consisting of four plethra*, Plb.6.27.2. **-πλευρος**, ον, *four-sided*, σχῆμα Str.5.1.2; κίων *AP*9.682; σῶμα Gal.8.894; *facing four ways*, τάγμα Ael.*Tact.*36.4, cf. Ascl.*Tact.*11.6, Arr.*Tact.*28.4: τετράπλευρον, τό, *figure with four sides*, Arist.*Mech.*848$^{b}$20, *Pr.*911$^{b}$3, Apollod.*Poliorc.*165.16; part of Sagittarius, Ptol.*Tetr.*25. **-πλῆ**, Adv. *in a fourfold manner, fourfold*, Il.1.128, Hero *Metr.*1.28, al. **-πλόος**, η, ον, contr. **-πλοῦς**, ῆ, οῦν, *fourfold*, Plu.*Luc.*2; τοῦ τετραπλοῦ μισθοῦ *PSI*9.1055.13 (iii A.D.); τὸ τ., = τετραμοιρία, X.*An.*7.6.7; ἀποδίδωμι τετραπλοῦν *Ev.Luc.*19.8. Adv. -πλῶς Lxx 3*Ki.*6.31(33). (Cf. ἁπλόος.) **-πνης**, ὁ, *with four nostrils*, τὸν τετράπνην ὕδρον Lyc.1313 (nisi leg. τετράπουν).

**τετρᾰποδ-ηδόν**, Adv. *on all fours*, ἑστάναι Ar.*Pax*896. **-ης**, ου, ὁ, *four-footed*, Man.4.26. **-ητί**, Adv. *on all fours*, Plb.5.60.7. **-ία**, ἡ, *a measure* or *length of four feet*, *IG*1².372.72, al., 4²(1).109 ii 84, al. (Epid., iii B.C.); κατὰ -δίαν ib.7.4255.33 (Oropus, iv B.C.). II. in Metric, τ. δακτυλική Heph.15.8. **-ίζω**, *go on all fours*, Arist.*HA*501$^{a}$3; = *quadripedo*, *Gloss.* **-ισμός**, ὁ, *a going on all fours*, Sch.Nic.*Al.*417. **-ιστής**, οῦ, ὁ, in pl., f.l. for τετραδισταί in *EM*754.15. **-ιστί**, Adv. = τετραποδητί, Plu.2.241f, Luc.*DMar.*7.2. **-ος**, ον, late form of τετράπους, found in codd. of Plb.1.29.7, etc., v.l. for τετράπεδος in Arr.*An.*6.29.5.

**τετρά-πολις** [ᾰ], εως (and in Androt.35 ιδος), ἡ, rarely ὁ, poet. **τετράπτολις** E.*Heracl.*80 (lyr.):—*of* or *with four cities*, τ. λαός, of the northern part of Attica, E. l. c., cf. Ar.*Lys.*285 (lyr.): ἡ τ. this part of Attica, the four cities being Oenoe, Marathon, Probalinthos, Tricorythos, Arist.*Fr.*491, Plu.*Thes.*14. 2. in Doris, Str.9.4.10. 3. in Syria, Id.16.2.4. 4. in Cephallenia, Th.2.30. ⊛ **-πολος**, ον, *turned up* or *ploughed four times*, Theoc.25.26. **-πορος**, ον, *with four passages* or *openings*, ἀψῖδες *AP*9.

696. II. *coming four ways*, ἄνεμοι ib.656. ⊛ -πος, ον, poet. for sq., Arat.214, Aenigm.ap.Asclep.Tragil.7 J.; Cret. nom. sg. **τετράπος** (from *-ποδs) *Schwyzer* 181 iii 7 (Gortyn). ⊛ -πους, ὁ, ἡ, πουν, τό, gen. ποδος, pl. ποδα, *four-footed*, Hdt.2.68, Pl.*Ti.*92a; λεία τ. a booty *of cattle*, Plb.4.75.7; τετράποδα ζῴδια, viz. Aries, Taurus, Leo, Sagittarius, *Cat.Cod.Astr.*1.166: cf. τετράποδος. 2. τετράπουν, τό, *quadruped, beast*, Pl.*Phdr.*250e, Arist.*PA*697$^{b}$23, etc.: pl., Hdt.3.106, Ar.*Nu.*659, Th.2.50, Arist.*HA*490$^{a}$29, etc.; πάντα τὰ τ. καὶ ἑρπετὰ τῆς γῆς *Act.Ap.*10.12. II. of things, δίφρος τ. Eup.58, *POxy.*646 (ii A.D.), cf. Epich.149. 2. *of four feet* in length or area, *IG*1$^{2}$.372.10, al., Pl.*Men.*83b; πάχος ποήσει τὸ στρῶμα τετράπουν *IG*2$^{2}$.1668.14. ⊛ -πρόσωπος, ον, *with four faces* or *fronts*, βωμός Plu.2.308a; ἀριθμός, of the τετράς, Herm. *in Phdr.* p.107 A. -πτερος, ον, *four-winged*, of winged ants, S.*Fr.*29; τετράπτερα, opp. δίπτερα, Arist.*HA*490$^{a}$16, *PA*682$^{b}$8. -πτερυλλίς, ίδος, ἡ, *four-wing*, i.e. *grasshopper* or *locust*, Boeot. word in Ar.*Ach.*871: Elmsl. thinks that by τῶν ὀρταλίχων ἢ τῶν τετραπτερυλλίδων is intended birds and *beasts*; no doubt this is so, τετραπτερυλλίδων being brought in παρ' ὑπόνοιαν for τετραπόδων. -πτῖλος, ον, *four-winged*, Ar.*Ach.*1082. -πτολις, poet. for τετράπολις (q.v.). -πτῠχος, ον, *fourfold*, Hp.*Off.*12 (and Gal. ad loc., 18(2).822), Gal.14.793. -πτωτος, ον, *with four cases*, Sch.D.T. p.231 H., Diom. p.309 K., *Gloss.* -πῦλον, τό, *archway entered from four sides*, *OGI*722.6 (Egypt, iv A.D.); = *quadrivium*, *Gloss.*: Adj. -πῦλος, ον, *with four gateways*, περίβολος πόλεως Str.12.4.7. ⊛ -πυργία, ἡ, *building with four towers, fortified country-house*, Plu.*Eum.*8: ἡ Τ., place-name in Cyrene, Plb.31.18.11, Str.17.3.22; perh. as pr. n. in *IG*2$^{2}$.2776.118, cf. Procop.*Aed.*4.1: as Adj. -πύργιος, ον, J.*AJ*13.2.1 (s.v.l.); πεδίον τ. Dam.*Isid.*63. -πώγων, ωνος, ὁ, a plant, = τραγοπώγων, Ps.-Dsc.2.143. -πωλία, ἡ, *team of four horses*, *Gloss.* ⊛ -πωλον, τό, = τέθριππον, Cyran.27 (-πολ- cod.), Lyd.*Mens.*1.12.

**τετρ-άρουρος** [ᾰ], ὁ, *tenant of four* ἄρουραι, *PMich.Zen.*96.2 (iii B.C.), *BGU*1213.18 (p.192, iii B.C.).

**τετρά-ρραβδος**, ον, *with four spokes*, Sch.Pi.*P.*2.73. -ρριζος, ον, *with four roots*, ὀδόντες Gal.2.753: -ρριζος = *dentium dolor*, *Gloss.* -ρρῖνος, ον, (ῥίς) *with four nozzles*, λύχνον τετράρινον (sic) *IG*11(2).199*B*87 (Delos, iii B.C.). -ρρυθμος, ον, *consisting of four metres*, Sch.Ar.*Ach.*665. -ρρῡμος, ον, *with four poles*, i.e. *eight-horsed*, ἅρμα X.*Cyr.*6.1.51, 6.4.2, Philostr.*VA*2.42. II. τετράρυμον ἀμφοδον = *complitus* (sic), *Gloss.* (from ῥύμη *street*).

**τετραρχ-έω**, *to be tetrarch*, τῆς Γαλιλαίας *Ev.Luc.*3.1, cf. J.*BJ*3.10.7. -ης, ου, ὁ, *tetrarch*, Str.12.5.1, Plu.*Ant.*56, *OGI*416 (Cos, i A.D.), 543.3 (Ancyra, ii A.D.), etc.; of rulers under the protection of Rome of lower grade than kings, e.g. in Palestine, *Ev.Matt.*14.1, al., J.*BJ*1.12.5, al.; generally, Sall.*Cat.*20.7, Hor.*Sat.*1.3.12, etc.: also **τέτραρχος**, Θεσσαλῶν *SIG*274 (Delph., iv B.C.): gen. -χου *OGI*606.4 (Syria, i A.D.), but -χα *IGRom.*4.1683 (Pergam.): cf. τετραρχία. II. *a leader of four* λόχοι, or 64 men, *Rev. Arch.*3 (1934).40 (Amphipolis, iii/ii B.C.), 6(1935).31 (ibid., ii B.C.), Ascl.*Tact.*2.8, Arr.*Tact.*10.1, Ael.*Tact.*9.2. -ία, ἡ, *tetrarchy, the province of a tetrarch*, esp. of Thessaly, the four provinces being Thessaliotis, Phthiotis, Pelasgiotis, Hestiaeotis, Hellanic.52 J., E.*Alc.*1154, D.9.26, Theopomp.Hist.201; also of the four divisions of each of the three Galatian tribes, Str.12.5.1; ἡ τῶν δώδεκα τ. βουλή v.l. ibid.; cf. τετράς II. 2. generally, of the divisions of Roman protectorates, e.g. Palestine under Augustus, J.*BJ*2.6.3; districts adjacent to Syria, *tetrarchiae regnorum instar singulae*, Plin.*HN*5.74. II. τ. ἱππική *the command of four* λόχοι, Arr.*An.*3.18.5, cf. Id.*Tact.*10.1, Ael.*Tact.*9.2, Ascl.*Tact.*2.8; Φιλίππου τετραρχίας ἔργον monument erected by Philip's τ., *IG*9(1).316 (Scarphea, Locr. Orient., iv B.C.). -ικός, ή, όν, *of a tetrarch*, τὸ τ. γένος Str.12.3.37. -ος, ὁ, = τετράρχης (q.v.).

⊛ **τετράς**, άδος, ἡ, *the number four*, Arist.*Metaph.*1081$^{b}$16, 1090$^{b}$23, Ph.1.22, Plu.*Lyc.*5, etc. 2. *the fourth day* of the month, *h.Merc.*19, Hes.*Op.*794, 798, Ar.*Nu.*1131, Th.5.54, *IG*1$^{2}$.304.50, 62, etc.; so Boeot. **πετράς** (q.v.); τετράδι γέγονας, prov. of one born to a life of labour (cf. τετραδισταί II), Pl.Com.100, cf. Aristonym.4, Sannyr.5. b. *the fourth day of the week, Wednesday*, *Cod.Just.*9.4.6.1. 3. *a space of four days*, Hp.*Prog.*20. 4. the four *quarters* of the moon, Thphr.*Sign.*5, 27, 38. II. = τετραρχία I, Hellanic.52 J. III. κατὰ τετράδα διατετάχθαι *in four divisions*, Ascl.*Tact.*3.1.

**τετρᾶς**, ᾶντος, ὁ, *quadrant of a circle*, Vitr.4.2.4, 4.3.4, 10.6.1. II. a coin, Lat. *quadrans*, Hsch.; cf. ἑξᾶς; on the accent cf. Hdn.Gr.1.56.

**τετρά-σειρον** [ᾰ], τό, *quadrangular barn, granary*, Hero *Geep.*197, *Stereom.*1.91 (better -σιρ-): but τετράσειροι, = τετράοροι, Eust.1734.2. -σημος, ον, in Music, *of four time-units*, Aristid.Quint.1.16; πούς Heph.6.1, cf. Quint.*Inst.*9.4.51; ἐπιπλοκή Sch.Heph. p.110 C. -σίριον, τό, *small quadrangular barn*, Hero *Mens.*49. -σκαλμος, ον, *four-oared*, D.S.40.1. -σκελής, ές, (σκέλος) *four-legged, four-footed*, τ. οἰωνός, of a kind of griffin, A.*Pr.*397; χέρσου τ. γονή, i.e. quadrupeds, S.*Fr.*941.10; τ. ὕβρισμα the wanton violence *of Centaurs*, E.*HF*181; τ. κενταυροπληθὴς πόλεμος ib.1272; of bandages, Heliod.ap.Orib.48.23.1, Sor.*Fasc.*41, Gal.18(1).774. ⊛ -σπαστος, dub. l. et dub. sens., ἐλέφαντα ἐπριάμεθα τ. *SIG*247 ii 5 (Delph., iv B.C.); perh. -στάσιον, in reference to the weight or size (cf. διστάσιος, τριστάσιος) of the piece of ivory.

**τετρ-άσσᾰρον**, τό, *coin worth four asses*, i.e. the Roman *sestertius*, Arr.*Epict.*4.5.17.

**τετρασσός**, ή, όν, *in four copies*, ἀποχή *BGU*817.17 (ii A.D.), *PLond.*3.978.6 (iii A.D.), etc.

**τετρά-στάδιος** [στᾰ], ον, *four stades in length*, πορθμός Str.8.6.3: τετραστάδιον, τό, *a length of four stades*, Id.7.7.6. -στάσιον, v. τετράσπαστος. -στάτηρος [στᾰ], ον, *costing four staters*, σωτηρία Ar.*Ec.*413. II. τετραστάτηρον, τό, *a four-stater piece*, Arist.*Fr.*520. -στεγος, ον, *with four stories*, D.S.20.85, J.*AJ*1.3.2; fem. -η, *PRyl.*153.8 (ii A.D.). -στῐχία, ἡ, *four rows*, ὀδόντων Philum.*Ven.*33.1. -στῐχος, ον, *in four rows* or *courses*, LXX *Ex.*28.17, 36.17 (39.10). -στοιχεί, Adv. *in four rows*, Ph.2.152. -στοιχία, ἡ, *four divisions* of the spindle berry, Thphr.*HP*3.18.13. -στοιχος, ον, *in four rows*, κριθαί ib.8.4.2. 2. τ. σῶμα alloy *of four metals*, Olymp.Alch. p.96 B. II. τετράστοιχον, τό, *four classes of* ζῷα, Procl. *in Cra.* p.22 P. -στομος, ον, *four-edged*, πέλεκυς Gal.2.643. ⊛ -στοον, τό, *hall with four rows of columns*, Hero *Stereom.*2.1, *TAM*2(1).179 (Sidyma), *BCH*56.293 (Stobi); ὁ ἐπὶ τοῦ -στόου, = *atriensis*, *Gloss.*:— -στοος, ον, as Adj., ἀγορά Zos.2.31. -στῡλος, ον, *with four pillars in front*, στοαί Phoen.6.11; of a temple, Vitr.3.3.7:— -στῡλον, τό, *colonnade*, *Jahresh.*26 *Beibl.*51 (Ephesus, i A.D.), *POxy.*2138.14 (iii A.D.), *CPHerm.*127$^{v}$*Fr.*1 i 8 (iii A.D.); dub. sens. in *PFlor.*335.2 (iii A.D.). -συλλᾰβέω, *have four syllables*, Eust.1020.21. -σύλλᾰβος, ον, *of four syllables*, Luc.*Gall.*29; πόδες Heph.3.3. Adv. -βως Phryn.*PS* p.16 B., St.Byz. s.v. Τελμησσός. -σχῐδής, ές, only in Adv. -δῶς, = *quadripertito*, Dosith. p.412 K. -σχιστος, ον, *split* or *parted into four*, *Gloss.* -σχοινος, ον, *four* σχοῖνοι (i.e. 240 *stades*) *long*, Str.12.3.35: neut. -σχοινον διέχειν Id.17.1.16. -σωμία, ἡ, *alloy of four metals*, Olymp.Alch. p.96 B. -σωμος, ον, *suitable for holding four bodies*, οἶκος *MAMA*1.235 (Laodicea Combusta).

**τετρᾰτία**, ἡ, dub. sens. in *PFay.*347 (ii A.D.).

**τετράτιος** [ᾰ], α, ον, = τέτρατος, *Supp.Epigr.*1.464.22 (Galatia, iii A.D.).

⊛ **τετρά-τομος** [ᾰ], ον, *cut into four pieces*, ξύλα *IG*1$^{2}$.313.99, 314.109. 2. *in four rolls*, χάρτας -μους *PLond.ined.*2134 (ii A.D.). -τονος, ον, *of four tones*, Cleonid.*Harm.*5, Bacch.*Harm.*47.

⊛ **τέτρᾰτος**, η, ον, poet. for τέταρτος, *fourth*, Pi.*P.*4.47; τὸ τέτρατον *the fourth time*, Il.13.20, 21.177, Hes.*Op.*596, *Sc.*363:—of a bandage, στηθοδεσμίδα, ἥν τινες τέτρατον καλοῦσι Gal.18(1).823 (s.v.l.).

**τετρά-τροπος** ἐνιαυτός, *with four turning-points*, *PMag.Lond.*122.79. -τροχος, ον, *four-wheeled*, *Edict.Diocl.*15.38a, Sch.Od.9.242, Apollon.*Lex.* s.v. τετράκυκλος. -τρῠφος, ον, (θρύπτω) *broken into four pieces*, Hes.*Op.*442; cf. ὀκτάβλωμος.

**τετραυγής**, ές, *four-eyed*, θεός Orph.*Fr.*77: also as epith. of a kind of stone, *shot with four colours*, Id.*L.*230.

**τέτρᾰφα**, v. τρέπω and τρέφω.

**τετρᾰφᾰλαγγ-άρχης**, ου, ὁ, *commander of a* τετραφαλαγγία, *EM* 729.5. -αρχία, ἡ, *his command*, Ael.*Tact.*9.10, Suid. -ία, ἡ, *corps of four phalanxes* or *a phalanx in four divisions*, i.e. of 16,384 men, Plb.12.20.7, Arr.*Tact.*28.6, Ael.*Tact.*36.6, Polyaen.4.7.12.

**τετρᾰφάληρος** [φᾰ], ον, *with four bosses* (φάλαρα, cf. Lat. *phalerae*), κυνέη Il.5.743, 11.41.

**τετράφᾰλος** [ρᾰ], ον, *with four horns*, epith. of κυνέη, κόρυς, Il.12.384, 22.315.

**τετρᾰφάρμᾰκος**, ον, *compounded of four drugs*:—as Subst., τετραφάρμακος, ἡ, *a compound of wax, tallow, pitch, resin*, Meno *Iatr.*14.19, Ph.1.433 (= *Stoic.*2.154), Gal.1.242; also -κον, τό, Id.12.328. II. -κος, ἡ, metaph., of the first four Κύριαι Δόξαι of Epicurus, Phld.*Herc.*1005.4.

**τετράφαται**, -φατο, v. τρέπω.

**τετρά-φορος** [ᾰ], ον, cited by Hdn.Gr.1.234 on account of its anomalous accent; so that its sense must be act., *bearing fourfold*. -φῡλος, ον, *divided into four tribes*, Hdt.5.66, D.H.4.14. -φυον· τετραπάλαιστον, Hsch.

⊛ **τέτρᾰχᾰ**, Adv. *in four parts*, τ. ἑαυτὴν διανείμασα Pl.*Grg.*464c.

**τετράχειρ** [ᾰ], χειρος, ὁ, ἡ, *four-handed*, of Apollo, *IG*5(1).259 (Sparta), Zen.1.54, Lib.*Or.*11.204, Hsch. s.v. κυνακίας.

**τετρᾰχῇ**, Adv. = τέτραχα, X.*HG*5.2.7, Plu.*Ant.*29, Luc.*Nav.*16, etc.

**τετραχθά** [θᾰ], Adv., poet. for τέτραχα, Il.3.363, Od.9.71; cf. διχθά, τριχθά.

**τετρᾰχίζω**, *engage to do for a fourth part* of the profit, Ar.*Fr.*870.

**τετρᾰχίτων** [ῐ], ωνος, ὁ, ἡ, *having four coats*, of arteries, Anon. Lond.28.27.

**τετρᾶχμον**, v. τετράδραχμον.

**τετρᾰχόθεν**, Adv. *on four sides*, Lib.*Or.*11.209, Eust.1572.24.

**τετρᾰχόθι**, Adv. *in four places*, δῆσαι τὸ σπογγίον λίνῳ τ. Hp.*Morb.*2.33.

**τετρᾰ-χοϊαῖος**, α, ον, = τετράχοος, *CIG*3071 (Teos). ⊛ -χοίνῑκος, ον, *holding four* χοίνικες, μέτρον *POxy.*836 (i B.C.), cf. Dsc.1.33, *PFlor.*19.11 (iii A.D.), Eust.1854.12, *AB*242, etc. -χοος, ον, contr. ⊛ -χους, ουν, *holding four* χόες, κάδος Hedyl.ap.Ath.11.473a; μέτρον *PGrenf.*2.24.13 (ii B.C.). II. as Subst., ὁ, or τό, *an amount of four* χόες, *Gp.*9.10.8. -χορδικός, ή, όν, *of* or *belonging to the tetrachord*, Plu.2.1145c. -χορδος, ον, (χορδή) *four-stringed*, ὄργανον Ath.4.183a; λύρα Str.13.2.4. II. Subst. -χορδον, τό, *tetrachord*, i.e. *scale of four notes*, comprising two tones and a half, Arist.*Pr.*922$^{b}$8, *Fr.*47, Plu.2.1021e, etc.: metaph., (sc. παθῶν) Aristo *Stoic.*1.85, cf. Jul.*Caes.*315c.

**τετρᾰχοῦ**, Adv. *in four places*, Choerob. *in Theod.*1.388 H.

**τετραχρον-έω**, *contain four time-units*, A.D.*Synt.*135.22, Charax in *AB*1150. **-ία**, ἡ, *a consisting of four time-units*, Eust.1407.44, Sch.Heph.p.110C. **-ος**, ον, *containing four time-units*, Heph.3.1, A.D.*Pron.*35.11; λέξις Anon.Rhythm.*Oxy.*9 v 11, Eust. 1407.43.

**τετρά-χυτρος** [ᾰ], ον, *made of four pots*, τρυφάλεια Batr.255. **-χωρος**, ον, *with four divisions*, Dsc.1.101. II. τ. μέτρον measure *of four* χῶρα, *PGen.*71.2, al. (iii A.D., cf. *Arch.Pap.*3.401).

**τετρᾰχῶς**, Adv. *in fourfold manner*, Arist.*Cat.*14$^{a}$26, *Metaph.* 983$^{a}$26, Hermog.*Stat.*7.

**τετράων**, ωνος, ὁ, = ὄρνις ποιός, Hsch. (cf. τέταρος, τέτραξ); Lat. *tetrao, guinea-fowl, Meleagris numida*, Suet.*Cal.*22; but also, *black grouse* and *capercaillie, Tetrao tetrix* and *urogallus*, prob. in Plin.*HN* 10.56.

**τετρᾰ-ώνῠμος**, ον, *having four names*, of the Moon-goddess, *PMag.Par.*1.2560. **-ωτος**, ον, *with four ears*, Zen.1.54; *with four handles*, ποτήριον Simarist.ap.Ath.11.483a.

**τετρεμαίνω**, redupl. form of τρέμω, τετρεμαίνειν Ἀττικῶς, τρέμειν Ἑλληνικῶς Moer.p.365 P.; cf. τετραμαίνω.

**τέτρημαι**, v. τετραίνω.

**τετρ-ήμερος**, ον, *of four days*: μετὰ τὴν τ. (sc. ἡμέραν) after *the fourth day*, Arist.*Pol.*1286$^{a}$13, cf. *PHib.*1.115.22 (iii B.C.); **τεθρήμερον** *for four days*, *AP*15.40.5 (Cometas): cf. τετραήμερος. **-ήρης** (sc. ναῦς), ἡ, *quadrireme*, Arist.*Fr.*600, Plb.1.47.5 (a model of one, *Inscr.Délos* 1432 *Ab*ii 55 (ii B.C.)); acc. τετρήρην *IG*2$^{2}$.1628.49, al.; but -ήρη ib.1629.272, *Inscr.Délos* l. c., Plb.1.47.7; gen. -ήρου *IG*2$^{2}$. 1629.705; but -ήρους ib.628, al.; also Dor. -ήρευς *Supp.Epigr.*4. 178.10 (Cedreae, ii B.C.):—hence **-ηρικὰ** πλοῖα, = τετρήρεις, Plb.2. 10.5; and **-ηρῐτικός**, *IG*2$^{2}$.1629.685.

**τέτρηχα**, v. ταράσσω III.

**τετρίγει, τετρῑγυῖα, τετρῑγῶτας**, v. τρίζω.

**τέτριξ**, ιγος, ἡ, a bird, also called οὔραξ by the Athenians, difft. from τέτραξ and τετράων, perh. *pipit*, Ital. *tiiro*, Arist.*HA*559$^{a}$ 2,12. II. *tetrix*, = *tristis*, Gloss.

**τετρόγυος**, v. τετράγυος.

**τετρόμμᾰτος**, ον, *four-eyed*, ἀριθμός, of the τετράς, Herm. *in Phdr.* p.107 A.

**τέτρομος**, ὁ, = τρόμος, Hp.ap.Gal.19.146, A.D.*Pron.*58.12, Hdn. Gr.2.190, Hsch.; cf. τέτραμος.

**τετρ-όργυιος**, ον, *of four fathoms*, *AP*6.223 (Antip.): cf. τετρώρυγος. **-όροφος**, v. τετρώροφος. **-ούγκιον**, τό, *coin of four unciae*, i.e. *triens*, *Dacia* 3/4.607 (Tomi).

**τέτροφα**, v. τρέπω, τρέφω.

**τετρωβολ-ιαῖος**, α, ον, = τετρώβολος, Sch.Ar.*Pax* 253, Suid. s.v. τετρώβολον. **-ίζω**, *receive four obols*, i.e. *to be a soldier* (v. sq. II), Theopomp.Com.55. ⊕ **-ος**, ον, *of four obols*, τόκος *IG*12(5).860.29 (Tenos). II. as Subst. **τετρώβολον**, τό, *four-obol piece*, τετρωβόλου τοῦτ' ἔστιν (as Kuster for τετρώβολον) Ar.*Pax* 254, cf. Plb. 34.8.8, *SIG*982.15 (Pergam., ii B.C.), etc.; it was a soldier's daily pay, hence τετρωβόλου βίος a *soldier's* life, Paus.Gr.*Fr.*307; so in masc. -ώβολος, of a common soldier, Men.*Pk.*203. 2. τετρώβολον, τό, *weight of four obols*, Dsc.4.159, Gal.12.628, etc.

**τετρῳδέομαι**, Pass., *to be of the fourth series* (cf. δευτερῳδέομαι), Iamb. *in Nic.*p.88 P.

**τετρώκοντα, τετρωκοστός**, v. τεσσαράκοντα, τεσσαρακοστός.

**τετρωκοντάλῑτρος** [ᾰ], ον, *weighing forty* λίτραι, πέδαι Dinol.4 (τετταρακ- codd., corr. Ahrens).

**τετρωκοστομόριον**, τό, Dor., *the fortieth part*, Archim.*Aren.*2.4, al.

**τετρώριστος**, ον, = τετράορος, S.*Fr.*958 codd.Str. (leg. τετραόρῳ).

**τέτρωρον**, τό, (ὅρος) *plot of ground marked out by four boundaries*, *Tab.Heracl.*1.90,159: also **τέτρωρος**, ὁ, *BGU*1060.18 (i B.C.).

**τέτρωρος**, ον, contr. for τετράορος (q. v.).

**τετρ-ώροφος**, ον, *of four stories*, Hdt.1.180 (v.l. for -οροφ-), Ph.2. 143, App.*Pun.*95. **-ώρῠγος**, ον, = τετρόργυιος, X.*Cyn.*2.5; cf. δι-, δεκ-ώρυγος.

**τέττᾰ**, expld. as ἑταίρου πρὸς ἑταῖρον γενικὴ προσφώνησις (Apollon. *Lex.*), or as a friendly or respectful address of youths to their elders (Hsch., Suid., Eust.490.36), or said to be untranslatable (ib.37), τέττα, σιωπῇ ἧσο Il.4.412.

**τετταράκοντα, τέτταρες**, etc., v. τεσσαρ-.

**τεττίγιον** [ῑγ], τό, *small* τέττιξ (v. τέττιξ I. 2), or more prob. *a coin stamped with a* τέττιξ, τεττίγια χρυσᾶ δύο *IG*11(2).158 *A* 5, cf. 36 (Delos, iii B.C.): in literal sense, Hsch. s.v. κερκώπη.

**τεττῑγομήτρα**, ἡ, *subterranean larva* or *nymph of the* τέττιξ, Arist. *HA*556$^{b}$7.

**τεττῑγόνιον**, τό, *a small and voiceless kind of* τέττιξ, a *leaf-hopper* or *cicadelle*, Arist.*HA*532$^{b}$17; fem. pl. *tettigoniae*, Plin.*HN*11.92; prob. everywhere f.l. for τιτιγόνιον (q. v.).

**τεττῑγότης**, ητος, ἡ, *cicala-hood*, Anon. *in Cat.*51.4, Simp. *in Cat.* 270.26.

**τεττῑγο-φόρας**, ου, ὁ, (φέρω) *wearing a* τέττιξ, as the Athenians were called, because in early times *they wore golden* τέττιγες, as a token that they were αὐτόχθονες (cf. τέττιξ I. 2, τεττιγομήτρα), Ar.*Eq.* 1331 (anap.): also **-φόρος**, ον, Eust.395.34: hence **-φορία**, ἡ, Tz. *H.*1.233.

**τεττῑγώδης**, ες, *like a* τέττιξ, Luc.*Bacch.*7.

**τεττίζω**, part. -οντας, read by Zenod. in Il.2.314, acc. to Eust. 490.41; cf. τιτίζω.

**τέττιξ**, ῑγος (but ῐκος Ar. and Theoc. acc. to Hdn.Gr.ap.Choerob. *in Theod.*1.292 H.), ὁ, *cicala*, *Cicada plebeia* or allied species, a winged insect fond of basking on trees, when the male makes a chirping or clicking noise by means of certain drums or 'tymbals' underneath the wings, whence the joke in Xenarch.14, εἶτ'. . οἱ τέττιγες οὐκ εὐδαίμονες, ὧν ταῖς γυναιξὶν οὐδ' ὁτιοῦν φωνῆς ἔνι; prov., τέττιγος ἐδράξω πτεροῦ Archil.143 (v. συλλαμβάνω II. 1). This noise is freq. used as a simile for sweet sounds, Il.3.151, Hes.*Op.*582, *Sc.*393, Simon.173, 174, etc.; and Plato calls them οἱ Μουσῶν προφῆται, *Phdr.*262d; but they also became a prov. for garrulity, λαλεῖν τέττιξ Aristopho10.7: τ. πολλοὶ γινόμενοι νοσῶδες τὸ ἔτος σημαίνουσι Thphr.*Sign.*54. They were thought to sing continually without food or drink, Ar.*Nu.* 1360, Pl.*Phdr.*259c; or on a diet of air and dew, Arist.*HA*532$^{b}$ 13, Theoc.4.16, *AP*6.120 (Leon.), *Anacreont.*32, Plu.2.660f. The Greeks ate τέττιγες to whet the appetite, Ath.4.133b, cf. Ar.*Fr.*51, 569.4, Alex.162.13 (anap.), Anaxandr.41.59 (anap., unless here the τέττιξ ἐνάλιος is meant, v. infr. II); and as a medical remedy, Dsc. 2.51, Orib.*Fr.*64. 2. gold ornament worn in the hair (cf. χρύσειαι δὲ κόρυμβαι ἐπ' αὐτῶν τέττιγες ὥς Asius *Fr.Ep.*13.5), esp. in early Attica, Th.1.6, Heraclid.Pont.ap.Ath.12.512c; ἀρχαῖα. . καὶ τεττίγων ἀνάμεστα, i.e. full of *old-fashioned notions*, Ar.*Nu.*984 (anap.), v. Sch.(980) and cf. τεττιγοφόρας; γυνὴ. . ἔχει τ. ἐπιχρύσους, in a list of votive offerings at Samos, *Michel* 832.51 (iv B.C.). 3. Com. name for *a foreign cook*, Ath.14.659a, Hsch., cf. Poll.4.148,150. 4. Ἀκάνθιος τ., prov. of a silent person, Zen.1.51, St.Byz. s.v. Ἄκανθος. II. τ. ἐνάλιος a kind of *lobster*, *Arctos ursus*, Ael.*NA*13. 26. III. part of the ear, τοῦ λοβοῦ τὸ περὶ τῇ κυψέλῃ Poll.2.86.

**τέτυγμαι, τετῠκεῖν**, v. τεύχω.

**τετῡφωμένως**, Adv., (τυφόω) *stupidly*, D.23.137.

**τετύχηκα**, v. τυγχάνω.

**τετώμενοι**· ὑστερούμενοι, ἐνδεῶς ἔχοντες, Hsch. (Cf. τητάομαι.)

**τεῦ**, Dor. gen. of σύ (q. v.). II. **τεῦ**, Ion., Ep., and Dor. gen. of τίς; *who?*, and **τευ** enclit., gen. of τις, *some one*, v. τίς, τις.

⊕ **τεῦγμα**, ατος, τό, *that which is made, a work*, Dosiad.*Ara* 9.

**τευθαλλίς**, ίδος, ἡ, = πολύγονον ἄρρεν, Dsc.4.4 (dub. l.).

**τευθενί**, v. ἐμμεντευθενί.

**τευθίδιον**, τό, Dim. of τευθίς, Pherecr.130.10, Ephipp.15.4, Eub. 110. [-ῐδ- Ephipp. l. c., -ῑδ- Eub. l. c., in almost identical passages, so that Eub. should perh. be emended from Ephipp.]

**τευθῐδώδης**, ες, *like a* τευθίς, Ath.7.318f.

**τευθίς**, ίδος, ἡ, *calamary* or *squid*, *Loligo vulgaris*, Semon.15, Ar.*Ach.*1156, *Eq.*929,934, Thphr.*Sign.*40, Gal.6.769, etc.; cf. τεῦθος:—in Philox.2.13, **τευθιάς**, άδος, ἡ. II. name of some sort of *pastry*, Iatrocl.ap.Ath.7.326e. [τευθῑς, ῑδος Ar. ll. cc., but also ῐδος, Ath.3.106c (s. v. l.).]

**τεῦθος**, ὁ, *calamary* or *squid*, of a larger kind than the τευθίς, perh. *Todarodes sagittatus*, Arist.*HA*490$^{b}$13, 524$^{a}$25, *Fr.*340.

**τευθός**, ὁ, a gregarious fish, Arist.*HA*610$^{b}$6 (s. v. l.).

**τεύθριον**, τό, = πόλιον, Dsc.3.110. 2. = ἐρυθρόδανον, ib.143.

**τεύκριον**, τό, *tree-germander*, *Teucrium flavum*, Dsc.3.97. II. = χαμαίρωψ, ib.98.

**τεύκριος**, ὁ, = σκολοπένδριον, Ps.-Dsc.3.134.

**τευκ-τήρ**, ῆρος, ὁ, *maker*, Hsch., Phot., Suid. **-τικός**, ή, όν, *able to attain to*, ἀγαθοῦ Arist.*EN*1142$^{b}$22; τῶν τελῶν Phld.*Rh.*1. 53 S.: Comp. -ώτερος ib.145 S. **-τός**, ή, όν, = τυκτός, Antiph. 52.2 (troch.), Hsch., Suid. **-τωρ**, ορος, ὁ, = τευκτήρ, Man.4.422: pl., Id.2.333.

⊕ **τευμάομαι**, Ep. aor. τευμήσατο *fashioned*, ἄντρον Antim.3: pres. only in Hsch. (Perh. cf. Avest. *šyaoman*- 'work'.)

**τεῦξις**, εως, ἡ, *making*, Hsch. II. (τυγχάνω) *attainment, acquisition*, opp. ἔφεσις, Plu.2.1071e, cf. Arr.*Epict.*2.5.8, S.E.*M.*11. 82, Plot.1.5.2, 6.8.5. 2. = ἔντευξις I, *AP*15.25.23 (Besant.).

**τεῦς**, Boeot. and Dor. gen. of σύ (q. v.).

**τευτ-άζω**, pf. τετεύτακα Pl.*R.*521e:—τ. περί τι *to be employed upon, engaged in, concerned with* a thing, Pl. l. c., *Phlb.*56e, *Ti.*90b: abs., *to be busy, bustling*, Telecl.36, Pl.Com.89 (anap.): c. inf., *bid* or *order* one *repeatedly* to do a thing, Pherecr.184 (anap.):- also Med., Phryn.Com.36, Luc.*Lex.*21, cj. in Them.*Or.*13.161c. **-ασμός**, ὁ, = στραγγεία, Hsch. **-άσσω**, = τευτάζω, Orac. in *Ath.Mitt.*25.399 (Aezani).

**τευτλίον**, τό, Dim. (in form) of τεῦτλον (q. v.), Ar.*Ra.*942, *Fr.*130, Thphr.*HP*7.2.6, *CP*2.5.3, Diocl.*Fr.*140:—**σευτλίον** in Diph.Siph.ap. Ath.9.371a, *PCair.Zen.*292.23, al. (iii B.C.), *PPetr.*3 p.3-8 (iii B.C.).

**τευτλίς**, ίδος, ἡ, = τεῦτλον, Thphr.*HP*7.7.2; τεῦτλα τευτλίδας καλῶν Diph.47 (prob. σευτλίδας).

**τευτλόεις**, εσσα, εν, contr. οῦς, οῦσσα, οῦν, *of* or *full of beet*: hence the island Τευτλοῦσσα, *Beet-island*, Th.8.42.

**τεῦτλον**, τό, Ion. and later Att. **σεῦτλον**, *beet*, *Beta maritima*, Batr.162, Hp.*Art.*63, Thphr.*HP*1.6.6, freq. in Com.; τέμαχος ἐν τεύτλου. . κρύπτεται στεγάσμασιν Antiph.181 (troch.); τεύτλῳ περὶ σῶμα καλυπτὰ ἔγχελυς Eub.35 (lyr.): more freq. in pl., τεύτλοισί τ' ἐγχέλεια συγκεκαλυμμένα Pherecr.108.12, cf. Ar.*Pax* 1014 (lyr.); ἐγχέλεις τεῦτλ' ἀμπεχόμεναι Eub.37, cf. 93:—the later Com. ridicule the use of the Ion. forms, ἐὰν μὲν τευτλίον [εἴπῃ], παρείδομεν· ἐὰν δὲ σεῦτλον, ἀσμένως ἠκούσαμεν,—ὡς οὐ τὸ σεῦτλον ταὐτὸν ὂν τῷ τευτλίῳ Alex.142.5; ἐπὰν δὲ καλέσῃ. . τὸ τευτλίον. . σεῦτλα Euphro 3;

τεῦτλα τευτλίδας (prob. σευτλ–) καλῶν Diph.47: the form τεῦτλον is used by Diocl.*Fr.*119, Gal.6.298, al.; σεῦτλον in *PPetr.*3p.326 (iii B.C.), *PCair.Zen.*232ᵛ (iii B.C.), *BGU*1118.17 (i B.C.), *PLond.*3.964.15 (iii A.D.), *Edict.Diocl.*6.14, *Gp.*8.33, al.; [σεῦ`τλος, τό, prob. in Bell-Nock-Thompson *Magical Texts from a Bilingual Papyrus* p.19 (iii/iv A.D.).

**τευτλόρριζον**, τό, *beetroot*, *Gp.*12.1.2.

**τευτλοφᾰκῆ**, ἡ, *dish of beet mixed with lentils*, Heraclid.Tar.ap. Gal.6.477,529.

**τευχεσφόρος**, ον, *wearing armour*, ἀνήρ, λαός, A.*Ch.*627 (lyr.), E.*Supp.*654.

*τευχέω, v. τετευχῆσθαι.

**τευχήεις**, εσσα, εν, *armed*, καρήατα Opp.*C.*3.4.

**τεύχ-ημα**, ατος, τό, *fabric*, A.*Fr.*375 codd.Sch.E. (τέχνημα Nauck). **–ήρης**, ες, *armed*, Orph.*A.*527. **–ηστήρ**, ῆρος, ὁ, (τεῦχος) *armed man*, *warrior*, ἄνδρες τ. A.*Pers.*902 (lyr.); also **–ηστής**, οῦ, ὁ, ἀνήρ Id.*Th.*644, cf. Call.*Jov.*77, A.R.3.415, Tryph.534.

**τευχῖτις**, ιδος, ἡ, = σχοῖνος Ἀραβική, Dsc.1.17, Plin.*HN*21.120.

**τευχοπλάστις**, ιδος, ἡ, *making vessels*, παρθένος Lyc.1379.

⊛ **τεῦχος**, εος, τό, (τεύχω) prop. *tool*, *implement*:—but mostly in pl. τεύχεα, I. *implements of war*, *armour*, *arms*, freq. in Ep.; more precisely, ἀρήϊα τεύχεα, πολεμήϊα τ., Il.14.381, 7.193; χρύσεια, χαλκήρεα, 10.439, 15.544; ποικίλα, αἰόλα παμφανόωντα, μαρμαίροντα, 3.327, 5.295, 18.617; always of a warrior's *whole armour*, *harness*, ἀρήϊα τεύχεα δύω 6.340, cf. 7.193, al.; ἐς τεύχε' ἔδυνον Od.24.498; κατὰ τεύχε' ἔδυν Il.4.222, cf. 6.504, al.; Πάτροκλον περὶ τεύχεα ἕσσε 18.451; ἀπέδυσε, ἐξεδύοντο, 4.532, 3.114, cf. 13.182, al.; also χαλκήρεα τεύχε' ἀπ' ὤμων συλήσειν 15.544; Ἕκτορι δ' ἥρμοσε τεύχε' ἐπὶ χροΐ 17.210: Trag. τεύχη A.*Myrm.* in *PSI*11.1211.17, S.*Aj.*572,577, E.*Andr.*617, etc.; uncontr. τεύχεα S.*Ph.*398 (lyr.). 2. pl. also, *the gear* of a ship, oars and the like, ἐγκοσμεῖτε τὰ τ. νηΐ μελαίνῃ Od.15.218; τ. δέ σφ' ἀπένεικαν 16.326. II. in Trag. (rarely in Prose, v. infr.) a *vessel* of any kind, e.g. *bathing-tub*, A.*Ag.*1128 (lyr., Blomf. κύτει, metri gr.); *cinerary urn*, τεύχη καὶ σποδός ib.435 (lyr.), cf. S.*El.*1114,1120, *Riv.Fil.*57.379 (Crete); *balloting-urn*, A.*Ag.*815, *Eu.*742; *vase for libations*, Id.*Ch.*99, E.*IT*168 (lyr.); *vase* or *ewer* for water, Id.*Hec.*609, *Andr.*167, Diocl.*Fr.*129; *cup*, E.*Ion* 1184; *amphora*, A.*Fr.*108; *scent-pot*, ib.180.5 (pl.); *matula*, S.*Fr.*565; *pot* or *jar*, X.*An.*5.4.28; ξύλινα τ. *chests*, ib.7.5.14; ἀλφίτων τ. a meal-*barrel*, Id.*HG*1.7.11; *bee-hive*, Arist.*HA*625ᵃ26; *capsule* of a poppy, Nic.*Fr.*74.52. III. Medic., of the *vessels* of the body, Hp.*Loc.Hom.*1.24; also, *the human frame*, *body*, as holding the intestines, Id.*Epid.*6.2.1, Arist.*Phgn.*810ᵇ19; τεῦχος νεοσσῶν λευκόν an egg, E.*Hel.*258. IV. *case* for holding papyrus rolls, α' τεύχους, α' τόμου, κολλήματος ρδ' *PRyl.*220.78 (ii A.D.); *roll* of writing-material, πεποίηται διπλῆν τὴν.. ἀναγραφὴν ἐν βυβλίνοις καὶ δερματίνοις τεύχεσιν *Inscr.Prien.*114.30, cf. 11 (i B.C.); κελεύσας εἰς τάξιν ἀποδοῦναι τὰ τ. Aristeas 179; καθὼς ἀνεγνώσθη τὰ τ. Id.310, cf. Sm.*Is.*8.1 (where LXX has τόμος); βίβλων.. ἐν τεύχεϊ τῷδε πεντάς *AP*9.239 (Crin.); τ. βιβλειδίων *BGU*970.4 (ii A.D.); τ. συγκολλησίμων βιβλειδίων *POxy.*2131.4 (iii A.D.); τ. = *volumen*, *Gloss.*: hence πεντάτευχος, ὀκτάτευχος. V. *masonry*, *fabric*, ἀνεκτίσθη τὸ τ. τοῦτο *Sammelb.*7439.7 (vi A.D.).

**τευχοφόρος**, ον, *bearing arms*, *armed*, E.*Rh.*3 (anap.).

**τεῦχρος**· ἀδελφὸς νόθος, Hsch. (fort. Τεῦκρος).

⊛ **τεύχω**, Il.1.110, S.*Tr.*756, etc.: fut. τεύξω Od.1.277: aor. ἔτευξα Il.14.338, etc.; Ep. τεῦξα 18.609, Od.8.276: pf. τέτευχα *AP*6.40 (Maced.), 9.202 (Leo Phil.), intr. once in Hom. (v. infr. I.3); in correct writers τέτευχα is the pf. of τυγχάνω (for in Il.13.346 ἡρώεσσι τετεύχατον or τετεύχετον is f.l. for ἐτεύχετον):—Med., fut. τεύξομαι in act. sense, Il.19.208 (dub. l. here and in A.*Ag.*1230), but prob. pass. in Il.5.653 (elsewh. fut. of τυγχάνω): aor. inf. τεύξασθαι *h.Ap.*76,221: redupl. aor. τετῠκεῖν, -έσθαι, v. infr. I.1:—Pass., 3 fut. τετεύξομαι Il.21.322,585: aor. ἐτύχθην 4.470, A.*Eu.*353 (lyr.); ἐτεύχθην Hp.*Decent.*17 (v.l.), *AP*6.207 (Arch.), etc. (but this belongs equally to τυγχάνω): pf. τέτυγμαι, plpf. ἐτετύγμην, freq. in Hom., etc., v. infr.; 3 pl. τετεύχαται, ἐτετεύχατο, τετεύχατο, Il.13.22, 11.808, 18.574: (v. τυγχάνω):—*make ready*, *make*, freq. in Ep. and Lyr.; also in A., but rare in S. and E. (once in Com., Eub.43); never in Prose. I. *produce by work* or *art*; esp. of material things, *make*, *build*, δώματα, θάλαμον, νηόν, etc., Il.6.314, 14.166, Od.12.347, etc.; of a worker in metal, τὸ μὲν [σκῆπτρον] Ἥφαιστος κάμε τεύχων Il.2.101; θώρηκα, τὸν Ἥφαιστος κάμε τεύχων 8.195; τρίποδας.. ἔτευχεν [Ἥφαιστος] 18.373; τ. δόλον, of the net which Hephaestus *wrought*, Od.8.276; τέκτονος υἱόν,.. ὃς χερσὶν ἐπίστατο δαίδαλα πάντα τεύχειν Il.5.61; of women's handiwork, εἵματα τ. Od.7.235; of a cook, δεῖπνον τετυκεῖν *dress* or *prepare* a meal, 15.77,94 (so in Med., *prepare* a meal or *have it prepared*, of those who are to eat it, 20.390; τετύκοντό τε δαῖτα Il.1.467, 2.430; τεύχοντο δαῖτα Od.10.182; τεύξεσθαι δόρπον Il.19.208; δόρπον τετύκοντο Od.12.307, cf. 283, al. (the Ep. aor. τετυκεῖν, τετυκέσθαι is used in this sense only)); also τεῦχε κυκειῶ Il.11.624; ἄλφιτα τεύχουσαι *preparing* meal (by grinding the grain), Od.20.108; αὐτὰρ ὁ εἴδωλον τεῦξ' *formed*, *created* it, Il.5.449: so also in Pi. and A., θεὸς ὁ τὰ πάντα τεύχων βροτοῖς Pi.*Fr.*141, cf. *O.*1.30; δαῖτ'.. ἔτευξεν A.*Ag.*731 (lyr.); φάρμακον τεύχουσα ib.1261; ὦ γαῖα κεραμί, τίς σε Θηρικλῆς ποτε ἔτευξε; Eub. l.c.:—Pass., δώματα τετεύχαται Il.13.22; ἐν βήσσῃσι τετυγμένα δώματα Od.10.210,252, cf. 21.215; θεῶν ἐτετεύχατο βωμοί Il.11.808; βωμὸς.. τέτυκτο Od.17.210; νηὸς γε τέτυκτο Il.5.446; οἱ.. σῆμα τετεύξεται for him a tomb *shall be built*, 21.322; εἵματα.. τετυγμένα χερσὶ γυναικῶν 22.511; ἱμάντα.., ᾧ ἔνι πάντα τετεύχαται in which all *are wrought*, *are to be found*, 14.220: τετύχθαι τινός to *be made of*.., βόες χρυσοῖο τετεύχατο κασσιτέρου τε 18.574; περόνη χρυσοῖο τέτυκτο Od.19.226, cf. Hes.*Sc.*208: c. dat. rei, τετυγμένα δώματα.. ξεστοῖσιν λάεσσι *built with* or *of*.., Od.10.210; αἱ μὲν γὰρ [πύλαι] κεράεσσι τετεύχαται, αἱ δ' ἐλέφαντι 19.563; but δόμον.. αἰθούσῃσι τετυγμένον *built* or *furnished with*.., Il.6.243. 2. pf. part. τετυγμένος freq. has the sense of an Adj., = τυκτός, *well-made*, *well-wrought*, τεῖχος, βωμὸς τετ., Il.14.66, Od.22.335, al.; σάκος, δέπας, κρητήρ, Il.14.9, 16.225, 23.741, al.; ἄγγεα Od.9.223; δῶρα 16.185; ἀγρός *wrought*, *tilled*, 24.206: metaph., νόος ἐν στήθεσσι τετυγμένος a *ready*, *constant* mind, 20.366. 3. pf. part. Act. occurs once in pass. sense, ῥινοῖο τετευχώς *made of* hide, 12.423. II. of natural phenomena, actions, events, etc., *cause*, *bring to pass*, τ. ὄμβρον ἠὲ χάλαζαν, of Zeus, Il.10.6; αἱ δὲ [πύλαι] πετασθεῖσαι τεῦξαν φάος 21.538; παλίωξιν τ. 15.70, cf. Hes.*Sc.*154 (Pass.); βοὴν διὰ ἄστεος Od.10.118; γέλω δ' ἑτάροισιν ἔτευχε 18.350; γάμον τ. 1.277; τ. πομπήν 10.18, cf. Pi.*P.*4.164; τ. πόλεμον καὶ φύλοπιν Od.24.476; θάνατόν τινι 20.11; ἄλγεα, κήδεά τινι, *work* one woe, Il.1.110, Od.1.244; ἐν δ' ἄρα οἱ στήθεσσι.. αἱμυλίους τε λόγους καὶ ἐπίκλοπον ἦθος τεῦξε Hes.*Op.*79, cf. 265, *Th.*570; τ. ξείνια Pi.*P.*4.129; τ. μέλος ib.12.19; τ. γέρας, τιμάν τινι, *get* him honour, Id.*I.*1.14,67; τ. κακά A.*Eu.*125; τ. στάσιν ἐν ἀλλήλαισι, i.e. to quarrel, Id.*Pers.*189; τ. φόβον Id.*Pr.*1090 (anap.); σφαγάς S.*Tr.*756; τάφον E.*Rh.*959; φίλοις ἔριν Id.*Andr.*644; κρυπτὸν δόλον Call. in *PSI*11.1218*a*6:—Pass., *to be caused*, and so, *arise*, *occur*, ἔργον ἐτύχθη ἀργαλέον Il.4.470, cf. 2.320; οὐ γὰρ ἔτ' ἀνσχετὰ ἔργα τετεύχαται Od.2.63, cf. Il.14.53, 22.450; τὰ δ' οὐ ἴσαν, ὡς ἐτέτυκτο Od.4.772, cf. 392; ἡμῖν νεῖκος ἐτύχθη Il.11.671; πὰρ Διὸς ἀθανάτοισι χόλος καὶ μῆνις ἐτύχθη 15.122; Ἀργείοισι.. νόστος ἐτύχθη 2.155; ὅμαδος ἐτ. 12.471, etc.; τετεύξεται αἰπὺς ὄλεθρος ib.345, cf. 5.653; εἰ δή μοι ὁμοίη μοῖρα τέτυκται *is ordained*, 18.120; ὁπποτέρῳ θάνατος καὶ μοῖρα τέτυκται 3.101; φόνος υἱι τέτ. Od.4.771; φίλοισι δὲ κήδεα.. τετεύχαται 14.138, cf. Il.21.585; ἐν βροτοῖς γέρων λόγος τέτυκται *there exists*, A.*Ag.*751 (lyr.), cf. E.*El.*457 (lyr.). III. c. acc. pers., *make* so and so, ὄφρα μιν.. ἄγνωστον τεύξειεν Od.13.191, cf. 397; τ. τινὰ ἰσοδαίμονα, μέγαν, εὐδαίμονα, Pi.*N.*4.84, A.*Eu.*668, E.*Heracl.*614 (lyr.): of things, οὐδέ κεν ἄλλως οὐδὲ θεὸς τεύξειε Od.8.177: c. dupl. acc., ὦ πούς, τί σε.. τεύξω; what *shall I make of* thee? S.*Ph.*1189 (lyr.):—hence in pf. and plpf. Pass. simply for γίγνεσθαι or εἶναι, Ζεὺς ταμίης πολέμοιο τέτυκται Il.4.84; [Ὠκεανὸς] γένεσις πάντεσσι τέτ. 14.246; ὅς ῥα Σκαμάνδρου ἀρητὴρ ἐτέτυκτο 5.78, cf. 16.605; οὐ μὲν γάρ τι καταθνητός γ' ἐτ. 5.402, cf. 16.622; νόον ἐν πρώτοισι.. ἐτ. *was* among the first in mind, 15.643; γυναικὸς ἄρ' ἀντὶ τέτυξο *thou wast* like a woman, 8.163; ἀντὶ κασιγνήτου ξεῖνός θ' ἱκέτης τε τέτυκται Od.8.546; Νύμφαις, ταῖς Δίος ἐξ αἰγιόχω φαῖσι τετυγμέναις Alc.85: also of things, τόδε σῆμα τετύχθω *let* this *be* the sign, Od.21.231, cf. Il.22.30: in aor. 1, πέπλων ἄκληρος ἐτύχθην A.*Eu.*353 (lyr.), cf. *Supp.*87 (lyr.).

⊛ **τέφρ-α**, Ep. and Ion. **τέφρη**, ἡ, *ashes*, as of the funeral pile, Il.23.251; νεκταρέῳ δὲ χιτῶνι μέλαιν' ἀμφίζανε τέφρη 18.25; ὁ ἀὴρ ὁ ἐγκατακλειόμενος ἐν ταῖς θήκαις (coffins).. διαλύει πάντ' εἰς τ. Thphr. *Ign.*47; τ. πηγνυμένη νιφετὸν [σημαίνει] Id.*Sign.*42; κηπὶ τὴν τέφρην οἰχνεῖ (sc. τὸ πῦρ) Call. in *PSI*11.1216.35; καταπάσας τέφραν, ἐμπάσαι τῆς τέφρας, Ar.*Nu.*177, Pl.*Ly.*210a; δόξαι τινὰ ψάμμον ἢ τ. ἐσθίειν Gal.6.782; ἐκκρίνεσθαι τὴν οἷον τ. τῶν ὑπεροπτηθέντων χυμῶν Id.18(2).279; τέφρᾳ τιλθῆναι, prob. *lime*, Ar.*Nu.*1083 (τίτανος is a form of τ. acc. to Gal.12.140); ἡ τ. ἡ Φρυγία was used for eye-disease, Arist.*Mir.*834ᵇ30 (cf. Pl. l.c.); so τ. κληματίνη Dsc.5.117: τῆς τ. πλυθείσης ἡ κονία (cf. κονία II) γίνεται Gal.12.222, cf. Thphr.*HP*5.9.5: prov., ὅρκους.. εἰς τέφραν γράφειν Philonid.7: *tefre*, = *nugacitas*, *Gloss.* (With τεφ– [from θεφ–] cf. Skt. *dáhati*, Lith. *degù* 'burn', Lat. *favilla*, Gr. θέπτανος.) **–αῖος**, α, ον, = τεφρός, Ael.*NA*6.38. **–ᾰκός**, ή, όν, *made from ashes*, of eye-salves, τὰ σποδιακὰ καὶ τὰ τ. καλούμενα Aët.7.105 (s. v.l.). ⊛ **–άς**, άδος, ἡ, *ash-coloured*, a kind of τέττιξ, Ael.*NA*10.44. **–ήεις**, εσσα, εν, poet. for τεφρός, Nonn.*D.*6.228. **–ίζω**, *to be ash-coloured*, Dsc.1.14, Aret.*SD*1.9. II. trans., ἐτέφρισεν· ἐνέπρησεν, Hsch. **–ῖνος**, η, ον, = τεφρός, χροιή Hp.*Anat.*1.

**τεφροειδής**, ές, *like ashes*, *ash-coloured*, Dsc.4.109, Aret.*SD*1.14.

**τεφρ-ός**, ά, όν, *ash-coloured*, Arist.*HA*519ᵃ2; χρῶμα ib.6.0ᵃ28; κόρση Herod.7.71; τεφρὴ γέρανος Babr.65.1, cf. *PSI*6.569.6 (iii B.C.): as Subst., –ον, τό, *ash-coloured ointment*, esp. for the eyes (cf. τέφρα), Cels.6.6.7, Aët.7.10,23. **–όω**, *burn to ashes*, Lyc.227; πόλεις 2 *Ep.Pet.*2.6:—Med., Nic.*Al.*534:—Pass., *to be burnt to ashes*, Thphr. *Ign.*20, *AP*5.187 (Leon.); *to be covered with ashes*, D.C.66.21. **–ώδης**, ες, *like ashes*, Thphr.*Ign.*39, Babr.85.14, Plu.*Them.*8; τ. γῆ Str.16.2.44. **–ωσις**, εως, ἡ, *a burning to ashes*, Sch.Ar.*Nu.*771, Dsc.1.86.

⊛ **τεχν-άζω**, *employ art*, *contrive*, ὅπως.. Arist.*EN*1140ᵃ11, cf. *MM* 1197ᵃ13. II. *use art* or *cunning*, *deal subtly*, *use subterfuges*, Hdt.3.130, 6.1; τί ταῦτα στρέφει τεχνάζεις τε; Ar.*Ach.*385, cf. *Ra.*957; τ. τε καὶ ψεύδεσθαι Pl.*Hp.Mi.*371d, cf. *Lg.*879a, etc.; τοὺς λαγὼς θηρῶντες πολλὰ τεχνάζουσιν X.*Mem.*3.11.7; of the hare, τ. τῇ βαδίσει Id.*Cyn.*8.3: c. acc. cogn., τ. ἀπάτην *use art* so as to deceive, Plu.*Tim.*10: c. inf., *contrive cunningly that*.., Arist.*Pol.*1259ᵃ32, Plu.*Alc.*19. 2. Med., aor. ἐτεχνασάμην, in same sense, Hdt.2.121.α', Aen.Tact.4.1; τεχνάζεσθαι ὅπως.. Plu.*Caes.*43. 3. Pass., in pf. part., ἅμαξαι τετεχνασμέναι ὥσπερ οἰκήματα *artificially contrived*, Hp.*Aër.*18; ἐπίνοια τετεχν. *cunningly devised*, Ps.-Luc.*Philopatr.*26:—τεχνήσασθαι τὸ μετὰ τέχνης τι κατασκευάσαι, τεχνάσασθαι δὲ τὸ κακουργῆσαι Ps.-Hdn.Gr.post Moer.p.477 P. **-άομαι,** fut. -ήσομαι: aor. ἐτεχνησάμην, Ep. τεχν-: pf. τετέχνημαι, Ion. 3 pl. τετεχνέαται cj. in Hp.*VM*22:—*make by art, execute skilfully*, Od.5.259, 11.613 (for μὴ ..μηδ', cf. οὐ c); πολλὰ τ. *practise* many *arts*, X.*Cyr*.8.2.5. 2. also as Pass., *to be made by art*, ὅ τι καλὸν αὐτοῖς τεχνῷτο ib.8.6.23; διαιτήματα τετεχνημένα *devised by art*, Hp.*VM*3.—On the supposed Act. τεχνῆσαι, v. τεχνήεις. II. *contrive* or *execute cunningly*, ταῦτα δ' ἐγὼν..τεχνήσομαι Il.23.415, etc.; χερσὶν ἀτεχνησάμην S.*Tr*. 534, cf. 928; τῶν μηδὲν ὀρθῶς..τεχνωμένων Id.*Ant*.494; τ. κακά Id. *Ph*.80; πόλεμος ἀφ' αὐτοῦ τὰ πολλὰ τεχνᾶται πρὸς τὸ παρατυγχάνον Th.1.122: abs., γένοιτο μέντἂν πᾶν θεοῦ τεχνωμένου if God *contrives*, S.*Aj*.86, cf. E.*Med*.369,382,402, Ar.*V*.176: c. inf., *contrive how to do*, Th.4.26; so also, followed by a clause, *contrive* or *devise means* for doing, τεχνήσομαι ὥς κε γένηται παῖς ἐμός *h.Ap*.326; τ. τί ἂν φάγοι X.*Ages*.9.3. 2. in pass. sense, ὁ ἐπὶ κακῷ τεχνηθεὶς δόλος Sch.Il.15.14. ⊛ **-άρχης,** ου, ὁ, *master of a craft*, Tz.ad Hes.*Op*. 260. ⊛**-ασμα,** ατος, τό, *anything made* or *done by art, handiwork*, κέδρου τεχνάσματα, of a cedar coffin, E.*Or*.1053; τ. σιδήρου *implement* of iron, Opp.*C*.2.174, cf. Semon. (?) in *PLit.Lond*.53$^v$.9, Hdn. 4.15.2. II. *artifice, trick*, E.*Or*.1560, Ar.*Th*.198, X.*HG*6.4.7, Ezek.*Exag*.41. **-ασμός,** ὁ, *cunning contrivance, artifice*, Man.4. 332 (pl.). **-αστέον,** *one must employ subtlety*, ὅπως ἂν εὐπορία γένοιτο Arist.*Pol*.1320$^a$35. **-αστός,** ή, όν, *made by art*, Id.*PA*639$^b$25, al. **-η,** ἡ, (τέκτων) *art, skill, cunning of hand*, esp. in metal-working, Od.3.433, 6.234, 11.614; also of a shipwright, Il.3.61; of a soothsayer, A.*Ag*.249 (pl., lyr.), *Eu*.17, S.*OT*389, etc.; τέχναι ἑτέρων ἕτεραι Pi.*N*.1.25; ὤπασε τ. πᾶσαν Id.*O*.7.50. 2. *craft, cunning*, in bad sense, δολίῃ τ. Od.4.455, Hes.*Th*.160: pl., *arts, wiles*, Od.8. 327,332, Hes.*Th*.496,929; δολίαις τέχναισι χρησάμενος Pi.*N*.4.58; τέχναις τινός by his *arts* (or simply by his *agency*), Id.*O*.9.52, *P*.3. 11; τέχνην κακὴν ἔχει he has a bad *trick*, Hes.*Th*.770, cf. Pi.*I*.4(3). 35(53), S.*Ph*.88, etc. 3. *way, manner*, or *means whereby a thing is gained*, without any definite sense of art or craft, μηδεμιῇ τ. in no *wise*, Hdt.1.112; ἰθέῃ τ. straight*way*, Id.9.57; πάσῃ τ. by all *means*, Ar.*Nu*.1323, *Th*.65, *Ec*.366; παντοίᾳ τ. S.*Aj*.752, etc.; οὐκ ἀποστήσομαι..οὔτε τ. οὔτε μηχανῇ οὐδεμιᾷ *IG*1$^2$.39.22; πάσῃ τ. καὶ μηχανῇ X.*An*.4.5.16; μήτε τ. μήτε μηχανῇ μηδεμιᾷ Lys.13. 95. II. *an art, craft*, πᾶσαι τέχναι βροτοῖσιν ἐκ Προμηθέως A.*Pr*. 506, cf. *IG*1$^2$.678; τὴν τ. ἐπίστασθαι to know the *craft*, Hdt.3.130; φλαύρως ἔχειν τὴν τ. ibid.; τῆς τ. ἔμπειρος Ar.*Ra*.811; ταύτην τέχνην ἔχει he makes this his *trade*, Lys.1.16, cf. 6.7; ἐν τῇ τ. εἶναι practise *it*, S.*OT*562, Pl.*Prt*.317c; ἐπὶ τέχνῃ μαθεῖν τι to learn a thing *professionally*, opp. ἐπὶ παιδείᾳ, ib.312b, cf. 315a; τέχναι καὶ ἐργασίαι X.*Mem*.3.10.1; τέχνην τὸ πρᾶγμα πεποιημένοι having made *a trade* of it, D.37.53; τέχνας ἀσκεῖν, μελετᾶν, ἐργάζεσθαι, to practise *them*.X. *Cyr*.1.6.26,41 (Pass.), *Oec*.4.3; πατρῴαν τέχναν ἐργάζεσθαι ἁλιεύεσθαι Πρακτικὰ Ἀρχ.Ἑτ.1932.52 (Dodona, iv B.C.); ἰατρὸς τὴν τ. *POxy*. 40.5 (ii A.D.); τεθεραπευκὼς ἀνεγκλήτως τῇ τ., of a barber, *PEnteux*. 47.3 (iii B.C.); παραμενῶ πρὸς ὑπηρεσίαν τῆς τ. (viz. weaving) *Sammelb*.7358.20 (iii A.D.); ἀπὸ τεχνῶν τρέφεσθαι live by *them*, X.*Lac*. 7.1. III. *an art or craft*, i.e. *a set of rules, system* or *method of making* or *doing*, whether of the useful arts, or of the fine arts, Epich.171.11, Pl.*Phdr*.245a, Arist.*Rh*.1354$^a$11, *EN*1140$^a$8; ἡ ἐμπειρία τέχνην ἐποίησεν, ἡ δ' ἀπειρία τύχην Polus ap.eund.*Metaph*. 981$^a$4; ἡ περὶ τοὺς λόγους τ. the *Art* of Rhetoric, Pl.*Phd*.90b; οἱ τὰς τ. τῶν λόγων συντιθέντες *systems* of rhetoric, Arist.*Rh*.1354$^a$12, cf. Isoc.13.19, Pl.*Phdr*.271c, Phld.*Rh*.2.50 S., al.; hence title of various treatises on Rhetoric (v. vi; but rather *tricks* of Rhetoric, in Aeschin. 1.117); τέχνῃ *by rules of art*, Pl.*Euthd*.282d; ἢ φύσει ἢ τέχνῃ Id.*R*. 381b; τέχνη καὶ ἐπιστήμη Id.*Ion*532c; ἄνευ τέχνης, μετὰ τέχνης, Id. *Phd*.89e: τ. defined as ἕξις ὁδοποιητική, Zeno *Stoic*.1.20, cf. Cleanth. ib.1.110. IV. = τέχνημα, *work of art, handiwork*, κρατῆρες.., ἀνδρὸς εὐχείρος τέχνη S.*OC*472; ὅπλοις.., Ἡφαίστου τέχνη Id.*Fr*. 156, cf. Str.14.1.14, *PLond*.3.854.4 (i A.D.), Paus.6.25.1, al. V. = συντεχνία, ἡ τ. τῶν λιθουργῶν, τῶν σακκοφόρων, Dumont-Homolle *Mélanges d'archéol. et d'épigr*.p.378 No.65,66 (Perinthus); τ. βυρσέων, συροποιῶν, *IGRom*.1.717,1482 (both Philippopolis); τοὺς καταλειπομένους ἀπὸ τῆς τ. *BGU*1572.12 (ii A.D.); ὁ χαλκεὺς ἀπὸ τῆς τ. *SIG* 1140 (Amphipolis). VI. *treatise* on Grammar, D.T. tit., or on Rhetoric, Anaximenes Lampsacenus tit.⊛ **-ήεις,** εσσα, εν, poet. Adj. *cunningly wrought*, δεσμοὶ τεχνήεντες..Ἡφαίστοιο Od.8.297, cf. Ael. *NA*1.59 (Comp.); αὐδὴ τεχνήεσσα λίθου *Supp.Epigr*.1.424 (Halic., V B.C.). Adv. τεχνηέντως *artfully, skilfully*, Od.5.270. II. of persons, *skilful*, γυναῖκες ἱστῶν (v.l. -ὸν) τεχνῆσσαι (vulg. τεχνῆσαι, but there is no act. verb τεχνάω) 7.110, cf. Q.S.8.296; as epith. of Hephaestus, dub. in *Epic.Alex.Adesp*.7.11. **-ημα,** ατος, τό, *that which is cunningly wrought, work of art, handiwork*, ἔκπωμα.., τεχνήματ' ἀνδρός S.*Ph*. 36 (where pl. is used of one thing). 2. of a man, πανουργίας τέχνημα *a masterpiece* of villainy, ib.928. II. *artful device, trick*, κάπηλα προσφέρων τ. A.*Fr*.322; δόλια τ. E.*IT*1355; opp. ἰσχύς, Hp.*Fract*.2 (pl.): generally, *device, contrivance*, Pl.*Prt*.319a; τὸ μνημονικὸν τ. Id.*Hp.Mi*.368d, al., cf. Ephor.54J. **-ήμων,** ον, gen. ονος, *cunningly wrought*, αὐλοί *AP*9.504. 2. *skilful*, of artists, Opp.*C*.1.326. **-ησις,** εως, ἡ, *artifice*, D.H.*Dem*.38. **-ητικός,** ή, όν, *artificial, refined*, ἀσωτία Plb.32.11.10 cod. A Ath. (Schweigh. τεχνιτικός). **-ητός,** ή, όν, *artificial*, opp. natural, αὐγῆς εἶδος Hp.*Off*.3; τ. σύμβολα, opp. θεῖα, Plu.*Per*.6; τὸ τεχνητόν *the product of a craft*, Plot.4.4.23; τὰ τεχνητὰ τῶν ὀργάνων *artificial* instruments (or perh. instruments *belonging to a craft*), as the builder's κανών, ibid. **-ήτωρ,** ορος, ὁ, *artificer, maker*, μύρων Man.2. 327. ⊛ **-ικός,** ή, όν, of persons, *artistic, skilful, workmanlike*, Epich. 171.11, Pl.*Smp*.186c, etc.; τ. περί τινος Id.*Tht*.207c; περί τι Id.*La*. 185e, etc.; εἴς τι ib.d; esp. of rhetoricians and grammarians, τ. λόγων πέρι Id.*Phdr*.273e; οἱ περὶ τοὺς λόγους τ. ib.a; ὁ τ. τε καὶ ἀγαθὸς ῥήτωρ Id.*Grg*.504d; Comp., *more proficient in one's craft*, Phld. *Mus*.p.74 K.; opp. θεωρητικός, *practical*, Arist.*EN*1180$^b$20; τ. περὶ τὸν βίον Id.*HA*622$^b$23 (Comp., v.l. Sup.); τ. τὴν ψυχήν Id.*Pol*. 1327$^b$27; τ. ὄμματα Ael.*VH*14.47; τ. πόημα Phld.*Po*.5.20; τὸ τ. *technical excellence*, ib.2.55; τ. ἐνέργειαι, οἷον αὐλεῖν ἢ σαλπίζειν ἢ κιθαρίζειν Gal.6.323; later, οἱ τεχνικοί *the grammarians*, Sch.D.T. p.4 H.; ὁ τ. freq. of Hdn.Gr., Choerob. in *Theod*.1.142 H., al.; also of D.T., Sch.D.T.p.204 H. b. φύσις = πῦρ τεχνικόν, Zeno *Stoic*.1. 34; τὸν τ. νοῦν the mind *of the Great Designer*, *Theol.Ar*.58; δύναμίς τις..ἣν..τεχνικὴν εἶναι λέγομεν Gal.*Nat.Fac*.1.6. 2. *artful, cunning*, Plb.16.6.6. II. of things, *artificial*, opp. αὐτόματος, Thphr. *Lap*.55; τ. ὕδατα an *artificial* water-supply, Gal.17(2).183. Adv. -κῶς ibid. 2. *done by rules of art, technical, systematic*, τοῦτο σοφὸν εὑρὼν ἅμα καὶ τ. Pl.*Phdr*.273b; ἡ περὶ τὸν πόλεμον ἀγωνία τ. Id.*R*.374b, cf. *Euthphr*.14e; πραγματεῖαι τ. Id.*Grg*.501b, etc.; ἡ τ. παιδεία Arist.*Pol*.1341$^b$9; ἔχειν τὸ τ. περί τι to be *technically* employed upon.., Id.*Rh*.1355$^b$35, cf. *Ph*.193$^a$32. III. Adv. -κῶς *according to the rules of art*, τ. εἰργασμένα, πεποιημένα, Pl.*Chrm*. 173c, Isoc.2.44; τ. ἐξηύρηται Pl.*Euthd*.303e; τ. ἔχειν Id.*Phdr*.271c; τ. πολιτεύεσθαι Isoc.3.52; ὁ δυνάμενος..τεκμαίρεσθαι τ. Gal.18(2). 257. **-ιον,** τό, Dim. of τέχνη, Pl.*R*.495d. 2. in bad sense, a *low art*, Diph.87.1, Antid.2.4, Polystr.p.17 W., Them.*Or*.21.246c.

**τεχνῖτ-εία,** ἡ, *artifice*, Epicur.*Ep*.2 p.40 U., Hippoloch.ap.Ath.4. 130a, S.E.*M*.5.86. **-ευμα,** ατος, τό, *a work of art, art*, Aristeas 78, Max.Tyr.34.3. II. *the theatrical profession* (cf. τεχνίτης II), *OGI* 51.11 (Ptolemais, iii B.C.). **-εύω,** *make* or *produce artificially, fabricate*, μεταφορὰς ἀπὸ τῶν φυτῶν Phld.*Rh*.1.171 S. (prob.); εἰκόνα Ph.1.35, cf. 374 (Pass.); λεξείδια Jul.*Mis*.345b; τ. τοῦτο *treat* it *secundum artem*, Olymp.Alch.p.98 B.; θάλπος Max.Tyr.36.5, etc.: in bad sense, *pervert by art*, δεινὸς τ. λόγους ἐπὶ τὰ πονηρότερα D.H. *Is*.4. II. intr., *use art* or *cunning*, περί τι S.E.*M*.2.64,88, cf. Muson.*Fr*.18$^A$p.97 H.: c. inf., J.*AJ*5.8.11. ⊛**-ης,** ου, ὁ, *artificer, craftsman*, opp. γεωργός, X.*Oec*.6.6, Arist.*Pol*.1262$^b$26, al.; opp. ῥήτωρ, Emp.ap.Thphr.*Sens*.11; of a potter, *PCair.Zen*.500.2,3 (iii B.C.); τεχνῖται οἱ χρήσιμόν τι ποιεῖν ἐπιστάμενοι, opp. οἱ ἐλευθερίως πεπαιδευμένοι, X.*Mem*.2.7.4,5, cf. *Act.Ap*.19.24: metaph., πόλις ἧς τ. καὶ δημιουργὸς ὁ θεός *Ep.Hebr*.11.10, cf. Lxx *Wi*.13.1. II. *one who does* or *handles* a thing *by the rules of art, skilled workman*, opp. ἄτεχνος, Pl.*Sph*.219a, cf. Hp.*VM*4, Arist.*Rh*.1397$^b$23, Gal.6.155, 18(2).245; opp. ἰδιώτης, Id.6.204; opp. ὁ ἔμπειρος, Arist.*Metaph*.981$^b$31; c. gen. rei, τ. τῶν πολεμικῶν *skilled* in.., X.*Lac*.13.5; also οἱ περὶ τοὺς θεοὺς τ. *persons versed* in religious practices, Id.*Cyr*.8.3.11; ἄνθρωπος τ. λόγων, as a sneer, Aeschin.1.170; οἱ Διονυσιακοὶ τ. or οἱ περὶ τὸν Διόνυσον τ., theatrical *artists*, musicians as well as actors, D. 19.192 (where τ. alone), Arist.*Rh*.1405$^a$24, *Pr*.956$^b$11, *SIG*399.12 (Amphict. Delph., iii B.C.), *CIG*2619, al. (Cyprus), *OGI*50 (Egypt, iii B.C.), Plb.16.21.8, Posidon.36 J., etc.; so perh. in οἷος τ. παραπόλλυμαι, = Lat. *qualis artifex pereo* (Nero's last words), D.C.63.29. III. *trickster, intriguer*, Luc.*DMort*.13.5. **-ικός,** ή, όν, *of* or *for a craftsman*, Phld.*Mus*.p.40 K.; [διάζωμα] prob. cj. in Herm.ap.Stob.1.49. 69: Sup., Phld.*Vit*.p.33 J. (s.v.l.). **-ις** (properisp.), ιδος, fem. of τεχνίτης, of an accomplished courtesan, *AP*11.73 (Nicarch.), cf. Luc. *Tox*.13. 2. *crafts-woman*, *Delph*.3(2).220, 3(3).54 (ii B.C.), Chor. 23.5 p.254 F.-R.: as Adj., ἡ πάντων τ. σοφία Lxx *Wi*.7.22; τούτου τοῦ ἐνεργήματος (sc. respiration) τεχνίτιδες φῦσαι Herm ap.Stob.1.49.69.

**τεχνογρᾰφ-έω,** *write a treatise on rhetoric*, Phld.*Rh*.1.170 S. **-ικός,** ή, όν: τὰ -κά *treatises on rhetoric*, D.H.*Is*.20. **-ος** (parox.), ὁ, *writer on the art of rhetoric*, Arist.*Rh.Al*.1421$^a$39, Phld.*Rh*.1.151 S., al., D.H.*Lys*.24, etc.

**τεχνο-δίαιτος** [ῐ], ον, *living in art*, of Hephaestus, Orph.*H*.66. 3. **-ειδής,** ές, *artistic*, D.L.7.156.

**τεχνολογ-έω,** *prescribe as a rule of art*, Arist.*Rh*.1354$^b$17: abs., τῶν τεχνολογούντων ib.1356$^a$11; τ. περί τινος ib.1354$^b$26; καθ' ἑαυτὸν τ. *Com.Adesp*.345:—Pass., τὰ τεχνολογούμενα *rules of art*, S.E.*M*. 11.40, *P*.2.247; -ουμέναις παρακλήσεσιν Iamb.*Protr*.21; τὴν θηριακήν, περὶ ἧς ἡμῖν ὁ πᾶς οὗτος λόγος..τετεχνολόγηται Gal.14.230. **-ητέον,** *one must treat systematically*, περί τινος Nicom.*Ar*.2.22. **-ία,** ἡ, *systematic treatment*, of grammar, etc., Phld.*Rh*.1.128 S. (pl.), Cic. *Att*.4.16.3, Anon.Lond.2.18, Plu.2.514a (pl.), S.E.*P*.2.205, Iamb. *Comm.Math*.7, etc. **-ος** (parox.), ὁ, *writer on the art of rhetoric*, Phld.*Rh*.1.203 S. (pl.).

**τεχνο-παίγνιον,** τό, *game of art*, esp. *a way of showing off one's powers of verse-making*, 'jeu d'esprit', title of a poem by Ausonius. **-παράδοτος,** ον, *transmitted by art*, Zos.Alch.pp.138 (prob. cj. for τεκνο-), 236 B. **-πωλικός,** ή, όν, *making a trade of art*, Pl.*Sph*.224c.

**τεχνοσύνα,** ᾶ, Dor., poet. for τέχνη, *AP*6.4 (Leon.).

**τεχνούργ-ημα,** ατος, τό, *a work of art*, *Corp.Herm*.3.4. **-ία,** ἡ, = foreg., Aristeas 80, *Corp.Herm*.3.4. **-ός,** όν, *industrial*, of Solon's third class, μοῖρα τεχνουργός (sc. πολιτείας) Lyd.*Mag*.1.47.

**τεχν-όω,** *instruct in an art*, Gal.1.227, 6.480, 13.656, Elias *in Porph*. 139.16; *make artistic*, Eustr.*in EN*1.5. 2. Med. -ώσατο, = -ήσατο, Nonn.*D*.25.413 (s.v.l.). **-ύδριον,** τό, Dim. of τέχνη, Pl.*R*.

475e. **-ύφιον**, τό, = foreg., in sense of *workshop, study*, Suet. *Aug.*72 (codd. τεχνόφυον). **-ωσις**, εως, ἡ, *becoming artistic*, Eustr. *in EN*322.37; *craftsmanship*, Fronto *Ep.Gr.*1.4.

**τέῳ**, Ion. dat. of τίς; *who?*, and **τεῳ**, Ion. dat. of τις, *any one*, v. τίς, τις.

**τέων**, Ion. gen. pl. of τίς; *who?*, and **τεων**, of τις, *any one*, v. τίς, τις. II. **τέων**, gen. pl. of ὅς, Nic.*Al.*2.

**τεωρεῖς**· δραπέται, κακοῦργοι, λῃσταί, Hsch. **τέωρος**· συκοφάντης καὶ τὰ ὅμοια, Id.; cf. τέναρος.

**τέως**, Ep. prob. **τῆος** (not in codd. of Hom., v. sub fin.):—Adv. of Time, *so long, in the meantime*, correlat. to ἕως, ἧος ἐγὼ.. ἠλώμην, τῆός μοι ἀδελφεὸν ἄλλος ἔπεφνεν Od.4.91, cf. Il.20.42; to ὄφρα, 19.189; so in Att., ἐσθίων τ. ἕως.. Ar.*Pax* 32: sts. without a Relat., *until then, during that time*, referring to a time already indicated, ἐς γάμου ὥρην..· τῆος δὲ.. παρὰ μητρὶ κεῖσθαι ἐνὶ μεγάρῳ Od.15.127; τελεσφόρον εἰς ἐνιαυτὸν..· ὁ δὲ τῆος (Nauck, for τέως μὲν)..δέδετο ib.231, cf. S.*Aj.*558; ποσσῆμαρ μέμονας.., ὄφρα τ... μένω, i. e. *for that number of days*, Il.24.658, cf. Od.16.370; ἐγὼ δ' οἴσω τ. E.*Heracl.*725, cf. Ar.*Pax* 687,729 (anap.). 2. rarely for ἕως, Hdt.4.165, Hp.*Int.*26, *Mul.*2.165, Pl.*Smp.*191e, D.19.326, 21.16, A.R.4.821,1617, *Sardis* 7(1)No. 1 ii 12,19. II. *for a time, a while* (cf. ἕως B), mostly with some answering word or phrase, as τῆος μὲν.., αὐτὰρ νῦν Od.16.139; τῆος.., ἀλλ' ὅτε δὴ 24.162 (Nauck, for τέως μὲν..); φίλον τ., νῦν δ' ἐχθρόν A.*Ch.*1001(993); τ. μὲν.., ὡς δὲ.. Th.6.61, Pl.*Phd.*117c; τ. μὲν.., ἐπεὶ or ἐπειδὴ δὲ.., X.*Cyr.*5.3.17, Lys.31.8; τ. μὲν.., ἡνίκα δὲ.. X.*HG*4.3.17; τ. μὲν.., μετὰ δὲ.. Hdt.1.11; τ. μὲν.., ἔπειτα δὲ.. Id.6.83; τ. μὲν.., τέλος δὲ.. Id.1.82; τ. μὲν.., νῦν δὲ.. Ar.*Th.*449; τ. μὲν.., ἔπειτα or εἶτα.., without δέ, Th.5.7, X.*HG* 2.2.17, Ar.*Nu.*66:—without answering phrase, A.R.2.132. III. *up to this time, hitherto*, Hdt.6.112, Ar.*Pl.*834, Pl.*Smp.*191b, *IG*1².57.21, 108.48; ἐν τῷ τ. χρόνῳ Lys.7.12, 27.16 (but ἐν τῷ τ. *in the meantime*, Polyaen.1.39.4, 8.47.1, Ael.*NA*2.25, 11.38, Steph. *in Hp.* 1.217 D., condemned by Hdn.*Philet.*p.434 P.; διὰ τὸ τ *for the present*, Zos.Alch.p.231 B.); φίλοι τ. ὄντες Is.1.9. IV. τ. εἰδέναι χρή you must know *to begin with*, *Gp.*9.11.1, 9.19.1; νυνὶ δ' αὐτὸ τὸ κεφάλαιον.. ἄκουσον εἰς ὀλίγους τ. ἀνενηνεγμένον σκοπούς Gal.15.764. [As a trochee before a vowel, Il.20.42, Od.16.370; as a trochee (spondee) before a consonant, Il.15.277 (Zenod.), Od.4.91, 15.127, 16.139; as an iambus, only Il.19.189 (sed leg. αὐτόθι τῆος, om. περ), 24.658, Od.18.190; as a monosyll., 15.231, 24.162, never in Il.; in codd. of Hom. written τείως, Od.4.91, al. (so in A.R.2.132, al.); τέως Il.24.658, al.; rarely τεῖος, one cod. in Il.20.42.] (Cret. **τάως** Hsch.: but the dialect forms of the correlative ἕως (ἇς etc.) indicate a primitive Gr. *τᾶος, Old Ion. *τῆος (cf. Skt. *tāvat* 'so great, so long'), whence later Ion. and Att. τέως.)

**τζάγγη**, ἡ, a kind of *shoe*, *misi.. zancas de nostris Parthicas paria tria*, Gallienus ap.Trebell.*Claud.*17; *usum tzangarum.. intra urbem ..nemini liceat usurpare*, *Cod.Theod.*14.10.2.

**τζαγκάριος**, ὁ, *maker of* τζάγγαι, *PLond.*5.1708.89 (vi A.D.); also [τ **σαγγάριος** (accus. -άριν) *MAMA*3.89 (Diocaesarea); and σαγγάριος (q. v.).

**τζάπιον**, τό, *bidens, ligo, raster*, *Gloss.*

⊛**τῆ**, old Ep. Interjection, *there!*, in Hom. always followed by imper., τῆ, σπεῖσον Διΐ.. Il.24.287; τῆ, πίε οἶνον Od.9.347; τῆ, τόδε φάρμακον ἐσθλὸν ἔχων ἔρχευ 10.287; τῆ νῦν.. ἱμάντα τεῷ ἐγκάτθεο κόλπῳ Il.14.219; τῆ νῦν, καὶ σοὶ τοῦτο κειμήλιον ἔστω 23.618; τῆ δὴ τοῦτο πόρε κρέας Od.8.477; τῆ δὲ τόδε κρήδεμνον.. τάνυσσαι 5.346: rare after Hom., τῆ νῦν τόδε πῖθι λαβὼν Cratin.141 (adapting Hom., anap.); τῆ νῦν καταδέχεσθε τοὺς φακοὺς Eup.359; τῆ, Γυλλί, πῖθι Herod.1.82: without imper., prob. in Call.*Epigr.*33,38: folld. by an acc., Simm.26.3 (but f.l. in *AP*9.316.11 (Leon.)): pl. τῆτε Sophr.156. (Prob. an old case-form (with pan-Hellenic η, cf. Sophr., Simm. ll. cc.) of demonstr. stem το-; cf. τῆδε: wrongly expld. by Gramm. as imper. (= λαβέ) of *τάω (Eust.980.4) or *τῆμι (Sch. Ar.*Av.*1310): the variant τῆ, found in some Mss. (including papyri) of Hom., and in the papyrus of Herod. l. c., is censured by Apollon.*Lex.*)

**τῇ**, as Adv., = ταύτῃ, *here, there*, v. ὁ A. VIII. 1.

**τῆβαι**, only in Lat. spelling *tebae* 'sine afflatu' (i.e. with unaspirated *t*), Boeot. for *colles*, Varro *RR*3.1.6, as etym. of Θῆβαι.

**τήβεννα**, ἡ, also **τήβεννος**, ἡ, D.H.3.61, Plu.*Rom.*26, *Cor.*9, etc., = Lat. *toga* (incl. its varieties the *trabea*, etc.), *Inscr.Délos* 1442 *B*34 (ii B.C.), Plb.10.4.8, D.H.2.70, 3.61, 5.47, 6.13, D.S.5.40; worn by Antiochus Epiphanes, Plb.26.1ᴬ.2, Ptol.Euerg.3 J.: said to be derived from Τήμενος (Τήβεννος Suid.) the Arcadian, Artem.2.3, cf. Poll.7.61 (where **τηβεννίς** is prob. cj. for τημενίς); but D.H.3.61 expressly doubts its Hellenic origin. (The form of the word, and the context in D.H. l. c., suggest that it is Etruscan, but K. O. Müller's conjecture Τυρρηνοί for τύραννοι in *EM*756.26 is doubtful.)

**τηβένν-ειος**, ον, *belonging to Tebennos*, ἐσθής Suid. (citing Artem. 2.3, where τημένιον codd., τημένειον Kuster). **-ικός**, ή, όν, *consisting of the* τήβεννα, Str.3.4.20. **-ίς**, **-ος**, v. τήβεννα.

**τηβεννοφορ-έω**, *wear the* τήβεννα, Ἀρχ.Ἐφ.1910.345 (Larissa, ii B.C.). **-ιον**, τό, = *togipurium*, etc., *Gloss.* **-ος** (parox.) (also **-ηφόρος**), ον, *wearing the* τήβεννα, ib.

**τηγάν-η** [ᾰ], ἡ, = τήγανον, *Gloss.* **-ητόν**, *frictum, frixum*, ib. **-ίζω**, *fry in a* τήγανον, Posidipp.5 (Pass.), Lxx 2 *Ma.*7.5, Dsc.5.3 (Pass.), J.*AJ*7.8.1: metaph., dub. in *BGU*665 ii 3 (i A.D.). **-ιον**, τό, Dim. of τήγανον, dub. cj. in Telecl.10: τυγάνιον in *POxy.*1290.4 (v A.D.) may be a different word. **-ισμός**, ὁ, *frying*, Men.251 (pl.). **-ιστός**, ή, όν, *fried in a* τήγανον, Diph.Siph.ap.Ath.3.90e, J.*AJ*7.8.1, *BGU*1668.4 (i A.D.), Gal.6.812 (v.l.). **-ίτης** [ῑ] (sc. ἄρτος), ου, ὁ, *pancake*, Hippon.36; Asiatic Gr. for Att. ταγηνίτης acc. to Gal.6.490; = *lucunculus*, *Gloss.*

**τήγᾰνον, τηγᾰνόστροφον**, v. τάγηνον, ταγηνοστρόφιον.

**τῆγμα**, ατος, τό, *colour, paint*, χρυσοῦν, cj. for στίγμα in Ps.-Democr.ap.Zos.Alch.pp.119,126 B.

**τῆδε**, Dor. and Ion. Adv. *here*, *IG*12(3).537*a*, 538*b*, 551.2 (Thera), 12(9).285.5 (Eretria, vi B.C.), *Schwyzer* 148 (Megara, v B.C.).

**τῇδε**, dat. fem. of ὅδε:—**τηδί**, dat. fem. of ὁδί.

**τῆδες**, v. τῆτες.

**τηθαλλᾰδοῦς**, ὁ, (τήθη) *nursed by a grandmother, spoilt child, mollycoddle*, ὀκνεῖς λαλεῖν; οὕτω σφόδρ' εἶ τ.; *Com.Adesp.*17, cf. Poll.3.20, Phryn.*PS*p.113 B., Hdn.Gr.2.928, Suid.:—but this interpr. constantly alternates with μαμμόθρεπτος, as if from τίτθη, not τήθη.—Other forms occur, viz. **τηθαλλωδοῦς** (-αμμω cod.) in Hsch., cf. *EM*756.31; **τηθελᾶς** Sch.Ar.*Ach.*49; **τηθελαδοῦς** Phryn.267; **τηθαλώδης** Zonar.

**τήθεον**, v. τήθυον.

**τηθεύομαι**, f. l. for τιτθεύομαι in Arist.*GA*754ᵃ13.

**τήθη** (sts. written τηθή; the Ion. voc. τῆθα, Sch.Il.3.130, prob. belongs to this word), ἡ, *grandmother*, Ar.*Ach.*49, *Lys.*549, And.1.128, Pl.*R.*461d, Is.3.23, *IG*2².1534.229, D.57.20 (v.l. τιτθῆς, -ῇ), Men.532.4 (τιθή codd.), Hierocl.p.61 A. (τιτθαί, τίθαι, τίτθαι codd.), Lib.*Or.*25.47 (vv. ll. τίτθη, τίθη), Thom.Mag.p.359 R. (τίθη codd. and prob. Thom.); title of play by Diphilus, *IG*2².2363.35: τίθη λέγεται ἡ μάμμη, τίτθη ἡ βυζάστρια, τιθήνη ἡ τροφός Ps.-Hdn.Gr. post Moer.p.479 P., cf. Ptol.Asc.p.394 H., etc. II. *nurse*; τῇ, ὅθεν καὶ τήθη ἡ λέγουσα "δέξαι, θήλασον" Sch.Il.14.219, cf. Sch.Ar.*Lys.*549; but this is an error, the word for *nurse* being τίτθη (q. v.).

⊛**τηθία**, ἡ, = τήθη, *old woman*, Eust.971.43.

**τηθίβῐος** [θῐ], ἡ, = foreg., Eust.971.44.

**τηθίς**, ίδος, ἡ, (τήθη) *father's or mother's sister, aunt*, Is.9.19, D.27.14, 43.29, Men.923.5, J.*AJ*3.12.1 (vv. ll. τιτθίσι, τιθίσι, τιτθαῖς), 16.10.5 (vv. ll. τιτθίδα, τητθίδα), 17.1.1 (v.l. τητθίδα, Lat. vers. *nutricem*), Plu.2.838b, Hierocl.p.61 A. (τιθίδες, τιθίδες codd.), Lib.*Decl.*5.52 (one cod., vv. ll. τητθίδα, τιτθίδα), 26.21 (τιτθίδας codd., τιθίδας as cited by Thom.Mag.p.360 R., who thinks it may mean *grandmothers* or *great-aunts*); ἡ πρὸς πατρὸς τη[θίς] *POxy.*503.3 (ii A.D.); τῆς τηθίδος μου κύριος *PSI*10.1065.28 (ii A.D.); οὐκ ἐξὸν Ῥωμαίοις ἀδελφὰς γῆμαι οὐδὲ τηθίδας *PGnom.*70 (ii A.D.); ὥσπερ οὐδὲ νῦν τιτθίδας (leg. τηθίδας) οὐδ' ἀδελφὰς γαμοῦσιν Plu.2.265d; τηθίδα *PStrassb.*41.8 (iii A.D.); dat. spelt τειθειδι *Supp.Epigr.*6.221 (Phrygia).

**τῆθος**, εος, τό, = τήθυον; sg. τῆθος is used by Ath. in citing Arist. *Fr.*304; pl. τήθη Nic.*Al.*396, Poll.6.47: for τήθεα v. τήθυον. (τῆθος was perh. a back-formation (originally Ion.) from τήθεα, τηθέων, which were forms of τήθυον, q. v.)

**τηθυνάκιον**, τό, Dim. of τήθυον, Epich.42 (**τηθύνια** Meineke, Kaibel; but τήθυα, κτένια (Ahrens) is prob. cj.).

**τήθυον**, τό, an animal of the kind called *ascidia* or *sea-squirt*, Arist.*HA*531ᵃ18 (v.l. τηθέου), *PA*680ᵃ5, al.; once in Hom., τήθεα διφῶν Il.16.747 (= εἶδος θαλασσίων ὀστρέων, Sch.), cf. Arist.*Fr.*304. (For the variation τήθυον: τήθεον, cf. πτύον: πτέον, etc.; *tethea* is pl. in Plin.*HN*32.117, nom. sg. fem. ib.151.) II. **τηθύα**· τενάγη, ἃ προχέουσιν οἱ ποταμοί, Hsch.

⊛**Τηθύς**, ύος, ἡ, *Tethys*, wife of Oceanus, nurse of Hera, Il.14.201, 302; daughter of Uranus and Gaia, mother of the river gods and Oceanides, Hes.*Th.*136,337, cf. A.*Pr.*137 (anap.), *Th.*311 (lyr.); Ὠκεανὸν.. καὶ Τηθὺν ἐποίησαν τῆς γενέσεως πατέρας Arist.*Metaph.*983ᵇ30; taken as type of a very old woman, prob. in Call.*Iamb.*1.248 (*Hermes* 60.174); cf. προτήθυς. II. in later writers, the *Sea*, Lyc.1069, *AP*7.214.6 (Arch.), Nonn.*D.*31.187, Orph.*A.*335, etc., cf. Porph.ap.Eus.*PE*3.11, Suid. [ῡ in disyll. cases, ῠ in trisyll.]

**Τήϊος**, α, ον, *of* or *from Teos* (Τέως), Eup.146ᵃ, etc.: this Ionic form is also the Attic form, written τειοι (pl.) in *IG*1².205.10.

**Τηϊουργής**, ές, *of Teian workmanship*, τηϊουργῆ δύο *IG*11(2).110.22, al. (Delos, iii B.C.).

**τηκεδονικός**, ή, όν, in neut., = *tabificabile*, *Gloss.*

**τηκεδών**, όνος, ἡ, *melting*, of snow, D.S.1.30. II. *wasting away, consumption*, Od.11.201; τοῦ σκήνεος Aret.*SD*1.14; νούσων τακεδόνες (Dor. form) *Supp.Epigr.*2.615 (Teos, metr.); νόσῳ τηκεδόνι χρώμενος App.*BC*1.107. 2. *a means for reducing one's weight*, Hp.*Mul.*2.180. 3. *putrefaction*, σαρκὸς τακεδόνες Ti.Locr.102c, cf. Pl.*Ti.*82e; τ. πιμελῆς Gal.16.703.

**τηκόλῐθος**, ον, *dissolving stones*, of a remedy for the stone, Plin. *HN*36.143, Aët.12.64, Paul.Aeg.3.45. II. a gem, Plin.*HN*37.184.

**τηκ-τέον**, *one must dissolve*, φοινικίνην δι' ἐλαίου Gal.13.667, cf. 523. **-τικός**, ή, όν, (τήκω) *able to dissolve*, τινος Arist.*PA*648ᵇ17 (Comp.), cf. *Pr.*907ᵇ8; τ. δύναμις S.E.*M.*8.198. 2. *suitable for reducing*, σπληνός Dsc.4.183. **-τός**, ή, όν, *melted, molten*, μόλυβδος E.*Andr.*267. II. *capable of being dissolved, soluble*, σώματα τ. καὶ ἄτηκτα Pl.*Sph.*265c, cf. Arist.*Metaph.*1015ᵃ10, Thphr.*Lap.*4; opp. στερεός, Pl.*Criti.*114e; opp. τεγκτός (q. v.), Arist.*Mete.*385ᵇ12; τηκτόν, = φάρμακον τηκόμενον, Hp.*VC*14.

**τήκω**, A.*Fr.*300.5, etc., Dor. **τάκω** [ᾱ S.*El.*123 (lyr.), Theoc.2.28: fut. τήξω *AP*5.277 (Agath.), (συν-) E.*IA*398 (troch.); Dor. 2 sg. ταξεῖς (κατα-) Theoc.*Ep.*6.1: aor. ἔτηξα Hdt.3.96, (κατ-) Od.19.206, etc.: pf. ἔτηκα, in intr. sense, Il.3.176, etc.; Dor. τέτακα E.*Supp.*1141 (lyr.), (προσ-) S.*Tr.*836 (lyr.): plpf. ἐτετήκειν X.*An.*4.5.15:—

Med., fut. τήξομαι (but in pass. sense) Hp.*Flat.*12: aor. ἐτηξάμην Nic.*Al.*63,164,350:—Pass., fut. τακήσομαι Lxx *Le.*26.39, al., *Anacreont.*10.16, (συν-) Plu.2.752e: aor. ἐτάκην [ᾰ] E.*Hel.*3, Pl.*Phdr.* 251b, *Ti.*83a; freq. in compds. ἐξ-, ἐν-, συν-; rarely ἐτήχθην, Hp. *Morb.*4.57, Pl.*Ti.*61b, once in Trag., συντηχθεὶς E.*Supp.*1029 (lyr.): pf. τέτηγμαι Plu.2.106d, *AP*5.272 (Agath.); but in early Gr. the pf. and plpf. Pass. are supplied by the intr. Act. pf. and plpf. τέτηκα, ἐτετήκειν (v. supr.). I. Act., *melt, melt down* (trans.), of metals, Hdt.3.96, etc.; τ. πετραίαν χιόνα A. l. c.; *bring* clouds *down in rain*, Hdt.2.25; *dissolve*, Pl.*Ti.*60e,84d, Gal.13.523, etc. 2. metaph., *dissolve, cause to waste* or *pine away*, μὴ θυμὸν τῆκε *let* it not *melt* or *pine away*, Od.19.264; τίν' ἀεὶ τάκεις ὧδ' ἀκόρετον οἰμωγὰν τὸν Ἀγαμέμνονα; (i.e. τί ὧδε τήκει οἰμώζουσα τὸν Ἀγ.;) S.*El.*123 (lyr.); τ. βιοτάν E.*Med.*141 (anap.); σῶμα Pl.*R.*609c; τ. καὶ λείβει [τὸ θυμοειδές] ib.411b; τ. ἧπαρ Call.*Aet.Oxy.*2079.8; διαφορεῖν καὶ τ. [σάρκα] carry off and *reduce* superfluous flesh, Gal.6.96, cf. *Vict. Att.*1; ἡ ταχεῖα κίνησις τὴν θερμασίαν ἐπὶ πλέον αὐξάνουσα τήκει τὸ σῶμα Id.15.191; ἔρωτες τήξουσιν κραδίην *AP*5.277 (Agath.). II. Pass., with intr. pf. Act. τέτηκα, *melt, be dissolved, melt away*, of snow, *thaw*, χιὼν τηκομένη Od.19.207; ῥέειν ἀπὸ τηκομένης χιόνος Hdt.2.22; λευκῆς τακείσης χιόνος E.*Hel.*3; ἡνίκ' ἂν τακῇ χιών Id. *Fr.*228.4; τὴν χιόνα τετηκέναι X.*An.*4.5.15; of metals, ἐτήκετο κασσίτερος ὣς Hes.*Th.*862; σίδηρος.. πυρὶ κηλέῳ τήκεται ib.866; also τετηκότα (sc. κρέα) *sodden* flesh, E.*Cyc.*246; ἄλφιτα πυρὶ τ. *is consumed*, Theoc.2.18; τήκεται κοιλίη, merely, *is relaxed*, Hp.*Aër.*7; of putrefying flesh, *fall away*, Pl.*Ti.*82e; of a corpse, κατθανὼν ἐτήκετο S.*Ant.*906; κηκὶς μηρίων ἐτήκετο ib.1008; πυρὸς τετακότας σποδῷ E.*Supp.*1141 (lyr.); εἰς τοῦτο τετηκυῖα *resolved* into.., Pl.*Ti.* 85d; στοιχεῖα καυσούμενα τήκεται 2 *Ep.Pet.*3.12; of fat, τακείσης πιμελῆς Gal.6.192, cf. 18(2).140; of food in the digestive organs, τήκεται μὲν ἡ πρότερον ῥηθεῖσα [πτισάνη], ἡ δ' ἑτέρα δύστηκτός ἐστι Id.6.784. 2. metaph., *melt* or *waste away, pine*, κλαίουσα τέτηκα Il.3.176; τήκετο χρὼς Od.19.204; τήκετο καλὰ παρήϊα δάκρυ χεούσης ib.208; ἐν νούσῳ.. δηρὸν τηκόμενος 5.396; τ. νούσῳ Hdt.3.99, cf. Theoc.1.66,82, etc.; Ὀδυσσεὺς τήκετο *was moved to tears*, Od.8.522; κλαίω, τέτηκα S.*El.*283; μὴ λίαν τάκου E.*Med.*159 (lyr.); ψυχὴν ἐτήκου Id.*Heracl.*645, cf. *El.*208 (lyr.); ἐτάκευ βασκαίνων Theoc.5.12; τὸ κάλλος ἐτάκετο Id.2.83; *come to naught*, δόξαι.. τακόμεναι κατὰ γᾶν μινύθουσιν A.*Eu.*374 (lyr.); ἐπί τινι τακεὶς *consumed for love of*.., *AP*7.31 (Diosc.), cf. Luc.*DMeretr.*12.1; βλέμμα τηκόμενον a *languishing* look, Plu.*Ant.*53. (Cf. Lat. *tābes*, OE. *þawian* 'thaw', Slav. *tajati* 'melt'.)

**τηλαύγ-εια**, ἡ, = λαμπρότης, Hdn.*Epim.*132. **-ημα**, ατος, τό, *brightness* or *whiteness seen far off*, of leprosy, Lxx *Le.*13.23, Suid. **-ής**, ές, (τῆλε, αὐγή) *far-shining, far-beaming*, πρόσωπον, of the sun, *h.Hom.*31.13; εἵματα, of the moon, ib.32.8; φάος, φέγγος, Pi.*P.*3.75 (Comp.), *N.*3.64; ἀκτίς, ἀκτίνων σέλας, Ar.*Av.*1092 (lyr.), 1711; στέφανοι Pi.*P.*2.6; πρόσωπον θέμεν τ. to make it *beam from afar*, Id.*O.*6.4: metaph., τ. νοῦς *luminous* meaning, D.H.*Th.* 30; σαφεῖς καὶ τ. αἰτίαι Jul.*Or.*5.174d; λέξεις ἐπὶ τὸ -έστερον ἀχθεῖσαι Erot.*Prooem.* II. of distant objects, *far-seen, conspicuous*, σκοπιή Thgn.550; κορυφά Pi.*Pae.*7.12; φᾶρος B.16.5; ὄχθος S.*Tr.* 524 (lyr.); of leprosy, Lxx *Le.*13.4, al. III. *far-seeing*, αἴσθησις, ψυχή, Hp.*Ep.*17,22 (Comp.). Adv. -γῶς, τηλαυγέστερον δρᾶν to see *more clearly*, D.S.1.50, cf. Str.17.1.30, Ph.1.540, *Ev.Marc.*8. 25.—Poet. word, used in late Prose: δηλαυγῶς seems to be a different word. **-ησις**, εως, ἡ, *brightness shining from afar*, Lxx *Ps.*17(18).13.

**τῆλε**, Boeot. **Πειλε-** in pr. names, Adv. = τηλοῦ (q.v.), *at a distance, far off*, Il.17.190, Od.2.183, 17.312; μάλα τ. Hes.*Th.*1015; τ. πρὸς δυσμαῖς A.*Pers.*232 (troch.). 2. *to a distance, afar*, τῆλε δὲ χαλκὸς λάμπε Il.10.153; τ. βάλε 20.482; τ. πεσόντα 18.395; ᾤχετο τ. διὰ προμάχων 11.358. 3. c. gen., *far from*, τ. φίλων καὶ πατρίδος αἴης ib.817, 16.539; τ. δ' ἀπεπλάγχθη σάκεος δόρυ 22.291; cf. Od.2. 333, 12.354, etc.; τ. δ' ἀπ' αὐτοῦ κάππεσε Il.23.880, cf. 16.117, 17. 301, Od.5.315, Hes.*Sc.*275; also τῆλ' ἐξ.. Il.2.863.—Ep. word, used once by Pi., *P.*11.23, and once in Trag. (A. l. c.); never in Prose, cf. τηλαυγής.

**τηλε-βᾰθής**, ές, *very deep*, Opp.*H.*1.633. **-βῐος**, ον, *long-lived*, δαίην ἀσπίδα τηλέβιον, of a sacred serpent, Puchstein *Epigr.Gr.*p.76 (Memphis, i B.C.). **-βόας**, ου, ὁ, *shouting afar* or *loud*, only as pr. n., Arist.*Frr.*473,546; οἱ Τ. an Acarnanian tribe, Hes.*Sc.*19, Epigr.ap.Hdt.5.59. **-βόλος**, ον, *striking from afar*, χερμάς Pi.*P.* 3.49; of a bow, Arist.*Pepl.*52; χρῆσθαι τηλεβόλοις (sc. ὅπλοις) Str. 10.1.12, cf. 4.4.3 (Comp.), etc.

**Τηλεγόνεια**, ἡ, name of a poem in the Epic Cycle, Eust.785.23, 1796.47; gen. sg. misspelt -γονίας in Procl.*Chr.*p.109 Allen.

**τηλέγονος**, ον, only found as pr. name, Hes.*Th.*1014, Arist.*Po.* 1453$^b$33, etc.; = *Proculus*, *Gloss.* (*Proculus* is expld. as *qui patre longius peregrinante nascitur*, ib.).

**τηλεδᾰπός**, ή, όν, *from a far country*, ἄνδρες, ξεῖνοι, Od.6.279, 19. 351, etc.: of places, *far off, distant*, νήσων ἔπι τηλεδαπάων Il.21.454, 22.45, cf. *Jahresh.*23 *Beibl.*178 (Thrace), *Sammelb.*7423.9. (On the termin. -δαπος, v. ἀλλοδαπός.)

**τηλεθάω**, lengthd. for θάλλω (cf. τέθηλα, θηλέω, θαλέθω), used only in pres., and (exc. in Theoc.*Ep.*4.6, and late Ep., as D.P. 836) only in part., *luxuriant, flourishing*, ὕλη τηλεθόωσα Il.6.148; ἔρνος τηλεθάον 17.55; ἐλαῖαι τηλεθόωσαι Od.11.590; δένδρεα τηλεθόωντα 7.114: metaph., παῖδες τηλεθάοντες *blooming* sons, Il.22. 423; χαίτη τηλεθόωσα *luxuriant* hair, 23.142; ἄστεα τηλεθάοντα Emp. 112.7: c. dat., κισσὸς ἄνθεσι τ. *blooming with* flowers, *h.Hom.*7.41.

**τηλέθροος**, v. τηλύθροος.

**τηλε-κλειτός**, όν, also ή, όν (A.R.3.1097):—*far-famed*, Φοῖνιξ Il. 14.321; Ἐφιάλτης Od.11.308; Ἰκάριος 19.546; so also as epith. of the Trojan ἐπίκουροι, Il.5.491, 6.111, 9.233, 11.564 (v.l.), 12.108; written -κλητοί in some codd. (-κλειτός fr. -κλεϝετος, cf. sq.) **-κλῦτός**, όν, = τηλεκλειτός, Ὀρέστης Od.1.30, cf. *Chron.Lind.C.*51; of horses, τ. τέκνα Ποδάργης Il.19.400. **-μᾰχος**, ον, *fighting from afar*, Ἄρτεμις Luc.*Lex.*12. II. in Hom. pr. n., Τηλέμαχος, ὁ, son of Odysseus: Arc. Τηλίμαχος (influenced by the opposite ἀγχίμαχος, as conversely ἀγχέμαχος by τηλέμαχος) *IG*5(2).1.53 (Tegea, iv B.C.). **-πλᾰνος**, ον, *far-wandering*. πλάναι τ. *devious* wanderings, A.*Pr.*576 (lyr., restored by Seidler metri gr. for τηλέπλαγκτοι). **-πομπος**, ον, *far-sent, far-journeying*, φάος A.*Ag.* 300. ❀ **-πορος**, ον, *far-travelling, far-reaching*, τ. βόαμα *Lyr. Adesp.*102. 2. *far-distant*, τ. ἐν ἄντροις S.*Ant.*983 (lyr.); ἅδης Orph.*H.*18.9; δίνη Id.*Fr.*236. **-πῦλος**, ον, *with gates far apart*, τ. Λαιστρυγονίην Od.10.82, 23.318; but it is now written Τηλέπυλον as a pr. n., Laestrygonian *Telepylus*.

**τηλεσίφαντος** [ῐ], ον, = τηλέφαντος, ἄστρα Orph.*A.*341 codd.

**τηλε-σκόπος**, ον, *far-seeing*, ὄμμα Ar.*Nu.*290 (lyr.). II. proparox. τηλέσκοπος, ον, *far-seen, conspicuous*, Hes.*Th.*566,569, S.*Fr.* 338 (Bentley, for τῇδε σκοπῶν), Limen.1, *AP*6.251 (Phil.); parox. in Max.436, Musae.237. **-φᾰής**, ές, *far-shining*, Ph.Epic.ap.Eus. *PE*9.37; *far-seen*, κόνις *Epigr.Gr.*234 (Smyrna, iii B.C.): elsewhere only found in the fem. pr. name **Τηλεφάεσσα**, contr. Τηλεφάσσα, Apollod.3.1.1. **-φᾰνής**, ές, Aeol. [π]ηλεφάνης [ᾰ] prob. in Alc. *Oxy.*1788 *Fr.*1.7:—*far-seen, conspicuous*, τύμβος Od.24.83; πῦρ Pi. *Fr.*129.7, Aret.*SD*2.13; πέτρα Men.312 (anap.); σκοπιαί Ar.*Nu.*281 (lyr.). 2. metaph. of hearing, *heard plainly from afar*, ἀχώ S. *Ph.*189 (lyr.), cf. τηλωπός 2. **-φαντος**, ον, = foreg. 1, Pi.*Fr.*5: cf. τηλεσίφαντος. **-φᾰτος**, ον, = τηλεφανής 1, ib.87.4 (-φαντον cj. Bgk.).

**Τηλέφειον** ἀγαθόν, i.e. *health*, Diog.*Ep.*34.3; ἕλκος Τ. a wound *of Telephus*, i.e. a *malignant* wound, Gal.7.727, 10.83, al.

**τηλέφῐλον**, τό, *love-in-absence*, the leaf of some plant used as a charm by lovers to try whether their love was returned; the leaf was laid on the hand or arm and struck smartly, and its adhesion (or a loud crack, or a red colour, acc. to Sch.) was a favourable omen, οὐδὲ τὸ τηλέφιλον ποτεμάξατο τὸ πλατάγημα Theoc.3.29, cf. Sch. ad loc., Poll.9.127; τηλεφίλου πλαταγήματος ἠχέτα βόμβος γαστέρα μαντῴου μάξατο κισσυβίου *AP*5.295 (Agath.).

**τηλέφῐον**, τό, *Andrachna telephioides*, Hp.*Nat.Mul.*32, *Mul.*2.201, Ps.-Dsc.2.186, Gal.12.140.

❀ **τηλεφόρος**, ον, *far-carrying*, δόρυ Nonn.*D.*19.149.

**τηλεφώνιον**, τό, = τηλέφιον, Dsc.2.186.

**τηλέχθων**, ονος, ὁ, ἡ, *far-away*, γαῖα Opp.*H.*4.336.

**τήλη**, ἡ, = τῆλις, *Gloss.*; gen. sg. τήλη (with loss of -ς) *PTeb.* 115.12 (ii B.C.); gen. written τίλης, Hsch. s. v. βούκερας; dat. τήλῃ *PTeb.*66.43 (ii B.C.).

**τηλία**, ἡ, *board* or *table with a raised rim* or *edge*, to prevent meal and pastry placed on it from falling off, *corn-seller's* or *baker's board*, Pherecr.126, Peithol.ap.Arist.*Rh.*1411$^a$14, cf. *HA*578$^a$1 (hence cj. for ἑστίας in *Hippiatr.*1), *BGU*1117.11 (i B.C.), Sch.Ar.*Pl.*1038 (citing Eup.194), *AB*275: but in Ar. l. c. (1037) apptly. *hoop of a corn-sieve*, κοσκίνου κύκλος Sch. 2. *table* or *stage whereon game-cocks and quails were set to fight*, Aeschin.1.53, Poll.9.108, Alciphr.3.53: generally, *gambling-table*, *AB* l. c. 3. *chimney board, trap-door*, Ar.*V.*147.—A form **σηλία** is cited in Sch.Ar. l. c., cf. σήμερον, τήμερον; v. σαλία.

**τηλίζω**, *resemble fenugreek* (in smell), Dsc.3.40.

**τηλίκος** [ῐ], η, ον, Dor. **τᾱλίκος**, *of such an age, so old* or *so young*, answering to relat. ἡλίκος and interrog. πηλίκος (τηλικόσδε, τηλικοῦτος being used in Att.); used with relatives, πατρὸς.. τηλίκου ὥς περ ἐγών Il.24.487; so perh. παῖς τ., ὃν.. Od.18.175: c. inf., οὐ γὰρ ἐπὶ σταθμοῖσι μένειν ἔτι τηλίκος εἰμί not *so young* as to stay at home, 17. 20, cf. 1.297, 19.88; οὔ τοι τ. εἰμὶ μαθεῖν Thgn.578: Sup. -ώτατος, = πρεσβύτατος, Hsch. II. *so great*, τὸν τ. *AP*7.2.9 (Antip. Sid.); ὄνομα ib.7.11.4 (Asclep.); φρύαγμα τὸ τ. ib.10.64.1 (Agath.). Adv. -κως Aristaenet.2.9 (s. v. l.).

**τηλῐκόσδε**, ήδε, όνδε, and **τηλῐκοῦτος**, αύτη, οῦτον (also τηλικοῦτος as fem., S.*OC*751, *El.*614; and -οῦτο in neut., Alex.244), strengthd. forms of τηλίκος (as ὅδε, οὗτος of ὁ, τημοῦτος of τῆμος, v. οὗτος A); the latter being more common in Prose: I. of persons, *of such an age*, usu. meaning *so old*, with a part., τηλικόσδ' ὤν E.*Alc.*643, cf. Pl.*Ap.*34e, etc.; γεγῶσα τηλικήδ' ὅμως E.*Fr.*533; τηλικοῦτος ὤν Ar.*Eq.*881, Antiph.261, Pl.*Grg.* 489b, etc.: without part., τηλικόσδε, τηλικοῦτος, S.*OC*735, *El.* 614; νοῦς τηλικοῦτος the mind *of one so old as he is*, Id.*Ant.* 767; τηλικῷδε ἀνθρώπῳ Pl.*Ap.*37d: pleonast., τηλικοίδε γέροντες ἄνδρες Id.*Cri.*49a (s. v. l.): with Art., διδάσκεσθαι βαρὺ τῷ τηλικούτῳ A.*Ag.*1620, v. infr. 3. 2. of degrees of youth, *so young*, τηλικάσδ' ὁρῶν πάντων ἐρήμους girls *of so tender age*, S. *OT*1508, cf. *OC*1116; ἀεί σε κηδεύουσα.. τηλικοῦτος ib.751; ὃν εἰ τηλικοῦτον ὄντα ἀπεκτείνατε.. Lys.14.16, cf. Pl.*R.*378d, *Prt.* 361e. 3. repeated in opp. senses, οἱ τηλικοίδε καὶ διδαξόμεσθα δὴ φρονεῖν ὑπ' ἀνδρὸς τηλικοῦδε τὴν φύσιν; shall we *old as we are* take lessons forsooth from *one so young?* S.*Ant.*726; σὺ ἐμοῦ σοφώτερος εἶ τηλικούτου ὄντος τηλικόσδε ὤν you *though so young* are wiser than I *though so old*, Pl.*Ap.*25d. II. *so great, so large*, = τόσος, τοσόσδε, ἐμὲ τηλικόνδε ὄντα *the size I am*, Id.*Tht.*155b; τ. κακά Lyc.819, cf. Ath.9.380d; τὰ τ. Pl.*Ax.*370c: mostly in the stronger form, ἡ τηλικαύτη [πόλις] Id.*R.*423b; ἀνὴρ τ. ὢν being *so great*, X.*HG*6.4.31; ἡ τ. ἀρχή, τ. ἔχθρα, Pl.*Lg.*755b, 928e; τ. κακά, τ. ἀγαθόν, X.*Mem.*2.1.5, 4.4.8; τ. [ἀδικήματα] D.18.13; τ. τιμωρίαι Aeschin.1.173; πεπραγμένα τ. τὸ μέγεθος Isoc.5.151, cf. 98; τηλικαύτην βλάβην *PCair.Zen.*378.11 (iii B.C.):—τηλικοῦτος is freq. conjoined with τοιοῦτος and τοσοῦτος, νησύδρια τοιαῦτα καὶ τ. *so small*, Isoc.12.70; τ. καὶ τοιοῦτον σύστημα Pl.*Lg.*686b; τ. καὶ τοσοῦτος θεός Id.*Smp.*177a; τοσοῦτοι καὶ τ. θόρυβοι Aeschin.1.174; τ. καὶ τοσαῦτ' ἀγαθά D.19.24; οἱ τ. καὶ τοιοῦτοι τῷ γένει Men.*Epit.*120.

**τηλῐκουτοσί**, strengthd. form of τηλικοῦτος, Pherecr.146, Phryn.Com.19.

**τηλίνη**, ἡ, = κύτισος, Ps.-Dsc.4.112.

**τήλῐνος**, η, ον, *of fenugreek*, μύρον Plb.30.26.2: so τήλινον, τό, Men.952, *PPetr.*2p.114 (iii B.C.), Dsc.1.47, Ath.15.689a.

**τῆλις**, ἡ, gen. εως Hp.*Mul.*2.194, *PTeb.*55.8 (ii B.C.), etc., also ιος Hp.*Epid.*5.68 (= 7.65), *PLille* 37.5, al., *PLond.ined.*2360, *PCair.Zen.*731.10 (all iii B.C.):—*fenugreek, Trigonella Foenum-graecum*, ll. cc., Thphr.*HP*3.17.2, *PLond.*1.131.290 (i A.D.), Dsc.2.102, Sor.1.56, al., Gal.6.537, *PHolm.*15.25, etc.; written **τίλ-** in good codd. of *Gp.*2.18.11, al.

***τῆλις**, ιδος, ἡ, v. τᾶλις.

**τήλιστος**, η, ον, (τηλοῦ) Sup. without Posit. or Comp., *farthest, most remote*, Parth.*Fr.*8 (-ίτων codd. St. Byz.), v.l. (ap.Eust.) for τρίλλιστος in D.P.485: neut. τήλιστα as Adv., *farthest*, Orph.*A.*181; cf. τηλωπός I.

**τηλίτης** [ῑ] οἶνος, ὁ, wine *flavoured with* τῆλις (*fenugreek*), *Gp.*8.14 (τιλ-, v.l. τηλ-).

⊛ **τηλόθεν**, Aeol. **[π]ήλοθεν** prob. in Alc.*Supp.*12.10:—Adv., (τηλοῦ) *from afar*, τ. ἦλθεν Il.5.651, cf. S.*Aj.*1318, *Ph.*454; εἰ καὶ μάλα τηλόθεν ἐσσί Od.6.312, cf. 7.194: in Hom. mostly folld. by ἐκ, τηλόθεν ἐξ ἀπίης γαίης Il.1.270, al.:—**τηλόθε**, Pi.*N.*3.81, *AP*9.246 (Marc. Arg.). 2. sts. in the sense of τηλόθι, σήμηνε δὲ τέρματ' Ἀχιλλεὺς τ. ἐν λείῳ πεδίῳ Il.23.359: so c. gen., Πελειάδων τηλόθεν *far from* them, Pi.*N.*2.12, cf. S.*Aj.*204 (anap.), E.*HF*1112.

**τηλόθῐ**, Adv. = τῆλε, τηλοῦ, *afar, at a distance*, Od.1.22, Il.8.285, al., Theoc.24.116 codd.: c. gen., τηλόθι πάτρης Il.1.30, al.; νηῶν Q.S.14.410.

**τηλοῖ** and **τήλοι**, *far*, are conjectures (prob. false) for **πηλοι**, the Ms. reading (unaccented) in A.D.*Adv.*197.15; v. τηλοῦ fin.

**τηλόμελι**, μέλιτος, τό, *mixture of* τῆλις *and honey*, Paul.Aeg.6.20.

**τηλοπέτης**, ες, *far-flying*, *AP*6.239 (Apollonid.).

**τηλορός**, όν, collat. form of τηλουρός, τηλορὸς ναίω E.*El.*251.

**τηλόσε**, Adv. *to a distance, far away*, Il.4.455, 22.407, E.*IT*175 (anap.): c. gen., Q.S.4.407.

**τηλοτάτω**, Adv., Sup. of τηλοῦ, *farthest away*, Od.7.322:—Comp. **τηλοτέρω**, *farther away*, ἀπεῖναι Hp.*Art.*53: c. gen., *farther from..*, Id.*Nat.Puer.*31, Arat.1050:—hence Adj. **τηλότερος**, *AP*14.120 (Metrod.).

⊛ **τηλοῦ**, Adv. *afar, far away, in a far country*, Hom., Hes., and later Ep.; τηλοῦ ἐπ' Ἀλφειῷ Il.11.712; τ. τῶν ἀγρῶν *in a far-away corner* of the country, Ar.*Nu.*138. b. of Time, *long ago, of old*, οὐ γάρ σε..ἀρχεύοντα νέον γεινώσκομεν ἀλλ' ἔτι τ. Epic.*Oxy.*1015.13; ἐξέτι τ. since *olden times*, *IG*5(2).173.1 (Tegea, iv B.C.); so perh. Ὀδυσῆϊ γε τ. ἀπώλετο νόστιμον ἦμαρ Od.17.253: c. fut., οὐδέ τι τ. ὄψεαι Opp.*H.*2.495. 2. c. gen., mostly, *far from*, Od.13.249, 23.68 (also τηλοῦ ἀπὸ.. Hes.*Th.*302); rare in Trag., τ. σέθεν *far from* thee, E.*Cyc.*689. (Opp. ἀγχοῦ, ἄγχι. An obs. Adj. τηλός may be taken as the source whence come the Advbs. τηλοῦ, τηλοῖ, τηλόθι, τηλόθεν, τηλόσε, τηλοτέρω, τηλοτάτω, and Adj. τηλότερος; also τηλύς, whence τήλιστος: a form τῆλυ = τῆλε is recognized by A.D.*Pron.*54.28, and occurs in τηλύ-γετος: an Aeol. form **πήλυι**, cited by Priscian.*Inst.*1.6.37, Theognost.*Can.*160, is restored in Sapph.1.6, where however **πήλοι**, which is v.l. and is recommended by A.D.*Adv.*197.15, shd. perh. be read.)

**τηλουρός**, όν, (ὅρος) *with distant boundaries*: hence, generally, *distant*, χθονὸς πέδον A.*Pr.*1; πεδία E.*Andr.*889; αἶα A.R.2.543: c. gen., τ. οὖσα δωμάτων E.*Or.*1325; cf. *IGRom.*4.360.38 (Pergam., ii A.D.), and v. τηλορός.

**τηλύγετος** [ῠ], η, ον, old Ep. epith. of children, of uncertain origin and sense; sts. clearly of *a darling son, petted child*, ἀλλ' οὐκ Ἰδομενῆα φόβος λάβε, τηλύγετον ὥς Il.13.470; τίσω δέ μιν ἶσον Ὀρέστῃ, ὅς μοι τ. τρέφεται θαλίῃ ἔνι πολλῇ 9.143, cf. 285; so of an *only* son, ὡς..πατὴρ ὃν παῖδα φιλήσῃ μοῦνον τηλύγετον ib.482; ὅς οἱ τ. γένετο Od.4.11; ὡς δὲ πατὴρ ὃν παῖδα..ἀγαπάζῃ..μοῦνον τηλύγετον 16.19; son *of one's old age*, τ. οἱ υἱός..ὀψίγονος τρέφεται *h.Cer.*164, cf. 283; also λιποῦσα παῖδά τε τηλυγέτην, of Hermione, *the only* daughter of Helen, Il.3.175; once of two sons, perh. twins, Φαίνοπος υἷε, ἄμφω τηλυγέτω 5.153: so in later Ep., A.R.1.719, Mosch.4.79; of a wife, ἄλοχον σαόφρονα τηλυγέτην τε *JHS*19.296 (Galatia): once in Trag., τηλύγετον [χθονὸς] ἀπὸ πατρίδος E.*IT*829 (lyr.), where it seems to mean τηλοῦ γεγονότα, born *far away, far-distant*, as it certainly does in Simm.1.1 τηλυγέτων..Ὑπερβορέων ἀνὰ δῆμον; similarly, τηλυγέτων ἀποικιῶν· τῶν μακρὰν ἀπεχουσῶν, Hsch. (= *Com.Adesp.*1315). (The best of the ancient interpretations is *latest-born*, i.e. *after whom no more are born* (= ὁ τῆς γονῆς τέλος ἔχων, μεθ' ὃν ἕτερος οὐ γίνεται, Sch.TIl.9.482), including *only children*, these being the best-beloved. The word was prob. thought to be derived from τέλος (τελευ-τή, cf. Orion in *Et.Gud.*616.37) and γίγνομαι; but this presents difficulties, and the sense *petted, well-beloved*, may equally well be the primary one.)

**τηλύθροος**, ον, *heard from afar, loud-voiced*, Hsch. (where however the alph. order requires τηλέθροος).

**τηλῶθεν**, Adv. = τηλόθεν, Theognost.*Can.*157.

**τηλωπός**, όν, (ὤψ) *seen from afar, far away*, τηλωπὸς οἰχνεῖ S.*Aj.*564; without context in *Supp.Epigr.*2.359 (Gomphi, Hymn to Isis), Lyr. in *Mitt. a. d. Papyrussamml. der Nationalbibliothek in Wien* 1 (1932) p.139; fem. **τηλῶπις**, Orph.*A.*900; in 1188, Herm. restored τήλιστον. 2. metaph. of sound, *heard from afar*, ἰωά S.*Ph.*216 (lyr.); cf. τηλεφανής 2.

**τημέλ-εια**, ἡ, *care, attention, attendance*, Hp.*Ep.*17, Hierocl.p.59A., prob. cj. in Hld.5.30; **τημελία**, Sch.Ar.*V.*604. **-έω**, *take care of, look after*, c. acc., χώρει πρὸς Ἄργος παρθένους τε τημέλει E.*IA*731; οὐδ' ἐργάτης σίδηρος..οἴνης ὀρχάτους ἐτημέλει Moschio Trag.6.12; αἱ γυναῖκες, ὅταν τέκωσι, τ. τοὺς ἄνδρας Nymphod.15; ἵνα μηδὲν ἄλλο ἢ ταύτην (sc. τὴν ἀρετὴν) καθάπερ ἀγαθὸς γεωργὸς τ. καὶ περιέπῃ Ph.1.52, cf. eund.ap.Eus.*PE*8.14; τημελοῦντες [τὴν ἀρχὴν] ὥσπερ νομεῖς Aristid.*Or.*26(14).18; τ. τὴν κεφαλήν Plu.*Art.*18, Artem.1.38, cf. Plu.2.148d, S.E.*M.*7.249: c. gen., σώματός τ' ἐτημέλει E.*IT*311, cf. Pl.*Lg.*953a:—Med., c. acc., D.H.4.67. **-η**, f.l. for τημέλει (E.*IA*731) in Phryn.*PS*p.114B. **-ής**, ές, *careful, heedful*, Hsch., Phot., Suid. Adv. -ῶς Max.Tyr.25.4; poet. -έως Aglaïas 28. (Origin uncertain: cf. ἀτημελής.) **-ητής**· ἐπιμελητής, Hsch.

**τημένιος**, v. τηβέννειος. **τημενίς**, v. τήβεννος. **τήμερα**, **τήμερον**, v. σήμερον.

**τῆμος**, Dor. **τᾶμος**, Adv. *then, thereupon*, answering to the relat. ἦμος (q.v.), Il.23.228, Hes.*Op.*488,585, S.*Tr.*533 (nowhere else in Trag.), Theoc.13.27: freq. folld. by another Particle, ἦμος.., τ. ἄρα Il.7.434, Od.4.401, etc.; τ. δή.. 12.441: also antec. to εὖτε, εὖτ' ἀστὴρ ὑπερέσχε.., τ. δή.. Od.13.95: without any corresponding relat., *h.Merc.*101, Hes.*Op.*559, A.R.4.1400; so τ. δέ.. Od.7.318, Hes.*Op.*670.—The Att. words are τηνικάδε, τηνικαῦτα. II. in A.R.4.252, καὶ τῆμος even *to-day*; Thess. **τᾶμος** (τᾶμον), q.v.

**τημόσδε**, Dor. **τᾱμόσδε**, Adv. = τῆμος, Theoc.10.49, Call.*Jov.*21, cj. in A.R.2.957:—also **τημοῦτος**, Hes.*Op.*576, Call.*Dian.*175, *Aet.*3.1.44, Nic.*Th.*926.

**τηνάκις** [ᾰ], *at that time*, *IG*7.2462 (Thebes, iv B.C.).

**τηνάλλως** or **τὴν ἄλλως**, v. ἄλλως II. 3.

**τηνεῖ**, Adv., Dor. for ἐκεῖ, *there*, Epich.99, Orac.ap.Plu.*Dem.*19, *Schwyzer* 323 *C* 37 (Delph., iv B.C.), *APl.*4.255; opp. ὧδε, Theoc.1.106, cf. 4.35; but perh. equiv. to ὧδε, *here*, Id.5.33 (dub.), *PCair.Zen.*509.2,11 (iii B.C.).

**τήνελλα**, a word formed by Archil. (*Fr.*119) to imitate the twang of a guitar-string (cf. θρεττανελό): he began a triumphal hymn to Heracles with τήνελλα, ὦ καλλίνικε χαῖρε; hence the words τήνελλα καλλίνικε became a common mode of saluting conquerors in the games, *Hurrah!*, Ar.*Av.*1764 (lyr.), *Ach.*1227 (cf. Sch.Pi.*O.*9.1):—hence II. Adj. **τήνελλος**, ον, *greeted with huzzas*, ἐὰν..νικᾷς.., τήνελλος εἶ Ar.*Eq.*276. (Written **τήνεβλα** and **τήνεβλος** in Hsch.)

⊛ **τηνεσμός**, ὁ, f.l. for τεινεσμός in Nic.*Al.*382, Hsch.

**τήνης**· ἕως (Tarent.), Hsch.

**τηνίκα** [ῐ], Dor. **τᾱνίκα**, Adv. *at that time, then*, prop. answering to Relat. ἡνίκα and Interrog. πηνίκα, ὁπηνίκα; εὖτε.., τηνίκα.. A.R.1.799: also with the Art., ὅτε.., τὸ τ... S.*OC*440. 2. abs., *at that time* [of day], Theoc.1.17: c. gen., τοῦ ἔτους τ. *at that time* of the year, Ael.*NA*15.5 codd.—The Att. forms are τηνικάδε, τηνικαῦτα.

**τηνῐκάδε**, Adv. = foreg., answering to a Relat., *at this time, then*, ἐπεὶ.., τ... Plb.16.11.6; ἐπειδή.., τὸ τ. Id.16.30.7, cf. Ph.*Bel.*66.13, 74.38; also after δρῶν = ἐπεὶ ἑώρα, Plb.10.28.5. 2. abs., *at this time of day, so early*, τοῦ ἕνεκα τ. ἀφίκου; Pl.*Cri.*43a, cf. *Prt.*310b; αὔριον τ. to-morrow *at this time*, Id.*Phd.*76b: c. gen., τ. τῆς ὥρας, τοῦ καιροῦ, *at this season* of the year, Ael.*NA*1.36, 4.27.

**τηνῐκ-αῦτα**, commoner form for τηνίκα, answering to a Relat., *at that time, then*, ἡνίκα.., τηνικαῦτα.. X.*Cyr.*7.1.9; answering to ὁπηνίκα, S.*Ph.*465; to ὅτε or ὅταν, Id.*OC*393, *OT*76, etc.; to ὁπότε, ὅκως, X.*Cyr.*1.6.26, Hdt.1.17; to ἐπεί, ἐπειδάν, ἐπειδή, X.*An.*4.2.3, *Cyr.*1.2.13, D.21.96: also with the Art., τὸ τ. D.S.1.98, etc. 2. without a Relat. expressed, Hdt.1.18,63, S.*Ant.*779, etc.; ἤδη τ. *by that time*, Hdt.2.51, 6.53; τ. ἤδη only *then*, Ar.*Ec.*789; τὸ τ. ἤδη Pl.*Alc.*2.150e; *at that time* of day, Lys.1.22; *at this hour*, τ. ἐχθὲς ἔπινον Men.*Epit.*166: c. gen., τ. τοῦ θέρους *at this time* of the summer, Ar.*Pax* 1171 (lyr.); τ. τοῦ ἔτους Luc.*Herod.*7. II. without reference to Time, *under these circumstances, in this case*, τί τ. δρῶμεν; Ar.*Pax* 1142 (troch.), cf. Pl.*Lg.*792b, X.*Mem.*3.11.14. (From τηνίκα, as ἐνταῦθα from ἔνθα.) **-αυτί** [ῑ], = foreg. I. 2, *UPZ*144.26 (ii B.C.).

**τηνόθι**, Adv. of τῆνος, *in that case, then*, Theoc.8.44.

**τῆνος**, τήνα, τῆνο, Dor. for Aeol. κῆνος, Ion. and Att. κεῖνος, ἐκεῖνος, *he, she, it*, *IG*4.7 (Aegina), Epich.35, Sophr.56, Erinn. in *PSI*9p.xii, *Tab.Heracl.*1.136, Ages.ap.Plu.*Ages.*11, Theoc.1.4,5,11, etc.: sts. with a strongly demonstr. force, like ὅδε or ὁδί, Id.1.1,8,23, etc. 2. *the famous*, Id.1.120,126, etc.; or *the notorious*, Id.5.1,15, etc. 3. in opposed clauses, τόκα μὲν ἐν τήνων.., τόκα δὲ πὰρ τήνοις Epich.147, cf. Theoc.1.36.

**τηνῶ**, Adv. of τῆνος, Dor. for ἐκεῖθεν, Theoc.3.25.

**τηνῶθεν**, Adv. of τῆνος, Dor. for ἐκεῖθεν, Ar.*Ach.*754; also **τηνῶθε**, Theoc.3.10, *AP*6.354 (Noss.).

**τηξῐ-μελής**, ές, *wasting the limbs*, νοῦσος *AP*7.234 (Phil.). **-πόθος**, ον, *wasting with desire*, Ἔρωτες Crates Theb.5a.

**τῆξις**, εως, ἡ, *melting*, Arist.*Mete.*382b30, Plu.2.692a; κηροῦ S.E.*M.* 9.251; χιόνων Eratosth.ap.Str.16.1.15 (pl.). **2.** *wasting, loss of flesh*, Hp.*Coac.*509; σαρκός Plu.2.658a. **3.** *a solution*, λίτρου Aret.*CA*2.7.

⊕ **τηρ-έω** (τη- also in Dor., Alcm.23.77, Pi.*P.*2.88, cf. διατηρέω), pf. τετήρηκα Epicur.*Sent.*24, etc.:—*watch over, take care of, guard*, δώματα *h.Cer.*142; πόλιν Pi. l. c., cf. Ar.*V.*210; τὰς κύνας X.*Cyn.*6. 1; τὴν ἀσφάλειαν τῆς ἐπιβουλῆς Antipho 2.2.8; rarely of persons, δαιμόνων.., αἵτινες τηροῦμεν ὑμᾶς Ar.*Nu.*579 (troch.); τ. τὴν ἀρχὴν *maintain* it, Plb.21.32.2; τὸ τῆς πόλεως ἀξίωμα D.S.17.15:—Pass., τὸ ἔξωθεν [τεῖχος] ἐτηρεῖτο *was constantly guarded*, Th.2.13: fut. Med. τηρήσομαι in pass. sense, Id.4.30. **2.** τ. ὅπως.. ἔσται *take care that*.., Arist.*Pol.*1309b16; ὅπως μηθὲν παρανομῶσι ib.1307b31; τ. μή.. *cavere ne*.., Ar.*Th.*580, Pl.*Tht.*169c; τ. ἐμέ, ὅπως μὴ ἐξαπατήσω D.18.276: also in Med., τηρώμεσθ', ὅπως μή..αἰσθήσεται Ar. *V.*372; τηροῦ μὴ λάβῃς ὑπώπια ib.1386. **3.** τηρεῖν ἀπὸ τοῦ πυρός *protect* them from the fire, i.e. cook them slowly, Bilabel Ὀψαρτ.p. 10. **II.** *give heed to, watch narrowly, observe*, τηρῶ αὐτοὺς οὐδὲ δοκῶν ὁρᾶν κλέπτοντας Ar.*Eq.*1145, cf. *V.*364; τὰς ἁμαρτίας Th.4.60; ἐκεῖνο τ. μή.. Ar.*Pax* 146, cf. Pl.*R.*442a; τ. ὅ τι καὶ δράσει Ar.*Ec.* 946. **2.** *watch for* a person or thing, with a part., παραστείχοντα τηρήσας S.*OT*808; ἔνδον ὄντα τηρήσαντες αὐτόν *having watched* for his being within, Th.1.134; τ. τὸν πορθμὸν κατιόντος τοῦ ἀνέμου *watching* for a crossing with the wind blowing down, Id.6.2; τ. τινὰ ἀνιόντα *watch for* one's coming up, D.53.17: c. acc. only, ἄνεμον τηρῆσαι Th.1.65; τ. νύκτα χειμέριον Id.3.22, cf. 4.27; νύκτα καὶ ὕδωρ D.59.103; τ. τοὺς ἀστέρας Arist.*Cael.*292a8; τὴν θήραν τ. Id.*HA*623a13; τ. καιρόν Id.*Rh.*1382b10:—Pass., ὁ καιρὸς ἐτηρήθη *was watched for*, Lys.12.71. **3.** abs., *watch, keep watch*, Th. 7.80, Arist.*EN*1167b13: c. inf., *watch* or *look out*, so as to.., ἐτήρουν ἀνέμῳ καταφέρεσθαι Th.4.26. **4.** *observe, notice*, [μετακόσμησιν σωμάτων] Sor.1.41; τὸν χαρακτῆρα τῆς φράσεως Id.*Vit. Hippocr.*13; τὸ πολὺ μὲν οὕτως ἀποβαίνειν τετήρηται Gal.18(2). 13. **5.** *test by observation* or *trial*, τετηρημένον βοήθημα an *approved* method of treatment, Antyll.ap.Orib.6.22.3; τετήρηνται χρησιμεύοντές τισι Id.ib.21.9; as Empiric term, τετηρημένης ἐπ' αὐτοῖς τῆς θεραπείας, οὐκ ἐνδεικτικῶς εὑρισκομένης Gal.6.361; Μηνόδοτος ὁ ἐμπειρικός, ἐπὶ μόνῃ τῇ πληθωρικῇ καλουμένῃ συνδρομῇ φάσκων τετηρῆσθαι φλεβοτομίαν Id.15.766. **III.** *observe* or *keep* an engagement, ὅρκους Democr.239; παρακαταθήκας Isoc.1.22; ἀπόρρητα Lys. 31.31; εἰρήνην D.18.89; τὸ πρέπον Phld.*Po.*5.35; τὴν πίστιν 2*Ep.Ti.* 4.7. **2.** *preserve, retain*, τὰς αἰσθήσεις dub. in Epicur.*Ep.*1 p.5 U., cf. Demetr.Lac.*Herc.*1055.9,10; ἰδιότητας Phld.*Rh.*1.154 S.; τὴν ποιότητα Sor.1.51; τὴν τροφὸν ἐπ' ὀλιγοποσίας..τ. ib.118, cf. 46, al.:—in Ph.1.125 there is a double use. **-ημα**, ατος, τό, *observation*, in Grammar, A.D.*Synt.*143.4; *preservation*, σεμνώματος *IG*2².1099.34 (Epist. Plotinae, ii A.D.), cf. *Riv.Ist.Arch.*3.40 (Latos). **-ησις**, εως, ἡ, *watching, safe-keeping, guarding*, ἀφύλακτος ἢ τ. E.*Fr.*162; τῆς πολιτείας Arist.*Pol.*1308a30, cf. *PA* 692a7; τῆς πόλεως *Supp.Epigr.*6.724 (Perga, ii/i B.C.); τῆς οἰκίας *POxy.*1070.51 (iii A.D.); ἀξιώματος Pl.*Def.*413e; τῆς ἡλικίας Epicur. *Sent.Vat.*80; [πλούτου] Phld.*Oec.*p.44 J.; *preservation*, e.g. of health, Gal.10.646, Pap. in *Stud.Ital.*12(1935).94 (iii A.D.); *observance*, νόμων, ἐντολῶν, Lxx *Wi.*6.18(19), 1*Ep.Cor.*7.19; λεξάντων πρὸς τὴν τήρησιν τοῦ ὕδατος *SIG*683.60 (Olympia, ii B.C.). **2.** *vigilance*, Th.7. 13, Plb.6.11a.10. **3.** *means of keeping* or *guarding*, τὰς λιθοτομίας.., ἀσφαλεστάτην τ. the most secure *place of custody*, Th. 7.86, cf. *Act.Ap.*4.3, *BGU*388 iii 7 (ii A.D.). **II.** *observing, observation*, τῶν καθόλου συμβαινόντων (as Empiric term) Sor.1.4, cf. Gal.15. 830, 16.550, 18(2).307, *Sect.Intr.*4, S.E.*P.*1.23, 2.246, A.D.*Synt.*37. 14, etc. **-ητέον**, *one must watch*, τ. τινὰς εἰ.. Pl.*R.*412e, cf. 413c, D.H.*Rh.*10.19; τ. ὅτι Ach.Tat.*Intr.Arat.*28; *one must preserve, retain*, τὸ φάντασμα ἑκάστου Epicur.*Ep.*2 p.37 U. **-ητήριον**, τό, = Lat. *servatorium*, Gloss. (written *tiritrion*). **-ητής**, οῦ, ὁ, *keeper, observer*, δίκης D.S.3.4. **2.** *guard, warden*, *PMich.Zen.*84.10 (iii B.C.), *PLond.*3.1171.57 (i B.C.), *PAmh.*2.126.22 (ii A.D.), etc. **-ητικός**, ή, όν, *observant*, Str.3.5.8; ἀκολουθία S.E.*M.*8.288, cf. Anon.Lond.36.49; τ. αἵρεσις, τ. ἄνδρες, = ἐμπειρική (-κοί), Gal. *Sect.Intr.*1. **2.** Pass., *needing to be observed*, D.L.9.108. Adv. -κῶς *by observation*, S.E.*M.*5.70. **3.** *retaining*, βωμὸς τ. θυσιῶν Ph.2.151; *preservative*, Ar.Did.*Epit.*33; τοῦ ὑγιαίνειν Sor.1.42; φύσεων *Theol.Ar.*5. **-ητρα**, τά, *expenses of guarding* an olive-yard, *PSI*1.33.22 (iii A.D.). **-ήτρια**, ἡ, fem. of τηρητής, dub. cj. for περήτρια (-ίτρια, -άτρια) in Hsch., Phot., Suid. **-ός**, ὁ, *warden, guard*, only in A.*Supp.*248.

**τῆτα**, v. τῆτες. **τητάνιος**, v. σητάνειος.

**τητάομαι**, Dor. **τᾱτ-**, (τήτη) Pass., only used in pres., *to be in want*, σὺ δὲ τητᾷ Hes.*Op.*408; τὸ τητᾶσθαι *privation*, S.*El.*265; τητῶνται shd. be read for ἡττῶνται (or ἀπατῶνται) in X.*Cyr.*8.4. 33. **2.** elsewh. always c. gen., *to be in want of, be deprived of* or *bereft of*, φίλων τατώμενος Pi.*N.*10.78, cf. E.*Hel.*274; [ἀνδρός], πατρός, νυμφίων, S.*OC*1618, E.*Heracl.*24, *Hec.*324; τῶν ἐμῶν τ. πρὸς τοῦ κακίστου S.*Ph.*383; ἀδέρκτων ὀμμάτων Id.*OC*1200; Ἑλλάδος τητώμενοι E.*Heracl.*31; χορῶν τ. Id.*El.*310; χαρμάτων τητώμεθα Id.*Or.* 1084; ῥυθμοῦ τε καὶ ἁρμονίας Pl.*Lg.*810b; εὐγενείας Arist.*EN*1099b 2; ἔργου Jul.*Or.*4.134c.

**τῆτες**, Adv. *this year, of* or *in this year*, esp. in Com., as Ar.*Ach.* 15, *V.*400 (anap.), *Fr.*148a, cf. Lys.*Fr.*216 S.; ἡ τ. ἡμέρα *this very day*, cited as an unusual phrase by Ath.3.98b:—a Dor. form **τῆδες** is cited by Sch.Ar.*Ach.*15, Suid. s.v. τῆτες, Eust.1618.39; Dor. **τᾶτες** Sch.Ar., Suid. ll. cc.; **τῆτα** Suid. (Cf. σῆτες, σᾶτες, σατινός; prob. related to ἔτος as σήμερον (τήμερον) to ἡμέρα.)

**τήτη**, ἡ, *want*, Hsch.

⊕ **τητινός**, ή, όν, (τῆτες) *of this year, this year's*, Luc.*Lex.*1, Hdn. Gr.2.233, Phryn.*PS*p.114 B., Poll.6.73. **2.** = χθεσινός, Suid.

**τῆτος**, εος, τό, = τήτη, only in Hsch. and Phot. (τήτει· σπάνει), unless we read in E.*Fr.*492, τήτει σοφῶν, for τι εἴ τι: cf. χῆτος.

**τηΰσιος** [ῠ], α, ον, Dor. **ταΰσιος** (Alcm.92, B.5.81), *idle, vain, undertaken to no purpose*, τηϋσίη ὁδός Od.3.316, 15.13; τηΰσιον ἔπος an *idle, rash* word, *h.Ap.*540; μὴ ταΰσιον προΐει οἰστόν B. l. c.; τ. πόδες A.R.3.651. Adv. τηϋσίως Theoc.25.230. Cf. αὔσιος.

**τιάλλακτον** (τη- cod., extra ordinem)· Σέλευκος παρὰ Ἐπαινέτῳ ἔμβαμμά τι, Hsch.

**τῐάρα** [ᾰρ], ἡ, and **τῐάρας**, ου, Ion. **τιήρης**, εω, ὁ (as in Hdt.8. 120):—*tiara*, the Persian head-dress, esp. on solemn occasions, Hdt.1.132, 3.12 (v. πῖλος), 7.61, 8.120; worn by the great king, A. *Pers.*661 (lyr.); whose tiara was upright, X.*An.*2.5.23, *Cyr.*8.3.13, Phylarch.22 J., Luc.*Pisc.*35.

**τῐᾰραφόρος**, ον, *wearing a tiara*, Max.Tyr.26.7 (v.l. τιαροφόρος).

**τῐᾱρις**, = τιάρα, Hsch.

**τῐᾱρό-δεσμον**, τό, *band for fastening the tiara behind*, Polyaen.7.11. 2. **-ειδής**, ές, *like* or *shaped like a tiara*, X.*An.*5.4.13. **-φόρος**, ον, v. τιαραφόρος.

**τιβάθων**· τιμώμενος, Hsch. **τίβδαινον**· φίλον, Id. **τιβδεῖ**· φοβεῖται, Id.

**Τίβειος** [ῐ], name of a slave, *IG*2².1672.69, 2937.7, 2940.8, Men. 1075, *Her.*21, al., prob. cj. in Thphr.*Char.*9.3; later **Τίβιος** [–⏑⏑] *AP*14.123.11 (Metrod., Τίμιος cod.): originally a Paphlagonian name, Str.7.3.12, 12.3.25, who implies that it was not the name of a people; cf. however Τίβειον ὄρος (v.l. τόπος) in Phrygia, St.Byz.; Τίβιοι καὶ Φρύγες Gal.10.4; **Τιβία**, = ὕλη ἢ Φρυγία, *App.Prov.*3.79.

**τιβήν**, ῆνος, ὁ, = τρίπους, Lyc.1104:—also **τίβηνος**· λέβης, τρίπους, Hsch.

**τιγάς**· εἶδος ἀμπέλου, Hsch.

**τιγγάβᾰρι** [γᾰ], τό, Att. for κιννάβαρι, Diocl.Com.9,10 (dub. l., -βαρυ cod.Hsch., Theognost.*Can.*120).

**τιγγᾰβάρῐνος** [βᾰ], η, ον, *of vermilion*, χρῶμα Dam.*Isid.*203.

⊕ **τ[ῐ]γρήϊος**, ον, or η, ον, *tiger-like*, τ. ἴχνος ἀείρει cj. in Euph. in *Riv. Fil.*13(1935).67.

**τίγρῐς**, ἡ, Philem.47, Plu.2.144d, also ὁ, Alex.204, Arist.*HA*607a 4, Thphr.*HP*5.4.7: gen. τίγριος Arist. and Thphr. ll. cc.; τίγριδος Opp.*C.*3.340; acc. τίγριν: pl. nom. τίγρεις, and τίγριδες D.C.54.9, 76.7; τίγριες Opp.*C.*1.323; τίγρητες Ar.Byz.*Epit.*95.10 (acc. to Choerob. *in Theod.*1.160 H. the river-name is both Τίγρης -ητος and Τίγρις -ιδος):—*tiger*, *Felis tigris*; Seleucus sent one to Athens, ὁ Σελεύκου τίγρις Alex. l. c., cf. Philem. l. c.

**τιγροειδής**, ές, *like a tiger, tiger-striped*, ἵπποι D.C.75.14.

**τίζω**, (τί;) *to be always asking* 'what?', Ar.*Fr.*871.

**τίη**, better τί ἤ (A.D.*Conj.*255.8, 256.3), Att. (?) τιή (v. infr.), strengthd. form of τί; *why? wherefore?* Il.1.365, 6.145, al., Hes.*Th.* 35, and Att. Comedy: folld. by a Particle, τίη δέ..; Il.6.55, 15. 244, Od.16.421, al.; τίη δή..; Il.21.436; doubled, τιὴ τί δή; standing alone, *why so, tell me?* Ar.*V.*1155, *Pax*1018, *Th.*84. (The oxyt. τιή is called Att. by Eust.118.36, cf. 45.4, but was unknown to A.D. and is prob. a fiction; τίη and τιή are dub. ll. in Ar.*Ach.*826; cf. ἤ 1.2, ὁτιή.)

**τί ἦν εἶναι**, τό, as a Subst., v. εἰμί (*sum*) F.

**τιήρης**, v. τιάρας.

**τῑθαιβώσσω**, of bees, *store up honey*, Od.13.106. **2.** generally, *store up, put away*, ἔνδοθι γωρυτοῖο τιθαιβώσσουσα κάλυψε Antim. in *PMilan.*17.37 (glossed τιθεῖσα καὶ ἀποθησαυρίζουσα ibid.). **II.** *supply with food, foster, cherish*, τέκνα τ. Nic.*Th.*199: metaph., γύας τ. ἀρδηθμῷ Lyc.622.

**τῑθαίνομαι**, v. τιθηνέω.

**τῑθὰς** ὄρνις, άδος, ἡ, *barn-door fowl, hen*, *AP*9.95 (Alph.).

**τῑθᾰσ-εία**, ἡ, *taming, domestication*, ἰχθύων Pl.*Plt.*264c (pl.); τὰ δεχόμενα τιθασείαν (codd. -άσιον) Thphr.*HP*3.2.2. **-ευμα**, ατος, τό, *device for taming*, Porph.*Abst.*1.9 (pl.). **-ευσις**, εως, ἡ, = τιθασεία, Plu.2.441e, Alex.Aphr. *in Top.*370.28. **-ευτέον**, *one must tame*, τινα Ph.2.285. **-ευτής**, οῦ, ὁ, *one who tames*, Ar.*V.* 704. **-ευτικός**, ή, όν, *easy to tame*, ἐλέφας Arist.*HA*488b 22. **-εύτωρ**, ορος, ὁ, poet. for τιθασευτής, Opp.*C.*2.543. **-εύω**, *tame, domesticate*, τὰ ἥμερα τρέφων καὶ τ. Pl.*R.*589b; τιθασεύοντες τὰ χρήσιμα τῶν ζῴων X.*Mem.*4.3.10:—Pass., τ. ὁ ἐλέφας καὶ πειθαρχεῖ Arist.*HA*610a29, cf. *GA*756b22. **2.** metaph., ὑμᾶς τιθασεύουσι χειροήθεις ποιοῦντες D.3.31; τ. ἀνθρώπους εἰς φιλότητας Phld.*Lib.*p. 40 O.; τὰ νοσήματα ἐλαφρύνει τε καὶ τ. Gal.19.211:—Pass., [ἡ γυνὴ] ἐτετιθάσευτο X.*Oec.*7.10, cf. Pl.*Plt.*264a; of a disease, *become milder*, Ruf.ap.Aët.11.29. **3.** of trees, *cultivate*, [κοτίνους] εἰς ἐλαίας ἐξημεροῦντες καὶ τ. Plu.*Fab.*20. Cf. τιθασός fin. **-ιον**, τό, f.l. for τιθασεία, Thphr.*HP*3.2.2 codd. **-ός**, όν, *tame, domestic, domesticated*; esp. of animals, *tame, domestic*, χὴν S.*Fr.*866, cf. Epicr.3.24; opp. ἄγριος, Pl.*Plt.*264a; πάντων τιθασσότατον (sic codd., v. ad fin.) καὶ ἡμερώτατον τῶν ἀγρίων ὁ ἐλέφας Arist.*HA*630b18; of persons, *tractable, docile*, *AP*5.177 (Mel.), Plu.2.51f, al.; of plants, *cultivated, reared in* gardens, Id.Cor.3. Adv., -σῶς πρὸς ἡμᾶς σχεῖν to be reclaimed, Pl. Ti.77a; τ. ἔχειν πρὸς τοὺς ἀνθρώπους Arist.HA608$^{b}$31; ἐπιτιμᾶν τινι cj. in Ph.1.676. 2. metaph., domestic, intestine, Ἄρης τιθασὸς ὢν A. Eu.356 (lyr.). (The spelling with single σ is found in the best codd., e.g. BT of Pl.Plt. l.c., and papyri (PCair.Zen.75.5 (iii B.C.), Phld. Lib.p.40 O., and the Philo papyrus), and corroborated by the short quantity of the second syllable in verse: the form τιθασσός (τιθασσεύω etc.) is freq. in medieval codd., as of Arist. ll. cc., Porph.Gaur. 4.4, 4.8, al., Chor.p.96 B., cf. Sup. τιθασσότατος Arist. supr. cit., but should be rejected.)

**τῐθᾰσοτρόφος**, ον, keeping tame animals, Opp.C.1.354.

**τιθή**, ἡ, = τίτθη (q.v.), Hsch. (dub.).

⊕ **τίθημι** [τῐ], 2 sg. τιθεῖς Pi.P.8.11, S.Ph.992 cod. B (τιθείς LA rec.), E.Cyc.545 codd. Lp (-θεὶς P, τίθης l), Alc.890 codd. pler., corrupted to τιθείς Pl.R.376e Stob., Arr.Epict.3.22.76, Pl.Euthd.301e (ἐπι-), Lib. Or.46.28 (προσ-); ἐν-τιθεῖς (v.l. -εὶς) Ar.Eq.717; περι-τιθεῖς BGU 1141.19 (i B.C.); but τίθης is found in Pl.R. l.c. codd. AD, Ar. l.c. cod. A, Lib.Or.27.11 (προσ-), etc., and is taught by Choerob. in Theod. 2.328 H.; Ep. τίθησθα Od.9.404, 24.476, and so in Aeol., Alc.Supp.4. 27 (τίθεισθα Hsch.); 3 sg. τίθησι Il.4.83, al., and Att.; Dor. τίθητι SIG 331.13 (Megara, iv B.C.), Theoc.3.48; 3 pl. τιθέασι Th.5.96, Alex.128; Ep. and Ion. τιθεῖσι Il.16.262, Hes.Th.597, Hdt.2.91 (also A.Ag.466 (lyr.)); Aeol. τίθεισι (προ-) Schwyzer 631 A 2 (ii B.C.); Dor. τίθεντι IG12(3).103.10 (Nisyrus); Ion. 3 sg. τιθεῖ Il.13.732, Mimn.1.6, Hdt. 1.113, also Arc., SIG559.16 (Megalop., iii B.C.) (τιθῶ Luc.Ocyp.43,81, διατιθῶ cited by A.D.Synt.290.6): impf. ἐτίθην Pl.Grg.500b; ἐτίθεις Id.R.528d, Ar.Nu.59 (ἐν-), etc.; ἐτίθει Il.18.541, al., Ar.Ach.532, Nu. 63 (προσ-), etc., Ep. τίθει Il.1.441, al.; Ep. 3 pl. τίθεσαν Od.22.456; τίθεν Pi.P.3.65; πρό-τιθεν Od.1.112 (Aristarch.); late ἐτίθουν Act. Ap.4.35; Ion. impf. τίθεσκον Hes.Fr.112; ἐτίθεα (ὑπερ-) Hdt.3.155: imper. τίθει Il.1.509, etc.; inf. τιθέναι, not in Hom. or Hes.; Ep. τιθήμεναι Il.23.83; τιθέμεν Hes.Op.744, Pi.P.1.40; τιθεῖν Thgn.286, IG12(9).189.5 (Eretria); written τιθῖν Byzantion 8.50 (Phrygia, iv A.D.); part. τιθείς, but Ion. pl. τιθεῦντες v.l. in Hdt.2.91: fut. θήσω, Ep. inf. θησέμεναι Il.12.35, θησέμεν Pi.P.10.58: aor.1 ἔθηκα, only used in indic., and mostly in sg., for though 3 pl. is common, the 1 and 2 pl. are rare, X.Mem.4.2.15, (ἀν-) Hyp.Eux.9; even ἔθηκαν is very rare in early Attic, ἀνέθηκαν IG2.1620d, 2$^{2}$.2971 (both iv B.C.), but is found in Plb.8.4.4, etc.; Ep. 3 pl. θῆκαν Il.24.795, etc.: aor. 2 ἔθην, not used in indic. sg., whereas pl. is very common, ἔθεμεν, ἔθετε, ἔθεσαν, Ep. θέσαν 12.29, etc.; imper. θές Ar.Lys.185, etc.; Lacon. 3 sg. σέτω ib.1081; subj. θῶ, Aeol. and Ion. θέω Sapph.12, (προσ-) Hdt.1.108, Ep. θείω Il.16.83, al. (for *θή-ω); Ep. 2 and 3 sg. θήῃς, θήῃ, 6.432, 16.96, Od.10.301,341 (sts. with the opt. forms θείῃς, θείῃ as v.l.); Ep. 1 pl. θέωμεν (disyll.) 24.485, θείομεν (for *θή-ο-μεν, short-vowel subjunctive) Il.23.244, Od.13.364; opt. θείην, 1 pl. θεῖμεν 12.347, Pl.Prt.343e (θείημεν codd. BT), προσ-θεῖμεν Id.R.370d, and κατα-θεῖτε D.14.27; 3 pl. θεῖεν S.OC865; inf. θεῖναι, Ep. θέμεναι Il.2.285, θέμεν Od.21.3, Hes.Op.61,67; Dor. θέμειν IG 12(1).677.13 (Rhodes, iv B.C.); part. θείς Il.23.254, etc.: pf. τέθηκα Att. Inscrr.. IG2$^{2}$.2490.7 (iv B.C.), (ἀνα-) ib.839.38, 1299.44, 1534.76, also at Delos, ib.11(2).161 A (iii B.C.), etc., and in Papyri, POxy. 1087.42 (i B.C.); τέθεικα PCair.Zen.324 (iii B.C.), (ὑπο-) PPetr.3 p.53 (iii B.C.), (ἐκ-) UPZ62.4 (ii B.C.), (ἀνα-) IG2$^{2}$.1011.71,80 (ii B.C.), (προσ-) Str.1.2.23; hence some editors restore τέθηκα for τέθεικα in Attic authors, as X.Mem.4.4.19, D.20.55, 22.16, 27.36, Alex.15.13; Phocian 3 pl. ἀνα-τεθέκαντι BCH59.202 (Daulis):—**Med.** τίθεμαι, 2 sg. τίθεσαι Pl.Tht.202c; τίθῃ or τίθη dub. in PTeb.768.9 (ii B.C.); as Pass., AP11.300 (Pall.); imper. τίθεσο Ar.Pax 1039, Pl. Sph.237b, τίθου A.Eu.226, Dor. τίθευσο cj. in AP9.564 (Nic., τιθεύσω cod., τίθεσσο Plan., cf. ἀφίκευσο); Ep. part. τιθήμενος Il.10.34: fut. θήσομαι 24.402, etc.: aor. 1 ἐθηκάμην, only in indic. and part., and never in Att.; 2 sg. ἐθήκαο Theoc.29.18; Ep. 3 sg. θήκατο Il.10.31, Hes.Sc.128; part. θηκάμενος Thgn.1150, Pi.P.4.29: aor. 2 ἐθέμην Il.2. 750, etc.; Ep. and Lyr. 3 sg. θέτο 10.149, Pi.N.10.89; imper. θέο Od. 10.333, θοῦ S.OC466; subj. θῶμαι E.HF486, etc.; Ep. 2 sg. θῆαι Od. 19.403; opt. θείμην S.Ant.188, etc.; 3 sg. θεῖτο Od.17.225, A.Pr.527 (lyr.), Pl.Tht.195c, etc. (πρόσ-θοιτο, -θοισθε, ἔν-θοιτο are found in D. 11.6, 21.188, 34.17, but προσ-θεῖτο Id.6.12 codd.; ἐπιθοίμεθα, -θοιντο, Th.6.34,11; cf. τιθοῖτο X.Mem.3.8.10): pf. (v. infr.):—**Pass.** τίθεμαι SIG57.25 (Milet., v B.C.), Pl.Lg.705e, 744a: fut. τεθήσομαι E.El. 1268, Pl.Lg.730b, D.24.17: aor. ἐτέθην E.HF1245, Lys.31.28, etc. (ἐθέθην IG14.862 (Cumae, vi B.C.)): pf. τέθειμαι, rare in early Gr., Lxx 1Ki.9.24, Ev.Marc.15.47, (προσ-) Arist.Mech.853$^{a}$35; inf. τεθεῖσθαι Ar.Fr.327 codd. (but f.l.); part. τεθειμένος Demad.12, (προ-) X.Hier.9.11, (δια-) Men.591; also used in med. sense, D.21.49, SIG705.17 (Delph., ii B.C.), BGU1735.11 (i B.C.), Luc.Somn.9, (ἐν-) D.34.16, (προ-) Supp.Epigr.7.62.6 (Seleucia Pieria, ii B.C.), (συν-) OGI229.62 (Smyrna, iii B.C.); ὑπεκ-τεθημένος (sic) BCH54.269 (Rhamnus, iii B.C.); ἀνα-τέθηται (pass. sense) Phld.Mus.p.81 K.; Phocian pf. part. (med. sense) ἀνα-τεθεμένος BCH59.202 (Daulis):—the Pass. never occurs in Hom., and is generally rare, κεῖμαι being used instead.

**A.** in local sense, *set, put, place*, λίθον Il.21.405, cf. IG1$^{2}$.373. 10, al.; θεμείλια Il.12.29; τέρματα τ. Od.8.193; κλισίην, θρόνον τ. τινί, *set a stool or chair for him*, 4.123, 8.65 (so in Med., *set for oneself*, δίφρον 20.387); ἐκελήσατο θέμεν τὰν κλίναν, ἐφ' ἃς τὰν Σωστράταν ἔφερον *lay down*, IG4$^{2}$(1).122.31 (Epid., iv B.C.); πόδα τ. *plant* the foot, i.e. walk, run, A.Eu.294, E.IT32: so in Med., τετράποδος βάσιν θηρὸς τιθέμενος, i.e. going on all fours, Id.Hec. 1059 (lyr.): the mode is expressed by Advbs. or Preps., a. with Advbs., τ. τι πυρὸς ἐγγύς, ἀπάνευθε πυρός, Od.14.518, Il.18.412; προπάροιθε ποδῶν 20.324; χαμαὶ τ. τὸν πόδα A.Ag.906; τὰ ἄνω κάτω and τὰ κάτω ἄνω τ. Hdt.3.3, cf. A.Eu.651, etc.: with Advbs. implying motion, ἄλλοσε θῆκε Od.23.184,204; ἔχεις.. ὅποι θήσεις Pl.R.479c:—Med., ὅποι.. τιθοῖτο X.Mem.3.8.10. b. with Preps. of local sense, θεῖσα στέφανον ἀμφὶ βοστρύχοις E.Med.1160 (Med., ἀμφ' ὤμοισι τιθήμενον ἔντεα Il.10.34); ἀνά τινι or τι, as ἂμ βωμοῖσι Il.8.441; ἀνὰ μυρίκην 10.466; ἐπί τινος, τινι, or τι, as εἵματα ἐπ' ἀπήνης Od.6.252, cf. Il.16.223, etc.; ἐπὶ κρατὶ κυνέην 15.480; πέπλον Ἀθηναίης ἐπὶ γούνασι 6.92 (v. infr. III. 2); ἐπὶ [θρόνον τὰ ἱμάτια] Hdt.1.9, cf. A.Supp.483, etc.: τὴν ἀρχὴν (sc. τοῦ ἐπιδέσμου) κατὰ μεσοφρύου, ἐπὶ ἰνίον, etc., Sor.Fasc.1.2, al.; ὑπό τινι or τι, as δέμνι' ὑπ' αἰθούσῃ Il.24.644; ἀμβροσίην ὑπὸ ῥῖνά τινι Od.4.445: most freq. with the Preps. ἐν or εἰς, *put in* or *put into*.., as θῆκεν ἐν ἀκμοθέτῳ ἄκμονα Il.18.476; τόξα ἐν πυρί 5.215; ἐν κίστῃ ἐδωδήν Od.6.76; ἐν λεχέεσσι θ. [τινά] Il.18.352 (so in Med., ἐς δίφρον ἄρνας θέτο *put into* the car, 3.310; ὁ θεὸς ἔθετο τὰ μέλη ἐν τῷ σώματι 1Ep.Cor.12.18); ἐς λάρνακα, ἐς κάπετον, Il.24.795,797; ἐς ταφὰς S.Aj.1110 (Med., ἐν τάφοισι θέσθε Id.OC1410), cf. Ant.504, Tr.1254. c. in Poets also with dat. only, χρήματα μυχῷ ἄντρου Od.13.364 (so in Med., κολεῷ ἄορ θέο 10.333), cf. S.Tr.691, E.Hel.1064.—The same constructions will be found under many of the following heads. **II.** Special phrases: **1.** θεῖναί τινί τι ἐν χερσίν, ἐν χειρί, *put* it in his hands, Il.1.441,585, etc.; ἐν χερσὶ or χείρεσσί τινος 6.482, 23.597; οἶνον Ὀδυσσῆϊ ἐν χείρεσσι Od.14.448; ἐς χεῖρά τινος *into* his hand, S.Aj.751. **2.** of women, θέσθαι παῖδα, υἱὸν ὑπὸ ζώνῃ, *to have a* child *put* under her girdle, i.e. to conceive, h.Ven.255,282. **3.** ἐν ὄμμασι θέσθαι *set* before one's eyes, Pi.N.8.43. **4.** *set* a plant, X.Oec.19.7,9. b. *lay* a mosaic, PCair.Zen.665.10,15 (iii B.C.). **5.** θέσθαι τὴν ψῆφον *lay one's* voting-pebble on the altar, *put* it into the urn, ἐς τεῦχος οὐ διχορρόπως ψήφους ἔθεντο A.Ag.816: hence simply, *give one's* vote, ἐπὶ φόνῳ for death, E.Or.756 (troch.); ἑωυτῷ in one's own favour, Hdt.8.123; σὺν τῷ νόμῳ X.Cyr.1.3.17; εὔφρονα, δικαίαν τὴν ψῆφον τ., A.Supp.640 (lyr.), Lycurg.128, etc.; and in Pass., ἔστω δὴ φανερὰ ἡ ψῆφος τιθεμένη Pl.Lg.855d: also γνώμην θέσθαι, c. inf., *give one's* opinion, Hdt.7.82; περὶ ἡμῶν And.3.21: τίθεσθαι abs., *vote*, γνώμῃ S.Ph.1448 codd. (anap., γνώμην Lambinus), Hld.2.29; μετά τινος A.Supp.644 (lyr.); ἐναντία τινί Pl.Phlb.58b; τινι S.E.P.2.37 codd., Lib.Decl.1.65. **6.** in Hom., θεῖναί τινί τι ἐν στήθεσσι, ἐν φρεσί, etc., *put* or *plant* it in his heart, ἐν στήθεσσι τιθεῖ νόον Il.13.732; βουλὴν ἐν στήθεσσι τ. 17.470; ἔπος ἐν φρεσί 19.121, al.; also μένος δέ οἱ ἐν φρεσὶ θῆκε 21.145:—Med., ἄγριον ἐν στήθεσσι θέτο θυμόν *laid up* wrath in *his* heart, *treasured* it there, 9.629; ἐν φρεσὶ θέσθε αἰδῶ καὶ νέμεσιν 13.121; τοῖσιν κότον αἰνὸν ἔθεσθε *harboured* enmity against them, 8.449; καθαρὸν θέμενος νόον Thgn.89; θέμενος ἄγναμπτον νόον A.Pr.164 (lyr.); ἐνὶ φρεσὶ θέσθαι, c. inf., *bear* in mind, *think* of doing a thing, Od.4.729; θ. [τι] ἐν καρδίᾳ Ev.Luc. 1.66. **7.** *deposit*, as in a bank, τὰ πρυτανεῖα πρὸς τοὺς ἄρχοντας IG1$^{2}$.22.33; θεὶς ἐπὶ τὴν τράπεζαν τὰς τετταράκοντα μνᾶς Hyp.Ath.5; ἐνέχυρον τιθέναι τι Ar.Pl.451, cf. Ec.755, D.41.11, PEnteux.32.7 (iii B.C.), etc.:—Med., τὰ ἡμίσεα τῆς οὐσίης θέσθαι παρά τινα Hdt.6.86.α', cf. Od.13.207; τὴν τιμὴν θήσονται ἐπὶ τὴν τράπεζαν, ἕως.. PCair. Zen.723.11 (iii B.C.); ἐγγύην θέσθαι A.Eu.898; συνθήκας παρά τινι Lycurg.23:—Pass., τὰ ληφθέντα καὶ τὰ τεθέντα D.49.5 (but Act. and Med. are sts. distd., ὁ θεὶς *the mortgagor*, ὁ θέμενος *the mortgagee*, τοὺς θέντας ἡμᾶς ἢ καὶ τοὺς θεμένους ὑμᾶς Pl.Lg.820e, cf. Hyp.Fr.169, D.53.10; τίθεσθαι seems to have the same meaning as ὑποτίθεσθαι in IG2$^{2}$.43.41, 2758.4, 12(7).55.12 (Arcesine, iv/iii B.C.), but the two are distd. in Supp.Epigr.3.760 (Euboea, iv B.C.)): metaph., χάριν or χάριτα θέσθαι τινί *deposit a claim for* favour with one, *lay* an obligation on one, Hdt.9.60,107, cf. A.Pr.783, etc. **8.** *pay down, pay*, τόκον, εἰσφοράν, μετοίκιον, D.41.9, 22.43, 29.3; τὸ γιγνόμενον Id.18. 104; τὸν πριάμενον ἑκατοστὴν τιθέναι τῆς τιμῆς Thphr.Fr.97.1; τὴν τιμὴν PRev.Laws 18.13 (iii B.C.); τὰ μέρη PCair.Zen.218.33 (iii B.C.); [τὰς δραχμὰς] εἰς ἀνήλωμα τοῦ πλοίου ib.753.64 (iii B.C.):—Med., θέμενος ἀρραβῶνα PFlor.303.3 (vi A.D.). **9.** *put down in writing*, θοῦ δ' ἐν φρενῶν δέλτοισι τοὺς ἐμοὺς λόγους S.Fr.597 (cj. Nauck):—Pass., τὰ ἐν γράμμασι τεθέντα Pl.Lg.793b. b. *place to account, reckon*, D.27.34,36, 28.13; θήσω εἰς δύο παῖδας χιλίας δραχμὰς ἑκάστου ἐνιαυτοῦ Lys.32.28, cf. ib.21:—metaph. in Med., ἀλλ' οὐκ ἀκριβῶς αὐτὸ θήσομαι λίαν E.Med.532; τἀγαθὰ ἐς ἀμφίβολον ἀσφαλῶς ἔθεντο *reckoned* as doubtful, Th.4.18. **10.** in military language, τίθεσθαι or θέσθαι τὰ ὅπλα has four senses, a. *rest arms*, i.e. halt, with arms in an easy position but ready for action, Th.4.44,93, 7.3; θέμενοι ἐς τὴν ἀγορὰν τὰ ὅπλα advancing to the market-place and *resting arms* there, Id.2.2, cf. Hdt.9.52, X.An.1.5.14,17, 1.6.4, etc.; εἰς τάξιν τὰ ὅπλα τ. ib.2.2.21, 5.4.11; ἐν τάξει ib.2.2.8; ἀντία τισί over against them, Hdt.5.74 (in 1.62 ἀντία ἔθεντο τὰ ὅπλα over against it (the temple)); poet., πάτρας ἕνεκα εἰς δῆριν ἔθεντο ὅπλα Inscr.ap.D.18.289. b. *bear arms, fight*, τὸ θυμοειδὲς.. ἐν τῇ τῆς ψυχῆς στάσει τίθεσθαι τὰ ὅπλα πρὸς τὸ λογιστικόν Pl.R.440e; τοῦ δήμου ..παρακαλοῦντος τοὺς στρατιώτας τίθεσθαι πρὸς τὴν πόλιν IG2$^{2}$.666.10; ὃς ἂν μὴ θῆται τὰ ὅπλα μηδὲ μεθ' ἑτέρων Arist.Ath.8.5, cf. Lys.31.14, D.21.145; so ὁπόσοιπερ ἂν ὅπλα ἱππικὰ ἢ πεζικὰ τιθῶνται who *serve* on horseback or on foot, Pl.Lg.753b, cf. 756a; ἐν ταῖς ναυσὶ τὰ ὅπλα θέσθαι Plu.Cim.5. c. *lay down one's arms, surrender*, D.S.20.31,45; so, without the idea of surrender, θέσθαι τὰς ἀσπίδας X.*HG*2.4.12 (but Act., τὰ ὅπλα θείς Plu.2.759a). d. τὰ ὅπλα εὖ τίθεσθε *keep* your arms *in good order*, X.*Cyr*.4.5.3; εὖ ἀσπίδα θέσθω Il.2.382. 11. *lay in the grave, bury*, ἐμὰ σῶν ἀπάνευθε τιθήμεναι ὀστέα 23.83 (freq. with words added, ἐν τάφοισι, ἐς ταφάς, etc., v. supr. 1b); ποῦ σφε θήσομεν χθονός; A.*Th*.1006 (lyr.):—Pass., τὰ δὲ ὀστᾶ φασι..τεθῆναι..ἐν τῇ Ἀττικῇ Th.1.138, cf. Pl.*Mx*. 242c, *Lg*.947e; ἄλλῳ δὲ μηδενὶ ἐξεῖναι ἐν τῷ πυργίσκῳ τεθῆναι μετὰ τὸ ἐνταφῆναι αὐτήν· ἐπεὶ ὁ θείς τινα ἀσεβὴς ἔστω θεοῖς καταχθονίοις *TAM* 2(1).51 (Telmessus), cf. 55, al., *AJP*48.30 (Apamea), *Supp.Epigr*. 6.221 (Phrygia), etc. 12. τιθέναι τὰ γόνατα *kneel down*, *Ev.Marc*. 15.19, *Ev.Luc*.22.41, al. III. *set up*, of the prizes in games, ἄεθλα Il.23.263, etc.; ἀέθλιον ib.748; νικητήρια S.*Fr*.537 (so in Pass., τὰ τιθέμενα *the prizes*, D.61.25); also with the object offered as the prize, τ. δέπας, βοῦν, σόλον, etc., Il.23.656,750,826, al., cf. Hdt. 1.144, S.*Aj*.573:—this is more fully expressed by ἐς μέσσον τ., Il.23. 704: after Hom. more generally, *lay before* people as common property, βούλομαι ὑμῖν εἰς τὸ μέσον αὐτὸ θεῖναι Pl.*Lg*.719a; ἐς μέσον ἀρχὴν τιθεὶς ἰσονομίην ὑμῖν προαγορεύω Hdt.3.142; so also τ. τι εἰς τὸ κοινὸν X.*Mem*.3.14.1; reading and sense are doubtful in A.*Ch*. 145. 2. *set up* in a temple, *dedicate*, ἀγάλματα Od.12.347; τάσδε ..θεοῖς ἀσπίδας ἔθηκε E.*Ph*.576; so perh. Il.6.92 (v. supr. 1b). IV. *assign, award*, τιμήν τινι Il.24.57; ὄνομά τινι Pl.*Sph*.244d: esp. in Med., ὄνομα (or οὔνομα) θέσθαι τινί *give* a child a name *at one's own discretion*, Od.18.5, 19.406 (in 19.403 with v.l. θείης), Hdt.1.107,113, cf. E.*Ph*.13: ellipt., without ὄνομα, ᾧ δὴ ἀθροίσματι ἄνθρωπόν τε τίθενται καὶ λίθον Pl.*Tht*.157b, cf. *Cra*.402b: pleonast., Ἴωνα δ' αὐτὸν ὄνομα κεκλῆσθαι θήσεται E.*Ion* 75. V. τιθέναι νόμον *lay down* or *give* a law, of a legislator, S.*El*.580, E.*Alc*.57, Ar.*Ach*.532, Pl.*R*.339c, D.24.99, etc.:—so in Med., of Solon, Hdt.1.29; of a people, state, or legislature, *give oneself* a law, *make* a law, Pl.*R*.338e, Isoc.3.6, Arist. *Pol*.1289a14 (Pass., τίθεται νόμος Ar.*Nu*.1425, Pl.*Lg*.705e,744a; τιμωρίαι..ἐτέθησαν ib.943d); also θήσω θεσμὸν A.*Eu*.484; κήρυγμα θεῖναι S.*Ant*.8; σκῆψιν τιθέναι *allege* an excuse, Id.*El*.584: c. acc. et inf., *order matters so that*.., [ὁ Λυκοῦργος] ἔθηκε θύειν βασιλέα πρὸ τῆς πόλεως τὰ δημόσια ἅπαντα X.*Lac*.15.2, cf. 1.5, 2.11; without inf., καλῶς ἔθεντο ταῦτα πατέρες οἱ πάλαι E.*Or*.512: c. dat. et inf., γυναιξὶ σωφρονεῖν..θήσει Id.*Tr*.1057. 2. Med., *agree upon*, ἡμέραν θέσθαι D.42.1,13; so θ. συγγραφήν, ὁμολογίαν, σύμβολόν τινι, etc., *PEleph*. 2.16 (iii B.C.), *PGoodsp.Cair*.6ii 2 (ii B.C.), *PRein*.11.9 (ii B.C.), etc. 3. *execute* a document, τ. διαθήκην *make* a will, *Stud.Pal*.1. 6.3 (v A.D.): so in Med., *PSI*10.1119.16 (ii A.D.); θέσθαι τινὸς ἀπαρχὴν *make out* a person's birth-certificate, ib.9.1067.15 (iii B.C.), etc. VI. *establish, institute*, ἀγῶνας A.*Ag*.845, cf. X.*An*.1.2.10; ἐν τοῖς ἀγώνοις οἷς ἁ πόλις τίφητι (sic) *Delph*.3(3).120.17 (ii B.C.); πενταετηρίδα Pi.*O*.3.21. VII. *dispose, order, ordain, bring to pass*, of gods, οὕτω νῦν Ζεὺς θείη Od.8.465, 15.180; ὡς ἄρ' ἔμελλον θησέμεναι Il.12.35; [Ζεὺς] τίθησ' ὅπῃ θέλει Semon.1.2; τὰ δ' ἄλλα πάντ' ἄνω τε καὶ κάτω στρέφων τίθησιν (sc. Ζεύς) A.*Eu*.651; πάντα παγκάκως θεοὶ θέσαν cj. in Id.*Pers*.283 (lyr.); τέλος δ' ἔθηκε Ζεὺς..καλῶς S.*Tr*. 26; κόσμῳ θέντες, as etym. of θεοί, Hdt.2.52; of human beings, *administer, manage*, [τι] κακῶς θέμεν, εὖ θέμεν, Thgn.845,846; τὰ δ' ἄλλα φροντὶς..θήσει δικαίως A.*Ag*.913; ἐγὼ καὶ σὺ θήσομεν κρατοῦντε τῶνδε δωμάτων καλῶς ib.1673 (troch.); ταῦτ' ἐγὼ θήσω καλῶς E.*Hipp*. 521, cf. *Andr*.737; τὰ παρ' ὑμῶν εὖ τίθει Ar.*Lys*.243; τ. τὰ τῶν φίλων ἀσφαλῶς X.*Ages*.11.12; τὰ πράγματ' ὀρθῶς ἂν τιθῇ πράξει καλῶς E.*Fr*.287:—Med., *administer for oneself*, οἶκον εὖ θέσθαι Hes.*Op*.23; ἄνδρας σοφοὺς χρὴ τὸ παρὸν πρᾶγμα καλῶς εἰς δύναμιν τίθεσθαι Cratin. 172 (lyr.), cf. D.23.134, Anon.ap Suid. s.v. τίθεσθαι, Hsch. s.v. τὸ παρὸν εὖ τίθεσο; ἐν ἀπόρῳ εἴχοντο θέσθαι τὸ παρόν Th.1.25; τὸ παρὸν εὖ θέσθαι *make the best of* one's resources or situation, Luc.*Nec*.21, M. Ant.6.2, cf. Aristid.2.35 J.; εὐτυχίαν τὴν παροῦσαν ἔξεστι καλῶς θέσθαι Th.4.17; τὰ παρόντα θέσθαι καλῶς Ach.Tat.5.11; τὰ σεωυτοῦ τιθέμενος εὖ Hdt.7.236; τὰ οἰκεῖα εὖ θέμενον Pl.*R*.443d; τὰ ἴδια ἕκαστοι εὖ βουλόμενοι δὴ θέσθαι Th.4.59; τὰ πάντα ὅπως ἂν αὐτῇ ἥδιστα ᾖ οὕτως τίθεσθαι X.*Mem*.1.4.17; εἰ μὴ θήσομαι τἄμ' ὡς ἄριστα E.*Andr*. 378; τὸ σαυτοῦ θέμενος εὖ Id.*IT*1003, cf. *Ba*.49, *HF*605,938, *Hipp*. 709, Dionys.Eleg.1.5; τὰ πρὶν εὖ θέμενος S.*El*.1434; συνετῶν ἀνδρῶν (sc. εἶναι), πρὶν γενέσθαι τὰ δυσχερῆ, προνοῆσαι ὅπως μὴ γένηται· ἀνδρείων δέ, γενόμενα εὖ θέσθαι Pittac.ap.D.L.1.78; τὸ κοινῶς φοβερὸν ἅπαντας εὖ θέσθαι that all should *face* the common danger, Th.4.61; of wars, quarrels, etc., *bring* them *to a successful issue*, but sts. *put a good face on* them, *patch* them *up*, ἕως ἂν τὸν πόλεμον εὖ θῶνται Id. 8.84; θήσονται τὸν πόλεμον ᾗ βούλονται Id.1.31; πόλεμον ἀραμένους οὐ ῥᾴδιον εὐπρεπῶς θέσθαι ib.82; ὅτῳ τρόπῳ..τὸ σφέτερον ἀπρεπὲς εὖ θήσονται Id.6.11; μεθ' ἧς τὸ νῦν παρεστὸς νεῖκος εὖ θέσθαι χρεών S. *OT*633; τὸν πρὸς τοὺς Ἐλευσῖνι πόλεμον ὡς μετρίως ἔθεντο Pl.*Mx*.243e; ἄμεινον ἢ τότε ἐθέμεθα τὸν πόλεμον ib.245e; τὰς γενομένας συμφορὰς πρὸς ἀλλήλους θέσθαι καλῶς And.1.140: abs., θέσθαι καλῶς S.*Fr*. 350:—Pass., εἰ τεθήσεται κατὰ νοῦν τὰ πράγματα Th.4.120. 2. in the game of πεττεία, κυβεία, Lat. *tesserae* (cf. Ter.*Adelph*.739), *to place as skilfully as possible* the pieces which have been assigned to one by the luck of the dice, πεττείᾳ τινὶ ἔοικεν ὁ βίος, καὶ δεῖ ὥσπερ ψῆφόν τινα τίθεσθαι τὸ συμβαῖνον Socr.ap.Stob.4.56.39; ὥσπερ ἐν πτώσει κύβων πρὸς τὰ πεπτωκότα τίθεσθαι τὰ αὑτοῦ πράγματα ὅπῃ ὁ λόγος αἱρεῖ βέλτιστ' ἂν ἔχειν Pl.*R*.604c, cf. Plu.*Pyrrh*.26; στέργειν δὲ τἀκπεσόντα καὶ θέσθαι πρέπει σοφὸν κυβευτὴν S.*Fr*.947; τὰ δεσποτῶν γὰρ εὖ πεσόντα θήσομαι I *will take advantage of* my master's good luck, A.*Ag*.32: many of the passages cited in A. VII. 1 may be metaph. applications of this sense.

B. *put in a certain state* or *condition*, much the same as ποιεῖν, ποιεῖσθαι, and so often to be rendered by our *make*: I. folld. by an attributive Subst., *make* one something, with the predicate in apposition, θεῖναί τινα αἰχμητήν, ἱέρειαν, μάντιν, etc., Il.1.290, 6.300, Od.15.253, etc.; θ. τινὰ ἀρχέπολιν Pi.*P*.9.54; θεῖναί τινα ἄλοχόν τινος *make* her another's wife, of a third person who negotiates a marriage, Il.19.298 (for Med., v. infr. 3); ἧτε με τοῖον ἔθηκεν ὅπως ἐθέλει who *has made* me such as she will, Od.16.208; σῦς ἔθηκας ἑταίρους *thou hast made* my comrades swine, 10.338; so [νῆα] λᾶαν ἔθηκε 13.163, cf. Il.2.319, etc.; ἕως ἂν θῶ τοὺς ἐχθρούς σου ὑποπόδιον LXX *Ps*.109(110).1; but γέλων ἔθηκε συνδείπνοις *caused* them laughter, E.*Ion*1172; λόγους εἰς μέτρα τ. *put* them into verse, Pl. *Lg*.669d. 2. with an Adj. for the attributive, θεῖναί τινα ἀθάνατον καὶ ἀγήρων *make* him undying and undecaying, Od.5.136; πηρόν, τυφλόν, ἀφνειόν τ. τινά, Il.2.599, 6.139, 9.483; τὸν μὲν..θῆκε μείζονά τ' εἰσιδέειν καὶ πάσσονα Od.6.229, cf. 18.195, Pl.*Prt*.344d. b. of things, ἅλιον πόνον, πόνον οὐκ ἀτέλεστον, πάντα μεταμώνια, Il.4.26,57, 363; ὄλεθρον ἀπευθέα θῆκε Κρονίων Od.3.88, cf. 11.274; ἀποίητον θέμεν ἔργων τέλος Pi.*O*.2.17; ἀρὰν τ. ἀλαθῆ A.*Th*.944 (lyr.); ἀναστάτους οἴκους τ. S.*Ant*.674; τ. λεῖον τὸν τραχὺν ἐχῖνον Ar.*Pax*1086; τὸ πραχθὲν ἀγένητον τ. Pl.*Prt*.324b. 3. freq. in Med., γυναῖκα or ἄκοιτιν θέσθαι τινά *make* her *one's* wife, Od.21.72,316, B.5.169; παῖδα τὸν αὐτᾶς πόσιν θ. *take* her own son as husband, A.*Th*.929 (lyr.). b. υἱὸν θέσθαι τινά, like ποιεῖσθαι, *make one's* son, *adopt*, Pl.*Lg*.929c, etc.: abs., θέσθαι τινά *adopt*, Plu.*Aem*.5. c. generally, προσφιλῆ θέσθαι τινά S.*Ph*.532; but φίλον ἐμαυτῷ θ. *deem* my friend, Id.*Ant*.188; γέλωτα θέσθαι τινά *make* him *one's* butt, Hdt.3.29, 7.209. 4. c. inf., *make* one do so and so, τιθέναι τινὰ νικᾶσαι *make* him conquer, Pi.*N*.10.48 (dub.); μετατραπεῖν Id.*Fr*.177; τὸν πάθει μάθος θέντα κυρίως ἔχειν A.*Ag*.178 (lyr.), cf. 1036,1174 (lyr.), E.*Med*.718, *Heracl*. 990, etc. II. in reference to mental action, when Med. is more freq. than Act., *lay down, assume, hold, reckon* or *regard as*.., τί δ' ἐλέγχεα ταῦτα τίθεσθε; Od.21.333; δαιμόνιον αὐτὸ τίθημ' ἐγώ S.*El*.1270 (lyr.); τοιοῦτον θέντες τὸν δίκαιον Pl.*R*.361b, cf. 430b (Med.); θὲς δή μοι.. now *suppose* so and so, Id.*Tht*.191c; εὐεργέτημά τι θεῖναι D.1.10; with ὡς, θέντες ὡς ὑπάρχον εἶναι ὃ βούλονται Pl.*R*. 458a, cf. *Phd*.100a; μὴ τοῦτο ὡς ἀδίκημα θῇς D.18.193. 2. folld. by Advbs., ποῦ χρὴ τιθέσθαι ταῦτα; in what light must we *regard* these things? S.*Ph*.451; οὐδαμοῦ τιθέναι τι *hold* of no account, E.*Andr*.210; πρόσθεν or ἐπιπροσθέν τινος τιθέναι τι, Id.*Hec*.129 (anap.), *Supp*.515; πόρρω τίθεσθαί τί τινων *set* far below.., D.18.299. 3. folld. by Preps., τ. τινὰ ἐν φιλοσόφοις Pl.*R*.475d; ἐν τοῖς φίλοις X.*Mem*.2.4.4; also εἰς ὁποτέραν (of two classes) Pl.*Sph*.264c; εἰς τὸν δῆμον, εἰς τοὺς πλουσίους, X.*Mem*.4.2.39; also οὐκ ἐν λόγῳ τίθεσθαί τινα Tyrt.12.1; ἐν τιμῇ τίθεσθαί τινα Hdt.3.3; ἐν αἰτίῃ τιθέναι τινά Id.8.99; ἐν οἰωνῷ τινι τοῦ μέλλοντος, ἐν ἐπαίνῳ, ἐν γέλωτι τίθεσθαι, Plu.*Alex*.31, *Cat.Ma*.20, *TG*17; θέσθαι παρ' οὐδὲν *set* at naught, A.*Ag*.230 (lyr.), E.*IT*732, cf. Pl.*Phdr*.252a (but ἐν οὐδενὶ *BGU*1816.23 (i B.C.), *Supp. Epigr*.7.1.6 (Susa, i A.D., Epist. Artabani)); ἐν παρέργῳ θοῦ με S.*Ph*. 473; πάντα ταῦτ' ἐν εὐχερεῖ ἔθου ib.876; ταῦτ' ἐν αἰσχρῷ θέμενος E. *Hec*.806; ἐν ἀδικήματι θέσθαι τι Th.1.35; ἐν ἀδικήματος μέρει τιθέναι τι D.23.148; θέσθαι τὰ δίκαια ἔκ τινος *estimate* them by.., Id.8. 8. 4. c. partit. gen., ἐμὲ θὲς τῶν πεπεισμένων *put* me *down as one of* the convinced, Pl.*R*.424c, cf. 376e, 437b; τῆς ἡμετέρας ἀμελείας ἄν τις θείη *might reckon* it as due to our carelessness, D.I. 10. 5. c. inf., οὐ τίθημ' ἐγὼ ζῆν τοῦτον I *hold* not that he lives, *count* him not as living, S.*Ant*.1166: so in Med., Pl.*Phd*.93c, D. 25.43,44: rarely c. part., θήσω ἀδικοῦντα [αὐτόν] Id.23.76, cf. Pl. *Prt*.343e, *Ap*.27c. 6. elliptically, *lay down, assume*, θῶμεν δύο εἴδη (sc. εἶναι) Id.*Phd*.79a, etc.; θήσω οὕτω (sc. εἶναί τι) D.23.85, cf. Arist.*Pol*.1290a30. 7. *affirm*, opp. αἴρω (deny), τὸ ἐπέκεινα ὄντος οὐ τόδε λέγει—οὐ γὰρ τίθησιν—the phrase 'beyond being' does not denote a 'this' (for it is not an *affirmation*), Plot.5.5.6.

C. without any attributive word following, *make, work, execute*, of an artist, ἐν δ' ἐτίθει νειόν Il.18.541, cf. 550,561,607; [δόρπον] θησέμεναι Od.20.394. 2. *make, cause, bring to pass*, ἔργα Il.3. 321; τ. κέλαδον καὶ ἀϋτήν 9.547; ὀρυμαγδόν Od.9.235; ἔριν μετ' ἀμφοτέροισιν 3.136; φιλότητα, ὅρκια μετ' ἀμφ., Il.4.83, Od.24.546: c. dat. pers., σῆμα τιθεὶς Τρώεσσι Il.8.171; Ἀχαιοῖς ἄλγε' ἔθηκεν 1. 2, etc.; πᾶσι δ' ἔθηκε πόνον 21.524, cf. 15.721, 16.262; φόως ἑτάροισιν 6.6, etc.; χάρματ' ἄλλοις ἔθηκεν Pi.*O*.2.99; πόλει κατασκαφὰς θέντες A.*Th*.47; εἰρήνην φίλοις Id.*Pers*.769; αἷμα θήσεις E.*Ba*.837 (s. v.l.). 3. freq. in Med., *make* or *prepare for oneself*, θέσθαι κέλευθον *make oneself* a road, *open* a way, Il.12.418; θέτο δῶμα Od.15.241; τίθεντο δὲ δαῖτα, δόρπα, Il.7.475, 9.88 (but δαῖτα τίθενται *are holding* a feast, Od.17.269); μεγάλην ἐπιγουνίδα θέσθαι *to make oneself, get* a large thigh, Od.17.225; θέσθαι μάχην *engage in*.., Il.24.402; δυσμενέεσσι πόνον καὶ δῆριν ἔθεντο 17.158; ἱδρῶτα τίθεσθαι *have an access of* perspiration, Hp.*Decent*.2; μαρτύρια θέσθαι *produce as* testimony, Hdt.8.55; ἀνδρὸς αἰδοίου πρόσωψιν θηκάμενος *putting on* the aspect of a reverend man, Pi.*P*.4.29, cf. Hsch. s.v. θήκατο; πόνον πλέω τίθου *work thyself* the more annoy, A.*Eu*.226; εὐκλεᾶ θέσθαι βίον S.*Ph*.1422, etc. 4. periphr. for a single Verb, μνηστήρων σκέδασιν θεῖναι *make* a scattering, Od.1.116; θέμεν κρυφόν, νέμεσιν, αἶνον, for κρύπτειν, νεμεσᾶν, αἰνεῖν, Pi.*O*.2.97, 8.86, *N*.1.5; μὴ σχολὴν τίθει A. *Ag*.1059; ὑμῖν ἔθηκε σὺν θεοῖς σωτηρίαν (v.l. προμηθίαν) E.*Med*.915:—also in Med., θέσθαι μάχην, for μάχεσθαι, Il.24.402; θέσθαι θυσίαν, γάμον, for θύειν, γαμεῖσθαι, Pi.*O*.7.42, 13.53; σπουδήν, πρόνοιαν θέσθαι, S.*Aj*.13,536, cf. Pi.*P*.4.276; θ. ἐπιστροφὴν πρό τινος S.*OT*134;

περὶ τούτων οἰκονομίας *PEnteux.*22.6 (iii B.C.); and c. gen., θ. λησμοσύναν, συγγνωμοσύνην τινῶν, S.*Ant.*151 (lyr.), *Tr.*1265 (anap.). (Cf. Lith. *dēti* 'lay (eggs, etc.)', Skt. *dádhāti* 'lay down, place', Lat. *-do* in *con-do*, etc., Engl. *do, doom.*)

**τῑθην-εία**, Ion. -είη, ἡ, = τιθηνία, Opp.*H.*1.663 (pl.). **-εύω**, = sq., Hsch. (Pass.). **-έω**, *take care of, tend, nurse,* Lxx *Si.*30.9, *BGU* 859.4 (ii A.D.), Orph.*H.*63.15:—Pass., Hp.*Art.*60. II. elsewh. in Med. (aor. ἐτιθήνατο, as if fr. τιθαίνομαι, Luc.*Trag.*94), *nurse, suckle,* Thgn.1231, Men.*Sam.*32; *tend as nurse,* παῖδα νεογνόν *h.Cer.* 142, cf. X.*Cyr.*8.5.19. 2. *tend, foster,* οὐ πότνιαι σεμνὰ τιθηνοῦνται τέλη θνατοῖσιν S.*OC*1050 (lyr.), cf. Simon.148,172. **-η**, ἡ, (θῆσθαι) *nurse,* Il.6.389,467, 22.503; παῖς ἄτερ ὡς φίλας τιθήνας S. *Ph.*703 (lyr.); Διόνυσος θείαις ἀμφιπολῶν τ. Id.*OC*680 (lyr.):—metaph., Etna is called χιόνος τιθήνα, Pi.*P.*1.20; space ἡ τῆς γενέσεως τ., Pl.*Ti.*52d, cf. 49a, 88d, Arist.*Top.*139$^{b}$33; the dinner-table βίου τ., Timocl.13.2. II. = μήτηρ, Coluth.379. **-ημα**, ατος, τό, *nursling,* E.*Hyps.Fr.*60 i 10; ῥόδα τ. ἔαρος Chaerem.13.2. **-ησις**, εως, ἡ, *nursing,* Pl.*Lg.*790c, Thphr.*CP*2.1.6, *BGU*297.15 (i A.D.). **-ητήρ**, ῆρος, ὁ, = τιθηνός, *AP*7.241 (Antip. Sid.), *APl.*4.179 (Arch.):—fem. ⊛**-ήτειρα**, = τιθήνη, *AP*9.19 (Id.), *APl.*4.296 (Antip.). **-ητήριος**, α, ον, *nursing,* οὖθαρ *AP*9.1 (Polyaen.). **-ία**, ἡ, = τιθήνησις, Lxx 4*Ma.*16.7 (pl.).

**τῑθηνοκομητέον**, *one must tend like a nurse,* Ph.2.470.

**τῑθηνόκομον**· γένος· τοὺς Αἰθίοπας, ἐπεὶ μέλανες καὶ κομῆται (μελανὶς καὶ κομήτις cod.), Hsch.: also **τιθωνόκομον**· ἔθνος μέλαν μὲν τὸ ὅλον σῶμα, λευκὸν δὲ τὰς κόμας, Id.

**τῑθηνός**, όν, (θῆσθαι) *nursing,* χθών Lyc.1398; πόνων τιθηνοὺς ἀποδιδοῦσά σοι τροφάς repaying thee nurture for thy *nursing* labours, i.e. rewarding thee for thy trouble in nursing me, E.*IA*1230. II. Subst. τιθηνός, ὁ, *one who nurses* or brings up, *foster-father,* Lxx *Nu.* 11.12, al., Nic.*Al.*31, Orph.*H.*54.1, etc.; τ. τοῦ υἱοῦ τοῦ βασιλέως *Sammelb.*1568.2 (ii B.C.): also τιθηνός, ἡ, = τιθήνη, Anon.ap.Longin. 44.2, Plu.2.322c. 2. *nursling,* παῖδα τιθηνὸν *IG*14.1437.

**τίθθη**, v. τίτθη.

**τῑθός**, ή, όν, = τιθασός, Arat.960.

⊛ **τῑθυμαλλίς**, ίδος, ἡ, = παράλιος, Dsc.4.164, cf. Hp.*Superf.*28. 2. = ἡλιοσκόπιος, Ps.-Dsc.4.14 (p. 312 W.). 3. τιθυμαλλὶς (sic) μυρσινίτης, = τιθύμαλλος θῆλυς, Afric.*Cest.*p.69 V.; τ. χαρακίτης, = τιθύμαλλος ἄρρην, ib.p.81 V.

⊛ **τῑθύμαλλος** [ῠ], ὁ, *spurge, Euphorbia Peplus,* Cratin.325 (lyr.), Ar. *Ec.*405, Thphr.*HP*9.8.2, *PHolm.*5.24, 25.1: heterocl. pl. τιθύμαλλα *AP*9.217 (Muc. Scaev.).—Seven kinds are enumerated by Dsc.4. 164; τ. ἄρρην, = χαρακίας, l.c., cf. Thphr.*HP*9.11.8; τ. θῆλυς, = μυρσινίτης or μυρτίτης, ib.9.11.9, Dsc. l.c.; used for poisoning water in warfare, Afric.*Cest.*p.15 V.

**τιθωνόκομον**, v. τιθηνόκομον.

**Τῑθωνός**, ὁ, *Tithonus,* brother of Priam, husband of Eos, and father of Memnon, Il.11.1, 20.237, Hes.*Th.*984, etc.: metaph. of a decrepit old man, because, as the tale went, Eos begged Zeus to grant immortality to Tithonus, but forgot to ask for eternal youth, Ar.*Ach.*688, Call.*Iamb.*1.249: prov. of great old age, ὑπὲρ τὸν Τ. ζῆν Luc.*DMort.*7.1.

**τικ-τικός**, ή, όν, *of* or *for childbirth,* (sc. φάρμακον) a medicine *used for women lying-in,* Ar.*Fr.*872. ⊛**-τω**, Od.4.86, etc.: fut. τέξω 11.249, *h.Merc.*493, Orac.ap.Hdt.5.92.β', A.*Pr.*851,869, E.*Tr.*747, Ar.*Eq.*1037 (Orac.), *Th.*509; also τέξομαι Il.19.99, Hes.*Th.*469,898, *h.Ap.*101, A.*Pr.*768, Hdt.7.49, Ar.*Lys.*744, etc.; poet. inf. also τεκεῖσθαι *h.Ven.*127; pl. τεξείεσθε Arat.124: aor. ἔτεκον, Ep. τέκον, Il.1. 352, 5.875, etc.: aor. 1 ἔτεξα only late, Orph.*H.*41.8 codd. (for ἐντήξῃ is prob. l. in Ar.*Lys.*553): pf. τέτοκα Hes.*Op.*591, Hp.*Aph.*5.39, Ar.*Pax*757, Pl.Com.64.5, X.*Cyn.*5.13, cf. ἐντίκτω:—Med., in same sense as Act., only in Poets, A.*Ch.*127, *Fr.*44: fut. (v. supr.): aor. ἐτεκόμην Ar.*Av.*1193 (lyr.), Ep. τεκόμην Il.4.59, al.; subj. τέκηαι A.R.1.905:—Pass., pres. indic. τίκτεται A.*Th.*437; inf. τίκτεσθαι Sor.2.53; part. τικτόμενος ib.54: fut. τεχθήσομαι J.*AJ*2.9.2, *Gp.*17. 6.1, etc.: aor. ἐτέχθην Hp.*Superf.*18, Ps.-E.*Fr.*1132.44, Lxx *Nu.*26. 60 (v.l.), al., *Gp.*17.6.2, etc.: pf. τέτεγμαι, inf. τετέχθαι, Ael.*NA*2.12, Paus.3.7.7, etc.—These pass. tenses seem not to have been used in correct Att.:—*bring into the world, engender;* of the father, *beget,* of the mother, *bring forth.* I. impf. Act. τίκτε, ἔτικτε, in Hom. usu. of the father, Il.2.628, 6.155,206, 11.224, cf. Hes.*Fr.* 44 (of the mother, Il.16.180, 22.428, 24.497, Od.23.325); in Hes. (*Fr.*17,142), Lyr., and Trag. the pres. and impf. are also used of the mother, ἃ Θήβαν ἔτικτεν Pi.*O.*6.85, cf. B.18.50; μᾶτερ, ἅ μ' ἔτικτες A.*Eu.*321 (lyr.), cf. *Ag.*763 (lyr., of Ὕβρις), S.*El.*533; δεινὸν τὸ τίκτειν ib.770, cf. Pl.*Tht.*151a, etc.; τ. καὶ γεννᾷ Id.*Smp.*206d; of both parents, Στάσις δὲ καὶ Κρόνος..τικτέτον τύραννον Cratin.240. 2. aor. Act. τέκε, ἔτεκε, mostly of the mother, Il.1.36,352, 2.513, etc. (also fut. Med. τέξεσθαι 19.99); τεκεῖν τινά τινι 2.658, 6.22, etc.; ὑπό τινι 2.714,728, etc.; τ. ἔκ τινος Plu.*Thes.*20; παρά τινος Luc. *Alex.*42; παρά τινι E.*El.*62: but τέκεν of the father, Il.13.450, Od.3.489, al., Hes.*Th.*208, *Fr.*99.2: metaph., τῷ τεκόντι ἀρετήν Pl. *Smp.*212a. 3. the aor. Med. τέκετο is commonly used of the father, as Il.2.741, 6.154, al., Hes.*Fr.*19: but τέκετο of the mother, Il.2.742, 15.187, 22.48, Hes.*Fr.*46; so τῶν τεκομένων of the mother, A.*Ch.*419 (lyr.). 4. the two are conjoined, ὃν τέκετο θάνατος, ἔτεκε δ' αἰόλος δράκων S.*Tr.*834 (codd., lyr.). 5. aor. Act. is used in pl. of both parents, Od.7.55, 8.554 (οὓς Ἑκάβη ἠδὲ Πρίαμος τέκε παῖδας Il. 22.234); aor. Med. τεκόμεσθα, Od.23.61, 24.293. b. οἱ τεκόντες the *parents,* A.*Th.*49, S.*OT*999, etc.; the Art. is rarely omitted, πατέρων τε καὶ τεκόντων A.*Ch.*329 (lyr.): c. gen., κιόντων τοῖς τεκοῦσι Id.*Pers.* 245 (troch.): ὁ τεκών *the father,* Id.*Ch.*690, S.*OC*1108; ἁ τεκοῦσα *the mother,* A.*Th.*926 (lyr.), cf. *Ch.*133, etc. (rarely ἡ τίκτουσα, S. *OT*1247, *El.*342); in Prose, Lys.10.8; ἡ τ. αὐτόν his *mother,* Hdt. 1.116; ὅ τ' ἐκείνου τεκών E.*El.*335. 6. freq. in Medic. and other Prose, of women, τίκτουσι ῥηϊδίως Hp.*Aër.*5, cf. Sor.2.54, al., Gal. 16.670; κόρον ἔτεκε *IG*4²(1).121.5, cf. 21 (Epid., iv B.C.). II. of female animals, *bear young, breed,* of mares, Il.16.150, 20.225; of cows, Hes.*Op.*591; of sheep, Od.4.86, etc.; τὰς τετοκυίας τοκάδας *PCair.Zen.*292.305, cf. 710.4 (iii B.C.); ἐὰν τέκῃ ἵππος ib.635.2 (iii B.C.); of the hare, τὰ μὲν τέτοκε, τὰ δὲ τίκτει, τὰ δὲ κύει X.*Cyn.*5. 13; of birds, *hatch,* Il.2.313; ᾠὰ τ. *lay* eggs, Hdt.2.68, Ar.*Fr.*185, Arist.*GA*718$^{b}$23, etc.; of fish, *spawn,* Id.*HA*568$^{a}$16, Gal.6.718, etc. III. of the earth, *bear, produce,* ἔμπεδα μῆλα (sheep) Od. 19.113; ἡ γῆ..τίκτουσα ποίαν E.*Cyc.*333:—Med., γαῖαν.., ἣ τὰ πάντα τίκτεται A.*Ch.*127, cf. *Fr.*44.4:—Pass., τίκτεσθαι δὲ φόρους γᾶς..εὐχόμεθ' ἀεί Id.*Supp.*674 (lyr.). IV. metaph., *generate, engender, produce,* λέγω τὴν χώρην λιμὸν τέξεσθαι Hdt.7.49; ἐπειχθῆναι πρῆγμα τίκτει σφάλματα ib.10.ζ'; of impiety, τὸ γὰρ δυσσεβὲς ἔργον μετὰ μὲν πλείονα τίκτει A.*Ag.*759 (lyr.), cf. 763 (lyr., cf. supr. 1.1), *Ch.*805 (lyr.); ἡ ἐπιθυμία τ. ἁμαρτίαν *Ep.Jac.*1.15; μὴ θράσος τέκῃ φόβον A.*Supp.*498; of Night as the mother of Day, τῆς..τεκούσης φῶς τόδ' εὐφρόνης Id.*Ag.*279; ὃν αἰόλα νὺξ..τίκτει.., Ἅλιον αἰτῶ S.*Tr.*95 (lyr.): generally, τ. [νόμους] Id.*OT*870 (lyr.); χάρις χάριν γάρ ἐστιν ἡ τίκτουσ' ἀεί Id.*Aj.*522; τ. ἀοιδάς E.*HF*767 (lyr.); ὕδωρ δὲ πίνων οὐδὲν ἂν τέκοι σοφόν Cratin.199; τ. ῥήματα Ar.*Ra.*1059 (anap.); also in Prose, νουσήματα Hp.*Hum.*12; ἃ ἀεὶ τίκτει πόλεμον καὶ ἔχθραν Pl.*R.*547a; πολλοὺς καὶ καλοὺς λόγους Id.*Smp.*210d; [δᾲς] πῦρ τέξεται X.*Cyr.*7.5.23, etc.:—Pass., τῷδε κέρδει (sic codd.) κέρδος ἄλλο τίκτεται A.*Th.*437. (τίκτω fr. τί-τκ-ω redupl. fr. τεκ- (τέκνον, etc.).)

**τίλα** [ῐ], ἡ, *plucking,* εἰς τὴν τ. τοῦ χόρτου *PFlor.*180.4 (iii A.D.). II. pl., *flocks* or *motes floating in the air,* Plu.2.722a; cf. τίλος.

**τῐλ-άω**, *to have a thin stool,* χολὴν τιλᾶν Hippon.55A, cf. *Hippiatr.* 56. **-ημα**, ατος, τό, *a thin stool,* *EM*187.25.

**τιλλάρια**, τά, v. τιτλάρια.

**τιλλοπώγων**, ωνος, ὁ, *one who plucks out his beard,* Com.Adesp.1163.

⊛ **τίλλω**, Il.22.78, etc.: fut. τιλῶ (ἀπο-) Cratin.123, (παρα-) Ar.*Eq.* 373: aor. ἔτῖλα Theoc.3.21, (ἀπ-) Ar.*Lys.*578, *Fr.*686: pf. τέτιλκα *PCair.Zen.*782(*b*).121 (iii B.C.):—**Med.**, Ep. impf. τιλλέσθην Il.24. 711: fut. τιλοῦμαι (παρα-) Men.363.5:—**Pass.**, aor. ἐτίλθην Ar.*Nu.* 1083: 2 aor. ἐτίλην [ῐ] Lxx *Da.*7.4; 3 sg. imper. τιλήτωι *PFay.*131. 18 (iii/iv A.D.); part. τειλείς (i.e. τιλ-) *PFlor.*322.36 (iii A.D.): pf. τέτιλμαι Lxx *Is.*18.7, (ἐκ-) Anacr.21.10, (ἀπο-) Anaxil.22.20, (παρα-) Ar.*Ra.*516:—*pluck* or *pull out* hair, etc., πολιὰς δ' ἄρ' ἀνὰ τρίχας ἕλκετο χερσί, τίλλων ἐκ κεφαλῆς Il.22.78; τίλλε κόμην ib.406; τρίχας Men. *Epit.*271, *Her.*5; ἐρέβινθον *PCair.Zen.*719.6 (iii B.C.); τ. στάχυας καὶ ἐσθίειν *Ev.Matt.*12.1; τ. χόρτον τοῖς κτήσι *PFlor.*321.47 (iii A.D.):— Med., χαίτας τίλλεσθαι *pluck out one's* hair, Od.10.567. 2. with acc. of that *from which* the hair or feathers *are plucked,* τίλλειν πέλειαν, of birds of prey, 15.527, cf. Hdt.3.76; κίρκον εἰσορῶ..χηλαῖς κάρα τίλλοντα A.*Pers.*209; τίλλουσι τὴν γλαῦκα, of small birds attacking the owl, Arist.*HA*609$^{a}$15; so of the cuckoo, ib.618$^{a}$29 (Pass.); as a description of an idle fellow, τίλλων ἑαυτόν Ar.*Pax* 546, cf. *Ra.*428; of a cook, *pluck* a fowl, Eub.150.5, cf. Plu.2.233a; also τ. λαγών Ar.*Fr.*212; τ. πλάτανον *pluck* its leaves *off,* Plu.*Them.* 18; τὸν στέφανον τίλαί με κατ' αὐτίκα λεπτὰ ποησεῖς Theoc.l.c.; κῴδια τ. *PPetr.*2p.108 = 3p.78 (iii B.C.); also, *pluck* live sheep, instead of shearing, τοῖς τίλλουσιν τὰ ὑποδίφθερα (sc. πρόβατα) *PCair. Zen.*430.3 (iii B.C.), cf. Suid. s.v. πεκτῆρες:—Pass., *have one's hair plucked out,* Ar.*Th.*593; τέφρᾳ τιλθῆναι, as a punishment of adulterers, Id.*Nu.*1083; v. παρατίλλω, τέφρα. 3. c. acc. cogn., τίλματα τ. Plu.2.48b, cf. Herod.2.70. 4. τ. μέλη pluck the harp-strings, *play* harp-tunes, Cratin.256 (lyr.). 5. *pick so as to extract fibre,* τετίλκασι στιππύου δέσμας ς' *PCair.Zen.* l.c. 6. νεφέλιον παρατεταμένον καὶ τιλλόμενον *cirrous,* Thphr.*Sign.*43. II. since tearing the hair was a usual expression of sorrow, τίλλεσθαί τινα *tear one's hair in sorrow for* any one, τόν γ' ἄλοχός τε φίλη καὶ πότνια μήτηρ τιλλέσθην Il.24.711: without acc., τιλλόμενοι καὶ κλαίοντες Phld.*Ir.* p.36 W. III. metaph., *pluck, vex, annoy,* Anacr.13B; στέφανον τ., = τοὺς νόμους λυμαίνεσθαι, Pythag.ap.Porph.*VP*42:—Pass., ὑπὸ συκοφαντῶν τίλλεσθαι, with allusion to a bird's feathers, Ar.*Av.*285. (Not found in Att. Prose.)

**τίλ-μα**, ατος, τό, *anything pulled* or *shredded, lint,* Hp.*Decent.*8, Heraclid.Tarent.ap.Gal.12.957. II. *anything that can be pulled* or *plucked,* Plu.2.48b. III. = τίλσις, Herod.2.69 (pl.). IV. in later Medic. language, τίλματα *sprains,* Gal.18(1).682. **-μάτιον**, τό, Dim. of foreg. 1, Archig.ap.Gal.12.578, Sor.2.11. **-μός**, ὁ, *plucking* or *pulling out,* of hair, A.*Supp.*839 (pl., lyr.), Men.*Epit.* 472; also, *pulling up,* καλάμου *POxy.*1692.10 (ii A.D.), 1631.9 (iii A.D.), cf. ὀλοτίλλω; joined with κνησμοί, as a symptom in sickness, Hp.*Epid.*1.23 (pl.). II. *extraction of fibre,* σησάμου *PCair.Zen.* 787.21 (iii B.C.); τ. ὀσπρίων, *evulsitio,* *Gloss.*

**τῖλος**, ὁ, *a thin stool,* as in diarrhoea, *stercus liquidum,* Sophr. in *PSI*11.1214*d*6, Poll.5.91.

**τίλος**, ὁ, (τίλλω) *anything plucked:* οἱ τίλοι *the fine hair of the eyebrows,* Poll.2.50; also τιλ[λ]ά· πτερά, Hsch.

**τίλ-σις**, εως, ἡ, *plucking out,* τριχῶν τίλσεις Arist.*EN*1148$^{b}$27;

*pulling up*, τοῦ χόρτου PLond.1.113(3).7 (vi A.D.). -τός, ή, όν, *plucked, gathered*, λάχανα POxy.2138.7 (iii A.D.). 2. *shredded*, τ. μοτός *lint*, Gal.11.125; ἐλλύχνιον Sor.2.11: also in neut. as Subst., διαμοτώσαντες ξηροῖς τιλτοῖς Paul.Aeg.6.5, cf. *Gloss*. 3. τὸ τ. (with or without τάριχος) salt fish *stripped of its scales* before curing, Nicostr.Com.5.5, Pl.Com.193. ⊛ -τρον, τό, *payment for plucking or extracting fibre*, PRyl.inv.575 i 3 (iv A.D.): pl., PGot.67 (late Byz.).

**τίλφη**, ἡ, = σίλφη, Luc.*Ind*.17; cf. τίφη.

**τίλων**, ωνος, ὁ, a fish of the Thracian lake Prasias, Hdt.5.16, Arist.*HA*568$^{b}$25, 602$^{b}$26 (with vv. ll. τύλων, ψίλων, ψύλων, τίλλων, τριλών).

**τιμαδία**· μικρὰ τιμή, Hsch.

**Τιμαιογραφέω**, *write a Timaeus*, used of Plato by Timo 54.3.

⊛ **τιμαῖος**, ον, *highly prized*, Diocl.Com.18:—mostly as pr. n. Τίμαιος.

**τιμαιρεσίαι**, αἱ, *election of magistrates*, SIG282 ii 3 (Priene, iv B.C.).

**τιμαλφ-έω**, *do honour to*, τ. λόγοις νίκαν Pi.*N*.9.54; θεοὺς τοῖσδε τ. χρεών A.*Ag*.922; μολόντα τ. *celebrate* any one's arrival, Id.*Eu*.15:—Pass., σκήπτροισι τιμαλφούμενος ib.626; ὑπ' ἀστῶν..τ. ib.807:—rare in Prose, τ. τοὺς θεούς Arist.*Pol*.1336$^{b}$19; and in later Poetry, τ. τὰν σὰν..θυμέλαν *Sammelb*.6699.2 (iii B.C.):—Epich.(*Fr*.214) ridiculed Aeschylus for his use of this word. -ής, ές, (τιμή, ἀλφεῖν) *fetching a prize, costly, precious*, A.*Fr*.56, Ion Trag.43; -έστατον κτῆμα Pl.*Ti*.59b; πρᾶγμα χρυσοῦ -έστερον Nicostr.ap.Stob.4.23.62, cf. Ph.1.157; πάντα μου τὰ -έστατα κτήματα Gal.14.66.

⊛ **τιμάξιος**, ον, *worthy of honour*: Sup. -ώτατος, as a title, POxy.943.9 (vi A.D.).

**τιμάορος**, ον, v. τιμωρός. **τιμάοχος**, ον, v. τιμοῦχος.

**τιμ-αρχία**, ἡ, = τιμοκρατία, Pl.*R*.545b, 550d. II. = τιμητεία, Lat. *censoria potestas*, D.C.52.21. -ασία [prob. μᾶ], ἡ, *assessment*, IG5(1).1433.24 (Messene), SIG306.17 (Arc., iv B.C.). -ασις, v. τίμησις. -ατάς, v. τιμητής.

⊛ **Τιμαχεῖον**, τό, *monument of* Τίμαχος (cf. Eust.584.22), *Docum. ant. dell' Africa Italiana* 1.91 (Cyrene, iv B.C.).

⊛ **τιμάω**, Il.23.788, etc.: fut. τιμήσω 9.155, etc., Dor. 3 pl. τιμασεῦντι Theoc.*Ep*.7.4: aor. ἐτίμησα Hdt.8.124, etc., Ep. τίμησα Hes.*Th*.399, Lyr. τίμᾶσα Pi.*N*.6.41, B.12.194: pf. τετίμηκα Lys.26.17, etc., Dor. τετίμακα Pi.*I*.4(3).37(55):—Med., fut. τιμήσομαι always in pass. sense, *h.Ap*.485, A.*Ag*.581, S.*Ant*.210, E.*Fr*.360.49, Th.2.87, X.*Cyr*.8.7.15 (reading δι' ἄνδρα with codd. DF), *Hier*.9.9, exc. in Pl.*Ap*.37b, where it is used in a technical sense (v. infr. III. 2): aor. ἐτιμησάμην in senses shared by Act., Od.19.280, 20.129, Il.22.235, Th.3.40; in sense III. 2, Pl.*Cri*.52c:—Pass., fut. τιμηθήσομαι Th.6.80, D.19.223, IG2$^{2}$.1182.9, etc.; τετιμήσομαι Lys.31.24 codd. (τιμήσεται Cobet): aor. ἐτιμήθην Hdt.5.5, etc.; Lyr. 3 pl. τίμαθεν Pi.*Parth*.2.41: pf. τετίμημαι Il.12.310, etc.; also Med. in technical sense, v. III. 2:—*honour, revere, reverence* (in this sense the Med. is used only by Hom.); of the honour rendered to superiors, as by men to gods, by men to their elders, rulers, or guests, περὶ κῆρι θεὸν ὣς τιμήσαντο Od.19.280, etc.; τίμα τὸν πατέρα σου Lxx *Ex*.20.12, al.; conversely of the honour bestowed by gods upon a man, μερμήριζε (sc. Ζεύς).., ὡς Ἀχιλῆα τιμήσῃ Il.2.4, cf. 15.612, Od.3.379; by a father on his son, 14.203, Hes.*Th*.532; by an elder brother, Il.22.235 (Med.): also in Pi., Hdt., and Att., ἐξόχως τίμασεν Pi.*O*.9.69; δαιμόνων τιμᾶν γένος A.*Th*.236; θεοὺς τιμῶντες S.*OC*277, cf. 1071 (lyr.), Hdt.2.29; σέβεσθαι καὶ τ. τοὺς θεούς X.*Mem*.4.3.13; ἱλασκομένοις καὶ τιμῶσιν..Δία Πατρῷον SIG1044.6 (Halic., iv/iii B.C.); τὸν φίλον τιμῶσιν ἐξ ἴσου πατρί S.*Ant*.644, cf. 516, E.*Med*.660 (lyr.), Hdt.7.107, etc.; θεοὶ δ' ὅταν τιμῶσιν, οὐδὲν δεῖ φίλων E.*HF*1338: abs., οἱ τύραννοι μάλιστα δύνανται τιμᾶν *bestow honours*, D.20.15 (τιμᾶν secl. Bake), cf. Pl.*Lg*.631e: hence simply, *reward*, X.*Cyr*.3.3.6, Isoc.9.42 (so in Pass., Hdt.7.213, Lys.12.64, 19.18); ἐπαινεῖν καὶ τ., τ. καὶ δωρεῖσθαι, δωρεῖσθαί τε καὶ τ., τ. καὶ χαρίζεσθαι, X.*Cyr*.1.2.12, 3.2.28, 8.2.10, 2.4.9: c. dat. modi, δωτίνῃσι θεὸν ὣς τιμήσουσι *will honour* him *with* gifts, Il.9.155; ξεῖνον ἐτιμήσασθ' ἐνὶ οἴκῳ εὐνῇ καὶ σίτῳ Od.20.129; τιμᾶν τινα τάφῳ, γόοις, A.*Th*.1051, *Supp*.116 (lyr.); πόλιν τ. συμμάχῳ δορί Id.*Eu*.773; ἐσθήμασι Th.3.58; χοροῖς E.*Ba*.220; δώροις X.*An*.1.9.14, *HG*6.1.6; στρεπτοῖς καὶ ψελίοις τ. καὶ κοσμεῖν τινα Id.*Cyr*.1.3.3:—Pass., mostly in pf. τετίμημαι, which alone is pass. in Hom., *to be honoured, held in honour*, Il.9.608, Od.7.69; ἐτιμήθη παρὰ Ξέρξῃ Hdt.8.105; ὑπό τινος Pl.*R*.426c, etc.; τετίμαται πρὸς ἀθανάτων Pi.*I*.4(3).59(77); σκήπτρῳ..ὦκε τετιμῆσθαι περὶ πάντων Il.9.38, cf. 12.310; τιμᾶσθαι προεδρίαις X.*Vect*.3.4, cf. *Cyr*.8.4.2; ἐκ τοῦ πολεμεῖν Th.5.16: c. acc. cogn. attracted to gen., ὥς μευ αἰεὶ μέμνησαι ἐνηέος, οὐδέ σε λήθω, τιμῆς ἧς τέ μ' ἔοικε τετιμῆσθαι Il.23.649 (but c. gen., τετειμημένος ὑπὸ τῶν αὐτοκρατόρων τετάρτης στρατείας (= Lat. *quattuor militiis*) *Supp.Epigr*.7.145 (Palmyra, ii A.D.)); οἱ τετιμημένοι *men of rank, men in office*, X.*Cyr*.8.3.9; οἱ τιμώμενοι ib.8.8.4, cf. E.*Or*.[913]; τῆς πόλεως τὸ τιμώμενον ἀπὸ τοῦ ἄρχειν *the honour enjoyed by* the city, Th.2.63. II. of things, *hold in honour* or *esteem, value, prize*, *h.Hom*.25.6, Pi.*O*.6.72, etc.; τί τὴν τυραννίδα τιμᾷς ὑπέρφευ; E.*Ph*.550; νόμους τ. Id.*Tr*.1211; τὴν εὐσέβειαν, ἁγνωμοσύναν, Id.*Ion*1046, *Ba*.885 (lyr.); ἰσότητα Id.*Ph*.536, cf. Pl.*Tht*.149c; τὸ σωφρονεῖν τ. τοῦ βίου πλέον A.*Supp*.1013. 2. c. gen. pretii, *estimate* or *value at* a certain price, Pl.*Lg*.917c, 921b, PCair.Zen.269.13,15 (iii B.C.), UPZ67.3 (ii B.C.), etc.; πλοῖα τετιμημένα χρημάτων Th.4.26: abs., τετιμῆσθαι ἕκαστον τὴν οὐσίαν χρεών that each man should *have* his property *valued* (for assessment), Pl.*Lg*.955d, etc.; οἱ ὑπὲρ τὰς μυρίας τιμώμενοι δραχμάς Plb.6.23.15; τὸ τιμηθέν the *estimate*, Pl.*Lg*.954b:—freq. in Med., διακοσίων ταλάντων ἐτιμήσατο (τὰ) αὐτοῦ *estimated* his property *at*.., Lys.19.48, cf. PPetr.2 intr.p.33 (iii B.C.); πρὸ παντὸς τιμᾶσθαί τι, like περὶ παντὸς ποιεῖσθαι (v. περί A. IV), Th.3.40, cf. 1.33; πλείονος, μείζονος τιμᾶσθαι, X.*Mem*.3.10.10, *Cyr*.2.1.13; τοσούτου τ. τὴν πολιτείαν D.22.45; μίαν ἡδονὴν θανάτου τ. Plu.2.5b: also with Preps., ἀντὶ παντὸς ἂν τιμησαίμην εἰπεῖν τοῦ βίου D.18.214: without a gen., ἐτιμήσαντο τήν τε χώραν καὶ τὰς οἰκίας Plb.2.62.7: simply, *value, estimate*, ἐν προικὶ Is.3.35, cf. D.47.57 (Pass.), 53.1; τινα Lxx *Le*.27.8, *Ev.Matt*.27.9. 3. rarely, *award* or *give as an honour*, Παιάν τέ σοι τιμᾷ φάος Pi.*P*.4.270; ταῦτά τῇδέ μοι τάδε τιμᾶτε S.*Aj*.688; ἐκείνῳ δυσσεβῆ τιμᾷς χάριν Id.*Ant*.514; πατρῴαν τιμῶν χάριν E.*Or*.829 (lyr.): hence, III. as Att. law-term (cf. τίμημα 4): 1. in Act. (later in Med., PHal.1.201 (iii B.C.), D.L.2.41, etc.), of the court, *estimate the amount of punishment due* to the criminal, *award the penalty*, τιμάτω τὸ δικαστήριον, ὅ τι ἂν δέῃ πάσχειν..τὸν ἡττηθέντα Pl.*Lg*.843b; τὴν ἀξίαν τῆς βλάβης ib.879b; τ. τὰς βλάβας ib.843d; τ. τὴν δίκην ib.880d (cf. infr. 2c); ἅπασι τ. τὴν μακράν (sc. γραμμήν) *award* them the long line, i.e. sentence of death, Ar.*V*.106, ubi v. Sch.: abs., ὡς ἐγὼ τιμᾶν βλέπω I carry *penalty* in my eyes, am itching for pains and penalties, ib.847: the sentence or judgement awarded is added in the gen., τ. τινὶ θανάτου (sc. δίκην) *give sentence* of death *against* a man, *condemn* him to death, Lys.27.7 (cf. 8), Pl.*Grg*.516a, D.24.103 (Pass.), 32.15; τ. τινὶ δέκα ταλάντων *mulct* him in ten talents, Id.58.31; τίνος τιμήσειν αὐτῷ προσδοκᾷς τὸ δικαστήριον; at what do you expect the court *to fix* his *penalty?* Id.21.151, cf. Pl.*Ap*.37c; ἡ ἡλιαία τιμάτω περὶ αὐτοῦ ὅτου ἂν δόξῃ ἄξιος εἶναι παθεῖν Lex ap.D.21.47: c. acc. pers., τιμάτωσαν αὐτὸν καθ' ὅτι ἂν δοκῇ τῷ κοινῷ IG2$^{2}$.1275.16:—Pass., τιμᾶσθαι ἀργυρίου *to be condemned* to a fine, τινος *for* a thing, Lys.6.22, Lex ap.D.21.47; ἐὰν..ᾖ τῳ θανάτου τετιμημένον if *sentence* of death *has been passed* upon one, Pl.*Lg*.946e, cf. Antipho 6.38. 2. in Med., of the parties before the court, a. of the accuser, τιμᾶταί μοι ὁ ἀνὴρ θανάτου (sc. τὴν δίκην) he *estimates* the penalty *at* death (gen. pretii) for me, Pl.*Ap*.36b; εἰ βούλοιτο θανάτου σοι τιμᾶσθαι Id.*Grg*.486b, cf. D.25.74,83, etc. b. of the person accused (cf. ἀντιτιμάω, ὑποτιμάω), τιμήσεσθαι τοιούτου τινὸς ἐμαυτῷ *estimate* the penalty for myself at so high a rate, Pl.*Ap*.37b, cf. 38b; ἐξῆν σοι φυγῆς τιμήσασθαι Id.*Cri*.52c; ἔδησεν ἑαυτὸν τιμησάμενος δεσμοῦ Lys.6.21: pf. Pass., θανάτου τετιμημένος ἑαυτῷ Din.1.1:—Arist.*Rh*.1375$^{a}$1 uses the Act. in this sense. c. the acc. of δίκη or of the offence is added, πέντε μυριάδων τιμησάμενος τὴν δίκην Plu.*Cic*.8, cf. *Lys*.13, D.L.2.42; θανάτου τιμῶμαι τὰ πεπολιτευμένα ἐμαυτῷ Plu.*Phoc*.34.

**τιμάωρ**, v. τιμωρός.

**τιμ-έω**, Dor., = τιμάω, prob. in IG5(1).962.39 (Cotyrta, ii B.C.); inf. τιμεῖν ib.14.952.16 (Acragas, iii B.C.), 5(1).1432.41 (Messene); part. fem. τιμίονσα GDI5150.22 (Crete, found at Delos, ii B.C.); masc. pl. τιμέοντες SIG637.6 (Delph., ii B.C.):—in Hdt.6.39 all codd. have ἐπι-τιμέων; similar forms in the Ionic writings of Luc. (*Dom*.20, *Astr*.1). ⊛ -ή, ἡ, (τίω, v. ad fin.). I. *worship, esteem, honour*, and in pl. *honours*, such as are accorded to gods or to superiors, or bestowed (whether by gods or men) as a reward for services, τιμῆς ἔμμοροί εἰσι Od.8.480; ὄφρ' ἂν Ἀχαιοὶ υἱὸν ἐμὸν τίσωσιν ὀφέλλωσίν τέ ἑ τιμῇ Il.1.510; ἐκ δὲ Διὸς τιμὴ καὶ κῦδος ὀπηδεῖ 17.251; ἐν δὲ ἰῇ τ. ἠμὲν κακὸς ἠδὲ καὶ ἐσθλός 9.319, cf. 4.410; ἐν τ. σέβειν A.*Pers*.166 (troch.); ἐν τ. ἄγεσθαί τινας Hdt.1.134; ἐν τ. τίθεσθαι or ἄγειν τινά, Id.3.3, Pl.*R*.538e; ἐν τιμαῖς ἔχειν Philem.199; τιμαῖς αὐξήσας τινάς X.*Cyr*.8.8.24; τιμὴν νεῖμαι, ἀπονέμειν τινί, S.*Ph*.1062, Pl.*Lg*.837c; τοῖς φίλοις τιμὰς νέμειν pay *due regard*, S.*Aj*.1351; τιμὰς ὤπασας, πορών, A.*Pr*.30,946; διδόναι E.*Hipp*.1424, etc.; ἀποδοῦναι Pl.*R*.415c; τὸ πρᾶγμ' ἐμοὶ τιμὴν φέρει E.*Hipp*.329; τινὶ τιμὰς προσάπτειν S.*El*.356; ἀφύων τιμὴν περιάψας Ar.*Ach*.640 (anap.); τ. εὑρίσκεσθαι, δέκεσθαι, Pi.*P*.1.48, 8.5; τιμὴν παρ' ἀνθρώποις φέρεσθαι Ar.*Av*.1278; τιμὰς ἔχειν Hdt.2.46, etc.; πρός τινος Id.1.120; ἐν μεγάλῃ τιμῇ εἶναι X.*An*.2.5.38; τιμῆς λαχεῖν, τυχεῖν, S.*Ant*.699, *El*.364 (v.l.); οἱ γεραίτεροι ταῖς τῶν νέων τιμαῖς ἀγάλλονται *paid to them by* the young, X.*Mem*.2.1.33: c. gen., χωρὶς ἡ τ. θεῶν *the honour due* to them, A.*Ag*.637, cf. *Ch*.200; τιμὰς τὰς θεῶν πατεῖν S.*Ant*.745; τιμαὶ δαιμόνων E.*Hipp*.107: τιμῇ *with honour, honourably*, S.*OC*381 codd.; τιμῆς ἕνεκα as *a mark of honour*, X.*An*.7.3.28; τιμῇ προέχουσ' S.*Ant*.208. 2. *honour, dignity, lordship*, as the attribute of gods or kings, Il.1.278, 9.498, etc.; θεῶν ἐξ ἔμμορε τιμῆς Od.5.335; τ. βασιληΐς Il.6.193, cf. Hes.*Th*.393, Pi.*P*.4.108, A.*Eu*.228 (pl.); Περσονόμος τ. μεγάλη Id.*Pers*.919 (anap.); δίθρονος..καὶ δισκήπτρος τ. Id.*Ag*.44 (anap.): generally, like γέρας, *prerogative* or *special attribute* of a king, and in pl. his *prerogatives*, Od.1.117, Hes.*Th*.203, Thgn.374, S.*OT*909 (lyr.), etc.; βασιλικαὶ τ. imperial *prerogatives*, Hdn.7.10.5; σκῆπτρον τιμάς τ' ἀποσυλᾶται A.*Pr*.172 (anap.). 3. *a dignity, office, magistracy*, and in pl., *civic honours* (τιμὰς λέγομεν εἶναι τὰς ἀρχάς Arist.*Pol*.1281$^{a}$31), Hdt.1.59, etc.; ἔν τε ταῖς ἀρχαῖς καὶ ταῖς ἄλλαις τ. Pl.*Ap*.35b, cf. *Ti*.20a, etc.; μὴ φεύγειν τοὺς πόνους, ἢ μηδὲ τὰς τ. διώκειν Th.2.63; τιμὴν ἔχειν X.*Cyr*.1.3.8, etc.; τὴν τιμὴν εἴληχε Pl.*Phlb*.61c; οἱ ἐν τιμαῖς men in *office*, E.*IA*19 (anap.), cf. Isoc.9.81; ἐκβαλῶ σε ἐκ τῆς τιμῆς X.*Cyr*.1.3.9; τιμὰς ἴσχειν hold the *office* of τιμοῦχος (q.v.), *Jahresh*.12.136 (Erythrae, v/iv B.C.): generally, *office, task*, ἄχαρις τιμή Hdt.7.36:—also, b. *a person in authority, an authority*, κλῦτε δὲ Γᾶ (Ahrens for τὰ) χθονίων τε τιμαί A.*Ch*.399 (lyr.); καὶ τὰ καρτερώτατα τιμαῖς ὑπείκει yield to *authorities*, S.*Aj*.670. 4. *present of honour, compliment, offering*, e.g. to the gods, Hes.*Op*.142, A.*Pers*.622; *reward, present*, ἢ ἀργύριον ἢ τιμή Pl.*R*.347a; τιμαὶ καὶ δωρεαὶ ib.361c; ὅσοι..ἄλλην τινὰ δωρεὰν ἢ τ. ἔχουσιν παρὰ τῶν Λεβεδίων SIG344.22 (Teos, iv B.C.); τῶν εὐεργεσιῶν τιμὰς φέρονται Pl.*Phd.*113e. **5.** ἡ Δάου τ. 'the worthy D.', Herod. 5.68. **II.** of things, *worth, value, price, h.Cer.*132, *IG*1².349.10, 15, al.; ἐξευρίσκοντες τιμῆς τὰ κάλλιστα at *a price*, Hdt.7.119; τῆς αὐτῆς τ. πωλεῖν Lys.22.12; πρίασθαι D.21.149; δεκαπλάσιον τῆς τ. ἀποτίνειν Pl.*Lg.*914c; ἀποδιδόναι τινὶ τὴν τ. ib.a; δύο εἰπεῖν τ. to name two *prices*, ib.917b; ἀξιοῦν τι τ. τινός ib.d; περὶ τῆς τ. διαφέρεσθαι Lys.22.15; ἐμοὶ δὲ τιμὰ τᾶσδε πᾶ γενήσεται; Ar.*Ach.*895; ἑστηκυῖαι τ. fixed *prices, PTeb.*703.176 (iii B.C.); ὑπὲρ τιμῆς πυροῦ payment of money representing the *value* of wheat, *Ostr.*663 (ii A.D.), al. **2.** *valuation, estimate*, for purposes of assessment, τοῦ κλήρου Pl.*Lg.*744e: generally, ὁ πλοῦτος οἷον τιμή τις τῆς ἀξίας τῶν ἄλλων Arist.*Rh.*1391ᵃ1. **III.** *compensation, satisfaction, penalty*, τιμὴν ἀρνύμενοι Μενελάῳ..πρὸς Τρώων Il.1.159, cf. 5.552; ἀποτινέμεν, τίνειν τιμήν τινι, pay or make *it*, 3.286,288; τιμὴν ἄγειν Od.22.57; Πάτροκλον, ὃς κεῖται ἐμῆς ἕνεκ' ἐνθάδε τιμῆς Il.17.92, cf. Od.14.70,117; οὐ σή..ἡ τ. the *penalty* is not yours, Pl.*Grg.*497b. (The spelling [τι- not τει- *IG*1².347.33, etc.] and the majority of the senses show that τιμή is cogn. with τίω 'value, honour'; sense III perh. arose from a later association with τίνω.) ⊛ **-ήεις**, εσσα, εν, acc. τιμῆϝεντα (τιμετε[ lapis) prob. in *Supp.Epigr.*4.44 (Sicily); contr. **τιμῆς** Il. 9.605; acc. τιμῆντα 18.475; Dor. τιμάεις *BCH*21.599 (Delph., iv B.C.); pl. τιμάεντες Pi.*I.*4(3).7(25); Pamphyl. fem. τιμάϝεσα *Schwyzer* 686.6:—*honoured, esteemed*, of men or gods, Il.9.605, Od.13. 129, 18.161: Comp., τιμηέστερος πέλεται 1.393. **2.** of things, *prized, costly*, χρυσός Il.18.475, Od.8.393; δῶρον 1.312: Sup., [δῶρον] τιμηέστατον 4.614, 15.114; ἐμπόλημα -έστατον *Com.Adesp.*1226: Dor. contr. Sup. τιμαστάτων (gen. pl.) may perh. be restored in Archyt. ap.Stob.1.48.6 (τιμαιέτατων, τιμαετάτων, τιμαοτάτων codd., τιμαεστάτων cj. Gaisf.). ⊛ **-ημα**, ατος, τό, *honouring, tending*, τύμβου A.*Ch.*511. **2.** *estimate, valuation*, τ. τῆς ἀξίας E.*Hipp.*622; τὸ τ. ἐστι τῆς χώρας ἑξακισχιλίων ταλάντων D.14.19, cf. Docum. ib.18.55, *POxy.* 1274.14 (iii A.D.), etc. **3.** *payment*, τίμαμα hoισοντι will make *payment*, *Tab.Heracl.*1.150, cf. *PGrenf.*2.67.12 (iii A.D.); τὸ τ. ἔχων having received the *price*, Alciphr.3.47; pretium = τ. ἐπὶ τοῖς ὠνίοις καταβαλλόμενον, *Gloss.* **4.** in legal sense, *estimate of damages* done: hence, *penalty, punishment, fine*, τ. κλῳὸς σύκινος Ar.*V.*897; τί τίμημ' ἐπιγράψω τῇ δίκῃ; Id.*Pl.*480, cf. Lys.27.16, etc.; καὶ ἐγώ τε τῷ τ. ἐμμένω, καὶ οὗτοι Pl.*Ap.*39b; τ. δὲ [ἔστω], ὅ τι χρὴ πάσχειν ἢ ἀποτίνειν Id.*Lg.*941a; τιμάτω τὸ δικαστήριον τὸ τ. ib.907e, etc.; εἰς τὸ τ. ἀναβάς rising to speak on *the matter of the penalty*, D.19. 290; πρᾶξαι Πειθίαν τὸ τ. τῆς ὕβρεως καὶ ἀποδοῦναί μοι the *damages* for the assault, *PEnteux.*74.17 (iii B.C.). **5.** *cost, expense*, τῷ ἑαυτῆς τ. at her own *expense*, *POxy.*1208.4 (iii A.D.); κινδύνῳ καὶ πόρῳ καὶ τ. τῆς παντοίας μου ὑποστάσεως *PStrassb.*40.20 (vi A.D.), cf. *PFlor.*297. 27 (vi A.D.). **6.** in political sense, *the value at which a citizen's property was rated* for taxation, his *rateable property*, *IG*1².98.11, 2². 2498.8, Lys.17.7, 19.48, Pl.*Lg.*945a, etc.; ἡ ἀπὸ τιμημάτων πολιτεία a government *where the magistrates were chosen according to property, a timocracy*, Id.*R.*550c; ἐκ τιμημάτων αἱ ἀρχαὶ καθίστανται X.*Mem.* 4.6.12, cf. Pl.*Lg.*698b; ἀπὸ τ. μακρῶν αἱ μεθέξεις τῶν ἀρχῶν Arist.*Pol.* 1278ᵃ23; ἐκκλησιάζειν οἱ μὲν ἀπὸ τιμήματος οὐθενὸς οἱ δ' ἀπὸ μακροῦ τ. ib.1294ᵇ3; δημοκρατικὸν τὸ μὴ ἀπὸ τιμήματος ὀλιγαρχικὸν δὲ τὸ ἀπὸ τ. ib. line 9, cf. 1306ᵇ13: the τ. was calculated at so many years' purchase of the οὐσία, πεντεκαίδεκα ταλάντων τρία τάλαντα τίμημα D. 27.9.

**τῑμῆντα**, v. τιμήεις. **τῑμήορος**, ον, v. τιμωρός. **τῑμηρύειν**· τιμιοπωλεῖν, Hsch. **τιμῆς**, gen. of τιμή. **II.** contr. for τιμήεις.

**τῑμήσιος**, ον, f.l. in Ael.*NA*11.7.

**τίμ-ησις** [τῐ], εως, ἡ, *holding valuable, honouring, esteeming*, Pl. *Lg.*696d, 728e. **II.** *estimation* or *valuation* of property or merchandise, *PRev.Laws* 29.12, al. (iii B.C.), *PCair.Zen.*12.1, al. (iii B.C.), Plb.31.28.3: pl., *SIG*364.66 (Ephesus, iii B.C.); τὰς τ. προσεξεπλήρωσεν, = Lat. *census explevit*, *Mon.Anc.Gr.*19.10: Dor. **τίμᾱσις**, καρπῶ *Docum.ant.dell' Africa Italiana* 1.88 (Cyrene, iv B.C.). **2.** *assessment of damages*, Pl.*Lg.*878e; τ. ποιεῖν τινι (opp. a capital charge) Antipho 5.10; ἀπαντᾶν εἰς τὴν τ. Aeschin.3.198, cf. D.53.18: Dor. **τίμᾱσις** *Foed.Delph.Pell.* 1A9. **3.** *rating* or *assessment* for political purposes, Arist.*Pol.*1308ᵇ2 (pl.); ἀπὸ τιμήσεως πολίτευμα D.S.18.18; τοὺς πολίτας συντάξαι..κατὰ τιμήσεις Plot.6.3.1; of the Roman *census*, D.H.1.74: pl., Str.3.5.3: pl. of one *census*, Plu. *Caes.*55. **4.** *payment*, *PSI*4.327.10 (iii B.C.). ⊛ **-ητεία**, ἡ, *censorship*, Lat. *censura*, Plu.*Cat.Ma.*16, *Aem.*38, D.C.41.14. **-ητέος**, α, ον, *to be honoured, valued*, etc., E.*Or.*484, Pl.*R.*561c, etc. **II.** τιμητέον, *one must honour, esteem, estimate*, etc., ib.509a, *Lg.*722b, X. *Mem.*1.4.10, etc. ⊛ **-ητεύω**, *to be censor*, Plu.*TG*14, D.C.41.14; *hold a census*, τῆς Ἰουδαίας (of Quirinius) J.*AJ*20.5.2. **-ητήρ**, ῆρος, ὁ, = τιμητής, *assessor* of taxable property, *Abh.Berl.Akad.*1925(5).6 (Cyrene). **-ητήριος**, ον, *honouring*, θυσίαι Jul.*Or.*5.177a, cf. *Gal.* 298c. **-ητής**, οῦ, ὁ, *valuer* or *assessor of damages* or *penalties*, Pl.*Lg.*843d; τ. τῆς ζημίας οἱ δικασταί Arist.*Rh.Al.*1427ᵇ6; *assessor* of property, *SIG*344.123 (Teos, iv B.C.); τῶν οὐσιῶν (of Quirinius in Syria) J.*AJ*18.1.1; Boeot. **τιμᾱτάς** *SIG*1185.16 (Tanagra, iii B.C., pl.). **II.** at Rome, = *censor*, Plb.6.13.3, D.H.19.16, Plu.*Cic.* 27; as an Imperial title, *SIG*821 *C* 2 (Epist. Domitiani), etc. **-ητικός**, ή, όν, *estimating*: **I.** *for determining the amount of punishment*, πινάκιον τ. Ar.*V.*167. **2.** ἀνὴρ τ., = Lat. *vir censorius, one who has been censor* (τιμητής), Plu.*TG*4; τ. οἶκοι, τ. ὑπομνήματα, D.H. 1.74; ἡ τ. ἀρχή, = τιμητεία, Plu.*Aem.*38; ἄρχοντα τὸν διὰ πέντε ἐτῶν τιμητικὸν (sc. ἀγῶνα) Ἀφροδίτης *IG*14.745 (Naples). **II.** *doing honour to*, τινων Plu.2.120a; πρὸς Ῥωμαίους τὸ -κὸν τηρῶν J.*AJ*19.8. 1: cf. τιμικόν. Adv. -κῶς, χρῆσθαί τινι Ph.1.613, cf. 273 (but, *in the manner befitting an assessor*, *OGI*565.20 (Oenoanda)). ⊛ **-ητός**, ή, όν, *valued*, opp. μετρητός, of land, J.*AJ*5.1.21: c. gen. pretii, *PLond.*2.316*b*3 (ii A.D.). **II.** *valuable*, τὸ τοῦ χρόνου τ. J.*AJ*16. 2.4; πάντα δὲ τιματὰ τὰ πὰρ φίλων Theoc.28.25. **III.** τούτῳ τιμητόν he enjoys *the privilege of having his penalty assessed in court*, D. 27.67. **-ιάζω**, *become dear, go up in price*, dub. rest. in *Rev.Ét.Gr.* 6.160*B*15 (Iasus, cf. *Wien.Sitzb.*179(6).52). **-ικόν**, τό, *honorarium*, *Gloss.* (also -ητικόν, ib.).

**τῑμιο-πωλέω**, *sell dear*, Hsch. s.v. τιμηρύειν. **-πώλης**, ου, ὁ, *one who sells dear*, Phryn.Com.52.

⊛ **τίμι-ος** [τῐ], α, ον, Pl.*Prt.*347c, al.; also ος, ον S.*Ant.*948 (lyr.), Arist. *Pol.*1283ᵃ36, Opp.*H.*2.651: (τιμή):—*valued*, **I.** *held in honour, worthy*, ὅδε πᾶσι φίλος καὶ τ. ἐστι Od.10.38, cf. Sapph.10,105, Alc. 49, Hdt.9.71, etc.; ἄνδρα τ. A.*Ch.*556; γενεᾷ τίμιος [Δανάη] S. l. c.; τίμιοι ἐν τῇ πόλει Pl.*Lg.*829d; νηὸν..πᾶσιν μάλα τ. ἀνθρώποισι *h.Ap.* 483, cf. Hes.*Fr.*134.7, etc.: freq. in Comp. and Sup., τιμιώταται θεῶν A.*Eu.*967 (lyr.); πασῶν Ἀθῆναι -ωτάτη πόλις S.*OC*108; -ώτερον ἐπιστήμη ὀρθῆς δόξης ἐστί Pl.*Men.*98a; as form of address, -ώτατε Dsc.*Eup.*1 *Prooem.*; τῷ -ωτάτῳ χαίρειν Luc.*Ep.Sat.*2.25, A.D.*Synt.*41.2, *Sammelb.*7347.29 (ii A.D.), etc. **II.** of things, *valuable, prized*, οὐδὲν κτῆμα -ώτερον S.*Ant.*702, cf. E.*Alc.*301, *Ph.* 439 (Sup.), *Apoc.*17.4. **2.** *of high price, costly, dear*, Hdt.3.23 (Sup.), 8.105 (Comp.), Lys.22.8, Pl.*Euthd.*304b, *Prt.*347c, Thphr. *Lap.*18 (Sup.); πωλεῖται τίμιος is sold *dearly*, ib.31; τίμιον ἀγοράζειν *PCair.Zen.*160.10 (iii B.C.); χρυσίον ὅταν πολὺ παραφανῇ, τὸ ἀργύριον -ώτερον ποιεῖ X.*Vect.*4.10: Comp. -έστερος dub. in *PCair.Zen.* 375.13 (iii B.C.). Adv. -ίως, πρίασθαι Lyd.*Mag.*3.35. **3.** *conferring honour, honourable*, τιμία ἕδρα a seat *of honour*, A.*Eu.*854, cf. *Th.*241 (lyr.); τ. γέρας an *honourable* privilege, Id.*Supp.*986; οὐπιρρέων γὰρ -ώτερος χρόνος ἔσται πολίταις *more full of honour*, Id.*Eu.* 853; -ωτέρα χώρα a *higher* place, X.*Cyr.*8.4.10; δῶρα Id.*An.*1.2.27: τὰ τίμια, = τιμαί, Pi.*Fr.*221 (cj.), *SIG*659.8 (Delph., ii B.C.), al., Plb.6. 9.8, *Supp.Epigr.*3.468.10, al. (Thess., i B.C.); τὰ τ. τῶν ἱερῶν *OGI* 90.33 (Rosetta, ii B.C.); also in sg., *SIG*591.6 (Lampsacus, ii B.C.); τὰ -ώτατα, = τὰ φίλτατα, D.18.215; αἱ καλούμεναι τίμιαι τέσσαρες γαῖαι Zos.Alch.p.239B. **-ότης**, ητος, ἡ, *dignity*, διαφέρειν τιμιότητι καὶ ἀτιμίᾳ ἀλλήλων Arist.*GA*736ᵇ31; δυνάμει καὶ τ. ὑπερέχειν Id.*EN*1178ᵃ1. **2.** *costliness*, *Apoc.*18.19. **II.** as form of address, ἡ σὴ τ. *PAmh.*2.145 (iv/v A.D.). ⊛ **-ουλκέω**, *raise in price*, σῖτον Al.*Pr.*11.26, cf. Hsch., Suid. **-όω**, *hold in honour*, τιμιωθήσεται v.l. for τιμηθήσεται in Aq.*Ps.*71(72).14. **-ώρα**, ἡ, *season of high prices*, *IGRom.*4.1269 (Thyatira), prob. for τειμωρίαν in *Supp. Epigr.*4.397 (Stratonicea); written **τιμιόρα** in *UPZ*52.17 (ii B.C.): pl. perh. to be read for τιμωρίαι in *Gp.*1.8.11, *Cat.Cod.Astr.*4.155.

⊛ **τῑμο-γρᾰφέω**, *tax by assessment*, τὴν γῆν Lxx 4*Ki.*23.35. **-γρᾰφία**, ἡ, *assessment* of payment due, *Supp.Epigr.*2.568.5 (Didyma, ii B.C.). **-εις**, εσσα, εν, v. τιμοῦς. **-καρίδες**, *cammariunculi*, *Gloss.* (s.v.l.). **-κράτης** [ᾰ], ου, ὁ, *a 'timocrat'* (cf. sq.), Asp.*in EN* 182.8. **-κρᾰτία**, ἡ, *state in which the love of honour is the ruling principle*, expld. by Pl. as ἡ φιλότιμος πολιτεία, *R.*545b; cf. τιμαρχία. **II.** *state in which honours are distributed according to a rating of property, timocracy*, Arist.*EN*1160ᵃ36, ᵇ17. **-κρᾰτικός**, ή, όν, *of* or *for a* τιμοκρατία I, *timocratical*, νεανίας Pl.*R.*549b, cf. 580b. **II.** ἡ τ. πολιτεία, = τιμοκρατία II, Arist.*EN*1160ᵃ34.

**Τῑμολεόντειον**, τό, *a gymnasium named after Timoleon*, Plu.*Tim.* 39.

**τῖμος**, ὁ, poet. form of τιμή II, Archil.78, A.*Ch.*916, *Com.Adesp.* 1164, Herod.7.78: also in late Prose, Ant.Lib.17.5.

**τῑμοῦς**, οῦσσα, οῦν, *high-priced*, Comp. τιμούστερος *IPE*1².32*A* 61 (Olbia, iii B.C.): acc. pl. τιμοῦντας glossed τιμίους ὄντας in Hsch., as if a participle.

⊛ **τῑμοῦχ-έω**, *to be a* τιμοῦχος II, *SIG*38.29 (Teos, v B.C.), written τιμοχ-). **-ία**, ἡ, *office of* τιμοῦχος II, in pl., τιμουχιῶν μετέχειν *SIG*286.8 (Milet., iv B.C.); ὀμόσαι τὰς τ. ἦ μὴν ἐμμενεῖν κτλ. *the authorities* (colleges of magistrates) shall swear.., ib.1007.31 (Pergam., prob. ii B.C.), cf. 1017.13 (Sinope, iii B.C.). **-ιον**, τό, *office of* τιμοῦχος, *Inscr.Prien.*12.4 (iii B.C.). ⊛ **-ος** (proper sp.), ον, (ἔχω) *having honour*, *h.Ven.*31, *h.Cer.*268 (in form **τιμάοχος**). **II.** the name of a magistrate in certain Greek cities, as Massilia, Str.4.1.5; Naucratis, Herm.Hist.2; Teos, *SIG*578.60 (ii B.C.); Lebedos, prob. in *BCH*52.165; Messene, Ael.*Fr.*39; applied to a woman, *IG*12(8). 526 (Thasos): prob. title of officials of the Ἑλλήνιον at Memphis, Wilcken *Chr.*30 i 16 (iii/ii B.C.):—Aeol. **τίμωχος** *Schwyzer* 631 *A* 2 (Methymna (found at Miletus), ii B.C.).

**τῑμόω**, = τιμάω, in Pass., *Schwyzer* 417.5 (Elis); but the Rhodian forms τιμοῦντες *IG*12(1).155 i 10 (ii B.C.), τιμοῦσα ib.1033.12 (iii B.C.) may be the contractions of τιμάοντες, etc., cf. Ἀγλούκριτος (from Ἀγλαό-) *GDI*4245.77, if not forms of τιμέω (q.v.).

**Τιμῶλος, Τιμωλίτης**, v. Τμῶλος.

**Τῑμώνιον**, τό, *a Timon's*, i.e. *a misanthrope's, dwelling*, Str.17.1.9.

⊛ **τῑμωρ-έω**, fut. -ήσω Hdt.4.119, Antipho 5.87, etc.:—Med., fut. -ήσομαι E.*Alc.*733, Th.3.58: aor. ἐτιμωρησάμην Pl.*R.*378a:—**Pass.**, pf. τετιμώρημαι Th.7.77, Lys.25.15: used in med. sense, Antipho 3.2.8, Lys.7.20, X.*Cyr.*7.5.32, and prob. Th.3.67: aor. ἐτιμωρήθην *PMich.Zen.*57.9 (iii B.C.):—*to be an avenger, exact* or *seek to exact vengeance for, avenge*, τινι Democr.261, Hdt.1.103, 8.144, E.*Hec.*749,

Pl.*Smp.*180a, etc.: abs., Hdt.1.4: c. dat. et gen., τιμωρήσειν σοι τοῦ παιδός..ὑπισχνοῦμαι dub. l. in X.*Cyr.*4.6.8: c. acc. rei, τ. τῷ ἑταίρῳ τὸν φόνον *avenge* his slaughter, Pl.*Ap.*28c, cf. E.*Ph.*935: also τ. ὑπέρ τινος (for τινι) *take vengeance for* him, Pl.*Lg.*907e, cf. Lys.13.1; ὑπὲρ τοῦ δήμου ib.51: c. dat. rei, τῷ θανάτῳ τοῦ πατρός D.H.4.77: abs., Pl.*Lg.*729e:—Med., *avenge* or *seek to avenge one's own* relative or friend, πατρὶ πάντα τιμωρουμένης S.*El.*349, cf. 399, E.*Or.*1117:—impers. in Pass., Λεωνίδῃ τετιμώρηται *vengeance has been taken* for him, he *has been avenged*, Hdt.9.79 (but τετιμωρήσεαι ἐς..Λεωνίδην must be taken in signf. I. 3b, *thou wilt have taken vengeance* in respect to L., ib.78). 2. τιμωρεῖν τινα *take vengeance on* him, S.*OT*140; τοὺς αὐτοέντας ib.107; κελεύειν τιμωρεῖν ὑπὲρ αὐτοῦ [τὸν Ἀγόρατον] ὡς φονέα ὄντα Lys.13.42, cf. 92; Παλαμήδους σε τιμωρεῖ φόνου (v.l. φόνον) *is taking vengeance on* you *for* the murder of P., E.*Or.*433:—Pass., *to be visited with vengeance, punished*, Pl.*Grg.*525b,d, etc.; τετιμωρημένος Lys.25.15; ὧν ἡμάρτομεν τετιμωρήμεθα we *have been punished*, *PCair.Zen.*495.2 (iii B.C.); ἱκανῶς τετιμώρημαι ib.639.15 (iii B.C.); εἰς τὸ -ηθῆναι αὐτοὺς *PMich.Zen.* l. c.:—this sense is more freq. in 3. Med., *avenge oneself upon, exact vengeance from*, τινα Hdt.3.53, 6.138, S.*Ph.*1258, E.*Hec.*756,882, Antipho 2.3.11, Th.1.121, etc.; ὡς..οὐχ ὅπως τιμωρήσαιντο, ἀλλὰ καὶ ἐπαινέσειαν τὸν Σφοδρίαν X.*HG* 5.4.34; Ἑαυτὸν τιμωρούμενος *Self-punisher*, name of a play by Menander, cf. X.*Cyr.*3.1.15; ἀπαγαγών με εἰς τὸ δεσμωτήριον τετιμώρηταί με εἰσπράσσων δραχμὰς ρ' *PCair.Zen.*492.7 (iii B.C.): c. gen. rei, τιμωρεῖσθαί τινά τινος *take vengeance on* one *for* a thing, Hdt.3.145, E.*IT*558, Lys.6.31, Pl.*Smp.*213d, etc.: also τ. τινὰ ἀντί τινων Hdt.6.135; περὶ (fort. ὑπὲρ) τῶν πεπραγμένων Lys.14.2: less freq. c. acc. rei, εἰ μή σ' ἀδελφῆς αἷμα τιμωρήσεται *will visit* his sister's blood *on* thee, E.*Alc.*733, cf. *Cyc.*695. b. abs., *avenge oneself, seek vengeance*, Hdt.3.49, 7.8.β', Lys.13.84, X.*Cyr.*5.5.19, etc.; ταῖς ἐσχάταις τιμωρίαις τ. *visit* with the extreme penalties, Pl.*R.*579a; τὸ τιμωρησόμενον *the power to exact vengeance*, D.26.4: the crime is sts. added in a relat. clause, τ. εἴ τι..ἠδίκησαν X.*An.*5.4.6; τ. ὅτι..Id.*Cyr.*5.3.30: also τιμωρεῖσθαι ὑπὲρ τῆς Ἑλλάδος *exact vengeance* for Greece, Id.*An.*1.3.4. II. esp. in pres. and impf., *succour* one who has been attacked or has suffered injury, *help* him *to retaliate*, τινι Hdt.1.141,152, 2.63, 3.32,65, S.*OT*136, E.*Or.*718, Th.1.86,127, al.; εἰ τύπτοιτό τις αὐτῶν ὑπ' ἐκείνων τινός, ἐβοήθεόν τε πάντες καὶ ἐτιμώρεον ἀλλήλοισι Hdt.6.138, cf. Ael.*NA* 1.4: abs., *lend aid, give succour*, Hdt.1.18. 2. of medical aid, τ. τῷ παθήματι *relieve* it, Hp.*Art.*11; cf. τιμωρία II. 2, and Gal.15.494. **-ημα**, ατος, τό, *act of vengeance*, τ. Κορινθίων εἰς Σαμίους Plu.2.860a. 2. *penalty*, διπλᾶ..ἔστω τὰ τ. τῷ ὀφλόντι Pl.*Lg.*866b, cf. *R.*363e. II. *aid, succour*, τὰ Μενέλεω τιμωρήματα *succour given* to him, Hdt.7.169 (Μενέλεῳ Wesseling). **-ησείω**, *wish to avenge*, -ησείοντες Agath.3.17. **-ησις**, εως, ἡ, *punishment*, Pl.*Lg.*874e (pl.). **-ητέον**, *one must visit with vengeance, punish*, τινας Isoc.15.174; τι Pl.*Lg.*867c. II. τιμωρητέος, α, ον, *that ought to be punished*, ὑπὲρ ἁπάντων τ. ὡς κοινὸς ἐχθρός D.21.142. III. -ητέον *one must assist*, Hdt.7.168: pl. τιμωρητέα, Th.1.86. 2. *one must defend*, τῷ ἐναντίῳ λόγῳ Hp.*Acut.*37.β'. **-ητήρ**, ῆρος, ὁ, *avenger*, Hdt.5.80. **-ητής**, οῦ, ὁ, = foreg., Lxx 2*Ma.*4.16. 2. *murderer*, ὁ εἰρημένος τ. Σενούθης ἀνείλετο αὐτόν *PMasp.*5.16 (vi A.D.). **-ητικός**, ή, όν, *revengeful*, opp. συγγνωμονικός, Arist.*EN*1126ᵃ2; τὰ τ. *acts of revenge*, Id.*Rh.*1369ᵇ12; τὸ τ. τῶν ἐχθρῶν Phld.*Ir.*p.67 W. Adv. -κῶς Chrysipp.*Stoic.*3.129. **-ία**, Ion. -ίη, ἡ, *retribution, vengeance* (differing from κόλασις, corrective punishment, Arist.*Rh.*1369ᵇ12), ἐς τ...παρασκευαζομένοισι Hdt.5.90; τ. καὶ τίσις Id.7.8.α', cf. *Ep.Hebr.*10.29, etc.; πατρὸς τ. *vengeance taken for* him, E.*Or.*425; μητρὸς αἵματος τιμωρίαι *for having shed* a mother's blood, ib.400; ἐπὶ τῇ ἡμετέρᾳ τ. for the purpose of *punishing* us, Th.3.63; Λεωνίδην ἐάν τις ἀποκτείνῃ..τὴν τ. εἶναι καθάπερ ἐάν τις Ἀθηναίων ἀποθάνῃ *IG*1².56.16, cf. 154.12; οὐκ ἔχει τιμωρίαν γὰρ τἀδίκημ', ἔγκλημα δέ Men.*Pk.*253; ἡ κατὰ τῶν προδιδόντων τ. *vengeance* against or upon.., Lycurg.140, cf. D.18.274, Din.1.105; τ. ἐσομένη ἔς τινα Hdt.1.123, cf. D.22.55; τ. ὑπὲρ τοῦ ἀδικηθέντος Antipho 6.6, cf. Isoc.20.19: with Verbs, of the avenger, ποιεῖσθαι τιμωρίαν *execute vengeance*, D.21.26, etc.; τινος on one, And.4.18; τ. ὑπὲρ ὧν ἐπεπόνθειν λαβεῖν D.24.8; but παρά τινος λαμβάνειν τ. exact *it* from him, Philem.88.14; of the wrongdoer, τ. Ἀθηνῶν ηὗρε found, i.e. suffered, *vengeance* at Athens' hand, A.*Pers.*473; τιμωρίας τυγχάνειν *to be punished*, Pl.*Grg.*472d, *PEnteux.*50.7 (iii B.C.), etc. (but also, obtain *vengeance*, Th.2.74, X.*Cyr.*4.6.7); τ. ἀντιδοῦναι Th.2.53; τίνειν Pl.*Lg.*905a, etc.; ὑπέχειν Th.6.80, Pl.*Lg.*716b, etc.; of persons in authority, αἱ τ. εἰσὶ παρὰ τῶν θεῶν Hdt.2.120; τ. δοῦναί τινι give him *right of vengeance*, D.23.7, cf. ib.54, 59.86; so τὰς τ. τοῖς ἰδιώταις ἐποίησε βραδείας Id.26.4: pl., *penalties*, λαμβάνειν τὰς ἀξίας τ. Antiph.247; ταῖς ἐσχάταις τιμωρεῖσθαι τ. Pl.*R.*579a, cf. *Lg.*943d, al.; of state-punishments, Lxx 2*Ma.*6.26, al.; οἱ ἐπὶ τῶν τ. Plu.*Art.*14,17; of divine punishments, ἐξορκίζω σε..κατὰ (τῶν ἐπὶ) τῶν τ. τεταγμένων *PMag.Lond.*121.303. II. *succour*, εὑρήσεται τ. Hdt.3.148; ἡ ἀφ' ὑμῶν τ. Th.1.69, cf. 5.112; τ. ποιεῖσθαί τινι Id.1.124; τ. τοῦ τεθνεῶτος *due* to him, Antipho 1.5. 2. of *medical aid*, Hp.*Acut.*18 (pl.); cf. τιμωρέω II. 2. **-ίζω**, = τιμωρέω, *Tab.Defix.Aud.*155*A* 55, al. (iv/v A.D., Pass.). **-ός**, όν, contr. from **τιμάορος** (v. sub fin.), which remains as a Dor. form in Pi.*O.*9.84 (trisyll.), A.*Ag.*514, al., E.*Fr.*318.4, *IG*14.1389 ii 29 (Rome), etc.; in late Ep. **τιμήορος**, A.R.4.709,1358,1730: A.*Supp.*42 (lyr.) has an acc. τιμάορα, as if from **τιμάωρ**, ορος, ὁ:—*avenging*, and as Subst. *avenger*, τ. τινός any one's *avenger*, A.*Ag.*1280,1324, 1578, S.*El.*811,1156, etc.: c. dat., τ. τινὶ γενέσθαι Antipho 1.2: c. gen. rei, *helping* one *to vengeance for* a thing, πατρὶ τ. φόνου S.*El.*14: abs., ἐπεὶ τιμάορος ἔστωρ the founder is the *avenger*, *IG* l.c. (cf. *Berl.Sitzb.*1928.19): not always of persons, δίκη κακῶν τ. S.*Fr.*107.9; ἡ τῶν συγγενῶν αἱμάτων τ. δίκη Pl.*Lg.*872e, cf. 716a; χείρ E.*Hec.*843; λόγος τ. a plea or argument *for vengeance*, Hdt.7.5. 2. *executioner*, Plb.2.58.8. 3. τιμωρόν, τό, = κώνειον, Ps.-Dsc.4.78. II. *succouring*, and as Subst. *succourer* of one who has been attacked or wronged, Hdt.2.141, 7.171, Th.4.2; τὸν ἐμὸν τιμάορον Ἑρμῆν my *tutelary* god, A.*Ag.*514; ἡρῷσσαι, Λιβύης τιμήοροι ἠδὲ θύγατρες A.R.4.1358; Ἀπόλλωνα..Ἀνάφης τιμήορον ib.1730. 2. metaph., ἦλθον τιμάορος Ἰσθμίαισι Λαμπρομάχου μίτραις I have come *to pay honour to*.., Pi. l.c. (τιμα-ορος perh. 'penalty-exactor', fr. τιμή III and ἄρνυμαι:—for the accentuations τιμάορος: τιμωρός, cf. λυρᾴοιδος: λυρῳδός, on which see Hdn.Gr.1.229.)

**τίν**, Dor. dat. and acc. of σύ (q.v.).

**τίνα** (= Lat. *tina* 'wine-vessel'?), in acc. sg. τίναν, v.l. for τιτάδα in Alex.Trall.*Febr.*2; but τιτίδα (acc. of τιτίς, q.v.) may be conjectured.

® **τίναγ-μα** [ῐ], ατος, τό, *a shake, quake*, Lxx *Jb.*28.26, *AP*9.139 (Claudian.). **-μός**, ὁ, *shaking*, Plu.2.258c, Sor.2.29. II. *shaking* fruit from trees, *PFay.*102.29 (ii A.D.), *PFlor.*246.12 (iii A.D.); σησάμου *PCair.Zen.*787.59 (iii B.C.); = *excussio*, *Gloss.*

**τῐνάκ-τειρα**, ἡ (τινακτήρ not being in use), *shaker*, γῆς τινάκτειρα νόσος, of Poseidon's trident, A.*Pr.*924. **-τοπήληξ**, ηκος, ὁ, ἡ, *shaking the helmet* or *crest*, Hsch. **-τωρ**, ορος, ὁ, *shaker*, τ. γαίας, of Poseidon, S.*Tr.*502 (lyr.), cf. Nonn.*D.*21.155: Adj., τ. παλμός ib.100.

® **τῐνάσσω**, Il.12.298, etc.: fut. -ξω (ἀπο-) E.*Ba.*253: aor. ἐτίναξα Il.20.57, Sapph.42, poet. τίναξα Pi.*O.*9.30:—Med. (v. infr.):—Pass., fut. τινάξεται (δια-) E.*Ba.*587 (lyr.): aor. ἐτινάχθην Plu.*Cim.*16; Ep. 3 pl. ἐτίναχθεν Il.16.348: 2 aor. part. τινᾰγείς Str.5.4.9 (s.v.l.): pf. 3sg. indic. τετίνακται Hp.*Flat.*14 (v.l. τετάρακται); inf. τετινάχθαι (δια-) Aesop.305:—*shake* or *brandish* a weapon, δύο δοῦρε τινάσσων Il.12.298; ἔγχος 20.163, Tyrt.11.25; φάσγανον Il.22.311; ἀστεροπήν 13.243; αἰγίδα 17.595; ἐν χεροῖν πύρπνουν βέλος A.*Pr.*917; τόξα καὶ λόγχας ῥόπαλόν τε S.*Tr.*512 (lyr.); λαμπάδας ἐν χερσί Ar.*Ra.*340 (lyr.), cf. 328 (lyr.):—Med., ἐτινάξατο δούρατος ἀκμάς Theoc.22.185. 2. generally, *shake*, γαῖαν, of Poseidon, Il.20.57; ἑανοῦ ἐτίναξε λαβοῦσα *shook* her by the robe (to make her attend), 3.385; ποσὶ θρόνον λακτίζων ἐτίνασσε *upset* it, Od.22.88; ὡς δ' ἄνεμος..θημῶνα τ. *scatters*, 5.368; νεῦρα (sc. κιθάρας) τ. *make* the strings *quiver*, by striking them, *AP*9.584.9; τὴν ἐσθῆτα συνεχῶς τ. (to air it) Gal.17(1).652: metaph., Ἔρος ἐτίναξέ μοι φρένας Sapph. l.c.: abs., *shake* fruit from trees, *PFay.*102.1 (ii A.D.):—Pass., ῥάβδῳ τινάσσεται τὸ μελάνθιον Lxx *Is.*28.27:—Med., τιναξάσθην πτερά *they shook their* wings, Od.2.151 (so τινάσσονται πτερύγεσσιν Arat.971; τιναξαμένου τοῖς ὅπλοις Plu.*Alex.*63, cf. *Dio* 39):—Pass., πήληξ τινάσσετο Il.15.609; πεδόθεν τινάσσετο μακρὸς Ὄλυμπος *shook* or *quaked*, Hes.*Th.*680; φόβῳ ἐτίναχθεν αὐτῆς *quaked* with fear, A.R.4.641.—poet. Verb, used by Hp. l.c. (s.v.l.), Arist.*Mu.*397ᵃ28, Plu. (v. supr.), Sor.1.46, Philostr.*VA*4.6.

**τίνη**, Tarent. Dor. for τίν, A.D.*Pron.*82.13.

® **τινθᾰλέος**, α, ον, = sq., ποτόν, λοετρά, Nic.*Al.*445,463, cf. Epic. in *Arch.Pap.*7.7, Nonn.*D.*2.501. (Cf. διατινθαλέος.)

**τινθός**, όν, *boiling-hot*, Hsch. (τιντόν cod.). II. as Subst., the *steam* of a cauldron, Lyc.36.

**τινθῠρίζω**, *twitter*, of birds, Call.*Iamb.*1.258.

**τίνῡμαι**, inf. τίνυσθαι Hes.*Op.*711:—poet. for τίνομαι (v. τίνω II), *punish, chastise*, c. acc. pers., [Ζεὺς] τίνυται ὅς τις ἁμάρτῃ Od.13.214; οἳ..ἀνθρώπους τίνυσθον, ὅτις κ' ἐπίορκον ὀμόσσῃ Il.3.279, cf. 19.260, Plu.*Crass.*21: c. acc. rei, λώβην τινύμενος *chastising* insolence, Od.24.326. 2. *avenge, take vengeance for*, Ὅρκον Hes.*Op.*804 (v.l.); αἵματος δίκαν, φόνον, E.*Or.*323 (lyr.): abs., *avenge oneself*, Hdt.5.77. 3. *repay*, of the punisher, δὶς τόσα Hes.*Op.*711; of the punished, ἔνδικα *AP*11.374 (Maced.). 4. *repay*, in good sense, τ. κομιδὴν παιδοτροφίης Opp.*C.*2.349. II. Act., *pay* penalty, only in late writers, δίκας τιννύοντες Plu.*Brut.*33; δίκην τιννύς Olymp.Hist.p.455 D.; gen. pl. ἐκ-τιννύντων v.l. in D.S.16.29; ἐκ-τιννύω, = *pendo*, *Gloss.*; δίκας τιννύω, = *pendo poenas*, ib. [The 1st syll. is prob. always long (even in E.*Or.*323); the spellings ἀποτεινύτω (Crete, v B.C.), ἀποτειννυέτω (Avrom., i B.C.) (v. ἀποτίνυμι), and the form of the root (τῑ-: τει-: ποι- (v. τίνω), never τῐ-, which belongs only to τίω) show that the true spellings are τεινυ-, later τειννυ-, still later τιννυ- with ι long by nature: the early forms ἀποτινύ[μεν (v. ἀποτίνυμι), [τ]ινυμε[νο] *GDI*5125*A* 3 (Crete) remain unexplained: τίν[υ]σθαι is uncertain in *IG*12(9).1273 (p. viii) (Eretria, vi B.C.): perh. τῑνυ- existed as well as τεινυ-.]

® **τίνω**, Il.3.289, al., (ἀπο-) *IG*5(1).1390.76 (Andania, i B.C.), etc.: Ion. impf. τίνεσκον A.R.2.475: fut. τείσω (ἐκ-) *IG*2².412.6 (iv B.C.), (ἀπο-) *Epigr.Gr.*1132 (Att. vase, iv B.C.), *PPetr.*3 p.55 (iii B.C.), *IG*7.3073.1 (Lebad., ii B.C.), etc., etc.; Cypr. 3 sg. πείσει *Inscr. Cypr.*135.12 H.: aor. ἔτεισα (ἀπ-) *SIG*47.15 (Locr., v B.C.), 663.25 (Delos, iii/ii B.C.), *PPetr.*3 p.41 (iii B.C.), etc.: freq. written τίσω ἔτισα in Hellenistic and later Inscrr. and Pap., and in codd. of all authors (fut., Od.8.348, A.*Ch.*277, S.*Aj.*113, etc.; aor., Od.24.352, Pi.*O.*2.58, S.*OT*810, etc.): in Hom. confused (both in codd. and printed texts) with τίσω ἔτισα fut. and aor. of τίω, and only to be distd. by the sense: pf. τέτεικα (ἀπο-) *SIG*437.6 (Delph., iii B.C.); part. τετεικώς Lyc.765 (τετικώς, τεθεικώς codd.) (v. ἐκτίνω):—Med., pres. first in Thgn.204 (only τίνυμαι in Hom.): fut. τείσομαι Od.13.15, al.: aor. ἐτεισάμην 3.197, 15.236, al. (τισ- codd.):—Pass., aor. ἐξ-ετείσθην *IG*2².1613.198, D.39.15, 59.7: pf. 3 sg. ἐκ-τέτειсται Pl.*Phdr.*257a, D.24.187. [τῖνω (from *τίνϝω) in Ep., also Thgn.204, Herod.2.51, *AP*7.657 (Leon.); τῑνω in Trag., as A.*Pr.*112, S.*OC*635, E.*Or.*7; also in Pi.*P.*2.24 (Med.) and Sol. 13.31; also in some Epigrammatists, as Simm.25.1, *AP*9.286 (Marc. Arg.).] **I.** Act., *pay a price* by way of return or recompense, mostly in bad sense, *pay* a penalty, with acc. of the penalty, τ. θωήν Od.2.193; τιμήν τινι Il.3.289; ποινάς Pi.*O.*2.58, A.*Pr.*112, Theodect. 8.9; δίκην S.*Aj.*113, *El.*298, *Fr.*107.9, 2*Ep.Thess.*1.9, etc.; also τ. ἴσην (sc. δίκην) S.*OT*810; διπλῆν Pl.*Lg.*946e; τὸ ἥμισυ ib.767e (s.v.l.); μείζονα τὴν ἔκτ(ε)ισίν τινι ib.933e; τὴν προσήκουσαν τιμωρίαν ib.905a, cf. *Trag.Adesp.*490:—but also **b.** in good sense, *pay* a debt, *acquit oneself of* an obligation, ζωάγρια τ. Il.18.407; τείσειν αἴσιμα πάντα Od.8.348; εὐαγγέλιον (reward for bringing good news) 14.166; τ. χάριν τινί *render* one thanks, A.*Pr.*985; τ. γῇ δασμόν S.*OC*635; ἰατροῖς μισθόν X.*Mem.*1.2.54:—also simply, **c.** *repay*, c. acc. rei, τροφάς τινι E.*Or.*109:—in various phrases, τ. ἀντιποίνους δύας *repay* equivalent sorrows, A.*Eu.*268 (lyr.); φόνον φόνου ῥύσιον τ. S.*Ph.*959; αἱμάτων παλαιτέρων τ. μύσος *send* one pollution *in repayment* for another, A.*Ch.*650 (lyr., Lachm., for τελεῖ); ἀρᾶς τ. χρέος Id.*Ag.*457 (lyr.).—Constr.: **1.** c. acc. of the thing paid or of the thing repaid (v. supr.). **2.** less freq. c. dat., κράατι τείσεις *with* thy head, Od.22.218; ψυχῇ A.*Ch.*277. **3.** c. dat. of pers. to whom payment is made (v. supr.). **4.** c. dat. of the penalty, τ. θανάτῳ ἅπερ ἦρξεν Id.*Ag.*1529 (anap.); τύμμα τύμματι ib.1430 (lyr.). **5.** with gen. of the thing for which one pays, τ. ἀμοιβὴν βοῶν τινι *pay* him compensation *for* the cows, Od.12.382; τ. τινὶ ποινήν τινος *pay* one retribution *for*.., Hdt.3.14, 7.134; τ. μητρὸς δίκας *for* thy mother, E.*Or.*531; ἀντὶ πληγῆς πληγὴν τ. A.*Ch.*313 (anap.): also with acc. of the thing for which one pays, the price being omitted, *pay* or *atone for* a thing, τείσειαν Δαναοὶ ἐμὰ δάκρυα σοῖσι βέλεσσι Il.1.42; τ. ὕβριν Od.24.352; τ. φόνον or λώβην τινός, Il.21.134, 11.142; κακά Thgn.735; διπλᾶ δ' ἔτεισαν Πριαμίδαι θἀμάρτια A.*Ag.*537: less freq. c. acc. pers., τείσεις γνωτὸν τὸν ἔπεφνες *thou shalt make atonement for* the brother thou hast slain, Il.17.34. **6.** abs., *make return* or *requital*, Sol.13.29; παθόντα οὐκ ἐπίστασθαι τίνειν S.*OC* 1203, cf. 230 (lyr.). **II.** Med., *have a price paid one, make* another *pay for* a thing, *avenge oneself on* him, *punish* him, freq. from Hom. downwards.—Constr.: **1.** c. acc. pers., Il.2.743, Od.3.197, Hdt.1.10, 123, S.*OC*996, etc. **2.** c. gen. criminis, τείσασθαι Ἀλέξανδρον κακότητος *punish* him *for* his wickedness, Il.3.366, cf. Od.3.206, Thgn. 204 (where ἀμπλακίης, v.l. -ίας), Hdt.4.118, etc.; τ. τινὰ ἐφ' ἁμαρτωλῇ Thgn.1248; ὑπέρ τινος Hdt.1.27, 73. **3.** c. acc. rei, *take vengeance for* a thing, τείσασθαι φόνον, βίην τινός, Il.15.116, Od.23.31; λώβην Il.19.208, etc. **4.** c. dupl. acc. pers. et rei, ἐτείσατο ἔργον ἀεικὲς ἀντίθεον Νηλῆα *he made* Neleus *pay for* the misdeed, *visited* it *on* his head, Od.15.236; Ζεῦ ἄνα, δὸς τείσασθαι, ὅ με πρότερος κάκ' ἔοργε, δῖον Ἀλέξανδρον Il.3.351; τείσασθαί τινα δίκην *exact* retribution *from* a person, E.*Med.*1316 (dub. l.). **5.** c. dat. modi, τίνεσθαί τινα ἀγαναῖς ἀμοιβαῖς, φυγῇ, *repay* or *requite* with.., Pi.*P.*2.24, A.*Th.*638. **6.** abs., *repay oneself, indemnify oneself*, ἡμεῖς δ' αὖτε ἀγειρόμενοι κατὰ δῆμον τεισόμεθ' Od.13.15. (Root $q^{u}ī$- [alternating with $q^{u}ei$- and $q^{u}oi$-] 'pay': τί-νϝ-ω, τί-σις, τεί-σω [Cypr. πείσει], ἔ-τει-σα [cf. ἀπτεισάτου s.v. ἀποτίνω], ποι-νή (q.v.): Skt. *cáy-ate* 'avenge, punish': *ápa-ci-tis* 'vengeance':—not related to τίω.)

**τίξον·** δεῖξον, Hsch.

**τιὸ τιό,** imitation of a bird's note, Ar.*Av.*237.

**τίοισι,** Aeol. dat. pl. of τίς (q.v.).

**τίος, τίως, τίω,** Dor. genitives of σύ (q.v.).

**τιός,** Boeot. for τεός, σός, A.D.*Pron.*106.11.

⊛ **τίπτε;** Ep. sync. form for τί ποτε; Il.6.254, al., A.*Ag.*975 (lyr.):—elided before an aspirate, τίφθ' Il.4.243, al.:—on τίπτε δέ σε χρεώ, v. χρεώ.

**τιρ,** Elean for τις, *SIG*9.7 (vi B.C.); also Lacon. acc. to Hsch. (s.v. τίτιρ, leg. τί τίρ or τιρ).

**τίριος·** θέρους, Κρῆτες, Hsch.

⊛ **τίρων,** ωνος, ὁ, = Lat. *tiro, recruit*, *PSI*9.1063.5, 25 (ii A.D.); written τείρων (q.v.) ib.12; found mostly in gen. pl.; the dat. pl. τιρόναις *BGU*21 ii 11, iii 4 (iv A.D.) points to nom. sg. **τιρόνης (τιρώνης).**

**τιρωνᾶτος,** ὁ, = Lat. *tironatus*, as item in list of charges, *PLond. ined.*2142 (iv A.D.).

⊛ **τις, τι,** Indef. Pron. *any one, any thing*, enclitic through all cases (for exceptions v. infr.):—but **τίς; τί;** Interrog. Pron. *who? what?*, oxyt. in the monosyll. cases, parox. in the others:—Dialectal forms: Cypr. **σις** (*sis se*) *Inscr.Cypr.*135.10 H.; Arc. **σις** (with Ͷ for σ) *IG*5(2).262.25 (Mantinea, v B.C.); Thess. **κις** ib.9(2).515.12 (Larissa), 1226.4, 1229.27 (Phalanna), pl. **κινες** ib.517.41 (Larissa), neut. **κι** in διεκί, ποκκί (qq.v.); neut. pl. Dor. **σά**, Boeot. **τά**, Aeol. dat. τίῳ, τίοισι (v. infr. B). (I.-E. $q^{u}i$-, cf. Lat. *quis, quid*, etc.; for σά, τά, v. ἅσσα, σά μάν; with τέο (v. infr. B) cf. OSlav. gen. *česo*.)

**A.** Indef. Pron. **τις, τι,** gen. Ion. **τεο** Od.16.305, Hdt.1.58; more freq. **τευ** Il.2.388, al., Hdt.4.30, al., Meliss.7, etc.; Trag. and Att. **του** A.*Pr.*21, Ar.*Ach.*329, Th.1.70, etc. (sts. fem., S.*Aj.*290, *OT*1107 (lyr.), E.*Hec.*370, etc.); του is rare after 300 B.C., never in Lxx or *NT*, but found in *IG*12(5).798.17 (Tenos, iii B.C.), *PCair. Zen.*250.6, 647.23 (iii B.C.), Plb.3.23.3, revived by the Atticists, D.H.8.29, Plu.*Fab.*20, etc.; τινος Pi.*P.*2.90, *IG*1².16.17, 65.41, A.*Eu.*5, *Ch.*102, S.*Ant.*698, al., Hdt.2.109, al. (*Rh.Mus.*72.483), etc.; dat. Ion. τεῳ Il.16.227, Od.11.502, Hdt.2.48, 5.86; Trag. and Att. τῳ (also in Hom., Il.1.299, 12.328, Od.13.308, 20.297, al., always in masc.) A.*Th.*1045, *IG*1².39.54, D.S.18.45; as fem., A.*Th.*472, S.*OT*80, etc.; τινι (Hom. in the form οὔ τινι Il.17.68, Od.14.96) Pi. *O.*9.26, al., B.17.12, Hdt.1.114 (elsewh. fem., 2.62, 3.69, 83, 4.113), A.*Th.*1041, S.*Aj.*443, 495, etc.; acc. τινα Il.1.62, 5.761, etc., neut. τι 2.122, etc.: dual τινε Od.4.26, Pl.*Sph.*237d, *Prm.*143c, 149e: pl. τινες (Hom. only in οὔ τινες Od.6.279, 17.587 and οἵτινες (v. ὅστις)); Dor. τινεν *SIG*527.127 (Drerus, iii B.C.); nom. and acc. neut. τινα (ὅτινα Il.22.450), never in Trag., Ar., Th., or Hdt., f.l. in Isoc.4.74, first in Pl.*Chrm.*163d, *Ep.*325a, D.47.63, Hyp.*Ath.*19, Alex.110, Sotad.Com.1.22, Arist.*EN*1094ᵃ5, *IG*4²(1).121.35 (Epid., iv B.C.), etc.; ἅσσα (q.v.) Od.19.218, never in Trag. or Hdt.; Att. ἄττα first in Th.1.113, 2.100, Ar.*Ra.*173, al., Pl.*R.*400a, etc., never in Lxx, Plb., D.S., Str., revived by the Atticists, D.H.*Comp.*3, etc.; gen. Ion. τεων Hdt.2.175, 5.57, τεῶν cj. for γε ὧν in 4.76; τινων not in Hdt., first in Ar.*Eq.*977 (lyr.); dat. τισι, τισιν, first in Hdt. 9.113, X.*Ath.*1.18; N.-W. Dor. τινοις *GDI*1409.5 (Delph., iii B.C.); Ion. τεοισι Hdt.8.113, 9.27 (for τεοις and τεον v. τεός); acc. τινας Il.15.735, Od.11.371 (also in οὔστινας, ὅτινας, v. ὅστις), etc.; neut. τινα (v. supr.):—*any one, any thing, some one, some thing*; and as Adj. *any, some*, and serving as the Indef. Art. *a, an*; θεός νύ τίς ἐστι κοτήεις Il.5.191; καί τις θεὸς ἡγεμόνευεν Od.9.142; οὐδέ τις αὐτὸν ἠείδη δμώων ib.205; ἤ τι ὀϊσάμενος, ἦ.. ib.339; μή τίς μοι ὑποδείσας ἀναδύῃ ib.377, cf. 405–410; εἴ τινά που μετ' ὄεσσι λάβοι ib. 418, cf. 421, al.; τις θεός construed as if τις θεῶν, 19.40, cf. 11.502, *IG*1².94.19, E.*Hel.*1039. **II.** special usages: **1.** *some one* (of many), i.e. *many a one*, ὧδε δέ τις εἴπεσκεν Il.7.201, etc.: sts. with meiosis, implying *all* or *men*, 13.638, Od.3.224; so in Prose, Hdt.5.49 fin., Th.2.37, etc. **2.** *any one concerned, every one*, εὖ μέν τις δόρυ θηξάσθω Il.2.382; ἀλλά τις αὐτὸς ἴτω let *every man* come himself, 17.254; ἵνα τις στυγέῃσι καὶ ἄλλος 8.515, cf. 16.209, 17.227, al.; so in Trag. and Att., even with the imper., τοῦτό τις.. ἴστω S.*Aj.*417 (lyr.), cf. E.*Ba.*346, Ar.*Av.*1187; ἀγορεύω τινὶ ἐμὲ μὴ βασανίζειν Id.*Ra.*628; τοὺς ξυμμάχους αὐτόν τινα κολάζειν that *every man* should himself chastise his own allies, Th.1.40, cf. 6.77; ὅ τι τις ἐδύνατο Id.7.75; ἄμεινόν τινος better than *any others*, D.21. 66, cf. 19.35:—this is more fully expressed by adding other pronominal words, τις ἕκαστος Od.9.65, Th.6.31, etc.; πᾶς τις A.*Ag.*1205, Hdt.6.80, Th.8.94, etc.; ἅπας τις Hdt.3.113, etc.; οὐδέν τι μᾶλλον Id.4.118. In these senses, τις is freq. combined with pl. words, οἱ κακοὶ.. οὐκ ἴσασι, πρίν τις ἐκβάλῃ, for πρὶν ἐκβάλωσι, S.*Aj.* 965; οἷς ἂν ἐπίω, ἧσσόν τις πρόσεισι, for ἧσσον προσίασι, Th.4.85; ἐτόλμα τις.., δρῶντες Id.2.53, cf. 7.75; esp. after εἴ or ἤν τις, X. *Mem.*1.2.62, al. **3.** in reference to a definite person, whom one wishes to avoid naming, οὐκ ἔφασαν λέναι, ἐὰν μή τις χρήματα διδῷ (i.e. Cyrus) Id.*An.*1.4.12, cf. Ar.*Ra.*552, Theoc.5.122; so also euphem. for something bad, ἤν τι ποιῶμεν Th.2.74; ἂν οὗτός τι πάθῃ D.4.11: hence for the 1st or 2nd pers. Pron., ἅ τιν' οὐ πείσεσθαι ὀΐω Il.1.289, cf. S.*Ant.*751; ποῖ τις τρέψεται; for ποῖ τρέψομαι; Ar.*Th.*603, cf. S.*Aj.*245 (lyr.), 1138, Th.4.59, X.*An.*3.4.40, 5.7.31, etc. **4.** indefinitely, where we say *they*, French *on*, sts. with an ironical force, φοβεῖταί τις A.*Ch.*59 (lyr.); μισεῖ τις ἐκεῖνον D.4.8; as voc., τὸν Πλοῦτον ἔξω τις κάλει call P. out, *somebody*, Ar.*Pl.*1196. **5.** τις, τι may be opposed, expressly or by implication, to οὐδείς, οὐδέν, and mean *somebody, something*, by meiosis for *some great one, some great thing*, ηὔχεις τις εἶναι you boasted that you were *somebody*, E.*El.*939; εἰσὶν ὅμως τινὲς οἱ εὐδοκιμοῦντες Arist.*Pol.*1293ᵇ13; τὸ δοκεῖν τιν' εἶναι Men.156; τὸ δοκεῖν τινὲς εἶναι D.21.213; ὡς σὲ μὲν ἐν τῇ πόλει δεῖ τινὰ φαίνεσθαι, τὴν πόλιν δ' ἐν τοῖς Ἕλλησι μηδενὸς ἀξίαν εἶναι Id.10.71; κἠγών τις φαίνομαι ἦμεν after all I too am *somebody*, Theoc.11.79, cf. *Act.Ap.*5.36; also in neut., οἴονταί τι εἶναι ὄντες οὐδενὸς ἄξιοι Pl.*Ap.*41e, cf. *Phd.*63c, *Phdr.*243a, *Euthd.*303c, etc.:—so τι λέγειν to be near the mark, opp. οὐδὲν λέγειν, Id.*Prt.*339c, *R.*329e, *Phdr.*260a, etc.; ἵνα καὶ εἰδῶμεν εἴ τι ὅδε λέγει Id.*Cra.*407e; οἴεσθέ τι ποιεῖν, οὐδὲν ποιοῦντες Id.*Smp.*173c. **b.** τις is sts. opp. to another word, ἀελλοπόδων μέν τιν' εὐφραίνοισιν ἵππων τιμαί.., τέρπεται δὲ καί τις.. Pi.*Fr.*221; τισὶ τῶν πολιτῶν ἀπορούσι συνεξέδωκε θυγατέρας.., τοὺς δ' ἐλύσατο ἐκ τῶν πολεμίων Lys.19.59; μέρος μέν τι σιδήρου, μέρος δέ τι ὀστράκινον Lxx *Da.*2.33 (more freq. with the Article, v. infr. 10 c); ἔστιν οὖν οὐ πᾶν τὸ ταχύ, ἀλλά τι (sic codd. BT) αὐτοῦ ἀγαστόν Pl.*Cra.*412c; ἀναγκαῖον ἤτοι πᾶσι τοῖς πολίταις ἀποδίδοσθαι πάσας ταύτας τὰς κρίσεις ἢ τισὶ πάσας.. ἢ τινὰς μὲν αὐτῶν πᾶσι τινὰς δὲ τισίν Arist.*Pol.*1298ᵃ9, cf. 1277ᵃ23; τὸ μεῖζον τοῦθ' ὅπερ ἐστὶν ἑτέρου λέγεται· τινὸς γὰρ λέγεται μεῖζον greater than *something*, Id.*Cat.*6ᵃ38; τὸ πρώτως ὂν καὶ οὐ τὶ ὂν ἀλλ' ὂν ἁπλῶς Id.*Metaph.*1028ᵃ 30; πότερον τῷ τυχόντι ἤ τισίν; Id.*Pol.*1269ᵃ26. **6.** with pr. names τις commonly signifies *one named* so-and-so, ἦν δέ τις ἐν Τρώεσσι Δάρης Il.5.9, cf. X.*An.*3.1.4, etc.; with a sense of contempt, Θερσίτης τις ἦν there was *one* Thersites, S.*Ph.*442. **b.** *one of the same sort*, converting the pr. name into an appellative, ἤ τις Ἀπόλλων ἢ Πάν *an* Apollo or *a* Pan, A.*Ag.*55 (anap.); [πόλιες] ταὶ μέλονται πρός τινος ἢ Διὸς ἢ γλαυκᾶς Ἀθάνας Lyr. in *PVat.*11ᵛ xi 7; Σκύλλαν τινά A.*Ag.*1233, cf. Ar.*V.*181, *Av.*512, *Ra.*912: so also ὥς τις ἥλιος A.*Ag.*288; ἰσθμόν τιν' Ar.*Th*.647. **7.** with Adjs. τις combines to express the idea of a Subst. used as predicate, ὥς τις θαρσαλέος καὶ ἀναιδής ἐσσι προΐκτης *a* bold and impudent beggar, Od.17.449, cf. 18.382, 20.140, Il.3.220; ἐγώ τις, ὡς ἔοικε, δυσμαθής *a* dull*ard*, Pl.*R*.358a, cf. *Prt*.340e; φόβου πλέα τις εἶ *a* cow*ard*, A.*Pr*.696, cf. *Th*.979 (lyr.), *Ag*.1140 (lyr.); ὡς ταχεῖά τις..χάρις διαρρεῖ in what swift *fashion* (=ταχέως πως), S.*Aj*.1266, cf. *OT*618, Hdt.4.198; δεινόν τι ποιεύμενος thinking it *a* terrible *thing*, Id.3.155, 5.33. **8.** with numerals and Adjs. expressing number, size, or the like, εἷς δέ τις ἀρχὸς ἀνὴρ..ἔστω *some* one man, Il.1.144; ἕνα τιν' ἂν καθεῖσεν Ar.*Ra*.911; δώσει δέ τι ἕν γε φέρεσθαι Od.15.83; τινὰ μίαν νύκτα Th.6.61; προσκαλεσάμενός τινας δύο τῶν ἑκατονταρχῶν *Act.Ap*.23.23; sts. the τις softens the definiteness of the numeral, ἑπτά τινες *some* seven, seven *or so*, Th.7.34; ἐς διακοσίους τινάς Id.3.111, cf. 7.87, 8.21; so without an actual numeral, ἡμέρας τινάς *some* days, i.e. *several*, Id.3.52; στρατῷ τινι *of a certain amount, considerable*, Id.8.3; ἐνιαυτόν τινα a year *or so*, Id.3.68; so οὐ πολλοί τινες, τινὲς οὐ πολλοί, A.*Pers*.510, Th.6.94, etc.; ὀλίγοι τινές or τινὲς ὀλίγοι Id.2.17, 3.7; οὔ τινα πολλὸν χρόνον no *very* long time, Hdt.5.48; τις στρατιὰ οὐ πολλή Th.6.61; so also ὅσσος τις χρυσός what *a* store of gold, Od.10.45, cf. Hdt.1.193, 2.18, etc.; κόσοι τινές Id.7.234; πηλίκαι τινὲς τιμωρίαι Isoc.20.3; πολλὸς γάρ τις ἔκειτο Il.7.156; ἐκ πολλοῦ τευ χρόνου Hdt.2.58. **9.** with Pronominal words, ἀλλά τί μοι τόδε θυμὸς..μερμηρίζει *something*, namely this, Od.20.38, cf. 380; οἷός τις what sort of *a* man, Il.5.638 (dub. l.), cf. Od.9.348, 20.377, Pl.*Prt*.313a, etc.; ποῖός τις S.*Ant*.42, *OC*1163, Hdt.3.34, X.*An*.7.6.24, etc.; ὁποῖός τις Id.*Cyr*.2.2.2, al.; εὐτυχίη τις τοιήδε Hdt.3.139, cf. X.*Mem*.1.1.1, etc.; τοιοῦτός τις Id.*An*.5.8.7. **10.** with the Article, **a.** when a noun with the Art. is in appos. with τις, as ὅταν δ' ὁ κύριος παρῇ τις when the person in authority, *whoever he be*, is here, S.*OC*289; τοὺς αὐτοέντας..τιμωρεῖν τινας (v.l. τινα) Id.*OT*107. **b.** in Philosophic writers, τις is added to the Art. to show that the Art. is used to denote a particular individual who is not specified in the general formula, although he would be in the particular case, ὁ τὶς ἄνθρωπος *the individual* man (*whoever he may be*), *this or that* man, opp. ἄνθρωπος (man in general), ὁ τὶς ἵππος, ἡ τὶς γραμματική, Arist.*Cat*.1$^b$4, 8; τὸ τὶ μέγεθος, opp. ὅλως τὸ μέγεθος, Id.*Pol*.1283$^a$4, cf. S.E.*P*.2.223; but in ἑνὸς γὰρ τό γε τὶ φήσεις σημεῖον εἶναι Pl.*Sph*.237d, the Art. is used as in ll.cc. s.v. ὁ, ἡ, τό B.I.5: later ὅ τις (or ὁ τὶς) much like ὁ δεῖνα, δεῦρο ὅ τις θεός, ὄφθητί μοι in a general formula of invocation, *PMag.Par*.1.236; αἴρω σε, ἥ τις βοτάνη ib.287; εἰς τήν τινα κρείαν (leg. χρείαν) ib.289. **c.** freq. in opposed clauses, ὁ μέν τις.., ὁ δὲ.. E.*Med*.1141, *Hec*.624, Pl.*Phd*.99b, etc.; ὁ μέν τις.., ἄλλος δὲ.. E.*IT*1407; ὁ μὲν.., ὁ δέ τις.. X.*Cyr*.1.4.15: pl., οἱ μέν τινες.., οἱ δὲ.. Hdt.1.127, cf. Th.2.91; οἱ μέν τινες.., οἱ δὲ.., οἱ δέ τινες X.*Cyr*.3.2.10, etc.; οἱ μὲν.., οἱ δέ τινες.. ib.6.1.26, etc.: also combined with other alternative words, ὁ μέν τις.., ὁ δέ τις.., ἕτερος δέ τις.. Id.*Smp*.2.6; ὁ μὲν.., ἕτερος δέ τις.., ὁ δὲ.., etc., Ar.*Pl*.162 sq.: also in neut., τὸ μέν τι.., τὸ δέ τι.. Pl.*Ep*.358a; τὸ μέν τι.., τὸ δὲ.. Hdt.3.40; in adverb. sense, τὸ μὲν.., τὸ δέ τι.. *partly.., partly..*, Plb.1.73.4; and τι remains unaltered even when the Art. is pl., τὰ μέν τι μαχόμενοι, τὰ δὲ καὶ ἀναπαυόμενοι X.*An*.4.1.14, cf. *HG*7.1.46; also τὸ δέ τι.. but *in some* measure.., without τὸ μέν preceding, Th.1.107, cf. 118, 7.48. **d.** later τις is used as in b supr. but without the Art., γράψον..ὅτι τι καί τι εἴληφας that you have received *such* and *such* things, *POxy*.937.22 (iii A.D.); κληρονόμους καταλείπω τὴν θυγατέρα μού τινα καὶ τὸν σύντροφον αὐτῆς τινα καί τινα ib.1034.2 (ii A.D.); τίς τινι χαίρειν *A* to *B* greeting (in a draft letter), ib.509 (ii A.D.). **11.** the neut. τι is used, **a.** collectively, ἦν τι καὶ ἐν ταῖς Συρακούσαις there was *a party*.., Th.7.48; so perh. τῶν ἄλλων οὔ πέρ τι πεφυγμένον ἔστ' Ἀφροδίτην, οὔτε θεῶν, οὔτ' ἀνθρώπων no *class*, *h.Ven*.34 (but masc. τις in *h.Merc*.143). **b.** euphem. for something bad, v. supr. 3. **c.** joined with Verbs, *somewhat, in any degree, at all*, ἦ ῥά τί μοι κεχολώσεαι Il.5.421; παρεθάρρυνέ τι αὐτούς X.*HG*6.4.7, etc.: with Adjs. or Adverbs, οὕτω δή τι ἰσχυραί, οὕτω δή τι πολύγονον, etc., Hdt.3.12, 108, cf. 4.52; so also ὀλίγον τι ἧσσον Od.15.365; οὐδέ τι μᾶλλον Hdt.6.123, etc.; ἧσσόν τι Th.3.75, etc.; οὐ πάνυ τι, πολύ τι, σχεδόν τι, v. πάνυ I.3, πολύς III.1a, 2a, σχεδόν IV; also in conjunction with οὐδέν, μηδέν, οὐδέν τι πάντως Hdt.6.3; οὐδέν, μηδέν τι μᾶλλον, E.*Alc*.522, S.*Aj*.280; μηδέν τι λίαν E.*Andr*.1234:—also καί τι καὶ..ὑποψίᾳ *in part* also from suspicion, Th.1.107; καί πού τι καί Pi.*O*.1.28. **12.** τίς τε freq. in Hom., ὡς ὅτε τίς τε Il.3.33, 4.141, v. τε B. **13.** ἤ τις ἢ οὐδείς *few* or none, *next to none*, Hdt.3.140, X.*Cyr*.7.5.45, D.C.47.5, 48.4; ἤ τι ἢ οὐδέν *little* or nothing, Pl.*Ap*.17b; ἢ οὐδεὶς ἤ τις D.C.41.62 (s.v.l.). **14.** τις is pleonast. in such phrases as οὐδέν τι or μηδέν τι, v. supr. 11c. **b.** repeated in successive clauses, ὅσα λέγει τις ἢ πράσσει τις ἢ ψέγειν ἔχει S.*Ant*.689; εἴ τις δύο ἢ καὶ πλέους τις ἡμέρας λογίζεται Id.*Tr*.944 (where however κἄτι πλείους is prob. cj.), cf. E.*Or*.1218 (whereas τις is sts. omitted in the first clause, οὔτε φωνὴν οὔτε του μορφὴν βροτῶν A.*Pr*.21, cf. S.*Tr*.3): but in E.*Andr*.734, ἔστι γάρ τις οὐ πρόσω..πόλις τις, the repetition is pleonastic, as also in A.*Supp*.57 sq. (lyr., s.v.l.). **15.** τις is sts. omitted, οὐδέ κεν ἔνθα τεόν γε μένος καὶ χεῖρας ὄνοιτο (sc. τις) Il.13.287; ὡς δ' ἐν ὀνείρῳ οὐ δύναται (sc. τις) φεύγοντα διώκειν 22.199, cf. S.*OC*1226 (lyr.), *Leg.Gort*.2.2, X.*Smp*.5.2, Pl.*Grg*.456d: τις must often be supplied from what goes before, ib.478c, *Prt*.319d. **b.** sts. also τις is omitted before a gen. case which must depend upon it, as ἢ [τις] τᾶς ἀσώτου Σισυφιδᾶν γενεᾶς S.*Aj*.189 (lyr.); ἣν γαμῇ ποτ' αὐτὸς ἢ [τις] τῶν ξυγγενῶν Ar.*Nu*.1128; ἐν τῶν πόλεων *IG*1$^2$.56.14.—Cf. ὅστις, οὔτις, μήτις, ἄλλο τι. **III.** Accentuation and position of τις: **1.** accentuation: τις is normally enclitic, but in certain uses is orthotone, i.e. theoretically oxytone (τίς, τινά, τινές, τινῶν, etc., cf. Choerob. *in Theod*.1.373 H.) and barytone when followed by another word (τὶς or τις, τινὰ, τινὲς, τινῶν, etc.). According to Sch. D.T.p.240 H. its orthotone accent is τίς (not τὶς), τίνα, τίνες, etc. The orthotone form is used in codd.: **a.** at the beginning of a sentence, τίς ἔνδον..; is *any one* within? A.*Ch*.654 (τὶς cj. Hermann); τί φημι; = λέγω τι; am I saying *anything?* S.*Tr*.865, *OT*1471; (τίς ἦλθε;) ἦλθέ τις has *anybody* come? *Somebody* has come. Sch.D.T. l.c.; τὶς κάθηται, τὶς περιπατεῖ, *so and so* is sitting (walking), S.E.*M*.8.97; τὶς αἰπόλος καλούμενος Κομάτας Sch.Theoc.7.78; τίς ποτε οἰκοδεσπότης..ἐκοπία Aesop. in *Gloss*. iii p.41; or after a pause, πῶς γὰρ ἄν, ἔφην ἐγώ, ὦ βέλτιστε, τὶς ἀποκρίναιτο Pl.*R*.337e; τί οὖν (τὶς ἂν εἴποι) ταῦτα λέγεις; D.1.14 (v.l.); ἔντοσθεν δὲ γυνά, τι θεῶν δαίδαλμα Theoc.1.32; οὐ γυμνὸν τὸ φίλαμα, τι δ' ὦ ξένε καὶ πλέον ἑξεῖς Mosch.1.5 (v.l. for τὺ). **b.** when τις is opp. to another τις or to some other word, τισὶ μὲν συμφέρει, τισὶ δ' οὐ συμφέρει Arist.*Pol*.1284$^b$40, cf. Th.2.92, Pl.*Cri*.49a, D.9.2; τινὲς μὲν οὖν.., ἡμεῖς δὲ.. Sor.1.1; τὸ τὶ μὲν ψεῦδος ἔχον, τὶ δὲ ἀληθές S.E.*M*.8.127; ἀλλὰ τινὰ μὲν.., τινὰ δὲ.. Gem.14.6; ποτὲ μὲν πρὸς πάντα, ποτὲ δὲ πρὸς τινά Sor.1.48: without such opposition, τοῦτ' εἰς ἀνίαν τοὔπος ἔρχεται τινί for *a certain person*, S.*Aj*.1138. Codd. are not consistent; in signf. II.5a, 10c, 13 they make it enclitic; in signf. II.5b sts. enclitic, sts. orthotone (v. supr.); sts. enclitic and orthotone in the same sentence, πάντα δὲ τὰ γιγνόμενα ὑπό τέ τινος γίγνεται καὶ ἔκ τινος καὶ τί Arist.*Metaph*.1032$^a$14, cf. Pl.*Chrm*.165c. **2.** position: **a.** τις is rarely first word in the sentence, and rarely follows a pause (v. supr. III.1a, b); it may stand second word, ἔσκε τις ἐνθάδε μάντις ἀνήρ Od.9.508, cf. Il.8.515, 23.331; but in general its position is not far before or after the word to which it belongs in sense, ἀλλ' ἄγε δή τινα μάντιν ἐρείομεν 1.62; φυλακὴ δέ τις ἔμπεδος ἔστω 8.521. **b.** in Ion. Prose it sts. stands between its genitive and the Article of that genitive, τῶν τις Περσέων Hdt.1.85; τῶν τις ἰρέων Id.2.38; τῶν τινες Φοινίκων Id.8.90; ἐς τῶν τι ἄλλο στομάτων τοῦ Νείλου Id.2.179; so also in late Prose, Ath.3.108d, Eust.1402.18, 1659.27, 1676.1. **c.** it stands between the Art. and Subst. in signf. II.10b. **d.** τίς τι is the correct order, not τί τις, *IG*1$^2$.110.46, Th.7.10, X.*An*.4.1.14 (codd. dett.), D.22.22, etc. **e.** whereas in Att. the order ἐάν τις is compulsory, in Dor. the usual order is αἴ τίς κα, *Leg.Gort*.9.43, al., *Tab.Heracl*.1.105, al. (but αἴ κά τις Epich.35, 159; αἰ δέ κα μή τις *Leg.Gort*.5.13): later Dor. εἴ τί κα *GDI*2101.3, al.; καἴ τι ἂν (= καὶ εἴ τι ἂν) *IG*5(1).1390.50 (Andania, i B.C., v. infr. B.II.1b):—this Dor. order influenced the Koine, as in the rare εἴ τις ἂν Plu.*TG*15.

**B.** Interrog. Pron. **τίς**, Elean and Lacon. **τίρ** (q.v.), τί:—gen. Ep. and Ion. τέο Il.2.225, Herod.8.1, etc., or τεῦ Od.15.509, Hdt.5.106, etc.; Trag. and Att. τοῦ A.*Pr*.614, Ar.*Nu*.1223, etc.; Ion., Trag., and Att. τίνος Simon.154, Hdt.6.80, A.*Pr*.563 (anap.), S.*Aj*.892, Ar.*Ach*.588, etc.; dat. Ion. τέῳ Hdt.1.11, al. (as fem., 4.155); no dat. in Hom. or Hes.; Trag. and Att. τῷ S.*Ant*.401, D.19.60, etc.; Aeol. τίῳ Sapph.104; τίνι first in Pi.*N*.7.57, A.*Pers*.715 (troch.). S.*OT*10, Ar.*Ach*.919, Hdt.3.38, Th.1.80, D.20.115, etc.; acc. τίνα Il.5.703, etc.; neut. τί 1.362, etc.: dual τίνε (elided) Ar.*Av*.107: pl., nom. τίνες Od.1.172, etc.; neut. τίνα Pl.*Phd*.102a, Aeschin.2.81, Hipparch.1.1.4, Gem.17.12, *Ep.Hebr*.5.12; gen. Ep. τέων Il.24.387, Od.20.192, and as monosyll. 6.119, 13.200; Trag. and Att. τίνων S.*El*.1476, *OC*2, Ar.*Nu*.1089, etc.; dat. τίσι first in S.*OT*1126, Ar.*Ra*.1455, Pl.*R*.332d, etc. (no dat. in Hom. or Hes.); also τοῖσι S.*Tr*.984 (anap.); Ion. τέοισι Hdt.1.37, cf. 2.82 (v.l. ὁτέοισι); Aeol. τίοισι Sapph.168; acc. τίνας S.*OC*115, Ar.*Av*.370 (troch.); neut. τίνα Arr.*Epict*.1.30.3; Boeot. τά Pi.*O*1.82 (Adv.); Megar. σά Ar.*Ach*.757, 784 (Adv.): of the pl. Hom. uses only nom. τίνες with gen. τέων; ποῖος (*what? which?*) is sts. preferred (esp. in neut. pl.) to the Adj. τίς, e.g. τὰ ποῖα ταῦτα χρήματα; Ar.*Nu*.1270, cf. 1337, *Th*.621, Pl.*Cra*.391e, 395d, 406d; v. ποῖος I.3 and IV: **I.** in direct questions, *who? which?* neut. *what? which?* ὦ ξεῖνοι, τίνες ἐστέ; Od.9.252; τί νύ μοι μήκιστα γένηται; 5.299; τίς δαίμων τόδε πῆμα προσήγαγε; 17.446; τίς ἀχώ, τίς ὀδμὰ προσέπτα μ' ἀφεγγής; A.*Pr*.115 (lyr.), cf. 561 (anap.), etc.; properly at the beginning of the sentence; but this position may be varied, **a.** for grammatical reasons, as between the Art. and part. or noun, τοὺς τί ποιοῦντας τὸ ὄνομα τοῦτο ἀποκαλοῦσιν; X.*Mem*.2.2.1, cf. Pl.*Smp*.206b; τῆς περὶ τί πειθοῦς ἡ ῥητορική ἐστιν τέχνη; Id.*Grg*.454a; ὁ σοφιστὴς τῶν τί σοφῶν ἐστιν; Id.*Prt*.312d. **b.** for emphasis, ἃ δ' ἐννέπεις, κλύουσα τοῦ λέγεις; S.*OC*412, cf. *El*.1191; πόλις τε ἀφισταμένη τίς πω..τούτῳ ἐπεχείρησε; Th.3.45; esp. when the Verb begins the sentence, δράσεις δὲ δὴ τί; E.*HF*1246; ἦλθες δὲ κατὰ τί; Ar.*Nu*.239; διαφέρει δὲ τί; D.18.205.—The person freq. follows in gen. pl., as τίς θεῶν; Il.18.182, etc.; and of things or conditions, τί is freq. with the genit. sg., of all genders, πρὸς τί χρείας; S.*OT*1174; ἐλπίδων ἐς τί; Id.*OC*1749 codd. (lyr.); κἀνήρετ' ἐν τῷ πράγματος κυροῖ ποτε Id.*Aj*.314, etc. **2.** sts. as the predicate, τίς ὀνομάζεται; *what* is he named? E.*Ph*.123; so also may be expld. the union of τίς with a demonstr. or possess. Pron., or with a Noun preceded by the Art., τί τοῦτ' ἔλεξας; S.*Ph*.1173 (lyr.); τί ἐστι τουτί; τίς ὁ τρόπος τοῦ τάγματος; Id.*Ichn*.114; also with Pron. in pl., τί ταῦτα; E.*Ph*.382, *Andr*.548, etc.; τί γὰρ τάδ' ἐστίν; Ar.*Nu*.200; τί ποτ' ἐστίν, ἃ διανοούμεθα; Pl.*Tht*.154e; τί ποτ' ἐστὶ ταῦτα; ib.155c; σκεπτέον τί τὰ συμβαίνοντα Id.*Grg*.508b; so τί is used as predicate of a masc. or fem. subject, τί νιν προσείπω; A.*Ch.* 983(997); τί σοι φαίνεται ὁ νεανίσκος; Pl.*Chrm.*154d :—also τίς δ' ὅδε Ναυσικάᾳ ἕπεται; *who* is this that follows N.? Od.6.276 ; τίς δ' οὗτος ἔρχεαι; Il.10.82, cf. Alc.84.1, S.*El.*328,388, *Ant.*7,218, E.*Hec.*501, Pl.*Cri.*43c; and in the reverse order, τήνδε τίνα λεύσσω..; *who* is this I see? E.*IA*821 ; τίνι οὖν τοιούτῳ φίλους ἂν θηρῴην; *with what means* of such kind..? X.*Mem.*3.11.9 ; τί τοσοῦτον νομίζοντες ἠδικῆσθαι; Id. *Smp.*4.53; τί με τὸ δεινὸν ἐργάσῃ; *what* is the dreadful thing which..? E.*Ba.*492, cf. S.*OC*598,1488, etc.; τίν' ὄψιν σὴν προσδέρκομαι; *what* face is this I see of thine? E.*Hel.*557; παρὰ τίνας τοὺς ὑμᾶς; *who* are 'you' to whom [I am to come]? Pl.*Ly.*203b :—the Art. is exceptionally added to τίς, when it leads up to a word which requires the Art., ληφθήσει.. Πανήμου εἰκάδι· καὶ Λῴου τῇ—τίνι; τῇ δεκάτῃ on the twentieth of the month Panemus and of Loüs on the —*what* day? the tenth, Call.*Epigr.*46 :—in Com. also τὸ τί; *what* is that? Ar.*Nu.*775, *Pax*696, *Av.*1039, *Pl.*902, etc.; τοῦ τίνος χάριν; *UPZ*6.29 (ii B.C.); and with pl. Art., τὰ τί; Ar.*Pax*693. 3. with prop. names treated as appellatives (v. τις indef. II. 6b), τίς ἄρα Κύπρις ἢ τίς Ἵμερος; S.*Fr.*874; τίς σε Θηρικλῆς ποτε ἔτευξε; Eub.43; τίς.. Χίμαιρα πύρπνοος; Anaxil.22.3. 4. τίς ἂν θεῶν.. δοίη; like πῶς ἄν, *would that some one..*, S.*OC*1100, cf. A.*Ag.*1448 (lyr.). 5. a question with τίς often amounts to a strong negation, τῶν δ' ἄλλων τίς κεν οὐνόματ' εἴποι; Il.17.260; τίς ἂν ἐξεύροι ποτ' ἄμεινον; Ar.*Pl.*498; τίνες ἂν δικαιότερον.. μισοῖντο; Th.3.64, etc. 6. sts. two questions are asked in one clause by different cases of τίς; ἡ τίσιν τί ἀποδιδοῦσα τέχνη δικαιοσύνη ἂν καλοῖτο; Pl.*R.*332d; τί λαβόντα τί δεῖ ποιεῖν D.4.36 :—a like doubling of the question lies in the union of τίς with other interrog. words, τίς πόθεν εἰς (εἷς codd.) ἀνδρῶν; Od.1.170, cf. S.*Tr.*421. 7. τίς with Particles:—τίς γάρ; *why who? who possibly?* τίς γάρ σε θεῶν.. ἧκεν; Il.18.182; v. infr. 8 f. b. τίς δέ; ὦ κοῦραι, τίς δ' ὔμμιν.. πωλεῖται; *h.Ap.*169. c. τίς δή; *who then?* τίς δή κεν βροτὸς.. ἄζοιτ' ἀθανάτους Thgn.747; τίς δῆτα; S.*Aj.*518. d. τίς ποτε; *who in the world? who ever?* τίς ποτ' ὢν γενεὰν καὶ ποίαν τινὰ φύσιν ἔχων; X.*Cyr.*1.1.6, cf. S.*El.*975; τίς δήποτε; Id.*Fr.*106 (but τίς ἄν ποτε is prob. cj.). 8. the usages of the neut. τί; are very various: a. τί; alone, as a simple question, *what?* τί γάρ; A.*Th.*336 (lyr.):—on ὅτι τί; ὅτι τί δή; ὅτι δὴ τί; v. ὅτι B. 1b; on ὡς τί; v. ὡς F. I. b. τί τοῦτο; τί ταῦτα; v. supr. 2. c. τί μοι; τί σοι; *what* is it to me? to thee? S.*Ph.*753, etc.; c. gen., τί μοι ἔριδος καὶ ἀρωγῆς; *what* have I to do with..? Il.21.360; τί δέ σοι ταῦτα; Ar.*Lys.*514, cf. *Ec.*521 (where the answerer repeats the question in indirect form, ὅ τί μοι τοῦτ' ἔστιν;); ἀλλὰ δὴ τί τοῦτ' ἐμοί; Diph.32.18; τί ἐμοὶ καὶ σοί; *what* have I to do with thee? Lxx *Jd.*11.12, Arr.*Epict.*2.19.19, *Ev.Jo.*2.4; τί σοὶ καὶ εἰρήνῃ; Lxx 4*Ki.*9.18, cf. *Ho.*14.9; τί πρὸς σέ; M.Ant.8.44, cf. *Ev.Matt.*27.4; σοὶ δὲ καὶ τούτοισι τοῖσι πρήγμασι τί ἐστι; *what* have you to do with these matters? Hdt.5.33; τί τῷ νόμῳ καὶ τῇ βασάνῳ; D.29.36 :—folld. by a clause, τί δὲ τίν, εἰ κωτίλαι εἰμές; Theoc.15.89; or with inf., τί γάρ μοι τοὺς ἔξω κρίνειν; 1*Ep.Cor.*5.12 :—v. εἰμί C. III. 2. d. τί μαθών; τί παθών; v. μανθάνω v, πάσχω III. 4. e. τί; also often stands abs. as Adv. *how? why? wherefore?* Il.1.362, etc.; so too in Att., Pl.*Cri.* 43c, etc.; δόμων γὰρ ζῶσι τῶνδε δεσπόται. Answ. τί ζῶσιν; *how do you mean* ζῶσι? ζῶσι *forsooth!* E.*Alc.*806; Κιθαιρών—Answ. τί Κιθαιρών; *what about* K.? Id.*Ba.*1177 codd., cf. 1182 (both lyr.); cf. τίη. f. τί with Particles:—τί γάρ; *why not? how else?* and so it came to mean *of course, no doubt*, A.*Ag.*1230, *Ch.*880, *Eu.*678, etc.; used in affirmative answers, Pl.*Phdr.*258d, *Tht.*209b, al.; to introduce an argument, Arist.*Pol.*1281$^{a}$14; v. γάρ I. 4 :—τί δαί; v. δαί :—τί δέ; serving to pass on quickly to a fresh point, Pl.*Hp.Ma.*288c, al.; τί δέ, εἰ..; *but what, if..?* E.*Hel.*1043; τί δ' ἄν, εἰ..; Ar.*Th.*773; τί δ' ἦν..; Id.*Nu.*1444; τί δέ, εἰ μή..; *what* else but..? X.*Oec.*9.1, cf. S.*OT* 941, *Ph.*421; so τί δὲ δή; τί δή; τί δή ποτε; *why ever? why in the world? what do you mean?* Pl.*R.*470e, *Grg.*469a, *Sph.*241d, S.*El.* 1184 :—so also τί δῆτα; *how, pray?* τί δῆτ' ἄν, εἰ..; Ar.*Nu.*154 :—(τί μή; f.l. in S.*Aj.*668) :—τί μήν; i.e. *yes certainly*, much like τί γάρ; Pl.*Tht.*162e, etc., prob. in S.*Aj.*668 :—τί μὴν οὔ; in reply to a question, Id.*El.*1280 (lyr.) :—τί νυ; *why* now? Il.1.414, etc. :—τί δ' οὔ; parenthetic, *why not?* as an affirmative answer, S.*Ant.*460; τί οὐ καλοῦμεν; i.e. let us call, Ar.*Lys.*1103; τί οὐ βαδίζομεν; etc., Pl.*Prt.*310e, etc. :—τί οὖν; *how so?* making an objection, A.*Th.* 208; but τί οὖν ἔτ' ἂν σαίνοιμεν.. μόρον; ib.704; τί οὖν οὐκ ἐρωτᾷς; Pl.*Ly.*211d :—τί ποτε; v. τίπτε; g. with Conjunctions following :—τί ὅτι..; *why* is it that..? Stratt.62 (f.l.), Lxx *Ge.* 3.1, *Ev.Luc.*2.49, etc. :—with Conjunctions preceding, ἵνα τί; v. ἵνα B. II. 3 c. h. with Preps. :—διὰ τί; *wherefore?* Ar.*Pl.*1111, etc. :—ἐκ τίνος; from *what* cause? X.*An.*5.8.4 :—ἐς τί; to *what* point? how long? Il.5.465; but also, to *what* end? S.*Tr.*403, cf. *OC*524 (lyr.) :—κατὰ τί; for *what* purpose? Ar.*Nu.*239 :—πρὸς τί; *wherefore?* S.*OT*766, 1027, etc. II. τίς is sts. used for ὅστις in indirect questions, εἰρώτα δὴ ἔπειτα τίς εἴη καὶ πόθεν ἔλθοι Od.15.423, cf. 17.368; δεῖξον τίς ἔσται τῇ ταλαιπώρῳ χρόνος A.*Pr.*623; οὐδ' ἔχω τίς ἂν γενοίμαν ib.905 (lyr.); οὐκ ἔχω τί φῶ Id.*Ch.*91, cf. S.*OC*48, etc.; ἐπισκεψώμεθα τίνες πέπανται σφενδόνας X.*An.*3.3.18; εἰπὲ τίνα γνώμην ἔχεις ib.2.2.10; freq. in later Gr., where ὅστις is very rare, εἰς τὸ λογιστήριον γράφων.. τί ὀφείλεται *PHib.*1.29.42 (iii B.C.), cf. *PCair.Zen.* 21.40, al. (iii B.C.); οὐθεὶς ἐσήμηνεν παρὰ τί ἂν τοῖς προστεταγμένοις.. οὐ κατηκολούθησαν nobody indicated *why* they should not have obeyed orders, *PTeb.*72.160, cf. 61(*b*).227 (ii B.C.); ὅστις and τίς are sts. combined, ὡς πύθοιθ' ὅ τι δρῶν ἢ τί φωνῶν ῥυσαίμην S.*OT*71, cf. A.*Pr.*489 sq., 617,623 :—later with inf., τί πράττειν οὐκ ἔχω I do not know *what* to do, Aesop.67, cf. Ps.-Luc.*Philopatr.*29. b. sts. not in indirect questions, *whoever, whatever*, αἰτοῦ τί χρῄζεις ἕν E.*Fr.*773. 2; ταῦτα οὐκ ἀπέστελλον πάντα, ἀλλ' ἐκλεγόμενοι τίνων αἱ τιμαὶ ἐπετέταντο *whatever* things had risen in price, D.56.24; τίνα δ' ἃ Κύπρις οὐκ ἐφίλησεν *whomsoever* K. has not loved, *AP*5.169 (Noss.); τίνι ἡ τύχη δίδωσι, λαβέτω Antiochus ap. Ptol.Euerg.3 J.; λαμβανέτω τί θέλει *AP*12.219 (Strat.); τὰν ὀνάλαν κίς κε γινύειτει *IG* 9(2).517.22 (Larissa, iii B.C.); καὶ τί ἂν εἶ (=ᾖ) λοιπόν ib.5(1).1390. 50 (Andania, i B.C., nisi leg. καί τι ἄν, v. supr. A. III. 2 e); τίς ἂν δὲ χεῖρα προσαγάγῃ *Epigr.Gr.*376a (Aezani); τίς σοφός, αὐτῷ προσκολλήθητι Lxx *Si.*6.34; οὐ τί ἐγὼ θέλω, ἀλλὰ τί σύ *Ev.Marc.*14.36; τίς σοφίῃ πάντων πρῶτος, τούτου τρίποδ' αὐδῶ Orac. ap. D.S.9.3 et ap. D.L. 1.28 codd. (ὃς Cobet from Sch.Ar.*Pl.*9); χαῖρε καὶ σύ, τίς ποτ' εἶ *IG*9 (2).953 (Larissa), cf. *CIG*1982 (Thessalonica); in other places, as S.*El.*1176, *Tr.*339, *OT*1144, E.*Ion*324, this constr. cannot be admitted. c. τίς = ὅστις after a neg., μή τίς ἐστιν ἐν ὑμῖν ἀνὴρ ἢ γυνή.., τίνος ἡ διάνοια ἐξέκλινεν κτλ. ; Lxx *De.*29.18. d. = ὅς or ὅσπερ, τέων.. Ζεὺς ἐπὶ σαλπίγγων ἱρὰ βοῇ δέχεται Κᾶρες ὁμοῦ Λελέγεσσι Call.*Aet.*3.1.60, cf. *Del.*185, *Epigr.*30.2, Nic.*Al.*2; Δωροθέαν, τίς τὸν ἐμὸν ἄνδρα εἶχε *Tab.Defix.Aud.*10.4 (Cnidus, ii/i B.C.), cf. 5.2,8; τίνας ἱερεωσύνας εἶχον ἐπενεγύων *SIG*705.43, cf. 56 (Senatus consultum, Delph., ii B.C.); τίνα με ὑπονοεῖτε εἶναι, οὐκ εἰμὶ ἐγώ *Act.Ap.* 13.25; τίς ἔζησεν ἔτη β' *who* lived.., *IG*14.1560 (Rome), cf. 1391 (ibid.); εὗρον γεωργόν, τίς αὐτὰ ἑλκύσῃ *BGU*822.5 (ii/iii A.D.). 2. τίς; τί; in direct or indirect questions may be construed with a part., σὺ δὲ τίς ὢν ταῦτα λέγεις; being *who*, i.e. who are you that..? Pl.*Grg.*452a; ἐπειρέσθαι.. τίνες ἐόντες ἄνθρωποι.. ταῦτα προαγορεύουσι Hdt.1.153; καταμεμάθηκας.. τοὺς τί ποιοῦντας τὸ ὄνομα τοῦτο ἀποκαλοῦσι; X.*Mem.*2.2.1; or in a subordinate clause, ἀλλ' ὅταν τί ποιήσωσι, νομιεῖς αὐτοὺς σοῦ φροντίζειν; ib.1.4.14; νῦν δ' ἐπειδὴ τίνος τέχνης ἐπιστήμων ἐστί, τίνα ἂν καλοῦντες αὐτὸν ὀρθῶς καλοῖμεν; Pl. *Grg.*448c. III. = πότερος; X.*Cyr.*1.3.17, Pl.*Phlb.*52d, *Ev.Matt.* 27.21, *Ev.Luc.*5.23. IV. τί as exclamatory Adv., *how..!* τί ὡραιώθησαν σιαγόνες σου ὡς τρυγόνες Lxx *Ca.*1.10, cf. 4.10; τί θέλω *how* I wish! *Ev.Luc.*12.49; τί στενή v.l. in *Ev.Matt.*7.14.

C. Prosody: τις and τίς keep ῐ in all cases (digamma operates in Il.6.462, etc.). II. τί was never elided; but hiatus is allowed after τί in Ep. τί ἦ (v. τίη), also in Com., as τί οὔ; Ar.*Av.*149; τί οὖν; Id.*Pl.*94; τί ἐστι; Id.*Nu.*82, *Av.*1036; τί, ὦ πάτερ; Id.*Nu.* 80 :—a licence which is rarer in Trag., τί ἐστιν; S.*Ph.*733; τί οὖν; A.*Th.*208,704, *Eu.*902, S.*Aj.*873 (lyr.), *Ph.*100, etc.; τί εἶπας; Id. *Tr.*1203, *Ph.*917.

**τισιγίτης**, ου, ὁ, *utensil, vessel*, Persian word, Alexander ap. Ath. 11.784a.

**τίσις** [τῐ], εως, ἡ, (τίνω; cf. Skt. *apa-citis* 'vengeance') *payment by way of return* or *recompense, retribution, vengeance*, Od.2.76, Il. 22.19, Hes.*Th.*210, Alcm.23.36, etc.; ἐκ γὰρ Ὀρέσταο τ. ἔσσεται Ἀτρεΐδαο *retribution for* his murder, Od.1.40; freq. in Hdt., τίσιν δοῦναί τινος suffer *punishment for* an act, 8.76; τίσιν τινὶ ἐκτεῖσαι 6.84; τ. ἥξει 2.152, cf. S.*OC*228 (anap.); τιμωρίη τε καὶ τ. Hdt.7.8.α'; πρὸς κασιγνήτου τίσιν *for* him, S.*OC*1329; τῶν τοιούτων τ. *retribution for* such things, Pl.*Lg.*870d: pl., Ὀροίτεα Πολυκράτεος τίσιες μετῆλθον (where it may be personified, *avengers* of P., like Ἐρινύες) Hdt.3.126, 128. 2. *power to repay* or *requite*, both in bad and good sense, φίλων Thgn.337, cf. 345.

**Τισιφόνη**, ἡ, (τίνω, φόνος) *Tisiphone, the Avenger of blood*, one of the Erinyes, Orph.*H.*69.2, *A.*968, Apollod.1.1.4. 2. daughter of Alcmeon and Manto, E. ap. Apollod.3.7.7 (Nauck *TGF* p.380). (Τεισιφόνη shd. prob. be read.)

⊛ **τιταίνω**, Ep. redupl. for τείνω, τανύω, only used in pres., impf., and aor. Act., impf. and aor. Med., pres. and impf. Pass. :—*stretch*, τόξα τιταίνων *bending* his bow, Il.8.266; ἕτερος δ' ἐπὶ πᾶσι (παισὶ Pap.; v. πᾶσις) ποικίλον τόξον τιταίνει B.9.43; so in Med., ἐτιταίνετο καμπύλα τόξα Il.5.97, cf. Od.21.259; Τυδεΐδῃ ἔπι τόξα τιταίνετο Il.11.370; φόρμιγγα τιτηνάμενος *having tuned my* harp, Orph.*A.*251 codd.; hence τιταίνει.. νόμον *plays* a tune *on the strings*, Ar.*Fr.*671 (troch.). 2. *stretch out*, περὶ μέσσῳ χεῖρε τιτήνας Il.13.534; χρύσεια πατὴρ ἐτίταινε τάλαντα *held* them *out*, 8.69; προπάροιθε θρόνων ἐτίταινε τραπέζας Od. 10.354 :—Pass., *extend*, τῇ καὶ τῇ D.P.637, cf. 92,116, al. 3. *draw at full stretch*, ἅρμα τ. Il.2.390; βόε οἴνοπε πηκτὸν ἄροτρον.. τιταίνετον 13.704 : abs., τιταίνετον *haste along*, 23.403. 4. Pass., *strain* or *exert oneself*, chiefly in part., ἂψ ὤσασκε τιταινόμενος *with vehement effort*, Od.11.599; γυῖα τιταινόμενος *APl.*4.105; of a horse galloping, τιταινόμενος πεδίοιο *stretching* over the plain, Il.22.23; ἵππος ἄνακτα ἕλκησιν πεδίοιο τιταινόμενος σὺν ὄχεσφι 23.518; of birds, τιταινομένω πτερύγεσσιν Od.2.149; of a man running at full speed, Hes.*Sc.*229; of rivers, τ. κατ' ὄρεσφι Opp.*H.*1.22. 5. in Hp., Aret., and late Ep., *strain*, ὄμμα τ. Man.4.496, etc.; τ. ὄμμα εἴς τι Nonn.*D.*7.283; τ. ψιθύρισμα whistle *loudly*, ib.1.31, etc. :—Pass., *to be strained* or *stretched*, as in convulsions, Hp.*Epid.*5.47, Nic.*Th.*722, Aret.*CA*1.5, etc.: metaph., ἡ ὀδύνη τ. *becomes intense*, Hp.*Mul.*2. 134 (unless τὰ σκέλεα is the subject). II. Hes. attempts to derive the name Τιτῆνες from τιταίνω (lengthd. *ad hoc*, but retaining its usual sense) and at the same time from τίσις, *Th.*207 sqq.: v. Τιτάν.

⊛ **Τιτάν**, ᾶνος, ὁ; mostly pl. Τιτᾶνες, Ep. and Ion. Τιτῆνες, οἱ :—*the Titans*, Il.14.279, *h.Ap.*335, Hes.*Th.*630, al., Cratin. in *PSI*11.

1212.11,19, etc.; Τ. Προμηθεύς S.*OC*56, E.*Ph.*1122; of Atlas, dub. in A.*Pr.*427 (lyr.); of the Sun-god, Emp.38, cf. Ezek.*Exag.*217, Orph.*A.*512; of Apollo, *IG*12(5).893.1 (Tenos, dub. l.), 9(1).882.4 (Corc.), *Schwyzer* 649.8 (Balbilla). II. τιτάν· παιδεραστής, Hsch. III. a kind of *comet*, Heph.Astr.1.24 (Lyd.*Ost.*p.169). (Derived by Hes.*Th.*207 sqq. partly from τιταίνω (*the Strivers*), partly from the root of τίσις (Οὐρανὸς .. φάσκε δὲ τιταίνοντας ἀτασθαλίῃ μέγα ῥέξαι ἔργον, τοῖο δ' ἔπειτα τίσιν μετόπισθεν ἔσεσθαι); the latter derivation also in Orph.*Fr.*57, Plu.2.996c, Hsch., in modified form. Perh. really connected with τίταξ = βασιλεύς, and τιτήνη = βασιλίς in Hsch.)

**Τῑτάν-ια** [τᾱ] (sc. ἱερά), τά, *festival of the Titans*, Theodos.Gr. p.69 Göttling. **-ικός**, ή, όν, *of* or *for the Titans*, φύσις Pl.*Lg.* 701c; πάθη Plu.*Galb.*1; ἄθεος καὶ τ. τόπος Id.2.975c. Adv. -κῶς, σπαράττειν Procl. *in Alc.*p.43C., al. **-ιος**, α, ον, = foreg., *An.Ox.*1. 101:—fem. **Τῑτᾱνιάς**, Ep. -ηνιάς, άδος, = Τιτανίς, Call.*Fr.*471. **-ίς**, Ion. Τιτηνίς, ίδος, ἡ, fem. of Τιτάν, Τ. Θέμις A.*Pr.*874; Τ. Φοίβη Id. *Eu.*6, cf. E.*Hel.*382 (lyr.); Τ. Τηθύς Call.*Del.*17.

**τίτᾰνις** [τῐ], εως, ἡ, = τίτανος, Lycus ap.Orib.9.42.1 codd., Adam. *Vent.*37, Alex.Trall.9.3.

**τιτανισμός**, ὁ, ὁ παιανισμὸς τῶν Θρᾳκῶν τ. ὑπὸ τῶν Ἑλλήνων λέγεται κατὰ μίμησιν τῆς ἐν παιᾶσι φωνῆς Str.7 *Fr.*40.

**Τῑτᾰνο-γρᾰφία**, ἡ, *a history of the Titans*, Sch.A.R.3.1179. **-κράτωρ** [κρᾰ], ορος, ὁ, *conqueror of the Titans*, Luc.*Tim.*4. **-κτόνος**, ον, *slaying Titans*, Batr.281.

**Τῑτᾰν-ολέτης**, ου, ὁ, *destroyer of Titans*, Aus.*Epigr.*49.

**Τῑτᾰνομᾰχία**, ἡ, *battle of Titans*, title of poem in the Epic Cycle, Phld.*Piet.*56, al., D.S.1.97, Ath.7.277d, etc.

**τῑτᾰνόομαι**, *to be whitened* or *plastered*, τιτανωμένας (sic)· γεγυψωμένας, Hsch.

**Τῑτᾰνόπᾰνες**, οἱ, name of a Comedy by Myrtilus, Suid. s. v. Μυρτίλος: sg. parox. acc. to Hdn.Gr.1.13.

**τίτᾰνος** [ῐ], also **τέτανος**, Hsch., ἡ, *a white earth*, prob. *gypsum*, Hes.*Sc.*141, Luc.*Hist.Conscr.*62, *Alex.*21: also, *chalk, lime*, Arist.*Mete.* 383ᵇ8, 389ᵃ28; mixed with χάλιξ, Str.5.4.6; τ. ἐσβεσμένη Aret.*CA* 2.3; opp. τ. ζῶσα Aët.1.393; οἴκου τὴν ἐκ τῆς τ. διασῴζοντος ποιότητα (a cause of insanity) Gal.16.531; τ. ὕδατι βραχεῖσα Id.18(2).202; λαβὼν τ. θερμὴν φύρασον ὄξει *PHolm.*4.9: meaning indeterm. in Poll.7.124; τ. μέλαινα *Hippiatr.*80; *tetanos*, = *galbanus*, *Gloss.*: also, *marble-scrapings*, Luc.*Somn.*6. (Perh. from the Thessalian placename Τίτανος, cf. Τιτάνοιό τε λευκὰ κάρηνα Il.2.735, not conversely as Sch.Il. l. c.)

**Τῑτᾰνώδης**, ες, *Titanic*, φρόνημα Agatharch.98; Τιτανῶδες βλέπειν, ἀπιδεῖν, Luc.*Tim.*54, *Icar.*23.

**τῑτᾰνωτός**, ή, όν, *whitened*, Hsch.

**τίταξ**· ἔντιμος, ἢ δυνάστης, οἱ δὲ βασιλεύς, Hsch.

**τίτας** [ῐ], ὁ, (τίνω) Dor. for *τίτης, = τιμωρός, *avenging*, φόνος A. *Ch.*67 (lyr.). II. at Gortyn, *a magistrate who inflicted fines* (upon other magistrates), *public prosecutor*, *Schwyzer* 175 (pl.), 183 (sg.): τίται· εὔποροι, ἢ κατήγοροι τῶν ἀρχόντων, Hsch.

***τιτεύω**, only in Cretan forms τιτουϝέσθω στατῆρα *let him pay a fine* of one stater, *GDI*5128.5 (Axos), and τιτοϝτός, dub. in *GDI* 4978.

**Τῑτῆνες**, οἱ, Ion. for Τιτᾶνες, v. Τιτάν.

**τιτήνη**, ἡ, = βασιλίς, A.*Fr.*272 (pl.).

**τιτθ-εία**, ἡ, *nursing*, D.57.42, Sor.1.88. **-εν**· τίκτειν (perh. Cretan), Hsch. **-εύω**, *to be a nurse*, D.57.35. II. trans., *suckle, nurse*, τινα ib.42,44, Plu.*Lyc.*16, Sor.1.116:—Pass., τ. ἀπὸ τῆς μητρός Arist.*GA*754ᵃ13; οἱ -όμενοι *sucklings*, Id.*HA*523ᵃ 10. **-η**, ἡ, *nurse*, Ar.*Eq.*716, *Th.*609, Pl.*R.*343a, Thphr. *Char.*16.12. 20.5, *IG*2.2729.3, al. (iii B.C.), etc.; prop. *wet-nurse*, αἱ τ. καὶ αἱ τροφοί Plu.2.3c, cf. Ptol.Asc.p.394H., Gal.6.686; sts. confused with τήθη (q.v.); written τιθή in Hsch., τίθθη in *Com. Adesp.Oxy.*1825.8 (Pap. of v A.D.); τίθθη = *matertera*, *Gloss.* (i.e. confused with τηθίς). II. = τιτθός I, Arist.*HA*587ᵇ17, 588ᵃ5, *IG* 2².1534.256. **-ίδιον** [θῐ], τό, = τιτθίον, Ar.*Fr.*325 (Brunck τὰ τιτθία). **-ίζω**, *suckle*, *Gloss.*:—Pass., *suck*, Aq.*Is.*53.2. **-ίον**, τό, Dim. of τιτθός I, Crates Com.40, Ar.*Ach.*1199, *Ra.*415 (lyr.), Men. *Sam.*51, Antiph.106.4. **-ίς**, f.l. for τηθίς (q.v.).

**τιτθολᾰβέω**, *take hold of the teats*, Aristaenet.2.16, Hsch. s. v. βλιμάζειν.

**τιτθός**, ὁ, a woman's *breast*, Hp.*Aph.*5.40, Ar.*Th.*640, Lys.1.10, *IG*2².1534.223,281; ἡ θηλὴ τοῦ τ. Gal.*UP*15.7: rarely the male *breast*, Id.4.600, *AP*12.95 (Mel.): pl., of an animal's *teats*, Gal.6. 673,684; οἱ ἐν τοῖς τ. ἀδένες καλοῦνται οὔθατα ib.774. II. *nurser, rearer*, = τροφός, Ph.1.166 (v.l. for τιτθαί); cf. τίτθη.

**τιτιγόνιον**, τό, *an insect like a* τέττιξ, Epil.4 (where τιττιγόνιον cod. Phot., the alphabetical order requiring τιτιγόνιον; τρυγονίῳ codd. AC Ath., cf. ζῷον ὅμοιον τέττιγι καὶ τριγονίῳ Eust.1282.40), prob. cj. in Arist.*HA*556ᵃ20 (where τεττιγόνια, with v.l. τριγόνια, cf. τιγόνιον· εἶδός τι Ἀριστοτέλει, Hsch., τιγόνιον· ἐπὶ νηπίου τίθεται, Phot); the word is correctly written in *EM*760.47, Paus.Gr.*Fr.* 87 (ap.Eust.396.2, where it is rightly connected with τιτίζω: it is prob. Dim. of *τιτιγών (τιτιγών: τιτίζω, = ὀλολυγών: ὀλολύζω, = τρυγών: τρύζω)). (Perh. to be restored for *tetogonia*, v. l. *tetigometrae*, in Plin.*HN*11.92.)

**τῑτίζω**, like πιππίζω, *cry 'ti, ti', cheep* like a young bird; τιτίζοντας was the reading of Zenod. for τετριγῶτας in Il.2.314. (Onomatop.)

**τῑτίς**, ίδος, ἡ, *a small chirping bird*, Phot. II. *pudendum muliebre*, Id. III. *full-sized bath-tub*, Alex.Trall.8.2, prob. cj. in *Febr.*2 (τίναν and τιτάδα codd.).

**τιτλάρια**, τά, a kind of *writing-tablets*, Arr.*Epict.*3.22.74 (as Dufresne for τιλλάρια, which is glossed γραφεῖα by Sch.; τυλάρια cj. Coraës); cf. *Et.Gud.*530.42.

⊕ **τίτλ-ος**, ὁ, Lat. *titulus*, *title, inscription*, *Ev.Jo.*19.20, *IG*2².1121. 26,41 (iv A.D.), al., Lyd.*Mag.*1.19: also the *stone* bearing the inscription, *IG*12(7).259.10 (Amorgos, iii A.D.), *Supp.Epigr.*6.305, al. (Lycaonia), Hsch.: also fem., ἀνεστήσαμεν τὴν τ. ταύτην *Supp.Epigr.*6. 370 (ibid., iv A.D.), cf. 284 (ibid.). 2. *tattoo-mark*, Sch.Hermog. in Rh.7(1).676W. II. *title, section*, Just.*Nov.*29.4. **-όω**, *tattoo* a slave, Sch.Hermog. in Rh.7(1).676W.; *entitle* a book of the Iliad, Eust.731.15.

**τιτουϝέσθω, τιτοϝτός**, v. τιτεύω. **τιτραίνω, τιτράω, τίτρημι**, v. τετραίνω.

⊕ **τιτρώσκω**, Hp.*VC*11 (Act. and Pass.), Pl.*Phlb.*13c, X.*Cyr.*5.4.5; Ep. pres. **τρώω** (v. infr. 3): fut. τρώσω Thgn.1287, Hp.*Mul.*2.133, E.*Cyc.*422, (κατα-) X.*HG*2.4.15: aor. ἔτρωσα Il.23.341, Pi.*N.*10.60, Antipho 3.2.4; Cret. aor. subj. τρωώσῃ, part. τρωωσάντων, *Historia* 5. 219,220 (Gortyn): pf. τέτρωκα Ach.Tat.2.22: plpf. ἐτετρώκει Philostr. *Her.*2.18:—Pass., fut. τρωθήσομαι Pl.*Cri.*51b; also in med. form τρώσομαι Il.12.66: aor. ἐτρώθην Hp.*VC*11, E.*Andr.*616: 3 fut. τετρώσομαι Luc.*Nav.*37: pf. Pass. τέτρωμαι Hdt.8.18, Pi.*P.*3.48, etc.:—*wound*, Il.23.341, Od.16.293, etc.; χαλκῷ μέλη τετρωμένοι Pi.*P.*3. 48; θνῄσκοντας ἢ τετρωμένους A.*Th.*242 (for *Ag.*868, v. τετραίνω); τὸ ἀκόντιον .. ἔτρωσεν αὐτόν Antipho 3.2.4; τιτρώσκεται τὸν μηρόν *is wounded* in the thigh, Hdt.6.5; εἰς τὴν γαστέρα X.*An.*2.5.33: c. acc. cogn., τρῶσαι φόνον *inflict* a death-*wound*, E.*Supp.*1205; τετρωμένους καιρίους (v. l. -ίας) σφαγάς Id.*Ph.*1431. b. *kill*, τετρωμένος *slain*, Lxx *Nu.*31.19. 2. generally, *damage, injure*, τινα Hecat.30J.; τ. πολλὰς [τῶν νεῶν] Th.4.14; αἱ ἡμίσεαι τῶν νεῶν τετρωμέναι Hdt.8.18; τ. ᾠὸν *break* it, Arist.*HA*562ᵇ20. 3. metaph., of wine, *do one a mischief*, οἶνός σε τρώει μελιηδής, ὅς τε καὶ ἄλλους βλάπτει Od.21.293; τρώσει νιν οἶνος E.*Cyc.*422; so of love, ἐπεί μ' ἔρως ἔτρωσεν Id.*Hipp.*392; οἱ καλοὶ τ. X.*Mem.*1.3.13; of a person, τρώσασαν ἡμᾶς *having injured* us, E.*Hipp.*703; τὰ παραδείγματα ἡμᾶς οὐδὲν τιτρώσκει Pl.*Phlb.*13c; διχοστασίῃ τρώει γένος Call.*Dian.*133:—Pass., τετρωμένος τὴν ψυχήν D.S.17.112. 4. = συνουσιάζω, A.*Fr.* 44; cf. τρώζω. 5. γυναῖκα τίκτουσαν ἢ τιτρωσκομένην (τρωσκcod. θ) in childbirth or *miscarriage*, Hp.*Morb.*1.5.

**τιττίο**, barbarism for τιτθίον, Ar.*Th.*1185.

**τιττῠβίζω**, prop. of the cry of the common partridge, distd. from κακκαβίζω (of the Greek partridge), Thphr.*Fr.*181: generally, like τιτίζω, of swallows and other small birds, *twitter, chirrup*, Babr. 131.7: c. acc. cogn., τ. κέλαδον παντομιγῆ *Lyr.Alex.Adesp.*7.5; cf. ἀμφιτιττυβίζω.

**τιτυννός**, f.l. for τυννός in Suid. s.v. ἐκ τιτυννῶν.

**Τῐτῠοκτόνος**, ον, *slaying Tityus*, Call.*Dian.*110, *AP*9.790 (Antip.).

**Τῐτῠός**, ὁ, *Tityus*, Od.7.324, 11.576.

**τιτύρας**· ὄρνις ποιός, Hsch. (cf. τατύρας).

**τῐτύρ-ῐνος** [ῠ] αὐλός, ὁ, a *shepherd's pipe*, Artem.Eph.ap.Ath.4. 182d, cf. Amerias ib.176c, Hsch. **-ίς**, v. Τίτυρος II. 2. **-ιστής**, οῦ, ὁ, *piper*, App.*Pun.*66.

**Τίτῡρος** [ῐ], ὁ, = Σάτυρος, Ael.*VH*3.40; Dor. acc. to Eust.1157. 39; Sicilian for Σιληνοί or Σάτυροι or τράγοι acc. to Sch.Theoc.3.2 (dub. l.); but Str. distinguishes Τίτυροι from Σάτυροι and Σιληνοί, 10.3.15. 2. a common shepherd's name, Theoc.3.2. II. τίτυρος, ὁ, 1. = σάτυρος I. 3, *short-tailed ape*, Thphr.*Char.*5.9, Sch. Theoc. l. c. 2. Lacon. name for *the bell-wether*, Serv. ad Verg.*E. Prooem.*; *he-goat*, Sch.Theoc. l. c.; also called τιτυρίς, Phot. 3. a kind of bird, also τιτύρας, Hsch.; cf. τατύρας. 4. *reed* or *pipe* (cf. τιτύρινος), Id.

**τιτύς**, ά, = τίσις, *penalty*, *GDI*4976 (Gortyn), in gen. τιτυϝος. [Prob. ῑ.]

**τῐτύσκομαι**, Ep. Verb, used only in pres. and impf., combining the senses of the kindred Verbs τεύχω, τυγχάνω. I. like τεύχω, *make, make ready, prepare*, τιτύσκετο πῦρ Il.21.342; ὑπ' ὄχεσφι τιτύσκετο ἵππω *he put* two horses to the chariot, 8.41, 13.23:—later in Act. τιτύσκω, νίκαν Ἱέρωνι τιτύσκων B.5.49, cf. Antim.*Fr.*44, Arat.418, Lyc.1403, Max.279, Opp.*H.*2.99:—Pass., τιτύσκεται Aglaïas 25. II. more freq., *try to hit* (τυχεῖν), *aim, shoot*, τινος *at* a person, τινι *with* a thing, Μηριόνης δ' αὐτοῖο τιτύσκετο δουρὶ Il. 13.159; ἐγχείῃ δ' αὐτοῖο τιτύσκετο 21.582, cf. 3.80, 11.350, etc.: abs., βάλλε τιτυσκόμενος Od.22.118; τιτύσκεσθαι καθ' ὅμιλον Il.13. 498,560; ἄντα τιτύσκεσθαι *aim* straight before one, at a mark right opposite, Od.21.421, 22.266; of one unlocking a door, ἄντα τιτυσκομένη 21.48; χερσὶ τιτυσκόμενος, of a boxer, Theoc.22.88: c. acc. cogn., φώριον ἀλλήλων βλέμμα τιτυσκόμεθα *cast* stolen glances at each other, *AP*5.220 (Paul. Sil.). 2. metaph., φρεσὶ τιτύσκεσθαι *aim at* a thing in mind, i. e. *purpose, design*, c. inf., Il.13.558; of the Phaeacian ships, ὄφρα σε τῇ πέμπωσι τιτυσκόμεναι φρεσὶ νῆες Od.8.556. (From τι-τυχ-σκ- or τι-τυκ-σκ-.)

**τῑτώ**, οῦς, ἡ, = ἡμέρα, *day*, Call.*Fr.*206, Lyc.941.

**τίφη**, ἡ, *one-grained wheat, einkorn*, *Triticum monococcum*, Arist. *HA*603ᵇ26 (pl.), Thphr.*HP*1.6.5, 8.1.1 (pl.), al., Diocl.*Fr.*113 (pl.), Gal.6.791, Plin.*HN*18.93; wrongly glossed by ὄλυρα, Hsch. II. a kind of beetle, Ar.*Ach.*920,925 (cf. Sch.Rav. ad loc., Suid. s. v. θρυαλλίς). 2. = σίλφη I, Poll.7.19, Phryn.268 (Lobeck for τίλφη, confirmed by cod. Laur.), Ael.*NA*8.13. (The quantity of ι is doubtful; pl. τίφαι is written in Thphr.*HP*8.1.1, Diocl. l. c., dat. τιφαῖς Arist. l. c. (v.l. στιφαῖς).)

**τίφθ'**, v. τίπτε.

**τίφινος**, η, ον, *of* τίφη I, Gal.6.504, Orib.1.8.

**τίφιος** [τῐ], α, ον, (τῖφος) *of* or *from the marsh*, ὄρνεα Hsch.

**τῖφος**, εος, τό, *standing water, pond, marsh*, Theoc.25.15, A.R.2.822; ἔγχωρα τίφη Lyc.267.

**τίφυον**, τό, *autumn squill, Scilla autumnalis*, Thphr.*HP*7.13.7 (τό τ' ἴφυον cj. Wimmer), *CP*1.10.5 (pl.).

**Τῖφυς**, ῠος, ὁ, *Tiphys*, the pilot of the ship Argo, Pherecyd.*Fr.*107 J., A.R.1.105, al., Lyc.890 (Ἶφυς A.*Fr.*21 (Ἶφις Schmidt)). II. *nightmare*, Did.ap.Sch.Ar.*V.*1033.

**τῑφώδης**, ες, (τῖφος) *marshy*, χωρίον Str.8.3.19 (τειφ-, τυφ- codd.).

⊛ **τίω**, Il.9.238, etc.; Ep. inf. τιέμεν Od.15.543: impf. ἔτιον Il.5.467, etc.; Ep. τῖον ib.536, 18.81; Trag. τίον A.*Th.*775 (lyr.); Ion. τίεσκον Il.13.461: fut. τίσω 9.142, τείσω Philic. in *Stud.Ital.*9.46 (iii B.C.): aor. ἔτισα Il.1.244, 9.118, al.; poet. τῖσα *Supp.Epigr.*3.553 (Thrace, v A.D.):—**Med.**, Hes.*Th.*428:—**Pass.**, Ion. impf. τιέσκετο Il.4.46; part. τιεσκόμενοι *IGRom.*4.360.12 (Pergam.): pf. τέτιμαι, part. τετιμένος (v. infr.). [In pres. and impf. Hom. uses both ῑ (sts. even in thesi before a long syll., Od.14.84, 22.414) and ῐ, e.g. τιέσκετο Il.4.46, τίω ib.257, 9.378 (but τῖω ib.238, al.); τειόμενοι is written in Keil-Premerstein *Erster Bericht* p.9 (Troketta); always short in Trag.: in fut., aor., and pf. Pass. ῑ always, v. fin.]:—poet. Verb, used like τιμάω, *honour, revere*, of the bearing of men towards gods, οὐδέ τι τίει ἀνέρας οὐδὲ θεούς (sc. Ἕκτωρ) Il.9.238; ὅτε με βροτοὶ οὔ τι τίουσιν, says Poseidon, Od.13.129, etc.; also of the gods towards men, ὃν ἀθάνατοί περ ἔτισαν (sc. Ἀχιλλέα) Il.9.110, cf. 1.508; ὁ πόντιος Ὀρσοτρίαινά νιν περίαλλα βροτῶν τίεν Pi.*Pae.*9.48 (so in Med., Ζεὺς τίεται αὐτήν Hes. l. c.); but more freq. of the respect paid by men to other men, kings, friends, guests, etc., ὅν τ' ἶσον ἐτίομεν Ἕκτορι δίῳ Il.5.467, cf. 9.142; οἵ σε θεὸν ὣς τίσουσ' ib.303; ἶσον γάρ σε θεῷ τίσουσιν Ἀχαιοί ib.603; ὁ δέ μιν τίεν ἶσα τέκεσσι 13.176, cf. 15.439; ὃν Τρῶες δμῶς Πριάμοιο τέκεσσι τῖον 5.536; ἄριστον Ἀχαιῶν οὐδὲν ἔτισας 1.244; οὐδέ με τυτθὸν ἔτισεν ib.354; τ. ξεῖνον Od.15.543; τ. τινὰ φιλότητι Il.9.631; opp. ἀτιμάω, ib.110, Od.16.306, 20.132; also of things, θεοὶ δίκην τίουσι they *honour* right, 14.84:—Pass., θεὸς δ' ὣς τίετο δήμῳ Il.5.78, etc.; τιοίμην δ' ὡς τίετ' Ἀθηναίη 8.540, 13.827; τάων μοι περὶ κῆρι τιέσκετο Ἴλιος ἱρή 4.46: esp. pf. part. Pass. τετιμένος *honoured*, of persons, οὔτε θεοῖσι τετιμένος οὔτε βροτοῖσιν 24.533, cf. Hes.*Th.*415; λαοῖσι τ. Od.13.28, etc.:—also in Trag. (never in S.), but only pres. and impf. in this sense, the other tenses being supplied from τιμάω, πόλις.. δαίμονας τίει A.*Th.*77; θεοὺς αἰεὶ τίοιεν.. βουθύτοισι τιμαῖς Id.*Supp.*705 (lyr.); Ἑρμᾶν.. τίομεν Id.*Fr.*273 (hex.); τὸν θεὸν μεῖζον τίουσα τῆς ἐμῆς ἔχθρας E.*Heracl.*1013; of persons, ὅσον τότ' Οἰδίπουν τίον A.*Th.*775 (lyr.); τίειν γυναῖκα Id.*Ag.*259; of things, τ. νίκην, βρότεα, ib.942, *Eu.*171 (lyr.); μέλος τ. *honour* (i.e. sing) the strain, Id.*Ag.*706 (lyr.):—Pass., τίεσθαι δ' ἀξιώτατος βροτῶν ib.531. II. = τιμάω II, *value, rate*, τὸν δὲ [τρίποδα] δυωδεκάβοιον.. τῖον Ἀχαιοί they *valued* it at twelve steers' *worth*, Il.23.703; τίον δέ ἑ τεσσαράβοιον *valued* her at four steers' *worth*, ib.705; τίω δέ μιν ἐν καρὸς αἴσῃ (v. κάρ) 9.378; λόγων τείσομεν ἔργα κρείσσω Philic. l. c. (Root τῑ-, cf. τῑ-μή, πολύ-τῑ-τος: I.-E. $q^{u}\bar{\imath}$- (full grade $q^{u}\bar{e}y$-) 'revere, honour', cf. Skt. *cāyati* 'respect', *cāyús* 'showing respect': not cogn. with τίνω or τίνυμαι (τείνυμαι): the fut. and aor. τίσω ἔτισα are so written in codd. whether they belong to τίω or to τίνω; this spelling is wrong for the fut. and aor. of τίνω (q. v.), but may be right for the fut. and aor. of τίω, if τείσομεν in Philic. l. c. is an error; the pr. names beginning with Τεισ- may all be derived fr. τίνω.)

**τίω, τίως**, Dor. forms for σοῦ, v. σύ. **τλάθυμος**, v. τλήθυμος. **τλαιπαθής**, ές, = τληπαθής, Hsch. **τλάμων**, v. τλήμων. **τλᾱσίφρων**, v. τλησίφρων.

***τλάω**, never found in pres. (exc. in very late writers, as Tz.*H.*9.133), this tense being supplied by the pf. τέτλαμεν, etc., or by τολμάω: fut. τλήσομαι Il.11.317, A.*Ag.*1290; Aeol. and Dor. τλάσομαι Sapph.75, Pi.*P.*3.41; later fut. ταλάσσω Lyc.746: Ep. aor. 1 ἐτάλασσα Il.17.166; subj. ταλάσσω 13.829, 15.164 (an aor. Med. ταλάσσατο, Opp.*C.*3.155); inf. τελάσσαι Hsch. (cf. τελα-μών): but the usu. aor. was ἔτλην, Il.18.433, etc., Ep. τλῆν 5.385, al., Dor. ἔτλᾱν A.*Ag.*224 (lyr.), etc.; 3 pl. ἔτλησαν E.*Supp.*171, Dor. ἔτλᾱσαν S.*Ph.*1201 (lyr.), Ep. ἔτλᾰν Il.21.608, Simon.107.7 (= *IG*7.53); imper. τλῆθι Thgn.1237, Orac.ap.Hdt.5.56, S.*Ph.*475, etc., Dor. τλᾶθι Pi.*P.*4.276; 2 sg. subj. τλῇς A.*Supp.*428 (lyr.); opt. τλαίην, 3 pl. τλαῖεν Il.17.490; inf. τλῆναι A.*Pr.*704, Ep. τλήμεναι Theoc.25.174; part. τλάς, τλᾶσα, A.*Ag.*1453 (lyr.), *Ch.*753, S.*OC*1077 (lyr.): pf. τέτληκα, in 2 sg., Il.1.228, 543, Ar.*Pl.*280, *Th.*544, 3 sg., Od.19.347; in shorter forms with pres. sense, Ep. 1 pl. τέτλαμεν 20.311; imper. τέτλᾰθι Il.5.382, τετλάτω Od.16.275; opt. τετλαίην Il.9.373; Ep. inf. τετλάμεναι Od.13.307, τετλάμεν 6.190, τετλάναι Metag.18 (hex.); Ep. part. τετληώς, fem. τετληυῖα Od.20.23, masc. dat. τετληότι 4.447, al., pl. τετληότες Il.5.873, -ῶτες Orph.*A.*1350: plpf. ἐτέτλαμεν A.R.1.807:—poet. Verb, used by Isoc.4.96 (quoted by Arist.*Rh.*1408ᵇ16), X.*Cyr.*3.1.3; but τολμάω is the common prose form (cf. τλήμων): I. *suffer, undergo* hardship, disgrace, etc. (never like φέρω, of bodily loads or burdens): 1. abs., ***hold out, endure, be patient, submit***, ἤτοι ἐγὼ μενέω καὶ τλήσομαι Il.11.317, cf. 19.308; ἔτι τλαίης ἐνιαυτόν Od.1.288, cf. 2.219; esp. in imper., τέτλαθι, μῆτερ ἐμή, καὶ ἀνάσχεο Il.1.586; τλῆτε, φίλοι 2.299; τέτλαθι δή, κραδίη Od.20.18: so in inf., σὺ δὲ τετλάμεναι καὶ ἀνάγκῃ 13.307: in part., τετληότι θυμῷ 4.447, etc.; κραδίη τετληυῖα 20.23: sts. folld. by a relat. clause, τλῆ μὲν Ἄρης, ὅτε μιν.. δῆσαν Il.5.385, cf. 392; δηρὸν ἐτέτλαμεν εἴ κε.. μεταστρέψωσι νόον A.R. l. c. 2. c. acc. rei, ἔτλην ἀνέρος εὐνήν *I submitted* to be wedded to a man, Il.18.433; ῥίγιστα.. τετληότες εἰμέν 5.873; τλῆ δ' Ἀΐδης.. ὀϊστόν *bore up under* the wound from it, ib.395; ἔτλαν πένθος Pi.*I.*7(6).37; οἷα χρὴ πάθη τλῆναι πρὸς Ἥρας A.*Pr.*704, cf. *Ag.*1453 (lyr.), *Ch.*753, S.*OC*1077 (lyr.), *Tr.*71, E.*Hec.*1251. II. c. inf., *dare* or *venture to do*, οὔτε λόχονδ' ἰέναι τέτληκας θυμῷ Il.1.228, cf. 7.480, 21.150, etc.; *bring oneself to do something contrary to one's feelings*, whether good or bad, *have the courage, hardihood, effrontery, cruelty*, or *the grace, charity, patience*, to do anything, ἔστε δὴ πατρὶ ἔτλην γεγωνεῖν νυκτίφοιτα δείματα *I took courage* to.., A.*Pr.*657; ἔτλα θυτὴρ γενέσθαι θυγατρός Id.*Ag.*224 (lyr.); ἔτλα.. φῶς ἀλλάξαι *submitted* to exchange.., S.*Ant.*944 (lyr.); πῶς ἔτλης σὰς ὄψεις μαρᾶναι; how *couldst thou* quench thy orbs of sight? Id.*OT*1327; οὐδ' ἔτλης.. ἐφυβρίσαι nor *hadst thou the cruelty* to.., Id.*Aj.*1384; μὴ τλῇς με προδοῦναι *be* not *so cruel* as to forsake me, E.*Alc.*275 (anap.); οὐ γὰρ ἂν τλαίην ἰδεῖν *I could* not *bear* to see, Ar.*Nu.*119, cf. 1387 (lyr.), *V.*1159, *Pl.*280; so also in Il.24.35, 505, 519, Hes.*Op.*718, Sapph.75, Pi.*P.*3.41, etc. 2. c. acc. rei, *dare* a thing, i.e. *dare to do* it, ἄτλητα τλᾶσα A.*Ag.*408 (lyr.). 3. c. part., τάδε τέτλαμεν εἰσορόωντες Od.20.311 (but in 5.362, Il.5.383 the part. is independent of the Verb), cf. Simon.85.14, A.*Ag.*1041 (s.v.l.), *Th.*756 (lyr.), S.*El.*943. (Root τελᾰ- (τᾰλᾰ-) alternating with τλᾱ-: also in πολύ-τλας, τάλας, τάλαντον, τολμάω, τελαμών, Lat. *tollo*, OE. *þolian* 'endure', etc.)

**τλήθα**· ὡραία, Κυρηναῖοι, Hsch.

**τλήθῡμος**, Dor. τλάθ- [ᾱ], ον, *of enduring soul, stout-hearted*, Ὀδυσσεύς *AP*9.472; τ. κύων a *staunch* hound, Pi.*Fr.*234; ἀλκὰ παγκρατίου τ. Id.*N.*2.15.

**τλημοσύνη**, ἡ, *misery, distress*, in pl., *h.Ap.*191. II. *endurance*, Archil.9.6, Plu.*Crass.*26.

⊛ **τλήμων**, Dor. τλάμων [ᾱ], ονος, ὁ, ἡ: voc. τλῆμον A.*Pr.*614, but ἰὼ τλάμων S.*Aj.*893 (lyr.); τλήμων ἀνήρ (ἄνερ codd.) E.*Andr.*348, cf. *Hipp.*554 (lyr.): (*τλάω):—poet. Adj., used by X. and Aret. (v. infr.): I. *patient, steadfast, stout-hearted*, ὁ τλήμων Ὀδυσεύς Il.10.231, 498 (to whom a τλήμων θυμός is ascribed, 5.670); θαρσαλέοι καὶ τ. 21.430; ψυχὴν καὶ θυμὸν τλήμονα παρθέμενος Tyrt.12.18; τλάμονι ψυχᾷ Pi.*P.*1.48; τλήμονες, οἷον ἀγῶνα.. τελέσαντες.. ψυχὰς.. ὠλέσατ' *Ath.Mitt.*57.142 (Athens, v B.C.); τλήμων οὐδ' ἀπ' εὐτόλμου φρενὸς A.*Ag.*1302; of patients, Aret.*CD*1.4; τ. ἐς παιδείην Id.*SD*2.6: Sup. -εστάτη E.*Heracl.*570. 2. in bad sense, *overbold, reckless*, Thgn.196; τλάμονι καὶ πανούργῳ χειρί A.*Ch.*384 (lyr.); τλημονεστάτη γυνή S.*El.*439, cf. 275, A.*Ch.*596 (lyr.); τλάμονι θυμῷ E.*Med.*865 (lyr.). II. *wretched, miserable*, of persons, A.*Pr.*614, S.*Ph.*161 (anap.), Ar.*Pax*723, X.*An.*3.1.29, *Mem.*2.1.30: c. gen., ὦ τλάμων ὑμεναίων E.*Hipp.*554 (lyr.); θανάτου τλήμων Ar.*Th.*1072 (anap.). 2. of conditions, acts, words, etc., τλήμονες φυγαί, τύχαι, E.*Hipp.*1177, *HF*921 (lyr.); τλημονέστατος λόγος Id.*Hec.*562; ὁδὸς τλημονεστάτη, -τέρα, Id.*Med.*1067, 1068: sts. also, as we use *wretched*, in a disparaging sense, τ. γαστρὸς ἔριθον *h.Merc.*296; οἶνος Call.*Epigr.*62. III. Adv. τλημόνως *patiently*, A.*Ch.*748, E.*Supp.*947, Gal.14.213. 2. *miserably*, E.*Tr.*40, Hsch.

**τληπάθ-εια** [πᾰ], ἡ, *patience, endurance*, Sor.1.3, Hierocl. *in CA* 11 p.442 M. **-έω**, *endure misery*, Hdn.*Epim.*134, Hsch. II. *labour*, τληπαθεῖ (sc. ἡ φύσις) πρὸς τὴν τοῦ ζῴου σωτηρίαν Sever.*Clyst.*7. **-ημα**, ατος, τό, *wretchedness*, Sch.rec.A.*Pr.*688 (pl.). **-ής**, ές, = ταλαίπωρος, *wretched, enduring*, Zos.4.50, Sch.rec.A.*Pr.*231, *Pers.*574, etc.

**τλησί-κάρδιος**, ον, *hard-hearted*, A.*Pr.*160 (lyr.). II. *enduring*, ⟨ἀ⟩πένθεια (v. Addenda) τ. Id.*Ag.*430 (lyr.; τηξικάρδιος Auratus from Sch., τὴν καρδίαν τήκουσα). Cf. ταλακάρδιος. **-πονος**, ον, *patient of toil*, Opp.*C.*4.4, *H.*1.35.

**τλῆσις**, εως, ἡ, *audacity*, Hsch. **τλησίφρων**, ον, gen. ονος, (φρήν) = τλήθυμος, Id. (in Dor. form τλᾱσ-).

**τλη-τέος**, α, ον, *that must be endured*, Orph.*Fr.*47. **-τικός**, ή, όν, *patient*, Ph.1.193; gloss on ταλαίπωρος, Sch.Ar.*Pl.*33: Comp., Ph.1.591: Sup., ib.664. Adv. -κῶς ib.543, al., Hsch. **-τός**, ή, όν, Dor. τλᾱτός, ά, όν: I. Act., *patient, steadfast in suffering* or *labour*, θυμός Il.24.49. II. Pass., *to be endured*, always with neg., οὐ τ. not *to be endured, intolerable*, οὐ γὰρ δή που τοῦτό γε τλητὸν.. ἔπος A.*Pr.*1065 (anap.); οὐκ ἔστι τοὔργον τ. S.*Aj.*466; οὐ τλητὸν [ἐστι], c. inf., E.*Med.*797, *Alc.*887 (anap.).

**τμάγεν**, v. τμήγω.

**τμήγας**· γατόμος, ἀροτήρ, Hsch. **τμῆγος**· ἀρότης (quod delendum), βουτμῆμα, i.e. *furrow*, Id.

⊛ **τμήγω**, Nic.*Fr.*72, D.P.1043, Man.2.75: fut. τμήξω (ἀπο-) Parm.2: aor. 1 ἔτμηξα *IG*5(2).473 (Megalop., iii A.D.); Dor. ἔτμαξα Theoc.8.24 (prob.): aor. 2 δι-έτμᾰγον Od.7.276:—Med., aor. ἐτμηξάμην Nic.*Al.*68, *AP*7.480 (Leon.):—**Pass.**, aor. 2 ἐτμάγην [ᾰ] in Ep. 3 pl. τμάγεν (cf. διατμήγω) Il.16.374; later ἐτμήγην Call.*Fr.*300, *AP*9.661 (Jul.): more freq. in comp. with ἀπό or διά:—Ep. collat. form of τέμνω, *cut, cleave*, σικύας, πυετίην, Nic. ll. cc.; κάλαμος [δάκτυλον] ἔτμαξεν prob. in Theoc. l. c.; *cut*, of a circle, Man. l. c.:—Med., ὁδὸν ἐτμήξαντο *cut their way*, *AP*7. l. c. 2. metaph. in aor. 2 Pass., *to be divided* or *dispersed, part*, ἐπεὶ ἄρ τμάγεν Il. l. c.

**τμήδην**, Adv., (τέμνω) *with cutting, so as to cut*, Il.7.262.

⊛ **τμῆ-μα**, ατος, τό, (τέμνω) *part cut off, section, piece*, Pl.*Smp.*191d, al.;

*segment* of a line, Id.*R.*509d, Euc.2.11, etc.; of a circle (i.e. portion cut off by a chord), Arist.*Metaph.*1035ᵃ34 (pl.), *APr.*41ᵇ18, *Mete.* 343ᵃ12, Euc.3 *Def.*6, etc.; also of the portion cut off by radii, *sector*, τὰ ἀφαιρούμενα ὑπὸ τῶν ἐκ τοῦ κέντρου [τμήματα] Arist.*Cael.*290ᵃ3, cf. Str.2.5.34; of *lunes*, ὁ τετραγωνισμὸς ὁ διὰ τῶν τμημάτων Arist.*Ph.* 185ᵃ16; of *segments* of other figures cut off by straight lines or planes, Democr.155, Archim.*Con.Sph.Prooem.*, al.; and of *segments* bounded by a circle and a circumscribed polygon, Papp.316.2. 2. *cut, incision, wound*, Pl.*Grg.*476c. 3. *section* of a book, Ps.-Ammon. *in APr.*67.39. 4. Astrol., *division* between two zodiacal signs, Serapio in *Cat.Cod.Astr.*8(4).230. **-μάτιον**, τό, *small piece*, γῆς Eust.1171.33. **-μᾰτώδης**, ες, *endued with a quality of cutting* or *parting*, Hp.*Loc.Hom.*45.

**τμῆσις**, εως, ἡ, (τέμνω) *cutting*, Arist.*de An.*412ᵇ28; τάφρων *PHal.* 1.107 (iii B.C.). 2. (τέμνω IV. 3) *ravaging*, γῆς Ἑλληνικῆς Pl.*R.* 470a. 3. *logical division*, Id.*Plt.*276d. II. = τμῆμα, *section*, Id.*Smp.*190e.

**τμησίχρους**, ουν, = ταμεσίχρως, ἀνέπτυξε ποιητικῶς τὸ τμησίχροας Sch.Il.13.340.

**τμη-τέον**, (τέμνω) *one must cut*, διχῇ Pl.*Sph.*219d, cf. *R.*510b. **-τήρ**, ῆρος, ὁ, *one who cuts* or *severs, destroyer*, Nonn.*D.*26.303: c. gen., ib.14.311: as Adj., σίδηρος ib.13.481. **-τής**, οῦ, ὁ, *one who cuts*, gloss on ἐκτομεύς, Hsch. ※ **-τικός**, ή, όν, *able to cut, cutting*, κίσηρις Thphr.*Lap.*22; -ώτατος Pl.*Ti.*56a, Sor.1.80; τὸ τ. Arist. *Metaph.*1020ᵇ29. Adv. -κῶς, gloss on τμήδην, Sch.D Il.7.262. 2. *cutting, piercing*, of cold, Thphr.*CP*5.13.7; *biting, pungent*, of smell, μύρα Id.*Od.*60(62); πνεῦμα δριμὺ καὶ τ. Plu.2.697b. b. *solvent*, τὰ δριμέα.. ἐστιν τ. καὶ λεπτυντικά Sor.1.46, cf. Gal.6.266 (Sup.), 11.41 (Comp.), al.; ῥάφανος τ. χυμῶν Alex.Aphr.*Pr.*1.42. 3. metaph., *concise, trenchant*, λόγος Hermog.*Id.*2.1; τ. βραχυλογίᾳ D.H.*Dem.*58. Adv. -κῶς, λέγεσθαι κατὰ τὸ μῆκος Hermog. l.c. **-τός**, ή, όν, *cut, shaped by cutting*, τ. ἱμάντες S.*El.*747, E.*Hipp.*1245; τμητοῖς ὁλκοῖς S.*El.*863 (lyr.); τυρὸς τ. Antiph.133.9 (anap.), cf. Anaxandr. 30.1. 2. *that can be cut* or *severed*, ὡς τὸ τμητικὸν πρὸς τὸ τμητόν Arist.*Metaph.*1020ᵇ29, cf. *Mete.*387ᵃ7, Theoc.25.275.

**τμητοσίδηρος** [ῐ], ον, *cut down with iron*, ὕλη *AP*14.19.

**Τμῶλος**, ὁ, *Mount Tmolus* in Lydia, Il.2.866, etc.; also **Τύμωλος** in St.Byz.; παραὶ νιφόεντι Τυμώλῳ Keil-Premerstein *Erster Bericht* p.9 (Troketta); hence φυλὴ **Τυμωλίς** *IGRom.*4.1503 (Sardis); **Τυμωλεῖ[ται]**, οἱ, *inhabitants of T., Sardis* 7(1) No.152; and **Τυμωλειτική**, ἡ, *jar* of fish-sauce *from T.*, *POxy.*1759.8, 1760.14 (ii A.D.): Dim. **-ίκιον**, τό, *PFay.*104.23 (iii A.D.):—**Τμωλίτης** [ῑ], ου, ὁ, *inhabitant of T.*, *CIG*3142 iii 21 (Smyrna); οἶνος **Τιμωλίτης** (sic) wine *of Tmolus*, Gal.6.802 (cf. Lat. *Timolus*, Ov.*Met.*6.15, Plin.*HN*5. 110):—Adj. **Τμώλιος**, α, ον, Diog.Ath.1.7.

**τοάκης**· χιτὼν σχιστός, Hsch. **τόβλικος**· κρουματίου μίμησις, Id. **τογέρα**· μοιχός, λαλαχός, Id.

**τόθεν**, poet. Adv., answering to relat. ὅθεν and interrog. πόθεν (from το-, Demonstr. stem):—*thence*, Hes.*Sc.*32; Δρεπάνη τόθεν ἐκλήϊσται *thence* it is called D., A.R.4.990. 2. for ὅθεν, A.*Pers.* 99 (lyr.). II. *thereafter, thereupon*, Id.*Ag.*220 (lyr.); also ἐκ τόθεν, ἐξότε.. *from the day when..*, A.R.4.520.

**τόθι**, poet. Adv., answering to relat. ὅθι and interrog. πόθι:—*there, in that place*, Od.15.239, *h.Ap.*244, Pi.*P.*9.59, al., A.R.1.210 (nisi leg. τότε). 2. also for relat. ὅθι, *where*, *h.Pan.*25, Mimn.11.5, Pi.*N.*4.52, B.3.19, Theoc.22.199, A.R.4.1475, etc.

**τοι**, prop. ethical dative of σύ (q.v.), but used as an enclit. Particle, *let me tell you, mark you, look you* (in Engl. we freq. convey the impression by means of emphasis or tone), implying a real or imagined audience, freq. in Hom. and always in speeches (exc. ὃς δή τοι Il.10.316, Od.20.289), αἰσχρόν τοι δηρόν τε μένειν κτλ. Il.2. 298; ἀλλ' ἐφομαρτεῖτε· πλεόνων δέ τοι ἔργον ἄμεινον 12.412 codd.; τοῦτο δέ τοι ἐρέουσα ἔπος.. εἶμι *surely* I will go, 1.419; ταύτης τοι γενεῆς.. εὔχομαι εἶναι (recapitulating) 6.211 (so at the close of a narrative, Theoc.11.80); οὗτός τοι.. ἀπὸ στρατοῦ ἔρχεται ἀνήρ here comes, *look you..*, Il.10.341 (vulg., οὗτός τις Aristarch., etc.); freq. it is hard to dist. from the Ep. dat., as in ποῦ τοι ἀπειλαὶ οἴχονται; 13.219; so in Hes.*Op.* (addressed to Perses) 287,347,719, cf. Emp.17.14 (addressed to Pausanias), Pi.*P.*2.72 (addressed to Hiero), al.; and so in Trag. dialogue, A.*Eu.*729, etc.; σέ τοι κικλήσκω S.*OC*1578 (lyr.); betw. chorus and actor, Id.*Ph.*855 (lyr.), etc.; folld. by a plural, Tyrt.10. 11 (cf. 13); so ἄρσενάς τοι τῆσδε γῆς οἰκήτορας εὑρήσετε A.*Supp.*952: hence, as addressed to an imaginary audience, without personal reference, introducing a general sentiment or maxim, Thgn.153; τὸ συγγενές τοι δεινόν A.*Pr.*39, al. II. in subordinate clauses, 1. temporal and causal, ἐπεί τοι *h.Merc.*138, Pi.*I.*2.45, S.*Tr.*321; freq. ἐπεί τοι καί E.*Med.*677, Ar.*Ach.*933, Pl.*Tht.*142b, etc.; ὅτι τοι Id.*R.*343a. 2. conditional, εἴ τοι.., ἐὰν δέ τοι.., S.*OT*549,551, *Ant.*327; in apodosi, εἰ γὰρ κτενοῦμεν.., σύ τοι πρώτη θάνοις ἄν Id.*El.*582, cf. Il.22.488. 3. final, ὅπως.. τοι S.*El.*1469, cf. Hp.*Morb.*2.33. III. freq. combined with other Particles, ἀλλά τοι Thgn.656, Pi.*P.*3.19, etc.; ἀλλὰ .. τοι A.*Pers.*795, *Ag.*1304, etc.; γάρ τοι (γάρ A. II. 9); γέ τοι (γε I. 5); ἤτοι, καίτοι (v. sub vv.); μέν τοι (μέν B. II. 4); μή τοι, οὔ τοι; cf. also τοιγάρ, τοιγάρτοι, τοιγαροῦν, τοίνυν; so in τοι ἄρα, τοι ἆρα, which however are mostly contracted by crasis into τἄρα; as also τοι ἄν into τἄν, μέντοι ἄν into μεντἄν.

B. Position: τοι usually stands early in the sentence (or clause), e.g. Ζεύς ἐστιν αἰθήρ, Ζεὺς δὲ γῆ, Ζεὺς δ' οὐρανός, Ζεύς τοι τὰ πάντα A.*Fr.*70, etc. 2. hence τοι is sts. placed betw. Art. and Subst. or Adj., or betw. Prep. and Subst., τό τ. μέγιστον Pl.*Sph.*261c; ἐπί τ. Ἀκράγαντι Pi.*O.*2.90, cf. Ar.*Ec.*972, etc.; also after Prep. in compd. Verb, ἔκ τ. πέπληγμαι E.*Hipp.*934, cf. *Or.*1047, Ar.*V.*784. 3. τοι repeated, σύ τ. σύ τ. κατηξίωσας S.*Ph.*1095 (lyr.).

**τοι**, Dor., Aeol., Ion., and Ep. dat. sg. of σύ (q.v.).

**τοί, ταί**, Ep. and poet. for οἱ or οἵ, αἱ or αἵ, nom. pl. of ὁ and ὅ, freq. in Hom. (relat., Od.3.73, 12.63, more freq. demonstr.), not in Ion. Prose, rare in Trag., e.g. A.*Pers.*424: but in Dor. and certain other dialects as the Article, Ἰάρων.. καὶ τοὶ Συρακόσιοι *SIG*35 *Ba* (Olympia, v B.C.), etc.

**τοιαυτί**, strengthd. form of τοιαῦτα, Pherecr.153.10, Ar.*Eq.*49.

**τοιγάρ**, an inferential Particle, *therefore, accordingly, well then*, κέλεαί με.. μυθήσασθαι μῆνιν Ἀπόλλωνος..· τοιγὰρ ἐγὼν ἐρέω Il.1.76, cf. 10.427, Od.3.254, 8.402, A.*Supp.*309, *Th.*1038, *Pers.*607, S.*Ant.* 931 (anap.), 994, *Aj.*666, etc.; rare in Com. (Ar.*Lys.*516 (anap.), 901,902) and Prose (Hdt.8.114, Hp.*Cord.*10 (s.v.l.)); never in Att. Prose. II. strengthd. by other Particles, **τοιγαροῦν**, Ion. **τοιγαρῶν**, *for that very reason, therefore*, Hdt.4.149, Pl.*Sph.*234e, 246b, X.*An.*1.9.9, al., D.18.40, Arist.*Pol.*1271ᵇ3, etc.; also in Poets, as S.*Aj.*490, *OT*1519 (troch.), *Ph.*341, Ar.*V.*1098, etc. 2. **τοιγάρτοι**, Hdt.3.3, Th.6.38, And.1.108, Pl.*Phd.*82d, etc.; rare in Poets, Emp. 145, A.*Supp.*654 (lyr.), Ar.*Ach.*643 (anap.):—Hom. always inserts a word between τοιγάρ and τοι, τοιγὰρ ἐγώ τοι Il.10.413, Od.1.179, 214, al.—These forms must begin the sentence, exc. in late Gr., where τοιγαροῦν may be postponed, as Cleom.1.8, Wilcken *Chr.*491. 7 (ii A.D.), Gal.*Libr.Ord.*2, Vett.Val.356.3, *Sammelb.*6222.12 (iii A.D.), Jul.*Caes.*318d. (It is doubtful whether τοι- contains the demonstr. stem το-.)

**τοιθορύσσω**, *shake violently*, with fem. Subst. **τοιθορύκτρια**, Hsch. (cf. τανθαρύζω). **τοῖιν**, v. ὁ, ἡ, τό. **τοῖν**· τί ποτε, Κρῆτες, Hsch. **τοινί**, Arc., = τῷδε, v. ὁνί.

**τοίνυν**, (τοι, νυν) *therefore, accordingly*, an inferential Particle (never in Hom. or Hes.), χρὴ τ. πύλας ὕμνων ἀναπιτνάμεν Pi.*O.*6.27, etc.; εἰ τ... Hdt.1.57; ἂν τ... D.4.7; introducing a logical conclusion (less freq. than οὖν), Pl.*Chrm.*159d; φανερὸν τ., δῆλον τ., Arist.*Pol.*1260ᵃ2, *PA*641ᵃ15; also to introduce a minor premiss, or a particular instance of a general proposition, Pl.*Cra.*399b, Isoc.4. 103, etc. 2. in dialogue, to introduce an answer, *well* or *well then*, ἄπειμι τ. S.*El.*1050, cf. Th.5.89, etc.; esp. an answer which has been led up to by the same speaker, Pl.*Men.*76a, *IG*4²(1).121.31 (Epid., iv B.C.); in response to an invitation to speak, Ar.*Nu.*961, etc.; in expression of approval, esp. in phrase καλῶς τ. Pl.*Cra.*433a, etc.; κάλλιστα τ. Ar.*V.*856; also of disapproval or criticism, ἀπόλοιο τ. Id. *Nu.*1236, cf. S.*OT*1067. 3. continuing an argument, *well then*, Pl.*Smp.*178d, X.*An.*3.1.36, 7.7.28, etc. b. resuming the thread of argument or narrative after a break, Pl.*R.*562b, *Plt.*275d, D.47. 64, etc. c. adding or passing to a fresh item or point, *further, moreover, again*, Pl.*Ap.*33c, D.8.73, 20.18; ἔτι τ. Hp.*VM*19, Pl.*Phd.* 109a, *Cri.*52c, D.20.8; καὶ τ. X.*Cyr.*2.2.25; καὶ τ. καί Pl.*Sph.*234a; μὴ τ. μηδέ.. *nay*, not even.., X.*An.*7.6.19; οὐ τ. οὐδέ *nor again*, Hp.*Art.*57, D.20.7. 4. sts. at the beginning of a speech, ἐγὼ μὲν τ..., referring to something present to the minds of the speaker and hearer, *now I..*, X.*An.*5.1.2, cf. *Cyr.*6.2.14. 5. with subj. of exhortation or imper., in signfs. 1,2,3, εὖ τ. ἐπίστασθε.. Id.*An.*3.1.36, cf. *Cyr.*2.4.8, *Ev.Luc.*20.25, etc.

B. Position: in early writers τοίνυν is never the first word in a sentence, but this is not uncommon in later authors, as Lxx *Is.*3. 10, *Mim.Oxy.*413.225, *Ev.Luc.* l.c., *Ep.Hebr.*13.13, Gal.2.526, S.E. *M.*8.429, *AP*11.127 (Poll.), *IG*4.620.13 (Argos), Chor.32.34 F.-R. cod. (⟨τῷ⟩ add. Kaibel); it is usually placed second, but sts. later, ἧκω φέρουσα συμβολὰς τ. ἅμα Alex.143.1, cf. Ar.*Pl.*863, etc. [ῠ regularly, as A.*Pr.*760, S.*Tr.*71: but sts. ῡ, as Ar.*Eq.*1259, Alex. l.c.; in anap., Ar.*Nu.*429,435, *Av.*481.]

**τοῖο**, Ion. and Ep. gen. sg. of ὁ, Hom.

※ **τοῖος**, τοία (Ion. τοίη), τοῖον:—demonstr. Pron., corresponding to the relat. οἷος, interrog. ποῖος, and indef. ποιός, *such, such-like*, common in Poets, but rare in Prose (where τοιόσδε or τοιοῦτος is used, v. infr.): prop. τοῖος requires an answering clause with οἷος, τοῖος ἐών, οἷος οὔ τις Ἀχαιῶν (sc. ἐστίν) Il.18.105, cf. Od.4.342, al.; τοῖος ἐών, οἷόν κε.. ἴδησθε ib.421, cf. 1.257, al.; οὐ γάρ πω τοίους ἴδον.., οἷον Πειρίθοον (= οἷος Πειρίθοος ἦν) Il.1.262; οἵηπερ φύλλων γενεή, τοίη δὲ (not τοιήδε) καὶ ἀνδρῶν 6.146: for οἷος we have ὁποῖος, Od.17.421; or simple relat. Pron., ἡμεῖς δ' εἰμὲν τοῖοι, οἳ ἂν σέθεν ἀντιάσαιμεν Il.7.231 (v. infr.), cf. 17.164, 24.153,182, Od.2. 286, al.: rarely a Conj. instead of a relat. Adj., τοῖον ὅπως ἐθέλει *such as..*, 16.208: but τοῖος is sts. abs., referring to something mentioned earlier, Il.4.289,390,399, 5.828, 17.170, Pi.*I.*6(5).14, A.*Eu.* 378 (lyr.), S.*Aj.*562, Ar.*Ra.*470 (paratrag.), etc. 2. with qualifying words, τεύχεσι τοῖον Il.5.450; τ... ἐν πολέμῳ 18.105; τ. ἰδεῖν Thgn.216. 3. in early Prose writers only used in such phrases as τοῖος ἢ τοῖος Pl.*R.*429b, 437e; τοῖα καὶ τοῖα Id.*Phdr.* 271d, cf. Longin.27.1; οἱ μὲν τ. οἱ δὲ τ. Epicur.*Ep.*1 p.14 U., cf. Arr. *Epict.*3.16.11; οὐ μᾶλλον τοῖον ἢ τοῖον εἶναι Plu.2.1108f, al.: in late Prose used alone, S.E.*P.*1.228, *M.*7.197, Ael.*NA*1.41, *POxy.*903.14 (iv A.D.). II. τοῖος c. inf., *such as* to do, i.e. *fit* or *able* to do, τοῖοι ἀμυνέμεν Od.2.60: cf. οἷος III. III. with an Adj. of the same gender and case, it emphasizes the sense of the Adj., *so very, just..*, ἐπιεικέα τοῖον *just* of moderate size, Il.23.246; πέλαγος μέγα τοῖον a sea *so* large, Od.3.321; κερδαλέον δὴ τ. *so very* knowing, 15.451; still stronger, ἀβληχρὸς μάλα τ. *so exceeding* gentle, 11.135, 23.282; μείδησε..σαρδάνιον μάλα τ. 20.302: rarely with Sup., τ. μέγιστος δοῦπος v.l. in Hes.*Th.*703. IV. in late Ep., = οἷος, Nic.*Th.*762, *Al.*232,293. V. neut. τοῖον as Adv., *thus, so much,* τοῖον γὰρ ὑποτρομέουσι Il.22.241, cf. Od.3.496; θάμα τ. *ever so* often, 1.209; ἀλλ' ἴθι σιγῇ τ. 7.30, cf. 4.776: in later Ep. τοίως, Theoc.24.72 codd., A.R.3.1399. VI. Sch.Il.7.231 (v. supr. I. 1) has οἱ γλωσσογράφοι τὸ τοῖοι ἀντὶ τοῦ ἀγαθοί· ὅθεν καὶ Καλλίμαχος τῷ "τοίων δεῖ" κέχρηται.

**τοιόσδε**, άδε (Ion. ήδε), όνδε, a form of τοῖος, bearing the same relation to τοιοῦτος as ὅδε to οὗτος, *such as this,* in Hom. not so common as τοῖος, but in Hdt. and Att. much more so; sts. anteced. to οἷος, as ἀοιδοῦ τοιοῦδ' οἷος ὅδ' ἐστί Od.1.371, cf. 17.313, Il.24.375: but more freq. abs., ἀλλ' ὅδ' ἐγὼ τ. here am I *such as you see,* Od.16.205, cf. 15.330; freq. with implications, *so great, so bad,* etc.; οὐ κε κακοὶ τοιούσδε τέκοιεν 4.64; τοιόσδε τοσόσδε τε λαός Il.2.120, 799; τοιάδε λαίφεα *such* clothes, i.e. *so bad,* Od.20.206; τοσόσδε καὶ τοιόσδε Hdt.2.73: after Hom. anteced. to οἷος, S.*Fr.*576.2, Pl.*Men.* 75e, etc.; to ὅς, Hdt.7.158; rarely to a Conj., as ὡς, A.*Pers.*179: with a qualifying word, τοιόσδ' ἠμὲν δέμας ἠδὲ καὶ ἔργα Od.17.313; τοιόσδ' ἐστὶ πόδας 19.359: with the Art., ὁ τ. ἀνήρ, αἱ τ. πράξεις, A.*Th.*547, S.*OT*895 (lyr.); ἐν τῇ τ. ἀνάγκῃ Th.4.10; οἱ τοιοίδε S.*Aj.* 330; τὸ τ. Pl.*Prt.*358b; ἐν τῷ τοιῷδε in *such* circumstances, Hdt. 9.27, Th.2.36, etc.: without Art., κατὰ τοιόνδε in *such* wise, Hdt. 4.48, 7.10.ε'; ἕτεροι τ. Id.1.207; φωνῆς ἐνεχθείσης τοιᾶσδε 2*Ep.Pet.* 1.17: the sense is made more indef. by τοιόσδε τις, *such a* one, Hdt. 3.139, 4.50, freq. in Att., Pl.*Smp.*173e, al.: in prose narrative τοιάδε is, prop., *as follows,* ταιαῦτα *as aforesaid,* Hdt.1.8, al. (cf. ὅδε, οὗτος); but this distn. is not strictly observed. Adv. τοιῶσδε Adam.*Vent.* 37,39, Eust. ad D.P.*Prooem.*p.82 B., etc. [τοῖ- in A.*Pr.*239, *Ag.* 1400, S.*OT*435, *Aj.*453; but not so freq. as in τοιοῦτος.]

**τοιοσδί**, αδί, ονδί, Att. strengthd. form of τοιόσδε, Ar.*Eq.*1376, Pl. Com.174.6, Arist.*Metaph.*1060ᵇ21. Adv. τοιωσδί Dam.*Pr.*96.

**τοιουτογνώμων**, ον, gen. ονος, *minded in such manner, An.Ox.* 4.32 (Tz. *in Hermog.*).

✻**τοιοῦτος**, αύτη, οῦτο, Att. also -οῦτον Th.7.21, Pl.*Hp.Ma.*281b, etc., which is the Ep. form (v. Od.7.309, 13.330), and seems to prevail in Hdt. (2.5,150, 3.27,85, 5.106 (v.l.), 7.103), Gem. (2.20, al.), etc., while we find τοιοῦτο in A.*Pr.*801, *Ag.*315, Ar.*Ra.*1399 cod. Rav., Men.*Sam.*160, *Pk.*236, v.l. in Th.7.86: both forms occur in Pap., τοιοῦτον *PAmh.*2.29.17 (iii B.C.), *UPZ*146.8,32 (ii B.C.), Phld. *Rh.*1.249, 2.270 S., *Ir.*p.33 W.; τοιοῦτο *PEnteux.*27.8 (iii B.C.), *PCair.Zen.*379.8, 482.13 (iii B.C.), Phld.*Ir.*p.42 W., *Rh.*2.243 S. (citing Metrod.):—Aeol. **τέοντος** *Lyr.Adesp.*51 (cod. A Heph.); fem. τεαύτα Sapph.*Supp.*13.4, Alc.*Supp.*8.5, 25.10:—a stronger form of τοῖος, bearing the same relation to τοιόσδε as οὗτος to ὅδε, *such as this,* in Hom. not so common as τοῖος, but in Att. the most common of the three forms; anteced. to οἷος, Od.4.269, Pl.*Smp.*199d, etc.; to ὡς, Il.21.428; to ὅς, ὅσπερ, S.*Ant.*691, Th.1.21, Lys.13.1, 30.14, X. *Lac.*7.5, Pl.*R.*349d, etc.; to οἱόσπερ, v.l. in X.*Cyr.*6.2.2; less freq. to a Conj., as ὥστε, A.*Ag.*1075, Pl.*Smp.*175d: freq. also abs., Pi. *O.*6.16, Hdt.2.2, etc.; freq. with implications, *so good, so noble, so bad,* etc., Il.7.242, etc.; τοιοῦτον..ἐστὶ τὸ..τέλειον ἄνδρα εἶναι *so great a thing* is it.., Pl.*Hp.Ma.*281b; τοιοῦτος ὢν being *such a wretch,* S.*Aj.*1298, cf. *Ph.*1049; εἴς τι τοιοῦτον ἐμπίπτειν οὗ.. into *such a condition* in which.., Pl.*Grg.*511c; freq. coupled with τοσοῦτος, Th.5.63, X.*Cyr.*2.4.6, etc.; with οὗτος, Pl.*R.*461e, X.*Cyr.* 8.2.26, etc. (so in the expression οὗτος τοιοῦτος, αὕτη τοιαύτη, *just as* he (she, it) is, of slaves or animals for sale, *POxy.*95.19 (ii A.D.), etc.); εἰς σὲ τοιοῦτος ἐγένετο, τ. γίγνου περὶ τοὺς γονεῖς, *so disposed* towards.., X.*Cyr.*5.2.27, Isoc.1.14: c. dat., τ. ἦσθα τοῖς λόγοισι *such* in thy words, S.*Ph.*1271: τ. ἕτερος *such* another, Hdt.3.47; ἕτερα τοιαῦτα, ἕτερον τοιοῦτον, Id.1.120, 2.5; referring to what precedes, Id.3.82, Pl.*Lg.*904d; used instead of repeating an Adj., ἀθάνατος εἶναι καὶ στρατιῆς τ. ἄρχειν Hdt.1.207, cf. 3.82, 7.10.ε', Th.3.58: with the Art., οἱ τοιοῦτοι A.*Pr.*952, *Ch.*291, S.*OC*642, Hp.*Art.*42; τὰ τ. Pi. *O.*9.40; ὀνόματι ὁ τοιοῦτος ἐμὲ προσαγορεύων Antipho 6.40 cod. A. 2. the sense is made more indef. in τοιοῦτός τις or τις τοιοῦτος *such a* one, Pi.*O.*6.16, Th.1.132, etc.; τοιαῦτ' ἄττα Pl.*R.*386a; in this case it may freq. be rendered by an Adv., ἡ διάρριψις τοιαύτη τις ἐγένετο took place *in this wise,* X.*An.*5.8.7; ἐγένετο ἡ διακομιδὴ τοιαύτη τις Plb.3. 45.6. 3. τὸ τ. *such a proceeding,* Th.1.76, etc.; διὰ τὸ τ. for *such a reason,* Id.7.21; ἐκ τοῦ τ. Id.3.37; ἐν τῷ τ. in *such a case,* ib.81, etc. (but also ἐν τῷ τ. in *such a place,* X.*Ages.*6.7; ἐν τ. τῆς οἰκίας Id.*Eq.*4.1); also ἐν τ. εἶναι τοῦ κινδύνου to be in *such a state* of peril, Id.*An.*1.7.5. 4. in narrative, τοιαῦτα prop. refers to what goes before, τοιαῦτα μὲν δὴ ταῦτα A.*Pr.*500; καὶ ταῦτα μὲν τ. S.*El.* 696, cf. X.*An.*2.5.12, etc.; cf. τοιόσδε fin. b. after a question, τοιαῦτα affirms like ταῦτα (v. οὗτος c. VII. 1), *just so, even so,* E.*Hec.* 776, *El.*645. 5. τοιαῦτα abs., τὰ πλοῖα, τὰ τοιαῦτα ships *and such-like,* D.8.25. 6. τοιαῦτα as Adv., *in such wise,* S.*OT*1327: regul. Adv. τοιούτως only late, *EM*650.42.—Cf. τοσοῦτος. [τοῖ- freq. in Trag. and Com., e.g. A.*Ag.*593, *Eu.*194,197,424, S.*OT*406, Ar. *Ra.*1399, etc.; cf. τοιόσδε fin.]

**τοιουτοσί**, αυτηί, οὑτοί or ουτονί, Att. strengthd. form of τοιοῦτος, Ar.*Ra.*66, *Lys.*1087, Pl.*Tht.*163e; neut. τοιουτοί Epicur.*Fr.*310 codd. S.E.*P.*2.25 (but τοιουτονί codd. S.E.*M.*7.267).

**τοιουτό-σχημος**, ον, or -σχήμων, ον, *of such shape,* S.E.*M.*7.209 (nom. sg. neut.), Eust. ad D.P.175 (dat. pl. -σχήμοσι). **-της**, ητος, ἡ, *quality,* Alex.Aphr. *in Top.*210.24, Simp. *in Cat.*222.33 (= *Stoic.*2.126). **-τροπος**, ον, *of such fashion* or *kind, such-like,* Hdt. 7.226, Hp.*Prog.*24, *Art.*42, Th.2.8,13, Pl.*Lg.*735e, Epicur.*Ep.*1 p. 29 U., etc. Adv. -πως Hp.*Art.*44, Tz. ad Lyc.492, *Gloss.* **-χροος**, ον, *of such-like colour,* Hp.*Epid.*7.11, Damian.*Opt.*13; φύματα Eust. 830.17.

**τοιουτώδης**, ες, *of such kind,* Luc.*Pisc.*20, S.E.*M.*8.206, etc.

**τοῖρ**, Elean for τοῖς, *SIG*9 (vi B.C.).

**τοίσδεσι**, Od.10.268, 21.93, Hp.*Mul.*2.124 (v.l. τοῖς εἴδεσιν), Critias 5, and **τοίσδεσσι(ν)**, Od.13.258, al.:—Ep. (and Ion., if rightly read in Hp.) dat. pl. forms of ὅδε. [Accent varies in codd.; in Od.13. 258 most codd. and Eust. have τοίσδεσσι, and Hdn.Gr.2.155 prescribes τοίσδεσσι.]

**τοιχ-αρχος**, ὁ, (τοῖχος 2) *overseer of the rowers on each side of the ship, boatswain,* Artem.1.35, 2.23; written *tutarchus* in *Gloss.* **-άς**, άδος, ἡ, in pl., epith. of ships in Nonn.*D.*39.7 (στοιχάδας Ludwich). **-ίδιον**, τό, Dim. of τοῖχος, Anon.*Prog.*ap.Rh.1.642 W. **-ίζω**, (τοῖχος 2) of a ship, *lie on her beam ends,* Ach.Tat.3.1, Eust.1021.12. ✻**-ίον**, τό, Dim. of τοῖχος, *IG*14.894. **-ιος**, α, ον, *of a wall,* παραστάματα *BCH*20.324 (Lebad.).

**τοιχο-βάτης** [ᾰ], ου, ὁ, *walker on walls, Cat.Cod.Astr.*8(4).215. **-γραφία**, ἡ, *a writing* or *painting on a wall,* Aret.*CA*1.2; *the art of wall-painting,* St.Byz. s. v. Βοῦρα. **-διφήτωρ**, ορος, ὁ, *one who creeps through a hole in the wall* (in order to steal), and so = τοιχωρύχος, Hsch. **-δομέω**, *build walls, IG*7.422 (Oropus, iv B.C.). **-κρᾶνον**, τό, *top of a wall, coping,* Ph.*Bel.*83.19. **-ομαι**, Pass., *possess the concept* or *idea of a wall,* Plu.2.1120d, 1121a; cf. ἱππόομαι. **-ποιία**, ἡ, = τειχ- (which is v.l.), Ph.*Bel.*81. 34. **-ποιός**, ὁ, = τειχ-, *Milet.*7.69. **-πυργίσκος**, ὁ, *cupboard in a wall, armarium, EM*147.5 (v.l. -πυργίους).

**τοιχ-ορύκτης**, ου, ὁ, = τοιχωρύχος, Sch.Pi.metr.p.13 Boeckh, Phot., Suid.

✻**τοῖχος**, ὁ, *wall of a house* or *enclosure,* abs., Od.2.342, Ar.*V.*130, etc.; ἅπαντ' ἐρευνῶν τ. dub. in E.*Hec.*1174; τ. δώματος Il.16.212; μεγάροιο 18.374, cf. Od.19.37; τ. καὶ θριγκοί (of the αὐλή) 17.267, cf. Hes.*Op.*732; τὸν τῆς αὐλῆς τ. *PEnteux.*12.3 (iii B.C.); *wall of a temple, IG*1².372.51, al.; οἰκίας Pl.*R.*574d; ἐν τοῖσι τ. ἔγραφ' "Ἀθηναῖοι καλοί" Ar.*Ach.*144, cf. Pl.*Lg.*859a; εἰς τὸν τ. ἀντεγγραψάτω *IG*1². 94.24; νόμους ἀναγράφειν εἰς τοῖχον Decr.ap.And.1.84; κοινοὶ τ. party-*walls, OGI*483.101, al. (Pergam., ii A.D.); τοίχῳ προσιστάμενοι γυμνάζονται Gal.6.144: of the *side* of a tent or hut, Il.9.219, 24.598, E. *Ion*1158. b. metaph., τοῖχε κεκονιαμένε, as a term of abuse, *Act. Ap.*23.3. 2. pl., *sides of a ship,* Od.12.420, Thgn.674, E.*Hel.* 1573, Th.7.36, Theoc.22.12; τοίχου ἄρχω τοῦ δεξιοῦ Luc.*DMeretr.*14. 3, cf. *JTr.*49. 3. of other things, as the human body, εἰς ἀμφοτέρους τοίχους (by metaph. from a ship) E.*Tr.*118 (anap.), cf. Luc. *Asin.*9; of a cup, Pherecr.143.2; of a vessel, Arist.*Mete.*359ᵃ3; of a bath (πύελος), Gal.15.709. 4. prov., τοίχους τοὺς δύο ἐπαλείφειν 'to run with the hare and hunt with the hounds', Paus.6.3.15, cf. Suid. s. v. δύο τοίχους; ὁ εὖ πράττων τ. 'the snug side of the ship', 'the right side of the hedge', Ar.*Ra.*537 (lyr.); ἐς τὸν εὐτυχῆ τ. χωρεῖν E.*Fr.*89. (Akin to τεῖχος, but used in a special sense; later = τεῖχος, Lxx *Is.*25.12, prob. so in *JHS*24.39 (Cyzicus).)

**τοιχοφορέω**, *carry a wall* on one's head, perh. of Cybele or ἡ Τύχη τῆς πόλεως, *IG*12(5).241 (Paros, i B.C.).

**τοιχωρῠχ-έω**, *dig through a wall like a thief, to be a housebreaker,* Ar.*Pl.*165, Pl.*R.*575b, X.*Mem.*1.2.62: c. acc., τοῖχον Arist.*EN*1138ᵃ 25. 2. metaph., οἷα ἐτοιχωρύχησαν περὶ τὸ δάνειον what *thievish tricks they played* with their loan, D.35.9; τοὺς λόγους τινός Philostr. *VS*2.1.6; πάντα Ph.2.527. **-ημα**, ατος, τό, *hole dug in the wall,* Phot., Suid. 2. metaph., *thievish trick,* Poll.6.180. **-ία**, ἡ, *housebreaking,* X.*Ap.*25, D.H.4.24. **-ική** (sc. τέχνη), ἡ, *housebreaker's craft,* S.E.*M.*2.12. ✻**-ος** (parox.), ὁ, (τοῖχος, ὀρύσσω) *one who digs through the wall,* i.e. *housebreaker, burglar,* sts. as term of abuse, Ar.*Nu.*1327, *Ra.*773, *Pl.*204, Amips.24, etc.; τ. καὶ ἱερόσυλοι Pl.*Lg.*831e: as Adj., of things, ὦ τοιχωρύχον λαγύνιον *rascally,* Diph. 3.1.

**τοιχωτός**, ή, όν, *provided with a wall,* κλίνη -ωτή, = *lectus parietalis,* prob. in *Gloss.* (-ων etc. codd.).

**τόκᾰ**, Dor. for τότε, Pi.*O.*6.66, *N.*6.10, Epich.147, Isyll.7, *SIG*527. 99 (Drerus, iii B.C.), *Berl.Sitzb.*1927.159 (Cyrene), etc.

**τοκ-ᾰδεία**, ἡ, *poultry-farming, PSI*1.101.5, *PRyl.*213.53 (ii A.D.), etc. **-άδερ** (Lacon. for τοκάδες)· ἔγκυοι, Hsch.

**τοκᾰρίδιον**, τό, *usurula, Gloss.*

**τοκ-άς**, άδος, ἡ, (τίκτω) *of* or *for breeding, brood,* σύες θήλειαι τοκάδες Od.14.16, cf. *PSI*4.379.21 (iii B.C.), *PCair.Zen.*152 (iii B.C.), Plb.12. 4.8, etc.; φόρος χηνῶν τοκάδων *PPetr.*3 p.286 (iii B.C.); ὀρνέθων τελείων τοκάδων *POxy.*1207.9 (ii A.D.); *prolific,* γυναῖκες Str.4.1.2; τοκάδα τὴν κεφαλὴν ἔχει, of Zeus, Luc.*DDeor.*9.1. 2. *having just brought forth,* Eub.149; τ. λέαινα *with cubs,* E.*Med.*187 (anap.); τ. κύνες *with pups,* Call.*Dian.*89 (τ. as Subst., *mothers, AP*9.268 (Antip. Thess.)); of goats, Theoc.8.63: rarely of women, ὅσαι δὲ τοκάδες ἦσαν E.*Hec.*1157; γενναίων τ' ἐκ τοκάδων born from noble *mothers,* Id.*Cyc.*42 (lyr.); τοκάδα τὰν..Βάκχου his *mother,* Id.*Hipp.*560 (lyr.); τ. κόνις one's *mother*land, Lyc.316. **-άω**, *to be near delivery,* τοκῶσα Cratin.449. **-ειος**, α, ον, *for breeding,* ἰβιῶν, i.e. *place for breeding ibises, BGU*1216.171 (ii B.C.). **-ετός**, ὁ, = τόκος, *childbirth, delivery,* Hp.*Aër.*4, etc.; including pregnancy, Arist.*GA*748ᵇ 22; μαστοὺς ἐν τ. ἐπαιρομένους Dsc.4.68: pl., πεπειραμένοι τῶν τ.

Sor.1.70ᵃ, cf. 2.31; τοκετῶν βάσανος *AP*9.311 (Phil.). **-εύς**, έως, ὁ, (τίκτω) *one who begets, father*, Hes.*Th.*138,155: generally, *begetter*, τέκνου τ. A.*Eu.*659:—in Hom. and Hes. mostly in pl., *parents*, Od.1.170, Hes.*Op.*185, al. (in dual, τοκῆε δύω Od.8.312); so in Trag., A.*Pers.*580 (lyr.), al., E.*Hec.*403, al. (not in S., exc. f.l. in *El.*187 (lyr.)); also in Prose, Hdt.1.122, 3.52, Th.2.44, Lys.2.75, X.*Mem.*2.1.33, etc.; of animals, Nic.*Th.*620, *Al.*563.—Hom. and Hes. commonly have the Ep. forms τοκῆες, τοκῆας, τοκήων (Il.15.663, al., more rarely τοκέων ib.660, 21.587); τοκεῦσι 4.477, al.; gen. τοκήων also in Alc.*Supp.*25.12, Sapph.*Supp.*5.10, A.*Ag.*728 (lyr., dub. l.); dat. τοκέσι *IG*3.1311. ❋**-εών**, ῶνος, ὁ, *parent*, Heraclit.74, elsewh. dub., Call.*Iamb.*1.137, *AP*7.79 (Mel.), 408 (Leon.). **-ήεσσα**, ἡ, of a woman, *having had children*, Hp.*Nat.Mul.*3; *fertile*, Id.*Steril.* 226. **-ίζω**, (τόκος II. 2) *lend on interest*, D.45.70; μὴ τοκίζειν πλέονος ἢ τριῶν ὀδελῶν τὰν μνᾶν τοῦ μηνὸς ϝεκάστου *Schwyzer*324.6 (Delph., iv B.C.); τ. τόκον *practise* usury, *AP*11.309 (Lucill.):—Pass., τοκίζεται αὐτῷ ἀργύριον Hyp.*Fr.*273, cf. *IG*9(1).694.12,29 (Corc.). ❋**-ιον**, τό, = τόκος II. 2, *interest*, *Schwyzer*323 *A* 56 (Delph., iv B.C.). **-ίς**, ίδος, ἡ, prob. = τοκάς, perh. of geese, *BGU*1212 *D* 26 (Ptolemaic royal edict). **-ισμός**, ὁ, *the practice of usury*, X.*Vect.*4.6, Arist.*Pol.*1258ᵇ 25. **-ιστής**, οῦ, ὁ, *money-lender, usurer*, *IG*2².1554.69 (iv B.C.), Pl.*Alc.*2.149e, *PEnteux.*33.2 (iii B.C.); τ. κατὰ μικρὰ καὶ ἐπὶ πολλῷ Arist.*EN*1121ᵇ34; *lender, creditor*, *SIG*364.10, al. (Ephesus, iii B.C.): fem. **-ίστρια** *PTeb.*761.11 (iii B.C.).

**τοκο-γλῠφέω**, *practise usury*, Plu.2.34d, Luc.*Nec.*2, etc. **-γλύφος** [ῠ], ὁ, *one who marks down his interest* (orig. perh. by *notching* a piece of wood), *usurer*, *Com.Adesp.*1165, Ph.1.550, al., Plu.2.18e, Luc.*Vit.Auct.*23, Alciphr.1.26, etc.; cf. γλύφω II. **-πράκτωρ**, ορος, ὁ, (πράσσω VI) *one who exacts interest*, *Com.Adesp.*1165.

❋**τόκος**, ὁ, (τίκτω) *childbirth, parturition*, of women, Il.19.119, *h.Cer.*101, *IG*4²(1).121.15,17 (Epid., iv B.C.), Herophil.ap.Sor.2.53; of animals, Il.17.5; πλὴν ὅταν τ. παρῇ S.*Fr.*477; ποιεῖσθαι τὸν τ. Arist.*HA*542ᵃ25, etc.: pl., τόκοισί τε ἀγόνοις γυναικῶν S.*OT*26, cf. 173 (lyr.), E.*Med.*1031, etc. **b.** *the time of parturition*, ὁ τ. τῆς γυναικός Hdt.1.111; *period of gestation*, ἐνιαύσιος ὁ τ. Arist.*GA*777ᵇ13. **c.** ἡ φύσις τοῦ παιδίου τοῦ ἐν τόκῳ in the *foetal stage*, Hp.*Nat.Puer.*tit. (as cited in *Mul.*1.1). **II.** *offspring*, of men or animals, πάντων Ἀργείων ἐρέων γενεήν τε τόκον τε Il.7.128, cf. 15.141; of an eagle, ἐλθὼν ἐξ ὄρεος, ὅθι οἱ γενεή τε τόκος τε Od.15.175; μήλων τ. E.*Cyc.*162; Οἰδίπου τ. his *son*, A.*Th.*372, cf. 407, etc. (but also, *daughter*, θεὰ γεγῶσα καὶ θεοῦ πατρὸς τ. E.*Andr.*[1254]); *fry* of fish, Arist.*HA*543ᵃ4; *litter* of pigs, πασῶν τῶν συῶν ἀπὸ τόκου χοῖρον λαμβάνειν X.*Lac.*15.5. **2.** metaph., *produce of money* lent, hence *interest* (cf. S.*Fr.*477 (punningly), Sophr. 35, Pl.*R.*555e, Arist.*Pol.*1258ᵇ5), Pi.*O.*10(11).9, etc.; τ. ἐπίτριτος, v. h.v.; τ. πεντώβολος interest at 5 obols per month on the mina, *IG* 11(2).146 *B* 17 (Delos, iv B.C.); τ. πεντεκαιδέκατος, i.e. $\frac{100}{15}=6\frac{2}{3}$ %, *SIG*672.23 (Delph., ii B.C.); sg. and pl., *IG*1².324.5, Ar.*Nu.*18, 20, 34, etc.; τόκους ἀποδοῦναι ib.739, etc.; κομίζεσθαι Pl. l. c., *PEnteux.* 32.13 (iii B.C.); λαμβάνειν ἀπό τινος Is.8.35; ἀπολαμβάνειν Lys.17.3; δανείζειν ἐπὶ τόκῳ Pl.*Lg.*742c; ὀφείλειν ἐπὶ τόκῳ Isoc.17.7; τόκοι τόκων *compound interest*, Ar.*Nu.*1156; τόκος τόκου Thphr.*Char.*10. 10; τῶν τόκων ἔχων τόκους Men.870:—Ar. plays on the double meaning of the word, *Th.*843 sq.; so also Pl.*R.*507a, Plu.2.433e. **3.** metaph., *interest*, [γῄδιον] ὅτι λάβοι σπέρμα.. δικαίως ἀπεδίδου αὐτό τε καὶ τόκον X.*Cyr.*8.3.38, cf. Philem.231, 88.10; οἱ δ' εἰς τὸ γῆρας ἀναβολὰς ποιούμενοι, οὗτοι προσαποτίνουσι τοῦ χρόνου τόκους Men.235.9; *offspring*, ἢ τίκτων λόγους ἢ τὸν ἑτέρων τόκον λαμβάνων Lib.*Or.*12.94; *bringing forth*, ib.17.38. **4.** *oppression*, as translation of Hebr. *tōḵ*, Lxx *Ps.*71(72).14, *Je.*9.6.

**τοκοφορέω**, *pay interest*, ἐπ' ἐννέα ὀβολοῖς D.59.52.

**τολάριον**, τό, dub. sens. in *Dura*⁴100 (pl., iii A.D.); perh. = Lat. *torale*.

❋**τόλμ-ᾰ**, ης, ἡ, also **τόλμη**, which Phryn.*PS*p.114 B. compares with πρύμνη for πρύμνα: but (apart from πρὸς τόλμην πεσεῖν S.*Ichn.* 11 (Pap.), which is not guaranteed by the metre) only the form τόλμᾰ (acc. τόλμᾰν, e.g. E.*IT*862) occurs in Att. and Trag., E.*Andr.*702, *Ion* 1264, *Fr.*426 (in E.*Ion* 1416, ἥ γε τόλμα σου (cj. Jodrell) is the prob.l.), Th.3.82, 6.59, Pl.*La.*193d, *R.*575a, Gal.15.144, *POxy.*1119. 8 (iii A.D.), etc.; so in Ion., Hdt.7.135; but τόλμη (nom.) in Clitarch. 35 J., acc. τόλμην Lxx *Ju.*16.10(12) cod.Alex.: **τόλμᾱ** is Dor., Pi. *O.*9.82, 13.11:—*courage, hardihood*, Pi. ll. cc., Hdt.2.121.ζ', Trag. and Att. (v. supr.); τόλμα καλῶν *courage for* noble acts, Pi.*N.*7.59; τῶνδε τόλμαν σχεθεῖν to have *courage* or *nerve* for this business, A.*Pr.*16. **2.** in bad sense, *over-boldness, recklessness*, Id.*Ch.*1004 (996); πῶς οὖν.. ἐς τόδ' ἂν τόλμης ἔβη; S.*OT*125, cf. E.*Ion* 1264, etc.; τόλμης ἔργα κἀναισχυντίας Ar.*Th.*702; τ. ἀλόγιστος Th.3.82, cf. 6. 59; τ. καὶ ἀναίδεια Antipho 3.3.5, Is.6.46; θρασύτης καὶ τ. Pl.*La.* 197b; τ. καὶ ἀναισχυντία Id.*Ap.*38d; ἡ ἄφρων τ. Id.*La.*193d. **II.** *a bold* or *daring act*, φίλτρα τόλμης τῆσδε A.*Ch.*1029; τόλμας (gen.), ἂν ἔρεξα E.*Andr.*838 (lyr.): pl., κακὰς δὲ τόλμας μήτ' ἐπισταίμην ἐγὼ S.*Tr.*582, cf. *Aj.*46; ἀνόσιοι πληγῶν τ. Pl.*Lg.*881a, cf. *Ep.*336d. **III.** Pythag. name for 2, Anatol.ap.*Theol.Ar.*8. (v. *τλάω.) **-άω**, Ion. **τολμέω** Hdt.8.77; Dor. 2 sg. τολμῇς Theoc.5.35: fut. τολμήσω S.*El.* 471, Dor. -ασῶ Theoc.14.67: pf. τετόλμηκα A.*Pr.*333, Dor. -ᾱκα Pi.*P.*5.117:—Med., Lys.*Oxy.*1606.420 (*Bodl. Quarterly Record* 5 (1928).303):—*undertake, take heart* either *to do* or *bear* anything terrible or difficult: **1.** mostly abs., *dare, endure, submit* (v. *τλάω), ἐνὶ φρεσὶ θυμὸς ἐτόλμα Il.10.232; σὺ δ' (sc. κραδίη) ἐτόλμας Od. 20.20; οὐδὲ οἱ ἵπποι τόλμων Il.12.51; ἐγὼ δ' ἐτόλμησ' A.*Pr.*237, etc.; αἱ συμφοραὶ τοὺς ἡσυχίους τολμᾶν βιάζονται Antipho 3.2.1; τ. καὶ ἐκλογίζεσθαι Th.2.40; τολμῶντες ἄνδρες ib.43, cf. S.*Tr.*583; χρὴ τολμᾶν.. ἐν ἄλγεσι κείμενον ἄνδρα Thgn.555; τόλμα κακοῖσιν Id.355, 1029; τόλμα S.*Ph.*82; τόλμησον ib.481: in part., τολμήσας.. παρέστη *he took courage* and.., Plu.*Cam.*22, cf. *Ev.Marc.*15.43. **2.** c. acc. rei, *endure, undergo*, τ. χρὴ τὰ διδοῦσι θεοί Thgn.591, cf. E. *Hec.*333, Pl.*Lg.*872e. **II.** c. inf., *to have the courage, hardihood, effrontery, cruelty*, or *the grace, patience*, to do a thing in spite of any natural feeling, *dare*, or *bring oneself*, to do, εἰ.. τολμήσεις Διὸς ἄντα .. ἔγχος ἀεῖραι Il.8.424, cf. 13.395, 17.68, Od.9.332, S.*Aj.*528, Ar.*Nu.* 550, Lys.32.2, etc.; τόλμησον ὀρθῶς φρονεῖν A.*Pr.*999, cf. Thgn. 81, 377, etc.; τ. κατακεῖσθαι *submit* to keep one's bed, Hp.*Fract.*10; τ. ἀποθανεῖν *Ep.Rom.*5.7; οὐδὲ ἀπαιτούμενοι τὸν λόγον ἐτόλμησαν ἡμῖν δοῦναι *PCair.Zen.*330.5 (iii B.C.). **2.** sts. c. part., ἐτόλμα.. βαλλόμενος *he submitted to be* struck, Od.24.162; τόλμα ἐρῶσα E. *Hipp.*476, cf. Thgn.442, E.*HF*756. **3.** c. acc., πόλεμον τολμήσαντα *undertaking, venturing on* it, Od.8.519; [ἐσόδους] τετόλμακε Pi.*P.*5.117; τ. πάντα, δεινά, ἔργον αἴσχιστον, etc., S.*OC*761, E.*IA* 133 (anap.), *Med.*695, etc.; ὦ πᾶν σὺ τολμήσασα καὶ πέρα S.*Fr.*189; also τ. τὰ βέλτιστα Th.3.56, 4.98; πικρὰν πεῖραν S.*El.*471; v. τόλμημα:—hence in Pass., οἷ' ἐτολμήθη πατήρ such things as my father *had dared* (or *done*) *against him*, E.*El.*277; τοῦτο τετολμήσθω εἰπεῖν *let us take courage* to say this, Pl.*R.*503b; τὰ τολμηθέντα J.*AJ*2.3.1; αἱ τετολμημέναι ἐπίνοιαι Ph.1.674; τὰ τετ. εἰς ἐμέ *PGoodsp.Cair.*15.3 (iv A.D.). **4.** so in Act., τετολμηκυῖαι [λέξεις] *daring* expressions, Phld.*Rh.*1.341 S. **-η**, ἡ, v. τόλμα. **-ήεις**, Dor. **-άεις** [ᾱ] Pi.*P.*4. 89, εσσα, εν, *enduring, steadfast*, Od.17.284; *daring, bold*, Il.10.205, Pi. l. c.: Sup. contr. τολμήστατε (v.l. τολμίστατε) is f.l. in S.*Ph.*984. The prose form is τολμηρός. **-ημα**, ατος, τό, (τολμάω) *adventure, enterprise, daring* or *shameless act*, freq. in E. (not in A. or S.), mostly in pl., *Or.*1064, *Ba.*1222, al.: sg., *Ph.*1676; τ. τολμᾶτον οὐκ ἀνασχετόν Ar. *Pl.*419, cf. Th.6.54, 7.43, Pl.*Lg.*636c, etc. **2.** in language, *a bold expression*, Hermog.*Inv.*4.12, *Meth.*6. **-ηρός**, ά, όν, usual prose form for τολμήεις, Antipho 3.3.1, And.1.110, Lys.7.19, etc.; οἱ -ότατοι Isoc. 3.21; προθυμία -οτάτη Th.1.74; τὸ τ. τινῶν their *hardihood*, ib.102; τὸ -ότερον your *greater daring*, Id.2.87; τ. πολλὰ δρᾶν Arist.*EN*1117ᵃ 2; κἂν εἰ -ότερον εἰρῆσθαι Pl.*Sph.*267d: also in Poets, E.*Supp.*305, Ar.*Nu.*445 (anap.), Bion 1.60; ἀνοίας οὐδὲν -ότερον Men.738; opp. εὔτολμος, Id.*Mon.*153. Adv. **-ρῶς** Th.3.74,83, X.*Smp.*2.12, etc.: Comp. -ότερον Th.4.126, Plb.1.17.7, *Ep.Rom.*15.15: Sup. -ότατα Poll.3.136. **-ησις**, εως, ἡ, *a reckless act*, Pl.*Def.*412c. **-ητέον**, *one must venture*, etc., τάδ' E.*Med.*1051, *Ion* 1387, cf. *Com.Adesp.* 18.16 D.: c. inf., E.*IT*111: abs., ib.121, Pl.*Lg.*888a. **-ητής**, οῦ, ὁ, *bold, venturous man*, Th.1.70, Ph.2.72, J.*AJ*20.9.1, Adam.2. 5; θυμὸς τ. *AP*9.678. **-ητίας**, ου, ὁ, = τολμητής, *Com.Adesp.* 1166, Adam.1.7, Agath.1.4, 4.27. **-ητικός**, ή, όν, = τολμηρός, in Sup., Hippod.ap.Stob.4.1.94. **-ητός**, ή, όν, also ός, όν E.*Hel.* 816:—*ventured, to be ventured*, πὰν τόλμᾱτον Sapph.2.17; ἔστ' ἐκείνῳ πάντα.. τολμητὰ *within the compass of his daring*, S.*Ph.*634, cf. Cratin.324b; ἐλπὶς τ. E. l. c. **-ιλλος**, ὁ, *dare-devil*, Theognost. *Can.Prooem.*

**τόλυξ**· αἰδοῖον, Hsch.

**τολύπ-ευμα** [ῠ], ατος, τό, = τολύπη, Phot., Suid. **-ευτικός**, ή, όν, *of* or *for accomplishing*, Hsch. (Sup.). **-εύω**, *wind off* carded wool *into a clew* for spinning, Ar.*Lys.*587 (anap.). **II.** metaph., *wind off, achieve, accomplish*, ἐγὼ δὲ δόλους τολυπεύω, of Penelope's web (with a play on the literal sense), Od.19.137; ἐπεὶ πόλεμον τολύπευσε 1.238, 4.490, al.; Θρῄκην πένθος τ. *work* them grief, E.*Rh.*744 (anap.); δόμον τ. *finish building* it, *AP*9.655; λίθον.. ἐκ θεμέθλων *Arch.Anz.*31.149 (Nicopolis). **2.** *endure*, ἐς γῆρας τ. ἀργαλέους πολέμους Il.14.86; ὁπόσα τολύπευσε σὺν αὐτῷ καὶ πάθεν ἄλγεα 24.7. (Poet. word, v.l. in J.*AJ*17.1.2 for πολιτεύω.) **-η**, ἡ, *clew, ball of wool ready for spinning*, or *of spun yarn*, S.*Fr.*1102, Ar.*Lys.*586 (anap.), *AP*6.160 (Antip. Sid.), 247 (Phil.), Dsc.5.75, Arr.*Ind.*7.3, Hsch., Eust.1336.18, 1414.26. **II.** *ball* of anything, τῶν πράσων Eub.42.3. **2.** *globular cake*, Ath.3.114f, 4.140a, Hsch. **3.** a kind of *gourd, pumpkin*, = κολόκυνθα ἀγρία, Lxx *4Ki.*4.39, Phot., Suid.

**τομ-αῖος**, α, ον, also ος, ον E.*Alc.*101 (lyr.): (τομή):—*cut, cut off*, βόστρυχος, χαίτα (cf. τομή I), A.*Ch.*168, E. l.c. **II.** *cut in pieces*, ἄκος τ. *cut* or *shredded ready for use*, A.*Ch.*539, *Supp.* 268. **-άριον**, τό, Dim. of τόμος II, *small volume, tract*, Eust. ad D.P.*Prooem.*p.74 B., *EM*790.8, etc.; the τομάρια of Aristonymus are freq. cited by Stob., as 2.31.85, 4.46.21.

**Τόμαρος**, ὁ, v. Τομοῦροι.

**τομ-αροφύλᾰκες** [ῠ], οἱ, gloss on Τομοῦροι (q.v.), Str.7.7. 11. **-άς**, ή, v.l. for ἀποτομάς, J.*AJ*3.1.2. **2.** *clearing* in a forest, *IG*5(2).343 *A* 6,12 (Arc., iv B.C.). **-άω**, *need cutting*, πρὸς τομῶντι πήματι for a disease *that needs the knife*, S.*Aj.*582. **-εῖον**, τό, = sq. I. 3, Hp.ap.Gal.19.146. **-εύς**, έως, ὁ, Dor. dat. pl. τομέεσσι (vv.ll. τομέσι, τομεσσι) Archim.*Spir.*25:—*one that cuts, a carver*, Poll.6.13, etc.; τ. σίδηρος Max.277; πέλεκυς αὐχένος τ. Trag. *Adesp.*412; *divider*, ὁ ἀόρατος τ., i.e. God, Ph.1.498; as Adj., ὁ τ. λόγος ib.491. **2.** *shoemaker's knife*, Pl.*Alc.*1.129c; *edge of a knife*, X.*Eq.Mag.*2.3. **3.** *forceps*, gloss on τομεῖον, Gal.19.146. **4.** pl. τομεῖς, οἱ, *cutting-teeth, incisors*, Anon.Lond.24.23, Cels.8.1, Gal. 2.754, Poll.2.91, *Gp.*16.1.13, Simp.*in Cael.*664.3. **II.** Math., *sector* of a circle, Euc.6.33, Hero *Deff.*34. **2.** τ. στερεός *sector* of a sphere (intercepted by cone with vertex at centre), Archim.*Sph.*

*Cyl.*1*Def.*5; but τ. ἐν τῇ ἐπιφανείᾳ, i.e. surface included betw. two great circles and a circle cutting each at right angles, Papp.268.1. **-εύω**, = τέμνω, Hsch. **⁎-ή**, ἡ, (τέμνω) *end left after cutting, stump* of a tree, ἐπεὶ δὴ πρῶτα τομὴν ἐν ὄρεσσι λέλοιπεν [τὸ σκῆπτρον] Il.1.235; ῥιζῶν τομαί *the ends* of the roots (*left by cutting away* the tree), S.*Fr.*534.5 (anap.); ὀπὸν.. στάζοντα τομῆς ib.2; δοκοῦ τ. *end* of a beam, Th.2.76; ἡ τοῦ καλάμου τ. Thphr.*HP*4.11.7, cf. Theoc.10.46; λίθοι ἐν τομῇ ἐγγώνιοι stones cut square, Th.1.93 (sed leg. ἐντομῇ); σκέψαι τομῇ προσθεῖσα βόστρυχον having fitted the lock to *the place from which it was cut*, A.*Ch.*229 (σκέψαιτο μὴ cod. M, distinxit Turnebus); πρὸς τὴν τ. μεταστρέφειν to the *cut*, Pl.*Smp.*190e, cf. Arist.*HA*532ᵃ4. **b.** Ταύροιο τ. prob. = προτομή 1, Arat.322. **2.** Math., *section*, as a circle is the *section* of a sphere, a conic section of the cone, Arist.*Mete.*375ᵇ32, *Pr.*912ᵃ13, cf. *App. Anth.*4.74 (Synesius); with or without κοινή, *the line in which two planes cut* each other, Arist.*Metaph.*1060ᵇ14, Euc.11.16, Archim. *Con.Sph.*11, al., Apollon.Perg.*Con.*1.4, etc.; *point of intersection* of two lines, Archim.*Spir.*20, al., Ptol.*Alm.*3.3, etc.: abstract use, περὶ διωρισμένης τ. *On determinate section*, name of lost treatise of Apollon.Perg.; τὰ περὶ τὴν τ. the theorems about the *section* (sc. in extreme and mean ratio), Procl. *in Euc.*p.67 F.:—in conic sections, τομαὶ ἀντικείμεναι opposite *sections*, i.e. branches of hyperbola, Apollon.Perg.*Con.*2.15; συζυγεῖς τ. conjugate *sections* of hyperbolas, ib.17. **3.** *incision* or *insection* between parts of an insect's body (whence their name of ἔντομα), Arist.*PA*682ᵇ25. **4.** ἡ εἰς ἄπειρον τ. infinite *divisibility*, Epicur.*Ep.*1 p.16 U. **II.** *cutting, cleaving*, ἐν τομᾷ σιδάρου by *stroke* of iron, S.*Tr.*887 (lyr.); πελέκεως τ. E.*El.*160 (lyr.); φασγάνου τομαί Id.*Or.*1101; *cutting off* or *down*, ξύλου S.*Tr.*700; vine-*cutting*, *PCair.Zen.*736.29 (iii B.C.); *cutting up*, εἰς τ. καὶ προσαγωγὴν χάλικος *PPetr.*3 p.290 (iii B.C.); *hewing*, λίθων *IG*1².336.7,11, *SIG*244 ii 58 (Delph., iv B.C.), *IG*4²(1).106 i 19, al. (Epid., iv B.C.). **2.** *use of the knife* in surgery, Hp.*VC*13; ἢ καύσει ἢ τομῇ χρησάμενος Pl.*R.*406d; οὔτε τ. οὔτε καῦσις Hp.*Art.*62; σιδήρου τ. Sor.1.80: pl., Pi.*P.*3.53, E.*Fr.*403.6; τὰς θεραπείας..διὰ καύσεών τε καὶ τομῶν Pl.*Prt.*354a, cf. *Ti.*65b. **3.** *castration*, Luc. *Philops.*2. **4.** τ. φαρμάκων *shredding* of drugs, Conon 23.2. **5.** *pruning*, ἀμπέλων Thphr.*CP*3.14.2, Paus.2.38.3. **6.** σκυτῶν τ. *cutting* or *shaping* of leather, Pl.*Chrm.*173d. **7.** αἱ τ. τῆς γῆς, i.e. *canals*, Lib.*Or.*18.232. **III.** *severance, separation*, τ. καὶ διάκρισις Pl.*Ti.*61d, cf. 80e; of number, *division*, Id.*Lg.*738a; τομὴν ἔχειν ἔν τινι to admit *a distinction* in.., ib.944b; χρονικαὶ τ. *distinctions* of tenses, A.D.*Synt.*10.18; *process of division* (sc. μεγέθους), Nicom. *Ar.*1.2. **2.** *logical division*, Pl.*Plt.*261a, Arist.*APo.*95ᵇ30, *Metaph.* 1038ᵃ28, Gal.10.899. **3.** metaph., *conciseness* or *precision* in expression, Eun.*VS*p.461 B. **4.** τ. πράγματος, = *decisio*, *Gloss.* **IV.** *a cut, wound*, Arist.*HA*632ᵃ18, Aen.Tact.11.14: metaph., *wound*, πόλις δεδεγμένη τ. Plu.*Cor.*16, cf. *Per.*11. **2.** *caesura* in verse, Aristid.Quint.1.24; more generally, *break between successive words*, Hermog.*Id.*2.10, Heph.15.2, al., Eust.740.1. **V.** *edge, cutting power*, σιδήρου Arr.*Tact.*12.2. **-ιαῖος**, α, ον, = sq., *Gloss.* **-ίας**, ου, ὁ, *one who has been castrated*, ὗς οὐ τ. Antiph.133.5 (anap.); οἱ τ. τῶν βοῶν, ὑῶν, Arist.*HA*575ᵇ1, 578ᵃ33: abs., τομίας (in a list of eatables) *PSI*6.553.2 (iii B.C.); of men, *eunuch*, Hdn.1.11.2. **II.** = τομεύς I. 4, ὅσοι τομίαι τῶν ὀδόντων Ph.2.238. **III.** v. ταμίας. **-ιον**, τό, *victim cut up* for sacrifice, over which oaths were taken, τόμιον ἐντέμνεσθαι to cut *such a victim* in pieces, Ar.*Lys.*192; τὰ τ. the *parts of the victim* used at this solemnity, ib.186, Antipho 5.88, Pl.*Lg.*753d, Arist.*Ath.*55.5; στὰς ἐπὶ τῶν τ. κάπρου καὶ κριοῦ καὶ ταύρου D.23.68, cf. Aeschin.2.87, Paus.5.24.9, al. **2.** *small log* or *block of wood*, *IG*11(2).199 *A* 55, 219 *A* 14 (Delos, iii B.C.). **-ιος**, = τομίας I, *PFrankf.*5.7,17 (iii B.C.); τομίου προβάτου *Gloss.* **-ίς**, ίδος, ἡ, *knife*, Lxx *Pr.*24.37 (30.14).

**τομοειδής**, ές, *sector-like*, Sch.Euc. vol. v p.260 H.

**τομός**, ή, όν, (τέμνω) *cutting, sharp*, Pl.*Ti.*61e, Timo 4 (Comp.); v.l. for τολμηρόν in D.25.24; ὁ μὲν σφαγεὺς ἕστηκεν ᾗ τομώτατος as it will *cut sharpest*, S.*Aj.*815. **2.** metaph., λόγος -ώτερος σιδήρου Ps.-Phoc.124, cf. *Ep.Hebr.*4.12; of persons, οἱ -ώτατοι the *sharpest, hottest*, Call.*Fr.*78 codd.; ἐρέω τι τομώτερον ἢ ἀπὸ δάφνης Id.*Del.*94 codd.; πράξεις -ώτεραι Luc.*Tox.*11; cf. τορός. Adv. -μῶς *sharply, clearly*, Hsch. s.v. τμήδην.

**τόμος**, ὁ, *slice*, τ. ἐκ πτέρνης Batr.37; γαστρός, πλακοῦντος, Ar.*Eq.* 1179, 1190; τῆς χορδῆς Cratin.192; ἀλλάντων, πνοῦ, Pherecr.108.8, 19; γογγυλίδος Alex.88; τυροῦ, ἠνύστρου, Eub.150.2, Mnesim.4.14 (anap.): generally, *piece*, κιθῶνος *Michel* 832.20 (Samos, iv B.C.); of wood, *beam*, *IG*11(2).161 *D* 123, 165.49 (Delos, iii B.C.). **2.** *piece of land*, ib.7.3170.12 (Orchom. Boeot.), cf. 1739, 1742 (Thespiae). **3.** Geom., τ. κυλίνδρου *frustum* of a cylinder, portion of right cylinder intercepted betw. two parallel oblique sections, Archim.*Con.Sph.Def.*; τ. ἀπὸ ὀρθογωνίου κώνου τομᾶς ἀφαιρούμενος *frustum* of the section of a right-angled cone, i.e. portion of a parabola cut off by two parallel double-ordinates, Id.*Aequil.*2.10. **II.** *roll* of papyrus, *PCair.Zen.*357.15 (iii B.C.), Lxx *Is.*8.1, *PSI*10.1146.1 (ii A.D.), *Sammelb.*7362.1 (ii A.D.), etc.; τ. συγκολλήσιμος *PGrenf.*2.41.18 (i A.D.); τιμῆς ἀπὸ τόμου ἀγραφίου *PMich. Teb.*123ᵛ vii 25 (i A.D.); *tome, volume*, *PMich.* in *Class.Phil.*22.10 (ii A.D.), D.L.6.15: metaph., ἐν καθαρῷ διανοίας τ. Porph.*Marc.*32.

**Τομοῦροι**, οἱ, *priests of Zeus* at Dodona, εἰ μέν κ' αἰνήσωσι Διὸς μεγάλοιο Τομοῦροι, an ancient reading for θέμιστες in Od.16.403, v. Str.7.7.11, who explains it as a shortd. form of Τομάρ-ουροι, *guardians of Mount Tomarus*, cf. Hsch. s.v. Τόμαρος; the variant is given as Τόμουραι by Eust.1760.47, 1806.37; τόμουρε = μάντι occurs in Lyc. 223, cf. Hsch.

**τον-αῖος**, α, ον, (τόνος) *stretched*, δρόμος Suid., Zonar. **II.** τοναία (sc. φωνή), ἡ, *strained, loud voice*, Alex.169. **III.** Τόναια, τά, v. Τόνεα. **-άριον** [ᾰ], τό, *pitch-pipe*, to give the key-note for singing or speaking, Quint.*Inst.*1.10.27; cf. ἐπιτόνιον.

**Τόνεα**, τά, festival of Hera at Samos, Menodot.1 (better Τόναια, as Kaibel).

**τον-έω**, = τονόω II, Eust.60.14 (Pass.). **-ή**, ἡ, *prolongation* of a note at the same pitch, Cleonid.*Harm.*14.

**τονθολυγέω**, v. sq.

**⁎τονθορύζω** or **-ίζω**, *speak inarticulately, mumble*, Ar.*Ach.*683 (troch.), *Ra.*747, *V.*614 (anap.), Luc.*Deor.Conc.*1, Aristaenet.2.6; *gurgle*, ἐτονθόρυζε ταῦρος ⟨ὡς⟩ νεοσφαγής A.*Fr.*298:—in all these passages the best codd. have the form in -ύζω; τονθορύξει (prob. 2 sg. fut.) occurs in Herod.7.77; both forms are cited by Hsch.; -ίζω is found in codd. of Gal.2.689, Thom.Mag.p.352 R., etc., but is never expressly mentioned by Gramm.; cf. ὑποτονθορύζω.—Rarer collat. forms, **τονθολῠγέω**, *gurgle*, Pherecr.108.4; distd. from τανθαρύζω (q.v.) by Ptol.Asc.p.410 H., Ammon.*Diff.*p.79 V.; **τονθρ-ύζω**, Herod.8.8, Opp.*C.*2.541, 3.169 (recognized as Att. along with τονθορύζω by Phryn.336, cf. *PS*p.115 B.); cf. -ύς, ἡ, *muttering*, Hsch.; **-υστής**, οῦ, ὁ, *mutterer*, = γογγυστής, Aq.*Pr.*16.28; **-υσμός** and **τονθορυσμός**, ὁ, Phryn.336. (Prob. onomatop.)

**τόνθων**· παρὰ Κορίννῃ (*Fr.*40), ἐπὶ νωτιαίου (cod. νοτιβίου) κρέως τὸ ὄνομα, Hsch.

**τον-ιαῖος**, α, ον, *consisting of one tone*, in Music, διάστημα Arist. *Pr.*922ᵇ6, cf. Plu.2.1018f, Aristox.(?) *Oxy.*667.20, Alex.Aphr. *in Top.* 113.12. **2.** τὸ τ. χρῶμα, = τὸ τονικὸν χ., Cleonid.*Harm.*7. **-ίζω**, *furnish with an accent*, Troil.*Proll.Hermog.*ap.Rh.6.45 W., *Cod.Vat.* 1751 in *AB*1169 (note), *Gloss.* **-ικός**, ή, όν, *of* or *for stretching, capable of extension*, ὄρνιθες κατὰ πτέρυγας τονικοί Arist.*PA*693ᵇ12. **2.** Mus., τὸ τονικὸν [χρῶμα] (opp. τὸ ἡμιτόνιον (fort. ἡμιόλιον, cf. Cleonid.*Harm.*7) and τὸ μαλακόν), one of the three forms of χρῶμα or chromatic scale, S.E.*M.*6.51. **3.** *of* or *for accents*, τονικὰ παραγγέλματα A.D.*Adv.*181.9 (so περὶ τ. π., treatise by Jo.Alex.); τὸ -κόν A.D.*Pron.*35.13. **4.** *resulting from* τόνος II. 4, κίνησις, of God, opp. μεταβατικῶς κινούμενος, *Stoic.*2.149, cf. 147, al. **5.** *contractile*, ἐνέργεια, of a muscle, Gal.4.436; [πέπερι] στομάχου -ώτερον Id.6.265. Adv. -κῶς Id.4.435. **-ιος**, α, ον, = foreg.: τόνια, τά, *'tractor' machines*, Heliod.ap.Orib.49.2.1, al.; τονία, ἡ, *rope of a pulley*, Poll.10.31. **-ιστέον**, *one must accentuate*, Sch.Pi.*P.*4.9.

**τονοειδής**, ές, of breath, *drawn with difficulty*, v.l. (ap.Erot.) for γονοειδές in Hp.*Epid.*2.3.11.

**τόν-ος**, ὁ, (τείνω) *that by which a thing is stretched*, or *that which can itself be stretched, cord, brace, band*, οἱ τ. τῶν κλινέων *the cords* of beds or chairs, Hdt.9.118, cf. Ar.*Eq.*532 (anap.), Philippid.12, *Michel* 832.48 (Samos, iv B.C.); sg., *bedcords*, Ar.*Lys.*923; ὠμολίνου μακροὶ τόνοι A.*Fr.*206; ἐκ τριῶν τ. of three *plies* or *strands*, of ropes, X.*Cyn.*10.2. **2.** in animals, τόνοι are *sinews* or *tendons*, Hp.*Art.*11 (= *nerves* acc. to Gal.18(1).380):—of pneumogastric *nerves*, Ruf.*Onom.*158. **3.** in machines, *twisted skeins of gut in torsion-engines*, Ph.*Bel.*65.34, al., Hero *Bel.*83.4, Plu.*Marc.* 15. **b.** in the γαστραφέτης, = αἱ ἐκ τῶν ἄκρων κάμψεις, Hero *Bel.* 75.7. **c.** in dockyard equipment, ὑποζωμάτων τέτταρας τόνους ἐγ νεωρίων *IG*2².1673.12; τ. αἰχμάλωτοι ib.1610.23; τ. αἰχμάλωτος ἀδόκιμος ib.1613.282. **4.** *row* or *line* of pillars, ib.1668.48. **II.** *stretching, tightening, straining, strain, tension*, ὁ τ. τῶν ὅπλων Hdt. 7.36; *power of contracting muscles*, Sor.1.112; τ. καὶ ῥώμη Id.2.48; τὸν τῆς ὁλκῆς τ. ὑπεκλῦσαι diminish the *strength* of the pull, ib. 61. **2.** of sounds, *raising* of the voice, Aeschin.3.209, 210, D.18.280, Phld.*Lib.*p.19 O., etc.: hence, **a.** *pitch* of the voice, Pl.*R.* 617b, Arist.*Phgn.*807ᵃ17, etc.; including *volume*, τόνοι φωνῆς· ὀξύ, βαρύ, μικρόν, μέγα X.*Cyn.*6.20; κλαυθμυρίσαι μετὰ τόνου τοῦ προσήκοντος, of a new-born baby, Sor.1.79; τῷ αὐτῷ τ. εἰπεῖν Arist.*Rh.* 1413ᵇ31; ἐν τ. ἀνιεμένοις καὶ βαρέσι Id.*Aud.*804ᵃ26; τὴν φωνὴν καὶ τὸν τ. ἐξάραντα Hieronym.ap.D.H.*Isoc.*13 (cf. Phld.*Rh.*1.198 S.); σῴζειν τὸν τ. Longin.9.13: pl., Phld.*Rh.*1.196 S.; of a musical instrument, Plu.2.827b, etc.; *diatonic scale*, *APl.*4.220 (Antip.): metaph. of colour, *'values'*, Plin.*HN*35.29. **b.** *pitch* or *accent* of a word or syllable, Arist.*Rh.*1403ᵇ29, D.T.629.27, A.D.*Pron.*8.8, al., Gal.16.495 (the meaning of the Adv. τόνῳ mentioned by A.D. *Adv.*167.2 is not given by him (= λίαν, Hsch.): τόνῳ, = μετὰ προθυμίας ἰσχυρᾶς, was read by Gal.(16.585) in Hp.*Prorrh.*1.36 (ξὺν τόνῳ or ξὺν πόνῳ codd.Hp.)). **c.** *measure* or *metre*, ἐν ἑξαμέτρῳ τ. Hdt. 1.47, 62, 5.60; ἐν τριμέτρῳ τ. Id.1.174. **d.** in Musical writers, *key*, Aristox.*Harm.*2 p.37 M., Plu.2.1134a, 1135a, etc. **3.** *mental* or *physical exertion*, τ. ἀμφ' ἀρετῆς, i.e. in praising it, Xenoph.1.20; *bodily energy*, ἰσχὺς καὶ τ. Luc.*Anach.*25, cf. 27; συστρέψαι τὸν τ. (by massage) Gal.6.91: generally, *force, intensity*, Plu.*Demetr.*21, 2.563f, etc.; τ. ὀργῆς Id.*Brut.*34; τ. πνεύματος Luc.*Dem.Enc.*7; ὁ τ. τῆς φαρμακείης its *efficiency*, Hp.*Ep.*16; τ. δυνάμεων, title of a work by Heras, Gal.13.416; τ. σοφιστικός Eun.*VS*p.497 B. **4.** in Stoic Philos., *'tension'*, *force*, in Nature and Man, πληγὴ πυρὸς ὁ τόνος ἐστί, κἂν ἱκανὸς ἐν τῇ ψυχῇ γένηται πρὸς τὸ ἐπιτελεῖν τὰ ἐπιβάλλοντα, ἰσχὺς καλεῖται καὶ κράτος Cleanth.*Stoic.*1.128; ὁ ζωτικὸς τ. *Stoic.*2.235, Gal.6.321; αἰσθητικὸς τ. *Stoic.*2.215; συνεκτικὸς τ. the *tension* which holds the universe together, ib.134. **III.** metaph., *tenor of* one's way, course, εὐθὺν τ. τρέχειν Pi.O.10(11).64; ἕνα τόνον ἔχειν Plu.Dem.13. IV. quarter of a city, IG12(5).872.36, al. (Tenos). **-όω**, brace up, τὰ σώματα καὶ τὰς ψυχάς Ti.Locr. 103d, cf. Plu.2.647c, Agathin.ap.Orib.10.7.7, Sor.1.47, al., Gal. 6.411; Ῥωμαίους ἐτόνωσεν αἰδὼς δόξης J.BJ5.11.6:—Pass., ἡ δεξιὰ τετόνωται ib.1.26.2; [οὐσίαι] ἐπὶ τὸ οἰκεῖον τῇ φύσει αὐτῶν παραγίνονται σχῆμα τετονωμέναι Stoic.2.149 (cf. τόνος II. 4); τοῦ ἀναπνεομένου ἀέρος..ὑφ' οὗ τονοῦται τὸ τῆς ψυχῆς εἶδος Nicom.ap.Theol.Ar. 48. II. place the accent on a word or syllable, accentuate it, Sch. Il.12.137; περὶ τῶν διαφόρως τονουμένων, title of work by Phlp. (ed. Egenolff, Vratisl. 1880). **-ώδης**, ες, = τονοειδής, Hp.Coac.635, Gal. 6.237, Archig.ap.eund.8.109, Paul.Aeg.1.20. **-ωσις**, εως, ἡ, strengthening, bracing, Aret.CD1.3; τοῦ βρέφους Sor.1.95; τοῦ πνεύματος ib.108; activity, force, Ruf.ap.Orib.8.24.19: abs., 'tone', Apollon.ap.Orib.7.19.1. 2. vehemence in rhetoric, τονώσεις καὶ περιπαθήσεις Ph.1.158. II. accentuation, Eust.341.21. **-ωτέον**, one must brace up, Herod.Med. in Hermes 40.591, Orib.Fr. 64. ⊛**-ωτικός**, ή, όν, bracing, strengthening, Sor.2.48, Gal.6.577: c. gen., Antyll.ap.Orib.6.32.10, 6.35.1, Sor.1.49.

**τοξ-άζομαι**, (τόξον) shoot with a bow, Od.8.220,228: c. gen. objecti, shoot at, εἰ καὶ..τοξαζοίατο φωτῶν ib.218; κακῶς ἀνδρῶν τοξάζεαι 22.27: later c. acc., τ. θῆρας Opp.C.4.54.—Poet. word, for which τοξεύω is usual in Prose, but τοξάζω (Act.) occurs in Heraclit. All.13. ⊛**-αλκέτης**, ου, ὁ, = sq., App Anth.1.95. **-αλκής**, ές, mighty with the bow, Orph.H.58.2. **-αλλίς**, v. τρωξαλλίς. **-άριον** [ᾰ], τό, Dim. of τόξον, Luc.DMort.14.2, Longus 1.7, al. ⊛**-αρχέω**, to be captain of the archers, Supp.Epigr.2.361 (Apollonia in Illyricum, iv/iii B.C.), IG4.698 (Hermione, ii A.D.). **-αρχος**, ὁ, lord of the bow, archer, of the Persians (cf. τόξον I. 1), A.Pers.556 (lyr.). II. captain of the archers, IG1$^2$.79.7, Th.3.98; also ⊛**τοξάρχης**, Arr.An.1.8. 4, 1.22.7. **-εία**, ἡ, archery, OGI339.37 (Sestos, ii B.C., pl.), D.S. 3.8, 5.74, Str.16.4.10, Ph.2.158 (pl.), J.AJ1.3.8, Hld.9.3 (pl.). II. collective for οἱ τοξόται, force of archers, Philostr.VA8.7: pl., bows, J.AJ5.5.4. **-ελκής**, ές, drawing the bow, Man.4.244. **-ευμα**, ατος, τό, arrow, Hdt.4.132, al., S.Fr.427, E.Fr.455, Dsc.3.32; τρωθεὶς εἰς τὸμ πλεύμονα τοξεύματι IG4$^2$(1).122.56 (Epid., iv B.C.); ὅσον τ. ἐξικνέεται the distance of a bow-shot, Hdt.4.139; πρὶν τ. ἐξικνεῖσθαι before an arrow reached them, X.An.1.8.19; ἐπειδὴ εἰς τ. ἀφίκοιντο came within shot, Id.Cyr.1.4.23; ἐντὸς τοξεύματος ibid., E.HF991; ἔξω τοξεύματος Th.7.30; ἔβαλλον Βακχίου τοξεύμασι κάρα γέροντος, of the cottabus, E.Fr.562; φαρέτρα τοξευμάτων a quiverful of arrows (as a prize), IG12(5).647.28 (Ceos, iii B.C.); missile of any kind, Ascl.Tact.1.2: metaph., of songs and words, Pi.I.5(4).47; so καρδίας τοξεύματα S.Ant.1085; ὀμμάτων θελκτήριον τόξευμα A.Supp.1005. II. collective in pl. for οἱ τοξόται, force of archers, Hdt.6.112, Plu.Pyrrh.21. **-εύς**, έως, ὁ, bowman: only as pr.n. Bowman, Hes.Fr.110.4. **-ευσις**, εως, ἡ, a shooting with the bow, metaph., ὀμμάτων Lib.Descr.30.8,9. **-ευτήρ**, ῆρος, ὁ, = sq. II, Arat.506,685; the Centaur, ib.400: = sq. I, c. gen., βελέμνων Orph. L.499: fem. **τοξεύτειρα**, Opp.C.3.22. II. a species of wolf, Ar. Byz.Epit.89.11, Opp.C.3.296. **-ευτής**, οῦ, ὁ, bowman, archer, Il. 23.850, Call.Fr.130, D.P.751. II. the constellation Sagittarius, Arat.306, al. **-ευτικός**, ή, όν, of archery, ἡ τ. (sc. τέχνη) Gal.Thras. 45, cf. Eust.40.22. **-ευτός**, ή, όν, struck by an arrow, ἐκ Φοίβου S.Ph. 335. **-εύω**, shoot with the bow, τινος at a mark, Il.23.855; πάντες, ὥστε τοξόται σκοποῦ, τοξεύετ' ἀνδρὸς τοῦδε S.Ant.1034; also τ. ἐπὶ σκοποῦ Pl.Sis.391a; ἐς ἀλλήλους Hdt.1.214, cf. X.Cyr.3.3.66; κατά τινων Luc.Pisc.7 (metaph.); ἐς χωρίον, ἐς τὰ γυμνά, Hdt.8.128, Th.3. 23; ἐπ' ἐκεῖνο Luc.Cal.15 (metaph.); πρὸς τὸν οὐρανόν Hdt.4.94: metaph., τοξεύσασα τῆς εὐδοξίας E.Tr.643, cf. Ion 1411: abs., use the bow, Hdt.1.136; τὸν παῖδα τοξεύσας ἀπολώλεκε by an arrow, Id.3.74, cf. Ar. Av.1187, Th.4.48, etc.; καθ' ὑπερβολὰν τοξεύσας having shot too high, S.OT1197 (lyr.); εὔστοχα or ἄσκοπα τ. with good or no aim, Luc. Nigr.36, Tox.62. II. c. acc. objecti, shoot or hit with an arrow, X.An.4.2.12; θηρίον Id.Cyr.1.2.10; ἔλαφον Arist.Mir.837$^a$15:—Pass., to be struck by an arrow, Th.3.98, X.An.1.8.20, 4.1.18, Dsc.3. 32. 2. metaph., Ἔρως ἐτόξευσ' αὐτόν E.Tr.255; ἡ τυραννὶς πάντοθεν τοξεύεται is aimed at, Id.Fr.850. 3. c. acc. rei, shoot from a bow, metaph., discharge, send forth, τ. ὕμνους Pi.I.2.3; γλῶσσα τοξεύσασα μὴ τὰ καίρια A.Supp.446; ταῦτα νοῦς ἐτόξευσεν μάτην hath shot these arrows in vain, E.Hec.603:—Pass., ἡμῖν γὰρ ἤδη πᾶν τετόξευται βέλος A.Eu.676. **-ήρης**, ες, (ἀραρίσκω) furnished with the bow, χεὶρ E.Alc.35 (anap.), cf. Rh.226 (lyr.). 2. = τοξικός, τ. σαγή Id.HF188; τ. ψαλμός the twang of the bowstring, ib.1063 (lyr.). ⊛**-ία**, ἡ, = τοξῖτις, Leg.Gort.3.9. **-ιᾱνοί**, οἱ, persons born under Sagittarius, Cat.Cod.Astr.7.112 (Τοξινιανοί cod.). **-ίας**, ου, ὁ, epith. of Apollo at Sicyon, Hsch., cf. Theognost.Can.42. ⊛**-ικός**, ή, όν, of or for the bow, τ. θῶμιγξ, ἄτρακτος, A.Pers.460, Fr.139; τ. στολή an archer's equipment, Pl.Lg.833b; τ. κάλαμος a kind of Cretan reed used for arrows, Thphr.HP4.11.11. 2. ἡ τοξική (sc. τέχνη) archery, Pl. Smp.197a, La.193b, al., SIG1060.5 (Tralles, iv/iii B.C.). 3. τὸ -κόν shot-hole, loophole, Lxx Jd.5.28, Sm.Ez.40.16: so -κή (sc. θυρίς) Ph.Bel.81.25. II. of persons, skilled in the use of the bow, [Πάνδαρος] Plu.2.405b; τοξικώτατοι X.Cyr.6.2.4. III. τὸ -κόν, collectively, the bowmen, for οἱ τοξόται, Ar.Lys.462, D.C.36.47; πηλίκα τοξικὰ ἔχουσι; Mim.Oxy.413.198. 2. τ. φάρμακον poison for smearing arrows with, Arist.Mir.837$^a$13, BGU21 ii 14 (iv A.D.), Orib.Fr.126: τὸ τ. Str.3.4.18, Dsc.1.106, Ael.NA9.15: pl., Dsc.2. 79. b. = venenum, Gloss. **-ιτησία**, v. τοξότις. **-ῖτις**, ιδος, ἡ, with or without νευρά, the bowstring in torsion-engines, Hero Bel. 110.9, cf. 75.14, Ph.Bel.65.51. II. epith. of Artemis in Cos, Maiuri Nuova Silloge 452.

**τοξο-βέλεμνος**, ον, = sq., of Apollo, Orph.H.34.6. **-βόλος**, ον, shooting with the bow, AP9.179 (Leon.), 12.181 (Strat.). ⊛**-δάμᾱς** [δᾰ], αντος, ὁ, = sq., A.Pers.26,30,926 (all anap.). **-δαμνος**, ον, subduing with the bow, τ. Ἄρης the war of archers, i.e. the Persians (cf. τόξον I. 1), ib.86 (lyr.); Ἄρτεμις E.Hipp.1451, cf. Diph.30, Lyc. 1331. **-ειδής**, ές, bow-shaped, Callix.1. **-θήκη**, ἡ, bow-case, quiver, Sch.Ar.Th.1209. **-κλυτος**, ον, famed for archery, Pi.Fr.312, B.10.39.

**τόξον**, τό, bow, Il.4.124, etc.: freq. in pl. τόξα for sg., τόξ' ὤμοισιν ἔχων ἀμφηρεφέα τε φαρέτρην 1.45, al., cf. Pi.P.3.101, S.Ph.654; sts. in Prose, Heraclit.51, Hdt.2.106, PEleph.5.8 (iii B.C.); ἐτιταίνετο.. τόξα drew the bow, Il.5.97; also τόξον τιταίνει B.9.43; τόξον ἕλκετ' (v.l. εἷλκεν) Il.11.582; τόξον πῆχυν ἀνέλκειν 13.583; τόξον τείνειν, ἐντείνειν, A.Ag.364 (anap.), Fr.83; τ.. ἐντανύσαι Od.21.245, cf. Hdt.2. 173; κυκλοτερὲς μέγα τ. ἔτεινε Il.4.124, cf. E.Ba.1066; τόξου ῥῦμα (i.e. the Persians, the bow being an oriental weapon), opp. λόγχης ἰσχύς (i.e. the Greeks), A.Pers.147 (anap.). 2. τόξῳ by guess, Id.Ch.1033. 3. bowmanship, archery, τόξων εὖ εἰδώς Il.2.718, al.; τόξοισιν πίσυνος 5.205, cf. 13.716; ἡ τέχνη τῶν τ. Hdt.1.73; πρὸς τόξου κρίσιν S Tr.266; τόξῳ (sc. νικῶν) SIG1061.10 (Samos, ii B.C.). II. in pl. also, bow and arrows, τόξα πεπτεῶτ' ἄλλυδις ἄλλα Il.21.502, cf. Hdt.3.78, S.Ph.68, al.; sts. in pl. for the arrows only, ib.652, Pl.Lg.815a. III. metaph., τόξα ἡλίου its rays, E.HF 1090; ἀμπελίνοις τόξοις δαμέντες, of the effects of wine, Pi.Fr.218; τόξον μερίμνης Trag.Adesp.354; κότταβος..ὃν σκοπὸν ἐς λατάγων τόξα καθιστάμεθα for shooting of liquor from the cup, Critias 2. 2. IV. rainbow, Aeschrio 4, Lxx Ge.9.13, Hsch. s. v. εἴρη. 2. arch, AP9.694. 3. curved support, cradle used in amputations, Archig.ap.Orib.47.13.6; part of a carriage or cart, PPetr.2 p.133, 3 p.144 (iii B.C.).

**τοξόομαι**, become arched, ἐς τὸ πρηνές Aret.SA1.5; ἐς τὸ πρόσθεν ib.6.

**τοξο-ποιέω**, make like a bow, arch, τ. τὰς ὀφρῦς, of a supercilious person, Ar.Lys.8, Alciphr.3.19; τὴν ὀφρὺν εἴς τινα Longus 4. 20. **-ποιία**, ἡ, the making of bows, Poll.7.156. ⊛**-ποιός**, ὁ, bow-maker, bowyer, ibid., Gloss. **-σύνη**, ἡ, bowmanship, archery, Il.13.314, E.Andr.1194 (lyr.).—Poet. word, ἡ τοξική being used in Prose. **-τευχής**, ές, armed with the bow, A.Supp.288.

⊛**τοξότης**, ου, Dor. **-τας**, α, ὁ, bowman, archer, Il.11.385, A.Ag.628, IG1$^2$.929.67, 949.79, Hdt.3.39, Th.4.28, etc.; τοὺς τ. τούς τε ἀστοὺς καὶ τοὺς ξένους IG1$^2$.79.3; ἀτράκτων τοξόται E.Rh.312; τ. στρατός Pi. O.13.89; as a device on Persian coins, Plu.Ages.15, Art.20. 2. the Archer, Sagittarius, a sign in the Zodiac, Eudox.ap.Hipparch. 1.2.20, Luc.VH1.18, Ptol.Alm.8.1, Vett Val.11.3, Supp.Epigr.7.363. 3 (Dura-Europus, ii A.D.). II. at Athens, οἱ τοξόται were the city-police, Ar.Ach.54,711 (troch.), Eq.665, And.3.5, Pl.Prt.319c, Arist.Ath.24.3; cf. Σκύθης II. 1. b. archer-cavalry, Ascl.Tact.1.3; cf. Σκύθης II. 2.

**τοξότις**, ιδος, ἡ, fem. of foreg., archeress, of Atalanta, Call.Dian. 223; of Artemis, Orph.H.36.2, etc.: as Adj., τ. χείρ AP6.188 (Leon.):—Τοξότιδες, name of a play by A. II. loophole for shooting arrows, Plb.8.7.3; cf. τοξικός I. 3. III. a plant, = ἀρτεμισία, Poet. de herb.26, Apul.Herb.10; also called **τοξιτησία**, Ps.-Dsc.3.113.

**τοξουλκός**, όν, (ἕλκω) drawing the bow, τοξουλκῷ λήματι πιστούς trusting to skill in archery, of the Persians (cf. τόξον I. 1), A.Pers.55 (anap.). II. τ. αἰχμή the bow-stretching arrow, ib.239 (troch.).

**τοξο-φορέω**, bear a bow, of Eros, AP12.162 (Asclep.). **-φόρμιγξ**, f.l. in Demetr.Eloc.85 (τόξῳ φόρμιγγα Nauck). **-φόρος**, ὁ, ἡ, bow-bearing, epith. of Artemis, Il.21.483, Simon.107.4 (= IG7.53), Ar.Th.970 (lyr.); of Apollo, h.Ap.13,126, Pi.Pae.Fr.19.30; of Heracles, E.Tr.804 (lyr.); of the Cretans, Pi.P.5.41; of the Medes and Persians, Simon.137.3, Orac.ap.Hdt.9.43, cf. Epigr.ap.Arist.Fr.674; of the Phrygians, E.Rh.32 (lyr.): Subst., οἱ τ., = τοξόται, Hdt.1. 103. **-χίτων** [ῐ], ωνος, ὁ, ἡ, equipped with bow and arrows, Epich. 123 (dub. l.).

**τοξωτός**, ή, όν, = arcuatus, Gloss.

**τοπάεις**, ὁ, governor, Sammelb.5231.2 (i A.D.), 5275.1 (i A.D.). (Egyptian word.)

**τόπαζος**, ὁ, a gem of green hue (Plin.HN37.107), hence prob. chrysolite or peridot, AP6.329 (Leon.Alex.), J.AJ3.7.5, D.P.1121, Orph. L.278:—also **τόπαζον**, τό, Eust.ad D.P. l.c.; **τοπάζιον**, Lxx Ex.28. 17, Ps.118(119).127, Str.16.4.6, D.S.3.39, Apoc.21.20:—Pliny (HN l.c.) gives the name of topazon (v.l. topazium) to two varieties. (From the Trogodyte language acc. to Plin. l.c.; perh. the same as ταβάσιος.)

**τοπάζω**, aim at, guess, divine, τὸ γὰρ τοπάζειν τοῦ σαφ' εἰδέναι δίχα A.Ag.1369; ἃ δὲ δόξῃ τοπάζω, ταῦτ' ἰδεῖν σαφῶς θέλω S.Fr.235; τοπάζετε Ar.V.73; τ. περί τινος Pl.Tht.155d: folld. by a relat. clause, ib.151b; εἴτε.., εἴτε μή.. Id.Chrm.159a: folld. by acc. et inf., Id. Grg.489d, Phdr.228d:—Pass., νέον τι γίνεσθαι ἐτοπάσθη D.C.78.25. (The literal sense to put in a place, given by Hsch., is not found in classical Gr.)

**τοπαρχ-εῖον**, τό, = pagus, Gloss. **-έω**, to be a τοπάρχης, PSI6. 617.20 (iii B.C.), PCair.Zen.322.3 (iii B.C.), Tz.H.10.426, etc. **-ης**, ου, ὁ, governor of a district, esp. in Egypt, Lxx Ge.41.34, PRev. Laws 37.3, 41.7, al. (iii B.C.), PTeb.48.6 (ii B.C.); elsewh., Lxx Da.3.

94(27), D S.6.1, J.*AJ*8.7.2, *IGRom.*3.901 (Cilicia, i B.C.), Procop.*Pers.* 2.12, *Cat.Cod.Astr.*5(3).89; cf. τοπογραμματεύς. **-ία**, ἡ, *district governed by a* τοπάρχης, *PSI*4.412 (iii B.C.), *PRev.Laws* 87.4 (iii B.C.), *PTeb.*24.62 (ii B.C.), Lxx 1 *Ma.*11.28, *OGI*669.49 (Egypt, i A.D.), J. *AJ*13.4.9, al., *POxy.*2118.3 (ii A.D.). **-ος**, ὁ, ἡ, *ruling over a place*, γυνή *mistress*, A.*Ch.*664 (ταπαρχος (suprascr. ὁ) cod. M). II. = τοπάρχης, *SIG*880.29, al. (Pizus, iii A.D.).

**τοπασ-τέον**, (τοπάζω) *one must conjecture*, Hsch. **-τικός**, ή, όν, *divinatory, sagacious*, Men.*Epit.*340.

**τοπεῖον**, τό, *rope, cord*, Archipp.33, Stratt.30, Is.*Fr.*24, *IG*2$^{2}$.1609. 64,101, 1611.299, *SIG*241 *A* 29 (Delph., iv B.C.); cf. τοπήϊον.

**τοπέω** or **-άω**, = τοπάζω, Eust.543.17; cf. ὑποτοπέω.

**τοπηγορία**, ἡ, *discussion on a* τόπος or *common-place, rhetorical treatment* of the same, Longin.11.2: pl., Id.12.5, 32.5.

**τοπήϊον**, τό, Ion. for τοπεῖον, Call.*Del.*315.

**τοπ-ίζω**, *localize*, in Pass., Simp. *in Ph.*631.8, al. ❀ **-ικός**, ή, όν, *of* or *for place, in respect to place*, ὕλη τ., = κατὰ τόπον κινητή, Arist. *Metaph.*1042$^{b}$6. Adv. -κῶς *Peripl.M.Rubr.*5, al., Plu.2.424e. 2. *local*, φυλαί D.H.4.14; ἄνεμοι Antyll.ap.Orib.9.9.1; τ. δυναστεία *local influence*, *PRyl.*114.16 (iii A.D.); τ. βία *PFlor.*58.8 (iii A.D.); *of local make*, ἀγγεῖον *TAM*2.437 (Patara). Adv. -κῶς *in the local dialect*, opp. συνήθως, Sch.Th.*Oxy.*853 xiii 3. 3. of medicines and medical treatment or ailments, *to be applied locally, topical*, Sor.2.15, Gal.12. 383; τ. συγκίνησις Sor.1.46 (τροπ- cod.); τ. ἕλκος, πόνος, Id.2.36, *Fract.*15; τ. διάθεσις Gal.16.710. Adv. -κῶς Ruf.*Anat.*30, Sor.1. 102. 4. τ. ἐπίρρημα adverb *of place*, D.T.641.32, A.D.*Conj.*243. 29. II. *concerning* τόποι or *common-places*, Arist.*Rh.*1396$^{b}$21; he wrote a treatise τὰ τοπικά, being (as he says) *the method* or *theory of drawing conclusions* ἐξ ἐνδόξων; τ. ἀντίθεσις Hermog.*Stat.*6; -ώτεροι λόγοι Id.*Id.*2.11. Adv. -κῶς Id.*Stat.*3,12. ❀ **-ιον**, τό, = τόπος I. 1, 5, *field*, *PLond.*1.131.199 (i A.D.); ἅγιον τ. holy *place*, i.e. monastery, ib.77.25 (vi A.D.); *burial-place, tomb*, written τόπην *MAMA*3.81 (Diocaesarea), 372 (Corycus); τόπιν ib.168 (Corasium). II. *topia*, neut. pl., *artistic representation in which natural or artificial features of a place are used as the medium*, Vitr.7.5.2: so, opus *topiarium*, Plin.*HN*16.140, al. **-ισμός**, ὁ, *localization*, Simp. *in Ph.*774.27. **-ίτης** [ῑ], ου, ὁ, *of* or *belonging to a place*, St.Byz. s.v. Ἀγρός, al.

**τοπογραμμᾰτ-εία**, ἡ, *office of* τοπογραμματεύς, *PTeb.*24.66 (ii B.C.), *PSI*1.101.16 (ii A.D.), etc. **-εύς**, έως, ὁ, *secretary of a* τόπος (v. τοπάρχης), an Egyptian official, *PPetr.*3 p.71 (iii B.C.), *PTeb.*27.2, al. (ii B.C.), *OGI*665.31, 666.14 (both i A.D.), etc.

**τοπογρᾰφ-έω**, *describe a place* or *country*, Ath.1.16d. II. *determine the site of* a place, Str.13.1.5. **-ία**, ἡ, *description of a country, topography*, Id.8.1.3 (pl.); τῶν ἠπείρων ib.1, cf. Ptol.*Geog.* 1.1.5. 2. Astrol., *description of a 'region'*, Petos.ap.Vett.Val. 125.22. ❀ **-ος** (parox.), ὁ, *topographer*, D.S.31.18.

**τοπο-θεσία**, ἡ, *topography*, τῆς κατ' Αἴγυπτον χώρας D.S.1.42, cf. Cic.*Att.*1.16.18, Ptol.*Geog.*1.1.3. 2. Astrol., *situation, arrangement of heavenly bodies in regions*, Vett.Val.42.12. II. *description of a place, topographical account*, Cic.*Att.*1.13.5. 2. *plan, survey*, *POxy.*100.10 (ii A.D.), etc. 3. *region, quarter*, *PMasp.*162.9 (vi A.D.). 4. = *canalis*, *Gloss.* **-θετέω**, *describe*, τὴν ὅλην οἰκουμένην Str.2.5.1, cf. 12.3.23 (Casaub.). **-κρᾰτέω**, *rule* or *be master of a place*, Ph.2.383. **-κράτωρ** [ᾰ], ορος, ὁ, = τόπαρχος I, Paul.Al.*O.* 1. **-μᾰχέω**, *wage war by seeking* or *holding strong positions* which the enemy dares not attack, Str.1.1.17, Plu.*Flam.*3, *Cleom.*20, etc.; *manœuvre for position*, Id.2.487f, *Demetr.*43; περὶ τῆς στάσεως D.S. 13.39.

❀**τόπος**, ὁ (fem. by attraction τόπον τὰν καλειμέναν Δαματρεῖαν *IG* 9(1).32.80 (Stiris, ii B.C.)), *place, region*, first in A. (v. infr.), afterwds. freq. in all writers; periphr., χθονὸς πᾶς τ., i.e. the whole earth, A. *Eu.*249; ἐς τὸν Ἑλλήνων τ. Id.*Pers.*790; ἐν Ἑλλάδος τόποις in Greece, ib.796; ἐν Αὐλίδος τ. Id.*Ag.*191 (lyr.); Πέλοπος ἐν τ. Id.*Eu.*703, cf. 292; πρὸς ἑσπέρους τ. towards the West, Id.*Pr.*350; πρόσθε Σαλαμῖνος τόπων before Salamis, Id.*Pers.*447; Θρῄκης ἐκ τόπων E.*Alc.*67; Διρκαίων ἐκ τ. Id.*Ph.*1027 (lyr.): so in Prose, *district*, ὁ τ. ὁ Ἑλληνικός Isoc. 5.107, cf. *Ep.*1.8; ὁ περὶ Θρᾴκην τ. D.20.59; ὁ ἐπὶ Θρᾴκης τ. Aeschin.2. 9, 3.73; ὁ τ. οὗτος, ἐν τούτοις τοῖς τ., X.*An.*4.4.4, *Cyr.*2.4.20; ὅλος τ. a whole *region*, D.19.230; κατὰ τόπους καὶ κώμας Pl.*Criti.*119a; οἱ τῆς χώρας τ. the *places* of a country, Id.*Lg.*760c, etc. (but ὁ τ. τῆς χώρας the *geographical position*, D.4.31; *region*, Pl.*Lg.*705c); ὁ ἅγιος τ., of Jerusalem, Lxx 2 *Ma.*2.18 (cf. infr. 5); the universe divided into three τόποι, Arist.*IA*706$^{b}$3, *Cael.*312$^{a}$8 (contrast *PA*666$^{a}$15, etc.); οἱ κοινοὶ τ. public *sites* or *buildings*, *IG*4$^{2}$(1).65.8 (Epid.); ἄσυλος τ. *BGU*1053 ii 9 (i B.C.), *PTeb.*5.83 (pl., ii B.C.); οἰκίαι καὶ τόποι houses and *sites*, ib.281.12 (ii B.C.); so ψιλοὶ τ. *sites* not built upon, *OGI*52.2 (Ptolemais, iii/ii B.C.). 2. *place, position*, οὐ τὸν τρόπον, ἀλλὰ τὸν τ. μόνον μεταλλάξαι Aeschin.3.78; ὑπολιποῦ τ. leave a *space* (in a document), *PCair.Zen.*327.83 (iii B.C.); περικήπῳ τ. καταλιπεῖν ib.193.8 (iii B.C.); τ. ἔχειν have a *place*, D.H.*Dem.*23, Plu.2. 646a; φίλου τ. ἔχειν hold *the place of*.., Arr.*Epict.*2.4.5; Μερόλας ὁ αἱρεθεὶς ὕπατος εἰς τὸν τοῦ Κίννα τ. D.S.38/39.3; ἐνεγράφη εἰς τὴν ἱερωσύνην εἰς τὸν Λευκίου Δομιτίου τ. τετελευτηκότος Nic.Dam.*Fr.* 127.4 J., cf. D.H.2.73; ἀναπληροῦν τὸν τ. τοῦ ἰδιώτου 1 *Ep.Cor.*14.16; τ. ἔχειν also = have *room* (to grow), Thphr.*HP*1.7.1; τόπῳ c. gen., *in place of, instead of*, Hdn.2.14.5; ἀνὰ τόπον on *the spot, immediately*, E.*Supp.*604 (lyr., dub.l.); so ἐν τόπῳ *IG*12(7).515.63 (Amorgos); ἐπὶ τόπου Plb.4.73.8; ἐπὶ τῶν τ. *PEnteux.*55.5 (iii B.C.), *UPZ*70.16 (ii B.C.), *CIL*3.567.3 (Delph., ii B.C.), *POxy.*2106.23 (iv A.D.), etc.; κατὰ τὸν αὐτὸν τ. S.E.*P.*3.1; παρὰ τόπον at a wrong *place*, Str.10.2. 21, Arr.*Epict.*3.21.16 (but παρὰ τ. καὶ παρὰ καιρόν by virtue of the *place* and the time, ib.3.21.14). 3. *place* or *part* of the body, Hp.*Aph.* 2.46, *Loc.Hom.*tit., Sor.2.40, al., Gal. in titles of works, e.g. περὶ τῶν πεπονθότων τόπων, περὶ συνθέσεως φαρμάκων τῶν κατὰ τόπους; esp. ὁ τόπος, *pudendum muliebre*, Arist.*HA*572$^{b}$28, 583$^{a}$15, cf. Sor.2.62 (pl.). 4. *place, passage* in an author, κατὰ τόπους τινὰς τῆς ἱστορίας Plb.12.25f.1, cf. Ph.2.63, *Ev.Luc.*4.17, Sor.2.57,58, etc.; the word is prob. interpolated in X.*Mem.*2.1.20. 5. *burial-place*, *IG*12(7). 401 (Amorgos), al., *Ev.Marc.*16.6; also in codd. of E.*Heracl.*1041 (fort. leg. τάφον); later ὁ ἅγιος τ. is freq. of the *grave* of a martyr, or of a *monastery* associated with it, *PMasp.*94.18 (vi A.D.), etc. 6. in Egypt, *district, department*, a sub-division of the νομός, = τοπαρχία, *PMich.Zen.*43.8 (iii B.C.), *Theb.Ostr.*27.2 (ii B.C.): but most freq. in pl., ὁ ἐπὶ τῶν τ. στρατηγός, πράκτωρ, etc., *PEnteux.*27.9 (iii B.C.), *PRein.*7.17,35 (ii B.C.), etc.; οἱ ἔξω τ. dub. sens. in *PEnteux.*87.2 (iii B.C.), *BGU*1114.6 (i B.C.), etc. 7. a *room* in a house, τόπον ἕνα ἄνευ ἐνοικίου ib.896.4 (ii A.D.); δύο τόπους ἤτοι συμπόσια *POxy.*1129. 10 (v A.D.), cf. 502.34 (ii A.D.), 912.13 (iii A.D.). 8. *position* on the zodiac, Vett.Val.139.13; esp. the twelve *regions* of 30°, Ptol. *Tetr.*128, Heph.Astr.1.12. 9. αὐτὸς ὁ θεὸς καλεῖται τόπος, τῷ περιέχειν τὰ ὅλα Ph.1.630, cf. *Corp.Herm.*2.12, Hippol.*Haer.*6.32. II. *topic*, Isoc.5.109, 10.38, Aeschin.3.216, Plb.21.19.2, Phld.*Rh.*1.119S., etc. 2. *common-place* or *element* in Rhetoric, ὁ τοῦ μᾶλλον καὶ ἧττον τ. Arist.*Rh.*1358$^{a}$14, cf. 1396$^{b}$30, 1397$^{a}$7; τὸ αὐτὸ λέγω στοιχεῖον καὶ τ. ib.1403$^{a}$18: pl., Phld.*Rh.*1.226S. b. = ὁμολογουμένου πράγματος αὔξησις, Hermog.*Prog.*11; κοινὸς τ. ib.6. c. generally, *sphere*, ὁ πραγματικὸς τ. D.H.*Comp.*1. III. metaph., *opening, occasion, opportunity*, ἐν τ. τινὶ ἀφανεῖ Th.6.54 (but τρόπῳ is prob. cj.); ὀργῇ διδόναι τ. Plu.2.462b; μὴ δίδοτε τ. τῷ διαβόλῳ *Ep. Eph.*4.27; δότε τ. τῇ ὀργῇ leave *room* for the wrath (of God), i.e. let God punish, *Ep.Rom.*12.19; μὴ καταλείπεσθαί σφισι τ. ἐλέους Plb.1.88.2; μετανοίας τ. οὐχ εὗρε *Ep.Hebr.*12.17; οὐδὲ φυγῆς τόπον εὐμοιρήσαντες Hld.6.13; τ. διδόναι τινί c. inf., give *occasion* to.., Lxx *Si.*4.5.

**τοποτηρ-έω**, *to be warden of a* τόπος I. 6, *Sammelb.*7433.3,7, al. (v A.D.), *PFlor.*295.11 (vi A.D.). **-ησία**, ἡ, *office of* τοποτηρητής, Preisigke *Berichtigungsliste* p.102 (vi A.D.). ❀ **-ητής**, οῦ, ὁ, *warden of a* τόπος I. 6, Baillet *Inscr. des tombeaux des rois à Thèbes* 482,788, *PMonac.*6.11 (vi A.D.), etc.

**τοράλλιον**, τό, = Lat. *torale, bedcover*, Cumont *Fouilles de Doura-Europos* 372 No.13; cf. τολάριον.

**τόρβηλος**· μεμψίμοιρος, Hsch.

**τόργος**, ὁ, *vulture*, Call.*Fr.*204, Lyc.357,1080, prob. cj. in Muson. *Fr.*18$^{A}$ p.98 H. II. τ. ὑγρόφοιτος, i.e. *swan*, Lyc.88.

**τορδύλιον**, τό, = sq., Dsc.3.54 (τόρδιλον, τορδίλιον codd.), *Eup.*2. 81.

**τόρδῠλον**, τό, *hartwort, Tordylium officinale*, Ruf.ap.Orib.7.26. 118, Gal.11.646, 13.176; *tordylon*, Plin.*HN*24.177; cf. ὄρδειλον.

**τορ-εία**, ἡ, *carving in relief*, i.e. *repoussé* or *chasing*, Aristeas 58, Ph.2.478, J.*AJ*8.3.3, Plu.*Aem.*32, *Dem.*25. 2. metaph. of *rhetorical art*, Poll.6.141. **-εῖον**, τό, *chased work*, Hdn.*Epim.*135.

**τορέλλη**· ἐπιφώνημα θρηνητικὸν σὺν αὐλῷ Θρακικόν, Hsch.

**τόρ-ευμα**, ατος, τό, *embossed work, work in relief* (cf. τορεύω II), in pl., Men.24, Sopat.19; τ. ἀργυρᾶ καὶ χρυσᾶ D.S.3.47; ὀστράκινα τ. Str.8.6.23. II. in E.*HF*978 τόρ.ευμα (L$^{2}$P$^{2}$ ut vid.) is f.l. for τόρνευμα (LP). **-εύς**, έως, ὁ, *boring tool* used in making wells, Philyll.18 as cited by Poll.7.192, cf. 10.149 (τόρος Eust., cf. Hsch., Phot.); γόμφων τ. for boring holes for dowels, *AP*6.205.8 (Leon.). **-ευσις**, εως, ἡ, = *caelatura*, *Gloss.*; cf. τόρνευσις. **-ευτής**, οῦ, ὁ, *one who works in relief*, Plb.26.1.2, *CIG*3306 (Smyrna), D.H.*Comp.*25, *Sardis* 7(1) No.56.10 (ii A.D.); cf. τορνευτής. **-ευτικός**, ή, όν, prop. *of* or *for metal-work, skilled therein*: but Lat. *toreutice*, *sculpture* in general, Plin.*HN*34.54; opp. *graphice* (painting), ib.35. 77; cf. τορεύω II, and v. τορνευτικός. ❀ **-ευτός**, ή, όν, *worked in relief, chased*, ποτήριον Men.977; σκύφος *OGI*214.54 (Milet., iii B.C.); ἅρμα D.S.18.27. II. metaph., *elaborate*, ἔπος *AP*9.545 (Crin.), cf. D.H. *Comp.*25. ❀ **-εύω**, (τόρος) prop. = τορέω, *bore through*: metaph., ᾠδὴν τ. *sing a piercing* strain, Ar.*Th.*986 (lyr., τορνεύειν cj. Bentley). II. *work* metal, whether *in repoussé* or *chasing*, c. acc. materiae, τ. σίδηρον Str.13.4.17; ἄργυρον *Anacreont.*3,4: abs., Plu.*Aem.*37. 2. c. acc. objecti, *represent in this manner*, πόντον *Anacreont.*55.1; μάχην Paus. 1.28.2; παιδίον Id.5.17.4; ἐρέβινθον Plu.2.204f; Σάτυρον Pl.*Epigr.*28; ζῷα τετορευμένα Callix.2 (-νευ- cod. A Ath., corr. Salm.); γράμμα τορευθὲν *AP*7.274 (Honest.). III. metaph. of style, D.H.*Th.*24.—Freq. confounded with τορνεύω, cf. Callix. l. c. and v. supr. I. **-έω**, the pres. only in Hsch. (except that ἀντιτοροῦντα occurs in *h.Merc.*283): fut. -ήσω (ἀντι-) ib.178: aor. 1 part. τορήσας *Sardis* 7(1) No.83, (ἀντι-) Il. 10.267: aor. 2 ἔτορον Il. (v. infr.); redupl. τετορήσας *h.Merc.*119, cf. Hsch. s. vv. τέτορεν, τετόρη:—Pass., pf. τετόρημαι Nonn. (v. infr.): (τόρος):—*bore, pierce*, ἔτορε ζωστῆρα Il.11.236; τορήσας, v. supr.:—Pass., σπλάγχνα.. τετορημένα χαλκῷ Nonn.*D.*5.26; ἔγχεϊ ib.13. 493. 2. metaph., *proclaim in shrill piercing tones*, irreg. fut. τετορήσω Ar.*Pax* 381; cf. τορεύω I, τορός. II. = τορνεύω, *work, shape*, χέλυν Arat.269, cf. *AP*9.162. **-ητός**, ή, όν, *liable to be pierced*: *vulnerable*, Lyc.456.

**τόρμᾰ**, ης, ἡ, *wheel-rut*, Lyc.262 (= τὸ χάραγμα τὸ ἀπὸ τοῦ τροχοῦ Sch.):—τόρμη· εὐθὺς δρόμος κατὰ τέχνην, καὶ στροφή, καὶ σύμπας (δρόμος), Hsch. II. *socket, joint*, βουβῶνος ἐν τόρμαισι Lyc. 487.

**τορμικά**, τά, *parts mortised*, Hero *Bel*.94.12.

**τορμίον**, v. τόρμος II. 2. **τορμίς**· ἡ δέσποινα, Hsch.

**τόρμος**, ὁ, *hole* or *socket*, in which a pin or peg is stuck, Hdt.4.72, D.S.2.8; *mortise*, *Inscr.Délos* 504 *A* 7 (iii B.C.), *IG*2².1672.175; *nave* of a wheel, like πλήμνη, Hsch., Phot. II. *tenon*, Ph.*Bel*.55.11, 64.15, Hero *Bel*.95.5, Apollod.*Poliorc*.178.2. 2. *projecting peg* or *pivot*, Hero *Bel*.88.4.—Dim. **τορμίον**, τό, small *projecting peg*, Ph.*Bel*.75.42.

**τορν-εία**, ἡ, *crooked timber for shipbuilding*, Thphr.*HP* 5.7.3. **-ευμα**, ατος, τό, *whirling motion*, as of a lathe; cf. τόρευμα II. 2. pl., *turner's chips* or *shavings*. Hp.*Ulc*.12, *IG*11(2).287 *A* 23 (Delos, iii B.C.), Dsc.1.80, Ruf.*Ren.Ves*.8.5. **-ευσις**, εως, ἡ, = τορεία I, Sch.D Il.18.590 (fort. τόρευσις). **-ευτήριον**, τό, *turner's chisel*, Thphr.*HP* 5.6.4. **-ευτής**, οῦ, ὁ, *turner*, *IG*1².374.355, Aristox.*Harm*.p.33 M., *Sammelb*.3950, 5480, v.l. for τορευ- in M.Ant.5.1; τορνευταί· γλύπται, Hsch. **-ευτικός**, ή, όν, *of* or *for turning on a lathe*: ἡ -κή (sc. τέχνη) v.l. for τορευ- in M.Ant.5.1. **-ευτο-λῦρ-ασπῐδο-πηγός**, ὁ, *lyre-turner and shield-maker*, Com. word in Ar.*Av*.491 (anap.). ❋**-ευτός** (also **τορονευτός**, q.v.), ή, όν, *turned on a lathe*, ποτήρια Men.977, cf. *PLond*.2.402ᵛ.31 (ii B.C.), Sch.Od.1.440: written **τορυνευτός**, *Arch.Pap*.1.64 (ii B.C.). II. *fit for turning*, λίθοι Thphr.*Lap*.5. **-εύω**, *work with a lathe* or *chisel, turn*, Pl.*Criti*.113d; κρίκους ἐκ πυρῆνος Thphr.*HP* 4.2.7, cf. 5.3.2 (Pass.); πομφόλυγας *IG*1².373.254; τοὺς πόλους τ. στρογγύλους ib.2².1675.22:—Med., κυκλοτερὲς αὐτὸ ἐτορνεύσατο Pl.*Ti*.33b:—Pass., Thphr.*Lap*.42, Hero *Aut*.26.7, J.*AJ* 3.7.6. 2. metaph. of verses, *turn neatly, round off*, Ar.*Th*.54, cf. Plu.*Aem*.37. II. *turn round*, as a carpenter turns an auger, E.*Cyc*.661 (lyr.).—Cf. τορεύω fin.

**τορνία** σταφυλή, ἡ, a kind of *grape*, Poll.6.82: hence **τόρνιος** οἶνος Hp.*Morb*.2.47.

**τορνίσκος**, ὁ, Dim. (in form) of τόρνος, Ph.*Bel*.53.4, *IG*11(2).161 *A* 105 (Delos, iii B.C.).

**τορνο-γρᾰφέω**, *describe a circle*, Sch.BT Il.23.255. **-ειδής**, ές, *shaped like a circle, rounded*, Eust.ad D.P.157.

**τορν-όομαι**, *mark off with the* τόρνος, *make round*, τορνώσαντο σῆμα *they rounded off* the barrow, Il.23.255; ὅσσον τίς τ' ἔδαφος νηὸς τορνώσεται large as the bottom of a ship which a man *shall round off*, with allusion to the round shape of a merchant vessel (cf. γαῦλος), opp. to a ship of war, Od.5.249, cf. D.P.1170, Tryph.64.—Act. τορνῶσαι· περιγράψαι, κυκλῶσαι, Hsch., who also has Pass. τορνοῦμαι δὲ πρὸς μέτρον· ἀντὶ τοῦ περιγράφομαι (perh. a Trag. fragment). **-ος**, ὁ, *carpenter's tool for drawing a circle*, like our *compasses*, prob. a pin at the end of a string, Lat. *tornus* (Plin.*HN* 7.198), Thgn.805; κυκλοτερὴς ὡς ἀπὸ τόρνου (of the representation of the earth in early maps) Hdt.4.36; τροχὸς τόρνῳ γραφόμενος E.*Ba*.1067 (perh. in signf. II); κύκλος τις ὡς τόρνοισιν ἐκμετρούμενος Id.*Fr*.382.3. 2. κύκλου τ. the *centre* of a circle, X.*Vect*.1.6. II. *turning-lathe*, βόμβυκας τόρνου κάματον A.*Fr*.57.3 (anap.); καθάπερ τῆς ἐν τόρνῳ κυκλοφορουμένης σφαίρας as of a ball being turned in a *lathe*, Arist.*Mu*.391ᵇ22; τὰ τοῖς τόρνοις γιγνόμενα ἐπίπεδά τε καὶ στερεά Pl.*Phlb*.51c, cf. 56c; ὁ Ἰουδαϊκὸς λίθος.. ἔχων γραμμὰς παραλλήλους ὡς ἀπὸ τόρνου Dsc.5.137; *metae..ex torno ita perfectae, ut alia in aliam inire convenireque possit*, Vitr.9.8.6, cf. 10.7.3; ἄξων ἀπὸ τόρνου εἰργασμένος Hero *Spir*.1.16, cf. *Aut*.11.2. III. *that which is turned, circle, round*, D.P.157. **-ωτός**, ή, όν, *rounded with the* τόρνος, *turned*, Hdn.Gr.1.221.

**τορογλῠφεύς**, έως, ὁ, *tool used by a worker in relief*, prob. *drill*, *IG*11(2).199 *A* 86 (Delos, iii B.C.).

**τορονευτός**, ή, όν, = τορνευτός, *Edict.Diocl*.15.43.

**τορόνος**· τόρνος, Ταραντῖνοι, Hsch.

❋**τορός**, ά, όν, (cf. τέρε-τρον, τετραίνω) *piercing*: I. of the voice, *piercing, thrilling*, Luc.*Bacch*.7, Alciphr.3.48; τὸ τ. τῆς φωνῆς Porph.*Plot*.2: metaph., τ. φόβος *thrilling* fear, A.*Ch*.32 (lyr.). Adv., τορῶς γεγωνεῖν E.*Ion* 696 (lyr.): neut. as Adv., τορὸν ἠχεῖν, βοᾶν, Philostr.*VS* 1.25.10, *Her*.19.12. b. of the ear, *acute, fine*, *AP* 7.409 (Antip. Thess.). c. of the eye, *piercing*, Opp.*C*.1.181. 2. metaph., *clear, distinct, plain*, ἑρμηνεύς A.*Ag*.1062, cf. 616; ἔπος, μῦθος, ib.1162 (lyr.), *Supp*.274; τορὸν γὰρ ἥξει Id.*Ag*.254 (lyr.); τ. ὕμνοι dub. cj. in *AP* 4.1.7 (Mel.); ἐρέω τι τορώτερον (cj. for τομώτερον) Call.*Del*.94. Adv., ἀλλὰ τορῶς ταῦτ' ἴσθι Emp.23.11; τ. τέκμηρον, λέξω, A.*Pr*.604 (lyr.), 609, etc.; προυξεπίστασθαι ib.699; ἐπεξελθεῖν ib.870; ἀπαγγεῖλαι, φράσαι, Id.*Ag*.632, 1584; οὐκ ἴσμεν τ. E.*Rh*.77; ἀκούσας οὐ τ. ib.656. II. of persons, *sharp, ready, smart*, X.*Lac*.2.11 (Sup.), D.H.*Rh*.11.5, cj. in Call.*Fr*.78 (Sup.). Adv., ἐπερείδεσθαι τορῶς Ar.*Ra*.1102 (troch.); τ. τε καὶ ὀξέως διακονεῖν Pl.*Tht*.175e, Luc.*Anach*.21, *Merc.Cond*.35: Sup. -ώτατα Ael.*NA* 1.43.

**τόρος**, ὁ, *borer, drill*, used in trying for water, etc., Philyll.18 (v. τορεύς), *IG*2².1673.36, 54.

**τοροτίξ**, imitation of *a bird's note*, Ar.*Av*.267; τοροτοροτοροτοροτίξ ib.260; τοροτοροτοροτορολιλιλίξ ib.262 (all lyr.).

**τόρτυρα**· τῶν κεραμίων προμήκης πυθμήν, Hsch. (perh. f.l. for γόργυρα). **τορτυρόμενον**· νιφόμενον, Id.

**τορῡν-άω**, = τορύνω, Hp.*Int*.44, Eub.86, Dsc.*Eup*.2.54, Dieuch.ap. Orib.4.7.18, Gal.6.498, etc. **-η**, ἡ, *stirrer, ladle* for stirring things while boiling, Sophr.110, Ar.*Eq*.984 (lyr.), *Av*.78; χρυσῆ τ. ἢ συκίνη Pl.*Hp.Ma*.290d. II. τορύνη· σιτῶδές τι, Hsch. [ῡ in Ar. ll.cc., but ῠ in *AP* 6.305 (Leon.): nothing can be proved from Eup.370.] **-ευτός**, v. τορνευτός. **-ητός**, ή, όν, *stirred about*, Cael.Aur.*TP* 1.1. **-ω**, *stir up* or *about*, Ar.*Eq*.1172. II. = *insculpo*, *Gloss*.

**τοσᾰ-ετής**, ές, *so many years long*, πόλεμος Eust.222.37. **-κῐς**, Adv., (τόσος) *so many times, so often*, Polyaen.4.3.9; Ep. **τοσσάκι** Il.21.268, 22.197, Simon.145, etc.; elided, τοσσάχ' ὕδωρ Od.11.586. **-πλᾰσίων**, ον, gen. ονος, = τοσαυταπλάσιος, Porph. *in Harm*. p.325 W.

**τοσαυτά-κις** [ᾰ], Adv. = τοσάκις, And.4.36, Pl.*R*.546c, Arist.*Ph*.237ᵇ32, etc. **-πλάσιος** [πλᾰ], α, ον, *so many fold, so many times* or *so much more*, corresponding to relat. ὁσαπλάσιος, Id.*Pr*.917ᵇ23, 929ᵇ14; *the same multiple as*, Euc.5.1, Archim.*Sph.Cyl*.1.2, etc.:—also **-πλᾰσίων**, ον, gen. ονος, Id.*Aequil*.1.6, al., Theo Sm. p.76 H. **-χῶς**, Adv. *in so many ways*, Arist.*APr*.48ᵇ3, *Metaph*.1022ᵃ11, Thphr.*HP* 8.7.5, D.H.*Lys*.14, Alex.Aphr. *in Top*.61.13.

**τόσνυν**, v. ὄνυ.

❋**τόσος**, Ep. **τόσσος**, η, ον (both forms in Hom. (v. infr.) and Hes.(*Op*.680, 711, *Th*.705), the latter form also in Trag. (lyr.), S.*Aj*.184), Demonstr. corresponding to the Relat. ὅσος and interrog. πόσος:—of Size, Space, and Quantity, *so great, so vast*: of Time, *so long*: of Number, pl., *so many*: of Sound, *so loud*: generally of Degree, *so much, so very*:—freq. answered by the Relat. ὅσος, οὔ τι τόσος γε ὅσος Τελαμώνιος Αἴας Il.2.528; κακὸν τόσον ὅσσον ἐτύχθη 17.410, cf. Hes.*Op*.680: sts. with an Adv. as relat., τόσων.. ὡς.. A.*Ag*.866: freq. abs., when it either refers to something already mentioned, *so great* or *so many*, Il.9.546, 21.321, or to a well-known magnitude, which may be great or small, acc. to the context, *just so much* or *just so many*, Od.14.100, 22.144, Hes.*Th*.705, etc.: with numeral Adverbs, τρὶς τόσσα.. δῶρα thrice *as many*, Il.1.213, cf. 9.379, 21.80, 24.686; δὶς τόσα τείνυσθαι Hes.*Op*.711; δὶς τόσον [κακόν] Thgn.1090; δὶς τόσ' ἐξ ἁπλῶν κακά S.*Aj*.277; τόσαι τρὶς Alex.187.1.—Τόσος is used thus only in Poets, τοσόσδε or τοσοῦτος being used in Att. Prose, exc. in the neut., v. infr. II. 2. rarely poet. for ὅσος, Pi.*N*.4.5, B.15.11, Call.*Ap*.94. II. in Hom. τόσον and τόσσον are common as Adv. with Verbs and Adverbs, *so much, so far, so very*; with a relat., τόσσον.., ὅσον Il.3.12, cf. 6.450, al.; τόσσον.., ὡς.. 22.424; τόσον.., ὡς ὅτε.. 4.130: freq. abs., λίην τ. so very, Od.4.371, 15.405; τόσσον πολλόν *so very* far, Il.20.178; τ. πλέες *so many* more, 2.129; τ. φέρτερος Od.21.372; τόσσον.. πεπείρημαι Hes.*Op*.660; δὶς τόσσον.. ἀπῆμεν Od.9.491, cf. A.*Ag*.140 (lyr.), *Eu*.896, etc.: in Prose, τόσον νυνὶ φρόνει.. ὅσονπερ τότε prob. in Lys.*Oxy*.1606.194 (*Bodl.Quart.Record* 5.303); τόσα καὶ τόσα *so* and *so many*, Pl.*Phdr*.271d; ἔτη τ. καὶ τ. D.57.29; ζημιοῦσθαι τόσῳ καὶ τόσῳ Pl.*Lg*.721d. 2. ἐκ τόσου *ever since* (*that*), always of Time, freq. in Hdt., as 5.88, 6.84, cf. Pl.*Lg*.642e; ἀπολήμψῃ ἐν τόσῳ *in the meantime*, *POxy*.298.17 (i A.D.). 3. ἐς τόσον *so far*, ὁκόταν ἐς τ. προϊωσι τοῦ χρόνου.., πρότερον ἢ ἐς τ. ἀφικέσθαι Hp.*Mul*.2.133; εἰς τόσον ἔδειξαν *IG*12(3).174.28 (Cnidus, i B.C., Epist. Augusti); ἐπὶ τόσσον A.R.3.1146. 4. ὅσῳ μᾶλλον.., τόσῳ.., with a Comp., Th.4.28; ὅσῳ ἐπὶ τὸ μεῖζον.., τόσῳ ἐχυρώτερον.. Id.8.24, cf. Pl.*Lg*.665e, etc.; ὅσῳπερ.., τόσῳ.. ib.902e; ὅσῳ.., τόσῳ δὲ.. (Hertlein for τοσῷδε) Th.1.37. 5. τόσον *only*, Opp.*C*.2.183; so τόσον *PSI* 9.1030.16 (ii A.D.). (Cf. Lat. *tantum*.) III. rarely as regul. Adv. τόσως, δὶς τ. ἐμὲ κτείνας ἀδελφῆς E.*El*.1092, cf. *Med*.1194.

❋**τοσόσδε**, Ep. **τοσσόσδε**, ήδε, όνδε, = τόσος in all senses, but like τοσοῦτος with stronger demonstr. sense: Hom. has both common and Ep. forms (Il.2.120, Od.5.100), but not so freq. as τόσος or τόσσος, while in Att. τοσόσδε and τοσοῦτος are the regul. forms, the latter being most freq. in Prose:—in Ep., τοιόσδε τοσόσδε τε joined, Il. l.c.:—τοσόνδε μέντοι χάρισαί μοι Pl.*R*.457e; ἀλλά μοι ἔτι τ. εἰπέ ib.330d, cf. Hdt.1.13, etc.; and with Art., τὸ δὲ τ. οἶδα, ὅτι.. Pl.*Lg*.672b: c. inf., τοσσήνδε θεοὶ δύναμιν περιθεῖεν τείσασθαι μνηστῆρας *sufficient* to punish.., Od.3.205: with an answering ὅσσος, Il.14.94, 18.430: τοσοίδε ὄντες being *so many only*, i.e. *so few*, X.*An*.2.4.4. II. neut. τοσόνδε, Ep. τοσσόνδε, as Adv., *so very, so much*, Od.21.253; folld. by ὅσσον, Il.22.41: also in Trag. (not in E.), S.*El*.403, etc.; τ. ὅσον.. A.*Th*.772 (lyr.), etc.; τ. ὥστε.. S.*Aj*.1335: of Time, *so long*, τ. ὅσον περ.. A.*Ag*.860; ἐς τ. S.*OT* 1212 (lyr.); τοσσάδε Pi.*O*.1.116. 2. as Subst., ἐς τοσόνδε τοῦ χρόνου S.*El*.961, cf. 14; τὸ τοσόνδε *quantity*, Arist.*Ph*.224ᵇ6.

**τοσοσδί**, τοσηδί, τοσονδί, = τοσουτοσί, Alex.16.11; in a mathematical demonstration, Pl.*Men*.83d; τ. μῆκος ἢ τ. Arist.*Cael*.276ᵇ24.

**τοσουτάριθμος** [ᾰ], ον, *of so large a number*, πλῆθος A.*Pers*.432.

**τοσουτοπλάσιος** [ᾰ], ον, *so many times as great*, Iamb. *in Nic*.p.97 P.

**τοσοῦτος**, αύτη, οῦτο (or τοσοῦτον, v. sub fin.); Ep. **τοσσοῦτος**; Aeol. **τεσσοῦτος** (q.v.); = τόσος in all senses, but like τοσόσδε with stronger demonstr. sense: Hom. has both common and Ep. forms, but not so freq. as τόσος or τόσσος, while in Trag. (not in E.) it is common, and in Prose the prevailing form, cf. τοσόσδε:—freq. answered by the Relat. ὅσος, S.*Ph*.1076, Pl.*R*.330b, etc.; by ὁπόσος, Id.*Smp*.214a, etc.; by ὅστις, Hdt.7.49; also by Adv. ὡς, Od.21.402; τ. ἐγένετο ὥστε.. X.*Cyn*.1.9: freq. also, like τοσόσδε, abs., ἄφενος τ. Od.14.99; of persons, *so large, so tall*, etc., καί σε τ. ἔθηκα Il.9.485; also, *so great* (in rank, skill, or character), S.*Tr*.1140, Pl.*Smp*.177c, etc.; τ. καὶ τοιοῦτον τὸ θεῖον ὥσθ' ἅμα πάνθ' ὁρᾶν X.*Mem*.1.4.18; τηλικοῦτος καὶ τ. Pl.*Smp*.177a: pl., *so many*, τ. ἔτεα Il.2.328; [χρήματα] Od.13.258: with a qualifying word, mostly in acc., μεγάθεα τοσοῦτοι so big, Hdt.7.103; τοσοῦτος τὸ βάθος *so deep*,

X.*An*.3.5.7; τοσοῦτοι τὸ πλῆθος Arist.*Pol*.1283$^{b}$12; τὴν ἡλικίαν Plu.*Arat*.50; also τοσοῦτος ἐν κακίᾳ (v.l. εἰς κακίαν) Luc.*Alex*.1; τοσοῦτος ἡλικίας Plu.*Cat.Mi*.69 (s.v.l.): with numeral Advbs., δὶς τ., πολλάκις τ., etc., Th.6.37, Pl.*R*.330b, etc.; also ἕτερον τοσοῦτο *of the same height*, Hdt.2.149; ἕτεροι or ἄλλοι τοσοῦτοι *to the same number*, And.3.7, X.*HG*4.1.21: εἰς τοσούτους τεταγμένοι drawn up *only so few* in file (opp. οὕτω βαθεῖα φάλαγξ), Id.*Cyr*.6.3.22, cf. Isoc.9.29. **II.** neut. as Subst., *so much, thus much*, τοσσοῦτον ὀνήσιος Od.21.402, cf. S.*OT*836, *OC*790; τ. οἶδα Id.*Aj*.748, cf. 441, etc.; referring to what precedes, τοσαῦτα..εἰρήσθω Hdt.3.113; τοσαῦτ' ἔλεξε A.*Pers*.372, cf. *Pr*.621, *Ag*.680, etc.: freq. with Preps., διὰ τοσούτου at *so small a distance*, so near at hand, Th.2.29; ἐς τοσοῦτο(ν) *so far*, Hdt.3.113, 6.134; ἐς τ. ἥκομεν, ὥστε.. Lys.27.10; ἐς τ. ἐλπίδων βεβώς S.*OT*771, cf. *OC*748, Ar.*Nu*.832, Pl.*Ap*.25e, etc.; ἐκ τ. from *so far, so far* off, X.*HG*4.4.16; ἐν τοσούτῳ in *the meantime*, Ar.*Eq*.420, Th.6.64; ἐπὶ τοσοῦτο *so far*, Hdt.6.97, Arist.*Pol*.1300$^{a}$9; κατὰ τοσοῦτον *so far*, Lys.31.8, Pl.*Prm*.129a, etc.; μέχρι τοσούτου ἕως ἂν.. *so far, so long*, Th.1.90, cf. X.*Cyr*.1.4.23; παρὰ τοσοῦτον ἐλθεῖν κινδύνου Th.3.49, 7.2, cf. 6.37: τοσούτου δέω, v. δέω (B) I.2. **III.** neut. also as Adv., *so much, so far*, ἢ τοσσοῦτον..ἢ ἔτι μᾶσσον Od.8.203; τ. ὀδύρομαι 21.250; σθένειν τ. ὥστε.. S.*Ant*.453, etc.; τοσοῦτον, ὅσον.. Th.3.49, cf. 1.11,88, X.*An*.3.1.45, etc.: pl., τοσαῦτα μάχεσθαι ὅσα ἀναγκάζονται Th.7.81, cf. Pl.*Alc*.1.108a: with Adjs., τοσοῦτον φιλέλλην Sor.*Vit.Hippocr*.8; νεώτατος τ. Il.23.476; τ. εὐτυχέστεροι Lys.2.16:—but τοσούτῳ is more freq. with Comparatives, Hdt.7.49, Pl.*R*.576b, X.*HG*4.8.4, etc.; or with words implying comparison, τοσούτῳ διέφερεν ὥστε.. ib.3.1.10, cf. *An*.1.5.9. (The neut. is τοσοῦτον (Ep. also τοσσοῦτον) in Il.23.476, Od.14.99, A.*Pr*.621, S.*OT*771, al., and Att. generally (very freq. in Pl., *Prt*.314b, al., but τοσοῦτο is found in *Tht*.153a as cited by Anon.*in Tht*.): τοσοῦτο is found in Pi.*I*.2.35 (τοσοῦθ' ὅσον) and in A.*Eu*.201,427, Ar.*Nu*.832, where τοσοῦτον (which is v.l. in Ar. l.c.) is metrically possible; also in Hdt. (passim) and as v.l. in cod. B of Th.7.59 and codd. CG of Id.8.76, in all codd. of Lys.3.34, 6.17 and in the first hand of cod. X in 14.2, also in D.28.12; so later, *PCair.Zen*.367.38, *PMich.Zen*.28.17 (both iii B.C.), Phld.*Ir*.p.47 W., *Rh*.1.206 S.; τοσοῦτ' ἐπ' αὐτούς D.S.14.23; τοσοῦτ' ἀπέχειν Aristid.*Or*.36(48).100.)

**τοσουτοσί,** τοσαυτηΐ, τοσουτονί, later Att. for τοσοῦτος, with a stronger demonstr. force, Ar.*Pl*.427, Pl.*Hp.Ma*.292c, D.18.279, etc.

**τόσσαις,** Aeol. for τόσσας, aor. part. of an unknown pres. = τυγχάνω, *happen* to be, Pi.*P*.3.27 (just as τυχών is used, ib.4.5); inf., τόσσαι καλῶν Id.*Fr*.22; cf. ἐπέτοσσε.

**τοσσάκι,** Ep. for τοσάκις.

**τοσσάτιος** [ᾰ], η, ον, late Ep. for τόσος, *so great, so much*, *AP*9.425 (Barb.), Androm.ap.Gal.14.41: neut. τοσσάτιον *so wide a tract*, τ. ναίοντες, ὅσον.. D.P.363; *so long*, χρόνος A.R.4.962: pl., *so many*, *AP*7.56. (No form τοσάτιος occurs.)

**τοσσῆνος,** Dor. for τοσοῦτος, Theoc.1.54, v.l. in Id.3.51. (No form τοσῆνος occurs.)

**τόσσος, τοσσόσδε,** Ep. for τόσος, τοσόσδε. **τοσσοῦτος,** αὐτη, οῦτον, Ep. for τοσοῦτος.

® **τότε,** Dor. **τόκᾰ** (q.v.) (both forms in Pi. (τότε *P*.2.89, τόκα *O*.6.66) and Theoc. (τότε 13.23, τόκα 7.154)); Aeol. **τότᾰ** Alc.*Oxy*.1789 *Fr*.1 i 12 (τόκα acc. to codd. of Theoc.29.39, cf. ποτα, ὅτα):—Adv. *at that time, then*, corresponding to Relat. ὅτε or ὁπότε (infr. I.5), and to interrog. πότε; mostly of some point in past time, opp. νῦν, Il.15.724, etc.: c. gen., τ. τοῦ χειμῶνος Th.7.31: also of a future time, τότε κέν μιν..πεπίθοιμεν Il.1.100, cf. 4.182; λέξεις καὶ τότ' εἴσομαι S.*OT*1517 (troch.) (or of imagined circumstances, *in that case* (cf. νῦν I.4), Pl.*R*.334c); sts., *then, next*, πρῶτον μὲν.., εἶτα.., καὶ τ... D.24.48:—in Trag. and Att. also in indef. sense, *formerly*, καὶ νῦν θ' ὁμοίως καὶ τότ' ἐξεπίσταμαι S.*El*.907, cf. *Ant*.391, *Aj*.650, Ar.*Pl*.1117, *Lys*.1023 (lyr.); ὃ δὴ καὶ τότε ἐλέγομεν *just now*, Pl.*Tht*.157a; τ. μὲν.., νῦν δὲ.. A.*Ag*.799 (anap.), cf. E.*Alc*.915 (anap.); νῦν..τότ' Id.*Med*.1402 (anap.); ὁμοῖοι καὶ τ. καὶ νῦν Th.1.86, cf. 3.40, D.6.12; also τότ' ἢ τόθ', ὅτε τὸ κύριον μόλῃ *at one time or other*, A.*Ag*.766 (lyr.); συμφοραὶ..βροτοῖσιν ἢ τότ' ἦλθον ἢ τ. E.*Andr*.853. **2.** joined with other Particles, καὶ τ. even *then*, or (at the beginning of a clause) and *then*, Il.16.691, Hes.*Op*.536, etc.; καὶ τ. δή Il.1.92, Od.8.299; καὶ τότ' ἔπειτα Il.1.426; καὶ τ. μέν 21.40; δὴ τ. Hes.*Op*.417, Pi.*O*.3.25, A.*Th*.214 (lyr.), etc.; τ. δή ῥα Od.9.52; τ. γ' Il.3.224, Od.12.250; δὴ τ. γ' 15.228; τ. δ' ἤδη by *that time*, Il.2.699; ἀλλὰ τότ' ἤδη when *that time* comes, Hes.*Op*.588, cf. A.*Pr*.911, Lys.12.66, etc.: repeated with emphasis, τότ' ἄρα τ. S.*Ant*.1273 (lyr.); τ. δὴ τ. D.18.47. **3.** with the Art., ἄνδρες οἱ τ. people *then* living, the men *of that time*, Il.9.559, etc.; οἱ τότ' ἐόντες ἀοιδοί Pi.*I*.4(3).27(45); ὁ τ. τυραννεύων Hdt.1.20; οἱ τ. ἄνθρωποι Id.8.8; ἡ τ. ἀρωγή A.*Ag*.73 (anap.); τῇ τόθ' ἡμέρᾳ S.*El*.1134; ὁ τ. κόσμος 2*Ep.Pet*.3.6; ἐν τῷ τ. Th.1.92, Pl.*Criti*.110d; ἐν τῷ τ. χρόνῳ ib.111e (χρόνῳ om. cod. A), *Plt*.270e; εἰς τὸν τ. χρόνον Id.*Lg*.740c. **4.** εἰς τ. with fut., *on the day, then* (v. εἰς II.2), ἔμπροσθεν τοῦ ἀγῶνος ἐμανθάνομεν..ἂν μάχεσθαι.., μιμούμενοι πάντα ἐκεῖνα ὁπόσοις ἐμέλλομεν εἰς τ. χρήσεσθαι ib.830b, cf. D.14.24, etc.; ἐκ τ. or ἔκτοτε (q.v.) from *that time*, Plu.*Caes*.48, Arr.*An*.1.26.4; so ἀπὸ τ. LXX *Ps*.92(93).2, *Ev.Matt*.4.17. **5.** in apodosi, answering to ὅτε, S.*OC*778, etc.; to ὅταν, A.*Ag*.971, Ar.*Av*.1116 (troch.); to ὁππότε, Il.16.244, Od.23.257; to ὁππότε κεν or ὁπότ' ἂν δή, Il.9.702, 21.341; to ἀλλ' ὅτε δή, ib.451; to εἰ, 4.36; to ἐπεί κε, 11.192; to ἡνίκα, S.*Aj*.773: also after a part., like εἶτα, πάντα ἐάσαντες καὶ μόνον οὐχὶ συγκατασκευάσαντες αὐτῷ τ...ζητήσομεν; D.3.17, cf. 9.73 (interpol.), etc.: freq. joined with other Particles, δὴ τ. after ἦμος, Il.1.476; after αὐτὰρ ἐπεί, 12.17; after ὁππότε κεν, Od.10.294; also καὶ τ. δή after ἦμος, Il.8.69, Od.9.59; after ἀλλ' ὅτε δή, Il.22.209, Od.4.461; δή ῥα τ. after εὖτ' ἄν, Hes.*Op*.565; τότ' ἔπειτα after αὐτὰρ ἐπὴν δή, ib.616; καὶ τότ' ἔπειτα after ἦμος, Il.1.478. **II.** later for ὅτε, Nic.*Al*.422,595.

**τοτέ** (with changed accent, cf. ὅτε, ὁτέ), Adv. *at times, now and then*, in answering clauses, τοτὲ μὲν.., τοτὲ δὲ.. (much like ποτὲ μὲν.., ποτὲ δὲ..) *at one time.., at another..*, Od.24.447, A.*Ag*.100 (anap.), S.*OC*1745 (lyr.), Ar.*Eq*.540 (anap.), Pl.*Plt*.270a, al.; τόκα μὲν.., τόκα δέ (Dor. parox.) Pi.*N*.6.10; τότ' ἄλλος, ἄλλοθ' ἅτερος S.*El*.739; τ. μὲν.., ἄλλοτε δὲ.. Pl.*Phdr*.237e, Poet.ap.X.*Mem*.1.2.20; τ. μὲν.., αὖθις δὲ.. Pl.*Grg*.491b, etc.; τ. μὲν δίκαιον, ὅταν δὲ βούληται, ἄδικον Id.*Phdr*.261d, cf. A.*Ch*.412 (lyr.):—τοτὲ μέν in the first clause is sts. omitted, Il.11.63, Pl.*Phd*.116a, *Tht*.192d.

**τοτοβρίξ,** imitation of *a bird's note*, Ar.*Av*.243.

**τοτοῖ,** Interj. in Trag. lyr., A.*Pers*.551,561; **τοτοτοῖ,** S.*Tr*.1010; cf. ὀτοτοῖ.

**τού, τούγα, τούν, τούνη,** v. σύ.

**τοὔνεκα,** crasis for τοῦ ἕνεκα, *for that reason, therefore*, Il.1.291, al., Hes.*Op*.49, Pi.*O*.1.65; also **τοὔνεκεν,** Xenoph.2.19, A.R.1.1354, D.P.950, etc. **II.** interrog., for τίνος ἕνεκα; *wherefore?* *APl*.4.275.11 (Posidipp.).

**τουράκισον,** τό, name of a herb, *Cat.Cod.Astr*.8(1).191.

**τούρπαινα,** ἡ, a fish, the *torpedo*, Alex.Trall.12, Paul.Aeg.3.78, 7.17; written **τούπαινα,** as Lat. for βατίς I, βάτος (B), Cyran.104.

**τουτᾶ,** Cretan Adv. *here*, Epimenid.ap.D.L.1.113.

® **τουτάκῐς** [ᾰ], poet. Adv. for τότε, antec. to ὁπόταν, Thgn.844: abs., Pi.*P*.4.255, 9.14, Call.*Cer*.33, etc.: also **τουτάκι,** Pi.*P*.4.28, Isyll.67, Call.*Jov*.44, *Hec*.1.2.8. **2.** = οὕτως, relative to ὡς (*as*), Ar.*Pax* 1079 (hex.). **II.** = τοσάκις, Hsch.

**τουτεῖ** (perispom. acc. to A.D.*Synt*.238.9, but apparently τουτεί in codd.), Dor. Adv. *here*, *IG*4$^{2}$(1).122.25 (Epid., iv B.C.), 9(1).977.3 (Corc., iii B.C.), Theoc.5.45,103: but τουτει prob. = τουτί in τουτει καλύπτει μνῆμα Μελανώπου δέμας *Supp.Epigr*.4.192 (Halic., i B.C.).

**τουτέστι,** = τοῦτ' ἔστι, *that is to say*, *Ev.Marc*.7.2, Plu.2.64c, Heph.12.1, A.D.*Synt*.29.13, *Cod.Just*.1.1.5.3, etc.; f.l. in Arist.*Fr*.94 (codd. SM Stob.).

**τουτί, τουτογί, τουτοδί,** v. οὗτος A.

**τοῦτις·** ὁ κόσσυφος, Hsch.

**τουτ-όθεν,** Adv. *from here*, A.D.*Adv*.163.24, 190.20, cj. in Erinn.3.1; also **τουτόθε,** Theoc.4.10. **-ῶ,** Adv. *from here, from there*, Sophr.85, *SIG*1025.28 (Cos, iv/iii B.C.), *GDI*5075 *A* 53, al. (Crete); Lacon. acc. to Hsch. **-ῶθεν,** Adv. *thence*, Theoc.4.48.

**τοῦφος·** τάφος, Hsch.

® **τοφιών,** ῶνος, ὁ, *a tufa quarry*, *Tab.Heracl*.1.137. (Lat. *tōfus*, prob. borrowed from an Italic dialect.)

**τόφρᾰ,** demonstr. Adv. of Time, *up to* or *during that time, so long*, Hom., answering to relat. ὄφρα, which follows, Il.11.754, Od.4.289 (so ὄφρ' ἄν with subj., Il.1.509, al.); but the relat. commonly precedes, ὄφρα.., τ... *in (the course of) that time, so long..*, 18.381, Od.20.330, *h.Cer*.37; ὄφρ' ἂν.., τ... Il.7.194, Od.5.362, al.; ὄφρα.. τ. δὲ.. Il.4.221, Od.10.126:—besides the regular ὄφρα.., τόφρα.. we find τ..., ἕως.. 5.122; τ..., ἕως κε.. 2.77; more freq. ἕως.., τ..., Il.15.392, Od.12.328, al.; ἕως.., τ. δὲ.. Il.10.507, Od.5.425, etc.; ἀλλ' ὅτε δὴ.., τ... 10.571; πρὶν.., τ... Il.21.101; εὖτε.., τ. δὲ.. Od.20.77. **b.** abs., *meanwhile*, Il.10.498, 13.83, Od.3.303, 464, al. **2.** in Alex. Poets as relat., = ὄφρα, A.R.4.1617, Orph.*A*.347: τ. μὲν (relat.).., τ. δὲ (demonstr.).. Call.*Del*.39. **II.** in Antim.3 and Alex. Poets also as a final Conjunction, *so that, that*, A.R.3.807, 4.1487, *AP*9.242 (Antiphil.), 13.22 (Phaedim.), Orph.*A*.939.

**τραβέα,** ἡ, = Lat. *trabea*, D.H.2.70, al.; written **τραβαία,** Lyd.*Mens*.1.21.

**τράγαινα** [ᾰγ], ἡ, *hermaphrodite*, Arist.*GA*770$^{b}$35.

**τράγαις·** Αἰολεῖς, Hsch. (Apparently belongs to τραγάω.)

**τρᾰγάκανθα** [ᾰκ], ης, ἡ, *tragacanth*, *Astragalus Parnassi* and *creticus*, Thphr.*HP*9.1.3, Dsc.3.20, Sor.1.123, Gal.6.636:—nom. also **τραγακάνθη,** *Milet*.1(7) No.210:—**τραγάκανθος,** ἡ, v.l. in Thphr.*HP*9.15.8, Gal.14.303.

® **τραγαλέον·** διερρωγότα, Hsch.

**τρᾰγᾰλ-ίζω,** = τρώγω, Ar.*V*.674. **-ιον,** τό, = τρωγάλιον, Theognost.*Can*.125. **-ισμός,** ὁ, gloss on αἶκλον, ib.5.

**τρᾰγᾰνός,** ὁ, = τράγος III, Hsch. s.v. χόνδρος. **II.** = τράγος V.2 (v.l. for τάργανον), Dsc.4.51.

**τρᾰγᾰνός,** ή, όν, (τραγεῖν) *eatable*, Hdn.Gr.2.912, *EM*731.15. **II.** *gristly, cartilaginous*, Ath.8.347e. **2.** Subst. τράγανον, τό, *gristle, cartilage*, esp. of the ear (cf. τράγος VI), Antyll.ap.Orib.7.7.2, Gal.16.135; or of the nose, *Hippiatr*.26,130.

**Τρᾰγᾰσαῖος,** α, ον, *of* or *from the Epirotic city* Τραγασαί, Hellanic.34 J., Str.13.1.48, Poll.6.63. **II.** in Ar.*Ach*.808 of swine, ὡς τραγασαῖα φαίνεται, with a play on τραγεῖν; and ib.853, πατρὸς Τραγασαίου, with a play on τράγος I.2.

**τρᾰγάω,** (τράγος) of men, = τραγίζω I, Gal.4.633, *UP*14.7, Alex.Aphr.*Pr*.1.125. **II.** of vines, *to be over-luxuriant, run to leaf*, Arist.*HA*546$^{a}$3, *GA*725$^{b}$34, Thphr.*HP*2.7.6, 4.14.6, al.

**τρᾰγεῖν**, v. τρώγω.

**τράγ-ειος** [ᾰ], α, ον, = τράγεος, *of* or *from a he-goat*, κρέα, κρέας, Gal. 6.486, Philostr.*Gym.*43; στέαρ Dsc.2.76.18; αἷμα *PHolm.*7.30 (-ιον Pap.), 10.6; ἡ τραγείη (sc. δορά) *a goat's skin*, Theoc.5.51. **-έλᾰφος**, ὁ, *goat-stag*, a fantastic animal, represented on Eastern carpets and the like, Ar.*Ra.*937; οἱ γραφῆς τραγελάφους καὶ τὰ τοιαῦτα μειγνύντες γράφουσιν Pl.*R.*488a, cf. Arist.*APr.*49ᵃ24, *APo.*92ᵇ7; ποῦ ἐστὶ τ. ἢ σφίγξ; Id.*Ph.*208ᵃ30. 2. *a drinking-cup*, which had such a creature worked in relief on the fore-part, or was itself in this shape, Antiph.224.4, Diph.80, Men.24, etc.; so θρόνος.. ἔχων τραγελάφων προτομὰς ἐκτύπους, ἐξ ὧν ἤρτηντο κρίκοι D.S.18.26; as a signet, *IG*2².1388.62, *Inscr.Délos*442*B* 191 (ii B.C.). 3. *a what's-its-name, thingumbob*, τίθεται (sc. σκινδαψός) καὶ κατ' οὐδενὸς (fort. καὶ ἐπὶ τοῦ δεῖνος legend.) ὡς τὸ τραγέλαφος St.Byz. s. v. Γαληψός. II. later, a real animal of Arabia, or on the Phasis, prob. a kind of *wild goat* or *antelope*, Lxx *Jb.*39.1, D.S.2.51, Plin.*HN*8.120, etc. **-εος**, α, ον, = τράγειος, δειπνήσας τ. πόδα *AP*11.325 (Autom.). II. τρᾰγέα (sc. δορά), ἡ, *a goat's skin*, Thphr.*Od.*62 (60), Plu.2.294f; also **τραγῆ**, Poll.4.118, Eust.276.10.

**τράγη**· πεπληγμένη, πεπηγυῖα, Hsch.

**τράγ-ημα** [ᾰγ], ατος, τό, mostly in pl., like τρωγάλια, *dried fruits* or *sweetmeats*, eaten as *dessert*, Ar.*Ach.*1091, *Ra.*510, X.*An.*2.3.15, Diocl.*Fr.*141, *POxy.*1070.31 (iii A.D.), etc.; ὀνομάζω τ. τὰ παρὰ τὸ δεῖπνον ἐσθιόμενα τῆς ἐπὶ τῷ πίνειν ἡδονῆς ἕνεκα Gal.6.550; called δευτέρα τράπεζα, Arist.*Fr.*104; κάρυα καὶ τ. Clearch.Com.4; κάρυα καὶ.. καστάναια καὶ κυάμους Αἰγύπτου.. καὶ εἴ τινα ἄλλα τ. *IG*2².1013.20 (ii B.C.); καὶ τ. που παραθήσομεν αὐτοῖς τῶν τε σύκων καὶ ἐρεβίνθων καὶ κυάμων Pl.*R.*372c: metaph., Lyc.*Fr.*3; τ. τῶν λόγων D.H.*Rh.*10.18: less freq. in sg., Alex.250, Diph.79, Crobyl.9, Arist. l. c., Aret.*CD* 1.2. **-ημᾰτίζω**, *eat* τραγήματα, ἐν τοῖς θεάτροις Arist.*EN*1175ᵇ12:—more freq. in Med., Men.518.14, Thphr.*Char.*11.4, Ath.4.140e, etc. **-ημάτιον** [μᾰ], τό, Dim. of τράγημα, *PMich.Teb.*123ʳ v 21 (i A.D., pl.). **-ημᾰτισμός**, ὁ, *eating of* τραγήματα, Arist.*Fr.*104. **-ημᾰτοπώλης**, ου, ὁ, *seller of* τραγήματα, Hsch. s. v. κεγχρανοπώλης. **-ημᾰτοπώλιον**, τό, *confectioner's shop*, *PLond.*3.897.16 (i A.D.). **-ημᾰτώδης**, ες, *like* τραγήματα, ἐδέσματα Eust.1141.15.

**τρᾰγηφόρος**, ον, *wearing the* τραγῆ (v. τράγεος II), Hsch.

**τρᾰγ-ίαμβος** [ῑ], ὁ, *tragic iambus*, Suid. s. v. Ἀπολλόδωρος. **-ίδιον** [ῐδ], τό, *young he-goat*, *Inscr.Délos* 290.7 (iii B.C.). **-ίζω**, of boys' voices, *break, grow rough and hoarse*, Hp.*Epid.*6.3.14, Arist.*HA*581ᵃ21, *GA*788ᵃ1, etc.; cf. τραγάω. II. *smell like a goat*, ὀσμῆς εἶδος τραγίζον Gal.14.57; f.l. for πρασίζω (ἐν τῇ ὀσμῇ) in Dsc. 1.13.

**τρᾰγῐκ-εύομαι**, *speak in tragic fashion*, Sch.Ar.*Pl.*601. **-ός**, ή, όν, (τράγος) *of* or *like a goat, goatish*, in this sense first in later authors, as Plu.*Pyrrh.*11, Luc.*DDeor.*22.1; in a double sense, τὸ ψευδὲς τραχὺ καὶ τ. *goatlike and tragic*, Pl.*Cra.*408c. II. commonly, *of* or *for tragedy, tragic*, χοροί Hdt.5.67; σκευή, σκηνή, etc., Pl.*R.*577b, X.*Cyr.*6.1.54, etc.; τ. ποιηταί Aeschin.3.231, cf. *SIG*692.32 (Delph., ii B.C.); τ. αὐλητής, συναγωνισταί, *OGI*51.62,56 (Ptolemais, iii B.C.); τ. ἀνήρ, = τραγῳδός III, Pl.*Phd.*115a; so οἱ τ. Arist.*Rh.*1415ᵃ18 (but ὁ τ. specially of Euripides, Ph.2.53,469; he is called -ώτατος τῶν ποιητῶν Arist.*Po.*1453ᵃ29); σπουδὴ τ. the seriousness *of tragedy*, Pl.*Lg.*838c; τ. λῆρος *tragic* trumpery, Ar.*Ra.*1005; ἡ τ. ποίησις *serious* poetry (cf. τραγῳδία II), Pl.*R.*602b; ἡ τ. Arist.*Rh.*1403ᵇ22; τὰ τ. Pl.*R.*595c, *Phdr.*269a. 2. generally, *tragic, stately, majestic*, ὅπως ἐφαίνου..-ώτερος Ar.*Pax* 136; τ. γάρ ἐστιν ἡ ἀπόκρισις Pl.*Men.*76e; διὰ τὸ σεμνὸν καὶ τ. *pathos*, Arist.*Rh.*1406ᵇ8, cf. *Po.*1456ᵃ21, *Pr.*918ᵃ10. 3. in bad sense, *pompous*, εἴσοδος Plb.5.26.9, cf. Plu.2.330a, Luc.*Im.*21; *ranting*, D.18.313: prov., τ. πίθηκος, ἐπὶ τῶν παρ' ἀξίαν σεμνυνομένων, Hsch. III. Adv. -κῶς *in tragic* or *stately style*, τ. λέγειν Pl.*R.*413b, 545e; ἵνα σοι καὶ -ώτερον λαλῶ Men.531.8; -ώτερον ποιεῖν Luc.*Pisc.*39, cf. *Hist.Conscr.*16; -ώτερον οἰκεῖν to be housed *in stately fashion*, Plu.*Publ.*10. **-ώδης**, ες, *of tragic kind*, μῦθος Palaeph.40.

**τράγ-ῐνος** [ᾰ], ον, = τράγειος, *of a he-goat*, κόραι *AP*9.558 (Eryc.). **-ιον**, τό, *a plant smelling like a he-goat, stinking tutsan, Hypericum hircinum*, Dsc.4.49. II. *pimpinell, Pimpinella Tragium*, ib.50.

**Τράγιος** [ᾰ], ὁ, name of month at Melitea in Thessaly, *IG*9(2). 206 I *b* 15.

**τρᾰγ-ίσκος**, ὁ, Dim. of τράγος, *young he-goat*, Theoc.5.141, *AP*9.317: also **-ίσκιον**, Hsch. s.v. ἐξάγω κῶλον τραγίσκιον (a game played at Tarentum). II. *ornament in form of a goat*, *Inscr. Délos* 461 *Bb* 19 (ii B.C.). III. *a sea-fish*, Marc.Sid.23. **-ιστάς**· τοὺς τὰ ἱερεῖα κλέπτοντας, Hsch.

**τρᾰγο-βάμων** [βᾰ], ον, gen. ονος, *goat-footed*, of Pan, Sch.Ar.*Ra.*232. **-ειδής**, ές, *like a he-goat*, Pl.*Cra.*408d. **-κερως**, ων, = τράγος v. 2, τράγιον I, Ps.-Dsc.4.49. **-κουρικός**, ή, όν, *for shearing he-goats*, μάχαιρα Luc.*Pisc.*46. **-κτονος**, ον, *of slaughtered goats*, αἷμα E.*Ba.*139 (lyr., -κτόνον codd.).

**τραγόλας**, ὁ, = Lat. *tragula*, Anon.ap.Suid.

**τρᾰγο-μάσχᾰλος**, ον, *with arm-pits smelling like a he-goat*, Γοργόνες Ar.*Pax* 811. **-πᾶν**, πᾶνος, ἡ, an Ethiopian bird, a large *hornbill*, Mela 3.88, Plin.*HN*10.136, *Gloss.* **-πους**, ποδος, ὁ, ἡ, *goat-footed*, Simon.133, *AP*6.315 (Nicod.). ⊛ **-πρόσωπος**, ον, *goat-faced*, Suid. s.v. Μένδην. **-πτισάνη** [σᾰ], ἡ, *gruel made from* τράγος III, Cael.Aur.*TP*3.2. **-πώγων**, ωνος, ὁ, *with a goat's beard*, Cratin.101 (but τραγοπώγωνος as nom. is cited from the same play in Sch.Il.*POxy.*1087.37); cf. τετραπώγων. II. Subst., *salsify, Tragopogon porrifolius*, Thphr.*HP*7.7.1, Dsc.2.143.

**τρᾰγ-ορίγᾰνος** [ῐ], ἡ, *goat's marjoram, Thymus Teucrioides*, Nic.*Al.*310, Cels.5.11, Dsc.3.30, Gal.12.91: also neut. **-ορίγᾰνον**, Ps.-Dsc.3.30, Cels.3.21.7, Plin.*HN*20.176:—**τρᾰγορῑγᾰνίτης** [ῑτ] οἶνος wine *flavoured therewith*, Dsc.5.45. II. τ. πλατύφυλλος *organy, Origanum heracleoticum*, Id.3.30, Plin.*HN*20.177. 2. τ. λεπτόφυλλος *rock savory, Micromeria Juliana*, Dsc. l. c., Plin. l. c.

**τράγος** [ᾰ], ὁ, *he-goat*, Od.9.239, Pi.*Fr.*201; opp. αἴξ (she-goat), Hdt.2.46, *PCair.Zen.*328.19 (iii B.C.), etc.; τῶν αἰγῶν τῶν τράγων Hdt.3.112; τράγος γένειον.. πενθήσεις you will mourn your beard like the *goat* in the proverb, A.*Fr.*207; Κιλίκιοι τράγοι, of long-haired men, *Com.Adesp.*806; of men, τράγου ὄζειν, τράγου πνεῖν, to smell *like a goat*, *AP*9.368 (Jul. Imp., perh. with play on signf. III), 11.240 (Lucill.), cf. Gal.17(2).152. 2. *the age when change of voice and other signs of puberty appear*, Hp.*Epid.*6.4.21, Gal.*UP*14.7. b. *the change of the voice which takes place at this age*, dub. in *PLond.*1821.150; cf. τραγάω, τραγίζω. 3. *lewdness, lechery*, Luc.*Ep.Sat.*28. II. the male of the fish μαινίς, Arist.*HA*607ᵇ14, Clearch.73, Gal.*Vict.Att.*8, Opp.*H.*1.108. III. *spelt*, Dsc.2.93, Sor.2.44, Gal.15.455, Artem.1.68. IV. a rough kind of *sponge*, Arist.*HA*548ᵇ5, Dsc.5.120. V. among the Messenians, *the wild fig*, = ἐρινεός, Paus.4.20.2, cf. Orac.ap.D.S.8.21 (where perh. = *goat*). 2. = ἐφέδρα III, Dsc.4.51, Plin.*HN*13.116, 27.142. 3. *stinking nard, Valeriana saxatilis*, Dsc.1.8. VI. part of the ear (cf. ἀντίτραγος), Poll.2.85,86, Ruf.*Onom.*44. VII. a kind of light Lycian ship, Poll.1.83. VIII. a kind of *comet*, Lyd.*Ost.*10ᵇ. 2. a constellation of the δωδεκάωρος, Teucer in *Cat.Cod.Astr.*7.204, 8(4).198, Id. in Boll *Sphaera* 48.

**τρᾰγο-σκελής**, ές, *goat-shanked*, applied to Pan, Hdt.2.46, Duris 21 J., Luc.*DDeor.*22.2, *App.Anth.*6.191, etc. **-φᾰγέω**, *eat he-goats*, Str.3.3.7.

**τρᾰγῳδ-άριον**, τό, Dim. of τραγῳδία, D.L.6.80. **-εύς**, έως, ὁ, = τραγῳδός, Sch.Od.8.542. **-έω**, *act a tragedy*, Ar.*Nu.*1091. 2. c. acc. objecti, *represent* or *exhibit in tragedy*, τινας Id.*Th.*85; τ. τὴν Ἀνδρομέδαν Luc.*Hist.Conscr.*1; τὰ παιδία..τ. ὅτι ἂν ἴδῃ καὶ θαυμάσῃ Arr.*Epict.*3.15.5:—Pass., *to be made the subject of a tragedy*, Isoc. 9.6, 15.136, Str.9.5.22, etc.; ὁ τραγῳδούμενος στέφανος *famous in tragedy*, Plu.*Alex.*35; τὰ τραγῳδούμενα *subjects of tragedy*, Id.2. 837c. 3. metaph., *make famous* or *well known*, τὸ τάχιστον τετραγῳδημένον ἐν τῷ διώκειν, of Achilles, Arist.*Ph.*239ᵇ25; ὅσα περὶ τὸ πρόσωπον φαίνεται τετραγῳδημένα κατὰ τὸ προγνωστικὸν ὑφ' Ἱπποκράτους Steph. *in Gal.*1.246 D. II. metaph., *tell in tragic style, declaim*, ἡλίκα νῦν ἐτραγῴδει D.18.13, cf. 19.189; ὀνόματα τ. *dress up* words, Pl.*Cra.*414c:—Pass., ib.418d, Phld.*Oec.*p.24 J.; also, *exaggerate*, τραγῳδεῖν ἂν δόξειε μᾶλλον ἢ ἀληθεύειν would seem *to be romancing*, Gal.*UP*16.4; μὴ τ. τὸ πρᾶγμα (sc. τὸ ἀποθανεῖν), ἀλλ' εἰπὲ ὡς ἔχει Arr.*Epict.*4.7.15; στολαὶ τετραγῳδημέναι *extravagant, flaunting* robes, Antiph.36; τετραγῳδημένοι *pompous, braggart*, D.S.5.31. **-ημα**, ατος, τό, *piece of play-acting*, Porph.*Chr.*69. **-ητής**, οῦ, ὁ, = τραγῳδός, Sch.Theoc.4.30. **-ητός**, ή, όν, *represented in tragedy, tragic*, Sch.E.*Ph.*1493. **-ία**, ἡ, (τραγῳδός) *tragedy*, Ar.*Ach.*464, al., And.4.23, Arist.*Po.*1447ᵃ13, etc.; τ. ποιεῖν compose a *tragedy*, Ar.*Ach.*400, etc.; κωμῳδίαν καὶ τ. ποιοῦντες Pl.*R.*395a; τραγῳδιῶν ποιηταί *OGI*51.31 (Egypt, iii B.C.), cf. *SIG* 1079.3 (Magn. Mae., ii/i B.C.); ποιητὴς τραγῳδιῶν *IG*2².1132.38 = *SIG* 399.34 (Decr. Amphict., iii B.C.), *OGI*352.7 (Athens, ii B.C.), *IG*7. 3197.28 (Orchom. Boeot.); π. τραγῳδίας ib.416.27 (Oropus, i B.C.); τραγῳδίας διδάσκειν (cf. διδάσκω III) D.L.1.59; τραγῳδίᾳ διδάξαντα τὴν Μιλήτου ἅλωσιν Plu.2.814b; ὀκτὼ τ. διαγωνίσασθαι to act in eight *tragedies*, ib.785c; τῇ τ. νικᾶν Pl.*Smp.*173a; expld. as 'goat-song', because a goat was the prize, *Marm.Par.*58, Sch.Hermog. in *Rh.Mus.*63.150; other explanations in *EM*764.1: cf. τρυγῳδία. 2. in a simile, μίμησις τοῦ καλλίστου καὶ ἀρίστου βίου, ὃ δή φαμεν.. ὄντως εἶναι τραγῳδίαν τὴν ἀληθεστάτην Pl.*Lg.*817b; ἡ τοῦ βίου τ. καὶ κωμῳδία Id.*Phlb.*50b. II. generally, *any grave, serious poetry*, opp. κωμῳδία, hence Homer is called a writer of tragedy, Id.*Tht.*152e; cf. τραγικός, τραγῳδοποιός. 2. *an exaggerated speech*, Hyp.*Lyc.*12 (prob.l.), *Eux.*26: hence of descriptions of horrors, Plb.6.56.11, D.S.19.8, etc. 3. *outward grandeur, pomp*, Plu.*Demetr.*41, *Arat.*15, Ps.-Zaleuc.ap.Stob.4.2.19 (pl.), Luc.*Gall.*24; τραγῳδίαν ἐπιθεῖναι τοῖς πράγμασι προσποιητήν D.H.6.70. **-ικός**, ή, όν, *befitting a tragic poet* or *tragedy*, τραγῳδικὸν βλέπει Ar.*Pl.*424: generally, like τραγικός, τ. χοροί Id.*Th.*391 (as cited by Sch.Pl.*Thg.*127c); τ. θρόνος Ar.*Ra.*769; τ. τέχνη ib.1495 (lyr.); ᾠδυνήθην τραγῳδικόν suffered a *tragic* woe, Id.*Ach.*9. Adv. -κῶς Eust.632.37.

**τρᾰγῳδιο-γράφος** [γρᾰ], ὁ, *writer of tragedies*, Plb.2.17.6, 3.48.8, D.S.14.43, A.D.*Adv.*188.27 (where the Ms. reading is corroborated by the context), Baillet *Inscr. des tombeaux des rois à Thèbes* 1547. **-ποιός**, v. τραγῳδοποιός.

**τρᾰγῳδο-γράφος** [γρᾰ], ὁ, = τραγῳδιογράφος, *IG*12(5).433 (Paros, i A.D.). **-διδάσκᾰλος**, ὁ, *tragic poet*, who trained his own chorus and actors, Ar.*Th.*88, Isoc.12.168, Arist.*Po.*1449ᵃ5:—τραγῳδιοδιδάσκαλος and τραγῳδιδάσκ- are ff.ll. in Luc.*Cal.*1, Ath.15.699b, etc. **-ποδάγρα**, ἡ, name of a serio-comic *drama descriptive of the miseries of the gout*, ascribed to Lucian. **-ποιητής**, οῦ, ὁ, *tragic poet*, Sch.Ar.*Ra.*941. **-ποιία**, ἡ, *composition of tragedies*, *Dialex.*3.10. **-ποιός**, ὁ, *tragic poet*, Ar.*Th.*30, Pl.*Cra.*425d, *R.*408b, Eratosth.ap.Eutoc. *in Archim.* iii p.88 H., Phld.*Po.*2.29, etc.:

generally, *writer of serious poetry* (cf. τραγῳδία II), e.g. of Homer, Pl.*R.*605c,607a; and of Pindar, Hermog.*Id.*1.6:—τραγῳδιοποιός is found in Metrod.*Herc.*831.3, in codd. BT of Pl.*Smp.*223d, cod. A of *R.*607a, etc., and many codd. of Lib.*Or.*64.112, but is f.l. (in Pl. at least) for τραγῳδοπ-, which codd. give correctly in *Cra.*425d, *R.*408b,597e: cf. κωμῳδοποιός.

**τρᾰγῳδός**, ὁ, late Boeot. **τρᾰγᾰϝυδός** (i.e. τραγαοιδός) *IG*7.3195.21 (Orchom.):—*member of the tragic chorus*, εἴ τις τ. φησιν ὀρχεῖσθαι καλῶς Ar.*V.*1498, cf. 1505: usu. in pl., τῶν τ. τὸν χορόν Id.*Pax*806 (lyr.); τοῖς χοροῖσι τῶν τ. Id.*Av.*787 (troch.); τ. καὶ χοροί dub.l. in *Th.*391 (v. τραγῳδικός); χορηγὸς τραγῳδῶν D.21.59; τραγῳδοὺς καταλέγειν *IG*1².187.9; τραγῳδῶν (sc. ἐνίκα χορὸς οὗ) Περικλῆς Χολαργεὺς ἐχορήγει ib.2².2318.9; παλαιὸν δρᾶμα πρῶτον παρεδίδαξαν οἱ τ. ib.203; Ἀριφράδης τοὺς τ. ἐκωμῴδει, ὅτι ἃ οὐδεὶς ἂν εἴποι ἐν τῇ διαλέκτῳ, τούτοις χρῶνται Arist.*Po.*1458ᵇ32; τοῖς δὲ τ. ἕτερος σεμνὸς πᾶσιν λόγος ἄλλος ὅδ' ἐστίν Crates Com.24; ὡς οἱ τ. φασιν οἷς ἐξουσία ἔστιν λέγειν ἅπαντα καὶ ποιεῖν μόνοις Diph.30.4. 2. pl. also, = *tragedy* or *a performance of tragedy*, ἐν τοῖσι τ. on the *tragic stage*, Ar.*Av.*512; τραγῳδοῖς Aeschin.3.36; οὐδὲ..ὑποκριταὶ κωμῳδοῖς τε καὶ τραγῳδοῖς οἱ αὐτοί Pl.*R.*395a; τεθέασαι τραγῳδούς Men.*Epit.*108; χορηγεῖν τραγῳδοῖς Is.6.60; οἱ ἐν ἄστει τ. Aeschin.3.41, cf. 154; καινοῖς τραγῳδοῖς at the performance of new *tragedies*, *IG*2².956.34, 1028, Docum.ap.D.18.54, cf. Aeschin.3.34; θεωμένων καινοὺς τ. Ἀθηναίων Plu.*Phoc.*19; νενικηκὼς τραγῳδοῖς And.4.42, cf. Thphr.*Char.* 22.2; Διονυσίων τραγῳδοῖς *Supp.Epigr.*1.362.29 (Samos, iv B.C.); Διονυσίων ἡ τραγῳδοί on the day of the Dionysia on which there is a *tragic performance*, *IG*12(8).640 (Peparethus, ii B.C.); τραγῳδῶν τῷ ἀγῶνι ib.12(5).1341 (Paros, iii B.C.), 2².1214; τραγῳδῶν τῷ ἀγῶνι τῷ καινῷ ib.682.76; τραγῳδὸς ἦν ἀγὼν Διονύσια Men.873 (fort. τραγῳδῶν or -δοῖς); τοὺς γὰρ τραγῳδοὺς πρῶτον, εἰ βούλει, σκόπει ὡς ὠφελοῦσι πάντας Timocl.6.8; εἰς τοὺς τραγῳδοὺς εὔθετ', οὐκ εἰς τὸν βίον Philem.105. II. *performer* (*actor and singer*) *of tragedy*, ἡ τῶν τ. ἐν τῇ σκευῇ πρὸς ἀλλήλους ὁμιλία Arist.*Oec.*1344ᵃ21; ὑπεκρίθησαν τ. μὲν Θεσσαλὸς κτλ. Chares 4 J., cf. Plu.2.334d; Νεοπτόλεμος ὁ τ. D.S. 16.92, cf. *IG*2².1132.39 (Delph., iii B.C.); Αἰσώπῳ τῷ τ. Plu.*Cic.*5; οἵδε ἐπεδείξαντο τῷ θεῷ..· τραγῳδοί· Θεόδωρος Μεγαρεύς, Φιλοκλείδης Χαλκιδεύς *IG*11(2).105.17 (Delos, iii B.C.); ὡς οἱ κακοὶ τ. μόνοι ᾆσαι οὐ δύνανται ἀλλὰ μετὰ πολλῶν Arr.*Epict.*3.14.1; οἱ τ. χοροῦ δέονται φίλων συνᾳδόντων Plu.2.63a; ἐπειδὴ Νίκων..τ...ἀξιωθεὶς ἐπέδωκε τῷ θεῷ ἁμέραν καὶ ἀγωνίξατο..· καλέσαι..αὐτὸν καὶ τοὺς μετ' αὐτοῦ τοὺς ἄρχοντας καὶ ἐν τὸ πρυτανεῖον *SIG*659.3 (Delph., ii B.C.), cf. 424.42 (ibid., iii B.C.), al., *OGI*51.47 (Egypt, iii B.C.), *IG*7.3196.19 (Orchom. Boeot.), D.Chr.33.8, Luc.*Nav.*46, *Anach.*23, *Hist.Conscr.*1,22, M.Ant.3.8; τραγῳδούς miswritten for -δός in *SIG*509.12 (Delph., iii B.C.), and perh. in *IG*7.1773.21 (Thespiae). III. *tragic poet*, *Vit.Aeschyli* p.123 Westermann, Sch.Ar.*Ra.*86; this sense is doubtful in Crates Com.24, Diph.30.4, Timocl.6.8, Pl.*R.*395a, Arist.*Po.*1458ᵇ32 (v. supr. I. 1 fin., 2).

❊ **τρακτ-αΐζω**, *whiten* or *bleach like wax*, *EM*763.53. II. = Lat. *tractare*, *handle*, *manage*, Men.Prot.p.16 D.: cf. τρωκταΐζω. **-ευτής**, οῦ, ὁ, = κλιματάρχης 1, *Cod.Just.*1.42.1, Just.*Nov.*30.2, Lyd.*Mag.* 3.68, *PMasp.*120.8 (vi A.D.), etc.: hence **-ευτικός**, ή, όν, Just.*Nov.* 30.3. **-εύω**, *administer*, ἐπαρχίαν *Cod.Just.*12.49.13.1; *investigate*, = διαψηλαφᾶν, Lyd.*Mag.*3.20; τρακτεύει· μηχανᾶται, Hsch. **-ὸς** κηρός, ὁ, *white*, *bleached* wax, Paul.Aeg.4.21, Aët.12.53:—so **τρακτόν**, τό, *EM*763.54; also, *dough drawn out* or *rolled for pastry*, Lat. *tractum* or *tracta*, Ath.3.113d. **-ωμα**, ατος, τό, *plaster of* τρακτὸς κηρός, *Hippiatr.*26.

**Τράλλεις** or **Τραλλεῖς**, οἱ, *Trallians* (from Τραλλία in Illyria, Theopomp.Hist.340), Thracian barbarians, sometimes employed as mercenaries, l.c., D.S.17.65 (Τραλλεεῖς codd.), Plu.*Ages.*16, Hsch.: —also called **Τράλλοι**, St.Byz., and **Τράλλιοι**, Str.14.1.42 (om. codd. plerique). II. **Τράλλεις**, αἱ, *Tralles*, a city in Caria, X.*An.* 1.4.8, etc.; also **Τράλλις**, ιος, ἡ, Epigr.ap.Agath.2.17, Choerob.*in Theod.*1.196 H., etc.; gen. Τράλλεος *Epigr.Gr.*946 (Tralles), *EM*632. 6; Τράλλεως Choerob.*in Theod.*1.195 H.:—**Τραλλιανός**, ὁ, *a Trallian*, Str.14.1.42, App.*Mith.*23.

**τραλλόν**· πικρόν, Hsch.

**τράμις** [ᾰ] (not found in gen. sg.), ἡ, *the perineum* or *line which divides the scrotum and runs on to the breech*, Archil.195, Hippon. 84, Ar.*Th.*246, Ruf.*Onom.*101, Luc.*Lex.*2:—the acc. τράμιν has a long ι, if Hippon. l.c. is sound; the acc. **τράμην** in *EM*763.56 is f.l. for τράμιν, cf. Sch.Luc.p.191 R.

**τράμμα**· *sicinia*, *Gloss.*

**τράμπις**, ἡ, *ship*, Lyc.97; gen. τράμπιδος Id.1299; in Nic.*Th.* 268 cod. Π has τράμβιδος, τράμπιος cett.

**τρᾱνής**, ές, *clear*, *distinct*, ἴσμεν γὰρ οὐδὲν τ., ἀλλ' ἀλώμεθα S.*Aj.* 23, cf. Demetr.Lac.*Herc.*1013.5; χρόαι τρανεῖς Phld.*Sign.*10: Comp. -έστερος Procl.*Inst.*145; -εστέρα ἡ ὄψις τῆς ἀκοῆς Phlp. *in de An.* 229.12: Sup. -έστατος Phld.*D.*3.14:—later **τρᾱνός**, ή, όν, Moschio Trag.8, D.H.*Comp.*22, Plot.6.6.17; διάνοια Metrod.*Herc.*831.4: Comp. -ότερος Ph.1.16, Plu.2.378a; -οτέρα ζωή Plot.1.4.2, 6.7.5; -ότερα τὰ περὶ τῶν περισκίων Str.2.5.43; -οτάτη κρίσις Ptol.*Judic.* 7; ἀλκυόνιον τὸ -ότερον *brighter*, Archig.ap.Aët.6.55. 2. of Hermes, Corn.*ND*16. II. Adv., τρανῶς εἰδέναι, ἐρεῖν, μαθεῖν, ἀποδεῖξαι, A.*Ag.*1371, *Eu.*45, E.*El.*758, *Rh.*40 (lyr.), cf. Plu.*Dem.*15, etc.; also τρανόν, μάλα τ. ἐπιδών με Hp.*Ep.*17: Comp. -ότερον, εἰπεῖν Phld.*Rh.*1.336 S., cf. Ph.2.326, *AP*9.298 (Antiphil.): Sup. -ότατα S.E.*M.*7.404, *Theol.Ar.*33 (dub.), Iamb.*in Nic.*p.118 P.

**τρανίαν**· αὐλὴν ἐν ὁδῷ μεγάλην, Hsch.

**τρᾱνοποιέω**, *pronounce clearly*, τὸ ρ̄ *Vit.Dem.*p.305 Westermann.

**τρᾱν-ός**, v. τρανής. **-ότης**, ητος, ἡ, *clearness*, *plainness*, Ph. 2.185, Muson.*Fr.*4 p.19 H., Plu.2.720e: pl., τῆς σελήνης Ph.2.61, cf. Plot.1.4.3. **-όω**, *make clear*, *plain*, *distinct*, Ph.1.30, Diog.Oen.21; τὸν νοῦν *App.Anth.*3.158:—Pass., pf. part. τετρανωμένος, opp. ἀτράνωτος, Diog.Oen.30. **-ωμα**, ατος, τό, *that which is made clear*, τρανώματα γλώσσης Emp.4.11. **-ωτικός**, ή, όν, *fitted for clearing up*, *Theol.Ar.*33.

**τράξ**, part of a magical formula, τ. τέτραξ τέτραγος *Stud.Ital.*N.S. 2.394 (Crete).

❊ **τράπεζ-α** [ρᾰ], ης, ἡ, Dor. **τράπεσδα** Alcm.74ᵇ:—*table*, esp. *dining-table*, *eating-table*, freq. in Hom., Τηλεμάχοιο τ., ἐμὴ τ., Od.17.333, 447, cf. *IG*1².330.4, Men.518.2; τ. παραθεῖναι Hdt.6.139, Alex.171; παρέκειτο τ. Il.24.476; τ. εἰσφέρειν, ἐπάγειν, Ar.*V.*1216, Anaxandr. 2 (but ἐσῄρετο is prob. cj.); ἡ τ. εἰσῄρετο Ar.*Ra.*518; τ. ἀφαιρεῖν Od. 19.61, X.*Smp.*2.1 (Pass.); αἴρειν Men.273, cf. 451; ἐκφέρειν Pl.Com. 69.2; ξενίη τ. the hospitable *board*, ἴστω Ζεύς..ξενίη τε τ. Od.14.158, cf. 21.28; ᾔσχυνε ξενίαν τ. κλοπαῖσι A.*Ag.*401 (lyr.), cf. 701 (lyr.); ὅρκον μέγαν, ἅλας τε καὶ τράπεζαν Archil.96, cf. Wilcken *Chr.*11.58 (ii B.C.); ἡ ξενικὴ τ. Aeschin.3.224; τοὺς τῆς πόλεως ἅλας καὶ τὴν δημοσίαν τ. Id.2.22; δέξασθαι τραπέζῃ καὶ κοίτῃ entertain at bed and *board*, Hdt.5.20; κοίτης μεθέξουσα καὶ τραπέζης μόνον Plu.*Brut.*13; ἐπὶ τὰς αὐτὰς τ. ἰέναι Antipho 2.1.10; τράπεζαν Περσικὴν παρετίθετο he kept *a table* in the Persian fashion, Th.1.130; τ. κοσμεῖν X. *Cyr.*8.2.6, etc.; εἰς ἀλλοτρίαν τ. ἀποβλέπειν live at other men's *table*, at their expense, Id.*An.*7.2.33; τὴν τ. ἀνατρέπειν upset the *table*, D.19.198; prov. of a spendthrift, And.1.130; *table dedicated to the gods*, on which meats and offerings were set out, *IG*1². 190.4, 840.19, 2².1245.6, 1534.163, 1933.2, Din.3.2; τ. ἱερά *PCair. Zen.*708 (iii B.C.); ἐπὶ τὴν τ. τῶν Διοσκόρων ib.569.24 (iii B.C.); τ. Κυρίου, τ. δαιμονίων, 1*Ep.Cor.*10.21. 2. *table*, as implying what is upon it, *meal*, ἄνομος τ. Hdt.1.162, cf. E.*Alc.*2, X.*An.*7.3.22; also βορᾶς τ. S.*OT*1464; Συρακοσίων τ., prov. of luxurious living, Ar.*Fr.* 216, cf. Pl.*R.*404d; Σικελικαὶ τ. prov.ap.Jul.*Or.*6.203a; πολυτελὴς τ. Epicur.*Ep.*3 p.64 U.; δεύτεραι τ. the second *course*, Plu.2.133e, Ath.14.639b; cf. τράγημα. II. *money-changer's counter*, ἐν ἀγορᾷ ἐπὶ τῶν τ. Pl.*Ap.*17c, cf. Plu.2.70f; αἱ τ. τῶν κολλυβιστῶν *Ev. Matt.*21.12; most freq. *bank*, Lys 9.5, etc.; ἡ ἐργασία ἡ τῆς τ. the right to operate the *bank*, D.36.6; ἡ ἐγγύη ἡ ἐπὶ τὴν τ. security given to the *bank*, Id.33.10; δοῦναι ἀργύριον ἐπὶ τ. *Ev.Luc.*19.23; τὸ ἐπὶ τὴν τ. χρέως D.33.24; οἱ ἐπὶ ταῖς τ. *bankers*, Isoc.17.2; κατασκευάζεσθαι τράπεζαν set up a *bank*, Is.*Fr.*66; τῆς τ. ἀνασκευασθείσης the *bank* having been broken, D.33.9; δημοσία τ. public *bank* at Delos, *IG*2².2336.180 (i B.C.); in Egypt, *POxy.*835 (Aug.), etc.; βασιλικὴ τ. in Egypt, *PEleph.*27.22 (iii B.C.), *PTeb.*27.70 (ii B.C.), etc.; χειριστὴς τῆς ἐν τῇ Πολέμωνος μερίδι τ. *PEnteux.*38.1 (iii B.C.); opp. ἰδιωτικὴ τ. *POxy.*305 (i A.D.), etc.; κολλυβιστικαὶ τ. ib.1411.4 (iii A.D.). III. *any table* or *flat surface on which a thing rests*: as, 1. *cross bench* in which the mast is fixed, Sch. Il.15.729; τ. δολωνική, v. δολωνικός. 2. *platform on which slaves were exposed for sale*, Ar.*Fr.*874. 3. *tablet* or *slab* with a relief or inscription, τ. χαλκῆ Orac.ap.D.21.53, cf. Paus.8.31.3; at a tomb, Plu.2.838c. 4. *plinth* of a statue, *CIG*4702.7 (Egypt, iv B.C.). b. lamp-*stand*, *PSI*4.428.39 (iii B.C.). 5. *nether millstone*, *BGU*251.17 (i A.D.), Poll.7.19. 6. *part of a torsion-engine*, prob. the *plinth*, Ph.*Bel.*54.2, Hero *Bel.*100.1. 7. *part of the liver*, Nic.*Th.*560, Polyaen.4.20, Ruf.*Onom.*180. 8. *shoulder-blade*, Poll.2.177. 9. *grinding surface of the teeth*, ib.93, Ruf.*Onom.*54. (The word is shortd. from τετράπεζα; hence the question καὶ πόθεν ἐγὼ τρίπουν τ. λήψομαι; as if this were an absurdity, Ar.*Fr.*530; τ. τρισκελεῖς Cratin.301:—so τρίπεζα, τρέπεδδα (qq.v.), of three-legged tables.) **-εῖον**, τό, = τραπέζιον I, *IG*2².1541.27 (iv B.C.). **-είτης**, v. τραπεζίτης. **-εύς**, έως, ὁ, *at*, *of a table*, in Hom. always κύνες τραπεζῆες dogs *fed from their master's table*, Il.22.69, 23.173, Od.17.309:—**τραπεζῆται** in Ibyc.60; cf. τραπεζίτης III. II. *parasite*, Plu.2.50c; Ἀίδου τ. Aristias Trag.3. **-ήεις**, εσσα, εν, *of*, *from*, or *for the table*, κύμβος Nic.*Th.*526; κύνες Opp.*C.* 1.473 (unless τραπεζήεσσι is dat. pl. of foreg.). **-ήτας**, v. τραπεζεύς. **-ία**, ἡ, = τραπεζοποιία (which shd. perh. be read), Thphr.*HP* 3.10.1. **-ίας**· παρὰ τῇ τραπέζῃ τρυφωμένους, Hsch. (leg. τραπεζῆας, τρεφ-). ❊ **-ιον**, τό, Dim. of τράπεζα, *small table*, Phylarch.44 J.: *table of a money-changer*, Lys.*Fr.*50. II. Geom., *trapezium*, Arist. *Pr.*911ᵃ7, Archim.*Sph.Cyl.*1.10, al., D.P.175, Str.2.5.33.

❊ **τρᾰπεζῖτ-εία**, ἡ, *money-changing*, *banking*, *Supp.Epigr.*4.668.15 (Lampsacus); τ. δημοσία *POxy.*1415.26 (iii A.D.). **-εύω**, *to be engaged in banking*, D.36.29, 45.32, *BCH*36.210 (Delos, ii B.C.). ❊ **-ης**, ου, ὁ, Dor. **-τας** *IG*9(1).110.10 (Elatea, iv B.C.), etc.: (τράπεζα II):—*money-changer*, *banker*, Lys.*Fr.*1.1, D.36.28, 49.5, Antiph.159.11, *PEleph.*10.2 (iii B.C.), etc.; οἱ ἀνεσκευασμένοι τῶν τ. broken *bankers*, D.49.68. 2. *director of a state-bank*, *SIG*577.17 (Milet., iii/ii B.C.), *UPZ*112 ii 5 (ii B.C.), *IG*12(5).880.11, al. (Tenos, i B.C.). II. τραπεζίτης Πάρις *violator of hospitality*, *Trag.Adesp.* 270 (s.v.l.). III. τραπεζεῖται κύνες, = τραπεζῆες (v. τραπεζεύς), Hdn.Gr.2.356, al. [Hdn.Gr. l.c. says -ειτ- is correct in signf. III, -ῑτ- otherwise; in signf. I -ῑτ- is found in *IG*9(1) l.c. (iv B.C.), 4²(1).98.13 (Epid., iii B.C.), *PEleph.* l.c. (iii B.C.), *PCair.Zen.*176. 63 (iii B.C.), -ειτ- ib.174 (iii B.C.), *SIG*742.55 (Ephesus, i B.C.), etc.: prob. only -ῑτ- is correct.] **-ικός**, ή, όν, *of* or *for a banker*; τ.

λόγος speech *against the banker*, name of an oration by Isoc.; τ. δίκαι Arist.*Ath.*52.2; ἡ τ. στοά *the bankers' colonnade*, *Ephes.*3.65 p.148; τ. τέχνη Vett.Val.4.11; -κόν, τό, *extract from banking account*, *Arch.Pap.*4.104 (i A.D.), *BGU*748 iii 1 (i A.D.), *POxy.*574 (ii A.D.); εἰρόμενον τ. running *extract from bank-register* of contracts, Mitteis *Chr.*211.22 (iii A.D.).

**τρᾰπεζο-ειδής**, ές, *trapezium-shaped*, λόφος Str.14.6.3, cf. *Placit.* 3.10.3. **-κόμος**, ὁ, *one who sets out a table* or *who waits at table*, Longin.43.4, Plu.2.616a, D.L.9.80, etc.; = Lat. *structor*, Juba 84. **-κορος**, ον, (from κορέννυμι) *filling oneself at another's table*, or (from κορέω) *sweeping the table*, epith. of parasites, Ps.-Phoc. 91. **-λοιχός**, όν, *table-licker*, *parasite*, Suid.; so **Τραπεζολείκτης** as a pr. n., Alciphr.3.45. **-πῖναξ**, *repositorium*, *Gloss.* **-ποιέω**, *set out tables with meats*, Diph.43.3. **-ποιΐα**, ἡ, *table-making*, Str.4.6.2 (pl.). ❋**-ποιός**, ὁ, = τραπεζοκόμος, *a slave who set out the table*, *IG*2².2403 (Piraeus, iv B.C.), Men.*Sam.*75, Antiph.152, Philem.61 (cf. Ath.4.170d,e), S.E.*P.*1.82, Them.*Or.*4.54c. **-ρήτωρ**, ορος, ὁ, *table-talker*, Ath.1.22e. **-της**, ητος, ἡ, *table-nature*, *tableness*, Pl.ap.D.L.6.53. **-φόρος**, ον, *bearing a table*: 1. τ., ὁ, *table-bearer*, Ar.*Fr.*124. 2. τ., ἡ, *priestess of Athene* at Athens, Lycurg.*Fr.*48, Ister 16. 3. -φόρον, τό, *sideboard*, Cic. *Fam.*7.23.3, Poll.10.69, *Dig.*33.10.3: also -φόρος, ὁ, Artem.1.74.

**τρᾰπεζ-όω**, *offer* to a god, ὅσα κα οἱ θύοντες.. τραπεζῶντι *IG*5(1).1390.86 (Andania, i B.C.); prob. rest. ib.12(2).72 (Mytil., Pass.): intr. in Act., *receive an offering*, of the gods, Jul.*Or.*5.176d (s. v. l.). II. Pass., *to be set upon a table*, S.*Fr.*611. **-ώ**, ἡ, = τραπεζοφόρος 2, Hsch. (τραπεζών cod.). **-ώδης**, ες, = τραπεζοειδής, χωρίον Str.17.1.37, cf. Ruf.*Oss.*24, Sor.*Fract.*14. **-ωμα**, ατος, τό, *what is set upon a table*, *dish*, Eust.1402.19: pl., *offerings* to gods, *SIG*1007.15 (Pergam., ii B.C.). **-ωνία**, ἡ, *hiring of tables*, *Inscr. Magn.*116.41 (ii A.D.). **-ωσις**, εως, ἡ, *a setting upon a table*, Plu. *in Hes.*79 (pl.).

**τρᾰπείομεν**, v. τέρπω II. 2.

**τρᾰπελίζομαι**, = τροπαλίζομαι, Hsch.

**τρᾰπέμπᾰλιν**, Adv. *turned backwards*, Pherecr.240; to be restored in Plu.2.924c, D.C.47.40.

**τράπεσδα**, Dor. for τράπεζα (q. v.).

**τρᾰπέω**, *tread grapes*, Od.7.125, Hes.*Sc.*301, Anan.5.4. (Cf. τραπητής, τραπητός, τροπήϊον, τροπέοντο (Hsch.), Lith. *trepénti* 'tramp', etc.)

**τρᾰπῆναι**, v. τρέπω. **τράπηξ**, v. τράφηξ.

**τρᾰπητέον**, *one must turn* (intr.), Luc.*Rh.Pr.*8.

**τρᾰπητής**, οῦ, ὁ, (τραπέω) *wine-presser*, Hsch. s. v. πατηταί; οἶνος ❋**τρᾰπητός**, wine *fresh from the press*, Id. **τράπω**, Ion. for τρέπω (q. v.). **τραρόν**· ταχύ, Id. (cf. ὀτρηρός).

**τρᾰσιά**, ἡ, (ταρσός) *hurdle*, *crate*, whereon to dry figs, Eup.451, Ael.*NA*3.10; ταρσιή (Ion.) in Semon.39; cf. τερσιά. b. *the dried figs* themselves, Ar.*Nu.*50, Poll.7.144. 2. *drying-place*, for corn, S.*Fr.*118; also for cheese, Suid.; or for bricks, *kiln*, Greg.Cor.p.514 S.

**τραυλ-ίζω**, *mispronounce a letter*, *lisp*, as Alcibiades made *r* into *l*, Ar.*V.*44; ψελλίζονται καὶ τραυλίζουσι· τοῦτο δ' ἐστὶν ἔνδεια τῶν γραμμάτων Arist.*PA*660ᵃ26; πασχούσης [τῆς γλώττης] τραυλίζειν καὶ ψελλίζειν συμβαίνει Gal.16.510; of children, Ar.*Nu.*862,1381, Arist.*HA*536ᵇ8; σοφὰ.. -ίζουσα χελειδονίς *IG*14.1934*f*7:—Med., Archipp.45. **-ισμός**, ὁ, *lisping*, Plu.2.53c; f.l. for τρυλισμός (q. v.) in Erot.

**τραυλοηχέω**, *twitter*, of birds, Cyran.42.

**τραυλ-ός**, ή, όν, *mispronouncing letters*, *lisping*, *stammering*, Hp. *Aph.*6.32, Call.Com.19, *PSI*3.220.18 (iii A.D.), etc.; esp. of children, παῖς ἰσχνόφωνος καὶ τ. Hdt.4.155, cf. Arist.*Aud.*801ᵇ7, *Pr.*902ᵇ22. II. of the swallow, *twittering*, *APl.*4.141 (Phil.); τραυλὰ μινύρεσθαι *AP*9.70 (Mnasalc.), cf. 57 (Pamphil.). III. τὸ τ. τῶν λίθων the *oily quality* in stones, Olymp.Alch.p.97 B. **-ότης**, ητος, ἡ, *lisping*, Arist.*Pr.*902ᵇ23, Plu.*Alc.*1, etc.

**τραυλόφωνος**, ον, *with lisping speech*, Hsch. s. v. Βάττος.

**τραύλωσις**, εως, ἡ, = τραυλότης, Gal.18(1).51.

**τραῦμα**, ατος, τό, Ion. **τρῶμα** Hdt.1.18, al., Hp.*VC*2, al.; Dor. also **τρῶμα**, Theoc.21.50:—*wound*, *hurt*, ἀποθνήσκειν ἐκ τῶν τ. Hdt.2.63; τελευτᾶν ἐκ τοῦ τ. Id.3.29; τραυμάτων ἐτύγχανεν A.*Ag.* 866; πολλὰ τραύματ' ἐν στέρνοις λαβών Id.*Fr.*362, cf. Plu.*Pyrrh.*7; ὑφ' ὧν πολλὰ τραύματ' εἰληφώς D.18.262; πολλὰ τραύματ' ἔχων X. *HG*4.3.20; τραύματα ὑπὸ τῶν πολεμίων τοσαῦτα ἔχων Id.*Mem.*3.4.1; φέρειν, ποιεῖν, E.*Or.*1487 (lyr.), Theoc.19.6; τυπτέσθω ἄνευ τραυμάτων Pl.*Lg.*845c; τὰ ἄνευ τραύματος κατάγματα Sor.1.28; αἱ χωρὶς τραυμάτων αἱμορραγίαι Gal.15.127; ἀδύνατον νεκρῶν τραύματα μύειν Arist.*Fr.*167. II. of things, *hurt*, *damage*, as of ships, Hdt.6. 16, Plb.16.4.12. III. in war, *heavy blow*, *defeat*, Hdt.1.18, 4. 160; τὸ ἐν Μαραθῶνι τ. γενόμενον Id.6.132; τὸ τ. τὸ Λακωνικόν Id.8. 66. IV. ἡ τοῦ τ. γραφή an indictment *for wounding* (with intent to murder), Aeschin.2.93; τραύματος ἐκ προνοίας γραφὰς γραφόμενος Id.3.212, cf. Lys.3.41; δίκαι τραύματος Arist.*Ath.*57.3.

**τραυμᾰτ-εία**, ἡ, *wounding*, Hdn.*Epim.*183. **-ιαῖος**, α, ον, *wounded*, *PTeb.*304.12 (ii A.D.), *PFay.*108.14 (ii A.D.). **-ίας**, ου, ὁ, Ion. τρωμ-, *wounded man*, Pi.*Fr.*223; οἱ τ. the *wounded* of an army, Hdt.3.79, Th.7.75, 8.27; ὁ τ. 'Οδυσσεύς, name of a play, prob. by S., Arist.*Po.*1453ᵇ34; of plays by Alex. and Antiph., also by Philocles, *IG*2².2323.234. II. *corpse of one slain*, Lxx *De.*21. 1, *Jd.*16.24. **-ίζω**, Ion. τρωμ-: pf. τετραυμάτικα Decr.ap.D.18. 155:—Pass. -ισμαι (v. infr.): aor. Pass. ἐτραυματίσθην E.*Fr.*705:—*wound*, Hdt.1.59, al., E.*Ba.*763, *PPetr.*3 p.59 (iii B.C.), *BGU*1780.11 (i B.C.), *Ev.Luc.*20.12, etc.:—Pass., Hdt.9.61, al., Th.4.35, etc.; τετραυματισμένον γὰρ ὡς κύων νεβρὸν.. ἐκμαστεύομεν A.*Eu.*246; τραυματισθεὶς πολλά Th.4.12. **-ικός**, ή, όν, *of* or *for wounds*, ἀντίδοτος, [ῥίζα], Dsc.1.99, 3.3, etc.; τὰ τ. (sc. φάρμακα) Id.1.72.5; ἔστι (ἡ κόλλα) τραυματική Id.3.87, cf. 145. **-ιον**, Ion. τρωμ-, τό, Dim. of τραῦμα, *slight wound* or *hurt*, Hp.*Epid.*3.4. **-ισμός**, ὁ, *wounding*, Ruf.ap.Suid. s. v. Ῥοῦφος.

**τραυμᾰτο-θερᾰπεύω**, *treat wounds*, pf. inf. τραυμαραπευκέναι (sic) *BGU*647.11,23 (ii A.D.). **-ποιός**, όν, *making wounds*, *Gloss.*

❋**τραύξανα**, τά, *dry chips*, *waste that falls from the manger*, Pherecr. 241 (cf. Phot. and Suid.); **τραύσανον**· ξηρὸν πᾶν, ἢ φρύγανον, Hsch. Cf. τρώξανον.

**τράφαλλος**· ὁ χλωρὸς τυρός, οἱ δὲ **τραφαλλίδα**, Hsch. (cf. τροφαλίς).

**τραφέμεν**, v. τρέφω B. II. τράφε, τράφεν, Dor. forms of τρέφω, v. τράφω.

❋**τρᾰφερός**, ά, όν, (τρέφω) *well-fed*, *fat*, οἱ τραφεροί or τὰ τραφερά the *fat ones*, i. e. fishes, Theoc.21.44. II. Hom. uses τραφερή (sc. γῆ), ἡ, as Subst., *dry land*, ἐπὶ τραφερήν τε καὶ ὑγρήν Il.14.308, Od.20.98, *h.Cer.*43:—in later Poets as Adj., νομὸς τ. Arat.1027; κέλευθος ὑγρή τε τ. τε A.R.2.545; τ. ἄρουρα Opp.*H.*1.204; ἤθεα τ. tracts *of dry land*, ib.5.334. (In this sense it is from τρέφω (A) I, *make thick*.)

**τράφη**, ἡ, v. τάφρη.

**τράφηξ** [ᾰ], ηκος, ὁ, *beam* in framework of ἑλέπολις, Bito 53.4. 2. *spear*, Lyc.1001. 3. *baker's board*, *EM*764.35:—so perh. in Lyc.641 (unless the sense is more general, v. Sch.). 4. *handle of an oar*, Hsch. s. v. τρόπηκος; or *gunwale* on which the rowlocks are fixed, *IG*2².1604.40 (iv B.C.), *EM*764.36.—τράφηξ seems to be the true form; but τράπηξ, τρόπηξ, τροφῆς are found in cod. of Hsch.

**τράφος**, = τάφρος (q. v.).

❋**τράφω**, Dor. for τρέφω, inf. τράφειν Pi.*I.*8(7).44, τράφεν Megar. in Ar.*Ach.*788 codd. (written τράπεν *Leg.Gort.*3.49); also τραφέμεν Hes.*Th.*480; part. τράφοισα Pi.*P.*2.44: impf. ἔτραφον Theoc.3.16.

**τράχε**· πορεύου, Hsch. (Cf. τρέχω.)

**τρᾱχεόστρᾰκος**, = τραχυ-, Eust.1485.37.

**τρᾱχέως**, v. τραχύς II.

**τρᾰχηλ-άγχη**, ἡ, *cord for strangling*, Eun.*VS* p.481 B. **-ια**, τά, *scraps of meat and gristle about the neck, which were thrown away with the offal*: hence, simply, *scraps*, *offal*, Ar.*V.*968, Pherecr. 54; βόεια Hp.*Epid.*7.62. **-ιαῖος**, α, ον, *of*, *on*, or *from the neck*, *Hippiatr.*92, Hsch. s. v. κόλλαπες, Eust.1915.13; perh. to be restored for τραχηλιμαῖος in Str.2.5.27, 16.4.11. **-ιάω**, *arch the neck proudly*, like a horse: metaph., *exalt oneself*, Lxx *Jb.*15.25, Method.ap.*EM*174.25. ❋**-ίζω**, fut. Att. -ιῶ *PPetr.*2 p.52 (iii B.C.):—*bend* or *twist the neck of* a victim, βοῦν Thphr.*Char.*27.5. II. in wrestling, '*scrag*' one's opponent, τοὺς νεανίσκους Plu.*Ant.*33:—Pass., Pl.*Amat.*132c, Teles p.50 H., Them.*Or.*23.291b. 2. metaph., *inflict hardship on* a combatant, τοὺς.. φίλους οἱ λειπόμενοι τραχηλιοῦσι πόλεμοι Ph.2.131:—Pass., ἐμφυλίῳ πολέμῳ καὶ διχονοίᾳ -ιζόμενοι J.*BJ*4.6.2. 3. metaph. in Pass., *to be overpowered*, *swept away*, ταῖς ἐπιθυμίαις Ph.2.127; of ships in a whirlpool, Str.6.2.3. III. in a pun on signfs. I, II. 1, and II. 3, ἰδὼν 'Ολυμπιονίκην εἰς ἑταίραν πυκνότερον ἀτενίζοντα, "ἴδε" ἔφη, "κριὸν 'Αρειμάνιον ὡς ὑπὸ τοῦ τυχόντος κορασίου -ίζεται" see how the ram's *neck is being twisted*, D.L.6.61, cf. Plu.2.521b; τοὺς πολυπράγμονας ἴδοις ἂν ὑπὸ παντὸς ὁμοίως θεάματος -ιζομένους καὶ περιαγομένους ibid. IV. Pass., *to be laid open*, *Ep.Hebr.*4.13; τετραχηλισμένα· πεφανερωμένα, Hsch. **-ιμαῖος**, v. τραχηλιαῖος. ❋**-ιον**, τό, Dim. of τράχηλος, *butt-end of a spear*, *EM*732.1, Harp. s. v. στύραξ. **-ίς**, *collare*, *Gloss.* **-ισμός**, ὁ, *seizing by the neck*, '*scragging*', a trick in wrestling and ball-play, Plu.2.526e, Luc.*Lex.*5, Gal.*Parv.Pil.*2 (pl.), Ath.1.14f (pl.). 2. *wry neck*, *stiff neck*, Diocl.*Fr.*141 (pl.). **-ιστήρ**, ῆρος, ὁ, a kind of *bandage*, Gal.18(1).822. **-ιώδης**, ες, *stiff-necked*, *EM*751.35.

**τρᾰχηλο-δεσμότης**, ου, ὁ, *chaining the neck*, κλοιούς *AP*6.107 (Phil.) (-δέγμονας Stadtm., -δεσπότας Meineke). ❋**-ειδής**, ές, *like the neck*, Hsch. s. v. δειράδες. **-κοπέω**, *cut the throat*, *behead*, Plu.2.308d:—Pass., Arr.*Epict.*1.1.18, 1.2.16, etc.; σώματα τετραχηλοκοπημένα *Lyr.Adesp.* in *PFay.*2 iii 24. **-κοπία**, *decollatio*, *Gloss.*

❋**τράχηλος** [ᾰ], ὁ, Dor. **τράχᾱλος** *IG*4²(1).122.3, al. (Epid., iv B.C.): heterocl. pl. τράχηλα Call.*Fr.*98 (= *Iamb.*1.147):—*neck*, *throat*, Hdt.2.40, Hp.*Aph.*4.35, E.*Cyc.*608 (lyr.), Sor.1.84, Gal.6. 151, etc.; distd. fr. αὐχήν by Pl.*Phdr.*253e (τράχηλος being, acc. to *Gp.*19.2.3, *the whole neck and throat*, αὐχήν the back part of the neck in human beings, the upper part in animals; this difference is observed in Sor.*Fasc.*37 (cf. αὐχήν in 38,39,40,41), Adam.2.21; but αὐχήν in Hp.*Prog.*23 is glossed τράχηλος by Gal.18(2).264, cf. Ruf. *Onom.*66, Poll.2.130; in Lxx, *NT*, and Pap. τ. is more freq. than αὐχήν); τ. σώματος χωρὶς τεμών E.*Ba.*241, cf. *Supp.*716; ἀποτεμεῖν, ἀποκόψαι, Plu.*Art.*29, *Flam.*18, etc.; βρόχον δ' ἐνίαλλε τραχήλῳ Theoc.23.51; ἐς τ. πεσεῖν break one's *neck*, E.*Tr.*755; ἐπὶ τ. ὠθεῖν τινα thrust *head-foremost*, Luc.*DMort.*27.1, *Merc.Cond.*39; εἰς τ. Poll.2.135; ἐπιπεσεῖν ἐπὶ τὸν τ. τινός Lxx *Ge.*46.29, *Ev. Luc.*15.20; ἐν βρόχῳ τὸν τ. ἔχων νομοθετεῖ with a halter round his *neck*, D.24.139; ἔδει σε ἐν τῷ σῷ τ. ἐμπαίζειν at the risk of your own *neck*, *PTeb.*758.2 (ii B.C.). 2. *neck* of animals, of the horse, X.*Eq*.1.8; the hare, Id.*Cyn*.5.30; the camel, Plu.2.1125b, *BGU*469.6 (ii A.D.); *the neck* as a joint of meat, Plu.*Demetr.* 11; of a fowl, Gal.6.788. II. of parts *resembling the neck*, e.g. *upper part of the murex*, Eub.66, Posidipp.14, cf. Arist.*HA*547ᵃ16, Ath.3.87f; in the κάραβος *the narrow part of the abdomen*, Arist.*HA* 526ᵃ3; the *neck* of the grasshopper, ib.556ᵃ2. 2. *neck* of a vessel, *BCH*35.286 (Delos), Hero *Spir*.1.19, al.; of a gourd, Arist.*HA*616ᵃ 23; of parts of the body, τ. μήτρας Hp.*Mul*.2.169, Poll.2.222; ὑστέρας Sor.1.7; κύστεως ibid., Gal.*UP*14.9, Poll.2.171; καρδίας *Placit*.4.5.8. 3. *middle part of a mast*, Asclep.Myrl.ap.Ath.11.475a.

**τρᾰχηλόσῑμος**, ον, *bull-necked*, *Com.Adesp*.908.

❀ **τρᾰχηλώδης**, ες, = τραχηλοειδής, Sch.Nic.*Th*.871.

**Τρᾱχίς**, Ion. **Τρηχίς**, ῖνος, ἡ, *Trachis* in Thessaly, Il.2.682, etc.; also **Τραχίν**, Str.9.4.13:—Adj. **Τρᾱχίνιος** [ῑν], α, ον, Ion. **Τρηχ-**, Hdt.7.198, S.*Ph*.491, etc.; also ος, ον Theoc.24.83; fem. **Τρᾱχῑνίς**, ίδος, Paus.10.22.1: οἱ Τραχίνιοι, Ion. Τρηχ-, *the people of T.*, Hdt. 7.175, Th.3.92, etc.; αἱ Τ., name of tragedy by S.: ἡ Τραχινία, Ion. Τρηχ-, *the country of T.*, Hdt.8.31, Th. l. c., etc.; but the country was also called Τραχίς, Id.3.100, 4.78, 5.51.

**τρᾰχόομαι**, = τραχύνομαι, v.l. for ἐτέτρυτο or ἐτετρύχωτο in J.*AJ* 17.12.2.

**τρᾶχος**, *duretum*, *Gloss.*

**τράχουρος** [ᾱ], or **τρᾱχοῦρος**, ὁ, (οὐρά) a sea-fish, '*rough-tail*', *the horse-mackerel*, *Caranx trachurus*, Numen.ap.Ath.7.326a, Phylotim. ap.Gal.6.727, Opp.*H*.1.99; = *sorus*, *Gloss.*

**τρᾰχῠ-βᾰτέω**, Ion. **τρηχ-**, *walk on rough, rocky ground*, Hp.*Ep.* 17. **-δερμος**, ον, = sq., Arist.ap.Ath.7.305d (om. Rose, Arist. *Fr*.294), Tz. ad Lyc.340. **-δέρμων**, ον, gen. ονος, *rough-skinned*, Epich.59.

**τρᾰχυν-τικός**, ή, όν, *making rough*, Arist.*Pr*.872ᵇ36: c. gen., τῆς ἀρτηρίας Dsc.3.74. **-ω**, Ion. **τρηχ-**: pf. τετράχῠκα (ἀπο-) D.H.*Comp*.22:—Pass., aor. ἐτρᾱχύνθην Pl.*Ti*.66c: pf. τετράχυσμαι Arist.*HA*536ᵇ23, (ἐκ-) Luc.*Pisc*.51; 3 sg. -υνται Arist.*Pr*.901ᵇ11; inf. -ύνθαι Pl.*Prt*.333e: (τραχύς):—*make rough, uneven*, Id.*Ti*.65d: c. acc., τ. τὸ κύτος ib.67a; αὔρη τρηχύνοι πέλαγος A.R.4.768:— Pass., *become rough*, Pl.*Ti*.66c, Plu.*Rom*.3, etc.; of the sea, Arist. *Col*.791ᵃ21; of the voice, Id.*Aud*.803ᵇ2; τ. τῇ φωνῇ use *rough, harsh* tones, Plu.*TG*2. 2. in A.*Th*.1050, τράχυνε refers to τραχύς γε μέντοι δῆμος just before, *call them harsh*. 3. metaph. in Pass., *to be angry, exasperated*, τετραχύνθαι τε καὶ ἀγωνιᾶν Pl.*Prt.* 333e; πρός τινα Plb.2.21.3, Plu.*Pel*.26; τινι Anon.*Oxy*.664.38; τ. ὅτι.. D.H.*Th*.43. 4. τ. τὰς ἀκοάς *grate roughly on* the ears, Id. *Comp*.22. II. intr., *to be rough*, ὁ τραχύνων τόπος D.S.1.32; τὰ τραχύνοντα τοῦ ποταμοῦ Plu.*Cat.Ma*.20.

**τρᾰχῠ-όδους**, οντος, ὁ, ἡ, *with rough teeth*, gloss on καρχαρόδοντες, Apollon.*Lex*. **-όστρᾰκος**, ον, *rough-shelled*, Arist.*HA*528ᵃ 23. **-πους**, ποδος, ὁ, ἡ, *rough-footed*, ib.544ᵇ4.

❀ **τρᾰχ-ύς**, εῖα, ύ: Ep. and Ion. τρηχύς, fem. -εῖα, -εῖαν, -είης, neut. -ύ (Hom. (v. infr.), Hes.*Op*.291, Theoc.25.74); in Ion. Prose fem. τρηχέα, acc. τρηχέαν, gen. τρηχέης, dat. τρηχέῃ (imperfectly preserved in codd.; in Hdt.4.23, 9.122, codd. ABCP have τρηχέη, -έην, -έης, RSV have -εῖα, -εῖαν, -είης; for codd. Hp. v. Kühlewein i p. lxxxvi); τρηχείην (before conson.) Simon.89 codd., A.R.2.375 codd.; τρηχείης (as pr. n.) Hippon.47; gen. pl. neut. ἐρίων..τρηχείων *GDI* 5633.14 (Teos); dual in Trag. τραχεῖ, Ion Trag.67:—*jagged*, λίθος Il. 5.308; χαλινοί, opp. λεῖοι, X.*Eq*.9.9, cf. 10.6; τ. καὶ γωνιοειδής Thphr. *Sens*.65; *prickly*, ἄκανθαι, ἄκανθα, Plu.2.32e, 138d (both Sup.); *rugged*, ἀκτή, ἀταρπός, Od.5.425, 14.1; as epith. of Ithaca, 9.27, 10.417; so γῆ λιθώδης καὶ τρηχέα Hdt.4.23; Χερσονήσου τῆς Τρηχέης καλεομένης, of the Crimea, ib.99; and freq. in Trag. and Att. of rocky districts, A.*Pr*.726, E.*Fr*.1083; τὰ τραχέα, τὰ τραχύτατα, X.*Cyn*.4.10, Plu.*Flam*.4; τ. καὶ χαλεπὴ ὁδός Pl.*R*.328e; also, *rough*, γλῶσσα Hp.*Morb*.2.63; ἔρια *GDI* l. c., *PCair.Zen*.287.2 (iii B.C.); σφόγγοι ib.12.56 (iii B.C.); χῆμαι ib.82.12 (iii B.C.); σινδόνες (towels, opp. μαλακαί) Gal.6.418; χερσὶ μὴ πάνυ μαλακαῖς, ὥσπερ αὖ μηδὲ τραχείαις, ἀνατρίβειν τὸ σῶμα ib.417; τὰ τ. κατὰ τὰς ἀνωμαλίας ἀλλήλοις ἐμπλεκόμενα ἑνοῦται, τὰ δὲ λεῖα κτλ. Diocl.*Fr*.26; βλέφαρα Sor. 2.16, *PTeb*.273 intr. (ii/iii A.D.); *shaggy*, τὰ κάτωθεν τ. καὶ τραγοειδής, of Pan, Pl.*Cra*.408d, cf. 420e; λάσιον καὶ τ. [τὸ κέαρ]..ἔχοντες Id.*Tht*.194e; τ. σώματα, opp. λεῖα, X.*Mem*.3.10.1; of the voice, *harsh*, Pl.*Ti*.67c, etc.; esp. of the voice of boys, when it breaks, μεταβάλλειν ἐπὶ τὸ -ύτερον Arist.*HA*581ᵃ18; τὸ τ. τῆς φωνῆς Plu. *Mar*.14; and of a person, τῇ φωνῇ τ. X.*An*.2.6.9; also τραχυτάτη γλῶσσα (cf. τραχύστομος) Str.14.2.28; of sounds and their combinations, *harsh*, opp. λεῖος, σύνθεσις, διάλεκτος, Phld.*Po.Herc*.994. 32,36:—on τραχεῖα ἀρτηρία, v. ἀρτηρία. 2. of battle and conflict, ὑσμίνη Hes.*Sc*.119; νιφὰς πολέμοιο Pi.*I*.4(3).17(35), cf. Simon.89; φάλαγγες Tyrt.12.22. 3. of natural forces, ῥόθιον A.*Pr*.1048 (anap.); -ύτερα τὰ νοσήματα ἀπεργάζεσθαι Pl.*Ti*.84c; of a river, Plu.*Alex*. 60, etc.; ἄελλαι A.R.1.1078. 4. of persons, their acts, feelings, or conditions, *rough, harsh, savage*, τ. ἔφεδρος Pi.*N*.4.96; οὐ τ. εἰμι καταθέμεν I am not *niggardly* in paying, ib.7.76; Ἡσυχία Id.*P*.8. 10; ἅπας δὲ τ. ὅστις ἂν νέον κρατῇ A.*Pr*.35, cf. 188 (anap.), 326; δικαστὴς τ. εἶ Id.*Ag*.1421; τ. γε..δῆμος Id.*Th*.1049; τ. καὶ τεθηγμένους λόγους Id.*Pr*.313; τ. ὀργή E.*Med*.447; λεῖον καὶ τ. πάθημα Pl.*Ti*.63e; νόμοι τραχύτατοι Id.*Lg*.864c; τὸ τ. τοῦ ἤθους, τοῦ νόμου, Id.*Cra*.406a, *R*.452c; -ύτερα πράγματα Isoc.7.18; εὐνομίη τραχέα λειαίνει smooths *the rough places*, Sol.4.35. II. Adv. τρᾱχέως, Ion. τρηχέως, rare in the literal sense, *roughly*, τ. ὑλακτεῖν Plu.*Arat*.8; neut. as Adv., τρηχὺ φωνῇ ἠπείλει Theoc.25.74; θάλασσα τραχὺ βοᾷ *AP*5.179 (Mel.). 2. of men's acts, τρηχέως περιέπειν τινά handle *roughly*, Hdt.1.73, 114; τραχέως ἔχειν to be *rough, harshly disposed*, Isoc.3.33; τινι D.19.45; -ύτερον ἄρχειν Isoc.3.55; τ. ἀποκρίνεσθαι Plu.*Phoc*.21, etc.; τ. φέρειν take *hardly*, Id.*Lys*.15; rarely τραχυτέρως, Pl.*Clit*.406a; περιέφθησαν τρηχύτατα Hdt.6.15. (Prob. cogn. with θράσσω, cf. ἐνθράσσω.) **-υσμα**, Ion. **τρήχ-**, ατος, τό, *a roughness*, Hp.*Epid*.2.3.1, Ath.11.475b (both pl.); of *roughnesses* or perh. *prickly pains* in the skin, Archig.ap.Gal.8.91, cf. Gal.8. 105. **-υσμός**, Ion. **τρηχ-**, ὁ, *a roughening*, τοῦ ἐντέρου Hp.*Acut.* 60; τῆς ἐπιφανείας Orib.*Fr*.79.

**τρᾰχύ-στομος**, ον, *of rough speech* or *pronunciation*, Str.14.2.28, where he couples it with παχύστομος, and in the same paragraph he writes παχυστομέω (τραχυστομέω cod. E, and so it is cited in Eust.367.29), παχυστομία. **-της**, ητος, ἡ, Att. **τρᾰχῠτής**, ῆτος (acc. to Hdn.Gr.1.83):—*roughness, ruggedness*, κώνων λαμβάνοντα τραχύτητας Democr.155; τῆς χώρας X.*Cyr*.7.5.67; *sharpness*, of a bit, Id.*Eq*.10.6; τραχύτησί τε καὶ λειότησιν Pl.*Ti*.65c, cf. Ti.Locr. 100d; περὶ τὴν ἀρτηρίαν Arist.*GA*788ᵃ27; τὰ ῥοφητὰ..τὰς ἐν τῇ φάρυγγι τ. ἐκλεαίνει Gal.6.706; βλέφαρα τὰ τ. ἔχοντά τινα Id. 16.510; τ. φωνῆς Arist. *de An*.422ᵇ31, cf. Phld.*Po.Herc*.994.32, 33. 2. of persons, *roughness, harshness*, ὀργῆς A.*Pr*.80; τ. δυσπρόσοδος Plu.*Dio* 8, etc. **-φλοιος**, ον, *with rough rind* or *bark*, Thphr.*HP*1.5.2. **-φωνέω**, *pronounce with rough sound*, Eust. 1598.27 (Pass.). **-φωνία**, ἡ, *roughness of voice*, Arist.*GA*788ᵃ 22. **-φωνος**, ον, Ion. **τρηχ-**, *with rough, harsh voice* or *speech*, Hp.*Epid*.1.19, D.S.5.31, etc.: Comp., Eust.229.25.

**τράχω** [ᾰ], Dor. for τρέχω (q. v.).

**τρᾱχ-ώδης**, ες, *of rough nature*, v.l. in Arist.*HA*549ᵇ14, interpol. in Dsc.3.13. **-ωμα**, ατος, τό, *trachoma* in the eyes, in pl., Id. 1.64, Gal.*UP*10.11, *PSI*4.299.6 (iii A.D.). **-ωματικός**, ή, όν, *of* or *for trachoma*, Gal.12.775, Aët.7.113; *suffering from trachoma*, Gal.12.773. ❀ **-ών**, ῶνος, ὁ, *a rugged, stony tract*, Str.4.1.5, D.H. 19.4, *PVat*.11ʳ v 6 (ii A.D.), Luc.*VH*2.30, *Tox*.49:—hence **Τράχων**, in Syria, J.*AJ*13.16.5; and **Τραχωνῖτις**, ιδος, ἡ, χώρα *Ev.Luc*.3.1, etc.; **Τραχωνῖται**, οἱ, *its inhabitants*, J.*BJ*3.10.10; Τ. Ἄραβες Ptol. *Geog*.5.14.20.

**τρέ**· σέ, Κρῆτες, Hsch. (Prob. τϝέ; perh. from Κρητῶν πόλις in Pisidia.)

❀ **τρεῖος**, ὁ, *tierce*, on dice, *JHS*30.261, 32.275 (Pamphylia).

❀ **τρεῖς**, οἱ, αἱ, **τρία**, τά: gen. τριῶν: dat. τρισί, also τριοῖσι Hippon. 51, and τρίεσσι *Delph*.3(5).80.21 (iv B.C.); Aeol. τρίσσι *Inscr.Perg.* 245 *B*18 (Pitana): acc. τρεῖς (written τρες *IG*1².24.16, 44.15, 188. 37, 1085, al.), τρία: Dor. nom. τρέες *Leg.Gort*.9.48; τρῆς *IG*12(3). 1640 (Thera); τρῖς *SIG*236 *A* 10 (Delph., iv B.C.), *Tab.Heracl*.1. 23; acc. τρίινς *Leg.Gort*.5.54, al. (for *τρίνς, lengthd. to correspond with the other cases); τρῖς *IG*1².838, 839 (vi B.C.), *SIG*239 *D* ii 28 (Delph., iv B.C.), *Berl.Sitzb*.1927.158 (Cyrene):—*three*, Il.15.187, etc.; τρία ἔπεα *three* words, prov. in Pi.*N*.7.48,—for from the earliest times *three* was a sacred and lucky number, esp. with the Pythagoreans (cf. τριάς), Arist.*Cael*.268ᵃ11; so τῶν τριῶν μίαν λαβεῖν εὔσοιαν S.*Fr*.122; εἰ καὶ τῶν τριῶν ἓν οἴσομαι ib.908; cf. σωτήρ I. 2:—διὰ τριῶν ἀπόλλυμαι I am *thrice*, i.e. *utterly*, undone, E.*Or*.434 (cf. τριάζω); ἡ διὰ τριῶν ἀγωγή the 'trivium', Simp. *in Ph*.1171.34; ἵνα δήσῃ τρία τρία *by threes*, *POxy*.121.19 (iii A.D.). (I.-E. stem *trĭ-*, fuller form *trey-*, nom. *tréy-es* (Skt. *tráyas*, Lat. *tres*), whence τρέες, contr. τρῆς and τρεῖς (written τρες *IG*1².295. 11); acc. *tri-ns* (Goth. *þrins*, Skt. *trīn*), whence τρῖς and τρίινς; in Gr. the nom. τρεῖς functions as acc. (as in Att.), or the acc. τρῖς as nom. (ll. cc.).)

**τρεισκαίδεκα**, οἱ, αἱ, τρια καίδεκα, τά, first as three words, later as one, *thirteen*: gen. τριῶν καὶ δέκα Th.2.97, *IG*1².372.87, etc.: dat. τρισὶ καὶ δέκα Th.8.108, D.9.25, *IG*2².1673.7, etc.: acc. neut. τριακαίδεκα (or τρία καὶ δέκα) Hdt.1.119, Ar.*Pl*.194, 846, *Pax* 990:—sts other words are interposed, τρεῖς τε καὶ δ. Pi.*O*.1.79, but μέν follows τρισκαίδεκα in B.10.92 and δέ in Th.3.79 (s.v.l., δέ om. codd. BM):—the form τρισκαίδεκα (acc. masc. and fem.) is found in codd. of Hom. Il.5.387, Od.24.340 (in Od. τρεισκαίδεκα, διὰ διφθόγγου γράφουσι τὰ τῶν ἀντιγράφων ἀκριβέστερα Eust. ad loc.); also of Pi.*Fr*.135 (v.l.), B. l. c. (Pap.), Ar.*Ra*.50, X.*HG*5.1.5, Th.3.69, 79, 8.88 (τρεῖς καὶ δέκα cod. B); τρισκαίδεκα as gen., Hp.*Mul*.2.133 (τρεισ- cod. D), Is.8.35; as dat., Th.8.22 codd.:—early Inscrr., however, never have τρισκαίδεκα, but τρεῖς [τρες] καὶ δέκα ἡμέραι *IG*1².295.11 (v B.C.); στατῆρας τρεισκαίδεκα *SIG*241 *B*101 (Delph., iv B.C.); τρε[ισκαί]δεκα πόλεων ib.368 *B*1 (iii B.C.); λίθων τρεισκαίδεκα *IG*7.3073.134 (Lebad., ii B.C.); so that τρισκαίδεκα should be corrected in all early texts (in spite of Choerob. in *An.Ox*.2.267) either to τριῶν καὶ δ., etc., or to τρεισκαίδεκα: the same applies to the following compds.: v. τρεισκαιδέκατος.

**τρεισκαιδεκά-γωνος** [ᾰ], ον, *thirteen-sided*, Hero *Geep*.163. **-έτης**, ες, *thirteen years old*, Is.12.10, Poll.1.55, *PSI*8.940.29 (iii A.D.): fem. -έτις, Phleg.*Fr*.36.6 J. **-κλινος**, ον, *with* or *large enough for thirteen couches*, οἶκος Callix.1. **-μετρος**, ον, *of thirteen* μέτρα, Sch. Ar.*Ach*.1142. **-μηνος**, ον, *containing thirteen months*, ἐνιαυτός Eudox.*Ars* 14.3, Ptol.*Alm*.6.2, prob. in *IG*11(2).199 *A*1 (Delos, iii B.C.). **-πάλαστος** [πᾰ], ον, *measuring thirteen* παλασταί, *PPetr.* 3p.125 (iii B.C., τρισ- Pap.). **-πηχυς**, υ, in Dor. and Aeol. form **τρισκαιδεκάπᾱχυς**, *thirteen cubits high*, Theoc.15.17, prob. in *IG*12(2).14.2 (Mytil.). **-πλάσιων**, ον, gen. ονος, *thirteen-fold*, Cleom.

2.1. -στάσιος [στᾰ], ον, (ἵστημι A. IV) *worth thirteen times its weight*, χρυσίον τ. (sc. πρὸς τὸ ἀργύριον) Hdt.3.95. -σύλλᾰβος, ον, *of thirteen syllables*, Heph.15.15.

**τρεισκαιδεκᾰτ-αῖος**, α, ον, *on the thirteenth day*, Hp.*Hum*.6. -ημόριον, τό, *thirteenth part*, Eudox.*Ars* 16.11. ※ -ος, η, ον, *thirteenth*, *PCair.Zen*.1.10 (iii B.C.), *IG*11(2).161*B*10 (Delos, iii B.C.), *GDI*2642.61 (Delph., ii B.C.), *UPZ*10.5 (ii B.C.), etc.: **τρισκ-** occurs mostly later, *IG*11(2).283.9 (Delos, iii B.C.), *Mon.Anc.Gr*.12.12, *POxy*. 73.1, al. (i A.D.), and should be corrected in Il.10.561, Od.8.391, Hes. *Op*.780, etc.; cf. A.D.*Synt*.200.13; Aeol. [**τρισ**]**καιδέκοτος** *IG*12(2). 82.1 (Mytil.).

**τρεισκαιδεκᾰ-φόρος**, ον, *fruiting thirteen times*, Luc.*VH*2.13. -χορδος, ον, *of thirteen notes*, Nicom.*Harm*.11.

**τρεισκαιδεκ-έτης**, ες, *thirteen years old*, Lys.10.4, *AP*12.4 (Strat.); also **τρεισκαιδεχέτης**, *IG*12(5).303(4).7 (Paros), and **τρεισκαιδεκαέτης** (q.v.). -ήρης, ες, perh. *a galley rowed by thirteen men to each pair of oars passing through the same porthole*, Callix.1, Plu.*Demetr*.31; v. τριήρης. -ώρῠγος, ον, *of thirteen fathoms*, prob. l. for -δεκόργυιος in Thphr.*HP*5.8.1: cf. τριώρυγος.

**τρείω**, late Ep. for τρέω (q.v.).

**τρέμῑθος**, ἡ, poet. for τέρμινθος, Nic.*Th*.844, cf. St.Byz. s.v. Τρεμιθοῦς.

**τρέμω**, only pres. and impf., exc. pf. τετρέμηκα *EM*606.50:— *tremble, quake, quiver*, τρέμε δ' οὔρεα μακρὰ καὶ ὕλη ποσσὶν ὑπ' ἀθανάτοισι Il.13.18, cf. Call.*Del*.137; ὠλένας τρέμων ἄκρας *quivering in..*, E.*IT*283; τρέμουσα κῶλα Id.*Med*.1169; τρέμει [ἡ φωνή] Arist.*Pr*.906ᵃ 17; of persons, τρέμειν τὴν φωνήν ib.948ᵃ35; *shiver*, in the cold stage of malaria, Hp.*Flat*.8. II. esp. *tremble with fear*, ὑπὸ δ' ἔτρεμε γυῖα Il.10.390, cf. Od.11.527; φόβῳ, φρίκῃ τ., E.*Ion* 1452 (lyr.), *Tr*. 1026: then simply, *tremble, be afraid*, δεδιὼς καὶ τ. D.18.263; τ. τῷ δέει τί πείσεται Alex.110.6. 2. c. inf., *tremble* or *fear to* do, A.*Th*. 419 (lyr.), S.*OC*128 (lyr.); also τρέμων τὸν ἄνδρ' ἔφευγε μὴ κτάνοι Id.*OT*947, cf. E.*Andr*.808, 1057. 3. c. acc., *tremble at, fear*, S.*OC*256, E.*El*.643, etc.; τ. τὸ πρᾶγμα Ar.*Ach*.494; τὰ πράγματα Id.*Eq*.265 (troch.); τὸ μέλλον Pl.*Prm*.137a; [τῆς εὐδαιμονίας] ἕνεκα τ. Antipho 2.4.9; περὶ τῆς εὐδαιμονίας Id.2.3.8, cf. Pl.*R*.554d. (Cf. Lat. *tremo*, Lith. *trimù, trìmti* 'shiver'.)

**τρέξι**, for θρέξομαι and θρέξεται, barbarism in Ar.*Th*.1222, 1225.

※**τρέπεδδα**, ἁ, Boeot., = τράπεζα II, *bank*, *IG*7.3172.139 (Orchom., iii B.C.); **τρεπεδδίτας** [ῑ], ὁ, = τραπεζίτης, ib.2420.34 (Thebes, iii B.C.). (Not from τράπεζα but from τρίπεζα, which Hsch. inaccurately calls Boeot. for τράπεζα.)

**τρεπ-τέον**, (τρέπω) *one must turn*, ποίαν ὁδὸν νῷ τ. Ar.*Eq*.72; ἐπί τι Pl.*R*.365c. -τικός, ή, όν, *causing change in*, δύναμις -κὴ τῆς ὕλης Plot.2.3.17: epith. of the sign Libra, Heph.Astr.1.1:—f.l. for θρεπτικός, Max.Tyr.10.2. 2. Adv. -κῶς, κινοῦσι τὴν γῆν οὐ μεταβατικῶς ἀλλὰ τρεπτικῶς τροχοῦ δίκην *by revolution*, *Placit*.3.13.3. -τός, ή, όν, *liable to be turned* or *changed*, Arist.*Mu*.392ᵃ33, S.E.*M*.7.434, etc.; εἰς ἄλληλα *Placit*.1.17.4. 2. *liable to be turned*, of persons, Ph.1.648; θεοί Them.*Or*.7.98c. -τότης, ητος, ἡ, = τροπή, Hsch.

※**τρέπω**, Il.8.399, etc.: fut. τρέψω 15.261, etc.: aor. 1 ἔτρεψα 18.469, etc., Ep. τρέψα 16.645: besides aor. 1 Hom. has aor. 2 ἔτρᾰπον, Od.4.294, al., also Pi.*O*.10(11).15 (sts. also intr., v. περιτρέπω II and perh. Il.16.657, cf. III fin.): Aeol. aor. ἔτροπον, v. ἀνατρέπω: pf. τέτροφα Ar.*Nu*.858, Anaxandr.51, (ἀνα-) S.*Tr*.1009 (lyr.), And.1.131; later τέτρᾰφα Din.1.108, (ἀνα-) ib.30, D.18.296 (cod. S), Aeschin.1. 190, 3.158 (but cf. Wackernagel *Studien zum griech. Perf*.15); ἐπι-τέτραφα Plb.30.6.6:—Med., fut. τρέψομαι Hdt.1.97, Hp.*Prog*.20, E. *Hipp*.1066, etc.: aor. ἐτρεψάμην Od.1.422, E.*Heracl*.842: also aor. 2 ἐτραπόμην Il.16.594, Hdt.2.3, al. (used also in pass. sense, (ἀν-) Il.6.64, 14.447, and once in Att., (ἀν-) Pl.*Cra*.395d); imper. τραποῦ Ar.*Ra*. 1248: pf. (v. infr.):—Pass., fut. τρᾰπήσομαι Plu.*Nic*.21, etc.; also τετράψομαι Ph.1.220, (ἐπι-) Pisistr.ap.D.L.1.54: aor. ἐτρέφθην Hom. *Epigr*.14.7, once in Trag., E.*El*.1046 (v. ἐπιτρέπω); Ion. τραφθῆναι Od.15.80, cf. Hdt.4.12: aor. 2 ἐτράπην [ᾰ] A.*Pers*.1029 (lyr.), Ar.*Ec*. 416, etc.; ἐτρέπην (ἐν-) *UPZ*5.24 (ii B.C.): pf. τέτραμμαι Pl.*R*.519b; 3 pl. τετράφαται Thgn.42, cf. Il.2.25 (ἐπι-); 3 sg. imper. τετράφθω 12.273; part. τετραμμένος 19.212, etc.: plpf., Ep. 3 sg. τέτραπτο Od.4.260; 3 pl. τετράφατο Il.10.189.—From the aor. 2 has been formed the pres. ἐπιτρᾰπέουσι, ib.421; cf. τραπητέον.—The Ion. forms used by Hdt. are pres. Pass. τράπονται 6.33, al.; 3 sg. impf. τρέπεσκε 4.128; aor. Pass. τραφθείς 9.56; but fut. ἐπιτράψομαι is f.l. in 3.155, and in the pres. Act. and Pass. codd. vary (both forms in codd. of 2.92 (Act.), τρέπεται 1.117, τράπεται 4.60):—Dor. forms, **τράπω** *EM*114.19; fut. ἐπι-τραψῶ *Schwyzer*198.21 (Crete):—*turn* or *direct* towards a thing, Hom., etc.; mostly folld. by a Prep., τ. [φύσας] ἐς πῦρ Il.18.469; ἐς ποταμὸν φλόγα 21.349; εἰς εὐνὴν τράπεθ' ἥμεας *show* us to bed, Od.4.294 (perh. with a punning reference to ταρπώμεθα in next line); λέκτρονδε τραπείομεν εὐνηθέντες 8.292 (as though τραπείομεν in Il.3.441 belonged to τρέπω and not to τέρπω; unless there is a pause after λέκτρονδε); θυμὸν εἰς ἔργον τ. Hes.*Op*.316; εἰς ἐχθροὺς βέλος A.*Th*.255; πόλεις ἐς ὕβριν Th.3.39; τὸν ἄνθρωπον..εἰς ἀθυμίαν D.23.194; πρὸς ἠέλιον κεφαλήν Od.13.29; πρὸς ὄρος πίονα μῆλα 9.315; πρὸς εὐφροσύναν ἦτορ Pi.*I*.3.10; τὰς γνώμας πρὸς χρηματισμόν Pl.*Ep*.355b; also ἐπ' ἐμπορίην θυμόν Hes.*Op*.646, cf. Pl. *Phdr*.257b, *R*.508c; δᾶμον ἐς ἡσυχίαν Pi.*P*.1.70; ἐπ' ἐχθροῖς χεῖρα S.*Aj*.772; κατὰ πληθὺν τ. θυμόν Il.5.676; ἀντίον Ζεφύρου πρόσωπον Hes.*Op*.594: with Advbs., πάντων ὁμόσε στόματ' ἔτραπε Il.12.24; οὐκ οἶδ' ὅποι χρὴ..τ. ἔπος S.*Ph*.897; ἐνταῦθα σὴν φρένα E.*IT*1322; τὴν διάνοιαν ἄλλοσε Pl.*R*.393a; ἐκεῖσε τ. τὰς ἡδονάς Id.*Lg*.643c; ἐπὶ τὴν θεραπείαν τὸν λόγον Sor.2.23: c. inf., σέ..ἔτραπε..ὀργὰ παρφάμεν *led* thee *to speak* crookedly, Pi.*P*.9.43:—also in Med., τραπέσθαι τινὰ ἐπί τι Pl.*Euthd*.303c, cf. *Chrm*.156c:—Pass., κεῖται ἀνὰ πρόθυρον τετραμμένος Il.19.212. 2. Pass. and Med., *turn one's steps, turn in a certain direction*, τραφθῆναι ἀν' Ἑλλάδα Od.15.80; τραφθέντες ἐς τὸ πεδίον Hdt. 9.56; ἐς Θήβας ἐτραπόμην Id.2.3; ἐπὶ Προκόννησον, ἐπ' Ἀθηνέων, Id.6. 33, 5.57: with Advbs., ἀμηχανεῖν ὅποι τράποιντο which way *to turn*, A. *Pers*.459; ἀμηχανῶ..ὅπᾳ τράπωμαι Id.*Ag*.1532 (lyr.); πᾷ τις τράποιτ' ἄν; Id.*Ch*.409 (lyr.); ποῖ τρέψομαι; E.*Hipp*.1066, cf. X.*An*.3.5.13; ποῖ χρὴ τραπέσθαι; Lys.29.2: c. acc. cogn., τραπέσθαι ὁδόν *take* a course, Hdt.1.11, cf. 9.69, Pl.*Sph*.242b; πολλὰς ὁδοὺς τραπόμενοι κατὰ ὄρη Th.5.10; ἐτρέφθην ἥνπερ ἦν πορεύσιμον E.*El*.1046. 3. in Pass. and Med. also, *turn* or *betake oneself*, εἰς ὀρχηστύν, εἰς ἀοιδήν, Od.1.422, 18.305; ἐπὶ ἔργα Il.3.422, etc.; ἐπ' ἀναιδείην Hom.*Epigr*.14. 7; ἐπὶ σωφροσύνην Thgn.379; ἐπὶ ψευδέα ὁδόν Hdt.1.117; ἐπὶ φροντίδας E.*IA*646; ἐφ' ἁρπαγήν Th.4.104; ἐπ' εἰρήνην X.*HG*4.4.2; ἐς τὸ μαίνεσθαι S.*OC*1537; ἐς ἀλκήν Th.2.84; εἰς ἁρπαγὴν ἐπὶ τὰς οἰκίας X.*HG*6.5.30; κατὰ θέαν τετραμμένοι Th.5.9; πρὸς ἀλκήν Hdt.3.78; πρὸς τὸ κέρδιον τραπείς S.*Aj*.743; πρὸς λῃστείαν Th.1.5; πρὸς ἄριστον τετρ. Hdt.1.63; πρὸς τὸν πότον Pl.*Smp*.176a, etc.; also τ. πρός τινα *betake oneself, have recourse* to him, Cratin.152, X.*An*.4.5.30, Pl.*Prt*. 339e; ἐφ' ἱκετείαν τ. τῶν διωκόντων Id.*Ap*.39a. 4. Pass. and Med., of places, *to be turned* or *look* in a certain direction, πρὸς ζόφον Od. 12.81; πρὸς ἄρκτον, πρὸς νότον, etc., Hdt.1.148, Th.2.15, etc.; also πρὸς τοῦ Τμώλου Hdt.1.84; ἄντ' ἠελίου τετρ. straight towards, Hes. *Op*.727. II. *turn*, i.e. *turn round* or *about*, πάλιν τρέπειν *turn back*, ἵππους Il.8.432; τινα ib.399; ὅσσε, δόρυ, 21.415, 20.439; τὰ καλὰ τ. ἔξω *turn* the best side outmost, show the best side (of a garment), Pi.*P*.3.83:—Pass., πάλιν ἐτράπετ' Il.21.468; μή τις ὀπίσσω τετράφθω 12.273; c. gen., *turn from*.., υἷος 18.138; ἐτράπετ' αἰχμή the point *bent back*, like ἀνεγνάμφθη, 11.237; of the sun having passed the meridian, πόστην ἥλιος τέτραπται; Ar.*Fr*.163, cf. Antig. *Mir*.60; also of the solstice, ἐπειδὰν ἐν χειμῶνι τράπηται [ὁ ἥλιος] (v. τροπή I) X.*Mem*.4.3.8, cf. Pl.*Lg*.915d; τραπείσης τῆς ὥρας Arist. *HA*628ᵇ26:—intr. in Act., περὶ δ' ἔτραπον ὧραι, v. περιτρέπω II. 2. τ. τι εἴς τινα *turn* upon another's head, τ. τὴν αἰτίαν, τὴν ὀργὴν εἴς τινα, Is.8.41, D.8.57; freq. in imprecations, ἐς κεφαλὴν τράποιτ' ἐμοί on my head be it! Ar.*Ach*.833, cf. Hdt.2.39; εἰς σεαυτὸν τρεπέσθω on your head be it! *IG*4.444 (Phlius); ἡ κατ' ἐμοὶ τρέποιτ' ἂν αἰτίας τέλος; A.*Eu*.434; κατὰ σεαυτόν νυν τρέπου *keep your ills to yourself*, Ar.*Ach*.1019, *Nu*.1263; πρὸς ὑμᾶς αὐτοὺς τρέψεσθε Lys.8.19. 3. *alter, change*, φρένας Il.6.61; τὰς γνώμας X.*An*.3.1.41; [τὸ χρῶμα] Sor.1.35; [τὸ γάλα] ib.92; ἔτραπεν κεῖνον μισθῷ χρυσός Pi.*P*.3. 55; *deceive*, Archil.166; ἐς κακὸν τ. τινά Pi.*P*.3.35; ἅττ' ἂν ὑμεῖς ἐξαμάρτητ' ἐπὶ τὸ βέλτιον τρέπειν Ar.*Nu*.589 (troch.); ἐς γέλων τὸ πρᾶγμ' ἔτρεψας Id.*V*.1261, cf. Hdt.7.105, etc.:—Med., πρὸς τὰς ξυμφορὰς τὰς γνώμας τρέπεσθαι *shift their* views, Th.1.140, cf. Plu. 2.71e, etc.:—Pass., *to be changed*, τρέπεται χρώς Il.13.279, cf. Od. 21.413, Hes.*Op*.416; τὴν χρόαν τρέπεσθαι, of animals, Plu.2.51d; τῷ χρώματι τρεπομένας, of women, Sor.1.35 (so abs., of a man, Id.*Vit.Hippocr*.5); ὁ οὕτω τρεπόμενος σφυγμός Gal.18(2).40; τρέπεται νόος Od.3.147; νόος ἐτράπετ' 7.263; Διὸς ἐτράπετο φρήν Il.10. 45; τράπομαι καὶ τὴν γνώμην μετατίθεμαι Hdt.7.18; ὁρῶν αὐτοὺς τετραμμένους seeing that they *had changed their minds*, Id.9.34, cf. Th.4.106; ἐπὶ τὰ βελτίω τρέπου Ar.*V*.986: c. inf., κραδίη τέτραπτο νέεσθαι Od.4.260; ἐτράποντο..τῷ δήμῳ..τὰ πράγματα ἐνδιδόναι Th. 2.65: c. acc. cogn., πλείους τραπόμενος τροπὰς τοῦ Εὐρίπου Aeschin. 3.90: οἶνος τρέπεται the wine *turns, becomes sour* (v. τροπίας), S.E. *P*.1.41; ἡ ξανθὴ χολὴ..εἰς τὸν ἰώδη τρέπεται χυμόν Gal.16.534; ἡ ἀδελφὴ ἐπὶ τὸ κομψότερον ἐτράπη *has taken a turn* for the better, *POxy*.935.5 (iii A.D.); ἐπὶ τὸ ῥᾷον ἔδοξεν τετράφθαι ib.939.17 (iv A.D.); τοῦ πατρὸς ἡμῶν εἰς ἄπορον τραπέντος *having become* destitute, *PMeyer*8.14 (ii A.D.):—intr. in Act., τοῦ ἄρχοντος τρέποντος εἰς δεσπότην Ph.2.562. III. *turn* or *put to flight, rout, defeat*, τρέψω δ' ἥρωας Ἀχαιούς Il.15.261; ἔτρεψε φάλαγγας Tyrt.12.21, cf. Pi.*O*.10 (11).15, Hdt.1.63, 4.128, Th.1.62, 4.25, 33, etc.; in full, φύγαδε τ. Il.8.157; εἰς φυγὴν ἔτρεψε τοὺς ἑξακισχιλίους X.*An*.1.8.24; τρέψαι καὶ ἐς φυγὴν καταστῆσαι Th.7.43 (but ἔτρεψαν ἐς φυγὴν πόδα *they fled*, E.*Supp*.718):—Med., pres., X.*An*.5.4.16, J.*AJ*13.2.4, Plu.*Cam*.29: fut., Ar.*Eq*.275 (troch.): aor. 1, E.*Heracl*.842, X.*An*.6.1.13:—Pass., *to be put to flight*, aor. 2 ἐτράπην A.*Pers*.1029 (lyr.), X.*Cyr*.5.4.7 (v.l. ἐτράποντο), etc.: also aor. 1 ἐτρέφθην Id.*An*.5.4.23, *HG*3.4. 14, *Cyn*.12.5: aor. 2 Med. ἐτραπόμην Hdt.1.80, 9.63, etc.; ἐς φυγὴν τραπέσθαι Id.8.91, Th.8.95; τραπόμενοι κατέφυγον Id.4.54; φυγῇ ἄλλος ἄλλῃ ἐτράπετο X.*An*.4.8.19; ἐτράποντο φεύγειν Plu.*Lys*. 28, *Caes*.45: rarely in pf. Pass., τετραμμένου φυγᾷ γένους A.*Th*.952 (lyr.):—also intr. in Act., φύγαδ' ἔτραπε Il.16.657 (unless it governs δίφρον). IV. *turn away, keep off*, οὐκ ἄν με τρέψειαν ὅσοι θεοί εἰσ' ἐν Ὀλύμπῳ 8.451; τ. τινὰ ἀπὸ τείχεος 22.16; ἑκάς τινος Od.17.73 (Med.); τῇ..νόον ἔτραπεν 19.479: abs., ἀλλὰ Ζεὺς ἔτρεψε Il.4.381; of weapons, βέλος..ἔτραπεν ἄλλῃ 5.187; ἀπὸ ἔγχεος ὁρμὴν ἔτραπε Hes. *Sc*.456. V. *overturn*, εὐτυχοῦντα μὲν σκιά τις ἂν τρέψειεν A.*Ag*. 1328 (s.v.l.); τ. ἄνω κάτω Id.*Fr*.311. VI. *turn, apply*, τ. τι ἐς ἄλλο τι Hdt.2.92; τὰς ἐμβάδας ποῖ τέτροφας; what *have you done with* your shoes? Ar.*Nu*.858; τὸν μόναυλον ποῖ τέτροφας; Anaxandr. 51:—Pass., ποῖ τρέπεται..τὰ χρήματα; Ar.*V*.665 (anap.).

**τρεσᾶς** or **τρέσας**, ὁ, v. τρέω I. 2.

**τρέστης**, ου, ὁ, (τρέω) *trembler, coward*, Hsch.

**τρέφος**, εος, τό, = θρέμμα (v.l. βρέφος), S.*Fr.*154, cj. in E.*Fr.*996.

**τρεφουργία**, ἡ, *rearing*, Greg.Cor. *in Hermog.Meth.* in Rh.7(2). 1126 W. (example of a παράδοξος λέξις).

* **τρέφω**, Il.5.52, etc.; Dor. **τράφω** (v. sub voce); 1 sg. opt. τρέφοιν E.*Fr.*903: fut. θρέψω *h.Ven.*257, etc.: aor. 1 ἔθρεψα, Ep. θρέψα Il.2. 548: aor. 2 ἔτρᾰφον (v. infr. B): pf. τέτροφα intr., Od.23.237, (συν-) Hp.*Morb.Sacr.*11; but trans., S.*OC*186 (lyr.); also τέτρᾰφα Plb.12. 25$^{h}$.5:—**Med.**, fut. θρέψομαι in pass. sense, Hp.*Genit.*9, *Nat.Puer.* 23, Th.7.49, etc.: aor. ἐθρεψάμην Pi.*O.*6.46, A.*Ch.*928, etc.:—Pass., fut. τρᾰφήσομαι Ps.-D.60.32, D.H.8.41, etc., but in early writers in med. form θρέψομαι (v. supr.): aor. 1 ἐθρέφθην, Ep. θρέφθη Hes.*Th.* 198, rare in Trag. and Att., E.*Hec.*351,600, Pl.*Plt.*310a; ἐθράφθη *IG*12(9).286 (Eretria, vi B.C.): aor. 2 ἐτράφην [ᾰ] Hom. (sed v. infr. B), A.*Th.*754 (lyr.), Ar.*Av.*335 (lyr.), etc.; Ep. 3 pl. ἔτραφεν, τράφεν, Il.23.348, 1.251: pf. τέθραμμαι Hp.*Nat.Hom.*5, E.*Heracl.*578, etc.; 2 pl. τέθραφθε Pl.*Lg.*625a (but συντέτραφθε [s. v.l.] in X.*Cyr.*6.4.14); inf. τεθράφθαι Pl.*Grg.*525a, X.*HG*2.3.24 (in both with v.l. τετρ-). I. *thicken* or *congeal* a liquid, γάλα θρέψαι *curdle* it, Od.9.246; τρέφε (impf.) πίονα τυρόν Theoc.25.106:—Pass., with pf. Act. τέτροφα, *curdle, congeal*, γάλα τρεφόμενον τυρὸν ἐργάζεσθαι Ael.*NA*16.32; περὶ χροῒ τέτροφεν ἅλμη Od.23.237. II. usu., *cause to grow* or *increase, bring up, rear*, esp. of children bred and brought up in a house, ὅ σ' ἔτρεφε τυτθὸν ἐόντα Il.8.283; ἥ μ' ἔτεχ', ἥ μ' ἔθρεψε Od.2.131, cf. 12.134; εὖ ἔτρεφεν ἠδ' ἀτίταλλεν Il.16.191, cf. Od.19.354; ἐγώ σ' ἔθρεψα, σὺν δὲ γηράναι θέλω A.*Ch.*908, cf. *Supp.*894; μέχρι ἥβης τ. Th.2.46; γεννᾶν καὶ τ. Pl.*Plt.*274a; τ. τε καὶ αὔξειν μέγαν Id.*R.*565c: c. acc. cogn., τ. τινὰ τροφήν τινα *bring up* in a certain way, Hdt.2.2; also τῶν πρώτων μαθημάτων, ἐν οἷς οἱ παλαιοὶ τοὺς παῖδας ἔτρεφον Gal.16. 691:—Med., *rear for oneself*, θρέψαιό τε φαίδιμον υἱόν Od.19.368; αὐτὸν ἐθρέψαντο δράκοντες Pi.*O.*6.46; τεκοῦσα τόνδ' ὄφιν ἐθρεψάμην A.*Ch.*928; οἱ γεννήσαντες καὶ θρεψάμενοι Pl.*Lg.*717c; τεκὼν ἀρετὴν καὶ θ. Id.*Smp.*212a; ἔτεκον μὲν ὑμᾶς πολεμίους δ' ἐθρεψάμην ὕβρισμα E.*HF*458:—Pass., *to be reared, grow up*, ὅς μοι τηλύγετος τρέφεται θαλίῃ ἔνι πολλῇ Il.9.143; τῇ δμοῦ ἐτρεφόμην Od.15.365; ἅμα τράφεν ἠδ' ἐγένοντο Il.1.251, etc.; κάρτιστοι τράφεν ἀνδρῶν *grew up* the strongest men, ib.266:—prop. a boy was called τρεφόμενος only so long as he remained in the charge of the women, i.e. till his fifth year, Hdt.1.136; ἐξ ὅτου 'τράφην ἐγώ from the time when *I left the nursery*, Ar.*Av.*322; but even of pre-natal growth, ἐν σκότοισι νηδύος τεθραμμένη A.*Eu.*665, cf. *Th.*754 (lyr.):—generally, in Trag., τραφεὶς μητρὸς εὐγενοῦς ἄπο S.*Aj.*1229; ὅπως πατρὸς δείξεις οἷος ἐξ οἵου 'τράφης ib.557; κρατίστου πατρὸς.. τραφεὶς Id.*Ph.*3: παῖδες μητέρων τεθραμμέναι *true nurslings of* your mothers, implying a reproach for unmanliness (s. v.l.), A.*Th.*792; μιᾶς τρέφει πρὸς νυκτὸς *art nursed* by night alone, i.e. art blind, S.*OT*374. 2. of slaves, cattle, dogs and the like, *rear and keep* them, κύνας Il.22.69, Od.14. 22, etc.; ἵππους Il.2.766; λέοντος ἶνιν (v. σίνις) A.*Ag.*717 (lyr.); μῆλα Id.*Eu.*946 (lyr.); ὄφιν S *Fr.*226 (cj. for στρέφουσι); ἰκτῖνα Ar. *Fr.*628; ὄρτυγας Eup.214; ὄρνιθας Pl.*Tht.*197c; οἱ τρέφοντες (sc. τοὺς ἐλέφαντας) the *keepers*, Arist.*HA*571$^{b}$33; τ. παιδαγωγούς Aeschin.1.187; also τ. γυναῖκα E.*IA*749; τ. [ἑταίραν], [πόρνας], *keep* .., Antiph.2, Diph.87; ὁ τρέφων one's *master*, Nicol.Com.1.11,36: metaph., αἰγιαλὸν ἔνδον τρέφει *he keeps* a sea-beach in the house, Ar.*V.*110:—Pass., *to be bred, reared*, δοῦλος οὐκ ὠνητός, ἀλλ' οἴκοι τραφείς S.*OT*1123; ἐν τῇ σῇ οἰκίᾳ γέγονεν καὶ τέθραπται was born and *bred*, Pl.*Men.*85e; 'Αγαθεῖνον θρεμένον (i.e. τεθρεμμένον, = θρεπτόν, v. θρεπτός 1) ἑαυτῶν *MAMA*4.275*B* (Dionysopolis, ii A.D.); Νείκην τὴν θρεμένην μου ib.276*A* (ibid., ii A.D.). 3. *tend, cherish*, τὸν μὲν ἐγὼ φίλεόν τε καὶ ἔτρεφον, of Calypso, Od.5.135, cf. 7.256; of plants, Il.17.53; θρέψασα φυτὸν ὥς 18.57, cf. Od.14. 175. 4. of parts of the body, *let grow, cherish, foster*, χαίτην ..Σπερχειῷ τρέφε Il.23.142; τῷ θεῷ [πλόκαμον] τ. E.*Ba.*494; ὑπήνην ἄκουρον τ. Ar.*V.*476 (lyr.); τ. κόμην, = κομᾶν, Hdt.1.82; [τρίχες] πολλῷ ἐλαίῳ τραφεῖσαι Hero *Bel.*112: also τά θ' ὕεσσι τρέφει ἀλοιφήν things which *put* fat *on* swine, Od.13.410; τεθραμμένη εἰς πολυσαρκίαν X.*Mem.*2.1.22. 5. in Poets, of earth and sea, *breed, produce, teem with*, οὐδὲν ἀκιδνότερον γαῖα τ. ἀνθρώποιο Od.18.130; ἄγρια, τά τε τρέφει οὔρεσιν ὕλη Il.5.52; φάρμακα, ὅσα τρέφει εὐρεῖα χθών 11.741; ὅσ' ἤπειρος..τρέφει ἠδὲ θάλασσα Hes.*Th.*582; πολλὰ γᾶ τρέφει δεινὰ A.*Ch.*585 (lyr.), cf. 128, E.*Hec.*1181; θάλασσα..τρέφουσα πορφύρας ἰσάργυρον κηκῖδα A.*Ag.*959; ὃν πόντος τ., i.e. the sailors, Pi.*I.*1.48: rare in Prose, ἀεί τι ἡ Λιβύη τρέφει καινόν Arist. *GA*746$^{b}$8. 6. in Poets also, simply, *have within oneself, contain*, ὅ τι καὶ πόλις τέτροφεν ἄφιλον S.*OC*186 (lyr.), cf. *Tr.*817; τρέφειν τὴν γλῶσσαν ἡσυχαιτέραν *to keep* his tongue more quiet, Id.*Ant.*1089; ἡ γλῶσσα τὸν θυμὸν δεινὸν τ. Id.*Aj.*1124; τἀληθὲς γὰρ ἰσχὺον τρέφω Id.*OT*356 (so in Pl., τ. ἰσχυρὸν τὸ ἐλεινόν *R.*606b); τ. νόσον S. *Ph.*795; ἐκ φόβου φόβον τ. Id.*Tr.*28; ἄταν Id.*Aj.*644 (lyr.); οἵας λατρείας..τρέφει what services..*she has as her lot*, ib.503; ἐν ἐλπίσιν τρέφω..ἥξειν I *cherish* hopes that.., Id.*Ant.*897; τὸν Καδμογενῆ τρέφει..βιότου πολύπονον [πέλαγος] *is his daily lot*, Id.*Tr.*117 (lyr., but Reiske's cj. στρέφει is prob.); πόνοι τρέφοντες βροτούς E.*Hipp.*367 (lyr.). III. *maintain, support*, τ. ἀνδρὸς μόχθος ἡμένας ἔσω A.*Ch.*921, cf. Pi.*O.*9.106; τοῦ τρέφοντος 'Ηλίου χθονὸς φύσιν A.*Ag.*633; τ. τὸν πατέρα Aeschin.1.13; τὴν οἰκίαν ὅλην D.59. 67; οὐ δίκαιον τρέφεσθαι ὑπὸ πατρὸς ὑὸν ἡβῶντα Pl.*R.*568e; τὰ κτήνη χιλῷ ἐτρέφοντο X.*An.*4.5.25; γάλακτι, τυρῷ, κρέασι τ., Id.*Mem.* 4.3.10; σίτῳ, ὄψῳ, Id.*Lac.*1.3; *feed* a patient, Gal.15.503, 19.185; *provide the food for* an employee, σοῦ τρέφοντος αὐτόν, ἐμοῦ δὲ ἱματίζοντος αὐτόν *BGU*1647.14 (ii A.D.); also τ. ἀπό τινος Pl.*Prt.*313c, X.*HG*2.1.1; ἔκ τινος A.*Ag.*1479 (lyr.), cf. Pl.*R.*372b. 2. *maintain* an army or fleet, Th.4.83, X.*An.*1.1.9 (Pass.); τ. τὰς ναῦς Th. 8.44, X.*HG*1.5.5, 5.1.24; τ. τὸ ναυτικὸν ἀπὸ τῶν νήσων ib.4.8.9; ἐκ τῶν κωμῶν τρέφεσθαι Id.*An.*7.4.11, etc. 3. of land, *feed, maintain* one, τρέφει γὰρ οὗτος [ὁ ἀγρὸς]..με Philem.98.2, cf. Men.63,466, al. 4. of women, *feed* or *suckle* an infant, συνεξομοιοῦται τὰ τρεφόμενα ταῖς τρεφούσαις Sor.1.88; γυνὴ τρέφουσα ib.87; ἡ τρέφουσα, = ἡ τροφός, Gal.6.44. 5. of food, *nourish*, τὰ 'Ηρακλεωτικὰ τρέφει οὐχ ὁμοίως τοῖς ἀμυγδάλοις Diocl.*Fr.*126, cf. 117; ἡ οὐκ ἐπιτηδείως τῷ σώματι διδομένη τροφὴ οὐ τρέφει Sor.1.49; πυρῶν..ὅσοι κοῦφοι..ἧττον τρέφουσι Gal.*Vict.Att.*6; τὸ δέρμα πᾶν αὐτοῖς ὡς ἂν ὑπὸ φλεγματώδους αἵματος τρεφόμενον οἰδαλέον γίνεται Id.18(2).118, cf. 106. IV. *bring up, rear, educate*, Hes.*Fr.*19, Pi.*N.*3.53, etc.; τῷ λόγῳ τ. καὶ παιδεύεις Pl.*R.*534d; θρέψαι καὶ παιδεῦσαι D.59.18; Δήμητερ ἡ θρέψασα τὴν ἐμὴν φρένα A.*Fr.*479; ἡ θρέψασα (sc. γῆ) the *motherland*, Lycurg. 47:—Med., ἐθρέψω Ξέρξην ἐν τοῖς αὐτοῖς ἤθεσιν Pl.*Lg.*695e; ἡ θρεψαμένη one's *motherland*, Lycurg.85:—Pass., ὀρθῶς, εὖ τραφῆναι, Pl. *R.*401e, *Alc.*1.120e; παιδείᾳ, ἐν ταύτῃ τῇ παιδείᾳ τ., Id.*Lg.*695c, X. *Cyn.*1.16; ἐν πολυτρόποις ξυμφοραῖς Th.2.44; ἐν φιλοσοφίᾳ Pl.*Tht.* 172c; ἐν χλιδῇ X.*Cyr.*4.5.54; ἐν ἐλευθερίᾳ Pl.*Tht.*175d, *Mx.*239a; ἐν ἄλλοις νόμοις Arist.*Pol.*1327$^{a}$14; ἐν φωνῇ βαρβάρῳ Pl.*Prt.*341c; πάσαις Μούσαισι *BCH*50.444 (Thespiae, iv A.D.). V. the Pass. sts. came to mean little more than *to be*, ἐπ' ἐμοὶ πολέμιον ἐτράφη (sc. τὸ γένος) Ar.*Av.*335 (lyr.), cf. *Th.*141, S.*OC*805.

B. Hom. uses an intr. aor. 2 Act. ἔτραφον in pass. sense (which is to τρέφομαι, τέτροφα (intr.) as ἔδρακον to δέρκομαι, δέδορκα, etc.), ὃς..ἔτραφ' ἄριστος Il.21.279; λέοντε ἐτραφέτην ὑπὸ μητρί 5.555; τραφέμεν (Ep. for τραφεῖν) 7.199, Od.3.28, al.; ἐπεὶ τράφ' ἐνὶ μεγάρῳ, i.e. when he *was well-grown*, Il.2.661:—as trans. the aor. 2 is used by Hom. only in Il.23.90, and τράφε in Pi.*N.*3.53 is Dor. impf.:—ἐτράφην is perh. post-Homeric; 3 sg. τράφη is v.l. in Il.2. 661, 1 pl. ἐτράφημεν and 1 sg. ἐτράφην (περ) vv. ll. in 23.84; τράφη is in all codd. of 3.201, 11.222, which should prob. be emended from 2.661; 3 pl. ἔτραφεν 23.348 (v.l. ἔτραφον), Od.10.417 (v.l. ἔτραφον); τράφεν in all codd. of Il.1.251,266, Od.14.201, also (with v.l. τράφον) in 4.723: the *vox nihili* ἐτράφεμεν, found in Il.23.84 as cited by Aeschin.1.149, was emended by Scaliger to ἐτράφομεν:—the redupl. 3 sg. τέτραφ' Il.21.279, 3 pl. τέτραφεν 23.348, are ff. ll, though found in many codd. Later this aor. became obsolete, except in Ep. imitators, as in Call.*Jov.*55, Opp.*H.*1.774.

**Τρεφώνιος**, v. Τροφώνιος.

**τρεχέδειπνος**, ον, *running to a banquet*, of parasites, Plu.2.726a (who cites the explanation *coming late*), Ath.1.4a, 6.242c; τρεχέδειπνα, τά, *light robe* or *shoes worn by parasites*, Juv.3.67.

**τρέχις**, ὁ, *runner* (perh. as pr. n.), dub. in S.*Ichn.*188.

**τρέχνος**, εος, τό, = τέρχνος, *AP*15.25.6 (Besant.*Ara*), Hsch.

* **τρέχω**, Od.9.386, etc.: fut. θρέξομαι (ἀπο-) Ar.*Nu* 1005 (anap.), (μετα-) Id.*Pax*261, (περι-) Id.*Ra.*193; θρέξω only in Lyc.108; but ἀπο-θρέξεις Pl.Com.232: aor. 1 ἔθρεξα (v. infr.):—but the usual fut. and aor. come from the root δραμ-, viz. δρᾰμοῦμαι E.*Or.*878, X.*An.* 7.3.45, etc.; Ion. δραμέομαι Hdt.8.102; late δραμῶ Lxx *Ca.*1.4; but ὑπερ-δραμῶ Philetaer.3 (dub. l.); δράμομαι in compd. ἀναδράμεται *AP* 9.575 (Phil.): aor. 2 ἔδρᾰμον (v. infr.): pf. δεδράμηκα [ᾰ] Philem. 38, Men.741, (ἀνα-) Hdt.8.55, (κατα-) X.*HG*4.7.6, (περι-) Pl.*Clit.* 410a, (συν-) D.17.9: plpf. ἐδεδραμήκεσαν (κατ-) Th.8.92: poet. pf. δέδρομα (ἀνα-, ἐπι-) Od.5.412, 20.357:—Pass., pf. δεδράμημαι (ἐπι-) X.*Oec.*15.1.—The Verb is not common in Hom., who has pres. in Il.23.520, Od.9.386; in Il.18.599,602, Ion. Iterat. θρέξασκον (ἔθρεξα was also old Att., Epigr.ap.Plu.*Arist.*20, E.*IA*1569 (s. v.l., ἔβρεξε Weil), (περι-) Ar.*Th.*657); but the common aor. was ἔδραμον, Il. 23.393, Od.23.207, al.—Dor. **τράχω** [ᾰ] Pi.*P.*8.32, Hsch., *EM*756.10: fut. θραξοῦμαι Hsch.:—*run*, of men, ἰθὺς δράμε Od.23.207, etc.; θρέξασκον ἐπισταμένοισι πόδεσσι Il.18.599; τρέχει Ὅρκος ἅμα..δίκῃσιν Hes. *Op.*219; ψῦχε τρέχων Epich.37,110 (τράχων cj. Ahrens); βαδίζειν καὶ τ. Pl.*Grg.*468a; τρέχων, opp. βάδην, X.*Cyr.*2.2.30; τ. χερσίν, οὐ ποδωκείᾳ σκελῶν A.*Eu.*37: of horses, Il.23.393,520: the part. is freq. added to another Verb, τί οὐ τρέχων σὺ τὰς τραπέζας ἐκφέρεις; why do you not *run and* carry out..? Pl.Com.69.2, cf. Pl.*R.*327b; v. infr. 2. 2. of things, *move quickly*, τὸ δὲ [τρύπανον] τ. ἐμμενὲς αἰεί Od.9.386, cf. Il.14.413; ναῦς παρὰ γῆν ἔδραμεν Thgn.856; πόλιν ..ἐξ οὐρίων δραμοῦσαν S.*Aj.*1083; τὸ δ' ἐν ποσὶ τράχον ἴτω let what is now before me go *trippingly*, Pi.*P.*8.32; ἐπὶ καρδίαν ἔδραμε.. σταγών A.*Ag.*1121 (lyr.); ἔρις δραμοῦσα τοῦ προσωτάτω *having run its course*, S.*Aj.*731; πυρετὸς..ἥκει τρέχων has come *quickly*, Nicopho 12. 3. οἱ τρέχοντες a constellation rising with Libra, Antiochus ap.Teucrum in Boll *Sphaera* 58. II. c. acc. loci, *run over*, ῥόθια πεδία E.*Hel.*1117 (lyr.); ὁ ἵππος τ. καὶ πρανῆ καὶ ὄρεια X.*Eq.* 8.1:—in Att. Prose θέω seems to be more freq. in the pres., and in some phrases used exclusively, e.g. θεῖν δρόμῳ, v. θέω (A) II. 1 and cf. Th.3.111, X.*An.*1.8.18. 2. c. acc. cogn., δραμεῖν ἀγῶνα, βῆμα, δίαυλον, δρόμον, *run* a course, a heat, E.*El.*883,954, Alex.235, Men. 741, etc.; λαμπάδας, i.e. torch-races, *IG*2$^{2}$.1028.14: freq. metaph., ἀγῶνα δρ. *run* a risk, E.*Alc.*489, cf. *IA*1455; ἀγῶνα θανάσιμον δραμούμενον Id.*Or.*878; πολλοὺς ἀγῶνας δραμέονται περὶ σφέων αὐτῶν *run* for their life or safety, Hdt.8.102; κινδύνων τὸν μέγιστον τ. D.H.4.47; τὸν ὑπὲρ ψυχῆς ἀγῶνα, κίνδυνον ὑπὲρ τῆς ψυχῆς τ., Id.7. 48, 4.4; ἐσχάτην τρέχοντες ταύτην Plb.1.87.3: sts. the acc. is omitted, περὶ ἑωυτοῦ τρέχων *running* for his life, Hdt.7.57; περὶ τῆς

ψυχῆς Id.9.37; φόνου πέρι E.*El.*1264; περὶ νίκης f.l. in X.*An.*1.5.8 (ἐπὶ νίκῃ Rehdantz); cf. θέω (A) I. 2, δρόμος I. 2, κρέας fin. 3. παρὰ ἓν πάλαισμα ἔδραμε νικᾶν he was within one fall or bout of carrying off the victory, Hdt.9.33; cf. παρά c. III. 5, τριάζω I. 4. *commit*, μηδ' ἑτέρας δραμεῖν ἀταξίας ἢ ἀσελγίας *PLond.*5.1711.34 (vi A.D.).

**τρέψις**, εως, ἡ, *turning*, τέρψις, οἷον τρέψις, προτροπή τις ψυχῆς ἐπὶ τὸ ἀνειμένον D.L.7.114.

**τρεψίχρως**, ωτος, ὁ, ἡ, *changing colour*, a name for the polypus (cf. τρέπω II. 3), Arist.*Fr.*306.

**τρέω**, Hom. (v. infr.), A.*Th.*790 (lyr.): Ep. impf. τρέον Hes.*Sc.*213, 2 dual τρεέτην ib.171: aor. ἔτρεσα Il.11.745, Ep. τρέσσα 17.603: later Ep. pres. **τρείω** Opp.*C.*1.417, (ὑπο–) Timo 58.4:—this Verb is never contracted, except when the contraction is into ει:—*flee from fear, flee away* (Aristarch. held this to be the usual meaning in Homer), τρεῖν μ' οὐκ ἐᾷ Παλλάς Il.5.256; μήτε.. τρέε μήτε τι τάρβει 21.288; τρέσσε δὲ παπτήνας 11.546, 17.603; τρεῖτ' ἄσπετον ib.332: the sense of *fleeing* is most apparent in the phrases ἔτρεσαν ἄλλυδις ἄλλος 11.745, τρέσσαν δ' ἄλλυδις ἄλλη Od.6.138, τ. τεῖχος ὕπο Il.22.143; τρεέτην Hes.*Sc.*171; μὴ τρέσητε A.*Supp.*711; μὴ τρέσας without *fear*, Id.*Th.*436; οὐδὲν τρέσας Pl.*Phd.*117b; but, 2. τρέσας (cf. ἀνδρῶν τρεσσάντων Il.14.522, Tyrt.11.14) was a technical term at Sparta, and sts. used where we might say *runaway, coward*, ὁ τρέσας Ἀριστόδημος Hdt.7.231, cf. Tyrt. l. c., *AP*7.230 (Eryc.); οἱ ἐν τῇ μάχῃ καταδειλιάσαντες, οὓς αὐτοὶ τρέσαντας ὀνομάζουσι Plu.*Ages.*30, cf. *Lyc.*21, 2.191c, etc.:—and later a real Subst. was used in Com., **τρεσᾶς**, τρεσᾶ, acc. τρεσᾶν, Eust.772.12, cf. Gramm.ap.Gaisford *Choerob.*1 p. 43. 3. in Argive Prose, like Att. φεύγω, *to be banished*, τρέτō καὶ δαμευέσσθō *IG*4.554 (vi/v B.C.). II. trans., *fear, dread, be afraid of*, c. acc., Il.11.554, Pi.*Pae.*4.40, A.*Th.*397, *Ag.*549, al., S. *Ant.*1042, E.*Ph.*1077; ἄρκτον.. οὐκ ἔτρεσεν X.*An.*1.9.6:—so also c. gen., κελάδοιο, δηϊοτῆτος, Hes.*Th.*850: τ. μὴ.. A.*Th.*790 (lyr.).—Rare in Prose. (Cf. Skt. *trásati* 'to be terrified', Gr. ἄτρεστος.)

**τρηγαλέον**· διερρωγότα, Hsch.

**τρηδών**, όνος, ἡ, word coined to expl. τερηδών, Gal.7.38, 19.443.

**τρῆμα**, ατος, τό, (τετραίνω) *perforation, aperture, orifice*, Ar.*V.*141, Pl.*Grg.*494b, Gal.6.178,580; τὰ τ. τῶν οὐάτων Hp.*Carn.*15; τ. τυφλόν the *foramen* caecum in the skull, Gal.2.838; τῆς ἀρτηρίας, [τοῦ αἰδοίου], Arist.*HA*495$^a$29, 497$^a$25; the *hole* in the beam of a balance, *Theol.Ar.*29. 2. = τρύπημα, sens. obsc., Ar.*Ec.*906 (lyr.), *Lys.*410. II. of *the holes* or *pips of dice*, Amips.20.

**τρημᾰτ-ίζω**, (τρῆμα II) *bet on the pips of dice*, Sophr.129, Poll.9.96:—hence Dor. **–ίκτας**, α, ὁ, *dice-player*, Poll. l. c., Hsch. (prob. from Sophr. l. c.; τρηματῖται (pl.) acc. to Eust.1084.5, 1397.22). **–ιον**, τό, Dim. of τρῆμα I. 1, Hero *Spir.*1.18, al., Sever.ap.Aët.7.87. **–όεις**, εσσα, εν, *porous*, λίθος τ. pumice-stone, *AP*6.62 (Phil.). **–ώδης**, ες, *having a vent to the intestinal canal*, ζῷα τ., opp. ἄτρητα, Arist. *HA*488$^a$25 (unless the sentence is interpolated).

**τρήμη**, ἡ, = τρῆμα, Ar.*Fr.*730.

**τρῆνυ**, τό, sine expl. (as example of neut. in υ), Theognost.*Can.*120.

**τρηρόν**· ἐλαφρόν, δειλόν, ταχύ, Hsch.

❀ **τρήρων**, ωνος, ὁ, ἡ, (τρέω) *timorous, shy*, in Hom. always epith. of doves (i. e. of περιστεραί, the genus of which πέλειαι are a species, acc. to Eust.1262.61), τρήρωσι πελειάσιν Il.5.778, *h.Ap.*114, cf. Ar. *Av.*575; πέλειαι τρήρωνες Od.12.63; τρήρωνα πέλειαν Il.22.140, 23.853, cf. A.R.3.541; κέπφοι τ. Ar.*Pax* 1067. II. fem. Subst. *trembler*, = περιστερά (metaph. of women), Lyc.87,423. (Since the Subst. is implied for Hom. in πολυτρήρων, τ. is perh. always a Subst., name of the genus, and τ. πελειάδες is to be compared with ἴρηξ κίρκος, σῦς κάπρος, etc.)

**τρῆσις**, εως, ἡ, (τετραίνω) *boring through, perforation*, Pl.*Plt.*279e: pl., Hp.*Steril.*222. II. *orifice*, Arist.*HA*495$^a$28 (pl.).

**τρητοκουρήτας**· γνησίας γυναῖκας, οἱ δὲ παρθένους, Hsch. (Fort. τριτο–, v. τριτοκούρη.)

**τρητός**, ή, όν, (τετραίνω) *perforated, with a hole in it*, λίθος Od. 13.77; ἐν τρητοῖσι λεχέεσσιν, prob. of *inlaid* bedsteads (cf. τορευτός), Il.3.448, cf. Od.1.440, al.; others expld. it of the *holes* through which the cords that supported the bedding were drawn, or of the *holes* in the bedposts which received the framework (ἐνήλατα), *EM* 765.3:—μελισσᾶν τρητὸς πόνος, i. e. the honeycomb, Pi.*P.*6.54; τρητά *mortised*, Pl.*Plt.*279e; τ. ὀστοῦν, opp. ἄτρητον, Arist.*HA*516$^a$27; λίθαξ τ. pumice-stone, *AP*6.66 (Paul. Sil.); τ. δόνακες shepherd's pipes, ib.78 (Eratosth.).

**τρηχᾰλέος**, η, ον, poet. for τρηχύς, Pancrat.*Oxy.*1085.11, Marc. Sid.27, *AP*5.291.6 (Agath.), 6.63 (Damoch.), 64 (Paul. Sil.), *APl.*4.113 (Jul.).

**τρηχῠβᾰτέω, τρηχύνω, τρηχύς, τρήχυσμα, τρηχυσμός**, Ion. for τραχ–.

**τρήχω**, wrongly assumed as pres. of Homeric pf. τέτρηχα, v. ταράσσω. II. in later Ep., *to be rough* or *uneven*, pres. part. τρήχων Nic.*Th.*72,521: for τέτρηχα in this sense, v. ταράσσω III.

**τρηχώ**, οῦς, ἡ, *a rough, stony country*, v.l. in Nic.*Th.*284.

**τρηχώδης**, ες, Ion. for τραχώδης, v.l. (ap.Sch.) for ῥηχώδης in Nic. *Al.*230.

**τρῐ–**, stem of τρεῖς, in compds. *three times, thrice*:—also indefinitely, to add emphasis, e. g. τρίδουλος, τριβάρβαρος, τρίβαφος.

**τρῐαγμός**, ὁ, or **τρῐαγμοί**, οἱ, *the triad* or *the triads*, a philos. work by Ion of Chios, Harp. s. v. Ἴων, cf. D.L.8.8, Clem.Al.*Strom.*1.21.131 (where τριαγμοῖς is restored for τριγράμμοις); **τρῐασμοί** Suid. s. v. Ὀρφεύς.

**τρῐάδελφος** [ᾰ], ον, *of three brothers*, πόθος Tz.*H.*2.323.

**τρῐᾰδ-ίζω**, *make triple*, Dam.*Pr.*117 (Pass.). **–ῐκός**, ή, όν, *of three*, ἀριθμός Syrian. *in Metaph.*126.22; *triadic, pertaining to a triad*, Dam.*Pr.*57,117, Procl. *in Prm.*p.602 S.; τ. τῶν κόσμων τομή (of Proclus) Simp. *in Ph.*617.22. II. in Metric, *consisting of three* περίοδοι, Heph.p.61 C.; τ. συζυγία Sch.Ar.*Pax* 1127.

**τρῐάζω** (pres. only in compd. ἀπο–), aor. ἐτρίασα Theo Sm., Iamb. (v. infr.), and **τρῐάσσω**, *EM*765.37, Att. **τριάττω** Zonar.:—*conquer, vanquish*, properly of a wrestler, who did not win until *he had thrice thrown* his adversary, or conquered him *in three bouts* (παλαίσματα), τριαχθῆναι Thugen.1, cf. Suid. (Hence τριακτήρ, ἀτρίακτος, ἀποτριάζω.) II. *multiply by three*, Theo Sm.p.29 H., Iamb. *in Nic.*p.60 P.

**τρίαινα** [ῐ], ἡ, *trident, three-pronged fish-spear*, the badge of Poseidon, Il.12.27, Od.4.506, 5.292, A.*Pr.*925, E.*Fr.*360.47; as a symbol of the empire of the sea, Ar.*Eq.*839; τρίαιναν ἐσθλὸς καὶ κυβερνήτης σοφός, i. e. a good fisherman.., Archil.45. II. *three-pronged fork*, Longus 4.40; cf. τριαινόω II. III. a constellation rising with Pisces, Teucer in Boll *Sphaera* 52. IV. a kind of cautery, Paul.Aeg.6.48.

**τρῐαινατῆρες**· ἀντὶ τοῦ ἀροτριοῦντος, Hsch.

**τρῐαινοειδής**, ές, (εἶδος) *trident-shaped*, *Placit.*1.3.18, Paul.Aeg. 6.48, *EM*456.6, etc. Adv. **–δῶς** Hsch. s.v. πεμπωβόλους, Sch.D Il.1. 463.

**τρῐαιν-οῦχος**, ον, (ἔχω) *wielding the trident*, Herm. *in Phdr.*p. 135 A., Procl. *in Cra.*p.86 P., Eust.889.26. **–όω**, prop. *heave with the trident*: then, generally, *heave* or *prise up, overthrow*, θάκους μοχλοῖς τ. E.*Ba.*348. II. τ. δικέλλῃ τὸ γήδιον *break* it *up* with a fork or mattock, Ar.*Pax* 570 (troch.).

**τρῐαινώδης**, ες, = τριαινοειδής, *An.Ox.*2.447.

**τρῐᾱκάδαρχος** [κᾰ], ὁ, *chief of a* τριακάς, *IG*14.209,211, al. (Sicily).

**τρῐᾱκαιδεκέτης**, ου, ὁ, ἡ, *thirteen years old*, Pl.*Lg.*833d.

❀ **τρῐᾱκάς**, Ep. and Ion. **τρῐηκάς**, άδος, ἡ, (τρεῖς, τρία) *the number thirty*, ἐς τριακάδας δέκα ναῶν A.*Pers.*339. II. *the thirtieth day of the month*, Hes.*Op.*766, *IG*1$^2$.845.2, 7.2712.69 (Acraeph.), *PCair.Zen.*150.8 (iii B.C.), Dsc.*Eup.*1.146, *Hippiatr.*97; τ. ἡ πικρή (when school fees were due) Herod.3.9; first used by Thales, acc. to D.L.1.24. At Athens the τριακάδες were dedicated to the memory of the dead, Harp., Poll.1.66, etc.; offerings were made to Hecate, Ath.7.325a, etc.; ἡ τῶν τ. ἀνιέρωσις *Tab.Defix.*99.12; ἐπαρᾶσθαι ταῖς τριακάσιν *SIG*286.13 (Milet., iv B.C.); of a festival in the cult of Zeus Panamaros, ib.900.36 (iv A.D.). 2. *a month*, containing 30 days, Luc.*Luct.*16, *Rh.Pr.*9. III. at Athens, *a religious association of thirty persons, fraction of the deme*, *IG*2$^2$.1214.18, cf. Poll.8.111. 2. at Sparta, either = 30 families ($\frac{1}{10}$ of an oba), or = 10 families ($\frac{1}{30}$ of an oba), or simply *a company of thirty*, Hdt. 1.65.

❀ **τρῐᾱκάσιοι** [κᾰ], οἱ, Arc. for sq., name of an assembly at Tegea, *IG*5(2).3.20, 6.8 (iv B.C.).

**τρῐᾱκάτιοι** [κᾰ], οἱ, Dor. for τριακόσιοι, *Tab.Heracl.*1.28,34, al., *IG*4$^2$(1).110 A6 (Epid., iv/iii B.C.), etc. II. title of the ἔφηβοι at Cyrene, Ammon.*Diff.*p.37 V., Hsch.; corrupted to τριακάπους (acc.) in Eust.727.18, 1592.57: they are associated with λοχαγοὶ πελτασταν, *Schwyzer* 234.53:—hence **τρῐᾱκᾰτιάρχας**, α, ὁ, ib.14 (Cyrene, iv/iii B.C.).

❀ **τρίᾰκις** [ᾰ], Adv. *three times, thrice*, Ar.*Fr.*769, cf. A.D.*Adv.*146. 20; Lacon., acc. to Hsch., and found in *IG*5(1).222 (cf. add.): τριάκις καὶ τριάκι Theognost.*Can.*160.

**τρῐᾱκοιστος**, v. τριακοστός.

**τρῐᾱκονθ-άμμᾰτος**, ον, *with* or *of thirty knots*, X.*Cyn.*2.5. ❀ **–ή-μερος**, *of thirty days*, θέα *IG*4$^2$(1).532 (Epid.); ἀνοχαί Plb.5.28.1; μῆνες Nicom.ap.*Theol.Ar.*48; Ion. **τρῐηκοντήμερος**, μήν Hdt.2.4: but Dor. ❀**τρῐᾱκοντάμερος**, τό (q. v.), is perh. a different word. 2. τριακονθήμερον, τό, *a time of thirty days*, Plb.21.13.12, etc. 3. *thirty days old*, χοιρίδιον *PCair.Zen.*478 (iii B.C.).

❀ **τρῐάκοντα** [ᾱκ], Ep. and Ion. **τρῐηκ–**, late Gr. **τριάντα** (q. v.), οἱ, αἱ, τά, indecl.; but gen. τριηκόντων Hes.*Op.*696, also in later Ep., Call.*Fr.*67; dat. τριηκόντεσσιν *AP*11.41 (Phld.):—*thirty*, Il.2. 516, *IG*1$^2$.1.9, etc.; τ. καὶ ἕνα *thirty-one*, ib.4$^2$(1).71.9 (Epid., iii B.C.). II. οἱ τ., esp., 1. at Sparta, *a council of war of thirty*, X.*Ages.*1.7, *HG*3.4.2,20, 4.1.5, al. 2. at Athens, *the Thirty*, commonly called *the thirty tyrants*, appointed on the taking of Athens (404 B.C.), ib.2.3.2, *IG*2$^2$.6.12, Pl.*Ap.*32c, Arist.*Rh.*1400$^a$ 18. 3. certain magistrates, v. τεσσαράκοντα; οἱ λογισταὶ οἱ τ. (*IG*1$^2$.91.8) are sts. called simply οἱ τ., *IG*1$^2$.191.1, 193.1. [In late Epigr. ᾰκ, *AP*11.298, etc.]

❀ **τρῐᾱκοντά-δραχμοι** πυροί, wheat *at thirty* δραχμαί, Poll.4.165. **–δύο**, *thirty-two*, Lxx 1 *Es.*5.15, *PSI*10.1142.6 (ii A.D.) (τριακ– *AP*9. 682): similarly **–είς**, **–ενός**, *PSI*10.1143.7 (ii A.D.); **–εννέα**, ib.6, J.*AJ*10.5.1; **–έξ**, Lxx *Jo.*7.5, *PSI*10.1134.6 (i A.D.); **–επτά**, *Tab. Heracl.*1.30. **–ετηρίς**, ίδος, ἡ, *period of thirty years* or *festival recurring every thirty years*, *OGI*90.2 (Rosetta, ii B.C.): in full, τ. ἑορτή D.C.62.26; cf. τριακοντετηρίς. **–έτης**, Ion. **τρῐηκ–**, ες, *thirty years old*, Pl.*Lg.*914b,961b (in the former place without a variant, in the latter codd. AO have τριακοντ' ἔτη), *PAmh.*2.84.12 (ii/iii A.D.), *Riv. Fil.*57.379 (Aptera, iii/iv A.D.); also in forms **τρῐᾱκοντέτης** (q. v.)

and **τριᾱκοντούτης**, ου, ὁ, acc. pl. τοὺς τριακοντούτας *the men of thirty years*, Pl.*R*.539a, *Lg*.670a; nom. sg. masc. -ούτης Gal.6.471; fem. **τριακοντοῦτις**, Is.6.14. *CRAcad.Inscr*.1932.85 (Tipasa in Mauretania). II. *of* or *for thirty years*, τριακονταέτεις σπονδαί Th.5.14, X.*HG*5.2.2; αἱ τριακοντούτεις σπονδαί Th.1.23, 115, 2.2 (whence 5.14 and X. l. c. have been corrected): in fem. form, σπονδὰς τριηκοντοέτιδας (v.l. -ταέτιδας) Hdt.7.149; σπονδαὶ τριακοντούτιδες Ar.*Ach*.194, cf. *Eq*.1388, Th.1.87 (though elsewh. he uses the form in -ης as fem., v. supr.). **-ετία**, ἡ, *period of thirty years*, D.H.2.67. **-ζῠγος**, ον, *with thirty benches of oars*, Ἀργώ Theoc.13.74. **-κῐς**, Adv. *thirty times*, Plu.*Cor*.25. **-κλῖνος**, ον, *of thirty couches*, οἶκοι Satyr.2, Plu.2.679b; καταχωριζέτωσαν τοὺς τῆς προσόδου λόγους εἰς τὸ τ. let them put the revenue accounts on (the walls of?) *the thirty-couch room*, prob. in *POxy*.34ᵛi5 (ii A.D., cf. Wilhelm *Beitr. zur gr. Inschriftenkunde* (1909).265). **-κωπος**, ον, *thirty-oared*, as Subst., [sc. ναῦς] Plb.21.43.13 (τριακοντόκωπον codd., τριάκοντα κωπῶν Mommsen).

⊕ **τριᾱκοντάμερος**, τό, Dor. word, dub. sens. in *IG*14.256.27 (Phintias Geloorum); cf. *Jahresh*.4*Beibl*.21.

**τριᾱκοντᾰ-μηνιαῖος**, ον, = sq., πῶλος *Hippiatr*.95. **-μηνος**, ον, *at thirty months*, Arist.*HA*545ᵇ21. **-μναῖος**, α, ον, *weighing thirty minae*, λίθοι Ph.*Bel*.51.40, Plb.9.41.8. **-μοιρία**, ἡ, *arc of thirty degrees*, Pancharius ap.Heph.Astr.2.11 (*Cat.Cod.Astr*.8(2).67), Paul.Al.*H*.1. **-μοιρος**, ον, *of thirty degrees*, Vett.Val.336.5: Subst. -μοιρον, τό, *arc of thirty degrees*, Procl.*Par.Ptol*.45. **-μόριος**, ον, *containing thirty degrees*, ζῴδια Gem.1.8. **-πεδος**, ον, *thirty feet wide*, [ὁδός] *Tab.Heracl*.1.16, 21, 25, al. **-πεντάπηχυς** [ᾰπ], υ, *thirty-five cubits long*, Tz.*H*.3.903. **-πέντε**, *thirty-five*, Lxx 1*Es*.5.42, *PSI*8.903.4 (i A.D.). **-πηχυς**, υ, *thirty cubits long*, πηδάλια Callix.1, cf. Philostr.*Her*.1.3 (but divisim τριάκοντα πηχῶν D.S.3.36). **-πλάσιος** [πλᾰ], ον, *thirty-fold*, Archim.*Aren*.1.9, Gal.5.47, Procl.*Hyp*.3.61; also **-πλᾰσίων**, ον, gen. ονος, Archim.*Aren*.2.1. **-πους**, ποδος, ὁ, ἡ, πουν, τό, *of thirty feet*. βάθος D.H.9.68.

**τριᾱκοντ-άρουρος** [ᾰρ], ὁ, *tenant of thirty* ἄρουραι, *PPetr*.2 p.121 (iii B.C.), *PEnteux*.37.1, al. (iii B.C.), *PTeb*.89.51, al. (ii B.C., all abbreviated), etc. **-άρχης**, ου, ὁ, a god *who presides over thirty days* (one month), *PMag.Leid.W*.16.40 (λ κοντραχας (sic) acc. pl. Pap.). **-αρχία**, ἡ, *rule of thirty*, X.*HG*6.3.8 (pl.). **-άς**, άδος, ἡ, *the number thirty*, Vett.Val.315.16.

**τριᾱκοντά-σημος** [τᾰ], ον, *of thirty times*, in metre, Heph.13.6. **-στάδιος** [στᾰ], ον, *thirty stades long*, σχοῖνος Str.17.1.24. **-σχοινος**, ον, *of thirty* σχοῖνοι; ἡ τ. (sc. χώρα) a district along the Nile, Ptol.*Geog*.1.9.7. **-τέσσᾰρες**, *thirty-four*, Lxx 1*Ch*.7.7, *PCair.Zen*.1.7 (iii B.C.), *SIG*900.17 (Panamara, iv A.D.). **-τρεῖς**, *thirty-three*, Lxx 3*Ki*.2.11, Plu.*Aem*.38 (divisim). **-φυλλος**, ὁ, *one who has never read more than thirty pages*, Tz.*H*.3.218. **-χοίνικος**, ον, *of thirty* χοίνικες, μέτρον *PSI*4.358.6 (iii B.C.); ἀρτάβη *PRev.Laws* 39.2–4 (iii B.C.). **-χους**, ουν, *producing thirty-fold*, Thphr.*HP*8.2.8; -χουν ἀποδιδόναι Str.7.4.6 (prob. cj.). **-χρονος**, ον, = τριακοντάσημος, Tz. in *An.Ox*.3.311.

**τριᾱκόντ-ερος**, v. τριακόντορος. **-ετηρίς**, ίδος, ἡ, = τριακονταετηρίς, Wilcken *Chr*.109.7 (iii B.C.). **-έτης**, ες, = τριακονταέτης, Arist.*HA*576ᵃ30. **-ήρης** (sc. ναῦς), ἡ, perh. *a galley rowed by thirty men to each group of oars passing through the same porthole*, Callix.1, *OGI*39.3 (Paphos, iii B.C.).

**τριᾱκοντό-δραχμος**, ον, *of thirty* δραχμαί, τέλος *Schwyzer* 366 *A* 22 (Tolophon, iii B.C.). **-έτης**, only in contr. form, v. τριακονταέτης. **-κωπος**, v. τριακοντάκωπος.

⊕ **τριᾱκοντ-όριον**, τό, Dim. of sq., *IG*2².1627.16, Arist.*Ath*.56.3. **-ορος** (sc. ναῦς), ἡ, *thirty-oared ship*, Th.4.9, X.*An*.5.1.16, etc.; so written in *IG*2².1629.121, 335 (iv B.C.); but **τριακόντερος** ib.1².23.4 (restd.), 2².1649.6 (iv B.C.), τριη- Hdt.4.148, 7.97: cf. πεντηκόντορος. **-ούτης, -οῦτις**, v. τριακονταέτης. **-ώρῠγος**, ον, *of thirty fathoms*, X.*Cyn*.2.5; cf. δεκώρυγος.

**τριᾱκοσιεξήκοντα**, *three hundred and sixty*, Tz.*H*.9.571.

⊕ **τριᾱκόσιοι**, Ep. and Ion. **τρῐηκ-**, Dor. **τριακάτιοι** (q.v.), αι, α, *three hundred*, Il.11.697, Hes.*Th*.715, Hdt.7.202, etc. II. οἱ τ. at Athens, the richest members of the συμμορίαι, D.2.29, 18.171, etc. 2. a judicial body at Megara, Id.19.295: cf. τριακάσιοι.

**τριᾱκοσιοστός**, ή, όν, *three-hundredth*, Ptol.*Alm*.3.1: also ⊕ **τριᾱκοσιαστός**, *JHS*33.338 (Maced., ii A.D.).

**τριᾱκοσιόχους**, ουν, *bearing three-hundredfold*, Str.16.1.14 (-σάχοα codd.).

**τριᾱκοσταῖος**, Ion. **τρῐηκ-**, α, ον, *on the thirtieth day*, Hp.*Prog*.15; *in thirty days*, τ. περιώδευσε τὴν Σύρτιν Str.17.3.20; δίκαι -ταῖαι cases *which must be tried within thirty days*, *Tab.Heracl*.1.49, al. II. *thirty days old*, παιδίον Phylarch.36 J.

**τριᾱκοστημόριον**, τό, Ion. **τρῐηκ-**, *a thirtieth part*, Hp.*Oct*.13.

**τριᾱκόστ[ια]**, Ion. **τρῐηκ-**, τά, *rites performed on the thirtieth day after a funeral*, prob. in *IG*12(5).593.20 (Iulis, v B.C.).

**τριᾱκοστό-δῠος**, ον, (δύο) *thirty-second*, in neut., τὸ τ. = $\frac{1}{32}$, Nicom.*Ar*.1.8, *PLeid.X*.18; τριακοστόδιν is prob. written for -δυον in *Supp.Epigr*.7.807 (Syria). **-πεμπτος**, ον, *thirty-fifth*, Hero *Geom*.17.32, al., Tz.*H*.13.286.

⊕ **τριᾱκοστός**, Ion. **τρῐηκ-**, ή, όν, *thirtieth*, Pi.*O*.8.66, *IG*1².304.29, Hdt.4.44, 5.89, Hp.*Aph*.4.36, X.*Cyr*.5.3.6, *PCair.Zen*.236.6 (iii B.C.), etc.; Aeol. **τρῐάκοιστος** [ᾱ] *IG*11(4).1064*b*23 (Delos). II. ἡ τ. *duty of one-thirtieth*, D.20.32.

**τριακτήρ**, ῆρος, ὁ, (τριάζω) *victor*, A.*Ag*.171 (lyr.).

**τρῐανδρ-ικὸν** σύστημα, *triumvirate*, Lyd.*Mag*.1.50, *Gloss*. **-ος**, ὁ, = Lat. *triumvir*, *IG*7.89 (Megara, ii A.D.), restored from a Latin inscr., *CIL*14.3599.

⊕ **τρῐάντα**, = τριάκοντα, *IG*4.649 (Argos, late), 12(7).295 (Amorgos, late).

**τρῐαν[τέτης]**, ες, *thirty years old*, *Supp.Epigr*.2.367 (Apollonia, i A.D.).

**τρῐάνωρ** [ᾱ], ορος, ἡ, *she that has had three husbands*, of Helen, Lyc.851.

**τρῐάξ**, ἡ, = τριακάς, Hsch.

⊕ **τρῐάριοι** [ᾱ], οἱ, = Lat. *triarii*, Plb.6.23.16.

**τρῐ-άρμενος**, ον, *with three sails* or *masts*, ὁλκάς Plu.*Marc*.14; πλοῖον Luc.*Nav*.14; ναύτης τῶν τ. Id.*Pseudol*.27, cf. Philostr.*VA*4.9. **-αρχία**, ἡ, = Lat. *triumviratus*, D.C.41.36.

⊕ **τρῐάς**, άδος, ἡ, (τρεῖς) *the number three, triad*, Ion Hist.12 note, Pl.*Phd*.104a, al.; on its significance in the Pythag. philosophy, v. Arist.*Cael*.268ᵃ13, *Metaph*.1081ᵃ34, ᵇ12; τρισσὴν.. ἐτέων τριάδα (sc. γεγονώς), i.e. nine years old, *Syria* 5.338 (Sidon); τ. ἡ ἀκατονόμαστος, of the mystical Man from heaven (θεός—ἄγγελος—ἄνθρωπος παθητός), Zos.Alch.p.230 B. 2. ἡ τ. *group of three days*, τελευτᾷ ἐν τῇ πρώτῃ τ. Thphr.*Vent*.49; the *third day*, Ph.1.13. 3. *system of three strophes*, Heph.p.61 C. 4. ἡ ἁγία Τ. the holy *Trinity*, *Cod.Just*.1.1.5.2, etc.

**τρῐᾶς**, ᾶντος, ὁ, a Sicilian coin, Lat. *triens*, Arist.*Fr*.510; τριᾶντος πόρνη Hsch.

**τρῐασμός**, ὁ, v. τριαγμός. **τρῐάσσω**, = τριάζω (q.v.).

**τριατέτταρα**, τά, $\frac{3}{4}$ *mina*, name given to a plaster by Philoxenus, Asclep.ap.Gal.13.742.

**τρῐ-αῦλαξ**, ᾰκος, ὁ, ἡ, *three-pronged*, *Gloss*. **-αύχενος**, ον, = sq., of the moon-goddess, *PMag.Par*.1.2525. **-αύχην**, ενος, ὁ, ἡ, *with three necks*, of Hecate, Lyc.1186.

**τρῑβαία**, ἡ, *a mortar*, Suid. and Zonar. s.v. ἴγδη, *Gloss*.

⊕ **τρῑβᾰκός**, ή, όν, (τρίβω) *rubbed, worn*, χλαμύς *AP*6.282 (Theod.); τρίβων Luc.*Gall*.9; ἱμάτια *PTeb*.230 (ii B.C.), cf. *PCair.Zen*.92.4, al. (iii B.C.), Gal.15.192, Sch.Ar.*Pl*.714; διφθέραι Gal.11.133; ῥάκος Id.10.703; τελαμῶνες Sor.1.83; τὰ ἐπιβλήματα πρὸς λόγον τῆς ὥρας θερμότερα ἔστω ἢ τριβακώτερα ib.85, cf. 2.46; θέρους ὄντος ὀθόνια καὶ τ. ἱμάτια δοκεῖν φορεῖν ἀγαθόν Artem.2.3. 2. sens. obsc., πάσσαλος *AP*5.128 (Autom.). 3. of persons, *experienced*, [ἰατρός] Gal.15.582 (Comp.); ἰατροὶ γέροντες Id.8.155; ὁ περὶ ταῦτα τ. ὤν Id.14.258; '*old hand*', *crafty fellow*, Eust.932.46. II. τριβακὴ ἀσέλγεια (v. τριβάς) Luc.*Am*.28.

⊕ **Τρῐβαλλοί** (on the accent, v. Hdn.Gr.1.158), οἱ, *the Triballi*, a people on the borders of Thrace (v. Hdt.4.49): hence as a Comic name for barbarian gods, Ar.*Av*.1529, 1533, 1627; οὐδ' ἐν Τριβαλλοῖς ταῦτά γ' ἐστὶν ἔννομα Alex.241; καὶ ποὺ μὲν καλὸν τὸν πατέρα θύειν, οἷον ἐν Τ. Arist.*Top*.115ᵇ23:—Adj. **Τρῐβαλλικός**, ή, όν, Hdt.4.49. II. a slang term for *young fellows who lounge about taverns*, etc., like the 'Mohocks' of Addison's time, D.54.39:—hence the Comic exaggeration **Τρῐβαλλο-ποπᾰνό-θρεπτα** μειρακύλλια, *tavern-bred Mohocks*, Eub.75.3 (Casaubon for Τριβαλλο-πανό-θρεπτα: Meineke suggests Τριβαλλο-μαμμό-θρεπτα, and Kock defends the Ms. reading).

**τρῖβᾰνον**, τό, = λήκυθος, Hsch.; a measure of capacity, = κοτύλη, τρυβλίον, Gal.19.774, cf. *POxy*.661ᵛ (ii/iii A.D.).

**τρῑβᾰνόω**, *wear away, consume*, Sm.*Ps*.6.8.

**τρίβαξ** [ῐ], ᾰκος, ὁ, ἡ, = τριβακός 1.3, Menodotus ap.Gal.*Subf.Emp*.7 p.50 B., *EM*765.48.

**τρῐβάρβᾰρος**, ον, *thrice-barbarous*, Plu.2.14b.

⊕ **τρῐβάς**, άδος, ἡ, *a woman who practises unnatural vice with herself* or *with other women*, Man.4.358, Ptol.*Tetr*.171, Vett.Val.111.7, *Gloss*. II. = *mortarium, tritorium*, ib.

**τρί-βασμος** [ῐ], ὁ, *flight of three steps*, *Inscr.Prien*.159. **-βᾰφος**, ον, *thrice-dyed*, i.e. *of genuine dye*, Lyd.*Mag*.1.7 (s. v.l.). **-βελής**, ές, *three-pointed*, δόρυ, of the trident, *APl*.4.215 (Phil.).

**τρῐβ-εύς**, έως, ὁ, *rubber, masseur*, *PCair.Zen*.675.1 (iii B.C.), *PLond.ined*.2087 (iii B.C.), Str.15.1.55. 2. = δοῖδυξ, *pestle*, Gal.13.850, *AB* 239, *Gloss*.; = ἀλειπτρίβανος, *EM*59.57. II. in Mechanics, a *rim* or *flange* to take the pressure of a nut, Ph.*Bel*.53.19; = ἐντορνία, Hero *Bel*.97.11. **-ή**, ἡ, *rubbing*:—mostly metaph.: I. *rubbing down, wearing away, wasting*, τριβᾷ βίου A.*Ag*.465 (lyr.); κτεάνων τριβάς Id.*Ch*.943 (lyr., sed leg. τριβᾶς); *wear and tear* of fixtures in a house, *BGU*1116.26 (i B.C.). II. *practice*, opp. theory, Hp.*Praec*.1, X.*An*.5.6.15; *study*, τ. καὶ ἱστορία τῶν πόλεως πραγμάτων Metrod.*Fr*.27, cf. Phld.*Rh*.1.121 S., *Po*.5.20, al.; also, *mere practice, routine*, opp. true art, οὐκ ἔστι τέχνη, ἀλλ' ἄτεχνος τ. Pl.*Phdr*.260e; τριβῇ καὶ ἐμπειρίᾳ, opp. τέχνη, ib.270b, cf. *Grg*.463b, Gal.6.143; τριβῇ ζητεῖν, opp. μεθόδῳ, Arist.*SE*184ᵇ2; τριβὴν ἔχειν τινός Damox.1.10, D.S.16.15; τ. ἐν τοῖς πολεμικοῖς ἔχειν Plb.1.32.1; ἀρετὴν ἔχειν ἐν χρήσει καὶ τριβῇ Plu.*Phil*.13; διὰ τῆς ἐν τοῖς ἔργοις σπουδαιοτέρας τριβῆς καὶ συγγυμνασίας Sor.1.3. III. *that about which one is busied, the object of care, anxiety*, or *love*, Ὀρέστην, τὴν ἐμῆς ψυχῆς τριβήν A.*Ch*.749. 2. *occupation*, μειράκιον.. οὐκέτι ἔπεμπες ἐπὶ τὰ διδασκαλεῖα καὶ τὰς προσηκούσας τοῖς νεανίαις τριβάς *POxy*.471.115 (ii A.D.). IV. of Time, *spending*, οὐ μακροῦ χρόνου τ. S.*Ant*.1078, cf. *Fr*.664; συνουσίᾳ καὶ χρόνου τριβῇ Pl.*R*.493b; ἀξίαν τριβὴν ἔχει 'tis time well spent, A.*Pr*.639; [βίος] οὐκ ἄχαρις ἐς τὴν τριβήν a pleasant enough life in the *spending*, Ar.*Av*.156. 2. *delay*, ἐς τριβὰς ἐλᾷ seeks *delays*, S.*OT*1160; πορίζεις τριβάς Ar.*Ach*.385 (lyr.); and with the Verb omitted, μὴ τριβὰς ἔτι no more *delays*,

S.*Ant.*577; τριβῆς ἕνεκα καὶ ἀνοκωχῆς Th.8.87; μετὰ τ. πάσης Pl. *Ep.*344b; ὁ πόλεμος τριβὴν λαμβάνει Plb.1.20.9.

**τρῐβήν**, ῆνος, ὁ, *tripod*, Hdn.Gr.1.16, 2.718.

**τρῐβίδιν** [i.e. -ίδιον], τό, gloss on δίδυξ (leg. δοίδυξ), Hsch. (Mod. Gr. τριβίδιν, = δοίδυξ.)

**τρῐβῐκός**, ή, όν, *founded on practice*, Crates Gramm.ap.S.E.*M.*1.249; πεῖρα τ. *test* of theory *in practice*, Empiric t.t. ap.Gal.*Sect.Intr.*2; *tribica experientia*, Id.*Subf.Emp.*9 p.55 B.

**τρίβῐκος** [ρῐ], ὁ, (βῖκος) *an alembic with three receiving vessels*, Maria ap.Zos.Alch.p.236 B.

* **τρῐβολεκτράπελος** [ᾰ], ον; τριβολεκτράπελα στωμύλλειν deal *in coarse rude jests*, Ar.*Nu.*1003 (anap.).

**τρῐβολοειδῶς**, Adv. *like a* τρίβολος III, τ. ἐσχηματισμένη, i.e. triangular in cross-section, of the collar-bone, Ruf.*Oss.*12.

* **τρίβολος** [ῐ], ὁ, name of various prickly plants, **a.** *water-chestnut, Trapa natans*, τ. ἔνυδρος Thphr.*HP*4.9.1, Dsc.4.15. **b.** *caltrops, Tribulus terrestris*, Ar.*Lys.*576; τ. περικαρπιάκανθος, χερσαῖος, Thphr.*HP*3.1.6, 6.1.3, Dsc. l.c.; ἄκανθαι καὶ τ. Lxx *Ge.*3.18; βάτοι καὶ τ. Ph.1.680, cf. *IG*14.1934*f* 1 (Rome):—Alc.47 calls sour wine ὀξύτερος τριβόλων. **c.** τ. φυλλάκανθος, *thorny trefoil, Fagonia cretica*, Thphr.*HP*6.5.3. **d.** τ. παραθαλάσσιος, *prickly samphire, Echinophora spinosa*, Hp.*Nat.Mul.*32. **II.** τρίβολοι, οἱ, *a threshing-machine, a board with sharp stones fixed in the bottom*, Ph.*Bel.*85.36, al., Lxx 2*Ki.*12.31, Longus 3.30; τ. ξύλινος (in the section περὶ κάρπων) *Edict.Diocl.*15.41; τριβόλους ἀχυρότριβας *AP*6.104 (Phil.). **III.** *caltrop*, i.e. a four-spiked implement thrown on the ground to lame the enemy's horses, Ph.*Bel.*100.7, Plu.2.200a, Polyaen.1.39.2, 4.3.17, Hdn.4.15.2, Procop.*Goth.*3.24. **b.** τ. πηχῶν ε' a larger contrivance for stopping boulders, etc., thrown down a slope, Ath.Mech.38.2. **c.** οἱ κατακρημνώμενοι τ. an instrument hung from the walls of a fortress as a defence against battering-rams, Ph.*Bel.*100.15. **d.** a kind of missile, τριβόλων σιδηρῶν σφενδονῆται D.H.20.1; οἱ τ. οἱ καιόμενοι a kind of incendiary missile, Ph.*Bel.*100.20, cf. 94.9. **IV.** part of the bit of a bridle, *PCair.Zen.*782(*a*).9 (iii B.C.), Poll.1.148, Hsch. **V.** dub. sens. in naval dockyard records, σίδηρος ἐκ τοῦ τ. *IG*2².1629.1154, 1631.338. **VI.** as Adj., *three-tiered*, πυρὰ πυργοειδὴς τ. D.C.74.5.

* **τρίβος** [ῑ], ἡ, but ὁ in E.*Or.*1251, 1258, *El.*103, Plu.*Arat.*22: (τρίβω):—*worn* or *beaten track*, ἐν τρίβῳ μάλιστα οἰκημένοι in the *path* (of the war), Hdt.8.140.β' (so ἐν τ. τοῦ πολέμου κείμενος D.H.6.34, 11.54); τ. ἁμαξήρης E.*Or.*1251; λεπτὴν τ. ἐξανύσαντες Theoc.25.156; ἡ τ. τῆς ἀτραποῦ *the track* of the path, D.S.17.49; διασχισθέντες [τῆς ὁδοῦ] τρίβῳ τινὶ by *following a track*, X.*Cyr.*4.5.13. **2.** metaph., *path*, *h.Merc.*448; ποίην τις βιότοιο τάμοι τρίβον; *AP*9.359 (Posidipp.); βιότου τ. ὁδεύειν *Anacreont.*38.2; ποίην τις πρὸς ἔρωτας ἴοι τρίβον; *AP*5.301.1 (Agath.); τῆς αἰτίας ἴχνος καὶ τ. *track*, Plu.2.680f: pl., τρίβοι ἐρώτων A.*Supp.*1042 (lyr.). **II.** *rubbing, attrition*, Id.*Ag.*391 (lyr.); τ. κρηπῖδος *the rubbing* of a shoe, Aret.*SD*2.12. **2.** *socket, friction-joint*, ἡ κεφαλὴ τοῦ βραχίονος.. τρίβον ἑωυτῇ πεποιημένη Hp.*Art.*7, cf. 55; τὸ ἔθος τρίβον ποιεῖ Id.*Mochl.*41; *area of friction* or *pressure* of a bandage, Id.*Off.*8. **3.** *delay*, A.*Ag.*197 (lyr.). **III.** *bodily exercise*, Nic.*Al.*592 (pl.).

**τρί-βρᾰχυς**, υ, *consisting of three short syllables*, Heph.3.2, al., Choerob. *in Theod.*1.232 H.; in full, τ. πούς interpol. in D.H.*Comp.*17. **-βροχος**, ον, (βροχή II) *prepared with a triple infusion*, Dsc.1.55.

**τριβυνάριον**, τό, dub. sens., written τρηβυνάρην in a list of stage-properties, Pap. in *Eos* 32.30 (v/vi A.D.).

**τρίβω** [ῑ], Hes.*Op.*251, etc.: Ep. impf. τρῖβον S.*Fr.*483, (ἀπο-) Od.17.232: aor. ἔτριψα Pherecr.181; inf. τρῖψαι Od.9.333, etc.: pf. τέτριφα M.Ant.9.10, (συν-) Eub.62:—Med., fut. τρίψομαι (προσ-) Antipho 4.2.8: aor. ἐτριψάμην Call.*Lav.Pall.*25, A.D.*Synt.*210.26:—Pass., fut. τριφθήσομαι App.*BC*4.65, etc.; τρῐβήσομαι Plu.*Dio* 25, (ἐκ-) S.*OT*428, (κατα-) X.*HG*5.4.60; also τετρίψομαι (ἐπι-) Ar.*Pax* 246; fut. Med. in pass. sense, Th.6.18, 7.42: aor. ἐτρίφθην Id.2.77, Hp.*Epid.*5.6, Antiph.102; (δια-) D.19.164: more freq. aor. 2 ἐτρίβην [ῐ] Arist.*Pr.*893ᵇ40; (δι-) Th.1.125; (ἐκ-) Hdt.7.120; (ἐπ-) freq. in Ar., *Th.*557, al.; (κατ-) Pl.*Lg.*678d; (συν-) Ar.*Pax* 71, etc.: pf. τέτριμμαι Pl.*Phd.*116d; Ion. 3 pl. τετρίφαται Hdt.2.93. [ῐ only in pf. Act. and Pass., and fut. and aor. 2 Pass.]:—*rub*, τριβέμεναι κρῖ, i.e. *thresh, thresh it out*, because this was done by trampling under the feet of oxen, Il.20.496; μοχλὸν τρῖψαι ἐν ὀφθαλμῷ *work round* the stake in his eye, Od.9.333; χρυσὸν -όμενον βασάνῳ *rubbed* on a touchstone, so as to test its purity, Thgn.450; τ. τὸ σκέλος *rub* the leg, Pl.*Phd.*60b; τὰς τῆς ψώρας ἰάσεις τῷ τρίβειν Id.*Phlb.*46a; τὸν ὀφθαλμόν Arist.*Pr.*957ᵃ38; ἀμφοτέρων τὸν πύνδακα ib.938ᵃ14; τ. τὴν κεφαλήν, in sign of perplexity, Aeschin.2.49; ταῖς χερσὶ [τὰς τρίχας] τ. X.*Eq.*5.5; τὸν πόδα μύροις τ. Eub.108 (hex.); of a masseur, Gal.6.151, 187; in blood-letting, Id.15.784:—Med., χρηστηρίοις ἐν τοῖσδε.. τρίβεσθαι μύσος *rub one's* pollution *upon* the shrines, *pollute* them with it, A.*Eu.*195:—Pass., τετριμμένοι τὰ ἐπ' ἀριστερὰ τῶν κεφαλέων Hdt.2.93; ὕλη τριφθεῖσα ὑπ' ἀνέμων πρὸς αὑτήν, so as to catch fire, Th.2.77; ὀδόντες τριβόμενοι πρὸς ἀλλήλους Arist.*PA*661ᵇ22. **2.** *bruise, pound, knead*, κεδρίδας, [κώνειον], Ar.*Th.*486, Pl.*Phd.*117b; ἐλλεβόρου ἄμαξαν Id.*Euthd.*299b; ποίαν *IG* 4²(1).122.121 (Epid., iv B.C.); καταπλαστόν, [μάζας], Ar.*Pl.*717, *Pax* 8, 16; κάρυα καὶ ἀμύγδαλα εἰς θυείαν τ. Chrysipp.Tyan.ap.Ath.14.648a, cf. Sor.1.62, τὸ μέλαν *grind*, D.18.258:—Pass., θυμιήματα τετριμμένα Hdt.2.86; ἄρτοι σφόδρα τετριμμένοι Arist.*Pr.*929ᵃ17, cf. ᵇ8; μηδὲν τετριμμένον, ἀλλὰ τεθλασμένων ὁ χυλός Diocl.*Fr.*138. **3.** *crush*, βότρυν Arist.*Fr.*571. **II.** *wear out* clothes (cf. τρίβων (A)), τῶν ὑποδημάτων τὰ τριβόμενα Plu.2.680a; τελαμῶνες μὴ λίαν τετριμμένοι Sor.1.83; of a road, *wear* or *tread* it *smooth*, ἀτραπὸς τετριμμένη ἡ διὰ θυείας, with a play on *pounding* in a mortar, Ar.*Ra.*123; τὴν τετρ. ὥσπερ ὁδὸν ἐπὶ τὸν μακάριον βίον Phld.*Rh.*1.260 S.; τρίβει οὐρανόν *goes his way* through heaven (cf. τρίβος), Arat.231; τ. κύματα, of a ship, *AP*9.34 (Antiphil.); πόδας τρίβειν Theoc.7.123. **2.** of Time, *wear away, spend*, δυστυχῆ τ. βίον S.*El.*602; νησιώτην τ. βίον E.*Heracl.*84; γεωργὸν βίον τ. Ar.*Pax* 589 (lyr.); ὀδυνηρότερον τρίψεις βίοτον Id.*Pl.*526 (anap.); τ. πόλεμον *prolong* a war, Plb.2.63.4: abs., *waste time, tarry*, A.*Ag.*1056, D.23.173 vulg. (διατρ. cod. S):—Pass., ἐν τούτοις τρίβεται χρόνος ἐνίοτε μακρός Gal.16.578; ἀμφισβήτησις.. τρειβομένη πολλῶν ἐτῶν *prolonged*, *OGI*502.3 (Aezani, ii A.D.). **3.** *waste* or *ravage* a country, E.*Hec.*1142. **III.** of persons, *wear out*, σκολιῇσι δίκῃσι ἀλλήλους τρίβουσι Hes.*Op.*251; τρίβεσθαι κακοῖσι *to be worn out* by ills, Il.23.735; ἄλλην γενεὰν τρίβειν θανάτοις A.*Ag.*1573 (anap.); τ. ἀμφοτέρους *wear* them both *out*, Th.8.56, cf. 7.48, Plu.*Caes.*40:—Med., τρίψεσθαι αὐτὴν περὶ αὑτήν *wear* itself *out* by internal struggles, Th.6.18, cf. 7.42:—Pass., τριβόμενος λεώς *oppressed*, Hdt.2.124; πολέμιοι τριφθησόμενοι ἐν σφίσιν App. l.c.; τρίβεσθαι μάτην περὶ (ἐπὶ codd.) τὴν δίωξιν Plu.*Pomp.*41. **2.** of money and property, *waste, squander* it, οὔτε τι τῶν οἰκηΐων τρίβουσι οὔτε δαπανῶνται Hdt.2.37. **3.** *use constantly*, κατώμοσα.. μὴ πολὺν χρόνον θεοὺς ἔτι σκῆπτρα τἀμὰ τρίψειν Ar.*Av.*636 (lyr.); κοινὰ ὀνόματα καὶ τετριμμένα D.H.*Comp.*25; ἡ τετρ. καὶ κοινὴ διάλεκτος Id.*Th.*23; τετρ. σχηματισμός *in common use*, A.D.*Pron.*115.16, cf. S.E.*M.*1.229. **4.** Pass., *to be much busied* or *engrossed* with a thing, πολέμῳ Hdt.3.134; ἀμφ' ἀρετῇ τ. *practise oneself in, use oneself to* it, Thgn.465; τρίβεσθαι περὶ τοὺς δυνατούς Philostr.*VA*4.41: esp. in pf. part. Pass. τετριμμένος, *practised, expert*, ἔμπειροι καὶ τ. Phld.*Rh.*2.281 S.; οἱ ἐν ποιήμασι τ. Id.*Po.*5.21; τ. ἀκοή a *trained, expert* ear, ib.24; πολεμικὸς καὶ τετρ. δι' ὅπλων Plu.*Eum.*11; ἀνὴρ φιλοπόνως ἐπὶ τῶν ἔργων τετρ. Gal.15.585, cf. 623.

**τρῐβώλετερ**, obscure word found only in Alc.38: cited by Heph.11.3, who attests its metrical form (– – ⏑ ⏑), and by Choerob. *in Theod.*1.262 H., al., who says it is an Aeol. voc., proparox., and means εἶδος ἀκάνθης: the quantity is against Bergk's derivation from *τρῐβολ-ολετηρ 'caltrop-devourer'. [τριβωλ- codd.Heph., τριβολ-, τρεβολ-, and τριβαλ- codd.Choerob.]

**τρίβωμος** [ῐ], ὁ, *threefold* or *triangular altar*, *IG*14.966.8 (Rome).

* **τρίβων** (A) [ῑ], ωνος, ὁ, but ἡ in *PGiss.*76.2 (ii A.D.): (τρίβω):—*worn garment, threadbare cloak*, E.*Fr.*282.12, Ar.*Ach.*184, 343 (troch.), al., *PCair.Zen.*92.19, 519.11 (iii B.C.), *Sammelb.*7451.149 (iii B.C.): worn by the Spartans, Λακωνίζειν καὶ τρίβωνας ἔχειν D.54.34, cf. Duris 14 J.; by Philosophers, as Socrates, Pl.*Smp.*219b, *Prt.*335d; esp. by the Cynics, Crates Theb.16, Arr.*Epict.*3.1.24, etc.; and the Stoics, Zeno *Stoic.*1.63; πήρα καὶ τ. Plu.2.332a, cf. Luc.*Peregr.*15, D.L.6.13; οἱ τὴν χλαῖναν ἐν τῷ θέρει κατατρίψαντες ἐν τῷ τ. τὸν χειμῶνα διάγουσι Ath.Med.ap.Orib.*inc.*21.17:— = στολή τις ἔχουσα σημεῖα ὡς γαμμάτια acc. to *EM*766.6.

* **τρίβων** (B) [ῐ], ωνος, ὁ, ἡ, Adj. *practised* or *skilled in* a thing, *used to* it, c. gen., τρίβων αὐτῆς (sc. τῆς καννάβιος) Hdt.4.74; τ. λόγων E.*Ba.*717; τ. ἱππικῆς Ar.*V.*1429; τῶν κρεμαθρῶν οὔπω τ. Id.*Nu.*869; τῶν ἔργων τῆς ἰατρικῆς Gal.15.169, cf. 18(2).35: c. acc., τρίβων τὰ τοιάδε E.*Med.*686: abs., Id.*El.*1127: Comp. -ότερος *EM*766.4:—hence **2.** Subst., '*old hand*', *rogue*, Ar.*Nu.*869, 870 (a pun).

* **τρῐβων-άριον** [ᾰ], τό, Dim. of τρίβων (A), *small cloak*, Clearch.26, Arr.*Epict.*3.22.47. **-εύομαι**, *practise roguery*, or *put off, delay*, Antipho *Fr.*33. **-ικῶς**, Adv. *in the fashion of a* τρίβων (A), χλαῖναν ἀναβαλοῦ τ. Ar.*V.*1132. **-ιον**, τό, Dim. of τρίβων (A), ib.33, 116, *Pl.*714, 842, al., Lys.32.16, *PSI*4.418.19 (iii B.C.), *PCair.Zen.*659.20 (iii B.C.), Alciphr.3.55; dub. in Is.5.11. **-ιώδης**, ες, *like a* τριβώνιον, restored for τριβωνίδες in Hsch. s. v. ληδιώδεις.

**τρῐβωνο-φορέω**, *wear a* τρίβων (A), Plu.2.52e. **-φορία**, ἡ, *the wearing of a* τρίβων (A), ib.52c, 352c (pl.). **-φόρος**, ον, *wearing a* τρίβων (A), Hsch., *EM*766.3.

**τρῐβωνώδης**, ες, *like a* τρίβων (A), Phot. s. v. λῄδιον (fort. τριβωνιώδης).

**τρί-γᾰμος** [ῐ], ον, *thrice-married*, with allusion to Helen, Stesich.26, cf. Theoc.12.5. **-γένεια**, ἡ, *a third generation*, εἰς τ. παραμένειν Str.2.1.14; οἱ ἐκ τριγενείας στιγματίαι v.l. in Ph.2.446; cf. τριγονία. **II.** *threefold gender* (implied in one form), A.D.*Synt.*212.23; τὰ διὰ μιᾶς φωνῆς τριγένειαν ὑπαγορεύοντα Id.*Adv.*141.22. **III.** τ. ἀγαθῶν *three kinds* of goods, *Stoic.*ap.S.E.*P.*3.181. **-γενής**, ές, *thrice-born*, of the three stages in the life of moths and the like, Arist.*GA*759ᵃ3. **II.** *of threefold gender*, Trypho ap.A.D.*Pron.*61.18, cf. *Pron.*105.23. **III.** *of three kinds*, ἀγγεῖα Gal.14.698; *threefold, triple*, Anatolius ap.*Theol.Ar.*35. **-γέννητος**, ον, *thrice-born*, epith. of Athena, Lyc.519 (variously expld. by Sch.). **-γερήνιος**, ον, *of thrice Gerenian age*, i.e. *thrice* as old as Nestor, M.Ant.4.50; cf. sq. * **-γέρων**, οντος, ὁ, ἡ, *triply old*, i.e. *very old*, τ. μῦθος τάδε φωνεῖ 'tis a *thrice-told* tale, A.*Ch.*314 (anap.); τ. Νέστωρ *AP*7.144, cf. 157. **-γῐγᾱς** [γῐ], αντος, ὁ, *a triple* (i.e. *huge*) *giant*, Orph.*A.*1351.

**Τριγκαῖος**, cited without interpretation by Theognost.*Can.*52.

**τρίγλη**, ἡ, *red mullet, Mullus barbatus*, Epich.64, Sophr.50, Cratin.

58,320, Philyll.13, Diocl.*Fr.*135, *PCair.Zen.*83.2 (iii B.C.), Sor.1.51, 94, Gal.6.715; τ. μιλτοπάρῃος Matro *Conv.*27:—in later writers **τρίγλᾰ** or **τρῖγλα** prevailed, and is sts. found in codd. of earlier authors, as Arist.*HA*543ᵃ5, 591ᵇ19; τρῖγλαν (v.l. τρίγλαν) ἀπ' ἀνθρακιῆς *AP*6.105 (Apollonid.); τρίγλαν Corn.*ND*34, Plu.2.730b,977f,983f; but only τρίγλη is recognized by Hdn.Gr.1.255 note, 1.318, Ath.7.324c.

⊛ **τρίγληνος**, ον, in Hom. as epith. of ear-rings, ἕρματα τρίγληνα Il. 14.183, Od.18.298: ancient critics (cf. Sch. ad loc.) expld. it (1) from γλήνεα (Il.24.192), = ἀξιοθέατα, or (2) = τρίκοκκα, i.e. with three berry-shaped ornaments, or (3) = ἐκ τριῶν ζῳδίων συγκείμενα, or (4) = τριόφθαλμα, like Att. τριοττίδες; and in other ways. It is prob. formed from γλήνη as τρίκλινος fr. κλίνη, etc., but the sense remains uncertain. II. *three-eyed*, of Hecate, Ath.7.325a.

**τριγλίζω**, = κιχλίζω, *giggle*, Hsch.

**τριγλ-ίον**, τό, = sq., *PCair.Zen.*82.8 (iii B.C.), *Gp.*20.46.1. **-ίς**, ίδος, ἡ, Dim. of τρίγλη, Antiph.68.15, Arist.*Fr.*194, Dorio ap.Ath. 7.300f. ⊛ **-ῖτις**, ιδος, ἡ, a kind of ἀφύη, *like the* τρίγλη, Id.ib.285a.

**τριγλοβόλος**, ον, *casting* (the net) *at mullets*, Plu.2.966a, prob. in 983e.

**τριγλοφία, τριγλοφίτης**, v. τριγλυφία.

**τριγλοφόρος**, ον, *bearing mullets*, τ. χιτών a net *for catching them*, *AP*6.11 (Satyrius).

**τριγλῠφία**, ἡ, in Dor. form τριγλοφία, = τρίγλυφος, ἡ, *SIG*244ii60 (Delph., iv B.C.): hence **τριγλοφίτης** [φῐ], ου, ὁ (sc. λίθος), *Delph.* 3(5).23ii60 (iv B.C.).

⊛ **τρίγλῠφος**, ον, *thrice-cloven*, αἰχμὴ τ. *the trident*, Opp.*H.*5. 377. II. as Subst., **τρίγλυφος**, ἡ, in Doric architecture, *the triglyph, a three-grooved tablet* placed at equal distances along the frieze; it seems orig. to have been the end of the beam (the spaces between being at first open and then called ὀπαί, afterwards filled up and called μετόπαι), παστάδων ὑπὲρ τέραμνα Δωρικάς τε τριγλύφους E.*Or.*1372 (lyr.); πασσαλεῦσαι κρᾶτα τριγλύφοις Id.*Ba.*1214; γεῖσα τριγλύφων (cj. Blomf. for γ' εἴσω) the cornice of (i.e. above) *the triglyphs*, Id.*IT*113; σὺν τῇ τ. *IG*2².1668.30; τριγλύφων γωνιηιᾶν *SIG* 247ii61 (Delph., iv B.C.):—pl. τρίγλυφα, τά, Diph.61.2.

**τριγλώχῑς**, ῖνος, ὁ, ἡ, *three-barbed*, ὀϊστός, ἰός, Il.5.393, 11.507; τριγλώχινα (sc. Σικελίαν) Pi.*Fr.*322; τ. ὑμένες *tricuspid* valves of the heart, Erasistratei ap.Gal.5.548, Gal.*UP*6.14: in later writers with a neut. Subst., ἄορι τ. Call.*Del.*31; τ. τόξα Anon.ap.Suid.; βέλη τ. Paul.Aeg.6.88.—The nom. form **τριγλώχιν** is cited from Simon. (*Fr.*248) and from Call. (*Fr.*382 (= *Aet.Oxy.*2079.36)) by Choerob. *in Theod.*1.267 H.

**τριγμός** or **τρισμός**, ὁ, *shrill cry, scream*, of the partridge, τριγμὸν ἀφίησι Arist.*HA*614ᵃ22; of some fish, τριγμοὺς ἀφιᾶσι ib.535ᵇ16; φθέγγονται οἷον τρισμόν Thphr.*CP*5.10.5 (but τριγμόν *HP*4.14.5 cod. U); τρισμὸς μυός Plu.*Marc.*5. 2. *a grating, grinding, rasping*, τρισμοὶ ὀδόντων Hp.*Acut.*(*Sp.*)6, cf. Sch.Ar.*Av.*1520; τρισμοὶ πριόνων Plu.2.654f; *crepitation* in bone-fractures, Zos.Alch.p.233 B.

**τριγόλας**, α, ὁ, a kind of *fish* (cf. τρίγλη), Sophr.50,66,67.

**τρίγομφος** [ῐ], ον, *with three nails*, or perh. *firmly bolted*, S.*Fr.*315 (dub.).

**τρῐγον-έω**, *to be in the third generation*, τριγονήσαντα [τὰ ζῷα] συνεξομοιοῦται Thphr.*CP*1.9.3, cf. 2.13.3. **-ία**, ἡ, *the third generation*, πονηρὸς ἐκ τριγονίας D.58.17; ὁ ἐκ τ. ὢν μυροπώλης Hyp.*Ath.* 19; εἰ Ἀθηναῖοί εἰσιν ἑκατέρωθεν ἐκ τ Poll.8.85 citing Arist. (who does not use the word in *Ath.*55.3); οἱ ἐκ τ. (v.l. τριγενείας) στιγματίαι Ph.2.446; ἐκ τ. βασιλεύς Hdn.1.7.4; εἰς τ. παραμένειν, προελθεῖν, Str.11.10.1, 12.2.11, cf. Jul.*Or.*4.131c; cf. τριγένεια. ⊛**-ος** (proparox.), ον, *thrice-born*, Διόνυσος Orph.*H.*30.2. II. in pl. simply = τρεῖς, *three*, τέκνα τ. E.*HF*1023; κόραι τ. Id.*Ion* 496 (both lyr.).

**τρι-γράμμᾰτος**, ον, *with* or *of three letters*, Eust.1878.59. **-γύον**, τό, *a piece of three* γύαι, *Tab.Heracl.*2.19, al.

**τριγχός, τριγχίον** (Eust.1748.47), **τρίγχωσις** (*Gloss.*), late forms for θριγκός, etc.

**τρίγων**, ωνος, ὁ, prob. *a game at ball* (cf. Lat. *trigon*), Hdn.Gr.1.23.

**τρῐγων-ίζω**, *multiply by three*, Plu.2.416b (Pass.). 2. *represent as a triangular number*, Nicom.*Ar.*2.8 (Pass.). II. intr., *to be triangular*, νῆσος τριγωνίζουσα Hld.10.5:—Pass., τετριγωνίσθαι *assume triangular form*, Plot.2.6.2; ὁ ὀδοὺς -ίζεται *Hippiatr.*95. III. Astrol., *to be in trine aspect*, Ptol.*Tetr.*115, Man.4.266: c. acc., Ἑρμῆς Δία -ίζων Vett.Val.73.26; Ζῆνα -ίζων Φαίνων Orph.*Fr.* 286. **-ικός**, ή, όν, *triangular*, Ptol.*Tetr.*38, Iamb. *in Nic.*p.58 P.; πυραμίδες, on triangular base, Nicom.*Ar.*2.14. Adv. -κῶς *An.Ox.* 3.195. **-ισμός**, ὁ, *disposition of numbers triangular-wise*, Nicom. *Ar.*2.8. **-ιστί**, Adv. *triangle-wise*, ibid. **-ίστρια**, ἡ, *a woman who plays the* τρίγωνον (II. 2), Luc.*Lex.*8.

**τρῐγωνο-δεσπότης**, ου, ὁ, = τριγωνοκράτωρ, *Cat.Cod.Astr.*2.187. **-ειδής**, ές, *triangular-shaped*, ῥαφαί Arist.*HA*516ᵃ19; Ἰταλία τῷ σχήματι τ. Plb.2.14.4; τ. δύναμις Theo Sm.p.37 H. Adv. -δῶς Eust. ad D.P.242. **-κρᾰτορέω**, *rule a zodiacal triangle*, *Cat.Cod.Astr.* 6.6: hence **-κρᾰτορία**, ἡ, ib.1.29. **-κράτωρ** [ᾰ], ορος, ὁ, *ruler of a zodiacal triangle*, Ps.-Ptol.*Centil.*72, Paul.Al.*O.*2.

**τρίγωνος** [ῐ], ον, *three-cornered, triangular*, τὴν τ. ἐς χθόνα Νειλῶτιν, of the Delta, A.*Pr.*813; τ. ῥυθμοί Id.*Fr.*78; βάσεις Pl.*Ti.*55b; of the hearts of certain fish, Arist.*Frr.*314,330,333; of Sicily, Plb.1.42. 3; of Britain, Str.4.5.1. 2. ἀριθμοὶ τρίγωνοι, *triangular* numbers, are those whose units can be disposed in a triangle, as 3 ∴, 6 ⁞., etc., being represented by the formula $n(n+1)/2$, Plu.2.1003f, cf. Nicom.*Ar.*2.8; these numbers are also called *triangles* (τρίγωνοι), Plu. 2.744b. 3. Astrol., *in triangular* or *trine aspect*, of planets when there are three signs of the zodiac between them, so that they are at the apices of an equilateral triangle, S.E.*M.*5.39, Plot.2.3.4; τ. σχηματισμοί Ptol.*Tetr.*35, cf. Man.3.344. II. as Subst., τρίγωνον, τό, *triangle*, Ti.Locr.98a, Pl.*Ti.*50b, etc. 2. *a musical instrument of triangular form*, with strings of equal thickness but unequal lengths, Eup.77, Pl.Com.69.13, Pl.*R.*399c, Arist.*Pol.*1341ᵃ41, Diog.Ath.1.9; called τ. ψαλτήρια in Arist.*Pr.*919ᵇ12:—also as masc., πολὺς δὲ Φρὺξ τρίγωνος S.*Fr.*412, cf. Ath.4.183e. 3. *one of the Athenian law-courts*, Din.*Fr.*89.35, Lycurg.*Fr.*10, Men.1076, Paus.1.28.8, Poll.8. 121. 4. the constellation *Triangulum*, Eudox.ap.Hipparch.1.2. 13. 5. τρίγωνος, ἡ, name of a *lozenge*, Orib.*Syn.*3.183; as masc., Paul.Aeg.7.12.

**τρῐγωνότης**, ητος, ἡ, *triangularity*, Plot.2.6.2, Porph. *in Cat.*137.19.

**τρίδακνος** [ῐ], ον, *eaten at three bites*, of large oysters, Plin.*HN* 32.63.

**τρῐδακτῠλ-ιαῖος**, α, ον, = sq. II, διάστημα S.E.*M.*10.156, cf. Heliod. ap.Orib.48.58.2, *Gp.*7.15.17 (-λαῖα), etc. **-ος**, ον, *three-fingered* or *-toed*, Arist.*Fr.*354. II. *three fingers long, broad*, etc., εὖρος Hp.*Art.* 33, cf. 72; ξύλον D.Chr.64.10, cf. *Inscr.Délos* 1443*C*116 (ii B.C.), Plb.10.44.3, Dsc.3.69, etc.; κατατέμνονται εἰς τριδάκτυλα Androm.ap. Gal.13.22. III. τριδάκτυλον, τό, = ἄγνος I, Ps.-Dsc.1.103. IV. *having three dactyls*, with a play on signf. I, *App.Anth.*7.23 (Jul.).

**τρί-δειρος** [ῐ], ον, *three-necked*, metaph. of Sicily, Lyc.966. **-δέσποτος**, ον, *with three masters*, Sch.Lyc.328. ⊛ **-δουλος**, ον, *thrice a slave*, Ach.Tat.8.1; by descent, οὐδ' ἐὰν τρίτης.. μητρὸς φανῶ τ. S.*OT* 1063; as slave of a slave's slave, Theopomp.Hist.244. II. ζεῦγος τ. a leash *of slaves*, Ar.*Fr.*576; cf. τριπάρθενος. **-δραχμος**, ον, *worth three drachmas*, Id.*Pax* 1202. II. τρίδραχμος, ἡ, the *three-drachma tax*, *PRyl.*216.25, al. (ii/iii A.D.). III. τρίδραχμον, τό, *three drachmas*, Poll.6.165. **-δῠμος**, ον, *threefold*, τρίδυμα *three born at a birth*, Plu.2.906b,c, Sor.1.43, Artem.5.12; τ. ἀδελφοί Demarat.ap.Stob.3.39.32; παῖδες D.H.3.22; λόγος Ph.1.302; Τρίδυμος Πύλη, = *Porta Trigemina*, D.H.1.32. **-δύνᾰμος** [ῠ], ον, *of three powers* or *faculties*, ψυχή Hierocl. *in CA*20 p.463 M., Ammon. *in APr.* 2.33; τὸ τ. Procl. *in Prm.*p.945 S. **-δωρος**, ον, (δῶρον II) *measuring three palms*, *Milet.*7.57 (Didyma). **-έγγονος**, = τριωίωνος, *trinepos*, *Gloss.* **-ειδος**, ον, (εἶδος IV) *composed of three ingredients*, ἔμπλαστρος Aët.15.15: cf. ἑξάειδος, ἑπτάειδος, τετράειδος. ⊛**-έλικτος**, ον, (ἑλίσσω) *thrice coiled*, ὄφις Orac.ap.Hdt.6.77; Μαιάνδρου τ. ὕδωρ *AP*6.110 (Leon. or Mnasalc.); τ. ἰχνοπέδαν a noose *of three threads*, ib.109 (Antip.); τ. νῆμα (of the Fates) ib.7.14 (Antip. Sid.); τ. θώρακες, of three 'crow's-nests' (cf. θωράκια Moschio ap.Ath.5.208e), *App. Anth.*3.82.9 (Archimelus). **-έλιξ**, ῐκος, ἡ, *triple wreath*, Chaerem.7 (dub.). **-έμβολος**, ον, *like three ship's beaks*, Ar.*Av.*1256. **-ενος**, ον, (ἔνος (A)) *within three years*, Thphr.*HP*4.11.5; *three-year-old*, βοῦς Orac. in *IGRom.*4.360.32 (Pergam., ii A.D.). **-έσπερος**, ον, (ἑσπέρα) *in three successive nights*, ὄνειρος Luc.*Somn.*17, *Gall.*12. 2. τ. λέων, i.e. Heracles, *who was begotten in a triple night*, Lyc.33; Subst., ἡ Ἡρακλέους τ. *the triple night*, Alciphr.3.38.

**τριετ-ήρ**, ῆρος, ὁ, = τριέτης, Orph.*H.*53.4. ⊛ **-ήρης**, ες, = τριέτης, *in his third year*, prob. = μικιζόμενος, *IG*5(1).1120 (Geronthrae, v B.C.). **-ηρικός**, ή, όν, *belonging to a* τριετηρίς, παντέλεια Plu.2.671d; ἀγῶνες τ. *IG*5(1).662.6 (Laconia), cf. *POxy.*2105.3 (ii A.D.). **-ηρίς** (sc. ἑορτή), ίδος, ἡ, *triennial festival*, i.e. *celebrated every third year* (inclusively), = *in alternate years*, Pi.*N.*6.40, *IG*2². 1672.258,262, *OGI*51.27 (Egypt, iii B.C.), 299.17, 331.8 (both Pergam., ii B.C.), *IG*12(1).730.15 (Camirus, ii/i B.C.): pl., Hdt.4.108, E.*Ba.*133 (lyr.), Pl.*Lg.*834e; in full, τ. θυσίαι D.S.4.3; τ. ἑορταί Artem.4.39. 2. (sc. περίοδος) *cycle* or *period of three* (*two*) *years*, *h.Hom.*1.11, Arist.*Pol.*1308ᵇ1, *IG*12(1).155.50 (Rhodes, ii B.C.), *PGrenf.*2.69.22 (iii A.D.): so τ. ὧραι Orph.*H.*54.3. 3. γυναῖκες τ. *celebrating the triennial festival*, Opp.*C.*4.235. **-ηρος**, ον, *three years old*, Call.*Dian.*72, Nonn.*D.*45.294, *AP*7.552 (Agath.). II. *triennial*, *IG*7.2727 (Acraeph.). ⊛**-ης**, ες, or **τριετής**, ές, (ἔτος) *of* or *for three years*, τριέτεα χρόνον Hdt.1.199; τ. φορά *IG*4²(1).121.9 (Epid., iv B.C.); πλέον ἢ τ. ἐγένευ φίλος Theoc.29.17, cf. *BCH*48. 518 (Palestine); τ. προθεσμία Pl.*Lg.*954d (in 793d τρί' ἔτη is restored by Bekker): τρίετες as Adv., *for three years*, Od.2.106, 13. 377. 2. *three years old*, ἵππος Arist.*HA*545ᵇ13; παιδίον Artem. 4.39: τρίετες, τό, *the age of three years*, ἀπὸ τριέτους μέχρι τῶν ἓξ ἐτῶν Pl.*Lg.*794a, cf. Arist.*HA*545ᵇ3:—fem. **-έτις**, *Supp.Epigr.*6.125 (Cotiaeum). II. *recurring every three years*, κῶμος Orph.*H.*53. 5. **-ία**, ἡ, *period of three years*, Plu.*CG*2; κατὰ τ. Thphr.*CP*1. 20.4, Arg. ii D.22, cf. Dsc.1 *Prooem.*8, *PAmh.*2.100.7 (ii/iii A.D.), etc.; ἐς τ. Luc.*Alex.*41. **-ίζω**, *to be three years old*, Lxx 1 *Ki.*1.24.

**τριζῠγής**, ές, **τρίζῠγος**, ον (η, ον S.*Ichn.*168), and **τρίζυξ**, ῠγος, ὁ, ἡ, *three-yoked, three in union*, Χαρίτων τριζύγων S.*Fr.*545; τρίζυγοι θεαί E.*Hel.*357 (lyr.); τριζυγέες Χάριτες *AP*11.27 (Maced.); also τρίζυγες κασίγνητοι ib.6.181 (Arch.). 2. *triple*, τριζύγης οἴμου βάσιν S.*Ichn.* l.c.; τρίζυγον ἑβδομάδα *Supp.Epigr.*3.216 (Attica, ii/i B.C.).

⊛ **τρίζω**, Od.24.5,7, Hp.*Morb.*2.55, Arist.*HA*504ᵃ19, al.; but pf. τέτριγα is more freq. in pres. sense, Ep. part. τετριγῶτες, for τετριγότες, Il.2.314:—prop. of sounds uttered by animals (cf. τριγμός, τρύζω), *utter a shrill cry*, of young birds, Il.2.314; of bats, Od.24.7, cf. Hdt.3.110; of the Τρωγοδύται, τετρίγασι κατά περ αἱ νυκτερίδες Id. 4.183; of partridges, Arist.*HA*536ᵇ14; of the ἴυγξ, ib.504ᵃ19; of locusts, Id.*Mir.*844ᵇ26; of young swallows, Luc.*Tim.*21; of the elephant, Id.*Zeux.*10; of mice, Arat.1132, Babr.108.23, etc.; of the fish called σελάχη, Arist.*HA*535ᵇ25: also applied to the noise made by ghosts, 'squeak and gibber', Il.23.101, Od.24.5,9; ἔτριζον δίκην ἀσπίδων (αἱ ψυχαί) Herm.ap.Stob.1.49.44. 2. of other sounds, τετρίγει (Ep. plpf.) δ' ἄρα νῶτα θρασειάων ἀπὸ χειρῶν the wrestlers' backs *creaked*, Il.23.714; so τρίζει, *crepitates*, of a broken collar-bone, Sor.*Fract.*13; τέτριγε δ' ὁ κυνόδων *grinds*, Epich.21; τὸ τρίζειν ἀκουσίως involuntary *gnashing*, Gal.7.150; τ. τοὺς ὀδόντας *Ev.Marc.*9.18; τοῖς ὀδοῦσι *Hippiatr.*86; of a musical string, *give a crack*, *AP*6.54 (Paul. Sil.); of an axle, *creak*, ἄξων τετριγὼς ὑπ' ἅμαξαν Call.*Hec.*1.4.14; so of a cart-wheel, Babr.52.2; of a shoe, Philostr.*Ep.*37 (τρύζοι codd.); ἡ κοιλίη τ. Hp.*Morb.*2.55; of *singing* in the ears, τὰ ὦτα τέτριγε ib.15; of the *hissing* or *crackling* of a person burnt in the fire, Eup.120.

**τρι-ζῳδία**, ἡ, *the space of three signs*, i.e. *a quadrant of the zodiac*, Vett.Val.302.4, Paul.Al.*A.*2, Procl. *in R.*2.32 K., *Cat.Cod.Astr.*1.143. **-ζωος**, ον, *three lives long*, Hsch.

**τριηκάς**, Ep. and Ion. for τριακάς (q.v.). **τριήκοντα, τριηκόσιοι**, etc., Ion. for τριακ-. **τριηκοντήμερος**, Ion. for τριακονθήμερος.

**τρῑημερ-ία**, ἡ, *period of three days*, Lxx *Am.*4.4. **-ος**, ον, *living for three days*, M.Ant.4.50: τριήμερον, τό, *space of three days*, Arist.*HA*553ᵃ10.

**τρῑημῐ-αρτάβιον** [τᾰ], τό, *one and a half artabae*, *PCair.Zen.*376.8 (iii B.C.). **-γῦον**, τό, *a γύης and a half*, *Tab.Heracl.*2.29. **-κοτύλιον** [ῠ], τό, *a measure of* 1½ *cotylae*, *IG*1².842 *D* 2, 11(2).287 *A* 54 (Delos, iii B.C.). **-ολία**, ἡ, *a light undecked vessel of war*, *PLond.*1.106.3 (iii B.C.), *Sammelb.*6261.20 (ii B.C.), Plb.16.2.10, 3.4, 7.3, D.S.20.93, *IG*2².3218.9, 12(1).58.20 (Rhodes), *Supp.Epigr.*3.679 (ibid.), Ἀρχ.Ἐφ.1913.10 (Nisyros), Hsch., Phot. s.v. ἡμιολία; to be restored for τριηρημιολία in Ath.5.203d. Cf. ἡμιόλιος III. **-πηχυς**, υ, *a cubit and a half long*, Callix.2. **-πλίνθιον**, τό, *a brick and a half*, *IG*2².463.43 (iv B.C.). **-πόδιον**, τό, *a foot and a half*, X.*Oec.*19.4, 5:—as Adj. **-πόδιος**, ον, *a foot and a half long*, *IG*1².372.12, 373.15, 2².1668.28, 1682.9, 7.4255.20 (Oropus); also **-ποδιαῖος**, α, ον, *Inscr.Délos* 1416 *A* i 85 (ii B.C.).

**τρῑημίσ[εον]** [μῐ], τό, *one and a half*, *Schwyzer* 644 (Aegae, iv/iii B.C.).

⊛ **τρῑημι-στᾰτῆρα**, *a stater and a half*, *IG*2².1673.51 (fort. τρί' ἡμιστάτηρα). **-τόνιον**, τό, *a tone and a half*: in Music, *minor third*, Cleonid.*Harm.*3, Plu.2.389e,430a:—hence **-τονιαῖος**, α, ον, διάστημα Gaud.*Harm.*3, Theo Sm.p.54 H., cf. p.141 H. **-τονον**, τό, = -τόνιον, Alex.Eph.ap.Theon.Sm.p.140 H. **-χοῖνιξ**, ῐκος, ὁ, ἡ, f.l. for τρί' ἡμιχοίνικα in Thphr.*HP*8.4.5. **-ωβόλιον**, τό, *an obol and a half*, Ar.*Fr.*48.

**τρῑηραρχ-έω**, pf. τετριηράρχηκα Isoc.15.145, Lycurg.139:—*command a trireme*, Hdt.8.46, Th.4.11: c. gen., τ. νεός Hdt.7.181; τῆς Παράλου Is.5.42; τ. ἐς Κύπρον Lys.19.25. II. at Athens, and in the empires of the Diadochi, *to be trierarch*, i.e. *fit out a trireme for the public service*, Ar.*Eq.*912 (lyr.), *Ra.*1065 (anap.); τ. πολλά Antipho 2.2.12; τριηραρχίας πολλὰς τ. Lys.13.62; Γνώμη,.. ἧς ἐτριηράρχει Ἀπολλόδωρος *IG*2².1627.250; εἰς τὴν ναῦν ἣν τριηραρχεῖ *PCair.Zen.*36.5 (iii B.C.); οἶκος τριηραρχῶν a family *wealthy enough for the trierarchy*, Is.7.32; ὅσοι..τετριηραρχήκασι (at Teos and Lebedos) *SIG*344.66 (iv B.C.):—Pass., τριηραρχοῦσιν οἱ πλούσιοι, ὁ δὲ δῆμος τριηραρχεῖται *has trierarchs found it*, X.*Ath.*1.13. III. in the cult of Isis, *equip the sacred ship*, τριηραρχήσαντα ἱεροπρεπῶς *LW*1143 (Cius): cf. ναυβατέω, ναυαρχέω. **-ημα**, ατος, τό, *expense of the* τριηραρχία, D.50.1 ap.Harp. (codd. ἐπιτρ-). 2. a tax levied in Egypt for the upkeep of the navy, *PMich.Zen.*100.2, *PCair.Zen.*12.47, al., *PGrad.*6.3, *PRev.Laws* 94.3, *PPetr.*3 p.276, *PHib.*1.104.3 (all iii B.C.). II. *trierarch's crew of seamen*, D.50.44. **-ης**, v. τριήραρχος. **-ία**, ἡ, *command of a trireme*, Arist.*Pol.*1322ᵇ4 (pl.). II. at Athens, *the fitting out of a trireme for the public service*, Lys.32.24, X.*Ath.*1.13, *Oec.*2.6, etc.: also at Priene, *SIG*1003.29 (ii B.C.). **-ικός**, ή, όν, *concerning the* τριηραρχία, νόμος D.18.312; τὸ τ., = τοὺς τριηραρχοῦντας, Decr.ap.eund.18.105. **-ος** (proparox.), ὁ, *captain of a trireme*, Hdt.8.93, Ar.*Th.*837 (troch.), Th.4.11, 7.70, X.*HG*1.1.25, *OGI*773.5 (Ios, iv B.C.), *IG*2².1631.343 (iv B.C.), 884.11 (iii/ii B.C.), *BGU*1744.11 (i B.C.), *POxy.*1508.4 (ii A.D.), etc. II. *trierarch, one who* (singly or jointly with other citizens) *had to fit out a trireme for the public service*, Ar.*Ach.*546, Th.6.31, 7.13, *IG*1².304.36, al., 2².1.27, 1609.57, 1612.133, 1629.3, 183, etc.—**-άρχης** is a later form, meaning *naval commander* in general, Gal.*Thras.*47.

⊛ **τριηρ-αύλης**, ου, ὁ, *flute-player who gave the time to the rowers in the trireme*, D.18.129, Phld.*Mus.*p.72 K., Poll.1.96, 4.71. **-έτης, -ετικός**, ff.ll. for τριηριτ-. **-ημιολία**, v. τριημιολία.

**τριήρ-ης** (sc. ναῦς), ἡ, gen. εος, Att. ους *IG*2².1629.615, Ion. ευς Hippon.49.2; acc. εα, Att. η *IG*2².1610.30, 1623.113, 1632.235,338 (but τριήρην ib.1628.35, 1629.862): nom. pl. εες, Att. εις; gen. τριήρων ib.1627.397, etc., Ion. τριηρέων Hdt.7.89; hence Choerob. *in Theod.*1.411 H. prescribes as the contr. form τριηρῶν, not τριήρων, as in codd. of Th.6.46, X.*HG*1.4.11, D.14.9, v. Hdn.Gr.1.428; Thom.Mag.p.356 R. prescribes sg. τριήρεος and pl. τριήρων ("τριήρεων γὰρ..λέγομεν"), citing Aristid.1.431 J.: gen. dual τριήροιν X.*HG*1.5.19:—*a trireme*, i.e. prob. *a galley with three men on each bench, each man rowing one oar, and three oars passing together through the* παρεξειρεσία (cf. Tarn *Hellenistic Military and Naval Developments*, Cambridge 1930, pp.122 sqq.), Hdt.2.159, 7.36, Th.1.13, 2.93, Arist.*Mete.*369ᵇ10, *HA*533ᵇ6, *Rh.*1411ᵃ23, *IG*2².1623.276, Gal.*UP*1.24, etc.; τ. ἱππηγοί *IG*2².1627.241. 2. metaph., *a ship-shaped drinking-vessel*, Antiph.224.4, Epin.2.8. 3. as Adj., = τριώροφος, οἰκίαι Aristid.*Or.*27(16).20. **-ικός**, ή, όν, = τριηριτικός, σκεύη D.47.19; λιμήν Str.14.2.15, cj. in 13.2.2; αὐλεῖν τὸ τ. (sc. μέλος) Ath.12.535d; but τὸ τ. *the class which serves in a trireme*, Arist.*Pol.*1291ᵇ23. **-ῑτεύω**, *row in a trireme*, Poll.1.98. **-ίτης** [ῑτ], ου, ὁ, *one who goes in a trireme*, esp. as a soldier or rower, Hdt.5.85, Th.6.46, X.*An.*6.6.7; τριηρέτης is f.l. in Poll.1.95. ⊛ **-ῑτικός**, ή, όν, *of* or *like a trireme*, ὑποζώματα *IG*2².1629.70,100,134: for τριηρετικὰ σκεύη App.*Praef.*10, *Pun.*96, and -ρετικοὶ φάσηλοι Id.*BC*5.95, τριηριτ- shd. be read.

**τρίηρον**· πλοῖον μικρόν, Hsch. (fort. τριήριον).

**τρῑηρο-νόμος**, ὁ, = τριήραρχος, Hsch. **-ποιικός**, ή, όν, *of* or *for trireme-building*, *IG*2².1627.391 (-ποϊκ-), 1628.534 (-ποιϊκ-), 1622.389 (-ποϊκ-): cf. sq. ⊛ **-ποιός**, όν, *building triremes*, ib.1².93.4, 97.20, al., Arist.*Ath.*46.1; but τῶν τριηροποι⟨ικ⟩ῶν ταμίας is prob. cj. in D.22.17.

**τρῐ-θάλασσος** [θᾰ], Att. **-ττος**, ον, *of three seas, touching on* or *connected with three seas*, Ephor.119 J. ⊛ **-θάλεια** [θᾰ], τά, epith. of λόχια, = πολυθαλῆ λοχεύματα, Antim. in *PMilan.*17.33. **-θαλής**, ές, *thrice-blooming*: τριθαλές, τό, = ἀείζωον μικρόν, Plin.*HN*25.160. **-θαλλίαι**· μεγάλως τοῦ θάλλειν αἰτίαι, Hsch. **-θέλυμνος**, gloss on τρίπτυχος, Eust.849.5. **-θετος**, ον, *thrice-placed, thrice-folded*, Id.1154.31.

**τρῐθ-ημέρῃ**, Adv. *three days ago*, Herod.3.24 (τριτ- 6.21, and so τριτημέρᾳ, *Gloss.*): **-ημερινός**, *nudiustertianus*, *Gloss.*

**τρί-θῠρον** [ῐ], τό, *building with three doors*, *Supp.Epigr.*4.446.15 (Didyma, iii B.C.), cf. *Gloss.* **-ιππον**, τό, = *triga*, ib.; also **τριίππιν** (i.e. -ιον), ib. **-κᾰλάμιος** [λᾰ], α, ον, *involving three reeds*, ὀνειροθαυπτάνη (sic, v. ὀνειραυτοπτικός) τρικαλαμία *PMag.Par.*1.3172. **-κᾰλίνδητος**, ον, = τρικυλίνδητος, *EM*766.22, Phot.

**Τρῐκάρᾱνος** [κᾰ], ὁ, *the Three-headed*, a satirical attack on three cities, Sparta, Athens, and Thebes, written by Anaximenes of Lampsacus (*Frr.*20 and 21 J.) and ascribed by him to Theopompus, Paus.6.18.5, Luc.*Pseudol.*29, *Fug.*32; also a satire by Varro on the coalition of Caesar, Pompeius, and Crassus, App.*BC*2.9.

**τρῐ-κάρηνος** [ᾰ], Dor. **-κάρᾱνος**, ον, poet. for τρικέφαλος, *three-headed*, Πτωΐου κευθμών Pi.*Fr.*101 (codd. Str., -καράνου Bgk.), cf. Coluth.14, etc.; τ. ὄφις Hdt.9.81. **-καρπος**, ον, *bearing fruit* or *crops thrice a year*, ἄρουραι D.H.1.37. II. = τριέτης, Hsch. **-κέλλαρον**, τό, a utensil of unknown nature, perh. = τριλάγυνον κελλάριον, *POxy.*1290.5 (v A.D.). **-κεντρον**, τό, *spherical triangle*, Hero *Stereom.*1.96. **-κεράμιον** [ᾰ], τό, Dim. of sq., *Sammelb.*6964. **-κέρᾰμον**, τό, a liquid measure, ib.6965, al. **-κέρβερος**, ον, *a threefold Cerberus*, κύων Tz.*H.*2.751. **-κέφᾰλος**, ον, *three-headed*, γῦπες Luc.*VH*1.11, etc.:—ὁ τ. a statue of Hermes at Athens, Is.*Fr.*59, Philoch.69, cf. Ar.*Fr.*553. [Penult. in Poets sts. long, as Hes.*Th.*287.]

**τρίκκος**· ὀρνιθάριον ⟨ὅ?⟩ καὶ βασιλεὺς ὑπὸ Ἠλείων, Hsch.

**τρικλᾱρία**, ἁ, Dor. for *τρικληρία, epith. of Artemis in Achaea, Paus.7.19.1, 7.22.11.

**τρικλῑν-αρχία**, ἡ, *directorship of feasts*, *BCH*11.385, 15.186, 204 (Panamara). **-ιάρχης**, ου, ὁ, in Lat. form *tricliniarches*, *director of a feast*, Petron.22; title of an imperial official, *CIL*3.536 (Corinth). **-ικός**, ή, όν, *for a* τρίκλινος II, τρίποδες *POsl.*60 (ii A.D.). **-ιον**, τό, = τρίκλινος II, Theopomp.Com.64. **-ος**, ον, *with three couches*, θάλαμοι Moschio ap.Ath.5.207c; τ. οἶκοι Ath.2.47f, cf. Poll.6.7. II. Subst. τρίκλινος (sc. οἶκος), ὁ, *AB*114, Eust.1573.29, *Gloss.*; also **τρίκλινον**, τό, *SIG*1097.29 (Athens, iv B.C.), Anaxandr.70, Arched.2.12, Plb.30.26.3, *BGU*388 ii 21 (ii A.D.):—*dining-room with three couches*, συναγαγὼν τρεῖς ὄντας εἰς τ. Antiph.299. 2. τ. συγγενείας a family *party*, Men.923.1; ὅλον τ. (acc.) a whole *dinner-party*, Dsc.5.71, cf. Anaxandr. l.c., Arched. l.c. 3. *set of three couches*, οὐχ ὑποστρώσεις τ.; Amphis 46, cf. *SIG* l.c., Plb. l.c., Plu.*Caes.*55, *POxy.*1277.7,23 (iii A.D.). III. τρίκλινος ἤτοι ὡρεῖον *a barn* (?) or a granary, Hero *Stereom.*1.46.

**τρί-κλυστος**, ον, *thrice washed* or *cleansed*, Ar.*Fr.*875. **-κλωνος**, ον, *with* or *of three shoots*, Sch.Theoc.3.29. **-κλωστος**, ον, *thrice-spun, three-twisted*, of a line, *AP*6.109 (Antip.). ⊛ **-κογχος**, ον, Archit., *with three* κόγχαι or *apses* (v. κόγχη IV), τὸ τ. σίγμα *Princeton Exp.Inscr.* III A No.561 (Syria, v A.D.). **-κόκκια**, = *terniones, tuberes*, *Gloss.* ⊛ **-κοκκος**, ον, *with three grains* or *berries*, Sch.Il.14.183:—τρίκοκκος, ὁ, = μέσπιλον, Dsc.1.118; = ἡλιοτρόπιον τὸ μέγα, Plin.*HN*22.60; ἡλιοτρόπιον τ. Aët.12.63. **-κόλλῠβον**, τό, *a three-κόλλυβος piece*, Poll.9.72, Hsch. **-κόλουρος**, ον, *thrice-docked* or *cut short*, πυραμίς Nicom.*Ar.*2.14. ⊛ **-κόλωνος**, ον, *three-hilled*, Orac.ap.Str.6.1.5. ⊛ **-κόνητος**, ον, *thrice deserving to be killed*, Hsch.; cf. ἐπικονέω, κονή. **-κορος**, ον, (κόρη III) = τρίγληνος, Sch.Il.14.183, Sch.Od.18.298. **-κόρῠθος**, ον, = sq., Αἴας E.*Or.*1480 (lyr.). ⊛ **-κορυς**, υθος, ὁ, *with triple plume*, Κορύβαντες Id.*Ba.*123 (lyr.). **-κόρῠφος**, ον, *three-pointed* or *-topped*, φρούριον Str.6.1.5; *with three peaks*, ὄρος Id.9.2.34, Polyaen.1.1.2. **-κόρωνος**, ον, *thrice a crow's age*, *AP*11.69 (Lucill.), Alciphr.1.28, *AP*5.288 (Agath.). **-κοτῠλιαῖος**, α, ον, = sq. I, Alex.Aphr.*de An.*141.10. ⊛ **-κότῠλος**, ον (η, ον *Inscr.Délos* 1432 *A* b ii 30 (ii B.C.)), *holding three* κοτύλαι, Ar.*Th.*743, Dionys.Com.5, Men.324. II. οἶνος τ. *costing an obol for three* κοτύλαι, Hsch. **-κουρος**· ὁ ἐπὶ τρία ἔτη κεκ[αθ]αρμένος κριός, ὁμοίως καὶ ὁ μὴ κεκ[αθ]αρμένος, Id. **-κρᾱνος**, ον, *three-headed*, Ἅιδου σκύλαξ, of Cerberus, S.*Tr.*1098, cf. E.*HF*611,1277; μήτηρ τ., of Rhea, prob. in *CIG*4121 (Galatia). **-κράσπεδος**, ον, *with triple border*, Archim.*Bov.*39. **-κροος**, α, ον, *three-cleft*, δίκραν ἢ τρίκραν (fort. δικρᾶν ἢ τρικρᾶν) Thphr.*HP*9.11.3; cf. δίκροος. ⊛ **-κροτος**, ον, *rowed with triple stroke*, of a trireme, Aristid.*Or.*25(43).4; sc. ναῦς, Sch.Ael.*Tact.*p.234K.-R.: cf. δίκροτος, μονόκροτος.

**τρίκτειρα, τρίκτευα, τρίκτοια**, v. τριττύα.

**τρικτῡαρχέω**, v. τριττυαρχέω.

**τρίκτῠπος**, ον, *triply resounding*, epith. of the Moon-goddess, *PMag.Par.*1.2524,2820.

**τρικτύς**, v. τριττύα.

**τρῐκύᾰθος** [ῠ], ον, *holding three* κύαθοι, Anacr.32.

**τρίκυζα**· πολλῆς δεόμενα λιτανείας, Hsch.

**τρῐ-κῠλίνδητος**, ον, *thrice-rolled*, gloss on τρικαλίνδητος, *EM*766.22, Phot. ⊛ **-κύλιστος** [ῠ], ον, = foreg.: metaph., *easily influenced*, Epicur.*Fr.*125. **-κῡμία**, ἡ, *group of three waves*, τὸ μέγιστον [κῦμα] τῆς τ. Pl.*R.*472a; ἑτέραν περιμεῖναι χατέραν τ. Men.536.8: then, *a mighty wave* or *swell*, E.*Hipp.*1213, *Tr.*83 (pl.), Id.ap.Satyr. *Vit.Eur.Fr.*38 iii 14, *Com.Adesp.* in *PSI*10.1176.11: metaph., κακῶν τ. A.*Pr.*1015; σῶσαι ἐκ τῆς τ. τοῦ λόγου Pl.*Euthd.*293a; ἐν ἁπάσαις τ. τῆς τύχης Luc.*Dem.Enc.*33; αἱ τῶν βασάνων τ. Lxx 4*Ma.*7.2. **-κώλιος**, ον, *three-limbed*, i.e. *three-pronged*, ὀβελὸς *SIG*1025.53 (Cos, iv/iii B.C.). **-κωλος**, ον, *three-membered*, περίοδος Hermog. *Inv.*4.3, cf. Demetr.*Eloc.*17: τρίκωλον, τό, *a sentence of three clauses*, D.H.*Comp.*9, Quint.*Inst.*9.3.77, cf. Donat. ad Ter.*Hec.*291.

**τρῐκώμ-αρχος**, ὁ, apparently, *chief official of a* τρικωμία, *IG*2².1213. **-ία**, ἡ, *group of three villages*, *IGRom.*4.1367 (Lydia); as place-name in Egypt, *PEnteux.*82.1 (iii B.C.), etc. **-ος**, ὁ, prob. *inhabitant of a* τρικωμία, *IG*2².1213.

**τρῐ-λάγῡνος** [ᾰ], ον, *holding three bottles*, Stesich.7, *POxy.*741.12 (ii A.D.). **-λεκτος**, ον, *thrice said*, gloss on τρίφατον, Sch.Nic.*Th.*102. **-λῐνος**, ον, *of three threads*: τὸ τ. *necklace of three strings of pearls*, *Gloss.* ⊛ **-λλιστος**, ον, poet. for *τρίλιστος, (λίτομαι, λίσσομαι) *thrice*, i.e. *often* or *earnestly*, *prayed for*, Il.8.488. Adv. **-τως** *AP*5.270 (Maced.). **-λοβος**, ον, *three-lobed*, ἧπαρ [τοῦ σκάρου] Arist. *Fr.*330. **-λογέω**, *use* a word *in three forms*, Eust.1798.25 (Pass.). **-λογία**, ἡ, *trilogy*, *group of three dialogues*, Ar.Byz.ap. D.L.3.61; *group of three tragedies*, Aristarch. et Apollon.ap.Sch.Ar. *Ra.*1155. **-λοφία**, ἡ, *triple crest*, Ar.*Av.*94, Str.3.3.6 (pl.), 10.4.6. II. *three-crested helmet*, Plu.*Arat.*32. **-λοφος**, ον, *with three crests*, κράνος Polyaen.8.59. II. *with three peaks* or *points*, Nonn. *D.*6.124. **-μάκαιρα** [μᾰ], as if from *τρίμακαρ, *thrice-blest*, *AP*9.396 (Paul. Sil.), 7.614 (Agath.). **-μακρος**, ον, in metre, *of three long syllables*, Choerob. *in Heph.*p.217C. **-μαστῑγίας**, ου, ὁ, in Lat. form *trimastigia*, = *triverbero*, *Gloss.* **-μάτιον** [ᾰ], τό, *measure of three* μάτια ($\frac{1}{15}$ ἀρτάβη), *Ostr.*1018 (i/ii A.D.).

**τρῐμάχιον**, τό, = ἵππουρις II.2, Ps.-Dsc.4.46, *Gloss.* (but τρι(χο)μάχιον cj. Wellm. (in Dsc.) from *tricamachion*, v.l. in Apul.*Herb.*39).

**τρῐμελής**, ές, *consisting of three* μέλη, νόμος Plu.2.1132d; v. τριμερής.

**τρῐμέρ-εια**, ἡ, *division into three parts*, Sallust.11, Procl. *in Alc.* p.216C., Herm. *in Phdr.*p.157A. ⊛ **-ής**, ές, *tripartite*, *threefold*, ἡ ψυχή Arist.*VV*1249ᵃ30, cf. *Top.*133ᵃ31; ποταμός Agatharch.95; of a country, Str.11.2.18; ὧραι D.S.1.11; στάσις J.*BJ*5.1.1; φιλοσοφία Plu.2.874e; δρᾶμα Gal. in *Abh.Berl.Akad.*1925(1).38; νόμος τ. a piece of music *in the three modes* (Dorian, Phrygian, Lydian), Plu.2.1134b (nisi leg. τριμελής). Adv. τριμερῶς *Gloss.* **-ίζω**, *divide into three parts*, τὰ ὅρια τῆς γῆς Lxx *De.*19.3.

**τρίμετρος** [ῐ], ον, of verses, *consisting of three* μέτρα; i.e. in iambics, trochaics, and anapaestics, of three συζυγίαι (of two feet each); but in dactylics, etc., of three single feet: hence the iambic verse of six feet is called by the Greeks ἴαμβος τρίμετρος, Hdt.1.12; so τόνος τ. *trimeter* verse, ib.174; ἔπη τ. Pl.*Lg.*810e; τρίμετρον, τό, Ar.*Nu.*642, Arist.*Po.*1447ᵇ11 (pl.). II. τρίμετρος, ὁ, a measure of capacity for oil, *IG*14.422 iii 44 (Tauromenium).

**τρίμηνια**, ἡ, *space of three months*, *PRev.Laws* 22.1, 34.21 (iii B.C.). **-ιαῖος**, α, ον, = τρίμηνος 3, κριθαί Hp.*Mul.*1.44, cf. Thphr.*CP* 3.24.2, Dsc.2.85; = τρίμηνος 2, D.L.8.78; τριμηνιαία, ἡ, *space of three months*, Vett.Val.98.23:—τριμηναῖος is a freq. f.l. ⊛ **-ος**, ον, (μήν) *of three months*, χρόνος S.*Tr.*164; so ἡ τ. *period of three months*, Hdt.2.124, *IG*2².1358 ii 7,11, al., *PCair.Zen.*124.5, 440.4 (iii B.C.); τὸ τ. Plb.1.38.6, etc.; τ. παιδία *born after three months*, *Com.Adesp.*213: neut. as Adv., τρίμηνα ἐκτιτρώσκειν Hp.*Aph.*5.45. 2. *three months old*, Arist.*HA*562ᵇ28. 3. πυροὶ τ. wheat sown in spring, *so as to ripen in three months*, Philyll.4, cf. Thphr.*HP*8.1.4, *CP*4.11.1, *PCair.Zen.*155.6 (iii B.C.).

**τριμήσιον**, τό, = Lat. *tremis(sis)*, *a coin worth* $\frac{1}{3}$ *of the aureus*, *PSI* 9.1073 (iv A.D.), *PLond.*1.77.73 (vi A.D.), etc.

**τρῐμίγμᾰτος**, ον, *consisting of a mixture of three ingredients*, τροχίσκος Heras ap.Gal.13.544.

**τριμίσκον**· ἱμάτιον, Ἀσπένδιοι, Hsch. (Cf. τρίμιτος; fort. τριμιτίσκος.)

⊛ **τρῐμῐτ-άριος**, ὁ, *maker of* τρίμιτοι II, *PLond.* in *Mém.Inst.Franç.* 67.109 (iv A.D.); = *triliciarius*, *Gloss.* **-ῐνος**, η, ον, = sq. 1, A.*Fr.*365, Crates Com.34. **-ος**, ον, *three-threaded*, i.e. perh. *made of drill*, δελματική..τρίμιτος *Edict.Diocl.*19.28, cf. *IGRom.*3.228 (Pessinus); but used of felt shoes (dub. sens.) in Lysipp.3. II. as Subst., τρίμιτος, ὁ, or τρίμιτον, τό, *garment of drill* or *ticking*, Cratin. Jun.5, cf. Poll.7.78: Dim. **τριμίτιον**, Id.6.165; cf. τριμίσκον.

**τρῖμμα**, ατος, τό, (τρίβω) *that which is rubbed*: metaph., like τρίβων (B) 2, *a practised knave*, Ar.*Nu.*260, *Av.*431. II. *a drink* or *brew prepared of pounded groats and spices*, Alex.188, Sotad.Com.1.4, Axionic.4.8 (anap.); τριμμάτων πλῆθος Diocl.*Fr.*138; ὅπως λαβὼν παρ ἐμοῦ..σησάμου τέταρτον τρίψῃ μοι..τ. *UPZ*62.21 (ii B.C.); = ἀρωματίζον πόμα ἐν γάμοις πινόμενον, Hsch. 2. *fragments*, μοχλῶν *IG*2².1672.303 (τριμματα lapis), cf. 7.3073.165 (Lebad., ii B.C.); *scrapings*, Hp.*Nat.Mul.*32. III. *abrasion*, Gal.13.181.

**τριμμάτιον**, τό, Dim. of foreg. II. 1, Sotad.Com.1.17, Diph.44.5. 2. *shampoo-powder*, Archig.ap.Aët.6.7.

**τριμμᾰτολογέω**, *smooth*, *polish*, τὰς βάσεις ἐκ χλόης *IG*7.3073.162 (Lebad., ii B.C.).

**τριμμός**, ὁ, *beaten track*, X.*Cyn.*3.7, 4.3, Ael.*Fr.*114, D.C.56.20.

**τρι-μναῖος**, α, ον, = sq., γόμφος *SIG*246 ii 41 (Delph., iv B.C.). **-μνους**, ουν, (μνᾶ) *worth* or *weighing three minae*, Poll.6.165. **-μνως**, ω, ὁ, (μνᾶ) *a three-mina piece*, Phot., Suid.

**τρῐμοιρ-ία**, ἡ, *triple pay*, X.*HG*6.1.6, Luc.*Tim.*57. 2. *arc of three degrees*, Vett.Val.139.15. **-ιαῖος**, α, ον, *amounting to three-fourths*, Apollod.*Poliorc.*162.8 codd. (τριτημοριαῖος Schneider). **-ίτης** [ῑτ], ου, ὁ, *a ship's officer receiving triple pay*, Luc.*JTr.*48. **-ος**, ον, *threefold*, *triple*, χλαῖνα A.*Ag.*872; *three parts* to one, Antyll.ap. Orib.10.13.13.

**τρῐ-μορος** [ῐ], ον, = τρίμοιρος, Orph.*A.*1056 (dub.). **-μορφος**, ον, *three-formed*, Ἑκάτη τριοδῖτι, τρίμορφε, τριπρόσωπε Chariclid.1, cf. Lyc.1176, Corn.*ND*34; τὸν τ. θεὸν ἔτι κυόμενον ἐν τῷ ᾠῷ Orph.*Fr.*60; χαῖρε πάτερ κόσμου, χαῖρε τρίμορφε θεός *CIG*4971 (Egypt), *Sammelb.*6128. II. pl., = τρεῖς, Μοῖραι τ. the *three* fates, A.*Pr.*516. **-μυξος**, ον, (μύξα) *with three wicks*, Metag.12, *Inscr.Délos* 1417*A*172 (ii B.C.), *IG*7.2422 (Thebes, ii/i B.C.), 3498.8 (Orop.).

**Τρῑνακρία**, ἡ, an old name of Sicily, older than Σικανία acc. to Th. 6.2; older than Θρινακία acc. to Str.6.2.1:—Adj. **Τρῑνάκριος**, α, ον, Call.*Fr.*18, etc.; fem. **Τρῑνακρίς**, ίδος, Opp.*H.*3.627.—Also written **Τρῑνᾰκίη**, D.P.467, Eust. ad loc. II. **Τρῑναχία** (sic Pap.), ἡ, *triple*, as epith. of the Moon-goddess, *PMag.Par.*1.2525; written Θρινακία ib.2822.

**τρίναξ**, ᾰκος, ἡ, (ἀκή (A)) like θρῖναξ, *three-pronged mattock*, *AP*6.104 (Phil.) [where ι is short].

**τρῐ-νήσαρχος**, ὁ, *lord of three islands*, Tz.*H.*2.328. **-νυκτον**, τό, (νύξ) *space of three nights*, *Gloss.* (formed like τριήμερον).

**τριξέλλας**, = *gryllus*, *Gloss.* (Cf. τρωξαλλίς.)

**τρίξεστον**, τό, *three sextarii*, *one semicongium*, *Gloss.*

**τριξός**, ή, όν, Ion. for τρισσός, Hdt.1.171, al.

**τρίξῠλος**, ον, *containing three sticks*, or *three* ξύλα (v. ξύλον v) *in length*, δέσμαι *Theb.Ostr.*144 (i A.D.).

**τριοβολιαῖος**, -**ιμαῖος**, ff.ll. for τριωβ- (q.v.): **τριόβολον**, τό, = τριώβολον, *Sammelb.*7378.11 (ii A.D.).

**τριόγδον**· μέτρον τι παρὰ Ταραντίνοις, Hsch.

**τριοδ-έομαι**, Pass., *to belong to a tertiary series*, Nicom.*Ar.*1.19 (v.l. τριωδ-, cf. τριῳδέομαι). **-ῆῐος**, α, ον, *belonging to Hecate* or *Cybele* (cf. τριοδῖτις), Cibeles triodeia signa, *CIL*6.511 (Rome, iv A.D.). **-ία**, ἡ, *meeting of three roads*, Lat. *trivium*, *Gloss.* ⊛ **-ιον**, τό, = foreg., in gen. pl., *AB*102. ⊛ **-ίτης** [ῑτ], ου, ὁ, *one who frequents cross-roads*: τριοδίτας· τοὺς ἐν τῇ τριόδῳ διαλοιδορουμένους, *AB*309; τριοδίτης τριπύλιος, title of Menippean Satire by Varro, Non.p.306L. II. **τριοδῖτις**, ιδος, ἡ, epith. of Hecate, *who was worshipped at the meeting of three ways*, Chariclid.1, cf. Corn.*ND* 34. b. epith. of the Moon, Plu.2.937f, Doroth. in *Cat.Cod.Astr.*2.82. 2. σοβὰς τ. *street-walker*, Ph.1.568. 3. generally, *common*, *vulgar*, Μοῦσα Tz.*H.*12.513. 4. Pythag. name of 6, Anatol. ap.*Theol.Ar.*37.

**τριοδοντ-ία**, ἡ, *fishing with a trident* or *leister*, Pl.*Sph.*220e, Poll. 7.139. **-ιον**, τό, Dim. of τριόδους II.1, *Gloss.*

⊛ **τρίοδος** [ῐ], ἡ, = τριοδία, *a meeting of three roads*, Thgn.911, Pi.*P.*11.38 (where the pl. [cj.] is used for the sg., cf. Mosch.1.2, *Epigr.Gr.*841 (Thrace), *IG*3.1418.2); τροχήλατος σχιστῆς κελεύθου τρίοδος A.*Fr.*173, cf. E.*Supp.*1212, Pherecr.130.3 (anap., pl.), Ar.*Fr.*204 (pl.), Pl.*Grg.*524a, etc. 2. [Ἑκάτη] ναίουσ' ἱερὰς τ. S.*Fr.*535 (anap.); ἁ θεὸς ἐν τριόδοισι Theoc.2.36; the τρίοδοι were frequented by fortune-tellers and loungers, Thphr.*Char.*16.5,14, Aristid.*Or.*22 (19).10; φαρμακοπώλης ἐκ τριόδου Gal.9.823; ἐκ τῆς τ. ἰατροί Id.10.786: hence οἷα ἐκ τριόδου, i.e. vulgar, Luc.*Hist.Conscr.*16, etc.; λοιδορίαι ἐξ ἐργαστηρίων καὶ τριόδων D.C.46.4; of certain women, τρίοδοί τινες.. ἐγένοντο Clearch.25 (τριοδίτιδες cj. Lobeck). 3. prov. also of persons in doubt, ἐν τριόδῳ δ' ἕστηκα Thgn.l.c.; στὰς.., καθάπερ ἐν τ. γενόμενος Pl.*Lg.*799c; ἐν τ. εἰμί Zen.3.78, etc. 4. a measure in Egypt, μέτρῳ τῷ καλουμένῳ τριόδῳ *BGU*920.21 (ii A.D.). 5. *the 'trivium'*, Simp. in *Cael.*131.28. 6. metaph., τὰς συμφωνούσας ἁρμονίας τ. Ion Eleg.3.2. II. perh. = τετραοδία, Chrysipp.ap. S.E.*P.*1.69 (cf. *Stoic.*2.206).

⊛ **τριόδους**, όδοντος, ὁ, ἡ, *with three teeth*, *three-pronged*, κρεάγρα Lxx 1 *Ki.*2.13. II. **τριόδους**, ὁ, as Subst., = τρίαινα, *trident*, Pi.*O.*9.30, *I.*8(7).37, *Pae.*4.43; Ποσειδάνιος τ. B.*Fr.*6; *trident*, *leister*, for spearing fish, Pl.*Sph.*220c, Epicr.7, Arist.*Fr.*338, Thphr.*Fr.*178, *Inscr.Délos* 1408*D*8 (ii B.C.), cf. *AP*11.126. 2. τ. πλάγιος, of the letter E, Agatho 4.4, Theodect.6.5.

**τριοειδής**, ές, *triple in form*, τὸ μεσότητι προσκεχρημένον τ. Pythag. ap.Porph.*VP*51.

**τρίοζος** [ῐ], ον, *with three branches* or *boughs*, Thphr.*HP*1.1.8, al.

**τριοῖσι**, v. τρεῖς.

**τρῐ-ολύμπιος**, ον, *consisting of three Olympian goddesses*, ἅρμα, of the goddesses judged by Paris (cf. τρίπωλος), S.*Fr*.511 (lyr.). **-ονία**, ἡ, *team of three donkeys*, *BGU*15 ii 13 (ii A.D.), *PFlor*.2.205,211 (iii A.D.).

**τριοπηλίς**· δέσμη σκορόδων, Hsch. (v. τρόπαλις).

**Τριόπιον**, τό, a headland of Caria, Hdt.1.174, Th.8.35; on which was a temple consecrated to the Dorian worship of Apollo, τὸ **Τριοπικὸν** ἱρόν, ὁ **Τριόπιος** Ἀπόλλων, Hdt.1.144.

**τριοπίς**, v. τριοττίς. II. = ὀρνεόν τι, Phot. (s. v. l.); ζῷον ὅμοιον ἀκρίδι, Hsch.

**τρῐ-όργυιος**, ον, f. l. for τριώρυγος (q. v.). **-όρχης**, ου, ὁ, *with three testicles*: metaph., *very lecherous*, Timae.145. II. a kind of hawk, perh. *buzzard*, *Buteo vulgaris*, Ar.*Av*.1181, cf. Arist.*HA* 592$^b$3, 609$^a$24, 620$^a$17, Thphr.*HP*9.8.7; τριόρχας αἰετούς Lyc.148; παῖδες τ. (with pun on ὀρχέομαι) Ar.*V*.1534 cod. B (-οις codd. RV) (lyr.); v. τρίορχος. III. = κενταυρίς I, Plin.*HN*25.69 (where *triorchis*, mistranslating Thphr. l. c.). 2. = σεραπιάς, Aët.15.13, Paul. Aeg.4.25. **-ορχος**, ὁ, = τριόρχης II, Semon.9, Ar.*Av*.1206, *Com. Adesp*.592; gloss on μέρμνης, Hsch.; cf. μερμνάδαι· οἱ τ. παρὰ Λυδοῖς, Andron ap.*Gloss.Oxy*.1802.46. II. v. l. for τριόρχης in Ar.*V*. 1534 (lyr.).

**τριοτό**, a sound imitative of a bird's voice, Ar.*Av*.243 (lyr.).

**τριοττίς**, ίδος, ἡ, necklace with *three* pendants like *eyes* (cf. τρίγληνος), Hdn.Gr.1.104, Eust.976.36; Dim. **τριόττιον**, τό, ibid.:— a form **τριόττης**, ὁ, is also cited in Phot. and *EM*766.33; and **τριοπίς** or **τρίοπις** by Poll.5.98, Sch.BT Il.14.183, Hsch.

*✻* **τρῐούγκιον**, τό, *a weight of three unciae*, *IGRom*.1.667 (Tomi, written τρειουνκιν), *Dacia* 3/4.607 (ibid., τριουνκιν); = *quadrans*, *Gloss*.

**τριούμβουρα** καπιτᾶλιν, = *triumvirum capitalem*, *Ephes*.3 No.35 p.123.

**τρῐ-οῦχος**, ον, *containing three* or *the* τριάς, μονάς Procl.ap.Lyd. *Mens*.2.6, cf. Dam.*Pr*.117. **-όφθαλμος**, ον, *three-eyed*, Orac.ap. Apollod.2.8.3, Plu.2.520c, etc. 2. ὁ τ., name of a precious stone, Plin.*HN*37.186.

**τριπαγισμός**, ὁ, perh. *page of three columns*, Tz.*H*.9.291.

**τριπαια**, v. τροπαία. **τριπαιδία**, v. sq.

**τρί-παις** [ῐ], παιδος, ὁ, ἡ, *having three children*, Plu.*Num*.10; τιμὰς διώκει τρίπαιδας, = Lat. *jus trium liberorum* (τριπαιδίας cj. Doehner), Id.2.493e. **-πᾰλαι**, Adv. *long long ago*, Ar.*Eq*.1153, Luc. *Lex*.2; cf. τετράπαλαι. **-πάλαιος** [ᾰ], α, ον, *very old*, Phryn.*PS* p.111 B.; cf. τριπάχυιος. **-πᾰλαιστιαῖος**, α, ον, = sq., Ath.Mech. 23.3. **-πάλαστος** [πᾰ], ον, *three hands broad, long*, etc., Hdt.1.50 (with v. l. -πάλαιστα), *IG*1$^2$.373.10, 2$^2$.1672.156, *Inscr.Délos* 1432 *Bb* ii 22, al. (ii B.C.); **τριπάλαιστος** Heliod.ap.Orib.48.57.1. **-παλτος**, ον, (πάλλω) *thrice-brandished*: metaph., *threefold, manifold*, A.*Th*. 990 (lyr., dub. l.). **-πᾰνάγορσις**, ιος, ἁ, perh. *three-day festival*, *IG*5(2).3.8 (Tegea, iv B.C.). **-πάνουργος** [ᾰ], ον, *triply base, an arch-rogue*, Ἔρως *AP*12.57 (Mel.). **-παππος**, ὁ, *ancestor in the sixth generation*, Lat. *tritavus*, *Gloss*. **-πάρθενος**, ον, *consisting of three virgins*, ζεῦγος E.*Fr*.357. **-πάροδος**, ον, *with triple entrance*, ναῦς Moschio ap.Ath.5.207c. **-πατρος**, ον, = sq. 1, *with three fathers*, Lyc.328. **-πάτωρ** [ᾰ], ορος, ὁ, ἡ, *having three fathers*, name of Tritogeneia, *AP*15.25.26 (Besant.); of Orion, Nonn.*D*.13. 99. **II. τριπάτορες**, οἱ, = πρόπαπποι or οἱ πρῶτοι ἀρχηγέται, *AB* 307. **-πάχυιος** [ᾰ], ον, (παχύς) *thrice-fattened, thrice-gorged*, epith. of the δαίμων of the Atridae (perh. in allusion to the *three* visitations mentioned in A.*Ch*.1065–74), *Ag*.1476 (lyr.):—the word is doubtful; Bamberger proposed τριπάχυντον, referring to *Th*.771; Blomf. τριπάλαιον; Bamberger (olim) τριπαλαιστήν. *✻* **-πεδος**, ον, (πούς) *three feet long*, διάμετρος Plb.6.22.2; θριγκοί *IG*7.3073.76 (Lebad., ii B.C.). **-πέδων**, ωνος, ὁ, ἡ, (πέδη) *a slave who has been often in fetters*, Ar.Byz ap.Hdn.*Epim*.289, Eust.725.30, 1542.49. **-πεζαν**· τὴν τράπεζαν, Βοιωτοί, Hsch. (v. τράπεζα fin.). **-πέμπελος**, ον, *childish from age*, Plu.2.1071c: cf. πέμπελος. **-πενθημῐμερής**, ές, *consisting of three* πενθημιμερῆ, Heph.15.12. **-πέρῠσιν**, Adv. *years ago*, a rather vulgar word acc. to Poll.6.165. **-πέτηλος**, ον, *three-leafed*, or perh. *three-branched*, of Hermes' wand, *h.Merc*. 530. II. Subst. **τριπέτηλον**, τό, = τρίφυλλον, Call.*Dian*.165, Nic. *Th*.522. *✻* **-πετής**, ές, (πετάννυμι) *triply spread, threefold*, νέκταρ v. l. in Id.*Al*.347 (τριέτει cod. Π). **-πηδος**, ὁ, or **-πηδον**, τό, *trot* of a horse, *Hippiatr*.34. **-πηχυς**, υ, gen. εος, *three cubits long* or *tall*, ὕπερον τρίπηχυν Hes.*Op*.423; εἴδωλον τρίπηχυ Hdt.1.51; παλλάδιον τρίπηχυ Apollod.3.12.3; ῥῖνα τρίπηχυν *AP*11.267; κροκόδιλοι ὅσον τε τριπήχεες Hdt.4.192; κλῳῷ τριπήχει E.*Cyc*.235; τόξα τριπήχη X.*An*.4.2.28; καταπάλτας τριπήχεις *IG*2$^2$.1467.53, Plb.5. 88.7; ῥάβδους τριπήχεις Dsc.1.100: metaph., ἔπη τριπήχη Crates Com. 19 (ἐπεὶ codd.Ath.):—also **τριπήχης**, ες, Hdn.Gr.1.82. **-πῐθήκῐνος**, η, ον, *thrice* or *thoroughly apish*, ῥύγχος *AP*11.196 (Lucill.). **-πλᾰνής**, ές, *wandered through by three*, ποδηγία, of the three Gorgons, Lyc.846. **-πλᾰνήτης**, ου, ὁ, in Dor. form **τριπλανάτας**, *much-wandering*, ὁ τ. ἐστὶ Λαρτίου γόνος *IG*9(1).880 (Corc.). **-πλαξ**, ᾰκος, ὁ, ἡ, *triple, threefold*, ἄντυξ Il.18.480; cf. δίπλαξ.

**τριπλᾰσῐ-άζω**, *to triple, take three times*, Apollod.2.4.8, Plu.2. 1028b, Dam.*Pr*.98:—Pass., Plu.*Arist*.24:—hence **-ασμός**, ὁ, *a tripling*, Id.2.1028c (pl.). **-επιδῐμερής**, ές, **-επίπεμπτος**, **-επιτέταρτος**, **-επιτετρᾰμερής**, **-επιτρῐμερής**, **-επίτρῐτος**, **-εφήμῐσυς**, $3\frac{2}{3}$, $3\frac{1}{5}$, $3\frac{1}{4}$, $3\frac{4}{5}$, $3\frac{3}{4}$, $3\frac{1}{3}$, $3\frac{1}{2}$ *times as great*—all in Nicom.*Ar*.1.22,23 (-επίτριτος Theo Sm.p.79 H.); **-εφέβδομος**, $3\frac{1}{7}$ *times as great*, c. gen., Simp. *in Cael*.413.31. **-ος**, α, ον, *thrice as many, thrice as much, thrice as great as*, c. gen., ὄρνις τ. Κλεωνύμου Ar.*Ach*.88, etc.; τριπλασίᾳ τῆς πρώτης ζημίας Pl.*Lg*.756d; τριπλασίοις αὐτῶν Id.*R*.422c; τριπλασίας τιμῆς ἢ πρότερον D.42.31: abs., τ. δύναμιν εἶχε (sc. τῆς προτέρας) X.*An*.7.4.21; τ. διαστήματα Pl.*Ti*.36a; τριπλάσιον, opp. τριτημόριον, Arist.*Metaph*.1020$^b$27. 2. neut. as Adv., τριπλάσιον κεκράξομαί σου *thrice as much as* you, Ar.*Eq*.285 (lyr.), cf. 718:— regul. Adv. -ίως Sch.B Il.21.80, v. l. in Lxx *Si*.43.4. **-ότης**, ητος, ἡ, *triplicity*, Nicom.*Ar*.2.5. **-ων**, ον, gen. ονος, = τριπλάσιος Archim.*Circ*.3, al., Arr.*Tact*.16.12, Procl.*Hyp*.4.101; λόγος Ph.1.22.

**τρί-πλεθρος**, ον, *three* πλέθρα *wide*, Pl.*Criti*.115d, X.*An*.5.6. 9, *Inscr.Cret*.1.v 21 (Arcades, ii B.C.). **-πλεκής**, ές, *thrice-plaited, threefold*, τ. εἶναι ἡμῶν τὸ σῶμα Sor.2.4; *three-dimensional* (?), σχῆμα Procl.*Theol.Plat*.5.37. *✻* **-πλευρος**, ον, *three-sided*, Str.5.1.2; Astrol., *trine*, of aspect, Max.52,447, *Cat.Cod.Astr*.1.146; *facing three ways*, of a column on the march, Arr.*Tact*.28.4,5, Ael.*Tact*. 36.4,5. II. **τρίπλευρα**, τά, perh. part of a victim, *SIG*982.22 (Pergam., ii B.C.).

**τριπλῆ**, v. τριπλόος.

**τριπληγόνος**, ον, *producing a triplet*, dub. l. in Dam.*Pr*.123$^{bis}$.

**τριπλόη**, ἡ, *triplicity*, Dam.*Pr*.117.

**τριπλοκ-ία**, ἡ, *triplicity, threefold division*, of ἀγγεῖα into νεῦρα φλέβες ἀρτηρίαι, Gal.14.697 (prob. Erasistr.). **-ος**, ον, = *triplex*, *Gloss*.

*✻* **τριπλ-όος**, η, ον, contr. **-λοῦς**, ῆ, οῦν, *triple, threefold*, καλλίνικος ὁ τ., because this hymn of victory was *thrice repeated*, Pi.*O*.9.2; ἐν τ. ἁμαξιτοῖς, = ἐν τριόδῳ, S.*OT*716; τ. ζεῦγος, of persons, E.*Fr*.773. 61 (anap.); ὄνομα τ. *compounded of three*, Arist.*Po*.1457$^a$34; τριπλοῦν ἀποτινέτω *PRev.Laws* 19.14 (iii B.C.); εἰσπράξαντα τριπλῆν τὴν πρᾶξιν *PMich.Zen*.71.7 (iii B.C.); χόριον τ. Sor.1.58; Att. neut. pl. τριπλᾶ A.*Pers*.1033 (lyr.), *Ch*.792 (lyr.), etc. Adv. **-πλῶς** Procl. *in Prm*.p.656 S.; gloss on τριχθά, Hdn.*Epim*.134: but dat. fem. τριπλῇ is used as Adv. in Il.1.128, Luc.*Pseudol*.32. **-όω**, *multiply by three, triple*, Sm.*Ec*.4.12, Hdn.Gr.1.448. **-ωσις**, εως, ἡ, *tripling*, *PLeid.X*.6, *PHolm*.2.15.

**τρῐποδ-ᾰβάκιον** [ᾰκ], τό, (ἄβαξ) *three-legged stand*, κάδον ἐπὶ -ου καθηλωμένον *Inscr.Délos* 1417 *A* ii 153 (ii B.C.). **-ειος**, Ion. **-ήϊος**, ον, *three-footed*, ἕδρη Call.*Del*.90: poet. fem. **τρῐποδηΐς**, ΐδος, Nonn. *D*.9.257. II. τριπόδειον, τό, part of a tripod, different from the πόδες, *Inscr.Délos* 1449 *A ab* ii 138. **-ης**, ου, ὁ, ἡ, *three feet long*, ὅλμον τριπόδην Hes.*Op*.423; βαθύτερον τριπόδου X.*Oec*.19.3.

**τρῐποδη-φορέω**, *bring a tripod, offer it as a sign of victory*, esp. in dramatic contests, Str.9.2.4:—also **τριποδοφορέω**, Sch.Pi.*P*.11. 5. **-φορικός**, ή, όν, *accompanying the carrying of a tripod in procession*, μέλος Poll.4.53, Procl.*Chr*.ap.Phot.*Bibl*.p.321 B. **-φόρος**, ον, *stamped with the device of a tripod*, δραχμή *Inscr.Délos* 1439 *A bc* ii 6, 1450.99 (ii B.C.).

**τρῐποδ-ία**, ἡ, *metrical phrase of three feet*, Aristid.Quint.1.17, Sch. Ar.*Nu*.651. **-ίζω**, = Lat. *tripedo*, *Gloss*. (cf. *tripedio* = χορεύω ib.; but perh. = *trot*, cf. τρίπηδος). **-ιον**, τό, Dim. of τρίπους, Antiph. 249, Men.250, *CIG*3071 (Teos), *PTeb*.793 vi 8 (ii B.C.), Phld.*Acad. Ind*.p.44 M.; τ. Δελφικόν *Inscr.Délos* 442 *B* 39 (ii B.C.):—so **τρῐπο-**
*✻* **δίσκος**, ὁ, *IG*1$^2$.658, 2$^2$.47.7, 7.303.65 (Oropus), etc.; and **τριποδίσκιον**, τό, Suid. s. v. ἀνθράκιον. II. = λωτὸς ἥμερος, Ps.-Dsc.4.110. **-ιος**, ον, *three-footed*, ἡμικάδια *PCair.Zen*.14(*a*).5 (iii B.C.).

**τρῐποδοειδής**, ές, *tripod-shaped*, Eust.1312.28.

**τρῐ-πόθητος**, Dor. **-ᾱτος** (s. v. l.), ον, *thrice* (i. e. *much*) *longed for*, ὦ τριπόθατε Bion 1.58, cf. Mosch.3.51; εἶαρ τ. Bion *Fr*.15.15; τ. Ἄδωνις Hymn.ap.Hippol.*Haer*.5.9; also in late Prose, as Luc.*Hist.Conscr*. 31, etc. **-ποκος**, ον, *with triple* (i. e. *thick*) *wool*, Dicaearch.2. 8. **-πολία**, ἡ, *committee representing three cities*, *Berl.Sitzb*.1927. 170 (Cyrene). **-πόλιον**, τό, *sea-starwort*, *Aster Tripolium*, Thphr.*HP* 9.19.2 (citing Hes. and Musae.), Dsc.4.132. **-πολις**, εως, Ion. ιος, ὁ, ἡ, *with three cities*, νᾶσος, of Rhodes, Pi.*O*.7.18, cf. Scyl.99, al. 2. Τρίπολις, ἡ, *league of three cities*, as in Achaea, Plb.4.81.7, etc.; in Arcadia, Paus.8.27.4; in Phoenicia, D.S.16.41, etc. II. a kind of cake, Hsch. **-πόλιστος**, ον, *thrice-told*, τριπόλιστον οἶτον, of Oedipus, S.*Ant*.858 (lyr.). (From *πολίζω = πολέω; cf. ἀναπολίζω = ἀναπολέω). **-πολῑτικός**, ὁ, title of a work of Dicaearchus, Cic.*Att*. 13.32.2, Ath.4.141a. **-πολῖτις**, ιδος, ἡ, fem. Adj. = τρίπολις, Πελαγονία, in Thessaly, Str.7.7.9. **-πολος**, ον, *thrice turned up, thrice ploughed*, νειός Il.18.542, Od.5.127, Hes.*Th*.971; ἴκελον τὸ ξύμπαν τριπόλῳ νειῷ (τριποδονίῳ codd.), of an elephant's skin, Aret. *SD*2.13. **-πόνητος** ἔρις, fruit of *threefold* rivalry in *toil*, *AP* 6.286 (Leon.). **-πορθος**, ον, *thrice-sacked*, Τευκρίς ib.15.26.18 (Dosiad.). **-πορνεία**, ἡ, *threefold whoredom*, by descent, Antiph. Jun.ap.Ath.13.587b. **-πορνος**, ον, *a whore in the third degree*, Theopomp.Hist.*Fr*.244.

**τρίπος** [ῐ], ὁ, poet. for sq., nom. sg., Il.22.164, Hes.*Sc*.312, *IG*4. 801 (Troezen, vi B.C.) (v. τρίπους fin.); acc. τρίπον *AP*3.6 (Inscr. Cyzic.); neut. τρίπον ib.14.64; gen. τρίπου *EM*20.18.

*✻* **τρίπους** [ῐ], ποδος, ὁ, ἡ, πουν, τό, *three-footed*, *of* or *with three feet*: and so, I. *measuring three feet*, τ. τὸ εὖρος Hdt.3.60; τ. πλάτος *IG*1$^2$.372.14, al.; ὅρους..μὴ ἔλαττον ἢ τρίποδας ib.2$^2$.2492.24; τ. [γραμμή] Pl.*Men*.83e; ἡ τ. [δύναμις] *the side of a square three feet in area*, Id.*Tht*.147d. II. *going on three feet*, prov. of an old man who leans on a staff, τρίποδι βροτῷ Hes.*Op*.533 (but τρίποδι βροτοὶ ἶσοι is prob. cj.); τρίποδας ὁδοὺς στείχει A.*Ag*.80 (anap.); cf. τριτοβάμων, and see the Sphinx's riddle in *AP*14.64. III. of tables,

vessels, etc., *three-legged*, τ. λέβης A.*Fr.*1; τράπεζα Ar.*Fr.*530; ὑπόβασις Semus 15:—but mostly IV. as Subst., τρίπους, ὁ, 1. *tripod*, i.e. *three-legged cauldron*, Il.18.344, Od.8.434, etc.; τ. ἐμπυριβήτης Il.23.702; ὑψίβατος τ. ἀμφίπυρος S.*Aj.*1405 (anap.); ἄπυροι τ. *tripods* untouched by fire, i.e. new, unused, Il.9.122, cf. Paus.4.32.1; used as κρατῆρες, Semus l.c., Phylarch.44J.; given as prizes, Il.11.700, 23.264, al.; as gifts of honour, 8.290, Od.13.13; in Crete used as currency, *GDI*4969.130; placed as votive gifts in temples, esp. in that of Apollo at Delphi, Th.1.132, *SIG*697*L*3 (Delph., ii B.C.), etc.; ἡ τοῦ τ. ἀνάθεσις Lys.21.2; these were then called τ. ἀναθηματικοί, Δελφικοί, Apollon.*Lex.*; a street at Athens adorned with these gifts was called οἱ Τρίποδες, Paus.1.20.1; or they were preserved in private houses, Pi.*I.*1.19; they were mostly of bronze, Paus.4.12.8, but sts. of precious metals, even of gold, Pi.*P.*11.4, Hdt.9.81, Ar.*Pl.*9, Paus.10.13.9; sts. of wood, ξύλινοι τ. Id.4.12.8; from a *tripod* the Delphic Priestess delivered her oracles, E.*Ion*91 (anap.), *Or.*164 (lyr.), Orac.ap.Ar.*Eq.*1016, etc.: metaph., ὁπόταν ἐν τῷ τ. τῆς Μούσης καθίζηται [ὁ ποιητής] Pl.*Lg.*719c: prov., ἐκ τρίποδος λέγειν, i.e. authoritatively, Ath.2.37f; τὰ ἀπὸ τ., τὰ ἐκ τ., Zen.6.3, Diogenian.8.21, cf. Plu.*Dem.*29. b. Τρίπους, name of a work by Nausiphanes, D.L.10.14; of a work by Glaucias the Empiric, Gal.*Subf.Emp.*p.63 B. 2. as a landmark, *SIG*826*E* 13,23 (Delph., ii B.C.), 827*D*15 (ibid., ii A.D.). 3. *three-legged table*, X.*An.*7.3.21, Plu.*Cleom.*13; κύκλος τρίποδος the circular top of.., Artem.5.20, cf. 1.74. 4. a kind of *ear-ring*, Poll.5.97. 5. a musical instrument, described by Artemo ap.Ath.14.637b. (The oldest nom. of stem τριποδ- is prob. τρίπος (q.v.), which comes from τριποδ-ς but was later regarded as an *o*-stem.)

**τρί-πρᾱτος**, ον, *thrice sold*, *Com.Adesp.*884, cf. Ph.2.47. **-πρόσωπος**, ον, *three-faced*, Chariclid.1, Cleom.2.5.

**τριπτέον**, (τρίβω) *one must rub* or *grind*, Gal.6.229, *Gp.*5.51.2.

**τρίπτερος**, ον, *having three wings*, ἀρχή Orac.ap.Procl. *in Cra.* p.96 P.

**τριπ-τήρ**, ῆρος, ὁ, (τρίβω) *pestle*, καρπὸν..λεαίνειν τριπτῆρι Nic. *Th.*95, cf. *Fr.*70.15; *mortar* for grinding ψιμύθιον, Thphr.*Lap.*56; *board under the screw of a wine-* or *oil-press*, Nic.*Al.*494, cf. *AB* 308. II. *vat into which wine* or *oil runs after being pressed out*, Is.*Fr.*24, cf. Poll.7.151; τ. δικῶν (παρὰ προσδοκίαν for ἐλαῶν), of a συκοφάντης treated as an ἄγγος, Ar.*Ach.*937. 2. *horse-trough*, τριπτῆρες τέτταρες τὰ ζεύγη ποτίζειν ἐν τῇ ὁδῷ *IG*2².1673.21. 3. = ἀκόνη, *AB*308. **-τήριον**, τό, *rubbing tool*, *Gloss.* (pl.). **-της**, ου, ὁ, *bath-rubber, shampooer*, Plu.*Alex.*40.

**Τριπτόλεμος**, ὁ, *Triptolemus*, an Eleusinian, who spread the worship of Demeter, *h.Cer.*153, etc.

**τριπτός**, ή, όν, (τρίβω) *rubbed* or *pounded*, ἡ ξηρὴ τ. (sc. μᾶζα) Hp.*Vict.*2.40; so τριπτή, Gal.6.510, Poll.6.76.

**τρίπτρον**, τό, = τριπτήριον, Tz. ad Lyc.874 (pl.).

**τριπτύς**, v. τριττύς.

**τρί-πτῠχος**, ον, (πτύσσω) *consisting of three layers, threefold*, τρυφάλεια Il.11.353; of surgical dressings, Gal.14.793, 18(2).822; πτυγματίῳ τριπτύχῳ Heliod.ap.Orib.44.10.8; metaph., θρῆνοι E. *Ph.*1635: sts. simply = τρεῖς, Id.*Or.*1513 (troch.), *HF*474, Lyc. 573. **-πτωτος**, ον, *with three case-forms*, Choerob. *in Theod.*1. 335 H., Priscian *Inst.*5.14.76, etc. **-πῡλιος**, v. τριοδῖτις. **-πῡλοειδής**, ές, *like a* τρίπυλον, Ael.*Tact.*31.4. **-πῡλον**, τό, *triple gate*, *IGRom.*4.847 (Laodicea ad Lycum), 1209 (Thyatira), *Milet.*1 (7) No.261. **-πυργος**, ον, *with three towers*, Orac.Sib. in *EM*147. 38. **-πωλος**, ον, *of* or *with three horses*, ἅρματα D.H.7.73; τ. ἅρμα δαιμόνων..καλλιζυγές, of the three goddesses on Mount Ida, E.*Andr.*277 (lyr.). **-ρριζος**, ον, *with three roots*, ὀδόντες Gal.2. 753. **-ρρυθμος**, ον, *of three feet*, κῶλα, applied to paeonic rhythm, Sch.Ar.*Ach.*665, *Pax* 345. **-ρρῡμος**, ον, *with three poles*, i.e. *with four horses abreast*, τέλη A.*Pers.*47 (anap.).

**τρίς**, Adv. of τρεῖς (q.v.), *thrice, three times*, τ. τόσσα *thrice* as much or many, Il.1.213, cf. 5.136; δὶς καὶ τ. Thgn.633, S.*Aj.*433, etc.; δὶς ἢ τ. Ar.*Pax* 1181 (troch.); τ. τετράκι τε Pi.*N.*7.104; ἐς τ. *thrice*, Id. *O.*2.68, Hdt.1.86, 5.105, *GDI* iv p.884 (Erythrae, iv B.C.), Theoc. 1.25, 2.43; ἐπὶ τρὶς *thrice*, *Act.Ap.*10.16, 11.10, Dsc.*Eup.*2.19; freq. used merely to intensify the notion, τ. λελουμένη Eub.102, etc.; esp. in compds., such as τρισάθλιος, τρίσμακαρ, etc., cf. τρι-, τριάζω, τρικυμία; but such words may sts. be written divisim, τρὶς ἄθλιος, etc.: prov., τ. ἓξ βαλεῖν throw *thrice* six (the highest throw, there being three dice), A.*Ag.*33, cf. Pl.*Lg.*968e; τρὶς ἓξ νικητήριος βόλος *App. Prov.*4.99; ἢ τ. ἓξ ἢ τρεῖς κύβοι Pherecr.124. [ῐ: in Hes.*Op.*173 long by position before (ϝ)έτεος.] (I.-E. *tris*, cf. Skt. *tris*, Lat. *ter.*)

**τρῐσ-άθλιος**, α, ον, *thrice-unhappy*, S.*OC*372, Ar.*Pax*242, Men. *Pk.*150, *Mis.*40, *Fr.*302, etc.: also in late Prose, as Luc.*Gall.*24, Theo Sm.p.100 H. **-άλαστος** [ᾰλ], ον, *thrice-accursed*, *AP*12.137 (Mel.), *APl.*4.265. **-ᾰλῑτήριος**, ον, *thrice-sinful*, Lxx 2*Ma.*8.34, *Es.*8.13:—also **-ἄλιτρος** [ᾰ], ον, Tz.*H.*13 No.479 tit. **-ἄλῡπος**, ον, *quite harmless*, Thphr.*HP*2.4.2.

**τρί-σᾱμος**, ον, Dor. for τρίσημος.

**τρῐσ-άνθρωπος**, ὁ, *thrice a man*, used by Diogenes cynically for τρισάθλιος, D.L.6.47. **-άποτμος**, ον, = τρισάθλιος, *AP*5.229 (Paul.Sil.). **-ᾰρειοπᾰγίτης** [ῑτ], ου, ὁ, *an Areopagite thrice over*, i.e. *a stern and rigid judge*, Cic.*Att.*4.15.4. **-ᾰριθμος** [ᾰρ], ον, *thrice numbered*, Orac.ap.Luc.*Alex.*11. **-ᾰριστεύς**, έως, ὁ, *thrice-conqueror*, Hermog.*Stat.*1, al. **-άσμενος**, η, ον, *thrice-pleased, most willing*, X.*An.*3.2.24.

**τρῐσατ]ῠχής**, ές, *thrice-luckless*, prob. in Men.*Kol.*31.

**τρῐσ-άωρος** [ᾰ], ον, *most untimely dead*, *AP*7.527 (Theodorid.). **-βδέλῠρος**, ον, *thrice-abominable*, Suid. s.v. Διονυσίων σκωμμάτων. **-δείλαιος**, ον, = τρισάθλιος, *AP*7.737. **-δύστηνος**, ον, = foreg., ib.9.574. **-εινάς** (sc. ἡμέρα), άδος, ἡ, *the thrice-ninth* (= 27th) *day* in a month, Hes.*Op.*814.

✻**τρῐ-σέληνος**, ον, *of three moons* or *nights*, epith. of Heracles (cf. τριέσπερος), *AP*9.441 (Pall.), Nonn.*D.*7.126; νύξ *APl.*4.102. 2. πλάτος τ. *of three moons* in breadth, of the earth's shadow, Plu.2.923b.

**τρῐσ-έλικτος**, ον, = τριέλικτος, Man.1.197, Nonn.*D.*7.128. **-εξάγιστος** [ᾰ], ον, *thrice-accursed*, Tz.*H.*10.71. **-εξώλης**, ου, ὁ, *thrice-accursed*, strengthd. for ἐξώλης, Eust.725.29. **-έπαρχος**, ὁ, *thrice an* ἔπαρχος, i.e. *Praefectus Urbis*, *AP*9.697. **-επιβάρβᾰρος**, ον, *thrice-barbarous*, Tz.*H.*10.72. **-ευδαίμων**, ον, gen. ονος, *thrice-happy*, B.3.10, Luc.*Sacr.*2, *Merc.Cond.*3, etc. **-εφθος**, ον, *thrice-boiled*, Orib.3.13.2, Alex.Trall.7.1, 9.2. **-έχθιστος**, ον, *thrice-detested*, Phryn.*PS*p.112 B. **-έωλος**, ον, strengthd. for ἕωλος, *very stale*, Ael.*NA*17.44. **-ήμερος**, ον, *tertian*, of a fever, prob. in *Arch.Pap.*1.425 (τρισοιμ- Pap.); τρισημεραι = *triduum* is f.l. for τρεῖς ἡμέραι in *Gloss.*

**τρί-σημος** [ῐ], ον, in Music and Prosody, = τρίχρονος, Aristox. *Rhyth.*2.10, Aristid.Quint.1.14. II. Dor. **Τρίσᾱμος**, epith. of the τριάς, Nicom.ap.Phot.*Bibl.*p.144 B.

**τρισ-καίδεκα** and compds., v. τρεισκαίδεκα and compds.

**τρισκαιδεκάκις** [ᾰ], Adv. *thirteen times*, Hero *Mens.*28.1, Gal.7.512.

✻**τρισκᾰκοδαίμων**, ον, gen. ονος, *thrice-unlucky*, Ar.*Ach.*1024, *Ra.* 19, Aeschin.1.59, Men.404.1: shd. perh. be written divisim, esp. in view of Ar.*Pl.*851, τρὶς κακοδαίμων καὶ τετράκις.

**τρί-σκαλμος**, ον, *with three tholepins*, σκάφη *PCair.Zen.*25.5 (iii B.C.); πλοῖον οὐδὲν αὐτοῖς τρισκάλμου μεῖζον ἀπέλιπε Plu.*Aem.*6; but τ. νᾶες are = τριήρεις, A.*Pers.*679 (lyr.), cf. 1074 (lyr.).

**τρισ-κατάπτυστος**, ον, *thrice-abominable*, Poll.6.165. **-κατάρᾱτος** [ᾰρ], ον, *thrice-accursed*, D.25.82, Men.71, *Epit.*540. **-κεκορημένος**, Anacr.5 ap.Eust.1542.47; sed leg. τρὶς κεκ., v. κορέω (A) II.

**τρι-σκελής**, ές, *three-legged*, τράπεζα Cratin.301; ξόανον Theoc.*Ep.* 4.3; βάσις Hero *Bel.*88.4; κτείς τ., name of a bandage, Sor.*Fasc.* 45. **-σκελίς**, ίδος, ἡ, *three-pronged fork*, Aq.1 *Ki.*13.21:—Dim. **-σκελίδιον**, *small tripod*, *POxy.*1066.13 (iii A.D.).

**τρισ-κοπάνιστος** [ᾰ], ον, *thrice-struck* or *-stamped*, ἄρτος τ. *thrice-kneaded*, i.e. *fine*, bread, Batr.35. **-λοπος**, ον, *thrice-peeled*, of trees *which lose their bark thrice a year*, Thphr.*HP*3.5.1.

**τρίσμα**, ατος, τό, = τριγμός, *creaking* of olive plants rubbing together, Sch.Aristid.3 p.78 Dind.

**τρίσ-μᾰκαρ**, ᾰρος, ὁ, ἡ, strengthd. for μάκαρ, *thrice-blest*, Od.6.154, 155, Ar.*Pax*1332, *AP*5.254.17 (Paul.Sil.), etc.:—the divided form τρὶς μάκαρ is supported by the phrase τρὶς μάκαρες καὶ τετράκις in Od.5.306 (τρισμάκαρες codd.), cf. Hes.*Fr.*81.7 and τρισμακάριστος. **-μᾰκάριος** [ᾰρ], α, ον, = foreg., Ar.*Ach.*400, Philem.93.1; χελῶναι τρισμακάριαι τοῦ τέγους Ar.*V.*1293, cf. *Nu.*166. **-μᾰκάριστος** [ᾰρ], η, ον, = τρίσμακαρ, Luc.*Vit.Auct.*12: Sup. -τότατος *MAMA*1.267 (near Laodicea Combusta). **-μᾰκάρῑτης** [ῑ], ου, ὁ, epith. of Pythagoras, *the thrice-dying one*, as a pun on τρίσμακαρ, Antiph.168.8. **-μάκᾰρος**, ον, = τρίσμακαρ, *IG*14.2258 (τρὶς μάκαρος is prob.). **-μεγας**, ὁ, = τρισμέγιστος, Ἑρμῆς *PFlor.*50.97 (iii A.D.), *PMag.Lond.*121.551; of Plato, Zos.Alch. p.230 B. **-μέγιστος**, η, ον, *thrice-greatest*, title of the Egyptian Hermes (Thoth), *CPHerm.*125 ii 8 (iii A.D.), *OGI*716 (Achmim, iii A.D.), Ph.Bybl.ap.Eus.*PE*1.10, *Corp.Herm.* passim. (The Egyptian title is translated μέγιστος καὶ μ. καὶ μ. in Wilcken *Chr.*109.6 (iii B.C.).)

**τρισμός**, v. τριγμός.

**τρισμύριοι** [ῡ], αι, α, *thrice ten thousand*, 30,000, Hdt.2.163, 7.184, Ar.*Av.*1179, X.*An.*7.8.[26], etc.:—in sg. with a collective Subst., ἵππος τρισμυρία *thirty thousand* horse, A.*Pers.*315.

**τρισμῡριό-πᾰλαι**, Adv. *thirty-thousand-times long-ago*, Ar.*Eq.* 1156; cf. τρίπαλαι, τετράπαλαι. **-πλᾰσίων**, ον, gen. ονος, *thirty-thousand-fold*, Archim.*Aren.*2.1.

**τρισ-νέᾱτος**, η, ον, dub. in Cratin.134; cf. νεάτη, παρανήτη. **-οιζυρός**, ά, όν, *thrice-wretched*, Archil.129, Cerc.17.13.—In *EM*279.17, *Et.Gud.*585.14, **τρισόζυος** is cited from A.(*Fr.*445), prob. f.l. for τρισσόζωος (cf. τρισόζωος in cod. M of *EM*) or τρισσόζοος. **-όλβιος**, ον, *thrice happy* or *fortunate*, S.*Fr.*837, Ar.*Ec.*1129, Philem.93.1, Luc. *Nigr.*1; divisim, τρὶς δ' ὄλβια κύματα *AP*12.52 (Mel.). **-ολυμπιονίκης** [νῑ], ου, ὁ, *thrice victorious at Olympia*, οἶκος Pi.*O.*13.1; Νέρων Philostr.*VA*5.8.

**τρί-σουφος**, ον, *containing three* σοῦφα (cf. ὀκτασοῦφος), *Sammelb.* 1958 (iii A.D.). **-σοφος**, ον, *thrice*, i.e. *very, wise*, Tz.*H.*5. 177. **-σπαστος**, ον, *drawn threefold*, τ. ὄργανον *a triple* pulley, Orib.49.22.1; so *trispastos*, Vitr.10.2.3; μηχανή Tz.*H.*2.107.

✻**τρισπερίοδος**, ὁ, *thrice a* περιοδονίκης (q.v.), κῆρυξ *Inscr.Olymp.* 243 (iii A.D.).

**τρί-σπερμον**, τό, with or without κατάπλασμα, name of a plaster, Cass.Fel.34, Paul.Aeg.3.43. **-σπῐθᾰμος** [πῐ], ον, *three spans long*, Hes.*Op.*426, X.*Cyn.*9.13.

**τρισπόλιον**· βοτάνη τις, Hsch. (perh. poet. form of τριπόλιον).

**τρίσπονδος**, ον, *thrice-poured*, τ. χοαί a *triple* drink-offering to the dead, of honey, milk, and wine, S.*Ant.*431.

**τρισπῡθιονίκης** [νῑ], ου, ὁ, *winner of three victories in the Pythian games*, *BGU*1074.23 (iii A.D.).

**τρισσ-άκις** [ᾰ], Adv. *thrice*, *AP*5.194 (Mel.), *PHamb.*23.25 (vi

A. D.): **τρισσάκι**, Doroth.84. **-άτιος** [ᾰ], η, ον, poet. for τρισσός (cf. μεσσάτιος), *AP*6.12 (Jul.). **-ᾰχῇ**, Adv. *in three places*, Arist. *Mete.*351ᵃ15. **-εύω**, *do* a thing *thrice* or *for the third time*, Lxx 1*Ki.*20.19,20; cf. τρισσόω.

**τρισσό-ζωος**, or **-ζοος**, ον, *with three lives*, v. τρισοιζυρός. **-θεν**, Adv. *on three sides*, *AP*9.651 (Paul. Sil.). **-κέφᾰλος**, ον, *three-headed*, Orph.*A*.976 [with the penult. long metri gr.].

⊛ **τρισσ-ός**, ή, όν; Att. **τριττός** Pl.*Lg.*782d, etc.; Ion. **τριξός** (q. v.): (τρίς):—*threefold*, Hes.*Fr.*191, E.*Fr.*285.3, etc.; τρισσὸν ζεῦγος τρισσῶν (sed leg. τριῶν) θεῶν Id.*Tr.*924; πρᾶσις τ. γραφεῖσα *POxy.*1208.24 (iii A. D.):—Adv. -ῶς Thphr.ap.D.H.*Lys.*14, Lxx *Pr.*22.20, al., *AP* 12.123. II. in pl., = τρεῖς, Pi.*P.*8.80, S.*OT*164 (lyr.), *OC*479, E.*Hec.*645 (lyr.), Pl.*R.*504a. III. = τρίτος, *IG*12(2).129.8 (Mytil.). IV. τρισσοί, = *shields*, misrendering of Hebr. *šᵉlāṭīm* through confusion with *šālōš* 'three', Lxx 4*Ki.*11.10. V. literal rendering of Hebr. *šālīš* 'measure containing third part (of unknown unit)', Aq.*Is.*40.12. **-όω**, = τρισσεύω, Lxx 3*Ki.*18.34, where ἐτρίσσευσαν (but -ωσαν cod. A) follows.

**τρι-στάδιος** [ᾰ], ον, *measuring three stades*, τὸ πλάτος Pl.*Criti.* 115e, cf. D.H.1.34. **-σταθμος**, ον, *thrice the weight*, Agatharch. 96. **-στάσιος** [ᾰ], ον:—τ. κατὰ τιμὴν πρὸς χρυσίον ὁ μαργαρίτης *worth thrice its weight* in gold, Arr.*Ind.*8.13. **-στάτηρος** [ᾰ], ον, *worth three staters*, χλαμύς Poll.6.165. ⊛ **-στάτης** [ᾰ], ου, ὁ, *one who stands next to the king and queen*, *vizier*, Lxx 4*Ki.*7.2, al., cf. Hsch. **-στεγος**, ον, *of* or *with three stories*, D.H.3.68, Ath.Mech.13.8, *POxy.*99.5 (i A. D.), etc. II. τὸ τ. (sc. οἴκημα) *the third story*, *Act.Ap.*20.9:—also **τριστέγη**, ἡ, Artem.4.46.

**τριστέταρτον**, τό, dub. in *PFlor.*50.57 (iii A. D.), where ἀρούρας τρεῖς τριστέταρτον is prob. an error for ἀ. τρεῖς τέταρτον.

**τρι-στῐχία**, ἡ, *triple row*, Gal.14.771. 2. *union of three verses*, τ. ἰαμβική Sch.Ar.*Ra.*326 (-στοιχ-). ⊛ **-στῐχος**, ον, = τρίστοιχος, κριθαί *three-row* barley, *Placit.*5.10.2. **-στοιχί** [ῐ], Adv. *in three rows*, Il.10.473; **τριστοιχεί**, Hes.*Th.*727, and many codd. of Il. l. c. (perh. rightly). **-στοιχος**, ον, *in three rows*, ὀδόντες Od.12.91, Ctes.ap. Arist.*HA*501ᵃ27; κριθαί Thphr.*HP*8.4.2; *equipped with three rows* (of teeth), χείλεα Opp.*C.*3.413. II. *threefold*, *triple*, μαστός, βόθρος, *AP*9.668.5 (Marian.), Orph.*A*.951; τ. κεφαλαί, of Cerberus, Hermesian.7.12. **-στομος**, ον, *three-edged* or *three-pointed*, αἰχμή *AP*6.167 (Agath.); τ. δόρυ, of the trident, Max.Tyr.10.8; *with three mouths*, Ῥοδανός Str.4.1.8. II. τρίστομον, τό, dub. sens., prob. place-name, in *PTeb.*112.2, al. (ii B. C., cf. ii p.405); σιτολόγοι Τριστόμου *Ostr.*1097 (ii A. D.), cf. *BGU*1072 iii 2 (ii A. D.), etc. ⊛ **-στοος**, ον, *possessing a triple colonnade*, *IGRom.*4.662 (Acmonia). **-στροφος**, ον, *thrice-twisted*, λίνον Meges ap.Orib.44.24.12. 2. *consisting of three strophes*, Sch.Pi.*O.*9.1. **-συλλᾰβέω**, *consist of three syllables*, Hdn.Gr.2.927. **-συλλᾰβία**, ἡ, *compass of three syllables*, οὐχ ὑπερβαίνει τὴν τ. Sch.D.T.p.137 H. **-σύλλᾰβος**, ον, *trisyllabic*, D.H.*Comp.*17, A.D.*Synt.*8.1, Heph.3.2, Luc.*Philops.*35. Adv. -βως A.D.*Pron.*78.23. **-σύνθετος**, ον, *compounded of three elements*, Sch.D Il.24.540.

**τρίσ-φυλλον**, τό, poet. for τρίφυλλον, Nic.*Th.*520.

**τρι-σχημάτιστος** [ᾰ], ον, = sq., *trischematisti dactylici*, series of two dactyls and one spondee *capable of being arranged in three orders*, Sacerd.p.506 K. **-σχημος**, ον, *of triple form*, *An.Ox.*2.307. **-σχῐδής**, ές, *cloven in three*, Xenophon Medicus ap.Orib.45.11.3, Antyll.ap.eund.45.18.22. Adv. -δῶς Dosith.p.412 K.

**τρισ-χῑλιέτης**, ες, *of three thousand years*, Hierocl.*Prov.*p.463 B., Simp. *in Ph.*499.36. ⊛ **-χίλιοι** [χῑ], αι, α, Dor. **-χήλιοι** *Abh.Berl. Akad.*1925(5).25 (Cyrene):—*three thousand*, Il.20.221, Hdt.7.97, etc.: in sg. with collective Subst., ἀσπὶς τρισχιλία Longus 3.1. II. οἱ τ., at Athens, the 3000 nominated by the 30 Tyrants, X.*HG*2.3.18. **-χῑλιοστός**, ή, όν, *three-thousandth*, τ. ἔτει Pl.*Phdr.* 249a.

**τρισχῑλιο-τρισμύριοι** [ῡ], αι, α, *thirty-three thousand*, Tz.*H.*3.67. **-φόρος**, ον, *holding three thousand (measures)*, ὁλκάδες D.H.3.44.

**τρί-σχιστος**, ον, *cloven in three*, Sch.Nic.*Al.*347, *An.Ox.*2.307:— **-σχίστη**, ἡ, gloss on Αἰγυπτία στυπτηρία, Gal.19.71. **-σχοινος**, ον, *three* σχοῖνοι *long* or *broad*, in neut., Str.17.1.31, cf. Plin.*HN*5.85. **-σώμᾰτος**, ον, *three-bodied*, of Geryon, A.*Ag.*870; κύων, of Cerberus, E.*HF*24; τ. ἀλκά, of the Chimaera, Id.*Ion* 204 (lyr.). **-σωμος**, ον, = foreg., *An.Ox.*2.307.

**τρῐτᾰγωνιστ-έω**, *to be a* τριταγωνιστής, D.18.262,265, etc.; τ. τινί *play the third part* to another, Plu.2.840a. **-ής**, οῦ, ὁ, on the stage, *player who took the third part*, name of a play by Antiphanes; applied by D. to Aeschines, 18.129,209.

**τρῐτ-αΐζω**, *have a tertian fever*, Dsc.4.60, Gal.7.466. **-αϊκός**, ή, όν, *belonging to a tertian fever* (τριταῖος πυρετός), *like one*, Dsc.*Eup.* 2.18, al. Adv. -κῶς Aët.12.13. **-αιογενής**, ές, *produced by tertian fever*, ἀλγήματα Hp.*Coac.*120. Adv. -νῶς ib.299. ⊛ **-αῖος**, α, ον, *on the third day*, used with Verbs so as to agree with the subject, τριταῖοι ἐγένοντο ἐν τῇ Ἀττικῇ Hdt.6.120, cf. Hp.*Aph.*4.36, Th.1.61, 3.3, etc.; τ. ἄνεμος *which will blow in three days*, Pi.*N.*7.17; τριταίαν καρύσσουσιν θυσίαν E.*El.*171 (lyr.); τ. ἐκφορά a funeral *three days after* death, Pl.*Lg.*959a; ἐσβεβληκὼς..τ. ἐς Μηλιέας *three days before*, Hdt.7.196, cf. Plb.15.33.11. II. *three days old*, ἰχθύδια τ. Ar.*Fr.*387.9; ᾠὰ τ. ὄντα Arist.*PA*665ᵃ35; φίλος τ. *of three days' standing*, Theoc.29.18; ἐπεὰν τ. γένωνται after being *three days* dead, Hdt.2.89. 2. τριταῖος (sc. πυρετός), ὁ, *tertian fever* or *ague*, Hp.*Aph.*3.21, *Nat.Hom.*15, Pl.*Ti.*86a; ὁ ἀκριβὴς τ. Gal.18(2).246; οἱ τ. πυρετοί Id.15.755; τ. ῥῖγος *POxy.*1151.37 (v A. D.). III. of days, *third*, τ. φέγγος, ἡμέρα, E.*Hec.*32, *Hipp.*275; ἐς τὴν τριταίην Hp.*Coac.*225. **-αιοφυής**, ές, *of the nature of a tertian fever*, Id. *Epid.*1.3 (interpol.),7, *Coac.*26.

**τρῐτᾰλαντ-ιαῖος**, α, ον, *holding three talents*, ἀγγεῖα Plu.*Aem.*33; *capable of throwing a weight of three talents*, [ὄργανον] Ph.*Bel.*51.44. **-ος**, ον, *of three talents*, βάρος Ar.*Lys.*338 (lyr.); λίθος τ. *weighing three talents*, Moschio ap.Ath.5.208c. 2. *worth three talents*, οἶκος Is.3.18,49. II. **τριτάλαντον**, τό, *sum of three talents*, Poll. 6.165.

**τρῐ-τάλᾱς** [τᾰ], τάλαινα, τάλᾰν, *thrice-wretched*, *AP*7.373 (Thall.), 583 (Agath.), etc. **-τάνυστος** [ᾰ], ον, *triply-stretched*, *very long*, δόναξ ib.6.192 (Arch.).

**τρῐταρτημόριον**, τό, *three quarters of an obol*, Poll.9.65.

⊛ **τρίτᾰτος** [ῐ], η, ον, lengthd. poet. for τρίτος, like μέσσατος for μέσος, Il.1.252, 14.117, E.*Hipp.*135 (lyr.), A.R.1.53; τριτάτην, abs., *in the third place*, *IG*4.682.14 (Hermione: so Boeckh; τρίτατ' ἦν Fraenkel).

**τρῐτάω**, only in Ep. part., τριτόωσα σελήνη the moon *when three days old*, Arat.796.

**τρῐτεῖα**, τά, *third prize* or *place* (formed like πρωτεῖα, δευτερεῖα, ἀριστεῖα), Pl.*Phlb.*22e: in sg., *CIG*2758,2759 (Aphrodisias).

**τρῐτεία**, ἡ, *office of* τριτευτής, *IGRom.*4.414 (Pergam.).

**τρίτειχος** [ῐ], ον, *with triple wall*, Choerob. in *An.Ox.*2.265.

**τρίτευμα** [ῐ], ατος, τό, *triad of gods*, Ramsay *Cities and Bishoprics* i p.337.

**τρῐτ-εύς**, έως, ὁ, *third part of a* μέδιμνος, *IPE*1².32 *A* 60 (Olbia, iii B. C.), Poll.4.168. **-ευτής**, οῦ, ὁ, *distributor of* τριτεῖς, *IGRom.* 4.477,1680 (Pergam.), *Rev.Phil.*37.311 (Thyatira, ii A. D.). **-εύω**, *hold the office of* τριτευτής, *CIG*3491, *IGRom.*4.1244 (both Thyatira), 414 (Pergam.); dub. sens. in *PStrassb.*114.6 (ii B. C.).

**τριτημέρη, τριτημέρᾳ**, v. τριθημέρη.

**τρῐτημορι-αῖος**, α, ον, = sq., δίεσις Aristid.Quint.1.9, cf. Apollod. *Poliorc.*162.8. ⊛ **-ος**, α, ον (ος, ον v. infr.), *equal to a third part*, c. gen., τριτημορίη ἡ Ἀσσυρίη τῆς ἄλλης Ἀσίης Hdt.1.192; ἡ τριτημόριος [δίεσις] Cleonid.*Harm.*7; λόγος τ. *a ratio of* 1:3, Theo Sm. p.76 H. II. as Subst., **τριτημόριον**, τό, *third part*, Hdt.9.34, Th. 2.98, Pl.*Phd.*105b, Euc.*Sect.Can.*6, etc. 2. *a coin*, = τριταρτημόριον, Poll.9.65.

**τρῐτημορ-ίς**, ίδος, ἡ, = τριτημόριον 1, Hdt.1.211,212, 7.121, D.C. 36.54. ⊛ **-ον**, τό, = τριτημόριον 2, Philem.63,74.

⊛ **τρῐτίρενες** [ιρ], οἱ, name applied to ἔφηβοι *serving their third year*, *IG*5(1).1386 (Thuria, ii B. C.).

**τρῐτο-βάμων** [ᾰ], ον, gen. ονος, *forming a third foot*, βάκτρον E.*Tr.* 275 (lyr.); cf. τρίπους II.

**Τρῐτο-γένεια**, ἡ, (γίγνομαι) *Trito-born*, a name of Athena, Il.4.515, 8.39, Od.3.378, Hes.*Th.*895,924, *IG*14.1389 ii 1. (Variously expld. in antiquity, from the lake Τριτωνίς in Libya, from which an old legend represents the goddess to have been born, E.*Ion*872 (anap.), cf. Hdt.4.180; or from Triton, a torrent in Boeotia, Paus.9.33.7, cf. Apollod.1.3.6; or from a spring in Arcadia, Paus.8.26.6; or from τριτώ, Aeol. word for κεφαλή (Sch.Ar.*Nu.*985, Tz.ad Lyc.519; Athamanian acc. to Nic.(*Fr.*145) ap.Hsch.), i. e. *head-born*; or, *born on the third day* of the month, Ister 26 (the 23rd, τρίτῃ φθίνοντος, Sch.BT Il.8.39); or, *the third child* after Apollo and Artemis, Suid. s. v. τριτογενής; or, as representing Nature, *born thrice* in the year, D.S.1.12; or because she was *author of the three main bonds* of social life, Democr.1ᵇ,2.) II. the Pythagoreans gave the name Ἀθηνᾶ τ. to *the equilateral triangle*, Plu.2.381e; cf. τρεῖς, τριάς. **-γενής**, έος, ἡ, collat. form of foreg., *h.Hom.*28.4, Orac.ap.Hdt.7.141, Ar.*Eq.* 1189, *IG*1².529, al. II. prov., παῖς μοι τριτογενὴς εἴη, μὴ τριτογένεια, apptly. of children born on the third or 23rd of the month ("ἀρρενώδεις γὰρ αἱ τοιαῦται γυναῖκες"), Sch.BT Il.8.39, cf. Suid. s. v. τριτογένεια.

**τρῐ-τοκέω**, *bear three times* or *three at a birth*, *AP*9.430 (Crin.); Adj. **-τόκος** in the Lemma.

**τριτοκούρη**· ἡ πάντα συντετέλεσται τὰ εἰς γάμους· τινὲς δὲ γνησία παρθένος, Hsch.; cf. τρητοκουρήτας.

**τρῐτολογέω**, in Pass., *have one third of one's property confiscated*, *PGnom.*165 (ii A. D.).

**τρῐτομηνίς**, ίδος, ἡ, for ἡ τρίτη τοῦ μηνός, *the third of the month*, at Athens sacred to Pallas, Lycurg.*Fr.*49, Ister 26. (Proparox. in *AB* 308, Suid.)

⊛ **τρί-τομος** [ῐ], ον, *thrice-cut*, *IG*1².314.108: τρίτομον, τό, *a kind of tunny*, Xenocr.ap.Orib.2.58.139, Plin.*HN*32.151; = *tricodatum*, *Gloss.*; also an object of value, used as a bribe (exact sense uncertain), *UPZ*62.12 (ii B. C., cf. Wilcken ad loc.). **-τονος**, ον, *of three tones*: τρίτονον, τό, in Music, *interval of three whole tones*, Cleonid.*Harm.*5, Bacch.*Harm.*47.

**Τρῐτο-πᾰτέρες**, οἱ, = sq., *ancestors*, *Berl.Sitzb.*1927.158 (Cyrene). **-πατρῆς**, έων, οἱ, at Athens, *divinities worshipped by* γένη, ὅρος ἱεροῦ Τριτοπατρέων Ζακυαδῶν *IG*2².2615, cf. 1358.32, 1².842 *D* 7, 870: mythical ancestors of the human race acc. to Philoch.2 (but Τριτοπάτρεις seems to be a mistake for Τριτοπάτορας). **-πάτωρ** [ᾰ], ορος, ὁ, *great-grandfather*, Arist.*Fr.*415 (but perh. Ar.Byz.): v. l. τριπάτωρ. II. Τριτοπάτορες, οἱ, divinities worshipped at Athens, to whom prayers were offered ὑπὲρ γενέσεως παίδων (v. Τριτογενής II), Phanod.4, cf. Clitodem.19, etc.; wind-daemons acc. to Demon 2, cf. Orph.*Fr.*318: sg., Τριτοπάτωρ Πυρρακιδῶν prob. the mythical ancestor of the P., Durrbach *Choix d' inscrr. de Délos* No.7 (v/iv B.C.). [The quantity of the ι is unknown.]

**τριτοπηλίς·** σκορόδων δέσμη, ἀπὸ τοῦ πεπιλῆσθαι καὶ συνεστράφθαι, Hsch. (v. τρόπαλις).

✱ **τρίτος** [ῐ], Aeol. **τέρτος** (v. τέρτα), η, ον, (τρεῖς) *third*, τοῖσι δ' ἐπὶ τρίτος ἦλθε Od.20.185, cf. 14.471; τρίτος αὐτός himself *the third*, i.e. *with two others* (v. αὐτός I. 6); τ. ἡμίδραχμον *two drachmae and a half*, Din.*Fr*.8.4; cf. ἡμιτάλαντον; τ. γενέσθαι to be *third* in a race, Isoc.16.34, cf. Plu.*Alc*.11:—*the third* freq. appears as *completing the tale*, e.g. *the third and last* libation was offered to Ζεὺς Σωτήρ, Διὸς σωτηρίου σπονδὴ τρίτου κρατῆρος S.*Fr*.425, cf. A.*Fr*.55; ἔγχει κἀπιβόα τρίτον παιῶν', ὡς νόμος ἐστίν Pherecr.131.5 (cf. τριτόσπονδος): metaph., Κράτος τε καὶ Δίκη σὺν τῷ τρίτῳ.. Ζηνὶ A.*Ch*.244, cf. *Eu*. 759, *Supp*.26 (anap.); τρίτην ἐπενδίδωμι (sc. πληγήν) *the third and finishing* stroke, Id.*Ag*.1386; Ἐρινὺς.. αἷμα πίεται, τρίτην πόσιν, i.e. the blood of Clytemnestra and Aegisthus, the first being that of the children of Thyestes, the second that of Agamemnon, Id.*Ch*.578, cf. 1066 (anap.). II. τρίτη, with or without ἡμέρα, *the day after to-morrow*, ἐς τρίτην ἡμέραν Ar.*Lys*.612; εἰς τρίτην Anaxandr.4; τῇ τρίτῃ X.*HG*3.1.17, etc.; τρίτῃ καὶ τετάρτῃ Id.*An*.4.8.21, etc.; but ἐχθὲς καὶ τ. ἡμέραν yesterday and *the day before*, Id.*Cyr*.6.3.11:—διὰ τρίτης *two days later*, Arist.*Fr*.368; but, *every other day*, Hp.*Fract*. 48, Gal.6.354. 2. with other Nouns omitted, ἡ τ. (sc. χορδή) *the third string* in the heptachord, = ἡ παραμέση, Arist.*Pr*.920ᵃ16, Plu.2. 1137b:—ἡ τ. (sc. πληγή) *the third blow*, v. supr. I:—ἡ τ. (sc. μερίς) *the third part* of a coin or weight, Hsch. s. v. ἕκτη, Phot. post Τριτοπάτορες; ἐγένετο ὁ μέδιμνος χρυσοῦ καὶ δύο τριτῶν *IPE*1².32 A 63 (Olbia, iii B.C.); *third of a stater*, Herod.2.64. III. τρίτον as Adv., *thirdly*, S.*Ant*.55, *Fr*.380; *a third time*, E.*Hel*.1417, Aristid.2.182 J.; πρῶτον μὲν.., δεύτερον δὲ.., τ. δὲ.. Pl.*R*.358c; τοῦτο τ. this *third time*, Lxx*Nu*.22.32, *Ev.Jo*.21.14:—in Hom. always τὸ τρίτον, Il.3.225, 6.186, al., cf. Hdt.1.55, Ar.*Ach*.997, Th.6.5, etc.:—also ἐκ τρίτου *in the third place*, Pl.*Ti*.54a (but = *the third time*, *Ev.Matt*.26.44, Dsc. 5.32); ἐκ τρίτων E.*Or*.1178, Pl.*Grg*.500a:—regul. Adv. τρίτως *in the third degree*, Id.*Ti*.56b. 2. τρίτον *thrice*, Syrian.*in Metaph*. 134.15, *Gp*.2.39.7, al., Sch.Pi.*O*.2.123; Elean ἐν τρίτον *Schwyzer* 412.4. IV. τὸ τ. μέρος Isoc.12.177, etc.; τὸ τ. Luc.*Tox*.46; τὸ τ. τοῦ ἀριθμοῦ Str.7.7.4, cf. Lxx*Nu*.15.6; ἐπὶ τῷ τ. at the *third* signal, X.*An*.2.2.4. V. τρίτα, τά, 1. (sc. ἱερά) *a sacrifice offered the third day after the funeral*, Ar.*Lys*.613, Is.2.37, Poll.8. 146. 2. τὰ τρίτα λέγειν τινί play *the third part* (like τριταγωνιστεῖν τινι), D.19.246, cf. Men.223.17. 3. πρῶτα δραμεῖν καὶ δεύτερα καὶ τ. win.. *third place* in the race, E.*Epigr*.3 (τρίτατα cj. Bgk.). (Cf. Skt. *tṛtī̆yas*, Lat. *tertius*, etc.)

**τρῐτό-σπονδος**, ον:—τ. παιῶνα (Hartung for αἰῶνα) paean *accompanying the third libation* (to Ζεὺς Σωτήρ), A.*Ag*.246 (lyr.); cf. τρίτος I. **-σπορος**, ον, *sown for the third time*, τ. γονή *the third* generation, Id.*Pers*.818. **-στάτης** [ᾰ], ου, ὁ, *standing third* (from the coryphaeus) *in the chorus*, Arist.*Metaph*.1018ᵇ28, Poll.4. 106, Simp.*in Ph*.1268.27:—fem. **-στάτις**, ιδος, Ar.*Fr*.487.

✱ **τρίτρα**, τά, *three times the amount*, *Leg.Gort*.1.36, *GDI*5000 i 18 (Gort.).

**τρίττοια**, v. τριττύα. **τριττός**, ή, όν, Att. for τρισσός.

**τριττύᾱ** [ῠ], ἡ, = τριττύς II, Epich.187 (acc. to Eust., but he prob. wrote τρίκτοια like Sophr. infr.), Ister 34; acc. pl. τριττύας χρυσόκερως Porph.*Abst*.2.60; also **τρικτεύα** or **τρίκτευα**, *IG*2².1126.34 (Amphict. Delph., iv B.C.); **τρίττοια** βόαρχος χρυσόκερως ib.1².76. 37, 845.6, cf. Theognost.*Can*.103; **τρίττοα**, *IG*1².5.5 (Eleusis, v B.C.); τρικτοι (sic cod. A Ath.) ἀλεξιφαρμάκων Sophr.3 (perh. τρίκτοι' ἀλ. rather than τρικτὺς ἀλ. as Schweigh., Kaibel): Hsch. also cites **τρίκτειρα** ( = θυσία Ἐνυαλίῳ, θύεται δὲ πάντα τρία καὶ ἔνορχα).

**τριττῠαρχ-έω**, *to be head of a* τριττύς III, Pl.*R*.475a; so **τρικτυαρχέω**, *IG*11(2).287 B 96,97 (Delos, iii B.C.), *Inscr.Délos*442 B 19, 55, al. (ii B.C.). **-ος**, ὁ, *chief of a* τριττύς III, *IG*2².641.31 (iii B.C.), Poll.8.109; = *tribunus*, D.H.2.7; of an officer in the army, Lib.*Or*.25.58; **τριττυάρχης**, *EM*768.13.

✱ **τριττύς**, ύος, ἡ (written **τριτύς** in Tim.*Lex*., Hsch.), Att. acc. pl. τριττῦς Arist.*Ath*.21.3, cf. Harp.:—*the number three*, Hsch., Phot.:—νικᾶν τριττύν win *three victories*, Philostr.*Gym*.33. II. *sacrifice of three animals*, used specially on making solemn oaths,—boar, goat, and ram, Sch.Ar.*Pl*.820; bull, boar, and ram, Call.*Fr*.403; bull, goat, and boar, Ister 34; two sheep and an ox, Epich.187 (v. τριττύα). III. at Athens, *a third of the* φυλή, *IG*1².190.7, 884, al., D.14.23, Aeschin.3.30, Arist.*Ath*.21.3: in form **τριπτύς**, *IG*12(5).594 (Ceos, iv B.C.). 2. *third part of the* πρυτάνεις, Arist. *Ath*.44.1.

**τριτώ**, ἡ, = κεφαλή, v. Τριτογένεια. II. **Τρῑτώ**, οῦς, ἡ, = Τριτογένεια, *AP*6.194.

**τριτωδέομαι**, *to be tertiary* (cf. δευτερῳδέομαι), Simp.*in Ph*.499.35.

**Τρίτων** [ῑ], ωνος, ὁ, *Triton*, son of Poseidon and Amphitrite, Hes. *Th*.931, Lyc.887, Plb.7.9.2:—later in pl. Τρίτωνες, *Tritons*, sea-gods with fishes' or (sts.) with horses' tails, Mosch.2.123, Paus.9. 21.1, etc. 2. the god of the Libyan lake Tritonis, Hdt.4.179, A.R.4.1552. II. a river in Libya, joining the lake Tritonis with the sea, A.*Eu*.293, Hdt.4.178,191; ποταμὸς Τρίτων, = Νεῖλος, A.R.4.269, cf. Lyc.576, Plin.*HN*5.53. 2. a mountain-stream in Boeotia, running into lake Copais, Str.9.2.18, Paus.9.33.7.

**Τρῑτων-ιὰς** λίμνη, ἡ, the Libyan lake *Tritonis*, E.*Ion* 872 (anap.). **-ιος**, α, ον, *Tritonian*, οἶδμα Orph.*H*.24.6. **-ίς**, ίδος, ἡ, *Tritonis*, a lake in Libya famous in old Greek legends, Pi.*P*.4.20, Hdt.4. 178; cf. Τριτογένεια. 2. a spring in Arcadia, also connected by legends with the birth of Athena, Paus.8.26.6. II. a name of Athena (cf. Τριτογένεια), A.R.1.109. III. vase in the form of a Triton, *PPetr*.2 p.54, prob. in 3 p.113 (iii B.C.). **-ίσκος**, ὁ, *small figure of a Triton*, on a sun-dial, *Inscr.Délos* 1417 A i 140 (ii B.C.).

**τρῐ-νίωνος**, ὁ, = τριέγγονος, *trinepos*, *Gloss*. **-ύφαντος** [ῠ], ον, *with triple web*, *PGrenf*.2.111.38 (v/vi A.D.). **-φᾰλαγγία**, ἡ, *triple phalanx*, i.e. *army marching in three phalanxes*, Plb.6.40.11, Arr. *Tact*.28.6, Ael.*Tact*.36.6, etc.

**τρῐφάλεια**, ἡ, f.l. for τρυφάλεια in Coluth.30, where the best cod. has φαλαρειαν.

**τρῐ-φάλης** [ᾰ], ητος, ὁ, title of a Comedy of Ar., in which prob. Alcibiades was attacked. (Prob. from φάλης, φαλλός.) **-φαλλος**, ὁ, (φαλλός) title of Menippean Satire by Varro περὶ ἀρρενότητος, Non.p.191 L.

**τρῐφάσιος** [ᾰ], α, ον, (τρεῖς) *triple*, μουνομαχίη Hdt.5.1. II. in pl., much the same as τρεῖς, Id.1.95, 2.17, al.; cf. διφάσιος. III. = τρίφωνος, Hsch.

**τρίφᾰτος** [ῐ], η, ον, *thrice-told*, *triple*, Nic.*Th*.102.

**τρί-φθογγος**, ἡ, *a triple vowel-sound*, Tz.*H*.12.242: as Adj. τρίφθογγος, ον, *having three voices*, *PMag.Par*.1.2820. **-φίλητος** [φῐ], ον, *thrice-beloved*, Ἄδωνις Theoc.15.86. **-φορέω**, *bear thrice*, esp. of fruit, Thphr.*CP*2.9.13:—Pass., *to be used in three forms*, of words, e.g. μήν, μάν, μέν, Eust.32.15. **-φόρος**, ον, *bearing thrice*, of fruit-trees, Thphr. paraphrased by Ath.3.77e. **-φυής**, ές, *of threefold form*, *with three stems*, of plants, Thphr.*HP*2.6.9; of the psoas muscle, Gal.2.308: generally, *threefold*, Orph.*H*.52.5, Procl.*in Prm*.p.945 S. **-φύλᾰκος** [ῠ], ον, *containing three watches*, νύξ Sch.Il.10.252. **-φῡλία**, ἡ, *committee representing three tribes*, *Berl.Sitzb*.1927.170 (Cyrene).

**τρῐφύλλινος** οἶνος, ὁ, an Italian wine, Gal.14.19; **τριφολῖνος** (v.l. -φαλ-) in Ath.1.26e.

**τρῐφύλλ-ιον**, τό, Dim. of τρίφυλλον, Aret.*CD*2.13. **-ίς**, ίδος, ἡ, = ὀξαλίς II, Dsc.*Eup*.2.60 codd. (-φύλλου Wellm.). **-ον**, τό, *clover*, *Trifolium fragiferum*, Hdt.1.132, Pherecr.109, *PLips*.97 xxxiii 16, 24 (iv A.D.); τρίφυλλος, ἡ, Dsc.2.147; cf. τρίσφυλλον. 2. *treacle clover*, *Psoralea bituminosa*, Id.3.109. 3. = σατύριον, ib.128; = ὠκύθοον, Hsch.; also (in acc. -ον) = Ἀντιοχικὴ ἰσχάς, Str.13.4. 15. II. *trefoil ornament*, *Inscr.Délos* 1441 A i 90 (ii B.C.); φύλλα τ. ib.1442 A 36 (ii B.C.). **-ος**, ον, *three-leaved*, λωτός Dsc.4.111; βοτάνη Hsch. s. v. βάλαρις. II. τρίφυλλα· πολύφυλλα, καὶ πόα δέ τις Μηδικὴ οὕτω καλουμένη, Id.

**τρί-φῡλος** [ῐ], ον, *of three tribes*, πόλις D.H.4.14; τριφύλους ποιῆσαί τινας divide them *into three tribes*, Hdt.4.161. **-φυόν·** τριπλοῦν, Hsch. **-φωνος**, ον, (φωνή) *three-voiced*, Id. s. v. τριφάσιοι.

**τρίχᾰ** [ῐ], Adv., (τρίς) *in three parts* or *ways*, διὰ τ. κοσμηθέντες Il.2.655; τ. σφισὶν ἥνδανε βουλή Od.8.506; c. gen., τ. νυκτὸς ἔην 'twas *in the third watch* of the night, 12.312, 14.483; τ. σχίσαι τι Hdt.4.67; διὰ γαῖαν τ. δασσάμενοι Pi.*O*.7.75; τ. διῄρηται Arist.*HA* 503ᵃ27; cf. τριχθά; the common Prose form is **τριχῇ** (q. v.).

**τρῐχάϊκες** [ᾱϊ], οἱ, *the threefold people*, Δωριέες, so called from their three tribes (Ὑλλῆς, Δυμᾶνες, Πάμφυλοι), Od.19.177; πάντες δὲ τριχάϊκες καλέονται τρισσὴν οὕνεκα γαῖαν ἑκὰς πάτρης ἐδάσαντο Hes. *Fr*.191. (Apollon.ap.Sch.Od. l. c. compares κορυθάϊξ -ικος and explains it as 'shaking the hair of their crests'; others rendered it τρίλοφοι, and others ὀρχησταί: more prob. Hesiod is right as to the sense; the first part is τρίχα (Adv.), the second not ἑκάς (as Hes. seems to suggest) but ϝῖκ- = Skt. *viś*- 'village', cogn. with ϝοῖκος; or ϝεικ-, another grade of the same root.)

**τρίχακτον**, τό, = κτένιον, Phot., Suid.

**τρῐ-χάλεπτος** [ᾰ], ον, *thrice-jealous*, Νέμεσις (with pun on θρίξ, λεπτός) *AP*12.229 (Strat.). **-χαλκία**, ἡ, *tax of three* χαλκοῖ, *PLille* 16.2 (iii B.C., abbrev.). **-χαλκον**, τό, *a coin worth three* χαλκοῖ, Thphr.*Char*.10.6, *IG*4²(1).109 iii 128 (Epid., iii B.C.), 5(1). 1433.33 (Messene), Vitr.3.1.7. **-χᾱλος**, ον, Dor. for *τρίχηλος (cf. τριχήν), *cloven in three*, κῦμα τ., = τρικυμία, A.*Th*.760 (lyr.).

**τρίχ-απτος** [ῐ], ον, (θρίξ, ἅπτω) *plaited* or *woven of hair*, ἀμπεχόναι Pherecr.108.28. II. τὸ τ. (sc. ἱμάτιον) *fine veil of hair*, *IG*11(2). 287 A 53 (Delos, iii B.C.), Lxx*Ez*.16.10,13, cf. Poll.2.24, 10.32, Hsch.

**τρῐχάρακτος** [χᾰ], ον, (χαράσσω) *divided in three places*, πίναξ τ. ζώναις Ps.-Callisth.1.4.

**τρῐχάς**, άδος, ἡ, *the song-thrush*, *Turdus musicus*, Arist.*HA* 617ᵃ20.

**τρῐχαστός**, ή, όν, *capable of trisection*, Anatol.ap.*Theol.Ar*.35.

**τριχέα**, v. τροχιά.

**τρί-χειλος** [ῐ], ον, *three-lipped*, *An.Ox*.2.291. **-χειρ**, χειρος, ὁ, ἡ, *three-handed*, Tz.*H*.7.902.

**τρῐχῇ**, Adv., common Prose form of τρίχα, τριχῇ δασάμενος τὴν πόλιν Hdt.3.39 (though he also uses τρίχα, q. v.); τ. διείλοντο τὰς βασιλείας Isoc.6.21, cf. Pl.*Phdr*.253c, Str.17.3.1; τ. διαστήσασθαι τῷ λόγῳ πόλιν, διανεῖμαι τὸ στράτευμα, Pl.*R*.564c, *Lg*.683d; τοὺς τοξότας τ. ἐποιήσαντο X.*An*.4.8.15; νενεμημένων τῶν ἀγαθῶν τ. Arist. *EN*1098ᵇ13. II. *in three ways*, *triply*, Pl.*Cri*.51e, Arr.*Tact*. 23.1; τ. διαστατός *of three* dimensions, S.E.*P*.2.30, Plot.6.1.26, cf. 2.1.6.

**τρῐχή-λᾰβον**, τό, poet. for τριχολάβιον, Marc.Sid.72.

**τριχήν·** τρικόρυφον, Hsch. (fort. τρίχη(λο)ν).

**τριχθ-ά**, Ep. Adv. = τρίχα, *into* or *in three parts*, τ. ᾤκηθεν Il.2.668;

τ. πάντα δέδασται 15.189; τ. τε καὶ τετραχθὰ διατρυφὲν *into three pieces*, 3.363, cf. Od.9.71. **-άδιος** [ᾰ], α, ον, *threefold*, Aesar.ap.Stob. 1.49.27, *AP*5.243 (Paul. Sil.), 259 (Id.), 9.482.23 (Agath.).

**τρῐχία**, ἡ, *rope*, *PLond*.1.131*.2, al. (i A.D.).

**τρῐχ-ίας**, ου, ὁ, *one that is hairy*, Poll.4.148 sq. II. *a smaller kind of* τριχίς, Arist.*HA*598ᵇ12, Mnesim.4.38 (anap.), Dorio ap.Ath. 7.328e. III. an unlucky throw of the dice, Poll.7.204. **-ίασις**, εως, ἡ, *a disease of the eyelids, when they are introverted, and the lashes irritate the eye* (opp. ἐκτρόπιον), Gal.19.437, Sever.ap.Aët.7.68. II. *a disease of the urethra, when the urine is full of small hair-like substances*, Gal.17(2).768. III. *a disease in the breasts of women giving suck, such that the nipples crack into fine fissures*, Erot. 2. *a fissure, scratch* in a bone, Pall. *in Hp.Fract*.12.273 C., [Gal.]14.782. ※ **-ιάω**, *suffer from* τριχίασις I, Gal.12.740. II. *suffer from* τριχίασις III. 1, Arist.*HA*587ᵇ26; of the breasts, ὁκόταν γυναικὶ μαζὸς τριχιήσῃ Hp.*Mul*.2.186 (τριχιάσηται Erot.).

**τρῐχ-ίδιον**, τό, Dim. of τριχίς, Alex.155.3. **-ῐνος**, η, ον, *of hair*, περικαλύμματα Pl.*Plt*.279e, cf. Poll.7.208; χιτῶνες X.*An*.4.8.3; σάκκοι, σάκκος, *PSI*4.427.3 (iii B.C.), *PTeb*.796.10 (ii B.C.), *Apoc*. 6.12, Sor.2.85, *PGoodsp.Cair*.30 xxxix 15 (ii A.D.); ἱδρῷα *BGU*1515 (iii B.C.); ῥάκη Alciphr.3.42. ※ **-ιον**, τό, Dim. of θρίξ, Arist.*Pr*.963ᵇ10, Plu. 2.727a (s.v.l.), M.Ant.6.13. **-ίς**, ίδος, ἡ, (θρίξ) a kind of *anchovy full of small hair-like bones*, Ar.*Ach*.551, *Eq*.662; τριχίδας ὠψώνησ' ἅπαξ, as a mark of a most thrifty person, Eup.154; cf. Arist.*HA* 569ᵇ25, and v. τριχίας II. **-ισμός**, ὁ, = τριχίασις III. 2, Paul.Aeg.6. 90. **-ῖτις**, ιδος, ἡ, a sort of *alum*, so called from its *fibrous* nature, Dsc.5.106.

**τρῐχό-βρως**, ωτος, ὁ, ἡ, *eating hair*: hence τριχόβρωτες, = σῆτες or θρῖπες, *moths*, Ar.*Ach*.1111 (τριχοβρῶτες Poll.2.24; both accents admitted by Sch.Ar. l. c. (1110)). **-δεσμος**, ὁ, *hair-band*, Hsch. s.v. ἄμπυξ. **-ειδής**, ές, *like a hair*, Hp.*Nat.Hom*.14, Arist.*HA* 620ᵇ14; of the veins, *capillary*, Gal.2.808; of nerves, ib.355; ῥωγμή Sor.*Fract*.2; στιγμαί, on reptiles, Aët.13.23. Adv. **-δῶς**, πολιοῦσθαι Dsc.4.96.

**τρῐχόθεν**, Adv. *from three sides* or *places*, J.*BJ*3.7.20, al., Sch.E. *Rh*.529.

※ **τρῐ-χοίνῐκος**, ον, *holding* or *measuring three* χοίνικες, ἄρτος X.*An*. 7.3.23: τριχοίνικον, τό, *a measure of three* χοίνικες, Poll.1.246; as tribute in Egypt, *PTeb*.61(*b*).319 (ii B.C.), al.:—in Comic phrase, τ. ἔπη *most capacious* words, Ar.*V*.481 (troch.).

**τρῐχο-κόλλημα**, ατος, τό, a depilatory or eye-salve for the eyelashes, Cass.Fel.29. **-κόμος**· τριχῶν ἐπιμελούμενος, Hsch. **-κοσμητής**, οῦ, ὁ, *hairdresser*, Id. s.v. κεροπλάστης. **-λάβιον** [ᾰ], τό, *tweezers for pulling out hairs*, Alex.Trall.3.3, Paul.Aeg.6.13, *Gloss*. **-λᾰβίς**, ίδος, ἡ, = foreg., Orib.*Eup*.4.20, *Gloss*.; also **-λάβον**, τό, *Hermes* 38.283, *Gloss*.; dat. -λάβῳ Aët.8.53. **-λογέω**, *pluck hairs*, as the dying do, Hp.*Epid*.3.17.ιε΄.

**τρῐ-χόλωτος**, ον, *thrice-detested*, *AP*9.168 (Pall.).

**τρῐχό-μαλλος**, ον, *fleecy*, ὄϊς *AP*9.150 (Antip.). **-μᾰνές**, τό, *water-wort*, *Asplenium Trichomanes*, Thphr.*HP*7.14.1, Dsc.4. 135. **-μάχιον** [ᾰ], τό, v. τριμάχιον.

**τρίχοον**, v. τρίχους II.

**τρῐχοποιέω**, *make*, i.e. *get, hair*, Cass.*Pr*.50. II. *cause hair to grow*, τοῦ ἐχίνου ἡ τέφρα τριχοποιεῖ χριομένη Alex.Trall.1.1, as v.l. for -φυεῖ.

※ **τρί-χορδος** [ῐ], ον, *of* or *with three strings*, βάρβιτος Anaxil.15 (but Poll.4.60 gives -χορδον as the name of the instrument); τρίχορδα (sc. ποιήματα) Plu.2.1137b (ὀλιγόχορδα cj. Volkmann). **-χορία**, ἡ, *triple chorus*, Poll.4.107.

**τρῐχο-ρροέω**, = sq., Dsc.2.74, Plu.2.642e. **-ρρυέω**, *shed the hair*, Ar.*Pax*1222, Andreas ap.Ath.3.115e, Poll.2.26. **-ρρυής**, ές, *shedding the hair*, παλαιὸν δέρμα καὶ τ. A.*Fr*.275. **-τομέω** (A), *cut the hair*, ἀπὸ τῆς κεφαλῆς τὰς τρίχας D.H.7.72. **-τομέω** (B), *trisect*, Papp.56.8, 272.13, Procl. *in Euc*.p.272 F. **-το[νος**, ον, *hair-strung*, καταπάλται prob. in *IG*2².1467.51, al. (iv B.C.). **-τρώκτης**, ου, ὁ, = τριχόβρως, Hsch.

**τρῐχοῦ**, Adv. *in three places*, Hdt.7.36 (dub. l.), Choerob. *in Theod*. 1.388 H.

**τρίχ-ουλος** [ῐ], ον, = οὐλόθριξ, Archil.196.

**τρῐ-χουνιαῖος**, α, ον, = sq., χύτρα Dsc.2.76.12. **-χους**, ουν, *holding three* χόες, Nicostr.Com.11. II. Subst. **-χοον**, τό, *measure of three* χόες, in pl. -χοα, *SIG*945.5 (Assus, iv B.C.).

**τρῐχό-φοιτος** ἴουλος, prob. the first down of youth *just passing into hair*, *AP*12.10 (Strat.). **-φορέω**, *to be bristly*, Eust.1657.10. **-φόρος**, ον, *bristly*, of pigs, Sch.Nic.*Th*.98, *Gloss*. **-φῠέω**, *grow* or *get hair*, Dsc.1.72, Cleopatra ap.Gal.12.404, *Gloss*. **-φυής**, ές, *growing* or *getting hair*, Dsc.2.76.18: τριχοφυές, = τριχομανές, Apul. *Herb*.47 (interpol.). **-φυΐα**, ἡ, *growth of hair*, Heliod.ap.Orib.46. 30.6, Gal.12.433. **-φυλλος**, ον, *with leaves like hairs*, of the pine tribe, Thphr.*HP*3.9.4; of the crocus, ib.6.6.10. II. τριχόφυλλον, τό, a kind of *seaweed*, *Cystoseira foeniculacea*, ib.4.6.3.

**τρῐχόω**, *furnish* or *cover with hair*, Dsc.5.149:—Pass., τριχοῦσθαι τὸ γένειον *to get* or *have* a beard, Arist.*APo*.96ᵃ10, cf. Gal.12.379, Adam.2.37; *to be mixed with hairs*, πηλὸς τετριχωμένος Thphr.*CPl*. 6.7, Polyaen.6.3. II. *unravel* a thread, Heliod.ap.Orib.47.17.2 (Pass.). III. τριχῶσαι· θάψαι, Hsch. (perh. cf. ταρχύω).

**τρι-χρονέω**, *to be of the measure of three times*, in Prosody, Charax in *AB*1150. **-χρονος**, ον, *of three times*: 1. in Prosody, *of three short syllables*, or (as an equivalent) *of one short and one long*, Heph.3.1, A.D.*Synt*.133.27: metaph. of rhythm of pulse, Ruf.*Syn. Puls*.4.4. 2. Medic., *passing through three stages*, Sor.1. 46. 3. Gramm., *in three tenses*, Herophil.ap.Gal.17(2). 480. **-χροος**, ον, contr. **-ους**, ουν, *of three colours*, Plin.*HN*37. 183 (*trichrus*). **-χρῦσον**, τό, *gold pentadrachm*, worth 60 silver drachmae, *PCair.Zen*.21.13, 22.6, al. (iii B.C.). **-χρώμᾰτος**, ον, *three-coloured*, βοῦς Apollod.3.3.1:—so **τρίχρωμος**, ον, Luc.*DMeretr*. 9.2, Porph.ap.Eus.*PE*4.14. **-χρως**, ωτος, ὁ, ἡ, = foreg., Arist. *Mete*.371ᵇ33, 375ᵃ1.

**τρῐχ-ώδης**, ες, *like hair, like a hair*, Arist.*HA*620ᵇ17, *PA*691ᵃ7, al., Thphr.*HP*4.9.2, 6.2.8. 2. metaph., φωνία τ. notes *fine as hairs*, Arist.*Aud*.803ᵇ24. 3. *mixed with hair*, πηλός Hp.*Morb*.3.17. 4. τριχώδη· ὄργανα πολιορκητικά, πρὸς χώρησιν (fort. ὀχύρωσιν) ἐπιτήδεια, Hsch. ※ **-ωμα**, ατος, τό, *a growth of hair, hair* generally, Hdt.7. 70, X.*Cyn*.5.30, Arist.*HA*630ᵃ26, al., Thphr.*Char*.2.3, Ephipp.14.6, Lxx *Ca*.4.1; τὰ τ. διαφέρουσι καὶ πρὸς αὐτὰ τοῖς ἀνθρώποις..καὶ πρὸς τὰ γένη τῶν ἄλλων ζῴων Arist.*GA*781ᵇ30; ἐν γενείου συλλογῇ τριχώματος, i.e. at the age of manhood, A.*Th*.666. **-ωμάτιον**, τό, Dim. of foreg., Arist.*Phgn*.807ᵇ4, Clearch.25.

※ **τρίχωρος** [ῐ], ον, *with three divisions* or *cells*, Dsc.1.101. II. τρίχωρον, τό, wine measure in Egypt, *BGU*248.26 (i A.D.). III. *tricorus vel trichorus locus prandii qui et sima* (i.e. σίγμα) *dicitur*; *trichorum sive trichorium locus prandii*; *tricora tres cameras sive tres absidas*, all in *Gloss*.

**τρῐχῶς**, Adv. *in threefold manner*, διῃρῆσθαι τ. Arist.*HA*590ᵃ13, cf. *APr*.67ᵇ4, al., D.T.636.21, Sor.2.55, Gal.15.525, Men.Rh.p. 331 S.

※ **τρίχ-ωσις** [ῐ], εως, ἡ, *a being hairy, growth of hair*, τινος *of* or *on* a part of the body, Arist.*HA*544ᵇ25, *GA*722ᵃ7; of Esau, J.*AJ*1.18. 1; *fresh growth of hair*, Asclep.ap.Gal.12.413. 2. *coiffure*, Menemach.ap.Orib.10.16.1. II. = τριχίασις I (nisi hoc leg.), Hp.*Acut*. (*Sp*.)61. **-ωτός**, ή, όν, *furnished with hair, hairy*, Arist.*HA* 491ᵃ30, *PA*692ᵇ11, Thphr.*Fr*.172.2: τὰ τ. *animals furnished with hair*, Arist.*PA*665ᵃ6.

**τριψ-είδιον**, τό, sine expl., Zonar. (Perh. a spice.) **-ημερέω**, *waste the day*, Ar.*V*.849.

**τρῖψις**, εως, ἡ, (τρίβω) *rubbing, friction*, Pl.*Tht*.153a, Arist.*EN* 1118ᵇ6, al.; νεφῶν Epicur.*Ep*.2 p.49 U.; πρὸς ἄλληλα Pl.*Tht*. 156a. 2. *wear and tear*, esp. of garments, *POxy*.1273.32 (iii A.D.), etc. II. *resistance to wear, durability*, Hdt.4.183. III. τρίψιες *potted meats*, *AP*9.642 (Agath.). IV. *massage*, Diocl.*Fr*. 141, Cic.*Fam*.16.18.1, Str.15.1.55, Sor.1.25, 2.32, al., Gal.6.76, al., Polyaen.6.1.7.

**τρίψορχις**, perh. name of a throw in dicing, *Bull.Inst.Fr.Arch. Orient*.30.7 (Alexandria).

**τρίψῡχος**, ον, *with three lives*, Lyd.*Mens*.1.11.

※ **τρῐωβολ-εῖος**, α, ον, *amounting to three obols* (sc. per mina per month), τόκος *POxy*.506.12 (ii A.D.), *BGU*362 xv 5 (iii A.D.). **-ιαῖος**, α, ον, *weighing three obols*, τροχίσκοι Dsc.1.99, Gal.14.161. **-ῐμαῖος**, α, ον, *worth three obols, worthless*, Eust.1405.28; τριοβ- Phot. **-ον**, Dor. **τριώδελον** (q.v.), τό, (ὀβολός) *three-obol piece, half-drachma*, οὐκ ἄξιος τριωβόλου Nicopho 12, cf. Ar.*Pl*.125; ὀψωνεῖν μέχρι τριωβόλου Eub.88, etc.—At Athens, this was 1. *pay of the dicasts* or *jurymen* for a day's sitting in court, Ar.*Eq*.51,800, etc. 2. *pay given to the members of the* ἐκκλησία whenever they chose to attend, first given about 392 B.C., Id.*Ec*.292,308. 3. *pay of the marine soldiery* (ἐπιβάται), Th.8.45, X.*HG*1.5.7, etc. 4. *a tax paid by* μέτοικοι (or perh. *by freedmen who became such*), Men.35. II. *a weight of three obols*, Sor.1.63.

**τριώδελον**, τό, Dor. for τριώβολον, *GDI*4957 a 3, al. (Crete); = τριῶν ἡμιμναίων σταθμός, Hsch.

※ **τριωδέομαι**, Pass., *to be tertiary* (cf. δευτερῳδέομαι), μονὰς τριωδουμένη, = 100, Iamb. *in Nic*. p.88 P.; cf. τριοδέομαι.

**τρῐ-ώδους**, οντος, ὁ, = τριόδους (which is v.l.), Arist.*HA*537ᵃ27, 608ᵇ17. **-ῶλαξ**· ἀγὼν παρθένων δρόμου, Hsch. (Apparently Lacon. for *τριαῦλαξ, *measuring three furlongs*.) **-ωνῠμία**, ἡ, *a having three names*, Eust.353.30. **-ώνῠμος**, ον, *having three names*, *PMag.Par*. 1.2546, Lyd.*Mag*.1.21 (in tit.), *Gloss*. **-ώνῠχος**, ον, (ὄνυξ) *with three nails* or *points*, Lyc.392. **-ώριον**, τό, *three hours*, Lat. *trihorium*, Aus.*Idyll*.10.87, *Ep*.14.62. **-ώροφος**, ον, (ὄροφος) *of three stories* or *floors*, Hdt.1.180 (v.l. -ορ-), Lxx *Ge*.6.16; οἰκίαι Aristid. *Or*.27(16).20; οἰκήματα Ph.2.143; πύργοι J.*AJ*13.8.2. II. τὸ τ., = τρίστεγον, *third story*, Lxx 3*Ki*.6.13(8), in pl. **-ώρῠγος**, ον, (ὄργυια) *of three fathoms*, restored in X.*Cyr*.6.1.52 by L. Dind. from the best codd. (which have τριώρων or τριώρυνον), others having τριόργυ(ι)ον: cf. διώρυγος, πεντώρυγος. ※ **-ωτον**, τό, *jar with three handles*, *BGU* 544.17 (ii A.D.).

**Τροία**, Ion. **Τροίη**, ἡ, *Troy*, whether of the city, '*Troy-town*', Il. 9.46, etc.; or the country, *the Troad*, Τροίην ἐριβώλακα 3.74, etc.:—also **Τροΐα** as trisyll., Sapph.*Supp*.5.9, *Scol*.17,18, dub. in S.*Aj*.1190 (lyr., v. ad fin.); Dor. **Τρωΐα** Pi.*N*.2.14, 3.60, A.*Ch*.363 (lyr.); contr. **Τρῴα** Pi.*O*.2.81 (cj. Boeckh for Τροίας):—hence **Τροίᾱθεν**, Ion. -ηθεν, *from Troy*, Od.3.257, etc.; ἀπὸ Τροίηθεν Il.24.492; Dor. **Τρωΐᾱθεν** Pi.*N*.7.41:—**Τροίανδε**, Ion. -ηνδε, *to Troy*, Il.7.390, etc.; Dor. Τρῴανδε Pi.*I*.4(3).36(54). II. a game, the Lat. *Troja* (Verg.*A*.5.602), Τροίαν ἱππεῦσαι D.C.59.7, cf. 11. [Zenod. and Aristarch. scanned Τροίη (Troy) as disyll. everywhere in Hom., but Aristarch. scanned (and wrote) (πόλιν) Τρωΐην as trisyll. in Il.1.129, Od.11.510, understanding 'a Trojan city (city of the Troad)', v. Sch.

Il. l. c.; cf. Τρῶϊος: Τροίη (-ης -η -ην) stands at the beginning of the line in the phrase Τροίῃ ἐν εὐρείῃ Il.24.256,494, Od.1.62, 4.99, 5.307; in the other 82 occurrences the trisyll. form is admitted by the metre, but should perh. not be restored, as disyll. Τροίη (-ης etc.) is almost inevitably so placed in a hexam.:—codd.Pi. (in contrast to codd.Hom.) have Τρωΐα *N.*4.25, al., and Τροΐα ib.2.14, al. (with either spelling the word may begin with ⏑⏑), cf. Eust.65.22.]

**τροια η κροκη**, = *hoc subtemen*, *Gloss.*; v. τρῶα.

**Τροιζήν**, ῆνος, ἡ, *Troezen* in Argolis, Il.2.561, Hdt.8.41, etc.:—Adj. **Τροιζήνιος**, α, ον, E.*Hipp.*12, etc.; fem. **Τροιζηνίς**, ίδος, τὴν Τ. γῆν Th.2.56: οἱ Τροιζήνιοι the people, Hdt.7.99. (Usu. **Τροζ-** in Inscrr. up to ii B.C., as *IG*2².1673.57, al.; so Dor. Τροζάν ib.4²(1).102.219 (Epid., iv B.C.), etc.: Τροιζ- first in Τροιζάνιος ib.4.727 *A* 2 (Hermione, iv B.C.), Τροιζήνιος *SIG*169.29 (Iasus, iv B.C.); rarely Τρυζήν *IG*4.619 (Argos):—Τροίζηνος, ὁ, father of Euphemos the Ciconian, Il.2.847, cf. Sch.Il.*Oxy.*1087.24.)

**τρομ-άζω**, v. τρομέω fin. **-αίνω**, = τετρεμαίνω, *AB*228.

**τρομᾰλεόφωνος**, ον, *with trembling voice*, Νέστωρ Eust.220.23.

**τρομ-ερός**, ά, όν, *trembling*, χεῖρες Hp.*Acut.*(*Sp.*)23 (where Gal.15.827 prefers τρομώδης); βάσις E.*Ph.*304 (lyr.); γῆρα τ. γυῖα Id.*HF*231; prob. so in Sapph.*Supp.*10.4. 2. *trembling for fear, quaking*, E.*Tr.*176 (anap.), al.; δεῖμα A.R.4.53. II. *fearful*, μάστιξ E.*Rh.*36 (anap.), cf. *PMag.Par.*1.266,357, *PMag.Leid.V.*4.30. **-έω**, like τρέμω, *tremble, quake, quiver*, esp. from fear, οἱ δὲ μάλ' ἐτρόμεον καὶ ἐδείδισαν Il.7.151; τρομέουσι δέ τε φρένα ναῦται 15.627; τρομέοντο δέ οἱ φρένες ἐντός 10.10: c. inf., *fear* to do, Theoc.27.29,31; τρομεῦσιν μὴ κακῶς ἀκούσωσι Call.*Iamb.*1.328: simply, *quiver*, τρόμεσκε δὲ πάντ' ἀπὸ τοῖο (sc. Βορέαο) Hes.*Fr.*96.89, cf. Q.S.12.506, Orph.*L.*560. II. c. acc., *tremble before* or *at* a person, *stand in awe of*, τόν τε τρομέουσι καὶ ἄλλοι Il.17.203; τοῦτόν γε τρομέεις καὶ δείδιας Od.18.80; θάνατον τρομέεσθαι 16.446, etc.—With and without acc. Hom. uses both Act. and Med., but only in pres. and impf.; Ep. and Ion. τρομεοίατο for τρομέοιντο, Il.10.492; Ion. part., ἤθη δεσποτῶν τρομευμένους Sol.36.12.—Poet. word, used in trans. sense by A.*Pr.*542 (lyr., Act.), *Pers.*64 (anap., Med.); but never by S. or E.: aor. ἐτρόμησα only late, Lxx 1 *Ma.*2.24 (v.l. ἐτρόμασαν), *POxy.*416.10 (iii A.D.). **-ητός**, ή, όν, *trembling, moderately boiled*, of eggs, Gal.6.706, al. **-ικός**, ή, όν, *trembling*, = *tremibundus*, *Gloss.*; in pl., gloss on Ταντάλειοι, Suid.

**τρομοποι-έω**, *tremefacio*, *Gloss.* **-ός**, όν, *causing fright*, Sch. E.*Ph.*1285.

**τρόμος**, ὁ, *trembling, quaking, quivering*, I. from fear, πάντας ἕλε τ. Il.19.14; ὑπό τε τ. ἔλλαβε γυῖα 3.34, etc.; τ. μ' ὑφέρπει A.*Ch.*463 (lyr.), cf. E.*Ba.*607 (troch.); τ. καὶ ἔκστασις *Ev.Marc.*16.8; from love, τ. δὲ παῖσαν ἄγρει Sapph.2.13: pl., *shiverings*, Hp.*Coac.*92. 2. from cold, τ. καὶ ῥῖγος Pl.*Ti.*62b, cf. 85e; γίνεται ὁ τ. διὰ κατάψυξιν Arist.*Pr.*871ᵃ33: generally, ἰνῶν ἀτονία καὶ τ. Phld.*Acad.Ind.*p.76 M.; περὶ τ. Gal.7.584. 3. of earthquakes, Arist.*Mete.*366ᵇ18, *Mu.*396ᵃ10; σεισμοὶ ἐν γῇ καὶ τρόμοι Plu.2.373d.

**τρομ-ός**, ή, όν, *trembling, unsteady*, δράμημα γηραιοῦ ποδὸς E.*Fr.*876. Adv. **-μῶς**, τρέμειν Tz.*H.*12.769. **-ώδης**, ες, *trembling, quivering*, τρομώδεις ἔθνησκον Str.15.2.6; σάρξ Plu.2.689c; of delirious persons, χεῖρες, γλῶσσαι, Hp.*Acut.*42, *Prorrh.*1.20; πυρετοί Id.*Fract.*11. Adv. **-δῶς** Gal.7.69, Steph. *in Hp.*1.99 D.

**τρόνα**· ἀγάλματα, ἢ ῥάμματα ἄνθινα, Hsch. (Cf. θρόνον I.) **τρόνοι**· στύππιοι, στήμων, ἁρπεδόνη, ἄτρακτος, Id.

**τρόπᾰ**, Adv. a game with the ἀστράγαλοι described by Poll.9.103, τ. παίζειν Cratin.170; *ludit tropa nequiore talo* (Brodaeus for *rota* or *popa*), Mart.4.14.9.

**τροπαγός**· ὁ ἀπητιμασμένος, Hsch.

**τροπαία** (sc. πνοή), ἡ, *an alternating wind*, esp. *one which blows back from sea to land*, opp. ἀπογεία, Arist.*Pr.*940ᵇ22, 945ᵃ6, Thphr. *Vent.*31,53; *tropaei* (*venti*), Plin.*HN*2.114; τ. is said to have meant ἡ ἐναντία πνοή in S.*Fr.*1103 (where τριπαία, τρίπαια, τριπαῖα codd.). II. metaph., λήματος, φρενὸς τροπαία, *a change in the spirit* of one's heart or mind, A.*Th.*706, *Ag.*219 (both lyr.); but τ. κακῶν *a change from, release from*.., Id.*Ch.*775.

**τροπαϊκιαῖος**, α, ον, *amounting to* 1 τροπαϊκόν *per* 100 *denarii per month*, τόκος *IGRom.*4.1342 (Magn. Sip., ii A.D.).

⊛ **τροπαϊκόν**, τό, *a half-denarius*, = 8 *asses*, Anon.ap.Hultsch *Metrol. Script.*i p.302.

⊛ **τρόπ-αιον**, τό, old Att. **τροπαῖον** Hdn.Gr.1.369:—*trophy*, i.e. a *monument of* the enemy's *defeat* (τροπή II), usu. made of wood (D.S.13.24), but sts. of bronze (Plu.*Alc.*29), or stone (Paus.1.33.2); τ. στῆσαι Th.2.92, etc.: freq. with gen., στῆσαι τροπαῖα τῶν κακῶν E.*Or.*713; τ. αὐτοῦ στήσομαι Id.*Andr.*763; ὅταν τροπαῖα πολεμίων στήσῃ στρατός ib.694; τ. ἂν στήσαιτο τῶν ταύτης τρόπων Ar.*Pl.*453; τροπαῖα τῶν πολεμίων ἀποδεῖξαι And.1.147; ἔστησαν τ. ὑπὲρ τῆς Ἑλλάδος τῶν βαρβάρων Lys.2.25, cf. X.*An.*7.6.36; also θήσειν τροπαῖα, θράσους θέσθαι τροπαῖον, A.*Th.*277, Ar.*Lys.*318; τροπαῖ' ἱδρύεται E.*Heracl.*786; τ. πῶς ἀναστήσεις Διί; Id.*Ph.*572; τ. ἐγεῖραι Luc.*Dem. Enc.*40; νίκης τ. S.*Tr.*751; στῆσαι τ. τῆς τροπῆς, τῆς ἱππομαχίας, *for, in memory of*.., Th.2.92, 6.98; so τροπαῖ' ἔστησε τῶν ἐμῶν χερῶν S.*Tr.*1102; χορῶν.. νίκης ἔστησε τροπαῖα Ar.*Eq.*521 (anap.); so στῆσαι τροπαῖα κατὰ or ἀπὸ τῶν πολεμίων, Lys.18.3, Aeschin.3.156, cf. Isoc.5.148, D.20.78. **-αῖος**, α, ον, *of a turning* or *change* (cf. τροπαία, ἡ). II. *of* or *for defeat* (τροπή II), τροπαῖά τ' ἐχθρῶν καὶ πόλει σωτήρια (sc. σφάγια) E.*Heracl.*402; Ζεὺς Τ., as *giver of victory*, S.*Ant.*143 (anap.), *Tr.*303, E.*Heracl.*867, *IG*2².1028.27; hence στήσαιεν Ζηνὶ τροπαῖον ἕδος ib.2.2717. 2. *causing rout, appalling*, Ἕκτορος ὄμμασι τροπαῖοι, i.e. *terrible* to the eyes of Hector, E.*El.*469 (lyr.), cf. 1174.—Cf. τρόπαιον.

**τροπαιουχ-έω**, gloss on κατορθώσειαν, Sch.Th.7.66. ⊛ **-ος** (properisp.), ον, (ἔχω) *having* or *gaining trophies*: Ζεὺς τ. the god *to whom trophies are dedicated*, Arist.*Mu.*401ᵃ23, *CIG*4340*f*, *g* (Pamphylia); = Lat. *Jupiter Feretrius*, D.H.2.34, Plu.2.306c; as an epith. of Roman Emperors, *OGI*723.2 (Antinoopolis, iv A.D.), *CIG*3992 (Iconium), 4350 (Pamphylia), *SIG*906*B* (Magn. Mae., iv A.D., τροπε-), al.; Δᾶτις ὁ τ. Polem.*Cyn.*41.

**τροπαιοφορ-έω**, *triumph*, Ph.2.34. **-ία**, ἡ, *bearing of a trophy*, Plu.*Comp.Pel.Marc.*3. ⊛ **-ος** (parox.), ον, *bringing trophies*, Κύπρι *AP*5.293.24 (Agath.); *bearing a trophy* or *emblem of victory*, Νίκη D.S.18.26; Ζεὺς τ., = Lat. *Jupiter Feretrius*, *Mon.Anc.Gr.*10.9; εἰκόνες Plu.*Rom.*16. 2. a coin, *Inscr.Délos* 1439 *Cb*1, 1443 *Ai*141 (ii B.C.). II. = Lat. *triumphalis*, πομπή D.H.3.31, etc.; ἁψίς D.C.49.15.

**τροπᾰλίζω**, poet. for τρέπω, Hsch.

**τρόπᾰλις**, ιδος, ἡ, *bundle, bunch*, σκορόδων τ. *a bunch* of garlic, Ar. *Ach.*813 (Megar.). (Dor. for τρόπηλις, which is given with this accent by Hdn.Gr.1.91; but in Ar. l.c. codd. RAΓ have τροπαλλίδος and Suid. τροφαλλίδος:—cf. τριοπηλίς and τριτοπηλίς.)

**τροπᾰλισμός**· μεταβολή, καὶ τὸ ἐκ συμβόλων ὑποδέχεσθαι, Hsch.

**τροπᾰλόν**· τραχύ, Hsch. (i.e. τροχαλόν· ταχύ).

**τροπάομαι**, v.l. for τρωπ- in Il.15.666, cf. Suid.

**τροπέω**, = τρέπω, *turn*, ἵπποι ἂψ ὄχεα τρόπεον Il.18.224.

**τροπ-ή**, ἡ, (τρέπω) *turn, turning*: I. τροπαὶ ἠελίοιο: a. ὅθι τροπαὶ ἠελίοιο apparently denotes a point on the horizon, prob. the West or place where the sun sets (so Eust.1787.20), Od.15.404. b. each of two fixed points in the solar year, *the solstices*, first in Hes., ἠελίοιο τροπῇς *at the time of the* (*winter*) *solstice*, *Op.*479; μετὰ τροπὰς ἠελ. ib.564,663 (with Dor. acc. pl. in -ᾰς); πεδὰ τὰς τροπάς Alcm.33.5:—later the two solstices were distinguished as τροπαὶ θεριναί and χειμεριναί, Hdt.2.19, Th.7.16, Pl.*Lg.*767c, Arist. *HA*542ᵇ4 sqq., Gal.6.405, etc. (rarely in sg., τροπὴ θερινή Arist.*Mete.*364ᵇ2, Gem.1.13; τ. χειμερινή ib.15); τροπαὶ νότιοι Arist.*HA*542ᵇ11; τ. βόρειοι, νότιοι, Plu.2.601a:—when τροπαί is used alone, it mostly refers to *the winter solstice*, but the sense is always determined by the context, v. Hes. ll. cc.; περὶ ἡλίου τροπάς (sc. χειμερινάς) Th.8.39; εὐθὺς ἐκ τροπῶν Arist.*HA*542ᵇ20:—sts. also of other heavenly bodies, Pl.*Ti.*39d; περὶ Πλειάδος δύσιν καὶ τροπάς Arist.*HA*542ᵇ23, etc.; ἄστρων ἐπιτολάς, δύσεις, τροπάς Alex.30.5; τροπὰς τῶν ἐνδεδεμένων ἄστρων Arist.*Cael.*296ᵇ4; τροπαὶ ἡλίου καὶ σελήνης Epicur.*Ep.*2 p.40 U.:—sts. four in number (the two equinoxes and two solstices), S.E.*M.*5.11, Gal.17(1).22; so (on a sun-dial) θερινὴ τ., ἰσημερινὴ τ., χειμερινὴ τ., Ἀρχ.Δελτ.12.236 (Samos). 2. *turn, change*, Arist.*Pol.*1316ᵃ17; πλείους τραπόμενος τροπὰς τοῦ Εὐρίπου Aeschin.3.90; τ. πρὸς τὸ βέλτιον *turn* for the better, Phld.*Rh.*2.25 S.; ὀξυτέρας τρεπόμενος τ. τοῦ χαμαιλέοντος Plu.*Alc.*23; αἱ τοῦ κόλακος ὥσπερ πολύποδος τ. Id.2.52f; αἱ τοῦ αἵματος τ. καὶ ἀλλοιώσιες Ti.Locr.102c; αἱ περὶ τὸν ἀέρα τ. *changes* in the air or weather, Plu.2.946f; of wine, a *turning sour*, ib.939f (cf. τροπίας); *going bad*, of food, τ. καὶ διαφθορὰ τῶν παρακειμένων Gal.19.208; of phonetic *change* in language, A.D. *Adv.*210.4, Hdn.Gr.2.932. 3. τροπαὶ λέξεως *a change* of speech by *figures* or *tropes* (τρόποι), Luc.*Dem.Enc.*6, cf. Hermog.*Inv.*4.10, al. 4. αἱ τροπαί, = αἱ τροπαῖαι, *alternating* winds, Arist.*Pr.*940ᵇ16,21, Thphr.*CP*2.3.1, *Vent.*26. II. *the turning about of the enemy, putting to flight* or *routing* him, τροπήν (or τροπάς) τινος ποιεῖν or ποιεῖσθαι put one to *flight*, Hdt.1.30, Ar.*Eq.*246 (troch.), Th.2.19, 6.69, etc.; οἵαν ἂν τροπὴν Εὐρυσθέως θείμην (θείην codd.) E.*Heracl.*743; τροπὴ γινομένη Hdt.7.167, cf. Th.1.49,50, etc.: poet., ἐν μάχης τροπῇ A.*Ag.*1237; ἐν τροπῇ δορὸς *in the rout* caused by the spear, S.*Aj.*1275, E.*Rh.*82. III. used by Democr. for θέσις, *position*, Arist.*Metaph.*985ᵇ17, 1042ᵇ14, cf. Plot.4.5.2, 4.5.6. IV. *a coin*, Hsch.; cf. τροπαϊκόν. **-ήϊον**, τό, Ion. for *τροπεῖον, *press*, Hippon.57; cf. τραπέω. **-ηλις**, ιδος, ἡ, v. τρόπαλις. **-ηξ**, ηκος, ὁ, *the handle of an oar, an oar*, Hsch.; cf. τράφηξ. **-ίας** οἶνος, ὁ, *turned*, i.e. *sour*, wine (cf. τρέπω II. 3, τροπή I. 2), Ar.*Fr.*213; cf. ἐκτροπίας. **-ίδειον**, τό, = τρόπις, τροπιδεῖα καταβάλλεσθαι to lay *the keel*, Pl.*Lg.*803a; v.l. τροπίδια, cf. Poll.1.85, Phot. **-ίζω**, *furnish with a keel*, ναῦς ἱκανῶς τετροπισμένη Hp. *Ep.*14. **-ικός**, ή, όν, (τροπή) *of the solstice*, ὁ τ. (sc. κύκλος) the *tropic* or *solstice* as marked on the sphere, Arist.*Mete.*343ᵃ14 (with κύκλος, Jul.*Or.*4.147c); τ. χειμερινός, θερινός, Porph.*Antr.*21; ζῶναι *Placit.*3.11.4; οἱ τ. (sc. κύκλοι) Arist.*Mete.*345ᵃ6, 346ᵃ14, al., cf. Arat.528, Plu.2.429f; τὰ τ. ζῴδια the signs of the zodiac *in which the solstices and the equinoxes are situated*, S.E.*M.*5.6; so τ. ζῷα Man.2.382; and abs., τροπικά Id.3.41, 6.359; but used of Cancer and Capricorn only, opp. ἰσημερινά (Aries and Libra), Ptol.*Tetr.*31, etc. 2. of Time, *of* or *at the solstice*, αἱ τ. ἡμέραι, οἱ τ. μῆνες, Arist.*HA*544ᵃ33, 558ᵇ14. II. Rhet., *tropical, figurative*, τ. λέξις a *figurative* expression, D.H.*Th.*23, etc.; τὸ ποιητικὸν καὶ τ. Phld.*Rh.*1.157 S.; αἱ τ. *tropes*, Longin.32.6. Adv. **-κῶς** Phld.*Rh.*1.154 S., Ath.3.76c. 2. in Stoic Logic τροπικόν = συνημμένον ἢ διεζευγμένον ἀξίωμα (v. συνάπτω A. III. 3, διαζεύγνυμι I), *Stoic.*2.77, al., Arr.*Epict.*1.29.40. ⊛ **-ις**, ἡ, gen. τρόπεως *Placit.*2.4.15, Hdn.*Epim.*135; Ion. gen. τρόπιος Od.19.278, Hdt.2.96; τρόπιδος *EM*811.21; dat. τρόπιδι A.R.1.388; acc. τρόπιν Hippon.50, Orph.*A.*271: pl. τρόπεις, dat. τρόπισι D.C.48.38: (τρέπω):—*ship's keel*, Od.5.130, 12.421, Hdt. l.c.; τ. νεός Od.7.252,

19.278; πλοίου τ. Arist.*Metaph.*1013ᵃ5; and poet. *ship*, S.*Fr.*143; τρόπεις θέσθαι lay down *keels* for building ships, Plu.*Demetr.*43; cf. τροπιδεῖον: metaph., λέγε νυν τὴν τ. τοῦ πράγματος Ar.*V.*30.

**τροπολογ-έω**, *expound allegorically*, Aristeas 150. **-ία**, ἡ, = *moralis intelligentia*, *Gloss.* **-ος** (parox.), ὁ, *reciter* of select passages (?), *MAMA*3.217,452 (Corycus).

**τροπομάσθλης**, ητος, ὁ, *supple cringing fellow*—a word ridiculed by Luc.*Pseudol.*24.

**τροπός**, ὁ, *twisted leathern thong*, with which the oar was fastened to the thole, τροποῖς ἐν δερματίνοισι Od.4.782, 8.53; τροπὸν αὐτόν, ἐπαρτέα δεσμὸν ἐρετμοῦ Opp.*H.*5.359; cf. τροπόω (B), τροπωτήρ.

❀ **τρόπος**, ὁ, (τρέπω) *turn, direction, way*, διώρυχες παντοίους τρόπους ἔχουσαι Hdt.2.108; διώρυχας τετραμμένας πάντα τ. Id.1.189, cf. 199: but, II. commonly, *way, manner, fashion, guise*, τρόπῳ τῷ παρεόντι χρεώμενοι going on *as we are*, ib.97; τ. ὑποδημάτων Κρητικός Hp.*Art.*62; πᾶς τ. μορφῆς A.*Eu.*192; τίς ὁ τ. τῆς ξυμφορᾶς; S.*OT*99; ἀσκεῖν τὸν υἱὸν τὸν ἐπιχώριον τ. Ar.*Pl.*47; ὁ αὐτός που τ. τέχνης ἰατρικῆς ὅσπερ καὶ ῥητορικῆς Pl.*Phdr.*270b; *tenor*, of documents, *PGen.*16.11 (iii A.D.), etc.: also in pl., κεχώρισται τοὺς τ. in its *ways*, in its *kind*, Hdt.4.28; ψυχῆς τρόποι Pl.*R.*445c, etc.; οἱ περὶ τὴν ψυχὴν τ. Arist.*HA*588ᵃ20:—in various adverbial usages: 1. dat., τίνι τρόπῳ; *how?* A.*Pers.*793, S.*OT*10, E.*Ba.*1294; τῷ τ.; S.*El.*679, E.*Hipp.*929,1008; ποίῳ τ.; A.*Pr.*763, etc.; τοιούτῳ τ., τ. τοιῷδε, Hdt. 1.94, 3.68; ἄλλῳ τ. Pl.*Phdr.*232b, etc.; ἑνί γέ τῳ τ. *in* one *way* or other, Ar.*Pl.*402, Pl.*Men.*96d; παντὶ τ. *by* all *means*, A.*Th.*301 (lyr.), Lys.13.25; οὐδενὶ τ., μηδενὶ τ., *in* no *wise, by* no *means, on* no *account*, Hdt.4.111, Th.6.35, Pl.*Cri.*49a, etc.; ἑκουσίῳ τ. willingly, E.*Med.*751; τρόπῳ φρενός by *way* of intelligence, i.e. in lieu of the intelligence which is lacking to the child, A.*Ch.*754 (s.v.l.): poet. in pl., τρόποισι ποίοις; S.*OC*468; τρόποισιν οὐ τυραννικοῖς not after *the fashion* of.., A.*Ch.*479; ναυκλήρου τρόποις S.*Ph.*128. 2. abs. in acc., τίνα τρόπον; *how?* Ar.*Nu.*170, *Ra.*460; τ. τινά *in* a *manner*, E.*Hipp.* 1300, Pl.*R.*432e; τοῦτον τὸν τ., τόνδε τὸν τ., Id.*Smp.*199a, X.*An.*1.1.9; ὃν τ. *how*, D.H.3.8; *as*, Lxx *Ps.*41(42).1; τ. τὸν αὐτὸν A.*Ch.*274; πάντα τ. Ar.*Nu.*700 (lyr.), etc.; μηδένα τ. X.*Mem.*3.7.8; τὸν μέγαν τ., οὐ σμικρὸν τ., A.*Th.*284,465; τὸν Ἀργείων τ. Pi.*I.*6(5).58; Σαμιακὸν τ. Cratin.13; βάρβαρον τ. (βρόμον ex Sch. Schütz) *in* barbarous *guise* or *fashion*, A.*Th.*463; πίτυος τρόπον *after the manner* of a pine, Hdt.6.37; ὄρνιθος τ. *like* a bird, Id.2.57, cf. A.*Ag.*49 (anap.), 390 (lyr.), etc.; later, ἐς ὄρνιθος τ. Luc.*Halc.*1, cf. *Bis Acc.*27: rarely in pl., πάντας τρόπους in all *ways*, Pl.*Phd.*94d. 3. with Preps., τὸν ἐγκώμιον ἀμφὶ τρόπον in *way* of praise, Pi.*O.*10(11).77:—δι' οὗ τρόπου Men.539.6; διὰ τοιούτου τ. D.S.1.66:—ἐς τὸν νῦν τ. Th.1.6; εἰς τὸν αὐτὸν τ. μετασκευάσαι X.*Cyr.*6.2.8; ἐς ὄρνιθος τ. (v. supr. 2):—ἐκ παντὸς τ. Id.*An.*3.1.43, Isoc.4.95, etc.; ἐξ ἑνός γέ του τ. Ar.*Fr.* 187, Th.6.34; μηδ' ἐξ ἑνὸς τ. Lys.31.30; μηδ' ἐξ ἑνὸς τ. Isoc.5.3:—ἐν τῷ ἑαυτῶν τ. Th.7.67, cf. 1.97, etc.; ἐν τρόπῳ βοσκήματος Pl.*Lg.* 807a: in pl., γυναικὸς ἐν τρόποις, ἐν τ. Ἰξίονος, A.*Ag.*918, *Eu.*441:—κατὰ τὸν αὐτὸν τ. X.*Cyr.*8.2.5; κατὰ πάντα τ. Ar.*Av.*451 (lyr.), X.*An.* 6.6.30, etc.; κατ' οὐδένα τ. Plb.4.84.8, etc.; κατ' ἄλλον τ. Pl.*Cra.* 417b; κατὰ τὸν Ἑλληνικὸν τ. X.*Cyr.*2.2.28: in pl., κατὰ πολλοὺς τ. ib.8.1.46, etc.:—μετὰ ὁτουοῦν τ. in any *manner* whatever, Th.8. 27:—ἑνὶ σὺν τ. Pi.*N.*7.14. 4. κατὰ τρόπον, a. *according to custom*, κατὰ τὸν τ. τῆς φύσεως Pl.*Lg.*804b; opp. παρὰ τὸν τ. τὸν ἑαυτῶν Th.5.63, cf. Antipho 3.2.1. b. *fitly, duly*, Epich.283, Isoc. 2.6, Pl.*Plt.*310c, etc.; οὐδαμῶς κατὰ τ. Id.*Lg.*638c; opp. ἀπὸ τρόπου *unreasonable, absurd*, Id.*Cra.*421d, *Tht.*143c, etc.; so θαυμαστὸν οὐδὲν οὐδ' ἀπὸ τοῦ ἀνθρωπείου τ. Th.1.76. 5. πρὸς τρόπου *fitting, suitable*, *PCair.Zen.*309.5 (iii B.C.). III. of persons, *a way of life, habit, custom*, Pi.*N.*1.29; μῶν ἡλιαστά; Answ. μᾶλλα θατέρου τ. Ar. *Av.*109; ἐγὼ δὲ τούτου τοῦ τ. πώς εἰμ' ἀεί Id.*Pl.*246, cf. 630. 2. a man's *ways, habits, character, temper*, ὀργὴν καὶ ῥυθμὸν καὶ τ. ὅστις ἂν ᾖ (v.l. ὅντιν' ἔχει) Thgn.964; τρόπου ἡσυχίου of a quiet *temper*, Hdt.1.107, cf. 3.36; φιλανθρώπου τ. A.*Pr.*11; γυναικὶ κόσμος ὁ τ., οὐ τὰ χρυσία Men.*Mon.*92; οὐ τὸν τ., ἀλλὰ τὸν τόπον μόνον μετήλλαξεν Aeschin.3.78; τρόπου προπέτεια, ἀναίδεια, D.21.38, 45.71; ἀφιλάργυρος ὁ τ. *Ep.Hebr.*13.5:—οὐ τοὐμοῦ τ. Ar.*V.*1002; σφόδρ' ἐκ τοῦ σοῦ τ. quite of your *sort*, Id.*Th.*93; ξυγγενεῖς τοὐμοῦ τ. ib.574:—πρὸς τρόπου τινός agreeable to one's *temper*, Pl.*Phdr.*252d, cf. *Lg.*655d; πρὸς τοῦ Κύρου τρόπου X.*An.*1.2.11:—opp. ἀπὸ τρόπου Pl.*Phdr.*278d, *R.* 470c:—after Adjs., διάφοροι ὄντες τὸν τ. Th.8.96; σολοικότερος τῷ τ. X.*Cyr.*8.3.21:—esp. in pl., Pi.*P.*10.38, S.*El.*397,1051; σκληρός, ἀμνοὶ τοὺς τρόπους, Ar.*Pax* 350,935; σφόδρα τοὺς τ. Βοιώτιος Eub.39; πουλύπους ἐς τοὺς τ. Eup.101; μεθάρμοσαι τ. νέους A.*Pr.*311; τοὺς φιλάνορας τ. Id.*Ag.*856; νέας βουλὰς νέοισιν ἐγκαταζεύξας τ. S.*Aj.* 736; τοῖς τρόποις ὑπηρετεῖν Ar.*Ra.*1432; opp. νόμοι, Th.2.39; ἤθη τε καὶ τ. Pl.*Lg.*924d. IV. in Music, like ἁρμονία, a particular *mode*, Λύδιος τ. Pi.*O.*14.17; but more generally, *style*, νεοσίγαλος τ. ib.3.4; ὁ ἀρχαῖος τ. Eup.303; ᾠδῆς τρόπος, μουσικῆς τρόποι, Pl.*R.* 398c, 424c; διθυραμβικοὶ τ. (distd. fr. ἦθος) Phld.*Mus.*p.9 K.; ὁ ἁρμονικὸς τῆς μουσικῆς τ. Aristid.Quint.1.12, cf. 2.1; of art in general, πάντες τῆς εἰκαστικῆς τ. Phld.*Po.*5.7. V. in speaking or writing, *manner, style*, ὁ τ. τῆς λέξεως Pl.*R.*400d, cf. Isoc.15.45: esp. in Rhet. in pl., *tropes*, Trypho *Trop.*tit., Cic.*Brut.*17.69, Quint.*Inst.*8.6.1. VI. in Logic, *mode* or *mood* of a syllogism, *Stoic.*3.269, cf. 1.108, 2.83: more generally, *method* of instruction or explanation, ὁ ἄνευ φθόγγων τ. Epicur.*Ep.*1 p.32 U.; ὁ μοναχῇ τ. the *method* of the single cause, opp. ὁ πλεοναχὸς τ. the *method* of manifold causes, Id.*Ep.*2 p.41 U.; *mode* of inference, ὁ κατὰ τὴν ὁμοιότητα τ., opp. ὁ κατ' ἀνασκευὴν τ. τῆς σημειώσεως, Phld.*Sign.*30,31; αἰτιολογικὸς τ. Epicur.*Nat.* 143 G. VII. *beam*, Moschio ap.Ath.5.208c (so in Mod.Gr., cf. *Glotta* 11.249).

**τροποφορέω**, c. acc., *bear with another's moods*, Sch.Ar.*Ra.*1479, Suid. s.vv. σκύμνος et οὐ χρή; τὸν τῦφόν μου Cic.*Att.*13.29.1; v.l. for τροφο– in Lxx *De.*1.31, *Act.Ap.*13.18.

❀ **τροπ-όω** (A), (τρόπος) like τρέπω, *make to turn, put to flight*, Lxx *Jd.*4.23, 20.35 (v.l.), Wilcken *Chr.*11 A 40 (ii B.C.):—so in Med., Lxx 2 *Ki.*8.1, al., D.H.2.50, *Sammelb.*5829.2. **-όω** (B), (τροπός) *furnish the oar with its thong*, in Med., ναυβάτης τ' ἀνὴρ τροποῦτο κώπην σκαλμὸν ἀμφ' εὐήρετμον *fastened his oar by its thong* round the thole, A.*Pers.*376; τροπώσασθαι ναῦν Poll.1.87:—Pass., of the oar, *to be furnished with its thong*, Ar.*Ach.*553, Luc.*Cat.*1. **-ωτήρ**, ῆρος, ὁ, = τροπός, Ar.*Ach.*549, Th.2.93:—φλεβὸς τ., v. φλέψ.

**τρούβλιον**, τό, = τρύβλιον, *Gloss.*; also cj. (as Boeot.) in Alex. 142.

**τρούεται**· ἰσχναίνεται, τήκεται, Hsch. (Prob. Lacon. for τρύεται.)

**τρούθιος**, v. στρούθειος. **τρούλιον**, v. sq.

❀ **τροῦλλα**, ἡ, *ladle* or *cup*, used as a liquid measure, Lat. *trulla*, *BMus.Inscr.*980 (Cyprus), Olymp.Hist.p.462 D., *Gloss.*; written **τροῦλα** in *Hippiatr.*77:—Dim. **τρούλλιον**, τό, Lat. *trulleum*, Hero *Spir.*1.8, Aët.3.177, 16.136; written **τρούλιον** in *BGU*814.10 (iii A.D.), *Hippiatr.*74; cf. τρύλλιον.

**τροῦλλος**, ὁ, a kind of vessel, ἐν τ. μεγάλῳ ὑελίνῳ περιπηλώσαντες Zos.Alch.p.164 B.; οὐκ ἐῶντες καπνὸν διὰ τοῦ τ. ἀναδοθῆναι ibid.

**τροῦροι**· δρόμοι, στάδιοι, Hsch. **τρουφωνίδαι**· εἶδος κροκωτοῦ, Id.

**τροφάλ-ιον** [ᾰ], τό, Dim. of sq., Alex.172.12. **-ίς**, ίδος, ἡ, *fresh cheese*, Eup.277, Antiph.49 (troch.); τροφαλίδα τυροῦ Σικελικὴν κατεδήδοκεν a *piece* of Sicilian cheese, Ar.*V.*838, cf. Herm.Hist.2; whence the joke, καλεῖ..τὴν..Τυρὼ τροφαλίδα *Com.Adesp.*393; τ. ὀβολιαῖαι Arist.*HA*522ᵃ31.—The form **τρυφαλίς** is common in later writers, as Luc.*Lex.*13, Hdn.Gr.2.18 (rejected in favour of τροφαλίς Id.1.91), Hsch.; τὰς δέκα στρυ*φαλίδας (sic cod. A, ν superscr. A¹) τοῦ γάλακτος Lxx 1 *Ki.*17.18; a form **τροφαλλίς** occurs in codd. of Eust.1535.22 (in citation of *Com.Adesp.* l.c.); Hsch. also cites **τραφαλλίς, τράφαλλος.** (From τρέφω 1 acc. to Hdn.Gr.1.91, but the spelling τρυφ–, which he mentions, remains unexplained: oxyt. acc. to Hdn.Gr. ll. cc., so that the accus. τρόφαλιν in Erot. s. v. τεθραμμένον must be an error.)

❀ **τροφ-εία**, ἡ, *service as wet-nurse*, *BGU*1058.14, 1106.35, al. (i B.C.). **-εῖα**, τά, *pay for rearing and bringing up, wages of a nurse*, θανὼν τ. πληρώσει χθονί A.*Th.*477; [πορσῦναι] E.*El.*626; ἀποδοῦναι, ἐκτίνειν, Id.*Ion* 852, Pl.*R.*520b; prov., κριὸς τὰ τ. (sc. ἀπέτεισεν) Men.905; ἀνταποδοῦναι Lys.6.49, cf. *IG*5(2).345.7 (Orchom. Arc., ii/i B.C.), *POxy.*37.10 (i A.D.); πράξασθαι D.S.9.13. II. βίου τ. one's *living, food*, S.*OC*341; τ. ματρός mother's milk, E.*Ion* 1493 (lyr.). III. *fodder*, *BGU*912.19 (i A.D.), *PAmh.*2.143.5 (iv A.D.). IV. *maintenance, board*, paid in money or kind, *PEleph.* 3.2, al. (iii B.C.), *PMich.Teb.*121ʳ vii 7, al. (i A.D.), *PRyl.*153.4 (ii A.D.); paid to a wet-nurse, *BGU*1106.38,47 (i B.C.), *PGrenf.*2.75.5 (iv A.D.). **-εῖον**, τό, = οἰκίσκος, ὀρνίθων τ. Suid. **-εύς**, έως, ὁ, *one who brings up, foster-father*, S.*Ph.*344, E.*El.*16, *Ph.*45, Theophil. 1; *tutor*, βασιλέως *OGI*148.2 (Cyprus, ii B.C.), 256.1 (Delos, ii B.C.), cf. *Sammelb.*1568.1 (ii B.C.), Gal.14.664, M.Ant.5.31; of a woman, *nurse*, A.*Ch.*760 (στροφεύς codd.). 2. in S.*Aj.*863, Ajax addresses the plains and fountains of Troy, χαίρετ' ὦ τροφῆς ἐμοί *ye who have fed* me, or *with whom I have lived*; so τροφέας παρέδωκε τὴν γῆν καὶ τὴν θάλασσαν Antipho 4.1.2. 3. *rearer, breeder*, ἵππων Pl.*Lg.*735b; ἅρματος τ. *one who keeps* a chariot, ib.834b; πάσης κακίας *one who fosters* all wickedness, Id.*R.*580a. 4. *one who gives free meals to the people*, *IGRom.*3.89 (Amastris, i A.D.), 4.1680 (Pergam.). 5. *personal attendant, slave*, Aristid.*Or.*49(25).3,15,20, 50(26).103. ❀ **-εύω**, *serve as a wet-nurse, suckle*, Lxx *Ex.*2.7, Ph.2.83, *BGU*297.16 (i A.D.), etc.: c. gen., τ. δουλικοῦ ἐγγόνου *PSI*10.1131.26 (i A.D.), cf. 1065.11 (ii A.D.):—so **-έω**, *BGU*1111.10 (i B.C., Pass.), 859.4 (iv A.D.); τροφέοντο (τροφόεντο cod., corr. Porson) was read by Aristarch. in Od.3.290, and τροφέοντα is v.l. in Il.15.621. **-ή**, ἡ, (τρέφω) *nourishment, food*, Hdt.3.48, S.*Ph.*32,953, Th.1.5, *Ev.Matt.* 3.4, Gal.6.35, Iamb.*VP*3.16, etc.; ἡ καθ' ἡμέραν ἀναγκαία τ. Th.1.2; *the means of maintaining* an army, *provisions, forage*, τροφὴν παρέχειν Id.8.57, cf. 6.93: pl., *OGI*56.70 (Canopus, iii B.C.), etc. 2. βίου τροφαί *way* of life, *livelihood, living*, S.*OC*338,446; τροφή alone, δουλίαν ἕξειν τροφήν Id.*Aj.*499, cf. *OC*362; φεῦ τῆς ἀνύμφου..σῆς τροφῆς Id.*El.*1183; τὰς ἐκ γῆς τ. ηὕρετο Pl.*Prt.*322a: then, simply, *mode of life*, δίκην τίνουσαι τῆς προτέρας τ. Id.*Phd.*81d, cf. 84b; βώμιοι τ. E.*Ion* 52. 3. *that which provides* or *procures sustenance*, as the bow of Philoctetes, χερὶ πάλλων τὰν ἐμὰν μελέου τροφάν S.*Ph.*1126 (lyr.). 4. *a meal*, τροφαῖς τέτταρσιν ἐχρῶντο Philem.Gloss.ap.Ath. 1.11d. II. *nurture, rearing*, παιδία..τρέφειν..τροφήν τινα τοιήνδε Hdt.2.2, cf. 3; χάριν τροφᾶς ἀμείβων v.l. in A.*Ag.*729 (lyr.); νέας τροφῆς στερηθεὶς S.*Aj.*511; μητρὸς τ. E.*Ion* 1377: freq. in pl., ἐν τροφαῖσιν *while in the nursery*, opp. ἐφηβήσας, A.*Th.*665; ἠντόμαν τροφαῖς Id.*Ag.*1159 (lyr.); ὦ δυσάθλιαι τ. S.*OC*330; αἱ ἐμαὶ τ. E.*Tr.*1187; τ. δημόσιαι Arist.*Rh.*1361ᵃ36; ἐκτίνων τροφάς, much like τροφεῖα, A.*Th.* 548; οἷς ὀδύνας ἀντὶ τροφῶν ἔλιπον *IG*12(5).973 (Tenos). 2. *education*, E.*Hec.*599 (pl.); τ. τε καὶ παιδεία Pl.*Alc.*1.122b, cf. Arist. *EN*1179ᵇ34, 1180ᵃ26, al. 3. *rearing* or *keeping of animals*, Hdt. 2.65; τροφαῖς ἵππων Pi.*O.*4.16. III. sts. in Poets for the concrete θρέμμα, *brood*. νέα τ. a new *generation*, S.*OT*1, cf. A.*Th.* 786 (lyr.); of animals, ἀρνῶν τροφαί, i.e. young lambs, E.*Cyc.* 189. IV. a *place in which* animals *are reared*, ἰβίων τροφαὶ *PTeb.* 5.70, cf. 62.19, al. (ii B.C.), *PPetr.*3 p.221 (iii B.C.), etc. -ημα, ατος, τό, f.l. for ῥυφ-, Hp.*Fist.*7; for ῥοφ-, Cael.Aur.*TP*4.8 (both pl.). -ητικός, ή, όν, *concerning maintenance*, *CPR*109.11 (iii A.D.). -ιά, ἡ, = σποδιά, Erot. s.v. τροφιωδέων. -ίας, ου, ὁ, *brought up in the house*, *stall-fed*, τ. ἵπποι, opp. φορβάδες, Arist.*HA* 604ᵃ29; βοῦς τροφίας (acc. pl.) *IG*2².1028.16, cf. Plu.*Aem.*33; κῶθον τροφίην (Ion. form) Numen.ap.Ath.7.304e. -ικός, ή, όν, *nursing*, *tending*, ἡ -κή (sc. τέχνη) Poll.7.209; τὰ τ. ὄργανα the *alimentary* organs, Gal.9.392. -ῐμαῖος, α, ον, *reared at home*: αἱ τ. *the daughters of the house*, Ph.2.443 (v.l. for τροφίμαις). ❀ -ῐμος, ον, also ος, η, ον, v. infr.:—*nourishing*, *nutritious*, γάλα -ώτατον Arist. *HA*523ᵃ11, cf. *Pr.*927ᵃ22 (Comp.), Phld.*Sign.*27, Sor.1.94, al., Gal. 6.382; opp. ἄτροφος, Thphr.*CP*6.4.5: c. gen., γᾶ τρόφιμε τῶν ἐμῶν τέκνων E.*Tr.*1302 (lyr.), cf. *Ion*235 (lyr.); also ὕδωρ τὸ περὶ κηπείας τ. Pl.*Lg.*845d; τ. κλυστῆρες *nutritive* enemata, Lycusap.Orib.8. 34 tit. II. Subst. τρόφιμος, ὁ, a slave's *young master*, ὁ τ. σου Men.*Epit.Fr.*1, cf. *Epit.*160, *Pk.*74, al., *Com.Adesp.*24.20, 25.41 D.; rendered *erilis filius* by Ter.*Andr.*602, *Eun.*289, *Phorm.*39, v. Donat. ad locc.: metaph., ἡ βουλὴ τὸν ἑαυτῆς τ. καὶ εὐεργέτην *SIG*879.10 (Erythrae, iii A.D.): ἡ τροφίμη *the mistress*, Poll.3.73. 2. neut. τρόφιμον, τό, *maintenance*, *sustenance*, *BGU*297.21 (i A.D.); τ. δουλικόν *PMich.Teb.*121ʳ I 18, al. (i A.D.): esp. *food-supply* of Alexandria, Just.*Edict.*13.26, *PKlein.Form.*328.4 (vi A.D., cf. *Arch.Pap.*5.294): τροφίμη σύνταξις contract *for board*, *AP*9.175 (Pall.). III. Pass., *nursling*, *foster-child*, παῖς τ. τίνος; E.*Ion* 684 (lyr.), cf. Archipp.23, Pl.*Plt.*272b; ὁ τ., freq. in Inscrr., *IG*2².3969, 3.3396, etc., and Pap., *POxy.*1491.10 (iv A.D.), etc.; τ. ἀδελφός *PCair.Preis.* 42.6 (iii/iv A.D.); fem. τροφίμη *POxy.*903.6 (iv A.D.): οἱ τ. *our nurslings*, *pupils*, Pl.*R.*520d, cf. *Lg.*804a; τ. τῆς ἀρετῆς Luc.*Bis Acc.*6, cf. *AP*10.52 (Pall.):—at Sparta, οἱ τ. were young persons too poor to pay their quota to the φιλίτια, and brought up as companions of the richer class, who paid for them, X.*HG*5.3.9:—also τ. κύνες dogs *kept in the house*, Ael.*NA*11.13, 16.31. 2. of bodies, *healthy*, *strong*, *well-nourished*, Hp.*Aër.*20 (Comp.); of plants, *flourishing*, *luxuriant*, Thphr.*CP*1.15.4 (Comp.). 3. τ. κύημα *viable*, *capable of life*, opp. ἀνεμιαῖον, Poll.2.6. -ῐμότης, ητος, ἡ, *nutritiousness*, Eust.742.24. -ιον, τό, *aliment*, *maintenance*, *Sammelb.*5349 (ii A.D.). 2. *diet*, Sor.ap.Gal.12.415: as Adj., ἐδάφη τ. *pastures* for the Hathor-cow, prob. in *BGU*1216.113 (ii B.C.). II. *circular pad* to prevent sores, Gal.18(2).457. -ιοῦται· παχύνεται, Hsch. -ις, ὁ, ἡ, τρόφι, τό, gen. ιος, (τρέφω) *well-fed*, *stout*, *large*, τ. κῦμα κυλίνδεται a *huge*, *swollen* wave, Il.11.307 (cf. τροφόεις); of men, ἐπεὰν γένωνται τρόφιες [οἱ παῖδες] when the children grow *big*, Hdt.4.9. II. *nursling*, Lyc.264; τρόφις Ἐννοσιγαίου *nursling* of the earth-shaker, epith. of the dolphin, Opp. *H.*2.634 (v.l. τρόχις). -ῖτις συγγραφή, contract *providing for aliment*, *PTeb.*51.8, 776.8 (both ii B.C.), *PMich.Teb.*121ᵛ I 6, al. (i A.D.); γυνὴ τ. either a *wet-nurse* (so *POxy.*37.9 (i A.D.)), or a *wife married according to a* συγγραφὴ τ., *PGiss.*37 ii 13, cf. 36.13 (ii B.C.). 2. τ. γῆ dub. sens. in *CPR*244.13 (iii A.D.). -ιώδης, ες, *containing coagulated matter*, οὖρα Hp.*Epid.*7.120; ἐκ τροφιώδεος.. ὑποπέλιον Id.*Coac.*567; and so prob. ἐκ τροφιωδέων should be restored for ἐκ στροφωδέων in Id.*Prorrh.*1.156:—cf. Gal. ad loc. (16. 819 K.): a different expl. is given by Erot., τροφιωδέων· σποδιωδῶν, τροφιὰ γὰρ ἡ σποδιὰ λέγεται; cf. ἐκ τροφωλέων· σποδοειδῶν, Hsch. Cf. τροφώδης II.

**τροφό-εις**, εσσα, εν, (τρέφω) *well-fed*, *stout*, *large*, *big*, κύματά τε τροφόεντα Il.15.621, Od.3.290 (v. τροφέω). -ποιός, όν, *rearing*, *bringing up*, ὀρνίθων Man.4.244.

**τροφός**, ὁ and ἡ, (τρέφω) *feeder*, *rearer*, Hom. only in Od. and always fem. of a *nurse*, φίλη τ. Εὐρύκλεια 2.361, al., cf. Hdt.2.156, 6. 61, Lxx*Ge.*35.8, *PCair.Zen.*292.157 (iii B.C.), *Glotta* 16.274 (Egypt), Sor.1.105, al., Gal.6.36, etc.; ἡ τ. βασιλέως *Sammelb.*4980 (i B.C.); of a mother, S.*Aj.*849.—The masc. was usu. τροφεύς (q.v.); but τροφός as masc. occurs in E.*HF*45, *El.*409, Pl.*Plt.*268a,c. 2. metaph., of a city, Συράκοσαι, ἀνδρῶν ἵππων τε δαιμόνιαι τροφοί Pi.*P.* 2.2; Γῇ τε μητρί, φιλτάτῃ τροφῷ A.*Th.*16; αἷματ᾽ ἐκποθένθ᾽ ὑπὸ χθονὸς τροφοῦ Id.*Ch.*66 (lyr.), cf. S.*OT*1092 (lyr.), *OC*760; μήτηρ ἁπάντων γαῖα καὶ κοινὴ τ. Men.*Mon.*617; νὺξ ἄστρων τ. E.*El.*54; τὴν γεωργίαν τῶν ἄλλων τεχνῶν μητέρα καὶ τ. X.*Oec.*5.17, cf. Pl.*Plt.*267d; of Miletus, τ. τοῦ.. Ἀπόλλωνος *SIG*906 A 5 (iv A.D.). 3. in neut., τὸ τροφόν *that which nourishes*, Pl.*Plt.*289a. 4. τροφός, ἡ, name of a plaster, Orib.*Fr.*99. II. Pass., *nursling*, τροφοί· ἀντὶ τοῦ θρέμματα (Meineke τροφαί), Hsch.

**τροφοσαρκωτική**, v.l. for τροφός, σαρκωτική in Paul.Aeg.7.17. 82.

**τροφοφορ-έω**, *bring* one *nourishment*, *sustain*, Lxx*De.*1.31, 2*Ma.* 7.27, *Act.Ap.*13.18 (v.l. ἐτροποφόρησε). -ος (parox.), ον, *nourishing*, Eust.773.50, 1401.45.

**τροφώ**, οῦς, ἡ, *nurse*, *IG*12(1).454 (Rhodes), *Ath.Mitt.*51.5 (ibid.), *Annuario* 2.128 (ibid.).

**τροφώδης**, ες, *nutritious*, Arist.*Pr.*871ᵇ19, Xenocr.ap.Orib.2.58. 40,50; τ. τῆς σαρκός Arist.*Pr.*893ᵃ29. II. = τροφιώδης; Hsch. explains σῦφαρ by τὸ ἐπὶ τοῦ γάλακτος τ.

❀ **Τροφώνιος**, ὁ, the legendary builder of the first temple of Apollo at Delphi, *h.Ap.*296; afterwards himself the possessor of a celebrated oracle, Pi.*Fr.*2, Hdt.1.46, 8.134; καταβαίνων ὥσπερ ἐς Τροφωνίου (sc. ἄντρον) Ar.*Nu.*508:—Ζεὺς τ. Str.9.2.38. II. **Τροφώνεια**, τά, *his festival*, *IG*7.49.10 (Megara, ii A.D.), 2².3169.18 (Athens, iii A.D.); written **Τροφώνια** in *IG*2².3147 (ii B.C.), Poll. 1.37 (v.l. -ωνίαι): both prob. contr. fr. *Τροφωνίεια. (An older form **Τρεφώνιος** in Boeot. Inscrr., *IG*7.3055 (Lebad.), 3080 (ibid.), 4136 (Ptoön, ii B.C.), al.)

**τροχᾰδ-άριος**, ὁ, (τροχάς) *shoemaker*, *IG*3.3463. -ην, Adv., (τρέχω) *running*, βαίνειν *Epigr.Gr.*288 (Cyprus), A.D.*Adv.*198. 4. ❀ -ια, τά, *walking-shoes*, *Edict.Diocl.*9.12.

**τροχάζω**, (τρέχω) *run quickly*, Hdt.9.66, X.*An.*7.3.46, etc.; τ. στάδια πλείω Σωτάδου Philetaer.3; ἵπποις τ., of a charioteer, E.*Hel.* 724; of a horse, Arist.*HA*604ᵇ12; τ. ἐν τοῖς ὅπλοις Plb.10.20.2; τὸν μακρὸν τ. δρόμον *Inscr.Prien.*112.111 (i B.C.); τροχάσαι τὴν λαμπάδα *run* the torch-race, *OGI*764.54 (Pergam., ii B.C.); *make a forced march*, App.*BC*3.88; Astrol., of the moon, τὰ μεγάλα, τὰ μείζονα, τὰ ἥττονα τ., Gal.19.556,562; ἐπὶ τὰ μείζονα τ. ibid.—The Verb was rejected by the Atticists, *AB*114.

**τροχᾱϊκός**, ή, όν, *trochaic*, Anon.Rhythm.3.13, Heph.3.3, al., Hermog.*Id.*1.3, 2.1, etc. Adv. -κῶς ibid., Eust.11.36. (The form **τροχαιικός** is recommended by Phryn.28.)

**τροχαιοειδής**, ές, *trochaic*, Aristid.Quint.1.17.

**τροχαῖος**, α, ον, (τρόχος) *running*, *spinning*, πανία (*spools*) *AP*6. 288 (Leon.). II. τροχαῖος (sc. πούς), ὁ, a *trochee* or *foot consisting of a long and a short syllable* (also called χορεῖος), Pl.*R.*400b, etc.; used in quick time, Arist.*Rh.*1408ᵇ36, cf. *Po.*1452ᵇ24, and v. τροχερός:—hence, 2. in Music, οἱ σαλπικταὶ τροχαῖόν τι συμβοήσαντες playing *a brisk march*, D.C.56.22; τ. νόμος a tune *in trochaic time*, invented by Terpander, Plu.2.1132d, cf. Poll.4.65. 3. *tribrach* (⏑⏑⏑), Quint.*Inst.*9.4.82. 4. τ. σημαντὸς ὁ ἐξ ὀκτασήμου θέσεως καὶ τετρασήμου ἄρσεως (⊔ ⊔ – –) Aristid.Quint.1.16; τ. ἀπὸ ἰάμβου (⏑ – | – ⏑ – ⏑ – ⏑) ibid. III. τροχαῖα· μέσα ἐν κύβοις, ἢ ὁδός, ὡς Ῥίνθων (*Fr.*26), Hsch. (perh. τρόχια and τροχιά).

**τροχαιοχόρειος**, ὁ, *trochee and tribrach* (– ⏑ | ⏑ ⏑ ⏑), Tz. in *An. Ox.*3.307.

**τροχαϊσμός**, ὁ, *trochaic metre*, Eust.1647.26.

**τροχᾰλ-εῖον**, τό, *globe* or *sphere*, Arat.530. -ία, v. τροχιλεία. -ίζω, *roll along*, in Pass., δίσκος -ισθεὶς Pherecyd.12 J. -ός, ή, όν, *running*, τροχαλὸν δὲ γέροντα τίθησιν makes him *run quick*, Hes.*Op.* 518 (but v. infr. II); Μοιράων τροχαλώτερε *AP*7.681 (Pall.); τ. ὄχοι *swift-rolling*, E.*IA*146 (anap.). Adv. -λῶς *Gloss.* II. *round*, *AP* 5.34 (Rufin.), Nic.*Th.*589, etc.; and in Hes. l.c., Eust. and others interpret it by κυρτός, *bowed*, *bent*; cf. τρόχμαλος.

**τροχαντήρ**, ῆρος, ὁ, in Anatomy, *trochanter*, i.e. either of two *processes* at the head of the thigh bone, Gal.*UP*15.8, cf. Id.2.309, 312, Epigr.ap.S.E.*M.*1.316 sq. II. part of the stern of a ship, Hsch. III. an instrument of torture, Lxx 4*Ma.*8.13 (v.l. -τήρια).

**τροχαρέα**, v. τροχιλεία.

**τροχάς**, άδος, ἡ, in pl., = σανδάλια ἀπὸ αἰγείου δέρματος, Hsch., cf. *Edict.Diocl.* in *IG*2².1120: sg., = *gallicula*, *Gloss.*

**τρόχ-ασμα**, ατος, τό, *course*, *running*, *App.Anth.*6.193 (pl.): also -ασμός, ὁ, *Hippiatr.*42 (pl.), Hsch. s.v. ὑπὸ δρόμον. -αστής, οῦ, ὁ, *one who works a water-wheel*, *PKlein.Form.*1197 (vi A.D.). -αστικός, ή, όν, later Greek for Att. θρεκτικός (Moer.p.187 P.), ἡ τ. ἕξις or δύναμις Arr.*Epict.*2.18.1. -άω, Ep. form of τροχάζω, Arat. 1105, *APl.*4.275 (Posidipp.), *Anacreont.*29.6, etc.; of the stars, *revolve*, Arat.227. -ειλέα, v. τροχιλεία. -εῖον, v. τρόχιον. -ελλέα, v. τροχιλεία. -εός, ή, όν, = τροχόεις, Nic.*Th.*658. -ερός, ά, όν, (τροχός) *running*, *tripping*, τ. ῥυθμὸς τὰ τετράμετρα Arist.*Rh.*1409ᵃ1; cf. τροχαῖος II. -εύομαι, = Lat. *rotor*, Dosith.p.432 K. -ή, ἡ, = τρόχος, *course*, *Trag.Adesp.*261.

**τροχηλ-ᾰσία**, ἡ, *locomotion*, metaph. of the *mutability* of human life, Hp.*Ep.*17. -ατέω, *drive a chariot*: metaph., *drive hither and thither*, τροχηλατεῖν τινα μανίαισι E.*Or.*36; Κῆρες τροχηλατήσουσ᾽ ἐμμανῆ πλανώμενον Id.*El.*1253. -άτης [ᾰ], ου, ὁ, (ἐλαύνω) *charioteer*, formed like ἱππηλάτης, S.*OT*806, E.*Ph.*39. 2. τ. ἵππος, = *currilis equus*, *Gloss.* -ᾰτος, ον, *wheel-drawn*, σκηναὶ A.*Pers.*1001 (lyr.); δίφροι S.*El.*49. 2. *dragged by* or *at the wheels*, σφαγαὶ Ἕκτορος τροχήλατοι E.*Andr.*399. 3. *ploughed with wheels*, κελεύθου τρίοδος A.*Fr.*173. 4. *formed on the potter's wheel*, λύχνος Ar.*Ec.*1, cf. Xenarch.1.9. 5. metaph., *hurried along like a wheel* or *chariot*, E.*HF*122 (lyr.); τ. μανία *whirling* madness, Id. *IT*82. -ιά, v. τροχιλεία.

❀ **τροχιά**, ἡ, *wheel-track*, *rut*, Hsch., Phot., etc. II. *the round of a wheel*, *AP*7.478 (Leon.), 9.418 (Antip.), Nic.*Th.*816. III. *path*, Lxx*Pr.*4.26 (= *Ep.Hebr.*12.13). IV. *elastic strand in the τόνος of a torsion-engine*, Ph.*Bel.*54.41, prob. for τριχέα in Hero *Bel.* 108.3.

**τροχιάζω**, *roto*, *rotor*, *Gloss.*

**τροχιαῖος**, α, ον, *worked by a wheel*, σφήν (perh. = τροχαντήρ III) Lxx 4*Ma.*11.10.

**τροχῐαμβικός**, ή, όν, *consisting of trochee and iambus*, Sch.Heph. pp.137,360 C.

**τροχίας**, ου, ὁ, *courier*, *messenger*, Hsch. II. τ. χαλκός *cast* brass (less correct for χυτός), Poll.7.105.

**τροχίασμα**, ατος, τό, = τροχός, *wheel-work*, Bito 66.10.

**τροχίζω**, fut. Att. -ιῶ *AP* (v. infr.): (τροχός):—*break on the wheel*, *torture*, D.S.20.71, *AP*5.180 (Asclep.):—Pass., Antipho 1.20, Arist. *EN*1153ᵇ19; = ὑπὸ τροχοῦ κατατμηθῆναι ἢ καταθραυσθῆναι, Phryn.*PS* p.114B. II. *furnish with wheels*, Bito 58.3 (Pass.). III. Pass., *run round*, or perh. *take carriage exercise*, Arist.*Pr*.935$^b$29.

**τροχικός,** ή, όν, *granulated*, χαλκός *PLeid.X*.82.

**τροχῐλ-εία,** ἡ, *block-and-tackle equipment*, *pulley* or *system of pulleys*, *roller of a windlass*, and the like, *IG*1$^2$.313.112, 314.123, 374.142, 2$^2$.1666.91, 1672.205, al., 11(2).161*A*98 (Delos, iii B.C.); the later spelling **τροχιλία** is found in codd. of Hp.*Art*.43, Ar.*Lys*.722 (where τροχιλείας is metrically prob.), Plb.1.22.5, 8.4.5, Plu.2.18c, *Eum*.11, Gal.*UP*7.14; the word is variously corrupted in Archipp. 33; the form **τροχιλέα** occurs in Arist.*Mech*.851$^b$19, Ath.Mech.14.8, Suid. (citing Socr.ap.D.L.2.36, where τροχιλία); **τροχειλέα** prob. in *PLond*.3.1177.216 (ii A.D.); **τροχαλία,** Arist.*Mech*.853$^a$36, $^b$2; **τροχηλιά** (oxyt.), Thphr.*HP*4.3.5, Gal.*UP*7.14 (as v.l.); **τροχελλέα,** *POxy*.502.35 (ii A.D.); **τροχιλλέα,** *BGU*1116.24 (i B.C.), *Gloss.*; **τροχαρέα,** *PLond*.1821.194: metaph., μετά τινος τροχιλίας with a certain *ease* or *glibness*, Ath.13.587f (s.v.l.). **-εῖον,** τό, *pulley-block*, *pulley*, *IG*4$^2$(1).102.49 (Epid., iv B.C.); for the gen. pl. τροχιλιῶν (v.l. τροχίλων) in Pl.*R*.397a, and τροχιλίων in Moschio ap.Ath.5.208e, Hero *Spir*.1.27 (v.l.), τροχιλείων shd. perh. be read. **-ίδιον,** τό, Dim. of foreg., Hero *Spir*.1.27 (fort. τροχιλείδιον).

**τροχίλος** [ῐ], ὁ, (τρέχω) *Egyptian plover*, *Charadrius melanocephalus* (or perh. *spur-winged plover*, *Hoplopterus spinosus*), said to pick leeches from the crocodile's throat by Hdt.2.68; or to pick the crocodile's teeth by Arist.*HA*612$^a$21; cf. Ar.*Av*.79, *Ach*.876, *Pax* 1004 (anap.), Clearch.73, Ael.*NA*3.11, 8.25, 12.15. 2. *wren*, *Troglodytes europaeus*, Arist.*HA*615$^a$17, Plu.2.405d; cf. τύραννος I.4. II. Archit., *hollow between the mouldings on the base of a column*, also called *scotia*, Vitr.3.5.2. III. *sheave* in block-and-tackle equipment, Pl.*R*.397a (v.l.), *IG*2$^2$.1672.156,241, Hero *Bel*.85.4, *Spir*.1.26, al., Eust.1534.8.

**τροχῐλώδης,** ες, *like a pulley*, Orib.25.16.3 (quoted from Gal.2.769), Gal.18(2).349 (ubi τραχηλώδης), *UP*2.15.

**τροχίμαλλον,** τό, *heap of stones*, Ar.*Fr*.876 (s.v.l., cf. τρόχμαλος).

**τρόχ-ῐμος,** ον, *running*, *hastening*, S.*Fr*.240 (lyr.). **-ιον,** τό, Dim. of τροχός, *IG*4$^2$(1).102.292 (Epid., iv B.C.), 2$^2$.1548.4, 1550.4, Hero *Aut*.10.2, *Spir*.1.16; cf. τροχεῖον, *rotella*, *Gloss.* **-ιός,** ά, όν, = τροχόεις, *round*, φθοΐς *AP*6.258 (Adaeus). **-ις,** ὁ, *courier*, *messenger*, acc. τρόχιν A.*Pr*.941, S.*Inach.* in *PTeb*.692 ii 6 (troch.), Opp.*H*.2.634 (v.l. τρόφιν).

**τροχισκ-άριον,** τό, Dim. of τροχίσκος, Orib.*Fr*.82. **-ιον,** τό, Dim. of sq., Sch.A.R.4.144. ✻ **-ος** (parox.), ὁ, Dim. of τροχός, *small wheel* or *circle*, Arist.*Mech*.848$^a$25, Apollod.*Poliorc*.155.9. 2. *troche* or *trochisk*, of honey, Arist.*Mir*.831$^b$27; of soap, medicine, etc., Thphr.*HP*9.9.3, Antyll.ap.Orib.10.24.1, Sor.2.41, Gal.12.276. 3. *ear-ring*, Lxx *Ez*.16.12. 4. *a metal ball*, let fall to mark time, Lyd.*Mag*.2.16.

**τροχίτης** [ῑ], ου, ὁ (sc. οἶνος), name of a wine made in Cyprus, Dsc.5.32.

**τρόχμᾰλος,** ὁ, *rolled stone*, *pebble*, Thphr.*CP*3.6.4: pl. τρόχμαλοι, *a heap of such stones*, *cobble-wall*, *dry dyke*, Eust.1259.33; also neut. τρόχμαλα Nic.*Th*.143: sg. in collect. sense, σῆμα χωστῷ τροχμάλῳ κατηρεφές Lyc.1064.

**τροχο-βόλος,** ὁ, = τροχαστής, *PMasp*.139 (p.53) (vi A.D.). **-δῑνέομαι,** Pass., *whirl* or *roll round*, τροχοδινεῖται δ' ὄμμαθ' ἑλίγδην A.*Pr*.882 (anap.); cf. στροφοδινέομαι. **-ειδής,** ές, *round like a wheel*, *circular*, λίμνη, of the lake of Delos, Thgn.7, Hdt.2.170; of the lake of Gennesaret, J.*BJ*3.10.7; πόλις τ., of Athens, Orac.ap.Hdt.7.140; of leaves, *arranged in a whorl*, Dsc.3.27. Adv. -δῶς *in a whorl*, ib.103. **-εις,** εσσα, εν, *round as a wheel*, *round*, λίμνη Call.*Del*.261 (cf. foreg.); κύλιξ *AP*11.58 (Maced.); μόλυβδος ib.6.65 (Paul. Sil.); ἀλφοί Nic.*Th*.332, etc. **-κουράς,** άδος, ὁ, ἡ, (κείρω) *shaven* or *shorn all round*, Choeril.4 (τροχοκουράδες ap.Eus., τροχοκούριδες (f.l.) ap.J.*Ap*.1.22). **-παικτέω,** *play with wheels* or *hoops*, of acrobats or jugglers, Artem.1.76 (perh. = τροχοὺς μιμεῖσθαι, cf. X.*Smp*.2.22). **-πέδη,** ἡ, *the drag* or *brake of a wheel*, Herodes Atticus ap.Ath.3.99c. **-ποιέω,** *make wheels*, Ar.*Pl*.513 (anap.).

✻ **τροχός,** ὁ, (τρέχω) *wheel*, Il.6.42, 23.394, etc.; γῆ ἐπημαξευμένη τροχοῖσιν S.*Ant*.252; ἐν πτερόεντι τ. . .κυλινδόμενον, of Ixion, Pi.*P*.2.22; τροχοὺς μιμεῖσθαι to imitate *wheels*, of one who bends back so as to form a wheel, X.*Smp*.2.22, 7.3: metaph. of fortune, πότμος ἐν. .θεοῦ τροχῷ κυκλεῖται S.*Fr*.871; also μανίας τροχῷ E.*Pirith.Oxy*.2078 *Fr*.1.14. 2. *potter's wheel*, Il.18.600; τροχῷ ἐλαθεὶς [λύχνος] (cf. τροχήλατος) Ar.*Ec*.4; τροχοῦ ῥύμαισι τευκτὸν. .κύτος Antiph.52.2, cf. Pl.*R*.420e. 3. *wheel of a stage-machine*, Ar.*Fr*.188; also of a water-*wheel*, ὁ τ. τῆς μηχανῆς *POxy*.1292.13 (i A.D.); τ. καὶ μηχανή *PSI*9.1072.9 (iii A.D.). 4. *wheel of torture*, Anacr.21.9; ἐπὶ τοῦ τ. στρεβλοῦσθαι Ar.*Pl*.875, *Lys*.846, D.29.40; ἕλκεσθαι Ar.*Pax*452; ἐπὶ τὸν τ. ἀναβῆναι Antipho 5.40; ἀναβιβάζειν τινὰ ἐπὶ τὸν τ. And.1.43; ἐν τῷ τ. ἐνδεδεμένον Plu.2.509c; τῷ τ. προσηλοῦν [Ἰξίονα] ib.19e, cf. Luc.*DDeor*.6.5. 5. rotating *wheels* used in sieges as a defence against projectiles, D.S.17.45. II. child's *hoop*, Antyll.ap.Orib.6.26.5, S.E.*P*.1.106. III. *round cake*, κηροῖο, στέατος τ., Od.12.173, 21.178; τ. ἡλίου the sun's *disk*, Ar.*Th*.17 (v. infr. B); *coil* of a serpent, Orph.*L*.136. 2. *large pill* (cf. τροχίσκος 2), Sor.1.65, *POxy*.2144.25 (iii A.D.). IV. θαλάττης γῆς τε τ. *circles* or *zones* of land and sea, Pl.*Criti*.113d, cf. 115c, 116a, 117c sq., Plu.*Luc*.39. V. *circuit of a wall* or *fortification*, Κυκλώπιος τ. S.*Fr*.227, cf. Sch.A Pl.*Lg*.681a (v. facsim. fol. 175$^v$). VI. *ring playing on the bit* of a bridle, X.*Eq*.10.6, Poll.1.184. 2. *ring for passing a rope through*, on board ship, ib.94. VII. *whirlwind*, Lxx *Ps*.76(77).18. VIII. *wash-pot* (?), Gal.18(2).671. IX. a fish or sea-monster (Lat. *rota*, Plin.*HN*9.8), Ael.*NA*13.20. X. metaph., ὁ τ. τῆς γενέσεως *Ep.Jac*.3.6; ὁ τῆς εἱμαρμένης τε καὶ γενέσεως τ. Simp. *in Cael*.377.14.

B. τρόχος, ὁ, *circular race*, Hp.*Vict*.2.63, 3.68, *Insomn*.89; μὴ πολλοὺς τ. ἁμιλλητῆρας ἡλίου not many racing *courses* of the sun, i.e. not many days (codd. τροχούς *wheels*), S.*Ant*.1065; παῖδες ἐκ τρόχων πεπαυμένοι E.*Med*.46. 2. *place for running*, *race-course*, Id.*Hipp*.1133 (lyr.). II. an animal, Herodor.58J. (Trypho ap.Ammon.*Diff*.p.131V. distd. the two senses as above.)

**τροχ-ός,** όν, *running*, *tripping*, μέλος Pi.*Fr*.177. II. *round*, ἀσπίδες Lyd.*Mag*.1.10 (Sup.); but τροχωταῖς is prob. cj. **-ώδης,** ες, = τροχοειδής, Apollon.*Lex.* s.v. ὀλοοίτροχος, Sch.Nic.*Th*.166; v.l. for χυτρώδης in S.*Ichn*.295 (χυτροιδης text, τροχοιδη[s] mg. Pap.). **-ωσις,** εως, ἡ, *circular motion*, [βρονταὶ] -ώσεις ἐμποιοῦσι τῷ κενῷ Lyd.*Ost*.21. ✻ **-ωτός,** όν, v. τροχός, όν, II.

✻ **τρύβλιον,** τό, *cup*, *bowl*, Ar.*Eq*.650, *Av*.77, al.; εἰρήνης ῥοφήσει τρύβλιον Id.*Ach*.278; μισθοῦ τ. ῥοφῆσαι Id.*Eq*.905: also in later Gr., Lxx *Nu*.7.13, al., *Ev.Matt*.26.23. II. in Medic. prescriptions, a measure, = ὀξύβαφον II, Hp.*Int*.1, *Mul*.2.109, Alex.142, Gal.19.752. III. = κεραμεοῦν ἄγγος ἐπιδεχόμενον ὡς εἴκοσι ἀρτάβας, Ptol.Euerg.9J. [Proparox. acc. to Hdn.Gr.1.357, and so in Ar. ll. cc., Lxx ll. cc. (cod. B), Suid.; τρυβλίον (s.v.l.) Hp. ll. cc., Gal.19.752, 753, Hsch., *Gp*.7.36.1.]

**τρυγαβόλια·** εἰς ἃ καρποὺς ξηροὺς ἀπετίθεντο, Hsch.

**τρυγάνη,** ἡ, = *tribula*, expld. as τ. ἡ τὸν σῖτον ἀλοῶσα, *Gloss.* (post τρυτ-); cf. τυκάνη.

✻ **τρῠγάω,** (τρύγη): I. with acc. of the fruit gathered, *gather in* the fruit or crop, ἑτέρας [σταφυλὰς] τρυγόωσιν Od.7.124, cf. *Ev.Luc*.6.44; σῦκα, σῖτον, *Com.Adesp*.812 (Pass.), 787 (anap.): metaph., τρυγήσομεν αὐτήν (sc. Εἰρήνην) Ar.*Pax*1338 (lyr.); τ. παίδων ἄνθος *AP*12.256 (Mel.); ὄμφακας ἡλικίης *IG*14.769 (Naples):— Pass., Hdt.4.199, Arist.*Pr*.925$^b$15, *PCair.Zen*.184.5 (iii B.C.); of honey, Mosch.3.35; καθ' ὥραν τετρυγημένοι (by death) Luc.*Cat*.5. 2. abs., θερίζουσι καὶ σπείρουσι καὶ τρυγῶσι ταῖς γλώτταισι Ar.*Av*.1698 (lyr.), cf. *Pax*912, Pl.*Lg*.844e, *PCair.Zen*.300.17 (iii B.C.). II. with acc. of that from which the fruit is gathered, *gather* or *reap off* the trees or ground, ὅτε τρυγόῳεν ἀλωήν (Ep. opt. for τρυγῷεν) Il.18.566; οἱ δ' ἐτρύγων οἴνας Hes.*Sc*.292; ἀμπέλους τρυγῶν *Com.Adesp*.437; τοὺς Ταντάλου κήπους ib.530; τ. ἑαυτήν (sc. τὴν ἄμπελον) X.*Oec*.19.19. 2. prov., ἐρήμας τρυγᾶν (sc. ἀμπέλους) *strip* unwatched *vines*, of one who is bold where there is nothing to fear, Ar.*Ec*.886, *V*.634, ubi v. Sch. 3. metaph., c. acc. pers., *strip* one, i.e. *rob* him, Luc.*DMeretr*.1.2: c. acc. rei, *rob*, βίᾳ τρυγήσαντες τὸν περιστερεῶνα *BGU*1855.13 (i B.C.).

**τρύγγας,** ὁ, v.l. for πύγαργος, Arist.*HA*593$^b$5.

**τρυγέρᾰνος,** ὁ, burlesque name of an animal, to be sent to Seleucus in exchange for his tiger, Philem.47.

**τρῠγερός,** ά, όν, (τρύξ) = τρυγώδης, *full of lees*, οὐ τρυγεροὺς τὰ φθέγματ' οὐδὲ γλύξιδας Polyzel.12.

**τρῠγέω,** = ξηραίνω, Hsch.; cf. τρύγη II and τρύγω. II. late form for τρυγάω, *POxy*.1859.4 (vi/vii A.D.).

✻ **τρύγ-η** [ῠ], ἡ, I. *grain-crop*, *corn*, οὐδὲ τρύγην οἴσεις *h.Ap*.55, cf. Theognost.*Can*.24, *EM*167.24, al., Eust.1003.59. 2. *vintage*, *AP*11.203, Ath.2.40b, *PRyl*.157.18 (ii A.D.), etc.; τ. ἀμπέλων Hierocl.p.63A.; οἱ ἐπὶ τρύγῃ *grape-gatherers*, Hsch. s.v. σταφυλοδρόμοι; cf. τρυγητήρ. II. *dryness*, Nic.*Th*.368. **-ημα,** ατος, τό, *crop*, of honey, Atticista ined.ap.Ruhnk.*Tim.* s.v. βλίττειν. **-ήσιμος,** ον, *ripe for gathering*, *EM*271.32, Hsch. s.v. διατρύγιος, *Gloss.* **-ησις,** εως, ἡ, *harvest*, *vintage*, *PCair.Zen*.300.21 (iii B.C.), Plu.2.646e (pl.). **-ητήρ,** ῆρος, ὁ, *one who gathers ripe fruit*, esp. *grapes*, Hes.*Sc*.293 [with ῡ metri gr.]. II. = προτρυγητήρ, Colum.11.2. **-ητήριον,** τό, *wine-press*, *Gloss.* **-ητής,** οῦ, ὁ, = τρυγητήρ I, Lxx *Je*.29.10(49.9), al., *PTeb*.120.8 (i B.C.), Corn.*ND*30, Poll.1.222. **-ητικός,** ή, όν, *of* or *for the vintage*, *PStrassb*.40.49 (vi A.D.), *PSI*8.953.19,65 (vi A.D.), *Gloss.* **-ητος,** ὁ, *gathering of fruits*, *vintage*, *harvest*, Lxx *Is*.24.13, *PCair.Zen*.355.113 (iii B.C.), *PTeb*.120.120, al. (i B.C.), Plu.2.671d, cf. Poll.1.61. 2. *time thereof*, *harvest* or *vintage*, Th.4.84, Thphr.*HP*5.1.2, 9.11.8, Lxx *Am*.4.7, al., Luc.*Philops*.22, Gal.6.577. II. = τρύγη, *fruit gathered*, *crop*, Lxx *Jl*.1.11, al. III. *wine-press*, καθάπερ εἰς τοὺς τρυγητοὺς ὁ πᾶς οἶνος ἐμβάλλεται Gal.*Nat.Fac*.1.15. IV. (oxyt.) *drying up* of a lake, Sch.Nic.*Th*.368. (τρύγητος ὁ καιρὸς μονογενῶς, τρυγητὸς δὲ τὸ τρυγώμενον Hdn.Gr.1.220, cf. Hsch.; but ὀξυτόνως ὁ καιρὸς τοῦ τρυγᾶν Ammon.*Diff*.p.17V.; Moschop. ad Hes.*Op*.386 denies the distinction.) **-ήτρια,** ἡ, fem. of τρυγητήρ, D.57.45, Poll.1.222.

**τρῠγη-φάγος** [ᾰ], ον, *devouring crops*, Plu.2.730b; also **ἀ-τρυγηφάγος,** Hsch.; **ὀ-τρυγηφάγος,** Archil.97. **-φάνιος οἶνος,** ὁ, *second* wine *pressed from the husks*, Poll.6.17; also **-φάνιον,** τό, Id.7.151: cf. δευτερίας. **-φόρος,** ον, *bearing corn* or *grapes*, *h.Ap*.529.

**τρῠγ-ία,** ἡ, = τρύξ II, *lees*, *sediment*, οἰνηρὰ τ. Ph.*Bel*.86.29, cf. *Mim.Oxy*.413.55, *Gp*.7.12.7; ἐλαίου Hsch. s.v. τρύγιος; ὄξεος Aret.*CA*2.3; τ. αἵματος Gal.19.490. 2. = τρύξ I, *new wine*, *BGU*531 i 22 (i A.D.). **-ίας,** ου, ὁ, *full of lees* or *sediment*, οἶνος Orac.ap.Plu.2.295e, Orib.*Fr*.76. II. Subst., = τρύξ II, Lxx *Ps*.74(75).9, Hdn.*Epim*.137. 2. = τρύξ I, *new wine*, *BGU*417.9 (ii/iii A.D.). **-ίζω,**

*look like lees* or *dregs*, Aret.*SD*2.9. **-ικός**, ή, όν, *of lees*, = κωμῳδικός, Ar.*Ach.*628 (anap.); τ. χορός cj. Jacobs in *AP*7.410.3 (Diosc.); cf. τρυγῳδικός. **-ῖνον**, τό, *made from lees*, name of a black pigment, Polygnot. et Micon ap. Plin.*HN*35.42.

**τρύγιος**· τρυγία οἴνου ἢ ἐλαίου, Hsch.

**τρύγις**, ή, = ὄλυρα, v. l. for τίφη in Hp.*Vict.*2.43.

**τρῠγο-δαίμων**, ονος, ὁ, in Ar.*Nu.*296, for τρυγῳδός, with a play on κακοδαίμων, *a poor-devil poet.* **-δίφησις** [δῐ], εως, ή, (διφάω) *diving into lees*, a game in which the players had to dip their heads into a bowl full of lees so as to get something out, Poll.9.122,124.

**τρῠγόζω**, f.l. for τρύζω, of doves, in Ps.-Hdn.ap.Boissonade *Anecd.Gr.*3.263 (cf. *Stud.Ital.*1.79, *Philologische Abhandlungen Martin Herz..dargebracht* (Berlin 1888) 227).

**τρῠγοιπ-έω**, *strain wine*, Suid. **-ος** (proparox.), ὁ, *straining-cloth* for wine, Ar.*Pax*535, *Pl.*1087, Phryn.270, Poll.6.19, 10.75.

**τρυγονάω**, v. θρυγονάω.

**τρῠγόν-ιον**, τό, Dim. of τρυγών I, Them.*Or.*22.273c; as a pet name for a girl, *AP*7.222 (Phld.). II. = περιστερεὼν ὀρθός, Ps.-Dsc.4.59, Poet.*de herb.*56. III. f.l. for τιτιγόνιον (q.v.). **-ιος**, α, ον, *of* or *from a* τρυγών II, Opp.*H.*2.480.

**τρύγος**, τό, later form for τρύγη, *Et.Gud.*536, Antioch.Astr. in *Cat. Cod.Astr.*7.126, *Gloss.*; **τρύγος**, ὁ, Hsch. s. v. τρυγητός.

**τρῠγοσώμᾰτος**, ον, perh. *wasting the body*, Lyr. in *Philol.*80.334.

**τρῠγόω**, = τρυγάω, pf. part. Pass. τετρυγωμένος, *Gloss.*

**τρυγυλίας**, = τετριμμένος, dub. in Hsch. s. v. λᾶς τρυγυλίας (λαστρ. cod.).

**τρύγω**, *dry*, τρύγει· ξηραίνει, Theognost.*Can.*24; but τρυγεῖ· ξηραίνει, Hsch.; τρύγει· ξηραίνεται, Zonar.:—ἔτρυγεν· ἐξηράνθη, ἐπὶ λίμνης, Hsch.

**τρῠγῳδέω**, = κωμῳδέω, Hsch.

**τρῠγώδης**, ες, *like lees* or *dregs, thick*, πτύσις Hp.*Coac.*542; πύον, αἷμα, ἕλκος, Aret.*SD*1.14, 2.9, 2.4, cf. Sor.2.44; of milk, in respect of smell, Id.1.91; of an eye-salve, Cels.6.6.8; τὸ τ. (sc. τοῦ οἴνου) Arist.*Pr.*926b35, cf. Plu.2.693e; τ. τὴν χροιάν Ruf.*Anat.*31.

**τρῠγῳδ-ία**, ή, Com. word (with parody on τραγῳδία) for κωμῳδία, Ar.*Ach.*499,500 (variously expld. by Gramm.: either because the actors smeared their faces with *lees* (τρύξ) or because *new wine* was given as a prize, cf. Sch. ad loc., Anon.*Proll.Com.* in *CGF* p.7 K., etc.; or because comedy was acted at the season of *vintage* (τρύγη), Ath. 2.40b). **-ικός**, ή, όν, = κωμῳδικός, χορός Ar.*Ach.*886; cf. τρυγῳδός.

**τρῠγῳδο-ποιο-μουσική** (sc. τέχνη), ή, *the art of comedy*, Ar.*Fr.* 333.

**τρῠγῳδός**, ὁ, (τρύξ, ᾠδή) prop. *must-singer* or *lees-singer*, = κωμῳδός, Ar.*V.*650 (anap.), 1537; v. τρυγῳδία.

**τρῠγών**, όνος, ή, (τρύζω) *turtle-dove, Columba turtur*, Ar.*Av.*302 (troch.), 979 (hex.), *Ev.Luc.*2.24, Gal.6.700, etc.; περιστεραὶ τρυγόνες Aristeas 145: prov. of a great talker, τρυγόνος λαλίστερος Men.416, cf. Alex.92.3, Theoc.15.88, Alciphr.3.29; πονηρὰ κατὰ τρυγόνα ψάλλεις, ἐπὶ τῶν ἐπιπόνως ζώντων, Diogenian.7.71, cf. Hsch. s. v. τρυγονοψάλλειν. II. a kind of fish, the *sting-ray*, τρυγόνες ὀπισθόκεντροι Epich.66, cf. Arist.*HA*489b31, Antiph.26.23, Cels.6.9.6, Gal.*Vict. Att.*8; cf. τρυγόνιος. III. an oviparous quadruped of uncertain kind, Arist.*HA*540a31.

**τρυεῖτις**, = θρυῖτις, *BGU*485.10 (ii A.D.).

**τρύζω**, Hp.*Mul.*2.131, al., Arat.948, etc.: Ep. impf. τρύζεσκον Theoc.7.140: aor. ἔτρυξα Sopat.5 codd.Ath. (ἔγρυξεν Schw., Kaibel), (ἐπ-) Babr.112.8: mostly used in pres. and impf.:—*make a low murmuring sound*, of the note of the ὀλολυγών, Theoc. l. c., Arat. l. c., *AP*5.291 (Agath.); of the τρυγών, Poll.5.89, Eust.229.24, Ps.-Hdn. in *Stud.Ital.*1.80 (cf. τρυγόζω): metaph., of men, *mutter, murmur*, Il.9.311. 2. of liquids, *squirt out with a noise*, of diarrhoea, Hp.*Prog.*11; but τ. τὸ οὖρον Id.*Mul.*2.131, cf. *Steril.*247, *Prorrh.* 2.4, seems to mean *comes by drops.* 3. *creak*, of shoes, only in Philostr.*Ep.*37 (dub.). (Onomatop.)

**τρυηλίς**, ίδος, ή, *ladle, spoon*, Luc.*Lex.*7: τρυηλίς· ζωμήρυσις (ζῷον ῥύσις cod.), Hsch.

**τρῠλ-ίζω**, *gurgle*, of the bowels, Hp.*Int.*6 (τρυλλίζει, v. l. τρύζει); of the cry of a quail, Poll.5.89. **-ισμός**, ὁ, *gurgling*, Hp.*Mul.*1. 32 (cod. θ, τραυλισμός codd.Erot.). (Onomatop., like τρύζω.)

**τρύλλιον**, τό, = τρούλλιον, *Stud.Pal.*20.67.10 (ii/iii A.D.).

**τρῦμα**, ατος, τό, = τρύμη, *hole*, Sch.Ar.*Nu.*447. II. **τρύμα**, = πόνος, Theognost.*Can.*24.

**τρῡμᾰλ-ιά**, ή, = τρύμη, *hole*, Sotad.1 (sens. obsc.), Lxx *Je.*13.4, al.; ή τ. τῆς ῥαφίδος the *eye* of the needle, *Ev.Marc.*10.25; βελόνης Maria ap.Zos.Alch.p.238 B.; *mesh*, Aesop.26. **-ῖτις**, ιδος, ή, epith. of Aphrodite, Hsch.

**τρῡμάτιον**, τό, Dim. of τρῦμα, *EM*752.51 (τρυμμ-, prob. f. l. for τρημάτιον).

**τρύμη** [ῡ], ή, (τρύω) *hole*, Sch.Ar.*Nu.*447. II. metaph., *sharp fellow, sly knave*, Ar.*Nu.*448.

⊛ **τρύξ**, ή, gen. τρῠγός, *wine not yet fermented and racked off, must*, Anacr.41, Ar.*Nu.*50, al.: hence, *new, raw wine*, Cratin.250, *PTeb.* 555 (ii A.D.): prov., κατ' ὀπώρην τρύξ *must* in autumn, i.e. a state of ferment, Cic.*Att.*2.12.3. II. *lees of wine, dregs*, οἶνος ἀπὸ τρυγός Archil.4; ἐπειδὴ καὶ τὸν οἶνον ἠξίους πίνειν, συνεκποτέ' ἐστί σοι καὶ τὴν τ. Ar.*Pl.*1085, cf. Pherecr.249; συὸς τρύγα προσενεγκαμένης καροῦται..τὰ γαλουχούμενα Sor.1.88, cf. 2.41 (s. v. l.); = στέμφυλα, Gal.6.576; κυλίκεσσι καὶ ἐς τρύγα χεῖλος ἐρείδων Theoc.7.70; ἐν τῇ τ. τοῦ πίθου Luc.*Tim.*19; of other liquors, τ. [τοῦ ἄσχυ] Hdt.4.23; ἐλαίου Poll.1.245; ὄξευς Nic.*Th.*932; γῆ ὑπόστασις καὶ τ. τοῦ ὕδατος Metrod.ap.*Placit.*3.9.5. 2. of metals, *dross*, σιδηρήεσσα τρύξ Nic. *Al.*51; χαλκοῦ Dsc.5.103. 3. *faecal matter* in the stomach, Hp. *Epid.*5.79; αἵματος Gal.18(1).730. 4. metaph., ἠχώ.., φωνῆς τρύγα *APl.*4.155 (Euod.): metaph. also of an *old man* or *woman*, Ar. *V.*1309, *Pl.*1086. III. τρύγες στεμφυλίτιδες *second wine* pressed out of the husks, *poor wine*, Hp.*Vict.*2.52; ή ἐκ [στεμφύλων] τρύξ *Gp.*6.13.2; without any addition, Gal.6.580; cf. τρυγηφάνιος. IV. τ. οἴνου κεκαυμένη, = φέκλη, *salt of tartar*, obtained from the matter deposited on the bottom and sides of wine-vats, Dsc.5.114, *Eup.*2. 164, Gal.12.490; τροχίσκοι τρυγὸς ἢ ῥυπτόμεθα scouring balls of this substance, Thphr.*HP*9.9.3.

**τρύος**, εος, τό, (τρύω) = πόνος, *distress, toil, labour*, Call.ap.*Et.Gen.* (= Powell *Coll.Alex.*p.96).

**τρῦπα**, ή, *hole*, Eust.1069.19 (ubi τρύπα), *Gloss.*; ή τοῦ μυὸς τ. Hdn. *Epim.*89; but **τρύπη**, ib.136, *AP*14.62; αἱ τῶν αὐλῶν τρῦπαι Hsch. s. v. παραπλασμός.

**τρῡπᾰλώπηξ**, εκος, ὁ or ή, *a fox that penetrates anywhere, sly knave*, *Com.Adesp.*1170.

**τρῡπάν-η** [ᾰ], ή, = τρύπανον, Hdn.Gr.2.924, Hsch. **-ία**, ή, *thong for working a* τρύπανον (cf. τρυπάω), Poll.10.146. **-ίζω**, *bore through*, Hsch. (Pass.). **-ικός**, ή, όν, *of trepanning*, τέχνη Pall. *in Hp.Fract.*12.275 C. **-ιον**, τό, Dim. of τρύπανον, Archig. ap.Gal.12.821, Phot. s. v. τέρετρον. **-ισμός**, ὁ, *boring, piercing*, Aq.*Is.*54.12.

**τρῡπᾰνοειδής**, ές, *like an auger*, κίνησις Sch.Ptol.*Tetr.*19. Adv. -δῶς ibid.

⊛ **τρύπᾰν-ον** [ῠ], τό, a carpenter's tool, *borer, auger*, rotated by a thong (cf. τρυπάω), Od.9.385, cf. Pratin.Lyr.1.14, E.*Cyc.*461, Pl. *Cra.*388a, Nicoch.9, *AP*6.205 (Leon.); the *boring-point* of a siege-engine, Aen.Tact.32.5. II. a surgical instrument, *trepan*, Hp. *VC*18; τ. ὀξὺ καὶ εὐθύ the straight-pointed *trepan*, Gal.19.129; τ. ἀβάπτιστον, another kind with a guard to prevent its piercing to the brain, Id.10.447. III. *fire-drill* (v. πυρεῖον I), ἀχάλκευτα τρύπανα S.*Fr.*708, cf. Thphr.*HP*5.9.7, *Ign.*64. IV. τρύπανα, τά, metaph., *fellows who will do nothing without driving*, Crates ap. Stob.3.4.50. 2. metaph. of Pan, sens. obsc., Call.*Fr.*412. **-οῦχος**, ὁ, (ἔχω) *handle of a borer*, Poll.7.113, 10.146. **-ώδης**, ες, *piercing*, συναίσθησις Paul.Aeg.3.43.

**τρῡπ-άω**, *bore, pierce through*, ὡς ὅτε τις τρυπῷ (opt.) δόρυ νήϊον ἀνὴρ τρυπάνῳ, οἱ δέ τ' ἔνερθεν ὑποσσείουσιν ἱμάντι (cf. τρυπανία) Od.9. 384, cf. Hp.*VC*18, Pl.*Cra.*387e; ἐτρύπησεν τῷ ποδὶ τὴν βελόνην (of a very thin man) *AP*11.102 (Ammian. or Nicarch.), 308 (Lucill.); with double acc., πόνος με τὸν πόδα τ. *is stabbing into*, Luc.*Ocyp.* 169; cf. ἀλία (B):—Pass., τετρυπήσθω τὸ τρῆμα *let* the hole *be bored*, Hp.*Steril.*222; δι' ὠτὸς..τρυπωμένου through *well-bored* ear, i.e. *open to hear*, S.*Fr.*858 (codd.Plu., but ῥυπωμένου is prob. cj.); τὰ ὦτα τετρυπημένος *having* one's ears *pierced for ear-rings*, X.*An.* 3.1.31; ψῆφος τετρυπημένη the pebble of condemnation *which had a hole in it*, opp. πλήρης, Aeschin.1.79, Arist.*Ath.*68.2, 69.1; ἐτετρύπητο ἄλλη ἔξοδος Luc.*Alex.*16. 2. sens. obsc., Theoc.5.42, *APl.*4.243 (Antist.). **-η**, v. τρῦπα. **-ημα**, ατος, τό, *that which is bored, a hole*, Eup.354; in the ψῆφος, Arist.*Ath.*69.1; τ. νεώς, i.e. one of the holes through which the oars worked, Ar.*Pax*1234; in the flute, Archyt.1, Plu.2.389d; in a gate-fastening, the hole for the βάλανος, Aen.Tact.18.3; ῥαφίδος (cf. τρυμαλιά) *Ev.Matt.*19. 24; μυρμήκων *AP*11.78 (Lucill.); sens. obsc., Ar.*Ec.*624, Hermog. *Id.*2.3, Procop.*Arc.*9. **-ημάτιον**, τό, Dim. of foreg., Hero *Spir.* 1.7, al. **-ησις**, εως, ή, *boring*, Arist.*EE*1242a18, Thphr.*HP*5. 3.3; τῶν αὐλῶν Aristox.*Harm.*p.37 M., cf. Apollod.*Poliorc.*149. 2. **-ητέον**, *one must bore*, Paul.Aeg.6.90. **-ητήρ**, ῆρος, ὁ, *pierced vessel*, Ph.*Bel.*90.28. **-ητής**, οῦ, ὁ, *borer*, Pl.*Cra.* 388d. **-ητός**, ή, όν, *pierced*, Arist.*Ath.*69.1.

**τρῡσάνωρ** [ᾱ], ορος, ὁ, ή, (τρύω) *of a weary man*, αὐδὰ S.*Ph.*209 (lyr.).

**τρῡσί-βιος** [σῐ], ον, (τρύω) = τετρυμένον βίον ἔχουσα, γαστήρ Ar. *Nu.*421.

⊛ **τρῡσ-ίππιον**, τό, (τρύω) *a mark branded on the jaw of a horse superannuated* in the public service, Eup.318, cf. Zen.4.41: the metre of Eup. shows that τρυσίππειον, as written in Ael.Dion.*Fr.*311, Poll. 7.186, *EM*771.16, is incorrect.—The horse was **τρύσιππος**, ὁ, Theognost.*Can.*24.

**τρῦσις**, εως, ή, (τρύω) = νόσος, πόνος, Hsch.

**τρύσκει**· τρύχει, ξηραίνει, Hsch. (Cf. τρυγέω.)

**τρυσμός**, ὁ, (τρύζω) *gurgling*, Hp.*Mul.*1.7, Gal.7.79, al.; synonym of τρισμός, both denoting a *thin sound*, ib.242; = γογγυσμός, Hsch.

**τρυσσόν**· νοσερόν, λεπτόν, ἀσθενές, Hsch.: written τρυσόν in Theognost.*Can.*24.

**τρῡτάνη** [ᾰ], ή, *balance, pair of scales*, Ar.*V.*39, D.5.12, Lyc.270, Herod.2.90, D.Chr.22.5, Plu.*Crass.*17, Luc.*Hist.Conscr.*49, *Am.*4:—hence **τρῡτᾰνεύω**, *weigh*, *Gloss.*

**τρύφακτος**, v. δρύφακτος.

**τρῠφάλεια** [ᾰλ], ή, *helmet*, Il.3.372, 12.22, al.; τρίπτυχος 11.352; αὐλῶπις 13.530; ἵππουρις 19.382; λευκολόφους τ., as an exaggerated Ep. phrase, Ar.*Ra.*1016. (τρυ- does not stand for τρι- '*three*' as supposed by Hsch. (v. sq.); -φάλεια is perh. related to φάλος, ἀμφίφαλος, ἄ-φαλος.)

**τρυφάλη**· περικεφαλαία, τρεῖς ἔχουσα λαμπροὺς ἀστέρας, ἢ ἥλους, Hsch. **τρυφαλίς**, v. τροφαλίς.

**τρύφαξ** [ῠ], ἄκος, ὁ, *a wanton, debauchee*, Hippod.ap.Stob.4.1.95.

**τρῠφάω,** (τρυφή) *live softly, luxuriously, fare sumptuously,* ἐν ἀγκάλαις μητρὸς τρυφῆσαι, of a child, E.*Ion* 1376, cf. *Ba.* 969; τ. ἐν ταῖς ἐσθῆσι Isoc.2.32; τ. καὶ μεγαλοπρεπῶς διαιτᾶσθαι X.*Ath.* 1. 11; λευκὸς ἄνθρωπος, παχύς, ἀργός.., εἰωθὼς τρυφᾶν Sosicr.1, cf. *Ep.Jac.* 5.5, Gal.6.416, etc.; παῖσον, τρύφησον, ζῆσον· ἀποθανεῖν σε δεῖ *Epigr.Gr.* 362.5 (Cotiaeum, ii/iii A.D.). 2. part. τρυφῶν as Adj., *effeminate, luxurious,* Ar.*Nu.* 48, etc.; τ. καὶ ἀμελής Pl.*Lg.* 901a; τὸ τρυφῶν *effeminacy,* Ar.*V.* 1455 (lyr.); also of things, *dainty, delicate,* βασιλικὴ καὶ τρυφῶσα παιδεία Pl.*Lg.* 695d; ἀσπίδα..τρυφῶσαν Aristopho 14, cf. Antiph.52.10 (troch.); ἄρτοι τ. Alc.Com.5. II. *to be licentious, run riot, wax wanton,* Ar.*Lys.* 405, etc.; *to be extravagant,* opp. γλίσχρως ζῆν, Arist.*Pol.* 1266$^b$26. 2. *revel* in, ἐν τοῖς ἀγαθοῖς τινος Lxx *Si.* 14.4; *delight* in, ἐν ἀγαθωσύνῃ σου ib.*Ne.* 9.25. III. *give oneself airs, be dainty, fastidious,* ἆρ' οὐ τρυφῶμεν..., οἷσιν οὐκ ἀρκεῖ τάδε; E.*Supp.* 214; τ. δ' ὁ δαίμων *is fickle,* ib.552; ἐπειδή μοι δοκεῖς σὺ τρυφᾶν *to hang back,* Pl.*Euthphr.* 11e, cf. *La.* 179d, *Alc.* 1. 114a; οἱ τρυφῶντες *spoiled pets,* Id.*Men.* 76b; ἐν ταῖς ἐκκλησίαις τ. καὶ κολακεύεσθαι, of the people, D.8.34; οὐκ ἀνεκτὸν εἶναι..αἰχμάλωτον οὖσαν τρυφᾶν Id.19.197; τρυφῶσιν ἕτεροι πρὸς ἑτέρους, of philosophers, Alex.221.14; followed by a modifying clause, νῦν δὲ τρυφᾷς διότι.. Pl.*Prt.* 327e; ἐν ταῖς..ἑτέρων..ἀτυχίαις τ. Euphro 12; later, τ. κατά τινος *make sport of..*, Him.*Ecl.* 12.2.

**τρῠφερ-αίνομαι,** Pass., *to be fastidious,* τρυφερανθεὶς *with a coxcomb's air,* Ar.*V.* 688 (anap.). **-αμπέχονος,** ον, *with soft garments,* of the Ionians, Antiph.91 (anap.). **-εύομαι,** Pass., = τρυφεραίνομαι, Lxx *Es.* 15.6:—hence **-ευμα,** ατος, τό, in pl., gloss on βαυκίσματα, *AB* 225. **-ία,** ἡ, *tenderness,* γλώττης, etc., Sor.1.10, al.; *voluptuousness,* Aq.*Ge.* 18.12.

**τρῠφερό-βῐος,** ον, *living delicately, luxurious,* Φαίακες Phld.*Hom.* p.23 O., cf. *AB* 322, Procl.*Par.Ptol.* 232. ***-δίαιτος** [δῐ], ον, = foreg., *Cat.Cod.Astr.* 8(4).175. **-ομαι,** Pass., gloss on τρυφεραίνομαι, Sch.Ar.*V.* 686.

**τρῠφερός,** ά, όν, *delicate, dainty,* αὐχήν Batr.66; πλόκαμος E.*Ba.* 150 (lyr.); χεῖρες, χρώς, σάρξ, *AP* 5.65 (Rufin.), 150 (Mel.), 12.136; of a *soft* material, *BGU* 1080.19 (iii A.D.); of almonds, Arist.*Fr.* 277; of fish, *tender, soft-fleshed,* Xenocr.ap.Orib.2.58.5 (Comp.), Sor.2. 15 (Comp.); of an infant, Id.1.82: τὸ τ. *dainty softness,* Ar.*Ec.* 901 (lyr.); Θεσσαλικὸς δὲ θρόνος, γυίων -ωτάτη ἕδρα Critias 2; ὀθόνια Sor. 1.49; τελαμῶνες ib.83; φύλλα -ώτερα Dsc.2.161:—τρυφερόν, τό, name of a medicine, Gal.12.757, cf. 844. II. of persons, their life and habits, *effeminate, luxurious, voluptuous,* Ar.*V.* 551 (Comp.), etc.; ἡ τ. Ἰωνία Call.Com.5 (anap.); ἡ τ. Λέσβος Antiph.174.5 (lyr.); τ. βίῳ σύνεστιν Men.*Kith.Fr.* 1.9; τ. τρόποι Pl.Com.178: τὸ τ. *effeminacy,* ἐς τὸ -ώτερον μετέστησαν Th.1.6. Adv., ἀκολάστως καὶ -ρῶς ζῆν Arist. *Pol.* 1269$^b$23: neut. as Adv., τρυφερόν τι διασαλακώνισον *voluptuously,* Ar.*V.* 1169; τ. καλέειν *call softly,* Theoc.20.7, cf. 21.18: Comp. -ώτερον *more wantonly,* D.C.60.31.

**τρῠφερό-σαρκος,** ον, *with soft, tender flesh* or *body,* Xenocr.ap. Orib.2.58.33. **-στήμων,** ον, gen. ονος, *of delicate warp* or *texture,* Sch.Lyc.863. **-της,** ητος, ἡ, *luxury,* Arist.*EE* 1221$^a$9, Lxx *De.* 28.56, Ath.12.544f.

**τρῠφερ-όφθαλμος,** ον, *with weak eyes,* Aët.7.108.

**τρῠφερό-χρως,** ων, gen. ωτος, *of tender skin* or *hue,* Dsc.1.69, Orib. *Fr.* 118.

**τρῠφερωδῶς,** Adv. *delicately,* Phot. s. v. νοσακερῶς.

**τρῠφ-ή,** ἡ, (θρύπτω) *softness, delicacy, daintiness,* E.*Fr.* 892.4, Pl.*Lg.* 900e, etc.; στολίδος κροκόεσσαν..τρυφάν (sic leg. pro στολίδα ..τρυφᾶς) E.*Ph.* 1491 (lyr.): pl., *luxuries, daintinesses,* τ. Τρωϊκαί Id. *Or.* 1113; τρυφὰς τοιάσδε [τρυφᾶν] Id.*Ba.* 970; αἱ ἄγαν τ. Id.*Fr.* 54. 2; εἰς πλούτους ἀποβλέψαι καὶ τ. Pl.*Alc.* 1.122c, cf. *Lg.* 637e. II. *luxuriousness, wantonness,* τῶν γυναικῶν ἡ τ. Ar.*Lys.* 387; τ. καὶ ἀκολασία, τ. καὶ μαλθακία, Pl.*Grg.* 492c, *R.* 590b; ἡ ἐν ἡμέρᾳ τ. 2 *Ep. Pet.* 2.13; ὑπερτεταμένη τ. Sor.2.54: personified, Τρυφῆς πρόσωπον Ar.*Ec.* 973 (lyr.), cf. Alex.230.3. III. *daintiness, fastidiousness,* ὑπὸ τρυφῆς Ar.*Pl.* 818; ὕβρις ταῦτ' ἐστὶ καὶ πολλὴ τ. Id.*Ra.* 21, cf. Pl. *Grg.* 525a, Arist.*Pol.* 1295$^b$17. **-ηλός,** ή, όν, rare form of τρυφερός, σάρκες *AP* 7.48, cf. Rhetor. in *Cat.Cod.Astr.* 8(4).168, Pall. in *Hp.* 2. 19 D. Adv. -λῶς Jul.*Or.* 6.181d, Suid. s. v. Συβαριτικαῖς. **-ημα,** ατος, τό, *the object in which one takes pride* or *pleasure,* λέκτρων τ. E.*IA* 1050 (lyr.); of some kind of garment, Ar.*Fr.* 320.7, Polyzel.11, *IG* 2$^2$.1518. 69, 1524.199: in pl., generally, *luxuries,* Alciphr.1.12, al. **-ήρης,** ες, = τρυφερός, of Virgo, Vett.Val.10.10. **-ητής,** οῦ, ὁ, *voluptuary,* D.S.8.18, Ptol.*Tetr.* 162, Ath.1.7a, Heph.Astr.1.1: also **-ητίας,** ου, ὁ, Hdn.*Epim.* 137. **-ητικός,** ή, όν, *voluptuous,* Eust.1910.39.

**τρῠφοκᾰλάσῐρις** [λᾰ], ιος, ἡ, *a soft, costly woman's garment,* Ar. *Fr.* 320.6.

***τρύφος** [ῠ], εος, τό, (θρύπτω) *that which is broken off, morsel, lump,* Od.4.508; ἄρτου *AP* 6.105 (Apollonid.), Anon.Hist.*Oxy.* 1798 *Fr.* 44iv5 (*FGrH* 148 p.817 J.): pl., Hdt.4.181, Pherecr.108.5; κύλικος τρύφος a *potsherd,* Choeril.9; τ. τῆς Κῶ Str.10.5.16.

**τρυφώματα·** θρέμματα, Ἰταλοί, Hsch. (fort. θρύμματα).

**τρῠχ-ηρός,** ά, όν, *ragged, tattered, worn out,* τρυχηρὰ περὶ τρυχηρὸν ..χρόα λακίσματα E.*Tr.* 496. II. *wearing, tormenting, grievous,* τρυχηρῇ καὶ πολυμερίμνῳ βασάνῳ περιπεσόντες Vett.Val.109.1. **-ῐνος,** η, ον, *of rags, ragged,* J.*AJ* 5.1.16, Gal.*Thras.* 18, Alciphr.1. 36. **-ίον,** τό, Dim. of τρῦχος, *tatter, shred,* Hp.*Art.* 47,78, Aret. *CA* 1.2 (cj.), 2.2.

**τρύχνον,** τό, = στρύχνον, Nic.*Th.* 878 cod.Π, cf. Gal.12.145; also **τρύχνος,** ἡ, Phot., *EM* 771.31; used as a symbol of sweetness, μουσικώτερος τρύχνου *Com.Adesp.* 605; ἁ φωνὰ δὲ τρύχνος Theoc.10. 37 (v.l. τρύχνα, also v.l. in Sch. in lemmate).

**τρυχνόω,** f.l. for τρυχόω (q.v.) in Gal.19.147.

**τρῦχος,** εος, τό, *worn out, tattered garment,* τρύχει καλυφθεὶς Θεσσαλῆς ἀπληγίδος S.*Fr* 777; τρύχει πέπλων E.*El.* 501, cf. Thphr.*HP* 3. 8.6: pl., *rags, tatters,* E.*El.* 185 (lyr.), *Ph.* 325 (lyr.), Ar.*Ach.* 418. II. *rent,* δι' ἱματίων..οἷον τ. ἐποίησεν Arist.*Mete.* 371$^a$28.

**τρῡχόω,** *wear out, emaciate,* τὸ πᾶν σῶμα Gal.6.488; τὴν Ἑλλάδα Hdn.3.2.8; τρυχνοῦν (fort. τρυχοῦν), = καταπονεῖν, ἰσχναίνειν, Hp.ap. Gal.19.147:—Pass., οἶκος τρυχοῦται Mimn.2.12; mostly in pf. part. τετρυχωμένος, Th.4.60, Hp.*Mul.* 1.61, Pl.*Lg.* 807b (v.l.), etc.; τῷ πολέμῳ κατὰ πάντα τετρ. Th.7.28; ὑπὸ τῶν πολέμων Plb.1.11.2; παλαιὸν καὶ τετρ. δίκτυον Alciphr.1.14; also τρυχωθῆναι τὸ σῶμα, viz. by disease, Hp.*Mul.* 1.5.

**τρύχω** [ῡ], Od.1.248, etc.: Ion. impf. τρύχεσκεν A.R.2.473: fut. τρύξω Od.17.387:—Pass., pres. and impf., v. infr.: the pf. is supplied by τρύω and τρυχόω: cf. κατατρύχω:—*wear out, waste, consume,* τρύχουσι δὲ οἶκον Od.1.248, 16.125; οἵ τε [κηφῆνες] μελισσάων κάματον τ. Hes.*Op.* 305; πτωχὸν οὐκ ἄν τις καλέοι τρύξοντα ἓ αὐτόν no one would invite a beggar *to eat* him *out of house and home,* Od. 17.387; τρύχω βίον ἐν κακότητι Thgn.913; τρύχει τὰ νουσήματα, i.e. *get the better of, cure,* the disease, Hp.*Morb.Sacr.* 18; τρύχουσιν ἔρωτες, τρύχει πόθος, *AP* 12.88,143; γᾶ φθίνουσα τρύχει ψυχάν *distresses, afflicts,* S.*OT* 666 (lyr.); τρύχουσα σαυτήν E.*Hel.* 1286; τ. στρατείαις τὴν πόλιν X.*HG* 5.2.4:—Pass., *to be worn out,* τρυχόμενος Od.1.288, 2.219, cf. Thgn.752; τρύχεσθαι λιμῷ Od.10.177; εὐναῖς ἀνανδρώτοισι τρύχεσθαι S.*Tr.* 110 (lyr.); χρόνῳ Id.*Aj.* 605 (lyr.); ἀμπλακίαις E.*Hipp.* 147 (lyr.); τῇ προσεδρείᾳ Th.1.126; κατ' οἶδμ' ἅλιον E.*Hel.* 521 (lyr.); ἐτρυχόμεσθα..ὁδοιπλανοῦντες Ar.*Ach.* 68; δυσμενέων ἄστυ τ. Sol.3.22: c. gen., σου τρυχόμεθ' ἤδη τρία καὶ δέκ' ἔτη *we have pined for* thee.., Ar.*Pax* 989 (anap.).

**τρύχωσις** [ῠ], εως, ἡ, *exhaustion, distress,* Max.Tyr.34.2 (pl.).

**τρύω** [ῠ], Keil-Premerstein *Erster Bericht* p.9 (Troketta), cj. in Orph.*Fr.* 270.5: fut. τρύσω [ῡ] A.*Pr.* 27:—used mostly in pf. Pass. τέτρῡμαι (v. infr.), other tenses being borrowed from τείρω and perh. τρύχω, τρυχόω: but aor. Med. κατα-τρύσαιο Nic.*Al.* 593: pres. Pass. τρύομαι Call.*Fr.* 5.4 P., *IGRom.* 4.360.21 (Pergam., ii A.D.): cf. ἀποτρύω:—*wear out, distress,* ἀχθηδὼν κακοῦ τρύσει σε A. l. c.:—Pass., *to be worn out,* τέτρυσαι Simon.144; τετρῦσθαι ἐς τὸ ἔσχατον κακοῦ Hdt.1.22, cf. 2.129; δάκρυσιν τετρύμεθα *AP* 9.549 (Antiphil.): mostly in part. τετρυμένος (freq. with v.l. τετριμμένος), τετρ. ταλαιπωρίῃσί τε καὶ ἡλίῳ Hdt.6.12; πόνοις τετρυμένα σώματα Pl.*Lg.* 761d; γήρᾳ *AP* 6.228 (Adaeus); γήραϊ καὶ πενίῃ ib.7.336; τετρ. ..εὗδεν Ἔρως *AP* 9.627 (Marian.); ἐκ πορείας Plu.*Eum.* 15; συνειδέναι τοῖς σφετέροις πράγμασι τετρυμένοις Plb.1.62.7, cf. 1.71.3; ὑπὸ τῆς κακοπαθείας Id.10.13.11; τετρυμένη κλίνη, = τρυφερῶς ἐστρωμένη, Sor. 1.68 (s. v.l.). (τρῡ-, found also in ἄ-τρῡ-τος, τρύ-χ-ω, τρῦχος, is the weak grade of τερῡ-, found in τερύσκεται, τέρυ (qq.v.); cf. also τείρω, ἀ-τερά-μων.)

**τρωα·** ἀρπεδόνη, Hsch.; cf. τροια.

***Τρῳᾰδεύς,** έως, ὁ, *dweller in the Troad,* St.Byz.:—Adj. **Τρῳᾰδικός,** ή, όν, Eust.313.26.

**Τρῳάς,** άδος, ἡ, v. Τρωϊάς.

**τρωγ-άλια** [ᾰλ], τά, (τρώγω) *fruits eaten at dessert, figs, nuts,* etc., like τραγήματα (which is the older word, acc. to Arist.*Fr.* 104 (where sg. -άλιον)), Ar.*Pax* 772, *Pl.* 798, *IG* 12(5).647.12 (Ceos, iii B.C.), Poll. 6.79:—sg. also in Pi.*Fr.* 124, Phld.*Mus.* p.76 K., Plu.2.133c.—Adj. **-άλιος,** = τρωκτός, Hsch. **-ᾰνα,** τά, = foreg., *IG* 5(1).363.13,16 (Sparta, i A.D.).

**τρώγλ-η** (also **τρῶγλα,** *Gloss.*), ἡ, (τρώγω) *hole formed by gnawing,* esp. *a mouse's hole,* Batr.52, Babr.31.17: generally, *hole,* Arist. *HA* 552$^b$28, al.; of a serpent, Herod.4.90: pl., *caves,* Lxx 1 *Ki.* 14. 11; *holes* (gnawed) in clothes, Batr.184; of *canals* in the flesh, Hp. *Carn.* 9. **-ίτης** [ῑ], ου, ὁ, a bird, prob. = τρωγλοδύτης II, Hdn.*Epim.* 136, Eust.228.36. **-ῖτις,** ιδος, ἡ, a kind of *myrrh,* *Edict.Diocl.* *Delph.* 21, al., *Gp.* 7.36.1, Alex.Trall.1.12: also **τρωγλοδύτις** [ῠ], ἡ, Gal.14.68, Alex.Trall.5.4; ἶρις τ. *Gp.* 7.30.1; and **τρωγλοδῠτική,** Dsc.1.64.

***τρωγλο-δύνων** [ῠ], οντος, ὁ, *creeping into a hole,* of a mouse, Batr. 52. **-δῠτέω,** *dwell in holes,* Arist.*PA* 669$^b$7, *IA* 713$^b$20. **-δύτης** [ῠ], ου, ὁ, (δύω) *one who creeps into holes,* of foxes and snakes, Id.*HA* 610$^a$12; of crabs, Id.*IA* 713$^b$28:—for οἱ Τρωγλοδύται, *Troglodytes, Cave-men,* v. Τρωγοδύται. II. *wren, Troglodytes europaeus,* Ruf.*Fr.* 117, Philagr.ap.Aët.11.11. **-δῠτικός,** ή, όν, *of* or *for dwellers in holes,* ζῷα τ. animals *that dwell in holes,* Arist.*HA* 488$^a$23, al. II. *of* or *belonging to the Troglodytes,* v. Τρωγοδυτικός. III. τρωγλοδυτική, v. τρωγλῖτις. **-δύτις,** v. τρωγλῖτις. **-δῦτος,** ον, = τρωγλοδυτικός I, Arist.*PA* 691$^a$26.

**τρωγλύδριον,** τό, Dim. of τρώγλη, *a small hole,* Hdn.Gr.1.366.

**τρῶγμα,** ατος, τό, = τρωγάλιον, Philox.3.11 (pl.).

**τρωγμός·** τὸ ἐπιθέσθαι τὴν ὕλην τρωγμόν, Hsch.

**Τρωγοδύται** [ῠ], οἱ, name of an Ethiopian people, Hdt.4.183 (codd. ABC), Lxx 2 *Ch.* 12.3 (cod. B), Pap. in *Class.Phil.* 19.233,234 (iii B.C.), *OGI* 70 (Egypt, iii B.C.), *PTheb.Bank* 9.2 (i B.C.), *Sammelb.* 4050, Cic.*Div.* 2.44.93, Plin.*HN* 6.173, al., Mela 1.23, Mart.Cap.6. 593, al., v.l. in D.S.1.37: sg. in *PCair.Zen.* 40.2 (iii B.C.), *PSI* 4.332. 14 (iii B.C.): hence **Τρωγοδῠτικός,** ή, όν, *belonging to the* Τρωγοδύται, σμύρνα, cf. τρωγλῖτις (where Τρωγλ-); -κή, ἡ, *their country,* D.S. 1.30 (cf. p.lxxi Vogel), Plin.*HN* 6.169, al.; also ἡ **Τρωγοδύτις** [ῠ]

(Τρωγλ- codd.), ιδος, Plu.2.939d, Ael.*NA*17.3:—the spelling **Τρωγλο-** (as if *Cave-dwellers*) is known to Str.1.2.34 (unless the passage is interpolated) and is freq. f.l. in codd. (so always in codd.Str., as 16.4.4, 17.1.13, al., although he wrote it ἄνευ τοῦ λ acc. to Str.*Chr.* 16.55), cf. Arist.*HA*597ᵃ9, Dsc.2.160, Hsch.

⊛ **τρώγω**, Od.6.90, etc.: fut. τρώξομαι Ar.*Ach.*806, X.*Smp.*4.8: aor. 1 ἔτρωξα (κατ-) Batr.182, Hp.*Nat.Mul.*8, Timo 66.6: aor. 2 ἔτρᾰγον, 3 sg. subj. τράγῃ Pherecr.67.5 (elsewh. only in compos. with ἐν- (q.v.), κατα-, παρα-):—Pass., pf. τέτρωγμαι (δια-) Ar.*V.*371, (παρεν-) Eub.15.8:—*gnaw, nibble, munch*, esp. of herbivorous animals, as mules, τ. ἄγρωστιν Od.6.90; of swine, ἐρεβίνθους τ. Ar. *Ach.*801, cf. 806; of cattle, τὸν θαλλόν, κόμαρον τ., Theoc.4.45, 9.11; rarely of dogs, Εὐριπίδην ἔτρωγον Sotad.15.15; of human beings in disease, λίθους τε καὶ γῆν τρώγουσι Hp.*Prorrh.*2.31. II. of men, *eat* vegetables or fruit, τοὺς γενομένους [κυάμους] οὔτε τρώγουσι οὔτε ἕψοντες πατέονται Hdt.2.37; τὸ κάτω [τῆς βύβλου] ib.92; τὸν καρπὸν τοῦ λωτοῦ Id.4.177; τ. βότρυς Ar.*Eq.*1077; βολβοὺς τρώγων, τυροὺς κάπτων Anaxil.18.3 (anap.); of dessert, *eat fruits*, as figs, almonds, etc., Hdt.1.71, Ar.*Pax* 1324, Pherecr.159 (v. τρωγάλια); ἴτρια, μελίπηκτα, Sol.38.1, Antiph.140.4; of small fish as hors-d'œuvres, κἂν ποίᾳ πόλει τοσοῦτος (ὢν) τὸ μέγεθος ἰχθῦς τρώγεται; Eup.23 D.: abs., πίνειν καὶ τ. drink and *eat dessert*, D.19.197: Com. metaph., γνώμας τ. Πανδελετείους Ar.*Nu.*924 (anap.):—Pass., τρώγεται ἁπαλὰ ταῦτα καὶ αὖα Hdt.2.92. III. later, simply *eat*, serving as pres. to ἔφαγον instead of ἐσθίω, ὁ τρώγων μου τὴν σάρκα καὶ πίνων μου τὸ αἷμα *Ev. Jo.*6.54 (cf. aor. φάγητε.. πίητε ib.53); τρώγοντες καὶ πίνοντες *Ev. Matt.*24.38; never in Lxx (ὁ ἐσθίων ἄρτους μου Lxx *Ps.*40(41).10 becomes ὁ τρώγων μου τὸν ἄρτον when cited in *Ev.Jo.*13.18); δύο τρώγομεν ἀδελφοί is dub. l. in Plb.31.23.9; ἔδωκεν εὔζωμον νήστῃ τρώγειν *SIG*1171.9 (Crete, perh. i B.C.); ἡ νὺξ τὴν ἡμέραν τ. (of a black man eating white bread) Diog.Cyn.ap.*Sammelb.*5730 (iv/v A.D.); ψυχρὰ τρώγοντα κατακαίεσθαι *PMag.Lond.*121.177; ἔμοιγε, ὅσσα παρ' ἀνθρώποις, τρώγειν ἔθος Batr.34; this usage is mentioned by *AB*114, censured by Phot.

**τρώζειν**· ψιθυρίζειν, συνουσιάζειν, Hsch.

**Τρω-ΐᾰθεν** [ῐ], Adv. *from Troy*, Pi.*N.*7.41. **-ϊάς**, contr. **Τρῳάς** (freq. written Τρωάς), ἄδος, fem. of Τρώϊος, *Trojan*, Od.13.263; Τρωϊάδας γυναῖκας Il.9.139, al.; Τρωϊάδες alone, 18.122, al.; Τρῶας καὶ Τρῳάδας Trojan men and *Trojan women*, 22.105. II. γῆ Τρῳάς *the Troad*, S.*Aj.*819, al.; ἡ Τρωάς alone, Hdt.5.122. **-ϊκός**, ή, όν, (Τρώς) *Trojan*, Il.10.11, S.*Aj.*862, etc.; Τρωϊκὴν ἀνὰ χθόνα A.*Myrm.* in *PSI*11.1211.3; τὰ Τ. the *times of Troy*, the *Trojan war*, Hdt.2.145, al., Th.1.3, etc. **-ϊος**, η, ον, *of Tros*, οἷοι Τρώϊοι ἵπποι Il.5.222; ἵππους δὲ Τρῴους ὕπαγε ζυγόν 23.291 (here oxyt. acc. to Hdn.Gr.2.122). II. *Trojan*, Il.13.262:—cf. Τρώς, Τρωϊκός. **-ΐς**, ΐδος, ή, = Τρωϊάς, Τρῳάς, D.H.1.52, St.Byz. **-ΐτης** [ῑ], ου, ὁ, *native of Troia* in Egypt, *PCair.Zen.*133.8 (iii B.C.).

**τρωκτά**, τά, v. τρωκτός.

**τρωκταΐζω**, = κακουργέω, *EM*770.53: vulg. τρακταΐσαι, v. τρακταΐζω.

**τρώκ-της**, ου, ὁ, (τρώγω) *gnawer, nibbler*: but in Od.14.289, 15.416, Phoenician traffickers are called τρῶκται, *greedy knaves*; so τ. σφόδρ' ἐστίν *Com.Adesp.*606; and Gramm. explain τρώκτης by φάγος, φιλοκερδής, πανοῦργος, ἀπατεών, Hsch., Phot., Eust.1757.51; φιλοχρήματοι καὶ τ. Philostr.*Her.Prooem.*1. 2. as Adj., τρῶκται χεῖρες *greedy* hands, of a usurer, *AP*9.409 (Antiphan., dub. cj.). II. *a sea-fish with sharp teeth*, = ἀμία (q.v.), Ael.*NA*1.5. **-τικός**, ή, όν, *greedy*, Ph.2.269, Tz. ad Lyc.213: pecul. fem. **-τίς**, ίδος, Id. ad Hes.*Op.*702. ⊛ **-τός**, ή, όν, *to be gnawed* or *eaten raw*: *eatable*, Hdt.2.92; κῆποι τ. *kitchen* gardens, Philostr.*VA*3.56; τ. λάχανα Artem.1.67. II. τρωκτά, τά, = τρωγάλια, *fruits eaten at dessert*, ὅσα ἐστὶ τ. X.*An.*5.3.12; τρωκτὰ σησάμου τε καὶ μέλιτος *sweatmeats* of sesame and honey, Hdt.3.48.

**τρῶμα, τρωματίζω, τρωματίης, τρωμάτιον**, Ion. for τραυμ- (q.v.).

**τρωμᾱ**, ἡ, Dor. for *τραύμη, τραῦμα, τ. ἕλκεος a festering *wound*, Pi.*P.*4.271.

**τρώξ**, τρωγός, ὁ, (τρώγω) *gnawer*, name of the *weevil*, Stratt. 80. II. = τρώγλη, Hsch.

⊛ **τρωξαλλίς**, ίδος, ἡ, *grasshopper* or *locust*, Alex.15.12; ἀκρὶς τ. Dsc.2.52; *troxallis* (v.l. *trixallis*, etc.), Plin.*HN*30.117; τρωξαλλίς (also τριξελλας, τοξαλλίς) = *grillus*, *Gloss.*

⊛ **τρώξᾰνον**, τό, *twig*, Thphr.*CP*3.2.2; cf. τραύξανα.

**Τρωξάρτης**, ου (Ep. αο), ὁ, *Bread-gnawer*, name of a mouse in Batr.28, al.

**τρώξῐμος**, ον, = τρωκτός, τὰν τ. (sc. σταφυλάν) *eating*-grapes, Theoc. 1.49, cf. *Dig.*50.16.205: τρώξιμα, τά, *vegetables eaten raw*, Hp.*Int.* 30; λαχανοφαγίη τρωξίμων πολλῶν ib.34, cf. *PTeb.*213 (ii B.C.), 117.74 (i B.C.).

**τρῶξις**, εως, ἡ, *gnawing, biting*, ὀνύχων τρώξεις Arist.*EN*1148ᵇ28; λίθων, γῆς, Hp.*Prorrh.*2.31.

**Τρῳός**, v. Τρώϊος. **Τρῶος**, v. Τρώς.

**Τρωοφθόρος**, ον, *destructive to the Trojans*, *AP*9.62 (Even.).

**τρωπάω**, poet. for τρέπω, *turn, change*, ἥ τε θαμὰ τρωπῶσα χέει πολυηχέα φωνήν, of the nightingale, Od.19.521:—Med., *turn oneself, turn about*, πάλιν τρωπᾶσθαι Il.16.95; πρὸς πόλιν Od.24.536; φόβονδε Il.15.666; Ep. Iterat., τρωπάσκετο φεύγειν 11.568; cf. τρωπασκέσθω· μεταβαλλέσθω, ἐπιστρεφέσθω, Hsch.

**Τρώς**, Τρωός, ὁ, *Tros*, the mythic founder of Troy, Il.5.265, 20.230, *h.Ven.*207; also **Τρῶος**, ου, ὁ, Hes.*Fr.*205(b). II. pl. **Τρῶες**, Τρώων, οἱ, *Trojans*, Il.1.152, etc.; Τρῶας καὶ Τρῳάς *Trojan men* and Trojan women, 22.57; cf. Τρώϊος.

**τρῶσις**, εως, ἡ, (τρώω) *wounding*, mostly pl., Hp.*VC*2, Arist.*Po.* 1452ᵇ13, Plu.2.20e, *Sammelb.*6003.13 (iv A.D.): sg., Phld.*Herc.*1251.6; *injury* to a tree, Thphr.*HP*4.16.1.

**τρωσμός**, ὁ, (τρώω) = ἐκτρωσμός, *miscarriage*, Hp.*Coac.*532: pl., Id.*Septim.*9, Dsc.5.72.

**τρω-τέον**, *one must wound*, Sor.2.64. **-τός**, ή, όν, *vulnerable*, Il.21.568, E.*Hel.*810, X.*An.*3.1.23, Eub.107.8, Phld.*Sign.*38; cf. τρωτός· παθητός (leg. πληκτός), Hsch.; τετρωτος (sic) = *vulnerarius*, *Gloss.*

**τρωχάω**, Ep. for τρέχω, *run, gallop*, ἵπποι ῥίμφα μάλα τρωχῶσι Il. 22.163, cf. Od.6.318, A.R.3.874.

**τρώω**, Ep., = τιτρώσκω (q.v.). **τσαγγάριος**, v. τζαγκάριος. **τύ**, τυ, v. σύ.

**τύβαρις**, ὁ, a Dorian *salad, celery pickled in vinegar*, Poll.6.71.

**τυβηκτίς**· κακοσχόλος, Hsch.

**τυβίον**, τό, Dim. of **τύβος**, sine expl., Sch.D.T.p.195 H. (Perh. connected with ἡμιτύβιον.)

**τυγάνιον**, v. τηγάνιον.

**τῠγάτριον**, for θυγάτριον, barbarism in Ar.*Th.*1184, 1210.

⊛ **τυγχάνω**, Thgn.253, Pi.*P.*3.104, *O.*2.47, etc.: Ep. impf. τύγχανον Od.14.231, (παρετ-) Il.11.74: fut. τεύξομαι 16.609, Od.19.314, Ar.*Eq.*112, Lys.18.23 (also as fut. Med. of τεύχω): aor. 2 ἔτῠχον, Ep. τύχον, Il.5.287, 587, etc.; Ep. subj. τύχωμι, -ῃσι, 7.243, 11.116; later also τετύχῃσι, Max.577; late Ep. opt. τετύχοιμι Man.3.299: Ep. also aor. 1 ἐτύχησα Il.15.581, al., Hes.*Fr.*15: pf. τετύχηκα (intr.) Od.10.88 (part. τετυχηκώς, v.l. τετυχηώς, Il.17.748), Tb. 1.32, (trans.) X.*Cyr.*4.1.2, Isoc.3.59; later also τέτευχα, D.21.150 (cod. S), Arist.*EN*1119ᵃ10, *PA*647ᵇ15, freq. later, *PEnteux.*6.7 (iii B.C.), *UPZ*123.30 (ii B.C.), *PStrassb.*98.10 (ii B.C.), *Inscr.Prien.*108.287 (ii B.C.), etc.; Dor. pf. inf. τετεύχεν *SIG*398.5 (Cos, iii B.C.); but Ion. plpf. ἐτετεύχεε Hdt.3.14; τέτυχα v.l. in *Ep.Hebr.*8.6, v.l. in J.*BJ*7.5.4, (συν-) Aristeas 180, etc.; part. τετυχώς *Jahresh.*29 *Beibl.* 163 (Stara Zagora):—Med., aor. 1 τεύξασθαι Lxx 2 *Ma.*15.7:—Pass., impf. ἐτυγχάνετο Ant.Lib.39.3 (dub.): elsewh. in compds., aor. 1 ἐτεύχθην (ἐν-) Plb.35.6.1: pf. τέτευγμαι (ἐπι-) Id.6.53.2.

A. *happen to be at* a place, εἴ πέρ τε τύχῃσι μάλα σχεδόν even if *she be* quite near, Il.11.116; μὴ σύ γε κεῖθι τύχοις *may'st* thou not *be* there, Od.12.106; πέτρη τετύχηκε διαμπερὲς ἀμφοτέρωθεν 10.88; πεδίοιο διαπρύσιον τετυχηκώς Il.17.748 (but in these last two places the meaning may be '*has been made*' (though not by human agency), cf. [γαῖα] οὐδ' εὐρεῖα τέτυκται Od.13.243; γυναικὸς ἄρ' ἀντὶ τέτυξο Il.8.163, etc.; v. ad fin.). 2. of events, and things generally, *happen to* one, *befall* one, *come to* one's *lot*, c. dat. pers., οὕνεκά μοι τύχε πολλά because much *fell* to me, Il.11.684; καί μοι μάλα τύγχανε πολλά Od.14.231; θέλοιμ' ἂν ὡς πλείστοισι πημονὰς τυχεῖν A.*Pr.*348, cf. *Pers.*706 (troch.); οἷ' αὐτοῖς τύχοι S.*Ph.*275; εἴ τι δεσπόταισι τυγχάνει E.*Alc.*138: abs., εἰ δ' αὖθ', ὃ μὴ γένοιτο, συμφορὰ τύχοι A.*Th.*5, cf. *Ag.*347, etc.; ἄριστα πρὸς τὸ τυγχάνον E.*Hel.* 1290, cf. *Ion* 1511. b. aor. part. ὁ τυχών, *the first one meets, any chance person*, Hes.*Th.*973, Pl.*R.*539d, etc.; οἱ τ. *everyday men, the vulgar*, X.*Mem.*3.9.10, etc.; εἷς ἦν τῶν τ. Isoc.10.21; οὐχ ὁ τ. ἀνήρ, of Moses, Longin.9.9: so of things, τὸ τυχόν *any chance* result, Pl.*Ti.*46e; ὃν ἐξαλείφει πρόφασις ἡ τυχοῦσ' ὅλον E.*Fr.*1041; οὐχ ὁ τ. λόγος no *common* discourse, Pl.*Lg.*723e; σύνεσιν οὐ τὰν τυχοῦσαν Archim.*Spir.Praef.*; οἱ τ. φόβοι *trifling* fears, Lycurg.37; καίπερ τὸ τ. καταβαλοῦσιν though they may have paid *a trifling sum*, Str.5.2.7:—Math., τυχὸν σημεῖον *any* point (at random), Euc.1.5, cf. 6.9; ἄλλα, ἃ ἔτυχεν, ἰσάκις πολλαπλάσια *any* other equimultiples *taken at random*, Id.5.4. 3. in 3 sg. aor. or impf., impers. (sts. also pers.) in relat. clauses, as (when, where, etc.) *it* (*he, she*, etc.) *happened* (*may happen*, etc.), i.e. *any*how, at *any* time, place, etc., καὶ ἀρχομένοις καὶ μεσοῦσι καὶ ὅπως ἔτυχέ τῳ at the beginning, middle, or *any* other point, Th.5.20; ὡς ἔτυχε ζημιοῦσθαι to be penalized just *any*how, X.*Mem.*3.9.13; οὐχ ὡς ἔτυχεν *in* no *ordinary manner*, Men. *Sam.*79, *BMus.Inscr.*4.481*.340 (Ephesus, ii A.D.); τὴν μὲν δικαίαν, τὴν δ' ὅπως ἐτύγχανεν just *any*how, E.*Hipp.*929; ἀποτετμάσθω δύο τμάματα ὡς ἔτυχεν let two segments be cut off *at random*, Archim. *Con.Sph.*24; χώρᾳ γ' ἐν ᾗ ἔτυχε X.*Oec.*3.3; ὅπου ἔτυχεν Id.*Cyr.*8.4.3; ὅπου ἂν τύχῃ Pl.*Prt.*242e; ὁπότε τύχοι *sometimes*, Pl.*Phd.*89b; ὅταν τύχῃ *sometimes*, E.*El.*1169 (lyr.); but, *at any odd time*, Th.1.142; ἡνίκ' ἂν τ. D.1.3; ἂν τύχῃ, εἰ τύχοι, *it may be*, Pl.*Cra.*430e, *Hp.Mi.*367a; τὸ δέ, εἰ ἔτυχεν, οὐχ οὕτως ἔχει Id.*Cra.*439c; εἰ οὕτως ἔτυχεν Arist.*Cat.*8ᵇ12; τὸ ὅπῃ ἔτυχεν *mere chance*, Pl.*Phlb.*28d: with attraction of the relat. Pron., τὸ οἷς ἔτυχε προσκρούειν Plu.*Cic.*27; ὡμίλει ᾧ τύχοι Plb.26.1.3; ὧν ἔτυχε πιμπλάμενος Luc.*Vit.Auct.*9; οὐδὲ γὰρ ὧν ἔτυχ' ἦν they were not *just any* acts, D.18.130. b. c. acc. et inf., ἔτυχε ὄμβρον συνεργῆσαι Plu.*Alc.*28, cf. Ael.*NA*5.6; ἔτυχεν ὥστε.. D.C.39.12. 4. sts. the Verb agrees in person and number with the subject of the principal clause, perhaps by assimilation, ἀπαίροντες ἀπὸ τῆς Πελοποννήσου ὁπόθεν τύχοιεν, for ὁπόθεν τύχοι, Th.4.26, cf. 93, 5.56, 7.70, Pl.*Tht.* 179c; ὅ τι ἂν τύχωσι, τοῦτο λέγουσι they say *just anything*, Id.*Prt.* 353a; ὅ τι ἂν τύχωσι, τοῦτο πράξουσιν Id.*Cri.*45d, cf. *Grg.*522c, *Smp.* 181b; ἀναφύονται ὁπόθεν ἂν τύχῃ ἕκαστος Id.*Tht.*180c; ὡς ἐτύγχανον ἕκαστοι, ηὐλίζοντο X.*An.*2.2.17, cf. 3.1.3; τάχ' ἄν, εἰ τύχοιεν, σωφρονέστεροι γένοιντο D.15.16; δουλεύειν μᾶλλον ἢ μεθ' ὁποτέρου ἂν τύχωσι τούτων ἐλευθέρους εἶναι Th.8.48; πρὸς ὀργὴν ἥν τινα τύχητε ἔστιν ὅτε σφαλέντες τὴν τοῦ πείσαντος μίαν γνώμην ζημιοῦτε yielding to *the impulse of the moment*, Id.3.43; εἶτ' οὐκ ἐλήρουν ὅ τι τύχοιμ' Ar.

*Ra.*945: with attraction of the relat. Pron., οὗς ἂν τύχῃς ἐπαινῶν Isoc.12.206. **5.** neut. part. τυχόν, used abs. like ἐξόν, παρόν, etc., *since it so befell*, οὕτως τ. Luc.*Symp.*43. **b.** as Adv., *perchance, perhaps*, Isoc.4.171, X.*An.*6.1.20, Pl.*Alc.*2.140a, 150c, D.18.221, 21.41, Men.*Pk.*184, 1*Ep.Cor.*16.6; τ. ἴσως Epich.277, E.*Fr.*953.9, Men. *Epit.*287, Plb.2.58.9; τυχὸν μέν.., τυχὸν δέ.. Arr.*An.*1.10.6, etc. **II.** joined with the part. of another Verb to express a coincidence, τύχησε γὰρ ἐρχομένη νηῦς a ship *happened to be*, i.e. *was just then*, starting, Od.14.334; ξεῖνος ἐὼν ἐτύχησε παρ' ἱπποδάμοισι Γερηνοῖς Hes.*Fr.*15.2, cf. Semon.7.19, Pi.*N.*1.49; πρυτανεία ἣ ἂν τυγχάνῃ πρυτανεύουσα *IG*1².63.27, cf. 52; τὰ νοέων τυγχάνω what I *happen* to have, i.e. have *at this moment*, in my mind, Hdt.1.88, cf. 8.65,68.α'; ἐτετεύχεε ἐπισπόμενος Id.3.14; ὃ τυγχάνω μαθών which I have *just* learnt, S.*Tr.*370; παρὼν ἐτύγχανον I was by *just then*, Id.*Aj.* 748; τυγχάνει καθεύδων he is sleeping *just now*, Ar.*V.*336 (troch.); ἔτυχον στρατευόμενοι they were *just then* engaged in an expedition, Th.1.104; ἔτυχε κατὰ τοῦτο καιροῦ ἐλθών he came *just* at this point of time, Id.7.2; ἥτις δέ τοι μάλιστα σωφρονεῖν δοκεῖ, αὕτη μέγιστα τυγχάνει λωβωμένη she *is just the one who*.., Semon.7.109; but freq. τυγχάνω cannot be translated at all, esp. in phrase τυγχάνω ὤν, which is simply = εἰμί, S.*Aj.*88, Ar.*Pl.*35, Pl.*Prt.*313c, etc. **2.** the part. ὤν is sts. omitted, ὁ γὰρ μέγιστος τυγχάνει δορυξένων S.*El.*46; εἴ σοι χαρτὰ τυγχάνει τάδε ib.1457; νῦν δ' ἀγροῖσι τυγχάνει ib.313; ἔνδον γὰρ ἄρτι τυγχάνει Id.*Aj.*9; εἴ τις εὔνους τυγχάνει Ar.*Ec.*1141; εἰ σὺ τυγχάνεις ἐπιστήμων τούτων Pl.*Prt.*313e, cf. *Grg.*502b, *R.*369b, al.: sts. τυγχάνειν is used much like εἶναι, Σωτὴρ γένοιτ' ἂν Ζεὺς ἐπ' ἀσπίδος τυχών A.*Th.*520; οὐκ ἀποδάμου τυχόντος not *being* absent, Pi.*P.*4.5 (cf. τόσσαις); ποῦ χρὴ τηνικαῦτα τυγχάνειν; E.*IA*730; τ. ἐν ἐμπύροις *to be engaged* in.., Id.*Andr.*1113; freq. in Arist., δύο μέρη τετύχηκεν ἐξ ὧν ἡ πόλις *Pol.*1318ᵃ31, cf. 1289ᵇ16, *Top.*151ᵇ11; also in later Gr., τὰ ἑπτάμηνα γόνιμα τυγχάνειν Sor.1.55, cf. 69, al.: νέος πάνυ τυγχάνων *PLips.*40 ii 7 (iv A.D.), etc.:—Phryn.244 rejects this usage in Attic. **b.** τυγχάνον, = τὸ ἐκτὸς ὑποκείμενον, the external *reality*, e.g. αὐτὸς ὁ Δίων as distd. both from the word (φωνή) Δίων and its meaning, *Stoic.*2.48. **c.** τὰ πράγματα τυγχάνοντα καλοῦσι (sc. οἱ Στωϊκοί), τέλος γὰρ τὸ τυχεῖν τούτων, ib.77. **3.** later c. inf., τυγχάνομεν ἐπιδεδωκέναι we *happen* to have handed in.., we *have just* handed in.., *PTeb.*796.13 (ii B.C.), cf. *PSI*10.1118.8 (i A.D.), 1.39.4 (ii A.D.), Heliod. et Antyll.ap.Orib.44.8.21,25, 44.23.21, Gal.18(2).394.

**B.** *gain one's end* or *purpose, succeed*, οὐκ ἐτύχησεν ἑλίξας Il. 23.466; εἰ τύχῃ τις ἔρδων Pi.*N.*7.11, cf. 55; τὸ τυχεῖν, = νίκη, Id. *O.*2.51; πείθειν.. τυγχάνειν θ' ἅμα E.*Hec.*819; εἰ τύχοιμεν Th.4.63; τυχόντες *if successful*, opp. σφαλέντες, Id.3.39, cf. 82, Pi.*P.*10.62; τυγχάνουσι καὶ ἀποτυγχάνουσι Arist.*Po.*1450ᵃ3; ὀρθῶς πράττειν καὶ τ. Pl.*Euthd.*280a; *gain one's request*, Hdt.1.213 (so τυχόντα γνώμης in Th.3.42); in speaking, *to be right*, τί νιν καλοῦσα.. τύχοιμ' ἄν; A.*Ag.*1233, cf. *Ch.*14,317 (lyr.), S.*Ph.*223, *OC*1580; Δίκαν νιν προσαγορεύομεν τυχόντες καλῶς A.*Ch.*950 (lyr.):—Pass., impers., αὐτῷ πρὸς τὸ ἔργον οὐδὲν ἐτυγχάνετο nothing *went right*, dub. in Ant.Lib. 39.3:—in part. τυχήσας or τυχών, combined with νύξε, βάλε, οὖτα, etc., pierce, wound, etc., *successfully*, so that the whole phrase means *hit*, ἔγχεϊ νύξε κατὰ κληῖδα τυχήσας Il.5.579, cf. 858, 12.394; βάλε δουρὶ κατὰ ζωστῆρα τυχήσας ib.189; ὑπὸ στέρνοιο τυχήσας βεβλήκει 4.106, cf. 5.98,582, 13.371,397, Od.19.452, al.; also conversely, θηρητὴρ ἐτύχησε βαλών Il.15.581; βαλὼν τύχω Hdt.3.35; also apart from such combinations, *hit*, c. gen., προβιβάντος Il.16.609; μηρίνθοιο 23. 857; τ. τοῦ σκοποῦ Pl.*Lg.*717b, cf. *R.*523b, Th.2.35, X.*An.*3.2. 19, *Ap.*1: c. dupl. gen., εἰ.. τοῦ παιδὸς.. τύχω μέσης τῆς καρδίης Hdt. 3.35: abs., ἤμβροτες οὐδ' ἔτυχες Il.5.287; αἴ κε τύχωμι 7.243, Od.22. 7. **II.** *hit upon, light upon*: **1.** *meet, fall in with* persons, Λακεδαίμονι.. τυχήσας *having met* [him] in Lacedaemon, Od.21.13: c. gen., θρηνητοῦ A.*Ag.*1075; τριακτῆρος ib.172 (lyr.); ἀγαθῶν ἀνδρῶν Lys.2.5; γυναικῶν X.*Smp.*9.7: with a predicate added, μή τευ μελαμπύγου τύχῃς Archil.110; προφρόνων Μοισᾶν τ. Pi.*I.*4(3). 43(61); θεῶν ἀμεινόνων τ. E.*Heracl.*351; ἐμοῦ.. οἰκητοῦ S.*OT*1450, cf. 677; ἡμῶν τ. οἵων σε χρή E.*Hel.*1300, cf. Lys.18.23; ἐρωτᾶτε αὐτοὺς ὁποίων τινῶν ἡμῶν ἔτυχον X.*An.*5.5.15; τοῦ δαίμονος.. κακοδαίμονος Ar.*Eq.*112. **2.** *light on* a thing, τύχε γὰρ β' ἀμάθοιο βαθείης Il.5.587; *attain, obtain* a thing, c. gen., πομπῆς καὶ νόστοιο Od.6.290; αἰδοῦς Thgn.253, cf. 256; [οἴκτου] A.*Pr.*241; ξυγγνώμης Th.7.15; τῆς ἀξίας Ar.*Av.*1223; of *meeting with* misfortunes, βίης τυχεῖν *meet with, suffer* violence, Hdt.9.108; τραυμάτων, κακῶν, A.*Ag.*866, E.*Hec.* 1280; δίκης, κρίσεως, Pl.*Grg.*472d, *Phdr.*249a, cf. *Lg.*869b: abs., *have the lot* or *fate*, ἄλλος μὲν ἀποφθίσθω ἄλλος δὲ βιώτω, ὅς κε τύχῃ Il.8. 430; τὴν παρὰ Δαρείου αἰτήσας ἔτυχε μισθὸν Hdt.5.23 (where τήν is governed by αἰτήσας). **b.** after Hom. also c. acc. of neut. Adj. or Pron., τὰ πρόσφορα A.*Ch.*711, cf. *Eu.*30, S.*OC*1106, *Ph.*509 (lyr.), E.*Med.*758, *Hec.*51: later the acc. is used more freely, τ. ἐπίστασιν *Sammelb.*5235.15 (i A.D.); ὑπογραφήν *BGU*615.23 (ii A.D.); βοήθειαν *PGoodsp.Cair.*15.14 (iv A.D.); εὐκαιρίαν *PSI*9.1082.5 (iv A.D.); τὰ γυναίκια δεσμὸν οὐδένα βούλεται τυγχάνειν Sor.1.70ᵇ. **c.** after either case a gen. pers. may be added, *obtain* a thing *from* a person, ὧν δέ σου τυχεῖν ἐφίεμαι S.*Ph.*1315; σου τοῦτο τ. Id.*OC*1168; or the pers. may be added with a Prep., τ. ἐπαίνου ἔκ τινος Id.*Ant.*665; παρὰ σεῖο τ. φιλότητος Od.15.158; τιμίαν ἕδραν παρ' ἀνδρῶν A.*Eu.*856 (dub.); αἰδοῦς ὑπό τινος X.*Cyr.*1.6.10, cf. *Mem.*4.8.10, etc.: abs., χρὴ πρὸς μακάρων τυγχάνοντ' εὖ πασχέμεν Pi.*P.*3.104. **d.** c. inf., οἶμαί σου τεύξεσθαι μεθεῖναί με Pl.*Phlb.*50d; ἐὰν ψαῦσαι τοῦ νεκροῦ τύχωμεν Plu.*Pel.*33; οὐ τυχὼν ἐπιδείξειν (= ἐπιδεῖξαι) not *having succeeded* in proving, *PPetr.*3 p.153 (iii B.C.). (Τυ-γ-χ-άνω, with ἐτύχησα, τετύχηκα, is formed from the aor. τυχ-εῖν, which was orig. the aor. Pass. (with act. form) of τεύχω 'make'; ἔτυχε = *factum est*, as ἔτραφον = *I was nourished* (v. τρέφω); senses A. I. 1–3 are the oldest and are parallel to τεύχω II (esp. Pass.); many of the forms belong equally to both verbs; τιτύσκομαι likewise belongs to both verbs; τ(ε)υχ- from *θ(ε)υχ-, cf. ἀποθύσκειν, ἐνθύσκει, συνθύξω, and perh. Germ. *taugen* 'to be capable, useful', Engl. *dow, doughty*.)

**τύδαι·** ἐνταῦθα, Αἰολεῖς, Hsch. (f.l. for τυίδε).

**Τῡδεύς**, ὁ, gen. Τυδέως, Ep. -έος (never -ῆος) Il.2.406, al.: acc. -έα (never -ῆα) 6.222, also -ῆ 4.384:—the hero *Tydeus*, one of the Seven against Thebes, ll. cc.

* **τυΐ·** ὧδε, Κρῆτες, Hsch. (Cf. υἱ.) **τῦϊγγα·** ὀρνιθάριόν τι, Id. (Cf. τρύγγας? or leg. ἴϋγγα.)

* **τυΐδε**, Aeol. Adv. *hither*, τυῒδ' ἔλθ' Sapph.1.5, cf. *Supp.*1.2, 25.2, Theoc.28.5, *Epigr.Gr.*988.3 (Balbilla), Sch.T Il.14.298.

**τύϊον**, τό, f.l. for θυῖον in Thphr.*HP*5.2.1.

**τυκάνη**, ἡ, *an instrument for threshing*, Theognost.*Can.*24, Eust. 967.18; = *tribula, trahea*, *Gloss.*; written **τυτάνη** in Hsch., and **τρυγάνη** (q.v.): also Dim. **τυκάνιον**, *PLond.*5.1657.7 (iv/v A.D.), *Gloss.* (-νιν).

**τῠκ-ίζω**, (τύκος) *work stones*, λίθους Ar.*Av.*1138. **-ίον**, τό, Dim. (only in form) of τύκος, Eust.136.23. * **-ισμα**, ατος, τό, *a working of stones*, in pl., κανόνων τυκίσματα, i.e. *walls of stone worked* by rule, E.*Tr.*814 (lyr.); λαΐνων τυκισμάτων Id.*Fr.*125.3, cf. *HF*1096.

**τῠκον**, τό, Boeot. for σῦκον, Stratt.47.5, cf. Luc.*Jud.Voc.*8.

**τύκος** [ῠ], ὁ, (τεύχω) *instrument for working stone, mason's hammer* or *pick*, βάθρα.. κανόνι καὶ τύκοις ἡρμοσμένα E.*HF*945, cf. Poll.7.118: also **τύχος**, ὁ, *IG*11(2).161*A*87, 199*A*87 (Delos, iii B.C.), *Supp. Epigr.*2.569.27 (Didyma, ii B.C.); **τύχοι·** λιθοξοϊκὰ ἐργαλεῖα, Hsch., cf. Paus.Gr.*Fr.*62 (τοιχοι Poll.10.147 codd.); = ὄρυξ, Theognost.*Can.* 4. **2.** τύχους καὶ τοὺς σφῆνας καλοῦσιν Hsch. s.v. τύχων πυλῶν: cf. eund. s.v. τύφοι. **II.** from the likeness of shape, *battle-axe, pole-axe*, Hdt.7.89 (τύκους codd.CP; τύχους rell.).

**τυκτά**, a Persian word, which Hdt.(9.110) translates by τέλειον δεῖπνον βασιλήϊον.

**τυκτός**, ή, όν, (τεύχω) *finished, wrought out*, i.e. *complete*, τυκτὸν κακόν, of Ares, Il.5.831; κρήνη τυκτή a fountain *made by man's hand*, Od.17.206: then, *well-made, well-wrought*, τυκτῇσι βόεσσι Il. 12.105; of a bowling-green, ἐν τ. δαπέδῳ Od.4.627, 17.169; τυκτὴ μάρμαρος, of a tombstone, Theoc.22.210.

**τῠλαίνιον**, τό, Dim. of τύλος I, Aret.*SD*2.9. (As if from a form τύλαινα, like φλύκταινα.)

* **τῠλάριον**, τό, Dim. of τύλη, *POxy.*1159.24 (iii A.D.), *Dura*⁴155 (iii A.D.), *Sammelb.*7033.41 (v A.D.), *PGrenf.*2.111.34 (v/vi A.D.). **2.** Dim. of τύλος II. 4, Eutoc. ad Archim. iii p.70 H.

**τυλᾰρος** [ῠ], ὁ, = μάνδαλος, and **τῠλᾰρόω**, = μανδαλόω, Hsch.

**τυλάς**, άδος, ἡ, a kind of *thrush*, also ἰλλάς, Eust.947.10; = *bubo* or *charadrius*, dub. in *Gloss.*

**τῠλεῖον**, τό, Dim. of sq. 3, S.*Fr.*468, *PRev.Laws* 94.10 (iii B.C.), Ael.*NA*2.11, Hsch. s.v. κνέφαλλον.

**τύλη**, ἡ, = τύλος I, *swelling, callus*, esp. a porter's *shoulder, which has grown callous* from carrying weights, ἔκαμόν γα τὰν τύλαν κακῶς, says the Boeotian laden with his wares, Ar.*Ach.*860; ὑπόκυπτε τὰν τύλαν ib.954, v. Sch. ad ll.; τραχήλου τύλα Telecl.50 (so Dor. acc. τύλαν *Dura*⁴155 (iii A.D.)); of the *hump* of a camel, Hsch.: also, in pl., *blisters* on the hands, Id. **2.** *pad for carrying burdens on, porter's knot*, invented by Protagoras, acc. to Arist.*Fr.*63. **3.** *cushion, mattress*, Sapph.50, Eup.170, Antiph.214, *PTeb.*765.2 (ii B.C.), *PLond.*2.402ᵛ.15 (ii B.C., prob.), D.S.13.84, *AP*11.14 (Ammian.), 315 (Lucill.), Artem.5.8, etc. (= Att. κνέφαλλον acc. to Phryn. 151). [ῠ prob. in Eup. and Antiph. ll. cc., cf. τῠλος: but ῡ later, *AP* ll. cc.]

**τῠληρός**, ά, όν, *callous*, cj. Wimmer in Thphr.*HP*3.18.11.

**τύλιγ-μα** [ῠ], ατος, τό, gloss on ἕλιξ, Hsch. **-μός**, ὁ, *wrapping*, ὑμενοειδὴς τ., of the diaphragm, Sch.rec.A.*Pr.*881.

**τυλίον**, τό, Dim. of τύλος, *small pin* or *peg*, Hero *Spir.*1.6, Eutoc. ad Archim. iii p.70 H. **2.** f.l. for τυλεῖον in Theognost.*Can.*24.

**τῠλίσσω**, Att. -ττω, *twist* or *roll up*, ἠλακάτη τὸ ξύλον ἐν ᾧ τυλίσσονται τὰ ἔρια Sch.Od.6.53. **2.** metaph., οἴμας τυλίσσων (= ὁδοὺς ἐρευνῶν paraphr.) perh. *unravel*, Lyc.11. **II.** *bend*: aor. Pass. ἐτυλίχθη v.l. for ἐλυγίχθη in Theoc.23.54.

**τύλλος**, ὁ, *box, chest*, D.C.79.20.

**τῠλο-ειδής**, ές, *like a lump* or *callus*, Asclep.Jun.ap.Gal.13.537, Hsch. s.v. κηλάς; cf. τυλώδης. **-εις**, εσσα, εν, *callous, knobby*, Nic.*Th.*272.

**τῠλο-πλόκος**, ὁ, *mattress-maker*, *Aegyptus* 15.224 (v A.D.). **-προσκεφάλαιον**, τό, = *capitale pilentum*, *Gloss.* (s.v.l.).

* **τύλος**, ὁ, = τύλη I, *callus*, X.*Mem.*1.2.54, Nic.*Th.*178, Dsc.3.80; inside the hands, τὼ χεῖρε τύλων ἀνάπλεως Luc.*Somn.*6; on the knees, Sch.Ar.*Ach.*553, etc.; cf. τυλόω II. **II.** *anything rising like a lump, knob* or *knot*; esp. **1.** *wooden bolt with a knob at the end, trenail*, Ar.*Ach.*553, Plb.*Fr.*82, Arr.*An.*2.3.7. **2.** *knob* on a club, ῥόπαλον τύλους ἔχον περισιδήρους D.S.3.33, cf. Str.16.4.17. **3.** *membrum virile*, Poll.2.176, Hsch. **4.** *knob* or *nose* on which the thread of a screw works, Hero *Spir.*1.5; *peg* on which a string is looped, Eutoc. ad Archim. iii p.60 H.; *knob* on an axle to which a cord is attached, Heliod.ap.Orib.49.3.3, 49.4.25,51, 49.8.4, Sor.1.68. [ῡ Nic. l. c.; cf. τύλη.]

**τῠλο-φάντης**, ου, ὁ, late spelling of τυλ-υφάντης, *PKlein.Form.* 823.1 (vi/vii A. D.); hence **-φαντία**, ἡ, ib.2.

**τῠλ-όω**, *make knobby*:—Pass., ῥόπαλα τετυλωμένα σιδήρῳ clubs *knobbed* with iron, Hdt.7.63; of the outside of the κίτριον, σκληρὸν καὶ τετ. Gal.6.618. II. *make callous*, τυλοῖ τὸ στόμα [ὁ χαλινός] X.*Eq.*6.9:—Pass., *to be made hard* or *callous*, τετυλωμένης τῆς μήτρας Orib.22.7.1, cf. Sor.1.10, al.; μακέλᾳ τετυλωμένος ἔνδοθι χεῖρας Theoc.16.32; τετυλωμένα βλέφαρα Dsc.5.99. 2. metaph., τὴν χεῖρα καὶ τὴν ἀκοὴν πρὸς τὰ ἐξαρτήματα Iamb.*VP*26.118, cf. Arr. *Epict.*2.18.9.—Cf. τυλωτός, and v. μυλδόομαι. **-ῠφάντης**, ου, ὁ, (τύλη 3, ὑφαίνω) *one who weaves cushion-covers*, Hyp.*Fr.*125. **-ώδης**, ες, *callous*, Plu.2.46d (metaph.), Dsc.2.154, Antyll.ap.Orib.10.23.24, Sor.1.10, Gal.6.775. **-ωμα**, ατος, τό, glossed by τύμμα, Hsch.; gloss on τύλη, Id. s. v. γονοτύλη. 2. *sole* of the foot, Poll.2.198. **-ων**, ωνος, ὁ, *one with a callous hide*, *Gloss.* ❀ **-ωσις**, εως, ἡ, *a making* or *becoming callous*, Gal.14.767, Poll.4.191. II. ἐπιτιμὰγ κρηπῖδος τυλώσιος perh. payment for *hardening* the κρηπίς (by coating it with something), *IG*4$^2$(1).103.51 (Epid., iv B.C.). **-ωτός**, ή, όν, *knobbed*, ῥόπαλα Hdt.7.69.

**τυμβ-άς**, άδος, ἡ, (τύμβος) *sorceress, witch*, so called from their haunting tombs, Hsch. ❀ **-αύλης**, ου, ὁ, *one who plays the flute* at a funeral, D.Chr.49.12, Ptol.*Tetr.*180, Gal.7.241, Ael.*VH*12.43, etc. **-εία**, ἡ, *burial*, Suid. **-ειος**, α, ον, *sepulchral*, κρηπίς Lyc.882; later written τύμβιος (q.v.). **-ευμα**, ατος, τό, *tomb, grave*, S.*Ant.*1220. II. *that which is* or *is to be buried, corpse*, E. *Ion*933. **-εύω**, *bury*, σῶμα τυμβεῦσαι τάφῳ S.*Aj.*1063, cf. E.*Hel.* 1245:—Pass., ποῦ δ' ἐτυμβεύθη τάφῳ; Ar.*Th.*885:—Med., Nonn. *D.*5.549, al. 2. πατρὶ τυμβεῦσαι χοάς *pour* libations *on* his *grave*, S.*El.*406. II. intr., *dwell entombed*, ἐν τοιαύτῃ ζῶσα τυμβεύειν στέγῃ Id.*Ant.*888. **-ήρης**, ες, *entombed, buried*, ib. 255. II. *grave-like, sepulchral*, θάλαμος ib.947 (lyr.); ἕδρα Ar.*Th.* 889 (= *Trag.Adesp.*65). (v. -ήρης.) **-ίδιος** [ῐδ], η, ον, *at a funeral* or *tomb*, ἀγών, Ἑκάτη, Τύχη, Orph.*A.*577, *H.*1.3, 72.5. **-ίον**, τό, Dim. of τύμβος, Sch.D.T.p.195 H. ❀ **-ιος**, ον, *in the tomb*, *CIG*1956 (Macedonia); also α, ον, θέσις *BCH*48.518 (Palestine). **-ίτης** [ῑ], ου, ὁ, *on* or *at the grave*, λᾶας *AP*7.198 (Leon.).

**τυμβο-γέρων**, οντος, ὁ, *old man on the edge of the grave*, Ar.*Fr.* 55 D., *Com.Adesp.*1172, Thphr.ap.Phot., Procop.*Arc.*6.11. **-ποιός**, ὁ, *grave-digger*, *Dialex.*1.3.

❀ **τύμβος**, ὁ, *sepulchral mound, cairn, barrow*, τῷ κέν οἱ τύμβον μὲν ἐποίησαν Παναχαιοί Od.1.239, cf. Il.2.604, 793, Hdt.1.45, etc.; τύμβον χεῦαι (cf. τυμβοχοέω) Od.4.584, 12.14, 24.80; χῶσαι S.*Ant.* 1203; στήλῃ κεκλιμένος.. ἐπὶ τύμβῳ Il.11.371. 2. generally, *tomb, grave*, Pi.*O.*1.93, A.*Ch.*92, etc.; θρηνεῖν πρὸς τύμβον, of one who will not hear, ib.926; ὥσπερ ἀπὸ τύμβου πεσών like an old man from the *grave*, as old Philocleon says scoffingly to his son, Ar.*V.* 1370. 3. *tombstone* with the figure of the dead, τ. ξεστός E.*Alc.* 836, cf. *AB*309. II. metaph., γέρων τύμβος, = τυμβογέρων, E. *Med.*1209, *Heracl.*167; ὦ τύμβε Ar.*Lys.*372. [Dat. sg. τυμοι, i.e. τύμῳ [ῠ], in three metr. epitaphs, *IG*9(1).869, 870 (Corc., vi B.C.), prob. in *IG*12(9).285.10 (Eretria, = *Supp.Epigr.*1.409).]

**τυμβοσύνη**, ἡ, name of a wall in Constantinople, which was repaired with tombstones, Hsch.Mil.*Fr.*4.27.

**τυμβοῦχος**, ον, (ἔχω) *placed on a tomb, sepulchral*, Κήρ *AP*7. 154.

**τυμβο-φάντης**, ου, ὁ, *one who shows a tomb*, *An.Ox.*2.416. ❀ **-χοέω**, like τύμβον χεῦαι or χῶσαι, *throw up a cairn* or *barrow*, Hdt.7.117, v.l. in Il.21.323. **-χόη**, ἡ, *the throwing up a cairn* or *barrow*, ibid. (nisi leg. τυμβοχοῆσ', v. foreg.). **-χόος**, ον, (χέω) *throwing up a cairn* or *barrow*: τ. χειρώματα *burial-cairns thrown up* by work of hand, A.*Th.*1027. **-χωστος**, ον, (χώννυμι) *heaped up into a cairn* or *barrow, high-heaped*, ἕρμα τάφου S.*Ant.*848 (lyr.).

**τυμβόω**, only in pf. part. Pass. τετυμβωμένος, = *decrepitus*, *Gloss.*

**τυμβωρῠχ-έω**, *break open graves*, D.S.22.12, Plu.2.1128c, *App. Anth.*2.691 (Cyzicus); of the hyena, Arist.*HA*594$^b$4. **-ία**, ἡ, *grave-robbing*, *IG*12(7).478 (Amorgos), *CIG*2690 (Iasus), al. ❀ **-ος** (parox.), ὁ, *grave-robber*, Ar.*Ra.*1149, Luc.*JTr.*52, *CIG*2826, al. (Aphrodisias), Charito 1.9, 3.3. II. *grave-digger*, S.E.*M.*7.45.

**τύμμα**, ατος, τό, (τύπτω) *blow, wound*, A.*Ag.*1430 (lyr.); esp. a *prick, sting*, or *snake-bite*, Hp.*Epid.*7.37, Arist.*HA*624$^a$16, Theoc.4. 55, Androm.ap.Gal.14.33; τύμματα πληγῶν *PSI*5.455.16 (ii A. D.).

**τυμμή**, ἡ, collat. form of foreg., Anon.ap.Suid.

**τυμνία**, ἡ, Xanthian for ῥάβδος, St.Byz. s. v. Τυμνησσός.

**τῦμος**, ὁ, v. τύμβος fin.

**τυμπᾰν-άριος**, ὁ, *drummer*, *PLond.*5.1722.7 (vi A. D.). **-εύς**, έως, ὁ, *hollow drum, barrel*, Hero *Mens.*13. **-ίας**, ου, Ion. -ίης, ὁ, = τυμπανοειδής, ὕδρωψ a kind of dropsy in which the belly *is stretched tight like a drum*, Gal.19.424, Aret.*SD*2.1. II. *one who suffers from* τυμπανίας ὕδρωψ, Herod.Med.ap.Orib.10.8.9. **-ίζω**, *beat a drum*, as was done in the worship of Cybele, Eup.77, Plu.2.60a:—Pass., τυμπανίζεσθαι κατὰ τὰς ἐξόδους *march out to the sound of drums*, Str. 15.1.58. 2. τ. ἐπὶ ταῖς θύραις *drum with the hand* on them, Lxx 1*Ki.*21.13. II. perh. = ἀποτυμπανίζω (which is v.l.), *Ep.Hebr.* 11.35 (Pass.); coupled with ἀνασκολοπίζεσθαι in Luc.*JTr.*19; cf. τύμπανον II. III. of orators, 'beat the big drum', Philostr.*VS*1. 21.5. ❀ **-ικός**, ή, όν, *suffering from* τυμπανίας ὕδρωψ, Alex.Trall. 10. **-ιον**, τό, Dim. of τύμπανον, *of a head-dress*, Str.3.4.17; of pearls (from their shape), Plin.*HN*9.109; in a machine, a *drum, roller*, Hero *Spir.*1.16, al., Theo Sm.p.180 H.; cf. τύμπανον III. **-ισμός**, ὁ, *beating of drums, drumming*, as the Galli did in the worship of Cybele, Ar.*Lys.*388; in the Dionysus-cult, Str.15.1.8; as a superstitious practice, in pl., Plu.2.171b, 338c. **-ιστής**, οῦ, ὁ, *one who beats the* τύμπανον, *drummer*, Str.15.1.52, *BGU*630 iv 1 (ii A. D.); Τυμπανισταί, name of a play by Sophocles:—fem. **-ίστρια**, of a priestess of Sabazius, D.18.284, Luc.*Somn.*12. II. gen. pl. -ιστῶν (from -ιστός?) = *membraneorum*, *Gloss.* **-ίτης** [ῑ], ου, ὁ, = τυμπανίας I, Cels.3.21.2, Gal.14.746, *Gloss.*

**τυμπᾰνό-δουπος**, ον, *sounding with drums*, Orph.*H.*14.3. **-ειδής**, ές, *like a drum*, Arist.*Cael.*293$^b$34, D.L.9.30 (Cobet, for -ῶδες), *Placit.* 3.10.4. **-εις**, εσσα, εν, = foreg.; ὕδρωψ τ., = τυμπανίας, Nic.*Al.*342.

❀ **τύμπᾰνον**, τό, also in the form **τύπανον** (q. v.): (τύπτω):—*kettle-drum*, such as was used esp. in the worship of the Mother Goddess and Dionysus, Hdt.4.76, E.*HF*892; τυμπάνων ἀλαλαγμοί, ἀράγματα, Id.*Cyc.*65 (lyr.), 205; τύμπανα, Ῥέας τε μητρὸς ἐμά θ' εὑρήματα, says Dionysus, Id.*Ba.*59, cf. 156 (lyr.), *IG*4$^2$(1).131.9, 10 (Epid.); in Corybantic rites, Ar.*V.*119; τ. ἀράσσειν, ῥήσσειν, *AP*6.217 (Simon.), 7.485 (Diosc.); καταυλήσει χρῆται καὶ τυμπάνοις Sor.2.29. 2. metaph., τύμπανον φυσᾶν, of inflated eloquence, *AP*13.21 (Theodorid.). II. name of some instrument of torture or execution, Ar. *Pl.*476 (ξύλα ἐφ' οἷς [ἐν οἷς Suid.] ἐτυμπάνιζον· ἐχρῶντο γὰρ ταύτῃ τῇ τιμωρίᾳ· ἢ βάκλα, παρὰ τὸ τύπτειν Sch.); τινῶν μὲν εἰς δεσμωτήριον, τινῶν δὲ ἐπὶ τύμπανον ἀπαγομένων S.E.*M.*2.30; τοὺς ἐκ τυμπάνου καὶ τοὺς ἀνεσκολοπισμένους Luc.*Cat.*6; ἐπὶ τὸ τ. προσῆγε Lxx 2*Ma.*6.19, cf. 28; cf. τύπανον. 2. = *tumix, sirimpio* (dub. sens.), *Gloss.* 3. *cudgel*, τὰς πολλὰς ἐπὶ τοῦ νώτου διὰ τῶν τ. πληγάς Dam.*Isid.*185; so perh. in Lxx ll. cc. III. in a machine, *drum*, Hero *Bel.*86, cf. Orib. 49.4.43; in Verg.*G.*2.444, *tympana* are *wagon-wheels made of a solid piece of wood, rollers*; similarly perh. in *PLond.*1821.204, possibly of the *wheel* of an irrigating machine: cf. τυμπάνιον. IV. Archit., *the sunken triangular space enclosed by the cornice of the pediment*, Lat. *tympanum fastigii*, Vitr.4.7.5; *the square panel of a door*, Id.4.6.4.

**τυμπᾰνόομαι**, Pass., *to be stretched tight like a drum*, *Hippiatr.*71.

**τύμπᾰνος**, ὁ, = τύμπανον III, Hero *Spir.*2.36; = τύμπανον I. 1, dub. in *AP*6.220 (Diosc.).

**τυμπᾰνο-τερπής**, ές, *delighting in drums*, Orph.*H.*27.11. **-τρίβης** [ῑ], ου, ὁ, *drummer*, esp. used of the Galli in the worship of Cybele, in Lat. form *tympanotriba*, Plaut.*Truc.*611. **-φορέομαι**, Med., *carry drums*, Clearch.10.

**τυμπᾰνώδης**, ες, *drum-like, as of a drum*, ἦχος Sor.2.31, 37; v. τυμπανοειδής.

**Τυμωλ-ίς**, **-ῑτική**, **-ιτίκιον**, **-ος**, v. Τμῶλος.

**Τυνδάρεος** [ᾰ], ὁ, *Tyndareos*, husband of Leda, Od.11.298, 24.199 (cf. Hdn.Gr.2.151), and E. in lyr. passages (*El.*117, 989) acc. to codd. (prob. f.l.); Att. **Τυνδάρεως** [ᾰ], εω, ὁ, A.*Ag.*83 (anap.), Th. 1.9, title of tragedy by S. (gen. -εω also in Hes.*Fr.*94.7, but -έος *Fr.* 96.21):—hence Patron. ❀ **Τυνδᾰρίδης** [ῐ], Dor. **-δας**, Pi.*N.*10.73, etc.; pl. οἱ Τυνδαρίδαι, of Castor and Pollux, *h.Hom.*17.2, Hdt.4.145, etc. —Adj. **Τυνδάρειος** [ᾰ], α, ον, E.*Hel.*137, *IT*5; also ος, ον Id.*Or.*1512 (troch.), Ar.*Th.*919:—fem. Patron. **Τυνδᾰρίς**, ίδος, ἡ, παῖς E.*Hel.* 1546, etc.

**τύνη**, v. σύ.

❀ **τυννός**, ά, όν, Dor. for μικρός, *so small, so little*, Call.*Fr.*420, Theoc.24.139, *IGRom.*4.235.2 (Mysia); ἐκ τυννῶν (ἐκ τιτυννῶν codd., corr. Ruhnken) *from childhood*, Suid. s. v. ἐκ τιτυννῶν.

**τυννοῦτος**, ον and ο, lengthd. form of τυννός, *so small, so little*, Ar. *Th.*745; commonly with ι demonstr., **τυννουτοσί**, **-ονί**, Id.*Ach.*367, *Eq.*1220; gen. and dat. τυννουτουί, -ῳί, Id.*Nu.*392 (anap.), *Ra.*139.

**τυντλ-άζω**, = πηλοπατέω or βωλοκοπέω (acc. to Sch.), or = σκάπτειν ἀμπέλους (acc. to Hsch.), Ar.*Pax* 1148 (troch.); = ἐπιρραίνειν πηλῷ, Phot.:—metaph. in Pass., ὁ δ' ἀγνοῶν ταῦτ' εἰκότως -άζεται Sosip.1. 35. **-ος**, ὁ, *mud*, Men.1078, Sch.Ar.*Pax* 1148. **-ώδης**, ες, *muddy*, λόγος (οἷον πεπατημένος καὶ κοινός) *Com.Adesp.*909.

**τύξις**, εως, ἡ, *artifice*, Μενανδρείων ἐπέων δεδαηκότα πάσας τύξιας *Ath.Mitt.*17.272 (Athens, ii A. D.); τύξιν· τεῦξιν, παρασκευήν, Hsch.

**τῡπάζω**, (τύπος) = τυπόω, of footprints, Opp.*C.*1.458 (Pass.). II. (τυπή) = κόπτω, Hsch.

**τύπᾰνον** [ῠ], τό, (τύπτω) = τύμπανον (chiefly poet., also in Arist. *Ath.*45.1, Phld.*Mus.*p.49 K.), *drum*, *h.Hom.*14.3, A.*Fr.*57.10 (anap.), E.*Hel.*1347 (lyr.), Diog.Ath.1.3, *AP*6.165.5 (Phal.). [τυμπ- is read against the metre in E. l. c., A. l. c. codd.Str., Diog. l. c. codd. Ath.] II. = τύμπανον II, ὁ ἀπὸ τοῦ τ. nickname of one Lysimachus who at the last moment escaped execution, Arist. l. c.; ἄξιοί εἰσι τυχεῖν πάντες ἑνὸς τ. *AP*11.160 (Lucill.); τύπανα is metrically possible in Ar.*Pl.*476, and is required there by the alphabetical order in Suid., as is τύπανον in Hsch. III. = *crusta*, *Gloss.* IV. name of a street, *BGU*917 (iii A. D.).

**τύπανος**, ὁ, an unknown bird, Arist.*HA*609$^a$27 (perh. f.l. for τύραννος).

**τῡπάριον** [ᾰ], τό, Dim. of τύπος, *small figure, image*, Tz.*H.*11.473.

**τῠπ-άς**, άδος, ἡ, *mallet, hammer*, S.*Fr.*844, cf. Hsch. **-αστήριον**· τὸ τῶν ἁλιέων στυμνίον, Id. (τυμπ- cod., τυπ- poscit ordo). **-ετός**, ὁ, like κοπετός, *beating the breast* for grief, *mourning*, D.H.4.67. **-ή**, ἡ, *blow, wound*, in pl., Il.5.887, A.R.3.848, etc.: sg., Nic.*Th.*129, 673. **-ης**, ου, ὁ, *striker*, Hsch., Theognost. *Can.*24. **-ητός**, ὁ, = τυπετός, *beating of the breast*, *Supp.Epigr.*4. 573.12 (Notium, metr.). **-ίας**, ου, ὁ, *hammered, wrought*, χαλκός, opp. τροχίας, Poll.7.105.

**τῡπ-ίδιον**, τό, *a little model*, *IG*2².1534.66 (pl.). **※ -ικός**, ή, όν, *impressionable*, Plu.2.442c; *conforming to type* (τύπος VII. 3), Gal. 7.471. Adv. -κῶς, νοσεῖν Ruf.ap.Orib.8.47.11. **2.** *typicum*, = *figuratum*, *Gloss.*; τὰ τ. perh. *seals* on a will, *PMasp.*154ᵛ.20 (vi A.D.). **3.** Adv. -κῶς *by way of example*, 1*Ep.Cor.*10.11. **※ -ιον**, τό, Dim. of τύπος III, *small model*, *IG*2².1534.205, al., 11(2).161*B* 119 (Delos, iii B.C.).

**※ τῡπίς**, ίδος, ή, = τυπάς, *hammer*, A.R.4.762, al., Call. in *PSI*9. 1092.50, Agatharch.25.

**[τ]ῠπογράφος** [ᾰ], ὁ, or **-ον**, τό, *certified copy*, —γράφου γαμικοῦ *copy of* marriage *lines*, *Jahresh.*18 *Beibl.*287 (Ephesus, i B.C.).

**※ τύπ-ος** [ῠ], ὁ, (τύπτω) *blow*, τ. ἀντίτυπος Orac.ap.Hdt.1.67; *beat* of horses' hoofs, v.l. for κτύπος in X.*Eq.*11.12; αἰθερίου πατάγοιο τ. βρονταῖον ἀκούων Nonn.*D.*20.351; so perh. νάβλα τ. Sopat.16. **II.** *the effect of a blow* or *of pressure*: **1.** *impression* of a seal, τύποι σφενδόνης χρυσηλάτου E.*Hipp.*862, cf. Pl.*Tht.*192a, 194b, Chrysipp. *Stoic.*2.23, Luc.*Alex.*21; τ. ἐνσημήνασθαί τινι Pl.*R.*377b; *stamp* on a coin, τὰ ἀκριβῆ τὸν τ. Luc.*Hist.Conscr.*10, cf. Hero *Mens.*60, Hsch. s.v. Κυζικηνοὶ στατῆρες; on a branding-iron, ὁ τ. τοῦ καυτῆρος ἔστω ἀλώπηξ ἢ πίθηκος Luc.*Pisc.*46: generally, *print, impression*, χύτρας τύπον ἀρθείσης ἐν σποδῷ μὴ ἀπολιπεῖν, ἀλλὰ συγχεῖν Plu.2.727c, cf. 982b, Iamb.*Protr.*21.κθ', *Gp.*2.20.1; στίβου γ' οὐδεὶς τ. no foot*print*, S.*Ph.*29 (v.l. κτύπος); ὡς ἡδὺς ἐν πόρπακι σὸς (sc. τοῦ βραχίονος) κεῖται τύπος thy *imprint*, (O arm), E.*Tr.*1196 (σῷ cj. Dobree); τ. ὀδόντων *imprint* of teeth, *AP*6.57.5 (Paul. Sil.); *print*, βάλω τὸν δάκτυλόν μου εἰς τὸν τ. τῶν ἥλων *Ev.Jo.*20.25; οἱ τ. τῶν πληγῶν Ath.13. 585c. **b.** *impressions* supposed by Democr. and Epicur. to be made on the air by things seen, and to travel through space, Thphr. *Sens.*52, Epicur.*Ep.*1 p.9 U., *Nat.*2.6, al.; ὁ θεὸς . . πνεῦμα ἐνεκέρασεν [τοῖς ὀφθαλμοῖς] οὕτως ἰσχυρὸν καὶ φιλότεχνον ὥστε ἀναμάσσεσθαι τοὺς τ. τῶν ὁρωμένων Arr.*Epict.*2.23.3. **2.** *hollow mould* or *matrix*, καθάπερ ἐν τύπῳ τὰ σχήματα πλασθῆναι Arist.*PA*676ᵇ9, cf. *Pr.* 891ᵇ2; used by κοροπλάθοι, D.Chr.60.9, Procl. *in Ti.*1.335, 394 D., cf. Hsch. s.v. χοάνη; by fruit-growers, to shape the fruit while growing, *Gp.*10.9.3; *die* used in striking coins, metaph., Κύπριος χαρακτὴρ τ' ἐν γυναικείοις τύποις εἰκὼς πέπληκται τεκτόνων πρὸς ἀρσένων A.*Supp.*282. **3.** *engraved mark, engraving*, δέλτον χαλκῆν τύπους ἔχουσαν ἀρχαίων γραμμάτων *engravings* of letters, i.e. engraved letters, Plu.*Alex.*17, cf. Pl.*Phdr.*275a; τὰ γεγραμμένα τύποις Id.*Ep.*343a; τὸ μέτρον τοῦ ποδὸς ὑποτέτακται τούτοις τοῖς τ. the length of the foot is subjoined in this *engraving*, *Rev.Bibl.*35.285 (Jerusalem). **4.** *the depression between the underlip and chin*, Poll.2.90. **5.** *pip* on dice, Id.9.95. **III.** *cast* or *replica* made in a mould, τ. κατάμακτος *IG*2².1534.87; τ. ἔγμακτος ib.64. **IV.** *figure worked in relief*, whether made by moulding, modelling, or sculpture, αἱμασιὴ ἐγγεγλυμμένη τύποισι Hdt.2.138, cf. 106,136,148, 153; θεοῦ τ. μὴ ἐπίγλυφε δακτυλίῳ Iamb.*Protr.*21.κγ'; σιδηρονώτοις ἀσπίδος τύποις E.*Ph.*1130; χρυσοκόλλητοι τ. Id.*Rh.*305; τ. ἀργυροῦς *IG*2².1533.30, 11(2).161*B*77, cf. 115 (Delos, iii B.C.); τύπους ἐργάσασθαι καὶ παρέχειν ib.4²(1).102.36 (Epid., iv B.C.); *tablet bearing a relief*, καθελέσθαι τοὺς τ. καὶ εἴ τι ἄλλο ἐστὶν ἀργυροῦν ἢ χρυσοῦν ib.2².839.30, cf. 56, al.; τ. Ἔρωτα ἔχων ἐπειργασμένον Paus.6.23.5; τῶν τ' ἄλλων ὧν τύπος εἰκόν' ἔχει *IG*2.2378, cf. 2².2021.8, 3.1330.5; ἐνταῦθά εἰσιν ἐπὶ τύπου γυναικῶν εἰκόνες Paus.9.11.3; πεποιημένα ἐν τύπῳ in *relief*, Id.2.19.17; *typos scalpsit*, Plin.*HN*35.128; *impressā argillā typum fecit*, ib.151; πρὸς Ναυσίαν περὶ τοῦ τ., title of speech by Lysias, Suid. s.v. λιθουργική; Γάλλοι . . ἔχοντες προστηθίδια καὶ τύπους Plb. 21.37.6, cf. 21.6.7. **V.** *carved figure, image*, ποιεῦνται ξύλινον τ. ἀνθρωποειδέα, ποιησάμενοι δὲ ἐσεργνῦσι τὸν νεκρόν Hdt.2.86; τ. ποιησάμενος λίθινον ἔστησε· ζῷον δέ οἱ ἐνῆν ἀνὴρ ἱππεύς Id.3.88; χρυσέων ξοάνων τύποι, periphr. for χρύσεα ξόανα, E.*Tr.*1074 (lyr.); γραφαῖς καὶ τ. paintings and *statues*, Plb.9.10.12; γραπτοὶ τ. prob. painted pediment-*figures*, E.*Fr.*764, cf. Isoc.9.74, *AP*7.730 (Pers.); *idol, graven image*, Lxx *Am.*5.26, J.*AJ*1.19.10. **2.** *exact replica, image*, as children are called the τύποι of their parents, Artem.2. 45; τ. λογίου Ἑρμοῦ, of Demosthenes, Aristid.2.307 J. **VI.** *form, shape*, οὐλῆς Arist.*GA*721ᵇ32; σώματος Id.*Phgn.*806ᵃ32; προσώπου Id.*Mir.*832ᵇ15; ἀγγείου Crates Gramm.ap.Ath.11.495b; τὸν ἄρτον ἔχειν ἴδιον τ. *OGI*56.73 (Canopus, iii B.C.); οἱ τ. τῶν γραμμάτων D.H.*Dem.*52; ὁ τ. τῶν χαρακτήρων Plu.2.577f; τοὺς τ. τῶν συλλαμβανομένων Sor.1.39; Ἱππομέδοντος σχῆμα καὶ μέγας τ., periphr. for H. himself, A.*Th.*488; Γοργείοισιν εἰκάσω τ. Id.*Eu.*49; ὅμφακος τ., = ὄμφαξ, S.*Fr.*255.5; βραχιόνων ἥβητῆς τ. E.*Heracl.*858; κάλλος ἔχουσα τύποισι *features*, *IG*14.2135 (Rome), cf. Max.Tyr.31.3, Adam. 1.4. **2.** *thing having a shape*, οὐλοφυεῖς . . τ. χθονὸς ἐξανέτελλον undifferentiated *forms* rose from the earth, Emp.62.4; τ. τις πορφυροῦς κατὰ χρόαν, τῷ σχήματι ἐμφερὴς κιβωρίου θύλακι (viz. the placenta) Sor.1.57. **3.** *form of expression, style*, ὁ πραγματικὸς τ. [τοῦ Ξενοφῶντος] D.H.*Pomp.*4; ὁ τ. τῆς γραφῆς Longin.ap.Porph. *Plot.*19; ὁ τ. ὁ πολιτικός Hermog.*Id.*2.11; οὐδ' ἀληθινοῦ τύπου μέτεστι τῷ ἀνδρί ibid.; ὁ διὰ τῶν συμβόλων προτρεπτικὸς τ. Iamb.*Protr.*21; ὁ αἰνιγματώδης τ. Id.*VP*23.103. **4.** Gramm., *mode of formation, form*, τ. πατρωνυμικῶν D.T.634.29; τ. παθητικός A.D.*Synt.*278. 25. **VII.** *archetype, pattern, model*, capable of exact repetition in numerous instances, αὐτὸν ἐκμάττειν . . εἰς τοὺς τῶν κακιόνων τ. Pl.*R.* 396e; οἰκισταῖς (sc. πόλεως) τοὺς μὲν τ. προσήκει εἰδέναι, ἐν οἷς δεῖ μυθολογεῖν τοὺς ποιητάς . . , οὐ μὴν αὐτοῖς γε ποιητέον μύθους· . . οἱ τ. περὶ θεολογίας τίνες ἂν εἶεν; ib.379a, cf. 380c. **2.** *character recognizable in a number of instances, general character, type*, πάντα ὅσα τοῦ τ. τούτου Id.*Tht.*171e; τοῦ αὐτοῦ μετέχοντα τύπου Id.*R.*402d; τοῦτον τὸν τ. ἔχοντα Id.*Phlb.*51d. **3.** *type* or *form of disease* (esp. fever) with reference to the order and spacing of its attacks and intervals, Gal.7.463, cf. 475,490,512. **VIII.** *general impression, vague indication*, γίνεται ἀμυδρὸς ὁ τ. τῆς ῥάχεως (in the foetus) Diocl.*Fr.*175; τ. ἀμυδροί, opp. ἀκριβὲς εἶδος, Gal.6.5; ἕως ἂν ὁ τ. ἐνῇ τοῦ πράγματος as long as there is an *approximate indication* of the thing, Pl.*Cra.*432e; of the *general type* or *schema* corresponding with a name, Epicur.*Fr.*255. **2.** *outline, sketch, general idea*, ὅσον τοὺς τ. ὑφηγεῖσθαι Pl.*R.*403e; περιγραφὴ καὶ τύποι Id.*Lg.*876e; ἔχεις τὸν τ. ὧν λέγω Id.*R.*491c; τοὺς τ. μόνον εἰπόντες περὶ αὐτῶν Arist.*Pol.*1341ᵇ31; ἐξηγεῖσθαι τύποις Pl.*Lg.*816c; ὁ τ. τῆς φιλοσοφίας τοιοῦτός τίς ἐστιν Isoc.15.186, cf. Phld.*Rh.*2.166 S.; ὁ τ. τῆς ὅλης πραγματείας Epicur.*Ep.*1 p.3 U.; pl., ib.p.4 U.; δέονται . . ὑγρᾶς διαίτης, ἧς τὸν τ. ἀρτίως ὑπέγραψα Gal.6.397; τύπῳ, ἐν τύπῳ, *in outline, in general*, ὡς ἐν τύπῳ, μὴ δι' ἀκριβείας, εἰρῆσθαι Pl.*R.*414a; ἵνα τύπῳ λάβωμεν αὐτάς ib.559a; ἐν ἑνὶ περιλαβόντα εἰπεῖν αὐτὰ οἷόν τινι τύπῳ Id.*Lg.*718c; τύπῳ, καὶ οὐκ ἀκριβῶς Arist.*EN*1104ᵃ1; παχυλῶς καὶ τ. ἐνδείκνυσθαι ib.1094ᵇ20; τ. καὶ ἐπὶ κεφαλαίου λέγομεν ib.1107ᵇ14; ὡς ἐν τ. Id.*Pol.*1323ᵃ10; ὅσον τύπῳ *in outline* only, Id.*Top.*101ᵃ22; ὡς τύπῳ λαβεῖν Thphr.*Char.*1.1. **3.** *outline*, ταῦτα ὅσα εἴρηται καθάπερ ἐν γραφαῖς ἀχρόοις γραμμῇ μόνῃ τύποι ἀνδρῶν εἰκασμένοι εἰσί Adam.2. 61. **IX.** *prescribed form, model to be imitated*, ἣν ἁμάρτωσι τοῦ πατρικοῦ τ. τοῦ ἐπιμελέος Democr.228; οὗτος . . εἷς ἂν εἴη τῶν περὶ θεοὺς νόμων καὶ τύπων, ἐν ᾧ δεήσει τοὺς λέγοντας λέγειν καὶ τοὺς ποιοῦντας ποιεῖν Pl.*R.*380c, cf. 383c; ἐν τοῖς τ. οἷς ἐνομοθετησάμεθα ib.398b; εἰς ἀρχήν τε καὶ τ. τινὰ τῆς δικαιοσύνης ib.443c; τ. εὐσεβείας . . παισὶν . . ἐκτέθεικα *OGI*383.212 (Nemrud Dagh, i B.C.); ὥστε γενέσθαι ὑμᾶς τύπον πᾶσι τοῖς πιστεύουσιν ἐν τῇ Μακεδονίᾳ 1*Ep.Thess.*1.7; κατὰ τὸν τ. τὸν δεδειγμένον σοι Lxx *Ex.*25.39(40), cf. *Act.Ap.*7.44. **2.** *general instruction*, δόντες τοὺς τ. τούτους ὑπὲρ τῆς ὅλης διοικήσεως, ἐξέπεμπον τοὺς δέκα Plb.21.24.9; *general principle* in law, τ. ἐστὶν καθ' ὃν ἔκρεινα πολλάκις *PRyl.*75.8 (ii A.D.). **b.** *rule of life, religion*, ἐξεταστέον ποταπῷ χρῆται τύπῳ ὁ νοσῶν (e.g. whether Jewish or Egyptian) Erot.*Fr.*33. **3.** *rough draft* of a book, βιβλίον γεγραμμένον ἐν τύποις Gal.18(2).875, cf. 15.587,624, Anon. ap.Phot.*Bibl.*p.491 B.; *draft* of an official letter, τύπον ποιεῖ he *drafted* a letter, *UPZ*14.135 (ii B.C.); τ. χειρογραφίας *PMich.Teb.* 123ʳ ii 38 (i A.D.); τ. ἐπιστολικοί *models* of letters, *Epist.Charact.* tit. **4.** *form* of a document, ἔστιν δὲ ὁ τ. τῆς εἰθισμένης διαγραφῆς ὁ ὑποκείμενος *PMich.Zen.*9ᵛ.3 (iii B.C.); σωματισθῆναι . . τύπῳ τῷδε· τί ἑκάστῳ ὑπάρχει κτλ. *POxy.*1460.12 (iii A.D.); κατὰ τὸν αὐτὸν τ. *PFlor.* 279.16 (vi A.D.). **5.** *text* of a document, ὁ μὲν τῆς ἐπιστολῆς τ. οὕτως ἐγέγραπτο Lxx 3 *Ma.*3.30, cf. Aristeas 34, *Act.Ap.*23.25, prob. cj. in Lxx 1 *Ma.*15.2. **6.** *written decision*, θεῖος τ. an imperial *rescript*, *Cod.Just.*1.2.20, al., Just.*Nov.*113 tit., cf. *PMasp.*32.41 (vi A.D.); αἰτῆσαι θεῖον καὶ πραγματικὸν τ. Mitteis *Chr.*319.47 (vi A.D.); given by a bishop, *Sammelb.*7449.14 (v A.D.); by the ἔκδικος, *PSI*9.1075. 11 (v A.D.); by others, χρὴ . . δοῦναι τ. εἰς τὴν συγχώρησιν *POxy.*1911. 145 (vi A.D.): in pl., of the *acta* of a πάγαρχος, ib.1829.2,12 (vi A.D.). **X.** as law-term, *summons, writ*, οἱ τ. γράμμα εἰσὶν ἀγορᾶς, ἐρήμην ἐπαγγέλλον τῷ οὐκ ἀποδιδόντι Philostr.*VS*1.25.9; δίκης λῆξις εἴη ἂν ὁ νῦν καλούμενος τ. Poll.8.29. **-ουργία**, ή, *forming, modelling*, Greg.Cor. in Rh.7(2).1126 W. **※ -όω**, *form by impress*, κόνιν τυπόων Nonn.*D.*6.21:—Pass., γράμμα τυπωθέν Maiist.28. **2.** *impress, stamp*, ἐπιστολὴν σφραγῖδι App.*Hann.*51; σφραγῖδες τ. κηρόν Ph.1.326; σφραγὶς τ. εἴδη ib.47:—Med. or Pass., *to be stamped with an impression*, metaph. of perception, Zeno *Stoic.*1.39, cf. *PMag. Lond.*121.562. **3.** *stamp* a coin, Poll.3.86; τοῦ νομίσματος ἐπὶ μὲν θατέρου Ἄμμωνα . . ἐτύπωσαν Suid. s.v. Βάττου σίλφιον:—Pass., ἀὴρ φθόγγοις ἐνάρθροις τυπωθείς Plu.2.589c, cf. Thphr.*Sens.*50. **4.** *seal up*, *PGiss.*54.14 (iv A.D.). **II.** *form, mould, model*, τυποῦσι [θνητὰ γένη] θεοί Pl.*Prt.*320d:—in Med., ἡ πειθὼ τὴν ψυχὴν ἐτυπώσατο Gorg.*Hel.*13; Κύπριδος παῖδα τυπωσάμενος *AP*12.56 (Mel.), cf. 15.51 (Arch.):—Pass., *receive a form, be modelled*, of sculpture, opp. painting, τὰ γεγραμμένα καὶ τὰ τετυπωμένα Pl.*Sph.*239d; μιμήματα τυπωθέντα ἀπὸ . . Id.*Ti.*50c; τοῦ τυποῦντος καὶ τοῦ τυπουμένου Plu.2.1024c; of the foetus, Sor.1.43, cf. 82; τυπωθεὶς χαλκός *Supp.Epigr.*3.441 (Stratos). **2.** Pass., of diseases, *assume a* certain *type* (cf. τύπος VII. 3), Gal.7.463, al.; of treatment, Id.6.92. **III.** *ordain, decree*, *PLond.ined.*2142 (iv A.D.), *Cod.Just.*1.3.38.6 (Pass.), *PMasp.*353.14 (vi A.D.). **IV.** *execute in due form*, *POxy.*67.11 (Pass., iv A.D.), *PLips.*35.19 (Pass., iv A.D.).

**τυπτητέος**, α, ον, *to be beaten*, D.54.44.

**※ τύπτω**, Il.11.561, etc.: fut. τύψω Nonn.*D.*44.160, Hierocl.*Facet.* 200: aor. 1 ἔτυψα, Ep. τύψα, Il.13.529, al., Emp.43, Hdt.3.64, but rare in Trag. and Att., as A.*Eu.*156 (lyr.), [Lys.] *Fr.*20 S.: Att. fut. τυπτήσω Ar.*Nu.*1443, *Pl.*21, Pl.*Grg.*527a, D.21.204: aor. 1 ἐτύπτησα first in Arist.*Pol.*1274ᵇ20 (as v.l.), then Philostr.*VS*2.1.8, Aesop.66, Hierocl.*Facet.*86: aor. 2 ἔτυπον E.*Ion* 766 (lyr.); Ep. part. τετυπόντες Call.*Dian.*61 (perh. pf. τετύποντες): pf. τέτυφα only in Theodos.*Can.*p.47 H.; τετύπτηκα Poll.9.129, Philostr.*VS*2.10.3:—Med., Hdt.2.61, Plu.*Alex.*3, etc., (κατ-) Sapph.62: aor. 1 ἐτυψάμην Luc.*Asin.*14, (ἀπ-) Hdt.2.40: fut. (in pass. sense) τυπτήσομαι Ar.*Nu.* 1379:—Pass., aor. 1 ἐτύφθην Plu.*Galb.*26, *Gp.*18.17.7, Hierocl. *Facet.*138, Zen.2.68; ἐτυπτήθην Ph.2.323: aor. 2 ἐτύπην [ῠ] Il.11. 191, Pi.*N.*1.53, A.*Pr.*363, Ar.*Ach.*1194 (lyr.), Alciphr.3.57: pf. τέτυμμαι Il.13.782, A.*Th.*889 (lyr.), *Eu.*509 (lyr.), inf τετύφθαι Hdt. 3.64; τετύπτημαι Luc.*Demon.*16, Arg.D.54:—In Att. and Lxx the fut. and aor. are supplied by *πατάσσω*, e.g. *τύπτει..καὶ καταβάλλει πατάξας* Lys.13.71; later sts. by *παίω*, e.g. *ὁ δὲ παίσας ἐπερωτᾷ ποτέρᾳ τετύπτηκεν* Poll.9.129; the pf. by *πλήσσω*; the Pass. partly (esp. in pf. and aor.) by *πλήσσω*: a complete paradigm of this verb is given by Theodos.*Can.*p.43 H., al.:—*beat, strike, smite*, *τύπτουσιν ῥοπάλοισι* (sc. *τὸν ὄνον*) Il.11.561; *ἀμφὶ δέ μιν σφυρὰ τύπτε καὶ αὐχένα δέρμα* 6.117; *ἴχνια τύπτε πόδεσσι πάρος κόνιν ἀμφιχυθῆναι* 23.764; *χθόνα τύπτε μετώπῳ* Od.22.86; *ἅλα τύπτον ἐρετμοῖς* 4.580, 9.104, al.; but in Hom. mostly with weapons of war, [*ξίφει*], *δουρί, ἄορι*, Il.4.531, 13.529, 20.378; *ἐγχείῃσιν* 13.782 (Pass.); *φασγάνῳ* Od.22.98; *σκήπτρῳ τυπεὶς ἐκ τῆσδε χειρὸς* S.*OT*811; *μάστιγι* Lex ap.Aeschin.1.139 (Pass.): c. acc. cogn., *τ. τινὰ σχεδίην* (sc. *πληγήν*) Il.5.830; *πληγὰς τ. τινά* Antipho 4.3.1, v. infr. III. 2: the part struck is sts. in acc., *γαστέρα γάρ μιν τύψε παρ' ὀμφαλόν* Il.21.180, cf. Pi.*N.*9.26, E.*Andr.*1150, etc.: with a Prep., *Φόρκυνα..κατὰ γαστέρα τύψε* Il.17.313; *ἐγκύμονά τις ἔτυψε κατὰ γαστρός* [Lys.] l. c.; *τ. τινὰ εἰς τὸν ὦμον* X.*Cyr.*5.4.5; *ἐπὶ κόρρης* Pl.*Grg.*527a; *ἐπὶ τὴν σιαγόνα* *Ev.Luc.*6.29; *τ. χαλκώματα* *beat* pots and pans (to make a noise), Sor.2.29: abs., *strike*, *τύπτε δ' ἐπιστροφάδην* Il.21.20, cf. Od.22.308, Ar.*Ra.*610; *τ. καὶ πνίγων* Antipho 4.1.6; *Ζέφυρος λαίλαπι τύπτων* *beating* with fury, Il.11.306, cf. Pi.*P.*6.14 (s. v.l.). **2.** even of missiles, *ἐκ χειρὸς τοῖς λίθοις τύπτοντες* Plb.3.53.4; whereas Hom. opposes *τύπτειν* to *βάλλειν*, *δουρὶ τυπεὶς ἢ βλήμενος ἰῷ* Il.11.191 = 206, cf. 15.495, al. **3.** later, *sting*, *ὄφις μ' ἔτυψε μικρός* *Anacreont.*33.10; *ὑπὸ σφηκῶν τύπτεσθαι* X.*HG*4.2.12, cf. *Gp.* l.c.; *πόδα κάκτος τ.* Theoc.10.4; *οἱ βασιλεῖς* [*μελιττῶν*]..*οὐ τύπτουσιν* Arist.*HA*553$^{b}$6. **4.** metaph., *τὸν δ' ἄχος ὀξὺ κατὰ φρένα τύψε βαθεῖαν* sharp grief *smote* him to the heart, Il.19.125; *Καμβύσεα ἔτυψε ἡ ἀληθείη* Hdt.3.64; *ἔτυπεν ὀδύνα με πλευμόνων ἔσω* E.*Ion*766 (lyr.); *ξυμφορᾷ τετυμμένος* A.*Eu.*509 (lyr.); *ἀνίαισι τυπείς* Pi.*N.*1.53; *τύπτειν τὴν συνείδησίν τινος ἀσθενοῦσαν* *wound* his conscience, 1 *Ep.Cor.*8.12; of divine punishment, *ἐγώ εἰμι Κύριος ὁ τύπτων* Lxx *Ez.*7.6(9); *τύπτειν σε μέλλει ὁ θεός* *Act.Ap.*23.3. **5.** *strike* a coin, *ἐξ ἀργύρου τυπτόμενον νόμισμα* Hero *Mens.*60. **II.** Med. *τύπτομαι*, *beat, strike oneself*, esp., like *κόπτομαι*, *beat one's breast* for grief, Hdt.2.61: c. acc. pers., *mourn for* a person, ib.42, 132. **III.** Pass., *to be beaten, struck*, or *wounded*, *δουρὶ τυπείς* Il.11.191; *ὑπὸ δουρί* ib.433; *δορὸς ὕπο* Ar.*Ach.*1194 (lyr.); *κράτων τυπτομένων* Od.22.309. **2.** c. acc. cogn., *receive* blows or wounds, *ἕλκεα..ὅσσ' ἐτύπη* Il.24.421; *τύπτομαι πολλάς* (sc. *πληγάς*) *I get* many *blows*, Ar.*Nu.*972 (anap.), cf. *Pax*644 (troch.), *Ra.*636, Lex ap.Aeschin.1.139: c. dat., *καιρίῃ* (sc. *πληγῇ*) *τετύφθαι* Hdt.3.64; v. supr. I. 1.

**τῠπ-ώδης**, *ες*, (*τύπος* VIII. 2) *like an outline*, *ὡς εἰς τ. μάθησιν* so far as belongs to *general* or *superficial* knowledge, Arist.*Mu.*397$^{b}$12. Adv. *-ωδῶς* *summarily*, Cic.*Att.*4.13.2, Str.2.1.24, 4.1.1, 2: Comp. *-ωδέστερον* Ph.2.419. ® **-ωμα**, *ατος, τό*, *that which is formed* or *moulded*, *τ. χαλκόπλευρον*, of a brazen urn, S.*El.*54; *figure, outline*, *μορφῆς τ.* E.*Ph.*162. **2.** *seal-impression*, Anon. in *Gött.Nachr.*1922.35 (cf. 40): hence, **b.** *impression* received in perception, = *φάντασμα*, Plu.2.1121c. **-ῶντες**· *χοροί τινες*, Hsch. **-ωσις**, *εως, ἡ*, *forming, moulding, impression*, Thphr.*Sens.*53; *modelling*, S.E.*M.*9.197; of the foetus, Hp.*Alim.*42. **2.** *delineation, sketching in outline*, Phld.*Rh.*2.34 S. **II.** *the making of a τύπωμα* 2 b, *φαντασία τύπωσις ἐν ψυχῇ* *Stoic.*2.229, cf. Cleanth.ib.1.108, al., Plot.4.3.26; the *impression* made, Plu.*Brut.*37. **-ωτής**, *οῦ, ὁ*, *one who forms* or *moulds*, *κόσμοιο τ.* Orph.*Fr.*247.8:—fem. **-ῶτις**, *ιδος*, *σφρηγὶς τ.* *seal*-ring, Id.*H.*34.26. **-ωτικός**, *ή, όν*, *able to form* or *mould, formative*, Euryph.ap.Stob.4.39.27: c. gen., S.E.*M.*7.383, 8.407, Ath.9.392a. **II.** '*sketchy*', *περίληψις* (*outline*) Eustr. *in EN*14.32. **III.** in pass. sense, *τυπωτικοὶ λόγοι*, i.e. *λόγοι* *which are copies* of the things which are seen, Procl. *in R.*2.177 K. Adv. *-κῶς*, *μετέχειν τὰ αἰσθητὰ τῶν εἰδῶν* Id. *in Prm.*p.657 S. ® **-ωτός**, *ή, όν*, *fashioned, moulded*, Lyc.262.

**τῡρᾰκίνης** [ῐ], *ου*, Dor. **-νας**, *ὁ*, a kind of *cheese-cake*, Philox.3.17.

**τῡράλφῐτον**, *τό*, *cheese-cake*, *Wien.Sitzb.*132(2).23 (Caria).

**τῠρανν-εῖον**, *τό*, *a tyrant's dwelling*, Str.13.1.67, J.*BJ*4.3.7, Plu.*Dio*13, etc.: pl., D.S.16.70, Plu.*Tim.*13. **-εύω** and **-έω**, the former always in Hdt. (v. infr.) and found in Alc.*Supp.*28.12 (prob.); both in Trag. and Com., as the metre required, cf. S.*OT*408 with *OC*449; E.*Med.*967, *Ph.*560 with *Hel.*786; Ar.*Av.*483 (anap.) with *Lys.*631 (troch.), *Fr.*357; and X. used both, cf. *Cyr.*1.1.1 with *HG*4.4.6; Pl. has *-έω* in *Lg.*693a, *R.*580c, al., *-εύω* in *Men.*76b, more freq. in aor.: fut. *-εύσω* E.*El.*877 (lyr.), Ar.*Lys.* l.c., *-ήσω* first in Plu.2.403c, App.*BC*2.139: aor. *ἐτυράννευσα* Sol.33.6, Hdt.1.14, Th.6.55, 59, Pl.*R.*576c, *Grg.*473d, *Phdr.*238b, etc., *-ησα* E.*HF*29, X.*HG*2.2.24: pf. *τετυράννευκα* Isoc.8.113, *-ηκα* first in Plb.2.59.1:—**Pass.**, fut. *-ηθήσομαι* Sopat. in Rh.8.335 W.; but Med. *τυραννήσομαι* in pass. sense, D.20.161: aor. *ἐτυραννεύθην* Th.1.18, Pl. (v. infr.), *-ήθην* D.H.4.82, Str.8.6.25:—*to be a monarch, absolute ruler*, and in aor. *to become such*, Hdt.1.14, 5.92.ε', Th.6.55, etc.; *ὡς χρὴ τυραννεῖν, Ἰσοκράτους ἠκούσατε* Isoc.3.11; *τυραννεύσασα ἡ ἐπιθυμία* Pl.*Phdr.*238b: in Poets, *to be a prince* or *princess*, E.*Med.*967. **2.** c. gen., *to be ruler of* a people or place, *τ. Ἀθηνῶν* Sol.33.6; *Σαρδίων, Μιλήτου, Ἀθηναίων, Μήδων*, Hdt.1.15, 20, 59, 73; *χθονός, γαίας*, S.*OC*449, E.*El.*877 (lyr.), etc.; *τῶν κακιόνων* Id.*Fr.*1048.6; *Σάμου* Th.1.13; *τᾶς πόλιος* (sc. Eresus) *IG*12(2).526*d*20 (iv B.C.): metaph., [*Κύπρις*] *Διὸς τυραννεῖ πλευμόνων* S.*Fr.*941.15. **3.** c. acc., *τὸ συμπόσιον* Luc.*DMeretr.*3.2 codd.; *Μεσσήνην* f.l. (cod. S) in D.17.7:—Pass., *to be under the sway of τύραννοι*, Hdt.5.55, 78, Th.1.18, etc.; *τυραννουμένη πόλις* Pl.*R.*545c, cf. Hdt.4.137, 5.92.α', X.*HG*2.3.48; *ὑπό τινος τυραννήσεσθαι* D.20.161; *τυραννευθεὶς ὑπὸ Ἔρωτος* Pl.*R.*574e. **II.** *to be of a tyrannical disposition, be imperious*, Id.*Alc.*1.135a, *Men.*76b. **-ησείω**, Desiderat. of *τυραννέω*, *aspire to sovereignty*, Sol.ap.D.L.1.65. **-ησις**, *εως, ἡ*, *tyranny*, Ptol.*Tetr.*197. **-ητέον**, *one must be tyrant*, Sol.ap.D.L.1.64. **-ία**, *ἡ*, = *τυραννίς*, Xenoph.3 (with penult. long); *tyrannous conduct*, Wilcken *Chr.*20 ii 12 (ii A.D.), *PAmh.*2.142.15 (iv A.D.). **-ιάω**, *smack of tyranny*, *οἱ λόγοι σου τ.* D.L.3.18:—Med., *behave tyrannously*, *PSI*6.686.5 (vi A.D.). **II.** = *τυραννησείω*, J.*BJ*4.7.1, Heraclid.*Pol.*4, Suid. **-ίζω**, *take the part of tyrants*, D.17.7. **-ικός**, *ή, όν*, *of* or *for a τύραννος, royal*, *αἷμα* A.*Ag.*828; *τρόποισιν οὐ τυραννικοῖς* Id.*Ch.*479; *κράτος τ.* S.*OC*373; *λῆμα* E.*Med.*348; *δόμος, στέγαι*, ib.740, *Andr.*882; *κύκλος τ.* the circle or assembly *of kings*, S.*Aj.*749; *τ. θέαμα* (in good sense) Phalar.*Ep.*122.1. **2.** *befitting a tyrant, despotic*, *τυραννικόν τοι πόλλ' ἐπίστασθαι λέγειν* E.*Fr.*335; *συμφοραὶ τ.* *that befall a tyrant*, Isoc.8.91; *smacking of tyranny*, *τὸ σῦκον* (sc. *τὸ Λακωνικὸν*) *ἐχθρόν ἐστι καὶ τ.* Ar.*Fr.*108 (troch.); *φρονῶν τυραννικά* Id.*V.*507 (troch.); *ξυνωμοσία τ.* *in favour of tyranny*, Th.6.60; *νόμοι* Pl.*R.*338e; *τι δρᾶσαι τῶν τ.* ib.574b; *μαθὼν ἀντὶ τοῦ βασιλικοῦ τὸ τ.* X.*Cyr.*1.3.18; *τὰ τ.* *the period of the tyrants*, Arist.*Pol.*1303$^{a}$38. **3.** *tyrannical*, of persons, Pl.*R.*574c, *Phdr.*248e, etc.; Sup. *-ώτατος* Id.*R.*575d, 580c; *fit for tyrannical government*, *οἱ τ.*, opp. *οἱ δημοτικοί*, X.*HG*2.3.49; *τυραννικὸν* [*δίκαιον*] *οὐκ ἔστι κατὰ φύσιν* Arist.*Pol.*1287$^{b}$39. **II.** Adv. *-κῶς*, *ζῆν* Pl.*R.*575a; opp. *βασιλικῶς*, Isoc.5.154; opp. *πολιτικῶς*, Arist.*Ath.*16.2: Comp. *-ώτερον* Id.*Pol.*1313$^{a}$2. **-ίς**, *ίδος, ἡ*, voc. *τυραννί* S.*OT*380:—*monarchy, sovereignty*, *μεγάλης οὐκ ἐρέω τ.* Archil.25, cf. Pi.*P.*2.87, 11.53 (pl.), S.*OT*535, E.*Ba.*43, etc.; of the *sovereignty* of Zeus, *ἡ Διὸς τ.* A.*Pr.*10, al., cf. infr. II. 2:—but more freq. **II.** *despotic rule*, obtained by force or fraud, *tyranny*, Simon.71, Hdt.3.53, 81, Ar.*V.*417, Th.1.13, etc.; *τυραννίδα ἔχετε τὴν ἀρχήν* (of the Athenians) Id.3.37; *τ. ὑμῶν* *lordship* over you, D.2.30: metaph., *ἡ ἐπιθυμιῶν ἐν ψυχῇ τ.* Pl.*Lg.*863e. **2.** in concrete sense, *ἡ Διὸς τ.* *royal* Zeus, S.*Fr.*345: pl., *αἱ τυραννίδες*, = *οἱ τύραννοι*, Hdt.8.137; *ἴδεσθε χώρας τὴν διπλῆν τ.* A.*Ch.*973. **3.** *territory* or *resources of a princeling*, Liv.38.14.12. **III.** fem. of *τύραννος*, *princess*, Lxx *Es.*1.18. **IV.** name of a medicine, Gal.14.165.

**τῠραννο-δαίμων**, *ονος, ὁ, ἡ*, *tyrant more than human*, perh. referring to Aspasia, *Com.Adesp.*99. **-δῐδάσκᾰλος**, *ὁ*, *teacher of tyrants*, Pl.*Thg.*125a, D.C.59.24.

**τῠραννοκτόν-ειος**, *ον*, = *-κτονικός*, *τὴν -ειον αἰτεῖ δωρεάν* Sch.Hermog. in Rh.7(1).400 W. **-έω**, *slay a tyrant*, Plu.2.1128f, Luc.*Tyr.*21, Rhet.Anon. in *PLit.Lond.*138 ix 9:—Pass., *to be slain as a tyrant*, Luc.*Tyr.*20. **-ία**, *ἡ*, *the slaying of a tyrant*, Ph.ap.Eus.*PE*8.14, J.*AJ*19.1.10, Plu.*Pel.*34, Luc.*Tyr.*22. **-ικός**, *ή, όν*, *of* or *for the slaying of a tyrant*, *γέρα* App.*BC*4.94. **-ος** (parox.), *ὁ, ἡ*, *slayer of a tyrant*, D.S.16.14, Plu.2.256f, Luc.*Tyr.*1, Lib.*Decl.*43.32:—as Adj., *πάθος, τιμαὶ τ.*, *of slaying a tyrant*, Phalar.*Ep.*70.1.

**τῠραννο-ποιός**, *ὁ*, *maker of tyrants*, Pl.*R.*572e. **-πολίτης** [ῑ], *ου, ὁ*, *citizen under a tyranny*, Sidon.Apoll.*Ep.*5.8 (*-tarum*, v.l. *-tanorum*).

**τύραννος** [ῠ], *ὁ*, also *ἡ* (v. infr. I. 2), *an absolute ruler*, unlimited by law or constitution, first in *h.Mart.*5 (unless the hymn is late), where it is used of a god, *Ἆρες,..ἀντιβίοισι τύραννε*; so *ὁ τῶν θεῶν τ.*, of Zeus, A.*Pr.*736, cf. Ar.*Nu.*564 (lyr.); *ὦ τύραννε τᾶς ἐμᾶς φρενός*, i.e. Apollo, S.*Tr.*217 (lyr.); *σὺ δ' ὦ τύραννε θεῶν τε κἀνθρώπων Ἔρως* E.*Fr.*136; *Μὴν Τύραννος*, a Phrygian deity worshipped in Attica, *IG*2$^{2}$.1366.2 (i A.D.), al.; *οὔ, τὴν τ.* (perh. Hera), in an oath, Herod.5.77: first used of *monarchs* in the time of Archil. (cf. *τυραννίς* I) acc. to Hippias 9 D.; *Φίττακον ἐστάσαντο τ.* Alc.37 A; *ἣν μή τις ἢ τ. ἢ σκηπτοῦχος ᾖ* Semon.7.69; *λαγέτας τ.* Pi.*P.*3.85; interchangeable with *βασιλεύς* in Isoc.2.4 (cf. 1), 35 (cf. 36); later, *chief, princeling*, *OGI*654.8 (Egypt, i B.C.); *τ. ἴδιοι καθ' ἕκαστον ἐμπόριον* *Peripl.M.Rubr.*14: c. gen., *Κροῖσος..τ. ἐθνέων τῶν ἐντὸς Ἅλυος* Hdt.1.6; *Κλεισθένης ὁ Σικυῶνος τ.*, *Ἱστιαῖος ὁ Μιλήτου τ.*, etc., Id.5.67, 7.10.γ', etc.; *ὁ τῶν Κυπρίων τ.* Sor.1.39; *οἱ τ.*, of the Sicilian *tyrants*, Th.1.14; of the Pisistratidae, X.*HG*6.5.33, Arist.*Ath.*13.5, *Pol.*1275$^{b}$36, cf. Th.6.54, Pl.*Smp.*182c; *τὸν τ. κτανέτην* *Scol.*9.3; *οἱ τ.* the *monarchical party*, *προδιδοὺς τοῖς τ. τὴμ πόλιν τὴν Ἐρυθραίων* *IG*1$^{2}$.10.32: freq. in a bad sense, *δημοφάγος τ.* Thgn.1181, cf. 823, Hdt.3.80, Pl.*Grg.*510b, *Plt.*301c, *R.*569b, etc.; *ὕβρις φυτεύει τύραννον* S.*OT*873 (lyr.). **2.** in a wider sense, of *members of the ruler's family*, *οἱ τ.* 'the royal house', Id.*Tr.*316, cf. *OC*851, Charito 1.2: *ἡ τύραννος* is used both of *the queen* herself and *the king's daughter, princess*, E.*Hec.*809, *Med.*42, 877, 1356, cf. infr. II; *πρέπει γὰρ ὡς τ. εἰσορᾶν*, of Clytemnestra, S.*El.*664; *αὐτὴ..τ. ἦ Φρυγῶν* E.*Andr.*204. **3.** metaph., *ἵνα Δίκη τ. ᾖ* that Justice may be *supreme*, Critias 25.6 D.; *Ἔρως τ. ἀνδρῶν* E.*Hipp.*538 (lyr.); *Πειθὼ τὴν τ. ἀνθρώποις μόνην* Id.*Hec.*816. **4.** *golden-crested wren, Regulus cristatus*, Arist.*HA*592$^{b}$23; cf. *τροχίλος* I. 2. **II.** *τύραννος, ον*, as Adj., *kingly, royal*, *τύραννα σκῆπτρα* A.*Pr.*761; *τ. σχῆμα* S.*Ant.*1169; *τύραννα δρᾶν* to act *as a king*, Id.*OT*588; *ἡ τύραννος κόρη* E.*Med.*1125; *τύραννον δῶμα* *the king's* palace, Id.*Hipp.*843 (lyr.), etc.; *τ. ἑστία* Id.*Andr.*3; *τ. δόμος* the *royal* house, Id.*Hel.*478, etc.; *ἐς τύραννν' ἐγημάμην* into *the royal house*, Id.*Tr.*474. **2.** *imperious, despotic*, *τ. πόλις* Th.1.122, 124; *αἱ τ. φύσεις* Luc.*Ner.*2. (Loan-word, prob. from Phrygian or Lydian.)

**τῠραννοφόνος**, *ον*, *slaying tyrants*, *AP*7.388 (Bianor), D.C.44.35.

**τυράσιον**, *τό*, dub. sens. in *PSI*6.606.6 (iii B.C.).

**τύρβᾰ**, Adv., (*τύρβη*) *pell-mell, in confusion*, [*ὗς*] *τρέπουσα τύρβ' ἄνω κάτω* A.*Fr.*311.3; also **σύρβα**, Hsch., cf. *συρβάβυττα*.

**τυρβ-άζω**, *trouble, stir up*, τὸν πηλὸν ὥσπερ ἀτταγᾶς τυρβάσεις βαδίζων Ar.*V*.257; τυφλὸς..Ἄρης συὸς προσώπῳ πάντα τυρβάζει κακά S.*Fr*.838:—Pass., πολὺς δὲ πηλὸς ἐκ πίθων τυρβάζεται *bursts in turbid stream* from.., ib.783; c. dat. pers., *jostle against*.., Ar.*Pax* 1007 (anap.); τ. περὶ πολλά (v.l. for θορυβάζῃ) *to be troubled* about.., *Ev.Luc*.10.41. II. *revel, enjoy oneself*, Alex.25.6. **-ασία**, ἡ, = τύρβη II, Poll.4.104, Hsch.; cj. Rzach for τυρβάξας in Hes.*Fr*. 96.60. **-ασμα**, ατος, τό, *trouble, confusion*, dub. in Anon.*Herc*. 418*Fr*.2.4.

**τύρβη**, ἡ, *disorder, confusion, tumult*, τύρβην παρέχειν τινί Hp. *Fract*.22; τὴν τύρβην ἐν ᾗ ζῶμεν Isoc.15.130, cf. X.*Cyr*.1.2.3, Plb. 1.67.3, etc. II. metaph., ἡ ποιητικὴ τ. the poetic *rout*, Epicur. *Fr*.228; so of a *Bacchic festival and its dance*, Paus.2.24.6: hence, acc. to Suid., = ἀπόλαυσις, *revelry*. [Oxyt. in some codd. of Hp. l.c.; the form σύρβη is cited by Suid., Eust.871.60.] (Cf. Lat. *turba*, ONorse *þyrpask* 'crowd together'.)

**τύρβησις**· ἠλιβατὸν ἀέρα, Hsch.

**τῡρ-εία**, ἡ, *cheese-making*, Arist.*HA*523$^a$6. 2. *cheese-press*, *Tab.Heracl*.1.71. 3. *a cheese* as an offering, φέρειν τυρείην τῷ Ἑρμῇ *Schwyzer* 721.9, cf. 11 (Mycale, iv B.C.). II. metaph., *intrigue, roguery*, Eust.620.13, Zonar. **-ευμα**, ατος, τό, *that which is curdled, cheese*, in pl., E.*El*.496, *Cyc*.162,190. II. metaph., *intrigue*, *Com.Adesp*.706. **-ευσις**, εως, ἡ, = τυρεία I. 1, Arist.*HA*522$^a$ 26. **-ευτήρ**, ῆρος, ὁ, *one who makes cheese*, Ἑρμῆς τυρευτήρ Hermes as god of goatherds, and giver of goat's-milk cheese, *AP*9. 744 (Leon.). **-εύω**, (τυρός) like τυρόω, *make cheese, make into cheese*, *Com.Adesp*.1173:—Pass., τυρεύεται τὸ γάλα Arist.*HA*522$^b$ 2: impers., τυρεύεται *cheese is made*, ib.521$^b$30. II. metaph. (cf. τυρόω I. 2), *mix up cunningly, contrive by trickery and intrigue*, κακόν τινι τ. Luc.*Asin*.31, cf. Nic.Dam.136.6 J., Adam.1.3,17: abs., *concoct mischief*, D.19.295:—Pass., ἡ ἐπί τινι τυρευθεῖσα ἐπιβουλή Ph. 2.66. **-έω**, = foreg., τυρὸν ἐτύρησας Alcm.34.6.

**τυρηνίς**, ίδος, ἡ, a Persian plaster, Aët.15.15.

**τυριάνθινος**, η, ον, *of Tyrian-purple dye*, Mart.1.53; *pallium tyrianthinum*, Vopisc.*Carin*.20.5: written -άντινος, *PHamb*.10.23,30 (ii A.D.).

**τῡρίδιον** [ρῐ], τό, Dim. of τυρός, dub. cj. in Epich.92, D.L.6.36 (Cobet).

**Τυρίμνεια**, τά, festival of the god Τύριμνος at Thyatira, *Ath.Mitt*. 24.238, *BCH*11.105, Keil-Premerstein *Zweiter Bericht* 62; Ἀπόλλων Τύριμνος, *JHS*37.108, etc.; Τυριμναῖος, Keil-Premerstein *Zweiter Bericht* 115; Σεβαστείου καὶ Τυριμνήου πανηγύρεως *Ath.Mitt*.19.535.

**τύρινος** [ῠ], η, ον, *of Tyrian purple*, [χρῶμα] *POxy*.1739.4 (ii/iii A.D.).

**τῡρίον**, τό, Dim. of τυρός, *small cheese*, Chionid.7 (cj. for τυρόν), Telecl.25, Chrysipp.Tyan.ap.Ath.14.647c, *POxy*.1684$^v$ (iv A.D.), etc.

® **Τύριος** [ῠ], α, ον, *Tyrian*, Hdt.2.112, etc.; πορφύρα *PHolm*.26.8,23.

**τῡρ-ίσκος**, ὁ, = τυρίον, Ael.*NA*8.5, Longus 1.19. **-ίτης**, ου, ὁ (sc. πλακοῦς), = *scriblita*, *Gloss*.

**τύρμα**, ἡ, = Lat. *turma*, *IGRom*.1.1334,1346, al. (Egypt); also **τούρμα**, ib.1332, al. (ibid., i A.D.).

**τυρνες**, = *luciolus*, a kind of fish, prob. f.l. in *Gloss*.

**τῡρο-βόλιον**, τό, *cheese-basket*, Sch.Ar.*Ra*.568, Sch.Theoc.11. 37. **-βόλος**, ὁ, or **-βόλον**, τό, = foreg., *PSI*6.606.4 (iii B.C.). **-γλύφος** [γλῠ], ὁ, *Cheese-scooper*, name of a mouse in Batr.137.

**τῡρό-εις**, εσσα, εν, contr. **τῡροῦς**, οῦσσα, οῦν, Dor. **τῡρῶς**, ῶσσα, ῶν: (τυρός):—*cheesy, like cheese*, ἄρτον τυρῶντα Sophr.14: ὁ τ. (sc. ἄρτος or πλακοῦς) *cheese-bread, cheese-cake*, or simply *cheese*, Theoc. 1.58, Hegem.ap.Ath.15.698f. [τῡρόεντα is trisyll. in Theoc. l. c.] **-κλεψ**, ὁ, *cheese-thief*, Hdn.Gr.1.246. ® **-κνηστις**, ἡ, acc. ιν Ar.*V*.938, etc., gen. ιδος Id.*Lys*.231 sq.: (κνάω):—*cheese-scraper, cheese-grater*, Ar.*V*. l.c., 963, *Av*.1579, Pl.Com.8, *IG*11(2).154*A*69 (Delos, iii B.C.):—τῷ **τυροκνηστεῖ** (as if from -τεύς) Gal.19. 112. **-κομεῖον**, τό, *cheese-crate, cheese-rack*, Poll.1.251, 7. 175. **-κομέω**, *make cheese*, Id.1.251, Sch.Od.9.219. **-κόσκῐνον**, τό, *cheese-cake*, Chrysipp.Tyan.ap.Ath.14.647f. **-μαντις**, εως, ὁ and ἡ, *one who divines from cheese*, Artem.2.69. **-νωτος**, ον, *cheese-backed*, i.e. *spread with cheese*, πλακοῦντος κύκλος Ar.*Ach*. 1125 (cf. τυροφόρος)—parodied from Γοργόνωτος. **-ξόος**, ον, (ξέω) *scraping cheese*, Sch.D Il.11.639.

**τῡροποι-έω**, *make cheese*, Str.3.5.4, 4.5.2, Nic.Dam.104 J., Longus 3.33. **-ία**, ἡ, *cheese-making*, *Gp*.18.19, Eust.620.10. **-ικός**, ή, όν, *of* or *for cheese-making*, Apollon.*Lex*. s.v. τάλαροι. ® **-ός**, ὁ, *cheese-maker*, J.*BJ*5.4.1, Gal.4.632.

**τῡροπρᾱσία**, ἡ, *sale of cheeses*, *Stud.Pal*.20.96.4 (iv A.D.).

**τῡροπωλ-έω**, *sell like cheese*, ποιητῶν τ. τέχνην Ar.*Ra*.1369: lit., *sell cheese*, Men.*Pk*.100. ® **-ης**, ου, ὁ, *cheesemonger*, Ar.*Eq*.854, Critias 70, Lib.*Or*.29.30. **-ικῶς**, Adv. *like a cheesemonger*, Sch. Ar.*Ra*.1416.

® **τῡρός**, ὁ, *cheese*, ἐπὶ δ' αἴγειον κνῆ τυρόν Il.11.639; οὐκ ἐπιδευὴς τυροῦ Od.4.88; τ. ἐξ Ἀχαΐης Semon.23; τ. Σικελικός Ar.*V*.896, etc.; for Sicilian cheese, cf. Hermipp.63.9, Antiph.236, Philem.76: pl., *PCair.Zen*.110.25 (iii B.C.), al. 2. ὁ χλωρὸς τ. the fresh *cheese*, hence *the cheese-market*, Lys.23.6.—Cf. βούτυρον.

**τῡρο-τάρῑχος** [ᾰ], εος, τό, *a dish of cheese and salt fish*, in Lat. form *tyrotarichum*, Cic.*Att*.4.8.1, *Fam*.9.16.7. **-τόμος**, ον, (τέμνω) *cutting cheese*, Sch.Il.11.639, Eust.871.60. **-φάγος** [ᾰ], ὁ, *Cheese-eater*, name of a mouse in Batr.223. **-φορεῖον**, τό, *stand for cheese-racks*, Poll.1.251, 7.175, 10.130. **-φόρος**, ον, *with cheese on it*, πλακοῦς *AP*6.155 (Theodorid.).

**τῡρόω**, *make into cheese, curdle*, in Pass., Sopat.8, Dsc.2.83, Gal. 6.683, Sch.Theoc.5.86: metaph., ἐτύρωσάς με ἴσα τυρῷ Lxx *Jb*.10. 10; ἐτυρώθη ὡς γάλα ἡ καρδία αὐτῶν ib.*Ps*.118(119).70. 2. *make a mess of* (cf. τυρεύω II), τυροῦντες ἅπαντα Archestr.*Fr*.45.13; τυρωθέντα· ταραχθέντα, Hsch. II. *make* or *season with cheese*, πλακοῦντες τετυρωμένοι Artem.1.72.

**Τυρρην-ίζω**, *imitate the Tyrrhenians*, τῇ φωνῇ Polyaen.8.8. **-ικός**, ή, όν, *Tyrrhenian, Etruscan*, σανδάλια T. Cratin.131; κρατῆρες *IG*2$^2$. 1648.36, 11(2).161*B*122, 219*B*69 (Delos, iii B.C.): T. λόγος, a speech by Dinarchus: cf. Τυρσηνικός. **-ικουργής**, ές, *of Tyrrhenian* or *Etruscan work*, Poll.7.93. **-ίς**, ίδος, ἡ, = Τυρσηνίς (q.v.), [νῆες] Thphr.*HP*5.8.3. **-ολέτης**, ου, ὁ, *destroyer of Tyrrhenians*, *AP*9. 524.20. **-ός**, ή, όν, *Tyrrhenian*, *IG*2$^2$.1629.223, Plb.1.6.4, etc.; cf. Τυρσηνικός.

**τυρρίδιον**, τό, Dim. of τύρρις (v. τύρσις), *IG*14.352 ii 65,77 (Halaesa).

**Τυρσηνός**, ή, όν, Ion. for Att. Τυρρηνός; Dor. **Τυρσᾱνός** Pi.*P*.1.72, *SIG*14 (Delph., vi/v B.C.), also **Τυρρᾱνός** (v. infr.):—*Tyrrhenian, Etruscan*, *h.Hom*.7.8, Hes.*Th*.1016, E.*Med*.1359, etc.; τῷ Δὶ Τυράν' ἀπὸ Κύμας *SIG*35 (Olympia, v B.C.), cf. Τυρρανοί ib. 24 (Delph.):—the people were **Τυρσηνοί, Τυρρηνοί**, Hdt.1.57, etc.; T. Πελασγοί S.*Fr*.270 (anap.):—Adj. **Τυρσηνικός**, ή, όν, σάλπιγξ, κώδων, A.*Eu*. 567, S.*Aj*.17; cf. κηρός I. 3: also fem. **Τυρσηνίς**, ίδος, Σκύλλα E. *Med*.1342.

® **τύρσις**, ἡ, gen. ιος Hp.*Art*.43, X.*An*.7.8.12; ιδος *IG*12(7).115.4 (Amorgos, ii/i B.C.); acc. τύρσιν Pi.*O*.2.70, Hp. l.c., X.*An*.7.8. 13: nom. and acc. pl. τύρσεις, gen. εων, dat. εσι, ib.4.4.2, *HG*4.7. 6, *Cyr*.7.5.10; acc. pl. τύρσιας Lyc.834, Maiist.2:—also **τύρρις**, Hsch. (whence Lat. *turris* is borrowed):—*tower*, Pi. l.c., Hp. l.c. (cf. Gal.18(1).518); esp. *tower on a wall, bastion*, X. ll. cc.; opp. προμαχών, J.*BJ*5.4.3 sq.; also, *walled city* or *fortified house*, Nic.*Al*.2; = *villa rustica*, πύργος, *IG* l.c.

**τύρσος**, ὁ, = foreg., Hsch., Suid.

**τύρχη**, ἡ, = *furca*, *Gloss*.; τ. διδδους ξυλίνη *Edict.Diocl*.15.47.

**τῡρ-ώδης**, ες, *like cheese*, σιτία Hp.*Aff*.47, cf. Mnesith.Cyz.ap. Orib.*inc*.15.13, Plu.2.131e, Sor.1.87, Gal.6.47 (Sup.), 684; *containing cheese* (cf. τυρόεις and Chrysipp.Tyan.ap.Ath.14.647c), ἄρτος *SIG* 1025.49 (Cos, iv/iii B.C.). **-ωσις**, εως, ἡ, *cheese-making*, Olymp. *in Mete*.311.23. **-ωτός**, ή, όν, *prepared with cheese*, *Gloss*.

**τύσσει**· ἱκετεύει, Hsch. **τυτάνη**, ἡ, v. τυκάνη. **τύτε**, Adv., said to be Aeol. for τότε, *An.Ox*.1.64. **τύτη**· τὸ αὐτόθι, Hsch.

**τυτθός**, όν, Il.22.480, also ή, όν Call.*Dian*.64, A.R.3.93, 4.832 (cf. Hdn.Gr.1.145):—Ep. for (σ)μικρός, which is rarer in Hom., *little, small, young*, in Hom. mostly of persons, τυτθὸν ἐοῦσαν Il. l.c.; τόν γ' ἔθρεψε δόμοις ἔνι τυτθὸν ἐόντα while yet *a little one*, 11.223, cf. Od. 1.435, al.; τυτθὸν ὄντ' ἐν σπαργάνοις A.*Ag*.1606; αἱ μάλα τυτθαί Call. l. c.: of animals, ἀπτῆνα, τυτθόν A.*Fr*.337; τ. θηρίον ἐντὶ μέλισσα Theoc.19.5, etc.: of things, A.R.4.832, Maiist.29, etc. II. τυτθόν as Adv., *a little, a bit*, esp. of Space, ἀνεχάζετο τυτθὸν ὀπίσσω Il.5.443; τ. ἀποπρὸ νεῶν 7.334, cf. Od.9.540; τ. ὑπεκπροθέων Il.21. 604, cf. 10.345; τ. ἀπ' ἀκροτάτης κορυφῆς Hes.*Th*.62: of measure or degree, κοτύλην τις τ. ἐπέσχεν, so as to give only a sip, Il.22.494; τ. ἔτι ζώων with but *little* life yet in him, 19.335, cf. 16.302; οὐδέ με τ. ἔτισεν 1.354: of the voice, *low, softly, gently*, τυτθὸν φθεγξαμένη 24.170. 2. *by a little, scarcely, hardly*, ἀπὸ τ. ἅμαρτεν 17.609; ἠλεύατο ἔγχος τ. 13.185, 17.306; τ. ὑπὲκ θανάτοιο φέρονται 15.628: also pl., τυτθὰ ἐκφυγεῖν A.*Pers*.564 (lyr.); τ. οἷον καὶ ὁκόσον ἂν λάθοι Hp.*Cord*. 2; παρὰ τ. ἰόν ibid. III. pl. τυτθά, in Hom. only τυτθὰ διατμήξας cut *small*, Od.12.174; κεάσαιμι split *small*, ib.388. (Rare in Prose, Hp. l.c.: Thessalian word acc. to Sch.T Il.13.466.)

**τυτώ**, οῦς, ἡ, *night-owl*, Hsch.

**Τῡφάων, Τυφαόνιος**, etc., v. Τυφῶν, Τυφώνιος.

**τῡφεδ-ᾱνός**, ή, όν, (τῦφος) *stupid*, Ar.*V*.1364 (στυφεδανός, in error, Suid.). **-ών**, όνος, ἡ, *nonsense, humbug*, Neophro (?) Trag. in *PLit.Lond*.77 *Fr*.2.16, Call.*Fr*.98b (where acc. -ῶνα for -όνα metri gr.), Oenom.ap.Eus.*PE*5.36. II. Τυφεδῶνος, ὄνομα κύριον, ἢ τῆς καύσεως, Suid., cf. Theognost.*Can*.39.

**τύφ-η** [ῡ], ἡ, a plant used for stuffing bolsters and beds, *reed mace, Typha angustata*, Thphr.*HP*1.5.3, 4.10.5, Str.5.2.9, Dsc.3.118: τύφι, Ps.-Dsc. l. c. II. a sort of *tiara*, Tz.*H*.8.307. **-ήρης**, ες, *made from τύφη*, λύχνος *AP*6.249 (Antip.).

® **τυφλ-άγκιστρον**, τό, *blunt hook*, Heliod.ap.Orib.45.6.6, 45.18.8, Paul.Aeg.6.5. **-ηγορέω**, dub. sens. in Zos.Alch.p.232 B. **-ην**, v. τυφλίνης II. **-ίας**, ου, ὁ, *a venomous snake*, Philum.*Ven*.29; = κωφίας, Hsch.; cf. sq. **-ίνης** or **τυφλῖνος** ὄφις, ὁ, a *blind* snake, perh. *Pseudopus pallasi*, τυφλῖναι ὄφεις Arist.*HA*567$^b$25; -ίνοις ὄφεσιν ib. 604$^b$25: called **τυφλώψ** in Nic.*Th*.492, Ael.*NA*8.13 (on the accent, v. Hdn.Gr.2.66); **τυφλίας** and **τυφλών** in Hsch. (unless these are errors for τυφλίνας, τυφλῶψ); τυφλητης, τυφλίς, and τυφαις = *caeciola, caecilia, ciccola*, *Gloss*. (fort. τυφλίνης, τυφλίας); τυφλείας = *caecula*, ib.:—cf. κωφίας. II. τυφλῖνος, ὁ, a Nile fish, Marc.Sid.25, Hsch.; also τυφλίνης (τυφλῆνις, τυφλενες codd.) Artem.4.56; τύφλην (nom.) Ath.7.312b: Dim. **τυφλινίδιον**, τό, Xenocr.ap.Orib.2.58.152 (-φλην- codd.).

**τυφλο-γενής**, ές, *born blind*, *Gloss*. **-πλαστέομαι**, Pass., *to be formed blind*, Phot., Suid.; cf. sq. **-πλαστέω, πλάστης**, v. τυφοπ-. **-ποιός**, όν, *blinding*, Sch.Theoc.10.19, Eust.1769. 51. **-πους**, ποδος, ὁ, ἡ, *with blind foot*, of Oedipus, E.*Ph*.1549 (lyr.).

**τυφλοπτεῖται**, = τυφλοπλαστεῖται, Suid. (s. v. l., fort. τυφοπλαστεῖται).

® **τυφλός**, ή, όν, *blind*, once in Hom., Il.6.139, cf. *h.Ap.*172, freq. in other writers; τυφλὸς ἐκ δεδορκότος S.*OT*454; τ. Ἄρης, Πλοῦτος, Id.*Fr.*838, Theoc.10.19; τ. ὄψις, ὀφθαλμοί, E.*Cyc.*697, Pl.*R.*518c, etc.: c. gen., τ. τινός *blind to*.., X.*Smp.*4.12, Plu.*Sol.*12; but τ. τῆς προνοίας *lacking* vision of the future, Id.2.975c; τὰ τ. τοῦ σώματος, i.e. one's *back*, X.*Cyr.*3.3.45; καὶ τυφλῷ γε δῆλον even a *blind* man can see that, Pl.*R.*550d; for Cratin.6, v. κωφός II. 2. 2. of the limbs of the blind, τ. πούς E.*Hec.*1050, *Ph.*834, etc. (cf. τυφλόπους); χείρ ib.1699; [βάκτρον], τοξεύματα, Id.*Ion* 744, *HF*199. 3. metaph. of the other senses and the mind, τ. ἦτορ Pi.*N.*7.23; τυφλὸς τά τ' ὦτα, τόν τε νοῦν, τά τ' ὄμματ' εἶ S.*OT*371; τὴν τέχνην ἔφυ τ. ib.389. 4. metaph., τ. ὄλβος E.*Fr.*776; ἡ φύσις ἄνευ μαθήσεως τυφλόν Plu.2.2b; τῇ τύχῃ.., ἣν τυφλὴν λοιδοροῦμεν ib.98a; τ. ἔδραμε πᾶσα τρόπις *AP*9.289 (Bass.). II. of things, *dark, dim, obscure*, ἐλπίδες A.*Pr.*252; ἄτη S.*Tr.*1104; τὸ δ' ἐς αὔριον αἰεὶ τ. ἕρπει Id.*Fr.*593.6 (lyr.); τ. σπιλάδες *blind* rocks, *AP*7.275 (Gaet.); αἱ ἄνευ ἐπιστήμης δόξαι τυφλαί Pl.*R.*506c; δεσμῶν τ. ἀρχαί *hidden*, Plu.*Alex.*18; τ. ὑπόνοια Id.2.587c; τ. κίνημα, of revolution, Id.*Galb.*18. 2. of passages or apertures, *blind, closed, with no outlet*, τοῦ ἐντέρου τυφλόν τι, of the *intestinum caecum* (τὸ τυφλόν in Gal.*UP*4.18, al.), Arist.*PA* 675ᵇ7, cf. 676ᵃ5; τ. ἔντερον Ruf.ap.Orib.7.26.25; τ. τρῆμα the *foramen caecum* (stylo-mastoid), Ruf.*Onom.*144, Gal.*UP*9.10; τ. στενωποί Str.1.1.17; τ. ὁδοί Anon.ap.Suid.; τ. ῥύμη a *blind* alley, *POxy.* 99.9 (i A.D.); of rivers and harbours, *choked with mud*, Plu.*Sull.* 20 (v. sq.), cf. *Caes.*58; of the halcyon's nest, *closed, tight*, Id.2. 983d; τυφλοὶ ὄζοι branches *without buds* or *eyes*, Thphr.*HP*1.8.4, cf. *CP*3.2.8; τ. κῦμα *dark, trackless*, *AP*7.400 (Serapio), 12.156; τ. μώλωψ a wound *without an outlet*, Plu.*Aem.*19; τὸ τ. ἅμμα καλούμενον the so-called *unescapable* knot, Gal.2.669; of a hook (cf. τυφλάγκιστρον), *blunt*, Orib.45.18.9. III. Adv., πρὸς τὸ ὠφέλιμον τυφλῶς ἔχειν to be *blind* to it, Pl.*Grg.*479b; καὶ ἀσκέπτως Antip.*Stoic.* 3.256; τ. καὶ οὐ γνωρίμως διασαφεῖ Str.9.5.21. [ῡ by nature, S.*OT* 389, E.*Hec.*1050, etc., freq. ῠ by position: prob. not connected with τύφω [ῡ]: perh. cf. Goth. *daufs*, OE. *déaf* 'stupid', OIr. *dub* 'black'.]

**τυφλό-στομος**, ον, *with blind mouth*, of rivers, Str.4.1.8; cf. τυφλός II. 2. **-της**, ητος, ἡ, *blindness*, νοῦ Democr.175, cf. Pl.*R.*353c, Gal.15.142, etc. II. *closedness* of the *foramen caecum* (cf. τυφλός II. 2), Id.*UP*9.10. 2. metaph. of syllables ending in a consonant, *closedness*, Plu.2.738c. **-φόρος**, ον, *carrying a blind person*:—in Theoc.*Syrinx* (*AP*15.21) said by Sch. to be = *πηροφόρος, *carrying a scrip* or *wallet*; jestingly, as if, because πηρός means *blind*, therefore τυφλή is = πηρά (πήρα). **-ω**, *blind, make blind*, τινα Hdt. 4.2; ὄμματα, ὄψιν, E.*Cyc.*470, *Ph.*764:—Pass., *to be blinded, to be* or *become blind*, Hdt.2.111; τυφλοῦμαι φέγγος ὀμμάτων E.*Hec.*1035; ἕλκος τυφλωθέν a *blinding* wound (Pass. of τυφλόω ἕλκος *inflict a blinding* wound), S.*Ant.*973 (lyr.). 2. metaph., *blind, baffle*, Democr. 72, v.l. in Critias 25.26; τετύφλωται μόχθος Pi.*I.*5(4).56; τῶν μελλόντων τετύφλωνται φραδαί Id.*O.*12.9, cf. Pl.*Ti.*47b; τὴν ψυχὴν τυφλωθῆναι Id.*Phd.*99e, cf. 96c; τ. περὶ τὸν φιλούμενον ὁ φιλῶν Id.*Lg.* 731e. II. *make blind* or *without passage, stop up*, τὰς διόδους ἁμάξαις Aen.Tact.2.5; τ. ὀφθαλμούς [ἀμπέλου] *Gp.*5.9.7; τ. τὸν μαστόν *make* it *cease to yield milk*, Ael.*NA*3.39:—Pass., βλάστησις τυφλουμένη Thphr.*CP*5.17.7; οὖρα τυφλοῦται Nic.*Al.*340; ἡ φωνὴ τυφλοῦται Plu. 2.721b; τυφλωθείσης τῆς τοῦ δέρματος τρώσεως Gal.1.388:—also in Med., τυφλώσατο νηδύς Nic.*Al.*285.

**τυφλ-ώδης**, ες, gloss on βλάνος, Hsch. **-ών**, v. τυφλίνης. **-ωσις**, εως, ἡ, (τυφλόω) *a making blind, blinding*, Isoc.12.122 (pl.), cf. Ph.1. 391; γερόντων Diog.Oen.70 (pl.). II. *blindness*, Hp.*Aph.*6.56, Sch.Ar.*Pl.*115. **-ώττω**, *to be blind*, ψυχὴ τ. Luc.*Nigr.*4, cf. Phld. *Po.Herc.*1676.4, Cic.*Att.*2.19.1, Gal.15.168, Chor. in *Rh.Mus.*49.504 (p.252 F.-R.); περὶ τὰ κάλλιστα Plb.2.61.12; ἀμφὶ [τὰς αἱρέσεις] Gal. *Libr.Ord.*1. 2. *to be dim, faded*, of paintings, Philostr.*Im.*1. 2. **-ώψ**, ῶπος, ὁ, ἡ, (ὤψ) *blind-eyed, blind*, v. τυφλίνης.

**τῡφο-γέρων**, οντος, ὁ, (τῦφος) *silly old man, dotard*, Ar.*Nu.*908 (anap.); τ. ἄνδρες Id.*Lys.*335 (lyr.):—perh. with a play on τυμβογέρων. **-μανία**, ἡ, *delirium* (defined as a combination of φρενῖτις and λήθαργος, Gal. 7.655), Hp.*Epid.*4.13, Gal.16.497: metaph., *mad delusion*, Plu.2. 830b. **-πλαστέω**, *invent a falsehood*, ὅσα αἱ κεναὶ δόξαι -οῦσι Ph. 1.521, cf. 654, eund.ap.Eus.*PE*8.14; -ῶν ἑαυτὸν *deceiving* himself, Ph. 2.568: with v.l. τυφλο- except ap.Eus.l.c. **-πλάστης**, ου, ὁ, *inventor of falsehood*, μυθογράφων ἢ μιμολόγων ἢ τυφοπλαστῶν τὰ μηδενὸς ἄξια σεμνοποιούντων Ph.2.345 (vv.ll. τυφλοπα-, τυφλοπλα-). **-ποιέω**, *construct an imaginary world*, Ptol.*Judic.*16 (τυποποιεῖν cj. Bullialdus, male).

® **τῦφος**, ὁ, name of four kinds of fever, one of which is accompanied by stupor, Hp.*Int.*39; τῦφοι = *frigidae febres*, *Gloss.*; cf. τυφώδης I. 2. *delusion* (defined as οἴησις τῶν οὐκ ὄντων ὡς ὄντων), S.E.*M.*8.5; in this sense Monimus the Cynic said τῦφος τὰ πάντα, S.E.l.c.; τὸ γὰρ ὑποληφθὲν τῦφον εἶναι πᾶν ἔφη (sc. Μόνιμος) Men. 249.7, cf. Metrod.*Fr.*31, Phld.*Piet.*21; opp. ἀλήθεια, Ph.2.299; τὰ μὲν τοῦ σώματος ποταμός, τὰ δὲ τῆς ψυχῆς ὄνειρος καὶ τ. M.Ant.2. 17, cf. 6.13; οἴημα καὶ τ. Plu.2.81f, cf. ib.c, Arr.*Epict.*1.8.6, Iamb. *Myst.*2.4, 3.31; τὸν τ. ὥσπερ τινὰ καπνὸν φιλοσοφίας εἰς τοὺς σοφιστὰς ἀποσκεδάσας Plu.2.580b; πολὺν αὐτοῖς (sc. τοῖς μυστηρίοις) ἐπῆγον τ. ὡς μὴ ῥᾳδίως τινὰ συνορᾶν τὰ κατ' ἀλήθειαν γενόμενα Ph.Bybl.ap.Eus. *PE*1.9. 3. colloquially, *nonsense, humbug, affectation*, τὸν τρόπον μὲν οἶσθά μου ὅτι τῦφος οὐκ ἔνεστιν there is no *nonsense* about me, Antiph.195.2, cf. Plu.*Per.*5; ταῦτα τὴν παλαιὰν ἀλαζονείαν ἤλεγξε τῶν Μήδων τῦφον ὄντα κενόν Jul.*Or.*1.28b, cf. Pl.ap.D.L.6.26:—similarly in Cynic parodies, Πήρη τις πόλις ἐστὶ μέσῳ ἐνὶ οἴνοπι τύφῳ Crates Theb.4, cf. Timo 38, Jul.*Or.*6.202c; τὸν τ. μου τροποφόρησον my *piece of nonsense*, my *hobby*, Cic.*Att.*13.29.2; τὰ δὲ πολλὰ καὶ ὄλβια τ. ἐμάρψεν Crates Theb.8 (vv.ll. τύμβος, τάφος). 4. *vanity*, Zeno *Stoic.*1.69, Plb.3.22.4, 3.81.9; = *inflatio cordis vel superbia*, *Gloss.*; *arrogance*, Onos.42.24; ὁ φρυαττόμενος μεγάλα τ. Ph.1.667; *pomp*, σεμνότερον ἦγεν αὐτόν—ἄρχοντι δὲ λυσιτελέστατον ὁ τ. Id.2.518.

**τῡφόω**, (τῦφος) *delude*, rare in Act., ἐτύφωσ' ἐκ δ' ἔλετο φρένας Alc. 68 (cj. Porson), cf. Plu.2.59a; τ. τινὰ εἰς ἐλπίδα μειζόνων πραγμάτων Hdn.6.5.10:—but mostly in pf. Pass. τετύφωμαι (aor. Pass. τυφωθείς S.E.*P.*3.193), *to be crazy, demented*, ὦ τετυφωμένε σύ Pl.*Hp.Ma.*290a; ληρεῖν καὶ τετυφῶσθαι D.9.20; οὐ δὴ ποιήσω τοῦτο· οὐχ οὕτω τετύφωμαι Id.18.11, cf. 24.158, Plb.3.81.1, Cic.*Att.*12.25.2, *1Ep.Ti.*6.4, al.; ἴσως ἔγωγε τετύφωμαι ταῦτα λέγων καὶ τὰ μὴ δεινὰ ἀξιῶ δεδιέναι D.H.6.52; ὁ οἶνος τετυφωμένους ποιεῖ Arist.*Pr.*873ᵃ23, cf. Phld.*Mus.*p.54K.; γόητες καὶ σοφισταὶ καὶ τετυφωμένοι καὶ φαρμακεῖς Jul.*Or.*6.197d; ἀνόητος καὶ τετυφωμένος Luc.*Nigr.*1, cf. *Icar.*7, Arr.*Epict.*4.1.150: c. dat. modi, τετυφωμένος τοσαύταις εὐτυχίαις *demented, rendered vain*, Str.15.1.5; ἐπὶ πλούτοις τε καὶ ἀρχαῖς *filled with insane arrogance*, Luc.*Nec.*12: Harp. expl. τετύφωμαι by ἐμβεβρόντημαι. II. τυφῶσαι· πνῖξαι, ἀπολέσαι, Hsch.

**τύφω** [ῡ], Hdt.4.196, etc.: aor. inf. θῦψαι Hsch., Suid. s. v. ἀτυφία: pf. τέθῡφα dub. cj. in Crobyl.4 (τέθαιφε cod.A Ath.), Plb.5.42.3 (ὑπο-):—**Pass.**, Arist.*Mete.*362ᵃ7, Call.*Del.*141, etc.: fut. τῠφήσομαι (ἐκ-) Men.505: aor. ἐτύφην (ἐπ-) Ar.*Lys.*221: pf. τέθυμμαι (ἐπι-) Pl.*Phdr.* 230a:—*raise a smoke*, D.37.36: c. acc. cogn., τύφειν καπνόν Hdt. l.c.: abs., *smoke*, ἐπὶ σποδῷ μυδῶσα κηκὶς μηρίων ἐτήκετο κἄτυφε κἀνέπτυε S.*Ant.*1009. II. trans., *smoke*, τύφε πολλῷ τῷ καπνῷ (sc. τοὺς σφῆκας) Ar.*V.*457 (troch.), cf. 1079 (troch.):—Pass., [μέλισσαι] καπνῷ τυφόμεναι A.R.2.134; τυφόμεθα (v.l. -ούμεθα) ὑπὸ τοῦ καπνοῦ Jul.*Caes.*310d. 2. *consume in smoke, burn slowly*, τυφέτω, καιέτω τὸν Αἴτνας μηλονόμον E.*Cyc.*659 (lyr.); τ. τὸν χόρτον D.S.3. 29 (as v.l. for πυροῦσι): metaph., Crobyl. l.c.:—Pass., *smoke, smoulder*, τύφεται Ἴλιον E.*Tr.*145 (lyr.), cf. *Ba.*8; [χθὼν] καπνῷ κατερείπεται τυφομένα Id.*Hec.*478 (lyr.); τυφέσθω Κύκλωψ Id.*Cyc.* 655; λίνον τυφόμενον *smouldering* flax, *Ev.Matt.*12.20 (= λ. καπνιζόμενον Lxx *Is.*42.3): metaph., τυφόμενος πόλεμος *smouldering*, but not yet broken out, Plu.*Sull.*6; also of the fire of love, πόθοις τυφόμενον γλυκὺ πῦρ *AP*12.63 (Mel.), cf. 92 (Id.), 5.123 (Phld.), 130 (Id.), 11.41 (Id.).

**τῡφώδης**, ες, (τῦφος) of persons in fever, *delirious*, Hp.*Epid.*4.2, al.; also of the fever, ib.2.5.16, Gal.6.850, Erot. II. metaph., *deceitful*, μονογνώμονες, τυφώδεις, δόλιοι Vett.Val.12.4, cf. 2.3.

**Τῡφωεύς**, ὁ, gen. έος Il.2.783, dat. εῖ ib.782, acc. έα Hes.*Th.*821; **Τῡφώς**, Pi.*P.*1.16, A.*Pr.*372, gen. Τυφῶ Id.*Th.*517, *Supp.*560 (lyr.), Ar. *Nu.*336 (anap.), acc. Τυφῶ Hdt.3.5, Ar.*Eq.*511 (anap.); also nom. **Τῡφῶν** (q. v.):—*Typhoeus* or *Typhos*, a hundred-headed giant buried by Zeus (εἰν Ἀρίμοις), Il.2.782; youngest son of Gaia and Tartarus, Hes.*Th.*821; Pi. gives his birthplace as Cilicia, but places him under Cyme and Sicily, and so accounts for the eruptions of Etna, l.c. [ῡ in disyll. cases, ῠ in the others, cf. Τυφῶν.]

® **Τῡφῶν**, ῶνος, ὁ, Pi.*O.*4.8, *Fr.*93, etc.; Ep. **Τῡφάων**, ονος, *h.Ap.* 306, 352, Hes.*Th.*306; gen. Τυφάωνος Opp.*H.*5.217:—*Typhon*, represented by Hes. as son of Typhoëus and father of the Winds, cf. *Th.*307 with 869; son of Hera without a father, *h.Ap.* ll. cc.: in later Poets Typhōn and Typhōs were confounded, cf. Pi. ll. cc. with *P.*1. 16, 8.16, A.*Pr.*372 with 356, *Th.*493, Sch.Pl.*Phdr.*230a; taken in jest as the personification of τῦφος, Pl. l.c., Plu.2.1119b; in Egypt identified with Set, Hdt.2.144, al., *POxy.*1449.14 (iii A.D.). II. as Appellat., = τυφώς II, *typhoon*, Anaxag.ap.*Placit.*3.3.4, Arist.*Mete.* 371ᵃ9, al., *Mu.*395ᵃ24, Thphr.*Vent.*34. 2. a kind of *comet*, Lyd. *Ost.*15ᵇ, *An.Ox.*3.406. 3. Astron., the *Great Bear* or part of it, Teucer in Boll *Sphaera* 47, cf. Plu.2.359d. 4. in magical formulae, *donkey*, *PMag.Par.*1.3260, prob. in *PMag.Lond.*125.1; cf. Τυφώνιος I. 3. [ῡ in the disyll. form Τυφῶν, ῠ in the trisyll. Τυφάων, but long in gen. Τῡφάωνος; ᾱ in the forms Τυφᾱονα, -ονος, etc.]

**Τῡφων-ικός**, ή, όν, *Typhonian, of* or *from Typhon*, Plu.2.421c. II. (τυφῶν II. 1) *tempestuous*, ἄνεμος *Act.Ap.*27.14. **-ιος**, α, ον, *AB*308, etc.; Ep. **Τῡφάονιος**, A.R.2.1210, Nonn.*D.*1.223, al.; neut. Τῡφάονιον as place-name, Hes.*Sc.*32; **Τυφώνειος**, Dam.*Isid.*5, Id.ap.Suid. s. v. Σαραπίων; fem. **Τῡφᾱονίς**, ίδος, Nonn.*D.*2.287:—*of Typhon*, πέτρη A.R. l.c.; ἄρκτος Nonn.*D.*2.287. 2. Τυφώνιοι were *people burnt* at certain seasons in Egypt, Manetho ap.Plu.2.380d, cf. Herm.ap.Stob.1. 49.68. 3. Τυφώνιον, τό, in a magical formula, *donkey*, *PMag.Lond.* 121.653 (διὰ τὸ πυρρὸν γεγονέναι τὸν Τυφῶνα καὶ ὀνώδη τὴν χρόαν Plu.2. 362f). 4. Τυφωνία, ἡ, the plant στοιχάς, Ps.-Dsc.3.26. II. = foreg. II, πνεύματα Harp. s. v. τετύφωμαι, Herm. *in Phdr.*p.75 A., *EM* 755.13; τ. σκηπτοί Herm. l. c.; τὰ τ. πνεύματα μανίαν ἐμποιεῖ ἐμπεσόντα *AB* l.c.

**τῡφωνοειδῶς**, Adv. *like a whirlwind*, Str.5.4.9.

® **Τῡφώς**, ῶ, ὁ, = Τῡφωεύς (q. v.). II. as Appellat. τυφώς, gen. τυφῶ A.*Ag.*656; dat. τυφῷ Ar.*Lys.*974 (anap.) (but later writers used the form τυφῶν, ῶνος, v. Τυφῶν II. 1):—*whirlwind, typhoon*, ll. cc., S.*Ant.*418.

**τύφωσις** [ῠ], εως, ἡ, *crazy vanity*, Tz.*H.*10.571.

**τῠχ-άδιον**, τό, Dim. of τυχαῖον, Eust.1552.31 (written -άδιον). **-άζομαι**, = στοχάζομαι, Hsch.: aor. part. τυχασάμενον in Erot. is prob. a variant for στοχασάμενον in Hp.*Art.*4. ® **-αῖος**, α, ον, *accidental*, Plu.*Num.*10, *Placit.*1.4.1, Procl. *in Alc.*p.78 C. Adv. -ως *casually*, J.*AJ* 5.9.2, *AP*12.222 (Strat.), *Theol.Ar.*53. II. Τυχαῖον, τό, *temple of Fortuna* (Τύχη), D.C.43.21, al., *IGRom.*1.800 (Thrace), *OGI*585.5 (Cyprus); at Constantinople, Hsch.Mil.*Fr.*4.15: late spelling Τυχέῳ (dat.) *BGU*9 i 21 (iii A.D.). III. ἔμπορος τυχαίων dub. l. in *IG*14.419 (Messana). IV. Τυχαία, ἡ, = Τύχη, *CIG*4556 (Palestine). **-εια**, τά, a festival in honour of Τύχη at Lampsacus, ib.3644; τυχῖα = *genialia*, *Gloss.*: sg. τυχεῖον dub. cj. for στοιχεῖον in expl. of *genialis*, ib.

❀ **τύχη** [ῠ], ἡ, Boeot. **τιούχα** *IG*7.2809.1 (Hyettus, iii B.C.), **τούχα** ib.3083 (Lebad., iii B.C.): (τεύχω, τυγχάνω A. I. 2):—the *act* of a god, τύχᾳ δαίμονος Pi.*O.*8.67; ἄπαιδές ἐσμεν δαίμονός τινος τύχῃ E.*Med.*671; τύχᾳ θεῶν Pi.*P.*8.53; σὺν θεοῦ τύχᾳ, σὺν Χαρίτων τύχᾳ, Id.*N.*6.24, 4.7; θείῃ τύχῃ Hdt.1.126, 3.139, 4.8, 5.92.γ'; ἐὰν θεία τις συμβῇ τ. Pl.*R.*592a; θείᾳ τινὶ τύχῃ Id.*Ep.*327e; ἐκ θείας τύχης S.*Ph.*1326; δαιμονίως ἔκ τινος τ. Pl.*Ti.*25e; πῶς οὖν μάχωμαι θνητὸς ὢν θείᾳ τύχῃ; S.*Fr.*196; ἆρα θείᾳ κἀπόνῳ τάλας τύχῃ [ὄλωλε]; Id.*OC*1585; ἐμὲ.. δαιμονία τις τύχη κατέχει Pl.*Hp.Ma.*304c: ἄσημα δ' οὐκέτ' ἐστὶν οἷ φθίνει τύχα Κύπριδος E.*Hipp.*371 (lyr.); ἐξεπλήσσου τῇ τ. τῇ τῶν θεῶν Id.*IA*351 (troch.); δαίμονος τύχα βαρεῖα Id.*Rh.*728 (lyr.); τὰς.. δαιμόνων τ. ὅστις φέρει κάλλιστα Id.*Fr.*37. b. the *act* of a human being, πέμψον τιν' ὅστις σημανεῖ—ποίας τύχας; will order—what *action?* Id.*IT*1209 (troch.). 2. esp. ἀναγκαία τύχη, as a paraphrase for Ἀνάγκη, *Necessity, Fate*, τέθνηκ' Ὀρέστης ἐξ ἀναγκαίας τύχης S.*El.*48; τῆς ἀ. τ. οὐκ ἔστιν οὐδὲν μεῖζον ἀνθρώποις κακόν Id.*Aj.*485; πρόστητ' ἀ. τ. ib.803; εἴ τις ἀ. τ. γίγνοιτο Pl.*Lg.*806a: also pl., ἀλλ' ἥκομεν γὰρ εἰς ἀναγκαίας τύχας θυγατρὸς αἱματηρὸν ἐκπρᾶξαι φόνον E.*IA*511. II. regarded as an agent or cause beyond human control: 1. *fortune, providence, fate*, πάντα τύχη καὶ μοῖρα, Περίκλεες, ἀνδρὶ δίδωσι Archil.16; ἡμῖν ἐκ πάντων τοῦτ' ἀπένειμε τύχη Simon.100; πύργοις δ' ἀπειλεῖ δεῖν', ἃ μὴ κραίνοι τύχη A.*Th.*426; ἐπ' εὐμενεῖ τύχᾳ Pi.*O.*14.15; μετὰ τύχης εὐμενοῦς Pl.*Lg.*813a; κατελθὼν δεῦρο πρευμενεῖ τύχῃ A.*Ag.*1647; ὁρμώμενον βροτοῖσιν εὐπόμπῳ τύχῃ Id.*Eu.*93: personified, Σώτειρα Τύχα Pi.*O.*12.2; Τ. Σωτήρ A.*Ag.*664, cf. S.*OT*80; ἐμαυτὸν παῖδα τῆς Τ. νέμων τῆς εὖ διδούσης ib.1080; ⟨Τύχα⟩.. Προμαθείας θυγάτηρ Alcm.62, cf. Pi.*Fr.*41, D.Chr.63.7; πάντων τύραννος ἡ Τύχη 'στὶ τῶν θεῶν *Trag.Adesp.*506, cf. 505; Τύχα, μερόπων ἀρχά τε καὶ τέρμα.. προφερεστάτα θεῶν *Lyr.Adesp.*139. 2. *chance*, regarded as an impersonal cause, τύχη φορὰ ἐξ ἀδήλου εἰς ἄδηλον, καὶ ἡ ἐκ τοῦ αὐτομάτου αἰτία δαιμονίας πράξεως Pl.*Def.*411b; coupled with τὸ αὐτόματον, Arist.*Ph.*195$^b$31, al.; defined as αἰτία ἄδηλος ἀνθρωπίνῳ λογισμῷ *Stoic.*2.281; πειρῶ τύχης ἄνοιαν ἀνδρείως φέρειν Men.812; τὰ τῆς τύχης φέρειν δεῖ γνησίως τὸν εὐγενῆ Antiph.281, cf. Apollod.Com.17, Alex.252, Men.205; οὐκ ἔχουσιν αἱ τ. φρένας Alex.287; τῆς ἀναγκαίας μέν, ἀγνώμονος δὲ τ. οὐχ ὡς δίκαιον ἦν, ἀλλ' ὡς ἐβούλετο, κρινάσης τὸν ἀγῶνα D.*Ep.*2.5; personified and said to be blind, Men.417b, *Kon.*14, Plu.2.98a; τί δ' ἂν φοβοῖτ' ἄνθρωπος, ᾧ τὰ τῆς τ. κρατεῖ, πρόνοια δ' ἐστὶν οὐδενὸς σαφής; S.*OT*977; ἂν μὲν ἡ τ. συνεπιλαμβάνηται.., ἂν δ' ἀντιπίπτῃ τὰ τῆς τ., Plb.2.49.7, 8; ἡ Τ. σχεδὸν ἅπαντα τὰ τῆς οἰκουμένης πράγματα πρὸς ἓν ἔκλινε μέρος Id.1.4.1, cf. 1.63.9, 2.38.5, 36.17.1; τῆς Τ. ὥσπερ ἐπίτηδες ἀναβιβαζούσης ἐπὶ σκηνὴν τὴν τῶν Ῥοδίων ἄγνοιαν Id.29.19.2, cf. 23.10.16, Dem.Phal.39 J.; οὐκ ἂν ἐν τύχῃ γίγνεσθαι σφίσι would not depend on *chance*, Th.4.73; ὁ πόλεμος φιλεῖ ἐς τύχας περιίστασθαι Id.1.78, cf. 69; τύχῃ by *chance*, S.*Ant.*1182, *Ph.*546, Th.1.144, etc.; opp. φύσει, Pl.*Prt.*323d; ἀπὸ τύχης, opp. ἀπὸ παρασκευῆς, Lys.21.10; opp. ἀπὸ φύσεως, Arist.*Metaph.*1032$^a$29; ἀπὸ τ. ἀπροσδοκήτου Pl.*Lg.*920d; ἐκ τύχης Id.*Phdr.*265c, *R.*499b, etc.; διὰ τύχην Isoc.4.132, 9.45; δίκαιος οὐδεὶς ἀπὸ τύχης οὐδὲ διὰ τὴν τ. Arist.*Pol.*1323$^b$29; κατὰ τύχην Th.3.49, X.*HG*3.4.13; τῆς τ. εὖ μετεστεώσης Hdt.1.118; τὸ τῆς τ. ἀφανές E.*Alc.*785, cf. D.4.45. III. regarded as a result: 1. *good fortune, success*, δὸς ἄμμι τ. εὐδαιμονίην τε *h.Hom.*11.5; μοῦνον ἀνδρὶ γένοιτο τ. Thgn.130; τ. μόνον προσείη Ar.*Av.*1315 (lyr.); εἴ οἱ τ. ἐπίσποιτο Hdt.7.10.δ', cf. 1.32; σὲ γὰρ θεοὶ ἐπορῶσι· οὐ γὰρ ἄν.. ἐς τοσοῦτο τύχης ἀπίκευ ib.124; ἐπειδήπερ ἐν τούτῳ τύχης εἰσί Th.7.33; σὺν τύχᾳ Pi.*N.*5.48, cf. S.*Ph.*775; σὺν τ. τινὶ A.*Ch.*138, cf. *Th.*472; τύχᾳ Pi.*N.*10.25, E.*El.*594 (lyr.); οὐ πεποιθότες τύχῃ not believing in our *good fortune*, A.*Ag.*668; γλῶσσαν ἐν τύχᾳ νέμων ib.685 (lyr.); σοφῶν γὰρ ἀνδρῶν ταῦτα, μὴ 'κβάντας τύχης, καιρὸν λαβόντας, ἡδονὰς ἄλλας λαβεῖν without stepping out of *success already attained*, E.*IT*907; τὰς γὰρ παρούσας οὐχὶ σῴζοντες τ. ὤλοντ' ἐρῶντες μειζόνων ἀβουλίᾳ Id.*Fr.*1077: c. gen. rei, Ζεῦ τέλει', αἰδῶ δίδοι καὶ τύχαν τερπνῶν γλυκεῖαν Pi.*O.*13.115. 2. *ill fortune*, τὰς ἐκ θεῶν τύχας δοθείσας.. φέρειν S.*Ph.*1317; κατὰ τύχας in *misfortune*, opp. κατὰ.. εὐπραγίας, Pl.*Lg.*732c; τοιαύτῃσι περιέπιπτον τύχῃσι Hdt.6.16; τύχῃ by *ill-luck*, opp. ἀδικίᾳ, Antipho 6.1; opp. προνοίᾳ, Id.5.6; ἔστιν ἡ τ. τοῦ ἄρξαντος the *ill-luck* is his who began the fray, Id.4.4.8; of death, ἣν χρήσωνται τύχῃ, i.e. if they are killed, E.*Heracl.*714, cf. And.1.120, X.*Cyn.*5.29; δεχομένοις λέγεις θανεῖν σε, τὴν τ. δ' αἱρούμεθα A.*Ag.*1653; τ. ἑλεῖν Id.*Supp.*380, cf. *Pr.*106, 274, 290 (anap.); ὦ τῆς ἀώρου θύγατερ ἀθλία τύχης E.*Hec.*425: personified, εἰ μὴ τὴν Τ. αὐτὴν λέγεις *Misfortune* herself, ib.786. 3. in a neutral sense, mostly in pl. 'fortunes', ποίαις ὁμιλήσει τύχαις Pi.*N.*1.61; πρὸς τὸ παρὸν ἀεὶ βουλεύεσθαι καὶ ταῖς τ. ἐπακολουθεῖν Isoc.6.34; τὴν ἐλπίδ' οὐ χρὴ τῆς τ. κρίνειν πάρος the *event*, S.*Tr.*724; ἐν τῇσι παρεούσῃσι τύχῃσι Hdt.7.236; ἐγὼ δὲ τὴν παροῦσαν ἀντλήσω τ. A.*Pr.*377; φέρειν ἀνάγκη τὰς παρεστώσας τ. E.*Or.*1024: c. gen. rei, κοινὰς εἶναι τὰς τ. τοῖς ἅπασι καὶ τῶν κακῶν καὶ τῶν ἀγαθῶν Lys.24.22. 4. the quality of the fortune or fate may be indicated by an Adj., ἀγαθὴ τ. or ἡ ἀγαθὴ τ., A.*Ag.*755 (lyr.), Ar.*Pax* 360, D.*Ep.*4.3, etc.; πολλῇ χρῷτ' ἂν ἀγαθῇ τ. Pl.*Lg.*640d; freq. in prayers and good wishes, εὐχώμεσθα Δι.. θεσμοῖς τοῖσδε τ. ἀγαθὴν καὶ κῦδος ὀπάσσαι Sol.[31]; θεὸς τ. ἀγαθάν (sc. δότω) *GDI*1930, al. (Delph., ii B.C.): in nom., θεός, τύχα ἀγαθά *IG*4$^2$(1).47.1, 121.1 (Epid., iv B.C.), 73.1 (ibid., iii B.C.): freq. in dat., ἀγαθῇ τύχῃ *by God's help*, Lat. *quod di bene vortant*, ἀγαθᾷ τύχᾳ ib.103.119 (ibid., iv B.C.); ἀλλ' ἴωμεν ἀγαθῇ τ. Pl.*Lg.*625c; ταῦτα ποιεῖτ' ἀγ. τ. D.3.18; τύχῃ ἀγαθῇ And.1.120, Pl.*Smp.*177e, *Cri.*43d, etc.; in Com. with crasis, ἡγοῦ δὴ σὺ νῷν τὐχἀγαθῇ Ar.*Av.*675, cf. 436, *Ec.*131, Nicostr.Com.19; as a formula in treaties, decrees, etc., Λάχης εἶπε, τύχῃ ἀγαθῇ τῇ Ἀθηναίων ποιεῖσθαι τὴν ἐκεχειρίαν Decr.ap.Th.4.118, etc.; ἀγ. τ. τῇ Ἀθηναίων *IG*1$^2$.39.40; also ἐπ' ἀγαθῇ τ. Ar.*V.*869, cf. Pl.*Lg.*757e; μετ' ἀγαθῆς τ. ib.732d; τύχῃ ἀμείνονι, ἐπ' ἀμείνοσι τύχαις, ib.856e, 878a; also τύχᾳ σὺν ἐσλᾷ Sapph.*Supp.*9.4; ἐπὶ τύχῃσι χρηστῇσι Hdt.1.119: with κακός or equivalent words, τ. παλίγκοτος A.*Ag.*571; ἡ δέ τοι τ. κακὴ μὲν αὐτὴ γ' ἀλλὰ συγγνώμην ἔχει S.*Tr.*328; ἐν τοιᾷδε κείμενος κακῇ τ. Id.*Aj.*323; τίς τῆσδ' ἔτ' ἐχθίων τύχη; A.*Pers.*438; πρὶν αἰσχρᾷ περιπεσεῖν τύχῃ τινὶ E.*Hec.*498; ὅταν τις ἡμῶν δυστυχῆ λάβῃ τ. Id.*Tr.*471, cf. Th.5.102; ἀλιτηριώδης τ. Pl.*Lg.*881e; ποινὴν καὶ κακὴν τ. S.E.*M.*5.16. 5. with gen. (or possess. Adj.) of the person who enjoys or endures the fortune or fate, τῶν ἐν Θερμοπύλαις θανόντων εὐκλεὴς μὲν ἁ τύχα, καλὸς δ' ὁ πότμος Simon.4.2; θεῶν δ' ὄπιν ἄφθιτον αἰτέω, Ξέναρκες, ὑμετέραις τύχαις Pi.*P.*8.72; ὤμοι βαρείας ἆρα τῆς ἐμῆς τ. S.*Aj.*980; κατεδάκρυσε τὴν ἑαυτοῦ τ. X.*Cyr.*5.4.31; ἐπὶ τῇ τῶν Ἀρκάδων τ. ἥσθησαν Id.*HG*7.1.32; πρὸς τὰς τ. τῶν ἐναντίων ἐπαίρεσθαι Th.6.11; τῆς ὑμετέρας τ. D.1.1; τὴν ἰδίαν τ. τὴν ἐμὴν καὶ τὴν ἑνὸς ἡμῶν ἑκάστου Id.18.255. IV. the τ. or ἀγαθὴ τ. of a person or city is sts. thought of as permanently belonging to him or it, as a *faculty for good fortune, destiny*, almost = δαίμων I. 2, II. 3, τὸν δαίμονα καὶ τὴν τ. τὴν συμπαρακολουθοῦσαν τῷ ἀνθρώπῳ φυλάξασθαι Aeschin.3.157; ἐπισφαλές ἐστι πιστεύειν ἀνδρὸς ἑνὸς τύχῃ τηλικαῦτα πράγματα Plu.*Fab.*26; νὴ τὴν σὴν τ. Arr.*Epict.*2.20.29: personified, θύειν Τύχῃ Ἀγαθῇ πατρὸς καὶ μητρὸς Ποσειδωνίου κριόν *SIG*1044.34 (Halic., iv/iii B.C.); a statue of the Τύχη of the City of Antioch executed by Eutychides, Paus.6.2.7: so of rulers, ἀγαθῇ τύχῃ τῇ Πτολεμαίου τοῦ Σωτῆρος *OGI*16 (Halic., iii B.C.); διὰ τὴν τ. τοῦ θεοῦ καὶ κυρίου βασιλέως *BGU*1764.8 (i B.C.); νὴ τὴν Καίσαρος τ. Arr.*Epict.*4.1.14; ὀμνύω τὴν.. Σεβαστοῦ τ. *Sammelb.*7440.19 (ii A.D.), cf. *BGU*1583.23 (ii A.D.); of officials, e.g. the ἐπιστράτηγος, ἐάν σου τῇ εὐμενεστάτῃ τύχῃ δόξῃ *Sammelb.*7361.21 (iii A.D.). 2. = Lat. *Fortuna*; Τ. Σωτήριος, = *Fortuna Redux*, *Mon.Anc.Gr.*6.7; Τ. Πρωτογένεια, = *F. Primigenia*, *SIG*1133 (Delos, ii B.C.). 3. *position, station in life*, ἐγὼ μὲν δὴ τοιαύτῃ συμβεβίωκα τύχῃ.., σὺ δ' ὁ σεμνὸς.. σκόπει.. ποίᾳ τινὶ κέχρησαι τύχῃ.. τὸ μέλαν τρίβων κτλ. D.18.258; πάσῃ τ. καὶ ἡλικίᾳ *BCH*15.184, 198, 204 (Panamara); οἰκέτης τὴν τ. Ael.*NA*7.48; ἀμφίβολόν ἐστι πότερον ἡλικίας τοὔνομα ἢ τύχης Poll.3.76; οἱ δουλικὴν τ. εἰληχότες *POxy.*1186.5 (iv A.D.), cf. 1101.7, 11, 21, 24 (iv A.D.), etc.; *rank*, βουλευτικὴ τ. *PLond.*3.1015.1, 4 (vi A.D.), cf. *Cod.Just.*1.3.52.1, 4.20.15.1, 9.5.2. V. Astrol. uses: 1. = Σελήνη, Vett.Val.126.15; ἀγαθὴ τ. the κλῆρος of the moon, *Cat.Cod.Astr.*4.81. 2. ἀγαθὴ and κακὴ τ. names of two of the twelve regions, Vett.Val.69.13, 14. VI. Pythag. name for 7, *Theol.Ar.*44.

**τῠχ-ηρός**, ά, όν, *lucky, fortunate*, A.*Ag.*464 (lyr.), Arist.*Pol.*1295$^a$28. Adv. -ρῶς Ar.*Ach.*250, *Th.*305. 2. *from* or *by chance*, πάθη D.H.7.68; τὰ τ. ἀγαθά the goods *of fortune*, Plu.2.6a, Alex.Aphr. *in Top.*147.22; τὰ τ. Phld.*Vit.*p.27 J., Plu.2.35a, etc.; τὸ τ. Phld.*Sign.*36, Plu.2.23f. 3. τὰ μικρὰ καὶ τ. *ordinary* trifles (like τὰ τυχόντα), Zeno *Stoic.*1.70. **-ικός**, ή, όν, *casual, fortuitous*, αἰτία Diogenian.Epicur.4.34; ἐπίπτωσις Phld.*Rh.*1.211 S.; τ. περίπτωσις, a term of the Empiric physicians, *BKT*3 p.29 (i/ii A.D.); τ. εἶδος τῶν ὠφελούντων ἢ βλαπτόντων, opp. φυσικόν, Gal.*Sect.Intr.*2; σύμπτωμα Plb.9.6.5. Adv. -κῶς Id.28.7.1, D.S.2.19, Diogenian.Epicur.4.17. **-ιμαίως**, Adv. *by chance*, *Gloss.*

**Τῠχίος**, ὁ, masc. pr. n. *Maker* (from τεύχω, for he made shields), Il.7.220.

**τῠχόν**, Adv., v. τυγχάνω A. I. 5.

**τῠχόντως**, Adv. part. aor. 2 of τυγχάνω, *by chance, at random*, Arist.*EN*1124$^b$6, *GA*770$^b$15. II. οὐ τ. *in no ordinary manner*, *PFay.*12.15 (ii B.C.).

**τύχος**, ὁ, v. τύκος.

**Τύχων** [ῠ], ωνος, ὁ, (τύχη) a name of Hermes, *Inscr.Magn.*203 (iii B.C.), Hsch., Theognost.*Can.*33; of Priapus, D.S.4.6 (v.l. Τυφῶνα); [Πρίαπος] ἔοικε.. Τύχωνι Str.13.1.12; defined as δαίμων περὶ τὴν Ἀφροδίτην, Choerob. in *Theod.*1.274 H.; he is the giver of small gifts to mortals, *AP*9.334 (Pers.), cf. Apolloph.1 D. 2. name of the deified lance of Alexander of Pherae, Plu.*Pel.*29.

**τύψις**, εως, ἡ, *beating*, δάκρυα καὶ τ. προσώπων J.*AJ*19.1.17. 2. = τύμμα, Nic.*Th.*921, 933.

**τῷ**, dat. sg. neut. of ὁ, ἡ, τό, used abs., *therefore, in this wise, then*, Hom., v. ὁ, ἡ, τό, A. VIII. 2 a, b; ἀλλ' οὔτε περισπᾶται οὔτε σὺν τῷ ῑ γράφεται (i.e. τώ) A.D.*Adv.*199.2: written τώ in Alc.*Supp.*26.11. II. τῷ; for τίνι; dat. sg. of τίς; *who?* but 2. τῳ, enclit. for τινί, dat. sg. of τις, *some one.*

**τωθ-άζω**, Ar.*V.*1368, Theoc.16.9, etc.: fut. τωθάσομαι Pl.*Hp.Ma.*290a (τωθάσω Ar.*V.*1362 is aor. subj.; τωθάσουσι as fut. is v.l. in Gal.6.234): aor. ἐτώθασα Ar. l. c., Arist.*Rh.*1381$^a$34, Jul.

*Or.*5.159a, (ἐπ-) Hp.*Ep.*17: also **θωτάζω** (q.v.):—*mock, jeer at, flout,* τινα Hdt.2.60, Ar.*V.*1362, Pl. l.c., Herod.7.103; πολλὰ τ. τινά Theoc. l.c.:—Pass., *to be mocked,* Pl.*R.*474a, Lib.*Decl.*19.33. **2.** abs., *jeer,* Ar.*V.*1368, Arist. l.c. **-ασμα,** ατος, τό, *jeer, taunt,* in pl., Suid. s.v. Ἀδάμ. **-ασμός,** ὁ, *scoffing, jeering,* Arist. *Pol.*1336ᵇ17, D.H.3.71, Ph.2.83, Suid. **-αστής,** οῦ, ὁ, *scoffer,* Poll.6.29,123, 9.149, Hsch. s.v. κόβαλος. **-αστικός,** ή, όν, *mocking, scornful,* ὄρχησις D.H.7.72; of persons, Poll.5.161. Adv. -κῶς D.L.4.2, etc.

**τωκάλιον,** τό, name of an unknown article, τωκάλια δύο *PMasp.* 340ᵛ.38 (vi A.D.).

**τῶνδεων,** Aeol. for τῶνδε (cf. τοίσδεσι), Alc.126.

**τωνί,** or **τῶνι,** Arc. for τοῦδε, v. ὁνί. **τῶννυ,** = τῶνδε, v. ὄνυ(ν).

⊛ **τώς,** demonstr. Adv., answering to the interrog. πῶς, and to ὡς, = ὧς, οὕτως, *so, in this wise,* Il.3.415, Od.19.234, Hes.*Sc.*219,478, *Th.*892, Parm.8.21; also in A.(chiefly lyr.), *Th.*484, *Supp.*68,670,691 (once in trim., *Th.*637, v. infr. II); once in S. (*Aj.*841, a spurious passage); never in E. **II.** = ὡς, *as,* S.*Ichn.*296, Ar.*Ach.*762 (Doric), A.*Th.*637, *Epigr.Gr.*992 (Balbilla); in *PCair.Zen.*73.15 (iii B.C.) ου τως (corrected to οὐδ' οὕτως above the line) stands for οὐδ' ὥς.

# Υ

**Υ υ,** τό, indecl., twenty-third letter of the Formello abecedarium, *IG*14.2420, but twentieth of the Ion. alphabet: as numeral υ' = 400, but ,υ = 400,000. It is called τὸ ὖ by Pl.*Cra.*393d, Callias ap.Ath.10.453d (prob., the line ends ταῦ, ⟨τὸ⟩ ὖ), *IG*2².2783.4 (iv B.C.), Hellad.ap.Phot.*Bibl.*p.530 B.; τό τ' ὖ or τό θ' ὖ might be read in Achae.33.3 for τοῦ ῦ codd.Ath.; later τὸ υ ψιλόν or τὸ ψιλὸν υ (as name of the first letter of ὕαλος, υἱός, etc.), Theognost.*Can.*18, Sch. Ar.*Pl.*896, Ps.-Hdn.*Epim.*116,137, al.: so named to distinguish it from ἡ οι δίφθογγος, υ and οι being pronounced alike in late Gr.; ὖ is aspirated in *AP*9.385.20 (Steph.Gramm.), 11.67.1 (Myrin.) cod.Pal.; the Coptic name *he* (cf. Arm. *hiun*) may indicate that the early name was ὗ, which seems also to be implied by Serv. ad Verg.*A.*1.744: *alii dicunt Hyadas dictas vel ab Y littera, vel* ἀπὸ τοῦ ὑός, cf. Sch.Il.18.486: the sign Y represents *hy* on coins of P. Plautius Hypsaeus (58 B.C.), which are inscribed *Ypsae, BMus.Cat.Republ.Coins, Plate* 48 Nos.2,3,4,5, but *Hupsae,* Nos.13,14, *Plate* 123 Nos.7,8,9.

**ὖ ὖ,** exclamation of admiration (cf. Sch.), Ar.*Pl.*895; of alarm, S.*Ichn.*125; ὖ ὖ ὖ ib.170. (Written without breathing or accent in Pap. and in most codd. of Ar., cf. Suid.; ὗ Ar. cod. M.)

**ὑάγχη** [ῠ], ἡ, (ὗς, ἄγχω) *angina with external swellings like those in scrofula,* Cael.Aur.*CP*3.1: v. κυν-άγχη.

**ὑαγών** [ῠ], όνος, ἡ, assumed by Eust.842.52 as the orig. form of σιαγών, cf. Ath.3.94f.

**Ὑάδες,** ων, αἱ (sg. in collect. sense, Ptol.*Tetr.*94, *Gloss.*), *the Hyades,* a group of stars in the head of the Bull, Il.18.486; their morning setting (in November) was a rainy season, Hes.*Op.*615; hence commonly derived fr. ὕω, Lat. *Pluviae,* Verg.*A.*1.744, 3.516, Ov.*Fast.*5.166, v. Ὕης II; but in Lat. usu. called *suculae, piglings,* as if fr. ὗς, ὑός, Tiro ap.Gell.13.9.4; ῠ is short in Ep., though ῡ in E.*Ion*1156, *El.*468 (lyr.). **II.** five Nymphs named by Hes.*Fr.*180; later of the Nymphs who reared Dionysus, Pherecyd.90 J.; τὰς Βάκχας Ὑάδας ἔλεγον Hsch. s.v. ἔναστρος.

**ὕαιν-ᾰ** [ῠ], ἡ, prop. a fem. of ὗς: **I.** the striped *hyena,* a carnivorous animal with a bristly mane like a hog (whence the name), *Hyaena striata,* Hdt.4.192, Arist.*HA*579ᵇ15, Ael.*NA*7.22, Opp.*C.*3.263; also called γλάνος, Arist.*HA*594ᵃ31; cf. κροκόττας. **2.** a kind of antelope, Ael.*NA*15.15 (s.v.l.). **II.** a sea-fish, Numen.ap.Ath.7.326f, Ael.*NA*13.27; also **ὑαινίς,** ίδος, ἡ, Epich.65; v. ὗς II. **III.** in Porph.*Abst.*4.16 ὑαίνας is most prob. an error for λεαίνας, as the corresponding masc. is λέοντες. **-ειος,** α, ον, *of the hyena,* Cyran.76. **-ιος,** α, ον, = foreg., *hyaeniae* (sc. *gemmae*), Plin.*HN*37.168.

**ὑαινίς,** v. ὕαινα II.

**ὑαινοψώνιον,** τό, = ὠκιμοειδές, Ps.-Dsc.4.28 (corr. Wellm., ὑενόψωδον, ὑαινόψολον codd.).

**ὑακίζει·** οἱ εἰς τὰ αὐχένια βρέχει ἢ ὑετίζει ἢ ὕει, Hsch. (prob. two glosses, the first on ὑακίδδι, Boeot. for οἰακίζει, cf. ὕαξ).

**Ὑᾰκίνθια** [ῠ], τά (sc. ἱερά), a Laconian festival in honour of Hyacinthus, Hdt.9.7,11, Th.5.23, X.*HG*4.5.11, etc.; Cretan Ϝακίνθια *SIG*56.17 (Argos, v B.C.).

**ὑᾰκινθίζω** [ῠ], *to be like the* ὑάκινθος, Plin.*HN*37.77, v.l. for ὑακινθοειδῆ in Dsc.3.9.

**ὑᾰκινθῐνοβᾰφής,** ές, *dyed hyacinth-colour,* X.*Cyr.*6.4.2, Aristobul. ap.Arr.*An.*6.29.6; ὕφασμα Charito 6.4.

⊛ **ὑᾰκίνθῐνος** [ῠ], η, ον, *hyacinthine,* ἄνθος Od.6.231; ἄνθεα E.*IA*1298 (lyr.); ἐξαστις *Michel*832.14 (Samos, iv B.C.); φύλλα Theoc.11.26; *blue,* θώρακες *Apoc.*9.17; ἔνδυμα Ph.2.225, J.*BJ*5.5.7; *lana, Cod. Just.*4.40.1; λίθοι *PSI*3.183.5 (v A.D.).

⊛ **Ὑᾰκίνθιος,** ὁ, name of a month in several Dorian communities, *IG*12(1).155.68 (Rhodes), 12(3).325.20 (Thera), etc.; Cret. **Βακίνθιος** *Schwyzer*195.3 (iii/ii B.C.), and **Ϝακίνθιος** (v. Ὑακίνθια).

**ὑᾰκινθοειδής,** ές, *hyacinth-like,* ἄνθη Dsc.3.9.

**Ὑάκινθος** [ῠᾰ], ὁ, *Hyacinthus,* a Laconian youth, beloved by Apollo, who killed him by an unlucky cast of the discus, E.*Hel.*1469 (lyr.), Apollod.3.10.3, Paus.3.1.3: cf. Ὑακίνθια.

**B.** as Appellat., **I.** ⊛ **ὑάκινθος,** ὁ, Il.14.348, Paus.1.35.4; but ἡ in Sapph.94, Thphr.*HP*6.8.2, Theoc., etc. (v. infr.):—*wild hyacinth, bluebell, Scilla bifolia,* Il. l.c., *h.Cer.*7, Thphr.*HP*6.8.1, Dsc.4.62. **2.** *blue larkspur, Delphinium Ajacis,* ὑ. σπαρτή Thphr. *HP*6.8.2; said to have sprung up from the blood of Hyacinthus or (acc. to others) of Telamonian Ajax: and the ancients thought they could decipher on the petals the initial letters **ΑΙ,** or the interj. **ΑΙΑΙ,** cf. Mosch.3.6; hence the epithets γραπτά Theoc.10.28; αἰαστής Nic.*Fr.*74.31; πολύθρηνος Id.*Th.*902; πολύκλαυτος *IG* 14.607; cf. Ps.-Dsc.3.73. **3.** ὑ. πορφυρέη, prob. *Lilium Martagon,* Euph.40, *AP*5.146 (Mel.). **II.** ὑάκινθος, ἡ Hld., ὁ Ph. and J.:—a precious stone, of blue colour (J.*AJ*3.7.7), perh. *aquamarine, Apoc.*21.20, *Peripl.M.Rubr.*56, Luc.*Syr.D.*32, Hld.2.30, *Cod. Just.*11.12.1, etc.; cf. Plin.*HN*37.125. **III.** name of a *blue* colour, J.*AJ*3.6.1, *PHolm.*17.3; *blue stuff,* Lxx *Ex.*28.8, Ph.2.148, J.*BJ*5.5.4; χιτώνια τὴν χροιὰν ὑακίνθου Arr.*Tact.*34.6.

**Ὑακινθοτρόφια,** τά, a festival at Miletus, Haussoullier *Milet* p. 280; cf. Ἰακυνθοτρόφος.

**ὑᾰκινθώδης,** ες, *hyacinth-like,* Dsc.3.17.

**ὑακτορίζων,** οντος, ὁ, name of a variety of σμάραγδος, Dionysius in *Wien.Stud.*20.319.

⊛ **ὑᾰλᾶς,** ᾶ, ὁ, *glass-worker, IG*3.3436 (gen. οἱαλᾶ lapis). **II.** ὑάλας perh. = γυάλας, *PLond.*2.402 ii 13 (ii B.C.).

⊛ **ὑάλεος** [ᾰ], α, ον, (ὕαλος) = ὑάλινος, *of glass,* κύλιξ *AP*6.33 (Maec.); ὄψις *glass-coloured,* ib.12.249 (Strat.):—contr. **ὑᾰλοῦς,** ῆ, οῦν, *of glass,* ὑαλᾶ σκεύη Str.4.5.3; ἐκπώματα Luc.*Hist.Conscr.*25; λάγυνοι *POxy.*1294.6 (ii/iii A.D.); also **ὑελοῦς,** ῆ, οῦν, Hippoloch.ap.Ath.4.129d, Antyll.ap.Orib.7.16.13, Sor.*Fract.*2, *PFay.*104.1 (iii A.D.).

**ὑάλη** [ᾰ], ἡ, = ὕαλος, Hsch., Phot., Suid.

**ὑάλη,** ἡ, = σκώληξ, Hsch., who also cites **ὑάλεται·** σκωληκιᾷ: these are prob. dial. forms of εὐλή, εὐλάζει (which he also explains by σκωληκιᾷ). **ὑαλιεύς,** alternative form of ὑαλίης, Id.

**ὑᾰλίζω** or **ὑελίζω,** *to be green like glass,* Dsc.1.71,101, Ph.Byz. *Mir.*2.4, Aët.7.53, prob. in Herm.Trism. in *Rev.Phil.*32.264.

**ὑαλίης·** εἰκαῖος, βλοσυρός, Theognost.*Can.*18, Hsch.: cf. ὑανέοος.

**ὑαλικὸς κώμη·** Διονύσιος, Hsch.

**ὑᾰλ-ικός,** ή, όν, *of* or *for glass,* ψάμμος ὑ. sand *for making glass,* J.*BJ*2.10.2. **-ῐνος,** η, ον, *of crystal* or *glass,* Corinn.42; ἐκπώματα Ar.*Ach.*74; σφραγίς *IG*2².1451.13; σκεύη Phld.*Mort.*39; φιάλαι *SIG*1106.153 (Cos, iv/iii B.C.), cf. Hp.*Ep.*16, *PPetr.*3 p.113 (iii B.C.), Paus.2.27.3; ὑ. χρῶμα, = *ferrugineus, Gloss.*; *hyalinum* is expld. as *vitreum, viridi colore,* ib.: also **ὑέλινος,** η, ον, *AP*14.52, Ael.*VH* 13.3. [On the quantity, v. ὕαλος fin.]

**ὑάλιος,** = πολέμιος, Suid., as etym. of Ἐνυάλιος.

**ὑᾰλῖτις,** ιδος, ἡ, *vitreous,* ἄμμος and ψάμμος ὑαλῖτις Str.16.2.25; γῆ ibid.; [γῆ] **ὑελῖτις** Thphr.*Lap.*49.

**ὑαλκάδαι·** χορὸς παίδων, Λάκωνες, Hsch.

⊛ **ὑᾰλο-ειδής,** ές, *like glass, glassy, transparent,* ὑγρόν *vitreous humour,* Gal.*UP*14.6, cf. Id.19.358; ἥλιος Philol.ap.*Placit.*2.20.12 (also **ὑελ-** ib.2.25.11); ὁ ὑ. χιτὼν ὀφθαλμοῦ *the crystalline* lens of the eye, Medici ap.Poll.2.71. **2.** ὑ. λίθος a precious stone, perh. *topaz,* Thphr.*Lap.*30; ὑαλοειδέες..τόπαζοι Orph.*L.*280. [v. ὕαλος fin.] **-εις,** εσσα, εν, *glass-coloured* (cf. μελίχρως), παρειή *AP*5.47 (Rufin.).

⊛ **ὕᾰλος** or **ὕελος** (v. infr.), ἡ, v. Ael.Dion.*Fr.*217; but in Thphr. *Lap.*49, ὁ:—the form **ὕαλος** is said to be Att., **ὕελος** Hellenic, Phryn.281, Id.*PS* p.118 B., Moer.p.373 P., Thom.Mag.p.365 R.; in Hdt. codd. vary between ὕελος and ὕαλος; ὕελος is read in Arist.*APo.* 88ᵃ14, Thphr. l.c., *Ign.*73, *PHolm.*10.7, but ὕαλος in Lxx *Jb.* 28.17, Anon.Lond.39.18, *Apoc.*21.18; cf. ὑάλινος:—originally *some kind of crystalline stone,* such as that used by the Ethiopians to enclose their mummies in, Hdt.3.24; ὕ. ἀργή *Peripl.M.Rubr.*49; ὕ. ὀρωρυγμένη *rock-crystal,* Ach.Tat.2.3. **2.** *a convex lens of crystal,* used as a burning-glass, λίθος διαφανὴς ἀφ' ἧς τὸ πῦρ ἅπτουσι Ar.*Nu.* 768, cf. Thphr.*Ign.*73. **II.** *glass,* first in Pl.*Ti.*61b, cf. Arist.*Mete.* 389ᵃ8, and ὑαλῖτις; *glass-ware, PFay.*134.4 (iv A.D.). **III.** ὕαλος χνοώδης, in Paul.Aeg.6.22, is *an absorbent* of some kind:—ὕαλος is also expld. by βόρβορος in Hsch. and Theognost.*Can.*18. [ῠᾰλος, as appears from Ar.*Nu.*768:—but late Poets make ῡ in some derivs. to bring them into dactylic verses, ὑάλεος *AP*6.33, 12.249; ὑέλινος ib.14.52; ὑαλόεις ib.5.47; ὑαλοειδής Orph.*L.*280; in iambic metre, ὑαλόχροα *AP*6.211.]

**ὑᾰλουργ-εῖον,** or **ὑελ-,** τό, *glass-house,* Dsc.5.161, *Gloss.*; also **-ιον,** ib. **-ικός,** ή, όν, *of* or *for making glass,* κάμινος *Gp.*20.16 (ὑελ-): ἡ -κή (sc. τέχνη) David *Proll.*20.11. ⊛ **-ός,** ὁ, *glass-worker,* Str.16.2.25, *PTeb.*278.20 (i A.D.), *Gloss.*; **ὑελ-,** *PGot.*7.4 (iv A.D.).

**ὑᾰλοῦς,** v. ὑάλεος.

**ὑᾰλόχρους,** ουν, *glass-coloured, AP*6.211 (Leon., in acc. -χροα). [v. ὕαλος fin.]

⊛ **ὑᾰλ-οψός,** ὁ, (ἕψω) *glass-smelter,* Sch.Luc.*Lex.*7. **-ώδης,** ες, = ὑαλοειδής, of urine, Hp.*Coac.*146; χυμός Praxag.ap.Gal.6.509; of persons born on Sunday, prob. *green,* Anatolius in *Cat.Cod.Astr.* 8(3).188; **ὑελώδης,** Dsc.3.82 (as v.l.). **-ωμα,** ατος, τό, *glazing of the eye,* a disease of horses, *Hippiatr.*11. **-ῶπις,** ιδος, ἡ, *glassy, crystalline,* ἴασπις Orph.*L.*613.

**ὕαμα·** βάθος, Hsch.

**ὑάμινος**, η, ον, = ὕειος, ὑάμινόν τι θύειν *IG*12(5).647.8 (Ceos, iii B.C.). **ὑανέοος**· εἰκαῖος, βλοσυρός, χαλεπός, ὕπτιος, Hsch. (Cf. ὑαλής.) **ὑανεῶς**· τὰ αὐτά, Id. **ὑανία**, v. ὑηνία. **ὑαξ**· πηδάλιον, ὁδηγός, Id. (perh. Boeot. for οἴαξ). **ὑάς** ἡ τοῦ ὀφθαλμοῦ, = *felles oculi*, *Gloss.*; ὑ. ἡ τοῦ ὀμφαλοῦ, = *felles umbilici*, ib. (dub. sens.). II. v. Ὑάδες.

**ὑβάζω** [ῠ], (ὑβός) *stoop forward and vomit*, Suid.

**ὑβάλης**, ὁ, = λάγνος, Hsch.; so **ὑβαλλήν**, Theognost.*Can.*18.

**ὑββάλλω**, Ep. for ὑποβάλλω, Il.19.80.

**ὑβόομαι**, *become humpbacked*, Gal.18(1).76.

**ὑβός** [ῡ], ή, όν, *humpbacked*, Hp.*Aph.*6.46, Theoc.5.43.

**ὗβος**, ὁ, *hump* of a camel, Arist.*HA*499ᵃ14; of Cyprian oxen, Id. ap.Serv.Dan.ad Verg.*G.*1.138. (Parox. in codd.)

**ὑβρίγελως** [ῐ], ωτος, ὁ, *a scornful laugher*, Man.4.280.446.

⊛ **ὑβρίζω**, Od.18.381, etc., Dor. -ίσδω Theoc.14.9: fut. Att. -ιῶ D. 21.221, (ἐν-) prob. in Ar.*Th.*720 (-ίσεις cod. R): aor. ὕβρισα Hdt. 6.87, S.*Aj.*560, etc.: pf. ὕβρικα Ar.*Lys.*400, D.21.128: plpf. ὑβρίκειν Id.3.14:—Med., fut. ὑβριοῦμαι Ar.*Ec.*666 (anap.):—Pass., fut. ὑβρισθήσομαι D.21.222: aor. ὑβρίσθην S.*Aj.*367, Pl.*Lg.*885a: pf. ὕβρισμαι E.*Cyc.*665, etc.: (ὕβρις):—*wax wanton, run riot*, in the use of superior strength or power, or in sensual indulgence, ὑβρίζοντες ὑπερφιάλως δοκέουσι δαίνυσθαι κατὰ δῶμα Od.1.227; ὑβρίζοντες ἀτάσθαλα μηχανόωνται 3.207, 17.588; ἀλλὰ μάλ' ὑβρίζεις 18.381; ὁππότ' ἀνὴρ ἄδικος καὶ ἀτάσθαλος.. ὑβρίζῃ πλούτῳ κεκορημένος Thgn. 751; ἐνταῦθα νῦν ὕβριζε A.*Pr.*82, cf. S.*Ant.*480, etc.; esp. of lust, X.*Mem.*2.1.30; opp. σωφρονεῖν, Id.*Cyr.*8.1.30, Antipho 4.4.2. 2. of over-fed asses, *neigh* or *bray and prance about*, ὑβρίζοντες οἱ ὄνοι ἐτάρασσον τὴν ἵππον Hdt.4.129; of horses, X.*Cyr.*7.5.62; of elephants, Ael.*NA*10.10. 3. of plants, *run riot, grow rank and luxuriant*, Thphr.*HP*2.7.6, *CP*3.15.4. 4. metaph., of a river that swept away and drowned a horse, Hdt.1.189; so γῆ ὕβριστο *had been carried away* by river-floods, Emp.(?)154. II. trans., ὑ. τινά *treat* him *despitefully, outrage, insult, maltreat*, ἡμέας ὑβρίζοντες ἀτάσθαλα μηχανόωντο (v. infr. 2) Il.11.695; ὑ. τοὺς ὑβρίζοντας χρεών A.*Pr.*970; ὑ. γυναῖκα τὴν ἑαυτοῦ And.4.15; με, ἐμέ, S.*Ant.* 840 (lyr.), Lys.1.4; τὰς νήσους Isoc.8.99: more freq. (esp. in Prose) ὑ. εἴς τινα(ς) *commit an outrage* upon or towards him (them), E.*Ph.* 620 (troch.), *Hipp.*1073, Ar.*Pl.*899; ὑ. εἰς (dub. l.) τοὺς θεούς Id.*Nu.* 1506; εἰς σὲ καὶ τὴν σὴν γυναῖκα Lys.1.16; εἰς τὰς πατρίδας Isoc.4. 111; εἰς ταύτην τὴν παροιμίαν Pl.*Smp.*174b (acc. to Luc.*Sol.*10, ὑ. τινά was *to do one a personal injury*, ὑ. εἴς τινα *to injure that which belongs to one*; but the distinction was not observed): also ὑ. ἐν κακοῖσιν A.*Ag.*1612, cf. S.*Aj.*1151. 2. freq. c. acc. cogn., ὑ. ὕβριν A.*Supp.*880 (lyr.); ὕβρεις E.*Ba.*247; ὕβριν ἐς ἡμᾶς ὑ. Id.*IA* 961, cf. *Heracl.*18; ὑ. ὑβρίζεις ἐπὶ θανοῦσι τοῖς ἐμοῖς Id.*HF*708; ὕβρεις ἃς κατὰ τὴν ἀγορὰν ὕβριζεν D.22.68: with neut. Adj., ὑ. τάδε *commit* these *outrages*, Hdt.3.118; ὑ. τἄλλα Ar.*Lys.*400; ὅσα περὶ θεοὺς ὑ. τις Pl.*Lg.*885b, cf. 761e: and with other Nouns, τῶν ἀδικημάτων.., τῶν ἐς Ἀθηναίους ὕβρισαν Hdt.6.87 (so prob. θεοὶ τεισαίατο λώβην, ἣν οἵδ' ὑβρίζοντες ἀτάσθαλα μηχανόωνται (v. supr. II. 1) Od. 20.170): and c. dupl. acc., τοιαῦτα ὑ. τινά S.*El.*613; τίνος δέ σ' οὕνεχ' ὕβρισ' Αἴγισθος τάδε; E.*El.*266, cf. Pl.*Smp.*222a, X.*An.*6.4.2, *Cyr.*5.2.28:—Pass., ὕβριν ὑβρισθεὶς E.*Ba.*1297, cf. D.23.121; τάλαιν' ἐγὼ τῆς ὕβρεος ἧς ὑβρίζομαι Ar.*Pl.*1044; ὧν δ' εἰς τὸ σῶμα ὑβρίσθαι φημί D.21.25. 3. in legal sense, *commit a physical outrage on one* (cf. ὕβρις II. 2,3), Lys.14.26, 24.18, *Fr.*44, D.21.6 (Pass.), etc.; so later, ἐμὲ δέ, ἐὰν δύνῃ, καὶ ὕβριζε καὶ ἄπαγε *PCair.Zen.*454.9 (iii B.C.), cf. *PEnteux.*79.7, al. (iii B.C.); γυναῖκες καὶ παῖδες ὑβρίζοντας Th.8.74; ὑβρισθῆναι βίᾳ Pl.*Lg.*874c; τὰς γνάθους ὑβρισμένη *mauled* on the cheeks, Ar.*Th.*903; ὑβριζομένους ἀποθανεῖν to die *of ill-treatment*, X. *An.*3.1.13; ὑβρίσθαι *to be mutilated*, of eunuchs, Id.*Cyr.*5.4.35: of acts, τὰ ὑβρισμένα *outrages*, Lys.3.7. 4. pf. part. Pass., of things, *arrogant, ostentatious*, σημεῖ' ἔχων ὑβρισμένα E.*Ph.*1112; στολὴ οὐδέν τι ὑβρισμένη X.*Cyr.*2.4.5.

**ὑβριοπαθέω**, *show indignation at..*, Hermog.*Inv.*4.13.

**ὕβρις** [ῠ by nature, ῡ by position in Ep. etc.], ἡ, gen. εως Ar.*Lys.* 425, *Th.*465 (lyr.), εος Id.*Pl.*1044, Eub.67.9, Ep. and Ion. ιος Hes.*Op.* 217, Hdt.1.189:—*wanton violence*, arising from the pride of strength or from passion, *insolence*, freq. in Od., mostly of the suitors, μνηστήρων, τῶν ὑ. τε βίη τε σιδήρεον οὐρανὸν ἵκει 15.329, 17.565; μνηστῆρες ὑπέρβιον ὑ. ἔχοντες 1.368, 4.321; λίην γὰρ ἀτάσθαλον ὑ. ἔχουσι 16.86, cf. Alc.*Supp.*27.10; ὕβρει εἴξαντες Od.14.262, 17.431; θεοὶ.. ἀνθρώπων ὕβριν τε καὶ εὐνομίην ἐφορῶντες ib.487; δίκη ὑπὲρ ὕβριος ἴσχει Hes. l. c., cf. Archil.88, *IG*1².394 (vi B.C.), 4²(1).122.98 (Epid., iv B.C.); joined with ὀλιγωρίη, Hdt.1.106; δυσσεβίας μὲν ὕβρις τέκος A.*Eu.*533 (lyr.); ἐπιθυμίας.. ἀρξάσης ἐν ἡμῖν τῇ ἀρχῇ ὑ. ἐπωνομάσθη Pl.*Phdr.* 238a; in Poets freq. joined with κόρος (v. κόρος (A) 2): predicated of actions, ἆρ' οὐχ ὕβρις τάδ'; S.*OC*883; ταῦτ' οὐχ ὕβρις δῆτ' ἐστίν; Ar.*Nu.*1299, cf. *Ra.*21, *Pl.*886; ὕβρις τάδ' ἐστί, κρείσσω δαιμόνων εἶναι θέλειν E.*Hipp.*474; ὕβρει *in wantonness* or *insolence*, S.*El.*881, Pl.*Ap.*26e; ἐφ' ὕβρει E.*Or.*1581, D.21.38, *PCair.Zen.*462.9 (iii B.C.), etc.; δι' ὕβριν D.21.42; διὰ τὴν ὑ. X.*HG*2.2.10; πρὸς ὕβριν Plu. *Alc.*37, etc. 2. *lust, lewdness*, opp. σωφροσύνη, Thgn.379, X.*Cyr.* 8.4.14. 3. of animals, *violence*, Hdt.1.189; ὕβρις ὀρθία κνωδάλων Pi.*P.*10.36, cf. *N.*1.50 (v. ὑβρίζω I. 2); ἡ ἐκ τοῦ χαλινοῦ ὑ. D.Chr.63. 5. II. = ὕβρισμα, *an outrage* (though it is freq. difficult to separate this concrete sense from the abstract), Il.1.203, 214; ὕβριν τεῖσαι Od. 24.352; ὑπὸ γυναικὸς ἄρχεσθαι ὑ. ἐσχάτη Democr.111, cf. Xenoph.1. 17: sts., like ὑβρίζω, folld. by a Prep., Ἥρας μητέρ' εἰς ἐμὴν ὕβρις her *outrage* towards.., E.*Ba.*9; ἡ κατ' Ἀργείων (-ους codd. Priscian.) ὑ. S.*Fr.*368; ἡ πρὸς τοὺς δημότας ὑ. Hdn.2.4.1: c. gen. objecti, ὑ. τινός towards him, Id.1.8.4, etc.: pl., *wanton acts, outrages*, Hes.*Op.*146, E.*Ba.*247, *HF*741, Pl.*Lg.*884a, etc.:—for ὕβριν ὑβρίζειν, cf. ὑβρίζω II. 2. 2. *an outrage on the person*, esp. *violation, rape*, Pi.*P.*2.28, Lys. 1.2, etc.; παίδων ὕβρεις καὶ γυναικῶν αἰσχύνας Isoc.4.114, cf. Plb.6.8. 5; τὴν ὑ. τὴν εἰς τὸ ἑαυτοῦ σῶμα Aeschin.1.116; τὴν τοῦ σώματος ὕβριν πεπρακώς ib.188; so τὸ σῶμα ἐφ' ὕβρει πεπρακώς ib.29; γυναῖκας ἤγαγε δεῦρ' ἐφ' ὕβρει D.19.309; γυναικῶν ὕβρεις ἢ εἰς αὐτοὺς ἢ εἰς υἱεῖς Arist.*Rh.*1373ᵃ35. 3. in Law, a term covering all *the more serious injuries done to the person*, Isoc.20.2, Aeschin.1.15, D.37.33, 45.4; see esp. D.21 (against Meidias); ὁ τῆς ὕβρεως νόμος ib.35 (the text is given ib.47); δίκη ὕβρεως ἢ πληγῶν *PHal.*1.115 (iii B.C.), cf. *PHib.*1.32.8 (iii B.C.), etc. III. used of *a loss by sea*, Pi. (v. ναυσίστονος), *Act.Ap.*27.21.

B. as masc., = ὑβριστής, *a violent, overbearing man*, κακῶν ῥεκτῆρα καὶ ὕβριν ἀνέρα Hes.*Op.*191.

**ὑβρίς**, ίδος, ἡ, a night bird of prey, perh. *the great eagle owl, Strix bubo*, Arist.*HA*615ᵇ10.

**ὑβρίσδω**, Dor. for ὑβρίζω (q. v.).

**ὕβρ-ισμα**, ατος, τό, *wanton* or *insolent act, outrage*, Hdt.7.160, E.*Ba.*516 (both pl.), etc.; ὕβρισμα.. ἐς τούτους εἶχε ἐκ τῶν Σαμίων γενόμενον Hdt.3.48; τόδ' ὑ. ἐς ἡμᾶς ἠξίωσεν ὑβρίσαι E.*Heracl.*18, cf. X. *Ath.*3.5; τὰ τούτων ὑ. εἰς ἐμέ D.21.80. II. *object of insolence*, ὕβρισμα θέσθαι τινά, = ὑβρίζειν, E.*Or.*1038. III. abstract for concrete, τετρασκελὲς ὑ., = τετρ. ὑβρισταί, of the Centaurs, Id.*HF* 181. **-ισμός**, ὁ, = foreg. I, ὕβριζ' ὑβρισμοὺς οὐκ ἐναισίους A.*Fr.* 179. **-ιστέος**, α, ον, *that may be insulted*, D.54.44. **-ιστήρ**, ῆρος, ὁ, poet. for sq., Opp.*C.*1.416; χόλος Nonn.*D.*46.5; ὑβριστῆρες ἴαμβοι *AP*7.352:—ὑβριστῆρσι is a v.l. for ὑβριστῇσι in Il.13. 633. ⊛ **-ιστής**, οῦ, ὁ, *violent, wanton, licentious, insolent man*, ὑβριστῇσι.. τῶν μένος αἰὲν ἀτάσθαλον, οὐδὲ δύνανται φυλόπιδος κορέσασθαι Il.13.633; ὑβρισταί τε καὶ ἄγριοι οὐδὲ δίκαιοι ἠὲ φιλόξεινοι Od.6.120, 9.175, 13.201; of the suitors (cf. ὕβρις I. 1), ὑ. καὶ ἀτάσθαλοι 24.282; στρατὸν ὑβριστὴν Μήδων Thgn.775; Πέρσαι φύσιν ἐόντες ὑ. Hdt.1.89; ἀνδρῶν δυναστέων παῖδες ὑβρισταί Id.2.32; στρατὸν θηρῶν ὑ., of the Centaurs, S.*Tr.*1096: also in Prose, And.4.14, Lys.24. 15, *Ep.Rom.*1.30, etc.; in a milder sense, *sarcastic*, Pl.*Prt.*355c. 2. esp., opp. σώφρων, *lustful, lewd*, Ar.*Nu.*1068 (anap.), X.*Cyr.*3.1.21, etc.; ὁ εἰς ὁτιοῦν ὑ. Aeschin.1.17; ὑ. πενίης *insolent* towards.., *AP*9. 172b (Pall.). 3. of animals, *wanton, restive, unruly*, ταῦροι E.*Ba.* 743; ἵπποι X.*Cyr.*7.5.62, cf. Pl.*Phdr.*254c. 4. of natural forces, ὑβριστὴς Τυφάων Hes.*Th.*307; Ὑβριστὴν ποταμὸν οὐ ψευδώνυμον A.*Pr.* 717. 5. of things, ὑ. οἶνος διὰ νεότητα Ael.*Ep.*8; μέλι Ἀττικὸν ποιεῖ ὑ. [τὸν πλακοῦντα] makes it *proud*, Archestr.*Fr.*62.18; νάρθηκας ὑ., of the Bacchae, E.*Ba.*113 (lyr.).—Cf. ὕβριστος fin. **-ιστικός**, ή, όν, *given to wantonness, insolent, outrageous*, of persons, Pl.*Cra.*396b, etc.; of words, acts, etc., ἔπος Id.*Phdr.*252b; ὑ. καὶ βάρβαρος ἐπιστολή Aeschin.3.238; ὑ. διάθεσις Arist.*Rh.*1385ᵇ31; ὑ. ἀδικήματα *such as proceed from wanton insolence*, ib.1391ᵃ19; ὑβριστικὰ καὶ μανικὰ λέγοντες Pl.*Plt.*307b; παθῶν ὑ. καὶ δεινά D.45.1; ὃ καὶ -κώτατον συμβέβηκεν Id.17.23: τὸ -κόν *an insolent disposition*, X.*Mem.*3.10.5: τὰ Ὑ., name of a festival at Argos, Plu.2.245e. Adv. -κῶς Pl.*Chrm.*175d, X.*Cyr.*8.1.33 (v.l.), etc.; -κῶς διακεῖσθαι Lys.*Fr.*53.3: Comp. -ώτερον D.22.54. 2. metaph., of vines, *wanton, luxuriant*, Thphr.*CP*3.15.4. II. *of* or *relating to an outrage*, διήγησις D.H.*Dem.*11. **-ιστις**, ιδος, ἡ, fem. of ὑβριστής, *EM*595.38. II. = ὕβρις, ib.697.56, Suid. ⊛ **-ιστοδίκαι** [ῐ], οἱ, *abusers of law*, i.e. corrupt jurymen, name of a Comedy by Eupolis. **-ιστος**, η, ον, = ὑβριστικός, *wanton, insolent, outrageous*, ἔργον Pherecr.162; ὑ. χρῆμα (sc. ἡ γυνή) Pl.Com.98:—hence Comp. ὑβριστότερος Hdt.3.81 (v.l. ὑβριστικώτερος), X.*Cyr.*5.5.41, Pl.*Lg.* 641c: Sup. ὑβριστότατος Ar.*V.*1303, X.*An.*5.8.22, *Mem.*1.2.12, Pl. *Lg.*808d.—In *AB*368 (where Pherecr. and Pl.Com. are cited) we are told that ὕβριστος is of the same type as Superlatives like βέλτιστος, κάλλιστος, κράτιστος, etc.; in which case ὑβριστότερος, -ότατος would have to be regarded as doubled forms of comparison:—ὑβριστός oxyt. is cited in *EM*697.56. **-ίστρια**, ἡ, fem. of ὑβριστήρ, Lxx *Je.*27(50).31.

**ὕβ-ωμα**, ατος, τό, (ὑβόομαι) = ὗβος, *hump*, Hp.*Art.*43, al. **-ωσις**, εως, ἡ, *condition of being humpbacked*, Id.*Mochl.*36, al., Gal.18(1).77, Sch.Theoc.5.43.

**ὕγγεμος**· συλλαβή, Σαλαμίνιοι, Hsch. (Cypr.).

**ὑγεία**, ἡ, v. ὑγίεια.

**ὑγείδιον**, τό, name of various ointments, Gal.12.761.

**ὕγειος**, α, ον, = ὑγιής, *sound, unbroken*, *POxy.*1294.6 (ii/iii A.D.); written **ὕγιος** in *Gloss.*

**ὑγῐ-άζω** [ῠ], fut. -άσω Lxx *Ez.*47.9: pf. ὑγίακα ib.*Le.*13.37: (ὑγιής): —*make sound* or *healthy, heal, cure*, Arist.*Pol.*1287ᵃ37, *Top.*101ᵇ9, *PCair.Zen.*34.11 (iii B.C.), *PSI*6.665.6 (iii B.C.), Polystr.p.24 W., Phld.*Rh.*1.370 S., Ti.Locr.104d:—Pass., *become healthy, get well*, Hp. *Aph.*6.6, *deArte*4,5, Arist.*Rh.*1392ᵃ11, *Top.*117ᵃ19, *Ph.*229ᵇ4, *PCair. Zen.*34.12 (iii B.C.), Lxx *Le.*13.18, al.; ὑγιασθεὶς ἐκ τοῦ τραύματος Plb. 3.70.5: also intr. in Act., *become healthy*, Lxx *Ez.*47.8,9. ⊛ **-αίνω**, Thgn.255, etc.: fut. -ανῶ Hp.*Insomn.*93, Arist.*Metaph.*1032ᵇ18: aor. ὑγίανα D.54.1, Ion. ὑγίηνα Hp.*Nat.Puer.*20, *Epid.*2.2.4. [ῠ, but ῡ in augmented tenses, *Com.Adesp.*115]:—*to be sound, healthy*, or *in health*, Thgn. l. c., *Scol.*8, Hdt.1.153, Hp.*Nat.Mul.*12 (but ἐκφυγγάνει cod. C, Littré), Ar.*Av.*605 (anap.); opp. νοσεῖν, κάμνειν, Pl.*Grg.*495e, 505a;

ὑγιάνας καὶ σωθεὶς D.54.1; part. ὑγιαίνων, = ὑγιής, δυνάμενος, Lys.24.13; ὀφθαλμοὶ ὑγιαίνοντες X.*Oec.*10.6: of things, ὑγιαίνων καὶ τεταγμένος βίος *healthy*, Plu.2.5a, cf. 43b; ὄψα τῶν λιτῶν καὶ ὑ. ib.660f: generally, *to be in a certain state of health*, ὑ. νοσηρότερον and ὑγιεινότερον Hp.*Aph.*6.2. 2. *to be sound of mind*, Ar.*Nu.*1275, *Av.*1214, Pl.*Tht.*190c, Men.*Pk.*220, etc.; in full, τὰς φρένας ὑ. Hdt.3.33. 3. of *soundness* in political or religious matters, esp. in part., τὸ ὑγιαῖνον τῆς Ἑλλάδος Id.7.157; οἱ ὑγιαίνοντες, opp. turbulent agitators, Plb.28.17.12; ὑγιαίνουσα διδασκαλία 1 *Ep.Ti.*1.10; ὑγιαίνουσα ἀριστοκρατία Plu.*Dio* 12; δόξαι περὶ θεῶν ὑ. Id.2.20f, etc. 4. ὑγίαινε, like χαῖρε, a form of taking leave, *farewell*, Ar.*Ra.*165, *Ec.*477; found on tombstones, *CIG*3706 (Cyzicus), *IG*14.2526, al. (Lugdunum), *BMus. Inscr.*1123a (inc. loc.); but σὺ δ' ὑγίαινέ μοι salutation at meeting, Achae.44, cf. Alex.297; freq. in letters, Μνησίεργος ἐπέστειλε τοῖς οἴκοι χαίρειν καὶ ὑγιαίνειν *SIG*1259 (Athens, iv B.C.); σεαυτοῦ ἐπιμελοῦ ἵν' ὑγιαίνῃς *POxy.*745.10 (i B.C./i A.D.). II. Causal, = ὑγιάζω, Dicaearch.2.11:—Pass., f.l. in Hp. *de Arte* 4.5. -ανσις, εως, ἡ, *restoration to health*, opp. νόσανσις, Arist.*Ph.*225$^b$31, al., cf. *Metaph.*1068$^a$30, *EE*1219$^a$15 (with v.l. ὑγίασις), Gal.*Thras.*27, Herm. *in Phdr.*p.66A. -αντός, ἡ, όν, = ὑγιαστός, Arist.*Ph.*224$^a$30. -ασμα, ατος, τό, *cure*, in pl., gloss on ἀκέσματα, *AB*364. -αστήριον, τό, *hospital*, *BGU*1564.7 (ii A.D.), *Gloss.* -αστικός, ή, όν, *capable of restoring health, curative*, Arist.*Ph.*257$^a$17, *de An.*414$^a$10, Str.14.1.6, Dsc.4.78, Gal.1.229. -αστός, ή, όν, *capable of restoration to health, curable*, Arist.*Ph.*257$^a$17, *Cael.*310$^b$29. -άτης [ᾱ], ου, ὁ, *Health-giver*, a name of Dionysus, Ath.2.36b, Eust.1624.37.

* ὑγίειᾰ [ῠ], ἡ, and sts. in Com. ὑγιειᾶ, Ar.*Av.*604 (anap.), 731 (lyr., in compd. πλουθυγιείαν), Men.*Mon.*522 (also Isyll.60); Ion. acc. ὑγιείην Hdt.2.77, Heraclit.111; gen. ὑγιίης (⏑⏑⏑–) Herod.4.94, dub. in 4.20; and the metre requires a similar form in A.*Ag.*1001 (lyr.): from about ii B.C. written ὑγεῖα (pronounced ὑγῖα, contr. from ὑγῐᾰ), *IG*2$^2$.4457 (ii B.C.), 12(5).168 (Paros), 2$^2$.3181 (i A.D.), 3187 (ii A.D.); Ὑγία ib.4479 (i A.D.), 4536, *PTeb.*413.3 (ii/iii A.D.), etc.; Ion. ὑγείη Procl.*H.*1.22,42, *IG*14.1935 (as pr. n., Rome): (ὑγιής):—*health, soundness* of body, Simon.70, Pi.*P.*3.73, Hdt.2.77, Pl.*R.*332d, etc.; ὑ. καὶ νοῦς ἀγαθὰ τῷ βίῳ δύο Men.*Mon.*519, cf. Philem.163: pl. ὑγίειαι, *healthy states* or *conditions*, Pl.*Prt.*354b, *R.*618b, *Ti.*87d, Arist.*HA*601$^a$25. 2. of the mind, ὑ. φρενῶν *soundness* of mind, A.*Eu.*535 (lyr.); ἡ περὶ τὸ σῶμα καὶ τὴν ψυχὴν ὑγίεια Isoc.12.7. II. a kind of *cake* used at sacrifices, Herod.4.94, Ath.3.115a, Hsch., Phot., *AB*313. III. *a medicine*, Alex.Trall.5.4: generally, *a cure*, ὕπνος δὲ πάσης ἐστὶν ὑ. νόσου Men.*Mon.*522. IV. Pythag. name for *six*, Anatol.ap.*Theol.Ar.*37.

B. Ὑγίεια, ἡ, personified, *Hygeia, the goddess of health*, Hp.*Jusj.*, Ariphron 1,7, Paus.1.23.4, etc.: the last cup was drunk to her, μετανιπτρίδα τῆς Ὑγιείας πίνειν Antiph.149 (hex.), cf. Call.Com.6 (hex.): ἄγαλμα τῆς Ὑ. Ἀθηνᾶς Plu.*Per.*13.

ὑγι-εινός [ῠ], ή, όν, *good for the health, wholesome, sound, healthy*, Hp.*Aph.*3.15 (Comp.), 3.9 (Sup.); χωρία ὑ. *healthy* countries, X.*Cyr.*1.6.16, cf. Pl.*R.*401c; of food, *wholesome*, X.*Mem.*1.6.5, Pl.*Ion* 531e, etc.; σιτία -ότατα Isoc.1.45; τὰ ὑ. ὑγίειαν ἐμποιεῖ Pl.*R.*444c, etc.; ὕδωρ ὑ. Id.*Phlb.*61c. 2. *of* or *relating to health*, τέχνη, πραγματεία, etc., Gal.6.135, 1.301, etc.; τὸ ὑ. Arist.*Metaph.*1003$^a$35, 1060$^b$37. b. of a person, *devoted to the preservation of health*, a *hygienist*, τὴν τοιαύτην διάθεσιν ἰατροῦ καὶ οὐχ ὑγιεινοῦ λύειν (sc. ἐστί) Erasistr. ap.Gal.*Thras.*38, cf. Gal.6.77. 3. of persons, *healthy, sound*, μὴ πάνυ ὑ. φύσει Pl.*R.*408e, cf. a; ὑ. σῶμα Id.*Lg.*728e; βίος ib.733e, etc.: ὑγιεινόν *health*, opp. νοσερόν, Arist.*Rh.*1355$^b$30. II. Adv., -νῶς ἔχειν, = ὑγιαίνειν, Pl.*R.*407c, 571d; ὑ. φέρειν τι *without injury to health*, Hp.*Art.*41 (v.l. ὑγιηρῶς); ὑ. ποιεῖν τι *from regard to health*, Pl.*Grg.*522a; but ὑ. βαδίζειν, = ὡς ἂν ὁ ὑγιαίνων, Arist.*EN*1129$^a$16: Comp. -οτέρως and -ρον, X.*Lac.*2.5, *Mem.*3.13.2: Sup. -ότατα ib.4.7.9. -εις, εσσα, εν, = ὑγιής, ὑγίεντα ὄλβον Pi.*O.*5.23. -ηρός, ά, όν (-ής f.l. in Hp.*Aër.*9), *wholesome*, ἄκος Pi.*N.*3.18; ἔτος ὑ., opp. νοσερόν, Hp.*Aër.*10. II. of persons, *healthy, hearty, sound* (opp. νοσερός), κεφαλαί ib.4; ὑγιηρότατοι Hdt.4.187: Sup. ὑγιηρέστατος (which may be from ὑγιηρός, cf. σπουδαιέστατος, etc.) Id.2.77 codd., but in *AB*115.7 ὑγιηρότατος is cited from Hdt. Bk.2. Adv. -ρῶς, εἶχον Hp.*Epid.*1.5, cf. *Art.*41 (v.l.). * -ής, ές, gen. Att. -οῦς; dat. ὑγιεῖ; acc., Ion. ὑγιέα Hdt.1.8, etc. (ὑγιᾶ, v.l. ὑγιέα, Hp.*Art.*33); Att. ὑγιᾶ Th.3.34, Pl.*Chrm.*155e, al., X.*Mem.*4.3.13; also ὑγιῆ *IG*2$^2$.1673.42, 4$^2$(1).121.38,60,85, 122.109 (Epid., iv B.C.), Pl.*Phd.*89d, *Lg.*857e, cf. *IG* 14.1014 (ii A.D.), erroneously called un-Attic by Moer.p.375 P., Thom.Mag.p.365 R.: dual ὑγιῆ Pl.*Ti.*88c: neut. pl. ὑγιᾶ *IG*2$^2$.120.59, Thom.Mag. l.c., but ὑγιῆ in Pl.*Lg.*684c, 735b, and freq. in Att. inscrr., *IG*2$^2$.120.52, 1541.8, etc.; acc. pl. masc. ὑγιᾶς ib. 1$^2$.74.20; but ὑγιεῖς ib.4$^2$(1).121.36 (Epid., iv B.C.), 12(5).572.13 (Ceos, iii B.C.), and as fem., E.*Ba.*948; gen. ὑγιῶν Pl.*Lg.*735c:—Comp. ὑγιέστερος Epich.154 (with v.l. ὑγιώστερον), Sup. -έστατος Pl.*Grg.*526d; irreg. Comp. ὑγιώτερος in Sophr.34, prob. cj. in Epich. l.c.:—*healthy, sound* in body, ὑγιέα ποιέειν or ἀποδέξαι τινά restore him *to health*, make him *sound*, Hdt.3.130,134; ὑγιῆ σώματα ἀπεργάζεσθαι Pl.*Lg.*684c; τὸ ὑ. τοῦ σώματος, opp. τὸ νοσοῦν, Id.*Smp.*186b, cf. X.*Mem.*1.3.13; πόλις (opp. φλεγμαίνουσα) Pl.*R.*372e: prov., ὑγιέστερος κολοκύντας or ὄμφακος '*sound* as a bell', Epich. l.c., Phot.; ὑγιέστερος κροτῶνος or Κρότωνος Men.318, cf. Str.6.1.12. 2. of one's case or condition, σῶς καὶ ὑ. safe and *sound*, Hdt.4.76, Th.3.34. 3. of things, *safe and sound, in good case*, of the Hermae, Lys.6.12; of ships, Th.8.107; κόσμος X.*Mem.*4.3.13; τὸ ἔδαφος καὶ οἱ τοῖχοι Arist.*Mir.*842$^a$33; σῶν καὶ ὑγιὲς μένειν Pl.*Ti.*82b; *in good condition, unbroken*, πίθοι, κώθων, λίθος, *IG*1$^2$.326.7, 4$^2$(1).121.85 (Epid., iv B.C.), 7.3073.32 (Lebad., ii B.C.); πίθοι ὑ., opp. ἀγγεῖα τετρημένα καὶ σαθρά, Pl.*Grg.*493e, cf. *Cra.*440c, *Men.*77a (v. infr. III. 1); ἱμάτια *POxy.*530.20 (ii A.D.); μύλος ὑ. καὶ ἀσινής ib.278.18 (i A.D.). II. *sound in mind*, Simon.5.4, etc.; φρένες ὑγιεῖς E.*Ba.*948; *virtuous*, Pl.*Phd.*89d; ἦθος Id.*R.*409d, etc.; ὡς ὑγιεστάτη ψυχή Id.*Grg.*526d; as a complimentary epithet, ὑγιέστατον ἀνθύπατον *OGI*568.6 (Tlos, iii A.D.). 2. of words, opinions, and the like, *sound, wholesome, wise*, μῦθος ὅς..νῦν ὑγιής the word which is now *fitting*, Il.8.524 (the only place where any of this family of words occurs in Hom.); ὑ. δόξαι Pl.*R.*584e; εἴ τι ὑ. διανοοῦνται Th.4.22, cf. Pl.*Tht.*194b; χεῖρας καὶ γνώμην καθαροὶ καὶ ὑγιεῖς *IG*12(1).789.5 (Lindus, ii A.D.). 3. freq. with a neg., λόγος οὐκ ὑ. Hdt.1.8; οὐδὲν ὑ. βούλευμα Id.6.100; so in Trag. and Att., ὦ μηδὲν ὑ. μηδ' ἐλεύθερον φρονῶν S.*Ph.*1006; ἑλικτὰ κοὐδὲν ὑ. E.*Andr.*448; οὐδὲν ὑ. διανοουμένων Th.3.75; μηδὲν ὑ. λέγειν E.*Ph.*201, cf. Ar.*Th.*636, *Pl.*274, etc.; φέρειν, ἀσκεῖν, Id.*Ach.*956, *Pl.*50; οὐδὲν ὑ. οὐδ' ἀληθὲς ἔχειν Pl.*Phd.*69b: also of persons, τὰς οὐδὲν ὑγιές Ar.*Th.*394; πανοῦργον, ἄδικον, ὑγιὲς μηδὲ ἕν Id.*Pl.*37: c. gen., οὐδ' ἦν ἄρ' ὑ. οὐδὲν ἐμπύρου φλογὸς there is nothing *sound* or *good* in it, E.*Hel.*746; φεῦ· ὡς οὐδὲν ἀτεχνῶς ὑ. ἐστιν οὐδενός Ar.*Pl.*362, cf. 870, Pl.*Phd.*90c, *Grg.*524e, *R.*584a, D.18.23, etc.; οὐχ ὑ. οὐδὲν ἔτι λέγω τῶν ὀργίων E.*Ba.*262, cf. *Cyc.*259; ἐπ' οὐδενὶ ὑγιεῖ οὐδ' ἀληθεῖ Pl.*R.*603b, cf. Lys.9.4. 4. logically *sound*, τὸ ὑ. συνημμένον S.E.*M.*8.118; ὑ. ἀπόδειξις Id.*P.*1.116, cf. Arr.*Epict.*2.1.4. III. neut. as Adv., ὑγιὲς φθέγγεσθαι ring *sound and clear*, opp. σαθρόν, Pl.*Tht.*179d: also in phrase ἐξ ὑγιοῦς, φροντίζειν ὅπως καὶ τἆλλα γένηται..ἐξ ὑ. *correctly, in order*, *PTeb.*27.60 (ii B.C.); οὐκ ἐξ ὑ. τὰς κτήσεις ποιοῦσιν, i.e. dishonestly, Vett.Val.90.32. 2. regul. Adv. ὑγιῶς, *healthily*, διάγειν Ath.2.46f; *soundly*, κρίνειν, φιλοσοφεῖν, Pl.*R.*409a, 619d; ὑ. πεπολίτευμαι D.18.298; ὑ. ἀπαγγεῖλαι Plot.4.4.19; ὑ. καὶ πιστῶς *honourably* and faithfully, freq. in Pap., *POxy.*1031.18 (iii A.D.), etc. (Prob. from ὑ-, cf. Skt. *su-* 'well', and -γιη-, I.-E. *gʷiyē-*, cf. *gʷiyō-* in βιῶναι.)

ὑγῐο-ζῠγία [ῠγ], ἡ, *sound, healthy combination*, gloss on ἀρτιζυγία, Sch.A.*Pers.*541. -ποιέω, *make sound, heal*, D.S.32.11. -πους, ὁ, ἡ, πουν, τό, gen. ποδος, *sound of foot*, Hsch. s.v. ἀρτίπους. -της, ητος, ἡ, *soundness*: in Logic, S.E.*M.*8.118. * -ω, aor. inf. -ιῶσαι, f.l. for γυιῶσαι in Hp.*VM*9.

ὑγλιῆναι· φυσῆσαι, Hsch.

ὑγρ-ά, ἡ, v. ὑγρός I. 2. -άζω, *to be wet* or *moist*, Hp.*Aff.*7, Antig.*Mir.*88:—Pass., *become moist*, Hp.*Mul.*2.119. -αίνω, *wet, moisten*, X.*Cyn.*5.3, Pl.*R.*335d; of a river, *water* a country, E.*Tr.*226 (lyr.), *Hel.*3; βλέφαρον ὑ. δάκρυσιν ib.673 (lyr.); πηγαῖς οὐχ ὑγραίνουσιν πόδας Id.*Fr.*367:—Pass., of water, *collect in pools*, and of solids, *to be liquefied*, Arist.*Mete.*382$^b$28; opp. ξηραίνεσθαι, Id.*PA*653$^b$3, *HA*557$^b$11, etc.; τὸ ὑγρανθὲν [μέρος] the part which *is liquefied*, Pl.*Ti.*51b. 2. *relax* the bowels, Hp.*Aph.*3.17:—Pass., ib.2.20. -ανσις, εως, ἡ, *wetting, watering*, cited by Gal. (4.792) from Arist. (*PA* 650$^b$23, where ὑγρότης is in our text), Alex.Aphr.*Pr.*1.90; freq. in Gal., 10.469, 11.740, al. -αντέον, *one must moisten*, Id.1.284, al. -αντικός, ή, όν, *fit for wetting* or *moistening*, τῆς ἕξεως Diph. Siph.ap.Ath.2.59b, cf. Gal.15.735, Ptol.*Tetr.*18. * -ᾰσία, ἡ, *moisture*, ἐν τῷ σώματι Arist.*HA*557$^a$1, cf. *GA*727$^b$36, al., Thphr.*HP*3.13.2, Epicur.*Ep.*2 p.50 U.; διεξόδους.., δι' ὧν τὴν ὑ. ἐκδέχεται Alex.124.10. -ασμα, ατος, τό, = foreg., Hp.*Art.*38 (pl.), *Cord.*1. -έμπλαστρον, τό, *a moist plaster*, Plin.*HN*34.155. -ηδών, όνος, ἡ, = ὑγρότης I, Hp.*Mul.*1.17.

ὑγρίην· τὸ οὖρον, Διονύσιος, Hsch.

ὑγρο-βᾰτέω, *move in the water, move softly, flowingly*, cj. in *AP*9.709 (Phil.). -βᾰτικός, ή, όν, *going in the wet*, prob. to be supplied in Ath.3.99b. * -βᾰφής, ές, *dipped in the wet, wetted*, Nonn.*D.*8.142, 23.183. -βηξ, βηχος, ὁ, *moist cough*, Cass.Fel.33. -βῐος, ον, *living on* or *by the water*, as a fisherman, Nonn.*D.*13.75. -βόλος, ον, *moistening*, σταγόνες E.*Fr.*839.3 (anap.). -γελως, ων, *softly laughing*, Phryn.*PS*p.117 B. -γονος, ον, *produced in the wet* or *in water*, Nonn.*D.*14.145. -δρῦα, τά, *juices, liquid extracts*, τῶν βοτανῶν Zos.Alch.p.107 B. -θηρική (sc. τέχνη), ἡ, *water-hunting*, i.e. *fishing*, Poll.1.97. -κέλευθος, ον, *having wet paths*, Τηθύς, Νηρηΐδες, Orph.*H.*22.6, 24.2; Ἰχθύες Max.62. II. *leaving a moist trail*, κοχλίας Poet.ap.Ath.2.63b; so, perh., metaph., νεφέλαι Orph.*H.*21.3 (ὑδρο- codd.). -κέφᾰλος, ον, *suffering from water in the head*, Arist.*Pr.*861$^a$17, Sor.2.55: neut. -κέφαλον, τό (sc. πάθος), Alex.Trall.10. -κήλη, ἡ, f.l. for ὑδροκήλη, Poll.4.203. -κοίλιος, ον, *having moist* or *loose faeces*, Arist.*HA*632$^b$11 (-κοιλος is f.l. in Cyran.56; cf. ὑδρόκοιλος). -κολλούρια, τά, = κολλούρια (or κολλύρια) ὑγρά, Alex.Trall.2, Paul.Aeg.7.16. -λειχήν, ῆνος, ὁ, name of a moist skin-disease, Aët.15.44 (pl.). -λῐθος, ὁ, *liquefied ore*, Zos. Alch.p.110 B. -μᾰνής, ές, *madly fond of the water*, Nonn.*D.*43.284. -μέδων, οντος, ὁ, *lord of the water*, ib.31.57. -μέλεια, ἡ, *suppleness of limb*, Adam.2.12. -μελής, ές, *with supple limbs*, X.*Cyn.*5.13, Poll.4.96. -μέτωπος, ον, *with soft, smooth brow*, *AP*5.35.7 (Rufin.). -μοθος, ον, *fighting in the water*, Nonn.*D.*39.272, 41.393 (-μόρων is f.l. in 39.88). -μῠρον, τό, for ὑγρὸν μύρον, *liquid ointment*, Aët.16.119 (= 129 Z.); but *hydromyri* in Lat. version (114). -νομος, ον, *watery*, ὑγρονόμοιο πόρος Ἕλλης Nonn.*D.*3.37. -νοος, ον, contr. -νους, ουν, *of soft, weak mind*, Poll.6.126. -πᾰγής, ές, (πήγνυμι) *with frozen water*, Nonn.*D.*8.92. II. *of watery, flaccid consistency*, opp. σκληρόσαρκος, Xenocr.ap.Orib.2.58.134, Gal.

13.216. **–περίβολος**, ον, *surrounded by water*, *PMag.Leid.W.*21. 28. **–πισσον**, τό, for ὑγρὰ πίσσα, *liquid pitch*, Sch.Nic.*Al.*115; also **–πισσα**, ἡ, *Gp.*18.8.2, etc. **–ποιέω**, *make moist*, pf. part. Pass. ὑγροπεποιημέναι Leonid.ap.Aët.15.5. **–ποιός**, όν, *producing moisture*, φῶς Plu.2.367d; καρπός Porph.ap.Eus.*PE*3.11. **–πόρευτος**, ον, = ὑγροκέλευθος, Orph.*H.*82.1. **–πορέω**, *go through the water*, of ships, *APl.*4.221 (Theaet.). ❋ **–πορος**, ον, = ὑγροκέλευθος, Nonn.*D.*10.123, 23.182, 25.67, 42.118, Orph.*H.*51.2. **–πῡρῐνόψυχρος**, ον, *moist, fiery, and cold*, *PMag.Par.*1.1146. **–ρροέω**, *to be liquid* or *fluid*, Arist.*Pr.*863ᵃ17.

❋ **ὑγρός**, ά, όν: Comp. ὑγρότερος Pl.*Tht.*162b, etc.: Sup. –ότατος X.*Eq.*7.7, etc.:—*wet, moist, fluid* (opp. ξηρός), ὑγρὸν ἔλαιον, i.e. olive-oil, opp. fat or tallow, Il.23.281, Od.6.79; ὑ. πίσσα, νᾶπυ, *raw* pitch, *liquid* mustard, *SIG*1171.14 (Lebena, i B.C.), *IG*4²(1).126.22 (Epid., ii A.D.); τὸ ὑ. ξύλον, opp. τὸ ξηρόν, *Ev.Luc.*23.31; ὑγρὸν ὕδωρ Od.4.458; ἄνεμοι ὑγρὸν ἀέντες winds blowing *moist* or *rainy*, 5.478, 19.440, Hes.*Op.*625, *Th.*869; ὑ. ἅλς, πέλαγος, θάλασσα, Pi.*O.*7.69, *P.*4.40, A.*Supp.*259; ὑγρὰ νύξ a *wet* night, Pl.*Criti.*112a; ἐφ' ὑγροῖς ζωγραφεῖν paint on *a wet ground*, Plu.2.759c. 2. ὑγρά, Ion. ὑγρή, ἡ, the *moist*, i.e. the *sea*, ἐπὶ τραφερήν τε καὶ ὑγρήν Il.14.308; ἡμὲν ἐφ' ὑγρὴν ἠδ' ἐπ' ἀπείρονα γαῖαν 24.341, Od.1.97; ἐφ' ὑγρᾷ Ar.*V.*678; πουλὺν ἐφ' ὑγρήν Il.10.27; so ὑγρὰ κέλευθα the *watery* ways, i.e. the sea, 1.312, Od.3.71. 3. τὸ ὑ. and τὰ ὑ. *wet, moisture*, Hdt.1.142, Hp.*Loc.Hom.*9, *Liqu.* tit.; *liquid*, Hdt.4.172; γῆ ὑγρῷ φυραθεῖσα Pl.*Tht.*147c; ἐξερρύα συχνὸν ὑγρόν a quantity of *fluid*, *IG*4²(1).122.4 (Epid., iv B.C.); μετρεῖν τὰ ὑγρά *liquids*, ib.2².1013.10; ἐπὶ ὑγροῖς οὐκ ἐξὸν δανείζειν *PGnom.*232 (ii A.D.). 4. μέτρα ὑγρὰ καὶ ξηρά *liquid* and dry measure, Pl.*Lg.*746e. 5. θῆρες ὑ. *water*-animals, opp. πεζοί, *AP*9.18 (Germ.); οἱ ὄρνιθες οἱ ὑ. Philostr.*Im.*1.9; ὑ. ἀοιδός, of a frog, *AP*6.43 (Plato). 6. of the bowels or faeces, *loose*, Hp.*Aph.*2.20, Arist.*HA*617ᵃ1. 7. ὑ. σφυγμός a *damp* pulse, defined by Gal.19.405. II. *soft, pliant, supple*, of the eagle's back, Pi.*P.*1.9; of the limbs and body, ὑγραῖς ἐν ἀγκάλαις E.*Fr.*941, cf. Babr.34.7; ὑγρὸς τὸ εἶδος, of Ἔρως, Pl.*Smp.*196a; νεώτερος καὶ ὑγρότερος, opp. σκληρός, Id.*Tht.*162b; χορῷ.. ἔτερπον κέαρ ὑγροῖσι ποσσί B.16.108; ὑ. ὀρχηστής Poll.4.96, cf. Arist.*PA*655ᵃ24 (Comp.); ὑγρὰ ἔχειν τὰ σκέλη, of a horse, X.*Eq.*1.6; of a horse's neck, Id.*Cyn.*4.1 (so in Adv. of colts, γόνατα ὑγρῶς κάμπτειν, ὑγρῶς τοῖς σκέλεσι χρῆσθαι, Id.*Eq.*1.6, 10.15); of the hare, Id.*Cyn.*5.31; of the jackal, ταχυτῆτι διαφέρει διὰ τὸ ὑγρὸς εἶναι καὶ πηδᾶν πόρρω Arist.*HA*580ᵃ30; also of plants, ὑ. ἄκανθος Theoc.1.55; ὑ. χολάδες Babr.1.10; σῶμα ὑγρὸν κείμενον lying *in an easy position*, Hp.*Prog.*3; ὑγρὸν χύτλασον σεαυτόν Ar.*V.*1213; κέρας ὑ., of a bow, Theoc.25.206. 2. *languid, feeble*, of one dying, ἐς ὑγρὸν ἀγκῶνα.. παρθένῳ προσπτύσσεται S.*Ant.*1236; κἀπιθεὶς ὑγρὰν χέρα E.*Ph.*1439. 3. of substance, *flaccid, flabby*, σάρκες Arist.*HA*598ᵃ9, 603ᵇ32, al. b. *tender*, νεοττοί Ael.*NA*7.9; βρέφος Nonn.*D.*1.4. 4. *moist with wine, tipsy*, ὑγρὴν τὴν ψυχὴν ἔχειν Heraclit.117; ἡ διάνοια ὑ. γεγενημένη Plu.2.713a; οἰνοβαρὴς.. ὑγρὸν ἀείδων, οὐ μάλα νηφάλιον κλάζων μέλος Opp.*H.*2.412. 5. of the eyes, *melting, languishing*, ὑ. βλέμμα *Anacreont.*15.21; ὑγρὰ δερκομένοισιν ἐν ὄμμασιν *AP*7.27 (Antip. Sid.); ἐπ' ὄμμασιν ὑγρὰ δεδορκώς *APl.*4.306 (Leon.); τῶν ὀφθαλμῶν τὸ ὑ. ἅμα τῷ φαιδρῷ Luc.*Im.*6; also πόθος ὑ. a *languishing, longing* desire, *h.Pan.*33. Adv., ὑγρῶς βλέπειν Philostr.*Ep.*33: Sup., ὑγρότατα καὶ πένθιμα μελῳδεῖν App.*BC*1.106. 6. of language, *smoothly flowing*, D.H.*Dem.*20. 7. metaph. of persons or their tempers, *facile, pliant, easy*, ὑγρός τις καὶ δημοτικός Plu.*Mar.*28; κόλαξ ὑγρὸς ὢν μεταβάλλεσθαι Id.2.51c; τὸ Κίμωνος ὑ. his *easy temper*, Id.*Per.*5; *pleasure-loving*, Hsch.; ὑγρότατος ἐς ταῦτα *prone* to.., App.*BC*5.8; ὑ. τῷ γελοίῳ Plu.*Brut.*29 (Comp.). b. *soft, dainty, luxurious, voluptuous*, Id.2.751a; ὑ. πρὸς τὴν δίαιταν Id.*Sol.*3; βίου.., ὃν πάντες εἰώθασιν ὀνομάζειν ὑγρὸν Alex.203; cf. ὑγρότης II. 2. 8. of the vowels α ι υ, *sometimes long and sometimes short*, S.E.*M.*1.100. b. of στοιχεῖα, *liquid* (viz. λ μ ν ρ), D.T.632.9, Heph.1.3, al. III. Adv. ὑγρῶς, v. supr. II. 1 and 5; also ὑγρότερον δαπανᾶν spend *more freely*, Phld.*Oec.*p.73 J.

**ὑγρό-σαρκος**, ον, *of flabby flesh*, Arist.*HA*603ᵇ16, 538ᵇ9 (Comp.), Hp.*Ep.*21. **–σκελής**, ές, *with supple legs*, ἵππος Lib.*Ep.*672.1. **–σπερμος**, ον, *with liquid semen*, Gal.1.339. **–της**, ητος, ἡ, Dor. **–τᾱς**, ᾶτος, Ti.Locr.100d, 102c: (ὑγρός):—*wetness, moisture*, either in abstract or concrete sense, *fluidity* or *a fluid*, Hp.*VM*22, *Aph.*3.24, Pl.*Phlb.*32a, Arist.*PA*653ᵃ33; ὑ. τῆς χειρός *dampness* (from sweat), Plu.*Cat.Ma.*20: pl., Arist.*GA*760ᵇ4, *Mete.*352ᵇ13. II. *pliancy, suppleness*, ἡ ἐκ τῶν ἄρθρων ὑ. Hp.*Art.*8, cf. X.*An.*5.8.15; τοῦ σώματος, of serpents, Arist.*GA*718ᵃ30; of bears, Id.*HA*594ᵇ6; τῆς χειρός Plu.2.67e. b. of a flame, *flickering motion, lambency*, E.*Ph.*1256. 2. metaph. of persons, *ductility* of disposition, *the quality of being easily moved*, ὑ. τοῦ ἤθους Lycurg.33, Arist.*VV*1250ᵇ32; ἕξεως Plu.2.680d; but ὑ. βίου *a voluptuous course* of life, Crobyl.4; cf. ὑγρός II. 7. 3. *fluency*, prob. for γυρ– in Phld.*Po.Herc.*1677 *Fr.*21 (of Homer). **–τόκος**, ον, *producing moisture* or *water*, Nonn.*D.*22.102, 32.295. **–τράχηλος** [ᾰ], ον, *with pliant neck*, prob. to be supplied in Adam.2.21. **–τροφικός**, ή, όν, *of* or *for aquatic animals*, Pl.*Plt.*264d.

**ὑγροφᾰνής**, ές, *of moist appearance*, σφυγμός Archig.ap.Gal.8.662 (cf. ὑγρός I. 7).

**ὑγρ-όφθαλμος**, ον, *with moist eyes*, opp. σκληρόφθαλμος, Arist.*PA*648ᵃ18, 658ᵃ3.

**ὑγρό-φθογγος** λάγυνος, a narrow-necked bottle *that gurgles when one pours from it*, *AP*6.248 (Marc. Arg.). **–φλοιος**, ον, *with moist, soft rind*, *Gp.*9.16.2. **–φοιτος**, ον, = ὑγροκέλευθος, Lyc.88. **–φόρητος**, ον, *borne by* or *on water*, Nonn.*D.*15.373, 43.356. **–φόρος**, ον, = ὑδροφόρος, Max.283; ὑμήν *Theol.Ar.*48. **–φυής**, ές, *soft, supple*, παρθένος Sch.Theoc.1.47. Adv. –ῶς, λυγίζεσθαι Aristaenet.1.1. **–χίτων** [ῐ], ωνος, ὁ, ἡ, *in wet garment*, Nonn.*D.*23.112, 311. **–χρως**, οος, ὁ, ἡ, *with moist surface*, ὑγρόχροος.. νώτου Jo.Gaz.*Ecphr.*1.283. **–χῠτος**, ον, (χέω) *pouring* or *poured forth wet*, Nonn.*D.*8.275.

**ὑγρώσσω**, *moisten*, A.*Ag.*1329.

**ὑγυλόν**· ὑγιές, Hsch. (betw. ὕγγεμος and ὑγρόν, ὑγιᾶ).

**ὑδᾰλέος**, α, ον, (ὕδωρ) *watery*: hence, *dropsical*, Hp.*Prorrh.*2.2, Gal.7.213, 19.487.

**ὑδαλίς**· ὑδρωπιῶν, Hsch. **ὑδάν**· ἀγορασθεῖσαν, Id.

**ὑδᾰρής**, ές, (ὕδωρ) *watery*, ὑδαρὲς διαχωρεῖν Hp.*Prog.*11; ἰχῶρες Arist.*HA*586ᵇ33, etc. 2. mostly of wine, *mixed with too much water*, ὑδαρῆ 'νέχεέν σοι;—παντάπασι μὲν οὖν ὕδωρ Pherecr.70, cf. Hp.*Aër.*9 (Sup.), X.*Lac.*1.3, Alex.226, 230, Gal.6.272 (Comp.); κεράννυται οὔθ' ὑδαρὲς οὔτ' ἄκρατον Antiph.24; κυλίκιον ὑ. Lyc.*Fr.*2: metaph., τὸ χρύσιον κέρναν ὑδαρέστερον, i.e. mix *with a higher proportion of alloy*, *IG*12(2).1.14 (Mytil., iv B.C.). 3. metaph., *washy, feeble, languid*, ὑδαρεῖ σαίνειν φιλότητι A.*Ag.*798 (anap.); φιλία Arist.*Pol.*1262ᵇ15; μῦθος Id.*Po.*1462ᵇ7; ὑ. καὶ ψυχρὸς λόγος D.H.*Din.*11. II. of colour, *watery, pale grey*, ὄμμα προβάτων Arist.*GA*779ᵃ32. III. of taste, *insipid*, as plums, Thphr.*HP*1.12.1.

**ὑδᾰρός**, ά, όν, late form of ὑδαρής, Hsch. s.v. ὑδαρές, Phlp. *in de An.*404 (cod. A in app. cr., and as cited by Suid. s.v. ἄγευστος).

**ὑδᾰσιστεγής**, ές, *water-proof*, πῖλος *AP*6.90 (Phil.). [ῡ l.c., metri gr.]

**ὑδᾰτ-αίνομαι**, Med., *to be dropsical*, Hp.*Epid.*2.1.10. II. Act., of women, *to have watery menses*, ib.6.1.6, cf. Gal.19.148. **–εινός**, ή, όν, *watery, moist*, πνεύματα ὑδατεινότατα Hp.*Aër.*6; χώρη ὑδατεινή ib.15: perh. to be read for ὑδατῑνός (fem.) in Matro *Conv.*79, and for ὑδάτινος in Thphr.*Vent.*7, 57. **–ηγός**, όν, *drawing water*, ἀνήρ Call.*Hec.*1.4.12. **–ηρός**, ά, όν, *of* or *for water*, μήτε κρωσσοὺς μήτ' οἰνηροὺς μήθ' ὑ. *water-ewers* or *pails*, A.*Fr.*96 (anap.), as cited by Poll.6.23; but ὑδρηροὺς πίθους καὶ οἰνηροὺς as cited in *AB*115. **–ικός**, ή, όν, = sq., σημεῖον Thphr.*Sign.*11, 17; πρόσοδος revenue *derived from water-rights*, *PSI*2.160.7 (ii A.D.); πόρος Sch.Ar.*Pl.*521; ἡ ὑ. σφαῖρα the globe *of waters*, in reference to tidal phases, Nicom.ap.*Theol.Ar.*45. ❋ **–ῐνος**, η, ον, *watery, wet, moist*, νότοι Thphr.*Vent.*57 (nisi leg. ὑδατεινός); ὑ. νάρκισσος *that loves the water*, *IG*14.2508 (Nemausus); τὸ ὑ. σῶμα the body *which is water*, Plot.2.7.2: τὸ ὑ. *an eye-lotion*, Gal.17(2).185. II. *transparent like water*, of thin, *gauze-like* Milesian garments, καίρωμα Call.*Fr.*205; ὑ. βράκη Theoc.28.11; [στολή] *POxy.*265.3 (i A.D.). III. = ὑγρός II. 1, *pliant, supple*, βραχίονες *AP*9.567 (Antip.). [ὑδάτῐνος: but in dactylic (incl. Asclepiadean) verses ῐ; for ὑδατῑνός see ὑδατεινός.] **–ιον**, τό, Dim. of ὕδωρ, *a little water, rivulet*, of the Ilissus, Pl.*Phdr.*229a, cf. Pap. in *Hermes* 40.546: pl., Pl.*Phdr.*229b, Arist.*HA*606ᵇ21; *runnels*, *PRyl.*81.18 (ii A.D.). II. *small rain*, Thphr.*CP*2.9.9 (pl.). III. *a small drink of water*, Sor.1.105; *a small quantity of water*, Hero *Spir.*1.15, al. **–ίς**, ίδος, ἡ, in pl., = σταγόνες, Hsch., Phot.; as a urinary disease, Cael.Aur.*TP*5.4. II. *watery vesicle, hydatid*, Sor.1.58, Gal.18(2).679, *UP*10.7. III. *a disease in the liver*, Id.18(1).165: also *in the hoofs of horses*, *Hippiatr.*77. IV. *a gem*, Mart.Cap.1.75. **–ισμός**, ὁ, *succussion splash* in the lungs, Cael.Aur.*TP*5.10.

**ὑδᾰτο-δόχος**, ον, *holding water*, Suid. s.v. φακὸς ὕδατος. **–ειδής**, ές, *like water*, Arist.*Col.*793ᵇ30, Epicur.*Ep.*2 p.49 U. II. τὸ ὑ. the *aqueous humour*, of the eye, Gal.7.97. ❋ **–εις**, εσσα, εν, *watery*, *AP*9.327 (Hermocr.), D.P.782, Nonn.*D.*11.47, 23.281, 39.373, al. II. *transparent as water, thin, fine*, καλύπτρα *AP*6.270 (Nic.); cf. ὑδάτινος II. [ῠ in dactylic verses.] **–θρέμμων**, ον, gen. ονος, *nurtured and living in water*, ἰχθῦς Emp.21.11, 23.7 [with ῠ, in dact. verse]. **–κλυστος**, ον, *washed with water only* (without soap), Plu.2.134e. **–πλήξ**, πλῆγος, ὁ, ἡ, *beaten by the waters*, ἄκρα Opp.*C.*2.142, in poet. dat. –πλήγεσιν [ῠ]. **–ποσία**, ἡ, *drinking of water*, Hp.*Acut.(Sp.)*24, Luc.*Rh.Pr.*9. **–ποτέω**, *drink water*, Id.*Icar.*7. **–πότης**, ου, ὁ, *water-drinker*, Phryn.Com.69; cf. ὑδροπότης. **–πωτέω**, *drink water*, Cratin.288; cf. ὑδροπωτέω. **–ριζος**, ον, *rooted in water*, Parm.15ᵃ. [ῠ in dact. verse.] **–ρρῠτος**, ον, *flowing with water*, Eust.268.29.

**Ὑδατοσύδνη**, ἡ, name of a Nereïd, Call.*Fr.*347; formed like Ἁλοσύδνη. [ῠ in dact. verse.]

❋ **ὑδᾰτο-τρεφής**, ές, *bred in water, growing in* or *by the water*, αἴγειροι Od.17.208. **–χλοος**, ον, (χλόη) *water-green, pale*, v. ὑδατόχολος. **–χλωρος**, ον, *water-green*, Gal.19.148. **–χολος**, ον, *watery and bilious in colour*, of excrements, Hp.*Epid.*3.17.β', *Prorrh.*1.81, *Coac.*67; the reading ὑδατόχλοα is found in *Epid.*3.17.ιβ' (cf. Gal.17(1).751, 19.148), *Coac.*596: cf. sq. **–χροος**, ον, *pale as water*, Id.*Epid.*1.26.ι' (as v.l. for ὑδατόχολα).

**ὑδᾰτ-όω**, in Pass., *to be liquid, watery*, *AP*9.709 (Phil.); of wine, *to be watered*, Gal.15.699. II. Pass., *to be dropsical*, Hp.*Epid.*6.7.4, Ruf.*Ren.Ves.*4.1. ❋ **–ώδης**, ες, *watery*, οὖρον Hp.*Prog.*12, cf. *Epid.*1.26.ι', Sor.1.59, al.; opp. αἱματώδης, Arist.*HA*586ᵃ29; [ἄνεμος] ὑ. Id.*Mete.*364ᵇ21; [νέφος] –έστερον ib.377ᵇ6; of signs of the Zodiac, Vett.Val.6.4; ὑ. κρύσταλλος, of melting ice, *wet, sloppy*, Th.3.23; of taste, *watery, insipid*, Thphr.*HP*4.10.3. II. *full* *of water*, φύλλα Id.*CP*2.19.2; σφαιρίον Id.*HP*3.7.5. 2. *dropsical*, Hp.*Epid*.6.7.4. ⊛-**ώλενος**, ον, dub. sens., νύμφαι *IG*14.219 (Acrae).

**ὑδείω**, Ep. for ὑδέω.

**ὑδερ-αίνω**, *suffer from dropsy*, Hp.*Nat.Mul*.2. **-ίασις**, εως, ἡ, = ὕδερος I, *dropsy*, *Hippiatr*.38. **-ιάω**, *suffer from dropsy*, Hp. *Coac*.447, Anon.ap.Stob.4.31.84, Gal.6.338, Ael.*NA*3.18, 14.4.—A form **ὑδεράω** is cited by Phot., Suid., and occurs as v.l. in Aristid.*Or*.34(50).27, Poll.4.187. **-ικός**, ή, όν, *dropsical*, διάθεσις Gal.8.380. Adv. -κῶς Id.15.167:—as Subst., ὁ ὑ. *dropsical patient*, Ruf.ap.Orib.7.26.129, Orib.9.42.1. **-ιώδης**, ες, *suffering from dropsy*, Antyll.ap.Orib.6.27.2. **-όομαι**, Pass., *to become dropsical*, Hp.*Mul*.1.36,60. **-ος**, ὁ, (ὕδωρ) = ὕδρωψ, *dropsy*, Id.*Int*.22, Arist. *EN*1150$^b$33, etc.; ὑδέρῳ νοσήματι Id.*Fr*.486. II. ὑ. εἰς ἀμίδα *diabetes*, Gal.8.394; cf. **ὑδεροῦν** (= τὸν ὕδερον), which is cited from Hp. by Erot. (but = τὸ ὑδρηλὸν χωρίον acc. to Epicles ap.eund.), prob. with ref. to ὕδρωπες in *Aër*.4. ⊛ **-ώδης**, ες, *of a dropsical nature*, Dsc.5.148, Gal.15.319.

**ὑδέω** [ῠ], (ὕδης) *call, name*, Call.*Fr.anon*.62, Nic.*Al*.47,525; Ep. also **ὑδείω**, Call.*Jov*.76:—Pass., *to be told of, to be called* so and so, Arat.257, A.R.2.528, 4.264:—Suid. and *Et.Gud*.539.56 also quote the form ὕδειν (from ὕδω), and Theognost.*Can*.19 has ὕδειν· τρέχειν, λέγειν:—ὑδεῖν should perh. be restored for ἰδεῖν in E.*Hyps*.iii 15, where it would mean *tell of, celebrate*; [ὑ]δέοντος is suggested in *PLit.Lond*.60.9 (Posidipp.).

**ὕδη**, = φήμη, ᾠδή, Theognost.*Can*.19.

**ὕδης**, ου, ὁ, = ποιητής, συνετός, Hsch., Theognost.*Can*.19: cf. ὕδνης I. (ὑδέω, ὕδης, ὕδη may be cogn. with αὐδή, Skt. *vádati* 'speak'.)

**ὕδιον**, τό, Dim. of ὗς, X.*Mem*.1.2.30 (ὑίδια codd.), restored from Phot. and Cyr.ap.*An.Par*.4.176.

**ὑδνέω**, *nourish*, Hsch., *EM*776.11.

**ὕδνης**, = εἰδώς, ἔμπειρος (cf. ὕδης), Hsch. II. ὕδναι, = ἔγγονοι, σύντροφοι, Id. (perh. as root of Ἀλοσ-ύδνη, Ὑδατοσ-ύδνη).

**ὑδνοβόλοισι** δρόσοις, dub. in *Epigr.Gr*.1036 (Bithynia); cf. ὑδροβόλος.

**ὕδνον**, τό, *truffle, Tuber cibarium*, Thphr.*HP*1.1.11, 1.6.5, *Fr*.167, Diocl.*Fr*.119, Diph.Siph.ap.Ath.2.62c, Hegesand.35, Dsc.2.145, Gal.6.655.

**ὑδνόφυλλον**, τό, *a herb said to grow over truffles* and mark the spot where they are, Pamphil.ap.Ath.2.62d.

**ὑδογενής**, ές, *sprung from the water*, cj. Scaliger for ὑλογ- in Orph.*Fr*.247.36. [ῡ in dact. verse.]

**ὕδος**, τό, v. ὕδωρ.

**ὕδρα**, Ion. **ὕδρη**, ἡ, (cf. ὕδωρ) *water-serpent*, but esp. of *the Lernaean hydra*, Hes.*Th*.313, S.*Tr*.574,836 (lyr.), 1094; Ὕδραν τέμνειν, prov. of *labour in vain*, because two heads sprang up for every one which was cut off, Pl.*R*.426e: pl., but still with reference to the Lernaean hydra, E.*Heracl*.950, *Ph*.[1136]: prov., ὕδρης ποικιλώτερος Herod.3.89 (ἐπὶ τῶν δολερῶν Diogenian.7.69). II. name of a constellation, = ὕδρος III, Arat.444, etc.

**ὑδραγέω**, perh. an error for ὑδραγωγέω, *PCair.Zen*.380.6 (iii B.C.).

**ὑδρᾰγωγ-εῖον**, τό, = ὑδραγώγιον, Str.13.1.67; gen. pl. -είων (vv.ll. -ίων, -ιῶν) Men.Eph.ap.J.*AJ*9.14.2. **-έω**, *conduct* or *convey water*, *Ostr.Bodl*. iii 390 (ii A.D., dub.):—Pass., ὕδωρ ὑδραγωγεῖται v.l. in Str.13.1.67, cf. *PRyl*.157.19 (ii A.D.). ⊛**-ία**, ἡ, *conveyance of water* or *liquids*, Pl.*Ti*.77e, Arist.*PA*668$^a$14, Duris 89 J.; cf. ὑδρεία I. 2. **-ιον**, τό, *aqueduct* or *conduit*, *IG*12(2).103 (Mytil.), *Inscr. Prien*.208 (i B.C.), *IG*4$^2$(1).26 (Epid., i A.D.), *SIG*813 C5 (Delph., i A.D.), *POxy*.901.7 (iv A.D.). ⊛ **-ός**, όν, *bringing water*, σείριος Plu.2.365f; ὑ. ἐν συνόδῳ ἡ σελήνη Porph.ap.Eus.*PE*3.12: ὑ. φάρμακα purgatives *producing watery motions*, Gal.11.325. II. Subst. ὑ., ὁ, *water-carrier*, Artem.4.74, *JHS*24.195 (Greek text of *Edict.Diocl*.7.31, where *aquarius*). 2. *maker* or *manager of aqueducts*, Plu.2.914b; *digger of a channel*, Man.1.84. b. *aqueduct* or *irrigation channel*, with or without irrigation-machinery, Lxx 4*Ki*.18.17, *Si*.24.30, *PCair.Zen*.268.36 (iii B.C.), *PMich.Zen*.45.23 (iii B.C.), *PTeb*.50.8, al. (ii B.C.), Wilcken *Chr*.461.21 (iii A.D.), etc.; ὑ. δαψιλής a copious *watercourse*, 1*Enoch* 28.3. 3. *one who drinks much water, dropsical person*, Hp.*Epid*.7.122. 4. a plant, = νυμφαία, Apul.*Herb*.68.

**ὑδρ-αίνω**, *water*, ὑ. [γᾶν], of a river, E.*Tr*.226 (lyr.); ὑ. τινά *wash, sprinkle with water*, Id.*IT*54:—Med., *wash oneself, bathe*, ὑδρηναμένη Od.4.750,759; λουτρὰ ὑδράνασθαι χροΐ *pour* water *over one's* body, E.*El*.157 (lyr.). II. ὑδραίνειν χοάς τινι *pour* libations to.., Id.*IT*161 (lyr.). **-αῖος**, α, ον, *of water*, δαίμονες Olymp. *in Phd*.p.189 N., al. II. οὐδραία· ὑδρία, μέτρον τι, Ἀττικοῦ μετρητοῦ ἥμισυ, Hsch. (Apparently Boeot. or Lacon.)

**ὑδρᾰλέτ-ης**, ου, ὁ, (ἀλέω A) *water-mill*, Str.12.3.30. II. *engineer in charge of such a mill*, *Sardis* 7(1).169 (iv/v A.D., gen. -αλέτα):—Hsch. s.v. ἰδρόμυλοι also cites **-αλετία**, ἡ, and in *Gloss*. we find **-αλέσιον** (prob. l.). **-ικός**, ή, όν, *of a water-mill*, μύλος *Edict. Diocl*.15.54.

**ὑδραλής**, ὁ, = (1) μετάβολος, (2) ὄφις ὕδατος, Hsch.

⊛ **ὑδράλμη**, ἡ, *salt water*, Antyll.ap.Orib.4.11.13.

**ὑδρανᾶ**, ἁ, or perh. **ὑδράν**, ὁ or ἁ, Dor., *vase for lustral water*, *IG* 5(1).1390.37 (Andania, i B.C.), cf. Rhinth.27 (dub.).

**ὑδράνη**· τὸ ἀκραιφνὲς καὶ καθαρόν, Hsch. **ὑδρανός**· ὁ ἁγνιστὴς τῶν Ἐλευσινίων, Id.

⊛ **ὑδραντικός**, ή, όν, *for irrigation*, ὄργανον dub. in *PFlor*.58.10 (iii A.D.).

**ὑδραργῠρ-ίζω**, *to be like quicksilver*, v.l. in Tz.*H*.8.449 (leg. ὑπερυδρ-):—Pass., *to become quicksilver*, Syn.Alch.p.69 B. **-ος**, ἡ, *quicksilver*, artificially prepared from cinnabar-ore, Dsc.5.95, Hero *Spir*.1.38, *PHolm*.4.33, Syn.Alch.p.68 B.; τὰ δύο ὑ. *quicksilver* and *metallic arsenic*, Id.p.69 B.; τὸ ὑ. *PHolm*.2.28.

**ὑδράρπαξ**, ἄγος, ὁ, = κλεψύδρα I, Simp. *in Cael*.524.20.

**ὕδρας**, α, ὁ, = ὕδραυλις (s.v.l.), Porph. *in Harm*.p.293 W. (= p.119 Düring).

**ὑδράστινα**, ἡ, *wild hemp*, = κάνναβις ἀγρία, Ps.-Dsc.3.149.

⊛ **ὑδρ-αύλης**, ου, ὁ, *one who plays the* ὕδραυλις, *POxy*.93.2 (iv A.D.), *Cod.Just*.10.48.4; also **ὕδραυλος**, ὁ, *SIG*737.4 (Delph., i B.C.).⊛ **-αυλις**, εως, ἡ, *hydraulic organ*, invented by Ctesibius, Ath.4.174b, cf. Aristocl.ib.c, Ph.*Bel*.77.43 (-ην codd.), Hero *Spir*.1.28, Simp. *in Ph*. 681.7; described by Hero *Spir*.1.42:—so τὸ **-αυλικὸν** ὄργανον Aristocl. l. c., Hero *Spir*.1.42. **-αυλος**, ὁ, v. ὑδραύλης. II. = ὕδραυλις, Nicom.*Harm*.4; *hydraulus* in Cic.*Tusc*.3.18.43, Plin.*HN* 9.24.

**ὑδρ-εία**, ἡ, *drawing water, fetching water*, Th.7.13, Pl.*Lg*.844b, Plb.2.9.2, etc.: in pl., Pl.*Ax*.371e. 2. *distribution of water, watering, irrigation*, Id.*Lg*.761c, Thphr.*HP*2.6.3: metaph., ἡ ἐκ τῆς κοιλίας ἐπὶ τὰς φλέβας ὑ. Pl.*Ti*.78b, cf. 77d. II. *watering-place*, Plu.*Them*. 9.—Cf. ὑδρία fin. ⊛ **-εῖον**, Ion. **ὑδρήϊον**, τό, *bucket* or *pitcher*, Hdt. 3.14, Dem.Phal.*Fr*.5 J., Ergias ap.Ath.8.360f, etc.; ὑ. ἀργύρειον *Supp.Epigr*.4.306.14 (Panamara); ὑ. χαλκοῦν *BGU*387 ii 15 (ii A.D.); cf. ὑδρίον I. II. *reservoir*, Plb.34.2.6 (s.v.l.), Str.12.3.39 (both pl.): sg. in Id.1.2.30, *Supp.Epigr*.6.181 (Sebaste), *Sardis* 7(1) No. 17.13. ⊛ **-εκδοχεῖον**, τό, *water-tank*, *BCH*14.612 (pl., Aphrodisias (-εγδ-)): more freq. ὑδροδοχεῖον (q.v.). **-έλαιον**, τό, *water mixed with oil*, Dsc.2.85, Plu.2.663c, Sor.1.76, Gal.11.534, Ruf.ap.Orib.8. 24.1. **-εντεροκήλη**, ἡ, *hernia complicated with hydrocele*, Gal. 19.448.

⊛ **Ὕδρεος**, ὁ, perh. name of a Syrian divinity, *SIG*1137 (Delos).

⊛ **ὕδρ-ευμα**, ατος, τό, *watering-place, well, tank*, Str.16.4.14, *Peripl.M. Rubr*.25,26, *Ostr.Bodl*. iii 245 (i A.D.), Ptol.*Geog*.1.10.2, Thd.*Je*.39(46). 10, *OGI*701.12 (Egypt, ii A.D., pl.), etc.; *irrigation-system*, *PFlor*.50. 15 (ii A.D.), etc. **-εύς**, έως, ὁ, poet. for ὑδρευτής, Man.4.251. **-ευσις**, εως, ἡ, = ὑδρεία I. 2, *irrigation*, Thphr.*CP*3.9.5. **-ευτής**, οῦ, ὁ, *drawer of water*, *Gloss*. **-ευτικός**, ή, όν, *of* or *for watering*, ὄργανα Alex.Polyh.ap.Eus.*PE*9.27. **-εύω**, *draw, fetch*, or *carry water*, Od. 10.105, Thgn.264:—freq. in Med., *draw water for oneself*, [κρήνη] ὅθεν ὑδρεύοντο πολῖται Od.7.131, 17.206, cf. Hdt.7.193, E.*Tr*.205 (lyr.); ὕδωρ ἀνασπάσαντας ὑδρεύεσθαι Th.4.97; παρὰ τῶν γειτόνων Pl.*Lg*. 844b; [ἀπὸ τελμάτων] ὑ. αἱ μέλιτται Arist.*HA*626$^a$11. II. trans., *water, irrigate*, Thphr.*HP*2.6.3. **-ηγός**, ὁ, *water-conduit*, Hsch. s.v. ἀπόρυγας, Suid. s.v. παροχετεύει: as Adj., Hsch. s.v. ῥοώδες, Suid. s.v. ὀχετηγός. II. *water-carrier*, *Ostr.Bodl*. i 316 (i B.C.). **-ήϊον**, τό, v. ὑδρεῖον. **-ηλός**, ή, όν, *watery, moist*, λειμῶνες Od.9.133; Σάμος h.*Ap*.41; νέφη, λιβάδες, A.*Supp*.793 (s.v.l., lyr.), *Pers*.613; κρωσσοί, σταγόνες, E.*Cyc*.89, *Supp*.206:—poet. word, used by Hp.*Ep*.16 (Comp.), *Mul*.1.1.

**ὑδρηρόν**, τό, = ἔρινος or ἔχῖνος, Ps.-Dsc.4.141.

**ὑδρηρός**, ά, όν, = ὑδατηρός, Sophr. in *PSI*11.1214 *d*12, *Trag.Adesp*. 546.6, Philum.*Ven*.14.5; ἡ ἕλιξ, τὸ ὑδρηρὸν ὄργανον Ph.1.410 (v.l. ὑδρηλόν).

**ὑδρήχοος**, ον, *of poured water*, πῶμα E.*Fr*.892. II. Ὑδρηχόος, ὁ, the sign *Aquarius*, *BGU*957.3 (i B.C.), *PSI*4.312.6 (iv A.D.), *PMag.Lond*.121.293, *Gloss*.

⊛ **ὑδρ-ία**, ἡ, (ὕδωρ) *water-pot, pitcher*, Ar.*V*.926, *Ec*.678 (anap.), Lxx *Ec*.12.6, *CIG*2855.10 (Branchidae), *Ev.Jo*.2.6, etc.; ὑδρίης πέρι δήρις (cf. ἀμφορίτης) A.R.4.1767: prov., ἐπὶ θύραις τὴν ὑδρίαν to break the *pitcher* at the door, 'there's many a slip 'twixt cup and lip', Arist.*Rh*.1363$^a$7. II. *vessel* of any kind, e.g. *wine-pot*, Ar.*Fr*. 136; *a pot of money*, Id.*Av*.602 (anap.) (ἐν ὑδρίαις γὰρ ἔκειντο οἱ θησαυροί Sch. ad loc.(603)), cf. *IG*11(2).161 *B*100 (Delos, iii B.C.); ὑ. χαλκῆ D.47.52; ὑ. χρυσῆ, ἀργυρᾶ, *IG*2$^2$.204.35; ὑδρίαι ἄρτων πέντε bread-*pans*, *POxy*.155.4 (vi A.D.). 2. *balloting urn*, esp. in law-courts, etc., *IG*9(1).334.45 (Locr., v B.C.), Isoc.17.33, Plu.*TG*11. 3. *cinerary urn*, Id.*Phil*.21, Luc.*Dem.Enc*.29, etc. 4. *water-clock*, S.E.*M*.5.75, Jul.*Caes*.325c. [ῑ in A.R. l.c., where ὑδρείης is v.l.] **-ιάς**, άδος, ἡ, *of the water*, Ὑδριάδες Νύμφαι Pl.*Epigr*.24, Porph.*Antr*.13, al., *AP*6.57 (Paul. Sil.). **-ιαφόρος**, ὁ, *pitcher-carrier*, Ar.*Ec*.738, Poll.3.55. **-ίδιον**, τό, Dim. of ὑδρία, *IG*2$^2$. 1424*a*274, *Inscr.Délos* 1442 *B*18 (ii B.C.). **-ινεῖον**, τό, = ὑδρία, *Stud.Pal*.20.67.44 (ii/iii A.D.); ὑ. κασσιτέρινον ib.46.14 (ii/iii A.D.). **-ίον**, τό, Dim. of ὑδρία, Hp.*Hum*.11, acc. to Gal.19.148 (sed leg. ὑδρήϊον; ὑδρίειον cod.A Hp.). 2. *cistern, reservoir*, *BGU* 117.5 (ii A.D.). **-ιος**, α, ον, *of water*, περὶ ὑδρίων ὡροσκοπείων *On water-clocks*, a lost treatise by Hero, mentioned by Hero *Spir*.1 *Prooem*., and by Procl.*Hyp*.4.73. ⊛ **-ίσκη**, ἡ, Dim. of ὑδρία, *Supp. Epigr*.4.187.9 (Halic., iii B.C.), Lxx 4*Ki*.2.20, Ptol.Euerg.3 J., *PLond*.2.193.12 (ii A.D.).

⊛ **ὑδρο-βᾰφής**, ές, *dipped in water*, Poll.7.56 (v.l.):—also ⊛**βάφος**, ον, Μουσ.Σμυρν.1878 p.93. ⊛**-βόλος**, ον, *throwing water, watering*, δρόσοι cj. Boeckh for ὑδνο- in *Epigr.Gr*.1036 (Bithynia). **-γάρον**, τό, *fish-sauce prepared with water*, Alex.Trall.1.12, Aët.3.85, Paul. Aeg.3.37, *Gloss*. **-γάστωρ**, ορος, ὁ, ἡ, *with water in the belly, dropsical*, Man.1.155. **-γνώμων**, ονος, ὁ, *water-finder*, *Gp*.2.10.6. **-γονι-**

**κός**, ἡ, όν, *of the production of water*, σημεῖα ib.2.5.16. **-δόκος**, ὁ, = λάκκος, Hsch. **-δοχεῖον**, τό, *reservoir*, *PTeb.*84.13 (ii B.C.), *PLond.*1821.208, etc. **-δόχος**, ον, *containing water*, φύσις ὑμενώδης ὑ., of the foetus, *Theol.Ar.*46. **-δρόμος**, ον, *running in water*, i.e. *swimming*, Orph.*H.*24.7. **-ειδής**, ές, *watery*, Στρυμών E.*Rh.*353 (lyr.). **-εις**, εσσα, εν, *fond of the water*, δόναξ Id.*Hel.*349 (lyr.):—Ὑδροῦσσα was a name of the island Tenos (διὰ τὸ κατάρρυτον εἶναι), Arist.*Fr.*595, and of an island near Attica, Str.9.1.21. **-θήκη**, ἡ, *reservoir, cistern*, Moschio ap.Ath.5.208a. **-θήρας**, ου, ὁ, *fisherman*, Ael.*NA*14.29, Eust.574.16. **-θηρία**, ἡ, *fishing*, Ael.*NA*1.19. **-θηρικός**, ή, όν, *of* or *for fishing*, ib.14.24, 15.1. **-κέλευθος**, v. ὑγροκέλευθος II. **-κέφἄλον**, τό, *water in the head, hydrocephalus*, Gal.14.782: as Adj., τὸ ὑ. πάθος Antyll.ap.Orib.46.27.1. **-κήλη**, ἡ, *water in the scrotum, hydrocele*, Gal.7.729, *Gloss.*; cf. ὑγροκήλη. **-κηλικός**, ή, όν, *suffering from hydrocele*, Heliod.ap.Orib.50.49.2, Gal.14.788. II. *for curing hydrocele*, Paul.Aeg.6.62. **-κιρνάω**, *mix with water*, Tz.*H.*5.535. **-κιρσοκήλη**, ἡ, *aneurysm of the vessels of the testicles*, Gal.19.448. **-κοιλος**, prob. f.l. for ὑγροκοίλιος, Cyran.64. **-κόμιον**, τό, *gum-water*, Zos.Alch.p.172 B. ※ **-κόμος**, ὁ, prob. *well-bucket*, *PLond.*1821.190. **-κύων** [κῠ], κύνος, ὁ, title of Menippean Satire by Varro, Gell.13.31.2. **-λάπᾰθον** [λᾰ], τό, *water-sorrel*, = ἱππολάπαθον, Plin.*HN*20.231. **-λόγιον**, τό, *water-clock*, Cleom.2.1, Ptol.*Tetr.*108, *PLond.*3.1177.245 (ii A.D.), Ach.Tat.*Intr.Arat.*25.6, Procl.*Hyp.*4.79. ※**-μαντεία**, ἡ, *water-divination*, Augustin.*De Civ.Dei* 7.35. **-μαντις**, εως, ὁ, ἡ, *one who divines from water*, Str.16.2.39, Man.4.212. **-μαστευτική** (sc. τέχνη), ἡ, *the art of seeking for water*, *Gp.*2.6.1. **-μέδουσα**, ἡ, *Water-queen*, name of a frog in Batr.19. **-μέλαθρος**, ον, *dwelling in water*, ἰχθύες Emp.20.6. ※ **-μελι**, ιτος, τό, *hydromel*, later Gr. for μελίκρατον, Dsc.5.9, Ath.Med.ap.Orib.*inc.*23.3, S.E. *M.*6.44, Sor.1.52, Gal.6.274. **-μέτριον**, τό, *vessel for measuring a flow of water*, Ptol.*Alm.*5.14 (cj. for -ιων), Procl.*Hyp.*4.71. **-μηλον**, τό, *drink of water and* μηλόμελι, Dsc.5.22, Gal.6.744, Artem.1.66, *Gp.*8.27, etc. **-μιγής**, ές, *mixed with water*, Aret.*CA*1.1. **-μύλη** [μῠ], ἡ, *water-mill*, *Gloss.*; also **-μύλον**, τό, ib., and **-μύλος**, ὁ, Hsch. (pl.). **-μυρον**, v. ὑγρόμυρον.

**ὑδρ-όμφᾰλον**, τό, *umbilical hernia* supposed to be *due to fluid*, Gal.19.444. **-όμφᾰλος**, ον, *suffering from* ὑδρόμφαλον, Id.14.786.

**ὑδρο-νομέομαι**, *measure out water*, Luc.*Lex.*9. **-πᾰγής**, ές, *icy*, Emp. in *Vorsokr.*[3] i p. 209. ※**-πάροχος**, ὁ, *one who furnishes water* for irrigation, *POxy.*729.13, 2128.2 (ii A.D., pl.), etc.:—hence ※**-παροχία**, ἡ, *Supp.Epigr.*4.515.10 (Ephesus, i A.D.), *POxy.*137.22 (vi A.D.); **-παρόχιον**, τό, *PLond.*3.776.19; **-παροχισμός**, ὁ, *POxy.*1590.10 (iv A.D.). **-πέπερι**, εως, τό, *smartweed, Polygonum Hydropiper*, Dsc.2.161, Gal.12.147. **-πλασμός**, ὁ, = *qui* (v.l. *quas*) *cantio componit organi* (with variants), *Gloss.* **-ποιός**, όν, *producing water, watery*, Plu.2.939f, Porph.ap.Eus.*PE*3.11. **-πορος**, ον, = ὑγρόπορος, *through which water passes*, χαράδραι Nonn.*D.*2.438; ἠήρ Orac.ap.Eus.*PE*4.9. **-ποσία**, Ion. -ίη, ἡ, *water-drinking*, Hp. *Acut.*37, *Int.*45 (v.l. -πωσίη), X.*Cyr.*1.5.12, Pl.*Lg.*674a, Sor.1.65, etc. **-ποτέω**, *drink water*, Hdt.1.71, X.*Cyr.*6.2.26, Pl.*R.*561c, Ephor.(?) in *PLit.Lond.*114, 1*Ep.Ti.*5.23, Sor.1.117, Arr.*Epict.*3.13.21.—**ὑδροπωτέω** is the more correct form acc. to Ammon. *Diff.*p.111 V. ※ **-πότης**, ου, ὁ, (πίνω) *water-drinker*, X.*Cyr.*6.2.29; used of a thin-blooded, mean-spirited fellow, *AP*11.20 (Antip. Thess.); cf. ὑδατοπότης. **-πωσίη**, ἡ, v. ὑδροποσία. **-πωτέω**, v. ὑδροποτέω. **-ρόδῐνον**, τό, *oil of roses mixed with water*, Antyll.ap.Orib.10.13.21, Sor.2.24, etc. **-ροσᾶτον**, τό, *rose-water*, Ps.-Orib.5.33.3, Alex.Trall.*Verm.*(2.591 P.), *Febr.*1. **-ρρόα**, ἡ, but in Att. also ὑδρορρόη acc. to Moer.p.381 P., and so Polyaen.1.37: (ῥοή):—*water-course*, whether on the ground, *conduit, sluice*, Ar.*Ach.*922,1186; or on the roof, *gutter, spout*, Id. *V.*126; ἀπὸ τῶν ὀφθαλμῶν ὑδρορρόαι δύο ῥέουσιν Eub.98.4. II. = ὕδρωψ, *AB*312. III. *a hidden rock in the sea*, acc. to (the error of) Sch.Ar.*Ach.*1181. **-ρροια**, ἡ, = foreg. I, Plb.4.57.8. **-ρρόος**, ὁ, (ῥέω) = ὑδρορρόα I, Alciphr.3.47, Hsch. s.v. ὑδροφόρους. **-ρύα**, ἡ, = ὑδρορρόα I, Id. s.v. κορκόδρυα.

※ **ὕδρος**, ὁ, (ὕδωρ) *water-snake, Coluber natrix*, Il.2.723, Hdt.2.76, Arist.*HA*487ᵃ23, 508ᵇ1; λευκὸς ὡς ὕδρου γαστήρ Call.*Iamb.*1.218 (= εἶδος δράκοντος, Sch. in mg.). II. a small water-animal, = φαλάγγιον or σαῦρος, Artem.4.56. III. the constellation *Hydra*, Eudox.ap.Hipparch.2.2.13. (Cf. Skt. *udrás*, OE. *oter* 'otter'.)

**ὑδρο-σεληνίτης** [ῑ], ου, ὁ, a fine kind of *selenite*, Dam.*Isid.*233. **-σέλῑνον**, τό, = ἐλειοσέλινον, Ps.-Dsc.3.64.

**ὑδροσκοπ-έω**, *to be a water-finder*, Heuzey-Daumet *Mission Archéol. de Macédoine* No.113 (Thessalonica):—Med., *search for water*, *Gp.*2.6.42. **-ία**, ἡ, *water-finding*, ib.2.5 tit. 2. = ὑδρολόγιον, Sch. Ptol.*Tetr.*90. **-ική** (sc. τέχνη), ἡ, *the art of finding water, well-sinking*, *Gp.*2.6.47: τὸ -ικόν, *a treatise on this art*, ib.2.4 tit., 6 tit. ※ **-ιον**, τό, a hydrostatic instrument, Gal.5.68 (leg. -ίων for -ιῶν). 2. = ὑδροσκοπία 2, Heph.Astr.3.4. **-ος** (parox.), ὁ, *water-seeker, well-sinker*, *Gloss.*

**ὑδρο-σπάταλος**, ὁ, *bestia marina*, *Gloss.* **-σπονδα** (sc. ἱερά), τά, *drink-offering of water*, Thphr.ap.Porph.*Abst.*2.20. **-στάσιμος** [ᾰ], ον, *of* or *with standing water*, τόποι Dsc.3.118. **-στάσιον** [ᾰ], τό, (στῆναι) *standing water, pond, pool*, Men.Prot.p.55 D. II. *tank*, *BGU*492.9 (ii A.D.), *PFay.*131.12 (iii/iv A.D.). **-στᾰτέομαι**, Pass., *to have stagnant water*, τόποι ὑδροστατούμενοι spots *with standing water, marshes*, Anon.ap.Suid. s.v. ἀξιόλογα. **-στάτης** [ᾰ], ου, ὁ, *hydrostatic balance*, Procl.ad Hes.*Op.*589. **-στόλος**, ὁ, *watering-place for ships*, λιμὴν μέγας, ὅρμος ναυσὶ καὶ ὑδροστόλος *Peripl.M.Eux.*29.

**ὑδρό-της**, ητος, ἡ, *moisture*, Procl.*Par.Ptol.*166. **-φάντης**, ου, ὁ, *water-finder*, Olymp. *in Mete.*99.21:—hence **-φαντική** (sc. τέχνη), ἡ, *the art of discovering water*, *Gp.*2.6.1; also **-φαντικά**, τά, ibid.

**ὑδροφόβ-ας**, α, ὁ, = ὑδροφόβος II, Cels.5.27.2, Dsc.2.47, Plu.2.731b, 732a, Philum.*Ven.*1.4, 4.11. II. = ὑδροφόβος I, Arr.*Epict.*4.4.20 (cod. S m.pr.), Philum.*Ven.*4.5,12. **-ία**, ἡ, *horror of water* caused by the bite of a mad dog, *hydrophobia*, v.l. for foreg. in Dsc.2.47; ascribed by Men. to wine-drinkers, *Fr.*959. **-ιάω**, *suffer from hydrophobia*, Dsc.*Ther.*1, = Philum.*Ven.*1. **-ικός**, ή, όν, *of* or *like hydrophobia*, τὸ ὑ. πάθος, = ὑδροφοβία, Dsc. *Ther.*3; *suffering from hydrophobia*, Cass.*Pr.*73. II. *curing hydrophobia*, Gal.14.208. ※ **-ος** (parox.), ον, *having a horror of water, having hydrophobia*, Arr.*Epict.*4.4.20 (cod. S m.rec.), Gal.10.627. II. as Subst., -φόβος, ὁ, or -φόβον, τό (gender uncertain), = ὑδροφοβία, Dsc.*Ther. Praef.*, Gal.16.621.

**ὑδροφορ-έω**, *carry water*, X.*An.*4.5.9, Arist.*HA*625ᵇ19. II. *serve as* ὑδροφόρος, *CIG*2886 (Branchidae), *Milet.*7.67. **-ησις**, εως, ἡ, *carrying of water*, Eust.1323.59. **-ία**, ἡ, *the office of* ὑδροφόρος II, *CIG*2885, *Milet.*7.68. II. *carrying of water*, Luc.*DMarin.*6.2. ※ **-ια**, τά, *water-carrying*, a festival of Apollo in Aegina, Sch.Pi.*N.*5.81; ἑορτὴ πένθιμος Ἀθήνησιν ἐπὶ τοῖς ἐν τῷ κατακλυσμῷ ἀπολομένοις, Suid. (citing 'Apollonius'); name of an ἀγών, Sch. Call. in Διηγήσεις viii 32. **-ικός**, ή, όν, *for carrying water*, ἀγγεῖον Suid. s.v. κρωσσός. Adv. -κῶς *like a water-carrier*, κινεῖσθαι Alex. Aphr. *in Top.*440.4. ※ **-ος** (parox.), ον, *carrying water*, κόρη Plu. *Them.*31; ἀγγεῖον Poll.8.66. II. Subst. ὑ., ὁ and ἡ, *water-carrier*, Hdt.3.14, X.*An.*4.5.10, *PCair.Zen.*702.24 (iii B.C.), Lxx *Jo.*9.33(27), Luc.*Vit.Auct.*7, etc.; Ὑδροφόροι, title of Tragedies by Aeschylus and by Sophocles; ὑ. Ἀρτέμιδος Πυθίης, title of priestess at Branchidae, *OGI*226.1 (iii B.C.); so in pl., *CIG*2885, *BMus.Inscr.*922.9; also at Athens, of maidens who served at the Dipolieia, Thphr.ap.Porph.*Abst.*2.30; cf. ὑδροφορέω II. III. ὑδροφόρους· ὑδρορρόους, Hsch.

**ὑδρο-φῠλᾰκέω**, *to be a* ὑδροφύλαξ, *PLond.*1.131ʳ.50 (i A.D.); *guard as* ὑ., τὸ ῥῆγμα ib.60; χώματα -πεφυλακημένα *POxy.*729.23 (ii A.D.). **-φῠλᾰκία**, ἡ, *office of* ὑδροφύλαξ, *PLond.*1.131ʳ.138 (i A.D.), *POxy.*729.7 (ii A.D.). **-φύλαξ** [φῠ], ᾰκος, ὁ, *guard* or *inspector of aqueducts* or *irrigation-works*, *PLond.*1.131ʳ.205 (i A.D.), *BGU*621.6 (ii A.D.), *Cod.Just.*11.43.10.4, etc. **-χᾰμαίμηλον**, τό, *chamomile-oil and water*, Alex.Trall.*Febr.*5. **-χᾰρής**, ές, *delighting in water*, Eust.254.11, etc. **-χᾰρις**, ὁ, *Grace of the waters*, name of a frog, Batr.227. **-χόα** (Moer.p.381 P.) or **-χόη** (*Ostr.Bodl.*i 393, *Gloss.*), ἡ, *conduit, aqueduct*, Xenocr.ap.Orib.2.58.3 (pl.), Hsch., etc.; less Att. than ὑδρορρόη, Moer. l.c. **-χοεῖον**, τό, *well, cistern*, Men.Prot.p.37 D.; = Lat. *aquale*, *Gloss.*:—wrongly written **ὑδροχεῖον** in Suid. **-χοεύς**, έως, ὁ, v. sq. **-χόος**, ὁ, (χέω) *water-pourer*, name of the constellation *Aquarius*, Eudox.ap.Hipparch.1.2.20, *Placit.*1.6.6, Euc.*Phaen.*p.12 M., cf. *AP*12.199 (Strat.); contr. **-χοῦς**, *Supp.Epigr.*7.363.5, al. (Dura-Europus, ii A.D.):—dat. ὑδροχοῆϊ (as if from ὑδροχοεύς), Ep. for the common ὑδροχόῳ, Arat.389, Nonn.*D.*23.315. II. name of an Egyptian month, = Φαρμοῦθι, *POxy.*465.11 (ii A.D.). **-χῠτος**, ον, *pouring* or *gushing with water*, κρῆναι E.*Cyc.*66 (lyr.). **-ψῡγεῖον**, τό, *cool-water tank*, *PRyl.*233.6 (ii A.D.); written **-ψυγιον** in *PLond.*2.394.3 (vi A.D.), *Gloss.* **-ψύκτιον**, τό, = foreg., *PCair.Zen.*764.30 (iii B.C.).

※ **ὕδρω**, apparently = ὕδωρ, *Supp.Epigr.*3.672 (Delos, graffito).

**ὑδρ-ώδης**, ες, *watery*, Thphr.*CP*5.12.3 (Comp.). **-ωμα**, ατος, τό, = ὕδρευμα, *CIG*4837 (Egypt). **-ών**, ῶνος, ὁ, *the month in which Aquarius rises*, Ptol.*Alm.*9.7.

**ὑδρωπ-ία**, ἡ, = ὕδρωψ, Vett.Val.105.27, (-οπ-) Orib.8.17.2 codd. **-ίᾱσις**, εως, ἡ, = ὕδρωψ, *Lex.Havn.ined.* s.v. ὕδερος. **-ιάω**, *have dropsy*, Hp.*Aph.*7.47, *Aër.*7, Arist.*GA*789ᵇ14, Thphr.*Lass.*5, etc. **-ικός**, ή, όν, *suffering from dropsy*, Hp.*Aph.*6.27, Arist.*Pr.*871ᵇ24, Plb.13.2.2, Dsc.1.103, *Ev.Luc.*14.2, *POxy.*1088.63 (i A.D.), Sor.2.63: metaph., ναῦς ὑ. *AP*11.332 (Nicarch.). **-ισμός**, ὁ, = ὑδρωπίασις, Asclep.ap.Cael.Aur.*CP*1.14. **-ιώδης**, ες, *like dropsy, dropsical*, Hp.*Coac.*444, al.; τὸ ὑ. *dropsy*, ib.298,417:—also **-οειδής**, ές, Id.*Int.*12, al.; but τὰ ὑ. simply *watery* discharges, Id.*Mul.*1.30.

※ **ὕδρωψ**, ωπος, ὁ, (ὕδωρ) *dropsy*, Hp.*Aph.*3.22 (pl.), *IG*4²(1).122.1, 123.33 (Epid., iv B.C.), Epicur.*Fr.*190, Sor.2.37, etc.; ὑ. ξηρός Hp.*Aph.*4.11; he distinguishes two kinds, ὁ ὑποσαρκίδιος (v.l. ὑπὸ τῇ σαρκί) and ὁ μετ' ἐμφυσημάτων, *Acut.*(*Sp.*)52. 2. ὑ. εἰς ἀμίδα *diabetes*, Gal.7.81. 3. *any watery discharge*, e.g. *discharge before parturition*, Arist.*HA*587ᵃ6, Cleophant.ap.Sor.2.53; cf. πρόφορος II. II. *a dropsical person*, Hp.*Int.*47 (dub. l.), *Epid.*2.5.13—in which sense Dsc.ap.Gal.19.148 read ὑδρώψ (oxyt.). III. one of the four humours, *aqueous humour*, Hp.*Morb.*4.32, al.

**ὕδω**, v. ὑδέω.

※ **ὕδωρ** [ῠ, v. fin.], τό, gen. ὕδατος: an Ep. dat. ὕδει in Hes.*Op.*61, Thgn.961; later nom. ὕδος Call.*Fr.*475; Boeot. **οὖδωρ** prob. in *IG*7.3169 (Orchom.):—*water*, of any kind, but in Hom. rarely of sea-water without an epith., ἄνεμός τε καὶ ὕ. Od.3.300, 7.277; but ἁλμυρὸν ὕ. 9.227, al., cf. Th.4.26; of rivers, ὕ. Αἰσήποιο, Στυγός, Il.2.825, 8.369, al.; so in Lyr. and Trag., ὕ. Ἀσώπιον Pi.*N.*3.3; ὕ. τὸ Νείλου A.*Supp.*561 (lyr.): freq. in pl. (but only once in Hom., ὕδατ' ἀενάοντα Od.13.109), Καφίσια ὕδατα *the waters* of Cephisus, Pi.*O*.14.1; ῥυτῶν ὑδάτων S.*OC*1599; ὕδασιν τοῖς Ἀχελῴου Id.*Fr*.271 (anap.): *spring-water, drinking-water*, οἶνον ἔμισγον καὶ ὕ. Od.1.110; ἀφυσσάμεθ' ὕδωρ 9.85; ὕδατα καὶ.. σῖτοι Pl.*R*.404a; πότιμον ὕ. X.*HG*3.2.19; ὕ. πίνων a *water*-drinker, D.6.30, cf. 19.46, Ar.*Eq*.349; ὕ. δὲ πίνων οὐδὲν ἂν τέκοι σοφόν Cratin.199, cf. Aristopho10.3, Bato 2.9, al.: ὕδωρ κατὰ χειρός *water* for washing the hands, v. χείρ; φέρτε χερσὶν ὕ. Il.9.171; ὕ. ἐπὶ χεῖρας ἔχευαν 3.270, Od.1.146, al.; λοέσσας ὕδατι λευκῷ Il.23.282:—on γῆν καὶ ὕδωρ αἰτεῖν and διδόναι, v. γῆ I. 2 b:—a curse was invoked upon those who refused fire (i.e. the right to borrow burning embers) or water or to direct a traveller on his way, Diph.62, cf. X.*Oec*.2.15:—prov., ὅρκους ἐγὼ γυναικὸς εἰς ὕ. γράφω S.*Fr*.811, cf. Men.*Mon*.25; ἐν ὕδατι γράφειν Pl.*Phdr*.276c; ὅταν τὸ ὕδωρ πνίγῃ, τί δεῖ ἐπιπίνειν; *if water chokes*, what more can be done? of a desperate case, Arist.*EN*1146ᵃ35, cf. ἐπιρροφέω I. 2. *rain-water, rain*, ὅτε λαβρότατον χέει ὕ. Ζεύς Il.16.385; ὕσαι ὕδατι λαβροτάτῳ Hdt.1.87; ἐγίνετο ὕ. ἄπλετον Id.8.12; πολὺ Th.6.70, D.59.99; ὕ. ἐπιγενόμενον πολὺ X.*HG*1.6.28; τὸ ὕ. τὸ γενόμενον τῆς νυκτός Th.2.5, cf. Hdt.8.13: more definitely, ὕδωρ ἐξ οὐρανοῦ X.*An*.4.2.2, Aristid.*Or*.50(26).35 (but ἐξ οὐρανοῦ is a gloss in Th.2.77): pl., ὕ. ὄμβρια Pi.*O*.11(10).2; τὰ Διός, or παρὰ τοῦ Δ., ὕ. Pl.*Lg*.761a,b; τὸ ἐκ Διὸς ὕ. Thphr.*HP*2.6.5; καινὸν ἀεὶ τὸν Δία ὕειν ὕδωρ, ὕδωρ τὸν θεὸν ποιῆσαι, Ar.*Nu*.1280, *V*.261 (lyr.), cf. Thphr.*Char*.3.4: abs., ἐὰν πλεῖω ποιῇ ὕ. Id.*CP*1.19.3: κεραύνια ὕ. thunder-*showers*, Plu.2.664f; ὕ. πολλά, συνεχέα μαλθακῶς Hp.*Epid*.1.1. 3. for ἐν ὕδατι βρέχεσθαι, Hdt.3.104, v. βρέχω. 4. in the law-courts, τὸ ὕδωρ was *the water of the water-clock* (κλεψύδρα), and hence *the time it took in running out*, ἂν ἐγχωρῇ τὸ ὕδωρ D.44.45; οὐχ ἱκανόν μοι τὸ ὕ. Id.45.47; ἐν τῷ ἐμῷ ὕ., ἐπὶ τοῦ ἐμοῦ ὕ., in the time allowed me, Id.18.139, 57.61; οὐκ ἐνδέχεται πρὸς ταὐτὸ ὕ. εἰπεῖν one cannot say (all) in one speech, Id.27.12; τὸ ὕ. ἀναλῶσαι Din.2.6; πρὸς ὕ. σμικρὸν διδάξαι Pl.*Tht*.201b; ἐν μικρῷ μέρει τοῦ παντὸς ὕ. D.29.9; ἐπίλαβε τὸ ὕ. stop the *water* (which was done while the speech was interrupted by the calling of evidence and reading of documents), Id.45.8; ἐγχεῖται τὸ μὲν πρῶτον ὕ. τῷ κατηγόρῳ.., τὸ δὲ δεύτερον ὕ. τῷ φεύγοντι Aeschin.3.197; ἀποδιδόναι, παραδιδόναι τινὶ τὸ ὕ., to give him the turn of speaking, Id.1.162, Din.1.114. 5. generally, *liquid*, ὕδατος εἴδη τὰ τοιάδε· οἶνος, οὖρον, ὀρός Arist.*Mete*.382ᵇ13, cf. Hp.*Cord*.12. II. part of the constellation Aquarius, Arat.399. 2. a name for the winter solstice, Paul.Al.*A*.4. III. Ὕδατα, τά, as the name of *places with hot* or *mineral waters*, Ὕ. Σέξτια, Lat. *Aquae Sextiae*, Ὕ. Νεαπολιτανά, etc., Ptol.*Geog*.2.10.8, 3.3.7, etc. [ῠ by nature, ὕδωρ Il.18.347, al. (usu. with ῡ when not at end of line), ὕδατος 16.229, al., ὕδατι Od.12.363, al., ὕδατ' 13.109, and so always in Att. (exc. sts. in dactylic verse, Ar.*Ra*.1339); Hom. freq. has ὕδωρ (always at end of line exc. in phrase Στυγὸς ὕδωρ Il.15.37), also ὕδατος Il.21.300,312, Od.5.475, ὕδατι Il.23.282, Od.22.439; later Ep. admits ὕδωρ more freely, A.R.4.601, so that we find ῡ in the second half of the foot in *h.Cer*.381, Batr.97, A.R.4.290, etc.; also in Alc.*Supp*.11.8.] (Cf. Skt. *udán-*, gen. *udn-ás* 'water', OE. *wæter*, ONorse *vatn*; I.-E. *u(e)d-* with suffix *r* alternating with *n* (ὕδ-ṇ-τος): cogn. with Skt. *u-ná-t-ti* (root *ud-*), 3 pl. *u-n-d-ánti* 'moisten', cf. Lat. *unda*.)

**ὑεικός** [ῠ], ή, όν, = ὑϊκός, Poll.6.55, Phot., etc.; ὑ. τι ποιεῖν, = ὑηνεῖν, Tim.*Lex*.

**ὕεινα**, = Lat. *verrina*, prob. an error for ὕεια (v. sq.), *Gloss*.

⊛ **ὕειος**, α, ον, (ὗς) *of* or *belonging to swine*, κοιλία ὑεία *pig's* tripe, Ar.*Eq*.356; ὕ. τρίχες *pig's* bristles, Arist.*HA*519ᵃ24; σαρκὸς ὑείας κρέας Philetaer.10; κρεῖσκος Alex.189; πλευρόν Hermipp.45; ἀκροκώλιον Stratt.4, Antiph.126.2, cf. Hecat.9 J. (where ὕεα): ῥύγχος Anaxil.11; κοιλία, σπλάγχνα, Arist.*HA*495ᵇ27, 507ᵇ37; ὕεια (sc. κρέα) Anaxandr.39.7, Diocl.*Fr*.141, Lxx *Ps*.16(17).14, 1*Ma*.1.47, cf. *IG*12(1).677.26 (Rhodes, iii B.C.):—θηρίον ὕ., as a type of brutish ignorance, Pl.*R*.535e; v. ὑηνός, ὑϊκός. (This form is censured by Thom.Mag.p.371 R., who recommends ὑεικός.)

**υεἱός**, late spelling of υἱός (q.v.).

**ὑελᾰκῡκάδες** [ῡ] ὄγχναι, dub. l. in *AP*6.232 (Crin.).

**ὑελέψης**, ου, ὁ, (ἕψω) *glass-smelter*, Hsch., Olymp. *in Mete*.331.17.

**Ὑέλη**, ἡ, *Velia* in Lower Italy, Hdt.1.167, Str.6.1.1: also called Οὐέλιαι (v.l. Βελίαι), Ptol.*Geog*.3.1.8; Οὐέλια D.H.1.20, who says this form is an old dialect word (Ϝέλια) for ἐλώδη = *marshy* places; but ἕλος prob. had no Ϝ. (The coins have υελητων, υελητεων, and Ϝελη(των), *BMus.Cat Coins Italy* pp.304,305,306; the Oscan name *Velia* was prob. adapted as *Ὑελέη (hence Ὑελῆ is more prob. than Ὑέλη) and Ἐλέα.)

**ὑελιάριος**, ὁ, *glass-worker*, *MAMA* 3.10 (Seleucia ad Calycadnum); also **ὑλιάριος**, ib.591 (Corycus).

**ὑελίζω, ὑέλινος**, v. ὑαλ-. **ὑέλιον**, τό, *small mirror*, Suid. s. v. σπέκλον. **ὑελῖτις, ὕελος, ὑελουργεῖον, ὑελουργός, ὑελοῦς**, v. ὑαλ-.

**ὑελ-οψικός**, ή, όν, (ὑελέψης) *of a glass-smelter*, καμίνια Zos.Alch.p.246 B. **-οψός**, ὁ, = ὑελέψης, Hdn.*Epim*.138 (ὑελλοψός).

**ὑελώδης**, v. ὑαλ-. **ὗεν**· εὗρεν, Hsch. **ὕεος**, v. ὕειος.

**ὑέργον**, written for Ϝέργον in *GDI*5072*b*5,8 (Crete, iii B.C.).

**ὕεσι**· στολή, Πάφιοι, Hsch. **ὑεστάκα**· ἱματισμός, Id.

**ὑετηρία**, ἡ, *rainfall, rainy weather*, *Cat.Cod.Astr*.1.132.

**ὑετής**· ὁ αὐτοετής, Μαρσύας, Hsch. (i.e. οἰετής).

**ὑετ-ία** [ῡ], ἡ, *rainy weather*, Gem.*Calend*.5, Ptol.*Phas*.p.14 H., al. **-ίζω**, *send* or *cause rain*, Lxx *Je*.14.22, *Jb*.38.26: c. acc., *water with rain*, θεὸν τὸν ὑετίζοντα τὴν γῆν *PMag.Par*.1.3049:—Pass., v. ὑλίζω. ⊛ **-ιος**, α, ον, *rainy, bringing rain*, ἄνεμοι Arist.*Pr*.940ᵇ33; Ζεὺς ὑ. Id.*Mu*.401ᵃ18, *SIG*1107.4 (Cos, iii/ii B.C.), Corn.*ND*9 (so ὁ Ὑ. alone, *Annuario* 8/9.321 (Rhodes)); ὑετιώτερος νότος Thphr.*Vent*.7; cf. ὑετός II. 2. *of* or *belonging to rain*, ὕδωρ ὑ. a fall *of rain*, Id.*Sign*.28; ὑ. ὕδατα *rain*-water, Plu.2.911f tit.; ὑέτια ἦν it was *rainy weather*, Hp.*Epid*.4.18; ὑετίων δὲ μὴ ἐκφέρειν wool shall not be brought out (for sale) *in rainy weather*, *GDI* iv p.876 (Ionia, iv B.C.). II. Subst. ὑέτιος, ὁ, name of a stone. Cyran.39.

**ὑετίς**, f.l. for ὑστις.

**ὑετόεις** [ῡ], εσσα, εν, = ὑέτιος I. 1, dub. l. in *AP*9.525.21.

**ὑετό-μαντις** [ῡ], εως, ὁ, ἡ, *prophet of rain*, κορώνη Euph.89; Ἶρις Poet.ap.Olymp. *in Mete*.235.2. **-ποιός**, όν, *rain-making*, ἀστέρες *Cat.Cod.Astr*.1.132.

**ὑετ-ός** [ῡ], ὁ, (ὕω) *rain*, Il.12.133, Hes.*Op*.545; ποιεῖν ὑετόν Ar.*V*.263 (lyr.); esp. *a heavy shower* (whereas ὄμβρος is continuous rain, ψεκάς or ψακάς drizzle), Antipho5.22, X.*Cyn*.5.4, Arist.*Mete*.347ᵃ12, *Mu*.394ᵃ31, Chrysipp.*Stoic*.2.203: pl., *rains*, Diog. Apoll.3, Arist.*PA*653ᵃ4. II. as Adj. in Sup., ἄνεμοι ὑετώτατοι the *rainiest* winds, Hdt.2.25 (where θυετιώτατοι cod. D, ὑετιώτατοι Hude). [ῡ Hom., Hes., Att.; later ῠ in ὑετοῖο Nic.*Th*.273.] **-ώδης**, ες, *rainy, showery*, J.*AJ*1.1.1.

**Ὑεύς**, v. Ὕης.

⊛ **ὑεύχομαι**, Cypr. for ἐπεύχομαι (Cypr. ὐ- = ἐπι- in compds.), *Inscr. Cypr*.120 H.: cf. ὑνεύχομαι.

**ὐϜαις**, Adv. *in perpetuity*, = εἰς ἀεί, *Inscr.Cypr*.135.10 H.

**ὕζω**, v. ὕξον.

**Ὕη**, ἡ, = Σεμέλη, Pherecyd.90 J.; Ὑή, Hsch.

**ὑην-εία**, ἡ, = ὑηνία, Dam.*Isid*.194,238. **-εύς**, έως, ὁ, *swinish* or *boorish fellow*, *hog*, Call.Com.31. **-έω**, *to be as stupid as a hog*, *play the hog*, Pl.*Tht*.166c; also συηνέω, Phot. **-ία**, ἡ, *swinishness, swinish stupidity*, Ar.*Pax*928, Pherecr.237; of the last stage of drunkenness, ἐκ δὲ πόσιος κῶμος, ἐκ κώμου δ'..ὑανία Epich.148; also συηνία, Phot. **-ός**, ή, όν, *swinish*, θρέμματα ὑ. *swinish* creatures, Pl.*Lg*.819d.

**Ὕης** [ῡ], ου, ὁ, (ὕω) epith. of Ζεὺς ὄμβριος (cf. ὑέτιος), Hsch., Theognost.*Can*.18. II. epith. of Dionysus, Cli(to)dem.21, Euph.14 (in Hsch. also **Ὑεύς**, in Sch.Ar.*Av*.874 **Ὕας**), *as the god of fertilizing moisture*, Plu.2.364d: cf. Ὑάδες II, Ὕη. The invocation Ὕης ἄττης in D.18.260 is of doubtful meaning; Ὕης is placed among ξενικοὶ θεοί by Ar.*Fr*.878 (cf. Apolloph.7). (Acc. to Hdn.Gr.1.59 Ὑῆς is the correct accent.)

**ὑθαράν**, dub. in *IG*4.742.20 (Hermione).

**ὑθλ-έω**, *talk nonsense, trifle, prate*, Ar.*Nu*.783; τοιαῦθ' ὑθλῶν δειπνεῖ καὶ ζῇ Ephipp.19 (anap.). [ῡ Ephipp. l. c., perh. long by nature, but the accent of ὕθλος, if correct, implies ῠ, and so apptly. Alex. in *Gloss.Oxy*.1801.52.]

**ὑθλορρήμων**, ον, gen. ονος, *talking nonsense, prating*, Tz.*H*.4.375.

**ὕθλος**, ὁ, *idle talk, nonsense*, Pl.*Ly*.221d, D.35.25; γραῶν ὕ. old wives' *gossip*, Pl.*Tht*.176b, Porph.*Abst*.4.16, cf. Jul.*Or*.5.161b (pl.): pl., ὕθλους λέγειν, Pl.*R*.336d.

**υἱ**, Adv. = οἷ (*whither*), *Schwyzer* 198.18, 199.16 (Crete): cf. υἱς.

**υἷα**, υἱάσι, v. υἱός.

**υἱάφιον** [ᾰ], τό, Dim. of υἱός, *Gloss*.

**υἱϊδῆ**, ἡ, fem. of υἱιδοῦς, *granddaughter*, *POxy*.261.5 (I A.D.), Poll.3.17, Hsch., etc.

**ὑΐδιον** (A), τό, Dim. of ὗς, X.*Mem*.1.2.30 codd., *IG*1².38.12 (prob.): v. ὕδιον.

⊛ **ὑΐδιον** (B), τό, Dim. of υἱός, Ar.*V*.1356 (so cod. R, not υἱίδιον).

**υἱϊδοῦς**, οῦ, ὁ, (υἱός) *son's son, grandson*, Pl.*Lg*.925a, X.*An*.5.6.37, D.43.73; written **υἱιδοῦς** in Arist.*HA*585ᵇ34, Paus.4.15.3.

**ὑΐζω**, (ὗς) *squeal like a pig*, Poll.5.87; v. ὑϊσμός.

⊛ **υἰήν**· τὴν ἄμπελον, ἢ υἱόν, Hsch. **υἰήν**· ποιὰ βοτάνη, Id.

⊛ **υἱιδεύς**, έως, ὁ, = υἱιδοῦς, Isoc.*Ep*.8.1; cf. υἱιδοῦς.

⊛ **ὑϊκός** [ῠ], ή, όν, (ὗς) *of* or *for swine*, δέρμα ὑ. *pig's* skin, Axionic.9; ὑ. πάσχειν to have something *of the swine's nature*, X.*Mem*.1.2.30; ἱερεῖον ὑϊκὸν *PCair.Zen*.91.3 (iii B.C.), cf. Plb.2.15.3, *Milet*.7.18; ὑϊκή, ἡ, *tax on swine*, *PSI*4.384.2 (iii B.C.), *PFay*.230, al. (I A.D.); τῶν ὑϊκῶν λόγον dub. in *PStrassb*.112.7 (ii B.C.):—cf. ὑεικός.

**ὕιλη**· ὅμιλος, Hsch.

⊛ **υἱο-θεσία**, ἡ, *adoption as a son*, Nic.Dam.130.18 J.; in a religious sense, πνεῦμα υἱοθεσίας *Ep.Rom*.8.15, cf. 23, *Ep.Gal*.4.5; freq. in Inscrr., in the phrase καθ' υἱοθεσίαν, *GDI*2581.218 (Delph., ii B.C.), *SIG*581.102 (Crete, ii B.C., ὑο-): pl., νεανίσκων υἱοθεσίας ποιεῖσθαι D.L.4.53. **-θετέω**, *adopt as a son*, *PLips*.28.22 (iv A.D.), *Cat. Cod.Astr*.6.68 (both Pass.). **-θετος**, ον, v.l. υἱοθετός, *adopted as a son*, Thom.Mag.p.362 R.; dat. written υοθετω in *Supp.Epigr*.6.624 (Pisidia). **-θρεπτος**, ὁ, *foster-son*, Keil-Premerstein *Dritter Bericht* No.31 (Lydia).

**υἱόν**· ἀναδενδράδα, Hsch.; cf. υἰήν.

**υἱοποι-έομαι**, Med., *adopt as a son*, Plb.36.16.5, *GDI*2202.24 (Delph., ii B.C.), D.S.4.60, Nic.Dam.66.7 J.:—Pass., **-ηθῆναι** *Cat. Cod.Astr*.6.71. **-ητος**, ον, *adopted as a son*, D.H.*Din*.12. ⊛ **-ία**, ἡ, *adoption as a son*, Ἀρχ.Ἐφ.1917.25 f. No.313 (Perrhaebia, in form ὑοποΐαν).

⊛ **υἱός**, ὁ (written Ϝhιός in Ἀρχ.Ἐφ.1931.103 (Nemea, vi B.C.)), declined regul. υἱοῦ, υἱῷ, υἱόν, but in Att. Inscrr. only after 350 B.C. (exc. υἱός *IG*1².529,530, 598,625; ὑός ib.585,828; ὑόν ib.70.8), and then always so:—in earlier Att. and other Inscrr. inflected as a ῠ-stem (like πῆχυς), nom. υἱύς (written *hυιhυς*) Klein *Vasen mit Meistersignaturen* 72 (*Brit.Mus.Cat.*701) (ὑύς *IG*1².571,670,686; contr. ὗς ib.663); gen. υἱέος (ὑέος *IG*2².4883); dat. υἱεῖ: dual υἱεῖ Lys.19.46, written *hυιε* in *IG*1².775 (corrupted to υἱέε in Pl.*Ap.*20a cod. B), υἱέοιν: pl. υἱεῖς (ὑεῖς *IG*1².115.14, al.), υἱέων, υἱέσι (S.*Ant.*571, Ar. *Nu.*1001 (anap.)), ὑέ[σιν] (*IG*1².54.14), υἱεῖς (ὑεῖς *IG*2².1.73): but gen. υἱέως, and acc. υἱέα, υἱέας, which are formed as though from nom. *υἱεύς, are rejected by Phryn.48,49, Thom.Mag.p.367R., as not Att., though the two latter forms are used by later writers (as υἱέα Euph. 5, Arr.*Cyn.*16, ὑέα *IG*4²(1).244.4 (Epid., ii B.C.), but υἱέως is f.l. in Th.1.13, J.*AJ*18.2.4, etc.): dat. pl. υἱεῦσιν is mentioned as a form that would be regular by Eust.1348.27:—Homer uses nom. υἱός (very freq.); gen. υἱοῦ only in Od.22.238, elsewh. υἱέος; dat. υἱέϊ or υἱεῖ; acc. υἱέα Il.13.350 (cf. *IGRom.*4.360.29 (Pergam., hex.)), elsewh. υἱόν (very freq.): pl., nom. υἱέες Il.5.10, al., or υἱεῖς Od.15.248, 24.387,497; gen. υἱῶν Il.21.587, 22.44, Od.24.223; dat. υἱοῖσι(ν) only Od.19.418, υἱάσι(ν) Il.5.463, al. (never υἱέσι); acc. υἱέας ib.149, al.:—he also uses the shorter forms, gen. υἷος, υἷι, υἷα, dual υἷε (distd. from the voc. sg. υἱέ by the accent), pl. υἷες, υἷας; but these were confined to Ep.: their accentuation (in which codd. agree with Hdn.Gr.1. 409) may preserve a trace of their Aeolic origin (v. infr.). The declension υἱῆος, υἱῆϊ, υἱῆα, υἱῆες, υἱήεσσι, υἱῆας (like βασιλῆος, etc., as though from *υἱεύς), belongs solely to later Ep. poets, as A.R.2. 1093,1119, Nic.*Fr.*110, *AP*9.23 (Antip.), etc. Dialect Inscrr. have the foll. archaic forms, nom. υἱύς *IG*5(1).720 (Lacon.), *Leg.Gort.*12. 17 (υιυις lapis); acc. υἱύν *Inscr.Olymp.*30, *Leg.Gort.*10.15; gen. υἱέος ib.6.3, *Schwyzer* 105 (Methana, vi B.C.); but υἱοῦ *IG*9(1).867 (Corc., vii B.C.); nom. pl. υἱέες *Leg.Gort.*7.25; acc. pl. υἱύνς ib. 4.40, *IG*1².407 (Cret. or Argive); dat. pl. υἱάσι *Leg.Gort.*4.37 (as in Hom., influenced by θυγατράσι, πατράσι, which have ρα = ṛ, cf. Skt. *pitṛ́ṣu*); ὑέεσσι *IG*14.10 (Syrac.); υἷος in *SIG*55 (Thessaly, v B.C.) is perh. the Aeol. gen. (ὑός is nom. rather than gen. in *IG*1².828); acc. ὗα *Schwyzer* 625 (Mytil., ii/i B.C.); a nom. ὑῖς (scanned –◡) *IG*1².472 (Boeotia, vi B.C.), cf. Simon.249 (v. infr.); nom. pl. ὗες *IG*2².3632.24 (hex., Eleusis, ii A.D.). The initial syll. is both υἱ- and ὑ- in Att. Inscrr. down to 400 B.C. (e.g. ὑεῖς *IG*1².115.14, ὑέ[σιν] ib.54.14, ὑόν v. supr.), afterwards ὑ-, but υἱός reappears under the Empire; in Plato cod. A usually has ὑ'ος, which is found also in T, cod. B always has υἱός, editors restore ὑός; acc. υἱόν is recommended by Phryn. l. c.; in Inscrr. of Pergamon, Magnesia, and Delphi, and in non-literary Papyri, ὑός is at all times less common than υἱός:—ὁ υειός *CIG* (add.) 3857*p*; dat. υειῷ ib.3846*z*⁸² (both Phrygia), cf. *BCH*11.471:—*son*, Il.6.366, etc.; υἱὸν ποιεῖσθαί τινα to adopt as *a son*, Aeschin.2.28; υἱεῖς ἄνδρες grown-up *sons*, D. 25.88: metaph., Κόρον Ὕβριος υἱόν Orac.ap.Hdt.8.77: rarely of animals, *Ev.Matt.*21.5. 2. periphr., υἷες Ἀχαιῶν, for Ἀχαιοί, Il. 1.162, al.; cf. παῖς 1. 3. 3. generally, *child*, and so υἱ. ἄρρην male *child*, *Apoc.*12.5, *PSI*9.1039.36 (iii A.D.). 4. freq. in Lxx in periphrases (Hebraisms with various meanings), υἱὸς ἐτῶν ἑκατόν 100 *years old*, *Ge.*11.10, al.; υἱοὶ ἀδικίας 2*Ki.*7.10; υἱοὶ θανατώσεως 1*Ki.* 26.16; υἱοὶ τῶν συμμίξεων *hostages*, 4*Ki.*14.14; so υἱὸς εἰρήνης *Ev. Luc.*10.6. 5. in some dialects, including the Ion. Prose of Hdt., υἱός is replaced by παῖς: υἱός is rare in Trag., A.*Th.*609, *Fr.* 320, E.*Or.*1689 (anap.), al., and 7 times in S.:—Hom. has both words in this sense. 6. as a general term of affection, *PGiss.*68.2 (ii A.D.), *POxy.*1219.2 (iii A.D.); υἱέ, an author's address to the reader, Lxx *Pr.*1.8, al. 7. δάμου υἱός, υἱὸς πόλεως, Ἑλλάδος, as titles of honour, *SIG*804.10 (Cos, i A.D.), 813*A*,*B* (Delph., i A.D.), 854 (Eleusis, i A.D.). 8. υἱοὶ ἀνθρώπων *sons* of men, periphr. for *men* (cf. supr. 2,4), Lxx*Ps.*89(90).3; οἱ υἱοὶ τῶν ἀ. ib.*Ge.*11.5, *Ev.Marc.*3. 28; υἱὸς ἀνθρώπου *man*, Lxx*Ez.*2.1,3, al.; of the Messiah, ib.*Da.*7. 13, *Apoc.*14.14; used by Jesus of himself, *Ev.Matt.*8.20, al. (by Stephen recalling the words of Jesus, *Act.Ap.*7.56). 9. υἱοὶ Θεοῦ *sons* of God, implying *inheritors of the nature* of God (cf. supr. 4), *Ev.Matt.*5.9, cf. 45, *Ev.Luc.*6.35; implying *participants in the glory* of God, ib.20.36. b. of Jesus, τὸ γεννώμενον κληθήσεται υἱὸς Θεοῦ ib. 1.35; ὁ Χριστός, ὁ υἱὸς τοῦ Θεοῦ, *Ev.Matt.*26.63, cf. *Ev.Jo.*1.34. c. Θεοῦ υἱός, = Lat. *Divi* (sc. *Caesaris*) *filius*, patronymic of Augustus, *BGU*543.3 (27 B.C.), *PTeb.*382.21 (i B.C.), *IG*12(3).174.2 (Epist. ad Cnidios, 5 A.D.). [Hom. sts. has the first syll. short in nom., voc. and acc. sg., οὐδὲ Δρύαντος υἱός Il.6.130; Ἀμφιτρύωνος υἱός Od.11.270; Ποδῆς υἱὸς Ἠετίωνος Il.17.575, cf. 590; Ἀνθεμίωνος υἱόν 4.473; Σελάγου υἱόν 5.612; Ἕκτορ, υἱὲ Πριάμοιο 7.47; and Πηλῆος υἱός, Μηκιστῆος υἱός seem to be the better readings in 1.489, 2.566: in these places some other form ought perh. to be restored, but none of the known forms has a short ῠ: ὑός has ῡ in *IG*1².585 (vi B.C.), 828 (v B.C.), 2. 2338, 2².4319 (both iv B.C.); Simon. l. c. seems to have used a monosyll. nom. υἷς, and Hdn.Gr. may have read it as ὗις (◡◡), but this is uncertain, as in Sch.Il.5.266 he seems to say that ὗις (υἷις cod.) does not occur.] (Prob. from *sū-yú-s, cf. Skt. *sūte* 'procreate', Tocharian (A-dial.) *se*, (B-dial.) *soyä* 'son'; different suffix in **sū-nu-s*, Skt. *sūnús*, etc., and in **sū-nu-s*, OE. *sunu*, etc (all = *son*); **sūyú-* perh. became **sūwyú-*, then **suiwú-*; υἱός and υἱόν perh. by dissimilation from υἱύς υἱύν, since the *o*-stem forms appear first where υ-υ would otherwise be repeated; ὑῖς (ὗις?) may be another dissimilation; the precise origin of υἷος υἷι υἷες etc. is uncertain.)

**υἱόω**, (υἱός) *make into a son*, Ael.*Fr.*180:—Med., *adopt as one's son*, Nic.Dam.128J.:—Pass., Suid.

**υἷς**, Adv. *as far as*, *SIG*1 (Abu-Simbel, vi B.C.): cf. υἱ, ὥσπερ. II. v. υἱός.

**ὑϊσμός**, ὁ, (ὑΐζω) *squealing* or *grunting of swine*, Poll.5.87.

**υἱων-εύς**, έως, ὁ, = sq., Hsch. ❀ **-ός**, ὁ, *grandson*, Il.2.666, Od. 24.515, Theoc.17.23, *IG*5(1).1450 (Messene, i A.D.), *POxy.*261.7 (i A.D.), *SIG*829*A* (Delph., ii A.D.), Plu.*Publ.*14, etc.:—fem. **υἱωνή**, ἡ, J.*BJ*1.22.1; less Att. than ὑϊδοῦς and ὑϊδῆ, Moer.p.379P., Thom. Mag.p.362R.

**υἵωσις**, εως, ἡ, = υἱοθεσία, Ael.*Fr.*180 (pl.).

❀ **ὑκερός**, ὁ, = ἐκυρός (with vowel-transposition), Keil-Premerstein *Zweiter Bericht* Nos.146,151; fem. **ὑκερά**, ἡ, ib.232.

**ὕκης** [ῡ], ὁ, *a sea-fish*, Antim.ap.Ath.7.304e (om. Kinkel), Philet. 20, Call.*Frr.*72,156; also as fem. (perh. fr. nom. ὕκη), ὕκας ἀγελήϊδας Numen.ap.Ath.7.327cd, 327b; also **ὗκος**, or **ὕκος**, ὁ, Hsch.: said by Zenod.ap.Ath.7.327c to be Cyren. for ἐρυθρῖνος, by Hermipp. Hist.ibid. (= *Fr.*74) to be = ἰουλίς.

**ὕκιστρον**, τό, = Lat. *ambitiones*, dub. in *Gloss.*

**ὑκσώς**, = βασιλεῖς ποιμένες, in the sacred language of Egypt, Man. ap.J.*Ap.*1.14.

**ὕλαγ-μα** [ῠ], ατος, τό, *bark* or *yelp of a dog*, κυνῶν ὑλάγματα E.*IT* 293: metaph., νηπίοις ὑλάγμασιν, of angry words, A.*Ag.*1631, cf. 1672 (troch.). **-μός**, ὁ, *barking, baying*, Il.21.575, Arist.*HA*536ᵇ30, Aen.Tact.22.14; κλαγγῇ καὶ ὑ. X.*Cyn.*4.5.

**ὑλᾰγωγ-έω** [ῡ], *carry wood*, D.42.7, Poll.7.109:—hence **-ία**, ἡ, *carrying of wood*, **-ός**, όν, *carrying wood*, ib.101.

**ὑλάδια**, τά, *a kind of figs*, f.l. in Ath.3.78a.

**ὑλάζομαι** [ῡ], *fetch* or *carry wood*, *IG*2².1035.38,59, 1177.19, Poll. 7.109, Hsch.

❀ **ὑλαῖος** [ῡ], α, ον, (ὕλη) *belonging to the wood* or *forest, savage*, θήρ Theoc.23.10; ἤθη Ael.*NA*16.10; ἀνθοσύνη, i.e. weeds, *AP*11.365 (Agath.):—**Ὑλαία**, Ion. **-αίη**, ἡ, a *wild* district on the Borysthenes, Hdt.4.9, etc. II. *material, corporeal*, Zos.Alch.p.114B., Procl.*H.* 1.3. b. *concerned with matter*, θεοί Iamb.*Myst.*5.14, Dam.*Pr.*134; *belonging to* ὕλη, opp. ἐμπύριος and αἰθέριος, Procl.*Theol.Plat.*4.39.

**ὑλᾰκ-άω**, poet. collat. form for ὑλάω, ὑλακτέω, only in Ep. part. ὑλακόωντες [ῡ], Opp.*C.*3.281. **-ή** [ῠ], ἡ, *barking, howling*, Poetae ap. Pl.*Lg.*967d, A.R.3.749, *AP*6.167 (Agath.), etc.; also in late Prose, Plu.*Cim.*18, Luc.*VH*1.32, prob. l. in Ant.Lib.23.2. **-όεις**, εσσα, εν, *howling*, χόλος Opp.*H.*1.721. [ῡ in dact. verse.]

**ὑλᾰκόμωρος**, ον, *always barking, howling*, κύνες Od.14.29, 16.4; μόθον ὑ. Nonn.*D.*36.197. (For the ending -μωρος, cf. ἐγχεσίμωρος, ἰόμωροι, σινάμωρος.) [ῡ in dact. verse.]

❀ **ὑλακτ-έω** [ῠ], used only in pres. and impf., exc. that Luc.*Nec.*10 has aor. ὑλάκτησα: (ὑλάω):—*bark, bay, howl*, of dogs, ἱστάμενοι δὲ μάλ' ἐγγὺς ὑλάκτεον Il.18.586; ἀγαθός γ' ὑλακτεῖν Ar.*V.*904; ὑ. περιτρέχων Eup.207 (of a man compared to a dog); of hounds, *give tongue*, ὑ. περὶ τὰ ἴχνη X.*Cyn.*3.5, cf. 9.2. 2. metaph., κραδίη δέ οἱ ἔνδον ὑλάκτει *howled for rage*, Od.20.13; of a hungry stomach, *yelp for food*, νηδὺς ὑλακτοῦσα *AP*6.89 (Maec.). b. c. acc. cogn., τοιαῦθ' ὑλακτεῖ S.*El.*299; ἄμουσ' ὑλακτῶν *howling* his uncouth songs, E.*Alc.*760. II. trans., *bark at*, τινα Ar.*V.*1402, Isoc.1.29, Theoc.6.29: metaph., *bark* or *snarl at*, Plb.16.24.6; hence Vespasian called the Cynic Demetrius κύνα ὑλακτοῦντα, D.C.66.13. **-ητής**, οῦ, ὁ, *a barker*, θεῖον ὑ. δήμου κύνα, of Heraclitus, *AP*7.479 (Theodorid.). **-ιάω**, = ὑλακτέω, Q.S.2.375, in Ep. part. ὑλακτιόωντες. **-ικός**, ή, όν, *disposed to bark*, Arist.*Phgn.*807ᵃ19, Luc. *BisAcc.*33; ζῷον Ph.1.352.

**ὑλᾰσία** [ῡ], ἡ, *gathering of wood*, *IG*2².1177.18.

**ὑλάσκω** [ῠ], = ὑλακτέω, prob. in A.*Supp.*877 (lyr.); pres. **ὑλάσσω** Charito6.4, Eust.1791.64; aor. ὕλαξα D.C.63.28.

**ὕλασμα** [ῠ], ατος, τό, = ὕλαγμα, Cyran.42 (pl., s. v. l.).

**ὕλασσα**· ἡ ξυλ(ε)ία, καὶ φρυγανισμός, Hsch. (Either f.l. or Thess. for ὑλασία; cf. γυμνασσαρχεἰσαντα *IG*9(2).620.3.)

**ὑλάστρια** [ῡ], ἡ, *she who gets* or *fetches wood*, Phot.

**ὑλάω** [ῠ], = ὑλακτέω, used only by Poets and only in pres. and impf., *bark, bay*, of dogs, κύνες οὐχ ὑλάουσιν, ἀλλὰ περισσαίνουσι Od. 16.9; κύνων.. ἄνδρ' ἀγνοιήσασ' ὑλάει 20.15; θεσπέσιον ὑλάοντες Theoc. 25.70:—Med., κύνες οὐχ ὑλάοντο Od.16.162. 2. metaph. of a man, *howl*, ἢ μάτην ὑλῶ (so Herm. for ὑλακτῶ); S.*Fr.*61 (lyr., dub.); of Cassandra, μάτην ὑλάουσα Tryph.421. II. trans., *bark* or *bay at*, τινα Od.16.5 (so perh. 20.15, v. supr.).

**ὑλειώτης** [ῡ], ου, ὁ, (ὕλη) *forester*, epith. of Pan, *AP*6.106 (Zon.).

**Ὑλέτης**, ου, ὁ, = *Silvanus*, *Gloss.*

**Ὑλεύς**, έως, ὁ, name of a dog, *Ringwood*, X.*Cyn.*7.5.

**ὕλη** [ῡ], ἡ, *forest, woodland*, Il.11.155, Od.17.316, *Ep.Jac.*3.5, etc.; γῆν.. δασέαν ὕλῃ παντοίῃ Hdt.4.21; ἀπ' ὕλης ἀγρίης ζώειν Id.1.203; ὕλα ἀεργός virgin *forest*, *Berl.Sitzb.*1927.167 (Cyrene); τὰ δένδρα καὶ ὕλη fruit-trees and *forest-trees*, Th.4.69 (cf. δένδρον); not only of *forest-trees*, but also of *copse, brushwood, undergrowth* (cf. ὕλημα), directly opp. to timber-trees, X.*An.*1.5.1, *Oec.*16.13, 17.12, *PSI*6.577.8 (iii B.C.), Sor.1.40: also in pl., *h.Cer.*386, Hecat.291J., Mosch.3.88, Plb. 5.7.10, D.S.3.48, D.H.*Th.*6, Str.5.1.12, 15.1.60, Plu.*Pyrrh.*25, *Cat. Ma.*21, *Comp.Cim.Luc.*3, Luc.*Prom.*12, *Sacr.*10, *Am.*12, Babr.12.2, al., Nonn.*D.*3.69,252, 16.91, 36.70, etc. II. *wood cut down*, Od.5. 257 (cf. III); *firewood, fuel*, Il.7.418, 23.50,111, al., Od.9.234, Hdt.4. 164, 6.80; *brushwood*, Id.7.36, Th.2.75, etc.; *timber*, ὕ. ναυπηγησίμη Pl.*Lg.*705c; ναυπηγήσιμος καὶ οἰκοδομική Thphr.*HP*5.7.1, cf. *IG*4²(1). 102.50 (Epid., iv B.C.); also, *twigs* for birds' nests, Arist.*HA*559ᵃ 2. III. *the stuff* of which a thing is made, *material*, (perh. so of wood), Od.5.257; rarely of other *material*, as metal, οἱ παρ' ἄκμονι.. ὕλην ἄψυχον δημιουργοῦντες Plu.2.802b (cf. S.*Fr.*844, but ὕλη is Plutarch's word): generally, *materials*, *PMasp.*151.91 (vi A.D.). 2. in Philosophy, *matter*, first in Arist. (Ti.Locr.93b, al. is later); defined as τὸ ὑποκείμενον γενέσεως καὶ φθορᾶς δεκτικόν, *GC*320a2; as τὸ ἐξ οὗ γίγνεται, *Metaph.*1032a17; οὐσία ἥ τε ὕ. καὶ τὸ εἶδος καὶ τὸ ἐκ τούτων ib.1035a2; opp. as δυνάμει τόδε τι to τόδε τι ἐνεργείᾳ, ib. 1042a27; opp. ἐντελέχεια, ib.1038b6: in later philosoph. writers, mostly opp. to the intelligent and formative principle (νοῦς), Procl. *Inst.*72, etc.; ὕ. τῶν ἀριθμῶν Iamb.*Comm.Math.*4. 3. *matter* for a poem or treatise, ὕ. τραγική, ποιητικαὶ ὗλαι, Plb.2.16.14, Longin. 13.4, cf. 43.1, Vett.Val.172.1, etc.; ἡ ὑποκειμένη ὕ. the subject-*matter*, Arist.*EN*1094b12, cf. Phld.*Rh.*2.124S. 4. ὕ. ἰατρική *materia medica*, Dsc.tit.; so ὕλη alone, *materia medica*, Id.1 *Prooem.*, Gal. 17(2).181; ὗλαι τῆς τέχνης ibid., cf. 6.77, Sor.1.83,110, 2.15,28; ἡ ὕ. τῶν ὁπλομαχικῶν ἐνεργειῶν Gal.6.157. b. ἡ μέση ὕλη the middle *range of diet*, Sor.1.46, 2.15; τροφιμωτέρα ὕλη Id.1.95, cf. 36. 5. pl., *material resources*, βασιλικαὶ ὗλαι Ph.1.640. IV. *sediment*, Ar.*Fr.*879, cf. Sch.Ar.*Pl.*1086,1088 (hence ὑλίζω (ἀφ-, δι-), ὑλώδης II); *mud*, *slime*, *UPZ*70.9 (ii B.C.); ὕλη, ὕλει, and ἰλυῖ are cj. for ὕδει in Thgn.961. 2. *matter* excreted from the human body, Sor.1.22,23,25, al.; ἡ ὕ. τῶν ἐμπυημάτων Gal.18(2). 256; *phlegm*, *catarrh*, *PMed.* in *Arch.Pap.*4.270 (iii A.D.).

**ὑλήεις** [ῡ], εσσα, εν, but ὑλήεις as fem. in Od.1.246; ὑλήειν as neut., Choerob. *in Theod.*2.214H., cj. in Archil.74.9; Dor. **ὑλάεις** (v. infr.): (ὕλη):—*woody*, *wooded*, πρών Il.17.748; Ζάκυνθος, Νήϊον, Od.1.246,186; ὄρος, Ἴδη, Hes.*Th.*484,1010; ὑλᾶεν πόντου πρόβλημα S.*Aj.*1218 (lyr.); ἀν' ὑλάεντα νάπη E.*Hel.*1303 (lyr.); πλόος, ἀταρπὸς ὑ., *through the wood* or *dense growth*, Antim.62, *AP*10.22 (Bianor). 2. *dwelling in the woods*, ib.9.524.21.

**ὑληκοίτης** [ῡ], ου, ὁ, *one who lodges in the wood*, Hes.*Op.*529.

**ὕλημα** [ῡ], ατος, τό, (ὕλη) mostly in pl., *woody plants*, esp. of *shrubs*, *bushes* (including τὰ φρυγανικὰ καὶ θαμνώδη), Thphr.*HP*1.5.3 (cj. for κλήματα), cf. 1.6.7, 1.10.6, 3.3.6; opp. δένδρα and ποώδη, ib. 4.4.5: sg., ib.9.16.4:—hence **ὑληματικός**, ή, όν, *belonging to the class of* ὕλημα, Id.*CP*6.11.10.

**ὑληνόμος** [ῡ], ον, = ὑλονόμος, S.E.*P.*1.56.

**ὑληουργός** [ῡ], όν, poet. for ὑλουργός, A.R.2.80.

**ὑληρεύς**· νομεὺς ἐν ὕλῃ φυλάττων, Hsch.

**ὑλησκόπος**, v. ὑλοσκόπος.

**ὑλητήρ**, ῆρος, ὁ, perh. *a kind of wine* (cf. sq.), *BGU*1069 ii 7 (iii A.D.).

**ὑλῆτις**· οἴνου εἶδος, Hsch. (Fort. ὑλίτης secund. ord. litt.)

**ὑλητόμος** [ῡ], ον, Dor. ὑλᾱτόμος, = ὑλοτόμος, Theoc.17.9.

**ὑληφορέω**, **-φόρος**, = ὑλοφορέω, -φόρος (qq.v.).

**ὑληώρης** [ῡ], ου, ὁ, = ὑλώδης, εὐναί Nic.*Th.*55.

**ὑληωρός** [ῡ], όν, (οὖρος (B)) *watching the wood*, of Pan and the Nymphs, A.R.1.1227, *AP*9.337 (Leon.): cf. ὑλωρός, ὑληρεύς.

**ὑλιάριος**, v. βελιάριος.

**ὑλίας**· τοὺς καρπατίνους τόμους, Hsch.

**ὑλῐβάτης** [ῡ, ᾰ], ου, Dor. **-τᾱς**, ὁ, epith. of τράγος (ταῦρος Eust., unmetrically), Antiph.133.3 (anap., cod.A Ath.; ἠλιβάτας Eust.); also δέλφακας **ὑλιβάτους** Anaxil.12 (lyr., cod.A Ath.): perh. = *mud-walker* (ὗλις), esp. in Anaxil. l.c., but ἠλιβάτας, -τους are prob. in both places: ὑλιβάταισι occurs with little context in *IG*2².4762 (i/ii A.D.).

**ὑλιγγες**· λόγχαι, Hsch.

**ὑλῐγενής** [ῡ], ές, dub. l. in Nicaenet.1.7.

**ὑλίζω** [ῡ], *filter*, *strain*, *PMag.Lond.*46.71, *PSI*4.297.17 (prob. v A.D.):—Pass., δι' ὀθονίου, διὰ τῆς τέφρας ὑλίζεσθαι, Dsc.3.7, *Placit.*3. 16.5; τὸ ἀφθόνως ὑλιζόμενον ἐν σπηλαίοις Dsc.5.98 codd. (ὑετιζόμενον cj. Wellmann): cf. ἀφ-, διυλίζω. II. ὑ. τὰς ῥῖνας *wipe* the nose (cf. ὕλη IV. 2), Cratin.354. (Acc. to Gramm. from ὗλις (q.v.), transposed for ἰλύς, *EM*180.10; cf. ὕλη IV.)

**ὑλικός** [ῡ], ή, όν, (ὕλη) *of* or *belonging to matter*, *material*, ὑλικὴ οὐσία Arist.*Metaph.*1044a15, 1049a36, *Stoic.*2.144, etc.; ὑ. ἀρχή Arist. *PA*640b5: τὸ ὑ. Id.*Metaph.*1035a8, Plot.1.6.5: Comp., Id.3.5.9. Adv. -κῶς, opp. ἐντελεχείᾳ, Arist.*Metaph.*1078a31:—cf. ὕλη III. 2. II. Subst. **ὑλικόν**, τό, perh. *woodwork*, εἰς τὰν ἐπισκευὰν τῶν τάφων κ[αὶ τοῦ] ὑλικοῦ *Annuario* 8/9.322 (Rhodes, i B.C.).

**ὑλίμη**· μάχη τις, Hsch.

**ὕλιμος** [ῡ], ον, *of the forest*, φόβη E.*Fr.*495.34; νάπη prob. in Id. *Ba.*1084.

**ὗλις**, εως, ἡ, *mud*, *IG*2².2498.9 (iv B.C.), *PLille* 3.19 (iii B.C., gen. υλ[..]s), Lxx *Ps.*39(40).3, *EM*180.10 (where ὗλις parox.): v. ὑλίζω fin., ὕλη IV. 1 fin. [υλιν may be an engraver's error in *IG* l.c. for ἰλύν, which is found in the similar passage *IG*1².94.20,23 (v B.C.).]

**ὑλισμός**, ὁ, *fusio*, *Gloss.*

**ὑλιστάγιον** [ᾰ], τό, *stand for a strainer*, *PLond.*2.191.15 (ii A.D.).

**ὑλισ-τήρ** [ῡ], ῆρος, ὁ, (ὑλίζω) *filter*, *colander*, Dsc.2.101, Ath.Med. ap.Orib.5.5.1, *PLond.*2.191.15 (ii A.D.). ❋**-τήριον** and **-τριον**, τό, = foreg., both in Sch.Nic.*Al.*493, the latter in *POxy.*599 (i/ii A.D., pl., s.v.l.). **-τήριος**, α, ον, *strained*, γλεῦκος prob. cj. for αὐλητήριον in *Trag.Adesp.*420. **-τικόν**, *fusionaticum*, *Gloss.* **-τός**, ή, όν, *strained* or *filtered*, Dsc.*Eup.*2.36, *Sammelb.*4425 ii 16, al. (ii A.D.), *PFay.*95.13 (ii A.D.). **-τριον**, τό, v. ὑλιστήριον.

❋**ὑλίτης**, v. ὑλῆτις.

**ὕλλος**, ὁ, a fish, Cyran.39. 2. the *Egyptian ichneumon*, *Pharaoh's rat*, Tim.Gaz. in *Hermes* 3.25.

**ὑλο-βάτης** [ῡ, ᾰ], ου, Dor. **-τας**, ὁ, *one who haunts the woods*, *APl.*4.233 (Theaet.), *AP*6.32 (Agath.). **-βίος**, ὁ, *living in the woods*, name of a sect of Indian devotees, being a literal translation of the Skt. *Vāna-prastha*, *one who retired to the forest*, being in the third stage of life, Megasth.ap.Str.15.1.60. **-γενής**, ές, *born in the forest* or *undergrowth*, Aenigm.ap.Ath.2.63b, Orph.*Fr.*247.36 (v. ὑδογενής).

**ὕλογος**· στρατός, Περγαῖοι, Hsch.

**ὑλο-γράφος** [ῡ, ᾰ], ον, *painting wood*, *writing upon wood*, Man.4. 342. **-δρόμος**, ον, *wood-ranging*, θῆρες Ar.*Th.*47; ἡ πιθήκη ὑλοδρόμος κέκληται Ael.*NA*6.26.

**ὕλοι**· σπόνδυλοι, Hsch. **ὑλοκάτοικος**, ὁ, *silvicola*, *Gloss.*

**ὑλό-κομος** [ῡ], ον, *thick-grown with wood*, νάπος E.*Andr.*284 (lyr.). **-κοπέω**, *peck wood*, of the σίττη, Arist.*HA*616b 25. **-κόπος**, ὁ, *woodcutter*, *Gloss.* **-κουρός** (on the accent, v. Hdn. Gr.1.202), ὁ, = ὑλοτόμος, Lyc.1111. ❋**-μᾰνέω**, *run to wood*, of the vine (cf. τραγάω II), Thphr.*CP*3.1.5, Sm.*Ho.*10.1, *Gp.*5.40.1, etc.; πεδία ὑλομανοῦντα *overgrown with thick wood*, Str.14.6.5: cf. φυλλομανέω. 2. metaph. of language, etc., *run riot*, ὑ. τὸ μυθῶδες Plu. 2.15e. **-μᾰνής**, ές, (μαίνομαι) *mad after the woods*, Hsch. (-μανεὶς cod.). **-μᾰχέω**, *fight in the woods*, App.*Mith.*103. **-μήτρα**· εἶδος σκώληκος, Hsch. ❋**-νόμος**, ον, *living in the woods*, θήρ Simon.(?)179.7; μέλιτται Arist.*HA*624b29; ζῷα ὑ. prob. for ἑλο- in Hp.*Vict.*2.49; Νύμφαι Orph.*H.*51.10: cf. ὑληνόμος.

❋**ὑλο-ξιδής**, gen. ῆ, ὁ, perh. *woodcutter*, *MAMA* 3.338 (Corycus). **-ομαι**, Pass., *to be materialized*, Dam.*Pr.*400, Simp. *in Ph.* 320.35. **-ποιὸς** αἰτία, *material* cause, Syrian. *in Metaph.*158. 26. **-ροδον**, τό, *wild rose*, *Gloss.* **-σκόπος**, ον, *watching over woods*, of Pan, *Inscr.Cret.*1.xvi 7 (Lato, ii/i B.C.), *AP*6.107 (Phil., ὑλησκόπῳ codd.). **-της**, ητος, ἡ, *materiality*, Plot.2.9.10, *Corp. Herm.*8.3, 12.22, Iamb.*Myst.*8.3.

**ὑλοτομ-έω** [ῡ], *cut* or *fell wood*, Hes.*Op.*422, D.H.4.44, Diusap.J. *AJ*8.5.3. **-ία**, ἡ, *felling of wood*, Arist.*Pol.*1258b31, *PLond.*3.1171. 58 (i B.C.), Ael.*NA*3.21. ❋**-ικός**, ή, όν, *of* or *for the felling of wood*: ἡ -κή (sc. τέχνη) *the woodman's art* or *trade*, D.L.3.100. **-ιον**, τό, *timber-market*, Str.13.1.51. **-ος** (parox.), ον, (τέμνω) *cutting* or *felling wood*, πελέκεις Il.23.114; τέκτων Lxx *Wi.*13.11. II. Subst. ὑλοτόμος, ὁ, *woodcutter*, *woodman*, Il.23.123, Hes.*Op.*807, S.*El.*98 (anap.), *IG*1².1084.5, Thphr.*HP*3.9.3, Gal.17(2).229, etc. III. τὸ ὑλότομον either *a plant cut in the wood* (cf. τέμνω III), used as a charm; or = *worm* (cf. φερέοικος), supposed to be the cause of pain in teething (οὐλοτόμοιο may be the right reading), *h.Cer.*229.

**ὑλο-τρᾰγέω** [ῡ], *eat wild roots and fruits*, Ael.*NA*16.21. **-τρᾰφής**, ές, *fed by matter*, *material*, Procl.*H.*3.9.

**ὑλουργ-έω** [ῡ], = ὑλοτομέω, Ael.*NA*7.22. **-ία**, ἡ, *the carpenter's art*, *carpentry*, Poll.7.101. **-ός**, όν, *working wood*, δρέπανα D.H. 3.73. II. Subst. ὑλουργός, ὁ, *carpenter* or *woodman*, E.*HF*241, J.*AJ*8.2.6.

**ὑλο-φάγος** [ῡ, ᾰ], ον, *feeding in the woods*, βοῦς Hes.*Op.*591, cf. Hp.*Vict.*2.49. II. *eating wood*, Agatharch.51 (of the Ethiopians), cf. D.S.3.24, Ant.Lib.22.5. **-φορβός**, όν, (φέρβομαι) *feeding in the woods*, E.*IT*261. **-φορέω**, *carry* or *gather wood*, Ph.2.86; **ὑληφορέω**, Phryn.*PS*p.116B. **-φόρος**, ον, *carrying wood*, *a wood-carrier*, *AP*9.335 (Leon.); οἱ ὑ., name of a play by Aristomenes:—also **ὑληφόρος**, ἡ, Ar.*Ach.*272. II. of a mountain, *wooded*, Plb.3.55.9. **-χᾰρέω**, (χαίρω) = ὑλομανέω, Aq.(?)*Is.*35.2.

**ὑλ-ώδης** [ῡ], ες, *woody*, *wooded*, νῆσος Th.4.8,29; πάγος S.*Ichn.* 215; ὄρος, λόφος, Dicaearch.2.1, Plu.*Marc.*29; ὁδοί Onos.6.7: τὰ ὑ. *wooded ground*, opp. τὰ ψιλά, X.*Cyn.*5.7. II. *turbid*, *muddy*, ὕδωρ Dsc.5.81; ποταμός, λίμναι, ῥεῖθρον, Plu.*Pyrrh.*21, *Sull.*20, *Brut.* 51: metaph., βίος David *Proll.*79.3: cf. ὕλη IV. 1. **-ῷος**, α, ον, *material*, ὑλῷοι λέγονται οἱ τήνδε τὴν ὕλην ἐξάπτοντες τῆς τῶν οὐρανίων Olymp. *in Alc.*p.19 C. (= Orph.*Fr.*353). ❋**-ωρέω**, *hold the office of* ὑλωρός, *IG*9(2).257 (Thessaly). **-ωρός**, ὁ, (οὖρος (B)) = ἀγρονόμος, *forester*, *ranger*, Arist.*Pol.*1321b30: cf. ὑληωρός.

**ὗμα**, ατος, τό, (ὕω) gloss on ὕσμα, Erot. (pl.).

**ὑμαί**, oxytone Adv. cited in Theognost.*Can.*158.

**ὑμᾶλιξ**, v. ὁμῆλιξ. **ὑμαρτέω**, v. ὁμαρτέω.

**ὑμεδᾰπός** [ῡ], ή, όν, (ὑμεῖς) *your countryman*, Hdn.Gr.1.478, Hld.10.11, Hsch., Phot., Suid.; cj. Casaubon in Ath.9.366a. (On the termination, v. ἀλλοδαπός, ποδαπός, ἡμεδαπός.)

**ὑμέες**, **ὑμεῖς**, etc., v. σύ. **ὑμέλαι**· στεῤῥαί, Theognost.*Can.* 22: **ὑμέλην**· στεῖραν, ἄγονον, Suid.

**ὑμεναϊκὸν** μέτρον, = – ◡◡ – ◡◡, Serv.*Centim.* (4.460 Keil).

❋**ὑμέναι-ος** [ῡ], ὁ, (Ὑμήν) *the wedding* or *bridal song*, sung by the bride's attendants as they led her to the bridegroom's house, Il.18. 493, Hes.*Sc.*274, A.*Ag.*707 (lyr.), E.*IA*1036 (lyr., s.v.l.): pl., παμφώνων ἰαχὰ ὑμεναίων Pi.*P.*3.17, cf. E.*Alc.*922 (anap.), etc.: Aeol. **ὑμήναος** Sapph.91, *Epigr.Gr.*418.7 (Cyrene): a form **ὑμήναιος** in Call. *Aet.*3.1.43. 2. *wedding*, S.*OT*422, E.*Ion*1475 (lyr.): pl., S.*Ant.* 813 (lyr.), E.*IA*123 (lyr.), Phld.*Mus.*p.68 K. II. = Ὑμήν, *Hymen*, the god of marriage, addressed in wedding-songs, freq. in Trag. and Com. (lyr.), Ὑμὴν ὦ Ὑμέναι' ἄναξ E.*Tr.*314; Ὑμὴν ὦ Ὑμέναι' Ὑμήν ib.331; Ὑμὴν Ὑμέναι' ὦ Ar.*Pax*1335; Ὑμὴν ὦ, Ὑμέναι' ὦ Id.*Av.*1736,1742; Dor. Ὑμὰν ὦ Ὑμέναιε Theoc.18.58; hence the two are used as one word, ὑμὴν ὑμέναιον ἀείδων Opp.*C.*1.341. **-όω**, *sing the wedding-song*, A.*Pr.*557 (lyr.). 2. *wed*, *take to wife*, κούρας Theoc.22.179: prov., πρίν κεν λύκος οἶν ὑμεναιοῖ Ar.*Pax*1076 (hex.).

**ὑμενήϊος** [ῠ], ὁ, epith. of Dionysus, *AP*9.524.21.

**ὑμέν-ϊνος** [ῠ], η, ον, (ὑμήν) *of skin* or *membrane*, περιγλωττίς Clearch.21. **-ιον**, τό, Dim. of ὑμήν, Arist.*HA*497a21, 529a17, Ruf.*Ren.Ves.*11.6.

**ὑμενο-ειδής** [ῠ], ές, *membranaceous*, Hp.*Mul.*1.11, *Epid.*2.2.17, Arist.*HA*519b13, Dsc.1.106; cf. ὑμενώδης. **-πτερος**, ον, *membrane-winged*, ὄφεις Str.15.1.37; μυῖα Luc.*Musc.Enc.*1.

**ὑμεν-όστρᾰκος** [ῠ], ον, *of ware thin as a membrane*, ποτήρια Luc. *Lex.*7. **-όω**, *cover with a film*, Steph. *in Hp.*1.155 D.:—Pass., *become skin* or *membrane*, Hp.*Nat.Puer.*12, Gal.4.526. ❋ **-ώδης**, ες, = ὑμενοειδής, πόροι Arist.*HA*514a32; ὑστέραι ib.510b23; πλεύμων Id.*PA*669a34; [μήτρα] Thphr.*HP*1.6.1; τύπος, σῶμα, Sor.1.57,82; σύνδεσμοι, τένων, etc., Gal.*UP*1.15, 2.7, al. II. of liquids, *full of membranous substances* or *fibres*, οὖρον Hp.*Coac.*571.

**ὑμές** [ῠ], Dor. for ὑμεῖς; v. σύ.

❋ **ὑμέτερος** [ῠ], α, ον, Dor. and Ep. **ὑμός** (q.v.): (ὑμεῖς):—*your, yours*, Hom., etc.; with a Pron. added in gen., ὑμέτερος ἑκάστου θυμός the courage of each of *you*, Il.17.226; ὑμέτερος θυμὸς αὐτῶν *your* own mind, Od.2.138; ὑμέτερόνδε *to your house*, Il.23.86: τὸ ὑ. *your part, your business*, ἢν μὴ τὸ ὑ. αἴτιον γένηται Hdt.8.140.α', cf. Pl.*Grg.*522c; τὸ δ' ὑ. πρᾶξαι *your character* is to.., Th.1.70; τὰ ὑ. *your goods*, X.*Cyr.*3.2.12: in Prose sts. with the Article, ταῖς ὑμετέραις πόλεσι Pl.*Lg.*836c; and objectively, αἱ ὑ. ἐλπίδες hopes *raised by you*, Th.1.69; ἐπὶ τῇ ὑ. παρακελεύσει for the purpose of advising *you*, Pl.*Ap.*36d. II. poet. (never in Att.) sts. for σός, Sol.19.2, Call.*Del.*204,227, Nonn.*D.*5.340, *AP*5.292 (Paul. Sil.).

**ὑμέτιαι**· αἱ ἐπὶ ἑνὸς γεγενημέναι, Theognost.*Can.*22.

❋ **ὑμήν**, ένος, ὁ, *thin skin, membrane, caul*, of those which enclose the brain and heart, Arist.*HA*494b29, 519b4, al.; the foetus, ib. 586a20, Sor.1.57, Porph.*Gaur.*10.3; the bowels, Arist.*PA*673b4; the eye, Sor.1.103, Gal.*UP*10.7,9; ὑ. περικάρδιος *the pericardium*, ὑ. περιτόναιος *the peritoneum*, Poll.2.217,224; ὑ. ὑγρός the large dorsal *sinew* of cartilaginous fish, Ael.*NA*14.26; *the membrana nictitans* of birds, Arist.*PA*657a30; *the wing* of insects, ib.682b18. 2. *capsule* or *seed-vessel* of plants, Thphr.*HP*1.11.2, *Gp.*5.2.11; ὁ ἔξωθεν ὑ., opp. ἡ ἔνδοθεν σάρξ, of a date, Sor.2.13. 3. *thin plate of metal*, Ph.1.503, Ath.6.230d. 4. *parchment*, Aristeas 176, J.*AJ*12.2.11 (pl.). 5. in Eub 67.5 Pors. restored ὕφεσιν for ὑμέσιν. [ῡ A.R.4.1648.]

❋ **Ὑμήν**, ένος, ὁ, *Hymen*, the god of marriages, v. ll. cc. sub ὑμέναιος:—voc. Ὑμέν is cited from Call. (*Fr.*461). II. = ὑμέναιος I, *wedding-song*, Poll.3.37. [ῡ Theoc.18.58, whereas in Ὑμέναιος υ is short; but ῠ Opp.*C.*1.341 (text doubtful in E.*Tr.*331 (lyr.)), cf. Lat. Hȳmen, Hўmenaeus.]

**ὑμήναιος, ὑμήνᾶος**, v. ὑμέναιος.

**ὕμμες, ὔμμΐ, ὔμμιν, ὔμμε**, Aeol. and Ep. for ὑμεῖς, ὑμῖν, ὑμᾶς:—ὔμμι is elided in Od.17.241, 22.62; cf. σύ.

**ὔμμος**, α, ον, Aeol. for ὑμός, ὑμέτερος, A.D.*Pron.*113.8.

**ὑμν-ᾰγόρης**, εω, ὁ, *singer of hymns*, *AP*9.525.21. ❋ **-αγωγός**, ὁ, *leader of a hymn*, Kourouniotes Ἐλευσινιακά 1.225 (i B.C.). **-αοιδός** [ᾰ], ὁ, = ὑμνῳδός, Hdn.Gr.1.229, *IG*12(2).68.12 (Mytil., ii A.D.). **-άριον**, τό, Dim. of ὕμνος, Lyd.*Mens.*2.6. ❋ **-έω**, Ep. ὑμνείω Hes.*Op.*2; Ep. 3 pl. ὑμνεῦσιν *h.Ap.*190; fem. part. ὑμνεῦσα Hes. *Th.*11; Aeol. inf. ὔμνην to be restored for ὑμνεῖν in Alc.5.2; Lacon. 1 pl. subj. ὑμνίωμες Ar.*Lys.*1305 (lyr.): Aeol. 3 pl. impf. ὔμνην Sapph. *Supp.*20c.6: fut. ὑμνήσω Pi.*Parth.*2.11: (ὕμνος): I. with acc. of person or thing sung of, *sing of*, first in Hes.*Th.*11,33, freq. in *h.Hom.* (*h.Ap.*178, al.), Lyr. (Sapph. l.c., Alc. l.c., Pi.*N.*10.2, al., B.10.13, al.), and Trag. (E.*IT*367, etc.; θρήνοις..σ' ὑμνήσομεν Id.*Rh.* 976): also in Prose, *celebrate in a hymn, commemorate*, Ὦπιν Hdt. 4.35; τὰς τούτων ἀρετάς Lys.2.2, cf. B.5.33; [Παλαμήδη] ὑμνοῦσιν ὡς ..ἀπόλλυται X.*Mem.*4.2.33, etc.; τὸν θεόν *Act.Ap.*16.25; of the hymn itself, οὔτε..μέ τις ὕμνος ὕμνησεν S.*Ant.*815 (lyr.): c. dupl. acc., ἃ τὴν πόλιν ὕμνησα the points wherein *I praised* our city, Th. 2.42:—Pass., *to be celebrated in hymns*, of gods, *OGI*56.66 (Canopus, iii B.C.), Paus.9.23.3, etc.; also Ἀργεῖοι..τὰ πολλὰ πάντα ὑμνέαται (Ion. for -ηνται) *are* everywhere *praised*, Hdt.5.67; ὑμνηθήσεται πόλις E.*Ion* 1590; ἡ ὑμνουμένη χρυσῆ πλάτανος *famous*, X.*HG*7.1.38; αἱ ὑμνούμεναι φιλίαι Arist.*EN*1171a15; σοφία ἐν ἐξόδοις ὑμνεῖται Lxx *Pr.* 1.20: impers., ὑμνεῖτο δ' αἰσχρῶς foul *songs were sung*, *Com.Adesp.* 1203.5. 2. *descant upon*, in song or speech, ἐν κατηρεφεῖ στέγῃ ..ὑμνήσεις κακά S.*El.*382; τὰν ἐμὰν ὑμνεῦσαι (Dor. for -οῦσαι) ἀπιστοσύναν *ever singing of* my want of faith, E.*Med.*423 (lyr.):—Pass., Ἐτεοκλέης ἂν..ὑμνοῖτο..φροιμίοις πολυρρόθοις A.*Th.*7. 3. c. acc. cogn., *sing*, ᾆσμα, ὕμνον, Heraclit.15, A.*Ag.*1191: c. dupl. acc., παιᾶνα..ὑμνοῦσι..τὸν Λατοῦς γόνον E.*HF*688 (lyr.), cf. *SIG*711 *L* 12 (Delph., ii B.C.). II. *tell over and over again, harp upon, repeat, recite*, Pl.*Prt.*317a, *R.*549e, *Tht.*174e, etc.; ὡς.. Id.*R.*364a; ὑμνοῦσι τὸ γῆρας ὅσων κακῶν αἴτιόν [ἐστι] ib.329b; τὸν νόμον ὑμνεῖν *recite the form of* the law, Id.*Lg.*871a:—Pass., ὁ δ' εἶπε πρός με βαί', ἀεὶ δ' ὑμνούμενα (Sch. τὰ πολυθρύλητα) S.*Aj.*292. III. intr., *sing, chant*, ὡς ποιηταὶ ὑμνήκασι περὶ αὐτῶν Th.1.21; ὑμνῶν οὔποτ' ἔληγεν ὡς.. X.*Ages.*11.2. 2. in pass. sense, φῆμαι..ὑμνήσουσι περὶ τὰ ὦτα *will ring* in their ears, Pl.*R.*463d. [On the quantity, v. ὕμνος.]

**ὑμνηπολέω, ὑμνηπόλος**, v. ὑμνοπ-.

❋ **ὕμν-ησις**, εως, ἡ, *lauding, praising*, Lxx *Ps.*117(118).14, D.S.4. 7. **-ήστρια**, ἡ, fem. of ὑμνητής, *Ath.Mitt.*37.287 (Pergam., ii A.D.). **-ητέον**, *one must celebrate*, Luc.*Dem.Enc.*19: c. dupl. acc., *one must glorify as*, Pl.*Epin.*983e, cf. Dam.*Pr.*2. **-ητήρ**, ῆρος, ὁ, = sq., *AP*7.19 (Leon.), Opp.*H.*3.7. **-ητής**, οῦ, ὁ, *one who sings of* or *praises*, τυραννίδος Pl.*R.*568b; *performer of hymns*, *IG*2².2361.3. **-ητικός**, ή, όν, *laudatory*, ἡ ποιητική Str.10.3.10. **-ητός**, ή, όν, *sung of, praised, lauded*, εὐδαίμων καὶ ὑ. Pi.*P.*10.22, cf. 11.61, Lxx *Da.*3. 56. **-ήτρια**, ἡ, = sq., *Ath.Mitt.*35.458 (Pergam.), *IG*2².5100, 5131. **-ητρίς**, ίδος, ἡ, fem. of ὑμνητής, Poll.1.35 (v.l. -ήτριαι). **-ικός**, ή, όν, *consisting of a song of praise*, ὑ. εἰς [τὴν Κόρην] προσαγόρευσις *Milet.*7.64 (Didyma, ii/iii A.D.), cf. Phryn.*PS* p.58 B.

**ὑμνίωμες**, v. ὑμνέω.

**ὑμνο-άνασσα** [ᾰν], ἡ, *queen of song*, B.11.1. **-βρῦής**, ές, *full of hymns*, χώρα Philod.Scarph.19. **-γράφος** [ᾰ], ὁ, *composer of hymns*, of the Psalmist, Ph.1.264, Lxx 4 *Ma.*18.15; Μάτρις ὁ Θηβαῖος ὑ. Ptol. Heph.ap.Phot.*Bibl.*p.148 B.; Πλησίρροος ὁ Θεσσαλὸς ὁ ὑ. ibid. **-δῐδάσκᾰλος**, ὁ, *teacher of hymns*, *SIG*1115.26 (Pergam., i A.D.), *Ath. Mitt.*37.302 (ibid., ii A.D.), *Jahresh.*15.46 (Notium), prob. in *IG*5(1). 363 (Sparta). **-θέτης**, ου, ὁ, *composer of hymns, lyric poet*, Theoc. *Ep.*11, *AP*7.428.16 (Mel.), 12.257 (Id.); ὑ. στέφανος a garland *of minstrelsy*, ib.4.1.2, cf. 44 (Id.):—also **-θετήρ**, ῆρος, ὁ, *EM*177. 25. ❋ **-λογέω**, *sing hymns* or *praise*, Sm.*Ps.*64(65).9, *PLond.*3. 1029.3 (iii A.D.). II. *proclaim by hymns*, ὅτι.. Phld.*Mort.* 17. **-λογία**, ἡ, *hymn-singing*, Sm.*Jb.*33.26. **-λόγια**, τά, *Carmentalia*, *Gloss.* **-λογίζω**, = -λογέω, Mart.Cap.1.2 (γυμν- codd.). **-λόγος**, ον, *hymn-singing*, ἄνδρες *Supp.Epigr.*7.897 (Gerasa). ❋ **-ποιός**, όν, *making hymns*, Μοῦσα E.*Rh.*651: Subst. -ποιός, ὁ, *minstrel*, Id.*Supp.*180:—hence **-ποιέομαι**, *sing hymns of praise*, Sm.*Ps.*55(56).11. **-πολεύω**, *to be composing songs of praise*, *PLit.Lond.*38.2 (iii A.D.):—also **ὑμνηπολέω**, Hsch., Phot. ❋ **-πόλος**, ον, *composing songs of praise*, κεφαλή Phalar.*Ep.*78. 3. II. Subst. -πόλος, ὁ, *poet, minstrel*, Emp.146, Simon.184, *AP* 7.18 (Antip.Thess.), etc.; **ὑμνηπόλος**, ὁ, Suid., prob. in *IG*14.1014.1.

**ὕμνος**, ὁ, *hymn, ode*, in *praise* of gods or heroes (καί τι ἦν εἶδος ᾠδῆς εὐχαὶ πρὸς θεούς, ὄνομα δὲ ὕμνοι ἐπεκαλοῦντο Pl.*Lg.*700b; ὕμνους θεοῖς καὶ ἐγκώμια τοῖς ἀγαθοῖς Id.*R.*607a, cf. Arist.*Po.*1448b27), once in Hom., ἀοιδῆς ὕμνος Od.8.429 (folld. by Demodocus' song of the Wooden Horse, 499 sqq.); ὕμνῳ νικήσαντα φέρειν τρίποδ' Hes.*Op.*657; ἀνδρῶν τε παλαιῶν ἠδὲ γυναικῶν ὕμνον ἀείδουσιν *h.Ap.*161; freq. in Pi., ὕμνος πολύφατος, ἐπικώμιος, etc., *O.*1.8, *N.*8.50, al.; Θήρωνος Ὀλυμπιονίκαν ὕμνον *O.*3.3; and in B., ὑφάνας ὕμνον 5.10, cf. 6.11, al.; ὕμνοι θεῶν *to* or *in honour of* the gods, Pl.*Lg.*801d; τιμῶν θεὰν ὕμνοισιν E.*Hipp.*56; τοὺς χορούς..καὶ τοὺς ὕ. τῷ θεῷ ποιεῖτε D.21.51, cf. Pl.*Smp.*177a; ὕμνοι Δαυεὶδ *psalms* of David, Lxx 2 *Ch.*7.6; ψαλμοὶ καὶ ὕ. καὶ ᾠδαί *Ep.Eph.*5.19: in Trag. also of *mournful songs*, addressed to gods or heroes, τὸν δυσκέλαδον ὕ. Ἐρινύος A.*Th.*868 (lyr.), cf. *Pers.*620,625 (anap.), *Ch.*475 (lyr.); ὕ. ἐξ Ἐρινύων, δέσμιος φρενῶν, ἀφόρμικτος Id.*Eu.*331 (lyr.), cf. 306; ἐν ἀλύροις κλέοντες ὕμνοις E.*Alc.*447 (lyr.); ὕ. Ἅιδου, of one whose songs are death, Phryn. Com.69 (lyr.).—On ὕμνοι of various kinds v. Men.Rh.p.333 S.; ὁ κυρίως ὕ. πρὸς κιθάραν ᾔδετο ἑστώτων Procl.*Chr.*ap.Phot.*Bibl.*p.320 B., cf. Did.ap.*EM*777.9. [Most commonly ῡ, but only by position; ῠ proved by εὔῠμνος (q.v.), ὑμνῳδεῖ A.*Ag.*990 (lyr.), ὑμνήσω E.*Ba.*72 (lyr.).]

**ὑμνοτήιαι**· σύνοδοι τῶν ἐπ' ἔτος γεγαμημένων, Hsch.

**ὑμνο-τόκος**, ον, *producing hymns, musical*, *IG*5(1).315 (Sparta), Nonn.*D.*26.204. **-φῐλος**, ον, *loving songs of praise*, [Μοῦσαι] *Inscr.Perg.*184.

**ὑμνῳδ-άρχης**, ου, ὁ, *choir-master*, *Jahresh.*15.48 (Notium). **-εῖον**, τό, *building for choral singing*, *IGRom.*4.353b (Pergam., ii A.D.). ❋ **-έω**, *sing a hymn* or *song of praise*, Pl.*Lg.*682a, Lxx 1 *Ch.* 25.6: generally, *sing*, θρῆνον A.*Ag.*990 (lyr.). II. = χρησμῳδέω, E.*Ion*6; cf. ὑμνῳδία 2. [ῠ in A. l.c., v. ὕμνος fin.]

**ὑμνώδης**, ες, apparently = ὑμνῳδός, ἐνθεάτερος καὶ ὑμνώδης Philostr. *VA*5.21.

**ὑμνῳδ-ία**, ἡ, *singing of a hymn, hymning*, *CIG*2715a22 (Stratonicea), Porph.*Abst.*2.34: pl., E.*Hel.*1434, Ps.-Luc.*Philopatr.*26, Artem.1.56. 2. = χρησμῳδία, *prophetic strain*, E.*Ion*682 (lyr.). ❋ **-ός**, όν, *singing hymns*, κόραι Id.*HF*394 (lyr.); σοφὴν θεῶν ὑμνῳδόν Diog.Ath.1.5; ὑμνῳδοί, οἱ, *choral singers*, *Jahresh.* 11.103 (Pergam., i A.D.), 15.48 (Notium), *BMus.Inscr.*481*.296 (Ephesus), *CIG*3148.39 (Smyrna), etc.

**ὔμοι**, Adv., Aeol. for ὁμοῦ, Sapph.*Supp.*23.13, *Epigr.Gr.*988.3 (Balbilla). **ὔμοιος**, α, ον, Aeol. for ὅμοιος (q.v.).

**ὑμολογία**, ᾱ, Aeol. for ὁμ-, *Schwyzer* 644.13 (Aegae, iv B.C.).

**ὑμός** [ῠ], ά and ή, όν, Dor. and Ep. for ὑμέτερος, *your*, Il.5.489, 13.815, Od.1.375, 2.140, Hes.*Th.*662, *SIG*685.127 (Crete, ii B.C.). II. also for σός, Pi.*P.*7.15, 8.66, Orac.ap.D.S.8.29. Cf. ἁμός (A).

**ὑνάκιον**, τό, name of a garment, *PMasp.*6 ii 61,96 (vi A.D.).

**ὕναν**· τὴν εἰρήνην, Hsch.

❋ **ὑνεύχομαι**, = ἐπεύχομαι, *Schwyzer* 682.12 (Cypr.): cf. εὔχομαι.

**ὑνθύω**, Arc., = ἀναθύω (B) 2, τᾷ Κόρϝαι *IG*5(2).554 (Melpea, vi/v B.C.).

**ὔνιον** [ῠ], τό, Dim. of ὕνις, *PAmh.*2.143.11 (iv A.D.).

**ὕνις**, εως (ιος Hdn.Gr.2.761), ἡ, *ploughshare*, *PPetr.*2 p.133 (iii B.C.), *PCair.Zen.*782(a).37 (iii B.C.), *PStrassb.*118.15 (i A.D.), Corn. *ND*28, Babr.37.2, Plu.*Rom.*11, Artem.2.24, *Gp.*2.2.3, Sm.1 *Ki.*13. 20, *PTeb.*406.19 (iii A.D.), *PFlor.*134.3 (iii A.D.); also **ὕννις**, ὁ, Sch. Hes.*Op.*425, Hsch.; **ὕννη**, ἡ, Aesop.98b. (Plu.2.670a derives the word from ὗς, from the hog's nozzling and rooting.) [ῠ, *AP*6.104 (Phil.), 7.175,176 (both Antiphil.), 280 (Isid.), Babr. l.c., Hdn.Gr. l.c.; Suid. is in error when he says τὸ δὲ υ μακρόν.]

**ὑννάς**· αἶξ ἀγρία, Hsch.: also ὑννή (ὑννῆς cod.)· αἶξ, Id.

**ὑννῑμάχος** [ᾰ], ον, *fighting with a ploughshare*, Max.Tyr.30.6.

* **ὕννος**· πῶλος ὁ ἐν τῇ γαστρὶ νοσήσας. πρὶν κυηθῆναι, Hsch. (cf. γίννος, ἴννος). **ὑντετράστιαν**· κατεαγέν, Σαλαμίνιοι, Id.

* **ὑντίθημι**, Cypr. for ἀνα-τ., aor. ὑνέθηκε *Schwyzer* 682.12.

**ὕντωσε**· συμπαρῆσαν, Hsch. **ὕξον**· βοήθησον, Id. (i.e. perh. ὕξον = σῦξον, σοῦξον, cf. ἀπέσοιξεν· ἀπέσωσεν, Λάκωνες, Id.).

* **ὑο-βοσκός** [ῡ], ὁ, *swineherd*, Arist.*HA* 603ᵇ5: hence **-βοσκέω**, Moer.p.355 P. **-βότης**· συοβόσκης, Hsch.

**ὑοειδής** [ῡ], ές, *shaped like the letter* Υ, φάλαγξ Ascl.*Tact.*11.7. Adv. -δῶς, of the fission of a vein, Antyll.ap.Orib.7.7.1. II. esp. ὀστοῦν ὑ. the *hyoid* bone, at the base of the tongue, Ruf.*Onom.* 155, Gal.18(2).957, *UP*7.19, al., Poll.2.202.

**ὑο-θεσία, -θετος**, v. υἱο-.

**ὑολλός**· τόπος συῶν βορβορώδης, Hsch. (s. v.l., before ὑοβότης).

**ὑομεμνία**· ἑορτή τις ἐν Ἄργει, Hsch.

**ὑομουσία** [ῠ], ἡ, *swine's music, swinish taste in music*, Ar.*Eq.*986 (lyr.).

**ὑοποιία**, ἡ, v. υἱοποιία.

**ὑό-πρωρος** [ῠ], ον, of a ship, *having a beak turned up like a swine's snout*, Σάμαινα ναῦς ἐστιν ὑόπρωρος τὸ σίμωμα Plu.*Per.*26. **-πώλης**, ου, ὁ, *dealer in pigs*, Poll.7.187.

**ὑός**, ὁ, v. υἱός.

**ὑοσᾰλᾰκωνία** [ῠ], ἡ, (ὗς, σαλακωνία) *piggish ostentation*, prob. cj. in Ath.15.691f (ὀσα- codd.).

**ὑόσερις**, ἡ, *swine's endive, hawk's-beard, Crepis neglecta*, Plin.*HN* 27.90.

**ὑοσκῠᾰμ-άω** [ῡο], *to be mad from taking henbane*: *to be raving mad*, Pherecr.72:—in Hsch. -έω. **-ινος**, η, ον, *of henbane*, ἔλαιον Dsc.1.35. **-ος**, ὁ, (ὗς) *henbane, Hyoscyamus niger*, Hp. *Morb.*2.43, X.*Oec.*1.13, Dsc.4.68, *POxy.*1088.39 (i A.D.), Plu.*Demetr.* 20, Sor.2.41, *PHolm.*21.12, 25.5; other varieties, ὑ. μηλινοειδής, *H. aureus*, ὑ. λευκός, *H. albus*, Dsc. l. c.: also **ὑοσκύεμος**, *PMag.Osl.* 1.327.

**ὑόφθαλμος**, ὁ, = ἀστὴρ Ἀττικός, Ps.-Dsc.4.119.

**ὑοφορβ-εῖον** [ῠ], *porcinarium*, *Gloss.*; in later spelling, οἰκίαν σὺν -ίῳ *PLond.*3.978.5, al. (iv A.D.). **-ία**, ἡ, *pigsty*, ἔπαυλις ἐν ᾗ ὑ. *CPHerm.*44 (iii A.D.). **-ιον**, τό, = συοφόρβιον, *herd of swine*, *PSI*6.669.7 (iii B.C.), Str.4.4.3, 5.1.12. II. v. ὑοφορβεῖον. **-ός**, ὁ, *swineherd*, *PCair.Zen.*152.6 (iii B.C.), *PTeb.*5.171 (ii B.C.), Poll.7.187.

**ὑοχαί**· τὸ βορβορῶδες ὕδωρ, Hsch.

**ὑπά**, Aeol. for ὑπό, v. ὑπό init.

**ὑπᾰγᾰνακτέω**, *become somewhat wroth*, D.H.*Dem.*54, Hdn.2.7.2.

**ὑπαγγελεύς**, έως, ὁ, *messenger*, ἑπόμενος ὡς βασιλεῖ..ὑπαγγελεύς Jul.Laod. in *Cat.Cod.Astr.*1.136.

**ὑπάγγελος**, ον, *summoned by a messenger*, οὐκ ἄκλητος, ἀλλ' ὑ. A.*Ch.*838.

**ὑπάγγελτος**, ον *informed against*, Anon.ap.Suid.

* **ὑπαγκᾰλ-ίζω**, *clasp in the arms, embrace*, E.*Cyc.*498 (lyr.):—Pass., γένος ὑπηγκαλισμένη *having* them *clasped in her arms*, Id.*Heracl.* 42. **-ιος**, ον, *in the arms*, of a child, D.H.7.67. * **-ισμα**, ατος, τό, *that which is clasped in the arms, a beloved one*, of a wife or mistress, S.*Tr.*540; of a child, E.*Tr.*757: cf. παραγκάλισμα.

**ὑπαγκώνιον**, τό, *elbow-cushion*, Poll.6.10, Gal.18(2).503, Sm.*Ez.* 13.18.

**ὑπάγνῡμι**, *break underneath*, Opp.*H*4.653 (Pass.).

**ὑπᾰγόρ-ευσις**, εως, ἡ, *suggestion, advice, counsel*, J.*AJ*3.8.8, 17.4. 3, *POxy.*1497.9 (iii A.D.). 2. *idea, notion*, Gal.1.201. **-ευτικός**, ή, όν, *suggestive*, τινος S.E.*M.*8.201: Comp. -ώτερος Gal.10. 493. **-εύω**, the aor. being in Att. (but not in later Gr., cf. J.*AJ*3.5.3, etc.) ὑπεῖπον (q.v.), pf. ὑπείρηκα:—*dictate*, X.*Oec.*15.7 (Pass.), Plu. *Caes.*17; freq. in Pap., *BGU*592 ii 4 (ii A.D.), etc.; γράψαιτο ὑπαγορευθὲν Arist.*Top.*142ᵇ32: more generally, ἃ δεῖ ποιεῖν D.17.29; ἡ ὑπαγορευομένη διάθεσις the *given* state of health, Alex.Trall.12. II. *suggest*, ἐλπίδα, πρόφασιν, Str.1.2.32,39, cf. Marcellin.*Puls.*172, Gal.6. 314, Posidon.ap.Aët.6.2, etc.; θυσίας καὶ καθαρμούς Plu.*Marc.*29: folld. by inf., D.H.*Th.*19:—impers. in Pass., Epict.*Ench.*30. III. *imply, indicate without the use of a special word or form*, ξὺν νηΐ..ὑπαγορεύει ξὺν μιᾷ νηΐ A.D.*Synt.*72.17, cf. 278.12 (Pass.), al. IV. *reply*, gloss on ἀντιβληθέντος in Dinarchus, Harp., *AB*409 (Pass.). V. *enumerate*, Anon.Lond.11.42; *name, call by a title*, ἐν τῷ "περὶ μετοχῆς" ὑπηγορευμένῳ A.D.*Synt.*302.10, cf. 337.11; ταῦτα φρενιτικὰ εἶναι ὑπαγόρευε Herod Med. in *Rh.Mus.*58.71.

**ὑπαγορία**· συμβουλία, Hsch. (Perh. Dor. ὑπᾱ-, but found also as gloss on μακρηγορία, Id.) **ὑπάγορον**· κατὰ βίαν ὑπερήφανον, Id.

**ὑπάγροικος**, ον, *somewhat clownish*, S.E.*M.*6.50, Plu.2.710d (Comp.), Marcellin.*Puls.*126, etc.; -οτέρα διάλεκτος Ar.*Fr.*685 (anap.).

**ὑπάγρυπνος**, ον, *somewhat sleepless*, Hp.*Coac.*171.

**ὑπάγω** [ᾰ]: A. trans., *lead* or *bring under*, ὕπαγε ζυγὸν ὠκέας ἵππους *brought* them *under* the yoke, *yoked* them, Il.16.148, cf. 23. 291; ἵπποις (acc.) δ' ἄνδρες ὕπαγον ὑπ' ἅρματα Sapph.*Supp.*20a.17, cf. E.*Hipp.*1194 in *PLit.Lond.*73 (ἐπῆγε codd.); also simply, ἡμιόνους ὕπαγον Od.6.73. 2. *bring under one's power*, [οἱ θεοί] σε ὑπήγαγον ἐς χεῖρας τὰς ἐμάς Hdt.8.106; ὑ. τινὰς εἰς δουλείαν Luc.*Apol.*3:—Med., *bring under one's own power, reduce*, πόλιν Th.7.46; τοὺς Θρᾷκας Luc.*DDeor.*18.1, etc. 3. *subsume*, ὑφ' ἓν μέρος λόγου τὰ ἄρθρα καὶ τὰς ἀντωνυμίας A.D.*Synt.*88.11, cf. 235.7 (Pass.); πάντα τῷ τῆς μανίας ὀνόματι Luc.*Abd.*29. 4. *bring forward in reply*, in Pass., A.D.*Conj.* 251.9, *Synt.*73.11. 5. *subject*, τὴν ἀρχομένην [διάθεσιν] τοῖς βοηθήμασιν Sor.2.38:—Pass., τῶν -ομένων τῇ διαίτῃ παθῶν Id.1.2. II. *bring* a person *before the judgement-seat* (the ὑπό refers to his being set *under* or *below* the judge), ὑ. τινὰ ὑπὸ δικαστήριον *bring* one *before* a court, i.e. *accuse, impeach* him, Hdt.9.93, cf. 6.72 (Pass.); ὑ. τινὰ ὑπὸ τοὺς ἐφόρους ib.82; οἱ -όμενοι εἰς ὑμᾶς X.*HG*2.3.28; ὑ. τινὰ ἐς δίκην Th.3.70; simply, ὑ. τινὰ ὡς ἐπιβουλεύοντα X.*HG*2.3.33; ὑ. τινὰ θανάτου on a capital charge, ib.2.3.12, 5.4.24; θανάτου ὑπὸ τὸν δῆμον Μιλτιάδεα *impeached* him before the commons on a capital charge, Hdt.6.136: c. dat., ὑ. τινὰς δικαστηρίοις Luc.*Fug.*11:—Med., τάνδ' ὑπάγεται Δίκα E.*El.*1155 (lyr., dub. l., δίκαν codd.):—Pass., Phld.*Rh.* 2.140 S.: c. dat., τοῖς τῆς..πεπρωμένης..νόμοις ὑπαχθέντα *IG*12(7). 240.24 (Amorgos, iii A.D.); ὁ πένης ὑπάγεται τῷ νόμῳ Lib.*Decl.*36 tit. III. *lead on by degrees*, τὰς κύνας X.*Cyn.*5.15, cf. 10.4; *draw* or *lead on* by art or deceit, Hdt.9.94; τινὰ ἐπὶ κῶμον E.*Cyc.* 507 (lyr.); ὑ. τοὺς πολεμίους εἰς δυσχωρίαν *draw* them *on* by pretended flight, X.*Cyr.*1.6.37; ὑ. τοὺς πολεμίους ὑποφεύγοντες ib.3.2. 8; τὸν ἐρῶντα τῷ ἐρωμένῳ ἀκολουθεῖν.., ὅπῃ ἂν ἐκεῖνος ὑπάγῃ Pl. *Euthphr.*14c; τίν' ὑπάγεις μ' ἐς ἐλπίδα; E.*Hel.*826; ὁ θεὸς ὑπῆγεν αὐτόν, ἵνα ἀφικόμενος..δοίη δίκην Lys.6.19; ἡ πέρδιξ..ἀπὸ τῶν ᾠῶν ὑπάγει (sc. ἄνθρωπον) Arist.*HA*613ᵇ32: c. inf., σ' ὑπήγαγον εἰς χεῖρας ἐλθεῖν *so as to* come, E.*Andr.*428:—Med., *lead on for one's own advantage*, but freq. much like the Act., *lead on*, ἐλπίσιν ὑπαγαγέσθαι τινά Isoc.5.91, cf. X.*An.*2.4.3; ὑ. Θετταλοὺς εἰς δουλείαν *reduce* them, D.8.62; ὑ. τινὰς ἐς μάχην, ἐς φιλίαν, D.C.36.4, 42.39; ἐς φόρου συντέλειαν Hdn.6.2.1; *give* one *a lead* in speech, E.*Andr.*906, cf. X.*An.* 2.1.18:—Pass., κατὰ μικρὸν ὑπαχθεὶς Isoc.5.1; [ἐλπίσι καὶ φενακισμοῖς] ὑπαχθέντες D.5.10 (v.l. ἐπ-); ὑπὸ τῆς ἀπάτης καὶ τῶν ἀλαζονευμάτων Aeschin.1.178, etc.; εἰς ἔχθραν ὑπηγμένος ὑπό τινος D.18.188; ἐκ λοιδορίας εἰς πληγάς Id.54.19. (In this sense, ἐπάγω is freq. v.l.) IV. *take away from beneath, withdraw*, τινὰ ἐκ βελέων Il.11.163; ὕπαγε τὰς ἀκροβελίδας Archipp.10:—Pass., ὑπαγομένου κάτωθεν τοῦ χώματος Th.2.76. 2. *draw off*, τὸ στράτευμα Id.4.127; ὑπήγαγεν Κύριος τὴν θάλατταν Lxx *Ex.*14.21. 3. *carry off below*, ὑ. τὴν κοιλίην *purge* the bowels, Hp.*Morb.*3.17, Aret.*CA*1.10; ὑ. τὴν γαστέρα Phryn.279, Gal.6.353, al.; v. infr. B. III. 4. *bring down* a bandage, Sor.*Fasc.*2: c. dat., *bring under*, τῷ κοίλῳ τοῦ ποδὸς ib.59.

B. intr., *go away, withdraw, retire*, ὑπάγω φρένα τέρψας Thgn. 921, cf. Ar.*Av.*1017, *AP*9.341 (Glauc.); of an army, *draw off* or *retire slowly*, Hdt.4.120,122, Th.4.126; of the lion, ὑπάγει βάδην Arist.*HA*629ᵇ17; ἂν φυτεύῃ καὶ ὑπάγῃ if he..*goes away*, *IG*12(7). 62.54 (Amorgos, iv B.C.); ὑπάγει αὔριον he *is going* (= *leaving, setting out*) to-morrow, *POxy.*1291.11 (i A.D.); ὑπάγοντι εἰς Ἑρμοῦ πόλιν *PLond.*1.131.155,218, al. (i A.D.). II. *go forwards, draw on*, ὕπαγ' ὦ, ὕπαγ' ὦ *on with you!* E.*Cyc.*52 (lyr.); ὕπαγε, τί μέλλεις; Ar. *Nu.*1298; ὑπάγεθ' ὑμεῖς τῆς ὁδοῦ Id.*Ra.*174; ὑ. εἰς τοὔμπροσθεν Eup.79: also of an army, X.*An.*3.4.48, 4.2.16. 2. later, in pres., simply *go*, opp. ἔρχομαι 'come', ὕπαγε Σατανᾶ *Ev.Matt.*4.10; ὕπαγε, δεῖξον.. *Ev.Marc.*1.44; ἦσαν οἱ ἐρχόμενοι καὶ οἱ ὑπάγοντες πολλοί ib.6.31; ποῦ ὑπάγεις; *Ev.Jo.*16.5; ἐν πλοίῳ ὑπάγοντι ἰς Ταπόσιριν *Sammelb.*7357.8 (iii A.D.); ὕπαγε ἰς πάντα τόπον ib.7452.7,19 (iii A.D.); καθ' ἡμέρα⟨ν⟩ ὑπάγω παρὰ Σεραπιάδα *BGU*38.17 (ii/iii A.D.): the aor. is ἀπῆλθον, ὕπαγε..καὶ ἀπῆλθε *Ev.Matt.*9.6:—αὐτόματα ὑπάγοντα automata *which go* (from place to place), opp. στατά (those which perform actions while standing still), Hero *Aut.*1.2:—rare in Lxx (and only in cod. ℵ), *To.*8.21, al., *Je.*43(36).19. III. Medic., of the bowels, *to be open*, κοιλίη ὑπάγουσα Hp.*Acut.*(*Sp.*)ᵒ, Gal.15.756; v. supr. A. IV. 3. IV. *sink down, squat*, Arist.*HA* 540ᵃ7; cf. ὑπαγωγή III. 2.

**ὑπᾰγωγ-εύς**, έως, ὁ, *tool for shaping and adjusting bricks* or *tiles, trowel*, Ar.*Av.*1149 (ubi v. Sch.); cf. Hermipp.69: v. ἐπαγωγεύς. 2. *plasterer*, *IG*2².1672.31. II. *the bridge of a stringed instrument*, = ὑποβολεύς, Nicom.*Harm.*10. **-ή**, ἡ, *leading on gradually*, τοῦ κυνηγεσίου X.*Cyn.*6.12; *leading on artfully*, D.19.322 (v.l. ἐπ-, pl.), Poll.4.50, Phot. 2. Gramm., *introduction, use* of a form, A.D. *Synt.*206.19. II. *clearing out* or *purging of the body downwards*, κοιλίας Dsc.3.25; γαστρός Gal.6.278, al. III. (ὑπάγω intr.) *retreat, withdrawal*, Th.3.97; *retreat* or *haven* for ships, Phot. 2. *sinking down, squatting* (cf. ὑπάγω B. IV), ἐξ ὑπαγωγῆς Arist.*HA*578ᵇ 7. IV. *irrigation-channel*, *Sammelb.*5126.25 (iii A.D.). V. *bringing down of a bandage*, Sor.*Fasc.*32. **-ίδιον**, τό, Dim. of ὑπαγωγεύς II, Ptol.*Harm.*2.2, Porph. *in Harm.*pp.296,3, 7 W. **-ικός**, ή, όν, *drawn slowly out*, περίοδος, opp. στρογγύλη καὶ πυκνή, D.H. *Dem.*4. II. *attractive, persuasive*, Id.*Comp.*4 (unless in sense I: v.l. ἐπαγ-). **-ιον**, τό, Dim. of ὑπαγωγεύς II, Ptol.*Harm.*1.8, 11. **-ός**, όν, *carrying off downwards, evacuating*, κοιλίας Dsc.2.33; οὔρων καὶ κοιλίης Aret.*CD*1.2: abs., *aperient*, κλύσμα Gal.18(1).250.

**ὑπᾰγωνιάω**, *to be somewhat anxious*, Phleg.*Mir.*3.

**ὑπαδύγια**, τά, Elean for ὑποζύγια, *Schwyzer* 411.8, cf. 417.3.

**ὑπᾴδω**, *sing by way of accompaniment*, Λίνον δ' ὑπὸ καλὸν ἄειδε (sc. τῇ φόρμιγγι) Il.18.570; ἡ δ' ὑπὸ καλὸν ἄεισε (sc. ἡ νευρή) Od.21.411; ταῖς Μούσαις τι μέλος ὑπᾴσατε Ar.*Ra.*874; without acc., *to accompany with the voice*, χοροῖσι ib.366; τινι Luc.*Salt.*30; in poet. form **ὑπαείδω**, aor. ὑπήεισαν Call.*Dian.*242; ὑ. νόμον Id.*Del.*304. [The α of ὑπαείδω used long by Call.*Del.* l. c.]

**ὑπαέριος**, ον, *living in the air*, of the *bird* τρυγών, as opp. to the fish, Ael.*NA*8.26. Cf. ὑπήριος.

* **ὑπάετος** [ᾰ], ὁ, a kind of *eagle* or *vulture*, Arist.*HA*618ᵇ34; cf. ὑψιαίετος.

**ὑπαί**, poet. for ὑπό (q. v.).

**ὑπαιάζω**, v.l. for ἐπαιάζω, *AP*9.372.

**ὑπαιδείδοικα**, Ep. for ὑποδέδοικα, v. ὑποδείδω.

**ὑπαιδέομαι**, c. acc., *show some respect for* another, X.*HG*5.3.20.

**ὑπαΐδιος** οἶκος, *eternal*, of the grave, *IG*5(1).734 (Sparta): or perh. *underground* (αἶα), cf. ὑπόγαιος and ὑπογαΐδιος, καταγαΐδιοι (ὑπ' ἀΐδιον *IG* l. c.).

**ὑπαιδράσειαν**· ὑπόψειαν, Hsch.: v. ὑποδρασίη.

**ὕπαιθᾰ**, Adv., (ὑπό, ὑπαί) *out under, under and away*, ὕ. λιάσθη yielded *before* him, *under* his attack, Il.15.520; ποταμὸς.. ὕ. ῥέων 21.271; ἡ δὲ [πέλεια] ὕ. φοβεῖται 22.141; κατακέκλιται ἤπειρόνδε κοίλη ὕ. νάπη A.R.2.735. II. Prep. with gen. *under*, αἱ μὲν ὕπαιθα ἄνακτος ἐποίπνυον (sc. αἱ ἀμφίπολοι) *under* him, so as to support him, Il.18.421; of one shrinking *under* an attack, ὕπαιθα δὲ τοῖο λιασθεὶς φεῦγ' 21.255. (Expld. as εἰς τὸ ἰθὺ καὶ ἀντικρὺ καὶ ἔμπροσθεν in Eust. 1030.20, cf. 1234.11, 1262.61; as ἐκ πλαγίου in Sch.A.R. l. c., denied or doubted by Eust. ll. cc.)

**ὑπαίθρ-ιος**, ον, also α, ον E.*Andr.*227: (αἰθήρ):—*under the sky, in the open air*. Pi.*O.*6.61; ὑ. κατακοιμηθῆναι Hdt.4.7, cf. Th.1.134; of troops, Hdt.7.119, X.*An.*5.5.21, 7.6.24: also of things, λύχνα καίειν ὑπαίθρια Hdt.2.62; τῶν ὑ. πάγων δρόσων τε A.*Ag.*335; ὑπαιθρίοις δεσμοῖς πεπασσαλευμένος Id.*Pr.*113; ὑ. δρόσος E. l. c.; ὑ. δεξαμεναί, opp. ὑπόστεγοι, Pl.*Criti.*117b; ἔστι.. ὑ. τὸ στιππύον ἐρριμμένον *PSI* 4.404.7 (iii B. C.); ὑ. ἔργα *outdoor* work, X.*Oec.*7.20:—*in the open, in public*, ὑπαίθριος πεῖραν αὑτοῦ διδούς Luc.*Apol.*14. II. as Subst., ἐν ὑπαιθρίῳ, = ἐν ὑπαίθρῳ, Gal.6.94, cf. Hdn.*Epim.*140. -ος, ον, = foreg., [κοίτη] Hp.*Acut.*45; ἱππεῖς καὶ στρατιῶται, i. e. encamped, opp. κάτοικοι, *OGI*229.14 (Smyrna, iii B. C.); ἔδοξεν Ἀθηναίων τοῖς τεταγμένοις ἐν Ἐλευσῖνι.. καὶ τοῖς ὑπαίθροις *IG*$2^2$.1304.3 (iii B. C.); παραχειμασία Plb.3.87.2; δυνάμεις Id.1.82.14, cf. *PCair.Zen.*545.5 (iii B. C.), *PMich.Zen.*90.3 (iii B. C.), *PTeb.*722.11 (ii B. C.); τὰ κτήνη μου ὕ. ἐστιν *PEnteux.*11.2 (iii B. C.); ἀγῶνες Phld.*Rh.*2.108 S.; πόλεμοι D.H.6.22; ὕπαιθρον ὕλην λεῖπε Babr.12.14. 2. *public, open*, ὑ. πράξεσι Plu.*Cat.Ma.*16; παραφροσύνην ὕ. Id.*Agis* 2. II. as Subst., ὕπαιθρον, τό, *open enclosure*, *IG*$2^2$.1035.47, Luc.*Symp.*20; ἐν ὑπαίθρῳ in *the open air*, Antipho 5.11, X.*Mem.*2.1.6, *Oec.*7.19: metaph., εἰς ὕπαιθρον into *the public view*, into *the daylight*, πρῶτον εἰς ὕ. ἐξεληλυθώς, of a youth, Plb.10.3.4; εἰς ὕ. ἕλκειν τινά Plu.2.501d; τὴν αὑτῶν ἀμαθίαν εἰς ὕ. ἄγουσι Erot.*Prooem.* 2. in military language, from Plb. downwds., τὰ ὕ. the *field*, the *open country*, opp. fortified places, τῶν ὕ. ἀντιποιεῖσθαι 1.12.4, 1.30.6; μάχεσθαι ἐν τοῖς ὕ. 18.3.4; ἐκχωρεῖν τῶν ὕ. retire from the *open country*, and shut themselves up in the towns, 9.3.6; ἡ ἐν ὑπαίθροις οἰκονομία 6.12.5. 3. ἡ ὕπαιθρος (sc. γῆ), = τὰ ὕπαιθρα, the *field*, D.H.8.63, 9.6. 4. *open to the sky*, Lat. *hypaethros, aedificia, ambulationes*, Vitr.1.2.5, 5.9.5; *hypaethros* (sc. ναός), *a temple with an open skylight*, Id.3.2.1. This form is not used by Att. writers except in the phrase ἐν ὑπαίθρῳ; the form employed by them in Adj. sense is always ὑπαίθριος; v. X.*Oec.*7.20, where αἱ ἐν τῷ ὑπαίθρῳ ἐργασίαι are synon. with ὑπαίθρια ἔργα.

**ὑπαίθω**, poet., = ὑποκαίω, S.*Tr.*1210: metaph., of love, *inflame*, Id. *Fr.*345.

**ὑπαικάλλω**, = ὑποσαίνω, Ael.*NA*4.45, *Fr.*107; prob. cj. for ὑπεκβάλλω in Plu.2.530d.

**ὑπαινίσσομαι**, Att. -ττομαι, *intimate darkly, hint at*, τι or τινα D.19.22, Plu.*Rom.*8, Chor.6.43 F.-R., etc. 2. *allude, glance*, εἴς τινα D.H.*Rh.*9.7.

**ὑπαιρέω**, Ion. for ὑφαιρέω (q. v.).

**ὑπαίρω**, aor. Pass. ὑπήρθη v.l. for ὑπερήρθη in Lxx 2 *Ch.*32.23.

**ὑπαισθάνομαι**, *observe*, Them.*Or.*7.89d, Aristaenet.2.5.

**ὑπαΐσσω**, Att. -ᾴσσω, *dart beneath*, c. acc., μέλαιναν φρῖχ' ὑπαΐξει (where ᾰ, v. l. ὑπαλύξει) Il.21.126. II. *dart from under*, c. gen., βωμοῦ ὑπαΐξας 2.310. III. abs., ὑπᾴξας διὰ θυρῶν S.*Aj.*301 (v. l. ἀπ-).

**ὑπαισχύνομαι** [ῡν], Pass., *to be somewhat ashamed*, τινά τι *of* a thing *before* a person, Pl.*La.*179c.

**ὑπαίτιος**, ον, *under accusation, called to account*, τινος or ὑπέρ τινος *for* a thing, Antipho 4.1.4, 2.2.6; ὑ. τινὶ *responsible to* one, *liable to be called to account by* him, X.*Mem.*2.8.5; ὑποπτεύσας μή τι πρὸς τῆς πόλεως ὑπαίτιον εἴη Κύρῳ φίλον γενέσθαι that it might be *reprehensible* in the eyes of the state, Id.*An.*3.1.5; *blameworthy*, τῆς ψυχῆς ἡ ἄλογος καὶ παρὰ φύσιν κίνησις ὑ. Ph.2.348, cf. 1.19, 136, 2.291; *guilty*, Agatharch.18; ὑπαίτια ζῴδια *hurtful* signs of the Zodiac, Ptol.*Tetr.* 150; τὸ ὑ. πάθος Aët.16.36. Adv. -τίως Ph.1.682, al., Poll.3.139. 2. ἵνα μὴ ὑ. γενώμεθα κινδύνῳ *exposed* to danger, *POxy.*1033.18 (iv A. D.).

**ὑπαιφοινίσσω**, Ep. for ὑποφοινίσσω, Nic.*Th.*178 (Pass.).

**ὑπακμάζω**, *flourish in succession to*, J.*Ap.*2.35.

**ὑπᾰκοή**, ἡ, (ὑπακούω) *obedience*, *Ep.Rom.*5.19, *PMasp.*159.24 (vi A. D.); *answer to prayer*, Lxx 2 *Ki.*22.36.

**ὑπᾰκολουθέω**, *follow closely*, τινι v. l. for ἐπακ- in Ph.1.224, etc.

**ὑπᾰκου-ός**, ὁ, *obedient to*, Πιερίδων A.R.4.1381. -σις, εως, ἡ, *sense* of a word, ὑ. καταχρηστική *misinterpretation*, Phld.*Rh.*1.89 S. II. *correspondence*, *Theol.Ar.*37. -στέον, *one must accept* an invitation, Pl.*Ep.*328b, Plu.2.709d. II. *one must answer*, τι περί τινος Pl.*Sph.*261d. 2. *one must understand something left out*, Phld.*Rh.*1.115 S., *Mort.*30, Sch.Pi.*O.*10.84, 11.19, etc.; ὅτι.. Plu.2.34b. ※ -ω, fut. -ακούσομαι Lxx *Ge.*41.40 (v. sub fin.); later -ακούσω *Mim.Oxy.*413.222: I. *hearken, give ear*, θεοὶ δ' ὑπὸ πάντες ἄκουον Il.8.4; ὁ δ' ἄρ' ἐμμαπέως ὑπάκουσε Od.14.485, cf. *h.Ven.*180: c. gen., ὅττις.. πλάσιον ἆδυ φωνείσας ὑπακούει Sapph.2.4; ὑμῶν Ar.*V.*318 (lyr.); τῆς κρίσεως Aeschin.3.56 (s. v. l.). 2. *answer* (by voice or act) when called, ἢ ἐξελθέμεναι ἢ ἔνδοθεν αἶψ' ὑπακοῦσαι Od.4.283, cf. 10.83, E.*Alc.*400 (lyr.), Ar.*V.*273 (lyr.), Theoc.13.59: in Prose, ὁ κῆρυξ ἐκήρυττε τίς τὴν ἱκετηρίαν καταθείη, καὶ οὐδεὶς ὑπήκουεν And.1.112; τῷ παιδίῳ Ar.*Lys.*878, cf. *Nu.*360 (anap.), X.*Ages.*3.4, Aeschin.1.49, D.19.266. b. in a dialogue, *answer* when questioned, σοι Pl.*Sph.*217d; τοῖς λόγοις Id. *Lg.*898c. 3. *listen to, heed, regard*, c. gen. rei, Id.*Tht.*162d, X.*Cyr.*8.1.20; ὑ. νόμων Pl.*Lg.*708d; ὑ. διαίτῃ *submit* to a regimen, Id.*R.*459c; λόγῳ Arist.*Pol.*1333$^{a}$18; ὑ. τῷ ξυμφόρῳ τινός *comply* with his interest, Th.5.98; δείπνῳ ὑ. *accept an invitation* to dinner, Ath.6.247d: abs., *give way, submit, comply*, Hdt.3.148, 4.119, Pl.*Prt.*325a, *PCair.Zen.*367.15 (iii B. C.): with a neut. Pron., μάλα γε τοῦτο ὑπήκουσεν in this matter he *obeyed*. X.*Cyr.*2.2.3; οὐδὲν τούτων ὑπήκουον Th.1.29, cf. 139, 140, etc.; ὑ. τινός τι or τινί τι, *obey* one *in* a thing, ib.26, Pl.*Lg.*774b. II. Special senses: 1. of porters, *answer* a knock at the door, ὑ. τινί Id.*Cri.*43a: abs., Id.*Phd.*59e, *Act.Ap.*12.13: ⟨παρὰ⟩ τὴν θύραν Thphr.*Char.*4.9, 28.3; ὁ ὑπακούσας the porter, X.*Smp.*1.11, cf. D.47.35. 2. of a judge, *listen* to a complainant, τινι X.*Cyr.*8.1.18; also of the parties in legal proceedings, *appear before the court*, Is.4.28, D.19.257, 290; ὑ. εἰς τὸ δικαστήριον Hyp.*Eux.*2, cf. *PSI*10.1100.10 (ii A. D.), *Sammelb.*7369.10 (ii/iii A. D.). 3. of dependants, subjects, etc., *obey, submit to*, Δαρείου οὐδαμὰ ὑ. Hdt.3.101; Ἀθηναίων Th.4.56, cf. 6.82; τοῖς πέλας Id.2.61. b. Astrol., *to aspect from South to North*, of the southernmost of two zodiacal signs equidistant from an equinoctial point, opp. προστάσσειν, Ptol.*Tetr.*35; = ἀκούω v, Paul.Al.*E.*2. 4. *answer one's expectations, succeed*, ὑπήκουέ μοι τὸ πρᾶγμα Luc.*Icar.*10; τῆς μεταλλείας ἀσθενῶς ὑπακουούσης Str.9.1.23. 5. ὑ. αὐγαῖς ἁλίου *to be subject* to the sun's rays, Pi.*O.*3.24; ταῖς ὥραις Thphr.*CP*1.15.1; τοῦ ψύχους ib. 5.4.2; ὑπακούουσι τῶν τῆς ἀρχῆς παθημάτων οἱ κατὰ τοὺς ὀφθαλμοὺς μύες *feel the effects of*.., Gal.18(2).68. 6. of ailments, *yield, give way* to a remedy, τινι Hp.*Epid.*3.8, Gal.6.354: abs., Hp.*Prorrh.*2.39, Sor.1.122, Gal.6.439: metaph., τὸ μυθῶδες ὑ. λόγῳ Plu.*Thes.* 1; τοῖς ἰσχυρῶς φερομένοις ὑ. ὁ ἀήρ Archyt.1; πληγαῖς ὑ., of metal, Plu.2.802b; τὸ χορόδιον ὑπακοῦον *yielding to pressure*, Hp.*Epid.*4.45; μὴ εὐθέως ὑπακούοντος εἰς ἐξολκὴν τοῦ ἐμβρύου Sor.2.62, cf. 86. 7. *concede a point in dispute*, Arist.*Top.*161$^{b}$15. 8. *correspond*, πᾶσα παραγωγὴ ἐπιρρηματικὴ.. μιᾷ ὑπακούει πτώσει κατὰ τὴν διάλυσιν every adverbial derivative *corresponds* to a case, e. g. οἴκοθι to ἐν οἴκῳ, A.D.*Adv.*206.21; *conform* to a theory, Id.*Synt.*236.14. III. κοινὸν ὑ. *understand under* the term κοινόν.., Pl.*Phlb.*31c, cf. Plu.2.23c:—Pass., κοινῶς ὑ. *to be understood* in a general sense, Phld.*Po.* 5.35. 2. in Gramm., *understand* a word omitted, A.D.*Synt.*22.21 (Pass.): τὸ -όμενον what one *has in mind*, the *subject*, Id.*Pron.*68.15, al. 3. *understand*, c. acc. et inf., Phld.*Mus.*p.72 K., *Po.*5.9. IV. fut. ὑπακούσεται in Th.6.69, if correct, must be Pass., if their *service shall be* lighter; but Sch. gives ὑπακούσονται, whence ξυγκαταστρεψάμενοι (for -οις) is conjectured.

**ὕπακρος**, ον, *nearly the highest*, Pl.*Amat.*136c, 138e, Longin.34.1.

**ὑπακ-τέον**, (ὑπάγω B) *one must go*, *EM*777.26, Zonar. II. (ὑπάγω A. IV. 3) *one must purge*, Archig.ap.Gal.12.976. III. *one must subsume*, τὰ ἐκεῖ ὑφ' ἓν γένος τοῖς ἐνταῦθα Plot.6.1.1. IV. *one must introduce* or *apply* (remedies), Aët.5.130. V. ὑπακτέον τι τῇ χειρουργίᾳ *one must subject* it to operation, Paul.Aeg.6.25. -τικός, ή, όν, (ὑπάγω A. IV. 3) *fit for carrying downwards, aperient, evacuant*, κοιλίας Mnesith.Ath.ap.Ath.3.92b; τῆς κοιλίας καὶ τῆς οὐρήσεως Id. ap.Ath.8.358a (Comp.); γαστρός Gal.6.265: abs., Diocl.*Fr.*141.

**ὑπαλγέω**, *have a slight pain*, Hp.*Epid.*4.41; f.l. for ὑπεραλγέω in Ael.*NA*2.43.

**ὑπᾰλεαίνω**, *warm somewhat* or *gradually*, Ael.*NA*15.12 (Pass.).

**ὑπάλ-ειμμα** [ᾰλ], ατος, τό, *salve*, Ar.Byz.*Epit.*17.4, Dsc.1.30. -ειπτος, ον, *that may be spread like a salve*, Hp.*Ulc.*22: ὑπάλειπτον, τό, *salve*, Gal.19.148. -ειπτρον, τό, *spatula for spreading a salve*, Hp.*Mul.*2.163, *Art.*11, etc.; also -ειπτρίς, ίδος, ἡ, Id.*Superf.* 28. -είφω, *lay on, spread like salve*: Med., ὑπαλείφεσθαι φάρμακον Pl.*La.*185c:—Pass., ὑπαλειφθὲν ἔλαιον Arist.*Pr.*967$^{a}$4. II. *anoint*, κόμμι τὴν γνάθον Hp.*Art.*33: metaph., εἰρήνῃ τινὰ τὠφθαλμὼ Ar.*Ach.* 1029:—Med., *anoint oneself*, Hp.*Acut.*(*Sp.*)58, Ar.*Pax* 898; ὑ. τοὺς ὀφθαλμούς *paint one's* eyes, X.*Oec.*10.5; μύροις τὰς ῥῖνας Alex.190 (v. l. ἐναλ-); ἅτερος πρὸς τὸν ἕτερον ὑπαλείφεται one *anoints himself* to fight with the other, *Com.Adesp.*401:—Pass., *have one's eyes anointed*, παρ' ἰατρῷ Ar.*Fr.*129; of the eyes, ὑπαληλιμμένοι *painted*, opp. ὑγιαίνοντες in their natural state, X.*Oec.*10.6. III. *line*, i.e. *be the lining of*, ὁ ἔνδον χιτὼν.. ὁ καὶ τὸν στόμαχον ὑπαλείφων Gal.*Nat.Fac.*3.8; ὁ χιτὼν.. ὁ ὑπαλείφων τὸ στόμα Id.15.746, cf. 16.571. -ειψις, εως, ἡ, *anointing*, Hp.*Vid.Ac.*9, Thphr.*Sud.*39.

※ **ὑπᾰλεύομαι**, aor. ὑπαλεύασθαι, = ὑπαλύσκω, ὑπαλευάμενος θάνατον Od.15.275, cf. Hes.*Op.*557; ὑπαλεύεο φήμην ib.760: cf. ὑπαλύσκω.

**ὑπαλλ-ᾰγή**, ἡ, *interchange, exchange*, Ph.1.13; γένους A.D.*Synt.* 209.6: pl., γάμους ἑλομένη τῶν κακῶν ὑπαλλαγάς E.*Hel.*294; v. l. for παρ-, Thphr.*CP*2.19.6. 2. *change* of régime, Gal.6.410; of colour, ἡ τῆς χροιᾶς ὑ. Id.15.535; of wine with age, ib.629. 3. *pledging as security, mortgage*, ἐδανείσατο ἐπὶ ὑπαλλαγῇ οἰκίας *BGU* 362 ix 17 (iii A. D.), cf. *PLips.*10 ii 2 (iii A. D.). II. *hypallage*, a figure of speech, D.H.*Comp.*3 (pl.); expld. as Rhet. equivalent of Gramm. μετωνυμία by Cic.*Orat.*27.93, Quint.*Inst.*8.6.23; = ἐπιτίμησις II. 2, Alex.*Fig.*2.28. -αγμα, ατος, τό, *that which is exchanged*, νόμισμα ὑ. τῆς χρείας money is *the exchangeable representative* of demand, Arist.*EN*1133$^{a}$29; *substitute*, Thphr.ap.Porph.*Abst.* 2.27. 2. *mortgaged property*, *PRyl.*177.13 (iii A. D.), etc.; expld.

in *AB*423 as = ἐνέχυρόν τι τῆς προικὸς ἀντάξιον—a usage censured by Phryn.275. ⊛ **-ακτέον,** *one must change* (poultices), Herod.Med. in *Rh.Mus.*58.84. ⊛ **-ακτικός,** ή, όν, only in Adv. **-κῶς,** *with hypallage,* Sch.Il.15.52, Ammon.*Diff.*p.100 V. **-αξις,** εως, ἡ, *interchange,* Gal.1.629, al.; *alteration, variation* in health, Id.6.403. **-άσσω,** Att. **-ττω,** *exchange,* Plb.5.8.9, Luc.*Sol.*10:—Med., θνητὸν βίον ἀντ' ἀθανάτου Ph.1.37; but τὸ μῖσος τῇ εὐνοίᾳ *by* the goodwill, J.*AJ*15.3.2. **2.** *change a little,* Plu.2.930c; τὸ τὴν οἰκείαν χώραν ὑπηλλαχὸς Gal.10.160; λουτρὰ καὶ θυμοὶ κτλ. ὑπαλλάττοντα τὴν κρᾶσιν Id.6.28, cf. 307, al.; *alter* the text of a book, τὰς παλαιὰς γραφὰς Id.15.21, cf. 16.679, al.:—Med., *change one's place,* Poll.6.194; *change one's bearing,* πρός τινας Phot., Suid. s.v. Κωρυκαῖος:—Pass., ὑπηλλάχθαι εἰς.. Arist.*Fr.*580; ὅταν [βιβλίον].. τινὰ.. ὑπηλλαγμένα ἔχῃ *altered* (from the first draft), Gal.15.424. **3.** *mortgage,* ἀρούρας *BGU*301.9 (ii A.D.), cf. *PStrassb.*56.8 (iii A.D.), etc. **II.** intr. in Act., *change gradually,* εἰς ἀνδρῶν ἡλικίαν Poll.2.10; of wine, Gal.15.629.

**ὑπάλληλος,** ον, *subordinate, subaltern,* Arist.*Metaph.*1018ᵇ1, Dam. *Pr.*87.

**ὑπᾰλοιφή,** ἡ, = ὑπάλειψις, of ships, *IG*2².1622.740; *greasing,* Ph. *Bel.*102.14.

**ὑπάλπειος,** α, ον, *under the Alps*: ἡ ὑ. (sc. χώρα) *sub-Alpine Italy,* Plu.*Marc.*3: so **ὑπαλπῖνος,** ἰατρός *IG*14.892 (Ischia).

**ὑπάλυξις** [ᾰ], εως, ἡ, Ep. Noun, *a shunning, escape,* οὔ τοι ἔτ' ἔσθ' ὑ. Il.22.270; κακῶν ὑ. Od.23.287, cf. A.R.4.1261, Keil-Premerstein *Erster Bericht* p.9 (Troketta).

**ὑπᾰλύσκω,** Ep. Verb, = ὑπαλεύομαι, used by Hom. only in aor., *flee from, escape,* τέλος θανάτοιο.. ὑπαλύξας Il.11.451; ὑπὸ κῆρας ἀλύξας 12.113, cf. 327, Od.4.512; τὸ μὲν ὥς ὑπάλυξε 5.430; ὑπάλυξεν ἀέλλας 19.189; χρεῖος ὑπαλύξας *having got quit of* a debt (without paying it), 8.355 (for Il.21.126, v. ὑπαΐσσω): abs., Hes.*Sc.*304, Thgn. 817: fut. ὑπαλύξειν A.R.3.336.

⊛ **ὑπᾰμάω,** *cut short off,* τί τινος Nic.*Th.*901.

**ὑπαμβής,** ές, (ἄμβη) *obliquely inclined downwards,* γένειον Ph.*Bel.* 65.8 (v.l. ὕπαμβλυ); τρῆμα Apollon.Cit.1.

**ὕπαμβλυς,** υ, *blunt,* v.l. for foreg. (q.v.), dub. l. in Phld.*Acad.Ind.* p.95 M.

**ὑπᾰμείβω,** in Med., πόντον ὑπαμείβεσθαι *exchange* land *for* sea, go into the sea, Opp.*H.*1.651.

**ὕπαμμος,** ον, = ὕφαμμος, Thphr.*Fr.*167.

**ὑπάμπελος,** ον, *planted with vines,* Cat.Cod.Astr.4.151.

**ὑπαμπέχω,** *keep under a cloak,* τὸ ἦθος Plu.2.562b (Pass.).

**ὕπαμπρος,** ον, dub. sens., σιδήριον ὕ. *IG*1².313.128, 314.145.

**ὑπαμφίβολος,** ον, *somewhat doubtful,* Ph.2.30,309.

**ὑπαμφιέννυμαι,** Med., *put on under* another garment, Ael.*NA*16.15.

**ὑπανα-βλέπω,** *gain one's sight gradually,* Ael.*NA*3.25. **-γιγνώσκω,** *read clause by clause,* Is.11.4, Aeschin.2.109; τὴν εἰσαγγελίαν Hyp.*Eux.*40; *read aloud,* Hierocl. *in CA*27 p.484 M.

**ὑπᾰναγκάζω,** *force under* or *in,* τι μεσηγὺ τῶν πλευρέων Hp.*Art.*5 (Pass.).

**ὑπανάγω** [ᾰγ], *withdraw,* τὴν δύναμιν J.*AJ*4.4.5; *lead gradually back,* ἡμᾶς καὶ ὑπανάγοντος is f.l. (cod. Med.) for ἡμᾶς ἐπανάγοντος in Hierocl. *in CA*15 p.454 M. (= p.103 M. ed. 1853).

**ὑπανα-δύομαι,** Med., *withdraw secretly from, endeavour to escape,* τὴν ἔξοδον D.H.7.13: abs., *Com.Adesp.*19.3 D. **-θλίβω** [ῑ], *squeeze up from below, Placit.*4.22.1.

**ὑπαναιρέω,** *withdraw, take away,* τὴν εὐφημίαν App.*BC*2.127.

**ὑπανα-κᾰθαίρω,** *purge gently,* cj. for ἢ ἀνακ- in Sor.1.86. **-κεῖμαι,** Pass., *recline below at table,* D.L.7.17. **-κῑνέω,** intr., *rise up and go away,* ἐπὶ τὸ δεῖπνον Ar.*Ec.*1165. **-κλάω,** *bend up under,* ὑπανακλωμένων τῶν σκελῶν Herod.Med. in *Rh.Mus.*58.75. **-κλίνω** and **-κλίνομαι** [ῑ], = *subcubo, Gloss.* **-κόπτω,** *check and throw back,* τινὰ τῆς ὁρμῆς Lib.*Decl.*43.15. **-λαμβάνω,** *skim off,* -ληφθείσης πτερῷ ῥυπαρίας Dsc.2.77.

**ὑπανᾱλίσκω,** *waste away, spend* or *consume gradually,* Hp.*Aff.*47, Th.3.17 (Act. and Pass.), Plu.*Sert.*13, etc. **2.** *spend* as a contribution, εἰς τὴν εἰκόνα.. Ἀλεξανδρείας δραχμὰς τρισχιλίας *BMus.Inscr.* 425 (= *Inscr.Prien.*25).

**ὑπανα-μέλπω,** *sing in accompaniment,* μεταξὺ ἐπιρροφῶν Ael.*NA* 14.5. **-μιμνήσκομαι,** *recall to mind once more,* τοῦ πατρὸς ὑπανεμνήσθη Aesop.157 H. (i p.237 Chambry). **-πείθω,** *exert undue influence upon,* Mitteis *Chr.*96 ii 11, cf. 18 (Pass.) (iv A.D.). **-πίμπλαμαι,** Pass., *to be filled gradually,* τινος with.., Ael.*NA*17.13. **-πλέω,** *rise and float on the surface,* Ph.1.320,565,593.

**ὑπαν-άπτω,** *kindle underneath,* φῶς Eustr. *in EN*8.20.

**ὑπανά-στᾰσις,** εως, ἡ, *rising up from one's seat,* ὑπαναστάσει τιμᾶν τοὺς πρεσβυτέρους Arist.*EN*1165ᵃ28, cf. Phld.*Hom.*p.36 O.: pl., Pl. *R.*425b, Porph.*Abst.*2.61: cf. ὑπανίσταμαι 2. **-στᾰτέον,** (ὑπανίσταμαι) *one must rise up,* esp. *to make room for another,* X.*Lac.*9.5. **-στρέφω,** *recur,* of an illness, Hp.*Morb.*2.12. **-τείνω,** *offer,* τὴν θηλήν, of a mother, Lib.*Decl.*43.56. ⊛ **-τέλλω,** *spring forth from below,* πηγὴ ὑ. Ael.*NA*15.4. **-τρέπω,** *upset,* τὸν στόμαχον Sor.1.44 (Pass.). **-τροπιάζω,** = ὑποτροπιάζω, ὑπαναστρέφω, Poll.3.107. **-φλέγομαι,** Pass., *to be heated gradually,* ἐκ τοῦ οἴνου Ael.*VH*14.41. ⊛ **-φύομαι,** *grow* or *swell up under* or *gradually,* ib.7, *NA*4.21. **-χωρέω,** *go back gradually, retire slowly,* Th.1.51; ἐκ τῆς ἀγορᾶς ὑπανεχώρησεν (cod. Vat. for παρεχ-) D.H.5.8, cf. S.E. *M.*9.293, D.C.63.26; τῶν ἐνταῦθα πραγμάτων, of death, *PMasp.*151.37 (vi A.D.). **-χώρησις,** εως, ἡ, *gradual retirement,* D.H.3.19 (pl.), Sor.1.68 (pl.), Hld.1.19.

⊛ **ὕπανδρος,** ον, (ἀνήρ) *under a man, subject to him, married,* γυνή LXX *Nu.*5.20, Plb.10.26.3, *Ep.Rom.*7.2, etc.; τὰς ὑ. τῶν γυναικῶν Polem.Hist.59; ὕ. γύναια Plu.*Pel.*9. **II.** *feminine,* ἀγωγὴ οἰκουρὸς καὶ ὕ. a *feminine* mode of life, D.S.32.10.

**ὑπάνειμι,** (εἶμι *ibo*) *come on, creep on,* Luc.*Merc.Cond.*39.

**ὑπανέλκω,** *draw up,* Tim.Gaz.ap.Ar.Byz.*Epit.*88.23.

**ὑπᾰνεμόω,** *breathe gently over,* ἔρωτι τὰς παρειάς Lib.*Descr.*30.18.

**ὑπαν-ερπύζω,** *creep up secretly* or *softly,* Ael.*NA*5.3. **-έρχομαι,** *recover gradually from,* τῆς θερμότητος Gal.19.149. **-εσις,** εως, ἡ, *remission* of fevers, Orib.46.25.7.

**ὑπανθ-έω,** *begin to flower* or *blossom,* Philostr.*Im.*1.31, Poll.1.60; ἰούλῳ ὑ. Id.2.10. **-ηρός,** όν, *slightly coloured* with blood, ὑπανθηρὸν πτύειν Hp.*Epid.*2.2.7.

**ὑπᾰνῐάομαι,** Pass., *to be somewhat distressed,* opt. -ιῷντο Ar.*Nu.* 1195.

⊛ **ὑπαν-ίημι,** *remit* or *relax a little,* τὸ λίαν ἀπάνθρωπον Plu.*Dio*7; ὑ. τῶν δεσμῶν *relax the strictness of..,* J.*AJ*2.5.1:—Pass., δύναμις ὑπανειμένη μᾶλλον Dsc.1.68. **II.** intr., τοῦ φόβου μικρὸν ὑπανέντος Plu.*Aem.*23:—so in Pass., Ph.2.87, al. **-ίσταμαι,** Pass. with aor. 2 and pf. Act., *rise, stand up,* Thgn.485; of game, *start up,* X.*Cyr.* 2.4.19; of land, ὑπανεστώς *rising slightly above the plain,* Ph.2.510. **2.** τοῖσι πρεσβυτέροισι.. ἐξ ἕδρης ὑπανιστέαται *rise up from* their seats *to make room* or *show respect to..,* Hdt.2.80, cf. Phld. *Vit.*p.38 J.; τῶν θάκων τοῖς πρεσβυτέροις ὑ. Ar.*Nu.*993 (anap.); ἕδρας ὑ. βασιλεῖ X.*Lac.*15.6; ὑ. ἀπὸ τῶν θάκων ὁδῶν τε παραχωρεῖν Id.*Hier.* 7.2, cf. *Smp.*4.31; καθήμενος ὑ. Id.*Mem.*2.3.16: metaph., θυμὸς ὑπανίστατο *gave way,* Callistr.*Stat.*13: cf. ὑπανάστασις. **3.** *withdraw,* ἐκ τῶν Ἀθηναίων Suid. s.v. Ἀρίσταρχος. ⊛ **-ίσχω,** *rise slowly,* of the moon, Ael.*NA*11.10; ὑ. τοῦ ὕδατος Philostr.*VA*3.1. **-οίγω** or **-οίγνυμι,** *open from below, tap* a cask, βῖκος ὑπανεῴγνυτο Ephipp.8.2, cf. Hermipp.82.7 (hex.). **2.** *open underhand* or *secretly,* [γράμματα] ὑπανέῳγεν D.32.28; τὸ δωμάτιον ὑπανοίξασα Luc. *Asin.*13. **3.** intr., *open underneath,* ἄντρον ὑπανοίγει J.*BJ*1.21.3.

**ὕπαντα,** Adv., c. dat., μολὼν ὕ. τοῖς ἐμοῖς βουλεύμασι *intervening in..,* cj. Hartung in E.*Supp.*398.

⊛ **ὑπαντάξ,** Adv., (ἄντα) = ἐξ ἐναντίας, Ar.*Fr.*616: cf. ἄνταξ.

⊛ **ὑπαντ-άω,** Ion. **-έω** *APl.*4.101: fut. -ήσομαι J.*AJ*1.20.1, A.D. *Synt.*149.15, S.E.*M.*10.61: aor. -ήντησα Plu.*Arat.*34, Dor. -άντᾱσα Pi.*P.*8.59:—*come* or *go to meet,* either as a friend, X.*Cyr.*3.3.2; or in arms, ib.1.4.22, 4.2.17; εἰς τὰς ὁδοὺς ὑ. Hyp.*Eux.*22, cf. *SIG*798.21 (Cyzicus, i A.D.); ὑ. τινί Pi. l.c., X.*Cyr.*6.3.15, *Ev.Matt.*8.28, etc.; ὑ. τῇ πόλει πρὸς τὴν χρείαν Plu. l.c.; πρὸς τὸ [βῆμα] *POxy.*1630.15 (iii A.D.): also c. gen., ἀνδρῶν ἀγαθῶν παιδὸς ὑ. S.*Ph.*719 (anap., s. v. l.):—in App.*BC*5.45 the acc. ὄντα (sic codd., ὄντι Schweigh., Mendelss.) refers to σε κατιόντα ὁρῶν just before:—later in Med., ὑπαντώμενος αὐτοῖς Hdn.2.5.5, cf. 3.11.3, 5.4.5, etc. **2.** *meet, encounter,* of a heavenly body, Ptol.*Tetr.*132. **II.** metaph., *meet,* i.e. *agree to,* ταῖς τιμαῖς Posidon.36 J.; *present oneself at,* τῇ ἀποδόσει *Sammelb.* 6.23 (iii A.D.); πρὸς τὴν ἀπόδοσιν *BGU*614.23 (iii A.D.). **2.** *meet,* i.e. *reply* or *object to,* τοῖς ἐμοῖς βουλεύμασι E.*Supp.*398 (s.v.l., v. ὕπαντα); πρός τινα or τι S.E.*M.*10.105, etc.; πρός τι ὑ. ὡς.. A.D. *Synt.*265.4: abs., εὐαρεστήσεως ὑπαντησομένης *come in response, ensue,* Herod.Med. in *Rh.Mus.*58.85, cf. 100. **3.** *occur* to one, τῷ ῥήτορι Longin.16.4. **4.** *fall in with,* ἀνωμαλίᾳ S.E.*M.*1.6; *correspond with,* A.D.*Conj.*232.23. **-η,** ἡ, = Lat. *obvia, Gloss.*; εἰς ὑπάντην = *obviam,* ib. **-ησις,** εως, ἡ, *coming to meet,* ἐξῆλθον εἰς ὑπάντησιν αὐτῷ *Ev.Jo.*12.13, cf. J.*AJ*11.8.4, App.*BC*4.6 (pl.); ψήφισμα -ήσεως *SIG*798.16 (Cyzicus, i A.D.). **2.** Astrol., *encounter* of a heavenly body, in ἄφεσις, Ptol.*Tetr.*132 (pl.). **II.** metaph., *retort, answer,* S.E.*M.*11.202; πρός τι ib.7.278, A.D.*Synt.*305.19. **2.** *counter-treatment,* Sor.2.41. **-ητέον,** *one must reply,* Sch.Il.3.440. **-ητικός,** ή, όν, *of meeting,* τόποι Ptol.*Tetr.*141. **-ήτωρ,** ορος, ὁ, *heavenly body encountered* in course of projection of vital quadrant, Heph.Astr.2.11 (*Cat.Cod.Astr.*8(2).72.28), Doroth. in *Cat. Cod.Astr.*2.198.15, Sch.Ptol.*Tetr.*169. **-ιάζω,** *come* or *go to meet, encounter,* without case, Il.6.17, Pi.*P.*4.135, A.*Pers.*407, X.*Cyr.*4.2.18: c. dat., Pi.*P.*8.11, *Pae.*2.32, A.*Pers.*834,850, X.*Cyr.*5.5.9: also c. acc., Pi.*P.*5.44, Hdt.4.121, J.*AJ*1.10.4, Plu.*Pomp.*71, App.*Mith.* 5, Luc.*VH*1.21. **-ιάω,** = foreg., only in Ep. part. ὑπαντιόωντος, Opp.*H.*2.565.

**ὑπαντλ-έω,** *draw up,* τὰ κύματα τῷ στέρνῳ (s.v.l.) Philostr.*Im.*2.13 (ἐπ- Kayser). **-ιον,** τό, *cask, jar, AB*411, Hsch.

**ὑπάντομαι,** only in pres. and impf., = ὑπαντάω, Hdn.4.11.2, 8.7.8.

**ὕπαντρος,** ον, (ἄντρον) *with caverns underneath, cavernous,* χώρα, γῆ, Arist.*Mete.*366ᵃ25, *Pr.*932ᵃ8, Str.9.2.16; νῆσος Theagen.17; πέτρα Ael.*NA*16.17. **II.** *underground,* οἶκοι Id.*VH*12.38. **2.** *dwelling under the earth,* Hsch.

**ὑπανύσθαι·** ὑπουργεῖν, Hsch.:—Act. aor., ἐνὶ γναθμοῖς ὑπανύσσας γλῶσσαν ἀναύδητον *subduing,* Maiist.57.

**ὑπανώμᾰλος,** ον, *rather uneven,* γάλα Sor.1.88.

**ὕπαξις,** εως, ἡ, *evacuation,* γαστρός Aët.5.135.

**ὑπαξόνιος,** ον, *under the axle,* σύριγγες Call.*Lav.Pall.*14.

**ὑπαπαίδευτος,** ον, *somewhat untaught* or *unpolished,* Phryn.*PS* p.120 B.

**ὑπαπαντ-άω,** = ὑπαντάω, τοῖς ἱεροῖς, τοῖς Ῥωμαίοις, *IG*2².1011.7, 18 (ii B.C.), cf. *PStrassb.*101.4 (i B.C.), *BGU*1768.3 (i B.C.), D.S.32.6. **-η,** ἡ, = Lat. *obviatio, Gloss.* **-ησις,** εως, ἡ, = ὑπάντησις I.1, *IG*2².1028.6 (ii/i B.C.).

**ὑπαπειλέω,** *hint threateningly,* τινι c. inf., X.*HG*4.6.3.

**ὑπάπειμι**, (εἶμι *ibo*) *withdraw, retreat*, Th.5.9; *withdraw stealthily*, κατ' ὀλίγους ὑπαπῆσαν Id.3.111; κατ' ὀλίγον Luc.*Icar.*14; ἐφήβου.. ἄρτι ὑπαπῄει *was past the age of*.., Philostr.*VA*6.3.

**ὑπαπέρχομαι**, = foreg., Ael.*NA*11.33.

**ὑπαπο-κῑνέω**, intr., *move off secretly* or *softly, sneak away*, c. gen., τῆς ὁδοῦ Ar.*Av.*1011. **-κινητέον**, *one must make off, sneak away*, Id.*Th.*924. **-κρύπτω**, *conceal under*, λόχμῃ ἑαυτήν Ael.*NA*5.40. **-λείπομαι**, Pass., *to be left behind* (al. ὑπολ.), ib.10.43. **-τρέχω**, *run away secretly, slip away*, Ar.*Ec.*284. **-ψήχω**, *scrape off by degrees*, πηλόν Ael.*NA*3.24.

**ὑπαπροσθίδιος**, ον, *former, earlier*, *Berl.Sitzb.*1927.8 (Locr., v B.C.).

**ὑπάπτω**, Ion. for ὑφάπτω (q. v.).

❀ **ὕπαρ**, τό, indecl. (gen. ὕπαρος, acc. to *EM*491.30):—*real appearance seen in a state of waking, waking vision*, opp. ὄναρ (a dream), οὐκ ὄναρ, ἀλλ' ὕ. no illusive dream, but *a* (*vision of*) *reality*, Od.19.547, 20.90; ἐξ ὀνείρου δ' αὐτίκα ἦν ὕ. Pi.*O.*13.67; ἵνα ὕ. ἀντ' ὀνείρατος γίγνηται Pl.*Plt.*278e. II. acc. abs. is used as Adv., *in a waking state, awake*, ὕ. ἀλλήλοις διαλεγόμεθα Id.*Tht.*158c, cf. *IG*4²(1).122.133, al. (Epid., iv B.C.); opp. ὄναρ, ἀμφισβήτημα.. περὶ τοῦ ὄναρ τε καὶ ὕ. a question.. about sleeping and *waking*, Pl.*Tht.* l. c.; οἷον ὄναρ εἰδὼς.. πάλιν ὥσπερ ὕ. ἀγνοεῖν knowing things in a dream.. not to know them *when one awakes*, Id.*Plt.*277d; ὄναρ ἢ ὕ. ζῆν to pass life asleep or *awake*, Id.*R.*476c, cf. *Ti.*71e; καὶ ὄναρ καὶ ὕ. both sleeping and *waking*, i. e. both *by day* and night, always, Hp.*Lex*4, cf. Democr.174; οὔτε ὄναρ οὔθ' ὕ. neither sleeping nor *waking*, i. e. not at all, Pl.*Phlb.*36e; οὐθ' ὕ. οὔτ' ὄναρ ib.65e, cf. *R.*382e; καθ' ὕπνον.., ἢ καὶ ὕ. ἐγρηγορώς *wide* awake, Id.*Lg.*800a; opp. ἐν τοῖς ὕπνοις, Arist.*Pr.*957ᵃ18; ὕ. καὶ μεθ' ἡμέραν, opp. κατὰ τὸν ὕπνον, Plb.10.5.5. 2. ὕπαρ *in reality, actually*, ἔκρινα πρῶτος ἐξ ὀνειράτων ἃ χρὴ ὕ. γενέσθαι A.*Pr.*486; ὕ. ἡ πόλις οἰκήσεται ἀλλ' οὐκ ὄναρ Pl.*R.*520c, cf. 574e, 576b, al.—The phrase καθ' ὕπαρ is censured by Phryn.395, and is f.l. for καθ' ὕπνους in Apollod.3.12.5.

**ὑπάρ**, Pamph. for ὑπέρ, in anastrophe **ὕπαρ**, *Schwyzer* 686.2.

**ὑπᾰραιόω** (ἀραιός), -ώσασα v.l. for ὑποχαλάσασα (= *slackening, lowering*, τὸν τόνον) in *Corp.Herm.*18.4: cf. ὑποχαυνόω.

**ὑπᾰράσσω**, Att. -ττω, *strike underneath*, τῆς γῆς τοῖς ποσὶν -ομένης Anon.ap.Suid.

**ὑπαργήεις**, εσσα, εν, = ὑπόλευκος, Nic.*Th.*663.

**ὑπάργῑλος**, ον, *somewhat clayey, argillaceous*, γῆ Thphr.*HP*9.4.8.

**ὕπαργμα**, ατος, τό, in pl., *property*, Parth.1.2, 8.3.

**ὑπαργύρ-ευσις** [ῠρ], εως, ἡ, *obaeratio*, *Gloss.* **-εύω**, dub. sens., perh. *use base money*, Plu.2.832a (s. v. l.). **-ίζω**, *to be silver-grey*, κόμη Eun.*VS*p.485 B. **-ος**, ον, *having silver underneath*: hence, I. of rocks and the like, *containing silver, veined with silver*, πέτρα, χθών, E.*Cyc.*294, *Rh.*970; γῆ, λόφοι, X.*Vect.*1.5, 4.2: metaph. of men, *containing a proportion of silver*, Pl.*R.*415c; cf. ὑποσίδηρος. 2. *silver underneath*, of gilded plate, πρόσωπον ὕ. κατάχρυσον *IG*1².280.76, cf. 92.60, al.; κρατὴρ ὕ. ἐπίτηκτος ib.2².1388*A*44; τὰ ὕ. χρυσία, of false gold coins, S.E.*P.*2.30, cf. Poll.7.104; ὑπέλαβον ἑαυτοὺς εἶναι τοὺς ὑπαργύρους καὶ ὑποχρύσους θεούς, νομίσματος κεκιβδηλευμένου τὸν τρόπον Ph.1.542. 3. *silver-plated*, δακτύλιοι *Inscr.Délos* 298.40 (iii B.C.), 442*B*61 (ii B.C.). II. *sold* or *hired for silver, mercenary, venal*, φωνά Pi.*P.*11.42; ὑπάργυρα λέγειν Tz.*H.*8.828: cf. καταργυρόω II. 2. = κινάμωμον, Hsch. (prob. so called because *worth its weight in silver*). **-όω**, *plate with silver*, *Inscr.Délos* 399*B*110 (ii B.C., Pass.).

**ὑπάρδω**, *moisten below* or *gently*, Sch.Nic.*Al.*139.

**ὑπαρκ-τέον**, *one must begin with*, τι Pl.*R.*467c; τῶν ἴσων ὕ. αὐτῷ he *must render* equal *initial services* (to others), Aristid.*Or.*23(42).29. **-τικός**, ή, όν, Gramm., *expressing existence, substantive*, τὰ -κὰ τῶν ῥημάτων A.D.*Synt.*65.13; -κὴ μετοχή, i. e. ὤν, ib.151.13. II. = ὑπαρκτός, f.l. in S.E.*P.*3.249, Gal.19.529.

**ὑπάρκτιος**, ον, (ἄρκτος) *towards the north*, Plu.*Mar.*11, *Sert.*17.

**ὑπαρκτός**, ή, όν, *subsisting, existent, real*, Epicur.*Fr.*27, Posidon.ap.D.L.7.91, Plu.2.1046c, etc.

**ὕπαρνος**, ον, *with a lamb under* it, i. e. *suckling a lamb* or (metaph.) *a babe*, E.*Andr.*557, Call.*Ap.*53; ὕπαρνοι ἀγέλης *PLond.*3.1171.5 (i B.C.); cf. ὑπόρρηνος.

**ὕπαρξις**, εως, ἡ, *existence, reality*, τοῦ θεοῦ Phld.*Piet.*114, cf. *D.*3.10; opp. ἀνυπαρξία, S.E.*P.*1.21, cf. 3.24; opp. νόησις, Plu.2.1067c, Gal.6.115; opp. ἀναίρεσις, A.D.*Conj.*221.17; εἴ τις.. ἐν οὐχ ὑπάρξει τὸν χρόνον λέγοι Plot.3.7.13. 2. in Logic, *existence in a subject*, Ammon.*in Cat.*6.16, al. 3. Gramm., τὰ τῆς ὑπάρξεως ῥήματα, = ὑπαρκτικὰ ῥ., A.D.*Pron.*25.2, cf. *Stoic.*2.46. 4. Math., *positive term*, λεῖψις ἐπὶ λεῖψιν πολλαπλασιασθεῖσα ποιεῖ ὕπαρξιν Dioph.1 *Def.*9; cf. ὑπάρχω B. IV. 3. II. *substance*, ἡ τοῦ κέρατος ὕ. S.E.*P.*1.129. 2. like τὰ ὑπάρχοντα, *substance, property*, Lxx *Pr.*18.11, Plb.2.17.11, Phld.*Oec.*p.69 J. (pl.), D.H.7.8, D.S.20.71, *Ep.Hebr.*10.34, *POxy.*1274.14 (iii A.D.); χρημάτων ὕ. Teles p.43 H.

**ὑπαρόω**, *plough just before sowing*, Thphr.*HP*8.11.8, *CP*3.20.8.

**ὑπαρπάζω**, Ion. for ὑφαρπάζω (q. v.).

**ὑπάρπεζος**, ον, *under a hedge*, Nic.*Th.*284.

**ὑπαρτάω**, *hang* or *bind on underneath*, Ael.*NA*5.7 (Pass., s. v. l.).

**ὑπαρχ-εία**, ἡ, *province, district*, *PAvrom.*1 *A* 6 (i B.C.), *CRAcad. Inscr.*1930.161 (Dura-Europos, ii A.D.). **-ή**, ἡ, *beginning*, ἐν τῇ τῆς ἐπιστήμης ὑπαρχῇ Arist.*Ph.*247ᵇ29. 2. ὅλως μηδεμίαν ὑπαρχὰν ἔχοντος ὀπτίλλου, ἀλλ' ἢ χώραμ μόνον not a *vestige* of an eye, *IG*4²(1).121.75 (Epid., iv B.C.). II. very freq. in the phrase ἐξ ὑπαρχῆς, from or in *the beginning*, Arist.*Pol.*1293ᵃ2, al.; ἡ ἐξ ὑ. γένεσις Id.*HA*590ᵃ21. 2. *afresh, anew*, ἐξ ὑ. αὖθις S.*OT*132; πάλιν ὥσπερ ἐξ ὑ. ἐπανίωμεν Arist.*de An.*412ᵃ4; πάλιν οὖν οἷον ἐξ ὑ. Id.*Rh.*1355ᵇ24; πάλιν ἐξ ὑ. Id.*PA*685ᵇ29, D.40.16. **-ία**, ἡ, = ὑπαρχεία, *OGI*238.1 (Eriza, iii/ii B.C.).

**ὑπαρχῐ-τέκτων**, ονος, ὁ, *deputy clerk of the works*, *IG*2².1678*aA*7 (iv B.C.), *Delph.*3(5).25 ii *A*13 (iv B.C.), *PPetr.*2 p.138, al. (iii B.C.), *IG*7.3073.160 (Lebad., ii B.C.). **-φῠλᾰκίτης** [ῑτ], ου, ὁ, *deputy chief of police*, *BGU*1222.61, al. (ii B.C.).

❀ **ὕπαρχ-ος**, ὁ, *subordinate commander, lieutenant*, ὕ. ἄλλων.. οὐχ ὅλων στρατηγός S.*Aj.*1105; ὕ. ὢν τῷ ἀδελφῷ Luc.*DMort.*12.2; ὑπάρχοις τοῖς ἐμοῖς E.*Hel.*1432. 2. *subordinate governor*, of satraps, etc., Hdt.3.70, 4.166, al., X.*An.*4.4.4; Ἰωνίας Th.8.31; Ἑλλησποντίων Sor.*Vit.Hippocr.*8; in the Seleucid kingdom, *OGI*225.36 (Didyma, iii B.C.). b. = Lat. *proconsul*, *Epigr.Gr.*906 (Gortyn); = *legatus*, ὕ. Αὐτοκράτορος Καίσαρος *Inscr.Prien.*247, cf. App.*BC*5.26, D.C.36.36, al.; ὕ. Αἰγύπτου, = *praefectus Aegypti*, Arr.*An.*3.5.7; ὕ. τοῦ ἱεροῦ πραιτωρίου, = *praefectus praetorio*, *IGRom.*3.435 (Pisidia), cf. Lyd.*Mag.*1.14, al., *Gloss.*; so ὕ. alone, in verse, of the *praefectus praetorio Illyrici*, *IG*2².4224 (v A.D.), cf. 4226 (v A.D.), 7.94 (Megara, v A.D.); ὁ τῆς πόλεως ὕ., = *praefectus urbi*, Lyd.*Mag.*1.38, cf. 2.19. II. *subject to* one, τῶν Καρχηδονίων Plb.7.9.5.

❀ **ὑπάρχω**, fut. -ξω Hdt.6.109, S.*Ant.*932 (anap.): aor. ὑπῆρξα (v. infr. 1):—Pass., fut. ὑπαρχθήσομαι *PTeb.*418.7 (iii A.D.): pf. ὑπῆργμαι, Ion. -αργμαι Hdt.7.11:—*begin, take the initiative*:—Constr.: 1. abs., Od.24.286, E.*Ph.*1223; ὑπάρχων ἠδίκεις αὐτούς Isoc.16.44; ὁ ὑπάρξας the *beginner* (in a quarrel), D.59.15, cf. 1; ἀμύνεσθαι τοὺς ὑπάρξαντας Lys.24.18; ἀμυνομένους, μὴ ὑπάρχοντας Pl.*Grg.*456e; ὡς οὐχ ὑπάρχων ἀλλὰ τιμωρούμενος Men.358:—Med., Pl.*Ti.*41c, Ael.*NA*12.41, etc. 2. c. gen., *take the initiative in, begin*, ἀδίκων ἔργων, ἀδικίης, Hdt.1.5, 4.1, cf. Th.2.74, etc.; ὕ. τῆς ἐλευθερίας τῇ Ἑλλάδι And.1.142, cf. Pl.*Mx.*237b. 3. c. part., *take the initiative in* doing, ἐμὲ ὑπῆρξαν ἄδικα ποιεῦντες Hdt.7.8.β', cf. 6.133, 9.78; ὑπάρχει εὖ (or κακῶς) ποιῶν τινα X.*An.*2.3.23, 5.5.9; τοῖς αὐτοῖς ἀμύνεσθαι οἷσπερ καὶ οἱ Λακεδαιμόνιοι ὑπῆρξαν retaliating by the means which the L. *had used first*, Th.2.67 (where οἷσπερ is expld. by the following ἀποκτείναντες and ἐσβαλόντες). b. in Med. c. inf., Ael.*NA*14.11: c. gen., βαδίσεως -ονται ib.4.34; ἡλίου -ομένου τῆς ἀκμῆς ib.1.20. 4. c. acc., ὕ. εὐεργεσίας εἴς τινα or τινι *take the initiative in* [doing] kindnesses to one, D.19.280, Aeschin.2.26; ὕ. τοῦτο (sc. τὸ εὐνοεῖν) Men.927:—Pass., ὑπηρεσίαι ὑπηργμέναι εἰς Φίλιππον αὐτῷ Aeschin.2.109; τὰ παρὰ τῶν θεῶν ὑπηργμένα D.1.10; τὰ ἔκ τινος ὑπαργμένα (Ion. for ὑπηργ-) Hdt.7.11; ὑπηργμένων πολλῶν κἀγαθῶν Ar.*Lys.*1159; οὐδέν μοι ὑπῆρκτο εἰς αὐτόν Antipho 5.58; ἀνάξια τῶν εἰς ὑμᾶς ὑπηργμένων Lys.21.25; ἄξιον τῶν ὕ. equivalent *to what was done for him*, Arist.*EN*1163ᵇ21: impers., ὑπῆρκτο αὐτοῦ (sc. τοῦ Πειραιέως) *a beginning* of it *had been made*, Th.1.93.

B. in Act. only, *to be the beginning*, παιδοβόροι μὲν πρῶτον ὑπῆρξαν μόχθοι τάλανες A.*Ch.*1068 (anap.); πολλῶν κακῶν, μεγάλων ἀχέων, E.*Ph.*1582 (v.l.), *Andr.*274 (lyr.), cf. *HF*1169. 2. *to be already in existence*, πημονῆς δ' ἅλις γ' ὑπάρχει A.*Ag.*1656 (troch.); φοίνισσα δὲ Θρηϊκίων ἀγέλα ταύρων ὑπᾶρχεν *was already there*, Pi.*P.*4.205; αὗται αἱ νέες τοῖσι Ἀθηναίοισι ὑπῆρχον *already existed*, opp. to those they were about to build, Hdt 7.144; εἰ τοίνυν σφι χώρη γε μηδεμία ὑπῆρχε if they *had* no country *originally existing*, Id.2.15; χωρὶς δὲ τούτων οἱ χίλιοι ὑπῆρχον the *original* thousand *existed*, X.*Cyr.*1.5.5; ἔδει πρῶτον μὲν ὑπάρχειν πάντων ἰσηγορίαν Eup.291 (lyr.); ὑπαρχούσης μὲν τιμῆς, παρούσης δὲ δυνάμεως X.*Ages.*8.1; τοῦτο δεῖ προσεῖναι, τὰ δ' ἄλλ' ὑπάρχει D.3.15, cf. 8.53; ταὐτὰ ὕ. αὐτῷ ἅπερ ἐμοί Antipho 5.60, cf. Lys.12.23; ὑμῖν.. ἐλευθερίαν τε ὑπάρξειν καὶ Λακεδαιμονίων ξυμμάχοις κεκλῆσθαι *there is in store* for you.., Th.5.9: c. gen., οἶκος δ' ὕ. τῶνδε.. ἔχειν *there is* store of these things for us to have, A.*Ag.*961 (s. v. l., οἴκοις Pors.): freq. in part., ἡ ὑπάρχουσα οὐσία the *existing* property, Isoc.1.28; τὰ ὕ. ἁμαρτήματα Th.2.92; τῆς ὕ. τιμῆς for the *current* price, Syngr. ap.D.35.12; οἱ ὕ. πολῖται the *existing* citizens, Id.18.295; τῆς φύσεως ὕ. nature *being what it is*, X.*Cyr.*6.4.4; also κρησφύγετόν τι ὑπάρχον εἶναι that there should be a refuge *ready prepared*, Hdt.5.124. 3. *exist really*, opp. φαίνομαι, Arist.*Cael.*297ᵇ22, *Metaph.*1046ᵇ10; ἀθεώρητοι τῶν ὑπαρχόντων Id.*GC*316ᵃ9; καταληπτικὴ φαντασία ἡ ἀπὸ τοῦ ὑπάρχοντος *Stoic.*2.25. 4. simply, *be*, τοῖσιν ἄγουσιν κλαύμαθ' ὑπάρξει S.*Ant.*932 (anap.); ὅθεν εὐμάρει' ὑπάρχοι πόρου Id.*Ph.*704 (lyr.): and with a predicate, θησαυρὸς ἄν σοι ναὸς ὑπῆρχ' οὑμός E.*Hec.*1229; τὸ χωρίον καρτερὸν ὕ. Th.4.4; φύσεως ἀγαθῆς ὑπάρξαι *to be* of a good natural disposition, X.*Oec.*21.11; κἂν σοφὸς ὑπάρχῃ Philem.102; μέγα ὕ. τοῖς τοιούτοις λόγοις *is* of great advantage to them, D.3.19; πολλῶν ὑπάρξει κῦρος ἡμέρα καλῶν, = κυρώσει πολλὰ καλά, S.*El.*919. b. τὰ ὑπάρχοντα, much like τὰ ὑπηργμένα (A. 4 Pass.), a man's *record*, ἀνάξιον τῶν ὕ. τῇ πόλει καὶ πεπραγμένων τοῖς προγόνοις D.8.49; τὰ κάλλιστα τῶν ὕ. your *past record*, Id.18.95; ἡ ὑπάρχουσα αἰσχύνη the disgrace *which has been incurred*, Id.19.217; τὰ ὑπάρχοντα [αὐτῷ] ἐγκλήματα Aeschin.1.179. 5. sts. with a part., much like τυγχάνω, τοιαῦτα [αὐτῷ] ὑπῆρχε ἐόντα Hdt.1.192; ἐχθρὸς ὕ. ὢν D.21.38; ὕ. δύναμιν κεκτημένοι Id.3.7, cf. 15.1. 6. προγόνων ὕ. τῶν ἐξ Ἰλίου *to be the descendant of*.., D.H.2.65. II. like ὑπόκειμαι II. 2, *to be laid down, to be taken for granted*, Pl.*Smp.*198d; τούτου ὑπάρχοντος, τούτων ὑπαρχόντων, *this being granted*, Id.*Ti.*30c, 29b; θέντες ὡς ὑπάρχον Id.*R.*458a. III. *belong to, fall to one, accrue*, ὑπάρξει τοι.. τὰ ἐναντία you *will have*, Hdt.6.109, etc.; τὸ μισεῖσθαι πᾶσιν ὕ. Th.2.64; τὴν ὑπάρχουσαν ἀπ' ἀλλήλων ἀμφοτέροις [σωτηρίαν] Id.6.86; ἡ ὑπάρχουσα φύσις your *proper* nature, its *normal* condition, Id.2.45; τῇ τέχνῃ ὑπάρχειν διδούς assigning *as a property* of art, Pl.*Phlb.*58c, cf. *Tht.*150b,c. 2. of persons, ὑ. τινί *to be devoted to* one, X.*An.*1.1.4, *HG*7.5.5, D.19.54, etc.; καθ' ὑμῶν ὑπάρξων ἐκείνῳ *he will be on* his *side* against you, ib.118, cf. 2.14. b. ἐν παντὶ . . πᾶς χωρίῳ, καὶ ᾧ μὴ ὑπάρχομεν every one in every place, even *outside our sphere of influence* (lit. *to which we do* not *belong*), Th.6.87. 3. in the Logic of Arist. ὑπάρχειν denotes *the subsistence* of qualities *in a subject*, *Metaph.*1025ᵃ14; ὑ. τινί, = κατηγορεῖσθαι τινος, *APr.*25ᵃ13, al.; ὑ. κατά τινος ib.24ᵃ27, *Int.*16ᵇ13; ἐπί τινος ib.16ᵃ32; ὑ. τινὶ ζῴῳ πεζῷ δίποδι εἶναι *Top.*109ᵃ14; ὑπάρξει τι [τῷ πρώτῳ] it *will have predicates*, Plot.5.6.2; ἡ γένεσις τῷ χρόνῳ . . ὑπάρχει Dam.*Pr.*142. IV. freq. in neut. pl. part., τὰ ὑπάρχοντα, 1. in signf. I, *existing circumstances, present advantages*, Democr. 191, D.2.2; ἀπὸ τῶν αἰεὶ ὑ. σφαλέντες Th.4.18, cf. 6.33; πρὸς τὰ ὑ. ib.31; ἐκ τῶν ὑ. *under the circumstances, according to one's means*, X. *An.*6.4.9, Arist.*Pol.*1288ᵇ33; ὡς ἐκ τῶν ὑ. Th.7.76, 8.1. 2. in signf. III, *possessions, resources*, Id.1.70,144, etc.; τὰ ἑκατέροις ὑ. ib.141; κινδυνεύειν περὶ τῶν ὑ. Isoc.3.57: as a Subst., τὰ ὑ. αὐτοῦ *Ev.Matt.* 24.47, cf. Lxx *Ge.*12.5; ὑποθέμενος τὰ ὑ. καὶ ὑπάρξοντα *present* and *future resources*, *POxy.*125.22 (vi A.D.), etc. 3. Math., ὑπάρχοντα εἴδη *positive* terms, Dioph.1 *Def.*10. V. impers., ὑπάρχει *the fact is that . .*, c. acc. et inf., ὑ. γάρ σε μὴ γνῶναί τινα S.*El.*1340; ὡς ὑ. τοῦ ἔχειν . . as *the case stands* with regard to having, Arist.*HA*516ᵇ 25; περὶ τοὺς μαστοὺς ὑπεναντίως ὑ. ib.500ᵃ14. 2. *it is allowed, it is possible*, c. dat. et inf., ὑ. ἡμῖν ἐπικρατεῖν Th.7.63, cf. And.2.19, etc.; ὑ. αὐτῇ εὐδαίμονι εἶναι Pl.*Phd.*81a, cf. *Prt.*345a, *Phdr.*240b, etc.: also without a dat., οὐχ ὑ. εἰδέναι Th.1.82; ὑ. τὴν αὐτὴν εἶναι μητέρα Is.7.25, etc.: abs., ὥσπερ ὑπῆρχε as well as *was possible*, Th.3.109. 3. in neut. part., ὑπάρχον ὑμῖν πολεμεῖν *since it is allowed* you to . ., Th. 1.124, cf. Pl.*Smp.*217a.

C. *to be* ὕπαρχος or *subordinate colleague*, D.C.36.36; τῷ . . Ἀντωνίνῳ Id.71.34. II. dub. in the sense of ἄρχω, *rule*: for Th.6. 87, where the Sch. is in error, v. supr. B.III.2b; in Arist.*Pol.*1291ᵇ 32 ὑπερέχειν is prob. l.

**ὑπᾰρωμᾰτίζω**, *have something of an aromatic flavour*, Dsc.3.8.

**ὑπασθενέω**, *to be a little unwell*, Phryn.*PS*p.120B.

**ὑπασπ-ίδιος** [πῐ], ον, (ἀσπίς) *covered with a shield*, in Hom. only as Adv., ὑπασπίδια προποδίζων and προβιβῶντι (-βῶντος) Il.13.158, 807, 16.609:—after Hom. as Adj., ὑ. πολεμιστής Asius*Fr.Ep.*13.7 K.; τὸν ὑ. κόσμον the *body*-armour and arms of Ajax, S.*Aj.*1408 (anap.); ὑ. κοῖτον ἰαύειν sleep an *armed* sleep, sleep *in arms*, E.*Rh.*740 (anap.). **-ίζω**, *serve as shield-bearer*, τινι Pi.*N.*9.34, E.*Heracl.* 216. **-ιστήρ**, ῆρος, ὁ, *shield-bearing*, ὄχλος A.*Supp.*182. ⊛ **-ιστής**, οῦ, ὁ, *shield-bearer, armour-bearer, esquire*, Hdt.5.111, E.*Rh.*2 (anap.), *Ph.*1213, X.*An.*4.2.20, etc. 2. pl., a brigade of guards in the Macedonian army, D.S.19.40, Arr.*An.*2.4.3, 2.20.6.

**ὑπάσσω**, Att. for ὑπαΐσσω.

**ὑπαστράπτω**, *flash* or *gleam by reflection*, Philostr.*VA*2.24.

**ὕπαστρος**, ον, *under the stars, guided by the stars*, ὕπαστρον μῆχαρ ὁρίζομαι γάμου φυγάν I mark out *by the stars* a plan for escaping marriage, i.e. I flee to escape marriage, guiding my course by the stars, A.*Supp.*393 (lyr.).

⊛ **ὑπασχολέομαι**, *to be a subordinate official*, *OGI*179.10 (Egypt, i B.C.).

**ὑπᾱσώδης**, ες, *feeling slight nausea*, Hp.*Coac.*508.

**ὑπᾰτ-εία**, ἡ, *the office* or *rank of* ὕπατος, *consulate*, Plu.*Publ.*10, al., *Sammelb.*7445.1 (iv A.D.), 7340.3 (vi A.D.), etc.; in late Inscrr. and Papyri freq. written ὑπατία, *CIG*3467.3, *TAM*2(1).187 (Sidyma, iv A.D.), *PLond.*1.113.5(*a*). II. = ἀνθυπατεία, App.*Hisp.*83. **-εύω**, *to be consul*, *Mon.Anc.Gr.*11.21, Plu.*Publ.*3, etc.; ὁ ὑπατευκώς, Lat. *consularis*, Posidon.36 J. 2. *to be consular governor*, τῆς ἐπαρχείας *Ath.Mitt.*48.102, *IGRom.*1.575 (both Nicopolis ad Istrum, ii A.D.): abs., ib.3.1277 (Arabia, ii A.D.). ⊛ **-η** (sc. χορδή), ἡ, *the highest of the three strings* which formed the framework of the musical scale (opp. νεάτη, μέση), but *the lowest* in pitch, Philol.6, Pl.*R.*443d, etc.; αἱ ὑπάται *the highest tetrachord*, Anon.*Oxy.*667.16; τὴν ἀπὸ τῶν ὑπάτων . . ἐπίτασιν raising of pitch from the *low notes*, Antyll.ap.Orib. 6.10.7; τὸ βομβυκέστερον τῶν ὑπατῶν Nicom.*Harm.*11; ὑπάτη ὑπατῶν ibid. (but ὑ. ὑπάτων Cleonid.*Harm.*4). **-ήϊος**, ον, = ὕπατος, φέγγεα Ῥώμης Nonn.*D.*41.366. **-ία**, v. ὑπατεία. **-ικός**, ή, όν, *of* or *for a consul, consular*, ἀρχή Str.17.3.25, D.S.20.91; δύναμις Plu.*Cam.*1, etc. II. *of consular rank*, Lat. *consularis*, ἄνδρες Str. l.c., Plu.*Sert.* 27; ὁ ὑ. D.H.6.96, Luc.*Salt.*83; ὑπατικὸς ἐπὶ τῶν ναῶν *consularis aedium sacrarum*, *IG*14.1045; c. gen., ὑ. τῶν ἱερῶν ναῶν ib.993.

**ὑπάτμενοι**· δοῦλοι, ὑποῦργοι, Hsch.

**ὑπατμ-ίζω**, *vaporize, inhale*, Dsc.3.25, 5.11,13, al. (Pass.). **-ισμός**, ὁ, *vaporization*, Id.3.23, Orib.*Syn.*9.53, Alex.Trall.1.16. **-ός**, ὁ, = foreg., Paul.Aeg.6.75.

**ὑπᾰτο-ειδής**, ές, *in the region of the* ὑπάτη, in Music, Aristid. Quint.1.12; φθόγγος Bacch.*Harm.*43.

**ὑπ-άτοπος**, ον, *somewhat absurd*, Arist.*PA*644ᵃ35; cf. ὑπεράτοπος.

⊛ **ὕπᾰτος**, η, ον, also ος, ον (v. infr. III. 1), *highest, uppermost*, in Hom. as epith. of Zeus, ὕπατε κρειόντων Od.1.45; θεῶν ὕπατος Il. 19.258, al.; θεοὶ ὕπατοι the gods *above*, opp. οἱ χθόνιοι, A.*Ag.*89 (anap.), cf. 55 (anap.); Ζεὺς Ὕ. at Athens, Paus.1.26.5, al., Orac. ap.D.21.52 (coupled with Ἀθηνᾶ Ὑ. Orac.ap.eund.43.66); ὑ. δῶμα Διός Pi.*O.*1.42; ὑ. τεθμός Id.*N.*10.32; ὑπάταν βασιλῆιδα τειμάν *Hymn.Is.*143. 2. simply of Place, ἐν πυρῇ ὑ. on the *very top* of the funeral pile, Il.23.165, 24.787; ὑ. ὅρος Epigr.ap.D.S.1.15. b. *lowest*, κευθμοί A.R.3.1213. c. *furthest*, κέρας ὠκεανοῖο Id.4. 282. 3. of Time, *last*, νοῦσος *AP*7.233 (Apollonid.): but οὐχ ὕπατον, πύματον δέ Puchstein*Epigr.Gr.*p.76 (Memphis, i B.C.). 4. of Quality, *highest, best*, Pi.*O.*1.100; ὑ. πρὸς ἀρετάν *most excellent*, Id.*P.*6.42; ὑ. [μόρος] S.*Ant.*1332 (lyr.). II. c. gen., ὕπατος χώρας Ζεύς *supreme over* the land, A.*Ag.*509; ὕπατοι λεχέων *high above* the nest, ib.50 (anap.); ὑ. τῶ σκάνεος ἅπαντος Ti.Locr.100a; σοφίας ὕπατος *IG*2².3632.7 (ii A.D.). III. as Subst., 1. ὕπατος, ὁ, = Lat. *consul*, Plb.6.12.1, al., D.H.4.76, 6.1, 7.1, al., *Mon. Anc.Gr.*5.1; cf. στρατηγός II. 4:—hence also, = ὑπατικός, τὰν ὑπάταν ἀρχάν Epigr.ap.Plu.*Marc.*30; but in this sense commonly with masc. termin., ὕπατον ἀρχὴν ἔχειν Plb.2.11.1 (pl.), cf. 3.40.9, Hdn.2.6. 6; ὕπατος τιμή J.*BJ*7.4.2. 2. ἡ ὑπάτη, v. sub voce.—For the form, cf. μέσατος, νέατος, μύχατος, etc.

**ὑπ-αττῐκός**, ή, όν, *somewhat Attic*, εἰρωνευτής Timo 25.

**ὑπ-ᾰτῦφος**, ον, *moderately free from* τῦφος, Timo 60.

**ὑπαυγάζω**, *shine under, gleam beneath*, χρυσοῦ ψῆγμα ποταμῷ ἀργυροδίνῃ ὑπαυγάζον Philostr.*VS*2.1.14; οἱ μαζοὶ ὀρθοὶ ὑπαυγάζουσι Id. *Im.*2.8. 2. *begin to shine, dawn*, of daybreak, Luc.*VH*2.47, Polyaen.7.8.2. II. trans., *light up*, ἀστὴρ ὁλκὸν ὑπαυγάζων A.R.3.1378, cf. Dam.*Isid.*63.

**ὑπαυγή**, ἡ, *shining through*, Orib.45.18.6.

**ὑπαυγής**, ές, f.l. in Iamb.ap.Stob.3.3.26.

**ὕπαυγος**, ον, of a heavenly body, *within* 15° *of the sun, combust*, Serapio in *Cat.Cod.Astr.*8(4).230, Paul.Al.*L.*1 (with Sch.), Steph. in *Hp.Aph.*2.363D. II. less technically, *exposed to rays*, Orph.*Fr.* 353.

⊛ **ὑπαυλέω**, *play on the flute in accompaniment*, μέλος τισί Alcm. 78; πένθιμόν τι D.C.74.5; ὑ. λυσιῳδοῖς Posidon.4J.; Πανδιονίδι Luc. *Harm.*1: abs., Id.*Salt.*83.

⊛ **ὕπαυλις**, εως, ἡ, = ἔπαυλις, *PLond.*1.113.5(*a*) (v A.D.).

⊛ **ὑπαυλισμός**, ὁ, *music for the flute*, *BGU*1125.3, al. (i B.C.).

**ὕπαυλος**, ον, (αὐλή) *under* or *in the court*, c. gen., σκηνῆς ὕπαυλος *under shelter of* the tent, S.*Aj.*796.

**ὑπαυστηρός**, όν, *somewhat harsh* or *sour*, ἐν τῷ γλυκεῖ ὑ. Dsc.4. 55, cf. Sor.1.95, Gal.6.583.

**ὑπαυχένιος**, α, ον *AP*6.41 (Agath.), ος, ον Hld.3.4:—*under the neck*, βύρσα *AP* l.c.; λέπαδνον ib.4.3ᵇ.1 (Agath.). II. ὑπαυχένιον, τό, *cushion* or *pillow for the neck*, Sm.*Ez.*13.18, Gal.18(1).420, Luc. *Gall.*11, Paul.Aeg.4.48, 6.99; προσκεφάλαια ὑ. Poll.10.38.

**ὑπαύχενον**, τό, *the lower part of the neck*, Arat.487,524.

**ὑπαφᾰνίζω**, *make away with gradually*, Ael.*NA*2.56.

**ὑπαφήτορες**· ὑποτεταγμένοι, Hsch.

**ὑπαφίσταμαι**, *step back, withdraw*, Antipho4.4.1; μικρὸν ὑπαποστήσομαι Men.*Sam.*153; ἐξ Ἀθηνέων Thales ap.D.L.1.44; τῆς ὁδοῦ ἀλλήλοις Ael.*NA*2.25.

**ὑπαφρ-ίζω**, *foam somewhat*, Eust.586.8. **-ος**, ον, *frothy*, πέλαγος Sch.BT Il.14.16; πτύσματα Gal.9.564. II. = κρυφαῖος, Heraclid.Tarent.ap.Erot., who cites Hp. *de Arte*10, S.*Frr.*236,312; so ὕπαφρον ὄμμ' ἔχων (of Odysseus) in E.*Rh.*711 (lyr.), acc. to Sch.; Hsch. explains by τὸ μὴ φανερόν, also κρύφιον καὶ ὕπουλον, and τὸ ὑγρασίαν ἔχον ἐμφερῆ ἀφρῷ (i.e. *blear*-eyed in E. l.c.). [ὕπαφρον codd. Hp., E., Hsch., Phot.; ὕποφρος (-ον) codd. Erot.; in Hp. this sense hardly fits, and Littré accepts Schneider's cj. ὑπόφορον 'pierced with ducts'.]

**ὑπάφρων**, ονος, ὁ, ἡ, *somewhat stupid* or *unintelligent*, ἐόντων τῶν Θρηΐκων ὑπαφρονεστέρων Hdt.4.95.

**ὑπάφωνος**, ον, *somewhat indistinct, obscure*, of a symptom, dub. in Hp.*Prorrh.*1.107 = *Coac.*315.

**ὑπαχλύνομαι**, Pass., *grow dark by degrees*, ὑπηχλύνθη οὐρανός Q.S. 1.67.

**ὑπέᾱσι**, Ion. for ὕπεισι, 3 pl. of ὕπειμι (q.v.).

**ὑπέατι**, perh. Ion. dat. of ὕπεας (q.v.).

**ὑπέγγυος**, ον, *under surety*: I. of persons, *having given surety, liable to be called to account* or *punished*, A.*Ch.*38 (lyr.); ὑ. πλὴν θανάτου *liable to any punishment* short of death, Hdt.5.71: c. dat., τὸ γὰρ ὑπέγγυον δίκᾳ καὶ θεοῖσιν *liability* to human and divine justice, E.*Hec.*1027 (lyr.). 2. of things, *legitimate*, γάμος ὑ., opp. ἀνέγγυος, Poll.3.34. II. *pledged, hypothecated*, *BGU*1792.7 (i B.C.), *POxy.*507.31 (ii A.D.).

**ὑπεγείρω**, *rouse gradually*, ἑαυτόν Philostr.*VS*1.21.5; βραχίονα Id. *Im.*1.24, cf. Ael.*NA*6.1.

**ὑπέγκειμαι**, *form an inner layer*, cj. for ὑπέρκ- in Sor.1.57.

**ὑπεγκλίνω** [ῑ], *turn a little* or *gradually*, οἰήϊον Orph.*A.*1205.

**ὑπεδέκτο**, Ep. 3 sg. aor. 2 of ὑποδέχομαι (q.v.).

⊛ **ὑπειδόμην**, aor. Med. (inf. ὑπιδέσθαι, part. ὑπιδόμενος, in codd. freq. written ὑπείδεσθαι, -ειδόμενος, as if from a pres. ὑπείδομαι, which is found in late Gr., v. infr. III):—*view from below, behold*, E. *Supp.*694; of a prophetic vision, τὴν τύχην θ' ὑπειδόμην τὴν σήν, ἃ πείσῃ τ' . . Id.*Hyps.Fr.*60.37. II. metaph., *mistrust, suspect*, Id.*Ion*1023, Plb.1.66.6, etc. 2. *perceive, detect*, ὡς . . Dam.*Pr.* 429. III. *seem*, ὃ ὑπείδεται πως εἰπεῖν which he *appears* to mean, ib.345.

**ὑπεικ-ᾰθεῖν**, aor. 2 of ὑπείκω, ὑπεικάθοιμι S.*El.*361, Pl.*Ap.*32a; 3 pl. ὑπείκαθον A.R.4.339; 3 sg. ὑποείκαθε Orph.*A.*706; pres. part. ὑπεικαθέων (as if from *ὑπεικαθέω) Opp.*H.*5.500. **-τέον**, *one must give way* or *yield*, S.*Aj.*668, Pl.*Cri.*51b. **-τικός**, ή, όν, *disposed to yield, yielding*, Arist.*GC*326ᵃ14. **-ω**, Ep. ὑποείκω, with impf. ὑπόεικον, Il.16.305: fut. ὑπείξω A.*Ag.*1362, S.*OT*625, D.15.24;

ὑπείξομαι Il.1.294, Od.12.117; Ep. also ὑποείξομαι Il.23.602: aor. 1 ὑπεῖξα X.*An.*7.7.31; Ep. ὑπόειξα Il.15.227: cf. ὑπεικαθεῖν:—*retire, withdraw, depart,* c. gen. loci, νεῶν *from* the ships, Il.16.305; ὑ. τινὶ ἕδρης *retire from* one's seat *for* another, make room for him, Od.16.42; ὑ. τοῦ ἀρχαίου λόγου *draw back* from.., Hdt.7.160; ὑ. τινὶ λόγων (cj. Valck. for λόγῳ) give one the first word, allow him to speak first, X.*Mem.*2.3.16; πολίταις ὁδῶν καὶ θάκων καὶ λόγων ὑπείκειν Id.*Cyr.*8.7.10. 2. *yield, give way,* ὑ. τινὶ Id.*An.*7.7.31: abs., of a seaman, ὅστις..πόδα τείνας ὑπείκει μηδέν S.*Ant.*716; of things, Il.20.266; ὅσα δένδρων ὑ. S.*Ant.*713; ὑ. ὑγρὰ οὖσα ἡ κνήμη X.*Eq.*7.6; ὑ. αἱ δάπιδες *are soft and yielding,* Id.*Cyr.*8.8.16; ἐν ὑπείκοντι in *a yielding substance,* Arist.*PA*694ᵇ15; πρὸς ἀντιπῖπτον.. καὶ οὐ πρὸς ὑπεῖκον Id.*Pr.*961ᵇ4; καθ' ἅπερ ἂν ὑπείκῃ Gal.2.711; τὸ ὑπεῖκον, = οἱ ὑπείκοντες, E.*IT*327. 3. c. acc., πάροιθε νεμεσσηθεὶς ὑπόειξε χεῖρας ἐμάς *he scaped* my hands, Il.15.227. II. metaph., *yield, give way, comply,* ib.211; θεοῖσιν ὑπείξεαι ἀθανάτοισι Od.12.117, cf. Il.23.602; ἀλλ' ἤτοι μὲν ταῦθ' ὑποείξομεν ἀλλήλοισι 4.62; σοὶ πᾶν ἔργον ὑπείξομαι *I will give way* to thee in.., 1.294: in Trag., Att., etc., sts. abs., *yield, submit,* S.*Aj.*371, *OT*625, Th.1.127, Pl. *Ap.*32a, *Ep.Hebr.*13.17, etc.: sts. c. dat., *submit to,* A.*Ag.*1362; τιμαῖς S.*Aj.*670; γήρᾳ ὑ. E.*IA*1140 (anap.); ὑ. θυμουμένοις Pl.*Lg.*717d, cf. *R.*336e, etc.; ἐπιθυμίαις Phld.*D.*1.25: c. inf., νῷν ὕπεικε τὸν κασίγνητον μολεῖν *concede* to us that.., S.*OC*1184; ὑ. δαμῆναι *submit* to be conquered, A.R.4.1676; but ὑ. μὴ πολεμίζειν *yield,* so as not to.., prob. l. ib.408 (ὑπείξομαι, -ωμαι codd.).

⊛ **ὑπειλέομαι,** Pass., *wriggle, creep under,* ὑπειλοῦνται πέτραν Ael. *NA*9.57; ὑπιλληθέωσιν, glossed by ὑποσυστραφῶσιν, Hp.ap.Gal. 19.148; of a bandage, *to be passed under,* Heliod.ap.Orib.48. 51.1.

**ὑπειλίσσω,** perh. implied by ὑπήλικται, v. ὑπελίσσω.

**ὑπείλλω,** or **ὑπίλλω** (both forms in codd.), aor. perh. ὕπιλα, *draw in, contract,* οὐρὰν δ' ὑπίλασ' ὑπὸ λεοντόπουν βάσιν καθέζετο E. *Fr.*540 (ὑπίλλας codd.Ael., ὑπῆλας codd.Ath., ὑπείλλει codd.Erot.); μηδεὶς μοχθηρὸς ἄπορος ὑπείλλων καὶ ὑποστέλλων ἀχρηματίας οἴκτῳ τὸ δίκην δοῦναι παρακρουέσθω *evading,* Ph.2.348. II. *keep shut,* σοὶ δ' ὑπίλλουσιν στόμα S.*Ant.*509.

**ὕπειμι,** (εἰμί *sum*) *to be under,* c. dat., φίλτατοι ἄνδρες ἐμῷ ὑπέασι μελάθρῳ *are under* my roof, Il.9.204; ὄνυχες χείρεσσιν ὑπῆσαν Hes.*Sc.*266; of young sucking animals, πολλῇσι [ἵπποις] πῶλοι ὑπῆσαν *under* many mares *were* sucking foals, Il.11.681; of horses, *to be under the yoke,* ὑπὸ τοῖσι ἅρμασι ὑ. Hdt.7.86. II. *to be* or *lie underneath,* ὕ. οἰκήματα ὑπὸ γῆν Id.2.127; κρηπὶς ὑπῆν λιθίνη X. *An.*3.4.7; μὴ στερεμνίου τινὸς ἡμῖν ὑπόντος if we had not some solid *support, basis,* Phld.*D.*3.11: metaph., κοὐδέπω κακῶν κρηπὶς ὕπεστι A. *Pers.*815 codd. 2. like ὑπόκειμαι II.2, *to be laid down,* ὑπόντος τοῦδε this *being granted,* E.*El.*1036. 3. *to be concealed, lurk,* δείσαντες μὴ ἐνέδρα τις ὑπείη X.*Cyr.*1.4.23; ἡ μὲν πρὸς τὴν τροφὴν ὄρεξις πολλάκις ὕπεστιν, ἐπισκοτεῖται δὲ ὑπὸ τῆς..λύπης Sor.1.37. 4. of things, *subsist, be available,* βίος ἀρκέων ὑπῆν Hdt.1.31; μεγάλα χρήματα..ὑπῆν τοῖς στρατιώταις Th.8.36; ὕπεστί μοι θάρσος S.*El.* 479 (lyr.); διὰ τὸ..ὑπεῖναι ἐλπίδα..ἀντιτυχεῖν Th.6.87; τοῖς μὲν γὰρ..ἐλπίδες ὕ. Isoc.12.10; ὑπούσης τῆς ἔχθρας Is.1.33; διὰ τὴν τόθ' ὑποῦσαν ἀπέχθειαν D.18.36; τοῖς μὲν ζῶσι πᾶσιν ὕ. τις..φθόνος ib. 315, etc. 5. *occur to* one, αὐτῷ δέ μοι ὑπῆν ὡς.. Pl.*Ep.*339e. 6. *follow, be subsequent,* A.D.*Synt.*16.22. III. *to be subjected* or *subject,* E.*Supp.*443; κτῆμα βασιλέων οἱ ὑπόντες *subjects,* A.D.*Synt.* 292.26.

**ὕπειμι,** (εἶμι *ibo*) used as fut. of ὑπέρχομαι, *steal secretly upon* one, *steal a march on,* c. acc., ἡ τυραννὶς ὡς λάθρα γ' ἐλάνθαν' ὑπιοῦσά με Ar.*V.*465 (lyr., s.v.l.); τοὺς βασιλέας ὑπῄει δέος Paus.7.1.7; ὑπῄει ἐπῶν ἡμᾶς..μνήμη Id.10.4.2; also ὕπεισί με.. it *occurs* (or *will occur*) *to* me, Aristid.1.448 J.: rarely c. dat., ὑπῄει μοι τὸ γιγνόμενον Plu.2.652b. 2. of persons, ὑ. τινά *insinuate oneself into* his *favour,* Id.*Cic.*45, D.Chr.4.10. II. *fall back, retire,* Hdt.4. 120. III. Medic., τὰ ὑπιόντα *motions,* Hp.*Aff.*11: impers., ταύτῃ ὕπεισι *the urine will pass* that way, Ruf.*Ren.Ves.*3.17.

**ὕπειξις,** εως, ἡ, (ὑπείκω) *yielding, compliance,* both in sg. and pl., Pl.*Lg.*815a, 727a, Hierocl. in *CA*5p.427 M.; δειλία..ὕ. τις ψυχῆς Thphr.*Char.*25.1: c. dat., ἡ τοῦ θήλεος ὕ. τῷ ἄρρενι Plu.2.751d.

**ὑπεῖπον,** aor. with no pres. in use (ὑπαγορεύω (q.v.) being used instead): fut. ὑπερῶ Ar.*Fr.*652: pf. Pass., v. infr. 2:—*say* or *repeat before* another, ἐγὼ δ' ὑπερῶ τὸν ὅρκον l.c. 2. *say by way of preface, premise, suggest,* ὑπειπεῖν τούσδε τοὺς αὐτοὺς λόγους E.*Supp.* 1171; ὀλίγ' ἄττ' ὑπειπὼν πρῶτον Ar.*V.*55; ὥσπερ ἐν ἀρχῇ ὑπείπομεν Th.1.35; τοσοῦτον ὑπειπών D.18.60; οὐδὲν ὑπειπὼν πῶς without *suggesting* the method, Id.23.53, cf. 60; τοιοῦτος.., ὃν ὑπεῖπες Pl.*Virt.*377d; so ἀκοὴν ὑπειπών, = προειπών (referring to the words of the proclamation, ἀκούετε, λεῴ), E.*HF*962:—Pass., καθάπερ καὶ ἐξ ἀρχῆς ἦν ὑπειρημένον Is.11.12. 3. *subjoin, add,* ὑπειπούσης ..ὅτι ἐς ἑσπέραν ἥξοιμι Ar.*Pl.*997, cf. Lys.*Fr.* in *PHib.*1.14.32; ὑπειπὼν τἄλλα ὅτι αὐτὸς τἀκεῖ πράξοι Th.1.90, cf. 2.102; τὸν ἐχθρὸν ..ὑπειπὼν τὸν αὑτοῦ *adding the name of* his personal enemy, D.25. 91; ὑπειπὼν τῆς Ὑγιείας τοὔνομα Philetaer.1. 4. *suggest an explanation, hint, give a clue,* ὥστ'..ἄν..ὑπείποις S.*Aj.*213 (anap.); οὑτωσί πως ὑπειπόντα τὸ τοῦ Πιττακοῦ Pl.*Prt.*343e.

**ὑπείρ,** poet. for ὑπέρ, used when a long syll. is needed before a vowel, e.g. ὑπεὶρ ἅλα: also in compds.

**ὑπειράλιος** [ᾰ], ον, Ep. form of *ὑπεράλιος, *on the sea,* D.P.851, 1085.

**ὑπειρέχω,** v. ὑπερέχω. **ὑπείροχος,** v. ὑπέροχος.

**ὑπ-είρω,** *insert underneath,* τοὺς δακτύλους Hp.*Art.*32.

**ὑπείσας,** v. ὑφεῖσα.

**ὑπεισ-βαίνω,** *steal into,* δόμους ὑπεσβαίνουσα cj. Housman in E. *Med.*382 (ὑπερβ- codd.). **-δύομαι,** Med. with aor. 2 Act. ὑπεισέδυν, *get in secretly, slip* or *steal in,* Hdt.1.12 (ὑπεκδύς is prob. cj.); *come* or *go in gradually,* Arist.*GC*325ᵇ4:—Act. pres. ὑπεισδύνω, *EM*290. 13. **-ειμι,** (εἶμι *ibo*) *enter upon, succeed to,* εἰς τὴν αὐτῶν τάξιν *Cod. Just.*1.3.41.1, cf. *PLond.*1.77.18 (vi A.D.). 2. *succeed to* an office, τὴν πρωτοκωμητίαν ib.5.1677.48 (vi A.D.). 3. Ἀγαθῖνος εἰς τὴν τοιαύτην ὑπεισῄει διδασκαλίαν *succeeded to,* i.e. came to give his authority to, this teaching, Gal.7.488. II. *enter imperceptibly,* ὑ. τί τινα *comes into* one's mind, Ach.Tat 8.17. **-έλευσις,** εως, ἡ, *succession* to an inheritance, *Cod.Just.*6.4.4.20a. **-ελευστέον,** = *obeundum, Gloss.* ⊛ **-έρχομαι,** *enter upon secretly,* λαθὸν ὑπεισῆλθεν τὸ γῆρας, v.l. for ὑπῆλθεν, *came on me unawares,* Pl.*Ax.*367b; πάντως ἂν οἶκτος αὐτὸν ὑπεισῆλθε pity would *have stolen over* him, Lib.*Decl.*6.38 (v.l. ὑπῆλθε). 2. *come into one's mind,* Luc.*Merc.Cond.*11. 3. *enter instead, be substituted,* τῶν συμφώνων τούτων, ἃ ὑπεισέρχεται εἰς τὸν τόπον τούτου the consonants which *are substituted* for it, Dosith. p.385 K. 4. *enter* a body *in one's turn,* εἰς τοὺς ἐμοὺς ἀνθρώπους *PGiss.*40 ii6 (iii A.D.); *succeed to* office, βουλευτικὸν φρόντισμα *PSI*6. 684.4 (iv/v A.D.). II. *slip into, assume,* πρᾶον σχῆμ' ὑπεισελθών Men.689. **-ρέω,** *flow in gradually,* Longus 1.1.

**ὑπέκ,** before a vowel ὑπέξ, (ὑπό, ἐκ) poet. Prep. with gen., *out from under, from beneath, away from,* ὑπὲκ κακοῦ, θανάτοιο, etc., Il. 13.89, 15.628, al.; ὑπὲξ ἁλός A.R.4.933, cf. Q.S.4.402.

**ὑπεκ-βαίνω,** *go out from below,* Anon.ap.Suid. s.v. κᾆτα; of a vein, Gal.2.793; ὑπεκβὰς τοῦ δεσμωτηρίου *escaping..,* Agath.4.28, cf. 5.1, 20. **-βάλλω,** *cast out, reject, AP*5.65 (Rufin.). II. *pass by,* ὑπὲκ ποταμοῖο βαλεῖν Ἀμύροιο ῥέεθρα A.R.1.596. III. f.l. for ὑπαικάλλω in Plu.2.530d. ⊛ **-δέχομαι,** *have under oneself,* of a cow, μαστῷ πόρτιν ὑ., of a calf at the udder, *AP*9.722 (Antip. Sid.). **-διδράσκω,** only in aor. ὑπεξέδραν, *run out, escape secretly from,* τοῦ Κύκλωπος Plu.2.642b; ἐκ Καρχηδόνος Id. *Flam.*20: abs., D.C.36.24. **-δύομαι,** Med., with aor. 2 and pf. Act., *slip out of, escape,* c. acc., πόνους Τρωϊκοὺς ὑπεξέδυν E. *Cyc.*347, cf. Plu.2.170f, Opp.*H.*3.384, etc.: metaph., ὑπεκδυόμενοι τὴν Στοάν Phld.*Sto.Herc.*339.13: also c. gen., Plu.*Dem.*9: abs., ὑπεκδὺς *having slipped out,* Hdt.1.10, Plu.*Arat.*9, etc.; ὑπεκδέδυκα δεῦρ' ἔξω λάθρα Men.*Epit.*483.—An Act. impf. ὑπεξέδυνε in Babr.4.4. **-δῠσις,** εως, ἡ, *slipping out* or *away, escape,* Opp.*H.* 3.395. **-θεμα,** ατος, τό, *supplementary item* of account, *IG* 5(1).1390.59 (Andania, i B.C., ὑπεχθ- lap.). **-θέσῐμος,** ον, of merchandise, *deposited for re-exportation, GDI*5040.25 (Crete, written ὑπεχθέσιμος); cf. ὑπεκτίθεμαι II. ⊛ **-θεσις,** εως, ἡ, *a removing secretly,* κτήσεως J.*BJ*4.7.2. **-θέω,** *run off secretly* or *gradually,* Emp.100.21, Plu.*Pomp.*80. **-κᾰθαίρω,** *purge from beneath,* in Pass., Hp.*Mul.*1.60, *Nat.Mul.*35. **-καίω,** *kindle,* Thphr.*Ign.*63: metaph., *stir up,* ὑ. τὴν γνώμην Luc.*Peregr.*26; *inflame,* ἔχθραν Plu.2.616e; πλῆθος Id.*Dio*22. ⊛ **-κᾰλύπτω,** *uncover from below* or *a little, AP*7.480 (Pass., Leon.). **-καυμα,** ατος, τό, *combustible matter, fuel,* X.*Cyr.*7.5.22, Arist.*Resp.*473ᵃ5, *Mete.*341ᵇ19, al.: metaph. of *food,* as supplying animal heat, Hp.*Aph.*1.14, Plu.2. 694f, Aët.9.19. b. the supposed *Sphere of Fire* surrounding the atmosphere, Simp. *in Cael.*20.26, al. (quoting Arist.*Mete.* l.c.). 2. metaph., *provocative, incentive,* ἔρωτος X.*Smp.*4.25; πολλοῖς ὑ. ἔστ' ἔρωτος μουσική Men.237, cf. Phld.*Mus.*p.80 K.; ὑ. τῆς νόσου Arist. *Pr.*859ᵇ19; πόθου καὶ χάριτος Plu.*Lyc.*15. **-καυσις,** εως, ἡ, *kindling,* Alex.Aphr. *in Mete.*33.18. **-καύστρια,** ἡ, *she who lights a fire underneath,* name of the priestess of Athene at Soli, Plu.2.292a (ὑπερκαύστρα (sic) Hsch.). **-κειμαι,** Pass., *to be carried out to a place of safety,* to be *stowed safe away,* Hdt.8.41, 9.73, Th.8.31; ἐς [Σαλαμῖνα] Hdt.8.60.β'; of money, Th.1.137; ὑ. παρά τισι Isoc.19.18.—Cf. ὑπεκτίθεμαι I. **-κενόω,** *empty out below,* D.C.69.4. **-κλέπτω,** *carry off secretly,* J.*AJ*14.11.6, Opp.*H.*4.48:—Pass., χρήματα ὑπεκκλαπέντα Plu.*Them.*25. **-κλίνω** [ῑ], *bend aside, escape,* Ar.*Eq.*272 (troch.): c. acc., *shun, avoid,* Plu.*Cam.*18. **-κομίζω,** *carry out* or *away to safety,* Th.4.123, Plu.*Cam.*21; *eliminate insensibly,* τὸ πλήρωμα Ruf.ap.Orib.45.30.51:—Med., ὑπεκκομίσασθαι πάντα *get* all *one's goods carried out to safety,* Hdt.9.6, cf. X.*Cyr.*2.4.13. **-κρίνομαι** [ῑ], Pass., *to be carried off insensibly,* D.L.9.76. **-λαμβάνω,** *carry off underhand,* ἔσω δόμων E.*HF*997. **-λείπω,** *fail* or *flag by degrees,* Thphr.*Ign.*55, Gal.8.489. **-λῠσις,** εως, ἡ, *reduction,* τῆς φλεγμονῆς Sor.1.122. **-λύω,** *loosen* or *weaken a little,* τὴν γνώμην Plu.*Nic.*14; τὴν σφοδρότητα τῆς ἐμβολῆς J.*BJ*7.8.5; τὸν τῆς ὁλκῆς τόνον Sor.2.61 (prob.); ἐπὶ συνουσίαν ὁρμὰς Ps.-Dsc.1.103; [ὁ οἶνος] στρατηγοὺς τῆς φρονήσεως ὑπεκλύει Sch.Il.6.260; *weaken the force of,* τὸν λόγον A.D.*Synt.*224.4:—Pass., *cease, become weaker and weaker,* παλμοὶ ὑπεκλυόμενοι Hp.*Mul.*1.25; οἶνος Sch.Ar.*V.*151; ὑπεκλυομένην ἴσχει τὴν ταραχήν S.E.*M.*11.214, cf. Sor.2.11: c. gen., *to be freed from,* τινος A.D.*Synt.*41.11. **-πέμπω,** *send out secretly,* δύο ναῦς Th.4.8; ὑ. τινὰ χθονός E.*Hec.*6; ὑ. [τινὰ] λάθρᾳ ἄλλους ἐς οἴκους Id.*Andr.*47:—Pass., c. acc. loci, τὸ Φωκέων πέδον ὑπεξεπέμφθην *to* Phocis, S.*El.*1350. **-περάω,** *go forth and pass over,* πόντον ναῦται ὑπεκπερόωσιν Q.S.5.246, cf. Orph.*A.*69. **-πηδάω,** *spring out from under,* Aristaenet.2.5. **-πίπτω,** *miss,* τοῦ καιροῦ J.*AJ* 16.11.5 (dub. l.). 2. *prolapse,* cj. in Sor.1.12. **-πλέω,** *sail out secretly,* Plu.*Lys.*11, Philostr.*VS*2.21.1. **-πνέω,** *exhale* or *evapo-*

*rate gradually*, metaph., Pl.*Ax.*365c. **-πονέω**, *work out under* another's command, Poll.9.110.

**ὑπεκπρο-θέω**, *run forth from under, outstrip*, Ἄτη.. πάσας (sc. τὰς Λιτὰς) πολλὸν ὑπεκπροθέει Il.9.506: abs., ὁ τὸν πεδίοιο διώκετο.. τυτθὸν ὑπεκπροθέοντα *running on before*, 21.604, cf. Od.8.125, A.R. 4.937. **-θρῴσκω**, aor. part. -θορών, *spring out from under*, Opp. *C.*4.160. **-λύω**, *loose from under*, ἡμιόνους μὲν ὑπεκπροέλυσαν ἀπήνης *loosed* the mules *from under* the carriage-yoke, *unyoked and let* them *go to graze*, Od.6.88. **-ρέω**, *flow up and out*, of water *running in and out of* a rock-basin, ib.87. **-τάμνω** (Ion. for -τέμνω), *go forth and cut*, ὑπεκπρὸ δὲ πόντον ἔταμνε νηῦς A.R.4. 225. **-φεύγω**, *flee away secretly, escape and flee*, ὑπεκπροφυγών Il. 20.147, 21.44; πῇ κεν ὑπεκπροφύγοιμι; Od.20.43: c. acc., εἴ πως.. ὑπεκπροφύγοιμι Χάρυβδιν 12.113; ὅτ' ἀνὴρ ὑπεκπροφύγῃ κακότητα Hes.*Sc.*42. **-χέομαι**, Pass., *stream forth from under*, ὕζον Q.S. 13.57.

**ὑπέκ-πῡρος**, ον, (πῦρ) *somewhat on fire*, Orph.*L.*140. **-ρέω**, *flow out from under*, τὰ ὄρη Philostr.*Im.*1.12. II. metaph., *pass away gradually*, Pl.*Smp.*203e; opp. προσέρχομαι, Arist.*GC*321ᵇ27, Plot.4.4.42; c. acc., τοὺς ἀμνήμονας ὑπεκρεῖ τὰ γιγνόμενα μετὰ τοῦ χρόνου Plu.*Mar.*46; of a person, ὑπεκρυεὶς τῆς σκηνῆς *having slipped out of* the tent, Id.*Pomp.*3. 2. *waste away*, νόσῳ, v.l. for ὑπορρέω, J.*BJ*1.33.2. **-ρήγνῡμαι**, Pass., *to be gradually broken away*, Plu.*Cam.*3. **-ρίπτω**, *dislodge by intrigue*, 'elbow out of..' Id. *Comp.Ages.Pomp.*1. **-σῴζω**, *save by drawing away from*, φίλους δ' ὑπεκσῴζοιεν ἐναλίων πόρων A.*Pers.*453: abs., αὐτὸν ὑπεξεσάωσεν (Ep. for -έσωσεν) Il.23.292. **-τελέω**, *accomplish secretly*, Q.S.1. 204. **-τήκω**, *cause to waste slowly away*, τύλους Gal.13.745; τὸν ὄγκον ib.242; ἀδένας ἢ ὑμένας Heras ap.eund.13.795:—Pass., ὑ. σάρκες Hp.*Flat.*12. **-τίθεμαι**, Med., *bring* one's property *to a place of safety*, of persons or things which one removes from the dangers of war, ἔστ' ἂν αὐτοὶ τέκνα τε καὶ τοὺς οἰκέτας ὑπεκθέωνται Hdt.8.4, cf. 41, Th.1.89; ἐκ χερῶν κλέψας' Ὀρέστην τῶν ἐμῶν ὑπεξέθου S.*El.*297; ὃν ἔξω δωμάτων ὑπεξέθου E.*Andr.*69; ὑπεκθέμενοι παῖδας ἐς Σαλαμῖνα Lys.2.34; ὑ. τὰ χρήματα X.*Cyr.*6.1.26; τοῖς ὑπεκτεθημένοις (sic) τὰ βοσκήματα διὰ τὸν πόλεμον *BCH*54.269 (Rhamnus, iii B.C.); *pueros* ὑπεκθέμενος *in Graeciam*, Cic.*Att.*7.17.4, cf. *OGI*437.64 (Pergam., i B.C.):—Pass., ὑπεκτιθέμενοι ἔξω τῆς χώρης οἱ παῖδες.. ἥλωσαν Hdt.5.65. II. *deposit for re-exportation*, εἰ δέ τί κα.. ὑπέχθηται (Cret. for ὑπέκ-θηται) *GDI*5040.21; cf. ὑπεκθέσιμος. III. Act. -τίθημι, *expose* a new-born child, Lib.*Decl.*34. 14: in Med. simply, *bring forth*, γεννᾶν καὶ ὑ. τὸν τόκον Jul.*Or.*4. 145a. **-τρέπω**, *turn gradually* or *secretly from* a thing, τῶν δ' ὑ. πόδα S.*Tr.*549:—Med., *turn aside from*, c. acc., Pl.*Phd.*108b: c. inf., ὑπεκτραποίμην μὴ οὐ συνεκσῴζειν *decline the task* of helping.., S.*OC*566. **-τρέχω**, fut. -δρᾱμοῦμαι Id.*Ant.*1086: aor. ὑπεξέδραμον Hdt.1.156:—*run out from under, escape from*, τὸ παρεὸν Hdt. l.c.; θάλπος οὐχ ὑπεκδραμεῖ S. l.c.; ὑ. τὴν σὴν.. γλωσσαλγίαν (where the metaph. is taken from a ship) E.*Med.*524; θεοὺς ὑπεκδραμούμενοι Id.*Ph.*873: abs., of horses, Plu.*Eum.*7: c. inf., ἢν ἐγὼ μὴ θανεῖν ὑπεκδράμω E.*Andr.*338. II. *run out beyond*, τοῦ χρόνου τέλος S. *Tr.*167. **-τροφή**, ἡ, *upbringing of a succession*, εἰς ὑ. πάτρας v.l. (ap.Gal.*Protr.*10) for εἰς ὑπερβολὴν πατρός in E.*Fr.*282.6. **-τρώγω**, aor. 2 ὑπεξέτρᾰγον, *gnaw secretly away*, Macho ap.Ath.13. 579d. **-φαίνω**, *show forth*, τὴν ὥραν τῶν ὀστῶν Philostr.*Im.*1. 24. **-φέρω**, *carry out a little*, ὑπεξέφερεν σάκος *lifted* it *a little outwards*, so that Teucer could take shelter under it, Il.8.268. II. *carry out from under, carry off*, so as to be out of danger, φίλον υἱὸν ὑπεξέφερεν πολέμοιο 5.318; τυτθὸν γὰρ ὑπὲκ θανάτοιο φέρονται 15. 628: generally, *carry away, bear onward*, ὑπέκφερον ὠκέες ἵπποι (sc. αὐτούς) Od.3.496; ἵππος ὑ. τὸν ἄνδρα Plu.*Luc.*17; πόδες αὐτὸν ὑπέκφερον A.R.1.1264. 2. *eliminate insensibly*, Ruf.*Ren.Ves.*3. 3. III. intr., ὑ. ἡμέρης ὁδῷ *get on before, have the start* by a day's journey, Hdt.4.125. IV. *endure*, πόνους Lesb.Rh.2. 7. V. v.l. for ὑπεξέφυγεν in Il.22.202. **-φεύγω**, *flee away* or *escape*, Il.8.243, 20.191, Od.23.320, S.*Ant.*553, Pl.*Euthd.*291b. II. mostly c. acc., *escape from*, ὑ. ὄλεθρον, κῆρα, κακότητα, Il.6.57, 16.687, Od.3.175, al.; μίασμα S.*Ant.*776; ἐπηρείας τοιαύτας Marcellin.*Puls.* 89; τὸ κέρας τῶν Πελοποννησίων.. ἐς τὴν εὐρυχωρίαν Th.2.90, cf. 91. **-φράζω**, *detail gradually*, Eust.1957.33. **-φυγγάνω**, = ὑπεκφεύγω, Hp.*Morb.*2.14. **-φύομαι**, Pass., *grow gradually out of*, ὑ. τῶν κροτάφων κέρας Philostr.*Im.*1.15. **-χᾰλάω**, *let oneself down from*, ἐκ θυρίδος αὐτόν *AP*11.200 (Leon., cj. Scaliger for ὑπερ-). II. Pass., *to be relaxed*, Sor.1.65 (cj. Rose for ὑπερ-). **-χέω**, in Pass., *well up*, ὑπεξέχυτ' αὐτίκα δάκρυ A.R.3. 705: metaph. in Act., *get rid of*, φθόνους καὶ ζηλοτυπίας Plu.2.78e.

**ὑπεκχωρ-έω**, *withdraw, retire*, (sc. ἐκ τῆς Ἀττικῆς) Hdt.9.13,14; ὑ. τοῦ βίου Pl.*Lg.*785b: c. dat., *retire and give place to* another, Id. *Phd.*103d; ὑ. τῷ θανάτῳ *make way for* death, *and so escape*, ib. 106e. 2. *to be purged*, ἐπὴν φάρμακόν τις πιὼν κάτω καὶ ἄνω ὑπεκχωρέῃ Hp.*Loc.Hom.*33. **-ησις**, εως, ἡ, *excretion by stool*, ib. 1,41. **-ητικός**, ή, όν, *purgative*, τὰ -κά ib.41.

**ὑπέλαιον**, τό, *sediment* or *lees of oil*, elsewh. γλοιός, Hsch. (-ος cod.).

**ὑπελάσσων**, ον, gen. ονος, *slightly smaller*, Gal.18(2).862.

**ὑπελάτη** [ᾰ], ἡ, a shrub, = χαμαιδάφνη, Plin.*HN*15.131.

**ὑπελαύνω** (sc. τὸν ἵππον), *ride up* so as to meet, X.*An.*1.8.15 (v.l. for πελάσας), cf. Demetr.*Eloc.*93. II. Pass., *to be purged downwards*, Aret.*CA*1.5.

**ὑπέλαφρος**, ά, όν, *somewhat light, unimportant*, S.E.*M.*1.63.

**ὑπελέγχω**, *refute gently*, μετρίως ὑ. Lyd.*Mag.*2.26.

**ὑπέλεθρος**, ὁ, *dung of swine*, Eust.1821.40.

**ὑπελθετέον**, (ὑπέρχομαι) *one must take shelter under*, ὑπὸ τὰς στοάς Str.13.3.6.

**ὑπελίσσω**, *turn up*, τὸν ὀφθαλμὸν κάτωθεν Ach.Tat.1.6:—Pass., 3 sg. pf. written ὑπήλικται *is* (*are*) *wrapped up*, *BGU*781 i 10, vi 6 (i A.D.).

**ὑπεμβάλλω**, *insert under*, τοῖς σκέλεσι προσκεφάλαιον Heliod.ap. Orib.50.49.3. 2. *insert after*, τῷ ο ὑπεμβάλλουσι τὸ υ (in νοῦσος, etc.) Greg.Cor.p.387 S.

**ὑπέμβρῠον**, τό, *foetus*, ὑ. ἐκβάλλουσιν Poet. *de herb.*104.

**ὑπεμβρῠόω**, *impregnate*, S.*Fr.*[1127.4].

**ὑπεμνήμῡκε**, in Il.22.491, πάντα δ' ὑπεμνήμυκε, of an orphan boy: Aristarch. interpreted it—*he hangs down his head* utterly, *he is* altogether *cast down*; so that it must be taken (cf. Sch.) as Ep. pf. of ὑπ-ημύω, for ὑπ-εμήμυκε (ν being inserted metri gr.):—the pres. is used by Coluth.338, ὑπημύουσι παρειαί *sink in, become hollow*.

**ὑπεμ-πίπρημι**, *put fire under, set on fire*, J.*BJ*2.19.4, D.C.62.16 (dub. l.). **-φαίνω**, *hint at, indicate*, S.E.*M.*1.4, Gal.19.556, etc. II. intr., *to be cogent*, of a proof, Papp.650.5.

**ὑπεναντιολογία**, ἡ, *contradiction*, Phld.*Rh.*1.p.64 S. (pl.).

**ὑπεναντιόομαι**, pf. ὑπηναντίωμαι Demetr.Lac.*Herc.*1012.37:—*do what one can to oppose*, ὑ. τῷ νοσήματι μετὰ τοῦ ἰητροῦ Hp.*Epid.*1. 11; *oppose secretly, thwart*, Plu.*Per.*34, *Caes.*1. II. Pass., *to be opposed* or *opposite*, Arist.*EE*1240ᵃ12, *Phgn.*807ᵃ26.

**ὑπεναντί-ος**, α, ον Arist.*Pol.*1327ᵃ17, Plu.*Ages.*24; but ος, ον Pl. *Alc.*2.139b:—*set over against, meeting*, ἵπποι ὑ. ἀλλήλοισιν Hes.*Sc.* 347. 2. *set against, opposite*, of enemies in battle, τοὺς σφίσιν ὑ. Th.2.2; οἱ ὑ. the *enemy*, X.*Cyr.*1.6.38, cf. D.18.148, etc. 3. *opposed, opposite, contrary*, γένη Pl.*Plt.*306e; of *contrary* properties, τὸ ὑ. Hp.*VM*13; ὑπεναντιωτάτοις.. πλείστοις χρώμενον endued with most qualities *most opposed to one another*, Alex.141.2; ἰχθὺς ὑ. αὐτοῖσι Damox.2.37: freq. c. dat., *opposite* or *contrary to*, ὁ ὑπεναντία τούτοισι λέξας Hdt.7.50, cf. X.*HG*4.8.24 (Sup.), Pl.*Tht.*176a, *Lg.*810d, Epicur.*Ep.*1 p.28 U., *Abh.Berl.Akad.*1925(5).7 (Cyrene, iii B.C.), *SIG* 613.28 (Delph., ii B.C.), Wilcken *Chr.*27.1 (ii A.D.), etc.; so ὑ. πρός τι Arist.*Pol.*1328ᵇ41; πρὸς δημοκρατίαν *IG*2².657.48: as Subst., τὸ ὑ. τούτου.. πέφυκε is in character the *opposite* of this, Hdt.3.80; τὰ ὑ. τούτων *on the contrary*, Id.7.153; τὰ ὑ. *incongruities*, Arist.*Po.*1455ᵃ 26, cf. 1461ᵇ23. 4. of logical propositions, *subcontrary*, Steph. *in Int.*30.38. Adv. -ίως ib.32.24. b. Math., *subcontrary*, τομή Apollon.Perg.1.5; of a mean, Archyt.2, Papp.84.14, etc. II. Adv. -ίως *in a manner contrary to*, τοῖς νόμοις Aeschin.3.8; ὑ. ἔχειν to be *opposed*, Arist.*GA*719ᵃ28; ὑ. κεῖσθαι ib.719ᵇ18; περί τινα ὑ. ὑπάρχει πρός τι Id.*HA*500ᵃ13, al., cf. Phld.*Po.*5.19; ὑ. θεραπεύσεις Aët.16.52: also neut. pl. ὑπεναντία as Adv., *IG*2².1258.8, 7.2225.36 (Thisbe, ii B.C., senatus consultum). **-ότης**, ητος, ἡ, *opposition*, Epicur.*Ep.*1 p. 28 U., *Nat.*117 G., Str.10.2.12; ἡ τούτων (v.l. τῶν ἱερῶν) ὑ. J.*Ap.*1. 25. II. Math., *subcontrariety*, Nicom.*Ar.*2.28. **-ωμα**, ατος, τό, *contradiction*, Arist.*Po.*1461ᵃ32. II. *self-contradiction*, Id.*SE* 181ᵇ5. **-ωσις**, εως, ἡ, *opposition*, like ὑπεναντιότης, Hp.*Aph.*2. 22, *Loc.Hom.*44, Arist.*SE*173ᵃ28, A.D.*Conj.*251.2; ὑπεναντιώσεις πρὸς ἄλληλα λαβοῦσα involving *contrarieties*, D.61.14; ὑ. ἔχειν Arist. *de An.*409ᵇ22; καθ' ὑπεναντιώσεις ἅμα ψύχεται κάεται Longin.10.3.

**ὑπένδεθεν** (sic), f.l. for ὑπένερθεν, Erot.

**ὑπενδίδωμι**, *give way a little*, Th.2.64, Ph.1.456; c. dat., φίλτροις Id.2.10; of the legs, Sor.1.113.

**ὑπέν-δῠμα**, ατος, τό, *undergarment*, *AP*6.201 (Marc. Arg.), 292 (Hedyl.). **-δύτης** [δῠ], ου, ὁ, = foreg., Str.15.3.19. **-δύω**, *put on underneath*, ὑπενέδυσ' ἐρραμμέν' αὐτήν Alex.98.11 (troch.):—Med., ὑ. τῷ θώρακι χιτῶνα Demoph.*Sim.*31:—Pass., ὁπλισμῷ ὑπενδεδυμένοι χιτῶνας *having* tunics *on under*, Plu.*Aem.*18, cf. Id.2.595e. **-ειμι**, (εἰμί *sum*) *to be in down below*, τῷδ' ὑπένεστι τάφῳ *Epigr.Gr.*238 (Smyrna).

**ὑπένερθε**, also **-θεν**, Adv. *underneath*, ζωστὴρ..., ἠδ' ὑ. ζῶμά τε καὶ μίτρη Il.4.186; σφυρὰ καλ' ὑ. ib.147, cf. 17.386; ὑ. δὲ γαῖα φάνεσκε Od.12.242; χιτῶνά γ' ἔχων.. ὑ. Ar.*Ra.*1067 (anap.); τὰν ὀροφὰν τάν ὑπένερθε *IG*4²(1).102.46 (Epid., iv B.C.); τὰν ὕλαν τὰν ὑπένερθεν ib. 51. 2. *under the earth, in the nether world*, Il.3.278, 20.61, Archil. 17; οἱ ὑ., opp. οἱ οὐράνιοι, Pl.*Ax.*371b, cf. A.R.2.259. II. c. gen. (which sts. goes before, sts. after), *under, beneath*, ποδῶν ὑ. Il.2. 150; ὑ. Χίοιο Od.3.172; ὑ. γενείου Hes.*Sc.*418; γαίας ὑ. Pi.*N.*10. 87; τοὐμφαλοῦ ὑ. Ar.*Nu.*977 (anap.); Ἀγρυλῆς ὑ. prob. in *IG*1².398. 16.

**ὕπενες**· εἰς τετάρτην, Hsch.

**ὑπεν-νοέω**, *have in mind, secretly purpose*, Ael.*VH*4.8. **-τρᾰγίζω**, v.l. (ap.Orib.12 s.v. νάρδος) for ὑπερτραγίζω in Dsc.1.7.

**ὑπέξ**, v. ὑπέκ.

**ὑπεξ-άγω** [ᾰ], *carry out from under* or *secretly*, esp. *out of* danger *into* safety, ἀλλά σε δαίμων οἴκαδ' ὑπεξαγάγοι Od.18.147; ὑπὲκ θανάτου ἀγάγωμεν Il.20.300:—Med., παῖδας καὶ γυναῖκας ὑπεξαγάγωνται ἐκ τῆς Ἀττικῆς Hdt.8.40; cf. ὑπεκτίθεμαι I. 2. in Medic. sense, *carry off*, κάτω ὑ. Hp.*Loc.Hom.*30, cf. Aret.*CA*2.6; ὑ. κοιλίαν *relax* the bowels, Plu.2.635b; τὰ σκύβαλα Artem.1.67. b. *extract*, τὸ ἔμβρυον Hp.*Foet.Exsect.*1. II. ὑ. πόδα E.*Hec.*812; ὑ. ἐμαυτόν Luc.*Nigr.*18. 2. intr., *withdraw, retire slowly*, Hdt.4.120, X. *Cyr.*3.3.60. b. of air, sound, and the like, *escape*, Arist.*Pr.* 883ᵃ5, *Aud.*804ᵃ19. III. *behave*, εὐνοϊκῶς καὶ φιλοδόξως πρὸς πάντας τοὺς πολίτας *BMus.Inscr.*925b14 (Branchidae, i B.C.). **-ἀγωγή,** ἡ, *withdrawal,* M.Ant.5.23; ἐκ τῶν Ἀθηνῶν Hld.6.8. **-αείρω,** *lift up,* ὑπὲκ ποδὸς ἴχνος ἀείραι Opp.*H.*2.5.

⊛ **ὑπεξαίρ-εσις,** εως, ἡ, *removal,* τοῦ ἀλγοῦντος Epicur.*Sent.*3 (ἐξαίρεσις a better reading, acc. to Demetr.Lac.*Herc.*1012.23); τοῦ ἀλλοτρίου Gal.14.681; τῶν ἀποφατικῶν *Stoic.*2.84; μεθ' ὑπεξαιρέσεως with *a reservation,* Epict.*Ench.*2.2, M.Ant.4.1, *Stoic.*3.149, cf. D.S. 12.21 (pl.), Artem.1.52; καθ' ὑπεξαίρεσίν τινος S.E.*M.*8.479; εἶχεν ὑ. τοῦ μὴ ὅμοιον εἶναι.. A.D.*Adv.*205.21: hence in Rhet., *a treating as exceptional,* Alex.*Fig.*1.7. 2. *refutation,* opp. πίστις, Phld.*Rh.* 1.202 S. (pl.). **-ετέος,** α, ον, *to be removed,* Hp.*Mul.*1.11. 2. ὑπεξαιρετέον, *one must remove,* Ph.1.362,399,521. **-ετος,** ον, *removable,* Phld.*Piet.*115. **-έω,** *take away from below* or *gradually,* αἷμ' ὑ. τῶν κτανόντων *drain away* their blood, S.*El.*1420 (lyr.); ἀντλεῖν καὶ ὑ. τὴν θάλατταν Plu.2.127c: Medic., βραχύ τι προστίθει ἢ ὑπεξαίρει *take away* (from the dose), Alex.Trall.*Febr.*7. 2. *make away with, destroy secretly* or *gradually,* τινας Pl.*R.*567b; ὄλβον δωμάτων -ελών E.*Hipp.*633; ὑ. τινὶ τὰ δεινά *set* him *quit of* all danger, Th.4.83; κεἰ μὲν φοβεῖται τοὐπίκλημ' ὑπεξελεῖν (-ελών codd.), αὐτὸς καθ' αὑτοῦ [σημαινέτω] and even if he fears [*thus*] *to do away with* the accusation, let him give evidence himself against himself, S.*OT*227 (other explanations are given in Jebb's commentary):—Pass., *to be made away with,* ἐπιτήδειοι ὑπεξαιρεθῆναι Th.8.70; τούτων ὑπεξαραιρημένων these *being out of the question,* Hdt.7.8.γ΄. II. Med., *take out privily for oneself, steal away,* ὑπὲκ μήλων αἱρεύμενοι (sc. ἄρνας, ἐρίφους) Il.16.353; *steal,* τὴν τιμὴν τοῦ σίτου Ph.2.71. b. *remove for one's own advantage,* γεωργὸς..τὴν ἀλλοτρίαν ὑπεξελόμενος ὕλην τότε σπείρει Sor.1.40. 2. *put aside, except, exclude,* τὴν πρώτην ἡμέραν Ph.1.3; κατηγορήσειν ἕνα..ὑπεξελόμενος δι' οἰκειότητα Plu.*Cat.Mi.*21; τὰ δόγματα Arr.*Epict.*4.7.35; *exempt,* τινὰ τῆς ὕβρεως Ph.2.328; οὐδεμίαν ὑ. πρόφασιν *making* no *exception,* Theopomp.Hist.118: hence in Rhet., Alex.*Fig.*1.7 (and in Act., Zonae. *Fig.*5 p.162S.). 3. *remove,* Pl.*Tht.*151c; τὸ ἄλγημα Sch.Epicur. *Sent.*29:—Pass., Diog.Oen.29. 4. *reserve, put aside in safety,* ἰδίων τι κτημάτων D.19.78:—Pass., χῶραι ὑπεξειρημέναι (sic) *reserved, IG*7.413.20, al. (Oropus, i B.C.); *to be excluded, excepted,* Gal.16.528, *PLond.*5.1708.159 (vi A.D.).

ὑπεξ-αίρω, *subtract,* Hero *Geom.*10.4, al. 2. Pass., *to be elated,* Arist.*VV*1251$^b$19 (nisi leg. ὑπεραίρεσθαι). **-ακρίζω,** *ascend to the summit,* βοσκήματ' ἄρτι πρὸς λέπας ὑπεξήκριζον E.*Ba.*678 (unless ὑ. is 1 sg., *I was driving* them *up*). **-αλέασθαι,** aor. 1 inf. of *ὑπεξᾰλέομαι, *flee out from under, avoid,* c. acc., Il.15.180. **-άλυξις** [ᾰ], εως, ἡ, *escape, Epigr.Gr.*1034.21 (Callipolis). **-ᾰλύσκω,** aor. -ήλυξα, = *ὑπεξαλέομαι, c. acc., Hes.*Th.* 615, A.R.3.551. **-αναβαίνω,** *step suddenly back,* ποδὶ σκαιῷ Theoc.22.197. **-ανάγομαι** [ᾰγ], Pass., *put out to sea secretly,* Th.3.74. **-αναδύομαι,** Med., with aor. 2 -έδυν, *dive out and emerge, come from under secretly* or *gradually,* λάθρῃ ὑπεξαναδὺς πολιῆς ἁλός Il.13.352; ὑ. κεφαλῇ *duck* or *stoop* so as to avoid a blow, Theoc. 22.123. **-ανίσταμαι,** aor. 2 -ανέστην, *arise,* διαβολὴ ὑ. Plu.*Cam.* 22, cf. Luc.*Merc.Cond.*39; ὑ. τινὶ *rise as a mark of respect for..,* Id. *Demon.*63, Plu.*Lyc.*20, etc. **-αντλέω,** *drain out from below, exhaust,* κακῶν..κῦμ' ὑπεξαντλῶν φρενί E.*Ion*927. **-άπτω,** *kindle secretly* or *gradually,* τινὶ πόθον τινός Ael.*NA*14.20:—Pass., ὑ. ἐκ τοῦ οἴνου Id.*VH*14.41. **-αφύομαι,** Pass., *to be drained off,* of streams that lose themselves in the sand, A.R.2.983. **-ειμι,** (εἶμι *ibo*) *withdraw gradually,* Hdt.4.120, 7.211: generally, *withdraw, disappear,* ὅταν μηθὲν ἔτι ὑπεξίῃ..λυπηρόν Metrod.*Fr.*28; of fire or snow, *disappear gradually,* Pl.*Phd.*103d,106a; of water, opp. ἐπιγίγνεσθαι, Arist.*Pol.*1270$^a$39: c. dat., *make way for,* τὰς ἕνας ἀρχὰς ταῖς νέαις ὑ. D.25.20. II. *go out to meet* or *against* one, Hdt. 1.176 codd. (leg. ἐπεξ-). 2. *issue forth from,* θαλάμων Anon.ap. Suid. III. *to be discharged,* of the faeces, Archig.ap.Aët.9. 42. **-ειρύω,** v. ὑπεξερύω. **-ελαύνω,** *drive away secretly* or *gradually,* Hdt.4.120 (where τὰς ἀγέλας or τὰ βοσκήματα must be supplied): intr., *march away,* ib.130. **-έλευσις,** εως, ἡ, *punishment,* Suid. (prob. an error for ἐπεξ-). **-ερεύγω,** *disgorge,* Nic.*Al.* 227. **-ερύω,** *drag out and away,* [τὸν νεκρὸν] ὑπεξείρυσαν Hdt.7.225:—Med., πατέρα..ὑπεξείρῡτο φόνοιο A.R.2.1181. ⊛ **-έρχομαι,** aor. 2 -ῆλθον, pf. -ελήλυθα:—*go out from under: go out secretly, withdraw, retire,* Th.8.70; Μέγαράδε, Ἀθήναζε, And.1.15, D.59.103; πόλεως Plu.*Publ.*7; ὑ. λέγοντος *slip away from..,* Pl.*Tht.*182d: rarely c. acc. pers., *withdraw from, escape from,* Th.3.34: c. acc. rei, νόσῳ ὑ. τὸν βίον App.*Reg.*2: also c. dat., *keep out of one's way, avoid,* Pl. *Lg.*865e; *give up one's right to,* τισι D.37.7. 2. *rise up and quit one's domicile, emigrate,* ἐς.. Hdt.1.73, 8.36. II. *go out to meet,* Id.1.176 (leg. ἐπεξ-). III. Medic., *to be discharged* from the bowel, Archig.ap.Aët.9.28. **-έχω,** intr., *withdraw* or *retire secretly,* Hdt.5.72; ἐκ τῆς Χίου Id.8.132; ἐς Θεσσαλίην Id.6.74 (always in aor. -εσχον). **-ηγητικός,** ή, όν, *serving as explanation,* Eust.584.30 (f.l. for *ἐπ-). **-ίστημι,** *alter gradually,* Hsch.; esp. for the worse, *perplex,* Callistr.*Stat.*2. II. Pass., with aor. 2 and pf. Act., *withdraw from,* τοῦ νεώ Luc.*Am.*17; τῆς πόλεως Plu.*Cat.Mi.*19; τῆς ἀγορᾶς Id.*CG*1; ὑ. τῆς ἀρχῆς *give up all claim to* it, Hdt.3.83: c. inf., ὑ. ἄρχειν Luc.*Sat.*6. 2. c. acc., *go out of the way of, avoid,* ὑπεκστῆναι βούλομαι τὸν λόγον Pl.*Phlb.*43a; cf. ὑπεξέρχομαι 1. 3. c. dat., *give place to, make way for,* X.*Ath.*1. 10; *yield to, give way to,* ταῖς ἀπορίαις, τῷ καιρῷ, Plu.*Sol.*25, *Cat.Mi.* 35. **-οδος,** ἡ, *diarrhoea,* Hp.*Prorrh.*2.23. **-ούσιος,** α, ον, but ος, ον *POxy.* (v. infr.), *subject to the power of* another, opp. αὐτεξούσιος, *Cod.Just.*6.4.4.25, Sch.E.*Andr.*411,628; θυγάτηρ *POxy.*129.2 (vi A.D.), cf. Mich.*in EN*45.33; = *filius familias, Gloss.* ⊛ **-ουσιότης,** ητος, ἡ, *subjection,* ib.

**ὑπεπιμόριος,** ον, an arithmetical term, the reciprocal of ἐπιμόριος, represented by the fraction $1/(1+\frac{1}{n})$ or $n/(n+1)$, Arist.*Metaph.* 1021$^a$2:—so **ὑφημιόλιος** is the reciprocal of ἡμιόλιος ($\frac{2}{3}$ of $\frac{3}{2}$), **ὑπεπίτριτος** of ἐπίτριτος ($\frac{3}{4}$ of $\frac{4}{3}$), **ὑπεπιτέταρτος** of ἐπιτέταρτος ($\frac{4}{5}$ of $\frac{5}{4}$), **ὑπεπόγδοος** of ἐπόγδοος ($\frac{8}{9}$ of $\frac{9}{8}$), etc., Nicom.*Ar.*1.19, *Exc.*2, Theo Sm.p.75 H., etc.; and so **ὑπεπιμερής** is the reciprocal of ἐπιμερής, Nicom.*Ar.* l.c.—These ratios are called ὑπόλογοι, ἐπιμόριος etc. being πρόλογοι.

**ὑπεπιστᾰτ-έω,** *to be sub-inspector, Sammelb.*4638.19 (ii B.C.). ⊛**-ης,** ου, ὁ, *sub-inspector, deputy-overseer, IG*11(4).1053 (Thessalonica, iii B.C.).

⊛ **ὑπέρ** [ῠ], Ep. also **ὑπείρ,** used by Hom. (metri gr.) only in the phrase ὑπεὶρ ἅλα (v. ὑπείρ); Arc. **ὀπέρ** (q.v.): in Aeol. replaced by περί (v. περί A. v): Prep. governing gen. and acc., in Arc. also dat. (Cf. Skt. *upári* 'above', Goth. *ufar,* OE. *ofer* 'over':—from it are formed the Comp. and Sup. ὑπέρτερος, -τατος, also Adv. ὕπερθεν, and Nouns ὑπέρα, ὕπερος.)

A. WITH GENIT., I. of Place, *over;* 1. in a state of rest, *over, above,* freq. in Hom., βάλε.. στέρνον ὑ. μαζοῖο Il.4.528; χιτωνίσκους ἐνεδεδύκεσαν ὑ. γονάτων *not reaching to* the knees, X.*An.*5.4. 13; ἔστηκε..ὅσον τ' ὄργυι' ὑ. αἴης Il.23.327; εἴθ' ὑ. γῆς, εἴτ' ἐπὶ γῆς, εἴθ' ὑπὸ γῆς Thphr.*Ign.*1; στῆ δ' ἄρ' ὑ. κεφαλῆς stood *over* his head as he lay asleep, Il.2.20, Od.4.803, al.; πασάων ὕ. ἥ γε κάρη ἔχει 6. 107; ὑ. πόλιος, ὅθι Ἕρμαιος λόφος ἐστίν, ἧα 16.471; ὑ. κεφαλῆς οἱ ἐγίνετο διεξελαύνοντι *over*head, i.e. over the gateway, Hdt.1.187; ὑ. τῆς ὀροφῆς *IG*1$^2$.373.246; ὑ. τοῦ ἀγάλματος ib.264; ὅρος τὸ ὑ. Τεγέης Hdt.6.105; τὰ ὑ. κεφαλῆς the higher ground, X.*Ages.*2.20; Ἰωνίας ὑ. ἁλὸς οἰκέων *on* the Ionian sea, i.e. on its shores, Pi.*N.*7.65; λιμὴν καὶ πόλις ὑ. αὐτοῦ κεῖται Th.1.46, cf. 6.4, D.C.40.14: of relative geographical position, *above, farther inland,* οἰκέοντες ὑ. Ἁλικαρνησσοῦ μεσόγαιαν Hdt.1.175; ἐξ Αἰθιοπίας τῆς ὑ. Αἰγύπτου Th.2.48; τοῖς ὑ. Χερρονήσου Θρᾳξίν X.*An.*2.6.2; ὑ. Μασσαλίας Plb.2.14.8, cf. 5. 73.3, al.: in Hellenistic Gr. the acc. is commoner in this sense, v. infr. B. I. b. of ships at sea, *off* a place, Th.1.112, 8.95; ναυμαχίην τὴν ὑ. Μιλήτου γενομένην Hdt.6.25; ὑ. τούτου (sc. Φαλήρου) ἀνακωχεύσαντες τὰς νέας ib.116. 2. in a state of motion, *over, across,* κῦμα νηὸς ὑ. τοίχων καταβήσεται Il.15.382; τὸν δ' ὑ. οὐδοῦ βάντα προσηύδα Od.17.575; πηδῶντος..τάφρων ὕ. S.*Aj.*1279; ὑ. θαλάσσης καὶ χθονὸς ποτωμένοις A.*Ag.*576; ἐκκυβιστᾶν ὑ. [τῶν ξιφῶν] X.*Smp.*2.11. 3. *over, beyond,* ἐν Κρήτῃ εὐρείῃ τηλοῦ ὑ. πόντου Od.13.257. II. metaph., *in defence of, on behalf of,* τεῖχος ἐτειχίσσαντο νεῶν ὕ. Il.7.449; ἑκατόμβην ῥέξαι ὑ. Δαναῶν 1.444: generally, *for the prosperity* or *safety of,* τὰ ἱερὰ ὑ. τῆς Εὐβοίας θῦσαι *IG*1$^2$. 39.65, cf. 45.5; ἱερὰ θυόμενα ὑ. τῆς πόλεως X.*Mem.*2.2.13; ἐπιτελεῖν τὰς θυσίας ὑ. τε ὑμῶν καὶ τῶν τέκνων *UPZ*14.27 (ii B.C.); in dedications (always with reference to living persons), Σμικύθη μ' ἀνέθηκεν.. εὐξαμένη..ὑ. παίδων καὶ ἑαυτῆς *IG*1$^2$.524, cf. 2$^2$.4403, 4$^2$(1).569 (Epid.); Ἀρτέμιδι Σωτείρᾳ ὑ. βασιλέως Πτολεμαίου Ἐπικράτης Ἀθηναῖος *OGI*18 (Egypt, iii B.C.), cf. 365 (Amasia, ii B.C.), al.; ὑ. τῆς εἰς αἰῶνα διαμονῆς Ἀντωνείνου Καίσαρος ib.702.3 (Egypt, ii A.D.); ὑ. τῆς τύχης..Ἀντωνείνου Σεβαστοῦ Εὐσεβοῦς ib.703.2 (Ptolemais, ii A.D.); ὑ. σωτηρίας τοῦ κυρίου ἡμῶν..Ἀντωνείνου ib.706 (Egypt, ii/iii A.D.); εὐδόντων ὕ. φρουρήμα A.*Eu.*705; ὑ. τινὸς κινδυνεύειν, μάχεσθαι, βοηθεῖν, Th.2.20, Pl.*Lg.*642c, X.*An.*3.5.6; ἧς ἔθνησχ' ὕ. S.*Tr.*708; ὑ. γῆς τῆς Ἀθηναίων ναυμαχέειν Hdt.8.70; ὑ. τῆς Ἑλλάδος ἀμῦναι Pl.*Lg.*692d; ἀμυνῶ ὑ. ἱερῶν καὶ ὁσίων Jusj.ap.Poll.8.105; νῦν ὑ. πάντων ἀγών A.*Pers.* 405; ὑ. δόξης τελευτήσαντες D.23.210, cf. Isoc.6.93; πάνθ' ὑ. ὑμῶν φανήσεται πράξας Χαβρίας, καὶ τὴν τελευτὴν αὐτὴν τοῦ βίου πεποιημένος οὐχ ὑ. ἄλλου τινὸς *in* your *interests,* D.20.80, cf. 83; ὑ. τῆς Ἀσίας στρατηγήσας Isoc.4.154; of things sought, ὑ. τοῦ νεκροῦ ὠθισμὸς ἐγένετο πολὺς Hdt.7.225; ἀφίκετο ὑ. γενεᾶς, ὑ. φωνᾶς, ὑ. τοῦ θησαυροῦ, *IG*4$^2$ (1).121.10,42, 123.11 (Epid., iv B.C.); γίνωσκέ με πεπορεῦσθαι εἰς Ἡρακλέους πόλιν ὑ. τῆς οἰκίας *UPZ*68.3 (ii B.C.); sts. even of the thing to be averted, ἱκέσιον λόχον δουλοσύνας ὕ. *about* slavery, A.*Th.*111 (lyr.), cf. Aeschin.3.10. 2. *for, instead of, in the name of,* ὑ. ἑαυτοῦ τι προϊδεῖν *on* his own *behalf,* Th.1.141; ὑ. τινὸς ἀποκρίνεσθαι Pl.*R.*590a; προλέγειν X.*An.*7.7.3; ἐπεὶ οὖν σὺ σιωπᾷς, ἐγὼ λέξω καὶ ὑ. σοῦ καὶ ὑ. ἡμῶν Id.*Cyr.*3.3.14, cf. S.*El.*554; ὑ. Ζήνωνος πράσσων *as* Zeno's *representative, PSI*4.389.8 (iii B.C.); ἔγραψεν ὑ. αὐτῶν διὰ τὸ φάσκειν αὐτοὺς μὴ εἰδέναι γράμματα *PGrenf.*2.17.9 (ii B.C.); θεάσασθε ὃν τρόπον ὑμεῖς ἐστρατηγηκότες πάντ' ἔσεσθ' ὑ. Φιλίππου as though *by commission from* P., D.3.6; so in other dialects c. acc., v. infr. B. v. 3. in adjurations, with verbs of entreaty, entreat one *as representative of* another, τῶν ὑ. ἐνθάδ' ἐγὼ γουνάζομαι οὐ παρεόντων, i.e. I entreat you as they would if they were here, Il.15.665, cf. 660; then more metaph., *by,* λίσσομ' ὑ. ψυχῆς (*as you value* your life) καὶ γούνων σῶν τε τοκήων 22.338, cf. 24.466; λίσσομ' ὑ. θυέων καὶ δαίμονος..σῆς τ' αὐτοῦ κεφαλῆς καὶ ἑταίρων Od.15.261; λίσσομ' ὑ. μακάρων σέο τ' αὐτῆς ἠδὲ τοκήων A.R.3.701; ὑ. ξενίου λίσσεται ὔμμε Διός *in the name of* Zeus, *AP*7.499.2 (Theaet.); so Aeol. περ (v. περί A. v). 4. of the cause or motive, *for, because of, by reason of,* ἀλγέων ὕ. E.*Supp.*1125 (lyr.); ὑ. παθέων Id.*Hipp.*159 (lyr.); ἔριδος ὕ. Id.*Andr.*490 (lyr.); of punishment or reward, *for, on account of,* τοῖσιν ἄγουσιν κλαυμαθ' ὑπάρξει βραδυτῆτος ὕ. S.*Ant.*932 (anap.), cf. Isoc.11.39, Lys.3.43, 4.20, 13.41,42, X.*An.*1.3.4; ἀτῆθθαι ὑ.

τῷ πατρὸς τὰ πατρῷϊα the father's property shall pay the fine *for* the father, *Leg.Gort.*11.42; ἀποτεισάτω ὁ δεσπότης ὑ. τοῦ δούλου *PHal.*1.198 (iii B.C.); τοῦτον (viz. a runaway slave) ὃς ἂν ἀναγάγῃ, λήψεται ὅσα καὶ ὑ. τοῦ προγεγραμμένου *UPZ*121.24 (ii B.C.); τὸ κατεσκευασμένον ὑ. τῆς ἡμετέρας σωτηρίας Ἰσιδεῖον *as a thank-offering for..*, *Sammelb.*3926.12 (i B.C.); ὑ. ὧν ἐτιμήσαμεν αὐτοὺς ταῖς μεγίσταις τιμαῖς Isoc.9.57; ἀποδοῦναι χάριν ὑ. ὧν..ἅπαντας ἀνθρώπους εὐεργέτησεν Id.4.56; of payment, ἡμιωβέλιον ὑ. ἑκάστου *IG*1².140.2; μέτρησον Ποσειδωνίῳ ὑ. Ἡρακλείδου *on account of* H., i.e. debiting H.'s account, *PFay.*16 (i B.C.); μετρήσω ὑ. σοῦ εἰς τὸ δημόσιον *for the credit of* your *account*, *PAmh.*2.88.22 (ii A.D.); ὑ. λαογραφίας *Ostr. Bodl.* iii 80 (i A.D.); ὑ. λόγου ἀννώνης *Ostr.*1479 (iii A.D.); ὑ. ὧν ἔμαθεν καταβαλεῖν μισθόν Jul.*Or.*3.126a, cf. Ael.*NA*3.39. 5. ὑ. τοῦ μή c. inf., *for the purpose of preventing* or *avoiding*, ὑ. τοῦ μηδένα..βιαίῳ θανάτῳ ἀποθνήσκειν X.*Hier.*4.3; ὑ. τοῦ μὴ ποιεῖν τὸ προσταττόμενον Isoc.7.64, cf. 12.80; τὴν πόλιν ἐκλιπεῖν ὑπέμειναν..ὑ. τοῦ μὴ τὸ κελευόμενον ποιῆσαι D.18.204: also without μή, *for the sake of*, ὑ. τοῦ τοῖς ἄλλοις ἐπιτάττειν ἐθέλειν ἀποθνήσκειν to be ready to die *for the sake of..*, Isoc.6.94; μὴ τοσαύτην ποιεῖσθαι σπουδὴν ὑ. τοῦ βλάψαι τοὺς πολεμίους ἡλίκην ὑ. τοῦ μηδὲν αὐτοὺς παθεῖν δεινόν Plb.3.94.9, cf. 5.32.1, 5.86.8: this constr. is found also in signf. A. III. III. *concerning*, ὑ. σέθεν αἴσχε' ἀκούω Il.6.524; κᾶρυξ ἀνέειπέ νιν ἀγγέλλων Ἱέρωνος ὑ. καλλινίκου ἅρμασι Pi.*P.*1.32; Σκύθαι μὲν ὧδε ὑ. σφέων τε αὐτῶν καὶ τῆς χώρης τῆς κατύπερθε λέγουσι Hdt.4.8; τὰ λεγόμενα ὑ. ἑκάστων v.l. in Id.2.123; τοὺς ὑ. τοῦ αἰῶνος φόβους Epicur.*Sent.*20; διαλεχθῆναι, ἀγορεύειν ὑ. τινός, Pl.*Ap.*39e, *Lg.*776e; περὶ μὲν οὖν τούτων τοσαῦτά μοι εἰρήσθω, ὑ. ὧν δέ μοι προσήκει λέγειν.. Lys.24.4, cf. 21, 16.20; ὑ. οὗ..ὁμολογῶ..διαφέρεσθαι τούτοις D.18.31; βουλευομένων ὑ. τοῦ ποίαν τινὰ [εἰρήνην ποιητέον] Id.19.94; ἔγραψάς μοι ὑ. τῶν καμίνων *PCair.Zen.*273.2 (iii B.C.); ἐνεκάλουν ὑ. σύκων *PSI*6.554.24 (iii B.C.); ἐπεδώκαμέν σοι ὑπόμνημα ὑ. τοῦ μὴ εἰληφέναι τὴν..ὄλυραν *UPZ*46.4 (ii B.C.); συλλαλήσαντες ὑ. τοῦ τὴν πόλιν ἐνδοῦναι τοῖς Ῥωμαίοις Plb.1.43.1; θροῦς ὑ. τοῦ τὸν Λυκοῦργον ἐκπέμπειν talk *of* sending L., Id.5.18.5, cf. 6; γνώμην ὑ. τῆς κοινῆς [δόξης] Isoc.6.93; ὑ. τῶν τούτου λητουργιῶν..ὡδὶ γιγνώσκω D.21.152; ἐκ τῶν ἐμφανῶν ὑ. τῶν ἀφανῶν πιστεύειν Jul.*Or.*4.138b; with vbs. expressing emotion, ποίας..γυναικὸς ἐκφοβεῖσθ' ὕ.; S.*OT*989; εἰ τὰ παρὰ σοὶ καλῶς ἔχει, θάρρει ὑ. ἐκείνων X.*Cyr.*7.1.17; οὐδεὶς ὑ. μου δαιμόνων μηνίεται κατασφαγείσης A.*Eu.*101 (approaching sense II. 1).

B. WITH ACCUS., I. of Place in reference to motion, *over, beyond*, freq. in Hom., e.g. ὑ. ὦμον ἦλυθ' ἀκωκή Il.5.16, cf. 851; ἀλάλησθε..ὑπεὶρ ἅλα Od.3.73, cf. 7.135, al., A.*Eu.*250, S.*Ant.*1145 (lyr.); ὑ. τὸν δρύφακτον ὑπερτιθέμενοι Plb.1.22.10: without such reference, ὑ. Ἡρακλείας στήλας ἔξω κατοικοῦσι Pl.*Criti.*108e, cf. Jul.*Or.*1.6d; τὰς κεφαλὰς ὑ. τὸ ὑγρὸν ὑπερίσχον Plb.3.84.9; τῶν ὑ. τὸ Σαρδῷον πέλαγος τόπων Id.2.14.6; ὑ. Μασσαλίαν Id.2.16.1; λόφον κείμενον ὑ. τὴν ὁδόν Id.2.27.5, cf. 3.47.2, al.; τῶν συριῶν ὑ. τὴν σκηνὴν οὐσῶν *PHib.*1.38.7 (iii B.C.); οὐλὴ..ὑ. ὀφρὺν δεξιάν *PCair.Zen.*76.13 (iii B.C.); τὸ ὑ. τὸν ἔσχατον..σπόνδυλον Sor.1.102; ὑ. τὸν οὐρανόν Jul.*Or.*4.135a. II. of Measure, *above, exceeding, beyond*, ὑ. τὸν ἀλαθῆ λόγον Pi.*O.*1.28; ὑ. τὸ βέλτιστον A.*Ag.*378 (lyr.); ὑ. ἐλπίδα S.*Ant.*366 (lyr.); ὑ. δύναμιν Th.6.16; μεγέθει ὑ. τοὺς ἐν τῇ νηΐ Pl.*R.*488b; ὑ. ἄνθρωπον εἶναι Id.*Lg.*839d, Luc.*Vit.Auct.*2; ὑ. ἡμᾶς *beyond* our powers, Pl.*Prm.*128b; ὑ. τὴν ἀξίαν E.*HF*146; ὑ. τὴν οὐσίαν Pl.*R.*372b; ὑ. τὸ ὕδωρ (cf. ὕδωρ I. 4) Luc.*Pr.Im.*29. b. after Comp., *than*, δυνατώτεροι ὑ... Lxx *Jd.*18.26: so after Posit., τοῖς ἀγαθοῖς ὑ. αὐτόν *better than* he, ib.3*Ki.*2.32. 2. of transgression, *in violation of*, ὑ. αἶσαν, opp. κατ' αἶσαν, Il.3.59, al.; ὑ. Διὸς αἶσαν 17.321; ὑ. μοῖραν 20.336; ὑ. μόρον (or ὑπέρμορον) ib.30; ὑ. θεόν 17.327; ὑ. ὅρκια 3.299, al. III. of Number, *above, upwards of*, τὰ ὑ. δέκα μνᾶς [ξυμβόλαια] *IG*1².41.23, cf. 22.48, al.; ὑ. τεσσεράκοντα ἄνδρας Hdt.5.64; ὑ. τετταράκοντα (sc. ἔτη) X.*HG*5.4.13; ὑ. τὰ στρατεύσιμα ἔτη γεγονόσι Id.*Cyr.*1.2.4; ὑ. ἥμισυ *more than* half, ib.3.3.47. IV. of Time, *beyond*, i.e. *before, earlier than*, ὁ ὑ. τὰ Μηδικὰ πόλεμος Th.1.41; ὑ. τὴν φθοράν Pl.*Ti.*23c. V. in some dialects, in sense A. II. 1, 2, *on behalf of*, ὑ. τὰν πόλιν *SIG*437 (Delph., iii B.C.), al., cf. *IG*4²(1).109 iv 113 (Epid., iii B.C.), 5(2).438–40, 442 (Megalop., ii B.C.), 4²(1).380, 665 (Epid., i A.D.), *IPE*4.71.10 (Cherson., ii A.D.); in sense A. III, *concerning*, ἐπικράνθη μοι ὑ. ὑμᾶς Lxx *Ru.*1.13.

C. WITH DAT., only Arc., μαχόμενοι ὑ. τᾷ τᾶς πόλιος ἐλευθερίᾳ fighting *for...*, *IG*5(2).16 (Tegea, iii B.C.).

D. POSITION: ὑπέρ may follow its Subst., but then by anastrophe becomes ὕπερ, Il.5.339, Od.19.450, al., S.*OT*1444, etc.

E. AS ADV., *over-much, above measure*, ὑπὲρ μὲν ἄγαν E.*Med.*627 (lyr.); also written ὑπεράγαν, Str.3.2.9, Ael.*NA*3.38, etc.; cf. ὑπέρφευ: as a predicate, διάκονοι Χριστοῦ εἰσι; ὑπὲρ ἐγώ I am *more* [than they], 2*Ep.Cor.*11.23.

F. IN COMPOS. ὑπέρ signifies *over, above*, in all relations, e.g., 1. of Place, *over, beyond*, as in ὑπεράνω, ὑπέργειος, ὑπερβαίνω, ὑπερπόντιος. 2. of doing a thing *for* or *in defence of*, as in ὑπερμαχέω, ὑπερασπίζω, ὑπεραλγέω. 3. *above measure*, as in ὑπερήφανος, ὑπερφίαλος.

⊛ **ὑπέρα** [ῠ], ἡ, (ὑπέρ) an *upper rope*: mostly in pl. ὑπέραι, the *braces* attached to the ends of the sailyards (ἐπίκρια), by means of which the sails are shifted fore and aft, acc. to the direction of the wind, Od.5.260, cf. Luc.*DMort.*4.1: prov. of those who drop the substance to grasp a shadow, ἀφεὶς τὴν ὑ. τὸν πόδα διώκει he lets go *the brace* to catch at the sheet, Hyp.*Fr.*181. II. ὑπέραι, = ὕπερα, τά, Hsch. (s.v.l.).

**ὑπερᾰβέλτερος**, ον, also α, ον Lib.*Decl.*26.32:—*excessively simple* or *silly*, προφάσεις D.48.42; γυνή Lib. l.c.

**ὑπεράγᾰθος** [ᾰγ], ον, *transcendently good*, Plot.6.9.6, *Supp.Epigr.*6.441 (Lycaonia).

**ὑπεράγᾰμαι** [ᾰγ], *to be exceedingly pleased*, Pl.*Smp.*180a. II. *admire above measure*, τινά τινος *for* a thing, Luc.*Dem.Enc.*33; τι Ael.*VH*12.1.

**ὑπεράγαν**, v. ὑπέρ E.

**ὑπερᾰγᾰνακτέω**, *to be exceedingly angry* or *vexed at*, τινος Pl.*R.*535e; πράγματι Aeschin.1.60, cf. Thphr.ap.Porph.*Abst.*2.29: abs., Arist.*Fr.*163, Ael.*VH*8.9.

**ὑπερᾰγᾰπάω**, *love exceedingly, make much of*, c. acc., D.23.196, Arist.*EN*1168ᵃ1; τινά τινος *for* a thing, J.*AJ*12.4.6.

**ὑπεράγνοια**, ἡ, *utter ignorance*, Dam.*Pr.*29.

**ὑπέραγνος**, ον, *of surpassing purity*, Jul.*Or.*5.178d.

**ὑπεραγοναστάς**· εἱμαρμένας κρόκας, οἷον ὑπερστήμονας, Hsch.

**ὑπεράγόντως**, Adv. *exceedingly*, Lxx 2*Ma.*7.20, *OGI*315.51 (Pessinus, ii B.C.), Hsch. s.v. ἐσχάτως.

**ὑπεραγρυπνέω**, *keep watch for*, τινος Ael.*NA*8.25.

**ὑπεράγω** [ᾰ], *lift up over*, τὸ πεπονθὸς [σκέλος] ὑπεραγάγωμεν ταύτης (the cross-bar) Paul.Aeg.6.118: metaph., *elevate, exalt*, τὴν ἡγεμονίαν εἰς ἄκραν εὐδαιμονίαν App.*BC*4.92. II. *excel, surpass*, c. gen., Plb.11.13.5; τοῖς ὀδοῦσι πάντων D.S.3.35: c. acc., ἡ πολιτείη ἡ ὑμετέρη ὑπερῆγε τὰς ἑτέρων Hp.*Ep.*27: mostly in part. ὑπεράγων, ουσα, ον, *eminent, principal*, αἰχμάλωτοι *SIG*588.67 (Milet., ii B.C.); *extravagant, excessive*, Phld.*Herc.*1251.5; *extraordinary*, D.S.13.90, etc.; ῥώμαις Id.5.17, etc.; c. acc., τοὺς ἄλλους κατά τι ὑ. v.l. in Id.3.44; ἐν πᾶσι τοῖς ἔργοις -ων Lxx *Si.*30.31 (33.23); ἡ ὑπεράγουσα ἐπιστροφή *excessive* twisting, Ph.*Bel.*58.21; cf. Lxx 1*Ma.*6.43, J.*AJ*15.7.6, al.

**ὑπερᾰγωνιάω**, *to be in great distress*, D.61.28; διὰ τὰ παιδικά Pl.*Euthd.*300c; τινος *for* one, J.*AJ*16.4.1, Hierocl. *in CA*13 p.448 M.

**ὑπερᾰγωνίζομαι**, Med., *fight for*, τινος J.*BJ*2.12.7, App.*BC*1.96, Jul.*Or.*2.55c; τινὶ ὑπέρ τινος Them.*Or.*2.37a.

**ὑπεραείρω**, = ὑπεραίρω:—Pass., aor. ὑπερηέρθη *was uplifted beyond measure*, *AP*5.298 (Agath.).

**ὑπεράης**, ές, gen. έος, (ἄημι) *blowing hard*, ἄελλα Il.11.297.

**ὑπεραθετέω**, f.l. for ἀνυπερθετέω, Aq.*Ps.*88(89).39.

**ὑπέραθλος**, ον, *extremely wretched*, Phld.*Mus.*p.23 K. (s. v. l.).

**ὑπεραιδέομαι**, *feel great shame before, stand in great awe of*, c. acc., A.R.3.978.

**ὑπεραιμ-έω** (not -όω, cf. πολυαιμέω), *have over-much blood*, σῶμα ὑπεραιμοῦν X.*Eq.*4.2: v. ὑπερεμέω. **-ωσις**, εως, ἡ, *over-fullness of blood*, Poll.1.209 (wrongly inferred, instead of **-ησις**, from foreg.).

**ὑπεραινετός**, όν, *to be praised exceedingly*, Lxx *Da.*3.(52).

**ὑπεραιόλιος**, ον, *hyper-Aeolian*, in Music, Alyp.*Diat.*6, al.

**ὑπεραίρω**, *lift* or *raise up over*, εἰς τὸν ἔξω τόπον τὴν τοῦ ἡνιόχου κεφαλήν Pl.*Phdr.*248a; τὴν ὀφρῦν ὑπὲρ τοὺς κροτάφους Luc.*Am.*54; ἑρμάτων ὑ. τὸ σκάφος *over* the rocks, Philostr.*VA*3.23; ὑ. τὸ φθέγμα *raise* it *very high*, Luc.*Ner.*9:—Med., *lift oneself* or *rise above*, πάντων Anon. in Rh.1.632 W.: abs., *to be lifted up*, 2*Ep.Cor.*12.7; *give oneself airs, be coy*, Aristaenet.1.17, 2.6; *exalt oneself above*, ἐπὶ θεόν 2*Ep. Thess.*2.4. 2. *heighten*, ναῦν τοίχοις Philostr.*VA*3.35. II. intr., 1. c. acc., *jump over*, τειχία X.*Eq.Mag.*8.3; *cross*, Ἄλπεις Plb.2.23.1; ὑ. τὸ πέλαγος *pass over*, Id.1.28.1; ὑ. τὴν ἄκραν *double* the cape, Id.1.54.7; κάμψαντες τὸν Πάχυνον ὑ. [τὸ πέλαγος] εἰς.. Id.1.25.8; also τὸν Καταράκτην *OGI*654.6 (Egypt, i B.C.): abs., *cross the sea*, Plb.1.47.2: as naval and military term, *outflank*, τὸ λαιὸν τῶν πολεμίων Plb.1.50.6, cf. 3.73.7, etc.: without a sense of motion, *rise above*, τὸ ὕδωρ Thphr.*HP*4.8.10; τὸ μέγεθος τοῦ δένδρου Id.*CP*5.14.9. 2. *excel*, τινι in a thing, D.18.220: c. acc., *excel*, Id.60.21, Aristeas 16, Philostr.*Her.*2.19; τοὺς πρὸ ἑαυτοῦ ἡγεμονεύσαντας *SIG*877 A 5 (Delph., ii/iii A.D.); νοῦν ὑπεραίρει Plot.6.7.22. 3. *overshoot, go beyond*, μήθ' ὑπεράρας μήθ' ὑποκάμψας καιρόν A.*Ag.*786 (anap.); ὑ. τὸν ὡρισμένον καιρόν Plb.9.14.11; τὴν συνήθειαν Id.28.14.2; *exceed*, ὑ. τῆς οὐσίας τὸ μέγεθος ὁ τῶν τέκνων ἀριθμός Arist.*Pol.*1266ᵇ11; οὐ ἡ πρόνοια τὰς πάντων εὐχὰς οὐκ ἐπλήρωσε μόνον ἀλλὰ καὶ ὑπερῆρε *BMus.Inscr.*894.8 (Halic., i A.D.); πυγωνιαῖον ἢ μικρὸν ὑπεραῖρον a little *more*, Thphr.*HP*4.6.8; τῶν ὑπεραιρόντων ἱερέων the priests *in excess* (of a certain number), *BGU*1.16 (iii A.D.); τῶν ὑπεραιρούντων (sic) τὸν ἀριθμὸν τῶν ἱερέων *PLond.*2.347.6 (iii A.D.); τὸ ὑπεραῖρον ἀργύριον the money (received) *in excess*, *SIG*976.27 (Samos, ii B.C.); τοσοῦτον ἐν [τοῖς δαπανηθεῖσιν] ὑπερῆρεν [αὐτόν] he so far *exceeded* him in his expenditure, D.C.37.8; λόγος ὑπεραίρων τοῖς ὀνόμασι καὶ ταῖς γνώμαις *overdone*, Philostr.*VA*8.6; τὸ ὑπεραῖρον *exaggeration*, Plb.16.12.9. III. c. gen., *pass beyond, double* a cape, τοῦ ἀκρωτηρίου Philostr.*VA*3.24; *rise above*, τῆς γῆς Id.*Her.*19.16. 2. *transcend, exceed*, μήτ' ὑπεραίροντα τῶν εἰθισμένων ὄγκων (τὸν εἰθ. ὄγκον Stob.) μήτ' ἐλλείποντα Pl.*Lg.*717d, cf. D.C.75.13 (c. gen.), etc.; ὑ. τῷ μεγέθει τινῶν D.S.20.91, etc.; *overcome*, τέχνῃ τοῦ ῥοθίου Philostr.*VA*7.26. 3. c. gen., *despise*, ib.1.2, Philostr.Jun.*Im.*7. IV. *overflow*, τὰ ἀγγεῖα Arist.*Mir.*835ᵃ32: abs., of a stream, ὑ. εἰς τὰ χωρία D.55.10. 2. ὑ. ὑπέρ τι *project* beyond.., Arr.*Tact.*12.9; οἱ ἐν τῷ τρίτῳ ζυγῷ ὑ. τοὺς πρωτοστάτας πήχεις ς', i.e. their σάρισαι *project beyond..*, Ael.*Tact.*14.4; ὑπεραίρει ἔξω τὰ βλέφαρα *project beyond* the eyelids, of a tumour, Aët.7.36, cf. 15; *overlap*, Aristarch.Sam.8. V. Ὑπεραίρων, οντος, ὁ, *Most Excellent*, = Lat. *Exsuperatorius*, name given to December by Commodus, D.C.72.15.

**ὑπεραίσιος**, ον, *excessive, immoderate*, prob. in *Lyr.Adesp.* in *PRyl.* 14.8, cf. *AB*359, *EM*39.21.

**ὑπέραισχρος**, ον, *exceedingly foul* or *ugly*, X.*Cyr.*2.2.28, Plu.2.632a (quoting X. l. c.).

⊛ **ὑπεραισχύνομαι** [ῡν], Pass., *feel much ashamed*, ὑ. μὴ.. Aeschin.3.151; ἐπὶ πράγματι Id.1.33: c. part., *to be ashamed at doing* a thing, Dromo 1.

**ὑπεραίτιος**, ον, *more than causative, transcendentally causative*, Procl. *in Prm.*p.753 S., Dam.*Pr.*6.

**ὑπεραιώνιος**, ον, *more than eternal*, Dam.*Pr.*101$^{bis}$.

**ὑπεραιωρέω**, *suspend* or *support above*, κατακεκλιμένος ὑπὸ δένδρων παντοίας ὑπεραιωρούντων χάριτας Lib.*Or.*1.53:—Pass., Hdt.4.103. 2. *hold up, raise*, τὴν κεφαλήν Aret.*CD*1.3:—Pass., of the overlapping end of a dislocated bone, ὑπεραιωρεῖσθαι τὴν κεφαλὴν τοῦ μηροῦ ὑπὲρ τῆς κοτύλης *to be lifted* or *drawn over*, Hp.*Art.*70; ὑ. ὑπὲρ τῆς ἀρχαίης ἕδρης ib.71, *Fract.*14, cf. 41: abs., Id.*Art.*22: Littré (following Apollon.Cit.) gives the Act. in same sense, *Art.*73; and so in the Subst.⊛**-αιώρησις**, εως, ἡ, αἱ ἐξ ὑ. [ἐμβολαί] ib.25, *Mochl.*15. 3. in nautical language, ὑπεραιωρηθῆναι c. gen. loci, *lie off* a place, τῇσι νηυσὶ ὑπεραιωρηθέντες Φαλήρου Hdt.6.116.

**ὑπερακμάζω**, *surpass in vigour* or *bloom*, τὴν οἰκετικὴν ἐπιφάνειαν Myro 2 J.: abs., τὰ οἰνάρια -ήκμακεν *PSI*6.666.18 (iii B. C.).

**ὑπέρακμος**, ον, *sexually well-developed*, 1*Ep.Cor.*7.36, Sor.1.22; = Lat. *exoletus*, *Gloss.*: neut. pl. as Adv., ἀκολασταίνοντες ὑ. Eust.1915.20.

**ὑπερᾰκοντίζω**, *overshoot*, i. e. *outdo*, Νικίαν ταῖς μηχαναῖς Ar.*Av.*363 (troch.); διακοσίαισι βουσὶν ὑπερηκόντισα *I overshot* him with my 200 kine, Id.*Eq.*659, cf. Diph.66.5; also κλέπτων τοὺς βλέποντας ὑπερηκόντικεν *has outdone* them in stealing. Ar.*Pl.*666:—Pass., [ἡ ἰατρικὴ] ὑπερηκοντίσθη κατὰ τὴν ἀξίαν πασῶν τῶν κατὰ τὸν βίον χρειῶν *has been made to excel*.., Alex.Aphr.*Pr.*2 *Prooem.*

**ὑπερᾰκούω**, pf. -ακήκοα, *hear exceedingly well*, Phryn.*PS*p.121 B. (= *Com.Adesp.*1175).

**ὑπερακρᾰτής**, ές, *very incontinent*, only in Adv. -τῶς, ζῆν D.61.45 (vv. ll. ὑπερακράτως, ὑπεράκρως).

**ὑπερακρῑβής**, ές, *exceedingly exact*, Luc.*Herm.*54.

**ὑπερακρίζω**, *mount and climb over*, c. acc., τειχία X.*Eq.Mag.*6.5. II. *project, beetle over*, c. gen., δόμων E.*Supp.*988 (anap.).

**ὑπεράκριος**, ον, (ἄκρα) over or beyond the heights, οἱ Ὑπεράκριοι, = οἱ Διάκριοι, *the poor inhabitants of the Attic uplands beyond the heights (which bound the plain of Athens)*, opp. to the richer classes of the plains and coasts (cf. πεδιακός II, πάραλος II), Hdt.1.59, D.H.1.13. 2. τὰ ὑ. the *heights above* the plain, the *uplands*, Hdt.6.20.

**ὑπέρακρος**, ον, *very precipitous*, λόφοι Ael.*NA*14.16. II. Adv. ὑπεράκρως, v. ὑπερακρατής.

**ὑπεράλγ-εινος**, ον, *in excessive anguish*, f. l. in Aristid.*Or.*48(24).63. **-έω**, *feel pain for* or *because of*, ἀπάτης S.*Ant.*630 (anap.), cf. E.*Alc.*883 (anap.), *Hipp.*260 (anap.), Ar.*Av.*466 (anap.). 2. *grieve exceedingly*, τινι at a thing, Hdt.2.129, Arist.*Rh.*1380$^{b}$33; ἐπί τινι Luc.*Asin.*38: abs., E.*Med.*118 (anap.); ὑπεραλγεῖν ἀλγοῦντι παρόντα Arist.*Rh.*1383$^{b}$33; ὑ. φροντίδα in mind, E.*Heracl.*619 (lyr.). **-ής**, ές, *exceedingly grievous*, τὸν ὑ. χόλον S.*El.*176 (lyr.). 2. *suffering excessively*, Plb.3.79.12. **-ύνω**, *grieve exceedingly*, App.*Hisp.*71.

**ὑπεραλκής**, ές, *exceedingly strong*, ἕδραι Plu.*Pomp.*65.

⊛ **ὑπεράλλομαι**, *spring* or *leap over*, or *beyond*, c. gen., αὐλῆς ὑπεράλμενον (aor. 2 part.) Il.5.138: also c. acc., πολλὰς στίχας ὑπερᾶλτο (aor. 2) 20.327; so in Prose, X.*An.*7.4.17, *Eq.*8.4; ὑ. πλοίων ἱστούς, of dolphins, Arist.*HA*631$^{a}$22; τὰς μαχαίρας, of sword-dancers, Phld.*Rh.*1.74 S.; τὴν σκιὰν τὴν ἑαυτῶν Plu.2.1071b. II. metaph., *leap to a high place*, Lxx *Si.*38.33.

**ὑπέραλλος**, ον, *above others, exceedingly great*, Pi.*N.*3.33.

**ὑπέραλμα**, ατος, τό, a *hurdle* for leaping over, Artem.1.55.

**ὑπεράλπιος**, ον, *beyond the Alps*, Lat. *transalpinus*, Str.4.3.3, 5.1.4, al.

**ὑπεραμερία**, -άμερος, v. ὑπερημ-.

**ὑπεραμπέχω**, *cover all in its embrace*, ὁ ὑπεραμπέχων οὐρανός Tim.*Fr.*8.

**ὑπεραμφισβητέω**, *dispute about* a thing, Poll.5.165.

**ὑπεραναβαίνω**, *pass over, cross*, τὰς Ἄλπεις Zos.2.53. 2. *rise above*, τὸν ἀέρα Gal.19.172. II. metaph., *transcend*, c. acc., Eust.18.25, Eustr. *in EN*32.36; ὑπεραναβεβηκὸς κριτήριον a *transcendent* or *superior* criterion, S.E.*M.*7.445.

**ὑπεραναιδεύομαι**, Pass., *to be surpassed in impudence*, Ar.*Eq.*1206 (cj. Anon. in Budaei et aliorum Dictionario Graecolatino, Basil. 1565, pro -αναιδεσθήσομαι); Dind. suggests ὑπεραναιδισθήσομαι, citing *AB*80: ἀναιδίζεσθαι· Ἀριστοφάνης Ἱππεῦσιν.

**ὑπεραναίσχυντος**, ον, *exceedingly impudent*, D.43.65. Adv. -τως Phld.*Rh.*1.227 S.

**ὑπερανάκειμαι**, Pass., *lie above another at table*, D.L.7.17 codd. (sed leg. ὑπανα-, q. v.).

**ὑπερανᾱλίσκω**, also -ανηλ-, *overspend, exceed estimate*, *PCair.Zen.*702.17, al. (iii B. C.), *PHib.*1.100.1 (iii B. C.), *Sammelb.*7451.65 (iii B. C.):—Pass., ὑπερανηλίσκονται *PCair.Zen.*176.2 (iii B. C.); ὑπερανηλῶσθαι *Supp.Epigr.*4.447.60 (Didyma, ii B. C.).

**ὑπερανάστης**, ου, ὁ, = μετανάστης, Hsch., Phot.

⊛ **ὑπερανα-τείνομαι**, *stretch oneself upward excessively*, Luc.*Pr.Im.*13. **-τίθεμαι**, *to be set upon*, τινι J.*AJ*3.7.7.

**ὑπερανέχω**, *rise up over*, τινος Eust.1020.28; *excel*, τῶν ἄλλων ἀνθρώπων Procl. *in Alc.*p.137 C.: abs., Id. *in Prm.*p.663 S. 2. *hold above*, Ἀπόλλων τόξον αὐτῶν ὑπερανασχών Conon 49.2.

**ὑπερανήλωμα**, ατος, τό, *excess of expenditure*, *PHib.*1.112$^{v}$ (cf. 100 note 1, iii B. C.), *Supp.Epigr.*4.447.62 (Didyma, ii B. C.).

**ὑπερανθέω**, *bloom exceedingly*, Arat.1060, Poll.3.71. 2. *to be over-prosperous*, D.C.*Fr.*39.3.

**ὑπεράνθρωπος**, ον, *superhuman*, D.H.11.35, Luc.*Cat.*16.

**ὑπεραν-ίεμαι**, *to be excessively diluted*, Crito ap.Gal.13.880. **-ίσταμαι**, Pass., with aor. 2 and pf. Act., *stand up* or *project over*, c. gen., D.H.1.15, 9.68: abs., Id.3.68, Luc.*Icar.*12: metaph., ταῶς ὑπερανεστηκὼς *strutting, conceited*, Philostr.*Her.*15. **-ίσχω**, = ὑπερανέχω I, κορυφὴ ὑπερανίσχουσα J.*BJ*7.6.1, cf. Eust.1020.27.

**ὑπεραντλ-έομαι**, Pass., *to be very leaky*, ὑ. ἅλμῃ to be water-logged, Luc.*Merc.Cond.*2. **-ος**, ον, prop. of a ship, *full of water* (ἄντλος), *water-logged*, *AP*5.203 (Mel.), Ph.1.670, Plu.*Luc.*13, Poll.1.92, etc.: metaph., of the ship of state, D.C.52.16. 2. of persons, φορτί' ἐξέρριψ' ὑ. γενόμενος Diph.43.12: metaph., *overcharged*, Luc.*Tim.*18; συμφορᾷ E.*Hipp.*767 (lyr.); ταῖς φροντίσιν Plu.*Mar.*45. II. *overflowing*, σιτοθῆκαι Them.*Or.*18.221b: metaph., ὕβρις Luc.*Tim.*4.

⊛ **ὑπεράνω** [ᾰ], Adv. *above*, opp. ὑποκάτω, *SIG*588.31 (Milet., ii B. C.); οἰκεῖν Luc.*DDeor.*4.2, etc.; *above the horizon*, Euc.*Phaen.*p.8 M.: mostly c. gen., ὑ. τούτων [τῶν μορίων] σχίζεται [ἡ φλέψ] Arist.*HA*513$^{b}$32, cf. *PSI*6.631.6 (iii B. C.), Lxx *Ez.*43.15, al.; ὑ. γίγνεσθαί τινος to get *the upper hand of*, Teles p.44 H., Plu.2.10b, Phld.*Mort.*34; ὑ. τεθεῖσθαι πάντων Id.*Piet.*102; ποιεῖν or ποιεῖσθαί τινα or τι ὑ. τινός, Plu.2.98e, 6b; πάντων ὑ. ποιεῖν act *more nobly* than all others, D.L.7.128. 2. οἱ ὑ. πλεονασμοὶ *excessive* repetitions, Plb.12.24.1; but μίαν ὑ. ποιότητα one *supreme* quality, Meno *Iatr.*14.18. 3. of time, *further back*, ἐκ τῶν ὑ. χρόνων *SIG*742.58 (Ephesus, i B. C.). 4. *above*, in a document, [ψηφίσματα] ὑ. γεγραμμένα ib.591.2 (Lampsacus, ii B. C.).

**ὑπεράνωθεν** [ᾰ], Adv. *from above*, Lxx *Ps.*77(78).23, Ph.Byz.*Mir.*1.1, Hsch. s. v. ὕπερθεν. II. c. gen., *above*, Lxx *Ez.*1.25, Aesop.4.

**ὑπεράνωρ**, Dor. for ὑπερήνωρ.

⊛ **ὑπεραπαιτ-έω**, *demand payment in excess of what is due*, *Cod.Just.*1.4.26.7:—hence **-ησις**, εως, ἡ, *demand for such payment*, ib.3.10.1.2.

**ὑπερᾰπᾰτάομαι**, Pass., *to be deceived excessively*, *AP*9.761.

**ὑπεραπλόομαι**, Pass., *to be super-simplified* or *transcendent in simplicity*, Iamb.*Myst.*7.2, Procl.*Inst.*93: c. gen., Id. *in R.*1.73 K., al., Eustr. *in EN*268.31.

**ὑπεραπο-δέχομαι**, dub. sens. in *Wiener Sitzb.*132(2).12 (Caria). **-δίδωμι**, *pay over and above*, *IPE*1$^{2}$.32 *A* 18 (Olbia, iii B. C.), Philostr.*VS*1.25.3. **-θνήσκω**, *die for*, τινος X.*Cyn.*1.14; ὑπέρ τινος Pl.*Smp.*208d, Arist.*EN*1169$^{a}$20, al.: abs., Pl.*Smp.*179b, 180a, Apollod.1.9.15. **-κρίνομαι** [ῑ], Med., *answer for* one, *defend* him, τινος Ar.*V.*951, *Th.*186.

**ὑπεραπόλλυμι**, *destroy and more than destroy*, v. l. for ὑπερβαλλόντως ἀπώλεσε in Sch.E.*Alc.*1082. II. Pass., *die for*, τινος Sch. Pi.*P.*6.30.

**ὑπεραπο-λογέομαι**, *speak for* any one, *defend* him, τινος Hdt.6.136, X.*HG*1.7.16; ὑ. τῆς ὑποψίας Antipho 2.4.2. **-τῖσις**, εως, ἡ, gloss on ὑπερέκτισις (-έκτησις cod.), Hsch. (better -τεισις in both, v. ἔκτεισις). **-φᾰσις**, εως, ἡ, *transcendent negation*, Procl. *in Prm.* p.913 S. (pl.). **-φᾰτικός**, ή, όν, *denying doubly*, ὑπεραποφατικὸν ἐστιν ἀποφατικὸν ἀποφατικοῦ *Stoic.*2.66. **-χράω**, *to be more than enough*, Poll.1.236, 6.149. Adv. pres. part. Act. **-χρώντως**, *more than enough*, Id.9.154.

**ὑπερᾰραιόομαι**, *become excessively rarefied*, Anon. *in EN*127.24.

**ὑπερᾰρέσκω**, *please above measure*, App.*BC*2.1.

⊛ **ὑπεράριθμος** [ᾰ], ον, *supernumerary*, Procop.*Arc.*24.

**ὑπεραρπάζομαι**, *to be 'rapt' above*, ὁ πρῶτος θεὸς ὑπερήρπασται πασῶν τῶν τοῦ ὄντος προόδων Procl. *in Prm.*p.839 S.

**ὑπεραρρωδέω**, Ion. for ὑπερορρωδέω, *to be afraid on behalf of*, τῇ Ἑλλάδι *for* Hellas, Hdt.8.72.

⊛ **ὑπέραρσις**, εως, ἡ, *exaltation*, Lxx *Ez.*47.11.

**ὑπεραρτάω**, *hang above*, of an amulet, Aët.2.36 (Pass.).

**ὑπεραρχαῖος**, α, ον, *very old*, Sch.Il.3.144.

**ὑπεράρχιος**, ον, *prior to* ἀρχαί, [πηγαί] Dam.*Pr.*130.

**ὑπερασθενής**, ές, *exceedingly weak*, Arist.*Pol.*1295$^{b}$8.

**ὑπερασθμαίνω**, *gasp exceedingly*, Arr.*Cyn.*14.3.

**ὑπέρασθμος**, ον, *panting exceedingly*, X.*Cyn.*10.20, Poll.5.80, 84.

**ὑπερασμενίζω**, *take exceedingly great pleasure*, ἐφ' ἡδοναῖς μικραῖς Plu.2.1094c.

**ὑπερασπάζομαι**, *to be exceedingly fond of*, τινα X.*Smp.*4.38, Plu.2.229e.

**ὑπερασπ-ίζω**, fut. -ιῶ Lxx *Pr.*2.7, al.: pf. -ήσπικα *OGI*441.80 (Lagina, senatus consultum, i B. C.):—*cover with a shield*, τινα Plb.6.39.6, D.S.17.99, D.H.6.12, Plu.*Cor.*3, Arr.*Fr.*56 J., etc.; τινος Id.*An.*6.28.4, Lxx *Ge.*15.1, al.; ὑπὲρ τῆς πόλεως ib.4*Ki.*19.34: metaph. c. gen., *defend*, Chor.32.1 (p.345 F.-R.). **-ισμός**, ὁ, *a covering with a shield, protection*, Lxx *Ps.*17(18).36, al. **-ιστής**, οῦ, ὁ, *one who holds a shield over, protector, champion*, ib.2.30, al., cf. Ph.1.374: fem. **-ίστρια**, ἡ, Lxx 4*Ma.*15.29 (-ίστεια cod. A).

⊛ **ὑπεράστειος**, ον, *exceedingly polished* or *witty*, Hegesand.9.

**ὑπεραστράπτω**, *flash exceedingly*, ὄμματα Arr.*Cyn.*4.5: metaph., Anon. in Rh.1.632 W. II. c. acc., *outshine*, τῇ αἴγλῃ τῶν λίθων τὸν ἥλιον Procop.*Aed.*1.4.

**ὑπεραστρονομέω**, *astronomize above and beyond*, οὐρανοῦ Procl. *Hyp.*1.1.

**ὑπερασχάλλω**, *to be exceedingly grieved*, τῷ συμβεβηκότι Aristid.*Or.*25(43).63.

**ὑπερασχημονέω**, *behave with great unseemliness*, Plu.2.45f.

**ὑπεράτοπος**, ον, *beyond measure absurd*, D.17.8, Cels.ap.Orig.*Cels.*2.46.

**ὑπεραττῐκ-ίζω**, *imitate the Attic dialect to excess*, Philostr.*VA*1.17 : metaph. of excessive subtlety in philosophy, Simp. *in Ph.*235.3. **-ός**, ή, όν, *excessively Attic, carrying imitation of the Attic dialect to excess*, Luc.*Lex.*25. Adv. -κῶς Id.*Demon.*26.

**ὑπεραυαίνω**, *dry excessively*, τὸν ἐγκέφαλον Hp.*Ep.*19 (*Hermes* 53.70).

**ὑπεραυγ-άζω**, *eclipse by superior light*, Eust.729.21 (Pass.). ❋ **-έω**, = foreg., in Pass., prob. l. in Str.16.4.6 (cod. E, cf. Eust. ad D.P. 1121). **-ής**, ές, *shining exceedingly*, Luc.*VH*1.29.

**ὑπεραυθεντέω**, = Lat. *exauctoro, auctoro*, *Gloss.*; λέγων καὶ ὑπεραυθεν[τῶν ὡ]ς ὑπὲρ ἰδίων πολειτᾶν dub. in *Bull.Soc.Roy. des Lettres de Lund* 1928/9 iv 16 (Thuria, i B.C./i A.D.; fort. ὑπὲρ αὐθεντῶν).

**ὑπεράϋλος**, ον, *purely immaterial*, only in Adv. -λως, Ph.1.103.

**ὑπεραυξ-άνω** and -ω, *increase above measure*:—Pass., *to be so increased*, Gal.14.226; *become over-powerful*, And.4.24, D.C.79.15. **2.** Pass. also, *grow above*, ὑπεραύξονται τῶν ἀμπέλων Sch.Ar.*V.*1282. **II.** intr. in Act., *grow* or *abound exceedingly*, ὑπεραυξήσας (of a fish) Callisth.ap.Stob.4.36.16; ὑπεραυξάνει ἡ πίστις ὑμῶν 2*Ep.Thess.*1.3. **-ημα**, ατος, τό, *product of overgrowth*, Praxag.Med. et Phylotim.ap.Gal.*UP*8.12. **-ησις**, εως, ἡ, *overgrowth*, τῶν ὀνύχων Gramm. in Harp.p.vii Dind. s.v. ἀπονυχίζειν; σαρκός Paul.Aeg.3.81, 6.85.

**ὑπεραύστηρος**, ον, *excessively severe*, *POxy.*471.93 (ii A.D.).

**ὑπεραυχ-έω**, *to be over-proud*, Th.4.19, D.C.57.12, etc. **-ής**, ές, = sq., νίκη Tryph.671. **-ος**, ον, *over-boastful, over-proud*, πληγὰς τῶν ὑπεραύχων S.*Ant.*1351 (anap.), cf. X.*Ages.*11.11; ὑπέραυχα βάζειν A.*Th.*483 (lyr.); τὰ ὑ. D.H.8.50; τὸ ὑ. Ph.1.458.

**ὑπεράφανος**, ον, Dor. for ὑπερήφανος (q.v.).

**ὑπεραφρίζω**, *froth over*, of a cup full of sparkling wine, Eub.56, Aristopho 14 (troch.).

**ὑπεραχθής**, ές, *overburdened*, Theoc.11.37. **II.** *very heavy*, φόρτος Nic.*Th.*342; πτερύγων ῥιπή Opp.*H.*5.263.

**ὑπεράχθομαι**, Pass., *to be exceedingly grieved at..*, c. dat., ὑπεραχθεσθέντες τῇ Μιλήτου ἁλώσι Hdt.6.21; μήθ' οἷς ἐχθαίρεις ὑπεράχθεο S.*El.*177 (lyr.).

**ὑπερβάθμιος**, ον, *stepping over the threshold*: metaph., *going beyond bounds, transgressing*, ἤρξαντο ὑ. τείνειν πόδα ὡς ἠδύνατο ἕκαστος, of satraps, Anon.Hist.(*FGrH*155) p.836 J.; ὑ. πόδα ἀποτείνειν, prov. of meddling with theology, Ascl.*in Metaph.*98.11; ὑ. π. τείνειν Marin.*Procl.*13, Agath.2.29, cf. Suid. s.v. ὑπερβάθμιος; ὑ. π. πέμπειν Phlp.*in Cat.*6.13.

❋ **ὑπερβαίνω**, fut. -βήσομαι Heraclit.94: aor. 2 ὑπερέβην, Ep. 3 pl. ὑπέρβᾰσαν Il.12.469:—*step over, mount, scale*, c. acc., τεῖχος Il. l. c.; οὐδόν Od.8.80; τείχη E.*Ba.*654, Th.3.20; γεῖσα τειχέων E.*Ph.*1180; τάφρους Id.*Rh.*111; ὑ. τοὺς οὔρους *cross* the boundaries, Hdt.6.108; τὰ ὄρεα, Αἷμον, Id.4.25, Th.2.96; δόμους *step over* the threshold of the house, E.*Med.*382 codd.; δῶμα Id.*Ion* 514 (troch., s.v.l.); ὑ. τέγος ὡς τοὺς γείτονας D.22.53; ὑ. τὴν οἰκίαν τινός, of burglars, *PTeb.*796.2 (ii B.C.); but more usu. ὑ. εἰς τὴν οἰκίαν ib.793 vi 21 (ii B.C.), cf. *BGU* 1007.10 (iii B.C.), *PSI*4.396.4 (iii B.C.) (the usage c. gen. is more than dub.; in Hdt.3.54 the best codd. have ἐπέβησαν; in E.*Supp.* 1049 Kirchhoff restored ὑπεκβᾶσ'; in *Ion* 220 Herm. supplied βᾶλόν): abs., ὑ. εἰς τὴν τῶν Θηβαίων X.*HG*5.4.59; τῶν [ἡδονῶν] εἰς τὸ ἐπέκεινα ὑ. Pl.*R.*587c; of rivers, *overflow*, ἐς τὴν χώρην, ἐς τὰς ἀρούρας, Hdt.2.13,14; εἰ ἐθελήσει ὑπερβῆναι ὁ ποταμὸς ταύτῃ ib.99. **2.** *overstep, transgress*, μέτρα Heraclit. l.c.; οὐ θέμιν οὐδὲ δίκαν Pi.*Fr.*1.5; νόμους τοὺς Περσέων Hdt.3.83, cf. S.*Ant.*449, al.; τοὺς ὅρκους D.11.2; τὸν τῶν ἀναγκαίων ὅρον Pl.*R.*373d; τῆς εἱμαρμένης ὅρον *IG*12(7).53.32 (Amorgos, iii A.D.); τἀληθές *exceed* the truth, Phld.*Po.*5.24: abs., *transgress, trespass, sin*, ὅτε κέν τις ὑπερβήῃ (Ep. aor. subj.) καὶ ἁμάρτῃ Il.9.501; ὑ. καὶ ἁμαρτάνοντες Pl.*R.*366a, cf. 1*Ep.Thess.*4.6. **3.** *pass* or *go beyond*, τοὺς προσεχέας Hdt.3.89; *leave out, omit*, Pl.*R.*528d, al., Epicur.*Ep.*3 p.63 U., Gal.15.592, etc.; ὑ. τι τῷ λόγῳ D.4.38; ὑ. τὸ σαφὲς εἰπεῖν Id.60.31; *pass over*, i.e. leave unmolested, the next heir, Is.3.57; ὑ. τῆς οὐσίας *omit* part of it, Arist.*APo.*$91^{b}27$. **4.** *jump across* an intervening space, Phld.*D.*3.9. **5.** of Time, *pass by, elapse*, ὑπερβάντων τῶν τῆς συμπαθείας χρόνων Sor.2.41. **II.** *go beyond*, ὑπερβὰς ἑβδομήκοντα [ἔτη] *after passing* the age of seventy, Pl.*Lg.*755b; ὑ. τοῦτο *go beyond* this, in their demands, Plb.2.15.6; *transcend*, τὸν νοῦν Plot.6.7.39: abs., *dies* ὑπερβαίνοντες *supernumerary* days in the calendar, Macr.*Sat.*1.13.10. **2.** *surpass, outdo*, πάσῃ παρὰ πάντας ἀνθρώπους ὑ. ἀρετῇ Pl.*Ti.*24d; ὑ. ἢ γνῶσιν σαφηνείᾳ ἢ ἄγνοιαν ἀσαφείᾳ Id.*R.*478c: abs., dub. l. in Thgn. 1015. **III.** *stand over, shield, protect*, c. dat., Opp.*H.*1.710. **IV.** in pf., *to be higher than*, δύο [ἐσχάρας] ὑπερβεβηκυίας τὴν ἐν τῷ μεταφρένῳ ἐσχάραν Paul.Aeg.6.44.

**B.** Causal in aor. 1, *put over*, ὑπερβησάτω ἐπὶ τὰς δεξιὰς πλευρὰς τὴν κνήμην, as a direction to one mounting a horse, X.*Eq.*7.2.

**ὑπερβακχεύω**, *express in over-Bacchic style*, τὰς πανηγυρικὰς ἐννοίας Philostr.*VS*2.26.1.

**ὑπερβαλλόντως**, v. sq. A. II. 5.

**ὑπερβάλλω**, fut. -βαλῶ, Ep. -βαλέω Od.11.597: Ep. aor. 2 ὑπειρέβαλον Il.23.637:—*throw over* or *beyond a mark, overshoot*, ὑπέρβαλε σήματα πάντων Il.23.843; τόσσον παντὸς ἀγῶνος (sc. σήματα) ὑπέρβαλε ib.847; δουρὶ ὑ. Φυλῆα *beat* him *in throwing* with it, ib.637. **2.** ὅτε μέλλοι ἄκρον [λόφον] ὑπερβαλέειν *force* the stone *over* the top, Od. l.c. **3.** intr., *run beyond, overrun* the scent, of hounds, X.*Cyn.*6.20. **4.** *outstrip* or *pass*, in racing, τινας S.*El.*716. **5.** Med., *throw* a stone *over* one's head, *SIG*1071 (Olympia). **II.** in various metaph. senses: **1.** *outdo, excel, surpass, overpower*, δέδοικα μὴ πρὶν πόνοις ὑπερβάλῃ με γῆρας E.*Fr.*453.5 (lyr.): c. gen., Pi.*Fr.*33; βροντῆς ὑπερβάλλοντα κτύπον A.*Pr.*923. **2.** *go beyond, exceed*, μήτ' ἄρ' ὑπερβάλλων βοὸς ὁπλὴν μήτ' ἀπολείπων Hes.*Op.*489; ὑ. πόσιος μέτρον Thgn.479; τὴν τοῦ μετρίου φύσιν Pl.*Plt.*283e; ὑ. τὰ ἱκανά X.*Hier.*4.8: of Time, ὑ. ἑκατὸν ἔτεα *exceed* 100 years, in age, Hdt.3.23; ὑ. τὰς τρεῖς ἡμέρας *delay longer than..*, Hp.*VC*14; ὑ. τὸν χρόνον *exceed* the time, i.e. be too late, X.*HG*5.3.21; ὑ. τὸν καιρὸν *exceed* reasonable bounds, Democr.235, D.23.122: in number, intensity, etc., ἡδοναὶ ὑ. λύπας Pl.*Lg.*734b, cf. *Prt.*356b (Pass.): c. dat. modi, *exceed* one *in..*, πάντας ἀνθρώπους τόλμῃ καὶ μιαρίᾳ X.*HG*7.3.6; ἅπαντας ἀνθρώπους ὠμότητι D.18.275: abs., ὑ. πρὸς ἀρετήν Pl.*Lg.*945c. **b.** c. gen. pro acc., ἆρα λύπῃ ὑ. τὸ ἀδικεῖν τοῦ ἀδικεῖσθαι; Id.*Grg.*475c, cf. *Lg.*734a; ὑ. τῆς συμμετρίας Arist.*Pol.*$1284^{b}8$, cf. *HA*$503^{b}22$. **3.** abs., *exceed*, αἱ μέσαι ἕξεις πρὸς μὲν τὰς ἐλλείψεις ὑπερβάλλουσι compared with their defects *are in excess*, Id.*EN*$1108^{b}17$; *exceed all bounds*, A.*Pers.*291, E.*Ba.*785, Th.7.67, Pl.*Tht.*180a; οὐχ ὑπερβαλών keeping within bounds, Pi.*N.*7.66; μή νυν ὑπέρβαλλ', ἀλλ' ἐναισίμως φέρε E.*Alc.*1077: c. dat. modi, ὑ. τῇ μοχθηρίᾳ Ar.*Pl.*109; ἀδυναμίᾳ τοῦ δοξάσαι Pl.*Tht.*192c, cf. X.*Mem.*4.3.7; ἀνοίᾳ D.8.16. **b.** freq. in part. ὑπερβάλλων, ουσα, ον, *exceeding, excessive*, ὑ. δαπάνη X.*Hier.*11.2; ἡδονή, ἔπαινοι, Pl.*R.*402e, *Phdr.*240e; θεάματα ταῖς δαπάναις ὑ. Isoc.4.45, cf. Pl.*Lg.*899a: οἱ ὑπερβάλλοντες, opp. οἱ καταδεέστεροι, Isoc.9.13; τὰ ὑ. *an over-high estate*, E.*Med.*127 (anap.); φεύγειν τὰ ὑ. ἑκατέρωσε *extremes*, Pl.*R.*619a; τὸ ὑ. αὐτῶν *such part* of them *as goes beyond that*, Th.2.35; οἱ ὑ. [λόγοι], title of work by Thrasymachus (*Fr.*7), perh. *overpowering* arguments. **4.** *overbid* or *outbid* at auction, ἀλλήλους Lys.22.8, *POxy.*1633.5 (iii A.D.); τὸ ὑπερβάλλον the *overbid*, *PPetr.*3 p.195 (iii B.C.): abs., *go on further and further*, in making offers, προέβαινε τοῖσι χρήμασι ὑπερβάλλων he went on *bidding more and more*, Hdt.5.51; ᾔτει τοσαῦτα ὑπερβάλλων Th.8.56, cf. And.1.133:—Pass., ἕνεκα τοῦ -βεβλῆσθαι τὴν οἰκίαν *POxy.*513.25 (ii A.D.); v. infr. B. I. 3. **5.** Adv. ὑπερβαλλόντως *exceedingly*, Pl.*R.*492b, Epicur.*Nat.*2.2, *SIG*685.36 (Crete, ii B.C.), Phld.*Lib.*p.7 O., 2*Ep.Cor.*11.23; written ὑπερβαλόντως in *IG*12(7).410.12 (Amorgos); opp. μετρίως, Isoc.1.28. **III.** *pass over, cross* mountains, rivers, and the like, πρῶνα A.*Ag.*307; κορυφάς Id.*Pr.*722; γῆς ὅρους E.*Or.*443; τὰς Ἄλπεις εἰς τὴν Ἰταλίαν Str.7.2.3: c. gen., θριγκοῦ τοῦδ' ὑ. ποδί E.*Ion* 1321 (where Dobree suggested θριγκοὺς τούσδ'): metaph., *surmount*, τάσδ' ὑ. τύχας Id.*Alc.*795. **b.** of ships, *double* a headland, ὑ. Μαλέην Hdt.7.168; τὴν ἄκραν Th.8.104. **c.** abs., *cross over*, ἐς τὴν ἄνω Μακεδονίην Hdt.8.137, cf. X.*An.*4.6.10; πρὸς τοὺς Θρᾷκας ib.7.5.1; κατὰ λόφους τινάς ib.6.5.7. **2.** of water, *run over, beat over*, c. gen., ὑπερβάλλει δὲ θάλασσα ἀμφοτέρων τοίχων Thgn.673; of rivers, *overflow*, τὰς ἀρούρας Hdt.2.111: abs., of a kettle, *boil over*, Id.1.59; of the sea, ἣν δ' ὑπερβάλῃ..πόντος E.*Tr.*691. **3.** of the sun, *to be very hot*, Hdt.4.184. **4.** *exceed*, i.e. overlap, a base, Euc.6.29; cf. ὑπερβολή IV.—Note, the case that follows is almost always the acc.; the gen. occurs in a few exceptional instances, v. supr. II. 2 b, III. 1 and 2.

**B.** Med., with pf. Pass., = A. II, *outdo, overcome, conquer*, τινα Hdt.5.124, Ar.*Eq.*758 (lyr.), *Nu.*1035; τὴν βασιλέος δύναμιν Hdt.8.24; μάχῃ ὑ. τινά E.*Or.*691; φίλτροις ὑ. τινά S.*Tr.*584, cf. Ar.*Eq.*413: abs., *to be conqueror*, Hdt.6.9, 7.168. **2.** *exceed, surpass*, τινα D.19.342, etc.; τοὺς ἀπ' αἰῶνος *OGI*542.11 (Ancyra, ii A.D.); πάντας τῷ ὕψεϊ καὶ τῷ μεγάθεϊ Hdt.2.175, cf. 110; τινὰ ἀναιδείᾳ Ar.*Eq.*409; θωπείαις ib.890; εἴς τι Pl.*Criti.*115d; ἔν τινι Str.1.1.2. **b.** δόσι χρημάτων ὑ. *surpass all*, Hdt.1.61; ἀρετῇ Id.9.71; ὑπερβαλλόμενος πλήθεϊ with *overpowering* numbers, Id.3.21: pf. part. Pass., ὑπερβεβλημένη γυνή an *excellent, surpassing* woman, E.*Alc.*153; φύσις ὑπερβεβλ. Pl.*R.*558b; ταφῆς τῆς μὲν ὑπερβεβλ., τῆς δὲ ἐλλειπούσης Id.*Lg.*719d: c. gen., γόγγροι τῶν παρ' ἡμῖν ὑπερβεβλ. κατὰ τὸ μέγεθος Str.3.2.7. **3.** *overbid, outbid* (v. supr. A. II. 4), τινὰ χρήμασιν Pl.*Phdr.*232c, cf. X.*Cyr.*5.3.32. **4.** *outflank*, τὸ κέρας τῶν πολεμίων Ascl.*Tact.*10.2, cf. 18. **II.** *put off, postpone*, τὴν ἀπόδοσιν Hdt.4.9; τὴν συμβολήν Id.9.45; εἰς ἄλλον καιρόν Phld.*Rh.*1.223 S.; but ἢν ὑπερβάλωνται ἐκείνην τὴν ἡμέραν..συμβολὴν μὴ ποιεύμενοι if *they let* that day *pass* without fighting, Hdt.9.51: abs., *delay, linger*, Id.3.71,76, 7.206; εἰς αὖθις ὑπερβαλέσθαι Pl.*Phdr.*254d, cf. Arist.*Rh.Al.* $1420^{a}8$, $1438^{b}6$.

**ὑπερβᾶν**· ὑπερῴαν, Hsch.

**ὑπερβᾰρ-έω**, *overweigh, outweigh*, Suid. s.v. ταλαντουμένην, *EM*744.16. **-ής**, ές, *exceedingly heavy*, δαίμων A.*Ag.*1175 (lyr.); τὰν τύχαν ..τὰν ὑπερβάρεα *IGRom.*4.1302 (Cyme, i B.C./i A.D.); ὑ. ἀνάβασις τοῦ Νείλου *POxy.*486.32 (ii A.D.):—but **ὑπέρβᾰρυς**, υ, in Hp.*Art.* 46, Gal.7.587.

**ὑπερβᾰσ-ία**, Ion. -ίη, ἡ, *passover*, given as equiv. to Πάσχα, J.*AJ* 2.14.6: but commonly, **II.** metaph., *transgression, trespass*, ὑπερβασίῃ Διὸς ὅρκια δηλήσηται Il.3.107; τίσασθαι μνηστῆρας ὑ. ἀλεγεινῆς Od.3.206; τεάν, Ζεῦ, δύνασιν τίς ἀνδρῶν ὑ. κατάσχοι; S.*Ant.*605 (lyr.): pl., Il.23.589, Od.22.168, Hes.*Op.*828. ❋ **-ις**, εως, ἡ, *a passing over*, ὄρη μόλις ἁμάξῃ μιᾷ καὶ ὀρικῷ ζεύγει τὴν ὑ. βιαζομένοις ξυγχωροῦντα Jul.*Or.*2.72a; *a pass* over mountains, Str.4.6.12; *passage* over a desert, Id.16.2.30. **2.** *overstepping*, of a dislocated joint, Hp.*Art.*80. **3.** καθ' ὑπέρβασιν, of bandaging which gives the appearance of winglets, Gal.18(1).790. 4. '*jumping over*' an intervening space, Phld.*D*.3.9. II. metaph., *transgression*, Thgn.1247. III. Act., = ὑπερβίβασις (nisi hoc legend.), *transport across* (the Isthmus), τῶν λέμβων Plb.4.19.8. 2. Rhet., *transposition*, Suid. s. v. Γοργίας (pl.).

**ὑπερβᾰτ-έον,** *one must pass over*, c. acc., Plu.2.709e. **-ήριος,** ον, *of* or *for passing over*, ὑπερβατήρια θύειν (sc. ἱερά) Polyaen.1.10.1; cf. διαβατήρια. **-ικός,** ή, όν, *delighting in hyperbata*, of Thucydides, Marcellin.*Vit.Thuc*.50. Adv. -κῶς *with hyperbaton*, ἀναγνῶναι Eust.1179.16. 2. *inclined to neglect*, τοῦ παραινοῦντος λόγου Chrysipp.*Stoic*.3.125. **-όν,** τό, *the figure hyperbaton*, i.e. *a transposition of words* or *clauses*, Phld.*Rh*.1.160 S. (pl.), Ph.1.580, Quint.*Inst*.8.6.65, A.D.*Synt*.311.26, Longin.22.1 (pl.), Hermog.*Inv*.4.3, etc.; of letters, A.D.*Adv*.167.6. **-ός,** ή, όν, later ός, όν (v. infr.), *that can be passed* or *crossed*, *scaleable*, of a wall, Th.3.25, *PEnteux*.13.5 (iii B.C.); *accessible* to trespassers, *PFay*.110.9 (i A.D.); ἐξ ὑπερβατῶν *PRyl*.138.16 (i A.D.). 2. *transposed*, of words, ὑπερβατὸν δεῖ θεῖναι..τὸ "ἀλαθέως" Pl.*Prt*.343e; σύνθεσις ὀνομάτων ὑπερβατή Arist.*Rh.Al*.1435$^a$37; νοήσεις ὑπερβατοί thoughts *expressed in inverted phrases*, D.H.*Th*.52. Adv. -τῶς *in inverted order*, Arist.*Rh.Al*.1438$^a$28, Str.8.3.10, 8.6.7; so δι' ὑπερβατοῦ D.H.*Th*.31; cf. foreg. 3. Subst. -τός, ὁ, name of a βρόχος, Heraclas ap.Orib.48.18.1. II. Act., *going beyond*, τῶνδ' ὑπερβατώτερα *going far beyond* these, A.*Ag*.428 (lyr.); *extravagant*, ἐνύπνια Arist.*Div.Somn*.463$^b$1. Adv. -τῶς *miraculously*, δημιουργεῖται Hp.*de Arte* 11.

**ὑπερβεβλημένως,** Adv. pf. part. Pass. of ὑπερβάλλω, *beyond all measure*, *immoderately*, Arist.*EN*1118$^a$7.

⊛ **Ὑπερβερεταῖος,** ὁ (sc. μήν), the last month of the Macedonian year, *PCair.Zen*.2.6 (iii B.C.), J.*AJ*8.4.1, etc.: prov. of those who exceed their term, Zen.6.30. II. name of a month in several Hellenistic calendars, *Hemerolog.Flor*.

**ὑπερβήῃ,** v. ὑπερβαίνω A. I. 2.

**ὑπερβῐάζομαι,** *press exceeding heavily*, of the plague, Th.2.52, cf. J.*AJ*9.10.2, Procop.*Vand*.2.4, al.

**ὑπερβίαιος** [ῐ], ον, *extremely violent*, ἐξολκή Orib.45.18.26.

**ὑπερβῐβ-άζω,** Causal of ὑπερβαίνω, *carry over*, *transport*, Plb.8.36.9, Luc.*VH*2.42. 2. in Music, *transpose higher*, opp. ὑποβιβάζω, Theo Sm.p.91 H. II. *transpose* the letters of a word, Ps.-Plu.*Vit.Hom*.9, A.D.*Synt*.342.6 (Pass.); *transpose* words, Longin.22.2, Anon.*in Tht*.51.40; ὁ Ἀλέξανδρος ὑπερβιβάζειν μᾶλλον ἀξιοῖ τὴν λέξιν prefers to *explain* the phrase *as a hyperbaton*, Simp.*in Cael*.352.3. **-ᾰσις,** εως, ἡ, v. ὑπέρβασις III. ⊛ **-ασμός,** ὁ, *transposition*, A.D.*Synt*.315.10, 341.24. **-αστέον,** *one must transpose*, Sch.Pi.*O*.6.40. **-αστήρ,** ῆρος, ὁ, a surgical instrument, *Hermes* 38.283.

**ὑπερβίη** [ῐ], ἡ, *overbearing might*, *arrogance*, Suid.

⊛ **ὑπέρβῐος,** ον, (βία) *of overwhelming strength* or *might*, Ἡρακλῆς Pi.*O*.10(11).15; δαῖμον, i.e. Apollo, B.3.37: c. gen., πάντων ὑπέρβιος Pi.*Oxy*.408.28. II. mostly in bad sense, *overweening*, *lawless*, *wanton*, οἷος κείνου θυμὸς ὑ. Il.18.262; ὑ. ὕβριν ἔχοντες Od.1.368; ὑ. ἦτορ ἔχοντες Orph.*Fr*.119: neut. ὑπέρβιον as Adv., Il.17.19, Od.12.379, 14.92,95: regul. Adv. -βίως Sch.A.R.4.1523.

**ὑπερβῐόω,** *outlive* another, τινος Plb.22.20.3.

**ὑπερβλαστ-άνω,** *shoot over-luxuriantly*, Thphr.*CP*1.20.6. **-ής,** ές, *shooting over-luxuriantly*, ibid.

**ὑπερβλέπω,** *overlook*, *neglect*, Phot. s. v. ὑπερορᾶν.

**ὑπερβλήδην,** Adv. *above measure*, Orph.*A*.257.

**ὑπέρβλημα,** ατος, τό, *portion of an area projecting beyond* a given line, Archim.*Con.Sph*.2, al.; *excess* of one magnitude over another, Simp.*in Ph*.973.9.

**ὑπερβλύζω,** *bubble* or *gush over*, *overflow*, χολὴ ὑπερβλύσασα Hp.*Ep*.23, cf. Q.S.5.324; τὸ -ύζον τοῦ νάματος Ph.1.174; ἐκ πηγῆς D.Chr.12.70; τοῦ βόθρου Philostr.*VA*3.14; τῆς φιάλης ib.25: metaph. of wine-drinkers, Ph.2.478 (prob. cj.): c. acc., φλέβες ὑ. αἷμα Q.S.11.192; ἔλαιον ὑ. τὸ κιβώτιον Procop.*Aed*.1.7: c. dat., τὰ θεῖα ὑ. τοῖς ἀγαθοῖς Herm.*in Phdr*.p.170 A.

**ὑπέρβλῠσις,** εως, ἡ, *a gushing over*, *eruption*, φθειρῶν Suid. s. v. Καλλισθένης; gloss on διαφλύξιες, Gal.19.92 (pl.).

**ὑπερβοάω,** *outroar*, τὴν θάλατταν Aristid.2.105 J.

**ὑπερβολ-άδην** [ᾰ], Adv. *immoderately*, *excessively*, Thgn.484. **-αῖος,** ὁ, *added*, *additional*; of notes or strings, Pherecr.145.26; fem., of *the highest tetrachord* in the two-octave scale, Aristox.(?) *Oxy*.667.18; in gen. pl., Euc.*Sect.Can*.10, Plu.2.1029a; **ὑπερβολαία,** ἡ, *the* νήτη *of the tetrachord* ὑπερβολαίων, Theo Sm.p.89 H., Ptol.*Harm*.3.8, cf. Ph.1.111. ⊛ **-ή,** ἡ, (ὑπερβάλλω) *a throwing beyond* others, δίσκων ὑπερβολαῖς Philostr.*Im*.2.19: in intr. sense, *altitude* of a star, Arist.*Mete*.342$^b$32. 2. *overshooting*, *superiority*, χερῶν ὑπερβολαῖς E.*Fr*.434; στρατιᾶς Th.6.31. 3. *excess*, τοῦ μεγέθεος Archyt.1; opp. ἔλλειψις or ἔνδεια, Pl.*Prt*.356a, 357a,b; θερμασίης Hp.*Vict*.2.65; ὑ. δισσή.., τῷ ποσῷ καὶ τῷ ποιῷ Arist.*PA*668$^b$14; ὑπερβολὴν τῆς ἐπιθυμίας ἔχειν c. acc. et inf., And.3.33, etc.: hence in various phrases, χρημάτων ὑπερβολῇ..πρίασθαι at an *extravagant* price, E.*Med*.232; ἐπέφερον τὴν ὑ. τοῦ καινοῦσθαι pushed on their *extravagance* in revolutionizing, Th.3.82; οὐκ ἔχον ἐστὶν ὑπερβολήν it can go no further, D.21.119, cf. 25.54; ἃ μηδὲ πιθανὰς τὰς ὑ. ἔχει Men.*Her*.62; so οὐδεμίαν or μηδεμίαν ὑ. λείπειν, Isoc.4.5,110, cf. D.3.25; οὐδεμίαν ὑ. καταλείπων φιλοτιμίας *SIG*545.13 (Delph., iii B.C.); εἴ τις ὑ. τούτου if there is *aught beyond* (worse than) this, D.19.66, cf. Isoc.5.42; ταῦτ' οὐχ ὑ.; is not this *the extreme*, *the last degree?* D.27.38; ὑπερβολὴν ποιήσομαι I will put *an extreme case*, Id.19.332; τοσαύτην ὑ. ποιεῖσθαι ὥστε.. to go so *far* that.., Id.18.190: folld. by a gen., ὑ. ποιεῖσθαι ἐκείνων τῆς αὑτοῦ βδελυρίας to carry his own rascality *beyond* theirs, Id.22.52, cf. 23.201, And.4.22, Lys.14.38; ὑ. ποιεῖν τῆς τιμῆς to *raise* the price, Arist.*Pol*.1259$^a$26; εἰς ὑ. εὐδαιμονίας ἥκειν Isoc.11.14; τοσαύτας ὑ. δωρειῶν παρέσχηται D.20.141; ὑ. ἀνοίας ἔχειν Polystr.p.27 W. 4. with Prep. in Adverbial phrases, = ὑπερβαλλόντως, εἰς ὑπερβολὴν *in excess*, *exceedingly*; εἰς ὑ. ἄμεινον E.*Fr*.494; ἀγαθὸς εἰς ὑ. Antiph.80.11; ἐς ὑ. ἐκθερμαίνεσθαι Hp.*Vict*.2.65: c. gen., κτήσαιτ' ἂν ὄλβον εἰς ὑ. πατρός E.*Fr*.282.6 (v.l. εἰς ὑπεκτροφὴν πάτρας); *far beyond*, τοῦ πρόσθεν εἰς ὑ. πανοῦργος, i.e. *far more* wicked, Id.*Hipp*.939, cf. D.61.33; ἀναλίσκειν πάντα εἰς ὑπερβολάς Pl.*Ep*.326d:—ἐξ ὑπερβολῆς Plb.8.15.8:—καθ' ὑπερβολὰν τοξεύσας *with surpassing* aim, S.*OT*1196 (lyr.); καθ' ὑ. ἐπαινεῖν *extravagantly*, Isoc.5.11; οἱ καθ' ὑ. ἐν ἐνδείᾳ ὄντες in *extremity* of need, Arist.*Pol*.1295$^b$18; αἱ καθ' ὑ. ἡδοναί Id.*EN*1151$^a$12; τὸ καθ' ὑ. τραχύ Phld.*Po.Herc*.994.35; καθ' ὑ. ἁμαρτωλός *Ep.Rom*.7.13: c. gen., καθ' ὑ. φιλοδοξίας *OGI*472.9 (Didyma, i A.D.):—so in dat., εὐτελὴς ὑπερβολῇ Men.615; παχεῖ' ὑ. Philem.41; ὑ. ἀγαθός Arist.*HA*625$^a$29, etc. 5. *pre-eminence*, *perfection*, without any notion of excess, δι' ἀρετῆς ὑπερβολήν Id.*EN*1145$^a$24, cf. *Rh*.1367$^b$1, *Pol*.1284$^a$4; ἡ ὑ. τῆς φιλίας *the best and noblest kind* of friendship, Id.*EN*1166$^b$1; but ἡ καθ' ὑ. φιλία, = ἡ καθ' ὑπεροχήν, Id.*EE*1238$^b$18. 6. *overstrained phrase*, *hyperbole*, ὑπερβολὰς εἰπεῖν Isoc.4.88; οἱ πρὸς ὑπερβολὴν πεπονημένοι λόγοι ib.11; ὑπερβολὰς εἰπεῖν make *strong statements*, Id.3.35, D.27.64; as a figure of speech, Arist.*Rh*.1413$^a$29, Demetr.*Eloc*.52, Str.3.2.9; πρὸς -ὴν εἰρημένος Id.1.2.33. 7. τὸ καθ' ὑπερβολήν *the superlative degree*, in Adjectives, Arist.*Top*.134$^b$24; τιθέναι ὑπερβολῇ ib.139$^a$9; καθ' ὑ. εἰπεῖν Id.*Cael*.281$^a$16. 8. *overbid* at auction, *PPetr*.2 p.44 (iii B.C.). II. *crossing over*, *passage* of mountains, etc., X.*An*.1.2.25, Plb.3.34.6, etc. 2. in sg. or pl., *place of passage*, *mountain-pass*, with or without τοῦ ὄρους, τῶν ὀρέων, X.*An*.3.5.18, 4.1.21, 4.4.18; ὑ. τοῦ Ταύρου Wilcken *Chr*.1 ii 14 (iii B.C.); αἱ τῶν Ἄλπεων ὑ. Plb.3.39.10; αἱ Ἄλπιαι ὑ. Str.7.1.5; ἡ κατὰ τὸν Αἷμον ὑ. D.S.19.73. III. (from Med.) *delay*, τοῦ κακοῦ Hdt.8.112, cf. Decr.ap.D.18.29, Plb.14.9.8; [τῆς κρίσεως] ὑ. λαβούσης *PEnteux*.65.3 (iii B.C.). IV. the conic section called *hyperbola*, because the square of the ordinate is equal to a rectangle with height equal to the abscissa applied to the parameter (as base) but *exceeding* (ὑπερβάλλον), i.e. overlapping, that base, Apollon.Perg.*Con*.1.12, Procl.*in Euc*.p.419 F. ⊛ **-ία·** ὕβρις, κόρος, Hsch. **-ικός,** ή, όν, *hyperbolical*, *extravagant*, Plb.18.46.13; ὑ. σχήματα *exaggerated* attitudes, Gal.18(2).57: fem. as Subst., μηδεμίαν ὑπερβολικὴν ποιουμένοις committing no *extravagance*, *Milet*.7.69 (Didyma, ii B.C.). Adv. -κῶς, ὑ. ἀποφαίνεσθαι Plb.2.62.9, cf. Phld.*Mus*.p.72 K., Gal.17(2).209, al.; -ώτερον εἰπεῖν Plb.7.11.8. **-ιμος,** ον, (ὑπερβολή III) *to be put off*, *delayed*, ὑπερβόλιμοι δίκαι *deferred* suits, *PHal*.1.139, al. (iii B.C.), cf. Sch.Ar.*V*.592. **-ιον,** τό, *overbid*, *PTeb*.72.418, 61(*b*).408,416 (ii B.C.), *UPZ*112 viii 8 (ii B.C.). 2. *increase of rent*, *PTeb*.302.14 (i A.D.), *POxy*.103.26 (iv A.D.).

**Ὑπερβόρ-εοι,** οἱ, *the Hyperboreans*, *a people* supposed to live *in the extreme north*, *h.Hom*.7.29, Pi.*P*.10.30, Hdt.4.32 sq., Str.15.1.57. 2. Adj., τύχη ὑπερβόρεος, prov. of *more than mortal* fortune, A.*Ch*.373 (anap.). (**ὑπερβόρειος** is a constant v.l. in codd.; but in the poetic passages ὑπερβόρεος is either necessary or at least admissible, as in Cratin.22, and this form is found in *IG*2$^2$.1636.8.) **-ίς,** ίδος, fem. of foreg., κόρη D.H.1.43.

**ὑπερβράζω,** *boil* or *foam over*, in aor. Pass., *AP*11.248 (Bianor).

**ὑπερβρῑθής,** ές, = ὑπερβαρής, ἄχθος S.*Aj*.951.

**ὑπερβρύω,** *to be full to overflowing*, καρποῖς Luc.*Rh.Pr*.6.

⊛ **ὑπερβώϊα** (sc. ἱερά), τά, name of a Cretan festival, *Inscr.Cret*.1.xix 1 (Malla, iii B.C.), 1.viii 13.13 (Cnosos, ii B.C.), *GDI*5040.41 (Hierapytna, ii B.C.).

**ὑπ-εργάζομαι,** *work under*: *plough up*, *prepare* for sowing, τῷ σπόρῳ νεὸν ὑ. X.*Oec*.16.10, cf. *IG*2$^2$.2498.20, Thphr.*HP*3.1.6; ἄρουραν εἰς σποράν D.H.10.17. II. *subdue*, *reduce*: pf. in pass. sense, *to be subdued*, ὑπείργασμαι ψυχὴν ἔρωτι E.*Hipp*.504. III. *do underhand* or *secretly*, Plu.*Galb*.9. IV. = ὑπηρετέω, *do a service*: pf. in pass. sense, πόλλ' ὑπείργασται φίλα E.*Med*.871. V. *produce gradually*, Philum.ap.Orib.8.45.7.

**ὑπεργᾰμία,** ἡ, *a late marriage*, Phot.

**ὑπεργᾰνάει** (sic, 3 sg.), prob. *exults much*, Sch.Pi.*Pae*.3.95.

**ὑπεργάνυμαι** [ᾰ], *exult much*, Philostr.*Im*.1.5; *rejoice over*, τινας Eun.*VS* p.468 B. (s. v.l.).

**ὑπέργειος,** ον, (γῆ) *above ground*, opp. τρωγλοδυτικός, of animals, Arist.*HA*488$^a$24, cf. *Gp*.10.18.8; opp. ὑπόγειος, Poll.5.150; *above the horizon*, σελήνη *Gp*.1.7.1; φορά (of the moon) Gal.9.906; ζῴδια Vett.Val.98.9; τὸ ὑ. ἡμισφαίριον *Cat.Cod.Astr*.4.150.

**ὑπεργέλοιος,** ον, *above measure ridiculous*, D.19.211.

⊛ **ὑπεργεμ-ίζω,** *overfill*, *overload*, X.*Vect*.4.39 (Pass.). **-ω,** *to be overfull*, τινος *of* a thing, Alex.83, Plb.4.75.8; χρημάτων *Trag.Adesp*.486: abs., Alex.216, D.S.3.17.

**ὑπεργεννάομαι,** Pass., *to be born besides*, Hsch. s. v. ὑπερφύς.

**ὑπεργηρ-άω,** *grow exceedingly old*, Poll.9.18, Men.*Mon*.608: pf. ὑπεργεγήρακα Apollod.ap.D.L.8.52, Aët.16.26. **-ως,** ων, *exceedingly old*, *of extreme age*, Ph.1.622, Babr.47.1, Luc.*DMort*.27.9, etc.; τὸ ὑ. *extreme old age*, A.*Ag*.79 (anap.); *past the age of service*, *PGiss*.59 iv 14 (ii A.D.): prob. proparox.: sts. **ὑπέργηρος,** ον, in codd. (so in *Gloss*.); pl. ὑπέργηροι Vett.Val.350.19.

**ὑπεργίγνομαι**, *have the superiority*, Phld.*Rh.*2.86 S. (written -γειν-). 2. of Time, *elapse*, τοῦ ὑπεργεγενημένου μετὰ ταῦτα χρόνου *BGU*1167.7 (i A. D.), cf. 1148.14 (i B. C.).

**ὑπεργνήσιος**, ον, *really genuine*, Steph. *in Gal.*1.289 D.

**ὑπέργομος**, ον, *overladen*, Str.17.1.50.

**ὕπεργος**, ον, *under cultivation*, [ἀγροί] Afric.*Cest.*p.70 V.

**ὑπεργρᾰφ-ή**, ἡ, *alteration* or *interlineation* in a document, *Rev.Ét. Gr.*19.246 (Aphrodisias). **-ω**, *sign instead*, ὑπέρ τινος dub. in *PLond.*2.311.24 (ii A. D.).

**ὑπεργυῖον**· ὑπέρμηκες, μέγα, Hsch.

**ὑπερδάκνω**, in Pass., *to be excessively irritated* (by a plaster), Archig.ap.Gal.13.255.

⊕**ὑπερδᾰπᾰν-άω**, v. ὑπερδάπανον. **-ημα**, ατος, τό, *sum overspent*, *PLond.*3.1171.22, al. (i B. C.), *POxy.*1578.8 (iii A. D.). ⊕ **-ον**, τό, = foreg., *PLond.* l.c. 21 (nisi leg. ὑπερδαπανῶι, = -ῶ, = ὑπερανηλίσκω, cf. *Sammelb.*7451.65,113).

**ὑπέρδᾰσυς**, υ, *very hairy*, ἀνήρ X.*Cyr.*2.2.28. II. *thick with leaves*, κιττός Ael.*NA*7.6.

**ὑπερδεής**, ές, Ep. acc. ὑπερδέᾰ, for ὑπερδεέα: (δέος):—*above all fear, undaunted*, ὑπερδέα δῆμον ἔχοντας Il.17.330, cf. Eust. ad loc.; but Apollon.*Lex.*, Hsch., derive it from δέομαι (to want), *much less, inferior*: neither expl. is satisfactory and Brocks' cj. ὑπὲρ Δία should perh. be accepted.

**ὑπερδείδω**, *fear for* one, ὡς ὑπερδέδοικά σου S.*Ant.*82; δράκοντας.. τέκνων ὑπερδέδοικε *fears* them *for* or *because of*.., A.*Th.*293 (lyr.). 2. *fear exceedingly*, τινας Them.*Or.*10.138c: abs., *to be in exceeding fear*, Hdt.8.94.

**ὑπερδειμαίνω**, *to be much afraid of*, τοὺς Πέρσας Hdt.5.19.

**ὑπέρδεινος**, ον, *exceedingly alarming* or *dangerous*, τὸ πρᾶγμα εἰς ὑπέρδεινόν μοι περιέστη D.21.111; *very hard*, Luc.*Tim.*13. 2. *very able*, ῥήτωρ Poll.4.20; ὑ. εἰπεῖν D.Chr.46.7.

**ὑπερδειπνέω**, *feast immoderately*, Men.*Her.*17, Hsch.

**ὑπερδεκα-πλάσιος** [πλᾰ], α, ον, *more than tenfold*, Eust.190.10 (or divisim). **-τάλαντος** [τᾰ], ον, *of more than ten talents*, βλάβη Phalar.*Ep.*137.1.

⊕ **ὑπερδέξιος**, ον, *lying above one on the right hand*, εἶχον ὑ. χωρίον.. χαλεπώτατον, καὶ ἐξ ἀριστερᾶς..ποταμόν, v.l. for ὑπὲρ δεξιῶν in X.*An.* 4.8.2. II. simply, *lying above* or *over*, ὑ. χωρίον *higher* ground, ib.3.4.37, etc.; τὰ ὑ. ib.5.7.31, cf. Aen.Tact.1.2; ἐξ ὑπερδεξίου *from above*, X.*HG*7.4.13, Plb.2.3.6, etc.; ἡ ἐξ ὑ. τάξις *up-stream*, Id.3.43. 3; ἐκ τῶν ὑ. X.*HG*4.2.14; ἐξ ὑπερδεξίων Luc.*Tim.*45, Paus.4.29.4: c. gen., *commanding from above*, or simply *above*, λόφος ὑ. τῶν πολεμίων Plb.1.30.7, cf. 10.30.7; τοῦ τείχους Id.8.4.9: also of streams, ἔστιν ἡ Σηστὸς ὑ. τοῦ ῥοῦ *up-stream* with regard to the current, Str.13.1. 22. 2. metaph., *superior, having the advantage in* a thing, τῷ πολέμῳ Plb.5.102.3, etc.; *victorious over*, ὑ. τῆς κακίας τὴν ἀρετήν Plu.*Num.* 20; ὑ. ἐγένετο τοῦ λοιμοῦ, i.e. he recovered, Ruf.*Fr.*114. 3. c. gen., *convenient for*, ὑ. χωρίον τοῦ ἀποκρούεσθαι τὴν ἔφοδον Arr.*Tact.*9.2.

**ὑπερδεόντως**, f.l. for ὑπεραγόντως in Apollon.*Lex.* s.v. ὑπερδέα.

**ὑπερδέω**, *bind upon*, τοῖς μηροῖς [κήλην] *AP*6.166 (Lucill.).

**ὑπερδια-ζεύγνυμαι**, *to be separated by an interval of an octave*, Bacch.*Harm.*87: hence **-ζευξις**, εως, ἡ, ibid. **-θήκη**, ἡ, *codicil*, L. Robert *Villes d'Asie Mineure* (Paris 1935) 226. **-τᾰσις**, εως, ἡ, *excessive tension*, Gal.1.168. **-τείνω**, *overstretch* or *-strain*, τὸν στόμαχον Archig.ap.Orib.8.1.5:—Pass., of the bladder, Gal.8. 407. 2. Pass., *strain* or *exert oneself above measure*, D.25.1 (also v.l. in 20.143), D.Chr.50.6, Luc.*Herm.*26, etc. **-φορέομαι**, Pass., *to be dissipated in excess*, -εῖσθαι τὰ ὑγρά Sor.2.54.

**ὑπερδίδωμι**, *give instead*, προπάντων μίαν ὑπερδοῦναι θανεῖν E.*Fr.* 360.18 (perh. ὕπερ δοῦναι); πλοῦτον ὑπερδώησι is dub. l. in Antioch. Astr. in *Cat.Cod.Astr.*1.112.

**ὑπερδῐκ-άζω**, *vindicate, defend*, τινος Al.*Ps.*9.5. **-αιόω**, *punish with severity*, Sch.Pi.*P.*10.68. ⊕**-έω**, Boeot. ὀπερδικίω (q.v.), *plead for, act as advocate for*, τοῦ λόγου Pl.*Phd.*86e; τὸ φεύγειν τοὐδ' ὑπερδικεῖς *advocatest* acquittal *for* him, A.*Eu.*652; ὑ. ὑπέρ τινος D.C. 38.10: abs., Plu.2.694e. **-ος**, ον, *more than just, severely just*, Νέμεσις Pi.*P.*10.44; of things, κἂν ὑπέρδικ' ᾖ though they be *never so just*, S.*Aj.*1119. Adv. **-κως** A.*Ag.*1396. II. *pleading for* another, Sch.Pl.*Phd.*86e.

**ὑπερδισκ-εύω**, *throw the discus farther than* another, c. acc., Phryn.*PS*p.117 B. **-έω**, = foreg., metaph., πονηρίᾳ πάντας Anon. ap.Phryn. l.c. Cf. ὑπερακοντίζω.

**ὑπερδῐσύλλᾰβος**, ον, *of more than two syllables*, Hdn.Gr.1.227.

**ὑπερδιψ-άω**, *to be exceedingly thirsty*, Gal.12.288,351, *UP*11. 10. **-ος**, ον, *exceedingly thirsty*, *Hippiatr.*6.

**ὑπερδοκέω**: impers., κἀμοὶ ὑπερδοκεῖ ταῦτα *I am more than of* your *opinion*, Philostr.*VA*1.40.

**ὑπερδομέομαι**, Pass., *to be built over*, τινος J.*BJ*6.3.2.

**ὑπέρδουλος**, ὁ, *a slave and more*, A.D.*Synt.*310.13.

**ὑπέρδρῑμυς**, υ, *exceedingly pungent*, Phryn.362 (only in Nuñez), v.l. for γοργόν in Luc.*DDeor.*7.3.

**ὑπερδύνᾰμ-ος** [δῠ], ον, *of higher power*, δύναμις Them.*Or.*1.8b. **-όω**, *prevail over*, τινας Lxx *Ps.*64(65).3.

**ὑπερδῠναστεύω**, *exercise predominance*, Heraclit.*All.*25.

**ὑπερδώριος**, ον, *hyper-Dorian*, τόνος Aristox.ap.Cleonid.*Harm.*12; τρόπος Alyp.*Diat.*15, *Chrom.*15.

**ὑπερεβδομηκοντᾰέτης**, ὁ, ἡ, *more than seventy years old*, *CIG*2721 (Stratonicea).

**ὑπερεγγυάω**, *betroth*, Ph.2.311.

**ὑπερεγρήγορα**, pf. 2 of *ὑπερεγείρω, *watch on behalf of*, τινος Philostr. *VA*8.12.

**ὑπερέγχριστος**, ον, *for smearing on above*, of an eye-salve, Cass. Fel.29.

**ὑπ-ερεθίζω**, *provoke somewhat, stimulate a little*, Babr.95.65 (but αἱρέτιζε is prob. cj.), App.*BC*2.94.

**Ὑπέρεια**, ἡ, *High-land*, the abode of the Phaeacians before they migrated to Scheria, Od.6.4. 2. name of a fountain, Il.2.734, 6.457.

**ὑπερείδεος**, α, ον, *above species*, Olymp. *in Phlb.*p.241 S., Dam.*Pr.* 7,86.

**ὑπερεῖδον**, inf. ὑπεριδεῖν, aor. without pres. in use; v. ὑπεροράω.

⊕ **ὑπ-ερείδω**, fut. -σω Diog.Oen.20: pf. Pass. ὑπερήρεισμαι Arist. *PA*695ᵃ7; ὑπήρεισμαι Str.17.1.37, D.S.1.47:—*put under as a support*, λᾶβρον ὑπερεῖσαι λίθον Pi.*N.*8.47; τὸν ἀέρα ὑ. (sc. τῇ γῇ) Pl. *Phd.*99b; ὑπερείδουσιν ἐσωτάτω τὸ σκέλος Gal.18(1).591:—Pass., τοῖς τετράποσι πρὸς τὸ βάρος σκέλη ἐμπρόσθια ὑπερήρεισται Arist. l.c., cf. *IA*710ᵇ30, J.*AJ*8.3.5. 2. *lean upon*, οἰκίαν Lxx *Jb.*8.15. 3. *lift, carry*, τινα Iamb.*VP*3.17. II. *under-prop, support*, τὴν ὀροφήν Plu.*Rom.*28; προβλήματα διὰ παραδειγμάτων Id.*Marc.*14; τοὺς νεανίας *Com.Adesp.*1302: abs., τὰ -ερείδοντα [σώματα] Epicur.*Ep.*1 p. 7 U.:—Pass., Str. l.c.

**ὑπ-έρεικος**, ἡ, (ἐρείκη) *St. John's wort, Hypericum crispum*, Nic. *Al.*603:—more freq. **ὑπερικόν**, τό, Dsc.3.154, Gal.12.148; also, *Hypericum revolutum*, Dsc.1.19.

**ὑπ-ερείκω**, in 2 sg. aor. ind. ὑπήρικας *thou hast torn* or *dashed down*, *Lyr.Alex.Adesp.*34.5.

**ὑπέρειμι**, (εἰμί sum) *to be superior*, Lyd.*Mens.*2.6, *EM*664.20.

**ὑπερειπεῖν**, *speak in defence of*, τινος Arist.*Oec.*1349ᵃ34.

**ὑπ-ερείπω**, *undermine, subvert*, metaph., Plu.2.71b:—Pass., Id. *Ant.*82. II. Pass., *to be unable to stand, totter*, of limbs, *fail*, Id. *Pomp.*74; so in aor. 2 ὑπήριπον, Il.23.691.

**ὑπ-έρεισις**, εως, ἡ, *supporting*, Epicur.*Ep.*1 p.8 U., Porph.ap.Eus. *PE*3.11, Iamb.*VP*3.17: pl., Epicur.*Nat.*11.9,12.

**ὑπ-έρεισμα**, ατος, τό, *under-prop, support*, Arist.*PA*655ᵃ10, Chrysipp.*Stoic.*2.168, Plu.2.132a, Sm.*Ps.*53(54).6.

**ὑπερεισοδιάζω**, *contribute on behalf of* (the state), τοὺς φόρους *IGRom.*3.739 iii 89 (Rhodiapolis, ii A. D.).

**ὑπ-ερειστικός**, ή, όν, *for propping* or *supporting*: Adv. **-κῶς** Eust. 236.14.

**ὑπερεκβλύζω**, *bubble* or *boil over, superabound*, Al.*Pr.*3.10.

**ὑπερεκδῐκέω**, *exact extreme vengeance for*, τὴν κιβωτόν J.*AJ*6.1.2.

**ὑπερέκεινα**, Adv. *beyond*, c. gen., 2*Ep.Cor.*10.16.

**ὑπερεκ-ζέω**, *bubble over*, of wine, Vett.Val.222.1 (prob.). **-θερᾰπεύω**, *seek to win by excessive attention*, Aeschin.2.154. **-κειμαι**, f.l. for ὕπαρ ἐκκ-, Plu.2.1066c. **-κρίσις**, εως, ἡ, *excessive secretion* or *evacuation*, Gal.12.678 (pl.). **-λάμπω**, *to be very bright*, of the eyes, Id.16.782. **-περισσοῦ**, Adv. *superabundantly*, *Ep.Eph.*3.20, 1*Ep. Thess.*3.10 (v.l. **ὑπερεκπερισσῶς**). **-πίπτω**, *extend beyond, exceed*, c. gen., τῶν δέκα *Placit.*1.3.8; *extend beyond*, Gal.*UP*3.8, al., 18(1). 84; of time, *PThead.*10.12 (iv A. D.). II. abs., *go beyond all bounds*, Luc.*Herm.*67; τοσοῦτον ὑ. ὥστε.. Id.*Salt.*83, cf. S.E.*M.*6. 6. 2. *to be exceptional*, μακροβιοτεία Phld.*Sign.*17. **-πλήσσω**, *astonish beyond measure*, τινα J.*AJ*8.6.5:—Pass., *to be amazed*, ἐπί τινι X.*Cyr.*1.4.25; ὑπερεκπεπληγμένος ὡς ἄμαχόν τινα τὸν Φίλιππον *astonished at* or *admiring* him *exceedingly*, D.2.5, cf. Plu.2.523d, etc.: abs., ὑπερεκπλᾰγείς *overwhelmed* (by error), ib.87ob. **-πτωσις**, εως, ἡ, *exaggeration, excess*, Andronic.Rhod.p.572 M., Longin.15. 8, Iamb. *in Nic.*p.54 P. **-τείνω**, *stretch out beyond measure*, ἑαυτούς 2*Ep.Cor.*10.14:—Pass., *stretch out beyond*, Procl.*Inst.*59, Dam.*Pr.*284; πόλλ' ὑπερεξετάθης cj. for πουλὺ παρεξ- in *AP*9.643 (Agath.). **-τίνω** [ῑ], *pay for* any one, τῶν νεκρῶν Luc.*DMort.* 22.2. **-τῐσις**, εως, ἡ, *payment for* any one, Hsch., *Gloss.* (nisi leg. **-τεισις**). **-τρέπομαι**, Pass., *feel utter aversion for*, τινα Aret. *SD*1.5 (ὕπαρ ἐκτ. Ermerins). **-φεύγω**, *survive* a certain period, c. acc., Hp.*Morb.*2.58; *escape from*, δίκτυον Plot.6.6.3. **-φρύττω**, *dry up* or *parch too much*, Sever.*Clyst.*pp.4,5 D. (Pass.). **-χέω**, *pour out over*, metaph., εἰς τὴν ἐπαρχίαν τὰς τιμάς J.*BJ*1.21.4:—Pass., *overflow*, Lxx *Jl.*2.24, D.S.11.89, Ph.1.362, Ael.*NA*12.41, etc.:—also **-χύνομαι** in *Ev.Luc.*6.38; fut. -χυθήσομαι v.l. in Lxx *Jl.*2.24. **-χῠσις**, εως, ἡ, *overflowing*, of the Nile, Hld.1.5; of the sea, Plu.2.731c (pl.); κοιλίας *Gloss.*

**ὑπερέλᾰσις**, εως, ἡ, = ὑπέρθεσις, ὑπερβολή, Hsch.

**ὑπερελαύνω**, *pass over*, ῥοάς Q.S.11.330.

**ὑπερέλαφρος**, ον, *exceedingly light* or *nimble*, X.*Cyn.*5.31.

**ὑπερελίσσω**, *whirl round above* one's head, κοντούς Arr.*Tact.*43.2.

**ὑπερεμέω**, *vomit violently*: metaph. of over-full veins, *cause suffusion*, ὑπερεμήσαντα τὰ φλέβια Hp.*Morb.*2.17; ἢν ὑπερεμήσωσιν αἱ φλέβες ib.18 (-εμέσ- ib.4): hence **ὑπερέμετος**, ὁ, *over-fullness of the veins*, ib.4 (vv.ll. ὑπερεμέειν, ὑπεραίμετον): but forms of ὑπεραιμέω (q.v.) shd. prob. be restored; the corruption has been helped by the words of Hp., τὸ μὲν οὔνομα οὐκ ὀρθὸν τῇ νούσῳ, οὐ γὰρ ἄνυστον ὑπεραιμῆσαι (-εμῆσαι codd.) οὐδὲν τῶν φλεβίων κτλ.; ὑπεραιμήσειε stands in *Morb.*2.4 cod.G.

**ὑπερεμ-πίπλημι**, in Pass., *to be over-full* or *very full*, τινος *of* a thing, Ael.*NA*14.25: abs., X.*Cyr.*1.6.17, Luc.*Symp.*35, Gal.6.132, 15.39. **-φορέομαι**, Pass., *to be filled quite full*, ὕψου Luc.*DMeretr.* 6.3: abs., Id.*Ep.Sat.*32.

**ὑπερένδοξος**, ον, *exceedingly glorious*, Lxx *Da.*3.(53); ὄνομα *POxy.* 1151.54 (v A. D.).

**ὑπερενῐαυτίζω,** *last above a year,* Jul.*Ep.*180 (p.392a).

**ὑπερενόομαι,** Pass., *to be completely one,* Iamb.*Myst.*2.11.

**ὑπερεν-τελής,** ές, *more than complete,* f.l. in D.C.47.17. **-τρῠφάω,** *to be exceedingly haughty,* ἡμῖν to us, Alciphr.1.37; τῇ καθ' Ἡρακλέους λοιδορίᾳ *in* or *by..,* Sch.S.*Tr.*281. **-τυγχάνω,** *intercede,* (sc. ὑπέρ τινος) *for* one, *Ep.Rom.*8.26.

**ὑπερένωσις,** εως, ἡ, *transcendental unification,* Procl. *in Prm.*p. 920 S.

**ὑπερεξαίρω,** *raise exceedingly*: Pass., Hp.*Epid.*4.31. II. *exalt* or *praise exceedingly,* Eust.1265.25. III. intr., *excel, be privileged,* –ουσαν τῇ ζωῇ τῇ ἀκραιφνεστάτῃ Porph.*Sent.*40 (but ὑπερζέουσαν ζωῇ in Plot.6.5.12).

**ὑπερεξᾰκισχίλιοι** [χῑ], αι, α, *above* 6000, D.59.89, J.*AJ*17.2.4.

**ὑπερεξ-ανθέω,** *sprout at the top,* Poll.6.54. **-άπτω,** *kindle above measure,* Ael.*NA*9.20. **-έχω,** *project,* Sch.Ar.*Nu.*10.

**ὑπερεξηκοντέτης,** ες, *above sixty years old,* Ar.*Ec.*982.

**ὑπέρεξις,** εως, ἡ, *a property* or *quality in excess,* Pl.*Ti.*87e.

**ὑπερέξοχος,** ον, *superior to,* c. gen., *Epic.Alex.Adesp.*9 ii 25.

**ὑπερεπαινέω,** *praise above measure,* τι or τινα Hdt.1.8, Ar.*Eq.* 680, *Ec.*186, Pl.*Euthd.*303b, al.

**ὑπερεπ-αίρω,** *exalt* or *exaggerate beyond measure,* App.*Pun.*42, *Syr.*12, *BC*1.11. ⊛ **-αρσις,** εως, ἡ, *excessive exaltation,* Aq.*Ps.*47 (48).4.

**ὑπερεπείγω,** *press hard,* App.*BC*2.114, D.C.59.21.

⊛ **ὑπερεπι-θῡμέω,** *desire exceedingly,* c. inf., X.*Cyr.*4.3.21, 6.1.5, Sm. *Ps.*118(119).174, Porph.*Plot.*19. **-κλίνω** [ῑν], *turn over,* Iamb.*Protr.* 21.ιθ'. **-στήμων,** ον, gen. ονος, *exceedingly wise, AB*312. **-τᾰτικός,** ή, όν, *doubly intensive,* of α in ἀάατος, Sch.Il.14.271. **-τείνω,** *strain too tight, to be too rigid,* intr., metaph. of philosophy, v.l. in Philostr.*VA*2.37. II. trans., *increase the force of,* τὰ σημαινόμενα Artem.3.59.

**ὑπερέπτα,** v. ὑπερπέτομαι.

**ὑπ-ερέπτω,** *eat away from below, cut away from under,* of a stream, κονίην ὑπέρεπτε ποδοῖιν Il.21.271. II. of mental suffering, *gnaw secretly,* Q.S.9.377.

**ὑπερέραμαι,** aor. –ηράσθην, *love beyond measure,* τινος Ael.*VH* 12.1.

**ὑπερερρωμένως,** Adv. *very vigorously,* Poll.4.89, 5.125.

**ὑπερέρυθρος,** ον, *very red,* Aët.7.6, 7.8 (ὑπερρυθρός ed. Ald., corr. Hirschberg; but ὑπέρυθρος should perh. be read: *subrubra,* Lat. version).

**ὑπερέρχομαι,** aor. 2 –ῆλθον, pf. –ελήλυθα:—*pass over, cross,* τὰς πηγὰς τοῦ ποταμοῦ X.*An.*4.4.3; τὰ ὄρη Ael.*NA*16.21; τὴν θάλατταν J. *AJ*3.1.5. II. *surpass, excel,* ἀρεταῖς Pi.*O.*13.15. III. *overcome* or *survive* a disease, ἣν ταύτην ὑπερέλθῃ ὁ νοσέων Aret.*SA*1.10.

**ὑπερεσθίω,** *eat immoderately,* X.*Mem.*1.2.4.

**ὑπερέσχεθον,** poet. aor. 2 of ὑπερέχω.

**ὑπερετής,** ὁ, ἡ, *past the age,* i.e. of liability to poll-tax, *POxy.* 1030.8 (iii A.D.), etc.

**ὑπ-ερέττω,** *row quietly,* Ael.*NA*13.2.

**ὑπέρευ,** Adv., (εὖ) *exceedingly well, excellently,* Pl.*Tht.*185d, X. *Hier.*6.9, D.18.10, Men.*Pk.*404, Zeno *Stoic.*1.27, Cic.*Att.*10.1.3:— **ὑπέρευγε,** Men.*Epit.*308, Luc.*Par.*9, Ael.*VH*9.38.

**ὑπερευγενής,** ές, *exceedingly noble,* Arist.*Pol.*$1295^{b}6$.

**ὑπ-ερεύγομαι,** *vomit up,* ἄχνην (ἄκρην codd., corr. Ruhnken) ἐς πόντον A.R.2.984.

**ὑπερευ-δαιμονέω,** *to be exceedingly happy,* Arist.*Rh.*$1385^{b}21$, Luc. *Gall.*20 (v.l. for ὑπερευδαίμονα εἶναι), Aristaenet.1.18. **-δαίμων,** ον, gen. ονος, *utterly blessed,* Plot.5.8.4,5; cf. foreg. **-δοκέομαι,** *to be well-pleased,* Plb.*Fr.*232. **-δοκῐμέω,** *enjoy exceedingly great renown,* Lys.8.7. **-ήθης,** ες, *extremely silly,* Phld.*Mus.*p.33 K., Id. *D.*3.14.

**ὑπ-ερευθής,** ές, poet. for ὑπέρυθρος, Arat.867, Opp.*H.*3.167.

**ὑπερευ-θύμως** [ῡ], Adv. *very confidently,* Poll.5.125. **-καιρέω,** *to be very convenient,* οἰκίη ὑπερευκαιρέουσα Hp.*Ep.*13. **-λᾰβέομαι,** *to be exceedingly cautious,* Eun.*VS* p.470 B. **-πρεπῶς,** Adv. *exceedingly becomingly,* Sch.S.*Ant.*696.

**ὑπερεύρεμα,** ατος, τό, *additional cost* on accepting a new tender, *IG*7.3073.2 (Lebad., ii B.C.), *BCH*20.323 (ibid.).

**ὑπερευρίσκω,** *fetch* or *cost a higher amount,* τοῦ ἐξ ἀρχῆς εὑρέματος *IG*7.3074.2 (Lebad., ii B.C.); διὰ τὸ ὑπερευρῆσθαι because *the expenses came to more,* dub. in *PLips.*97 xxvii 21, xxxii 16 (iv A.D.).

**ὑπερευρύβᾰτος** [ρῠ], ὁ, *a super-Eurybatus, Com.Adesp.*1176.

**ὑπερευ-τῠχής,** ές, *exceedingly lucky,* Vett.Val.29.19. **-τῠχία,** poet. –ίη, ἡ, *exceedingly good luck, AP*5.46 (Rufin.). **-φραίνω,** *delight exceedingly,* Phld.*Po.*2.17, Lib.*Ep.*243:—Pass., *rejoice exceedingly,* Luc.*Am.*5; αὐτὸ τοῦτο *at..,* Id.*Icar.*2; ἐπί τινι J.*BJ*7.1. 3. **-χᾰριστέω,** *to be extremely thankful, PTeb.*12.24 (ii B.C.).

**ὑπερεύχομαι,** *wish* or *pray for,* τινος Hierocl. *in CA*7 p.429 M., *PMasp.*205.10 (vi A.D.), etc. II. *pray earnestly to,* τὸν θεόν J.*AJ* 11.4.3.

**ὑπερεύωνος,** ον, *exceedingly cheap,* Ael.*VH*14.44.

**ὑπερεχθαίρω,** *hate exceedingly,* Ζεὺς γὰρ μεγάλης γλώσσης κόμπους ὑ. S.*Ant.*128 (anap.).

**ὑπερεχθραίνω,** = foreg., Ptol.*Tetr.*64.

**ὑπερεχόντως,** Adv. *pre-eminently, especially,* Eust.4.13.

**ὑπερέχω,** Ep. **ὑπειρ-** Thgn. (v. infr. I. 2): Ep. impf. ὑπείρεχον Il.2. 426: aor. ὑπερέσχον, and in poet. form –έσχεθον, 11.735, 24.374: fut. –έξω *PCair.Zen.*60.6 (iii B.C.), Hsch.:—*hold over,* σπλάγχνα.. ὑπείρεχον Ἡφαίστοιο *held* them *over* the fire, Il.2.426; μου τὸ σκιάδειον ὑπέρεχε Ar.*Av.*1508; ἡμῶν ὑπερεῖχε τὴν χύτραν Id.*Eq.*1176; ὑπερέχοντα τὸν αὐλὸν τῆς θαλάσσης *holding* it *up out of* the sea, Arist.*HA* $537^{b}1$. 2. ὑ. χεῖρά (χεῖράς) τινος *hold* one's hand *over* him, *so as to protect,* μάλα γάρ ἑθεν εὐρύοπα Ζεὺς χεῖρα ἑὴν ὑπερέσχε Il.9.420,687; τις..ἐμεῖο θεῶν ὑπερέσχεθε χεῖρα 24.374; Ζεὺς τῆσδε πόληος ὑπειρέχοι..χεῖρα Thgn.757; so πόλεως ἵν' ὑπερέχοιεν ἀλκάν A.*Th.*215 (lyr.), cf. *Fr.*199.7: c. dat. pers., οἱ..ὑπείρεχε χεῖρας Ἀπόλλων Il. 5.433; αἴ κ' ὔμμιν ὑπέρσχῃ χεῖρα Κρονίων 4.249, cf. Od.14. 184. 3. *hold above,* ὑ. τὸ ῥύγχος, ὅπως ἀναπνέῃ, of the dolphin, Arist.*HA*$589^{b}11$, cf. $566^{b}15$, $599^{b}27$, al.; ὑ. ὀφρύν *elevate, AP*5.298 (Agath.). II. intr., *to be above, rise above the horizon,* εὖτ' ἀστὴρ ὑπερέσχε φαάντατος Od.13.93; αὐτῆς [Αἰγύπτου] εἶναι οὐδὲν ὑπερέχον no part of it *was above water,* Hdt.2.4; ὕδωρ, ..ὃ μόλις ὑπερέχοντες ἐπεραιώθησαν which they crossed, *with their heads* only just *above* it, Th.3.23; ἕψεται ἄχρι ἂν ὑπερέχῃ τὸ ὕδωρ till it *sticks out above* the water, Dsc.3.7; but ἐπιχέας ὕδωρ ὥστε ὑπερέχειν till it *covers* (sc. the contents of the vessel), Id.5.87; τὸ κέρας τὸ ἕτερον ἢ καὶ ἀμφότερα ὑπερέχοντα *projecting above the ground,* Hdt.2.41; γεῖσον.. ὑπερέχον τρία ἡμιπόδια *projecting* a foot and a half, *IG*$2^{2}$.1668.34, cf. 7.3073.71 (Lebad., ii B.C.): c. gen., ὑπερέσχεθε γαίης *rose above, overlooked* the earth, Il.11.735; ὄμμ' ὑπερσχὸν ἴτυος E.*Ph.*1384; [σταυροὺς] οὐχ ὑπερέχοντας τῆς θαλάσσης Th.7.25; σκεύη ὑπερέχοντα τοῦ τειχίου Pl.*R.*514c, cf. X.*An.*3.5.7; ὤφθη..ὁ δεξιὸς ὀφθαλμὸς ὑπερέχειν θατέρου παμπόλλῳ δή τινι Gal.18(2).301. 2. *overtop, be prominent above,* στάντων μὲν Μενέλαος ὑπείρεχεν εὐρέας ὤμους, i.e. stood (head and) shoulders above them, Il.3.210; ὅκως τινὰ ἴδοι τῶν ἀσταχύων ὑπερέχοντα Hdt.5.92.ζ', cf. Arist.*Pol.*$1284^{a}37$; φιλέει ὁ θεὸς τὰ ὑπερέχοντα πάντα κολούειν Hdt.7.10.ε', cf. X.*Cyr.* 6.2.17; ⟨ᾧ⟩ ὁ πρῶτος ὅρος ὑ. τοῦ δευτέρου..μέρει by the fraction by which the first term *exceeds* the second, Archyt.2: τὸ ὑπερέχον the *excess,* Dioph.1.6. 3. in military phrase, *outflank,* τῶν πολεμίων ὑ. τῷ κέρατι X.*HG*4.2.18, cf. Th.3.107. 4. metaph., c. acc., *overtop, excel, outdo,* βροτῶν πάντων ὑπερσχὼν ὄλβον A.*Pers.*709 (troch.); σωφροσύνῃ πάντας ὑ. E.*Hipp.*1365 (anap.); πελταστικῷ εἰκὸς ὑ. τὴν ἡμετέραν δύναμιν X.*HG*6.1.9. b. c. gen., πάντων ὑ. μεγέθει καὶ ἀρετῇ Pl.*Ti.*24e, cf. *Prm.*150e, *Grg.*475c; ὑ. τῶν πολλῶν D.23.206, cf. *Ep.Phil.*2.3; ἁπάντων ὑπερέχουσι τῶν κακῶν Anaxil. 22.7 (troch.). c. abs., *prevail,* θεῶν ὑπερέσχε νόος Thgn.202; οἱ ὑπερσχόντες the *more powerful,* A.*Pr.*215; τῶν πόλεων αἱ ὑπερέχουσαι Isoc.4.95; οἱ ὑπερέχοντες *those in authority,* D.L.6.78, cf. Vett.Val. 61.30, al.; ἐπειδὰν ἡ θάλαττα ὑπέρσχῃ *has prevailed,* D.9.69; ἐν τοῖς πολεμίοις ὑ. *excel* in.., Men.642; ἐνδέχεται..μὴ τοσοῦτον ὑ. τῷ ποσῷ, ὅσον λείπεσθαι τῷ ποιῷ *exceed* so much.., Arist.*Pol.*$1296^{b}23$; ὑπὲρ ὧν πλειονάκι ἐντετευχυιῶν ὑπερέχων ἡμᾶς ἀπράκτους καθίστησι *being too strong for* us, *Sammelb.*4638.18 (ii B.C.); πᾶν κρύφιον οὐχ ὑπερεῖχέ σέ *was beyond* thee (i.e. thy comprehension), Thd.*Ez.*28.3. d. Pass., *to be outdone,* ὑπό τινος Pl.*Phd.*102c,d; τὴν δύναμιν τοῦ ὑπερέχειν καὶ ὑπερέχεσθαι Id.*Prm.*150d; κατὰ πλοῦτον ὑπερέχειν κατ' ἀρετὴν δ' ὑπερέχεσθαι Arist.*Pol.*$1281^{a}7$, cf. Gal.15.805. 5. in Logic, *have a wider extension,* Arist.*APo.*$99^{a}24$, cf. *Rh.*$1363^{b}8$ (Act. and Pass.). 6. ἐπὶ τοῖς ὑπερέχουσι δανεῖσαι to lend on the security of *excess value,* of a second mortgage, *SIG*364.33 (Ephesus, iii B.C.). III. c. gen. rei, *rise above, be able to bear,* τῆς ἀντλίας Ar.*Pax*17; τῶν ἀναλωμάτων D.S.4.80 (v.l. for ὑπερεῖδον). IV. *have over,* ὑπερέχει he *has in hand, PCair.Zen.*292.498, cf. 790.25 (iii B.C.); ὑπερέξομεν πρὸς τὸ διὰ χερός ib.355.93 (iii B.C.).—Cf. ὑπερίσχω.

**ὑπερέψω,** *overboil,* Sor.1.86, Alex.Aphr.*Pr.*2.70 (both Pass.).

**ὑπερέω,** contr. **ὑπερῶ,** fut. with no pres. in use; v. ὑπεῖπον.

**ὑπέρ-ζεσις,** εως, ἡ, *boiling over,* Arist.*Pr.*$936^{b}1$, *Theol.Ar.*27. **-ζεστος,** ον, *boiling over,* ὕδατα Arist.*Mu.*$395^{b}25$. **-ζέω,** *boil over,* Id.*GA*$753^{a}33$, *Pr.*$936^{a}37$, *PHolm.*18.23: metaph., ἀνὴρ παφλάζει..ὑπερζέων Ar.*Eq.*920 (lyr.); τὰ παιδία ὑ. τῷ πάθει Arist.*Pr.*$861^{b}$8; of anger, Eun.*Hist.*p.240 D.; φύσιν..ἐν αὐτῇ οἷον ὑπερζέουσαν ζωῇ Plot.6.5.12. 2. *ferment thoroughly,* Dsc.5.7, Herod.Med.ap. Aët.9.2.

**ὑπέρζωος,** ον, *supervital, above life,* Procl.*Inst.*115 (v.l. **ὑπέρζως**).

**ὑπέρηβος,** ον, *past early youth,* Gal.19.489.

**ὑπερηγορ-έω,** *speak for,* τινος Dam.ap.Suid., cf. Ascl. *in Metaph.* 201.11. **-ία,** ἡ, *defence,* Thom.Mag.p.318 R.

**ὑπερήδομαι,** Pass., *rejoice beyond measure at* a thing, τοῖσι χρηστηρίοισι Hdt.1.54; τῷ πόματι Id.3.22: c. part., ἀκούων ὑπερήδετο he *rejoiced much* at hearing, Id.1.90, X.*Cyr.*3.1.31: also ὑ. ὅτι.. ib.8. 3.50. II. Act., *please exceedingly,* Hdn.2.3.11.

**ὑπέρηδυς,** υ, *exceedingly sweet,* used in Sup. by Luc.*Tim.*41, etc. Adv. –έως *very gladly* or *pleasantly,* X.*Cyr.*1.6.21, Phld.*Lib.*p.43 O.: Sup. –ήδιστα Luc.*DMort.*9.1.

⊛ **ὑπερήκω,** *to have got beyond,* τι Gal.2.461.

**ὑπερηλίθιος** [ῐθ], ον, *exceedingly foolish,* Phld.*Po.*5.10.

**ὑπερῆλιξ,** ῐκος, ὁ, ἡ, *above a certain age,* Luc.*Am.*10, App.*Pun.* 114; *too old* to have children, Ph.2.17: Comp. –έστερος Ocell.4.6.

⊛ **ὑπερημερ-ία,** ἡ, Boeot. **ὑπερᾱμερία** (v. infr.), **οὑπερᾱμερία** *IG*7. 3172.58, al. (Orchom., iii B.C.), **ὀπερᾱμερία** ib.3054.10,13 (Lebad.): —*a being over the day,* i.e. as law-term, *default caused by non-observance of the latest term* for payment, μελλούσης μοι ἤδη ἐξήκειν τῆς ὑ. the *term of* my *borrowing* (my *stay of execution*) being about to expire, D.47.49; ἀναβάλλεσθαι τὴν ὑ. defer *it,* ib.50:—hence, 2. *forfeiture of recognizances, distress,* εἰληφότες τῇ ὑπερημερίᾳ having seized it *by virtue of this right*, Id.33.6; κατὰ τὴν ὑ. Id.30.27; also, *the amount so forfeited*, ὑπερημερίαν πρᾶξαι Thphr.*Char.*10.10; and, *a document declaring such forfeiture*, τᾶν ὑπεράμεριάων (Boeot. gen. pl.) τᾶν ἰωσάων (i.e. οὐσῶν) κὰτ τᾶς πόλιος *IG*7.3172.115 (Orchom., iii B.C.); also, *penalty for unpunctual delivery*, ib.$4^2$(1).113.7 (Epid.), 103.74, al. (ibid., iv B.C.), καταστήσας τὸ σῶμα ἀφείσθω τῆς ὑ. *PMich. Zen.*70.9, cf. 14 (iii B.C.). **-ος**, ον, *over the day for payment*, after which the debtor became liable to have his goods seized, Lex ap. D.21.10, Syngr.ap.eund.35.12, *IG*5(2).6.44 (Tegea, iv B.C.); ὑ. γενέσθαι τινί D.47.75; ὑ. γενόμενος ἑπτὰ μνῶν Antipho 5.63, cf. Lys. 23.14; τὸ ὑπεράμερον τῶν ὀδέων the *penalty for unpunctual delivery* of.., *IG*$4^2$(1).109 ii 150 (Epid., iii B.C.); λαβὼν ὑπερήμερόν τινα, i.e. having a right to *distrain upon* him, D.21.81; ἑάλω ὑ. Ach.Tat.4.42: c. gen., ὑ. τῆς προθεσμίας Luc.*Pisc.*52; also of the debt, τῆς δίκης ὑ. γίγνεσθαι Plu.2.548d; ὑ. δικαιωτής *adjourning the penalty*, ib.549d. II. metaph., ὑ. μοι τῶν γάμων αἱ παρθένοι *past the time* of marriage, Anaxandr.68; ὑ. τῆς ζωῆς *past the term* of life, Luc. *Philops.*25; ὑ. τῆς ἀκροάσεως *too old* to listen, Philostr.*Ep.*68. 2. of things, τοῦ ἰδίου βίου φθέγξασθαί τι ὑ. *lasting beyond* one's own life, Longin.14.3; ὡς ὑ. γίγνεσθαι τἀληθὲς τοῦ ἑκάστου βίου the search for truth *lasts longer than* the individual's life, Luc.*Herm.*67. b. *time-expired*, μήπω τοῦ πένθους ὑπερημέρου..γεγονότος Ph.2.169.

**ὑπερήμῐσυς**, υ, *above half, more than half*, ὑπερημίσεες ἦσαν Hdt. 7.40; Γελῴων ὑπερημίσεας..τὠυτὸ..ἐποίησε ib.156; ὄντες ὑπερημίσεις *Inscr.Prien.*28.30 (ii B.C.); ὑπερήμισυ (or ὑπὲρ ἥμισυ) τοῦ στρατεύματος X.*An.*6.2.10; χρηματιζόντωσαν ὑπερήμισυ γινόμενοι *IG*$4^2$(1). 68.74 (Epid., iv B.C.).

**ὑπ-έρημος**, ον, *somewhat desolate*, Plu.*Publ.*4, *Aem.*8, *Pomp.* 28.

**ὑπερήνεμος**, ον, (ἄνεμος) *above the wind*, Plu.*Fr.inc.*150, Alex. Aphr. *in Mete.*16.13.

**ὑπερηνορ-έη**, ἡ, *exceeding spirit, haughtiness*, A.R.3.65. ❀**-εος**, ον, Dor. **-ᾱνόρεος**, = sq., Theoc.29.19, but f.l. for ὑπὲρ ἀνορέαν (Ahrens). **-έων**, οντος, ὁ, *exceedingly manly*: but always used in bad sense (though ἠνορέη is = ἀνδρεία, *manliness, courage*), *overbearing, overweening*, of the Trojans, Il.4.176; of Deïphobus (the Trojan), 13.258; of the Cyclopes, Od.6.5; in Od. mostly of the suitors, 17.482, al.; κακῶς ὑπερηνορέοντες 2.266, cf. 4.766. II. Com., *thinking oneself more than man*, Ar.*Pax* 53. (No Verb ὑπερηνορέω occurs: cf. ὑπερμενέων.)

**ὑπερήνωρ**, Dor. **-άνωρ**, ορος, ὁ, ἡ, (ἀνήρ) = foreg., *overbearing, overweening*, of the tyrant Pelias, Hes.*Th.*995; θήρ Orph.*A.*944; also μεγαλαγορία E.*Ph.*184 (lyr.); θυμός Orph.*A.*671.—In Hom. only as pr. n.

**ὑπερηφᾰν-εύω**, *behave arrogantly*, J.*AJ*4.8.23 (s.v.l.), Sch.Theoc. 1.66, *EM*778.49, etc.; also **-εύομαι**, πρὸς πάντας Phld.*Vit.*p.23 J., cf. Lxx *Ne.*9.16, al., Sch.Pi.*N.*11.55. **-έω**, used by Hom. once in part., much like ὑπερηνορέων, *overweening, arrogant*, ὑπερηφανέοντες Ἐπειοί Il.11.694: hence later writers formed the Verb, *to be arrogant*, ἐπί τινας Lxx *Ne.*9.10, cf. Hp.*Ep.*17, Plb.6.10.8, Phld.*Vit.* p.11 J., al., J.*BJ*3.1.1, etc. II. later writers also used it in a trans. sense, *treat disdainfully*, c. acc., D.S.23.15, J.*AJ*6.3.4, al., X.Eph.1.16, *POxy.*1676.16 (iii A.D.), etc.: c. gen., Them.*Or.*21.249b, prob. in Luc.*Nigr.*31: c. acc. et inf., *scorn* that.., Longus 4.19. 2. ὑ. ἑαυτούς *extol* themselves, Plb.5.33.8. **-ία**, ἡ, *arrogance*, Sol.ap. Arist.*Ath.*5.3, And.4.13, Pl.*Smp.*219c, Thphr.*Char.*24, Men.252, Aristeas 262, Phld.*Vit.*p.16 J., al., *Ev.Marc.*7.22; ὑ. τοῦ τρόπου X. *Cyr.*5.2.27; τοῦ βίου D.21.137: also c. gen. objecti, *contempt towards* or *for*.., Pl.*R.*391c, D.21.195 ([πάντων ἀνθρώπων] secl. Blass). **-ος**, ον, Dor. **ὑπερά-** Pi.*P.*2.28, B.16.49:—mostly in bad sense, *overweening, arrogant*, Hes.*Th.*149, Pi., B. ll. cc., A.*Pr.* 405 (lyr.), Isoc.12.196, D.4.9, Phld.*Vit.*p.10 J., etc.; Κύριος ὑπερηφάνοις ἀντιτάσσεται Lxx *Pr.*3.34; ὑβρισταὶ καὶ ὑ. Arist.*Rh.*$1390^b$33; -ώτεροι..καὶ ἀλογιστότεροι ib.$1391^a$33; οἰκίαι -ώτεραι D.13.30. Adv., **-νως** ἔχειν bear oneself *proudly*, Pl.*R.*399b, *Tht.*175b; ὑ. ζῶντες living *sumptuously, prodigally*, Isoc.4.152, Pl.*Lg.*691a; ὀψωνεῖν.. οὐχὶ μετρίως.., ἀλλ' ὑ. Diph.32.20; of a dish, ὑ. ὄζειν Alex.261.6 (but also, *insolently, brutally*, μαστιγοῦν τινα prob. in *PCair.Zen.*80. 4 (iii B.C.)).—This sense appears in Hom. in the part. ὑπερηφανέων (q.v.). 2. rarely in good sense, *magnificent, splendid*, σοφία, ἔργον, Pl.*Phd.*96a, *Smp.*217e; ὑ. τι διαπραττομένη Id.*Grg.*511d; ποτήρια χρυσᾶ.., ὑπερήφανα Philippid.27; πράξεις ὑ. τὸ μέγεθος Plu.*Fab.*26; *sublime*, Dam.*Pr.*3. Adv. **-νως**, ἀγωνιζόμενος Plu.*Ages.* 34.

**ὑπερηχέω**, *outroar*, τὸν Αἰγαῖον Aristid.1.123 J.

**ὕπερθα**, v. ὕπερθεν.

**ὑπερθάλασσος** [θᾰ], ον, *over the sea, overseas*, βασιλεῖς ὑπερθάλασσοι (sic codd., -θαλάσσιοι Hercher) Alciphr.2.4.

**ὑπερθαρσέω**, Att. **-θαρρῶ**, *to be over-confident*, Phld.*Vit.*p.20 J.

**ὑπερθαυμάζω**, Ion. **-θωμάζω**, fut. -άσομαι Luc.*Pr.Im.*18:—*feel* or *express great admiration*, Hdt.3.3, *Sammelb.*1912, Luc.*VH*1.34; ἐπί τινι Id.*Am.*52. II. c. acc., *wonder greatly at, admire greatly*, J.*BJ*2.9.3, Luc.*Zeux.*3, Gal.18(1).401, Ath.12.523d.

**ὑπερθαύμαστος**, ον, *most admirable*, *AP*15.16 (Const. Rhod.).

**ὑπέρθειος**, ον, *more than divine*, ἀρχαί Dam.*Pr.*118 (Sup.).

**ὑπέρθεμα**, ατος, τό, *overbid*, *Gloss.*

**ὑπερθεμᾰτ-ίζω**, *overbid*, *Gloss.*, Dosith.p.431 K., Priscian. *de xii vers.Aen.*116 (p.486 K.). **-ισμός**, ὁ, *overbidding*, *Gloss.*, Charis. p.553 K. **-ιστής**, οῦ, ὁ, *one who overbids*, *Gloss.*

**ὑπερθεμιστοκλῆς**, ὁ, *a super-Themistocles*, *Com.Adesp.*1177: cf. ὑπερπερικλῆς, ὑπερσωκράτης, etc.

❀ **ὕπερθεν**, also **ὕπερθε** Il.5.503, Od.14.476, (ὕπερθ') A.*Th.*228 (lyr.), *PHib.* (v. infr.); Aeol. **ὕπερθα** A.D.*Adv.*193.13: Adv.: (ὑπέρ):—*from above* or (more freq.) merely *above*, τάφρος καὶ τεῖχος ὕ. Il.12.4, etc.: of the body, *above, in the upper parts*, ὕ. φοξὸς ἔην κεφαλήν 2.218; ἔνερθε πόδες καὶ χεῖρες ὕ. 13.75, cf. 5.122; τὰ ματρόθεν μὲν κάτω, τὰ δ' ὕ. πατρός Pi.*P.*2.48: rare in Prose, X.*An.*1.4.4, *Mem.*1.4.11, Sor. 1.18; τὸ ὕ. [τῆς γῆς] Arist.*Mu.*$391^b$14; Ὀξυρύγχων πόλις ἡ ὕπερθε Μέμφεως *PHib.*1.95.5 (iii B.C.). 2. *from heaven above*, Od.24. 344, *h.Cer.*13; i.e. from the gods, Il.7.101. 3. of Degree, τοτὲ μὲν ἄπορα, τοτὲ δ' ὕ. sometimes *yet more*, S.*OC*1745 (lyr.). II. c. gen., *above, over*, Pi.*P.*4.192, Simon.37.9, A.*Ag.*232 (lyr.), etc.; ὕ. μόχθων ἐγένεθ' got the *better* of.., E.*Ba.*904 (lyr.); also **ὕπερθεν ἤ..** *above* or *beyond*, i.e. worse than.., Id.*Med.*650 (lyr.).

**ὑπέρθεος**, ον, *more than God*, μὴ φρονεῖθ' ὑπέρθεα Men.*Mon.*243 codd. (ὑπὲρ θεούς Brunck, Meineke).

**ὑπερθερᾰπεύω**, *cherish* or *court exceedingly*, Poll.4.49, Hld.1.9.

**ὑπερθερμ-αίνω**, *warm* or *heat excessively*, Hp.*Morb.*1.2:—Pass., ib.2.1, Arist.*Pr.*$860^b$19, *EE*$1239^b$35, Thphr.*HP*4.14.6, Alex.Aphr. *Pr.*1.89, *Placit.*5.30.6. **-ᾰσία**, Ion. **-ίη**, ἡ, *immoderate warming, heating*, Hp.*Morb.*2.3. **-ος**, η, ον (*Gp.*6.8.1), or ος, ον (Sor.2.57), *over-warm, hot*, *Gp.* l.c., Sor. l.c., Gal.11.674.

**ὑπερ-θεσία**, ἡ, = sq. III, *PStrassb.*53.5 (ii A.D.). **-θεσις**, εως, ἡ, *putting over* or *across*, τῆς χειρὸς ὑπὲρ τὸν στρωτῆρα Apollon.Cit. 1. 2. = ὑπέρβασις 1.1, *pass*, Str.16.2.8, al. II. *transposition*, of words or propositions, παθητικαὶ ὑ. Phld.*Rh.*1.198 S., cf. Chrysipp.*Stoic.*2.83; distd. fr. παρένθεσις, Hermog.*Id.*1.12; also, = μετάθεσις 1.4, *EM*3.25, al. III. *delay, postponement*, Plb.3.112.4, *Sammelb.*7404.55 (ii A.D.), *POxy.*2106.5 (iv A.D.); ὑ. σχεῖν to be *put off*, Plb.2.51.7; ὑ. ἔλαβε τὸ διαβούλιον ἐπὶ τοὺς δέκα *was postponed* for the sake of consulting them, was referred to them, Id.18. 42.7; μηδεμίαν ὑ. ποιησάμενος *IG*7.2712.62 (Acraeph., i A.D.), cf. 9 (2).517.37 (Larissa, iii B.C.), D.S.16.94, Ph.2.2; ἄνευ πάσης ὑ. freq. in Pap., *PTeb.*386.23 (i B.C.), etc.:—a usage censured by Poll.9.137:—εἶναι τὴν ἀναβολὴν ὑπέρθεσιν ἐνεργείας δι' ὄκνον· ὑπερτίθεσθαι δέ τινα μόνον, ἀνεγκλήτου τῆς ὑ. οὔσης *Stoic.*3.163. IV. like ὑπερβολή, *excess, extraordinary character*, κατὰ τὴν ὑ. τῆς ἐπιβολῆς Plb.30.5.10; καθ' ὑπέρθεσιν *in an ascending scale*, D.S.19.34; μηδεμίαν ὑ. καταλιπεῖν no *power of exceeding*, Id.17.114; τὸ καθ' ὑ. αὐτοῦ μεγαλομερές his *superlative* munificence, prob. in *IGRom.*4.293 *a* ii 53 (Pergam., ii B.C., cf. *Wiener Sitzb.*214(4).38). V. Gramm., *the superlative degree*, Poll.5.106, Phryn.*PS*p.1 B., Procl. *in Prm.*p.943 S.

**ὑπερθέσμος**, ον, perh. *decreed as additional*, ἐτάξατο τῆς ὑπερθέσμου ἑβδομαίας ἡμέρας θεᾶς Βερνίκης Εὐεργέτιδος τὴν καθήκουσαν ἀπαρχήν *PSI*6.690.12 (i/ii A.D.), cf. *Sammelb.*6995.19 (ii A.D.), 6996.32 (ii A.D.).

**ὑπερθετ-έον**, *one must transpose*, Sch.Pl.*Grg.*499a. 2. *one must put over*, of a bandage, Sor.1.56. II. *one must put off*, Ph. 1.15, *Hippiatr.*14. **-ικός**, ή, όν, *superlative*, τὸ ὑ. εἶδος τῆς συγκρίσεως Sch.Hermog.*Stat.* in Rh.7(1).430 W.; τὸ ὑ. alone, Poll.3. 136, cf. Asp. *in EN*110.30, Simp. *in Cael.*713.28; ὑ. ὄνομα *EM*143.12, cf. A.D.*Adv.*167.26, etc. Adv. **-κῶς** *in the superlative*, Gal.9.619, 12. 814, Sch.Ar.*Pl.*83, etc. II. *dilatory*, Ph.2.269, Hsch., Phot., Suid. s.v. μελληταί. 2. *requiring* or *causing delay*, Vett.Val.182. 17, al. ❀**-ος**, ον, *placed above*, Sch.Od.3.65.

**ὑπερθέω**, *run beyond*, ὑ. ἄκραν *double* the headland, prov. of escaping from danger, A.*Eu.*562 (lyr.), cf. E.*Fr.*230 (anap.). 2. *outstrip, surpass, outdo*, [τινὰ] τύχῃ Id.*Andr.*195; δύναμιν Pl.*Lg.* 648e; *transcend*, τὸ καλόν Plot.6.9.11.

**ὑπερθῐγής**, ές, = ὑπερήφανος, Anon.ap.Suid.

**ὑπερθνῄσκω**, *die for*, τινος E.*Alc.*682; χθονός Id.*Ph.*998, cf. *Andr.* 498 (anap.): abs., Id.*Alc.*155.

**ὑπερθορεῖν**, **-θορέομαι**, v. ὑπερθρῴσκω.

**ὑπερθρᾰσύνομαι**, Pass., *act with great audacity*, D.C.41.28.

**ὑπερθρησκεύω**, *worship superstitiously*, Cels.ap.Orig.*Cels.*8.12.

**ὑπερθρῴσκω**, fut. -θοροῦμαι, Ep. -θορέομαι: aor. -έθορον, Ep. ὑπέρθορον; inf. -θορεῖν Hdt.6.134, Ep. -θορέειν Il.12.53 (v.l. in Hdt. l.c.): —*overleap, leap* or *spring over*, c. acc., τάφρον ὑπερθορέονται Il.8.179; ὑπέρθορον ἑρκίον αὐλῆς 9.476, cf. 12.53; so ὑπερθ. τοὺς ἀνθρώπους, τὸ ἕρκος, Hdt.2.66, 6.134; πεδίον Ἀσωποῦ A.*Ag.*297; πύργον ib.827; βᾶριν οὐχ ὑπερθορεῖ *will* not *escape from* it, Id.*Supp.*873 (lyr.): also ὑπὲρ ἕρκος ὑ. Sol.4.29: c. gen., πόλεως ὑ. E.*Hec.*823.

**ὑπερθῡμόομαι**, Med., *to be ὑπέρθυμος*, inf. -οῦσθαι Poll.5.125; impf. ὑπερεθυμοῦντο D.C.43.37 (s.v.l.).

**ὑπέρθῡμος**, ον, *high-spirited, high-minded, daring*, freq. in Hom., in good sense, Il.2.746, 5.376, al., cf. Hes.*Th.*937, Pi.*P.*4.13, B.12. 103, etc.: irreg. Sup., ὑπερθυμέστατος ἀνδρῶν Stesich.95. II. in bad sense, *overweening*, Od.7.59, Hes.*Th.*719, *AP*6.332 (Hadr.); *over-spirited*, of a horse, X.*Eq.*3.12. III. *vehemently angry*, Poll.6.124. Adv., ὑπερθύμως ἄγαν *in over-vehement wrath*, A.*Eu.* 824. IV. in Adv. also, *eagerly, readily*, *IGRom.*4.1302.12 (Cyme, i B.C./i A.D.).

**ὑπερθύριον** [θῠ], τό, (θύρα) *lintel of a door* or *gate*, Od.7.90; ὑπερθυρίοις ἀραρυῖαι ἑπτὰ πύλαι Hes.*Sc.*271:—in Prose ❀**ὑπέρθῠρον**, τό, Hdt.1.179, *IG*$1^2$.372.201, $4^2$(1).103 *B*97 (Epid., iv B.C.), 11(2).145.19 (Delos, iv/iii B.C.), *Inscr.Délos* 442 *B*70 (ii B.C.), J.*BJ*5.5.3, Plu.2. 684a, etc.; also in Parm.1.12, Herod.2.65 (pl.). II. Lat. *hyperthyrum, frieze over the lintel*, Vitr.4.6.2.

**ὑπερθῠρόω**, *provide with a* ὑπέρθυρον, Pass., -ωθῆναι τὴν εἴσοδον *IG*4.558.26 (Argos).

**ὑπερθύω**, *foam, boil over*, of wine, Alex.5: in form **ὑπερθυίω**, ἅλμα στόματος ὑπερέθυιεν Tim.*Pers.*75.

**ὑπερθωμάζω**, Ion. for -θαυμάζω.

**ὑπερῐάστιος**, ον, *hyper-Ionian*, τρόπος Alyp.*Diat.*12, *Chrom.*12, Mart.Cap.9.935; τόνος Cleonid.*Harm.*12.

**ὑπεριάχω** [ᾰ], *shout above, out-shout*, αὐλῶν *APl.*4.305 (Antip.).

⊕ **ὑπεριδρύω**, in Pass., *to be established above, superior to*, Hero *Deff.* 136.23, Procl.*Inst.*98, Dam.*Pr.*26.

**ὑπεριζάνω**, *sit on*, Nonn.*D.*41.308; *settle upon*, νεφέλη ὑ. τοῦ στρατοπέδου J.*AJ*3.5.2.

**ὑπερίημι**, *send farther, send beyond the mark*, οὔτις Φαιήκων τόδε γ' ἵξεται οὐδ' ὑπερήσει Od.8.198. II. Med., *go on high*, ἠέλιος ὑπεριέμενος Xenoph.31.

**ὑπερικόν**, τό, v. ὑπέρεικος.

**ὑπερικταίνοντο**, 3 pl. impf. Pass., *hobbled along beneath*, in the phrase γούνατα δ' ἐρρώσαντο, πόδες δ' ὑπερικταίνοντο Od.23.3: according to Aristarch. it meant ἄγαν ἐπάλλοντο, and other ancient critics gave other explanations, v. *EM*779.9; a reading ὑποακταίνοντο (= ἔτρεμον) is mentioned in Hsch.; cf. ἀκταίνω.

**ὑπερῑν-άω**, *purge violently*, Hp. as cited by Erot. (cf. ὑπέρινος), Poll.4.179 (Pass.). **-ησις**, εως, ἡ, *violent purging*, Hp.*Loc.Hom.* 47. **-ος**, ον, *purged violently*, Id.*Epid.*6.5.15, Demetr.Com.Vet.6, Ruf.ap.Orib.7.26.168; ὑπέρινον ἄνω ποιεῖν Thphr.*HP*9.14.2; ὑ. γὰρ γίνονται καὶ οἱ ὄρνιθες καὶ τὰ φυτά *exhausted* by production, Arist. *GA*750ᵃ29.

**Ὑπερῑονίδης**, ου, ὁ, Patron. of Ὑπερίων, *Hyperion's son*, i.e. Ἥλιος, Od.12.176, *h.Cer.*74, Hes.*Th.*1011:—fem. **Ὑπερῑονίς**, ίδος, ἡ, Pythagorean name for *unity*, Lyd.*Mens.*2.6: also, *female eagle*, Cyran.98.

**ὑπερίππια**· ἀγών τις παρθένων, Hsch.

**ὑπερίπταμαι**, later form for ὑπερπέτομαι, Arist.*Mir.*836ᵃ33, Plu. *Num.*8; πᾶσαν γῆν Max.Tyr.6.6.

**ὑπερισθμίζω**, *draw* or *convey over an isthmus*, πλοῖα Plb.4.19.9, 5.101.4, al.

⊕ **ὑπερίστᾰμαι**, Pass., with aor. 2 and pf. Act.:—*stand over*, ὄνειρον ὑπερστὰν Ἀρταβάνου Hdt.7.17. 2. *stand over* one *for protection, protect*, τινος S.*El.*188 (lyr.): abs., A.R.4.370. 3. *surpass*, τινος J.*BJ*5.10.3.

**ὑπερίστιον**, τό, *top of distaff*, *EM*424.48.

**ὑπερίστωρ**, ορος, ὁ, ἡ, *knowing but too well*, c. gen., S.*El.*850 (lyr.).

**ὑπερίσχνος**, ον, *very thin, jejune*, of style, Hermog.*Id.*2.12.

**ὑπερίσχῡρος**, ον, *exceedingly strong*, ἔρυμα X.*Cyr.*5.2.2; of persons, Arist.*Pol.*1295ᵇ6.

**ὑπερισχύω** [ῡ], *to be exceedingly strong*, of fire, Thphr.*Ign.*10; ὁ λόγος Lxx 2*Ki.*24.4; οἶνος ib.1*Es.*3.10, cf. 4.41; of trees, *to be too luxuriant*, Thphr.*CP*3.18.2. 2. of persons, *to be overbearing*, *Sammelb.* 4638.6 (ii B.C.). II. c. gen., *to be stronger than, prevail over*, τοῦ πάθους J.*BJ*1.29.4, cf. Lxx *Jo.*17.18: also c. acc., *PPetr.*2 p.58 (iii B.C., cf. 3 p.66), *PRyl.*119.30 (i A.D.).

**ὑπερίσχω**, = ὑπερέχω, *hold above*, ἱκέτησι χεῖρ' ὑ. A.R.3.986; τὰς κεφαλὰς ὑπὲρ τὸ ὑγρόν Plb.3.84.9. II. intr., *to be* or *rise above*, Thphr.*CP*2.19.4; *project*, Aret.*SA*2.6. 2. *to be superior, prevail*, τῷ ἰσχύειν Thphr.*CP*1.15.3: c. gen., *prevail over*, δίκη δ' ὑπὲρ ὕβριος ἴσχει Hes.*Op.*217: c. acc., ὑ. τὴν αἰδῶ τὸ πάθος Aret.*SA*2.12. 3. *protect*, τινος *AP*6.268 (Mnasalc., dub. l.).

⊕ **Ὑπερίων** [ῑ], ονος, ὁ, *Hyperion*, in Hom. *the Sun-god*: he always joins Ὑπερίων Ἠέλιος (Il.8.480, Od.1.8, al.), or Ἠέλιος Ὑπερίων (Od. 12.133), exc. Il.19.398, Od.1.24, *h.Ap.*369, where Ὑπερίων stands alone for Ἥλιος; in *h.Hom.*31.4 Ὑπερίων is father of Ἥλιος. II. Ὑπερίων (derived from ὑπὲρ ἰών) is Pythag. name for 9, *Theol.Ar.* 58.

**ὑπερκαγχάζω**, *laugh to excess*, D.L.7.185.

**ὑπερκᾰθαίρομαι**, Pass., *to be purged excessively*, Hp.*Aph.*7.41, cf. Gal.18(1).144.

**ὑπερκάθαρσις**, εως, ἡ, *excessive purging*, Hp.*Aph.*5.4, *Coac.*554 (pl.); of menorrhagia, Orib.*Fr.*143, Aët.16.62: pl., interpol. in Dsc. 2.49.

**ὑπερκαθ-έζομαι**, Med., *sit over*, τῆς κεφαλῆς J.*AJ*19.8.2 (v.l. -καθίζ-). **-εύδω**, *sleep for one*, τινος, opp. ὑπερεγρήγορα, Philostr. *VA*8.12. **-ημαι**, *to be posted over* or *upon*, ἐπὶ τῶν ἄκρων X.*An.*5. 2.1. II. *sit over and watch, keep an eye on*, ἡμῶν ib.5.1.9, cf. Plot. 3.4.5. **-ίζω**, *sit upon*, Antig.*Mir.*163. **-ίστημι**, Dor. inf. -καπιστάμεν, *pay on another's behalf*, ἄταν *Leg.Gort.*11.35.

**ὑπέρκαιρος**, ον, *beyond the time, at wrong times*, Ath.14.613c, citing X.*Ages.*5.1; but codd. of X. give ὑπὲρ καιρόν. 2. ὑ. πρὸς τὸν τόπον *otiose, superfluous*, Phld.*Rh.*1 p.119S.

**ὑπερκαίω**, *burn violently, be exceedingly hot*, of the sun, Philostr. *Gym.*58; [χωρίον] Poll.5.110:—Pass., *to be burnt up*, γῆ Alex.Aphr. *Pr.*2.74: metaph., τῷ θυμῷ ὑ. Sch.Il.9.421.

⊕ **ὑπερκᾰκέω**, *to be quite luckless*, Hsch.

**ὑπερκαλλής**, ές, = sq., X.*Cyr.*5.1.18 (v.l. καλήν), D.C.59.28.

**ὑπέρκᾰλος**, ον, *exceedingly beautiful*, Arist.*Pol.*1295ᵇ6; *more than beautiful*, Plot.1.8.2, 6.7.33; fem. ὑπερκάλη, like παγκάλη, Poll.3.71. Adv. -λως Hsch. s.v. ὑπέρευγε.

**ὑπερκάμνω**, *suffer* or *labour for* any one, πόλεως E.*Ba.*963, cf. *IA* 918. II. in pf., gloss on ἀπεῖπεν, Sch.S.*Tr.*791.

**ὑπερκαρπέω**, *bear overmuch fruit*: in aor., *to be exhausted by fruiting*, Thphr.*CP*2.11.2, Ath.Med.ap.Orib.*inc.*7.5.

**ὑπερκατα-βαίνω**, *get down over, get quite over*, μέγα τεῖχος ὑπερκατέβησαν ὁμίλῳ Il.13.50,87: c. gen., *AP*9.533. **-βακχεύω**, *talk arrogantly*, prob. cj. in *Com.Adesp.*1380 (for -βαπτύ- Hsch.). **-γέλαστος**, ον, *exceedingly absurd*, Aeschin.3.192, Plu.2.4a. **-κειμαι**, Pass., *lie* or *sit above*, at table, c. gen., Id.*Mar.*3, Luc.*Symp.*31, etc. **-ληκτος**, ον, *hypercatalectic*, Heph.4.4, Aristid.Quint.1.23.

**ὑπερκατεργάζομαι**, aor. 1 part. -κατεργασθείς in pass. sense, *over-digested*, Gal.6.255.

**ὑπερκατηφής**, ές, *exceedingly downcast*, Luc.*Am.*52; ὑ. πρᾶγμα *very distressing*, Id.*Nec.*10.

**ὑπέρκαυσις**, εως, ἡ, *extreme virulence*, τοῦ ἰοῦ Philum.*Ven.*31.2.

**ὑπερκαχλάζω**, *run bubbling* or *boiling over*, Luc.*DMar.*11.2; ἐμβόλου Philostr.Jun.*Im.*11.

**ὑπέρκειμαι**, Pass., *lie above*, esp. of place, *to be placed* or *situated above* or *beyond*, οἱ ὑπερκείμενοι τῆς Μακεδονίας βάρβαροι Plb.4.29.1, cf. 5. 44.10, Str.9.5.19; ἡ ὀφρὺς ὑ. τοῦ ὄμματος Philostr.Jun.*Im.*2, cf. Sor.1. 8, al., Gal.6.344, al.: rarely c. dat., ἔν τινι ὑ. αὐτοῖς νησιδίῳ Arist.*Mir.* 832ᵃ23: abs., Hp.*Fract.*8; mostly in part., *lying* or *situated above*, ἡ ὑπερκειμένη χώρα Isoc.4.163; τῶν ὑ. κρημνῶν *overhanging*, Plb.10.30.2. 2. metaph., *to be placed above* (in rank), ὁ -μενος [δαίμων] *superior*, Plot. 3.4.3, cf. Procl.*Inst.*56; *transcend*, τῆς διακρίσεως Dam.*Pr.*164: c. acc., *excel*, τινα Lxx *Ez.*16.47. 3. εἰς πρᾶσιν ὑπερκείμενα *put up* for sale, *PAmh.*2.97.5 (ii A.D.), restd. in *PGen.*5.8 (ii A.D.). II. *to be delayed, postponed*, Luc.*Bis Acc.*23; τὰς εἰς τὸ τρίτον ἔτος ὑπερκειμένας (sc. ἀρτάβας) *BGU*1760.24 (i B.C.); cf. ὑπερτίθημι II. 5.

**ὑπερκεν-όω**, *purge completely* or *excessively*, Gal.17(2).365:—Pass., Id.7.602, Phryn.*PS* p.120B. **-ωσις**, εως, ἡ, *excessive evacuation*, Gal.13.154, Orib.*Eup.*3.11.3.

**ὑπερκέρ-ᾰσις**, εως, ἡ, *an outflanking on one wing*, Plb.1.27.5, Ascl. *Tact.*10.2, Arr.*Tact.*29.9, Ael.*Tact.*25.1, 38.1; cf. sq. and ὑπερφαλάγγησις. ⊕ **-άω**, (κέρας v. 3) *outflank*, τοὺς πολεμίους Plb.11.23.5, cf. Plu.*Brut.*41, Onos.21.1, etc.: metaph., *stretch beyond*, ἡ ἤπειρος ὑ. *Peripl.M.Rubr.*38; ὑ. ὕδωρ τῆς ἀντλίας Sch.Ar.*Pax*17. **-ως** (proparox.), ων, *with immense horns*, ἔλαφος Poll.5.76. **-ωσις**, εως, ἡ, = ὑπερκέρασις, Agath.2.9 (pl.).

**ὑπερκέφᾰλα**, Adv. *over the head*, ὑ. μ' ὑπερεβάλετο *SIG*1071 (Olympia).

**ὑπερκηλέω**, *charm beyond measure*, Luc.*Am.*1.

**ὑπερκλύζω**, *overflow*, Str.9.5.19, Isid.Char.1:—Pass., Str.10.2.15.

**ὑπερκλῠσις**, εως, ἡ, *overflow*, Eun.*VS* p.459B.

**ὑπερκολᾰκεύω**, *flatter immoderately*, τινα D.19.160, D.C.44.7, etc.

**ὑπερκομίζω**, *carry over*, Str.2.1.15 (Pass.).

**ὑπέρκομπος**, ον, *overweening, arrogant*, τὸν ὑ. θρῶσα Φάων' Men. 312 (anap.); ταῖς ὑπερκόμποις σαγαῖς A.*Th.*391; σῆμ' ὑπέρκομπον τόδε ib.404; τῶν ὑπερκόμπων ἄγαν φρονημάτων Id.*Pers.*827; ὑπερκόμπῳ θράσει ib.831: c. dat. modi, αἱ δ' ὑπέρκομποι τάχει [νῆες] *extraordinary*, ib.342 (s. v. l.). Cf. sq.

**ὑπέρκοπ-ος**, ον: (κόπτω, cf. παράκοπος):—*overstepping all bounds, extravagant, arrogant*, δόρυ A.*Th.*455 (lyr.); ὑπέρκοπον μηδέν ποτ' εἴπῃς αὐτὸς ἐς θεοὺς ἔπος S.*Aj.*127. Adv. -πως *extravagantly, excessively*, οἱ δ' ὑ. ἐν τοῖσι σοῖς πόνοισι χλίουσιν μέγα A.*Ch.*136; and Grotius' cj. ὑπερκόπως (for -κότως) is generally received in Id.*Ag.* 468 (lyr.), τὸ δ' ὑπερκόπως κλύειν εὖ.—Since ὑπέρκοπος is required by the metre in the above passages, whilst in those cited under foreg. (exc. Men. l. c.) either ὑπέρκομπος or ὑπέρκοπος might stand, Blomf. proposed to read -κοπος everywhere in Trag. II. *overtired, worn out*, ὑ. γενομένη [ἡ πάρδαλις] Arist.*Mir.*831ᵃ9, cf. Poll.5. 84. **-όω**, in Pass., *to be overtired, worn out*, Aët.5.66,91.

**ὑπερκορ-έννυμι**, *over-fill* or *glut*, τινά τινος one *with* a thing, Thgn.1158, in aor. opt. ὑπερκορέσαις:—Pass., pf. inf. ὑπερκεκορέσθαι Poll.7.23. **-ής**, ές, *over-full, glutted*, οἴνου D.C.51.24, cf. 59.17, 60.34, Poll.5.151: metaph., sens. obsc., Herod.5.1:—**ὑπέρκορος**, ον, Ptol.Euerg.3J. Adv. -ρως Poll.5.151.

**ὑπερκορύφωσις** [ρῠ], εως, ἡ, *projecting point* or *end*, Hp.*Anat.*1 (pl.).

**ὑπερκόσμιος**, ον, *supramundane*, Iamb.*Myst.*5.20, Hierocl.*Prov.* p.464B., Procl. *in Prm.* p.927S., *Inst.*164, Ammon. *in Int.*36.13, Dam.*Pr.*43; also **ὑπέρκοσμος** (s. v. l.), ib.98.

**ὑπέρκοτος**, ον, *exceedingly angry, cruel*, πάγαι A.*Ag.*822. Adv. -τως, ἐχθῆραι E.*HF*1086; cf. ὑπέρκοπος.

**ὑπερκράζω**, *outshout*, τινα Philostr.*Im.*1.28, in 3 fut. -κεκράξομαι.

**ὑπερκρᾰτέω**, *overpower*, τὸν λαόν Lxx 3*Ki.*16.22 (v.l.): c. gen., ὁ οἶνος ὑ. πάντων J.*AJ*11.3.3. 2. intr., *prevail*, ib.6.10.2 (where codd. SP have ὑπερκρατοῦς ὄντος, cf. Hsch. s. v. ὑπερμενεῖ).

**ὑπερκρεμάννυμι**, *hang up over*, ὑ. ἄταν τινί Pi.*O.*1.57 (nisi ὕπερ κρ. leg.); ὑπερκρεμνῶσιν (sic) (sc. τὸ ζῴδιον) τοῦ λύχνου *PMag.Berol.* 2.49:—Pass., ὑπὲρ κεφαλῆς γῆρας ὑπερκρέμαται Thgn.1022, cf. Mimn.5.

**ὑπερ-κρίνομαι** [ῑ], Pass., *to be judged superior*, Aq.*Ps.*50(51).6, Phryn.*PS* p.119B. **-κρῐσις**, εως, ἡ, *extra crisis*, Gal.18(2). 235. 2. prob. f.l. for ὑπερέκκρισις in Id.16.810.

**ὑπερκτάομαι**, *acquire over and above*, πολὺ γάρ τι κακῶν ὑπερεκτήσω *thou hast brought* much *excess* of evil *on thyself*, i.e. *more* than was needful, S.*El.*217 (anap.).

**ὑπερκυάνεος**, ον, *very dark blue*, Hsch.

**ὑπερκῠβιστάω**, *plunge headlong into danger*, Plb.28.6.6.

**ὑπερκύδας** [κῡ], αντος, ὁ, (κῦδος) *exceedingly famous* or *renowned*, only found in acc., ὑπερκύδαντας Ἀχαιούς Il.4.66,71; ὑπερκύδαντα Μενοίτιον Hes.*Th.*510.

**ὑπερκύπτω**, *pop one's head up, bob up, peep over*, Hom.*Epigr.*14.22, J.*AJ*12.7.4; ἐπὶ δένδρεόν τι ἀμβὰς ὑπερέκυπτε εἰς τὸ ἄβατον *IG* 4²(1).121.91 (Epid., iv B.C.); ὑπερκύψας..κατεῖδον Pl.*Euthd.*271a; (the cake) ὑπερέκυπτε τοῦ κανοῦ Nicostr.Com.15; τοῦ στομίου Luc. *Luct.*16; ἀνανήξασθαι καὶ ὑπερκῦψαι (sc. κλύδωνος) Ph.1.210, cf. 2.85; of water-plants, τοῦ ὕδατος Dsc.4.100, cf. 113; of a muscle, *emerge, come to the surface*, Gal.*UP*11.3,5; ὑπερκύπτει τις [τῶν φρενῶν] μοῖρα πρὸς ὑποχόνδριον οἷον χάραξ ib.7.21: c. acc., τὴν κυρτότητα τῆς θαλάττης *look over the top of*, Theo Sm.p.123 H. 2. *command a view of*, σκοπιάν, ἡ ὑπερκύπτει τὸν οὐρανόν Them.*Or.*23.293b. II. *put one's head over*, c. acc., ταῦρον..μέγαν, ὃς ὑπερκύψας τὸ Ταΰγετον ἀπὸ τοῦ Εὐρώτα πίεται Plu.*Lyc.*15; ὅταν ὑπερκύψῃ (sc. ἡ φλέψ) τὸν ἀμνειόν when it *passes* the inner membrane, Gal.5.555: metaph., *overtop, transcend*, πολλῶν ὄλβον *AP*6.250 (Antiphil.); θεὸς ὑ. τὰς δυνάμεις ἑαυτοῦ Ph.1.173.

**ὑπερλᾰλέω**, *speak too much*, Philostr.*Dial.*1. II. *speak for*, Ὁμήρου Eust.2.14, cf. 836.60.

⊛ **ὑπέρλαμπ-ρος**, ον, *exceedingly bright*, ἀκτῖνες Ar.*Nu.*571 (lyr.). 2. *very splendid*, ἀγορά Aristid.*Or.*18(20).6. II. of sound, *very clear* or *loud*: neut. as Adv., ὀλολύζειν οὐχ ὑπέρλαμπρον D.18.260. III. *very distinguished*, Plu.*Pomp.*14; in titles, ἡ ὑ. ὑμῶν εὐσέβεια, τὸ ὑ. ὑμῶν ὕψος, *PLips.*34.21 (iv A.D.), *PMasp.*8.9 (vi A.D.). -**ρύνομαι**, *outshine*, ἐσθῆτι ἢ κόσμῳ τοὺς ὑποτεταγμένους J.*BJ*2.8.7. II. *show great eagerness*, ἐφ' ὅτῳ ἂν τύχωσι, of hounds, X.*Cyn.*3.7. -**ω**, *shine exceeding brightly*, Poll.9.20. II. *surpass in splendour*, c. acc., πάντας Aristid.*Or.*26(14).84. III. *shine over*, c. gen., θέατρον ὑπερλάμπον τῆς ὅλης (sc. πόλεως) Lib.*Or.*61.10.

**ὑπέρλεπτος**, ον, *exceedingly thin, fine* or *delicate*, Philostr.*Im.*2.28; χυμός Alex.Trall.*Febr.*3.

**ὑπερλευκ-αίνομαι**, *to be exceedingly white*, Eust. ad D.P.248. -**ος**, ον, *exceeding white*, Hp.*Mul.*2.111, Luc.*Am.*41.

**ὑπερλίαν**, Adv. *beyond measure, exceedingly*, σοφός Eust.1396.42; τὸ ὑ. Id.1184.18; οἱ ὑ. ἀπόστολοι the '*super*-Apostles', 2*Ep.Cor.*11.5, 12.11.

**ὑπέρλοφος**, ον, *with high crest*, ἐλάτη Nonn.*D.*28.219.

**ὑπερλύδιος** [λῡ], ον, *hyper-Lydian*, τρόπος Gaud.*Harm.*23, Alyp. *Diat.*3, al.

**ὑπερλῡπέομαι**, Pass., *to be displeased beyond measure*, Hdt.8.90.

⊛ **ὑπερμαζάω**, *to be overfull of barley bread* (μᾶζα), *to be wanton from high feeding*, Ath.14.663b, Alciphr.1.18, etc.: metaph., Luc.*Nav.*15; ἐπὶ τῷ ἀξιώματι D.C.57.22: cf. κριθάω.

**ὑπέρμαζος**, ον, *above the breasts*, Paul.Aeg.6.44.

**ὑπερμαίνομαι**, aor. -εμάνην [ᾰ], Pass., *to be* or *go stark mad*, Ar. *Ra.*776.

**ὑπερμάκης**, v. ὑπερμήκης.

**ὑπερμαντεύομαι**, f.l. for ὕπερ μ. in E.*Ion* 431.

**ὑπερμᾰχ-έω**, *fight for* or *on behalf of*, πόλεως S.*Ant.*194, E.*Ph.*1252, cf. J.*AJ*3.14.4; σὺ ταῦτα..τοῦδ' ὑπερμαχεῖς ἐμοί; *dost* thou *fight* thus *for* him against me? S.*Aj.*1346 (in Luc.*Pisc.*23, τούτου is prob. to be restored): abs., Id.*JTr.*17. -**ησις**, εως, ἡ, *defence*, Sm.*Ex.*12.11, *EM*89.4. -**ητικός**, ή, όν, *inclined to fight for*, c. gen., Plu.*Num.*16, Corn.*ND*20. -**ικός**, v.l. for foreg. in Plu.*Num.* l. c. -**ομαι**, = ὑπερμαχέω, τῆς ἐλευθερίας Id.*Cat.Mi.*53; τάδ' ὡσπερεὶ τοὐμοῦ πατρὸς ὑπερμαχοῦμαι *will fight* this battle *for* him, S. *OT*265. -**ος**, ὁ, *champion, defender*, Lxx *Wi.*16.17, *AP*7.147 (Arch.); τᾶς ἁμᾶς πόλεος *Inscr.Cret.*1.xix 3.29 (Malla, ii B.C.); τοῦ δικαίου Ph.2.33; τῆς ἐλευθερίας Lyd.*Mag.*2.8.

**ὑπερμεγάθης**, v. ὑπερμεγέθης.

**ὑπέρμεγας**, άλη, α, *immensely great*, Ar.*Eq.*158, Ael.*NA*6.63, etc.

**ὑπερμεγεθ-έω**, f.l. for ἑτερομεγ-, Artem.1.31. ⊛ -**ης**, Ion. -**άθης** [ᾰ], ες, = ὑπέρμεγας, [λίθοι], ὄφιες, κέρεα, Hdt.2.175, 4.191, 7.126; κυούμενον Sor.2.55; ἀδίκημα Aeschin.3.7; παρασκευάς Isoc.9.61; εὐεργεσίαι, ψεῦδος, D.18.316, 43.29; μηδὲν ὑ. τὴν πόλιν βλάψειν Id.23.190; ὑ. ἔργον *exceedingly difficult*, X.*Cyr.*1.6.8. Adv. -θως Ph. 1.103; κολάζεσθαι Phld.*Ir.*p.57 W.

**ὑπερμεθύσκομαι**, aor. ὑπερεμεθύσθην, Pass., *get excessively drunk*, Hdt.2.121.δ', Heraclid.Cum.2.

**ὑπερμεν-έτης**, ου, ὁ, poet. for ὑπερμενής, *h.Mart.*1. -**έων**, οντος, ὁ, *exceedingly mighty*, ἄνδρες ὑπερμενέοντες, for ὑπερμενέες, Od. 19.62. (No Verb ὑπερμενέω occurs: cf. ὑπερηνορέων.) ⊛ -**ής**, ές, (μένος) *exceedingly mighty*, epith. of Zeus, Il.2.116,350,403, al., Hes. *Cat.Oxy.*1358 *Fr.*1.11, al.; ὑπερμενέες βασιλῆες Il.8.236, al.; ἐπίκουροι 17.362.

**ὑπερμέση** (sc. χορδή), ἡ, = λίχανος, Nicom.*Harm.*3.

**ὑπέρμεστος**, ον, *full to overflowing*, Ph.2.533, Hsch. s.v. ὑπερχειλῶν.

⊛ **ὑπερμετρ-έω**, *pass all measure*, Hsch. s.v. ὑπερχειλές (Pass.). 2. ὑπερμετρῶν ἀμὲ τοῖς δικαίοις, i.e. *giving* us *more than* our due, *IG*5(1). 1145.31 (Gythium, i B.C.):—Pass., *PSI*4.425.7 (iii B.C.). -**ία**, ἡ, *a passing all measure, overflow*, Ptol.*Tetr.*84. II. *a going beyond the metre*. Eust.353.35. -**ος**, ον, *beyond all measure, excessive*, κτῆσις X.*Ep.*4; γῆρας Pl.*Lg.*864d; κολάσεις, ὀργαί, Phld. *Ir.*pp.52,61 W.; of a tumour, Leonid.ap.Aët.15.5. Adv., μηδ' ὑπερμέτρως ἄλγει E.*Fr.*418. II. *going beyond the metre*, Luc.*JTr.*6, Heph.6.2.

**ὑπερμετώπιος**, ον, *over the forehead*, *EM*212.12.

**ὑπερμήκης**, ες, Dor. -**μάκης** [ᾱ] Pi.*O.*7.37: (μῆκος):— *exceedingly long*, δρόμοι A.*Pr.*591; ἡ βασιλέος..χεὶρ ὑ. the king's arm is *very long*, reaches *very far*, Hdt.8.140.β'. 2. *exceedingly high*, of mountains, Id.7.128,129. 3. ὑπερμάκης βοά a cry *exceeding loud*, Pi. l. c.

**ὑπερμιξολύδιος** [λῡ], ον, *higher than the mixo-Lydian*, ἁρμονία Ath. 14.625d; τόνος Cleonid.*Harm.*12; -**λύδια**, τά, ib.13.

**ὑπερμῑσέω**, *hate exceedingly*, Lys.31.19.

**ὑπέρμορ-α**, Adv. = ὑπέρμορον or ὑπὲρ μόρον (v. μόρος I), Il.2.155. -**ως**, Adv. = foreg., Sch.Il.20.30, *EM*779.47.

**ὑπερνέμομαι**, *range the hills above*, Λιβύης ἄκραν Philostr.*VA*5.1.

**ὑπερνέφελος**, ον, *above the clouds*, Luc.*Icar.*2, *Herm.*5; [πόλις] μικροῦ ὑ. Poll.9.20.

**ὑπερνεφής**, ές, (νέφος) = foreg., Plu.*Fr.inc.*150, Hdn.8.1.5, etc.

**ὑπερνέω**, *float over the top of*, Sch.Luc.*JTr.*47.

**ὑπερνεωλκέω**, *haul over land*, τὰς νῆας, τὰ πλοῖα, Plb.8.34.12, Str. 6.3.1 (Pass.), cf. 8.2.1; στῦλον ἰσθμοῦ Plu.*Ant.*69.

**ὑπερνῑκάω**, *prevail completely over*, Hp.*Hebd.*50, Gal.19.645; *to be more than conqueror*, *Ep.Rom.*8.37: c. acc., τὰς Χάριτας, μίμημα, Lib.*Descr.*30.9.4.

**ὑπερνο-έω**, *think further, trouble oneself further*, S.*OC*1741 codd. (lyr.). -**ησις**, εως, ἡ, *super-thought*, Plot.6.8.16. -**ος**, ον, contr. -**νους**, ουν, *superintellectual*, θεός Procl.*Inst.*115.

**ὑπερνοσέω**, *to be extremely ill*, f.l. in Hp.*Loc.Hom.*33 for ὑπέρινος.

**ὑπερνότιος**, ον, also η, ον D.P.151:—*beyond the south wind*, i.e. *at the extreme south*, opp. ὑπερβόρεος, Hdt.4.36, Str.1.3.22.

**ὑπερξανθ-ίζω**, *to be very fair* or *flaxen*, of hair, Eust.975.60. -**ος**, ον, *very yellow*, Ruf.ap.Orib.8.24.64.

**ὑπερξηρ-αίνω**, *dry up exceedingly*, Hp.*Vict.*2.66, *Morb.*1.2, al.:—Pass., *to be dried up*, Arist.*Mete.*352ᵃ7, Gal.*UP*14.11. -**ᾰσία**, Ion. -**ίη**, ἡ, *excessive dryness*, Hp.*Morb.*1.28. -**ος**, ον, *exceedingly dry*, *droughty*, Arist.*Resp.*477ᵇ28, Dsc.2.84.

**ὑπερογκ-έω**, *become exceedingly large, swell*, Hp.*Art.*51:—also Pass. -**όομαι**, Poll.4.187. -**ος**, ον, *of excessive bulk* or *size*, γενομένης τῆς κνήμης ὑ. *swelled to a great size*, X.*HG*5.4.58; [μαστοὶ] οἱ ὑ. Sor.1.88; πιμελὴς καὶ ὑ. Luc.*Tim.*15; δύναμις ὑ., opp. ταπεινή, D.4.23; τὰ ὑ. τῶν βελῶν Arist.*Aud.*802ᵇ34. 2. *immoderate, excessive*, οὐσίαι Pl.*Ep.*317c; τιμαί, εὐτυχίαι, etc., Plu.2.820f, *Aem.*34, etc.; φρόνημα Id.*Luc.*21; τὰ ὑ., opp. τὰ ἐλλείποντα, Pl.*Lg.*728e; of style, *ponderous, verbose*, Plu.2.7a (but also ὑπέρογκα λαλεῖν talk 'big', *Ep.Jud.*16, cf. 2*Ep.Pet.*2.18): generally, *exceedingly great*, πρᾶγμα Luc.*DMort.*23.2. Adv. -κως Ph.1.103, Plu.*Demetr.*30: neut. as Adv., ὑπέρογκον φρονεῖν Iamb.*Protr.*14. 3. *difficult*, Lxx 2*Ki.*13.2.

**ὑπερόδιον**, = *pergula*, *Gloss.* (fort. ὑπερῷον vel ὑπερῴδιον).

**ὑπεροδῠνέω**, prob. f.l. for ὑπερωδυνέω in Hp.*Epid.*6.3.8.

**ὑπερο-ειδής**, ές, *pestle-shaped*, Hp.*Art.*47,73, Dsc.2.167, prob. in *PMed.Lond.*155 ii 26,32.

**ὑπεροιάζομαι**, v. ὑπεροίομαι.

**ὑπεροιδαίνω**, *to be much swollen*, *AP*5.59 (Rufin.).

**ὑπεροιδάω**, *swell unnaturally*, of the breasts, Luc.*Am.*53: also -**οιδέω**, -οιδοῦντος αἵματος, in gloss on αἱματοφλοιβοιστάσιες, Gal.19.71.

**ὑπεροικέω**, *dwell above* or *beyond*, c. gen., Hdt.4.13,21,37, Str.7.7.8: also c. acc., ὑ. τὸ Πάγγαιον πρὸς βορέω ἀνέμου Hdt.7.113, cf. Paus.4.35.5, Luc.*Alex.*9.

⊛ **ὑπεροικοδομέω**, *build over* or *above*, J.*AJ*15.9.6 (Pass.).

**ὑπέροικος**, ον, *dwelling above* or *beyond*, τῆς χώρης Hdt.4.7.

**ὑπέροινος**, ον, *immoderately fond of wine*, Polyaen.8.25.1.

**ὑπεροίομαι**, *to be very self-conceited*, aor. part. -ησάμενοι, Hsch.:— also **ὑπεροιάζομαι**, Phot., Suid., prob. in Hsch.

**ὑπεροκνέομαι**, *to be very hesitant*, Phld.*Lib.*p.39 O.

**ὑπερομβρία**, ἡ, *a violent storm of rain, heavy rain*, Arist.*HA*602ᵃ7: mostly in pl., Id.*Mete.*366ᵇ9, 368ᵇ17, Thphr.*CP*5.3.7.

⊛ **ὑπερον**, τό, v. ὕπερος, ὁ, and ὕπερα, τά.

**ὑπερόντως**, Adv. *super-essentially, transcendentally*, Plot.6.8.14.

**ὑπέροξυς**, υ, *very acute*, πυρετοί Hp.*Fract.*11.

**ὑπεροπ-εύς**, = ὑπερόπτης, and -**εύει**· ψεύδεται, ff. ll. for ἠπ- in Hsch.

**ὑπεροπλ-ήεις**, εσσα, εν, Ep. for ὑπέροπλος, A.R.2.4, in Sup. ὑπεροπληέστατος. -**ία**, ἡ, *insolence, presumptuousness*, ᾗς ὑπεροπλίῃσι Il.1.205: in sg., Rhian.1.12. II. *high courage*, Theoc.25.139. [Always with ῑ, metri gr.] -**ίζομαι**, (ὅπλίζω) *vanquish by force of arms*, οὐκ ἄν τίς μιν ἀνὴρ ὑπεροπλίσσαιτο Od.17.268, acc. to Aristarch.; others expld. it as *treat haughtily* or *scornfully*:—Act. in Suid. (-ῆσαι Hsch.). ⊛ -**ος**, ον, *insolent, presumptuous* (never of persons in Hom. or Hes.); in Hom. only ὑπέροπλον εἰπεῖν to speak *insolently*, *presumptuously*, Il.15.185, 17.170; in Hes., ἠνορέη, βίη ὑπέροπλος, *Th.* 516,619,670; ἀτασθαλίη Orph.*Fr.*120; ἦβα Pi.*P.*6.48; of persons, Λαπίθαι ὑ. ib 9.14. II. *big, mighty*, ἀνὴρ ὑ. a *monstrous* man, Theoc. 22.44; of fishes, Opp.*H.*1.103, etc. III. of conditions, *overwhelming*, ἄτα Pi.*O.*1.57; μηδὲν μέγα μηδ' ὑ. Ps.-Phoc.59 (v.l. ὑπέρφρυ, cf. Hsch.).—Ep. word.

**ὑπεροπτάω**, *over-bake, bake at too fierce a fire*, in Pass., Gal.6.484, Poll.7.23, Alex.Aphr.*Pr.*1.104,110. II. *over-heat*, in Pass., Prodic. 4 ap.Gal.*Nat.Fac.*2.9, Id.5.682; ὑπερωπτημένη χολή Id.16.512.

**ὑπεροπτέον**, (ὑπερόψομαι) *one must despise, esteem lightly*, πραγμάτων Isoc.*Ep.*9.18; τὴν τοιαύτην τιμήν Jul.*Or.*2.70d.

**ὑπεροπτεύω**, = ὑπεροράω, Socr.*Ep.*37.

**ὑπερόπτης**, ου, ὁ, (ὑπερόψομαι) *contemner, disdainer*, χρυσοῦ κανάχης ὑπερόπτας (dub. l.) S.*Ant.*130 (anap.); ὑ. τῶν εἰωθότων Th.3.38: abs., *disdainful, haughty*, πρὸς πάντα παλίγκοτος ἠδ' ὑ. Theoc.22.58; ὑ. καὶ ὑβρισταί Arist.*EN*1124ᵃ29, cf. Phld.*Vit.*p.36 J., Jul.*ad Them.*264d.

**ὑπερόπτησις**, εως, ἡ, *over-heating*, Gal.18(2).176, 19.490, Alex. Trall.*Febr.*2.

**ὑπεροπτικός**, ή, όν, *contemptuous, disdainful*, Isoc.1.30, 12.241, Luc.*Nigr.*1, etc.; ἠπείλησεν ὑπεροπτικά Id.*DDeor.*21.1; τὸ -ώτατον D.17.26. Adv. -κῶς X.*HG*7.1.18, Str.8.6.23: Comp. -ώτερον Plb. 5.46.6: Sup. -ώτατα D.C.49.7. 2. c. gen., ἀδικία ἕξις ὑ. νόμων Pl.*Def.*416a.

**ὑπέροπτος** (A), ον, *disdainful*, ὀφρύς *AP*12.186 (Strat.); gloss on ὑπέροφρυς, Hsch.: neut. pl. as Adv., S.*OT*883 (lyr.). Regul. Adv. -τως Poll.9.147. II. *great, excessive*, Hsch., cf. Phot., Suid.

**ὑπέροπτος** (B), ον, (ὀπτάω), *over-heated*, Gal.19.426.

**ὑπερόρ-ᾱσις**, εως, ἡ, *overlooking, disdaining*, τῶν αἰσθητικῶν κινήσεων M.Ant.8.26: abs., *contempt, disdain*, Lxx *Nu.*22.30. **-ᾱτικός**, ή, όν, = ὑπεροπτικός, Poll.9.147. **-άω**, fut. -όψομαι: aor. ὑπερεῖδον, inf. -ϊδεῖν: aor. Pass. ὑπερώφθην:—*look over, look down upon*, c. acc., τὴν θάλασσαν ὑπερορῶντα Hdt.7.36. II. *overlook, take no notice of*, τοὺς πονηροὺς ὑπερορᾷ Lys.2.77; τὴν ὕβριν ὑπερεώρακε Aeschin.1.116; οὐκ ὀλίγα τῶν προσόδων ὑ. *remit*, *OGI*56.16 (Canopus, iii B.C.); δι' ὄνειρον..ὑπεριδεῖν τὸ συμφέρον Sor.1.4: c. part., οὐχ ὑπεροψόμενοί τινας ἀφαιρεθέντας D.H.5.52. 2. *despise, disdain*, ὑπεριδὼν Ἴωνας Hdt.5.69, cf. Phld.*Vit.*p.27 J.; λόγους ὑπεριδεῖν Th.4.62; σφῶν τὸ πλῆθος ὑπεριδών Id.5.6, cf. 6.11; ὑπερείδετε τὴν ἐμὴν ὁμιλίαν Lys.8.7; πλὴν ἀρετῆς πάντα ὑ. Pl.*Criti.*120e; πάντα τἀνθρώπινα ὑπερεώρα πρὸς τὴν παρὰ τῶν θεῶν ξυμβουλίαν X.*Mem.*1.3.4:—Pass., ἡ Λακεδαίμων κακῶς ἤκουσε καὶ ὑπερώφθη Th.5.28, cf. 7.42; ὑπ' ἐκείνων ὑπερορᾶσθαι Pl.*Phdr.*232d. b. less freq. c. gen., ὑπερορῶ τῆς ἀπολογίας Antipho 3.3.4; ὑμῶν D.19.338; τῶν νόμων X.*Mem.*1.2.9; πενίας Gorg.*Pal.*32; τῶν μὲν ζῴων φροντίσαι, τῶν δ' οὕτω τιμίων (sc. τῶν ἄστρων) ὑ. Arist.*Cael.*290$^{a}$32; ὑπερεῖδε τῶν ἀνθρωπείων ἀγαθῶν Luc.*Demon.*3, cf. Gal.6.108,312.

**ὑπερογίζομαι**, Pass., *to be exceedingly angry*, D.C.50.25.

**ὑπεροργώντως**, Adv., (ὀργάω) *with eager desire*, Hsch. s.v. περιόργως.

**ὑπερορέγομαι**, Pass., *long exceedingly for*, c. gen., Poll.5.165.

**ὑπερορ-ία**, ἡ, v. ὑπερόριος I. 2. **-ίζω**, *drive beyond the frontier, banish*, τοὺς πολίτας D.C.57.15: c. gen., τῶν βασιλείων θυρῶν Lib. *Or.*18.135:—Pass., Aeschin.3.131,252; ἐξ ἁπάσης τῆς οἰκουμένης ὑπερωρίσθησαν Isoc.6.32. II. of things, μετριότητα ὑ. Pl.*R.*560d; τὰ ξύλα, τὸν σίδηρον, Aeschin.3.244. ※**-ιος**, ον, also α, ον (v. infr.), poet. **-ούριος** Theoc. (v. infr.): (ὅρος):—*over the boundaries, abroad*, D.46.7; ῥιψάτω ὑπερούριον Theoc.24.95, cf. Anon.ap Suid.; ὑ. ἀσχολία occupation *in foreign parts, abroad*, Th.8.72; ὑ. ἀρχή, opp. ἔνδημος, Lex ap.Aeschin.1.19; δικαστήρια, opp. ἐπιχώρια, *PMonac.* 14.83 (vi A.D.); τὰ ὑ. *foreign affairs*, opp. τὰ κατὰ πόλιν and τὰ ἔνδημα, Arist.*Pol.*1285$^{b}$14. 2. ἡ ὑπερορία (sc. γῆ) *the country beyond one's own frontiers, foreign land*, *IG*1$^{2}$.56.7, And.3.36, Lys.31.9, Pl.*Phdr.*230d; also εἰς τὰν ὑπερόριον στρατεύεσθαι *Foed.Delph.Pell.* 2 B 22; opp. τὰ ἔνδημα, X.*An.*7.1.27; ἐκ τῆς ὑ. ἀνακαλεῖσθαι, i.e. from the land where he had been in exile, Plu.2.508a; hence, actually, *banishment*, φόνοις καὶ ὑπερορίαις D.C.67.3; τὰ ὑ. (sc. χωρία) X.*Ath.* 1.19, *Smp.*4.31. II. *foreign to the purpose, outlandish, alien*, λαλιά Aeschin.2.49; ἀρχαὶ ἐνυπνίων ὑπερόριαι ἢ τοῖς χρόνοις ἢ τοῖς τόποις ἢ τοῖς μεγέθεσιν Arist.*Div.Somn.*464$^{a}$1, cf. Aristid.1.128 J.; τὸ τῶν ἀέρων ἄηθες καὶ ὑ. Anon.ap.Suid. III. c. gen., ὑ. τοῦ νομοῦ *beyond the boundaries of* the nome, *PPetr.*2 p.16 (iii B.C.): metaph., λιμὸς.. βρώσεις ὑποβάλλων..τῆς φύσεως ὑπερορίους Procop.*Goth.*3.17: abs., ἰσχναίνειν καὶ γυμνάζειν τὸ σῶμα,..ποιεῖν δὲ ὡς μὴ ὑπερόριοι ἀπέλθωμεν go *over the mark*, Pall. *in Hp.*2.77 D. **-ισμός**, ὁ, *banishment*, Poll.9.158. **-ιστέον**, *one must banish*, Aristid.*Or.*46(3).33.

**ὑπερόρκιος**, ον, *beyond an oath*, δυναμένη ὑπερόρκια *more* powerful *than any oath*, Cels.ap.Orig.*Cels.*1.1.

**ὑπερορμαίνω**, *break forth over*, Man.4.131.

**ὑπερόρνυμαι**, Pass., *rise up over, hang over*, ἄτας ὑπερορνυμένας πόλει S.*OT*165 (lyr., cj. Musgr., ἄτας ὑπερ codd.).

**ὑπερορρωδέω**, *to be afraid on behalf of*, τινος E.*Supp.*344: cf. ὑπεραρρωδέω.

※ **ὕπερος**, ὁ, or **ὕπερον**, τό, v. infr.:—*pestle*, ὕπερον δὲ τρίπηχυν Hes. *Op.*423; λεήναντες ὑπέροισι Hdt.1.200; ὑπέρου μοι περιτροπὴ γενήσεται, prov. of never-ending and ineffectual labour, Pl.Com.1, cf. Pl.*Tht.*209e, Philem.30, Plu.2.1072b; so εἰ ἐς ὅλμον ὕδωρ ἐκχέας ὑπέρῳ σιδηρῷ πτίττοι Luc.*Herm.*79; ὕπερα σιδηρᾶ Poll.7.107, with which Bgk. compared ..έροις σιδηροῖς, the mutilated title of a successful comedy in *IG*14.1097. II. *anything shaped like a pestle*, 1. *club, cudgel*, Plu.*Alex.*63, Luc.*Demon.*48. 2. *lever for stretching dislocated joints*, Hp.*Fract.*13, al. III. like πηνίον, a pupa of a geometrid moth, Arist.*HA*551$^{b}$6.—The form **ὕπερον, τό**, is found in *Hesperia* 5.383 (Athens, v B.C., pl.), Hp.*Art.*5,78, Plb.1.22.7, *PRyl.*167.14 (pl., i A.D.), Luc.*Philops.*35, Poll.1.245, 7.107, 10.114, *EM*779.48; whereas none of the other passages in which the word occurs prove anything about the gender, except Hes. l.c.; whence it has been suggested that τρίπηχυ should be read there, and ὕπερον, τό, received as the only form.

**ὑπερουράνιος** [ᾰ], ον, *above the heavens*, Pl.*Phdr.*247c, Poll.1.23; θεοί Iamb.*Myst.*8.7; θεός, κύκλα, Cels.ap.Orig.*Cels.*6.19,38.

**ὑπερούριος**, ον, Ion. and poet. for ὑπερόριος (q.v.).

**ὑπερούσιος**, ον, *above Being*, Them.*Or.*1.8b, Procl.*Inst.*115, *Theol. Plat.*3.21, Syrian. *in Metaph.*5.34. Adv. -ίως Procl.*Inst.*118,145, Eustr. *in EN*40.7.

**ὑπερουτάω**, *wound on account of*, τευχέων Q.S.5.289 (Pass., s. v.l.).

**ὑπέροφρυς**, υ, *supercilious*, prob. in Ps.-Phoc.59, cf. Hsch., Phot., Suid.

**ὑπεροχ-έω**, *carry above, support*, μηροῦ κεφαλὴ ὑ. τὸ ὕπερθεν τοῦ σώματος Hp.*Fract.*18. **-ή**, ἡ, (ὑπερέχω II) *projection, prominence*, οὐ κνῖσα κρούει ῥινὸς ὑπεροχὰς ἄκρας; Ephipp.3, cf. *Gp.*9.10.4; αἱ ὑ. τῶν βουνῶν, τῶν ὀρῶν, their *prominent points*, Plb.10.10.10, Plu. 2.936a; *top* of an upright beam, Ath.Mech.17.4; ὑ. λιθοειδεῖς, of the mastoid processes of the skull, Ruf.*Onom.*139; τὰς ὑ. αὐτῶν (sc. τῶν μαστῶν) Sor.1.55: abs., *an eminence*, Plb.3.104.3. 2. *rising* of a star, ἀνατολὴν εἶναι..ὑ. ἄστρου ὑπὲρ γῆς Chrysipp.*Stoic.*2.200; *raising*, τῆς ἑαυτῶν κεφαλῆς Plot.5.8.3. II. metaph., *pre-eminence, superiority*, ὑπεροχῆς ἐπιθυμεῖ ἡ νεότης, ἡ δὲ νίκη ὑ. τις Arist.*Rh.*1389$^{a}$13; ἡ ἰσχὺς καὶ ἡ ὑ. Id.*Pol.*1297$^{b}$18; τὴν ὑ. ἀπονέμειν τοῖς ἀρίστοις ib. 1293$^{b}$41; τὴν ὑ. τῆς πολιτείας λαμβάνειν *superiority in* the government, ib.1296$^{a}$31; διὰ τὴν ὑ. τοῦ πλήθους because of *superiority* in multitude, ib.1293$^{a}$4; ἡ ἐν τῷ ἐπιτηδεύματι ὑ. *IG*2$^{2}$.3800: pl., πρὸς τὰς ὑ. οὕτω διακεῖσθαι Isoc.12.16; διαφέρεσθαι ἐν τῷ ποσῷ καὶ ταις ὑ. Arist.*Pol.*1323$^{a}$35. 2. like ὑπερβολή, *excess*, opp. ἔλλειψις (defect), in many senses, as in Arithm., one of the ἀριθμοῦ ᾗ ἀριθμὸς πάθη, Id. *Metaph.*1004$^{b}$12, cf. Archim.*Spir.*11, *Aequil.*1.2, Dioph.1.6, al.; ἐν ἴσῃ ὑ., of an arithmetical progression, Papp.76.21, al., cf. Archyt.2, Porph. *in Harm.*p.266 W.; *excess*, of a sum of money, *SIG*976.66 (Samos, ii B.C.); in Physics, Arist.*Ph.*187$^{a}$16, 189$^{b}$10, *HA*486$^{b}$8, al.; διαφέρειν καθ' ὑπεροχήν Id.*PA*644$^{a}$17, al.; τάχος τὸ ὑ. [ἔχον] κινήσεως Id.*Metaph.*1052$^{b}$30; ἡ κατὰ τὴν ἀρετὴν ὑ. Id.*EN*1098$^{a}$11, cf. *Rh.*1368$^{a}$25; τῶν ἠθῶν (sc. τοῦ Ἐπικούρου) *IG*2$^{2}$.1099.27 (Epist. Plotinae), cf. 4$^{2}$(1).86.18 (Epid., prob.); φιλίας εἶδος τὸ καθ' ὑ., where one *exceeds* the other in rank, etc., Arist.*EN*1158$^{b}$12, cf. 1161$^{a}$20: pl., κατὰ πλούτων ὑπεροχάς Pl.*Lg.*711d; οἱ ἐν ὑπεροχαῖς εὐτυχημάτων ὄντες Arist. *Pol.*1295$^{b}$14. 3. alone, *supremacy, authority, dignity*, Plb.1.64.1; τὴν Σελεύκου τοῦ βασιλέως ὑ. Antiph.187.4; δαιμόνων ὑ. *OGI*383.75 (Nemrud Dagh, i B.C.); οἱ ἐν ὑπεροχαῖς νεανίσκοι D.S.4.41; οἱ ἐν ὑπεροχῇ ὄντες *PTeb.*734.24 (ii B.C.), 1*Ep.Ti.*2.2; ἀνὴρ ἐν ὑ. κείμενος Lxx 2*Ma.*3.11. 4. of language, *periphrasis, prolixity*, opp. ἔλλειψις, Pl.*Plt.*283c. 5. as a title, *Excellency*, Just.*Nov.*25.5; ἡ ὑμετέρα Ὑ. *POxy.*130.20 (vi A.D.). **-ικός**, ή, όν, *involving pre-eminence*, Heliod. *in EN*180.2, Eust.1384.44. Adv. -κῶς *pre-eminently*, Eustr. *in EN* 29.25. ※ **-ος**, Ep. and Ion. **ὑπείρ-**, ον, (ὑπερέχω II) *prominent, eminent, distinguished above* others, c. gen., ὑπείροχον ἔμμεναι ἄλλων Il.6.208, 11.784: abs., ὑπείροχον εἶδος *h.Hom.*12.2; οἱ ὑπέροχοι (v.l. ὑπείροχοι) τῶν ἀστῶν Hdt.5.92.η'; θῆρες ἐν πελάγεϊ ὑπέροχοι *mighty*, Pi.*N.*3.24; ὑπέροχον σθένος A.*Pr.*428 (lyr.); ὑπέροχος βία *overbearing* force, S.*Tr.*1096 codd. (sed leg. βίᾳ); ὑ. Νίκα B.3.5; συρικτὰν μέγ' ὑπείροχον Theoc.7.28; οἰωνῶν μέγ' ὑ. ἀγγελιώτην Call. *Jov.*68: Sup. ὑπεροχώτατος Pi.*P.*2.38 (as a title, *PMasp.*4.5 (vi A.D.)): neut. pl. ὑπείροχα as Adv., *IG*12(5).678.21 (Syros, metr.).

**ὑπεροψία**, ἡ, *contempt, disdain*, τῶν νόμων Th.1.84; τῶν συμμάχων Isoc.8.96; ἡ πρὸς τὰς κολάσεις ὑ. J.*BJ*3.7.33: abs., Lys.12.93, Isoc. 12.242, Phld.*Vit.*p.29 J., Alex.Aphr. *in Top.*254.26, etc.

**ὑπέροψις**, εως, ἡ, *taking no notice*, Lxx *Le.*20.4.

**ὑπερόψομαι**, v. ὑπερoράω.

**ὑπεροψωνέω**, *outbid in the purchase of provisions*, Phryn.*PS*p. 117 B. (*Com.Adesp.*1181), where however the Ms. reading ὑποψόνην (leg. ὑποψωνεῖν) may be a quotation of Ar.*Ach.*842.

**ὑπερπᾰγής**, ές, *very frosty*: τὸ ὑ. *excessive frost*, X.*Cyn.*8.2.

**ὑπερπᾰθ-έω**, *to be grievously distressed*, ὑπερπαθήσασ' E.*Ph.*1456; ὑπερεπάθησε J.*AJ*7.2.1. ※ **-ής**, ές, *grievous*, Phleg.*Fr.*36.1 J., Tz. *H.*1.784 (Sup.). Adv. -θῶς Sch.Ptol.*Tetr.*158.

※ **ὑπερπαίω**, mostly used in pf. -πέπαικα, *overstrike, surpass, exceed*, c. gen., πολὺ δ' ὑπερπέπαικεν τούτων Ar.*Ec.*1118: c. acc., τοσοῦτον ὑπερπέπαικας πλούτῳ τοὺς ἄλλους D.50.34, cf. Plb.14.5.14, J.*Ap.*1.24, Luc.*Im.*9, Aristocl.ap.Eus.*PE*15.2, Hld.7.9, Iamb. *in Nic.*p.32 P.; τὰ -παίοντα χρήματα *Supp.Epigr.*3.509 (Thrace, iii A.D.).

**ὑπερπᾰλύνω**, *overspread* or *smear over*, ὑπὲρ καλαμίδα παλύνας *AP* 10.11 (Satyr.).

**ὑπερπάσχω**, *to be over-passionate*, Ptol.*Tetr.*188 (s. v.l., ὑπερπαθῶς lemma ap.Sch.).

**ὑπερπαφλάζω**, *bubble* or *boil over*, Luc.*Lex.*8.

**ὑπερπᾰχ-ύνομαι**, Pass., *to be* or *become exceedingly fat*, Thphr. *CP*5.11.3. **-υς**, υ, *exceedingly fat*, Hp.*Aër.*15, Plu.*Cat.Ma.*9; *very thick*, πλῆθος ὑ., of πτισάνη, Hp.*Acut.*11; of ships, *with very thick timbers*, D.C.49.1. (In Hp.*Aër.* l.c. nom. pl. -πάχητες, v.l. -πάχυτες.)

**ὑπερπείθομαι**, Pass., *to be more than convinced*, Poll.5.152; -πεποιθώς *Gloss.*

**ὑπερπεινάω**, *to be excessively hungry*, Gal.12.288,351.

**ὑπερπέλομαι**, *to be superior to*, ἄλλων νήσων A.R.4.1637.

**ὑπερπενθέω**, *mourn exceedingly*, c. acc., Philostr.*VS*2.1.8.

**ὑπερπεπαίνομαι**, Pass., *to be* or *become over-ripe*, Apollon.*Lex.* s.v. πέπον, *EM*661.55.

**ὑπερπεράω**, *pass beyond*, τὸν σφιγκτῆρα Paul.Aeg.3.43.

**ὑπερπερικλῆς**, ὁ, *a super-Pericles*, *Com.Adesp.*1178.

**ὑπερπερισσ-εύω**, *abound much more, be in great excess*, χάρις *Ep. Rom.*5.20:—Med., ὑ. τῇ χαρᾷ 2*Ep.Cor.*7.4. **-ῶς**, Adv. *beyond all measure*, *Ev.Marc.*7.37.

**ὑπερπέσσω**, *digest very quickly*, Hp.*Loc.Hom.*44 (vulg. -πεσεῖν).

**ὑπερπέταμαι**, = ὑπερπέτομαι, *AP*5.258 (Paul. Sil.), 7.546, 12.249 (Strat.).

**ὑπερπετάννυμι**, *stretch over*, παραπετάσματα ὑπέρ τινων D.C.43.

24. II. ὑπερπετασθῆναι is aor. of ὑπερπέτομαι (q.v.) in D.S.4.51, Luc.*Rh.Pr.*6.

**ὑπερπετής**, ές, *flying over* or *above*, τοῦ τείχους ὑπερπετῆ γιγνόμενα τὰ βέλη Aen.Tact.32.10; βέλη ὑ. τῶν πρωτοστατῶν φερόμενα darts *flying over* their *heads*, Plb.18.30.3, cf. 8.7.3, D.S.14.23; ὑ. ὄρνεις Str.5.4.5; τὸ ὑ. *all that flies over*, Id.15.1.38; ὑ. πνεῖν, of winds, Id. 15.3.10: metaph., *high-flying*, Luc.*Pr.Im.*17. II. *stretching beyond, reaching high*, θωράκια Plb.8.4.4; φάλαγξ *outflanking*, D.H.9. 11: c. gen., ὑ. τῆς πνοῆς *far above*, D.S.17.7; κορυφὴ -εστέρα τῆς καμήλου *reaching higher*, Str.16.4.16; ἐὰν βίᾳ τις τὸ κλύσμα ἐνθλίβων ὑπερπετὲς αὐτὸ ποιήσῃ *too high*, Mnesith.ap.Orib.8.38.9.

**ὑπερπέτομαι**, also -**πέταμαι**, -**ίπταμαι** (qq.v.): Ep. aor. -πτάμην, in Prose -επτόμην Arist.*HA*597ᵃ12: aor. Act. -έπτην S.*Ant.* (v. infr.), Ph.1.165: in late Prose also -επετάσθην (v. infr.): (v. πέτομαι):—*fly over*, of a spear, ὑπέρπτατο χάλκεον ἔγχος Il.13.408, 22. 275, cf. Od.22.280; of birds, Arist.*HA*541ᵃ28, Philostr.*VA*2.10: aor. Act., ἀετὸς ἐς γᾶν ὑπερέπτα S.*Ant.*113 (anap.). 2. c. acc., *fly over* or *beyond*, ὁ δ' [λᾶας] ὑπέρπτατο σήματα πάντων Od.8.192; of birds, ὑ. τὸ ὄρος Arist.*HA*597ᵃ12; ὑπερπετασθῆναι πολλὰ μέρη τῆς οἰκουμένης D.S.4.51, cf. Luc.*Rh.Pr.*6: also c. gen., A.R.2.1252, Plu.*Pomp.*25. 3. metaph., *skip over*, εἴδη καὶ γένη Ph.1.165.

**ὑπερπήγνυμαι**, Pass., with pf. -πέπηγα, *to be fixed above*, Hp. *Epid.*6.3.8. II. *become exceedingly thick*, Orib.*Fr.*116; ὑποχύματα ὑπερπεπηγότα Paul.Aeg.6.21.

**ὑπερπηδ-άω**, *leap over*, τοὺς δρυφάκτους Ar.*Eq.*675; τὸν ποταμόν Luc.*Ind.*7. II. metaph., *overleap*, in various senses, 1. *escape from*, θεοῦ..πληγὴν οὐχ ὑ. βροτός S.*Fr.*961. 2. *overstep, transgress*, νόμιμα D.23.73, cf. Aeschin.3.12,200, Hyp.*Lyc.* 12. 3. *surpass*, ὑ. τῷ μηχανήματι τοὺς σύμπαντας Pl.*Lg.*677e, cf. Ael.*NA*6.25. 4. abs., *pass over*, εἴς τι Arist.*Metaph.*1027ᵇ6. 5. of a roller, *skip* a point, Id.*Mech.*855ᵇ26; so, *pass over, omit*, ἑκόντα ὑ. Lib.*Or.*59.80, cf. *Ep.*925.1. -**ησις**, εως, ἡ, *a leaping over*, Plu. 2.371b codd. (leg. ὑπεκ-).

**ὑπερπιαίνω**, *make exceedingly fat*, Gal.*Protr.*12.

⊛ **ὑπέρπικρος**, ον, *exceedingly sharp in temper*, τὸν πικρῶς ὑ. A.*Pr.* 944.

**ὑπερπίμπλημι**, *overfill*, τοὺς ποταμοὺς Ael.*NA*16.12:—mostly in Pass., *to be overfull*, Hp.*Int.*10: διὰ τὸ ὑπερπεπλῆσθαι Arist.*HA*625ᵇ4; πίνειν ἕως ἂν ὑπερπλησθῇ Id.*EN*1118ᵇ17: c. gen., ὑπερπλησθεὶς μέθης S.*OT*779; ὕβρις, εἰ πολλῶν ὑπερπλησθῇ ib.874 (lyr.).

**ὑπερπίνω** [ῑ], *drink overmuch*, X.*Cyr.*8.8.10.

**ὑπερπίπτω**, *fall over, run over*, of water, Plb.4.39.8; *run over, project*, τῶν τροπικῶν εἰς.. Str.2.2.2, cf. 2.5.27; *fall over the edge, roll off*, Arr.*Tact.*11.6. 2. *fall beyond* a point, *pass over*, [ὁ νότος] ὑ. [τῆς Αἰγύπτου] Arist.*Pr.*945ᵃ25; ὄρεα ὑπερπίπτοντα [πνεύματα] winds *which pass over* mountains, Hp.*Vict.*2.38; of missiles, Aen. Tact.32.9; of a badly adjusted νευρά in a torsion-engine, ἤτοι ὑπελεύσεται τὸν λίθον ἢ ὑπερπεσεῖται αὐτόν *will slip over the top of* the projectile, Hero *Bel.*112. 3. of a number, *exceed*, Vett.Val.352. 13; also τὸν -πίπτοντα ἄρσενα the *excess* of males, *PTeb.*701.45 (iii B.C.), cf. *PCair.Zen.*327.46, 569.131 (iii B.C.). II. of Time, *to be past, gone by*, ἣν ὑπερπέσῃ ἡ νῦν ἡμέρη Hdt.3.71, cf. Hp.*Mul.*2. 133; but ὁ -πεσὼν χρόνος *over*time for which interest is due, *PPetr.* 3 p.160 (iii B.C.), *PAmh.*2.50.19 (ii B.C.), *POxy.*1040.25 (iii A.D.), etc.

**ὑπερπλάζω**, *toss on high*, τὰς χεῖρας Euph.44.

**ὑπερπλεονάζω**, *abound exceedingly*, 1 *Ep.Ti.*1.14, Vett.Val.85.17; ὁ -άζων ἀὴρ Hero *Spir.*1.10.

**ὑπέρπλεος**, ον, = ὑπέρπλεως, *abundant*, Tz.*H.*8.652; *additional*, μηδὲν λάβῃς ὑ. *BGU*412.20 (iv A.D.).

**ὑπέρπλεως**, ων, *overfull, surfeited*, γαστριμαργίαις Luc.*Am.*42, cf. Poll.4.186: cf. foreg.

**ὑπερπληθής**, ές, *superabundant*, Nicoch.11; ὑπερπληθῆ ἐξημαρτηκώς having done *more than enough* misdeeds, v.l. for παμπληθῆ in D.26.7.

**ὑπερπλημμυρέω**, *overflow*, *Gloss.*

**ὑπερπλήρ-ης**, ες, *overfull*, Plot.5.2.1, Jul.*Or.*4.140b, Procl.*Inst.* 131, Dam.*Pr.*307, etc. -**όω**, *fill overfull*, X.*Cyr.*8.2.22:—Pass., *to be overfull, gorged*, Id.*Lac.*5.3, Arist.*HA*594ᵇ20, *GA*738ᵃ12, Gal.15. 39. -**ωσις**, εως, ἡ, *excessive repletion*, Id.4.756, Orib.8.32.6, al.

**ὑπερπλούσιος**, ον, *over-wealthy*, Arist.*Pol.*1295ᵇ7.

**ὑπερπλουτ-έω**, *to be exceedingly rich*, Ar.*Pl.*354, Luc.*Tim.*10, etc.; τὸ ἱερὸν ὑ. ἐν τοῖς ἀναθήμασιν Id.*Phal.*2.9. -**ος**, ον, = ὑπερπλούσιος, χλιδή A.*Pr.*466, cf. Pl.*R.*552b.

**ὑπερπνέω**, *blow beyond*, ἄνεμοι τῆς ὥρας ὑ. *beyond* the season, Philostr.*VA*8.7 (πέρα πν. cj. Kayser). II. metaph., c. acc., *raise oneself proudly above*, τοὺς Ἀθηναίους Id.*VS*2.10.2; *despise*, Theoc. 29.19 (tm., dub.).

**ὑπερπνιγής**, ές, = ὑπέρασθμος, Anon.ap.Suid., cf. eund. s. v. ἐκτραχηλίζω.

**ὑπερποθέω**, *desire excessively*, Aristid.*Or.*42(6).1, Sch.rec.Pi.*O.*8. 81 (Pass.).

**ὑπερπολάζω**, *overflow*, Str.1.3.6, Hsch. s. v. ζέσεν; εἰς.. Str.17.1. 37.

**ὑπέρπολυς**, -πόλλη, -πολυ, Ion. **ὑπέρπολλος**, η, ον, *overmuch*, and in pl. *over many*, A.*Pers.*794, Hp.*Epid.*4.38, X.*HG*3.2.26, D.43. 69:—ὑπέρπουλυ in Hp.*Epid.*2.2.23.

**ὑπερπον-έω**, *toil* or *labour beyond measure, undergo excessive strain*, X.*Mem.*1.2.4, *Eq.Mag.*4.1; ὑ. τῷ πολέμῳ Plu.*Nic.*21. II. *bear* or *endure for* others, σφὼ δ' ἀντ' ἐκείνων τἀμὰ δυστήνου κακὰ ὑπερπονεῖτον S.*OC*345; ὠδῖνας Pl.*Lg.*717c. 2. in Med. c. gen. pers., τοῦδ' ὑπερπονουμένῳ θανεῖν S.*Aj.*1310. -**ος**, ον, *quite worn out*, διὰ γῆρας Plu.*Alex.*61, cf. Anon.ap.Suid. s.v. ὑπερπνιγεῖς.

**ὑπερπόντιος**, ον, also α, ον Pi.*P.*5.59, A.*Ag.*414 (lyr.):—*over the sea*, πόθῳ δ' ὑπερποντίας, i.e. for Helen, A. l.c., cf. *Supp.*41 (lyr.); φοιτᾷς ὑπερπόντιος S.*Ant.*785 (lyr.); ὑπάρχοντα..ὑ. properties *overseas*, *IG*12(7).67.44 (Amorgos, iv/iii B.C.). 2. *from beyond the sea*, i.e. *foreign, strange*, γλῶσσα Pi. l.c.

**ὑπερποτάομαι**, poet. for ὑπερπέτομαι, Lyc.17.

⊛ **ὑπερπράξιον**, τό, *over-exaction, extortion*, *CIG*2712.7 (Mylasa).

⊛ **ὑπερπράσσω**, Att. -ττω, *extort more than is due*, τῷ ὑπερπραχθέντι to the person *from whom too much has been extorted*, *Cod.Just.*1.4. 29.10.

**ὑπερπρόθεσμος**, ον, = ὑπερήμερος, Suid. s. h. v.

**ὑπέρπτᾰτο**, v. ὑπερπέτομαι.

**ὑπέρπτωχος**, ον, *exceedingly poor*, Arist.*Pol.*1295ᵇ7.

**ὑπερπυππάζω**, *acclaim beyond measure*, τινα Ar.*Eq.*680.

⊛ **ὑπέρπῡρος**, ον, *exceedingly fiery*, Arist.*Resp.*477ᵇ29, Thphr.*CP*1.21. 5. 2. *put over* or *on the fire*, ἀπαρχαί D.H.2.31, 6.14.

**ὑπερπυρριάω**, aor. -ίᾱσα, *blush scarlet for* another, τινος Ar.*Ra.* 308.

**ὑπερπώρωσις**, εως, ἡ, *excessive callus-formation* in fractures, Paul. Aeg.6.108.

**ὑπερπωτάομαι**, poet. for ὑπερπέτομαι, Theoc.15.120.

**ὑπερρέω**, aor. ὑπερερρύην, *overflow*, Plot.5.2.1.

**ὑπερρίπτω**, *throw* the arm *over* a cross-bar, Apollon.Cit.1.

⊛ **ὑπερσαρκ-έω**, *have* or *get an excess of flesh*, ὑ. τὸ ἕλκος *grows proud* or *fungous flesh*, Hp.*VC*15 (ὑπερσαρκίσῃ is f.l.), cf. Poll.4.191. 2. of persons, ὑπὸ τρυφῆς καὶ ἀδηφαγίας ὑ. Nymphis 16, cf. Ael.*VH*9. 13. -**ημα**, ατος, τό, = ὑπερσάρκωμα, Orib.*Fr.*10 (pl.). -**όω**, = ὑπερσαρκέω, ἕλκος -ῶσαν Sor.2.36, cf. Ps.-Gal.14.772. -**ος**, ον, *covered with flesh*, [ἵπποι] ῥάχιν ὑπέρσαρκοι Ar.Byz.*Epit.*147. 26. -**ωμα**, ατος, τό, *overgrown flesh*, in pl., Dsc.2.73, Vett.Val.109. 33, Aët.7.66. -**ωσις**, εως, ἡ, *overgrowth of flesh*, Hp.*Epid.*5.100, Dsc.1.107 (pl.).

**ὑπερσέβω**, *reverence excessively*, Sch.Ptol.*Tetr.*61.

**ὑπερσέληνος**, ον, *above the moon*, f.l. for ὑπο-, Dam.*Pr.*110.

**ὑπερσεμν-ος**, ον, *exceedingly grave, very solemn* or *holy*, ὑ. χρῆμα, of the Temple, Ph.2.589, cf. Ael.*NA*2.6. -**ύνομαι**, *to be exceedingly solemn* or *pompous*, X.*Smp.*3.11:—Act. -ύνω, *extol*, D.C.57.24.

**ὑπερσεύομαι**, pf. -έσσυμαι, *hasten over*, ὀρέων ἄκρας Q.S.2.183.

**ὑπερσῑτίζω**, *eat largely*, Philostr.*Gym.*48 codd. (-σιτήσ- Cobet).

**ὑπερσκελής**, ές, *with one leg too long*, σῶμα Pl.*Ti.*87e.

**ὑπερσκληρως**, Adv. *with excessive severity*, *PRein.*47.13 (ii A.D.).

**ὑπερσοφιστ-εύω**, *to be an arch-sophist*, Philostr.*VS*2.2. -**ής**, οῦ, ὁ, *arch-sophist*, Phryn.Com.69.

**ὑπέρσοφος**, ον, *exceedingly wise* or *clever*, Ar.*Ach.*972 (lyr.), Pl. *Euthd.*289e; τὸ ὑ. τῆς τέχνης Philostr.*Her.*10.1.

**ὑπερσπεύδω**, *hasten excessively*, Diogenian.6.26, Sch.Ar.*Ra.*1180.

**ὑπέρσπονδος**, ον, *truce-breaking*, gloss on ὑπερφίαλος, Sch.Il.15. 94.

**ὑπερσπουδ-άζω**, *take exceedingly great pains*, περί τι Luc.*Anach.* 9, Philostr.*VA*5.26; ὑπερεσπουδακὼς τὰ τοῦ γάμου πράττειν Men. *Sam.*4, cf. J.*AJ*15.3.6:—Pass., τῇ κωμῳδίᾳ τὸ τοιοῦτον ὑπερεσπούδασται Eust.1277.48. -**ος**, ον, *exceedingly nervous* or *earnest*, Poll. 6.29.

**ὑπερστατέω**, *protect*, ἡ δίκη γε ξυμμάχων ὑπερστατεῖ A.*Supp.*343.

**ὑπερστείχω**, *walk* or *pass over*, κολώνην Heliod.ap.Stob.4.36. 8.

**ὑπερστένω**, *groan for*, σῶν ὑ. πόνων A.*Pr.*66 (nisi leg. ὕπερ στένω).

**ὑπερστέργω**, *love excessively*, Poll.5.113.

**ὑπερστερητικός**, ή, όν, *doubly privative*, of ἀάατος, Eust.985.16.

**ὑπερστήμων**, dub. sens. in Hsch. s. v. ὑπεραγοναστάς.

**ὑπερστίλβω**, *shine exceedingly*, Poll.3.71.

**ὑπερσυνεχής**, ές, *more than continuous*, Simp. *in Ph.*879.5.

**ὑπερσυντέλικος** χρόνος, Gramm., *pluperfect* tense, D.T.638.24, A.D.*Synt.*281.6, Choerob. *in Theod.*2.12 H., etc.; without χρόνος, A.D *Adv.*124.18, *EM*483.51, etc.; ὑ. διάθεσις is f.l. for συντ. in A.D. *Synt.*70.8.

**ὑπερσχεθεῖν, ὑπέρσχῃ, ὑπέρσχοι**, v. ὑπερέχω.

**ὑπερσχετικόν**, *superabile*, *Gloss.* (ὑπερεσχ- codd.).

**ὑπερσωκράτης**, ὁ, *a super-Socrates*, *Com.Adesp.*1179.

**ὑπερτᾰλαντάω**, *outweigh*, *EM*744.15.

**ὑπέρταξις**, εως, ἡ, *superior order*, Dam.*Pr.*359.

**ὑπέρτᾰσις**, εως, ἡ, *excessive tension*, Anon.Lond.2.28. 2. ὑ. ὑπέρ τι *elevation* above.., M.Ant.10.8.

**ὑπέρτᾰτος**, η, ον, poet. Sup. of ὑπέρ, *uppermost, highest*: I. mostly of Place or position, ἧστο ὑ. Il.23.451; κεῖτο ὑ. 12.381; ὑ. δώματα, θρόνος, etc., Hes.*Op.*8, Pi.*O.*2.77 (dub. l.), etc. 2. of gods, partly in reference to their abode, partly to their power, ib. 4.1, A.*Supp.*672 (lyr., nisi leg. -τως, v. infr. 4): then simply, 3. of rank or power, θεῶν τὰν ὑ. S.*Ant.*338 (lyr.); δαιμόνων ὑ. Ar.*Av.* 1765 (lyr.); ἄνασσα Περσίδων ὑ. A.*Pers.*155 (troch.). 4. of things, ὑ. ὄλβος, ἀνορέαι, Pi.*P.*3.89, *N.*3.20; μόχθοι, σέβας, S.*OC*105, *Ph.*402 (lyr.), etc.; τὰν ἐκ πασᾶν ὑ. πόλεων Id.*Ant.*1138 (lyr.); φρένας, πάντων ὅσ' ἐστὶ χρημάτων ὑ. ib.684; τοῦτο κερδέων ὑπέρτατον B.3.84: in late Prose, ἀρετή *PStrassb.*40.41 (vi A.D.). Adv. -τως *above all*, A. *Supp.*672 (Ahrens from Sch.); *above all measure*, Sch.rec.Pi.*O.*1.

1. II. of age, *eldest*, Pi.*N*.6.21 :—Pi. has also **ὑπερώτατος**, *N*.8. 43 : cf. ὑπέρτερος III fin.

**ὑπερτείνω**, I. trans., *stretch* or *lay above*, ξύλα Hdt.4.71 ; *hold out over*, σῷ κάρᾳ κύκλον E.*El*.1257 ; ὑ. σκιὰν σειρίου κυνός *stretch over* [the house] a shade from the sun, A.*Ag*.967, cf. E.*El*.1022 ; ὑ. χεῖρά τινος *stretch* the hand *over* one *for protection*, Id.*IA*916 (troch.) ; also ὑ. πόδα ἀκτῆς *stretch* one's foot *over* the beach, i. e. pass over it, Id.*Med*.1288, cf. *Fr*.676. 2. *strain to the uttermost*, τὴν ἐπιθυμίαν J.*AJ*4.6.1 ; τιμωρίαν Plu.*Publ*.12 :—Pass., τὸ ὑπερτεταμένον *high-strained language*, Longin.12.5 ; τὰ ὑ. Id.10.1, cf. 38.1 ; = signf. II.2 infr., ὑπερτεταμένη ἔκλυσις, τρυφή, λύπη, *extreme* relaxation, etc., Sor.1.34, 2.54,58. II. intr., *stretch* or *jut out over*, ὑπὲρ τοῦ τείχους Th.2.76 ; εἰς τὸ ἔξω X.*Cyn*.9.15 ; but also c. acc., ὑ. τὸ κέρας *outflank* the enemy's wing, Id.*HG*4.2.19. 2. metaph., *go beyond, exceed the measure* or *number of*.., c. gen., D.61.16, Arist.*Pol*.1319$^b$13 : c. acc., *exceed*, τὴν ἀνθρωπίνην φύσιν Id.*EN*1110$^a$25 ; ὑ. τοῖς χρόνοις τὴν Μίνω βασιλείαν Id.*Pol*.1329$^b$24 ; τὸ ἀλγοῦν -τεῖνον τὸ ἡδόμενον Epicur.*Sent*.4 : c. dat. modi, *exceed others* in a thing, ταῖς οὐσίαις Arist.*Pol*.1293$^a$30 ; τῷ πλήθει ib.1296$^a$16 (but ἐὰν τὸ τῶν γεωργῶν -τείνῃ πλῆθος ib.1296$^b$28) ; ὑ. τῷ καλῷ *exceed* in.., Id.*EN*1165$^a$3, cf. 1171$^b$8 ; ὑ. ὁ κίνδυνος *is extreme*, ib.1116$^b$16. 3. in Logic, *exceed, comprehend more than*, τὸ Β ὑ. τοῦ Α, opp. ἀντιστρέφει (is convertible), Id.*APr*.33$^a$39, cf. 68$^b$24.

**Ὑπερτελεάτας** [ᾰτ], α, ὁ, epith. of Apollo at Cotyrta, *IG*5(1).961, al.

⊛ **ὑπερτέλ-ειος**, ον, (τέλος) *beyond completeness* or *perfection*, αὐλοὶ ὑ., = ἀνδρεῖοι, Poll.4.81, cf. Aristox.*Fr.Hist*.67. 2. of numbers, = ὑπερτελής II.1, Theo Sm.p.45 H. **-έω**, *overleap*, δουλείας γάγγαμον A.*Ag*.359 (anap.). II. *pay in addition*, *Stud.Pal*.22.183.42 (ii A.D., Pass.), *PSI*1.66.22 (v A.D.). **-ής**, ές, *overleaping* : of a beacon, *leaping over the strait*, A.*Ag*.286. 2. c. gen., *rising* or *appearing above*, τίς οἴκων..ὑ...θεῶν; E.*Ion*1549; ἄθλων ὑ. *one who has reached the end* of his labours, S.*Tr*.36. II. of numbers the sum of whose factors (including unity) *is greater than themselves* (such as 12, because 1 + 2 + 3 + 4 + 6 = 16), opp. ἐλλιπεῖς, Nicom.*Ar*.1.14, cf. Mart.Cap.7.753 ; of the μονάς, *Theol.Ar*.3 ; cf. ὑπερτέλειος 2. 2. of payments, *due*, *PSI*1.66.21 (v A.D.).

**ὑπερτέλλω**, *rise over* or *above*, ὁ ἥλιος ὑπερτείλας the sun *when he has risen above the horizon* and reached a certain height, Hdt.3. 104 ; φλὸξ -τέλλουσα γῆς E.*Fr*.772 ; τοὺς -τείλαντας ἐκ γαίας *sprung* from the ground, Id.*Ph*.1007 : c. gen., φαρέων μαστὸς ὑπερτέλλων *appearing above* her dress, Id.*Or*.841 (lyr.) ; κορυφῆς ὑπερτέλλων πέτρος the stone *hanging over* the head [of Tantalus], ib.6, cf. *AP*5.235 (Paul. Sil.) : rarely c. dat., ib.9.656 (v/vi A.D.) ; ὥρα ὥρας μυρία (fort. μορίῳ) ὑπερτείλασα Vett.Val.343.16 :—also in Med., Opp.*H*. 5.126.

**ὑπερτενής**, ές, *stretching over, laid over*, χαλκὸν..ἀσπίδος ὑ. A.*Fr*. 128. II. abs., *tall*, πίτυς Apollod.1.4.2 ; but ὑπερτενῆ κρεμάσας ἐκ πίτυος Zen.4.81.

⊛ **ὑπερτερ-έω**, *surpass*, ὁ θεὸς δυνάμει πάντων ὑ. Them.*Or*.13.170a ; εἴς τι Sch.Luc.*Pro Merc.Cond*.12. 2. Astrol., = καθυπερτερέω, *Cat.Cod.Astr*.2.171. **-ία**, Ion. **-ίη**, ἡ, *the upper part* or *body of a carriage*, opp. to the axle and wheels, Od.6.70, *IG*1².313. 114, al., Pl.*Tht*.207a. II. *pre-eminence*, Thgn.418. III. = ὑπερηφανία, Hsch.(pl.). ⊛ **-ος**, α, ον, poet. Comp. from ὑπέρ (used also in late Prose) : I. mostly of Place, *over* or *above, upper*, κρέ' ὑπέρτερα flesh *from the outer parts of a victim, outside* pieces (opp. the σπλάγχνα or inwards), Od.3.65,470, cf. Arat.576 (cf. Sch.) : generally, *higher*, τὰ δ' ὑ. νέρτερα θήσει Ζεύς Ar.*Lys*.772 (hex.). 2. metaph., *nobler, more excellent*, εὖχος, κῦδος, Il.11.290, 12.437 ; γενεῇ ὑ. 11.786 (where Eust. takes it as an Ion. form for νεώτερος, 884.33, cf. Archil.28, and v. ὑπέρτατος II). b. *stronger, mightier*, ἐξ ὑπερτέρας χερός S.*El*.455. 3. c. gen., *victorious* or *triumphant over*, δαΐων Pi.*N*.4.38 ; ἀντιπάλων Wilcken *Chr*.109.4 (iii B.C.), *OGI*90.2 (Rosetta, ii B.C.) ; ἡμῶν γε..Νέμεσίς ἐσθ' ὑ. A.*Fr*.266, cf. E.*Med*. 921 ; εἰ τἄδικ' ἔσται τῆς δίκης ὑ. Id.*El*.584 ; πρᾶγμα καὶ ἀσχολίας ὑπέρτερον θήσομαι I will prefer *above*.., Pi.*I*.1.2, cf. *P*.2.60 ; εἴ τι τῶνδ' ἔχοις ὑ. *better than*.., A.*Ch*.105 ; τὰ πάντα, χὤτι τῶνδ' ὑ. Id. *Fr*.70 ; οὐδὲν οἶδ' ὑ. nothing *further*, S.*Ant*.16. II. of Time, *longer*, ζωὴν ζήσω δορκάδος ὑπερτέραν Aesop.16$^b$. III. neut. as Adv., μάντεων ὑ. *better than*.., S.*Ant*.631, cf. A.*Th*.530 :—also -έρως, Apollon.*Lex*. ; -έρω Them.*Or*.11.152c ; cf. ἀνωτέρω.—A second Comp. form ὑπερτερώτερος is cited from A. (v. Nauck ad *Fr*. 434), whence it is conjectured by Weil for ὑπερβατώτερα in *Ag*. 428 (lyr.) : cf. ὑπέρτατος fin.

**ὑπερτετρᾰκισχίλιοι** [χῑ], αι, α, *above* 4000, J.*AJ*18.1.5 : sg., πλῆθος -χίλιον Ph.2.457.

**ὑπέρτεχνος**, ον, *exceedingly artificial* or *ingenious*, Hsch.

**ὑπερτήκω**, *melt exceedingly*, Str.3.2.8, Lxx 4 *Ma*.7.12 (Pass.).

⊛ **ὑπερτίθημι**, I. the literal senses only in late writers, 1. *set higher, erect*, βωμόν *IG*14.1020 (Rome). 2. *set on the other side, carry over*, τὸ ἄροτρον Plu.*Rom*.11 ; ὑ. τὸ βῶ *transpose* it, Paus. 3.13.5 :—so in Pass., A.D.*Synt*.8.20 ; of accent, *to be shifted*, Id.*Adv*. 189.26 :—Med., ὑπερθέσθαι τινὰ πέραν ποταμοῦ Plb.21.39.9. 3. c. acc. loci, *cross, pass over*, τὸν Ταῦρον Str.14.4.3 :—Med., ὑπερθέσθαι τὴν ἄκραν *double* it, D.S.13.3 : cf. ὑπέρθεσις I.2. b. *shoot over*, ταῖς βολαῖς τὸ τῆς φάλαγγος βάθος Ael.*Tact*.4.3. 4. Med., *hold over*, so as to protect, παιδὸς ὑπὲρ χέρα θηκαμένα *AP*6.280. II. metaph., παντὶ θεὸν αἴτιον ὑπερτιθέμεν *set* God *over* all as cause, Pi.*P*.5.25. 2. *hand over* or *communicate* a thing to another, εἰ..τοὶ ὑπερετίθεα (Ion. for -ετίθην) τὰ ἔμελλον ποιήσειν Hdt.3.155, cf. 5.32 :—so in Med., esp. in order to ask advice, Γύγῃ τὰ σπουδαιέστερα τῶν πρηγμάτων Id.1.8 ; τοῖσι ὀνειροπόλοισι τὸ ἐνύπνιον ib.107, cf. 5.56 ; ἐπεί τε ἐμοὶ ὑπερέθεσθε [ταῦτα] Id.3.71, cf. 5.24, 7.18. 3. Med., *set oneself above, surpass, exceed, excel*, τινὰ ταῖς χορηγίαις, κατὰ τὴν ὠμότητα, Plb.2.63.3, 18.17.3 ; ἀτὸν (= αὐτὸν) ἐν τῇ πρὸς τὸν δῆμον εὐεργεσίᾳ *IG*12 (5).860.27 (Tenos, i B.C.), cf. 2².1304.19 (iii B.C.), *OGI*339.61 (Sestos, ii B.C.) : abs., ὑ. τῇ μεγαλοψυχίᾳ *IG*2².1043.65 ; ὑ. τῇ φιλοπονίᾳ ib.12 (5).129.10, cf. 27 (Paros, ii B.C.) :—Act., ὑπερτ[ιθ]εὶς..ἑατὸν τῇ πρὸς τὰ κοινὰ σπουδῇ καὶ φιλοτιμίᾳ *Ath.Mitt*.35.413 (= *IGRom*.4.293a ii 3, Pergam., ii B.C.). 4. of Time, *outlast, outlive*, τὰ τετταράκοντα ἔτη σπανίως ὑπερτιθέασιν Str.16.4.12, cf. Gal.19.565 :—Med., μόνην τὴν νύκτα ὑπερθεμένη *having let* it *pass*, Hld.1.10. 5. Med. also, *put off, defer*, *PEleph*.11.5 (iii B.C.), etc. ; ὑ. τὴν ἐπανόρθωσιν ποιῆσαι Epict.*Ench*.51.1 ; ὑ. τι εἰς τὴν ἐσομένην σύνοδον *IG*7.2711.49 (Acraeph., i A.D.) ; εἰς ἄλλον καιρὸν ἐπιτηδειότερον Phld.*Rh*.1.212 S. ; τὴν ταχθεῖσαν ἡμέραν Plb.5.29.3, etc. : abs., *delay*, Id.4.30.2, etc. :—Pass., *to be put off*, *Gp*.2.49.1. b. Med., *omit*, τὴν ῥαφὴν ὑπερθέμενοι Paul.Aeg.6.16. 6. Gramm., *to be formed as a superlative*, Δαναώτατος ὑπερτίθεται A.D.*Pron*.64.12, cf. *Adv*.168.1.

**ὑπερτῑμ-άω**, *honour exceedingly*, τινα S.*Ant*.284, Lxx 4 *Ma*.8.5 ; *prize overmuch*, Ph.1.112 :—Pass., Luc.*JTr*.48. **-ιος**, ον, *overdear*, ὑ. ἀγοράζειν τι Arist.*Oec*.1352$^b$7.

**ὑπερτοκέω**, in aor. *to be exhausted by breeding*, Thphr.*CP*2.11.4 ; cf. ὑπέρινος.

**ὑπέρτολμος**, ον, (τόλμα) *overbold*, ἀνδρὸς φρόνημα A.*Ch*.594 (lyr.).

**ὑπερτόν-αιον**, τό, *lintel* of a door or window, *IG*2².1672.164 : pl., ib. 463.56 (iv B.C.), 1668.31, 11(2).158*A*78 (Delos, iii B.C.), Poll.7.122. **-έω**, *to be overstrained*, Hp.*Mul*.1.1. **-ος**, ον, *strained to the utmost, at full pitch, exceeding loud*, γῆρυμα A.*Eu*. 569 ; βοά Ar.*Nu*.1154 (lyr.), Phryn.Com.46 (lyr.) : metaph., δύναμις ὑ. Plu.*Fab*.19 ; ὑ. τῷ κόπῳ *Hippiatr*.10. II. ὑπέρτονον (sc. ξύλον), τό, *main-beam*, *EM*576.16, Eust.249.20, 780.28. (Cf. διάτονος.)

**ὑπερτοξ-εύσιμος**, ον, *to be shot beyond*, μίασμ' ἔλεξας οὐχ ὑ. an abomination not *to be outdone*, A.*Supp*.473. **-εύω**, *overshoot*, Arr.*Tact*.5.5 (Pass.).

**ὑπερτρᾰγίζω**, *smell very rank like a he-goat*, τῇ ὀσμῇ Dsc.1.7.

**ὑπερτρέχω**, fut. -δρᾰμοῦμαι, and in Philetaer.3 (s.v.l.) -δραμῶ : aor. -έδρᾰμον : cf. ὑπερθέω :—*run over* or *beyond, outrun, escape from*, ἄκρην πενίην Thgn.620. 2. *prevail against*, ὥστε..θεῶν νόμιμα..θνητὸν ὄνθ' ὑπερδραμεῖν S.*Ant*.455 ; πῶς τὰ κρείσσω θνητὸς ὢν ὑπερδράμω; E.*Ion*973, cf. *Hel*.1524 ; ἣν δ' αὖ κρατηθῇς καὶ τὰ τοὔδ' ὑπερδράμῃ if..his fortune *prevail*, Id.*Ph*.578. 3. *excel, surpass*, εἰ θεὰς ὑπερδράμοι κάλλει Id.*Tr*.930, cf. Philetaer. l.c.

**ὑπερτρῐσύλλᾰβος**, ον, *of more than three syllables*, Hdn.Gr.1.131, *EM*459.48.

**ὑπέρτροπα**, τά, name of a way of tuning the cithara, Ptol.*Harm*. 1.16, 2.16.

**ὑπερτροχάζω**, *outstrip, go beyond*, Ph.1.173.

**ὑπερτρῠφάω**, *to be excessively luxurious and haughty*, Luc.*JTr*.48, D.C.62.28.

**ὑπερυβρίζω**, *maltreat excessively*, Poll.8.75, D.C.59.4.

**ὑπερυγραίνω**, *make too wet*, Hp.*Morb*.1.2 :—Pass., *become so*, Arist.*Mete*.365$^b$11.

**ὑπέρυγρος**, ον, *excessively liquid*, of sputum, Gal.17(2).395.

**ὑπερυδραργῠρίζω**, *outdo Hydrargyrus*, a famous thief, Tz.*H*.8. 449.

**ὑπέρυδρος**, ον, *overfull of water* : *very dropsical*, Hp.*Aff*.22.

**ὑπ-ερυθραίνω**, of a cosmetic, *impart a blush to*, τὸ πρόσωπον Aët.8. 6 :—Pass., *to be turned red*, αἵματι [Chor.]*Fr*.7 (p.283 B.). **-ερυθριάω**, aor. 1 -ίᾱσα, *grow rather red, blush a little*, Ar.*Pl*.702. **-έρυθρος**, ον, *reddish*, Hp.*Prog*.12, *Art*.86, Th.2.49, Pl.*R*.617a.

**ὑπερυμν-έω**, *extol exceedingly*, Thd.*Da*.3.(54) (Pass.). **-ητος**, ον, *highly extolled*, Lxx *Da*.3.(53).

**ὑπερῠπάται** (χορδαί), αἱ, *notes higher than the ὑπάτη*, Aristid.Quint. 1.6 : sg., Theo Sm.p.88 H.

**ὑπερυποκειμαι**, *to be over-mortgaged*, *PLond*.2.154.13 (i A.D.).

**ὑπερύψηλος**, ον, *exceeding high*, X.*An*.3.5.7, Arr.*An*.1.5.12, Ael. *VH*3.1, etc.

**ὑπερυψόω**, *exalt exceedingly*, τινα *Ep.Phil*.2.9 :—Pass., Lxx *Ps*. 36(37).35, 96(97).9.

**ὑπερφαίνομαι**, Pass., *appear, show oneself over* or *above*, τοῦ λόφου Th.4.93 ; τοῦ ποταμοῦ, i.e. on its bank, Plu.*Pyrrh*.16, cf. Arist.*HA* 550$^b$3, Euph.44 : also c. acc., ὑ. τὰ τείχη Plu.*Dio*39 : abs., *appear in the air above*, Arist.*HA*620$^b$2, Jul.*Or*.2.62d :—so in Act., δοιοὶ δὲ σκυνίοισιν ὑπερφαίνουσι μέτωπον οἷα τύλοι Nic.*Th*.177. 2. metaph., *to be superior*, Them.*Or*.1.11a.

**ὑπερφᾰλαγγ-έω**, *extend the line of one's phalanx so as to outflank the enemy on both wings*, Ascl.*Tact*.10.18, Arr.*Tact*.29.10, Ael.*Tact*. 38.1 : generally, *outflank*, X.*Cyr*.7.1.5, etc. : c. gen., ὑ. τοῦ στρατεύματος ib.6.3.20 ; ὑ. ὑπὲρ τὸ κέρας Arr.*Tact*.25.9. **-ησις**, εως, ἡ, *outflanking of the enemy's line on both wings*, ib.29.8,9, cf. ὑπερκέρασις :—so **-ίωσις**, Anon.ap.Suid. ; and **-ωσις**, *An.Ox*.3.163.

**ὑπερφᾰνής**, ές, (ὑπερφαίνομαι) *appearing over* or *above, out-topping*, δόρατα ταπεινὰ καὶ μὴ ὑπερφανῆ X.*Eq.Mag*.5.7 (cod.B, ὑπερηφανῆ cett.) : coupled with ὑπέργεια, Poll.5.150 (v.l. ἐπι-), cf. 9.20.

**ὑπέρφᾰσις**, εως, ἡ, = ὑπερηφανία, Hsch.

**ὑπέρφᾰτος**, ον, (φατός, φημί) *above speech, ineffable*, νιφετοῦ σθένος Pi.*Pae*.9.15; ὑ. ἀνὴρ μορφᾷ τε καὶ ἔργοισι Id.*O*.9.65.

**ὑπερφέγγεια**, ἡ, (φέγγος) *excessive shining*, Iamb.*VP*15.67.

**ὑπερφέρεια**, ἡ, (ὑπερφερής) *haughtiness, pride*, Aq.*Jb*.37.4, al.

**ὑπερφερέτης**, ου, ὁ, *the supreme one*: in D.H.2.34, = Lat. *Jupiter Feretrius*.

**ὑπερφερής**, ές, *pre-eminent, excellent*, Lxx *Da*.2.31, Hsch.: Comp., Anon.ap.Suid., Dionysius in *Wien.Stud*.20.319.

**ὑπερφέρω**, *bear* or *carry over*, ὑ. τὸν ἰσθμὸν τὰς ναῦς Th.3.81, cf. 15,87:—Pass., [νῆες] ὑπερενεχθεῖσαι τὸν ἰσθμόν Id.4.8; ὑπερενεχθῆναι τὰς δίνας D.H.3.56; νυκτὸς ὑπερφέρεσθαι (sc. τὸν Ταῦρον) Plu.2.510b; ὑ. ὑπὲρ.. X.*Oec*.18.7: c. gen., *to be transferred from*, τὰς τῶν..ζῴων διαφορὰς μὴ δυναμένας ὑπερενεχθῆναι τῶν κατὰ φύσιν τόπων Ptol.*Geog*.1.12.2. II. mostly intr., *to be prominent, stand out*, Plu.2.591c. 2. metaph., *surpass, excel, have the advantage over*, τινός τινι one in a thing, ῥόδα ὀδμῇ ὑπερφέροντα τῶν ἄλλων Hdt.8.138, cf. 9.96, Ar.*Eq*.584 (lyr.), Th.1.81: c. gen. only, τέχνη τέχνης ὑπερφέρουσα S.*OT*381, cf. X.*Lac*.15.8: c. dat. modi only, κάλλεϊ καὶ ἀρετῇ μέγα ὑ. Hdt.8.144, cf. 4.74, E.*Hec*.268; πλούτῳ X.*Lac*.15.3. b. sts. c. acc. pro gen., ὑπερφέρεις τόλμῃ τε τόλμαν καὶ λόγῳ χρηστῷ λόγον E.*Heracl*.554; ὑ. τὴν ἀνθρωπίνην φύσιν Isoc.4.60; μεγέθει καὶ ῥώμῃ πάντας Plu.*Rom*.7. c. abs., τοῦθ' ὑπερφέρει *has* this *pre-eminence*, S.*OC*1007 (s.v.l.); πολὺ ὑπερενεγκεῖν X.*Mem*.3.5.13. d. part., in honorific expressions, ἡ σὴ -φέρουσα ἐξουσία *PSI*4.292.5 (iii A.D.), etc.

**ὑπέρφευ**, Adv. = ὑπερφυῶς, *excessively, overmuch*, φλεόντων δωμάτων ὑ. A.*Ag*.377 (lyr.); οὐχ ὑ. θνητὸν ὄντα χρὴ φρονεῖν Id.*Pers*.820; τί τὴν τυραννίδα τιμᾷς ὑ.; E.*Ph*.550; φέρεις ὑ. τὰς τύχας Id.*HF* 1321:—Hsch. explains it by ὑπεράγαν; and in Phryn.*PS*p.89B. (= Cratin.359) we have μηδὲν ὑπέρφευ· ἐπὶ τοῦ μηδὲν ἄγαν.

**ὑπερφεύγω**, *escape beyond, survive*, τὰς ἑπτὰ ἡμέρας Hp.*Morb*.2.20, cf. 27; in tmesi, οὐκ ἔστιν ὑπὲρ (ὑπὲκ Herm.) θανατὸν φυγεῖν A.*Pers*.100 (lyr.).

**ὑπερφθέγγομαι**, *speak louder than*, τὰ ἔργα ὑ. τοὺς λόγους Luc.*Tox*.35; τῷ λόγῳ ὑπερφθέγγονται τὴν ἀλήθειαν they *shout down* the truth, Gal.8.808, cf. *UP*8.2; εὐεπείᾳ τὸν Ὅμηρον ὑ. *excel* Homer therein, Plu.2.396d.

**ὑπερφθίνομαι** [ῐ], Pass., *die for* or *in behalf of*, ὑπερέφθιτο πατρός Pi.*P*.6.30.

**ὑπερφίᾰλος** [ῐ], ον, *overbearing, overweening, arrogant*, of persons, freq. in Homer, in Il. of the Trojans, 13.621, 21.459, al.; in Od. of the Cyclopes, 9.106 (of the Cyclopes in good sense, B.10.78); more freq. of the suitors, Od.1.134, 2.310, al.; Γίγαντες B.14.62; ὑ. γόνος, of a Centaur, Pi.*P*.2.42, cf. *O*.10(11).34, *P*.4.111; also θυμὸς ὑ. an *arrogant* spirit, Il.15.94; ἔπος, μῦθοι ὑ., Od.4.503,774.—Orig. the word seems only to have signified *puissant*, without any bad sense, as is prob. from Od.21.289, where Antinous uses it of himself and the rest of the suitors, ὑπερφιάλοισι μεθ' ἡμῖν δαίνυσαι; and Aristarch. read ὑπερφίαλον for ὑπέρθυμον in Il.5.881: later writers also used it without any bad sense, δεσμὸς ὑ. a *huge* bond, Pi.*Fr*.92; οἶνον ὑπερφίαλον κελαρύζετε pour *the noble* wine, or pour it *without stint*, Ion Trag.10:—this notion appears most clearly in the Adv. ὑπερφιάλως, *exceedingly, excessively*, ὑ. νεμεσᾶν Il.13.293, Od.17.481, 21.285; ἀνιάζειν Il.18.300: but the Adv. also passed into the sense of *haughtily, arrogantly*, Od.1.227, 4.663, etc. (The old deriv. from ὑπὲρ φιάλην, *running over* (cf. Ion l.c.), is improbable, but modern explanations are unconvincing.)

**ὑπερφῐλέω**, *love beyond measure*, Ar.*Pl*.1072, X.*Cyr*.1.4.6, etc.

⊕**ὑπερφῐλοσοφέω**, *philosophize exceedingly*, Hp.*Ep*.17.

**ὑπερφῐλότῑμος**, ον, *over-ambitious*, only in Adv. -μως, Theopomp. Hist.111.

**ὑπερφλεγμαίνω**, *to have excess of juices*, Hp.*Loc.Hom*.9,27.

**ὑπερφλέγω**, *overheat, inflame*, Gal.19.514 (Pass.).

**ὑπέρφλοιος**, ον, *luxuriant, succulent*, μῆλα Emp.80 (scanned ⏑ – ⏑ ⏑).

**ὑπερφλοισμοὶ** ὑγροί, gloss on διαφλύξιες, Hsch.

**ὑπερφλῠᾱρέω**, *talk* or *chatter very absurdly*, Phryn.*PS*p.119B.

**ὑπερφλύζω**, *boil* or *bubble over*, Hsch.

**ὑπερφοβ-έομαι**, Pass., with fut. Med., *to be over-frightened, fear exceedingly*, A.*Th*.238; ὑ. μή.. X.*Cyr*.1.4.2. **-ος**, ον, *very fearful, timid*, Id.*Eq*.3.9; τὸ ὑ. D.C.58.6. II. causal, *very terrible*, λέγειν τὰ φαῦλα μείζω καὶ τὰ δεῖν' ὑπέρφοβα Men.497 (v.l. for ὑπὲρ φόβον, ap.Stob.4.38.3a), cf. Lxx *Da*.7.19.

**ὑπερφορέω**, = ὑπερφέρω I, *carry over*, τι ὑπέρ τινος X.*Cyn*.8.4.

**ὑπερφρον-έω**, (ὑπέρφρων) *to be over-proud, have high thoughts*, μηδ' ὑπερφρόνει A.*Ag*.1039, cf. Plb.6.18.7; μὴ ὑ. παρ' ὃ δεῖ φρονεῖν, ἀλλὰ φρονεῖν εἰς τὸ σωφρονεῖν *Ep.Rom*.12.3: c. dat. modi, *to be proud in* or *of* a thing, πλούτῳ Hdt.1.199; τὸν λόγον, ᾧ ὑπερπεφρόνηκας Pl.*Alc*.1.104a. 2. c. acc., *overlook, look down upon, despise*, ὑπερφρονήσας τὸν παρόντα δαίμονα A.*Pers*.825; τοὺς θεούς Ar.*Nu*.226; πέφυκε ἄνθρωπος τὸ..θεραπεῦον ὑπερφρονεῖν Th.3.39; ἑτέρους Aristeas 122:—Pass., *to be despised*, ὑπὸ τῶν εὐπραγούντων Th.6.16. 3. c. gen., *think slightly of*, δαιμόνων E.*Ba*.1325; τῶν καθεστώτων νόμων Ar.*Nu*.1400; τοῦ ἐπιτηδεύματος Pl.*Phdr*.258b. II. *surpass in knowledge*, ὑ. ἱστορίᾳ τὸν δῆμον (v.l. for περιφρ-) Aeschin.1.141: c. acc. cogn., πάντα ὑ. *excel in* all *wisdom*, Hp.*Ep*.17. **-ησις**, εως, ἡ, *contempt*, θανάτου Plu.2.238b, cf. Poll.9.146.

**ὑπερφροντίζω**, *to be exceedingly concerned*, Hld.10.29.

**ὑπερφροσύνη**, ἡ, *arrogance*, Plu.2.19d, 827a.

**ὑπερφρύγιος** [ῠγ], ον, *hyper-Phrygian*, ἁρμονία Ath.14.625d; τόνος Cleonid.*Harm*.12; τρόπος Alyp.*Diat*.9, al.

⊕**ὑπέρφρων**, ον, gen. ονος, (φρήν) *haughty, arrogant*, σῆμα, λόγοι, A.*Th*.387,410; φρονήματα E.*Heracl*.388: neut. pl. ὑπέρφρονα as Adv., S.*Aj*.1236. Regul. Adv. ὑπερφρόνως D.C.37.5,49 (this Adv. is censured by Poll.9.147). 2. in good sense, ἐκ τοῦ ὑπέρφρονος from *a sense of superiority*, Th.2.62, D.C.45.43.

**ὑπερφύ-εια** [φῠ], ἡ, *magnificence*, τῶν πυραμίδων *OGI*666.26 (Egypt, i A.D.); *excellency*, as a title, *POxy*.135.12 (vi A.D.), etc.; cf. ὑπερφυΐα. **-ής**, ές, Att. acc. sg. ὑπερφυᾶ Ar.*Eq*.141, *Nu*.76: Att. neut. pl. ὑπερφυῆ Pl.*Grg*.467b, -φυᾶ Ar.*Ra*.611: (φύομαι): I. literally, *growing above* the ground, Dsc.4.73, Luc.*Lex*.6; *growing higher than* the rest, οἱ ὑ. τῶν ἀσταχύων D.L.1.100. 2. *overgrown, enormous*, σμίνθος A.*Fr*.227 (troch.); λίθοι ὑ. τὸ μέγαθος Hdt.2.175, cf. Ar.*Pax*229, *Pl*.734; ὑ. τῷ μεγέθει ψόφος Arist.*Cael*.291ᵃ21. II. without a distinct sense of bulk, *monstrous, extraordinary*, in good and bad sense, ἔργον ὑ. μέγαθός τε καὶ κάλλος Hdt.9.78; ἔργον ὑ. ἐργάσατο Id.8.116; ἀτραπὸς δαιμονίως ὑ. Ar.*Nu*.76; ὑ. τέχνη Id.*Eq*.141; πῶς οὐχ ὑπερφυές; is it not *most strange*? D.29.14; κἀκεῖν' ὑ., εἰ.. Isoc.17.30; τὸ δὲ πάντων -έστατον, ὅτι.. Lys.27.12, cf. Ar.*Th*.831 (troch.): freq. joined with a relat., ὄχλος ὑπερφυὴς ὅσος Id.*Pl*.750; ὑπερφυεῖ τινι..ὡς μεγάλῃ βλάβῃ Pl.*Grg*.477d: freq. also joined with other Adjs., in which case, as a rule, it stands second, σχέτλια λέγεις καὶ ὑ. ib.467b; δεινὸν ὡς ἀληθῶς καὶ ὑ. D.21.88, etc.; but it stands first in Plu.2.12b, 155a, al. 2. Sup. -έστατος, as an honorific title, *Stud.Pal*.20.129.3 (v A.D.), etc.: also in Posit., ἡ ὑ. ὑμῶν ἐξουσία *PMasp*.2 i 1 (vi A.D.), etc. III. Adv. -ῶς *marvellously, strangely, exceedingly*, φιλαθήναιος ἦν ὑ. Ar.*Ach*.142; ὑ. σπουδάζειν Pl.*Grg*.481b; in affirm. answers, ὑ. μὲν οὖν Id.*R*.525b: Comp. -εστέρως Philostr.*Gym*.36. 2. ὑ. ὡς.., before a Verb, ὑ. ὡς χαίρω Pl.*Smp*.173c, cf. *Tht*.155c; before an Adj., ὑ. ὡς ἀληθῆ λέγεις Id.*Phd*.66a. **-ΐα**, ἡ, *marvellousness*, Suid.; esp. as an honorific title, *PMasp*.4.2 (vi A.D.), etc.; cf. ὑπερφύεια.

**ὑπερφύομαι**, Pass., with aor. 2 and pf. Act., *grow upon* or *over*, [ἔρως] ἔνδον τῆς ἐμῆς ὑπερεφύετο ψυχῆς Aristaenet.1.6 (sed leg. ὑπεφύετο); τινι Gal. *in Pl.Ti*.p.6D. II. metaph., *surpass, excel*, c. acc. pers. et dat. rei, ὑπερφὺς Ἕλληνας ἰσχύϊ Hdt.6.127, cf. D.C.56.2: c. gen. pers., Aristid.2.151J.

**ὑπερφῡσάομαι**, Pass., *to be inflated excessively*, Luc.*Cont*.19.

**ὑπερφωνέω**, *speak exceedingly well*, Philostr.*VS*1 *Prooem*. II. trans., *outbawl*, τινα Luc.*Rh.Pr*.13; οἰμωγῇ ὑ. τὸν τῶν σαλπίγγων ἦχον J.*AJ*11.4.2: metaph., *outdo*, Philostr.*VA*5.7, cf. Jul.*Or*.6.182a; τὸ Θηβῶν πάθος ὑ. τοὺς Ἕλληνας Him.*Ecl*.2.4. 2. *sing loudly*, αἴνεσιν Lxx *Ju*.15.14(16.1).

**ὑπερχαίρω**, aor. -εχάρην Hp.*Morb.Sacr*.17, late aor. -έχηρα Procop.Gaz.p.147B.:—*rejoice exceedingly at* a thing, δώροις E.*Med*.1165; ἐπὶ τοῖς γάμοις Plu.2.1098b; τούτων ἀκούσας ὑπερέχηρεν ὁ Πηλεύς Procop.Gaz. l.c.: c. part., μανθάνων ὑ., ὁρῶν ὑ., X.*Cyr*.1.3.3, Luc.*Nec*.12: also ὑ. ὅταν.., ὅτι.., X.*HG*4.1.10, *Cyn*.4.4: abs., Hp.*Morb.Sacr*.17, Plu.*Ages*.33, Luc.*VH*1.30.

**ὑπερχᾰλ-αστικός**, ή, όν, *very relaxing*, ὕπνοι prob. cj. in Hp.*Ep*.24 (ὑπερκολαστικοῖς, ὑπερκαλυστικοῖς codd.). **-άω**, *loosen too much*, Sor.1.65 (Pass.); f.l. for ὑπεκχ- in *AP*11.200 (Leon., corr. Scaliger).

⊕**ὑπερχᾰρής**, ές, *overjoyed*, Plb.8.17.2, Man.ap.J.*Ap*.1.26, Lxx *Es*.5.9, etc.; ἐπί τινι Plb.1.44.5.

⊕**ὑπερχειλής**, ές, *over the brim, running over*, κρατῆρες Ath.1.13d, cf. Poll.5.133, Them.*Or*.19.229a, etc.

**ὑπέρχειρ**, ὁ, ἡ, gen. χειρος, = μακρόχειρ, Philostr.*Gym*.38.

**ὑπερχειρία**, ἡ, *protectress*, a name of Hera in Laconia, Paus.3.13.8.

**ὑπερχέω**, *cause to overflow*, τὸ ὕδωρ (accus.) Aesop. in *Gloss*. vol. iii p.43:—Pass., *overflow, overrun*, of liquids, Arist.*Pr*.876ᵃ18, *Mir*.837ᵇ9; ὑπὲρ τὸ ἀγγεῖον D.C.66.16; of the air, Hp.*Aph*.7.51; ὑπερχεῖται εἰς τὸ ἀχανές Arist.*Mete*.367ᵃ19; *flow over*, τρίχες τῶν ἀκρωμίδων ὑπερκεχυμέναι Alciphr.*Fr*.5.4; τὰς -ομένας τοῦ ὄντος ἀρχάς Dam.*Pr*.61.

**ὑπερχθόνιος**, ον, *above the earth*, Man.2.26.

**ὑπερχλίω**, *to be over-wanton* or *arrogant*, S.*Tr*.281 (v.l. -χλιδῶντες).

**ὑπερχολάω**, *to be over-charged with bile*, Hp.*Morb*.2.41; *to be* or *become very angry*, Ar.*Lys*.694 (lyr.), Philostr.*Im*.2.11.

**ὑπέρχολος**, ον, *exceedingly bilious* or *wrathful*, Antiph.309; *overcharged with bile*, Meno *Iatr*.19.41.

**ὑπ-έρχομαι**, aor. ὑπῆλθον, Ep. -ήλυθον, the only tense used by Hom. (in both forms); Dor. subj. ὑπένθῃ *Berl.Sitzb*.1927.158 (Cyrene); pf. ὑπελήλυθε Men.498:—*go* or *come under, get under*, c. acc., ὑπήλυθε θάμνους Od.5.476; ὑπήλθετε δῶμ' Ἀΐδαο 12.21; ἐπεί κε μέλαθρον ὑπέλθῃ 18.150, cf. *Berl.Sitzb*. l.c.; ὄφρ' ἂν γᾶν ὑπέλθῃ A.*Eu*.339 (lyr.); [ἡ μήτρα] ὅλη [τὴν κύστιν] ὑπελήλυθεν Sor.1.7: with a Prep., ὑπὸ τὴν φορὰν τοῦ ἀκοντίου *come within* its range, Antipho 3.2.5; εἰς τὴν ὁδὸν τοῦ ἀκοντίου Id.3.4.5; ὑπὸ τὸ βέλος ibid.: rarely c. dat., τοῖς στενοῖς *enter* (come under the mountains), Plu.*Comp.Per.Fab*.2. II. of involuntary feelings, *come upon, steal over* one, c. acc., Τρῶας δὲ τρόμος αἰνὸς ὑπήλυθε γυῖα Il.7.215, 20.44; φρίκης αὐτὸν ὑπελθούσης Hdt.6.134; ὥς μ' ὑπῆλθέ τις φόβος S.*Ph*.1231, cf. *El*.1112; θαυμά τοί μ' ὑπέρχεται ib.928; ὥσθ' ἵμερός μ' ὑπῆλθε.. E.*Med*.57, cf. Philem.79.1; οὐ γάρ τις οἶκτος σῆς μ' ὑ. φυγῆς E.*Hipp*.1089; ἐς δ' ἄκραν δεῖμ' ὑπῆλθε κρατὸς φόβαν, of fear causing the hair to stand up, S.*OC*1465 (lyr.); ἐκ ποδῶν δ' ἄνω ὑ. σπαραγμὸς εἰς ἄκρον κάρα A.*Fr*.169; ὑπελήλυθέν τέ μου νάρκα τις ὅλον τὸ δέρμα Men.498. III. of persons, *creep* or *insinuate oneself into* another's *good graces*, *fawn upon*, εἶδες οἷ' ὑπέρχεται ἡμᾶς; Ar.*Eq.*269 (troch.); οἱ κριταὶ ὑ. 'Αλκιβιάδην And.4.21; ὑ. τὰς ἀρχάς, τοὺς πολεμίους, X.*Lac.*8.2, *Ath.*2.14; ὑ. πάντας ἀνθρώπους καὶ δουλεύων Pl.*Cri.*53e; ὑ. καὶ θεραπεύειν D.23.8; ὑ. δώροις καὶ κολακείαις Plu.*Luc.*6. **2.** *entrap, beguile*, λάθρᾳ μ' ὑπελθών S.*OT* 386; οἷ αὖ μ' ὑπῆλθες Id.*Ph.*1007; δόλῳ μ' ὑπῆλθες E.*Andr.*435, cf. *Supp.*138, *IA*67; τὸν ἄνδρα ποικίλως ὑ. ἐν λόγοισιν Ar.*Eq.*459. **IV.** c. acc. rei, *seek by base arts*, τυραννίδα Plu.*Dio* 7; φιλίαν D.Chr.74.5. **V.** *advance slowly*, of an army, X.*An.*5.2.30; cf. ὑπάγω A. III. **VI.** *recede, give way*, ὑπελθόντος τοῦ ἀέρος Arist.*Cael.*295$^{a}$22 (s. v. l.). **VII.** of excrements, *pass*, Gal.18(2).147, Orib.*Eup.*1.9.10; ὑπέρχεται ῥᾳδίως, of laxative food, Gal.6.629; also of semen, καθεύδοντι ὑπέρχεται Ruf.ap.Orib.6.38.29. **VIII.** *undertake, assume*, ὑπελθεῖν τοὔνομα καὶ τὸ ἔργον *assume* the title and the duty, Lib.*Or.*49.5.

® **ὑπέρχρεως**, ων, *over head and ears in debt*, D.27.25.

**ὑπερχρήμᾰτος**, ον, *very rich*, Ocell.4.6.

**ὑπερχρον-έω**, *to be overdue*, *IG*5(1).11 (Sparta). **-ίζω**, *to be over the time*, Hsch. s. v. χρονιώτερον. **-ιος**, ον, *beyond the usual time* of life, *very old*, Zen.6.30. **2.** *overdue*, *PFlor.*86.21 (i A. D.). **b.** ὑπερχρονία, ἡ, = ὑπερημερία, *PLips.*120.8 (i A. D.): but, *pay for overtime*, *BSA* 27.234 (Sparta, ii A. D.). **-ος**, ον, *super-temporal*, Simp. *in Ph.*1158.30.

**ὑπέρχυε**, used in a mystic invocation (perh. addressed to a fountain), ὕε κύε ὑ. *IG*2$^{2}$.4876.

**ὑπέρχῠμα**, ατος, τό, *overplus, surplus*, Hero *Mens.*61.7.

**ὑπέρχῠσις**, εως, ἡ, *overflow*, Eratosth.ap.Str.16.1.15, Plu.2.502a, Philum.*Ven.*20.2, etc.

**ὑπερχωρέω**, *pass beyond* a mark, Arist.*Phgn.*813$^{b}$33 (inserting ⟨οὐχ⟩).

**ὑπέρψῡχος**, ον, *too strong for the soul*, σῶμα Pl.*Ti.*88a.

**ὑπέρψυχρος**, ον, *very cold*, of the season, Sor.2.57; *very frigid*, of bad wit, Luc.*Hist.Conscr.*16.

**ὑπερψύχω** [ῡ], *strike with a violent chill*, Hp.*Morb.*1.2:—Pass., Id. *Aff.*1, Arist.*EE*1239$^{b}$34; *to be over-chilled*, Gal.1.372.

**ὑπερῶ**, Att. fut. of ὑπεῖπον.

**ὑπερῴα**, Ion. -η, ἡ, *palate*, Il.22.495, Hp.*Mochl.*39, Plu.*Cat.Ma.*9, Gal.6.828, 17(2).439, *UP*11.11, Aristid.*Or.*47(23).69, al.; ὑπερῷα (v. l. -ῴα) Arist.*HA*492$^{b}$26:—elsewh. οὐρανός, οὐρανίσκος (καὶ οὐρανίσκου καὶ ὑπερῴας Gal.18(2).286, where one cod. omits καὶ οὐρανίσκου). (Cf. ὑπερῷος.)

**ὑπερῴδιον**, τό, Dim. of ὑπερῷον, ὑ. δύο τεθυρωμένα *Inscr.Délos* 351.7, cf. *IG*11(2).287*A*146, al. (Delos, iii B. C.).

**ὑπερωδῡν-έω**, *feel excessive pain*, Hp.*Epid.*6.3.8. **-ία**, ἡ, *excessive pain*, Anon.ap.Suid. s. v. ἀκληρούντων. **-ος**, ον, *very painful*, Hp.*Liqu.*1.

**ὑπ-ερωέω**, *start back, recoil*, Il.8.122,314, 15.452.

**ὑπερωϊόθεν**, Adv. *from an upper room*, v. ὑπερῷον. **ὑπερώϊον**, τό, v. ὑπερῷον. **ὑπερώϊος**, η, ον, v. ὑπερῷος.

**ὑπερωκεάνιος** [ᾰ], ον, *beyond the ocean*, Ph.2.547: metaph., *hyperoceanic, monstrous*, ὑ. καὶ μετακόσμιος ἀσέβεια Id.1.425, cf. 675.

**ὑπερωμία**, ἡ, (ὦμος) *the part above the shoulders*, ὑπερωμίαν καὶ ἐπάνω ὑψηλός *by the head and shoulders*, Lxx 1*Ki.*9.2, cf. 10.23.

**ὑπερωνέομαι**, *buy too dear, bid high*, Them.*Or.*21.261b:—Pass., [ὑπε]ρωνηθεῖσι *farmed out at excessive rates*, *IGRom.*4.1211 (Thyatira, i B. C.).

**ὑπερῷον**, Ep. and Ion. **-ώϊον**, τό, *the upper part of the house*, where the women resided, παρθένος αἰδοίη ὑπερώϊον εἰσαναβᾶσα Il.2.514; εἰς ὑπερῷ' ἀναβάς 16.184, cf. Od.1.362; ὑπερωϊόθεν φρεσὶ σύνθετο θέσπιν ἀοιδὴν..Πηνελόπεια *from her chamber* she heard it, ib.328; approached by a κλῖμαξ, ib.330: so in later Gr., *upper chamber* or *story*, *Act.Ap.*1.13, *Supp.Epigr.*2.754 (Syria, ii A. D.), *POxy.*2146.7 (iii A. D.). **2.** *attic, garret*, Ar.*Eq.*1001, *Pl.*811, Men.*Sam.*17, *IG*2$^{2}$.1638.27; ἄνωθ' ἐξ ὑ. Ar.*Ec.*698 (anap.); of *a spare room*, Antipho 1.14.

**ὑπερῷος**, α, ον, Ion. and Ep. **-ώϊος**, η, ον: also ος, ον (v. infr.):—*upper*, στοαὶ ὑπερῷοι D.H.3.68, Paus.5.10.10; περίπατοι Lxx *Ez.*42.5, cf. *IG*4$^{2}$(1).126.11 (Epid., ii A. D.); [τόποι (rooms)] *POxy.*76.19 (ii A. D.); ὑ. θάλαμος, = ὑπερῷον, Plu.*Pel.*35; so ὑ. οἶκος Gal.14.47; οἴκημα *OGI*483.110 (Pergam., ii B. C.), Plu.*Arat.*26. **2.** Thess. **Ὑπεροῖος**, ὁ, name of a month in Perrhaebia, *IG*9(2).1231.8 (Phalanna, ii B. C.).

**ὑπέρωρος**, ον, *over-ripe*, Dsc.1.64, Poll.6.54; κάλλος Them.*Or.*13.165c.

**ὑπερωρόφιος**, ον, *over* or *above the roof*, v. l. in Poll.1.80.

**ὑπερώσιος**, ον, = περιώσιος, *EM*665.29.

**ὑπερώτατος**, η, ον, poet. Sup. for ὑπέρτατος (q. v.).

**ὑπερωτ-άω**, *reply by a question*, Pl.*Grg.*483a. **2.** *ask artfully*, or *slip in a question*, Arg.D.1.5, and so perh. in Pl. l. c.: perh. simply *ask*, μαρτυροῦντας τὰ ὑπερωτώμενα *IG*2$^{2}$.1237.73 (iv B. C.). **-ησις**, εως, ἡ, *question in reply*, A.D.*Conj.*227.4.

**ὑπεσθίω**, *eat away under* or *secretly*, Sch.Il.21.271.

**ὑπεσταλμένως**, Adv., (ὑποστέλλω) *obscurely*, ἀλληγορῆσαι Heraclit.*All.*29; opp. μετὰ παρρησίας, Sch.S.*Aj.*82.

**ὑπέσχεθον**, v. ὑπέχω. **ὑπέσχημαι**, v. ὑπισχνέομαι.

**ὑπετῠμολογέω**, *suggest an etymology*, Sch.Ar.*Av.*181.

**ὑπεύδιος**, ον, *under the calm sky*, γέρανοι Arat.1012; τὰ ὑπεύδια καὶ κατασκιαζόμενα τῶν δένδρων *sheltered*..trees, Plu.ap.*EM*103.53 = Sch.Il.15.625. **II.** *somewhat calm*, ἀκτή A.R.1.584, cf. 3.1202; ὑ. καὶ λεία θάλαττα Ael.*NA*1.41, etc.; τὸ ὑ. τῆς θαλάσσης *a tolerable calm*, Plu.*Them.*32. [ῑ in Arat. l. c. metri gr., cf. εὔδιος.]

® **ὑπεύθῡνος**, ον, *liable to give account for* one's *administration* of an office, *responsible*, ὑ. ἀρχή, opp. μουναρχίη, Hdt.3.80; τραχὺς μόναρχος, οὐδ' ὑ. κρατεῖ A.*Pr.*326, cf. *Ch.*715; οὐχ ὑπεύθυνος πόλει Id.*Pers.*213; ὑ. τὴν παραίνεσιν ἔχοντας πρὸς ἀνεύθυνον τὴν ὑμετέραν ἀκρόασιν we who advise are *responsible*, while you who hear are irresponsible, Th.3.43; οἱ ὑ., at Athens, magistrates who, on quitting office, *had to give an account* of their administration to examiners (εὔθυνοι) and (if they had handled public funds) to auditors (λογισταί), Ar.*Eq.*259, *V.*102, Antipho 6.43, etc.; ὁπόσοι ἄρχοντες ἐν μιᾷ πόλει γεγένηνται, ὑ. εἰσιν And.4.30; ἄνδρες λογισταὶ τῶν ὑ. χορῶν, addressed to the spectators, who were 'auditors' and judges of the performance, Eup.223. **2.** c. gen., *under liability for, answerable for*, ὑ. ἑτέρας ἀρχῆς Jusj.ap.D.24.150; προκλήσεως Id.45.43; of slaves, σῶμα ὑ. ἀδικημάτων their body is *liable for* their misdeeds, i. e. they *must pay for* them with their body, Id.22.55; τῆς ἀγνοίας ὑ. *held responsible for* it, Id.18.196; τῆς φωνῆς Luc.*Salt.*27. **3.** c. dat., ὑ. κινδύνῳ, ὑ. τιμωρίᾳ, Lycurg.129,148, cf. *BCH*17.242 (Phrygia): c. dat. pers., *responsible to* another, *dependent on* him, ὑ. ὢν οὐδενί D.18.235; διδόναι ἑαυτὸν ὑ. τῇ τύχῃ, etc., ib.189, cf. Aeschin.2.170; τῇ γνώμῃ τῶν πολλῶν Phld.*Ind.Sto.*21. **II.** Adv. -νως Poll.3.139.

**ὑπευθυντηρία**, ἡ, *levelled surface beneath a pavement*, *IG*7.3073.105, al. (Lebad., ii B. C.).

® **ὑπευλᾰβέομαι**, *to be somewhat afraid*, c. inf., Lxx 2*Ma.*14.18 (v. l. ἐπ-).

**ὑπευν-άζομαι**, v. sq. I, II. **-άομαι**, Pass., (εὐνάω) only in fem. part. aor. ὑπευνηθεῖσα, *in wedlock with*, Φοίβῳ ὑ. (v. l. ὑπευνασθεῖσα) Orac.ap.Eus.*PE*3.14. **II.** *to be under-bedded with* a thing, i. e. *lying* or *sitting upon*, ὀρταλὶς..ὑπευνηθεῖσα νεοσσοῖς Nic.*Al.*294 (ὑπευνασθεῖσα cod. opt.).

**ὑπεφηβαρχέω**, *to be under-officer of the ephebi* (at Cyzicus), *CIG* 3665.

**ὑπέχ-θεμα, -θέσιμος**, v. ὑπεκ-.

**ὑπέχω**, fut. ὑφέξω S.*OT*552, etc.: aor. ὑπέσχον, poet. also ὑπέσχεθον, Aeol. inf. ὑποσκέθην *IG*12(2).526*A*40 (Eresus, iv B. C.):—*hold under*, **a.** *put* a mare *under* or *to* a horse, ὑποσχὼν θήλεας ἵππους Il.5.269. **b.** of *holding out* the hand *to receive* something, ὑπέσχεθε χεῖρα 7.188; προτείνειν καὶ ὑ. [τὴν χεῖρα], to receive bribes, D.19.255; ὑ. χρυσίῳ τὴν χεῖρα Men.309: prov. of a greedy person, ὑ. τὴν χεῖρα ἀποθνήσκων Diogenian.3.12. **c.** ῥημάτων ὑ. οὖας *lend* an attentive ear, Simon.37.14; σὺ δὲ μείλιχον οὖας ὑπόσχες Procl.*H.*7.52; ὑ. τὰ ὦτά τινι Aristid.2.230J., etc. **d.** *hold* a cup *under* another vessel, while something is poured into it, Hdt.2.151, Ar.*Ach.*1063, *Pax*431, cf. 909: also intr., ὑ. κρουνοῖς *stand under* shower baths, Antyll.ap.Orib.10.3.10. **e.** *put under*, like wax under a seal, τι ταῖς αἰσθήσεσι Pl.*Tht.*191d. **f.** ὑ. μαστόν, of mother or nurse giving suck, E.*Ion* 1372; νηπίοις θηλὴν ὑ. Plu.*Rom.*21. **2.** *supply, afford, furnish*, νεφέλην A.*Fr.*199.7 (ὑπερσχών Casaubon); πλοῦτος ὑ. μέριμναν Pi.*O.*2.54; πάντα Ar.*Lys.*841; ὑ. τὸ αὐτὸ τοῖς ἐναντίοις (sc. fear) Th.7.21; ὑ. ἑαυτόν *submit* oneself to another, so as to be at his disposal or follow his advice, X.*Cyr.*7.5.44, v. l. in Pl.*R.*399b: also c. inf., ὑπόσχες Σωκράτει ἐξελέγξαι *allow* Socrates to examine you, Id.*Grg.*497b. **II.** *uphold, support*, τοὺς ὤμους Hdt.4.72. **2.** *undergo, suffer*, τήνδ' ἄτην S.*Tr.*1274 (anap.); ζημίαν E.*Ion* 1308; κακόν Ar.*Th.*196; τιμωρίαν τινός *for* a thing, Th.6.81, Aeschin.3.221, Lycurg.91, cf. Pl.*Lg.*716b; πυρὸς αἰωνίου δίκην *Ep.Jud.*7; κόλασιν Plu.2.198d, etc.; also τούτων τὰς αἰτίας *to be subject to* accusation for.., Antipho 5.67; τούτων..οὐκ ἂν δικαίως τὴν αἰτίαν ὑπέχοιμι Pl.*Ap.*33b; ψόγον ἀμουσίας ὑ. Id.*R.*403c. **3.** in law-phrases, ὑ. δίκας [τινός] *to have to give* an account of a thing, or *suffer* a penalty, Hdt.2.118; δίκην ὑπόσχες αἵματος.. Εὐμενίσι E.*Or.*1649; ὑ. φόνου δίκας Pl.*Lg.*872c (poet. also φόνον μητρὸς ὑφέξω in the same sense, E.*El.*1318 (anap.)); δίκην ὑ. τῶν πεπραγμένων D.19.95; ὑφέξειν τὴν δίκην S.*OT*552; ὑφέξω τοῖς κακίοσιν δίκην E.*Hec.*1253; ὑ. τῇ πόλει δίκην Pl.*Phd.*99a; τοιάνδε δίκην ὑφέξειν *undergo* such a trial, Th.3.53, cf. *IG*12(2) l. c.; τοῖς χρήμασι τὰς δίκας ὑ. *to have to pay* the penalty with one's property, Isoc.20.17; ὑ. δίκας, ἐὰν.. D.23.77; ὑ. κρίσιν περὶ ὧν ἄν τις ἐγκαλῇ Id.21.125:—ὑ. καὶ λαμβάνειν τὸ δίκαιον ἐπὶ τῶν χρηματιστῶν, i. e. to have the right of suing or being sued, *PTeb.*5.213, al. (ii B. C.); λαμβάνω ἐγὼ καὶ ὑπέχω τὸ δίκαιον ὑπὲρ τοῦ Πολυκλείτου *PEnteux.*8.6 (iii B. C.); ἐπαναγκάσαι αὐτὸν τὸ δίκαιον ἡμῖν ὑποσχεῖν ib.59.11 (iii B. C.). **b.** ἐμοὶ λόγον ὑποσχέτω *let him render* account to me, Pl.*Prt.*338d; οὐδενὶ θέλων ὑπέχειν λόγον X.*Mem.*4.4.9; ὑ. τῇ πόλει περὶ τοῦ βίου λόγον And.4.37; ὑ. εὐθύνας [ἀρχῆς] Lys..24.26, cf. 9.11, 30.3. **4.** *sustain, maintain*, λόγον an argument, Arist.*Rh.*1354$^{a}$5, *Metaph.*1011$^{a}$22, al.; ὑπόθεσιν Id.*Top.*158$^{a}$31; θέσιν καὶ ὁρισμόν ib.160$^{b}$14. (For the Med., v. ὑπισχνέομαι.)

**ὑπέωρος**, perh. f. l. for *ὑπεῷος (= ὑπηοῖος) in *Gloss.*

**ὑπήβολος**, ον, v. ὑπώβολος.

**ὑπηέριος**, ον, *exposed to the air*, δρόμοι, opp. ἐν τῷ ἱματίῳ, Hp.*Vict.*2.63 (v. Loeb ed.). **2.** *misty*, A.R.4.1577.

**ὑπηθέω**, *sift*, Hsch. s. v. ὑποσακίζειν.

**ὑπήκοον**, τό, *horned cummin*, *Hypecoum procumbens*, Dsc.4.67, Plin.*HN*27.93.

**ὑπήκοος**, ον, (ἀκοή) *hearkening*, ἀμφοτέροισι perh. *answering* with both gifts, *AP*9.46 (Antip. Thess.); *a hearer, scholar*, Poll.4.44, Iamb.*VP*26.121. **II.** *obeying, subject*, c. gen., Πέρσας Μήδων ὑπηκόους ἐποίησε Hdt.1.102, cf. 4.167, 7.111,149, A.*Pers.*234,242 (both troch.),

Th.4.78, 6.20, etc.; ὑ. τῶν νόμων Arist.*EN*1102$^{a}$10. 2. c. dat., E.*Heracl.*287, X.*Cyr.*2.4.22; ἅπαντα τῷ πλουτεῖν ὑπήκοα Ar.*Pl.*146; γλῶττα ὑ. τῷ λογισμῷ Plu.2.90b; also ναυσὶ καὶ οὐ φόρῳ ὑ. *liable to furnish*.. (cf. ὑποτελής), Th.7.57; τροφὴ ὑ. τῇ πέψει *easy of* digestion, Plu.2.661b; ὕλη ὑ. phlegm *easily brought up*, Steph. *in Hp.*1.181 D. III. abs. as Subst., ὑπήκοοι, οἱ, *subjects*, X.*HG*4.1.36, etc.; ἡ ὑ. (sc. χώρα) D.C.36.53; τὸ ὑ. = οἱ ὑ., τὸ ὑ. τῶν ξυμμάχων Th.6.69, cf. D.C.37.25, etc.; *the subject allies* of Athens were called ὑπήκοοι, opp. αὐτόνομοι, Th.7.57, cf. 6.22, 8.2.

**ὑπήλᾰτος**, ον, (ἐλαύνω) *carrying off downwards*, φάρμακα ὑ. *purging* medicines, Hp.*Acut.*23, *Morb.*4.56, Gal.6.152, 244.

**ὑπηλῐφής**, ές, (ὑπαλείφω) *pitched*, *caulked*, of a ship, *EM*61.6.

**ὑπημάτιος** [ᾰ], α, ον, (ἦμαρ) *towards day*, *in early morning*, like ὑπηῷος, Opp.*H.*4.640.

**ὑπημύω**, v. ὑπεμνήμυκε.

**ὑπηνέμ-ιος**, ον, (ἄνεμος) *lifted* or *wafted by the wind*, ὑπᾱνέμιοι φορέονται Theoc.5.115; ὑ. τανύοιτο, of the Sun, Arat.839. 2. *swift as the wind*, Plu.*Sert.*12. II. *full of wind*, ὑ. ᾠὰ *wind*-eggs, which produce no chickens, Ar.*Fr.*186, Pl.Com.19 (ἀνεμιαῖον ᾠόν was considered better Att., Moer.p.73 P.); of eggs laid by hens without impregnation, Arist.*HA*559$^{b}$24; so κυήματα ὑ. Id.*GA*749$^{b}$1; in Ar.*Av.*695 (anap.), ὑ. ᾠόν is the egg produced by Night *alone*, without impregnation; and Luc.*Sacr.*6 calls Hephaestus the ὑ. παῖς of Hera; λοχεῖαι καὶ ὠδῖνες Plu.2.38e (s. v.l.): hence 2. metaph., *empty*, *idle*, ὄνειροι ib.735e, cf. Luc.*Harm.*4; πλοῦτος Id.*Gall.*12. **-ος**, ον, (ἄνεμος) *sheltered from the wind*, S.*Ant.*411; ἀκτή Theoc.22.32; λιμήν Poll.1.100; [τόποι] Thphr.*CP*3.6.9; opp. προσήνεμος, ἐκ τοῦ ὑπηνέμου on *the lee-side*, X.*Oec.*18.7; ὑπηνέμους ποιεῖσθαι τὰς νεοττεύσεις to make the nests *in sheltered places*, Arist.*HA*559$^{a}$3; ἐν ὑπηνέμοις (sc. τόποις) ib.568$^{b}$26: metaph., *gentle*, αὔρα E.*Cyc.*44 (lyr.). II. *swift as the wind*, *APl.*4.54; epith. of Mars, *Cat.Cod.Astr.*2.81. III. = foreg. II. 2, ἐπιθυμίαι, δόξαι, D.Chr.20.24 codd., Alciphr.2.2.

⊛ **ὑπήν-η**, ἡ, prop. *hair on the upper lip* (which is the first to grow, cf. sq.), *moustache*, distd. from πώγων, Eub.100, cf. Phot., Suid.: generally, *beard*, A.*Fr.*27; τὴν ὑ. ἄκουρον τρέφων Ar.*V.*476 (lyr.); μολύνων τὴν ὑ. Id.*Eq.*1286 (troch.); ἕλκοντες ὑπήνας letting the *beard* grow long, trailing *beards*, Id.*Lys.*1072; ἄναξ ὑπήνης, of one *with a huge beard*, Pl.Com.122. 2. in Arist.*HA*518$^{b}$18, it seems to mean *the upper lip*, καὶ τὴν ὑ. καὶ τὸ γένειον δασὺ ἔχειν, cf. Theoc.20.22. **-ήτης**, ου, ὁ, *one that is just getting a beard* (cf. foreg.), πρῶτον ὑ. a youth *with his* first *beard*, Il.24.348, Od.10.279, cf. Pl.*Prt.*309b (quoting Homer), Him.*Ecl.*13.24, al.; Ἑρμῆς ὑ., opp. Ζεὺς γενειήτης, Luc.*Sacr.*11: generally, *bearded*, τράγος *AP*6.32 (Agath.).

**ὑπηνόβῐος**, ον, *living by his beard*, i.e. by bullying, Pl.Com.124.

**ὑπηοῖος**, η, ον, (ἠώς) Ep. Adj. *towards dawn*, *early*, Il.18.277 = 303, Od.4.656; στίβη ὑπηοίη *early* rime, *morning* frost, 17.25: cf. ὑπηῷος.

**ὑπήρατος**· λογομάχος, ὑπέρλαμπρος, Hsch.

**ὑπηρ-έα** and **-ία**, ἡ, = ἐπήρεια, *PFlor.*189.3 (iii A.D.), *BGU*908.10 (ii A.D.). **-εάζω**, = ἐπηρεάζω, *PSI*4.350.3 (iii B.C.), *PFlor.*189.14 (iii A.D.).

**ὑπηρέμᾰ**, Adv. *softly*, *gently*, D.P.1122 (nisi leg. ὑπ' ἠρέμα πορφυρέουσαν, i.e. ὑποπορφυρέουσαν).

⊛ **ὑπηρεσ-ία**, ἡ, (ἐρέτης) *body of rowers*, *ship's crew*, οἵ τε ναῦται καὶ οἱ ἐπιβάται καὶ ἡ ὑ. D.50.30, cf. 10, 25, al.; ὑ. κρατίστην ἐμισθωσάμην ib.7; εἶχον κυβερνήτην Φαντίαν.., παρεσκευασάμην δὲ καὶ τὸ πλήρωμα πρὸς ἐκεῖνον καὶ τὴν ἄλλην ὑ. ἀκόλουθον Lys.21.10; κυβερνήτας ἔχομεν πολίτας καὶ τὴν ἄλλην ὑ. πλείους καὶ ἀμείνους ἢ ἅπασα ἡ ἄλλη Ἑλλάς Th.1.143; τῆς ἄλλης ὑ. *IG*1$^{2}$.98.22; χρεία πλοίων ἐστὶ καὶ τῆς κατὰ θάλατταν ὑ. Plb.5.109.1: pl., *crews*, Th.6.31, 8.1, Isoc.4.142; pl. of naval *equipment*, [ναῦς] εὖ ταῖς ὑ. ἐξηρτυμένη Plb.1.25.3; ἡ θρὶξ [τῶν αἰγῶν] ἀναγκαία.. εἰς ναυτικὰς ὑπηρεσίας *Gp.*18.9.3. II. generally, *service*, δουλεία καὶ ὑ. Ar.*V.*602 (anap.); ἰατρικὴ ὑ. Pl.*Lg.*961e; αἱ σωματικαὶ ὑ. Arist.*Pol.*1259$^{b}$26; μόρια τὰ πρὸς ταύτην τὴν ὑ. (sc. πορεύεσθαι) Id.*Juv.*468$^{a}$19; αἱ ὑ. αἱ ἔξωθεν κινητικαί Id.*PA*684$^{b}$33; τέχναι καὶ γοητεῖαι καὶ ὅλως ὑ. τινές *all kinds of service*, D.*Prooem.*52 (s. v.l., *deceptions* seems to be the sense); πᾶσαν λειτουργίαν καὶ ὑ. ἐκτελεῖν *CIG*2786 (Aphrodisias); παρέχειν τι εἰς ὑ. τινί Pl.*Lg.*717c; ἡ ἐμὴ τῷ θεῷ ὑ. Id.*Ap.*30a; τίς αὕτη ἡ ὑ. ἐστὶ τοῖς θεοῖς; Id.*Euthphr.*14d; τὰς ἐκείνων ὑ. εἰς αὑτόν Id.*Lg.*729d, cf. Arist.*EN*1158$^{a}$17; ἄλλας ὑ. ὑποστάντα τῇ πόλει *IG*4.609 (Argos), cf. 12(5).946.23 (Tenos, i/ii A.D.), *CIG*2767 (Aphrodisias), etc. 2. in concrete sense, in pl., *the class of servants* or *attendants*, Pl.*Lg.*956e, *Ep.*350a, cf. *IG*5(1).1390.98 (Andania, i B.C.): also in sg., *retinue*, Lxx *Jb.*1.3, *OGI*139.8 (Philae, ii B.C.); of *shop-assistants*, *Sardis* 7(1).168 (iv A.D.). 3. ὑ. σοι παντελὴς.. κεραμίων 'a dinner-*service*', Axionic.7. **-ιον**, τό, *cushion on a rower's bench*, Th.2.93, Isoc.8.48, *PCair.Zen.*54.44 (iii B.C.); εἰς ὑ. καὶ κώπην, i.e. to rowers' service, Plu.*Them.*4. 2. *riding-pad* or *saddle-cloth*, D.S.20.4. II. *rowers' pay*, *AB*312, Phot. III. = ὑπηρετικὸν πλοῖον, Eratosth. ap.Str.2.1.23.

**ὑπηρετ-εία**, ἡ, = ὑπηρεσία II. 1, μακάρων *App.Anth.*2.263. **-εύω**, = sq., *IG*5(1).1360 (Messenia), *IGRom.*4.1046 (Cos). ⊛ **-έω**, fut. -ήσω Alex. (v. infr.), etc.: plpf. ὑπηρετήκειν X.*HG*3.3.9:—prop. *do service on board ship, as a rower* (cf. ὑπηρέτης, ὑπηρεσία), *SIG*524.33, 47 (Praesus, iii B.C.):—Pass., πλοῖον ὑπὸ δύο ἀνθρώπων ὑπηρετεῖσθαι δυνάμενον D.S.2.55. II. *to be a servant*, *do service*, S.*El.*996, *Ph.*990; opp. ἄρχω, Ar.*V.*518 (troch.); τοὺς διὰ φόβον ὑ. X.*Hier.*1.38. 2. c. dat., *minister to*, *serve*, τῷ παρόντι δαίμονι S.*El.*1306, cf. E.*Ph.*1708, Th.4.108, etc.; ὑ. τῷ χρηστηρίῳ *submit to* its ruling, Hdt.8.41, cf. Pl.*Lg.*914a; ἔργοις ἀνοσίοις ὑ. S.*OC*283; [νόμῳ, λόγῳ], Lys.2.19; ὑ. τοῖς τρόποις *humour* his ways, Ar.*Ra.*1432; τῷδ' ὑ. λόγῳ *second*, *support* it, E.*Med.*588; ὢν ἄνθρωπος ἀνθρώπου τύχαις ὑπηρετήσω Alex.150. 3. ὑ. τινὶ εἴς or πρός τι, Hdt.1.109, X.*Eq.*8.7, etc.; also ὑ. τινί τι *serve* one in a thing, οἷς σὺ ταῦθ' ὑπηρετεῖς S.*Ph.*1024, cf. Ar.*Pl.*979, Pl.*Smp.*196c, X.*Cyr.*5.1.20, D.18.138, 59.35. b. in financial sense, τὸν δὲ ταμίαν εἰς τὸ ἀνάλωμα ὑπηρετῆσαι *Supp.Epigr.*1.351.30 (Samos, iv B.C.), cf. 363.43 (ibid., iii B.C.), *Inscr.Prien.*3 (iv B.C.), 18 (iii B.C.), al. c. at Athens, *serve as* ὑπηρέτης of the Council, D.19.70. d. in the Mithraic cult, *to be a* ὑπηρέτης or *servitor*, *Rev.Hist.Rel.*109.63 (Rome). e. *render military service*, *BGU*180.14, 613.23 (both ii A.D.). 4. abs., *serve*, *be subordinate*, opp. προστάττω, Arist.*Top.*129$^{a}$13; ἡ ὑπηρετοῦσα ἐπιστήμη Id.*Metaph.*982$^{b}$5: c. neut. pl. of Adj., etc., τὰ λοίφ' ὑ. *help in* what remains to be done, S.*Ph.*15; ὑ. τὰ περὶ τὸν πόλεμον Pl.*R.*467a; and with cogn. acc., ὑ. τὰς διακονικὰς πράξεις Arist.*Pol.*1277$^{a}$36:—Pass., *to be done as service*, τὰ ἀπ' ἡμέων ἐς ὑμέας ὑπηρετέεται Hdt.4.139; χρὴ δὴ τό γε ἐμὸν ὑπηρετέεσθαι *that* my *service should be rendered*, Id.1.108; ἢν τὰ παρ' ὑμῶν ὑπηρετῆται Isoc.3.63; τὸ πρᾶγμα τὸ ὑπηρετηθέν Arist.*EE*1243$^{a}$16, cf. X.*HG*5.2.34.—The Med. occurs in late texts, as Hld.7.19, al., and Alciphr.1.11, dub. in *Supp.Epigr.*1.327.19 (Callatis, i A.D.); τὸ -ούμενον the *retinue*, Memn.2.4; fut. -ήσομαι *POxy.*58.24 (iii A.D.); but in S.*El.*1306, ὑπηρετοίην was rightly restored by Musgrave and Elmsl. for -οίμην. **-ημα**, ατος, τό, *service rendered*, Antipho 1.15, Pl.*Alc.*1.106b, Chaerem.ap.Porph.*Abst.*4.8; ποδῶν ὑ. feet *that serve* one, S.*El.*1358. ⊛ **-ης**, ου, ὁ, (ἐρέτης) Dor. **ὑπηρέτας** *IG*4$^{2}$(1).122.40, 112 (Epid., iv B.C.), *SIG*1000.31 (Cos, i B.C.):—*rower*, τοὶ ὑ. τᾶν μακρᾶν ναῶν *SIG* l. c. (dub. sens.). II. *underling*, *servant*, *attendant*, Hdt.3.63, 5.111; δοῦλοι καὶ πάντες ὑ. Pl.*Plt.*289c; ὑ. [τῆς πόλεως], opp. ἄρχων, Id.*R.*552b; ἡ πόλις εἰς ὑπηρέτου σχῆμα.. προεληλυθεν D.23.210; τῶν ἰατρῶν, τῶν δικαστῶν ὑ., Pl.*Lg.*720a, 873b; used in Trag. and Att. to express all kinds of *subordinate* relations, as Hermes is ὑ. θεῶν, A.*Pr.*954, cf. 983; the Delphians are Φοίβου ὑπηρέται, S.*OT*712; Neoptolemus is ὑ. to Odysseus, Id.*Ph.*53; the αὐλός is ὑ. to the Chorus, Pratin.Lyr.1.7: sts. c. dat., τῷ θεῷ ὑ. Pl.*Lg.*773e; τοῖς νόμοις ib.715c, Arist.*Pol.*1287$^{a}$21; also οἱ περὶ τυράννους καὶ πόλεις ὑ. E.*Tr.*426; opp. οἰκέτης, X.*Mem.*2.10.3: c. gen. objecti, ὑ. παντὸς ἔργου *a helper in* every work, Id.*An.*1.9.18. 2. at Athens, a. *the servant who attended each man-at-arms* (ὁπλίτης) to carry his baggage, rations, and shield, Th.3.17; sts. light-armed as slingers or bowmen, Ar.*Av.*1186. b. ὁ τῶν ἕνδεκα ὑ. the *assistant* of the Eleven, employed in executions of state-criminals, Pl.*Phd.*116b, cf. X.*HG*2.3.54, 2.4.8. c. a *petty officer* of the Council, *IG*1$^{2}$.879 (pl.), *Hesperia* 3.63 (iv B.C.). 3. pl., *staff-officers in immediate attendance on the general*, *aides-de-camp*, *adjutants*, X.*Cyr.*2.4.4, 6.2.13, etc.: sg., D.50.31; also, *officer attached to* τάξις, σύνταγμα, or ἑκατονταρχία, Ascl.*Tact.*2.9, 6.3, Ael.*Tact.*9.4, 16.2, Arr.*Tact.*10.4, 14.4. 4. *servitor* in the cult of Mithras, *Rev.Hist.Rel.*109.64 (Rome). **-ησία**, ἡ, = sq., *Gloss.* **-ησις**, εως, ἡ, *service*, τὰ εἰς -ήσεις σώματος Arist.*Rh.*1384$^{a}$18. **-ητέον**, *one must serve*, φίλῳ Id.*EN*1164$^{b}$25. **-ικός**, ή, όν, *menial*, ἐν ὑ. μοίρᾳ τινί Pl.*Plt.*290c; ὅπλα ὑ. the arms *of the hired soldiery*, X.*Cyr.*2.1.18. 2. *of* or *for service*, *doing service*, τὸ μὲν -ώτατον.. τῷ σώματι, τὸ δὲ ἀρχικώτατον Pl.*Lg.*942e; ἐπιμέλειαι ὑ. *of public servants*, Arist.*Pol.*1299$^{a}$24; ἡ θεοῖς ὑ. (sc. τέχνη) Pl.*Euthphr.*13e; ἡ ἰατροῖς ὑ. εἰς τίνος ἔργου ἀπεργασίαν τυγχάνει οὖσα ὑ.; ib.d; *serviceable*, τοῖς τῆς ψυχῆς ἔργοις -ώτατον.. τὸ θερμόν ἐστιν Arist.*PA*652$^{b}$10. 3. opp. ἀρχικός, *subordinate*, Id.*Pol.*1260$^{a}$23, cf. 1256$^{a}$5; ἀγαθά, opp. προηγούμενα, Arr.*Epict.*2.8.6, cf. Iamb.*Myst.*1.5. 4. ὑ. κέλης a cock-boat, *attending on* a larger vessel, X.*HG*1.6.36; -κόν, τό (sc. πλοῖον), *dispatch-boat*, *tender*, D.50.46, Decr.ap.eund.18.106; in full, ὑ. [πλοῖον] restd. in *SIG*1053.12 (Samothrace, i B.C.); ὑ. νῆες D.S.13.14; ὁ ἐπὶ τῶν ὑ. Aeschin.2.73. **-ις**, ιδος, fem. of ὑπηρέτης II, E.*IA*322 (troch.), Pl.*Plt.*305c, Sor.1.73, al., Sch.Ar.*Ra.*206: metaph., δυνάμεις θρέψεως -έτιδες Gal.8.367, cf. *Nat.Fac.*3.9.

**ὑπήτιον**, τό, *subula*, *Gloss.* (cf. ὄπεας).

**ὑπήτριον**, τό, *the part of the body below the* ἦτρον, *paunch*, θύννων Theopomp.Com.51.

**ὑπηχέω**, *sound in answer*, *echo*, *respond*, ὑπὸ δ' ἤχεεν οὔρεα μακρά Hes.*Th.*835; ἔρρηξε δ' αὐδήν, ὥσθ' ὑπηχῆσαι χθόνα E.*Supp.*710; ὥστε τὴν κώμην ὑπηχεῖν so that the village *rang again*, Pherecr.10 (troch.); θερινὸν ὑπηχεῖ τῷ τῶν τεττίγων χορῷ *echoes* summer-like with the cicada-choir, Pl.*Phdr.*230c; of musical strings, Arist.*Pr.*921$^{b}$15: metaph., with neut. Adj., ἄλλο ὑ. Luc.*DMar.*1.4; σαθρὸν καὶ ἀγεννές Plu.2.64e. 2. *prompt*, *suggest*, esp. of an inner voice, Ph.1.599, 645, 659, 692, 2.12; καθάπερ ὑποβολέως ἔνδοθεν ὑπηχοῦντος ib.416.

**ὑπηῷος**, η, ον, (ἠώς) = ὑπηοῖος, A.R.4.841, Q.S.4.111, etc.

**ὑπίημι**, **ὑπήσω**, Ion. for ὑφ- (q.v.).

**ὑπίλλω**, v. ὑπείλλω, ὑπειλέομαι.

**ὕπισθα**, Aeol. for ὄπισθε, A.D.*Adv.*193.13.

**ὑπίσσω**, v. ὀπίσω. **ὑπίστημι**, Ion. for ὑφίστημι.

**ὑπισχνέομαι**, Ion. and Ep. **ὑπίσχομαι** Od.8.347, Hdt.5.30, al., also A.*Eu.*804, Ar.*Fr.*615, *IG*2$^{2}$.1126.11 (Delph. Amphict.), *Schwyzer*323*A*14 (Delph., iv B.C.); impf. ὑπίσχετο Il.23.195, ὑπίσχεο 20.84, ὑπίσχοντο Hdt.7.168; but Hdt. also has ὑπισχνέετο 9.109 (v.l. for -έεται); ὑπισχνεύμενος 2.152; ὑπισχνοῦμαι S.*Ichn.*2; imper. ὑπισχνοῦ Ar.*V.*750 (anap.): fut. ὑποσχήσομαι D.19.324: aor. ὑπεσχόμην Il.9.263, etc.: pf. ὑπέσχημαι Th.8.48, X.*Oec.*3.1, D.

7.33, etc.: plpt. ὑπέσχητο Id.19.121:—Act. ὑπισχνέω Aesop.205.—A collat. form of ὑπέχομαι, which supplies several of its tenses, and even in pres. is used = ὑπισχνέομαι, App.*Mith.*16,20, *PBrem.*36.10, *PRyl.*96.9, *PGiss.*5.10 (all ii A. D.), etc. (ὑπίσχομαι was replaced by ὑπισχνέομαι under the influence of the opposite ἀρνέομαι):—*take upon oneself*, i. e. *undertake to do*, δείδω μὴ οὔ τίς τοι ὑπόσχηται τόδε ἔργον Il.10.39; τροφαῖσι βασιλικαῖσι καὶ παιδεύμασιν ἅπανθ' ὑπισχνεῖθ' ὡς ἀπὸ σπλάγχνων ἐῶν Ezek.*Exag.*38 (s.v.l.): more freq., *promise*, ὑποσχέσθαι δ' ἑκατόμβας Il.6.115, cf. 23.195; ὅσσα τοι..ὑπέσχετο δῶρα 9.263; βουλέων, ἅς τέ μοι αὐτὸς ὑ. 12.236, cf. 20.84; ὑ. δαπάνην τῇ στρατιῇ Hdt.5.30; [πόλεσιν] ὀλιγαρχίαν Th.8.48, etc.: with a thing as subject, τῆς τῶν ὀδόντων ἀναφυήσεως ὑπισχνουμένης τὴν τῶν στερεμνιωτέρων διαίρεσιν καὶ λείωσιν Sor.1.116; τὰ στύφειν ὑπισχνούμενα ib.120. b. c. inf. fut., ὑπό τ' ἔσχετο—καὶ κατένευσε—δωσέμεναι Il.13.368, cf. Od.4.6; ὑ.—καὶ κατένευσεν—Ἴλιον ἐκπέρσαντ'.. ἀπονέεσθαι (for this Verb has a fut. sense) Il.2.112, 9.19; ὑ. Ἑλένην.. δωσέμεν Ἀτρεΐδῃσιν ἄγειν 22.114; ὑ. δυοκαίδεκα βοῦς..ἱερευσέμεν 6.93; so in Trag. and Att., S.*Ph.*615, E.*Tr.*930, Pl.*Phdr.* 235d, etc.; also ὑ. ἦ μήν.., c. inf. fut., X.*Cyr.*6.2.3: c. acc. et inf. fut., ἐγὼ δέ τοι αὐτὸν ὑπίσχομαι..τείσειν Od.8.347, cf. A.*Eu.*804. c. c. inf. aor., only f.l., as in X.*An.*1.2.2, 2.3.19 (where the variants παύσεσθαι, βουλεύσεσθαι are now accepted), while in *Cyr.*2.2.12, 6.1.21, *An.*7.2.24 he uses inf. fut.; in D.42.17, for ἀποφαίνειν Cobet restores ἀποφανεῖν. d. freq. with a neut. Adj., μεγάλα ὑ. Hdt. 2.152, al.: without acc., ὑπίσχεται ἀνδρὶ ἑκάστῳ *she makes promises* to each man, Od.2.91; ὑπισχνέεται καὶ ὄμοσε Hdt.9.109, cf. 5.51; ἠρώτα αὐτὴν εἰ ἐθελήσει διακονῆσαί οἱ, καὶ ἡ ὑπέσχετο τάχιστα Antipho 1.16; ὑποσχόμενος.., ἃ ὑπεδέξατο οὐκ ἐπετέλει Th.2.95. 2. c. inf. pres., *profess that* one is, *profess* to be, ὑ. οἷός τε εἶναι Hdt.7. 104; οὐδεὶς ὑπέσχετο εἰδέναι Id.2.28, cf. Pl.*Sph.*234b, *Tht.*178e; also, *profess* to do a thing, ὑ. ποιεῖν ἄνδρας ἀγαθοὺς πολίτας Id.*Prt.* 319a, cf. *Sph.*232d; θεοὺς ὑ. πείθειν Id.*Lg.*909b; ὑ. συστρατεύεσθαι X.*An.*7.7.31 (-σεσθαι Cobet); with ὡς, ὑ. ὡς.. ἐπίσταται Pl.*Ion* 541e. 3. *consent*, οὐχ ὑπέσχετο λαβεῖν τιμὴν (price) ἀλλ' ἐχαρίσατο *Sammelb.*7457.8 (ii B. C.).

**ὕπισχνος**, ον, *somewhat thin*, φλοιός Dsc.3.128.

**ὑπίχνιος**, ον, *under the foot*, ἕλκος Q.S.9.383.

**ὑπν-ᾰλέος**, α, ον, (ὕπνος) = ὑπνηρός, Nic.*Th.*162, *Al.*85, Aret.*SD* 2.13; *seen in sleep*, ὄνειροι *AP*5.242 (Maced.); τέρας ὑπνα[λέον] is prob. in Pi.*Pae.*8.34. II. Act., *sending to sleep*, κόπος *AP*5.46 (Rufin.). **-ἀπάτης** [πᾱ], ου, ὁ, *cheating of sleep*, ib.164 (Mel.), 196 (Id.). **-ηλός**, ή, όν, *drowsy*, Nic.*Th.*189, Gal.1.329, D.L.6.77, Jul.*Or.*2.87a, Lib.*Or.*15.68. 2. *like sleep*, ὑ. ὁ θάνατος ἐντρέχει Philostr.*Im.*2.6: metaph., *indolent*, Aristid.1.424 J. 3. *soporific*, Philostr.*VA*8.7.7. **-ηρός**, ά, όν, = foreg. I: τὸ ὑ. *drowsiness*, Hp. *Aër.*24. **-ίδιος**, α, ον, = foreg., *AP*7.198 (Leon.), dub. cj. for ὑμνιδίῳ. **-ίζω**, *put to sleep*, Phryn.*PS*p.119 B. **-ικός**, ή, όν, *of* or *for sleep*, *producing sleep*, Hp.*Liqu.*1, Aret.*CA*1.10: ὑπνικόν, τό, name of a plant, Zopyr.ap.Orib.14.50.2:—**ὑπνιακός**, in Hsch. s. v. *μυστικός*.

**ὑπνο-δότης**, ου, ὁ, *giver of sleep*, ὀτοβεῖ δόναξ..ὑπνοδόταν νόμον A. *Pr.*575 (lyr.):—fem. **-δότειρα**, *she that gives sleep*, E.*Or.*175 (lyr.); Ion. -δοτείρη *Epigr.Gr.*312.1 (Smyrna):—a form *ὑπνοδῶτις, ιδος, ἡ [with ῠ], occurs in Orph.*H.*57.8. **-μᾰχέω**, *fight with sleep*, *withstand sleep*, X.*Cyr.*2.4.26, D.C.72.8; rejected by Moer.p.376 P. and Thom.Mag.p.365 R.

**ὕπνον**, τό, a kind of *lichen*, Aët.1.75, and cited by Cornarius *Comm. ad Gal.Pharm.sec.locos*, Basil.1537, p.290, from Aët.12.44 (= 55 Kostomiris), 13.117,118.

**ὑπνο-ποιέω**, *cause* or *bring sleep*, Sever.ap.Aët.7.96, Alex.Trall.1. 11. **-ποιός**, όν, *causing sleep*, Dsc.1.1, al., Gal.1.585, 19.382, Ael.*NA*6.14, *Gp.*8.3.

***ὕπνος**, ὁ, *sleep*, *slumber*, Od.11.245, al. (v. infr.); *of the sleep of death*, κοιμήσατο χάλκεον ὕ. Il.11.241; Κάλχανθ' ὕ. θανάτοιο κάλυψεν Hes.*Fr.*160 codd.Str.; ὕπνῳ καὶ καμάτῳ ἀρημένος Od.6.2, cf. 12.281; τάπητες μαλακώτεροι ὕπνω Theoc.15.125, cf. 5.51.—Special phrases: I. of going to *sleep*, μιν ἐπήλυθε..ὕ. Od. 4.793; ἐπὶ..ὕ. ὄρουσεν Il.23.232; ἱκάνει 1.610; ἔχει 10.4, etc.; τὸν ὕ. ἔμαρπτε 23.62, al.; ᾕρει 24.4, al.; λαμβάνει S.*Ph.*767; opp. ὕπνος ἀνῆκέ τινα Il.2.71, Od.19.551, Pl.*Prt.*310d: of persons, ὕπνον ἀωτεῖν Il.10.159, etc.; ὕπνου δῶρον ἕλοντο Od.16.481, etc.; λαβεῖν Pl.*Smp.*223b; κοιμᾶσθαι X.*Hier.*6.7; ἡδὺν ὕπνον καθεύδειν Men.*Kith.Fr.*1.5; ὕπνου τυχεῖν Ar.*Ach.*713; μικρὸν ὕπνου λαχών X. *An.*3.1.11; ὕπνου λαχεῖν μέρος Cratin.218; ἐν ὕπνῳ or ὕπνῳ πεσεῖν to fall a-*sleep*, Pi.*I.*4(3).23(41), A.*Eu.*68; εἰς ὕπνον πεσεῖν S.*Ph.*826; οὐχ ὕπνῳ γ' εὕδοντα (so Badham for εὕδοντά) μ' ἐξεγείρετε Id.*OT*65; also ὕπνῳ δεδμημένος, δαμείς, Il.10.2, 14.353, etc.; νικώμενος, κρατηθείς, A.*Ag.*290, *Eu.*148 (lyr.); κάτοχος S.*Tr.*978 (lyr.); σκεδάσαι.. ἀπὸ βλεφάρων ὕπνον ib.991 (lyr.). 2. of waking from sleep, ἐγεῖραί τινα ἐξ ὕπνου Od.15.44, etc.: of the sleeper, ἀνόρουσε, ἔγρετο, ἐξ ὕ. Il. 10.162, 2.41; ἐξ ὕ. στῆναι S.*Ph.*277; ἀπολακτίσασ' ὕπνον A.*Eu.*141; ἀποσείσασθαι Luc.*Tim.*6. 3. with Preps., when the pl. also is not uncommon, ἐν ὕπνῳ in *sleep*, in *a dream*, E.*IT*44, Pl.*R.*476c; ἐν τοῖς ὕ. ib.572b, *Sph.*266b, Isoc.9.21, *PCair.Zen.*34.5 (iii B. C.); καθ' ὕπνον ὄντα S.*Tr.*970 (lyr.), cf. Pl.*Lg.*800a; καθ' ὕπνον, κατὰ τοὺς ὕπνους, Plu.2.717e, 555b, *Alex.*50; περὶ πρῶτον ὕ. about one's first *sleep*, Ar.*V.*31, Th.2.2; περὶ πρώτους ὕ. Eub.13; ἀπὸ πρώτου ὕ. Th.7.43; διὰ μέσων τῶν ὕ. Plu.*Them.*28; ἐκ τῶν ὕ. ἐγείρεσθαι Pl.*R.*330e: pl., *dreams*, ὕ. ἀγένητοι Phld.*D.*1.22. II. *Sleep*, as a god, twin-brother of Death, Il.14.231, 16.672,682; acc. to Hes.*Th.*212, son of Night without father. [ῠ by nature, A.*Th.*3, *Ag.*14,912, etc.; ῡ by position in Ep., etc.] (Cf. Skt. *svápati* 'sleep', Subst. *svápnas* 'sleep, dream'; Lat. *somnus*, *sopor*, etc.)

**Ὑπνοτράπεζος** [ᾰ], ὁ, *Table-sleeper*, name of a parasite, Alciphr. 3.60.

**ὑπνο-φᾰνής**, ές, *appearing in sleep*, Man.4.364. **-φόβης**, ου, ὁ, *driving away sleep*, of Dionysus, *AP*9.524.21. **-φόρος**, ον, *bringing sleep*, Plu.2.657d, Lycusap.Orib.9.46.2.

***ὑπν-όω**, fut. -ώσω *Gp.*18.14.3: aor. ὕπνωσα Hp.*Epid.*3.1.γ', Plb.3. 81.5, Lxx *Si.*46.20, J.*AJ*1.12.1, Plu.*Alex.*76, etc.: pf. ὕπνωκα Id.2. 236b, (καθ-) J.*AJ*5.9.3:—Med., fut. ὑπνώσομαι ibid.:—Pass., pf. part. ὑπνωμένος Hdt.1.11, 3.69: aor. ὑπνώθην Plu.2.313a:—*put to sleep*, only in Dsc.4.63:—Pass., *fall asleep*, *sleep*, Hdt. ll. cc.:—so in Med., J. l. c. II. intr., like Pass., Hp.*Epid.*3.1.γ', 7.11 (ὑπνώσσουσα Littré, with cod. C), Arist.*Somn.Vig.*454ᵃ2, *Fr.*10, J.*AJ*1.12.1; Lacon. inf. ὑπνῶν, for -οῦν, Ar.*Lys.*143. III. *die*, Lxx l. c. (Cf. ὑπνώω.) **-ώδης**, ες, *drowsy*, E.*HF*1049 (lyr.), Arist.*Phgn.*808ᵃ 28, cf. *Pr.*909ᵇ37 (Comp.); ἕξις Pl.*R.*404a. 2. *asleep*, ὑ. εἶδεν ὄναρ *Epigr.Gr.*774.1 (Priene, iv/iii B. C.). 3. *inducing sleep*, Thphr. *HP*9.11.5. **-ωδία**, ἡ, *sleepiness*, *drowsiness*, Iamb.*Protr.*21.κε' p. 110 P. **-ώσσω**, Att. -ττω, *to be sleepy* or *drowsy*, ἄγαν ὑπνώσσεις A.*Eu.* 121, cf. 124, Hp.*Epid.*7.11 (v. ὑπνόω II), Pl.*R.*534c, Arist.*PA*653ᵃ14, Gal.4.436,439: simply, *sleep*, E.*Or.*173 (lyr.), *Cyc.*454 (where Herm. ὑπνώσσῃ for -ώσῃ): metaph., φόβῳ δ' οὐχ ὑπνώσσει κέαρ my heart *knows* not *sleep*, A.*Th.*288 (lyr.). **-ωτικός**, ή, όν, *inclined to sleep*, *sleepy*, *drowsy*, Arist.*Somn.Vig.*457ᵃ26; μετὰ τὰ σιτία -ώτατοι Id.*Pr.* 874ᵇ17, cf. 876ᵃ20 (Comp.). Adv. -κῶς Gal.19.149. II. Act., *putting to sleep*, *narcotic*, μηκώνιον Hp.*Mul.*2.201; θρίδαξ Diph.Siph. ap.Ath.2.69f; φάρμακα Plu.2.652c; πότημα *POxy.*1088.66 (i A. D.): as Subst., -κὸν πίνειν *a narcotic*, Plu.*Caes.*34; pl., Arist.*Somn.Vig.* 456ᵇ29, Porph.*Abst.*1.27. **-ώω**, Ep. Verb, perh. *to be drowsy*, *tired*, τοὺς δ' αὖτε καὶ ὑπνώοντας ἐγείρει Il.24.344, Od.5.48, 24.4; ὅτε..ἐπὶ κοῖτον ἐκ νομοῦ ὑπνώουσα κίῃ Nic.*Th.*127; but elsewh., *sleep*, τὴν εἴσιδον ὑπνώουσα Mosch.2.24; ἔννυχον ὑπνώοντι Maiist.22; ὑπνώοντες ῥέγκουσιν Nic.*Th.*433; ὀφθαλμοῖσιν ἀμοιβαδὸν ὑπνώεσκε, of Argus, Q.S.10.191: metaph. of the stars, Coluth.349 (s. v. l.).

***ὑπό** [ῠ], Prep. with gen., dat., and acc.: Aeol. ὑπά Alc.39; Boeot. ὑπά Ἀρχ.Δελτ.14 Pl. ii 19 (Thespiae, iii B. C.); Ion. *hυπύ* only in *IG* 14.871 (Cumae, v B. C.); Arc. ὀπύ *Schwyzer* 664.15,21 (Orchom. Arc., iv B. C.); in Ep. Poets (also B.12.139) ὑπαί: this is found in Hom. only six times as a well-attested reading (ὑ. πόδα Il.2.824, ὑ. δέ 3. 217, 11.417, 12.149, ὑ. δείους 10.376, 15.4); elsewh. (before λ ν ρ ϝ) it is weakly attested as v.l. for ὑπὸ (⏑ –), e.g. ποσσὶ δ' ὑπὸ (v. l. ὑπαὶ) λιπαροῖσι Il.2.44, al.; but ὑπαὶ νεφέων is given by most codd. in Il.15. 625, 16.375 (v. Allen ed. maj.), and ὑπαὶ νεφέεσσι Anon.ap.Plu.2.38e; also in compds., ὑπαιδείδοικα *h.Merc.*165, ὑπαιφοινίσσω (q. v.); it is not freq. in Trag. Poets, A.*Ag.*892,944,1164 (lyr.), *Eu.*417, S.*El.* 711,1418 (lyr.), *Inach.* in *PTeb.*692 ii 5 (lyr.), E.*El.*1188 (lyr.), Ar. *Ach.*970 (paratrag.). (With ὑπό (ὕπο) cf. Skt. *úpa* 'towards, near to, etc.', Goth. *uf* 'under'.)

A. WITH GENITIVE, I. of Place, with Verbs of motion, *from under*, αὖτις ἀναστήσονται ὑ. ζόφου they will rise again *from under* the gloom, Il.21.56; ὑ. χθονὸς ἧκε φόωσδε Hes.*Th.*669; ῥέει κρήνη ὑ. σπείους Od.9.141, cf. Pl.*Phdr.*230b; ὄσσε δεινὸν ὑ. βλεφάρων ἐξεφάανθεν Il.19.17; ἐσιδόντες ὑπαὶ χειμῶνος αἴγλαν *from under* the storm-cloud, B.12.139; esp. of rescuing *from under* another's power, after the Verbs ἐρύεσθαι, ἁρπάζειν, ῥύεσθαι, ἐρύειν, Il.9.248, 13.198, 17.224,235; ἤγαγεν ὑμέτερόνδ' ἀνδροκτασίης ὑ. λυγρῆς *from the consequences of*, 23. 86; also ἵππους μὲν λῦσαν ὑ. ζυγοῦ *from under* the yoke, 8.543, Od.4. 39; ὑπ' ἀρνειοῦ λυόμην I loosed myself *from under* the ram, 9.463; σπλάγχνων ὕπο ματέρος μόλεν, i. e. was born, Pi.*N.*1.35, cf. *O.*6.43; rarely in Trag., ὑ. πτερῶν σπάσας E.*Andr.*441; περᾷ γὰρ ἤδ' ὑ. σκηνῆς πόδα Id.*Hec.*53; once in Hdt., τὰς δέ οἱ ἵππους ὑ. τοῦ ἅρματος νεμομένας ἀφανισθῆναι 4.8; αἴ τις ὑ. τῶν νομίων τῶν ἐπιϝοίκων ἀνχωρέῃ *SIG*47.27 (Locris, v B. C.); cf. ὑπέκ. 2. of the object *under* which a thing is or is placed, *under*, *beneath*, with collat. sense of motion, as μοχλὸν ὑ. σποδοῦ ἤλασα πολλῆς thrust it *in under* the embers, Od. 9.375; ὑ. στέρνοιο τυχήσας Il.4.106; τοὺς μὲν ὑ. χθονὸς εὐρυοδείης πέμψαν Hes.*Th.*717: also without the sense of motion, ὑπ' ἀνθερεῶνος ὀχεὺς τέτατο Il.3.372; βάθιστον ὑ. χθονός ἐστι βέρεθρον 8.14; ἐτέθαπτο ὑ. χθονὸς Od.11.52; κεκευθὼς πολεμίας ὑ. χθονὸς A.*Th.*588; ὑπ' ἀγκῶνος βέλη Pi.*O.*2.83; νέρθεν ὑπ' ἐγκεφάλοιο Il.16.347; τὰ ὑ. γῆς δικαιωτήρια Pl.*Phdr.*249a; δεξιὰν ὑφ' εἵματος κρύπτειν E.*Hec.*342; φέρειν ζώνης ὕπο ib.762: Thom.Mag.p.375 R. says that ὑ. = *under* takes gen. in Att., acc. in 'Hellenic' Greek; κατακρύψας ὑ. κόπρου, which is v.l. in Od.9.329 for ὑ. κόπρῳ, is called by Eust.1631. 36 Ἀττικώτερον, ὁποῖον καὶ τὸ φέρειν τι ὑ. κόλπου ἢ ὑ. μάλης (v. κόλπος, μάλη); but in Att. Prose, Hdt., and the Koine ὑ. c. gen. in signfs. 1. 1, 2 is almost limited to these and a few other phrases, esp. ὑ. γῆς; it is not found at all in Th., Lxx, Ptolemaic papyri, and *NT*; X. has ὑ. ἁμάξης (= *from under*) *An.*6.4.22,25; the Orators have only ὑ. μάλης, Lys.*Fr.*54, D.29.12; ὑ. γῆς is found in Pl.*Ap.*18b, *Mx.* 246d, *R.*414d, al., Arist.*Mete.*352ᵇ6, al., Hipparch.2.2.45, Plb.18.18. 10 (ὑ. τῆς γῆς), 21.28.3,10. b. metaph.. ἀρετῶσι δὲ λαοὶ ὑπ' αὐτοῦ *under* his rule, Od.19.114. II. of Cause or Agency, freq. with pass. Verbs, and with intr. Verbs in pass. sense, μή πως τάχ' ὑπ' αὐτοῦ δουρὶ δαμήῃς Il.3.436, cf. 4.479; ἡνίοχοιο ἐν κονίῃσι πεσόντος ὑφ' Ἕκτορος 17.428; εὖτ' ἂν πολλοὶ ὑφ' Ἕκτορος θνήσκοντες πίπτωσι

1.242; τὸν..τοκέα ὑ. τοῦ..παιδὸς ἀποθνήσκειν Hdt.1.137; οἵαις ὑπ' αὐτοῦ πημοναῖσι κάμπτομαι A.*Pr.*308, cf. *Th.*7, al.; πέλεκυς..ὅς τ' εἶσιν διὰ δουρὸς ὑπ' ἀνέρος Il.3.61; ὑπ' Ἀχαιῶν..φοβέοντο..ἀπὸ νηῶν 16.303; πάσχειν δὲ κακῶς ἐχθρὸν ὑπ' ἐχθρῶν A.*Pr.*1042 (anap.); ὑ. τοῦ Μήδου δεινότερα τούτων πάσχοντες Th.1.77; ἐκπεσόντες ὑ. τοῦ πλήθους Id.4.66; ἀναστάτων Καμαριναίων γενομένων ὑ. Συρακοσίων Id.6.5; ὑφ' ὑμῶν αὐτῶν καὶ μὴ ὑ. τῶν πολεμίων τοῦτο παθεῖν Id.4.64; κλύοντές ἐσμεν αἰσχίστους λόγους..τοῦδ' ὑπ' ἀνδρὸς ἀρτίως we have been called shameful names *by*.., S.*Aj.*1321; κακῶς ὑ. τῶν πολιτῶν ἀκούειν to be ill spoken of *by*.., Isoc.4.77, cf. Pl.*Hp.Ma.*304e, X.*An.*7.7.23; of a subordinate agent, ὑ. κήρυκος προαγορεύειν, ἀπειπεῖν κηρύκων ὕπο, Hdt.9.98, E.*Alc.*737, cf. Th.6.32; ἐμῶν ὑπ' ἀγγέλων..πορεύεται S.*Tr.*391; ὑ. ἀγγέλων πέμπων Pl.*Phlb.*66a: sts. with a verbal Subst., τὸ ὑ. νόμου ἐπίταγμα (i.e. ἐπιταττόμενον) Id.*R.*359a; ἐκφορὰ φίλων ὕπο A.*Th.*1029; ἡ ὑπ' ἀρετῆς Ἡρακλέους παίδευσις X.*Mem.*2.1.34; ἡ ὑ. πάντων τιμή Id.*Cyr.*3.3.2; Ἥρας δεσμοὶ ὑ. υἱέος Pl.*R.*378d; so ἄτρωτον ἦν ὑ. στύγους (=οὐ τετρωμένον) prob. in A.*Ch.*532. 2. also in pregnant phrases, not only of the immediate act of the agent, but also of its further result, ὅθ' ὑ. λιγέων ἀνέμων σπέρχωσιν ἄελλαι hasten driven on *by* them, Il.13.334; ὑφ' Ἕκτορος..φεύγοντες fleeing *before* him, 18.149; χάσσονται ὑπ' ἔγχεος 13.153, cf. 7.64, 11.119,424, Od.5.320, 7.263, al.; πράγματα εἶχον ὑ. λῃστῶν X.*HG*5.1.5; ἔπαινον, αἰτίαν ἔχειν ὑ. τινῶν, Hdt.9.78, A.*Eu.*99; οὐκέτι ἀποχωρεῖν οἷόν τ' ἦν ὑ. τῶν ἱππέων Th.7.78, cf. Ar.*V.*1084. 3. freq. of things as well as persons, ὡς διάκειμαι ὑ. τῆς νόσου Th.7.77; κεῖμαι νούσου ὕ. στυγερᾶς *IG*4$^2$(1).125.8 (Epid., iii B.C.): χαλεπῶς ἔχειν ὑ. τραυμάτων Pl.*Tht.*142b; ὑ. δόρατος πλαγείς *IG*4$^2$(1).122.64 (Epid., iv B.C.); ὑ. ἔχιος φῦμα ib.123.4 (ibid., iv B.C.); ἰάθη ὑ. ὄφιος ib.121.113 (ibid., iv B.C.); κατεσκεύασαν τὰς πύλας κλείεσθαι ὑ. σφύρας τε μεγάλης καὶ κτύπου παμμεγέθους γιγνομένου Aen.Tact.20.4: of the agency of feelings, passions, etc., ἀνόρουσ' ὑ. χάρματος *h.Cer.*371; ἐνδακρύειν, ἀνολολύξαι χαρᾶς ὕπο, A.*Ag.*541,587; μαίνεται..ὑφ' ἡδονῆς S.*El.*1153; χλωρὸς ὑπαὶ δείους Il.10.376; ὑ. δέους ἔρρηξε φωνήν Hdt.1.85, cf. Th.6.33; οὐ δυνατὸν τὸν δῆμον ἐσόμενον ὑ. τῶν κακῶν καρτερεῖν Id.4.66; ὑ. κακοῦ ἀγρυπνίῃσι εἴχετο Hdt.3.129; ὑπ' ἄλγους A.*Eu.*183; ὑπ' ὀργῆς Ar.*V.*1083; ὑ. λύπης S.*OT*1073: hence ὑπό is used even with active Verbs, where a passive word may be supplied, e.g. ὑ. ἀρετῆς καὶ προθυμίης συνεπλήρουν τὰς νέας *from* courage, i.e. impelled *by* courage, Hdt.8.1; ὤρυσσον ὑ. μαστίγων Id.7.22, cf. 56; οὐδὲ σέ γε δόλος ἔσχ' ὑ. χειρὸς ἐμᾶς *by* my agency, S.*Ph.*1118 (lyr.); αἰ μήτις αὐτὸς δοίη, μὴ ὑπ' ἀνάγκας not *under* compulsion, *GDI*5128.5 (Vaxos). 4. ὑπό freq. serves to denote the attendant or accompanying circumstances, νέφος ἐρχόμενον κατὰ πόντον ὑ. Ζεφύροιο ἰωῆς Il.4.276, cf. 16.591, etc.: sts. with part. added, ἀμφὶ δὲ νῆες σμερδαλέον κονάβησαν ἀϋσάντων ὑπ' Ἀχαιῶν *at* their shouting, i.e. when they shouted, 2.334, 16.277; ἴαχε σάλπιγξ ἄστυ περιπλομένων δηΐων ὕ. 18.220. 5. of *accompanying* music, to give the time, κώμαζον ὑπ' αὐλοῦ Hes.*Sc.*281, cf. 278; ᾄδων ὑπ' αὐλητῆρος Archil.123, cf. Thgn.825, Charon *Fr.*9; πίνειν ὑ. σάλπιγγος Ar.*Ach.*1001: generally, of anything *attendant*, δαΐδων ὕ. λαμπομενάων ἠγίνεον *by* torch-light, Il.18.492, cf. E.*Hel.*639 (lyr.), *Ion* 1474 (lyr.); καταθάψομεν..ὑ. κλαυθμῶν A.*Ag.*1554 (anap.); ὑπ' εὐκλείας θανεῖν E.*Hipp.*1299; εἴσειμ' ὑπαὶ πτερύγων κιχλᾶν καὶ κοψίχων Ar.*Ach.*970; ὑπ' εὐφήμου βοῆς θῦσαι offer a sacrifice *accompanied by* it, S.*El.*630; ὑ. φανοῦ πορεύεσθαι *by* lantern-light, X.*Lac.*5.7; ὑ. πομπῆς ἐξάγειν τινά *in* or *with* solemn procession, Hdt.2.45, cf. Ar.*Th.*1030; ὑ. βίης βήξας coughing *with* violence, violently, Hdt.6.107; ἐτόξευον ὑ. μαστίγων, i.e. they shot and lashed, X.*An.*3.4.25: v. infr. B. II. 4, C. IV. 1. 6. ὑ. Ἑλλανοδικᾶν, = ἐπί c. gen., *SIG*171 (Olympia, iv B.C.). 7. Math., ἡ ὑ. ΘΔΗ *the angle* ΘΔΗ (= ἡ ὑ. τῶν ΘΔ, ΔΗ περιεχομένη γωνία), Procl.*Hyp.*2.26; but also τὸ ὑ. τῶν ΑΓ, ΓΒ *the rectangle contained by* ΑΓ, ΓΒ, = ΑΓ × ΓΒ, Euc.2.4. 8. ναῦλον ὄνων γ' εἰς τὴν πόλιν ὑ. οἴνου *laden with* wine, Pap. in *Hermes* 28.163 (ii A.D.), cf. ib.479, and infr. C. IV. 2.

B. WITH DATIVE (esp. in Poets, never in Lxx (*Jb.*12.5 is dub. l.) or *NT*, not common in Arist., Ptolemaic papyri, or Plb.), of Position *under*, ὑ. ποσσί Il.2.784, al.; ὑ. πλατανίστῳ ib.307, cf. 18.558; ὑ. Τμώλῳ *at* its *foot*, 2.866, cf. Od.1.186; Βερύσιοι ὑ. τῇ Ἴδῃ *IG*1$^2$.191.11, cf. 373.118, al.; ὑ. τῇ ἀκροπόλι Hdt.6.105; τῶν θανόντων ὑπ' Ἰλίῳ *under* its walls, E.*Hec.*764, cf. A.*Ag.*860; πέτρῃ ὕ. γλαφυρῇ εὗδον, Βορέω ὑπ' ἰωγῇ Od.14.533; ὑ. τοῖς ὄρεσιν ἔχειν τὰς πηγάς Arist.*Mete.*350$^b$27; ὑ. πέτρᾳ παῖς *IG*4$^2$(1).122.19 (Epid., iv B.C.); ὑ. τῷ ναῷ ἀστραγαλίζοντος αὐτοῦ ib.121.25 (ibid., iv B.C.); hυπὺ τῇ κλίνῃ τούτῃ ληνὸς (or Λῆνος) hύπυ ib.14.871 (Cumae, v B.C.); στρουθοὶ ὑ. τῇ τραπέζῃ *Michel* 832.33 (Samos, iv B.C.); ὑ. τῇ μασχάλῃ Hp.*Art.*11; χέλυν δ' ὑ. μασχάλῃ εἶχεν *h.Merc.*242; ὑ. ταῖς μασχάλαις Arist.*PA*688$^b$5,14; ὁ ὑ. τῇ γῇ ἀήρ *under* the earth, Id.*Cael.*295$^a$28; ἐὰν ὑ. σοὶ κατακλινῇ lies *next below* you, Pl.*Smp.*222e; ὑφ' ἅρμασι *under*, i.e. *yoked to*, the chariot, Il.8.402, 18.244; εἶχε μάχαιραν ὑφ' αὐτῷ παρεσκευασμένος Plb.8.20.6 codd., cf. *POxy.*1800 *Fr.*2.36 (*Vit.Aesop.*); ὑ. τοῖς χιτωνίσκοις περιζώματα φοροῦσιν Plb.12.26$^a$.4, cf. 13.7.9; τά τε θηρία καὶ τὰς ὑπ' αὐτοῖς σχεδίας *under* them, on which they stood, Id.3.46.8; τῆς γῆς τῆς ὑ. τῷ κόσμῳ κειμένης Timae.ap.eund.12.25.7; οἱ ὑ. τῇ ἄρκτῳ, τῇ μεσημβρίᾳ, οἰκοῦντες Adam.2.31, cf. Arist.*Pr.*940$^a$37, *Phgn.*806$^b$16; ὑ. τῷ μετώπῳ ὀφρύες Id.*HA*491$^b$14; ὑ. τῷ γενείῳ Plb.34.10.9; τὰ ὑ. τοῖς ὕδασι καὶ ὑμέσι καὶ ὑέλοις Hero *Deff.*135.12; ὑ. τῷ δέρματι Gal.18(2).102. 2. with Verbs of motion, where rest or position follows, εἷσαν ὑ. φηγῷ set [him] *down under* it, Il.5.693; ἔζευξαν ὑφ' ἅρμασιν..ἵππους Od.3.478, cf. Il.24.782; ὑ. δ' ἄξοσι..ἔπιπτον 16.378, cf. X.*Cyr.*7.1.37; δέμνι' ὑπ' αἰθούσῃ θέμεναι Il.24.644. 3. in such phrases as ὑ. χερσί τινος ἁλῶναι, δαμῆναι, 2.374,860, al.; ἐμῇς ὑ. χερσὶ δάμασσον 3.352; ὑ. δουρὶ δαμῆναι 5.653, etc.; ἔκπεσον ἵππων Ἀτρεΐδεω ὑ. χερσί 11.180; ὤλετο..ὑ. γαμφηλῇσι λέοντος 16.489; πέπληγμαι δ' ὑπαὶ δάκει φοινίῳ A.*Ag.*1164 (lyr.); ἐν κονίῃσι πέσοιεν ὑπ' ἀνδράσι Il.6.453; ὑ. τινὶ κτείνεσθαι 16.490. 4. *behind*, ὑ. φάλαγγι Ascl.*Tact.*6.1; *under the cover* or *protection of*, ὑ. τούτῳ τῷ φράγματι τοὺς ὑπορύσσοντας εἶναι Aen.Tact.37.9; ὑ. ταῖς αὐτῶν ἀσφαλείαις Plb.1.57.8, 4.12.10, 16.6.1. II. of the person *under whose hand, power*, or *influence*, or the thing *by* or *through which* a thing is done, ὑπ' Ἀργείοισι φέβοντο fled *before* them, Il.11.121; freq. in Hom. with intr. or pass. Verbs, ἐφόβηθεν ὑφ' Ἕκτορι Il.15.637; ὁρμηθέντες ὑ. πληγῇσιν ἱμάσθλης Od.13.82; βῆ..θεῶν ὑ. πομπῇ Il.6.171; ὦρτο δὲ κῦμα πνοιῇ ὕπο 23.215; ὑ. λαίλαπι βέβριθε χθών 16.384; τεκεῖν, τεκέσθαι ὑ. τινί, 2.714,728,742; ἀτῆθαι ὑ. τῷ μεμφομένῳ *GDI*4994.8 (Crete); ὁ χρησμὸς ὁ γεγονὼς ὑ. τοῖ Ἀπόλλωνι *Inscr.Magn.*38.5, cf. 12,31,52. 2. expressing *subjection* or *dependence*, ὑ. τινί *under* one's *power*, δέδμητο δὲ λαὸς ὑπ' αὐτῷ Od.3.305, cf. Il.9.156; ὑπ' ἀνδράσιν οἶκον ἔχουσιν Od.7.68; εἶναι ὑ. τισί to be *subordinate, subject to* them, Th.1.32; ὑ. Χείρωνι τεθραμμένος *under the eye of*.., Pl.*R.*391c; ἔχειν ὑφ' ἑαυτῷ have *under* one, *at* one's *command*, X.*Cyr.*2.1.26; τὰ θηρία τὰ ὑ. τοῖς ἀνθρώποις Pl.*R.*563c; ὑ. τινὶ στρατεύσασθαι Plu.*Cic.*44: in pregnant sense, ἵνα..πάντα ὑ. Πέρσῃσι γένηται Hdt.7.11, cf. Th.7.64; ὑπ' ἑωυτῷ ποιήσασθαι Hdt.7.157; κινδυνεύσαιμ' ἂν ὑ. τῇ δυσχερεστάτῃ γενέσθαι τύχῃ Lys.24.6; ὑ. τῷ Μακεδόνι ταττομένων Plb.18.11.4; τοὺς τραφέντας ὑ. τούτοις Id.6.7.2. 3. of the subordination of things coming *under* a class, αἱ ὑ. ταῖς τέχναις ἐργασίαι Pl.*Smp.*205c; τὸ ὑ. ταῖς γεωμετρίαις Id.*R.*511b; ὄργανα..τὰ ὑ. τῇ μουσικῇ Id.*Hp.Ma.*295d. 4. as in A. II. 5, ὑπ' αὐλητῆρι πρόσθ' ἔκιον advanced *to the music of* the flute-player, Hes.*Sc.*283; ὑπ' αὐλῷ, ὑ. κήρυκι καὶ θεολόγῳ, Luc.*DDeor.*2.2, *Alex.*19; ὑ. μάστιξι διορύττειν τὸν Ἄθω Plu.2.470e: generally, of attendant circumstances, ἐξ ἁλὸς εἶσι..πνοιῇ ὕπο Ζεφύροιο Od.4.402; ὑ. ῥάβδοις καὶ πελέκεσι κατιών *escorted by* the lictors, Plu.*Publ.*10; ὑ. σκότῳ, νυκτί, A.*Ag.*1030 (lyr.), A.R.1.1022, etc.; λάμπει δ' ὑ. μαρμαρυγαῖς ὁ χρυσός B.3.17; αἰθομένα δᾲς ὑ. ξανθαῖσι πεύκαις Pi.*Fr.*79; ὑ. φωτὶ πολλῷ προσῄει Plu.*Galb.*14; ὑ. λαμπάσιν ἡμμέναις Hld.10.41; ὑ. πολλῷ στρατῷ *escorted by* a great host, Nic.Dam.10 J.; ὑ. δικαιοσύνῃ διαγαγεῖν τὸν βίον Pl.*Ep.*335d.—ὑπό has no sense c. dat. which it has not also c. gen.; but all its senses c. gen. do not belong to the dat.:—later ὑπό c. dat. is found as a mere periphr. of the dat., στέφος..αὐτὸς ὑφ' ἡμετέραις πλεξάμενος παλάμαις *AP*5.73 (Rufin.), cf. 85 (Claudian.); λέων ὑπ' ἄκοντι τετυμμένος A.R.2.26, cf. Man.2.131.

C. WITH ACCUSATIVE, of Place; to express motion *towards and under* an object, ὑ. σπέος ἤλασε μῆλα drove them *under*, i.e. *into*, the cave, Il.4.279; ὑ. ζυγὸν ἤγαγεν Od.3.383; σεῦ ὕστερος εἶμ' ὑ. γαῖαν, i.e. shall die, Il.18.333; νέεσθαι ὑ. ζόφον 23.51, cf. Od.3.335; κατακρύπτειν τινὰ ὑ. τὴν αὐτὴν θύρην *under shelter* of it, i.e. *behind* it, Hdt.1.12; πάϊς ὣς ὑ. μητέρα δύσκεν εἰς Αἴαντα Il.8.271; ὅκως ἔωσι ὑ. τὸν πεζὸν στρατὸν τὸν σφέτερον Hdt.9.96; ὑ. τὸν πρῶτον λόχον τῶν ὁπλιτῶν τὸν πρῶτον λόχον τῶν ψιλῶν τετάχθαι Ael.*Tact.*15.2; of coming *close up under* a lofty citadel, ἤλθεθ' ὑ. Τροίην *up to* T., Od.4.146; ὅτ' ἔμελλεν ὑ. πτόλιν αἰπύ τε τεῖχος ἵξεσθαι Il.11.181; παυρότερον λαὸν ἀγαγόνθ' ὑ. τεῖχος ἄρειον 4.407; ὑ. τὰ τείχη φεύγειν Plb.1.74.11; ὑ. τὰς ἴλας φεύγειν Id.3.65.7, cf. 3.105.6, 11.21.5, al.; ὑ. ταὐτὸ στέγος εἰσελθεῖν *GDI*3536 *B* 3 (Cnidus); πᾶν ὃ ἐὰν ἔλθῃ..ὑ. τὴν ῥάβδον Lxx *Le.*27.32, cf. *De.*4.11, al.; so ὑ. δικαστήριον ὑπαχθείς, ἀγαγόντες, Hdt.6.72,104 (cf. ὑπάγειν ὑ. τοὺς ἐφόρους ib.82) prob. refers to the elevated seats of the judges in court, cf. ὑπάγω A. II. 2. of Position or Extension *under* an object, without sense of motion, Ἀρκαδίην ὑ. Κυλλήνης ὄρος Il.2.603, cf. 824, etc.; ἰκριώσασι ὑ. τὴν ὀροφήν *IG*1$^2$.374.76; ἐργασαμένοις τὸ ἄνθεμον ὑ. τὴν ἀσπίδα ib.371.9; τὰ μὲν ὑ. τὸν λόφον καὶ τὰμ φάραγγα *Inscr.Prien.*37.162 (ii B.C.); ἀνθέντω ὑ. τὸν ναὸν τᾶς Δάματρος *IG*5(1).1498.13 (loc. inc., ii B.C.); ὅσσοι ἔασιν ὑπ' ἠῶ τ' ἠέλιόν τε everywhere *under* the sun, Il.5.267; ὑπ' αὐγὰς ἠελίοιο φοιτῶσι Od.2.181; τῶν ὑ. τοῦτον τὸν ἥλιον..ἀνθρώπων D.18.270; τὰ ὑ. τὴν ἄρκτον Hdt.5.10, cf. Arist.*Mete.*362$^a$17; οἴκησις ἡ λεγομένη ὑ. τὸν πόλον Gem.5.38, cf. 16.21, al.; ὑ. τὸν οὐρανόν Lxx *Ex.*17.14, al., *UPZ*106.14 (i B.C.); τὸ ὑ. τὴν ἀκρόπολιν Th.2.17; ὁ ὑ. γῆν λεγόμενος εἶναι θεός Hdt.7.114, cf. Il.19.259; ὑ. γῆν is more freq. than ὑ. γῆς in Arist., *Mete.*349$^b$29, al., in Hipparch., 1.3.10, al., and entirely supersedes ὑ. γῆς in Hdt., 2.124,125,127,148,150, 3.102, 4.195, 7.114, and Gem., 2.19, al.; it is found also in Plb.21.28.11, etc.; ὑ. γῆν *the nadir*, opp. μεσουράνημα, *PLond.*1.98$^r$.49, 110.33 (i/ii A.D.); also ἄγχε δέ μιν..ἱμὰς ἁπαλὴν ὑ. δειρήν Il.3.371; Τρῶες..πτῶσσον ὑ. κρημνούς 21.26; ἀγέροντο..ἄλσος ὕ. σκιερόν Od.20.278; τρωθεὶς ὑ. τὸν ὀφθαλμόν *IG*4$^2$(1).122.120 (Epid., iv B.C.); οὐλὴ ὑπ' ὀφθαλμὸν δεξιόν *PCair.Zen* 76.13 (iii B.C.); ὑ. τὸ μέρος τοῦ ἐνοφειλομένου ὑπογραψάτω ὅσον ἰδίᾳ ἔχει *PRev.Laws* 19.2 (iii B.C.); κείμενος ὑ. τὸν ὀμφαλόν Sor.1.7, cf. 67, al.; ὑ. τὰς πύλας ἵππων πόδες φαίνονται Th.5.10; μὴ ὑποτιθέναι κύλικα ὑ. τὴν κλίνην *IG*12(5).593 *A* 21 (Ceos, v B.C.); ὑ. τὸν ὀδόν ib.4$^2$(1).102.249 (Epid., iv B.C.); καταψύξατε ὑ. τὸ δένδρον Lxx *Ge.*18.4; ὑ. τὸν λέβητα ib.*Ec.*7.7(6); ὑ. τοὺς πόδας ib.*La.*3.34; εἰς τοὺς ὑ. πόδα χωρεῖ τόπους Dsc.5.75 (v. πούς I. 6 g); ἡ ὑ. πόδα (sc. γραμμή) the *base* of a triangle, Hero *Mens.*55; also ὑπ' αὐγὰς..λεύσσουσαι πέπλους *holding* them *up to* the light, E.*Hec.*1154; also ὑ. τὸν ὀφθαλμόν *close to* the eye, Arist.*Pr.*874$^a$9; ὑποκειμένης τῆς Εὐβοίας ὑ. τὴν Ἀττικήν Isoc.4.108; ὑπ' αὐτὴν ἐσχάτην στήλην ἔχων ἔχριμπτ' ἀεὶ σύριγγα S.*El.*720; εἰ θεωρήσειεν ὑπ' αὐγὰς τὸν ἀνθρώπειον βίον Iamb.*Protr.*8 (cf. αὐγή 1): of subordinate position, κατακλίνεσθαι ὑ. τινά Luc.*Symp.*9; τίς ὑ. τίνα; who is *next to* whom, Onos.10.2. b. Math., ὁ κύβος ὁ ὑ. τὴν.. σφαῖραν *inscribed in* the sphere, Papp.440.5; εἶναι ὑ. τὸ αὐτὸ ὕψος Euc.11.29, Archim.*Sph.Cyl.*1.19; ὑ. τὰν αὐτὰν γωνίαν *subtending*.., Id.*Aren.* 1.20 (cj.), cf. 21; αἱ γωνίαι ὑφ' ἃς αἱ ὁμόλογοι πλευραὶ ὑποτείνουσι Euc.6.6, al. 3. of the logical subordination of things *under* a class, τῶν ἑτερογενῶν καὶ μὴ ὑπ' ἄλληλα τεταγμένων Arist.*Cat.*1ᵇ16, etc.; οἱ ὑ. τὸ ψεῦδος τεταγμένοι *in the category of*.., Luc.*Ind.*20. II. of *subjection, control, dependence*, never in Hom., once in Hdt., ὑ. βασιλέα δασμοφόρος 7.108; ὑ. σφᾶς ποιεῖσθαι Th.4.60, cf. Pl.*R.*348d, Arist. *HA*488ᵃ10, etc.; ἕως κα ᾖ ὑ. τὸν πατέρα *Test.Epict.*3.29; ὑ. τιν' ἦν τῶν βασιλέων Men.340; τί δ' οὐ κρατέοντος ὑπ' ἰσχύν; Call.*Jov.*75, cf. 74; ὑ. Δία Γῆν Ἥλιον *Sammelb.*5616 (i A.D.), *POxy.*722.6 (i/ii A.D.), etc. (v. ἥλιος II. 1); ὑ. θεὸν καὶ ἄνθρωπον *Michel*854.52 (Halic., iii B.C.); τοῦ τοπαρχοῦντος ὑ. σέ *PCair.Zen.*322.3 (iii B.C.); στρατευσάμενον ὑ. ἄρχοντα Ἀντίοχον *IG*12(1).43.7 (Rhodes); μηδὲ ὑ. δεσπότην ὤν LXX *Pr.* 6.7, cf. *Ps.*143.2; for ὑ. χεῖρα, v. χείρ; οἱ ὑ. τινά X.*Cyr.*3.3.6, 8.8.5, etc.; τοῖς ὑφ' αὐτὸν τεταγμένοις *GDI*3750.75 (Rhodes). III. of Time, *in the course of, during*, or to be left untranslated in English, ἐκέλευε Τρωσὶ ποτὶ πτόλιν ἡγήσασθαι νύχθ' ὕ. τήνδ' ὀλοήν Il.22.102; ὑ. τὴν νύκτα ταύτην Hdt.9.51, cf. 58; ὑ. τὴν πρώτην ἐπελθοῦσαν νύκτα ἀπέδρη Id. 6.2; τῆς κολοκύνθης.. ἣ ἐγενήθη ὑ. νύκτα καὶ ὑ. νύκτα ἀπώλετο LXX *Jn.*4.10: rarely with stress on the *duration*, πάνθ' ὑ. μηνιθμόν *throughout* its continuance, Il.16.202; ὑ. τὸν παρεόντα τόνδε πόλεμον Hdt.9.60; οὐδὲν τῶν κατ' Αἴγυπτον ὑ. ταῦτα ἑτεροιώθηναι *during* that time, Id.2.142; ὑ. τὸν χρόνον ὃν οἱ ἑξήκοντα καὶ τριηκόσιοι ἦρχον οἴδε ἐθεάρεον *IG*12(8).276.4 (Thasos). 2. also of Time, *about*, sts. more precisely *at*, and of events, *about* or *at the time of*, ὑπ' αὐτὸν τὸν χρόνον ὅτε.. Ar.*Ach.*139, cf. Hdt.7.165; ὑπ' αὐτὸν τὸν καιρόν Plb. 11.27.4, 16.15.8; ὑφ' ἕνα καιρόν *at* one time, Diog.Oen.38; ὑ. τὸν αὐτὸν χρόνον Th.2.26; ὑ. τοὺς αὐτοὺς χρόνους Id.1.100; ὑ. τὸν σεισμόν Id.2.27, cf. Plb.4.33.5, Plu.*Alex.*14; ὑ. τὴν ἑωθινήν, ὑ. τὴν ὄρφνην, Plb. 18.19.5,7; ὑ. τὸν ὄρθρον *Act.Ap.*5.21, *Gp.*2.4.3; ποιεῖσθαι τοὺς περιπάτους ὑ. τὸ ψῦχος *in* the cool of the morning, Plb.5.56.10; ὑφ' ἓν πάντες all *at* once, *at* the same time, Arr.*Epict.*3.22.33, cf. S.E.*M.* 10.124, Sor.1.103, al.; παιδάριον ὑ. τὴν ἀναπνοὴν ἑπτὰ καὶ πέντε στίχους συνεῖρον *in* one breath, Plb.10.47.9; ὑφ' ἓν ἐκτρῖψαι *at* one blow, LXX *Wi.*12.9; ὑ. μίαν ἄρσιν καὶ θέσιν ἀνατείνοντες καὶ καταπιθέμενοι, of a squad of diggers, *Gp.*2.45.5; ὑ. μίαν φωνήν Aristeas 178; πῶς γὰρ ἂν ὑ. τὰς αὐτὰς ἡμέρας ἔν τε τῇ Ἰταλίᾳ καὶ ἐν τῇ Κιλικίᾳ.. πολεμήσειε; *at* the same time, D.C.36.35; sts. c. part., ὑ. τὸν νηὸν κατακαέντα *at the time of* its burning, Hdt.1.51; ὑ. τὴν κατάλυσιν τοῦ πολέμου *just at* the end, X.*Mem.*2.8.1, cf. Plu.*Mar.*46; ὑ. τὸν θυμὸν ἐκ χειρὸς ἐπιστρατευσαμένων *at the very time of* their anger, Plb. 2.19.10; ὑ. παροξυσμόν Gal.19.215; παραδόντω τοῖς αἱρεθεῖσι εἰς τὸν ὑπ' αὐτὰ (or ὕπαντα as Adv. = ἑξῆς) ἐνιαυτὸν *IG*9(1).694.60 (Corc., ii/i B.C.); ὑ. κύνα Arist.*HA*547ᵃ14, Thphr.*CP*1.13.3, D.S.19.109; ὑ. τὰς θερινὰς [τροπὰς] καὶ τοῦ κυνὸς τὴν ἐπιτολήν *Gp.*2.6.17. IV. of accompaniment, ὑπὸ ὄρχησίν τε καὶ ᾠδήν Pl.*Lg.*670a; ὑ. αὐλὸν διαλέγεσθαι X.*Smp.*6.3 codd. (ὑ. τοῦ αὐλοῦ Cobet); ὑ. κήρυκα (v. κῆρυξ 1.3).—Compare A. II. 5, B. II. 4. 2. ὄνον ἕνα ὑ. λαχανόσπερμον *laden with*.., Meyer *Ostr.*81.2 (i A.D.), cf. *PFay.*p.324 (i A.D.); ὄνοι ὑ. δένδρα *BGU*362.16, al. (iii A.D.); cf. supr. A. II. 8.

D. Position: ὑ. can follow its Subst., becoming by anastrophe ὕπο. It is freq. separated from the Subst. by intervening words, as in Il.2.465, Od.5.320, 7.130:—ὑπαί is placed after its case in A. *Eu.*417, S.*El.*1418, *Inach.* l.c., although acc. to Hdn.Gr.1.480 it cannot suffer anastrophe.

E. As Adv., *under, below, beneath*, freq. in Hom.; esp. of young animals, *under the mother*, i.e. *at the breast*, Od.4.636, 21.23. 2. *behind*, Hdt.7.61: cf. C. I. II. ὑπ' ἐκ or ὑπέκ, v. ὑπέκ.—In Hom. the separation of the Prep. from its Verb by tmesis is very freq., and sts. it follows, in which case it suffers anastrophe, φυγὼν ὕπο νηλεὲς ἦμαρ Od.9.17.

F. In Composition: I. *under*, as well of rest as of motion, as in ὕπειμι, ὑποβαίνω, etc. 2. of the *casing* or *covering* of one thing with another, as ὑπάργυρος, ὑπόχρυσος. 3. of the *agency* or *influence under which* a thing is done, to express subjection or subordination, ὑποδαμνάω, ὑποδμώς, ὑφηνίοχος, cf. ἐπί G. III. II. denoting what is in small degree or gradual, *somewhat, a little*, as in ὑποκινέω, ὑποδεής, ὑπόλευκος (so in tmesi, ὑ. τι ἀσεβῇ Pl.*Phdr.* 242d, cf. *Grg.*493c; ὑ. τι μικρὸν ἐπιθήκισα Ar.*V.*1290 (lyr.)). III. *underhand, secretly*, as in ὑποθέω, ὑποθωπεύω, ὑποκορίζομαι, ὑπόρνυμι.

**ὑποακραῖος**, ον, (ἄκρα) *under the height*, epith. of Apollo, *IG*2². 2914.

**ὑποακταίνομαι**, v. ὑπερικταίνοντο.

**ὑποάμουσος**, ον, *somewhat estranged from the Muses*, Pl.*R.*548e.

**ὑποβαθ-μός**, ὁ, = ὑπόβαθρον, Phot., Suid. **-ρα**, ἡ, *plinth, pedestal*, *Supp.Epigr.*6.319 (Laodicea Combusta). II. metaph., ὑ. τῶν συλλογισμῶν S.E.*P.*2.166, cf. Procl.*Inst.*71; αἱ τῶν ἄλλων τεχνῶν ὑ. τε καὶ ἀρχαί Aristid.Quint.3.10; ἡ ὕλη ὑ. καὶ ἕδρα δοκεῖ τῷ εἴδει εἶναι Plot.6.3.4, cf. Ruf.*Anat.*2. 2. pl., ὑποβάθραι *stages* in the pursuit of virtue, Max.Tyr.40.4. **-ρον**, τό, *anything put under, a base*: 1. *footstool*, Thphr.*HP*5.7.6, App.*Pun.*111, D.L.1.94; ὑ. νυμφικά *IG*2².1485.54. 2. *a wooden framework* to support a couch, a kind of *rocking apparatus*, X.*Mem.*2.1.30, Antyll.ap. Orib.6.23.3, Anon.ap.Stob.4.31.84. 3. *keel* of a ship, prob. for ὑποβάραθρον in Gal.19.169. 4. *step*, δι' ὑποβάθρων Lyd.*Mag.*2.11, 3.41.

**ὑποβαίνω**, *stand under*, τὸ ὑποβαινόμενον σκέλος the leg *which is stood on*, opp. τὸ ἔξω ἀποβαινόμενον (the lame leg which is pointed outwards to relieve it from the weight of the body), Hp.*Art.*52. 2. *serve as a base* or *foundation*, ὑποβεβηκυῖαι ἀρχαί S.E.*M.*3.94 (v. l. ἀπο-). 3. in pf., *fall under the head of*, [τῇ σαφηνείᾳ] ὑποβέβηκε τὸ καθαρὸν καὶ εὐκρινές Hermog.*Id.*1.1; ὑποβεβηκώς logically *subordinate, low in the descent from the universal to the particular*, ὑποβεβηκυῖαι ἰδέαι ibid., cf. Phld.*Sign.*29, S.E.*P.*1.39, Sor.1.2, 2.1,6, Aristid. Quint.3.24; πάντα τὰ ὑποβεβηκότα προσεχῶς ὕλαι τῶν ἐπαναβεβηκότων (cf. ἐπαναβαίνω III. 2) Porph. *in Harm.*p.197 W.; of numbers, *lower* in the scale, S.E.*M.*9.306. II. *go under* or *down*, Ph.*Bel.* 100.8 (s. v. l.); of the tide, *ebb*, *Placit.*3.17.1. III. *step back*, opp. προϊέναι, Gal.*Parv.Pil.*2; ὑπέβη εἰς τοὐπίσω Hld.2.5; of a gladiator, Artem.2.32: in pf., *stand further back*, πήχεσι δυσὶν ὑποβεβηκότες Ascl.*Tact.*5.1, cf. Ael.*Tact.*14.4, Arr.*Tact.*12.8. IV. metaph., τεσσεράκοντα πόδας ὑποβὰς τῆς ἑτέρης [πυραμίδος] τὠυτὸ μέγαθος *going* 40 feet *below* the like size of the other pyramid, i.e. building it 40 feet lower, Hdt.2.127; ὑ. αὐχήματος *descend from* boasting, D.H.8.48; τῆς ἀρχαίας εὐδαιμονίας ὑποβεβηκότες *fallen from* it, J.*AJ*11.4.2; ὑποβαίνοντι πρὸς τὰ ἄλλα *coming down to* the details, Thphr.*Metaph.*27; in Neoplatonism, of the descent (cf. ὑπόβασις 1. 2) from the universal to the particular, from unity to plurality, or from eternity to the world, οἱ (sc. θνητοὶ) τῶν ἡρώων ὑποβεβήκασιν *are inferior to*.., Hierocl. *in CA*27 p.483 M., cf. Moderatus ap.Simp. *in Ph.*231.5, Porph.*Gaur.*6.2, Iamb.*Comm.Math.*8, Simp. *in Ph.*784. 15: also c. acc., *fall below*, δοκεῖς μοι οὐδένα τῶν πρὸ σοῦ ἐν οὐδενὶ -βεβηκέναι Pl.*Chrm.*158b; τὰ φυσικά.., διὰ τὸ πᾶσαν τὴν.. ἀσώματον οὐσίαν ὑποβεβηκέναι Simp. *in Ph.*286.13: abs., *to be lower* or *less*, καθάπερ ὑ. τὸ τίμημα Pl.*Lg.*775b; τούτῳ νοσήσαντι ὑπέβη τὰ δεξιά interpol. in Philostr.*Gym.*41. 2. ὑποβὰς *a little below* (in the book), Str.1.2.40, 6.2.4; μικρὸν ὑποβάς Parth.21.3; ὑποβαίνων ἐρεῖ Hermog. *Inv.*4.10; v. ὑποκαταβαίνω 4.

**ὑποβάκχειος**, ὁ (sc. πούς), *the metrical foot* ⏑ – –, D.H.*Comp.*17, Choerob. *in Heph.*p.216 C. 2. *the foot* – ⏑ ⏑ –, ib.p.218 C.

**ὑπόβακχος**, ον, *under the influence of Bacchus, frenzied*, Philostr. *VS*1.19.1.

**ὑποβάλημα**, τό, dub. sens. in *Ostr.Strassb.*713, 753 (farm accounts, ii A.D.).

***ὑποβάλλω** (Ep. ὑββάλλω, v. infr.). *throw, put*, or *lay under*, as cloths, carpets, and the like, ὑπένερθε δὲ λῖθ' ὑπέβαλλεν Od.10.353; κάτω μὲν ὑποβαλεῖτε τῶν Μιλησίων ἐρίων *carpets of* Milesian wool, Eub.90.2, cf. X.*Cyr.*5.5.7; ὑ. πλευροῖς πλευρά E.*Or.*223, etc.; ὑπὸ τοὺς πόδας ὑ. τι X.*Oec.*18.5; ὑ. ταῖς μασχάλαις τὰς χεῖρας Sor.2.59; ὑ. αἶγας τοῖς τράγοις, of breeders, Longus 3.29; ὑ. τοῖς ξίφεσι τὰς σφαγάς Plu.*Brut.*31; ὑ. τινὰς τοῖς θηρίοις *throw* them *under* the elephants' feet, Plb.1.82.2; ὑ. τοὺς δακτύλους, of a flute-player, *put down*, Luc.*Harm.*1; ὑ. [φάρμακον] ὑπὸ τὰ βλέφαρα *insert* under the eyelids, Sever.ap.Aët.7.32; τοῖς φορείοις τῶν γυναικῶν ὑ. τὰ ὄμματα *cast furtive* glances at, Plu.2.522a, cf. Eust.1406.36:—Med. and Pass., *place under oneself* or *have placed under one*, λυκοφάνους ὑποβάλλεσθαι Plu.2.237b; πορφυρίδας ὑποβεβλημένοι Luc.*Symp.*13. 2. *lay under*, as a beginning, foundation, Aeschin.1.24 (cj. Reiske for ὑπολαβών):—in Med., θεμέλιον ὑ. τυραννίδος Plb.13.6.2; ὁ πρῶτος ὑποβεβλημένος the first *founder*, Str.12.3.30. 3. *subject, submit*, ἐχθροῖς ἐμαυτόν E.*HF*1384, cf. Aeschin.3.90; ὑπὸ τοσαύτας συμφορὰς σφᾶς αὐτούς Isoc.8.113. II. Med., *bring in* another's child *as one's own*, Hdt.5.41, Ar.*Th.*340, 407, 565, Pl.*R.*538a, D.21.149, etc.; or *palm off one's own* child as another's, ἡ ὑποβεβλημένη τὸν αὑτῆς υἱόν Arist.*Rh.*1400ᵃ24:—Pass., τῶν ὑποβαλλομένων (sc. παίδων) Id.*Rh.Al.*1421ᵃ29:—the origin of this phrase is plain from the words of E., μαστῷ γυναικὸς σῆς ὑπεβλήθην λάθρᾳ *Alc.*639, cf. *Supp.* 1160 (lyr.), X.*Cyn.*7.3; v. ὑποβολιμαῖος. 2. Med., of a drama, [Εὐριπίδης] τὸ δρᾶμα (sc. Μήδειαν) δοκεῖ ὑποβαλέσθαι Arist.*Fr.*635: metaph., ὑποβαλλόμενοι κλέπτουσι μύθους *with false suggestions* they spread secret rumours, S.*Aj.*188 (lyr.); cf. Isoc.15.21 and v. ὑπόβλητος. 3. *suborn*, *Act.Ap.*6.11:—Pass., of an informer, App. *BC*1.74. III. *suggest, whisper*, as a prompter does, ἑσταότος μὲν καλὸν ἀκούειν, οὐδὲ ἔοικεν ὑββάλλειν Il.19.80 (where Sch.B expl. *it to interrupt*); ὑποβαλεῖν δυνήσεσθε, ἣν τι ἐπιλανθάνωνται X.*Cyr.*3. 3.55, cf. Pl.*Grg.*491a, D.21.204, Aeschin.3.48; ὑ. ὁ νόμος ἃ χρὴ γράφειν ib.22; ἐγώ σοι λόγον ὑποβαλῶ καλόν Id.1.121; ὑ. παιδὶ λόγον *dictate*, Isoc.12.231, cf. 5.149; ὑ. ὀνόματα, of an informer, Lys.13. 25; τὸν -οντα τῇ Πυθίᾳ τοὺς χρησμούς Plu.2.404b; τὰς ἀνειμένας [ἁρμονίας] ἡ φύσις ὑ. τοῖς τοιούτοις Arist.*Pol.*1342ᵇ22; ταῦτα ἡ αἴσθησις ὑ. Epicur.*Ep.*2 p.39 U.; so, *provoke, produce*, ib.1 p.29 U., etc.: cf. ὑποβλήδην I. 1, ὑποβολή I. 3. IV. Med., *appropriate to oneself*, ἀλλότρια Str.17.1.5; δόξαν Plu.*Pomp.*31. 2. *attempt* a work, σύνταξιν καὶ ἱστορίαν Id.*Dem.*2.

**ὑποβάπτω**, *dip* or *dye a little*, ὑποβεβαμμένος = *suffectus*, Gloss.

**ὑποβαρβᾰρ-ίζω**, *speak rather like a foreigner, speak rather broken Greek*, Pl.*Ly.*223a, Aristid.2.95 J.; τοὔνομα βραχύ τι ὑποβαρβαριζόμενον Eust.365.21. **-ος**, ον, *speaking somewhat barbarously*, Id.1914.37.

**ὑποβᾰρύνομαι**, *to be weighed down*, ὑπό τινων Plu.*Nob.*12 (Wytt. for ὑποβρυομένους).

***ὑπόβᾰσις**, εως, ἡ, (ὑποβαίνω) *going down, retiring*, of the Nile floods, Str.17.1.4; καθ' ὑπόβασιν *downwards*, in bandaging, Sor. *Fasc.*58; καθ' ὑπόβασιν τῆς τῶν πρωτείων τάξεως *downwards through the series*, Ptol.*Tetr.*46; οὕτω καθ' ὑπόβασιν μέχρις ἀπείρου and so *on* ad infinitum, S.E.*M.*9.306, cf. *P.*3.87; *successive diminution*, of the terms in a series, opp. προκοπή, Iamb. *in Nic.*p.19 P. 2. in Neoplatonism, *declension, descent* from eternity to the world, etc. (v. ὑποβαίνω IV), Procl. *in Prm.*p.492 S., *Inst.*21,97, al., *in Ti.*2.206 D., al., Aristid.Quint.3.10; ὑ. ἑβδοματική Dam.*Pr.*205; ἡ κατ' οὐσίαν αὐτῶν ὑπεροχή τε καὶ ὑ. Hierocl. *in CA*1 p.419 M., cf. Simp. *in Ph.* 774.21. 3. *moral declension,* Plot.1.8.7; *declension* from perfect health, Aët.4.1. II. *stooping* or *crouching down,* esp. of a horse that lowers itself to take up the rider, X.*Eq.*1.14; cf. ὑποβιβάζω II. III. *basement, pedestal, foot,* Semus 15, *Test.Epict.*8.23, *IGRom.*4.685.16 (Sebaste), J.*AJ*8.3.6.

**ὑποβάσκᾰνος**, ον, *somewhat envious,* Man.5.45 codd. (ὑπὸ β. Rigler).

**ὑποβασμός**, ὁ, Ion. for ὑποβαθμός, Phot., Suid., prob. in Hsch. (ὑποβάσιμον· ὑπόβαθρον cod.).

**ὑποβαστάζω**, *bear from under, underprop,* Charito 3.6, Gal.14.717 (Pass.).

**ὑποβαστακτήρ**, ῆρος, ὁ, *underbearer,* Hsch. s. v. ἐρείσματι.

**ὑποβᾰτήρ**, ῆρος, ὁ, *pedestal* or *support* for a στήλη, *IG*7.3073.8 (Lebad., ii B. C.).

**ὑποβάτης** [ᾰ], ου, ὁ, = ὑπόβαθρον, Hsch.; dub. sens. in *IG*2².1425.390.

**ὑποβδύλλω**, *break wind secretly,* Luc.*Lex.*10.

**ὑποβεβηκότως**, Adv. *downwards, by a non-recurring succession,* Ocell.1.14. 2. *in a subordinate way,* opp. γενικῶς, Nicom.*Ar.*2.20.2.

**ὑποβένθιος**, ον, (βένθος) = ὑποβύθιος, *AP*7.636 (Crin.).

**ὑποβήσσω**, Att. -ττω, *have a slight cough,* Hp.*Coac.*372,438, Gal.10.361, Luc.*Gall.*10, etc.

**ὑποβῐβ-άζω**, Causal of ὑποβαίνω, *draw* or *bring down*: Medic., *carry off downwards,* i. e. *by purging,* ὑ. τὰ χολώδη Dsc.3.30, cf. Antyll.ap.Orib.6.6.1. II. Med., *stoop* or *crouch down,* of a horse that lowers itself to take up the rider, X.*Eq.*6.16, Poll.1.213; cf. ὑπόβασις II. III. *lower, humble,* Hsch., Phot., Suid. IV. Music., *transpose lower,* opp. ὑπερβ., Theo Sm.p.92 H. V. Pass., of numbers, *to be in a descending series,* Iamb. *in Nic.*p.53 P. **-ασμός**, ὁ, *a carrying off downwards, purging,* κοιλίας Xenocr.ap.Orib.2.58.124: more generally, *passing down,* τῆς τροφῆς Herod.Med.ap.Aët.9.13. **-αστικός**, ή, όν, *purgative,* Dsc.4.1, Antyll.ap.Orib.6.34.3. Adv. -κῶς, μετατιθέναι τὰς ὀξείας *nearer to the end of the word,* Eust.980.52.

❀**ὑποβιβλιοθηκοφύλαξ** [φῠ], ᾰκος, ὁ, *sub-librarian, BGU*660.9 (iii A. D.).

**ὑποβιβρώσκομαι**, Pass., *to be eaten away underneath,* D.S.3.44, Q.S.9.382.

**ὑποβῑνητιάω**, *have aphrodisiac properties,* ὑποβινητιῶντα βρώματα Men.462.11.

**ὑπόβλαισος**, ον, *somewhat bandy,* σκέλη Arist.*IA*713ᵃ30.

**ὑποβλαστάνω**, *grow from below,* of the hydra's heads, J.*BJ*1.30.3.

**ὑποβλάττα**, ἡ, *purplish cloth, Edict.Diocl.*19.9, al.

**ὑποβλεπτικῶς**, Adv. *with look askance,* gloss on ὑπόδρα, Eust.59.2; so **-βλεμμᾰτικῶς**, gloss on ὑποδράξ, Sch.Nic.*Th.*457.

**ὑποβλέπω**, fut. -ψομαι Pl.*Cri.*53b:—*look up from under* the brows *at, look askance at, eye suspiciously* or *angrily* (cf. ὑπόδρα), Pherecr.153.2 (hex.), Ar.*Lys.*519 (anap.), *Th.*396; ὑ. αὐτὸν ὡς καταφρονοῦντα σφῶν Pl.*Smp.*220b; ὑποβλέψονταί σε διαφθορέα ἡγούμενοι Id.*Cri.* l.c., cf. Luc.*Symp.*6, App.*Syr.*45; also, *cast stolen looks at,* of lovers, Plu.2.521b:—Pass., ὑποβλεπώμεθ' ὡς ἐγνωσμένοι E.*HF*1287. 2. of *menacing* looks, ἀπειλητικόν τι ὑ. Luc.*Vit.Auct.*7; δεινόν τι καὶ θηριῶδες Id.*Am.*29; ταυρηδὸν ὑ. πρὸς τὸν ἄνδρα *look mischievously,* Pl.*Phd.*117b. 3. ὑ. ἐλεεινὰ *APl.*4.199 (Crin.); ἐς τὸν βάρβαρον Philostr.Jun.*Im.*2. II. *look with the eyes half open, blink,* of persons half asleep, Hp.*Coac.*64, Arist.*Insomn.*462ᵃ22, *Pr.*958ᵃ21. III. *look under,* ὑ. τοῖς λῃτοῖς Plu.2.994c.

**ὑποβλέφᾰρα**, τά, *eyelids,* prob. in *PLond.*1821.24.

**ὑπο-βλήδην**, Dor. -βλήδαν Dius ap.Stob.4.21.17:—Adv. *by way of interruption,* ὑ. ἠμείβετο Il.1.292; v. ὑποβάλλω III, ὑποβολή I. 3,4. 2. *in answer,* A.R.1.699, 3.400, Q.S.2.147. 3. *speaking in turn,* Coluth.146. II. *supposititiously,* ὑ. ἐτέκοντο Man.6.292. III. *askance,* ὑ. ἐσκέψατο *h.Merc.*415. **-βλημα**, ατος, τό, *anything put under, bedding, Hippiatr.*10 (pl.). 2. dub. sens. in list of naval equipment, *IG*2².1621, al. **-βλητέος**, α, ον, *to be put under,* γῇ φυτῷ ὑ. X.*Oec.*19.9. II. ὑποβλητέον *one must put under,* πίθῳ ἄμμον *Gp.*6.2.4, cf. Sor.2.46, Aët.7.26; *one must cause to lie* in the bath, Herod.Med.ap.Orib.10.37.14. 2. *one must lay the foundation of,* λόγον D.H.*Rh.*7.4. **-βλητικῶς**, Adv. = ὑποβλήδην, Eust.106.1. ❀**-βλητος**, ον, *put in another's place, counterfeit,* οὐδεὶς ἐρεῖ.. ὡς ὑπόβλητον λόγον.. ἔλεξας S.*Aj.*481; τὸ σὸν.. ὑ. στόμα *suborned, false,* Id.*OC*794; *supposititious,* of a child, Apollod.3.5.7, Nic.Dam.*Fr.*103 (*x*) J. Adv. -τως Sch.S.*Aj.*188.

**ὑποβλίττω**, *cut out secretly,* as honey from a hive, metaph., Philostr.*VA*6.36.

**ὑποβλώψ**, ῶπος, ὁ, ἡ, *one who takes stolen glances* (cf. παραβλώψ), Eust.1406.38.

**ὑποβοηθέω**, *furnish, supply,* esp. arms in war, *Gloss.*

**ὑποβοηθός**, ὁ, = *subadjuva,* Lyd.*Mag.*2.16; = *adjutor,* ib.1.46 (pl.).

**ὑπόβοικος**, v. ὕποικος.

**ὑποβολ-εύς**, έως, ὁ, (ὑποβάλλω) *suggester, reminder* (v. ὑποβολή I. 3), Ph.1.591; in a theatre, *prompter,* Plu.2.813f. 2. *interpreter,* Eust.106.12. II. = ὑπαγωγεύς II, Theo Sm.p.71 H. **-ή**, ἡ: I. actively, *a throwing* or *laying under,* στρωμάτων, opp. περιβολή, Pl.*Plt.*280b; μεθ' ὑποβολῆς πλείονος φλογός Sor.1.50; ἡ τῶν ἐνεδρευόντων ὑ. *setting* men *in ambush,* Plb.3.105.1; ἐπανάγονται τρισὶ τριήρεσιν ἐξ ὑ. Id.15.2.12. 2. *substitution by stealth,* esp. *of supposititious children,* Pl.*R.*538a, Satyr.*Vit.Eur.Fr.*39 vii 10 (pl.), Luc.*Salt.*37; ὑποβολῆς γράφεσθαί τινα charge one with *being supposititious, AB*312, cf. sq.; also ὑ. κλειδῶν *substitution of false* keys, Plu.*Rom.*22. 3. *suggesting, reminding,* ἐξ ὑποβολῆς by *admonition,* X.*Cyr.*3.3.37; ἐξ ὑπομνήσεως καὶ ὑ... τοῦ ἐπισκόπου on the *suggestion* of .., *Sammelb.*7475.8 (vi/vii A. D.); τίνος ὑποβολῇ; = *cujus impulsu? Gloss.*; ὑ. ἡ πρὸς ἄρχοντα ἢ βασιλέα γινομένη ἀναφορὰ ἤτοι διδασκαλία, = *suggestio,* ib.; τὰς τῶν περιστάσεων ὑ. the *influence* of circumstances (on Hannibal's actions), Plb.9.24.3; ἐξ ὑ. διιέναι τὸν ὅρκον *at the dictation* of another, Polem.Hist.83; ἐξ ὑ. λέγειν deliver a speech *with a prompter at hand* (= λέγειν τὸ ἐξ ἀναγνώσεως καὶ γραφῆς ὑποβαλλόμενον), Apollon.ap.Sch.B Il.19.80:—τὰ Ὁμήρου ἐξ ὑ. γέγραφε ῥαψῳδεῖσθαι (sc. Σόλων), οἷον ὅπου ὁ πρῶτος ἔληξεν, ἐκεῖθεν ἄρχεσθαι τὸν ἐχόμενον Solon enacted that the poems of Homer should be recited from a *cue*.., D.L.1.57: ὑποβολή perh. = ῥαψῳδία in *Michel* 913 (Teos, ii B. C.): cf. ὑποβάλλω III, ὑποβλήδην, ὑπόληψις I. 1. 4. *interruption,* διακόπτειν ἐξ ὑ. τὸν λόγον Sch.B Il.19.80. 5. Medic., αἱ ἐξ ὑ. ἐγχρίσεις anointing *by interposition* or *beneath* (the eyelid), opp. αἱ κατ' ἐκτροπήν, Antyll.ap.Orib.10.23.24; καθ' ὑποβολήν Sever.ap.Aët.7.32. II. passively, *that which is put under, foundation, groundwork,* πρὸς τὴν Ῥωμύλου.. αὔξησιν τὴν μὲν Τύχην ὑποβολὰς κατατεθεῖσθαι, τὴν δ' Ἀρετὴν ἐξῳκοδομηκέναι Plu.2.320b; ἀρχὴ καὶ ὑ. τοῦ σωφρονεῖν ἡ ἐν σίτοις καὶ ποτοῖς ἐγκράτεια Muson.*Fr.*18ᴬp.94 H.; φυσικὴν εἶναι ὑ. τῇ ψυχῇ πρὸς καλοκἀγαθίαν a natural *foundation* or *capacity* for.., Id.*Fr.*2 p.7 H.; ἐν πολλοῖς [τῶν ζῴων] ὑποβολὰς ἔχων πρὸς τὸ τέλειον [ὁ λόγος θεωρεῖται] Porph.*Abst.*3.2; *subject-matter* of discourse, Luc.*Dem.Enc.*21. **-ῐμαῖος**, α, ον, (ὑποβολή I. 2) *brought in by stealth, supposititious,* of children, Pl.*R.*537e, Plb.2.55.9; τὰ ὑ. (sc. τέκνα) Hdt.1.137, etc.; ὑ. ποιεῖ τοὺς ἑαυτοῦ νεοττοὺς ὁ κόκκυξ Arist.*HA*618ᵃ28: Ὑποβολιμαῖος, name of plays by Cratinus Jun., Alexis, and others. 2. metaph., ὑ. σύνεσις *Com.Adesp.*345; εὔνοια Plu.2.3c; κάλλος Sch.B Il.14.170. **-ος**, f.l. for ὑπόβολος (q.v.).

**ὑποβομβέω**, *murmur gently,* Anon. in Rh.3.579 W.

**ὑποβορβόριον**, τό, *sediment, dregs,* Hsch.

**ὑποβορβορύζω**, *rumble a little,* of the bowels, Hp.*Epid.*4.7, *Coac.*62,285; κοιλίη Aret.*SA*2.6, 11.

**ὑποβόσκομαι**, *feed upon,* σάρκα.. ὑ. ὕδρης ἰός Nic.*Al.*247.

**ὑποβουκόλος**, ὁ, *under-cowherd, PLips.*97 vi 7, al. (iv A. D.).

**ὑπόβραγχος**, ον, *somewhat hoarse from cold,* φθέγγεται -ότερον Hp.*Loc.Hom.*14.

**ὑποβρᾰχεῖν**, aor. 2 inf., *crack under,* μέγ' ὑπέβραχε γαῖα Q.S.10.72.

**ὑπόβρᾰχυς**, εια, υ, *rather short* in stature, Phld.*Acad.Ind.* p.51 M. II. in Metric, ὑπόβραχυς (sc. πούς), the foot ⏑⏑⏑⏑–, Diom.p.481 K.

**ὑποβρέμω**, *roar* or *rumble beneath,* ὑποβρέμει μυχὸς γᾶς A.*Pr.*433 (lyr.), cf. Orph.*A.*1267:—Med., Nic.*Al.*290.

**ὑποβρέχω**, of a toper, οἰναρίοις τῆς ἡμέρας τὸ λοιπὸν ὑποβρέχει μέρος *soaks away* the rest of the day, Alex.275; ἀκτὴν ταῖς κοτύλαις ὑ. *AP*11.3; ὑποβεβρεγμένος *somewhat drunk,* μειρακύλλια Men.*Inc.* 2.34, cf. Ph.1.260, Luc.*DDeor.*23.2:—in sense *treat, moisten,* prob. cj. in Thphr.*HP*5.3.3.

**ὑποβρομέω**, = ὑποβρέμω, Nic.*Al.*287.

**ὑπόβροχος**, ον, *somewhat wet,* τόπος *EM*752.3. II. (βρόχος) *under a noose* or *slip-knot,* ἔλαβόν σου ἐπιστόλιον.. ὑπόβροχον *BGU* 531 i 4 (i A. D.).

**ὑπόβρῠχα**, Adv. *under water,* τὸν δ' ἄρ' ὑ. θῆκε Od.5.319; ὥστε Θεσσαλίην.. ὑ. γενέσθαι Hdt.7.130; ὑ. ναυτίλλονται Arat.425, cf. Opp.*H.*1.145, Q.S.13.485, 14.619, etc.

**ὑποβρῡχάομαι**, *roar* or *bellow a little,* Luc.*Am.*6, Tryph.319, etc.; of the breathing of one in a passion, Adam.2.41.

**ὑποβρύχιος** [ῠχ], ον, also α, ον, *under water,* τὴν δ' ἄνεμος.. καὶ κῦμα θαλάσσης θῆκαν ὑποβρυχίην *h.Hom.*33.12; ὑποβρυχίον.. φέρων (sc. τὸν ἵππον) Hdt.1.189; ὑ. θάνατοι *Cat.Cod.Astr.*2.161: metaph., ἡ Ἑλλὰς ὑ. φερομένη Aristid.*Or.*23(42).46. II. *below the surface,* ὑποβρύχιαι συμπεριφέρονται Pl.*Phdr.*248a; opp. ἐπιπολάζων, Luc.*Dips.*3; *deep-seated,* ἐκπυήσιες Hp.*Art.*12; ὑ. πυρετός *a hidden* fever, one *that shows itself by degrees,* Id.*Epid.*1.25 (so Littré with Gal.9.560; ἄρχεται μαλακῶς καὶ ὑποβρύχια [Adv.] codd., Kühl.); πυρετοὶ -ιοι Aret.*SD*2.9; ὀφθαλμῶν ὑ. πόνος ib.1.2; πῦρ Id.*SA*2.7. 2. *deep,* θάλασσα, βυσσός, Opp.*H.*1.49, 5.159.—Cf. βρύχιος, περιβρύχιος. III. = ὑποβρυχώμενος, of oxen, *h.Merc.*116.

**ὑποβρύχω** [ῡ], = ὑποβρυχάομαι, Polem.*Phgn.*30.

**ὑπόβρωμος**, ον, *stinking a little,* τῇ ὀσμῇ Dsc.1.64.

**ὑποβῠθ-ίζω**, *submerge, Gloss.* **-ιος**, ον, (βυθός) *under the depths,* gloss on ὑπόβρυχα, Erot.

**ὑποβώμ-ιον**, τό, Dim. of sq., *Inscr.Grecques et Latines de la Syrie* 1.153 (Cyrrhus). **-ίς**, ίδος, ἡ, *base of an altar, Jahresh.*18 *Beibl.*23 (Cilicia, ii A. D.).

**ὑπογάιδιον**· ὑπόγειον τύμβον, Hsch. (fort. -γαΐδιον, cf. καταγαΐδιοι).

**ὑπόγαιος**, ον, v. ὑπόγειος.

**ὑπογᾰμ-έω**, *marry thereupon* or *after,* τὴν γυναῖκα Ael.*NA*7.

25.  -ιον, τό, *illicit intercourse with a betrothed person*, Ph.2.311.

**ὑπογαστρ-ίδιον**, τό, Dim. of ὑπογάστριον II, Eub.139 (lyr.). **-ίζομαι**, *eat oneself pretty full*, ὑπεγαστρίζετο (v.l. -ιζε) *Com.Adesp.* 1174. ⊛ **-ιον**, τό, *the lower belly from the navel downwards, the paunch*, Hp.*Aph.*4.80, Arist.*HA*503$^{a}$17, Sor.2.48, etc. II. *the belly of a sea-fish*, esp. of the tunny, a favourite dish at Athens, Stratt. 4,31 (hex.), Ar.*Fr.*364, etc.; whence the joke in Id.*V.*195. **-ιος**, ον, *sexual*, οἶστροι, ἡδοναὶ ὑ., Ph.1.38, 2.294. **-ίς**, ίδος, ἡ, *paunch*, Philox.2.23 codd. (-ιδίοις Bgk.).

**ὑπογείνομαι**, aor. 1 ὑπεγείνατο *brought forth*, Euph.90.

**ὑπόγειος**, also **ὑπόγαιος**, ον, (γῆ) *underground, subterraneous*, οἴκημα ὑπόγαιον Hdt.2.100,148 (vv.ll. -γεον, -γεα); ὀρύγματα ὑπόγαια *mines*, Id.4.200 (v.l. -γεα); ὑπογαίου (v.l. -γείου) βροντῆς A. *Fr.*57.10 (anap.); ὑπόγειον ὕδωρ *Gp.*2.6.33; ὑ. οἶνος *stored in a cellar*, Gal.19.95. II. ὑπόγειον or -γαιον, τό, *an underground chamber*, Plu.2.770e, Hdn.1.15.6. III. Astron., *under the earth*, Man.3.27, *Gp.*1.7.1; [ἄστρα] τὴν ὑ. φορὰν ἐνεχθέντα *Placit.*1.6.8: τὸ ὑ. *the nadir*, Vett.Val.75.24.—The form **ὑπόγεως**, ων, cited in Hdn.*Epim.*208 and Suid., occurs in codd. of Paus.2.2.1, 2.36.7; cf. ὑπογάιδιον.

**ὑπόγεισον**, τό, = ἀείζωον τὸ μέγα, Plin.*HN*25.160 (-geson).

**ὑπογελάω**, *laugh a little, smile*, Pl.*Chrm.*162b, Polem.*Phgn.*19.

**ὑπογενει-άζω**, *entreat by touching the chin*, Aeschin.1.61. **-άσκω**, *to have a beard beginning to grow*, Hdn.*Philet.*p.444 P. **-ον**, τό, *the part under the chin*, Eust.548.3.

**ὑπογεωργ-έω**, *farm as* ὑπογεωργός, in Pass., τῶν ὑπογεωργουμένων κωμῶν prob. in *Sammelb.*7193$^{v}$iii 12 (ii A.D.). **-ός**, ὁ, *sub-lessee and farmer of state land*, *POxy.*1661.4,7 (i A.D.).

**ὑπόγεως**, ων, v. ὑπόγειος.

**ὑπογηράω**, *grow rather old*, Ael.*NA*7.17.

**ὑπογίγνομαι**, Ion. and later Gr. **-γίνομαι** [ῑ], *grow up after* or *in succession*, ὑπαὶ δέ τε κόμπος ὀδόντων γίγνεται Il.11.417; ἵνα σφι γενεὴ ὑπογίνηται Hdt.3.159; of inflammation following a hurt, Hp.*Art.* 38, cf. Ti.Locr.104a; of feelings and thoughts, Plb.2.44.1, 6.6.7, etc.

**ὑπ-ογκόομαι**, Pass., *to be somewhat swollen*, Poll.3.49, 4.68.

**ὑπόγλαυκ-ος**, ον, *somewhat grey*, of eyes, X.*Cyn.*5.23; of leaves, Dsc.2.180, 4.60. **-ωσις**, εως, ἡ, *slight cataract*, Aët.7.115 (pl.).

**ὑπογλαύσσω**, *glance from under, glance furtively*, like ὑποβλέπω, of the eyes, Call.*Dian.*54, Mosch.2.86.

**ὑπόγλισχρος**, ον, *somewhat slippery* or *clammy*, Hp.*Epid.*3.1.γ′; *somewhat tough*, φύλλον Thphr.*HP*7.13.1. II. metaph., *somewhat stingy*, Numen.ap.Eus.*PE*14.7 (Comp.).

**ὑπογλουτίς**, ίδος, ἡ, (γλουτός) *the exterior junction of the buttocks and thighs*, Arist.*HA*493$^{b}$10, Ruf.*Onom.*116.

**ὑπογλῠκ-αίνω**, *sweeten a little*: metaph., *coax and smooth down*, δῆμον ῥηματίοις Ar.*Eq.*216. **-υς**, υ, *sweetish*, Hp.*Mul.*1.109, Ath. 14.625a, Philagr.ap.Orib.5.21.9.

**ὑπογλώσσ-ιος**, Att. **-ττιος**, ον, (γλῶσσα) *under the tongue*, ὑ. βάτραχος, = sq. I. 1, Orib.*Fr.*22, Aët.8.39. II. Subst., τὸ ὑ. *the region under the tongue*, Arist.*HA*506$^{a}$28, Heliod.ap.Orib.45.6.5. 2. = ὑπόγλωσσον II, Plin.*HN*15.131. III. pl., = ὑπογλωσσίδες III, Paul.Aeg.2.47. **-ίς**, Att. **-ττίς**, ίδος, ἡ, *swelling on the under side of the tongue*, Hp.*Morb.*2.11,31. 2. *the under surface of the tongue*, Poll.2.105, Hsch. II. a kind of *chaplet* (prob. made from the ὑπόγλωσσον), Pl.Com.51. III. pl., *cough lozenges*, Gal.13.7. **-ον**, τό, *horse-tongue, Ruscus Hypoglossum*, Dsc.4.129, cf. Plin.*HN*27.93. II. ὑπόγλωττον, τό, = δάφνη Ἀλεξάνδρεια, Dsc. 4.145. **-ος**, ον, *somewhat talkative*, Polem.*Phgn.*35 (Comp., s.v.l.). II. *under the tongue*, οἴδημα Poet.*de herb.*46.

**ὑπογνάμπτω**, *bend*, ψυχῆς ὁρμὴν *h.Mart.*13.

**ὑπόγνυθα**· τὸ καθῆσθαι τὰς χεῖρας ἔχοντα ὑπὸ γνάθον, Hsch.

**ὑπογογγ-ύζω**, *murmur* or *mutter to oneself*, Sch.D.19.197, Dosith. p.430 K. **-υστής**, οῦ, ὁ, *a murmurer*, *Gloss.*

**ὑπογόνιον**, τό, *the part under the knee*, *BGU*394.6 (ii A.D.).

**ὑπόγραμμα**, ατος, τό, *inscription on the base* of a στήλη, Lycurg. 118. II. *pigment* used *for painting under* the eyelids, Ar.*Fr.* 320.5, cf. Phryn.*PS*p.118 B., *EM*782.8: v. ὑπογραφή III.

**ὑπογραμμᾰτ-εία**, ἡ, *the office of* ὑπογραμματεύς, Plu.2.840f. ⊛ **-εύς**, έως, ὁ, *under-clerk, under-secretary*, Antipho 6.35, Lys.30.27, *IG*1$^{2}$. 374.110,258; restored by Dind. in Ar.*Ra.*1084 (anap.) for ὑπὸ γραμματέων. ⊛ **-εύω**, *serve as under-secretary*, τινι Antipho 6. 49; τῇ ἀρχῇ Lys.30.29, cf. D.19.70.

**ὑπογραμμός**, ὁ, *writing-copy, pattern, model, outline*, Lxx 2*Ma.* 2.28, 1*Ep.Pet.*2.21; ὑ. παιδικοί *copy-heads* for children, containing all the letters of the alphabet, of which three forms have been preserved by Clem.Al.*Strom.*5.8.49,48—μάρπτε σφὶγξ κλὼψ ζβυχθηδόν, βέδυ ζὰψ χθὼμ πλῆκτρον σφίγξ, and κναξζβὶ χθύπτης φλεγμὼ δρόψ, which last was wrongly ascribed to Thespis (*Fr.*4). II. *outline*, σκιὰ καὶ ὑ. Ph.*Fr.*7 H.; πρὸς ἣν ἕκαστος ἔχει παρασκευὴν τὸν τακτικὸν δεῖ ὑπογραμμὸν τιθέναι τοῦ πλήθους Ael.*Tact.*8.1.

**ὑπογραπτέον**, *one must sketch out*, συντόμως Phld.*Oec.*p.38 J., cf. Str.13.4.12.

⊛ **ὑπογρᾰφ-εύς**, έως, ὁ, *one who writes under another's orders, secretary, amanuensis*, *PCair.Zen.*647.50 (iii B.C.), Plu.*Crass.*2, Luc.*Dem. Enc.*44; *military secretary, adjutant*, *PStrassb.*105.5 (iii B.C.). 2. *person who has drafted* or *signed a deed on behalf of another*, ὑ. τῶν ὁμολογούντων *PAmh.*2.110.24 (i A.D.), cf. *PMeyer* 13.17 (ii A.D.), etc.; παρεχούσης ὑπογραφέα ὑπὲρ αὐτῆς καὶ μάρτυρας τοὺς ἑξῆς ὑπογράφοντας *PMasp.*23.10 (vi A.D.). 3. at Athens and elsewh., *the clerk of the Assembly*, = ὑπογραμματεύς (the clerk of the Council being ἀντιγραφεύς), Sch Ar.*Eq* 1253 (but in the text (1256), ὑ. δικῶν appears to mean *a signer* of accusations *on behalf of another*), cf. *IG*14.209 (Acrae). 4. = Lat. *scriba*, Lyd.*Mag.*2.30. ⊛ **-ή**, ἡ, *written accusation*, Pl.*Tht.*172e (but perh. in signf. II. 2), *IG*9(2).522.20 (Larissa, iii/ii B.C., dub. sens.); cf. ὑπογράφω I. 2. b. in Egypt, an unknown form of legal procedure before a court, *PEnteux.*50.8 (iii B.C.), *PPetr.*2 p.55 (iii B.C.). c. *decision* of an official on a petition handed to him, *PTeb.*45.28 (ii B.C.); of a court (perh. orig. so called because written below a petition), *including a record of the legal proceedings*, *UPZ*118.1, 162 vii 33, ix 24 (ii B.C.), *BGU*1759.4, 1827.12 (i B.C.). 2. *admission of liability in writing*, *IG*12(7).3. 35 (Amorgos, iv B.C.), *Mél.Navarre* 357 (Thespiae), *PEnteux.*35.7 (iii B.C.). 3. *copy*, Phld.*Acad.Ind.*p.6 M. (pl.). 4. *entering* of horses at the Olympic games, D.S.13.74 codd. (ἀπογρ- Schaefer). 5. pl., = Lat. *commentarii*, App.*Pun.*136, *BC*4.132. II. *outline, contour*, Arist.*GA*764$^{b}$30; τενόντων ὑπογραφαί *traces* of feet, foot-*prints*, A.*Ch.*209. 2. architect's *plan*, *SIG*1156 (Priene, iii/ii B.C.); *diagram*, Ascl.*Tact.*11.7: metaph., *outline, sketch, general description*, opp. τελεωτάτη ἀπεργασία, Pl.*R.*504d, cf. 548d, *Lg.*737d; θεωρείσθω ἐκ τῆς ὑ. Arist.*Int.*22$^{a}$22, *Mete.*346$^{a}$32, *HA*510$^{a}$30: Medic., as Empiric t.t., Gal.8.720. 3. in Logic, *description, general illustration*, opp. definition, *Stoic.*2.75. 4. *example, illustration*, ὑπογραφῆς ἕνεκα Ael.*Tact.*8.3. III. *painting under* of the eyelids, X.*Cyr.*1. 3.2, Nicostr.ap.Stob.4.23.62; cf. ὑπόγραμμα II, ὑπογράφω V, ὑποχρίω. **-ικός**, ή, όν, *descriptive*, opp. definitory, Porph. *in Cat.*64.16, Simp. *in Cat.*22.16, Ascl. *in Metaph.*385.12. Adv. **-κῶς** Olymp. *in Cat.*44.1. **-ίον**· τῶν ἐπὶ τῷ σώματι δεδανεισμένων, Hsch. **-ίς**, ίδος, ἡ, *pencil*, Poll.7.128. II. *a surgical instrument*, Id.4.181, 10.149. ⊛ **-ω**, *write under* an inscription, *subjoin* or *add to* it, τῇ στήλῃ ὑ. ὅτι "οὐκ ἐνέμειναν τοῖς ὅρκοις" Th.5.56; τὰς πόλεις..ὧν εἷς ἕκαστός ἐστιν *IG*2$^{2}$.237.34; ὁ ὑπογεγραμμένος the *undermentioned*, *CIG* 1957g (Maced.), cf. *PTeb.*61(*a*).10, al. (ii B.C.); ἐπὶ τῶν ὑπογεγραμμένων μαρτύρων *PAvrom.*1 A 7 (i B.C.; but κατὰ τὰ ὑπογεγραμμένα *as has been indicated* (above), *PCair.Zen.*173.10 (iii B.C.), v. infr. II. 4). 2. *sign, subscribe*, τὸ ψήφισμα αὐτοῦ ὑπέγραψα Hyp.*Eux.*30, cf. *PTeb.* 35.11 (ii B.C.):—Med., ὑ. τὰς καταβολάς *sign and so make oneself liable for* the payment, D.*Ep.*3.40; τοὺς ἵππους ἰδίους ὑ. *signed his name as* their *owner*, D.S.13.74 codd. (better ἀπεγράψατο as Peiresc and Plu.*Alc.*12); ὑπογράψας ἐπιβουλεῦσαί με *having accused* me of plotting, D.37.23 (v.l. in 23.220); ὑ. κρίσεις τινί *lodge* accusations against one, Plb.22.4.6 (s.v.l.); ὑ. τὴν ἀντωμοσίαν κατά τινος Them.*Or.*26. 313c; *bring an accusation* against one, εἴπ' εἴ τι καινὸν ὑπογράφῃ τὠμῷ βίῳ E.*HF*1118. 3. *write under orders* or *from dictation*, οὐκ ἔχων οὐδὲ τὸν ὑπογράφοντα *an amanuensis*, Jul.*Ep.*28, cf. Plu.*Caes.* 17. II. *write under*, i.e. *trace* letters for children *to write over*, οἱ γραμματισταὶ τοῖς μήπω δεινοῖς γράφειν τῶν παίδων ὑπογράψαντες γραμμὰς τῇ γραφίδι Pl.*Prt.*326d: metaph., ἡ πόλις νόμους ὑ. *traces out* laws as guides of action, ibid., cf. *Lg.*734e: abs., πάντα ὑ. τῷ πράττειν *give* all *directions* for acting, ib.711b; ᾗ ἡμεῖς ὑ. as we *sketched out*, Id.*Tht.*171e: folld. by relat. clause, τοὺς..ὑπογράψαντας τίνα τρόπον.. Phld.*Mus.*p.86 K. 2. *trace in outline, sketch out*, οἱ γραφεῖς ὑπογράψαντες ταῖς γραμμαῖς οὕτως ἐναλείφουσι τοῖς χρώμασι τὸ ζῷον Arist.*GA*743$^{b}$24; καθάπερ ζωγράφον ὑ. ἔργα Pl.*Lg.*934c; ὡς λόγῳ σχῆμα πολιτείας ὑπογράψαντα μὴ ἀκριβῶς ἀπεργάσασθαι Id. *R.*548c; ὑ. τοῖς ἐξεργάζεσθαι καὶ διαπονεῖν δυναμένοις Isoc.5.85; *sketch*, τὸ σχῆμα τῆς Σικελίας Plu.*Nic.*12; *mark* on a map, πόλεις Ptol.*Geog.*1.18.5:—Med., οἷον δή τις ναυπηγὸς..καταβαλλόμενος τὰ τροπιδεῖα ὑπογράφεται τῶν πλοίων σχήματα *has* their forms *traced out*, Pl.*Lg.*803a; ὑ. τὸ σχῆμα τῆς πολιτείας Id.*R.*501a; ὑ. σκιάν Poll. 7.129 (v.l.):—Pass., τὰ ὑπογεγραμμένα the *symptoms described*, Hp. *Epid.*1.3, cf. 19, Phld.*Piet.*19. 3. σπληνίσκος ὑπογεγραμμένος ἱππέα *with an outline sketch* of a horseman *upon it*, *Michel* 832.24 (Samos, iv B.C.). 4. metaph. senses taken from II. 1, II. 2, *trace, indicate*, τοῖς τιμιωτέροις ὑπέγραψεν ἡ φύσις τὴν βοήθειαν Arist.*PA*658$^{a}$23; τὰς δύο φλέβας..ἡ φύσις ὑπέγραψεν Id.*GA*740$^{a}$28; ἡ τῶν τόπων θέσις ὑπογράφει τὴν ἡγεμονίαν ταύτην Str.8.1.3; ὑπογράφων αὐτῷ μεγάλας ἐλπίδας *hinting at*.., Plb.5.36.2, cf. 5.62.1, Aët.9.42; ἐλπίδα παραιτήσεως ὑπογράφει θεῶν διὰ τιμῆς Epicur.*Ep.*3 p.65 U.; τὴν αὐτὴν ἀπορίαν ὑπογράφουσιν *present* or *suggest* the same problem, Str.17. 1.34; *indicate*, τὸν χαρακτῆρα τῆς λέξεως D.H.*Dem.*40; τὴν μετὰ κίσσαν ἐπιμέλειαν Sor.1.54: c. dupl. acc., νομάδας αὐτοὺς ὑπογράφων Str.1.1.6:—Pass., ἡ κοινὴ τοῦ θεοῦ νόησις ὑπεγράφη *was traced*, Epicur.*Ep.*3 p.59 U.; μέχρι τοῦ πρῶτον ὑπογραφέντος αὐτοῖς χνοῦ till *the* first *signs* of their beard *appeared*, Luc.*Am.*10. 5. Med., *describe generally*, ὑ. τὴν διόρθωσιν τοῦ νόμου D.S.12.18:—Pass., τύπῳ..ὑπογεγράφθω περὶ ψυχῆς (impers.) Arist.*de An.*413$^{a}$10, cf. *SE*181$^{a}$2. III. Med., ὑ. ἑαυτῷ εἰς μνήμην c. inf., *make a memorandum* that.., App.*Pun.*136. IV. Med., *pledge, mortgage*, ὑπογράψονται τὼς χώρως *Tab.Heracl.*1.149. V. ὑπογράφειν or -γράφεσθαι τοὺς ὀφθαλμούς *paint under* the eyelids, Nic. Dam.4 J., J.*BJ*4.9.10, Poll.5.102, Luc.*Bis Acc.*31; ὑπεγέγραπτο τοὺς ὀφθαλμούς Ath.12.529a: abs., ὑπογεγραμμένη Ar.*Fr.*880, Hsch.; cf. ὑπογραφή III, ὑπόγραμμα II.

**ὑπογρύζω**, *mutter privately*, Lib.*Decl.*43.60.

**ὑπόγρῡπος**, ον, *with a rather hooked nose*, Philostr.*Her.*15.

⊛ **ὑπόγυιος** or (v. sub fin.) **ὑπόγῠος**, ον, *nigh at hand, imminent*, ὑ. μοι τῆς τοῦ βίου τελευτῆς οὔσης Isoc.15.4, ὑπόγυον ἐνδείκνυται θάνατον

Gal.18(2).69; ὑπόγυον, used abs., *near the end, at the approach of death*, Hp.*Epid*.7.51,52; εἴ τινων ὑ. ἡ ἀφαίρεσις τῶν καρπῶν Thphr. *CP*1.13.10; τοῦτ' ἔστιν ὑπογυιότατον (v.l. -γυώτατον) πρὸς αὐτάρκειαν *the readiest means*, Arist.*Pol*.1321$^{b}$16; ὑπογύου οὔσης τῆς ἑορτῆς Id. *Oec*.1347$^{a}$28, cf. *IG*5(2).265.10 (Mantinea, i B.C.); τῶν χρόνων ὑ. ὄντων D.28.17; ἡ ὑπόγυος πρόσταξις the *immediate* command (i.e. that something shall be done immediately), A.D.*Synt*.253.2; ἡ ἐκεῖνος καὶ ἡ οὗτος..τὴν ὑπόγυιον γνῶσιν τοῦ προσώπου παριστᾶσιν Id. *Pron*.61.4. Adv. ὑπογύως *immediately, in the immediate future*, ἐὰν γένηται ἡμᾶς μὴ ὑ. ἀναπλεῖν *PAmh*.2.135.10 (ii A.D.). II. *recent*, ὁ πόλεμος ὁ ὑπογυιότατος Isoc.14.17; ὑπογυωτέροις παραδείγμασι χρῆσθαι D.61.46; τὰ ὑπογυιότατα Ps.-Philipp.ap.eund.12.12; ὑπογυώτερα τοῖς χρόνοις D.60.9; ὑπόγυιόν ἐστι ἐξ οὗ.. it is *a very short time* since.., Isoc.18.29; ἐν τοῖς ὑ. λόγοις, opp. τοῖς ἄνω, Arist.*GA*757$^{a}$28; ταῖς ὑ. ἀπεψίαις Gal.6.195; ὑπόγυοι αἰτίαι νοσημάτων Id.15.162. Adv. ὑπογυίως or -γύως *recently, lately*, Ath.5.206d, Dsc.*Ther.Prooem*., *BGU*731 ii 5 (ii A.D.); ἔχων ὑ. ἐν μνήμῃ τὰς τιμὰς ὧν ἀγοράζει having *freshly* in his mind, *PRyl*.233.12 (ii A.D.): neut. -γυον as Adv., *Gloss*.; τὸ ὑπογυιότατον Isoc.9.81. III. *sudden*, ὅσα θάνατον ἐπιφέρει ὑπόγυια ὄντα Arist.*EN*1115$^{a}$34; ἐξ ὑπογύου *off-hand, on the spur of the moment*, X.*Cyr*.6.1.43, Pl.*Mx*.235c, Isoc.4.13; ἐξ ὑ. γίγνεσθαι, opp. ἐκ πολλοῦ χρόνου σκέψασθαι, Arist.*Rh*.1354$^{b}$3; ἐξ ὑπογύου τινὸς χρόνου *OGI*13.7 (Samos, iv B.C.). 2. of persons, ὑ. τῇ ὀργῇ *in the first burst* of anger, Arist.*Rh*.1380$^{b}$6. 3. *actual, present*, διὰ τὴν ὑπόγυιον ἰσχνότητα Gal.*Nat.Fac*.2.6.—The forms ὑπό-γυιος and -γυος vary continually in codd., and the erroneous Comp. and Sup. forms ὑπογυιώτερος -ώτατος, and ὑπογυότερος -ότατος occur; in Papyri and Inscrr. we have ὑπογύως *POxy*.237 vi 6, vii 32 (ii A.D.), etc., ὑπογυίως *PSI* 10.1103.8 (iii A.D.), ὑπόγυιος *IG*5(2) l.c., *CPR*220.5 (i A.D.).

**ὑπογυμνάζω**, *practise*, τὰς πολεμιστηρίους ἀσκήσεις Heraclit.*All*. 11.

**ὑπογυμνᾰσί-αρχος**, ὁ, *under-gymnasiarch*, *IG*12(5).39 (Naxos), 232 (Paros):—hence -**αρχέω**, *to be under-gymnasiarch*, ib.12 (2).258 (Mytil.), 12(3).1314 (Thera), etc.; -**αρχία**, ἡ, *Sammelb*. 7473.7 (iii A.D.).

**ὑπογυμνόω**, *make partly bare*, τὸ σκέλος Aristaenet.1.27.

**ὑπόγυος**, ον, = ὑπόγυιος (q.v.).

**ὑπογύπωνες**, οἱ, *a sort of dancers*, Poll.4.104.

**ὑπόγῡρος**, ον, *somewhat curved*, νῶτα Philostr.*Gym*.35.

**ὑποδαίω**, *light, kindle under*, ὑπὸ δὲ ξύλα δαῖον Il.18.347.

**ὑποδάκνω**, *bite privily*, φθεῖρες γεωργὸν ὑ. App.*BC*1.101. II. *to be somewhat pungent*, τῇ γεύσει Dsc.4.142: metaph., *to be mordant*, Demetr.*Eloc*.260.

**ὑπόδακρυς**, gloss on γλαμυρός, Hsch.

⊛ **ὑποδακρύω**, *weep a little* or *secretly*, Luc.*DDeor*.6.2, Chor.*Lyd*. 39. 2. *ooze*, of blood, Antyll.ap.Orib.7.21.8.

**ὑποδαμνάω**, *master* or *weaken beneath* one, ποταμὸς ὑπὸ γούνατ' ἐδάμνα Il.21.270:—Pass. ὑποδάμνᾰμαι (from *ὑποδάμνημι), *to be overcome, overpowered*, εἰπέ μοι ἠὲ ἑκὼν ὑποδάμνασαι Od.3.214, 16.95; aor. 1 part. ὑποδμηθεῖσα, of a woman, *subdued* by a man, *yielding to* his *embrace*, *h.Hom*.17.4, Hes.*Sc*.53, *Th*.327,374; also ὑποδμηθείς, of a man, *subdued by love*, *AP*5.299 (Paul. Sil.); ἀλλήλοις ὑποδεδμῆσθαι *to be married*, Eust.1418.38:—Med., Ἔρος φρένας ὑποδάμναται Theoc.29. 23, cf. Q.S.1.336, 6.284.

**ὑπόδᾰσυς**, υ, *somewhat hairy*, Dsc.2.139, 3.103.

**ὑποδεδιώς**, ὁ, (ὑποδείδω) Comic name of a bird in Ar.*Av*. 65.

**ὑποδέδρομε**, v. ὑποτρέχω.

**ὑποδεής** (A), ές, (δέομαι) *somewhat deficient, inferior*; used only in Comp. ὑποδεέστερος. I. of persons, *lower in degree*, Hdt.1.91, 134; κυνίδια τῶν ἀνθρώπων καὶ τῇ γνώμῃ καὶ τῇ γλώσσῃ ὑ. X.*Oec*.13. 8. b. *younger*, *PMasp*.23.16 (vi A.D.), *PLond*.5.1708.37 (vi A.D.). 2. of things, ἐκ πολλῷ ὑποδεεστέρων with *resources* much *inferior*, Th.2.89; αὐτὸς ἑωυτοῦ ῥέει -έστερος, of the Nile, Hdt.2.25; τέχνη ἐκείνης -τέρα Pl.*Euthd*.289e; δηλοῦται..ὑποδεέστερα ὄντα τῆς φήμης *inferior* to report, i.e. exaggerated, Th.1.11; ἔστι δὲ τοῦτο ὑ., of bee-bread, Arist.*HA*623$^{b}$24. II. Adv. -εστέρως Th.8.87, Antipho4.4.6: neut. pl. ὑποδεέστερα as Adv., Id.3.3.9.

**ὑποδεής** (B), ές, (δέος) *somewhat fearful*, Hsch., Phot., Suid.

⊛ **ὑπόδειγ-μα**, ατος, τό, *sign, token, indication*, v.l. in X.*Eq*.2.2 (pl.); φιλαγαθίας *IG*2$^{2}$.1011.81. 2. *illustration, picture showing how something is to be done*, Apollon.Cit.2,3. II. *pattern*, Plb.3.17.8; μετανοίας Lxx *Si*.44.16, cf. 2*Ma*.6.28; ὑ. καὶ σκιά *Ep.Hebr*.8.5, cf. 9.23; τὸ ὑ. τοῦ οἴκου Lxx *Ez*.42.15: in Inscrr., πρὸς ὑπόδειγμα ἀρετῆς *CIG*2769,2774,2775d (add.), al. (Aphrodisias); καλὸν ὑ. τῆς ἰδίας προαιρέσεως καταβαλλόμενος *BMus.Inscr*.925 *b* 22 (Branchidae, i B.C.): but also ὑ. ἀπειθίας *BGU*747 ii 14 (ii A.D.); ὑ. μελλόντων ἀσεβεῖν 2*Ep.Pet*.2.6. III. *example, instance*, *AP*6.342, Ph.*Bel*.69.10, D.H. *Comp*.17, Hp.*Ep*.17, Herm. *in Phdr*.p.185 A.; ὑποδείγματος χάριν Nicom.*Ar*.1.8; *specimen*, *BGU*1141.43 (i B.C.), etc.: pl., Phld.*Rh*. 1.8 S., al.:—rejected as less correct than παράδειγμα by the Atticists, Phryn.4. -**μᾰτίζω**, *give an example*, Heph.Astr.2.10. -**μᾰτικός**, ή, όν, *by way of example*, διδασκαλία S.E.*M*.4.23. Adv. -κῶς ib.1.154, 4.3. -**μᾰτισμός**, ὁ, dub. sens., ταραχὰς οὐκ ὀλίγας ποιήσει καὶ ὑποδειγματισμοὺς *Cat.Cod.Astr*.8(4).142.

**ὑποδείδω**, I. trans., *shrink in fear under, cower before*, c. acc., Hom., who uses mostly the aor. (usu. written with double δ for δϝ, v. δείδω), ὑπέδδεισαν, ὑποδδείσαντες, Il.1.406, 12.413, al.; ὑποδείσατε Od.2.66: Ep. pf. 2 and plpf., ὑποδείδια 17.564, Philet.8, ὑπεδείδισαν Il.5.521: Ep. pf. 1 ὑπαιδείδοικα *h.Merc*.165: literally, of birds, *cower beneath*, μέγαν αἰγυπιὸν ὑποδείσαντες S.*Aj*. 169 (anap.). II. abs., *fear*, μή τίς μοι ὑποδδείσας ἀναδύῃ Od.9. 377; ὑποδεδοικώς Luc.*Salt*.63; cf. ὑποδεδιώς.

**ὑποδείελος**, ον, (δείλη) *towards evening*, Arat.826.

**ὑποδείκ-νῡμι** and -**νύω** (v. infr.), *show, indicate*, οὗτοι.. πάντα θεοὶ θνητοῖσ' ὑπέδειξαν Xenoph.18.1; πολλοῖσι ὑποδέξας (Ion. aor.) ὄλβον ὁ θεός *having given a glimpse of* happiness, Hdt.1.32; ἄλλο τι τῶν χρησίμων ὑ. *show* any other good *symptom*, Hp.*Coac*.483; ὑποδεικνύεις μὲν ἦθος ἀστεῖον Nicom.Com.1.1; ὑ. ἐλπίδας Plb.2.70.7, etc.; τὰς χώρας ὑποδείκνυμεν we *indicate, cite* the passages, Phld.*Rh*.1. 98 S.; ὑ. τινὰ τοῖς ἀνδράσι *introduce*, Plu.2.710c. 2. abs., *indicate one's will, intimate*, οἱ θεοὶ οὕτως ὑποδεικνύουσι X.*Mem*.4.3.13, cf. *An*. 5.7.12; *warn*, τίς ὑπέδειξεν ὑμῖν φυγεῖν; *Ev.Matt*.3.7. 3. *lay an information*, τῷ βασιλεῖ περί τινος Lxx *To*.1.19; ὑποδέδειχέν σε τὰ σύμβολα ἀπεστράφθαι he *has reported* that.., *BGU*1755.4 (i B.C.): c. acc., *report*, σοι τὴν τῆς οἰκίας σου διάθεσιν ib.1881.3 (i B.C.): also ὑπόδειξον αὐτῷ ὅτι ἀναβαίνω *PSI*9.1079.5 (i B.C.):—Pass., *to be brought to the notice* of a court, *produced* in evidence, *PTeb*.27.78 (ii B.C.), etc. II. *show by tracing out, mark out*, διώρυχας Hdt.1.189; Ὅμηρος καὶ τὰ τῆς κωμῳδίας σχήματα..ὑπέδειξε Arist.*Po*.1448$^{b}$37, cf. *Rh*.1404$^{b}$25, *Ath*.41.2: abs., *set a pattern* or *example*, τοῦ διδασκάλου πονηρῶς τι ὑποδεικνύοντος X.*Oec*.12.18; οὐχ οἷόν τε μὴ καλῶς ὑποδεικνύντος καλῶς μιμεῖσθαι unless *some one sets* a good *example*, Arist.*Oec*. 1345$^{a}$9. 2. generally, *teach, indicate*, ὑ. αὐτοῖς οἵους εἶναι χρή.. Isoc.3.57, cf. 5.111, *Ep*.2.11; ὡς ἔμπροσθεν ὑπεδείξαμεν Sor.1.16, cf. 54, al., Ael.*Tact*.28.1. 3. *make a show of, pretend to*, ἀρετήν Th. 4.86, cf. Plb.2.47.10. -**τέος**, α, ον, *to be pointed out*, Id.3.36. 5. II. ὑποδεικτέον, *one must point out, indicate*, Sor.1.53, S.E. *M*.7.167, Aët.9.38. -**της**, ου, ὁ, *one who points out*, Sm.*Ps*.83(84). 7, *Gloss*.

**ὑποδειλιάω**, *to be somewhat cowardly*, ὑποδεδειλιακότες ἄνθρωποι *poor cowardly* fellows, Aeschin.1.181. II. = ὑποδείδω, πόλεμον, f.l. for ἀπο-, Plb.35.3.4.

**ὑποδειμαίνω**, = ὑποδείδω, *stand in secret awe of*, τὸν [νόμον] Hdt.7. 104, cf. Plu.2.986d.

**ὑπόδειξις**, εως, ἡ, *intimation, indication*, ὑπόδειξιν ποιεῖσθαι τίνα πότ' ἐστιν.. Phld.*Rh*.1.52 S.; θεῖα ὑ. Phleg.36.3 J., cf. *PMag.Leid. W*.18.27; ὑποδείξεως ἕνεκα γεγράφθω διάγραμμα Nicom.*Ar*.2.3:— f.l. in Plu.*Demetr*.38.

**ὑποδειπνέω**, *dine as a substitute for* another, τινι Luc.*Gall*.10.

**ὑποδειρίς**, ίδος, ἡ, *base of neck in front*, Ruf.*Onom*.66.

**ὑποδέκομαι**, v. ὑποδέχομαι.

**ὑποδεκ-τέον**, *one must receive*, Pl.*Lg*.953b. -**τήριον**, τό, v.l. for ὑποδυτήριον in Str.14.5.6. -**της**, ου, ὁ, *receiver, steward*, a financial official, = καταπομπός, τῶν κελευσθέντων ἀπαιτηθῆναι *PLips*.ap. Wilcken *Chr*.43 intr. (iv A.D.); ἐσθῆτος, οἴνου, *Stud.Pal*.20.87.1, 91.1 (iv A.D.): abs., *POxy*.136.15 (vi A.D.), *PLond*.5.1667.1 (vi A.D.), Just.*Nov*.163.2, etc. -**τικός**, ή, όν, *of* or *for receiving*, -κὸς τοῦ σώματος τόπος S.E.*M*.10.20, cf. Gal.2.542, 4.722; ἀγγεῖον ὑ. ταρίχων Sch.Ar.*V*.674. II. δεῖπνον ὑ. an entertainment *by way of welcome*, Plu.2.727b.

**ὑποδελεάζω**, dub. l. in Ph.*Bel*.100.39 codd.: ὑποδενδρυάζοντας (= *divers*) cj. Diels.

**ὑπόδεμα**, ατος, τό, = Lat. *perna*, dub. in *Gloss*.

**ὑποδέμω**, *lay as a foundation*, τὸν πρῶτον δόμον Hdt.2.127:—Med., *found*, πόλιν ὑποδείμασθαι Str.7 *Fr*.35.

**ὑποδενδρυάζω**, = ὑποδῦναί που καὶ πτῆξαι ὑπὸ σκέπην, Phot., Suid.; but = τὸ ἐξ ἀφανοῦς καὶ αἰφνιδίως ἐπιφαίνεσθαι, Hsch.:—cf. ὑποδελεάζω.

**ὑποδέννω**, v. ὑποδέω.

**ὑποδεξίη**, ἡ, = ὑποδοχή 1.2, *reception of a guest, means of entertainment*, πᾶσά τοί ἐσθ' ὑποδεξίη [ῐ] Il.9.73.

**ὑποδέξιος**, α, ον, (ὑποδέχομαι) *able to receive, capacious, ample*, λιμένες Hdt.7.49; = ὑποδοχεύς, Phot.:—in E.*Rh*.364 (lyr.), for ὑποδεξίαις ἁμίλλαις (codd.) ἐπιδεξίοις and ὑποδεξιᾶν are conjectured.

**ὑπόδεξις**, εως, ἡ, = ὑποδοχή, *care, attention*, Hp.*Decent*.16. II. *undertaking* to contribute to public funds, *AJP*56.362 (Colophon, iv B.C.).

**ὑποδέρ-αιον**, τό, = sq., Poll.5.98, Hsch., etc. -**ίδιον**, τό, = sq. II, *IG*2$^{2}$.1424 *a* 84. -**ίς**, ίδος, ἡ, *the lower part of the neck*, Poll.2.130, 235, 5.56. II. *necklace*, *IG*1$^{2}$.313.54, al., Ar.*Fr*.320.14, Arist.*HA* 558$^{b}$2, *IG*2$^{2}$.1388.17, al.

**ὑποδέρκομαι**, = ὑποβλέπω, Q.S.3.252.

**ὑποδερμᾰτῖτις**, ιδος, ἡ, *a disease of horses*, *Hippiatr*.69.

**ὑποδερμίς**, ίδος, ἡ, = κλειτορίς, Ruf.*Onom*.111.

**ὑποδέρω**, *strip off the skin a little* or *below*, Gal.2.700, 18(2).103, Orib.46.15.5.

**ὑποδεσ-ίδιον**, τό, Dim. of sq. II.2, ὑ. ἀγροικικόν = *soccus*, *Gloss*. (s. v.l.). -**ις**, εως, ἡ, (ὑποδέω) *under-bandaging*, Hp.*Off*.11. II. *putting on one's shoes*, Arist.*Pol*.1257$^{a}$9, *Cael*.271$^{a}$33, Luc.*Gall*. 26. 2. concrete, = τὰ ὑποδήματα, *foot-gear*, Pl.*Chrm*.173b, X. *Mem*.1.2.5, Duris14 J., Str.10.4.16: pl., Pl.*Prt*.322a, *R*.425b, D.S. 5.45:—also ὑπόδησις (q.v.). -**μα**, ατος, τό, *pledge*, in pl., Hsch. ⊛ -**μεύω**, = ὑποδέω, Sch.Ar.*Ec*.269. -**μέω**, = foreg., in Med., -εῖται τὰ πέδιλα Sch.A.R.4.1515: abs., Sch.S.*Tr*.779. -**μιος**, ον, *pledged*, Hsch. -**μίς**, ίδος, ἡ, *under-bandage*, Hp.*Fract*.27, *Art*.69. ⊛ -**μός**, ὁ, = ὑπόδημα, *foot-gear*, Plb.11.9.4. II. = ὑποδεσμίς, Gal.18(2).538.

**ὑποδεύω**, *moisten*, dub. rest. in Epigr.Gr.808 (Pamphylia: [ὑπ]οχεύοι Kaibel).

**ὑποδέχνυμαι**, poet. for sq., ὑποδέχνυσο Orph.A.83.

⊛ **ὑποδέχομαι**, in Ion. and Dor. Prose **-δέκομαι** Hdt. (v. infr.), IG4$^2$(1).121.46 (Epid., iv B.C.) · fut. -δέξομαι Od.16.70, Dor. -δεξοῦμαι SIG 558.22 (Ithaca, iii B.C.): aor. -εδεξάμην Il.6.136, rarely -εδέχθην E. Heracl.757 (lyr.; used in pass. sense by Poll.1.74, D.C.48.15, PLond. 5.1659.6 (iv A.D.), Sch.Il.14.323; -δεχόμενος in pass. sense, D.C. 55.10, POxy.1894.14 (vi A.D.)): 3 sg. Ep. aor. 2 or impf. ὑπέδεκτο Od.14.52,275, Hes.Th.513, Pi.P.9.9; 2 pl. imper. ὑπόδεχθε cj. Bentl. in Call.Epigr.42; inf. ὑποδέχθαι Il.7.93; part. ὑποδέγμενος Od.13. 310:—*receive into one's house, welcome*, ὁ δέ με (sc. Φοίνικα) πρόφρων ὑπέδεκτο Il.9.480; χαῖρε δ' Ὀδυσσεὺς ὅττι μιν ὣς ὑπέδεκτο Od.14.52; τὸν δ' οὐχ ὑποδέξομαι αὖτις Il.18.59, Od.19.257; ξεῖνον..ὑποδέξομαι οἴκῳ 16.70; Θέτις δ' ὑπεδέξατο κόλπῳ Il.6.136, cf. 18.398; Διὸς πλαστὴν ὑπέδεκτο γυναῖκα Hes. l.c.; οἰκίοισι ὑ. τινά Hdt.1.41; ὑπέδεκτο ξεῖνον ὀχέων *received* the stranger [as he lighted] from his chariot, Pi. l. c.; ὁ ὑποδεξάμενος the man *who had received him*, Isoc.9.20; ἱκέτας ὑ. E.Heracl.757 (lyr.), cf. Berl.Sitzb.1927.167 (Cyrene), Ep.Jac.2.25; φυγάδας Th.5.83, cf. PRev.Laws 44.14 (iii B.C.); *harbour* a runaway slave, POxy.1643.12 (iii A.D.); [ξένον] ἀγοραῖς καὶ λιμέσι καὶ δημοσίοις οἰκοδομήμασιν ἔξω τῆς πόλεως Pl.Lg.952e, cf. 953b,d, OGI49.5 (Ptolemais, iii B.C.); ὑ. φρουράν *admit* an enemy's garrison, D.58. 38, cf. 67, IG1$^2$.87.10, Arist.Pol.1303$^a$36; λῃστάς, πειρατάς, *harbour* brigands, pirates, SIG38 B21 (Teos, v B.C.), Supp.Epigr.3.378 B11 (Delph., ii/i B.C.), cf. POxy.1408.23 (iii A.D.); γυναῖκάς τινι εἰς τὸ αὐτὸ φοιτώσας ὑποδέχεσθαι Plu.Per.32; αἱ Θίβρωνα ὑποδεξάμεναι πόλεις those who *admitted* him *as a friend*, X.HG4.8.21, cf. Th.3.111, 6.34: with a thing as subject, γαῖα..ὑπέδεκτο μάντιν Οἰκλείδαν the earth *opened up to receive* the seer O., Pi.N.10.8; αἰθὴρ μὲν ψυχὰς ὑπεδέξατο σώμ[ατα δὲ χθών] IG1$^2$.945.6; τῆς τεκούσης καὶ θρεψάσης καὶ ὑποδεξαμένης [χώρας] Pl.Mx.237c. 2. *entertain* to a meal, θύων Διὶ Κτησίῳ κἀκεῖνον ὑποδεχόμενος Antipho 1.18, cf. IG4.679.15 (Hermione, iii/ii B.C.); ἵνα ἔχῃ ἡ στρατιὰ τὰ ἐπιτήδεια (πολλὴ γὰρ οὖσα οὐ πάσης ἔσται πόλεως ὑποδέξασθαι) Th.6.22; ὁ ὑποδεχόμενος the *host* (at a dinner party), Epict.Fr.17; τὸ πλῆθος λαμπρῶς ὑπεδέξατο D.S. 17.115, cf. Plu.Alex.23. 3. *give ear to, hearken to*, εὐχάς Hes. Th.419; τοὺς λόγους Hdt.8.106; ὑ. διαβολάς *give ear to* accusations, Lys.25.11 codd. (leg. ἀπο–). 4. *admit, allow* a thing with which one is taxed, Hdt.4.167; οὐκ ὑ. *refuse to admit, deny*, Id.3.130, 6. 69. II. *take up* a burden, ἡ γυνὴ ὑποδεξαμένη φέρει τὸ φορτίον τοῦτο X.Mem.2.2.5; of ships, *take on board*, τὰ εἴδη POxy.1412.10 (iii A.D.); of dolphins, Luc.DMar.8.1. 2. *bear patiently*, βίας ὑποδέγμενος ἀνδρῶν Od.13.310, 16.189; *submit to*, τὰς κατὰ νόμους παραγγελίας POxy.67.11 (iv A.D.); μέτρον, i.e. *accept* it *as correct*, ib. 157.5 (vi A.D.); τροφὴ θλίβουσα πᾶν τὸ δοκοῦν αὐτὴν ὑποδέχεσθαι Sor. 1.115. III. *undertake, promise*, αἴδεσθεν μὲν ἀνήνασθαι, δεῖσαν δ' ὑποδέχθαι Il.7.93, cf. Hdt.9.21,22; ὁ δέ οἱ πρόφρων ὑπέδεκτο (sc. δώσειν) Od.2.387; ὑποδέκομαι (sc. ἐνιαυτοῦ ἀποθυσεῖν τὰ ἴατρα) IG4$^2$(1).121. 46 (Epid., iv B.C.); c. inf. fut., h.Cer.443, Hdt.3.69, 4.119,133, 6.11, 7.158, 8.29,102, Th.2.29 (inf. aor. is v.l. for fut. in Hdt.1.24, 6.2); c. inf. pres., Antipho 3.3.6 (s. v. l.); ὑ. τινὶ ἦ μὴν.. c. inf. fut., Th.8.81; Κορίνθιοι ὑπεδέξαντο τὴν τιμωρίαν *undertook* to champion their cause, Id.1.25; ὥσπερ ὑπεδέξασθε, βοηθήσατε ib.71; ὑ. μεγάλα τινί *make* him great *promises*, Hdt.2.121.ζ'; τὴν ἀτραπὸν ἐθελονταὶ Φωκέες ὑποδεξάμενοι Λεωνίδῃ ἐφύλασσον Id.7.217; ἃ ὑπεδέξατο οὐκ ἐπετέλει Th.2.95; *undertake to contribute*, ὅσον ἂν ἕκαστος θέλῃ AJP56.362 (Colophon, iv B.C.); abs., ibid.; ὑπεδέξαντο εἰς τὰ τείχη ib.363; also τὰ ἐκφόρια ἅπερ ὑπεδέξω the rents which you *undertook to collect*, POxy.1134.7 (v A.D.). 2. *accept as a responsibility, take in charge*, as a nurse, h.Cer.226; of officials, shippers, farm bailiffs, etc., *take over, receive as agent* (cf. ὑποδέκτης), τοὺς νεολέκτους..ὑποδεξάμενοι κατὰ διαδοχὴν..παραπέμψατε Wilcken Chr. 469.5 (iv A.D.); καταπιστεῦσαι Αὐρηλίῳ Πέτρῳ..σιτομέτρῃ..ὑποδέξασθαι τὸν δημόσιον σῖτον Sammelb.5273.4 (v A.D.), cf. Wilcken Chr.434.12 (iv A.D.), PLips.34$^v$.7, 58.9, al. (iv A.D.), POxy.1899. 16, 1982.17 (v A.D.), Cod.Just.1.5.18.11; τὴν ὑποδοχὴν πᾶσαν τοῦ μακαρίου Ἰούστου αὐτὸς ὑπόδεξαι POxy.1838.1 (vi A.D.); *accept* (as a liability) a dowry or donatio ante nuptias, Cod.Just.5.17. 12, Just.Nov.22.19. IV. *receive in succession, take up*, μέλος A.Supp.1022 (lyr.); περαιωθέντας..λειμὼν ὑποδέχεται Luc.Luct.5, cf. VH2.44; τὴν εἰς τὸ στόμα φορὰν τῶν περιττωμάτων ὑποδέχεται στόμαχος Gal.6.421, cf. 432, 18(2).163,176,218; ὁ ὑποδεξάμενος the *receiver* of stolen goods, Cat.Cod.Astr.1.96. 2. intr., of a place, *come next*, τὸ πρὸς τὴν ἠῶ θάλασσα ὑποδέκεται καὶ τενάγεα Hdt.7.176; of rank, *come next in order*, ὅταν πλείονες συνδειπνῶσι, ..μέσος ὁ κράτιστος (sc. κάθηται), ὁ δ' ὑποδεχόμενος παρ' αὐτόν Posidon. 15J. 3. *intercept*, ὁ μὲν..ἐπόρουσεν, ὁ δ' ἐμμαπέως ὑπέδεκτο Hes. Sc.442; ἐν δυσχωρίᾳ [τοὺς πολεμίους] X.Cyr.1.6.35; of hunters, *intercept* beaten-up game, ib.2.4.20; *catch*, τὸ πήδημα τῆς σφαίρας Poll. 9.105; ὑπτίαις ταῖς χερσὶ [τὸ μῆλον] Philostr.Im.1.6; τὸ ἐνθεῦτέν μιν οἱ ἐχθροὶ ὑποδεξάμενοι καὶ ὑπὸ δικαστήριον ἀγαγόντες Hdt.6.104; *catch as in a trap*, στυγερὸς δ' ὑπεδέξατο κοῖτος a hateful resting-place *receives* (*entraps*) them, Od.22.470; ἔτι γάρ νύ με πῆμ' ὑπέδεκτο still more sorrow *was in store for* me, 14.275; ἀκλεὴς νιν δόξα πρὸς ἀνθρώπων ὑποδέξεται *will be her lot*, E.Heracl.624 (lyr.); ὑποδεξαμένης αὐτοὺς πολλῆς ῥύσεως ὕδατος when a rush of water *takes* them *by surprise*, Pl.Lg.944b. 4. *catch, collect* a liquid. παιδίον θεασάμενος, ἐπειδὴ κατέαξε τὸ σκεῦος, τῷ κοίλῳ τοῦ ψωμίου τὴν φακῆν ὑποδεχόμενον D.L.6.37; of channels, *receive*, τὸ στόμα τῶν μητρέων οὐχ ὑποδέχεται τὸν γόνον Hp.Aër.21; τὴν ἐσομένην τῶν ὑδάτων εἴσροιαν POxy.1409.19 (iii A.D.); κατεφίλει καὶ ὑπεδέχετο τὰ δάκρυα X.Eph.1.9; ποταμὸς πάσας ὑποδεχόμενος τὰς ἀνθρωπείας λύμας Plb.5.59.11, cf. Gp.12.2.4, al.; ἀγγεῖον τὸ μέλλον ὑποδέξεσθαι τὸ ὕδωρ v.l. in Hero Spir.1.24, cf. 30.

**ὑποδέω**, late Gr. **-δέννω** Gloss., Dosith.p.435 K.:—*bind* or *fasten under*, ἁμαξίδας ὑ. τῇσι οὐρῇσι, of long-tailed sheep, Hdt.3. 113. II. esp. *underbind* the feet, i.e. *shoe*, because the ancient sandals or shoes were bound on with straps, [καμήλους] ὑ. καρβατίναις Arist.HA499$^a$29, cf. Plu.Pomp.24, Paus.10.25.4; so Cobet restores ὑποδῶν τὰ μὲν ὁπλαῖς, for ὑπὸ ποδῶν, in Pl.Prt.321b:—mostly in Med., *bind under one's feet, put on shoes*, Ar.Av.492 (anap.), Pl. Smp.220b; ὑποδουμένη *as I was putting on my shoes*, Ar.Ec.36, cf. Thphr.Char.10.14; ὑποδεῖται, for the purpose of going away, Pherecr.153.4 (hex.); οἱ ἔμπαλιν ὑποδούμενοι (v. ἔμπαλιν II.1) Pl.Tht. 193c; ὑποδούμενος τὸν ἱμάντα..τῆς ἐμβάδος ἀπέρρηξα Men.109. III. in Med. and Pass., also, c. acc., 1. of that which one puts on, κοθόρνους ὑποδέεσθαι Hdt.1.155, cf. 6.125; ὑπόδημα ib.1; τὰς Λακωνικάς Ar.Ec.269; Σκυθίκαις (Aeol. accus.) Alc.103; τὰς ἐμβάδας Eub. 30, cf. Theopomp.Com.52; τὰ σανδάλια Act.Ap.12.8; cf. ὑποδύω II. 1b:—so in pf. Pass., ὑποδήματα, βλαύτας ὑποδεδεμένος, *with* shoes, slippers *on one's feet*, Pl.Grg.490e, Smp.174a; ἁπλᾶς ὑποδέδενται D. 54.34: abs., ὑποδεδεμένοι ἐκοιμῶντο *with their shoes on*, X.An.4.5.14; ὥσπερ ὑποδεδ. Arist.PA687$^a$28. 2. of the foot, ὑποδεδεμένοι τὸν ἀριστερὸν πόδα *with* the left foot *shod*, Th.3.22, cf. Arist.Fr.74; θάτερον [πόδα] σανδάλῳ ὑποδεδ. Luc.Hist.Conscr.22, cf. Ael.VH1.18; ὑποδησάμενοι τοὺς πόδας ἐν ἑτοιμασίᾳ τοῦ εὐαγγελίου Ep.Eph.6.15. IV. ὑποδῆσαι· ἐνεχυρασθῆναι, Ἰταλιῶται, Hsch.

**ὑποδηλ-όω**, *show privately*, σημεῖον Ar.Th.1011; *hint at, suggest*, θεῖόν τι Philostr.Her.Prooem.3; τὸ ἀθαρσές τινος Plu.Nic.4; *imply*, Ael.NA5.45; *foreshadow*, ib.7.7. **-ωσις**, εως, ἡ, *insinuation*, a rhetorical phrase ascribed to Evenus of Paros in Pl.Phdr.267a, cf. Poll.4.33 (pl.).

⊛ **ὑπόδημ-α**, ατος, τό, (ὑποδέω) *sole bound under the foot with straps, sandal*, ποσὶν..ὑποδήματα δοῦσα Od.15.369; ποσὶν..ὑποδήματα δοίην 18.361, cf. Hdt.1.195, etc.; ποδὸς ὑ. Pl.Alc.1.128a, etc.; whereas ὑπόδημα κοῖλον is a *shoe* or *half-boot*, which covered the whole foot (v. κοῖλος I.1); ὑπόδημα is sts. used alone in this sense, cf. Ar.Pl. 983 (and Sch. ad loc.), Arist.Rh.1392$^a$32; εἰς ὑποδήματα γράφειν put down as paid for *shoes*, Lys.32.20 (Pass.); δεξιὸν εἰς ὑ., ἀριστερὸν εἰς ποδάνιπτρα, of one who is ready for anything, perh. alluding to Theramenes (v. κόθορνος 3), Ar.Fr.914 (perh. Ar.Byz., cf. Did. and Polem.Hist.(Fr.101 M.) ap.Hellad.ap.Phot.Bibl.p.533 B.); similar words are ascribed to Pythag. by Iamb.Protr.21.ια' (where ὑπόδησις is used); τὸ ὑ. ἔρραψας μὲν σύ, ὑπεδήσατο δὲ Ἀρισταγόρης Hdt.6.1, cf. Lib.Ep.52; ὁ σπάρτος, ἐξ οὗ πλέκουσιν ὑποδήματα τοῖς ὑποζυγίοις Gal. 6.502. **-ἄτάριος**, ὁ, *sandalmaker, shoemaker*, IG9(2).16.16 (Hypata, ii A.D.), Gloss. **-άτιον**, τό, Dim. of ὑπόδημα, Hp.Art.62; of the *shoes* of an ass, Arr.Epict.4.1.80. ⊛ **-ἄτοποιός**, ὁ, *sandalmaker*, Gloss., prob. in IG2$^2$.1576.37. **-ἄτορράφος** [ρᾰ], ὁ, (ῥάπτω) *shoemaker*, Hdn.Gr.1.225, al., Gloss. **-ἄτουργικός**, ή, όν, *of* or *for sandal-making*: -κή, ἡ (sc. τέχνη), Olymp. in Alc.p.197 C. ⊛ **-ἄτουργός**, ὁ, *sandalmaker*, JHS22.124 (Pisidia), prob. in Wiener Denkschr.44.27 No.59 (Cilicia).

**ὑπόδημον**, τό, = ὑπόδημα, ὑ. λευκόν PRoss.-Georg.2.41.15 (ii A.D.): pl., ὑπόδημα πορφυρᾶ ib.32.

**ὑποδηόομαι**, Pass., *to be treated in hostile manner*, ὑποδηωθείς Q.S. 2.260, 3.355.

**ὑπόδησις**, εως, ἡ, = ὑπόδεσις, *foot-gear*, Philum.ap.Orib.45.29.33, Iamb.Protr.21.ια'.

**ὑποδια-βάλλω**, *slander somewhat*, Artem.5.53. **-βιβρώσκομαι**, Pass., *to be somewhat corroded*, Hp.Cord.6. **-ζευκτικός**, ή, όν, Gramm., *subdisjunctive*, of certain conjunctions, An.Ox.1.188, EM 415.24, Suid. s.v. ἤ.

**ὑποδιαίρ-εσις**, εως, ἡ, *subdivision*, Diog.Bab.Stoic.3.215, Gal.14. 689, Hermog.Inv.3.10, S.E.M.11.15, Vett.Val.98.10, Procl.Hyp.3.10, etc. **-έω**, *subdivide*, Hermog.Inv.1.2, S.E.P.3.75, M.7.35, D.L.7.84.

⊛ **ὑποδιᾱκονέω**, *serve under another*, CIG1947.8 (loc. inc.):—Med., ὑποδιακονεῖσθαι ταῖς ἱερουργίαις Poll.4.92, cf. Arg.Theoc.2.

**ὑποδιᾱκονικός**, ή, όν, *of* or *for a* ὑποδιάκονος, Ph.2.94.

⊛ **ὑποδιάκονος** [ᾱ], ὁ, *underservant*, Posidipp.26.10, Ph.2.17, al., MAMA3.462, al. (Corycus).

**ὑποδιακρίνω** [ρῑ], *distinguish* as subdivisions. Dam.Pr.86 (Pass.).

⊛ **ὑποδιάκων** [ᾱ], ονος, ὁ, = ὑποδιάκονος, Supp.Epigr.6.377 (Lycaonia), MAMA3.109 (Cilicia).

**ὑποδια-λαμβάνω**, *distinguish in succession*, Phld.Rh.2.64 S. **-λείπω**, *intermit a little*, of the pulse, Gal.8.487. **-νοέομαι**, Med., *design secretly*, v.l. in Jul.Ep.107. **-πήγνῡμαι**, Pass., with pf. 2 -πέπηγα, *to be fixed across below*, Ph.Bel.74.11. **-σπάομαι**, Pass., *to be somewhat dispersed*, ἐναιώρημα ὑποδιεσπασμένον Hp.Epid. 1.26.ι'. **-στολή**, ἡ, *slight stop*, between words in speaking or reading. Quint.Inst.11.3.35. II. *mark to divide words from one another* (most Greek writing being continuous), e.g. ἔστιν, ἄξιος to distinguish it from ἔστι Νάξιος, Ps.-D.T.674, Sch.D.T.p.24 H., al., Eust.701.56, 1465.16. III. *slight change* in positions of the planets, Vett.Val.73.17. **-σύρω** [ῡ], *sneer at a little*, IG4$^2$(1).121. 24 (Epid., iv B.C.). **-τρίβω** [ῑ], *delay a little*, Gal.Libr.Propr. Prooem. **-φθείρω**, *corrupt gradually*, J.AJ15.8.1, D.C.66.13, Hdn.2.6.14. **-φορος**, ον, *subdivided*, Gal.19.602.

**ὑποδῐδακτής**, οῦ, ὁ, = sq., *Gloss.*

**ὑποδῐδάσκᾰλος**, ὁ, *under-teacher*, of a chorus, Pl.*Ion* 536a; ὑ. τραγικός *SIG*692 *A* 31 (Delph., ii B.C.), al.: generally, Cic.*Fam.*9.18.4.

**ὑποδιδράσκω**, Ion. **-διδρήσκω**, *escape secretly, evade*, Aret.*SD*1.1.

**ὑποδῐδωμι**, intr., *give way*, Arist.*MA*698ᵇ15; ὑ. οἱ πόδες, ἡ γῆ, Aristid.*Or.*31(11).12, Philostr.*VA*3.20; of power and empire, *decay*, Aristid.2.187 J., Philostr.*VS*1.21.4; τὴν ἰσχὺν ὑποδεδωκότες in strength, Id.*Gym.*48.

**ὑποδιήγησις**, εως, ἡ, *narrative with inclusion of motives and causes*, Ruf.Rh.25; *narrative of a similar case*, Eust.771.9.

⊕ **ὑπόδῐκος**, ον, (δίκη) *brought to trial* or *liable to be tried*, Lex ap. Lys.10.9, Pl.*Lg.*954a, al., *PHal.*1.72, al. (iii B.C.); οὐχ ὑ. [ἐστι] τὰ εἰκότα not *liable to action*, Arist.*Rh.*1376ᵃ22; τινος *for* a thing, ὑ. γενέσθαι χερῶν A.*Eu.*260 (lyr.); ἀνδραποδισμοῦ Pl.*Lg.*879a; οὐδενὸς τούτων And.4.31; τῆς κακώσεως Is.8.32 (ἐπίδ– codd.); φόνου D.54.25; τοῦ βλάβους *PHal.*1.101 (iii B.C.): with the person injured in dat., ὑ. τῷ παθόντι Lex ap.D.21.10; ὑ. τῷ ἐθέλοντι τιμωρεῖν γιγνέσθω Pl.*Lg.* 871b; τῶν διπλασίων ὑ. ἔστω τῷ βλαφθέντι let him be *liable to forfeit* twice the amount to the person damaged, ib.846b (but ὑ. ποτὶ διπλοῦν *IG*5(1).1390.78 (Andania, i B.C.)); ὑ. ἀσεβείας γιγνέσθω τῷ ἐθέλοντι Pl.*Lg.*868d; ἵνα ὑ. γένηται πᾶς ὁ κόσμος τῷ θεῷ *Ep.Rom.*3.19.

**ὑποδῐμερής**, ές, *in the ratio of* ⅗, converse of ἐπιδιμερής, ὅρος Iamb. *in Nic.*p.42 P.

**ὑποδῑνέομαι**, Pass., *become dizzy*, Call.*Del.*79.

**ὑποδιοικητής**, οῦ, ὁ, *sub-διοικητής*, *PSI*6.632.11 (iii B.C.), *PCair. Zen.*403.12 (iii B.C.), *PGrenf.*2.23.2 (ii B.C.), etc.

**ὑποδιπλ-άσιος** [ᾰ], ον, *the inverse of double*, i.e. ½, Nicom.*Ar.*1.18. **-όω**, = *duplico*, *Gloss.*:—Pass., *to be folded double*, Gal.*UP*4.11. ⊕ **-ωσις**, εως, ἡ, *a fold* of skin, *EM*594.18.

**ὑποδίφθερος**, ον, or α, ον, (διφθέρα) *clothed in skins*, Luc.*Tim.*7; so of sheep, *bratted, wearing leather coats* to protect their fleeces, *PCair.Zen.*430.3, *PHib.*1.32.12, *PPetr.*3 p.269, *PLond.ined.*2308 (all iii B.C.); ὑποδιφθέρας τρέφουσι ποίμνας ἱκανῶς ἀστείας ἐρέας Str.4.4.3; ἔχει (sc. ἡ χώρα) προβατείαν ὑποδιφθέρου καὶ μαλακῆς ἐρέας Id.12.3.13.

**ὑποδιψ-άω**, *to be somewhat thirsty*, Hp.*Epid.*3.1.γ'. **-ιος**, ον, *exciting thirst in some degree*, Man.5.188. **-ος**, ον, *somewhat thirsty*, Ps.-Plu.*Fluv.*10.1.

**ὑποδμώς**, ῶος, ὁ, *servant*, Ποσειδάωνος Od.4.386, Matro *Conv.*62.

**ὑποδόκιον**, τό, *beam on which the rafters rest*, *SIG*247 ii 72 (Delph., iv B.C.), *IG*4²(1).102.59 (Epid., iv B.C.).

**ὑποδομ-ή**, ἡ, Dor. **-δομά**, *supporting wall*, = ἀνάλημμα II, *IG*4.823.36 (Troezen, iv B.C.), 11(2).146 *A* 72 (Delos, iv/iii B.C.), 158 *A* 72 (iii B.C.), al. **-ησις**, εως, ἡ, = foreg., εἴργεται ὑποδομήσεσι τειχίων ἡ τῆς θαλάττης ἐπιδρομή Dion.Byz.11.

**ὑπ-οδόντιος**, ον, *under the teeth*, ἄλγος *IG*12(2).489.5 (Lesbos).

**ὑπόδοξος**, ον, *slave to opinion*, Phld.*D.*1.16.

**ὑποδορ-ά**, ἡ, *gradual stripping of the skin*, Heliod.ap.Orib.46.15.5, Antyll.ib.45.25.5, Aët.15.8. **-ίς**, ίδος, ἡ, = ὑποδερμίς, Hsch. s.v. κλειτορίς, Suid. s.v. μύρτον; cf. ἐπίδερις.

**ὑπόδοσις**, εως, ἡ, *decrease, remission*, μόχθων A.*Eu.*505 (lyr.).

⊕ **ὑπόδουπος**, ον, *reverberating*, νοῦθος δὲ ποδῶν ὑ. ὀρώρει Hes.*Fr.*48 (as understood by Hdn.Gr.2.947, but Hes.*Th.*70 prob. shows that νουθὸς (Adj., cf. Addenda) and ὕπο δοῦπος shd. be read).

⊕ **ὑποδοχ-εῖον**, τό, *reservoir*, Aristeas 89, 91, *PTeb.*733.8 (ii B.C.); used for storage of (live?) fish, *PHamb.*6.10 (ii A.D.); of wine, *PSI*8.918.2 (i A.D.), *POxy.*729.28 (ii A.D.); τοῦ ὑπάρχοντος λέμβου Ἀντικλεῖ ἐν τῷ βασιλικῷ ὑ. *PPetr.*2 p.64 (iii B.C., perh. = *dock*); coupled with διῶρυξ, *PSI*9.1056.6 (vi A.D.); perh. also, *store-house, barn*, οἰκόπεδα καὶ ὑποδόχιον *BGU*301.11 (ii A.D.), cf. *PTeb.*86.15, al. (ii B.C.), etc.: metaph., *entrepôt*, Ἀπάμεια τῶν ἀπὸ τῆς Ἰταλίας καὶ τῆς Ἑλλάδος ὑ. κοινόν ἐστι Str.12.8.15, cf. 17.1.13; ὑ. τροφῆς, of the stomach, Gal.19.361. II. *socket* of door-hinge, *IG*11(2).287 *A* 116 (Delos, iii B.C.). (In signf. I written **ὑποδόχιον** (less prob. **ὑποδοχῖον**) in *PPetr.*2 pp.24, 64 (iii B.C.), *PTeb.*733.8 (ii B.C.), but **ὑποδοχεῖον** (**ὑποδόχειον**) in *PSI*10.1126.13 (iii A.D.), and codd. Aristeas, Str., Gal. ll. cc.; in signf. II **ὑποδοχεῖον**.) **-εύς**, έως, ὁ, *receiver, host*, Luc.*Fug.*30, Charito 3.2, Phot. s.v. ὑποδέξιος: Astrol., of a planet *entertaining* another, Vett.Val.103.1. ⊕ **-ή**, ἡ, *reception*, χῶραι εἰς ὑποδοχὴν ἕτοιμοι τοῖς.. περιττώμασι Gal.6.173, cf. Sor.1.84; χρῶνται [τοῖς ὕδνοις] πρὸς ὑποδοχὴν ἀρτυμάτων Gal.6.655; βόθρος εἰς ὑ. ῥίψεως πεποιημένος Poll.9.103; τὴν δοθεῖσαν ὑπόθεσιν εὐφυᾶ πρὸς ὑ. γυμναστικῆς a subject fit for *reception* of gymnastic training, Luc.*Hist.Conscr.*35. 2. *entertainment, hospitality*, Ar.*Pax* 530 (v. VI infr.), Pl.*Lg.*919a (pl.); κτήνεα σιτευέσκον.. ἐς ὑποδοχὰς τοῦ στρατοῦ Hdt.7.119; ἐσδέξομαι.. ὑποδοχαῖς δόμων E.*IA* 1229; ὑποδοχὰς ποιεῖσθαι Ath.5.210e; τὰν ὑποδοχὰν ἐποήσαντο τῶν δαμοτᾶν *SIG*1107.12 (Cos, iii/ii B.C.); also ἐς ὑποδοχὴν τοῦ στρατεύματος ἐτάσσοντο for the *reception* of the army (in hostile sense), Th.7.74. 3. *harbouring*, ἀνδραπόδων τῶν ἀφισταμένων Id.1.139, cf. Pl.*Lg.*955b. 4. *means for entertaining*, Plu.*Alc.*12; ὑποδοχὰς τὰς ἐπιβαλλούσας Teles p.40 H.; so perh. in *IG*4²(1).92.6 (Epid., iii/iv A.D.). II. *acceptance, support*, εἰς ὑποδοχὴν ἅπαντα λέγειν καὶ πράττειν τινί by way of *playing up to, supporting*, or *seconding* him, Aeschin.3.62, cf. Plb.31.25.10. III. *an admission*, D.7.13. b. *expectation*, Id.*Ep.*3.34. IV. *resort, quarter*, for troops, Pl.*Lg.*848e; for ships, X.*Vect.*3.1. 2. *receptacle, reservoir*, Arist.*Pol.*1330ᵇ6, *Mete.*349ᵇ7; ἡ τῆς μισγαγκείας ὑ. Pl.*Phlb.* 62d; of the vessels of the body, ὁ μαστὸς ὑ... ἐστι γάλακτος Arist. *PA*692ᵃ12; of the stomach, ὑ. τροφῆς ib.682ᵃ17; of the womb, Id. *GA*722ᵇ14, etc. 3. metaph., πάσης γενέσεως ὑ. Pl.*Ti.*49a, cf. 51a; ἀρθρῖτις καὶ ποδάγρα πολλῶν ἄλλων κακῶν ὑποδοχαί εἰσιν *substitutes, diversions*, Ruf.ap.Orib.45.30.62. V. *stewardship, office of the* ὑποδέκτης, ἀννωνῶν *PSI*1.44.1 (v A.D.); λόγος ὑποδοχῆς (including ἀνάλωμα) ib.8.959.1 (iv A.D.); τὴν ὑ. πᾶσαν τοῦ μακαρίου Ἰούστου αὐτὸς ὑπόδεξε (leg. -ξαι) *POxy.*1838 (vi A.D.), cf. *PLond.*5.1667.3 (vi A.D.), *PFlor.*290.3 (vi A.D.), etc. 2. *taking over, receipt by an agent, acceptance of responsibility for*, πρὸς ἀπόδειξιν ὑποδοχῆς *PSI*1.60.28 (vi A.D.), cf. 72.4 (vi A.D.); παντὶ δημοσίων ἀπαίτησιν καὶ ὑ. ποιησαμένῳ Just.*Nov.*163.2. VI. *continuous succession*, ὑποδοχῆς Διονυσίων Ar.*Pax* 530 (as expld. by Sch.). **-ιον**, v. ὑποδοχεῖον. **-ον**, τό, *receptacle*, f.l. for ὑποδοχή in Gal.*UP*14.14.

**ὑπόδρᾰ**, Ep. Adv., used only in the phrase ὑ. ἰδών looking *from under* the brows, *looking askance, grimly*, Il.1.148, al.; cf. ὑποδράξ. (Prob. from ὑπό, *δρακ, cf. δέρκομαι.)

**ὑποδρᾱμᾰτουργέω**, = ὑποτραγῳδέω, v.l. in Luc.*JTr.*1.

⊕ **ὑποδράξ**, Adv., later form for ὑπόδρα, Call.*Fr.anon.*63, Nic.*Th.* 457, 765.

**ὑποδρασίας**· τὰς ἔχθρας, Hsch.: ὑποδρασίη· ὑποψία, Id.: cf. ὑπαιδράσειαν.

**ὑποδράσσομαι**, Att. **-ττομαι**, Med., *try to get hold of*, Plu.*Caes.* 14 codd.

**ὑποδρέω**, Ep. **ὑποδρώω**, *serve*, c. dat., οἵ σφιν ὑποδρώωσιν Od.15.333; οἱ ὑποδρῶντες τῷ θεῷ (sc. Ἀσκληπιῷ) Ael.*NA*9.33.

**ὑποδρήσσω**, = foreg., A.R.3.274, Musae.143.

**ὑποδρηστήρ**, ῆρος, ὁ, (ὑποδράω) *attendant, assistant*, τινος Od.15.330, Coluth.152.

**ὑπόδρῖμυς**, υ, *somewhat acrid* or *pungent*, Dsc.1.18, al., Sor.1.91, Gal.11.835.

⊕ **ὑποδρομ-έω**, = ὑποτρέχω, c. acc., Sapph.2.10, in pf. ὐπαδεδρόμακεν. **-ή**, ἡ, *running under* or *into the way of* a thing, Antipho 3.2.5; αἱ σελήνης ὑπὸ τὸν ἥλιον ὑ. Cleom.2.3; ὀστέου ῥαγέντος ὑπὸ τὸ ἀντικείμενον ὑ. Sor.*Fract.*5; ὑ. αἵματος *suffusion*, Dsc.*Eup.*1.37, Archig.ap.Orib.46.23.1, Sch.Theoc.5.99. II. *place to run down into, burrow*, Ael.*NA*16.15; *bower*, Id.*VH*3.1. III. *cringing*, ib. 14.48, Poll.4.50. IV. = ὑπόδρομος (B), ὁ, Ael.*NA*14.26. ⊕ **-ος** (A), ον, *running under*, ὄχθησιν ὑ. Orph.*A.*802; πέτρος ἴχνους ὑ. a stone *in the way of* his foot, E.*Ph.*1391. 2. name for a venomous *spider*, = ψύλλα, Ael.*NA*6.26. **-ος** (B), ὁ, = ὑποδρομή IV, *a place* for ships *to run into, cove*, Ph.1.14, al., Ptol.*Geog.*4.6.2 (pr. n., v.l. Ἱππόδρομος).

⊕ **ὑπόδροσος**, ον, *somewhat dewy*, Theoc.25.16.

**ὑπόδυμα**, ατος, τό, *tunic, undergarment*, *IG*5(1).1390.19 (Andania, i B.C.): Medic., = ὑπεζωκὼς χιτών, *the lining membrane of the chest (pleura)*, Cael.Aur.*TP*1.4.

**ὑποδύνω**, v. ὑποδύω.

**ὑπόδῠσις**, εως, ἡ, *getting under* a place, Arist.*IA*713ᵃ20. II. *retiring place, place of shelter*, Agatharch.32, J.*BJ*3.7.22, Muson.*Fr.* 14 p.71 H. III. *imperceptibility*, σφυγμῶν Sor.2.61. IV. = *submersio*, *Gloss.*

**ὑποδύσκολος**, ον, *rather awkward* or *difficult*: σημεῖον ὑ. a *rather troublesome* symptom, Hp.*Coac.*185; ὑποδύσκολόν [ἐστι] Eust.219.23. Adv. -λως *rather irritably*, Id.360.17.

**ὑποδύστροπος**, ον, *somewhat stubborn*, Poll.4.145.

**ὑποδυσφορ-έω**, *to be somewhat restless* or *impatient*, Hp.*Epid.*3.17.γ', Pl.*Ep.*357e. **-ος**, ον, *rather impatient*, Hp.*Prorrh.*1.39, *Coac.*49.

**ὑποδυσχεραίνω**, = ὑποδυσφορέω, Plu.2.711c, Aristid.*Or.*50(26).62, 51(27).65.

**ὑποδῠσώδης**, ες, *somewhat rank-smelling*, Dsc.4.184, 5.112.

**ὑποδῠσωπέομαι**, Pass., *look somewhat askance at*, τι Plu.2.646b.

**ὑποδῠτ-ήριον**, τό, (ὑποδύω) in pl., *coves*, places for ships to run into, Str.14.5.6 (v.l. ὑποδεκτηρίων). **-ης**, ου, ὁ, *garment worn under a coat of mail*, *PEnteux.*32.6 (iii B.C.), D.S.17.44, Plu.*Phil.*11; simply *undergarment*, Lxx *Ex.*28.(27)31, *IG*5(1).1390.20 (Andania, i B.C.), J.*BJ*5.5.7.

**ὑποδύω**, **ὑποδύνω**, *put on under*, κιθῶνας ὑποδύνειν τοῖσι εἵμασι Hdt.1.155. 2. metaph., κίνδυνον ὑποδύνειν *undergo* danger, Id.3.69; ταῦτα ὑποδύνειν Id.7.10.θ'. 3. intr., *slip in under*, ὑποδύνουσι ὑπὸ τοὺς πίλους Id.4.75: c. acc., *slip into, insinuate oneself into*, ὑπέδυνε τῶν Ἰώνων τὴν ἡγεμονίην Id.6.2; τὸ "δὶς παῖδες οἱ γέροντες" ὑποδῦνον αὐτοὺς νύττει Phld.*Lib.*p.64 O.: v. infr. II. 1d. 4. *slip from under*, ἧττον ἂν ὑποδύοι ὁ ἵππος X.*Eq.*8.7 (the only place in which pres. Act. ὑποδύω is found). II. mostly in Med. **ὑποδύομαι**, fut. -δύσομαι Od.20.53, Arr.*Fr.*126 J.: aor. 1 -εδυσάμην, Ep. 3 sg. -δύσετο Od.4.570 (tm.): also aor. 2 Act. -έδυν, pf. -δέδῦκα:—*go* or *get under* or *down into*, c. acc., ὑποδῦσα θαλάσσης κόλπον *having plunged into*.., Od.4.435, cf. 570 (tm.), Il.18.145 (tm.); ὑ. ὑπὸ τὴν ζεύγλην Hdt.1.31; ὑπὸ τὴν φοινικίδα Ar.*Pl.*735; -δεδυκότος τοῦ ἄρθρου εἰς χωρίον Hp.*Art.* 10; ὑ. ὑπὸ τῶν κεραμίδων *creep under*, Ar.*V.*205; φέρει τιν' ὑποδεδυκότα *underneath it*, like Odysseus under the ram of Polyphemus, ib. 182; ὑπὸ παντὶ λίθῳ σκορπίος ὑποδύεται *Scol.*23; εἰς τὴν θάλατταν Luc. *Herm.*71: c. dat., ὑ. τῇ πέλτῃ Id.*DMort.*27.3. b. *put one's* feet *under* a shoe, *put on*, ἀνύσας ὑπόδυθι τὰς Λακωνικάς Ar.*V.*1158; ὑποδύσασθαι.. δυσμενῆ καττύματα ib.1159; ὑποδυσάμενος ib.1168 (but in these places Scal. restored ὑποδοῦ (ὑ. δ' ἀνύσας τι Van Leeuwen), ὑποδήσασθαι, -δησάμενος, cf. ὑποδέω III. 1). c. metaph., *put on* a character (because the actor's face was *put under* a mask), ἡ κολακευτικὴ.., ὑποδῦσα ὑπὸ ἕκαστον τῶν μορίων, προσποιεῖται εἶναι τοῦθ' ὅπερ ὑπέδυ pretends to be the character which *it puts on*, Pl.*Grg.* 464c; οἱ σοφισταὶ ταὐτὸν ὑποδύονται σχῆμα τῷ φιλοσόφῳ Arist.*Metaph.*1004$^b$18; ὑποδύεται ὑπὸ τὸ σχῆμα τὸ τῆς πολιτικῆς ἡ ῥητορική Id.*Rh.*1356$^a$27; τὴν ἡδονὴν ὑποδύεται τὸ βλάπτον Ath.Med.ap.Orib. *inc.*23.25; also ὑ. τὸν Δία, τὴν Ἀθηνᾶν, Luc.*Pisc.*33: c. dat., προγόνων ἀρεταῖς Plu.*Arat.*1, cf. Gal.*Thras.*36; for ὀνόματι ὑ. συμμάχων in D.H.15.7, ὄνομα is prob. cj. d. metaph., *insinuate oneself into favour with*, τὸν δῆμον Plu.*Cat.Mi.*32, cf. 57: abs., *creep*, θαύματα καὶ τότε ὑπεδύετο Pl.*Lg.*967b: v. supr. I. 3. 2. c. gen., *come from under, come forth from*, θάμνων ὑπεδύσετο Od.6.127: metaph., κακῶν ὑποδύσεαι 20.53. 3. *go under so as to bear, bear on one's shoulders*, τὸν μὲν ἔπειθ' ὑποδύντε Il.8.332, 13.421. b. metaph., *undergo* labour or toil, *take* it *on oneself*, c. acc., ὑπέδυσαν τὸν πόλεμον Hdt.4.120, cf. supr. I. 2; πόνον, κίνδυνον, X.*Cyr.*1.5.12, etc.; τὸν Ἀριστοφάνην *tackle*, Luc.*Ind.*27; ὑ. αἰτίαν *make oneself subject to..*, D. 23.12. c. c. inf., *submit, undertake*, ὑποδύεσθαι διδάσκειν X.*Oec.*14. 3. 4. of feelings, *steal into* or *over* (cf. ὑφέρπω), τίς μ' ὑποδύεται πλευρὰς ὀδύνα; A.*Eu.*842 (lyr.): rarely c. dat., πᾶσιν δ' ὑπέδυ γόος sorrow *stole upon* all, Od.10.398; ἀλλά μοι ἄσκοπα κρυπτά τ' ἔπη..ὑπέδυ S.*Ph.*1112 (lyr.); ὑποδύεται..ταῖς ψυχαῖς ὁρμή Luc.*Anach.*37: abs., of diseases, X.*Eq.*4.2. 5. abs., *slip* or *slink away*, D.25.28. 6. *submit to*, τισι Arr.*Parth.Fr.*87 Roos; ὑποδύσεται τοῖς ἐκ Ῥωμαίων.. ἀξιουμένοις Id.*Fr.*126 J.: also c. acc., ὑπέδυσαν τὰ ἐπαγγελλόμενα Id. *Fr.*3 J.; μηκέτι τὸ εἱμαρμένον ἢ παρὸν δυσχερᾶναι ἢ μέλλον ὑποδύεσθαι (sic cod. P) M.Ant.2.2 (vv. ll. ἀπο-, ἀνα-: ὑπιδέσθαι cj. Wilamowitz). 7. abs., ὀφθαλμοὶ ὑποδεδυκότες *sunken, hollow* eyes, Luc. *Tim.*17, *Hippiatr.*34.

**ὑποδώρ-ιος**, ον, *hypo-Dorian*, ἁρμονία Ath.14.625a; τόνος Plu.2. 1142f:—Adv. **-ιστί**, *in the hypo-Dorian mode*, Arist.*Pr.*920$^a$8, 922$^b$ 10.

**ὑποεικᾰθε, ὑποείκω**, v. ὑπεικ-.

**ὑποεικτός**, όν, *readily yielding*, v.l. in Opp.*H.*1.526 (ed. J. G. Schneider, Lips. 1813).

**ὑπο-επιμερής**, ές, = ὑπεπιμερής, λόγοι Ph.2.183 cod. M, cf. Iamb. *in Nic.*p.37 P. **-επιμόριος**, ον, = ὑπεπιμόριος, Iamb. l. c.

**ὑποεργεπιστάτης** [ᾰ], ου, ὁ, *sub-overseer of works*, *LW*1743 o (Abydos).

**ὑποεργός**, όν, contr. ὑπουργός (q. v.), A.R.1.226, Cleanth.1.9.

**ὑποέστης**· χιτών, Hsch.

**ὑποζάκορος** [ᾰ], ὁ or ἡ, *under-priest* or *priestess*, Hdt.6.134,135, *IG*2$^2$.2245.36, al.:—hence **ὑποζᾰκορεύω**, ib.4073, 7.2523 (Thebes).

**ὑποζατηθείς**· ὑποκατασχών, Hsch.

**✱ὑποζεύγνῡμι**, pf. ὑπέζευχα Orus ap.*EM*786.5:—*yoke under, put under the yoke*, I. of the animals yoked, ὑ. ἵππους Od.15.81; βοῦς Hdt.4.69; ἡμιόνους..ζεῦξαν ὑπ' ἀπήνῃ Od.6.73:—Med., οὐρῆας ὑποζεύξασθαι ἀπήνῃ A.R.3.841. b. metaph., *subjugate*, Orus l. c.:—Pass., *submit* to, τῷδ' ὑπεζύγην πόνῳ S.*Aj.*24. 2. of the chariot, ἄρμ' ὑπαζεύξαισα Sapph.1.9; ὑποζεύξασθαι τέθριππον Plu. *Cam.*7. II. *bring under* a class, εἰς τὸ δουλικὸν ὑ. γένος Pl.*Plt.* 309a:—Pass., ὑπεζεῦχθαι ἑνὶ γένει *to be brought under* one and the same class, Arist.*PA*644$^a$18.

**ὑποζευκτικὸς** σύνδεσμος, *subordinative* conjunction, Dosith.p. 418 K.

**ὑπόζευξις**, εως, ἡ, *a subjoining*, figure of speech illustrated by Verg.*Aen.*10.149 sq., Charis.p.280 K., Diom.p.444 K., Donat.ad Ter. *Phorm.*162.

**ὑποζέω**, *ferment a little, begin to ferment*, *Gp.*6.12.2.

**ὑποζηνην** (acc. sg. masc.), dub. sens. in *Sammelb.*7357.15 (iii A. D.).

**ὑποζητέω**, *search for*, dub. in *BGU*1024 iv 21 (iv A. D., Pass.).

**ὑποζοφόεις**, εσσα, εν, *somewhat dark* or *black*, Nic.*Th.*337, in fem., with v.l. **ὑποζοφόωσα**.

**ὑποζῠγ-έω**, *to be a* ὑποζύγιον, Hsch. s. v. ἀστράβη (s. v. l.). **-ή**, ἡ, *enslavement*, *Schwyzer* 701 C 7 (Erythrae, v B. C.).

**ὑποζύγι-ον** [ζῠ], τό, *beast for the yoke, beast of draught* or *burden*, Thgn.126, Hdt.9.39, Pl.*Lg.*873e, etc.: pl., Hdt.1.167, 3.25, 9.24,39, 41, etc.; ὑποζύγια καλούμενα πάντα ὁμοίως, βοῦς, ἡμιόνους, ἵππους X.*Oec.*18.4: as Adj., ὑποζύγιαι ἡμίονοι Ar.Byz.ap.Eust.1625.41; ὑ. ζῷα *PMasp.*2 ii 3 (vi A. D.). II. later specifically *an ass*, Lxx *Za.* 9.9, *Ev.Matt.*21.5, 2*Ep.Pet.*2.16: ἡμίονοι καὶ ὑποζύγια *PCair.Zen.*158 (iii B. C.); βοῦς ἢ ὑ. ἢ πρόβατον *PPetr.*3 p.56 (iii B. C.); οὖρον οἷον ὑποζυγίου Hp.*Aph.*4.70. **-ώδης**, ες, *like a beast of burden*, Ar.*Fr.* 731. 2. *as of an ass*, οὖρον Archig.ap.Aët.13.120 (Wellmann *Pneumatische Schule* p.30).

**ὑπόζῠγ-ος**, ὁ, the *pleura*, Cael.Aur.*TP*2.1,11, 5.10. **-όω**, = ὑποζεύγνυμι: Med., *bring under one's power*, τι Luc.*Am.*28:—Pass., ὑπεζύγωται πρὸς τῷ ὑπὸ τὸ οὖς ὀστέῳ Hp.*Art.*30.

**ὑποζῡμόομαι**, Pass., *ferment slightly*, Dieuch.ap.Orib.4.5.1.

**ὑποζωγρᾰφέω**, *depict*, [τὸν Ὠρίωνα] δι' ἄστρων ἐν τῷ οὐρανῷ Sch. Od.5.121, cf. *PLeid.X.*73.

**ὑπόζωμα**, ατος, τό, (ὑποζώννυμι) *diaphragm, midriff*, Arist.*HA*509$^b$ 17, 514$^a$30, *PA*674$^a$9, al. 2. in insects, *division between thorax and abdomen*, Id.*HA*535$^b$8, *PA*659$^b$16, al. II. in pl., *ropes* or *braces used to strengthen the hull of a trireme* (cf. ὑποζώννυμι II), Pl.*R.*616c (where a beam of light passing through heaven and earth is compared to τὰ ὑ. τῶν τριήρων), *Lg.*945c, *IG*2$^2$.1479.49, 1609.108, 1611. 335,410, 1612.319, 1622.287,640, 1627.410, 1668.74, 1673.12,13, etc.; ὑ. ἐλάμβανε δώδεκα (sc. ἡ τεσσαρακοντήρης ναῦς)· ἑξακοσίων δ' ἦν ἕκαστον πηχῶν Callix.1; ὁ στόμαχος καθάπερ νεὼς τοῦ σώματος ὑ. ὑπάρχει Herod.Med. in *Rh.Mus.*58.99; cf. ζώμευμα.

**ὑποζώνη**, ἡ, *girdle*, *BGU*717.10 (ii A. D.), *Gloss.*; also **ὑπόζωνον**, τό, *BGU*1670.2 (i/ii A. D.), *PHamb.*10.25 (ii A. D.): Dim. **ὑποζώνιον**, τό, *Gloss.*

**ὑποζώνιος**, ον, *under the girdle*, ξίφος Lyd.*Mag.*2.9.

**ὑποζώννῡμι** (inf. ὑποζωνύναι in *IG*1$^2$.73.9) and **-ύω** Plb.27.3.3, *undergird*, τοὺς ἵππους ῥυτῆρσι Plu.*Eum.*11; ὑ. τινὰ τοῖς ποσσίν *AP*12.222 (Strat.); ὁ ὑπεζωκὼς τὰς πλευράς (sc. ὑμήν), or abs. ὁ ὑπεζωκώς, *the pleura*, Alex.Aphr.*Pr.*1.53, Gal.2.591 (ὑμήν is expressed in Diocl.*Fr.* 64, Antyll.ap.Orib.44.23.45, Orac.Chald.ap.Dam.*Pr.*265); ὑπεζωκότες foetal *membranes*, Sor.1.58; *lining* of the intestines, Orib.*Fr.* 58:—Pass., esp. in pf. part., ζειρὰς ὑπεζωμένοι (v.l. -ζωσμ-) *girt* with ζειραί (q. v.), Hdt.7.69; ὑπεζωσμένοι ἱμάντας Plu.*Rom.*26: abs., ὑπεζῶμέναι (οἱ) *girt up*, Hdt.2.85 (with vv. ll.):—esp., II. *brace* a ship, so as to make her seaworthy (cf. ὑπόζωμα II), *IG* l. c., Plb. l. c., *Act. Ap.*27.17; ὑπέζωται *IG*2$^2$.1621.68. III. ὑπεζῶσθαι· τὸ εἰς ἄνδρας ἐλθεῖν, Φιλητᾶς, Hsch. (prob. = *come to man's estate*).

**ὑπόζωσμα**, ατος, τό, later form for ὑπόζωμα II, Plu.*Rom.*7.

**ὑποθάλπω**, *heat inwardly*, ὑπό μ' αὖ..μανίαι θάλπουσ' A.*Pr.*878 (anap.); ὑ. τινὰ τέχνῃ Philostr.*VA*1.34; *warm up*, in literal sense, Ruf. *Sat.Gon.*22. 2. *light* or *kindle secretly*, ἐλπίδα τινός Ael.*Fr.* 306:—Pass., *glow under*, τέφρη (sc. ἁρπάζουσα) πῦρ ὑποθαλπόμενον *AP*12.92 (Mel.).

**ὑποθαρρέω**, *pluck up courage*, Ael.*NA*16.11.

**ὑποθεάτρους** αὐλοὺς τοὺς ἐπὶ τοῖς νόμοις τοῖς αὐλητικοῖς ἐκάλεσαν, Poll.4.82; perh. cf. ὑπόθετρον.

**ὑποθειάζω**, *to be divinely inspired*, τὴν φιλοσοφίαν (acc. of respect) Philostr.*VA*1.3, cf. 6.11.

**✱ὑπόθεμα**, ατος, τό, = ὑπόθημα, *base*, Ph.*Bel.*53.24, 57.34, Hero *Bel.* 97.8, Apollod.*Poliorc.*143.10, Plu.2.1011d. II. ἐπὶ ὑποθέματι ἀγρῷ *on the security* of land, *SIG*672.25 (Delph., ii B. C.), *CIG*2048 (Philippopolis); ἐπὶ ὑποθέμασιν ἀξιοχρέοις *Inscr.Cos* 383.9, cf. *SIG*976.48 (Samos, ii B. C.); ὑποθέματα (corrected to ὑποθήκας) λαβεῖν τῶν τε οἰκιῶν καὶ κτημάτων *PCair.Zen.*640.11 (iii B. C.); ἔχω τῶν μωστίων ὑπόθεμα δραχμὰς τ' *BGU*1523.7 (iii B. C.).

**ὑποθεμᾰτιαῖος**, ον, *belonging to a base*, λίθοι *Inscr.Délos* 372 *A* 166 (200 B. C.).

**ὑποθέναρ**, τό, *the part of the palm next the fingers*, Ruf.*Onom.* 87, Poll.2.143. 2. = στῆθος III. 2, *base of the thumb*, Orib.25.1. 29. 3. *the part opposite the* στῆθος, *inner ridge of palm*, Gal.14. 704.

**ὑποθεραπεύω**, *to be disposed to worship*, τὸ θεῖον Philostr.*VA*4.40; *bribe*, ὑ. τινὰ χρυσοῖς Memn.24.

**ὑποθερμ-αίνω**, *heat a little*, Gal.11.417:—Pass., *grow somewhat hot*, ὑπεθερμάνθη ξίφος αἵματι Il.16.333, 20.476, cf. Hp.*Ulc.*26: metaph., Luc.*DMeretr.*8.3. **-ος**, ον, *somewhat hot*, Gal.6.240, Poll. 5.108: of persons, *somewhat hot* or *passionate*, ὑποθερμότερος τῷ ἔργῳ Hdt.6.38, cf. Luc.*Cal.*5; ὑ. βλέμμα, of a horse, Poll.1.192; οἴνου ὑ. δύναμις Plu.2.1146f.

**ὑπόθεσις**, εως, ἡ, (ὑποτίθημι, ὑποτίθεμαι) *proposal, proposed action*, τὴν ἐν φίλοις δικαιοτάτην ὑ. ἔχω ὑποτιθέναι X.*Cyr.*5.5.13; ἵνα σὺ τὰ σαυτοῦ κατὰ τὴν ὑ. ὅπως ἂν βούλῃ περαίνῃς Pl.*Grg.*454c; *intention, policy*, πολλὰ πρᾶξαι πρὸς τὴν ὑ. τῆς πατρίδος ὡς συχνῆς ἀδικίας δεομένην Thphr.*Fr.*136; διὰ τὴν ὑ. τῆς πολιτείας..ἠναγκάζετο χρῆσθαι τοῖς ὑπουργοῦσι Plu.*Caes.*51; πρὸς ὑ. τινα ἀγαθῶν ἀνδρῶν men good for a particular *policy*, Arist.*Pol.*1293$^b$4; ὑ. τῆς δημοκρατικῆς πολιτείας ἐλευθερία ib.1317$^a$40; ἡμῖν ἡ τῶν νόμων ὑ. ἐνταῦθα ἔβλεπεν, ὅπως.. Pl.*Lg.*743c; περὶ τῶν αὐτῶν οὐχ ὁμοίως ἅπασι βουλευτέον, ἀλλ' ὡς ἂν ἐξ ἀρχῆς ἕκαστοι τοῦ βίου ποιήσωνται τὴν ὑ. Isoc.6.90; τοῖς φαύλοις ἐνδέχεται τὰ τυχόντα πράττειν· εὐθὺς γὰρ τοῦ βίου τοιαύτην πεποίηνται τὴν ὑ. Id.1.48; ἀνάγκη τοῖς περὶ ὅλων τῶν πραγμάτων καλὰς τὰς ὑ. πεποιημένοις καὶ τὰ μέρη τὸν αὐτὸν τρόπον ἔχειν ἐκείνοις Id.7.28; πρὸς ταύτην τὴν ὑ. ἀποβλέποντες ἄμεινον βουλευσόμεθα καὶ περὶ τῶν ἄλλων Id.8.18; ἐξέστητε τῆς ὑ. ἐφ' ἧς ὑμᾶς οἱ πρόγονοι κατέλιπον D.10.46; οἱ τῆς αὐτῆς ὑ. προεστῶτες those who advocated the same *policy*, Plb.30.32.12; ἅπαντας ἀπονεύσειν ἐπ' ἐκείνην τὴν ὑ. Id.24.9.7; Ἀχαϊκωτέραν εἶναι..ταύτην τὴν ὑ. καὶ νικητικωτέραν ἐν τοῖς πολλοῖς ib.4; τὸ τῆς ἰδίας ὑ. λαμπρὸν Id.21.23.1; τὸ τῶν σαρισῶν μέγεθός ἐστι κατὰ μὲν τὴν ἐξ ἀρχῆς ὑ. ἑκκαίδεκα πηχῶν, κατὰ δὲ τὴν ἁρμογὴν τὴν πρὸς τὴν ἀλήθειαν δεκατεττάρων Id.18.29.2; τηροῦντες τὴν αὐτῶν ὑ. Id.5.5.5; πρὸς ταύτην ἁρμοζόμενοι τὴν ὑ. Id.3.16.1, cf. 3.50.7; κατασκέψασθαι τὴν τῶν ὑπεναντίων ἐπίνοιαν καὶ τὴν ὅλην ὑ. ib.6; Φάβιος..κατὰ τὴν ἐξ ἀρχῆς ὑ. οὐδαμῶς κρίνων ἐκκυβεύειν οὐδὲ παραβάλλεσθαι τοῖς ὅλοις Id.3.94.4. 2. *suggestion, advice*, ἐδώκαμεν ἄν σοι ὑποθέσεις δι' ὧν οἱ ἀντίδικοι ἂν οἴμωζον *PMich.Zen.*57. 7 (iii B. C.); διελέγοντο..κατὰ τὰς ἐντολὰς τὰς Ἀράτου καὶ τὰς ὑ. Plb. 2.48.8, cf. 2.52.6, 4.24.2; κροτηθείσης τῆς ὑ. Id.28.16.5; πολυτέχνους ὑ. ἔργων elaborate *proposals* for works, Plu.*Per.*12. 3. *purpose*, τῆς στρατηγίας ὑπόθεσιν τὴν τυραννίδα πεποιημένος Id.*Tim.*2; λόγῳ μὲν ἀποδώσων.., ἑτέραν δὲ τῆς ἀποδημίας ἔχων ὑ. λανθάνουσαν τοὺς πολλοὺς Id.*Mar.*31; ἐξ αὐτῆς τῆς αἰτίας τῆς τε ὑ. τοῦ πολέμου ἀξιολογώτατος ἀγὼν συνηνέχθη D.C.41.56; ὑ. τοῦ πολέμου καὶ πρόφασιν διδόντων ἐλευθεροῦν τοὺς Ἕλληνας Plu.*Flam.*15; τὸ χωρὶς ὑποθέσεως πολεμεῖν..τί ἄλλο ἢ μανία; D.Chr.38.17; [οἱ ἐλέφαντες] ἴσασι τῆς ὁδοῦ τῆς ἐπ' αὐτοὺς τὴν ὑ...εἶναι..τοὺς ὀδόντας Ael.*NA*6.56. 4. *occasion, excuse, pretext*, οὕτω γὰρ ἂν αὐτοῖς ἡ ἀπολογία προαναιροῖτο καὶ ἡ πρώτη ὑ. τῆς ἐθελοδουλείας Luc.*Merc.Cond.*5; τοιαύτης αὐτοῖς τῆς ὑ. οὔσης ib.10; ἀεὶ χρὴ ἐπί τινι λυπεῖσθαι καὶ μὴ ἄνευ ὑ. Artem.

2.60; ὑ. ἀργυρισμοῦ καὶ φόνων εἰληφέναι ἐδόκει D.C.63.26; μή με νομίσῃς ἀπὸ τῆς παρούσης ὑ. ἀπαρτᾶν τὸν λόγον Id.52.18. **5.** actor's *role*, τοὺς ὑποκριτὰς..οὓς ὁρῶμεν οὔτε κλαίοντας ἐν τοῖς θεάτροις, ὡς αὐτοὶ θέλουσιν, ἀλλ' ὡς ὁ ἀγὼν ἀπαιτεῖ πρὸς τὴν ὑ. Plu.*Dem.*22; ἰδεῖν τί μου ποιεῖ ὁ ἀθλητής, πῶς μελετᾷ τὴν ὑ. Arr.*Epict.*1.29.38, cf. 41; τὴν τοῦ πατρὸς καὶ τῆς μητρὸς ὑ. λαβεῖν Iamb.*VP*8.39. **6.** *function, occupation, station in life*, [Διονύσιος] ἐκ δημοτικῆς καὶ ταπεινῆς ὑ. ὁρμηθείς Plb.15.35.2; [Ἀγαθοκλῆς] ὁρμηθεὶς ἀπὸ τοιαύτης ὑ. Id.12.15.7; τὸ μὴ εἶναι ἄλλην βίου ὑ. εἰς τὸ φιλοσοφεῖν οὕτως ἐπιτήδειον ὡς ταύτην ἐν ᾗ νῦν ὢν τυγχάνεις M.Ant.11.7, cf. 8.1, Paul. Aeg.3.17. **7.** *practical problem*, κοινὴ ἡ ὑ. καὶ τῷ καθ' ἡμᾶς βίῳ πάνυ πολλή, βαλανείου κατασκευή Luc.*Hipp.*4; ἡ μὲν οὖν ὑ τοιαύτη Hero *Aut.*21.2. **II.** *subject proposed* (*to oneself or another*) *for discussion*, κελεῦσαι τὴν πρώτην ὑ. τοῦ πρώτου λόγου ἀναγνῶναι Pl. *Prm.*127d; ἐπὶ τὴν ὑ. ἐπανάγειν τὸν λόγον X.*Mem.*4.6.13; ἐπὶ τὴν ὑ. πάλιν ἐπανελθεῖν Isoc.4.63, cf. Gal.6.124; τὴν ὑ. περὶ ἧς βουλεύεσθε οὐχὶ τὴν οὖσαν παριστάντες D.3.1; τοὺς δικαστὰς ἀπαγαγὼν ἀπὸ τῆς ὑ. Id. 19.242; ἐπὶ τῆς ὑ. μεῖναι Aeschin.3.76; ἔξω τῆς ὑ. λέγειν Isoc.7.63, cf. 12.161; μὴ πόρρω λίαν τῆς ὑ. ἀποπλανηθῶ Id.7.77, cf. 12.88, Aeschin. 3.176,190; ὅτ' ἔγραφον περὶ τὴν αὐτὴν ὑ. Isoc.5.83; περὶ [τῆς πόλεως] τὴν ὑ. ποιησάμενος Id.12.35; τοῦ πράγματος ἐν κεφαλαίῳ..δήλωσις, ἵνα γινώσκωσι περὶ ὧν ὁ λόγος παρακολουθῶσί τε τῇ ὑ. Arist.*Rh.Al.* 1436$^{a}$36, cf. Pl.*Def.*415b; ἡ ὑ. ἐλάττων Arist.*Rh.*1404$^{b}$15; πρὸς ὑπόθεσιν λέγειν, opp. πρὸς ἀμφισβητοῦντα, ib.1391$^{b}$13; πολλὰ πρὸς τὴν ὑ. οἰκείως διαλεχθείς D.S.13.53: *haec erat* ὑ., *de gravitate ordinis*, etc., Cic.*Att.*1.14.4. **2.** *case at law, lawsuit*, γράφει ὁ Μαιίστας εἰς τὴν ὑ. ταύτην *IG*11(4).1299.29 (Delos, iii B.C.), cf. *OGI*665.18, 669.41 (both Egypt, i A.D.), *POxy.*237 vii 34, viii 22 (ii A.D.), 486.26 (ii A.D.); τὰ περὶ ταύτης τῆς ὑ. πεπραγμένα *PLips.*34.18 (iv A.D.). **3.** *subject* of a poem or treatise, Zeno *Stoic.*1.23, Plb.1.2.1, D.H.*Pomp.*3, Longin. 38.2, Plu.*Pomp.*42, Luc.*Charid.*14, *Pseudol.*5, al.; of a picture, Id. *Zeux.*5,7; of an impromptu declamation, ἐπειδὰν οἱ παρόντες ὑποβάλωσί τινας ὑ. καὶ ἀφορμὰς λόγου Id.*Rh.Pr.*18; *plot, story*, μῦθοι καὶ ὑποθέσεις Phld.*Po.*2.62, cf. 5.5, al., Arg.Men.*Oxy.*1235.113 (ii A.D.), Dicaearch.ap.S.E.*M.*3.3, Artem.4.59, Sch.S.*Aj.Prooem.*, Arg.Ar. *Ach.* tit., etc. **4.** *speech*, αἱ δικανικαὶ καὶ δημηγορικαὶ ὑ. Theon *Prog.*1; = ἐπίδειξις I.3, ἀρξαμένων (v.l. -ῳ) τῆς ὑ. Lxx 4*Ma.*1.12; ἀνδρὸς ἀρετὰς ὅλην πληρούσας ὑ. providing matter for a whole *speech*, Chor.p.34 B. **b.** *speech* or *subject of a speech in which the person, occasion, etc. are particularized*, opp. θέσις v.2, Aphth.*Prog.* 13, cf. Quint.*Inst.*3.5.7. **5.** a kind of *play* or *pantomime*, μῖμοί τινές εἰσιν ὧν τοὺς μὲν ὑποθέσεις τοὺς δὲ παίγνια καλοῦσιν Plu.2.712e; μιμολωγοι η υποθησις εικυρα (i.e. μιμολόγοι· ἡ ὑπόθεσις Ἑκυρά), i.e. 'theatrical performance: *play*, the Hecyra', *Ath.Mitt.*26.4 (inscr. on lamp, iii B.C.); κλάειν ἤρξαντο πάντες καὶ μετέβαλε τὸ συμπόσιον εἰς σκυθρωπὴν ὑ. into a *tragedy*, Charito 4.3; so perh. in Luc.*Nigr.*8; of Aesop's *fables*, χρῆται [τῇ ἀλώπεκι] ὁ Αἴσωπος διακόνῳ τῶν πλείστων ὑ. Philostr.*Im.*1.3. **III.** *supposition*, ἢ βούλεσθε..ἀπ' ἐμαυτοῦ ἄρξωμαι καὶ τῆς ἐμαυτοῦ ὑ., περὶ τοῦ ἑνὸς αὐτοῦ ὑποθέμενος, εἴτε ἕν ἐστιν εἴτε μὴ ἕν, τί χρὴ συμβαίνειν; Pl.*Prm.*137b; αὕτη ἡ ὑ., εἰ ἓν μὴ ἔστιν ib.160b; χρὴ..μὴ μόνον εἰ ἔστιν ἕκαστον ὑποτιθέμενον σκοπεῖν τὰ συμβαίνοντα ἐκ τῆς ὑ., ἀλλὰ καὶ εἰ μὴ ἔστι τὸ αὐτὸ τοῦτο ὑποτίθεσθαι ib.135e, cf. 136a; [σκοπεῖν] τί ἐφ' ἑκατέρας τῆς ὑ. συμβήσεται ib. 136b; εἰ ὀρθὴ ἡ ὑ. ἦν, τὸ ψυχὴν ἁρμονίαν εἶναι Id.*Phd.*94b, cf. 92d, *Sph.*244c; πρὸς μὲν τὴν ὑ. ὀρθῶς λέγουσιν, ὅλως δ' οὐκ ὀρθῶς Arist. *Metaph.*1082$^{b}$32; ἐξ ὑποθέσεως σκοπεῖσθαι examine by starting from an *assumption*, of reasoning by analysis in geometry, Pl.*Men.* 86e; τῶν τὴν τέχνην ζητεύντων ἐξ ὑποθέσιος λόγων arguments seeking to derive the (medical) art from an *assumption*, Hp.*VM*13; ὑ. αὐτοὶ αὑτοῖς ὑποθέμενοι τῷ λόγῳ ib.1; ἄγοντες ἐπὶ ὑπόθεσιν τὴν τέχνην ib. 15; χρῆσιν ἀρετῆς τελείαν, καὶ ταύτην οὐκ ἐξ ὑ. ἀλλ' ἁπλῶς· λέγω δ' ἐξ ὑ. τἀναγκαῖα, οἷον..τιμωρίαι καὶ κολάσεις..τὸ καλῶς ἀναγκαίως ἔχουσι Arist.*Pol.*1332$^{a}$10; ἡ πολιτεία ἡ ἐξ ὑ. (= ἡ δοθεῖσα) the constitution based on a *presupposition*, ib.1288$^{b}$28; of currency, ἓν δή τι δεῖ εἶναι, τοῦτο δ' ἐξ ὑ.· διὸ νόμισμα καλεῖται according to a *presupposed convention*, Id.*EN*1133$^{b}$21 (cf. $^{a}$29–31, *APr.*41$^{a}$40); of reductio ad impossibile, ἢ δεικτικῶς ἢ ἐξ ὑ. τοῦ δ' ἐξ ὑ. μέρος τὸ διὰ τοῦ ἀδυνάτου Id.*APr.*40$^{b}$25-6, cf. 41$^{a}$25; δυνατοῦ δεξάμενον ὑπόθεσιν ἐπ' ἀδύνατον ἀπαχθῆναι Arr.*Epict.*1.7.25, cf. Procl.*in Euc.*pp.76,252 F.; καθ' ὑπόθεσιν by way of *supposition*, '*let us suppose*', Phld.*Rh.* 1.95 S., *Sign.*12, Cleom.1.7. **IV.** = τὸ ὑποκείμενον (cf. ὑπόκειμαι II. 8), the *presupposition* of an action, *that which has been settled* before it begins, περὶ τοῦ τέλους οὐθεὶς βουλεύεται, ἀλλὰ τοῦτ' ἐστὶν ἀρχὴ καὶ ὑ. Arist.*EE*1227$^{a}$8, cf. $^{b}$30; τῶν πράξεων τὰς ἀρχὰς καὶ τὰς ὑ. ἀληθεῖς καὶ δικαίας εἶναι προσήκει D.2.10; of a thing, *that without which it cannot exist* or *be what it is*, its *essence*, αὕτη (sc. τὸ στέλεχος) οἷον ὑ. καὶ φύσις δένδρων Thphr.*HP*4.13.4 (cf. οὐσία καὶ φύσις τοῦ δένδρου ibid.); ἐπὶ τοῖς χυμοῖς μόνοις σηπομένοις ἔχοντος τὴν ὑ. ὅλου τοῦ νοσήματος, ὅπερ ἐστὶ πυρετώδους ὄντος Gal.18(2).299. **2.** in the syllogism, the *preliminary statements of fact* (whether proved or not) from which inference starts, i.e. the premisses (προτάσεις), τῶν ἀποδείξεων αἱ ὑ., equivalent to ἀρχαί, Arist.*Metaph.*1013$^{a}$16; αἱ ἀρχαὶ καὶ αἱ λεγόμεναι ὑ. Id.*APo.*81$^{b}$15; ὅσα δέδεικται δι' ἐκείνων ὑποθέσεις ποιησάμενοι taking as *premisses* (here) what has been proved in those other works, Gal.6.7, cf. 25,224; ἴστω..τῆς ὑγιεινῆς πραγματείας ἀνατρέπων τὴν ὑ. ib.17; ὑπόθεσιν, αἴτησιν οὖσαν πράγματος εἰς κατασκευήν τινος S.E.*M.*3.4; λαμβάνειν ἀναποδείκτους ὑ. Plu.2.720f, cf. 721d; ἀναγκαῖον ἢ τὰς ὑ. εἶναι τὰς πρώτας ψευδεῖς, ἢ τὰς ὑπὲρ τῶν συμβαινόντων ἀποφάσεις Plb.1.15.9, cf. 11. **b.** *assumption of existence* of any one of the fundamental objects of a particular science, ὁ ὁρισμὸς θέσις μέν ἐστι..ὑ. δ' οὐκ ἔστι· τὸ γὰρ τί ἐστι μονὰς καὶ τὸ εἶναι μονάδα οὐ ταὐτόν Arist.*APo.*72$^{a}$23; ἐν ταῖς πράξεσι τὸ οὗ ἕνεκα ἀρχή, ὥσπερ ἐν τοῖς μαθηματικοῖς αἱ ὑ. Id.*EN*1151$^{a}$ 17. **3.** *starting-point*, ἐκ ταύτης τῆς ὑ. λαβεῖν τὸν λόγον τὴν εἰς ἑκάτερον μέρος ὁρμήν Iamb.*VP*27.130; *beginning*, τὰς μὲν ἐλπίδας οὐ τελειοῖ (sc. ὁ ὄνειρος), τὰς δὲ ὑ. τῶν πραγμάτων ταῖς περιοχαῖς ὁμοίας ποιεῖ (referring to a birth of twins which died), Artem.4.47. **4.** *raw material*, τὴν δοθεῖσαν ὑ. εὐφυᾶ πρὸς ὑποδοχὴν γυμναστικῆς.. ἀμείνω ἀποφαίνειν Luc.*Hist.Conscr.*35; οἵαν ὕλην καὶ ὑ. φεύγεις· .. μένε οὖν μέχρι ἐξοικειώσῃς σαυτῷ καὶ ταῦτα M.Ant.10.31. **V.** *mortgage*, Thphr.*Fr.*97.1 (pl.). **VI.** *placing under*, πτύγματος Sor.1.70$^{a}$; προσκεφαλαίου Id.2.86. **2.** *thing placed under, base*, τὰς ὑ. (signf. III) ποιούμενος οὐκ ἀρχὰς ἀλλὰ τῷ ὄντι ὑ., οἷον ἐπιβάσεις τε καὶ ὁρμάς Pl.*R.*511b, cf. Arr.*Epict.*1.7.22; in D.2.10 (v. supr. IV. 1) the ἀρχαί and ὑποθέσεις (i.e. basic principles) of actions are compared to the foundations (τὰ κάτωθεν) of a house or a ship; Τριπτόλεμος..τὰς πρώτας ὑ. βαλόμενος τῇ πόλει Lib.*Or.*11.52.

**ὑποθετ-έον**, *one must suppose, assume*, Pl.*Ti.*61d, Arist.*Pol.*1278$^{b}$ 15, al.; *one must place underneath*, Sor.1.56; ἄνθρακας Dsc.1.71; *one must apply a suppository*, c. dat., Aët.9.41. **-ήριον, τό**, = *suppostorium*, *Gloss.* **-ης, ου, ὁ**, *one who suggests, prompter, adviser*, Anon.ap.Suid. ⊛ **-ικός, ή, όν**, *hypothetical*, λόγοι Arr. *Epict.*1.7.22, Asp.*in EN*18.27, etc.; σχῆμα Eust.186.27; distd. from ἐκθετικός, *Stoic.*2.62. Adv. -κῶς Gal.4.609, S.E.*M.*3.12, etc. **II.** *belonging to the subject*, ὑ. ἐξήγησις Sch.Plb.14 init. **III.** *suggestive, hortatory*, λόγοι Muson.*Fr.*17 p.91 H. Adv. *-κῶς by way of suggestion*, Demetr.*Eloc.*296. **-ος, ον**, *placed under*: Medic., ὑπόθετον, τό, *suppository, pessary*, Antiph.208, Alex.Trall.9.3.

**ὑπόθετρον, τό**, a kind of musical performance, *BGU*1125.4,28 (i B.C.); perh. cf. ὑποθεάτρους.

**ὑπόθευτον**· Ῥόδιοι ἐπὶ θυσίας, Hsch.

**ὑποθέω**, fut. -θεύσομαι, *make a secret attack*, ποτὶ ἐχθρόν..λύκοιο δίκαν ὑποθεύσομαι Pi.*P.*2.84. **2.** *cut in before*, in running a race, *supplant*, Ar.*Eq.*1161; of a solar eclipse, ἐκλείπει..τῆς σελήνης ὑποθεούσης αὐτόν Cleom.2.3; ἡ σελήνη ὑποθεύσεται τὸν ἥλιον Them. *Or.*26.317b. **II.** of dogs, *run in too hastily*, X.*Cyn.*3.8.

**ὑποθεωρ-έω**, *hold up and look at*, τορεύματα Plu.2.42c. **-ησις, εως, ἡ**, prob. f.l. for ἐπιθ-, τῶν ἀστέρων Ptol.*Tetr.*193.

**ὑποθήγω**, *whet*, χαυλιόδοντας Ael.*NA*5.45; *sharpen, make acute*, ὄμμα τινί ib.9.16; *stimulate*, τινὰ μύωπι ib.5.39: metaph., ὑ. τὸν σὺν εἰς ἀνάστασιν *provoke* him to rise, ib.8.2:—Pass., ὑποθήγεσθαι ἐπὶ τὸν φόνον Id.*Fr.*81.

**ὑποθηκ-άριος, α, ον**, *of* or *for a mortgage*, Just.*Nov.*4.2, Procop. *Arc.*28: in Lat. form *hypothecarius*, *Cod.Just.*4.32.26, al. ⊛ **-η, ἡ**, (ὑποτίθημι) *suggestion, counsel, warning*, Hdt.1.156,206, al.; ποιέειν τὰς Κροίσου ὑποθήκας ib.211; ὑποθήκαις διακονεῖν Antipho 1.17; κατὰ τὴν Βίαντος ὑ. Arist.*Rh.*1389$^{b}$23, cf. 1368$^{a}$2 (pl.); applied to didactic poems, such as Hesiod's, Isoc.2.3,43, Phld.*Po.*5.27, Hierocl. *in CA Praef.*p.417 M.; *instructions*, Cic.*Att.*2.17.3; ὑ. ἄνευ νόμων Ruf. ap.Orib.*inc.*20.19; οὐ κατ' ἰατρικάς ἐστιν ὑ. is not a matter for medical *advice*, Sor.1.126; ὑποθήκας διδόναι Gal.6.307; ποιήσασθαι ib.405. **II.** *pledge, deposit, mortgage*, D.34.50, Arist.*Oec.*1348$^{b}$21, *Supp.Epigr.*1.366.39 (Samos, iii B.C.), *PCair.Zen.*504.4 (iii B.C.), *PEnteux.*15.4 (iii B.C.), etc.; συγγραφὴ -θήκης *PRein.*18.11 (ii B.C.); ἐπὶ ὑποθήκαις upon *securities given*, *SIG*742.39, cf. 51 (Ephesus, i B.C.), al.; ὑ. ἔγγαιοι *mortgages* on land, *Test.Epict.*5.6; also ἐν ὑποθήκῃ on *deposit*, *PGrenf.*2.17.3 (ii B.C.). ⊛ **-ῐμαῖος, α, ον**, *relating to a mortgage*, συγγραφή, ἀσφάλεια, *PMasp.*23.11 (vi A.D.), 96.15 (vi A.D.); = *fiduciarius*, *Gloss.*: neut. -αῖον, τό, *pledge*, *PMasp.*96.38 (vi A.D.).

**ὑπόθηλυς, εια, υ**, *effeminate*, διάλεκτος ὑποθηλυτέρα Ar.*Fr.*685 (anap.).

**ὑπόθημα, ατος, τό**, *stand, base*, *IG*11(2).144 *A* 60,67 (Delos, iv B.C.), Paus.10.16.2, Ath.5.210a, etc., cf. Poll.10.114; ὑ. κεφαλῆς, of a pillow, Chaerem.ap.Porph.*Abst.*4.7: cf. ὑπόθεμα I: = Att. θρανίον, acc. to Paus.5.11.7. **II.** = ὑποθήκη II, *AJP*56.374 (pl., Colophon, iv B.C.), Men.*Epit.*288, *SIG*976.13 (Samos, ii B.C.); cf. ὑπόθεμα II.

**ὑποθημοσύνη, ἡ**, *advice, counsel, warning*, in pl., ὑποθημοσύνῃσιν Ἀθήνης Il.15.412, Od.16.233: also in later Ep., A.R.2.1146, cf. Afric. *Cest.*38, etc.: sg., Ἑρμοῦ ὑποθημοσύνῃ X.*Mem.*1.3.7, cf. Luc.*Astr.*1.

**ὑποθήμων, ονος, ὁ, ἡ**, *suggesting advice*, Hsch.

**ὑποθιγγάνω**, *touch lightly*, Hp.*Art.*40 (Pass.).

**ὑπό-θλασμα, ατος, τό**, *fragment, splinter* of bone, v.l. for περίθλασμα in *Hippiatr.*104. **-θλάω**, *crush slightly*, Ael.*NA*1.15.

**ὑποθλίβω** [ῑ], *press under* or *gently*, Nic.*Th.*296 codd. (ἐπι-Schneider), *Al.*30, Dsc.1.43, Luc.*VH*2.14, Cass.*Pr.*28.

**ὑποθοιναρμόστρια, ἡ**, *assistant-*θοιναρμόστρια, *IG*5(1).1390.30 (Andania, i B.C.).

**ὑποθολόω**, *make rather muddy*, τὸ ὕδωρ Ael.*NA*4.31.

**ὑποθορῠβέω**, *begin to make a clamour*, ὑ. ἐς τὸν Κλέωνα, ὅτι οὐ καὶ νῦν πλεῖ Th.4.28.

**ὑποθράττω**, = ὑποταράσσω, Plu.*Pomp.*68, *Fab.*2.

**ὑποθραύω**, *break* (in spirit), Lxx 2*Ma.*9.11 (Pass.).

**ὑποθρεπτέος, α, ον**, *needing to be nourished up*, τὴν ἰσχὺν -τέοι Philostr.*Gym.*52.

**ὑποθρόνιον, τό**, *footstool*, poet. for ὑποπόδιον, *EM*718.40.

**ὑποθρύπτομαι**, Pass., *to be nerveless* or *emasculated*, -ομένη δημαγωγία Plu.*Per.*15:—Act., ὑ. ἑαυτόν *languish*, Philostr.*VA*1.12. **II.** ὑπεθρύφθην μετώπῳ *I wantoned* with her face—by stealing kisses, *AP* 5.293.15 (Agath., dub.l.).

**ὑποθῡμί-ᾱμα,** Ion. **-ημα,** *ατος, τό, fumigation,* Hp.*Mul.*2.206, Dsc.1.13, Sor.1.72. **-άς,** *άδος, ἡ,* v. ὑποθυμίς I. 1. **-ᾱσις,** *εως,* Ion. **-ησις,** *ἡ, fumigation,* Hp.*Nat.Mul.*103 (pl.), Dsc.1.67, Sor.2.33, *Hippiatr.*22. **-ᾱτέον,** *one must fumigate, Gp.*16.7.1, Antyll.ap.Orib.10.19.3. **-άω,** *fumigate,* τι θείῳ Luc.*DMeretr.*4.5 :—Med., aor. 1, Hp.*Mul.*2.128 :—Pass., *to be burnt for fumigation,* Dsc.1.6,76, 3.112. II. abs. in Act., *make a thick smoke,* Aen.Tact.32.1.

**ὑποθῡμίς,** Aeol. **ὑπά-,** *ίδος, ἡ, garland worn on the neck, that one may enjoy the sweetness of the flowers,* Anacr.39, Sapph.*Supp.*23.15, Alc.36 (ὑποθυμιάδας codd.). 2. = ὑπογλωττίς II, Philet.ap.Ath.15.678d. II. **ὑποθῡμίς,** an unknown bird, Ar.*Av.*302 (troch.).

**ὑπόθυψις,** *εως, ἡ,* (ὑποτύφω) *incentive, provocation,* Plb.6.11$^{a}$.9.

**ὑποθωπεύω,** *win by flattery,* Ar.*Ach.*639 (anap.), *V.*610 (anap.), D.H.7.34, Philostr.*VS*1.21.4: abs., οὐδὲν ὑποθωπεύσας without *using any flattery,* Hdt.1.30; εἴργασταί μοι μηδὲν -εύσας ὁ λόγος Chor.3.84 p.69 F.-R.

**ὑποθωρήσσομαι,** Med., *arm oneself in secret,* λόχῳ ὑπεθωρήσσοντο Il.18.513.

**ὑποθωΰσσω,** *call to* a person *softly,* Ael.*NA*8.2.

**ὑποϊάστιος,** *ον, hypo-Ionian,* τόνος Aristox.ap.Cleonid.*Harm.*12, Aristid.Quint.1.10; τρόπος Alyp.*Diat.*11.

**ὑποϊάχω** [ᾰ], *sound forth a little* or *in answer,* κράνα ὑ. *AP*9.314 (Anyt., s. v.l.).

**ὑπ-οίγνῡμι,** *open a little* or *secretly,* τὴν θύραν Ar.*Th.*424, cf. *Ec.*15.

**ὑποιδ-αίνω,** = -οιδέω, dub. cj. in Orib.8.6.3. **-ᾰλέος,** *η, ον, somewhat swollen,* Hp.*Morb.*2.52, *Int.*12. **-έω,** intr., *swell up somewhat,* Id.*Coac.*136 (om. Littré), *Superf.*17, Ael.*VH*14.7, Philostr.*VA*3.46, etc. **-ος,** *ον,* = -αλέος, Gal.11.11, al.

**ὑποίζεσθαι·** ὑπονοεῖν, Hsch.

**ὑποικ-έω,** *dwell under,* τῷ βορέᾳ (Sylburg for ὑπείκειν) Arist.*Pr.*945$^{a}$9, cf. Ael.*NA*16.17. 2. ὑποικοῦντες, = γείτονες, Poll.6.113. II. *lie hidden,* ἐν ὀφθαλμοῖς ὑ. δάκρυ *APl.*4.111 (Glauc.). **-ίζομαι,** in aor. 1 Med., = foreg. I, βῶλον ὑπῳκίσατο *AP*7.372 (Bass.). ⊛ **-οδομέω,** *build under,* γεισηποδίσματι *IG* 2$^{2}$.463.114; τοῦ τείχους, f.l. for ἐπ-, Luc.*Hist.Conscr.*3. **-ος,** *ὁ,* = γείτων, οἱ ὑπόβοικοι (= ὑπόϝοικοι) *Inscr.Cret.*1 xvi 1.33 (Lato, iii B.C.). **-ουρέω,** *keep house, stay at home,* Ael.*NA*11.32: metaph., κακὸν ὑ. ἐν τῇ ψυχῇ *lurks, lies hidden,* Luc.*Abd.*6; ἢν μὴ ὑποικουρέωσι φλεγμοναί Aret.*CA*2.3; esp. in part., ἀμορφία ὑποικουροῦσα Luc.*Gall.*24; μῖσος τὸ ὑποικουροῦν J.*AJ*17.5.5, cf. D.S.31.17. II. trans., *engage in* or *plot underhand,* ἃ.. -εῖτε τοῖσιν ἀνδράσιν Ar.*Th.*1168, cf. Plu.*Pomp.*42 :—Pass., ὑποικουρουμένη ὀργή anger *secretly cherished,* Plb.4.49.4, cf. 3.11.3: τὰ -ημένα the *plot, intrigue,* Ph.2.202. 2. c. acc. pers., *work secretly upon,* τὴν στρατιάν Plu.*Luc.*34; χρήμασι πολλοὺς ἄρχοντας Id.*Pomp.*58; νόσος ὑ. αὐτούς *crept in among* them, Id.*Cam.*28. 3. abs., *intrigue,* Id.*Oth.*3. **-ουρία,** *ἡ, inherence,* Simp. *in Ph.*1328.3.

**ὑπ-οιμώζω,** *wail softly, whimper,* Luc.*Merc.Cond.*27.

**ὕπ-οινος,** *ον, under the influence of wine,* Phryn.*PS* p.118 B. 2. *full of wine,* βότρυς Philostr.*Im.*1.31; πέτραι ib.18.

**ὑποϊππαρχέω,** *to be subpraefectus equitum, IGRom.*3.680 (Patara, i A.D.).

**ὑποιστέον,** *one must endure,* Aphth.*Prog.*13.

**ὑποιστός,** *ή, όν,* (ὑποφέρω) *tolerable,* Hsch., Phot., Suid.

**ὑποϊσχάνω,** poet. for ὑπίσχω, ὑπέχω, *hold under,* ὑπὸ μαζῷ χειρὸς ἀγοστόν A.R.3.120.

**ὑποΐσχομαι,** Med., *catch by holding under,* αἷμα A.R.4.473; σεληναίην αἴγλην ἑανῷ ib.169.

**ὑποίσω,** *perfero, Gloss.*; cf. ὑποφέρω.

**ὑποκαγκελίζω,** dub. sens., ἔχοντες φακούς, ὑποκαγκελίζοντας τοὺς ὀφθαλμούς *Cat.Cod.Astr.*7.221.

**ὑποκᾰθαίρω,** *purge downwards,* τὴν κοιλίην Hp.*Aph.*7.68, cf. Thphr.*HP*7.12.3, Plu.2.127c, Gal.6.248.

⊛ **ὑποκάθαρσις** [κᾰ], *εως, ἡ, purging downwards,* Hp.*Ulc.*3.

**ὑποκαθ-έζομαι,** *lie in ambush,* Anon.ap.Suid., Onos.6.7; late aor. ὑποκαθεσθῆναι, *sink, settle down,* Sch.Th.3.89, *Gp.*6.18 (v.l. ἐπικ-). ⊛ **-ημαι,** Ion. **-κάτημαι,** prop. pf. of ὑποκαθέζομαι, *to be seated down in* a place, *station oneself* there, ἐν ταύτῃ τῇ πόλι Hdt.7.27. 2. *sit below,* τινι Philostr.*VA*3.16; *to be placed under,* ὄμμα ὑ. τῇ ὀφρύϊ ib.8. II. *lie in ambush,* Str.15.1.42: metaph., Philostr.*VA*7.14; ὑποκαθήμενον δρᾶν to have an *insidious* look, Id.*Im.*2.18; but also ἡ -καθημένη ἀοριστία the *fundamental* indeterminacy, Carneisc.*Herc.*1027.14. 2. c. acc. pers., *lie in wait for,* τὸν βάρβαρον Hdt.8.40, cf. Philostr.*VS*2.2, *Her.*2.11: metaph., φθόνος ὑ. τινά Id.*VS*2.26.3: abs., *lurk,* Plu.2.556b: c. dat., ὑποκαθημένης αὐτῷ τῆς ὀργῆς Plb.4.29.7. III. *sit idle,* D.H.11.37. **-ίζω,** *place in ambush,* λόχον ἐν ὕλαις Id.9.56 :—Med., *lie in ambush,* ὑ. ὑπὸ τῷ τείχει X.*HG*7.2.5. II. intr. in Act., *lie in ambush,* Plb.12.4.14, etc. 2. *sink down, form a sediment,* Gal.13.285, *Placit.*1.4.2. 3. *sit down under,* ὡς.. ἐκ τῆς σκιᾶς (sc. τῆς σμίλακος) τοὺς ὑποκαθίσαντας.. βλάπτεσθαι Dsc.4.79. ⊛ **-ίημι,** *let down by degrees,* τὰς ὀφρῦς ὑ., i.e. resume one's calmness, Phryn.*PS* p.120 B.; τὸ ἰσχίον Philostr.*Gym.*31; ὑ. πώγωνος βάθη *let* the beard *grow long,* Ephipp.14.7. II. Med., *leave behind at large, leave untouched,* Plb.23.10.8. **-ισμα,** *ατος, τό, ambush,* Hsch. s.v. ἐνέδρα. **-ίστᾰμαι,** Pass., *settle at the bottom,* of sediment, Gal.19.605. 2. *subside,* of symptoms, Aret.*CA*1.1. II. *take the place of* another, Hdn.8.8.2: Act. in *Gloss.* **-ιστής,** *οῦ, ὁ,* = *subsessor,* ib.

**ὑποκαίω,** Att. **-κάω,** *burn by applying fire below,* τινὰς ζῶντας D.S.20.71, cf. 19.108; *burn underneath,* ὀστέα Hdt.4.61; ξύλα ὑ. τῷ τρίποδι *under* the tripod, Anon.ap.Eust.1146.37; *light sacrificial fires,* cf. ὑποκλαίω. 2. *light under,* πῦρ Luc.*Phal.*1.11 :—Pass., Arist.*Mete.*355$^{a}$17. 3. ὑ. λέβητα, [κακκάβην], *light a fire under* it, Gal.13.37, 6.707. 4. *heat* a bath, *PFlor.*127.4 (iii A.D.), *PGiss.*40 ii 19 (iii A.D.). II. metaph. in Pass., ὑ. τινός *to be inflamed by love for..,* Parth.12.1, 23.2; *to be inflamed,* φλύκταιναι -όμεναι Ph.2.101.

**ὑποκᾰκοήθης,** *ες, somewhat malignant,* Hp.*Mul.*1.36, Ph.2.570.

**ὑποκακχέω,** poet. for ὑποκαταχέω (q.v.).

**ὑποκάλυμμα** [κᾰ], *ατος, τό,* v. ὑποκόλαμμα.

**ὑποκαμίσιον,** *τό, under-shirt, Stud.Pal.*20.245.20, *PKlein.Form.*83 (vi A.D.); but expld. as *vestis super camisiam, Gloss.*

**ὑποκαμπή,** *ἡ, bend,* Gal.18(2).564.

**ὑποκάμπτω,** *bend short back,* ὑπὸ γλωχῖνα δ' ἔκαμψαν they *turned in* the strap-end *under* the strap itself, Il.24.274; ὑποκεκαμμένα [τὰ σκέλη] Philum.ap.Aët.16.23. II. intr., *turn back, double* as a hare, X.*Cyn.*5.16. III. metaph., c. acc., *fall short of,* καιρὸν χάριτος A.*Ag.*786 (anap.).

**ὑποκάπηλος** [ᾰ], *ὁ, petty huckster,* Philostr.*VA*8.7.11.

**ὑποκαπν-ίζω,** *burn* for purpose of fumigation, ζειάς Hp.*Mul.*2.117, cf. Gal.14.551. **-ισμα,** *ατος, τό, that with which one fumigates,* Alex.Trall.5.4. **-ισμός,** *ὁ, fumigation,* Dsc.*Eup.*1.210, Antyll.ap.Orib.8.12.1, Sor.2.33, Gal.16.147. **-ιστέον,** *one must fumigate,* Herod.Med. in *Rh.Mus.*58.73,79. **-ιστός,** *ή, όν, to be used for fumigation,* Alex.Trall.5.4.

**ὑποκάπτω,** *snap up,* Arist.*HA*618$^{a}$23.

**ὑποκάρδιος,** *ον, in the heart,* ἕλκος, ὀργά, Theoc.11.15, 20.17.

**ὑποκᾰρόω,** *reduce to a state of stupor,* Dsc.*Eup.*1.26 :—Pass., Hp.*Epid.*1.26.ια', Dsc.4.75.

**ὑποκάρπιος,** *ον, under the wrist,* ἀρτηρία Aristaenet.1.13.

**ὑπόκαρπος,** *ον, bearing fruit,* φοίνικες *CPR*45.26 (iii A.D.).

**ὑποκάρφω,** *dry a little* or *gradually,* Nic.*Al.*80 (Pass.).

**ὑποκᾰρώδης,** *ες, somewhat lethargic,* Hp.*Prorrh.*1.154, *Coac.*254.

**ὑποκατα-βαίνω,** *descend by degrees,* Hdt.2.15, Hp.*Prog.*11, Th.7.60, Clearch.ap.J.*Ap.*1.22, Gal.18(2).145; *come down,* X.*An.*7.4.11, D.C.40.26. 2. *go back gradually,* i.e. *relax* severity of régime, Hp.*Aph.*1.7. 3. *settle down,* Arist.*Pr.*938$^{b}$31, Alex.Aphr.*Pr.*2.20. 4. ὑποκαταβάς, *lower down in the text,* Eust.1351.43, al. **-βάλλω,** *throw down under,* -κάββαλε (Ep. aor.) τέφρῃ τινά Q.S.10.484. **-βᾰσις,** *εως, ἡ, gradual descent,* εἰς εὐτέλειαν Eust.1402.16; glossed by παραχώρησις, Phot., Suid.; ὑ. τῆς διαίτης *reduction,* Gal.17(2).378. **-γελάω,** *laugh in one's sleeve at,* τινων Arr.*Epict.*4.6.21. **-κλάω,** *break gradually,* Apollon.*Lex.* s.v. ὑπερικταίνοντο. **-κλείω,** *enclose underneath,* Cyran.15, al. **-κλίνω** [ῑ], *lay down under* :—Pass., *lie down under,* Plu.2.50d; of a wrestler allowing himself to be beaten, ib.58f. II. Pass. also, *lie* or *sit lower* at table, τινι ib.618e; πάντων J.*AJ*12.4.9 (so, more rarely, in Act., *seat under* another *at table,* τινα Luc.*Gall.*11). 2. metaph., *give way, submit, be complaisant,* τινι *to* one, Pl.*R.*336c; ἀλλήλοις ἐν τῇ ζητήσει ib.e; ὑ. τισὶ τῆς ἀξιώσεως D.H.6.24,71: abs., *give in,* D.9.64, Plu.*Pomp.*75, etc.; θεραπεύων καὶ -όμενος D.Chr.6.57. 3. ὑ. τοῦ εἰς πλέον ἐναντιοῦσθαι *desist from* further opposition, J.*AJ*18.1.1. **-κλῐσις,** *εως, ἡ,* metaph., *taking a lower place, compliance, servility,* Plu.2.58c (pl.); *a humiliation,* Hld.10.25. **-λείπω,** *leave behind,* μνημόσυνον Hp.*Prorrh.*2.20. **-πίπτω,** *sink down under,* Ep. aor. -κάππεσε Q.S.1.588.

**ὑποκατ-άρᾱτος** [ᾰρ], *ον, subject to a curse, CIG*(add.)3882*b*(Phrygia).

**ὑποκατα-σκευάζω,** *prepare secretly,* ἐνέδραν J.*AJ*15.4.2; μῖσος ib.16.1.2 (Pass.); *prepare beforehand,* Iamb.*Myst.*3.27 (Pass.); δεῖ -εσκευάσθαι μᾶλλον τοῦ διαλόγου τὴν ἐπιστολὴν *should be somewhat* more *studied,* Demetr.*Eloc.*224. **-σκευή,** *ἡ, gradual preparation,* τῆς ψυχῆς Iamb.*Protr.*1. ⊛ **-στᾰσις,** *εως, ἡ, substitution, Gloss.* ⊛ **-στάτης** [στᾰ], *ου, ὁ, substitute,* ἐπιμελητὴς ἤτοι ὑ. Ἀπολλωνίου Ἥρωνος *PLips.*55.9 (iv A.D., = *Arch.Pap.*3.566), cf. *PFlor.*325.3 (v A.D.). ⊛ **-στᾰτος,** *ον,* = *obstinatus, substitutus, Gloss.* **-στέλλω,** *moderate, mitigate,* Agatharch.99. **-φρονέω,** apptly., *to be a little irrational,* of a patient, ἴσως ἄλλως ὑποκατεφρόνει Hp.*Epid.*4.31. II. *despise a little,* τινος Aristox.*Harm.*p.31 M. **-χέω,** *pour gently forth,* πτερύγων ὑποκακχέει ἀοίδαν Alc.39; but πτερύγων δ' ὕπα κακχέει, *pours forth from beneath* his wings (of the cricket), is prob. cj.

**ὑποκάτ-ειμι,** (εἶμι *ibo*) *go down:* ὑποκατιών *further on, lower in the text, AB*156, Syn.Alch.p.59 B., Sever.*Clyst.*p.32 D. **-έρχομαι,** = ὑποκαταβαίνω, τὸ ὑποκατελθόν, = ἐναιώρημα, of urine, Gal.19.606. **-εσθίω,** *devour* or *consume secretly,* gloss on ὑπέρεπτε, Apollon.*Lex.* **-έχω,** *subject,* τινὰ τιμωρίαις *IG*14.872.38 (Tab. Defix.). **-ορύσσω,** *bury under,* Sophr.3 (Pass.).

**ὑποκάτω** [ᾰ], Adv. *below, under,* c. gen., ὑ. τῆς ἐκροῆς Pl.*Phd.*112d; ὑ. ἐμοῦ κατακλίνου Id.*Smp.*222e; τὸ ὑ. τοῦ νοηθέντος Epicur.*Ep.*1 p.18 U.; τὸ Λητῷον, ὃ ὑ. Πουρέου ἐστί *SIG*826 *E*34 (Delph., ii B.C.): abs., Pl.*Lg.*844c, *IG*12(5).872.19 (Tenos, iii B.C.); ὑ. παραγράψαι τι Hyp.*Eux.*30. II. in Logic, τὸ ὑ. γένος the *subordinate* genus, opp. τὸ ἐπάνω, Arist.*Top.*143$^{a}$21; τὰ ὑ. ib.122$^{a}$9, al.

**ὑποκάτωθεν** [ᾰ], Adv. *from below* or *underneath,* Arist.*GA*773$^{a}$22: c. gen., ὑ. τοῦ οὐρανοῦ Lxx *De.*9.14. II. = ὑποκάτω, οἱ ὑ. ἀγροί the *lower* lands, Pl.*Lg.*761b.

**ὑποκατώρῠχος,** *ον, sunk beneath the earth,* Thphr.*CP*5.9.11 (v.l. ἀποκατώρυγες).

**ὑπό-καυσις,** *εως, ἡ, burning underneath,* Dieuch.ap.Orib.4.5.2. 2. *burning* of bricks, ὑ. τῆς ὀπτῆς (sc. πλίνθου) *POxy.*2153.12

(iii A.D.). II. *the fire of the hypocaust*, Vitr.5.10.1, Plu.2.658e; *heating* by this means, *IGRom.*4.1210 (Thyatira); βαλανείου *POxy.*2127.8 (ii A.D.). **-καυστήριον**, τό, *heating-chamber*, βαλανείου *PLond.*3.1166.7 (i A.D.), *PMag.Lond.*121.469. **-καύστης**, ου, ὁ, *bath-heater*, *PLond.* l. c., *POxy.*1146.10 (iv A. D.). **-καυστον**, τό, *the hot-air space under the sweating-room in a bathing establishment, hypocaust*, Plin.*Ep.*2.17, Stat.*Silv.*1.5.59. **-καυστος**, ον, *heated by a hypocaust*, ἀλειπτήρια Herod.Med. in *Rh.Mus.*58.112. **-καύστρα**, ἡ, *the hot-air space of a hypocaust*, *Gloss.*: written **ὑποκαστρα** three times in *PMag.Berol.*2.48, al.

* **ὑπόκειμαι**, used as Pass. of ὑποτίθημι, fut. ὑποκείσομαι Pi.*O.*1.85, etc., but aor. ὑπετέθην:—*lie under*, ὑπὸ δὲ ξύλα κεῖται Il.21.364; θεμέλιοι ὑ. Th.1.93; τὸν μηρὸν ὑποκείμενον ἔχειν Arist.*IA*712$^b$32, cf. *PA*686$^a$13, 689$^b$18: c. dat., τοιαύτης τῆς κρηπῖδος ὑποκειμένης ταῖς πολιτείαις Pl.*Plt.*301e: τὰ ὑποκείμενα, opp. τὰ ὑπερκείμενα, Sor.1.8. 2. of places, *lie close to*, ὑποκειμένης τῆς Εὐβοίας ὑπὸ τὴν Ἀττικήν Isoc. 4.108; ὑ. τὸ πεδίον τῷ ἱερῷ Aeschin.3.118; λόφος ὑποκείμενος τοῖς Σιννάκοις Plu.*Crass.*29; τὸ τὴν οἰκουμένην ὑποκεῖσθαι πρὸς τοῦτον τὸν τόπον Arist.*Mete.*364$^a$7, cf. *Pr.*941$^b$39; (τὰ) πρὸς βορρᾶν καὶ ἄρκτον ὑποκείμενα μέρη τῶν ὀρέων *Gp.*2.5.1; τὰ ὑποκείμενα ἐδάφη the *adjacent* soil, D.S.3.50; ἡ -κειμένη χώρα the *adjacent* country, ibid. (but, the *adjacent low* lands, Id.2.37, Plu.*Sert.*17); ὅρος ὑπόκειται Plb.5.59.4 codd. (ἐπίκ- Schweigh.); ὁ ὑποκείμενος ποταμός Id.3.74.2; ὑποκεῖσθαι πρὸς τὴν ὄψιν *to be presented* to the sight, Demetr.Lac.*Herc.*1013.17. 3. *to be given below* in the text, κατὰ τὴν.. συγγραφήν, ἧς τὸ ἀντίγραφον ὑπόκειται *PCair.Zen.*355.122 (iii B.C.); γράψον.. τοὺς χαρακτῆρας ὡς ὑπόκειται as *below*, *PMag.Par.*1.408; λέγε τὸν λόγον τὸν ὑποκείμενον ib.230; ὡς ὑπόκειται as *below*, *Sammelb.*5231.11 (i A. D.), etc.; also, as *set forth*, *PKlein.Form.*78 (v/vi A. D.). II. in various metaph. senses, 1. *to be established, set before* one (by oneself or another) as an aim or principle, ἐμοὶ μὲν οὗτος ἄεθλος ὑποκείσεται *shall be* my *appointed* task, Pi. l. c.; δυοῖν ὑποκειμένοιν ὀνομάτοιν two phrases *being prescribed, having legal sanction*, D.23.36; ὑπόκειται πρῶτον μὲν διωμοσία, δεύτερον δὲ λόγος *the prescribed course is*.., ib.71; μένειν ἐπὶ τῶν ὑποκειμένων to abide by one's *resolves*, Plb.1.19.6, 2.51.1; μένειν ἐπὶ τῆς ὑ. γνώμης Id.1.40.5; ἐμοὶ ὑπόκειται ὅτι.. for me *it is a fixed principle* that.., Hdt.2.123, cf. Arist.*Oec.*1343$^b$9; νομίζω συμφέρειν.. τοῦθ' ὑποκεῖσθαι D.14.3; τῶν πραγμάτων ἐν οἷς τὰ ὑποκείμενα διαφέρει τῷ εἴδει things of which the *principles* differ in kind, Arist.*Pol.*1275$^a$35; τὰς ὑποκειμένας μοίρας τξ' the *conventional* 360°, Ptol.*Alm.*5.1. 2. *to be assumed as a hypothesis* (cf. ὑπόθεσις III), Pl.*Cra.*436d, al.; ὑπέκειτο μὴ οἷόν τε εἶναι.. Id.*Erx.*404b; τούτων ὑποκειμένων Id.*Prt.*359a, *R.*478e; τὴν ἐκ τῶν -κειμένων ἀρίστην [πολιτείαν] the best (possible) *in the circumstances*, opp. to τὴν κρατίστην ἁπλῶς and to τὴν ἐξ ὑποθέσεως, Arist.*Pol.*1288$^b$26; ὑποκείσθω τι *let it be taken for granted*, Id.*EN*1103$^b$32, cf. 1129$^a$11, al., Gal.15.175; ὑποκείσθω ὅτι.. *let it be taken for granted* that.., Arist.*Pol.*1323$^b$40; ὑ. εἶναι τὴν ἡδονὴν κίνησιν Id.*Rh.*1369$^b$33: so with a nom., ὑ. ἡ ἀρετὴ εἶναι.. Id.*EN*1104$^b$27, cf. *Rh.*1357$^a$11: c. part., τοιόνδε ζῷον ὑ. ὄν Id.*GA*778$^b$17: without any Verb, ἡ τοῦ δέρματος φύσις ὑ. γεώδης (sc. εἶναι or οὖσα) ib.782$^a$29, etc.: cf. ὑποτίθημι IV. 1. 3. *to be suggested*, τρόπῳ τῷ ἐξ ἐμεῦ -κειμένῳ Hdt.3.40. 4. *to be in prospect*, ἐλπὶς ὑπόκειται σφαλεῖσι κἂν αὐτοὺς διασῴζεσθαι Th.3.84; αἱ ὑποκείμεναι προσδοκίαι καὶ αἱ ἐλπίδες D.19.24; παρ' ὑμῖν ὀργὴ μεγάλη καὶ τιμωρία ὑπόκειται τοῖς τὰ ψευδῆ μαρτυροῦσι *is reserved* for them, Id.34.19, cf. Lycurg.130; δυοῖν κινδύνοιν -κειμένοιν ibid.; ὁρᾶν τὸν θάνατον ὑποκείμενον *PPetr.*3 p.73 (iii B.C.); φόβου ὑποκειμένου ὅτι οὔσει τι βέβαιον παρὰ σοῦ *PSI*4.380.3 (iii B.C.); τοῦτο καὶ τοῖς μηθὲν ἀσεβὲς ἐπιτελεσαμένοις κατὰ τοὺς τοῦ πολέμου νόμους ὑπόκειται παθεῖν Plb.2.58.10. 5. *to be subject to, submit to*, τῷ ἄρχοντι Pl.*Grg.*510c; βασιλεῖ Philostr. *VA*3.20; πατρῳνίῳ *POxy.*237 vii 16 (ii A.D.); ἐξετάσεσιν *PFlor.*33.14 (iv A.D.); βασάνοις *POxy.*58.25 (iii A.D.): abs., *pay court to* one, ὑποκείσονται δεόμενοι καὶ τιμῶντες Pl.*R.*494c; τῷ λόγῳ *to be captivated* by the story, Philostr.*VA*6.14; θρῆνοι -κείμενοι *subdued*, Id.*VS*2.4.2. 6. *to be subject to, liable to* a penalty, *Supp.Epigr.*6.424, cf. 415,421, al. (Iconium), *PLond.*1.77.53 (vi A.D.): also c. acc., ὑποκείσεται τῷ φίσκῳ δηνάρια πεντακόσια *Rev.Phil.*36.61 (Iconium). 7. *to be pledged* or *mortgaged*, c. gen., *for* a certain sum, Is.6.33, D.49.11,35; ναῦς ὑποκειμένη ἡμῖν Id.56.4; τὰ ὑποκείμενα the *articles pledged*, Syngr. ap.D.35.12; the *mortgaged property*, *SIG*1044.28 (Halic., iv/iii B. C.); ἐνέχυρα -κείμενα *IG*12(7).58 (Amorgos); ὑποκείμενοι, of slaves *pledged for* a sum of money, D.27.9. b. of payments, *to have been granted* or *allocated*, ἀποφαίνουσιν ὑποκεῖσθαι ἐν τῇ γραφῇ τῶν εἰς τὰ ἱερὰ (sc. ὑποκειμένων) δίδοσθαι κτλ. *UPZ*21.4 (ii B.C.), cf. 23.21 (ii B.C.), *BGU* 1197.4, 1200.28 (both i B.C.): Subst. ὑποκείμενα, τά, = φιλάνθρωπα, *salary* (*ear-marked proceeds of taxes*), τὰ ἐπιβάλλοντά μοι ἐκ τοῦ ἱεροῦ ὑ. *PLond.*2.357.9, cf. 5 (i A. D.); ὑ. αἰτεῖ ἀπὸ τῶν κωμῶν *BGU*23.12 (ii/iii A. D.), cf. *OGI*665.19,26 (Egypt, i A. D.): c. dat., as part of name of specific taxes, ὑ. βασιλικῇ γραμματείᾳ *ear-marked for the benefit of*.., *PPar.*17.22 (ii A. D.); ὑ. τοπογραμματείᾳ *PSI*1.101.18 (ii A. D.), cf. *POxy.*1436.23 (ii A. D.), etc.: also in sg., ὑποκείμενον ἐπιστρατηγίᾳ *BGU* 199.14 (ii A. D.), cf. *PFlor.*375.22 (ii A. D.), etc.: also c. gen., ὑ. ἐννομίου *PRyl.*213.72, al. (ii A. D.): τοπαρχίας ib.73, etc. 8. in Philosophy, *to underlie, as the foundation in which something else inheres, to be implied or presupposed by something else*, ἑκάστῳ τῶν ὀνομάτων.. ὑ. τις ἴδιος οὐσία Pl.*Prt.*349b, cf. *Cra.*422d, *R.*581c, Ti.Locr.97e: τὸ ὑποκείμενον has three main applications: (1) to the matter which underlies the form, opp. εἶδος, ἐντελέχεια, Arist.*Metaph.*983$^a$30; (2) to the substance (matter + form) which underlies the accidents, opp. πάθη, συμβεβηκότα, Id.*Cat.*1$^a$20,27, *Metaph.*1037$^b$16, 983$^b$16; (3) to the logical subject to which attributes are ascribed, opp. τὸ κατηγορούμενον, Id.*Cat.*1$^b$10,21, *Ph.*189$^a$31: applications (1) and (2) are distinguished in Id.*Metaph.*1038$^b$5, 1029$^a$1-5, 1042$^a$26-31: τὸ ὑ. is occasionally used of what underlies or is presupposed in some other way, e. g. of the positive termini presupposed by change, Id.*Ph.*225$^a$3-7. b. *exist*, τὸ ἐκτὸς ὑποκείμενον the external *reality*, *Stoic.*2.48, cf. Epicur.*Ep.*1 pp.12,24 U.; φῶς εἶναι τὸ χρῶμα τοῖς ὑ. ἐπιπῖπτον Aristarch.Sam.ap.*Placit.*1.15.5; τὸ κρῖνον τί τε φαίνεται μόνον καὶ τί σὺν τῷ φαίνεσθαι ἔτι καὶ κατ' ἀλήθειαν ὑπόκειται S.E.*M.*7.143, cf. 83,90,91, 10.240; = ὑπάρχω, τὰ ὑποκείμενα πράγματα the *existing* state of affairs, Plb.11.28.2, cf. 11.29.1, 15.8.11,13, 3.31.6, Eun.*VS*p.474 B.; Τίτος ἐξ ὑποκειμένων ἐνίκα, χρώμενος ὁπλισμοῖς καὶ τάξεσιν αἷς παρέλαβε Plu.*Comp.Phil.Flam.*2; τῆς αὐτῆς δυνάμεως ὑποκειμένης Id.2.336b; ἐχομένου τοῦ προσιόντος λόγου ὡς πρὸς τὸν ὑποκείμενον A.D.*Synt.*122.17. c. ὁ ὑ. ἐνιαυτός the year *in question*, D.S.11.75; οἱ ὑ. καιροί the time *in question*, Id.16.40, Plb.2.63.6, cf. Plu.*Comp.Sol.Publ.*4; τοῦ ὑ. μηνός the *current* month, *PTeb.*14.14 (ii B.C.), al.; ἐκ τοῦ ὑ. φόρου in return for a reduction from the *said* rent, *PCair.Zen.*649.18 (iii B. C.); πρὸς τὸ ὑ. νόει according to the *context*, *Gp.*6.11.7. 9. in logical arrangement, *to be subject* or *subordinate*, τῇ.. ἰατρικῇ.. ἡ ὀψοποιικὴ.. ὑ. Pl. *Grg.*465b; ὁ τὴν καθόλου ἐπιστήμην ἔχων οἶδέ πως πάντα τὰ ὑποκείμενα Arist.*Metaph.*982$^a$23, cf. *APo.*91$^a$11; ἑκάστη [τέχνη] περὶ τὸ αὐτῇ ὑ. ἐστι διδασκαλική Id.*Rh.*1355$^b$28. b. ἡ ὑ. ὕλη the *subject*-matter of a science or treatise, Id.*EN*1094$^b$12, 1098$^a$28, Phld.*Po.Herc.*1676.3 (pl.); τὸ ὑ. the *part affected* by a disease, Plb.1.81.6. III. trans., = ὑποτέθειμαι, I *have appended*, ὧν τὸ καθ' ἓν ὑπόκειμαι *PTeb.* 140 (i B.C.); cf. παράκειμαι (Addenda).

**ὑποκείρω**, *cut off below*, μύες.. τοὺς στάχυς.. ὑποκείροντες Ael.*NA* 6.41, cf. 17.17. 2. *cut off, take away*, Ph.1.327. II. metaph., ὑ. τοὺς χρεώστας *tear, mangle* them, Plu.2.829a.

**ὑποκεκορισμένως**, Adv. = ὑποκοριστικῶς, Anon.*Prog.* in Rh.1. 598 W.

**ὑπο-κελεύω**, *do the duty of a boatswain, give the time in rowing*, Luc.*Cat.*19:—hence **-κέλευσμα**, ατος, τό, Sch. ad loc.

**ὑπόκεν-ος**, ον, *somewhat hollow*, Ruf.*Onom.*139, v.l. in Dsc.2.131; simply, *hollow*, πλάσον Ἑρμῆν ὑπόκενον *PMag.Par.*1.2361; *somewhat flabby*, Mnesith.ap.Orib.*inc.*15.8: metaph., ᾠδή Hsch. s. v. ἴθυμβος (-κυνος cod.); ὑ. καὶ ψυχρόν Hermog.*Id.*2.9; δόξα Hierocl. *in CA*23 p.470 M. **-όω**, *empty below, purge*, τὴν κοιλίην Hp.*Prog.*23, al.; ὑποκεκενωμένος *purged*, Id.*Prorrh.*2.4. 2. *carry off by purging*, τὴν κόπρον Id.*Int.*20 (Pass.).

**ὑποκεντά**· ὑπομονητικά, Hsch.

* **ὑποκεντέω**, *pierce underneath*, τινὰ δόρασιν App.*Ill.*20; τινὰ ὑπὸ τὸ γένειον D.C.65.21.

**ὑποκέρᾰμος**, ον, *tiled*, of a roof, *IG*4$^2$(1).106 ii 136 (p.144, Epid., iv B. C.).

**ὑποκερχᾰλέος** or **-κεγχνᾰλέος**, α, ον, *with a rattle in the throat*, Hp.*Epid.*7.12.

**ὑποκεφάλαιον** [φᾰ], τό, *pillow, cushion*, σκύτινον ὑ. Hp.*Fract.*8, *Art.*30, cf. *Michel*832.23 (Samos, iv B. C.), Sor.1.67, Aret.*CA*1.1; cf. προσκεφάλαιον.

**ὑπόκηρος**, ον, f.l. for ἐπίκηρος in Hp.*Morb.Sacr.*1 (Sup.).

**ὑποκήρ-υγμα**, ατος, τό, *proclamation by herald*, *Dacia* 2.206 (Histria). **-ύσσω**, *proclaim by herald*, c. inf. fut., *PRev.Laws*53.18 (iii B. C.), cf. *AB*312:—Med., *have a thing proclaimed* or *cried*, esp. for sale, Aeschin.3.41; σεαυτὸν ὑ. εἰς πάντας *advertising* yourself, Pl. *Prt.*349a; σιωπὴν ὑ. D.H.9.48: c. acc. et inf., J.*AJ*3.6.1.

**ὑποκῐθᾰρίζω**, *play an accompaniment on the harp*, Sch.Il.18.570.

**ὑποκῐναιδέω**, *talk suggestively*, Phld.*Vit.*p.41 J.

**ὑποκινδῡν-εύω**, *run some risk*, f.l. for ἀποκ- in Plu.*Pel.*2 (corr. Reiske). **-ος**, ον, *somewhat dangerous*, Pl.*Lg.*830e.

**ὑποκῑνέω**, *move softly* or *lightly*, Ζεφύρου ὑποκινήσαντος (sc. τὸ κῦμα) Il.4.423 (better ὕπο κ., v. Sch. A), cf. Plu.2.596c, etc.:—Pass., of the apparent *vibration* of the moon, Ptol.*Tetr.*101. 2. metaph., *urge gently on*, so as to make him speak, Pl.*Chrm.*162d, Plu.*Arat.* 9; ὑ. ἔγκλημα Luc.*Eun.*13; cf. κινέω A. II. 2. II. intr., *move a little*, οὐδεμία πόλις ἂν ὑπεκίνησε not a single city *would have stirred a finger*, Hdt.5.106, cf. Ar.*Ra.*644, X.*Cyn.*3.6; ἐπ' ἑφέδρου ὅτι μὴ ὑποκινήσει on a chair which *will* not *shake*, Hp.*Morb.*2.47. 2. metaph., *to be deranged in mind*, ὁ.. μαινόμενος καὶ ὑποκεκινηκὼς Pl. *R.*573c.

**ὑπόκινυμι** [κῐ], Ep. for ὑποκινέω, impf. ὑπεκίνυον Q.S.4.510 (s.v.l.):—Pass., ποσὶν δ' ὑπεκίνυτο γαῖα Id.3.36.

**ὑποκῐνύρομαι** [ῡ], *hum a tune*, Ael.*VH*9.11.

**ὑποκίρνᾰμαι**, Pass., *to be mixed*, Arist.*Insomn.*460$^a$30.

**ὑπόκιρρος**, ον, *somewhat yellow*, Hp.*Epid.*7.11, Dsc.2.83, Gal.19.129; of stars (viz. those now called *red*), Ptol.*Alm.*7.5, al., *Tetr.* 23,90.

**ὑποκιρσόω**, in Pass., of veins, *to be swollen*, Hp.*Ulc.*10.

**ὑποκιστίς**, ἴδος, ἡ, *hypocist, Cytinus Hypocisthis*, Dsc.1.97 (v.l. -κισθίς), cf. Plin.*HN*26.49, Sor.1.50, Gal.8.114, 12.27.

**ὑπόκκινος**, ον, prob. misspelling for *ὑποκόκκινος, *reddish*, *PGrenf.* 2.28.5 (ii B. C.).

**ὑποκλαγγάνω**, v. ὑπο-κλάζω.

**ὑποκλ-ᾰδόν**, Adv. *with the knees somewhat bent, inclined a little* or *gradually*, Opp.*C.*4.205. **-άζω**, *bend the knees under one, sink down*, Hld.7.7, Nonn.*D.*43.47; ὑ. τινι *bow the knee before*.., ib.47.

627; ἄρνες ταῖς μητράσιν ὑποκλάσαντες τὴν θηλὴν ἔσπασαν Longus 3.13 (ὑ. αὐτοὺς codd.); ὑπώκλασε γαῖα χανοῦσα (in an earthquake) Epic. in *BKT*5(1) p.85 (iv B.C.): metaph. of an expiring lamp, *AP* 5.278 (Paul. Sil.); of a *declining* fever, Paul.Aeg.2.47; τὰ δ' ὑπείροχ', ὀπανίκα νεύσω, κῦρος ὑποκλάζοισ' the mighty, when I nod, *bow down before* my power, *Hymn.Is.*143.

**ὑπο-κλάζω** or -**κλαγγάνω**, *cry out a little, groan*, τί μάτην ὑπέκλαγες; S.*Ichn.*171 (lyr.).

**ὑποκλαίω**, Att. -**κλάω** [ᾱ], *shed secret tears*, A.*Ag.*69 (anap., Casaubon ὑποκαίων).

**ὑπόκλαστος**, ον, in personal descriptions, either *slightly curly-haired*, or *slightly bent, stooping*, *PGrenf.*2.32.4, al. (ii B.C.), *PStrassb.* 87.14 (ii B.C.), *PLond.*3.1208.13 (i B.C.).

**ὑποκλάω** [ᾰ], *break underneath*, γούνων ὑποέκλασε δεσμά Nic.*Th.* 728. 2. *break by degrees, break down*, ὑπέκλασε δεῖμα..ἠνορέην Q.S.4.483:—Pass., ὑποκλώμενοι τὰς ψυχάς J.*BJ*7.8.7; θυμὸς ὑποκλασθείς *AP*5.215 (Agath.). 3. *enclose in a bend*, γραμμὴν τὴν -κλῶσαν τοὺς τρεῖς δακτύλους (in palmistry) *Cat.Cod.Astr.*7.238.

**ὑποκλείω**, *shut up*, *PGiss.*67.16 (ii A.D.).

❀ **ὑποκλέπτω**, *steal from under*, ᾠά Dionys.*Av.*1.11; *draw off* superfluous humours, κατὰ μέρος ὑ. Alex.Trall.12.1, cf. 1.10, *Febr.*5,7; ὑ. ἑαυτόν *steal away* from another's company, Luc.*DMeretr.*10.3:—Pass., *to be stolen away*, αἰδὼς ὑπὸ κρύφα κλέπτεται Pi.*N.*9.33, cf. *PFreib.*11.6 (iii A.D.). 2. ὑποκλέπτεσθαι εὐνάς *suffer dishonour by stealth*, S.*El.*114 (anap.). II. *keep secret*, ἕλκος Musae.85; *conceal from notice*, ἐρευθιόωσαν παρειήν Id.161; εἰ διὰ βραχύτητα τοῦ πνεύματος ὑποκλέπτοι καὶ κωλύοι τὰ λεγόμενα *muffle* his words, Antyll.ap. Orib.6.10.7; ὑ. ὀπωπήν *take a stolen* look, *AP*5.220 (Paul. Sil.), cf. 289 (Id.); φιλίη ὑποκλεπτομένη ib.266 (Agath.). 2. *cheat, beguile*, ζῆλόν τινος ib.268 (Id.). 3. Med., *disregard*, τὰς παρὰ μικρὸν διαφοράς Dam.*Pr.*88.

**ὑπόκλημα**, ατος, τό, dub. sens. in *BGU*329.22 (ii A.D.).

**ὑποκλῑνής**, ές, *subject, subordinate*, Sch.A.*Pers.*21.

**ὑποκλίνω** [ῑ], *bend under* or *in subjection to*, γόνυ τινί Nonn.*D.*15.124: but usu. in Pass., *recline* or *lie down under*, c. dat., σχοίνῳ ὑπεκλίνθη Od.5.463, cf. *AP*9.71 (Antiphil.), etc.; Βάκχῳ νύμφη ὑποκλινθεῖσα, = ὑποδμηθεῖσα, Orph.*A.*195; μαζὸς ὑπεκλίνθη *has grown flaccid*, *AP*5.272 (Agath.); ὑποκεκλιμένων τῶν σκελῶν with the legs *bent*, Aët.16.111. 2. *give way to*, ὅταν τὸ ἐπιθυμητικὸν -κλίνηται τῷ θυμικῷ Herm. *in Phdr.*p.157 A.: so intr. in Act., εἰ..ὑποκλίνοιτε φάλαγγι Orph.*A.*848. 3. *turn aside*, Phlp. *in Mete.*85.39.

**ὑποκλονέομαι**, Pass., *to be driven in confusion before* one, Ἀχιλῆϊ Il.21.556. II. *to be shaken so as to fall*, Q.S.14.572.

**ὑποκλοπέομαι**, Pass., *lurk in secret places*, εἴ τις ἔτ' ἀνδρῶν ζωὸς ὑποκλοπέοιτο Od.22.382.

**ὑπόκλοπος**, ον, *guileful*, λόγος B.14.30.

**ὑπο-κλύζω**, *wash from below*, πόντος ὑ. χθονὸς ἕδρανα *AP*9.663 (Paul. Sil.); ὑ. τὸ σῶμα *purge* the body *by a clyster*, Plu.2.127c, cf. Hp.*Morb.*2.40; τὴν κοιλίην Aret.*CA*1.2; ὑ. τὴν πόλιν *flush* it, J.*AJ* 15.9.6. II. Pass., *to be submerged*, A.R.1.533 (s.v.l.): metaph., *to be flooded* with mischief, Luc.*Nigr.*16. -**κλυσις**, εως, ἡ, = *sublavies*, *Gloss.* -**κλυσμός**, ὁ, *purging from below*, as by a clyster, Plu.2.974c.

❀ **ὑποκλύω**, *hear*, Q.S.1.509 (v.l. ἐσέκλ-); τινος *from* one, A.R.3.477.

**ὑποκλωπάω**, v. ὑπολωπάω.

**ὑποκνήθω**, *scratch a little*, Ael.ap.Ar.Byz.*Epit.*113.6, Tz.*H.*6.89.

**ὑποκνίζω**, *tickle* or *excite a little*, ἀκκισμὸς ὑ. τὰς ὁρμάς Ph.2.127, cf. Aristaenet.2.1,10; τοὺς ἀκούοντας Chor.p.125 B., cf. Id.30.2 p.342 F.-R.:—Pass., *to be somewhat excited*, X.*Mem.*3.11.3; ὑποκεκνισμένος *'smitten'*, Plu.*Sull.*35.

**ὑποκνυζάομαι**, *growl a little*, Nonn.*D.*15.200.

**ὑποκοιλ-αίνω**, *become hollow*, J.*AJ*3.7.6. -**ιον**, τό, *the lower belly*, *Gloss.* -**ίς**, ίδος, ἡ, *the lower eyelid*, Aret.*SD*1.7; cf. κύλα. -**ος**, ον, *slightly concave*, Hp.*VC*13, Dsc.3.90, Ruf.*Oss.*18: Comp., -ότερον μέτωπον Arist.*Phgn.*809ᵇ21.

**ὑποκολακεύω**, *flatter a little*, Plb.6.18.5 (Pass.).

**ὑποκόλαμμα**, ατος, τό, *the fold-over* of a garment, *subsumen, subsutio*, *Gloss.*: written ὑποκάλαμμα in *PMag.Osl.*1.40, and ὑποκάλυμμα in *PMag.Lond.*121.190: cf. ἀνακολαφή and ἀνακολαφίς (Addenda).

**ὑποκολλάω**, *glue underneath*, Hero *Spir.*1.32, *Aut.*26.5, *PAmh.*2.137.13 (iii A.D.), *PLips.*36.10 (iv A.D.), *PMag.Lond.*46.208.

**ὑποκόλοβος**, ον, *dwarf*, of a plant, Dsc.1.1.

**ὑποκολπ-ίδιος**, ον, = sq. I. 2, ξίφη Hdn.7.6.7. ❀ -**ιος**, ον, *lying on the bosom, in the lap*, ἄλλος τοι γλυκίων ὑποκόλπιος; Theoc.14.37; ἐραστὴν..ἔχονθ' ὑποκόλπιον ἄλλην *AP*5.129 (Maec.), cf. 274 (Paul. Sil.); Κυδίλλης ὑποκόλπιος ib.24. 2. *worn* or *concealed in the fold of the robe*, ξίφη Hdn.7.11.3; βιβλίδιον *AP*12.208 (Strat.). II. *in the mother's womb*, Ἀπόλλων ὑποκόλπιος αἰνὰ χολώθη Call.*Del.*86.

**ὑποκολυμβάω**, *dive under*, Gal.19.149.

**ὑποκομίζω**, f.l. for ὑπεκκ- (corr. Niese) in J.*Vit.*23 codd.

**ὑπόκομμα**, ατος, τό, *a gathering in at the waist*, Hsch. s.v. ὀρθοστάδιοι χιτῶνες.

**ὑποκομπέω**, *sound under* one, ἐν τῷ βαδίζειν Plu.2.672a.

**ὑπόκομψος**, ον, *rather neat* or *elegant*, Polem.*Phgn.*66.

**ὑποκόν-ῑσις**, εως, ἡ, *a putting dust to the roots*, esp. *by digging round*, Thphr.*CP*3.16.3. -**ίω** [ῑ], *put dust to the roots*, esp. *by digging* (cf. ὑποσκάπτω), Id.*HP*2.7.5. II. Med., of wrestlers, *sprinkle oneself with dust*, in preparation for the contest, τὼ χεῖρε ὑποκονίεται *Com.Adesp.*401: metaph., Plu.2.614d.

**ὑπόκοπος**, ον, *somewhat tired*, X.*Cyn.*6.25, Erasistr. ap.Gal.*Consuet.*1, Anon.Vat.1.

❀ **ὑπόκοπρος**, ον, *slightly faecal*, Hp.*Epid.*4.27.

**ὑποκόπτω**, *cut under* or *beneath*, στέλεχος Str.16.4.10; *hamstring*, τὴν ἰγνύαν τινός Plu.*Eum.*7; τένοντας ποδῶν D.H.6.33; ὑποκεκομμένος τὰ νεῦρα J.*BJ*6.8.4: metaph., ὑ. τὰ νεῦρα τῆς δυνάμεως ib. 5.1.4; τὴν ἐλπίδα ib.6.1.3.

**ὑποκορ-ίζομαι**, aor. ὑπεκορισάμην Aristid.1.493 J., Charito 3.7: in dialects **ὑποκουρίζομαι** (q.v.). I. trans., *call by endearing names*, of lovers, νηττάριον ἂν καὶ φάττιον ὑπεκορίζετο *he would call* me *coaxingly* little duck and little dove, Ar.*Pl.*1011; ψυχὴν ὑ. τινά *call* him *dear* soul, Plu.2.692e; τὴν Ἑκάλην ἐτίμων, Ἑκαλίνην ὑποκοριζόμενοι Id.*Thes.*14; [Κωλώτην] Ἐπίκουρος εἰώθει Κωλωτάραν ὑ. καὶ Κωλωτάριον Id.2.1107e; τὸν πύκτην Ἡρακλείδην Ἡρακλοῦν ὑπεκορίζοντο ib.624b, cf. Ath.13.585f. 2. *call by a soft name*, esp. *call* something bad *by a fair name, gloss over*, εὐηθείᾳ..ἣν ἄνοιαν οὖσαν ὑποκοριζόμενοι καλοῦμεν Pl.*R.*400e; ἐραστοῦ ὑποκοριζομένου καὶ εὐχερῶς φέροντος τὴν ὠχρότητα ib.474e; ὑποκοριζόμενοι, ὕβριν μὲν εὐπαιδευσίαν καλοῦντες κτλ. ib.560e; δουλείαν Φιλίππῳ ξενίαν καὶ ἑταιρίαν καὶ τοιαῦθ' ὑποκοριζόμενοι *calling* their slavery *by the fair names* of friendship, etc., D.19.259; *fuga quam tu peregrinationem* ὑποκορίζῃ Cic.*Att.*9.10.4; προθυμίας τὰς ἐπιθυμίας ὑ. Plu.2.449a, cf. 56d, *Sol.*15, Aristid.2.112 J., etc.; ὑ. καὶ σκώπτει θάνατον Arr.*Epict.*4.1.166. 3. reversely, *call* something good *by a bad name*, οἱ μὲν φίλοι καλοῦσί με Εὐδαιμονίαν, οἱ δὲ μισοῦντες ὑποκοριζόμενοι ὀνομάζουσί με Κακίαν but my enemies *nickname* me Vice, X.*Mem.*2.1.26 (unless ὑποκοριζόμενοι has been transposed from the former clause). 4. *make a pretence of, imitate, mimic*, φθέγμα Philostr. *VS*2.10.2:—Pass., ὑποκεκορισμένη πρεσβεία *pretended*, Anon.ap. Suid. II. intr., *use diminutives*, Arist.*Rh.*1405ᵇ28. III. Act. (signf. II) first in Dam.*Isid.*76, Eust.1196.13:—Pass., *to become in the diminutive form*, τὸ γήδιον -ιζόμενον ἐφύλαξε τὸ η τοῦ γῆ A.D. *Adv.*174.27. -**ῐσις**, εως, ἡ, *use of the diminutive form*, καθ' ὑ. Eust.1196.14; *euphemism*, Gal.18(2).236 (-κρισις codd., corr. Cornarius). -**ισμα**, ατος, τό, *a coaxing* or *endearing name*, as Dem. said that his nickname Βάταλος was a ὑ. τίτθης, Aeschin.1.126. 2. *a fair name* for something base, as παράσιτος for πολυφάγος, Alex. 178.2, cf. 219.5; σεισάχθεια for χρεῶν ἀποκοπή, Plu.2.807e; so φυγῆς ὑ. καὶ παρακάλυμμα Id.*Galb.*20. 3. *diminutive*, Eust.1540.54. -**ισμός**, ὁ, *blandishments, use of endearing names*, Plu.*Thes.*14, Alciphr.3.33. 2. *use of diminutives*, Arist.*Rh.*1405ᵇ28. -**ιστικός**, ή, όν, *diminutive*, τὸ ὑ. (sc. ὄνομα) Ath.14.650e, cf. D.T.634.25. Adv. -κῶς Str.5.4.12, Ath.7.308f; *by a pet name*, Plu.2.847e.

**ὑποκοσμήτης**, ου, ὁ, *under*-κοσμητής, *IG*2².2037.6, 2047.10.

**ὑποκουρίζομαι**, dialect-form of ὑποκορίζομαι, *coax* or *soothe with soft names*, ἑσπερίαις ὑ. ἀοιδαῖς, of the serenades sung by girls on the evening of a friend's marriage, Pi.*P.*3.19; cf. Hsch. s.v. κουριζομέναις.—Suid. cites Act. with the expl. κολακεύω.

**ὑποκουφίζω**, intr., *to be lighter, easier*, of fevers, Hp.*Epid.*1.7: so in Pass., Orib.*Syn.*9.26.3.

**ὑπόκουφος**, ον, *somewhat light*, ῥίζα Dsc.3.2; *fickle*, Plu.2.205a; ὑ. τὴν γνώμην Id.*Pel.*14, etc.

**ὑποκρᾱτήριον**, Ion. **ὑποκρητ**-, τό, *stand of a* κρατήρ, κρητὴρ καὶ ὑποκρητήριον *SIG*2 (Sigeum, vi B.C.: = κρατῆρα κἀπίστατον in the Attic version), cf. 1121 (Naucratis); so βάθρον ὑ. *IG*4.39.11 (Aegina):—also **ὑποκρᾱτηρίδιον**, Ion. **ὑποκρητ**-, τό, Hdt.1.25, Philostr. *VA*6.11.

**ὑποκράτησις** [ᾰ], εως, ἡ, *mastering, overcoming* of poisonous bites, ἡ ὑ. δι' ἀκρατοποσίας Dsc.*Ther.Praef.*

**ὑποκρέκω**, of stringed instruments, *answer in sound*, i.e. *sound in harmony with*, τὸ καυχᾶσθαι παρὰ καιρὸν μανίαισιν ὑποκρέκει Pi.*O.*9.39. 2. trans., ὑ. τι *play an accompaniment*, Luc.*DMeretr.*15.2; τὸ ἡδὺ καὶ τὸ πρὸς χάριν ὑ., of a flatterer, Plu.2.55d.

**ὑποκρεμάννυμι**, *underpin, shore up*, τὰ τείχη ξύλων κορμοῖς App. *BC*1.112. II. Pass., *to be hung underneath*, dub. l. in Plu.2.624b.

❀ **ὑπόκρημνος**, ον, *precipitous*, Str.14.1.31,33 (prob. pr. n.).

**ὑπόκρηνος**, ον, (κάρηνον) *under the head*, Call.*Fr.anon.*64.

**ὑποκρητηρίδιον**, **ὑποκρητήριον**, Ion. for ὑποκρατ-.

**ὑποκρίζω**, *squeak a little*, τάρνοπα ὑποκρίζοντα Ael.*NA*6.19; *gibber*, in 2 sg. aor. 2 ὑπέκρῐγες, S.*Ichn.*171 (lyr.).

**ὑποκρίνω** [ῑ], *separate gradually*, Suid., Eust.687.20. II. *subject to inquiry, interrogate*, τοὺς ἀντιδίκους *AB*449, Suid. s.v. ἄρχων. B. Med. ❀ **ὑποκρίνομαι**, fut. -κρινοῦμαι, Ion. -έομαι Hdt.1.164: aor. ὑπεκρινάμην Od.15.170, Hdt.3.119 (v.l. -ετο): later also aor. and pf. Pass. in med. sense, ὑπεκρίθην [ῐ] Ctes.*Fr.*29.41, Plb.5.25.7, App.*BC*4.46; ὑποκέκρῐμαι D.19.246:—*reply, make answer*, Il.12.228; τινι 7.407, Od.2.111, 15.170, cf. Hdt.1.2,164, Hp.*Fract.*16, etc.; of an oracle, Hdt.1.78,91:—the Att. word was ἀποκρίνομαι (ὑποκρ- is given by all codd. of Th.7.44, as, vice versa, ἀποκρ- appears in all codd. of Hdt.5.49, 8.101; cf. ὑπόκρισις I). 2. *expound, interpret, explain*, ὄνειρον Od.19.535,555; ὀνείρατα Ar.*V.*53, cf. Philostr.*VA*2.37, Hp.*Ep.*15; ὑ. ὅπως.. Theoc.24.67. II. Att., *speak in dialogue*, hence *play a part* on the stage, the part played being put in acc., τὴν Ἀντιγόνην Σοφοκλέους ὑποκέκριται D. l. c.; [ἥρωα] Luc.*Nigr.*11: abs., *play a part, be an actor*, οἱ ὑποκρινόμενοι Arist.*EN*1147ᵃ23; ὑ. τραγῳδίας, κωμῳδίαν, *play* tragedies, comedy, Id.*Rh.*1403ᵇ23, Luc.*Merc.Cond.*30, cf. *Nigr.*24, etc.; ὑπεκρίθησαν τραγῳδοί tragedians *acted*, Chares *Fr.*4 J.; μισθῶν ἐλασσόνων συνεχώρησεν ὑποκρινεῖσθαι τῷ δήμῳ *Supp.Epigr.*1.362.10 (Samos, iv B.C.): also ὑ. τὰ πάντα [προσωπεῖα] *play* all the characters, Luc.*Salt.*66; ὑ. μανίαν ib. 83. **2.** *deliver a speech, declaim*, of orators and rhetoricians, Arist. *Rh.*1413$^{b}$23, Phld.*Rh.*1.195 S., al.: c. acc., τὰ Ὁμήρου Ath.14.620d; ἀλλοτρίους λόγους Luc.*Pseudol.*25; *represent dramatically*, ἐρωτικῶν δραμάτων ὑποθέσεις, of Hld., Ach.Tat., and Iamb., Phot.*Bibl.*p.73B.; *ape, mimic*, τὸ τῶν Ἰνδῶν ἔργον Philostr.*VA*3.4; *represent* in art, Philostr.Jun.*Im.Prooem.*, cf. Callistr.*Stat.*7. **3.** of an orator, *use histrionic arts, exaggerate*, D.18.15. **4.** metaph., *play a part, feign, pretend*, ib.287, Lxx *Si.*1.29, al.; ὑ. τὸν βασιλικόν *take* the king's *part, play* the king, Arist.*Pol.*1314$^{a}$40; ὑπολαμβάνειν καὶ ὑποκρίνεσθαι ib. 1310$^{a}$10; μεγαλοψυχίαν Phld.*Vit.*p.24 J.: c. inf., D.31.8, Plb.2. 49.7, Lxx 4*Ma.*6.15; ὑ. ὡς ἐσθίοντα ib.2*Ma.*6.21; ὑποκριθεὶς νεκρὸς διέφυγε Vett.Val.275.19. **5.** c. acc., *deceive*, App.*Pun.*13 (s. v.l.).

⊛ **ὑπο-κρῐσία**, poet. **-ίη**, ἡ, rarer form for ὑπόκρισις II, *APl.*4.289. **-κρῐσις**, εως, ἡ, **I.** Ion. (and perh. in Porph.*Chr.*35.10), *reply, answer* (cf. ὑποκρίνω B. 1), Hdt.1.116, 9.9; τῶν χρηστηρίων Id.1.90; but the Att. word ἀπόκρισις occurs in codd. at 1.49, 5.50. **II.** Att., *playing a part* on the stage, Arist.*EN*1118$^{a}$8, Phld.*Mus.*p.91 K. **2.** an orator's *delivery*, Arist.*Rh.*1386$^{a}$32, 1403$^{b}$22, 1413$^{b}$18, Chrysipp. *Stoic.*2.96, Phld.*Rh.*1.195 S., 201 S. (pl.); οἱ κατὰ τὴν ὑ. ῥήτορες orators who depend on their *delivery*, opp. to the authors of written speeches, Arist.*Rh.*1404$^{a}$18. **b.** *tone* or *manner* of an animal's cry, ὁ κυνηγέτης ἀπὸ τῆς ὑ. ᾔσθετο τοῦ κυνὸς ὑλακτοῦντος νῦν μὲν ὅτι ζητεῖ τὸν λαγών, νῦν δὲ ὅτι εὗρεν.. Porph.*Abst.*3.5. **3.** metaph., *playing a part, hypocrisy, outward show*, Phoc.2 B, Plb.35.2.13, Lxx 2*Ma.*6.25, *Ev. Matt.*23.28, al., Luc.*Somn.*17. **4.** ὑπόκρισιν, as Adv., *after the manner of*, δελφῖνος ὑ. Pi.*Oxy.*408.69 (= *Fr.*235). **-κρῐτήρ**, ῆρος, ὁ, rarer form for sq., Herm.Iamb. (p.237 P.) ap.Ath.13.563e. **-κρῐτής**, οῦ, ὁ, *one who answers*: **I.** *interpreter* or *expounder*, τῆς δι' αἰνιγμῶν φήμης Pl.*Ti.*72b; ὀνείρων Luc.*Somn.*17, etc. **II.** in Att., *one who plays a part* on the stage, *actor*, Ar.*V.*1279, Pl.*R.*373b, *Chrm.* 162d, *Smp.*194b, X.*Mem.*2.2.9, etc. **2.** of an orator, ποικίλος ὑ. καὶ περιττός (of Dem.) Phld.*Rh.*1.197 S.; *one who delivers, recites, declaimer*, ἐπῶν Tim.*Lex.* s.v. ῥαψῳδοί; *rhapsodist*, D.S.14.109, 15.7; this sense or sense II. 1 is possible in *PCair.Zen.*4.44 (iii B.C.). **3.** metaph., *pretender, dissembler, hypocrite*, Lxx *Jb.*34.30, 36.13, *Ev. Matt.*23.13, al. **-κρῐτικός**, ή, όν, *belonging to* ὑπόκρισις II, *skilled therein*, ἔστι φύσεως τὸ ὑ. εἶναι *having a good delivery*, Arist.*Rh.*1404$^{a}$ 15. **2.** *suited for speaking* or *delivery*, λέξις -κωτάτη ib.1413$^{b}$9, cf. Demetr.*Eloc.*193: ἡ -κή (sc. τέχνη) *the art of delivery*, Arist.*Rh.* 1404$^{a}$13, *Po.*1456$^{b}$10, al. (but, *the actor's art*, Hp.*Vict.*1.24 (v.l. ὑποκριταί), Phld.*Mus.*p.91 K., Gal.*Thras.*27). Adv. -κῶς Chamael.ap. Ath.9.407a. **3.** metaph., *acting a part, pretending to*, ὑ. τοῦ βελτίονος Luc.*Alex.*4, cf. Vett.Val.42.25, al. Adv. -κῶς id. 38.19.

**ὑποκρουνιδία**· θυσία τις παρὰ Κνιδίοις, Hsch.

**ὑπό-κρουσις**, εως, ἡ, *interruption*, Hsch. s.v. κροῦσις:—Adv. **-κρουστικῶς**, *EM*781.8.

**ὑποκρουσταλίς**· εἶδος τοῦ λίνου σπέρματος, Hsch.

**ὑποκρούω**, *strike gently*, [λίθον] χερμάδι *APl.*4.279; *beat time, give the time*, Plu.*Dem.*20; ὑ. τοῖς λέγουσι Longin.41.2. **2.** sens. obsc., Ar.*Ec.*256 (with play on signf. II. 1), 618 (anap.). **II.** metaph., *break in upon, interrupt*, c. acc., Id.*Ach.*38, *Ec.*588 (anap.), Alex. 32, Henioch.5.4, Plb.18.4.3: abs., ὑποκρούσας (sc. εἶπε) Pl.*Erx.*395e. **2.** ὑπέσχοντο εἰς τὰ μηνιαῖα αὐτοῦ ὑποκροῦσαι ταύτην τὴν δόσιν *to credit* this payment to his monthly account, *PFlor.*132.10 (iii A.D.). **III.** in Med., *find fault with, attack*, Ar.*Pl.*548 (anap.).

**ὑποκρύπτω**, *hide under* or *beneath*, ἄχνῃ ὑπεκρύφθη [the ship] *was hidden beneath* the spray, Il.15.626:—Med., ὑποκρύπτεσθαί τινα *keep* something *secret from* him, v.l. in X.*An.*1.9.19, cf. J.*BJ*1.31.4:—Pass., διὰ τὸ ἄνω τὸ κεφάλιον ὑποκεκρύφθαι Sor.2.64.

**ὑποκούφιος** [ῠ], η, ον, *hidden under*, Nonn.*D.*29.107.

**ὑπόκρῠφος**, ον, = foreg., Sch.Ar.*Ach.*96.

**ὑποκρώζω**, *croak faintly*, as a sick person, Luc.*DMort.*6.4.

**ὑποκτῠπέω**, *crash*, Ael.*NA*3.13.

**ὑποκυάνεος**, ον, *rather dark-blue*, Alex.Mynd.ap.Sch.Theoc.5.96.

**ὑποκῠβερνάω**, *to be under-pilot*, νεώς of a ship, Poll.1.98.

**ὑποκῡδής**, ές, *covered with shoal-water*, εἱαμενή Euph.138, cf. Ctes. *Fr.*23, Din.*Fr.*17.6; ὑποκυδεῖς τίνες εἰσί; κοῖλοι τόποι *AB*312, cf. Harp.; ὑποκυδές· ὑποφρύδιον (leg. ὑποβρύχιον) Hsch.: perh. διακυδόμεναι is related.

**ὑποκύκλιος** (sc. πούς), ὁ, in metre, the *ionic a minore*, Sch.Heph. p.302 C., al.

**ὑπόκυκλος**, ον, *running on wheels*, τάλαρος Od.4.131. **II.** ὑπόκυκλον, τό, *ball on the foot of a tripod*, Hsch.

**ὑπόκῠλος**, ον, (κύλα) dub. sens., a term in carpentry, *Inscr.Délos* 504 *A* 10 (iii B.C.).

**ὑποκῡμαίνω**, *wave gently, ripple*, of sand, Philostr.*Im.*2.22; of the arms, ib.18: trans., τὰς [κόμας] ταῖς αὔραις ἀφῆκεν ὑποκυμαίνειν Him. *Or.*1.4.

**ὑποκῡμᾰτίζω**, *cause to surge*, τό τοι ῥόθιον τοῦτο πηγαὶ -ίζουσι ζέουσαι Philostr.*Im.*2.17. **II.** intr., dub. sens., of tunnies swimming in shoals, one above another, -ίζουσιν ἀλλήλοις ib.1.13.

**ὑποκύπτω**, *stoop under a yoke*, Μῆδοι ὑπέκυψαν Πέρσῃσι *bowed to the* Persian *yoke*, Hdt.1.130, cf. 6.25, 109; κύνες τοῖς ἀνθρώποις ὑποκύπτοντες Aesop.266: abs., of suppliants, *bow down, bow low*, ἱκετεύουσιν ὑποκύπτοντες Ar.*V.*555 (anap., where cod. R has ὑποπίπτοντες), cf. Luc.*Nav.*30, *Nigr.*21; so of animals drinking, ὑποκύψαντα..πιεῖν ὥσπερ βοῦν (v.l. ἐπικ-) X.*An.*4.5.32; of the victim at a sacrifice, θύεται δέ, αἲ μέγ κα ὑποκύψει, τᾷ Ἱστίᾳ prob. in *SIG*1025. 20 (Cos); also ὑ. ἐπὶ τὰ ὀπίσθια σκέλη Arist.*Mir.*831$^{a}$25; *stoop* to look at a thing, Plu.2.470e. **II.** c. acc., ὑ. τὰν τύλαν *stoop* it so as to let a load be put on, Ar.*Ach.*954.

**ὑποκυρτόομαι**, Pass., *to be* or *become somewhat curved*, Callisth.ap. Eust.918.40:—Act. in *Gloss.*

**ὑπόκυρτος**, ον, *gibbous, humped*, *Placit.*2.22.2, Dsc.3.158, v.l. in Hp.*Art.*54 (Comp.).

**ὑπόκῡφος**, ον, = ὑπόκυρτος, Str.6.1.12.

**ὑποκῡφώνιον**, τό, *part of a chariot* (v. κύφων I), Poll.1.143.

**ὑποκύω**, used only in Med. ὑποκύομαι, of the woman, *conceive, become pregnant*, ὑποκῡσᾰμένη Il.6.26, Od.11.254, Hes.*Th.*308; so of animals, Il.20.225.

**ὑποκωθωνίζομαι**, *indulge in deep potations*, Anon.ap.*An.Ox.*2.414.

**ὑποκώλιον**, τό, (κῶλον) *thigh* of an animal, in pl., X.*Cyn.*4.1, 5.10, Arr.*Cyn.*5.9.

**ὑποκωμῳδέω**, *play up* to a lead, Luc.*Tox.*14.

**ὑπόκωφος**, ον, *somewhat deaf, rather deaf*, Hp.*Coac.*172, Ar.*Eq.* 43, Pl.*Prt.*334d, *R.*488b. **II.** *absurd, foolish*, σφόδρα ὑπόκωφον προσπίπτειν ἔοικε (sc. the reading συναγείρεται in Il.15.680) Philem. Lex.ap.Porph.*ad Il.*p.287 S., cf. Phld.*Rh.*1.330 S.

**ὑπολάζυμαι**, = ὑπολαμβάνω, in Boeot. form οὐπολάδδουνθη, = ὑπολάζυνται, they *think, consider*, c. acc. et inf., *Supp.Epigr.*1.132.12 (Thespiae, ii B.C.).

**ὑπολαιμίζω**, *cut the throat*, Zonar.

**ὑπολᾱΐς**, ΐδος, ἡ, an unknown small bird, Arist.*HA*564$^{a}$2, cf. 592$^{b}$22 (v.l. ἐπιλαΐς), Thphr.*CP*2.17.9, Antig.*Mir.*100 (cj.), Hsch.; also **ὑποληΐς**, Id.

**ὑπολακτίζω**, *kick stealthily*, Luc.*Asin.*28.

**ὑπολᾰλέω**, *whisper*, τινί τι Apollod.*Poliorc.*137.4.

**ὑπολαμβάνω**, also **ὑπολάζυμαι** (q.v.), late Dor. 3 pl. fut. -λαμψοῦνται Anon.*Oxy.*410.99:—*take up by getting under*, as the dolphin did Arion, Hdt.1.24, Pl.*R.*453d; τοὺς νεοττοὺς ὑ. ἡ φήνη Arist.*HA*619$^{b}$ 34; τὸ κῦμα ὑ. τινά Clearch.73; νεφέλη ὑ. τινά *Act.Ap.*1.9. **b.** *bear up, support*, Hdt.4.72; ὑ. τοὺς ἐνδεεῖς Str.14.2.5, cf. D.S.19.67; ὑπέλαβές με πέμψας μοι τὰ κριθάρια *BGU*48.3 (ii/iii A.D.). **2.** *take up, seize* or *come suddenly upon*, ὑπὸ τρόμος ἔλλαβε γυῖα Il.3.34, Od.18.88; of a storm of wind, Hdt.4.179; of a fit of madness, Id. 6.75; of a pestilence, ib.27; of a river *taking up* earth thrown into it, Id.2.150; of winds *taking up* water, ib.25; of soldiers marching, δυσχωρία ὑπελάμβανεν αὐτούς, i.e. they came suddenly into difficult ground, X.*HG*3.5.20: abs., ὑπολαβὼν πυρετός Hp.*Epid.*5.20; of events, *follow next, come next*, ὑπέλαβε ναυμαχίη καρτερή Hdt.8.12, cf. 6.27. **3.** in discourse, *take up* what is said, *interpret* or *understand* it in a certain way, ταύτῃ ὑπολαμβάνεις ᾗ ἂν κακουργήσαις μάλιστα τὸν λόγον Pl.*R.*338d; ὃν μὴ σὺ φράζεις, πῶς ὑπολάβοιμ' ἂν λόγον; E. *IA*523, cf. Pl.*Euthd.*295c; ὑ. τι εἴς τινα *understand* it of, i.e. apply it to, him, Aeschin.1.157; ὥσπερ ὁ ἀκούων ὑ. Arist.*Rh.*1412$^{a}$30; *rejoin, retort*, Pl.*Lg.*875d, D.22.10, etc.; πρός τι Th.5.85; τι πρός τινας D.20.146, cf. 23.93; ὑ. τινὶ ὅτι.. Pl.*R.*598d; ὑ. ὡς.. X.*Ath.*3.12, etc.: c. acc. et inf., *reply that..*, Th.5.49; ὑπολαμβάνειν χρὴ εἰ.. *retort by asking* whether.., Lys.13.82: abs., in dialogue, ἔφη ὑπολαβών, ὑ. ἔφη, ὑ. εἶπεν, he said *in answer*, Pl.*R.*331d, Hdt.101, Th.3.113, etc. **b.** *take up, interrupt*, μεταξὺ ὑ. X.*An.*3.1.26; ἔτι λέγοντος αὐτοῦ ὑ. Id. *Cyr.*5.5.35. **4.** *take up* the conqueror, *fight with* him, Th.8.105. **5.** *take up* a charge, Id.6.28; ὑ. τὴν ἐπιθυμίαν τινός *take up and turn* it to their own use, Luc.*Cal.*17. **II.** = ὑποδέχομαι, *receive and protect*, ὁ Κῦρος ὑπολαβὼν τοὺς φεύγοντας (the exiles) X.*An.*1.1.7; *admit* a visitor, Pl.*Smp.*212d; of a doctor, *take in hand, treat* a patient, Hp. *Morb.*1.15 (Pass.). **2.** *accept* or *entertain* a proposal, Hdt.1.212, 3. 146; δυσχερῶς ὑ. D.57.35; μηδεὶς ὑπολάβῃ δυσκόλως ἐάν.. *take it amiss*, ib.59. **III.** *take up* a notion, *assume, suppose*, freq. of an ill-grounded opinion, ὑ. θεῖον εἶναι τὸ ἐπαγγελλόμενον Hdt.2.55; οὐκ ἂν ὑπέλαβον τοῦτον ἀντειπεῖν Antipho 3.3.2, cf. Pl.*Phd.*86b, *Prt.*343d; ἐὰν ὑπολάβῃ..Ἀθήνησιν εἶναι, ὢν ἐν Λιβύῃ Arist.*Metaph.*1010$^{b}$10: an Adv. is freq. added to give the word a good sense, ὀρθῶς ὑ. Pl.*Grg.* 458e, Arist.*EN*1145$^{b}$21, καλῶς Id.*Rh.*1404$^{a}$1, etc.; βέλτιον ὑπελάβομεν εἶναι πάλιν γράψαι *PCair.Zen.*36.15 (iii B.C.): with εἶναι omitted, *assume* or *understand* a thing to be so and so, τὰ φύματα τεχνικώτατον ὑπειληφέναι (sc. εἶναι) δεῖ δύνασθαι διαλύειν Hp.*Medic.* 10; τὸ χαλεπὸν κακὸν (sc. εἶναι) ὑ. Pl.*Prt.*341b; ὑ. τὸν Ἔρωτα ἕν τι τῶν ὄντων Id.*Phdr.*263d; ὑ. τι ὡς ὄν.. Id.*Prm.*134c; τὸν αἰθέρα τῇδέ πῃ ὑ. *conceive of* the word αἰθήρ somewhat in this way, Id.*Cra.* 410b; οὕτως ὑ. περί τινος Isoc.3.26, cf. D.18.269: simply c. acc., καίπερ ὑπειληφὼς ταῦτα though *I assume* this to be so, Id.19.3, cf. Arist.*Metaph.*1005$^{b}$26; τίς σε ἀναγκάσαι δύναται ὑπολαβεῖν τι ὧν οὐ θέλεις; Arr.*Epict.*2.6.21; ὃ βούλει, ὑπολάμβανε ib.1.10.4; ὑ. πλῆθος ὡρισμένον Arist.*Metaph.*1073$^{b}$13; ὑ. ὅτι.. Id.*Pol.*1301$^{a}$25:—Pass., τοιοῦτος ὑπολαμβάνομαι Isoc.12.5, cf. Arist.*Rh.*1366$^{a}$26; ὑ. μειζόνως ἢ κατὰ τὴν ἀξίαν Isoc.11.24, cf. D.23.6; ἡ ὑπειλημμένη ἀρετή Id.14. 1; ὅπως ποθ' ὑπείλημμαι περὶ τούτων ἀρκεῖ μοι I am content with whatever *opinion* of me *has been formed* in these matters, Id.18.269: c. inf., τῇ φιλανθρωπίᾳ ἣν ἔχειν ὑπείληψαι παρὰ τοῖς ἀνθρώποις Isoc. *Ep.*4.9, cf. Arist.*Rh.*1383$^{b}$8; ὑπολαμβάνεται δεδωκέναι *is understood* to have granted, Id.*SE*178$^{a}$20: τὸ ὑποληφθὲν πᾶν, = πᾶσα ὑπόληψις (II), Men.249.7. **2.** *suspect, disbelieve*, X.*Ages.*5.6, unless ὅ τι ὑπολαμβάνουσί τινες ταῦτα οὐκ ἀγνοῶ means 'I know how some people *regard* it'. **IV.** *draw away, seduce*, ὑ. μισθῷ μείζονι τοὺς ναυβάτας Th.1.121, cf. 143; Κέρκυραν ib.68. **2.** *take away, remove*, *seize*, τοῖς ἐπικούροις φράσας τὰ ὅπλα ὑπολαβεῖν ordering his body-guard to *remove* the arms (of the citizens), Id.6.58. 3. *receive*, ἀποτίσει..ὃ ὑπείληφεν..ἀργυρικὸν κεφάλαιον Mitteis*Chr.*220.21 (i A.D.), cf. *BGU*709.19 (ii A.D.). V. ὑ. ἵππον, as a term of horsemanship, *hold up* the horse, *check* him in his course, X.*Eq.*7.15, 9.5.

**ὑπολαμπ-άς**, άδος, ἡ, part of a στοά, possessing ἐπιστύλια, δοκοί, παραστάδες, a roof, and tiles, *Inscr.Délos* 366*A* 14. al., cf. 338*Ab*84 (iii B.C.); κλεῖθρον τῆς ὑ. ib.442*B*219 (ii B.C.); [Πτολεμαῖος] κατεῖδεν διά τινων ὑ. τοὺς Αἰγυπτίους παρὰ τὸν ποταμὸν ἀριστοποιουμένους Phylarch.40 J. **-ής**, ές, *shining with inferior lustre*, σάκος..ἠλέκτρῳ θ' ὑπολαμπὲς ἔην, χρυσῷ τε φαεινῷ λαμπόμενον Hes.*Sc.*142. **-ρος**, ον, *rather bright*, of stars in a constellation, Vett.Val.6.9. **-τειρα**· Ἑκάτη ἐν Μιλήτῳ, Hsch. **-ω**, *shine under*, ὁ ἥλιος εἰς τὰς παστάδας ὑ. X.*Mem.*3.8.9; ὑ. τὰ ὄμματα καθεύδοντος, of a lion, Plu.2.670c:—Med., τέφρῃ πῦρ ὑπολαμπόμενον *AP*12.80 (Mel.). II. *begin to shine*, ὡς τὸ ἔαρ ὑπέλαμπε Hdt.1.190, cf. Ael.*NA*8.22; ἕως ὑ. ib.10.50; ὑ. ἡ ἡμέρα Plu.*Ant.*49: metaph., ὑ. τὸ ἦθος ταῖς παρειαῖς Poll.2.87.

**ὑπόλαμψις**, εως, ἡ, *shiny appearance*, Hp.*Epid.*4.31; *gleam*, Thphr.*Sign.*53.

⊕ **ὑπολανθάνω**, *lie concealed under*, Ael.*VH*3.1, Lyd.*Ost.*9$^{b}$.

**ὑπολάπαρος** [λᾰ], ον, *somewhat flabby* or *loose*, Hp.*Epid.*1.26.β', al.

**ὑπολαπάσσω**, *empty from below*, *purge*, Ael.*NA*14.14, Phot.

**ὑπολέγω**, *dictate*, *prompt*, τισί τι Plu.2.46b. 2. *consider*, *take into account*, ὑ. εἰ.. D.C.54.15. 3. *take as a basis for*, τὰ ἔργα τοῖς λογισμοῖς Id.46.35.

**ὑπ-ολέθριος**, ον, *almost fatal*, *dangerous*, Hp.*Coac.*7.

⊕ **ὑπολείβω**, *pour libations*, A.*Ag.*69 (anap.):—Pass., *percolate*, *trickle down*, Hp.*Mul.*1.34, Nic.*Al.*24.

**ὑπόλειμμα**, ατος, τό, *remnant*, *remainder*, Hp.*Prorrh.*2.42, Arist.*HA*559$^{b}$21, *GA*744$^{b}$15,31, Thphr.*CP*1.11.3, al., Lxx 4*Ki.*21.14, al.

**ὑπολειπ-τέον**, *one must leave remaining*, Ph.1.184, Plu.2.813a. **-τικός**, ή, όν, *possessing direct motion only* (i.e. Eastward along the ecliptic), of the sun and moon, Adrastus ap.Theon.Sm.p.147 H.

**ὑπολείπω**, also **-λιμπάνω** (q.v.), *leave remaining*, ἅ ῥα τῇ προτέρῃ ὑπέλειπον ἔδοντες Od.16.50; ὑ. λόγον αὐτοῖς, ὡς..οἷοί τ' ἔσονται Th.8.2 (cf. infr. III); πολεμίους τινὰς ὑ. Id.6.17; τὸν πόλεμον τοῖς παισί Id.1.81; οὐδεμίαν ὑπερβολὴν ὑ. τινί *leave* him no possibility of exceeding, Isoc.6.105 (f.l. for κατα-); τοῖς ἔγγιστα τιμωρεῖσθαι ὑ. Antipho 4.4.11. 2. of things, *fail* one, ὑπολείψει ὑμᾶς ἡ μισθοφορά Lys.27.1 (ἐπι- Reiske, Hude), cf. Arr.*Ind.*26.9 (ἐπι- Ellendt); ὑ. τινὰ ὁ λόγος Gorg.17; ὑπολείποι γὰρ ἂν ὁ αἰὼν διαριθμοῦντα Arist.*Rh.*1374$^{a}$33; [τὰ ὕδατα] ὑ. τινάς Id.*Pol.*1330$^{b}$7. 3. intr., *fail*, *fall short*, θεοὶ..ὑπέλιπον οὐ πώποκα Epich.170.1; ὅταν ὑπολίπωσιν αἱ βάλανοι Arist.*HA*615$^{b}$22; ὑ. τὸ μέλι ib.626$^{b}$6; αἱ τρίχες Id.*GA*745$^{a}$15, cf. *PA* 650$^{a}$36 (c. dat.); ἡ φωνὴ ὑπολελοίπει *had ceased*, Hp.*Epid.*5.10, etc.: also, *fail in* what is expected of one, *come short*, Lys.31.4 (ὑπολίπωμαι codd.). II. Pass., c. fut. Med., *to be left remaining*, ἐν μεγάρῳ ὑπελείπετο *he was left behind*.., Od.7.230, cf. Hdt.1.105, 2.15,86; ἐγὼ δ' ὑπολείψομαι αὐτοῦ Od.17.276, 282, etc.; ὑπολειφθείς Hdt.5.61, 8.67, X.*HG*4.1.39, cf. Isoc.4.70. 2. of things, πέμπτον δ' ὑπελείπετ' ἄεθλον Il.23.615; ἐμοὶ δ' ἅπαξ ἀποφυγόντι ὁ αὐτὸς κίνδυνος ὑπολείπεται Antipho 5.16; μὴ ὑπολείπεσθαι [τοὺς νόμους], εἴ ποτε.. *so that they do* not *remain in force*, in case that.., Th.3.84; οὐδὲν ὑπολείπεται ἀλλ' ἤ.. Pl.*Phdr.*231b; μηκέτι ὑπολείπεσθαι αὐτοῖς περὶ μηθενὸς ἔνκλημα μηθέν *SIG*712.29 (Crete, ii B.C.). 3. c. gen., ὑπολείπεσθαι τοῦ στόλου *stay behind* the expedition, i.e. not to go upon it, Hdt.1.165, cf. A.*Ag.*73 (anap.). 4. *to be left behind* in a race, Ar.*Ra.*1092; *lag behind*, κατὰ τὴν ὁδὸν πορεύεσθαι -όμενον Pl.*Smp.*174d; of stragglers in an army, X.*An.*1.2.25, etc.; ὑ. μικρὸν τοῦ στόματος *fall behind* the front rank, ib.5.4.22 (s. v.l.); of fixed stars, *lie to the East* of a point in the celestial sphere, Hipparch.3.5.6, al.; of the apparent motion of planets, Arist.*Mete.*343$^{a}$24, al., cf. Epicur.*Ep.*2 p.53 U., Gem.12.22, Ptol.*Alm.*12.1, Theo Sm.p.147 H. 5. metaph., *to be inferior*, ταῖς ἡλικίαις τῶν πατέρων Arist.*Pol.*1334$^{b}$39, cf. 1254$^{b}$35. 6. abs., *fail*, *come to an end*, ὁπόταν..νὺξ ὑπολειφθῇ S.*El.*91 (anap.), cf. Arist.*Mete.*356$^{b}$5, al. III. Med., *leave behind one*, τὰ πρόβατα Hdt.4.121; μηδεμίαν τῶν νεῶν Id.6.7; ὑ. τούτων ὡς χιλίους *leaving* about 1000 of them *unburied*, Id.8.24; ὑπολείπεσθαι αἰτίαν, ὡς.. *to leave* cause for reproach *against oneself*, in thinking that.., Th.1.140 (v. sub init.); πόνους Isoc.9.45. 2. *retain*, [τοῦ ὕδατος] περὶ ἑωυτόν Hdt.2.25; δόρυ ἓν ὧν ἔσχον Arr.*Tact.*4.6, cf. 39.1; *reserve*, ἑαυτῷ ἑκατὸν ἅρματα Lxx 2*Ki.*8.4; σαυτῷ ταύτην τὴν ὅλυραν *PHib.*1.50.4 (iii B.C.); τὸν ὑπάρχοντα χόρτον τοῖς προβάτοις *PCair.Zen.*645.6 (iii B.C.); ὑπολιποῦ τόπον *leave* a space, ib.327.83 (iii B.C.): but in D.18.219 the Act. ὑπέλειπε..ἑαυτῷ..ἀναφοράν (*left* himself a means of escape) is the best reading. 3. *deduct* from a payment, *IG*7.3073.50,56 (Lebad., ii B.C.):—Pass., ib.58; ὑπολειπέσθω τῆς τιμῆς τὸ ὀφειλόμενον *Philol.*83.204 (Euboea, iii B.C.).

**ὑπολειτουργός**, ὁ, = λειτουργός IV, Herm.ap.Stob.1.21.9.

**ὑπόλειψις**, εως, ἡ, *failure*, *deficiency*, τοῦ θερμοῦ *Placit.*5.30.4; τῶν ὀδόντων Arist.*GA*745$^{a}$33. II. *falling behind*, in growth, Thphr.*CP*5.1.11. III. Astron., *direct motion*, i.e. Eastwards along the ecliptic, Gem.12.19, Ptol.*Alm.*1.8, 12.1, Theo Sm.p.147 H. 2. *occultation*, Iamb.*VP*6.31.

**ὑπόλεπρος**, ον, *somewhat rough*, *scaly*, Thphr.*HP*3.14.2.

**ὑπολεπτολόγος**, ον, *rather too subtle*, Cratin.307.

**ὑπόλεπτος**, ον, *somewhat thin*, ῥόος Aret.*SD*2.11, cf. Luc.*Philops.*34, Ael.*NA*16.15.

**ὑπολεπτύνω**, *make rather fine*, Tz.*H.*3.419.

**ὑπολευκ-αίνομαι**, Pass., *become white underneath* or *somewhat white*, Il.5.502, cf. Arat.927, Luc.*DMeretr.*11.3, etc. **-ανθίζω**, *become whitish on the surface*, Ruf.ap.Orib.8.24.64, Philum.*Ven.*35.2. **-ίζω**, = ὑπολευκαίνομαι, Sch.Pi.*O.*6.91. **-ος**, ον, *whitish*, Hp.*Epid.*3.14, Arist.*HA*526$^{a}$11, Sor.2.85, etc. **-όχρως**, ωτος, ὁ, ἡ, *of whitish skin* or *complexion*, Hp.*Epid.*1.19.

**ὑπολήγω**, *desist gradually*, Hp.*Epid.*1.22; κατὰ μικρὸν ὑ. Ael.*VH* 14.29; ὑ. τινός Id.*NA*12.44.

**ὑποληΐς**, v. ὑπολαΐς.

**ὑποληκάω**, in Hsch., = ὑποκρούω I.2 (sens. obsc.).

**ὑπόλημμα**, ατος, τό, *supposition*, Pl.*Def.*413b.

**ὑπόλημψις**, v. ὑπόληψις.

**ὑπολήνιον**, τό, *vessel placed under a press* to receive the wine or oil, *vat*, Lxx *Jl.*3(4).13, *Is.*16.10, *Ev.Marc.*12.1, Poll.10.130; dub. sens. in *POxy.*1735.5 (iv A.D.): as Adj., κρατῆρας -ίους dub. sens. in *OGI* 383.147 (Commagene, i B.C.).

**ὑποληνίς**, ίδος, ἡ, = ὑπολήνιον, Call.*Dian.*166.

**ὑπόληξις**, εως, ἡ, *tip* of a handle, Ath.11.491e.

**ὑποληπ-τέον**, (ὑπολαμβάνω) *one must suppose*, *understand*, *regard*, τἆλλα..τὸν αὐτὸν τρόπον ὑ. Pl.*Tht.*156e; οὕτως ὑ. περί τινος Id.*R.* 613a: c. inf., Arist.*PA*648$^{a}$14; τίνα..ἔχον δύναμιν αὐτὸ ὑ.; Pl.*Ti.* 49a. II. *one must answer*, Eust.1172.26. **-τικός**, ή, όν, *of* or *for understanding*, δύναμις ὑποληπτικὴ τινος Pl.*Def.*414c, cf. M.Ant.3.9. Adv. -κῶς Id.7.16. **-τός**, όν, = δοξαστός I, Arist.*APr.*49$^{b}$6, Simp. *in Epict.*p.8 D. II. *determinate*, χρόνοι Anon.Lond.3.19.

**ὑποληρέω**, *to be slightly imbecile*, Ael.*VH*3.37.

**ὑπολησμοσύνη**, ἡ, *forgetfulness*, *Srpska Kraljevska Akademija*, *Spomenik* 71.312 (Požarevatz).

**ὑποληψείδιον**, τό, *small assumption*, Arr.*Epict.*4.1.140.

⊕ **ὑπόληψις** (later -λημψις Anon. in *Tht.*3.14, etc., v. infr. II.3b), εως, ἡ, (ὑπολαμβάνω) *taking up*, esp. *taking up the cue*, *taking up the matter* where another leaves off, ἠνάγκασε τοὺς ῥαψῳδοὺς..ἐξ ὑπολήψεως ἐφεξῆς αὐτὰ διιέναι Pl.*Hipparch.*228b; cf. ὑποβολή I.3. 2. *rejoinder*, *reply*, ὑ. ποιεῖσθαι Isoc.11.30, cf. 12.150 (ἐπι- Cobet, Blass, in both places). II. *taking in a certain sense*, *assumption*, *notion*, Pl.*Def.*413a sq., Arist.*MM*1235$^{a}$20 (pl.); ὑ. λαμβάνειν Id.*Rh.*1417$^{b}$10; τῆς ὑπολήψεως διαφοραὶ ἐπιστήμη καὶ δόξα καὶ φρόνησις Id. *de An.* 427$^{b}$25; but distd. fr. νόησις, ib.$^{b}$17; fr. ἐπιστήμη, Id.*Top.*149$^{a}$10; joined with δόξα, Id.*EN*1139$^{b}$17, Epicur.*Fr.*239; ὑ. ψευδεῖς, μοχθηραί, Id.*Ep.*3 p.60 U., Phld.*Mus.*p.49 K.; μὴ τοιαύτης οὔσης τῆς ὑπαρχούσης ὑ. περὶ ἑκατέρου unless such had been the existing *impression*, D.18.228: Chrysipp. wrote περὶ ὑπολήψεως, *Stoic.*2.9; οἱ τῆς ἐναντίας ὑ. Sor.1.31. 2. *hasty judgement*, *prejudice*, *suspicion*, ὑ. εἰς τοὺς δικαστὰς οὐ δικαία Hyp.*Eux.*32, cf. Luc.*Cal.*5. 3. *estimate formed of* a person or thing, *good* or *bad reputation*, *public opinion*, Hdn.7.1.6; ἐν ὑπολήψει τυγχάνοντες being in *high repute*, Marcellin.*Puls.*118. b. *conceit*, πολλοὺς ἐπλάνησεν ἡ ὑπόλημψις αὐτῶν Lxx *Si.*3.24. 4. *estimate*, *plan*, Epict.*Ench.*1.1. III. perh. *subvention*, *subsidy*, *Sammelb.*7193$^{v}$ ii 14, al. (ii A.D.), *PTeb.*341.12 (ii A.D.). 2. ὑ. ἑτέρου ἐλαιουργίου perh. *taking over*, *BGU*612.7 (i A.D.). 3. perh. *payment in advance*, *PLond.*3.895.12 (i A.D.), *PRyl.*2.127.25 (i A.D.).

**ὑπολιγαίνω**, *make to sound a little*, κρουμάτιον Ach.Tat.1.5.

**ὑπ-ολίζων**, v. ὀλίγος VI.1.

**ὑπόλιθος**, ον, *stony*, γήδιον Luc.*Tim.*31, *Abd.*27.

**ὑπόλιμνος**, f.l. in Heraclit.*All.*65, where ὑπόλημνον codd. AG; the correction of G$^{1}$ ἀτύπωτος ὕλη μόνον ἦν should be accepted.

**ὑπολιμπάνω**, collat. form of ὑπολείπω, *leave behind*, 1*Ep.Pet.*2.21, Them.*Or.*10.139d. 2. Med., *leave over*, μὴ ὑπολιμπάνεσθε *leave* no *arrears* (uncollected), *PHib.*1.45.13 (iii B.C.); *reserve*, κερμάτιον εἰς τοὺς προστάντας τῆς σωτηρίας ἡμῶν *PSI*4.392.4 (iii B.C.). II. intr., *fail*, τὰ νάματα ὑ. D.H.1.23.

**ὑπολιμώδης**, ες, *somewhat hungry*, δεῖπνα Plu.2.643d.

**ὑπόλινον**· τὸ δρμινον, Hsch.

**ὑπολιπαίνω**, *anoint a little*, Hp.*Liqu.*3 (Pass.).

**ὑπολίπαρος** [ῐ], ον, *rather fat* or *greasy*, Dsc.2.83, Erot. s.v. νεφέλαι, prob. in *IG*5(1).364 (Sparta): *rather shiny*, Thphr.*HP*3.12.9; of the eyes in fever, Archig.ap.Orib.46.23.3.

**ὑπολιπής**, ές, *left remaining*, Thphr.*HP*3.13.2, Theopomp.Hist.101, Clearch.25. II. *deficient*, Brut.*Ep.*20: τὸ ὑ. the *deficit*, prob. in *Supp.Epigr.*2.580.15 (Teos, ii B.C.).

**ὑπ-ολισθάνω** and (later) **ὑπ-ολισθαίνω**, *slip* or *slide slightly*, Hp.*Art.*5, Poll.2.15: metaph., ὑ. εἰς ὕπνον Ael.*VH*2.35; εἰς τὰς τέρψεις Luc.*Dem.Enc.*12.

**ὑπόλισπος**, Att. **-λισφος**, ον, *flat underneath*, πυγίδια Ar.*Eq.*1368; τὰ ὑπὸ τῷ ἰσχίῳ μήτε ὑπόλισφα ἔστω μήτ' αὖ περιττά Philostr.*Gym.*35; of persons, *flat-hipped*, Poll.2.184, Phryn.*PS* p.117 B.; [παρθένοι] Ruf.ap.Orib.*inc.*2.24.

**ὑπόλιχνος**, ον, *somewhat lickerish* or *dainty*, Luc.*Icar.*29.

**ὑπολογ-έω**, *take account of*, τινος Arist.*Pol.*1325$^{a}$39 (cod.S$^{b}$, -ιεῖν cett.; ὑπόλογον ποιεῖσθαι Madvig). II. *deduct*, esp. from a sum due, ὑπολογεῖν αὐτοῖς τὰς ζημίας ἐκ τῶν μισθῶν *IG*12(9).207.73 (Eretria, iii B.C.), cf. *PCair.Zen.*257.12, 317.11, al. (iii B.C.), *PRev.Laws* 28.16 (iii B.C.), *PTeb.*61(*b*).391, 72.396 (ii B.C.): Poll.2.122 cites ὑπολογεῖν (dub. sens., v.l. ὑπολέγειν) from Theopomp.Com.96. ⊕ **-ή**, ἡ, = ὑπολογισμός, *BGU*422.5 (ii A.D.). II. *foundation*, τείχους *IG* 2$^{2}$.1672.8. **-ίζομαι**, *take into account*, *take account of*, ὑ. εἰς τὴν μίσθωσιν *put* the payment *to the account of*.., ib.2492.28:—Pass. in pass. sense, -ισθεισῶν τῶν γεγενημένων προσόδων *SIG*364.92 (Ephesus, iii B.C.); –ισθήσεται ἡ τιμὴ εἰς τὰς γινομένας ἀναφοράς *PRev. Laws* 34.9 (iii B.C.). 2. τὴν τιμὴν ἐκ τῶν ὀψωνίων ὑ. *deduct* the price from.., Plb.6.39.15: so in Act., Ptol.*Geog.*1.14.6, and Pass., ib.1.13.3. 3. metaph., *take into account*, κίνδυνον ὑ. τοῦ ζῆν ἢ τεθνάναι Pl.*Ap.*28b; τοὺς παρεληλυθότας πόνους Id.*Phdr.*231b; τὸ ἀλγεινόν Id.*Grg.*480c, cf. D.18.99,197; οὐδὲν ὑπελογίζοντο τὰς νίκας (sc. τοῦ Κίμωνος) And.4.33, cf. Din.1.5; μηδὲν ὑ. τὸ ξενικὸν [τῶν νόμων], ἂν βελτίους φαίνωνται Pl.*Lg.*702c; ὑ... εἰ ἀποθνῄσκειν δεῖ πρὸ τοῦ ἀδικεῖν Id.*Cri.*48d. **–ιμαῖος,** = *subditivus*, *Gloss.* **–ισμός,** ὁ, *consideration*, *reason*, Chrysipp.*Stoic.*3.173 (pl.); πονηροὺς ὑ. κατὰ μικρὸν ἐλάμβανον *became* gradually *demoralized*, D.H.15.3. **–ιστέον,** *one must take into account*, ὅτι.. Pl.*R.*341d: c. acc. et inf., Id.*Plt.*293d. **–ος,** ον, *held accountable* or *liable*, *Tab.Heracl.*1.138, dub. in Lys.30.15. Adv. **–γως** *responsibly*, *as a responsible person*, ὀμνύω *POxy.*87.14 (iv A.D.). 2. *reckoned to one's account*, either to one's credit or against one, οὐδέν σοι ὑ. τίθεμαι ἐάν.. Pl.*Prt.*349c, cf. D.36.48; οὐδὲ ἀδίκως τούτοις φημὶ ἂν εἶναι ὑ. τὴν ἐκείνων φυγήν Lys.28.13; μηδὲν τὴν ἡμετέραν ἡλικίαν ὑ. ποιούμενος Pl.*La.*189b. **–ος,** ὁ, *a taking into account*, *reckoning*, *account*, μηδένα ὑ. ποιεῖσθαί τινος D.25.66; ἐν ὑπολόγῳ τὰς προκλήσεις ποιεῖσθαι Lys.4.18; οὐχ ὑ. ποιεῖσθαί τινί τινος to give him no *credit for*.., Din.1.14; εἰς ὑ. λαμβάνειν τι Ath.4.145f; οὐδεὶς ὑ. γίγνεταί τινι Din.*Fr.*6.12; μὴ ἔστω ὑπόλογος τῇ πόλει τοῦτο τὸ ἀργύριον the city shall not take *credit for* this money, *IG*12(7).67*B*14 (Amorgos, iv/iii B.C.). 2. *deduction*, μηθένα ὑ. ποιούμενος ἀβρόχου taking no *account of*, i.e. making no *deduction for*.., *PHib.*1.85.24 (iii B.C.). 3. *what is deducted*, in gen. sg. ὑπολόγου, *subtract*, *minus*, Wilcken *Chr.*385.36 (iii B.C.); ἀπὸ τῆς ἀναφερομένης.. ἐν ὑπολόγῳ γῆς, i.e. unproductive land, the rent which it ought to have produced being *deducted* from the general revenue, *PTeb.*10.4, al. (ii B.C.); ὑπόλογος κουρεῖ *deduction* for barber, *PCair.Zen.*176.219 (iii B.C.), cf. 320.6 (iii B.C.); ἀνυπόλογα παντὸς ὑπολόγου free from any *deduction*, ib.371.7 (iii B.C.). II. the converse of πρόλογος, *the consequent in a ratio in which the former number is the smaller*, as 5 in $\frac{3}{5}$, Nicom.*Ar.*1.19, Dam.*Pr.*374; but simply the *second-named term in a ratio*, Mich. *in EN*16.14.

**ὑπολοιπ-άς,** άδος, ἡ, *remainder*, τοῦ οἴνου *POxy.*1223.29 (iv A.D.). **–ος,** ον, *left over*, μετὰ τῶν ὑ. with the *survivors* or *remaining descendants*, Hdt.7.171; τοὺς ὑ. Πεισιστρατιδέων Id.6.123. 2. of things, = λοιπός, ὑ. τὸ βάραθρόν σοι γίγνεται still *remains* for you, Ar.*Pl.*431; τί ὑμῖν ὑπόλοιπόν ἐστι τῆς ἐκείνων ἀρετῆς; And.1.109; τὸ ὑ. *the residue*, Pl.*R.*427e, *POxy.*$1252^{v}$.36 (iii A.D.), etc.; ὅσα ἦν ὑ. all that *remained to be done*, Th.4.90; τῆς ὑ. Ἀθηναίων καταλύσεως what *remained to effect* their destruction, Id.8.26; ἔστι δ' ἡ ἐνέργεια ἐν ταῖς ἐπιθυμίαις τῆς ὑπολοίπου ἕξεως καὶ φύσεως, i.e. the pleasure declared to be a γένεσις εἰς φύσιν is really the ἐνέργεια of the healthy *remainder* of the organism, Arist.*EN*$1152^{b}$35; ἡ ὑ. ἰσημερία the *other* equinox, Gal.17(1).15. (In codd. ὑπό- and ἐπί-λοιπος are often interchanged.)

**ὑπόλοξ-ος,** ον, *somewhat oblique* or *obscure*, Eust.805.3. Adv. **–ξως** *obliquely*, Sor.*Fract.*10. **–όω,** *turn somewhat obliquely*, τὰς ὄψεις Phlp.*in Mete.*85.23; *express somewhat ambiguously*, τὴν ἔννοιαν Eust.777.41.

**ὑπολοπάω,** *peel*, *lose the bark*, cj. Schneid. in Thphr.*HP*5.1.4.

**ὑπολόχᾱγος,** ὁ, *under*-λοχαγός, X.*An.*5.2.13.

**ὑπολοχάω,** *lie in ambush for*, τινας J.*BJ*6.7.2.

**ὑπολῡγίζομαι,** Pass., *to be concealed*, *EM*571.24.

**ὑπολύδιος** [ῡ], ον, *hypo-Lydian*, τόνος Plu.2.1141b; διὰ πασῶν Cleonid.*Harm.*9; τρόπος Alyp.*Diat.*2.

**ὑπολύζω,** *hiccup*, *sob a little*, Gal.19.80.

**ὑπολῡπέομαι,** *to be grieved at heart*, Lxx 2*Ma.*4.37.

⊛ **ὑπολύριος** [ῠ], ον, (λύρα) *under the lyre*, δόναξ ὑ. a *cross reed to which* (in early lyres) *the lower ends of the strings were attached*, Ar.*Ra.*233, cf. Poll.4.62.

**ὑπόλῠσις,** εως, ἡ, *relaxing underneath*, γονάτων Lxx *Na.*2.11, Aret.*SD*2.9.

**ὑπολυσσάω,** Ion. **–έω,** *have a kind of madness*, Hp.*Hebd.*51.

**ὑπόλυσσον,** τό, = ἀρτεμισία, Ps.-Dsc.3.113.

**ὑπολύχνιον,** τό, *lamp-stand*, *POxy.*1645.10 (iv A.D.).

**ὑπολύω,** *loosen beneath* or *below*, ὑπέλυσε δὲ γυῖα *made* his limbs *give way under him* (by giving him a deadly wound), Il.15.581; πολλῶν ἀνδρῶν ὑπὸ γούνατ' ἔλυσε Od.14.236; ὑπέλυσε μένος καὶ φαίδιμα γυῖα *made* courage and strength *fail*, Il.6.27; of wrestlers, ὑπέλυσε δὲ γυῖα 23.726:—Pass., ὑπέλυντο δὲ γυῖα 16.341; λύθεν δ' ὑπὸ φαίδιμα γυῖα ib.805; ὑπολύεταί μου τὰ γόνατα Ar.*Lys.*216. II. *loose from under* the yoke, ὁ δ' ἔλυεν ὑφ' ἵππους Il.23.513, cf. Od.4.39; ὑ. ζεύγη βοεικά Th.4.128; *loose from under* the sheep, ἑταίρους Od.9.463:—Med., σὺ τόν γ'.. ὑπελύσαο δεσμῶν thou *didst set* him *free* from bonds, Il.1.401. 2. *untie* a person's sandals *from under* his feet, *take off* his shoes, ὑπαί τις ἀρβύλας λύοι A.*Ag.*944; τὰς Περσικάς Ar.*Nu.*152, cf. *Th.*1183:—Med., *take off one's own* sandals or shoes, or *have* them *taken off*, τὰς ἐμβάδας Id.*V.*1157 (prob. cj. for ὑποδύου): abs., ὑπολύεσθαι, opp. ὑποδεῖσθαι, Id.*Lys.*950, *Pl.*927, cf. X.*An.*4.5.13:—also b. c. acc. pers., ὑ. τινά *unshoe* him, *take off his shoes*, οὐχ ὑπολύσεις αὐτόν; Pherecr.153.6 (hex.); ὑπολύετε, παῖδες, Ἀλκιβιάδην Pl.*Smp.*213b. 3. Med., *disarm oneself*, Ael.*VH*14.48 (v.l. ἀπελύσατο). III. Pass., *to be released*, of mortgaged properties or pledges, *AJP*56.375 (Colophon, iv B.C.).

**ὑπολωπάω,** f.l. in Heraclit.*All.*70, where Κύκλωψ is called ὁ τοὺς λογισμοὺς ὑπολωπῶν (v.l. ὑποσυλῶν: ὑποκλωπῶν cj. Hase).

**ὑπολωφάω,** *abate*, intr., Eust.45.18.

**ὑπομάζιος,** ον, *under the breast*, *sucking*, μηδ' αὐτῶν τῶν ὑπομαζίων φειδόμενοι D.S.34.2; also as v.l. for ὑπομάσθιος (q.v.). II. τὸ ὑ. *waist-band*, ἄλλην τε πολλὴν περιέκειτο φλυαρίαν ὑπομάζιόν τε καὶ ἀμφωλένιον Aristaenet.1.25 (unless Adj. with φλυαρίαν).

**ὑπόμαζος,** ον, *under the breast*, f.l. for ὑπέρμαζος in Paul.Aeg.6.44.

**ὑπομαίνομαι,** Pass., *to be somewhat mad*, Hp.*Vict.*1.35, Men.*Epit.*457.

**ὑπόμακρος,** ον, *longish*, ῥάβδος Ar.*Pax*1243; πρόσωπον Arist.*Phgn.*$807^{b}$26, cf. Alex.333; ἔντασις Hp.*Prorrh.*1.144; φλεγμονή Gal.16.808: cf. ἐπίμακρος.

**ὑπομᾰλᾰκ-ίζομαι,** Pass., *grow cowardly by degrees*, X.*An.*2.1.14. ⊛**–ος,** ον, *somewhat soft*, Ptol.*Tetr.*166.

**ὑπομᾰλάσσω,** Att. **–ττω,** *soften by degrees* or *gently*, φύλλον Aristaenet.1.3; ὑ. τὴν κοιλίαν *relax*, Dsc.5.7:—Pass., *to be gradually softened*, Luc.*DMeretr.*4.2.

**ὑπομᾰνιώδης,** ες, *somewhat mad*, Sch.Ar.*Av.*989.

**ὑπομαντεύομαι,** *divine partly*, τὴν διάνοιάν τινος Pl.*Sis.*388b; *hint prophetically*, ὡς.. Eust.777.49.

**ὑπομᾰραίνομαι,** Pass., *wither* or *waste gradually*, Ph.2.252, Plu.2.411e, Ptol.*Tetr.*101.

**ὑπόμαργος,** ον, *somewhat mad*, *crazy*, only in Comp. ὑπομαργότερος, Hdt.3.29,145, 6.75, D.H.3.2, App.*BC*5.49.

**ὑπομαρμαίρω,** *gleam under*, Opp.*C.*3.70 (nisi lg. ὕπο μαρμ–).

⊛ **ὑπομαρτῠρέω,** in Pass., *receive testimony*, ἐπὶ τῇ σεμνότητι τοῦ βίου *CIG*4415 (Cilicia).

**ὑπομάσθιος,** ον, (μασθός) = ὑπομάζιος, Conon 44, Lxx 3*Ma.*3.27, J.*BJ*6.3.4. (–μάσθιος cod. R, –μαστιαιος cod. A, Lxx l.c.; –μάστιος and –μάζιος vv. ll. in J. l.c.; –μάζιον v.l. in Conon l.c.: [ὑπο]μάστιος occurs in *IG*12(7).53.6 (Amorgos, iii A.D.).)

**ὑπομάσσω,** Att. **–ττω,** *smear* or *rub underneath*, Theoc.2.59; ὑπομεμαγμένος *lying close under*, ταῖς πέτραις Anon.ap.Suid.

**ὑπομάστιος,** v. ὑπομάσθιος.

**ὑπόμαστρος,** ον, = ὑπεύθυνος, ἔστωσαν ὑπόμαστροι.. διπλασίου *IG*5(1).1390.51 (Andania, i B.C.).

**ὑπομάσχᾰλος,** ον, *under the arm-pits*: τὸ ὑ. perh. *a wallet slung under the arm*, *POxy.*1923.4 (v/vi A.D.), *Gloss.*

**ὑπόμαυρος,** ον, *somewhat dark* or *gloomy*, *Gloss.*

⊛ **ὕπ-ομβρος,** ον, *mixed with rain*, θέρος ὕ. a *rainy* summer, Plu.*Cam.*3 (as v.l. for ἔπομβρον); ἔαρ *Gp.*1.12.21; νύξ *EM*450.49; γῆ Philostr.*Im.*1.9, cf. Ph.*Bel.*82.28, 97.27; *impregnated*, ἀσφάλτῳ Philostr.*VA*1.24. II. ὕπομβρον ὀστέον Hp.ap.Erot., who explains it as ὑπόνομον καὶ κάθυγρον γεγονός, and ap.Gal.19.149, who says ὕφυγρον, ὑπόπυον, where the reference is to Hp.*VC*15; μόλις ὕπομβρον γενόμενον καὶ κατακλυσθὲν τὸ ἱερεῖον apparently *drenched*, as t.t. in divination, Plu.2.438a.

**ὑπομεθύω,** *to be somewhat drunk*, Hsch. s.v. βεβρεγμένος.

**ὑπόμειγμα,** ατος, τό, *mixture*, Plu.2.934d.

**ὑπομείγνυμι,** *mix in*, *add by mixing*, ζύμωμά τισι Pl.*Ti.*74d, cf. 71b; τὸ ὑπομεμιγμένον τῆς λύπης the *admixture*, Id.*Phlb.*47a. II. intr. and metaph., *come near secretly*, ὑπὸ τῇ Χερσονήσῳ Th.8.102.

**ὑπομειδιάω,** *smile a little* or *gently*, *Anacreont.*$27^{A}$.14, Phld.*Vit.*p.31 J., Plu.*Dio*20, Hld.7.10, Alciphr.3.3, etc.; ὑ. σαρδάνιον Plb.18.7.6.

**ὑπομειόομαι,** Pass., *to be diminished a little* or *gradually*, Gal.19.375.

**ὑπομείων,** ον, gen. ονος, *inferior*:—ὑπομείονες, among the Spartans, were *citizens of inferior right*, opp. ὅμοιοι, X.*HG*3.3.6; in an army, οἱ ὑ. *the subaltern officers*, D.C.38.35.

**ὑπομέλαθρα·** Ἀρτέμιδος ἐπίθετον, ὡς ὁ Μύνδιος (i.e. Alex.Mynd.), Hsch.

**ὑπομελαίνω,** *to be blackish*, Ruf.ap.Orib.7.26.15, *Gp.*15.2.16. 2. *make blackish*, of hair-dye, Crito ap.Gal.12.436.

**ὑπομελανδρῠώδης,** ες, *somewhat like the* μελάνδρυον, Epich.102 (–μαλ– Hsch.).

**ὑπομελᾰν-ίζω,** = ὑπομελαίνω I, Gal.16.763, Aret.*SA*1.8, *SD*1.10. **–όω,** *make rather black*, [κύων] γηράσκων ὑπομελανοῖ τοὺς ὀδόντας Ar.Byz.*Epit.*78.10.

**ὑπομέλᾱς,** μέλαινα, μέλᾰν, *blackish*, Hp.*Epid.*1.26.β', Gal.16.714, Aret.*SD*1.15.

**ὑπομέμφομαι,** *blame a little* or *secretly*, Plu.*Cat.Mi.*15, Nonn.*D.*15.289, etc.

**ὑπομεμψίμοιρος** [ῐ], ον, *querulous*, Cic.*Att.*6.1.2.

**ὑπομενε-τέον,** (ὑπομένω) *one must sustain*, *abide*, *endure*, Th.2.88, Isoc.6.7, Pl.*Lg.*770e, Arist.*EN*$1110^{a}$30; –μενετέα Zeno *Stoic.*1.49, Cleanth.ib.129, cf. *Stoic.*3.22,64,72.—The form **ὑπομενητέον** is v.l. in Isoc. l.c., etc.; **ὑπομονητέος** occurs (with vv. ll.) in D.L.7.126. **–τικός,** ή, όν, *disposed to undergo*, *patient of*, τῶν δεινῶν Arist.*EN*$1115^{a}$25 (Comp.); κινδύνων Id.*EE*$1232^{a}$26; πρὸς λύπας ib.$1229^{b}$5. 2. *obstinate*, διδασκαλίαι Demetr.Lac.*Herc.*1012.47. Codd. also have **ὑπομενητικός** or **–μονητικός,** Hp.*Decent.*3, Pl.*Def.*412b,416a, Arist.*VV*$1250^{b}$14, Chrysipp.*Stoic.*3.125, Andronic.Rhod. p.576 M., Hierocl. *in CA*7 p.429 M. Adv. **–κῶς** *Stoic.*3.72. **–τός,** ή, όν, *endurable*, ib.22.

**ὑπομενητός,** ή, όν, *endurable*, Phld.*Ir.*p.80 W., J.*AJ*17.6.5 (with v.l. –μονητός), cf. Hdn.*Epim.*141 (–μον–).

⊛ **ὑπομένω,** fut. –μενῶ cj. in Epicur.*Ep.*1 p.7 U.:—*stay behind*, Od.10.232, 258, Th.5.14, Lys.13.12, etc.; ἐν Σπάρτῃ Hdt.6.51, 7.209; ὑπομεινον ἕως ἂν παραγένηται *PSI*4.322.4 (iii B.C.): also, *remain alive*, Hdt.4.149: of things, *to be left behind, remain*, ὑπέμεινε τὸ παχύτερον Gal.7.664, cf. Sor.1.88, al.: generally, *to be permanent*, Arist.*Cat.* 5$^a$28. II. trans., 1. c. acc. pers., *abide* or *await* another, διὰ τοῦτό σε οὐχ ὑπέμενον X.*An.*4.1.21; esp. *await* his attack, *bide* the onset, Il.14.488, 16.814, al., Hdt.3.9, 4.3, al., App.*BC*5.81; ὑ. τὰς Σειρῆνας *abide* their *presence*, X.*Mem.*2.6.31; of evils, κακῶν ὅσα ἡμᾶς ἐν ὑστέρῳ χρόνῳ ὑ. Pl.*Phdr.*250c, cf. Plb.1.81.3. 2. c. acc. rei, *to be patient under, abide patiently, submit to* any evil that threatens one, δουλείαν Th.1.8; πόνον X.*Mem.*2.1.3; ἀλγηδόνα Pl. *Grg.*478c; αἰσχρόν τι Id.*Ap.*28c, cf. *Ti.*49e; δούλειον ζυγόν Id.*Lg.* 770e; τοὺς ἄλλους λόγους Isoc.8.65; *face*, τὴν μέλλουσαν δουλητὴν Hdt. 6.12; τὸ ἀγώνισμα τόλμης δεῖται τὸν κίνδυνον ὑπομεῖναι Gorg.8, cf. Isoc. 6.70; ἀπειλάς D.21.3; *face up to*, λόγον Pl.*Hp.Ma.*298d; οὐχ ὑπέμειναν τὰς δωρεάς they *could* not *abide* the gifts, i.e. scorned to accept them, Isoc.4.94; ὑ. τὴν κρίσιν *await* one's trial, Aeschin.2.6, cf. And.1.121, Lys.20.6: generally, *wait for*, τὴν ἑορτήν Th.5.50; μακρὸν οὐχ ὑπέμεινεν ὄλβον *could* not *endure* his great bliss, i.e. it turned his head, Pi.*P.*2.26. 3. abs., *stand one's ground, stand firm*, Il.5.498, 15.312, Hdt.6.96; ἐς ἀλκὴν ὑ. Th.3.108; ἐς χεῖρας Id.5.72; ἀνδρικῶς ὑ. Pl.*Tht.*177b; ὑπομένων καρτερεῖν endure *patiently*, Id.*Grg.*507b; ὑ. καὶ καρτερεῖν Id.*La.*193a. 4. c. inf., *submit, bear*, or *dare* to do a thing, *wait* to do, οὐδ' ὑπέμεινε γνώμεναι *he did* not *wait* for us to know him, Od.1.410; ὑ. πονεῖν he *submitted* to toil, X.*Mem.*2.2.5, cf. 2.7.11, Pl.*Lg.*869c, D.18.204, *PCair.Zen.*8.22 (iii B.C.), Phld.*Ir.* p.46 W., etc.; ἀξιωθεὶς ὑπέμεινε γυμνασιαρχῆσαι *IG*12(3).331.16 (Thera, iii/ii B.C.). 5. with part. relating to the subject, εἰ ὑπομενέουσι χεῖρας ἐμοὶ ἀνταειρόμενοι if they *shall dare* to lift hand against me, Hdt.7.101, cf. 209; ὑπομένεις με κηδεύων you *persist* in.., S.*OT* 1323 (lyr.); οὐχ ὑπομένει ὠφελούμενος he *submits* not to be helped, Pl.*Grg.*505c; πολύποδες ὑ. τεμνόμενοι Arist.*HA*534$^b$28. 6. with part. relating to the object, ὑ. Ξέρξην ἐπιόντα *await* his coming, Hdt. 7.120, cf. Pl.*Phd.*104c, *Mx.*241a; οὐ.. γὰρ ἀπ' αὐτοῦ χωριζόμενον τὸ βρέφος ὑπέμενεν (sc. τὸ θηρίον) *it* (the elephant) *could* not *bear* the infant's being removed, Phylarch.36 J.: c. gen. part., φιλοῦντος ὑ. *submit* to his kissing, Ael.*VH*12.1. 7. in App.*BC*5.54, ὑ. τῇ Ἀντωνίου γνώμῃ is prob. f.l. for ἐπιμεμενηκώς. 8. *promise*, c. fut. inf., Iamb.*VP*8.36. 9. *admit of*, like δέχομαι III. 3, D.H.*Isoc.*2; φοινίκων βάλανοι αἱ κατὰ τὴν Ἀλεξάνδρειαν.. οὐδὲ τὴν ἀπόθεσιν ὑπομένουσιν Gal.*Vict.Att.*12. 10. τὴν ναυτίαν οὐχ ὑπομένουσιν *do* not *suffer from* seasickness, Sor.1.49; ἀλλοκότους φαντασίας τῆς ψυχῆς ὑπομενούσης *experiencing*, ib.39, cf. 31, al.; ὅταν ἔμφραξιν ὑπομένῃ ὁ πόρος χωρὶς αἰτίας *undergoes* obstruction, Aët.7.50.

**ὑπομερισμός**, ὁ, *subdivision*, Nicom.*Ar.*1.8. 2. Astrol., = διαίρεσις τῆς χρονοκρατορίας Heph.Astr.2.27 bis. II. a figure in Rhetoric, = ὑποδιαίρεσις, Hermog.*Inv.*3.15.

**ὑπόμεστος**, ον, *rather full*, ἀργυρίου Ph.2.67; βιβλιδίων Eun.*VS* p.471 B.

**ὑπομεταφέρομαι**, Pass., *slip gradually into*, ὑπὲρ τοῦ μὴ ῥᾳδίως εἰς νόσους -εσθαι τὸ σῶμα Gal.6.40 (v.l. ὑποφέρεσθαι).

**ὑπομετέωρος**, ον, *slightly wanting support*, of a limb unevenly bandaged, Hp.*Fract.*23.

⊕ **ὑπομήκης**, ες, gen. εος, = ὑπόμακρος, Hero *Aut.*30.3, Sor.1.12, D.L.7.1; φύλλα Dsc.4.119: Comp., Arist.*Fr.*339, Dsc.3.106.

**ὑπομηκύνω**, *lengthen somewhat*, τὰ κέρα Agath.2.9.

**ὑπομηλᾰφάω**, *probe to the bottom, probe thoroughly*, Hsch., Phot., *EM*783.12.

**ὑπομηλίζω**, *to be* or *look yellowish*, τῇ χρόᾳ Dsc.3.68.

**ὑπομήλινος**, ον, *yellowish*, Dsc.3.69.

⊕ **ὑπομηλίς**, ίδος, ἡ, *Eastern Thorn, Crataegus orientalis*, Pallad. *Agric.*13.4.

**ὑπομήρια**, = *intertrigines, Gloss.*

**ὑπομήτριος**, ον, *in the mother's womb*, Max.186.

**ὑπομίᾰρος** [ῐ], ον, of a word, *unclassical*, Poll.9.143.

**ὑπομιλτόομαι**, Pass., *to be covered with ruddle*, Sch.Od.5.245.

**ὑπομῑμέομαι**, *imitate a little*, f.l. in D.S.13.95 (Reiske ἀπομιμ-).

⊕ **ὑπομιμνήσκω** (not -μιμνῄσκω, cf. *PCair.Zen.*15$^v$.35 (iii B.C.), Phld.*Ir.*p.63 W.), fut. ὑπομνήσω, aor. ὑπέμνησα: I. Act., 1. c. acc. pers., *put* one *in mind* or *remind* one of, ὑπέμνησέν τέ ἑ πατρός Od.1.321, cf. 15.3, Th.6.19; also ὑ. τοὺς Ἀθηναίους τάδε Id. 7.64, cf. X.*Cyr.*3.3.37, Pl.*Criti.*108a, etc.; ὑ. ἡμᾶς τί βούλει δηλοῦν.. Id.*Phlb.*31c; τὸν εἰδότα περί τινος Id.*Phdr.*275d; τινὰ ὅτι.. Id. *Phd.*88d; πῶς Id.*Phdr.*277b; ὑ. τινά *put* him *in mind*, Id.*La.*181c; ἐὰν.. σεαυτὸν ὡς ἄνθρωπος ὢν ὑπομιμνήσκῃς Isoc.1.21. 2. *bring to one's mind, mention, suggest*, c. acc., Hdt.7.171, 9.6, S.*Ph.*1170 (lyr.), Pl. *Phdr.*241a, etc.; ὅτι.. Phld.l.c. b. Medic., *provoke* a dormant process, τὴν ἔκκρισιν Sor.2.59; αἱμορροΐδας ἢ ἔμμηνα γυναιξὶν Aët.3.136; cf. ὑπομνηστέον 3. 3. c. gen. rei, *make mention of*, πατρίδος τῆς ἐλευθερωτάτης Th.7.69, cf. Aeschin.3.156, Theoc.21.50. 4. c. acc. cogn., ἀληθῆ ὑ. Pl.*R.*427e: abs., καλῶς, ὀρθῶς ὑπέμνησας, Id.*Phdr.* 266d, *Tht.*187e; ἀναστὰς ὑπομνησάτω *let him* get up and *remind* me, And.1.70; ὑ. ὅτι.. *suggest* that.., Pl.*R.*452c, etc. II. Pass. or Med., fut. -μνησθήσομαι Phld.*Sign.*27:—*call to mind, remember*, τι Pl.*Phlb.*47e, *La.*188a, X.*Cyr.*6.1.24, etc.; τινων Luc.*Cat.*4. 2. *make mention*, περί τινος A.*Pers.*329; ὡς ὑπέμνησται as *has been observed* above, Procl.*in Prm.*p.657 S. (v.l. ὑπομέμνησται).

**ὑπόμισθ-ος**, ον, *serving for pay, hired*, of persons, Luc.*Merc.Cond.* 53 ὑ. ὀβολῶν δ' *hired for* 4 obols, Id.*Tim.*6. 2. ὑ. ἔργον *farmed out*, Id.*Alex.*49. **-ωσις**, εως, ἡ, *sub-lease*, *CPR*244.5 (iii A.D.). **-ωτής**, οῦ, ὁ, *sub-lessee*, *BGU*512.19, 1047 iv 5,17 (both ii A.D.), *CPR*243.8,20 (iii A.D.).

**ὑπομνάομαι** [ᾰ], *court clandestinely*, ζώοντος ὑπεμνάασθε (impf.) γυναῖκα Od.22.38.

**ὑπομνεία**, ἡ, *remembrance*, ὑπομνείας χάριν *CIG*2032 (Thrace).

⊕ **ὑπόμνημα**, ατος, τό, *reminder, memorial*, ἔχειν ὑπομνήματά τινος Th.2.44; ἵν' ὑ. τοῖς ἐπιγιγνομένοις ᾖ τῆς τῶν βαρβάρων ἀσεβείας Isoc. 4.156, cf. 73; τῆς ἀρετῆς ὑ. μᾶλλον ἢ τοῦ σώματος καταλιπεῖν Id. 2.36, cf. D.23.210; τοιούτοις χρώμενος ὑπομνήμασιν such *means of remembrance*, Pl.*Phdr.*249c; freq. in Inscrr., e.g. ὅπως ὑ. τῆς ἡμέρας ταύτης ᾖ,.. στεφανηφορεῖν Ἐρετριεῖς πάντας *IG*12(9).192.5 (Eretria, iv B.C.); ἀνθέμεν ὑν ἀργύρεον ὑπόμνᾱμα τᾶς ἀμαθίας ib.4$^2$ (1).121.39 (Epid., iv B.C.). 2. *tomb*, *Ath.Mitt.*29.294, al. (Mysia). II. *reminder, mention*, in a speech, Th.4.126; in a letter, X.*An.*1.6.3; esp. *written reminder, memorandum*, ὑ. Ζήνωνι παρὰ Διονυσίου, τῷ φέροντί σοι τὸ ὑ., *PCair.Zen.*307.1,19 (iii B.C.), cf. 301.1, al. (iii B.C.). 2. *note* or *memorandum* entered by a tradesman in his day-book, ὑπόμνημα ἀπεγράψατο he had a *note* made of it, D.49.30, cf. 28.6; of bankers, εἰώθασιν ὑπομνήματα γράφεσθαι ὧν διδόασι χρημάτων.. Id.49.5. 3. mostly in pl., *memoranda, notes*, Hp.*Art.*34 (but prob. a gloss), Pl.*Phdr.*276d; ὑ. γράφειν, γράψασθαι, Id.*Plt.*295c, *Tht.*143a. 4. *minutes* of the proceedings of a public body, *public records*, τὰ κατ' ἄρχοντας ὑ. Plu.2. 867a, cf. D.S.1.4, Luc.*Dem.Enc.*26, etc.; τὰ τῆς βουλῆς ὑ. the *acts* of the Senate, D.C.78.22; ἐπὶ τῶν ὑ. τῆς συγκλήτου, = Lat. *a commentariis*, *IG*4.588 (Argos, ii A.D.), 5(1).533 (Sparta, ii A.D.); ἐπὶ τῶν ὑ. καταστῆσαί τινα J.*AJ*7.5.4, cf. Lxx 2*Ki.*8.16 (quoted by J. l. c.); *records* of a magistrate, *POxy.*1252$^r$.26 (iii A.D.), etc.; including his *decisions*, Mitteis *Chr.*372 iv 20 (ii A.D.), *POxy.*911.8 (iii A.D.), etc. 5. *dissertations* or *treatises* written by philosophers, rhetoricians, and artists, Archyt.ap.D.L.8.80 sq., Sotad.Com.1.35, Demetr.Lac.*Herc.*1014.67, Longin.44.12, D.L.4.4; of historical or geographical works, Plb.1.1.1, 1.35.6, 3.32.4, Ptol.*Geog.*1.6.2, etc.; of medical works, Gal.6.460,691, al. (the same work is called ὑ. and σύγγραμμα in 15.1). b. *division, section*, 'book' of such a treatise, Phld.*Mus.*p.92 K., *Po.*5.26, *PMed.* in *Arch.Pap.*4.270. c. *explanatory notes, commentaries*, Sch.Ar.*Av.*1242, etc.; of the Homeric *commentaries* of Aristarch., Sch.Il.2.420, al.; εἰ γὰρ τὰ συγγράμματα (Aristarchus' independent treatises on Homeric questions) τῶν ὑπομνημάτων προτάττοιμεν.. Did.ap.Sch.Il.2.111; so Gal. distinguishes ὑπομνήματα (clinical *notes*) from συγγράμματα of Hippocrates, 16.532,543; and the συγγράμματα of Hp. from his own *commentaries* (ὑπομνήματα) on them, ib.811; *commentary*, οὕτω Θέων ἐν ὑ. τῷ εἰς Θεόκριτον *Et.Gud.d.* s.v. γρῖπος. III. *draft* or *copy* of a letter, Pl.*Ep.*363e. IV. *memorial, petition*, addressed to a magistrate, whereas the ἔντευξις 4 is in form addressed to the king, *IG*12(3).327.4 (Egypt, iii B.C.), *BGU*1007.1 (iii B.C.), *PTeb.* 30.10, al. (ii B.C.), *UPZ*23.2, 28.3 (ii B.C.), etc. 2. *notification*, e.g. of birth, *PFay.*28.12 (ii A.D.); of removal, *POxy.*251.29 (i A.D.), etc.

⊕ **ὑπομνημᾰτ-ίζομαι**, Med., *note down for remembrance, make a memorandum of*, τι Plu.2.120d, etc. 2. *write memoirs* or *annals*, Plb.5.33.5; ὑ. τὰς Ἀλεξάνδρου πράξεις Str.2.1.9:—Pass., *to be recorded*, ἐν ᾧ ὑπεμνημάτιστο τάδε Lxx 1*Es.*6.22(23); so freq. in Pap., ἀξιοῦσιν -ισθῆναι τὴν ἔντευξιν αὐτῶν *PHamb.*29.15 (i A.D.), cf. *PRyl.* 77.46 (ii A.D.), etc. b. *write a treatise*, ὑ. τι περὶ ὕψους Longin.1.2; *treat of* a subject, Demetr.Lac.*Herc.*1055.23. 3. *explain, interpret*, οἱ ὑπομνηματισάμενοι *commentators*, A.D.*Synt.*156.12, Sch.S. *OC*390: so in Act., ὁ τὴν Ὀδύσσειαν -ίζων, ὁ Ὅμηρον -ίσας, St.Byz. s. vv. Δωδώνη, Ἐρυθραί, cf. Syrian. *in Hermog.*1.1 R. ⊕ **-ικός**, ή, όν, *serving for memoirs* or *dissertations*, διάλογοι *memoirs* in the form of dialogue, D.L.4.5; γραφή Phld.*Rh.*1.99 S.; χαρακτὴρ τοῦ λόγου Ap.Ty.*Ep.*19, cf. Ammon. *in Int.*213.31 (Comp.): neut. -κόν, τό, = ὑπόμνημα II. 5, Phld.*Rh.*2.196 S. 2. *serving for notes* or *commentary*, τρόπος *abbreviated* style, Simp. *in Ph.*60.29. Adv. -κῶς Gal. 18(1).529; *by way of reminder*, Anon. *in EN*229.17. **-ιον**, τό, Dim. of ὑπόμνημα, Parth.*Epist.Dedic.*2, *PMich.Teb.*123$^r$ ii 19, al. (i A.D.), M.Ant.3.14. ⊕ **-ισμός**, ὁ, *memorandum*, of a shopping-list, *PFreib.*ap.Wilcken ad *UPZ*62.12 (Ptolemaic); *minute*, Plb.23. 2.4, 25.4.5; *royal decree*, *OGI*262.3 (Baetocaece); στρατηγοῦ (in Roman Egypt) his *official diary*, in pl., *Sammelb.*7404 ii 31 (ii A.D.), Wilcken *Chr.*41 i 1, iv 1, vi 1 (iii A.D.); of other officials, e.g. ἐπιστρατήγου *PSI*10.1100.1 (ii A.D.); ἀναγραφὴ -ισμῶν list (register) of *records*, *PLips.*123.2 (ii A.D.); *a decree of the Areopagus*, because these were kept as *written records*, Cic.*Fam.*13.1.5, *Att.*5.11.6, *IG* 2$^2$.3952,4012, 4$^2$(1).83.18 (Epid., i A.D.), *SIG*1008.2 (Eleusis, iii A.D.). b. *note-taking*, Ath.Med.ap.Orib.*inc.*21.6. 2. = ὑπόμνημα II. 3, *memoirs, annals*, Plb.2.40.4; *treatise*, Phld.*Rh.*1.120 S., al., Stob.2.7.5, etc. 3. *commentary* on an author, Eust.746. 29. **-ιστής**, οῦ, ὁ, *commentator*, τοῦ Ἱπποκράτους Steph. *in Hp.* 2.458 D. 2. = ὁ ὑπόμνημα λέγων, Hsch.

**ὑπομνημᾰτογρᾰφ-εῖον**, τό, *office of the* ὑπομνηματογράφος 2, *PTeb.* 58.12 (ii B.C., abbrev.). ⊕ **-έω**, *discharge function of* ὑπομνηματογράφος 2, ib.64(*a*).89, al. (ii B.C.). II. Med., *write down as a memorandum*, Theano *Ep.*6.4. **-ος** (parox.), ὁ, in pl., *memoir-writers* or *historians* (incl. τὰ τῶν Γαλιλαίων.. βιβλία), opp. φιλόσοφοι, Jul.*Ep.* 106; παρὰ Ἑρμοῦ τοῦ πάντων ἔργων -γράφου Herm.ap.Stob.1.49. 44. 2. *recorder*, name of a great official in the Egyptian king's household, and the corresponding official in the office of the minister of finance (διοικητής), and prob. in those of other high officials, *PMich.Zen.*55.24 (iii B.C.), *OGI*147 (Paphos), al., *UPZ*14.127 (ii B.C.), Wilcken *Chr.*11 *B*1 (ii B.C.), *Sammelb.*6155.24, 7259.37 (both i B.C.), Str.17.1.12 (hence of David and Hezekiah, Lxx 1*Ch.*18.15, *Is.*36.3); also of a lesser local official, *PTeb.*58.33, 112.87 (both ii B.C.), *Sammelb.*7434.9 (ii A.D.), etc.

**ὑπομνημᾰτοφύλαξ** [ῠ], ἄκος, ὁ, *keeper of archives*, *Cod.Just.*12.37 (38).19 *Intr.*

⊕**ὑπόμνησ-ις**, εως, ἡ, *reminding*, Th.4.17,95; ἐπιστολὴ ὑπομνήσεως τῶν ἔργων *PGiss.*67.3 (ii A.D.); so Pl. calls the art of writing οὐ μνήμης ἀλλ' ὑπομνήσεως φάρμακον *Phdr.*275a; τινων of things, Id. *Lg.*732d (pl.); ὑπόμνησίν τινος ἔχειν to be able *to suggest* a thing, X.*Cyr.*3.3.38; αἰωνία ὑ. *CIG*(add.) 2809*b* (Aphrodisias); ὅσον ὑπομνήσεως ἕνεκα εἰρήσεται Gal.15.221. 2. *mention*, ὑ. ποιεῖσθαί τινος to make *mention* of a thing, Th.2.88, 3.54, etc.: pl., ποιεῖσθαι τὰς ὑ. Phld.*Lib.*p.33 O.; ὑ. κακῶν *a tale* of woe, E.*Or.*1032. 3. Medic., *provocation* (cf. ὑπομιμνήσκω I. 2b), τῆς ὀρέξεως Sor.1.106, cf. 100; *return*, *revival* of natural functions, Alex.Trall.4.1. b. *recurrence*, *relapse*, Dsc.*Eup.*1.26. 4. = ὑπόμνημα II. 5, *treatise*, Phld. *Rh.*1.8,32 S. **-κω**, late form of ὑπομιμνήσκω, Orph.*H.*77.6; cf. μνήσκομαι. **-τέον**, *one must remind*, τινά τινος S.E.*P.*3.70; *one must warn*, τινα Ph.1.383. 2. *one must make mention*, τινος Arist.*Rh.Al.*1436b29. 3. *one must provoke*, τὰς ἐκκρίσεις Herod. Med. in *Rh.Mus.*58.75. **-τεύομαι**, Med., *betroth* one's daughter, Arist.*Pol.*1304a14:—Pass., ὁ ὑπομνηστευθεὶς *one betrothed*, ib.a15. **-τικός**, ή, όν, *awakening the recollection*, *suggestive*, S.E. *P.*2.99, *M.*8.202, etc.; τῶν συμβαινόντων M.Ant.11.6: **-κόν**, τό, *reminder*, Lemma to *AP*5.291; -κὸν χορηγίας *memorandum* of stage properties, Pap. in *Eos* 32.30 (v/vi A.D.), cf. *PGen.*79.1 (iv A.D.), *PMasp.*32.33 (vi A.D.), *POxy.*1343 (vi A.D.). Adv. **-κῶς** Gal.1.149, S.E.*M.*8.289: Comp. **-ώτερον** ib.2.106. 2. Medic., *provocative* (cf. ὑπομιμνήσκω I. 2b), τοῦ πάθους Herod.Med. in *Rh. Mus.*58.88. **-τριαι**, αἱ, expld. in *AB*312 as αἱ ὑμνοῦσαι τὴν θεὸν ἱέρειαι.

**ὑπ-όμνῡμι**, *interpose by oath*, φὴς ὑπομνὺς S.*Fr.*339 codd. (ἐπομνὺς Pearson). II. Med., in Att. law, *make oath* (for oneself or another) that something serious prevents a person's appearing in court at the due time, and so *apply for a postponement of the trial*, D.47.39, etc.; ὑ. τινὰ δημοσίᾳ ἀπεῖναι στρατευόμενον Id.48.25; τὸν Δημοσθένην τις ὑπωμόσατο ὡς νοσοῦντα *applied for an extension of the term* for Demosthenes on the plea of sickness, Id.58.43: hence, comically, ὑπώμνυτο ὁ μὲν οἶνος ὄξος αὐτὸν εἶναι γνήσιον, τὸ δ' ὄξος οἶνον αὐτὸ μᾶλλον θατέρου Eub.65:—Pass., ὑπομοθέντος τούτου this *affidavit being put in by way of excuse*, D.48.25; ὑπομοθείσης ταύτης τῆς γραφῆς Hyp.*Fr.*202. 2. in the Assembly or Boule, *make an objection on oath*, X.*HG*1.7.34, Plu.2.848d, Poll.8.44.

⊕**ὑπομονή**, ἡ, *remaining behind*, Arist.*Rh.*1410a4, D.H.1.44. II. *endurance*, τῶν ἀκουσίων πόνων Democr.240; λύπης Pl.*Def.*412c; ἡ μὴ ὑ. ἀτιμαζομένων Arist.*APo.*97b24, cf. *Rh.*1384a21; εὐχερὴς τῆς ἀποτέξεως ὑ. Sor.1.46; πολέμου Plb.4.51.1; [θανάτου] Plu.*Pel.*1; ἡ τῆς μαχαίρας ὑ. τῶν πληγῶν the sword's *power to sustain* blows, Plb. 15.15.8. 2. in bad sense, *obstinacy*, Demetr.Lac.*Herc.*1012.47. 3. of plants, *power to endure*, Thphr.*CP*5.16.3. III. *enduring to do*, αἰσχρῶν ἔργων Id.*Char.*6.1.

**ὑπομονητέος**, **ὑπομονητικός**, **ὑπομονητός**, v. ὑπομεν-.

**ὑπομορφάζω**, *pretend*, Ph.1.604 codd., ἐπιμ. corr. Mangey.

**ὑπομοσχεύω**, (μόσχος (A)) *propagate by layers*: metaph., *propagate*, τὸν πόλεμον Eun.*Hist.*p.271 D.

**ὑπομόχθηρος**, ον, *baddish*, *rather hard*, *Com.Adesp.*476; ἔριον Philostr.*Im.*2.28; of a word, Poll.2.109.

**ὑπομοχλ-εύω**, *act as a lever*, Hp.*Mochl.*38. **-ιον**, τό, *the fulcrum* of a lever, Arist.*Mech.*850a35, al., Ph.*Bel.*59.21.

**ὑπομύζω**, f.l. in Diph.43.23.

**ὑπομῡκάομαι**, *bellow in answer*, A.*Fr.*57.8 (anap.).

**ὑπομυκτηρίζω**, *sneer at*, τινα Nicol.Com.1.38.

**ὑπόμυξις**, εως, ἡ, *cartilage of the nose*, between the nostrils, *Gloss.*

⊕**ὑπόμυξ-ος**, ον, *somewhat charged with mucus*, Hp.*Art.*8, al.; so ⊕**-ώδης**, ες, Gal.18(1).363.

**ὑπομύσᾰρος** [ῡ], ον, *rather filthy* or *fetid*, Hp.*Epid.*7.92.

**ὑπομύω**, only pf. part., ὄμματα ὑπομεμυκότα *half-closed* eyes, Alciphr.3.55.

**ὑπόμωρος**, ον, *rather stupid* or *silly*, Luc.*Icar.*29, Ptol.*Tetr.*163.

⊕**ὑποναίω**, *dwell under*, χῶρον *IG*14.902.

**ὑποναύσιος**, ον, *slightly nauseated*, Philum.*Ven.*16.8.

**ὑπονεάζω**, *begin to grow young again*, i.e. to be restored to strength, Philostr.*Her.*3.3, *Gym.*35.

**ὑπονεάω**, *break up fallow ground* with the plough, Thphr.*HP*3.1.6.

**ὑπονείφω**, *snow a little*, impers. ὑπένειφε *it was snowing a little*, Th.4.103:—Pass., νὺξ ὑπονειφομένη a *snowy* night, Id.3.23.

**ὑπονεκρόομαι**, *become torpid*, Lyd.*Mag.*1.42.

**ὑπονέμομαι**, Med., *eat away beneath* or *secretly*, ἔλαθεν πῦρ ὑπονειμάμενον *AP*7.444 (Theaet.); but ὑπονεμησαμένη, though found in cod. in Hp.*Oss.*18, is f.l. for ὑπονησαμένη, v. ὑπονέω. II. *undermine* (cf. ὑπόνομος): metaph., *deceive*, γυναῖκας Epich.9.

**ὑπονεφέλ-η**, ἡ, *cloudy appearance* in urine, Gal.19.617. **-ίζω**, *to be clouded* or *turbid*, ib.625. **-ος**, ον, *under the clouds*, Luc. *Fug.*25; *in cloudy weather*, Antyll.ap.Orib.6.21.35. II. *cloudy in appearance*, of urine, Hp.*Coac.*521.

**ὑπονέω**, *swim under*, Arist.*HA*631a18, Ael.*NA*9.35; τοῖς φρυγάνοις ib.5.23:—Med., ὑπονησαμένη *having dived under*, *passed under*, Hp.*Oss.*18, as restored from Gal.19.149, cf. Erot.

**ὑπονήϊος**, ον, *under the promontory* Νήϊον, *lying at its base*, Ἰθάκη Od.3.81, cf. 1.186 (v.l.).

**ὑπονήφω**, *to be somewhat sobered*, πρός τι J.*BJ*5.6.1.

**ὑπονήχομαι**, *swim under*, ταῖς πέτραις Paus.1.44.8: abs., *swim under* water, *dive*, Plu.*Ant.*29, *Brut.*30. II. *swim below* or *second*, τινι to one, Ael.*NA*2.6.

**ὑπονίζω**, *wash slightly* or *beneath*, πόδας ὑπονίψαι Hierocl.p.58 A.

**ὑπονιτρώδης**, ες, *somewhat alkaline*, Phylotim.ap.Ath.3.79b.

**ὑπονο-έω**, *suspect*, τι Hdt.9.88, E.*IA*1132; μηδὲν εἴς τινα Ar.*Pl.*361; ὑ. αὐτῶν τὴν διάνοιαν Th.7.73; ψεῦδος Pl.*Lg.*679c; πονηρά Phld. *Lib.*p.61 O.: c. acc. pers. et inf., ὑπονοήσαντες τοὺς Σαμίους τὰ τῶν Ἑλλήνων φρονέειν Hdt.9.99; ὑ. εἶναί τι θεῖον (v.l. θεόν) Arist.*Fr.*10: so ὑ. ὅπως.., ὅτι.., X.*Cyr.*3.3.20, *HG*4.8.35; τῶν λεγόντων ὑπενοεῖτε.., ὡς λέγουσι you *felt suspicious of* the speakers, thinking that.., Th.1.68; ὑ. περί τινος And.3.35; ὑ. τὰ λεγόμενα *watch* my words *captiously*, Id.1.9, Antipho 6.18. II. *surmise*, *conjecture*, *guess at*, Ar.*Eq.*652, *Lys.*1234; τὰ τῶν θεῶν And.1.139: c. acc. et inf., ὑ. ὧδ' ἔχειν τι Cratin.Jun.10: abs., ἀλλ' ὑπονόησον σύ μοι Ar. *Lys.*38; ὑπονοοῦντες προαρπάζειν *by conjecture*, Pl.*Grg.*454c; οὐδεὶς οἶδε.., ἀλλ' ὑπονοοῦμεν πάντες ἢ πιστεύομεν Men.261; ἐάσας ὑπονοεῖν εἰς τοὔνομα leaving us *to guess at*.., Alex.267.6. III. simply, *suppose*, *consider*, τινὰ μακαρίως ἐζηκέναι Phld.*Mort.*36:—Pass., **-νοούμενος** ἅπαντα γινώσκειν Id.*Piet.*101. IV. Med. in signf. I, ὅτι.. *POxy.*1680.14 (iii/iv A.D.). **-ημα**, ατος, τό, *supposition*, Hp. *Prorrh.*2.3 (pl.), Lxx *Si.*25.7. **-ητέον**, *one must suppose*, Chrysipp.ap.Gal.5.435, Str.16.4.27, Ph.1.581. **-ητής**, οῦ, ὁ, *suspicious person*, Adam.1.7. **-ητικός**, ή, όν, *suspicious*, Arr.*Epict.*1.23.3, Poll.9.152. 2. in pass. sense, στροφῆς ὅλης.. ὑπονοητικὰ *open to the suspicion of* being a whole strophe, Heph.*Poëm.*5.2.

**ὑπονόθ-ευσις**, εως, ἡ, *seduction*, *corruption*, *CIG*2695*b* (Mylasa), Procl.*Par.Ptol.*271. **-ευτής**, οῦ, ὁ, *seducer*, Ptol.*Tetr.*160, 164. **-εύω**, *procure by corruption*, τὴν ἀρχιερωσύνην Lxx 2*Ma.*4.7, cf. *Cat.Cod.Astr.*1.98 (Act. and Pass.).

**ὑπόνοια**, ἡ, (ὑπονοέω) *suspicion*, *conjecture*, *guess*, Ar.*Pax* 993 (pl., anap.); τοῦ μὴ συνειληφέναι Sor.2.54, cf. Gal.6.663; ὑπόνοιαι τῶν μελλόντων *notions formed* of future events, Th.5.87; ἡ ὑ. τῶν ἔργων Id.2.41, cf. E.*Ph.*1133; in bad sense, ὑπόνοιαι πλασταί D.48.39, cf. Men.*Mon.*732. 2. *suggestion*, Phld.*Mus.*p.71 K.; *imputation*, Id.*D.*1.13. II. *the real meaning which lies at the bottom* of a thing, *deeper sense*, τὰς ὑ. οὐκ ἐπίστανται X.*Smp.*3.6; esp. *covert meaning* (such as is conveyed by myths and allegories), ὁ.. νέος οὐχ οἷός τε κρίνειν ὅτι τε ὑ. καὶ ὃ μή Pl.*R.*378d, cf. Plu.2.19e; opp. αἰσχρολογία, Arist.*EN*1128a24; καθ' ὑπόνοιαν *by insinuation*, *covertly*, Plb.28.4.5, D.H.*Rh.*9.1; δι' ὑπονοιῶν Alciphr.2.4.

**ὑπονομ-εύς**, έως, ὁ, *worker on underground channels*, *PLond.*3.1177.312,335 (ii A.D.). **-ευτής**, οῦ, ὁ, = foreg., Ptol.*Tetr.*179. **-εύω**, *undermine*, *sap*, Din.ap.Phot., Anon.ap.Suid.; τὴν στερεὰν γῆν J.*BJ*7.2.2. 2. metaph., *stir up by secret arts*, *stratagems*, or *intrigues*, ὑ. Ῥωμαίοις πόλεμον D.H.3.23:—Pass., v.l. for -νοθ-, Lxx 2*Ma.*4.26. **-ή**, ἡ, *underground passage*, *mine*, Str.13.1.67, D.S.20.94. II. metaph., in pl., *secret stratagems* or *intrigues*, Hsch. III. *burrowing* of rabbits, Str.3.5.2. **-ηδόν**, Adv. *underground*, *by means of pipes*, Th.6.100. ⊕**-ος**, ον, (ὑπονέμομαι) *undermined*, τόπος D.S.3.37; χώρα ὑ. πυρὶ καὶ ὕδατι Str.12.8.17. 2. *underground*, ὑ. τάφροι *sewers*, App.*BC*4.13; ὀρύγματα J.*AJ*7.9.6; ὑ. ἄντρον Str.13.1.67; ὑ. τὴν ἀποφορὰν ἔχει, of a lake, Id.12.8.19 (s. v.l.). 3. ὑ. ἕλκος a *spreading* ulcer *with undermined edges*, Dsc. 5.120; κόλποι ὑ. Id.1.128, cf. Heras ap.Gal.13.815. II. ὑπόνομος, ὁ, as Subst., *underground passage*, *mine*, Th.2.76; οὐκέτι ὑπονόμοις, ἀλλ' ἤδη μηχαναῖς αἱρεῖν τὴν πολιτείαν Plu.*Caes.*6. 2. *water-pipe*, *conduit*, X.*HG*3.1.7, Arist.*Mete.*350a1, *IG*2².2491.11, *PCair. Zen.*745.19 (iii B.C.). 3. *sewer*, Str.5.3.8, App.*BC*4.40. 4. *vein* of minerals, X.*Vect.*4.26.

**ὑπονοσέω**, *to be somewhat affected* (*by illness*), of the spleen, Hp. *Morb.*4.57; *sicken*, of a person, Id.*Epid.*1.3, Luc.*Tox.*29, *Merc. Cond.*42.

**ὑπονοστ-έω**, *go down*, *sink*, Arist.*Mete.*367a24, Plu.*Them.*15; *settle*, of a stack of wood, Hdt.4.62; of the earth in an earthquake, Arist.*Mete.*365b12; of a river, ὑ. ἀνδρὶ ὡς ἐς μέσον μηρὸν Hdt.1.191, cf. Th.3.89, Plu.2.366e; of humours, εἰς τὸ βάθος Gal.6.254. 2. *settle*, *turn into* a thing, εἰς χλευασμὸν καὶ γέλωτα Plu.2.811e: metaph., *sink*, *decline*, ἐκ τοῦ φοβεροῦ ὑ. πρὸς τὸ εὐκαταφρόνητον Longin.3.1; πρὸς τὸ μὴ ὄν Dam.*Pr.*440; of the aged, *decline* in years, Poll.2.21. ⊕**-ησις**, εως, ἡ, *retirement*, *sinking*, *subsiding*, θαλάσσης Plu. *Ant.*3; of the Nile, Hld.9.22 (pl.); ὑ. ἀέρος εἰς γῆν, as a definition of an earthquake, Anaxag.ap.D.L.2.9; τοῦ θερμοῦ Gal.1.689: metaph., ἀλαζονείας Ph.*Fr.*102 H.

**ὑπονόσφιος**, ον, *surreptitious*, ὑπονόσφιον ἔγχος ἑλοῦσα Il.21.397 as read by Antimachus (πανόψιον vulg.); also written above the line in a Homer-Pap. of iii B.C. (*PGrenf.*2.4(*a*)).

**ὑπονοτίζω**, *moisten underneath* or *a little*, Hp.*Epid.*7.83, *Placit.*2.20.15 (Pass.).

**ὑπονουθετέω**, *admonish gently*, Ael.*NA*7.15.

**ὑπονυμφίς**, ίδος, ἡ, (νύμφη) *bridesmaid*, Sch.Ar.*Eq*.647.

**ὑπονύσσω**, *prick* or *sting underneath*: generally, *sting*, Theoc.19.3; *prick*, Ael.*NA*2.50; *prod, goad*, ταῦρον Hld.10.28; τοὺς ὑποχειρίους Lxx *Is*.58.3:—Pass., ὑπονύσσεται· καταπονεῖται, Hsch.

**ὑπονυστάζω**, *nod a little, fall asleep gradually*, Pl.*Smp*.223d, Plu.2.178f.

**ὑπόνωθρος**, ον, *somewhat dull*, Eust.3.39:—also **-νωθής**, ές, Dam.*Isid*.83 (in Comp. -έστερος).

**ὑπόξανθος**, ον, *yellowish* or *lightish-brown*, Hp.*Epid*.3.1.ιβ', Thphr.*HP*9.12.2, Dsc.1.11, Gal.6.481, etc.

**ὑποξενίζω**, *talk in a curious way of*, τι Luc.*Icar*.1.

**ὑποξέω**, *scrape underneath*, τὰς ὁπλὰς *Hippiatr*.104; ὑποξέοντες.. τῷ σμιλίῳ Aët.7.95. 2. *wipe underneath*, στρέψαντες σπόγγῳ ὑποξέουσι τὸ βλέφαρον ib.11.

**ὑποξηρ-αίνω**, trans., *dry up a little*, in Pass., Hp.*Morb*.1.15, 3.16, Thphr.*HP*4.2.4, Gal.6.434. **-ασία**, ἡ, f.l. for ὑπερ-, Hp.*Int*.20. **-ος**, ον, *somewhat dry*, πτύσματα, γλῶσσα, Id.*Coac*.363, *Epid*.7.22; ἐν τοῖς ὑ. *in dry places*, Plu.2.915e. 2. *lean, slender*, of parts that have not much flesh over them, Hp.*Fract*.4 vulg. (-ξυρα codd. opt.), v.l. for ὑπόξυροι in Id.*Art*.77.

**ὑπ-οξίζω**, *to be sourish*, Ath.3.114c.

⊛ **ὑπόξῠλος**, ον, *wooden underneath*, i.e. *of wood covered with a coat of some precious metal*, A.*Fr*.286, X.*Oec*.10.3, cf. *IG*1².280.78, al., 2².1388.76, Ar.*Fr*.881, Alex.192; κοίτη ὑ. κατάχρυσος *IG*1².280.79; βωμὸς J.*AJ*3.6.8; [θεοὶ] τὰ ἔνδον ὑ. Luc.*JTr*.8. 2. metaph., *spurious, counterfeit*, Men.*Per*.*Fr*.7; of poets, etc., Phryn.*PS*p.115 B.

**ὑπ-οξύνω**, in Pass., *form a sub-acute angle*, Gal.18(2).855.

**ὑποξῠρ-άω** or **-έω**, *shave* or *cut off some of the hair*, τὸν τόπον *Hippiatr*.77:—Pass., ὑπεξυρημένος Archil.58; ὑπεξ. τὸ γένειον, τὴν γνάθον, Luc.*DMort*.9.4, *Tim*.22. **-ιος**, α, ον, *on which shears* or *razors are rubbed*, *AP*6.307 (Phan.). **-ος**, ον, *cut away as if by a razor*, of an aquiline nose, Hp.*Epid*.6.8.26; γαστέρας, i.e. *flattened*, Id.*Prorrh*.2.23, as Littré (for ἀποξύμους of most codd.) after Gal.19.149, cf. *Art*.77 (v. ὑπόξηρος).

**ὑπ-οξυς**, υ, *sub-acid*, Dsc.2.80.

**ὑπόξυσμα**, ατος, τό, *scraping, shaving*, *Hippiatr*.33.

**ὑποξύω** [ῡ], *scrape a little* or *below*, λίθον, v.l. for ἀπο-, Dsc.5.141; ποταμὸς πέζαν ὑποξύων νάπης *AP*9.669 (Marian.); cf. D.P.61,385.

⊛ **ὑποοπλομάχος** [ᾰ], ὁ, *assistant* ὁπλομάχος, *SIG*697 *E*14 (Delph., ii B.C.), *Hesperia* 2.507 (Athens, iii A.D.).

**ὑποπαιδοτρίβ-ης** [ῐ], ου, ὁ, *under*-παιδοτρίβης, *IG*2².2086,2097, al. (ii A.D.):—hence **-έω**, ib.2993,2996 (i B.C.), al.

**ὑποπαίζω**, *play* or *joke a little*, Ael.*NA*12.21. II. trans., *poke fun at*, τὰ μεγάλα πάθη τῆς τραγῳδίας Sch.Ar.*Ach*.331.

**ὑποπᾰλαίω**, *go down voluntarily in wrestling*, Luc.*Ner*.8.

**ὑποπάλλω**, *rebound, 'repeat'*, of swallowed food, Ruf.ap.Orib.7.26.21. 2. Pass., *throb a little*, Agath.4.25.

**ὑποπαράβορρος**, ον, *exposed to other than due North winds*, Thphr.*HP*5.1.11.

**ὑποπαραιτ-έομαι**, *beg off*, γράμματα δι' ὧν ὑποπαρῄτου διὰ τὸ τοῦ ποδὸς ἄλγημα *Sammelb*.4630.4 (ii A.D.); *to be an excuse*, -ουμένης ἀσθενείας (from military service) Ph.2.379; *disclaim*, Phld.*Herc*.1457.8. **-ησις**, εως, ἡ, *excuse*, A.D.*Synt*.145.27. **-ία**, ἡ, *denial, refusal to recognize*, τῆς ἐκείνων θειότητος dub. l. in *Sammelb*.3924.42 (i A.D.).

**ὑποπαρα-κρούω**, = sq., Hp.*Epid*.7.83. **-ληρέω**, *wander, be slightly delirious*, ib.5. **-φέρομαι**, = foreg., Gal.17(2).107.

**ὑποπαρενθῠμέομαι**, *flag in attention*, Arr.*Epict*.4.3.5.

**ὑποπάρθενοι**, αἱ, *'demi-vierges'*, opp. ἑταῖραι, Ar.*Fr*.141.

**ὑποπαρωθέω**, *thrust aside underhand*, Is.8.38.

**ὑποπάσσω**, *strew under*, ποίην Hdt.1.132; ἡδύσματα Alex.186.7. II. *plaster under*, ἄργιλον Thphr.*Sign*.49.

**ὑπόπαστον**, τό, = ὑπόστρωμα, Ps.-Plu.2.839a.

**ὑποπάσχω**, *suffer slightly* or *secretly*, in part. -παθών, Hsch.

**ὑποπᾰτᾰγέω**, *clatter underneath*, Philostr.*Her*.1.3.

**ὑποπάτριος**, ὁ, *filius familias*, *Gloss*.

**ὑποπαύομαι**, Pass., *cease gradually*, τῆς πληρώσεως, of the Nile, Ath.7.301c.

**ὑποπᾰχύνομαι**, Pass., *grow thick, curdle*, Ph.2.397.

**ὑπόπᾰχυς**, υ, *somewhat fat* or *thick*, Hp.*Epid*.1.26.β', *Morb*.1.31, Gal.18(1).363 (Comp.).

**ὑποπέζιος**, α, ον, *inferior in rank*, οἱ ἄχραντοι θεοὶ δυνάμει ὑ. τῶν πατέρων Procl.*Theol.Plat*.5.38; *subordinate*, τῇ νοητῇ (sc. διακρίσει) Dam.*Pr*.198. II. Subst. **ὑποπεζία**, ἡ, *humiliation*, Hsch.

**ὑποπείθω**, *persuade gradually*, Men.Prot.p.121 D.:—Pass., Hld.7.2.

**ὑποπεινάω**, *begin to be hungry*, Ar.*Pl*.536 (anap.).

**ὑποπειράω**, *try to seduce*, Ael.*NA*14.5, Alciphr.3.52.

**ὑποπελιάζω**, *to be* or *grow* ὑποπέλιος, Gal.14.769.

**ὑποπέλιδνος**, ον, *somewhat black, wan*, or *livid*, Hp.*Epid*.3.1.ια':—also **ὑποπέλιος**, ον, Id.*Art*.86, *Epid*.1.26.η', Thphr.*HP*3.11.1, Dsc.1.67.

**ὑπόπεμπτος**, ον, *sent covertly*, as a scout or spy, X.*An*.3.3.4.

**ὑποπέμπω**, *send under, to*, or *into*, c. acc., γᾶς ὑποπεμπομένα σκότον E.*Hec*.209 (lyr.). II. *send secretly*, Th.4.46, X.*Cyr*.2.4.21, Arist.*Oec*.1352ᵃ3:—Pass., Lys.1.15. 2. *send as a spy, send in a false character*, X.*An*.2.4.22, cf. Th. l. c., and v. foreg.

**ὑποπεπτηῶτες**, Ep. pf. part. of ὑποπτήσσω (q.v.).

**ὑποπεπτωκότως**, Adv. pf. part. Act. of ὑποπίπτω, *submissively*, ὑ. καὶ ταπεινῶς Plb.35.2.13.

**ὑποπέπων**, ον, gen. ονος, *moderately concocted*, πτύαλα Hp.*Epid*.3.1.α'.

**ὑποπεράτωσις** [ᾰ], εως, ἡ, *gradual completion*, Hsch.

**ὑποπέρδομαι**, Med., *break wind a little*, Ar.*Ra*.1097 (anap.).

**ὑποπερι-κλάομαι**, Pass., *to be broken* or *bent round a little*, Dsc.3.68. **-πλύνομαι** [ῡ], Pass., *have slight diarrhoea*, Hp.*Prorrh*.1.98. **-ψύχω** [ῡ], *shiver a little*, Id.*Prorrh*.1.81 = *Coac*.131.

**ὑποπερκάζω**, *begin to assume a dark colour, begin to turn*, of grapes, ἕτεραι δ' ὑποπερκάζουσιν Od.7.126, cf. Ph.2.54:—Med., ὁ βότρυς ὑποπερκάζεται Ach.Tat.2.3; cf. περκνός.

**ὑποπέσσιον**, τό, *the space under the* πεσσός III, *PFlor*.15.17, *PLond*.5.1722.20, *PMonac*.11.27, 12.22 (all vi A.D.).

**ὑποπετάννῡμι**, *spread out under, lay under*, ὑπὸ λῖτα πετάσσας Od.1.130; ὑ. τι κάτωθεν Hp.*Fist*.7:—Pass., πεδίον ὑποπεπταμένον Luc.*Fug*.25.

**ὑποπέτασμα**, ατος, τό, *a cloth to spread under, carpet*, Pl.*Plt*.279d.

**ὑποπέτομαι**, *fly under*, Paus.4.18.5.

⊛ **ὑποπετρίδιος**, ον, *winged*, ὄνειροι Alcm.23.49, cf. *EM*783.24.

**ὑπόπετρος**, ον, *rocky*, γῆ Hdt.2.12, Thphr.*CP*3.20.5, *PTeb*.72.14 (ii B.C.), cf. Str.16.2.36; χωρία Dsc.4.33.

**ὑποπετρόω**, *change into stone*, *PMag.Leid.W*.19.36 (Pass.).

**ὑποπέττευμα**, ατος, τό, *beguilement, deception*, a doubtful word in Plu.2.987e.

**ὑποπήγνῡμι**, in Pass., *become hard* or *firm*, of fledgelings, Ael.*NA*3.30; of chickens in the egg, ib.14.7. II. *fix below*, Hero *Aut*.23.1, 24.4, Ael.*NA*1.58.

**ὑποπηδάω**, *leap forth* or *up*, J.*BJ*4.1.9, Ael.*NA*12.15.

**ὑποπιάζω**, f.l. for ὑπωπιάζω in *Ev.Luc*.18.5, 1*Ep.Cor*.9.27.

**ὑποπιέζω**, f.l. for ὑπωπιάζω (which Turnebus restored) in Plu.2.921f.

⊛ **ὑποπῐθηκίζω**, *play the ape a little*, ὑπό τι μικρὸν ἐπιθήκισα Ar.*V*.1290; cf. πιθηκίζω.

**ὑπόπικρος**, ον, *somewhat bitter*, Diocl.*Fr*.43, Thphr.*HP*3.11.4, 9.11.3, al., Gal.6.612.

⊛ **ὑποπίμελος** [ῑ], ον, *somewhat fat* or *fatty*, Diph.Siph.ap.Ath.3.121c, Dsc.5.75, Gal.19.359.

**ὑποπίμπλημι**, *fill*, φωτὸς τὰς διαστάσεις Ael.*NA*1.23; ὑ. τινὰ ἐλπίδος Philostr.*Her*.19.4; τὰς ψυχὰς ἡδονῆς Lib.*Or*.11.17:—Pass., πώγωνος ἤδη ὑποπιμπλάμενος *now beginning to have* a beard, Pl.*Prt*.309a; γαργαλισμοῦ ὑποπλησθῆναι Id.*Phdr*.253e; ὑποπίμπλαμαι τοὺς ὀφθαλμοὺς δακρύων *have my* eyes *filling* with tears, Luc.*DMarin*.12.2: later also c. dat., ὑ. δάκρυσιν *AP*5.274 (Paul. Sil.). II. Pass., of women, τέκνων ὑποπλησθῆναι *become mothers of many* children, Hdt.6.138: abs., *become pregnant*, Ael.*NA*12.21, Poll.3.49.

**ὑποπίμπρημι**, aor. 1 -έπρησα (the only tense in Hdt.):—*set fire to*, [ὕλην] Hdt.2.107; [τὰ φρύγανα] Id.4.69; ἤν τις ἐκείνας [τὰς ἕδρας] ὑποπίμπρησι Ar.*Lys*.348 (lyr.); the pres. also in Plu.*Nic*.16, *Dio*44. 2. *burn as on a funeral-pyre*, τινας Hdt.2.111, 3.45.

**ὑποπίνω** [ῐ], *drink a little, drink moderately*, μηκέθ' οὕτω.. Σκυθικὴν πόσιν..μελετῶμεν, ἀλλὰ καλοῖς ὑποπίνοντες ἐν ὕμνοις Anacr.63.11; ὑποπεπώκαμεν Ar.*Fr*.496; μετρίως ὑ. Pl.*R*.372d; ἐχθὲς ὑπέπινες, εἶτα νυνὶ κραιπαλᾷς Alex.286, cf. Antiph.271. 2. *drink at dessert*, Ar.*Av*.494 (anap.), Pherecr.153.5 (hex.), X.*Cyr*.8.4.9, etc. 3. ὑποπεπωκώς *rather tipsy*, Ar.*Pax*874, *Lys*.395, X.*An*.7.3.29.

**ὑποπῑπίσκω**, = ὑποποτίζω, aor. inf. -πῖσαι, Hsch.

⊛ **ὑποπίπτω**, fut. -πεσοῦμαι Phld.*Mort*.32:—*fall under* or *down, sink in*, ὑ. ἡ σάρξ Longus 1.13: metaph., τὸ θράσος ὑ. Plu.*Crass*.18. 2. *fall down, cringe before* any one, Pl.*R*.576a, X.*Cyn*.10.18: hence, *to be subject to* him, *fall under* his power, τῆς Ἑλλάδος ὑπὸ τὴν πόλιν -πιπτούσης Isoc.7.12: also of a flatterer, *cringe to, fawn on*, τινι Is.6.29, D.45.63,65, 59.43, Arr.*Epict*.4.1.55: abs., καταντιβολεῖτον αὐτὸν ὑποπεπτωκότες Ar.*Fr*.625, cf. Plu.2.525d; ὑποπεσὼν τὸν δεσπότην ᾔκαλλ' Ar.*Eq*.47, cf. Aeschin.3.116; of dogs, προσδέχονται καὶ ὑ. ἥκοντας Philostr.*Her.Prooem*.1; of suppliants, ὑποπεσεῖν ἐπὶ δεήσει J.*AJ*16.4.4; ὑποπίπτοντα καὶ δεόμενον Plu.2.540d. 3. [τὸ λουτρὸν] ὑποπῖπτον τῇ τοῦ σώματος ἀραιώσει *following immediately upon*.., Sor.1.46. 4. *fall under*, ἄνισοι περιφέρειαι τοῦ ἡλιακοῦ κύκλου ὑπὸ ἴσας περιφερείας τοῦ ζῳδιακοῦ κύκλου ὑποπεπτώκασιν Gem.1.38: metaph., *fall under* a class or system, ὑπὸ τὴν τάξιν Iamb.*VP*34.241, cf. Phld.*Rh*.1.75 S.; c. dat., Plu.2.777b, Gal.15.453; τὰ μὲν καθόλου.., τὰ δ' ὑποπίπτοντα *cases falling under* the rule, Plu.2.569e. II. *get in under* or *among*, ἐς τοὺς ταρσοὺς τῶν νεῶν Th.7.40; φονεύειν τοὺς ὑποπίπτοντας *those who fall in one's way*, Plb.3.86.11. III. of accidents, *happen to, befall*, τινι E.*Fr*.223: intr., *happen, fall out*, κατὰ τὸ ὑποπῖπτον *as occasion arises*, Archim.*Eratosth.Prooem*.; τὰ ὑποπίπτοντα *events, circumstances*, Plb.1.68.3; τὰ ὑπὸ τὸν αὐτὸν ὑποπεπτωκότα καιρὸν Id.2.58.14; ὅταν ὁ καιρὸς ὑ., ἐάν τις ὑ. χρεία, Id.10.17.1, 31.8.8: also, *come into one's head, suggest itself*, Isoc.5.85, Archim.*Sph.Cyl*.1 *Prooem*.; πᾶν τὸ ὑποπεσόν D.L.7.180; *enter the mind*, of ideas or impressions, Phld.*Mort*.39, S.E.*P*.1.35,40, etc.; *come under observation*, Id.*M*.8.60, Zeno *Stoic*.1.19; τοῖς αἰσθητηρίοις Phld.*D*.3.15; τῇ ἁφῇ Sor.2.21, cf. 1.58, al.; τῇ δυνάμει τῇ ὁρατικῇ Arr.*Epict*.1.6.4; ταῖς ὄψεσι *Gp*.2.10.2; τοῖς ἰδιώταις Gal.19.218; τῇ μαίᾳ Sor.1.1,2; οἱ σολοικισμοὶ ἀκοῇ -ουσιν A.D.*Synt*.199.2. 2. of persons, *to be subjected to*, τῷ ὀστράκῳ Plu.*Arist*.1, cf. *Nic*.11; αἰτίαις Hdn.6.1.7. 3. *surrender*, D.S.13.21, 14.46, Nic.Dam.127.7 J.; *succumb*, ἐν τῷ παλαίειν

Plu.2.58e. IV. *collapse underneath*, of a substructure, Pl.*Lg.* 793c. V. of places, like ὑπόκειμαι, *lie under* or *below*, τοῖς ὄρεσιν Plb.3.54.2, cf. Str.9.1.15; *lie behind*, Plb.6.31.1. 2. *to be exposed to attack from*, τοῖς πολεμίοις Id.12.21.5, cf. Str.6.2.5. 3. of persons or their actions, *to be exposed* or *liable to*, ζημίᾳ *PFlor.*278 ii 12, 27, al. (iii A. D.); συγκρίματι *PAmh.*2.68.34 (i A. D.); ἐγκυκλίῳ (a tax) *POxy.*1462.29 (i A. D.). VI. of revenue, *belong, accrue to*, τινι *Sammelb.*5245.9 (i A. D.), cf. *PSI*4.288.9 (ii A. D.); τῷ ἰδίῳ λόγῳ *PLond.*2.355.8 (i A. D.).

**ὑποπισσόω**, Att. -ττόω, *pitch underneath*, Ar.*Pl.*1093 (sens. obsc.).

**ὑποπλάγιος** [ᾰ], ον, *somewhat oblique*, Hp.*Mochl.*1.

**ὑποπλάκιος** [ᾰ], α, ον, *under the Trojan mountain Placus*, Θήβη Il.6.397, cf. Demetr.Sceps.ap.Ath.14.644a.

**ὑπόπλᾰκος**, ον, = foreg., Str.13.1.65, Hsch. (from false joining of ὑπὸ Πλάκῳ Il.6.396).

**ὑποπλάσσω**, *invent, feign*, Lib.*Descr.*14.9:—in Arist.*Fr.*216, ὑποσπασθῇ or ἐπικλασθῇ seems to be required (for ὑποπλασθῇ codd. Plu.).

**ὑποπλᾰτᾰγέω**, *rattle* or *roar under*, Q.S.3.178.

**ὑποπλᾰτ[υπρόσωπος]**, ον, *rather broad-faced*, dub. in *Arch.Pap.* 5.386 (ii A. D.).

**ὑπόπλᾰτυς**, υ, *somewhat extended*, ἐν τοῖσι στήθεσι ἐρυθήματα ὑ. Hp.*Coac.*410. 2. *rather flat*, σπέρμα [ἀλύσσου] Dsc.3.91; σχῆμα ὑ. ὁμοίως τοῖς φακοῖς Gal.6.551. II. *somewhat salt, brackish*, Dicaearch.1.27.

**ὑποπλᾰτωνικός**, ὁ, *a Platonic pretender*, Ephipp.14.2 (cj. for ὑπὸ Πλάτωνα καί).

**ὑποπλέκω**, *weave, plait*, Ael.*NA*17.21, al.

**ὑπόπλεος**, ον, Att. -πλεως, ων, *full*, c. gen., ἔτι.. δειματός εἰμι ὑ. am still afraid, Hdt.7.47; δακρύων τοὺς ὀφθαλμοὺς ὑ. Luc.*Somn.* 4. 2. *filled underhand*, ἀργυρίων Timocr.1.10.

**ὑπόπλευρον**, τό, = *armus*, *Gloss.*

**ὑποπλέω**, *sail under*, τὴν Κύπρον, i.e. *under the lee of* C., *Act.Ap.* 27.4: c. dat., ὑ. τενάγεσσι *AP*9.296 (Apollonid.):—Pass., Philostr. *Im.*2.17. II. *sail underground*, ἐς τὸν Τίβεριν δι' [ὑπονόμων] D.C. 49.43.

**ὑποπληρ-όω**, = ὑποπίμπλημι, ὑ. τινὰ τύφου Ael.*VH*9.17; *complete*, τεσσαρεσκαιδέκατον ἔτος Gal.5.41:—Subst. -ωσις, εως, ἡ, *completion*, Procl. *in Prm.*p.656 S.

**ὑποπλήσσω**, *strike beneath*, ποδὶ μηρόν Q.S.4.229 codd.

**ὑπόπλους**, ὁ, *passage-way for ships*, Pl.*Criti.*115e.

**ὑπόπλουτος**, ον, *wealthy underneath*, i.e. *rich in metals*, χώρα Posidon.47 J.

**ὑποπλύνω** [ῡ], = *sublavo*, *Gloss.*

**ὑποπλώω**, poet. and Ion. for ὑποπλέω, τενάγεσσιν *AP*9.14 (Antiphil.).

**ὑποπνέω**, *blow underneath*, Arist.*Pr.*887$^b$30: used for ὑποπέρδομαι, Hsch. s. v. ψιβδεῖ. II. *blow gently*, *Act.Ap.*27.13.

**ὑποπόδ-ία**, ἡ, *base*, Hero *Mens.*54. -ίζω, = ἀναποδίζω, Sch. Ar.*Av.*382; of planets, *retrace their path*, Paul.Al.*C.*1, al., Procl. *Hyp.*1.14, al. ⊕-ιον, τό, *footstool*, *IG*2$^2$.1394.15 (iv B. C.), Chares 2 J., *Schwyzer* 200 (Crete, ii B. C.), *PTeb.*45.38 (ii B. C.), Lxx *Ps.*98(99). 5, Luc.*Hist.Conscr.*27, Sor.1.68, Sch.Call. in Διηγήσεις vii 29. -ισμός, ὁ, *retrograde motion*, Procl.*Hyp.*7.4 (pl.), Lyd.*Mens.*2.8.

**ὑποποιέω**, *put under, assign to*, Διόνυσον τοῖς Ἑβραίων ἀπορρήτοις Plu.2.671c:—Med., *subject to oneself*, Luc.*Tox.*13. 2. *produce gradually*, μύξαν Hp.*Art.*40; ζῆλον καὶ συνήθειαν Plu.*Per.*5. 3. Med., *gain by underhand tricks, win by intrigue, win over*, [τοὺς Λακεδαιμονίους] D.19.76, cf. Arist.*Pol.*1303$^b$24, *PSI*5.452.12 (iv A. D.); [τοῖς χρήμασιν] ὑ. τινὰς ἐπί τινα Philostr.*Her.*10.6. II. Med., *assume, affect, put on*, τὴν τοῦ Κάτωνος παρρησίαν Plu.*Caes.* 41, cf. *Alex.*5.

**ὑποποικίλος**, ον, *somewhat variegated*, Hp.*Epid.*6.7.1, *Coac.*200; φλοιός Dsc.1.22.

**ὑπόποκος**, ον, *under wool, woolly*, Ph.1.20.

**ὑποπόλιος**, ον, *somewhat grey*, Anacr.25, Poll.2.12.

**ὑπόπολις**, εως, ἡ, *the lower city*, opp. ἀκρόπολις, *AB*212.

**ὑποπολῑτ-εύομαι**, *make one's measures subservient to*, τοῖς ἐχθροῖς Poll.4.36. -ικός, ή, όν, *indirectly connected with the state*, Sch. Hermog. in Rh.7(1).9 W. ( = *Prolegomenon Sylloge*, Lips. 1931, p. 192 Rabe).

**ὑποπολλαπλάσῐος** [πλᾰ], ον, of a number, *submultiple of another*, Nicom.*Ar.*1.17,18,19:—also **ὑποπολλαπλᾰσῐ-επιμόριος**, ον, *submultiple-superparticular*, i.e. *contained in another number several times with one fractional part remaining*:—and -επιμερής, ές, *submultiple-superpartient*, i.e. *contained in another several times with two or more fractional parts remaining*, ib.1.17,21 (cf. 23).

**ὑποπονέω**, *labour* or *suffer a little*, Hp.*Epid.*3.13 vulg. (ἐπόνεον cod. V, Kühl.).

**ὑποπόνηρος**, ον, *somewhat wicked* or *bad*, Ptol.*Tetr.*67; ὑποπόνηρά [ἐστι] Hp.*Epid.*6.7.1.

**ὑποπορ-εύομαι**, *go secretly*, Plu.*Tim.*18; διὰ τῶν ὑπονόμων Id.*Cam.* 5. -ευσις, εως, ἡ, *underground way*, Id.2.968b.

**ὑπόπορτις**, ιος, ἡ, *with a calf under her*, of a cow: metaph. of *a mother with a child at the breast*, Hes.*Op.*603; cf. ὕπαρνος.

**ὑποπορφῠρέω**, *to be somewhat purple*; v. ὑπηρέμα.

⊕ **ὑποπορφῠρ-ίζω**, *to be somewhat purple*, Dsc.1.103. -ος, ον, *somewhat purple*, χρῶμα Arist.*HA*616$^a$15; ῥόδον *AP*5.83; ἄνθη Dsc. 3.7.

**ὑποποτίζω**, *give to drink a little*, Hsch. s. v. ὑποπῖσαι.

**ὑπόπους**, ὁ, ἡ, neut. -πουν, gen. -ποδος, *furnished with feet*, ζῷον Arist.*Metaph.*1038$^a$11, cf. *IA*708$^a$21; τὰ ὑπόποδα (sc. ζῷα) Id.*HA* 511$^a$32, al., cf. Gal.10.21.

**ὑποπρᾱΰνω**, Ion. -πρηΰνω, *appease by degrees*, *AP*5.254.5 (Paul. Sil.).

**ὑπόπρεμνος**, ον, *with part of the stock attached* (cf. ὑπόρριζος II), Thphr.*HP*2.1.3.

**ὑποπρεσβύτερος** [ῠ], ον, *elderly*, Ar.*Fr.*350.

**ὑποπρήθομαι**, Pass., *begin to swell*, Ael.*NA*9.43.

**ὑποπρίαμαι**, *buy under the price*, Thphr.*Char.*30.12.

**ὑποπρίω** [ῑ], *gnash secretly*, τοὺς ὀδόντας Luc.*DMort.*6.3.

⊕ **ὑποπρό**, or ὑπὸ πρό, Prep. c. gen. *just before*, ποδῶν A.R.4.178; cf. ἀποπρό. II. Thess. ὑππρό, of Time, *before*, τὰ ψαφίσματα τό τε ὑππρὸ τᾶς γενόμενον καὶ τὸ τᾶμον the *former* decree [i. e. that of four years earlier] and the present one, *IG*9(2).517.43 (Larissa, iii B. C.), cf. 512.30 (ibid.): with τᾶς perh. supply ἀμέρας, but the sense of the whole phrase is simply that of Att. πρὸ τοῦ.

**ὑποπροάγων** [ᾰ], οντος, ὁ, *sub-προάγων*, *Papers of Amer. Sch. at Athens* iii No.465 (Seleucia Sidera), nisi leg. ὑπὸ προάγοντα.

**ὑπόπροσθεν**, Adv. *just before*, οἱ ὑ. χρόνοι Hp.*Epid.*3.2, cf. *Theol. Ar.*13,16.

**ὑποπρόστ(ε)ιμος**, ον, *liable to pay a fine*, τῷ ταμείῳ *BSA*17.226 (Pamphylia).

**ὑποπροτίθημι**, *push forward under*, [θύραν] κλίμακι Aen.Tact.36.2.

**ὑποπροχέω**, *pour forth under*, cj. in *AP*9.314.4 (Anyt.).

**ὑποπρύτᾰνις** [ῠ], εως, ὁ, *vice-president*, *IG*9(1).486.5 (Acarnania, ii/i B. C.).

⊕ **ὑπ-οπτάζομαι**, *to be suspected*, τῆς ἀλγηδόνος -αζομένης διὰ τῶν ἀρτηριῶν τῆς ἀναδόσεως *being suspected* (to arise) through.., Paul. Aeg.3.5 (s. v. l.).

**ὑπ-οπτάω**, *roast a little*, dub. for ὑποπτίσσω, Thphr.*HP*4.8.14.

**ὑποπτερίδιος**, ον, = ὑπόπτερος, Dionys.ap.*EM*783.20 sq.; cf. ὑποπτερίδιος.

**ὑποπτερνίς**, ίδος, ἡ, *knob* against which the butt-end (πτέρνα) of the arm of a torsion-engine came to rest, Ph.*Bel.*66.2, Hero *Bel.*93.8.

**ὑπόπτερος**, ον, *winged*, ὄφιες Hdt.3.107; πέλειαι S.*Ph.*288; νῶτα, δέμας, E.*Hec.*1264, *Hel.*618; τίς ἦν ὁ γράψας πρῶτος..Ἔρωθ' ὑπόπτερον; Eub.41.2, cf. Pl.*Alc.*1.135e; also of a ship, *whose sails are wings*, Pi.*O.*9.24, cf. Mimn.12.7, Pherecyd.Syr.2; also σύμφυτος δύναμις ὑποπτέρου ζεύγους τε καὶ ἡνιόχου Pl.*Phdr.*246a; ὄχημα Lib. *Ep.*1457.1. 2. metaph., ὑ. ἀνορέαι *soaring* spirits, Pi.*P.*8.91; ἴτω ὑπόπτερον (sc. τὸ νεῖκος) let it pass *swift as flight*, E.*Hel.*1236; ὑ. φροντίσιν *light*-minded, A.*Ch.*603 (lyr.); δόμον..κλῄσον ὑπόπτερος *fly* and shut it, Ion Trag.14 (lyr.): prov., ὑ. δ' ὁ πλοῦτος wealth *has wings*, E.*Fr.*420.4.

**ὑπόπτ-ευμα**, ατος, τό, *suspicion*, dub. rest. in Epicur.(?)*Oxy.*215 iii 12 (*Berl.Sitzb.*1916.886). -ευτέον, *one must suspect*, Gal.6. 317. -ευτής, οῦ, ὁ, *one who suspects*, Adam.2.36. ⊕-εύω, *to be suspicious*, X.*Hier.*2.17, Lys.1.10; ὑ. ἔς τινας c. inf. fut., *have suspicions* of them that..., Th.4.51. 2. merely, *suspect, guess, suppose*, opp. ἱκανῶς συννοῶ, Pl.*Tht.*164a, cf. X.*HG*5.4.29; *have an inkling of*, Pl.*Grg.*453b; ὁ ἵππος ὑ. τι X.*Eq.*6.14:—Pass., *to be conjectured*, Pl.*Lg.*967b. II. trans., *suspect, hold in suspicion*, τινα S.*El.*43, Th.8.39; θὴρ ὑ. κυναγώς Theoc.23.10; ὑ. τινὰ ἔς τι of something, Hdt.3.44:—Pass., *to be suspected, mistrusted*, Th.4.86; εἴς τι Id.6.92, Arist.*Rh.Al.*1437$^a$1: impers., ὡς ὑπωπτεύετο as *was generally suspected*, X.*HG*5.4.20. 2. c. acc. pers. et inf., *suspect that* he.., ὑ. αὐτὸν δρησμὸν βουλεύειν Hdt.8.100, cf. 127, Th.4.126, Pl. *Tht.*151b: c. inf. fut., ἄν τινας ὑποπτεύῃ μὴ ἐπιτρέψειν αὐτῷ ἄρχειν Id.*R.*567a, cf. Hdt.3.77: also ὑ. τινὰ ὡς.. *suspect of* him that.., ib.68; ὑ. μὴ.. Id.9.90. 3. c. acc. rei, *look with suspicion* or *apprehension on*, τὸ πρῆγμα Id.6.129; τὸ μέλλον E.*Rh.*49 (lyr.): also ὑ. τι *suspect* something, Id.*IT*1036, etc.; δεινὸν προσδοκᾶν ἢ ὑ. Epicur.*Ep.*1 p.30 U.; τι περί τινος Pl.*Cra.*409d; τι κατά τινος Plb. 8.20.2: c. acc. et inf., ἀλογώτατα ὑ. ἀεὶ λέγεσθαι Phld.*Ir.*p.44 W. III. *observe, notice*, δεῖ ἀκριβῶς ὑποπτεύειν ἥτις ἐστὶν ἡ ποιητικὴ αἰτία (of a gout-attack) Alex.Trall.12:—Med., τὸν ἄρρωστον ὑ. εἰ πάρεστι πυρετός Id.*Verm.*init. ⊕ -ης, ου, ὁ, (ὑφοράω, fut. ὑπόψομαι) *suspicious, jealous*, ἀνδρ' ὑπόπταν (Dor.) S.*Ph.*136 (lyr.); ἔς τινα Th.6.60; οὐδενὸς Arist. *HA*629$^b$10. 2. of a horse, *shy*, X.*Eq.*3.9, Sch.Th. l. c.

**ὑποπτήσσω**, *crouch* or *cower beneath*, like hares, birds, etc., πετάλοις ὑποπεπτηῶτες (Ep. pf. part. from shorter stem πτη-, cf. κατα-, προσ-πτήσσω) Il.2.312; ὑποπτήξας τάφῳ E.*Hel.*1203; ὑπέπτηχε *cowers*, Luc.*Musc.Enc.*4. II. metaph., *crouch before* another, *bow down to*, τινι X.*Cyr.*1.5.1; also ὑ. τοὺς νέους θεοὺς A.*Pr.*960, cf. 29, X.*Cyr.*1.6.8; τὸ τῶν Ἀθηναίων ἀξίωμα Aeschin.2.105: abs., *to be modest* or *shy*, X.*Cyr.*1.3.8.

**ὑπόπτιλλος**, ον, (πτίλος) *with somewhat inflamed eyes*, *CPR*218.3 (iii A. D.), *Gloss.*

**ὑποπτίσσω**, *crush slightly*, aor. part. -πτίσαντες Thphr.*HP*4.8. 14 Gaza (ὑποπτήσαντες codd.).

⊕ **ὕπ-οπτος**, ον, (ὑφοράω, fut. ὑπόψομαι) *viewed with suspicion* or *jealousy*, of persons, A.*Ag.*1637; opp. πιστός (trusted), Th.3.82; c. dat., *an object of suspicion to* one, πόλει E.*El.*644, cf. Th.4.103, 104, etc.; ὑ. τινὸς *suspected* in relation to a thing, Plu *Pomp.*56; ἐπί τινι Luc.*Cal.*29: c. inf., ὑ. αὐτοῖς μὴ προθύμως πέμψαι *suspected* by them of not having sent.., Th.6.75. 2. of things, τάδ' ἦν ὕποπτα E.*IT*1334; τούτων ὑπόπτων ὄντων Antipho 2.2.4, cf. Epicur.*Sent.*13, *Sammelb.*5761.22 (i A. D.); ὑ. ἂν γένοιτο X.*Cyr.*2.4.16; ὑ. καθειστήκει

c. inf., it was *matter for suspicion* to.., Th.4.78: τὰ ὕ. *suspected defects*, Plu.*Galb*.24. b. *expected, foreseen*, of ague fits, ὕ. ἡμέρα, προσβολή, Ruf.*Fr*.68, Dsc.5.113. 3. Adv., -τως διακεῖσθαι or ἔχειν to lie *under suspicion*, τινι Th.8.68, X.*HG*2.3.40. II. Act., *suspecting, fearing*, c. gen., ἁλώσεως E.*Hec*.1135; πρὸς φαρμακίην ὕ. Aret.*SD*1.5, etc.: τὸ ὕ. *suspicion, jealousy*, τὸ ὕ. τῆς γνώμης Th.1.90, cf. Plu.*Cleom*.36, Hdn.4.1.1; τῷ ὕ. μου *from suspicion* of me, Th.6.89; εἰς ὕποπτα μὴ μόλῃς ἐμοί E.*El*.345. Adv., *with suspicion*, -τως ἀποδέχεσθαι πάντα Th.6.53, cf. 8.66; ὕ. ἔχειν πρός τινα Isoc.8.112, D.19.132; περὶ τὰ προσφερόμενα Arist.*Pr*.926$^b$22. 2. of a horse, = ὑπόπτης 2, Poll.1.197.

**ὑποπτύσσω**, *fold, wrinkle under* or *a little*, Hp.*Nat.Mul*.7 (Pass.), Gal.*UP*10.9 (Pass.), al.

**ὑποπτῠχίς**, ίδος, ἡ, *joint*, τοῦ θώρακος Plu.*Alex*.16.

**ὑπόπτωσις**, εως, ἡ, *falling down*: metaph., καθ' ὑπόπτωσιν *submissively*, *Stoic*.3.169. 2. *incidence on the senses*, τοῦ χρώματος S.E.*M*.7.85, cf. 161,215, Gal.8.509.

**ὑποπτώσσω**, = ὑποπτήσσω, Q.S.5.368, 7.132. II. *give way a little*, ὑποπτώξασα ἡ νοῦσος Aret.*CD*1.5.

**ὑπο-πτωτικός**, ή, όν, *servile, submissive*, *Stoic*.3.155. -πτωτος, ον, *falling under, incident on*, ταῖς αἰσθήσεσι Diog.Oen.7, cf. Hierocl. p.23A., Alex.Aphr.*de An*.131.29, Porph.*Sent*.44, Procl. *in Prm*. p.659S.

**ὑποπύγιον**, τό, v.l. for ὀρροπύγιον, Arist.*PA*694$^b$19.

**ὑποπυθμένιος**, ον, = sq., Ath.11.492a: neut. as Subst., *bottom*, or perh. *base*, Ῥοδιακὴ κύλιξ -ιον οὐκ ἔχουσα *IG*11(2).287*B*90 (Delos, iii B.C.).

**ὑποπύθμην**, ενος, ὁ, ἡ, *under the bottom*, read by some in Il.11.635, for ὑπὸ πυθμένες ἦσαν, v. Ath.11.492a, Eust.869.8: glossed as ὑποβάσεις in Sch.T Il. l.c.

**ὑποπυθμίδιος**, ον, *at the bottom of the vessel*, *AP*6.300 (Leon.).

**ὑποπῡΐσκω**, (πύον) in Pass., *begin to suppurate*, Hp.*VC*18.

**ὑποπυκν-άζω**, *indulge somewhat frequently in*, [οἴνῳ] Luc.*Lex*.14 codd. (πυκνὰ ἐπιψεκάζοιμι Sommerbrodt). -ος, ον, *somewhat quick*, πνεῦμα (respiration) Hp.*Epid*.2.3.11. -όω, *condense* or *harden somewhat*, Gal.1.169:—Pass., *become somewhat dense*, Ptol.*Alm*.8.2.

⊛ **ὑπόπῡος**, ον, *tending to suppuration*, Hp.*VC*15: τὸ ὕ. a kind of *ulcer*, Gal.12.759. II. *mixed with pus*, γάλα Arist.*HA*522$^a$10.

**ὑποπῡρεταίνω**, *to be somewhat feverish*, Hp.*Epid*.7.26.

**ὑπόπῡρος**, ον, (πῦρ) *with fire under, with secret fire*, πάγαι, of Nauplius' signals, S.*Fr*.435 (lyr.); λιγνύς Adam.*Vent*.34. 2. metaph., ὑποπύρου τὰς φρένας, opp. ψυχῆς ὑγιαινούσης, of St. Paul, Porph.*Chr*.27.

**ὑποπυρρ-ίζω**, *to be reddish*, Dsc.2.146, Alex.Mynd.ap.Ath.9.387f. ⊛ -ος, *reddish*, Hp.*Prog*.11, Arist.*HA*616$^a$21, *PGrenf*.1.33.10 (ii B.C.).

**ὑποπύρωπος** [πῠ], ον, *rather fiery-eyed*, *PSI*6.569.8 (iii B.C.).

**ὑπόπωλος**, ον, *with a foal at foot*, of a mare, Str.8.3.28, *Hippiatr*.114; κάμηλος *PGen*.30.7 (ii A.D.); cf. ὕπαρνος.

**ὑποράβδωσις**, εως, ἡ, *fluting*, [κίονος] *Supp.Epigr*.4.447.19 (Didyma, ii B.C.).

**ὑποράπτω, ὑπορᾰφή**, v. ὑπορρ-.

**ὑπ-οργάζω**, *knead a little* (sens. obsc.), Hippon.84.

**ὑποργηθεῖσα**· ὑποχρισθεῖσα, Hsch.

**ὑπορέγχω**, *snore slightly* or *gently*, Hp.*Coac*.18.

**ὑπόρειος**, v. ὑπώρειος.

**ὑπορέμβομαι**, *wander*, πρὸς τὴν ἀγορὰν ἀσμένως Chor.p.122B.

**ὕπορθ-ος**, ον, *more or less upright, propped up in bed*, Herod. Med. in *Rh.Mus*.58.96. 2. τὰν οὖσαν ὑπ[ορ]θον ἐν τὰν Κρυβέλαν (sc. ὁδόν) perh. *almost direct to*.., Ἀρχ.Ἐφ.1927/8.123 (Thessaly, ii B.C.). ⊛ -όω, *prop up, support*, Sm.*Ps*.43(44).19, Sch.D Od.8.66, Dosith.p.435K. -ριος, α, ον, *towards morning, early*, φωναὶ [τῆς χελιδόνος] *Anacreont*.9.9. -ωμα, ατος, τό, *prop, stay*, *Gloss*. -ωσις, εως, ἡ, *renewal*, εἰς ὕ. τιμωρίας as expl. of *ad subrigenda*, ib. (cf. *Abh.Berl.Akad*.1865.268).

**ὑπ-όρνῡμι**, aor. 1 -ῶρσα, aor. 2 -ώρορε (v. infr.):—*rouse secretly* or *gradually*, mostly in tmesi, πᾶσιν ὑφ' ἵμερον ὦρσε γόοιο Il.23.108, cf. Od.4.113; in aor. 2, τοῖον γὰρ ὑπώρορε Μοῦσα such *was the* Muse's *power to move*, 24.62:—Pass., *rise secretly* or *gradually*, τοῖσιν ὑφ' ἵμερος ὦρτο γόοιο 16.215: so in plpf. Act. (intr.), πολὺς δ' ὑπὸ κόμπος ὀρώρει 8.380.

**ὑπόροφος**, ον, (from ὄροφος, reed) ὕ. βοά *the soft* note *of the pipe*, E.*Or*.147 (lyr.).

**ὑπόρραιβος**, ον, *somewhat crooked* or *bandy-legged*, Sch.B Il.8.164.

**ὑπορρᾰπίζω**, *put in rapid motion*, v.l. for ἀπορριπίζω or -ραπίζω in D.H.*Comp*.14 (Pass.).

**ὑπο-ρράπτω**, *patch*, θεώμενος ὑπερραμμένον τὸν χιτῶνα J.*AJ*17.5.7; [κάδος] τὸν πυθμένα ὑπέραπται *has a mend* in the bottom, *IG*2$^2$.1542.22; also φαῦλα ὑπέρραπτο ὑποδήματα *was wearing patched* shoes, Them.*Or*.20.237b. II. metaph., ὕ. λόγον *make up* a story, E.*Alc*.537. ⊛ -ρρᾰφή, ἡ, = *subsutio*, *Gloss*. -ρρᾰφος, ὁ, *cobbler*, dub. in *Wiener Denkschr*.44(6).44 (Cilicia).

**ὑπορρᾰχίς**, ίδος, ἡ, *hollow above the hip*, Poll.2.136.

**ὑπορρέω**, *flow under* or *beneath*, Arist.*Mir*.843$^a$21, Plu.*Crass*.4, 2.949d. 2. *infiltrate*, Hp.*Loc.Hom*.29. II. metaph., 1. *slip* or *glide into unperceived*, παρανομία ἠρέμα ὑπορρεῖ πρὸς τὰ ἤθη Pl.*R*.424d; λόγος τις ἅμα καὶ φήμη ὕ. πως Id.*Lg*.672b; ἁμαρτία κατὰ μικρὸν -ρέουσα D.19.228: c. dat., τἄδικον πολλαῖς ὑπερρύηκε E.*Fr*.497.5: c. acc., τὴν ψυχὴν ὕ. δυσχέρειαι Plu.2.437d: hence, *undermine*, ὑπὸ [τοῦ Φαβίου] ὑπορρέοντος ἀψοφητὶ καὶ παρεμπίπτοντος ἐνδελεχῶς ὑπερειπόμενος καὶ δαπανώμενος ἐλάνθανε [ὁ Ἀννίβας] Id.*Fab*.19; ὑπέρρει αὐτὸν τὸ νόσημα Parth.13.1; τοὺς ἐν ἁπάσῃ καθεστάναι δοκοῦντας εὐδαιμονίᾳ πάντα ταῦτα.. ὑπέρρει D.20.49. 2. *slip away*, ἐρείσματα ἐκ μέσου ὑπορρέοντα Pl.*Lg*.793c; τό τοι καλὸν ἄνθος ὕ. v.l. for ἀπο- in Theoc.7.121; of the hair, *fall off*, Luc.*Ep.Sat*.24; of friends, Id.*Vit.Auct*.27: of Time, *slip away, glide on*, ὑπορρέοντος τοῦ χρόνου Ar.*Nu*.1289: of persons, ὕ. εἴς τινα *sink to the level of*.., Plu.*Nic*.1; ὕ. εἰς ἰδιωτισμὸν *fall* into.., Epict.*Ench*.33.6.

**ὑπορρήγνῡμι**, in Pass., οὐρανόθεν ὑπερράγη αἰθήρ the air *is cleft beneath* from heaven on high, Il.8.558, 16.300.

**ὑπόρρηνος**, ον, (ῥήν, ἀρήν) poet. for ὕπαρνος, Il.10.216.

**ὑπόρριζος**, ον, (ῥίζα) *under* or *below the root* (sc. navel), Arist.*HA*493$^a$18. II. *with piece of root attached*, Thphr.*HP*2.1.3, *CP*1.2.2. III. Subst. ὑπόρριζον, τό, *secondary root*, Dsc.1.11.

**ὑπορρίν-ιον** [ρῑ], τό, (ῥίς) *part below the nose*, Hp.*Acut.(Sp.)*25, Ruf.*Onom*.40. 2. *moustache*, Poll.2.80. -ος, ον, *under the nose*: ὑπόρρινα, τά, *moustaches*, Ctes.*Fr*.29.53 (unless this be acc. sg. from a subst. ὑπόρρις). II. *speaking through the nose*, Hsch.

**ὑπορρῑπίζω**, *fan from below* or *gently*, πῦρ *AP*9.443 (Paul. Sil., with single ρ):—metaph. in Pass., ὑπορριπίζεσθαι ἐπὶ στάσεις App.*BC*1.105; πολλοῖς κόποις εἰς τὸ πέλαγος τοῦτο Syn.Alch.p.66B.

**ὑπορρίπτω**, *throw down* or *under*, ὕ. τινὰ τοῖς θηρίοις *throw* him to the wild beasts, Plu.*Eum*.17; πικροῖς δεσπόταις ὕ. ἑαυτούς Ph.1.376; so **ὑπορριπτέω**, App.*Mith*.38; πᾶν γένος δελέατος ὑπερρίπτει prob. cj. in Plb.29.8.3. 2. *insert under*, ὑπορρίπτειν τὸ σπαθίον ὑπὸ τοὺς χιτῶνας *Hippiatr*.20.

**ὑπορροιζέω**, *whirr* or *plash gently*, Plu.2.590c, Sch.Theoc.1.7.

**ὑπόρροος**, contr. -ους, ὁ, (ὑπορρέω) *runnel* or *channel to draw off* moisture *below*, in fomentations, Hp.*Fract*.29.

**ὑπόρρυθμος**, ον, *of right measure* or *proportion*, Ptol.*Tetr*.143 (= εὐάρμοστος Procl.*Par*.). II. of a hexameter, *in which each foot ends with a word*, Sch.Heph.p.293C., al.

**ὑπορρῠπαίνω**, dub. in S.*Ichn*.153: v. ἀπορρυπαίνω.

⊛ **ὑπόρρῠσις**, εως, ἡ, (ὑπορρέω) *surface-drain* for streets, Str.14.1.37 (pl.). 2. *drainage* of wounds, Heliod.ap.Orib.50.49.1. II. metaph., *falling away* of flesh, Hp.*Off*.3 (dub. sens.).

**ὑπόρρῡσος**, ον, *rather wrinkled*, βλαστήματα Aët.12.42.

**ὑπ-ορρωδέω**, *to be a little afraid of*, τὸ κακόν Eup.98.

**ὑπ-όρυγμα**, ατος, τό, *hole dug underneath, mine*, Aen.Tact.32.8 (pl.), *PLond*.2.245.11 (iv A.D.).

**ὑπορυκ-τικός**, ή, όν, *of* or *for mining*, Ph.*Bel*.97.36. -τον, τό, *funeral vault*, *IGRom*.1.804 (Heraclea-Perinthus).

**ὑπ-όρυξις**, εως, ἡ, *undermining*, τειχῶν Ph.*Bel*.99.11 (pl.), cf. Ath.Mech.31.6.

⊛ **ὑπ-ορύσσω**, Att. -ττω, *dig under, undermine*, τὸ τεῖχος, τὰ τείχεα, Hdt.5.115, 6.18, *PRyl*.127.11 (i A.D.); μέρος τοῦ ἐξαγωγοῦ *PTeb*.13.10 (ii B.C.); τὸ σταθμόν, of burglars, ib.804.12 (ii B.C.); σύριγγα Polyaen.6.17: abs., Ath.Mech.20.3: metaph., τὰς κοινὰς διαλύσεις ὕ. Plu.*Ages*.35; τὰ τῆς διαίτης Luc.*Merc.Cond*.31; ὕ. τῶν ἀπορρήτων ἔνια *find* them *out*, Plu.2.490c.

**ὑπορχ-έομαι**, *dance with* or *to music*, πρὸς δὲ καρδίᾳ φόβος ᾄδειν ἕτοιμος ἠδ' (fort. ἡ δ') ὑπορχεῖσθαι A.*Ch*.1025: c. acc. cogn., ὄρχησιν ὕ. Plu.*Num*.13; ὕ. γόους *sing and dance* a lament, Hld.6.8. II. *sing and dance* a character, of a pantomimic actor, Luc.*Salt*.16. -ημα, ατος, τό, *song accompanied by dancing and pantomimic action*, Pl.*Ion*534c, D.H.*Dem*.7, Plu.2.1134c, Luc.*Salt*.16. -ημᾰτικός, ή, όν, *of* or *for* a ὑπόρχημα, D.H.*Dem*.43; ποίησις ὕ. (compared to the κόρδαξ) Ath.14.630d,e; παίων τέταρτος, ὁ -κός, ὁ καὶ κρητικός, ⏑⏑⏑–, Choerob. *in Heph*.p.218C. -ησις, εως, ἡ, *dancing in accompaniment to song*, Sch.Ar.*Ra*.924. -ηστής, οῦ, ὁ, = *pantomimus*, dub. in *Gloss*.

**ὑπόσαθρος**, ον, *somewhat rotten*, Luc.*DMort*.10.1, *Fug*.32.

**ὑποσαίνω**, *fawn*, of dogs, Ael.*NA*17.17; ὕ. τῇ γλώττῃ, of a lion, ib.9.1, etc. II. c. acc., *fawn upon*, of men, Plu.2.65c; in Ep. form **ὑποσσαίνω** A.R.3.396.

**ὑποσαίρω**, *grin a little*, ὕ. ὀδόντας *show* one's teeth *a little*, Opp.*C*.2.243, τὰ χείλη ὑποσέσηρε Poll.4.145. II. *burst*, of over-ripe fruit, Philostr.*Im*.1.31.

**ὑποσᾱκίζω**, *strain* or *filter away* (cf. σακεύω), Hsch.:—metaph. in Pass., ὑποσακίζεται τὰ χρήματα *Com.Adesp*.645. II. *trot*, ὕ. τῆς ὁδοῦ *go briskly forward*, Ael.Dion.*Fr*.296 (corrupted to ὑποσκιάζειν in *EM*783.26).

**ὑποσᾰλεύω**, *agitate and urge on gradually*, in Pass., ὕ. εἰς ὀργὴν ὁ δῆμος App.*BC*2.143.

**ὑπόσᾰλος**, ον, *under the sea*, νησίον *Stad*.72. II. *shaken underneath, undermined*, γῆ Plu.2.434c (ὑπὸ σάλου codd.); ὀδόντες ὕ. *loose* teeth, Dsc.1.105.5.

**ὑποσάνδᾰλος**, ον, *in the form of a sandal*, ὑπόδημα Lyd.*Mag*.1.17.

**ὑποσᾰνίδιον** [ῐδ], τό, *under-side of a plane*, Hero *Aut*.30.4.

**ὑπόσαπρος**, ον, *somewhat putrid* or *rotten*, Hp.*Prog*.13, *Int*.1.

**ὑποσαρκ-α**, in Lat. form *hyposarca*, a cause or kind of dropsy, *Gloss*. -ίδιος [ῐδ], ον, *under the flesh* or *skin*, Hp.*Morb*.1.3, v.l. in *Acut.(Sp.)*52, Dsc.3.45. -ιος, ον, v.l. for foreg. in Dsc. l. c. -όω, *form flesh* or *heal up from below*, τὸν κόλπον Gal.11.129:—Pass., Id.10.325.

**ὑποσείραιος**, ον, *dragged alongside*, like a σειραῖος ἵππος, cj. Musgr. in E.*HF*445 (anap.).

**ὑπόσεισμα**, ατος, τό, *dust, crumbs*, τοῦ τεθραυσμένου κατὰ τὰ φορτία λιβάνου, = μάννα 1, Aët.7.40; ὑ. λιβανωτοῦ Gal.10.887, al.

⊛ **ὑποσείω**, Ep. ὑποσσ-, *rotate, spin round*, οἱ δέ τ' ἔνερθεν ὑποσσείουσιν ἱμάντι, of a stake, compared to an auger, Od.9.385; τὰ ὑποσείοντα κεφαλάς (vv.ll. -ήν, -ῆς), perh. a form of *paralysis agitans*, Hp.*Coac.*159. 2. *sift out*, v. ὑποσήθω. II. *hold out* or *throw to*, ἄρτους Ael.*NA*7.13.

**ὑποσελήν-ιος**, ον, *under the moon, sublunary*, ἡ ὑ. σφαῖρα Porph. ap.Eus.*PE*3.11. **-ος**, ον, = foreg., Xenocr.ap.Stob.1.1.29b; κόσμος Dam.*Pr.*88.

**ὑπόσεμνος**, ον, *mildly venerable* or *grave, impressive*, Philostr.*VS* 2.5.3, *Im.*1.29, *VA*8.6, Aristaenet.2.18.

**ὑποσευαντήρ**, ῆρος, ὁ, *driver-away*, λοιμοῦ *Ath.Mitt.*38.64 (Callipolis).

**ὑποσήθω**, *sift out*, ὑποσήσας τὸ λεπτότατον ἄλευρον Gal.6.481 (v.l. -σείσας).

**ὑποσημαίνω**, *throw out hints of, intimate*, τι Th.1.82; χρεῶν ἀποκοπάς Pl.*R.*566a; χελιδὼν ὑ. τι Ael.*NA*1.52, cf. Plu.*Per.*11: abs., *indicate*, καθάπερ τοὔνομα αὐτὸ ὑ. Arist.*EN*1122a23, cf. 1112a 16. 2. in military sense, σάλπιγγι ὑ. *make signal* by sound of trumpet, τῇ σάλπιγγι σιωπὴ ὑπεσημάνθη Th.6.32; also ὑπεσήμηνεν ἡ σάλπιγξ ἀνακλητικόν Plu.*Comp.Pel.Marc.*3: abs., ἡ σάλπιγξ ὑ. D.C.49.9, cf. Polyaen.1.35.1. 3. intr., *to be just visible*, of the whites of the eyes, Archig.ap.Orib.46.26.4. II *sign*, ἐπιστολῇ *PSI*5.471.3 (v/vi A.D.); πιττάκιον *PKlein.Form.*1033 (vi A.D.). III. Med., *observe*, τὠυτὸ σχῆμα ἔχοντα Hp.*Morb.*3.16.

**ὑποσημει-όομαι**, Med., *note down*, τὰ λεγόμενα D.L.2.48. II. *undersign, sign*, *BGU*287.14 (iii A.D.), *POxy.*1115.8 (iii A.D.), etc. III. *mark by numbers*, v.l. for παρασ- in Ptol.*Geog.*1.24. 7. **-ωσις**, εως, ἡ, *noting down*, ὑποσημειώσεις ποιεῖσθαι take *notes* of a conversation, D.L.2.122, cf. Nicom.*Harm.*1, Iamb.*VP*23.104 (pl.). 2. *signature*, *PMeyer*15.14 (iii A.D.), *PLips.*33 ii 17 (iv A.D.), Lyd.*Mag.*3.3, al.

⊛ **ὑποσήπω**, *cause to fester*, σάρκα Ael.*NA*6.5:—Pass., ib.1.51.

**ὑποσῑγάω**, *to be silent at* or *during*, Aeschin.2.162.

**ὑποσίδηρ-ος** [ῐ], ον, *having a mixture* or *proportion of iron in it*, Pl. *R.*415b. 2. *shod with iron*, σκύταλον Ar.*Fr.*402b (codd. Poll., σκυτάλιον Bgk. fr. Sch.Ar.*Av.*1283). **-όω**, in pf. part. Pass., δακτύλιοι χρυσοῖ -σεσιδηρωμένοι, i.e. iron rings gilded, *Inscr.Délos* 399 *B* 14 (ii B.C.).

**ὑποσῑμ-ος**, ον, *somewhat flat-nosed*, *PCair.Zen.*76.11 (iii B.C.), Ael. *NA*12.27, Philostr.*Her.*11, *BGU*316.14 (iv A.D.). 2. *somewhat concave*, Sor.1.12. **-όω**, *curve* or *bend upwards a little*, Alciphr.1.39.

**ὑποσιωπ-άω**, *pass over in silence*, Aeschin.3.239. II. *keep silent*, Ph.2.178, Ael.*VH*8.16. ⊛ **-ησις**, εως, ἡ, *a passing over in silence*, Greg.Cor. in Rh.7(2).1184 W., cf. Sch.D.1.2 (where its difference from ἀποσιώπ- is explained), 1.9. **-ητέον**, *one must be silent upon, suppress*, Ph.ap.Eus.*PE*8.14.

**ὑποσκάζω**, *limp a little*, Plu.2.4a, Luc.*Tim.*20, *Cont.*1.

**ὑπόσκαιος**, ον, *somewhat sinister*, Phot. s.v. ἴθυμβος.

**ὑποσκαίρω**, *spring* or *jump up*, c. acc. cogn., ἴχνος πεδίλῳ Nonn. *D.*8.21.

**ὑποσκᾰλεύω**, *stir up*, τὸ πῦρ Ar.*Ach.*1014.

**ὑποσκάλλειν**· ὑπεργάζεσθαι, Phot.

**ὑποσκαλμίς**, ίδος, ἡ, *the lower part of a* σκαλμός, *EM*715.22.

**ὑπόσκαμβος**, ον, *somewhat crooked*, Tz. ad Lyc.96.

**ὑποσκάπτω**, *dig under, dig about*, τὰς συκᾶς Thphr.*HP*2.7.5: metaph., τὸν τῆς ἡδονῆς τοῖχον ὑ. *undermine*, Eratosth.ap.Ath.13. 588a; ὑ. μακρὰ ἅλματα *mark* a long leap, Pi.*N.*5.20.

**ὑποσκαριφισμός**, v. ὑποσκαφισμός.

**ὑποσκᾰφή**, ἡ, *undermining*, σπηλαιώδεις ὑ. τῆς θαλάσσης Dsc.5.91.

**ὑποσκᾰφἴόκαρτος**, ον, (κείρω) of hair, *cut somewhat in the* σκάφιον *fashion* (v. σκάφιον (A) II), Nicostr.Com.32.

**ὑποσκᾰφισμός**, ὁ, (σκαφίς (A) II) *cleaning of corn with a shovel, winnowing*, Plu.2.693e; v.l. ὑποσκᾰρῐφισμός, *scraping lightly* to get rid of stones (cf. Paton in *CR*15.250).

**ὑποσκελ-ίζω**, *trip up one's heels, upset*, D.54.8; ἀλλήλους Luc. *Anach.*1; [οἶνος] ὑ. τοὺς πεπωκότας Eub.94.12:—Pass., Ph.2.39, Plu.2.6e; ὁ πρέσβυς ἐκ μέθας ὑπεσκέλισται *APl.*4.307 (Leon.). 2. metaph., ὑ. καὶ ἀνατρέπων Pl.*Euthd.*278b; ὑ. καὶ συκοφαντεῖν D.18.138, cf. Phld.*Vit.*p.24 J.:—Pass., Lxx *Ps.*36(37).31, Ph.2.58, al. **-ισμα**, ατος, τό, *fall given by tripping up*, Lxx *Pr.*24.17. **-ισμός**, ὁ, *tripping up, supplanting*, ib.11.3.

**ὑποσκεπάω**, *conceal, hide*, *Hymn.Mag.*5.18.

**ὑποσκέπτομαι**, *to be on the look-out for*, Hp.*Prog.*7, al.; *see underneath*, Arat.96 codd. (sed leg. ποσσὶν ὕπο σκ.).

**ὑποσκευάζω**, *repair*, dub. l. in *PTeb.*5.74 (ii B.C.).

**ὑποσκευή**, ἡ, *foundation*, Lat. *substructio*, *Gloss.*, *IGRom.*4.766 (Mossyna).

**ὑποσκήνιον**, τό, (σκηνή) in a theatre, *room under the stage*, Poll.4. 124 (pl. in 123), Ath.14.631f.

**ὑποσκηνόω**, *take shelter under*, δέρρεις αἷς ὑπεσκήνουν J.*BJ*3.7.17.

**ὑποσκῐ-άζω**, *overshadow gradually*, τῆς ὥρας ὑποσκιαζούσης as the time of day *gradually made it dark*, i.e. as it began to grow dark, Hippoloch.ap.Ath.4.130a. II. f.l. for ὑποσακίζω (q.v.). **-ἀσις**, εως, ἡ, *overshadowing*, Hp.*Ep.*12 (pl.). **-άω**, poet. for -άζω, ἣν ὑποσκιάησι..ἠέλιον νεφέλη Arat.854:—Pass., σκοπέλοισιν ὑποσκιόωνται ἄρουραι A.R.1.451. **-όεις**, = sq., χῶρος Nic.*Th.*96 (v.l. ὑπὸ σκ.). **-ος**, ον, (σκιά) *overshadowed, shaded*, ὑ. ἐν ψυκτηρίοις A.*Fr.* 146; νιφάδι..ὑ. θήσει χθόνα ib.199.8; ὑ. στόματα, of suppliants, *shaded by their olive-branches* (ἱκετηρίαι), Id.*Supp.*656 (lyr.); opp. ὑπαίθριος, Thphr.*CP*1.17.3; ὑ. περίπατοι Plu.*Alex.*7.—In Alciphr. 1.39, leg. ὑπόσκιος (-οις codd.)..δάφναις..κατάκλισις.

**ὑποσκιρτάω**, *leap up*, Ael.*NA*7.8, Philostr.*Im.*1.9; Πὰν ὑ. Εὔιον *dances* the Evian fling, ib.14.

⊛ **ὑπόσκληρ-ος**, ον, *somewhat hard*, Hp.*Fract.*11, *Art.*86. **-ύνομαι**, Pass., *become hardish*, Thphr.*Vent.*58.

**ὑπόσκνῑπος**, ον, *somewhat shortsighted*, *PPetr.*3p.8, al. (iii B.C.); also **ὑπόσκνιφος**, ib.p.15 (iii B.C.), *PSI*8.907.21 (i A.D.); **ὑπόσκιφος**, *Sammelb.*6822.12 (ii B.C.); **ὑπόσχνιφος**, *PTeb.*816 i 18 (ii B.C.).

**ὑποσκόλιος**, ον, *somewhat crooked*, Aret.*SD*1.8.

**ὑπόσκοπος**, ον, *looked under*, χείρ, of a hand *held so as to shade the eyes*, A.*Fr.*339, cf. σκώψ 2.

**ὑποσκότ-εινος**, ον, *somewhat dark*, *Gloss.* **-ιος**, ον, (σκότος) *overshadowed*, τῷ πλήθει τῶν βελῶν Sch.E.*Or.*1485.

**ὑποσκύφιος** [κῠ], ον, *beneath the scalp* or *pericranium*, Paul.Aeg.3. 22, 7.16.

**ὑποσκῠφισμός**, ὁ, v.l. for περισκυφισμός in Paul.Aeg.6.7.

**ὑποσκώπτω**, *banter*, τινας Alex.Aphr. *in Mete.*66.24.

**ὑποσμᾰρᾰγέω**, *resound under*, Q.S.12.97.

**ὑποσμήχω**, *rub* or *wipe a little*, Them.*Or.*20.235b, Paul.Aeg.3. 22, Alex.Trall.*Febr.*2 (sed leg. -σμύχεται).

**ὕπ-οσμος**, ον, (ὀσμή) *subject to*, i.e. *guided by, the smell*, Arist. *de An.*421b12, cf. S.*Ichn.*91, Hsch., Phot.

**ὑποσμύχω** [ῡ], *cause to smoulder away, consume slowly*, prob. in Aët.7.39:—Pass., ὑποσμύχονται ὀπωπαί A.R.2.445: metaph., ὑποσμύχουσα· ἔνδον ἐρεθίζουσα, Hsch., ἐνδιερεθίζουσα, ὑποκαίουσα, θλίβουσα, καταπονοῦσα, Phot., Suid. II. Pass., of fire, *smoulder*, Eust.864. 50, 1012.13; of itching, prob. in Alex.Trall.*Febr.*2: metaph., ὁ νοῦς ..ζωπυρεῖται -σμυχόμενος Eust.1656.47; ὑποσμύχεταί τι ἀπειλῆς Id. 717.51.

**ὑποσοβέω**, *swagger under*, πλατυνομένοις ἐναλλὰξ τοῖς ἀγκῶσι τοὺς πήχεις ὑποσοβῶν Hld.10.30.

**ὑποσόλοικος**, ον, *in somewhat bad taste*, Cic.*Att.*2.10.1, 14.21.3, Plu.2.615d (Comp.).

⊛ **ὑπόσομφος**, ον, *somewhat spongy* or *porous*, Erot. s.v. σπόγγοι, Sor.2.34, Gal.6.571, Them.*Or.*18.222d. 2. of the pulse, *rather soft*, Marcellin.*Puls.*297.

**ὑποσορικόν**, τό, *lower part of a tomb*, *JHS*6.357 (Aperlae): cf. ὑποστολικός.

⊛ **ὑποσόριον**, τό, *vault below the* σορός, *TAM*2.437.13, 438.5 (Patara), *JHS*6.356 (Aperlae).

**ὑπόσοφος**, ον, *sub-scientific*, τέχναι Philostr.*VA*8.7.3.

**ὑποσπᾰδίας**, ου, ὁ, *one who has the orifice of the urethra too low*, Gal.19.445: also **ὑποσπᾰδιαῖος**, Id.*UP*15.3, Heliod.ap.Sch.Orib. 50.3(p.54c D.), Paul.Aeg.6.54.

**ὑποσπᾰθ-ίζομαι**, Pass., *undergo an operation on the skull* (v. sq.), *PMed.* in *Arch.Pap.*4.270 (iii A.D.). **-ισμός**, ὁ, *an operation* for eye-affections, *wherein a spatula* (cf. sq.) *is introduced under the skin* of the scalp to produce lines of scar tissue on the forehead, Gal.14.784, Paul.Aeg.6.6: cf. ὑπο-, περι-σκυφισμός. **-ιστήρ**, ῆρος, ὁ, *spatula*, ibid.

**ὑποσπαίρω**, *gasp* or *struggle*, esp. in death, Anon.ap.Suid.; of hysterical respiration, ἀτάκτως ὑ. *draw short and irregular breaths*, Paul.Aeg.3.71.

**ὑποσπᾰνίζομαι**, Pass., used by Trag. only in pf. part., *to be scant* or *stinted of*, ὑπεσπανισμένοι βορᾶς A.*Pers.*489, cf. *Ch.*577. 2. of things, *to be lacking, to be left undone*, τί δ' ἐστὶ χρείας τῆσδ' ὑπεσπανισμένον (cf. χρεία II. 4) S.*Aj.*740. II. Act. in signf. I. 1, Procop.*Goth.*2.20, 3.25; in signf. I. 2, Ph.2.64,73.

⊛ **ὑποσπασ-μός**, ὁ, *drawing secretly away*, Aq.*De.*15.1. **-τέον**, *one must withdraw*, *Gp.*14.7.25. **-τος**, ον, *capable of being pulled out from under*, κλίνας..ἐχούσας τραπέζια ὑπόσπαστα ἐξ ἑαυτῶν *Inscr.Délos* 1403 *Bb* i 30,34 (ii B.C.).

**ὑποσπάω**, *draw away from under*, στρώματα D.24.197; τὰ σκολύθριά τινων ὑ. Pl.*Euthd.*278b; τὸν κίονα Arist.*Ph.*255b25; ὑ. τινὰ ἐκ τῶν ποδῶν, i.e. trip him up, Luc.*Asin.*44, cf. Plu.2.535f. 2. *draw off*, τὴν ὑποστάθμην Protagorid.4; τὸ πῦρ Dsc.1.30; ὑ. τῆς ποσότητος τοῦ γάλακτος *reduce* the baby's ration of milk, Sor.1. 116. II. metaph., *withdraw secretly, filch away*, ποίμνης νεογνὸν θρέμμ' ὑποσπάσας E.*El.*495; ὑπέσπασεν φυγῇ πόδα *withdrew* his foot *secretly*, stole away, Id.*Ba.*436:—Med. ὑποσπάσασθαι in X.*Eq.*7.8 is (prob.) *to draw one's skirts from under one*, of a horseman after mounting:—Pass., *to be withdrawn*, Arist.*Somn.Vig.*457b24. 2. εἰπεῖν ὑ. *refuse* to say, Phld.*Lib.*p.23 O.

**ὑπόσπειρα**, ἡ, *a kind of hair-dressing*, Poll.2.31.

**ὑποσπείριον**, τό, *base in the form of a* σπεῖρον III, Hero *Spir.*1.10.

**ὑπόσπειρον**, τό, *plinth of Ionic base*, *Supp.Epigr.*4.453.7,23 (Didyma, ii B.C.), *Rev.Phil.*36.71 (Iconium).

**ὑποσπείρω**, *sow, implant*, πραπίδεσσι πόθον Melanipp.7; ὕδασι μειλιχίην *APl.*4.333 (Leont.), cf. Ph.2.13, Plu.*Lys.*5; *introduce, interweave*, λόγους Πλάτωνος Id.*Dio*11; οὐρανομήκεις ἐλπίδας ὑ. Eun. *Hist.*p.251 D.:—Pass., *to have plants sown in the midst*, φοινικῶν -όμενος *CPR*45.7 (iii A.D.), cf. *Sammelb.*5670.7 (ii A.D.); *to be overspread*, ῥίζαις ὑπεσπαρμένον λεπταῖς Dsc.1.3: metaph., πνεύματα ὑπέσπαρται ἐν τῷ σώματι Cass.*Pr.*43.

**ὑπόσπῖλος**, ον, *rather spotted*, Philum.*Ven.*15.4.

**ὑποσπλην-ίζομαι**, Pass., *have a plaster* or *compress laid upon one's* *wound*, Sch.Ar.*Pl.*1082; but ὑπεσπληνισμένον· ὑπωπιασμένον (ὑποπ- cod.), ἢ πεποικιλμένον, Hsch. (i. e. *having a black eye*). **-ος, ον,** *suffering in the spleen*, Hp.*Epid.*3.17.ϛʹ, Gal.6.630.

**ὑποσπογγίζω,** *wipe with a sponge*, *Gp.*6.12.1.

**ὑποσποδίζω,** *to be* or *become somewhat ash-coloured*, Dsc.5.79.11.

**ὑποσπονδορχηστής,** οῦ, ὁ, like ἐπι-, a kind of *priest*, *Inscr.Olymp.*80.11 (i A. D.), 122.16 (iii A. D.).

**ὑπόσπονδος,** ον, (σπονδή) *under a truce* or *treaty*, *secured by treaty*, ὑπόσπονδοί τε ἔφασαν εἶναι ἕτοιμοι..ἐκχωρῆσαι ἐκ τῆς νήσου Hdt.3.144; ὑ. ἐξέρχονται ἐκ τῆς χώρης Id.5.72, cf. 126; κατελθεῖν ἐπὶ τὰ ἑωυτοῦ ὑ. Id.6.103, cf. E.*Ph.*81; ὑ. ἀφιέναι τοὺς ἀφεστῶτας X.*HG*1.2.18, cf. 2.2.1; τὴν Ταυρικὴν ὑ. λαβών *IPE*2.423 (Tanais): esp. in phrases of taking up the dead from a field of battle, τοὺς νεκροὺς ὑ. ἀποδοῦναι to allow a truce for taking up the dead, Th.1.63, 6.103, X.*HG*2.4.19; τοὺς νεκροὺς ὑ. κομίσασθαι, ἀνελέσθαι, etc., to demand a truce for so doing, which was an acknowledgement of defeat, Th.2.79, 4.44, etc.

**ὑποσπονδοφόρος,** ὁ, = ὑποσπονδορχηστής, *Inscr.Olymp.*121.19 (iii A. D.).

**ὑποσπουδάζω,** dub. l. in J.*AJ*19.2.5, D.C.39.25 (leg. ὑπερεσπούδαζε).

**ὑποσσαίνω, ὑποσσείω,** Ep. for ὑποσαίνω, ὑποσείω.

**ὑποστάζω,** intr., *drop slowly*, *Gloss.*; ὑ. ἐκ ῥινῶν *to have a running at the nose*, v.l. in Hp.*Coac.*205.

**ὑποστάθμη,** ἡ, *foundation*, D.S.3.44 (pl.). **II.** = ὑπόστασις B. I. 1, *sediment*, Pl.*Phd.*109c, Protagorid.4, Dsc.5.103, Plu.2.130b, etc.; ἐν τῇ Ῥωμύλου ὑποστάθμῃ, as a translation of Cicero's *in faece Romuli*, Plu.*Phoc.*3, cf. Cic.*Att.*2.1.8; ὑ. τροφῆς, almost = περίττωμα, Hp.*Vict.*2.45; of matter, ἡ πάντων ὑ. Dam.*Pr.*36, cf. Zeno *Stoic.*1.29, Procl. *in Alc.*p.181C.

**ὑποστάθμιος,** ον, *by weight* (?), ὑποστάθμιον ἀγόρασον ἡμικοτύλην ξηρομύρου *POxy.*1142.1 (iii A. D.).

**ὑποσταθμίς,** ίδος, ἡ, = ὑποστάθμη II, Zos.Alch.p.218 B., Phot., Suid.

**ὑπόσταλσις,** εως, ἡ, *drawing in*, *contraction*, τῆς κοιλίας prob. l. in Arist.*HA*$499^{a}21$.

⊛ **ὑπόστἄσις,** εως, ἡ, (ὑφίστημι, ὑφίσταμαι): **A.** as an act, *standing under*, *supporting*, ἡ κεφαλὴ τοῦ μηροῦ καὶ ὁ αὐχὴν τοῦ ἄρθρου..ὑπὸ συχνῷ μέρει τοῦ ἰσχίου τὴν ὑ. πεποίηται Hp.*Art.*55; [τοὺς προσθίους πόδας] ἔχουσιν..οὐ μόνον ἕνεχ' ὑποστάσεως τοῦ βάρους Arist.*PA*$659^{a}24$; ἐνεπάγην εἰς ἰλὺν βυθοῦ, καὶ οὐκ ἔστιν ὑ. Lxx *Ps.*68(69).3. **2.** *resistance*, τοῦ κύματος Arist.*Mete.*$368^{b}12$ (unless = *settling down*); so perh. in Hp.*Off.*3, Ael.*Fr.*59. **3.** *lying in ambush*, S.*Fr.*719.

**B.** as a thing, **I.** in liquids, *that which settles at the bottom*, *sediment*, Hp.*Steril.*242, Arist.*HA*$551^{b}29$, *Mete.*$382^{b}14$, Thphr.*HP*9.8.3; esp. of *sediment* in the urine, Hp.*Coac.*146,389, *Aph.*4.69, al., Gal.6.252, al.; but the urine itself is called ἡ ὑ. ἡ εἰς τὴν κύστιν, Arist.*Mete.*$358^{a}8$; ἡ τῆς ὑγρᾶς τροφῆς ὑ. Id.*PA*$647^{b}28$; ἐκ τῶν νεφρῶν ἡ γιγνομένη ὑ. ib.$671^{b}20$; also of the dry excrement, ἡ τῆς ξηρᾶς τροφῆς ὑ. ib.$647^{b}28$, cf. $677^{a}15$, *Mete.*$358^{b}9$. **b.** *an accumulation of pus*, *abscess*, Hp.*Art.*40. **2.** νέφους ὑποστάσεις cloud-*cumuli*, D.S.1.38. **3.** a kind of *jelly* or *thick soup*, in pl., Men.462.10 (cf. Poll.6.60), Orib.4.8.1. **4.** metaph. of time, *duration*, ἡ στιγμιαία τῶν καιρῶν ὑ. Gal.19.187; μνήσθητι τίς μου ἡ ὑ. remember how short my *time* is, Lxx *Ps.*88(89).48; ἡ ὑ. μου ὡσεὶ οὐθὲν ἐνώπιόν σου mine *age* is as nothing before thee, ib.38(39).6; ἐφ' ὅσον αὐτοῦ (sc. Ἕκτορος) ἡ ὑ. τῶν χρόνων ὑπῆρχεν as long as his *store* of years lasted, Vett.Val.347.14. **5.** *coming into existence*, *origin*, ἡ ὑ. μου ἐν τοῖς κατωτάτω τῆς γῆς Lxx *Ps.*138(139).15; περὶ τοῦ γένους..τῶν Ἰουδαίων..ὅτι..τὴν πρώτην ὑ. ἔσχεν ἰδίαν J.*Ap.*1.1; ἀκμὴ οὐδὲ ἔχει γενέσεως ὑ. καθ' ἑαυτήν has no *power* of originating by itself, Hermog.*Id.*1.10. **II.** *foundation* or *substructure* of a temple, etc., Lxx *Na.*2.7, D.S.1.66, 13.82; ὑποστάσεις ἐπάλξεων *lower part* of a crenellated wall, Ph.*Bel.*84.9; ὑ. ξύλου is f.l. for ὑπότασις ξ. in Hp.*Mochl.*25. **2.** metaph. of a narrative, speech, or poem, *groundwork*, *subject-matter*, *argument*, Plb.4.2.1, D.S.1.3, etc. **3.** *plan*, *purpose*, Id.16.32; κατὰ τὴν ἰδίαν ὑ. Id.1.28, 15.70; πρὸς τὴν ἰδίαν ὑ. Id.1.3; οἱ Αἰγύπτιοι..ἰδίᾳ τινὶ ὑ. κεχρημένοι εἰσί (sc. in their calendar) Gem.8.16, cf. 25; κατὰ τὴν Καίσαρος ὑ. *BMus.Inscr.*892.21 (Halic., i B.C./i A. D.). **4.** *confidence*, *courage*, *resolution*, *steadiness*, of soldiers, Plb.4.50.10, 6.55.2; *hope*, ἔστι μοι ὑ. τοῦ γενηθῆναί με ἀνδρί Lxx *Ru.*1.12; ἀπώλετο ἡ ὑ. αὐτῆς ib.*Ez.*19.5, cf. *Ep.Hebr.*3.14; ἡ ὑ. τῆς καυχήσεως 2*Ep.Cor.*11.17, cf. 9.4; ἔστιν δὲ πίστις ἐλπιζομένων ὑπόστασις *confidence* in things hoped for, *Ep.Hebr.*11.1 (unless *substance* be the right sense here). **5.** *undertaking*, *promise*, οἱ ὑπογεγραμμένοι γεωργοὶ ἐπέδωκαν ἡμῖν ὑπόστασιν *PEleph.*15.3 (iii B.C.), cf. *PTheb.Bank* 1.8 (ii B.C.), *PTeb.*61(*b*).194 (ii B.C.). **6.** Astrol., τὰ τούτου (sc. κλήρου τύχης) τετράγωνα ὑπόστασις (fort. -στάσεις) [λέγεται] Serapio in *Cat.Cod.Astr.*8(4).227. **III.** *substantial nature*, *substance*, δύσσχιστα, τῷ κολλώδη τὴν ὑ. ἔχειν woods hard to cleave, because of their resinous *substance*, Thphr.*CP*5.16.4; ἡ τοῦ γεώδους ὑ. ib.6.7.4. **2.** *substance*, *actual existence*, *reality* (οἱ νεώτεροι τῶν φιλοσόφων ἀντὶ τῆς οὐσίας τῇ λέξει τῆς ὑ. ἐχρήσαντο Socr.*HE*3.7), opp. semblance, φαντασίαν μὲν ἔχειν πλούτου, ὑ. δὲ μή Artem.3.14; τῶν ἐν ἀέρι φαντασμάτων τὰ μέν ἐστι κατ' ἔμφασιν, τὰ δὲ καθ' ὑπόστασιν (*substantial*, *actual*), Arist.*Mu.*$395^{a}30$, cf. *Placit.*3.6, D.L.7.135, 9.91; so ὑποστάσεις are the *substances* of which the reflections (αἱ κατοπτρικαὶ ἐμφάσεις) appear in the mirror, *Placit.*4.14.2; ὑ. ἔχειν have *substantial existence*, Demetr.Lac.*Herc.*1055.14, S.E.*P.*2.94,176, M.Ant.9.42; ἰδίᾳ χρησάμενον ὑποστάσει (ὑποτάσει cod.), πρὸς ἰδίαν ὑ. φυτευθέντα, a separate *existence*, Sor.1.96, cf. 33; ὑπόστασιν μὴ ἔχειν Id.2.57; ὑποστάσεις τε καὶ μεταβολαί M.Ant.9.1, cf. 10.5; [ἡ παρασιτική] διαφέρει καὶ τῆς ῥητορικῆς καὶ τῆς φιλοσοφίας..κατὰ τὴν ὑ. (in respect of *reality*)· ἡ μὲν γὰρ ὑφέστηκεν, αἱ δὲ οὔ Luc.*Par.*27; κατ' ἰδίαν ὑ. καὶ οὐσίαν S.E.*M.*9.338. **3.** *real nature*, *essence*, χαρακτὴρ τῆς ὑ. *Ep.Hebr.*1.3. **IV.** as a Rhet. figure, *the full expression* or *expansion* of an idea, Hermog.*Id.*1.11, Aristid.*Rh.*1 p.479 S., Syrian. *in Hermog.*1.60 R. **V.** = ὑπόστημα III, *camp*, Lxx 1*Ki.*13.23, 14.4. **VI.** *wealth*, *substance*, *property*, ib.*De.*11.6, *Je.*10.17, *POxy.*1274.15 (iii A. D.), *BGU*1020.16 (vi A. D.), etc. **2.** pl., *title deeds*, *documents recording ownership of property*, *POxy.*237 viii 26 (ii A. D.).

**ὑποστᾰτ-έον,** *one must suppose* or *assume*, Sch.Il.11.24: Adj. **-έος,** *subeundus*, *Gloss.* ⊛ **-ης,** ου, ὁ, *that which stands under*, *support*, *prop*, Plu.*Cor.*24; *stand* of a bowl, etc., Paus.10.26.9. **II.** *one that gives substance*, *creator*, Procl.*Theol.Plat.*3.7, *Inst.*53, Simp. *in Ph.*1327.5. **-ικός,** ή, όν, *able* or *willing to face*, c. gen. rei, ὑ. τῶν δοκούντων δεινῶν Muson.*Fr.*8 p.39 H. **2.** abs., *patient*, *steadfast*, *firm*, Arist.*EE*$1222^{a}33$ (Comp.); ἔν τινι D.S.20.78. Adv **-κῶς** Plb.5.16.4. **II.** *belonging to substance*, *substantial*, Arr.*Epict.*1.20.17. **2.** c. gen. rei, *giving substance to*, *causing the existence of*, τῶν ὅλων Procl. *in Prm.*p.537 S., cf. *Inst.*25, Herm. *in Phdr.*p.136 A., Dam.*Pr.*300; opp. φθαρτικός, Ammon. *in Porph.*103.15. **III.** *-κόν, τό*, *entrance-fee* paid by initiates, *IG*5(1).1390.50 (Andania, i B.C.). ⊛ **-ις,** ιδος, ἡ, fem. of ὑποστάτης II, Procl.*Theol.Plat.*3.7. **-ός,** όν, or **ὑπόστᾰτος,** ον, (ὑφίσταμαι) *set under*: as Subst., ὑπόστατον, τό, *stand*, = ὑποστάτης, *IG*$2^{2}$.1388.43, 11(2).161 *B* 126 (Delos, iii B.C.), Paus.10.26.9, Demiopr.ap.Poll.10.46. **II.** *to be borne* or *withstood*, οὐχ ὑποστατόν E.*Supp.*737; θεὸς..θνητοῖς οὐδαμῶς ὑ. Id.*Fr.*177.2 (as Scal. for -της). **III.** *substantially existing*, *Stoic.*2.114, A.D.*Synt.*201.9, S.E.*M.*10.60, Iamb.*Comm. Math.*8. **-ρια,** ἡ, *an under-handmaid of a temple*, *IG*5(1).248 (Amyclae).

**ὑποστᾰχύομαι,** Pass., *yield increase like ears of corn*: metaph., ὑποσταχύοιτο βοῶν γένος Od.20.212.—Later we find an Act., ὑποσταχύεσκον ἴουλοι as v. l. (ap.Sch.) in A.R.1.972 (ἐπι- codd.A.R.).

**ὑποστέγ-ασμα,** ατος, τό, v. l. for ὑποπέτασμα in Poll.7.208. **-ή,** ἡ, = *casula*, dub. in *Gloss.* **-ιον,** τό, = *suggrunda*, ib. **-νόομαι,** Pass., *to be made air-tight*, Ph.*Bel.*102.14. **-ος,** ον, (στέγη) *under the roof*, *in the house*, S.*Ph.*34: also with Verbs of Motion, βεβᾶσιν δωμάτων ὑπόστεγοι Id.*El.*1386; εἰσδέδεγμαι πημονὴν ὑπόστεγον Id.*Tr.*376. **2.** *covered over*, ἄντρον Emp.120; δεξαμεναί Pl.*Criti.*117b; καθέδραι D.H.3.68. **3.** βίος ὑ. *indoor* life, Them.*Or.*30.350a; ἡ ὑ. φιλοσοφία Jul. *ad Them.*262d. **-ω,** *cover up*, X.*Cyn.*5.10; *contain*, *hold*, *Placit.*4.22.2.

**ὑποστείχω,** *go under*, τὸν ποταμόν Philostr.*VA*1.25.

**ὑποστελεύς,** έως, ὁ, dub. sens., τοῖς ὑποστελεῦσι (in accounts of a trading cruise) *PCair.Zen.*753.25 (iii B.C.): ὑποστολεῦσι may be meant.

⊛ **ὑποστέλλω,** *draw in*, *contract*, ὑπέστειλ' ἱστίον *made* him *furl* his sail, Pi.*I.*2.40, cf. Arist.*Mech.*$851^{b}10$ (Med.); ὑ. τὴν οὐράν *tuck down* the tail, of dogs, Ammon.*Diff.*p.27 V.; τοῖς δακτύλοις ὑπεσταλμένοις with *closed* fingers, Aristaenet.1.10; γαστὴρ ὑπεσταλμένη Philostr.*Gym.*34. **2.** *reduce*, in Pass., *to be reduced*, ὑποστέλλεται τὸ πλῆθος (sc. τῆς καθάρσεως) Sor.1.22; *to be limited*, τῷ λεχθέντι ἀριθμῷ Ph.1.29. **3.** *draw back for shelter*, ὑπὸ βουνόν τινα τοὺς ἱππεῖς Plb.11.21.2, cf. Plu.*Crass.*23,26; ὑ. ἑαυτόν *shelter* oneself *behind*, τινι or ὑπό τι, Id.*Arat.*47, Plb.7.17.1; with ἑαυτόν omitted, Id.6.40.14, etc.: metaph., ἑαυτόν *Ep.Gal.*2.12, cf. Hld.7.26. **b.** *cover*, τᾷδ' ὑπεστάλη κόνει (in a dog's epitaph) *PCair.Zen.*532.24 (iii B.C.). **4.** intr., *to be reduced in size*, Callix.1; *to be subordinate*, οὐδενὶ ἑτέρῳ S.E.*M.*8.32, cf. Ph.2.335,357. **5.** *draw back*, φασὶ τοὺς θορυβώδεις καὶ προυνίκους ὑποστέλλειν αὐτοῦ τῇ παρόδῳ *drew back* to let him pass, D.L.4.6; of troops, ὑπεσταλκότες *a little in the rear*, Ael.*Tact.*19.7; ἔχειν ὑπεσταλκότας ταῖς ῥαξὶν τοὺς ὄνυχας have the nails *not projecting beyond* the finger-tips, Sor.1.3, cf. 18. **6.** *take away*, *remove*, in Pass., A.D.*Adv.*203.22; *to be excepted*, Id.*Pron.*30.8, al. **7.** *belong*, c. dat., *POxy.*486.22 (ii A. D.), $1502^{v}.3$ (iii A. D.), *PFlor.*47.8,29 (iii A. D.); τῇ συγγραφοδιαθήκῃ *POxy.*1102.14 (ii A. D.); τῷ νυνὶ ἀμφοδογραμματεῖ, i. e. *fall within* his *authority*, ib.2131.13 (iii A. D.); *to be subjected*, ποιναῖς πρός τινος Lyd.*Mag.*3.70. **II.** in Med., *place restrictions on oneself* or *another*, *reduce diet*, Hp.*Aph.*1.11: c. gen., *abstain from*, τῆς τροφῆς Arist.*Pr.*$864^{b}36$; ὀπώρας Aret.*CA*1.1. **2.** *avoid*, χειμῶνα Hp.*Aph.*4.6; *shrink from*, οὐδένα..κίνδυνον *SIG*442.10 (Erythrae, iii B.C.), cf. *IG*12(8).53.6 (Imbros, ii B.C.); τι τῶν ἀγαθῶν πρὸς τὸ μὴ εἶναι αὐτῷ Arist.*MM*$1208^{a}1$; ὁ μηδὲν ὑποστειλάμενος πρὸς ὕβριν one who has *stuck at* nothing, D.21.70. **3.** *shrink before*, *hold in undue awe*, τὴν Δημάδου δύναμιν Din.1.11; οὐ γὰρ μὴ ὑποστείληταί σε Lxx *Ex.*23.21, cf. *De.*1.17, *Wi.*6.7; ὑποστείλασθαί τι δεῖ πρὸς τὸν τοιοῦτον ὑμᾶς καὶ αἰσχυνθῆναι; need you *hold back*..? Din.3.13: abs., Ael.*NA*7.19; *draw back*, *Ep.Hebr.*10.38. **4.** ὑποστέλλεσθαι λόγῳ *place restrictions on oneself* in speech, E.*Or.*607 (only here in Trag.); without λόγῳ, *refrain from saying*, οὐ μὴν οἶμαι δεῖν..ὑποστείλασθαι περὶ ὧν ὑμῖν συμφέρειν ἡγοῦμαι D.1.16; οὐδὲν ὑπεστειλάμην τῶν συμφερόντων τοῦ μὴ ἀναγγεῖλαι ὑμῖν *Act.Ap.*20.20, cf. 27; οὔτε μέγα οὔτε μικρὸν ἀποκρυψάμενος..οὐδ' ὑποστειλάμενος Pl.*Ap.*24a; οὐδὲν or μηδὲν ὑποστειλάμενος *with* no *reserve*, Isoc.6.89, 8.41, 9.39, D.4.51; *make reservations*, Phld.*Rh.*1.109, 110 S.; ὀμνύω μὴ ὑπεστάλθαι *POxy.*246.26 (i A. D.); περὶ τῶν μόσχων,

..οὗ ἕνεκεν ὑπεσταλμένοι εἰσίν dub. sens. in *PCair.Zen.*412.24 (iii B.C.). 5. = διαλανθάνω, *delitesco*, *Gloss.*; so perh. in Gal.7.646.

***ὑπόστεμα**, v. ὑπόστημα III.

**ὑποστενάζω**, = ὑποστένω, *utter low moans*, S.*Aj.*322, 1001. II. [Ἄτλας] οὐράνιον πόλον νώτοις ὑποστενάζει *groans under* the weight of heaven, A.*Pr.*430 (lyr.).

***ὑποστενᾰχίζω** (v.l. -στονᾰχίζω), *groan beneath*, γαῖα δ' ὑπεστενάχιζε Διί Il.2.781.

**ὑπόστενος**, ον, *somewhat narrow*, Dsc.2.176, 3.38.

**ὑποστένω**, *moan in a low tone*, S.*El.*79; ὑποστένοι μέντἂν ὁ..λεώς *would grumble*, Ar.*Ach.*162, cf. Charito 6.2; gloss on ὑποστεναχίζω, Sch.Il.*Oxy.*1086.45.

**ὑποστερν-ίζομαι**, Med., *place under one's breast*, φελλούς Plu.2.324f. **-ος**, ον, *under the breast*, glossed by ὑπογάστριον, Hsch.

***ὑπόστη**, ἡ, prob. part of a tomb (cf. ὑπώστη, εἰσώστη), *Supp.Epigr.*4.194,195 (Halic.), *BCH*12.280,281 (Myndus).

***ὑπόστημα**, ατος, τό, (ὑφίστημι) *that which sinks to the bottom, sediment*, esp. in urine, Hp.*Judic.*3; of excrement and urine, τὰ ὑ. τῆς κοιλίας καὶ τῆς κύστεως (cf. ὑπόστασις B. I. 1) Arist.*HA*487ᵃ6, cf. *PA*653ᵇ11; ὑ. τὸ λευκόν, of birds, ib.679ᵃ18. II. *that which is set under, support*, Id.*IA*708ᵇ2. 2. *base, stand*, Callix.2, Hegesand.45, *IG*3.1418,1419,1421; cf. ὑπόθημα. III. *a station of soldiers, camp*, Lxx 2*Ki.*23.14 (with v.l. ὑπόστεμα). IV. = περίνεος, Poll.2.171, Ruf.*Onom.*101. V. *multitude*, Hsch.

**ὑποστηρ-ιγμα**, ατος, τό, *underprop*, Lxx 3*Ki.*7.11(24), 10.12, al., J.*AJ*8.7.1. **-ίζω**, *underprop, sustain*, Lxx *Ps.*36(37).17, al., Luc.*Hist.Conscr.*3, *VH*1.32, Gal.18(2).433; τῷ λαιῷ βραχίονι τὸ τόξον ὑπεστήρικτο Hld.1.2.

**ὑποστιγμή**, ἡ, Gramm., *comma*, D.T.630.14, Quint.*Inst.*11.3.35, Simp. *in Cael.*316.20; ὑ. ἐνυπόκριτος, ἀνυπόκριτος (qq.v.), Nicanor ap.Sch.D.T.pp.24,27 H.

**ὑπο-στίζω**, *make somewhat variegated* or *spotted*, Nonn.*D.*1.333; ὑπεστιγμένοι ὀφθαλμοί Philostr.*Gym.*25. II. Gramm., *put a comma*, Phlp. *in Mete.*99.10. **-στικτέον**, *one must put a comma*, Simp. *in Cael.*316.19, etc.

**ὑποστίλβω**, *shine a little, glisten*, Dsc.5.85, Philostr.*VA*3.11, Charito 1.4; *shine under*, of eyes, Opp.*C.*1.421.

**ὑποστιμμίζω**, *paint with* στίμμι, Aët.7.79.

**ὑπόστιφρος**, ον, *rather harsh*, φωνή Ar.ap.*Gloss.Oxy.*1803.3.

**ὑποστολεύς**, v. ὑποστελεύς.

**ὑποστολή**, ἡ, *fasting*, Plu.2.129c, Heliod.ap.Orib.46.20.6. 2. *omission of a letter*, τοῦ ῑ A.D.*Adv.*187.22: generally, *removal*, Id.*Pron.*91.26, al. II. *shrinking, timidity, evasion*, *Ep.Hebr.*10.39, Hsch.; δι' ὑποστολῆς *holding back*, Ascl.*Tact.*10.21; μετά τινος ὑ. with a certain *reserve*, Phld.*Rh.*1.108 S. III. *concealment, dissimulation*, J.*BJ*2.14.2.

**ὑποστολίζω**, = ὑποστέλλω, *furl*, λαῖφος *Lyr.Adesp.*132 = *Trag.Adesp.*377.

**ὑποστολικός**, ή, όν, perh. *underground*, or misspelling of ὑποσορικός, ποιαλίς (i.e. πυαλίς) *TAM*2.706 (Araxa).

***ὑπόστολοι**, οἱ, officials of the Serapeum at Demetrias in Thessaly, τὸ κοινὸν τῶν ὑ. *IG*9(2).1107, cf. Ἀρχ.Δελτ.1.148 (Eretria).

**ὑποστόμια**, τά, *small tags of iron on the bit*, Poll.1.184; cf. ἐχῖνος v.

**ὑποστοναχίζω**, v. ὑποστεναχίζω.

**ὑποστόρεσμα**, ατος, τό, = ὑπόστρωμα, Gal.6.447, *UP*12.3, al.

**ὑποστόρνυμι**, Philostr.*VA*3.27, also in Pass., X.*Cyr.*8.8.16 (with v.l.), Gal.*UP*2.7 (with vv.ll.), Med. in Ael.*NA*9.26; also **ὑποστρώννυμι** or **-ύω**, Plu.*Art.*22, Phan.Hist.11, Gal.6.447: fut. ὑποστορῶ Eub.90.1; also -στρώσω Amphis 46: aor. -εστόρεσα Od.20.139; also -έστρωσα E.*Hel.*59, etc. (v. infr.): plpf. ὑπεστρώκει Babr.34.2 (ap.Suid.): pf. Pass. ὑπέστρωμαι Orac.ap.Hdt.1.47; 3 sg. ὑπεστόρεσται and inf. ὑπεστορῆσθαι Anon.ap.Suid.; part. ὑπεστορεσμένος Gal.16.749, *Gp.*10.44.1:—*spread, lay*, or *strew under*, esp. of bedclothes, ἡ μὲν δέμνι' ἄνωγεν ὑποστορέσαι δμῳῇσιν Od. l. c.; ὑποστρώσεις τρίκλινον Amphis 46; προσκεφάλαια ὑποστρῶσαι Thphr.*Char.*2.11 (so in Med., ὑποστόρεσαι..τῆς ὀριγάνου *strew me* some of it *under*, Ar.*Ec.*1030, cf. Nic.*Th.*63); λέκτρα ὑποστρῶσαί τινι *make* his bed for a man, i.e. serve him as a wife, E. l. c.; ὑπεστρώννυον τὰ ἱμάτια αὐτῶν ἐν τῇ ὁδῷ *Ev.Luc.*19.36: abs., *make a bed*, οὔκουν ὑποστορεῖτε μαλακῶς τῷ κυνί; Eub. l. c., cf. Phan.Hist. l. c.:—Pass., εὗδ', ὑπὸ δ' ἔστρωτο ῥινὸν βοός Il.10.155; δάφνην ὑπέστρωται Call.*Iamb.*1.223; τὰς εὐνὰς..ὑποστόρνυσθαι X. l. c.; ὑ. στρῶμαθ' ἁλουργῆ Anaxandr.41.6 (anap.); ᾗ χαλκὸς ὑπέστρωται which *has* copper *laid under* it, Orac. ap.Hdt.1.47. 2. metaph., κέρδεσιν χεῖρας ὑ., of the action of the hand in receiving money, *APl.*4.272 (Leont.); γαλήνην ὑ. ταῖς τριήρεσιν Them.*Or.*10.133b; ὕδατίς οὐσία τις ἐστι..ὑπεστρωμένη τῷ..δέρματι Paul.Aeg.6.14. II. *bestrew with* a thing, ἅλω οἰνάροις Babr. l. c. III. metaph. in pf. Pass., *to be subject to*.., τῶν τοῖς θεοῖς κλήρων ὑπεστρωμένων Dam.*Pr.*398, cf. Procl.*Inst.*132: so in Act., *subject*, πάντα -στρώσαντες ἑαυτοῖς ib.121.

**ὑποστοχάζομαι**, *have a fundamental aim*, Gal.18(2).441.

**ὑποστρᾰβ-αινίζω**, *have a slight squint*, *PPetr.*3 p.27 (iii B.C.). **-ος**, ον, *squinting a little*, *BGU*1258.7 (ii B.C.), *PGrenf.*1.33.7 (ii B.C.), *POxy.*99.3 (i A.D.), Vett.Val.110.16.

**ὑποστρᾰτεύομαι**, *perform military service under*, τινι App.*BC*1.29.

**ὑποστρᾰτηγ-έτης**, ου, ὁ, = ὑποστράτηγος, Tz.*H.*5.219. **-έω**, *serve as subordinate commander*, τινι X.*An.*5.6.36, Luc.*Bacch.*2, App.*BC*5.54. **-ος** (proparox.), ὁ, *subordinate commander*, X.*An.*3.1.32; = Lat. *legatus*, D.H.19.14(18), App.*Hann.*10, al., D.C.59.21, etc. II. title of an official at Tenos, *IG*12(5).883.9, al. (i B.C.); in Magnesia, ib.9(2).1111.7; in Egypt, *UPZ*124.33 (ii B.C.), *PTheb.Bank* 8.9 (ii B.C.), *BGU*1060.2 (i B.C.), 1778.6, al. (i B.C.).

**ὑποστρᾰτοφύλαξ** [φῠ], ᾰκος, ὁ, *subordinate commander*, Str.12.5.1.

**ὑποστρεπ-τέον**, *one must return*, Suid., Zonar. s.v. ἀποπορευτέα. **-τικῶς**, Adv. = ὑποτροπάδην, Sch.Opp.*H.*1.636.

**ὑποστρέφω**, *turn round about* or *back*, ἵππους Il.5.581, cf. 505; πάλιν ὑ. βίοτον εἰς Ἅιδαν E.*HF*736 (lyr.); ὁ κισσὸς..Βακχίαν ὑποστρέφων ἅμιλλαν *bringing back* the Bacchic struggle, i.e. the swift and eager dance, S.*Tr.*220 (lyr., s.v.l.). 2. *roll up*, Arist.*Pr.*895ᵇ10 (Pass.). 3. Pass., *revolve beneath*, τινι Arat.73: c. acc., Id.512 (better γαῖαν ὕπο σ.). II. intr., *turn about*, esp. of persons flying or retreating, Il.12.71, Hdt.7.211, 9.14, Th.3.24; φύγαδ' αὖτις ὑ. Il.11.446; δεῦρ' ὑ. πάλιν E.*Alc.*1019; τοὔμπαλιν ὑ. X.*An.*6.6.38; πάλιν ὑποστρέψαντα φεύγειν Antipho 2.4.5:—Pass., αὖτις ὑποστρεφθείς Il.11.567, cf. Hdt.4.129; -στρᾰφείς S.*OT*728. 2. generally, *return*, αὖτις ὑ. Od.8.301, cf. Hdt.4.120,124, al.; ἐπὶ ζήτησιν ib.140; εἰς τὰς πατρίδας τὰς ἰδίας *PGiss.*40 ii 8 (iii A.D.), cf. *PFlor.*247.10 (iii A.D.); in fut. Med., οὐ μὲν γάρ τί σ' ὑποστρέψεσθαι ὀΐω Od.18.23; of a disease, *return, recur*, Hp.*Epid.*1.3, Gal.15.751. 3. *turn away*, and so *elude* an attack, E.*IA*363 (troch.), X.*An.*2.1.18: metaph. in Med., c. inf., *refuse*, τὸν ἀΐδιον ἐπιγινώσκειν Θεὸν ὑπεστρέφοντο (sc. οἱ Βλέμυες) *PMasp.*4.9 (vi A.D.). 4. ὑποστρέψαντες *reversely*, Ar.*Av.*1283. 5. *retract the accent*, A.D.*Synt.*308.8.

**ὑποστροβέω**, *agitate inwardly*, ὑπ' αὖ με δεινὸς ὀρθομαντείας πόνος στροβεῖ A.*Ag.*1215.

**ὑποστρόγγῠλος**, ον, *somewhat round*, Thphr.*HP*8.8.5, Dsc.3.4, al., Apollod.*Poliorc.*178.1.

**ὑποστροφ-άς**, άδος, ἡ, *a screw working a crane*, Ath.Mech.37.1. **-ή**, ἡ, *turning about, wheeling round*, of cavalry, Hdt.9.22: generally, *return march*, D.C.71.2. 2. in the phrase ἐξ ὑποστροφῆς, of the chariot, *turning round* the meta at the far end of the δίαυλος, i.e. *turning sharply round*, S.*El.*725: so in military sense, *wheeling right about*, Plb.2.25.3, 3.14.5, D.H.2.41, etc. b. *on the contrary*, Epist. Philipp.ap.D.18.166. 3. *return*, J.*AJ*2.14.3. II. *recurrence, relapse*, ὀδυνημάτων Hp.*Art.*50, cf. *Prog.*22, *Epid.*1.3, Gal.6.815. 2. Rhet., τὸ καθ' ὑποστροφὴν σχῆμα *recurrence* to a subject, after a parenthesis, Hermog.*Id.*2.1, cf. Aristid.*Rh.*2 p.514 S. 3. Gramm., *throwing back* of the accent, A.D.*Synt.*134.18. ***-ος**, ον, *turning back*, Them.*Or.*34 p.462 Dind., Hsch.; cf. ὑπόφορος. **-ώδης**, ες, *causing a relapse*, Hp.*Acut.*14, *Epid.*2.3.8, etc.

**ὑπόστρυφνος**, ον, *somewhat astringent*, Hp.*Int.*30, Dsc.2.5.

**ὑπό-στρωμα**, ατος, τό, *that which is spread under, bedding, litter*, ἵππου X.*Eq.*5.2, cf. Dsc.1.103, *Peripl.M.Rubr.*65. **-στρώμνιος**, ον, *laying on a bed*, Phot. **-στρώννῡμι** and **-ύω**, v. ὑποστόρνυμι. **-στρωσις**, εως, ἡ, *flooring* of a vault, Hero *Mens.*16. **-στρωτέον**, *one must spread under*, τινί τι *Gp.*14.18.5.

**ὑποστύλ-ιον** [στῡ], τό, perh. *lowest course* of a building, *PCair.Zen.*445.6 (iii B.C.). **-ισμός**, ὁ, *propping up*, of vines, *PFlor.*369.3 (ii A.D.). **-όομαι**, Pass., *to be underpinned*, Apollod.*Poliorc.*155.8. **-ος**, ον, *resting on pillars set underneath*, οἶκος Hecat.Abd.12. **-ωμα**, ατος, τό, *a dwarf pillar* as support in a ἑλέπολις, Bito 52.5. II. *shore, support*, of an undermined wall, Apollod.*Poliorc.*146.1.

**ὑποστύφω** [στῡ], *to be somewhat astringent*, Dsc.1.118; ὑποστῦφον ἥδυσμα Plu.*Ant.*24; of astringent tastes, *screw up* the mouth, οὖλα Nic.*Al.*17. 2. *treat* a part *with an astringent*, οἴνῳ v.l. in *Hippiatr.*106. 3. *make astringent*, ἄρωμα Thphr.*Od.*22 (Pass.). II. *thicken somewhat*, τὸ ἔλαιον ib.17.

**ὑπόστυψις**, εως, ἡ, *a making astringent*, Thphr.*Od.*22.

**ὑποσύγ-γρᾰφος**, ὁ, *party to a contract*, *PRyl.*128.8 (i A.D.). **-κόπτω**, in Pass., *to be syncopated a little*, A.D.*Adv.*142.11. **-χέω**, *confuse*, τὴν Πίσαν καὶ τὴν Ἦλιν Sch.Pi.*O.*1.28:—mostly in Pass., τὰ -κεχυμένα Ph.1.300, cf. 320 (cj.); ταῦτα ὑποσυγκέχυται Luc.*Sol.*10; ὑποσυγκεχυμέναι φωναί *somewhat confused*, Arist.*Aud.*802ᵃ4; of a person, J.*AJ*16.4.4. **-χρίω**, *anoint underneath*, Gal.6.228. **-χῠτος**, ον, *confused*, Ph.1.440. Adv. -τως ib.180, Phot.

**ὑποσυλάω**, *take away secretly* or *gradually*, Alex.Trall.4.1 (cf. ὑπολωπάω):—Pass., Pall. *in Hp.*2.78 D.

**ὑποσυλλέγω**, *collect gradually*, Ph.2.211 (Pass.), Heliod.ap.Orib.46.22.2 (Pass.), Sor.1.27.

**ὑποσυλλογιστικός**, ή, όν, name of a type of syllogism, *Stoic.*2.83,88.

**ὑποσυμ-βαίνω**, *to be inferior, weaker*, Gal.19.408. **-βολος**, ον, *veiled under symbols*, dub. l. in Plu.2.673b. II. of foreigners, *living under conditions embodied in special treaties* (σύμβολα), *IG*5(1).1433.14,46 (Messene) as read by Wilhelm *Jahresh.*17.57 (ὑπὸ συμβόλων ed. *IG*). **-μῐγής**, ές, *partly mixed*, Gal.6.94,137, Hierocl. *in CA* 3 p.425 M. **-πᾰθέω**, *sympathize in some degree*, v.l. in Sch. Od.2.70.

**ὑποσυν-ᾰλείφομαι**, Pass., *suffer a synaloephe*, as αὑτοῦ for ἑαυτοῦ, A.D.*Synt.*142.24; or *crasis*, as κἆτα, Id.*Conj.*231.3. **-άπτω**, *combine*, and **-ᾰφή**, ἡ, *combination*, of tetrachords separated by the interval of a fourth, Bacch.*Harm.*85. **-θετος**, ον, of words, *formed from compounds*, e.g. λιθοβολεῖ, ψευδοδοξεῖ, βουκολεῖ (from λιθοβόλος etc.), Simp. *in Cat.*71.27, cf. 10.29, Dexipp. *in Cat.*12.7. **-θημα**, ατος, τό, *a sign accompanying a watchword*, Ph.*Bel.*93.44.

**ὑποσῡρ-ιγμός**, ὁ, *whistling* of the dragon when slain, part of the

Pythian Nomos, Demetr.Lac.*Herc.*1014.53. **-ίζω**, Att. **-ίττω**, *whistle, rustle,* αἰθὴρ..πτερύγων ῥιπαῖς ὑ. A.*Pr.*126 (anap.); *make a whistling sound,* ἡ ἀρτηρία..ὑπεσύριζε Hp.*Epid.*7.25, cf. 7, al.; of snakes. Id.*Ep.*15, Ael.*NA*2.7. 2. *make a signal by whistling,* τινι Aristaenet.2.4.

**ὑποσυρμός**, ὁ, *purging,* Archig.ap.Aët.8.7.

**ὑποσύρω** [ῡ], *drag down,* τὰς ἁμάξας εἰς τὸν ποταμόν Plu.*Pyrrh.* 28; ὑ. τὰ σκέλη *trip* them *up,* D.S.17.100; ὑ. τὸν πόδα Luc.*Anach.* 27:—Pass., ὑποσυρέντων τῶν ἵππων if the horses *were tripped up,* Sch. Il.*Oxy.*221 xii 33; ὑπεσύρησαν εἰς τὸ βαθὺ τῆς λίμνης Ach.Tat.4.14: metaph., ὑποσυρῆναι εἰς τὸν ἔσχατον μεριστόν *to be brought down,* Dam. *Pr.*106; ὅταν..οἱ κάμνοντες εἰς τὴν τοιαύτην ὑποσύρωνται τοῦ σώματος διάθεσιν Gal.15.607:—Med., *draw off downwards, undermine,* χώματα App.*Mith.*76 (so the Act., v.l. in *J.BJ*2.19.5); ὑποσύρεσθαι νηδύν *purge,* Nic.*Al.*367 (so in Pass., ὑποσυρέσθω ἡ κοιλία Archig.ap.Aët.6. 7). II. metaph., *trip up,* Plu.2.446b (Pass.); *draw away gradually, seduce,* in Pass., S.E.*M.*8.241, Gal.1.317, 17(1).619; *entrance, beguile,* τὴν ἀκοήν Procop.Gaz.*Ep.*128 (Act.), 33 (Pass.). 2. *reduce, diminish, abridge,* τὴν γραφήν D.H.1.7 (v.l. for ἐπι-).

**ὑποσυστρέφω**, *roll up tight underneath,* Gal.19.148 (Pass.).

**ὑπόσυχνος**, ον, *somewhat frequent,* Hp.*Epid.*1.26.γ', Alciphr.3.42: neut. as Adv., *a good deal,* Thphr.*HP*3.12.7.

**ὑπόσφαγμα**, ατος, τό, *the blood of an animal mixed with various ingredients,* like *black-puddings,* expld. by ὑπότριμμα, Erasistr.ap.Ath. 7.324a. II. *a suffusion of blood in the eye* from a blow, S.E.*P.*1. 44, Gal.7.99, Cass.*Pr.*27; a *compression-mark* on the arm, v.l. for -σφιγμα in Antyll.ap.Orib.7.9.4. III. *the ink of the cuttle-fish,* Hippon.68B, cf. Gal.19.149.

**ὑποσφάξ**, ᾶγος [ᾰγ], ἡ, *cleft,* Opp.*H.*1.744 (Schneid. διασφάγες, from Eust.134.21, 897.60, 1476.59), Eust.897.61.

**ὑποσφίγγω**, *bind tight below,* Nonn.*D.*26.262.

**ὑπόσφιγμα**, v. ὑπόσφαγμα II.

**ὑποσφόνδῠλον**, τό, = ἱερὸν ὀστοῦν, Ruf.*Onom.*114.

**ὑποσφρᾱγίζω**, *subsigno, Gloss.*:—Med., f.l. for ἐπ- in Phalar. *Ep.*10.

**ὑπ-οσφραίνομαι**, *get scent of* a thing, interpol. in Suid.

**ὑποσφῡρίζομαι**, (σφῦρα II. 1) *cover in the seed when sown* (cf. ὑπαρόω), Poll.7.145.

**ὑποσχάζω**, *trip up,* ὑποσχάσει πτέρναν σου LXX *Si.*12.17.

**ὑποσχεθεῖν**, v. ὑπέχω.

**ὑποσχεσάριος**, ὁ, *tax-farmer* (cf. ὑπόσχεσις II), *POxy.*1432.5 (iii A.D.).

**ὑποσχέσθαι**, v. ὑπισχνέομαι.

**ὑποσχεσ-ίη**, ἡ, Ep. for ὑπόσχεσις, pl. in Il.13.369, A.R.2.948, Id. *Fr.*12.14: sg. in Call.*Epigr.*58. **-ιον**, τό, = sq., *AP*12.24 (Laureas). **-ις**, εως, ἡ, (ὑπισχνέομαι) *undertaking, engagement, promise,* οὐδέ τοι ἐκτελέουσιν ὑπόσχεσιν ἥν περ ὑπέσταν Il.2.286; τέλεσόν μοι ὑ. ἥν περ ὑπέστης Od.10.483; τὴν ὑ. ἐκτελέσαι Hdt.5.35; κραίνειν A.*Supp.*368; ἀποδιδόναι Isoc.15.75, cf. Pl.*Men.*77a; ὑ. ἀπολαβεῖν to receive the fulfilment of *a promise,* X.*Smp.*3.3; ἀπαιτεῖν τὰς ὑ. to demand *their* fulfilment, Arist.*EN*1164ᵃ17; ὑ. ψεύσασθαι to fail in *its* performance, Aeschin.1.143; μεγάλας ποιεῖσθαι τὰς ὑ. Isoc.4. 14; ἡ ὑ. ἀπέβη was accomplished, Th.4.39; δύο ὑποσχέσεις, τὴν μὲν ἀναπρᾶξαι, τὴν δὲ αὐτὸς ἀποδοῦναι Id.2.95; ἐξ ὑποσχέσεως according to *engagement, CIG*2713 (Labranda), cf. 2779 (Aphrodisias), *IG*4. 203 (Isthmus). II. *promise* to pay, ὀκτὼ δραχμῶν *PCair.Zen.* 736.25 (iii B.C.), cf. *POxy.*91.11 (ii A.D.); *contract* to execute work, farm land, etc., ib.1117.6 (ii A.D.), *PTeb.*10.7 (ii B.C.). III. *profession* of principles, Luc.*Pisc.*31.

**ὑποσχετικός**, ή, όν, *inclined to promise,* Phot., Suid. s. v. προδωσίκομπος, Eust.710.12.

**ὑποσχημᾰτίζομαι**, Med., glossed by οἷον προσποιεῖσθαι καὶ πλάττεσθαι, Phryn.*PS* p.119B.

**ὑποσχῐδᾰκώδης**, ες, (σχίδαξ) *apt to splinter,* Dsc.5.160.

**ὑποσχίζω**, *split underneath,* Ael.*NA*17.44, v.l. for ἀποσχάζω in Arist.*HA*512ᵃ30:—Pass., Poll.9.127; *to be forked,* of a blood-vessel, Hp.*Oss.*12. II. *break up* ground, *PFay.*112.5 (i A.D.), etc. (but also, *damage* land, *BGU*2.13 (iii A.D.)).

**ὑπόσχισ-μα**, ατος, τό, a kind of *man's shoe,* Poll.7.91. **-μός**, ὁ, *breaking up* of ground, *PFay.*112.3 (pl., i A.D.), *PAmh.*2.91.11 (pl., ii A.D.), etc.

**ὑπόσχνιφος**, v. ὑπόσκνιπος.

**ὑπόσχολος**, ὁ, *under-teacher,* Sch.D.18.129.

**ὑποσχόμενος**, v. ὑπισχνέομαι. **ὑποσχών**, v. ὑπέχω.

**ὑποσῴζω**, *rescue,* gloss on ὑπελύσατ', Sch.A.R.3.997:—Med., f.l. for ἀπο- in Jul.*Or.*1.25a.

**ὑποσωμᾰτόω** τινά, *renew* his *body gradually,* Herm.ap.Stob.1. 41.8.

**ὑποσώρ-ευσις**, εως, ἡ, *accumulation,* Ruf.ap.Orib.8.24.61. **-εύω**, *heap up under,* Erot. s. v. ὑπονησαμένη, Sor.1.31 (Pass.).

**ὑποσωφρονιστής**, οῦ, ὁ, *assistant-trainer* of Athenian ἔφηβοι, *IG* 2².2054.12, 2085.16, al.

**ὑποτᾰγή**, ἡ, *subordination, subjection,* D.H.3.66, 2*Ep.Cor.*9.13, *Ep.Gal.*2.5; ἐν ὑποταγῇ in a *subordinate position, BGU*96.7 (iii A.D.): pl., *Cat.Cod.Astr.*8(4).143. 2. *post-position,* ἐν ὑποταγῇ A.D.*Pron.*35.23, cf. *Synt.*306.8. 3. *copy,* ψηφισμάτων..καὶ ἐπιστολῆς *IGRom.*3.705 (Lycia, ii A.D., pl.).

**ὑπόταγμα**, ατος, τό, *registration, register, BGU*55 ii 5 (ii A.D.).

**ὑποταίνιος**, ον, *forming a long narrow strip of land,* ἄμμος Ph.1. 647; αὐχήν, of the island of Pharos, Id.2.139; (sc. γῆ), cf. ταινία II. 2) ib.524.

**ὑποτακ-τέον**, *one must subsume,* τινί τι Arr.*Epict.*2.17.7, cf. D.T. 641.27. 2. *one must subjoin,* Archig.ap.Aët.12.1. ⊛ **-της**, ου, ὁ, *one who brings into subjection,* ὦ τῶν ὑπερεχόντων ἐπιτάκται (ὑποτάκται cj. Dieterich recte)· ὦ τῶν ὑποτεταγμένων ὕψωταί *PMag.Leid. V.*7.11. ⊛ **-τικός**, ή, όν, *post-positive, necessarily placed after* something with which it is combined, e.g. μοι, opp. ὑποτασσόμενος (capable of being placed after, e.g. ἐμοί), A.D.*Pron.*35.22, cf. *Adv.* 126.21; ὑ. συλλαβαί, e.g. γμ, κμ, χμ, Id.*Synt.*7.9, cf. 58.3; ὑ. φωνῆεν a vowel *which must come second* in a diphthong, *EM*203.47, al.; στοιχεῖα (i.e. ι and υ) D.T.631.8; οὐχ ὑ. τῷ ν̄ τὸ π̄, π cannot follow ν, D.H.*Comp.*22. Adv. **-κῶς**, opp. προτακτικῶς, A.D. *Synt.*227.15. 2. ὑ. ἄρθρον, i.e. ὅς, ἥ, ὅ, D.T.640.6, A.D.*Pron.* 110.14, Greg.Cor.p.385S.; τὸ "ὅς" ὑποτακτικόν Ath.11.493b; ὑ. σύνταξις τῶν ἄρθρων A.D.*Synt.*87.2. 3. of Verbs, ὑ. ἔγκλισις *subjunctive* mood, D.T.638.8, A.D.*Synt.*246.15, al.; τὰ καλούμενα ὑ. ῥήματα verbs *in the subjunctive,* ib.265.25, cf. *Conj.*243.13, 244.18, al.; ἐὰν τοῦτο -κὸν ᾖ if this is *subjunctive,* Phryn.337; ὑ. σύνδεσμος conjunction *requiring the subjunctive,* Thom.Mag.p.132R. 4. **-τακτικόν**, τό, a charm *for bringing* people *into subjection, PMag. Lond.*121.940; ὑ. Ἀπόλλωνος ib.124.36. 5. ὑποτακτικὰ ζῴδια the *feminine* ζῴδια, i.e. even numbers beginning with Taurus, *Cat.Cod.Astr.*1.165, 5(1).187. 6. *submissive, obedient,* τέκνα *PMasp.*97ᵛD37 (vi A.D.). **-τος**, ον, *agreed,* φόρος *CPR*247.12 (iv A.D.).

**ὑποτᾰμιεύω**, *to be deputy-treasurer, OGI*473.10 (Didyma, i A.D.).

**ὑποταμνόν**, τό, *a plant cut off at bottom* for magic purposes, *h.Cer.* 228; or perh. ὑποτάμνον *borer, worm* (part. of sq.); but the word is prob. corrupt.

**ὑποτάμνω**, Ion. for ὑποτέμνω.

**ὑποτᾰνύω**, = ὑποτείνω (A) I. 1 a, ὑπὸ δ' ἕρματα..τάνυσσαν Il.1.486, cf. Ruf.ap.Orib.*inc.*20.2.

**ὑπόταξις**, εως, ἡ, *subjection, submission,* Phld.*Rh.*2.206S., D.H. 1.5, D.L.7.122. II. *drawing up* of light-armed *behind* the phalanx, Ascl.*Tact.*6.1, Ael.*Tact.*24.3, Arr.*Tact.*20.3. III. Gramm., *postposition,* A.D.*Pron.*116.5, al.

**ὑποτᾰράσσω**, contr. **-θράσσω**, Att. **-ττω**:—*stir up, trouble,* Ar.*V.* 1285, Plu.*Fab.*2, etc.:—Pass., κοιλίη..ὑπεταράχθη f.l. in Hp.*Epid.*1. 26.ε'; ὑ. πρός τι *to be somewhat troubled* at.., Luc.*DMort.*7.2. 2. ὑ. τι *cause* some *trouble,* D.C.39.56, cf. 79.4.

**ὑποταρβέω**, *to be somewhat afraid of, shrink before,* τοὺς ὑποταρβήσαντες Il.17.533.

**ὑποταρτάριος** [ᾰ], ον, *under Tartarus,* of the Titans, Il.14.279, Hes.*Th.*851, Luc.*Herc.*1.

**ὑπότᾰσις**, εως, ἡ, (ὑποτείνω) *a stretching under*: *extension,* Hp. *Fract.*18; ξύλου Id.*Mochl.*25; πεδίων ὑποτάσεις the plains *that stretch below,* E.*Ba.*749.

⊛ **ὑποτάσσω**, Att. **-ττω**, Pass., fut. ὑποτᾰγήσομαι Cyran.15: aor. 2 ὑπετάγην [ᾰ] Phryn.Com. (v. infr.), etc.:—*place* or *arrange under, assign,* τινί τι Plb.3.36.7, Plu.*Nic.*23, etc.; ὑ. ὑπὸ τὸ τῆς προδοσίας ὄνομα Plb.18.15.4:—Pass., τὸ ὑποτεταγμένον (sc. ὀστέον) the *inferior* bone, i.e. the ulna, Hp.*Off.*16. II. *post in the shelter of,* ὑποτάσσεσθαί τινι Luc.*Par.*49; *draw up behind,* Ael.*Tact.*15.1 (Pass.), Arr.*Tact.*26. 7. 2. *subject,* ἑαυτοὺς οὐδενί Phld.*Rh.*2.204S., cf. Plu.*Pomp.*64; *subdue, make subject,* Θηβαΐδα *OGI*654.7 (Egypt, i B.C.), cf. 199.10, al. (Adule, i A.D.); ἔθνη Hdn.7.2.9; αὐτῷ τὰ πάντα *Ep.Phil.*3.21; πάντα ὑπὸ τοὺς πόδας αὐτοῦ *Ep.Eph.*1.22:—Pass., *to be obedient,* τινι *Ep.Col.* 3.18, al.; ὑποτάγητε τῷ θεῷ *Ep.Jac.*4.7, cf. Arr.*Epict.*3.24.65; ἄγρια θηρία ὑποταγήσεται αὐτῷ Cyran.15; ὑποτάξονται *they will submit,* Hdn.2.2.8; τὸ πλῆθος -όμενον Onos.1.17, cf. Palaeph.38: abs., κοὐχ ὑποτᾰγεὶς ἐβάδιζεν ὥσπερ Νικίας *dejectedly, timidly,* Phryn.Com.59 (s. v.l.); οἱ ὑποταττόμενοι *subjects,* Plb.3.13.8, etc.; ὑποτεταγμένοι *subordinates,* Phld.*Oec.*p.72J.; ἐδούλευσας, ὑπετάγης Arr.*Epict.*4.4. 33; ὑποτεταγμέναι ἀρεταί *subordinate* virtues, i.e. the sub-divisions of the four cardinal (πρῶται) virtues, *Stoic.*3.64. 3. Pass., c. dat., *underlie, to be implied in* or *associated with,* τὰ -τεταγμένα τοῖς φθόγγοις Epicur.*Ep.*1p.4U., cf. *Nat.*28p.13V.; τὰ -τεταγμένα, ἡ -τεταγμένη διάνοια, of the content or meaning which *underlies* a writer's words, Phld.*Po.*5.26,27. III. *put after,* Plu.2.737f; *subjoin, append,* ὑποτετάχαμέν σοι..τὸ ἀντίγραφον *SIG*664.11 (Delos, ii B.C.), cf. *POxy.*34ᵛ iv 7 (ii A.D.):—Pass., τὰ -τεταγμένα *what follows, OGI*629. 6 (Palmyra, ii A.D.); οἱ -τεταγμένοι [ἀριθμοί] the numbers *that follow,* Plu.2.1020a, etc.; οἱ ὑποτεταγμένοι the *following* persons, *SIG*880. 11 (Pizus, iii A.D.); κῶμαι αἱ ὑποτεταγμέναι the *following* villages, Ptol. *Geog.*6.7.27. 2. *take as a minor premiss,* Arr.*Epict.*4.1.61. IV. *govern the subjunctive, EM*471.16.

**ὑποταύριον**, τό, *the part below the* ταῦρος (III) or κοχώνη, *Hippiatr.* 48, prob. in Erot. s. v. τράμιν; also **ὑπόταυρος**, ὁ, Sch.Luc.*Lex.*1.

**ὑποταφρεύω**, *undermine,* χώματα App.*Pun.*16.

**ὑποτείνω** (A), *stretch under, put under,* ὀθόνιον Hp.*VC*14, Pl.*Ti.*74a; δοκίδα ὑπὸ τὴν κλίνην Hp.*Fract.*13; ἀντηρίδας..ὑ. πρὸς τοὺς τοίχους *fixed* stay-beams *to strengthen* the ship's sides, Th.7.36:—Pass., *to be extended beneath,* Arist.*PA*695ᵃ2. b. intr., *extend under, subtend,* ὑπὸ τὴν μείζω γωνίαν ὑ. τὴν τοῦ τριγώνου (sc. ἡ γραμμή) Id. *Mete.*376ᵃ13; ἡ τὴν ὀρθὴν γωνίαν ὑποτείνουσα (sc. γραμμή or πλευρά) the *hypotenuse* or *line subtending* the right angle, Apollod.ap.Ath.10. 418f; so ἡ ὑποτείνουσα alone, Pl.*Ti.*54d, Arist.*IA*709ᵃ1,20; of a chord, *subtend* an arc, Euc.3.29; ἡ τὴν ΜΝΞ περιφέρειαν ὑποτείνουσα εὐθεῖα Theodos.Tripol.*Sphaer.*2.33 Heiberg. 2. *strain, pull hard*, [τοὺς κάλως] Ar.*Pax* 458: metaph., μεγάλας ὀδύνας ὑ. *intensifies*, S.*Aj.* 262 (anap.). II. *hold out hopes, offer*, c. inf., ὑ. τὰ ἐμπόρια συνελευθεροῦν Hdt.7.158, cf. Th.8.48; also ὑ. [τινὶ] μισθούς Ar.*Ach.*657; ἐλπίδας, ὑποσχέσεις, D.13.19, 23.14:—Med., D.C.38.31. 2. *lay* or *put before one, present, suggest*, ὑ. τοῖς λόγοις μέμψιν Paus.7.9.4; ὑ. λόγους τινὶ τοιούτους λέγειν E.*Or.*915 (tm.); ἀπάτην Plu.*Tim.*10:—Med., Pl.*Tht.*179e; also, *propose a question*, Id.*Grg.*448e; τὸ προοίμιον δύο ταῦτα ὑποτείνεται *has as its subjects*, Steph. *in Gal.*1.233 D.

**ὑποτείνω** (B), v. ὑποτίνω.

**ὑποτειχ-ίζω**, *build a wall under* or *so as to intercept, build a cross-wall*, Th.6.99, App.*Ill.*19. **–ῐσις**, εως, ἡ, *the building of a cross-wall*, Th.6.100. **–ισμα**, ατος, τό, *cross-wall*, ibid.

**ὑποτεκμαίρομαι**, *guess at* a thing, Ar.*Fr.*198.7.

**ὑποτέλ-ειος**, α, ον, *less than complete*: as Subst., ὑποτελεία, ἡ (sc. στιγμή), name of one of eight punctuations, Nicanor ap.Sch.D.T.p. 24 H. II. ὑ. ἀριθμοί numbers *which exceed the sum of their factors*, Mart.Cap.7.753. **–έω**, *pay, discharge*, of a tribute or tax, φόρον ὑ. Hdt.1.171, X.*HG*1.3.9, etc.; συντάξεις, συντάξεις καὶ φόρους, Isoc. 7.2, 12.116; τὸν φόρον ὑποτελῶ Ἀθηναίοισιν *IG*1².39.26: abs., *pay tribute*, Th.3.46, Luc.*Anach.*30, etc.: also ὑ. ἀξίην βασιλέϊ Hdt.4. 201; ὑ. ἔρανον, δῶρα, D.10.40, Plu.2.830d; μίσθωμα *IG*12(7).55.15 (Amorgos); ὑ. τι *discharge* a duty, Luc.*Rh.Pr.*23:—Pass., ὁ -τελεσθησόμενος ὅρκος *PLond.*5.1708.260 (vi A.D.). ⊛**–ής**, ές, (τέλος I. 8) *subject to taxes, tributary*, Th.2.9, 5.111; in full, ὑποτελὴς φόρου Id.1.19, 56,66, 7.57; ὑ. φόρων or φόροις (φόρου Schaefer) Plu.*Art.*21, *Pyrrh.* 23; of persons employed in government monopolies (exact sense uncertain), τοὺς ὑποτελεῖς τῇ τε ἰχθυηρᾷ κτλ. *UPZ*110.97 (ii B.C.), cf. *PTeb.*5.210, 40.24, al. (ii B.C.); τὰ ὑποτελῆ γενήματα *PRev.Laws* 28. 18 (iii B.C.), cf. 33.14, etc. II. Act., *receiving payment*, c. gen., μισθοῦ Luc.*Merc.Cond.*36. **–ίς**, ίδος, ἡ, a name given by Herillus *Stoic.*1.91 to *a subordinate object, which ought to be only held as a means towards attaining the chief good* (τέλος), cf. Stob.2.7.3ᶜ (Madvig, ὑποτελές codd.), Suid.

**ὑποτέλλομαι**, *arise*, Arat.723, A.R.2.83.

**ὑποτεμενίτης** [ῑ], Dor. **–τας**, acc. (fem.?) *-ταν*, *pertaining to the region under the* τέμενος, dub. in *SIG*247 $I^{2}$69 (Delph., iv B.C.); perh. ὑπὸ Τεμενίταν.

**ὑποτέμνω**, Ion. **–τάμνω** Aret.*CA*1.8: fut. -τεμῶ *IG* (v. infr. b):—*cut away under* or *underneath*, ὑπὸ γλῶσσαν τάμε χαλκός Il.5.74; ταμὼν ὕπο πυθμέν' ἐλαίης Od.23.204; ὑ. τὰς ἀγκύρας Plu.*Ant.*32:—Pass., ὑποτέτμηται τὰ νεῦρα τῶν πραγμάτων D.ap.Aeschin.3.166; τὰς ῥίζας ὑποτετμημένος *having* them *cut away below*, Luc.*Tim.*8; ὑποτμηθεὶς τὴν ἰγνύαν hamstrung, Id.*Tox.*60. b. *trim* the surfaces of blocks of stone, *IG*7.3073.110 (Lebad., ii B.C.). 2. *cut underhand*, i.e. *in a cheating way*, of a roguish leather-seller, Ar.*Eq.*316 (troch.). II. *cut off, intercept*, ὑ. πηγάς Pl.*Lg.*844a; ὑ. τὴν ἐλπίδα X.*HG*2.3.34; [τὰς ῥίζας] Diog.Oen.29:—more freq. in Med., ὑποταμέσθαι τὸ ἀπὸ τῶν νεῶν (sc. αὐτοῖς) Hdt.5.86; ὑποτεμοῦμαι τὰς ὁδούς σου *I will cut off* your way, *stop* you *short*, Ar.*Eq.*291, cf. Arist.*Mete.*$356^{a}27$; ὑ. τὸν πλοῦν X.*HG*1.6.15; ὑποτέμνεσθαί τινας *intercept* them, Id.*Cyr.*1. 4.19, cf. *HG*7.1.29; τοὺς χρόνους ὑμῶν ὑ. Aeschin.3.67; τὰς ὁρμάς, τὴν ἐπίνοιαν, Plb.18.38.1, 36.3.1, etc.; *forestall*, τὴν ἀκόντισιν αὐτῶν.. δρόμῳ..προσπεσόντες ὑπετέμοντο D.C.38.49; *prevent, guard against*, ὑποτέμνεσθαι τὸν φόβον (the risk of gangrene, by excision) Paul.Aeg. 6.107; ὑ. τὴν διάγνωσιν *prevents*, Id.3.78; in pf. Med., ὑποτετμημένος πάσας αὐτῶν τὰς ὠφελείας Plb.5.107.6.

**ὑποτερετίζω**, *hum the key-note* while tuning the κιθάρα, Sch.Pi.*O.* 9.59.

**ὑποτέταρτος**, ον, *contained* $1\frac{1}{4}$ *times*, i.e. *standing to another number in the ratio* 4:5, Mart.Cap.7.761.

**ὑποτετράγωνος** [ᾰ], ον, *almost square* or *rectangular*, Adam.2.23.

**ὑποτετρᾰμερής**, ές, *in the ratio of* $1:1\frac{4}{5}=\frac{5}{9}$, Iamb. *in Nic.*p.42 P.: —**ὑποτετραπλᾰσιεπίτρῐτος**, ον, *contained* $4\frac{1}{3}$ *times*, i.e. *in the ratio of* $\frac{3}{13}$, Domnin. in Boisson.*Anecd.*4.420; and **ὑποτετραπλάσιος** [πλᾰ], ον, '*subquadruple*', i.e. *in the ratio of* $\frac{1}{4}$, Nicom.*Ar.*1.18.

**ὑπότευξις**, εως, ἡ, *rejoinder, reply*, S.E.*M.*9.251.

**ὑπότεφρος**, ον, *somewhat ash-coloured*, Dsc.5.155, Ruf.*Anat.*51.

**ὑποτεχνάομαι**, *come to aid by art*, Alex.Trall.1.17.

**ὑποτήκομαι**, Pass., *waste, pine away*, Man.5.191, Max.Tyr.34.2, Ael.*NA*15.4.

**ὑποτηρέω**, *notice beforehand, foresee*, τὴν σύνοδον Sch.A.R.2.321.

⊛ **ὑποτίθημι**, *place under*, ὑπὸ κύκλα ἑκάστῳ πυθμένι θῆκεν Il.18.375; τὰ φρύγαν' ὑ. *puts* the firewood *under*, Telecl.40; θεοῦ βάσεις ὑποτιθέντος *putting* legs or feet *under* them, Pl.*Ti.*92a, cf. Arist.*PA*$686^{a}34$; σιδηρᾶς κανονίδας ὑ. Ph.*Bel.*57.11, cf. 60.31, al.; ὑπὸ ποταμοὺς πολλοὺς..πόλιν ὑ. Pl.*Lg.*682c; κύλικα ὑπὸ τὴν κλίνην *IG*12(5).593. 21 (Iulis, v B.C.); ὀχετὸν ἐκποιήσαντι καὶ ὑποθέντι ib.1².373.66; [φοίνικας] ὑ. X.*Cyr.*7.5.12; ἀλεκτορίδι ὑ. τὰ ᾠά Arist.*HA*$564^{b}3$; ἑαυτὴν [τῷ ἄρρενι] ib.$540^{a}11$; ὑ. ⟨τι⟩ ὑπὸ τὸν ὀφθαλμόν Id.*Pr.*$874^{a}9$; of a prancing horse, ὑ. τὰ ὀπίσθια σκέλη ὑπὸ τὰ ἐμπρόσθια X.*Eq.* 11.2; τὰ ὄπισθεν σκέλη διὰ πολλοῦ ὑ. *bring up* his hind legs far apart from one another, ib.1.14; κατακλίνεται [ὁ λαγὼς] ὑποθεὶς τὰ ὑποκώλια ὑπὸ τὰς λαγόνας Id.*Cyn.*5.10: metaph., ὑποχειρίους τοῖς ἐχθροῖς ὑ. τὰς αὑτῶν πατρίδας Pl.*Plt.*308a; ἔστε ὑπέθηκε Ἀΐδᾳ until he *handed him over* to Hades, of a hound attacking a boar, *PCair.Zen.*532.11 (iii B.C.):—Med., *place under one's feet*, τι X.*Cyr.*8.1.41; τοὺς μηροὺς ὑφ' αὑτά Arist.*IA*$713^{a}23$. 2. *place under* a certain class, γεωργικῇ, θηρευτικῇ, etc., Pl.*Plt.*289a. b. *subjoin, enclose, append* a document, ὑποτέθεικά σοι τὸ ἀντίγραφον *PLille*4.2 (iii B.C.), cf. *Sammelb.*5675.2 (ii B.C.), etc.: so in Med., *PLond.*3.921.10 (ii/iii A.D.). II. *set before* one, *offer, suggest*, τὴν ἐν φίλοις δικαιοτάτην ὑπόθεσιν ἔχω ὑποτιθέναι X.*Cyr.*5.5.13; *hold out* hope, ὑποτιθεὶς τίν' ἐλπίδα; E.*Or.*1186, cf. X.*HG*4.8.28, D.23.58, Plu.2.256a, *Lys.* 23, Aristid.1.379 J.; τοῦ Ἑλληνικοῦ ἐλπίδα ἣν ὑπετίθει αὐτῷ δουλώσειν Th.1.138; ἡ εὐπραγία ὑ. ἰσχὺν τῆς ἐλπίδος Id.4.65; ὑπέθηκας ὀρθῶς τοὺς λόγους, i.e. you have given good advice, E.*IA*507; τὸν ὑποθέντα τὰς τέχνας γυναιξὶ τόνδε he who *proposed* these tricks to the women, Id.*Ba.*675:—earlier in Med., *suggest*, βουλὴν Ἀργείοις ὑποθησόμεθ' ἥ τις ὀνήσει Il.8.36; ὄφρα οἱ ἤ τι ἔπος ὑποθήσεαι ἠέ τι ἔργον Od.4.163, cf. Il.11.788; δόλον ὑπεθήκατο Hes.*Th.*175; ἄλλα μὲν αὐτὸς ἐνὶ φρεσὶ σῇσι νοήσεις, ἄλλα δὲ καὶ δαίμων ὑποθήσεται Od.3.27; Κροῖσος ταῦτά οἱ ὑπετίθετο Hdt.1.156, cf. 3.36; ἔπεμψέ με σωτηρίην ὑποθησόμενον ὑμῖν, ἥν περ βούλησθε πείθεσθαι Id.5.98, cf. 7.237; σμικρὸν ὑποθέσθαι τοῖς κριταῖσι βούλομαι Ar.*Ec.*1154: c. dat. pers. only, *advise, counsel, admonish* one, Od.2.194, 5.143, Ar.*Av.*1362, *Lys.* 522 (anap.), Pl.*Chrm.*155d: with an Adv., ἀλλά μοι εὖ ὑπόθευ Od. 15.310, cf. Hdt.1.90; αὐτάρ τοι πυκινῶς ὑποθησόμεθ', αἴ κε πίθηαι Il. 21.293. 2. Med., in stronger sense, *enjoin*, ταῦτα τοῖσι ὑπολειπομένοισι ὑποθέμενος ὁ Δαρεῖος Hdt.4.135; of a doctor, Pl.*Plt.*295c; of Nestor, Id.*Hp.Ma.*286b; [Μέττιος Ῥοῦφος] τῷ στρατηγῷ περὶ τούτου ὑπέθετο *POxy.*237 vi 40 (ii A.D.); gloss on ἐπιστέλλει, Sch.S.*OT*106; of Pythagoras, τὴν εἰς τὸ σπονδειακὸν μεταβολὴν ὑπέθετο τῷ αὐλητῇ Iamb.*VP*25.112; τοῖς ἀπὸ τοῦ νομοῦ ὑπόδειγμα τῆς ἀπειθίας ὑ. *BGU* 747 ii 14 (ii A.D.); δύο σκοποὺς ὑποθέσθαι τῆς φλεβοτομίας *prescribe* two conditions of (successful) venesection, Gal.15.765. 3. Med., *instruct, demonstrate*, γραμματικόν τι ποιῆσαι ἄλλου ὑποθεμένου Arist. *EN*$1105^{a}23$; δεῖ ὑποθέσθαι τί λέγομεν τὸ βαρύ *as a preliminary* we must *explain*, Id.*Cael.*$269^{b}20$; ὑ. ὡς χρὴ μάχεσθαι Philostr.*Her.*10.5; Φινεὺς..τοῖς Ἀργοναύταις..περὶ τῶν συμπληγάδων ὑπέθετο πετρῶν Apollod.1.9.22; ὁ ὑποθέμενος αὐτῷ τὴν ἀνάγνωσιν Arr.*Epict.*1.26.13, cf. 2.2.21; παλαισμάτων εἴδη ὁπόσα ἐστί, δηλώσει ὁ παιδοτρίβης, καιρούς τε ὑποθέμενος κτλ. Philostr.*Gym.*14: c. acc. et inf., ὑ. τῷ ἐπιεικεῖ παιδὶ ῥᾴδιον πεφυκέναι κτλ. Iamb.*VP*10.51. III. Med., *propose to oneself as a task*, πολεμιστήριον [ἵππον] ὑπεθέμεθα ὠνεῖσθαι X.*Eq.*3.7; δεῖ ὑποτίθεσθαι κατ' εὐχήν, μηδὲν μέντοι ἀδύνατον Arist. *Pol.*$1265^{a}17$; *make up one's mind, adopt as a policy*, παρὰ τὸ δίκαιον τὸ ξυμφέρον λέγειν ὑπέθεσθε Th.5.90; τοῦθ' ὑπέθετο, δεινότατον πρᾶγμα, οἶμαι, ὅπως ἐν ἐκείνῳ εἴη..φάναι And.1.39; ἕνα τοῦτον ὑποθέμενος τὸν σκοπόν, ἅπαντας ἡμᾶς ἀγορεύειν κακῶς Luc.*Pisc.*7; πρὶν τὴν ἀρχὴν ὀρθῶς ὑποθέσθαι, μάταιον ἡγοῦμαι περὶ τῆς τελευτῆς ὁντινοῦν ποιεῖσθαι λόγον D.3.2:—Pass., ὁ ὑποτεθεὶς σκοπός Arist.*EN*$1144^{a}24$. 2. *propose to oneself as a subject of discussion* or *argument*, ἀπ' ἐμαυτοῦ ἄρξωμαι καὶ τῆς ἐμαυτοῦ ὑποθέσεως, περὶ τοῦ ἑνὸς αὐτοῦ ὑποθέμενος, εἴτε ἕν ἐστιν εἴτε μὴ [ἕν], τί χρὴ συμβαίνειν; Pl.*Prm.*137b, cf. *Ti.*26a; ἵνα μὴ δοκῶ περὶ τὰ μέρη διατρίβειν, ὑπὲρ ὅλων τῶν πραγμάτων ὑποθέμενος Isoc. 4.51, cf. 12.119; ὥσπερ ὑπεθέμην Thphr.*Char.Prooem.*5; περὶ ἀέρος εἰπόντες, ὥσπερ ὑπεθέμεθα Arist.*Mete.*$340^{a}23$, cf. *Rh.*$1432^{b}5$, Aeschin. 1.37, 2.102; ὑποθησόμεθα ταύτης ἀρχὴν τῆς βύβλου τὴν πρώτην διάβασιν ἐξ Ἰταλίας Ῥωμαίων Plb.1.5.1:—Pass., οἱ ὑποτεθέντες λόγοι Pl. *Lg.*812a. IV. Med., *assume as a preliminary*, ταύτην μὲν δὴ πυρὸς ἀρχὴν καὶ τῶν ἄλλων σωμάτων ὑποτιθέμεθα Id.*Ti.*53d; ὑποθέμενος ἑκάστοτε λόγον.., ἃ μὲν ἄν μοι δοκῇ τούτῳ συμφωνεῖν, τίθημι ὡς ἀληθῆ ὄντα Id.*Phd.*100a; οἱ περὶ τὰς γεωμετρίας..ὑποθέμενοι..τὰ σχήματα, .. ποιησάμενοι ὑποθέσεις αὐτά Id.*R.*510c; ὑπόθεσιν Id.*Phd.*101d; ὃ ἐξ ἀρχῆς ὑπετιθέμεθα Id.*Chrm.*171d; ἐὰν ὡς ὂν ὑποθῇ ὃ ὑπετίθεσο Id.*Prm.* 136c; ὑ. περί τινος ὡς ὄντος ib.136b, cf. 137b, *Plt.*284c; ὑ. ὡς τούτου οὕτως ἔχοντος Id.*R.*437a: c. acc. et inf., *assume* or *suppose that..*, Id.*Phd.*100b, *Prt.*339d: without inf., [τὴν ἀρετὴν] διδακτὸν ὑ. *assume* it to be teachable, ib.361b; τἀναντία οἷς ὑπεθέμην Id.*Tht.*165d; ὥσπερ ὑπέθου as you *began by requiring*, Id.*R.*346b (referring to 336d):—Pass., esp. in aor. ὑπετέθην (cf. ὑπόκειμαι II. 2), Id.*Ti.*48e, 61d; τὰ ὑποτεθέντα Id.*Prm.*136b; τῶν καλῶν τι ἡ σωφροσύνη ὑπετέθη *was assumed* to be.., Id.*Chrm.*160d (referring to 159c); τοῦτο δ' ἀδύνατον, ὥστε ψεῦδος τὸ ὑποτεθέν Arist.*APr.*$61^{a}31$; εἰ τοῦτό τις ὑποτεθείη γινώσκειν if it were *assumed* that one knew this, Phld.*Rh.*2. 17 S. 2. later, *assume, suppose, estimate*, παρέσομαι πρὸς ὑμᾶς, ὡς ὑποτίθεμαι, τῇ ιζ *PCair.Zen.*247.4 (iii B.C.); ὑποτιθεμένου τοῦ ποδὸς δραχμῆς the foot *being reckoned* at one drachma, *Supp.Epigr.*4.446. 14 (Didyma, iii/ii B.C.), cf. *PCair.Zen.*$15^{r}$.34 (iii B.C.); τὸν χιλιάρουρον (sc. ἀμπελῶνα) ὑποτιθέμεθα ἐπὶ τὸ ἔλαττον we *assess* at the reduced sum, ib.361.9 (iii B.C.); νεώτερον αὐτὸν ὑ. *put* him *down* as younger, D.H.4.6; ταῦτα τὸν Ὅμηρον ὡς συστρατιώτην ἔφη εἰρηκέναι καὶ οὐχ ὡς ὑποτιθέμενον not as a *composer of fiction*, Philostr.*Her.*4.4. V. Act., *establish as a preliminary, premise*, ταῦθ' ὑποθεὶς ἐπεῖπεν ὡς.. Aeschin.2.157; τοῦθ' ὑποθέντες ἀκούετε τῇ γνώμῃ, τί ἄν, εἴ τις ἔπασχε ταῦθ' ὑμῶν, ἐποίει *after deciding* in your own minds, D.21.108; ῥυθμοὺς καὶ σχῆμα ἐλευθέριον ὑποθεῖσαι μέλος ἢ λόγον ἐναντίον ἀποδοῦναι Pl.*Lg.*669c. 2. *represent as* ὑποκείμενον (v. ὑπόκειμαι II. 8), εἰ μή τις ἑτέραν ὑποθήσει τοῖς ἐναντίοις φύσιν Arist.*Ph.*$189^{a}28$; [ἀρχὴν] ἄν τε μίαν ἄν τε πλείους Id.*Metaph.*$988^{a}24$. VI. *couch, present*, τὴν σάρισαν Luc. *DMort.*27.3. VII. *put down as a deposit* or *stake, pawn, pledge, mortgage*, τοῦτο τὸ ἐνέχυρον Hdt.2.136; τὴν οἰκίαν, τὴν οὐσίαν, Isoc.21.2, D.28.17, 49.12; ὑπέθεσαν αὐτῷ τοῦ ταλάντου τὰς προσόδους *mortgaged* their revenues for the talent, Aeschin.3.104; τῷ πατρὶ τἀνδράποδα D.27.25; δραχμὴν ὑπόθες Diph.73.2; ὑποθέμενοι χρυσίον *IG*1².313. 177; τὴν οἰκίαν πωλοῦντα καὶ ὑποτιθέντα selling and *mortgaging*, i.e. having full ownership of, the house, *PCair.Zen.*588.1, cf. 9 (iii B.C.),

*PRyl.*162.28 (ii A.D.); cf. ὑποθήκη II:—Med., of the mortgagee, *lend* money *on pledge*, D.28.18; ὑποθέσθαι τὰ σκεύη τῆς νεώς Id.50.55:—but the Med. is used for the Act. in later writers, Plu.*Cat.Mi.*6:—for the Pass., ὑπόκειμαι is used, except in aor. 1, πόρους (revenues) ὑποκεῖσθαι αὐτοῖς τούς τε ὑποτεθέντας εἰς τὸ βουλευτήριον.. *OGI*46.10 (Halic., iii B.C.), cf. *AJP*56.375 (Colophon, iv B.C., Med. and Pass.); cf. τίθημι. 2. *stake, hazard, venture*, εἰς οἷον κίνδυνον ἔρχῃ ὑποθήσων τὴν ψυχήν Pl.*Prt.*313a; τὸν ἴδιον κίνδυνον ὑποθεὶς *at* his own risk, D.19.252; also ἑαυτὸν ἔγγυον ὑποθείς Plu.*Crass.*7: τὴν ψυχὴν ταῖς τύχαις Luc.*Dem.Enc.*41; τὰ σὰ τοῖς ἐκτός Arr.*Epict.*2.2.12; τὸν τράχηλον ib.4.1.77; ἑαυτὸν τῷ νόμῳ, i.e. risked the penalties of the law, Philostr.*Gym.*24; οὐδὲ αὐτοὺς ταύταις ὑποθήσομεν ταῖς αἰτίαις Jul.*Or.*3.112a; νομίμοις ποιναῖς ὑποθεῖναι [αὐτούς] *PMasp.*24.50 (vi A.D.); ἑαυτὸν [ὀργῇ] Plu.*Them.*24; τοῖς κινδύνοις σφᾶς αὐτούς Aristid.1.467 J.

**ὑποτίλλω**, *pluck up*, τὴν βοτάνην Thphr.*HP*2.7.5.

**ὑποτῑμ-άω**, *name the price of* what one offers for sale, ἰχθύν Alex. 125.4. II. Med., 1. *make a return* or *assessment of one's property*. Arist.*Oec.*1347ᵃ22, 1353ᵃ12. 2. as law-term, = ἀντιτιμάομαι, X.*Ap.*23, Arr.*Epict.*3.24.61, D.Chr.56.14; ἀποθνῄσκειν ὑποτιμῶ Arist.*Rh.Al.*1437ᵃ17; cf. τιμάω III. 2b. 3. *allege, plead in excuse*, ἀμβλυωπίαν Gal.5.192; γῆρας, ἀσθένειαν, Nic.Dam.*Fr.*130.17 J.; ἀγνοίας πρόφασιν *POxy.*1119.11 (iii A.D.); πενίαν Iamb.*VP*5.23, cf. Apollod.2.5.3. 4. *under-estimate, tone down*, εἰρωνεύεσθαι καὶ ὑ. D. Chr.32.90. —ημα, ατος, τό, *estimated value*, *IG*7.3073.9, al. (Lebad., ii B.C.). ⊛—ησις, εως, ἡ, *estimate of one's own liability* for taxation, damages, etc., *self-assessment*, *PSI*5.502.26 (iii B.C.), Arg D.21, Ph. ap.Eus.*PE*8.7. 2. *plea for release, excuse*, Ph.2.325, Plu.*Cam.*40, Ael.*NA*4.43, etc. —ητής, οῦ, ὁ, as transl. of Lat. *subcensor*, D.C. 52.21, 24, 33. ⊛—ητος, η, ον, *assessed*, δίκαι dub. in *IG*5(1).1336 (Laconia).

**ὑποτίνω**, *pay*, ὑποτεινέτω (sic) ζημίας *JRS*18.154 (Jerash, ii A.D.).

**ὑποτιτθ-ίδιος**, ον, = ὑποτίτθιος, παιδάριον *GDI*1954 (Delph.). —ικόν, τό, *a child at the breast*, Mitteis *Chr.*372 vi 10 (ii A.D.). —ιος, ον, *under the breast*, τὰ ὑ. *children at the breast*, Lxx *Ho.*14.1, Ath. 2.46e; θυγάτριον, παιδίον, *PCair.Zen.*292.302 (iii B.C.), *BGU*1058.12 (i B.C.), etc.; of an animal, ib.629.14 (ii A.D.): ὑπότιτθος in Phot., Suid.

***ὑποτλάω**, aor. ὑπέτλην, *endure*, *AP*5.301.6 (Agath.).

**ὑποτμήγω**, Ep. for ὑποτέμνω, Q.S.5.244, 9.380:—Med., A.R.4. 328.

**ὑπότμη-σις**, εως, ἡ, *cutting from underneath*, σκελῶν Ph.*Bel.*100.2 (pl.). —τέος, α, ον, *to be cut at the base*, Orib.45.16.5.

**ὑπ-οτοβέω**, *sound in answer, echo*, ὑπὸ δὲ.. ὀτοβεῖ δόναξ.. νόμον A.*Pr.*574 (lyr.).

**ὑποτομ-εύς**, έως, ὁ, *a cutting instrument*, Lxx 2*Ki.*12.31. —ή, ἡ, *a cutting off below*, Plu.2.980c; *cutting away underneath*, Thphr. *HP*9.2.7, Heliod.ap.Orib.45.6.3, Leonid.ap.Aët.7.71: pl., *trimmed surfaces* of blocks of stone in architecture, *IG*7.3073.113, 114 (Lebad., ii B.C.). II. *a smaller incision* or *line*, Procl.*Hyp.*3. 11; ὑποτομῆς μόριον *sub-division*, *Theol.Ar.*4. —ος, ον, *null and void, rescinded*, *IG*5(2).344.14 (Orchom. Arc., iii B.C.).

**ὑπότονα**, τά, *ropes* holding a swinging ladder, Ath.Mech.36.9.

**ὑποτόναιον**, τό, *threshold*, *IG*2².1672.66 (pl.).

**ὑποτονθορύζω** (sts. incorrectly written -ίζω, as in Lib.*Decl.*43. 60), *murmur in an under-tone*, Luc.*Merc.Cond.*26, *Bis Acc.*4, al., Agath.4.7; ἐπῳδήν Luc.*Nec.*7.

**ὑποτοξεύομαι**, Pass., *to be exposed to arrows*, Aen.Tact.36.1.

**ὑποτοπ-άζω**, = ὑποτοπέω, Ph.2.480, Hld.9.5. —ασμός, ὁ, *suspicion, surmise*, J.*AJ*17.4.2. —εύω, = sq., τινα v.l. in Th.8.76: c. acc. et inf., f.l. in Id.5.35. 2. Gramm., *doubt the genuineness of a passage*, v.l. in Chaeris ap.Sch.Od.7.80. —έω, pf. —τετόπηκα D.C. 38.42:—*suspect, surmise*, τι Th.1.56; c. acc. et inf., ib.20, 51, Alciphr. 3.72, Procop.*Vand.*1.18; ὑ. μή.. Th.2.13. 2. c. acc. pers., *suspect* him, Id.5.116 (s.v.l.). II. Med. **ὑποτοπέομαι**, aor. ὑπετοπήθην in med. sense:—*suspect* a thing, οὐδὲν ὑποτοπηθέντα Hdt.9.116; κἀχ' ὑποτοπεῖσθαι Ar.*Ra.*958: c. inf., ὑποτοπηθέντες Δημάρητον δρησμῷ ἐπιχειρέειν Hdt.6.70, cf. Ar.*Th.*496, Lys.9.4 (Scal. for ὑπετυπούμην); ὑποτοπεῖσθαι χρὴ ἐκ τῶν γεγραμμένων one must *form an idea*, Hp.*Art.* 33.—In Att. Prose the word generally used was ὑποπτεύω. —ητέον, *one must suspect*, Ph.1.143. —ος, ον, *suspicious*, Polem.*Phgn.* 37 (sed leg. καχύποπτοι).

**ὑποτορεύω**, *engrave in toreutic work*, ὀρόφοις γυπῶν πτέρυγας Ael. *NA*10.22.

**ὑποτρᾰγῳδέω**, *play tragic parts in subordination to..*, τινι Philostr. *VS*1.18.1; *play up to* another's *tragic acting*, v.l. in Luc.*JTr.*1.

**ὑποτραυλ-ίζω**, *lisp somewhat*, Luc.*Tim.*55. —ος, ον, *lisping a little*, Hp.*Epid.*7.3.

**ὑποτρᾰχήλ-ιον**, τό, *the back just below the neck*, Poll.2.136. II. *neck of a column*, Vitr.3.3.12, al. —ος, ον, *under the neck*, Hsch. s.v. ὑποθυμί[ο]ς.

**ὑποτρᾰχ-ύνω**, *affect with a somewhat grating sensation*, τὴν ἀκοήν D.H.*Comp.*22. —υς, Ion. and Ep. —τρηχυς, υ, *somewhat rough*, Hp.*Epid.*2.1.8, Archestr.*Fr.*32 (—τρηχυν fem.), Orph.*L.*363, Dsc.3. 44, Gal.19.514.

**ὑποτρέμω**, *tremble a little*, Pl.*R.*336e, Plu.2.973f, Marcellin.*Puls.* 291, etc.

**ὑποτρέπομαι**, Pass., *turn back*, Plu.2.77d, Opp.*H.*3.516.

**ὑποτρέφω**, *rear, nourish*, σκύλακας D.H.4.81; πώγωνας D.S.3.63; ῥίζεα.. ὑποτέτροφε λίμνη Nic.*Al.*589: metaph., *cherish, nurse*, τὴν χολήν Luc.*Cal.*24; *foster, encourage*, παχὺν καὶ γλίσχρον ὑποθρέψει χυμόν Gal.*Vict.Att.*6; ὑποθρέψαι πλῆθος χυμῶν Id.1.302, cf. 6.239, al.:—Med., *cherish*, τόλμαν X.*Cyr.*2.1.17:—Pass., *grow up in succession*, Pl.*R.*560a; ὑ. τιμωρὸς ἐπὶ τοὺς τυράννους Plu.2.595c; ὁ ἐκ Βερενίκης -όμενος Polyaen.8.50, cf. Nic.Dam.51 J.; θάμβος ὑπετρέφετο my wonder *grew*, Call.*Aet.Oxy.*2080.87.

**ὑποτρέχω**, aor. -έδρᾰμον (v. infr.): poet. pf. -δέδρομα *h.Ap.*284; -δεδρ(ά)μηκα (v. infr. IV):—*run in under*, ὑπέδραμε καὶ λάβε γούνων *ran in under* the spear or sword and clasped his knees, Il.21.68, Od. 10.323 (though it may be only, *ran up to* him); ὑ. πρὸς στέρνα πατρός E.*IA*631, cf. [636]; ὑπὸ τοὺς πόδας τοῦ ἵππου ὑπέδραμε Hdt. 7.88; ὑ. ὑπὸ τὴν τοῦ ἀκοντίου φοράν *in under, within* the dart's range, Antipho 3.2.4: later c. acc., νησίον ὑ. *run under the lee of..*, *Act.Ap.* 27.16; ὑ. πρῶνας Them.*Or.*13.168b; τὸν τρίβωνα Philostr.*Ep.*7: c. dat., [ταῖς πλατάνοις] Plu.2.185e; ναυλόχοις ib.243e. II. *run under, stretch away under*, ὑποδέδρομε βῆσσα *h.Ap.*284. III. *run in between, intercept*, λῃστάς X.*Cyr.*1.2.12; τὰ κορίανν' ἐπριάμην ὑποδραμών Ar.*Eq.*676; ἐν ταῖς συνόδοις ἡ σελήνη τὸν [τοῦ ἡλίου] κύκλον ὑποτρέχουσα Jul.*Or.*2.80d (cf. ὑποθέω I. 2); ὅταν [ἡ σελήνη] ὑπὸ τὴν φλόγα [τοῦ ἡλίου] ὑποδράμῃ D.C.60.26; *pass between* a star and the earth, Ptol.*Alm.*8.4. 2. = ὑποσκελίζω, *trip up, overreach*, τῶν στρατηγῶν ὑποδραμὼν τοὺς (Bentl. for τῶν) ἐκ Πύλου Ar.*Eq.*742 (dub. l.). 3. *interrupt*, Dius ap.Stob.4.21.17. 4. *usurp*, τὴν Ἡρακλέους προσηγορίαν S.E.*M.*9.36; τὴν τῶν θεῶν τιμήν ib.38:—Pass., τὰς ὑποδεδραμημένας ἐπιστατείας the posts *into which they have crept*, *PTeb.*24.67 (ii B.C.). IV. *overrun, steal over*, ἔρευθος ὑ. *steals over* the skin, Hp.*Fract.*27; καί τις οἷον ἀπελπισμὸς ὑπέδραμεν τοὺς ἀνθρώπους a kind of despair *came over* people, Plb.30.32.11; καί τις ἔλεος αὐτὸν ὑποτρέχει Id.9.10.7: also c. dat., αὐτίκα χρῷ πῦρ ὑπαδεδρόμακεν Sapph.2.10; in slightly different sense, ὑπέδραμέ τις ἔννοια.. τοῖς ἀνθρώποις *occurred to* people, Plb.16.6.10; οὐχ ὑπέδραμε δέ *it did* not *occur to* him, Str.12.3.27, cf. Arr.*Epict.*4.2.2: c. acc. et inf., Plb.14. 12.5. V. *insinuate oneself into any one's good graces, flatter, fawn upon*, ὑ. τινὰ θωπείᾳ E.*Or.*670, cf. Aeschin.3.162; ὃς δ' ἂν.. χαρίζηται ὑποτρέχων Pl.*R.*426c; θωπείαις ὑποδραμών Id.*Lg.*923b; ὑ. καὶ κολακεύειν Phld.*Ir.*p.66 W. VI. Medic., ἦν οἷον λίθοι ὑποτρέχωσιν if what seem to be stones *get into* the eye, Hp.*Loc.Hom.*13; but ὡς τὸ δάκρυον συμπεπηγὸς ὑποτρέχειν ποιέῃς so as to make the coagulated tears *run off*, ibid.

**ὑποτρέω**, Ep. 3 pl. pres. -τρείουσι Timo 58.4: Hom. only in aor. -έτρεσα:—*shrink back, give ground*, Il.7.217, 15.636, 17.275; ὑποτρέσαι Pi.*Fr.*224: c. acc., *shrink before, flee before*, Il.17.587. Poet. word, used in late Prose, Plu.*Mar.*7, M.Ant.11.9.

**ὑπότρητος**, ον, *bored* or *pierced through below*, αὐλοί Ath.4.176f.

**ὑπότρηχυς**, Ion. for ὑπότραχυς.

**ὑποτρῑβή**, ἡ, *a rubbing off below*, ἵπποι χωλεύοντες ἐξ ὑποτριβῆς App.*Mith.*75: cf. sq.

**ὑποτρίβω** [ῑ], *rub a little* or *gently*, Hp.*Genit.*1. 2. *rub down* for mixing in a dish, σήσαμ' ὑ. εἰς ταύτην (sc. ἅλμην) Damox.2.38, cf. Cratin.27; v. ὑπότριμμα. II. *rub off beneath* or *gradually*:—Pass., ὑποτρίβεσθαι τὰς ὁπλάς, of horses, *wear their* hoofs *off*, D.S. 17.94: so intr. in Act., ὑποτρίβουσι τοῖς ποσί *Hippiatr.*53: cf. foreg. III. in Pass., *to be aggravated* or *become chronic*, of diseases, Aët.9.35.

⊛**ὑποτρίζω**, *cry, squeak*, or *chirp*, of fowls, Ael.*NA*7.7; of cats, ib.7.8. 2. of things, λεπτὸν ὑ. Nonn.*D.*11.219, *AP*11.352 (cod. Plan., Agath.). 3. *crepitate*, Antyll.ap.Orib.45.3.4:—freq. with v.l. ὑποτρύζ-.

**ὑποτρῐήραρχος**, ὁ, *sub-trierarch*, *PPetr.*3 p.184 (iii B.C.).

**ὑποτρῐμερής**, ές, *contained* $1\frac{3}{4}$ *times, the converse of* ἐπιτριμερής (q.v.), *less by* $\frac{3}{7}$, Iamb. *in Nic.*p.42 P.

**ὑπότριμμ-α**, ατος, τό, *a dish compounded of various ingredients grated and pounded up together*, Hp.*Vict.*2.56, 3.80, Gal.6.650, cf. ὑποτρίβω I. 2; ἐν ὑ. ζέσαι Antiph.222.3; ὑποτρίμμασι καρυκεύσῃ Jul. *Or.*6.192a, cf. 7.226a: its general taste was sour or piquant, hence βλέπων ὑπότριμμα looking *sharp and sour*, Ar.*Ec.*292; ὑ. χλωρά, of green herb sauces or soups, also called φυλλάδες, Poll.6.71. Cf. ὑπόσφαγμα. —άτιον, τό, Dim. of foreg., Telecl.1, cf. Poll.6.68.

**ὑποτριόρχης**, ου, ὁ, a kind of *hawk*, Arist.*HA*620ᵃ19; cf. τριόρχης II.

**ὑποτριπλᾰσι-επιδίπεμπτος**, ον, *contained* $3\frac{2}{5}$ $(\frac{1}{\frac{17}{5}})$ *times*, Domnin. in Boisson.*Anecd.*4.420. —ος, ον, '*subtriple*', i.e. *in the ratio* 1:3, *contained three times*, Nicom.*Ar.*1.18.

**ὑποτρίπους**, ποδος, ὁ, v. ὑπότριψις II.

**ὑποτρίταιος** [ῐ], α, ον, $\frac{1}{3}$ *less than full*, of the moon, Antioch.Astr. in *Cat.Cod.Astr.*7.115.

**ὑπότρῐτος**, ον, *contained* $1\frac{1}{3}$ *times, standing to another number in the ratio* 3:4, Mart.Cap.7.761.

**ὑπότριψις**, εως, ἡ, *a rubbing under*, e.g. of a horse's hoof, *Hippiatr.*54. II. dat. pl. ὑποτρίψεσιν, *under parts*, lower framework of tables, trestles, etc., Ph.*Bel.*74.14 codd. (ὑποτρίποσιν 'supports for tripods', Diels).

**ὑποτρομ-έω**, = ὑποτρέμω, *tremble under*, τρομέει δ' ὑπὸ γυῖα Il.10. 95. II. c. acc., *tremble before* any one, μιν.. ὑποτρομέεσκον ὁρῶντες 20.28: without acc., ὑποτρομέουσιν ἅπαντες 22.241. —ος, ον, *quivering, shaking*, Plu.2.435b; *somewhat afraid* or *timid*, Aeschin.3.159, Luc. *DDeor.*19.1, etc. —ώδης, ες, *somewhat tremulous*, Hp.*Epid.*4.45.

**ὑποτροπ-άδην** [ᾰ], Adv. *turning back, returning*, Opp.*H.*1.636, 3.

274. **-άζω,** in Pass., *return*, πάλιν ὑπετροπάσθην μῆνας τέσσερας *PCair.Zen.*34.17 (iii B.C.). II. in Pass., = ὑποτροπιάζω, *have a relapse*, *PSI*4.435.17 (iii B.C.). **-ή,** ἡ, *a turning back, repulse*, Plu. *Alex.*32. II. *relapse, recurrence*. Id.2.565d; τῶν ἔμπροσθεν νοσημάτων Id.*Luc.*7; cf. Hp.ap.Gal.19.150 (defined as οὐ μόνον ἡ ὑποστροφὴ ἀλλὰ καὶ ἡ ἐναλλὰξ μεταβολή). **-ιάζω,** *return again, recur*, esp. of an illness, Hp.*Aph.*4.61, *Int.*2, al.; ἐπὶ τὴν ἀρχαίαν ὑ. νόσον Ph.1.459. **-ιασμός,** ὁ, *relapse* in illness, Hp.*Aph.*4.36, Gal.19.517. **-ίη,** ἡ, poet. for ὑποτροπή, πολέμοιο *turning* of the fight, A.R.1.1052. **-ικός,** ή, όν, *indicating relapse*, Hp.*Coac.*79,581. **-ιον,** τό, dub. sens., perh. *fishery-rights, temple-tribute from fisheries*, *IG*11(2).161 *A* 26, 162 *A* 30 (Delos, iii B.C.).

**ὑποτρόπιος,** α (Ep. η), ον, (τρόπις) *under the keel*, Opp.*H.*1.224, Orph.*A.*267.

**ὑπότροπος,** ον, (ὑποτρέπομαι) *turning back, returning*, ὑπότροπον ἐκ πολέμοιο ἵξεσθαι Il.6.501; ὑ. ἵκετο δῶμα Od.20.332; ὑ. ἵξομαι αὖτις Il.6.367; οὐκ ἔθ' ὑπότροποι αὖθις ἔσεσθε *h.Ap.*476; ὑ. οἴκαδ' ἱκέσθαι Od.21.211. 2. *rallying* from the effect of a blow, Theoc.25.263.

**ὑποτροφ-ή,** ἡ, *supply of nourishment, sustenance*, Max.Tyr.27.5, etc.; ἡ τῆς σωμασκίας ὑ. Iamb.*VP*5.21. II. *growth*, ὑ. γῆς Max. Tyr.29.1. ⊛ **-ος,** ον, *reared at the breast*, νεᾶνις E.*IA*1204 (v.l. ὑπόστροφον).

**ὑποτροχ-άζω,** = ὑποτρέχω III.1, of moon and sun, c. dat., Gem.9.10; *overlap*, ὑποτροχάζουσι δὲ ἀλλήλαις αἱ τῶν ἠπείρων ἄκραι (in the Bosporus) Dion.Byz.3. **-ἄλος,** ον, *somewhat round*, v.l. for περιτρόχαλος in Hdt.3.8. **-άω,** poet. for ὑποτρέχω, Mosch.*Fr.*3.5. **-ίζω,** *lay under the wheel, torture*, Suid. **-ος,** ον, *on wheels*, μηχανήματα Ph.*Bel.*85.39; πορεῖα Plb.8.34.11; σχεδία Ath.Mech.9.15, cf. D.S.20.48,91, Onos.42.3; δίφρος (for babies) Sor.1.114.

⊛ **ὑπότρῠγος,** ον, (τρύξ) *full of lees* or *sediment*, Hp.*Epid.*4.25.

⊛ **ὑποτρύζω,** *murmur, hum in an undertone*, [ὑποτρύ]ζουσιν ἀοιδῇ prob. in Call. in *PSI*11.1219.1; νήτη..λεπτὸν -τρύζουσα, of a chord, *AP*11.352 (cod. P, Agath.); cf. ὑποτρίζω.

**ὑποτρῡπάω,** *bore*, prob. in *IG*$2^2$.463.77.

**ὑποτρύω** [ῡ], *become fatigued*. καμάτοισι Nic.*Al.*83.

**ὑποτρώγω,** *eat with other things*, Xenoph.22.3. II. *eat by way of preparation*, X.*Smp.*4.9. III. metaph., *eat away from below*, τοῖχον ὑ. ποταμός Call.*Epigr.*45.4.

**ὑποτυγχάνω,** *interrupt, reply, answer*, Hp.*Ep.*17, D.H.6.87, 7.16, J.*AJ*6.11.9, Plu.2.113b, Aesop.46, *PRyl.*77.39 (ii A.D.).

**ὑποτύμβιος,** ον, *in the tomb*, *IG*14.1592 (Rome).

**ὑπότῠπ-ος,** ον, *subject to a claim*, *IG*12(5).872.77 (Tenos). **-όω,** *sketch out, outline*, Arist.*EN*1098$^{a}$21, Plb.21.30.6 (Pass.):—Med., *draft*, συγγραφὴν -τυπώσασθαι καὶ γράψαι *PSI*4.429.10 (iii B.C.). 2. *predispose*, πρὸς σωφροσύνην Phld.*Mus.*p.57 K., cf. p.77 K. 3. *prescribe*, τροφὴν αὐτάρκη καὶ λουτρά Paul.Aeg.6.110. II. Med., ἐν ἀνθρώποις εὐθὺς γιγνομένοις ὑπετυπώσαντο τὴν τῶν ὀνύχων γένεσιν *took care to have* nails *formed in a rudimentary way*, Pl.*Ti.*76e; ὑποτυπωσάμενος τὴν οὐσίαν..τί ἐστι *having formed a notion of* it, Arist.*Metaph.*1028$^{b}$31, cf. Hdn.1.3.5, Philostr.*VS*1 *Prooem.*

**ὑποτύπτω,** *strike* or *push down*, κοντῷ ὑ. ἐς λίμνην *push down* into the lake with a pole, Hdt.2.136; ὑποτύπτουσα..φιάλῃ ⟨ἐς⟩ τοῦ χρυσοῦ τὴν θήκην *dipping* with a cup into.., Id.3.130; ὑποτύψας τούτῳ (sc. ἡμίσει ἀσκοῦ) ἀντλέει he draws it *dipping* with the vessel into the water, Id.6.119; οἱ χῆνες ὑ. ὥσπερ ταῖς ἄμαις..τοῖν ποδοῖν Ar.*Av.*1145. 2. *strike downwards* with the feet, *strut*, χέρσῳ (codd., χερσαῖ' Maass) ὑπέτυψε κορώνη *struts upon* the land, Arat.950:—Med., *gush downwards*, of wine, ὅπως ὑπετύψατο ληνοῦ Nic.*Al.*163. II. *strike underneath*, *Placit.*3.15.11 (Pass.).

**ὑποτύπ-ωσις** [ῠ], εως, ἡ, *sketch, outline*, Str.2.5.18, Ph.2.12, Anon.Lond.7.17, Hermog.*Prog.*6, Poll.7.128; ὑ. ἕνεκα συγγράμματος *draft* for a book, Gal.15.760; as Empiric term, Id.8.709, al.; opp. ἐξεργασία, Plot.6.3.7; ὑπογραφάς τε καὶ ὑποτυπώσεις, opp. ὅρους, *Stoic.*2.76: αἱ Ὑποτυπώσεις was the name given by Sextus Empiricus to his *Outlines* of the Pyrrhonic Philosophy, cf. D.L.9.78, Gal.*Libr. Propr.Praef.*: Proclus calls one of his works ἡ ὑ. τῶν ἀστρονομικῶν ὑποθέσεων, *Hyp.*7.50. 2. *model, pattern*, 1*Ep.Ti.*1.16, 2*Ep.Ti.*1.13; εἰς ὑποτύπωσιν ἀρετῶν Phld.*Mus.*p.77 K. 3. a Rhet. figure, *by which a matter was vividly sketched in words*, Quint.*Inst.*9.2.40. **-ωτικός,** ή, όν, *by way of outline, compendious*, τρόπος τῆς συγγραφῆς S.E.*P.*1.239. Adv. -κῶς ib.2.1.

**ὑποτύραννος** [ῠ], ὁ, *princeling*, Prisc.p.333 D. (agnovit Wilcken, ὑπὸ τυράννων codd.), *Sammelb.*6257 (v/vi A.D.).

**ὑποτῡρίς,** ίδος, ἡ, (τυρός) a kind of *cheese-cake, milk curdled and pressed in moulds with honey*, Chrysipp.Tyan.ap.Ath.14.647f.

**ὑπότυφλος,** ον, *purblind*, Plu.2.53f, Hierocl.p.29 A.

**ὑποτῡφ-όομαι,** Pass., *become somewhat arrogant* or *deluded*, ὑπ' αἰώρας φρενῶν καὶ κενοῦ φυσήματος Ph.1.665. **-ος,** ον, *puffed up*, Ion Chius ap.Plu.*Per.*5; f.l. for ὑπάτυφος in Timo 60.

**ὑποτύφω** [ῡ], *burn with a smouldering fire beneath*, πῦρ ὑ. τὴν νῆσον Philostr.*Im.*2.17: metaph., *kindle into a smouldering fire, cause to burn secretly*, ὑποθύψας τὴν διαβολὴν Plb.5.42.3:—Pass., ἔχθρα ὑπετύφετο Ctes.*Fr.*29.46; ὑπετέθυπτο Apolloph.10; λύπη, ὀργή, Luc.*Abd.*30; εἰρωνεία Ph.1.142; ὀργή Id.2.584, πόλεμος Plu.*Per.*32, Jul.*Or.*1.13b; of persons, ὑποτετύφθαι *burn with a hidden fire* (of love), Poll.3.68; -όμενος ἐς τὸν ἔρωτα Ael.*VH*9.41.

**ὑπότυψις,** εως, ἡ, dub. sens., part of a tripod and of a table, *Inscr. Délos* 1403 *Ab*i72, 1423 *Aa*i11, 1442 *B*45 (all ii B.C.).

**ὑπουάτιος** [ᾰ], ον, (οὖας) *under the ears*, Orph.*A.*221.

**ὑπόϋγρος,** ον, = ὕφυγρος, *rather damp*, *Gloss.*

**ὑπουδαῖος,** α (Ion. η), ον, (οὖδας) *subterranean*, Plu.2.266e, Opp.*H.*3.487.

**ὑπουθᾰτίας,** ου, ὁ, *under the udder*, hence *sucking*, *AP*10.101 (Bianor).

**ὑπούλ-η,** ἡ, *subgingivae*, *Gloss.* (dub.). **-ος,** ον, of sores, *extending inwards, under the surface of the flesh, enclosed*, τὰ συριγγώδη καὶ ὅσα ὕ. ἐστι καὶ ἔντοσθε κεκοιλασμένα Hp.*Medic.*11; ὅσα μὲν ἔχει στόμα μέγα καὶ οὐ ταχὺ συμφύεται, ταῦτα καίειν δεῖ, ὅπως ἡ ἐσχάρα ἐκεῖ πέσῃ· οὕτως γὰρ οὐκ ἔσται ὕπουλα, i.e. there will be no internal accumulation of pus, Arist.*Pr.*863$^{a}$12; also of the part affected, *festering, purulent*, σῶμα Cratin.351, cf. Plu.*Lyc.*4; ἐπιληψίαι Gal.*Vict.Att.*1; σπλήν Pl.*Ti.*72d. 2. metaph., *with festering sores underneath, unsound, hollow*, οἰδεῖ καὶ ὕ. ἐστιν [ἡ πόλις] Id.*Grg.*518e; ὕ. τὴν ψυχὴν ποιήσει ib.480b; ὕ. τέλμα *treacherous*, Plu.*Rom.*18; ὕ. εὐνομία (v.l. αὐτονομία) *hollow, unreal*, Th.8.64; ὕ. ἡσυχία D.18.307; applied to the Trojan horse, S.*Fr.*1105; κάλλος κακῶν ὕπουλον a fair outside, but *fraught* with ills *below*, Id.*OT* 1396; ὕ. μάντευμα *false, fallacious*, Paus.3.7.3; φαντασίαι Gal.7.203; λόγοι Babr.44.4; of persons, *false, deceitful*, ἀνὴρ ὕ. δίκτυον κεκρυμμένον Men.*Mon.*587; δόλιοι καὶ ὕ. Phld.*Ir.*p.60 W., cf. Plu.*Caes.*60, etc.; ὕ. οἱ Ἀττικοί Dicaearch.1.4; *concealed*, [δόξαι], ἔχθρα, Phld.*D.*1.24, D.H.3.28; of evils, *festering within*, οἴημα Plu.2.44a; στάσεις ib.329b. Adv., -ως διακεῖσθαί τινι to be *secretly hostile* to one, Plb.10.35.6; ὑ. ἀκροᾶσθαι render a *hollow* obedience, Plu.*Luc.*21; joined with δολίως, *Epigr.Gr.*387 (Apamea Cibotus). (Perh. from ὑπείλλω, lit. *shut up, suppressed*; ὕπουλον = a 'gathering'.) **-ότης,** ητος, ἡ, *treachery*, Phld.*D.*1.25, Hsch. s v. ὑπόκρισις.

**ὕπουρα·** ὑπὸ τὰ ὄρη, Hsch. (Cf. ὑπ' οὔρει· ὑπὸ τῷ ὄρει, Phot., Suid.)

**ὑπουράνιος** [ᾰ], ον, and in Arat.134 η, ον:—*under heaven, under the sky*, ὀξύτατον δέρκεσθαι ὑπουρανίων πετεηνῶν Il.17.675; εἴδωλα Arat.616; τόπος Dam.*Pr.*56; οἱ ὑ. *heavenly* beings, Phld.*Piet.*58. II. *as far as heaven covers*, μέγα κέν οἱ ὑπουράνιον κλέος εἴη Il.10.212, cf. Od.9.264.

⊛ **ὑπουργ-έω,** Ion. **ὑποργέω,** like ὑπηρετέω, *render service* or *help* to one, *assist*, c. dat., Hdt.8.110, Democr.255, *PCair.Zen.*176.297 (iii B.C.), etc.; ὑ. τισὶ ἔργῳ Th.6.88:—Pass., μὴ κάμνων ὑπὸ καμνόντων ὑ. *receive assistance*, Epict.*Gnom.Fr.*24. 2. c. acc. rei, χρηστὰ ὑ. (sc. τοῖς Ἀθηναίοισι) *do* them good *service*, Hdt.8.143, cf. 7.38, S.*Aj.*681, *El.*461, *Ph.*143 (lyr.), Antipho 4.3.4, Th.7.62; τὰ δίκαια Gorg.*Fr.*21; ὑ. χάριν τινί A.*Pr.*635, E.*Alc.*842; of a woman, τισὶ ὑ. πρὸς χάριν Anaxil.21.2; *furnish*, βεβαίαν κατάληψιν Aristid.Quint.1.3:—Pass., τὰ ὑποργημένα *services done* or *rendered*, Hdt.9.109. 3. abs., S.*Ph.*53; τὰ τῆς κοιλίης ὑ. *do* their *duty*, Hp.*Morb.*3.15. 4. c. dat. rei, *assist* or *promote*, τῇ καθάρσει ibid. **-ημα,** ατος, τό, *service done* or *rendered*, Hdt.1.137, And.2.17, X.*Hier.*8.7. **-ημᾰτικός,** ή, όν, *making use of such service*, Sch.D.T.p.111 H. **-ητέον,** *one must serve* or *be kind to*, Luc.*Cont.*2, Hld.7.17. ⊛ **-ία,** ἡ, *service rendered*, S.*OC*1413, X.*Hier.*1.38, Arist.*Rh.*1385$^{a}$29, Luc.*Pseudol.*25, *Rev.Ét.Anc.*33.210 (Theangela), *BGU*197.17 (i A.D.), etc.; sens. obsc., Amphis 20.5. 2. pl., *medical duties, services*, Hp.*Decent.*12, al.; *duties of a midwife*, Sor.1.4 (pl.). **-ικός,** ή, όν, = sq., δύναμις Procl. *in Alc.*p.68 C.; γένος Jul.*Gal* 143b. **-ός,** όν, contr. for ὑποεργός (q.v.), *rendering service, serviceable, conducive to*, τῷ ἀποπήγνυσθαι X.*An.*5.8.15: οἱ ὑ. the *assistants*, Hp.*Acut.*67, *IG*$1^2$.344.80, al., Plb.5.89.3; ὑ. τινός *a servant of* any one, *PCair.Zen.*176.220 (iii B.C.), LXX *Jo.*1.1, Plb.30.8.4; δρατῶν Hld.2.16. Adv. -γῶς Aristaenet.1.3 (parox. codd.), s.v.l.

**ὑπουρέω,** *make a little water*, *Hippiatr.*22.

**ὑπόφαιδρος,** ον, *somewhat cheerful* or *gay*, Poll.4.143.

**ὑποφαίνω,** *bring to light from under*, θρῆνυν ὑπέφηνε τραπέζης *he drew* the stool *from under* the table, Od.17.409. 2. *show a little, just show*, θύννοι..τὰ λευκὰ ὑποφαίνοντες Arist.*HA*537$^{a}$21; αἱ παρειαὶ ὑ. τὴν τῆς αἰδοῦς χροιάν Poll.2.87: metaph., *give indications of*, μικρὰν ἐλπίδα D.19.123; πρᾳότητα Plb.27.12.3, cf. v.l. in 23.5.5: c. part., ὑπέφαιν' ἐσομένη..λαμπρὰ (Dobree for -ὸν) πάνυ Anaxandr.9.6; ὑ. ὥσπερ ἐπιθησόμενος Ael.*NA*5.19: c. acc. et inf., Sor.2.61. II. Pass., *to be seen under*, ὑπὸ τὰς πύλας πόδες πολλοὶ ὑποφαίνονται Th.5.10; cf. v.l. in Thphr.*Char.*4.4. 2. *just show oneself, be half seen*, as the half-opened eyes (cf. ὑπόφασις I), ἤν τι -ηται τοῦ λευκοῦ Hp.*Prog.*2, *Aph.*6.52; of teeth, Arist.*HA*502$^{a}$12; εἴ τι τῆς χώρας ἔρημον χιόνος ὑ. Arr.*An.*4.19.1; ὑ. σελήνη Ael.*NA*4.10; ἡ ὠλένη διὰ τῆς ἐσθῆτος Philostr.*Im.*2.8; ὑ. σωτηρία Isoc.4.93, 6.44; ὅπως πιστότερα ὑμῖν ὑποφαίνοιτο Lys.13.19 codd. (ὅπως -οτέρα ἡ μήνυσις φαίνοιτο corr. Francken); ἀμφισβήτησις Arist.*EN*1096$^{b}$9; ἡμέρα, ἔαρ (v. infr. III), X.*Cyr.*4.5.14 (as v.l.), *HG*5.3.1. III. intr. in Act., of the dawn of day, ὑπέφαινε ἡμέρα, ἕως, the day *gradually breaks* or *just begins to break*, Id.*An.*3.2.1, 4.3.9, cf. *Cyr.*4.5.14, etc.; ἤδη ὑπέφαινέν τι ἡμέρας (impers.) Pl.*Prt.*312a: so ἔαρ ὑπέφαινε X.*HG*3.4.16; γίνωσκε τὸν καρπὸν καλῶς ὑποφαίνοντα *PCair.Zen.*329.13 (iii B.C.). 2. metaph., τὰ νῦν ὑποφαίνοντα the difficulties now *dawning upon us*, Pl.*Sph.*245e; τοσαύτας ὁρῶν ὑποφαινούσας ἐλπίδας Din.1.21; ἐὰν ὑποφαίνῃ ἀπορία μέλιτος Arist.*HA*625$^{a}$23.

**ὑπόφαιος,** ον, *somewhat grey*, Erot. s.v. πελλόν (ubi ἱππόφαιον codd.), Phot. s.v. κίαλον.

**ὑπόφαιστον,** τό, variant for ἱππόφαιστον (q.v.), Ps.-Dsc.4.160, Paul.Aeg.7.3.

**ὑποφᾰκώδης,** ες, *somewhat of a lentil colour*, Hp.*Epid.*2.1.10.

**ὑποφάλακρος** [φᾰ], ον, *somewhat bald*, *PGrenf.*2.20 ii 12 (ii B.C., prob.), Physiogn.ap.Hippol.*Haer.*4.19,24.

**ὑπόφαντις**, v. ὑποφῆτις.

**ὑποφαρμάσσω**, Att. **-ττω**, *spice, drug, adulterate*, [οἶνον] Plu.2.614b, cf. 672b.

**ὑπόφᾰσις**, εως, ἡ, *a being half seen*, ὑ. τῶν ὀφθαλμῶν, of the eyes, when in sleep they show through the half-opened eyelids, Hp.*Prog.*2 (v.l. ὑποφαύσιας), *Aph.*6.52, cf. Aret.*SA*1.5; *trace, slight indication*, ἱδρῶτος Gal.10.541. II. *symptom, sign*, χρησταὶ ὑποφάσιες Aret.*CA*1.4. 2. *appearance*, σολοικισμοῦ ὑπόφασιν ποιεῖσθαι A.D.*Pron.*22.22; οὐδὲ ὑ. not a *trace*, Dam.*Pr.*84; ἡ ὑ. τῶν μερῶν ib.157.

**ὑποφᾶτις**, v. ὑποφῆτις.

**ὑπόφαυλος**, η, ον, *somewhat low*, δίαιτα Hp.*Fract.*7; of a word, Poll.10.98.

**ὑπόφαυσις**, εως, ἡ, *narrow opening*, in the bridge across the Hellespont, Hdt.7.36; in a testudo, Ph.*Bel.*99.39; αἱ θυρίδες δικτυωταί, ὑποφαύσεις κύκλῳ LXX *Ez.*41.16. II. ὑποφαύσιας was read for ὑποφάσιας in Hp.*Prog.*2 by Artemidorus and Dioscurides ap.Gal.18(2).52, but rejected by Gal. l.c.

**ὑποφαύσκω**, *begin to shine*, ὑποφαύσκοντος *at daybreak*, Arist.*Pr.*888$^b$27; ὑποφαυσκούσης ἕω v.l. ib.938$^a$32; cf. ὑποφώσκω.

**ὑποφείδομαι**, *spare a little*, X.*An.*4.1.8; c. gen., Plu.2.707b; ὑ. μὴ ἕλκειν Luc.*Peregr.*6; *to be moderate* or *restrained* in speech, Phld.*Lib.*p.24 O.

**ὑποφειδομένως**, Adv. *somewhat sparingly, restrainedly*, Plu.*Alex.*28.

⊛ **ὑποφέρω**, fut. ὑποίσω S.*El.*834 (lyr.), Phld.*Lib.*p.28 O.: aor. ὑπήνεγκον Arist.*Pol.*1267$^a$27, Ep. ὑπήνεικα Il.5.885:—*carry away under*, esp. *bear out of danger*, ἀλλά μ' ὑπήνεικαν ταχέες πόδες Il. l.c.:—Pass., *to be taken from under*, ἐὰν [τὸ ὑποκείμενον] ὑποφέρηται Arist.*IA*705$^a$9. 2. *bring close together*, τὰ ὀπίσθια σκέλη (sc. ἐπὶ τὰ ἔμπροσθεν) Id.*HA*604$^b$1. II. *bear* or *carry by being under, bear a burden*, τὰ ὅπλα, of an armour-bearer, X.*Cyr.*4.5.57; τῶν τὰ σημεῖα δοράτων ὑποφερόντων Plu.*Sull.*7:—Pass., *to be supported*, τοῖς σκέλεσι Arist.*Pr.*882$^b$29. 2. metaph., *endure, submit to*, πόνους καὶ κινδύνους Isoc.3.64, cf. X.*Eq.Mag.*1.3; κινδύνους καὶ φόβους Pl.*Tht.*173a; ῥαθύμως ὀργήν Id.*Lg.*879c; τὸν τῶν ὁμιλητικῶν τρόπον Isoc.1.30; γῆρας καὶ πενίαν Aeschin.1.88 (v.l. ἀμύνεσθαι); εἰσφοράς X.*Oec.*2.6; ἀναλώματα D.59.42; πόλεμον ὑπενεγκεῖν Arist.*Pol.*1267$^a$27; ὑ. παρρησίαν Phld.*Lib.*p.62 O.; ἀδικίας *Sammelb.*5238.22 (i A.D.); τὰ φυτὰ.. ἀνέμων ἐμβολὰς ὑ. Sor.1.96; οὐ γὰρ αὐτὸς ὑποφέρω κίνησιν I *do* not *trouble* to move, *PFlor.*362.10 (ii A.D.). III. *bear* or *carry behind*, δίφρους τινί Ael.*VH*4.22. 2. *subjoin, add* in speaking, D.H.7.16, Longin.16.4. IV. *hold out, present*, δᾷδα Plu.*Publ.*23; τὰ σεσιδηρωμένα μέρη ταῖς πληγαῖς Id.*Cam.*41; πληγὰς ὑ. *inflict* them, Id.*Eum.*7; οὐκ ὀλίγην βλάβην ὑποφέρει με (= μοι?) *inflicts*, *POxy.*488.19 (ii/iii A.D.). 2. metaph., *hold out, suggest, proffer*, εἰ τῶν.. οἰχομένων.. ἐλπίδ' ὑποίσεις S.*El.*834 (lyr.); ὑπέφερον τοὺς μῆνας *proposed* the (holy) months, i.e. a truce, X.*HG*4.7.2; σπονδὰς ἀδίκως ὑποφερομένας ibid. b. ὑποφέρονται γραμμαί τινες αἱματώδεις *there are suggestions of* lines (in the foetus), Ath.Med.ap.Orib.22.9.1. V. *carry down*, of a river, Plu.2.325a, Poll.1.111; κοιλίη ὑποφέρει χολώδεα Aret.*SA*2.4; *cause to slip* or *fall*, Plu.2.459b, Poll.1.187:—Pass., *to be borne down*, τοῖς ποταμοῖς Plu.*Alex.*63; *slip down*, κατὰ κρημνῶν Id.*Mar.*23; of the legs, *give way under* a person, Hp.*Int.*36. 2. metaph., *bring down* in numbers, App.*BC*5.6; in Pass., *decline gradually*, of consumptive people, Hp.*Epid.*1.2; ὀρθοστάδην ὑ. ib.3.13, 17.ιγ'; εἰς πενίαν App.*BC*2.2; πόλις ὑποφερομένη πταίσμασι Plu.*Comp.Per.Fab.*1; στάσιν ὑποφερομένην ἀνακαλεῖσθαι to revive an *expiring* faction, Id.*Sert.*4, cf. *Lyc.*2; of festivals, *fall after their due time*, Id.*Caes.*59. VI. *bring* to a certain point, ὑ. τινὰ εἰς διόρθωσιν Id.*Lyc.*25:—Pass., *to be carried away*, ὑ. εἰς ὕβριν Id.*Alc.*18; πρὸς τὸ κομπῶδες Id.*Alex.*23.

**ὑποφεύγω**, Ion. Iterat. ὑποφεύγεσκε v.l. in Hdt.2.174:—*flee from under, shun*, τινα Il.22.200, E.*El.*1343 (anap.); φυγὼν ὕπο νηλεὲς ἦμαρ Il.21.57; ὑ. τὸν πλοῦν *withdraw from, endeavour to evade*, Th.4.28. II. abs., *retire a little, withdraw*, Hdt.4.111,120, Th.3.97; *evade*, Pl.*Lg.*762b. 2. of land, *recede*, *Peripl.M.Rubr.*26. 3. *pass under* or *through*, τὴν λῆξιν καὶ τὴν αὔξησιν δι' ἧς ὑ. ἡ φύσις Zos.Alch.p.108 B.

**ὑπόφεως**, ὁ, = ὑπήκοον, Ps.-Dsc.4.67.

**ὑποφητ-εία**, ἡ, *an expounding of present* or *past events*, opp. προφητεία, Zonar. **-εύω**, *act as* ὑποφήτης, τισι Luc.*Philops.*6; τινι Id.*Bis Acc.*1. ⊛ **-ης**, ου, ὁ, (φημί) *suggester, interpreter, expounder*, esp. of the divine will or judgement, e.g. *priest who declares an oracle*, Il.16.235; Μουσάων ὑποφῆται, i.e. *poets*, Theoc.16.29, 17.115; ἑτέρων ὑ. Id.22.116; Γλαῦκος.. Νηρῆος ὑ. A.R.1.1311, cf. Porph.ap.Iamb.*Myst.*5.1, Orib.*Syn.*8.2.1. **-ις** (properisp.), ἡ, fem. of ὑποφήτης, Ἀφροδίτης (of Phryne) Ath.13.590e; Ἐνυαλίοιο καὶ Εἰράνας ὑποφᾶτιν.. σάλπιγγα *AP*6.46 (Antip. Sid.):—διᾱβολιᾶν ὑποφάτιες prob. *purveyors* of slander (= ἑρμηνευταὶ καὶ διάβολοι Sch.), perh. in reference to the ποταγωγίδες of Hiero, Pi.*P.*2.76: v.l. ὑποφάντιες (lemma in Sch. *E*), which might be taken as *suggestions* (Dor. for *ὑποφάνσεις). **-ωρ**, ορος, ὁ, ἡ, = ὑποφήτης, Μοῦσαι.. ὑποφήτορες.. ἀοιδῆς A.R.1.22; Πιερίδων ὑ., of poets, *AP*14.1 (Socr.), cf. Epic.*Oxy.*1015.1; μύθων ὑ. Man.3.326.

**ὑποφθᾰδόν**, Adv. *striving to be first, in rivalry*, Opp.*H.*3.145, 618. II. *taking one unawares*, ib.5.387.

**ὑπ-οφθάλμιος**, ον, *under the eyes*, φρουρά Poll.2.87; τὰ ὑ. the *parts under the eyes*, Hp.*Coac.*136, *Mul.*1.11, 2.110; sg. as expl. of ὑπώπιον, Aët.8.2.

**ὑποφθάνω** [ᾰ], aor. ὑπέφθην A.R.4.307; part. ὑποφθάς Il.7.144; also in Med. aor. part. (v. infr.): later aor. 1 ὑπέφθᾰσα (v. infr.):—*haste before, be* or *get beforehand*, ὑποφθὰς δουρὶ μέσον περόνησεν *getting beforehand* he pierced him through the middle, Il. l.c.; ἔγραψεν ὑποφθάσας Plu.*Pomp.*21:—also in part. Med., κτεῖνεν ὑποφθάμενος Od.4.547. II. c. acc., *to be beforehand with* one, A.R. l.c., Plu.*Aem.*26, etc.:—Med., τὸν ὑποφθαμένη φάτο μῦθον Od.15.171, cf. *AP*9.227 (Bianor).

⊛ **ὑποφθέγγομαι**, *speak in an undertone*, ἐντὸς ὑ., of an ἐγγαστρίμυθος, Pl.*Sph.*252c; ἡσυχῇ, ἠρέμα ὑ., Luc.*Nigr.*13, Longus 1.25; ὑ. τινί τι *hint gently, suggest*, Plu.2.88c. 2. *reply*, τινι Id.*Brut.*36. 3. *speak from underground*, J.*BJ*3.2.3. II. of birds, Ael.*NA*7.7, Longus 3.12; of a dog, Plu.*Arat.*8, Gal.18(1).291; also ὑ. κερκίς Philostr.*Im.*2.28.

**ὑποφθείρω**, *destroy* or *corrupt gradually*, in Pass., Gal.19.316; πολλῆς ὑποφθειρομένης νεότητος Arg.Lib.*Decl.*25.

**ὑποφθίνω** [ῐ], *waste away, pine gradually*, Heraclit.*All.*61, Dsc.*Eup.*2.30.

**ὑποφθον-έω**, *feel secret envy at*, τινι X.*HG*3.2.13; Κυαξάρης, ὅτι ἐκεῖνοι ἦρχον τοῦ λόγου, ὥσπερ ὑπεφθόνει (v.l. ὑπό τι ἐφθόνει) Id.*Cyr.*4.1.13. **-ος**, ον, *somewhat jealous*, only in Adv., ὑποφθόνως ἔχειν πρός τινα behave *somewhat jealously* towards one, Id.*HG*7.1.26.

**ὑποφθορ-ά**, ἡ, *corruption, decay*, Heliod.ap.Orib.44.23.27: pl., *seductions*, Vett.Val.118.5. **-εύς**, έως, ὁ, *corrupter, seducer*, *Gloss.* **-ιος**, ον, *decayed*, of teeth, Gal.12.880.

**ὑποφῐάλιον** [ᾰ], τό, *stand for a* φιάλη, *Inscr.Délos* 1441 *A* ii 35 (ii B.C.).

**ὑποφῐλέω**, *kiss slily*, ἀλλήλους Aristaenet.1.25.

**ὑπόφῑμος**, ον, *covered with a lid*, ἔλαιον Zos.Alch.p.114, cf. p.165 B.

**ὑποφλεγέθω**, f.l. for ἐπι-, Nic.*Al.*282.

**ὑποφλεγ-μαίνω**, *to be somewhat inflamed*, Orib.9.37.10, prob. to be read in Hp.*Loc.Hom.*9 (ὑπερ- vulg.). **-μᾰτίζω**, *to be salivated*, Alex.Trall.1.15. **-μᾰτώδης**, ες, *suffering somewhat from phlegm*, Hp.*Coac.*592.

**ὑποφλέγω**, *heat from below*, λαμπάδι ὕδωρ *AP*9.626 (Marian.).

**ὑποφοβ-έομαι**, Pass., *to be somewhat frightened*, Men.*Georg.*2, v.l. in Sch.E.*Hipp.*433. **-ος**, ον, *somewhat frightened, shy*, Phot. and Suid. s.v. ὑποδεής.

**ὑποφοινίζω**, *to be purplish*, Dsc.4.24 (ὑποφοινικοῦν cj. Wellm.).

**ὑποφοίνιος**, η, ον, *reddish*, λιβάδες *AP*15.25.3 (Besant. *Ara*).

⊛ **ὑποφοινίσσομαι**, poet. ὑπαιφ-, Pass., *become somewhat purple*, Nic.*Th.*178,720, Dsc.3.67, etc.

**ὑποφόν-ια**, τά, at Athens, *price paid by the murderer* to the relations of the deceased, to buy off their vengeance, *were-geld*, Din.(*Frr.*10.4, 18.11) et Thphr.ap.Harp.; καταθεὶς τὰ ὑ. Philostr.Jun.*Im.*10.8, cf. Aristid.2.436 J.: metaph., *blood-money*, ὑ. τοῖς στρατιώταις ἐδεδώκει τῆς σφαγῆς D.C.77.12. **-ιος**, ον, *murderous*, cj. in S.*Tr.*839 (lyr.).

**ὑποφορ-ά**, ἡ, (ὑποφέρω) *carrying off below, purging*, Hp.*Coac.*304, 511 (pl.), Heliod.ap.Orib.44.8.21. 2. *draining off*, Sor.1.58. II. *putting forward*, by way of excuse, ἡ τῶν μηνῶν ὑ. X.*HG*5.1.29. 2. Rhet., = ὁ τοῦ ἐχθροῦ λόγος, Hermog.*Inv.*3.4, cf. 13 (pl.), Tib.*Fig.*39. III. *drain*, *Gp.*2.6.8, v.l. in Arr.*Epict.*1.29.40. IV. in Str.5.4.9 ἀποφοράς is the true reading (ὑπ- codd. plerique). **-έω**, perh. *drain off*, dub. in *IG*2$^2$.463.93. ⊛ **-ος**, ον, *subject to tribute*, τισι *Peripl.M.Rubr.*16, Plu.2.774c. II. *with hollow passages, fistulous*, Gal.14.681; dub. cj. in Hp.*de Arte* 10 (ὕπαφρον (q.v.) codd.).

**ὑποφράζομαι**, Med. with aor. Pass. **-σθείς**, *note, observe*, A.R.1.462.

**ὑποφράσσω**, Att. **-ττω**, *stop* or *block up*, Mnesith.ap.Orib.8.38.3, Hero *Aut.*26.2 (both Pass.).

**ὑπόφρῑκος**, ον, (φρίξ) *shuddering a little*, LXX 3 *Ma.*6.20.

**ὑποφρίσσω**, Att. **-ττω**, *to be rather bristly*, γενειὰς ὑποφρίττουσα Philostr.Jun.*Im.*8; *shudder a little*, Luc.*Peregr.*39, *JConf.*4, *Pr.Im.*12, Aët.12.68; of an artery, Archig.ap.Gal.8.90. 2. c. acc., *feel dread before* or *of*, Euph.78, Gal.*UP*14.4. 3. *bristle*, πολιῇσιν ἐθείραις Nonn.*D.*35.55.

**ὕποφρον**, v. ὕπαφρος.

**ὑποφρύγ-ιος** [ῠ], ον, *hypo-Phrygian*, of modes and keys in music, ἁρμονία Ath.14.625d; διὰ πασῶν εἶδος Cleonid.*Harm.*9; τόνοι ib.12; τρόπος Bacch.*Harm.*47. Adv. **-ιστί**, *in the hypo-Phrygian mode*, Arist.*Pr.*922$^b$10, al.

**ὑποφῠγή**, ἡ, *refuge*, θέρους *from* heat, J.*AJ*8.5.2, cf. 15.10.1 (pl.), Poll.9.16 (pl.).

**ὑποφῠλ-ᾰκέω**, *serve as deputy*-ἀρχιφύλαξ, τοῦ Λυκίων ἔθνους *IGRom.*3.516 (Cadyanda). ⊛ **-ᾰκία**, ἡ, *office of deputy* ἀρχιφύλαξ, ib.489.16 (Oenoanda). **-αξ**, ᾰκος, ὁ, *deputy*-ἀρχιφύλαξ, *TAM*2(1).189 (Sidyma).

**ὑποφῠλάσσω**, = ὑποφυλακέω, *CIG*4332.12 (Phaselis).

**ὑποφυλλίς**, ίδος, ἡ, in acc. pl., v.l. for ἐπιφυλλίδας, LXX *Ob.*1.5.

**ὑποφῡράω**, *throw into confusion*, ὑπό τι πεφυρακέναι τὰς ψήφους *to have done* some *cooking* of the accounts, Cic.*Att.*6.5.1.

**ὑποφῡσάω**, *blow gently*, *EM*818.57:—Pass., *to be flatulent*, *Hippiatr.*46. 2. metaph., *elate*, Ph.1.339 (Pass.).

**ὑπόφῠσις**, εως, ἡ, *attachment underneath*, τένοντος Gal.*UP*2.6. 2. *growth by way of substitution*, θατέρου [φλοιοῦ] Thphr.*HP*4.15.1;

καθ' ὑπόφυσιν αὔξονται [οἱ ὄνυχες], καθάπερ αἱ τρίχες Gal.2.337. **3.** *sucker*, *EM*784.28, Phot.

**ὑποφῠτεύω**, *plant under*, *Gp*.10.50:—Pass., ὑ. ὑπό τινι Thphr.*CP* 3.10.5.

**ὑποφύω**, *cause to grow up under*, τοῖσι δ' ὑπὸ χθὼν φύεν ποίην Il. 14.347:—Pass., fut. -φύσομαι Diog.Oen.29: aor. 2 -εφύην Arist. *HA*501ᵇ9: pf. -πέφυκα Gal.2.277:—*grow up below* or *as a substitute*, of flesh, Hp.*VC*17, *Fract*.33; of teeth, Arist. l. c.; of hoofs, ib.604ᵃ25: metaph., ἂν [τὰς ῥίζας] ὑποτέμωμεν, οὐδὲν τῶν κακῶν ἡμῖν -φύσεται Diog.Oen. l. c.:—ὑποφύει = ὑποφύεται is f.l. in Thphr.*HP* 4.15.2. **2.** Pass., of muscles, *to be inserted under*, τῷ δέρματι Gal.2.246, *UP*3.11, cf. 4.10, al. **II.** Pass. also, *to be in process of growth*, ἐξειργάσατο τὴν τέχνην τὴν γραφικὴν ὑποφυομένην ἔτι Ael. *VH*8.8.

**ὑποφώγω**, *roast slightly*, Dsc.4.116 (Pass.).

**ὑποφωλεύω**, *lie hidden in the shelter of*, τοίχοις *AP*7.375 (Antiphil.).

**ὑποφων-έω**, *call out in answer*, Plu.*Pomp*.25, 2.53b; *sing in answer*, Mosch.3.48. **II.** ὑ. τινά *echo* his *name*, *BMus.Inscr*.789 (Cnidus, dub.). **-ησις**, εως, ἡ, *answer*, *retort*, Plu.2.33d (pl.).

**ὑποφώσκω**, = ὑποφαύσκω, ὑποφωσκούσης ἕω Arist.*Pr*.938ᵃ32 (v.l.); τῆς ἡμέρας ὑ. D.S.13.18 (v.l. ἐπιφ-).

**ὑποφωτίζω**, *throw light upon*, metaph., Diog.Oen.30.

**ὑποχάζομαι**, aor. -κεκαδόμην (v. infr.):—*give way before* some one, ὑπὸ δὲ Τρῶες κεκάδοντο Il.4.497; καί οἱ . . Ζεὺς . . ὑποχάζεται A.R. 1.1101.

**ὑποχαίρω**, *rejoice secretly*, εἰς τὸ κακόν Polem.*Phgn*.40.

**ὑποχᾰλᾰρός**, ά, όν, *somewhat slack* or *loose*, Hp.*Mochl*.38.

**ὑποχάλ-ᾰσις** [χᾰ], εως, ἡ, *a sinking down*, Suid. s. v. ὀφιζήσεις. **-άω**, *slacken a little*, *lower*, τὸν τόνον *Corp.Herm*.18.4 (v.l. ὑπαραιώσασα); τοῦ μέλους (partit. gen.) Ael.*NA*12.46:—Pass., *to be relaxed*, Sch.S.*Ant*.531. **II.** intr. = Pass., Anon.*Prog*. in Rh.1.621 W.

**ὑποχᾰλεπαίνω**, *become a little angry*, Sch.S.*OC*117.

**ὑποχᾰλῑνίδιος** [ῐδ], α, ον, *under the bridle*: ἡ ὑποχαλινιδία (sc. ἡνία) prob. *chin-strap attached to each end of the bit*, X.*Eq*.7.1.

**ὑποχαλκ-ίζω**, *look somewhat copper-coloured*, *EM*805.49. **II.** trans., *change for copper*, Hsch. **-ος**, ον, *containing a mixture of copper*, Pl.*R*.415b; κανοῦν χρυσοῦν ὑπόχαλκον *bronze gilt*, *IG*2².1407. 21; ὑπόχαλκον δέ σου τὸ χρυσίον *Com.Adesp*. (?) ap.Suid. s. v. ὑπόχαλκον: metaph., Plu.2.1b, 65a: cf. ὑπάργυρος, etc. **2.** *sounding like copper*, ὑ. ἠχὼ φέρειν Philostr.*VA*3.8. **3.** *of a copper colour*, ζῷον ὑπόχαλκον τὴν μορφήν (sc. the οἶστρος or μύωψ) Sch.Od.22.299.

**ὑποχᾰράσσω**, Att. -ττω, *engrave under*, Plu.*Alex*.69.

**ὑποχᾰροπός**, όν, *rather blue-eyed*, X.*Cyn*.5.23 (v.l.), Dicaearch. Hist.10, Ptol.*Tetr*.144; also **ὑποχάροψ**, *PTeb*.816 i 14 (ii B.C.).

**ὑποχάρτωσις**, εως, ἡ, = *tectoria*, *Gloss*.

**ὑποχάσκω**, aor. 2 ὑπέχᾰνον, pf. ὑποκέχηνα (v. χάσκω):—*gape a little*, Ar.*Pl*.314, X.*Eq*.6.8; κακὸν ὑποχάσκειν it is bad for the patient *to have the mouth a little open*, Hp.*Epid*.4.46; μικρὸν ὑποκεχηνυῖαι τὸ στόμα Ach.Tat.1.1; σῦκα ὑ. *open a little* (as they ripen), Philostr. *Im*.1.31.

**ὑπόχαυν-ος**, ον, *somewhat porous*, Archig.ap.Orib.8.2.3. **II.** *somewhat conceited*, Ath.14.624e, Procl.*Par.Ptol*.233, Adam.2.21,23 (Comp.). **-όω**, *make somewhat conceited*, *puff up*, Plu.2.21c; ἡμιτελῆ τὸν λόγον ὑ. τῷ πάθει *letting* his words *die away* half-finished (of one just falling asleep), Procop.Gaz.p.159 B.

**ὑπόχειρ**, ὁ, ἡ, = sq., S.*El*.1092 (lyr., Musgr. for ὑπὸ χεῖρα).

**ὑποχείρ-ιος**, ον, Pl.*Tht*.198a, *Plt*.308a; ος, α, ον, Id.*Erx*.392c, Hdt.5.91: (χείρ):—*under the hand*, *in hand*, χρυσὸν ὅτις χ' ὑποχείριος ἔλθῃ Od.15.448, cf. Anon.ap.Suid., and v. πρόχειρος. **2.** mostly of persons, *under* any one's *hand* or *control*, *under command*, *subject*, τινι Hdt.6.33,44; ὑ. εἶναι, γενέσθαι τινί, ib.119, A.*Supp*.392 (lyr.), X.*An*.3.2.3, Pl.*Lg*.683d; ὑποχειρίους ποιέεσθαί τινας make *subject*, bring *into subjection*, Hdt.1.106; ὑποχειρίας παρέξειν τὰς Ἀθήνας Id.5.91; ὅταν δ' ὑποχείριος ἔλθῃ Thgn.363; λαβεῖν τινα ὑποχείριον to get *into one's power*, E.*Andr*.736, Lys.4.5, etc.; ὑ. ἔχειν τινάς Th. 3.11, etc.; τὰ ὑ. τέκνα *POxy*.1642.5 (iii A.D.); ὑ. τὸν ἵππον ἔχειν keep him '*well in hand*', X.*Eq*.8.12; τὴν χώραν ὑ. τοῖς πολεμίοις παραδόντα Lycurg.8, cf. X.*Cyr*.5.3.13; ὑ. τοῖς ἰητροῖσι *in the power* of . ., Hp.*Medic*.1; of wild birds, ὑ. ποιήσασθαι keep them *in captivity*, Pl.*Tht*.197c; ὑ. τὰς ἐπιστήμας ἔχει ib.198a. **-ισμός**, ὁ, *treatment* of a subject, Gal.18(2).661.

**ὑποχειρογρᾰφέω**, *sign*, ὅρκος ὃν ὤμοσεν καὶ ὑπεχειρογράφησεν *PTheb.Bank* 11.1,19 (ii B.C.), *PTeb*.811.11 (ii B.C.); written ὑποχυρ-, *Dura*⁶ 432 (iii A.D.):—Pass., *PMeyer* 6.25 (ii B.C.), *POxy*.1473.38 (iii A.D.).

**ὑπόχευμα**, ατος, τό, *gentle stream*, *soft sprinkling*, v.l. in Pi.*P*.5.101 (pl.); ὑπὸ χεύμασιν codd. opt.

⊕**ὑποχεύς**, έως, ὁ, *trulla*, *Gloss*.

**ὑποχέω**, aor. ὑπέχεα, Ep. ὑπέχευα—the only form of the word used by Hom.:—*pour* into a cup placed *under*, *pour out*, Χίου (οὐχὶ Ath.cod. A) δύο κυάθους, ἀνεβόησέν τις, ὑπόχει (ὑποχεῖς Cobet) Sophil.4.3, cf. Men.8:—Med., ὑποχέασθαι πλείονας *have* more cups *poured out*, Diph. 5; ὑ. τρίτην ὕδατος μοῖραν Hp.*Nat.Mul*.15: metaph., οἷον βαφὴν (βαφῇ or -ῇ codd.) τῇ ῥητορικῇ τὴν φυσιολογίαν ὑποχεόμενος Plu.*Per*.8. **2.** in Hom. only of dry things, *strew* or *spread under*, βοείας, ῥῶπας, Il. 11.843, Od.14.49, cf. 16.47:—Pass., φύλλα ὑποκεχυμένα ὑπὸ τοῖσι ποσί the leaves *fallen and scattered under* the feet, Hdt.7.218. **3.** metaph., τῷ μὲν ἀπιστίῃ ὑπεκέχυτο he *was secretly full of* unbelief, *steeped in* it, Id.2.152, cf. 3.66. **II.** Med., *pour back one's own into*, πάλιν δ' ὑπεχεύατο παῖδας σπλάγχνοις Opp.*H*.1.740. **III.** Pass., *to be spread beneath*, as the air beneath the ether, Arist.*Mu*.392ᵇ6. **2.** *to be suffused*, *suffer from cataract* (cf. ὑπόχυσις), of persons, Chrysipp. *Stoic*.2.52; τὰ τῶν ὑποχεομένων συμπτώματα Gal.6.425; ὑποχυθέντες τὰς ὄψεις Ph.2.50; τοὺς ὑποκεχυμένους καὶ ἀμβλυωποῦντας Dsc.2.164, cf. *POxy*.39.9 (i A.D.); ἀρχόμενοι ὑποχεῖσθαι Dsc.2.151, cf. Cass.*Pr*. 19: metaph. of the mind, ὑποκεχύσθαι πολλὴν ἀχλύν Max.Tyr.16.3.

**ὑποχή**, ἡ, (ὑπέχω) *a round fishing-net*, Plu.2.977f, M.Ant.10.10, Opp.*H*.3.81, Ael.*NA*13.17, *Gp*.20.25.2. (Parox. in *Gp*. l. c.)

**ὑπόχηλα**, τά, (χηλή) *part of the hand near the fingers*, Poll.2. 144.

**ὑποχθόνιος**, η, ον, Call. (v. infr.): (χθών):—*under the earth*, *subterranean*, Hes.*Op*.141 (v.l. ἐπιχθ-), A.R.1.647, etc.; θεοῖς ὑ. *Rendic. Pont.Accad*.III vol.6.43, cf. Phld.*Piet*.58; ἴθ' ὑποχθόνιοι E.*Andr*. 515 (anap.); γύπη ὑπ[οχθονίῃ] Call.*Aet.Oxy*.2080.73 (= *Fr*.172); ἐχώρει -ιος, of one entering the cave of Trophonius, Philostr.*VA*8. 19; ὑ. γενέσθαι Luc.*Cont*.22: cf. καταχθόνιος, χθόνιος.

**ὑπόχθων**, ονος, ὁ, ἡ, = foreg., [Arist.]*Pepl*.41, *Supp.Epigr*.7.213.7 (Tab. Defix., Berytus, ii/iii A.D.).

**ὑπ-οχλέομαι**, Pass., *to be rolled beneath*, Il.21.260, in tmesi.

**ὑποχλιαίνω**, *warm a little* or *by degrees*, Hp.*Epid*.2.2.7 (Pass.), Plu.2.658d.

**ὑπ-οχλίζω**, *lift with a lever*, κληῖδας ὑποχλίσσασα πυλάων A.R.*Fr*.12.

**ὑπόχλοος**, ον, *of a palish yellow*, παρειή Call.*Del*.80.

**ὑποχλωρομέλᾱς**, ᾰνος, ὁ, *rather dark green* or *yellow*, of persons, Hp.*Epid*.6.3.13.

**ὑπόχλωρος**, ον, *greenish yellow*, *pale*, Hp.*Prog*.11, *Fract*.11, Arist. *HA*616ᵃ18, Sor.1.44,91.

**ὑποχοινικίς**, ίδος, ἡ, *base on which the* χοινικίς *rests*, in a torsion-engine, Ph.*Bel*.62.20.

**ὑποχοιρίς**, ίδος, ἡ, *swine's succory*, *cat's ear*, *Hypochoeris radicata*, Thphr.*HP*7.7.1, 11.4 (cj.), Plin.*HN*21.89.

**ὑπόχολ-ος**, ον, *somewhat bilious*, *yellowish*, of colour, Hp.*Morb*. 3.16, *Aff*.9, Aret.*SA*2.1, S.E.*M*.1.308. **-ώδης**, ες, *rather bilious*, Hp.*Epid*.3.1.έ.

**ὑποχονδρ-ιᾰκός**, ή, όν, *of the* ὑποχόνδριον, νόσημα Gal.8.185. **-ιος**, ον, (χόνδρος) *under the cartilage of the breastbone*, πάθη ὑ. ailments *in that part*, Arist.*Pr*.953ᵇ25. **II.** ὑποχόνδριον, τό, in sg. and pl., *the soft part* or *parts of the body below the cartilage and above the navel*, *abdomen*, τὸ δεξιὸν ὑ. Hp.*Aph*.4.64, al., cf. Arist.*HA*493ᵃ20, Thphr. *Od*.59(61), Sor.1.93, al., Gal.6.56, al.

**ὑποχορηγ-έω**, *furnish*, *supply*, τῇ Ῥώμῃ ἕκαστα Str.6.2.7. **-ία**, ἡ, *supply*, ποταμοὶ παρέχουσιν ὑ. Id.5.3.7.

**ὕποχος**, ον, (ὑπέχω) *subject*, *under control*, θεοῖς X.*An*.2.5.7; βασιλῆς βασιλέως ὕποχοι μεγάλου his *subjects* or *officers*, A.*Pers*.24 (anap.). **2.** = ἔνοχος, *liable to*, ἐξωλείας D.57.53; ὕποχοι ἐόντω τοῦ ἐνκλήματος *IG*5(2).357.92 (Stymphalus); *responsible for*, διανοίας Ph. 1.429; πλημμελείας *PLit.Lond*.138 viii 31.

⊕**ὑποχραίνω**, f.l. in Coluth.232.

**ὑποχρεμετίζω**, *neigh to* or *with*, Q.S.8.57 codd. (ἐπιχρ- Koechly).

**ὑποχρέμπτομαι**, *expectorate gently*, Hp.*Morb*.2.27, 3.15.

**ὑπόχρεως**, ων, gen. ω (masc. and fem.) *BGU*239.5 (ii A.D.), *PFlor*. 86.13 (i A.D.): also **ὑπόχρεος**, ον, *IG*2².1132.22 (Decr. Amphict., iii B.C.); gen. ου *Sammelb*.4415.8 (ii A.D.): pl. ὑπό-χρεοι, -χρέους, Plb.9.29.7, D.H.4.10: (χρέος):—*indebted*, *in debt*, Ar.*Nu*.242; ὁ δῆμος ὑ. τῶν πλουσίων *in their debt*, Plu.*Sol*.13. **2.** ὑ. τινί *dependent upon* him, Plb.6.17.1, cf. 4.51.2. **3.** of property, *involved*, *encumbered*, Is.10.16,17 (sed leg. ὑπέρχ-), D.49.11, 50.61. **4.** *obliged*, *bound*, c. gen., φιλίας καὶ χάριτος ὑ. *bound by ties of* love and favour past, Plu.*Pomp*.76, cf. D.S.19.44: also c. dat., ὑ. χάριτι Plb. 21.19.10, cf. 9.29.7.

**ὑποχρήστης**, ου, ὁ, *assistant oracle-giver*, *Milet*.7.50 (Didyma, i B.C.), 1(7) No.263 (ii A.D.).

**ὑπό-χρισμα**, ατος, τό, *foundation-layer* for artificial gems, *PHolm*. 14.12. **-χριστέον**, *one must anoint*, τοὺς πεπονθότας τόπους Orib. *Fr*.58. **-χρίω** [ῑ], *smear under* or *on*, *besmear*, *anoint*, τινί τι Hdt. 2.86, Hp.*Fract*.21; *paint* another's *face under the eyes*, X.*Cyr*.8.8. 20:—Med., *paint oneself*, ὑποχρίεσθαι τοὺς ὀφθαλμούς (cf. ὑπογράφω V) ib.8.1.41; *anoint oneself slightly*, Aret.*CD*1.3.

**ὑπόχρονος**, ον, *temporary* (?), *IG*2².2776.156 (ii A.D.).

⊕**ὑπόχρῡσ-ος**, ον, *containing a mixture* or *proportion of gold*, γῆ Poll.3.87: metaph. of persons, Pl.*R*.415c; cf. ὑπάργυρος, etc. **II.** *laden with gold*, *very rich*, ἔμπορος Hld.2.8; νεανίσκος '*gilded youth*', Luc.*Tox*.16. **III.** *gleaming with gold*, μῆλα Philostr.*Im*.1.31; *gilded*, Men.*Epit*.170; [δακτυλίους] σιδηροῦς ὑ. *Inscr.Délos* 298.33 (iii B.C.); κονδύλιον ὑ. ib.442 *B* 61 (ii B.C.). **-όω**, *gild*, δακτύλιοι σιδηροῖ ὑποκεχρυσωμένοι ib.421.43, 439*a* 13, 442 *B* 15, cf. 96 (all ii B.C.).

**ὑποχρώννῡμι**, in pf. part. Pass. ὑποκεχρωσμένος, *with high complexion*, of a comic mask, Poll.4.146.

**ὑποχῡλίζω**, *extract the juice from*, Dsc.*Eup*.2.30,34 (both Pass.).

**ὑπό-χῠμα**, ατος, τό, *cataract* in the eye, Dsc.3.81, Gal.10.119, Aq. *Le*.21.20. **-χύνω** ὀφθαλμούς, *cause cataract* in the eyes, Cyran. 25. **-χυρογραφέω**, v. ὑποχειρογραφέω. **-χῠσις**, εως, ἡ, (ὑποχέω III. 2) *cataract*, Dsc.1.73 (pl.), 2.12 (pl.), Ael.*NA*7.14, Iamb.*Myst*. 3.25 (pl.).

**ὑποχῠτήρ**, ῆρος, ὁ, *vessel to pour* oil into a lamp, Lxx *Je*.52.19, Phot., *EM*784.30.

**ὑπόχῠτος**, ον, (ὑποχέω) *having* something *poured in*, ὑ. οἶνος wine *that has been 'doctored'*, Phryn.Com.65, cf. Timachid.ap.Ath.1.31e: metaph. of a person, = ὁ κακῶς γεγονώς, Poll.3.56 (= *Com.Adesp.*100).

**ὑποχωλ-αίνω,** *to be somewhat lame*, Hp.*Epid.*7.47, Ph.1.606. **-εύω,** = foreg., *Gloss.* **-ος,** ον, *somewhat lame*, Vett.Val.110.15.

**⊛ὑποχωρ-έω,** fut. -ήσομαι Luc.*Tox.*11:—*go back, retire, withdraw*, Il.6.107, 22.96; χώρησαν δ' ὑπό τε πρόμαχοι.. 4.505; ὑ. ἐς τὴν Σάμον, εἰς Σικυῶνα, Th.8.79, Is.6.20; πρὸς αἱμασιάν Th.4.43; παρὰ Τισσαφέρνην Id.8.45; freq. in part., ὑποχωρῶν ᾤχετο, ὑποχωρήσαντες φεύγουσι, Is.4.28, D.22.66; of a lion, βάδην ὑ. Arist.*HA*629ᵇ14; of long-horned kine, νέμεσθαι ὑποχωροῦντας Id.*PA*659ᵃ20; εἰς τὰ βαθέα ὑ., of eels, Id.*HA*592ᵃ27, etc. 2. c. gen., *withdraw from*, ὑ. τῆς χώρης Hdt.1.207; ὑ. τοῦ πεδίου X.*Cyr.*2.4.24; τοῦ βίου *IG*12(7).395.9 (Amorgos): c. dat., τὸ δημοκρατικὸν ὑπεχώρησε τῷ ὀλιγαρχικῷ *gave way to*, Pl.*R.*560a; τὸν ἥσσω τῷ κρατοῦντι ὑ. Th.1.77; but ὑ. τῷ δαίμονι *try to escape from..*, Plu.*Brut.*40. b. κἀκεῖνος ὑπεχώρησεν αὐτῷ τοῦ θρόνου he (Aeschylus) *gave* Sophocles *a share of* the throne, Ar.*Ra.*790 (not *surrendered* it, which would be παρεχώρησεν); τοὺς πρεσβυτέρους ἐντρέπεσθαι.. ὁδῶν ὑποχωροῦντας *making way for them* on the streets (not '*retiring from* the streets'), Plu.2.237d. 3. c. acc., *avoid, shun*, μηδένα ὄχλον [νεῶν] Ἀθηναῖοι ὄντες ὑποχωρεῖν Th.2.88; so perh. to be taken in Il.13.476, μένει.., οὐδ' ὑποχωρεῖ, Αἰνείαν ἐπιόντα; cf. Pl.*Sph.*240a, D.H.6.93, Luc.*Tox.*36. b. *cede, yield*, τὴν δεσποτίαν αὐτοῖς *POxy.*67.19 (iv A.D.). II. *pass off below*, esp. by way of stool, σάρκες Hp.*Aph.*4.26, etc.; εἰ ταχέως ὑποχωρεῖ τῶν ὑποχονδρίων Gal.6.56, cf. 253:—in Med., Hp.*Aph.*7.67. III. *go on steadily*, εἰρεσία ὑπεχώρησεν ἐκ παλαμᾶν the rowing *went on*, stroke *after* stroke, Pi.*P.*4.202. IV. Ἡγέλοχος οὕτω προηνέγκατο (sc. γαλην ὁρῶ) ὥστε μὴ ὑποχωρῆσαι ἐκ τῆς συναλοιφῆς τὸ γαληνά, ἀλλὰ διαχωρῆσαι μᾶλλον, ὥστε δόξαι τὴν γαλῆν εἰπεῖν Sch.Ar.*Ra.*305 (dub. sens.). **-ημα,** ατος, τό, *downward evacuation*, Hp.*Aph.*7.68 (pl.), Thphr.*Char.*20.6 (pl.), etc. **⊛-ησις,** εως, ἡ, *retirement, retreat*, πεδιναὶ ὑ. *retirements* by the plains, Plb.1.34.8; πελαγίαν ποιεῖσθαι τὴν ὑ. make one's *retreat* by sea, Id.1.28.9; αἰδὼς τολμήσεως ὑ. Pl.*Def.*412c. b. *ebb* of the tide, Aristid.Quint.3.7 (pl.). c. *cession* of property, *POxy.*67.20 (iv A.D.). 2. *retiring-place, retreat*, Luc.*Hipp.*5, *CIG*3705 (Apollonia ad Rhyndacum). II. ὑ. τῆς γαστρός *an evacuation* of the bowels *by stool*, Hp. *Morb.*3.16, Gal.6.649: abs., Hp.*Aph.*4.83, *Epid.*7.3,5, Dieuch.ap. Orib.4.7.15, Mnesith.ib.8.38.3. III. *the vent*, Arist.*HA*594ᵃ13. **-ητικός,** ή, όν, *relaxing, evacuating*, Hp *Loc.Hom.*13, al. **-ίζω,** *separate, divide before* some one, Sch.Il.24.96 (Pass.).

**ὑποψάθυρος** [ᾰ], ον, *somewhat crumbling* or *friable*, διαχωρήματα Hp.*Prorrh.*1.116 (codd. and Gal.), cf. *Coac.*598 (-ψάφαρον codd.).

**ὑποψακάζω,** v. ὑποψεκάζω.

**ὑποψᾰλάσσω,** *handle* or *feel gently*, as one feels a beast to see if it is fat, Ar.*Lys.*84.

**ὑποψάλλω,** *touch softly*, prop. of the strings of the lyre: metaph., ὑ. τοὺς τέττιγας ἡ ὥρα *invites* them *to sing*, Philostr.*VA*7.11.

**ὑπόψαμμος,** ον, like ὕφαμμος, *having sand under* or *in* it, *sandy*, γῆ ὑποψαμμοτέρη *somewhat sandy*, Hdt.2.12, cf. Paus.4.36.5; τὸ ἀραιὸν καὶ ὑ. Ephor.65(c) J.; λίμνη X.*HG*3.2.19; θάλαττα Plu. *Pomp.*78.

**ὑπόψᾱρος,** ον, *somewhat dappled*, ἵπποι Posidon.52 J.

**ὑποψαύω,** *touch below* or *slightly*, τινος Plu.2.368e, cf. Hld.1.26 (ubi v.l. ἐπιψ-).

**ὑποψάφᾰρος,** ον, = ὑποψάθυρος (q.v.).

**ὑποψάω,** *scrape gently*, τὸν χῶρον τοῖς ποσὶ Ael.*NA*14.5.

**ὑποψεκάζω,** metaph., *tipple a little*, Poll.6.30, in phrase πυκνὸν ὑ., prob. cited from X.*Smp.*2.26, where codd. have ἐπιψακ- or ἐπιψεκ-; ὑπεψεκάζομεν Alciphr.*Fr.*6; ὑποψακ- is found in Poll.6.20 and as v.l. in 6.30.

**ὑποψελλίζω,** *lisp* or *stammer a little*, τὴν γλῶσσαν Lib.*Decl.*43.21.

**ὑποψεύδομαι,** *lie a little*, Eust.1955.26.

**ὑποψέφᾰρος,** ον, cj. by Diosc.Gloss. for ὑποψάθυρος in Hp., Gal. 16.763, cf. 19.150.

**ὑποψηλᾰφάω,** gloss on ὑπομηλαφάω, *EM*783.11, Phot.

**ὑποψηνίζω,** *prick from below*, like the ψήν (q.v.): metaph., ὑπεψηνισμένη, = ἀκμαῖα πρὸς τόκον (prob. from a Comic poet), Suid. (-μένοι and ἀκμαῖοι *Et.Gen.*, Phot.).

**ὑποψήφ-ῐσις,** εως, ἡ, *calculation*; and **-ιστής,** οῦ, ὁ, *calculator*, *Gloss.*

**ὑποψήχω,** *scrape up*, σώματα σὺν ταῖς ἄμμοις Posidon.48 J.

**ὑπ-οψία,** later **ὑφοψία** (first in *PSI*4.340.14 (iii B.C.)), Ion. ὑποψίη, ἡ: (ὑφοράω, fut. ὑπόψομαι): I. of the subject, *suspicion, ill-feeling*, ὑποψίην ἔς τινα ἔχειν Hdt.3.52, cf. Th.4.27, And.1.68; τὰ ἴχνη τῆς ὑ. φέροντα εἴς τινα Antipho 2.3.10; μεστὸς ὑποψίας Lys.1.17; ὑ. πρός τινα D.48.18, Plu.*Cic.*43; ὑ. λαμβάνειν κατά τινος D.29.24; αἱ τῶν μετεώρων ὑ. Epicur.*Sent.*11; τὸ σκότος ἐν ὑποψίᾳ ποιούμενος Aeschin.1.10; ἐν ὑποψίαις, δι' ὑποψίας ἔχειν τινά, Plu.*Pyrrh.*23, *Cat.Ma.*23; ὑ. γίγνεται, εἰσῆλθέν τινι, Th.2.13, Pl.*Ly.*218c; ἐς ὑ. καθιστάναι τινά to bring him into *suspicion*, Th.5.29; ὑποψίαν πρὸς ἀλλήλους ποιεῖν Lys. 25.30; opp. εἰς ὑποψίας ἐμπεσεῖν, Antipho 2.2.3. 2. of the object, ὑ. εἶχον were regarded with *suspicion*, Hdt.9.99; πολλὰς ἔχει ὑ. admits of *suspicions*, Pl.*Phd.*84c; ὑ. ἐνδιδόναι ὡς.. Id.*Lg.*887e; ὑ. παρέχειν Th.1.132, cf. Phld.*Piet.*111; ὑ. παρέχειν μὴ εἶναί τι Pl.*Mx.*247e: Astron., ἡ πρώτη ὑ. the first time the observer *suspects* he has seen a star rising, the first *glimpse*, Ptol.*Alm.*8.6. b. *apprehension*, ὁ κατὰ τὴν ὑ. φόβος Epicur.*Sent.*34; φόβος καὶ ὑ. Polystr.p.7 W.; αἱ τῶν μετεώρων ὑ. καὶ αἱ περὶ θανάτου Epicur.*Sent.*11. II. *jealous, censorious watch*, ἡ πρὸς ἀλλήλους τῶν ἐπιτηδευμάτων ὑ. Th.2.37.

**ὑποψιαστικῶς,** *suspiciously*, Zen.6.2, Sch.Ar.*V.*641.

**ὑποψῐθύρ-ίζω,** *whisper softly*, of fingers on the lyre, Ach.Tat.1.5. **-ισμα,** ατος, τό, *whispering*, Anon.*Prog.* in Rh.1.640 W.

**ὑπόψῑλος,** ον, *somewhat bald*, Ptol.*Tetr.*143, al.

**ὑπ-όψιος,** ον, (ὑφοράω, fut. ὑπόψομαι) *viewed from beneath* the brows, i.e. *viewed with suspicious looks*, λώβην τ' ἔμεναι καὶ ὑπόψιον ἄλλων Il.3.42 (where, however, Ar.Byz. read ἐπόψιον, v. ἐπόψιος), cf. Q.S.13.289. II. *under the eye* or *view, conspicuous*, Opp.*H.*1.30.

**ὑποψοφέω,** *make a slight noise*, ἐν τοῖσι ποτοῖσι Hp.*Coac.*62, cf. *Epid.*5.63; of water under ice, Ael.*NA*6.24. 2. ἐπορχουμένην ἑαυτῇ.. καὶ τοῖς δακτύλοις.. ὑποψοφοῦσαν *snapping* her fingers *in accompaniment*, Plu.2.336c.

**ὑπόψυχρος,** ον, *somewhat cold, coolish*, Hp.*Epid.*1.18, Gal.6.655. 2. *chilling*, Hp.*Acut.*62. 3. metaph., ὑ. τὰς φύσεις Ptol. *Tetr.*56. 4. *rather lacking in humour, flat*, κωμικοί Suid. s. v. Λύκις; προοίμιον Anon. in *Tht.*3.30; *rather absurd*, ζήτημα ὑ. Hermog.*Stat.*12; ὑ. τὸ λέγειν ὡς.. A.D.*Pron.*83.22; σύμπτωσις φωνηέντων ὑπόψυχρος Phld.*Rh.*1.163 S.

**ὑποψύχω** [ῡ], *cool a little*, Dsc.2.136:—Pass., Ath.7.297a.

**ὑπ-οψωνέω,** *underbid in the purchase of victuals* or *buy up underhand*, Ar.*Ach.*842 (lyr.).

**ὑποψωρώδης,** ες, *somewhat itchy* or *mangy*, Hp.*Epid.*4.20.

**ὑπτπρό,** v. ὑποπρό.

**ὑπτι-άζω,** (ὕπτιος) *lay oneself back, fall back*, Hdn.1.4.7, Procop. *Goth.*4.31, Eust.249.5; ὑπτιάζων βόλος an *unlucky* cast, opp. πρανής, Poll.7.204. II. metaph., of haughty persons, *carry oneself with languid arrogance*, Aeschin.1.132. 2. *to be supine, careless*, or *negligent*, Hdn.2.12.2, etc.; πρὸς τὴν ἐπιμέλειαν Id.2.8.9; of literary style, ὑπτιάζων λόγος *languid* style, τὸν ὑ. λόγον ὀρθοῖ καὶ γοργὸν ποιεῖ Hermog.*Id.*2.1. B. trans., *bend back*, ὑ. τὰς χεῖρας (cf. ὕπτιος II) Lxx *Jb.*11.13:—Pass., κάρα γὰρ ὑπτιάζεται his head *lies supine*, S.*Ph.*822; ὑπτιαζόμενοι *lying on their backs*, J.*BJ*3.7.29; ἐπ' αὐτὸν ἄνοδος ἠρέμα προσάντης ὑπτίαστο the approach *sloped gently upwards* (cf. ὕπτιος IV), ib.5.5.6. 2. Pass., *diverge*, of light rays, Phlp. *in Mete.*21.11. 3. *upset*, ὑπτιάζειν καὶ ἀνατρέπειν τὴν γαστέρα Gal.6.593; *relax*, [τὸ στόμα τῆς γαστρός], opp. ῥωννύειν, Id. 15.461. II. metaph., *make subservient*, Lyd.*Mag.*2.26. **-ασμα,** ατος, τό, *that which is laid back*, ὑπτιάσματα χερῶν *attitudes of supplication* with hands *upstretched*, A.*Pr.*1005; ὑ. κειμένου πατρός his father's *body* as it lies *supine*, Id.*Ag.*1285. **-ασμός,** ὁ, *laying oneself backwards*, Luc.*Salt.*71, Philostr.*Im.*2.6 (pl.), Vett. Val.3.12. 2. *lying supine*, of bedridden people, Hp.*Fract.*11. II. metaph., *sluggish appetite, aversion from food, nausea*, Gal.8.378, 13.140. **-άω,** only in Ep. part. ὑπτιόωσα and 3 sg. subj. ὑπτιάησι, poet for ὑπτιάζω, intr., of the moon's crescent, *lean backward*, Arat. 789, 795. **⊛-ος,** α, ον, *laid on one's back*, freq. in Hom., esp. of one falling *backwards*, opp. πρηνής, πολλοὶ δὲ πρηνεῖς τε καὶ ὕπτιοι ἔκπεσον Il.11.179; ὁ δ' ὑ. ἐν κονίῃσι.. πέσε 15.434, cf. 4.522, al., S.*OT* 811; τὸν δ' ὑ. ὦσ' ἀπὸ δουρός Il.16.863; ἄλλοτ' ἐπὶ πλευρὰς κατακείμενος, ἄλλοτε δ' αὖτε ὑ., ἄλλοτε δὲ πρηνής, of Achilles in his grief, 24.11; ὑ. ἀποθανέειν to die *lying on one's back*, Hdt.4.190; ῥέγκει.. ὑ. Ar.*Eq.*104; ὕπτιον καθεύδειν οὐδενὶ βέλτιόν ἐστιν Diocl. *Fr.*141; κατεκλίνη ὑ. Pl.*Phd.*117e, cf. Sor.2.87, al., Gal.18(2).56, al.; ὑ. ἀνατετραμμένος Pl.*Euthd.*278c; of a quadruped, ὀρθοῦ ἑστεῶτος.. καὶ ὑπτίου standing upright and *lying on its back*, Hdt.2.38, cf. *AP*5.202 (Asclep.). II. ὑ. μέρη, in animals, *the under parts*, i.e. *the belly*, opp. τὰ πρανῆ (the upper parts, the back), Arist. *PA*658ᵃ16, al., cf. πρανής II: hence Thphr.*HP*1.10.2, 3.14.2 uses ὕπτιος of the *smoother* upper surface of leaves, opp. πρανής of the rougher and under: γαστὴρ ὑ. the belly *uppermost*, E.*Cyc.*326; of the hand, ἐκτείνειν τὴν χεῖρ' ὑ. to hold out the hand *with the under side uppermost*, to hold out *the hollow of* the hand, so as to receive something, Ar.*Ec.*782; τὴν χεῖρα νῦν μὲν ὑ., νῦν δὲ πρηνῆ προτείνας Plu.*Tim.*11; τῆς χειρὸς ὑ. τὸ μέσον Id.*Crass.*18; ὑ. ταῖς χερσὶν ὑποδέχεσθαί τι Philostr.*Im.*1.6; ἐδέξαντο ὑπτίαις χερσὶ τὸν τῶν πολεμίων στρατόν Procop.*Goth.*3.16.19; οὐλὴ καρπῷ δεξιῷ ὑπτίῳ *PLond.* 2.259.81 (I A.D.); ὑ. χεῖρας ἀνατείνειν lift the *upturned* hands in prayers, Plu.*Comp.Phil.Flam.*2, cf. Philostr.*Im.*2.1; ταῖς χερσὶν ὑπτίαις διαλέγεσθαι D.Chr.33.52; ἐξ ὑπτίας νεῖν swim or float *on one's back*, Ar.*Fr.*665, Pl.*R.*529c. III. generally, of anything *turned downside up*, πάλος ἐξ ὑπτίου 'πήδησεν.. κράνους from the *upturned* helmet, *with the hollow uppermost*, A.*Th.*459 (cf. Il.7.176); παράθες νυν ὑ. αὐτὴν ἐμοί (sc. τὴν ἀσπίδα) Ar.*Ach.*583, cf. *Lys.* 185, Th.7.82; ἀψῖδος ἥμισυ ὕπτιον a half-wheel *with the concave side uppermost*, Hdt.4.72; but κύλιξ ὑ. a cup *with the bottom uppermost*, Ar.*Lys.*195; ὑπτίοις σέλμασιν ναυτίλλεται he sails with the benches *upside down*, i.e. suffers shipwreck, S.*Ant.*716; κεῖσθαι ὥσπερ γάμμα ὑ. X.*Oec.*19.9; σχαλίδες Id.*Cyn.*6.7; περιφέρεια κοίλη καὶ ὑ., opp. πρηνὴς καὶ κυρτή, Arist.*Mete.*350ᵃ11. 2. ἐξ ὑπτίας ἀνάπαλιν διανεῖν τὸν λόγον *trace* the argument *backwards* from the conclusion, Pl.*Phdr.*264a, cf. Herm. *in Phdr.*p.187 A.; ἐξ ὑπτίας *backwards, in reverse order*, ἀπὸ τῶν ἐσχάτων ἐπὶ τὰ πρῶτα ἐπανιόντες Dam.*Pr.*81; ἐξ ὑπτίας χωροῦντες Procl.*Hyp.*7.57. IV. of land, *flat, horizontal*, Hdt.2.7, Thphr.*CP*5.12.7, App.*BC*4.2, *Mith.*42, Ael.*NA*16.15, Plu. 2.193e, 530a; ἐν ὑπτίῳ τοῦ ὄρους Paus.8.13.1; ὑ. μᾶλλον ἢ ὄρθιος, of a flight of shallow steps, Luc.*Hipp.*5; of the sea, *smooth*, Philostr. *Im.*2.17, Lib.*Descr.*7.5. V. metaph., *supine, lazy, careless*, Aristid. *Or.*31(11).5, Id.2.112 J., Poll.1.158, etc.; ἔστω.. μὴ ὑ. ὁ τράχηλος his neck should not be *relaxed*, Zeno *Stoic.*1.58; δεῖ αὐτῷ καὶ αὐχένος ὀρθοῦ καὶ βλέμματος οὐχ ὑπτίου Lib.*Or.*64.103; προσφέρομαι τῶν αὐστηρῶν τι.. ὅταν αἴσθωμαί ποθ' ὕ. [τὸν στόμαχον] γεγονότα καὶ πλησίον ἥκοντα ναυτίας Gal.6.601, cf. 15.460; of language, *flat, tedious*, D.H.*Isoc.* 15, *Din.*8, Hermog.*Stat.*3, etc. Adv., ὑπτίως ἔχειν to be *flat and dull*, Ph.1.305; ὑ. καὶ οὐ ποιητικῶς ᾖσεν Philostr.*Her.*2.19. VI. *passive*, of Verbs, D.L.7.43,64; cf. ὀρθός v. -ότης, ητος, ἡ, *supine position*, of leaves, Thphr.*HP*1.10.2. II. of a river, *flatness*, Str.8.3.19. III. metaph., *supineness, calmness*, Poll.3. 122; of style, *flatness*, Hermog.*Id.*1.11, 2.1. 2. *slackness*, Iamb. *VP*15.64 (pl.). -όω, only in Pass., *to be turned on one's back*, ὑπτιωθέντος [τοῦ βρέφους] Sor.1.100, cf. 106; to be *turned downside up, to be upset*, ὑπτιοῦτο σκάφη νεῶν A.*Pers.*418; of leaves, *to be laid back*, Dsc.4.88. 2. of land, *slope gently upwards*, λόφος.. ὑπτιούμενος ἐπὶ τὴν κορυφὴν ἄκραν J.*AJ*15.11.3. 3. metaph. of the appetite (cf. ὑπτιασμός II), *to be sluggish*, ὄρεξιν.. ὑπτιωμένην ἀνεγεῖραι Gal.14.302; -οῦσθαι τὸν στόμαχον Archig.ap.Gal.13.140, cf. Sor.1. 50. -ωσις, εως, ἡ, = ὑπτιασμός II, στομάχου Id.2.8: abs., Herod. Med.ap.Orib.5.27.21 codd.

**ὑπῳάδιος** [ᾰ], ον, (ᾠόν) *from the egg, hatched*, ὄφρα γένωνται παῖδες ὑ. Opp.*H.*1.752 (v.l. ἐπῳάδιοι).

**ὑπώβολος**, ον, (ὀβολός) *mortgaged* ἐπὶ *ὀβολιμαίῳ τόκῳ, Pherecr. 58 (Porson, for ὑπόβολον); Dor. **ὑπώδελος** Epich.79 (dub. sens.).

**ὑπωθέω**, *push* or *thrust away*, ὦσεν ὑπ' ἐκ δίφροιο Il.5.854. 2. *push up from beneath*, τὴν κεφαλὴν τοῦ ξύλου ὑπὸ τὴν μασχάλην Hp. *Art.*7.

**ὑπωλένιος**, ον, (ὠλένη) *under the arm*, φαρέτρη Theoc.17.30; f.l. for ἐπωλ-, *h.Merc.*510 codd.

**ὑπώμ-αιος**, ον, (ὦμος) *under the shoulder*, πόδες the *forefeet*, Arat.144, cf. 1115; -ώμαια, τά (sc. κρέα), *SIG*1025.53 (Cos, iv/iii B.C.). -ία, Ion. -ίη, ἡ, (ὦμος) *the part under the shoulders*, Hp. ap.Gal.19.150.

**ὑπωμοσία**, ἡ, *oath taken in court to delay proceedings* (v. ὑπόμνυμι II), 1. *oath* or *affidavit showing good ground for the absence* of a party to a suit, *application for delay*, D.21.84 (pl.), v. Harp. s.v.; ὑπωμοσίαν παραδέχεσθαι Hyp.*Eux.*7; cf. ἀνθυπόμνυμι. 2. *oath* taken by the prosecutor in a γραφὴ παρανόμων (v. παράνομος II. 2), with the effect of suspending the proposed law or decree, ἐὰν [τὸν νόμον] ἐν ὑ. to leave it in *the condition caused by the* ὑπωμοσία, to let it drop, D.18.103; cf. *AB*313, Poll.8.56.

**ὑπωπι-άζω**, *strike* one *under the eye, give* him *a black eye*:—Pass., *have a black eye*, ὑπωπιασμέναι Ar.*Pax*541, cf. Arist.*Rh.*1413ᵃ20, D.L.6.89. II. metaph., *bruise, mortify*, 1*Ep.Cor.*9.27; also, *annoy greatly, wear out*, τινα *Ev.Luc.*18.5, cf. Plu.2.921f (corr. Turnebus for ὑποπιέζω). -ασμός, ὁ, = *suggillatio*, *Gloss.* -ον, τό, (ὤψ) *the part of the face under the eyes*, νυκτὶ θοῇ ἀτάλαντος ὑπώπια like night in *countenance*, i.e. dark, gloomy, Il.12.463, cf. Hp.*Int.*12 (v.l. ὑπόπνα), Philostr.*Gym.*48. II. *a blow in the face, black eye*, E.*Fr.*374, Ar.*Ach.* 551, *V.*1386, Apolloph.3, Lys.4.9, etc.: then, *any bruise* or *weal*, Thphr.*HP*9.20.3, cf. Gal.12.804; improperly applied to *a bruise on the foot*, as is shown by the joke in Ath.3.97f. 2. metaph., *blot, disgrace*, Cic.*Att.*1.20.5. III. a plant, the root of which was bruised and applied *as a cure for black eyes*, = θαψία, Ps.-Dsc.4. 153. -ος, α, ον, *with a black eye*, Poll.8.79.

**ὑπωπίς**, ίδος, ἡ, = ὑπώπιον III, Hsch.

**ὑπώρ-εια** (in some passages of Hdt. (v. infr.) the best codd. give **ὑπώρεα**), ἡ, *the foot of a mountain, skirts of a mountain range*, mostly c. gen., ὑπωρείας ᾤκεον.. Ἴδης Il.20.218; οἰκέουσι ὑπώρεαν ὀρέων ὑψηλῶν Hdt.4.23, cf. 1.110, 2.158, 7.199; [ὄρεα] συμμίσγοντα τὰς ὑπωρέας (-είας codd.) ἀλλήλοισι ib.129; ἐπὶ τῆς ὑπωρέης (-είης codd.) τοῦ Κιθαιρῶνος Id.9.19, cf. 25 (-είης codd.); ἐν ταῖς ὑ. Pl.*Lg.* 681a. -ειος, ον, *under the mountains*, καμπή Callistr.*Stat.*1: but ὑπόρειος θάλασσα ib.14.

**ὑπώρορε**, v. ὑπόρνυμι.

❋ **ὑπωρόφ-ιος**, ον, also α, ον Pi.*P.*1.97, *AP*7.424 (Antip. Sid.): (ὄροφος):—*under the roof, dwelling under it, under cover, in a house*, Il.9.640; τόξα.. νηῷ κεῖται ὑπωρόφια Simon.143; φόρμιγγες ὑ. the harps *sounding in the hall*, Pi.*P.*1.97; parodied, ὑ. φάλαγγες (spiders) Ar.*Ra.*1313 (lyr.); ὑ. δόμοι, = ὑπερῷα, Mosch.2.6. 2. ὑπωροφία (sc. χώρα), ἡ, *the woodwork of a tiled roof*, *IG*11(2).161 *A* 51 (Delos, iii B.C.); Dor. **ὑπωρυφία** ib.4²(1).102.42 (Epid., iv B.C.); *the space under the roof* or *canopy*, D.S.18.26; καπνώδεις ὑ. App.*BC*4. 13. -ος, ον, = foreg., E.*El.*1166, *Ph.*299, *HF*107 (all lyr.), Call. *Iamb.*1.414; of a swallow's nest, *under the eaves*, *AP*10.2 (Antip. Sid.): c. dat., ὑ. τῷ ἀνδρί *Berl.Sitzb.*1927.164 (Cyrene).

**ὑπωρυφία**, v. ὑπωρόφιος 2.

**ὑπωρυχία**, ἡ, *the part undermined*, App.*BC*4.111 (pl.).

**ὑπώστη**, ἡ, = εἰσώστη, *CIG*2667 (Halic.), Newton *Halicarn.*ii p. 710; also written ὑπόστη (q.v.).

**ὕπωχρος**, ον, *pale yellow*, Arist.*HA*586ᵇ33, Dsc.3.152, Gal.6.336, 16.588; *sallow*, Hp.*Int.*4, Arist.*Phgn.*807ᵇ7, Philostr.*Gym.*49, Luc. *Tox.*19.

**ὗραξ** [ῠ], ᾶκος, ὁ, *mouse* or *shrew-mouse*, Nic.*Al.*37. (Cf. Lat. *sorex* 'shrew'.)

**ὑράξ**, Adv. *promiscuously*, Hsch.; Aeol. **ὕρραξ** Theognost.*Can.* 23, interpol. in Suid. **ὕργα**· πτύον, Theognost.*Can.*23: cf. ὕριγγα. **ὑργαί**, αἱ, = ἐπιθέματα πρὸς κουφισμὸν τῶν φορτίων, ibid.; cf. ὑρχή. **ὑργάλαι**· ἀεὶ ἔρρωσο, ibid. **ὑρεῖ**· φοβεῖται, Hsch. (leg. τρεῖ). **ὑρειγαλέον**· διερρωγός, Id. (leg. ϝρηγ- or [Boeot.] ϝρειγ-). **ὑριατόμος**· ὁ τὰ κηρία τέμνων τῶν μελισσῶν, Id.; cf. ὗρον. **ὕριγγα**· πτύον, Σαλαμίνιοι, Id. (Cypr. for σύριγγα, accus.). **ὑρίς**, v. ὕσταξ. **ὑρίσιδα**· σπυρίδιον, σπυρίς, Hsch. (leg. ὑρίς and ὑρίδα): cf. ὑρρίς.

❋ **ὑρῖχός** [ῠ], ὁ, *wicker basket, hand-basket*, Ar.*Fr.*569.5; **σύριχος**, Alex.128.3; written also **ὑρισσός**, Theognost.*Can.*23 (**ὑρίσσος** Hsch.); **ὑρίσκος** and **συρίσκος**, Hsch.; **ὕρισχος**, Phryn.*PS*p.116B. (**βρίσχος** ibid.); **σύρισσος**, Poll.10.129.

**ὑρμίνη**· μάχη, πόλις, Theognost.*Can.* 23 (cf. ὑσμίνη, and Ὑρμίνη, Il. 2.616). **ὗρον**, = σμῆνος, Hsch.; cf. **ὗρους**, = σίμβλον, Theognost. *Can.*23: hence ὑριατόμος (q.v.). **ὕρραδα**· σπυρίδιον, ibid. **ὑρράδιος**· προγονίος ἢ ἄδοξος, ibid., cf. Hsch.: Ὑρράδιος, *son of* Ὕρρας, i.e. Pittacus, D.T.634.31, cf. Call.*Epigr.*1. **ὕρραξ**, v. ὑράξ. **ὑρραπλέα**· ῥηγαλέα, Theognost.*Can.*23 (cf. ὑρειγαλέον). **ὑρραχα**· πρίσχη, Hsch. **ὑρρίς**· σπυρίς, Zonar.; cf. ὑρίσιδα. **ὑρρώφθαι**· φληναφᾶν, Hsch. **ὑρτακός**· ὄστρεον, Id. **ὑρτάνα**· ἀπομάχυτρας, Id. (fort. πῶμα χύτρας). **ὑρτήρ**· πλυνεύς, Id.

❋ **ὑρχη**, ἡ, *jar*, for pickles, in acc. pl. ὕρχας, Ar.*V.*676 (anap.); nom. sg. ὕρχη (twice corr. from ὕρχης) ταρίχου, ὑπογαστρίων ὕρχη, *PSI*4.428. 8, 84 (iii B.C.); for wine, in acc. pl. ὕρχας, Ar.*Fr.*423. (Aeol. acc. to Poll.6.14, Sch.D.T.p.143 H.; ψιλοῦται Sch.D.T. l.c.; ὑρχή ('ἐφ' ἧς τὰ φορτία φέρουσιν οἱ ναῦται, Hsch.) is perh. a diff t. word.)

**ὗς**, = ὑός, υἱός (q.v.).

❋ **ὗς** (A), ὗν, gen. ὑός [ῠ]; or **σῦς**, σῦν, gen. συός, ὁ and ἡ: Hom. prefers σῦς, and uses ὗς only metri gr.: in Hdt. and Att. ὗς is the prevailing form, as also at Rhodes, *IG*12(1).905, Myconos, *SIG*1024. 16 (iii/ii B.C.), etc., and ὑῶν ὄρος is an Argive place-name, ib.56.25 (v B.C.); ὗς Alc.99 (s.v.l.); both forms in Pi., v. infr.; ὗς in *PCair.Zen.* 462.7 (iii B.C.), Lxx *Le.*11.7, al. (σῦς only as v.l. in *Ps.*79(80).14), and Plb.8.29.4, 31.14.3, 34.8.8 (συναγρειον f.l. in 8.26.10, B.-W.ii *Praef.* p.lxxvii); but σῦς (acc. σῦν) in *IG*5(1).1390.34, al. (Andania, i B.C.): pl., nom. ὕες, σύες; acc. ὕας, σύας, Att. ὗς Pl.*Tht.*166c, Plb.12.4.5,8, *GDI*5633.9 (Clazomenae) (σῦς Od.14.107); gen. ὑῶν, συῶν; dat. ὑσί (συσί Il.5.783, 7.257), but Ep. also ὕεσσι Od.13.410, σύεσσι (v. infr.):—*the wild swine*, of the *boar*, σῦν ἄγριον ἀργιόδοντα Il.9.539, cf. 8.338, al.; ἀργοτέρῳ συῒ καπρίῳ 11.293; ἀγροτέροισι σύεσσιν ἐοικότε 12.146; ἀργιόδοντος ὑός 10.264; also called σῦς κάπριος or κάπρος, v. sub vocc.; cf. also χλούνης; of the *sow*, συὸς ληϊβοτείρης Od.18.29; ὗς ἄγριος Hdt.4.192, cf. X.*Cyr.*1.6.28, etc.; ὕες (v.l. ὗς) ἄγριαι Arist.*HA*578ᵃ25. 2. of the domesticated animal, Od. 14.14; the hogs being eaten, ὕες θαλέθοντες ἀλοιφῇ Il.23.32; they were fed on acorns, Od.10.243; also on μῆλα πλατανίστινα, Gal.6. 597; τοκὰς ὗς *sus foeta*, Luc.*Lex.*6, cf. Od.14.16; ὗς ἐπίτεξ Alciphr. 3.73. 3. provs., Βοιωτία ὗς, of stupidity (cf. Συοβοιωτοί), Pi.*O.*6. 90, cf. *Fr.*83 (σύας); ὗς ποτ' Ἀθαναίαν ἔριν ἤρισεν (or more shortly ἡ ὗς τὴν Ἀθηνᾶν, Lat. *sus Minervam*, Plu.*Dem.*11), of dunces *setting themselves up* against wise men, Theoc.5.23; οὐκ ἂν πᾶσα ὗς γνοίη Pl. *La.*196d; ὗς διὰ ῥόδων 'a bull in a china-shop', Crates Com.4; ὗς ἐκώμασε, of arrogant and insolent behaviour, Theognost.*Can.*24; ὗς ὑπὸ ῥόπαλον δραμεῖται, of one who runs wilfully into destruction, Dinoloch.14; παχὺς ὗς ἔκειτ' ἐπὶ στόμα (cf. βοῦς VIII) Men.21; λύσω τὴν ἐμαυτῆς ὗν I will give my *rage* vent ('*go the whole hog*'), Ar.*Lys.* 684. II. = ὕαινα II, Epich.68, Archestr.*Fr.*22.1. III. v. ὕσγη. (Cf. Lat. *sūs*, OE. *sú*, *sw-in*: perh. I.-E. *sū-s* fem. 'mother', cf. Skt. *sū-s* 'mother', *sū-te* 'bring forth (young)'; change of meaning as in Polish *maciora* (1) 'mother', (2) 'sow', and in Sardinian *mardi* 'sow', from *mater*; Skt. *sū-s* is also masc., and σῦς is difficult.)

**ὗς** (B), Dor. for οἷ, *whither*, *IG*4.498.4 (Mycenae, ii B.C.). II. Dor. for ἐκεῖ(σε), in the gloss ὕσειμι· ἐκεῖ βαδίζω, Hsch. (cf. ὕσπερ).

**ὑσαλιβάτης**· ὁ Σκύθαι ἀλείμματι χρῶνται στέατι μοσχείῳ καὶ αἰγείῳ Theognost.*Can.*24: cf. ὗς· ἀλείφαβοῦς· οἱ γὰρ Σκύθαι ἀλείματι χρῶνται ὑείῳ καὶ μοσχίῳ στέατι, Hsch.

**ὕσγη**, ἡ, a shrub from which comes the dye ὕσγινον, prob. *kermes-oak*, *Quercus coccifera*, Suid.; prob. cj. for ὗς in Paus.10.36.1 (who says it is a Galatian word, = κόκκος).

**ὑσγίνη**, ἡ, = ἰσάτις, dub. cj. in Ps.-Dsc.2.184.

**ὑσγῖνο-βαφής**, ές, (βάπτω) *dipped* or *dyed in* ὕσγινον, i.e. *scarlet*, X.*Cyr.*8.3.13, Clearch.25: τὰ ὑ. *scarlet cloths*, Luc.*Gall.*14, Ath.12. 539e. -ειδής, ές, *scarlet in appearance*, σελήνη *PMag.Par.*2.249 = 556 (written εἰσγηνονιδη).

**ὑσγῖνόεις**, εσσα, εν, *scarlet*, ὑσγινόεντας Nic.*Th.*870. [v. sq.]

❋ **ὕσγῖνον**, τό, a vegetable dye of bright crimson or scarlet colour, perh. the *kermes* (v. ὕσγη), Nic.*Th.*511, *AP*6.254 (Myrin.); *hysginum*, Vitr.7.14.1 (*excygno* codd.), Plin.*HN*9.140, 21.170, 35.45 (*hygino, yyg-, yog-, id genus*, codd.), *Dig.*32.1.78.5, Isid.*Etym.*19.17.15 (*iscino*): gen. sg. ισγινης *Edict.Diocl.*19.8; ισγενης, ib.24.9–12. 2. *scarlet cloak*, τὸ ἄλλο ζεῦγος τῶν ὑσγείνων *POxy.*531.17 (ii A.D.). [ῑ Nic. and *AP* ll.cc.; but ὑσγῐνόεις Nic.*Th.*870: the forms ισγινη, ισγενη point to a naturally short ι, lengthd. metri gr.]

❋ **ὑσγῖνόσημος**, ον, *with crimson stripes*, only in the form **ισγινοσημων** (gen. pl.), *Edict.Diocl.*29.36, al.; *isginosema*, ib.9.

**ὕσδος**, for ὄσδος, Aeol. for ὄζος, Sapph.4,93.

**ὕσθην, ὑσθῆναι**, v. ὕω.

**ὑσθλός**· σαλός, φλύαρος, Hsch. (cf. ὕθλος).

**Ὕσῖρις**, = Ὄσιρις, Hellanic.176J. (Plu.(2.364d) derives it ἀπὸ τῆς φύσεως (ὕσεως Salmasius) καὶ τῆς εὑρέσεως.)

**ὕσις**, εως, ἡ, (ὕω) *a raining*, Hsch. s.v. Ὑή; cf. foreg.

**ὕσκας**, prob. misspelling of ἴσκας (v. ἴσκαι) in Aët.7.91.

**ὑσκίνιοι**· ὑσκάνιοι, Hsch.

**ὕσκλ-ος**, ὁ, *the latchet* or *eyelets of a sandal*, ὕσκλοι· ἀγκύλαι, βρόχοι, οὓς ἡμεῖς ὕσκλους τῶν ὑποδημάτων καὶ τὰς λέγνας τῶν ἱματίων, Hsch.; **ὕσκλοι**· ἀγκύλοι, Theognost.*Can.*24; written **ὕσχλος** in Poll.7.80; τὸ ὕσχλος δασύνεται, ἔστι δὲ τῶν ὑποδημάτων, ὅθεν οἱ ἱμάντες ἐξάπτονται πρὸς τὸ συνέχειν τὸν πόδα, Phryn.*PS* p.25 B. · hence ἐπτύσχλος, ἐννήϋσκλοι. **-ωτός**, ή, όν, *having a* ὕσκλος, ὑπόδημα Dicaearch.1.19.

**ὑσκυθά**· ὑὸς ἀφόδευμα, Hsch. (cf. ὑσπέλεθος).

**ὕσμα**, ατος, τό, (ὕω) *rain*, in pl., Hp.*Epid.*1.1.

**ὑσμῆθες**· οὐσίαι, Hsch. (fort. θυσίαι).

**ὑσμίνη** [ῑ], ἡ, Ep. Noun, *fight, battle, combat*, κατὰ κρατερὴν ὑ. Il.5.84, al.; κατὰ κρατερὰς ὑ. ib.200; ἐν σταδίῃ ὑ. 13.314; ἐν ὑ. δηϊοτῆτος 20.245; πρώτῃ ἐν ὑ. in the front *of the fight*, 15.340; ὑσμίνηνδε to *the fight*, 2.477; ὑσμίναν φέροντες B.12.144:—in Il.2.863, 8.56, we have a metaplast. Ep. dat. ὑσμῖνι as if from ὑσμίν or ὑσμίς. (Cf. Skt. *yúdh* fem. 'battle', *yúdhyati* 'fight'.)

**ὑσόβρυον**, τό, = μᾶρον, prob. f.l. in Dsc.3.42.

**ὑσπέλεθος**, ὁ, *swine's dung*, Poll.5.91, D.C.46.5; ὕσπελθος· υἱὸς (leg. ὑὸς) ἔκπατος, Theognost.*Can.*24. (From ὑ-σπέλεθος.)

**ὕσπερ** or **ὕσπερ**, Dor. for οἷπερ, *whither*, Epich.99.5: cf. υἷς, ὗς (B).

**ὑσπλᾱγίς**, ίδος, ἡ, Dor. for ὕσπληξ 3, ἀπὸ μιᾶς ὑσπλαγίδος, i.e. starting all at once, with one consent, Ar.*Lys.*1000.

**ὕσπλαγξ, ὕσπλαξ**, v. ὕσπληξ.

**ὑσπλήγγιον**, τό, = sq. 2, Hero *Aut.*24.4.

**ὕσπληξ**, ηγος, ἡ (Phryn.54, etc., but ὁ *CIG*2824.14 (Aphrodisias), Eust.598.23), *IG*1².313.116, 314.129, *Inscr.Perg.*10.3 (iii B.C.), Pl. *Phdr.*254e, Eust. l. c., etc.: rarely **ὕσπληγξ**, ηγγος, ἡ (ὁ Hero *Aut.* 24.4), D.P.121, Dionys.*Av.*3.18; Dor. **ὕσπλαγξ** Theoc.8.58; gen. **ὑσπλᾶκος** *IG*4²(1).98.2 (Epid., iii B.C.): dat. pl. ὑσπλῆξιν Plu.2.588f, Ep. ὑσπλήγεσσι *AP*6.259 (Phil.): Dor. **ὑσπλᾱγίς** (q.v.):— *snare* or *gin* of a bird-catcher, Theoc. l. c.; *wolf-trap*, Hsch.; also *the part of a springe or noose trap which slips down when touched*, Dionys.*Av.* l. c., cf. 3.13; = ῥόπτρον, Hsch.; = πάσσαλος, κρίκος κεράτινος, Id., Sch.Pl.*Phdr.*254e. 2. a *twisted strand*, the untwisting of which releases motive power in an automaton (cf. στρέβλη 1. 2), Hero *Aut.*2.8 (also, a *piece of wood made to rise or fall* by this or similar means, ib.6, cf. 24.4); ψυχὴ ἀνθρώπου μυρίαις ὁρμαῖς οἷον ὕσπληξιν ἐντεταμένη Plu.2.588f; [τὸ θερμὸν] ἀθροῖσαν ἑαυτὸ καὶ οἷον συνεσπειραμένον γεγονός, . . σφοδρᾷ τῇ φορᾷ χρώμενον καὶ οἷον ἀπὸ ὕσπληγος ἐξαλλόμενον Gal.7.623; ὥσπερ ἀπὸ ὕ. ἀναπεσών throwing himself back as from a ὕ., i.e. violently, Pl.*Phdr.*254e; ὥσπερ ἀπὸ ὕ. θέοντες, i.e. running at top speed, Luc.*Cat.*4. 3. a *contrivance* (of uncertain nature, but prob. on the principle of ὕ. 1 or 2; = Lat. *transenna, Gloss.*) *for starting a race, starting-machine* (κυρίως τὸ μηχάνημα τὸ ἀποκροῦον τὸν κανόνα τοῦ δρομέως Sch.D.P.121; cf. σχαστηρία 1), ὕσπληγος ἀγκῶνας τρεῖς, παραστάδας ὑσπλήγων τέτταρας καὶ κίονας δύο, σύριγγας τῶν ὕ. δύο, in a list of wooden objects, *Inscr. Délos* 1400.9 (ii B.C.), cf. 1409 *Ba*ii 43 (ii B.C.); ὕσπληγα λαμπαδίειον (for the torch-race) *IG*11(2).203 *B*96 (Delos, iii B.C.); ἀφέσεις τὰς ἀπὸ τῶν ὑσπλήγων τοῦ Παναθηναϊκοῦ σταδίου ib.2².1035.50 (i B.C.); ἔπεσεν ἡ ὕ. Luc.*Tim.*20; τῆς ὕ. εὐθὺς καταπεσούσης Id.*Cal.*12; ἑστᾶσιν ὥσπερ ἐφ' ὕσπληγος ἐξορμᾶν ἕτοιμοι J.*BJ*3.5.4 (v.l. ὑφ' ὕσπληγος); διήκει πρὸ αὐτῶν καλῴδιον ἀντὶ ὕσπληγος Paus.6.20.11; χαλῶσιν αἱ ὕ. ib.13; ἀθρόα δ' ὕσπληξ πάντα (sc. τὰ ἅρματα) διὰ στρεπτοῦ τεῖνα [τ' ἔ]χουσα κάλω· [ἣ] μέγ' ἐπαχήσασα θοὰς ἐξήλασε πώλους *Inscr.Perg.* l. c.; ψόφος ἦν ὕσπληγος ἐν οὔασιν, i.e. the race had just started, *AP*11.86, cf. Plu.2.804e; ἔσχατο ἡ ὕ. Hld.4.3; ψαλιδωτὰς ἱππαφέσεις διὰ μιᾶς ὕ. ἅμα πάσας ἀνοιγομένας D.H.3.68: metaph., κἀπὸ γῆς ἐσχάζοσαν ὕσπληγας were loosing the *starting-machine* from land, i.e. were starting out from land, Lyc.22. 4. = καμπτήρ II, metaph., D.P.121, cf. Eust. ad loc.; ὕσπληγας ὑποφήνας τῶν κατὰ φιλοσοφίαν λόγων setting *limits* to.., dub. in Metrod.*Herc.*831.11. 5. part of a burial-place, perh. *gate*, *CIG* l. c. 6. = μύωψ II. 2 or μάστιξ, Herm. *in Phdr.*p.170 A., Hsch., Suid.; = **ὑστριχίς** 1, Eust.ad D.P.121 (deriving it from ὗς and πλήσσω).

**ὑσπολέω**, *keep swine*, Hsch.

⊕**Ὕσ-πορος**, ὁ, *Swineford*, name of a river, Nonn.*D.*26.168; cf. Βόσπορος.

**ὕσσακος**· ὑστακός, Hsch.; ὑσσάκους· πασσάλους, *EM*785.7, Phot. (cf. ὕσταξ); dub. in *Lyr.Adesp.*46 A; but, = *pudenda muliebria*, Ar. *Lys.*1001: Dor. word acc. to Phot.

**ὑσσός**, ὁ, *javelin*, = Lat. *pilum*, Plb.6.23.8 sq., D.H.5.46, Str.10.1.12, Plu.*Pyrrh.*21, etc.

⊕**ὑσσωπίτης** [ῑ] οἶνος, ὁ, *wine prepared with hyssop*, Dsc.5.40; written *hysopites* in Plin.*HN*14.109; ὑσω-, v.l. in *Gp.*8.15.

**ὕσσωπος**, ἡ, *hyssop, Origanum hirtum*, Hebr. *'ēzōb*, *IG*12(5).593.16 (Iulis, v B.C.), *PCair.Zen.*704.8 (iii B.C.), LXX *Ex.*12.22, al., Ezek. *Exag.*185, Nic.*Al.*603, *Th.*872, *Ev.Jo.*19.29, *Ep.Hebr.*9.19, Dsc.3.25, Ath.4.156e:—also **ὕσσωπον**, τό, Cels.4.14.2, 4.15.3, Plin.*HN*25.136, 26.114, 124, Ps.-Dsc.3.25, Sor.2.32, al., Gal.6.638, 12.149, *Hippiatr.* 130.10; cf. ὑσωπίς. (Written **ὑσω-** in *IG* l. c., Cels. and Plin. ll. cc. (*hyso-*), Gal.6.279, *Vict.Att.*6, 12, Ath. l. c., and as v.l. in LXX 3 *Ki.*4.29(5.13), *Ps.*50(51).9, *Ev.Jo.* l. c., *Ep.Hebr.* l. c., Gal.6.572, 638, 656, *Gp.*13.8.2, *Hippiatr.*130.14 (f.l. for οἰσύπου ib.130.49); **ὑσσω-** in *PCair. Zen.* l.c. and freq. in codd.; **ὑσσ-** is a long syll. in Ezek. and Nic. ll. cc.; gen. written **ἰσσύπου** in *PGoodsp.Cair.*30 xlii 8 (ii A.D.).)

**ὑστακητεῖ**· φενακίζει, Hsch. **ὑστακός**, = πάσσαλος, in Theognost. *Can.*24: v. ὕσσακος. **ὑσταλωπιᾷ**· νυστάζει, Hsch. **ὕσταξ**· πάσσαλος κεράτινος, Id. (ὕστα· ξυρίς in Theognost.*Can.*24 shd. perh. be ὕσταξ· ὑρίς).

⊕**ὕσταριν**, Adv. = ὕστερον, *Schwyzer* 424 (Elis, iv B.C.).

**ὑστάς**· πλαστὰς (leg. παστὰς) ἀμπέλων, Hsch.; cf. **ὑστάδα**· ἡ δασεῖα ἄμπελος, Id. (Perh. Cypr. for συστάς, cf. ξυστάδες.)

**ὑστάτιος** [ᾰ], η, ον, poet. for ὕστατος (cf. μεσσάτιος for μέσσος, τοσσάτιος for τόσσος), Il.15.634; τί πρῶτόν τοι ἔπειτα τί δ' ὑστάτιον καταλέξω; Od.9.14, cf. Euph.23, A.R.1.139: neut. as Adv., *at last*, Il.8.353; *for the last time*, Call.*Ap.*79:—**ὑστᾰτίη**, ἡ, *the end*, βιότοιο Q.S.14.315.

**ὕστᾰτος**, η, ον, v. ὕστερος B.

**ὑστέρα**, Ion. **ὑστέρη**, ἡ, *womb*, Hp.*VM*22, *Aph.*5.22, Arist.*HA* 493ᵃ25, Thphr.*HP*9.13.3, Sor.1.2, etc.; freq. in pl. ὑστέραι, Ion. gen. -έων, Hdt.4.109, Hp.*Coac.*515, Pl.*Ti.*91c:—with a play on the Adj. ὑστέρα (the second woman), Ath.13.585d. 2. *ovary* of animals, Arist.*GA*720ᵃ26, *HA*511ᵃ22; of birds, ib.564ᵇ21; reptiles, ib.508ᵃ13; fishes, ib.566ᵃ7. (Lit. *the upper* or *protruding* part, Skt. *úttaras* 'upper', Comp. of *úd* 'upwards'; so also Skt. *udáram* 'belly'; cf. ὕστρος· γαστήρ, Hsch.; or perh. ἡ ὑ. (sc. μήτρα or δελφύς) *the back part.*)

**ὑστεραῖος**, α, ον, *following, next*, qualifying ἡμέρα, τῇ ὑστεραίῃ ἡμέρῃ on the *following* day, Hdt.8.22; but mostly without ἡμέρα, Id.1.77, 126, al., Antipho 5.23, Th.7.52, *IG*1².63.36, 66.19; also ἐς τὴν ὑστεραίην (-αν) ἐλθεῖν, ἀναβαλέσθαι, Hdt.4.113, D.21.84; ἐν τῇ ὑ. Pl. *Prt.*318a; τῆς ὑ. καὶ ἐπὶ τῆς ἄλλης ὑστέρης on the *morrow* and the day following, Aret.*CA* 2.2: c. gen., τῇ ὑ. τῶν μυστηρίων And.1.111; τῇ ὑ. τῆς μάχης Pl.*Mx.*240c: folld. by ἤ, τῇ ὑ. ἢ ᾗ ἂν ἔλθῃ Id.*Cri.* 44a; τῇ ὑ. ἢ ᾗ ἔθυεν Id.*Smp.*173a; and prob. ᾗ should be inserted in the foll. places, τῇ ὑ. ᾗ ἐθάπτετο Antipho 6.37; τῇ ὑ. ᾗ ἂν προθῶνται Lex ap.D.43.62. II. = ὕστερος, *later, subsequent*, ἡ ὑ. ἐπιστρατηΐη v.l. in Hdt.9.3, cf. D.H.*Th.*6 (but the vv.ll. ὑστέρην, ὑστέρας are to be preferred): elsewh. it may mean *of* or *on the next day*, μάχῃ τῇ μὲν πρώτῃ.., τῇ δὲ ὑ... in *the next day's* fight, Th.7.11; τῇ μὲν προτέρᾳ [ἐκκλησίᾳ].., ἐν δὲ τῇ ὑ. Id.1.44, cf. Aeschin.2.65, 67 (ὑστέρᾳ corr. Bekker), Luc.*VH*1.19; τῇ ὑ. προσβολῇ X.*HG*2.1.15.

**ὑστεραλγ-ής**, ές, *causing pains in the womb*, ὄξος Hp.*Acut.*61. **-ία**, ἡ, *pains in the womb*, Gal.10.82.

**ὑστερ-έω**, fut. -ήσω LXX *Ps.*83(84).12, al.: aor. ὑστέρησα (freq. with v.l. ὑστέρισα) Hdt.1.70, etc.: pf. ὑστέρηκα D.S.15.47, *Ep.Hebr.*4.1: plpf. ὑστερήκειν Th.3.31:—Pass., aor. ὑστερήθην 2 *Ep.Cor.*11.9, J.*AJ*15.6.7: (ὕστερος):—*to be behind* or *later, come late*, opp. προτερέω or φθάνω, ὑστέρησαν οἱ ἄγοντες Hdt.1.70, cf. E.*Ph.*976, X.*HG* 5.1.3, Pl.*Grg.*447a: c. dat. modi, ὑ. τῇ διώξει Th.1.134; τῇ βοηθείᾳ D.59.3: simply, *occur later*, of thunder after lightning, Epicur.*Ep.*2 p.46 U. II. c. gen. rei, *come later than, come too late for*, ὑστέρησαν (v.l. ὑστέρισαν) ἡμέρῃ μιῇ τῆς συγκειμένης *came* one day *after* the appointed day, Hdt.6.89; ὑ. τῆς μάχης ἡμέραις (sic leg. cum cod. C[1], pro -ρας) πέντε *came too late for* the battle by five days, X.*An.*1.7.12; ὑστερήσαντες οὐ πολλῷ Th.8.44; ὑ. δείπνου Amphis 39; ἐπειδὴ τῆς Μυτιλήνης ὑστερήκει *had come too late* to save M., Th.3.31; ὑ. τῆς πατρίδος *fail to assist* it, X.*Ages.*2.1; τῶν λέμβων ὑ. *miss* them, Plb.5.101.4; τῶν καιρῶν Arist.*SE*175ᵃ26; τῆς ἐργασίας *PCair.Zen.* 25.12 (iii B.C.); ταύτης [τῆς ὥρας] Gal.7.362; τῆς βοηθείας D.S. 13.110. 2. c. gen. pers., *come after* him, ὑ. εἰς Ἁλίαρτον τοῦ Λυσάνδρου X.*HG*3.5.25: also c.dat., *come too late for* him, Th.7.29. 3. ὑ. ἔς τι Hp.*Epid.*6.7.3. III. metaph., *lag behind, be inferior to*, τῶν.. ἀποστόλων 2 *Ep.Cor.*11.5; ἐμπειρίᾳ ὑ. τῶν ἄλλων Pl.*R.*539e; μηδ' ἐν ἄλλῳ μηδενὶ μέρει ἀρετῆς ὑ. ib.484d; ἵνα γνῶ τί ὑστερῶ ἐγώ LXX *Ps.*38(39).5. 2. *fall below, fail to do justice to* a theme, ὑστερήσας οὐδὲν τῆς τέχνης Luc.*Par.*60. IV. *fail to obtain, lack*, τἀγαθοῦ Clearch.Com.3.5; τοῦ δικαίου *PEnteux.*86.11 (iii B.C.); ξύλων ἀκανθίνων οὐχ ὑστεροῦσι, ἀλλ' ἢ ἔχουσιν ἱκανά *PCair.Zen.* 270.5 (iii B.C.):—Med. (with aor. Pass.), ὑστερεῖσθαί τινος D.S.18.71, *Ep.Rom.*3.23, J.*AJ*15.6.7, *PMasp.*2 iii 14 (vi A.D.); ὑστερηθεὶς τῆς ὁράσεως *having lost* his sight, *PLond.*5.1708.85 (vi A.D.); δάνιον δανιεῖς αὐτῷ ὅσον ἂν ἐπιδέηται καὶ καθ' ὅσον ὑστερεῖται LXX *De.*15.8 (cod. A); in fut. Med., παιδὸς ὑστερήσομαι (ἐστερήσομαι corr. Reiske) E.*IA* 1203. 2. abs., *fail, come to grief*, Phld.*Oec.*p.50 J.; *fall short of supplies*, ἵνα μηθὲν ὑστερῇ τὰ ἐλαιουργια *PHib.*1.43.6 (iii B.C.):—Med., *to be in want*, *Ev.Luc.*15.14, 1 *Ep.Cor.*8.8; pf. part. ὑστερημένοι those *who have failed*, Phld.*Herc.*1457.9. V. of things, *fail, be wanting*, Dsc.5.75.13, *Ev.Jo.*2.3; ἕν σε (v.l. σοι) ὑστερεῖ *Ev.Marc.* 10.21; ὡς μὴ ὑστερεῖν τι ὑμῖν τῶν ὑπαρχόντων δικαίων *BGU*1074.7 (iii A.D.).—Cf. ὑστερίζω throughout. ⊕ **-ημα**, ατος, τό, *shortcoming, deficiency, need*, LXX *Ps.*33(34).10, *Ev.Luc.*21.4, *Corp.Herm.* 13.1, etc. **-ησις**, εως, ἡ, = foreg., *Ev.Marc.*12.44, *Ep.Phil.*4.11. **-ησμός**, ὁ, *arrears*, οὐδέποτε ἐν ὑ. γενάμενοι τῶν βασιλικῶν φόρων *PMasp.*2 ii 19, cf. 19.13, 283.4, *PFlor.*296.52 (all vi A.D.). **-ητικὸς** τύπος, of a fever, *which comes on later* in the day at each following attack, Gal.9.553 (pl.); παροξυσμὸς Id.7.359. **-ίζω**, fut. Att. -ιῶ D.4.32, Arist.*Ph.*262ᵇ17: aor. ὑστέρισα (v. ὑστερέω, which is a freq. v.l.):—like ὑστερέω, *come after, come later* or *too late*, Th.6.69, X.*An.*6.1.18, Men.364.5, *Sam.*325; of attacks of fever, Gal.7.353; ὑ. ἐν [τοῖς καιροῖς] X.*Cyr.*8.5.7, cf. 7.5.46, Arist.*Ph.* l. c., *GA*770ᵃ22; αἱ ὧραι ὑ. the seasons *are late*, Plu.*Luc.*31; of the mind, Arist.*SE*174ᵃ19; c. gen., ὑ. τῶν καιρῶν *to be behind, come too late for*, D.4.35, 18.102; τῶν ἔργων Id.4.38, cf. ib.32; τῶν πραγμάτων Isoc.3.19; τῶν βαρβάρων Id.4.164; ὑ. τῶν συλλογισμῶν *to be behind-hand* in apprehending them, Arist. *Rh.*1400ᵇ32, cf. 1410ᵇ25; τὸ ναυτικὸν πρὸς ἅπασαν ὑστερίζον βοήθειαν Plu.*Ant.*63; κραυγῇ οὐδὲν ὑστεριζούσῃ τοῦ λαγῶ *lagging behind* it,

X.*Cyr.*1.6.40. II. metaph., *lag behind, be* or *become inferior to*, c. gen., ἀθληταί τινες..ὑ. τῶν ἀντιπάλων Id.*Mem.*3.5.13; τοῖς λόγοις ὑ., opp. τοῖς ἔργοις πρωτεύω, Arist.*Rh.Al.*1420ᵃ18. III. ὑ. τῆς ἀκμῆς τῆς ἐμαυτοῦ *I am later than*, i.e. *past*, my prime, Isoc.9.73; ἂν ὑστερίζῃ τῆς τεταγμένης ἀκμῆς if the guest *is later than* the appointed time, Alex.149.10.

**ὑστερ-ικός**, ή, όν, (ὑστέρα) of women, *suffering in the womb, hysterical*, Hp.*Prorrh.*1.119, Arist.*GA*776ᵃ10; ὑ. πνὶξ *passio hysterica, hysterics*, Sor.2.26, Gal.11.47; also in pl., Id.14.181; so τὰ ὑστερικά (sc. πάθη) Hp.*Aph.*5.35. Adv. -κῶς, πνιγόμεναι Dsc.2.8. 2. *of* or *belonging to the womb*, σκληρύσματα Hp.*Coac.*517; ὑμένες, πόρος, Arist.*GA*717ᵃ5, 720ᵇ31; σπερμάτια remedial *for the womb*, Hp.*Mul.*1.45. II. ἐν ὑ. τόπῳ dub. sens. in *PLond.*3.755ᵛ.7 (iv A.D.). **-ιος**, α, ον, neut. pl. -ια, τά, *afterbirth*, Cyran.56; cf. ὕστερον.

**ὑστερο-βουλία**, ἡ, *deliberation after the fact*, Lxx *Pr.*24.71 (31.3). **-γενής**, ές, *not appearing until after the birth*, Arist.*HA*518ᵃ21, 521ᵇ18, *GA*772ᵇ30, al. 2. generally, *later in origin*, τὰ ὑ., opp. ἀρχαί, Id.*Metaph.*1091ᵃ33, cf. Nicom.*Ar.*1.4, S.E.*M.*7.225, Iamb.*Comm.Math.*10, Herm. *in Phdr.*p.154A.; *later in date*, μυθοποιία Str.11.5.5. **-γονία**, ἡ, *posterity*, *Gloss.* **-ληπτος**, ον, gloss on παλινάγρετος, Phot. **-λογία**, ἡ, Rhet., = πρωθύστερον, Choerob.*Trop.*27, Eust.80.16, al. **-λόγος**, ον, *speaking last*: esp. *the actor who plays the last part*, opp. πρωτολόγος, Teles p.5 H. codd.Stob. (δευτερολόγος Meineke, prob. rightly). **-μαντις**, εως, ὁ, ἡ, *prophesying too late*, Sch.Lyc.200. **-μηνία**, Thess. ὑστερομειννία, Boeot. οὑστερομεινία, ἡ, *the last day of the month*, *IG*9(2).517.40 (Larissa, iii B.C.), *Schwyzer* 462 *A* 1 (Tanagra, iii B.C.). **-μῦθος**, ον, *speaking later*, στόμα Nonn.*D.*42.155.

**ὕστερον**, τό, *the afterbirth*, Hp.*Mul.*1.46, Arist.*HA*587ᵃ8, Sor.1.57: pl., Hp. l.c., *Aph.*5.49.

**ὑστερο-πάθεια** [πᾰ], ἡ, *secondary affection*, Gal.8.31. **-περίοδος**, ον, *with postponed principal clause*, Sch.Il.14.169. **-ποινος**, ον, *avenging after* the act, *late-avenging*, Ἐρινύς, Ἄτη, A.*Ag.*58, *Ch.*383 (both lyr.). ⊛**-ποτμος**, ον, *supposed dead, and then appearing alive*, Plu.2.265a, Hsch. **-πους**, ὁ, ἡ, neut. πουν, gen. ποδος, *coming late*, ὑ. βοηθῶ Ar.*Lys.*326 (lyr.); ὑ. Νέμεσις *AP*12.229 (Strat.); Ἐρινύς Orph.*A.*1164. **-πρωτος**, ον, = Lat. *praeposterus*, *Gloss.*

⊛**ὕστερος, ὕστᾰτος**, *latter, last*, Comp. and Sup. without any Posit. Adj. in use. (The Posit. must be looked for in Skt. *úd* 'up'; with ὕστερος, ὕστατος cf. Skt. Comp. and Sup. *úttaras, uttamás* 'higher, (later)', 'highest, (latest)'; cf. ὑστέρα.)

**A. ὕστερος**, α, ον, *latter*: I. of Place, *coming after, behind*, ὑστέρῳ ποδί E.*Hipp.*1243, *HF*1040; ὑστέρας ἔχων πώλους keeping them *behind*, S.*El.*734; ὑ. λόχος X.*Cyr.*2.3.21; ἐν τῷ ὑ. λόγῳ Antipho 6.14, cf. Pi.*O.*11(10).5, Pl.*Grg.*503c, etc.; τὰ ὕ. the *latter clauses*, Plu.2.742d (s. v. l., δεύτερα Turnebus): c. gen., ὕστεροι ἡμῶν *behind* us, Pl.*Ly.*206e, cf. Th.3.103; οὐδὲν ὑστέρα νεώς not a whit *behind* (*slower than*) a ship, A.*Eu.*251. II. of Time, *next*, ὁ δ' ὕστερος ὄρνυτο χαλκῷ Il.5.17, 16.479; τῷ ὑ. ἔτει in the *next* year, X *HG*7.2.10; τῇ ὑ. Ὀλυμπιάδι Hdt.6.103; ὑ. χρόνῳ in *after* time, Id.1.130, A.*Ag.*702 (lyr.), etc.; ἐν ὑ. χρόνοις Pl.*Lg.*865a; ἐν ὑστέραισιν ἡμέραις A.*Ag.*1666 (troch.); δεκάτῃ ὑ. or ὑ. δεκάτῃ, on the 21st day, Decr.ap.D.L.7.10, cf. Longin.*Rh.*p.192 H.: c. gen., *later than, after*, σεῦ ὕστερος εἶμ' ὑπὸ γαῖαν Il.18.333, cf. Ar.*Ec.*859, Pl.*Phd.*87c, al.: ὑ. χρόνῳ τούτων Hdt.4.166, 5.32, cf. Th.2.54. 2. *later, too late*, ὑ. ἐλθὼν Il.18.320; κἂν ὑ. ἔλθῃ Ar.*V.*691 (anap.); μῶν ὕστεροι πάρεσμεν; Id.*Lys.*69; ὑ. ἀφικνεῖσθαι Th.4.90; ὑ. (sc. ἐλθών) S.*OT*222, *Tr.*92; Διονύσιος ὁ ὕ. D. the *second*, Arist.*Pol.*1312ᵃ4. 3. c. gen. rei, *too late for*, ὕστεροι ἀπικόμενοι τῆς συμβολῆς Hdt.6.120; ὑ. ἐλθεῖν τοῦ σημείου Ar.*V.*690 (anap.); κακῶν ὑ. ἀφῖγμαι E.*HF*1174; ὑ. ἀφίκοντο τῆς μάχης μιᾷ ἡμέρᾳ Pl.*Lg.*698e. 4. as Subst., οἱ ὕ. *posterity*, E.*Supp.*1225; ἄνδρες ὕ., ὑ. βροτοί, Id.*Tr.*13, 1245. III. of inferiority in Age, Worth, or Quality, γένει ὕ., i.e. younger, Il.3.215; c. gen., οὐδενὸς ὕ. *second* to none, S.*Ph.*181 (lyr.), cf. Th.1.91; γυναικὸς ὕ. S.*Ant.*746; μηδ' ἔμπροσθεν τῶν νόμων, ἀλλ' ὕ. πολιτεύου not putting yourself above the laws, but *below* them, Aeschin.3.23; σῶμα δεύτερον καὶ ὕ. (sc. ψυχῆς) Pl.*Lg.*896c; νομίσας πάντα ὕστερα εἶναι τἄλλα πρός τι that all things were *secondary* to.., Th.8.41. 2. logically *posterior*, ὁ τόπος ὕ. τῆς ὕλης Plot.2.4.12. IV. Adv. ὑστέρως is found only in Eccl. writers, the ascription to Plato by Ammon. *Diff.*p.115 V., Thom.Mag.p.284 R. being now corrected from Ptol. Ascal.p.405 H., where codd. have δευτέρως: the neut. ὕστερον was used, rarely of Place, *behind*, ὀπαδεῖν ὕ. A.*Fr.*475; ὕ. τῶν ἱππέων γίγνεσθαι X.*Cyr.*5.3.42. 2. of Time, *later, afterwards*, Parm.8.10, Hdt.6.91, etc.; also τὸ ὕ., opp. τὸ παλαιόν, Lycurg.61; ὕστερα Od.16.319; freq. with other words, ὕ. αὖτις Il.1.27; οὔποτ' αὖθις ὕ. S.*Aj.*858; ἔπειτα δ' ὕ., after μέν, Antiph.270; εἶτα..ὕ. Id.53.4; χρόνῳ ὕ. πολλῷ a long time *after*, Hdt.1.171; ὕ. χρόνῳ or χρόνῳ ὕ. some time *later*, Th.1.8, 64; χρόνοις ὕ. Lys.3.39; βραχεῖ χρόνῳ ὕ. X.*Cyr.*5.3.52; οὐ πολλαῖς ἡμέραις ὕ. Id.*HG*1.1.1; ὀλίγῳ or ὀλίγον ὕ. Pl.*R.*327c, *Grg.*471c; πολλῷ ὕ. Th.2.49, Pl.*Phd.*58a; οἱ ἄνθρωποι οἱ ὕ. *posterity*, Id.*R.*415d; τὰ ὕ. γράμματα the *later* inscriptions, Id.*Chrm.*165a. b. c. gen., ὕ. τούτων Hdt.1.113, etc.; ὕ. ἔτι τούτων Id.9.83; τῆς ἐμεωυτοῦ γνώμης ὕ. *after* my own opinion was formed, Id.2.18; τοῦ δέοντος ὕ. *later than* ought to be, Ar.*Lys.*57: c. dat. et gen., ἔτεσι πολλοῖσι ὕ. τούτων Hdt.6.140, cf. 1.91; πολλῷ ὕ. τῶν Τρωϊκῶν Th.1.3, cf. Isoc.19.22: folld. by ἤ, τεσσαρακοστῇ ἡμέρᾳ ὕ...ἢ Ποτείδαια ἀπέστη Th.1.60, cf. 6.4. 3. in Adv. sense with Preps., ἐς ὕστερον Od.12.126, Hes.*Op.*351, Hdt.5.41, 74, S.*Ant.*1194, E.*IA*720, Pl.*Ti.*82b, etc.: ἐν ὑστέρῳ Th.3.13, 8.27: ἐξ ὑστέρου D.S.14.109, D.H.4.73; also ἐξ ὑστέρης Hdt.1.108, 5.106, 6.85.

**B. ὕστᾰτος**, η, ον, *last*: I. of Place, ἅμα θ' οἱ πρῶτοί τε καὶ ὕστατοι Il.2.281; εὐθυντὴρ ὕστατος νεὼς *hindmost*, of a rudder, A.*Supp.*717; ἡμῖν τοῖς ὑ. κατακειμένοις Pl.*Smp.*177e. II. of Time, τίνα πρῶτον, τίνα δ' ὕ. ἐξενάριξεν; Il.11.299, cf. 5.703, E *HF*485, etc.; ὁ δ' ὕ. γε..πρεσβεύεται A.*Ag.*1300; ἡλίου..πρὸς ὕ. φῶς ib.1324; τὸν ὕ. μέλψασα γόον ib.1445; τοὖπος ὕ. θροεῖ S.*Aj.*864; ἡ ὑστάτη (sc. ἡμέρα) τῆς ὁρτῆς the *last day* of.., Hdt.2.151; ἐν τοῖσιν ὑ. φράσω Ar.*Ra.*908; οὐκ ἐν ὑστάτοις not among *the last*, E.*Ion*1115; οἱ ὕστατοι εἰπόντες D.1.16, etc.; ὕστατος ἁλώσιος ἀντάσαις meeting with his downfall *at last*, Pi.*O.*10(11).41. III. of Rank or Degree, οὐκ ἐν ὑστάτοις S.*Tr.*315; τὰ ὕ. πάσχειν, like τὰ ἔσχατα, Luc.*Phal.*1.5. IV. for regul. Adv. ὑστάτως (which occurs only in *Hippiatr.*20), the neut. sg. and pl. are used, πύματόν τε καὶ ὕστατον Od.20.116; ὕστατα καὶ πύματα 4.685, 20.13; νῦν ὕστατα Il.1.232, Od.22.78; ὕστατα ὁρμηθέντες Hdt.8.43; καὶ πρῶτον καὶ ὕ. Pl.*Mx.*247a; ὕ. δή σε προσορῶ, τὸ ὕ. προσειπεῖν, Id.*Phd.*60a, Luc.*VH*1.30. 2. in Adv. sense with Preps., ἐν ὑστάτοις *at last*, Pl.*R.*620c; εἰς τὸ ὕ. *extremely*, γέρων ἐς τὸ ὕ. Luc.*Herm.*9.

**ὑστερο-φᾰνής**, ές, *brought to light later*, Eust.864.15. **-φημία**, ἡ, *posthumous fame*, Plu.2.85c, M.Ant.2.17, Longin.14.3. **-φθόρος**, ον, *destroying after the act, late-destroying*, Ἐρινύες S.*Ant.*1074. **-φωνος**, ον, *sounding after, echoing*, *APl.*4.153 (Satyr.). **-χρονία**, ἡ, *a later time*, Eust.642.3. **-χρονος**, ον, *later in time*, ὑ. οἱ νόμοι τοῦ λόγου Sch.Hermog.*Stat.* in Rh.7(1).208 W.

**ὑστήρια**, τά, (ὗς) *a festival* at Argos *in which swine were sacrificed* to Aphrodite, Zenod.ap.Ath.3.96a. (Suspiciously like a pun on μυστήρια.)

**ὑστιακόν**, τό, a kind of *drinking-cup*, Rhinth.3 (codd.Ath.); **ὑστιακκός** (masc.) in Hsch. **ὑστίς**· ὑδρίς, Id. (ὑετ- cod.).

**ὕστριξ**, ῐχος (but in Opp.*C.*3.391 ὑστρίγγων, from **ὕστριγξ**), ὁ and ἡ, *porcupine, Hystrix cristata*, Hdt.4.192, Arist.*HA*490ᵇ29, 579ᵃ29, 600ᵃ28, Ael.*NA*1.31. II. in pl., something obtained from pigs, prob. *bristles*, Pl.Com.28. III. ὕστριχας (acc. pl.) ἢ σίδηρον as instruments of punishment, prob. *whips, the cat*, Ph.ap.Eus.*PE* 8.14; cf. sq. I.

**ὑστρῐχίς**, ίδος, ἡ, (ὕστριξ III) *whip for punishing slaves*, Ar.*Ra.*619, *Pax*746 (anap.), cf. Poll.2.24, 3.79, Ph.2.287 (ὑστριχίσι with v.l. ὑστρίξι dat. pl.). II. *disease of the horse's tail*, *Hippiatr.*59 tit.

**ὕστρος**· γαστήρ, Hsch. **ὕσχλος**, v. ὕσκλος. **ὑσωπίς**· ἡ σάμψυχος, Id. **ὕσωπος**, v. ὕσσωπος.

**ὑύζω**, *make the sound* υ υ, of owls, v. l. for ἰύζω in Poll.5.90 (fort. ὑΰζω).

**ὑύς**, έος, ὁ, = υἱός (q.v.).

**ὕφα**, indecl., = ὕφασμα, *EM*60.53, 785.26.

**ὑφᾱγέο**, or **ὑφᾱγεῦ**, Dor. for ὑφηγοῦ, imper. of ὑφηγέομαι, Theoc.2.101.

**ὑφάδιον**, τό, Dim. of ὑφή, gloss on κρόκος and κρόκη, Sch. rec. A.*Th.*858, Sch.E.*Hec.*468.

**ὑφαδρος**, ον, *somewhat thick, stout*, or *strong*, ἱμάτιον Poll.7.57.

**ὑφάζω**, assumed as = ὑφαίνω, *EM*785.26, Eust.1436.51.

⊛**ὕφαιμος**, ον, (αἷμα) *suffused with blood, blood-shot*, Hp.*Aph.*5.23; of the nails, Orib.*Syn.*7.18; ὑγρασία Sor.1.19; βοῦς Id.2.43; οἱ βραχίονες καὶ οἱ καρποὶ τῶν χειρῶν D.47.59; esp. of the eyes, S.E.*P.*1.44, Gal.18(2).301, Philostr.*Gym.*25, Philostr.Jun.*Im.*15; βλέφαρα ὕ. Arist.*Phgn.*807ᵇ29; ὕφαιμον βλέπειν Men.*Epit.*479, Ael.*NA*3.21; ῥίζα ὑ. τὴν χρόαν Dsc.4.23. II. of complexion or temperament, *sanguine*, Hp.*Epid.*3.14; ὕ. ἵππος *hot-blooded*, Pl.*Phdr.*253e; θερμὸς καὶ ὕ. Arist.*Phgn.*806ᵇ4, cf. 807ᵇ32.

**ὑφαίμων**, ον, gen. ονος, *containing blood*, ῥόοι Hp.*Loc.Hom.*47.

⊛**ὑφαίνω** [ῠ], Ion. impf. ὑφαίνεσκον Od.19.149: fut. ὑφᾰνῶ Ar.*Ec.*654 (anap.): aor. ὕφηνα Od.4.739, 13.303, Ar.*Lys.*586, etc.; later ὕφᾰνα, Lxx *Jd.*16.14, *Inscr.Délos* 442 *A* 206 (ii B.C.), *AP*6.265 (Noss.), *Hymn.Is.*14; as Dor. form, B.5.9, al.: pf. ὕφαγκα (συν-) D.H.*Comp.*18, (παρ-) Ph.Byz.*Mir.*2.5:—Med., v. infr.: aor. ὑφηνάμην Pl.*Phd.*87b, X.*Mem.*3.11.6:—Pass., aor. ὑφάνθην Pl.*Ti.*72c, (ἐν-, συν-) Hdt.1.203, 5.105: pf. ὕφασμαι Antiph.99, Luc.*VH*1.18, (ἐν-) Hdt.3.47, (παρ-) X.*Cyr.*5.4.48, but 3 sg. ὕφανται S.E.*M.*8.129; a form ὑφήφασμαι is cited in Suid., ὑφήφανται in Phryn.*PS* p.32 B., ὑφήφασται Choerob. *in Theod.*2.91 H., ὑφύφασται Zenod.ap.*EM*785.46, Eust.1436.51: cf. ἐξυφαίνω. [ῠ exc. in augm. tenses.]:—*weave*, freq. in Hom., who always joins ἱστὸν ὑφαίνειν (cf. ὑφάω), Il.6.456, Od.2.104, al.; except in 13.108, φάρε' ὑφαίνουσιν; so ὑ. ὕφασμα E.*Ion*1417; χλαῖναν Ar.*Lys.*586; ἱμάτιον Pl.*Hp.Mi.*368c; ἐν εὐπήνοις ὑφαῖς ὑ. τι E.*IT*814; ἐν Ἐκβατάνοισι ταῦθ' ὑφαίνεται Ar.*V.*1143; ἀράχνια ὑ., of spiders, Arist.*HA*542ᵃ13, cf. 623ᵃ8: abs., *weave, ply the loom*, Hdt.2.35; αἱ ὑφαίνουσαι Arist.*GA*717ᵃ36; αἴγειροι πτελέαι τε εὔσκιον ἄλσος ὕφαινον Theoc.7.8 (cj. Heinsius for ἔφαινον):—Med., ἱμάτιον ὑφαίνεσθαι Pl.*Phd.*87b, cf. X.*Mem.*3.11.6 sq.:—Pass., λίθος ὑφαινομένη, i.e. asbestos, Str.10.1.6. II. *contrive, plan*, of all schemes, good or bad, which are craftily imagined, freq. in Hom.; πυκινὸν δόλον ἄλλον ὕφαινε Il.6.187; ἔνδοθι μῆτιν ὑ. Od.4.678; ἐνὶ φρεσὶ μῆτιν ὑφήνας ib.739; μῆτιν ὕφαινε μετὰ φρεσίν Hes.*Sc.*28, cf. B.16.51; δόλους καὶ μῆτιν ὑ. Od.9.422; μύθους καὶ μήδεα πᾶσιν ὑ. Il.3.212, cf. Call.*Fr.*3 ii 10 P. (Pass.); ταῦθ' ὕφηναν ἡμῖν ἐπὶ τυραννίδι this was *the plot they laid* against us to bring in tyranny, Ar.*Lys.*630; πάντα..ἐκ φρενὸς ὑφάνασα *Hymn.Is.*14:—Med., Nicopho 5:

but ὑφαίνεται is f.l. for ὑφαίνετε in *Lyr.Adesp.*ap.Stob.1.5.11 (v. Nauck*TGF*² p.xx). III. generally, *create, construct*, οἰκοδομήματα Pl.*Criti.*116b; ὄλβον Pi.*P.*4.141; θεμείλια Φοῖβος ὑφαίνει he *lays* the foundation, Call.*Ap.*57; κηρὸν ὑ. Tryph.536:—Pass., ἀναίμου ὑφανθέντος [τοῦ σπληνός] Pl.*Ti.*72c. 2. *compose, write*, ποικίλον ἄνδημα metaph. of an ode) Pi.*Fr.*179; ὕμνον B.5.9. (ὑφ-αίνω, cf. ὑφή, ὕφος, OE. *wefan* 'weave', Skt. *ubhnāti* 'hold together, cover, bind'.)

**ὑφαίρ-εσις**, εως, ἡ, *taking away from under*, ἰγνυῶν ὑ., in wrestling, Sopat.ap.Sch.T.Il.23.729. 2. *purloining, pilfering*, τοῦ γραμματείου from the clerks' office, Test.ap.D.45.61; ζεύγους χεροψελίων ὑ. ποιεῖσθαι *PSI*10.1128.23 (iii A.D.), cf. Mitteis*Chr.*372 ii 8, iii 5 (ii A.D.). 3. *subtraction*, ἑνός Ph.1.574; *reduction*, τοῦ μεγέθους Diog.Oen.39; οἴνου καὶ τροφῆς Sor.1.46. II. ὑφαίρεσιν ποιεῖσθαι τῶν ὑποκειμένων to undertake the *moderation* or *mitigation* of.., Plb.15.8.13. III. in Gramm., *omission* of a letter, Sch. Ar. *Av.*149, *EM*389.6: opp. συγκοπή (which involves loss of a syllable), Hdn.Gr.2.247. **-ετέον**, *one must take away*, τροφῆς Plu.2.132c, cf. Ptol.*Tetr.*132, Sor.1.55, Ath.Med.ap.Orib.*inc.*21.13. **-έτρια**, ἡ, *midwife*, Hsch. **-έω**, fut. -ήσω (ὑφελῶ in Aq.*Ex.*5.19): aor. ὑφεῖλον (aor. 1 Med. ὑφειλάμην Lxx *Jb.*21.18): Ion. ὑπαιρέω, etc., Hdt.3.65, al.:—*seize underneath* or *inwardly*, τοὺς δ' ἄρ' ὑπὸ τρόμος εἷλεν Il.5.862, cf. Od.24.450. II. *draw* or *take away from under*, ὑπὸ δ' ᾕρεον ἕρματα νηῶν Il.2.154; ἄνθεμον ποντίας ἐέρσας Pi.*N.*7.79; [τὸ παιδίον τῆς μητρός] Pl.*Tht.*161a; τὴν χεῖρα ὑφῄρει *tried to draw* it *away*, Ar.*Pl.*689. 2. *take away underhand, filch away*, [τῶν Ἀθηναίων] τοὺς ξυμμάχους Th.3.13; ὑ. τὴν πρόσοδον, τὴν εὐπορίαν, *diminish* it *gradually*, ib.31,82; *purloin, steal*, βοῦν *PSI*4.366.2 (iii B.C.); ταῦτα (sc. ζεῦγος χεροψελίων κτλ.) ib.10.1128.30 (iii A.D.); of a doctor, ὑ. τὸ οἰνάριον καὶ τὸ λουτρόν *remove* from the regime, Sor.2.15; ὑ. τῆς ὑποψίας *gradually to take away* part of.., Th.1.42; so ὑ. τοῦ πλήθεος Hp.*VM*5; τοῦ τόνου Luc.*Philops.*8; τῆς ὀργῆς Phalar.*Ep.*72 codd. (ὑφῆκα Valckenaer):—Pass., ὑφῃρέθη σου, κάλαμος ὡσπερεὶ λύρας S.*Fr.*36; ὑπαραιρημένος *put secretly away, made away with*, Hdt.3.65:—also Med., *filch, purloin*, Ar.*Eq.*745, *Nu.*179, *Pl.*1140, D.45.58, *PCair.Zen.*350.4 (iii B.C.), etc.; ὑ. τοὺς καιροὺς τῆς πόλεως Aeschin.3.66; τὴν δημοκρατίαν ἄρδην ὑ. ib.145; ὑ. τί τινος *filch* it *from* him, Hdt.5.83, Lys.14.37, etc.; χρήματα ἐξ Ἐλαιοῦντος Hdt.9.116; ὑ. μου τὴν ἀπολογίαν Hyp.*Lyc.*11; ὑ. τι ἐξ ἱερῶν ἢ ὁσίων Pl.*Lg.*857b: abs., Ar.*V.*556. 3. Med. also c. acc. pers., ὑ. τινά τινος *rob* him of.., Aeschin.3.222; σιγῇ τοῦθ' ὑφαιρούμεσθά νιν *keep* it *from* him.., E.*El.*271. 4. *subtract, deduct*, ὑφαιρεθέντος τοῦ ἐπιδεκάτου *IG*4²(1).103.325, al. (Epid., iv B.C.); ὑφαιρουμένης τῆς προικὸς τῆς προδεδομένης *POxy.*1102.10 (ii A.D.).

**ὑφᾰλικός**, v.l. for ὕφαλμος in Dsc.3.136: cf. ὑφαλυκός.

**®ὕφᾰλμ-ος**, ον, *somewhat salt*, Dsc.3.136 (ὑφαλικός codd.CN, Orib.); also ibid. as f.l. for ὑφάμμοις (τόποις). **-ῠρίζω**, *to be* or *taste somewhat salt*, Id.1.14, Plu.2.669b. **-ῠρος**, ον, *somewhat salt*, Dsc.2.122; f.l. for ὑφάμμοις (τόποις), Id.3.136.

**®ὕφᾰλ-ος**, ον, (ἅλς) *under the sea*, ἔρεβος ὕ. the darkness *of the deep*, S.*Ant.*589 (lyr.); ὕ. πέτραι *AP*11.390 (Lucill.), cf. Ael.*NA*14.28, Jul.*Or.*1.41a; μὴ περὶ τὴν ὕφαλον (without πέτραν) ῥαγῇ τὸ σκάφος Lib.*Ep.*308, cf. Id.*Or.*62.32; νῆσοι Luc.*DMar.*10.1; τὸ ὕ. (sc. ἔδαφος), Str.1.3.5; τὰ ὕ. τῆς νεώς the *parts under water*, opp. τὰ ἔξαλα, Luc.*JTr.*47; ὕ. πληγή, τραύματα, damages to a ship *under water*, Plb.16.3.2, 16.4.12. 2. metaph., *secret, crafty*, of men, *EM* 785.44; ὑ. ἡλικία καὶ μνησίκακος Gal.19.489. II. *somewhat salt*, ὕδατα v.l. for ὑφαλυκά, Hp.*Aër.*3. **-ῠκός**, ή, όν, *somewhat salt, brackish*, ib.7, Olymp. *in Mete.*100.30, al. **-ώδης**, ες, *somewhat shallow*, D.S.24.1.

**ὕφαμμα**, ατος, τό, = ὕφασμα (but prob. a metal object), *IG*2². 1424*a* 397, 1425.402.

**ὕφαμμος**, ον, like ὑπόψαμμος, *mixed with sand, sandy*, Thphr.*HP* 1.6.12, 6.5.2, *CP*2.16.8, *PAmh.*2.85.16 (i A.D.); ὕφαμμος, ἡ (sc. χώρα), *PCair.Zen.*269.9 (iii B.C.), 352 (iii B.C.).

**ὑφᾰνάω**, poet. for ὑφαίνω, φαρέα θ' ὑφανόωντας Man.6.433 [ῠ].

**ὕφαν-σις**, εως, ἡ, *weaving*, Gal.*Thras.*27, Poll.7.33. **-τάριος**, ὁ, = ὑφάντης, *MAMA*3.516 (Corycus). **-τεῖον**, τό, *weaving-shed*, *PTeb.* 703.88 (pl., iii B.C.). **-της**, ου, ὁ, *weaver*, Pl.*Phd.*87b, *R.* 369d, Arist.*Pol.*1291ᵃ13, Lxx*Ex.*26.1, *PCair.Zen.*80.10 (iii B.C.), etc. **-τικός**, ή, όν, *skilled in weaving*, Pl.*Cra.*388c sq.; τὸν -ώτατον Id.*Grg.*490d. Adv. -κῶς *in weaver-like fashion*, Id.*Cra.* l.c. II. ἡ ὑφαντική (sc. τέχνη) *the art of weaving*, Democr.154, Pl.*Grg.*449d, Arist.*Pol.*1256ᵃ6, Phld.*Mus.*p.103 K.; in full, ὑ. τέχνη *PSI*3.241.8 (iii A.D.). 2. τὸ τέλος τοῦ -κοῦ tax *on weaving*, *Ostr.Bodl.* i 127 (ii B.C.).

**ὑφαντο-δόνητος**, poet. -δόνᾱτος, ον, *swung in the weaving, woven*, ἔσθος Ar.*Av.*943 (lyr.). **-ποιέομαι**, Med., *weave a web*, gloss on σκευωρούμενον, Sch.D.9.17 (vol. viii p.186 Dindorf).

**ὑφαν-τός**, ή, όν, (ὑφαίνω) *woven*, χρυσὸν.., ἐσθῆτά θ' ὑφαντήν Od. 13.136, 16.231; ὑφαντά τε εἵματα καλά 13.218; ὑφανταὶ γράμμασιν τοιαίδ' ὑφαί E.*Ion* 1146; ὑφαντοῖς ἐν πέπλοις Ἐρινύων *woven* by them, of Clytemnestra's net, A.*Ag.*1580; Ἐρινύων ὑ. ἀμφίβληστρον, of the Centaur's robe, S.*Tr.*1052; γυίων εἶδος ὑφαντόν, of the human frame, Tim.*Pers.*148; ὅσα ὑφαντά τε καὶ λεῖα *brocaded* and plain stuffs, Th. 2.97. **-τρια**, ἡ, fem. of ὑφάντης, M.Ant.10.38, Ael.*NA*6.57, Poll.7. 33. **-τρον**, τό, *wage for weaving*, *PSI*6.599.8 (iii B.C.): pl., *PEnteux.*4.4 (iii B.C.), *PTeb.*117.47, al. (i B.C.), *PLond.*3.1168 intr. p.136 (i A.D.). **-τών**, ῶνος, ὁ, *weaving-shed*, *PAmh.*2.131.12 (dub., ii A.D.).

**ὑφάπᾰλος** [ᾰπ], ον, gloss on ὑπολάπαρος (vv.ll. ὑπελάπαρος, ὑπεράπαλος), Erot.p.63 N.

**ὑφαπλ-όω**, *spread*, ὄρνιθες -ώσασαι τὰς πτέρυγας Him.*Or.*12.3; *spread under*, δέρμα [τοῖς ἐρίοις] μαλακόν Paul.Aeg.6.62 (v.l. for ἐφ-):—Pass., *to be spread under*, τινι Heraclit.*All.*39:—metaph. in Act., ὑ. μῦθον τῷ λόγῳ Them.*Or.*22.279d. **-ωσις**, εως, ἡ, *spreading under*, Sch.Hermog.*Stat.* in Rh.7(1).268 W.

**®ὑφάπτω**, Ion. ὑπάπτω, *set on fire from underneath*, ὑπῆψαν τὴν ἀκρόπολιν Hdt.1.176; ὑφῆψε δῶμ' ἀνηφαίστῳ πυρί E.*Or.*621, cf. 1618; ὑ. πυράν Th.2.52:—Pass., πόλις ὑφάπτεται πυρί E.*Tr.*1274; ἃς (sc. ἁμάξας) ἔδει ἐν καιρῷ ὑφαφθῆναι Aen.Tact.28.7; εὕρωμεν (i.e. -ομεν) τὰς θύρας.. ὑφημ(μ)ένας φωτί *BGU*1201.10 (i A.D.). 2. metaph., *inflame unperceived*, τοὺς θεωμένους X.*Cyr.*5.1.16. II. *light underneath*, πῦρ, φλόγα, Luc.*Phal.*1.12, Aristaenet.2.4; ὁ νικέων ὑφαπτέτω τὰ ἱερά the winner (in the race) *shall light* the sacred lamps, *SIG*671.16 (Delph., ii B.C.): abs., *light a fire under* or *in* a place, Ar.*Th.*730. B. Med., *tie* or *bind under*, ὑπὸ δειρὴν ἁψαμένη *tying a rope round* her neck, hanging herself, Alex.Aet.3.33.

**ὑφαρμόζω**, Att. -ττω, *fit under* (intr.), τῇ μασχάλῃ Hp.*Art.*7:—Pass., Ptol.*Alm.*5.1; τρόπις ὑφήρμοσται τῇ νηΐ Philostr.*Im.*2.15.

**ὑφαρπ-άζω**, Ion. ὑπαρπάζω Hdt. (v. infr.):—*snatch away from under*, τὴν ἕδραν τινός X.*Cyr.*8.4.16. 2. *take away underhand, filch*, μᾶζαν Ar.*Eq.*56; Κύπριν Id.*Th.*205, *Ec.*722:—Med., οὐκ ἂν ὑφαρπάσαιο τἀμὰ παίγνια ib.921 (lyr.); *snap up the meaning* of a sentence, Id.*Nu.*490. 3. ὑ. τὸν ἐπίλοιπον λόγον *snatch away* the rest of what one is going to say, *cut* it *short*, Hdt.5.50, 9.91: abs., ἔφη ὑφαρπάσας, *interposing hastily*, Pl.*Euthd.*300d. **-άμενος**, poet. for ὑφαρπασάμενος, *AP*9.619 (Agath.). **-ᾰσις**, εως, ἡ, = *usurpatio, Gloss.*

**ὑφᾰσία**, ἡ, = ὕφανσις, *EM*785.26.

**ὕφασ-μα** [ῠ], ατος, τό, *woven robe, web*, Od.3.274, A.*Ag.*1492 (lyr.), *Ch.*27 (lyr.), 231, 1015, E.*Hel.*1243, *Ion* 1417, Pl.*Plt.*310e, Archestr. *Fr.*15.6, *POxy.*1428.10 (iv A.D.), etc.; ἀραχνίων ὑ. Aret.*CA*2.6 (pl.), cf. ὕφαμμα. **-μάτιον**, τό, Dim. of ὕφασμα, Hsch. s.v. προγωνίαν.

**ὑφαύω**, *light underneath*, aor. 3 sg. ὑφηῦσε (v.l. ὑφηῦνε) Sch.D.T. p.112 H.

**ὑφάω** [ῠ], poet. for ὑφαίνω, αἱ δ' ἱστοὺς ὑφόωσι Od.7.105, cf. D.P. 1116.

**ὕφεαρ**, αρος (not ᾰτος), τό, Arcadian name for *mistletoe, Viscum album*, growing on the πρῖνος (here = *Quercus coccifera*), Thphr.*HP* 3.16.1, *CP*2.17.1: ὕφεαρ· τὸ ἐπιφυόμενον ταῖς πεύκαις καὶ ταῖς ἐλάταις, Hsch.

**ὑφεδρ-εύω**, *lurk beneath*, τὰς γεφύρας App.*Ill.*20: metaph., *to be latent*, Heraclit.*All.*17; *lie in wait*, Procop.Gaz.p.163 B. **-ία**, ἡ, *a sitting under, lower seat*, opp. προεδρία, Suid.

**ὑφέζομαι**, Pass., = ὑφεδρεύω, *lurk beneath*, Opp.*H.*2.302.

**ὑφειλήτης**, ου, ὁ, *one who filches away*, to expl. φιλήτης, Eust. 194.34.

**ὑφειμένως**, Adv. pf. part. Pass. of ὑφίημι, *in a subdued tone* or *manner*, X.*An.*7.7.16, Philostr.*VS*1.25.5; ὑ. ἔχειν πρός τινα Aristid. 2.137 J.

**ὑφείρω**, *fasten under*, ξίφος πήχει Philostr.*VA*8.25.

**ὑφεῖσα**, Ion. ὑπεισα, *I placed under* or *secretly*, ὑπείσας ἄνδρας (Ion. part.) *having set* them *in ambush*, Hdt.3.126, cf. 6.103; λόχον ὑφείσας Nic.Dam.55 J.: but as (ὑφ-)εἷσα is the augmented aor. of ἑδ- (cf. καθίζω, Att. fut. καθέσω), the part. must be unaugmented, and ὑπέσας, ὑπέσαντες shd. be restored in Hdt. ll.cc., and either ὑφέσας or the later form ὑφίσας [ῑ] (cf. ὑφίζω) in Nic.Dam. l.c.

**ὑφεκτέον**, (ὑπέχω) *one must support, submit to*, δίκην Pl.*R.*457e; ὑ. τινὶ τῆς ἀνανδρίας αἰτίαν X.*Lac.*9.5; ὑ. λόγον τινὶ *one must give* account, Arist.*APo.*77ᵇ5.

**ὑφελίσσω**, only in form ὑπελίσσω (q.v.).

**ὑφελκ-τέον**, *one must draw away under* or *underhand*, τῶν δαδίων *some of* them, Ar.*Eq.*920 (lyr.). **-υσμός**, ὁ, *withdrawing, Gloss.* **-ω**, *draw away under, draw away underhand* or *gently*, ὑ. [τινὰ] ποδοῖιν *draw* one *away* by the two feet, Il.14.477; *draw away by undermining*, ὑ. παρὰ σφᾶς τὸν χοῦν Th.2.76, cf. D.C.66.4; ὑ. κάτωθεν τὸ κλιμάκιον Plu.2.781e; ὑ. τοὺς πόδας, i.e. to be slippery, Poll.1.187:—Med., Περσικὰς ὑφέλκομαι *I trail* Persian slippers *under my feet*, Ar.*Ec.*319:—Pass., ὑφελκέσθω τὸ ὑποπόδιον Heliod.ap.Orib.49. 8.19.

**ὑφέν**, earlier ὑφ' ἕν, Adv. *in one, as a single word*, ἀναγιγνώσκειν ὑφ' ἕν Plu.2.31e; πῶς.. πληθυντικὸν καὶ ἑνικὸν ὑφ' ἓν κεκλήσεται; how can a plural and a singular be addressed *in one and the same word?* A.D.*Pron.*22.7. 2. ἡ ὑφέν the *hyphen*, a sign (‿) written below two consecutive letters to show that they belong to the same word, D.T.*Supp.*674.4, Sch.D.T.p.126 H., Diom.p.434 K., *PAmh.* 2.21.6 (iii/iv A.D.).

**ὑφεξαιρέω**, = ὑπεξαιρέω, *make an exception of*, *PLond.*1.113 iv 22 (vi A.D., Pass.); *eliminate*, Zos.Alch.p.157 B. (Pass.).

**ὕφεξις**, εως, ἡ, *promise*, Sch.Ar.*V.*337 (dub. l.).

**ὑφέπομαι**, *follow behind*, impf. ὑφείπετο v.l. for ἐφ- in App.*Mith.*88.

**ὑφέρπω**, (v. ἕρπω) *creep on secretly*, ὑφεῖρπε γὰρ πολύ the report *spread* far, S.*OT*786; φθονερὸν ὑπ' ἄλγος ἕρπει Ἀτρείδαις angry feelings *creep abroad* against them, A.*Ag.*450 (lyr.). II. c. acc., ὑ. εὐνήν Philostr.*VA*1.37; ὑ. σκοπὸν *secretly aim at*, Hld.10.19. 2. like ὑπέρχομαι II, of involuntary feelings, *steal upon, come over*, χαρά μ' ὑφέρπει A.*Ag.*270; τρόμος μ' ὑ. Id.*Ch.*463 (lyr.).

⊛ **ὕφεσις**, εως, ἡ, (ὑφίημι) *letting down, slackening*, of strings in music, Plu.2.389e; τῆς φωνῆς Antyll.ap.Orib.6.9.5; *relaxation*, σωμάτων μυωδῶν Gal.19.403; of the pulse, Ruf.*Syn.Puls*.6.5; *lowering*, τῶν ἀκοντίων Arr.*Tact*.38.3. **2.** *complaisance*, ἐπὶ τῶν πραγμάτων Plu. *Ant*.24; πρὸς τοὺς φίλους Id.2.808c; χάρις.. ὕφεσις ἀκριβείας ἐν δέοντι Favorin.ap.Gell.1.3.27. **II.** = ὑφαίρεσις III, A.D.*Pron*.51.5, *EM* 36.33; ἡ ὕ. τῆς προθέσεως A.D.*Conj*.247.12. **2.** Arithm., *subtraction*, David *Proll*.54.20; *lowering* of numbers, Ph.1.187. **III.** *descent in the scale, abasement*, Procl. *in Prm*.p.618 S., *Inst*.29, al.; joined with ὑπόβασις (q.v.), Aristid.Quint.3.10; κατὰ ὕφεσιν Dam. *Pr*.34, cf.69,91; *subordination, subjection* as a form of relation, Elias *in Porph*.203.5:—ἐν ὑφέσει· ἐν ἐλαττώσει, Hsch.

**ὑφεσμούς**· συμποδισμούς, Hsch.

**ὑφεσπέρ-ιος**, ον, *towards evening, western*, στῆλαι D.P.450. ⊛ **-ος**, ον, = foreg.: ὑφέσπερα as Adv., *AP*5.304 (better divisim).

**ὑφή** [ῠ], ἡ, *web*, mostly in pl., A.*Ag*.949, E.*Ion* 1146, *IT*814, Pl. *Plt*.281a, etc.; πέπλων ὑφαί E.*IT*312: a spider's *web*, Arist.*HA* 623$^{a}$21 (sg.). (v. ὑφαίνω.)

**ὑφηγ-εμών**, Dor. **ὑφᾱγ-**, όνος, ὁ, = ἡγεμών, *AP*12.56 (Mel.). **-έομαι**, pf. ὑφήγημαι (v. infr.):—*go just before, guide, lead*, τινι E.*El*. 664, Pl.*Euthd*.278c, etc.: abs., *go first, lead the way*, ὑφηγοῦ S.*El*. 1502, cf.Th.1.78, Pl.*Phd*.82d; τοῦτο εὐθὺς ὑφήγηται this *is the guiding principle*, Arist.*Pol*.1260$^{a}$4; κατὰ τὸν ὑφηγημένον τρόπον according to the *normal* plan, Id.*EN*1108$^{a}$3, *Pol*.1256$^{a}$2; κατὰ τὴν ὑ. μέθοδον ib. 1252$^{a}$17 (it is not necessary to regard these usages as pass.). **II.** c. acc. cogn., ὑ. τὴν ὁδόν *show* the way, Plu.*Pomp*.76, etc.; ὑ. ταῦτα *gave* these *instructions*, Lys.33.3:—Pass., τὰ δι' ἡμῶν ὑφηγούμενα the *precepts laid down* by us, Ael.*Tact.Prooem*.6:—but, **2.** c. acc. rei, *show the way to, instruct in*, ἀγαθά X.*Cyr*.8.7.15; χρήματα Id. *Ages*.1.19; τύπους Pl.*R*.403e; ὑ. γόνον *indicate* or *describe* it, D.H. 1.78, cf. Ph.1.14; τινί τι Plu.2.147c, D.L.8.60; also τινί τινος Plu. 2.582b. **III.** *lead to* a thing, *indicate* that it is so, A.*Eu*. 192. **-ημα**, ατος, τό, *direction*, Iamb.*VP*31.213 (pl.). **-ημᾰτικός**, ή, όν, of argument, *expository*, opp. ἀπορητικός, Syrian. *in Metaph*.54.3, cf. Olymp.*Proll*.11.13; τρόπος [διδασκαλίας] Steph. *in Hp*.1.56 D.: **-κά**, τά, *books of instruction, commentaries*, Dam.*Pr*. 341. ⊛ **-ησις**, εως, ἡ, *leading, guidance*, Hp.*Nat.Puer*.18, *OGI*267. 13 (Pergam., iii B.C.), *SIG*827 iii 4 (Delph., ii A.D.); ὑ. ὁδοῦ Poll.3. 95; κατὰ τὴν ὑ. τινός D.18.151, cf. Arist.*Rh.Al*.1420$^{b}$25, Plb.10.27. 3; γράφειν κατὰ τὴν ὑ. τῶν γραμμῶν by the *guiding pattern* of lines, Pl. *Prt*.326d; *sketch, outline* of a subject, Gal.*Libr.Propr.Praef*. (pl.). **II.** *direction*, Onos.*Praef*.3 (pl.), Iamb.*VP*21.96:—in Paus.7.24.8 ὑπήχησις is prob. cj. **-ητέον**, *one must guide, teach*, Ph.2.127. **-ητήρ**, ῆρος, ὁ, = sq., S.*OC*1588, *AP*11.319 (Autom.). **-ητής**, οῦ, ὁ, *guide, leader*, ὑφηγητοῦ δίχα S.*OC*502; ὧν ὑφηγητῶν under whose *guidance*, Id.*OT*966; ὡς ὑφηγητοῦ τινος (sc. ὄντος) as if led by some (invisible) *guide*, ib.1260. **2.** *teacher, master*, Plu.*Dem*.5, Ph.1. 36, al. ⊛ **-ητικός**, ή, όν, *fitted for guiding*, οἱ ὑ. διάλογοι Plato's *expository* dialogues, opp. οἱ ζητητικοί, D.L.3.49. Adv. -κῶς Poll.4. 42.

**ὑφήλιος**, ον, *under the sun*, πᾶσαν τὴν ὑ. the whole *world*, Porph. *Chr*.49.

**ὕφημαι**, Pass., *sit under*, αἰγείροισι D.P.292.

**ὑφημιόλιος**, ον, of a number, *standing to another number in the ratio of* 1 *to* $1\frac{1}{2}$, i.e. $\frac{2}{3}$, the reciprocal of ἡμιόλιος ($\frac{3}{2}$), Arist.*Metaph*. 1021$^{a}$1, Nicom.*Ar*.1.19.

**ὑφηνιοχ-έω**, *to be a* ὑφηνίοχος, and generally, = ἡνιοχέω, v.l. in Luc.*Somn*.15:—Pass., *drive after* or *behind*, of chariots, D.61. 28. **-ος**, ὁ, *charioteer* (as *subordinate to the warrior* in his chariot), Il.6.19, X.*Cyr*.6.4.4, 7.1.15.

**ὑφήσσων**, ον, gen. ονος, *of lesser stature*, Hes.*Sc*.258.

**ὑφιδρόω**, *perspire slightly*, Hp.*Epid*.3.1.η'.

**ὑφιδρύω**, *subordinate, place under control of*.., τὴν ψυχὴν τὴν αὑτοῦ νῷ Plot.6.9.3.

**ὑφιέρεια**, ἡ, *assistant priestess*. *IG*11(2).287 *B* 61 (Delos, iii B.C.), *Inscr.Délos* 1444 *Aa* 48 (ii B.C.), *SIG*1012.23 (Cos, ii/i B.C.).

**ὑφιζάνω**, = ὑφίζω, Arist.*HA*637$^{b}$8; κατὰ τὸν θᾶκον Pyrgio ap.Ath.4. 143e; ὑφίζανον κύκλοις *were crouching beneath*.., E.*Ph*.1382. **II.** *sink, settle down*, τὸ χῶμα ὑ. App.*Mith*.36, cf. Arr.*An*.2.27.4, Gal.10. 973, Procop.*Goth*.4.11.

**ὑφίζησις**, εως, ἡ, *a settling* or *sinking*, Str.1.3.5, Anon.ap.Suid. (pl.).

**ὑφίζω**, *sit down, crouch*, E.*Rh*.730 (troch.). **II.** *sink down, fall in*, D.C.68.25:—Med., Opp.*H*.4.246; τὸ πρὸς ἁφὴν -όμενον σῶμα Ocell.2.3. **III.** v. ὑφεῖσα.

⊛ **ὑφίημι**, Ion. **ὑπίημι** Hdt.1.156, al.:—*let down, lower*, ἱστόν Il.1. 434, *h.Ap*.504, cf. Poll.1.107; ὑ. τὸ ἱστίον *lower* sail, Sch.S.*El*.335 (v. infr. III); ὑ. τὰς ῥάβδους, of lictors, Plu.*Pomp*.19. **2.** *put under*, ὑπὸ δὲ θρῆνυν ποσὶν ἥσει Il.14.240, cf. Od.19.57; ὑφείσθωσαν ὑπὸ τοὺς βρόχους X.*Cyn*.10.2; *put* a young one *under its dam, put* it *to suck*, ὑπ' ἔμβρυον ἧκεν ἑκάστῃ Od.9.245,309; ὑφίητι (Dor.) τὰ μοσχία Theoc.4.4:—but in Med., μαστοῖς ὑφεῖτο *put* it *to her own* breasts, to suckle it, E.*Ph*.31. **b.** *put female to male*, Palaeph.39. **3.** ὑ. τινά *engage* any one *secretly, prepare* him *to play a part, suborn*, ὑφεὶς μάγον τοιόνδε S.*OT*387, cf. Pl.*Ax*.368e: hence in pf. part. Pass., ὡς ἔχιδν' ὑφειμένη like a snake *lurking*, S.*Ant*.531: also ἐνέδρας πολλὰς ὑφείς Plu.*Pyrrh*.30, cf. Anon.ap.Suid. s.v. ὑφέντες; ἐνσχεθεὶς ταῖς πάγαις ἃς ἄλλοις ὑφῆκε Ael.*Fr*.22; δέλεαρ αὐτῷ δέκα σπείρας ὑφῆκεν Plu. *Pomp*.20, cf. *Per*.13. **4.** *give up, surrender*, σῶμ' ὑφεῖσ' ἀλγηδόσι E.*Med*.24; ὑ. τὴν χώραν ἡμετέραν εἶναι X.*An*.3.5.5. **5.** *let down, relax*, τὸ ἄγαν τινός Plu.2.68e. **II.** intr., *slacken, relax*, or *abate from* a thing, c. gen., ὑπεὶς τῆς ὀργῆς Hdt.1.156; τῆς ἀγνωμοσύνης Id.9.4, cf. E.*Ion*847; πολὺ τῆς ὁρμῆς ὑφεικώς D.Chr.11.95: abs., *give in, abate*, οὐδὲν ὑπιέντες Hdt.7.162:—Med., ὑπίεσθαι τῆς ὀργῆς Id.2.121.δ'; ὕφεσθε τοῦ τόνου Ar.*V*.337; τοῦ μέγα φρονεῖν X.*Cyr*.7. 5.62; τῆς δυνάμεως μηδέν Id.*Mem*.4.3.17; of things, [τὸ ὕδωρ] ὑπίεται τοῦ ψυχροῦ *abates from*.., Hdt.4.181; οὐ πόνων ὑ. X.*Ages*.7.1; τοῦ στόματός γε ὑ. *I give way* as to it, Id.*Smp*.5.7: *yield, give way*, D.H. 8.84; τοῖς πολεμίοις Id.*Cyr*.5.2.12; φρονήματος οὐδενὶ.. ὑφιέμενος *inferior* to none in spirit, Plu.*Cat.Mi*.1, cf. Id.2.54c; ὑ. τῆς ἐμπειρίας Jul.*Or*.2.53d; ὑ. τινὶ τῆς ὁδοῦ Luc.*Luct*.2; *give up*, τῶν ἐκ τῆς ἀρχῆς προσόδων Jul.*Or*.1.19c: c. dat. et inf., οὐδενὶ ὑφείμην ἂν ἥδιον ἐμοῦ βεβιωκέναι X.*Mem*.4.8.6, cf. *HG*7.4.9, *Oec*.12.14. **III.** Med. and Pass., *lower one's sails* (v. supr. I.1), Archil. (?) in *PLit.Lond*.54, Ar.*Ra*.1220: mostly in pf. part., ἐν κακοῖς μοι πλεῖν ὑφειμένῃ δοκεῖ to run *with lowered sails*, i.e. *to lower* one's tone, S.*El*.335; so ὑφειμένοις πλέων ἱστίοις καὶ ταπεινοῖς Plu.*Luc*.3: metaph., τῆς φωνῆς ὑφειμένης ἐπαρθείσης δὲ μή Phld.*Rh*.1.199 S., cf. Philostr.*Im*.1.22, Aristaenet.1.3; τὸ ὑφειμένον *diminution*, Thphr.*CP*6.14.12; μισθῶν ὑφειμένων at *reduced* wages, *PTeb*.5.251 (ii B.C.); ὑφειμένα χρώματα *pale* colours, Steph. *in Gal*.1.250 D.: c. gen., ὑφεῖσθαί τινος *to descend lower in the scale than, be inferior to*, Procl.*Inst*.18, Dam.*Pr*.34: abs., -ειμένος Plot.6.4.11, Procl.*Inst*.24, al. **2.** σῴζω νεοσσοὺς ὄρνις ὣς ὑφειμένη like a *cowering* hen,—or perh. *with my* nestlings *under me*, E.*HF*72. **3.** *submit*, X.*An*.3.1.17, 3.2.3, al.: c. inf., κατθανεῖν ὑφειμένη *submissively prepared* to die, E.*Alc*.524.

**ὑφῑκάνω** [ᾱ], = ὑπέρχομαι II, *steal over* one, αὐτὴν ὑπὸ τρόμος αἰνὸς ἱκάνει Il.11.117.

**ὑφιστάω**, late form of ὑφίστημι, Sch.Il.18.600; also ⊛ **ὑφιστάνω**, Dam.*Pr*.270.

⊛ **ὑφίστημι**, Ion. **ὑπίστημι** Hdt.5.16, al.: fut. ὑποστήσω E.*El*.983: aor. ὑπέστησα, Dor. ὑπέστᾱσα Pi.*O*.8.26:—Causal, *place* or *set under*, ὑποστήσαντες [τῷ χαλκηΐῳ] τρεῖς κολοσσούς *having set* them *under* it, *to support* it, Hdt.4.152; ὑ. προθύρῳ κίονας Pi.*O*.6.1: metaph., χώραν ὑπέστᾱσε ξένοις κίονα ib.8.26: without dat., τρεῖς σταυροὺς ὑπίστησι *plants* three piles in the lake *to support* a house, Hdt.5.16; ὑ. κλῶνας X.*Cyn*.10.7; ἐρείσματα Arist.*HA*625$^{a}$12, etc.: metaph., γνώμας ὑποστήσας σοφάς *having laid* them *as a foundation, having begun with* them, S.*Aj*.1091; ὑ. δόλον E. l.c.; v. infr. B.I.1. **2.** *post secretly* or *in ambush*, τοὺς δορυφόρους Hdt.5.92.η'; ταξιάρχους X.*HG*4.1. 26. **3.** *bring to a halt, hold up*, ὑποστήσαντες (sc. τοὺς στρατιώτας) ἐν τῷ στενῷ οἱ στρατηγοί Id.*An*.4.1.14 (v.l. ὑποστάντες, v. infr. B. III); ὑπέστησε τὴν ἑαυτοῦ ναῦν ἀντίπρῳρον τοῖς πολεμίοις *stationed* it, Plb.1. 50.6. **4.** *give substance to, cause to subsist*, '*hypostatize*', Plot.6.7.40, al.; *treat as subsisting*, ὁ νοῦς κατὰ τὸ νοεῖν ὑφιστὰς τὸ ὄν Id.5.1.4; ὑφίστησι μὲν τὸ ὅλον, ὑφίσταται δὲ τὰ μέρη Dam.*Pr*.271, cf. Procl. *Inst*.28. **II.** Med. also in causal sense, mostly fut. and aor. 1, *lay down, premise*, εἰ μή τι πιστὸν τῷδ' ὑποστήσει στόλῳ A.*Supp*. 461; ἀρχὰς ψευδεῖς ὑποστήσασθαι Plb.3.48.9; ἐπειδὰν ὑποθέσεις εὐπεριλήπτους.. ὑποστήσωνται Id.7.7.6. **2.** *substitute* one thing for another, τὸν τρόπον τῇ τοῦ Πέρσου ἀλαζονείᾳ X.*Ages*.9.1. **3.** *conceive, suppose*, c. acc. et inf., τῷ -στησαμένῳ τοὺς θεοὺς.. εἶναι Phld.*D*.1.17; τοὺς θεοὺς ὑφίστανται τὸν κόσμον διοικεῖν D.S.1.11, cf. Heraclit.*Incred*.13; but the inf. is mostly omitted, ἄφθαρτον ὑποστησάμενοι τὸν κόσμον D.S.1.6, cf. 12, D.L.2.86:—Pass., τοὺς θεούς, ἂν φρονοῦντες -σταθῶσιν Phld.*D*.1.7. **4.** *set before oneself* as a model, τινα Isoc.5.113.

**B.** Pass., with aor. 2 and pf. Act. (Hom. uses only aor. 2):—*stand under as a support*, ὑπεστᾶσι κολοσσοὶ.. τῇ αὐλῇ Hdt.2.153; τοὺς σταυροὺς τοὺς ὑπεστεῶτας τοῖσι ἰκρίοισι Id.5.16; τὸ ὑφεστὸς τῷ βάρει Arist.*IA*708$^{b}$31; v. supr. A. I. 1. **2.** *sink, settle*, τὸ ὑπιστάμενον the milk, opp. τὸ ἐπιστάμενον (the cream), Hdt.4.2; opp. τὸ ἐπιπολάζον, Arist.*Cael*.311$^{a}$17; of a *sediment, deposit*, ἐν οὔρῳ ψαμμώδεα ὑφίσταται Hp.*Aph*.4.79, cf. Arist.*Mete*.357$^{b}$3; opp. ἐπιπλεῖν, Thphr. *HP*3.15.4; of the sun, *set*, Emp.48 (cj.). **II.** *place oneself under an engagement, promise* to do, folld. by fut. inf., ὅσσ' Ἀχιλῆϊ.. ὑπέστημεν δώσειν Il.19.195, cf. Hdt.9.94; θύσειν ὑπέστης παῖδα E.*IA*360 (troch.), cf. Ar.*V*.716 (anap.), Pl.*Lg*.751d; by aor. inf., ὑφεστακὼς μοι ἦν ὁ Διόδωρος φιλάνθρωπον δοῦναι *BGU*1141.45 (i B.C.); by pres. inf., ὑπέστησαν ποιέειν ταῦτα Hdt.3.128; ὑ. τὴν τάξιν ἔχειν X.*Cyr*.6.3.35: the inf. is sts. omitted, ὡς.. ὑπέστην καὶ κατένευσα (sc. ἔσεσθαι) Il.4.267: abs., ἢ ἔπος ἠέ τι ἔργον ὑποστὰς ἐξετέλεσσε *after promise given*, Od. 3.99, cf. Il.21.457, Hdt.3.127, 9.34, Lys.19.19, X.*An*.4.1.26; ὥσπερ ὑπέστη as *he promised*, Th.4.39, 8.29: c. dat. pers., ὥς οἱ ὑπέστην as *I promised* him, Il.15.75: sts. with acc. of object (but an inf. may be supplied), πάντα τελευτήσεις ὅσ' ὑπέστης.. Πριάμῳ 13.375; τρίποδας φέρον, οὕς οἱ ὑπέστη 19.243, cf. 11.244; ἐκτελέουσιν ὑπόσχεσιν ἥνπερ ὑπέσταν 2.286, cf. Od.10.483; ἦ ῥ' ἅλιον τὸν μῦθον ὑπέστημεν.., ἀπονέεσθαι vain was the promise *we made*.., that he would return, Il.5.715. **2.** *submit*, c. dat., τινι 9.160: with aor. inf., ὑ. θανεῖν, κατθανεῖν, E.*HF*706, *Ion* 1415. **3.** c. acc. rei, *submit to, consent to*, ὁ τὸ ἐλάχιστον ὑπιστάμενος *who offers to take* the least, Hdt.1.196; ὑ. τὸν πλοῦν *undertake* it *unwillingly*, Th.4. 28; ὑ. τὸν κίνδυνον Id.2.61, Lys.9.7, cf. Th.4.59, Isoc.3.28; ἀγῶνας Th.3.57, *OGI*763.9 (Milet., ii B.C.); πόνον E.*Supp*.189; βέλος Id. *HF*1350; ἔρωτα Id.*Tr*.415; ἀπεχθείας Plu.*Them*.3; πόλεμον Plb. 1.6.7, Alciphr.3.45; πράγματα ib.61; τὴν πρᾶξιν Plu.*Pel*.8; τὸν ἆθλον Luc.*Rh.Pr*.24: also c. inf., *consent, bring oneself to*, οὔ τίς με.. ὑπέστη σαῶσαι Il.21.273; πᾶν ἂν ὑποστὰς εἰπεῖν D.21.114; ὑ. ἐξαπατᾶν τινα Id.

19.69: abs., *submit patiently*, Id.*Prooem*.5.1; ὑφίστασθαι συμβαίνει τὸν κερατοειδῆ the cornea *yields* (to pressure), Aët.7.36. b. *undertake* an office, τὴν ἀρχὴν X.*An*.6.1.19,31; γυμνασιαρχίαν *IG*5(1).535.12 (Sparta), cf. *OGI*494.6 (Milet., ii A.D.); ὑφέστη (sic) τὴν στρατηγίαν *SIG*876.6 (Smyrna, ii/iii A.D.), cf. Plu.*Cam*.37: also ἐθελοντὴν ὑποστῆναι τριήραρχον Lys.29.7; χορηγὸς ὑπέστην D.21.69; ἐμὲ τοῦ λόγου διάδοχον..ὑποστάντα Pl.*Phlb*.19a; poet., ὑπέστης αἵματος δέκτωρ A.*Eu*.204: metaph., ψυχὴν Τέλητος ὑπέστης, i.e. you promised to be as brave as T., Hermipp.46 (anap.). c. *make an offer* in a public auction, ἔδοξεν..μοι μηθὲν ὑποστῆναι I decided to *make* no *bid*, *commit myself to* nothing, *PCair.Zen*.371.9 (iii B.C.), cf. *PMich.Zen*.60.10 (iii B.C.); δώδεκα ἀρταβῶν ὑπέστη he *undertook* (to supply the produce) of 12 artabae, ib.36.5 (iii B.C.), cf. *PCair.Zen*.199.4 (iii B.C.), *PEleph*.21.16 (iii B.C.); ὑφίστατο..τάξεσθαι ἑκάστου πήχεως [x] *PTheb. Bank* 1.2 (ii B.C.); οὐ δυνόμενος (= -άμενος) οὐκέτι ὑποστῆναι τὴν γεωργίαν *Sammelb*.7468.11 (iii A.D.). d. ὑπέστη πολλὰς ἀπορίας *laid himself open to* many doubts, Plot.3.6.12. III. *lie concealed* or *in ambush*, Hdt.8.91, E.*Andr*.1114, v.l. in X.*An*.4.1.14; v. supr. A. I. 2, ὑφίημι I. 3, ὑφεῖσα. IV. *resist, withstand*, c. dat., A.*Pers*.87 (lyr.), X.*An*.3.2.11, *HG*7.5.12: ξυμφοραῖς ταῖς μεγίσταις ὑ. Th.2.61, cf. E.*HF*1349: c. acc., Id.*Cyc*.200, *Rh*.375 (lyr.), Th.1.144, Plb.9.35.1: abs., *stand one's ground, face the enemy*, E.*Ph*.1470, Th.4.54, 8.68, Plb.4.80.5; opp. φεύγω, X.*Cyr*.4.2.31, Plu.*Demetr*.25; ὑποστᾰθείς, opp. φεύγων, E.*Rh*.315; of clouds, opp. προωθεῖσθαι, Arist.*Pr*.940$^b$36. 2. *subsist, exist* (cf. ὑπόστασις B. III), κατ' ἰδίαν ὑφεστώς Arist.*Fr*.188; ὑφέστηκε τό τε ὁρᾶν ἡμᾶς καὶ ἀκούειν ὥσπερ τὸ ἀλγεῖν Epicur.*Fr*.36; τὸ ὑφεστηκὸς τέλος Id.*Sent*.22, cf. Diog.Oen.5, Arr.*Epict*.3.7.6; ἐκ τοῦ μηκέτ' ὄντος μηδ' ὑφεστῶτος Plu.2.829c, cf. Luc.*Par*.27; τὸ παρῳχημένον τοῦ χρόνου καὶ τὸ μέλλον οὐχ ὑπάρχειν ἀλλ' ὑφεστηκέναι φησί (sc. Χρύσιππος) *Stoic*.2.165; the Stoic distinction betw. τὸ ὂν and τὸ ὑφεστός is pettifogging acc. to Gal.10.155 (= *Stoic*.2.115); τὰ ὑφεστῶτα *business in hand*, Plb.6.14.5. b. ὑφεστηκότος παρὰ τῷ ταμίᾳ κατ' ἰδίαν λόγου the treasurer *having* a special bank-account, *IG*12(9).236.64 (Eretria, ii B.C.); τὸ ἥμισσυ ἀναπεμπόντω ἐπὶ τὰν δαμοσίαν τράπεζαν ἐς τὸν ὑφεστᾱκότα τᾶς θεοῦ λόγον *Arch.f.Religionswiss*.10.211 (Cos, ii B.C.); ὑποστησαμένους λόγον πόλεως "τῶν..χρημάτων" ἐγγράφεσθαι τὸ διδόμενον they shall *open* a municipal account (entitled) 'the..fund' and place this gift to its credit, *SIG*577.13 (Milet., iii/ii B.C.). V. ἡ κοιλία ὑφίσταται the bowels *are costive*, lit., *are obstructed* or *stopped*, Plu.2.134e. VI. *arise within*, τῷ πλήθει τοιοῦτον ὑπέστη δέος Plb.11.30.2 codd. (παρέστη is prob. cj.).

**ὑφόδιον**, τό, = ἐφόδιον, dub. l. in *Ath.Mitt*.44.23 (Samos, iii B.C., v. *Supp.Epigr*.1.363.43).

**ὑφοδόω**, *guide*, Philippid.22 (ὑφοδώσεις cj. for ὑφ' ὁδοῦ ὡς εἶναι).

**⁎ὑφόλμιον**, τό, (ὅλμος II. 1) *mortar-stand*, Ar.*Fr*.61. II. *part of the* ὅλμος (in a flute, v. ὅλμος II. 5), Pherecr.242, Poll.4.70.

**ὑφόρ-ᾱσις**, εως, ἡ, = ὑποψία, *suspicion*, Plb.30.4.3, Phld.*Ir*.p.49 W., Plu.2.479b, D.L.2.99: c. gen., κινδύνων J.*AJ*17.12.2. **-ᾱτέον**, *one must suspect*, Plu.2.50b, M.Ant.7.53, Herod.Med.ap.Orib.6.20.3. **-άω**, aor. ὑπεῖδον (v. infr.), *look at from below, eye stealthily, view with suspicion* or *jealousy, suspect*, τινα X.*An*.2.4.10; τί μάτην ..ὑπό μ' ἴδες; S.*Ichn*.172 (lyr.):—Pass., D.11.4, Plu.*Rom*.8:—freq. in Med., ὑφορῶμαι (aor. ὑπειδόμην, v. sub voce), in same sense, Th.3.40, X.*Mem*.2.7.12, Is.2.7, D.18.43, Arist.*HA*629$^b$10: folld. by μή, Plb.3.18.8, etc.: abs., Luc.*DDeor*.19.1.—Cf. ὑποβλέπω, ὑποψία, ὕποπτος.

**ὑφορβ-έω**, *herd pigs*, *SIG*986.5,10 (Chios, v/iv B.C.). **-ός**, ὁ, v. συφορβός, and add *PPetr*.2p.113 (iii B.C.).

**ὑφορθ-όω**, late form of ὑπορθόω, *re-erect*, prob. in *PHamb*.23.27 (vi A.D.). **-ωσις**, εως, ἡ, *restoration*, *PMasp*.69.12 (vi A.D.).

**ὑφορμάω**, *to be in motion under*, metaph., ἀμφιβολία τις ὑφορμῶσα τῇ διανοίᾳ Adam.*Vent*.36 (fort. ὑφορμοῦσα, v. ὑφορμέω I fin.):—Pass., aor. part. ὑφορμηθέντα *darting back*, read by Ar.Byz. for ἐφ- in Il.16.313.

**ὑφορμ-έω**, *lie at anchor in wait for* others, Plb.3.19.8, 34.3.2, Ael.*NA*11.19, Charito 3.7, etc.: metaph., αἱ πόλεις ὑ. ἀλλήλαις D.Chr.38.42; ὁ τοῦ κόλακος λόγος..ὑ. τινὶ πάθει Plu.2.61e; τὸ ὑφορμοῦν *suspicion*, Lib.*Decl*.40 (προθεωρία).2, 46 (προθεωρία).2; τὰ ὑφορμοῦντα Sch. D.1.1 (viii p.30 Dindorf). II. lit., *anchor under*, ὑπὸ τὸ τεῖχος D.Chr.11.116, cf. 7.2. **-ίζομαι**, Pass. and Med., *come to anchor*, Th.2.83 codd. (ἀφ- Blomfield); τῇ Σαλαμῖνι Plu.*Sol*.9: metaph., *to be found under* or *in* a place, Philostr.*Her*.1.3.

**ὑφόρμιον**, τό, (ὅρμος I) *necklace*, Ael.Dion.*Fr*.417.

**ὑφόρμ-ισις**, εως, ἡ, *harbour, anchorage*, *AP*7.699. **-ιστήρ**, ῆρος, ὁ, *one who makes fast below*, of a stone fastened to steady a raft, Opp.*H*.4.421. **-ος**, ὁ, (ὅρμος II) *anchorage*, Arist.*HA*542$^b$23 (pl.), Str.6.1.1 (pl.), 14.1.8, etc. II. Adj., *fit for anchoring in*, αἰγιαλός Id.14.1.35; τόπος St.Byz. s. v. λιμήν. 2. *at anchor*, ναῦς Ph.2.521.

**ὕφος** [ῠ], εος, τό, = ὑφή, *web*, Pherecr.243, Eub.67.5 (= 84.4, cf. ὑμήν), Str.10.1.6, Plu.2.396b; ἐριοῦν ὕ. Dsc.1.19; of a spider, Id.2.63; of a *net*, *AP*9.370 (Tib. Ill.). 2. metaph., τὸ τῶν λόγων ὕ. Longin.1.4, cf. Hermog.*Inv*.3.13; τὰς ποιήσεις οἷον ὑφῆ Phld.*Po*.5.11; of the *text* of an author, Gal.17(1).80; τὸ φυσικὸν ὕ. τοῦ ἀριθμοῦ the natural *series* of numbers, Nicom.*Ar*.1.9.

**ὑφοψία**, v. ὑποψία. **ὑφόωσι**, Ep. 3 pl. of ὑφάω (q.v.).

**ὕφυγρος**, ον, *somewhat moist*, Arist.*Pr*.867$^b$35. II. *filled with fluid*, Poll.4.197; gloss on ὕπομβρον, Gal.19.149.

**ὕφυδρος**, ον, *under water*, of a diver, Th.4.26, D.C.42.12, etc.; ὕφυδρος νεῖν Ael.*NA*15.1. II. *full of water*, λειμωνία cj. in Thphr.*CP*3.11.3; χωρίον Str.4.1.6. 2. *dropsical*, Hp.*Morb*.1.7, as expld. by Gal.19.150.

**ὑφυπνόομαι**, *become sleepy*, Hld.9.12 codd. (ἀφυπν- cj. Koraes).

**ὑφωμᾰδόν**, Adv. = ὁμοθυμαδόν, Phot., Suid.

**Ὑχαῖος**, ὁ (sc. μήν), name of a month at Physkos, *GDI*1842.2 (Delph., ii B.C.).

**⁎ὔχηρος**, ἡ, = ἐπίχειρον II. 1, ἀ(ν)τὶ τᾶ ὐχήρων (= τῆς ἐπιχείρου) instead of the *gratuity*, *Inscr.Cypr*.135.5 H. (Idalium).

**ὑψᾰγόρας**, Ion. -ης, ου, ὁ, (ἀγορεύω) *boaster, braggart*, Od.1.385, 2.85, al.: in late Prose, Men.Prot.p.6D.

**ὑψαυχεν-έω**, *carry the neck high, show off*, D.H.7.46, Ph.1.145, al., Lxx 2*Ma*.15.6, Plu.2.324e, Poll.2.135; of the cock, Ael.*NA*4.29. **-ία**, v. ὑψηλαυχενία. **-ίζω**, = ὑψαυχενέω, *AP*9.777 (Phil.). **-ος**, ον, = ὑψαύχην, Ἄραβες Tim.Gaz.ap.Ar.Byz.*Epit*.147.27.

**ὑψαυχέω**, = μεγαλαυχέω, ὑψηλοφρονέω, S.*Fr*.1106, Chrysipp.*Stoic*.3.141, Ps.-Phoc.62.

**⁎ὑψαύχην**, ενος, ὁ, ἡ, *carrying the neck high*, ἵππος Pl.*Phdr*.253d, cf. Them.*Or*.21.248c; θυμός Ph.1.311; v. ὑψηχής. 2. metaph., *stately, towering*, ἐλάτη E.*Ba*.1061; θῶκος *Epigr.Gr*.903 (Sardis, iv A.D.); of a wine-bottle, *AP*5.134. 3. in moral sense, *stately, haughty*, ib.250 (Iren.), 9.641 (Agath.), etc.

**ὑψαυχής**, ές, *high-vaunting*, κόρα B.12.84.

**ὑψερεφής**, ές, *high-roofed, high-vaulted*, ὑ. μέγα δῶμα Il.5.213, 19.333; χαλκοβατὲς δῶ ὑψερεφές Od.13.5; δώματα 4.757; ναός Ar.*Nu*.306 (lyr.):—also **ὑψηρεφής**, ές, ὑψηρεφέος θαλάμοιο Il.9.582.

**ὑψηγορ-έω**, *talk big*, Ph.1.365. **-ία**, ἡ, *stateliness of phrase, lofty expression*, ib.206, Longin.8.1. **-ος**, ον, *grandiloquent, vaunting*, A.*Pr*.320,362; *sublime*, Ph.1.473.

**ὑψήεις**, εσσα, εν, poet. for ὑψηλός, Nic.*Fr*.74.62, *AP*9.525.21 (Brunck for ὑψόεντα).

**ὑψηλ-αυχενία**, ἡ, *carrying the neck high*, X.*Eq*.10.13 (ὑψαυχ- cj. Dind.).

**ὑψηλο-γνώμων**, ον, gen ονος, *high-minded, proud*, Them.*Or*.15.190d. **-κάρδιος**, ον, *high-hearted, proud*, Lxx *Pr*.16.6(5), Sm.*Ec*.7.9(8). **-κρημνος**, ον, *with lofty cliffs*, πέτραι A.*Pr*.5.

**ὑψηλολογ-έομαι**, *speak proudly*, Pl.*R*.545e, Them.*Or*.23.291a:—Act., ib.31.354c. **-ία**, ἡ, *vaunting*, Poll.2.121, 6.148. **-ος** (parox.), ον, *talking high, vaunting*, Them.*Or*.2.26d, 21.262a.

**ὑψηλό-λοφος**, ον, v. ὑψίλοφος. **-νοος**, ον, contr. **-νους**, ουν, *high-minded*: τὸ ὑψηλόνουν Pl.*Phdr*.270a (cf. Plu.*Per*.8); ῥήτορες Them.*Or*.26.329c. **-νωτος**, ον, *high-backed*, Sch.A.*Pr*.830. **-πέτης**, ες, *high-flying*, Lat. *praepes*, *Gloss*. **-ποιός**, όν, *producing loftiness or sublimity*, Longin.28.1, 32.6. **-πους**, ὁ, ἡ, neut. πουν, gen. ποδος, *high-footed*, of beds, Antyll.ap.Orib.9.14.2.

**⁎ὑψηλός**, ή, όν (also -ός, όν Demetr.Troezen.1 Diels): Comp. and Sup. -ότερος, -ότατος, and irreg. -έστατος Paus.5.13.9: (ὕψι, ὕψος):—*high, lofty*, θάλαμος Od.1.426; πύργος Il.3.384, etc.; of a *highland* country, χώρη ὀρεινή..καὶ ὑψηλή Hdt.1.110; ὑψηλὰ χωρία Th.3.97; and ὑψηλά alone, Pl.*Lg*.732c; ἐφ' ὑψηλοῦ εἶναι, καθῆσθαι, X.*HG*4.5.4, Luc.*Rh.Pr*.6; ἐν ὑψηλῷ τινι καταστάς Plu.*Eum*.17; ἀπὸ ὑψηλοῦ κρεμασθείς Pl.*Tht*.175d; ἀφ' ὑψηλοτέρου καθορῶντες X.*HG*6.2.29; ἐποικοδομήσαντες ὑψηλότερον [τὸ τεῖχος] Th.7.4. Adv., -λῶς καθήμενος Pherecr.64. II. metaph., *high, lofty, stately, proud*, ὄλβος, ἀρεταί, κλέος, Pi.*O*.2.22, 5.1, *P*.3.111; τέχνη θεσπεσία τις καὶ ὑ. Pl.*Euthd*.289e; ὑ. καὶ χαύνη ἐλπίς Id.*Ep*.341e; ὑψηλὰ κομπεῖν talk *high* and boastfully, S.*Aj*.1230. 2. of persons, opp. δυσδαίμων, E.*Hel*.418; ἀφ' ὑψηλῶν βραχὺν ᾤκισε Id.*Heracl*.613 (lyr.); ἐπὶ τοῖς ἐμοῖς κακοῖς ὑ. εἶναι Id.*Hipp*.730; ἐπὶ τούτοις ὑ. ἐξαρεῖν αὐτόν Pl.*R*.494d, cf. And.3.7, Aeschin.2.174; [δαίμονα] ὑ. αἴρειν E.*Supp*.555; τὸ νέον ἅπαν ὑ. καὶ θρασύ Metrod.*Fr*.57; αὑτὸν παρέχειν -ότερον λημμάτων Luc.*Nigr*.25; ὑ. τῷ ἤθει Plu.*Dio* 4. 3. *upraised*, i.e. *mighty*, ἐν βραχίονι -λῷ Lxx *Ex*.6.1, al. 4. of poets, *sublime*, Longin.40.2; τὰ -ότερα the *loftier, sublimer* thoughts or language, Id.43.3; ὑ. λέξις, λόγος, D.H.*Lys*.13, Plu.*Per*.5. Adv. -λῶς Gal.10.12.

**ὑψηλο-τάπεινος** [ᾰ], ον, *now high, now low*, τὸ ὑ. καὶ μεγαλόμικρον Ph.2.61. **-τάπείνωμα**, ατος, τό, *ups and downs of fortune, vicissitudes*, Paul.Al.*M*.3: cf. ὑψοταπείνωμα. **-της**, ητος, ἡ, *loftiness, sublimity*, S.E.*M*.7.17, *AB*342, *Gloss*. **-τράχηλος** [ᾰ], ον, *high-necked*, Hsch. s. v. δανήλοφα. **-φᾰνής**, ές, *appearing sublime*, Longin.24.1 (in Sup. -έστατος). **-φόρος**, ον, *exalted*, Hsch. s. v. ἐρισφάραγος (s. v. l.).

**ὑψήλοφος**, ον, v. ὑψίλοφος.

**ὑψηλο-φρονέω**, *to be high-minded*, *Ep.Rom*.11.20, 1*Ep.Ti*.6.17. **-φρονία**, ἡ, *haughtiness*, Suid. s. v. ἑωροκοπίαις. **-φρων**, ονος, ὁ, ἡ, *high-minded, high-spirited*, ἀνήρ Pl.*R*.550b; *haughty*, θυμός E.*IA* 919. **-φυής**, ές, *of a high growth*, Thphr.*HP*3.12.3 (Comp.). **-φωνος**, ον, *with high or loud voice*, Sch.rec.S.*El*.243.

**ὑψήλωσις**, εως, ἡ, *a rising, swelling up*, τῶν μελῶν Gal.19.546.

**ὑψήνωρ**, ορος, ὁ, ἡ, *raising* or *exalting men*, Nonn.*D*.17.169.

**ὑψηρεφής**, v. ὑψερεφής.

**ὑψηχ-έω**, *sound high* or *loud*, Sch.Il.6.507. **-ής**, ές, (ἦχος) *making a loud* or *ringing sound*, ὑψηχέες ἵπποι, because of their *loud neighing*, or their '*high-resounding pace*' (cf. ἐρίγδουπος), Il.5.772 (v.l. ὑψαύχενες ap.Longin.), 23.27; τὸ ὑ. τῶν λόγων Philostr.*VS*1.25.7.

**ὕψι**, Adv. *on high, aloft*, ὑ. δ' ἀναθρώσκων πέτεται Il.13.140; ὑ. βιβάς ib.371; Ζεὺς ἥμενος ὑ. 20.155, cf. Od.16.264; ἴρηξ..ἀηδόνα..ὑ. μάλ' ἐν νεφέεσσι φέρων Hes.*Op*.204; ἐμάχοντο..ἀπὸ νηῶν ὑ. μελαινάων ἐπιβάντες from *high on* the ships, Il.15.387; ὕ. . . ἀέλλη σκίδνατο 16.374; ὕ. . . ὁρμίσσομεν *out at sea*, 14.77. (Hence ὑψίων, ὑψίτερος, ὕψιστος,—all prob. connected with ὑπέρ.)

**ὑψῐάγυια** [ᾰγ], fem. Adj. *with stately streets*, πόλις B.12.71.

**ὑψιαίετος**, ὁ, f.l. for ὑπάετος (q.v. in Addendis), Ant.Lib.20.6.

**ὑψῐ-βάμων** [ᾱ], ον, gen. ονος, = sq., Hsch. **-βᾰτος**, ον, *set on high*, πόλιες Pi.*N*.10.47; τρίπους S.*Aj*.1404 (anap.). ⊛**-βίας** [βῐ], ου, ὁ, Boeot. **οὐψ-** or **οὑψ-**, *high and mighty*, Corinn.13. **-βόας**, ου, ὁ, *loud-shouter*, name of a frog in Batr.202. **-βρεμέτης**, ου, ὁ, *high-thundering*, epith. of Zeus, Il.1.354, 12.68, Od.5.4, Hes.*Op*.8, etc.; in mock heroic lines, Ar.*Lys*.773, cf. Luc.*Tim*.4. ⊛**-βρομος**, ον, = foreg., Orph.*H*.19.1. **-γέννητος**, ον, *born on high*, ἐλαίας ὑψιγέννητος κλάδος its *topmost* shoot, A.*Eu*.43. ⊛**-γονος**, ον, *produced on high*, Nonn.*D*.27.98. **-γυιος**, ον, *high-stemmed*, ἄλσος Pi.*O*.5.13. **-δαίδαλτος**, ον, *high and richly wrought*, τρίποδες B.3.18. **-δειρος**, ον, *with high cliffs*, χθών (of Delphi) Id.4.4. (Apptly. formed from δειρή in the sense of δειράς.) **-δομος**, ον, *high-built*, πύλαι Coluth.391. **-ζῠγος**, ον, prop. of a rower, *sitting high on the benches*: metaph. of Zeus, *high-throned*, Il.4.166, 7.69, al., Hes.*Op*.18, B.10.3. **-ζωνος**, ον, *high-girded*, f.l. for Ὑψιζώρου, pr. n., Call.*Fr*.19.1. **-θρονος**, ον, *high-throned*, of gods, Pi.*N*.4.65, *I*.6(5).16. **-κάρηνος** [ᾰ], ον, *high-topped*, δρύες Il.12.132, *h.Ven*.264; ἄγκος Call.*Fr.anon*.1. **-κέλευθος**, ον, *on a lofty path*, ψυχή *AP*9.207. **-κέρᾱτα**, v. ὑψίκερως. ⊛**-κέρης**, ητος, = sq., Choerob. *in Theod*.1.166 H. ⊛**-κερως**, ων, gen. ω, (κέρας) *high-horned*, ἔλαφος Od.10.158; ὑψίκερω. . φάσμα ταύρου S.*Tr*.507 (lyr.): metaplast. acc., ὑψικέρᾱτα πέτραν a *high-peaked* rock, Pi.*Fr*.325: acc. fem., ὑψικέραν βοῦν B.15.22. **-κόλωνος**, ον, *high*, κίων Opp.*C*.4.87. **-κομος**, ον, also η, ον Q.S.5.119: (κόμη):—*with high-bound tresses*, Ἑλένα Pi.*Pae*.6.95. 2. *with lofty foliage, towering*, δρύες Il.14.398, Od.9.186, Hes.*Sc*.376; ὄρη Asius *Fr.Ep*.8. **-κομπος**, ον, *boasting, arrogant*, Eust.1687.49. Adv. -πως S.*Aj*.766. **-κρᾰν[ά]εσσα** [νᾰ], fem. Adj. *high and rugged* (cf. κραναός), Antim. in *PMilan*.17.49. **-κρᾰτέω**, *rule aloft* or *on high*, Phot., Suid. **-κρεμής**, ές, *suspended on high*, Opp.*C*.4.93. ⊛**-κρημνος**, ον, *with high crags*, Μίμας Hom.*Epigr*.6.5. II. *built on a high crag*, πόλισμα A.*Pr*.421 (lyr.), cf. *Fr*.32. **-κροτος**, ον, *loftily resounding*, ποδῶν χορεῖαι Tim.*Pers*.214. **-λοφος**, ον, *high-crested*, Αἴτνα Pi.*O*.13.111; θυρίδες *AP*5.152 (Asclep.); v.l. in Ar.*Ra*818 (hex.) for ἱππολόφων; in Hp.*Ep*.16 the best codd. have ὑψηλόλοφος (v.l. ὑψήλοφος). **-λυχνος αὐγή**, illumination *by a light hung on high*, Philox.2.3. **-μέδων**, οντος, ὁ, *ruling on high*, Ζεύς Hes.*Th*.529, B.14.51; ὕ. θεῶν τύραννον Ar.*Nu*.563 (lyr.). II. metaph., *towering*, Παρνασός Pi.*N*.2.19. **-μέλαθρος**, ον, *high-built*, *h.Merc*.103, 134, 399; Διὸς ὕ. κράτος Orph.*H*.5.1. **-νεφής**, ές, *dwelling high in the clouds*, Ζεύς Pi.*O*.5.17, cf. Nonn.*D*.26.147; Ταῦρος ib.48.376. **-νομος**, ον, *feeding on high places*, of the goat, Eust.472.11. **-νοος**, ον, *arrogant*, ὕβρις B.12.44; *high-minded*, Nonn.*D*.9.207, *Epigr.Gr*.440.10 (Namara). ⊛**-πᾰγής**, ές, *high-built, towering*, Σίπυλος *APl*.4.132 (Theodorid.). 2. *set on high*, ὅπλα ὑ. κρεμάσασα Nonn.*D*.2.712. **-πεδος**, ον, *with high ground, high-placed*, Pi.*I*.1.31. **-πέτᾰλος**, ον, = ὑψίκομος 2, Com. of κράμβαι, Polyzel.9. **-πετήεις**, εσσα, εν, = ὑψιπέτης, Il.22.308, Od.24.538:—irreg. acc. pl. ὑψιπετῆεις, as if from ὑψιπετήης, κίχλας Matro *Conv*.78. **-πέτηλος**, ον, Ion. and Ep. for ὑψιπέτᾰλος, used like ὑψίκομος, of trees, Il.13.437, Od.4.458, 11.588. **-πέτης**, ου, Dor. **-πέτας**, α, ὁ: (πέτομαι):—*high-flying, soaring*, αἰετός Il.12.201, 219, Od.20.243; ὑψιπετᾶν ἀνέμων Pi.*P*.3.105; γενοίμαν αἰετὸς ὑψιπέτας S.*Fr*.476 = Ar.*Av*.1337 (lyr.): Comp. -έστερος Herm.ap.Stob.1.49.45:—some unnamed Gramm. (in opposition to Aristarchus) wrote ὑψιπετῆς (contr. from ὑψιπετήεις), v. Sch. AIl.12.201; the acc. sg. ὑψιπετῆ ὄρνιθα in Ant.Lib.16.2 belongs in sense to this word, in form to the next. **-πετής**, ές, (πίπτω) *fallen from heaven*, Παλλάδιον Eust.1520.62, cf. Suid. 2. *lofty*, ἀμπτάμενος οὐράνιον ὑ. ἐς μέλαθρον E.*Hec*.1101 (lyr.). 3. v. foreg. fin. ⊛**-πόδης**, ου, ὁ, poet. for ὑψίπους, Nonn.*D*.20.81, 37.686. ⊛**-πολις**, ιδος or εως, ὁ, ἡ, *citizen of a proud city*, opp. ἄπολις, S.*Ant*.370 (lyr.). **-πολος**, ον, *soaring on high*, ὑψιπόλοις ἀγέλαισιν οἰωνῶν Opp.*C*.3.111. **-πορος**, ον, *with lofty path*, of the planet Saturn, prob. for -πολος in Nonn.*D*.41.350; Ἥλιος ib.10.141; κέλευθος ib.2.126, al., cf. Opp.*C*.3.497. **-πότητος**, ον, = ὑψιπέτης, *flying aloft, soaring*, Nonn.*D*.5.295, al. ⊛**-πους**, ὁ, ἡ, gen. ποδος, *high-footed*, i.e. *high-reared, lofty*, νόμοι S.*OT*866 (lyr.). **-πρυμνος**, ον, *with high stern*, Str.4.4.1. **-πρῳρος**, ον, *with high prow*, ibid. (ubi ὑψόπρ- codd.); ὑψίπρῳρον αἶρε ταρσόν Orac.ap.Porph.ap.Eus.*PE*5.9. ⊛**-πῠλος**, ον, *with high gates*, Il.6.416, 16.698, E.*HF*1030 (lyr.), B.8.46. **-πυργος**, ον, *high-towered*, Simon.112, A.*Eu*.688, S.*Tr*.354, E.*Tr*.376, etc.: metaph., ὑ. ἐλπίδες *towering* hopes, A.*Supp*.97 (lyr.). **-στολος**, ον, (στολή II) *high-girded, well girt*, Hsch.

**ὕψιστος**, η, ον, Sup. without any Posit. in use: (ὕψι, ὑψοῦ):—*highest, loftiest*, of places, A.*Pr*.720, A.R.2.1026, etc.; ἐν τοῖς ὑ., i.e. in heaven above, *Ev.Matt*.21.9, *Ev.Luc*.2.14. 2. of Zeus, *highest*, Pi.*N*.1.60, 11.2, A.*Eu*.28; Ζηνὸς ὕψιστον σέβας S.*Ph*.1289: one of the gates of Thebes was called Ὕψισται from his temple there, Paus.9.8.5: of Jahweh, ὁ θεὸς ὁ ὕ. Lxx *Ge*.14.18, cf. *De*.32.8, *OGI* 96.7 (Egypt, ii B.C.), *SIG*1181 (Rhenea, ii B.C.), etc. 3. of things, στέφανος, κέρδος, Pi.*P*.1.100, *I*.1.51; κακῶν ὕψιστα A.*Pers*.331, 807; ὕ. ἐν βροτοῖς φόβος Id.*Supp*.479.

**ὑψῐ-τέλεστος**, ον, prob. f.l. for ὀψιτέλεστος, *late-finished*, φάος (of the moon born after the sun) Nonn.*D*.41.94. **-τενέω**, *aim high*, Theoctist.ap.Stob. vol. v p.1146 Hense. **-τενής**, ές, *stretched on high*, πόδες Opp.*C*.3.492; αὐχήν Nonn.*D*.4.376; *on high*, δαίμων ib.40.83. **-τένων**, οντος, ὁ, *with high-strained sinews, strong-necked*, ταῦροι Ps.-Phoc.202.

**ὑψίτερος** [ῐ], α, ον, Comp. of Adv. ὕψι, *loftier*, δρύες Theoc.8.46.

**ὑψῐ-τέχνης**, ου, Dor. **-τέχνᾱς**, α, ὁ, *of lofty art*, Ἀσκλαπιός *IG*4²(1).129.5 (as read by P. Maas *Epidaurische Hymnen* 128). **-τῠχος**, ον, *reaching a height of fortune*, Paul.Al.*M*.2. ⊛**-φᾰής**, ές, *high-shining, far-seen*, τάφος *AP*7.701 (Diod.); οὐρανὸς ὑ. *PMag.Leid.V*.8.2:—also **-φᾰνής**, ές, μνῆμα *IG*2².3639.1: metaph., *eminent*, B.13.5:—also **-φάεννος** [ᾰ], ον, Ph.Epic.ap.Eus.*PE*9.37. **-φοίτης**, ου, ὁ, *one who wanders or moves on high*, Hsch., Phot.; = ὑψίφρων, Id. **-φόρητος**, ον, *high-borne, lofty*, ἀταρπός Procl.*H*.4.14. **-φρων**, ονος, ὁ, ἡ, = ὑψηλόφρων, *haughty*, Pi.*P*.2.51. **-χαίτης**, ου, ὁ, perh. = βαθυχαίτης, ib.4.172; cf. εὐρυχαίτης.

**ὑψίων** [ῑ], ον, gen. ονος, poet. Comp. of ὕψι, *loftier*, Pi.*Fr*.213; cf. ὑψίτερος.

**ὑψόθεν**, Boeot. **οὑψόθεν** prob. in Corinn.*Supp*.1.32, Adv.: (ὕψος):—*from on high, from above*, Il.11.53, 15.18, Hes.*Th*.704, Pi.*P*.8.81, A.*Supp*.175 (lyr.), *Fr*.275, E.*Ba*.1111, *Fr*.420.3; ὑ. ἐκ κορυφῆς Od.2.147; ἐκ πέτρης 17.210: rare in Prose, καθορῶντες ὑ. τὸν τῶν κάτω βίον Pl.*Sph*.216c. II. = ὑψοῦ, *aloft, on high*, ὁ ὑ. σκοπός A.*Supp*.381 (lyr.); τὰ ὑ., opp. τὰ ἔνερθε, *AP*12.97 (Antip.). 2. c. gen., *above, over*, Pi.*O*.3.12, Arat.26, A.R.2.806, *IG*2².4225.2.

**ὑψόθι**, Adv., (ὕψος) like ὑψοῦ, *aloft, on high*, ὑψόθ' ἐόντι Διί Il.10.16, cf. 17.676, Call.*Jov*.30, D.P.134; ὑψόθ' ὄρεσφιν Il.19.376.

**ὕψοι**, Adv. *upwards*, v.l. for ἴψοι in Sapph.91.

**ὑψο-κράτωρ** [ᾰ], ορος, ὁ, *lord of the* ὕψωμα, Doroth. in *Cat.Cod.Astr*.5(3).86. **-πρῳρος**, ον, v. ὑψίπρῳρος.

**ὑψ-όροφος**, ον, *high-roofed, high-ceiled*, θάλαμος Il.3.423, 24.192, Od.2.337, al.; οἶκον ἐς ὑψόροφον (with v.l. οἶκον ἐϋκτίμενον) 10.474, al.: cf. ὑψερεφής, ὑψώροφος.

⊛**ὕψος**, εος, τό, (ὕψι) *height*, ὕψος κρεῖσσον ἐκπηδήματος A.*Ag*.1376; εἰς ὕ. αἴρειν τινά E.*Ph*.404; κυπαρίττων ὕψη καὶ κάλλη Pl.*Lg*.625c; ὕ. ἔχειν, λαμβάνειν, rise some *height*, Th.1.91, 4.13, cf. 2.75; ἀφ' ὕψους [με] δισκοβόλησε *Epigr.Gr*.336 (Alexandria Troas): pl., Pi.*Ti*.44d: abs. ὕψος, *in height*, opp. μῆκος, εὖρος, πλάτος, Hdt.1.50, 178, *IG*1².372.24, 2².1666 *A*79, *PMich.Zen*.38.12, al. (iii B.C.); so ἐς ὕψος Hdt.2.13, 155. II. metaph., *summit, crown*, ὕ. ἀμαθίας Pl.*Ep*.351d; σεμνότητος Arist.*Mu*.398ᵃ12. 2. *sublimity, grandeur*, τῶν λόγων Metrod.*Herc*.831.8, cf. Longin.1.1, al.: pl., Id.3.4, 7.4.

**ὑψόσε**, Adv. of motion, *aloft, on high*, ὑψόσ' ἄειρας Il.10.465, Od.9.240; ὑψόσ' ἀνέσχεθε χειρί Il.10.461; ὑ. δ' αὐγὴ γίγνεται ἀΐσσουσα 18.211; τοῦ δ' ὑ. γούνατ' ἐπῆδα 21.302, cf. 324; ὑ. δ' ἄχνη σκίδναται 11.307, cf. Od.12.238; κίονες ὑ. ἔχοντες *high* reaching, 19.38. The two editions by Aristarchus gave ὑψόσε and ὑψοῦ respectively in Il. 10.465, 505, cf. Od.12.249.

**ὑψοτᾰπείνωμα**, ατος, τό, *variation of fortune, vicissitude*, Vett.Val.10.24, al., Critodem. in *Cat.Cod.Astr*.8(1).259: cf. ὑψηλοταπείνωμα.

**ὑψοτάτω**, Adv., Sup. of ὑψοῦ, *most highly*, B.*Fr*.16.6.

**ὑψοῦ**, Adv., (ὕψος) *high*, νῆα . . ἔρυσσαν ὑ. ἐπὶ ψαμάθοις Il.1.486; ὑ. δ' ἐν νοτίῳ τήν γ' ὅρμισαν [νῆα] *out* from the beach, Od.4.785, 8.55; τῆς πόλιος . . ἐκκεχωσμένης ὑ. having the soil raised *to a great height*, Hdt.2.138; ὑ. πατεῖν Pi.*O*.1.115, cf. *P*.10.70, B.5.18; ὑ. κρέμασθαι Hermipp.55 (anap.); ὑ. φέρεσθαι Anaxil.22.30. II. metaph., ἐξάρας με ὑ. having praised me *highly*, Hdt.9.79; ὑ. αἴρειν θυμόν S.*OT*914. Cf. ὑψόσε.

**ὑψ-όφθαλμος**, ον, *with prominent eyes*, Procl.*Par.Ptol*.230 (s.v.l., ῥιψ- Ptol.)

**ὑψόφωνος**, ον, *with high, shrill voice*, Hp.*Epid*.1.19 (om. Littré with Gal. and 3 codd.).

⊛**ὑψόω**, *lift high, raise up*, Batr.81, *APl*.4.41 (Agath.):—Med., τάφον ὑψώσαντο *AP*7.55 (Alc.):—Pass., μάκελλος ἐκ θεμελίων ὑψοῦτο *IG* 5(2).268.45 (Mantinea, i B.C.). II. metaph., *elevate, exalt*, opp. ταπεινόω, Lxx *Ex*.15.2, al., Plb.5.26.12, *Ev.Matt*.23.12, al.; πονοῦντα τὸν ἴδιον ὑψῶσαι βίον [Men.] ap.Clem.Al.*Strom*.5.14.120:—Pass., *to be exalted*, μὴ ὑψωθῇς τῇ καρδίᾳ Lxx *De*.8.14; τὰ χθαμαλὰ ὑψοῦται Plu.2.103e; ὑ. κάλλεϊ *AP*5.91 (Rufin.); ἐκ ποδὸς ὑψούμενοι, of suddenly *exalted* persons, Hp.*Praec*.7. 2. *represent in the 'grand manner'*, Longin.14.1. 3. Pass., Astron., of planets, *mount* to the north of the ecliptic, Theo Sm.p.135 H. 4. Pass., Astrol., of planets, *attain exaltation*, i.e. maximum apotelesmatic efficacy, Vett.Val.140.7.

**Ὑψώ**, όος, ἡ, a name for Hypsipyle, A.*Fr*.247.

**ὕψ-ωμα**, ατος, τό, *elevation, height*, οὐ χθὼν οὐρανίοις ὑψώμασι [φθονέει] Ps.-Phoc.73; ὕ. τοῦ ἀέρος Ph.2.408; τὸ ὕ. τῆς ῥινός the *bridge* of the nose, Gal.18(1).796, 806. 2. Astrol., *exaltation* of a heavenly body, opp. ταπείνωμα, Plu.2.149a, 782d, S.E.*M*.5.33, Ptol.*Tetr*.37. II. metaph., *exaltation*, Vett.Val.92.29. **-ωμᾰτικός**, ή, όν, dub. sens., ἀπὸ ὑ. ζῳδίου εἰς ὑψωτικόν Id.228.19. **-ώροφος**, ον, = ὑψόροφος, *Rev.Phil*.46.114 (Yazili Kaya). **-ωσις**, εως, ἡ, *a raising high*, τοῦ βραχίονος Gal.18(1).324, cf. 18(2).472. 2. *hill, eminence*, Str.7.5.10 (pl.). II. metaph., *exalting, glorifying*, αἱ ὑ. τοῦ Θεοῦ Lxx *Ps*.149.6. **-ωτής**, οῦ, ὁ, *one who exalts*, *PMag.Leid.V*.7.11 (pl.). **-ωτικός**, ή, όν, *containing the exaltation of a planet*, ζῴδιον Vett.Val.228.20.

⊛**ὕω** [ῡ in pres. exc. in Herod.7.46]: fut. ὕσω [ῡ] Cratin.121, Ar.*Nu*.1118, 1129 (both troch.): aor. ὗσα Pi.*O*.7.50, Hdt.2.22, Thphr.*CP*4.14.3, etc. (v. infr.):—Med., fut. (as Pass.) ὕσομαι Hdt.2.14:—**Pass.**, aor. ὕσθην Id.3.10: pf. part. ἐφ-υσμένος X.*Cyn*.9.5:—*rain*, ὗε Ζεύς Il. 12.25, Od.14.457, cf. Hes.*Op*.488, Thgn.26; κῆν ὕῃ [ῠ] Ζεύς Herod.7.46; ὗσον, ὗσον, ὦ φίλε Ζεῦ, κατὰ τῆς ἀρούρας Votum ap.M.Ant.5.7; [ὕει] ὁ θεὸς Hdt.2.13; τίς ὕει; Ar.*Nu*.368 (anap.), cf. 370 sq.; ὕσομεν πρώτοισιν ὑμῖν, of the clouds, ib.1118 (troch.):—but, 2. after Hom. ὕει was used impers. (cf. νείφω, etc.), *it rains*, Hes.*Op*.552, Hdt.2.22, 4.28; ὕσαι ὕδατι λαβροτάτῳ Id.1.87; εἰ ὗε *if it rained*, Id.4.185; ὕοντος *when it is raining*, Ar.*V*.774; ὕοντος πολλῷ *as it was raining* heavily, X.*HG*1.1.16 (where Eust. read πολλοῦ, 1769.39); πολὺ ὕσαντος *after it had rained* heavily, Thphr.*CP*4.14.3; ὕε, κύε, prayer addressed by hierophants to sky and earth, *BCH*20.79 (Athens, i A.D.), Procl. *in Ti*.3.176 D. 3. sts. c. acc. loci, ἑπτὰ ἐτέων οὐκ ὗε τὴν Θήρην *it did* not *rain on* Thera, Hdt.4.151; τὴν χώραν ὗεν ὁ θεός Paus.2.29.7; ὄμβρος ὗε πόντον καὶ νῆσον A.R.2.1115 (hence the pass. usage, v. infr. II.1.). 4. freq. c. acc. cogn., ὗσε χρυσόν *it rained* gold, Pi.*O*.7.50; καινὸν ἀεὶ τὸν Δία ὕειν ὕδωρ Ar.*Nu*.1280; ὗσεν ὁ θεὸς ἰχθύας, βατράχους, Phan.Hist.1, Heraclid.Lemb.3; ὕεις εὐσεβέσιν χύδην χρυσεόρρυτον ὄλβον *Supp.Epigr*.7.14.23 (Susa, Hymn to Apollo, i A.D.); νεφέλαι ὕουσι [μύρον] Luc.*VH*2.14: also c. dat. modi, ψακαζέτω δ' ἄρτοισιν, ὑέτω δ' ἔτνει Nicopho 13; ὕσαντα τὸν θεὸν ἰχθύσι Ath.8.333a. II. Pass., with fut. Med., *to be drenched with rain*, λέων ὑόμενος Od.6.131; ὕσθησαν αἱ Θῆβαι Thebes *was rained upon*, i.e. it rained there, Hdt.3.10; ὕεται ἡ χώρη Id.2.13, cf. 14,22,25; ἡ γῆ ὕεται ὀλίγῳ *it rains* little or seldom there, Id.1.193; σῖτος ὑσθείς Thphr.*HP*8.11.4; ὑόμενος μύρῳ Alex.62.8; ὄνος ὕεται he is like an ass in rain, prov. of an obstinate person, Cratin.52 (troch.); ἐγὼ δὲ τοῖς λόγοις ὄνος ὕομαι Cephisod.1. 2. sts., *fall down in rain, in a shower*, ὑσθῆναί φασιν χρυσόν Str.14.2.10; ὕδωρ ὑόμενον Plu.2.912a. (Cf. Skt. *sunóti* 'press out juice'.)

**ὑ-ώδης** [ῡ], ες, *swinish*, πάθος Plu.2.535f. **-ωδία**, ἡ, *swinishness*, Ath.3.96f. **-ών**, ῶνος, ὁ, *pig-pen*, *PCair.Zen*.468.2 (iii B.C.).

**ὑωνός**, ὁ, = υἱωνός, *PFlor*.71.235 (iv A.D.).

# Φ

**Φ φ, φεῖ** (q.v.), τό, indecl., twenty-first letter of the Ion. alphabet: as a numeral φ' = 500, but ,φ = 500,000.

**φᾶ**, Dor. for ἔφα, ἔφη, v. φημί. **φάανθεν, φαάνθη**, v. φαίνω.

⊛**φαάντερος**, α, ον, Ep. Comp. of φαεινός, *more brilliant*, *AP*9.210: Sup. **φαάντατος**, η, ον, *brightest*, ἀστήρ Od.13.93.

⊛**φάβα**, ατος, τό, (Lat. *faba*) *beans*, *Edict.Diocl*.1.9 (CIL iii p.2328[58]), 6.38, *Hippiatr*.7,104,129,130.134, *Gloss*.

**φάβα**· μέγας φόβος, Hsch.

**φᾰβατάριον**, τό, *tureen for lentil-soup*, *POxy*.1657.6 (iii A.D.).

**φᾰβάτινος**, η, ον, *made of beans*, from Lat. *faba*, ἄλευρον Alex.Trall.3.7.

**φᾰβο-κτόνος**, ὁ, (φάψ) *dove-killer*, Hsch. **-μελι**, v. φακόμελι. **-τύπος** [ῠ], ὁ, *dove-striker*, a kind of *hawk*, Arist.*HA*592$^b$2.

**φάγαινα** [φᾰ], ἡ, = ἡ μετὰ τὰς νόσους πολυφαγία, Ammon.*Diff*. p.136 V. II. = φαγέδαινα I. 1, Hsch.

**φᾰγάνθρωπος**, ον, = ἀνθρωποφάγος, Hsch., Phot.

**φᾰγᾶς**, ᾶ, ὁ, *glutton*, Cratin.451.

**φᾰγέδαιν-α**, ἡ, *cancerous sore, canker*, A.*Fr*.253, E.*Fr*.792, Hp.*Aër*.10, D.25.95, *IG*4$^2$(1).123.135 (Epid., iv B.C.), Gal.7.727. 2. a disease of bees, Colum.9.13.10. II. = **φάγαινα** I, Gal.19.419. **-ικός**, ή, όν, *of the nature of a cancer*, πάθη Plu.2.1087e; ἕλκη Dsc.2.78, 5.112, cf. Heliod.ap.Orib.46.22.3, Gal.6.750, 815. II. *of morbid hunger*, *Gloss*. **-όομαι**, Pass., *suffer from cancer*, Hp.*Epid*.4.19, 5.44: later in Act., Aq.*De*.7.23, dub. in Phld.*Sto.Herc*.339.20. **-ωμα**, ατος, τό, = φαγέδαινα I, Pall.*Febr*.7.

**φᾰγεῖν**, inf. of ἔφαγον, with no pres. in use (exc. in late Gr., φαγεῖ Anon. *in EN*448.16; φαγέοις in edd. of Ps.-Phoc.157 is v. dub.), used as aor. 2 of ἐσθίω; later 1 pl. ἐφάγαμεν Lxx 2*Ki*.19.42 cod. B, 3 pl. ἐφάγοσαν ib.*Ge*.18.8: later fut. is φάγομαι, ib.*Si*.36.23, *Ev.Luc*.14.15; 2 sg. φάγεσαι Lxx *Ru*.2.14, *Ev.Luc*.17.8; φάγῃ Lxx *Ge*.3.14; also φαγοῦμαι ib.2 (v.l.); fut. φαγήσω is v. dub. in Lib.*Or*.53.29:—*eat, devour*, both of men and beasts, freq. in Hom.; ἀζηχὲς φαγέμεν καὶ πιέμεν Od.18.3, cf. 15.378, Pl.*Lg*.831e; reversely, πιόντα ἢ φαγόντα Id.*Prt*.314a, cf. *Phd*.81b, E.*Cyc*.336 (dub. l.): mostly c. acc., Il.21.127, 24.411, etc.: c. gen., *eat of* a thing, Od.9.102, 15.373; ὄρνιθος ὄρνις πῶς ἂν ἁγνεύοι φαγών; A.*Supp*.226; ἀπό τινος Lxx *Ge*.2.16. II. *eat up, devour, squander*, Od.2.76, 4.33. (Cf. παματοφαγέω and Skt. *bhájati* 'apportion, (Med.) enjoy'.)

**φαγέσωρος**, ὁ, *glutton*, and γαστὴρ **φαγεσωρῖτις**, *Com.Adesp*.1183, 1184.

**φαγηλός**, v. φάγιλος.

**φάγ-ημα** [φᾰ], ατος, τό, *food, victuals*, Anon.ap.Suid., Demetr.Sceps.ap.Ath.3.91d, *PMag.Berol*.1.23. **-ήσια** (sc. ἱερά), τά, *an eating-festival*, and **φαγησιπόσια**, τά, *an eating and drinking festival*, Clearch.62.

**φάγῐλος**, ὁ, *a lamb*, either *when it begins to be eatable* or *to eat alone*, Arist.*Fr*.507; written **φαγηλός, φαναός** in Hsch., **φαυλλός** in Eust.1625.38.

**φαγλαός**· χειμαρρός, Hsch.

**φᾰγολοίδορος**, ὁ, *swallower of insults*, *Gloss*.

**φάγος** [ᾰ], ὁ, *glutton*, *Ev.Matt*.11.19, *Ev.Luc*.7.34, Zen.1.73.

**φάγρος**, ὁ, *sea-bream* or *braize*, *Pagrus vulgaris*, Hp.*Int*.1, Eup.38 (lyr.), Pl.Com.56.2, Antiph.193, Arist.*HA*598$^a$13, 601$^b$30, Speus. ap.Ath.7.327c, Numen.ib.322f, *BGU*1095.18 (i A.D.), Phylotim.ap. Gal.6.726, 12.800: written **φαγρώριος** in Str.17.2.4; **φάγωρος** in Hsch. II. Cret., *whetstone*, Simm.27.

**φάγυλοι**· μαστοί, μάρσιπποι, Hsch.; cf. **φαγύλιον**· μαρσίππιον, Phot.

**φάγων** [ᾰ], ωνος, ὁ, *glutton*, Varro ap.Non.p.69 L., Vopisc.*Aurel*. 50. II. **φαγών**, όνος, ἡ, *jaw*, Hsch. (pl.).

**φάγωρος**, v. φάγρος. **φαδάσαι**· γνάψαι, Hsch.

**φᾰεθοντ-ιάς**, άδος, ἡ, = sq., Opp.*C*.1.219. **-ίς**, ίδος, (φαέθων) *of Phaethon*, i.e. *the Sun*, φ. αἴγλη, μαρμαρυγή, *AP*9.782 (Paul. Sil.), *APl*.4.77 (Id.).

**φᾰέθω**, (φάω) *shine*, only in part. φαέθων (exc. 3 sg. φαέθει, Hsch.), *radiant*, epith. of the sun, Il.11.735, Od.5.479, 11.16, Hes.*Th*.760, S.*El*.824 (lyr.), E.*El*.464 (lyr.). 2. abs., *the sun*, *AP*5.273 (Paul. Sil.), 9.137 (Hadr.); πάννυχα καὶ φαέθοντα nights and *days*, S.*Aj*.929 (lyr.). b. of the moon, φαέθουσα καὶ αὐγάζουσα *PMag.Par*.1.2558. II. as pr. n., 1. **Φαέθων**, ὁ, one of the *light-bringing* steeds of Eos, Od.23.246. 2. son of Eos and Cephalus, Hes.*Th*.987. 3. son of Helios, famous for his unlucky driving of the sun-chariot, E.*Hipp*.739 (lyr.), Arist.*Mete*.345$^a$15; subject of play by E. b. the *Sun*, Doroth. in *Cat.Cod.Astr*.2.82, Nonn.*D*.5.81. c. the constellation *Auriga*, ib.1.357, 38.424. 4. the planet *Jupiter*, Arist.*Mu*.392$^a$24, Eudox.*Ars* 5.14, Cic.*ND*2.20.52.

⊛**φαεινός**, ή, όν (so always in Ep.), Aeol., Lyr., and Trag. (even in dialogue, E.*Ph*.84, al.) **φαεννός**, Att. **φᾱνός** (q.v.):—poet. Adj., *shining, radiant*, πῦρ Il.5.215; σελήνη 8.555; Ἠώς Od.4.188; ὄσσε Il.13.3; χαλκός 12.151; κασσίτερος 23.561; ὀρείχαλκος, χρυσός, Hes.*Sc*.122,142; κρητήρ Il.3.247, al.; δόρυ 4.496; ἀσπίς, σάκος, 3.357, 8.272; πήληξ 13.805; θώρηξ φαεινότερος πυρὸς αὐγῆς 18.610; ὅπλα E.*Andr*.1146; μάστιξ Il.10.500; θύραι Od.6.19; of *bright* colours, ζωστὴρ φοίνικι φαεινός Il.6.219, cf. 15.538; φ. πέπλος, τάπης, 5.315, 10.156; φ. πλόκαμοι *bright, glossy*, 14.176; εἶδος, of the stars, Sapph.3.2; ἄστρον Pi.*O*.1.6, cf. E.*Cyc*.353, al.; ἔρεβος ὦ φαεννότατον ὡς ἐμοί darkness *bright as the day* to me, S.*Aj*.395 (lyr.); of the Dawn, *AP*5.227 (Paul. Sil.). 2. of the voice, *clear, distinct, far-sounding*, Pi.*P*.4.283. 3. *splendid, brilliant*, ἀρεταί, θυσίαι, Id.*N*.7.51, *I*.5(4).30; κρηπὶς ἐλευθερίας Id.*Fr*.77.—Very rare in Prose, ἐν τοῖς φαεινοῖς χρόνοις, of *clear* nights, Aen.Tact.25.2; Φάεννος is pr. n. at Rhodes, *Chron.Lind*.B.34.

**φαείνω**, poet. form of φαίνω, *shine, give light*, freq. of the sun, ἠέλιος δ' ἀνόρουσε.., ἵν' ἀθανάτοισι φαείνοι Od.3.2, cf. Hes.*Op*.528, Call. in *PSI*11.1218a7; [ἠὼς] ἐπιχθονίοισι φ. Hes.*Th*.372; also ἐν νεκύεσσι, μετ' ἀθανάτοισι φ. Od.12.383,385; λαμπτῆρας τρεῖς ἵστασαν ἐν μεγάροισιν, ὄφρα φαείνοιεν 18.308; λαμπτῆρσι φαείνων *giving light* by.., ib.343:—Pass. in same sense, A.R.2.42; *appear*, ib.4.1362, Call.*Ap*.9. 2. metaph., λόγος περὶ τοῦδε φαείνει Orph.*Fr*.247.9. II. trans., *bring to light*, ὁπόσ' ἑρπετὰ γαῖα φαείνει Nic.*Th*.390.

**φαεννός**, v. φαεινός.

**φαέσασθαι**· ἰδεῖν, μαθεῖν, Hsch.

⊛**φᾰεσίμβροτος**, ον, *bringing light to mortals, shining on them*, ἠώς Il.24.785, B.12.128; Ἥλιος Od.10.138,191, Hes.*Th*.958; Ἀπόλλων *IG*14.2524 (Autun); Ἠριγένεια ib.3.1326; ὄργια.. φαεσίμβροτα Δηοῦς ib.2$^2$.3661 (Eleusis, ii/iii A.D.); once in Trag., θεοῦ φαεσίμβροτοι αὐγαί E.*Heracl*.750 (lyr.).

**φᾰεσφορ-έω**, *bring light*, of the moon, Nech.ap.Vett.Val.154.31. **-ία**, Ion. **-ίη**, ἡ, *bringing of light, illumination*, Call.*Dian*.11, Musae.302. **-ος** (parox.), ον, (φάος, φέρω) *light-bringing*, λαμπάδες A.*Ag*.489; Κύκλωπος ὄψις E.*Cyc*.462; ἐν μακρᾷ φλογὶ φαεσφόρῳ, i.e. after many days, Id.*Hel*.629 (lyr.), cf. Call.*Dian*.204; Ἠώς A.R.4.885; of Artemis, *IG*14.2524 (Autun). Cf. φωσφόρος.

**φάζαινα**, ἡ, a *disease* in horses, *Hippiatr*.130.119 (acc. sg. written φαζάναν cod. B, φαζάνην cod. M).

**φαζακηνίαις**· δειλαῖς, Hsch. (leg. φυζακιναῖς). **φαζάλη**, ἡ, a *disease* contracted in the Red Sea, Id.

**φάηκες**· ὀφθαλμοί, Hsch.

**φαθί** or **φάθι**, v. φημί.

**Φαίαξ**, ᾱκος, Ion. **Φαίηξ**, ηκος, ὁ, *Phaeacian*, Od.5.35, etc. II. pr. n. of an architect, who gave his name to *conduits* or *sewers* (**φαίακες** or **φαιακοί**), D.S.11.25.

**φαίδει**· ὄψει, Hsch.

⊛**φαιδῐμ-όεις**, εσσα, εν, = sq., Il.13.686. **-ος**, ον, also α, ον Pi.*P*.4.28, *N*.1.68 (not used by Hom. in fem.): (φαιδρός): *shining, radiant, glistening*, esp. of men's limbs, φ. ὦμος Od.11.128, Pi.*O*.1.27; γυῖα Il.6.27, Hes.*Th*.492; κόμα Pi.*N*.1.68; πρόσοψις Id.*P*.4.28 (s.v.l.); *sleek, glossy*, ἵπποι Id.*O*.6.14. 2. of heroes, *famous, glorious*, φαίδιμ' Ἀχιλλεῦ Il.9.434; φαίδιμ' Ὀδυσσεῦ Od.10.251; φαίδιμος Ἕκτωρ, Αἴας, Il.4.505, 5.617, etc.—Used by Trag. only in Ep. phrases, φαίδιμ' Ἀχιλλεῦ A.*Fr*.131 (anap., ap.Ar.*Ra*.992); ἀμφὶ φ. ὤμοις S.*Fr*.453; so φ. βραχίονες Achae.4.

**φαίδρα**, ἡ, = ἵππουρις, f.l. for ἐφέδρα in Ps.-Dsc.4.46.

**φαιδρο-είμων**, ον, gen. ονος, (εἷμα) *in bright attire*, Agath.5.15. **-νους**, ουν, *with bright, joyous mind, light-hearted*, A.*Ag*.1229 (s.v.l.).

**φαιδρ-όομαι**, Pass., *beam with joy*, X.*Cyr*.2.2.16. **-ός**, ά, όν, *bright*, *beaming*, φάος Pi.*Fr*.109; ἀλίου σέλας A.*Eu*.926 (lyr.); σελήνη Id.*Ag*.298; τράπεζαι Cratin.301 (troch.); κρατήρ Alex.119.1; of *sparkling* water, λευκῶν φαιδροτέρην λιβάδων (of a woman), *AP*7.218 (Antip. Sid.); ἀήρ Poll.9.20. **2.** metaph., *beaming with joy*, *bright*, *cheerful* (opp. στυγνός, X.*An*.2.6.11), φ. πρόσωπον Sol.42.3, S.*El*.1297, etc.; φ...ὄμμασι δέξασθε..βασιλέα A.*Ag*.520; φ. φρενὶ δέξασθαι Id.*Ch*.565; φ. κάρα S.*El*.1310; ὄμμα φ. ὡς εἶδον τέκνων E.*Med*.1043; φαιδροῖς ὠσίν, of a horse pricking his ears, Ar.*Pax*156 (anap.); of persons, *of glad countenance*, *cheerful*, X.*Cyr*.3.3.59, Gal.6.186, 16.615 (Comp.), etc.; φαιδρὸς λάμποντι μετώπῳ Ar.*Eq*.550 (anap.); ὄμμασι καὶ σχήμασι καὶ βαδίσματι φαιδρός X.*Ap*.27; κυνὲς ἀπὸ τῶν προσώπων φ. Id.*Cyn*.4.2; ἐπί τινι φ. *glad* at a thing, D.18.323. Adv. -δρῶς *joyously*, *cheerily*, φ. βιοτεύων X.*Cyr*.4.6.6, cf. 4.2.11; neut. pl. φαιδρά as Adv., φ. γοῦν ἀπ' ὀμμάτων σαίνει με *with happy smile*, S.*OC*319, cf. *Fr*.766 (anap.). **II.** masc. pr. n., properisp. Φαῖδρος: fem. Φαίδρα, Ion. Φαίδρη, parox. (Cf. Lith. *giẽdras* 'fair, clear (weather, sky)'.) **-ότης**, ητος, ἡ, *brightness*, *brilliance*, ὀφθαλμῶν Poll.6.199; λίθων Lib.*Or*.11.89, cf. 221. **2.** metaph., *joyousness*, Isoc.15.133, Plu.2.595d.

**φαιδρυν-τής**, οῦ, ὁ, *cleanser*, Poll.7.37. **II.** φαιδρυνταί, οἱ, descendants of Phidias, who had charge of the statue of Zeus at Elis, Paus.5.14.5, *Inscr.Olymp*.466.5, cf. *AB*314: written **φαιδυνταί** in Inscrr., *Sammelb*.2536 (Naucratis), *IG*2$^2$.1078.16, al., *IGRom*.4.1680. **-τικός**, ή, όν, *of* or *for cleaning*, Poll.7.37. **-τρια**, ἡ, fem. of φαιδρυντής, σπαργάνων φ. *washer* of baby-linen, A.*Ch*.759. **-ω**, Ep. impf. φαιδρύνεσκεν A.R.4.671:—*make bright*, *cleanse* (coupled with ἀποπλύνειν καὶ διαπλύνειν by Poll.7.40), τινὰ λουτροῖσι φ. A.*Ag*.1109 (lyr.); θεαὶ μορφὰν ἐφαίδρυναν *gave* me *a bright* form, says Helen, E.*Hel*.678 (lyr.); φ. χρόα Call.*Jov*.32; δέμας, εἵματα, A.R.3.1043, 4.671; στεφανοῦντα καὶ φαιδρύνοντα τὸν Ἑρμῆν καὶ τὴν Ἑκάτην Porph.*Abst*.2.16; χεῖρας *AP*5.227 (Paul. Sil.); τῇ γλώττῃ τὸ πρόσωπον Ael.*NA*3.21; [Ἥλιος] κοσμῶν καὶ φαιδρύνων Jul.*Or*.4.142a:—Med., λουτρῷ χρόα φαιδρύνεσθαι *to wash one's* skin *clean*, Hes.*Op*.753, cf. Mosch.2.31. **II.** metaph., *cheer*, A.*Ag*.1120:—Med., τὸν ἑαυτοῦ βίον φαιδρύνασθαι Pl.*Lg*.718b:—Pass., *beam* or *brighten up with joy*, X.*Cyr*.5.5.37; ἐπί τινι at a thing, Callistr.*Stat*.9; τὼ ὀφθαλμώ Poll.6.199. **III.** Pass., *become more glaring*, of a fever, ἀεὶ μᾶλλον ἐφαιδρύνετο Gal.14.653.

**φαιδρωπός**, όν, (ὤψ) *with bright*, *joyous look*, of a young lion (cf. χαροπός), A.*Ag*.725 (lyr.); ὄμμα φ. E.*Or*.894.

**φαιδυντής**, v. φαιδρυντής.

**φαίκανον**, τό, = πήγανον, Hsch.

**φαικ-άς**, άδος, ἡ, a kind of *shoe*, worn by Athenian gymnasiarchs, Egyptian priests, and others, *AP*6.254 (Myrin.). **-άσιον** [ᾰ], τό, = foreg., Eratosth.9, Wilcken *Chr*.20 iii 7 (ii A.D.), App.*BC*5.11, Plu.*Ant*.33, etc.

**φαίκλα**, ἡ, = Lat. *faecula*, *PHolm*.16.2 (φακλαν Pap.); cf. φέκλη, σφέκλη.

**φαικός**, ή, όν, = λαμπρός, S.*Fr*.1107. Adv. -κῶς Hsch.

**φαιλόνη**, ἡ, and **φελόνη**, ἡ, = sq., *Gloss*.

**φαιλόνης**, = φαινόλης, 2*Ep.Ti*.4.13 (wrongly expld. by γλωσσόκομον, εἰλητάριον μεμβράϊνον, Hsch.); written **φελόνης** in *PFay*.347 (ii A.D.), v.l. in 2*Ep.Ti*. l.c.:—Dim. **φαιλόνιον** *POxy*.933.30 (ii A.D.); written **φ[ε]λόνιον** in *PGen*.80.14 (iv A.D.).

**φαινίνδᾰ παίζειν**, to play *at ball*, Antiph.283, Juba 81, Ath.1.14f, Poll.9.105: written **φενίνδα** in *Com.Adesp*.711.

**φαινίς**, ίδος, ἡ, Laced. for ἀνεμώνη, Sosib.ap.Sch.Theoc.5.92.

**φαινόλη**, Dor. **-όλα**, ἡ, = Lat. *paenula*, *thick upper garment*, *cloak*, Rhinth.7, cf. **φαινόλα·** τὸ ὕφασμα, Hsch.; **φαίνουλα** *Edict.Diocl*.19.51 (Megalop.), **παίνουλα** ib.52, **πένουλα** ib.51 (Megar.):—but usu. **φαινόλης**, ου, ὁ, Arr.*Epict*.4.8.34, Ath.3.97e, Artem.2.3, Poll.7.61, *POxy*.736.4 (i A.D.).

**φαινόλις**, ἡ, (φαίνω) *light-bringing*, *light-giving*, ἠώς *h.Cer*.51, Mosch.4.121; αὔως Sapph.95.

**φαινομένως**, Adv., *apparently*, opp. ὡς ἀληθῶς, Procl. *in Prm*.p.499 S.; opp. ἀφανῶς, ib.p.618 S.; φ. καὶ εἰδωλικῶς Id. *in R*.1.77 K.

**φαινο-μηρίς**, ίδος, ἡ, *showing the thigh*, *with bare thigh*, Ibyc.61; cf. φανόμηρις. **-πους**, ποδος, ὁ, ἡ, *with shining feet*, Theognost.*Can*.12. **-προσωπέω**, *show one's face*, *put in an appearance*, coined by Cic.*Att*.7.21.1:—hence **-προσωπητέον**, *one must put in an appearance*, ib.14.22.2.

**φαινοῦκλον**, τό, Lat. *foeniculum*, = μάραθρον, *Et.Gud*. s. h. v.

**φαῖνοψ**, οπος, ὁ, ἡ, (ὤψ) *bright-eyed*, *conspicuous*, ἀέλιον *Hymn.Is*.31, cf. Man.4.239: in Il. only as pr.n.

⊛ **φαίνω**, Od.7.102, etc., Ep. also **φαείνω** (q.v.):—fut. φᾰνῶ, A.*Fr*.304.5, Ar.*Ach*.827, etc. (φᾱνῶ acc. to A.D.*Adv*.187.26, but φᾱνῶ, Ar.*Eq*.300, and ἀναφᾱνῶ, E.*Ba*.528, are dub.); Ion. φᾰνέω (ἀπο-) Hp.*Steril*.213, opt. φᾰνοίην S.*Aj*.313 (cod. rec., rightly): aor. 1 ἔφηνα Il.2.318, Hdt.1.95, etc.; Dor. ἔφᾱνα Pi.*I*.4(3).2, *IG*4$^2$(1).123.28 (Epid., iv B.C.), also later Att., subj., ἀπο-φάνῃ dub. l. in *IG*2$^2$.1631.379 (= 2.811*c* 133); φάνῃς Philem.233 (ἐκ-φάνῃς Men.*Mon*.418 = Chares Iamb.4*b*20); so in late Prose, (ἐξ-) Ael.*VH*12.33, (ἐπι-) *Ev.Luc*.1.79, (ἀνα-) *Act.Ap*.21.3; Ep. iter. φάνεσκε (intr.) Il.11.64, al., Hes.*Fr*.14.3: pf. πέφαγκα Ps.-Callisth.2.10, (ἀπο-) Din.1.15, al.: intr. pf. πέφηνα (v. infr. A III.2), Dor. 3 pl. ἐκ-πεφάναντι Sophr.83; plpf. ἐπεφήνειν D.C.46.10:—Med., fut. inf. φᾰνεῖσθαι Od.12.230, Ion. φᾰνέομαι Hdt.3.35; opt. φανοῖσθε Lys.26.10 (nisi leg. φανεῖσθε); the forms φανῆσθον and Dor. imper. φάνευ are corrupt in Pl.*Erx*.399e, Teles p.58 H. (leg. φαίνευ): aor. 1 ἐφηνάμην (trans.) S.*Ph*.944, (ἀπ-) Hdt.7.52, etc.:—Pass., Ion. impf. φαινέσκετο Od.13.194: fut. φᾰνήσομαι Hdt.8.108, Sicilian Dor. (inf.) φᾰνήσειν (fort. -ησεῖν) Archim.*Aren*.4.20; Ep. fut. πεφήσεται Il.17.155: aor. 1 ἐφάνθην A.*Pers*.263 (lyr.), S.*OT*525, etc.: rare in Prose, X.*HG*6.4.11, D.58.13, (ἀπο-) *IG*1$^2$.10.35, D.19.44; Ep. 3 sg. φαάνθη Il.17.650, 3 pl. φάανθεν 1.200: aor. 2 ἐφάνην [ᾰ], Ep. φάνην Il.1.477, etc.; Ep. 3 pl. φάνεν Od.18.68; Ep. subj. φανήῃ Il.19.375; Ep. inf. φανήμεναι 9.240: pf. πέφασμαι S.*OC*1543, 3 sg. πέφανται Il.2.122, 16.207, Pi.*P*.5.115, A.*Ag*.374 (lyr.); πέφᾰται in B.9.52, Perict.ap.Stob.4.28.19 belongs either to φαίνω in sense A. I.5, or to φημί; inf. πεφάνθαι Pl.*Euthd*.294a, etc.; part. πεφασμένος Il.14.127, Thgn.227, A.*Pr*.843, S.*OC*1122, Pl.*Phdr*.245e, etc.; 3 pl. plpf. ἐπέφαντο Hes.*Sc*.166.

**A.** Act., *bring to light*, *cause to appear*, in physical sense, τέρας τινὶ φ. *make* a sign *appear* to one, Il.2.324, cf. Od.3.173, etc.; σήματα φαίνων Il.2.353; γέννσι φ. ὀπώραν Pi.*N*.5.6; δύο μορφὰς φ. A.*Fr*.304.5; τὸν αὐχένα Hdt.2.132; ἔφην' ἄφαντον φῶς, i.e. fire, S.*Ph*.297; λαμπάδας Ar.*Ra*.1524 (anap.); φ. θησαυρόν E.*El*.565; φ. μηρούς, ἐπιγουνίδα, *show by baring*, i.e. *uncover*.., Od.18.67,74; φαίνοισα πρόσωπον ἀλάθεια Pi.*N*.5.17; *reflect* an image in water, τὰ δέ νιν καλὰ κύματα φαίνει Theoc.6.11:—Med., τὰ τόξα..τοῖσιν Ἀργείοισι φήνασθαι θέλει *exhibit* them *as his own*, S.*Ph*.944. **b.** *make known*, *reveal*, *disclose*, ἐς τὸ φῶς φανεῖ κακά Id.*OT*1229; κακῶν ἔκλυσιν E.*IT*898 (lyr., prob.); τὸν μιαρὸν τῷ χρόνῳ ἀποδόντες φῆναι Antipho 4.4.11; ὁδόν τινι Od.12.334; τὰ ὀνείρατα καὶ τὸν πόρον X.*An*.4.3.13, cf. *Cyr*.6.4.13, S.*OT*725; τοῖς πολεμίοις σύνθημα Din.3.10, etc.; φανεῖ..κωκύματα wailings *will show forth* [the truth of what I say], S.*Ant*.1078: with a predic. added, ἡμᾶς σὺ δειλοὺς φανεῖς wilt *make* us *appear*.., Id.*Aj*.1362; τὸν Λαΐου φόνον φανεῖ δικαίως ὀρθόν Id.*OT*853. **c.** γόνον Ἑλένῃ φ. *show* her a child, i.e. *grant* her to bear one, Od.4.12; φ. παρακοιτίν τινι *show* (i.e. *give*) one a wife, 15.26. **2.** of sound, *make* it *clear* to the ear, *make* it *ring clear*, ἀοιδὴν φαίνειν 8.499; σάλπιγξ..ὑπέρτονον γήρυμα φαινέτω στρατῷ A.*Eu*.569. **3.** *show forth*, *display* in action, ἀρετήν Od.8.237; ἀεικείας 20.309; βίην Hes.*Th*.689; εὐμαχανίαν Pi.*I*.4(3).2; εὔνοιαν Hdt.3.36; ὕβριν ib.127; ὀργάς A.*Ch*.326 (lyr.). **b.** *set forth*, *expound*, νοήματα Il.18.295; λόγον Hdt.1.116; τριφασίας λόγων ὁδούς Id.1.95; but τὰ λαμπρὰ..φ. ἔπη *make* them *good*, S.*OC*721. **4.** *inform against* one, *denounce*, φανῶ σε (σε φανῶ codd.) τοῖς πρυτάνεσι Ar.*Eq*.300 (lyr.), cf. *Ach*.824, S.*Ant*.325: *denounce* a thing *as contraband*, Ar.*Ach*.542,819, al.; φαίνειν πλοῖον D.58.9; τὰ φανθέντα articles *denounced* as contraband, ib.13: abs., *give information*, ὁ φήνας ἢ ὁ γραψάμενος *IG*1$^2$.45.3, cf. 4.24, Isoc.18.20, X.*Cyr*.1.2.14, Phld.*Rh*.2.207 S., etc. **5.** φαίνειν φρουράν, *call up* a levy, at Sparta, X.*HG*3.2.23, al.; also φ. θυσίαν *proclaim*, *order* a sacrifice, Philod.Scarph.112:—Pass., πέφαται θνατοῖσι νίκας ὕστερον εὐφροσύνα has been *ordained*, B.9.52. **II.** abs., *give light*, *shine*, φαίνοντες νύκτας..δαιτυμόνεσσι Od.7.102, cf. 19.25; of the sun, moon, etc., φ. τινί Ar.*Nu*.586 (troch.); εἰς ἅπαντα φ. τὸν οὐρανόν Pl.*Ti*.39b; ἀλλά, σελάνα, φαῖνε καλόν Theoc.2.11; οἱ λύχνοι φ. ἧττον Thphr.*Ign*.11; cf. φάω: so ἦρι μὲν φαίνοντι in spring *when it shines forth*, A.*Fr*.304.4 codd. (leg. φανέντι); of the Dioscuri *shining* in mid-air, E.*El*.1234 (anap.): metaph., ἀγανὴ φαίνουσ' ἐλπίς soft *shining* hope, A.*Ag*.101 (anap., dub.). **b.** Φαίνων, οντος, ὁ, the planet *Saturn*, Arist.*Mu*.392$^a$23, Cic.*ND*2.20.52, etc.; Φ. ὁ τοῦ Ἡλίου Eudox.*Ars* 5.19; acc. -ωνα *Placit*.2.15.4. **III.** Ep. iter. φάνεσκε *appeared*, μετὰ πρώτοισι φάνεσκε Il.11.64; ὑπένερθε δὲ γαῖα φάνεσκε Od.12.242, cf. 11.587, Hes.*Fr*.14.3. **2.** pf. 2 πέφηνα is also used intr., S.*OC*328, etc.; less freq. in Prose, Hdt.9.120, D.3.22, Plb.9.13.8.

**B.** Pass., *come to light*, *appear*, φάνεν δέ οἱ εὐρέες ὦμοι, being stripped bare, Od.18.68, cf. Il.22.324, Od.19.39: freq. of fire, *shine brightly*, πυρὰ φαίνετο Ἰλιόθι πρό Il.8.561; ἕκαθεν δέ τε φαίνεται αὐγή 2.456; δεινὼ δέ οἱ ὄσσε φάανθεν *shone like fire*, Il.1.200: freq. of the *rising* of heavenly bodies, ἄστρα φαεινὴν ἀμφὶ σελήνην φαίνετ' ἀριπρεπέα 8.556, cf. Hes.*Op*.598; of the first *gleam* of daybreak, ἦμος δ' ἠριγένεια φάνη ῥοδοδάκτυλος Ἠώς Il.1.477, Od.2.1, al.; ἅμ' ἠοῖ φαινομένηφι at *break* of day, Il.9.618, cf. Od.4.407, al.; ἀκτὶς ἀελίου, τὸ κάλλιστον..φανὲν..τῶν προτέρων φάος, ἐφάνθης ποτ' S.*Ant*.100 (lyr.): of a *rising* wind, οὐδέ ποτ' οὖροι πνείοντες φαίνονθ' ἁλιαέες Od.4.361; of a vapour, ἐκ νεφέων ἐρεβεννὴ φ. ἀήρ Il.5.864. **2.** of persons, οἴῳ φαινομένη *appearing* to him alone, Il.1.198, cf. Od.15.517, etc.; ἐφάνη λὶς εἰς ὁδόν Il.15.275; οὗπερ κἀφάνης where *thou didst first appear*, S.*OC*77; χρόνιος φανείς Id.*Ph*.1446 (anap.); ὁδὸν φανῆναι a pregnant expression for ἐλθεῖν ὁδὸν ὥστε φανῆναι, Id.*El*.1274 (lyr.); κέλευθον φανείς *Aj*.878 (lyr.); πόθεν φαίνῃ; whence *come you?* Pl.*Prt*.309a, X.*Mem*.2.8.1; οὐδαμοῦ φ. *is* nowhere *to be seen*, Id.*An*.1.10.16. **b.** *come into being*, φανεὶς δύστηνος *born* to misery, S.*OC*974, cf. 1225 (lyr.); *become*, ἐκ βασιλέως ἰδιώτην φανῆναι X.*An*.7.7.28; δυοῖν ἐφάνη τριήραρχος D.18.104; *to be made out*, δοῦλος λόγοισιν..φανείς S.*Aj*.1020, cf. 1241. **3.** of events, *come about*, τέλος οὔ πώ τι πέφανται Il.2.122; φάνη βιότοιο τελευτή 7.104; ἔργον, ἄεθλον, etc., 16.207, Od.21.106, etc.; τὸ φανθέν S.*Tr*.743; of sayings, *to be set forth*, λόγος ἀρχαῖος φανείς ib.1, cf. *OT*474 (lyr.), 848. **II.** *appear to be* so and so, c. inf., δμῳάων ἥ τίς τοι ἀρίστη φαίνεται εἶναι Od.15.25, cf. 11.336; οὐ γάρ σφιν ἐφαίνετο κέρδιον εἶναι 14.355; τοῦτό μοι θειότατον φαίνεται γενέσθαι Hdt.7.137; εὖ σὺ λέγειν φαίνει Ar.*Nu*.403 (anap.), cf. A.*Pr*.319, etc.: freq. with inf. omitted, οὐ καὶ πρόσθεν ἀρίστη φαίνετο βουλή Il.9.94, cf. 2.5; ὃς τις φαίνηται ἄριστος Od.14.106; σμερδαλέος αὐτῇσι φάνη 6.137; ἕρμαιον ἂν ἐφάνη Pl.*R.*368d, etc.: but in Hdt., etc., also c. part., *to be manifest*: thus, ἐμοὶ σὺ πλουτέειν μέγα φαίνεαι you *appear* to me to be very rich, Hdt.1.32; but εὔνοος ἐφαίνετο ἐών he was *manifestly* well-inclined, Id.7.173, cf. 175, Th.1.2; οὐκ ἄκαιρα φαίνεται λέγειν he *appears* to be speaking.., A.*Pr.*1036; but φανέονται λέγοντες οὐδέν it *will be manifest* that they talk nonsense, Hdt.3.35; φαίνομαι δύο καθορᾶν εἴδη Pl.*Sph.*235d; but οὐκ ἂν φανεῖμεν πῆματ' ἔρξαντες A.*Pers.*786; πλαγκτὸς οὖσ' ἐφαινόμην Id.*Ag.*593, cf. Hdt.9.89, E.*Andr.*343; ἐφάνησαν πεπονθότες Pl.*Ap.*22c: with part. omitted, πέφανται ἁρματηλάτας σοφός (sc. ὤν) Pi.*P.*5.115, cf. *N.*6.14; κρατηθεὶς ἡμερώτερος φανεῖ A.*Ag.*1632; Κᾶρες ἐφάνησαν (sc. ὄντες) *they were seen* to be Carians, Th.1.8; τί φαίνομαι (sc. ὤν) δῆτ'; what *do I look like?* E.*Ba.*925; ὡς ἀγαθοὶ.. ἐφάνησαν Pl.*R.*408a: hence φαίνεσθαι, opp. εἶναι, εἶναι μὲν ὅσπερ εἰμί, φαίνεσθαι δὲ μή E.*Fr.*698 (ap.Ar.*Ach.*441); στρατηγὸς ἀγαθὸς μὴ ὢν φαίνεσθαι X.*Mem.*1.7.3; ὀλίγοι καὶ ὄντες καὶ φαινόμενοι Id.*HG*6.5.28. 2. in Philosophy, φαίνομαι (abs.) is sts. used of what *appears* to the senses, φαίνεται δ' οὐδὲν *is observed*, Arist.*Ph.*204$^b$35, cf. *Cael.*312$^b$30; φ. κατὰ τὴν αἴσθησιν Id.*GA*716$^a$31: sts. of what *is* mentally *manifest*, Id.*EN*1175$^a$29; *to be evident*, Id.*APr.*24$^b$24: esp. *appear* to the imagination (cf. φαντασία 2), Pl.*Sph.*264b; φ. καὶ μύουσιν ὁράματα Arist.*de An.*428$^a$16; φ. δέ τι.. οἷον τὰ ἐν τοῖς ὕπνοις ib.$^a$7: distd. from αἰσθάνεσθαι and δοξάζειν, ib.$^b$1: esp. in part. φαινόμενος, η, ον: a. *appearing* in sense experience, τὰ φ. κατὰ τὴν αἴσθησιν Id.*Cael.*303$^a$22, al.; εἴτε τὰ δοκοῦντα πάντα ἐστὶν ἀληθῆ καὶ τὰ φ. Id.*Metaph.*1009$^a$8, cf. *de An.*404$^a$29 (sg.); τὰ φ. *sense-data*, Id.*PA*639$^b$8, Epicur.*Ep.*1pp.9,10 U., al.: Astron., τὰ φ. = celestial *phenomena*, title of a work by Eudoxus, versified by Aratus, Hipparch.1.1.8, cf. Arist.*Cael.*293$^b$27; πρός τινας δόξας αὑτῶν τὰ φ. προσέλκοντες ib.293$^a$26: generally, τὸ μὴ ἐκ φαινομένων τὸ βλεπόμενον γεγονέναι *Ep.Heb.*11.3. b. mentally *apparent*, opp. ὄντα τῇ ἀληθείᾳ, Pl.*R.*596e, cf. Arist.*Top.*100$^b$24, *EN*1113$^a$24; τὰ οὖν ἐμοὶ φαινόμενα οὕτω φαίνεται Pl.*R.*517b; [νοῦς] τῶν φ. θειότατον Arist.*Metaph.*1074$^b$16; τὸ φ. εἰπεῖν to express one's *opinion*, Plu.2.158c: hence, *specious, fallacious*, φ. ἐνθυμήματα, opp. ὄντα, Arist.*Rh.*1402$^a$28. c. τὰ φ. *what is to be seen, show*, Lib.*Or.*30.28. 3. freq. in answers in Plato's dialogue, φαίνεται, *yes*, *Prt.*332e, *R.*333c, al.; ὥς γέ μοι φ. *Prt.*324d, cf. *R.*383a, al.: [τοῦτο] φῂς εἶναι; Answ. φαίνομαι (sc. λέγειν) X.*Mem.*4.2.20. b. later impers. c. dat. pers. et inf., *it seems good*, ἐάν σοι φαίνηται Wilcken *Chr.*304.11 (iii B.C.), cf. *PCair.Zen.*44.7,16 (iii B.C.), etc.; ὁπότε αὐτῷ φανείη στρατιὰν ἐξάγειν D.H.2.14, cf. 4.85. 4. joined with δοκέω, εἰ δή κακός τε φ. δοκῶ τέ σοι E.*Hipp.*1071; δοκοῦμεν ἂν.. χείρους φαίνεσθαι Th.1.122, cf. Pl.*Phdr.*269d, *Erx.*399c, X.*Mem.*2.1.22. 5. οὐδαμοῦ φαίνεσθαι 'to be nowhere', metaph. from racing, Pl.*Phd.*72c, cf. *Grg.*456b, D.18.310. III. τὰ φανθέντα, v. supr. A. I. 4.

**Φαίνων**, ὁ, v. foreg. A II. b.

**φαινῶπις**, ιδος, ἡ, pecul. fem. of φαῖνοψ, Man.4.177.

**φαιός**, ά, όν, *grey*, of any colour mixed of black and white, Pl.*Ti.*68c, cf. Arist.*Cat.*12$^a$18, *Top.*106$^b$6, al.: opp. to both μέλας and λευκός, in a negative sense, Pl.*R.*585a; φ. ἄρτοι, opp. to λευκοί, Alex.120; τὸ ξανθὸν ἢ φ. Jul.*Or.*4.138d; of mourning, φ. ἱμάτια Plb.30.4.5; ἀποθέσθαι τὰ φ. Id.15.25.11; φ. ἐσθής *SIG*1219.5 (Gambreion, iii B.C.)), D.H.5.17, D.C.49.12, al.; ἰώδης καὶ φ. χολή (καλοῦσι δ' αὐτὴν ἰσατώδη) Gal.15.35; *dark-complexioned*, *P.Strassb.*79.2 (i B.C.). 2. of sound, *harsh*, Arist.*Top.*106$^b$7, *Aud.*802$^a$2, Poll.2.117, S.E.*M.*6.41. II. φαιά, ἡ, name of a plaster, Androm.ap.Gal.13.906, etc. (Cf. Lith. *gaĩsas* 'reflected light of a blazing fire'.)

**φαιουρός**, όν, (οὐρά) *sable-tailed*, Lyc.334.

❀ **φαιοχίτων** [ῐ], ωνος, ὁ, ἡ, *dark-robed*, A.*Ch.*1049 (where the second syll. is apparently long metri causa).

**φαιρίδδω**, Lacon. or Boeot. for σφαιρίζω, and **φαιρωτήρ** for σφαιρωτήρ, Hsch.

**φακαρίς**, ίδος, ἡ, prob. an error for φαλαρίς, *Gloss.*

**φᾰκᾶς**, ᾶ, ὁ, (φακός II. 2) a nickname of Dioscorides, Suid. s. v. Διοσκουρίδης.

**φακέα**, ἡ, v. φακῆ.

**φᾰκεινοπώλιον** (i.e. φακῖνο-), τό, *shop where lentil soup is sold*, *BGU*9 i 8 (iii A.D.).

**φάκελος** [ᾰ], ὁ, *bundle, faggot*, φρυγάνων, ῥάβδων, Hdt.4.62,67; ξύλων E.*Cyc.*242; δονάκων Opp.*H.*4.419 (σφακέλους codd.); ὕλης Th.2.77; οἱ φ. τῶν ῥάβδων, = Lat. *fasces*, D.C.53.1; also written φάκελλος Arist.*Metaph.*1016$^a$1 (but φάκελος codd. EJ and Alex.Aphr. and so all codd. in 1042$^b$17), Aen.Tact.33.1, D.H.7.11, J.*AJ*5.7.4 (v.l. φακέλους), Polyaen.7.6.9, but the form φάκελος is corroborated by Phld.*Rh.*1.74S., *Edict.Diocl.*32.26, and required by the metre in E. and Opp. ll. cc.; distd. from σφάκελος by Ptol.Asc.p.406H.; cf. κομποφακελορρήμων. II. = φακιόλιον, Phot., Suid.

**φακεψός**, ὁ, *one who boils lentil soup*, *PPetr.* cited in *PHib.*1.112.77 note (iii B.C.), *PPar.*67.16 (Ptol.), *PBouriant* 13.1 (i A.D.), *PLond.*3.944.2 (iii A.D.).

❀ **φακῆ**, ῆς, ἡ, contr. for φακέα, a form found in Epich.33, ridiculed by Euphro 3:—*dish of lentils* (φακοί), *lentil-soup*, Ar.*Eq.*1007, *V.*811, al., Diocl.*Fr.*141, *PHib.*1.112.77 (iii B.C.), etc.; in parodies of *Trag. Adesp.*89,92 ap.Ath.4.156f: prov. τοὐπὶ τῇ φ. μύρον 'pearls before swine', Sopat.14, Clearch.53, Cic.*Att.*1.19.2; title of Menippean satire by Varro; ὅταν φακῆν ἕψητε μὴ 'πιχεῖν μύρον Stratt.45.

**φάκηλος** [ᾰ], ὁ, *the middle finger*, *PLond.*1821.297.

**φακηψός**, ὁ, = φακεψός, *PSI*4.402 (iii B.C.).

**φακιάλιον** [ᾰλ], τό, (Lat. *faciale*) *face-cloth, turban, towel*, *Dura*[4] 100 (iii A.D.), *PTeb.*406.18 (iii A.D.), *Edict.Diocl.*26.99,114, 29.38, Lyd.*Mag.*1.32; also written -άριον, τό, *POxy.*114.7 (ii/iii A.D.), etc., and πακιάλιον, φακιόλιον (qq.v.).

**φᾰκῖνᾶς**, ᾶ, ὁ, *lentil-seller*, *BGU*9 iv 20, 1087 ii 13, v 15 (iii A.D.).

**φᾰκῖνοπώλιον**, v. φακεινοπώλιον.

**φάκῖνος** [ᾰ], η, ον, *made of lentils*, ἄρτος Sopat.1; φάκινον δεῖ ποιεῖν i.e. of the consistency of φακῆ, Zos.Alch.p.172B.

**φᾰκιόλιον**, τό, = φακιάλιον, Sch.Ar.*Pl.*729; written **φακιώλιον** *Stud.Pal.*20.245.23 (vi A.D.).

**φάκιολος**, f.l. for φάκελος D.H.10.16.

❀ **φάκιον** [ᾰ], τό, *decoction of lentils*, used as an emetic, Hp.*Morb.*2.43.

**φᾰκο-ειδής**, ές, *lentiform*, Arist.*Cael.*287$^a$20, Str.17.1.34, Dsc.4.139, Gal.10.448; esp. φ. χιτών, of the capsule of the lens of the eye, Ruf.*Onom.*153. II. φακοειδές, τό, = ἔμπετρον Dsc.4.179. **-μελι**, ιτος, τό, a *compound of lentils and honey*, as a desiccative application, Paul.Aeg.6.22 (v.l. φαβόμελι). **-πτῐσάνη** [σᾰ], ἡ, *a decoction of lentils and barley*, Gal.6.527,540. **-πώλιον**, τό, *lentil-shop*, *PTeb.*402.38 (ii A.D.).

**φᾰκός**, ὁ (φακόν, τό, Pap. in *Philol.*80.340 (s. v.l.)), *lentil*, *Ervum Lens*, and *its fruit*, Solon 38.3, Hdt 4.17, *IG*1$^2$.334.7, Thphr.*HP*8.1.4, Diocl.*Fr.*117, etc.; φακὸν ἕψειν Theoc.10.54; ἕψημα φακοῦ LXX *Ge.*25.34; ἀφέψημα φακοῦ Sor.1.121. b. pl. = φακῆ, *lentil-soup*, Pherecr.67.3, Amphis40, Gal.6.770, *Vict.Att.*7. 2. φ. ὁ ἐπὶ τῶν τελμάτων, *duckweed*, *Lemna minor*, Dsc.1.12, 4.87. II. *anything shaped like lentils*: 1. *hot-water bottle*, *POxy.*1088.46 (i A.D.); φ. ὀστράκινος Hp.*Nat.Mul.*34; πυρίῃ φακῶν τῶν κεραμήων Aret.*CA*2.5; φ. τοῦ ἐλαίου *oil-flask*, LXX 1 *Ki.*10.1; τοῦ ὕδατος ib.26.11. 2. *spot* on the body, *mole, birthmark*, *PPetr.*3 p.2, al. (iii B.C.), Dsc.1.13, 5.118, Plu.2.563a, 800e, Gal.11.845, etc. 3. *ornament on beds*, Theodor.Hierap.ap.Ath.10.413b. (Cf. Albanian *bathe* 'Vicia Faba'.)

**φάκ-οψις** [ᾰ], εως, ὁ, ἡ, *with moles* or *freckles on the face*, *Gloss.*

**φακουσιακός**, ή, όν, *from* Φακοῦσσαι (later Φακοῦσαι) in Egypt, ἀφρός Aglaïas 20 (i.e. νίτρον, which was called **φακούσιον** acc. to Sch. l. c.).

**φάκται**· ληνοί, σιπύαι, πύελοι, Hsch.

❀ **φακτωνάριον**, τό, perh. = *πακτωνάριον, Dim. of πάκτων, *PLond.*5.1904.6 (v/vi A.D.).

**φᾰκ-ώδης**, ες, *lentil-coloured*, Hp.*Epid.*3.14; of the kidneys, Ruf.*Anat.*51. 2. *freckled*, Diocl.*Fr.*179. **-ωσις**, εως, ἡ, *a being freckled*, Heph.Astr.1.1 (pl.). II. *discoloration* of the white of the eye, Gal.14.768. **-ωτός**, ή, όν, *lentil-shaped*, of hot-water bottles, Archig.ap.Aët.9.28, Orib.*Fr.*116; *provided with a lenticular terminal guard*, [ἐκκοπεύς] Gal.10.449; *provided with a lenticular screw-thread*, κοχλίας Hero *Mech.*2.5 (ii p.286 Schmidt).

**φάλα**· ἡ μικρὰ κάρα, Hsch.

**φᾰλαγγ-άρχης**, ου, ὁ, *commander of a* φαλαγγαρχία I, Arr.*Tact.*10.6, Ascl.*Tact.*2.10, Ael.*Tact.*9.8. II. *commander of a* φαλαγγαρχία II, Ascl.*Tact.*9, Ael.*Tact.*23. **-αρχία**, ἡ, *corps of* 4096 *men*, Ascl.*Tact.*2.10, Ael.*Tact.*9.8, Arr.*Tact.*10.6. II. *contingent of* 64 *elephants*, Ascl.*Tact.*9 (cf. Ael.*Tact.*23). **-ηδόν**, Adv. *in phalanxes*, Il.15.360, Plb.3.115.12, Polyaen.7.44.2, Onos.21.6. **-ιάω**, *to be venomous*, prob. l. in Hsch. for φαλαγγῶσα.

**φᾰλαγγιόδηκτος**, ον, *bitten by a venomous spider*, Dsc.4.52,115, Gal.14.180.

**φᾰλάγγιον**, τό, (φάλαγξ v) a kind of *venomous spider*, esp. *Lathrodectus* or *malmignatte*, Pl.*Euthd.*290a, X.*Mem.*1.3.12, Thphr.*HP*8.10.1, Diocl.*Fr.*145; distd. from ἀράχνιον, Arist.*HA*622$^b$28, cf. 555$^b$12. II. *spider-wort*, *Lloydia graeca*, a herb, said to cure this spider's bite, Dsc.3.108. III. *log* or *roller put under a ship*, Hsch., Eust.140.9, 469.20: written -εῖον, *EM*786.45.

**φᾰλαγγιόπληκτος**, ον, *stung by a venomous spider*, Gal.13.66.

**φᾰλαγγ-ίτης** [ῑ], ου, ὁ, *soldier in a phalanx*, Plb.4.12.12, D.S.18.2, D.H.4.18. II. = φαλάγγιον II, Gal.12.150:—also fem. **-ῖτις**, ιδος, ἡ, Dsc.3.108. **-ῑτικός**, ή, όν, *armed like the phalanx*, σπεῖρα Plb.18.28.10.

**φᾰλαγγο-μᾰχέω**, *fight in a phalanx*; generally, *fight in the ranks*, opp. ἱππομ-, πυργομ-, X.*Cyr.*6.4.18, cf. D.S.19.30. **-μάχης** [μᾰ] ἐλέφας *fighting in the* φάλαγξ, *AP*9.285 (Phil.).

**φαλαγγοστορύναι**· ὄργανα πολεμικά, Hsch.

**φᾰλαγγ-όω**, (φάλαγξ II. 2) *furnish with rollers*, Polyaen.5.2.6: τὰς προσαγωγὰς τοῖς μηχανήμασι Ph.*Bel.*98.5. **-ωμα**, ατος, τό, *roller*, Phryn.*PS*p.124B. II. *a Dionysiac procession*, Hsch. **-ωσις**, εως, ἡ, an eye-disease, *relaxation* or *fall of the eyelid*, Sever.ap.Aët.7.68, Paul.Aeg.6.8. 2. = διστιχία or τριστιχία *of the eyelashes*, Ps.-Gal.14.767,771.

**φᾰλαγκτήριον**, τό, *block of wood*, *SIG*57.33 (Milet., v B.C.).

**φάλαγξ** [φᾰ], αγγος, ἡ, (v. sub fin.) *line of battle, battle-array*, Hom. only in Il., once in sg., Τρώων ῥῆξε φάλαγγα Il.6.6: elsewh. pl. *the ranks of an army in battle*, Δαναοὶ ῥήξαντο φάλαγγας 11.90; φάλαγγες ἀνδρῶν 19.158, Hes.*Th.*935; τῶν κάτω Διὸς φαλάγγων S.*Inach.* (lyr.) in *PTeb.*692 iii 10. 2. *heavy infantry* (ὁπλῖται) *in battle-order*, X.*An.*1.8.17, al.; ἡ φ. τῶν ὁπλιτῶν ib.6.5.27, cf. D.9.49; opp. πελτασταί, X.*An.*6.5.25; opp. ἱππεῖς, Id.*Cyr.*6.3.2, *Ages.*2.9; τοὺς ἱππεῖς πρὸ τῆς φ. ἔστησαν D.S.20.10, cf. Plu.*Crass.*23; but οἱ Ἕλληνες ἱππεῖς ὥσπερ φ. ἐπὶ τεττάρων παρατεταγμένοι X.*HG*3.4.13: esp. *line of battle*, opp. κέρας (column in marching order), ἐπὶ φάλαγγος ἄγειν, opp. κατὰ κέρας or ἐπὶ κέρως ἄγειν, Id.*Cyr.*1.6.43; of ships, Id.*HG*6.2.30; ἐκ κέρατος εἰς φ.

καταστῆσαι to form from column into *line*, Id.*Cyr.*8.5.15; παρ' ἀσπίδα παραγαγόντας τὴν ἐνωμοτίαν ἐπὶ φάλαγγος Id.*An.*4.3.26; ἐπὶ φάλαγγος καθίστασθαι Id.*Cyr.*6.3.21, cf. *An.*6.5.7,25. b. *main body, centre*, opp. the wings (κέρατα), Id.*Cyr.*7.1.6, al. c. *camp*, εἴσω, ἔξω φάλαγγος, Id.*Ages.*2.15, *Lac.*12.3, cf. *Eq.*8.12. 3. esp. of the Macedonian *phalanx*, Plb.18.29sqq., etc. 4. in writers on Tactics: a. *corps of* 16384 ὁπλῖται, Ascl.*Tact.*2.7, Ael.*Tact.*8.3. b. *corps of* 8192 ψιλοί (= ἐπίταγμα, q.v.) Ascl.*Tact.*2.7, Arr.*Tact.*14.2. c. *contingent of* 64 *chariots* (= two κέρατα), Ascl.*Tact.*8, Ael.*Tact.*22.2. d. *contingent of* 64 *elephants*, ib.23. 5. metaph., λοπάδων παρατεταγμένη φ. Diph.44.3; of a *band* of pupils, Lib.*Ep.*145.1; of a governor's *staff* (Lat. *officium*), Id.*Or.*46.11. II. *round piece of wood, trunk, log*, φάλαγγες ἐβένου Hdt.3.97; ἐκ κοτίνοιο φ. A.R.2.843; φ. πύξιναι *IG*11(2).287*B*145 (Delos, iii B.C.). 2. pl., *rollers* for moving heavy loads, A.R.1.375sq., Orph.*A.*270: sg., Phryn.*PS*p.124B. 3. *arm of a balance*, Arist.*Mech.*849b36; *arm of the Danish steelyard*, ib.853b25. III. = φάραγξ, *BGU*282.18 (ii A.D.). IV. *bone between two joints* of the fingers and toes, Id.*HA*493b29; pl., Ruf.*Onom.*84 (but *metacarpals*, [Ruf.]*Oss.*22). 2. *row* of eyelashes, Paul.Aeg.6.8. V. = φαλάγγιον I, Ar.*V.*1509, *Ra.*1314 (lyr.), Pl.Com.22, X.*Mem.*3.11.6: masc. in Arist.*HA*609a5. (The orig. sense was prob. *log*, cf. *OHG balcho* 'beam', Lat. *sufflamen* (for *sub-flag-men*) 'brake'.)

**φάλαι·** ὅρα, σκόπει, Hsch.

**Φαλαίκειον** (sc. μέτρον), τό, metre *used by the poet Phalaecus*, Anon.Metr.*Oxy.*220 viii 8, Heph.10.3, etc.

**φάλαινα,** v. φάλλαινα.

**φᾰλάκρ-α,** ἡ, *bald bare hill*, St.Byz.:—hence freq. as a place-name. **-ιάω,** *to be baldheaded*, Suid. s.v. ἀωρόλειος.

**φᾰλακροειδής,** ές, *rather bald*, D.C.76.8.

**φᾰλακρ-όομαι,** Pass., *become bald*, Hdt.3.12, Arist.*HA*518b26, *GA*783b8:—later in Act., φαλακρώσουσι φαλακρώματα Lxx*Ez.*27.31 cod.A. ⊛**-ός,** ά, όν, (φαλός, ἄκρος) *baldheaded*, Anacr.68, Hdt.3.12, 4.23, Hp.*Aph.*6.34, Pl.*R.*495e, *Sammelb.*4637.16 (ii B.C.), etc.; prop. *bald on the crown*, Arist.*HA*518a27; φ. τὴν κεφαλήν Luc.*Luct.*16; πρόσωπον φαλακρόν E.*Cyc.*227; οἱ φαλακροί Ar.*Nu.*540 (lyr.), *Pax*767 (lyr.), etc.: prov. of labour in vain, φαλακρῷ κτένας δανείζειν Plu.*Prov.*26; φαλακρὸν τίλλειν Suid. 2. *like a bald head, blunt, knobbed*, φ. σιδήρια of cauterizing irons, Hp.*Art.*11; στρογγύλωσις ib.61; φαλακρότερος (v.l. -ώτερος) εὐδίας Sophr.108. 3. *bald spot*, ἔχειν φαλακρόν τινα Anon.*Incred.*17. II. ὁ φ. name of a fallacy, D.L.2.108. [φᾰλᾰκρός E.l.c., Ar.*Nu.*540.] **-ότης,** ητος, ἡ, *baldness on the crown*, opp. ἀναφαλαντίασις (in front), Arist.*HA*518a28. II. *smoothness*, φ. κεφαλῆς of a bone, Hp.*Mochl.*41. **-ωμα,** ατος, τό, *bald head*, used for *a bald man*, Cic.*Att.*14.2.3. II. *bald place*, Lxx*Le.*13.42, al.: pl., ib.*Ez.*27.31 cod. A. **-ωσις,** εως, ἡ, *a becoming bald, baldness*, Plu.2.652f (pl.), 919c, Aq., Sm.*Mi.*1.16, Alex.Aphr.*Pr.*1.2, Sor.ap.Gal.12.420 (pl.).

**φαλακτόνοιο·** εἶδος ἱέρακος, Hsch.; cf. φαβοκτόνος.

**φαλάμεσσιν,** written for παλάμαισιν in *MAMA*1.382 (Phrygia, iv/v A.D.).

**Φαλάνθειος,** ὁ, epith. of Hermes, *IG*2².4855.

**φαλάνθη·** ἐριουργός, Hsch.

**φάλανθος** [φᾰ], ον, *bald in front*, βρέγμα *AP*9.317, cf. D.L.7.160, Phryn.*PS*p.124B. cod.; neut. φάλανθον, τό, *bald patch*, οὐλὴ φαλάνθῳ δεξιῷ *PStrassb.*81.29 (ii B.C.).

**φᾰλαντ-ίας,** ου, ὁ, *bald man*, Luc.*Philops.*18. **-ωμα,** ατος, τό, *bald place*, v.l. in Lxx*Le.*13.43.

**φᾰλᾰρίς,** Ion. **φαληρίς,** ίδος, ἡ:—*coot, Fulica atra*, so called from its *bald white head*, Ar.*Ach.*875, *Av.*565 (anap., in Ion. form), Arist.*HA*593b16 (v.l. φαληρίς), *Fr.*350, Alex.Mynd.ap.Ath.9.395e; φαληρίδες ταριχηραί Cleomenes ap.eund.9.393c. II. *canary grass, Phalaris nodosa*, Dsc.3.142 (both forms in codd.); *phaleri* (sic), Plin.*HN*27.126.

**Φᾰλᾰρισμός,** ὁ, *tyranny, like that of Phalaris*, Cic.*Att.*7.12.2.

**φᾰλᾰρῖτις,** ιδος, ἡ, *furnished with* φάλαρα, name of Athena, Call.*Fr.*503.

**φάλᾰρον** [φᾰ], τό, (φάλος) *boss* or *disc*, mostly in pl., once in Hom., βάλλετο δ' αἰεὶ κὰπ φάλαρ' εὐποίηθ', of metal *bosses* on a helmet, Il.16.106; βασιλείου τιάρας φάλαρον πιφαύσκων A.*Pers.*662 (lyr.). II. pl., *cheek-pieces* of a horse's head-stall (expld. by παραγναθίδες Hsch., τὰ τῶν γνάθων σκεπάσματα Phot.), Hdt.1.215, E.*Supp.*586, X.*HG*4.1.39, Ptol.Euerg.9J.; but φάλαρα is a gloss in ἀμπυκτήρια φ. πώλων S.*OC*1069 (lyr.); cf. Lat. *phalerae*. 2. *bandages for the cheek*, Heliod.ap.Orib.48.44, Sor.*Fasc.*18. III. metaph., *ornaments*, Plu.2.528a, D.Chr.78.26.

**φάλᾰρος** [φᾰ], α, ον, (or **φαλᾰρός,** ά, όν Hsch.), Dor. for the Ion. φάληρος (v. infr. II), *having a patch of white*, ὁ κύων ὁ φάλαρος the dog *with a white spot*, Theoc.8.27; ὁ Φάλαρος, as a ram's name, Id.5.103. II. ὄρη χιόνεσσι φάληρα hills *patched* with snow, Nic.*Th.*461. (Cf. φαλός, φαλακρός.)

**φᾰλεροῦχος** (φάλαρον, cf. Lat. *phalera*), ὁ, *wearing* φάλαρα, epith. of the Sun, *PMag.Berol.*2.90.

**φᾰληριάω,** *to be patched with white*, κύματα φαληριόωντα waves *crested with white foam*, Il.13.799; φαληριῶσαν σπίλον *white with breakers*, Lyc.188; φ. στόρθυγξ *white with foam*, Id.491; λίθον λευκὰ φαληριόωντα *App.Anth.*3.79 (Posidipp.).

**φᾰλήριον,** τό, = φαλαρίς II, Ps.-Dsc.3.142.

**φᾰληρίς,** v. φαλᾰρίς.

**Φάληρον** [ᾰ], τό, *Phalerum*, the western harbour of Athens, Hdt.5.63, etc.: **Φαληροῖ** *at Ph.*, X.*Eq.Mag.*3.1, Plu.*Thes.*17; **Φαληρόθεν** *from Ph.*, Pl.*Smp.*172a; **Φαληρόνδε** *to Ph.*, Th.1.107:—**Φαληρεύς,** έως, ὁ, *a Phalerian*, Hdt.5.63, etc.; fem. **Φαληρίς,** ίδος, St.Byz.: Adj. **Φαληρικός,** ή, όν, Th.2.13, Ar.*Ach.*901, al.

**φάληρος,** v. φάλᾰρος.

**φᾰλῆς,** ῆτος, or **φάλης,** ητος (φάλεω Hippon.14 Diehl), ὁ, = φαλλός, S.*Ichn.*145 (pl.), Ar.*Lys.*771 (hex.), Theoc.*Epigr.*4.3. II. **Φᾰλῆς,** ῆτος, ὁ, *Phales*, Φ. ἑταῖρε Βακχίου Ar.*Ach.*263 (lyr.): also written Φάλης, ητος (which acc. to Sch.Ar. l. c. was the Dor. form), Sophr.39, Luc.*JTr.*42.

**φαλίζει·** θέλει, Hsch. **φαλικρόν·** ἄκρατον, Id. (cf. χαλ-). **φᾰλιόπους,** ὁ, ἡ, neut. πουν, gen. ποδος, *white-footed*, Id.

**φαλιός,** ά, όν, = φάλαρος, Call.*Fr.*176, *PPetr.*2 pp.115,117 (iii B.C.), Procop.*Goth.*1.18.

⊛**φαλίπτει·** μωραίνει, Hsch. **φαλίσσομαι,** (φαλός) Pass., *to be white*, Id. **φάλκη,** ἡ, *bat*, Id.; also = ὁ τῆς κόμης αὐχμός, Id.

**φάλκης,** ου, ὁ, part of a ship, *rib*, acc. to Poll.1.85,86 τὸ τῇ στείρᾳ προσηλούμενον. (Cf. ἐμφαλκόομαι.)

**φαλκίδιον,** τό, *the minimum share of an estate which must be left to the heirs under the Lex Falcidia*, *PMasp.*97v71 (vi A.D.), al.

**φαλλ-ᾰγωγεῖον,** τό, *platform* or *wagon used in the* φαλληφόρια, *IG*11(2).144*A*34, al. (Delos, iv B.C.). **-ᾰγώγια** (sc. ἱερά), τά, = φαλληφόρια, Corn.*ND*30. **-ᾰγωγία,** ἡ, *carrying of the phallus*, *IG*2².673*b*7.

⊛**φάλλαινα,** ἡ, *whale*, A.*Dict.* in *PSI*11.1209.9, Arist.*HA*489b4, 521b24, 537a31, al., Str.3.2.7, Ael.*NA*9.50, 16.18, Philostr.*VA*2.14, Nonn.*D.*6.298, Babr.39.1, Gal.6.728,737, *UP*3.12, al., Porph.*Abst.*3.20. 2. of *any devouring monster*, Ar.*V.*35,39, Lyc.841. II. *moth*, Nic.*Th.*760 (Rhodian in this sense acc. to Sch.).—In late codd. (as those of Gal.) freq. written φάλαινα; but cod.Rav. of Ar., and the best codd. of Arist., Str., Babr., Lyc., Nic., Philostr., and Nonn. (the Pap. of A.*Dict.* is indistinct) have φαλλ-; cf. sq.; the metre requires a long first syll. in Babr., Nic., Nonn., and admits it elsewhere; in Lat. the best spelling is *ballaena*.

**φάλλη,** ἡ, = foreg. I, Lyc.84,394. II. = foreg. II, Hsch.

**φαλλήν,** ῆνος, ὁ, (φαλλός) a name of Dionysus, Paus.10.19.3 (κεφαλῆνα codd., corr. Lobeck); cf. Φαλῆς:—Adj. **φαλληνός,** όν, φαλληνὸν τιμῶσι Διωνύσοιο κάρηνον Orac.ap.Eus.*PE*5.36 (s.v.l., φαληνοτιμῶσι cod.A, Φαλλῆνος τιμῶσι Lobeck).

**φαλληφορ-έω,** *carry a phallus in procession*, Plu.2.365c. **-ια,** τά, *festival* of Dionysus *in which a phallus was carried in procession*, ib.355e.

**φαλλικός,** ή, όν, *of* or *for the* φαλλός: τὸ φ. (sc. μέλος) *the phallic song*, Ar.*Ach.*261, Arist.*Po.*1449a11; restd. in *IG*1².187.33; also a dance, Poll.4.100.

**φαλλοβάτης** [ᾰ], ου, ὁ, (βαίνω) *one who mounts on a phallus-shaped pillar, phallic priest*, Luc.*Syr.D.*29.

**φαλλός,** ὁ, *membrum virile, phallus*, or *a figure thereof*, borne in procession in the cult of Dionysus as an emblem of the generative power in nature, *IG*1².45.13, Hdt.2.48,49, Ar.*Ach.*243, Luc.*Syr.D.*16.

**φαλλοφορ-έω,** = φαλληφορέω, Philomnest.2. **-ος** (parox.), ον, *bearing a phallus*, Semus 20; fem. in *AJA*37.252 (Latium, ii A.D.).

**φᾰλός,** ή, όν, *white*, Hsch. (Cf. Skt. *bhālam* 'brightness, forehead', Welsh *bal* 'having a white spot on the forehead', etc.) II. *stammering, deaf, stupid*, Id. (Cf. φαλίπτει and perh. Old Slav. *zŭlŭ* 'wicked', Skt. *hvárate* 'to be crooked', etc.)

**φάλος** [ᾰ], ὁ, *horn* of a helmet, Il.3.362, 4.459, 13.132,614, 16.216, 338; cf. ἀμφίφαλος, τρυφάλεια. (Expld. as a *boss* or *ornament* by Gramm., Apollon.*Lex.*, etc.)

**φαλύγματα·** ὑγράσματα, Hsch. **φαλύνει·** λαμπρύνει, Id.

**φάλυρα** [φᾰ], τά, = λάφυρα (q.v.), *SIG*56.9 (Argos, v B.C.).

**φαλύσσεται·** καταρρήσσει, περιέρχεται, Hsch. **φαλωθείς** (i.e. Dor. for φηλ-, unless φᾰλ-)· παρατραπείς, Id.

**φᾰλωτός,** ή, όν, *furnished with* φάλοι, περικεφαλαῖαι Eust.425.44.

**φάμα,** ἡ, Dor. for φήμη. **φαμάξαι·** φάσεις, Hsch.

**φᾰμίλ-ία,** ἡ, = Lat. *familia*, *BCH*14.370 (Caria), *Gp.*2.7.2; φ. μονομάχων *Inscr.Cos* 141.1, *IGRom.*4.1454 (Smyrna); στρατιωτῶν *BGU*316.10 (iv A.D.). **-ιαρικός,** ή, όν, = sq., *Edict.Diocl.*26.31; also **φαμελ-** ib.10, al.; **φαμηλ-** *MAMA*3.100 (Diocaesarea). **-ιάριος,** ὁ, = Lat. *familiaris*, *Edict.Diocl.*26.96,117, *PStrassb.*40.11,24 (vi A.D.); also **φαμελ-** *Edict.Diocl.*26.75, al. **-ιαρίς,** ίδος, ἡ, = fem. of foreg., ib.28.43,53.

⊛**φᾱμιστός,** ά, όν, Dor. for *φημιστός (which is not found), *famous*, *Bull.Soc.Arch.Alex.*7.245 (i B.C./i A.D.).

**φαμμάστρια·** τὰ ψαιστά, καὶ ἑορτή τις, Hsch. **φάμμη·** ἄλφιτα, Id.

**φάν,** poet. for ἔφασαν, v. φημί. **φάναι** [ᾰ], inf. of φημί; but **φᾶναι,** inf. aor. of φαίνω.

**φᾰναῖος,** α, ον, (φανή) *giving* or *bringing light*, of Zeus, E.*Rh.*355 (lyr.); of Apollo, in Chios, Achae.35.

**φάναξ,** = *lanterna*, prob. an error for φανός, *Gloss.*

**φανάός,** v. φάγιλος.

**φᾰνάπτης,** ου, ὁ, *lamplighter*, *Stud.Pal.*10.251*A*2 (vi A.D.), etc.

**φᾰνάριον,** τό, Dim. of φανός, Eust.1571.4, Sch.Opp.*H.*5.430.

**φᾰνάω,** = ⟨φαίνειν⟩ θέλω, Hsch.

**φανδόν,** Adv. *openly*, Hdn.Gr.1.509.

**φάνδουρος,** ὁ, = πανδούρα (q.v.), Nicom.*Harm.*4.

**φᾰνερο-μῑσής,** ές (v.l. -μῖσος, ον), *openly hating*, opp. φανερόφιλος,

Arist.*EN*1124$^{b}$26. **-ποιέω,** *explain, reveal,* Heph.Astr.3.37(*Cat.Cod.Astr.*5(3).85); τὰ πράγματα Sch.Ar.*Eq.*1253, *PLond.*5.1708.70, 1729.40 (vi A.D.). **-ποίησις,** εως, ἡ, *illustration, explanation, Gloss.*

⊛**φᾰνερός,** ά, όν, but ός, όν, E.*Ba.*991 (lyr.): (φαίνω):—*visible, manifest,* ἡ στήλη ἔχει πάντα φ., i.e. all that is in it can be plainly seen, Hdt.3.24; φ. ὄμμασιν ἐμοῖς E.*Ba.*501; φ. τι δεῖξαι S.*Tr.*608 (v.l.); θήσω φανέρ' ἀθρό' Pi.*O.*13.98; φ. ποιῆσαι Pl.*Lg.*630b, etc.; ἐς φ. ὄψιν βαίνειν E.*El.*1236 (anap.); τοὔργον παρέσται φ. S.*Ph.*1291; φ. χαρακτὴρ ἀρετᾶς E.*HF*658 (lyr.); φ. πηγαί Th.2.15; ἐσβολαὶ ἐς Αἴγυπτον Hdt.3.5; φ. ἔχθραν κτήσασθαι Th.1.42; διαφορὰ φ. ἐγένετο ib.102; φ. θάνατος, ὄλεθρος, opp. ἀφανής, Antipho 3.3.7, And.1.53; φ. ὑποψία εἰς ἐμὲ ἰοῦσα Antipho 2.2.6; φ. γενόμενος *if detected,* Lys.7.12:—Constr.: φανερός εἰμι c. part., ἀπικόμενοι φανεροί εἰσι they are *known* to have come, Hdt.3.26; ἐπισπεύδων φανερὸς ἦν Id.7.18; ὁ μέν ἐστι φ. ἐκβὰς ἐκ τοῦ πλοίου καὶ οὐκ εἰσβὰς πάλιν Antipho 5.23: folld. by Conj., φανεροὶ γιγνόμενοι ὅτι ποιοῦσιν X.*Cyr.*2.2.12; φ. ἦν ὅπως ἐγίγνωσκεν Id.*Mem.*1.1.17: impers., φανερόν [ἐστιν] ὅτι.. ib.3.9.2; εἰ φανερὸν γίγνοιτο ὅτι.. Pl.*Phd.*70d. 2. *shining, illustrious,* προεδρίη Xenoph.2.7; ὁδός Pi.*O.*6.73; *conspicuous, remarkable,* φ. μηδὲν κατεργάζεσθαι Th.1.17. 3. φ. οὐσία *real* property, opp. personalty (ἀφανής), Lys.32.4, *Fr.*79, D.50.8. b. property *in possession* (opp. *in action*), And.1.118, Is.6.30, D.38.7. c. *in hand, in cash,* μηδὲν φανερὸν κεκτῆσθαι to have no *cash in hand,* Din.1.70; λαβὼν ἀργύριον φ. καὶ ὁμολογούμενον D.56.1; πόρος φ. Id.14.24; φ. οὐσία Id.27.57; φ. χρήματα Lys.12.83; φ. ποιεῖν D.28.4; φανερόν τι *a certain sum of money,* Sch.Ar.*Pl.*330, Sch.Aeschin.1.102. 4. of votes, φ. ψήφῳ by *open* vote, opp. κρύβδην (ballot), D.43.82, cf. Arist.*Ath.*68.2; ψῆφον φ. διενεγκεῖν Th.4.74; τὴν ψῆφον φ. φέρειν Pl.*Lg.*767d; φ. ἡ ψῆφος τιθεμένη ib.855d. 5. Adv. -ρῶς *openly, manifestly,* βουλόμενος φ. Hdt.9.71; στείχειν A.*Pr.*1090 (anap.); οἴχεσθαι S.*El.*833 (lyr.); ἀκοῦσαι Ar.*Nu.*291 (anap.); ἀποδείκνυσθαι τὴν γνώμην Th.1.87; φ. ἐρᾶν, opp. λάθρᾳ, Pl.*Smp.*182d; τὸ φ. ἐξεῖναι Isoc.2.3: Comp., φανερώτερον ἐκπολεμεῖν Th.6.91; -τέρως Arist.*PA* 657$^{a}$2: but, b. τὸ φ. freq. with Preps. in advb. sense, ἐκ τοῦ φ. *openly,* Hdt.5.96, 8.126; πολέμιος οὐκ ὢν ἐκ τοῦ φ. not *openly declared,* Th.4.79; ἐκ τοῦ φ. τὴν μάχην ποιεῖσθαι X.*HG*6.5.16; ἐκ τοῦ φ. ἀποφεύγειν Id.*Mem.*3.11.8; ἀπὸ τοῦ φ. D.H.4.4; also ἐν τῷ φ. σαυτὸν παρεῖχες X.*Cyr.*7.5.55; ἀκοῦσαι ἐν τῷ φ. Id.*An.*1.3.21; βουλεύεσθαι D.18.235 (rarely ἐν φ. X.*Ages.*5.7); ἐς τὸ φ. ἀποδῦναι Th.1.6; αἱ ἐς τὸ φ. λεγόμεναι αἰτίαι, Id.1.23; τὸν σῖτον φέρειν ἐς τὸ φ. into *public,* Id.3.27, cf. Pl.*Grg.*480c, etc.; εἰπεῖν κατὰ τὸ φ. Ar.*Th.*525 (lyr.); ἐπὶ φανεροῖς ξυνελθεῖν on *public, acknowledged* terms, Th.1.69. II. of persons, *manifest, conspicuous,* εἰ [Διόνυσος καὶ Πὰν] φ. ἐγένοντο ἐν τῇ Ἑλλάδι Hdt.2.146; φανερὰ.. ἦλθε κόρα S.*OT*507 (lyr.); Κύπρις.. φανερὰ τῶνδ' ἐφάνη πράκτωρ Id.*Tr.*861 (lyr.); πάντων -ώτατος Βρασίδας ἐγένετο Th.4.11, cf. X.*Cyr.*7.5.58; οἱ -ώτεροι *persons of distinction,* Philostr.*VA*2.20. 2. *open, frank,* opp. ἐπίβουλος, Arist.*EN*1149$^{b}$15. III. = τις, φ. χρέα *certain* debts, Mitteis *Chr.*71.3 (v A.D.), cf. *PMasp.*167.10, 194.5 (vi A.D.), etc.

**φᾰνερότης,** ητος, ἡ, *display, show,* Ph.ap.Eus.*PE*8.14.

**φᾰνερόφῐλος,** ον, *open friend,* opp. φανερομισής, Arist.*EN*1124$^{b}$27.

**φᾰνερ-όω,** *make manifest,* σεαυτὸν τῷ κόσμῳ *Ev.Jo.*7.4, cf. 2.11, 2*Ep.Cor.*5.10 (Pass.); *reveal, make clear,* τινὶ τὴν ἀλήθειαν *POxy.*925.4 (v A.D.); ἀληθῆ πεφανέρωται *have been demonstrated,* Olymp. Alch.p.88 B. II. *make known* or *famous,* D.H.10.37:—Pass., *become so,* ἐφανερώθη ἐς τοὺς Ἕλληνας δαπάνῃσι μεγίστῃσι Hdt.6.122. **-ωσις,** εως, ἡ, = σημασία I, Hsch. (φ. διὰ σάλπιγγος Phot., Suid.). 2. *disclosure,* ἡ ἀπὸ τοῦ οἴνου φ. τοῦ λογισμοῦ Anon.*Incred.*17. II. *manifestation,* τοῦ πνεύματος 1*Ep.Cor.*12.7, cf. 2*Ep.Cor.*4.2. 2. Astron., *becoming visible,* Jul.Laod. (?) in *Cat.Cod.Astr.*5(1).189 (pl.). **-ωτής,** οῦ, ὁ, *one who makes manifest,* τῶν ἀποκεκρυμμένων *PMag.Leid.V.*7.12 (pl.).

**φᾰνή,** ἡ, *torch,* Hes.*Fr.*47. II. φαναί, αἱ, *torch-processions,* such as took place in the cult of Dionysus, E.*Ion* 550 (troch.); μυστηρίων τε τῶν ἀπορρήτων φανὰς ἔδειξεν Ὀρφεύς Id.*Rh.*943.

**φᾰνήῃ,** Ep. for φανῇ: **φανήμεναι,** Ep. for φανῆναι; v. φαίνω.

**Φάνης** [ᾰ], ητος, ὁ, a divinity in the Orphic system, representing the first principle of life, Φάνητα.., πρῶτος γὰρ ἐφάνθη Orph.*A.*15.

**φᾰνητι-ασμός,** ὁ, *love of show and ostentation,* Eust.894.8, 904.62.

**φᾱνίον,** τό, Dim. of φανός, *AP*12.82,83 (Mel.). 2. name of several *eye-salves,* Gal.12.755. II. **Φανίον** (or **Φάνιον**), name of a courtesan, Men.ap.Ath.13.567c.

**φᾰνοίην, φάνοισθε,** fut. opt. Act. and Med. of φαίνω.

**φανόμηρις,** ιδος, ἡ, = φαινομηρίς, Poll.2.187.

**φᾰνόπτης,** ου, ὁ, *opening for light, window,* Sch.Lyc.98. II. gloss on ξυνοικία, Sch.Ar.*Eq.*997.

⊛**φᾱνός,** ή, όν, (contr. fr. φαεινός) *light, bright,* Parm.8.41, Phryn. Com.93; ἅμα φανοτάτῳ τινὶ πυρί Pl.*Phlb.*16c; ἵνα ὡς φανότατον ᾖ τὸ ἔσω X.*Cyn.*10.7; τὸ φ. *brightness, light,* ib.5.18; στρέφειν πρὸς τὸ φ. ἐκ τοῦ σκοτώδους Pl.*R.*518c, cf. 478c (Comp.); φανά τε καὶ καλά ib.506d, cf. Phld.*Po.*2.45; φανότατος ἀήρ Gal.18(2).285; τοῖς φανοτάτοις θεῶν Ἡλίῳ καὶ Σελήνῃ Hld.10.4. 2. of garments, *washed clean,* χλαῖνα Ar.*Ach.*845 (lyr.); σισύρα Id.*Ec.*347. 3. *bright, joyous,* φαναῖς ἐν εὐφροσύναις A.*Pr.*538 (lyr.); φ. βίον διάγειν Pl.*Phdr.*256d. 4. *conspicuous,* ἐλλόγιμος καὶ φ. Id.*Smp.*197a. 5. Adv. -νῶς *clearly*: Comp. φανότερον Jul.*Or.*4.145b; Sup. φανότατα, Luc. *Hist.Conscr.*44. II. Φᾶνος, ὁ (properisp., cf. Hdn.Gr.1.175), name of a συκοφάντης, Ar.*Eq.*1256.

**φᾱνός,** ὁ, *torch,* Ar.*Lys.*308; ὑπὸ φανοῦ πορεύεσθαι X.*Lac.*5.7; ποῖος φ. τοιοῦτος οἷος ὁ ἥλιος; Alex.87; distd. from **λύχνος,** Anaxandr.48, cf. Phryn.40; but prob. = λύχνος in *UPZ*5.18, 6.15 (ii B.C.), *Stud.Pal.*10.251.2 (vi A.D.); μετὰ φανῶν καὶ λαμπάδων *Ev.Jo.*18.3, cf. *PLond.*3.1159.59 (ii A.D.): the form **πᾱνός** (prob. a different word) is found in A.*Ag.*284, S.*Fr.*184, E.*Ion* 195 (lyr.), *Fr.*90, Diph.6, Men.62. II. φ. ὑελοῦς glass *cover,* Olymp.Alch.p.75 B. 2. a form of *still,* Zos.Alch.p.224 B.

**φᾱνότης,** ητος, ἡ, *brightness, clearness,* Aristid.*Or.*43(1).24, Gal. *UP*10.1, Iamb.*Comm.Math.*34: metaph. in pl. of words, αἱ φ. τῶν ὀνομάτων Phld.*Po.*2.45. 2. *visible appearance,* ἡ γνῶσις φ. [τοῦ γιγνωσκομένου] Dam.*Pr.*6.

**φάνσις,** εως, ἡ, = φάσις (A) II.1, Porph.ap.Eus.*PE*3.4, Suid. s.v. ἐπιτολῆς. II. *morning twilight, Gloss.*

**φαντάζω,** (φαίνω) *make visible, present to the eye* or *mind,* τι Alex.Aphr.*Pr.*2.18, Hsch.: but, φ. τὴν αἴσθησιν, *deceive,* Callistr. *Stat.*14:—Med., with aor. Pass., *place before one's mind, picture* an object *to oneself, imagine,* τι Longin.15.2,8, M.Ant.10.28, Porph. *Sent.*33, Iamb.*Myst.*3.20, Chor.p.16 B.; χωρίον Id.*Milt.*29 F.-R.; κύνα ἐν ὕδατι Hp.*Ep.*19 (*Hermes* 43.68); περί τῆς φύσεως Him.*Or.*14.24; *fancy, imagine,* ὅτι.. Arr.*Epict.*1.5.6; ὄναρ ἐφαντάσθην Hp.*Ep.*15; τοῖς μηδὲ φαντασθεῖσιν ὡς καλόν.. Plot.1.6.4; c. acc. et. inf., Polem. *Phgn.*36, Iamb.*Myst.*2.10. II. in early writers only in Pass., fut. φαντασθήσομαι Pl.*Smp.*211a: aor. ἐφαντάσθην Id.*Phil.*51a:—*become visible, appear,* σφι Hdt.4.124; ὄνειρον φαντάζεταί μοι Id.7.15; μηδὲ φαντάζου δόμων πάροιθε E.*Andr.*876, cf. *Ph.*93; φ. ἄλλοτε ἐν ἄλλαις ἰδέαις Pl.*R.*380d; also, *to be heard,* μυκαὶ σηκοῖς ἔνι φ. A.R.4.1285; φοβερὸν ἦν τὸ -όμενον *Ep.Hebr.*12.21. b. *to be terrified by visions* or *phantasms,* *PMag.Lond.*121.888. 2. *make a show,* Hdt.7.10.ε'. 3. φαντάζεσθαί τινι *make oneself like* some one, *take his form,* φανταζόμενος.. γυναικί A.*Ag.*1500 (anap.). 4. *appear* so and so, *to be imagined,* Pl.*Hp.Ma.*300c; ἡδοναὶ φαντασθεῖσαι Id. *Phil.*51a; τῷ νοηθῆναι ἢ φαντασθῆναι Arist.*de An.*433$^{b}$12. 5. com. for συκοφαντεῖσθαι, *to be informed against,* Ar.*Ach.*823 (Megar. φαντάδδομαι).

**φαντᾰσί-α,** ἡ, verbal noun of φαντάζομαι and (in sense) of φαίνομαι, *appearing, appearance,* = τὸ φαίνεσθαι, πάντες ἐφίενται τοῦ φαινομένου ἀγαθοῦ, τῆς δὲ φ. οὐ κύριοι do not control the *appearing.* Arist *EN* 1114$^{a}$32; usu. with less verbal force, *appearance, presentation* to consciousness, whether immediate or in memory, whether true or illusory, φαίνεται μὲν ὁ ἥλιος ποδιαῖος, ἀντίφησι δὲ πολλάκις ἕτερόν τι πρὸς τὴν φ. Id.*Insomn.*460$^{b}$19; ἡ τοῦ γάλακτος φ. the *appearance* of the milky way, Id.*Mete.*339$^{a}$35; ἡ τοῦ προσώπου φ. Phld.*Acad.Ind.* p.50 M.; esp. of visual *images,* ἐπεὶ ἡ ὄψις μάλιστα αἴσθησίς ἐστι, καὶ τὸ ὄνομα ἀπὸ τοῦ φάους εἴληφεν [ἡ φ.] Arist.*de An.*429$^{a}$2; κατοπτρικὴ φ. *image* reflected in a mirror, *Placit.*3.1.2; also of other sense-perceptions, φ. καὶ αἴσθησις ταὐτὸν ἔν τε θερμοῖς καὶ πᾶσι τοῖς τοιούτοις *appearance* is the same as perception, whether we are talking of hot things or of anything else like them, Pl.*Tht.*152c, cf. Chrysipp.*Stoic.*2.21; ταῦτα ἔστι μέν τι, ἀλλ' οὐχ ὧν ἐμποιεῖ τὴν φ. Arist.*Metaph.*1024$^{b}$24; ἡ φ. ἐστὶν αἴσθησίς τις ἀσθενής.. κἂν τῷ ἐλπίζοντι ἀκολουθοῖ ἂν φ. τις οὗ ἐλπίζει Id.*Rh.*1370$^{a}$28; αἱ [αἰσθήσεις] ἀληθεῖς ἀεί, αἱ δὲ φ. γίνονται αἱ πλείους ψευδεῖς Id.*de An.*428$^{a}$12; φ. ἀληθεῖς ἁπάσας Epicur.*Fr.*254; ἀπελθόντων τῶν αἰσθητῶν ἔνεισιν αἱ αἰσθήσεις καὶ φ. ἐν τοῖς αἰσθητηρίοις Arist.*de An.*425$^{b}$25; διὰ τὸ ἐμμένειν [τὰς φ.] καὶ ὁμοίας εἶναι ταῖς αἰσθήσεσι ib.429$^{a}$5; τῆς αἰσθήσεως ἀλλοιουμένης ἐξ ἧς γίνεσθαι τὴν φ. Thphr.*Sens.*63; ἐλέγχειν τὰς ἀλλήλων φ. καὶ δόξας Pl.*Tht.*161e; freq. in later Philos. esp. in meaning psychic *image,* Epicur.*Ep.*1 p.12 U., S.E.*M.*7.152, M.Ant.4.24, al.; defined as τύπωσις ἐν ψυχῇ Chrysipp.*Stoic.*2.23; φ. καταληπτική Zeno *Stoic.*1.17, etc.; [φ. κ.] ἣν κριτήριον εἶναι τῶν πραγμάτων φασί, τὴν γιγνομένην ἀπὸ ὑπάρχοντος κατ' αὐτὸ τὸ ὑπάρχον ἐναπεσφραγισμένην *Stoic.*2.21, cf. 26, al.; διανοητικαὶ φ. mental *images,* Cic.*Fam.*15.16.1; νυκτεριναὶ φ. Phlp. *in de An.*486.13, cf. *Gp.*12.17.15; *apparition,* Arist.*Mir.*846$^{a}$37. b. less scientifically, *appearance,* ἐμποιοῦντα τὴν φ. (sc. τοῦ ἐλέγχειν) Id.*SE* 165$^{b}$25; τὸ παράδοξον τῆς τῶν ζῴων φ. Plb. 3.53.8, cf. 5.48.9, App.*BC*4.102, *Hann.*15; κατὰ τὴν πρώτην φ. Plb.11.27.7; συναύξειν τὴν φ. [τῆς νίκης] Id.16.8.3; δουλεύοντες τῇ τῶν ἐκτὸς φ. Id.30.19.4; φ. ποιεῖν καὶ προσδοκίαν Id.18.10.7, cf. 14.2.4; ζῷα.. μέχρι φ. φαινόμενα (in a conjuring trick) Cels.ap.Orig.*Cels.*1.68; κατὰ τὴν πρόχειρον οὑτωσὶ φ. Gal.6.105, cf. 15.17,115, 19.206; τῶν ἀπεπτούντων ἐνίοις φ.. γίνονται Id.18(2).73, cf. 71, al. 2. *imagination,* i.e. the *re-presentation* of appearances or images, primarily derived from sensation (cf. αἴσθησις II), ὅταν μὴ καθ' αὑτὸ ἀλλὰ δι' αἰσθήσεως παρῇ τινι τὸ τοιοῦτον αὖ πάθος (sc. δόξα) ἆρ' οἷόν τε ὀρθῶς εἰπεῖν ἕτερόν τι πλὴν φ.;.. "φαίνεται" δὲ ὃ λέγομεν (i.e. φαντασία) σύμμειξις αἰσθήσεως καὶ δόξης Pl.*Sph.*264a,b; οὐδὲ δόξα μετ' αἰσθήσεως οὐδὲ δι' αἰσθήσεως οὐδὲ συμπλοκὴ δόξης καὶ αἰσθήσεως φ. ἂν εἴη Arist.*de An.*428$^{a}$26; ἡ φ. καθ' ἣν λέγομεν φάντασμά τι ἡμῖν γίγνεσθαι ib.428$^{a}$1; ἔστι δὲ φ. ἡ ὑπὸ τῆς κατ' ἐνέργειαν αἰσθήσεως γινομένη κίνησις Id. *Insomn.*459$^{a}$17, cf. *de An.*429$^{a}$1; εἰ ἔστι καὶ τοῦτο [τὸ νοεῖν] φ. τις ἢ μὴ ἄνευ φ. ib.403$^{a}$8; c. gen., μέλλοντος κακοῦ Id.*Rh.*1382$^{a}$21, cf. 1370$^{a}$30, $^{b}$33, al.; αἰσχροῦ φ. Cic.*Att.*9.6.5; also περὶ ἀδοξίας φ. ἐστὶν ἡ αἰσχύνη Arist.*Rh.*1384$^{a}$23; γίγνεται ἑκάστῳ φ. ὅτι τοιοῦτός [ἐστι] ib.1371$^{a}$9; ἡ κατὰ τὴν σύλληψιν φ. τῆς γυναικός *Placit.*5.12.2, cf. Sor.1.39 (pl.); τὰ πρὸς τὴν φ. χρώματα colours as judged by the φ., *apparent* colours, *Placit.*1.15.8; φωτίζεσθαι πρὸς τὴν φ. ib.2.28.6. b. in Aristotle, *faculty of imagination,* both presentative and representative, opp. αἴσθησις, [φ.] οὐκ ἔστιν αἴσθησις Arist.*de An.*428$^{a}$5; opp. δόξα, because πίστις is absent, ib.22,24; opp. ἐπιστήμη, νοῦς, διάνοια, οὐδὲ [φ.] τῶν ἀεὶ ἀληθευόντων οὐδεμία ἔσται, οἷον ἐπιστήμη ἢ νοῦς ib.428ᵃ17; φ. ἕτερον καὶ αἰσθήσεως καὶ διανοίας· αὐτή τε οὐ γίγνεται ἄνευ αἰσθήσεως καὶ ἄνευ ταύτης οὐκ ἔστιν ὑπόληψις ib.427ᵇ14; φ. γίνεται ἢ διὰ νοήσεως ἢ δι' αἰσθήσεως Id.*MA*702ᵃ19; ὀρεκτικὸν [τὸ ζῷον] οὐκ ἄνευ φ., φ. δὲ πᾶσα ἢ λογιστικὴ ἢ αἰσθητική Id.*de An.*433ᵇ28. c. *creative imagination*, φ. σοφωτέρα μιμήσεως δημιουργός Philostr.*VA*6.19. 3. the *use of imagery* in literature, τεθορύβηται ταῖς φ. μᾶλλον ἢ δεδείνωται Longin.3.1; ἡ ῥητορικὴ φ. Id.15.2; ἀπὸ τοῦ ἀποδεικτικοῦ περιελκόμεθα εἰς τὸ κατὰ φαντασίαν ἐκπληκτικόν Id.15.11; αἱ ποιητικαὶ φ. Plu.2.759c; ἐς τὰς φ. τῶν λεγομένων τῷ σχήματι τοῦ σώματος συνεφέροντο App.*Pun.*134, cf. *Hisp.*26, *Syr.*40. 4. *prestige, reputation*, μεγάλην ἐφείλκετο φ. ὡς μόνος εἰδὼς τί λέγει Plb.22.9.12, cf. 24.7.2, 24.11.5, *Fr.*233; ἐκ τοῦ τοὺς ἄλλους ἐλέγχειν φ. ἀπενέγκασθαι προαιρούμενος Hipparch.1.1.6; *parade, ostentation*, ποιέειν μηδὲν περιέργως μηδὲ μετὰ φαντασίης Hp.*Decent.*7, cf. Plb.15.25.22, 16.21.1, 31.26.6, Posidon.36J., D.S.12.83, Vett.Val.38.26, al.; ἡ ἐφήμερος τῆς ἀρχῆς φ. Sopat.ap.Stob.4.5.55; μετὰ πολλῆς φ. *Act.Ap.*25.23, cf. D.L.4.53. **-άζομαι**, *to be presented to the mind*, τὸ ὂν φαντασιαζόμενον δόξῃ Ph.1.464. **-αστής**, οῦ, ὁ, *one who is fond of display*, cj. in Polem.*Phgn.*27. **-αστικός**, ή, όν, *receptive of impressions* or *images*, Epicur.*Nat.Herc.*1398.1, Plu.2.431b; τὸ φ. ib.432c. Adv. **-κῶς**, τοῦ μέλλοντος ib.433c.

**φαντᾰσιο-κοπέω**, *indulge vain fancies*, Lxx *Si.*4.30(35). **-κόπος**, ον, *conceiving vain fancies* or *hopes*, *EM*673.46, Eust.1700.53. **-πλήκτως**, Adv. *like one who is mad on showing off*, M.Ant.1.7.

**φαντᾰσ-ιόω**, *bring images before the mind of*, τινας S.E.*M.*8.406: abs., ib.397. II. mostly in Med., *have* or *form images* or *presentations*, Aristocl.ap.Eus.*PE*14.21, S.E.*M.*8.406; πεφαντασιωμένος *subject to hallucinations*, Ruf.*Fr.*79; ἔμψυχον φαντασιούμενον *having the faculty of presentation*, opp. ἀφαντασίωτον, Plu.2.960d; τὸ φαντασιούμενον τῆς ψυχῆς Gal.4.445; φ. ἡ διάνοια διὰ τῶν αἰσθήσεων S.E.*P.*2.72, cf. *Stoic.*2.22, al. 2. c. acc. rei, φαντασιωθείς δαιμόνιόν τι Plu.2.236d, cf. Ph.1.55, al. **-ις**, εως, ἡ, = φαντασία, φήμη καὶ φ. Pl.*Ti.*72b, cf. Demetr.Lac.*Herc.*1055.3, Plot.3.6.7,13: pl., *portents*, τερατολόγοι φαντάσεις ἐς ἀεὶ προὔλεγον Procop.*Pers.*2.30. **-ιώδης**, *fantastic*, πτοῖαι Philostr.*VA*7.14; *unreal, imaginary*, Dam.*Pr.*7. 2. φ. ὕπνοι *troubled by dreams*, Gal.1.361 (Comp.); of persons, φ. τοῖς ὀνείρασιν ib.327. II. *showy, pompous*, of persons, Vett.Val.39.1; δόξα ib.355.12; ἔνδυμα *EM*506.47, Suid. s.v. κεστός. Adv. **-δῶς**, Eust.1699.35. **-μα**, ατος, τό, = φάσμα, *apparition, phantom*, ἐνύπνια φαντάσματα A.*Th.*710; νυκτέρων φ. ἔχουσι μορφάς Id.*Fr.*312; φ. δαίμονος Plu.*Dio* 2, cf. E.*Hec.*54,94 (anap.), 390, Chrysipp.*Stoic.*2.22, *Ev.Matt.*14.26; περὶ τὰ μνήματα ..ὤφθη ἄττα ψυχῶν σκιοειδῆ φ. Pl.*Phd.*81d; *vision, dream*, Arist.*EN* 1102ᵇ10(pl.), Theoc.21.30. b. pl., *phenomena*, τὰ ἐν ἀέρι φ. Arist.*Mu.*395ᵃ29: pl., *portents*, D.H.4.62. II. = φαντασία 1, Pl.*Prt.*356e, *Tht.*167b, *Prm.*166a, *R.*598b, Arist.*de An.*428ᵃ1, Epicur.*Ep.*2 pp.37, 51 U.; distd. from εἰκών, Pl.*Sph.*236c. **-μάτιον**, τό, *miserable phantom*, Plu.2.766b. **-μός**, ὁ, *mental image*, Epicur.*Ep.*1 p.12 U. 2. pl., of the *vain imaginings* of philosophers, Timo 45. 3. *vision*, φαντασμοὶ ὀνείρων *PMag.Lond.*124.25 (iv/v A.D.). **-τής**, οῦ, ὁ, *one who makes a parade, boaster*, Polem.*Phgn.*27 codd. **-τικός**, ή, όν, *able to produce the appearance* of something, Pl.*Sph.*266d, 268c: ἡ -κή (sc. τέχνη), *the art of producing appearances*, opp. εἰκαστική, ib.236c; φ. ἐπιβολὴ τῆς διανοίας Epicur.*Sent.*24, cf. *Ep.*1 p.13 U., Phld.*Sign.Fr.*1 (pl.): τὸ φ. Arist.*de An.*432ᵃ31, Plot.4.3.29: the *imaginative faculty, faculty of being deluded by images*, Chrysipp.*Stoic.*2.22. Adv. **-κῶς**, *by means of mental images*, Epicur.*Nat.*28.7; τυποῦσθαι M.Ant.3.16, S.E.*M.*7.373, cf. Jul.*Or.*5.164c, Syrian. *in Metaph.*115.37, etc. **-τός**, ή, όν, *acting upon the* φαντασία (q.v., signf. 2), Arist.*Mem.*450ᵃ24; only of real objects acc. to Chrysipp.*Stoic.*2.22; τὸ ὑποπῖπτον φ. M.Ant.3.11. Adv. **-τῶς** Syrian. *in Metaph.*117.14.

**φάντης**, ου, ὁ, = συκοφάντης (for which it is perhaps f.l.), Phot. s.v. ποταγωγίδες (pl.). **φαντί**, Dor. 3 pl. pres. of φημί.

**φαντικός**, ή, όν, *significant*, Ammon. *in Int.*59.25.

**φαν-τός**, ή, όν, (φαίνομαι) *visible*, Orph.*Fr.*75. **-τωρ**, ορος, ὁ, *one who displays*, σεμνῶν φ. νυκτῶν *IG*2².3411 (ii A.D.).

**φανυλός**, v. φάγιλος.

**φάο**, Ep. imper. pres. Med. of φημί, Od.16.168, etc.

**φαορκίς**· τρυγίς, Hsch.

⊕**φάος**, φάεος, τό, Att. contr. **φῶς**, φωτός, and resolved Ep. **φόως** (φόωσδε, though read by Ar.Byz. and Aristarch., is to be rejected in Il.16.188); Aeol. **φάος** Sapph.*Supp.*25.9, but cf. φανοφόρος:—Hom. uses φάος and φόως, never φῶς; of the oblique cases he uses only dat. sing. φάει and acc. pl. φάεα; dat. pl. φαέεσσι Hes.*Fr.*142.4, Call.*Dian.*211, etc.:—φάος is the only form used by Pi.: Trag. use φάος or φῶς, both in lyr. and dialogue, as metre requires: Com. use φάος in lyr. only, Ar.*Eq.*973, *Ra.*1529; φῶν is a late acc. in *BCH*51.380 (Cyme, Hymn to Isis); in Prose φῶς is the only form used in nom. and acc.: gen. φάους X.*Cyr.*4.2.9,26, *Oec.*9.3, Arist.*de An.*429ᵃ3; dat. φάει A.*Ag.*575, *Ch.*62 (lyr.), S.*Ph.*415,1212 (lyr.), etc.: pl., φάη B.8.28, Gal.18(2).250, *AP*7.373 (Thall.); gen. φαέων Arat.90; dat. φάεσι Call.*Dian.*71; in Prose gen. φωτός Pl.*R.*518a, *Ax.*365c; dat. φωτί Luc. *Musc.Enc.*9, etc. (φῷ E.*Fr.*534); pl., φῶτα *IG*11(2).203 *A* 33 (Delos, iii B.C.), etc.; gen. φώτων ib.4²(1).110.43 (Epid., iv B.C.); dat. φωσί (v. infr. 1.2): (φάω). [ᾰ regularly; but Hom. always has ᾱ metri gr. in φᾱεα; and so dat. pl. φᾱεσι in Call.*Dian.*71]:—*light*, esp. *daylight*, ἤδη φ. ἦεν ἐπὶ χθόνα Od.23.371; φ. οἴχεθ' ὑπὸ ζόφον 3.335; κατέδυ λαμπρὸν φ. ἠελίοιο Il.1.605; Ἠὼς..Ζηνὶ φόως ἐρέουσα 2.49; ἀθανάτοισι φόως φέροι Od.5.2; νὺξ ἀποκρύψει φάος A.*Pr.*24; τὸ τοῦ ἡλίου φῶς Pl.*R.*515e; πρὸς τὸ φῶς βλέπειν ib.; οὐράνιον φῶς, αἰθέρος φῶς, S.*Ant.*944 (lyr.), E.*Ph.*809 (lyr.); ἡμέρας ἁγνὸν φάος Id.*Fr.*443; ἡμερήσιον φάος A.*Ag.*23; τὸ ἡμερινὸν φῶς Pl.*R.*508c; ἐν φάει by *daylight*, Od.21.429; ἕως ἂν φῶς γένηται till *daybreak*, Pl.*Prt.*311a; ἅμα φάει at *daybreak*, Plu.*Cam.*34; ἅμα τῷ φωτί Plb.1.30.10, al.; ἕως ἔτι φῶς ἐστιν while there is still *light*, Pl.*Phd.*89c; ἔτι φάους ὄντος X.*Cyr.*4.2.26; κατὰ φάος νύκτας τε E.*Ba.*425 (lyr.); κατὰ φῶς, opp. νύκτωρ, X.*Cyr.*3.3.25; also, of moon*light* and star*light*, φαέεσσι σελήνης Hes. l.c., cf. Pi.*O.*10(11).75, Bion *Fr.*8.5, etc.; ἀστέρος τηλαυγέστερον Pi.*P.*3.75; τὰ φῶτα, sc. sun and moon, Ptol.*Tetr.*37,38. b. in Poets, freq. in phrases concerning the life of men, ζώει καὶ ὁρᾷ φ. ἠελίοιο Il.18.61, cf. Od.4.540, etc.; λείπειν φ. ἠελίοιο Hes.*Op.*155, Thgn.569; ἐς φάος οὐκ ἀνίεσκε, ἀφίκεσθε, Hes.*Th.*157,652; ζῇ τε καὶ βλέπει φάος A.*Pers.*299; ὅστις φῶς ὁρᾷ S.*OT*375; ὄντα ἐν φάει Id.*Ph.*415, etc.; Διὸς ἐν φάει E.*Hec.*707 (lyr.); πέμψατ' ἔνερθεν ψυχὴν ἐς φῶς. ἀναγαγεῖν εἰς φῶς, A.*Pers.*630 (anap.), Ar.*Av.*699 (anap.); πρὸς φῶς ἀνελθεῖν S.*Ph.*625; πρὸς φῶς ἄγειν Pl.*Prt.*320d; λείπω φάος Ar.*Ach.*1185 (paratrag.); εἰ στερήσομαι τοῦδε τοῦ φωτός Pl.*Ax.*365c: but also εἰς φῶς ἰέναι to come into *the light*, i.e. into *public*, S.*Ph.*1353; εἰς φῶς λέγειν ib.581; τὸ φῶς κόσμον παρέχει *light* (i.e. *publicity*) is a guarantee for order, X.*Ages.*9.1. c. simply *a day*, φῶς ἐν ἡλίου καταρκέσει E.*Rh.*447; νόστιμον βλέπειν φάος, = ἦμαρ, A.*Pers.*261: pl., κρισίμων φαέων of critical *days*, *AP*11.382.11 (Agath.). 2. *the light* of a torch, lamp, fire, etc., τίς τοι φάος οἴσει; Od.19.24, cf. 34,64; φάος πάντεσσι παρέξω 18.317; φῶς δαΐων A.*Ch.*863 (anap.); ποιεῖν X.*HG*6.2.29; πρὸς φῶς πίνειν to drink by *the fire*, Id.*Cyr.*7.5.27; *a light*, φῶς ἔχων..ἀφηγεῖτο Id.*HG*5.1.8: pl., Plu.*Pel.*12, *Ant.*26, etc.; τὰ φ. the *illuminations*, *IG*11(2).203 *A* 33 (Delos, iii B.C.); μέσοις φωσίν at a moderate *fire*, Ps.-Democr.Alch.p.46 B., cf. Zos.Alch.pp.147, 155 B. 3. *the light* of the eyes, φάος ὀμμάτων, ὄσσων, Pind.*N.*10.40, Opp.*H.*4.525: pl., φάεα *eyes*, Od.16.15, 19.417; τίεσκον ἴσον φαέεσσιν ἐμοῖσι Mosch.4.9; φάη Gal. l.c.: sg., of the Cyclops' *eye*, E.*Cyc.*633. 4. *window*, *IG*4²(1).110.43 (Epid., iv B.C.), Plu.2.515b; *opening* in a machine, Heliod.ap.Orib.49.7.14. II. *light*, as a metaph. for deliverance, happiness, victory, glory, etc., καί τῷ μὲν φάος ἦλθεν Il.17.615; φόως δ' ἑτάροισιν ἔθηκεν 6.6; ἐπὴν φάος ἐν νήεσσι θήῃς 16.95; ἐν χερσὶ φόως 15.741; [πύλαι] πετασθεῖσαι τεῦξαν φάος 21.538; φ. ἀρετᾶν Pi.*O.*4.11; δώμασιν φάος μέγα A.*Pers.*300, cf. S.*Ant.*600 (lyr.). *Aj.*709 (lyr.); λαμπρὸν φ. γένους *Trag.Adesp.*9; of persons, ἤν πού τι φόως Δαναοῖσι γένωμαι Il.16.39, cf. 8.282, etc.; esp. in addressing persons, ἦλθες, Τηλέμαχε, γλυκερὸν φάος Od.16.23; ὦ φάος Ἑλλήνων Anacr.124; Ἀκραγαντίνων φάος Pi.*I.*2.17; ὦ φίλτατον φῶς S.*El.*1224,1354; ὦ μέγιστον Ἕλλησιν φάος E.*Hec.*841; in late Prose, Anon.ap.Suid. s.v. ὦ φῶς: pl., *AP*7.373 (Thall.). b. of God, ὁ θεὸς φ. ἐστί 1*Ep.Jo.*1.5; φ. καὶ ζωή ἐστιν ὁ θεὸς καὶ πατήρ *Corp.Herm.*1.21; of Christ, φ. εἰς ἀποκάλυψιν ἐθνῶν *Ev.Luc.*2.32, etc. 2. with reference to *illumination* of the mind, τῆς ἀληθείας τὸ φῶς E.*IT*1026; φ. ἐν τῷ φιλοσοφεῖν Plu.2.77d, cf. 47c; τὸ φ. τὸ ἐν σοί *Ev.Matt.*6.23; τὸ φ. τῆς ζωῆς *Ev.Jo.*8.12; ἐν τῷ φ. εἶναι 1*Ep.Jo.*2.9; τέκνα φωτός, ὅπλα τοῦ φ., *Ep.Eph.*5.8, *Ep.Rom.*13.12. III. *the dark ring round the nipple*, Poll.2.163.

**φᾰοστᾰσία**, ἡ, coined as etym. of φαντασία, Sophon. *in de An.*121.19, interpol. in Ph.1.279.

**φάρ**, φαρός, τό, Lat. *far, spelt*, Sor.1.98, Aret.*CA*2.2, Alex.Trall.5.5 (prob.). B. φᾶρ, τό, apoc. form of φᾶρος, Hdn.Gr.1.394.

**φᾰραγγ-αῖον**· τῆς φαρέτρας τὸ κάλυμμα, Hsch. ⊕ **-ίτης** [ῑ], ου, ὁ, *of, from a gully* or *ravine*, of the wind Iapyx, Arist.*Vent.*973ᵇ15. **-όω**, *convert into gullies* or *ravines*, [γῆ] πεφαραγγωμένη (by the Nile floods), *PGurob* 26 intr.p.44 (iii B.C.), *PTeb.*151 (ii B.C.). **-ώδης**, ες, *full of chasms* or *ravines*, τόποι Arist.*HA*578ᵃ27, cf. D.S.1.32, J.*AJ*5.2.11, Corn.*ND*27. II. *found in ravines*, of the plant ὄστρυς, Thphr.*HP*3.10.3.

**φάραγξ** [ᾰ], αγγος, ἡ, *cleft, chasm*, esp. in a mountain side, *ravine, gully*, Alcm.60.1 (pl.); φ. πρὸς δυσχειμέρῳ A.*Pr.*15, cf. 142 (anap.), al., E.*IT*277, X.*HG*7.2.13, Thphr.*HP*9.5.2 (pl.), *Schwyzer* 289.161 (Priene, ii B.C.), etc.; πᾶσα φ. πληρωθήσεται Lxx *Is.*40.4; πάντας.. ἐς φάραγγα ἐσέβαλον Th.2.67; ἐν πύλαισι γὰρ σταθεὶς φάραγγος *of the cave*, E.*Cyc.*668; φάραγγα δακτύλου πιάσματι σύρει, of shaping a roll before it is baked, Eub.75.11:—metaph., of Cleon, φάραγγα καὶ Χάρυβδιν ἁρπαγῆς Ar.*Eq.*248 (troch.). II. metaph., of the anus, Sotad.2.2.

**φάραι**· ὑφαίνειν, πλέκειν, Hsch. **φαραιδάκη**· μυρίκη, Id.

**φαραν-ίτης** [ῑ], ου, ὁ, *native of* Φαράν (between Palestine and Egypt), ἀννῶνα τῶν φ. β' ἄλης *PFlor.*297.192,219 (vi A.D.). **-ῖτις**, ιδος, ἡ, *a kind of amethyst found at* Φαράν, Plin.*HN*37.122.

**φαρατρίτας**, v. φαρετρίτης.

**φᾰράω**, *plough*, ἄφαρον φαρόωσι (sc. γῆν) Call.*Fr.*183 (ap.E.M.788.24); cf. φαρόω.

**φαρβό**, v. φαρυμός.

**φάργ-μα**, ατος, τό, *enclosure, precinct*, *Schwyzer* 89.8 (Argos, iii B.C.), cf. Hsch. **-νῦμι**, v. φράγνυμι.

**φαρεός**, ὁ, = φᾶρος, *Chron.Lind.*D.36.

**φᾰρέτρ-α**, Ion. **-η**, ἡ, (φέρω) *quiver* for arrows, ἰοδόκος Il.15.443; ὡς εἴ τε φαρέτρῃ πῶμ' ἐπιθείη Od.9.314; ἀμφηρεφής Il.1.45; βέλη ἔνδον ἐντὶ φαρέτρας Pi.*O.*2.84, cf. E.*Rh.*979, *HF*969; ὥσπερ ἐκ φαρέτρας ῥηματίσκια..ἀνασπῶντες Pl.*Tht.*180a; φ. τοξευμάτων a *quiver-full of..*, *IG*12(5).647.28 (Coressus, iii B.C.). **-εών, ῶνος,** ὁ, = foreg., Hdt.1.216, 2.141, 7.61. **-ιον,** τό, Dim. of φαρέτρα, Mosch.1.20. **-ίτης** [ῑ], ου, Boeot. **-τας,** ὁ, = τοξότης, *member of a military club*, *Supp.Epigr.*3.354 (Thisbe, iii B.C.), *IG*7.2714.2 (Acraeph.); also written **φαρατρ-** *Schwyzer* 463(3).5 (Tanagra).

**φᾰρετροφόρος,** ον, *quiver-bearing*, *AP*5.176 (Mel.): but **φαρετρήφορος** ἰός *borne in the quiver*, *Ath.Mitt.*56.122 (Smyrna).

**φαρθένος,** = παρθένος, *IG*5(2).262.28,31 (Mantinea, v B.C.), 1².555, 650.

**φαρία,** ἡ, a *vessel* of some kind, *PRyl.*224(*a*) introd. (ii A.D.).

**φᾱρικόν,** τό, some kind of *poison*, Nic.*Al.*398, Dsc.5.6; **Φαριακὸν** φάρμακον in Phylarch.10 J.

**φάρινος,** η, ον, *of cloth*, χιτών *Schwyzer* 462 *B* 42 (Tanagra, iii B.C.).

**φάριον,** τό, Dim. of φᾶρος: = ἐρεοῦς κεκρύφαλος, Poll.7.66.

**φαρκάζω,** = κλέπτω, Hsch. **φάρκες·** νεοσσοί, Id.

**φαρκῑδ-όομαι,** (φαρκίς) Pass., *to be wrinkled*, expld. by στυγνάζοντες, Hsch. **-ώδης,** ες, *wrinkled*, Hp.ap.Erot.; to be restored for φορακιώδης in Id.*Mul.*2.172.

⊛ **φαρκίς,** ίδος, ἡ, *wrinkle*, S.*Fr.*1108 (φαρμακίδα cod. Phot.), Erot. s. v. φαρκιδῶδες.

**φαρκτ-όομαι,** *guard oneself*, Hsch., Phot. (-εσθαι cod.). **-ός,** ή, όν, = φρακτός, *EM*667.23.

**φαρμᾰκ-άω,** *suffer from the effect of drugs* or *charms*, D.46.16, Thphr.*Fr.*105, Plu.2.1016e, etc. II. *require a remedy*, Luc.*Lex.* 4. **-εία,** ἡ, *use of drugs*, esp. of *purgatives*, Hp.*Aph.*1.24, 2.36 (both pl.), *PCair.Zen.*18.5 (iii B.C.), Gal.15.447, etc.; αἱ ἄνω φ., i.e. emetics, Arist.*Pr.*962a3; of abortifacients, Sor.1.59: generally, *the use of any kind of drugs, potions,* or *spells*, Pl.*Lg.*933b: pl., Id.*Prt.* 354a, *Ti.*89b, Men.535.9. 2. *poisoning* or *witchcraft*, D.40.57, Plb.6.13.4, *POxy.*486.21 (ii A.D.); αἱ περὶ τὰς φαρμακείας, = αἱ φαρμακίδες, Arist.*HA*572a22. II. metaph., *remedy*, παιδιὰς προσάγειν φαρμακείας χάριν Id.*Pol.*1337b41. **-ειά,** ἡ, = φαρμακίς, name for σίττη (διὰ τὸ πολύιδρις εἶναι), Id.*HA*616b23. **-εργάτης** [γᾰ], ου, ὁ, *apothecary*, Tz.*H.*8.918. **-εύς,** έως, ὁ, *poisoner, sorcerer*, S.*Tr.*1140, Pl.*Smp.*203d, etc.; γνήσιοι σοφισταὶ καὶ φ. Jul.*Or.*6.197d. II. *druggist, apothecary*, Aret.*CD*2.12. **-ευσις,** εως, ἡ, = φαρμακεία, in pl., Hp.*Prorrh.*2.4, Pl.*Lg.*845d. **-ευτέον,** *one must use a purge*, Gal.16.123, 17(2).665. **-ευτής,** οῦ, ὁ, later form for φαρμακεύς, Ph.1.449, Ptol.*Tetr.* 161, Vett.Val.17.10, etc. **-ευτικός,** ή, όν, *of* or *by means of drugs* or *pharmacy*, κάθαρσις Pl.*Ti.*89b: ἡ -κή (sc. τέχνη), = φαρμακεία, opp. surgery, Gal.15.425, D.L.3.85; φ. ἰατρός *one who prescribes drugs*, Gal.*Thras.*24. **-εύτρια,** ἡ, fem. of φαρμακευτής, Eust. 1415.64; pl., title of the 2nd Idyll of Theoc. **-εύω,** *administer a drug* or *medicine*, Pl.*R.*459c, *Ti.*89d. 2. *use enchantments, practise sorcery*, φαρμακεύσαντες ταῦτα ἐς τὸν ποταμόν *having used* this *charm* upon the river, Hdt.7.114. II. c. acc. pers., *purge*, τινα Hp.*Acut.*(*Sp.*)55; φ. ἄνω κούφῳ φαρμάκῳ *purge* upwards, i.e. by an emetic, Id.*Art.*67, cf. *Aph.*4.12:—Pass., *to be purged*, ib.2.37, Men.*Her.Fr* 5; *to be physicked*, Arist.*Top.*111a2. 2. *drug* a person, *give* him *a poisonous* or *stupefying drug*, E.*Andr.*355, *SIG*1181.4 (Rhenea, ii B.C.); φ. τινὰ ἐπὶ βλάβῃ μὴ θανασίμῳ Pl.*Lg.*933d:—Pass., οὐ πεφαρμάκευσαι ἀλλὰ μεμάγ(ε)υσαι Astramps.*Orac.*25.4 (ii A.D.), cf. *POxy.*472.1 (ii A.D.). 3. *season* in cookery, [ἰχθὺν] πεφαρμακευμένον τυροῖσι Philem.79.5. 4. metaph., πειθοῖ κακῇ τὴν ψυχὴν φ. Gorg.*Fr.*11 D. **-ή·** ἡ χύτρα ἣν ἡτοίμαζον τοῖς καθαίρουσι τὰς πόλεις, Hsch. **-ηρός,** ά, όν, (φάρμακον III) *treated with preservatives*, κωπῶν ζεύγη *BGU*544.21 (ii A.D.). 2. *glazed*, of bronze vessels, ib. 17. **-ία,** Ion. -ίη, = φαρμακεία, Hp.*Decent.*10, Lxx *Ex.*7.11 (pl.), Man.2.310. **-ικός,** ή, όν, *of* or *for a* φάρμακον, Tz.ad Lyc. 1137. **-ιον,** τό, Dim. of φάρμακον, *mild remedy*, Pl.*Phdr.*268c, *Tht.* 149c, *PPetr.*3 p.115 (iii B.C.), Plu.2.43b; *AP*11.333 (Callicter). 2. *purgative*, f.l. for φαρμακείῃσι in Hp.*Aph.*1.20. **-ίς,** ίδος, fem. of φαρμακεύς, *sorceress, witch*, D.25.79, Arist.*HA*577a13, A.R.4.53:—as Adj., γυνὴ φ. Ar.*Nu.*749; irreg. Sup., φαρμακιστόταται γυναικῶν J.*AJ*17.4.1, cf. Suid. s. v. Μήδεια. II. fem. Adj., *poisonous, venomous*, σαύρα Nic.*Al.*538. **-ίστρια,** ἡ, = foreg. 1, Hsch. s. v. βαμβακεύτριαι. **-ίτης** [ῑ], ου, ὁ, *drugged* or *medicated*, δακτύλιος φ. a ring *containing poison*, Eup.87; οἶνος φ. Semus 5a; fem. φαρμακῖτις γῆ, = ἀμπελῖτις II, Dsc.5.160; φ. σαύρα Aët.13.56; also ἡ φ. (sc. βίβλος) *On Drugs*, title of lost work by Hippocrates, Hp.*Aff.*9,15, 28, al.; φαρμακίτιδες βίβλοι, by Andromachus, Gal.13.891. II. = ἀδηφάγος, Hsch.; cf. φαγεσωρῖτις. **-ίων,** ωνος, ὁ, *pharmacist*, nickname of Asclepiades Junior, Gal.13.441.

**φαρμᾰκο-δοσία,** ἡ, *poisoning*, Mich. *in EN*17.23. **-εις,** εσσα, εν, = φαρμακώδης, *poisoned*, ἰός Mosch.4.30: *poisonous*, Nic.*Al.*4; of a person, *sorcerer*, Nonn.*D.*21.144.—In Nic.*Al.*293, we have nom. pl. fem. φαρμακόεις for -όεσσαι. **-θήκη,** ἡ, *medicine-chest*, *POsl.*54.6 (ii/iii A.D.), *Cat.Cod.Astr.*1.104. **-μαντις,** εως, ὁ, either *one who is at once* φαρμακός and μάντις, or *who uses* φάρμακα *to divine from*, title of play by Anaxandrides.

⊛ **φάρμᾰκον** [v. sub fin.], τό, *drug*, whether healing or noxious: in Hom. the sense is freq. determined by an epith., φάρμακα, πολλὰ μὲν ἐσθλὰ.., πολλὰ δὲ λυγρά Od.4.230; τόδε φ. ἐσθλόν 10.287, cf. 292; φ. ἤπια, ὀδυνήφατα (v. infr. 2); κακὰ φ. ib.213; φ. λυγρὰ ib. 236; φ. οὐλόμενον ib.394; ἀνδροφόνον 1.261; θυμοφθόρα φ. 2.329; so, after Hom., προσανέα φ. Pi.*P.*3.52; παιώνια A.*Ag.*848; χρήσιμον Pl.*R.*382c; θανάσιμα Ph.*Bel.*103.31; ὀλέθριον Luc.*Herm.* 62. 2. *healing remedy, medicine*, in Hom. mostly of those applied outwardly, ἐπιθήσει φάρμαχ' ἅ κεν παύσῃσι μελαινάων ὀδυνάων Il.4.191; ἐπ' ἄρ' ἤπια φάρμακα πάσσε ib.218; ὀδυνήφατα φ. πάσσων 5.401,900, cf. 11.515,830, 15.394; προσάλειφεν ἑκάστῳ φ. Od.10.392; φ. περιαλείφειν Ar.*Eq.*906; also of potions, πιὼν φάρμακ' Od.10.326; φ. πεπωκώς Hdt.4.160, cf. Pi. l. c.; παρὰ τοῦ ἰατροῦ Pl.*R.*406d, cf. *Grg.*467c; φ. χριστόν E.*Hipp.*516; ἔγχριστον Theoc.11.1; ἐπίχριστον Str.17.1. 10; ἐπίπαστον Theoc. l. c.; καταπλαστόν Ar.*Pl.*716; ποτόν E.*Hipp.* l. c.; freq. in Medic. writers, Sor.1.4, Gal.6.265, etc.; of *medicines* for cattle, *PFlor.*222.11 (iii A.D.). b. c. gen. (v. infr. II), φ. νόσου *a medicine for* it, *remedy against* it, A.*Pr.*251,606 (lyr.); βηχὸς Phryn.Com.60: κεφαλῆς *for* a head-ache, Pl.*Chrm.*155b; στραγγουρίας Arist.*HA*612b16, cf. 624a16; μέθης Amphis 37; δίψης *AP* 6.170 (Thyill.); but ὑγιείας φ. *a medicine to restore* or *maintain* health, Aristid.*Or.*37(2).11. 3. *enchanted potion, philtre*: hence, *charm, spell*, Od.4.220 sq., Ar.*Pl.*302, Theoc.2.15, *PSI*1.64.20 (i B.C.); φαρμάκοις τὸν ἄνδρ' ἔμηνεν Ar.*Th.*561; τοιαῦτα ἔχω φ. such *charms* have I, Hdt.3.85, cf. *Apoc.*9.21. 4. *poison*, S.*Tr.* 685, E.*Med.*385; πιεῖν τὸ φ. Antipho 6.15, Pl.*Phd.*57a, 115a; φάρμακα ἐσβεβληκέναι ἐς τὰ φρέατα Th.2.48; φ. δηλητήρια *SIG*37 *A* I (Teos, v B.C.); τοξικὸν φ. *BGU*21 ii 14 (iv A.D.). 5. *lye* for laundering, *Stud.Pal.*22.56.12 (iii A.D.). II. generally, *remedy, cure*, Hes.*Op.*485, Alc.35, etc.; μεῖζον..τῆς νόσου τὸ φ. *the cure* too strong for, i.e. worse than, the disease, S.*Fr.*589.4, cf. *Com.Adesp.* 455; φ. πραΰ, of a bridle, Pi.*O.*13.85; φ. τινι *for* a thing, Thgn. 1134 (pl.), Archil.9; πρός τι Arist.*Pol.*1321a16; ποττὸν ἔρωτα Theoc. 11.1; but most freq. φ. τινός *remedy against*.. χλαῖνα..φ. ῥίγευς Hippon.19; Ζεὺς πάντων φ. μοῦνος ἔχει Simon.87; τὸ σιγᾶν φ. βλάβης ἔχω A.*Ag.*548; φ. πόνων, λύπης, E.*Ba.*283, *Fr.*1079; δόλοι.. χρείας ἀνάνδρου φ. ib.288; φόβου Pl.*Lg.*647e; λήθης φάρμακα (of γράμματα) E.*Fr.*578.1; v. εὐδιανός. 2. c. gen. also, *a means of producing* something, φ. σωτηρίας Id.*Ph.*893; μνήμης καὶ σοφίας φ. Pl.*Phdr.*274e; ὑπομνήσεως ib.275a, cf. 230d; ἀθανασίας Antiph.86. 6; ἡσυχίας Arist.*Pol.*1273b23; φ. μανίας, of the oil applied to wrestlers, D.L.1.104. 3. ἐπὶ θανάτῳ φ. ἑᾶς ἀρετᾶς εὑρέσθαι *a remedy* or *consolation in* his own virtue, Pi.*P.*4.187. III. *dye, paint, colour*, Emp.23.3, Hdt.1.98, A.*Fr.*134, Ar.*Ec.*735, Pl.*R.*420c, *Plt.*277c, *PCair.Zen.*789.13 (iii B.C.), etc. IV. *chemical reagent*, *PLeid.X.*25, *PHolm.*13.46, 22.10, Ps.-Democr.ap.Zos.Alch.p. 160 B.; *used by tanners*, Sch.Ar.*Eq.*44,368.—Cf. φαρμάσσω. [μᾰ; but μᾱ in φαρμακός.]

**φαρμᾰκο-ποιέω,** *prepare dyes* or *colours*, Suid. s. v. βάψας. **-ποιία,** ἡ, *preparation of drugs*, D.L.7.117. **-ποιός,** όν, *preparing drugs*, ἔθνος φ. A.*Eleg.*2, cf. *Cat.Cod.Astr.*8(4).211. ⊛ **-ποσία,** Ion. -ίη, ἡ, *drinking of medicine*, Hp.*Aph.*4.19 (pl.), X.*An.*4.8.21 (unless in signf. 2), Pl.*Sph.*227a, etc. 2. *drinking of poison*, Luc.*Nec.*18, Porph.*Chr.*96. **-ποτέω,** *drink medicine*, Hp.*Aff.*27,41, Thphr.*HP*9.15.4. **-πωλέω,** *to be a druggist*, Ar.*Fr.*28 (anap.), Epicur.*Fr.* 171. **-πώλης,** ου, ὁ, *druggist, apothecary*, Ar.*Nu.*767, Critias *Fr.* 70 D., Theopomp.Com.2, Aeschin.3.162, Phld.*Rh.*1.34 S., etc.

**φάρμᾰκος** (on the accent v. Hdn.Gr.1.150), ὁ, ἡ, *poisoner, sorcerer, magician*, Lxx *Ex.*7.11 (masc.), *Ma.*3.5 (fem.), *Apoc.*21.8, 22.15.

**φαρμᾱκός** [v. ad fin.], ὁ, *one sacrificed* or *executed as an atonement* or *purification* for others, *scapegoat*, Hippon.5, al., Ar.*Ra.*733 (troch.), Ister 33; and, since criminals were reserved for this fate, a general name of reproach, Ar.*Eq.*1405, Lys.6.53, Call. in Διηγήσεις ii 29, D. 25.80. [ᾰ Hippon. and Call., ᾱ Ar.*Eq.* l. c.; on the accent v. Hdn. Gr.1.150; φαρμᾰκός Did.ap.Harp.]

**φαρμᾰκο-τρίβης** [ῐ], ου, ὁ, *one who grinds drugs* or *colours*, D.48. 12, Ael.*NA*9.62. **-τρίπτης,** ου, ὁ, = foreg., *AB*314.

**φαρμᾰκουργός,** όν, = φαρμακοποιός, Lyc.61.

**φαρμᾰκοφόρος,** ον, *producing drugs*, Eust.1415.54.

**φαρμᾰκ-όω,** *medicate*, φαρμακώσαισ' ἀντίτομα ὀδυνᾶν *having endued* them *with healing power* against pains, Pi.*P.*4.221. II. in Pass., *to be poisoned*, μελίκρατον πεφαρμακωμένον Plu.2.768d; of an arrow, Dsc.*Eup.*2.144 (v.l.). 2. *to be bewitched*, *POxy.*1477.20 (iii/iv A.D.). **-τήρ,** ῆρος, ὁ, = φαρμακεύς, Opp.*H.*2.483. **-τήριος,** α, ον, = φαρμακευτικός, Lyc.1138. **-της,** ου, ὁ, = φαρμακτήρ, Opp.*H.* 4.648,693. **-τός,** ή, όν, *poisoned*, βέλη Str.11.2.19; γένος Man.4. 540. 2. *poisonous*, δόλος Id.4.52. **-ώδης,** ες, *of the nature of a* φάρμακον, 1. *medicinal*, Arist.*HA*624a18, *Mir.*835b32, *Pr.*863b 32; γάλα Thphr.*HP*9.15.4 (Sup.); χυμοί Id.*CP*6.4.6 (Comp.); ποτήματα Sor.2.29; τὰ -ωδέστερα φάρμακα ib.33. 2. *poisonous*, Plu.*Ant.* 47, 2.974c; *poisoned*, τοξεύματα Dsc.3.80; τὸ φ. Plu.2.17b. 3. of places, *rich in medicinal herbs*, Thphr.*HP*9.15.4 (Posit. and Sup.). **-ών,** ῶνος, ὁ, *dye-house*, S.*Fr.*1109. **-ωνῖτις** Ἀνδρομάχου βίβλος, = φαρμακῖτις (which shd. perh. be read), Gal.13.890.

**φάρμαξις,** εως, ἡ, *medical treatment*, Pl.*Phlb.*46a. 2. *witchery*, Numen.ap.Eus.*PE*14.8. 3. = Lat. *veneficium*, *Gloss.* II. *treatment* of metals, φ. περὶ τὸν χαλκόν Plu.2.395b.

**φαρμάσσω,** Att. -ττω, prop. *treat by using* φάρμακα: generally, *treat*, once in Hom., ὡς δ' ὅτ' ἀνὴρ πέλεκυν..εἰν ὕδατι ψυχρῷ βάπτῃ.. φαρμάσσων Od.9.393; cf. foreg. II. II. after Hom., *heal* or *relieve by medicine*, Pl.*Lg.*933b, A.R.4.1512. b. φ. μέθυ *medicate it*, Nic.*Th.*619. 2. *enchant* or *bewitch by potions* or *philtres*, A.R.3. 478, 4.61 (and in Med., Id.3.859): *bewitch by flattery*, Pl.*Smp.*194a, *Men.*80a:—Pass., οἱ πεφαρμαγμένοι Hp.*Morb.Sacr.*1; πεφάρμαχθε Ar.*Th.*534: metaph., of a lamp, φαρμασσομένη χρίματος..παρηγορίαις A.*Ag.*94 (anap.). 3. *poison*, κρέα Plu.*Art.*19 (Pass.); βέλη, τὸ ὕδωρ Id.2.681f (Pass.), 978c: ἀπεψίας, δι' ἃς φαρμάσσεται τὸ γάλα Sor.1.94. 4. *dye, colour*, ἔρια Poll.7.169: metaph., φαρμασσομένη εὐμορφία *painted, false*, Philostr.*Ep.*27. **5.** *season*, τηγανίτας σησάμοισι φ. Hippon.36.

**φαρμιανὸν** μάλαγμα, a plaster, Asclep.ap.Gal.13.975.

**Φαρνάκειος** [ᾰ], α, ον, *of Pharnaces*, τετρᾶχμον *Inscr.Délos* 1444 *A a* 17 (ii B.C.). **2.** Φαρνάκειον, τό, in Lat. form *Pharnaceon*, = πάνακες Κενταύρειον, Plin.*HN*25.33; cf. *Gloss.*

⊛ **φάρξις**, εως, ἡ, *fencing*, ναοῦ *IG*4²(1).102.75 (Epid., iv B.C.).

⊛ **φᾶρος**, εος, τό, later also **φάρος** [v. sub fin.]:—*a large piece of cloth, web*, φάρε' ἔνεικε Καλυψώ.., ἱστία ποιήσασθαι Od.5.258, cf. E.*Hec.*1082 (lyr.). **II.** commonly, *a wide cloak* or *mantle* without sleeves, μαλακὸν δ' ἔνδυνε χιτῶνα..περὶ δὲ μέγα βάλλετο φ. (of a man) Il.2.43; πορφύρεον μέγα φ. ἔχων ἐν χερσὶ 8.221, cf. Od.15.61, Xenoph.3.3, Pherecyd.Syr.2, Hdt.9.109, E.*El.*1221 (lyr., pl.); also worn by women, Od.5.230, Hes.*Op.*198, A.*Ch.*11, etc.; drawn over the head, μέγα φ. ἑλὼν..κὰκ κεφαλῆς εἴρυσσε Od.8.84, cf. E.*Supp.*286, Ar.*Th.*890; used as a *shroud* or *pall*, Il.18.353, 24.580, S.*Aj.*916; πύματον φ. my last *rag*, Pl.*Eleg.*12; εἰς ὅ κε φ. ἐκτελέσω..Λαέρτῃ ἥρωϊ ταφήϊον Od.2.97, 24.132; also of *bed-spread*, δεμνίοις..στρωτὰ βάλλουσαν φάρη S.*Tr.*916: ἀναιδείας φ. (expld. by Hsch. from Il.2.262), S.*Fr.*291.—Ep., Trag. (for Ar. l.c. is paratrag. and Philetaer.19 is corrupt), and twice in Hdt. (Corinthian acc. to *AB*1096). [ᾱ in Hom. and mostly in later Ep.; φᾰρέεσσι Hes.*Op.*198 codd., A.R.3.863. A. has ᾱ always; S. has ᾱ in *Tr.*916, *Frr.*360, 373, 586, and never certainly ᾰ; E. has both ᾱ, *El.*191, *Hec.* l.c., *IT*1149 (all lyr.), al., and ᾰ, *HF*414 (s. v. l.), *Andr.*831, *Or.*840, *Hipp.*133 (all lyr.), *Supp.*286, cf. Hdn.Gr.2.942.]

⊛ **φάρος** [ᾰ], ὁ, = φάρυγξ, Lyc.154.

⊛ **φάρος** [ᾰ], τό, *plough*, Alcm.23.61 (cf. Sosiph.ap.Sch.), Antim. *Eleg.*p.293 B. **II.** = ἄροσις, *ploughing*, Hsch. s. v. βούφαρον, *EM*175.36. (Cf. Lat. *foro*, OE. *borian* 'bore'.)

**Φάρος** [ᾰ], ου, ἡ, *Pharos*, an island in the bay of Alexandria, Od. 4.355, E.*Hel.*5, Th.1.104, etc.; famous for its lighthouse, Str.17.1.6, etc.: hence σκοπιαὶ **Φάριαι** the watch-tower *of Pharos*, Alciphr.2.4. **II.** as Appell., φάρος, ὁ, *lighthouse*, *AP*9.671, 11.117 (Strat.).

**φαροφόρος**, v. φαυροφόρος.

**φαρόω**, = φαράω, Hsch.

**φάρσος**, εος, τό, *any piece cut off* or *severed, portion*, (= τρύφος, κλάσμα, πτερύγιον, ἀκρωτήριον, Hsch.; part of a house, Poll.7.121); φάρσεα πόλιος *the quarters* of a city, Hdt.1.180; ἐν φάρσεϊ ἑκατέρῳ ib. 181, cf. 186; φ. βότρυος *AP*6.299 (Phan.); φ. δραχμαῖον Nic.*Th.*664; σχίζειν τὸ ἱμάτιον εἰς δώδεκα φ. J.*AJ*8.7.7. **2.** = *velamen, Gloss.*; ῥούσιον φ., = *vexillum*, ib.; φ. σκεπαστήρια protective *sheets* or *coverings*, J.*AJ*3.8.2; ὡραῖον τὸ φ. ἄνθεσι παντοίοις ib.3.6.4; λίνεον φ. ibid.

**φαρσοφόρος**, ὁ, = *signifer, vexillarius, Gloss.*

**φάρσωμα**, ατος, τό, *ship's timbers*, Demetr. in *Cat.Cod.Astr.*8(3).98.

**φᾰρύγγεθρον**, τό, = φάρυγξ, Hp.*Anat.*1, Ruf.*Onom.*62, Aret.*SA* 1.7:—**φαρύγεθρον** Poll.2.207 (with v.l. -ετρον ib.99); **φαρύγαθρον** Hsch.

**φᾰρυγγίζω**, = λαρυγγίζω, Poll.2.207.

**φᾰρυγγοτομία**, ἡ, *laryngotomy*, Asclep.ap.Cael.Aur.*CP*1.14, Antyll.ap.Paul.Aeg.6.33.

**φᾰρῠγίνδην**, Adv. *like a gulf*, Com.Adesp.1185.

**φάρυγξ** [ᾰ], ἡ, less freq. ὁ (v. sub fin.), also **φάρυξ** Ar.*Ra.*259 (lyr.), 571; gen. φάρῠγος (always in Hom., Trag. and Com. (exc. φάρυγγος E.*Cyc.*356 (lyr.)), as ib.410,592, Cratin.186,257 (troch.), Telecl.1.12 (anap.), Ar.*Fr.*614), later φάρυγγος Nic.*Al.*363: (φάρος):—*throat*, φάρυγος δ' ἐξέσσυτο οἶνος Od.9.373; φάρυγος λάβε δεξιτερῆφιν 19.480; ὁ φ. εὐτρεπὴς ἔστω, for dinner, E.*Cyc.*215, cf. ll. cc.; ὦ μιαρὰ φ., of a glutton, Ar.*Ra.*571; ηὔξατό τις ὀψοφάγος ὢν τὸν φ. αὐτῷ μακρότερον γεράνου γενέσθαι Arist.*EN*1118a33: of singing, κεκραξόμεσθά γ' ὁπόσον ἡ φ. ἂν ἡμῶν χανδάνῃ Ar.*Ra.*259 (lyr.), cf. Hp.*Carn.*16, 18, *Acut.*59, al.—Used of the *windpipe* by Arist.*PA*664a16, 665a10, cf. *de An.*421a4, Gal.6.176; opp. παρίσθμια and λάρυγξ, ib.674, cf. 15.789,792, Aret.*CA*1.9; τὴν φ. κέρχνειν Diocl.*Fr.*147; of the *oesophagus* by *EM*557.17; of the *pharynx* by Hp.*Prog.*23 (cf. Gal.18(2).264), Poll.2.207; both of *pharynx* and *windpipe* by Gal.*UP*8.1. **II.** *dewlap* of a bull, Hld.2.1. **III.** pl., of *diseases of the throat*, Hp.*Aph.*3.5.—The gender is indeterm. in Hom.: fem., in Att., Phryn.46, cf. Cratin.and Ar. ll. cc., Pherecr.69, Th.2.49, Call.(?) *Fr.*331 (cf. *Fr.*51 P.); masc. in Epich.21, Telecl.1.12, E.*Cyc.*215, etc.: both genders in Hp., Arist., etc., and later writers (ἡ Aristid. *Or.*48(24).57, Ael.*NA*1.30, Paus.8.37.8, ὁ Plu.2.698f, Luc.*Asin.*38).

**φαρυμός**, = τολμηρός, θρασύς, Hsch.: also **φαρβό** (sic), Id.

**φαρύνει**· λαμπρύνει, Hsch.

**φάρχμα**, ατος, τό, = φράγμα, *IG*4²(1).102.253 (pl., Epid., iv B.C.).

⊛ **φάρω**, Locr. and Dor. for φέρω, *IG*9(1).334.5 (Locr., v B.C.), *EM* 114.20.

**φάσαξ**, ακος, ὁ, *informer*, = συκοφάντης, Com.Adesp.1186.

**φασγάν-ιον** [γᾰ], τό, = φάσγανον II. 1, Dsc.4.20, Corn.*ND*35, Plin. *HN*25.137. **II.** = ξάνθιον, Gal.12.87. **-ίς**, ίδος, ἡ, in pl., barber's *knives and scissors*, *AP*6.307 (Phan.). **-ιῶσαν**· ἐξιφισμένην, Hsch. ⊛ **-ον**, τό, poet. Noun, *sword*, δῶκεν μέγα φ. ἥρως σὺν κολεῷ τε φέρων καὶ ἐϋτμήτῳ τελαμῶνι Il.23.824; κολεοῦ γυμνὸν φ. Pi.*N.*1.52b; ἀμφιπλῆγι φ. S.*Tr.*930, cf. E.*Fr.*373 (Cypr. acc. to *AB* 1095). **II.** = ξιφίον, *corn-flag, Gladiolus segetum*, Thphr.*HP*7.12.3, 7.13.1, Nic.*Fr.*74.63. **2.** = ξάνθιον, Dsc.4.136. **3.** = ἀσπάλαθος, f.l. for σφάγνον in Id.1.20. **III.** = ξίφος II, Opp.*H.*3.556. **-ουργός**, όν, *forging swords*, Αἶσα A.*Ch.*647 (lyr.). **-ω**, *slaughter with the sword*, Hsch. (Pass.).

⊛ **φασήλιον**, τό, Dim. of φάσηλος, *POxy.*1656.8 (iv/v A.D.), *Gloss.* **2.** = ἰσόπυρον, Dsc.4.120.

**φασηλοειδής**, ές, *like the* φάσηλος I, Choerob. *in Thd.*1.288 H.

⊛ **φάσηλος** [ᾰ], ὁ (cf. Ath.2.56a, 4.139a: Lat. *phaselos* is fem., Colum.10.377), a kind of bean, *calavance, Vigna sinensis*, Epich. 151, Ar.*Pax* 1144 (troch.), Demetr.Com.Vet.5, Wilcken *Chr.*198.18 (iii B.C.), etc.; cf. φασίολος. **II.** hence Lat. *phaselus*, *a light boat, canoe, skiff*, from its likeness to a bean-pod, Catull.4, Hor.*Od.*3.2.29.

**φάσθαι**, inf. pres. Med. of φημί, Il.1.187, Od.11.443.

⊛ **Φᾱσιᾱνός**, όν, *from the river Phasis* (v. Φᾶσις):—ὁ φ. (sc. ὄρνις), *the Phasian bird, pheasant, Phasianus colchicus*, Mnesim.9, Ar.*Nu.* 109 (where some took it for *a Phasian horse*, cf. Sch.ad loc., Ath.9.387a, and cf. Φασιανοὶ ἵπποι, Φασιανικοὶ δὲ ὄρνεις Hdn.Gr. post Phryn. p.459 Lobeck), Arist.*HA*557a12, 633b2, Thphr.*Fr.*180, Ptol.Euerg. 2(b) J., *Edict.Diocl.*4.17 (*Aeg.*); Φ. ὄρνιθες Callix.2, cf. Ath.14.654c, etc.:—also **Φασιανικός**, Ar.*Av.*68 (with a play on συκοφαντικός, as **Φασιανὸς ἀνήρ** represents συκοφάντης in Id.*Ach.*726), Paul.Aeg.1.83; Φ. ὄρνιθες Poll.6.52; Φ. στέαρ Aët.5.118.

**φάσιμος** [ᾰ], η, ον, *denounced, informed against*, *GDI* iv p.885 (Erythrae, iv B.C.). **2.** dub. sens., φ. κύλιξ, παρὰ τὴν φάσιν τὴν ἔνδειξιν, Phot., *EM*789.2.

⊛ **φᾰσίολος**, ὁ, = φάσηλος I, Poll.1.247, Gal.6.542,545,557, 11.891, interpol. post Dsc.2.107: **φασίωλος** *Edict.Diocl.*1.21 (*Aeg.*); **πασίολος** ib.6.33: **φασιούλνος** *Hippiatr.*130,134.

**φάσις** (A) [ᾰ], εως, ἡ: (φαίνω):—*denunciation, information laid*, γραφαὶ ἢ φάσεις ἢ ἐνδείξεις ἢ ἀπαγωγαί And.1.88, cf. Lys.*Fr.*209 S., Din.*Fr.*89.36, D.25.78, Lex ap.eund.35.51; ἡ περὶ τὸ πλοῖον φ. Id. 58.5, cf. *SIG*695.83 (Magn.Mae., ii B.C.). **II.** (φαίνομαι) *appearance*, of stars, Ti.Locr.97b, Arist.*Mete.*342b34, Nic.*Th.*122, Phld.*D.*3.10, etc.: special uses, **a.** πρὸς τὸν ὁρίζοντα φ. *appearance* above the horizon, opp. ὑπὸ τὸν ὁρίζοντα κρύψις, Gem.13.2. **b.** *heliacal rising*, opp. κρύψις, φ. ἑῷαι, ἑσπέριαι, Ptol.*Tetr.*99, cf. *Alm.*8.6, al. **c.** including the previous signf. and κρύψεις, Id.*Phas.*p.3 H., al. (pl.), Vett.Val. 241.30 (pl.). **d.** pl., *phases* of the moon, Gem.8.11, Gal.9.904, Man. 2.491,497. **2.** *an appearance, trace*, τινος Anon.ap.Suid. s. v. φασί.

⊛ **φάσις** (B) [ᾰ], εως, ἡ: (φημί): **I.** *utterance, expression*, Arist. *Int.*16b27, 17a17. **II.** *statement, proposition*, comprehending both κατάφασις and ἀπόφασις (*affirmation* and *denial*), these being αἱ ἀντικείμεναι φ., ib.21b18, *Metaph.*1011b14, 1062a6; ἀναπόδεικτοι φ. Id.*EN*1143b12: opp. ζήτησις, ib.1142b14. **2.** = κατάφασις, *affirmation*, opp. ἀπόφασις, Pl.*Sph.*263e, Arist.*APr.*51b20, 62a14, *Metaph.* 1008a9. **3.** *mere assertion*, without proof, *PCair.Zen.*620.20 (iii B.C.), Hipparch.2.2.23, Phld.*Rh.*2.296 S.: pl., Mitteis *Chr.*31 ix 8 (ii B.C.), Hipparch.1.1.9, Phld.*Mus.*p.77 K. **4.** *judgement, sentence*, Greg.Cor. *in Hermog.* in Rh.7(2).1121 W. **5.** *rumour*, *Act.Ap.* 21.31; but, *tidings*, καλαὶ φ. *POxy.*805 (i B.C.); πέμψον μοι τὴν φ. send me *word*, ib.2149.17 (ii/iii A.D.), cf. 293.4,8 (i A.D.), 530.30 (ii A.D.). **6.** in Music, dub. sens., ἐνῆς (= ἐνῆν) ἐν τῷ μέλει πολλὰ φ. *IG*7.1818.7 (Thespiae, iii B.C.).

**Φᾶσις**, ιος, also ιδος Arist.*Fr.*83, ὁ, *the river Phasis* in Colchis, Hes.*Th.*340, Hdt.1.2, etc.; χθονὸς Εὐρώπης μέγαν ἠδ' Ἀσίας τέρμονα Φᾶσιν A.*Fr.*191 (anap.).

**φασκαίνω**, = βασκαίνω, *EM*190.28.

**φασκάς**, άδος, ἡ, a kind of *duck*, Alex.Mynd.ap.Ath.9.395d, cf. βασκάς.

⊛ **φασκία**, ἡ, = Lat. *fascia, bandage, strip*, Sor.1.56, Poll.2.166, *Dura*⁴ 93 (iii A.D.), *Edict.Diocl.*28.37 (**φασκίνια** *Geronthr.*),38, *BGU*814.10 (iii A.D.):—hence **φασκιόω**, *bind with bandages*, Dsc.*Eup.*2.69 (v.l.), Cyran.55.

**φάσκον, φάσκος**, v. σφάκος II. **II. φάσκος**, τό, = Lat. *fascis, bundle*, *Edict.Diocl.*14.7,12.

**φάσκω**, used by Ep. only in impf. ἔφασκον Il.13.100; Ep. φάσκον Od.24.75, Hes.*Th.*209: freq. in Trag. and Com. (but perh. never in pres. indic., v. infr.): as impf. of φημί S.*OT*110, etc., also Ar. *Ra.*742; also imper. φάσκε E.*Hel.*1077, Arist.*Rh.Al.*1429a6; subj. φάσκω A.*Ch.*93, Ar.*V.*561 (anap.), Antipho 3.4.3, Lys.25.11, Is.10.11, *PHal.*1.134 (iii B.C.); opt. φάσκοιμι S.*Aj.*1037, D.30.27; inf. φάσκειν S.*El.*9, *OT*462, *Ph.*1411 (anap.), Ar.*Ra.*695 (troch.), X.*Mem.*1.2.52, al., Isoc.8.1; part. φάσκων *IG*1².66.6, E.*HF*1382 (the only part of the Verb used in Th.(3.70) and Pl.(*R.*337e, al.), exc. ἔφασκεν Id.*Lg.*901a):—Pass. is not found, ἐφάσκετ' is for ἐφάσκετε S.*Ph.*114. Rare in pres. indic. before iii B.C.: φάσκει Is.6.16 (φάσκοι Reiske, Wyse), *PMich.Zen.*82.6 (iii B.C.), *PSI*8.921.7 (ii A.D.), dub. in S.E.*P.* 1.17 (v.l. φάσκοι), Gal.15.35, *Gp.*9.14.2, Hsch; φάσκεις *PSI*9.1011.10 (iii B.C.); φάσκουσι(ν) Aeschin.*Ep.*11.11, *PCair.Zen.*21.25, 244.5, al. (iii B.C.), Plu.*Ant.*86, Ath.10.429b, *Gp.*5.2.9, etc.; φάσκομεν is dub. cj. (for πάσχομεν) in Alex.146.4:—*say, affirm, assert*, c. acc. et inf., Od.4.191, 8.565, al.; φάσκειν as imper., in this constr., S.*OT* 462, *Ph.*1411 (anap.); οὐ φασκόντων χρήσειν *saying* they *would* not.., Hdt.3.58; οὐ φάσκων ἀνεκτὸν εἶναι Th.8.52; the inf. is freq. to be supplied, ἐν τῇδ' ἔφασκε γῇ (sc. εὑρεθήσεσθαι) S.*OT*110; φησίν γε· φάσκων δ' (sc. ἥξειν) Id.*El.*319; τῶν φασκόντων γονέων (sc. εἶναι) Pl. *R.*538a, etc.; rarely φ. ὡς.., ὅτι.., Mosch.2.12, Plu.2.215f: c. acc., τοῦτο φ. τοὔπος A.*Ch.*93, cf. E.*HF*1382, etc.: abs., ὡς ἔφασκεν S.*OT* 114; φάσκουσα καὶ οὐ φάσκουσα Pl.*Tht.*190a. **2.** *think, deem, expect*, ὃ οὔ ποτ' ἔγωγε τελευτήσεσθαι ἔφασκον Il.13.100; οὔ μ' ἐφάσκεθ'..οἴκαδ' ἱκέσθαι Od.22.35; φάσκειν..δρᾶν *believe that* you see, S.*El.*9. **3.** *say, promise*, c. inf. fut., με..ἔφασκε θήσειν ἀθάνατον Od.7.256; φάσκων προσποιήσειν αὐτὴν Th.2.85, cf. Pl.*Ion* 541e.

**φάσκωλος**, ὁ, *leathern bag, wallet, scrip*, Ar.*Fr.*319:—also **φάσκωλον**, τό, Lys.*Fr.*90S., Is.*Fr.*171S.: a Dim. **φασκώλιον**, τό, Teles p.38H., D.Chr.7.55, Ael.*NA*7.29, Gal.2.559, Agath.4.22 (Phot. and *EM*789.5 distinguish φασκώλιον *bag* from φάσκωλον *purse*).

**φάσμα**, ατος, τό: (φαίνω):—*apparition, phantom*, Hdt.6.69, 117, A.*Ag.*415 (lyr.), etc.; φ. ἀνθρώπου *spectral appearance* of a man, Hdt. 4.15; φ. γυναικός Id.8.84, cf. Pl.*Smp.*179d; φ. νερτέρων E.*Alc.*1127; *vision* in a dream, ὀνείρων φάσματα A.*Ag.*274, cf. S.*El.*644, etc.; φ. νυκτός ib.501 (lyr.); νύχια φ. E.*IT*1263 (lyr.). 2. *appearance, phenomenon*, Pl.*Tht.*155a; ἀνατολῆς φ. καὶ δύσεως Epicur.*Nat.*11.8 (pl.), al.: so, of *strange phenomena* in the heavens, Arist.*Mete.* 338$^b$23, 342$^a$35; of *images* apprehended by sense, Diog.Oen.*Fr.* 7. 3. of *shows* or *mysteries*, as *images* or *types* of realities, εὐδαίμονα φ. μυούμενοι Pl.*Phdr.*250c. 4. *sign from heaven, portent, omen*, Hdt.3.10, 4.79, 7.37,38, 8.37, S.*El.*1466, Pl.*Plt.*268e, etc.; φ. Κρονίδα Pi.*O.*8.43, cf. A.*Ag.*145 (pl., lyr.); Παλλάδα.. εὔσημον φ. ναυβάταις Eur.*IA*252 (lyr.). 5. *monster, prodigy*, periphr., φάσμα ταύρου, ὕδρας, *a monster* of a bull, of a hydra, S.*Tr.* 509 (lyr.), 837 codd. (lyr.); of the Sphinx, *Epigr.Gr.*1016.3.

**φασμᾰτιάω**, *see visions* or *hallucinations*, Hp.*Ep.*19 (*Hermes* 53.68).

**φασμᾰτο-λογέω**, *to speak of prodigies*, Sch.Luc.*Icar.* init. **-φάνεια** [φᾱ], ἡ, *spectral apparition*, Sch.Aristid.p.343D.

**φασμᾰτώδης**, ες, *like a vision*, Sch.Luc.*Icar.* init.

**φάσουλος**, = φάσηλος I, Cyran.30 (cf. φασίουλος v.l. in Gal.6.542).

⊕**φάσσα**, Att. **φάττα**, ἡ, *ringdove* or *cushat, Columba palumbus*, Ar.*Ach.*1104, *Av.*303 (troch.), *Pax* 1004 (anap.). Arist.*HA*544$^b$5, Sor.1.51, 2.41, Gal.6.700, *Vict.Att.*8, Aret.*CD*1.2, *Gp.*15.1.19; λαβεῖν φ. ἀντὶ περιστερᾶς *a wild pigeon* for a tame one, Pl.*Tht.*199b, cf. Alex. Aphr. *in Top.*117.9.—Luc.*Sol.*7 coined a masc. form **φάττος**.

**φάσσιον**, τό, = *palumbina*, *Gloss.*

**φασσο-φόνος**, ον, *dove-killing*, ἴρηξ Il.15.238:—as Subst., the name of a kind of hawk, Arist.*HA*615$^b$7, 620$^a$18, Gal.*UP*11.18, Porph.*Abst.*3.8:—so **-φόντης**, ου, ὁ, = foreg., Ael.*NA*12.4.

**φᾰτειός**, η, όν, *speakable*, οὔ τι φατειός *unutterable, unspeakable*, of horrid objects, Κέρβερος, Φόβος, ὄφιες, Hes.*Th.*310, *Sc.*144,161; φάσμα καρτερὸν οὔ τι φ. Menoph.Damasc.ap.Stob.4.21.7.

**φᾰτέον**, (φημί) *one must say*, Pl.*Lg.*864a, *Sph.*237e, Plb.2.21.8; *one must call*, εὐγενεῖς Jul.*Or.*2.83b: abs., *one must say 'yes', assent*, Pl.*Phlb.*40b, etc.

**φάτης** [ᾰ], ου, ὁ, (φημί) *talker, liar*, Hsch.

**φᾱτί**, Dor. 3 sg. pres. of φημί.

⊕**φᾰτίζω**, Ion. and Dor. Verb, used also in Trag., *tell of*, διάκοσμον Parm.8.60; ἐφάτισαν [τὰ γράμματα].. Φοινικήϊα κεκλῆσθαι *they spoke of* them by the name of Phoenician, Hdt.5.58; οὐδὲν ἀναύδατον φατίσαιμ' ἄν S.*Aj.*715 (lyr.): generally, *say*, φατίζω πάλιν "ἀγάλλευ" Dius ap.Stob.4.21.17, cf. Hsch.; *make a statement* in court, *PGrenf.* 2.78.22 (iv A.D.):—Pass., *to be expressed*, πεφατισμένον ἐστὶν Parm. 8.35; *to be said* to do, c. inf., A.R.1.24, Eus.Mynd.63; τὸ φατιζόμενον *as the saying is*, S.*OC*139 (lyr.); κατὰ τὰ φατιζόμενα Eus.Mynd. l.c. II. *promise, engage, betroth*, παῖδά τινι E.*IA*135 (anap.):—Pass., ἐμὴ φατισθεῖσα *my promised bride*, ib.936. III. Pass., *to be called, named*, Ἱερὴ δὲ φατίζεται A.R.1.1019; πεφάτισται Call. *Jov.*39, A.R.4.658, Nic.*Fr.*74.30; Θέμις φατίζεται παρὰ τοῖς οὐρανίοις θεοῖς, Δίκα δὲ παρὰ τοῖς χθονίοις Theag.ap.Stob.3.1.117.

**φᾰτικός**, ή, όν, (φημί) *assertory*: esp. of unsupported *assertion*, Phld. *Rh.*1.8, 2.119S. Adv. **-κῶς** ib.1.120S.; φ. μόνον χωρὶς πίστεως ib.1.40S.

**φατιρίς**· εἶδος ὀρχήσεως, Hsch.

⊕**φάτις** [ᾰ], ἡ: acc. φάτιν: voc. φάτι S.*OT*151 (lyr.), φάτις Id.*Aj.* 173 (lyr.): contr. acc. pl. φάτῑς Pi.*P.*3.112 (s.v.l.): not found in any other cases: (φημί):—poet. Noun, used also by Hdt., I. *voice from heaven* (not in Hom.), *oracle*, φ. Διός S.*OT*151 (lyr.), cf. 1440, E.*Supp.*834 (lyr.); ἀπὸ θεσφάτων τίς ἀγαθὰ φ. βροτοῖς στέλλεται; A.*Ag.*1132 (lyr.); ἀπ' οἰωνῶν S.*OT*310; Μουσάων Ar.*Av.*924 (lyr.); of a dream, A.*Pers.*227 (troch.); of the interpreter of dreams, ib. 521. 2. *voice* or *saying* among men, *common talk, rumour*, αἰσχυνόμενοι φάτιν ἀνδρῶν ἠδὲ γυναικῶν Od.21.323, cf. Sol.2.3; φ. ἀνθρώπους ἀναβαίνει ἐσθλή *good report*, Od.6.29; εὐκλεής E.*Fr.*242; φ. βαρεῖα A.*Ag.*456 (lyr.); ἐπίψογος ib.611; κακὰ S.*Aj.*186 (lyr.); φ. ἔτυμος, νημερτής, E.*IA*794 (lyr.), Lyc.1051; μαψίδιος, ψευδής, Id.*Hel.*251 (lyr.), *AP*7.239 (Parmen.); in Doric Prose, *PSI*9.1091.5: c. gen. objecti, φ. μνηστήρων *a report of* the suitors, Od.23.362: but κατὰ τῶν ἱρέων τὴν φάτιν as the priests' *story* runs, Hdt.2.102; ὡς φ. ὁρμηται Id.7.189; φ. κρατεῖ A.*Supp.*294; ὥσπερ ἡ φ. S.*OT*715; ὡς φ. ἀνδρῶν Id.*Ant.* 829 (lyr.); οὕτω φ. αὐδᾷ E.*Ion* 225 (lyr.): ἡ φ. μιν ἔχει *the report* goes of him.., Hdt.7.3, cf. 8.94; ἐχθρὰ Φάλαριν κατέχει φάτις Pi.*P.* 1.96: reversely, in same sense, ἔχει τινὰ φάτιν ἀνὴρ Ἐφέσιος Hdt.9. 84, cf. E.*Hel.* l.c.: φάτιν ἀγγέλλειν, φέρειν, Batr.138, A.*Ag.*9, etc.; ἆραι S.*Aj.*191 (lyr.); καταβαλεῖν φ. ὡς.. Hdt.1.122; κλύειν φάτιν S.*Aj.*850; φ. ἐπέρχεται, ἦλθέ τινι, Id.*Ant.*700, E.*Hipp.*130 (lyr.); ἐς τοὺς δήμους φ. ἀπίκετο ὡς.. Hdt.1.60; ἐνθεῦτεν φ. κεχώρηκε ib.122; ἦ σ' ἐπίανέν τις ἄπτερος φ.; A.*Ag.*276; *proverb*, φ. αὐτοῖσιν μαρτυρεῖ Heraclit.34 (cf. *Trag.Adesp.*517). 3. *subject of a saying* or *report*, Νέστορα καὶ Σαρπαδόν', ἀνθρώπων φάτις *themes* of many a tale, Pi.*P.*3.112 (s.v.l.); δέρκομαι φάτιν ἄφραστον *a thing* unspeakable, S.*Tr.*693. II. *speech, words*, of a single person, Id.*Ph.*1045, *El.* 329, 1213. 2. *speech, language*, Ἕλλην' ἐπίσταμαι φάτιν A.*Ag.* 1254. III. *a name*, Id.*Fr.*6.

**φᾰτν-εύω**, *feed at the manger*, Thd.*Pr.*14.4 (Pass.), Oenom.ap. Eus.*PE*5.34 (Pass.). **-η**, ἡ, *manger, crib*, [ἵππους] ἀτίταλλ' ἐπὶ φάτνῃ Il.5.271; ἵππος ἀκοστήσας ἐπὶ φ. 6.506; ἵππους μὲν κατέδησαν.. φάτνῃ ἐφ' ἱππείῃ 10.568; ἐυξέστῃ ἐπὶ φ. 24.280; ἡ φ. τῶν ἵππων Hdt.9.70, cf. E.*Ba.*510 (pl.), X.*Cyr.*3.3.27 (pl.), *Ev.Luc.*2.7, al.; φάτναι Ζηνός, of the *manger* of Pegasus, Pi.*O.*13.92: also of oxen, ὥς τίς τε κατέκτανε βοῦν ἐπὶ φ. Od.4.535, 11.411. 2. βοῦς ἐπὶ φ., proverb. of ease and comfort, Philostr.*Im.*2.10; also πλουσίαν ἔχειν φ. E.*Fr.*378; φάτναις ἀργυραῖς χρῆσθαι Str.3.2.14; ἡ ἐν τῇ φ. κύων 'the dog in the manger', Luc.*Tim.*14, cf. *AP*12.236 (Strat.); θεραπεύειν τὴν φ. τινός to court one who feeds you, Ael.*Fr.*107; τοὺς ἐκ τῆς αὐτῆς οἱονεὶ φ. ἐδηδοκότας ib.39: τὴν αὐτὴν φ. ζητεῖν to return to their old *haunts*, Eub.120. II. = φάτνωμα I, *IG*11(2). 161 *A* 46 (Delos, iii B.C.): pl., ib.4²(1).109 iii 85, al. (Epid., iii B.C.), D.S.1.66. III. *socket of tooth*, Poll.2.93. IV. the *Manger*, name of the nebula (star-cluster) between the ὄνοι in Cancer, Thphr. *Sign.*23, al., Arat.892,898, Eratosth.*Cat.*11, Ptol.*Tetr.*23. (Later Gr. πάθνη acc. to Moer., but φάτνη in Attic and Delian Inscrr., *IG*2². 1487.37, 11(2). l.c., *Inscr.Délos* 504 *A* 6, *B*9: *bhṇdh*, cf. Skt. *badhnāti* 'tie', Celt. *benn* 'wicker chariot'.) **-ίζομαι**, Pass., *to be kept at rack and manger*, ἵππος φατνιζόμενος Hld.7.29:—also **-άζομαι**, Aq. *Pr.*14.4. **-ίον**, τό, Dim. of φάτνη, *socket* of a tooth, Sor.1.118, Gal. 2.754, *UP*11.8: *gum*, τὸ ἀνωτέρω φ. Ph.2.238. **-ιος**, ὁ, epith. of Zeus at Laodicea Combusta, *MAMA*1.7. **-όω**, (φάτνη) *roof, ceil*, Lxx 3*Ki.*7.40(3):—Pass., ib.*Ez.*41.15. **-ωμα**, ατος, τό, *coffered work* in a ceiling, A.*Fr.*78: pl., *coffers* or *compartments*, Plb. 10.27.10, Callix.2; ξύλινα φ. *IGRom.*4.556 (Ancyra). II. *projecting platform*, Moschio ap.Ath.5.208b. III. = φατνίον, Gal.14. 778, Simp. *in Ph.*371.21, Eust.547.4; = *mandibulum*, *Gloss.* ⊕**-ωμᾰτικός**, ή, όν, *coffered*, στέγης παρασκευή Plu.2.227c; in form **παθνωματικός** (cf. φάτνη fin.) *MAMA* 4.293 (Dionysopolis, i A.D.). **-ωσις**, εως, ἡ, *ceiling in coffers*, Lxx 3*Ki.*6.14(9) cod.A (pl.), Sm.*Ca.*1. 17. **-ωτός**, ή, όν, *coffered*, Hsch., Phot.

**φᾱτός** (A), ή, όν, (φημί) *spoken* or *that may be spoken*, mostly with negat., οὐ φ. *unspeakable, unutterable, ineffable*, Hes.*Sc.*230, Parm. 8.8, Pi.*O.*6.37, *I.*7(6).37; τὸ μὴ φ. μηδὲ ῥητὸν κάλλος Plu.2.383a; pleon., κάλλος οὐ φ. λέγειν Ar.*Av.*1713. Adv. οὐ φατῶς, = ἀφάτως, Hsch. 2. *famous, notable*, ἄνδρες ἄφατοί τε φ. τε Hes.*Op.*3.

**φᾰτός** (B), ή, όν, (θείνω II) *slain, dead*, Hsch.

**φάτρα, φατρία, φατριάρχης**, v. φρατρ-.

**φατριά**, ἡ, *brother's wife*, *Gloss.*

**φάτριν**· τόπον ὕπαιθρον, ἐρείπιον, φάνα, Hsch.

**φάττα**, ἡ, Att. for φάσσα.

**φαττάγης**, ου, ὁ, perh. *pangolin* or *scaly ant-eater*, *manis*, Ael. *NA*16.6.

**φάττιον**, τό, Dim. of φάττα, νηττάριον ἂν καὶ φ. ὑπεκορίζετο Ar.*Pl.* 1011, cf. Ephipp.15.8.

⊕**φάττος**, v. φάσσα.

**φαύζω**, = φρύγω, Hsch., Phot.; cf. φαῦσιγξ.

**φαυλεπίφαυλος**, ον, *bad upon bad, bad as bad can be*, *AP*11.238 (Sup., Demod.).

**φαυλ-ία**, ἡ, v. φαύλιος. **-ίζω**, *hold cheap*, νομοθέτας Pl.*Lg.*667a; τὴν δίαιτάν μου X.*Mem.*1.6.5, cf. 4.4.14; τὰ πρωτοτοκεῖα Lxx *Ge.*25. 34. **-ιος**, α, ον, = φαῦλος, only used of fruits, *coarse*, μῆλα φ. Telecl.4, Theopomp.Com.19; φ. ἐλαία, and φαυλία alone, *a coarse kind of olive*, produced from the κότινος or wild-olive, Thphr.*CP*6. 8.3, *HP*2.2.12 (prob.), *Od.*15, Luc.*Lex.*5, Poll.6.45. **-ισμα**, ατος, τό, *disparagement, contempt*, Lxx *Ze.*3.11. **-ισμός**, ὁ, = foreg., ib.*Is.*51.7, al. **-ίστρια**, ἡ, *she that despises*, ib.*Ze.*3.1.

**φαυλό-βιος**, ον, *living disreputably*, Sch.Ar.*Ra.*425. **-νους**, ουν, *ill-disposed*, Sch.Ar.*Nu.*629. **-ρρημόνως**, (ῥῆμα) Adv. *speaking evilly* or *ill*, Poll.8.81.

⊕**φαῦλος**, η, ον, also ος, ον E.*Hipp.*435, *Fr.*1083.9, Th.6.21: (cf. φλαῦρος):—*cheap, easy, slight, paltry*, first found commonly in E., twice in Hdt.1.26,126 (Comp., elsewh. φλαῦρος), six times in Democr., *Fr.*87, al., twice in S., *Frr.*41,771: Adv. φαύλως once in A., *Pers.* 520. I. of things, *easy, slight*, φ. ἀθλήσας πόνον E.*Supp.*317; φαυλότατον ἔργον ''tis as easy as lying', Ar.*Eq.*213; φ. πρᾶγμα Id.*Lys.*14; τὸ ζήτημα οὐ φ. Pl.*R.*368c; φ. ἐρώτημα Id.*Phlb.*19a; φαῦλον αὐτοῖς προστάξομεν Id.*R.*423c: freq. with negat., οὐ φ., ἀλλὰ χαλεπὸν πιστεῦσαι ib.527d; μάχη οὐ φ. Id.*Tht.*179d; οὐ φ. τέχνη Id.*Sph.*223c; οὔτοι βασιλέα φαῦλόν [ἐστι] κτανεῖν 'tis no *slight matter* to kill a king, E.*El.*760; νυκτὸς γὰρ οὔτι φ. ἐμβαλεῖν στρατόν no *easy* matter, Id. *Rh.*285; οὐ φ. πληγαί D.54.13; φιλοῦσιν ἰατροὶ λέγειν τὰ φαῦλα μείζω Men.497; φαῦλα ἐπιφέρειν bring *paltry* charges, Hdt.1.26; τὰ φ. νικήσας ἔχω have gained *petty* victories, S.*Fr.*41 (wrongly glossed by μέγα in Phot., Suid., and *EM*789.43, cf. Hsch.); σύμμαχον Τροίᾳ μολόντα Ῥῆσον οὐ φαύλῳ τρόπῳ, i.e. with no *trivial* force, E.*Rh.* 599; παρὰ φαῦλον ποιεῖσθαί τι D.H.*Rh.*4.2, cf. Lib.*Or.*14.26. Adv. **-λως** εὑρεῖν, τυχεῖν, Ar.*Eq.*404 (troch.), 509 (anap.); φ. πάνυ Id.*Lys.* 566 (anap.); φ. ἐκφυγεῖν to get off *easily*, Id.*Ach.*215 (lyr.); φ. ἀποδρὰς Id.*Th.*711 (lyr.); φαυλότατα καὶ ῥᾷστα Id.*Nu.*778; οὔτι φαύλως ἦλθε *with* no *trivial force*, E.*Ph.*112; φ. βοηθήσειν D.15.13; φαύλως καὶ γλίσχρως παρείχοντο χρήματα *Hell.Oxy.*14.2; τὰς ἐλπίδας φ. ἔχειν to be *slight*, Hdn.1.3.1. 2. *simple, ordinary*, δίαιτα Hp.*Fract.*36, *Art.*49, Eur.*Fr.*213.4; σῖτα καὶ ποτὰ φαυλότατα X.*Mem.*1.6.2, cf. Hp. *Vict.*3.68 (Comp.); but freq. with sense *poor, indifferent*, στρατιά Th.6.21; ἀσπίδες, τείχισμα, παρασκευή, Id.4.9.115, 6.31; ἱμάτιον X. l.c. Adv. **-λως**, διατρίβειν ἐν φιλοσοφίᾳ Pl.*Tht.*173c; μὴ φ. μηδὲ ἰδιωτικῶς Id.*Lg.*966e. 3. *mean, bad*, πρῆξις Democr.177; λόγοι E. *Andr.*870, ψόγος Id.*Ph.*94 (perh. both in signf. I.1 and in I.3);

οὐ φ. ὄψις Pl.*R*.519a; φ. δόξα D.24.205; τὰ πράγματ' ἐστὶ φ. Id.19.30; φαῦλα διαπεπραγμένος Philem.229; ὁ φαῦλα πράττων *Ev.Jo*.3.20; μηδὲ πραξάντων τι ἀγαθὸν ἢ φ. *Ep.Rom*.9.11; τὸ φ. *evil*, E.*IT*390; τὰ φ., opp. τὰ ἀγαθά, X.*Smp*.4.47; τύχη φ., opp. ἀγαθή, Arist.*Ph*.197$^{a}$26, cf. *Metaph*.1065$^{a}$35; τὴν πόλιν μηθὲμ φ. παθεῖν *OGI*765.35 (Priene); κομίσασθαι... εἴτε ἀγαθὸν εἴτε φ., of rewards and punishments, 2 *Ep.Cor*.5.10; φ. μαίωσις Sor.2.17, cf. 1.91, al. II. of persons, *low* in rank, *mean*, *common*, E.*Fr*.688; οἱ φαυλότατοι *the commonest sort* (of soldiers), Th.7.77; [γάμος] ὁ ἐκ τῶν φαυλοτέρων, opp. ἐκ μειζόνων, X.*Hier*.1.27, cf. Pl.*R*.475b; of outward looks, αἱ φαυλότεραι *the plainer ones*, Ar.*Ec*.617, cf. 626 (Comp., both anap.). 2. *inefficient*, *bad*, διδάσκαλος S.*Fr*.771.3; τὸ φ. καὶ τὸ μέσον καὶ τὸ πάνυ ἀκριβές *the inefficient*, the middling, and the perfect, Th.6.18; φ. αὐλητής, opp. ἀγαθός, Pl.*Prt*.327c; τοξότης Id.*Tht*.194a; οὐ δὲ φαύλων ἀνδρῶν οὐδὲ τῶν ἐπιτυχόντων Id.*Cra*.390d; opp. σπουδαῖος, Isoc.1.1, Pl.*Lg*.757a, etc.; esp. in point of education and accomplishments, opp. σοφός, οἱ γὰρ ἐν σοφοῖς φαῦλοι παρ' ὄχλῳ μουσικώτεροι λέγειν E.*Hipp*.989, cf. *Ph*.496, *Ion* 834, Pl.*Smp*.174c, *Alc*.1.129a; τὸ πλῆθος τὸ -ότερον E.*Ba*.431 (lyr.); οἱ -ότεροι, opp. to οἱ ξυνετώτεροι, Th.3.37; οἱ φαυλότεροι γνώμην ib.83; τὰ γράμματα φαῦλοι Pl.*Phdr*.242c (so in Adv., φαυλοτέρως πεπαιδευμένοι Id.*Lg*.876d); generally, *inferior*, Id.*Grg*.483c: c. inf., φαῦλοι μάχεσθαι Eur.*IT*305; φ. λέγειν, φ. διαλεχθῆναι, Pl.*Tht*.181b, *Prt*.336c: of animals, φ. κύων D.26.22; φαυλότατοι ἵπποι X.*Mem*.4.1.3. 3. *careless*, *thoughtless*, *indifferent*, E.*Med*.807:—esp. in Adv., φαύλως ἐκρίνατε judged *lightly*, A.*Pers*.520; φ. εὕδειν E.*Rh*.769; οὐχ ὧδε φ. Id.*Ion* 1546; φ. παραινεῖν *off-hand*, Id.*HF*.89; λόγισαι φαύλως μὴ ψήφοις ἀλλ' ἀπὸ χειρός *off-hand*, *roughly*, Ar.*V*.656 (anap.); φ. εἰπεῖν *casually*, Pl.*R*.449c; φ. φέρειν to bear *lightly*, E.*IA*850, Ar.*Av*.961. 4. in good sense, *simple*, *unaffected*, φαῦλον, ἄκομψον, τὰ μέγιστ' ἀγαθόν E.*Fr*.473 (anap.), cf. D.L.3.63. Adv. -λως, παιδεύειν τινά *by a very simple method*, X.*Oec*.13.4; φ. καὶ βραχέως ἀποκρίνασθαι Pl.*Tht*.147c. 5. of health, etc., φαύλως ἔχειν to be *ill*, Hp.*Aph*.2.32; φ. πράττειν to be *in sorry plight*, Men.*Sam*.165; φ. ἔχει τὰ πράγματα D.10.3, al.

**φαυλότης**, ητος, ἡ, *meanness*, *poorness*, *badness*, of persons and things, Pl.*Lg*.646b, Isoc.4.146 (pl.); τῆς στολῆς X.*Cyr*.2.4.5; τῶν βρωμάτων ib.5.2.16; φ. χώρας, opp. ἀρετή, *poorness* of soil, Pl.*Lg*.745d; opp. ἐπιείκεια, Arist.*EN*1175$^{b}$25; φ. μοναρχίας ἡ τυραννίς ib.1160$^{b}$10: in pl., *states of bad health*, Dsc.2.49. 2. *want of accomplishments* or *skill*, Hp.*Art*.77 (v.l. for φλαυρότης), E.*Fr*.641; στρατηγῶν φ. D.18.303; ἡ ἐμὴ φ. my *lack of judgement*, my *poor judgement*, X.*Mem*.4.2.39, Pl.*Hp.Ma*.286d. 3. in good sense, *plainness*, *simplicity of life*, ἡ ἀμφὶ τὸ σῶμα φ. X.*Ages*.11.11, cf. *HG*4.1.30.

**φαυλουργός**, όν, *working ill*, Ar.*Fr*.882: cf. φλαυρουργός.

**φαῦνος**· φαίνων ἑαυτόν, Hsch.; φαυόν· ἀκανθῶδες φυτόν, Id.

**φαυοφόρος**, ἡ, Aeol. = ἱέρεια, Hsch. **φαῦρος**· κοῦφος, Id.

⊛**φαυροφόρος**, ον, dub. sens., πάντες φαυροφόροι πόκτοισι φέρον Call.*Fr.anon*.132 (= *Lyr.Adesp*.73) ap.*Et.Gen*.cod.A (φαυροτέροις cod.B); **φαροφόροι**, referring to sheep *clad in leathern coats*, cj. Reitzenstein Ind.Lect.Rost.1891/2 p.4.

**φαῦσιγξ**, ιγγος, ἡ, (φαύζω) *blister from burning*, also *any blister* or *pustule*, Ar.*Fr*.883 (pl., φαύστιγγες Phot.), Hp.ap.Gal.19.150, Poll.7.110.

**φαυσίμβροτος**, ον, = φαεσίμβροτος, Pi.*O*.7.39.

**φαῦσις**, εως, ἡ, (φάω) *lighting*, *illumination*, τῆς γῆς Lxx *Ge*.1.15, cf. *Ju*.13.13. 2. Astron. = φάσις, φ. ἐκ τῶν τοῦ ἡλίου αὐγῶν heliacal *rising*, Theo Sm.p.137 H.

**φαύσκω**, cited in *EM*673.51, al., but only found in the compds. δια-, ἐπι-, ὑπο-φαύσκω, and in redupl. πιφαύσκω.

**φαῦσμα**· σπλάγχνα ἐκ σίτων πεποιημένα καὶ αἱ ἀπαρχαὶ τῶν πεμμάτων, Hsch.

⊛**φαυστήρ**, ῆρος, ὁ, *lamp* or *candelabrum*, or perh. *large window*, *IG*4$^{2}$(1).109 ii 105, 147 (Epid., iii B.C.).

**φαυστήριος**, ὁ, epith. of Bacchus, from the torches used in his orgies, Lyc.212.

⊛**φαύω**, Aeol. form of φάω, Hsch., *EM*789.28, Eust.1728.6.

**φάψ**, ἡ, gen. φᾰβός, *wild pigeon*, A.*Frr*.210, 257, Arist.*HA*593$^{a}$15, al., Lyc.580.

**φάω** [ᾰ], *shine*, φάε δὲ χρυσόθρονος Ἠώς Od.14.502; Χηλαὶ λεπτὰ φάουσαι Arat.607:—Hsch. also cites a part. φῶντα = λάμποντα, and Ep.aor. 2 πέφη = ἐφάνη. (φαϝ-, cf. φάος, φαῦσις.)

**φαωτός**, ά, όν, = φαιός, χλαῖνα *Schwyzer* 323 *C* 24 (Delph., iv B.C.).

**φέβομαι**, poet. Pass., only pres. and impf., = φοβέομαι, *to be put to flight*, *flee in terror*, οἱ δ' ἐφέβοντο κατὰ μέγαρον Od.22.299; ἔνθα καὶ ἔνθα φέβοντο Il.15.345; ἔνθα καὶ ἔνθα διωκέμεν ἠδὲ φέβεσθαι 8.107; αἴ κε φέβωμαι πληθὺν ταρβήσας 11.404; μένον ἔμπεδον οὐδὲ φέβοντο 5.527; ὑπ' Ἀργείοισι φέβοντο 11.121; πεδίονδε φέβεσθαι A.R.3.1345: c. acc., *flee from*, φεβώμεθα Τυδέος υἱόν Il.5.232. (Cf. φόβος, φοβέω, φοβερός, Lith. *bėgti* 'run'.)

**φεγγαῖον**, prob. f.l. for φεγγέων (gen. pl. of φέγγος) in Aen.Tact.10.26.

**φεγγίτης** [ῑ], ου, ὁ, = σεληνίτης, Plin.*HN*36.163, Alex.Aphr. *in Sens*. 29.7, Tz.ad Lyc.98.

**φεγγοβολέω**, = ἀκτινοβολέω, ἀκτῖσι Σελήνην Man.4.367, cf. 264, 571: *shine*, ib.527.

⊛**φέγγος**, εος, τό, *light*, *splendour*, *lustre*, τῆλε δὲ φ. ἀπὸ χροὸς ἀθανάτοιο λάμπε θεᾶς *h.Cer*.278; τὸ φ. τῆς χρόας Duris 14 J.; τὸ φ. τῆς δόξης Κυρίου Lxx *Ez*.10.4; φ. ἀστραπῆς ὅπλων ib.*Hb*.3.11: freq. like φάος, of *daylight*, either abs. or with some word added, φ. ἡλίου A.*Pers*.377, S.*Tr*.606, etc.; τὸ φ. τοῦ θεοῦ E.*Alc*.722; without the Art., φ. εἰσορᾶν θεοῦ Id.*Or*.1025, cf. S.*Aj*.673; ὦ φέγγος ib.859, E.*El*.866; ὦ φ. ἡμέρας A.*Ag*.1577; δεκάτῳ φέγγει ἔτους in the tenth year, ib.504. b. *moonlight*, X.*Cyn*.5.4; νυκτερινὰ φέγγη, opp. ἡμερινὸν φῶς, Pl.*R*.508c; ἐὰν τὸ φ. ἐκλείψῃ *Cat.Cod.Astr*.4.172, cf. Nonn.*D*.38.255; φῶς ἡμέρας, φέγγος σελήνης Hsch. s.v. φέγγος; τὸ φ. [τοῦ γάλακτος], of the milky way, Arist.*Mete*.346$^{a}$26. c. of men, φ. ἰδεῖν, προσιδεῖν, to see *the light*, come into the world, ἐπεὶ πάμπρωτον εἶδον φ. Pi.*P*.4.111; ἀελίου προσιδεῖν φ. B.5.162; λιπεῖν φ. E.*Or*.954; ὄλωλα, φ. οὐκέτ' ἔστι μοι S.*Tr*.1144. d. *day*, τριταῖον ἤδη φ. E.*Hec*.32, cf. Sosiph.3.1; μοιρίδιον φ. = μ. ἦμαρ, E.*Eleg*.2. 2. *the light* of torches or fire, φ. λαμπάδων A.*Eu*.1022; πυρός ib.1029, *Ch*.1037: *a light*, *torch*, Ar.*Ra*.448, X.*Smp*.1.9; pl. φέγγη *torches* or *watch-fires*, Aen.Tact.10.26 (cj.), Plu.*Cam*.25, etc. 3. *the light* of the eyes, φ. ὀμμάτων E.*Hec*.368, 1035; ὄσσων Theoc.24.75; τυφλὸν φ., i.e. blindness, E.*Hec*.1068 (lyr.). II. *light*, as a metaph. for delight, glory, pride, joy, Pi.*P*.8.97, *N*.3.64, 4.13; τί γὰρ γυναικὶ τούτου φ. ἥδιον δρακεῖν, ἀπὸ στρατείας ἀνδρὶ σώσαντος θεοῦ πύλας ἀνοῖξαι; A.*Ag*.602; of persons, Pi.*N*.9.42; μέγα βροτοῖσι φ. Ἀσκληπιόν Ar.*Pl*.640 (lyr.); Μουσέων φ. Ὅμηρον *AP*7.6 (Antip. Sid.); ὦ ταῖς ἱεραῖς φ. Ἀθήναις Ar.*Eq*.1319 (anap.); πλοῦτος.. ἀνδρὶ φ. Pi.*O*.2.56; φ. ὀπώρας, of wine, Id.*Fr*.153. 2. *lustre*, δικαιοσύνης καὶ σωφροσύνης Pl.*Phdr*.250b; φ. ἐλέους Lxx 3 *Ma*.6.4; τῆς ψυχῆς τὸ γάνωμα καὶ τὸ φ. Plu.2.792a, etc.

**φέγγω**, = φαίνω, *make bright*, Hsch.:—Pass., *shine*, *gleam*, φλογὶ φέγγεται λειμών Ar.*Ra*.344 (lyr.). II. intr., *shine*, ὁ λαμπτὴρ φεγγέτω Aen.Tact.26.3, cf. A.R.4.1714, J.*AJ*3.8.3.

**φεῖ**, τό, name of the letter φ, Callias ap.Ath.10.453d, Hellad.ap.Phot.*Bibl*.530 B.; φεῖ shd. be restored for φῖ in Pl.*Cra*.427a, etc.; a pun on φφ = Φιδίς (leg. Φειδίς) in *AP*7.429 (Alc.).

**φειδαλφιτέω**, *to be sparing of barley*: hence, *to be thrifty*, *Com.Adesp*.1187. Adv. -τως, *thriftily*, Phryn.*PS*p.180 B.

⊛**Φειδιᾰκός**, ή, όν, *made by Phidias*, ἀνδριάς Arr.*Epict*.2.19.23.

**φειδ-ίτης** [ῑ], **-ίτια**, v. φιδ-ίτης, -ίτιον.

⊛**φείδομαι**, Anacr.101, etc.: impf. φείδοντο (without augm.) even in S.*El*.716 after a diphth. at the end of the preceding line: fut. φείσομαι Ar.*Ach*.312 (troch.), Pl.*Ap*.31a, etc., Ep. πεφῐδήσομαι Il.15.215, later fut. Pass. in med. sense φ⟨ε⟩ισθήσομαι *PUniv.Giss*.21.6 (ii A.D.): aor. 1 ἐφεισάμην Sol.32.1, A.*Th*.412, And.2.11, etc., Ep. 3 sg. φείσατο Il.24.236: Ep. redupl. aor. 2 πεφῐδόμην, used by Hom. in opt. πεφῐδοίμην, πεφίδοιτο, Od.9.277, Il.20.464, inf. πεφιδέσθαι 21.101: pf. part. πεφεισμένος Luc.*Hist.Conscr*.59 (in med. sense, D.C.50.20); Ep. imper. πεφίδησο *IG*14.1363.16; part. πεφιδημένος Nonn.*D*.12.392:—*spare*: I. *spare* persons and things, e.g. in war, i.e. *not destroy* them, c. gen., Τρώων Il.21.101; ἀνδρός 24.158, cf. Od.9.277, 22.54, Pl.*Ap*.31a; Ἰλίου Il.15.215; Ἄρης οὐκ ἀγαθῶν φ. Anacr. l.c.; ἀπ' ἀνδρῶν ὧν Ἄρης ἐφείσατο A.*Th*.412; γῆς πατρίδος Sol. l.c.; μὴ φείσῃ βίου *spare* not my life, S.*Ph*.749; μὴ φείδεσθε.. στρατοῦ Id.*Aj*.844; φ. μήτε ἰδίου μήτε δημοσίου οἰκοδομήματος Th.1.90, cf. 3.74: abs., *spare*, *be merciful*, ib.59. II. *spare* persons and things in using them, *use sparingly*, ἵππων φειδόμενος, i.e. *taking care* of them, Il.5.202; πίθου μεσσόθι φ. Hes.*Op*.369; φ. ὃν εἶχε βίον (βίον by attraction to the relat.) Thgn.908; ἰδίᾳ μὲν τῶν ⟨ὄντων⟩ φείδομαι δημοσίᾳ δὲ λῃτουργῶν ἥδομαι Lys.21.16; φείδεσθε τοὐλαίου σφόδρα Pl.Com.190: in this sense, most freq. with a negat., οὐ φ. not *to spare*, i.e. *to use* or *give freely*, οὐδέ νυ τοῦ περ [δέπαος] φείσατο Il.24.236; μὴ φείδεο σίτου Hes.*Op*.604; θνῄσκωμεν ψυχέων μηκέτι φειδόμενοι Tyrt.10.14; τᾶς ζωᾶς Id.15.5; σφετέρας οὐ φείσατο νευρᾶς Pi.*I*.6(5).33; φείδεο τῶν νεῶν, μηδὲ ναυμαχίην ποιέο Hdt.8.68.α'; τούτων φ. μηδενός Id.9.41, cf. 39; φείδοντο κέντρων οὐδέν S.*El*.716; οὐδὲν φ. αὐτῶν οὔτ' ἐν πόνοις κτλ. X.*Cyr*.4.2.1, cf. 7.1.29; οὔτε τοῦ σώματος οὔτε τῶν ὄντων And.2.11; οὐδενὸς ἂν ἐφείσατο τῶν ἑαυτοῦ Lys.19.24; οὔθ' ἱερῶν κτεάνων οὔτε τι δημοσίων φ. Sol.4.13; μήτε χρημάτων μήτε πόνων Pl.*Phd*.78a: later also c. acc., τῶν συμμάχων and τὰ τῶν συμμάχων both in D.C.50.20. 2. abs., *to be sparing*, *live thriftily*, φείδεσθαι μὲν ἄμεινον Thgn.931; τοὺς φειδομένους καὶ τοὺς ἀκριβῶς διαιτῶντας And.4.32; οἱ γεωργοῦντες καὶ φ. D.24.172, cf. Antipho Soph.53; freq. in part. φειδόμενος, η, ον, *thrifty*, Ar.*Pl*.247, 553 (anap.), etc.; ὄμμασι φειδομένοις with *shrinking*, *shy* eyes, *AP*12.21 (Strat.), cf. 5.215 (Agath.), 268 (Id.); αἱ μὴ φ. (sc. μέλισσαι) the un*thrifty* ones, Arist.*HA*627$^{a}$20: also ἔπαινοι πάνυ πεφεισμένοι Luc.*Hist.Conscr*.59; πεφιδημένα δάκτυλα Nonn.*D*.12.392; cf. πεφεισμένως, φειδομένως. III. *have consideration for*, τῆς τοῦ λόγου συμμετρίας Plu.2.114b: with neg., *pay* no *heed to*, οὔτ' ἀνθρώπων φείδεται οὔτε θεῶν *AP*5.278 (Paul.Sil.), cf. 7.706 (Diog.). IV. *draw back from*, *refrain from*, θαλάσσας Alc.*Supp*.4.13 (prob.); κελεύθου Pi.*N*.9.20; κινδύνου X.*Cyr*.5.5.18; τᾶς θήρας Bion *Fr*.10.12; τοῦ λέγειν, τοῦ ἀκολουθεῖν, X.*Cyr*.1.6.19 (v.l.), *HG*7.1.24; φείδου μηδὲν ὧνπερ ἐννοεῖς S.*Aj*.115, cf. E.*Med*.401, etc.; οὐδενὸς φεισάμενος οὔτε τῶν πρὸς τοὺς θεοὺς οὔτε τῶν πρὸς τοὺς πολίτας δικαίων *SIG*708.36 (Istropolis, ii B.C.): (abs., μὴ φείδεσθε E.*Tr*.1285; φείδου μηδέν Id.*Hec*.1044; μὴ φείδου, εἴ τι ἔχεις διδάσκειν X.*Cyr*.1.6.35): c. inf., *spare* to do, *forbear* from doing, dub. in E.*Or*.393 (fort. abs., post φείδου δ' distinguendum); also φ. μή τι δρᾶσαι τῶν τυραννικῶν Pl.*R*.574b; τί φειδόμεσθα τῶν λίθων.. μὴ οὐ καταξαίνειν τὸν ἄνδρα; Ar.*Ach*.319 (troch.). V. in Lxx, with Preps., φ. ἐπί τινι *have mercy upon*.., *Je*.15.5, 21.7; ἐπί τινα Id.28(51).3; φ. περί τινος *to keep one's hands off*.., 2 *Ki*.12.6 (but φ. περὶ κακώσεως *spare* to hurt, ib.*Si.*13.12); φ. ὑπὲρ τῆς κολοκύνθης *Jn.*4.10; ἀπό τινος 1 *Ki.*15.3, *Ez.* 24.21; φ. τι ἀπό τινος *keep* it *off*, *Jb.*30.10; φ. τῆς ψυχῆς ἀπὸ θανάτου ib.33.18, cf. *Ps.*18(19).14; φειδεύμενοι (from contr. **φειδέομαι**) is cj. for φιλεύμεναι in Eus.Mynd.17.

**φειδομένως**, Adv. *sparingly, thriftily*, 2 *Ep.Cor.*9.6, Plu.*Alex.*25; cf. πεφεισμένως.

**φειδ-ός**, ή, όν, *sparing, thrifty*, *Com.Adesp.*101: written **φιδός** by Call. (*Fr.*460) acc. to *EM*791.12 (cod. V): Comp., φειδότερος ἐς τὰ χρήματα Democr.279: hence Com.pr.n. **Φειδύλος**, Philippid.6. **-ώ**, όος, contr. οῦς, ἡ: *sparing*, νεκύων Il.7.409; βίου E.*Fr.*438 (dub.); ἄνευ παντὸς οἴκτου καὶ φειδοῦς Lxx *Es.*3.13; οὔτε φ. τῶν παίδων οὔτ' ἔλεον ἔσχον D.H.8.79 (but τῆς αἰδοῦς ὀλίγην ποιήσασθαι φειδὼ *consideration for*.., S.E.*M.*2.27); φειδὼς (sic cod. P) τῶν παραδειγμάτων ἔστω Longin.22.4; ὀπώρας φ. ἔστω Orib.*Fr.*55; φ. τις ἐγίγνετο.. μὴ προαναλωθῆναι (sc. τὴν εὐπραγίαν) Th.7.81. II. abs., *thrift, sparing*, κτήματα δαρδάπτουσιν ὑπέρβιον, οὐδ' ἔπι φειδώ Od.14.92, cf. 16.315, Hes.*Op.*369; φ. καὶ λιμός Democr.229; φ. πονηρά E.*Fr.*407; opp. ἀσωτία, Arist.*Rh.*1390b1.

**φειδωλ-ή**, ἡ, = foreg., Il.22.244, Sol.13.46, *AP*12.31 (Phan.). ®**-ία**, ἡ, = φειδώ II, Ar.*Nu.*835, *Ec.*750, Pl.*R.*572c, etc. II. = ἀκρίβεια, τόξου χρώμενος φειδωλίᾳ *Trag.Adesp.*569. **-ιον**· δίφρος, σφέλας, χόρτος, Hsch. **-ός**, ή, όν, also ός, όν Ar.*Nu.*421 (anap.), Lys.1.7:—*sparing, thrifty*, and as Subst., *niggard, miser*, Ar.*Pl.*237, Eup.154, Democr.228, Pl.*R.*554a, al.; φ. γαστήρ Ar.*Nu.* l.c.; φ. γλῶσσα *a niggard* tongue, i.e. sparing of words, Hes.*Op.* 720: c. gen., φ. χρημάτων Pl.*R.*548b; τόξων Anon.*Trop.*p.209 S. (cf. φειδωλία II); φ. περί τινα Eus.Mynd.6; τὸ φ. αὐτοῦ τῆς ψυχῆς Pl.*R.*560c; τὸ φ. ἐν δαπάναις Plu.*Galb.*3; θνητά τε καὶ φ. οἰκονομοῦσα pursuing earthly and *niggardly practices*, Pl.*Phdr.*256e; φ. μέτρῳ Alciphr.3.57 (nisi leg. Φειδωνίῳ, cf. sq. II). Adv., τεθραμμένος.. ἀπαιδεύτως τε καὶ φειδωλῶς Id.*R.*559d. II. *merciful*, *PMag.Leid.V.*9.3.

**φείδων**, ωνος, ὁ, *oil-can with a narrow neck, that lets only a little run out*, Poll.10.179, cf. II. 1. II. as pr.n. **Φείδων**, king of Argos, the author of Peloponnesian weights and measures, Hdt.6.127:—hence Adj. **Φειδώνειος** or **Φειδώνιος**, α, ον, μέτρα Arist.*Ath.*10.2, *Fr.*480, Thphr.*Char.*30.11, Str.8.3.33 (Poll. l.c. connects signf. 1 with the Adj.); μέδιμνοι Φ. *Delph.*3(5).3 ii 3 (iv B.C.). 2. name of an old man in Com., *Thrifty*, Antiph.191.21, etc.:—hence Com. patron. **Φειδωνίδης** [ῐ], ου, ὁ, *Thrifty-son*, Ar.*Nu.*65.

**φειδώς**, *parsimonia*, *Gloss.* **φειράω**, v. θηράω.

**φεισμονή**, ἡ, *sparing, mercy*, Phot., Suid.

**φειστέον**, *one must spare*, Isoc.14.15. II. *one must use sparingly*, ἐπαίνου Plu.2.91a; κλυσμῶν Ruf.ap.Orib.8.24.31, cf. Archig.ap.Aët.9.42, Philum.ib.12.

**φέκλη**, ἡ, = Lat. *faecula*, Ruf.*Fr.*115, Crito ap.Gal.12.490; cf. σφέκλη, φαίκλα.

**φελγύνει**· ἀσυνετεῖ, ληρεῖ, Hsch.

**φελίζω**, dub. sens. in Hippon.14.3.

**φελλᾰγωγία**, ἡ, perh. due to a confusion with φαλλ-, Suid. (expld. as a Roman festival).

**φελλάς**· τὸ τῶν βιβλίων ἔξωθεν σκέπασμα, Hsch. s.v. φελλός, Suid.

**φελλάτᾱς** [λᾱ] λίθος, gen. α Polem.Hist.73, ὁ:—a kind of *stone*, of which statues were made, Polem.Hist. l.c., Hsch.; also **φελλεάτας**, called Dor. and expld. by κισσηρώδεις λίθοι in Sch.Ar.*Nu.*71 (**φελλέτας**, Suid.); prob. the same as *pilates* and *pelastes* cited (acc. to codd.) fr. Cato by Fest.p.268 L. (Cf. sq.)

®**φελλεύς**, έως, ὁ, *stony ground*, Cratin.271 (pl.), Is.8.42 (acc. sg., χωρία ἄττα delendum), *IG*2².1582.53; φέλλερα is corrupt in *AB* 315 and φελλός in Hsch. II. **Φελλεύς**, name of a *rocky district* of Attica, Ar.*Ach.*273, *Nu.*71, Pl.*Criti.*111c:—**Φελλείτης**, ου, ὁ, *a man of Phelleus*, St.Byz.

**φελλεύω**, (φελλός) *float like a cork*, Hsch.

**φελλεών**, ῶνος, ὁ, = φελλεύς I, Arr.*Cyn.*17.

**φελλίνας**· κοῦφος, ἀπὸ τοῦ φελλοῦ, Hsch.:—pl. **φελλῖναι** (fort. **φελλίναι**) as name of a kind of water-fowl, Dionys.*Av.*3.23.

**φελλίνιοι**· ὀροβάκχαι, Hsch.

**φέλλῐνος**, η, ον, *made of cork*, Luc.*VH*2.4.

**φελλίον**, τό, = φελλεύς I, X.*Cyn.*5.18 (pl.).

**φελλὶς** γῆ, = foreg., Poll.1.227: Φελλεΐδα is pr.n. of a piece of land in *IG*2².2492.1,32 (the older form was prob. φελλῆϊς (φελλῆς): ἀφελλής is v.l. in Poll. l.c.).

**φελλόδρῡς**, ῠος, ἡ, *holm-oak*, *Quercus Ilex* var. *agrifolia*, Thphr. *HP*1.9.3, 3.3.3, 3.16.3.

**φελλόπους**, ὁ, ἡ, πουν, τό, gen. ποδος, *cork-footed*, Luc.*VH*2.4.

**φελλός**, ὁ, *cork-oak*, *Quercus Suber*, Thphr.*HP*1.2.7, 1.5.2, al. 2. *cork*, φελλῶν καὶ βίβλων καὶ δεσμῶν ἐργαστικαὶ [τέχναι] Pl.*Plt.*288e: esp. of the *corks* on a net, Pi.*P.*2.80, A.*Ch.*506; in a cistern or bowl, Hero *Spir.*1.20, *POxy.*2146.7 (iii A.D.).

**φελλοχᾰλαστέω**, *loosen corks* which hold nets (?), apptly. function of an official in a guild of worshippers of Isis, *IGRom.*1.817.10 (Callipolis).

**Φελλώ**, οῦς, ἡ, *Cork-land*, Com. word in Luc.*VH*2.4.

**φελλώδης**, ες, *of cork* or *bark*, Poll.10.85.

**φελόνης, φελόνιον**, v. φαιλόνης, φαιλόνιον.

**φέλων**, = ἀλαζών, Theognost.*Can.*12.

**φέναγμα**, ατος, τό, (as if from *φενάσσω) = φενάκισμα, Phot.

**φενάκη** [ᾱ], ἡ, = πηνήκη, *false hair, wig*, Luc.*Alex.*59, *D.Meretr.* 11.3.

**φενᾱκ-ίζω**, *play the* φέναξ, *cheat, lie*, Theopomp.Com.8, Ar.*Pl.*271; of the *deceptive appearance* of certain unripe figs, S.*Fr.*731; with neut. Adj., ταῦτ' ἄρ' ἐφενάκιζες σύ Ar.*Ach.*90, cf. D.19.66, Hyp. *Ath.*2: abs., φ. ἀτηρῶς Phld.*Mus.*p.104 K. 2. trans., *cheat, trick*, τινα Ar.*Pax* 1087 (hex.), D.2.7, Men.*Sam.*100; ὧν πεφενάκικε τὴν πόλιν (by attraction for ἅ) D.19.72:—Pass., *to be cheated*, Id.6.29; οἷ' ἐφενακιζόμην ὑπ' αὐτοῦ Ar.*Ra.*921. **-ικῶς**, Adv. *with a pun*, *EM* 402.39. **-ισμα**, ατος, τό, = sq., Hsch. s.v. πηληκίσματα: τὰ περὶ τοῦ ἀγαθοῦ φ. Socr.*Ep.*36. **-ισμός**, ὁ, *cheating, quackery, imposition*, D.24.194, Jul.*Ep.*202: freq. in pl., Ar.*Eq.*633, D.5.10, Din.1. 92. **-ιστής**, οῦ, ὁ, = φέναξ, Phld.*Piet.*27, Sch.Ar.*Ach.*88. **-ιστικός**, ή, όν, *cheating*, Poll.4.21. Adv. -κῶς, ib.24,51, 9.135.

**φενακνίς**, ίδος, ἡ, = φιδακνίς, Demioprat.ap.Poll.10.74.

**φέναξ**, ᾱκος, ὁ, *cheat, quack, impostor*, Ar.*Ra.*909, Heraclit.*Ep.*6.3, Porph.*Chr.*29, etc.; in Ar.*Ach.*89, perhaps with a play on φοῖνιξ (the bird); in *Eq.*634 Φένακες are addressed as the tutelary gods of cheats.

**φενίνδα**, v. φαινίνδα.

**φενν-ησία**, ἡ, *office of* φεννῆσι, *Ostr.*416, al. (i A.D.). **-ῆσι**, ὁ, transcription of Egypt. *p-hn-n-ēse*, 'the priest of Isis', ib.416 (i A.D.); nom. sg. also -ήσιος ib.413 (i A.D.) and -ῆσις ib.420 (i A.D.).

**φεννίον**· Μηδικὴ ὁδός (Pamphyl.), Hsch. ®**φεννίς**, ίδος, ἡ, *a game of ball*, Id. (Perh. corrupted from φαινίνδα, since Hsch. gives acc. φεννίδα as well as nom.; cf. φενίνδα.) **φέννος**· θάνατος, ἐνιαυτός (i.e. ϝένος), Id. ***φένω**, v. θείνω II.

**φεόγω**, = φεύγω, *SIG*194.3,24 (Amphipolis, iv B.C.), 283.11 (Chios, iv B.C.).

**φεραϊκός**, dub. sens. in Herod.Med. in *Rh.Mus.*58.90.

**φεραῖος**, ὁ, a kind of κεστρεύς, Arist.*Fr.*318 (cf. περαίας).

**φερ-άλιος** [ᾰ], ον, Dor. for *φερήλιος, *bringing sunshine*, *Hymn.Is.* 30. **-ανθής**, ές, *flower-bringing*, ἔαρ *AP*9.363 (Mel.). **-ασπις**, ιδος, ὁ, ἡ, *shield-bearing*, *h.Mart.*2, A.*Ag.*693 (lyr.), *Pers.*240 (troch.), *AP*7.152. **-αυγής**, ές, *bringing light*, Nonn.*D.*38.81, al., *PMag. Berol.*2.92.

**φερβήτης**, ου, ὁ, *herdsman*, Hsch. (-τας cod.).

**φέρβω**, only pres. and impf., exc. plpf. ἐπεφόρβειν (v. infr.):—Poet. Verb (used by Hp. (v. infr.) and v.l. in Pl.*Criti.*115a, and later Prose, ἔφερβε φονέα ἑαυτοῦ App.*Syr.*62); *feed, nourish*, of the earth, *h.Hom.*30.2; [ἄνθεμα] ὕδωρ φέρβει Pi.*O.*2.73; μ' ἔφερβε σὸς δόμος E.*Or.*869; of shepherds, φ. βοτά Id.*Hipp.*75; c. gen. rei, ἐπεὶ βοτάνης ἐπεφόρβει βοῦς *h.Merc.*105. 2. *preserve*, πατρῷον οἶκον Hes. *Op.*377. II. Pass., *to be fed, feed upon* a thing, παρέξω δαῖθ' ὑφ' ὧν ἐφερβόμην shall make food for those by whom *I fed myself*, S.*Ph.* 957; τάδε φέρβεται ἐκ σέθεν ὄλβου *h.Hom.*30.4. 2. *eat, consume*, c. acc., ἡ ψυχὴ τὸ σῶμα φέρβεται Hp.*Epid.*6.5.2; metaph., *feed on*, σοφίαν E.*Med.*827 (lyr.): c. dat., ἐλπίσιν Hp.*Ep.*17: abs., *to be fed, live*, A.R.4.1016. 3. *enjoy, have*, κρέσσονα ἁλικίας νόον Pi.*P.*5. 110:—late in Act., φέρβειν πρηΰτατον.. νόημα Opp.*H.*2.643.

**φερε-αυγής**, ές, poet. for φεραυγής, *AP*9.634. **-βοτρυς**, υ, gen. υος, *bearing bunches of grapes*, Nonn.*D.*19.55.

**φερέγγυος**, ον, (ἐγγύη) *giving surety*:—hence, generally, *to be depended upon, trusty*, φρουρήμα, προστάται, σθένος, A.*Th.*449,797, *Eu.*87: c. inf., *capable, sufficient*, οὐ φ. εἰμι δύναμιν παρασχεῖν τοσαύτην Hdt.5.30; λιμὴν φ. διασῶσαι τὰς νέας Id.7.49, cf. A.*Th.*396,470: c. gen. rei, *warrant for* a thing, *able to answer for*, τί.. κελεύεις, ὧν ἐγὼ φ.; S.*El.*942; *trusty* in face of danger, πρὸς τὰ δεινὰ φερεγγυώτατος Th.8.68.—Cf. ἐχέγγυος.

**φερε-γλᾰγής**, ές, *bringing* or *giving milk*, Orph.*L.*218. ®**-ζῠγος**, ον, *bearing the yoke*, ἵππος Ibyc.2. **-ζωος**, ον, *bringing life*, Nonn. *D.*12.6. **-κᾰκος**, ον, *inured to toil* or *hardship*, Plb.3.71.10, 3.79. 5. **-καρπος**, ον, *yielding fruit*, σπέρματα, γαῖα, Plu.2.495c, *AP*9. 778 (Phil.); Βάκχος, Σελήνη, Orph.*H.*50.10, 9.5, cf. *Fr.*44. **-κλεής**, ές, *renowned*, prob. in Euph.79. **-κοσμος**, ον, *ornamental*, Sor.1. 2.

**Φερεκράτειον** μέτρον, metre *used by Pherecrates*, Heph.10.2.

**φερε-κῡδής**, ές, *renowned*, νᾶσος B.12.182; γένος *IG*12(9).1179 (Chalcis). **-μηλος**, ον, = πολύμηλος, νᾶσοι Pi.*Pae.*5.38.

**φερεμμελίης**, ου, ὁ, poet. for *φερεμελίας, *spear-bearing*, φώς Mimn. 14.4.

**φέρενα**, Aeol. = φερνή, Hdn.Gr.2.939, *EM*790.43.

**φερέ-νῑκος**, ον, *carrying off victory, victorious*, name of a race-horse of King Hiero, Pi.*O.*1.18, etc. (The fem. pr.n. Βερενίκη is Maced. for Φερενίκη.) ®**-οικος**, ον, *carrying one's house with one*, of the Scythians in Hdt.4.46. II. Subst., *house-carrier*, i.e. *snail*, Hes.*Op.*571: acc. to others, a kind *of wasp*, or *a tortoise*, Hsch., *EM*790.35, cf. φέροικος. **-οινος**, ον, *wine-bearing*, γῆ A.D.*Synt.*8. 24. **-πολις**, ιος, ὁ, ἡ, *upholding the city*, Τύχη Pi.*Fr.*39; poet. also **φερέπτολις**, Opp.*H.*1.197, Nonn.*D.*2.86, al. **-πονέω**, *endure toil* or *hardship*, Eustr. *in EN*90.10. **-πονία**, ἡ, *patience in toil* or *hardship*, App.*Prooem.*11,12, al., Iamb.*Protr.*21.κα'. **-πονος**, ον, *bringing toil and trouble*, ἀμπλακίαι Pi.*P.*2.31. II. *bearing toil* or *hardship, patient thereof*, ἐν ταῖς μάχαις App.*Gall.*1.3; τὸ φ. τῆς ψυχῆς Them.*Or.*11.149d, cf. Eust.1488.44. Adv. Sup. -ώτατα App.*Mith.*74. **-πτερος**, ον, *bearing wings, winged*, Max.610: gen. pl. φερεπτερύγων from -πτέρυγος, ον, or -πτέρυξ, ὁ, ἡ, Opp.*H.* 2.482. ®**-πτόλεμος**, ον, poet. for *φερεπόλεμος, *warlike*, γαῖα *Jahresh.*18 *Beibl.*35 (Olba); νησοὶ φ. ships *of war*, prob. in Orac.ap. Paus.10.9.11. **-πτολις**, v. φερέπολις.

**φερεσ-ανθής**, ές, = φερανθής, χοροί prob. in *h.Hom.*30.14. ® **-βίος**, ον, *life-bearing, life-giving*, γαῖα *h.Ap.*341, Hes.*Th.*693; οὖθαρ ἀρούρης *h.Cer.*450; ἄρουρα *h.Hom.*30.9; Ἥρη Emp.6.2; Δήμητρος στάχυς A.*Fr.*300.7; Δηώ Antiph.1:—Poet. word, used in Arist.*Mu.*391$^b$13. **-σᾰκής**, ές, gen. έος, *shield-bearing*, of men, Hes.*Sc.*13, Nonn.*D.*26.291, al.; also ποταμός, νῆες, ib.23.11, 36.447; τελαμῶνες Tryph.11.

**φερεσσίπονος** [ῐ], ον, = φερέπονος, *IG*14.1015.

**φερε-στάφῦλος** [ᾰ], ον, *bearing bunches of grapes*, Ἐρυθραί Archestr.*Fr.*4.17; of Dionysus, *AP*9.363.11 (Mel.), Opp.*C.*3.79. **-στᾰχυς**, υ, *bearing ears of corn*, αὖλαξ Nonn.*D.*42.330, al. **-στέφᾰνος**, ον, *bringing victory*, Χάριτες B.18.6. II. *winning the crown of victory*, *IG*2$^2$.3118.

**φερετρεύομαι**, Pass., *to be carried on a φέρετρον*, Plu.*Marc.*8.

**Φερέτριος**, ὁ, Lat. *Feretrius*, epith. of Zeus, D.H.2.34, etc.

**φέρετρον**, τό, (φέρω) *bier, litter, frame*, Plb.8.29.4; cf. φέρτρον.

**φέριστος**, η, ον, v. φέρτατος.

**φέρμα**, ατος, τό, (φέρω) *that which is borne, fruit of the womb*, A.*Ag.*119 (pl., lyr.). 2. *fruit of the earth*, Id.*Supp.*690 (lyr.).

**φερν-άριον**, τό, Dim. of sq., *BGU*1052.10, 1101.18, etc. (i B.C.). **-ή**, ἡ, (φέρω):—*that which is brought by the wife, dowry*, Hdt.1.93, E.*IA*47 (anap.), *Hipp.*629, X.*Cyr.*8.5.19, Aeschin.2.31, *OGI*218.65 (Ilium, iii B.C.), etc.; θεραποντὶς φ. *a dowry* of handmaids, i.e. *given as a dowry*, A.*Supp.*979 (anap.); pl., of *a dower*, as consisting of divers presents, E.*Or.*1662, Anaxandr.41.23 (anap.); φερναὶ πολέμου, of a wife won in battle, E.*Ion* 298; also, *bridal gifts*, λάζυσθε φ. τάσδε, παῖδες, of Medea's presents to Creüsa, Id.*Med.*956. II. Dor. ⊛ φερνά, *portion* of victim reserved for the God, *IG*4$^2$(1).40.6, 41.7 (Epid., v/iv B.C.). **-ίζω**, fut. ιῶ *UPZ*2.15 (ii B.C.):—*portion, endow*, φερνῇ φερνιεῖ παρθένον LXX *Ex.*22.16:—Pass., πεφερνισμένη ὑπὸ τοῦ πατρός *PEnteux.*9.8 (iii B.C.), cf. *PLond.*1.177.15 (i A.D.).

**φέρνιον**, τό, (φέρω) *fish-basket*, Men.717, *Com.Adesp.*1342, Ael. *NA*17.18, Alciphr.1.9, Poll.6.94:—in Hsch. written **φέρμια, τά**.—On the accent, v. Hdn.Gr.1.360.

**φέρ-οικος**, ὁ, a white animal like a *squirrel*, Cratin.94 (ὅμοιον γαλῇ Phot., cf. Hsch. s.v. φερέοικος, *EM*790.36, sed fort. γαλεώτῃ). **-όλβιος**, ον, *bringing happiness*, Orph.*H.*64.12, 68.2. **-όμβρον**, τό, = σίκυς ἄγριος, Ps.-Dsc.4.150; = πέπλιον, ib.168. **-οπλος**, ον, *bearing arms*, *Pae.Delph.*8, Max.380.

**φερρεύει**· ἀποφέρει, Hsch.

**Φερρεφάττιον** (-εῖον *AB*314), τό, *sanctuary of Persephone*, D.54.8.

⊛ **Φερσέφασσα**, ἡ, = Περσέφασσα, Περσεφόνη, S.*Ant.*894, E.*Hel.*175 (lyr.): Att. **Φερρέφαττα**, Ar.*Th.*287, *Ra.*671 (with vv. ll.), Pl.*Cra.*404c,d, *Hesperia* 4.21 (Athens, iv B.C.); also Dor. τὰν Φερρέφατταν Epicr.9.3; **Φερσεφάασσα** Epigr.ap.Arist.*Mir.*843$^b$27:—hence **Φερσεφάσσια**, τά, festival at Cyzicus, *IGRom.*4.949 (Chios). (Etym. uncertain: παρὰ τὸ φέρβειν τὴν φάτταν Porph.*Abst.*4.16.)

⊛ **Φερσεφόνη**, poet. for Περσεφόνη, Pi.*O.*14.21; Φερσεφόνας ἕδος, of Acragas, Id.*P.*12.2, cf. Pl.*Cra.*404c; **Φερσεφόνεια** Orph.*H.*24.11, al.:—Adj. **Φερσεφόνειος**, α, ον, δώματα *AP*7.483. (Expld. as τὸ διὰ τῶν καρπῶν φερόμενον καὶ φονευόμενον πνεῦμα Cleanth.*Stoic.*1.124.)

**φερτάζω**, collat. form of φέρω, Hsch.

⊛ **φέρτᾰτος**, η, ον, *bravest, best*, πολὺ φ. Il.1.581, etc.; μέγα φ. 16.21, cf. *Lyr.Alex.Adesp.*25, etc.: c. dat. modi, χερσίν τε βίηφί τε φ. ἦσαν Od.12.246; περὶ δ' ἔγχει Ἀχαιῶν φ. ἐσσι Il.7.289; ὄλβῳ φ. Pi.*N.*10.13: of things, κακῶν φέρτατον *the best*, i.e. *least bad*, among evils, Il.17.105; λόγοι φ. *best*, Pi.*P.*5.48; ὅ τι φέρτατον ἀνδρὶ τυχεῖν Id.*O.*7.26. 2. in form **φέριστος**, ἄνδρα φέριστον Il.9.110; μὴ φῦναι φέριστον B.5.160, cf. Pi.*Fr.*126 (φέρτ- cj. Boeckh): mostly voc. φέριστε, Il.6.123, 15.247, Theoc.7.125, etc.; φέριστοι Il.23.409; φέριστε Καδμείων ἄναξ A.*Th.*39; ὦ φ. δεσποτῶν S.*OT*1149; εἶεν, ὦ φ. Pl.*Phdr.*238d; II. Comp. **φέρτερος**, α, ον, *braver, better*, of persons, πολὺ φ. Il.4.56, etc.: c. dat. modi, βίῃ καὶ χερσὶ καὶ ἔγχεϊ φ. 3.431, cf. Od.6.6; φ. οὐκ ὀλίγον ἔγχει Il.19.217: c. inf., θεοὶ.. φέρτεροί εἰσι νοῆσαι Od.5.170; φ. γόνος πατρός Pi.*I.*8(7).35; παῖδα φ. πατρός A.*Pr.*768: of things, ἀγών, νόστος, Pi.*O.*1.7, *P.*1.35; πολὺ φέρτερόν ἐστιν 'tis much *better*, Il.1.169; τί φ. ἢ.. c. inf., B.4.18: c. inf., Od.12.109, 21.154; εἰς τὸ φ. τίθει τὸ μέλλον E.*Hel.*346 (lyr.). Adv., τέττιγος φέρτερον ᾄδεις Theoc.1.148. (From root φερ- 'bring', 'produce': ἀπὸ τοῦ φέρειν βέλτιον Hsch.)

**φερτός**, ή, όν, *endurable*, οὐ τλατᾶς οὐ φερτᾶς E.*Hec.*158 (lyr.).

**φέρτρον**, τό, = φέρετρον, Il.18.236, Ael.*VH*12.64.

**φέρτρυς**· ἆθλος (Thurii), Hsch.

⊛ **Φερφερέτας**, ὁ, epith. of Zeus in Thessaly (cf. Περφεραῖος), *IG*9(2).1057.1 (Mopsium, i B.C.).

⊛ **φέρω** (Locr. **φάρω** [ᾰ], *IG*9(1).334.5 (Oeanthea, v B.C.)), only pres. and impf. (late 1 aor. 3 pl. ἤφεραν *IG*3.1379), Il.21.458, etc.: Ep. forms, 2 pl. imper. φέρτε Il.9.171; 2 sg. subj. φέρῃσθα Call.*Dian.*144; 3 sg. subj. φέρῃσι Il.18.308, Od.5.164, al.; Ep. inf. φερέμεν Il.9.411, al.: impf. ἔφερον, Ep. φέρον 3.245; also φέρεσκε, φέρεσκον (3 pl.), Od.9.429, 10.108. II. fut. οἴσω Il.7.82, etc.; Dor. οἰσῶ Theoc.3.11; 1 pl. οἰσεῦμες Id.15.133; 3 pl. *hoίσοντι Tab.Heracl.*1.150: the foll. act. forms are not fut. in sense, imper. οἶσε Od.22.106, 481, Ar.*Ach.*1099, 1101, 1122, *Ra.*482; οἰσέτω Il.19.173, Od.8.255; 3 pl. οἰσόντων Antim.15; inf. οἴσειν Pi.*P.*4.102, Ep. οἰσέμεν Od.3.429, οἰσέμεναι Il.3.120, Od.8.399, etc.: aor. 1 inf. οἶσαι Ph.1.611 codd. (ἀν-οῖσαι is prob. in Hdt.1.157):—Med., fut. οἴσομαι Il.22.217, S.*El.*969, etc. (in pass. sense, E.*Or.*440, X.*Oec.*18.6; so Dor. οἰσεῖται Archim.*Fluit.*1.7, al.): fut. Pass. οἰσθήσομαι D.44.45, Arist.*Ph.*205$^a$13, Archim.*Fluit.*1.3, al., (ἐξ-) E.*Supp.*561:—Pass., pf. προοῖσται Luc.*Par.*2; cf. οἰστέον, οἰστός (ἀν-οιστός). III. from ἐνεγκ- (not found in Hom. or Hdt., exc. as v.l. in Il.19.194, but in Pi.*O.*13.66, *I.*8(7).21, (προσ-) Id.*P.*9.36, also B.16.62, and normal in Att. and Trag., also in codd.Hp., *Epid.*1.1.2, al.) come aor. 1 ἤνεγκα, and aor. 2 ἤνεγκον:—Indic., 1 sg. ἤνεγκον S.*OC*521 (lyr.), 964, Ar.*Ra.*1299, *Th.*742, *Lys.*944, (δι-) Isoc.18.59, but ἤνεγκα S.*El.*13, E.*Ion*38, Aeschin.2.4, and in compos. with Preps.; 2 sg. always ἤνεγκας Ar.*Av.*540 (lyr.), (ἐξ-) S.*Tr.*741 (in Ar.*Th.*742, δέκα μῆνας αὔτ' ἐγὼ ἤνεγκον is answd. by ἤνεγκας σύ;); 3 sg. ἤνεγκε, common to both forms; dual δι-ηνεγκάτην Pl.*Lg.*723b; pl. always ἠνέγκαμεν, -ατε, -αν (3 pl. ἀπ-ήνενκαν *IG*2$^2$.1620.37, al., once ἀπ-ήνεγκον ib.1414.2; δι-ηνέγκομεν is f.l. in X.*Oec.*9.8): imper., 2 sg. ἔνεγκε E.*Heracl.*699, Ar.*Eq.*110, X.*Mem.*3.6.9 (ἔνεγκον cj. Pors. in Anaxipp.8); 3 sg. ἐνεγκάτω Ar.*Pax*1149 (troch.), *Th.*238, Pl.*Phd.*116d, (προσ-) X.*Smp.*5.2; but ἐξ-ενεγκέτω *IG*1$^2$.63.33, 76.61; Dor. 3 pl. ἐνεγκόντω ib.5(1).26.16 (Amyclae, ii/i B.C.); 2 pl. ἐξ-ενέγκατε Ar.*Ra.*847: subj. ἐνέγκω common to both forms: opt., 1 sg. ἐνέγκαιμι E.*Hipp.*393, Pl.*Cri.*43c: 3 sg. ἐνέγκαι (cod.A, but -κοι cod.Laur.) S.*Tr.*774, but ἐνέγκοι Id.*Fr.*84 (anap.), Pl.*R.*330a, (ξυν-) Th.6.20, etc.; 2 pl. ἐνέγκαιτε (ἐνέγκατε codd.) E.*Heracl.*751 (lyr.): inf. ἐνεγκεῖν A.*Supp.*766, S.*OC*1599, *IG*2$^2$.40.18, etc., (προσ-) Pi.*P.*9.36, Hp.*VM*15; Hellenistic ἐνέγκαι Arist.*Oec.*1349$^a$27 (εἰσ-), *PAmh.*2.30.35 (ii B.C.), *Ev.Marc.*2.4 (προσ-), etc., found also in codd.Hp., *Aff.*3 (προσ-), *Nat.Mul.*19 (δι-): part. ἐνεγκών Pi.*I.*8(7).21, S.*El.*692, Th.6.56, etc., ἐνέγκας *IG*2$^2$.1361.21 (εἰσ-), 333.4, D.49.51 (and later, Demetr.Com.Nov.1.10 (εἰσ-), Arist.*Oec.*1351$^a$14, etc.; in X. we find ἐξ-ενεγκόντες *Mem.*1.2.53, and δι-ενεγκοῦσα, συν-ενεγκόντες, vv.ll. in ib.2.2.5, *An.*6.5.6):—Med., only ἠνεγκάμην, Ar.*Ec.*76 (ἐξ-), etc. (exc. imper. ἐνεγκοῦ S.*OC*470); 2 sg. ἠνέγκω E.*Supp.*583, X.*Oec.*7.13; 3 sg. ἠνέγκατο S.*Tr.*462, Pl.*R.*406b, etc.; 1 pl. ἠνεγκάμεθα Id.*Ion*530b, (προ-) *Phlb.*57a; inf. εἰσ-ενέγκασθαι Isoc.15.188: part. ἐνεγκάμενος Aeschin.1.131, (ἀπ-) X.*Ages.*6.2. IV. from ἐνεικ- comes aor. 1 ἤνεικα, found mostly in Ion. (but not in codd.Hp.), Ep. and Lyr., also at Cos (v. infr.) and implied elsewh. in pass. forms (v. infr. v):—the endings are those of aor. 1, exc. in imper. ἔνεικε Od.21.178, inf. ἐνεικέμεν (v.l. ἐνεγκέμεν) Il.19.194, ἐνείκην (v. infr.), and part. μετ-ενεικών, ἐξ-ενικοῦσι (v. infr.), cf. συνενείκομαι:—1 sg. ἀν-ένεικα Od.11.625; 2 sg. ἀπ-ένεικας Il.14.255; 3 sg. ἤνεικε Od.18.300, al., Hdt.2.146, Ep. ἔνεικε Il.15.705, al.; 1 pl. ἐνείκαμεν Od.24.43; 3 pl. ἤνεικαν Hdt.3.30, Ep. ἔνεικαν Il.9.306; imper. 2 sg. ἔνεικον Anacr.62.3; 2 pl., ἐνείκατε Od.8.393; 3 pl. ἐνεικάντων *Schwyzer* 688*B*3 (Chios, v B.C.); inf. ἐνεῖκαι Il.18.334, Pi.*P.*9.53, Hdt.1.32; ἐνεικέμεν (v. supr.); Aeol. ἐνείκην Alc.*Oxy.*1788 *Fr.*15 ii 20; part. ἐνείκας Il.17.39, (ἀν-) Hdt.2.23; μετ-ενεικών *Abh.Berl.Akad.*1928(6).22 (Cos, iii B.C.):—Med., 3 sg. ἀν-ενείκατο Il.19.314; 3 pl. ἠνείκαντο 9.127, Hdt.1.57, (ἐσ-) 7.152; part. ἐνεικάμενος Alc.35.4. 2. aor. 1 ἤνῐκα is found in the foll. dialect forms: 3 sg. ἤνικε *IG*4$^2$(1).121.110 (Epid., iv B.C.); ἤνικεν *SIG*239 *B*i11 (Delph., iv B.C.); ἀν-ήνικε *IG*4.757*A*12, al. (Troezen, ii B.C.); ἀπ-ήνικε ib.4$^2$(1).103.16, al. (Epid., iv B.C.); but ἤνῑκε is prob. written for ἤνεικε in *IG*4.801.3 (Troezen, vi B.C.); 1 pl. ἀν-ηνίκαμες[ῐ] *GDI* 3591*b*21 (Calymna); 3 pl. ἤνικαν *SIG*239*B*i17 (Delph., iv B.C.), *IG*12(2).15.15 (Mytil., iii B.C.); 3 sg. subj. ἐνίκει *Berl.Sitzb.*1927.161 (Cyrene); ἐσ-ενίκη, and inf. ἐσ-ένικαι, *IG*12(2).645*b*43, 39 (Nesus, iv B.C.); part. (dat. pl.) ἐξ-ενικοῦσι *IG*4.823.49 (Troezen, iv B.C.); so in later Gr., εἰσ-ήνικα *Supp.Epigr.*7.381, 382 (Dura-Europos, iii A.D.); ἤνιγκα ib.383 (ibid., iii A.D.):—Med., part. ἐξ-ε[νικ]άμενος *IG*12(2).526*a*5 (Eresus, iv B.C.). b. Boeot. aor. 1 in 3 pl. εἴνιξαν *IG*7.2418.24 (Thebes, iv B.C.); 1 sg. ἤνειγξα Hdn.Gr.2.374. V. other tenses: pf. ἐνήνοχα D.21.108, 22.62, (ἐξ-) Luc.*Pr.Im.*15, 17, (μετ-) Pl.*Criti.*113a, (συν-) v.l. in X.*Mem.*3.5.22:—Pass., fut. ἐνεχθήσομαι Arist.*Ph.*205$^b$12, Archim.*Fluit.*2.2, al., (ἐπ-) Th.7.56, (κατ-) Isoc.13.19: aor. ἠνέχθην X.*An.*4.7.12 and freq. in compds.; Ion. ἀπ-ηνείχθην Hdt.1.66, etc.; (περι-) ib.84; 3 pl. written ἠνείχτθησαν in *Schwyzer* 707*B*9 (Ephesus, vi B.C.); Dor. part. ἐξ-ενειχθείς *IG*4$^2$(1).121.115 (Epid., iv B.C.); Hellenistic ἐνεγχθείς *PCair.Zen.*327.42 (iii B.C.), (συμπερι-) *IPE*1$^2$.32*A*31, 78, *B*70 (Olbia, iii B.C.); in dialects, 3 sg. indic. ἀπ-ηνίχθη *IG*4$^2$(1).103.111 (Epid., iv B.C.); 3 sg. subj. ἐξ-ενιχθῇ ib.12(5).593*A*23 (Ceos, v B.C.), *Abh.Berl.Akad.*1928(6).21 (Cos, iii B.C.); Boeot. ἐν-ενιχθεῖ *IG*7.3172.150 (Thespiae, iii B.C.); part. (neut.) ἐπ-ενιχθέν *Abh.Berl.Akad.*1928(6).53 (Telos, iv B.C., ined.); Att. pf. ἐνήνεγμαι, ἐνήνεκται Pl.*R.*584d, εἰσ-ενήνεκται E.*Ion*1340; ἀν-ενήνεγκται *IG*1$^2$.91.4; ἐπαν-ενήνειγκται ib.2$^2$.1607*a*7; Ion. ἐξ-ενηνειγμένος Hdt.8.37; Att. plpf. προσ-ενήνεκτο X.*HG*4.3.20; part. κατ-, μετ-ενηνεγμένος Plb.10.30.2, Str.13.1.12. (With φέρω cf. Lat. *fero*, OE. *beran*, Skt. *bhárati* 'bear'; οἴσω is of uncertain origin; ἐνεγκ- is prob. redupl. ἐγκ- (ἐνεκ- in Pass. forms and in δουρηνεκής, etc.), cogn. with Skt. *náśati* 'attain,' Lat. *nanciscor*, Lith. *nèšti* 'carry, bear'; ἐνεικ- (ἐνῐκ-) is of uncertain origin; the glosses ἐνέεικαν· ἤνεγκαν, and ἐνεείκω· ἐνέγκω (Hsch.) are not corroborated.)

A. Act., I. *bear* or *carry* a load, ἐν ταλάροισι φέρον μελιηδέα καρπόν Il.18.568; μέγα ἔργον, ὃ οὐ δύο γ' ἄνδρε φέροιεν 5.303; ἦγον μὲν μῆλα, φέρον δ' εὐήνορα οἶνον Od.4.622; χοάς A.*Ch.*15; φ. ἐπ' ὤμοις S.*Tr.*564; χερσὶν φ. Id.*Ant.*429; φ. ὅπλα βραχίονι E.*Hec.*14; *bear* (as a device) on one's shield, A.*Th.*559, etc.; γαστέρι κοῦρον φ., of a pregnant woman, Il.6.59; φ. ὑπὸ ζώνην or ζώνης ὕπο, A.*Ch.*1000(992), E.*Hec.*762: in Trag. stronger than ἔχω, ἁγνὰς αἵματος χεῖρας φ. *to have* hands clean from blood, E.*Hipp.*316 (v.l. φορεῖς); ἀλαὸν ὄμμα φέρων Id.*Ph.*1531 (lyr.); γλῶσσαν εὔφημον φ. A.*Ch.*581, cf. *Supp.*994; καλὸν φ. στόμα S.*Fr.*930 codd. (nisi leg. φορῇ); ἄψοφον βίσιν φ. Id.*Tr.*967 (lyr.). II. *bear, convey*, with collat. notion of *motion*, freq. in Hom., πῇ δὴ..τόξα φέρεις; Od.21.362; πρόσω φ. ib. 369; εἴσω φέρω σ' ἐντεῦθεν Ar.*V.*1444, cf. Pl.*Lg.*914b; πόδες φέρον Il.6.514; πέδιλα τά μιν φέρον 24.341, etc.; of horses, 2.838; ἵππω.. ἅρμα οἴσετον 5.232, etc.; of ships, Od.16.323, cf. Il.9.306; τὰ σώματα τῶν ζῴων συνέστηκεν ἐκ τοῦ φέροντος καὶ τοῦ φερομένου Diocl. *Fr.*17. b. of persons, *bring to bear*, μένος or μένος χειρῶν ἰθύς τινος φέρειν *hurl* one's strength right upon or against him, Il.16.602, 5.506; φ. τὴν ὀργήν, τὴν αἰτίαν ἐπί τινα, Plb.21.31.8, 33.11.2. c. *lead, direct*, τὴν πόλιν Plu.*Luc.*6. 2. of wind, *bear along*, [πνοιὴ Ζεφύρου] φ. νῆάς τε καὶ αὐτούς Od.10.26; [σχεδίην] ἄνεμοι φέρον ἔνθα καὶ ἔνθα 5.330, cf. 4.516, Il.19.378, etc.; ἐπέλασσε φέρων ἄνεμος Od.3.300, 7.277, cf. 5.111, etc.: abs., ὁ βορέας ἔξω τοῦ Πόντου εἰς τὴν Ἑλλάδα φέρει *is fair* for Greece, X.*An.*5.7.7: metaph., ὅπῃ ἂν ὁ λόγος ὥσπερ πνεῦμα φ. Pl.*R.*394d; φ. τινὰ φρένες δύσαρκτοι A.*Ch.*1023, cf. *Th.*687 (lyr.):—Pass., v. infr. B. III. *endure, suffer*, λυγρά Od.18.135; ἄτην Hdt.1.32; χαλινόν, ζυγόν, A.*Ag.*1066,1226; πημονάς, τύχας, Id.*Pers.*293, E.*Or.*1024; ξυμφοράς Th.2.60; τὰς οὐ προσηκούσας ἁμαρτίας Antipho 3.2.10; also of food, ἐσθίουσι πλείω ἢ δύνανται φ. X.*Cyr.*8.2.21; of strong wine, *bear, admit*, καὶ τὰ τρία φέρων καλῶς, i.e. three parts of water, instead of ἴσον ἴσῳ, Ar.*Eq.*1188, cf. *Ach.*354; so τὰς ἐπιδείξεις..φέρουσιν αὐτοῦ (sc. Ἰσοκράτους) οἱ λόγοι, τοὺς δὲ ἐν ἐκκλησίαις..ἀγῶνας οὐχ ὑπομένουσι D.H.*Isoc.*2: metaph., ἣ φέρειν πέφυκε Pl.*Ti.*48a. 2. freq. with modal words, πήματα κόσμῳ φ. Pi.*P.*3.82; σιγῇ κακά E.*Hec.*738; ὀργῇ τὸν πόλεμον Th.1.31; θυμῷ φ. Id.5.80; χαρᾷ φ. τι J.*AJ*19.1.13: esp. with an Adv., [ὕβριν] ῥηϊδίως φ. Hes.*Op.*215; δεινῶς, βαρέως, πικρῶς, χαλεπῶς φέρειν τι, *bear* a thing impatiently, *take* it ill or amiss, Hdt.2.121.γ', 5.19, E.*Ion*610, Pl.*R.*330a, etc.; δυσπετῶς, βαρυστόνως φ., A.*Pr.*752, *Eu.*794; προθύμως φέρειν τὸν πόλεμον *to be* zealous *about* the war, Hdt.9.18,40; προθύμως τὰ τοῦ πολέμου ἔφερον Th.8.36; αἶσαν φέρειν ὡς ῥᾷστα A.*Pr.*104; συμφορὴν ὡς κουφότατα φ. Hdt.1.35; ῥᾳδίως φ. Pl.*Grg.*522d, al.; εὐπετῶς φ. S.*Fr.*585, X.*Mem.*2.1.6; εὐπόρως (εὐφόρως Brunck) ἐνεγκεῖν S.*Ph.*873; εὐμενῶς, εὐχερῶς φ., D.*Ep.*3.45, Pl.*R.*474e; these phrases are used mostly c. acc. rei; also c. part., βαρέως ἤνεικε ἰδών Hdt.3.155, cf. Ar.*Th.*385, etc.; φ. ἐλαφρῶς..λαβόντα ζυγόν Pi.*P.*2.93; ῥᾳδίως φέρεις ἡμᾶς ἀπολείπων Pl.*Phd.*63a: c. gen., τοῦ ἐνδεοῦς χαλεπώτερον φ. Th.1.77, cf. 2.62; ἐπί τινι, χαλεπῶς φ. ἐπὶ τῇ πολιορκίᾳ X.*HG*7.4.21, cf. Isoc.12.232; πράως ἐπὶ τοῖς γιγνομένοις φ. D.58.55: c. dat. only, βαρέως φέρειν τοῖς παροῦσι, τῇ ἀτιμίᾳ, X.*An.*1.3.3, *HG*3.4.9, cf. 5.1.29; later, χαλεπῶς φ. διά τι, πρός τι, D.S.17.111, Jul.*Or.*1.17c codd. IV. *bring, fetch*, εἰ..θεὸς αὐτὸν ἐνείκαι Od.21.196; φ. ἄποινα Il.24.502; ἄρνε 3.120, cf. Sapph.95; ὕδωρ, οἶνον, Anacr.62.1; ἔντεα Il.18.191; τόξα Od.21.359; κνημῖδας A.*Th.*675; δᾷδα Ar.*Nu.*1490, etc.; γῆν τε καὶ ὕδωρ Hdt.7.131:—Med., *carry* or *bring with* one, or *for one's own use*, ποδάνιπτρα Od.19.504; οἶνον Alc.35, cf. Hdt.4.67, 7.50, X.*Mem.*3.14.1; φερνὰς δόμοις E.*Andr.*1282; *fetch*, Od.2.410; χοὰς ἐκ κρήνης S.*OC*470. 2. *bring, offer, present*, δῶρα Od.8.428, etc.; μέλος Pi.*P.*2.3; χοάς τινι A.*Ch.*487; φ. πέπλον δώρημά τινι S.*Tr.*602; πρός τινα δῶρα X.*An.*7.3.31; χάριν τινὶ φ. *grant* any one a favour, *do* him a kindness, Il.5.211, Od.5.307, al.; ἐπὶ ἦρα φ. τινί Il.1.572, Od.3.164, etc.; φ. τισὶ εὐνοίας, ὄνησιν ἀστοῖς, A.*Supp.*489, S.*OC*287; but after Hom., χάριν τινὶ φ. *show* gratitude to him, Pi.*O.*10(11).17; μῆνιν φ. τινί *cherish* wrath against..A.*Niob.* in *PSI*11.1208.12. b. = ἄγω IV. 1, ἄχρι νῦν καθ' ὥραν ἔτους λέγονται πένθος ἐπὶ Μελεάγρῳ φέρειν Ant.Lib.2.7; Ἰάλεμος· ὁ ἐπὶ τοῖς ἀπολωλόσιν ἀνίαν φέρων, Suid.:—Med., τοῦ γονέως ἐφ' ᾧ γε τὸ πένθος φέρεσθε Phalar.*Ep.*103.1. 3. *bring, produce, cause*, [ἀστὴρ] φέρει πυρετὸν βροτοῖσιν Il.22.31; ὄσσαν..ἥ τε φ. κλέος ἀνθρώποισι Od.1.283, cf. 3.204; φ. κακόν, πῆμα, ἄλγεα, etc., *work* one woe, Il.8.541, Od.12.231,427, etc.; δηϊοτῆτα φ. *bring* war, 5.203; ἐπ' ἀλλήλοισι φ. Ἄρηα Il.3.132, cf. 8.516; πόλεμον Hes.*Sc.*150; θάνατον φ. B.5.134; τοῦτο εὐδοξίαν σοι οἴσει Pl.*Ep.*312c; τὸ σωθῆναι τὸ ψεῦδος φέρει S.*Ph.*109; τέχναι..φόβον φέρουσιν μαθεῖν A.*Ag.*1135 (lyr.); ὥσπερ τὸ δίκαιον ἔφερε as justice *brought with it, brought about*, i.e. as was just, no more than just, Hdt.5.58; ἀν' ὅ κα φέρῃ ὁ λόγος ὁ ταμία Φιλοκλέος *IG*4$^2$(1).77.13 (Epid., ii B.C.); of a calculation, *yield* a result, Vett.Val.349.27; *produce, adduce, bring forward*, παραδείγματα Isoc.7.6, etc.; πάσας αἰτίας D.58.22; ἁρμόττουσαν εἰκόνα Id.61.10:—Pass., εἰς τὴν συνηγορίαν..τοιαῦτά τινα φέρεται Sor.2.3. b. *bring* or *carry with one, involve*, τὸ πᾶν ἡμῖν τοῦ πολέμου φέρουσιν αἱ νέες Hdt.8.62; οὐ ξύλων ἀγὼν ὁ τὸ πᾶν φέρων ἐστὶ ἡμῖν, ἀλλ' ἀνδρῶν ib.100. 4. μῦθον φ. τινί *bring* one word, Il.10.288, 15.202; ἀγγελίην φ. *bring* a message, ib.175, Od.1.408; λόγον Pi.*P.*8.38; ἐπιστολὰς φ. τινί S.*Aj.*781, cf. *Tr.*493; ἐπιστολήν X.*Ages.*8.3: hence, *tell, announce*, πευθώ, φάτιν, A.*Th.*370, *Ag.*9; σαφές τι πρᾶγος Id.*Pers.*248 (troch.), cf. *Ag.*639, etc.; *report*, ἀγήν (breakages) *PCair.Zen.*15$^r$27 (iii B.C.); φ. κεχωνευκώς *reports* that he has.., ib.741.26, cf. 147.4, 268.24 (all iii B.C.); *enter, book* a payment made, *PBaden*47.12:—Med., λόγους φ. E.*Supp.*583; but also ἀγγελίας ἔπος οἴσῃ thou *shalt have* it *brought* thee, *receive*, Id.*Ph.*1546 (lyr.); μαντήϊα..φέρονται Hes.*Fr.*134.9:—Pass., θάνατον ἀνάγκη φέρεσθαι τοῦ διαθεμένου the death of the testator must be *announced*, *Ep.Heb.*9.16. 5. *pay* something *due* or *owing*, φόρον τέσσαρα τάλαντα φ. *pay* as a tax or tribute, Th.4.57, cf. *IG*1$^2$.57.9, Pl.*Plt.*298a, *PCair.Zen.*467.7 (iii B.C.); δασμόν X.*An.*5.5.10; σύνοδον φ. *subscribe to the expense* of a meeting, *IG*2$^2$.1012.14, 1326.6; χρήματα πᾶσι τάξαντες φ. Th.1.19; μισθὸν φ. X.*Cyr.*1.6.12 (but usu., *receive, draw*, pay, μισθὸν δύο δραχμὰς τῆς ἡμέρας Ar.*Ach.*66; τέτταρας τῆς ἡμέρας ὀβολοὺς φέρων Men.357; αἱ νῆες μισθὸν ἔφερον Th.3.17, cf. X.*An.*1.3.21, *Oec.*1.6); φ. ἐννέα ὀβολοὺς τῆς μνᾶς τόκους Lys.*Fr.*1.2, cf. Lycurg.23; also of property, *bring in, yield* as rent, φ. μίσθωσιν τοῦ ἐνιαυτοῦ Is.5.35. 6. *apply, refer*, τι ἐπί τι Pl.*Ti.*37e, *Chrm.*163d, *R.*478b, cf. Plb.3.36.7, al.; φ. τὰ πράγματα ἐπί τινα *confer* powers upon, Id.2.50.6. 7. ψῆφον φ. *give* one's vote, A.*Eu.*674,680, And.1.2, Is.11.18; ψῆφος καθ' ἡμῶν οἴσεται (Pass.) E.*Or.*440; περὶ ταύτης ἡ ψῆφος οἰσθήσεται D.44.45; ὑπὲρ ἀγῶνος Lycurg.7, cf. 11: hence φ. τινά *appoint* or *nominate* to an office, φ. χορηγόν D.20.130, 39.7, cf. Pl.*Lg.*753d, Arist.*Pol.*1266$^a$10:—Pass., ibid.; ὅπως φέρηται ἐν τῷ στρατιωτικῷ *UPZ*15.10 (ii B.C.); τῶν φερομένων ἐν Κλεοπάτρᾳ κληρούχων *PRein.*10.13, al. (ii B.C.); φερομένου μου ἐν τῇ συνοχῇ since I *am enrolled* in prison, i.e. am in prison, *BGU*1821.21 (i B.C.):—Med., *choose, adopt*, ταύταν φ. βιοτάν E.*Andr.*785 (lyr.). V. *bring forth, produce*, whether of the earth or of trees, φ. ἄρουρα φάρμακα Od.4.229; ἄμπελοι φ. οἶνον 9.110; [νῆσος] φ. ὥρια πάντα ib.131, cf. Hes.*Op.*117; [οὐ] γῆ καρπὸν ἔφερε Hdt.6.139; γύαι φ. βίοτον A.*Fr.*196.5, cf. Pi.*N.*11.41, E.*Hec.*593, etc.: abs., *bear fruit, be fruitful*, εὖτ' ἂν τάδε πάντα φέρῃσι *h.Merc.*91; ἡ γῆ ἔφερε (καρπόν add. codd. quidam) Hdt.5.82; αἱ ἄμπελοι φέρουσιν X.*Oec.*20.4; also of living beings, τόπος ἄνδρας φ. Pl.*Ti.*24c; ἤνεγκεν αὐτὸν Λαοδίκεια Philostr.*VS*1.25.1; ἡ ἐνεγκοῦσα *one's country*, Hld.2.29, Lib.*Or.*2.66, al., Chor.p.81 B., Lyd.*Mag.*3.26, dub. in *Supp.Epigr.*4.439 (Milet.) without Art. (also ἡ ἐνεγκαμένη Jul.*Ep.*202); or *Mother Earth*, M.Ant.4.48: generally, *create, form*, Πηνειὸς Τέμπη φ. Philostr.*Im.*1.25; [τὰ βρέφη] ἄρχεται φέρειν τοὺς ὀδόντας Aët.4.9; φ. τοὺς κυνόδοντας *Gp.*16.1.14. VI. *carry off* or *away*, Κῆρες ἔβαν θανάτοιο φέρουσαι Il.2.302; φ. τινὰ ἐκ πόνου 14.429, 17.718, etc.; of winds, [ἔπος] φέροιεν ἀναρπάξασαι ἄελλαι may the winds *sweep away* the word, Od.8.409; of a river, Hdt.1.189:—Med., *carry off with one*, Od.15.19. 2. *carry away as booty* or *prize*, ἔναρα, τεύχεα, Il.6.480, 17.70; αἶγα λέοντε φ. 13.199; δεῖπνον φ., of Harpies, A.*Eu.*51; ἐνέχυρα βίᾳ φ. Antipho 6.11; in the phrase φέρειν καὶ ἄγειν (cf. ἄγω I. 3), *IG*1$^2$.69.19; φέροντα ἢ ἄγοντα Lex ap. D.23.60; αἴ κα..ἄγῃ ἢ φέρῃ *Leg.Gort.*5.37; ἥρπαζον καὶ ἔφερον Lys.20.17; κείρων ἢ φέρων *IG*12(9).90.10 (Tamynae, iv B.C.); αἴ τίς κα..φέρει τι τῶν ἐν τᾷ ἱαρᾷ γᾷ *Tab.Heracl.*1.128; of a divorced wife, αἰ δέ τι ἄλλο φέροι τῶ ἀνδρός, πέντε στατῆρανς καταστασεῖ κὤτι κα φέρῃ αὐτόν *Leg.Gort.*3.2; φέρειν alone, *rob, plunder*, θεῶν ἱερά E.*Hec.*804; ἀλλήλους Th.1.7; abs., *SIG*38.23 (Teos, v B.C.):—Pass., φερόμενοι Βακχῶν ὕπο E.*Ba.*759:—Med. in same sense, ἔναρα Il.22.245; πελέκεας οἰκόνδε φ. 23.856; ἀτερπέα δαῖτα Od.10.124, cf. 15.378. 3. *carry off, gain*, esp. *by toil* or *trouble, win, achieve*, both Act. and Med., ἤ κε φέρῃσι μέγα κράτος ἦ κε φεροίμην Il.18.308; φέρειν τρίποδα Hes.*Op.*657; τἀπινίκια S.*El.*692; τιμήν Ar.*Av.*1278; τἀριστεῖα, τὰ νικητήρια, Pl.*R.*468c, *Lg.*657e; πέρα..οὐδὲν φ. S.*OC*651; ἐκ σοῦ πάντ' ἄνευ φόβου φ. Id.*OT*590; τίς..πλέον τᾶς εὐδαιμονίας φέρει ἤ..; ib.1190 (lyr.), cf. *El.*1088 (lyr.); in bad sense, μείζω τὴν αἰσχύνην φ. Pl.*Lg.*671e: also, *receive one's due*, φ. χάριν S.*OT*764; ὡς τοῦτό γ' ἔρξας δύο φέρῃ δωρήματα Id.*Ph.*117; μισθὸν φέρειν (v. supr. IV.5); of a priest's perquisites, φέρει ὁ ἱαρεὺς γέρη σκέλη κτλ. *BMus.Inscr.*968 *A*9 (Cos), cf. *IG*1$^2$.24.10, al., *SIG*56.35 (Argos, v B.C.):—Med. (v. ad init.), *win for oneself*, κῦδος οἴσεσθαι Il.22.217; δέπας, τεύχεα, *carry off as a prize*, 23.663,809, al.; ἀέθλια or ἄεθλον φ. *carry off, win* a prize, 9.127, 23.413; τὰ πρῶτα φέρεσθαι (sc. ἄεθλα) 23.275,538; οὐ σμικρὸν ἆθλον τῆς ἐρωτικῆς μανίας φέρονται Pl.*Phdr.*256d; of perquisites, τὸ..σκέλος τοὶ ἱαρομνάμονες φερόσθω (i.e. φερούσθω from *φερόνσθω) *IG*4$^2$(1).40.13 (Epid., v/iv B.C.): hence οὐ τὰ δεύτερα Hdt.8.104; πλέον φέρεσθαι *get* more or a larger share *for oneself, gain* the advantage over any one, τινος Hdt.7.211, cf. S.*OT*500 (lyr.), E.*Hec.*308; ταῦτα ἐπὶ σμικρόν τι ἐφέροντο τοῦ πολέμου this *they received* as a small help towards the war, Hdt.4.129; ἠνείκατο παρὰ Ἐγεσταίων τὰ οὐδεὶς ἄλλος 5.47; ἴδια κέρδεα προσδεκόμενοι παρὰ τοῦ Πέρσεω οἴσεσθαι 6.100; χάριν φέρεσθαι παρ' ὑμῶν And.2.9; φ. τὴν ἀπέχθειαν αὐτῶν Antipho 3.4.2; ὀνείδη Pl.*Lg.*762a; εὐσέβειαν ἐκ πατρὸς οἴσῃ S.*El.*969; δάκρυ πρὸς τῶν κλυόντων A.*Pr.*638; ἀπό τινος βοσκάν Id.*Eu.*266 (lyr.); ἐξ ἀνανδρίας τοὔνομα Aeschin.1.131: generally, *get for one's own use and profit, take and carry away*, esp. *to one's own home*, τοῦ..πάμπρωτα παρ' ἀγλαὰ δῶρα φέροιο Il.4.97: hence φέρειν or φέρεσθαι is often used pleon., v. infr. XI. VII. abs., of roads or ways, *lead* to a place, ὁδὸν φέρουσαν ἐς ἱρόν Hdt.2.122, cf. 138; τὴν φέρουσαν ἄνω (sc. ὁδόν) Id.9.69; τῆς μὲν ἐς ἀριστερὴν ἐπὶ Καρίης φ., τῆς δὲ ἐς δεξιὴν ἐς Σάρδις Id.7.31; ἐπὶ Σοῦσα X.*An.*3.5.15; ἁπλῆ οἶμος εἰς Ἅιδου φέρει A.*Fr.*239; ἡ ἐς Θήβας φέρουσα ὁδός Th.3.24 (but ἡ ἐπ' Ἀθηνῶν φέρουσα ibid.); also ἡ θύρα ἡ εἰς τὸν κῆπον φ. the door *leading* to the garden, D.47.53; αἱ εἰς τὴν πόλιν φ. πύλαι, αἱ ἐπὶ τὸ τεῖχος φ. κλίμακες, X.*HG*7.2.7, cf. *PMich.Zen.*38.27 (iii B.C.), Plb.10.12.3. 2. of a district or tract of country, *stretch, extend* to or towards, φέρειν ἐπί or ἐς θάλασσαν Hdt.4.99; ἐς τὴν μεσόγαιαν ib.100; πρὸς νότον Id.7.201; ἡ ἀπὸ δυσμῶν αὐτῆς (sc. τῆς Κιμβρικῆς) καὶ ἐπὶ τὸν Ἄλβιν φέρουσα Ptol.*Geog.*2.11.2, cf. 3. b. of time, τῇ νυκτὶ τῇ φερούσῃ εἰς τὴν β' τοῦ Παχών *PPetr.*3 p.x (iii B.C.), cf. *PTeb.*61 (*b*) 288 (ii B.C.), *BGU*1832.5 (i B.C.), etc. 3. metaph., *lead* to or towards, *be conducive* to, ἐς αἰσχύνην φέρει Hdt.1.10; τὰ ἐς ἄκεσιν φέροντα Id.4.90; ἐς βλάβην, ἐς φόβον φέρον, S.*OT*517, 991; εἰς ὄκνον E.*Supp.*295: esp. in good sense, *tend, conduce* to one's interest, ἐπ' ἀμφότερά τοι φέρει (impers.) ταῦτα ποιέειν Hdt.3.

134; so τὰ πρὸς τὸ ὑγιαίνειν φέροντα X.*Mem.*4.2.31; τροφαὶ μέγα φ. εἰς ἀρετάν E.*IA*562 (lyr.); μέγα τι οἰόμεθα φέρειν (sc. κοινωνίαν γυναικῶν τε καὶ παίδων) εἰς πολιτείαν Pl.*R.*449d; τὰ καλὰ ἐπιτηδεύματα εἰς ἀρετῆς κτῆσιν φ. ib.444e, cf. X.*Cyr.*8.1.42; τοῦτο ἔφερεν αὐτῷ *was for* his *good*, M.Ant.5.8. b. *point* to, *refer* to a thing, ἐς τί ὑμῖν ταῦτα φαίνεται φέρειν; Hdt.1.120; φωνὴ φέρουσα πρός τινα *addressed* to him, Id.1.159; ἐς ἀρηΐους ἀγῶνας φέρον τὸ μαντήϊον Id.9.33, cf. 6.19; [ὕψις] φέρει ἐπὶ πᾶσαν γῆν *refers* to.., *extends* over.., Id.7.19; τὰ ἴχνη τῆς ὑποψίας εἰς τοῦτον φ. *point* to him, Antipho 2.3.10; πρός τινας Pl.*R.*538c; ταύτῃ ⟨ὁ⟩ νόος ἔφερε Hdt.9.120; ἡ τοῦ δήμου φέρει γνώμη, ὡς.., the people's opinion *inclines* to this, that.., Id.4.11; ἐπὶ τὸ αὐτὸ αἱ γνῶμαι ἔφερον Th.1.79: c. inf., τῶν ἡ γνώμη ἔφερε συμβάλλειν whose opinion *inclined to* giving battle, Hdt.6.110, cf. 5.118; πλέον ἔφερέ οἱ ἡ γνώμη κατεργάσεσθαι his opinion *inclined* rather to the view.., Hdt.8.100, cf. 3.77. VIII. *carry* or *have in the mouth*, i.e. *speak of*. πολύν τινα ἐν ταῖς διαβολαῖς φέρειν Aeschin.3.223; *use* a word, οὐκ οἶδα καθ' ὁποτέρου τούτων οἱ παλαιοὶ τὸ τῆς ζειᾶς ἔφερον ὄνομα Gal.*Vict.Att.*6, cf. 7.644, 15.753,876; *record* an event, οἱ δευτέρῳ μετὰ τὴν ἔξοδον..ἔτει φέροντες αὐτὴν D.H.1.63: more freq. in Pass., πονηρῶς, εὖ, φέρεσθαι, *to be* ill or well *spoken of*, X.*HG*1.5.17, 2.1.6; ἀτίμως ὑπὸ τῶν ἀνθρώπων φ. Pl.*Ep.*328e; abs., φέρεται [the report] *is carried about*, i.e. *it is said*, c. acc. et inf., τοιόνδε φέρεται πρῆγμα γίνεσθαι Hdt.8.104 (v.l.); ἐν χρόνοις φέρεται μνημονευομένοις *is recorded as occurring* within historical times, Str.1.3.15; ὅτε καὶ Δημόκριτος φέρεται τελευτήσας Sor.*Vit.Hippocr.*11; κρίνομεν..τὰ γραφέντα ὑφ' ἡμῶν προστάγματα ἐν τοῖς ἱεροῖς νόμοις φέρεσθαι παρ' ὑμῖν *OGI*331.60 (Pergam., ii B.C.); ὧν τὰ ὀνόματα φέρεται *are in use*, Ptol.*Geog.*7.4.11; of literary works, *to be in circulation*, ἐπιστόλιον αὐτοῦ τοιοῦτον φέρεται Plu.2.808a, cf. 209e, 832d, 833c, al., Jul.*Or.*6.189b, *Gp.*2.35.8, Eun.*VS* p.456 B.; πρόλογοι διττοὶ φέρονται Arg.E.*Rh.*; ὁ στίχος οὗτος ἔν τισιν οὐ φέρεται Sch.E.*Ph.*377, cf. Sch.Il.8.557. 2. of words, φέρεσθαι ἐπί τι to *refer* to something, A.D.*Pron.*61.5, *Synt.*21.14, al. IX. imper. φέρε like ἄγε, as Adv., *come, now, well*, 1. before another imper., φέρε γὰρ σήμαινε A.*Pr.*296 (anap.); φέρ' εἰπὲ δή μοι S.*Ant.*534; φ. δή μοι τόδε εἰπέ Pl.*Cra.*385b; so φέρετε..πειρᾶσθε Hdt.4.127. 2. before 1 sg. or pl. of subj. used imperatively, φέρε ἀκούσω, φέρε στήσωμεν, Hdt.1.11,97; φ. δὲ νῦν..φράσω Id.2.14; φέρ' ἴδω, τί δ' ἥσθην; Ar.*Ach.*4; φέρε δὴ κατίδω Id.*Pax* 361, cf. 959; φ. δὴ ἴδωμεν, φ. δὴ σκεψώμεθα, Pl.*Grg.*455a, *Prt.*330b, cf. E.*Or.*1281 (lyr.), *Ph.*276, etc.: less freq. before 2 pers., φέρε..μάθῃς S.*Ph.*300. 3. before a rhetorical question, φέρε..τροπαῖα πῶς ἀναστήσεις; E.*Ph.*571; φ. δὴ νῦν..τί γαμεῖθ' ἡμᾶς; Ar.*Th.*788 (anap.), cf. *Ach.*541, Pl.*R.*348c; φ. μῶν οὐκ ἀνάγκη..; Id.*Lg.*805d; φ. πρὸς θεῶν πῶς..; Id. *Grg.*514d; freq. in phrase φέρε γάρ, φέρε τίς γὰρ οὗτος; Ar.*Nu.*218; φ. γὰρ πρὸς τίνας χρὴ πολεμεῖν; Isoc.4.183, cf. Antipho 5.36; also φ. δή Pl.*Grg.*455a, al.: usu. first in a sentence, but τὴν ἀνδρείαν δὲ φ. τί θῶμεν; Id.*Lg.*633c, etc. 4. φέρε δή, ἐάν πῃ διαλλαχθῶμεν.. *come* let us see if we can.., Id.*Cra.*430a. 5. φέρε c. inf., *suppose, grant* that..φ. λέγειν τινά Plu.2.98b; φ. εἰπεῖν *let us* say, D.Chr.31.93, 163, Porph.*Abst.*3.3; οἷον φ. εἰ. Iamb. *in Nic.*p.47 P., al. (οἷον φέρε alone, Hierocl. *in CA*11 p.439 M.). X. part. neut. τὸ φέρον, as Subst., *destiny, fate*, τὸ φ. ἐκ θεοῦ [καλῶς] φέρειν [χρή] ye must bear nobly *what* heaven *bears to you, awards you*, S.*OC*1693 (lyr., codd., sed secl. καλῶς, χρή); εἰ τὸ φέρον σε φέρει, φέρε καὶ φέρου *AP* 10.73 (Pall.). 2. part. φέρων in all genders freq. joined with another Verb: a. to express a subsidiary action, φέρων ἔδωκε *he brought and* gave, Od.22.146; δὸς τῷ ξείνῳ ταῦτα φέρων *take* this *and* give it him, 17.345; ἔγχος ἔστησε φέρων *brought* the spear *and* placed it, 1.127; σῖτον παρέθηκε φέρουσα ib.139, al., cf. S.*Tr.*622; τοῦτο ἐλθὼν οἴκαδε φέρων τῷ πατρὶ ἔδωκα Pl.*Hp.Ma.*282e, cf. *R.*345b; so ὁ μὲν Ἐπίχαρμον..εἰς δέκα τόμους φέρων συνήγαγεν Porph.*Plot.*24; ἑκάστῃ ἐννεάδι τὰ οἰκεῖα φέρων συνεφόρησα ibid., etc.; sts. translatable by *with*, ᾤχοντο φέροντες τὰ γράμματα Th.7.8. b. intr., in pass. sense, to denote unrestrained action, νῦν σε μάλ' οἴω..φέροντα..φιλητεύσειν *h.Merc.*159; φέρουσα ἐνέβαλε νηῒ φιλίῃ she *went and* rammed, rammed *full tilt*, Hdt.8.87; ὅταν ἐπὶ θάτερ' ὥσπερ εἰς τρυτάνην ἀργύριον προσενέγκῃς, οἴχεται φέρον *down* it sinks, D.5.12; τὰ μὲν ἄλλα μέρη τοῦ πολέμου παρῆκαν, φέροντες δὲ παντὶ τῷ στρατεύματι πρὸς αὐτὸν Ἀκράγαντα προσήρεισαν *hurling themselves*, Plb.1.17.8; εἰς τοῦτο φέρων περιέστησε τὰ πράγματα Aeschin.3.82; ὑπέβαλεν ἑαυτὸν φέρων Θηβαίοις ib.90, cf. 1.175, 3.143,146; in the foll. passages φέρων accompanies a Verb of throwing, giving, entrusting, or dedicating, and expresses wholehearted action, whether wise or unwise; there is always an accus., freq. of the reflex. Pron., governed by the principal Verb (or perh. by φέρων): ἐπεὶ ἐς τοὺς κρατῆρας ἐμαυτὸν φέρων ἐνέβαλον (sc. ὁ Ἐμπεδοκλῆς) when I *went* (or *took*) *and* threw myself.., Luc.*Icar.*13, cf. *Fug.*1, Plu.*Comp.Arist.Cat.*1, *Fab.*6, *Per.*12, Paus.1.30.1, Ael.*VH*8.14, *Frr.*10,69, Philostr.*VA*3.4; τὴν κατασκευὴν..φέρων ἐδωρήσατο τῇ μητρί D.S.31.27, cf. Ach.Tat.1.7; σεαυτὸν..φέρων ἀπημπόληκας Luc.*Merc.Cond.*24; τί παθόντες..τοῖς ἀτέκνοις τῶν γερόντων ἐσποιεῖτε φέροντες αὐτούς; Luc.*DMort.*6.3, cf. *Ind.*19, *Lap.*22; ταύτῃ (sc. τῇ ὀργῇ) φέρων ὑπέθηκεν ἑαυτόν Plu.*Them.*24, cf. *Per.*7; τούτῳ φέροντες ὑποβάλλουσι τοὺς υἱοὺς Id.2.4b, cf. *Luc.*6, *Pomp.*27, Ael.*VH*6.1, Max.Tyr.1.2; προσέθετο φέρων ἑαυτὸν ἐκείνῳ Eun.*VS* p.456 B., cf. pp.461,465 B., Dam.ap. Suid. s.v. Σεβηριανός; ἀλλὰ σοὶ μέν, ὦ θεῶν πάτερ, ἐμαυτὸν φέρων ἀναθήσω Jul.*Or.*7.231b. 3. ἔκκρισις..ἐκ μικρῶν φέρουσα διαστημάτων *occurring* at short intervals, Sor.2.45. XI. φέρειν, φέρεσθαι are freq. added epexegetically to δίδωμι and similar Verbs, δῶκεν ..τρίποδα φέρειν Il.23.513, cf. 16.665, 17.131; τεύχεα..δότω φέρεσθαι 11.798, cf. Od.21.349, E.*Tr.*419,454 (troch.).

B. Pass. is used in most of the above senses:—special cases: I. *to be borne* or *carried* involuntarily, esp. *to be borne along* by waves or winds, *to be swept away*, φέρεσθαι ἀνέμοισι, θυέλλῃ, Od.9.82, 10.54, cf. A.*Pers.*276 (lyr.), etc.; πᾶν δ' ἦμαρ φερόμην, of Hephaestus *falling* from Olympus, Il.1.592; ἧκε φέρεσθαι he sent him *flying*, 21.120; ἧκα πόδας καὶ χεῖρε φέρεσθαι I let *go* my hands and feet, let them *swing free* [in the leap], Od.12.442, cf. 19.468; μέγα φέρεται πὰρ σέθεν, of a word uttered, *comes* with weight, Pi.*P.*1.87; βίᾳ φέρεται Pl.*Phdr.*254a; πνεῦμα φερόμενον Id.*R.*496d; τὸ πνεῦμα κατὰ τὰς ἀναπνοὰς εἴσω τε καὶ ἔξω φέρεται Gal.16.520; ῥεῖν καὶ φέρεσθαι Pl.*Cra.*411c; φ. εἰς τὸν Τάρταρον Id.*Phd.*114b; simply, *move, go*, ποῖ γᾶς φέρομαι; S.*OT*1309 (anap.); οὐκ οἶσθ' ὅποι γῆς οὐδ' ὅποι γνώμης φέρῃ Id.*El.*922, cf. E.*Hec.*1076 (anap.), etc.; of the excreta, τὰ φερόμενα..εἰ μὲν αὐτομάτως φέροιτο Philum.ap.Aët.9.12; πρὸς κοιλίαν φερομένην Aët.4.19: metaph., εἰς τὸ λοιδορεῖν φέρῃ E.*Andr.*729; πρὸς τὴν τοῦ κάλλους φύσιν Pl.*Phdr.*254b, cf. X.*Mem.*2.1.4; ἐπὶ ταὐτὸ φέρονται *have* the same *tendency*, Phld.*Vit.*p.42 J.; ἀπὸ δογμάτων καὶ ἀπὸ θεωρημάτων φ. Vett.Val.238.30; of veins, *to be conveyed*, Gal.15.531; also ἡ φερομένη οὐσία (the doctrine of) *universal motion*, Pl.*Tht.*177c; οἱ φερόμενοι θεοί the *moving* gods, i.e. the stars and planets, Plot.2.3.9. 2. freq. in part. with another Verb of motion, φερόμενοι ἐσέπιπτον ἐς τοὺς Αἰγινήτας they fell into their hands *with a rush, at full speed*, Hdt.8.91; ἀπὸ..ἐλπίδος ᾠχόμην φερόμενος Pl.*Phd.*98b; ἧκε φερόμενος εἰς τὴν ἑαυτοῦ φύσιν Aeschin.3.89. 3. of voluntary and impulsive motion, ἰθὺς φέρεται μένει Il.20.172; ὁμόσε τινὶ φέρεσθαι *come* to blows with him, X.*Cyn.*10.21; δρόμῳ φ. πρός τινα Id.*HG*4.8.37; φυγῇ εἰς ἑαυτοὺς φ. Id.*Cyr.*1.4.23; ἥξει ἐπ' ἐκεῖνον τὸν λόγον φερόμενος Lycurg.59; φερόμενος ὑπ' ὀργῆς D.H.*Comp.*18. II. metaph., καλῶς, κακῶς φέρεσθαι, of things, schemes, etc., *turn out, prosper* well or ill, *succeed* or *fail*, οὔτ' ἂν..νόμοι καλῶς φέροιντ' ἄν S.*Aj.*1074; κακῶς φ. τὰ ἑαυτοῦ X.*HG*.3.4.25; εὖ φέρεται ἡ γεωργία Id.*Oec.*5.17; ὀλιγώρως ἔχειν καὶ ἐᾶν ταῦτα φέρεσθαι to neglect things and let them *take their course*, D.8.67; less freq. of persons, *fare* well or ill, εὖ φερόμενος ἐν στρατηγίαις *being generally* successful.., Th.5.16, cf. 15; καλῶς φερόμενος τὸ καθ' ἑαυτόν Id.2.60; φ. ἐν προτιμήσει παρά τινι D.S.33.5; χεῖρον φερομένη παρὰ τἀδελφῷ J.*AJ*16.7.6; of euphonious writing, σύνθεσις καλῶς φερομένη Phld.*Po.*5.26. 2. *behave*, ὑποκριτικῶς, ἀστάτως, etc., Vett.Val.38.20, 197.8, al. 3. *have an opinion*, ὅπως ἠνέχθη περὶ τοῦ σφυγμοῦ what *his opinion was* about.., Marcellin.*Puls.*233.

C. Med.: for its chief usages, v. supr. A. VI. 3.

**φερωνῠμ-έομαι**, Pass., *bear a name from*.., Eust.656.62. **-ία**, Ep. -ίη, ἡ, *name received from* an event or action, Opp.*H.*1.243: *accordance of a name with an event*, Eust.776.49. **-ος**, ον, *bearing the name of, named after*, τινός Nic.*Th.*666, Orph.*A.*719, Coluth.246, *Theol.Ar.*19, Nonn.*D.*13.69; ἔκ τινος Id.5.71: *well-named*, like ἐπώνυμος, Ael.*NA*17.8. Adv. -μως Arist.*Mu.*399ᵃ19, Heraclit.*All.*22.

**φεσκάσιον**· μάγγανον πλοϊκόν, Phot., Suid.

⊛ **Φετιάλιοι**, οἱ, = Lat. *Fetiales*, D.H.2.72; written **Φιτιαλεῖς** in Plu.*Num.*12; **Φητιαλεῖς** Id.*Cam.*18: sg. **Φητιάλιος** D.C.50.4.

**φεῦ**, exclamation of grief or anger, *alas!* freq. in Trag.; φ. τάλας S.*Aj.*983, etc.: freq. c. gen., φ. τοῦ ὄρνιθος..A.*Th.*597, cf. S.*El.*920, 1183; φ. βροτείας [φρενός] E.*Hipp.*936: joined with other exclam., οἰοῖ δᾶ φ. A.*Eu.*841 (lyr.); παπαῖ φ. or φ. π., S.*Ph.*785,792; φ. ὦ Ἑλλάς X.*Ages.*7.5, cf. *Cyr.*7.3.8. II. of astonishment or admiration, *ah! oh!* E.*Heracl.*552, *El.*262, *Ph.*1740 (lyr.), Pl.*Phdr.*273c, etc., cf. Sch.Ar.*Av.*162, etc.; doubled, φ. φ. E.*Heracl.*535, Ar. l.c., Theoc.5.86: c. gen., φ. φ. τῆς ὥρας, τοῦ κάλλους Ar.*Av.*1724 (lyr.); φ. τοῦ ἀνδρός *oh*, what a man! X.*Cyr.*3.1.39 (where, however, there is also a sense of *grief*): also φ. τὸ καὶ λαβεῖν πρόσφθεγμα τοιοῦδ' ἀνδρός *oh*, but to get speech of such a man! S.*Ph.*234; folld. by a relat., φεῦ, ὅσῳ λέγεις κτλ. Pl.*Phdr.*263d; φ. ὡς εὖ λέγεις Id.*Hp.Ma.*287b.—φεῦ in Trag. and Com. Poets sts. stands extra versum, A.*Ag.*1307, *Ch.*194, Ar.*Nu.*41, etc.; when it forms part of the verse, it is usu. at the beginning, but not so in S.*Ph.*234,1302.

**φεύγυδρος**, ον, (ὕδωρ) *shunning water*, Polybus ap.Cael.Aur.*CP*3.9.

**φεύγω**, Il.21.472, etc.: Ep. inf. φευγέμεν, φευγέμεναι, 10.147, 21.13; impf. ἔφευγον 22.158, etc., Poet. φεῦγον 9.478, Tyrt.5.8, Pi.*N.*9.13: iter. φεύγεσκον Il.17.461, Hdt.4.43: fut. φεύξομαι Il.18.307, etc.; also φευξοῦμαι in E. and Com., E.*Med.*341,346, *Hel.*500,1041, *Ba.*659, Ar.*Ach.*203 (cod. R), 1129, *Pl.*447, *Av.*932 (ἀπο-), Men.283 (but dub. where found in Att. Prose, Pl.*Lg.*635c, al., D.38.19; φευξεῖται is dub. l. in *IPE*1².24.11 (Olbia, iv B.C.); fut. Act. ἐκ-φεύξω only late, v.l. in Aesop.349ᵇ, cf. Chambry ii p.479): aor. ἔφυγον, Ion. φύγεσκον Od.17.316: pf. πέφευγα Hdt.7.154 codd. (v. infr. II. 1a); opt. πεφεύγοι Il.21.609 (ἐκ-πεφευγοίην S.*OT*840), part. πεφευγότες Od.1.12; part. pf. Pass. πεφυγμένος in act. sense, Il.6.488, Od.1.18, etc. (in pass. sense, Epicur.*Fr.*423); Ep. πεφυζότες (cf. φύζα) Il.21.6,528,532, 22.1, later sg. πεφυζώς Nic.*Th.*128; Aeol. πεφύγγων, v. φυγγάνω:—Med., μὴ φεύγησθε Anon.Hist. in *PLit.Lond.*115: aor. 1 δια-φεύξασθαι Decr.Ath. in Hp.*Ep.*25. I. abs., *flee, take flight*, opp. διώκω, Il.22.157, etc.; βῆ φεύγων ἐπὶ πόντον 2.665; πῇ φεύγεις; 8.94; πόσε φεύγετε; 16.422; ποῖ φύγωμεν..χθονός; A.*Supp.*777 (lyr.); ποῖ τις οὖν φύγῃ; S.*Aj.*403 (lyr.); ἐνθένδε ἐκεῖσε φ. Pl.*Tht.*176b:

with Preps., φ. ἀπό τινος Od.12.120; φεύξονται ἀφ' ἑαυτῶν εἰς φιλοσοφίαν Pl.*Tht.*168a, etc.; ἐκ πολέμοιο, ἐκ θανάτοιο, Il.7.118, 20.350; ἐκ κακῶν πεφευγέναι S.*Ant.*437, cf. Hdt.1.65; ὑπὲκ κακοῦ Il.15.700, cf. 17.461 (rarely c. gen. only, πεφυγμένος ἦεν ἀέθλων (v. infr. II) Od.1.18; τῆς νόσου πεφευγέναι S.*Ph.*1044); φ. ἐς πατρίδα γαῖαν Il.2.140, 159, al.; ἐπὶ Σάρδεων, ἐπὶ τὸν Ἑλικῶνα, X.*Cyr.*7.2.1, *Ages.*2.11; πρὸς τὸ ὄρος Id.*HG*3.5.19; ὑπὸ γᾶν A.*Eu.*175 (lyr.); ὑπὸ δελφῖνος ἰχθύες φ. Il.21.23, cf. 554 (cf. infr. III. 2): c. acc. cogn., φύγε λαιψηρὸν δρόμον *ran* the course full swiftly, Pi.*P.*9.121; τίνα φυγὴν φευξούμεθα; E.*Hel.*1041; φ. τὴν παρὰ θάλασσαν (sc. ὁδόν) *flee* by the shore route, Hdt.4.12; cf. infr. III; for φυγῇ φεύγειν, v. infr. II. 1, φυγή I. 1. 2. pres. and impf. tenses prop. express only *the purpose* or *endeavour to get away*: hence part. φεύγων is added to the compd. Verbs καταφεύγω, ἐκφεύγω, προφεύγω, to distinguish *the attempt* from *the accomplishment*, βέλτερον, ὃς φεύγων προφύγῃ κακὸν ἠὲ ἁλώῃ it is better that one should *flee and* escape than stay and be caught, Il.14.81; φεύγων ἐκφεύγει Hdt.5.95, cf. Ar.*Ach.*177; φ. καταφυγεῖν Hdt.4.23. 3. φ. εἰς.. *have recourse* to.. *take refuge* in.., ἐς τοὺς ἀφώνους μάρτυρας E.*Hipp.*1076. 4. c. inf., *shun* or *shrink from* doing, Hdt.4.76, Antipho 1.13, Pl.*Ap.*26a; with inf. omitted, φεύγουσι γάρ τοι χοἰ θρασεῖς *shrink back*, S.*Ant.*580. II. c. acc., *flee, avoid, escape*, Ἕκτορα Il.11.327, etc.; φ. τινὰ ἐκ μάχης Hdt.7.104; φ. ἐς τὴν Ἀσίην τοὺς Σκύθας Id.4.12; φ. θάνατον Il.1.60; ἔνθ' ἄλλοι μὲν πάντες, ὅσοι φύγον αἰπὺν ὄλεθρον, οἴκοι ἔσαν πόλεμόν τε πεφευγότες ἠδὲ θάλασσαν Od.1.11; ἔφυγον κακόν, εὗρον ἄμεινον, formula used by μύσται, D.18.259; with modal dat., φ. ὄνειδος λόγοις, ἀμαχανίαν ἔργῳ, Pi.*O.*6.90, *P.*9.92; *avoid, shun*, χρὴ ..φεύγειν τὰ παχύνοντα Gal.*Vict.Att.*12; τὴν ἀργίαν καὶ τὴν ἀκινησίαν τοῦ σώματος Sor.1.93, cf. 46, al.; φόνον φ. *flee the consequences of* the murder, E.*Med.*796; αἷμα συγγενὲς φ. χθονός Id.*Supp.*148; τὰν Διὸς μῆτιν φ. A.*Pr.*906 (lyr.); ὀσμὴν.., μὴ βάλῃ, πεφευγότες S.*Ant.*412; φεύγων φυγῇ τὸ γῆρας Pl.*Smp.*195b; ἐς πόντον..φύγε πέτρας νηῦς Od.10.131; οὐδεμία [πόλις] πέφευγε (sed fort. leg. ἀπέφυγε) δουλοσύνην πρὸς Ἱπποκράτεος at the hands of.., Hdt.7.154: part. pf. Pass. also retains the acc. in Hom. in periphrastic phrases, μοῖραν δ' οὔ τινά φημι πεφυγμένον ἔμμεναι ἀνδρῶν Il.6.488; πεφυγμένον ἔμμεν ὄλεθρον Od.9.455; οὐ οἱ νῦν ἔτι γ' ἔστι πεφυγμένον ἄμμε γενέσθαι Il.22.219, cf. *h.Ven.*34:—but in pass. sense, τὸ πάραυτα πεφυγμένον κακόν Epicur. l. c. b. *seek to avoid, shirk*, στρατείαν D.21.162; εἰ τοῦτο φεύξονται καὶ μὴ 'θελήσουσι ποιεῖν Id.20.138; so in aor., ἢν φύγῃ τις, ζημιοῦν Ar.*Ach.*717. 2. of things, ἡνίοχον φύγον ἡνία *escaped, slipped from his hands*, Il.23.465; Νέστορα δ' ἐκ χειρῶν φύγον ἡνία 8.137, cf. 11.128; τὸ φεῦγον the *part which slips*, X.*Eq* 10.9, cf. Hp.*Off.*9, Gal.18(2).735: c. dupl. acc., ποῖόν σε ἔπος φύγεν ἕρκος ὀδόντων Il.4.350, Od.1.64, etc. b. of wine, '*go off*', *turn sour*, *Gp.*7.7.8. III. *flee one's country*, Il.9.478, Od.13.259; οἱ φεύγοντες the *exiles*, Th.1.24, X.*Ages.*7.6; πατρίδα φ. Od.15.228, X.*Cyr.*3.1.24; τὴν αὑτοῦ Th.5.26; ἅπασαν τὴν Ἀθηναίων ξυμμαχίδα *IG*1².10.30; φ. ἐξ Ἄργεος Od.15.224, cf. Th.8.85; ἐξ Ἀθηνέων, ἐκ τῆς πατρίδος, Hdt.6.103, X.*An.*1.3.3. 2. φ. ὑπὸ Σκυθέων *to be expelled, driven out* by..Hdt.4.125: but esp. *to be exiled*, φ. ὑπὸ τοῦ δήμου Id.5.30, X.*HG*1.1.27; φ. ἐξ Ἀρείου πάγου by their sentence, Din.1.44: also c. acc., φ. Πεισιστρατίδας Hdt.5.62. 3. abs., *go into exile, live in banishment*, A.*Ag.*1668 (troch.), Antipho 2.2.9, Pl.*Mx.*242b; δύο ἔτη φευγέτω Id.*Lg.*867c; φ. ἀειφυγίαν *to be banished* for life, ib.871d, al.; φεύγειν Ἀμφίπολιν ἀειφυγίην *SIG*194.3, cf. 24 (Amphipolis, iv B. C.); but also ἐν ἀειφυγίᾳ Pl.*Lg.*877e; φεύγων ἀπ' οἴκων ἃς ἐγὼ φεύγω φυγάς E.*Andr.*976; φεύγοντες *being in exile*, opp. φυγόντες *having gone into exile*, Lys.14.33; with play on words, "μέχρι τίνος φεύξῃ, Ἀρκαδίων;" καὶ ὅς, "ἔς τ' ἂν τοὺς ἀφίκωμαι οἳ οὐκ ἴσασι Φίλιππον" Duris 3 J. IV. as law-term (mostly in pres. and impf., but cf. Lys.12.4 (v. infr.)), *to be accused* or *prosecuted at law*: ὁ φεύγων the *accused, defendant*, Ar.*V.*893, Pl.*R.*405b, etc.; opp. διώκω, οὔτε φεύγων ἁλοὺς οὔτε διώκων ἡττηθείς D.23.66; c. acc., φ. γραφάς, δίκην, Ar.*Eq.*442 (lyr.), *Nu.*167; ὑπό τινος δίκας φ. Pl.*Ap.*19c, cf. D.49.1; οὐδενὶ πώποτε οὔτε ἡμεῖς οὔτε ἐκεῖνος δίκην οὔτε ἐδικασάμεθα οὔτε ἐφύγομεν Lys. l. c.; φ. ἀπολογίας Aeschin.3.201; the crime being added in gen., φόνου δίκην φ. Antipho 5.9; γραφὰς φ. παρανόμων D.18.235; more freq. c. gen. only, φ. φόνου *to be charged with* murder, Lys.10.31, Lycurg.133, etc.; φ. δειλίας Ar.*Ach.*1129; ξενίας Id.*V.*718 (anap.); with gen. of the penalty, ἐὰν.. φεύγῃ δεσμῶν *OGI*218.92 (Ilium, iii B. C.); also περὶ θανάτου φ. Antipho 5.95; φ. ἐπὶ μηνύσει τινός And.1.18; ἀσεβείας φ. ὑπό τινος *is accused of* impiety by.., Pl.*Ap.*35d; rarely of things, τὸ φεῦγον ψήφισμα the decree *that is on its defence*, the decree *in question*, D.23.58:—in Hdt.7.214 αἰτίην φ. has the older sense, *flee from* a charge, *quit one's country* on account of a charge. 2. *plead in defence*, δεῖ τοί σε φεύγειν..ὡς οὐκ ἔχουσι κῦρος [οἱ νόμοι] A.*Supp.*390; ἔφευγε μὴ εἰδέναι *pleaded* ignorance, S.*Ant.*263. (Cf. Lat. *fugio*, Goth. *biugan* 'bend', etc.)

**φεύζω**, *cry* φεῦ, *cry woe*, τί τοῦτ' ἔφευξας; A.*Ag.*1308.

**φευκ-ταῖος**, α, ον, = ἀποτρόπαιος, Hsch. **-τέον**, *one must flee*, ἀπό τινος Pl.*Phd.*62d; δεῦρο τοῖς κακοῖσι φ. they *must flee*, E.*Heracl.*259, cf. Ar.*Av.*392 (lyr.): pl., Sch.Il.10.149. II. c. acc., ἀκολασίαν Pl.*Grg.*507d, cf X.*Mem.*2.6.4, etc. III. φευκτέος, α, ον, *to be avoided*, Gal.18(2).850; τὰ φ. Iamb.*VP*31.190. **-τιάω**, Desiderat. from φεύγω, *wish to flee*, Arist.*Fr.*130. **-τικός**, ή, όν, *inclined to avoid*, opp. ὀρεκτικός, c. gen., Arist.*de An.*$431^{a}13$; opp. αἱρετικός, Phld.*Mus.*p.93 K. **-τός**, ή, όν, *to be shunned* or *avoided*, Arist.*EN* $1153^{b}2$; opp. αἱρετός, ib.$1119^{a}23$, $1172^{b}19$, Epicur.*Ep.*3 p.63 U., Phld.*Herc.*1251.13: Comp., Arist.*Top.*$116^{b}5$. 2. *that can be escaped* or *avoided*, ἀγγελίαν ἄτλατον οὐδὲ φευκτάν S.*Aj.*224 (lyr.), cf. Pl.*Ax.*369b; cf. φυκτός.

**φευξασπίδιον**, τό, = πόλιον, Ps.-Dsc.3.110.

**φευξείω**, = φευκτιάω, prob. for φευξιῶ in E.*HF*628.

**φεύξῐμος**, ον, later form of φύξιμος, τόπος Plb.13.6.9; ἔστι δούλῳ φ. βωμός Plu.2.166e. II. = φευκτός, Hsch.

**φευξῐπ..**, dub. in Cerc.6.7 (fort. φευξιπήμον' or φευξίπονον *avoiding trouble* or *toil*).

**φεῦξις**, εως, ἡ, = φύξις, S.*Ant.*362 (lyr.).

**φεψᾰλόομαι**, Pass., *to be burnt to ashes*, A.*Pr.*364.

**φέψᾰλος**, ου, ὁ (also **φέψελος**, gloss on φεψάλυξ, Hsch.):—*spark, piece of the embers*, Ar.*Ach.*668 (lyr.), *V.*227, Arist.*Mete.*$367^{a}5$:—**φεψάλυξ** [ᾰ], ῠγος, ὁ, Archil.126, Ar.*Lys.*107, Plb.1.48.6: prov. phrases, ἀσπὶς ἐν τῷ φεψάλῳ κρεμήσεται, i.e. will be hung in the chimney, of things laid by and unused, Ar.*Ach.*279; οὐδὲ φεψάλυξ not so much as.., Id.*Lys.* l. c.

**φέως**, ω, ὁ, = στοιβή, *Poterium spinosum*, Thphr.*HP*6.1.3.

**φή**, enclit. for φησί, Anacr.40:—but **φῆ**, Dor. **φᾶ**, for ἔφη.

**φή** (**φῆ** Aristarch.) = ὡς, *as, like as*, read by Zenodotus in Il.2.144, 14.499, said by Sch.A on 14.499 to occur in Antim. (he cites *Fr.*79) and in Call. (v. *Frr.*366,518), φὴ ῥα prob. for δή ῥα (v.l. θῆρα) in *h.Merc.*241.

*⁕***φηγῐνέος**, η, ον, = sq. κρητήρ, νηῦς, *AP*6.33 (Maec.), Orph.*A.*67.

**φήγῐνος**, η, ον, *oaken*, ἄξων Il.5.838; ὄζος Call.*Epigr.*36, cf. Dsc.*Eup.*1.102.

**φηγός**, Dor. **φᾱγός** Theoc.9.20, ἡ, = δρῦς ἀγρία, *Valonia oak, Quercus Aegilops*, Thphr.*HP*3.3.1, 3.8.2, etc.: freq. in Il. (not in Od.), Διὸς περικαλλέϊ φηγῷ Il.5.693; φηγῷ ἐφ' ὑψηλῇ..Διός 7.60; ἡ παλαιὰ φ., of *the oak* of Dodona, S.*Tr.*171, cf. Hes.*Frr.*134.7, 212 (but δρῦς S.*Tr.*1168). II. *acorn of the same tree*, Ar.*Pax* 1137 (lyr.), Pl.*R.*372c, Theoc. l. c., D.Chr.6.62. (Cf. Lat. *fāgus* 'beech', OE. *bóc* 'beech'.)

**φηγότευκτος**, ον, *oaken*, μόσσυν Lyc.1432.

**φηγών**, ῶνος, ὁ, *oak-grove*, Lat. *aesculetum*, *Gloss.*

**φήῃ**, Ep. 3 sg. pres. subj. of φημί (q. v.).

**φηληκίζω**, = φηλόω, *EM*160.41.

**φηληκόθρεπτος**, ον, = ἐριναστός, Hsch.

*⁕***φήληξ**, ηκος, ὁ, *a wild fig* (perh. from φῆλος, *deceitful*, because it seems ripe when it is not really so), Ar.*Pax* 1165 (cf. S.*Fr.*731).

**φηλητεύω, φηλήτης**, v. φιλητεύω, φιλήτης.

**φῆλ-ος**, ον (φηλός is prob. an error in Theognost.*Can.*61), *deceitful*, *EM*130.51, 160.45, Sch.Ar.*Pax* 1165, Suid. (The connexion with Lat. *fallere* is doubtful.) **-όω**, *cheat, deceive*, ἐφήλωσεν φρένας A.*Ag.*492; ἐπέεσσιν A.R.3.983; λώβαισι καὶ κλαυθμοῖσι Lyc.785, cf. Men.17:—Pass., γλώσσαις φηλούμενοι E.*Supp.*243. **-ωμα**, ατος, τό, *deception, cheat*, Antipho Soph.71. **-ωσις**, εως, ἡ, *deceit*, *EM*791.33.

**φῆμα**, ατος, τό, (φημί) *that which is said, word*, Hsch. (pl.).

*⁕***φήμη**, ἡ, Aeol. and Dor. **φάμα**, Sapph.*Supp.*20*a*.12, Pi.*O.*7.10; pseudo-Dor. **φήμα** B.5.194, al., Isyll.80: (φημί). I. *utterance prompted by the gods, significant* or *prophetic saying*, χαῖρε δὲ φήμῃ Ὀδυσσῆος φίλος υἱός Od.2.35, ubi v. Sch.; in the prayer of Odysseus to Zeus, φήμην τίς μοι φάσθω Od.20.100; folld. by φήμην δ' ἐξ οἴκοιο γυνὴ προέηκεν ἀλετρίς ib.105; φ. and κλεηδών are interchanged, Hdt.5.72, cf. S.*El.*1109 sq.; φ. about a τέρας, Hdt.3.153; εἴτε του θεῶν φήμην ἀκούσας εἴτ' ἀπ' ἀνδρὸς οἶσθα S.*OT*43, cf. 86, 475 (lyr.); τοῦ ὀνείρου ἡ φ. the *message* of the dream, Hdt.1.43; φ. μαντικαί S.*OT*723; φ. θεσφάτων Id.*Tr.*1150; μάντεων φῆμαι E.*Hipp.*1056, cf. *Ion* 180 (lyr.); φήμη τις οἴκων ἐν μυχοῖς ἱδρυμένη Id.*Hel.*820; φήμας τε καὶ μαντείας Pl.*Phd.*111b, cf. Isoc.9.21; φήμας καὶ ἐνύπνια καὶ οἰωνούς X.*Smp.*4.48, cf. *Cyr.*8.7.3, etc.; φήμης ἕνεκα *ominis causa*, Pl.*Lg.*878a, cf. 908a; τῇ πόλει (sc. Aquileia) ἀετὸς οἰκιζομένῃ τὴν αὑτοῦ φ. χαρίζεται Jul.*Or.*2.72a; hence, comically, φήμη γ' ὑμῖν ὄρνις ἐστί Ar.*Av.*720; φ. ἀγαθὴν λέξομεν = εὐφημίαν παρέξομεν, Id.*V.*865 (anap.). 2. *report, rumour*, usu. of uncertain and mysterious origin, φήμη οὔ τις πάμπαν ἀπόλλυται, ἥν τινα πολλοὶ λαοὶ φημίξωσι· θεός νύ τίς ἐστι καὶ αὐτή Hes.*Op.*763, cf. Aeschin.1.128 (citing φήμη δ' ἐς στρατὸν ἦλθε as from Il.); Φήμης βωμός Sch. ad loc., Paus.1.17.1; *common report*, opp. συκοφαντία, Aeschin.2.145; φάμα δ' ἦλθε κατὰ πτόλιν Sapph. l. c.; ἄμβροτε Φ. S.*OT*158 (lyr.); φ. ἐσέπτατο ἐς τὸ στρατόπεδον Hdt.9.100; φ. δημόθρους A.*Ag.*938; τίν' ἔχων φ. ἀγαθὴν ἥκεις; Ar.*Eq.*1320 (anap.); φ. ὑπορρεῖ Pl.*Lg.*672b; φήμην κατασκεδάσαι Id.*Ap.*18c. 3. *report* of a man's character, *repute*, δεινὴν δὲ βροτῶν ὑπαλεύεο φήμην· φ. γάρ τε κακὴ πέλεται, κούφη μὲν ἀεῖραι—ῥεῖα μάλ', ἀργαλέη δὲ φέρειν, χαλεπὴ δ' ἀποθέσθαι Hes.*Op.*760; ὑποδεέστερα τῆς φ. Th.1.11; περὶ τὸν τῶν ἀνθρώπων βίον..καὶ πράξεις ἀψευδής τις πλανᾶται φ. Aeschin.1.127; τοιαύτην φ. σαυτῷ περιφυομένην Isoc.5.78: pl., ἐπιφέρειν γυναικείους ἑαυτοῖς φήμας Pl.*Lg.*935a; ἐπώνυμος ἐν φήμαις βροτῶν Antiph.105:—esp. of *good report, fame*, περιχαρὴς τῇ φ. Hdt.1.31; κατὰ τὴν εὐλογίαν καὶ τοὺς ἐπαίνους καὶ τὴν φ. Isoc.5.134, cf. 4.186; ὁ δ' ὄλβιος ὃν φᾶμαι κατέχοντ' ἀγαθαί Pi.*O.*7.10: but also φ. πονηραί A.*Ch.*1045; αἰσχρὰ φ., opp. καλὴ δόξα, Isoc.1.43; ψευδῆ φ. ὑμνεῖν κατὰ θεῶν Pl.*Lg.*822c, cf. *R.*463d. 4. φᾶμαι *songs of praise*, Pi.*P.*2.16; φάμα φιλοφόρμιγξ A.*Supp.*697 (lyr.), cf. *Th.*866 (anap.). II. *any voice* or *words, speech, saying*, λόγων φ. poet. periphr. for λόγοι, S.*Ph.*846 (lyr.); esp. *common report, tradition, legend*, ἀλλ' ἔστι φήμη.. A.*Supp.*760; πολιαὶ φῆμαι E.*El.*701 (lyr.), cf. Pl.*Phlb.*16c, *Lg.*713c; αἱ ἀρχαῖαι φ. Plb.12.3.2; μνήμην παρὰ τῆς

φήμης λαβών Lys.2.3. b. *common report* or *parlance*, Chrysipp.*Stoic.*2.242; ὅσους ἡ κοινὴ φ. παραδέδωκεν [θεούς] Phld.*Piet.*17. 2. *message*, A.*Ch.*741, S.*El.*1155, E.*Hipp.*158 (lyr.).

❊**φημί**, φῄς, φηις *PCair.Zen.*316.1 (iii B.C.), *PSI*7.846.7 (Pap. of Ar. (?), ii/iii A.D.), cf. Hdn.Gr.2.147,419; φησί (apocop. φή Anacr.40); pl. φᾰμέν, φᾰτέ, φᾱσί; Dor. **φᾱμί**, φᾱσί or φᾱτί (Ar.*Ach.*771, Anon. in *PSI*9.1091.11,18), 3 pl. φαντί; Aeol. **φᾶμι** Sapph.32, 2 sg. φαῖσθα Alc.*Supp.*20.6, 3 sg. φαῖσι ib.26.5, Sapph.66, 3 pl. φαῖσι Sapph.*Supp.*5.2: aor. 2 ἔφην, Ep. φῆν Il.18.326; ἔφησθα 1.397, al., Ar.*Lys.*132, X.*An.*1.6.7, Pl.*Cra.*438a, Aeschin.3.164, etc. (rarely ἔφης Il.22.280, X.*Cyr.*4.1.23), Ep. φῆσθα Il.21.186, Od.14.149 (v.l. φῇσθα), φῆς Il.5.473, Od.7.239 (v.l.); ἔφη, Ep. φῆ, Dor. φᾶ Pi.*I.*2.11; 1 pl. ἔφᾰμεν Isoc.3.26 (ἔφημεν A.D.*Adv.*184.7, Gal.1.158, Papp.524.16, Choerob. *in Theod.*2.341 H.); 2 pl. ἔφᾰτε And.2.25; 3 pl. ἔφασαν, Ep. φάσαν Il.2.278, also ἔφᾰν, φάν, 3.161, 6.108; imper. φαθί (on the accent v. Hdn.Gr.1.431, al., A.D.*Synt.*264.4; φάθι is found in codd. of Pl. *Grg.*475e, al.); subj. φῶ, φῇς, φῇ, Ep. φῇσιν Od.1.168, φήῃ 11.128, 23.275; Dor. 3 pl. subj. φᾶντι *Tab.Heracl.*1.116; opt. φαίην, 1 pl. φαῖμεν Il.2.81, 24.222, Pi.*N.*7.87, 3 pl. φαῖεν Th.3.68, etc.; inf. φάναι, Hdt.1.27, etc., poet. φάμεν Pi.*N.*8.19; part. φάς Il.9.35, Hdt.1.63,141, *SIG*279.18 (Zeleia, iv B.C.), φᾶσα Hdt.6.135, pl. φάντες Il.3.44, 14.126, Pl.*Alc.*2.139b: fut. φήσω, Dor. φασῶ Ar.*Ach.*739, etc.; 1 pl. φασοῦμες Diotog.ap.Stob.4.1.133: aor. 1 ἔφησα Cratin. in *PSI*11.1212.9, Hdt.3.153, *PCair.Zen.*19.3 (iii B.C.) (ἔφασεν is dub. ib.140.7); Dor. 3 sg. φᾶσε Pi.*N.*1.66; 2 sg. subj. (Dor.) φάσῃς [ᾱ] Simon.32 (φήσῃς etc. codd. Stob., corr. Bgk.); opt. φήσειε Hdt.6.69, A.*Pr.*503, part. φήσας X.*Mem.*3.11.1, Isoc.12.239, inf. φῆσαι Thphr. *Char.*2.7:—**Med.** (chiefly poet. in early writers), impf. and aor. 2 ἐφάμην, ἔφατο (also *SIG*437.6 (Delph., iii B.C.), *PCair.Zen.*343.8 (iii B.C.), *PSI*4.437.8 (iii B.C.), Parth.4.5, etc.), Ep. φάτο Il.20.262, φάσθε Od.6.200, 10.562, ἔφαντο, Ep. φάντο 24.460; imper. φάο 16.168, 18.171, φάσθω, φάσθε; inf. φάσθαι; part. φάμενος (also Archim. *Spir. Prooem.*, *Eratosth.Prooem.*, *SIG*364.83 (Ephesus, iii B.C.), *PCair.Zen.*236.4 (iii B.C.), *PHamb.*4.14 (i A.D.), J.*AJ*17.12.2, Gal.6.228, etc.): Dor. fut. φάσομαι [ᾱ] Pi.*N.*9.43:—**Pass.**, pf. 3 sg. πέφαται A.R.2.500; 3 sg. imper. πεφάσθω Pl.*Ti.*72d; but part. πεφασμένος Il.14.127, A.*Pr.*843 shd. be referred to φαίνω: aor. ἐφάθην (ἀπ-, κατ-) Arist.*Int.*$18^{b}$39. The pres. indic. φημί is enclit., exc. in 2 sg. pres. φῄς: φαμέν is 1 pl. pres., φάμεν poet. inf.: φαντί is 3 pl., φάντι part. II. φάσκω supplied all moods of pres. except the indic., also impf. ἔφασκον; cf. ἠμί. [ᾰ, except in φᾶσι, and in masc. and fem. part. φάς, φᾶσα: in inf. φάναι ᾰ always; φᾶναι is corrupt in Eub.119.11 codd. Ath.]:—*say, affirm, assert*, either abs., or folld. by inf., e.g. Λυσίθεος Μικίωνα φιλῖν (=-εῖν) φησι *IG*$1^2$.924, cf. 57.48, or acc. et inf.; the inf. is freq. omitted, σὲ κακὸν καὶ ἀνάλκιδα φήσει (sc. εἶναι) Il.8.153; also Κορινθίους τί φῶμεν; what *shall we say of* them? X.*HG*3.5.12; φ. πρός τινα, πρὸς ξεῖνον φάσθαι ἔπος ἠδ' ἐπακοῦσαι Od.17.584: less freq. c. dat., αὐτοῖς *Ev.Matt.*13.28; κατά τινος φ. to *speak* against him, X.*Ap.*25: sts. folld. by ὡς, Lys.7.19, v.l. in X.*HG*.6.3.7; by ὅτι, Pl.*Grg.*487d, Corn.*ND.*30; by an interrog. clause, μή ποτε φάσῃς ὅ τι γίνεται αὔριον Simon. l.c.; by part., dub. in Pl. *Grg.*481c (fort. leg. θῶμεν); also parenthetic, τίνες, φῄς, ἦσαν οἱ λόγοι; Pl.*Phd.*59c. b. since what one says commonly expresses a belief or opinion, *think, deem, suppose*, φῆ γὰρ ὅ γ' αἱρήσειν Πριάμου πόλιν Il.2.37; φαίης κε ζάκοτόν τέ τιν' ἔμμεναι ἄφρονά τε *you would say, would think*, he was.., 3.220; ἶσον ἐμοὶ φάσθαι *to say* he is (i.e. *fancy* himself) equal to me, 1.187, 15.167; μὴ..φαθὶ λεύσσειν *think* not that you see, Theoc.22.56; τί φῄς; what *say you?* i.e. what *think you?* (v. infr. II. 5); λέγ' ἀνύσας ὅ τι φῄς Ar.*Pl.*349:—so φ. δεῖν, φ. χρῆναι, *deem* it right, And.3.34, Isoc.3.48. c. *say*, i.e. *write*, of an author, ὡς ἔφημεν Gal.1.158, etc.—The Med. has all these senses as well as the Act. II. Special Phrases: 1. φασί, *they say, it is said*, Il.5.638, Od.6.42, etc.; parenthetically, Arist.*EN*$1109^{a}$35, Men.*Epit.*223, etc.: Prose writers use φησί when quoting, D.23.89, etc.; φησίν *saith* He, 1 *Ep.Cor.*6.16; esp. of an opponent's objection, Plu.2.112c; even after a plural, ὃ τοίνυν μέγιστον ἔχειν οἴονται.. "καὶ αὐτός", φησί, "τῶν εἰσιόντων ἦσθα" Lib.*Or.*52.39; "τὸν δὲ μετ' εἰσενόησα", ἔφη Ὅμηρος as H. *said*, Pl.*Prt.*315b. 2. joined with a synon. Verb, ἔφη λέγων, ἔφησε λέγων, Hdt.3.156, 6.137, etc.; ἔλεγε φάς Id.1.122; λέγει οὐδέν, φαμένη..Id.2.22; τί ἐροῦμεν ἢ τί φήσομεν; D.8.37, cf. 25.100; τί φῶ; τί λέξω; E.*Hel.*483. 3. in repeating dialogues the Verb commonly goes before its subject, ἔφην ἐγώ, ἔφη ὁ Σωκράτης, *said* I, *said* S., but the order is sts. inverted, ἐγὼ ἔφην, ὁ Σωκράτης ἔφη, I *said*, S. *said*. 4. inserted parenthetically, though the sentence has been introduced by λέγει, εἶπεν, etc., ὁ Ἰσχόμαχος.. εἶπεν· ἀλλὰ παίζεις μὲν σύ γε, ἔφη X.*Oec.*17.10, cf. Pl.*Chrm.*164e; ἡ κρίσις..διαρρήδην λέγει "διότι", φησίν, "ἔδοξε τἀληθῆ εἰσαγγεῖλαι" Lys.13.50. 5. τί φημί; S.*OT*1471, and τί φῄς; *Ph.*804, E.*Hel.*706 (dub.), are used extra metrum, as exclamations. 6. κυριώτατα φάναι, in parenthesis, strictly *speaking*, Ph.2.374; ὡς οὕτω φάναι, = ὡς εἰπεῖν, ἅπασαι ὡς οὕτω φάναι *practically* all, Gal.*Vict.Att.*9; συνελόντα (v.l. -όντι) φάναι, = συνελόντι εἰπεῖν, Id.16.502. 7. Οἰδίπουν..ἂν μόνον φῶ if I only *mention* Oedipus, Antiph.191.6, cf. Pl.*Cra.*411a, 435a. III. like καταφημι, *say yes, affirm, assert*, καὶ τοὺς φάναι and they *said yes*, Hdt.8.88; καί φημι κἀπόφημι S.*OC*317; ἔγωγέ φημι Pl.*Grg.*526c; φάναι τε καὶ ἀπαρνεῖσθαι Id.*Tht.*165a: c. inf., φῄς ἢ καταρνεῖ μὴ δεδρακέναι τάδε; S.*Ant.*442; but οὔ φημι means *say no, deny, refuse*, c. inf., ἡ Πυθίη οὐκ ἔφη χρήσειν *said* she would *not*.., Hdt.1.19, cf. 8.2; οὐκ ἔφασαν ἐπιτρέψαι Lys.13.15,47 (leg. -τρέψειν): c. acc. et inf., οὔ φημ' Ὀρέστην σ' ἐνδίκως ἀνδρηλατεῖν A.*Eu.*221, cf. Hdt.2.63: abs., κἂν μὲν μὴ φῇ if he *says no*, Ar.*Av.*555 (anap.); ἢ φάθι ἢ μὴ ἃ ἐρωτῶ answer me *yes* or no, Pl.*Grg.*475e; so in answers, φημί or οὕτως φημί *yes*, Id.*Phdr.*270c, al., *Grg.*500e; οὐκ ἔφη he *said no*, Id.*Phd.*118a.—In this sense Att. writers, besides pres., mostly use fut. φήσω and aor. ἔφησα, but in impf., inf., and part. pres., to avoid ambiguity, they prefer ἔφασκον, φάσκειν, φάσκων (v. φάσκω): φάναι is distd. fr. φάσκειν, e.g. ἔφη σπουδάζειν *he said* he was in haste, ἔφασκε σπουδάζειν *he alleged* he was in haste; but ἔφησθα is found in this sense, X.*An.*1.6.7. IV. *command, order*, ἔφην τῷ Ὀρθοβούλῳ ἐξαλεῖψαί με Lys.16.13 (so ἔφασαν, v.l. for ἔφρασαν in X.*Cyr.*4.6.11).

❊**φημίζω**, aor. ἐφήμισα A. (v. infr.), E. (v. infr.), Ep. subj. -ίξω Hes.*Op.*764, Dor. ἐφάμιξα (κατ-) Pi.*O.*6.56:—**Med.**, aor. ἐφημισάμην A. (v. infr.), Ep. -ιξάμην D.P.90, Nonn.*D.*3.276:—**Pass.**, fut. φημισθήσομαι Lyc.1082: aor. ἐφημίσθην Plu.2.264d, etc.: pf. πεφήμισμαι Str.1.2.12: (φήμη). I. *prophesy, utter*, ἣ καὶ Λοξίας ἐφήμισε A.*Ch.*558. 2. *spread a report*, φήμην φ. Hes.*Op.*764; διαβολάς J.*BJ*1.23.2, cf. Q.S.13.538, etc.:—Pass., οἱ τεθνάναι φημισθέντες Plu. l.c., cf. J.*BJ*1.29.4, Arr.*Peripl.M.Eux.*6, *PGiss.*19.4 (ii A.D.); Μίνως ὀαριστὴς τοῦ Διὸς ἐφημίσθη εἶναι Plot.6.9.7: abs., *to be slandered*, *Supp.Epigr.*4.648.12 (Lydia, ii A.D.). 3. *call, name*, τινά τι Call.*Aet.*3.1.14,58, Nonn.*D.*9.23; οὔνομα φ. Opp.*H.*5.476:—Med., Euph.57. 4. *promise*, ἣν (sc. εὐνήν) ἐφήμισεν πατήρ μοι E.*IA*1356; ὃ ἐφήμισεν..παρασχέσθαι Sch.Call. in Διηγήσεις xi 3. II. Med., *express in words*, συντόμως ἐφημίσω A.*Ag.*629, cf. 1162 (lyr.), 1173 (lyr.):—Pass., Zos.Alch.p.169 B.

**Φήμιος**, ὁ, name of a minstrel in Od. (1.154, al.). 2. epith. of Zeus, *SIG*1014.27 (Erythrae, iii B.C.); Φημία, epith. of Athena, ibid.

**φῆμις**, ιος, ἡ, poet. for φήμη, *speech, talk*, Il.10.207; but ἐς θῶκον πρόμολον δήμοιό τε φῆμιν the *place of talk* Od.15.468. 2. *common opinion* or *judgement expressed in talk*, χαλεπὴ δ' ἔχε δήμου φ. 14.239, cf. 16.75; τῶν ἀλεείνω φῆμιν ἀδευκέα their 'bitter *gossip*', 6.273; Κασσάνδραν..φᾶμις ἔχησι βροτῶν Ibyc.9. b. φ. ἀοιδῶν their *praise*, Euph.40: hence, 3. *reputation*, χαλεπὴν δέ τε φῆμιν ὀπάσσει..γυναιξί Od.24.201; later of *good report*, Man.3.183,237.

**φημισμός**, ὁ, = φήμη, Suid.

**φημοσύνη**, ἡ, *oracular utterance*, *Inscr.Cret.*1.xvi 7 (Lato, ii/i B.C.).

**φήνη**, ἡ, a kind of *vulture*, perh. *lammergeyer, Gypaëtus barbatus*, φῆναι ἢ αἰγυπιοί Od.16.217, cf. 3.372, Ar.*Av.*304, Arist.*HA*$592^{b}$5, $619^{b}$23, cf. φίνις; sacred to Athena, Ael.*NA*12.4.

**φηνός**, = λαμπρός, Hdn.Gr.1.176.

❊**φήρ**, ὁ, gen. φηρός, Aeol. (cf. Hsch.) for θήρ, pl. φῆρες Simon.59 (cf. *Rh.Mus.*38.378); of *the Centaurs*, Il.1.268, 2.743; in sg., Pi.*P.*3.4, 4.119:—in Ion. writers of *Satyrs* (v. sq.), Gal.17(2).38; of Marsyas, Telest.1.5.

❊**φήρεα**, τά, *swelling of the parotid glands*, so as to be like the budding horns of Satyrs (φῆρες), Hp.*Epid.*6.3.6 (nisi leg. φηρεῖα), cf. Gal. ad loc.: hence Adv. **φηρεατικῶς**, Gal.19.151.

**φηρία**, Aeol. for θηρία, Hsch.

**φηρομᾰνής**, ές, *madly fond of wild animals*, epith. of Dionysus, *AP*9.524.22. **φῆρος**· ἡ τῶν ἀρχαίων θεῶν τροφή, Hsch.; φῆρον Hdn.Gr.1.385.

**Φητι-αλεῖς, -άλιοι**, v. Φετιάλιοι. **φήτρη, φητρία**, v. φράτρα.

**φθάζω**, = φθάνω, Sch.A.R.2.1219.

**φθαίρω**, Dor. for φθείρω, Eust.1648.6, *EM*269.50.

**φθάνω**, Il.9.506, impf. ἔφθανον X.*HG*6.2.30, *AP*9.272 (Bianor): fut. φθήσομαι Il.23.444, Th.5.10, Pl.*R.*375c, etc.; but φθάσω [ᾰ] Hp.*Morb.*3.13 (s. v.l.), X.*Cyr.*5.4.38: aor. ἔφθᾰσα Hdt.7.161, A.*Pers.*752 (troch.), Th.3.49, X.*Cyr.*7.1.19, etc.; imper. φθάσον J.*AJ*6.11.7; opt. 3 sg. φθάσειε Isoc.8.120, pl φθάσειαν X.*HG*7.2.14 (this tense prevails in later Gk., Plb.3.66.1, etc.); Dor. ἔφθασσα Theoc.2.115: but the only Ep. aor. is ἔφθην, not found in A. or S., but the more usual form in E. and Ar., less freq. in Th., X., D.; pl. ἔφθημεν, -ητε, -ησαν, E.*Ph.*1468, Isoc.5.7, Antipho 2.2.5, Ep. pl. 3 φθάν Il.11.51; subj. φθῶ, Ep. 3 sg. φθήῃ, φθῇσιν, 16.861, 23.805; Ep. 1 pl. φθέωμεν Od.16.383; 3 pl. φθέωσι 24.437; opt. φθαίην, Ep. 3 sg. φθαίησι (παρα-) Il.10.346; inf. φθῆναι Hdt.6.115, Th.4.4; part. φθάς Hdt.3.71; Ep. part. Med. φθάμενος Il.5.119, al., Hes.*Op.*554: pf. ἔφθᾰκα Philipp.ap.D.18.39, Lxx 2 *Ch.*28.9, *IG*12(9).906.26 (Chalcis, iii A.D.); πέφθακα Ps.-Callisth.2.10 (v.l): plpf. ἐφθάκει Plu.*Galb.*17, Luc.*Philops.*6:—**Pass.**, Arist.*Mu.*$395^{a}$18: impf. ἐφθάνετο *AP*9.278 (Bianor); ἐφθάνοντο J.*BJ*5.2.4 (v.l. ἐφονεύοντο): aor. ἐφθάσθην D.H.6.25, *Epigr.Gr.*315 (Smyrna), *IPE*2.197 (Panticapaeum, ii A.D.), J.*AJ*8.12.4. Gal.4.560. [φθᾰνω always in Att. (so also in *AP*9.272 (Bianor), *APl.*4.382,384); φθᾱνω in Il.9.506, 21.262 (where Zenod. read φθανέει for φθάνει)]:—*come* or *do first* or *before* others: I. c. acc. pers., *to be beforehand with, overtake, outstrip*, in running or otherwise, φθάνει δέ τε καὶ τὸν ἄγοντα Il.21.262; φθῇ σε τέλος θανάτοιο 11.451, cf. Hes.*Op.*554,570, Hdt.7.161, E.*Heracl.*120, *IT*669, Isoc.9.42, etc.; οὐ μὴ φθάσωμεν τοὺς κοιμηθέντας 1 *Ep.Thess.*4.15; so ἔφθησαν τὸν χειμῶνα they *anticipated* the storm, Hdt.7.188; φθάσας τὸν λογισμόν D.21.38:—Pass., *to be overtaken*, ὑπό τινος Arist.*Mu.*$395^{a}$18, *AP*9.278 (Bianor); ἐφθάσθην (v. supr.). II. abs., *come* or *act first*, opp. ὑστερέω or ὑστερίζω, E.*Ph.*975, X.*An.*6.1.18, cf. Th.4.121; τοῦ φθάσαντος ἁρπαγή the prey of *the first comer*, A.*Pers.*752 (troch.), cf. *Fr.*23 (lyr.); πρὶν ἐλθεῖν αὐτοὺς φθάσαι βουλόμενοι Th.7.36; μὴ φθάσῃ ἐς τὸν Ἑλλήσποντον ἐσπλεύσας Id.8.100; φθάσαι πρὶν ἀδικηθῆναι Arist.*Pol.*$1302^{b}$23, cf. *Rh.*$1373^{a}$23;

in later writers, τὰ φθάσαντα the things *before mentioned*, Ael.*VH* 1.34, Arg.D.46; part. φθάνων, φθάσας *previous*, τῶν φθασάντων δυεῖν βιβλίων Porph.*Abst.*3.1; ἐν τοῖς φθάνουσιν ἔργοις Dex.Hist.*Fr.*26 J.; τοῖς φθάνουσι κατορθώμασι Id.*Fr.*6 J.; οἱ φθάσαντες πόνοι Agath.5.16; τὸ φθάνον *previous time*, Ael.*VH*14.6; τὸ φθάσαν, τὰ φθάσαντα, the *past*, Agath.3.2, al., Procop.Gaz.*Ep.*32; ὁ φθάσας χρόνος Men. Prot.p.127 D. 2. with Preps., *come* or *arrive first*, ἕως τῶν οὐρανῶν Lxx 2 *Ch.*28.9; ἔφθασεν ἐφ' ὑμᾶς *Ev.Matt.*12.28, *Ev.Luc.*11.20, cf. 1 *Ep.Thess.*2.16: φ. εἰς.., simply, *arrive at, attain to*, *Ep.Rom.*9.31, *Ep. Phil.*3.16, Plu.2.338a; φθάσομεν εἰς Πηλούσι(ον) *PPar.*18.14 (ii A.D.): abs., of Time, *arrive*, καιρὸς τῆς τομῆς ἔφθακε (v.l. ἔφθασεν) Lxx *Ca.* 2.12; ἔφθασεν ὁ μὴν ὁ ἕβδομος ib.2 *Es.*3.1. b. *extend*, μέχρ. γῆς Plot.3.2.7; εἰς βορρᾶν *PFlor.*50.87 (iii A.D.). c. *reach*, αἰθέρα *APl.*4.384. d. Gramm., *to be applied* or *applicable*, ἐπ' ἀμφοτέρας τὰς διαθέσεις A.D.*Synt.*211.22, cf. 217.23, al. III. the action in which one *is beforehand* is expressed by the part. agreeing with the subject, [Ἄτη] πολλὸν ὑπεκπροθέει, φθάνει δέ τε πᾶσαν ἐπ' αἶαν βλάπτουσ' ἀνθρώπους and *is beforehand* in doing men mischief, Il.9.506; ἀλλ' ἄρα μιν φθῆ Τηλέμαχος κατόπισθε βαλών Telemachus *was beforehand* with him *in* striking, i.e. struck *first*, Od.22.91, cf. 16.383, Il.10.368; ἔφθασέν με προαπελθὼν Χάρμος *PCair.Zen.*16.3 (iii B.C.); ἔφθησαν ἀπικόμενοι arrived *first*, Hdt.4.136, cf. 6.115; so φ. εὐεργετῶν *to be the first* to show a kindness, X.*Mem.*2.3.14; ὅπως φθάσειαν βοηθήσαντες Id.*HG*7.2.14; ἔφθασαν προκαταλαβόντες Th.3.112; φθάνουσιν αὐτοὺς προκαταφυγοῦσαι Id.2.91; ἣν φθάσωσιν πρότερον διαφθείραντες τὸ στράτευμα Id.7.25; φ. γόνασι προσπεσὼν πατρός E.*HF*986, etc.: part. Pass. is also used, ἤ κε πολὺ φθαίη πόλις ἁλοῦσα, i.e. it would be taken *first*, Il.13.815; εἴ κε φθήῃ τυπείς shall be wounded *first*, 16.861; φθαίητε γὰρ ἂν.. ἐξανδραποδισθέντες ἤ.. Hdt.6.108; μὴ φθάσωσι προεπιβουλευόμενοι Th.3.83; ἔφθη κατακωλυθείς X.*HG*1.6.17; φθάνειν δεῖ πεφραγμένους τοὺς πόρους they must *first* be blocked up, Id.*Cyr.*2.4.25: these clauses, being compar. in sense, are folld. by a gen., φθὰν δὲ μέγ' ἱππήων.. κοσμηθέντες were drawn up *before* the drivers, Il.11.51; more freq. by πρὶν.. or ἤ.., ἔφθη ὀρεξάμενος, πρὶν οὐτάσαι 16.322, cf. Antipho 1.29, X. *Cyr.*3.2.4; φθήσονται τούτοισι πόδες καὶ γοῦνα καμόντα ἢ ὑμῖν Il.23.444; ἔφθης πεζὸς ἰὼν ἢ ἐγὼ σὺν νηΐ Od.11.58; ἔφθησαν ἀναβάντες πρὶν ἤ.. Hdt.9.70; ἔφθησαν ἐκπεσόντες πρότερον ἤ.. Id.6.91. b. in later Gr., c. part. to express *previous* action or happening, φθάνω ὑμῖν πρότερον γεγραφηκώς I have *already* written to you, *POxy.*1666.3 (iii A.D.), cf. 237 vi 30 (ii A.D.), etc.; ἔφθασα εἰρηκώς Luc.*Pisc.*29; ὡς ἔφθην εἰπών Id.*Par.*3; cf. III.2b. 2. in the same sense, part. φθάς or φθάσας, Ep. φθάμενος, is used like an Adv. with a principal Verb, ὅς μ' ἔβαλε φθάμενος, for ὅς μ' ἔφθη βαλών, Il.5.119, cf. 13.387, Od. 19.449; οὐκ ἄλλος φθὰς ἐμεῦ κατήγορος ἔσται no other shall be an accuser *before* me, Hdt.3.71; ἀνέῳξάς με φθάσας you opened the door *before* me, Ar.*Pl.*1102; φθάσας προσπεσοῦμαι Th.5.9, cf. 2.91, X.*Cyr.* 1.5.3, etc.; even with a part., φθάσας.. ἁρπάσας Hdt.6.65; rarely part. pres., φθάνοντες δῃοῦμεν X.*Cyr.*3.3.18. b. in signf. III. 1 b, φθάσαντες ἐπληρώσαμεν αὐτούς we had *already* paid them, *POxy*.1103.6 (iv A.D.); but ὡσεὶ καὶ ὁμογενῆ φθάσας εἶπον as if I *had* said (not *had already* said) ὁ., Gal.16.502. 3. rarely c. inf., ὁ φθάσας θαρσῆσαι he that *first* gains confidence, Th.3.82; σπεύδειν ὅπως.. φθαίης ἔτ' εἰς ἐκκλησίαν ἐλθεῖν (v.l. ἐλθών) hurry *to be in time* to get to.., Ar.*Eq.*935 (lyr.), cf. *Nu.*1384 (v. infr. IV. 1); μόλις φθάνει θρόνοισιν ἐμπεσοῦσα μὴ χαμαὶ πεσεῖν hardly *manages* by falling *first* on the seat not to fall on the ground, E.*Med.*1169; more freq. in later writers, of actions which one *manages* to do, *does before* or *has done first* or *already*, A.R.1.1189, D.H.4.59,61, Sor.1.111, Gal.15.2,93, Luc. *D.Mort.*13.2, *Harm.*2; ἐὰν φθάσω πρὸ τῆς τρύγης ἀνελθεῖν *PSI*8.971.10 (iii/iv A.D.); ἐὰν ὁ ἰατρὸς αὐτὸ φθάσῃ κενῶσαι Gal.16.499; φθάνοντος ἤδη πυρέττειν ἐκ τεττάρων ἡμερῶν τοῦ νοσοῦντος *having already begun*, ib.498; μὴ φθάνων προσηκόντως τρέφεσθαι if he *is* not *first* suitably nourished, Id.18(2).36, cf. 84,103; συμβαίνει φθάνειν ἀποθνήσκειν τοὺς νεωτέρους the young die *first*, ib.222; εἰ φθάσαιμεν παλαιοὺς πίθους ἔχειν μεγάλους if we *already* have.., *Gp.*6.3.11, cf. 10.22.2, al., A.D.*Pron.*90.1; ἔφθακεν οὖν ταῦτα ἐψηφίσθαι καὶ τῇ βουλῇ *IG*12(9).906.26 (Chalcis, iii A.D.). IV. with negatives, 1. with οὐ and part. (inf. is v.l. in Ar.*Nu* 1384), folld. by καί or καὶ εὐθύς, of two actions following close on each other, οὐ φθάνειν χρὴ συσκιάζοντας γένυν καὶ.. ὁρμᾶν you must *no sooner* get your beard than you march, E.*Supp.*1219; οὐ φθάνει ἐξαγόμενος καὶ εὐθὺς ὅμοιός ἐστι τοῖς ἀκαθάρτοις *no sooner* is he brought out than he becomes unclean, X.*Eq.*5.10, cf. Ar.*Nu.*1384; οὐκ ἔφθημεν εἰς Τροιζῆν' ἐλθόντες καὶ τοιαύταις νόσοις ἐλήφθημεν ἐξ ὧν.. *no sooner* had we come to Troezen than.., Isoc.19.22, cf. 5.53, 8.98, 9.53; οὐκ ἔφθη μοι συμβᾶσα ἡ ἀτυχία καὶ εὐθὺς ἐπεχείρησαν διαφορῆσαι τἄνδοθεν *scarcely* or *no sooner* had misfortune befallen me when.., D.57.65, cf. 43.69, Isoc.4.86. 2. οὐκ ἂν φθάνοις, οὐκ ἂν φθάνοιτε, with part. pres., express a strong exhortation or urgent command, οὐκ ἂν φθάνοιτε τὴν ταχίστην ὀπίσω ἀπαλλασσόμενοι you could not *be too quick* in departing, i.e. *make haste and* be off, Hdt.7.162; οὐ φθάνοιτ' ἔτ' ἂν θνήσκοντες *make haste and* die, E.*Or.*936, cf. 941, *Alc.* 662, *Heracl.*721, *Tr.*456 (troch.), *IT*245; οὐκ ἂν φθάνοιτον τοῦτο πράττοντε Ar.*Pl.*485; ἀποτρέχων οὐκ ἂν φθάνοις ib.1133; εἰς ἀγορὰν ἰὼν ταχέως οὐκ ἂν φθάνοις ib.874, cf. *Ec.*118; οὐκ ἂν φθάνοις λέγων Pl. *Smp.*185e, X.*Mem.*2.3.11; these phrases are not to be treated as questions, cf. οὐκ ἂν φθάνοιμι (sc. λέγων) Pl.*Smp.*214e, cf. *Phd.*100c, D.25.40, Luc.*Fug.*26, *Symp.*2, *Anach.*14: c. part. aor., once in Luc., *Vit.Auct.*26. b. in 1, 2, or 3 pers., to express immediate futurity, οὐκ ἂν φθάνοις ἀκούων you *shall* hear *in a moment*, Pl.*Euthd.* 272d; οὐκ ἂν φθάνοι τὸ πλῆθος τούτοις τοῖς θηρίοις δουλεῦον *will soon* (or *inevitably*) be enslaved to.., D.24.143; also to express what is logically inevitable, οὐκ ἂν φθάνοιεν αὐτοὺς προσκυνοῦντες they *will soon be* (or *cannot logically help*) worshipping them, Aristeas 137; τοῦτο μὲν οὐκ ἂν φθάνοις καὶ Ἐμπεδοκλεῖ πρὸ αὐτοῦ ἐγκαλῶν Luc.*Fug.*2; οὐκ ἂν φθάνοι κἀμὲ μάντιν λέγων Id.*Hes.*8; οὐκ ἂν φθάνοι τις ἁπάσας ἀναιρῶν τὰς τοιαύτας προστασίας Id.*Apol.*11: c. part. aor., Id.*Tox.*2.

**φθάρ-μα**, ατος, τό, *corruption*, Lxx *Le.*22.25. II. *outcast, castaway*, J.*BJ*5.10.5. **-σία**, ἡ, *destruction*, Thales ap.Fulg.*Myth.*2.11. **-τικός**, ή, όν, *destructive*, c. gen., φθαρτικὰ ἀλλήλων τὰ ἐναντία one of another, Arist.*Ph.*192$^a$21; ἡ κακία φ. ἀρχῆς Id.*EN*1140$^b$19; πόλεως φ. Id.*Pol.*1281$^a$20: abs., Id.*Po.*1452$^b$11; opp. ποιητικός, γεννητικός, Id.*Top.*114$^b$17, 124$^a$25; ζῷα οὐ φ. Porph.*Abst.*1.11; φ. φαρμακεῖαι Plu.2.134e; φάρμακα *deadly* poisons, Dsc.3.45; ἐμβρύων φ., v.l. for φθόριος, Id.2.166, cf. 1.105; φ. δύναμις Gal.11.764. Adv. **-κῶς** Arist.*Top.*153$^b$32. **-τός**, ή, όν, *destructible, perishable*, opp. ἀΐδιος, Id.*APo.*75$^b$24, 85$^b$18, *Metaph.*992$^b$17, 1058$^b$26, Ocell.1.4, Plu. 2.106d, S.E.*M.*9.141, etc.; gloss on θνητός, Sch.Theoc.24.171 (Antinoë Pap.).

**φθαστέον**, (φθάνω) *one must anticipate*, Herod.Med.ap.Orib.7.8.2.

**φθᾰτέω**, aor. subj. φθατήσῃ, glossed φθάσῃ, Hsch.; cf. καταφθατόομαι (or rather -έομαι); also **ψᾰτᾶσθαι**, = προκαταλαμβάνειν, Id.; ψατῆσαι, = προειπεῖν, Id.

**φθέγγομαι**, Od.10.228, etc.: fut. φθέγξομαι Il.21.341: aor. ἐφθεγξάμην, Ep. and poet. φθεγξάμην 18.218, Pi.*O.*6.14: pf. ἔφθεγμαι, 2 sg. ἔφθεγξαι Pl.*Lg.*830c, 3 sg. ἔφθεγκται (trans.) Arist.*APo.*77$^a$2, (Pass.) Id.*Cael.*279$^a$23:—*utter a sound* or *voice*, esp. *speak loud and clear*, freq. in Hom., φθεγξάμενος παρὰ νηός Il.11.603, cf. 10.67, al., Pl. *R.*336b (properly of all animals that have lungs, Arist.*HA*535$^a$30): I. of the human voice, ἀνθρωπηΐῃ φωνῇ φ. Hdt.2.57; ἀπὸ γλώσσας Pi.l.c.; διὰ τοῦ στόματος Pl.*Sph.*238b; [ψυχῆς] φθεγξαμένης ἀΐων Xenoph.7.5; φθεγξαμένου τευ ἢ αὐδήσαντος Od.9.497; with a part. expressing the kind of cry, φθέγξομ' ἐγὼν ἰάχουσα Il. 21.341; τοὶ δ' ἐφθέγγοντο καλεῦντες Od.10.229, cf. 12.249; so σφοδρῷ τῷ πνεύματι φ. Archyt.1; φ. μετὰ βοῆς Pl.*Lg.*791e, etc.; μέγιστον ἁπάντων D.19.206; καλὸν καὶ μέγα ib.216, cf. 337; ἐλεύθερον καὶ μέγα Pl.*Grg.*485e; also of weak, small voice, φθεγξάμενος ὀλίγῃ ὀπί Od.14.492; τυτθὸν φθεγξαμένη Il.24.170; of the battle-cry, X.*An.* 1.8.18; of the recitative of the chorus, Id.*Oec.*8.3; οὐκέτι πόρρω διθυράμβων φ. Pl.*Phdr.*238d; οὐδ' ἂν φθέγξασθαι δυνηθείη would not be able to *utter a syllable*, Isoc.15.192, cf. Pl.*R.*368c; opp. silence, X.*Mem.*4.2.6; εἶτα σὺ φθέγγει..; *open your mouth..?* D.18. 283; of children just born, Arist.*HA*587$^a$27:—Constr.:—c. acc. cogn., *utter*, ἔπος Hdt.5.106; ἀγέλαστα Heraclit.92; ὀδυρμοὺς καὶ γόους ἀνωφελεῖς A.*Pr.*34; καίρια S.*Ph.*862 (lyr.); ἀράς, λόγους, βλασφημίαν, E.*Ph.*475, *Med.*1307, *Ion* 1189; ῥῆμα μοχθηρόν *SIG*1175.19 (Piraeus, Tab.Defix., iv/iii B.C.); τἀληθῆ Pl.*Phlb.*49b; ὑπέρογκα ματαιότητος φ. 2 *Ep.Pet.*2.18: the pers. addressed added with a Prep., φ. εἰς ἡμᾶς E.*Ph.*l.c.; πρός τινα Pl.*Ion* 534d; later τισί, Plu.*Crass.*27; φ. τι περί τινος Isoc.10.13; τὸ φθεγγόμενον, abs., that *which uttered the sound*, Hdt.8.65. 2. of animals, as a horse, *neigh, whinny*, Id.3.84,85; of an eagle, *scream*, X.*An.*6.1.23; of a raven, *croak*, Thphr.*Sign.*16; of a fawn, *cry*, Theoc.13.62; of birds, opp. ἄφωνοί εἰσι, Arist.*HA*618$^a$5; ἐν τῷ θέρει ᾄδει [κόττυφος], τοῦ χειμῶνος.. φ. θορυβῶδες ib.632$^b$17; of worms, φ. οἷον τριγμόν Thphr. *CP*5.10.5; of certain fish, Arist.*Fr.*300, Opp.*H.*1.135. 3. of inanimate things, of a door, *creak*, Ar.*Pl.*1099; of thunder, X.*Cyr.* 7.1.3; of trumpets, Id.*An.*4.2.7, 5.2.14; of the flute, Id.*Smp.*6.3, Thgn.532; of the lyre, φόρμιγξ φ. ἱρὸν μέλος Id.761, cf. Arist. *Metaph.*1019$^b$15; of an earthen pot, εἴτε ὑγιὲς εἴτε σαθρὸν φ. whether it *rings* sound or cracked, Pl.*Tht.*179d; φ. παλάμῃσι *to clap* with the hands, Nonn.*D.*5.106, cf. *AP*9.505.17 (dub.). II. = ὀνομάζω, *to name, call by name*, Pl.*R.*527a, *Phlb.*25c, 34a; τῷ πλέγματι τούτῳ τὸ ὄνομα ἐφθεγξάμεθα λόγον *gave* it the name of λόγος, Id.*Sph.*262d; φ. εἴδωλον ἐπὶ πᾶσιν ὡς ἓν ὄν ib.240a; φ. γιγνόμενα *speak of* things as coming into existence, Id.*Tht.*157b; καὶ τὸν κύλλαστιν φθέγγου *use the word* κ., Ar.*Fr.*257; also τῇ δυνάμει ταὐτὸν φ. *have* the same *meaning*, Pl.*Cra.*394c. III. c. acc. pers., *sing*, or *celebrate* one *aloud*, Pi.*O.*1.36; also, *tell of, recount*, θεῶν ἔργα Xenoph.12.1.

**φθεγγώδης**, ες, corrupt word in Hp.*Praec.*7, cf. Erot.*Fr* 7.

**φθεγκ-τικός**, ή, όν, *vocal*, Max.Tyr.14.2. **-τός**, ή, όν, *capable of being sounded*, Plu.2.1017f.

**φθέγ-μα**, ατος, τό (written **φθέγγμα** in late Inscrr., *Epigr.Gr.*1002, 1003), *sound of the voice, voice*, Pi.*P.*8.31, A.*Pr.*588 (lyr.), S.*OC*1623, Ar.*Nu.*319 (anap.), etc.; periphr. of a person, ὦ φθέγμ' ἀναιδές, for ὦ φθεγξάμενε ἀναιδῆ, S.*OC*863, cf. *Aj.*14, *El.*1225. b. *language, speech*, Id.*Ant.*354 (lyr.). c. *saying, word, utterance*, Id.*OC*1177, Pl.*R.*616a, Lxx *Wi.*1.11: pl., *accents, words*, Pl.*Lg.*655a, Polyzel. 12. 2. of other sounds, as of birds, *cries*, S.*El.*18, E.*Hel.*747; of a bull, *roaring*, Id.*Hipp.*1215; βροντᾶς φ. Pi.*P.*4.198; θυείας φ. the *grinding* of the mortar, Ar.*Pax* 235; of *musical notes*, Id.*Av.*683 (lyr.), Pl.*Lg.*812d; of the nightingale's *song*, Ar.*Av.*204,223. **-ματικός**, ή, όν, *vocal*, μαντεῖον Max.Tyr.41.1.

**φθέγξις**, εως, ἡ, *speech, utterance*, Hp.*Epid.*2.6.4, Aret.*CA*1.1, Porph.*Abst.*3.3, *EM*430.55.

⊛**φθείρ**, ὁ, later ἡ, Phryn.277: gen. φθειρός: dat. pl. φθειρσί:—

*louse*, Archil.137, Heraclit.56, Hdt.2.37, 4.168, Ar.*Pax*740, al., *IG* 4²(1).122.45 (Epid., iv B.C.), etc.: prov., πρὸς φθεῖρα κείρασθαι, i.e. to be close shaven, Eub.32; of the *morbus pedicularis* (φθειρίασις), τὴν σάρκα εἰς φθεῖρας μεταβάλλειν Plu.*Sull.*36; τοῦ σώματος διαλυθέντος εἰς φθειρῶν πλῆθος D.S.34/5.2.23; ὁ γευσάμενος..φθειρσὶν ἐξέζεσεν Ael.*NA*9.19. 2. of *lice* that infest animals, Arist.*HA*556$^{b}$22; birds, ib.557$^{a}$11; fish, ib.557$^{a}$22; also vegetables, μὴ ὁ σῖτος φθειρὶ ζέσῃ Luc.*Ep.Sat.*26, cf. Ctes.*Fr.*57.21, Gal.6.572; οὐ ποιήσει φθεῖρας ἡ ἄμπελος *Gp.*5.30.1. II. *sea-fish* attendant on the dolphin, *Naucrates ductor*, Arist.*HA*557$^{a}$31, Marc.Sid.86, Ael.*NA*9.7. III. *the seed* of a kind of pine, Phot. IV. *middle part of the rudder*, Poll.1.89.

**φθειρ-άριος,** *α, ον, lousy, Gloss.* **-ίᾱσις,** εως, ἡ, *morbus pedicularis*, Dsc.4.152, 5.105, Archig.ap.Gal.12.463, Plu.*Sull.*36, Porph.*VP*55; of fowls, *Gp.*14.17.3. **-ιάω,** *to be lousy*, D.L.5.5: esp. *have the morbus pedicularis*, *Com.Adesp.*280, Archig.ap.Gal.12.463, Plu.*Sull.*36; τοῖς ἐκ νόσου φθειριῶσι Dsc.1.37; of bees, *Gp.*15.2.13; of oxen, ib.17.29; also φθειριῶσα ἄμπελος Str.7.5.8. **-ίζομαι,** Pass., *pick the lice off oneself*, Arist.*Fr.*76, Thphr.*Sign.*16, Apollod.ap.Ath.13.586a:—Act. (with fut. -ιῶ) Lxx *Je.*50(43).12. **-ιασμός,** ὁ, = φθειρισμός, *Gloss.* **-ιον,** τό, = σταφὶς ἀγρία, Ps.-Dsc.4.152. **-ισμός,** ὁ, *picking lice, Gloss.* **-ιστικός,** ή, όν, *seeking lice*:—ἡ -κή (sc. τέχνη), *the art of louse-hunting, vermin-killing*, Pl.*Sph.*227b.

**φθειρό-βρωτος,** *ον, lice-eaten*, Hsch.Mil.69. **-γράφος** [ᾰ], name of a *plaster*, Androm.ap.Gal.13.913. **-κομίδης** [ῐ], ου, ὁ, *lousy fellow*, *Com.Adesp.*1188. **-κτονέω,** *kill lice*, ib.1189. **-κτόνον,** τό, = σταφὶς ἀγρία, Ps.-Dsc.4.152. **-ποιός,** όν, *producing lice*, λίνον Plu.2.352e; ἔριον ib.642c, *Gp.*15.1.5. II. (φθείρ III) πίτυς φ. *pine that bears small edible seeds, Pinus brutia*, Thphr.*HP*2.2.6. III. *destructive*, πνεῦμα δαιμόνιον φ. *PMasp.*1884 (vi A.D.). **-πύλη** [ῠ], ἡ, nickname of the courtesan Phanostrate, ἐπειδήπερ ἐπὶ τῆς θύρας ἑστῶσα ἐφθειρίζετο Apollod.ap.Ath.13.586a. **-τρᾰγέω,** *eat lice*, or perh. *pine-seeds* (φθείρ III), Hdt.4.109. **-τρωκτέω,** = foreg., Arr.*Peripl.M.Eux.*18. **-φάγοι** [ᾰ], οἱ, *lice-eaters*, name of a tribe in the Caucasus, Str.11.2.19 (but perh. *eaters of fir-cones*, as they lived near Πιτυοῦς), Porph.*Chr.*69. **-φόρος,** ον, (φθείρ III) = φθειροποιός II, Thphr.*CP*1.9.2.

®**φθείρω,** Aeol. **φθέρρω** Hdn.Gr.2.303, al.; Arc. **φθήρω** *IG*5(2).6.17 (Tegea, iv B.C.): Ion. impf. φθείρεσκε (δια-) Hdt.1.36: fut. φθερῶ X.*HG*7.2.11, (δια-) A.*Ag.*1266, etc.; Ion. φθερέω (δια-) Hdt.5.51; Ep. φθέρσω (δια-) Il.13.625: aor. 1 ἔφθειρα A.*Pers.*244 (troch.), X.*HG*7.2.4; poet. ἔφθερσα Lyc.1402; Arc. 3 sg. opt. (?) φθέραι *IG*5(2).6.8 (Tegea, iv B.C.): pf. ἔφθαρκα Din.1.64, (δι-) E.*Med.*226; Arc. part. ἐφθορκώς *IG*5(2).6.10 (Tegea, iv B.C.):—Med., fut. φθεροῦμαι (in pass. sense) S.*OT*272, E.*Andr.*708, Th.7.48; Ion. φθερέομαι (δια-) Hdt.8.108 (v.l. δια-φθαρέεται), 9.42 (vv. ll. δια-φθαρέονται, δια-φθορεῦνται); later φθαροῦμαι Archig.ap.Orib.8.23.5:—Pass., fut. φθᾰρήσομαι Hp.*VM*13, Arist.*Metaph.*1066$^{b}$30, Epicur.*Ep.*1 p.7 U., (δια-) E.*Hec.*802, etc., Dor. -ησοῦμαι Ti.Locr.94d: aor. ἐφθάρην [ᾰ] S.*OT*1502, Th.7.13, Pl.*Lg.*708c; poet. 3 pl. ἔφθαρεν Pi.*P.*3.36: also part. κατα-φθερείς Epich.35.13: pf. ἔφθαρμαι S.*El.*765, 3 pl. ἐφθάραται Th.3.13; inf. ἐφθάρθαι Arist.*Metaph.*1021$^{b}$27, (δι-) Is.9.37, Aeol. ἔφθορθαι Eust.790.8: plpf. 3 pl. ἐφθάρατο App.*BC*3.15, (δι-) Hdt.8.90. The compd. διαφθείρω is much more freq. than the simple Verb:—*destroy* things, μῆλα κακοὶ φθείρουσι νομῆες Od.17.246; φ. τῶν Συρίων τοὺς κλήρους *waste* them, Hdt.1.76, cf. X.*HG*7.2.11, *An.*4.7.20; τοὺς θεῶν νόμους S.*Aj.*1344; τὰς ναῦς v.l. in Th.2.91; τὴν πόλιν καὶ νόμους Pl.*Lg.*958c, cf. X.*Mem.*1.5.3; εὐδαιμονίαν Din.l.c.; ἔμβρυα Dsc.2.163; τὸ συλληφθέν Sor.1.60 (also abs., *miscarry*, ib.59); τὸν κοινὸν οἶκον Mitteis *Chr.*284.11 (ii B.C.):—Pass., *to be destroyed*, S.*Aj.*25, etc.; ἐκ τῶν αὐτῶν καὶ διὰ τῶν αὐτῶν καὶ γίνεται πᾶσα ἀρετὴ καὶ φθείρεται Arist.*EN*1103$^{b}$8; εἰς τὸ μὴ ὂν φ. *pass away, cease to be*, Epicur.*Ep.*1 p.5 U.; δυὰς προσθέσει μονάδος εἰς τριάδα φθείρεται μηκέτι μένουσα δυάς Ph.2.509; of animals, *perish*, *PStrassb.*24.15 (ii A.D.). 2. of persons, μαψαῦραι...ναύτας φ. *destroy* them, Hes.*Th.*876 (but perh. only Act. of signf. II.4); στρατόν A.*Pers.*244 (troch.), *Ag.*652:—Pass., Id.*Pers.*272, 283 (lyr.); γειτόνων πολλοὶ ἁμᾷ..ἔφθαρεν Pi.*P.*3.36; νόσῳ ἐφθάραται Ἀθηναῖοι Th.3.13, cf. 7.48; πρόρριζον ἔφθαρται γένος S.*El.*765; ἔφθαρμαι *I am undone!* Men.*Her.*13; μὴ φθαρῶσιν *PMich.Zen.*80.4 (iii B.C.). 3. *corrupt, bribe*, τινα D.S.4.73; *lure, entice, trap*, κημοῖσι πλεκτοῖς πορφύρας φθείρει γένος S.*Fr.*504 (s.v.l.); φθείρει γὰρ ἡ πρόνοια τὴν ἀβουλίαν *entices to its ruin, entraps*, *Trag.Adesp.*484 (s.v.l.); *pervert*, φθείρουσιν ἤθη χρήσθ' ὁμιλίαι κακαί E.*Fr.*1024:—Pass., v. infr. II.3. b. *seduce* a woman, ὑπὸ τῆς θυγατρὸς ἀδικούμενον καὶ Διονυσίου τοῦ φθείραντος αὐτὴν κιναίδου *PEnteux.*26.11 (iii B.C.):—Pass., E.*Fr.*485, D.Chr.11.153 (but not Att. acc. to Phryn.53, Moer.p.103 P.), Artem.5.17. 4. *ruin, spoil*, ποσὶν φθείροντα πλοῦτον ἀργυρωνήτους θ' ὑφάς, of one who treads on rich carpets, A.*Ag.*949; βαφὰς φθείρουσα τοῦ ποικίλματος, of blood, Id.*Ch.*1013; of a poison, ὧνπερ ἂν θίγῃ, φθείρει τὰ πάντα S.*Tr.*716; φαρμάκων φθείρειν πεφυκότων τὰ σώματα Gal.15.541; δούλην (wet-nurse) μὴ φθείρουσαν τὸ γάλα *BGU*1058.29 (i B.C.), cf. Sor.1.88; τοῦ σώματος (sc. τῶν νοσούντων) φθείροντος τὸ θρέψαι δυνάμενον ib.90, cf. 63, al. 5. τὰ μιγνύμενα τῶν χρωμάτων οἱ βαφεῖς "φθείρεσθαι" καὶ "φθοράν" τὴν μῖξιν ὀνομάζουσιν Plu.2.393c (where μιαίνω I is compared). II. Pass. (cf. supr. I.1, 2), 1. φθείρεσθε (as a curse) *may you perish! ruin take you!* Il.21.128, Sannyr.10; φθείρου as an imprecation, *go to the devil! be off!* Ar.*Ach.*460, *Pl.*598, 610 (anap.), E.*Fr.*610; ἐκποδὼν ἡμῖν φθείρεσθε Herod.6.16: c. gen., φθείρεσθε τῆσδε *off from* her! unhand her, let her go, E.*Andr.*715 (so in fut. indic., εἰ μὴ φθερῇ τῆσδ' ὡς τάχιστ' ἀπὸ στέγης if thou *dost* not *depart*... ib.708). b. with a Prep., φθείρεσθαι πρὸς τοὺς πλουσίους, of hangers-on and flatterers, D.21.139, cf. Plu.*Phoc.*21, *Eum.*14, *Ant.*24; εἰς ἡδονὰς ἀπὸ..πόνων Anon.ap.Stob.4.31.84; ἀκούω σε λυρῳδοῦ γυναικὸς ἐρᾶν καὶ εἰς ἐκείνης φθειρόμενον πᾶσαν τὴν ἐφήμερον ἄγραν κατατίθεσθαι Alciphr.1.18. 2. Medic., ἡ κοιλίη φθαρήσεται *will be deranged, disordered*, Hp.*VM*13. 3. *to be morally corrupted*, ἐφθάρη ἡ γῆ ἐναντίον τοῦ θεοῦ Lxx *Ge.*6.11, cf. *Ho.*9.9, al.; ἔστι ἐν Ἀλεξανδρείᾳ σκηνῶν ἐν τοῖς Ἀριστοβούλου φθειρόμενος *PCair.Zen.*37.7 (iii B.C.); φθαρεὶς Εὔτυχος ὑπὸ τῆς Ἀρσινόης ib.620.7 (iii B.C.); but ἐν Σικυωνίαι ἐφθαρμένους is f.l. for ἐν Σικυῶνι διεφθ. (cj. Sintenis) in Plu.*Arat.*40. 4. of seafarers, *wander, drift* (cf. supr. I.2, πολύφθορος II.2, φθορά 8), πόσον χρόνον πόντου 'πὶ νώτοις ἅλιον ἐφθείρου πλάνον; E.*Hel.*774; ναυτίλους ἐφθαρμένους sailors *driven out of their course*, Id.*IT*276; ἱκέτας δέχεσθαι ποντίους ἐφθαρμένους Id.*Cyc.*300; of shipwrecked persons, νεῶν (ἐκ νεῶν Elmsl.) φθαρέντες A.*Pers.*451; also of travellers or wanderers by land, οὐχ ἕνα νομίζων φθείρεται πόλεως νόμον (v.l. τόπον) E.*El.*234; ὁ Μενέλαος χρόνον πολὺν ἐφθείρετο πανταχόσε τῆς Ἑλλάδος D.Chr.7.95; οὐδὲν δεῖ φθείρεσθαι περιόντα (= περιιόντα) τὴν ἀρχὴν ἅπασαν Aristid.*Or.*26(14).33; ἄνω κάτω διαθέοντας τὴν Ἑλλάδα καὶ φθειρομένους Id.1.420 J.; τῶν μετοίκων τῶν ἐξ Ἑρμιόνης οὐκ οἶδ' ὅπως εἰς Πειραιᾶ φθαρέντων Alciphr.1.13; μὴ περιΐδῃς ἀγαθοὺς γείτονας εἰς στενὸν τοῦ καιροῦ φθειρομένους ib.24; [Ἀλέξανδρον] ὑπὲρ τὸν Ἰνδὸν κτλ. φθειρόμενον Arr.*An.*7.4.2; φθαρῆναι εἰς βάρβαρα ἔθνη (ἐν βαρβάροις ἔθνεσι or ἔθεσι codd.) Phalar.*Ep.*49; φθαρέντων ἐς ἀλλήλους *falling foul* of one another, App.*Praef.*10 (s.v.l.). 5. of women, χέρσους φθαρῆναι *pine away in* barrenness, S.*OT*1502, cf. *El.*1181 (unless *wander*, cf. supr. II.4). (Cf. Skt. *kṣárati* 'flow', later 'wane, perish', Avest. *γžar-* and *žgar-* 'flow'.)

**φθειρώδης,** ες, *infested by lice, lousy*, κεφαλαί, γυναῖκες, Arist.*HA*557$^{a}$7, 9.

**φθεῖσαι, φθείσει, φθεῖτο, φθεῖσθαι,** v. φθίω.

**φθερσί-βροτος,** ον, = φθισίμβροτος (q.v.), Epigr. in Paus.3.8.9. **-γενής,** ές, *destroying the race*, Ἐρινύες A.*Th.*1059 (anap.).

**φθέωμεν, φθέωσι, φθήῃ, φθῇσιν,** v. φθάνω.

**Φθία** [ῑ], ας, Ep. and Ion. **Φθίη,** ης, ἡ, *Phthia* in Thessaly, the home of Achilles, Il.1.155, al.; **Φθίηνδε** *to Phthia*, 1.169, etc.; **Φθίηφι** *at Phthia*, 19.323.—Hence **Φθῑώτης,** ου, ὁ, *a man of Phthia*, Hdt.7.132, Th.8.3, etc.; Φθιῶτ' Ἀχιλλεῦ A.*Fr.*132, cf. E.*Tr.*575 (anap.), *IA*237 (lyr.): as Adj., Πηνειὲ Φθιῶτα Call.*Del.*112:—**Φθῑῶτις** γῆ, *the land of Phthia*, E.*Andr.*664, etc.; ἀκταὶ Φ. Id.*Tr.*1125; γυναῖκες Id.*Andr.*1047:—Adj. **Φθῑωτικός,** ή, όν, Str.9.5.8:—also Adj. **Φθῖος,** α, ον, whence Φθῖοι = Φθιῶται, Il.13.686; with pecul. fem. **Φθῑάς,** άδος, ἡ, E.*Hec.*451 (lyr.), etc.

**φθίδιος,** α, ον, (φθίω) *perishable*, Hsch. (post φθόσις). **φθίνα,** ἡ, *mildew*, Id. II. a kind of *olive*, Id.

**φθῐν-άς,** άδος, ἡ, (φθίνω) intr., *wasting, waning*, μηνῶν φ. ἁμέρα E.*Heracl.*779 (lyr.); φ. ὥρα Heraclit.*All.*71; ἕως διχοτόμου φθινάδος Str.3.5.8. II. Act., *wasting*, νόσοι S.*Ant.*819 (anap.); τηκεδόνες Ph.2.432; φ. νόσος, technically, *consumption*, = φθίσις, Hp.*Gland.*14 (pl.), Paus.5.26.5; and without νόσος, Hp.*Mul.*1.2; also, = *empyema*, Ruf.*Ren.Ves.*2.36. **-ασμα,** ατος, τό, *declining, sinking*, ἡλίου φθινασμάτων A.*Pers.*232 (troch.). **-άω** or **-έω,** collat. form of φθίνω, fut. φθινήσω *Gp.*1.12.34: aor. ἐφθίνησα Hp.*Epid.*7.122, Luc.*Par.*57, (κατ-) Plu.2.117c: pf. ἐφθίνηκα Dsc.1 *Praef.*6, (κατ-) Plu.*Cic.*14.

**φθῐνό-καρπος,** ον, *having lost its fruitfulness*, of a tree *stripped of its branches*, Pi.*P.*4.265. **-κωλος,** ον, *with wasting limbs*, Man.4.500. **-μετόπωρον,** τό, = μετόπωρον, τό, *An.Ox.*1.108, *EM*371.50.

**φθῐν-οπωρικός,** ή, όν, = sq., σήσαμον *PLille*41.4, al. (iii B.C.). **-οπωρῑνός,** ή, όν, *autumnal*, Hp.*Aph.*2.25, Plu.2.735b, Gal.6.443; ἰσημερία ἡ φ. Arist.*HA*543$^{b}$9, *PHib.*1.27.170 (iii B.C., without ἡ), Plb.4.37.2. ®**-οπωρίς,** ίδος, pecul. fem. of foreg., ἀνέμων πνοά Pi.*P.*5.120. II. ἡ φθινοπωρίς (sc. ἐλαία), = κολυμβάς, *an olive*, Call.*Fr.*50. **-οπωρισμός,** ὁ, = sq., Anan.5.3 [φθῑ-, metri gr.]. **-όπωρον,** τό, *the waning of* ὀπώρα (also called μετόπωρον or *the season following* ὀπώρα), *autumn*, Hdt.4.42, 9.117, Hp.*Aph.*1.18, Th.2.31, Arist.*HA*601$^{b}$25, al., *PCair.Zen.*20.4 (iii B.C.), Sor.1.22, Gal.6.127; metaph. νεηνίης φθινόπωρον, γέρων χειμών Pythagoras ap.D.L.8.10:—φθινόπωρον (fem.) ἰσημερινήν is dub. l. in Orph.*Fr.*285.34.

**φθῐν-ύθω** [ῠ], poet. for φθίνω, only pres. and impf.; Ep. impf. φθινύθεσκε Il.1.491. 1. trans., *waste*, φθινύθουσιν ἔδοντες οἶκον ἐμόν Od.1.250; οἶνον δὲ φ. 14.95; οἵ μευ φ. φίλον κῆρ *cause* it *to pine away* 10.485 (so perh. Il.1.491); ἵνα μηκέτ' ὀδυρομένη..αἰῶνα φθινύθω *waste* my life, Od.18.204; in later Ep., μαψίδιον φ. πόνον Opp.*C.*4.186. 2. intr., *waste away, decay, perish*, of men, λαοὶ μὲν φ. περὶ πτόλιν Il.6.327, cf. 21.466, Od.12.131; παυρότεροι...φθίνυθον Il.17.364; τούσδε ἔα φθινύθειν, as an imprecation, 2.346; also ἄχεϊ φ. παρειαί Od.8.530, cf. 16.145. **-υλλα,** ἡ, (φθίνω) nickname for a thin or delicate woman, *starveling*, Ar.*Ec.*935, cf. φθῖσα. **-ω,** v. φθίω. **-ώδης,** ες, *consumptive*, οἱ φ. Hp.*Aph.*4.8, etc.; τὸ φ. *a consumptive habit*, Id.*Epid.*1.2; φ. διάθεσις, νόσος, Androm.ap.Gal.13.18, Gal.17(1).62; τὰ φ. πάθη Id.6.775, Paus.10.2.4. Adv. -δῶς Gal.17(1).61, al. **-ωδικός,** ή, όν, = foreg., Id.17(1).722, al.

**Φθῖος,** α, ον, v. Φθία.

**φθῖσα,** ἡ, = φθίνυλλα, Hsch.

**φθῑσήνωρ**, *ορος*, *ὁ*, *ἡ*, (*φθίω*, *ἀνήρ*):—*destroying* or *killing men*, *πόλεμος* Il.2.833, 9.604, al., Hes.*Th.*431; *θυμός* *AP*9.457. [ῑ perh. metri gr., but in Il.2.833 *φθεισ-* is found in some codd. (including *πολλὰ τῶν παλαιῶν ἀντιγράφων* ap.Eust.356.20), and Choerob. in *An.Ox.*2.273, and shd. perh. be read.]

**φθίσθαι**, v. *φθίω*.

**φθῐσιάω**, *to be consumptive*, Hp.*Aph.*5.12, Arist.*Pr.*949$^a$27.

**φθῐσῐκ-εύομαι**, *to be consumptive*, Androm.ap.Gal.13.17. **-ός**, *ή*, *όν*, *consumptive*, Arist.*Pr.*884$^a$11, Dsc.1.72, Sor.*Vit.Hippocr.*5, Plu.2.674b, Arr.*Epict.*3.13.20, etc.: metaph., *σε..φθόνος φθισικὸν πεποίηκε* Men.540.7.

**φθῑσίμβροτος**, *ον*, (*φθίω*, *βροτός*) *destroying* or *killing men*, *μάχη*, *αἰγίς*, Il.13.339, Od.22.297; **φθῑσῐβρ-** in Epigr.ap.Plu.*Lys.*22 (sed **φθερσῐβρ-** (q.v.) ap.Paus.3.8.9). [ῑ perh. metri gr., unless *φθεισ-* shd. be read.]

**φθίσις** [ῐ], *εως*, *ἡ*, (*φθίω*):—*wasting away*, *perishing*, *decay*, *καρποῦ* Pi.*Pae.*9.14; of the *κόσμος*, Ocell.1.4; opp. *αὔξησις*, Hp.*VM*6, Pl.*Phd.*71b; opp. *αὔξη*, Id.*R.*521e: pl., Id.*Phlb.*42d. 2. of the moon, *waning*, Arist.*HA*582$^b$2, *GA*767$^a$4. II. of persons, *atrophy*, *emaciation*, Hp.*Art.*1. 2. esp. *consumption*, Hdt.7.88, Hp.*Epid.*1.24, *Aph.*5.11 (pl.), Arist.*HA*518$^b$21 (pl.), *EN*1150$^b$33, *IG*4$^2$(1).122.69 (Epid., iv B.C.), cf. *φθόη*. 3. *contraction of the pupil of the eye*, Gal.19.435, Aret.*SD*1.7, Aët.7.55.

**φθῐσίφρων**, *ονος*, *ὁ*, *ἡ*, *destroying the mind*, Opp.*C.*2.423 (*φθεισ-*).

**φθῖτο**, v. *φθίω*.

**φθῐτός**, *ή*, *όν*, (*φθίω*) Trag. (never in S.), only pl. *φθιτοί* (always without Art.) *the dead*, A.*Pers.*220 (troch.), 523, *Eu.*97, E.*Alc.*100 (lyr.), *Hipp.*1437, *HF*1026 (lyr.); also in later Prose, Plu.2.955b: with the Art., Luc.*DDeor.*26.2: sg., *AP*9.117 (Stat.Flacc.), Sch. Call. in *Διηγήσεις* vi 4, Id. in *PSI*9.1094.28, dub. in *IG*9(1).881.4 (Corc.). II. *liable to decrease*, *decline*, opp. *αὐξητός*, Arist.*Ph.*201$^a$13.

**φθῐτόω**, = *φθίνω* (*φθίω*) II, Lyc.1159 (Pass.).

***φθίω**, *ἔφθιον*, each once in Hom. (v. infr. I. 2), the common pres. being **φθίνω**, Od.5.161, al. (also **φθινύθω**, q.v.): impf. *ἔφθῐνον* Hdt.3.29, Pl.*Ti.*77a: fut. and aor. *φθ(ε)ίσω*, *ἔφθ(ε)ισα* and *ἔφθῖσα* (v. infr. II): pf. *ἔφθῐκα* v.l. in Dsc.*Praef.*6 (cf. *φθινάω*), (*ἀπ-*) Them.*Or.*28.341d:—Med. and Pass. (in same sense), fut. *φθίσομαι* (leg. *φθείσομαι*, in view of *φθείσω*, v. infr. II) Il.11.821 (*φθειται* *PGen.* (ii B.C.)), 19.329, 24.86 (v.l.), Od.13.384: aor. I *φθίσασθαι* (*ἀπο-*) Q.S.14.545: 3 pl. aor. Pass. *ἔφθῐθεν*, v. *ἀποφθίνω*: aor. 2 *ἐφθίμην*, *ἔφθῐσο* A.*Th.*971 (lyr.); *ἔφθῐτο* Il.18.100, Thgn.1141 (nisi leg. *ἔφθιται*), A.*Eu.*458, S.*OT*962, E.*Alc.*414 (lyr.); 3 pl. *ἐφθίατο* Il.1.251; imper. 3 sg. *φθίσθω* (*ἀπο-*) 8.429; Ep. subj. *φθίεται* 20.173, *φθιόμεσθα* 14.87; opt. *φθίμην* (*ἀπο-*) Od.10.51, *φθῖτο* (*φθῖτ'*) 11.330 (the v.l. *φθεῖτ'* is incorrect); inf. *φθίσθαι* Il.9.246, 13.667, Od.14.117, 15.354, (*κατα-*) 2.183 (always with incorrect v.l. *φθεῖσθαι*); part. *φθίμενος*, v. infr. I.2: rare in pf., *ἔφθιται* Od.20.340, 3 pl. *ἐξ-έφθινται* A.*Pers.*679 (lyr.). [Hom. has ῑ in *φθίῃς* (infr. I. 2), ῐ in *ἔφθιεν* (infr.), *φθιόμεσθα*, *φθίεται*: ῑ always in fut. and aor. *φθίσω*, *φθίσομαι*, *ἔφθισα* (sed v. infr. II), cf. *φθῑσήνωρ*, *φθισίμβροτος* (qq.v.): ῐ always in aor. and pf. Pass. (v. supr.), exc. in opt. (v. supr.):—Hom. also uses ῑ in *φθίνω* (prob. fr. **φθῐ-νϝω*, cf. *φθίνυθω*) whereas ῐ always in *φθῐνω* in Pi. and Trag., who use ῐ even in *ἔφθισα*, v. infr. II.] (Cf. *ψίνω*, *ψινάς*, *ψίσις*: *φθῐ-* and *ψῐ-* correspond to Skt. *kṣi-*, pres. *kṣiṇā́ti*, *kṣiṇóti*, 'he destroys', Pass. *kṣīyante* 'they perish', *ákṣitas* (= *ἄφθιτος*) 'imperishable', fut. stem *kṣesya-* (= *φθεισο-*), aor. stem *kṣeṣ-* (= *φθεισ-*).) I. *decay*, *wane*, of Time, *πρίν κεν νὺξ φθῖτο* (opt. aor.) first would the night *be come to an end*, Od.11.330: *τῆς νῦν φθιμένης νυκτός* S.*Aj.*141 (anap.); in this sense mostly in pres. *φθίνω*, *φθίνουσιν νύκτες τε καὶ ἤματα* they *wane* or *pass away*, Od.11.183, etc.; *μηδέ τοι αἰὼν φθινέτω let* not thy life *be wasted*, 5.161: esp. b. of the moon, *wane*, [*σελήνη*] *αὐξανομένη καὶ φθίνουσα* Arist.*Cael.*291$^b$20; hence, in monthly reckoning, *μηνῶν φθινόντων* in the moon's *wane*, i.e. towards the month's end, 10.470, etc.; later, *μὴν φθίνων*, the last *decad*, *IG*1$^2$.298.17, 328.13, Th.5.54, etc.; opp. *ἱστάμενος* (*ἵστημι* B. III.4), *μεσῶν*, but in Hom., the *second half* of the month (*τοῦ μὲν φθίνοντος μηνός*, *τοῦ δ' ἱσταμένοιο*), Od.14.162, 19.307. c. of the stars, *decline*, *set*, A.*Ag.*7 (prob. interpol.). 2. of persons, *waste away*, *pine*, *perish*, *ὥς κε δόλῳ φθίῃς* Od.2.368 (perh. aor. subj. with ῑ metri grat.); *ἦτοι ὁ τῆς ἀχέων φρένας ἔφθιεν was wasting away* in mind, Il.18.446 (perh. trans., *causing* his heart *to pine*; prob. impf., but possibly aor.); *φθίνει καὶ μαραίνεται νόσῳ* E.*Alc.*203; *ἐκ φόνων* S.*Tr.*558; *οἱ φθίνοντες consumptive* people, Hp.*Aph.*3.10, cf. *Epid.*1.24. b. of life, strength, etc., *οὐ φθίνει ἀρετά* Pi.*P.*1.94; *φθίνει μὲν ἰσχὺς γῆς φ. δὲ σώματος* S.*OC*610, cf. *OT*665 (lyr.); *ὕβρις..ἀνθεῖ τε καὶ πάλιν φ.* Id.*Fr.*786; *ἥβην τὴν μὲν ἕρπουσαν πρόσω, τὴν δὲ φθίνουσαν* Id.*Tr.*548; *τοῖς μὲν αὔξεται βίος, τῶν δὲ φθίνει* E.*Fr.*415.5, cf. Pl.*Phd.*71b, *Ti.*81b, etc.; c. dat. modi, *πόλις φθίνουσα μὲν κάλυξιν..*, *φθίνουσα δ' ἀγέλαις* S.*OT*25; of things, *fade away*, *disappear*, *ἐδεστὸν ἐξ αὐτοῦ φ. καὶ ψῇ* Id.*Tr.*677; *τὸ σῶμα φθίνει* Hp.*Loc.Hom.*24; metaph., *φθίνοντα Λαΐου θέσφατα* S.*OT*906 (lyr.), cf. *Ant.*1013:—Pass., *αὐτὸς φθίεται* Il.20.173, cf. 14.87; more freq. in fut. and aor., *ἤδη φθ(ε)ίσονται* 11.821, cf. 19.329, Od.13.384; *τηλόθι πάτρης ἔφθιτο* Il.18.100; *δύο γενεαὶ μερόπων ἀνθρώπων ἐφθίατο* 1.251; *νούσῳ ὑπ' ἀργαλέῃ φθίσθαι* 13.667; *νόσοις ὁ τλήμων ἔφθιτο* S.*OT*962; *πρὸς φίλου ἔφθισο wast slain* by.., A.*Th.*971 (lyr.), cf. E.*Med.*1414 (anap.): freq. in part. *φθίμενος*, *slain*, *dead*, Od.11.558, al.; *χερσὶν ὑπ' Ἀργείων φθίμενος* Il.8.359; *ἐν πολέμῳ φθίμενον* *IG*1$^2$.976; *φθίμενοι the dead*, *φθιμένοισι μετείην* Od.24.436; *πενθήσει βασιλῆ φ.* Orac.ap.Hdt.7.220, cf. Euph.21; *φθιμένων ζῳῶν τε φωτῶν* Pi.*I.*4(3).10(28), cf. B.5.83; *φθιμένοισιν* A.*Th.*732 (lyr.); *φθίμενος* S.*Tr.*1161, cf. *Ant.*836 (anap.); *μηδέτιν' εἰπεῖν...φθιμένων* E.*Hec.*137 (anap.): less freq. c. Art. (cf. *φθιτός*), *τὸν φθίμενον* A.*Th.*336 (lyr., codd.); *τῶν φ.* Id.*Ag.*1023 (lyr.); *τῶν πρότερον φ.* Id.*Ch.*403 (anap.); *φ. δέμας*, *σῶμα*, *mortal*, *IG*9(1).882.9,12 (Corc.); *Φθιμένη Perishing*, personified as a goddess, *Φυσώ τε Φ. τε* Emp.123.1: rare in Prose, *τοῖς φθιμένοις* X.*Cyr.*8.7.18. II. Causal, in fut. *φθ(ε)ίσω*, aor. I *ἔφθ(ε)ισα* (usu. written *φθίσω*, *ἔφθισα* in codd., but correctly *φθεισαν* (Od.20.67) in *PHib.*1.23 (iii B.C.), *φθείσει* (Il.6.407) in cod. A and *Et.Gen.*cod.B (Miller *Mélanges* 300)), *cause to decay* or *pine away*, *consume*, *destroy*, *φθ(ε)ίσει σε τὸ σὸν μένος* Il.6.407; *τὸν Πάτροκλος ἔμελλε φθ(ε)ίσειν* 16.461, cf. 22.61; *οἳ μεμάασιν Ὀδυσσῆος φθ(ε)ῖσαι γόνον* Od.4.741; *ἵνα φθ(ε)ίσωμεν ἑλόντες αὐτόν* 16.369; *τόν ῥ' ἔθελον φθ(ε)ῖσαι* ib.428; *τοκῆας..φθ(ε)ῖσαν θεοί* 20.67: rare in Trag. (only lyr., and in the form *ἔφθῖσα*), *Μοίρας φθίσας* A.*Eu.*173; *τὸν...ὑπὸ σῷ φθίσον κεραυνῷ* S.*OT*202; *φυτὸν ἥμερον μήτε φθίνειν μήτε σίνεσθαι* Pythag.ap.D.L.8.23; *νῦν σε μοῖρα...φθίνει*, *φθίνει* dub. in S.*El.*1414 (lyr., fort. *σοι*).

**φθίωσις**, f.l. for *φθίσις* in Dam.*Pr.*86.

***Φθιώτης**, **-ῶτις**, etc., v. *Φθία*.

**φθογγ-άζομαι**, = *φθέγγομαι*, *Παλλάδος αἰγὶς μυρίων φθογγάζεται κλαγγαῖς δρακόντων* Pi.*Dith.*2.18, cf. Ion Trag.53 (lyr.); *Κύκλωψ φθογγάζετο μύρμηξ* *AP*9.539. **-άριον**, *τό*, Dim. of *φθογγή*, *sounding-pipe*, Hero *Spir.*2.35. ***-ή**, *ἡ*, poet. form of *φθόγγος*, *voice* of men, Il.2.791, A.*Supp.*197, etc.; of the Sirens, v.l. for *φθόγγον* in Od.12.198; *οἶκος εἰ φθογγὴν λάβοι σαφέστατ' ἂν λέξειεν* A.*Ag.*37, cf. E.*Hipp.*418; *τῶν ἁλόντων καὶ κρατησάντων..φθογγάς* A.*Ag.*325; of the voice of Orpheus, *ἦγε πάντ' ἀπὸ φθογγῆς* ib.1630; *βάλλει με..φ. του* S.*Ph.*206 (lyr.); of birds and animals, *ὥστ' ἀηδόνος στόμα φθογγὰς ἱεῖσα* E.*Hec.*338; *φ. ὀΐων τε καὶ αἰγῶν* Od.9.167; *μόσχων* E.*IT*293 (pl.). **-ήεις**, *εσσα*, *εν*, contr. **φθογγῆς**, *sounding*, Hdn.Gr.2.618, al.; *φωνήεντας καὶ φθογγήεντας*, of vowels, Nicom.*Exc.*6. **-ος**, *ὁ* (both Poet. and Prose), *any clear*, *distinct sound*, esp. *voice* of men, Il.5.234, etc.; of the Sirens, Od.12.41,159; *φθόγγῳ ἐπερχόμεναι* 18.199; *φ. ἀραῖον οἴκοις* A.*Ag.*237 (lyr.); *γόων οὐκ ἀσήμονες φ.* S.*OC*1669; *φ. οἰκείου κακοῦ voice*, *telling* of.., Id.*Ant.*1187; *τὸν Αἵμονος φ.* ib.1218, cf. 1214; of birds, *ἀλεκτρυόνων φ.* Thgn.864; *ἀγνῶτα..φ. ὀρνίθων* S.*Ant.*1001, cf. 424; *φθόγγος οὔτ' ὀρνίθων οὔτε θαλάσσης* E.*IA*9 (anap.); *κυνῶν καὶ προβάτων καὶ ὀρνέων* Pl.*R.*397a. 2. *speech*, *Ἑλλάδος φθόγγον χέουσαν* A.*Th.*73; *φ. ἔμμετρος*, opp. *πεζά*, poetical *speech*, Phld.*D.*3.13; *utterance*, *saying*, *Trag.Adesp.*417. II. generally, *sound*, *ἀνέμων* Simon.37.11; *δαίμονος πεδαρσίου..πτερωτὸς φ.* Ar.*Av.*1198 (= *Trag.Adesp.*47); *φωνῆς μὲν οὔ, φθόγγου δὲ μετέχοντά τινος*, of semi-vowels, Pl.*Phlb.*18c, cf. Arist.*Aud.*801$^b$2, 804$^b$9; *ἄνευ φθόγγου καὶ ἠχῆς* Pl.*Ti.*37b, cf. Epicur.*Ep.*1 p.32 U.; *εἰς τοὺς φ. καὶ τὰς συλλαβάς* Pl.*Cra.*389d, cf. Plu.*Alex.*27, Gal.15.6. 2. of musical *sounds*, *λωτὸς φθόγγον κελάδει* E.*El.*716 (lyr.); *λύρας* Pl.*Lg.*812d, etc., cf. *φθόγγους ἀλύρους θρηνοῦμεν* Alex.162.6 (anap.). b. pl., *notes* on a musical instrument; *strings* of lyre, D.Chr.10.19; *stops* of flute, Philostr.*VA*5.21; cf. Corn.*ND*14.

**φθόη**, *ἡ*, Att. = *φθίσις* (q.v.), Pl.*Lg.*916a, Pl.Com.184, Isoc.19.11, D.*Ep.*3.30, Luc.*Cont.*17, *Tab.Defix.*98.5, Gal.6.421, etc.; esp. of *empyema*, Aret.*SD*1.8. (**φθοϝ-ᾱ* from root of *φθίω*, *φθίνω*.)

***φθόϊς**, *ϊος*, *ὁ*: acc. sg. *φθόϊν* (*φθόϊγ καὶ ἑρμητήν*) *GDI* iv p.883 (Erythrae, iv B.C.); nom. et acc. pl. *φθόεις* Hp.*Mul.*1.104, Ath.11.489d (written *φθόϊς* in Plu.2.292f); Att. acc. pl. *φθοῖς* Ar.*Pl.*677; dat. *φθοῖσι* Eup.373; Dor. and poet. acc. pl. *φθόϊας* *SIG*1025.31,38 (Cos, iv/iii B.C.), Call.*Fr.*337:—also Att. **φθοΐς**, *ΐδος*, *ἡ*, acc. *φθοΐδα* *AP*6.258 (Adaeus); nom. pl. *φθοΐδες* or *φθοῖδες* *IG*1$^2$.301.103,109,116:—*a* kind of *cake*, Ar. l.c., *GDI* l.c., *SIG* l.c., Chrysipp.Tyan.ap.Ath.14.647d, Porph.*Abst.*2.7: Lat. abl. pl. *pthoibus* *CIL*6.32323.140, 145 (Rome, i B.C.); nom. *fthois* = *uuum* (i.e. *libum*), *Gloss.* 2. Medic., *pastille*, used for fumigation, Hp. l.c. 3. *bar* of precious metal, *χρυσίου Σκαπτησυλικοῦ* *IG* l.c., cf. 2$^2$.1443.20, al.; but *φ. χρυσίου* gold-*dust*, Hsch. II. a kind of *cup*, prob. the same as *φιάλη ὀμφαλωτή*, Eup. l.c., cf. Ath.11.502b; *φθόεις κυκλοτερεῖς* ib.489d.

**φθοΐσκος**, *ὁ*, Dim. of foreg. I.2, Hp.*Mul.*1.51; used as a pessary, ib.74.

**φθονερ-ία**, *ἡ*, *enviousness*, Arist.*MM*1192$^b$18, *Stoic.*3.103, *PMich.Zen.*23.4 (iii B.C.); *περὶ φθονερίας*, title of work by Cleanthes, *Stoic.*1.107. **-ός**, *ά*, *όν*, *envious*, *jealous*, of persons, *σοφίης μὴ φ. τελέθειν grudging* of wisdom, Thgn.770, etc.; *ὕψον λόγοι φθονεροῖσιν* Pi.*N.*8.21; *φ. ταῖς ἑτέρων εὐτυχίαις* D.H.6.46: Sup., *ὀρνίθων -ώτατος* *AP*5.2 (Antip.Thess.). Adv., *-ρῶς ἔχειν πρὸς τὰ παιδικά* to be *enviously* disposed, Pl.*Phdr.*243c, cf. Isoc.15.302, X.*Cyr.*1.4.15, etc. 2. of the gods, *jealous* of those who abuse their gifts, or who enjoy unbroken felicity, *ὁ φ. δαίμων* Corinn.4; *τὸ θεῖον πᾶν ἐὸν φ.* Hdt.1.32; *ἐμοὶ αἱ σαὶ μεγάλαι εὐτυχίαι οὐκ ἀρέσκουσι, ἐπισταμένῳ τὸ θεῖον ὡς ἔστι φ.* Id.3.40, cf. 7.46; *φθονεραῖς ἐκ θεῶν μετατροπίαις* by *jealous* changes of purpose, Pi.*P.*10.20; cf. *φθόνος* I.2. II. of feelings, etc., *φ. γνῶμαι*, *ἐλπίδες*, Id.*I.*1.44, 2.43; *ἄλγος* A.*Ag.*450 (lyr.); *ὀδύνα* S.*Ph.*1141 (lyr.); *φ. ὁδοί full of envy*, Id.*Fr.*353 (lyr.); *φ. τέχνη* *Anacreont.*16.38.

**φθον-έω**, aor. *ἐφθόνησα*, later *ἐφθόνεσα* Lxx *To.*4.7, *JHS*46.45 (Athens, iii/iv A.D.), *AP*5.303, 7.607 (Pall.), Nonn.*D.*3.159:—Med., fut. in pass. sense φθονήσομαι D.47.70:—**Pass.**, fut φθονηθήσομαι X.*Hier.*11.15: aor. ἐφθονήθην E.*El.*30, X.*Mem.*4.2.33, etc.: pf. part. ἐφθονημένος J.*AJ*6.11.10, Vett.Val.330.2: (φθόνος):—*bear ill-will* or *malice, grudge, be envious* or *jealous*, I. abs., εἴ περ γὰρ φθονέω τε καὶ οὐκ εἰῶ διαπέρσαι, οὐκ ἀνύω φθονέουσα Il.4.55,56; κρείττων δόξα τῶν φθονούντων too high for *envy*, D.3.24; εἰ πέφυκε φθονεῖν τὸ θεῖον (cf. φθονερός I.2) Arist.*Metaph.*982b32: c. acc. et inf., οὔτε τινὰ φθονέω δόμεναι I do not *grudge* that any should give thee, Od.18.16; οὐ φθονῶ σ' ὑπεκφυγεῖν S.*Ant.*553; τὸ μὲν σὸν οὐ φθονῶ καλῶς ἔχειν E.*Med.*312; ἐφθόνησαν [οἱ θεοὶ] ἄνδρα ἕνα βασιλεῦσαι Hdt.8.109; ἔφη (sc. ὁ Σωκράτης) φθονεῖν τοὺς ἐπὶ ταῖς φίλων εὐπραξίαις ἀνιωμένους X.*Mem.*3.9.8; ὁ φθονῶν ἐπὶ κακοῖς τοῖς τῶν πέλας ἡδόμενος Pl.*Phlb.*48b. 2. c. dat. pers., πτωχὸς πτωχῷ φθονέει καὶ ἀοιδὸς ἀοιδῷ Hes.*Op.*26; οὐ φ. ἀγαθοῖς Pi.*P.*3.71; φ. φασὶ μητρυιὰς τέκνοις E.*Ion* 1025; τισὶ φ. καὶ δυσμενῶς ἔχειν Isoc.12.241, cf. 8.13; freq. with part. added, φ. τινὶ εὖ πρήσσοντι *to envy* him for his good fortune, Hdt.7.236,237; παιδικοῖς φ. οὐσίαν κεκτημένοις Pl.*Phdr.*240a, cf. Lys.27.11; without a Noun expressed, καλῶς πράττουσι, πλουτοῦντι φ., Isoc.1.26, Lys.21.15, etc.: c. dat. rei, φ. τοῖς ἀγαθοῖς τινος X.*Cyr.*2.4.10 (v.l. ἐπὶ τοῖς ἀγ., cf. Isoc. 1.26; ἐφ' οἷς ἕτεροι ποιήσαντες ἐτιμήθησαν φ. D.20.151): c. gen. rei, τοῦ εὐτυχέειν φθονέουσι καὶ τὸ κρέσσον στυγέουσι Hdt.7.236; οὐδέ τί σε χρὴ ἀλλοτρίων φθονέειν *to be envious* because of other men's goods Od.18.18: c. dat. pers. et gen. rei, *bear a grudge* against a person on account of a thing, E.*HF* 1309. 3. *resent*, c. gen., τῆς δοκήσεως τῶν κερδῶν Th.3.43: c. dat. rei, *feel righteous indignation at*, ταῖς εὐπραγίαις τινῶν Isoc.8.124; also c. dat. pers., Id. 4.184, D.28.18. b. φ. τινὶ folld. by εἰ.., or ἐάν.. *take it ill* or *amiss* that.., Hdt.3.146, X.*HG*2.4.29; μή μοι φθονήσητ', εἰ.. Ar.*Ach.*496: abs., φ. ἐάν τις.. Lys.3.9; φθονεῖς ἄπαις οὖσ', εἰ.. E.*Ion* 1302; also φ. τινὶ ὅτι.., X.*Cyr.*3.1.39; φ. ὅτι.. Lys.24.3, dub. l. in 18.16. II. *refuse from feelings of envy* or *ill-will*, *grudge*, c. inf., οὐκ ἂν φθονέοιμι ἀγορεῦσαι Od.11.381; μὴ φθόνει κιρνάμεν Pi.*I.*5(4).24; φράσαι E.*Med.*63; σαυτὸν ἐπιδοῦναι Ar.*Th.*249; μὴ φθονήσῃς is freq. in dialogue, *do not refuse* to do a thing, μὴ φ. διδάξαι Pl.*R.*338a, cf. *Hp.Mi.*372e, *Smp.* 223a; also μὴ φθόνει μοι ἀποκρίνασθαι Id.*Grg.*489a; μὴ φθονήσῃς alone, Id.*Prt.*320c; δῆλον ὅτι οὐ φθονήσει Ἱππίας ἀποκρίνεσθαι Id. *Hp.Mi.*363c; οὐδενὶ πώποτε ἐφθόνησα Id.*Ap.*33a: c. part., μηδέ μοι φθόνει λέγων A.*Th.*480 (nisi leg. λόγων): c. acc. et inf., τί φθονέεις.. ἀοιδὸν τέρπειν; Od.1.346: c. dat. et inf., τῇ δ' οὐκ ἂν φθονέοιμι ..ἅψασθαι 19.348; οὔτοι φθονῶ σοι δαιμόνων τιμᾶν γένος A.*Th.* 236. 2. *grudge, refuse to grant* a thing, φθονήσας μήτ' ἀπ' οἰωνῶν φάτιν, μήτ' εἴ τινα.. μαντικῆς ἔχεις ὁδόν S.*OT*310: c. dat. pers. et gen. rei, οὔ τοι ἡμιόνων φθονέω Od.6.68; μηδέ μοι φθονήσῃς εὐγμάτων A.*Pr.*583 (lyr.), cf. E.*Hec.*238; μή μοι φθονήσῃς τοῦ μαθήματος Pl.*Euthd.*297b, cf. X.*Cyr.*8.4.16; φ. τοῖς ἑαλωκόσι τῆς σωτηρίας Plb.6.58.5: c. gen. rei only, *to be grudging of* a thing, πέπλων, καρποῦ, E.*HF*333, Pl.*Mx.*238a; μηδ' ὀλίγης φθονέσῃς γαίης *JHS* l.c. III. Pass., *to be envied* or *begrudged*, Hdt.3.52, S.*Fr.*188, E.*El.*30; διὰ σοφίαν φ. ὑπό τινος X.*Mem.*4.2.33; ἐπ' ἐσθλοῖς E.*Fr.* 814 (lyr.); φθονηθέντα ὑπὸ Μοίρης *JRS*18.30 (Phrygia): c. gen., *to be grudged* a thing, φ. τοῦ γάμου ὑπὸ δαιμονίου τινός Plu.2. 772b. **-ησις**, εως, ἡ, *jealous refusal*, S.*Tr.*1212. **-ητέον**, *one must envy*, οὐδενί Ph.1.319, Ap.Ty.*Ep.*91. **-ητικός**, ή, όν, *envious*, ἕξις Plu.2.682d; φθονητική, ἡ, Phld.*Vit.*p.43 J. Adv. -κῶς Plu. l.c.

**φθονόλετρος**, ον, dissim. fr. *φθονόλεθρος, *enviously destructive*, δαίμων *Jahresh.*23 *Beibl.*402 (Prusa).

⊛**φθόνος**, ὁ, *ill-will* or *malice*, esp. *envy* or *jealousy* of the good fortune of others (Pl.*Def.*416b, Arist.*Rh.*1387b22), Pi.*O.*8.55, etc.; φθόνῳ *through envy*, Hdt.3.30, 9.71; opp. εὔνοια, Pl.*Lg.*635b; opp. ἔπαινος, Lys.24.1; ἴσχει ὄλβος φθόνον incurs *envy*, Pi.*P.*11.29, cf. Isoc.5.68; φθόνον πρὸς ἀστῶν ἀλφάνουσι E.*Med.*297; φθόνῳ χρῆσθαι πρὸς τὰ παιδικά Pl.*Phdr.*253b; κρέσσων οἰκτιρμοῦ φθόνος better *to be envied* than pitied! Pi.*P.*1.85, cf. And.2.6; πρὸς γὰρ τὸν ἔχονθ' ὁ φ. ἕρπει S.*Aj.*157 (anap.), cf. *OT*382; ἐς τἀπίσημα δ' ὁ φ. πηδᾶν φιλεῖ E.*Fr.*294; φ. συνεστιώμενος, of wealth, Secund.*Sent.*9; φ. [ἐστὶ] τοῖς ζῶσι πρὸς τὸ ἀντίπαλον Th.2.45; κατὰ φθόνον A.*Eu.*686, Pl.*Grg.* 457d; σὺν φθόνῳ E.*Andr.*780 (lyr.); διὰ φθόνον *Ep.Phil.*1.15: c. gen. objecti, *envy for, jealousy of*, τῶν πεπραγμένων Lys.2.48; φθόνον δὲ σωμάτων ἕξει θεός i.e. *will grudge, deny*, A.*Pr.*859: c. gen. subj., *envy* or *jealousy felt by* another, Pl.*Hp.Ma.*282a; also φ. ἐφ' ἑτέροις Plu.2.39e, etc.; εἴς τινα *AP*6.257 (Antiphil.); πρός τινα Luc.*Rh.Pr.*22: pl., *envyings, jealousies, heartburnings*, Isoc.15.163, Pl.*Lg.*679c, 801e, etc. b. a *cause for indignation*, a *reproach*, ἀποκτείνειν φθόνος [ἐστὶ] γυναῖκας E.*Hec.*288. 2. esp. *jealousy* of the gods (cf. φθονερός I.2), θεῶν φ. A.*Pers.*362, *Ag.*947; φ. μὴ γένοιτό τις θεῶν E.*Alc.*1135: hence abs., τὸν φ. δὲ πρόσκυσον S.*Ph.*776; εὐλαβούμενος φθόνον D.18.305. II. *refusal from feelings of ill-will* or *envy, grudging*, φθόνος μὲν οὐδείς.. A.*Pr.*628; οὐδεὶς φ. or φ. οὐδείς, c. inf., said in granting a request willingly, ἃ τυγχάνω ἀκηκοώς, φ. οὐδεὶς λέγειν Pl.*Phd.*61d; οὐδεὶς.. φ. αὐτῷ διελθεῖν αὐτά Id.*Sph.*217a, cf. b, *Lg.*641d, 664a.

**φθορ-ά**, Ion. **φθορή**, ἡ, (φθείρω) *destruction, ruin*, Hdt.2.161, 7.18, Hp.*Vict.*1.5, A.*Ag.*406 (lyr.), etc.; of persons, *death*, esp. by some general visitation, as pestilence, Th.2.47, Pl.*Lg.*677a (pl.), *GDI* 5104c11 (Crete, pl.); ἀνδροθνῆτας Ἰλίου φθοράς A.*Ag.*814. b. of animals, *loss by death*, *PStrassb.*24.26,31 (ii A.D.). 2. Philos., *passing out of existence, ceasing to be*, γενομένῳ παντὶ φ. ἐστι Pl.*R.* 546a; περὶ γενέσεως καὶ φθορᾶς Id.*Phd.*95e, title of work by Arist., cf. Pl.*Phlb.*55a, Arist.*Ph.*229b13, Gal.6.6; ἡ φ. μεταβολή τίς ἐστι τῶν φθειρομένων εἰς τοὐναντίον ἑκάστῳ Plu.2.948f: pl., Pl.*Phd.*96b, *R.*490e, al.: with dat. (instrumental), ἡ μεγίστη φθορὰ ὕδασιν Id.*Ti.*23c, cf. 22d. 3. *deterioration*, εἰς καρπογονίαν in respect of.. Thphr.*CP* 5.8.2. b. *loss by deterioration*, ἐκφορίου.. ἀνυπολόγου πάσης φθορᾶς *PTeb.*105.3,18 (ii B.C.); *damage*, ἐκτεῖσαι τὴν γεγονυῖαν ὑπ' αὐτῶν τοῦ χόρτου.. φ. *BGU*1824.29 (i B.C.); misspelt φθαρά ib.1866.3 (i B.C.). 4. *seduction*, ἐλευθέρων Lex ap.Aeschin.1.12; παρθένων, γυναικῶν, Plu.2.712c (pl.), Vett.Val.2.37 (pl.), cf. Parth.35.3, D.H.2.25; *rape*, Str.6.1.6. 5. *abortion* or *miscarriage*, *IG*2².1365.22, 1366.7, Sor.1.56, Gal.17(1).800; τοῦ ἐμβρύου Sor.1.59. 6. *gradation of colours* in painting, Plu.2.346a; τὰς μίξεις τῶν χρωμάτων οἱ ζωγράφοι φθορὰς ὀνομάζουσι ib.725c, cf. 393c. 7. = φθόη, Hp.*Aph.*7.80. 8. *storm-tossings* or *shipwrecks*, τί τοι λέγοιμ' ἂν τὰς ἐν Αἰγαίῳ φθοράς; E.*Hel.*766; cf. φθείρω II.4. **-εῖον**, το, *drug for producing abortion*, *SIG*985.20 (Philadelphia, i B.C.): pl., *IG*12 (1).789.12 (Lindos, ii A.D.); cf. φθόριος I. **-εύς**, έως, ὁ, *corrupter, seducer*, Ph.2.53, al., Plu.2.18c, Arr.*Epict.*2.22.28, Vett.Val.119.12, Jul.*Caes.*336a, *AP*5.256 (Pall.), etc.: metaph., φ. ἀγαθῶν Ph.1.412.—Hellenistic acc. to Moer.p.390 P.

**φθορηγενής**, ές, *breeding corruption*, *PMag.Par.*1.2865 (fort. leg. φθορηγόνε metri gr.).

⊛**φθορ-ία**, ἡ, *corruption, mischief*, Hp.*Jusj.* **-ικός**, ή, όν, *destructive*, c. gen., Horap.2.79 (φθορόοικον ed. Pauw, φθορικὸν cod.Vat. ap.Bast.*Ep.Crit.*p.83). **-ῐμος**, η, ον, *destructive*, Man.2.346. II. *perishable*, τὸ φ. τῶν σωμάτων Herm.ap.Stob.1.49.44. **-ιος**, ον, *destructive*: esp. of means *to produce abortion*, πεσσός Hp.*Jusj.*; φ. ἐμβρύων Dsc.5.67, cf. Sor.1.60: φθόρια, τά, = φθορεῖα, Dsc.2.164, Plu.2. 134f. II. φθόριον ἕδνον sum given to a bride as compensation for loss of virginity, *PSI*9.1075.6 (v A.D.).

**φθορο-εργός**, όν, = φθοροποιός, Dam.*Isid.*204. **-ποιέω**, *commit injury*, Dsc.*Ther.Praef.*, Suid. s. v. λοιμεύεται. **-ποιός**, όν, *causing destruction*, Boëth.*Stoic.*3.265, Petos.ap.Vett.Val.80.7, Dsc.*Alex. Praef.*, *Placit.*5.30.1, Doroth. in *Cat.Cod.Astr.*2.196; δύναμις Ph.2.96; πάθος Simp. *in Cael.*436.26: c. gen., Ph.2.327, al.; τῶν ζῴων *Gp.*2. 27.5; μεταβολὴ φ. τοῦ μεταβαλλομένου Dam.*Pr.*414. 2. *abortifacient*, Ps.-Dsc.1.1.

**φθόρ-ος** (on the accent v. Hdn.Gr.1.191), ὁ, = φθορά, Thgn.833, Th.2.52, Pl.*Euthd.*285b, Arist.*Pr.*879b26; πολὺς ἐγένετο φ. τῶν πολεμίων Plb.3.51.3: mostly in phrases, ἴτ' ἐς φθόρον = φθείρεσθε (v. φθείρω II.1), A.*Ag.*1267; οὐκ ἐς φθόρον..; Id.*Th.*252; ἄπαγ' ἐς τὸν φθόρον [Epich.] ap.Ath.2.63d. II. like ὄλεθρος, *pestilent fellow*, Ar.*Eq.*1151, D.13.24; of a woman, Ar.*Th.*535; φθόρος ἀργυρίῳ Theoc.15.18. **-ώδης**, ες, *corrupt, pestilent*, τὸ φ. τοῦ ἀέρος Hdn.1. 12.2; αὐχμοί Lyd.*Ost.*36.

**φθόσις**· φθίσις, Hsch.

**φθοώδης**, ες (φθόη), *consumptive*, νόσος Paus.10.2.6.

**φθύζω**, only in compd. ἐπιφθύζω (q. v.). **φιν**, **σφιν**, v. σφεῖς.

**-φῐ, -φῐν**, case-suffix with locative, ablative and instrumental sense, freq. in Ep.; also Aeol. acc. to Sch.D, Gen.Il.3.338, Sch. Opp.*Hal.*1.709; Boeot. acc. to Hsch. s.v. πασσαλόφιν (who cites Ἴδηφιν = Ἴδης); found in Lyr., σὺν ὄχεσφι Ibyc.2.6; Μῶσα.., ὠρανίαφι Alcm.59 (voc. acc. to A.D.*Adv.*165.8); πασσαλόφιν in a Com. parody, Hermipp.55 (anap.).

⊛**φῐάλη** [ᾰ], ἡ, *bowl* or *pan* used as a saucepan for boiling liquids, ἀμφίθετος φ. ἀπύρωτος Il.23.270; also used as a *cinerary urn*, [ὀστέα] ἐν χρυσέῃ φ. καὶ δίπλακι δημῷ θείομεν ib.243, cf. 253. 2. after Hom., *broad, flat bowl* or *saucer* for drinking or pouring libations, φιάλας τε καὶ ἄλλα ἐκπώματα Hdt.9.80, cf. 2.151, 7.54; δωροφοροῦσιν.. φιάλας Ar.*V.*677 (anap.); οἰνοδόκον φ. χρυσῷ πεφρικυῖαν Pi.*I.*6 (5).40; ἀργυρωθέντες σὺν οἰνηραῖς φ. Id.*N.*10.43; of gold, Hdt.2.151, 7.54, Pi.*I.*1.20, Pl.*Criti.*120a (pl.), *PCair.Zen.*21.16 (iii B.C., s. v. l.), *Apoc.*5.8, etc.; ἔλαβε σύμβολον παρὰ βασιλέως τοῦ μεγάλου φ. χρυσῆν Lys.19.25; of silver, Pi.*N.*9.51, *IG*1².313.15, al., Lys.12.11, *PCair. Zen.*327.5, al. (iii B.C.); ἀργυρηλάτους χρυσέας τε φ. E.*Ion* 1182; φ. λυκιουργεῖς D.49.31; as a votive offering, Hdt.1.50, *PTeb.*6.27 (ii B.C.), etc.; πίνειν ἐκ φ. μεγάλης ἐπὶ δεξιά Pl.*Smp.*223c, cf. X.*Smp.* 2.23; φ. καρυωτή, v. καρυωτός II. b. used for unguents, ἄλλος δ' εὐώδες μύρον ἐν φ. παρατείνει Xenoph.1.3; for administering medicines, *IG*4²(1).122.125 (Epid.. iv B.C.). c. τὸ ἐκ φιάλης revenue, perh. from a *collecting-bowl*, *IG*11(2).161*A*116 (Delos, iii B.C.), cf. *Inscr.Délos* 442*A*156 (ii B.C.). II. from its broad flat shape, φιάλη Ἄρεως metaph. for ἀσπίς, *shield*, cited from Tim. (*Fr.*22) by Antiph.112, cf. Anaxandr.80, Arist.*Rh.*1412b35. III. *ornament used in a coffered ceiling*, Agatharch.102.—The form **φιέλη** was less Att., Moer.p.389 P.

⊛**φῐᾰληφόρος**, ἡ, *cup-bearer*, title of a Locrian priestess, Plb.12.5. 9; name of play by Anaxandr.

**φῐᾰλ-ίδιον**, τό, Dim. of φιάλη, Hero *Spir.*1.12:—also⊛**-ιον**, τό, Eub.69, Arist.*Mir.*832b26, *IG*7.303.58 (Orop.), 11(2).161*B*27, al. (Delos, iii B.C.), etc.; **-ίς**, ίδος, ἡ, Luc.*Lex.*7; **-ίσκη**, ἡ, Dor. **-ίσκα**, *Schwyzer* 182*a*8 (Gortyn, v/iv B.C.), Sch.Ar.*Ra.*1403; **-ίσκος**, ὁ, prob. in *BSA*18.184 (Maced.). **-ίτης** ἀριθμός [ῑτ], an arithmetical puzzle *concerning a number of bowls*, Procl. *in Euc.* p.40 F., Sch.Pl.*Chrm.*165e, Hero *Deff.*135.5 (all pl.).

⊛**φῐάλλω**, fut. φῐᾰλῶ, *undertake, take in hand, set about* a thing, found twice in codd. of Ar., οὐδὲ φιαλεῖς *V.*1348; ὅπως ἔργῳ φιαλοῦμεν *Pax* 432: acc. to Eust.1403.16 it is shortd. for ἐφιάλλω; hence Bentley restored οὐδ' ἐφιαλεῖς and ἔργῳ 'φιαλοῦμεν.

**φῐᾰλο-βωμός**, ὁ, *bowl-shaped altar* or *libation-table*, Zos.Alch.

p.108 B. **-ειδής**, ές, *bowl-shaped*, Hero *Spir.*2.24, Hsch. s.vv. πατάνια, πέδαχνα; βωμός Zos.Alch.p.108 B. **-μαντεία**, ἡ, *divination by* gazing into *a saucer*, prob. in *PMag.Par.*1.3243 (-εῖον, τό, prob. ib.3209).

**φῐᾰλ-όω**, *excavate into the form of a* φιάλη, βόθροι *Gp.*9.5.7. **-ώδης**, ες, = φιαλοειδής, ποτήριον Ath.11.488f, Sch.Ar.*Ach.*1227. **-ωτός**, ή, όν, *saucer-shaped*, θυμιατήριον *IG*11(2).161 *B*36,37 (Delos, iii B.C.); θρίδακες φιαλωταί lettuces *with a broad flat head*, *Gp.*12.13.8.

**φῐᾰρ-ός**, ή, όν, a word used by Alex. Poets, *gleaming, shining*, of the dawn, Call.*Fr.*257; αἴγλῃσιν φιαρῇσι Max.594; generally, *bright*, of a young girl, φιαρωτέρα ὄμφακος ὠμᾶς Theoc.11.21; φιαρὸν δέμας Max.443; *sleek*, of a bird, Nic.*Al.*387; of cream, φιαρὴ γρῆϋς ib.91. **-ύνω**, *make bright and clean*, Hsch.

**φῐβάλεως** [ᾰ], ω, ἡ, a kind of *early fig*, found in Com. in pl., nom. φιβάλεῳ (φιβαλέοι codd.Ath.) Telecl.5: gen., τῶν φιβάλεων σύκων Pherecr.80; φιβάλεων alone, Hermipp.51: acc., φιβάλεως ἰσχάδας Ar.*Ach.*802; φιβάλεως alone, Apolloph.5.—Sch.Ar. l. c. has γένος συκῆς ἡ φίβαλις (taking φιβάλεως as gen. sg.) and explains as the name for a district in Megaris or Attica; *EM*793.26 has φιβάλεως· γένος συκῆς· λέγουσι δὲ οὕτω καὶ τὰς μυρρίνας. II. *a lean, dried-up person*, Telecl. l. c., Sch.Ar. l. c., Suid.

**Φιβί**, ὁ, name of the Ibis, = Hermes Thoth, *Cat.Cod.Astr.*1.167.

⊕**φίβλ-α**, ἡ, = Lat. *fibula*, *Supp.Epigr.*2.776 (Dura), Sch.Call.*Ap.* 32, Sch.Gen.Il.18.401:—also -ίον *Gloss.* **-όομαι**, Pass., = πορπόομαι, Phot., Suid.

**φῐδάκν-η**, -ίς, v. πιθάκνη.

**φῐδ-ίτης** [ῑτ], ου, Dor. -ας, α, ὁ, *member of a* φιδίτιον, Sphaer. *Stoic.*1.142, Ath.4.140e (φειδ- codd.Ath. in both places). **-ίτιον** [ῑτ], τό, *common mess* at Sparta, later name for the earlier ἀνδρεῖον (v. ἀνδρεῖος III), Arist.*Pol.*1271$^a$27, 1272$^a$2, $^b$34, *Rh.*1411$^a$25, Antiph.44.3, Dicaearch.Hist.23, Phylarch.44 J., D.H.2.23, Cic. *Tusc.*5.34.98, Ἑλληνικά 1.18,19 (Gytheum, I A.D.), Plu.*Lyc.*12 (hence Porph.*Abst.*4.4), *Agis* 8, *Cleom.*13, *Phoc.*20, Paus.7.1.8, *IG*5(1).128. 13, al. (ii A.D.), Philostr.*VA*4.27, Them.*Or.*19.227b, Hsch. s.vv. διαφοιγοιμόρ, φιδίτια, Phot. s. v. συσσιτίαι, Suid. s. v. Λυκοῦργος, φιλίτια, Eust.1413.23. II. *dining-hall* in which the meals took place, X.*HG*5.4.28, *Lac.*3.5; 5.6, Phld.*Mus.*pp.18,86 K., D.Chr.2. 44, Plu.*Lyc.*26, *Ages.*20, Id.2.697e, Ath.4.139c. [Quantity given by εἰς τὰ φιδίτια (φειδ- codd.Ath.) at end of iambic line in Antiph. l. c., where φῑδῑ- is possible but involves an unlikely φιδίτης.] (Written φιδείτια in Ἑλληνικά l. c., φειδείτιον (or -α) in *IG*5(1) ll. cc. (exc. φειδίτιον in 1507); but dat. φιλιτείοις and φιλειτείοις in Phld. ll. cc. (Pap.); this contradiction in the early evidence is unexplained; the form φιδ- or φειδ- is corroborated by Plu.*Lyc.*12, where it is suggested that the word comes from φιλία with substitution of δ for λ, or from φειδώ, or from *ἐδίτια ('eatings', cf. ἐδωδή) with prefixed φ. Codd. have φιδίτια (or -ον) in Arist.*Pol.* (v.l. φιλίτια), Plu. (exc. φιτιδίοις v.l. in *Cleom.* l. c., φιλιτίων all codd. in *Phoc.* l. c., φιλίτια all codd. in 2.714b, φιλέοτιον in 2.697e), Hsch.; φειδίτια in Paus., Ath. (who cites Antiph., Dicaearch.Hist., Phylarch.), Eust.; φιλίτια in X. (v.l. φιδίτια in *HG* l. c.), Arist.*Rh.* (φιδίτια Sch.), D.H., D.Chr., Philostr., Them., Suid.; *philitiis* in Cic.)

**φιέλη**, v. φιάλη.

⊕**φικιδίζω**, = παιδεραστέω, Suid.: ⊕**φικιῶ**, sine expl., Id.

⊕**φικοπήδαλος**, ὁ, dub. sens. in *PMon.*4.11 (vi A.D.), *PLond.*5. 1714.33 (vi A.D.).

**φικοτύχη**, ἡ, = φυκοτύχη, Paul.Aeg.3.59, v.l. in Aët.15.35.

**φῐλ-άβουλος**, ον, *wilfully unadvised*, *AP*12.80 (Mel.), *APl.*4.133 (Antip.). **-αβρος**, ον, *loving delicacy* or *refinement*, Hld.7.12.

**φῐλᾰγᾰθ-έω**, *love good men* or *goodness*, *IG*2$^2$.1006.89 (ii B.C.), *Michel* 509.7 (Nacrasa, iii B.C.), *BCH*5.326 (Maeonia), *PTeb.*124.17 (ii B.C.), *Supp.Epigr.*7.62.18 (Seleucia in Pieria, ii B.C.). **-ία**, ἡ, *love of goodness*, Ph.2.136, *PMon.*6.72 (vi A.D.); *benevolence*, *Sardis* 7 No.4.30 (ii B.C.), *BMus.Inscr.*1032.48 (Teos, i B.C./i A.D.); εἴς τινας *Sammelb.*1106.6 (Ptol.): pl., *Mém.Inst.Franç.*67.34 (Aphroditopolis, i B.C.). **-ος**, ον, *loving goodness*, Arist.*MM*1212$^b$18, Lxx *Wi.* 7.22, Scymn.104, Ph.2.136, Plu.*Comp.Thes.Rom.*1, Wilcken *Chr.*20 ii 11 (ii A.D.); as honorary epithet in inscrr. of religious associations, etc., *IG*2$^2$.1326.8, etc.; so in Adv. -θως ib.12(5).860.6 (Tenos), *SIG*762.13 (Odessus, i B.C.), prob. in *Supp.Epigr.*2.485 (Panticapaeum, iii A.D.).

**φῐλάγλᾱος**, ον, *loving splendour, resplendent*, Pi.*P.*12.1, B.17.60; Ἔρως *AP*12.77 (Asclep. or Posidipp.).

**φῐλάγρ-αυλος**, ον, *fond of the country*, Πάν *AP*6.73 (Maced.), cf. Nonn.*D.*8.15. **-έτις**, ιδος, ἡ, *fond of the chase, huntress*, Ἄρτεμις *AP*9.396 (Paul.Sil.). **-ευτής**, οῦ, ὁ, *lover of the chase*, Babr.107. 10. **-έω**, *love the country*, Epicurei ap.D.L.10.120.

**Φιλάγριον** or **-ίανον**, τό, a kind of *bandage*, invented by Philagrius, Alex.Trall.1.12; also τὸ Φιλαγρίανον (sc. μάλαγμα) Paul.Aeg. 7.18.

**φίλαγρ-ος** [ῐ], ον, *fond of the country*, Luc.*Lex.*3. 2. (ἄγρα) *fond of the chase*, Δίκτυννα φ. *Mnemos.*4(1936).11 (Athens). **-ότις**, ιδος, ἡ, = φιλαγρέτις, Orph.*H.*36.6.

**φῐλάγρυπνος**, ον, *wakeful*, λύχνος *AP*5.196 (Mel.); παννυχίδες *APl.*4.309; πόθος *AP*5.165 (Mel.).

**φῐλ-άγων** [ᾰ], ωνος, ὁ, ἡ, *loving contests*, κισσός *AP*7.708 (Diosc.). **-ᾰγωνιστής**, οῦ, ὁ, *fond of contests*, Ptol.*Tetr.* 63. **-ᾰγωνιστικός**, ή, όν, = foreg. Sch.Pi.*I.*4.47.

**φῐλᾰδελφ-εια** (sc. ἱερά), τά, name of a festival in honour of Ptolemy Philadelphus, *Inscr.Délos* 314 *B*169 (iii B.C.), *IG*2$^2$.2197.15; also in sg., *Sardis* 7(1).79 *C*8 (iii A.D.). **-έω**, *show brotherly affection*, *Not.Scav.*1919.66 (Jewish). ⊕**-ία**, ἡ, *brotherly love*, Alex. 334, Ph.2.558, J.*AJ*2.6.9, Babr.47.15; in *NT*, *love of the brethren*, *Ep.Rom.*12.10, al. **-ιον**, το, name of a *plaster*, Gal.12.756. ⊕**-ος**, ον, *loving one's brother* or *sister, brotherly, sisterly*, φ. δάκρυα S.*Ant.* 527 (anap.); of persons, X.*Mem.*2.3.17, Plu.*Sol.*27: Sup., Id.*Luc.* 43; freq. as a title of kings, as of Ptolemy II and Arsinoe, Wilcken *Chr.*106, etc.; of Ptolemy XIII, *OGI*185, etc., and of Attalus II, ib.329.38 (Aegina, ii B.C.), etc.; τῆς Φ. Κύπριδος, of Arsinoe, Posidipp.ap.Ath.7.318d; of Antoninus and Verus, *IG*2$^2$.3405, al.; τὸ φ. τῆς ψυχῆς D.S.17.34. Adv. -φως Sch.S. l. c. 2. in *NT*, *loving the brethren*, 1*Ep.Pet.*3.8. II. φιλάδελφον, τό, *mock orange*, *Philadelphus coronarius*, Apollod.ap.Ath.15.682c. III. φιλάδελφοι, οἱ, name of fabulous *stones*, Ps.-Plu.*Fluv.*11.4.

**φῐλ-αδύνᾰμος** [ῠ], ον, *soon weakening*, ὕδωρ Hp.*Acut.*62 (Sup.). **-άεθλος** [ᾰ], ον, poet. for φίλαθλος, *AP*12.143, *IG*7.2244 (Thisbe). ⊕**-ᾰθήναιος**, ον, *fond of the Athenians*, Ar.*Ach.*142, *V.* 283 (lyr.), Pl.*Ti.*21e: Sup., D.19.308. **-αθλητής**, οῦ, ὁ, *fond of athletes*, Plu.2.140c,631a, D.C.*Fr.*110.4. **-αθλος**, ον, *fond of games* (i.e. as a competitor), Ph.1.268, Ptol.*Tetr.*166; θεός Plu. 2.724b: metaph., *fond of exertion*, διάνοια, νοῦς, Ph.1.543,523; also γυμνάσια φ. *IG*3.1344.

**φίλαι**, Ep. 2 sg. imper. aor. I Med. of φιλέω, Il.5.117, 10.280.

**φῐλ-αίακτος**, ον, *lamentable*, πόνοι A.*Supp.*803 (lyr.). **-αιδήμων**, ον, gen. ονος, *loving modesty*, *AP*7.450 (Diosc.). **-αιδής**, ές, = foreg., Vett.Val.14.25. **-αίμᾰτος**, ον, *fond of blood, bloodthirsty*, Φόβος A.*Th.*45; ἀλκαί E.*Rh.*932; γῆς φιλαίματοι (v.l. -του) ῥοαί Id.*Ph.*174; Ἄρης Anacr.100. **-αιμος**, ον, = foreg., Procl. *Par.Ptol.*230. **-αίμων**, ον, gen. ονος, = foreg., Hsch.

**φῐλαίτερος, φιλαίτατος**, irreg. Comp. and Sup. of φίλος (q. v. sub fin.).

**φῐλαίτιος**, ον, *fond of bringing accusations, fault-finding, censorious*, A.*Supp.*485, *PAmh.*2.65.22 (ii A.D.); distd. from φιλεπιτιμητής by Isoc.1.31; πονηρὸν ὁ συκοφάντης.. καὶ φιλαίτιον D.18.242; opp. εὐγνώμων, X.*Mem.*2.8.6; τῷ φ. τῆς ἀμελείας πέρι θεῶν *fond of bringing charges* of neglect in their case, Pl.*Lg.*903a; τὸ φ. *censoriousness*, Plu.*Sol.*25, cf. 2.813a. Adv. -ίως Str.2.1.41, Poll.3. 139. II. *liable to censure*, D.10.70.

⊕**φῐλᾰκανθίς**, ίδος, ἡ, *fond of thorn bushes*, χαλκίδες prob. in *AP*6. 304 (Phan.).

**φιλακίζομαι**, = χαριεντίζομαι, *EM*793.29, Phot.

**φῐλ-ακόλαστος**, ον, *fond of sensual indulgence*, Plu.*Tim.*14; τὸ φ. Id.*Galb.*19. **-ᾰκόλουθος**, ον, *readily following*, Ar.*Ra.*417, Aristomen.15. ⊕**-ἄκρᾱτος**, Ion. -ητος, ον, *fond of sheer wine, given to wine*, of Anacreon, Simon.183.5; Διόνυσος *AP*6.169; also φ. ἔρπυλλος ib.4.1.53 (Mel.); ἁρμονίη ib.7.26 (Antip. Sid.). **-ακρῑβέω**, *to be very precise*, Phld.*Po.Herc.*994 *Fr.*19 (dub.), Hsch.

**φῐλ-ᾰλειπτέω**, *to be fond of anointing oneself*, of athletes, Hdn. Gr.1.433, al., *EM*61.13. **-ᾰλεξανδρεύς**, έως, ὁ, *well-disposed towards Alexandria*, *IGRom.*1.1075 (Alexandria). **-ᾰλέξανδρος**, ον, *admirer of Alexander, fond of A.*, Str.13.1.27, Plu.*Pomp.*2; as epith. of Apollo, D.S.17.46, etc.: Sup. φιλαλεξανδρότατος D.C.77.9.

**φῐλᾰλήθ-εια**, ἡ, *sincerity, ingenuousness*, τρόπου Them.*Or.*15. 198b. **-ειος**, ον, v. sq. **-ης**, ες (parox., on the accent v. Hdn.Gr. 1.80), *loving truth, a lover of truth*, Arist.*EN*1127$^b$4, Phld.*Rh.*1.361 S., D.S.1.76, Ph.1.192, Plu.*Mar.*28; opp. φιλοψευδής, Charond.ap.Stob. 4.2.24: Sup., φιλοσοφώτατος καὶ -έστατος Jul.*Ep.*97:—certain philosophers are called φιλαλήθεις by D.L.1.17, who seems to intend the Epicureans; also applied to the physician Alexander of Laodicea, Anon.Lond.24.32 (where -ειος), Sor.2.2, etc. Adv. -θως Phld.*Piet.*123, D.S.2.32, Gal.19.348; *frankly*, Cic.*QF*2.15(16).5.

⊕**φῐλαλληλ-ία**, ἡ, *mutual love*, Tz.ad Hes.*Op.*42: metaph. of numbers, *affinity*, Nicom.*Ar.*2.19, Iamb.*in Nic.*p.30 P. **-ος**, ον, *of mutual affection*, πάθος Ph.2.386; ἀγάπησις Plu.2.979f; τὸ φ., = φιλαλληλία, ib.977c; *fond of one another*, Babr.124.9, J.*BJ*2.8.2, Iamb. *Protr.*21.λ'; φ. ζῷον Arr.*Epict.*4.5.10: metaph. of numbers (cf. foreg.), Nicom.*Ar.*2.20. Adv. -λως Eust.1126.29.

**φίλ-αλμος** [ῐ], ον, *fond of leaping*, Eustr. *in EN*82.33. **-άλῡπος**, ον, *liking to be free from pain* or *grief*, Orph.*H.*50.7. **-ᾰλυστής**, οῦ, ὁ, *easily bewildered*, Hp.*Praec.*13. **-ᾰμαρτήμων**, ον, gen. ονος, *loving sin*, Lxx *Pr.*17.19. **-αμπελέω**, *love the vine*, Tz.*H.*6.73. **-άμπελος**, ον, *loving the vine*, θεῶν φιλαμπελωτάτη Ar.*Pax* 308 (troch.), cf. Nonn.*D.*12.41. II. *rich in vineyards*, D.H.1.37. **-αναγνωστέω**, *to be fond of reading*, D.S.1.3,77. ⊕**-αναγνώστης**, ου, ὁ, *fond of reading*, Plu.*Alex.*8. **-ᾰνᾱλωτής**, οῦ, ὁ, *fond of spending, prodigal*, c. gen. rei, φ. ἀλλοτρίων δι' ἐπιθυμίαν Pl.*R.*548b; ἐς τοὺς στρατιώτας D.C.77.9. ⊕**-ανδρία**, ἡ, *love for a husband*, Ph.2.36, Luc.*Halc.*2, *IG*5(1).1249 (Cyparissia), 14.1976, Lib.*Or.*29.14: pl., *examples of wifely affection*, App.*BC*4.36. II. *wifely jealousy*, E. *Andr.*229. 2. in later Gr. in bad sense, *love of the male sex*, Hermog. *Id.*2.5. **-ανδριος**, ον, late form for sq. II. 3, *JRS*18.30 (Phrygia). **-ανδρος**, ον, *loving men*; of a country, *loving its men*, πέδον A.*Th.*902 (lyr.). II. *loving masculine habits*, of Atalanta, S.*Fr.*1111; Ἀμαζόνες Plu.*Thes.*26. 2. of women, *lewd*, Pl. *Smp.*191e. 3. *loving one's husband*, *Ep.Tit.*2.4, Ph.2.431, Plu. *Alc.*8, Iamb.post Polem.p.48 Hinck, Luc.*Halc.*8; freq. in epitaphs, *Epigr.Gr.*387.12 (Apamea), *IG*14.1976; ψυχῇ φιλανδροτάτῃ *IG*14.

607*f* (Caralis). Adv. -ρως, ἔζησε ib.12(3).280 (Anaphe). **-άνθεμος**, ον, = sq., E.*Fr.*896, Nonn.*D.*17.83. **-ανθής**, ές, *fond of flowers*, μελισσα *AP*5.31 (Marc. Arg.); στέφανοι ib.71 (Pall.). **-ανθρᾰκεύς**, έως, ὁ, *friend of colliers*, Ar.*Ach.*336 (lyr.).

**φῐλανθρώπ-ευμα**, ατος, τό, *humane act*, Plu.*Sol.*15, Jul.*Ep.*184, etc.; πρός τινα Plu.2.970a; *piece of courtesy*, ib.816c. ⊛**-εύομαι**, *act humanely* or *courteously*, πρός τινας D.19.139: c. acc. rei, *to show kindness by granting* a thing, Hld.9.27, D.C.50.20; τι περί τινα Aristid.*Or.*21(22).10; τὰ θαυμαστά Id.2.234 J. 2. Astrol., = sq. I. 2, Procl.*Par.Ptol.*200. II. c. acc. pers., *treat humanely*, J.*AJ* 13.2.3; φ. τινά τι *do* one a *kindness*, Hld.9.2:—Pass., φιλανθρωπευθέντες D.S.18.18, cf. Phld.*Herc.*1457.9. 2. *conciliate*, τὸν δῆμον δώδεκα ἀποικίαις App.*BC*1.23. **-έω**, = foreg., *show kindness*, τὰ πρὸς ἡμᾶς *PCair.Zen.*428.14 (iii B.C.); τὰ λοιπὰ φ. τῇ πόλει *SIG*456.8 (Ziaelas, iii B.C.); ταῖς ἑαυτοῦ δυνάμεσιν πεφιλανθρώπηκε *OGI*90.12 (Rosetta, ii B.C.). 2. abs. in Astrol., *to be favourable*, φιλανθρωποῦντος τόπου Ptol.*Tetr.*141. II. trans., *treat kindly, deal kindly with*, τινα Plb.3.76.2, al.; τὸν τόπον Lxx 2*Ma.*13.23, cf. *POxy.*532.20 (ii A.D.):—Pass., προαιρούμενος..τὸν δῆμον φιλανθρωπεῖσθαι *Rev.Phil.*10(1936).253 (Ilium); φιλανθρωπηθείς Plb.38.20.11 (ap.Suid.); ἵν' ὦ πεφιλανθρωπημένος that I may *obtain redress*, *PTeb.*31.21 (ii B.C.). **-ία**, ἡ, *humanity, benevolence, kind-heartedness, humane feeling*, or, in a weaker sense, *kindliness, courtesy*, I. of men, Hp.*Praec.*6, Pl.*Euthphr.*3d, X.*Cyr.*1.4.1, *Act.Ap.*28.2, etc.; opp. σεμνότης, Isoc.15.133; opp. φθόνος, D.20.165; opp. ὠμότης, ib.109; joined with εὔνοια, Isoc.5.114, D.18.5; with πραότης, Isoc.5.116; with χρηστότης, Iamb.ap.Stob.4.5.76; φ. λόγων *courtesy*, D.18.298; τῆς παρὰ τουτωνὶ τιμῆς καὶ φ. ib.209; φ. διὰ τῶν λόγων Plb.28.17.11; φ. προσάγειν τινί Id.1.81.8; φ. εἰς or πρὸς τοὺς αἰχμαλώτους, ib.79.8,11; ὑπὸ φιλανθρωπίας Pl. l.c.; μετὰ φ. Isoc.15 l.c.; *clemency*, X.*Cyr.*7.5.73; so φιλανθρωπίᾳ Id.*Ages.*1.22; *the intercourse* of lovers, Aeschin.1.171: pl., *acts of kindness, courtesies*, D.8.70, 25.86, Plb.36.17.13, Phld.*Rh.*2.160 S., etc. b. ἡ σὴ φ. as a form of address, your *Clemency*, *PRyl.*296 (ii A.D.), etc. 2. of God, *love to man*, *Ep.Tit.*3.4, al. II. of things, ἡ τοῦ ὀνόματος (i.e. νόμος) φ. its *mildness*, D.24.156; ἡ φ. τῆς τέχνης, of agriculture, X.*Oec.*15.4, cf. Aeschin.2.15; χώρα πάσης φ. ἐστερημένη, of a desert country, D.S.17.50; in disease, *mild symptoms*, Gal.19.219. III. *concession, privilege*, *UPZ*162 vii 21 (ii B.C.), *OGI*139.20 (Egypt, ii B.C.), *Rev.Phil.*10 (1936).253 (Ilium); θεία φ. imperial *grant*, *SIG*888.102 (Scaptopara, iii A.D.). **-ινος**, η, ον, = sq., *IG*7.2711.110 (Acraeph., i A.D.). Adv. -νως dub. l. in Plb.33.18.3. **-ιον**, τό, *present*, '*douceur*', *Gloss.*, cf. Ulp. in *Dig.*50.14.2. ⊛**-ος**, ον, *loving mankind, humane, benevolent, tender-hearted*, and, in weaker sense, *kind, courteous*, Epich.[274]; φ. καὶ φιλαθήναιος καὶ φιλόσοφος Isoc.*Ep.*5.2; φ. καὶ φιλόπολις Id.2.15; δημοτικὸς καὶ φ. X.*Mem.*1.2.60; ψυχὴν φιλανθρωπότατος Id.*Cyr.*1.2.1; φ. δὲ παύεσθαι τρόπου, of Prometheus, A.*Pr.*11, cf. 28; of animals that attach themselves to men, as of dogs, *gentle*, X.*Cyn.*6.25; of horses, Id.*Eq.*2.3; τὸ φιλάνθρωπον, = φιλανθρωπία, Plu.*Cat.Ma.*3, etc.; τὸ φ. καὶ μεταδοτικόν Phld.*Oec.*p.54 J.; τὰ φιλάνθρωπα *humane treatment*, τῶν φ. τυχεῖν *PCair.Zen.*638.13 (iii B.C.); *kindnesses*, Plb.10.38.3, 12.5.3, etc. 2. of the gods, *loving men*, Pl.*Smp.*189c (Sup.), *Lg.*713d, Plu.*Num.*4. II. of things, *humane, humanizing*, χάρις δικαία καὶ φ. E.*Fr.*953.41; γεωργία X.*Oec.*19.17; ψηφίσματα Id.*Vect.*3.6; λόγοι D.45.4; τρόπος, in Music, Plu.2.1135c, etc.; of wines, *generous*, Id.*Cleom.*13 (Comp.), cf. 2.680b. 2. *appealing to human feeling*, of situations, Arist.*Po.*$1452^{b}$38, al. (less prob., *satisfying the sense of poetic justice*). 3. Medic., of diet, *generous*, τροφὴ -οτέρα, opp. ὀλίγη, Gal.1.211; but of a medical treatise, *popular*, Id.15.551 (Comp.). III. φιλάνθρωπα, τά, *concessions, grants, privileges, immunities*, *OGI*221.14 (Ilium, iii B.C.), *PCair.Zen.*37.11 (iii B.C.), *SIG*548.3 (Delph., iii B.C.), Plb.4.26.8, *UPZ*162 v 22, al. (ii B.C.), *OGI*331.42 (Pergam., ii B.C.), Epist.Jul.Caes.ap.J.*AJ*14.10.2, D.S.32.4, etc.; Thess. **φιλάνθρουπα** *IG*9(2).517.16 (Larissa, iii B.C.). b. sg., *benefaction, endowment, gratuity*, *BGU*1202.10 (i B.C.), *Mon.Anc.Gr.*9.10, etc. c. sg., *letter expressing friendly feelings*, *PSI*4.439.32, *PCair.Zen.*56.10 (both iii B.C.). IV. Adv., -ως τινὶ κεχρῆσθαι D.19.225; φ. διακεῖσθαι πρός τινα Plb.1.68.13; φ. καὶ δημοτικῶς D.24.24; θεοφιλῶς καὶ φ. Isoc.9.43, cf. 15.132, Phld.*Herc.*1251.14, etc.: Sup. -ότατα D.24.191, D.C.69.2. V. **-ον**, τό, = ἀπαρίνη, Dsc.3.90, Plin.*HN*24.176; **φιλανθρώπειος** βοτάνη in Archig.ap.Gal.12.574.

**φῐλάνωρ** [ᾱ], ορος, ὁ, ἡ, Dor. for φιλήνωρ, *fond of a man, amorous, conjugal*, στίβοι, τρόποι, A.*Ag.*411 (lyr.), 856; πόθος Id.*Pers.*136 (lyr.):—**φιλήνωρ** only in late Ep., Musae.267, Coluth.213. II. *kindly*, ξείνων φ. τιμά B.1.40; *fond of men*, of dolphins, βιοτά Pi.*Fr.*236.

**φίλαξ**, Elean for δρῦς, Hsch.

⊛**φῐλ-άοιδος** [ᾰ], ον, *fond of singing* or *singers*, Theoc.28.23; τέττιξ *AP*9.372; *musical*, κερκίς ib.6.47 (Antip. Sid.): Sup. -ότατος Epic.ap.D.Chr.32.84. **-ᾰπελλῆς**, ὁ, *admirer of Apelles*, Hdn.Gr.1.82; Dor. **-απελλᾶς** cj. Lobeck for φιλοπελλᾶς (v.l. φιλοπελᾶς), ib.57.

**φῐλάπεπτος**, ον, *subject to bad digestion*, Antyll.ap.Orib.6.8.3.

⊛**φῐλᾰπεχθ-ημοσύνη**, ἡ, *fondness for making enemies, quarrelsomeness*, D.54.37; περὶ τοὺς λόγους Aristid.2.297 J.: pl., *quarrelsome attempts*, Isoc.15.317. ⊛**-ήμων**, ον, gen. ονος, *fond of making enemies, quarrelsome*, Lys.24.24, Isoc.8.65, D.24.6: Sup., Jul.*Mis.*342d. Adv. -νως, ἔχειν to be *quarrelsome*, Pl.*R.*500b; πρός τινα Ph.2.381. **-ής**, ές, = foreg., Plb.12.25.6; λοιδορία Id.5.28.4. Adv. -θῶς, κατηγορεῖν Id.32.10.3.

**φῐλαπλοϊκός**, ή, όν, *fond of simplicity*, Luc.*Pisc.*20.

**φῐλᾰπόδημος**, ον, *fond of travelling*, X.*HG*4.3.2, Dicaearch.1.30, Ael.*NA*7.24; of Hippocrates, Sor.*Vit.Hippocr.*12.

**φῐλαργεῖος**, ον, *loving the Argives*, Them.*Or.*27.335c.

**φῐλαργικός**, ή, όν, (ἀργός) *contemplative*, dub. in Fulg.*Myth.*2.1.

**φῐλαργῠρ-έω**, *love money*, Epicur.*Sent.Vat.*43, Lxx 2*Ma.*10.20, *IG*9(2).338.12 (Epist. Flaminini), Phld.*Herc.*1457.12, Alciphr.1.40, S.E.*M.*11.122. **-ία**, ἡ, *love of money, avarice*, Hp.*Ep.*16, Democr.222, Isoc.8.96, Din.1.22, Diph.94, Plb.9.25.4, al., 1*Ep.Ti.*6.10, etc. **-ος**, ον, *fond of money, avaricious*, S.*Ant.*1055, *Fr.*587, Pl.*R.*347b, *PPetr.*3 p.150 (iii B.C.), Phld.*Ind.Sto.*19, *Ev.Luc.*16.14, etc.; Sup. -ώτατος X.*Mem.*3.1.10, 3.13.4.

**φῐλ-άρετος** [ᾰ], ον, *lover of virtue*, Arist.*EN*$1099^{a}$11; θεός Ph.1.19; generally, *virtuous*, Alex.Trall.8.2. **-ᾰριστείδης**, ου, ὁ, *admirer of Aristides*, *APl.*4.315 (Thom.Schol.). **-ᾰριστοτέλης**, ου, ὁ, *admirer of Aristotle*, Phld.*Ind.Sto.*6.1, Str.13.1.54. **-άρμᾰτος**, ον, *fond of chariots* or *the chariot-race*, πόλις Pi.*I.*8(7).22; Θῆβαι E.*HF*467; as name of a horse, *Mélanges Beyrouth* 15.111 (Berytus). **-άρπαξ**, αγος, ὁ, ἡ, *fond of rapine, ravenous*, *AB*1199. **-αρσάκης** [ᾰκ], ου, ὁ, *devoted, loyal to the Arsacid house*, Str.16.1.28. **-άρτεμις**, ὁ, ἡ, *lover of Artemis*, *Ephes.*2.29 (ii A.D.). **-άρχαιος**, ον, *fond of what is old, fond of antiquity*, Phld.*Rh.*1.157 S., Plu.2.1107e, Ath.3.126b: Rhet., *old-fashioned*, ἁρμονία D.H.*Dem.*36, al.

**φῐλαρχ-έω**, *to be fond of rule*, Plb.6.9.6, D.S.15.5, Plu.*Cat.Mi.*44, etc. **-ία**, ἡ, *love of rule, lust of power*, Thphr.*Char.*26.1, Plb.6.49.3, Phld.*Piet.*22, Lxx 4*Ma.*2.15, Gal.*Anim.Pass.*1.7, Jul.*Caes.*308d, freq. in Plu., as *Mar.*2, al.: in pl., Id.*Eum.*13; *efforts to gain power*, Id.*Cic.*10. **-ιάω**, *to be lustful of power*, Cels.ap.Orig.*Cels.*7.18. **-ικός**, ή, όν, *of* or *for an ambitious man*, Pherecr.14 (troch.(?), Posit. and Comp., φιλορχ- Meineke). **-ος**, ον, *fond of rule* or *power, ambitious*, Pl.*Phd.*82c, *R.*549a, Plb.6.48.8 (Sup.), Phld.*Ir.*p.37 W., etc.: τὸ φ. = φιλαρχία, Plu.2.793e. **-ων**, οντος, ὁ, *loving the rulers*, Aristox.ap.Stob.4.1.49.

**φῐλ-ασκητής**, οῦ, ὁ, *lover of training* or *exercise*, Vett.Val.46.28. **-αστράγᾰλος** [ᾰγ], η, ον, *fond of playing at knucklebones*, *AP*6.276 codd. (Antip.). **-αστρόλογος**, ον, *loving astrology*, Ptol.*Tetr.*66. **-άσωτος**, ον, *fond of a profligate life, profligate, wanton*, *AP*5.174 (Mel.), 190 (Id.).

**φῑλᾱτία**, ἁ, = Dor. for φιλησία, *Foed.Delph.Pell.*1 *B*8, 2 *A*13 (iii B.C.).

**φίλᾰτο** [ῑ], Ep. 3 sg. aor. Med. of φιλέω, Il.20.304, Call.*Aet.Oxy.*2080.55:—as Pass., A.R.3.66.

**φῐλ-αυθόμαιμος**, ον, = φιλάδελφος, Lyc.566. ⊛**-αυλος**, ον, *fond of the flute*, Μοῦσαι S.*Ant.*965 (lyr.); δελφίς E.*El.*435 (lyr.); οἱ φ. Arist.*EN*$1175^{b}$3. **-αύστηρος**, ον, *devoted to austerity*, βίος Ph.1.39.

**φῐλαυτ-έω**, *to be fond of self*, Ph.2.558. **-ία**, ἡ, *self-love, self-regard*, Cic.Att.13.13.1, Plu.2.48f; in bad sense, *selfishness*, *UPZ*42.10 (ii B.C.), Ph.1.173, al., Porph.*Abst.*3.2, Jul.*Caes.*316d, *Mis.*349b. **-ος**, ον, (αὑτοῦ) *loving oneself*, in good sense, τὸν ἀγαθὸν δεῖ φ. εἶναι Arist.*EN*$1169^{a}$12: more freq. in bad sense, *selfish*, Id.*MM*$1212^{a}$29, Phld.*Ir.*p.60 W., Ph.1.171, al., 2*Ep.Ti.*3.2, Plu.*Arat.*1, al., Arr.*Epict.*1.19.11; φ. μᾶλλον ἢ δεῖ Arist.*Rh.*$1389^{b}$35; τὸ φ. = φιλαυτία, Id.*EN*$1168^{b}$14, Plu.2.40f, etc. Adv. -τως Luc.*Am.*27, S.E.*M.*7.314. **-ότης**, ητος, ἡ, = φιλαυτία, Vett.Val.345.9.

**φίλ-αυχος** [ῐ], ον, *boastful*, Sch.Il.10.249. ⊛**-ᾰχαιός**, ὁ, ἡ, *friend of the Achaeans*, Hdn.Gr.1.228. **-ᾰχιλλεύς**, έως, ὁ, *friend of Achilles*, Eust.1696.63. **-αψευδής**, ές, *truthful*, dub. l. in Ph.1.644 (Sup.). **-έβδομος**, ον, *fond of the number seven*, ib.27; πάντα φ. everything '*goes by sevens*', *Theol.Ar.*42. **-έγγῠος**, ον, *readily giving security* or *bail*, E.*Fr.*923, Str.5.1.9. **-εγκλήμων**, ον, gen. ονος, *fond of fault-finding*, Ph.1.310, Poll.3.139, Gal.13.485, Sch.Il.1.354, Sch.Ar.*Pl.*874, etc. Adv. -μόνως Poll. l.c. **-εγκώμιος**, ον, *loving praises*, Sch.Ar.*Pl.*773. **-έθειρος**, ον, *attached to the hair*, σινδών *AP*6.307 (Phan.). **-ειδήμων**, ον, gen. ονος, *fond of learning*, Str.1.1.23, al., prob. in Cic.*Att.*12.6.2; τὸ φ. Str.1.2.29. ⊛**-εκᾱγᾰθία**, ἡ (sic), = φιλοκαγαθία (nisi hoc legend.), *love of honourable conduct*, *Rev.Arch.*20(1912).461 (Coptos, ii A.D.). **-εκδημητής**, οῦ, ὁ, = sq., Vett.Val.45.32. **-έκδημος**, ον, = φιλαπόδημος, τὸ φ. Str.1.2.29, 2.3.5. **-ελεήμων**, ον, gen. ονος, *compassionate*, Lxx *To.*14.9; also contr. **φῐλελήμων** *IG*$2^{2}$.4514.20. **-ελευθέριος**, ον, *loving liberality*, Lib.*Decl.*43 *Prooem.*; v.l. for sq. in D.H.11.15. **-ελεύθερος**, ον, *loving freedom, liberal*, Plb.4.30.5; πόλις Plu.*Tim.*2, etc.; τὸ φ. Plb.2.55.9, D.S.2.1, D.H.11.15 (cf. foreg.), etc. **-έλλην**, ηνος, ὁ, ἡ, *fond of the Hellenes*, mostly of foreign princes, as Amasis, Hdt.2.178, cf. Plu.*Ant.*23; of Parthian kings, *BMus.Cat.Coins*, *Parthia* p.14, etc.; φ. Ἀρσάκης *PAvrom.*1 *A*2 (i B.C.); also of Nero, *SIG*814.41 (Acraephiae, i A.D.); also of Hellenic tyrants, as Jason of Pherae, Isoc.5.122: generally of Hellenic patriots, Pl.*R.*470e; of Hippocrates, Sor.*Vit.Hippocr.*8; καλὸν Ἕλληνα ὄντα φιλέλληνα εἶναι X.*Ages.*7.4; μᾶλλον φ. ib.2.31, Isoc.4.96; μάλιστα φ., of the subjects of Evagoras, Id.9.50; coupled with φιλοβασιλεύς, *Com.Adesp.* in *Gött.Nachr.*1922.31. **-ελπις**, ιδος, ὁ, ἡ, *readily hoping, always hoping*, Phryn.*PS* p.121 B. **-έμπορος**, ον, *fond of traffic and travel*, Hld.6.7, Nonn.*D.*9.88; name of a comedy ascribed to Naevius, Fulg.*Serm.Ant.*21.

**φῐλεν-δεικτέω**, *to be fond of showing off*, Eust.702.20. **-δοξος**, ον, *fond of the great, snobbish*, Cic.*Att.*13.19.3. **-δοτος**, ον, expld. as = ἐλεήμων, Hsch. **-θεος**, ον, *filled with divine influence*, δειράς Limen.22; of a person, *religious*, *IG*3.1384; of Pan, *lover of inspired frenzy*, Orph.*H.*11.5. **-τολος**, ον, *loving the commandments*, *CIG*9904 (Jewish), *Sammelb.*1540 (v A.D.).

**φῐλέξοδος**, ον, *fond of going out* or *gadding about*, Axiop.4.4 codd. Stob.

**φῐλεορτ-αστής**, οῦ, ὁ, = sq., Poll.1.20. **-ος**, ον, *fond of feasts*, εἰρήνη Ar.*Th.*1147 (lyr.); Σύροι Hdn.2.7.9.

**φῐλεπαινος**, ον, *loving praise*, Phld.*Herc.*1457.11.

**φῐλεπι-στήμων**, ον, gen. ονος, *fond of knowledge* or *science*, Ph.2.374. Adv. -νως ib.300. **-στροφος**, ον, *tending to recur*, πάθος Herod.Med. in *Rh.Mus.*58.90. **-τῑμητής**, οῦ, ὁ, *censorious person*, Isoc.1.31, Ath.9.385a. **-τῑμος**, ον, *fault-finding*, *censorious*, τὸ Τιμαίου φ. Plb.12.4$^{A}$.6.

**φῐλεραστ-έω**, *to be amorous*, Poll.3.68. **-ής**, οῦ, ὁ, *fond of a lover*, or *fond of having lovers*, Pl.*Smp.*192b, Arist.*Rh.*1371$^{b}$24. **-ία**, ἡ, *devotion to a lover*, Pl.*Smp.*213d, Aristaenet.1.18. **-ος**, ον, *amorous*, Plb.23.5.7, *AP*5.143 (Mel.), etc. II. *dear to lovers*, ῥόδον *AP*5.135 (Mel.); πακτίς *IG*14.793.5 (Naples). **-ρια**, ἡ, *amorous*, *AP*5.3 (Phld.), 10.18 (Marc.Arg.).

**φῐλεργ-έω**, *love work*, *be industrious*, D.H.5.66, Plu.2.13a; of the spider, Ael.*NA*1.21. **-ία**, ἡ, *industry*, X.*Oec.*20.26, D.36.5, Arist.*Rh.*1361$^{a}$8, *OGI*669.33 (Egypt, i A.D.). **-ός**, όν, *industrious*, D.36.44, Plu.2.552a, etc.: τὸ φ., = φιλεργία, Ael.*VH*13.1. Adv. -γῶς ib.12.45.

**φῐλ-ερημία**, ἡ, *love of solitude*, *Cat.Cod.Astr.*2.161. ⊛**-έρημος**, ον, *fond of solitude*, Hp.*Ep.*12, *Lyr.Alex.Adesp.*7.10, Ph.1.490,506, Corn.*ND*30, Orph.*H.*56.2, Vett.Val.43.14, *AP*5.8 (Rufin.), 9.373. **-έρῑθος**, ον, *fond of wool-spinning*, κούρη Παλλαντιάς *AP*6.247 (Phil.): metaph., φ. ἀλακάτα Theoc.28.1. **-ερις**, ιδος, ὁ, ἡ, *fond of strife*, *disputatious*, *quarrelsome*, Arist.*SE*171$^{b}$26, Axionic.6.9, Phld.*Piet.*95, Muson.*Fr.*16 p.86 H.

**φῐλεριστ-έω**, *love strife*, *EM*793.32, Phot., Suid. **-ής**, οῦ, ὁ, = φίλερις, Alex.335. **-ία**, ἡ, *disputatiousness*, Simp. in *Ph.*88.30. **-ικός**, ή, όν, *pugnacious*, *combative*, φύσις Sch.Ar.*Pax* 788. **-τος**, ον, *pertinax*, *Gloss.*

**φῐλερνέω**, cj. for λιφερνέω in Hsch.

**φίλερος**, perh. f.l. for φιλέρ⟨ιστ⟩ος, Vett.Val.18.9.

⊛**φῐλ-ερως** [ῐ], ωτος, ὁ, ἡ, *prone to love*, *amorous*, *AP*5.170 (Mel.), 196 (Id.), Luc.*Am.*12, *Cat.Cod.Astr.*2.170. **-έσπερος**, ον, *fond of evening*, ἄνθος *AP*7.31 (Diosc.). **-εστιάτωρ** [ᾰ], ορος, ὁ, *lover of feasting*, Ph.2.70.

**Φῐλεταίρ-ειος**, α, ον, *of Philetaerus*. I. Φιλεταίρειον, τό, with or without ἀργύριον, *treasure dedicated by P.*, *Inscr.Délos*320 *B*84 (iii B.C.), *IG*11(2).224 *A*4 (Delos, iii B.C.). II. **-εια** (sc. ἱερά), τά, *festival in his honour*, *Inscr.Délos*366 *A*57 (iii B.C.), 442 *B*54 (ii B.C.): **-ειος**, ὁ (sc. μήν), name of a month at Pergamon, prob. in *Yale Classical Studies* 2.205: **-ειος** πούς a foot containing 16 δάκτυλοι, Hero *Geom.*4.3, al. **-ία**, ἡ, *attachment to one's comrades*, X.*Ages.*2.21, Alex.334, Arist.*Rh.*1364$^{b}$2. II. = φιλεταίριον, Plin.*HN*25.64. **-ικός**, ή, όν, *of comradely affection*, Sch.Il.4.412. **-ιον**, τό, or **-ιος**, ὁ, = πολεμώνιον, Dsc.4.8 (also **φῐλεταιρίς**, ίδος, ἡ, Plin.*HN*25.99; but = ῥάμνος, a spinous buckthorn, Nic.*Th.*632, where φιλέταιριν codd.). II. = ὠκιμοειδές, Dsc.4.28. 2. = κληματίς, Ps.-Dsc.4.7. **-ος**, ον, *fond of one's comrades* or *partisans*, *true to them*, Pl.*Ly.*211e, Arist.*Rh.*1389$^{a}$37, Thphr.*Char.*29.4; ἀνδρεία, τρόπος, ἦθος, Th.3.82, X.*Cyr.*8.3.49, Cratin.Jun.12; τὸ φ., = φιλεταιρία, Timocl.8.4, Plu.*Lys.*5. Adv. -ρως, in bad sense, Aeschin.1.110.

**φῐλ-έτνος** [ῐ], ον, *fond of pulse-soup*, *Com.Adesp.*1190 (fort. -ετνής). **-εύδῐος**, ον, *loving clear weather*, Ἀμφιτρίτα *Hymn.Is.*145. **-εύηχος**, ον, *fond of loud cries*, Διόπαν *Epigr.Gr.*827.5 (Caesarea Panias). **-εύιος**, ον, *loving the cry of* εὐοῖ, epith. of Dionysus, *AP* 9.524, Nonn.*D.*12.114. **-εύλειχος**, ον, (λείχω) *fond of dainties*, *AP*6.305 (Leon., Brunck for φιλεύχειλος; φιλεύλοιχος Lobeck, φιλεύχυμος Hecker). ⊛**-ευνος**, ον, *fond of the marriage-bed*, *Anacreont.*1.7. **-ευποιία**, ἡ, v. φιλοποιία.

**φῐλευρῑπίδης** [ῐδ], ου, ὁ, *fond of Euripides*, Plu.2.755b; name of a comedy by Axionicus, Ath.4.175b; by Philippides, Poll.9.38.

⊛**φῐλεύ-τακτος**, ον, devoted to discipline, ἐφηβοσύνα *AP*6.282 (Theod.). **-τράπελος** [ᾰ], ον, *loving wit*, Arist.*VV*1251$^{a}$20, v.l. *Rh.*1389$^{b}$11. **-φρόσῡνος**, ον, *fond of good cheer*, Vett.Val.104.14, Heph.Astr.1.1. **-χειλος**, ον, v. φιλεύλειχος. **-ώδης**, ες, *loving sweet smells*, Tz.*H.*5.399.

**φῐλέφηβος**, ον, *fond of youths*, *AP*12.161 (Asclep.).

**φῐλεχθ-ής**, ές, *quarrelsome*, Theoc.5.137. **-ρέω**, *exercise enmity*, Lxx *Pr.*3.30, Procl.*Par.Ptol.*171. **-ρος**, ον, *disharmonic*, μῖξις Gal.19.486. II. *prone to enmity*, Ptol.*Tetr.*119. Adv., -ρως ἔχειν πρός τινα to be *hostile* towards any one, D.L.3.36; φ. διακείμενοι Ptol.*Tetr.*191.

**φῐλέψιος**, ον, (ἐψιάομαι) *fond of play*, *sportive*, Nonn.*D.*10.378.

**φῐλέω**, Aeol. **φίλημμι** Sapph.79, cf. Ead.*Oxy.*1787 *Fr.*1 + 2.24; 2sg. φίλησθα Ead.22; late 3 pl. φιλεισι *Epigr.Gr.*990.12 (Balbill.): Boeot. **φίλειμι** Hdn.Gr.2.930: Ep. inf. φιλήμεναι Il.22.265: Ion. and Ep. impf. φιλέεσκε 3.388, al.: fut. φιλήσω, Ep. inf. φιλησέμεν Od.4.171: aor. 1 ἐφίλησα Pi.*P.*2.16, etc.: pf. πεφίληκα ib.1.13:—**Med.**, Poet. 1 aor. ἐφῑλάμην; 3 sg. ἐφίλατο, φίλατο, Il.5.61, 20.304, Call.*Aet.Oxy.*2080.55; 3 pl. φίλαντο Lyc.274; imper. φῖλαι Il.5.117, 10.280; subj. φίλωνται *h.Cer.*117, Hes.*Th.*97; but φίλατο as Pass., A.R.3.66; also part. φιλάμενος *IG*14.1549 (Rome):—**Pass.**, fut. Med. φιλήσομαι in pass. sense, Od.1.123, 15.281, Antipho 1.19: fut. 3 πεφιλήσομαι Call.*Del.*270: aor. ἐφιλήθην E.*Hec.*1000, Pl.*Phdr.*253c: Ep. 3 pl. ἐφίληθεν Il.2.668: pf. πεφίλημαι Pi.*N.*4.45, X.*An.*1.9.28; Dor. part. πεφιλᾱμένος Theoc.3.3. [ῐ except in the forms ἐφίλατο, φῖλατο, etc.]: (φίλος):—*love*, *regard with affection*, opp. μισεῖν, Pl.*R.*334c, Arist.*Rh.*1380$^{b}$34; φιλήσω τὸν δῆμον τὸν Ἀθηναίων *IG*1$^{2}$.15.36; (on its relation to *sexual love* v. infr. 3); of the love of gods for men, φ. δέ ἑ μητίετα Ζεύς Il.2.197; πέρι γάρ μ' ἐφίλει (of the love of the master for his swineherd) Od.14.146; (also ὃν περὶ κῆρι φ. Ζεὺς..παντοίην φιλότητα Od.15.245, cf. Il.9.117); μάλα τούς γε φ. ἑκάεργος Ἀπόλλων Il.16.94; εἰ..Ἕκτορά περ φιλέεις καὶ κήδεαι αὐτοῦ 7.204, etc.; of love for a child reared, Od.15.370; αἱ δὲ μὴ φίλει, ταχέως φιλήσει κωὐκὶ θέλοισα Sapph.1.23; λόγοις φιλοῦσαν οὐ στέργω φίλην S.*Ant.*543; φιλέων φιλέοντα Pi.*P.*10.66; ὃν δ' ἐχρῆν φιλεῖν στυγεῖς A.*Ch.*907; μάλιστά σ'..ἤχθηρα κἀφίλησ' ἐν ἡμέρᾳ μιᾷ S.*El.*1363; ὃν οἱ θεοὶ φιλοῦσιν ἀποθνῄσκει νέος Men.125; ὅσα θεοὶ ἀνθρώποις οὓς φιλοῦσιν [διδόασιν] *SIG* 985.48 (Philadelphia, i B.C.); οἱ φιλοῦντές τινα his *friends*, freq. in messages and letters, *OGI*184.10 (Philae, i B.C.), *Ep.Tit.*3.15, *PSI*8.971.30 (iii/iv A.D.), etc.; φιλεῖν ἐμαυτήν, αὑτόν, E.*Hel.*999, *Med.*86, etc.:—Pass., *to be beloved* by one, ἐκ Διός Il.2.668; παρ' αὐτῇ 13.627, etc.; τινι E.*Hec.*1000. 2. *treat affectionately* or *kindly*, esp. *welcome*, *entertain* a guest, Od.4.29, 5.135, Il.3.207, etc.; φίλος δ' ἦν ἀνθρώποισιν, πάντας γὰρ φιλέεσκεν ὁδῷ ἔπι οἰκία ναίων Il.6.15; ξεῖνον ἐνὶ μεγάροισι φ. Od.8.42; ξεῖνον ἄγων ἐν δώμασι..φιλέειν καὶ τιέμεν 15.543, cf. 14.322; θεὸς (i.e. Calypso) ἥ με..ἐφίλει τε καὶ ἔτρεφεν 7.256; τίς ἂν φιλέοντι μάχοιτο; who would quarrel with *a kind host?* 8.208; etc.:—Pass., παρ' ἄμμι φιλήσεαι *welcome shalt thou be* in our house, Od.1.123, cf. 15.281. 3. opp. ἐρᾶν, τούτους μάλιστά φασι φιλεῖν ὧν ἂν ἐρῶσι *regard with affection* those for whom they have a passion, Pl.*Phdr.*231c; ὥστε οὐ μόνον φιλοῖο ἄν, ἀλλὰ καὶ ἐρῷο ὑπ' ἀνθρώπων X.*Hier.*11.11, cf. *Smp.*8.21; εἰκὼ, τὸ φιλεῖν τοὺς ἐρωμένους Arist.*APr.*70$^{a}$6; but φ. is used of lovers, ἥ γ' Εὐρυμάχῳ μισγέσκετο καὶ φιλέεσκεν Od.18.325; Λυσίθεος Μικίωνα φιλῖν φησι μάλισστα τῶν ἐν τῇ πόλει *IG*1$^{2}$.924; οὐκ ἔστ' ἐραστὴς ὅστις οὐκ ἀεὶ φιλεῖ E.*Tr.*1051, cf. Hdt.4.176 (Pass.), Ar.*Lys.*905; of the *love* of man for wife, ὅς τις ἀνὴρ ἀγαθὸς..τὴν αὐτοῦ φιλέει (*cherishes* her) καὶ κήδεται ὡς καὶ ἐγὼ τὴν ἐκ θυμοῦ φίλεον Il.9.343, cf. 486; τὴν αὐτὸς φιλέεσκεν *loved and cherished* as his wife, ib.450; but ἐμὲ..ἀτιμάζει, φιλέει δ' ἀΐδηλον Ἄρηα (Hephaestus speaks of Aphrodite) Od.8.309: Com., ὦ Δῆμ', ἐραστής εἰμι σὸς φιλῶ τέ σε καὶ κήδομαί σου Ar.*Eq.*1341. b. of sexual intercourse, Hsch. s.v. βαίνειν. 4. *show outward signs of love*, esp. *kiss* (not in Hom.), φ. τοῖσι στόμασι *kiss* on the mouth, opp. τὰς παρειὰς φιλέονται, Hdt.1.134, cf. X.*Cyr.*1.4.27, *Smp.*9.5; κατὰ τὸ στόμα *AP*5.284 (Agath.); φιλήσω..τὸ σὸν κάρα S.*OC*1131; πατέρα..περὶ χεῖρε βαλοῦσα φιλήσει A.*Ag.*1559 (anap.), cf. Ar.*Av.*671,674, Pl.*Phdr.*255e, *Ev.Marc.*14.44, etc.: c. dupl. acc., τὸ φίλαμα, τὸ..τὸν Ἄδωνιν..ἀποθνᾴσκοντα φίλασεν the kiss wherewith *she kissed* him, Mosch.3.69:—Med., τὰς παρειάς *kiss each other's* cheeks, Hdt.l.c. 5. of things as objects of love, *like*, *approve*, σχέτλια ἔργα Od.14.83; ἀοιδάν Pi.*N.*3.7; οὐθ' ἴστων ἐφίλησεν ὁδοὺς οὔτε δείπνων..τέρψιας *P.*9.18, etc.; αἰσχροκέρδειαν S.*Ant.*1056, cf. 312; τὰς λευκοτάτας [μάζας] Telecl.1.6 (anap.); Πράμνιον οἶνον Ephipp.28. 6. of things as the subject, ἡσυχία δὲ φιλεῖ συμπόσιον Pi.*N.*9.48; ἡ [μίτρη] μαστοὺς ἐφίλησε Call.*Epigr.*39. 7. in making a request, οἶσθ' ὅτι ἢ φιλῶ σ' ἐγώ, κἀμοὶ πιθόμενος ὑπαποκίνει τῆς ὁδοῦ Ar.*Av.*1010; so τί πράσσει Φηλικίων ὁ ἀγαθός; φιλῶ σε *pray*, how goes it with the worthy Felicio? Arr.*Epict.*1.19.20; so perh. in Herod.1.66, πείσθητί μευ, φιλέω σε (but rather '*I speak as a true friend*'). II. after Hom., c. inf., *love to do*, *be fond* of doing, and so *to be wont* or *used to* do, φιλέει ὁ θεὸς τὰ ὑπερέχοντα κολούειν Hdt.7.10.ε'; ἣν ἁμάρτωσι τοῦ πατρικοῦ τύπου..φιλέουσι διαφθείρεσθαι Democr.228; Μοῖσα μεμνᾶσθαι φ. Pi.*N.*1.12, cf. *P.*3.18; φιλεῖ δὲ τίκτειν ὕβρις..ὕβριν A.*Ag.*763 (lyr.); τοῖς θανοῦσί τοι φιλοῦσι πάντες κειμένοις ἐπεγγελᾶν S.*Aj.*989, etc.; rarely with part. for inf., φιλεῖς δὲ δρῶσ' αὐτὸ σφόδρα Ar.*Pl.*645. 2. of things, events, etc., αὔρη ἀπὸ ψυχροῦ τινος φιλέει πνέειν Hdt.2.27; φιλεῖ ὠδῖνα τίκτειν νύξ A.*Supp.*769; ἐμπόρων ἔπη φ. πλανᾶσθαι S.*OC* 304; φιλεῖ γάρ πως τὰ τοιαῦθ' ἑτέρᾳ τρέπεσθαι Ar.*Nu.*813 (lyr.); φιλεῖ μεγάλα στρατόπεδα ἐκπλήγνυσθαι Th.4.125; ὃ δὴ φ. ὁ ἔρως ἐμποιεῖν Pl.*Smp.*182c: esp. with γίγνεσθαι of what *usually* happens, ἀπὸ πείρης πάντα ἀνθρώποισι φιλέει γίνεσθαι everything comes to man by experience, Hdt.7.9.γ', cf. 7.10.ζ', 7.50, Th.3.42, Isoc.6.104, Pl.*R.*494c, al.; οἷα φ. γίγνεσθαι Th.7.79, cf. Hdt.8.128; without γίγνεσθαι, οἷα δὴ φιλεῖ as *is wont*, Pl.*R.*467b; ὁποῖα φ. Luc.*Am.*9. 3. impers., φιλέει δέ κως προσημαίνειν (sc. ὁ θεός), εὖτ' ἂν..Hdt.6.27; ὡς δὴ φιλεῖ..λόγον ἔχειν ἀνθρώπους as *it is usual* for.., Plu.*Pomp.*73.

**φίλη**, ἡ, v. φίλος I.1b.

**φίληβος** [ῐ], ον, (ἥβη) *loving youth*: only as pr. n. *Philebus*.

⊛**φῐληδ-έω**, *find pleasure in*, *take delight in*, c. dat., μάχαις Ar.*Pax* 1130 (lyr.); ταῖς ὁσίν Antiph.126.3; μίζῃ Plb.34.10.4; Φοῖβος ἀεὶ πολίεσσι φ. Call.*Ap.*56; μὴ φ. τῇ περιωδευμένῃ προφορᾷ Phld.*Rh.*1.158 S.; φ. ἐρημίαις *to like to dwell in*.., Andreas ap. Ath.7.312e; πρὸς τὴν ψύξιν Gal.7.611; φ. πρὸς τοῖς μυροπωλίοις Alciphr.3.24; ἐπὶ τῇ χώρᾳ Suid. s.v. πενέσται: c. part., φ. ἐσθίων Ael.*NA*4.21: abs., Thphr.*HP*9.16.1. **-ής**, ές, *fond of pleasure*, Arist.*EN*1157$^{a}$33. II. *easily pleasing*, τινι Sch.Pi.*P.*2.133. **-ία**, ἡ, *delight*, γρυλίζειν ὑπὸ φιληδίας, of pigs, Ar.*Pl.*307 (lyr.), cf. 311 (lyr.). **-ονία**, ἡ, *fondness for pleasure*, Democr.159 (pl.), Agatharch.*Fr.Hist.*11, Hp.*Ep.*17, Epict.

*Gnom.*45, Plu.2.12c, 21c, *Sull.*2, Max.Tyr.31.5, S.E.*M.*11.120, etc. **-ονικός,** ή, όν, *advocating hedonism,* λόγοι Olymp. *in Grg.* p.7N. **-ονος,** ον, (ἡδονή) *fond of pleasure,* Plb.39.1.10, 2*Ep.Ti.*3.4, Epict.*Gnom.*46, Plu.*Galb.*1, al., Luc.*Herm.*16, Max.Tyr.4.2, etc.: τὸ φ., = φιληδονία, Plu.2.1094a. 2. *wont to bring delight,* Βάκχοιο νᾶμα *AP*10.118.

**φῐληκο-έω,** *to be attentive,* Plb.3.57.4. **-ΐα,** ἡ, *fondness for listening to,* τῶν λόγων Isoc.1.18: abs., Plu.2.40a, 44a, Jul.*Mis.*358d, prob. in Satyr.*Vit.Eur.Fr.*2 i 16. **-ος,** ον, (ἀκοή) *fond of hearing* conversation, discourses, etc., φ. καὶ ζητητικός Pl.*R.*535d; φιλόμουσος καὶ φ. ib.548e; οἵ τε φιλοθεάμονες οἵ τε φ. ib.475d; ἀνὴρ φ. καὶ ἱστορικός Plu.*Alc.*10:—τὸ φ., = φιληκοΐα, Id.2.704e: but also, *fond of hearing* for mere pastime, opp. οἱ φιλομαθοῦντες, Plb.7.7.8. Adv. -ως, ἔχειν Hld.5.16, Aristid.2.230 J., Chor.6.34 p.95 F.-R.

**φῐλ-ηλάκᾰτος** [ᾰκ], ον, *fond of the spindle,* καλαθίσκος *AP*6.160 (Antip. Sid.); prob. in B.1.74 p.439 Jebb. **-ηλῐάς,** άδος, ἡ, (ἥλιος) *loving the sun,* ᾠδή Telesill.2. **-ηλῐαστής,** οῦ, ὁ, *one who delights in the trials of the Heliaea,* Ar.*V.*88.

**φίλημ-α** [ῐ], ατος, τό, Dor. **φίλᾱμα** Mosch.1.5:—*kiss,* A.*Fr.*135, X.*Mem.*1.3.12, etc.; φ. δοῦναι E.*IA*679, 1238; φ. παρὰ γέννυν τιθέντα σόν Id.*Supp.*1154; πατρὶ..διὰ φιλημάτων ἰών Id.*Andr.*416; of kisses as prizes in a game, παίζωμεν περὶ φιλημάτων Pl.Com.46, cf. S.*Fr.*537, Eub.3.4; as a symbol of Christian love, 1*Ep.Cor.*16.20. II. pl., *cosmetics,* Ach.Tat.2.38 (fort. φαρμάκων). **-άτιον,** τό, Dim. of foreg.; only as pr. n., Luc.*D.Meretr.*11.2. **-η,** ἡ, = φιλία, Theognost.*Can.*112, *EM*216.3. **-μι,** v. φιλέω. **-ονίειος** (written **-ιηος**) ἀγών, festival *in honour of Philemon,* at Aphrodisias, *CIG*2811: -ίηα, τά, prob. ib.2812. **-οσύνη,** ἡ, *friendliness, affection,* Thgn.284 (v. l. συνημοσύνη), *IG*1$^{2}$.1016. **-ων,** ον, gen. ονος, *kindly, affectionate, EM*259.57: elsewh. as pr. n.

**φῐλ-ήνεμος,** ον, (ἄνεμος) *loving the wind,* πίτυς Plu.2.676a; (of bellows) αὐλός *AP*6.92 (Phil.). **-ήνιος,** ον, (ἡνία) *accepting the rein,* ἵπποι A.*Pr.*465. **-ήνωρ,** v. φιλάνωρ. **-ηραϊστής,** οῦ, ὁ, *friend of the* Ἡραϊσταί (guild of Hera-worshippers), *IGRom.*4.1732 (Samos). **-ήρεμος,** ον, *lover of silence,* epith. of the moon, *PMag.Par.*1.2808.

**φῐλήρετμος,** ον, (ἐρετμός) *fond of the oar,* of the Phaeacians, Od.8.96, etc.; of the Taphians, 1.181; κυδοιμός Nonn.*D.*39.214.

**φῑλησία,** ἡ, *thievishness,* Hsch. (pl.); cf. φιλήτης.

⊛ **Φῐλήσιος,** ὁ, epith. of Apollo, Conon 33.4 (prob. for Φιλίου), Varr. ap.Sch.Stat.*Theb.*3.283, Macr.*Sat.*1.17. II. φιλήσια, τά, = φιλοτήσια, προσφιλῆ, Hsch.

**φῐλ-ησίμολπος** [σῐ], ον, = φιλόμολπος, Pi.*O.*14.13. **-ησίμως,** Adv. *in love,* Hellanic.19(*b*) J. **-ησις,** εως, ἡ, *loving, affection,* Arist.*EN*1166$^{b}$32, 1156$^{a}$6 (pl.), Alex.Aphr. *in Top.*347.18, Plot.2.3.11. **-ησιστέφᾰνος,** ον, = φιλοστέφανος, δαίς Pi.*Pae.*1.8, cf. Aristid.*Or.*49(25).31. **-ήσῠχος,** ον, *fond of rest, peaceful,* Paul.Al.*M.*4. **-ητέον,** *one must love,* S.*Ant.*524, Arist.*EN*1165$^{b}$14.

**φῑλητεύω,** *to be a* φιλήτης, *h.Merc.*159 (v. l. φηλ-).

⊛ **φῑλήτης,** ου, ὁ, *thief,* voc. φιλῆτα Archil.46, *h.Merc.*446; φῶτες φιλῆται ib.67; φιλητέων ὄρχαμος ib.175 (prob.); φιλήτης ἀνήρ A.*Ch.*987 (1001); ὅρκος γὰρ οὐδεὶς ἀνδρὶ φιλήτῃ βαρύς S.*Fr.*933, cf. *Ichn.*332; ὃς δὲ γυναικὶ πέποιθε, πέποιθ' ὅ γε φιλήτῃσι Hes.*Op.*375; Ἑρμῆς φιλήτης Hellanic.19(*b*) J.; Ἑρμῆς φιλητῶν ἄναξ E.*Rh.*217; τῶν φιλητέων..ἄνακτα (sc. Ἑρμῆν) *Epigr.Gr.*1108 (Chios, date unknown); φιλήτης δ' Ἔρως καλοῖτ' ἄν *AP*5.308 (Dioph.); οὐκέτι χεῖρες ἔπαγροι φιλητέων Call.*Hec.*1.4.11; *latronum more, quos* φιλήτας (*hostilistas, stilistas, psti*[*l*]*listas,* codd.) *Aegyptii vocant,* Seneca *Ep.*51.13. (The spelling φιλ-, which is proved correct by φιλατία (q. v.), is found in *Epigr.Gr.* l. c., the Papyri of S.*Ichn.* l. c., Hellanic. l. c., Call. l. c. (tab. lign.), and the best codd. of the remaining Gr. passages, cf. Trypho and Hdn.Gr.ap.Choerob. in *An.Ox.*2.271; φιλ- also in Hsch., Suid.; φηλ- has MS. authority in Hes. l. c. (φιλ- Sch.Vett. cited by Eust.194.31), E. l. c., etc.)

**φῐλ-ητής,** οῦ, ὁ, *lover, AP*5.270 (Maced.). **-ητήσιος,** α, ον, *productive of love* or *friendship,* φυλακτήριον φ. Cyran.40 codd. (fort. φιλοτήσιον). **-ητικός,** ή, όν, *disposed to love,* τινος Arist.*EN*1117$^{b}$30, *Pol.*1327$^{b}$39: abs., *affectionate,* Id.*EE*1239$^{a}$27, *HA*488$^{b}$21, Plu.2.3d (Comp.): τὸ φ. Id.*Per.*1. II. *fond of kissing,* Arist.*Pr.*953$^{b}$15. ⊛ **-ητός,** ή, όν, *to be loved, worthy of love,* Id.*EN*1168$^{a}$15; τὰ φ. *objects of love,* ib.1156$^{a}$8. II. Adv. -τῶς *in a friendly spirit,* Eust.1490.47. ⊛ **-ητρον,** τό, the primary form of φίλτρον, acc. to *EM*795.17; f. l. in *AP*11.218 (Crates). ⊛ **-ήτωρ,** ορος, ὁ, *lover* (Cretan), Str.10.4.21, Hsch. 2. as fem., ἡ δὲ..κεῖται φ. τοῦδε here lies his *paramour,* A.*Ag.*1446 (τῷδε Sch., who derives φιλήτωρ from ἦτορ (cf. μεγαλήτωρ), the one *dear to* his *heart,* his *darling*). II. as Adj., *loving,* ἀγοστός, κόλπος, Nonn.*D.*3.398, 21.27. **-ήφαιστος,** ὁ, *friend of Hephaestus,* Eratosth.(?)ap.Apollod.(*FGrH*244)*Fr.*85 J.

**φῐλί-α,** Ion. -ίη, ἡ, (φιλέω) *affectionate regard, friendship* (not in A. or S.), usu. betw. equals, ἄνδρεσσι κακοῖς συνθέμενοι φ. Thgn.306, *IG*1$^{2}$.1037; ἐπαγγέλλεσθαι φ. Hdt.7.130; εἰς ἀλλήλους φιλίας ἀνακίρνασθαι E.*Hipp.*254 (anap.), cf. Democr.109, al., Hippias 17, Antipho Soph.64 (pl.), And.3.29, Pl.*Smp.*179c, etc.; φιλίας, inscr. on a bowl (perh. *loving*-cup), *BSA*32.194 (Haliartus, Hellenistic), etc.; ἡ τῆς ψυχῆς φ. διὰ τὸ ἁγνὴ εἶναι, opp. ἔρως, X.*Smp.*8.15, cf. Pl.*Phdr.*255e; opp. ἔχθρα, Isoc.1.33, Plot.3.2.2; ἡ φ. τοῦ κόσμου ἔχθρα τοῦ θεοῦ ἐστιν *Ep.Jac.*4.4; opp. μῖσος, Isoc.15.122; φ. θεῶν καὶ ἀνθρώπων Pl.*Smp.*188d; of family *affection,* X.*Hier.*3.7 (pl.); ἐν ταῖς φ. in the *family circle,* Arist.*Po.*1453$^{b}$19; of the *regard* of dependents towards their superiors, X.*An.*1.6.3; φ. ἡ πρὸς τὸν δῆμον Isoc.16.28; of *friendship* between States, ἐχρημάτισε περὶ φιλίας τοῖς Ἀθηναίοις Th.5.5; φ. καὶ ξυμμαχία Id.6.34; τῆς φ. ἀφέσθαι, τὴν φ. διαλύσασθαι, of communities, Isoc.6.11, 14.33: various εἴδη distd. by Arist.*EN*1156$^{a}$7 ff.; by the Stoics, *Stoic.*3.24, 27, 181: phrases, φ. πρός τινας ποιήσασθαι X.*Mem.*2.6.29; παρά τινων φ. λαβεῖν Id.*Cyr.*3.1.28; τισὶ διὰ φιλίας ἰέναι Id.*An.*3.2.8; εἰς φ. ἰτέον, ἔρχεται, Pl.*Phdr.*237c, *Ly.*214d; ἔστιν ἡμῖν ἐν φ. *PMich.Zen.*33.3 (iii B. C.); ἀνανεούμενος τὴν φ. καὶ ξενίαν τὴν πρότερον ὑπάρχουσαν Isoc.*Ep.*7.13; προλιπόνθ' ἡμετέρην φ. Thgn.1102; ἔλιπε φ. E.*Alc.*930 (lyr.); τῆς φ. ἐξίστασθαί τινι Lys.8.18: with Preps., διὰ φιλίας Pl.*Plt.*304e; μετὰ φιλίας X.*Mem.*1.2.10; διὰ φιλίαν, v. infr.; κατὰ φιλίαν Pl.*Lg.*823b:—the person is commonly expressed by πρός τινα, Isoc.5.32; πρὸς ἀλλήλους Id.9.57, etc.; less freq. εἰς ἀλλήλους E.*Hipp.* (v. supr.); also by object. gen., διὰ φιλίαν αὐτοῦ through *friendship for* him, Th.1.91; φ. ξυνετοῦ *friendship with* a wise man, Democr.98; so ἡμετέρη φ. *friendship with* us, Thgn.600, 1102 (v. supr.), Isoc.6.11 (v. supr.); φιλία ἡ σή X.*An.*7.7.29, E.*Or.*138, etc.: pl., φ. ἰσχυραί Hdt.3.82, Pl.*Smp.*182c. 2. *friendliness, amiability,* φ. ἄνευ τοῦ στέργειν Arist.*EN*1126$^{b}$22, cf. 1108$^{a}$28. 3. later, of lovers, *fondness,* Lxx *Pr.*5.19, *Lyr.Alex.Adesp.*1.8, *AP*5.266 (Agath.). 4. c. gen., of things, *fondness, liking for,* κέρδους Pl.*R.*581a; [τῶν ἀρχῶν] Arist.*Cael.*306$^{a}$12. 5. *the natural force which unites discordant elements and movements,* opp. νεῖκος, Emp.18, al., Isoc.15.268. II. Pythag. name for *three, Theol.Ar.*16 (not for *six,* Iamb. *in Nic.*p.34 P.). **-άζω,** *to be a friend,* τινι Lxx 2*Ch.*20.37, *BGU*1141.18 (i B. C.), Olymp. Hist.p.470 D.; φιλιάζουσαι, title of mime by Herodas. ⊛ **-ᾰκός,** ή, όν, = φιλικός, διάθεσις Plot.2.3.11. 2. **-ᾰκόν,** τό, *friendly society, funeral club, MAMA*3.580, 780, 788 (Corycus). **-αστής,** οῦ, ὁ, *reconciler,* Hsch. s. v. συναλλακτής.

**φῐλιᾱτρ-έω,** *to be an amateur doctor,* Dsc.5.19 (s. v. l.), *Alex.Praef.*, Plu.2.58a, Apollon.Cit.3, Orib.*Eup.Praef.* **-ης,** perh. gen. sg. fem. of sq., Dain *Inscr.du Louvre* 52. **-ος,** ον, *friend of the art of medicine,* A.D.*Pron.*12.10, Gal.6.269, 13.636, Ptol.*Tetr.*160. Adv. -ρως Apollon.Cit.1, cf. φιλοΐατρος.

**φῐλίδρως,** ων, gen. ωτος, *loving sweat* or *toil,* κυνηγεσία *Inscr.Cret.*1.xxii 59 (Olus, ii A. D.).

⊛ **φῐλῐκός,** ή, όν, *friendly,* ξενία Pl.*Lg.*919a; ἔργα X.*Cyr.*8.7.15; of persons, Arist.*EN*1157$^{b}$14; μεγαλόψυχος καὶ φ. Phld.*Rh.*1.209 S.; -ώτερόν ἐστι X.*Cyr.*2.4.32; τὸ -ώτατον ἦθος Id.*Mem.*3.10.3: φιλικά *proofs* or *marks of friendship,* φιλικὰ παθεῖν ὑπό τινος Id.*Cyr.*4.6.6; τὰ φ. Id.*Mem.*2.6.21, Arist.*EN*1166$^{a}$1, al.; φ. καὶ ποιητικὰ φιλίας ib.1158$^{a}$4; φιλικὸν οὐδὲν ἐποίουν X.*An.*4.1.9; φ. ἔργον Phld.*Lib.*p.59 O.; φ., τό, perh. *contribution,* 'benevolence', τὸ φ. τοῦ βοηθοῦ τῆς τάξεως *PSI*4.301.16 (v A. D.); τὸ φ. τῆς ἐμβολῆς *PFlor.*297.345, al. (vi A. D.). Adv. -κῶς, ἔχω πρὸς σέ Pl.*Grg.*485e; opp. πολεμικῶς ἔχειν, X.*HG*4.8.17; πρὸς ἑαυτὸν φ. διακεῖσθαι Arist.*EN*1166$^{b}$26; ἔχειν πρός τινα Is.7.8; -κῶς σοι ποιήσομεν *PCair.Zen.*15$^{v}$.38 (iii B. C.): Comp. -κώτερον X.*Mem.*4.3.12: Sup. -κώτατα Id.*Smp.*9.4.

⊛ **φίλιος** [ῐ], α, ον, also ος, ον E.*Hel.*629 (lyr.), Arist.*Fr.*675.13 (lyr.): (φίλος): I. Act., *friendly,* ὕμνος, ἔπη, Pi.*P.*1.60, 4.29; λόγοι, γνῶμαι, Hdt.7.163, 9.4; φρήν, ὄμματα, A.*Ag.*1491 (anap.), *Ch.*810 (lyr.); χείρ S.*OC*201 (lyr.), E. l. c. (lyr.); c. dat., *friendly to..*, φ. βροτοῖς φέγγος E.*Tr.*849 (lyr.): esp. opp. πολέμιος, *friendly,* [ἡγεῖσθαι] τοὺς αὐτοὺς πολεμίους καὶ φ. *IG*1$^{2}$.116.13; φ. πόλις, etc., Th.5.44, etc.; Ῥίον φ. τοῖς Ἀθηναίοις Id.2.86; φ. τοῖς συμμάχοις X.*Cyr.*6.1.19; οὐδεμίαν πόλιν Ἄργεος φιλιωτέρην Hdt.7.151; φ. τριήρης a *friendly* ship, i. e. one *belonging to a friendly power,* Th.4.120; (for 8.102, v. ἐπίπλοος); πρεσβεῖαι φ. καὶ πολέμιαι *to friends* and foes, X.*Lac.*13.10; πολλῶν..φιλίων καὶ πολεμίων ναυαγίων wrecks of many ships both *of friends* and enemies, Lys.2.38: ἡ φιλία (sc. γῆ, χώρα) *friendly country,* opp. ἡ πολεμία, X.*Cyr.*1.6.9, *An.*5.5.3, D.18.301; τὰ φίλια, ἀναχωρίζειν τὰ φ. *property of friends,* X.*Eq.Mag.*7.6; τισὶ φ. ἦν πρός τινας *friendship,* Hdt.3.49 (v. l. φίλα); for φίλια τέμνειν τινί, v. τέμνω II. 2: Comp. φιλιώτερος Id.7.151. 2. Ζεὺς φ., Ζεύς *as god of friendship* (his temple at Megalopolis, Paus.8.3.14), Diod.Com.2.5, 20; πρὸς Διὸς φιλίου Pl.*Phdr.*234e; μαρτύρομαι τὸν φίλιον..Δία Men.54: in familiar language without Ζεύς, ναὶ τὸν φίλιον Ar.*Ach.*730; νὴ τὸν φ. Pherecr.96 (lyr.); πρὸς φιλίου Pl.*Grg.*500b, 519e, *Euthphr.*6b; μὰ τὸν φ. τὸν ἐμόν τε καὶ σόν Id.*Alc.*1.109d; τὸν σὸν λιποῦσα φ. E.*Andr.*603:—of other divinities, φ. δαίμονες Luc.*Tox.*7; οἱ φ. θεοί Aristaenet.2.14; *kindly, gracious,* Κύπρι φ. *AP*5.10; ὦ Ζεῦ βασιλεῦ καὶ νὺξ φιλία A.*Ag.*355 (anap.). II. Pass., *beloved, dear,* of persons and things, γυνή Id.*Supp.*533 (lyr.); δμωΐδες *Ch.*719 (anap.); ὦ φ. γενέθλα S.*El.*226 (lyr.); φ. ἄλοχος E.*Alc.*876 (lyr.), 917 (anap.); βρέφη Id.*Tr.*557 (lyr.). III. Adv. -ίως Th.3.65, X.*Cyr.*6.3.13, Pl.*Lg.*768e.

**φῐλιόω,** *make a friend of,* ἐχθρούς Cyran.22:—Pass., *become friends,* Aesop.298, Sch.A.*Th.*767; censured by Poll.1.154: metaph., φιλιοῦται ψυχῇ σῶμα Alex.Aphr.*Pr.*2.67.

⊛ **Φῐλίππειος,** ον, also α, ον, ἠνορέη, κεφαλή, *AP*9.288 (Gem.), 519 (Alc.); πηγή prob. in Paus.8.7.4:—*of Philip,* ll. cc., etc. II. Φ. στατῆρες *gold didrachms coined by Philip,* Poll.9.59, 84, cf. *SIG*826 *I*15 (Delph., ii B. C.), D.S.16.8. III. **Φιλίππειον,** τό, his temple at Olympia, Paus.5.20.9. 2. **Φιλίππεια,** τά, festival in his honour, *BCH*32.110 (Delos).

**φῐλιππ-έω,** *to be fond of horses,* Theodos.Gr.p.37 G. **-ία,** ἡ, *love of horses* or *riding,* Stob.2.7.5$^{b}$11.

**Φῐλιππῐδόομαι**, *turn into a very Philippides*, πεφιλιππίδωσαι *you have become as thin as a lath*, Alex.144 (cf. Ael.*VH*10.6).

**Φῐλιππ-ίζω**, *to be on Philip's side, of his party*, D.18.176, Aeschin. 3.130. **-ικός**, ή, όν, *of* or *against Philip*, πόλεμος Plb.3.32.7: Φ. ἱστορίαι, of Theopompus: Φ. λόγοι, name of twelve speeches by Demosthenes. **-ιον**, τό, Dim. of Φίλιππος, Sch.Il.2.235. **-ισμός**, ὁ, *siding with Philip*, Sch.D.18.143. ⊛ **-ος**, ον, *fond of horses, horse-loving*, Pi.*N*.9.32, S.*Fr*r.582,859 (lyr.), E.*Hec*.9, Pl.*Ly*.212d, Ocell.4.14, etc.; φ. ἄστυ Θῆβας restd. in Pi.*Pae*.1.7, etc.:—Sup. φιλιππότατος X.*An*.1.9.5. **II.** as masc. pr. n., *Philip*.

**φῐλιπποτρόφος**, ον, *fond of keeping horses*, Phalar.*Ep*.77.3.

**φῐλίσκος**, ὁ, Dim. of φίλος, only as pr. n., Telesp.46 H., etc.

**φῐλίστιον**, τό, a plant, perh. *cleavers*, *Galium Aparine*, Hp.*Nat. Mul*.32, *Mul*.2.201: identified with ἀπαρίνη and φιλεταίριον by Gal. 19.151.

**φῐλιστορέω**, *love research*, Str.17.1.5, v.l. for φιλιατρέω in Dsc.5. 19. 2. *to be curious*, Sch.Od.9.174,229.

**φίλιστος**, ον, v. φίλος IV.

**φίλιστωρ**, ορος, ὁ, ἡ, *fond of learning*, Vett.Val.17.24; φ. λόγοι, title of work by Hierocl., Tz.*H*.7.716; without λόγοι, St.Byz. s. vv. Βραχμᾶνες et Ταρκυνία.

**φιλιτιανοί**, οἱ, dub. sens. (= *Feliciani*?) in *PMasp*.57 i 9 (vi A.D.).

**φιλίτιον**, v. φιδίτιον.

**φίλιχθυς** [φῐ], υος, ὁ, ἡ, *fond of fish*, Polem.Hist.66, Ath.8.358d.

**φῐλίων** [λῑ], ον, v. φίλος IV.

**φῐλί-ωσις** [λῐ], εως, ἡ, *making friendly*, Sch.E.*Ph*.375, al. **-ωτής**, οῦ, ὁ, *one who reconciles*, Suid. s. v. διαλλακτής. **-ωτικός**, ή, όν, *reconciling*, τῶν διαφορωτάτων dub. in *Theol.Ar*.5 (v.l. φιλωτική).

**φιλλῠρέα**, ἡ, v. φιλυρέα.

**φῐλο-**, very freq. in compos., cf. Ar.*V*.77.

**φῐλό-βακχος**, ον, *loving Bacchus* or *wine*, *AP*7.222 (Phld.). **-βαρβᾰρίζω**, *enjoy barbarisms of speech*, Phld.*Herc*.994.6. **-βάρβᾰρος**, ον, *fond of barbarians* or *foreigners*, Plu.2.857a. **-βάρβῐτος**, ον, *fond of the lyre*, Ἀνακρείων Critias 1.4 D. **-βᾰσίλειος** [σῐ], ον, *loving monarchy*, Plu.*Aem*.24. **-βᾰσῐλεύς**, έως, ὁ, *a friend to the king*, *Com.Adesp*. in *Gött.Nachr*.1922.31, D.S.17.114, Plu.*Alex*. 47, Jul.*Ep*.89b, etc. **-βᾰσῐλισταί**, οἱ, '*the King's Own*', regiment in Egypt, *UPZ*161.4 (ii B.C.), *PAmh*.2.39.12 (ii B.C.). ⊛ **-βάσκᾰνος**, ον, *envious*, Ptol.*Tetr*.161. **-βήδιοι**, οἱ, *admirers of Vedius*, *Ephes*.3 No.55. **-βιβλος**, ον, *fond of books*, Str.13.1.54. **-βοιωτός**, όν, *fond of the Boeotians*, Hdn.Gr.1.228. **-βορος**, v. φιλόβρωτος. **-βορρᾶς**, ᾶ, ὁ, *loving the North wind*, ib. 57. **-βοτρυς**, υ, *fond of bunches of grapes*, Phanocr.ap.Ath.7. 276f, Plu.2.668a. **-βουλος**, ὁ, *patron of the Senate*, *POxy*.1305 (iii A.D.). **-βούπαις**, ὁ, ἡ, gen. παιδος, *loving full-grown boys*, *AP*12.255 (Strat.). **-βρωτος**, ον, *voracious*, dub. in Herm.ap. Stob.1.49.44 (Sup. -βρωτάτου, v.l. -βορωτοτάτου; -βορωτάτου cj. Meineke). **-γᾱθής**, ές, Dor. for φιλογηθής (q.v.). **-γαιος**, ον, *loving the earth*, ὕνις *AP*6.104 (Phil.). **-γάϊος** [ᾱ], ὁ, *friend of Gaius* (i.e. Caligula), *Milet*.7.65. **-γαλλοβρᾰχειονοτύμπᾰνος**, ον, *loving the drum beaten by the arms of* Γαλλοί, Lyr. in *Philol*.80.334. **-γᾰμος**, ον, *longing for marriage*, μνηστῆρες E.*IA*392 (troch.). **-γᾰρέλαιος**, ὁ, *fond of fish-pickle and oil*, pr. n. of a parasite in Alciphr. **-γείτων**, ον, gen. ονος, *friendly to one's neighbours*, *Sammelb*.6651 (written -γίτων). **-γελοιαστής**, οῦ, ὁ, *a friend of jesters*, Poll.5.161. **-γέλοιος**, ον, *fond of the ludicrous, given to jesting*, Arist.*Rh*.1390ª23, *VV*1251ª19, Phld.*Hom*.p.26 O. **-γελως**, ὁ, ἡ, gen. ωτος, *laughter-loving*, Παρθένος Νίκη Men.616: acc. pl. φιλογέλωτας Pl.*R*.388e, cf. Arist.*Rh*.1389ᵇ10; ἐναντίον τὸ ὀδυρτικὸν τῷ φιλογέλωτι ib.1390ª24:—also acc. sg. φιλόγελων Jul.*Caes*.308d (but dat. -γέλωτι Id.*Mis*.346a): gen. sg. neut. φιλόγελω Philostr.*VS*1.21.5; nom. pl. φιλόγελω (leg. -γελῳ) Att. for φιλογέλωτες acc. to Moer.p.385 P.: acc. pl. φιλόγελως Thphr.*Fr*.124. **II.** as Subst., *jest-book*, title of work by Hierocles. **-γένεσις**, fem. Adj. *with an impulse towards generation*, οὐσία Plot.3.4.6. **-γενναῖος**, ον, *loving what is noble*: τὸ φ. D.L. 4.19. **-γερμᾰνικός**, ὁ, *loyal to Germanicus*, *IPE*2.400 (Gorgippia). ⊛ **-γέρων**, οντος, ὁ, *loyal to the Senate*, *IGRom*.4.783 (Apamea). **-γεωμέτρης**, ου, ὁ, *fond of geometry*, Ptol.*Tetr*. 163. **-γεωμετρία**, ἡ, *fondness for geometry*, Stob.2.7.5ᵏ. **-γεωργία**, ἡ, *fondness for husbandry*, X.*Oec*.20.25. **-γέωργος**, ον, *fond of husbandry*, ib.27,28, Arist.*Fr*.571, Lxx 2 *Ch*.26.10, Gal.6.552: Sup. -ότατος X.*Oec*.20.26. **-γηθής**, ές, only in Dor. form -γᾱθής: (γῆθος, γᾶθος) :—*loving mirth, mirthful*, A.*Th*.918 (lyr.). **-γλῐχέω**, *to be fractious, perverse*, Phld.*Rh*.2.190 S. **-γλῠκυς**, υ, *loving sweet things*, μέλισσα Plu.2.673e: esp. *fond of sweet wine*, Arist.*Top*.111ª3, *Pr*.875ᵇ3, Alex.Aphr.*in Top*.155.28; **φιλόγλῠκος**, ον, is prob. f.l. in Arist.*EE*1227ᵇ10, cf. Eustr.*in EN*82.33. **-γονία**, ἡ, *love of children*, Callistr.*Stat*.13. **-γονος**, ον, *loving one's children*, f.l. in Lxx 4 *Ma*.15.5 (Comp.).

**φῐλογραμμᾰτ-έω**, *love books*, Plu.*Aem*.28, 2.742a. **-ία**, ἡ, *love of books*, Stob.2.7.5ᵏ. **-ος**, ον, *loving books*, Plu.2.963b, D.L. 4.30, Ptol.*Tetr*.63.

**φῐλογρᾰφέω**, *love painting*, Plu.2.1093d.

**φῐλογυμναστ-έω**, *love gymnastic exercises*, Pl.*Prt*.342c,e, *R*.452b, Gal.17(1).211. **-ής**, οῦ, ὁ, *fond of gymnastic exercises*, Hp.*Aër*.1, Pl.*R*.535d, Ph.2.356. **-ία**, ἡ, *fondness for gymnastic exercises*, Pl. *Smp*.182c, 205d. **-ικός**, ή, όν, *of* or *for a* φιλογυμναστής, Id.*R*.456a; ἕξεις Arist.*EE*1222ª31. **-ος**, ον, f.l. for -γυμναστής, Ph.1.657.

**φῐλογύν-αιος** [ῠ], ον, *fond of one's wife*, *Sammelb*.411 (iii/iv A.D.): but usu. 2. *fond of women*, Theopomp.Hist.240, Arist.*Phgn*. 808ª36, Lxx 3 *Ki*.11.1 cod. Alex., Asp.*in EN*91.22. **-ης**, ου, ὁ, = foreg.2, Antiph.102, Lxx 3 *Ki*.11.1 cod. Vat., Ath.13.603e: acc. sg. -γύνην Plb.10.19.3: acc. pl. -γύνας Chrysipp.*Stoic*.3.167: but in early writers pl. φιλογύναικες (no sg. φιλογύναιξ occurs), Pl.*Smp*. 191d, interpol. in Aristaenet. 1.12. **-ία**, ἡ, *love of women*, Cic. *Tusc*.4.11.25, Plu.2.706b, Stob.2.7.10ᵉ; written **φιλογυναία** Sch. Gen.Il.21.498 (perh. fr. φιλογύναιος).

**φῐλο-γώνιος**, ον, *lurking in corners*: *retired*, βίος Tz.*H*.1.283. **-δαιτύμων** [ῠ], ονος, ὁ, ἡ, *fond of guests*, Hdn.Gr.2.727. **-δακρυς**, υ, gen. υος, *loving tears, given to weeping*, Poll.2.63, 6.202. **-δαμοῦσα**, f.l. for φιλόδημος οὖσα in Plu.2.745c. **-δάρειος** [ᾰ], ον, *friend of Darius*, Them.*Or*.7.95d. **-δάρτης**, ου, ὁ, *flagitiosus, plagosus*, Gloss. **-δαφνος**, ον, *loving the laurel*, epith. of Dionysus, E.*Fr*.477 (lyr.). **-δειπνιστής**, οῦ, ὁ, *one who likes giving dinners*, D.L.3.98. **-δειπνος**, ον, *fond of good dinners*, Alex.163.1, Ath. 1.6d; τὸ φ. Plu.2.726a. **II.** *fond of giving dinners, hospitable*, Ph.2. 70. ⊛ **-δέμνιος**, ον, *loving the bed, amorous*, Opp.*C*.1.161. **-δενδρος**, ον, *fond of trees* or *the wood*, *APl*.4.233 (Theaet.). **-δεπαστής**, οῦ, ὁ, *lover of cups*, Eust.868.58.

**φῐλοδεσποτ-έω**, of a slave, *love his master*, Ph.2.340. **-ος**, ον, *loving one's lord* or *master*, ἀνδράποδα φ. *slaves that hug their chains, cringing* slaves, Hdt.4.142, cf. *Com.Adesp*.24.13 D.; φύσει φ. D.S.17. 66; φιλόδουλοι καὶ φιλοδέσποτοι J.*BJ*4.3.10; δῆμος φ. Thgn.849; in good sense, φ. ἀπελεύθερος *MAMA*4.336 (Eumeneia); of dogs, Plu. 2.491c: τὸ φ. Luc.*Fug*.16; φ. θεραπεῖαι Ph.1.474: as Subst., title of plays by Timostratus, *AB*80 (where dat. -τῃ), Theognetus, Ath. 14.616a, and Sogenes, *IG*2².2323.157.

**φῐλοδημ-ία**, ἡ, *love of the people, popularity*, Poll.3.65. **-ος**, ον, *friend of the commons*, Ar.*Nu*.1187, Poll.4.34; φ. ἔργον *a popular* act, Ar.*Eq*.787 (anap.). Adv. -μως Poll.3.66. **-οτικός**, ή, όν, *inclined to be* φιλόδημος, dub. l. in D.H.8.90. **-ώδης**, ες, = foreg., D.L.4.22.

**φῐλοδίκ-αιος** [δῐ], ον, *loving the right, loving justice*, Arist.*EN*1099ª 11, Cic.*Fam*.15.19.3, Plu.*Arist*.22; θεός Ph.1.495: τὸ φ. M.Ant.1. 14. **-αστής**, οῦ, ὁ, *one who likes being a judge*, name of a play by Timocles, Ath.6.245b. **-έω**, *to be fond of litigation*, Th.1.77, Arist.*Rh*.1373ª35. **-ία**, ἡ, *litigiousness*, Sch.Ar.*Ach*.374, *Pl*. 171. **-ος**, ον, *litigious*, Lys.10.2, D.56.14, Arist.*Rh*.1400ª19.

**φῐλ-οδίτης** [ῑ], poet. voc. -ῖτα, ὁ, *friend of travellers*, Πρίηπε *AP* 6.102 (Phil.).

**φῐλοδοξ-έω**, *love fame, seek honour*, ἐπί τινι *for* or *in* a thing, Arist.*Rh*.1387ᵇ35; σωφροσύνῃ Plb.31.28.10; φ. εἰς τοὺς Ἕλληνας *seek credit* amongst them, Id.1.16.10; εἰς τὸ κοινόν, εἰς τὴν σύνοδον, *JHS*54.142 (Delos, ii B.C.); εἰς τὸν δῆμον *IG*2².1304.40; ἐν τῇ πρὸς Εὐμένην διαφορᾷ Plb.31.6.5; ἐν ἀριστοκρατικῷ πολιτεύματι Id.23.14. 1; πρός τι Id.27.9.7, Plu.2.125d; abs., Metrod.*Fr*.56, Plb.35.4.12, Phld.*Vit*.p.7 J., al.: prov., πεφιλοδοξηκὼς ἐν Σικελίᾳ καθάπερ ἐν ὀξυβάφῳ, i.e. to be a great man in a small way, Plb.12.23.7. **-ία**, ἡ, *love of fame* or *glory*, *SIG*577.3 (Milet., iii/ii B.C.), Plb.3.104.1, 24.9.8; in bad sense, *concern for one's reputation*, Phld.*Rh*.1.139 S., al., Ph.2.5, al., Gal.15.450: pl., Plu.2.1050d. ⊛ **-ος**, ον, (δόξα) *loving fame* or *glory*, Pl.*R*.480a, Phld.*Lib*.p.61 O. (prob., Comp.); περί τι Arist.*Rh*.1387ᵇ33; in bad sense, Ph.2.32, al.; εἰς τοὺς Ἕλληνας Plb.7.8.6: Sup., Id.32.8.5; τὸ φ. Luc.*Peregr*.38. Adv. -ξως *JHS*54.141 (Delos, ii B.C.), *OGI*339.98 (Sestos, ii B.C.), etc.: Sup. -ότατα *Supp.Epigr*.1.397.9 (Samos, i A.D.).

**φῐλο-δοσία**, ἡ, = φιλοδωρία, in pl., *IGRom*.4.791 (Apamea), 1572 (Teos). **-δοτος**, ον, *bounteous*, Dain *Inscr. du Louvre* 53 (near Smyrna, φιδολοτος lapis). **-δουλος**, ον, *loving slavery*, φ. καὶ φιλοδέσποτοι J.*BJ*4.3.10. **II.** in good sense, *loving one's slaves*, δεσπότης Ph.1.126. **-δουπος**, ον, *loving noise, noisy*, *AP*6.297 (Phan.). **-δρήριος**, ὁ, *friend of Dreros*, *SIG*527.47 (Cret., iii B.C.). **-δρομος**, ον, *loving the course*, Orph.*H*.14.11. **-δροσος**, ον, *loving the dew*, Nonn.*D*.1.357.

**φῐλόδυρ-μος**, ον, *fond of lamentation*, v.l. for sq. in Poll.6.202. **-τος**, ον = foreg., A.*Supp*.68 (lyr.); cf. foreg.

**φῐλοδωρ-ία**, ἡ, *fondness for giving, bounteousness*, *IG*7.101 (Megara), Luc.*Vit.Auct*.18, Ael.*VH*9.1, *CIG*2870 (Branchidae). **-ος**, ον, *bountiful*, Cratin.328, X.*Mem*.3.1.6, Plu.*Alex*.48, etc.; of God, Ph.1.50, al.; τὸ φ., = φιλοδωρία, Plu.*Ant*.43. Adv. -ρως Pl.*Tht*. 146d. 2. c. gen., *giving bountifully of*, εὐμενείας Id.*Smp*.197d. **II.** *fond of receiving gifts* or *bribes*, πόλις App.*Sam*.11. **III.** of actions, etc., *munificent*, πρᾶγμα φιλάνθρωπον καὶ φ. D.18.112.

**φῐλο-εθνής**, ές, *patriotic*, πάθος Ph.2.386. **-εργός**, όν, or **φιλόεργος**, ον, *fond of work, industrious*, κερκίς *AP*6.48, cf. 7.423 (Antip.Sid.): Sup., ib.6.288 (Leon.). ⊛ **-ζέφῠρος**, ον, *loving the west wind*, ib. 10.16 (Theaet.), 12.195 (Strat.). **-ζήλως**, Dor. **-ζάλως**, Adv. *zealously*, διατίθεσθαι ποτ' αὐτούς Hippodam.ap.Stob.4.1.95.

**φῐλοζω-έω**, = φιλοψυχέω, *love life*, παρὰ τὸ δέον, παρὰ τὸ καθῆκον, Plb.11.2.11, 30.7.8; πρὸς ἀπεγνωσμένας ἐλπίδας Id.30.8.3, cf. *Fr*.164, D.S.17.13, Ph.2.600. **II.** *desire long life*, Aristo *Stoic*.1.89. **-ία**, ἡ, *love of life*, esp. of an ignoble kind, *clinging to life*, διὰ φιλοζωΐαν Plb.15.10.5, cf. Andronic.Rhod.p.572 M.; διὰ τῆς συγγενοῦς φ. D.S.2.50; ὑπὸ φ. D.L.6.19; τὸν ἔνδοξον θάνατον τῆς ἀγεννοῦς φ. ἠλλάξαντο D.S.17.84. ⊛ **-ος**, ον, (ζωή) *fond of one's life*, with collat. sense of *cowardly*, βροτοί E.*Fr*.816.6, cf. Pl.Com.19 D., Charito 3.3, 5.2; φ. οἱ πρεσβύτεροι Arist.*Rh*.1389ᵇ32; τὸ φ. Phld.*Mort*.39

(misspelt -ζωιον, s. v.l.), *Ind.Sto.*27: as Subst., *coward*, Ph.2.269. b. of patients in disease, *desirous of living*, Aret.*SD*2.1. 2. of plants, *tenacious of life*, Thphr.*HP*7.13.4. b. *evergreen*, Nic.*Th.*68, *Al.*274.591. II. **φῐλόζῳος**, ον, (ζῷον) *fond of animals*, δημιουργός X.*Mem.*1.4.7; θεός Ph.2.305. 2. *delighting to produce life*, φύσις Cleom.1.2. **-ωτέον**, *one must cling to life*, Olymp. *in Grg.*p.183N. (sed leg. -ητέον).

**φῐλό-θᾰκος**, ον, *sedentary*, Hsch. **-θεᾱμοσύνη**, ἡ, *fondness for shows*, J.*AJ*19.1.15. **-θεάμων** [ᾰ], ον, gen. ονος, *fond of seeing, fond of shows* or *spectacles*, Pl.*R.*476a, b, Ph.1.38, al.; c. gen., ἀθλητῶν φ. Luc.*Herod.*8; generally, τὸ φ. Plu.2.704e. 2. *fond of contemplating*, τῆς ἀληθείας Pl.*R.*475e; μαθηματικῶν εἰδῶν Iamb.*Comm. Math.*20: abs., *contemplative*, Plot.3.8.4. **-θεΐα**, ἡ, *love of God, piety*, *Cat.Cod.Astr.*2.177. ⊛ **-θεος**, ον, *loving God, pious*, Arist.*Rh.*1391$^b$2, Ph.2.8, al., 2*Ep.Ti.*3.4, Demoph.*Sent.*44, Luc.*Cal.*14: Adv. -ως Poll.1.22. **-θεότης**, ητος, ἡ, *the love of God*, Men.Rh.p.361S.; condemned by Poll.1.21. **-θερμος**, ον, *loving warmth*, Thphr.*CP*2.3.3, Plu.2.648d. **-θερσίτης** [ῑ], ου, ὁ, *admirer of Thersites*, ὦ φ. φιλοκέρτομε, misquotation of Od.22.287 by Choerob. *in Theod.*1.164H.

**φῐλοθεωρ-έω**, *love speculation*, v.l. for φιλοθέωρον in Iamb. *in Nic.* p.90P. **-ητής**, οῦ, ὁ, gloss on φιλοθεάμων, Hsch., Phot. **-ος**, ον, = φιλοθεάμων 1, Alex.336, Arist.*EN*1099$^a$10, Plu.2.604c, Alex. Aphr. *in Top.*245.18; *sightseer*, Cic.*Fam.*7.16.1. II. *fond of contemplation*, Arr.*Epict.*1.29.58, Ptol.*Tetr.*203, Iamb. *in Nic.*p.90P.

**φῐλο-θήβαιος**, ον, *friend of Thebes*, name of a play by Antiphanes, cf. Them.*Or.*7.96a. **-θηλυς**, υ, *loving the female sex* or *females*, Ael.*NA*2.43. **-θήξ**, θῆγος, ὁ, ἡ, *often sharpened*, Theognost.*Can.*40. **-θηρ**, θηρος, ὁ, prob. f.l. for φιλόθηρος, Polem. *Phgn.*44.

**φῐλοθηρ-έω**, *to be fond of hunting*, Ael.*VH*9.3. **-ία**, ἡ, *love of the chase*, X.*Cyr.*2.4.26, Plu.2.633a. **-ος**, ον, *fond of hunting*, X.*Cyn.*5.25, Pl.*R.*535d, 549a: Sup. -ότατος X.*An.*1.9.6. **-θήσαυρος**, ον, *fond of accumulating treasure*, Vett.Val.18.11.

**φῐλο-θόρῠβος**, ον, *fond of noise* or *uproar*, Ptol.*Tetr.*159, *Cat.Cod. Astr.*2.173. **-θουκῡδίδης** [ῐδ], ου, ὁ, *fond of Thucydides*, *APl.*4.315 (Thom.Schol.) [ῠ l. c., wrongly]. **-θρέμμᾰτος**, ον, = sq. (or perh. *loving foster-children*), *Ath.Mitt.*24.206 (Pergam.). **-θρέμμων**, ον, gen. ονος, *fond of rearing animals*, Max.Tyr.7.7. **-θρεσκος**, ον, *loving ceremonies, pious*, βασιλῆες *Hymn.Is.*5; cf. θρεσκός, θρησκεία. **-θρεψ**, ὁ, *dear foster-child*, dub. in Keil-Premerstein *Zweiter Bericht* No.157 (Lydia, ii A.D.). **-θρηνής**, ές, = sq., Mosch.4.66. **-θρηνος**, ον, *fond of wailing, given to lamentations*, Poll.6.202, Ptol.*Tetr.*71, Nonn. *D.*9.294. **-θυρσος**, ον, *loving the thyrsus*, of Silenus, Orph.*H.*54.11; Γαλλαί *Lyr.Adesp.*121. ⊛ **-θύτης** [ῠ], ου, ὁ, *fond of sacrifices*, Ar.*V.*82, Antipho 2.2.12, Plu.*Rom.*7, etc.; φ. περὶ τὸ θεῖον Thphr. *Fr.*152. **-θῠτος**, ον, ὄργια φ. *offered by zealous worshippers*, A.*Th.*179 (lyr.).

**φῐλοΐατρος**, ον, = φιλίατρος, Procl.*Par.Ptol.*225.

**φῐλ-οίκειος**, ον, *loving one's relations*, Arist.*VV*1251$^b$35, *OGI*335.20 (Pergam., ii B.C.), prob. in Arist.*Rh.*1389$^a$37, Hierocl.p.61A.; τὸ φ. τῆς προαιρέσεως Plb.31.28.9, cf. *Cat.Cod.Astr.*2.161; πάθος *family* feeling, Ph.2.74: as Subst., title of play by Timostratus, *IG*2$^2$.2323.155. **-οικοδόμος**, ον, *fond of building*, X.*Oec.*20.29, Arist.*EN*1175$^a$34. **-οικτίρμων**, ον, gen. ονος, *prone to pity, compassionate*, E.*IT*345, Pl.*Mx.*244e, Plu.*Cam.*17, Aristid.*Or.*46(3).39, etc.: τὸ φ. Plu.2.959f, Ael.*VH*1.30. Adv. -νως Poll.8.11. **-οίκτιστος**, ον, = φιλοικτίρμων, κάρτα τοι φιλοίκτιστον γυνή S.*Aj.*580. **-οικτος**, ον, = foreg., Sch.Il.22.88. 2. *moving pity*, ἀπ' ὄμματος βέλει φιλοίκτῳ with *piteous* glance shot from her eyes, A.*Ag.*241 (lyr.). **-οινία**, Ion. -ίη, ἡ, *love of wine*, Hdt.3.34, D.S.5.26, Ath.10.430a. **-οινος**, ον, *fond of wine*, μοῦσα E.*Fr.*184 (s. v.l.), cf. Theopomp.Com.78, Pl.*Ly.*212d, *R.*475a, Arist.*Rh.*1371$^a$18, Jul. *Caes.*330c: Sup., Plu.*Cic.*27; ἔθνος Ael.*VH*3.13. **-οιστρομᾰνής**, ές, = sq., Orph.*H.*14.3. **-οιστρος**, ον, *loving frenzy*, ib.27.13. II. *loving to inspire with frenzy*, ib.32.9.

**φῐλοΐστωρ**, ορος, ὁ, ἡ, = φιλίστωρ, Steph. *in Gal.*1.265D., Hsch.

**φῐλ-οίφᾱς**, α, ὁ, Dor., (οἰφάω) *loving sexual intercourse, lecherous*, Theoc.4.62, Eust.1597.29:—also **-οιφος**, ον, Hsch.

**φῐλο-κᾰγᾰθία**, ἡ, *love of the good*, *Supp.Epigr.*6.68 (Ancyra), Bell *Jews and Christians in Egypt* 1927.40 (iv A.D., -εια), cf. φιλεκἀγαθία. **-κᾰγᾰθος**, η, ον, *loving the good*, *PLond.*5.1677.5 (vi A.D.). (Prob. short for *φιλοκαλοκάγαθος.) **-κάθᾰρος** [ᾰρ], ον, *loving cleanliness*, Vett.Val.3.24, Procl.*Par.Ptol.*90:—also ⊛ **-κάθᾰρος**, ον, Ptol.*Tetr.*63: τὸ φ. ib.62. **-κάθολος**, ον, *loving generalization*, Olymp. *in Alc.*p.160C.: also **-καθόλου** Id. *in Mete.*2.11, Ammon. *in APr.*53.32. **-καινος**, ον, *loving novelty* or *innovation*, Plu.2.731b, etc.: τὸ φ. D.H.15.6(7), Ph.2.115, Luc.*Icar.*24. **-καισαρ**, αρος, ὁ, *loyal to the Emperor*, *SIG*804.11 (Cos, i A.D.), etc.; as epithet of Zeus Polieus, *Mnemos.*55.265 (Coptos, iii A.D.). **-κᾰκος**, ον, *loving the bad* or *base*, Phld.*Lib.*p.24O., Sch.Pi.*P.*4.507.

⊛ **φῐλοκᾰλ-έω**, *love the beautiful*, Th.2.40; φιλοκαλεῖν τὴν φύσιν.. εἰκός ἐστι Chrysipp.*Stoic.*2.334. 2. *to be enthusiastic*, esp. for the beautiful or the good, περὶ τὰς εὐωχίας λαμπρυνόμενοι Str.14.1.20; εἰς ταύτην τὴν ἐπιβολήν this *project* (sc. of a beautiful tomb), D.S.1.66, cf. 13.90; περὶ παιδοτροφίαν J.*Ap.*1.12; περὶ τὴν τῶν λόγων ἐμπειρίαν D.Chr.18.1: c. inf., φ. Ἑλληνικαῖς φυτείαις διακοσμῆσαι τὰ βασίλεια Plu.*Alex.*35. 3. *beautify, elaborate*, τὰ περὶ τὴν ἐκφορὰν βασιλικῶς D.S.20.37; τοῖς πλούτοις πεφιλοκαληκότων [τὰς κτήσεις] πρὸς ἀπόλαυσιν ib.8; in literary style, *study effect*, Philostr.*VS*2.4.2. 4. Arithm., *elaborate, work out* a calculation, ὡς ἔνεστί τινα δι' ἑαυτοῦ φιλοκαλήσαντα κατανοῆσαι Iamb. *in Nic.*p.110P., cf. p.98P. 5. *repair, put in good order*, φ. καὶ βελτιοῦν *PLond.*3.1044.22 (vi A.D.):—Pass., of a church, *Palestine Dept. of Antiquities Quarterly* 3.97 (vi A.D.). **-ία**, ἡ, *love for the beautiful*, D.S.1.51. 2. *love of cleanliness*, Hsch. 3. Arithm., *calculation, working out*, Vett.Val.361.22. 4. *care, attention*, *Hippiatr.*68. **-ιον** (written -ιν), τό, *scopa*, *Gloss.*

**φῐλο-καλλωπιστής**, οῦ, ὁ, *one who loves ornament*, Ptol.*Tetr.*70. **-κᾰλος**, ον, *loving the beautiful* (both of personal and moral beauty), *loving beauty and goodness*, Pl.*Phdr.*248d, *Criti.*111e, *Com.Adesp. Oxy.*1239.18, etc.; τὸ φ. Plu.2.61d, 1026d. 2. *fond of effect and elegance*, X.*Cyr.*1.3.3; φ. περὶ ὅπλα ib.2.1.22; τὰ περὶ τὴν ἐσθῆτα φ. Isoc.1.26, cf. 10.57; of the peacock, Arist.*HA*488$^b$24. Adv., -λως ἔχειν περί τι J.*AJ*12.2.1, cf. Gal.14.218, etc.: Comp. -καλώτερον κοπρίσαι *more elaborately*, *Gp.*5.26.10. II. *fond of honour, seeking honour*, φιλοκαλώτεροι ἐν τοῖς κινδύνοις X.*Smp.*4.15, cf. Arist.*EN*1125$^b$12, 1179$^b$9. III. κατὰ τὸ φ. πειραθέντα κατανοῆσαι to see by *working out the calculation*, Iamb. *in Nic.*p.124P. **-καμπής**, ές, *easily bending, lithe*, κίρκος *AP*6.294 (Phan.). **-καρποφόρος**, ον, *bearing fruit abundantly*, θέρος ib.6.42. **-κατάσκευος**, ον, *fond of elaborate diction*, λόγος Phld.*Rh.*1.164S., cf. Procl.*Chr.*ap.Phot.*Bibl.* p.318B. **-κενος**, ον, *loving emptiness*, στόμα (= ματαιολόγον) Suid.

**φῐλοκέρδ-εια**, ἡ, *love of gain, greed*, Pl.*Lg.*649d, X.*Cyn.*13.12:—written -κερδία in D.S.5.35, Luc.*Sat.*14, cf. *EM*462.16. **-έω**, *to be greedy of gain*, X.*An.*1.9.16, *Cyr.*1.6.32. **-ής**, ές, *loving gain, greedy of gain*, Thgn.199, Pi.*I.*2.6, Ar.*Pl.*591 (anap.), X.*Oec.*14.10, etc.; φιλοχρήματος καὶ φ. Pl.*R.*581a: τὸ φ., = φιλοκέρδεια, ib. 586d. **-ία**, v. φιλοκέρδεια.

⊛ **φῐλο-κέρτομος**, ον, *fond of jeering*, Od.22.287, Theoc.5.77, *APl.*4.247 (Nilus Schol.). **-κηδεμών**, όνος, ὁ, ἡ, *fond of one's relatives*, X.*Ages.*11.13. **-κηδής**, ές, = κηδεμονικός, Ar.*Fr.*732. **-κηπος**, ον, *fond of a garden*, D.L.9.112. **-κῐθᾰριστής**, οῦ, ὁ, *lover of the cithara*, Plu.2.633a. **-κίνδῡνος**, ον, *fond of danger, adventurous*, X.*An.*2.6.7, *Cyr.*2.1.22, D.11.22; ἐπίπονος καὶ φ. βίος Isoc.10.17; θυμοειδὴς καὶ φ. Plu.*Arist.*17: Comp., Luc.*Peregr.*23: Sup., πρὸς τὰ θηρία φιλοκινδυνότατος X.*An.*1.9.6: τὸ φ. *adventurousness*, Plu.2.966a, Luc.*DMort.*14.5, etc.: Adv. -νως X.*Smp.*4.33, *OGI*248.39 (Pergam., ii B.C.); φ. ἔχειν Aristid.1.394J.: Comp. -ότερον Onos.1.24. 2. in bad sense, *foolhardy*, -ότατος πάντων ἀνθρώπων εἶ D.20.145, cf. Ael.*VH*12.23, Lib.*Ep.*14.2. Adv. -νως Luc.*DMort.*19.2; διετέθησαν Isoc.8.97. **-κισσοφόρος**, ον, *fond of wearing ivy*, of Dionysus, E.*Cyc.*620 (lyr.). **-κλαύδιος**, ον, *friend of Claudius*, *IGRom.*4.1048, *Supp.Epigr.*3.740 (both Cos, i A.D.). **-κλαυτος**, ον, *fond of weeping*, ὑάκινθοι Nonn.*D.*19.188. **-κλέαρχος**, ὁ, *friend of Clearchus*, Plu.*Art.*13. **-κλεια**, τά, festival at Delos, *endowed by Philocles* king of Sidon, *IG*11(2).287*A* 57 (iii B.C.); ἱερὸν Φιλόκλειον *Inscr.Delos* 370.39 (iii B.C.); Φ., τό (sc. ἀργύριον), *fund set up by P.*, ib.399*A* 124. **-κνήμῑς**, ῑδος, ὁ, ἡ, *fond of wearing greaves, fond of arms*, Hsch. **-κνῖσος**, ον, (κνίζω) *fond of pinching, prurient*, *AP*11.7 (Nic. or Nicarch.). **-κνῖσος**, ον, *delighting in the savour of banquets*, Nonn.*D* 19.179. **-κνώσιος**, ὁ, *friend of the Cnossians*, *SIG*527.48 (Crete, iii B.C.). **-κοινος**, ον, *liking to share the common lot*, *AP*9.546 (Antiphil.). II. *loving the common weal*, τὸ φ. Sch.S.*OT*669. **-κόλαξ**, ᾰκος, ὁ, ἡ, *fond of flatterers*, Arist.*EN*1159$^a$14, *Rh.*1371$^b$23, Phld.*Herc.*1457 *Fr.*15, Plu.2.49a. **-κόμοδος**, ὁ, *friend of Commodus*, Hdn.1.17.3. **-κομος**, ον, *fond of one's hair*, D.Chr.Κομ.Ἐγκ.p.386B. **-κονίμων** [ῑ], ὁ, ἡ, gen. ονος, (κόνις) *fond of rolling in the dust*, Epich.45 (φοινικείμονας cj. Porson). **-κοπρος**, ον, *requiring manure*, Thphr.*HP*2.7.1, 6.7.6; ζῷον *Gp.*12.9.2. **-κορίνθιος**, ὁ, *loving the Corinthians*, Them.*Or.*27.335d. **-ία**, v. φιλοκορινθιάζω. **-κοσμία**, ἡ, *love of ornament* or *show*, Plu.*Phil.*9. **-κόσμιος**, ον, *fond of orderly behaviour*, εἰς γυναῖκας *Cat.Cod.Astr.*2.171. **-κόσμος**, ον, *loving ornament*, Ael.*VH*12.1; γυνή Sext.*Sent.*513, cf. *Cat. Cod.Astr.*2.175; φ. περὶ κόμην Plu.2.976f. **-κουρος**, *attonsus*, *Gloss.* (sed leg. ψιλόκουρος). **-κρᾶτον**, τό, name of a *medicine*, Gal.14.161. **-κρημνος**, ον, *haunting steep rocks*, of goatherds, *AP*6.221.4 (Leon.). **-κρῑνέω**, v. φυλοκρινέω. **-κρότᾰλος**, ον, *loving the* κρόταλα, θυμέλαι *AP*9.505.8. **-κροτος**, ον, *loving noise*, of Pan, *h.Pan.*2. **-κτέᾰνος**, ον, *loving possessions, greedy of gain, covetous*, Il.1.122 (Sup.). **-κτήμᾰτος**, ον, = foreg., Ptol.*Tetr.*64. **-κτημοσύνη**, ἡ, *covetousness*, ib.177. **-κτήμων**, ονος, ὁ, ἡ, = φιλοκτέανος, Sol.36.19, Ptol.*Tetr.*158. ⊛ **-κτίστης**, ου, ὁ, *fond of building*, Horap.2.119, Critodem. in *Cat.Cod.Astr.*8(1).259, Theodos. Gr.p.37G. **-κτῖτος**, ον, = foreg., Nonn.*D.*40.505. **-κῠβος**, ον, *fond of dice*, Ar.*V.*75, Arist.*Phgn.*808$^a$31, Poll.6.167. **-κυδής**, ές, *loving glory, glorious*, ἥβη, κῶμος, h.*Merc.*375, 481. **-κύμαιος** [ῡ], ον, *friend of the Cymaeans*, *IGRom.*4.1302.32 (Cyme, i B.C./i A.D.).

**φῐλοκῠνηγ-έτης**, ου, ὁ, = φιλοκύνηγος, X.*Cyn.*5.14, 12.11. **-ία**, ἡ, *love of the chase*, Stob.2.7.5$^b$11. ⊛ **-ος**, ον, *loving the chase*, D.S.4.45, Plu.2.310f, Parth.10.1, Palaeph.6, *Supp.Epigr.*3.499 (Philippi, ii/iii A.D.), etc.; φ. ἐνέργεια Sostrat.4J.

**φῐλό-κῠνος**, f.l. for -κυβος in Adam.*Phgn.*1.9. **-κύριος** [ῡ], ὁ, *loyal to one's master*, of a slave, *TAM*2.466 (Patara): as pr.n., *IG*14.2074 (Rome), etc. **-κῡρος**, ὁ, *friend of Cyrus*, Str.11.11.4. **-κύων** [ῠ], -κῠνος, ὁ, ἡ, *fond of dogs*, Pl.*Ly.*212d, Ocell.4.14. ⊛ **-κωθωνιστής**, οῦ, ὁ, *fond of tippling*, f.l. for κωθωνιστής, Ath.10.433b. ⊛ **-κωμος**, ον, *fond of feasting and dancing*, epith. of Anacreon, Simon.183.5; πηκτὶς *AP*5.174 (Mel.), cf. Polem.*Phgn.*13, 67. **-κώμῳδος**, ον, *loving comedies*, title of a work by Dionysiades of Mallos, Suid. **-κωπος**, gloss on φιλήρετμος, Hsch. **-λαγνος**, ον, *fond of sexual intercourse*, Hp.*Morb.*2.51. **-λάκων** [ᾰ], ωνος, ὁ, ἡ, *fond of the Lacedaemonians*, Plu.*Art.*13, etc.; epith. of Cimon, Id. *Per.*9, *Cim.*16; name of a Comedy by Stephanus:—also **-λᾰκεδαιμόνιος**, ον, Them.*Or.*7.96a. **-λᾰλία**, ἡ, *talkativeness*, Lib.*Decl.*2. 18. **-λᾰλος**, ον, *fond of talking*, D.L.1.92. **-λάμπᾰδος**, ον, *loving torches*, epith. of Artemis, Hsch. ⊛ **-λᾱος**, ον, *loving the people*, title of Asclepius in Laconia, Paus.3.23.9. **-λήϊος**, ον, Ep. for *φιλόλειος, *loving booty*, *h.Merc.*335. **-λῐθος**, ον, *fond of precious stones*, Plu.2.462d. **-λιχνος**, ον, *loving dainties, lickerish, dainty*, *AP*6.295 (Phan.), 302 (Leon.).

**φῐλολογ-έω**, *love learning, pursue learning, study*, Sopat.6.6, Plu. 2.133b, *Cat.Mi.*6, Arr.*Epict.*3.10.10:—Pass., τὰ φιλολογηθέντα *learned discourses*, Plu.2.612e; ἅλις ὑπὲρ τῆς..τῶν σχημάτων χρήσεως..τοσαῦτα πεφιλολογῆσθαι Longin.29.2. **-ία**, ἡ, *love of argument* or *reasoning*, Pl.*Tht.*146a, Phld.*Ir.*p.18 W., Hierocl. *in CA* 12 p.446 M. 2. *learned conversation*, Antig.Car.ap.Ath.12. 548a. II. *love of learning and literature*, εὐτραπελία καὶ φ. Isoc. 15.296, cf. Arist.*Pr.*18 tit., Cic.*Fam.*16.21.4, Plu.2.645c, Arr.*Epict.* 4.4.1. ⊛ **-ος**, ον, *fond of words, talkative*, οἶνος φιλολόγους ποιεῖ Alex. 284; φ. καὶ πολύλογος, opp. βραχύλογος, of Athens, opp. Sparta, Pl.*Lg.*641e; *fond of speaking*, of Socrates, Id.*Phdr.*236e. II. *fond of dialectic, fond of philosophical argument*, opp. μισόλογος, Id.*La.* 188c; φ. γ' εἶ καὶ χρηστὸς Id.*Tht.*161a; ὁ φιλόσοφός τε καὶ ὁ φ. Id. *R.*582e, cf. Epicur.*Sent.Vat.*74, Phld.*Lib.*p.48 O. 2. *fond of learning and literature, literary*, Λακεδαιμόνιοι..ἥκιστα φ. ὄντες Arist.*Rh.*1398$^b$14; φύσει Ἀθηναῖοι φ. Str.2.3.7: opp. λογόφιλος (lover of reason), Zeno *Stoic.*1.67; φιλολόγῳ ὑποκατακλίνεσθαι φιλομαθῆ Plu. 2.618e, cf. 419d; opp. ἀπαίδευτος, Stob.4.22.107: opp. πολιτικός, Plu.*Luc.*42. 3. *student, scholar*, first used by Eratosthenes of himself, Suet.*Gramm.*10, cf. Str.14.5.15, D.H.*Comp.*25, Arr.*Epict.*2.4.1, Gal.*Libr.Propr.Prooem.*: but φιλόλογος ὁ φιλῶν λόγους καὶ σπουδάζων περὶ παιδείαν· οἱ δὲ νῦν ἐπὶ τοῦ ἐμπείρου τιθέασιν, οὐκ ὀρθῶς Phryn. 371. 4. of books, *learned*, Cic.*Att.*13.12.3 (Comp.): *suitable for a literary man, connected with learning*, ib.15.15.2. Adv. -λόγως *learnedly*, Poll.4.11, Arg.Ar.*Ra.* 5. φ. *multa*, much *learned conversation*, Cic.*Att.*13.52.2. III. *studious of words*, opp. φιλόσοφος, Plot.ap.Porph.*Plot.*14, et ap.Procl. *in Ti.*1.86 D., etc. (Freq. written parox. φιλολόγος in codd., as Pl.*Tht.*161a (cod.B), *EM*406. 10: but φιλόλογος Hdn.Gr.1.233 (from λόγος, not λέγω).)

**φῐλο-λοιδορία**, ἡ, *love of abuse*, *EM*463.43. ⊛ **-λοίδορος**, ον, *fond of reviling, abusive*, D.18.126, Arist.*HA*608$^b$10, *Pr.*875$^a$35, *Phgn.*808$^a$32, Dionys.*Av.*1.28. Adv. -ρως Poll.3.139, etc. **-λουστέον**, *one must be too fond of bathing*, οὐ φ. Aët.7.50. ⊛ **-λουτρέω**, *to be fond of bathing*, Hp.*Acut.*68. ⊛ **-λουτρος**, ον, *fond of bathing*, ib.66, Arist.*HA*605$^a$12. 2. of an eye-salve, *suitable for the bath*, ἔστι δὲ φ., ὅθεν ἐγχρίσας κέλευε λούεσθαι Aët.7.102. **-λῡπος**, ον, *fond of pain*, Plu.2.600c. **-λῡρος**, ον, *lyre-loving*, Epich.91.

**φῐλομάθ-εια** [μᾰ], ἡ, *love of learning* or *knowledge, curiosity*, Pl. *R.*499e, *Ti.*90b, Arist.*EN*1117$^b$29; φιλομαθείας χάριν Str.14.1.16: in codd. of Pl.*Ti.* l.c. and later writers (as Phld.*Mort.*33, Asp. *in EN*88.9) freq. **-μᾰθία**. **-έω**, *to be fond of learning, eager after knowledge*, Pl.*Lg.*810a, Plb.1.13.9, Phld.*Mort.*38, Corn.*ND*14; φ. περί τινος Plb.3.59.4. **-ής**, ές, *fond of learning, eager after knowledge*, Pl.*Phd.*67b, 82d, al.; ἐὰν ᾖς φ., ἔσει πολυμαθὴς Isoc.1.18: Sup. -έστατος X.*Cyr.*1.2.1: τὸ φ., = φιλομάθεια, Pl.*R.*376b, cf. 411d: Adv. -θῶς, ἔχειν Ant.Diog.11. 2. c. gen. rei, *eager after*, τῶν εἰς τὸν πόλεμον ἔργων X.*An.*1.9.5 (Sup.). **-ία**, ἡ, v. φιλομάθεια.

**φῐλο-μᾰκεδών**, όνος, ὁ, *friend of Macedonia*, Them.*Or.*10.132b. ⊛ **-μάλᾰκος** [μᾰ], ον, *loving effeminacy* or *delicacy*, Ptol.*Tetr.*162.

**φῐλομαντ-εία**, ἡ, *observance of omens*, *PMag.Par.*1.3243; v. φιαλομαντεία. **-ευτής**, οῦ, ὁ, *one who takes note of divinations* or *omens*, Pl.*Lg.*813d. **-ις**, εως, ὁ, ἡ, *devoted to oracles*, Luc.*Cont.*11, *Astr.*27.

**φῐλόμαστος**, ον, *loving the breast*, of young animals, A.*Ag.*142 (lyr.), 719 (lyr.).

**φῐλομᾰχ-έω**, *to be fond of fighting, eager to fight*, Plu.*Pomp.*65, *Caes.*52, *Fab.*5, etc.; φ. πρὸς τὸν Ἀννίβαν Id.2.195d: metaph. of argument, ib.122b, etc. **-ος** (proparox.), ον, *loving the fight, warlike*, Pi.*Fr.*164, A.*Th.*128 (lyr.); *pugnacious*, φίλερις καὶ φ. Phld.*Piet.*95, A.*Ag.*230 (lyr.).

**φῐλ-ομβρος** [ῐ], ον, *rain-loving*, νάρκισσος *AP*5.143 (Mel.):—also **-όμβριος**, ον, of a frog, Pl.*Eleg.*5.

⊛ **φῐλόμβροτος**, ον, *pleasing to mortals*, Max.456, Orph.*Fr.*280.

**φῐλο-μειδής**, ές, v. φιλομμειδής. **-μειράκιος** [ᾰ], ον, *fond of boys*, Phld.*Acad.Ind.*p.48 M., D.L.4.40. **-μεῖραξ**, ᾰκος, ὁ, ἡ, = foreg., Ath.13.603e: epith. of Artemis, Paus.6.23.8. **-μεμφής**, ές, *fond of finding fault, censorious*, Democr.109, Plu.2.707a:—irreg. Sup. φιλομεμφότατος Id.*Comp.Cim.Luc.*1. **-μετάβολος**, ον, *fond of change, variable*, φιλομετάβολόν τί ἐστιν ὁ αἰών S.E.*M.*1.82. ⊛ **-μέτριος**, ον, *loving moderation*, *POxy.*41.6, al. (iii/iv A.D.).

**φῐλομήδιον**, τό, = χελιδόνιον τὸ μέγα, Ps.-Dsc.2.180 codd. (fort. φιλομήλειον).

**φῐλόμηλος**, ον, *fond of apples* or *fruit*, Doroth.Hist.ap.Ath.7.276f.

**φῐλ-όμηρος**, ον, *fond of Homer*, of Alexander, Str.13.1.27; of Cassander, Caryst.8; of Sophocles, Eust.440.38, 851.58.

**φῐλο-μήτηρ**, ερος, ὁ, ἡ, = φιλομήτωρ, *Sammelb.*343, 5025. **-μητόρειος**, ὁ (cf. φιλομήτωρ II), *member of a deme called after Ptolemy X*, *OGI*169. **-μητορία**, ἡ, *love of one's mother*, *PMasp.*314 iii 12 (vi A.D.). **-μήτωρ**, ορος, ὁ, ἡ, *loving one's mother*, Ph.1.362, Plu.*Sol.*27, Lib.*Or.*1.58, etc.; name of a comedy by Antiph. II. title of Ptolemy VI of Egypt, *OGI*103, etc.; of Ptolemy X, ib.168.1, etc. (pl. θεοὶ Φ., of Ptol. X and his consort, ib.167, etc.); of Attalus III, ib. 764.39, Plu.*TG*14: of queen Pythodoris, *IG*2$^2$.3433. **-μίσως** [μῑ], Adv. *with hearty hatred*, Hsch. s. v. φιλαπεχθημόνως. **-μμειδής**, ές, poet. for φιλομειδής, *laughter-loving*, epith. of Aphrodite, Od.8.362, Il.3.424, Cypr.*Fr.*5, Hes.*Th.*989; Γλαυκονόμη φ. ib.256; μήτε φ. μάλα γίγνεο Naumach.ap.Stob.4.23.7: of Dionysus, *AP*9.524.22, in the form φιλομειδής also found in prose, Corn.*ND*24, Luc.*Im.*8, Aret.*CA* 2.3. Cf. sq. **-μμηδής**, ές, epith. of Aphrodite in Hes.*Th.*200 (ὅτι μηδέων ἐξεφαάνθη): acc. to Eust.439.36, Hes. here ἐκ τῶν τοῦ Κρόνου μηδέων ἐτυμολογεῖ as if Boeot.: in later Boeot. (from about iv B.C.) μηδ- would be written μειδ-. ⊛ **-μολπος**, ον, *loving the dance and song*, Pi.*N.*7.9. ⊛ **-μόνᾰχος**, ον, prob. f.l. for -μονόμαχος, *fond of gladiators*, or for -μαχος, *fond of fighting*, *Cat.Cod.Astr.*8(2).86.

**φῐλομουσ-έω**, *love music*, Phld.*Mus.*pp.17, 90 K., Ath.14.633b. **-ία**, ἡ, *love of music* or *of the Muses*, Agatharch.7, Str.14.2.21, Plu.2. 238b, Luc.*DMar.*8.2, etc. **-ος**, ον, *loving music* or *the Muses*, δελφῖνες Arion 1.8, cf. Theoc.14.61: generally, *loving music and the arts, accomplished*, Pl.*Phdr.*259b, *R.*548e, X.*Cyr.*5.1.1; μουσικοὶ καὶ φ. Phld.*Mus.*p.62 K., etc.; λόγοι φ. Ar.*Nu.*358 (anap.): τὸ φ., = φιλομουσία, Plu.2.984b, etc.

**φῐλο-μόχθηρος**, ον, *loving bad men*, Philonid.13. 2. *loving evil*, Eustr. *in EN*16.11. II. *fond of toil* or *labour*, v.l. for φιλόθηρος in Pl.*R.*535d (ap.Stob.). **-μοχθος**, ον, = φιλόπονος, Phalar. *Ep.*126, Ptol.*Tetr.*158, *Jahresh.*23 *Beibl.*178 (Thrace): neut. pl. as Adv., φιλόμοχθα Man.4.277.

**φῐλομῡθ-έω**, *to be fond of legends* or *fables*, Str.1.2.8, 9.3.11, 10.3. 23. **-ία**, ἡ, *love of legends* or *fables*, Id.11.6.2. **-ος**, ον, *fond of legends* or *fables*, ὁ φ. φιλόσοφός πώς ἐστιν Arist.*Metaph.*982$^b$18, cf. Jul.*Gal.*39b: τὸ φ., = φιλομυθία, Str.1.2.8, Longin.9.11. II. *talkative*, Arist.*EN*1117$^b$34, *Fr.*668 (Comp.).

**φῐλό-μῡρος**, ον, *loving unguents*, Alex.68: τὸ φ. *fondness for them*, Ael.*NA*16.24. **-μυρτοφᾰγηκόμος**, ον, dub. in Lyr. in *Philol.*80. 334. ⊛ **-μωμος**, ον, *given to censure, censorious*, Pl.*Prt.*346c, Ptol. *Tetr.*162, etc. **-νάμᾰτος** [νᾱ], ον, *loving water*, Orph.*H.*8.16. **-ναύτης**, ου, ὁ, *kind to sailors*, *AP*6.38 (Phil.); *loving ships*, Hsch. s. v. φιλήρετμοι.

**φῐλονεικ-έω, -ία, -ος**, v φιλονικ-έω, -ία, -ος.

**φῐλό-νεος**, ον, *loving youth* or *youths*, Luc.*Am.*24, Hld.7.20; written **φιλόνειος** *PSI*4.340.15 (iii B.C.). **-νέρων**, ωνος, ὁ, *friend of Nero*, *SIG*804.11 (Cos, i A.D.), Herzog *Koische Forschungen* 198 (Calymna).

⊛ **φῐλονῑκ-έω**, *to be fond of victory, engage in rivalry, be contentious*, mostly in bad sense, φρονήματι φιλονικῶν ἠναντιοῦτο *out of contentiousness, party spirit*, Th.5.43 (-νεικ- codd.), cf. Lys.22.8 (-νεικ- codd.); φιλονικοῦντας, ἀλλ' οὐ ζητοῦντας τὸ προκείμενον Pl.*Grg.*457d, cf. *R.*499e, Lys.33.4 (-νεικ- codd.); οἵτινες..νενικηκότες ἤδη..οὕτω φιλονικοῦσιν (v.l. -νεικ-), ὥστε..X.*HG*6.3.16: of the state, φ. παρὰ τὸ ἐπιεικές Democr.252; φ. ἄνευ γνώμης Thrasym.1.—Constr., abs., v. supr.; φ. περὶ παιδικῶν πρὸς ἀλλήλους Lys.3.40 (-νεικ- codd.); πρὸς ἀρετὴν Pl.*Lg.*731a; οὐ πρός γε αὐτὸ τοῦτο (ὃ add. codd. opt.) φιλονικοῦμεν, ὅπως..Id.*Phlb.*14b; φ. περὶ πάντων, περὶ κάλλους, Isoc.2.25, 10.48; ἀριστείων πέρι Pl.*Lg.*935c, cf. D.5.25: simply c. acc., φ. τὸ ἐμὲ εἶναι τὸν ἀποκρινόμενον *to be eager* that I should be the answerer, Pl.*Prt.*360e; the acc. is mostly a neut. Adj., τὰ χείρω φ. *to be so obstinate as to choose* the worst, Th.5.111 (-νεικ- codd.); μηδὲν φιλονίκει D.20.144 (-νεικ- codd.); φ. ὅπως..X.*Mem.*2.3.17: c. inf., φ. ἐπιδεῖξαι Plu.*Pomp.*31; ἐφιλονίκησαν (v.l. -νεικ-) αὐτοὺς is dub. in Arist.*Pol.*1306$^b$1. 2. in good sense, ἁμιλλώμενοι καὶ φ. X. *Cyr.*1.4.15; περὶ καλλίστων φ. Isoc.4.85; φ. ὅπως..Id.5.113. **-ηδόν**, *certatim*, *Gloss.* **-ητέον**, *one must strive*, ὑπέρ τινων Isoc.6.92; *one must continue one's endeavours*, Aët.9.12. ⊛ **-ία**, ἡ, *love of victory, rivalry, contentiousness*, mostly in bad sense, φ. ἕνεκα τῆς αὐτίκα Th.1.41, cf. 3.82; φ. ἀνόητος Democr.237; φ. ἢ φιλοτιμίας ἕνεκα Pl.*Lg.*860d, cf. *Alc.*1.122c; ἐκ μέθης καὶ φιλονικίας Lys.3.43; διὰ στάσιν καὶ τὴν πρὸς ἀλλήλους φ. Id.33.4; εἰς πόλεμον καταστᾶσαι πρὸς ἀλλήλας καὶ φ. Isoc.12.158; ἡ πρὸς ἀλλήλους ἔρις καὶ φ. D.9. 14, cf. Pl.*Ti.*88a; ἀλλά τίς με φ. εἴληφεν πρὸς τὰ εἰρημένα Id.*La.* 194a; ὑπὸ τῆς πρὸς τὰμὰ ἔργα φ. X.*Cyr.*8.7.12; οὐ φιλονικίᾳ γε ἐρωτῶ Pl.*Grg.*515b; ἐάν τις φιλονικίᾳ κριθῇ..δρᾶν, τεθνάτω Id.*Lg.*938c; εἰς τοσοῦτον φιλονικίας ἐλθεῖν πρὸς τὴν πόλιν, ὥστε..Id.*Mx.*243b; ἐγένετο φ. ἐν αὐτοῖς τὸ τίς αὐτῶν δοκεῖ εἶναι μείζων *Ev.Luc.*22.24: pl., φ. καὶ φιλοτιμίαι Pl.*R.*548c, cf. *Ti.*90b, D.18.246; περὶ ὁπόσων ἂν ἐγγένωνται ἀνθρώποις φ. X.*Cyr.*2.1.22; αἱ περὶ τὰς χορηγίας φ. Isoc. 7.53; φ. καὶ στάσεις Arist.*Pol.*1308$^a$31. 2. in good sense, *competition, emulation, emulous eagerness*, ἔστω τούτων..κατὰ νόμον ἅμιλλά τε καὶ φ. Pl.*Lg.*834c; φ. αὐτοῖς ἔμβαλλε X.*Cyr.*7.1.18; φιλονικίας ἐμποιεῖν περὶ τῶν καλῶν ἔργων ib.8.2.26; φ. ἐνέβαλε πρὸς ἀλλήλους τισὶ Id.*Ages.*2.8; esp. in the games, πολλὴ φ. ἐγίγνετο X.*An.*4.8.27, cf. *Lac.*4.2; διὰ φιλονικίαν Id.*Hier.*9.6; τῶν ἐργατῶν φ. πρὸς ἀλλήλους καὶ φιλοτιμία Id.*Oec.*21.10, cf. *SIG*685.12, 36 (Magn. Mae., ii B.C., found in Crete).—On the form φιλονεικία, v. φιλόνικος fin. **-ος**, ον, *fond of victory, contentious*. 1. in bad sense, οὔτε δύσηρις ἐὼν οὔτ' ἂν φ. ἄγαν Pi.*O.*6.19 (-νεικ- codd. vett.); φ. ἐστι πρὸς ὃ ἂν ὁρμήσῃ Pl.*Prt.*336e; coupled with φιλότιμος, Id.*R.*545a, 582e (v.l. -νεικ-), cf. 550b; ἐπίπονον καὶ φ. καὶ φιλότιμον..καταστήσας τὸν βίον Lys.2.16. 2. in good sense, of spirited horses, X.*Eq.*9.8 (Sup.): of persons, φ. πρὸς τὸ μὴ ἐλλείπεσθαι Id.*Mem.*2.6.5, cf. Plu.*Ages.*2 (Sup.); τὸ φ., = φιλονικία, ἔσῳζον τὸ φ. ἐν ταῖς ψυχαῖς X.*Cyr.*7.5.64. Adv. -κως *in eager rivalry*, παραθεῖν Id.*Cyn.*6.16; φ. ἔχειν πρὸς ἀλλήλους Id.*Cyr.*3.3.57, 8.4.4; φ. ἔχειν πρὸς τὸ εἰδέναι Pl.*Grg.*505e; opp. ἀνθρωπίνως, D.*Ep.*3.41. (In codd. the forms φιλόνικος, -νικέω, -νικία and φιλόνεικος, -νεικέω, -νεικία occur, without any distn. of meaning, e.g. in Isoc. we find περὶ τῶν καλλίστων ἐφιλονίκησαν 4.85, but τὰς θεὰς περὶ τοῦ κάλλους φιλονεικούσας 10.48; μὴ δύσερις ὢν.., μηδὲ πρὸς πάντας φιλόνικος 1.31; τῆς πρὸς ἡμᾶς φιλονικίας 4.19, but **φιλονεικία** in the same sense, 12.158; φιλόνῑκος is implied by Arist.*Rh.*1389$^{a}$12 (where -νεικ-, though found in good codd., as also in 1363$^{b}$1, 1368$^{b}$21, 1370$^{b}$33, *Phgn.* 809$^{b}$35, must be f.l.), καὶ φιλότιμοι μέν εἰσι [οἱ νέοι], μᾶλλον δὲ **φιλόνικοι**· ὑπεροχῆς γὰρ ἐπιθυμεῖ ἡ νεότης· ἡ δὲ **νίκη** ὑπεροχή τις, cf. Poll. 1.178, *AB*315; the compd. of φιλο- and νεῖκος would be *φιλονεικής; the sense *contentious* arises naturally from *fond of victory*; in *SIG* 685 (v. φιλονικία sub fin.) we have φιλονικίαν ll.12,36, and φιλονικίᾳ in *OGI*335.7 (Pergam., decree of Pitane, ii B.C.); -νῑκ- is also found in late documents, as *POxy.*157.1 (vi A.D.).) **-νομος**, ον, *loving the Jewish law*, *Supp.Epigr.*4.144 (Rome). **-νοσέω**, *to be usually sick*, Alciphr.2.2. **-νύμφιος**, ον, *loving the bridegroom* or *bride*, *AP* 10.21 (Phld.). **-ξεινος**, ον, poet. for φιλόξενος.

**Φῐλοξένειος**, ον, *invented by Philoxenus*, πλακοῦντες Ath.1.5d; wrongly written **-ξένιοι** in Poll.6.78.

**φῐλοξεν-έω**, *entertain hospitably*, Phld.*Hom.*p.63 O., D.S.31.18, Eust.1654.56, *EM*402.8; φ. τινὰς χρηστοῖς ἤθεσι *IPE*1$^{2}$.39.22 (Olbia, iii(?) A.D.):—Pass., ὑπό τινος Ant.Diog.3. II. *love foreign fashions*, περί τι φ. Str.10.3.18. ⊛ **-ία**, Ion. **-ίη**, ἡ, *hospitality*, *IG* 1$^{2}$.530, Pl.*Lg.*953a (pl.), A.R.3.1108, Plb.4.20.1, *Ep.Rom.*12.13, *BMus.Inscr.*1061 (Cyrene, ii A.D.), *AP*9.160, Chor.32.148 p.378.21 F.-R. **-ικός**, ή, όν, *hospitable*, Eust.158.37. **-ος**, poet. **-ξεινος**, ον:—*loving strangers*, *hospitable*, Od.6.121, 8.576, al., Pi.*O.*3.1, *N.*1.20, X.*HG*6.1.3, 1*Ep.Ti.*3.2, etc.; παθεῖν φιλόξενον ἔργον to meet with an act *of hospitality*, Pi.*I.*2.24; τὸ εἶναι φ. Arist.*VV*1250$^{b}$34, cf. 1251$^{b}$35; φιλόξεν' ἐστὶν (sc. τὰ δώματα) Αἰγίσθου διαί A.*Ch.*656: Sup. -ώτατος Id.*Fr.*196, Cratin.1.2; -έστατος E.*Fr.*879. Adv. -νως Isoc.4.41.

**φῐλοξενοφῶν**, ῶντος, ὁ, *fond of Xenophon*, Hdn.Gr.1.40.

**φῐλ-οξύτονος** [ῠ], ον, *usually oxytone*, προθέσεις Eust.72.39.

**φῐλό-οινος**, ον, poet. for φίλοινος, *AP*5.260 (Agath.). **-πᾰθής**, ές, *devoted to one's passions*, *sensual*, Ph.1.85, al. **-παιγμοσύνη**, ἡ, *love of play* or *sport*, Poll.5.161. **-παίγμων**, ον, gen. ονος, (παίζω) *fond of play*, *sportive*, ὀρχηθμός Od.23.134; ὀρχηστῆρες Hes.*Fr.*198, cf. Ar.*Ra.*333 (lyr.), Them.*Or.*24.301c, Lib.*Decl.*30.68: of the lion, πρὸς τὰ σύντροφα καὶ συνήθη σφόδρα φ. Arist.*HA*629$^{b}$11: epith. of Pan, *BCH*50.240 (Thasos, iii/ii B.C.). The more Att. form **φιλοπαίσμων** occurs in Pl.*R.*452e, *Cra.*406c; cf. Poll.5.161. Adv. -μόνως ibid. **-παίγνιος**, ον, *fond of toys*, Vett.Val.3.25.

**φῐλοπαιδ-εία**, ἡ, *love of boys*, Plu.2.1073c. **-ία**, ἡ, *love of one's children*, Sch.Il.3.259.

**φῐλοπαίκτης**, ου, ὁ, = φιλοπαίγμων, Vett.Val.75.6, Poll.5.161; also **φιλοπαίστης**, ibid.

⊛ **φῐλό-παις**, παιδος, ὁ, ἡ, *loving boys*, Pl.*R.*474d, Theoc.12.29, Phld. *Acad.Ind* p.48 M.; φ. χέλυς *singing the love of boys*, Simon.183.6; φ. νόσος Call.*Epigr.*47.6. 2. *loving one's children*, Aristaenet.1.13, *IG*12(5).292.7 (Paros), Jul.*Ep.*89b; χελιδών *AP*10.16 (Theaet.). 3. φ. νόμοι laws *which favour children*, Luc.*Abd.*18, 19. II. = πράσιον, Plin.*HN*20.241, Ps.-Dsc.3.105. **-παίσμων**, v. φιλοπαίγμων. **-παίστης**, ου, ὁ, = φιλοπαίγμων, Poll.5.161, Ael. *NA*4.34, 5.39, Suid. s.v. Θεόπομπος..κωμικός. **-πάλαιστρος** [πᾰ], ον, *loving the palaestra*, Vett.Val.43.17, 201.27, Rhetor. in *Cat.Cod. Astr.*8(4).214, Critodem. in *Cat.Cod.Astr.*8(1).259, Hsch. s.v. φιλέψιος. **-πάννῠχος**, ον, *friend of all-night festivals*, *AP*5.122 (Phld.), Orph.*H.*3.5. ⊛ **-παππος**, ὁ, *loving one's grandfather*, title of Antiochus of Commagene, *IG*2$^{2}$.3451; -παπποι θεοί *loving their grandparents*, title of Ptolemy XI and Tryphaena, *Bull.Inst.Ég.*1912.176. **-παράβολος**, ον, *fond of daring*, *venturous*, Plu.*Phil.*9; φ. θεραπεία *heroic* treatment, Asclep.ap.Cael.Aur.*CP*1.15. **-πάρθενος**, ον, *loving virgins*, Ach.Tat.8.13, Nonn.*D.*14.66, al.; as name of a horse, *Mélanges Beyrouth* 15.111 (Beyrout). II. *loving virginity*, Nonn.*D.*2.122, al. **-παρρησιαστής**, οῦ, ὁ, *lover of frankness*, Phld.*Lib.*p.56 O. **-πάρυγρος**, ον, *loving damp*, φιλογεώργους καὶ φ. *Cat.Cod.Astr.*8(4).167. **-πάτηρ** [ᾰ], ερος, ὁ, ἡ, = φιλοπάτωρ, *Sammelb.*343.14. **-πατρία**, ἡ, *love of one's country*, *patriotism*, Ar.*V.*1465 (lyr.). **-πατρις**, ιδος, ὁ, ἡ, but acc. φιλόπατριν Plb.1.14.4, *AP*7.235 (Diod.Tars.), Plu.*Cleom.* 10, Luc.*Peregr.*15, etc.:—*loving one's country*, *patriotic*, Plb. l.c., *AP* l.c., Cic.*Att.*9.10.5, Plu.*Fab.*12, etc.; freq. as honorary title, *SIG*804.12 (Cos, i A.D.), etc.; φιλοπάτριδας (acc. pl.) καὶ φιλοπάτορας *Sardis* 7(1).No.41*.10, etc.; τὸ φιλόπατρι, = φιλοπατρία, Plu.2.119c. **-πάτρως**, ω, ὁ, ἡ, *lover of one's uncle*, *Sammelb.*2007. ⊛ **-πάτωρ** [ᾰ], ορος, ὁ, ἡ, *loving one's father*, E.*Or.*1605, *IA*638, Arist.*EN*1148$^{a}$34, Jul.*Ep.* 89b; title of Ptolemy IV, *OGI*89, al. (θεοὶ Φ., of himself and his consort, ib.93, etc.); of Ptolemy IX, ib.739; of Ariobarzanes II, ib.354; of Ariarathes V, ib.352. **-πενθής**, ές, *indulging in mourning*, γυναῖκες Plu.2.113a (Comp.), etc.; πόθος φ. Gorg.*Hel.*9; τὸ φ. Plu.2. 822c. **-πένταθλος**, ον, *fond of the* πένταθλον, Sch.Pi.*N.*7.9. **-πέρσης**, ου, ὁ, *friend of the Persians*, of Cyrus, Them.*Or.*10.132b, cf. Men.Prot.p.88D. **-πευθής**, ές, *fond of inquiring*, *curious*, φύσει φ. ἄνθρωπος S.E.*M.*1.42; τὸ φ. Plu.2.515f.

⊛ **φῐλοπευστ-έω**, *to be fond of inquiry*, Plb.3.59.6, D.S.25*Fr.* 11, Ph.1.242, Vett.Val.355.22, etc.: c. acc., *inquire curiously about*, τὰ μὴ προσήκοντα Str.14.1.32, cf. Procop.Gaz.p.164 B. **-ης**, ου, ὁ, = φιλοπευθής, Ptol.*Tetr.*160. **-ία**, ἡ, *fondness for inquiry*, *curiosity*, Phld.*Rh.*1.96 S., Plu.2.518c. **-ος**, ον, = φιλοπευθής, Phot., Suid. (nisi leg. -πευστικός).

**φῐλό-πικρος**, ον, *fond of what is bitter*, Arist.*EE*1227$^{b}$11. **-πιστεύομαι**, *trust a friend*, Phld.*Vit.*p.16 J. **-πλάκουντος** [ᾰ], ον, *cake-loving*, *Com.Adesp.*31 D. **-πλάτᾰνος** [πλᾰ], ὁ, *Plane-lover*, name of a lover, Aristaenet.1.3. **-πλάτων** [ᾰ], ωνος, ὁ, ἡ, *fond of Plato*, Phld.*Ind.Sto.*61, Alex.Aphr. *in Top.*530.11, D.L.3.47, Attic. ap.Eus.*PE*15.4. **-πλεκτος**, ον, *usually braided*, κόμα *AP*6.206 (Antip.Sid.; fort. **-πλαγκτος** 'errant'). **-πληκτικός**, ή, όν, *given to striking*, γυνὴ ἀνδρὸς -ώτερον Ar.ap.Sch.Il.20.252 et ap. Eust. 1206.55 (misquotation of Arist.*HA*608$^{b}$10). **-πλόκᾰμος**, ον, *loving tresses* or *curls*, Euph.47. **-πλοος**, ον, contr. **-πλους**, ουν, *familiar with sailing*, *AP*6.236 (Phil.).

⊛ **φίλ-οπλος**, ον, *loving arms*, *AP*11.195 (Diosc.), *Epigr.Gr.*223.7 (Milet.), *Ephes.*3 Nos.55,70, Vett.Val.17.24, Ptol.*Tetr.*61,69.

**φῐλοπλούσιος**, ον, = φιλόπλουτος, Hld.5.12.

**φῐλοπλουτ-έω**, *love* or *seek riches*, Plu.2.524f. **-ία**, ἡ, *love of riches*, Hierocl.p.55 A., Plu.*Lyc.*30, *Crass.*2, etc. **-ος**, ον, *loving riches*, *eager to grow rich*, Plu.2.140f, Luc.*Dom* 5; φ. ἅμιλλα *eager* pursuit *of wealth*, wealth eagerly sought for, E.*IT*412 (lyr.); τὸ φ., = φιλοπλουτία, Plu.2.793e.

**φῐλοποι-έω**, *make a friend of*, *AB*428:—mostly in Med., *make one's friend*, *attach to oneself*, τινα Plb.3.42.2, 32.1.7, Aristeas 209, Phld. *Hom.*p.63 O., D.S.19.96, dub. in *SIG*656.27 (Abdera, found at Teos, ii B.C., leg. ἐφιλοπονοῦντο), v.l. in D.H.8.34. **-ησις**, εως, ἡ, = *conciliatio*, *Gloss.* **-ητής**, οῦ, ὁ, *a friend of poets*, Pl.*R.*607d. **-ητικός**, ή, όν, *good at making friends*, *conciliatory*, only in Adv. φιλοποητικῶς Phld.*Herc.*1251.14. **-ία**, ἡ, *making friends*, εἶναι τὸν ἔρωτα ἐπιβολὴν φιλοποιΐας *Stoic.* (Zeno(?)) 3.180 (v.l. φιλευποιΐα), cf. 181, Phld.*Herc.*1251.22, Andronic.Rhod.p.572 M., S.E.*M.*7.239. **-ός**, όν, *making friends*, τράπεζα Plu.*Cat.Ma.*25; νόμος Hierocl. *in CA* 6 p.428 M.; τὸ φ. Plu.2.612d, 632e. II. = φιλεργός, Hsch.

**φῐλοπόλεμος**, ον, poet. **φιλοπτ-** (so always in Hom., as also in *IG*2$^{2}$.3606.4), *fond of war*, *warlike*, Il.16.65,90, al. (never in Od.), Pl.*Ti.*24c; freq. in bad sense, opp. πολεμικός, Plu.*Comp.Eum.Sert.* 2, cf. Id.*Fab.*19, *Marc.*1; τὸ φ. D.S.2.21, Plu.*Num.*8, etc. Adv. -μως Isoc.8.97.

⊛ **φῐλόπολις**, ὁ, ἡ, poet. **φιλόπτολις** E.*Rh.*158: acc. φιλόπολιν Pi.*O.* 4.18, Pl.*Ap.*24b, Isoc.2.15, X.*Hier.*5.3, etc.; pl. φιλοπόλεις A.*Th.* 176 (lyr.); also pl. -πόλιδες, -πόλιδας, Pl.*R.*470d, 503a. I. *loving the city*, δαίμονες A. l.c. II. *loving one's city*, *patriotic*, δαίμων Ar.*Pl.*726 (where there is a play on the first sense), cf. 900, Th.2.60, 6.92, Pl. ll.cc., etc.; φ. Ἡσυχία Pi. l.c.; φ. ἀρετή *patriotism*, Ar.*Lys.* 547 (lyr.); so τὸ φιλόπολι Th.6.92.

⊛ **φῐλοπολίτης** [ῑτ], ου, ὁ, *loving one's fellow-citizens*, Lxx 2 *Ma.*14.37, D.Chr.1.28, Plu.*Lyc.*20, *Flam.*13.

**φῐλοπολύγελως** [ῠ], ωτος, ὁ, ἡ, *loving much laughter*: poet. φιλοπουλύγελως *AP*5.242 (Maced.).

**φῐλόπομπος**, ον, *amator jactantiae*, *Gloss.* (sed leg. φιλόκομπος).

**φῐλοπον-έω**, *love labour*, *be laborious* or *industrious*, X.*Lac.*5.8, Phld.*Rh.*1.35 S.: c. acc., τὰ διὰ τοῦ σώματος Pl.*R.*535d; τὸ φιλοπονεῖν, = φιλοπονία, X.*Oec.*21.6, Philem.238; τὸ περὶ τὴν ἀρετὴν φ. Isoc.1. 46; *take great care of*, βρέφος *POxy.*1069.23 (iii A.D.); *take heed to*, τὰ γράμματά μου *PIand.*97.6 (iii A.D.); *build as a labour of love*, μνημεῖον *Docum. Ant. dell' Africa Italiana* 2.118 (Cyrene):—Med., φιλοπονεῖσθαι περί τινος Arist.*Rh.*1405$^{a}$6, cf. Theopomp.Hist.226:—Pass., *to be elaborated*, ἐμμέτρως φιλοπονηθέντα *Cat.Cod.Astr.*8(1). 141. **-ηρία**, ἡ, *love of bad men and actions*, Thphr.*Char.*29.1. **-ηρος**, ον, *friend to bad men*, ibid., Din.*Fr.*89.37, Arist.*EN*1165$^{b}$16, Plu.*Alc.*24. II. *lover of evil*, Ph.2.4. **-ία**, ἡ, *love of labour*, *industry*, Pl.*R.*535d, *Stoic.*3.64,171, Phld.*Rh.*1.115 S., *TAM*2(1).283 (Xanthus); καρτερία καὶ φ. Pl. *Alc.*1.122c; ἡ περὶ τὴν παιδείαν φ. Isoc. 1.45; pl., Id.15.291, Plb.8.10.6, etc.; ἡ τῶν δρόμων φ. *laborious practice* of.., D.61.24; φ. ἐν τοῖς γυμνασίοις ib.26; so, as an event in competitions of ἔφηβοι, *SIG*1061.5 (Samos, ii A.D.). **-ος**, ον, *laborious*, *industrious*, Hp.*Aër.*1, S.*Aj.*879 (lyr.), Pl.*Phdr.*248d, etc.; πρός τι Ael.*VH*1.12; opp. ἄπονος, Pl.*R.*535d; τῷ σώματι φ. Isoc.1.40; φ. περὶ τὰ αὑτῶν ἔργα X.*Mem.*3.4.9: of dogs, ib.4.1.3, Poll.5.60; τὸ φ., = φιλοπονία, Plu.2.88d. Sup., -ώτατος τῶν Ἑλλήνων Isoc.6.56. 2. of things, *toilsome*, *laborious*, πόλεμος X.*Cyr.*7.5.47 (Sup.); φ. βίος Ocell.4.10; φιλόπονόν [ἐστι], c. inf., X.*Cyn.*6.8. 3. Adv., -νως ἔχειν πρὸς τοὺς πολέμους Id.*HG*6.1.6; φ. ἔπραξα D.18. 193; φ. καὶ φιλοκινδύνως *OGI*553.6 (Xanthus, i B.C.); τὴν σταφίδα κόπτε φ. Gal.12.868: Comp. -ώτερον Isoc.9.73: Sup. -ώτατα Plb. 10.41.3, 12.26$^{D}$.5, Demetr.Lac.*Herc.*1012.52.

**φῐλο-ποσία**, ἡ, *love of drinking*, *fondness for wine*, X.*Mem.*1.2.22, Arist.*Pr.*872$^{a}$6, Jul.*Caes.*327c; pl., Pl.*Phd.*81e. **-ποτέω**, *to be fond of drinking*, Phan.Hist.15, Poll.6.20. **-πότης**, ου, ὁ, *lover of drinking*, *fond of wine*, Hdt.2.174, Hp.*Aër.*1, Ar.*V.*79, Eup.208 (of Cimon), Antipho Soph.76, Arist.*HA*559$^{b}$2, *Pr.*874$^{a}$37 (wrongly accented -πότων), Ath.10.430c. **-ποτία**, ἡ, = φιλοποσία, Phryn. *PS* p.35 B. **-πότις**, ιδος, fem. of φιλοπότης, Ael.*VH*2.41. **-ποτμος**, ον, *fond of misery*, *unfortunate*, Plu.2.986d (Sup.).

**φῐλοπουλύγελως**, v. φιλοπολύγελως.

**φῐλοπραγμ-ᾰτίας**, ου, ὁ, = φιλοπράγμων, Cratin.27D., D.C.61.4. **-ονέω**, *busy oneself about*, τὰ ἄλλα D.C.77.17, cf. *PMasp.*3.9 (vi A.D.); *seek busily after*, v.l. for φιλοφρονέω, Nicostr.ap.Stob.4.22.102. II. *to be meddlesome*, *PMasp.*4.5 (vi A.D.). **-ονία**, ἡ, = sq., Sch.E.*Hipp.*73. **-οσύνη**, ἡ, *busy disposition, meddlesomeness, restless habit of life*, φεύγοντος τάς τε τιμὰς καὶ ἀρχὰς καὶ δίκας καὶ τὴν τοιαύτην πᾶσαν φιλοπρ. Pl.*R.*549c; of Philip of Macedon, D.1.14, 4.42; of Meidias, Id.21.137; synon. with πολυπραγμοσύνη, Arist.*Top.*111ª10. **-ων**, ον, gen. ονος, *fond of business*; mostly in bad sense, like πολυπράγμων, *meddlesome, a busybody*, Lycurg.3, Is.4.30, Jul.*Caes.*315c; name of a comedy by Crito; τὸ φ., in good sense, Plu.2.515f. Adv. Comp. -έστερον, φ. ἀναφέρειν τι εἰς τὰ ἱερὰ γράμματα Str.17.1.5.

**φῐλό-πρακτος**, ον, = φιλοπράγμων, Ptol.*Tetr.*160. **-πρεπής**, ές, *fond of propriety* or *decorum*, f.l. for μεγαλοπρεπής in D.H.*Rh.*3.4. **-πρόβᾰτος**, ον, *loving sheep*, *IG*2.2453.

**φῐλοπροσηγορ-ία**, ἡ, *easiness of address, affability*, Isoc.1.20, D.H.*Rh.*5.1. **-ος**, ον, *affable*, Isoc.1.20, Poll.5.137, Plu.2.10a, etc. Adv. -ρως Poll.5.139.

**φῐλο-προσηνής**, ές, *courteous*: Sup. Adv. -έστατα Cic.*Att.*5.9.1.

**φῐλοπρωτ-εία**, ἡ, *love for the first rank*, Zos.4.51; written -πρωτία in Phld.*Rh.*2.159S., Jul.*Caes.*319d, Porph.*Plot.*10. **-εύω**, *wish* or *strive to be first*, 3*Ep.Jo.*9. **-ος**, ον, *fond of being first*, Plb(?).*Fr.* (post 29.18) ap.Suid. s.v. πρωτόπειρος, Plu.2.471d, Artem.2.32, etc.; τὸ φ., = φιλοπρωτεία, Plu.*Sol.*29, *Alc.*2, etc.

**φῐλοπτόλεμος, φῐλόπτολις**, poet. for φιλοπόλεμος, φιλόπολις.

**φῐλό-πτορθος**, ον, *loving young shoots*, epith. of bees, Nonn.*D.*13.261. **-πτωχία**, ἡ, *love for the poor*, *AP*15.34 [χῐ, Arethas]. **-πῡγιστής**, οῦ, ὁ, = Lat. *paedico*, *PTeb.*1.17 (i B.C.). **-πῡρος**, ον, *loving wheat*, of Demeter, *AP*6.36 (Phil.). **-πυστος**, ον, glossed by φιλοπράγμων, Hsch.

**φῐλ-οπωριστής**, οῦ, ὁ, *loving autumn-fruits*, *AP*9.563 (Leon.).

**φῐλ-οργής**, ές, *passionate*, Nic.*Al.*175. **-όργιος**, ον, *loving passionate rites*, Κύπρις *AP*10.21 (Phld.); with ref. to Dionysus, *IG*2².5021.

❀ **φῐλορήτωρ**, ορος, ὁ, *fond of rhetoric*, Cic.*Att.*1.13.5. 2. *loving rhetoricians*, Phld.*Rh.*2.218S.

**φῐλ-όρθιος**, ον, *friend of straightness*, σελίδων κανόνισμα *AP*6.295 (Phan.). **-οριστία**, ἡ, *fondness for definition*, Gal.8.698. **-ορμίστειρα**, ἡ, *she who loves to bring to harbour*, Κύπρις *AP*10.21 (Phld.). **-ορνῑθία**, ἡ, *fondness for birds*, Ar.*Av.*1300, Philostr.*VA*6.36. **-ορνις**, ῑθος, ὁ, ἡ, *fond of birds*, Ocell.4.14, Plu.*Num.*4, Opp.*C.*1.78, Ael.*NA*6.29, Iamb.*VP*31.212. II. *loved* or *haunted by birds*, πέτρα A.*Eu.*23.

**φῐλο-ρρημᾰτία**, ἡ, *love of choice expressions*, D.Chr.12.66. **-ρρυθμος**, ον, *loving rhythm* in music, Plu.2.1138b. **-ρρώθων**, ωνος, ὁ, ἡ, *attached to the nose*, κημός *AP*6.246 (Phld. or Marc.Arg.). **-ρρώξ**, ῶγος, ὁ, ἡ, (ῥώξ (B), ῥάξ) *loving grapes*, ἄμπελος ib.7.22 (Simm.).

**φῐλ-όρτυξ**, ῠγος, ὁ, ἡ, *fond of quails*, Pl.*Ly.*212d. **-ορχήμων**, ον, gen. ονος, = sq., Arr.*An.*6.3.5. **-ορχηστής**, οῦ, ὁ, *loving the dance*, D.Chr.32.59, Aristid.Quint.2.6, Ptol.*Tetr.*164. **-ορχικός**, ή, όν, *loving the dance*, v. φιλαρχικός.

❀ **φῐλορώμαιος**, α, ον, *a friend to the Romans*, *SIG*804.12 (Cos, i A.D.), *IPE*2.34.8 (Panticapaeum, iii A.D.), Str.14.2.5, Plu.*Crass.*21, etc. The accent φιλορωμαῖος, found in *EM*396.45, etc., is condemned by Hdn.Gr.1.133 (φιλορρώμαιος occurs as v. l. in codd.).

❀ **φῖλος**, εος, τό, = φιλία, *Epigr.Gr.*289.6 (Caria, written φεῖλος).

❀ **φίλος**, η, ον, also ος, ον Pi.*O.*2.93: [ῐ: but Hom. uses the voc. φίλε with ῑ at the beginning of a verse, v. infr.]: I. pass., *beloved, dear*, Il.1.20, etc.; παῖδε φίλω 7.279; freq. c. dat., *dear* to one, μάλα οἱ φ. ἦεν 1.381; φ. ἀθανάτοισι θεοῖσι 20.347, etc.: voc., φίλε κασίγνητε (at the beginning of the line) 4.155, 5.359; with neut. nouns, φίλε τέκνον Od.2.363, 3.184, etc.; but φίλον τέκος Il.3.162; also φίλος for φίλε (Att., acc. to A.D.*Synt.*213.28), φίλος ὦ Μενέλαε Il.4.189, cf. 9.601, 21.106, al., Pi.*N.*3.76, A.*Pr.*545 (lyr.), E.*Supp.*277 (lyr.), Ar.*Nu.*1168 (lyr.): gen. added to the voc., φίλ' ἀνδρῶν Theoc.15.74, 24.40; ὦ φίλα γυναικῶν E.*Alc.*460 (lyr.): as Subst.: a. φίλος, ὁ, *friend*, κουρίδιος φίλος, i.e. husband, Od.15.22; φίλοι *friends, kith and kin*, νόσφι φίλων Il.14.256; τῆλε φίλων Od.2.333, cf. 6.287; φ. μέγιστος my greatest *friend*, S.*Aj.*1331; φίλοι οἱ ἐγγυτάτω, οἱ ἔγγιστα, Lys.1.41 codd., Plb.9.24.2; after Hom. freq. with a gen., ὁ Διὸς φίλος A.*Pr.*306; τοὺς ἐμαυτοῦ φ., τοὺς τούτων φ., Aeschin.1.47; φ. ἐμός S.*Ph.*421; τῶν ἐμῶν φ. ib.509; τοὺς σφετέρους φ. X.*HG*4.8.25: prov., ἔστιν ὁ φ. ἄλλος αὐτός *a friend* is another self, Arist.*EN*1166ª31; κοινὰ τὰ τῶν φ. Pl.*Phdr.*279c, cf. Arist.*EN*1159ᵇ31; οὐθεὶς φ. ᾧ πολλοὶ φ. Id.*EE*1245ᵇ20; also of *friends* or *allies*, opp. πολέμιοι, X.*HG*6.5.48; φ. καὶ σύμμαχος D.9.12, etc.; of *a lover*, X.*Mem.*3.11.4 (in bad sense, *Lac.*2.13); φίλε *my friend*, as a form of courteous address, *Ev.Luc.*14.10, etc.; in relation to things, οἱ μουσικῆς φ. E.*Fr.*580.3; ἀληθείας Pl.*R.*487a; τῶν εἰδῶν Id.*Sph.*248a; Χίους φ. ποιῆσαι Lys.14.36, etc.; ποιεῖσθαι Luc.*Pisc.*38; κτᾶσθαι Isoc.2.27, cf. Th.2.40; φίλους τιθέντες τούς γε πολεμιωτάτους E.*Hec.*848; φίλῳ χρῆσθαί τινι Antipho 5.63; ἡμᾶς ἔχειν φίλους And.1.40; for Hdt.3.49, v. φίλιος. b. φίλη, ἡ, *dear one, friend*, κλῦτε, φίλαι Od.4.722; λόγοις ἐγὼ φιλοῦσαν οὐ στέργω φίλην S.*Ant.*543; of a *wife*, φίλην τινὰ ἄγεσθαι take as one's *wife*, Il.9.146, 288; ἡ Ξέρξου φ., of his *mother*, A.*Pers.*832; of a *mistress*, X.*Mem.*2.1.23, 3.11.16; φίλην ποιήσασθαί τινα Antipho 1.14. c. φίλον, τό, *an object of love*, τὸ φ. σέβεσθαι to reverence *what* the city *loves*, S.*OC*187 (lyr.): addressed to persons, *darling*, φ. ἐμόν Ar.*Ec.*952 (lyr.); so φίλτατον ib.970; τὰ φίλτατα *one's nearest and dearest, dear ones*, such as wife and children, A.*Pers.*851, *Eu.*216, S.*OT*366, *OC*1110, E.*Med.*16: v. φίλτατος; τἀμὰ φίλα, τὰ σὰ φ., Id.*Ion* 523 (troch.), 613. d. οἱ πρῶτοι φίλοι, a title at the Ptolemaic court, *OGI*99.3, *PTeb.*11.4 (ii B.C.), etc.; or simply οἱ φ. τοῦ βασιλέως *OGI*100.1; or οἱ φ. alone, ib.115.4; τῶν φ. καὶ διοικητοῦ one of the king's *friends* and dioecetes, *PTeb.*79.56 (ii B.C.). 2. of things, *pleasant, welcome*, δόσις ὀλίγη τε φ. τε Od.6.208, cf. Il.1.167: c. dat. pers., αἰεὶ γάρ τοι ἔρις τε φίλη 5.891, cf. Od.8.248, 13.295; οὐ φίλα τοι ἐρέω Hdt.7.104; δαίμοσιν πράσσειν φίλα their *pleasure*, A.*Pr.*660, cf. infr. II. b. freq. as predic., φίλον ἐστί or γίγνεταί μοι *pleases* me, it is *after* my own *heart*, εἴ πού τοι φίλον ἐστί Od.7.320; μὴ φ. Διὶ πατρὶ γένοιτο ib.316, cf. Il.7.387; εἰ τόδε πᾶσι φ. καὶ ἡδὺ γένοιτο 4.17; καί τοι φ. ἔπλετο θυμῷ Od.13.145, etc.; τοῦτο μὲν ἴτω ὅπῃ τῷ θεῷ φίλον Pl.*Ap.*19a: less freq. c. inf., οὐ μὲν Τυδεΐ γ' ὧδε φίλον πτωσκαζέμεν Il.4.372; πεφιδέσθαι ἐνὶ φρεσὶ φίλτερον ἦεν Τρώων 21.101, cf. 24.334, Od.14.378; so ταῦτα δαίμονί κου φίλον ἦν οὕτω γενέσθαι Hdt.1.87, cf. 108, 4.97: rarely c. part., εἰ τόδ' αὐτῷ φίλον κεκλημένῳ if it *please* him to be so called, A.*Ag.*161 (lyr.): agreeing with pl., αἰεί τοι τὰ κάκ' ἐστὶ φίλα φρεσὶ μαντεύεσθαι Il.1.107, cf. Od.17.15; ἔνθα φίλ' ὀπταλέα κρέα ἔδμεναι Il.4.345; σοὶ δ' ἔργα φίλ' ἔστω μέτρια κοσμεῖν Hes.*Op.*306. c. in Hom. and early Poets, *one's own*; freq. of limbs, life, etc., φίλον δ' ἐξαίνυτο θυμόν he took away *dear* life, Il.5.155, cf. 22.58; κατεπλήγη φίλον ἦτορ 3.31; εἰς ὅ κε..μοι φίλα γούνατ' ὀρώρῃ 9.610; φίλον κατὰ λαιμόν 19.209; esp. of one's nearest kin, πατὴρ φ. 22.408, Sapph.*Supp.*20a.11; ἄλοχος φ. Il.5.480: cf. φίλτατος: as a standing epith. when no affection is implied, μητρὶ φίλῃ Ἀλθαίῃ χωόμενος κῆρ angry with *his own* mother, Il.9.555: simply to denote possession, φίλα εἵματα 2.261; φ. πόνος *their wonted* labour, Theoc.21.20. d. applied to the numbers 284 and 220, Iamb. *in Nic.*p.35P. II. less freq. (chiefly poet.) in act. sense, *loving, friendly*, Od.1.313, cf. Il.24.775: c. gen., φίλαν ξένων ἄρουραν *friendly* to strangers, Pi.*N.*5.8, cf. *P.*3.5: of things, *kindly, pleasing*, φίλα φρεσὶ μήδεα εἰδὼς Il.17.325; φίλα φρονέειν τινί feel *kindly*, Il.4.219; φ. ἐργάζεσθαί τινι Od.24.210; φ. εἰδέναι τινί 3.277; φ. ποιέεσθαί τινι deal with one in *friendly* fashion, do one a *pleasure*, Hdt.2.152, 5.37. 2. *fond of* a thing, *attached to*, ἄλλων νόμων Arist.*Fr.*543; δειλίας φίλον Pl.*R.*604d. III. Adv. φίλως, once in Hom., φίλως χ' ὁρόῳτε ye would *fain* see it, Il.4.347, cf. Hes.*Sc.*45, A.*Ag.*247 (lyr.), [1591], etc.; φ. ἐμοὶ *in a manner dear* or *pleasing* to me, ib.1581. 2. *in a friendly, kindly spirit*, τήνδε τὴν πόλιν φ. εἰπών S.*OC*758; φ. δέχεσθαί τινα X.*HG*4.8.5, cf. Pl.*Epin.*988c. IV. φίλος has several forms of comparison: 1. Comp. φιλίων [λῐ], ον, gen. ονος, Od.19.351, 24.268: Sup. φίλιστος, η, ον, interpol. in S.*Aj.*842. 2. Comp. φίλτερος, Sup. φίλτατος, v. sub voce. 3. Comp. φιλαίτερος X.*An.*1.9.29, Call.*Del.*58: Sup. φιλαίτατος X.*HG*7.3.8, Theoc.7.98. 4. regul. Comp. φιλώτερος X.*Mem.*3.11.18 codd., Call.*Fr.*146. 5. also as Comp., μᾶλλον φίλος A.*Ch.*219, S.*Ph.*886; φ. μᾶλλον Thphr.*CP*6.1.4; Sup., μάλιστα φ. X.*Cyr.*8.1.17.

❀ **φῐλο-σάρᾱπις** [σᾰ], ιδος, ὁ, *lover of Sarapis*, *Sammelb.*4275. **-σαρκία**, ἡ, *love of the flesh*, *Cat.Cod.Astr.*2.177. **-σέβαστος**, ον, *loyal to the Emperor*, *SIG*804.11 (Cos, i A.D.), *OGI*493.9 (Ephesus, ii A.D.), etc. **-σιγμᾰτος**, ον, *fond of the letter* σῖγμα, of Euripides, Eust.1170.53. **-σῖτος**, ον, *fond of corn, occupied about it*, ἔμποροι X.*Oec.*20.27. II. *fond of food, fond of eating*, Pl.*R.*475c, Poll.6.34. **-σκαρθμος**, ον, *fond of dancing*, Nonn.*D.*5.115, 10.222. **-σκεπος**, ον, *fond of shelter*, Thphr.*CP*2.7.3 (cod. Urb., fort. φυλλό-). **-σκηπτρος**, ον, *sceptred*, βασιλεύς *AP*9.691. **-σκήπων**, ωνος, ὁ, ἡ, *loving a staff*, of Pan, dub. in *AP*6.232 (Crin.). **-σκῐος**, ον, *fond of the shade*, Thphr.*HP*6.7.6, *CP*3.7.1, Opp.*H.*4.422. **-σκόπελος**, ον, *loving rocks*, Πάν *AP*6.32 (Agath.), cf. Marcell.Sid.70, Nonn.*D.*5.230, etc. **-σκοπος**, ον, (σκοπός II) *usually hitting the mark*, τόξα Him.*Or.*14.1 (leg. ἐπίσκοπα). **-σκύλαξ** [ῠ], ᾰκος, ὁ, ἡ, *fond of dogs*, Nonn.*D.*3.74. **-σκωμμοσύνη**, ἡ, *fondness for scoffing* or *jesting*, Poll.5.161. **-σκώμμων**, ον, gen. ονος, *fond of scoffing* or *jesting*, Hdt.2.174, Plu.*Sull.*2, App.*Samn.*7.2, Luc.*Tim.*46. Adv. -μόνως Poll.5.161. **-σκωπτέω**, *to love scoffing* or *jesting*, Ath.14.616b. **-σκώπτης**, ου, ὁ, = φιλοσκώμμων, Arist.*VV*1251ª19, Chrysipp.*Stoic.*3.199, Plu.*Brut.*29, Sext.*Sent.*278. **-σμάρᾰγος** [σμᾰ], ον, *loving noise* or *din*, Nonn.*D.*3.77. **-σμηνος**, ον, *loving beehives* or *swarms of bees*, ib.5.251.

❀ **φῐλοσοφ-έω**, pf. πεφιλοσόφηκα X.*Cyr.*6.1.41, D.48.49:—*love knowledge, pursue it*, φιλοσοφέων γῆν πολλὴν..ἐπελήλυθας (sc. Solon) Hdt.1.30; φιλοσοφοῦμεν ἄνευ μαλακίας Th.2.40; φιλοσοφήσετε καὶ σκέψεσθέ τι..Isoc.8.116, cf. 12.236; θεῶν οὐδεὶς φιλοσοφεῖ οὐδ' ἐπιθυμεῖ σοφὸς γενέσθαι, ἔστι γάρ Pl.*Smp.*204a; ὑπέλαβον φιλοσοφοῦντά με δεῖν ζῆν, says Socrates, Id.*Ap.*28e; φ. περὶ τῆς ἀληθείας Arist.*Metaph.*983ᵇ2; περὶ τοὺς ποιητάς Isoc.15.45, cf. Arist.*Pol.*1279ᵇ13; ὑπέρ τινος Luc.*Am.*31; διὰ τὸ θαυμάζειν οἱ ἄνθρωποι..ἤρξαντο φιλοσοφεῖν Arist.*Metaph.*982ᵇ12; φιλοσοφεῖν λέγεται καὶ τὸ ζητεῖν..εἴτε χρὴ φιλοσοφεῖν εἴτε καὶ μὴ Id.*Fr.*51; φ. γνησίως τε καὶ ἱκανῶς Pl.*R.*473d; ἀδόλως Id.*Phdr.*249a; καθαρῶς τε καὶ δικαίως Id.*Sph.*253e; ὀρθῶς Id.*Phd.*67e; ὑγιῶς Id.*R.*619d. b. in bad sense, *quibble*, περί τινος Lys.8.11. 2. *teach philosophy*, οἱ παιδεύοντες καὶ φιλοσοφοῦντες Isoc.3.9, cf. Plu.2.192a; νουθετεῖς καὶ φιλοσοφεῖς you are *lecturing* me, ib.69b. 3. *lead a well-regulated life*, Gal.5.462. II. c. acc., *discuss, investigate, study*, μελετᾶν καὶ φ. τι Isoc.8.5; φιλοσοφεῖν φιλοσοφίαν δι' ἧς.. *pursue* a philosophy.., X.*Mem*.4.2.23; φιλοσοφίαν καινὴν..οὗτος φ. (sc. Zeno) Philem.85; τὴν πολιτικὴν φ. Arist.*EN*1152$^b$2; πρὸς τὴν ὀλιγοσιτίαν πολλὰ πεφιλοσόφηκεν ὁ νομοθέτης Id.*Pol*.1272$^a$22; φ. τὰ Στωικὰ S.E.*P*.1.235; τὰ τοῦ βίου πράγματα D.H.*Rh*.11.2; *treat scientifically*, θαλάσσας Philostr.*VA*4.24; metaph., φ. ἡ γραφὴ τὰ τῶν μύθων σώματα painting *represents truly*, Philostr.*Im*.1.3:—Pass., *to be examined scientifically*, Plu.*Caes*.59; τὰ φιλοσοφούμενα *subjects of speculation*, Cic.*Fam*.11.27.5, Philostr.*VS*1 *Prooem*., D.L.4.49. 2. generally, *study, work at* a thing, φ. λόγον Isoc.4.6; ὅσοι φιλοσοφοῦντες ἐκμοχθοῦσί τι *Trag.Adesp*.522. 3. *devise ingeniously, contrive*, φ. τοῦτο, ὅπως..Lys.24.10, Isoc.15.121, Men.242; οὕτω πεφιλοσόφηκεν ὥστε..D. l.c. **-ημα**, ατος, τό, *a subject of scientific inquiry* or *a philosophic treatise*, ἐν τοῖς ἐγκυκλίοις φ. Arist.*Cael*.279$^a$30; of the poems of Homer as allegorized, Plb.34.4.4. 2. in Logic, *demonstration*, ἔστι φ. συλλογισμὸς ἀποδεικτικός Arist.*Top*.162$^a$15. 3. *philosophic principle, rule of conduct*, Plu.2.1125b, Gal.*Anim.Pass*.1.3. 4. *shrewd device* or *invention*, Plu.2.269b. **-ητέον**, *one must pursue knowledge*, Pl.*Euthd*.288d, Isoc.15.285, Epicur.*Ep*.3 p.59 U., Cic.*Att*.1.16.13, Iamb.*Protr*.12; ἥντινα [φιλοσοφίαν] φ. Luc.*Herm*.45; φ. περὶ μουσικῆς Ath.14.632b, cf. Plot.3.5.2. ***-ία**, ἡ, *love of knowledge, pursuit thereof, speculation*, Isoc.12.209, Pl.*Phd*.61a, *Grg*.484c, al.; ἡ φ. κτῆσις ἐπιστήμης Id.*Euthd*.288d; defined as ἄσκησις ἐπιτηδείου τέχνης, Stoic. in *Placit*.1 *Prooem*.2. 2. *systematic, methodical treatment* of a subject, ἐμπειρίᾳ μέτιθι καὶ φιλοσοφίᾳ Isoc.2.35; ἡ περὶ τὰς ἔριδας φ. *scientific treatment* of argumentation, Id.10.6; ἡ περὶ τοὺς λόγους φ. the *study* of oratory, Id.4.10: pl., οἱ ἐν ταῖς φ. πολὺν χρόνον διατρίψαντες Pl.*Tht*.172c; τέχναι καὶ φ. Isoc.10.67. 3. *philosophy*, Id.11.22, Pl.*Def*.414b, etc.; ἱστορία φ. ἐστὶν ἐκ παραδειγμάτων D.H.*Rh*.11.2:—Isoc. usu. prefixes the Art., 2.51, 5.84, 7.45 (but cf. 2.35 supr.); sts. also in Pl. and Arist., as Pl.*Grg*.482a, Arist.*Metaph*.993$^b$20, *EN*1177$^a$25, and so later, διὰ τῆς φ. καὶ κενῆς ἀπάτης *Ep.Col*.2.8; but more freq. without Art., τοῖς ἐν φιλοσοφίᾳ ζῶσιν Pl.*Phd*.68c, al., cf. Arist.*Pol*.1341$^b$28, al. (cf. Πλάτων καὶ φ. Plu.2.176d); exc. when an Adj. or some qualifying word is added to ἡ θεία φ. Pl.*Phdr*.239b; ἐκείνου τῇ φ. Id.*Ly*.213d; ἡ περὶ τὰ ἀνθρώπεια φ. Arist.*EN*1181$^b$15; ἡ τῶν Ἰταλικῶν φ. Id.*Metaph*.987$^a$31 (and pl., αἱ εἰρημέναι φ. ib.29); so later ἡ Ἰωνικὴ φ. D.L.1.122; ἡ δογματική, Ἀκαδημαϊκή, σκεπτικὴ φ. S.E.*P*.1.4, etc.; ὁ Ἐμπεδοκλῆς ἐν ἀρχῇ τῆς φ. Plu.2.607c, etc.; esp. ἡ πρώτη φ. *metaphysic*, Arist.*Metaph*.1026$^a$24, cf. 18. **-ικός**, ή, όν, *concerned with* φιλοσοφία, λόγοι Artem.5.83.

**φῐλοσοφοκλῆς**, ὁ, *a lover of Sophocles*, Phld.*Acad.Ind*.p.55 M., D.L.4.20.

**φῐλοσοφομειρᾰκίσκος**, ὁ, *young man of science* (a word perhaps coined with an allusion to φιλομεῖραξ), Ath.13.572b.

***φῐλόσοφος**, ὁ, *lover of wisdom*; Pythagoras called himself φιλόσοφος, not σοφός, Cic *Tusc*.5.3.9, D.L.*Prooem*.12; τὸν φ. σοφίας φήσομεν ἐπιθυμητὴν εἶναι πάσης Pl.*R*.475b, cf. Isoc.15.271; ὁ ὡς ἀληθῶς φ. Pl.*Phd*.64e sq.; φ. φύσει, τὴν φύσιν, Id.*R*.376c; φ. τῇ ψυχῇ, opp. φιλόπονος τῷ σώματι, Isoc.1.40: used of all *men of education and learning*, joined with φιλομαθής and φιλόλογος, Pl.*R*.376c, 582e; opp. σοφιστής, X.*Cyn*.13.6,9; later, *academician*, of the members of the Museum at Alexandria, *OGI*712 (ii A.D.), etc. 2. *philosopher*, i.e. *one who speculates on truth and reality*, οἱ ἀληθινοὶ φ., defined as οἱ τῆς ἀληθείας φιλοθεάμονες, Pl.*R*.475e; ὁ φιλόσοφος, of Aristotle, Plu.2.115b; ὁ σκηνικὸς φ., of Euripides, Ath.13.561a; as the butt of Com., Philem.71.1, Bato 5.11, Anaxipp.4, Phoenicid.4.16. II. as Adj., *loving knowledge, philosophic*, ἄνδρες Heraclit.35; ἀνήρ Pl.*Phd*.64d; τὸ φ. γένος Id.*R*.501e; φ. φύσις ib.494a; ψυχή ib.486b; διάνοια ib.527b; πειθώ Phld.*Rh*.1.269 S.; σύνεσις ib.p.211 S. (Comp.); οἱ φιλοσοφώτατοι Pl.*R*.498a, cf. *IG*5(1).598 (Sparta). 2. of arguments, sciences, etc., *scientific, philosophic*, λόγοι Pl.*Phdr*.257b; λόγοι -ώτεροι, of *instructive* speeches, Isoc.12.271; -ώτερον ποίησις ἱστορίας Arist.*Po*.1451$^b$5; τὸ φ., opp. τὸ θυμοειδές, as an element of the soul, Pl.*R*.411e, but = φιλοσοφία, Plu.2.355b. 3. *ingenious*, Ar.*Ec*.571 (hex.). III. Adv. -φως, διακεῖσθαι πρός τι Isoc.15.277; φ. ἔχειν περί τινος Pl.*Phd*.91a, cf. Cic.*Att*.13.20.4, etc.; opp. ῥητορικῶς, Phld.*Rh*.2.134 S.; Comp. -ωτέρως Arist.*Sens*.436$^a$20; -ώτερον Cic.*Att*.7.8.3. [Ar. l.c. has the penult. long, nowhere else found in poetry.]

**φῐλο-σπήλυγξ**, υγγος, ὁ, ἡ, *fond of grottoes*, *AP*11.194 (Lucill.). **-σπονδος**, ον, *used in drink-offerings*, φιλοσπόνδου λιβός, of libations, A.*Ch*.292. **-σπούδαστος**, ον, *worthy of eager pursuit*, Iamb.*VP*6.32 (sed leg. περισπ.). **-σπουδος**, ον, *eager, zealous*, *OGI*339.39 (Sestos, ii B.C.), *AP*5.45 (Phld.). **-στάφῡλος** [ᾰ], ον, *loving the grape-bunches*, Nonn.*D*.29.234.

**φῐλοστεφᾰν-έω**, *love crowns*, i.e. *honour and glory*, περὶ τοὺς ἀγῶνας Plb.7.10.2; φιλοστεφανῶν καὶ φιλοδοξῶν εἰς τοὺς Ἕλληνας *laying oneself out for crowns of honour* among them, Id.1.16.10, cf. Plu.2.1005b. **-ος**, ον, *loving crowns, garlanded*, Ἀφροδίτη *h.Cer*.102; Εὔκλεια B.12.184; κῶμοι E.*Fr*.453.8 (lyr.); ἄνδρες Ion Lyr.1.13, cf. *Sammelb*.7271 (i B.C.); prob. for πολυστ. in Cratin.317 (hex.).

**φῐλό-στολος**, ον, dub. sens. in *IG*14.479. **-στονος**, ον, *delighting in groans*, Eust.832.34. Adv. -νως A.*Th*.280.

**φῐλοστοργ-έω**, *love tenderly*, freq. of family *affection*, Pl.*Lg*.927b, cf. *Princeton Exp.Inscr*.787$^1$.3 (Syria), etc.; φ. διαφερόντως τὸν ἀδελφόν D.S.31.19; ἐπεφιλοστοργήκει τὴν παρθένον Plb.5.74.5: abs., τὸ φιλοστοργεῖν Phld.*Herc*.1457.13:—Pass., ἐγὼ (sc. Isis) ὑπὸ τέκνων γονεῖς -στοργεῖσθαι ἐνομοθέτησα *IG*12(5).p.305 (Ios, iii A.D.). 2. of sexual *love*, Clearch.49, *Gp*.14.2.2. **-ία**, ἡ, *tender love, affection*, Antipho *Fr*.73, Plb.9.13.2, Phld.*Hom*.p.8 O., *BMus.Inscr*.481*.79 (Ephes.), etc.; ἡ ἄγαν φ. Antip.*Stoic*.3.254; πρὸς τὸ θρέψαν ἔδαφος Demad.37; πρὸς ἀλλήλους Plb.31.25.1; πρὸς τὴν πατρίδα Id.16.17.8; πρὸς τὸν βασιλέα *Arch.Pap*.6.9 (Delos); ἡ φυσικὴ τῶν γονέων εἰς τέκνα φ. D.S.4.44; of an elephant, δεινή τις φ. γέγονε τοῦ θηρὸς πρὸς τὸ παιδίον Phylarch.36 J. 2. *affectionateness*, X.*Cyr*.1.4.3. 3. of sexual *love*, D.S.1.64. **-ος**, ον, (στέργω, στοργή) *loving tenderly, affectionate*, freq. of family *affection*, X.*Cyr*.1.3.2, Theoc.18.13, etc.; of a nurse, Sor.1.88; of horses, Arist.*HA*611$^a$12; γένος ἀετῶν πρὸς τοὺς τρέφοντας φ. Ael.*NA*2.40; title of two queens named Athenais, *IG*2$^2$.3426.3, 3428.5; φ. εἰς ἀλλήλους *Ep.Rom*.12.10; περί τινα Plu.*Cleom*.1 (dub. constr.); φ. πρὸς τὰ τηλικαῦτα Id.2.608c: Comp., *nihil* -ότερον Cic.*Att*.13.9.1: Sup., -οτάτη διαφερόντως πρός τινα *OGI*331.46 (Pergam., ii B.C.):—τὸ φ., = φιλοστοργία, X.*Ages*.8.1, Plu.*Sol*.7; τὸ ποτὶ τὰν πατρίδα φ. *Abh.Berl.Akad*.1925(5).28 (Cyrene, i B.C./i A.D.). Adv. -γως Arist.*HA*621$^a$29; εὐσεβῶς τὰ πρὸς τοὺς θεοὺς διακείμενος καὶ φ. πρὸς τοὺς γονεῖς *OGI*229.6 (Smyrna, iii B.C.), cf. *BMus.Inscr*.925$^b$12 (Branchidae, i B.C.), Plu.*Fab*.21; φ. ἔχειν πρός..J.*AJ*4.6.8; *literae φ. scriptae*, Cic.*Att*.15.17.2: Comp. -ότερον *Gp*.16.21.6: Sup. -ότατα Iamb.*VP*7.34.

**φῐλο-στρᾰτιώτης**, ου, ὁ, *the soldier's friend*, X.*An*.7.6.4, D.Chr.1.28, Plu.*Luc*.34, Poll.1.41, Jul.*Or*.2.86d, Eun.Hist.p.227 D. II. *fond of military affairs*, Plu.*Phil*.3. **-στροφος**, ον, *loving change, changeable*, Poll.6.168. 2. *fond of returning* to a place, of bees, Porph.*Antr*.19. 3. *inclined to return*, of symptoms, Aret.*CA*2.2.

**φῐλοσύγ-γᾰμος**, ἡ, *loving her husband*, *IG*5(1).734 (Sparta). **-γενής**, ές, *loving one's relatives*, Hierocl.p.56 A.: Sup. -έστατος D.Chr.3.113.

**φῐλό-σῡκος**, ον, *fond of figs*, Phanocritus ap.Ath 7.276f, Plu.2.668a. II. = συκοφάντης, Sch.Ar.*Pl*.874, *EM*733.57. **-σῡκοφαντία**, ἡ, *love of sycophancy*, Sch.Hermog.in Rh.7(1).265 W. **-συμβίωτος** [βῐ], ον, *lover of one's spouse*, Vett.Val.46.25. **-σύμμᾰχος**, f.l. for φιλόμαχος in Hsch.

**φῐλοσυν-άγωγος** [ᾰγ], ὁ, *lover of the synagogue*, *Not.Scav*.1919.66. **-έστιος**, ον, *loving those who share one's home*, Vett.Val.9.3. **-ήθης**, ες, *loving one's associates*, Plu.2.56c, Vett.Val.40.14, *Gloss*. **-ουσιάζω**, *promote social intercourse*, D.L.3.98. **-ουσιαστής**, οῦ, ὁ, *fond of sexual intercourse*, Sch.rec.Theoc.4.62, *EM*241.45. **-τομος**, ον, *loving brevity*, Ph.2.351, Plu.2.511b, Gal.19.185 (Comp.), Sch.Hermog. in Rh.7(1).105 W.

**φῐλοσωκράτης** [ᾰ], ου, ὁ, *friend of Socrates*, Ath.5.215f.

**φῐλοσωμᾰτ-έω**, *love, cherish the body*, Poll.3.137, Plot.2.9.18. **-ία**, ἡ, *love of the body*, Andronic.Rhod p.572 M., Poll.2.235, 3.137, Porph.*Marc*.25, Hierocl. *in CA*13 p.448 M. **-ος**, ον, *loving the body, indulging it*, οὐ φιλόσοφος, ἀλλά τις φ. Pl.*Phd*.68c, cf. Ph.2.16, al., Ptol.*Tetr*.158, Demoph.*Sent*.44; ψυχαί Porph.*Antr*.11; distd. fr. φιλήδονος, Plu.2.140c (but φιλήδονοι καὶ φ. D.Chr.4.115): τὸ φ., = φιλοσωματία, Plu.2.593d, *Fr*.18.1. Adv. -τως Poll.3.137.

**φῐλο-σώφρων**, ον, gen. ονος, *loving moderation*, διοίκησις Hdn.2.3.9. **-τᾰλαίπωρος**, ον, *loving hardship*, Steph. *in Hp*.1.87 D. **-τάπεινος** [ᾰ], ον, *loving humility*, Gal.17(2).148. **-τάρᾰχος** [τᾰ], ον, *tumultuous*, φ. χρῆμα ὁ δῆμος Men.Prot.p.66 D. **-τάρῑχος** [τᾰ], ον, *fond of salt-fish*, Antiph.178.

**φῐλοτεκν-έω**, *love one's children*, Philostr.*VA*2.14. ***-ία**, ἡ, *love of one's children*, Lxx 4 *Ma*.14.13, *Vit.Philonid*.p.4 C., Plu.2.14b, Poll.3.14, Hdn.6.5.8. ***-ος**, ον, *loving one's children* or *offspring*, Hdt.2.66, E.*HF*636, *Ph*.356, Ar.*Th*.752, *Ep.Tit*.2.4; ἦθος φ. D.S.34/5.11: Comp., αἱ μητέρες -ότεραι Arist.*EN*1168$^a$25; Sup. -ότατος Plu.*Aem*.6: τὸ φ., = φιλοτεκνία, Id.2.93f.

**φῐλοτερπής**, ές, *fond of pleasure*, Nonn.*D*.40.366.

**φῐλοτεχν-έω**, pf. Pass. πεφιλοτέχνημαι (v. infr. III):—*love art, practise an art*, of Athena and Hephaestus, Pl.*Prt*.321e; περὶ [ἐμπειρίας] Phld.*Mus*.p.89 K.; περὶ τὰ ἔξω Epict.*Ench*.29.7; περὶ τὴν παρρησίαν Plu.2.74c, etc.; ὑπέρ τινος Ael.*VH*2.2; φ. πρὸς τορευτὰς καὶ τοὺς ἄλλους τεχνίτας *to converse* with them *on art*, Plb.26.1.2; *use terms of art*, Phld.*Sign*.7. II. *use* or *employ art* or *artifice*, Plb.16.30.2, Plu.2.142b, 2.1050c, etc.: c. inf., D.S.13.82. III. *treat* or *arrange artistically*, συλλαβὰς ποικίλως φ. D.H.*Comp*.15; *represent in art*, ἀγέλην (in a mosaic) Chor.1.33 p.11 F.-R., cf. 3.6 p.49 F.-R.; *treat by the rules of art* (i.e. alchemy), Olymp.Alch.p.91 B. (Pass.):—Pass., *to be made* or *furnished by art*, παράδεισος τοῖς ἄλλοις πολυτελῶς πεφιλοτεχνημένος D.S 14.80; πρός τι Id.3.37; θηλὴ πεφιλοτεχνημένη an *artificial* teat, Sor.1.115; *to be represented artistically*, πᾶσα ἀπόνοια ἐν ἐκείνοις πεφιλοτέχνηται, in Trag., Jul.*Or*.7.211a. IV. *invent, devise*, λίνα καὶ ἄρκυς Str.15.3.18. **-ημα**, ατος, τό, *chef-d'œuvre*, Cic.*Att*.13.40.1, Aristid.*Or*.44(17).13, Hld.5.18, Chor.35.35 p.399.3 F.-R. II. ἐκπηδῆσαι ἐκ τοῦ φ. *the cunningly devised trap*, D.S.3.37. **-ης**, ου, ὁ, = φιλότεχνος, Polem.*Phgn*.21,22. **-ητέον**, *one must contrive as best one can*, Herod.Med.ap. Orib.10.8.16; *one must use art*, Eutoc. *in Archim.Sph.Cyl*.p.94 H. **-ία**, ἡ, *enthusiasm for art*, Pl.*Criti*.109c, Poll.6.167; ἡ περὶ [τὴν μουσικὴν] φ. Phld.*Mus*.p.19 K.; *craftsmanship*, of sculptors, D.S.1.98; of the pyramid-builders, ib.64; ἡ περί τι φ. Arr.*Epict*.2.5.21; περὶ τὰς κόμας Str.10.3.8; *ingenuity, artifice*, φ. καὶ δόλῳ, of hunters, D.S.3.37; in good sense, φ. ἡ περὶ τὸ ἱερόν *IG*2$^2$.1023, cf. Antyll.ap.Orib.6.10.7. II. of things, *artistic* or *ingenious construction*, D.S.2.8. **-τεχνῖται**, οἱ, *friends of the artists*, i.e. honorary members of a troupe, *OGI*51.73 (Ptolemais, iii B.C.). ***-ος**, ον, *fond of* *art* or *an art, artistic,* Pl.*R.*476a, Plu.2.41f, Ath.15.700c, etc.: τὸ φ., = φιλοτεχνία, *ingenuity,* Plu.*Demetr.*20, etc. Adv. -ως D.S.2.8, D.H. *Comp.*18, J.*AJ*12.2.10, Plu.2.104b, Antyll.ap.Orib.6.10.23. 2. of things, *artificial, curious,* D.S.1.33, 17.44: Sup., Papp.648.19.

*φῐλότης, ητος, ἡ, *friendship, love, affection,* μηνιθμὸν μὲν ἀπορρῖψαι φιλότητα δ' ἑλέσθαι Il.16.282; ξεῖνοι δὲ διαμπερὲς εὐχόμεθ' εἶναι ἐκ πατέρων φιλότητος Od.15.197, cf. S.*Ph.*1122 (lyr.); κατ' ἡλικίην τε καὶ φ. ἰλαδὸν συγγίνεσθαι Hdt.1.172: pl., Thgn.860; φιλότητι *in, with, from friendship* or *affection,* Il.3.453, Od.3.363, 10.43; ἐν φ. διέτμαγεν ἀρθμήσαντε Il.7.302; φιλότητί γε yes, *in affection* [we are brothers], E.*IT*498; φιλότητι χειρῶν with *friendly* services, Id.*Or.* 1048; φιλότητα μετ' ἀμφοτέροισι βάλωμεν Il.4.16; φ. μετ' ἀμφοτέροισι τίθησι ib.83, cf. Od.24.476; παρὰ σεῖο τυχὼν φιλότητος 15. 158; φιλότητα παρασχεῖν Il.3.354, Od.15.55; ἄγειν ἐς φ. Sapph. 1.19; εἰς ἀρθμὸν ἐμοὶ καὶ φιλότητα..ἥξει A.*Pr.*193 (anap.); ὑδαρεῖ σαίνειν φ. Id.*Ag.*798 (anap.); φ. τινός *friendship with, affection for,* Od.14.505, S.*Aj.*1410 (anap.); διὰ τὴν λίαν φ. βροτῶν by his overgreat *love* for men, A.*Pr.*123 (anap.); ξενίαι καὶ φιλότητες πρός τινας And.1.145: in addressing persons, ὦ φιλότης, = ὦ φίλος, *my dear friend,* Pl.*Phdr.*228d, Philox.2.7,34; without ὦ, Hp.*Ep.*17. 2. of *friendship between states,* φιλότητα καὶ ὅρκια πιστὰ ταμόντες Il.3.73, cf. 94,323; ναυμαχεῖν ὑπὲρ τῆς φ. Lys.2.35; φ. ἀντὶ διαφορᾶς ἐθέλοντες ποιεῖσθαι And.3.30. 3. prov., ἰσότης φιλότητα ἀπεργάζεται Pl.*Lg.*757a; more shortly, ἰσότης φ. Arist.*EN*1168$^b$8. 4. in Hom., freq. of *sexual love* or *intercourse,* in various phrases: μίγη φιλότητι καὶ εὐνῇ Il.6.25, cf. 3.445, al.; ἵνα μίσγεαι ἐν φ. 2.232; καθεύδετον ἐν φ., παραλέξομαι ἐν φ., Od.8.313, Il.14.237; ὕπνῳ καὶ φ. δαμείς ib.353, cf. 207, 13.636: less freq. c. gen., ἀείδειν ἀμφ' Ἄρεος φιλότητος ἐϋστεφάνου τ' Ἀφροδίτης Od.8.267; φ. γυναικός Hes. *Sc.*31, cf. *Th.*374,405,625,822: pl., Pi.*P.*9.39, *N.*8.1, Antipho Soph. 49. 5. personified, = φιλία I.5, opp. νεῖκος, Emp.17.20, al., cf. Hes.*Th.*224. (φιλία is the common prose form.)

*φῐλοτήσιος, α, ον, also ος, ον Thgn.489: Dor. φῐλοτάσιος [ᾰ], ον, S.*El.*1073 (lyr.):—*of friendship* or *love, promoting it,* φ. ἔργα Od.11. 246; φ. δίαιτα S.l.c.; φ. χορός Ar.*Fr.*675 (lyr.); τέρψις Phld.*Hom.* p.25 O.; μέλος Plu.2.329e; εὐνή Opp.*C.*3.375. II. ἡ φιλοτησία, with or without κύλιξ, the cup *sacred to friendship,* the *loving-cup,* ἡ μὲν γὰρ φέρεται φιλοτήσιος Thgn. l.c.; πῖνε, κατάκεισο, λαβὲ τήνδε φιλοτησίαν Ar.*Ach.*985 (lyr.); κύλιξ φ. Id.*Lys.*203; φ. σοι τήνδ' ἐγὼ..κύλικα προπίομαι Alex.291; φιλοτησίαν δὲ τήνδε σοι προπίομαι Theopomp.Com.32.9; φιλοτησίαν παρέχειν Luc.*Sat.*18: pl., φιλοτησίας προπίνειν D.19.128, Luc.*Herm.*11, *Gall.*12: hence in Alex. 58, τῆς φιλοτησίας ἐγὼ μεστὰς προπίνω, Meineke read τρεῖς for τῆς: jestingly, ἡ τοῦ φαρμάκου φ. Theopomp.Hist.177.

φῐλο-τῐβέριος, ὁ, *friend of Tiberius,* Ph.2.551. -τίμαιος [τῐ], *admirer of Timaeus,* Plb.12.25$^a$3 (Comp., cj. Orelli for -τιμότερον).

*φῐλοτῑμ-έομαι, fut. ήσομαι Pl.*Phdr.*234a, D.20.103; later, -ηθήσομαι D.S.11.18 codd.: aor. ἐφιλοτιμήθην X.*Mem.*2.9.3, Pl.*La.*182b, Isoc.4.44, Is.2.42; later, ἐφιλοτιμησάμην Plb.20.8.2, Ael.*VH*3.1 (written ἐφιλοτειμήσετο *Ephes.*3 No.13): pf. πεφιλοτίμημαι D.42.24, Porph.ap.Stob.2.1.32:—pf. in pass. sense, Aristid.1.446 J.: (φιλότιμος):—*love* or *seek after honour,* Pl.*Alc.*2.146a, Is.l.c., D.20.103, etc.: hence, *to be ambitious, emulous,* Ar.*Ra.*281; φ. ὅτι.. *to be jealous* because.., X.*An.*1.4.7, Lys.14.21; φ. πρὸς ἀλλήλους, πρὸς τοὺς ἄλλους, *vie emulously with, rival,* Pl.*Smp.*178e, *Phdr.*234a, cf. Lys.29.14. 2. the object of ambition, etc., is mostly added with a Prep., φ. ἐπί τινι *to place one's fame* in a thing, *glory* or *pride oneself* upon it, Pl.*R.*553d, X.*Mem.*2.6.12, Lys.14.42; ἐπὶ τοῖς πεπραγμένοις Isoc.3.46, al.; ἔν τινι Pl.*La.*182b; ὑπὲρ τῆς δόξης Isoc.8.93; περὶ τῶν καλῶν *contend in rivalry* for, Plu.2.760c; περὶ τὴν θήραν, δεῖπνα, D.S.3.18, Plu.*Phil.*9; ἀφ' ἑτέρων ἀρετῶν Id.2.819c: c. neut. pron. in acc., πρὸς ἃ ἐγὼ φιλοτιμοῦμαι X.*HG*1.6.5: c. acc. cogn., φ. φιλοτιμίας ἀκάρπους Plu.2.830e; τὴν ἀγαθὴν ἔριν J.*BJ*1.10.5; φ. πρὸς τὴν πόλιν *show patriotic zeal* for.., Lycurg.140, cf. *IG*2$^2$.1176.26, etc.; εἰς τὴν αὔξησιν D.S.1.50, cf. 25, D.L.4.44, Aristid. l.c. II. c. inf., *strive eagerly to* do a thing, *endeavour earnestly, aspire,* οὐ πάνυ ἂν φιλοτιμηθεῖεν φίλῳ σοι χρῆσθαι X.*Mem.*2.9.3, cf. *Oec.*21.6, *PPetr.*3p.115 (iii B.C.), *PCair.Zen.*578.2 (iii B.C.), etc.; φιλοτιμούμενοι ἐπιδείκνυσθαι πρὸς ἅπαντας Pl.*Phdr.*232a: c. part., φ. ἐλέγχων Id.*R.*336c, cf. X.*Eq.Mag.* 9.6: c. acc. et inf., *to be anxious that..,* ib.1.25: c. acc., ἀεὶ ἕν γέ τι φιλοτιμούμενος Id.*Oec.*4.24: with ὅπως, καλῶς ἂν ποιήσαις φιλοτιμηθεὶς ὅπως ἂν παρὰ τοῦ Θεοδώρου λάβῃς τὰ ἐπιστόλια *PCair.Zen.*41.19 (iii B.C.), cf. *PMich.Zen.*6.3 (iii B.C.). III. c. dat. rei, *present with* a thing, χρήμασί τινας v.l. in Procop.*Goth.*1.5: but c. acc. rei, *lavish upon,* τινί τι Aristaenet.1.1; πόλεμος..νίκας ἀδίκους φ. Chor.35.71 p.410 F.-R. -ημα, ατος, τό, *an act of ambition* or *ostentation,* Ph. 2.589, Plu.*Alc.*16 (pl.), 2.822a (pl.). 2. *thing on which one prides oneself,* Luc.*Tim.*43 (pl.), *Nav.*40 (pl.). *-ητέον, *one must seek distinction,* Plu.2.125c. *-ία, Ion. -ίη, ἡ, *love of honour* or *distinction, ambition,* freq. in bad sense in early writers, Pi.*Fr.*210, E.*IA*527, Ar.*Th.*383, Arist.*EN*1125$^b$22; κακίστη δαιμόνων φ. E.*Ph.* 532; ἄκαιρος Isoc.*Ep.*2.9; πλεονεξία καὶ φ. Th.3.82; with φιλονικία, Pl.*Lg.*860e; also in good sense, Isoc.5.110, X.*Mem.*3.3.13, *Hier.*7.3, Pl.*R.*553c: the object is added in gen., φ. τῶν καλῶν ib.555a, cf. X.*Cyr.*8.1.35; also φ. ἐπὶ τοῖς καλοῖς Pl.*Smp.*178d; ὑπὲρ τῶν ὅλων, περί τι, Plb.1.52.4, 5.71.6; πρὸς τὰ καλά Id.6.55.4, cf. Pl.*Lg.*834b; but φ. πρός τινα *ambitious rivalry* with him, φ. πρὸς ἀλλήλους φ. καὶ στάσις Plb.4.87.7 (but αἱ πρὸς σφᾶς αὐτοὺς φ. is f.l. for φιλονικίαι (ap.Stob.) in Isoc.3.18); φ. ἐμβάλλειν τινί, ὅπως..X. *Cyr.*8.1.39: freq. with Preps., διὰ φιλοτιμίαν Pl.*R.*586c, Isoc.5.86, etc.; φιλοτιμίας ἕνεκα Lys.19.56; ὑπὸ φιλοτιμίας Pl.*Phdr.*257c, etc.; simply φιλοτιμίᾳ D.2.18; φ. τινὶ καὶ φιλονεικίᾳ Plu.2.856a: pl., *jealousies, rivalries,* κατ' ἰδίας φ. Th.8.89; φιλονικίαι καὶ φ. Pl.*R.*548c, etc.; αἱ φ. τῶν συγγραφέων *party-feelings,* Plb.3.21.10. 2. *conceited obstinacy,* ἡ φ. κτῆμα σκαιόν Hdt.3.53; ὑπὸ φιλοτιμίας, ἣν ὀνομάζουσιν οἱ νῦν Ἕλληνες κενοδοξίαν Gal.6.415. 3. *ambitious display, ostentation,* πλούτου Lys.33.2: but freq. 4. *lavish outlay for public purposes, munificence,* ἡ πρὸς ὑμᾶς φ. Aeschin.3.19, cf. *POxy.* 1153.16 (i A.D.), *Dacia* 1.273 (Tomi), *BCH*51.99 (Panamara), etc.: pl., *occasions for munificence,* Plu.*Nic.*3. II. the object coveted, *honour, distinction, credit,* ἔστιν τὸ γράμμα ἐκείνῳ μὲν φ. πρὸς ὑμᾶς D.20.69; φ. παρέχειν τινί X.*Hier.*1.27; ἐκείνῳ ἔχει φ. is to his *credit,* D.2.3; ψευδῆ φ. κτᾶται Aeschin.3.45; ἐνὶ τὴν φ. συνεχώρησεν Plu. *Phoc.*20; both in sg. and pl., ἀποστερεῖσθαι τῆς φιλοτιμίας or τῶν -ιῶν, D.24.210, 19.223, cf. 24.91 (pl.); στέφανος φιλοτιμίας διὰ βίου, as an honour, *Rev.Arch.*22(1925).62 (Callatis); φιλοτιμίας χρυσίον *charitable* fund, ib.34(1931).347 (Stobi). III. punningly, *the conduct of one Philotimus,* Cic.*Att.*6.9.2, 7.1.1. *-ος, ον, *loving honour* or *distinction, ambitious,* mostly in bad sense (cf. Pl.*R.*347b, Arist.*EN* 1125$^b$9), E.*Ph.*567; τὸ μαντικὸν πᾶν σπέρμα φ. κακόν Id.*IA*520; joined with φιλοχρήματος, Pl.*Phd.*68c; with φιλόνικος, Id.*R.*551a, etc.; also in good sense, φ. καὶ ἐλευθέριος X.*Mem.*2.3.16; φ. καὶ μεγαλόψυχοι Isoc.9.3:—with abstr. Nouns (in both senses), εὐχά A.*Supp.*658 (lyr.); ἦθος E.*Supp.*907; σοφίαι φιλοτιμότεραι Κλεοφῶντος Ar.*Ra.*679 (lyr.); αἱ φ. τῶν φύσεων X.*Oec.*13.9; βίος Lys. 2.16; πολιτεία Pl.*R.*545b; φ. ἐπί τινι *emulous in regard to, eager for distinction in..,* ἐπὶ σοφίᾳ, ἐπ' ἀρετῇ, Id.*Prt.*343c, *Lg.*744e; περὶ τἀναγκαῖα φιλοτιμότατος Plb.9.20.6; ἱππικὸν φιλοτιμότερον πρὸς ἀλλήλους περὶ ἀνδραγαθίας X.*Eq.Mag.*9.3: c. inf., φιλοτιμότατοι καλόν τι ποιεῖν ib.2.2: c. acc. modi, τὰς ψυχὰς -ότεροι ib.7.3; -ότεροι τὰ ἤθη Arist.*Rh.*1391$^a$22: τὸ φ., = φιλοτιμία, E.*IA*22 (dub. l., anap.), 342 (troch.), Th.2.44, Pl.*Lg.*841c, etc. b. *rejoicing in worship,* Νυκτὸς παῖδες A.*Eu.*1033 (lyr.). 2. *prodigal, lavish,* λαμπρὸς καὶ φ. D.21.159; *munificent, generous,* πρός τινα Aristeas 227· περὶ ξένους Plu.*Crass.*3. 3. φιλότιμος, title of an official member of a guild or corporation at Histria, γερουσίας φ. *Analele Acad.Române* 38. 596 (pl.); so at Tomi, ὁ προστάτης καὶ δισφύλαρχος καὶ φ. *Dacia* 1. 273. 4. neut. pl., *gifts, endowments,* τὴν μὲν τοῖς ἑαυτῆς φ. κεκόσμηκεν Ἀφροδίτη Aristaenet.1.10. II. Adv. -μως *ambitiously, emulously,* Lys.16.18, Is.7.39; φ. πρός τινα ἔχειν to vie *emulously* with.., Pl.*Chrm.*162c; πρὸς ἀλλήλους Isoc.4.85; φ. ἔχειν πρός τι to strive, exert oneself *eagerly* after a thing, X.*Cyr.*1.6.26, etc.; τὰ λοιπὰ συσπεύσας φ. *zealously,* *PCair.Zen.*62(*b*)8 (iii B.C.); φ. πρὸς τοὺς λόγους διακεῖσθαι Isoc.15.277; *with public spirit, generously,* *IG*2$^2$.505.35, etc.: Comp. φιλοτιμότερον Lys.16.20, *PTeb.*23.10 (ii B.C.); or -οτέρως Isoc.9.5: Sup. -ότατα Plu.*Caes.*3.

φῐλο-τοιοῦτος, ὁ, *fond of so and so,* representing any compd. Adj. with φιλο-, Arist.*EN*1099$^a$9, 1118$^b$22, 1125$^b$14, cj. in *Rh.*1363$^b$ 1. -τόλμως, Adv. *daringly,* Onos.32.3. -τρᾰγήμων, ον, gen. ονος, *fond of sweetmeats* or *dessert,* Eub.45. -τρᾰγῳδός, όν, *fond of tragedies,* name of a comedy by Alexis. -τράπεζος [ᾰ], ον, *fond of the table,* Ath.3.113e. -τρᾰφής, ές, = φιλότροφος, E.*Fr.* 281. -τροπος, ον, *attached to* a person's *character,* Phld.*Lib.* p.21 O.

φῐλοτροφ-έω, *to be fond of feeding* or *keeping,* φ. κύνας Plu.2.685d:—Pass., *to be well fed, fatted,* Sm.1 *Ki.*28.24. -ία, ἡ, *breeding of animals,* *Gp.*14 Arg. -ιον, τό, *banqueting-hall,* *Supp.Epigr.*4.268. 6 (Panamara, ii A.D.). -ος (proparox.), ον, *fond of rearing* or *nurture,* Orph.*H.*2.5, Vett.Val.18.34, 46.28; *fond of one's foster-children,* *IG*12(8).472 (Thasos). II. *breeder of animals, fancier,* ἄνδρες φ. prob. in *Lyr.Alex.Adesp.*4.20.

*φῐλότρῠφος, ον, *loving luxury,* Ptol.*Tetr.*162.

φῐλοττάριον, τό, poet. Dim. of φιλότης, *little pet,* Ar.*Ec.*891.

φῐλο-τύραννος [ῠ], ον, *friend of tyranny,* Plu.*Per.*4, etc.; Sup. -ότατος Id.*Dio* 36; τὸ φ. *love of tyranny,* D.H.4.83. -τῡφος, ον, *loving pride, arrogant,* Ph.1.671. -τώθαστος, ον, *fond of fault-finding,* prob. in Hp.*Ep.*17 (for φιλοτωθάσσοντα vulg., -τώθασον codd.). -ῡγιής [ῠ], ές, *loving health,* Arist.*EE*1222$^a$32. -φαίαξ, ᾶκος, ὁ, ἡ, *friend of the Phaeacians,* Choerob. *in Thd.*1.287 H. -φάρμᾰκος, ον, *fond of drugs,* Gal.16.322: in bad sense, *Cat.Cod.Astr.*8(4).158; τὸ φ. ἔθος Paul.Aeg.2.11. -φθογγος, ον, *loving noise, noisy,* σκύλακες Anyte ap.Poll.5.48. -φθονία, ἡ, *love of envy,* Varro ap. Non.p.767 L. -φθονος, ον, *given to envy,* ἔστι τινὰ τῶν ἀνθρωπίνων φ. καὶ μικρόσοφα D.S.26.1; τὸ φ. Plu.2.91b. -φῐλία, ἡ, *love of one's friends,* v.l. in Arist.*EN*1155$^a$30. *-φῐλος, ον, *loving one's friends,* Id.*Rh.*1381$^b$27, *EN*1159$^a$34, Plb.1.14.4, Phld.*Lib.*p.40 O., Dain *Inscr. du Louvre* 174 (Egypt), *Cat.Cod.Astr.*7.205. -φόρμιγξ, ιγγος, ὁ, ἡ, *loving,* i.e. *accompanying, the lyre,* of song, A.*Supp.*697 (lyr.).

φῐλοφρον-έομαι, fut. ήσομαι, Luc.*Tim.*48, etc.: aor. ἐφιλοφρονησάμην and -φρονήθην, v. infr.: (φιλόφρων):—*treat* or *deal with kindly, show favour to,* τινα Hdt.3.50, Pl.*Lg.*738d, al.; τὰ ἄγρια ὄντα τῶν θηρίων Gal.19.211; φ. τινὰ τῇ δικέλλῃ *salute* him with a blow of the mattock, Luc. l.c.; also φ. περί τινα Epicur.*Ep.*2 p.35 U.; φιλοφρονήσασθαι ἀλλήλους *greet* or *embrace* one another, X.*An.*4.5.34 (so in aor. Pass. φιλοφρονηθῆναι Id.*Cyr.*3.1.40): metaph., ἤθη κακὰ φ. *embrace* bad habits, Pl.*Lg.*669c: also, 2. c. dat., φιλοφρονήσασθαί τινι *show a favour* to one, X.*Cyr.*3.1.8, *Oec.*4.20; πρὸς ἅπαντας, πρὸς τοὺς Ἕλληνας, D.S.16.89,91: metaph., φ. θυμῷ *indulge* passion,

Pl.*Lg.*935c. 3. abs., *to be of a kindly, cheerful temper*, X.*Ap.*7; *show a favour*, τοῖς -ησαμένοις εὐχαριστεῖ Phld.*Herc.*1251.22. II. of things, *cheer, please, be welcome to*, τινας Pl.*Lg.*820e. III. Act. φιλοφρονέων is found in D.S.27.4, but is f.l. for φίλα φρονέων in Od.16.17; so φιλοφρονοῦσι Plu.2.750d (leg. φίλα φρονοῦσι), and φιλοφρονεῖν v.l. for φιλοπραγμονεῖν in Nicostr.ap.Stob.4.22.102; 2 sg. imper. φιλοφρό[νει] is restd. in *SIG*1268 ii 2 (Miletopolis). **-ημα**, ατος, τό, *act* or *proof of kindness*, Aeschin.*Ep.*5.3 (pl.). **-ησις**, εως, ἡ, *kind treatment, courtesy*, Aristeas 246 (pl.), D.H.10.57 (pl.), J.*AJ*2.9.7, al., Plu.2.212f, Hld.3.11, Chariton 4.3. **-ητικός**, ή, όν, *friendly, kind*, Corn.*ND*24, Procl.*Par.Ptol.*225; φ. ἀρετή Sch.Pi.*P.*1.184.

**φῐλο-φροσύνη**, ἡ, (φιλόφρων) *friendliness, kindliness*, Il.9.256; τινος *towards* one, Hdt.5.92.γ'; εἰρήνη πρὸς ἀλλήλους καὶ φ. Pl.*Lg.*628c; κοινωνεῖν φιλοφροσύνης ib.640b; τυχεῖν Plu.*Pyrrh.*11; δέχεσθαι φιλοφροσύνην Id.*Mar.*40; νέμειν τινί Id.*Cat.Mi.*3; διὰ φιλοφροσύνην Pl.*Lg.*740e; μετὰ φιλοφροσύνης Plu.2.124c: pl., *friendly greetings, welcomes*, σὺν φιλοφροσύναις δέξασθαι Pi.*O.*6.98; ποικίλαι φ. Phld.*Lib.*p.29 O.; φιλοφροσύνας φιλοφρονεῖσθαι ἡδίους Luc.*Im.*21. II. *cheerfulness, gaiety*, X.*Smp.*2.24 (pl.), Plu.2.128d. **-φρόσῡνος**, η, ον, = sq., *Epigr.Gr.*815.2 (Crete), Epigr. in *Arch.Pap.*1.221 (Ptolemaic). **-φρων**, ον, gen. ονος, (φρήν) *kindly disposed, friendly*, Κροῖσου φ. ἀρετά Pi.*P.*1.94; φ. Ἡσυχία ib.8.1; φ. σαίνουσα.. Ἄτα A.*Pers.*97 (lyr.); φ. γένος E.*IT*1061; τὸν στρατηγὸν εἶναι χρὴ φ. καὶ ὠμόν X.*Mem.*3.1.6, cf. *Smp.*8.16; φιλοφρονέστατοι, of the Athenians, Id.*Mem.*3.5.3; φ. πρός τινα Phld.*Lib.*p.35 O.; τὸ φ., = φιλοφροσύνη, Plu.2.1102e. Adv. -νως, ἀσπάζεσθαί, δέξασθαί, δέκεσθαί τινα to greet *kindly*, welcome, Hdt.2.121.δ', 3.13, 5.18, cf. S.*Aj.*751; φ. ἔχειν πρὸς ἀλλήλους, πρὸς τὸ συγγενὲς θεῖον, to be *kindly minded* towards.., X.*Cyr.*3.3.10, Pl.*Criti.*120e; φ. βλέπειν to wear *a kind, friendly* look, X.*Mem.*3.10.4; φ. ὑπάρχει τᾷ πόλει *Supp.Epigr.*2.277.6 (Delph., ii B.C.): Comp. -εστέρως ἔχειν τὰ ὄμματα X.*Smp.*1.10. **-φῠσικός**, ὁ, *lover of nature, naturalist*, Gal.13.102. **-φωνος**, ον, *fond of talking, noisy*, Plu.2.1125c; τὸ φ. ib.967b. **-χᾰρής**, ές, *grace-loving*, *Cat.Cod.Astr.*2.171. 2. -χᾰρές, τό, = πράσιον, Plin.*HN*20.241, *Gloss.* **-χηρος**, ον, *kind to widows*, *Stud.Pont.*3.72 (Neoclaudiopolis); fem. φιλοχήρα *Supp.Epigr.*2.521.6 (Rome). **-χλαινος**, ον, *fond of a cloak*, νίκη φ., of the games at Pellene, Nonn.*D.*37.150.

**φῐλ-οχλος** [ῐ], ον, *loving popular favour*, Ptol.*Tetr.*16, D.L.4.41; τὸ φ. ib.42.

**φῐλοχορ-ευτής**, οῦ, ὁ, *friend of the choral dance*, of Dionysus, Ar.*Ra.*404 (lyr.). **-ος**, ον, *loving the choir* or *choral dance*, epith. of Pan, A.*Pers.*448: of Pallas, Ar.*Th.*1136 (lyr.); κῶμοι φ. ib.989 (lyr.); κιθάρα E.*IA*1037 (lyr.).

**φῐλοχρημᾰτ-έω**, *love money*, Antipho Soph.103, Pl.*Lg.*737a, Is.10.17, Iamb.*Protr.*20. **-ία**, ἡ, *love of money*, Poet.ap.Zen.2.24, Pl.*R.*391c, *Lg.*747b, 938b, Eus.Mynd.13, etc.; ἁ φ. Σπάρταν ὀλεῖ, a Spartan proverb, Arist.*Fr.*544. **-ιστής**, οῦ, ὁ, *fond of money-making*, φιλοχρηματισταὶ καὶ φιλοχρήματοι Pl.*R.*551a: perh. to be read in Arist.*Pol.*1316ᵃ40. **-ιστικῶς**, Adv., Poll.3.113. **-ιστος**, ον, = sq., dub. in Them.*Or.*2.35b. **-ος**, ον, *loving money*, And.4.32, Pl.*Phd.*68c, 82c, etc.; ὁ φ. Id.*R.*549b, Hierocl. *in CA*2 p.422 M.; φ. καὶ χρηματισταὶ οἱ ἐν ταῖς ἀρχαῖς Arist.*Pol.*1316ᵃ40 (s. v. l.); τὸ φ., = φιλοχρηματία, Pl.*R.*436a: Comp. -ώτερος X.*Smp.*4.45: Sup. -ώτατος D.S.1.94. Adv., -τως ἔχειν, = φιλοχρηματεῖν, Isoc.1.23.

**φῐλοχρημ-ονέω**, = φιλοχρηματέω, Pl.*Lg.*729a. **-οσύνη**, ἡ, = φιλοχρηματία, Ps.-Phoc.42, Pl.*Lg.*938c, *AP*11.270. **-ων**, ον, gen. ονος, = φιλοχρήματος, Dam.*Isid.*238, Lyd.*Mag.*3.53.

**φῐλό-χρησμος**, ον, *fond of oracles*, cj. in Rhetor. in *Cat.Cod.Astr.*8(4).147. **-χρηστος**, ον, *loving goodness* or *honesty*, X.*Mem.*2.9.4, D.H.7.62. **-χρήστωρ**, ορος, ὁ, perh. a mistake for sq., Calder *Philadelphia and Montanism* 32. **-χριστος**, ον, *loving Christ*, *IG*4.205 (vi A.D.), *Supp.Epigr.*8.231 (Palestine, vi/vii A.D.). **-χρύσης** [ῠ], ου, ὁ, *lover of Chryses*, Choerob. *in Thd.*1.186 H. **-χρῡσία**, ἡ, *love of gold*, Poll.3.113. **-χρῡσος**, ον, *fond of gold*, Luc.*Gall.*13, Rhetor. in *Cat.Cod.Astr.*8(4).147 codd.

**φῐλοχωρ-έω**, *to be fond of a place* or *country, haunt* it, Hdt.8.111; ἐκεῖσε φ. Ar.*Fr.*149.5: c. dat., φ. τόποις Plb.4.46.1; ὄρεσιν D.H.1.13; τῷ λόφῳ Id.1.34, cf. 3.9, 5.63; τοῖς ἀλλοτρίοις Id.8.47 (but ἐν τοῖς ἀλλοτρίοις ib.35 codd.); φ. περὶ ταφάς Plu.2.612a: metaph., φ. ἐπὶ τῇ παρανόμῳ δυναστείᾳ, ἐπὶ [τῇ φιλοσοφίᾳ], D.H.11.11, Iamb.*Protr.*6; περὶ τοὺς ἐθισμούς Plu.2.714b: c. inf., φιλοχωροῖμεν ἂν μένειν D.H.6.79 (s. v. l.). **-ία**, ἡ, *fondness for a place, local attachment*, Ar.*V.*834, D.H.1.27, Poll.6.167: metaph., *fondness for* a thing, ἡ ἐς τὰ μὴ σπουδαῖα τῶν μελῶν φ. Aristid.Quint.2.6, cf. 15. **-ος**, ον, *fond of a place*, Poll.6.167.

**φῐλο-ψάμαθος** [ψᾰ], ον, *fond of sand*, φώκη Nonn.*D.*43.251. **-ψευδής**, ές, *fond of lies* or *lying*, Il.12.164; παιδία Gal.*Anim.Pass.*1.7; φ. φύσις, opp. φιλόσοφος, Pl.*R.*485d: name of a dialogue by Luc.; τὸ φ., = sq., Plu.2.61d. **-ψευδία**, ἡ, *propensity to lying*, Hp.*Ep.*17. **-ψευδολόγος**, ον, *fond of telling lies*, Tz.*H.*5.140. **-ψεύστης**, ου, ὁ, = φιλοψευδής, Hsch.

**φῐλ-οψία**, ἡ, *fondness for dainties*, esp. *fish*, Plu.2.730b, 750d.

**⊕φῐλό-ψῑλος**, ον, *loving the last place in the chorus*, Alcm.152; cf. ψιλεύς. **-ψογος**, ον, *censorious*, E.*Ph.*198, *El.*904, Pl.*Prt.*346c, Eus.Mynd.1. Adv. -γως Poll.3.139.

**φῐλ-οψος** [ῐ], ον, *fond of dainties*, Plu.2.665e, 668c (Sup.), D.Chr.66.1.

**⊕φῐλοψῡχ-έω**, *love one's life*, with collat. sense of *to be cowardly* or *faint-hearted*, Tyrt.10.18, E.*Hec.*315, *Heracl.*518, 533, D.60.28, etc.; φ. ὑπὲρ τῆς ἀρετῆς Lys.2.25. **-ητέον**, *one must love life*, Pl.*Grg.*512e, = M.Ant.7.46. **-ία**, Ion. -ίη, ἡ, *love of life*, Iamb.*Protr.*20; φιλοψυχίην ἀναιρέεται he conceives a *desire for life*, Hdt.6.29; πολλὴ μεντἄν με φ. ἔχοι, εἰ.. Pl.*Ap.*37c; φιλοψυχίας ἕνεκα Id.*Lg.*944f. **-ος**, ον, *loving one's life*, with collat. sense of *cowardly, faint-hearted*, γυνή E.*Hec.*348, cf. M.Ant.10.8; δειλὸν δ' ὁ πλοῦτος καὶ φ. κακόν E.*Ph.*597 (troch.). Adv. -χως Poll.3.137; φ. ἔχειν Chor.35.139 p.429 F.-R. II. *loving men's lives* or *souls*, δέσποτα φιλόψυχε Lxx *Wi.*11.26.

**φῐλόψῡχρος**, ον, *loving the cold*, Thphr.*CP*2.3.3, Plu.2.648d.

**φῐλόω**, = φιλιόω, Lyd.*Mag.*2.25.

**φιλτάτιον**, τό, *darling*, Com. Diminutive in Ar.*Ach.*475 codd.

**⊕φίλτᾰτος**, η, ον, irreg. Sup. of φίλος, mostly poet., Il.6.91, al., Pi.*P.*9.98, A.*Th.*16, Ar.Ach.885, etc.; τὰ φ. *one's nearest and dearest*, v. φίλος I.1c; οἱ φ. A.*Ch.*234; less freq. in Prose, Pl.*Prt.*314a, *Grg.*513a, *Lg.*650a, X.*Cyr.*4.3.2, etc.; τὰ φ. σώματα, opp. τοὺς ἀλλοτρίους, Aeschin.3.78; cf. φίντατος.

**φίλτερος**, α, ον, irreg. Comp. of φίλος, Il.11.162, Od.11.360, Hes.*Op.*309, Pi.*I.*1.5, E.*El.*243, *Alc.*432, *Hipp.*185 (anap.) (not in A. or S.): in later Prose, D.C.64.14, Jul.*Or.*2.89a.

**φιλτρίς**, ίδος, ἡ, fem. Adj., name of a supposedly self-moving stone, prob. *used as a love-charm*, λίθος Dam.*Pr.*283.

**φιλτρο-δότις**, ἡ, = περιστερεὼν ὀρθός, Ps.-Dsc.4.59; = σκολοπένδριον, Id.3.134. **⊕-κατάδεσμος**, ὁ, *love-spell*, *PMag.Par.*1.296; perh. to be read in *PMag.Lond.*122 tit. **-κίνητος** [κῐ], ον, *excited by love-potions*, Tz.*Proll.Hes.*p.9.

**φίλτρον**, τό, (φιλέω) *love-charm*, whether a potion, or any other means, ἔστιν.. φίλτρα μοι θελκτήρια ἔρωτος E.*Hipp.*509, cf. *Ph.*1260, *Andr.*540 (anap.), Arist.*MM*1188ᵇ32, Theoc.2.1, Dsc.2.164, Alciphr.1.37, etc.; οὐκ ἐπὶ θανάτῳ διδόναι [φάρμακον] ἀλλ' ἐπὶ φίλτροις Antipho 1.9: of the robe of Nessus by which Deïanira hoped to win back the love of Hercules, S.*Tr.*584, 1142. 2. generally, *charm, spell*, οἱ φ. ἐν θυμῷ ὕμνοι τίθεν Pi.*P.*3.64; φ. ἵππειον, of the bit, Id.*O.*13.68; φίλτρα τόλμης *spells to produce* boldness, of oracles, A.*Ch.*1029; δεινὸν τὸ τίκτειν καὶ φέρει φ. μέγα E.*IA*917, cf. *Fr.*103 (anap.), *HF*1407; αἱ ξυγγενεῖς ὁμιλίαι.. φ. οὐ σμικρὸν φρενῶν Id.*Tr.*52; of ἀρεταί, Id.*Andr.*207; φίλτρα γάμου *AP*9.422 (Apollonid.); ἔν ἐστ' ἀληθὲς φ. εὐγνώμων τρόπος Men.646; εἰρήνης φ. a *charm* to promote peace (i. e. γεωργία), Plu.*Num.*16; [παῖδες] νήπιοι ψυχῆς εἰσιν ἰσχυρὰ φ. ἐξομηρεύσασθαι δυνάμενα στρατηγὸν πρὸς πατρίδα Onos.1.12. 3. *love, affection*, in pl., τὰ θεῶν δὲ φίλτρα φροῦδα Τροίᾳ E.*Tr.*859 (lyr.), cf. *El.*1309 (anap.), *AP*7.623 (Aemil.): also in sg., τὸ πρὸς τὴν πατρίδα φ. *SIG*876.7 (Smyrna, Epist.Severi et Caracallae); πᾶσι δὲ φ. κάλλιπεν *AP*15.45, cf. Ael.*NA*10.17, Opp.*C.*3.108, Lib.*Or.*3.22; τὸ πρὸς ἀμφοτέρους φ. Id.*Ep.*297.1. II. *dimple in the upper lip*, Bion 1.48, Ruf.*Onom.*39, Poll.2.90. III. = σταφυλῖνος, Eust.1163.9.

**φιλτρο-ποιός**, όν, *preparing love-charms*, Aristaenet.2.18. **-πόσιμον**, τό, = sq., Cyran.37, al. **-ποτον**, τό, *love-potion*, Cael.Aur.*TP*1.5.

**φίλ-υβρις** [φῐ], ὁ, ἡ, *fond of wanton violence*, Crates Theb.5a. **-υβριστής**, οῦ, ὁ, = foreg., *AP*5.48 (Gall.). **-ῠγιής**, ές, v.l. for φιλοῦγιής (q. v.). **-ύδρηλος**, ον, *loving moisture*, κῆπος ib.6.21. **-υδρίας**, ου, ὁ, = sq., Phot., *EM*795.1. **-υδρος**, ον, *loving water*, of the horse, Arist.*HA*605ᵃ13; λάχανα Thphr.*HP*7.5.1, cf. 6.7.6.

**φιλύκη**, ἡ, a shrub, *evergreen, privet, Rhamnus Alaternus*, Thphr.*HP*1.9.3, 3.3.1, al.

**φίλ-υμνος** [ῐ], ον, *loving song*, *Anacreont.*32.16 (cj. Steph. for φίλυπνε). **-υπήκοος**, ον, *loving one's subjects*, Plu.*Art.*30. **-υπνος**, ον, *loving sleep*, Theoc.18.10, Arist.*Somn.*457ᵃ22. **-υπόδοχος**, ον, *fond of entertaining*, D.L.2.133. **⊕-υπόστροφος**, ον, *apt to return*, of certain complaints, Hp.*Prorrh.*1.105, *Mochl.*37 (Comp.), Gal.18(2).272. **-υποστροφώδης**, ες, = foreg., Hp.*Epid.*4.7.

**φῐλύρ-α** [ῠ], Ion. -ρη, ἡ, *lime tree, Tilia platyphyllos*, Hdt.4.67, Thphr.*HP*1.12.4, al., Dsc.1.96, Corn.*ND*24. 2. φ. ἄρρην, = φιλυρέα, and φ. θήλεια *silver lime, Tilia tomentosa*, Thphr.*HP*3.10.4. II. *the bass underneath its bark*, used for writing on, Gal.18(2).630, Hdn.1.17.1, D.C.72.8; for garlands, φιλύρας.. ἀφύλλος στέφανος Xenarch.13. **-έα**, ἡ, *mock privet, Phillyrea media*, Thphr.*HP*1.9.3; but **φιλλυρέα** is f.l. for φιλύρα in Dsc.1.96. **-ῐνος**, η, ον, *of lime wood*, σανίς Hp.*Art.*47, cf. *Ostr.Bodl.* iii 267 (i A.D.), D.C.67.15, Heliod. (Leonid.Sch.) ap.Orib.44.20.74; *light as lime wood*, of Cinesias, Ar.*Av.*1377, cf. Sch. ad loc.; but Ath.12.551d thinks it means that *he wore stays of lime wood*. **-ιον**, τό, Dim. of φιλύρα, *tablet of lime wood*, Ael.*VH*14.12, prob. for φιλύρινον in *PMag.Par.*1.2695.

**φῐλ-ῳδία**, ἡ, *love of song*, τεττίγων Ael.*NA*5.13. **⊕-ῳδός**, όν, (ᾠδή) *song-loving*, Ar.*V.*270, *Ra.*240 (lyr.), Eub.84.1, Plu.2.633a, cj. in Arist.*EE*1238ᵃ37.

**φίλων**, ωνος, ὁ, perh. = φέλων, Alc.*Fr.*48 Lobel (= *Supp.*23.4).

**φῐλώνειος**, ον, *invented by Philo* of Tarsus, ἀντίδοτος Orib.*Fr.*82, etc.

**Φῐλωνίδειον** [ῐδ], τό, *trust-fund, dedicated by* Φιλωνίς, *Inscr.Délos* 396 *A* 62 (ii B.C.). II. **Φῐλωνίδεια** [ῐδ], τά, *festival in honour of P.*, ib.366 *A* 134 (iii B.C.).

**φῐλωνίζω**, *imitate Philo*, Suid. s.v. Φίλων.

**φῐλ-ώραιος**, ον, *loving the beautiful*, Tz.*H.*1.234. **-ωρείτης**, ου, Dor. -τας, ὁ, (ὄρος) *a lover of mountains*, Πάν *AP*6.96 (Eryc.).

**φίλωσις** [ῑ], εως, ἡ, older form of φιλίωσις, Iamb. *in Nic.*p.34 P., Megillus ap. *Theol.Ar.*27. II. Pythag. name for *six*, ib.37.

**φῑλωτερίς**, ίδος, ἡ, = κασταναία, Hsch.

**φῑλωτικός**, ή, όν, = φιλιωτικός, *Theol.Ar.*5.

**φῑμάριον**, τό, Dim. of φιμός, *mask*, only in Lat. form *fimarium*, *Gloss.*

**φῑμοκάτοχον**, τό, *charm to keep* men and dogs *silent*, Cyran.57, al.

⊛**φῑμ-ός**, ὁ, heterocl. pl. φιμά *AP*6.312 (Anyte):—*any instrument for keeping the mouth closed*: I. *muzzle*, for dogs, calves, etc., φιμὸν περιτιθέναι τινί Luc. *Vit.Auct.*22, cf. *APl.* c., Lxx *Si.*20.29. 2. *gag*: hence, *silencing* by a spell, *Tab.Defix.Aud.*25.13 (Curium, iii A.D.). II. *nose-band* of a horse's bridle, fitted with pipes, φ. δὲ συρίζουσι βάρβαρον βρόμον A.*Th.*463; πώλους.. φιμοῖσιν αὐλωτοῖσιν ἐστομωμένας Id.*Fr.*326; ἐμβαλῶ φ. εἰς τὴν ῥῖνά σου Lxx *Is.*37.29. III. a kind of *cup*, used as a *dice-box*, Aeschin.1.59, Diph. 76, cf. Poll.7.203, 10.150. IV. *tightening*, *constriction* by means of ropes, Apollod.*Poliorc.*161.1. V. = φίμωσις II. 2, φ. τοὺς ἐν αἰδοίοις χαλᾷ Dsc.4.91, cf. Androm.ap.Gal.13.311; *imperforation* of the anus, Heliod.ap.Orib.44.20.72. (Connected with σφίγγω, σφιγμός by *EM*795.21.)⊛-όω, *muzzle*, οὐ φιμώσεις βοῦν ἀλοῶντα Lxx *De.*25.4; *shut up as with a muzzle*, φ. τῷ ξύλῳ τὸν αὐχένα *to make fast* his neck in the pillory, Ar.*Nu.*592 (troch.); *close*, *seal up*, στόμα [ἄγγους] Asclep. ap.Gal.12.984: metaph., *muzzle*, *put to silence*, τινα *Ev.Matt.*22.34:—Pass., *to be put to silence*, *be silent*, φιμώθητι, πεφίμωσο, *Ev.Marc.*1.25, 4.39, cf. Luc.*Peregr.*15, *Mim.Oxy.*413.122; τινι *by* or *because of* a thing, J.*BJ*1.22.3, cf. 5.1.5; φιμοῦσθαι πρός τι *to be mute* in a matter, ib.*Prooem.*5, S.E.*M.*8.275. **-ώδης**, ες, *like a muzzle*: metaph., *astringent*, μύρτα Nic.*Th.*892. ⊛**-ωσις**, εως, ἡ, *muzzling*, *silencing*, of death, πρὶν φθάσαι τὴν φ. Vett.Val.257.13. II. *stopping up an orifice*, e.g. of the eye, Gal.18(2).812, *PMed.Strassb.*p.6. 2. *contraction* of the prepuce, Antyll.ap.Orib.50.5.1. ⊛**-ωτικός**, ή, όν, *silencing*; -κόν, τό, *spell for silencing*, *PMag.Lond.*121.396. **-ωτρον**, τό, *instrument for stopping up*, Suid.

**φιν**, = σφιν, v. σφεῖς A.II.

⊛**-φιν**, v. -φι.

**φίνις**, ὁ, v.l. for φήνη, Dsc.2.53.

**φίντατος**, Dor. for φίλτατος, Epich.56.

**Φίξ**, v. Σφίγξ.

⊛**φίσκος**, ὁ, Lat. *fiscus*, *basket*, *crate*, ἀργυρωμάτων *Ostr.Bodl.* iii 290 (i A.D.). II. *the Imperial Treasury*, χωρία τὰ ὑπὸ τοῦ φ. πραθέντα *IG*2².1100.4, cf. *OGI*669.21 (Egypt, i A.D.), *PRyl.*157.23 (ii A.D.), etc.

**φισκοσυνήγορος**, ὁ, = Lat. *advocatus fisci*, *PKlein.Form.*1028 (vi A.D.), *PMasp.*57 ii 23 (vi A.D.).

**Φιτιαλεῖς**, v. Φετιάλιοι.

⊛**φιτρός**, ὁ, *block of wood*, *log*, φιτρῶν καὶ λάων Il.12.29, 21.314; φιτροὺς αἶψα ταμόντες Od.12.11, cf. A.R.1.405, Call.*Fr.*246 (= *PSI*11.1218*a*2); *bole* or *trunk* of a tree, Q.S.12.137. II. *firebrand*, B. 5.142, Lyc.913.

**φίττᾰ**, f.l. for ψίττα (q.v.).

**φιττάκια**, v. πιττάκιον. 2. v. sq.

**φιττακίδες**, αἱ, a kind of *woman's shoes*, Poll.7.94 (v.l. **φιττάκια**).

⊛**φῖτυ**, τό, poet. for sq., Ar.*Pax*1164 (lyr.), Pherecr.244, Eup. 49, prob. in Epich.207.

**φίτῡμα** [ῑ], ατος, τό, (φῑτύω) *shoot*, *scion*, of a son, A.*Ag.*1281; οὐκ ἐμὸν τὸ φ., said a Spartan mother of a cowardly son, Plu.2.241a, cf. Epigr. ibid.

**φῑτῠποίμην**, ενος, ὁ, poet. for φυτοκόμος, *tender of plants*, *gardener*, ἀνδρὸς φ. δίκην A.*Eu.*911.

**φῖτυς**, υος, ὁ, *begetter*, *father*, Lyc.462,486.

**φῑτύω**, fut. ύσω [ῡ], E.*Alc.*294: aor. ἐφίτυσα (v. infr.):—*sow*, *plant*, *beget*, A.*Pr.*235, *Supp.*313, S.*Ant.*645, E. l. c.; ὁ φιτύσας πατήρ S.*Aj.*1296, *Tr.*311; also used by Pl., *R.*461a, *Lg.*879d, *Criti.*116c:—Med., of the woman, *bear*, Ἠὼς.. Κεφάλῳ φιτύσατο υἱόν Hes.*Th.* 986, cf. A.R.4.807, Opp.*C.*1.4; Ep. 2 sg. fut. φιτύσεαι Mosch.2. 160.

**φλαβίλλιον**, τό, = Lat. *flabellum*, Chrysipp.Tyan.ap.Ath.14.647f.

⊛**φλαγέλλιον**, τό, = Lat. *flagellum*, *PLond.*1.191.11 (ii A.D.), Hsch. s.v. σκυτάλαι.

**φλᾰδιάω**, = φλάω, Hsch.

***φλάζω**, intr. form of φλάω, *to be rent with a noise*, aor. 2 ἔφλᾰδον (cf. *EM*403.47), λακίδες ἔφλαδον A.*Ch.*28 (lyr.).—Pres. only in redupl. παφλάζω.

⊛**φλᾱμέντας**, ου, ὁ, = Lat. *flamen*, App.*BC*1.65; so **φλαμήν** *IG*2².5206, *CIG*4340*f* (add.): acc. sg. φλάμινα *Supp.Epigr.*6.588 (Pisidia): pl. **φλάμονες** D.H.2.64; **φλάμινες** Plu.*Num.*7; **φλαμίνιοι** Id.*Marc.* 5: fem. **φλαμινίκα**, ἡ, Lat. *flaminica*, Id.2.285a.

**φλανύσσω**, = φλυαρέω, Hsch.

**φλάσις** [ᾰ], εως, ἡ, (φλάω) Ion. for θλάσις, Hp.*VC*18.

**φλάσκη**, ἡ, *wine-flask*, Isid.*Etym.*20.6.2; also **φλάσκων**, ωνος, ὁ, *a flagon*, Hsch. s.v. ἀρυβάσσαλον, Tz.*H.*13.643:—Dim. **φλασκίον**, τό, Suid. s.v. πυτίνη, Sch.Od.2.349.

**φλάσ-μα**, ατος, τό, Ion. for θλάσμα, Hp.*Art.*36, al. **-μός**, ὁ, = τῦφος, Hsch. **-τός**, ή, όν, Ion. for θλαστός, v.l. Arist.*HA*523ᵇ7,11.

**φλαττόθρατ** and **φλαττοθραττοφλαττόθρατ**, Com. words in Ar. *Ra.*1296,1286; meant to parody an empty high-flown style—'sound and fury signifying nothing'.

**φλαυρίζω**, = φαυλίζω, Plu.*Caes.*52, 2.1118c.

⊛**φλαῦρος**, α, ον, = φαῦλος (*EM*128.57), first in Sol.13.15, Pi.*P.*1.87, prevailing in Ion. Prose, and freq. in Att. (v. infr. I. 2 and III): I. mostly of things, *petty*, *paltry*, *trivial*, Sol., Pi. ll. cc.; ἀποσκήψαντος τοῦ ἐνυπνίου ἐς φλαῦρον having come to *a trivial ending*, Hdt.1. 120. 2. *indifferent*, *bad*, χώρην τῆς νῦν ἐκτήμεθα οὐκ ἐλάσσονα οὐδὲ φλαυροτέρην Id.7.8.α'; φ. σημεῖον Hp.*Aph.*6.52; εἴ τι φ. εἶδες A.*Pers.*217 (troch.); opp. ἀγαθός, Pl.*Men.*92c; opp. καλός, Democr. 63; φλαῦρ' ἔπη μυθούμενος S.*Aj.*1162; κλύειν φλαῦρα ib.1323; φλαῦρον ἐργάσασθαί τινα to do one *a mischief*, Ar.*Nu.*1157; φλαῦρον εἰπεῖν τινας speak *disparagingly* of them, ib.834, cf. *Lys.*1045 (lyr.); περί τινος Antipho 5.30, Isoc.5.76; τῆς δόξης ταύτης φ. τι καταγιγνώσκειν Id.15.297; φ. τι ἀπολαῦσαί Id.8.81; γέροντα δ' ὀρθοῦν φλαῦρον ὃς νέος πέσῃ it is a *poor* thing, S.*OC*395. II. less freq. of persons, οὐ φλαυροτάτους.. τιμωρούς not *the least distinguished*.., Hdt. 7.171; τῆς στρατιῆς τὸ -ότατον the *least serviceable part*, Id.1.207; οἰκίης οὐ -οτέρης not *meaner*, Id.1.99. 2. *shabby*, *plain*, of personal appearance, τὸ εἶδος φ. Id.6.61. 3. *bad*, opp. χρηστός, E.*Med.*1103 (anap.). III. Adv., -ρως ἔχειν to be *ill*, Hp.*Mul.*1.26, Hdt.3.129, 6.135, Pl.*Sph.*228b; φ. ἔχειν τινός to be *ill off* for a thing, Th.1.126; φ. ἔχειν τὴν τέχνην have a *slight* knowledge of.. Hdt.3.130; φ. πρῆξαι τῷ στόλῳ to fare *badly* with.. Id.6.94; φ. ἀκούειν to be *ill* spoken of, Id.7.10.η'; φ. λέγειν ὑπέρ τινος Ael.*VH*8.17; φ. ἰέναι, of the καταμήνια, Hp.*Steril.*241.

**φλαυρότης**, ητος, ἡ, *poorness*, cf. φαυλότης, Plu.2.962a; condemned by Poll.4.12.

**φλαυρουργός**, όν, *working badly*, φλαυρουργοῦ τινος.. ἀνδρός of some *sorry* workman, S.*Ph.*35.

⊛**φλάω**, Ar.*Pl.*784, impf. 3 sg. ἔφλα Id.*Nu.*1376: fut. φλάσω [ᾰ], Dor. φλασσῶ Theoc.5.148 (Ahrens, φλασῶ codd.): aor. ἔφλᾰσα Hp. *VC*11, poet. φλάσα Pi.*N.*10.68, Dor. opt. φλάσσαιμι Theoc.5.150 (Ahrens, φλάσαιμι codd.):—Pass., aor. ἐφλάσθην Hp. l. c., etc.; pf. πέφλασμαι ib.5, (συμ-) *IG*2².1425.351:—= θλάω, *crush*, οὔ νιν φλάσαν Pi. l. c.; πουλύπουν φλάσασα ἐσθιέτω Hp.*Superf.*33, cf. *VC*2 (Pass.); ἔφλα ἐν τῇ θυείᾳ.. σκόροδα καὶ σχῖνον Ar.*Pl.*718; φλῶσι τἀντικνήμια ib. 784; ἔφλα με Id.*Nu.*1376, cf. Theoc. ll. cc.: metaph., πᾶσι κακοῖσιν ἡμᾶς [τὰς γυναῖκας] φλῶσιν.. ἄνδρες Ar.*Fr.*10 (lyr.). 2. Com., *bruise with the teeth*, *eat up*, Id.*Pl.*694, *Pax*1306, Antiph.190.19, Men.607. II. sens. obsc., = *masturbari*, Hsch.

**φλεβάζω**, = φλέω, *EM.*795.43; = βρύω, Phot.

⊛**φλεβ-ικός**, ή, όν, *of a vein*, *of the veins*, φ. πόροι the channels *of the veins*, Arist.*HA.*510ᵃ14, *PA*647ᵇ2; οἱ πόροι οἱ φ. Id.*HA*561ᵃ 17.

**φλέβιον**, τό, Dim. of φλέψ, *any one of the smaller vessels*, Hp.*VC* 1, Pl.*Ti.*65c,84e, Arist.*HA*514ᵃ19,ᵇ27; φλεβίου ῥῆξις Hp.*Aph.*4. 78. II. of *veins* in the earth, Str.8.6.21.

**φλεβο-δονώδης**, ες, f.l. for φλεδονώδης (q.v.). **-νευρώδης**, ες, *made up of veins and sinews*, Arist.*Resp.*478ᵇ8. **-νώδης**, f.l. for φλεδονώδης (q.v.). **-πᾰλία**, ἡ, *beating of the pulse*, Democr.120, Gal.9.499. **-περιμέτριος**, ον, perh. *imitating the veining* of alabaster, *PCair.Zen.*445.7 (iii B.C., dub. l.). **-ρραγία**, ἡ, *bursting of a vein*, Hp.*Acut.*(*Sp.*)40. **-σφυγμος**, ὁ, = *pulsus venae*, dub. in *Gloss.* (φλευτμονος cod.). **-τμής**, ὁ, ἡ, gen. τμῆτος, *having a vein opened*, Hdn.Gr.2.98.

⊛**φλεβοτομ-έω**, *open a vein*, *bleed*, Hp.*Ulc.*26, *Aph.*6.47, Arr.*Epict.* 2.17.9:—Pass., Hp.*Aph.*5.31, *PPetr.*2p.73 (iii B.C.). **-ησις**, εως, ἡ, *blood-letting*, Antyll.ap.Orib.7.14.2. **-ητέον**, *one must open a vein*, Archig.ap.Orib.47.13.5, Herod.Med.ap.eund.7.8.1; *bleed*, τινα Artem.2.70. II. Adj. -τέος, α, ον, Gal.10.611. **-ία**, Ion. -ίη, ἡ, *blood-letting*, Hp.*Coac.*288, *Nat.Hom.*11, Aristid.*Or.*49(25).34 (pl.), Gal.6.256; φλεβοτομίας ποιεῖσθαι Polybus ap.Arist.*HA*512ᵇ17. **-ική** (sc. τέχνη), ἡ, *the art of blood-letting*, Cael.Aur.*CP*1.3. **-ος** (parox.), ον, *opening veins*: φλεβοτόμον (sc. σμιλίον), τό, *lancet*, Luc.*Ind.*29, Cael.Aur.*CP*2.19, Steph. *in Int.*17.19, etc.

**φλεβοτονέομαι**, Pass., *to have the veins swollen in* great exertion, Phryn.*PS*p.121B.

**φλεβώδης**, ες, *full of veins*, or *with large veins*, Hp.*Morb.*4.40, Arist.*HA*494ᵃ7, 582ᵃ15; of plants, Thphr.*HP*1.5.3: Sup. -έστατος Arist.*Spir.*484ᵃ4. II. *like a vein*, ἀρτηρία Gal.*UP*6.10.

**φλεγέθω**, poet. form of φλέγω, only pres.: I. trans., *scorch*, *burn up*, πῦρ πόλιν φλεγέθει Il.17.738:—Pass., ὄφρα πυρὶ φλεγεθοίατο νεκροί 23.197. II. intr., *blaze*, *flare up*, πυρὶ φλεγέθοντι 21.358, cf. Orph.*Fr.*194; πυρσοί τε φλεγέθουσι Il.18.211; κεραυνοῦ φλεγέθοντος Hes.*Th.*[846]; [Ἅλιος] λαμπρᾷ στεροπᾷ φλεγέθων S.*Tr.*99 (lyr.), cf. E.*Ph.*169 (lyr.): metaph., *blaze forth*, *shine*, A.*Supp.*88 (lyr.).

**φλεγιάω**, = φλέγω, Hdn.Gr.2.949.

**φλέγμα**, ατος, τό, (φλέγω) *flame*, *fire*, *heat*, Il.21.337. II. Medic. 1. *inflammation*, *heat*, Hp.*Prog.*18, *Morb.*2.27, Gal.*Nat.Fac.*2.9. 2. *phlegm*, one of the four *humours* in the body, Hdt.4.187, Hp.*Nat.Hom.*4, *Aph.*7.54, Phryn.Com. l. c., Thphr.*HP*9.11.9; φ. ὀξὺ καὶ ἁλμυρὸν πηγὴ πάντων νοσημάτων ὅσα γίγνεται καταρροϊκά Pl.*Ti.*85b, cf. 83c sq.; ἡ χολὴ μέν ἐστι θερμόν, τὸ δὲ φ. ψυχρόν Arist.*Pr.*862ᵇ28, cf. Pl.*R.*564ᵇ; τὸ πικρὸν φ. Phld.*Vit.*p.18J.: pl., Pl.*Ti.*82e; φ. ἁλυκά ib.86e. 3. λευκὸν φ., a kind of dropsy, *anasarca*, Hp.*Aph.*7.75 (but λευκὸν φ., in the common sense, Pl.*Ti.*83d, 85a). 4. in Poets, *malignant*, *angry humour*, ἄγριον Ἀρχιλόχου φ. *AP*7.70 (Jul.), cf. 377 (pl., Eryc.).

**φλεγμ-ᾰγωγός**, όν, (φλέγμα II. 2) *carrying off phlegm*, Ruf.ap. Orib.8.47.46, Gal.11.325. ⊛**-αίνω**, aor. ἐφλέγμηνα Ar.*V.*276 (lyr.), D.C.64.4, M.Ant.4.49; later -ᾶνα Lxx *Na.*3.19: I. trans., *cause to swell up*; of food, *fill*, *nourish*, opp. ἰσχναίνω, Hp.*Loc.Hom.*34. II.

intr., *to be heated, inflamed, fester*, Id.*Aph*.5.58, *Prog*.7, Lxx l. c.; πληγὴ φλεγμαίνουσα ib.*Is*.1.6, cf. Ar. l. c., Pl.*Ti*.85b. b. *to be swollen*, Hp.*Loc.Hom*.13. 2. of the sea, *seethe*, M.Ant. l. c.; κῦμα φλεγμαῖνον Hld.5.17. 3. metaph., φλεγμαίνουσα πόλις, opp. ὑγιής, Pl. *R*.372e; ἀρχὴ φλεγμαίνουσα, = σπαργῶσα καὶ θυμουμένη, Id.*Lg*.691e; τὰ φ. τῶν πραγμάτων Plu.*Pomp*.21; of feelings, etc., Plb.3.86.6, Plu.*Per*.6, al., Hld.7.21; οἱ στρατιῶται ἐφλέγμηναν D.C. l. c.; also of luxury, πολυτελεῖς καὶ φλεγμαίνουσαι τράπεζαι Plu.2.660f; also τὰ ἐν Βαβυλῶνι φλεγμαίνοντα, of *extravagant* court ceremonial, Philostr.*VA*2.25. **-ανσις**, εως, ἡ, = φλεγμονή, Hp.*Mul*.1.40. **-ᾰσία**, Ion. -ίη, ἡ, = foreg., Id.*Acut*.35, Arist.*GA*746ᵃ5, etc. 2. *turgescence*, Hp.*Loc.Hom*.42. **-ᾰτιαῖος**, α, ον, (φλέγμα II. 2) *suffering from phlegm*, v.l. in *Gp*.12.22.2. **-ᾰτίας**, Ion. **-ίης**, ου, ὁ, (φλέγμα II. 2) = foreg., Hp.*Aër*.10, *Acut*.34, etc. 2. *one suffering from anasarca*, Id.*Epid*.7.6. **-ᾰτικός**, ή, όν, (φλέγμα II. 2) *abounding in phlegm*, ἔδεσμα, of the brain as food, Gal.6.676 (Comp.), cf. Alex.Aphr.*Pr*.1.2 (Comp.). **-άτιον**, τό, = φλέγμα II. 2, Sotad.ap.Stob.3.22.26. **-ᾰτισμός**, ὁ, as Lat. word, *flegma spissa, pinguis et glutinosa*, *Gloss*.

**φλεγμᾰτο-ειδής**, ές, (φλέγμα II. 1) *pituitous*, Hp.*Mul*.1.30. ⊛**-εις**, εσσα, εν, *fiery*, Hsch. **-ομαι**, Pass., *become phlegm*, Gal.15.90.

**φλεγμᾰτώδης**, ες, *full of phlegm*, κεφαλαί Hp.*Aër*.3. 2. of food, *nourishing*, Id.*Loc.Hom*.41. b. *inflammatory*, Pl.*R*.406a. 3. of persons, *phlegmatic*, Hp.*Epid*.3.14, Arist.*Pr*.860ᵇ9. II. *like phlegm*, κάθαρσις Id.*HA*574ᵇ5, 578ᵇ19; τὸ αἷμα.. ῥέει -έστερον Hp. *Nat.Hom*.6. 2. *apt to produce phlegm*, ὕδατα Id.*Aër*.7 (Sup.).

**φλεγμον-άομαι**, *become inflamed*, Alex.Trall.2. **-ή**, ἡ, *fiery heat*, dub.l. in Plu.2.398e (pl.). II. *inflammation*, Pl.*Ax*.366a (pl.), Philem.113, Plu.2.699e, *Alex*.35, etc. 2. Medic., *inflamed tumour, boil*, Hp.*VM*18, *Epid*.3.4, Pl.*Ax*.368c, Gal.10.66. III. metaph., *heat, passion, excess*, παθητικὴ φ. Chrysipp.*Stoic*.3.118; ἡ φ. τῶν παθῶν ib.124, cf. Lxx 4*Ma*.3.17 (pl.), Plu.2.994a, Ath.1.10e. **-ικός**, ή, όν, *inflammatory*, ῥεῦμα Gal.9.181. **-ώδης**, ες, *like an inflamed tumour* (φλεγμονή II. 2), *attended by them*, Id.15.727; αἴσθησις, κόπος, Id.16.593.

**φλεγμός**, ὁ, *blood*, Hsch.; Βρομίου φ. Thespis 4.6 (anap.).

**φλεγμώδης**, ες, = φλεγματώδης, χυμοί Gal.9.460 (s. v. l.).

**φλέγος**, τό, = φλόξ, Hsch.

**Φλέγρα**, Ion. -ρη, ἡ, *Phlegra*, an ancient name for Pallene in Thrace, prob. from its *volcanic* nature, Hdt.7.123, Str.7*Fr*.27; Φλέγρας πεδίον, in which the giants are said to have been conquered by the gods, Pi.*N*.1.67, Ar.*Av*.824; Φλεγραία πλάξ A.*Eu*.295: pl. Φλέγραι Pi.*I*.6(5).33.

**Φλεγραῖα**, τά (cf. foreg.), the *volcanic* plain of Campania, Plb.2.17.1, etc.

**φλεγύας** [ῠ], αο, ὁ, perh. *fiery red, red-brown*, epithet of the eagle μόρφνος, Hes.*Sc*.134.

**φλεγυάω**, = ὑβρίζω, Phocian word in Ephor.93J., cf. Eust.933.14.

**φλεγῠρός**, ά, όν, *burning, inflamed*, Hp.ap.Gal.19.152. II. metaph., *hot, ardent*, Μοῦσα Ar.*Ach*.665 (lyr.). 2. = ὑβριστικός, Hsch.; ψῆφος Cratin.57 (lyr.).

**φλέγω**, Il.21.13, etc.: fut. φλέξω S.*Fr*.1128.5, A.R.3.582, Lxx *De*.32.22, etc.: aor. ἔφλεξα A.*Pr*.582 (lyr.):—**Pass.**, fut. φλεγήσομαι (συμ-) J.*BJ*.7.8.5: in 4.6.3 the readings κατα-φλέξεσθαι, -φλεχθήσεσθαι, and -φλεγήσεσθαι are found in codd.; κατα-φλεχθήσεται Ach.Tat.*Intr.Arat*. p.61 M.: aor. ἐφλέχθην Hom.*Epigr*.14.23, (κατ-) Th.4.133: aor. 2 ἐφλεγην (ἀν-) Luc.*DDeor*.9.2, (ἐξ-) *AP*12.178 (Strat.): pf. πέφλεγμαι Lyc.806.

A. trans., *burn, burn up*, Il.21.13; πυρί ⟨με⟩ φλέξον A.*Pr*.582 (lyr.): φλέγων ἀκτῖσιν ἥλιος χθόνα Id.*Pers*.364, cf. 504:—Pass., *take fire, blaze up*, ῥέεθρα πυρὶ φλέγετο Il.21.365, cf. *BMus.Inscr*.1036 (Caria, ii/i B. C.). 2. Pass., *to be inflamed*, κάεσθαί τε καὶ φ. Pl. *Ti*.85b; ἡ πεφλεγμένη ποδαλγία *PLond*.5.1676.16 (vi A. D.). 3. metaph., *kindle, inflame* with passion, Ἄρεα..ὃς..φλέγει με *OT*192 (lyr.), cf. Mosch.*Fr*.2.3, *AP*5.122 (Phld.), 287 (Paul.Sil.); αἷμα δάϊον φ. E.*Ph*.241 (lyr.):—Pass., *burn with passion*, S.*OC*1695 (lyr.), Ar.*Nu*.992 (anap.), Pl.*Chrm*.155d; νεότητι καὶ ἀνοίᾳ φλέγεται τὴν ψυχήν Id.*Lg*.716a; ὑπὸ τοῦ πάθους D.H.11.28: ὑπὸ δίψης Id.9.66; ὑπὸ τοῦ λιμοῦ Ael.*NA*14.27; ἐπί τινι Id.*Fr*.52. II. *light up*, φ. λαμπάσι τόδ' ἱερόν E.*Tr*.309 (lyr.); Ζεὺς διὰ χερὸς βέλος φλέγων *making* it *blaze* or *flash*, A.*Th*.513; πυρὸς φλέξον μένος *Trag.Adesp*.90: metaph., ἄταν οὐρανίαν φλέγων *letting* the flame of mischief *blaze up* to heaven, S.*Aj*.195 (lyr.):—Pass., *blaze up, burst* or *break forth*, βωμοὶ δώροισι φλέγονται A.*Ag*.91 (anap.): metaph., ὕμνοι φλέγονται B.*Fr*.3.12. 2. metaph., *make illustrious* or *famous*, σὲ φλέγοντι Χάριτες Pi.*P*.5.45:—Pass., *to be* or *become so*, ἀρεταῖς, Μοίσαις φλέγεσθαι, Id.*N*.10.2, *I*.7(6).23.

B. intr., *burn, blaze*, of fire, torches, etc., A.*Ag*.308, *Th*.433, S.*Aj*.1278; of lightning, Id.*OC*1467 (lyr.); of the sun, Id.*Aj*.673; φλέγονθ' ὑπ' ἄστροις οὐρανόν A.*Th*.388: of armour, *flash*, νέφος ἀσπίδων φ. E.*Ph*.251 (lyr.); ἄνθεμα χρυσοῦ φλέγει Pi.*O*.2.72; γυναικὸς φλέγων ὀφθαλμός A.*Fr*.243; of fire-breathing bulls, φλέγει δὲ μυκτήρ S.*Fr*.336. 2. metaph., *burst* or *break forth*, of passion, θυμὸς ἀνδρείᾳ φλέγων A.*Th*.52, cf. 287; φ. λύσσῃ Ar.*Th*.680 (lyr.); of grief, A.R.3.773. 3. *shine forth, become famous*, Pi.*N*.6.38.—Poet. in early writers, exc. Pl. ll. cc. (Cf. Lat. *fulgeo, flagro, flamma*, Lett. *blāzma* 'glare of light or fire'.)

**φλεδον-εία**, ἡ, *idle talk*, *EM*796.3. **-εύομαι**, Med., *babble*, Hsch.:—Act. in *EM*796.4. **-έω** = foreg., Hsch. **-ώδης**, ες, *loquacious*, Erot.; to be read, for φλεβοδονώδης or φλεβονώδης, in Hp.*Prorrh*.1.101, *Coac*.20, *Epid*.4.45.

**φλέδων**, ονος, ὁ, ἡ, (φλέω) *idle talker, babbler*, Timo 28 (pl.), 37; of a woman, A.*Ag*.1195. II. **φλεδών**, όνος, ἡ, *idle talk*, Anon. ap.Gal.16.733 (pl.), Plu.2.420c (pl.).

**φλειά**, v. φλιά.

**φλεΐνος**, η, ον, *made from the plant* φλέως, Phryn.262.

**φλειός**, ὁ, = φλιά, *Jahresh*.28.55 (Sivrihissar).

**Φλειοῦς**, οῦντος, ὁ later **Φλιοῦς** (as spelt in codd. of Th.5.58, X. *HG*7.2.11, al., v.l. in Hdt.7.202), *Phlius* in the Peloponnese, B.8.4, Hdt. l. c., etc.:—Adj. **Φλειάσιος** [ᾱ], later **Φλι-**, *SIG*31 (Delph., v B. C.), *IG*1².82.15, etc., Ion. **Φλειήσιος** *SIG*239*B*49, 51 (Delph., iv B. C.), in codd. of Hdt. **Φλιάσιος** 8.72, al. (v.l. **Φλειάσιος** in 9.69, al.).

**φλενός**, v. φληνός II.

**φλέξις** (A), ιδος, ἡ, an unknown bird, Ar.*Av*.884.

**φλέξις** (B), εως, ἡ, *ardor, flammatus*, *Gloss*.

**φλέος**, ὁ, = φλέως, φλοῦς, Hsch. II. = βασκανία, φθορά, Id. (φλεός cod., Theognost.*Can*.49). III. **Φλέος**, epith. of Dionysus, *SIG*1003.1 (Priene, ii B. C.).

⊛**Φλεύς**, ὁ, epith. of Dionysus, Hdn.Gr.1.400, 2.911; cf. Φλέω· Διονύσου ἱερόν, Hsch.

***φλεύω**, only found in compds., v. ἐπι-, περι-φλεύω.

⊛**φλέψ**, ἡ, gen. φλεβός: also masc., φλέβες οἰδαίνοντες (nisi leg. οἰδαίνοντος) Nonn.*D*.47.111:—*blood-vessel*, whether *vein* or *artery*, Il.13.546, Hdt.4.2, 187, A.*Fr*.230, S.*Ph*.825; distd. from artery, Hp. *Alim*.31; φλὲψ κοίλη *vena cava*, Id.*Vict*.1.9, E.*Ion* 1011, Arist.*HA* 497ᵃ14; also called φ. μεγάλη, μεγίστη, ib.495ᵇ7, 496ᵃ26; φ. σπληνῖτις, ἡπατῖτις, ib.512ᵃ6; φλέβες σπερματίτιδες Diog.Apoll.6 (also used of the *ureters*, Hp.*Oss*.4); γονίμη φλέψ *membrum virile*, *AP* 6.218 (Alc.), cf. Neophro (?) in *PLit.Lond*.77*Fr*.2.7: so abs., *APl*.4.261 (Leon.); φλεβὸς τροπωτήρ Xenarch.1.8; φλέβα σχάζειν *to open a vein*, X.*HG*5.4.58; λύειν Posidon.72J.; οὗ ἂν ἡ φ. σφύζῃ where the *vein* throbs, Hp.*Epid*.2.5.16; αἱ φ. ἐξανίστανται Luc.*BisAcc*.11. 2. *vein* of metal, X.*Vect*.1.5, Arist.*GC*326ᵇ35, D.S.2.36, D.P.1104: *spring of* water, Arist.*Pr*.935ᵇ10; αἱ φ. τῆς πηγῆς Plb.34.9.7, cf. *Supp.Epigr*.4.467.5 (Didyma, iii A. D.), *Gp*.2.5.6. 3. *vein* in plants, Arist.*PA*668ᵃ25, Thphr.*HP*1.2.1.

**φλέω**, *teem with abundance, abound*, φλεόντων δωμάτων A.*Ag*.377 (lyr.); μήλων φλεόντων εὐπόκοις νομεύμασιν ib.1416; cf. *EM* 796.3. II. *babble*, Hsch.

**φλέως**, ω, ὁ, *wool-tufted reed, Erianthus Ravennae*, Ar.*Ra*.244 (lyr.), *Fr*.24, Pherecr.127, Arist.*HA*627ᵃ8, Thphr.*HP*4.8.1, etc.:—Ion. **φλοῦς**, acc. φλοῦν, q. v. (II), cf. φλόϊνος.—Thphr. has nom. φλεώς *HP*4.10.1, acc. φλεῶ 4.8.1, but φλεών 4.10.4, gen. φλεῶ ibid., al.; gen. φλέως is f.l. in Pherecr. l. c. II. = ἀπόκυνον, Ps.-Dsc.4.80.

**φληδάω**, = sq., Hsch.

**φληνάφ-άω**, *chatter, babble*, Ar.*Eq*.664, *Nu*.1475; τί ταῦτα ληρεῖς, φληναφῶν ἄνω κάτω; Alex.25.1, cf. Oenom.ap.Eus.*PE*5.24, Procl. *in Ti*.1.90D.:—Pass., Phld.*Rh*.1.246 S., *Ir*.p.69 W. **-ημα**, ατος, τό, = φλήναφος, E.*Ep*.5.2 (pl.). ⊛**-ία**, ἡ, *chattering, babbling, nonsense*, Phld.*Po.Herc*.994.38, Suid. ⊛**-ος**, ὁ, *idle talk, nonsense*, ἡ πρόνοια δ' ἡ θνητὴ καπνὸς καὶ φ. Men.482.6, cf. *Kol*.21, Luc.*Dem.Enc*.35, Amelius ap.Porph.*Plot*.17; τοὺς θεοὺς ἡγεῖτο εἶναι φλήναφον Lib.*Ep*.803.4: pl., Phld.*Rh*.2.267 S., Luc.*Somn*.7, *Pisc*.25, etc. II. *babbler*, ὦ φλήναφε Men.109, cf. Poll.6.119. ⊛**-ώδης**, ες, *chattering, babbling*, Hp.ap.Gal.19.152.

**φλῆνος**, εος, τό, = φλήναφος, prob. for φλῆφος in Hsch. II. **φληνός** and **φλενός** are assumed as etym. of φλήναφος in *EM*796.9, 10.

**φληνύω**, *babble*, Hp.ap.Gal.19.152.

⊛**φλῐά** (later φλειά, prob. in *Jahresh*.28.54 (Oropus, i B. C.)), ἡ, mostly in pl. φλιαί, *doorposts, jambs*, Od.17.221, Bion 1.87, Lxx *De*.6.9, Plb.12.11.2, J.*AJ*5.8.10: in sg., *IG*1².386.6, Theoc.23.18; παρὰ φλιῇ Call.*Iamb*.1.220; τὸ ψάφισμα..ἀναγράψαι ἐς τὰν φλιάν *IG*12(3).170.24 (Astypalaea), cf. 12(7).237.50 (Amorgos). 2. *lintel*, A.R.3.278; τᾶς φ. καθ' ὑπέρτερον Theoc.2.60. 3. *standing posts in which a windlass works*, Hp.*Art*.47. 4. *support*, φ. πιοειδής Ruf.ap.Orib.49.27.7, cf. Hp.*Art*.73.

**φλῐᾰρός**, ά, όν, = χλιαρός, Hsch.

⊛**Φλῐάσιος** [ᾱ], ὁ (sc. μήν), name of a Spartan month, St.Byz. s.v. Φλιοῦς; [Φλ]ειάσιος prob. in *IG*5(1).363.17 (Sparta, i A. D.); cf. Φλυήσιος.

**φλίβω** [ῑ], = θλίβω, Act., only impf. in Hsch.:—Med., ὃς πολλῇς φλιῇσι παραστὰς φλίψεται ὤμους Od.17.221 (θλίψεται codd. plurimi):—Pass., Hp.*Loc.Hom*.13, Theoc.15.76.

**φλῐδάω**, *overflow with moisture, be ready to burst*, συὸς φλιδόωντος ἀλοιφῇ Nic.*Al*.557; σηπεδόσι φλιδόωσα Id.*Th*.363; τοῖς δέρμασι φ. καὶ ῥακοῦσθαι Plu.2.642e.—Hsch. also has **φλιδάνει**· διαπίπτει, διαρρεῖ, **φλιδιόωντο**· διέποντο, ἐτέμνοντο, and **ἔφλιδεν**· διέρρεεν, ἐρρήγνυεν.

**φλιδών**, όνος, ἡ, *fold, wrinkle*, Hsch. (pl.). **φλίεθος**· καρποφόρος, Id.

**φλιμέλιον**, τό, f. l. for φλέμινα, the Lat. *flemina*, *Hippiatr*.51.

**Φλιοῦς**, v. Φλειοῦς.

**φλῖψις**, εως, ἡ, (φλίβω) = θλῖψις, Hsch.

**φλόα**, v. φλόος.

**φλόγ-εος**, α, ον, (φλόξ) *bright as fire*, ὄχεα Il.5.745, 8.389. 2. *burning, flaming*, πυρὸς αὐγαί E.*Hec*.1104 (lyr.); φλογέας δαλοῖσι χέρας Id.*Tr*.1257 (lyr.); λαμπάδες Ar.*R*.340 (lyr.). 3. *inflamed, red*,

**φλόγεαι**, = ἐρυθραί, dub. in Hp.ap.Gal.19.152; v. φλόγιος. **—ερός**, ά, όν, = foreg., *blazing, flaming, fiery-red*, σέλας E.*Hel*.1127 (lyr.); αἰθήρ Id.*El*.991 (anap.); ἀκτῖνες A.R.4.126: Comp. -ώτερον ἔγχος *IG*14.2012.20 (Sulp.Max.): metaph. of love, φ. πῦρ, ὀϊστός, *AP*5.238 (Paul.Sil.), 9.443 (Id.). **—ερῶνυξ**, ὕχος, ὁ, ἡ, (ὄνυξ) *with fiery hoofs*, Jo.Gaz.*Ecphr*.2.187. **—ετός**, ὁ, *burning, heat*, *Gloss.* **—ιά**, ἡ, Ion. -ιή, poet. for φλόξ, Nic.*Th*.54, *Al*.393,534,586. **—ιάω**, *become inflamed and red*, Hp.*Morb*.2.66, *Morb.Sacr*.15. **—ίδιον**, τό, in pl., = αἱ κεγχρίδες δι' ἐλαίου σκευαζόμεναι, Hsch. **—ίζω**, fut. φλογίσω Id., but -ιῶ LxxPs.96(97).3:— = φλέγω, *set on fire, burn*, S.*Ph*.1199 (anap.), Lxx l.c., al.: *singe*, Sch.Ar.*Eq*.1233:—Pass., *to be set on fire, blaze, flame*, φλογιζόμενον ἅλιον S.*Tr*.95 (lyr.): *to be burnt up, consumed*, Arist.*Mu*.$397^{a}29$: metaph., of the tongue, *Ep.Jac*.3.6 (Act. and Pass.). II. intr., *burn, blaze*, LxxEx.9.24. **—ικός**, ή, όν, *apt to scorch*, τῆς καρδίας *PMag.Par*.1.1505. ⊛**—ῖνος**, η, ον, *flaming, fiery*, ῥομφαία LxxGe.3.24; of colour, D.S.2.52, *POxy*.1739.5 (ii/iii A.D.): τὰ φλόγινα (sc. ἱμάτια) *flame-coloured garments*, Phylarch.41J., Ael.*VH*9.3. II. φ., τό (perh. sc. ἴον), *wallflower, Cheiranthus Cheiri*, Thphr. *HP*6.8.1. ⊛**-ίον**, τό, Dim. of φλόξ, Longin.35.4. **—ιος**, α, ον, dub. for φλόγεος or φλόγινος, Hp.*Int*.4, Orph.*H*.66.2. **—ίς**, ίδος, ἡ, *piece of broiled flesh*, Poll.6.55, Hsch.; ταύρου..φλογίδες *beef-steaks*, Archipp.11 (lyr.); κάπρου φλογίδες Stratt.11 (lyr.). **—ισμα**, ατος, τό, prop. *blister of a burn*: hence, generally, *blister*, as on bread, Hsch. s. v. οὐδ' ἅλα. **—ισμός**, ὁ, gloss on φλογμός, Id. II. a musical term of dub. import, Jo.Sic. in Rh.6.293W. **—ιστός**, ή, όν, *burnt up*, S.*El*.58. 2. *inflammable*, Arist.*Mete*.$387^{b}18$. **—ίστρα**, ἡ, *place where swine are singed*, Sch.Ar.*Eq*.1233, Eust.1286.20. **—ίτης** [ῐ], ου, ὁ, a precious stone like *the carbuncle*, Solin.37.23. **—ῖτις**, ιδος, ἡ, = foreg., Plin. *HN*37.189. II. epith. of a kind of ἀνεμώνη, *PMag.Leid.V*.3.24. **—μός**, ὁ, *flame, blaze*, as of lightning, πυρὸς φ. ὁ Διός E. *Supp*. 831 (lyr.), cf. 1019 (lyr.), *Hec*.474 (lyr.), f.l. in *Hel*.1162 (lyr.); *fiery heat*, A.*Eu*.940 (lyr.); of *burning lava*, Arist.*Mu*.$400^{b}4$: of the funeral pyre, prob. in *Supp.Epigr*.4.719 (Bithynia); pl., Eratosth. ap. Sch.Il.18.468. b. *fire*, Ph.1.118. 2. *inflammation*, Hipp.*VM*19, *VC*15, al.; *feverish heat*, Luc.*Peregr*.44. 3. metaph., *heat of passion*, Ph.1.166,238.

**φλογμοτύραννος** [ῠ], ὁ, *ruling the fire*, λαμπηδών Orac.ap.Eus. *PE*.5.13.

**φλογμόω**, *burn up, consume*, prob. in *PMag.Berol*.1.126.

**φλογο-βαφής**, ές, *flame-coloured*, δέρματα Lyd.*Mag*.2.13. **—δερπνοι**· ἄνθρακες, Hsch. (leg. vel -τερπνοι vel -δειπνοι). **—ειδής**, ές, *like flame, fiery-hot*, Plu.2.695c, etc.; φέγγος Ph.2.107; of colour, *flame-coloured, fiery-red*, Arist.*Col*.$791^{a}8$, $792^{a}28$, *Phgn*.$812^{a}23$, Thphr. *Sens*.78. 2. *inflamed*, Hp.*Morb*.3.7. **—εις**, εσσα, εν, = φλόγεος, πῦρ Alex.Eph.ap.Theon.Sm.p.140H.; Ζεύς Orph.*H*.20.2; of the eyes, *flashing*, Mosch.1.8; κύων *AP*12.225 (Strat.); σέλας Opp.*H*.2.536.

**φλογοιδέομαι**, (οἰδάνω) *to be inflamed and swell*, as etym. of φλοιδούμενος, Tz.adLyc.35.

**φλογο-λαμπής**, ές, *flaming*, of the planet Mars, Doroth. in *Cat. Cod.Astr*.2.81. **—λευκος**, ον, *flame-coloured mixed with white*, Poll.7.129, Hsch.

**φλογ-όω**, = φλέγω, *set on fire*, φάκελλον Aen.Tact.33.1, cf. Sch. Il.13.341:—Pass., *blaze, burn*, of fire, Thphr.*Ign*.71; of a stone, Id.*Lap*.20. **—ώδης**, ες, *like flame, fiery-hot*, Arist.*Mir*.$833^{a}17$, *Mu*.$392^{a}35$, Luc.*Anach*.16, etc.: Comp., ἥλιος -έστερος ἑαυτοῦ Them. *Or*.10.134a: Sup., -έστατα θέρη Ph.2.226: of colour, *fiery-red*, D.S. 2.50, Dsc.5.94 (Sup.): τὸ φ. *fiery heat*, D.C.48.51. 2. of the effect of inflammation, *fiery-red*, Hp.*Coac*.614; τὸ φ. ἐν προσώπῳ ib.7. 3. metaph., τὸ φ. ἐν τῇ διαλέκτῳ Phld.*Po*.2.41. **—ωμα**, ατος, τό, *that which is overbaked*, of bread, Hsch. (pl.). **—ωπός**, όν, (ὤψ) *fiery-looking, flaming-red*, πῦρ A.*Pr*.255; φ. σήματα omens or tokens *by fire* (not *lightning*), ib.498; *bloodshot*, of the eyes in anger, Eust.58.14. ⊛**-ωσις**, εως, ἡ, *burning*, Thphr.*Ign*.69; opp. πῆξις, Iamb. *Myst*.1.18. 2. *burning heat, inflammation*, Th.2.49, Ph.2.101, Gal.7.853, Procop.*Pers*.2.22. 3. *warming, heating*, βαλανείων Them.*Or*.4.61c (pl.). **—ώψ**, ῶπος, ὁ, ἡ, = φλογωπός, ἀντολαί A.*Pr*.791.

**φλόη**, ἡ, = χλόη, *viriditas*, *Gloss.*

**φλοίαξ**, ᾶκος, ὁ, f.l. for φλύαξ (q.v.).

**φλοιδέω**, **φλοιδιάω**, *seethe*, φλοιδούμενος Lyc.35: but part. pf. πεφλοιδώς· τὸν φλοιὸν ἀποβαλών, Hsch. Cf. φλυδάω.

**φλοΐζομαι**, (φλοιός) Pass., *have the bark stripped off*, Thphr.*HP* 3.16.3, 5.4.6, 5.9.5, [Gal.]14.393.

**φλόϊνος**, η, ον, *made from the plant* φλόος II, = φλέως, ἐσθὴς φλοΐνη garments *thereof*, Hdt.3.98; φ. ἡνίαι E.*Fr*.284; σπυρίς, ψίαθος, Poll.10.178.

**φλοιο-βαρής**, ές, *heavy with bark*, Sch.Il.13.390, Eust.939.5. **—ρραγέω**, *have the bark burst*, Dsc.4.181. **—ρραγής**, ές, *with the bark* or *rind burst*, Thphr.*HP*4.15.2, *CP*3.18.3, Dsc.1.13. **—ρριζος**, ον, *having roots covered with coats of rind*: τὰ φ. *bulbous plants*, Thphr. *Od*.63.

⊛**φλοιός**, ὁ, (φλέω) *bark* of trees, esp. *smooth bark* (such as one can cut one's name on, Theoc.18.47, Call.*Fr*.101), Il.1.237, Emp.81, Hdt.4.67, X.*Cyn*.9.18, Thphr.*HP*1.5.2, Sor.1.62; eaten in famine, Plb.7.1.3, Plu.*Ant*.17: pl., Call. l.c., Str.11.8.7, 15.1.60. b. *husk* or *skin* of certain fruits, Plu.2.684a, Aët.12.1. 2. *membrane enclosing the eggs* of certain animals, Arist. *HA*$558^{a}28$. 3. *tissue* from which spiders spin their webs, ib.$623^{a}32$. 4. metaph., of *superficial* or *useless coverings*, *redundancy*, ὁ Λακωνικὸς λόγος οὐκ ἔχει φλοιόν Plu.2.510f; φωνὴν..φλοιοῦ μεστήν Crantor ap. D.L.4.27; γυμνὸς τῶν φλοιῶν stripped of all *outsides*, M.Ant.12.2,8; περὶ τὸν φ. ἀσχολεῖσθαι Luc.*Herm*.79.

**φλοιόω**, *change into bark*, Nonn.*D*.36.310.

**φλοῖσβος**, ὁ, *any confused roaring noise*, in Hom. of *the noise of battle*, Il.5.322,469, 10.416 (never in Od.): τὸν μὲν ἄρ' ἐκ φλοίσβου.. ῥύσαντο Euph.23; of the sea, πόντου περῶσα φλοῖσβον A.*Pr*.792, cf. S.*Fr*.479, *Hymn.Is*.166; φλοίσβων δίναις Lyc.379; ἰλυόεις φ. Opp. *H*.1.777.—Poet. word.

**φλο-ϊσμός**, ὁ, *stripping off the rind, peeling*, Thphr.*HP*5.1.1. **-ϊστικός**, ή, όν, *of or for peeling off the rind*, φλοϊστικὴ φυτῶν (sc. ἡ τέχνη) *the art of stripping the inner bark* of trees, for making mats, etc., Pl.*Plt*.288d, cf. Poll.7.209.

**φλοίω**, (φλέω) *burst out, swell, be in full vigour* or *bloom*, Antim. 36, cf. Plu.2.683f.

**φλοι-ώδης**, ες, *like rind* or *bast*, Arist.*HA*$554^{b}27$, Thphr.*HP*1.6.7, 5.5.2, Dsc.1.23, Plu.2.640e, etc. 2. metaph., *showy, superficial*, Longin.3.2; τὸ σοβαρὸν καὶ φ. Plu.2.81b. **—ῶτις**, ιδος, ἡ, *made of rind, rind-covered*, σκέπη Lyc.1422.

**φλοκτίς**, ίδος, ἡ, = φλυκτίς, Lat. *papula, pustula*, *Gloss.*

**φλομίς**, ίδος, ἡ, *phlome, Phlomis samia*, Dsc.4.103 (three kinds distd., one used for lamp-wicks, φ. λυχνῖτις, θρυαλλίς, ibid.), cf. Plin.*HN*25.121.

**φλόμος**, ἡ (ὁ Dsc.1.28), *mullein. Verbascum sinuatum*, Cratin.325 (lyr.), Eup.14.5 (anap.), Thphr.*HP*9.12.3, Dsc.4.103 (who distinguishes four kinds, incl. φ. ἀγρία *sage of Jerusalem*, *Phlomis fruticosa*); φ. ὁ στενόφυλλος, distd. fr. φ. Ἰδαῖος (= ἐλένιον), Dsc.1.28; cf. πλόμος. 2. φ. Ἰουδαία, = ὀξυλάπαθον τὸ μέγα, Ps.-Dsc.2.114.

**φλομώδης**, ες, *like mullein*, Hsch. s.v. αἰθιοπίς, prob. for φλογμώδης in Gal.19.152.

**φλονίς**, ίδος, ἡ, = φολίς, λεπίς, Hsch., cj. in Emp.82.

**φλονῖτις**, ιδος, ἡ, = ὄνοσμα, *golden drop*, *Onosma echioides*, Ps.-Dsc.3.131.

**φλόνος**, ὁ, = φλόμος, Ps.-Dsc.4.103.

⊛**φλόξ**, ἡ, gen. φλογός: (φλέγω):—*flame* of fire, Od.24.71, etc.; δεινὴ δὲ φλὸξ ὦρτο θεείου καιομένοιο Il.8.135; τῆς δὲ [νηὸς] κατ' ἀσβέστη κέχυτο φλόξ 16.123; κατὰ πῦρ ἐκάη καὶ φλὸξ ἐμαράνθη 9.212; more fully, φλὸξ Ἡφαίστοιο Il.17.88, Od. l.c.; πυρός Pi.*P*.4.225, E.*Ba*.8, *Heracl*.914 (lyr.), Pl.*Ti*.83b, etc. (but also φλογὸς αἰθέριον πῦρ Parm.8.56); φλογὸς σπέρμα, of live charcoal, Pi.*O*.7.48; ἀναιθύσσειν, θύειν, E.*Tr*.344, *IT*1331; ἐγείρειν, παρακαλεῖν, X. *Smp*.2.24, *Cyr*.7.5.23; ἐμβαλεῖν τινι E.*Alc*.4, *Rh*.120; σβέσαι Th.2.77; φ. ἀπέσσυτο Hes.*Th*.859; ἀπορρέουσα Pl.*Ti*.67c; φλογὸς ἀποσβεσθείσης ib.58c: later in pl., *flames, meteors*, Arist.*Mete*.$341^{b}2$, *Mu*.$392^{b}3$, $400^{a}30$, Orph.*L*.178, Nic.*Fr*.74.48. 2. *fire* as an element, φλογὸς αἶσα Parm.12.2; φ. ἰλάειρα Emp.85. 3. of other kinds of *flame*, φ. κεραυνία, οὐρανία, of lightning, A.*Pr*.1017, E.*Med*. 144 (anap.); of the *heat* of the sun, A.*Pr*.22, *Pers*.505, S.*Tr*.696; *flash* of a miraculous cloud, Il.18.206; of precious stones, ψυχρὰ φ. Pi.*Fr*. 123.5; the *blade* of a sword, LxxJd.3.22, Aq., Thd.1*Ki*.17.7. 4. in similes and metaphors, φλογὶ εἴκελος, ἶσος, of *fiery* warriors, Il.13.330, 39; φ. οἴνου *the fiery strength* of wine, E.*Alc*.758; φ. πήματος S.*OT*166 (lyr.). II. *wallflower*, *Cheiranthus Cheiri*, Thphr.*HP*6.6.2.

⊛**φλόος**, ὁ, metaplast. acc. φλόα Nic.*Al*.302: contr. φλοῦς *PCair.Zen*. 229.10 (iii B.C.), *BGU*1122.17,20 (i B.C.), v.l. in Dsc.3.147: (φλέω):—rarer form of φλοιός, παρθένιός μοι ἔπι φ., of a tree, *AP*9.706 (Antip.), cf. *PCair.Zen*. l.c. (iii B.C.). 2. the human *skin*, Nic. l.c.; also of the *slough* of serpents, Id.*Th*.355,392. II. **φλοῦς**, Ion. for φλέως, Hdt.3.98. III. *bloom of a plant*, Arat.335, cf. Plu.2.683f.

**φλόρος**, ὁ, a bird, either *bee-eater* or *golden oriole*, Suid.; written **φλῶρος** in Sch.Opp.*H*.1.157.

**φλουάζω**, = φλυαρέω, Hsch.

**φλούδιον**, τό, Dim. of φλόος, φλοῦς, *Gloss.*, Zonar.

⊛**φλουμαρικός**, ή, όν, = πλουμαρικός, *PSI*9.1082.14 (iv A.D.).

**φλοῦς**, v. φλόος II.

**φλῦ**, a sound made by certain shellfish, Sch.rec.A.*Pr*.504.

**φλῠᾱκο-γραφία**, ἡ, *composition of* φλύακες, Suid. s.v. Ῥίνθων. **-γράφος** [γρᾰ], ὁ, *writer of* φλύακες, Ath.3.86a, al.

**φλύαξ** [ῠ], ᾱκος, ὁ, 1. = ἱλαροτραγῳδία, *tragic burlesque*, invented by Rhinthon, φλύακες τραγικοί *AP*7.414 (Noss.). 2. of persons, *jester*, St.Byz. s.v. Τάρας, Poll.9.149, Eust.884.26 (ubi **φλοίακες**).

**φλῠᾰρ-έω**, Ion. **φλυηρέω**:—*talk nonsense, play the fool*, ταῦτα λέγουσι φλυηρέοντες Hdt.2.131, cf. 7.104, Ar.*Eq*.545 (anap.), *V*.85, *Pl*. 360,575 (anap.); παῦσαι φλυαρῶν Philem.213.1 (troch.); φλυαρεῖς πρός με Men.*Pk*.146; οὐ φλυαρῶ (parenthetically) 'no joke', 'seriously', ib.153: c. acc. cogn., φάσκοντα..ἀεροβατεῖν καὶ ἄλλην πολλὴν φλυαρίαν φλυαροῦντα Pl.*Ap*.19c; πολλὰ φλυηρέεις Hdt.7.103; ταῦτα φ. Isoc.5.75; τοιαῦτα Pl.*R*.337b; ἄφες ἃ φλυαρεῖς ταῦτα Men.*Sam*.313. c. part., οὐ μὴ φλυαρήσεις ἔχων Ar.*Ra*.202; φλυαρεῖς ἔχων Pl.*Grg*. 490e; ἔχων φ. Id.*Euthd*.295c; Αἰσχύλος φ. φάσκων Id.*Smp*.180a; Δερκυλίδας φ. διατρίβων X.*HG*3.1.18. II. trans., *prate against*, ἡμᾶς 3*Ep.Jo*.10:—Pass., φλυαρηθέντες καὶ κατακερτομηθέντες Ph.2.599; *to be made a fool of*, D.L.7.173. **—ημα**, ατος, τό, *nonsense, futility*, in pl., D.H.*Comp*.18, Ph.2.495, J.*Ap*.2.9. ⊛**-ία**, ἡ, *nonsense, foolery*, in word or deed, Timocr.10, Ar.*Lys*.159, Pl.*Tht*.162a, etc.; παιδιὰ καὶ φ. Id.*Cri*.46d; καπνὸς καὶ φ. Id.*R*.581d; χρωμάτων καὶ ἄλλης πολλῆς φ. θνητῆς Id.*Smp*.211e, cf. *Phd*.66c: φ. καὶ λῆρος *Com.Adesp*.5.7D.: freq. in pl., *fooleries*, λῆροι καὶ φ. Pl.*Hp.Ma*.304b; εἴτε ληρήματα.., εἴτε φλυαρίας Id.*Grg.*486c ; περὶ σιτία καὶ ποτὰ καὶ ἰατροὺς καὶ φ. ib. 490c, cf. 519a ; ἄνηθα καὶ σέλινα καὶ φ. Eub.36.

**φλῠᾱρο-γρᾰφέω**, confused with *φλυακογραφέω by Sch.Nic.*Al.* 214. **-κοπέω**, *talk folly*, Zonar. s.v. Σαγγάριος. **-κοπία**, ἡ, *tomfoolery*, Id. s.v. Παιάν. **-λογέω**, = φλυαρέω, Sch.Ar.*Nu.* 1009. **-λογία**, ἡ, = φλυαρία, Pl.*Ax.*369d.

**φλῠᾱρ-ος** [ῠ], ὁ, *silly talk, foolery, nonsense*, τἄλλα πάντ' ἐστὶ φ. Ar.*Nu.*365 (anap.), cf. Men.541.2, Pl.*Ax.*365e, Plu.*Cic.*2, etc.: pl., *fooleries*, πολλῶν φλυάρων καὶ ταῶν ἀντάξια Stratt.27. II. *tattler, babbler*, Pl.*Ax.*369a, 1 *Ep.Ti.*5.13, Str.1.2.5, etc.: as Adj., ἡ φ. φιλοσοφία Lxx 4 *Ma.*5.10; φ. λόγος D.H.*Comp.*26 ; φ. γλῶττα Alciphr.3.69 : Comp. φλυαρότερος Arr.*Epict.*2.19.10. Adv. φλυάρως Sch.Ar.*V.* 855. **-ώδης**, ες, *foolish*, Plu.*Lyc.*6, Id.2.615a ; ῥῆμα Porph.*Chr.*61.

**φλυάσσω**, = φλυαρέω, Hsch. ; cf. φλουάζω.

**φλῠδᾰρός**, ά, όν, *soft, flabby*, Hp.ap.Gal.19.152.

**φλῠδάω**, *have an excess of moisture, become soft* or *flabby*, Hp. *Morb.Sacr.*13 (cf Erot., Gal.19.152), *Ep.*19 (*Hermes* 53.70); cf. φλοιδέω, φλοιδιάω.

✻**φλυζάκιον**, τό, Dim. of φλύκταινα, Hp.*Coac.*112, *Acut.*(*Sp.*)26, Cels.5.28.15 ; cf. φυσάκια.

**φλυζογράφος** [ᾰ], ον, = φλυαρογραφῶν, Sch.Nic.*Al.*214.

**φλύζω**, v. φλύω.

**φλύκταιν-α**, ἡ, *blister* made by a burn, Hp.*VM*16, Thphr.*Ign.*57, *IG*4²(1).126.25 (Epid., ii A.D.), Luc.*DMort.*20.4 ; *blister* caused by rowing, Ar.*V.*1119(troch.), *Ra.*236(lyr.); ἐξ αἵματος φ. blood-*blister*, Id.*Ec.*1057; caused by the bite of the μυγαλῆ, Arist.*HA*604ᵇ 20. 2. *pustule*, Hp.*Prog.*17, Th.2.49. **-ίδιον**, τό, Dim. of foreg., Hp.*Epid.*1.26.θ', Diocl.*Fr.*82. **-ίς**, ίδος, ἡ, = foreg., Hp. *Int.*1, *Epid.*2.1.1, Diocl.*Fr.*82.

**φλυκταινοειδής**, ές, *blister like*, Hp.*Mul.*2.116.

**φλυκταιν-όω**, *cause blisters on* or *in*, τὸ στόμα Dsc.2.173, cf. Archig.ap.Gal.12.406 :—Pass., *have blisters*, Hp.*Coac.*479, Dsc.1. 101. **-ώδης**, ες, = φλυκταινοειδής, Philum.*Ven.*17.1, Orib.*Fr.* 105. **-ωσις**, εως, ἡ, *blistering*, Hp.*Fract.*21, Dsc.*Eup.*2.8, Gal.14.163.

**φλυκτίς**, ίδος (but acc. pl. φλύκτεις Dsc.2.101), ἡ, = φλύκταινα, Thphr.*Ign.*39 ; *boil*, Lxx *Ex.*9.9, Gal.13.357.

**φλύος** [ῠ], εος, τό, = φλύαρος, *idle talk, foolery*, Archil.197.

**φλύσις** [ῠ], εως, ἡ, *breaking out, eruption*, Hp.ap.Gal.19.152.

✻**φλύω** [ῡ. cf. ἐπιφλύω] and **φλύζω**, aor. 1 ἔφλῠσα v. infr. II : (φλέω) :—*boil over, bubble up*: hence, *burst out*, ἐν τῇσι φλυζούσῃσι αἱμορραγίῃσι (Foes for σφύζουσι αἱμορραγέσι) Hp.*Epid.*2.3.14, cf. Hsch., Suid. ; φλύω expld. by πολυκαρπέω, Ael.*VH*3.41. II. metaph., *overflow with words, babble*, μάτην φλύσαι A.*Pr* 504 ; γράμματα ἐπ' ἀσπίδος φλύοντα Id.*Th.*661 : c. acc. cogn., φήμην στυγερὴν ἔφλῠσεν *AP*7.351 (Diosc.) ; ἔφλυσε v.l. for ἔβλυσε, ib.352 (Mel.(?)); μανίης ὕπο μυρία φλύζειν Nic.*Al.*214 ; φλύοντ' ἀνθηρῇ σὺν κακοδαιμονίῃ prob. in Alex.Aet.5.8 :—Med. or Pass., φλύεται, = ὑγραίνεται, Hp. ap.Gal.19.152.

**φνεί**, Comic imitation of the sound *phn*, Luc.*Lex.*19 ; expressing the note of a bird, Ar.*Fr.*885.

**φόα**, τά, = ἐξανθήματα, Hsch.

**φοβερ-ίζω**, *terrify, scare*, Lxx*Ne.*6.9, al. :—Pass., *Cat.Cod.Astr.* 8(4).194. **-ισμός**, ὁ, *a terrifying*, Lxx*Ps.*87 (88).17 (pl.).

**φοβερο-διακράτορες** [κρᾰ], οἱ, variant for φοβοδιάκτορες (q. v.), *PMag.Par.*1.1357. **-ειδής**, ές, *terrible to behold*, Lxx 3.*Ma.*6. 18. **-ποιέω**, *make formidable*, Onos.14 1.

**φοβερός**, ά, όν, (φόβος) *fearful*, whether Act. or Pass.: I. Act., *causing fear, terrible*, χρηστήρια φ. Hdt.7.139, cf. A.*Pr.*127 (anap.), *Th.* 78 (lyr.), etc.; ὅμιλος πλήθει -ώτατος *formidable* only from numbers, Th.2.98 (but τὰ τῷ πλήθει φ. things which are *fearful to* the multitude, Isoc.1.7, cf. Pl.*Ph.*67e): c. inf., φ. ἰδεῖν, φ. προσιδέσθαι, *fearful* to behold, A.*Pers.*27 (anap.), 48 (anap.); φ. εἰσιδεῖν E.*Ph.*127 (lyr.); φ. προσπολεμῆσαι D.2.22 ; φ. Πολυδεύκεα πὺξ ἐρεθίζειν Theoc. 22.2. 2. *regarded with fear*, esp. with respect to consequences, οὔτε ὅρκος φ. Th.3.83 ; ἵππος φ. μὴ ἀνήκεστόν τι ποιήσῃ a horse *that makes one fear* he will do some mischief, X.*Hier.*6.15 ; σεμνότερος εἶναι καὶ φοβερώτερος δοκεῖ And.4.18 ; φοβεροὶ ἦσαν μὴ ποιήσειαν X. *An.*5.7.2 ; τοῖς πολεμίοις φοβερώτεροι Id.*Eq.Mag.*4.11, cf. *Ages.*11. 10 (Sup.): τριήρης φοβερὸν πολεμίοις Id.*Oec.*8.8; τὸ πρὸ τῶν λυπηρῶν [προσδόκημα] φ. Pl.*Phlb.*32c ; φοβερώτατον ἐρημία X.*An.*2.5.9 ; τὸ φ. *terror, danger*, Id.*Lac.*9.1 ; τῶν φοβερῶν ὄντων τῇ πόλει γενέσθαι the things which were *dreaded* as likely to happen.., Id.*HG.*1.4.17 ; φοβερόν [ἐστι] μὴ.. there is *reason to dread* that.., Id.*Hier.*1.12, cf. *Cyr.*7.5.22 ; ἀγγέλλεσθαι ἐπὶ τὸ φοβερώτατον to be *fearfully exaggerated*, D.H.1.57. 3. Rhet., of style, *impressive, awe-inspiring*, τὸ κάλλος τὸ Θουκυδίδου φ. Id.*Pomp.*3 ; τὸ φ. Id.*Lys.*13 ; Ὅμηρος παίζων -ώτερος Demetr.*Eloc.*130. II. Pass., *afraid, timid*, ἐκτέταμαι φοβερὰν φρένα S.*OT*153 (lyr.), cf. Alc.97, Pherecr.245 ; ὄμμα E.*IA*620 : opp. θαρσαλέος, Th.2.3, X.*Cyr.*3.3 19(Comp.); φ. τὴν ψυχὴν Id.*Oec.*7.25 ; σκοπεῖν εἰ φοβεροί (sc. οἱ πῶλοι) Pl.*R.*413d ; φ. ποιεῖν τινα Id.*Lg.*647c, φ. εἰς τὸ τολμᾶν ib.649d. 2. *caused by fear, troubled, panic*, ἀναχώρησις Th.4.128 ; φοβερὰ ὄσσοις ὀμίχλα προσῇξε A.*Pr.*144 (lyr.) ; φ. φροντίδες *anxious* thoughts, Pl.*Thg.*127b. III. Adv. -ρῶς *threateningly, in a terrifying manner*, Lys.24.15, cf. Lxx 3*Ma.*5.45, etc.: Comp., -ώτερον φθέγγεσθαι X.*Smp.*1.10 : Sup., -ώτατα ἰδεῖν Id.*Cyr.*8.3.5. 2. *timidly*, -ώτατα ἔχειν Id.*Eq.Mag.*8.20. **-ότης**, ητος, ἡ, *terribleness*, Arist.*Rh.*1361ᵇ12, J.*BJ*7.8.3. **-ωπός**, όν, *terrible of aspect*, Orph.*Fr.* 58.2. **-ώψ**, ῶπος, ὁ, ἡ, = foreg., Id.*H.*70.10.

**φοβεσιστράτη** [ᾰ], ἡ, *scarer of hosts*, epith. of Athena, Ar.*Eq.*1177.

**φοβέστρᾰτος**, ον, = foreg., αἰγίς, of Athena, Hes.*Th.*ap.Chrysipp.*Stoic.*2.257, cf. *EM*797.54.

✻**φοβέω**, 3 pl. impr. φοβεόντων Hdt.7.235 : Ion. impf. φοβέεσκον Hes.*Sc.*162 : fut. -ήσω E.*Heracl.*357 (lyr.), (ἐκ-) Th.4.126 (dub.): aor. ἐφόβησα Il.15.15, etc.:—Pass. and Med., Ion. 2 sing. φοβέαι Hdt.1.39 ; Ion. imper. φοβεῦ or φοβέο, Id.1.9, 7.52 : Ep. 3 pl. impf. φοβέοντο Il.6.41 : fut. φοβήσομαι 22.250, Pl.*Lg.*649c, D.15.23, etc.; φοβηθήσομαι X.*Cyr.*3.3.30, Plu.*Brut.*40, Luc.*Zeux.*9, v.l. in Pl.*R.* 470a : aor. Pass. ἐφοβήθην Hdt.8.27, etc., Ep. 3 pl. ἐφόβηθεν or φόβηθεν, Il.15.326, 5.498 ; aor. Med. ἐφοβησάμην only *Anacreont.*31.11 : pf. πεφόβημαι Il.10.510, etc. : plpf. 3 pl. ἐπεφόβηντο X.*HG*7.4.32, Th.5.50, Ep. πεφοβήατο Il.21.206.

A. Act., in Hom. (never in Od.) always in the sense *put to flight*, [ἴρηξ] ἐφόβησε κολοιούς Il.16.583 ; [Ζεὺς] καὶ ἄλκιμον ἄνδρα φοβεῖ ib. 689 ; Τρώων οὓς ἐφόβησας 22.11 ; φοβῆσαί τε στίχας ἀνδρῶν 17.505 ; σὸς δόλος.. ἐφόβησε δὲ λαοὺς 15.15 ; σέ γέ φημι.. δουρὶ φοβῆσαι 20.187 ; once in Hes., φοβέεσκον ἐπὶ χθονὶ φῦλ' ἀνθρώπων l. c. II. *terrify, alarm*, Hdt.7.235, etc.; μὴ φίλους φόβει A.*Th.*262 ; ᾧ μή 'στι δρῶντι τάρβος οὐδ' ἔπος φοβεῖ S.*OT* 296, cf. 1013, E.*Hipp.*572 (lyr.) ; ἡ δύναμις τῶν νέων φοβοῦσά τινας Antipho 4.3.2 ; αἱ κάμηλοι ἐφόβουν τοὺς ἵππους X.*Cyr.*7.1.48 ; τὸν Ἀλκιβιάδην ἐφόβουν, μὴ.. ἐπαγάγωνται Th.5.45 : c. dat. modi, λόγοις A.*Pers.*215 (troch.); μεγαληγορίαισι φρένας E.*Heracl.* 357 (lyr.) ; τῷ μὲν Τισσαφέρνει τοὺς Ἀθηναίους φ., ἐκείνοις δὲ τὸν Τισσαφέρνην *to frighten* the Athenians with T., and T. with the Athenians, Th.8.82 : c. part., λέγοντες φ. τινάς *by* saying, X.*Eq.Mag.*1.8 ; λέγοντες ὡς ἥξει βασιλεύς D 14.25 : abs., πόνος ὁ μὴ φοβῶν κράτιστος S.*Ph.*864 (lyr.), φοβήσαντες κατεστήσαντο τὴν πολιτείαν *by terror*, Pl.*R.*551b. 2. c. acc. rei, *threaten with*, φ. λιμὸν D.H.6.51.

B. Pass. and Med., in Hom. always in the sense *to be put to flight* (cf. Sch.A Il.5.223, al.), once in Od., κύνες.. διὰ σταθμοῖο φόβηθεν 16.163 ; freq. in Il., ὑπέμειναν ἀολλέες οὐδὲ φόβηθεν 5.498 ; τοὶ δ' ἐφόβηθεν.. θεσπεσίῳ ὁμάδῳ 16.294 ; κὰμ μέσσον πεδίον φοβέοντο βόες ὣς ἅς τε λέων ἐφόβησε 11.172 : also part., μὴ καὶ πεφοβημένος ἔλθῃς 10.510, cf. 15.4, 21.606 ; φοβηθεὶς δύσεθ' ἁλὸς κατὰ κῦμα *in flight*, 6.135 ; βῆ δὲ φοβηθεὶς 22.137 : ὑπό τινος φοβέεσθαι *to flee* before him, 8.149 ; ὑπό τινι 15.637 ; c. acc., οὔ σ' ἔτι.. φοβήσομαι ὡς τὸ πάρος περ 22.250. II. *to be seized with fear, be affrighted*, Hdt. 9.70, E.*Tr.*1166, etc.—Constr., 1. abs., πεφόβημαι πτηνῆς ὡς ὄμμα πελείας S.*Aj.*139 (anap.); φοβηθέντες ᾤχοντο φεύγοντες flying *in terror*, Aeschin.1.43 ; ἃ μὴ οἶδα.. οὐδέποτε φοβήσομαι οὐδὲ φεύξομαι, Pl.*Ap.*29b, etc. : c. dat. instrum., μάστιγι φ. E.*Rh.*37 (anap.): c. acc. cogn., φ. αἰσχροὺς φόβους Pl.*Prt.*360b ; ἐφοβήθησαν φόβον μέγαν *Ev.Marc.*4.41 ; τὸν φόβον αὐτῶν μὴ φοβηθῆτε 1*Ep.Pet.*3.14. 2. folld. by Preps., φ. ἀπό τινος *to be afraid of* one (prob. a Hebraism), Lxx*Le.*26.2, *Je.*1.8, *Ev.Matt.*10.28, *Ev.Luc.*12.4 ; ἔκ τινος *from* some cause, S.*Tr.*671 ; εἴς τ. *to be alarmed* at a thing, Id.*OT*980 ; πρός τι Id.*Tr.*1211, Luc.*Prom.Es*4, Lib.*Or.*50.18 ; ἐπί τινι *fear* for.., Luc. *DMar.*14.4 ; but φ. ἀμφὶ γυναικί *fear* about.., Hdt.6.62 ; περὶ ἡμῶν X. *Cyr.*5.2.35, etc.; περί τινι Pl.*Euthd.*275b (περὶ σφίσιν αὐτοῖς τὸ κατάδηλον Th.4.123) ; περὶ χωρίῳ Id.2.90 ; ὑπὲρ τῶν μελλόντων And.4.36 ; περί τι Pl.*Cra.*404e : πρὸς ἀνδρὸς ἢ τέκνων S.*Tr.*150. 3. folld. by a relat. clause, φοβεῖσθαι μὴ.. *fear* lest a thing will be.., E.*Or*770 (troch.), Ar.*Pax*606 (troch.), Th.1.95, etc. ; φ. ὅπως μὴ.. Id.6.13, X.*Mem.*2.9. 3 ; φ. μὴ οὐ.. Id.*Oec.*16.6 ; freq. c. acc. folld. by μή, ταῦτ' οὖν φοβοῦμαι, μὴ .. S.*Tr.*550, cf. X.*An.*7.1.2 ; φ. τοὺς οὐσίαν κεκτημένους, μὴ.. Pl.*Phdr.* 232c, cf. Th.1.88, etc.; φ. ὑπέρ τινος, μὴ.. Id.*R.*387c ; c. inf. folld. by μή, φοβοίμην ἂν τῷ ἡγεμόνι ἕπεσθαι, μὴ ἀγάγῃ κτλ. X.*An.*1.3.17, cf. Pl.*Tht.*143e, *Grg.*457e : also φ. ὅτι.., = φ. μή.., in a more positive sense, X.*Cyr.*3.1.1, D.C.52.26 ; φ. τόδε, ὅτι.. Th.7.67 (but φ. τὸ κάεσθαι, ὅτι ἀλγεινόν because.., Pl.*Grg.*479a): διὰ τοῦτο φ. τινας, ὅτι.. Isoc.6.60 ; less freq. φ. ὡς.. X.*Cyr.*5.2.12 ; φ. πῶς χρὴ.. ib.4.5. 19 ; φ. εἰ δεήσει.. ib.6.1.17. 4. c. inf. with Art., φ. τὸ ἀποθνήσκειν Pl.*Grg.*522e, etc. : more freq. c. inf. alone, *fear to* do, *be afraid of* doing, A.*Ch.*46 (lyr.), S.*Aj.*253 (lyr.), E.*Ion*628, etc. : c. inf. fut., Th. 5.105. 5. c. acc. pers., *stand in awe of, dread*, δαίμονας τοὺς ἐνθάδε A.*Supp.*893 ; στρατὸν Ἀχαιῶν S.*Ph.*1250 ; τοὺς ἄνω θεοὺς Pl.*Lg.* 927b, cf. Isoc.1.16, etc. ; τὰς κύνας X.*Cyn.*5.16, etc. 6. c. acc. rei, *fear* or *fear about* a thing, βρόμον A.*Th.*476 ; τὸ προσέρπον S.*Aj.*227 (lyr.) ; μέμψιν E.*Alc.*1057 ; τὸ τοιοῦτον σῶμα Pl.*Phdr.*239d ; δουλείαν καὶ δεσμὸν X.*Cyr.*3.1.24. 7. c. gen., πεφοβημένος νυκτός, θαλάσσης, Arat.290, 766. 8. c. part., προδιδοὺς φοβηθεὶς Lycurg.17.

**φόβη**, ἡ, *lock* or *curl of hair*, Sapph.78 (pl.), A.*Ch.*188 ; βοστρύχων ἄκρας φόβας S.*El.*449, cf. *OC*1465 (lyr.) ; δρακόντων φόβαι, i.e. the Gorgon's snaky *locks*, Pi.*P.*10.47. 2. *mane* of a horse, S.*Fr.* 659.7, 10, E.*Alc.*429, *Ba.*1188 (lyr.). II. metaph., *leafage, foliage*, S.*Ant.*419, E.*Alc.*172, *Ba.*684, etc. ; ἴων φόβαι *tufts* of violets, Pi.*Fr.*75.18 ; ἀνθοῦσκου Cratin.98.6 (lyr.) ; εὐπέταλοι φόβαι *AP*6.158 (Sabin.) ; of *the plumy heads* of reed, Thphr.*HP*8.3.4, cf. 4.4.10.

**φόβ-ημα**, ατος, τό, *cause of terror*, ἐγχέων φ. δαΐων to them, S.*OC* 699 (lyr.), cf. Aq.*De.*4.34. **-ητέον**, *one must fear*, Pl.*R.*452b, *Lg.* 891a, etc. 2. φοβητέος, α, ον, *to be feared*, ib.746e. **-ητικός**, ή, όν, *fearful, timid*, Arist.*Pol.*1342ᵃ12. **-ητός**, ή, όν, *to be feared*, τινι S.*Ph.* 1154 (lyr.). **-ητρον**, τό, *scarecrow, bugbear, terror*, Lxx *Is.*19.17 : elsewh. always in pl. *terrors*, Hp.*Morb.Sacr.*1 (s. v. l.), Pl.*Ax.*367a, *Ev.Luc.*21.11 ; Τισιφόνης τὰ φ., prob. *tragic masks* of the Furies, *AP*11.189 (Lucill.). **-ίζω**, *terrify, scare*, *Delph.*3(2).129 (1 B.C.).

**φοβο-διάκτορες**, οἱ, name of demons, *PMag.Lond.*121.354 ; cf. φοβεροδιακράτορες. **-δίψος**, ον, = ὑδροφόβος, *like one bitten by a mad* *dog*, Cael.Aur.*CP*3.9. **-ειδής,** ές, *fearful*, Pempel.ap.Stob.4.25.52. **-θεΐα,** ἡ, = δεισιδαιμονία, Hsch. **-ποιέω,** *cause fear*, Sch.Hes.*Op*.1.

**⊛ φόβος,** ὁ, (φέβομαι) *panic flight*, the usual sense in Hom., cf. Sch. Il.11.71 (but cf. φύζα, φόβου κρυόεντος ἑταίρη Il.9.2); once in Od., οἱ δ' ἔσχοντο φόβου 24.57; freq. in Il., Δαναῶν γένετο ἰαχή τε φ. τε 15.396; πρῶτος Πηνέλεως..ἦρχε φόβοιο 17.597; ἐς φόβον ἀνδρῶν 15.310; φόβονδε = φύγαδε, ἑστάμεναι κρατερῶς, μηδὲ τρωπᾶσθε φόβονδε ib.666; φόβονδ' ἔχε μώνυχας ἵππους 8.139; μή τι φόβονδ' ἀγόρευε counsel not *to flight*, 5.252; ἀΐξαντα φόβονδε 17.579; ὦρσαν φόβον Δαναοῖς B.12.145. 2. Φόβος personified, as son of Ares, Il.13.299; Δεῖμός τε Φ. τε 11.37, cf. 4.440, 15.119, Hes.*Th*.934, A.*Th*.45; worshipped at Selinus, *IG*14.268.2. II. *panic fear*, [στρατῷ] φ. ἐμβάλλειν Hdt 7.10.έ; ἐν τῷ γινομένῳ φ. Id.9.69: generally, *fear, terror* (distd. from δέος (q.v.)), τορὸς ὀρθόθριξ φ. A.*Ch*.32 (lyr.); διάτορος φ. Id.*Pr*.183 (lyr.); ταρβόσυνος Id.*Th*.240 (lyr.), νεανικός E.*Hipp*.1204; joined with δέος and δεῖμα, v. sub vocc.; opp. θάρρος, Pl.*Lg*.644c; sts. in milder sense, *doubt, scruple*, Pl.*Phd*.101b; ἔχει πολλὴν ὑποψίαν καὶ φ. ὡς..Id.*Sph*.268a: also, *awe, reverence*, for a ruler or divine being, τοῦ ἡγεμόνος *POxy*.1642.17 (iii A. D.); θεοῦ Lxx *Ps*.35(36).1, *PLond*.2.418.4 (iv A. D.): τοῦ κυρίου *Act.Ap*.9.31.—Construction, a. c. gen. obj., *fear* or *dread of*.., A.*Pers*.116 (lyr.), Th.3.54, etc.; φ. τοῦ στρατεῦσαι X.*An*.3.1.18: c. dupl. gen., ὀμμάτων εἰληφότας φόβον..τῆς ἐμῆς ἐπεισόδου S.*OC*730: with Preps., φ. ἀπό τινος X.*An*.7.2.37 codd.; ὁ ἀπὸ τῶν πολεμίων φ. Id.*Cyr*.3.3.53; οὐξ ὀνειράτων φ. A.*Ch*.929; πρός τινος S.*El*.783; πρός τινας D.16.10, 25.93; φ. περὶ τοῦ καρποῦ *fear* for or concerning.., Th.4.88; φ. ἑκάστων πέρι Pl.*Phlb*.20b; ὑπὲρ τοῦ μέλλοντος Th.7.41; τὸν ἐκ τῶν Ἑλλήνων εἰς τοὺς βαρβάρους φ. X.*An*.1.2.18; τῷ καθ' ἑαυτὸν φ. from personal *fear*, D.19.2: c. inf., φόβῳ εἰσορᾶν *from fear* to see, E.*IT*1342:—for τεθνάναι τῷ φόβῳ τινά, v. θνῄσκω I. 2. b. with Verbs, τεύχειν φόβον A.*Pr*.1090 (anap.); κλάζουσι κώδωνες φ. Id.*Th*.386; φ. ποιεῖν τοῖς ἵπποις X.*An*.1.8.18; παρασχεῖν E.*Hec*.1113, etc.; παρασκευάζειν D.59.86; φόβους ἐμβάλλειν, φόβον ἐνθεῖναί τινι, to strike *terror* into one, X.*Cyr*.8.7.18, *An*.7.4.1; ἐνεργάσασθαί τινι Isoc.7.38, 11.25; ἔδωκ' Ἀπόλλων θῆρας φόβῳ Pi.*P*.5.61; of the person who feels fear, φόβον λαβεῖν, ἔχειν, E.*El*.39, X.*Hier*.11.11; ἐκ φόβου φ. τρέφω S.*Tr*.28: acc. cogn., φόβους φοβεῖσθαι, δεδοικέναι, Pl.*Prt*.360b, E.*Supp*.548; τὸν σὸν οὐ ταρβῶ φ. I fear not with thy *fear*, i.e. not like thee, S.*Ph*.1251; Ταντάλου φ. φοβεῖσθαι Sch.E.*Or*.6; ἐς φ. κατιστέατο Hdt.8.12, cf. Th.2.81; ἐν φ. γενέσθαι Pl.*R*.578e; φ. μ' ἔχει A.*Ag*.1243, cf. E.*Or*.1255; μοι φ. τις εἰσελήλυθ', μ' ὑπῆλθέ τις φ., ib.1324, S.*Ph*.1231; τοῖς Ἕλλησι φ. ἐμπίπτει X.*An*.2.2.19, etc.; διὰ φόβου ἔρχομαι, διὰ φόβων γίγνομαι, E.*Or*.757 (troch.), Pl.*Lg*.791b: opp. φόβον λύειν A.*Th*.270, E.*Or*.104; διαλῦσαι Pl.*Mx*.241b; φόβους ἐξαίρει τῶν πολιτῶν Isoc.2.23; ἀπεληλακέναι τινί X.*Cyr*.4.2.10; φόβου ἀπαλλάξεσθαι to get rid of *it*, ib.5.2.32; φόβου ἐκλύσασθαί τινα S.*OT*1002; φόβους ἀπολύεσθαι Arist.*Rh*.$1415^{b}18$; φόβου μεθεῖσα (Valck. φόβον) E.*Hel*.555; φόβου ἔξωθεν εἶναι Id.*El*.901; ἵνα φόβος εἴη στρατεύειν X.*An*.2.4.3; οὐ φ. μή.. Id.*Mem*.2.1.25; φ. ἐστὶν ὅπως μή..Pl.*Smp*.193a; but φόβος εἰ πείσω I *fear* I shall not persuade.., E.*Med*.184 (anap.); ἡμέας ἔχει φ. τε καὶ δέος ὅκως χρή..Hdt.4.115 (φόβος ἦν ὥστε μὴ τέγξαι is corrupt in E.*IT*1380): adverbial usages, φόβῳ *by* or *through fear*, A.*Supp*.786 (lyr.), *Th*.240 (lyr.), etc.; ἀνάγκῃ καὶ φ. Pl.*R*.554d: with Preps., διὰ φόβον, διὰ τὸν φ., Democr.41, X.*Hier*.1.38, *Cyr*.3.1.24; ἐκ τίνος φόβου; S.*OC*887; μετὰ φόβων Isoc.2.26; ἄρχειν ξὺν φόβοισι S.*OT*585; προαποθνῄσκειν ὑπὸ τοῦ φ. X.*Cyr*.3.1.25; Poet., ἀμφὶ φόβῳ E.*Or*.825 (lyr.): pl., not only in Poets, as Pi.*N*.9.27, A.*Th*.134 (prob. l.), S.*Aj*.531, etc., but also in Prose, φόβους καὶ δείματα Th.7.80; πόνους καὶ φ. Pl.*Lg*.635c; κινδύνους καὶ φ. Id.*Tht*.173a. 2. *object* or *cause of terror*, S.*OC*1652; φόβος ἀκοῦσαι *a terror* to hear, Hdt.6.112: pl., ἢν φόβους λέγῃ S.*OT*917; πολλῶν φ. προσαγομένων X.*An*.4.1.23.

**φοιβ-άζω,** (Φοῖβος) *prophesy*, *AP*9.525.22: c. acc., φ. ὄπα Lyc.6; Κασσάνδρη φοίβᾰσε μύθους *AP*9.191. 2. *inspire*, πάθος φοιβάζον τοὺς λόγους Longin.8.4:—Pass., Antioch.Astr. in *Cat.Cod.Astr*.7.112, Hld.2.22. II. = φοιβάω I, Lyc.731, 875, 1166. **-αίνω,** *clean*, Hsch.; φοιβανάτω (aor. imper.) δέ τις ἀσάμινθον Anon.ap. *EM*797.7. 2. = φοιβάζω I. 1, Hsch. **-άς,** άδος, ἡ, *priestess of Phoebus*: generally, *inspired woman, prophetess*, E.*Hec*.827: as fem. Adj., = φοιβάζουσα, Tim.*Fr*.3. **-αστής,** οῦ, ὁ, *vaticinator*, *Gloss.* **-αστικός,** ή, όν, *like inspiration, enthusiastic*, Longin.13.2, Ptol.*Tetr*.159: c. gen., φ. ἐμμέτρων χρησμῶν *uttering* oracles in verse, Plu.*Rom*.21. **-άστρια,** ἡ, *prophetess*, Lyc.1468. **⊛ -άω,** *cleanse, purify*, χεῖρας φοιβήσασα μύροις Theoc.17.134, cf. A.R.2.302, Call.*Lav.Pall*.11:—Pass., Hsch. 2. dub. sens. as v.l. in Lxx *De*.14.1. II. = φοιβάζω I, Sch.S.*Aj*.332.

**Φοίβ-ειος,** α, ον, Ion. **Φοιβήϊος,** ον E.*Ion*461 (lyr.):—*of Phoebus, belonging* or *sacred to him*, ἱρόν Hdt.6.61; δάπεδον Id.*IA*756 (lyr.); λατρεῖαι Id.*Ph*.225 (lyr.); γυνή Id.*Fr*.867:—pecul. fem. **Φοιβηΐς,** ΐδος, τέχνη *AP*9.201 (Leo Phil.). **⊛ -η,** ἡ, *Phoebe*, daughter of Uranus and Gaia, Hes.*Th*.136, 404, A.*Eu*.7: acc. to others the mother of Phoebus, ib.8; later, epith. of Artemis, Virg.*G*.1.431, etc.

**φοιβηλάλος** [ᾰ], ον, *uttering the oracles of Phoebus*, τρίπους, μάντις, Ps.-Callisth.1.45; Φοιβηλάλος, ἡ, = Πυθία I, ibid.

**φοίβ-ησις,** εως, ἡ, *inspiration*, Vett.Val.110.31 (pl.). **-ητεύω,** *to be a prophet*, Hsch. **-ητήρ,** ῆρος, ὁ, = sq., *PMag.Lond*.47.17 (dub. l.). **-ητής,** οῦ, ὁ, *prophet*, Man.1.237, *CIG*4990, al. (Ethiopia, iii A. D.). **-ητός,** ή, όν, *inspired, prophesying*, Man.4.550. **-ήτρια,** ἡ, = καθάρτρια, *purifier*, Hsch.; ἡ Φ., perh. Isis, *CIG*4987 (Ethiopia). **-ήτωρ,** ορος, ὁ, = φοιβητής, Orph.*L*.389.

**Φοιβό-ληπτος,** Ion. **-λαμπτος,** ον, *possessed by Phoebus*, Hdt.4.13, Lyc.1460, Plu.*Pomp*.48, Plot.5.8.10. **-νομέομαι,** Pass., *to be ruled by Phoebus*, i.e. *to be purified*, Thessalian word in Plu.2.393c.

**⊛ φοῖβος,** η, ον (accented φοιβάν in B.12.139 Pap.):—*pure, bright, radiant*, ὕδωρ Hes.*Fr*.274, Lyc.1009; ἡλίου φοίβῃ φλογί A.*Pr*.22; αἴγλα B. l. c. II. as pr. n., Φοῖβος, ὁ, *Phoebus*, i.e. *the Bright* or *Pure*, an old epith. of Apollo, Φ. Ἀπόλλων Il.1.43, al.; rarely inverted, Ἀπόλλων Φοῖβος 20.68, Hes.*Fr*.194: then alone as pr. n., Il.1.443, Alcm.61, etc. 2. *prophet*, *BCH*55.85 (Panamara).

**φοΐδες,** v. φωΐς.

**φοίνᾱ,** ἡ, Lacon. for θοίνη, Alcm.22.

**φοιν-άς,** άδος, ἡ, = ἐρυσίβη, Theognost.*Can*.25. **-ήεις,** εσσα, εν, (φοινός) *blood-red, deep red*, δράκων Il.12.202; αἷμα Mosch.2.58: *bloody*, ἀσπίς Nic.*Th*.158. **-ιγμα,** ατος, τό, *that which is red*, Lib.*Descr*.30.12. **-ιγμός,** ὁ, *the irritation* of the skin *by rubefacients*, Sor.2.15, al., Gal.10.466, Orib.*Fr*.56. **-ίζω,** v.l. for φοινίσσω, Nonn.*D*.12.323.

**Φοινῑκ-αιγύπτιος,** ὁ, *person of mixed Phoenician and Egyptian descent*, *PSI*5.531.1 (iii B. C.). **⊛ -αῖος,** ὁ (sc. μήν), name of month at Corinth, *Corinth* 8(1).2.

**φοινῑκάνθεμος,** ον, *with bright flowers*, ἔαρ Pi.*P*.4.64.

**Φοινῑκάρχ-έω,** *to be* Φοινικάρχης, *Rev.Bibl*.1895.386 (Gerasa, iii A. D.). **-ης,** ου, ὁ, *president of the provincial assembly of Phoenicia*, $IG2^{2}$.3817 (Eleusis, iii A. D.), Just.*Nov*.89.15. **-ια,** ἡ, *his office*, *Cod.Just*.5.27.1.

**φοινῑκ-άς,** άδος, ἡ, = ῥάφανος (Euboean), Hsch. (pl.). **-ασπις,** ιδος, ὁ, ἡ, *bearing red shields*, ἡμίθεοι B.8.10. **-είμων,** ον, gen. ονος, *with garment of red*, v. φιλοκονίμων. **-ειος,** ον, *of the palm-tree*, οἶνος D.S.1.91, Suid.; cf. φοινικήϊος.

**Φοινῑκελίκτης,** οῦ, ὁ, = ἀπατηλός, *Com.Adesp*.1293.

**⊛ φοινίκεος** [ῑ], έα, εον: (φοῖνιξ B. I):—*purple-red, crimson*, and (generally) *red*, νέφος Xenoph.32.2; ῥόδα Pi.*I*.4(3).18(36); προμαχεῶνες Hdt.1.98; εἷμα Id.2.132, cf. 7.76, 9.22; ὄνυχες Hp.*Int*.29; σύκινα φ., a variety of fig, *PCair.Zen*.33.12 intr. (iii B. C.); metaph., *blushing*, αἰδώς Erinn.*Fr*.1 B 34 Diehl$^{2}$; contr. **φοινῑκοῦς,** ῆ, οῦν, Hp.*Mul*.1.95, X.*An*.1.2.16, *Cyr*.7.1.2, Arist.*HA*$592^{b}24$, Dsc.3.153; σκηναί Plb.6.41.7; χιτών, as signal for battle, Plu.*Pomp*.68, *Brut*.40; γράμματα D.C.40.18; τὸ φ. *dark red*, Arist.*Metaph*.$1057^{a}25$, al.; less bright than τὸ ἁλουργές, Id.*Col*.$792^{a}14$ (φοινικά must be corrected to φοινικᾶ in Dsc.2.176, cf. Suid. s. v. φοινικᾶ (but φοινικιᾶ Id. s. v. ἁπλᾶ)). II. prob. f.l. for Φοινικικός, Thphr.*HP*3.12.3.

**φοινῑκεών,** ῶνος, ὁ, = φοινικών, *Gloss.*

**Φοινίκη** [ῑ], ἡ, *Phoenicia*, Od.4.83, Hdt.1.2, etc. II. *the country of Carthage*, E.*Tr*.221 (lyr.). III. *the constellation Ursa Minor*, Eratosth.*Cat*.2.

**⊛ φοινῑκ-ήϊος,** η, ον, Ion. for φοινίκειος, = φοινίκινος I, *of the date-palm*, ἐσθὴς φ. clothing *of palm leaves*, Hdt.4.43; οἶνος φ. *palm-wine*, Id.2.86; βίκους φοινικηΐους (–ηΐου Valla)..οἴνου πλέους 1.194; φοινικηΐη νοῦσος, = ἐλεφαντίασις, Hp.ap.Gal.19.153. II. *Phoenician*, Hdt.3.37, 8.90, 97; γράμματα Φοινικήϊα, of the ancient Ionic alphabet, Id.5.58, cf. Scamon 2; Φ. alone, *SIG*38.37 (Teos, v B. C.). **-ηΐς,** ΐδος, ἡ, = φοινικίς, Hsch. 2. = ἀνεμώνη 2, Id. **-ηρόν** μέτρον, measure *used for dates*, prob. in *BGU*604.15 (φοινικη[ Pap., ii A. D.), 732.1 (–ηγός Pap., ii A. D.).

**Φοινῑκ-ίας** ἄνεμος, ὁ, *the Phoenician* (i.e. *the south-east*) *wind*, Arist.*Mete*.$364^{a}4$, Gal.16.408. **-ίδιον,** τό, Dim. of Φοῖνιξ, *young* or *little Phoenician*, D.L.7.3. II. *ornament in shape of palm*, κόσμος or ὅρμος χρυσοῦς ἐπὶ φοινικιδίου Ἐριφύλης *Inscr.Délos* 399 *B* 139, 407.10 (ii B. C.). **⊛ -ίζω,** *imitate the Phoenicians*, of unnatural vice, Luc.*Pseudol*.28, Gal.12.249. II. (φοῖνιξ B. I. 2) *to be dark red* or *bay*, *Gp*.16.2.3. **⊛ -ικός,** ή, όν, *Phoenician*, Epich.54, Hdt.6.47, Th.6.46; κέδρος Thphr.*HP*9.2.3; γράμματα *Chron.Lind*.B.15; σήματα Κάδμου Timo 61; Φ. τι a tale of Cadmus the Phoenician, Pl.*R*.414c; later, also, *Punic*, to express craft and treachery, Φ. στρατήγημα Plb.3.78.1; ψεῦδος Φ. Eust.1757.59. Adv. *-κῶς in Phoenician fashion*, D.L.7.25. II. = φοινίκεος, *red*: metaph., κακὰ φ. 'of deep dye', Ar.*Pax*303 (troch., sed leg. φοινικίδων). III. = sq. I, φ. ἄρτοι *date-bread*, Ph.*Bel*.86.27; καρποί *BGU*603.10 (ii A. D.), etc.

**⊛ φοινίκ-ῐνος** [νῐ], η, ον, (φοῖνιξ B. II) = φοινικήϊος I, *of the date-palm*, φ. μύρον *palm*-unguent, Antiph.106.4; οἶνος ὁ φ. *palm*-wine, Ephipp.24; without οἶνος, Id.8.2; φ. καρποί *PHamb*.5.11 (i A. D.); φοινικίνη, ἡ, name of a plaster, Gal.13.375. b. *made of palm-wood*, Ath.Mech.17.14. II. Φοινίκινος, η, ον, *Phoenician*, ἡ Φ. νόσος *elephantiasis*, Gal.19.153. **⊛ -ιον,** τό, = φοῖνιξ B. II. 3, *POxy*.1656.12 (iv/v A. D.), etc. II. = φοῖνιξ B. IV, Arist.*Pr*.$918^{b}8$. III. *palm-wine* (?), *Supp.Epigr*.1.414.5 (Crete, v/iv B. C.). **⊛ -ιος,** α, ον, = φοινίκεος I, Epich.31, X.*An*.1.2.16 (v.l.), $IG2^{2}$.1514.41, Arist.*Mete*.$372^{a}4$, Plb.6.23.12 (nisi leg. φοινικοῖς); φ. οἶνος *palm*-wine, *Schwyzer*$182^{a}5$ (Gortyn, v/iv B. C.). II. = Φοινικικός I, S.*Fr*.514, D.S.3.67 codd., 5.74 codd. **-ιοῦς,** οῦν, = φοινίκεος, Ar.*Av*.272, Arist.*Col*.$792^{b}2$, al.; ταινίδιον *SIG*1018.4 (Pergam., iii B. C.). (Usu. second declension, prob. by 'contamination' of φοινίκιος and φοινικοῦς; once third declension, φοινικιοῦντα Arist.*Col*.$796^{a}32$, prob. by 'contamination' of φοινίκιος and φοινικόεις.) II. **φοινικιοῦν,** τό (sc. δικαστήριον), a court of justice at Athens, named from the colour of its walls, Paus.1.28.8. **–ίς,** *ίδος, ἡ, red* or *purple cloth*, Ar.*Pl.*731,735; used for horses, X.*Cyr.*8.3.12. **2.** *red cloak*, Ar.*Ach.*320 (troch.); φοινικίδ' ὀξεῖαν πάνυ a *red cloak* as bright as bright can be, Id.*Pax* 1173, cf. 1175 (both troch.): esp. the *dark-red military cloak* of the Lacedaemonians, Id.*Lys.*1140, X.*Lac.*11.3, Arist.*Fr.*542; also worn by Persians, X.*Cyr.*6.4.1, cf. φοινικιστής II; by Macedonians, Plu. *Aem.*18, etc.; distd. from πορφυρίς, X.*Cyr.*8.3.3. **3.** *red curtain* or *carpet*, Aeschin.3.76 (pl.). **4.** *red flag* hung out as the signal for action, Plb.2.66.11, D.S.13.77, etc.; generally, *red banner*, φοινικίδας ἀνασείειν, a form in solemn curses or excommunications, Lys.6.51. **5.** *ornamental palm-tree*, *Inscr.Délos* 314*B* 137 (iii B.C.). **–ισμα,** *ατος, τό*, in pl., = τὰ διὰ φοινίκων ἐπιθέματα, cj. in Aët. 9.10 (φοινίσματα codd.). ❋ **–ιστής,** *οῦ, ὁ*, (φοῖνιξ B.II) *dyer of purple* or *red*, Zonar. **II.** among the Persians, *wearer of purple*, opp. παραλουργής (q.v.), i.e. *one of the highest rank*, X.*An.*1.2.20; cf. Hsch. **III.** = Φοινικίζων I, Sch.Ar.*Pax* 883, *EM*235.47.

**Φοινῑκιστί,** Adv. *in the Phoenician* or *Punic tongue*, Plb.1.80.6.

**φοινῑκίτης** [κῑ], *ου, ὁ*, (φοῖνιξ B. II) φ. οἶνος *palm*-wine, Dsc.5.31.

**φοινῑκο-βάλᾰνος** [βᾰ], *ἡ, palm-nut*, i.e. *date*, the fruit of the date-palm, Plb.12.2.6, 26.1.8, Dsc.1.109, Gal.6.779, *IG*2².1013.20. **–βαπτος,** *ον, purple-dyed*, ἐσθήματα A.*Eu.*1028. **–βᾰτέω,** *climb palms*, Luc.*Syr.D.*29. **–βᾰφής,** *ές*, = φοινικόβαπτος, Hld. 3.3, Sch.Ar.*Ach.*319, Philostr.*Ep.*3,36. **–γενής,** *ές, Phoenician-born*, E.*Fr.*472 (anap.). **–γράφος** [ᾰ], *ὁ*, title of official at Mytilene, *IG*12(2).96, 97. **–δάκτῠλος,** *ον, crimson-fingered*, coined by Arist.*Rh.*1405$^{b}$20, on the analogy of ῥοδοδ–. **–εις,** *εσσα, εν*, (φοῖνιξ B. I) = φοινίκεος, *dark-red, purple* or *crimson*, χλαῖνα Il.10.133, Od.14.500; ἡνία Hes.*Sc.*95; σμώδιγγες..αἵματι φοινικόεσσαι *red* with blood, Il.23.717; αἵματι φοινικόεις Hes.*Sc.*194. [In Hom. and Hes. φοινικόεσσαι, -όεσσαν, -όεντα, must be pronounced as if contracted, cf. Nonn.*D.*41.352.] **–θριξ,** *ὁ, ἡ*, gen. τρῐχος, *with red hair*, βόες B.10.105. **–κρήδεμνος,** *ον*, Dor. **–κράδεμνος** [ᾱ], *with purple kerchief*, [Μοῖσαι] Id.12.222; Λατώ Id.10.97. **–κροκος,** *ον*, (κρόκη) *of purple woof*, ζώνα Pi.*O.*6.39. **–λεγνος,** *ον, red-streaked*, of the bird πηνέλοψ, Ion Trag.68. **–λοφος,** *ον, purple-* or *crimson-crested*, δράκων E.*Ph.* 820 (lyr.); ὄρνιθες Theoc.22.72; ἀλεκτρυόνες *Gp.*14.16.2. **–νωτος,** *ον, red-backed*, βόες B.5.102. **–παραδεισος,** *ὁ, palm-grove*, *CPHerm.*7 ii 24, *PSI*2.240.10. ❋ **–πάρῃος** [ᾰ], *ον, red-cheeked*, epith. of ships, the bows of which were painted red, Od.11.124. **–πάρῠφος,** *ον, with crimson border*, πορφυραῖ φ. τήβενναι, = Lat. *trabeae*, D.H.6.13. **–πεδος,** *ον, with red bottom* or *ground*, of the Red Sea, φοινικόπεδόν τ' Ἐρυθρᾶς..χεῦμα θαλάσσης A.*Fr.* 192 (anap.). **–πεζα,** *ἡ, ruddy-footed*, epith. of Demeter; prob. from the colour of ripe corn, Pi.*O.*6.94; also of Hecate, Id.*Pae.*2.77. **–πτερος,** *ον, red-feathered*: as Subst., φ., *ὁ, flamingo, Phoenicopterus antiquorum* Ar.*Av.*273 (troch.); also ὄρνις φ. Cratin. 114. **II.** = φοῖνιξ III. 4, Ps.-Dsc.4.43. ❋ **–πτερυξ,** *ῠγος, ὁ, ἡ, red-winged*, νύμφα Lyr. in *Mitteil. aus der Papyrussamml. d. Nationalbibliothek in Wien* 1(1932).139. **–πώλης,** *ου, ὁ, date-seller*, *PMasp.*58 viii 6 (vi A.D.). **–ροδος,** *ον, red with roses*, λειμῶνες Pi.*Fr.*129.2. **–ρυγχος,** *ον, with a red bill*, κορακίας Arist.*HA*617$^{b}$17. **–σκελής,** *ές, red-legged*, χηλαί E.*Ion* 1207. **–στερόπας,** *α, ὁ*, Dor. for *-στερόπης, *hurling red lightnings*, Ζεύς Pi.*O.*9.6. **–στολος,** *ον*, epith. of ἔγχεα, i.e. ἔγχεα τοῦ τῶν Φοινίκων στόλου, Id.*N.*9.28. **–τρόφος,** *ον, bearing palms*, τόπος Str.17.3.23.

**φοινίκ-ουρος** [ῑ], *ὁ*, perh. *red-start* (i.e. *red-tail*), *Luscinia phoenicurus*, Arist.*HA*632$^{b}$28, *Gp.*15.1.22. **–οῦς,** *ῆ, οῦν*, v. φοινίκεος.

**φοινῑκο-φᾰής,** *ές, ruddy-glancing*, πούς E.*Ion* 163 (lyr.). **–φόρος,** *ὁ, bearer of palms*, title of official in religious guild, *IG*5(2).47.10 (Tegea, φοινεικ– lapis). **II.** *bearing a palm as device*, νόμισμα *Inscr.Délos* 1429*B* ii 34 (ii B.C.). **–φῠτος,** *ον, grown with palms*, D.S.2.48, 19.98, J.*AJ*4.8.1.

**φοινικ-τέον,** *one must redden*, Ruf.ap.Aët.11.29. **–τικῶς,** Adv. *by having a sensation of redness*, πάσχειν S.E.*M.*7.198. **–τός,** *ή, όν, dyed purple*, ἔριον J.*AJ*4.4.6. **–ών,** *ῶνος, ὁ, palm-grove*, *PEnteux.*18.3 (iii B.C.), *P.Amh.*2.31.3 (ii B.C.), Lxx *Ez.*47.18, Str. 16.2.41, J.*BJ*4.8.2, Ael.*NA*16.18, etc.; written **φοινεικών,** *IGRom.* 4.1431 (Smyrna). **II.** *palm-bearing region*, Procop.*Pers.*1.19, al.

❋ **Φοῖνιξ,** *ῑκος, ὁ, ἡ, Phoenician*, Φοῖνιξ ἀνὴρ ἀπατήλια εἰδώς Od.14.288, cf. 13.272, 15.415; ὡς Φ. ἀνήρ, Σιδώνιος κάπηλος S.*Fr.*909. **2.** fem., γυνὴ Φοίνισσα Od.15.417; Φοίνισσαι, name of plays by Euripides, Phrynichus, etc.; also Φ. ἐμπολά Pi.*P.*2.67; χθών, νᾶσος, etc., E.*Ph.*6,204 (lyr.), etc.; Φ. βοά ib.301 (lyr.); κώπη Id.*Hel.*1272; Φ. ἄμπεχος *PCair.Zen.*33.14 (iii B.C.). **II.** *Carthaginian*, ἀλαλατός Pi.*P.*1.72; also fem., Φοίνισσαι νῆες Th.1.116, D.S.13.80.

**B. φοῖνιξ,** *ῑκος, ὁ, purple* or *crimson*, because the discovery and earliest use of this colour was ascribed to the Phoenicians, Il. 4.141, 6.219, Od.23.201, etc.:—hence, **2.** as Adj. (fem. φοίνισσα Pi. (v. infr.); φοῖνιξ as fem., E.*Tr.*815), *blood-bay*, of a horse, Il. 23.454; of *red* cattle, φοίνισσα ἀγέλα Pi.*P.*4.205, cf. Theoc.25.128: of the colour of fire, φοίνισσα φλόξ Pi.*P.*1.24; πυρὸς φ. πνοά E. l.c.; also φ. ἱμάντες Simon.17; πέπλοι E.*Hel.*181 (lyr.), etc. **II.** *date-palm, Phoenix dactylifera*, Od.6.163, *h.Ap.*117, Pi.*Fr.*75.14 (dub.), E. *Hec.*458 (lyr.), D.S.2.53; τόξα ἐκ φοίνικος σπάθης πεποιημένα Hdt.7.69, etc.: the male and female distd. by Hdt. as [ὁ φ.] ἔρσην and [ἡ φ.] βαλανηφόρος, 1.193 (but the latter is masc., ibid. and in 4.172, 182); φοινίκων..τῶν καρπίμων οἱ μὲν ἄρρενες αἱ δὲ θήλειαι Thphr.*HP*2.6.6, but αἱ ἀπὸ τῶν ἀρρένων πρὸς τοὺς θήλεις [βοήθειαι] ib.2.8.4. **2.** *palm-frond*, as a *badge of victory*, Arist.*MM*1196$^{a}$36, Plu.2.723b, etc.; τὸν φ. τινὶ ἀποδοῦναι Chrysipp.*Stoic.*3.175. **3.** *date*, Hellanic.56 J., Epich. 18, Antiph.65, Ephipp.24; more correctly, τοῦ φοίνικος ὁ καρπός Hdt.1. 193; καρπὸς φοίνικος Hermipp.63.22 (hex.); cf. φοινικοβάλανος. **III.** ὁ χαμαιρριφὴς *dwarf-palm, Chamaerops humilis*, Thphr.*HP*2.6.11. **2.** a Bactrian tree, *Mazri palm, Nannorhops ritchieana*, ib.4.4.8. **3.** a sea-plant, *Callophyllis laciniata*, ib.4.6.2, 10. **4.** *rye-grass, Lolium perenne*, Dsc.4.43. **IV.** a musical instrument, like a *guitar*, invented by the Phoenicians, Hdt.4.192, Ephor.4 J., Phillis 2 (pl.), Scamon 3; but so called because made from the Delian palm, acc. to Semus 1. **V.** the fabulous bird *phoenix*, Hes.*Fr.*171.4, Antiph.175; from Arabia acc. to Hdt.2.73; but from India, Philostr. *VA*3.49: prov., φοίνικος ἔτη βιοῦν Luc.*Herm.*53. **VI.** an *ornament*, Lxx *Ez.*41.25. **VII.** *perfume prepared from the fronds of the date-palm*, Thphr.*Od.*28. **VIII.** a *fish*, Ael.*NA*12.24. **IX.** a *bandage*, Heliod.ap.Orib.49.11.2. **X.** = εὐρύνοτος, Agathem.2.7. **XI.** φ. ἐν ὁπλῇ, a disease of the hoof, *Hippiatr.*10. **XII.** an eye-salve, Aët.7.116. [In all senses of the word ῑ in gen., but nom. φοῖνιξ, not φοίνιξ, Hdn.Gr.ap.Choerob. *in Thd.*1.292.]

**φοίνιξις,** *εως, ἡ*, = φοινιγμός, Antyll.ap.Orib.7.16.3, Dsc.2.154.

❋ **φοίνιος,** *α, ον*, also *ος, ον* Pi.*I.*4(3).35(53):—poet. Adj., used for φόνιος, when the first syll. is to be long, *of* or *like blood, blood-red*, αἷμα Od.18.97, A.*Th.*737 (lyr.), S.*Ph.*783; δρόσος A.*Ag.*1390; φ. στάλαγμα, i.e. blood, S.*Ant.*1239. **II.** *bloody, blood-stained*, φ. ἀλκά, of Ajax, Pi. l.c.; φ. ξυνωρίς, prob. of public and private loss, A.*Ag.*643; χεὶρ φ. S.*Aj.*772; χεῖρες Id.*OT*466 (lyr.); κοπίς prob. for κόνις in Id.*Ant.* 601 (lyr.). **2.** *bloody, murderous*, Σκύλλα A.*Ch.*614 (lyr.); πέπληγμαι ..δήγματι (prob. δάκει) φοινίῳ Id.*Ag.*1164 (lyr.), cf. 1278; φ. Ἄρης S.*El.*96 (anap.); ἔχιδνα Id.*Tr.*770: metaph., φ. σάλος, of pestilence, Id.*OT*24, cf. *Aj.*352.—Rare in Com., Ar.*Th.*694.

**φοινίσκη,** *ἡ*, dim. of φοῖνιξ, *small palm*, *BGU*227.10 (ii A.D.).

**Φοίνισσα, φοίνισσα,** fem. of Φοῖνιξ, φοῖνιξ.

❋ **φοινίσσω,** E.*Or.*1285 (lyr.), etc.; fut. ξω B.12.165, etc.: (φοινός):—*redden, make red*, αἵματι Ἄρης πόντον φοινίξει Orac.ap.Hdt.8.77, cf. B. l.c.; χεῦμα Καΐκου *Epic.Alex.Adesp.*3.15; σφάγια φ. E. l.c.; φοινίσσουσα παρῇδ' ἐμὰν αἰσχύνᾳ Id.*IA*187 (lyr.); *empurple*, μόρον S.*Fr.*395:—Pass., *to be* or *become red*, μάστιγι νῶτα φοινιχθείς S.*Aj.* 110; αἵματι φ. E.*Hec.*151 (anap.); πόντος ναΐοις ἐφοινίσσετο σταλαγμοῖς Tim.*Pers.*33, cf. Hp.*Epid.*7.92; καὶ χρόα φοινίχθην ὑπὸ τὤλγεος Theoc.20.16; νᾶμα δ' ἐφοινίχθη Id.23.61; τεμνόμενοι, φοινισσόμενοι, καόμενοι Porph.*Abst.*1.56:—Med., [σκίλλα] φοινίξατο σάρκα Nic.*Al.* 254, cf. Nonn.*D.*34.143. **2.** in the Perrhaebian dialect, = αἱμάσσω, Arist.*Mir.*843$^{b}$14. **3.** causal, θερμὸν ἔρευθος φοινίσσει *causes a hot flush*, Opp.*H.*2.428. **II.** intr., *become blood-red*, Nic.*Th.*238; ἄνθη μετὰ τοῦ λευκοῦ φοινίσσοντα ἐκ μέρους Dsc.4.159.

❋ **φοιν-ός,** *ή, όν*, (φόνος) *blood-red*, παρήϊον αἵματι φοινόν Il.16.159: *blood-red*, θυμὸν ἀποπνείων *h.Ap.*362. **2.** *deadly*, δάκη, ὄλεθρος, Nic.*Th.*146, 675; ποτόν Id.*Al.*187. **–ώδης,** *ες, of blood-red aspect*, ib.489.

❋ **φοΐς,** *ΐδος, ἡ*, v. φῴς.

**φοιτ-άζω,** = φοιτίζω, Hellad.ap.Phot.*Bibl.*p.532 B. ❋ **-ᾰλέος,** *α, ον*, also *ος, ον* E.*Or.*327 (lyr.):—*roaming wildly about*, Mosch.2.46, Opp.*H.*1.45; φοιταλέαι *distraught*, *AP*9.603 (Antip.) **II.** Act., *maddening*, κέντρα A.*Pr.*598 (lyr.); λύσσα E. l.c.; μάστιξ Opp.*H.* 2.513.—Poet. word. **-ᾰλιεύς,** *έως, ὁ*, = sq., Opp.*C.*4.236. **-ᾰλιώτης,** *ου, ὁ*, epith. of Bacchus, *the maddener*, *AP*9.524.22. **–άς,** *άδος, ἡ*, = φοιταλέος, of the βάκχαι, E.*Ba.*165 (lyr., pl.) **II.** as Adj., φ. ἀγύρτρια, of Cassandra, A.*Ag.*1273; φ. νόσος *madness, frenzy*, S.*Tr.*980 (anap.); φ. πλάνη Lyc.610; φ. ῥιπή, of the *flickering* of fire, Tryph.231; φ. ἐμπορίη, of commerce *by sea*, *AP*7.586 (Jul.): also with neut. Subst., φοιτάσι πτεροῖς on *wandering* wings, E.*Ph.* 1024 (lyr.): late also with masc., φοιτάδι μόχθῳ Jo.Gaz.*Ecphr.*1.90; φ. ἵπποι Nonn.*D.*38.260. **III.** *much trodden, frequented*, ὁδοί Anon. ap.Suid. ❋ **-άω,** Il.2.779, etc.; Ion.**–έω** Hdt.1.37, 7.126 (also late, ἐπεφοίτεε Nonn.*D.*1.321); Dor. inf. φοιτῆν Bion *Fr.*2; impf.Dor. 3 sg. ἐφοίτη Theoc.2.155; Ep. 3 dual φοιτήτην Il.12.266; Ion. φοίτεσκον Asius 13.1: Aeol. aor. subj. 2 sg. -άσῃς Sapph.68:—*go to and fro, backwards and forwards*, and generally, with notion of repeated motion, *stalk*; ἀν' ὅμιλον ἐφοίτα θηρὶ ἐοικώς Il.3.449, cf. 13.760; φοίτα δ' ἄλλοτε μὲν πρόσθ' Ἕκτορος, ἄλλοτ' ὄπισθε 5.595; φοίτων ἔνθα καὶ ἔνθα κατὰ στρατόν 2.779; ἐφοίτων ἄλλοθεν ἄλλος Od.9.401., cf. 10.119; πάντῃ φοιτήσασα Il.20.6; φοίτα μακρὰ βιβάς 15.686, cf. Od.11.539; διὰ νηὸς φ. *keep going* from one part to another, 12.420; ἀφάνης κἀν Ἀΐδα δόμῳ φοιτάσῃς Sapph. l.c.; of birds *on the wing*, Od.2.182, E.*Hipp.* 1059, *Ion* 154 (lyr.); of horses going to feed, Hdt.1.78; of hounds *casting about* for the scent, X.*Cyn.*4.4, 6.19; φοιτᾷς ὑπερπόντιος ἔν τ' ἀγρονόμοις αὐλαῖς, of love *frequenting* both sea and land, S.*Ant.* 785 (lyr.), cf. E.*Hipp.*447; of young men *strutting about* to show their persons, λαμπροί τ' ἐν ἥβῃ καὶ πόλεως ἀγάλματα φοιτῶσ' Id.*Fr.* 282.11. **2.** *roam wildly about*, Il.24.533; οἱ δὲ μεγάλα στενάχοντες φοίτων Od.14.355; φοιτῶν μανιάσιν νόσοις S.*Aj.*59, cf. *OT*476 (lyr.), 1255: hence, *roam about in frenzy* or *ecstacy*, ἐς Διόνυσον, of a Bacchant, *AP*6.172. **3.** of sexual intercourse, *go in* to a man or woman, εἰς εὐνὴν φοιτῶντε Il.14.296; πρὸς ἀλλήλους Pl.*R.*390c; πρὸς τὴν γυναῖκα Lys.1.19; παρ' αὐτήν ib.15; παρὰ τὸν ἑωυτῆς ἄνδρα Hdt.2.111; παρὰ τοὺς δούλους Id.4.1; ἐν περιτροπῇ αἱ γυναῖκες φοιτῶσι τοῖσι Πέρσῃσι Id.3.69. **4.** *resort* to a person as a friend, φ. παρά τινα *visit* him, Pl.*Phd.*59d, *Euthd.*295d, *La.*181c, etc.; παρ' ἡμᾶς φ. ὡς παρὰ φίλους Id.*R.*328d; πρὸς τὴν συνουσίαν τινός Id.*Lg.*624a; σφιν ἑκατέρωσε Id.*Grg.*523b. b. *resort* to a person or place for any purpose, ἐφοίτων παρὰ τὸν Δηϊόκεα..δικασόμενοι Hdt.1.96; παρά τινα φ. ἐς λόγους Id.7.103; φ. ἔς τε πολέμους καὶ ἐς ἄγρας, ἔς τε ἀγορὴν καὶ ἐξ ἀγορῆς, Id.1.37; ἐς τὰ χρηστήρια Id.6.125; εἰς τὸ ἱερὸν ἑκάστης ἡμέρας Pl.*Lg.*794b; φ. πρὸς τοὺς Ἀθηναίους, of embassies from the subject states, Th.1.95; φοιτᾶν ἐπὶ τὰς θύρας τινός *frequent, wait* at a great man's door, Hdt.3.119, X.*Cyr.*8.1.8, *HG.*1.6.10; later, φ. ἐπὶ θύρας Plu.*Aem.*10, Luc.*DMort.*9.2, etc.; ἐπὶ θύραις Plu.*Cat.Mi.*21 (s. v. l.); ἐπὶ τὴν ἐμὴν οἰκίαν Lys.3.29, cf. Aeschin.1.58; εἰς τὸ ἱερόν *IG*7.235.2 (Oropus, iv B.C.); also φ. εἰς συσσίτια Pl.*R.*416e; ἄκλητος φοιτᾷς ἐπὶ δεῖπνον Cratin.45 (anap.), cf. Eup.162 (lyr.); εἰς καπήλου φ. Plu.2.643c; εἰς Ἱπποθωντίδ' ἐφοίτα φυλὴν χορεύσων D.39.23; of a company of actors, φ. τισι εἰς τὴν πόλιν Pl.*Lg.*817a.: abs., of a suitor, φοιτῶν ἐναργὴς ταῦρος, ἄλλοτ' αἰόλος δράκων.. ἄλλοτ' ἀνδρείῳ κύτει βούπρῳρος S.*Tr.*11. c. of a dream that *visits* one *frequently, haunts* one, ἐν ὀνείρασι φοιτῶσα E.*Alc.*355; πολλάκις μοι φοιτῶν τὸ αὐτὸ ἐνύπνιον Pl.*Phd.*60e. 5. *resort to* a person as a teacher, παρά σε ταῦτα μαθησόμενος Id.*Smp.*206b; παῖς ὢν ἐφοίτας ἐς τίνος διδασκάλου (sc. οἶκον); Ar.*Eq.*1235, cf. Pl.*Prt.*326c, *Alc.*1.109d; τῶν διδασκάλων ὅποι ἐφοιτῶμεν Is.9.28; εἰς τὰ διδασκαλεῖα φ. X.*Cyr.*1.2.6; εἰς παλαίστραν Pl.*Grg.*456d; πρὸς τὰς τοῦ γραμματιστοῦ θύρας Id.*Erx.*398e: later, c. dat., τοῖς μάγοις Philostr.*VA*1.26; διδασκάλοις Jul.*Or.*7.219c: abs., *go to school*, Ar.*Nu.*916, 938 (anap.); ἐδίδασκες γράμματα, ἐγὼ δ' ἐφοίτων D.18.265: οἱ φοιτῶντες the *schoolboys*, Pl.*Lg.*804d, Isoc.15.183. 6. of a physician, *practise*, Hp.*Lex*4. II. of things, esp. of objects of commerce, *to come in constantly* or *regularly, be imported*, ἐξ ἐσχάτης (sc. Εὐρώπης) ὅ τε κασσίτερος ἡμῖν φοιτᾷ καὶ τὸ ἤλεκτρον Hdt.3.115; κέρεα τὰ ἐς Ἕλληνας φοιτέοντα *which are imported* into Greece, Id.7.126; σῖτος δέ σφι πολλὸς ἐφοίτα corn *came in* to them in plenty, ib.23, cf. Lys.32.15, X.*HG*1.1.35; *come in*, of tribute or taxes, τάλαντον ἀργυρίου Ἀλεξάνδρῳ ἡμέρης ἑκάστης ἐφοίτα Hdt.5.17, cf. 3.90: generally, ἀκάμας χρόνος..ἀενάῳ ῥεύματι φ. E.*Fr.*594.2 (anap.); ᾧ μία τις πήρα, μία διπλοΐς, εἷς ἅμ' ἐφοίτα σκίπων *travelled*, *AP*7.65 (Antip.); of reports, λόγος ἐφοίτα *was current*, Plu.*Fab.*21; τὸ Σερτωρίου κλέος ἐφοίτα πανταχόσε Id.*Sert.*23; ἀρεταὶ πάντῃ φ. διὰ τῆς φήμης D.S.10.12; of *fits* of pain, ἥδε [νόσος] ὀξεῖα φοιτᾷ καὶ ταχεῖ' ἀπέρχεται S.*Ph.*808, cf. Hes.*Op.*103; of the καταμήνια, Arist.*HA*582$^{b}$4, *GA*727$^{b}$27; of *recurrent* καθάρσεις, Id.*HA* 583$^{a}$26; τὰ οὖρα καθαρὰ ἐφοίτα *came* clear, Hp.*Epid.*7.115; ἄνω φοιτᾷ ἡ ὀδύνη Id.*Mul.*1.63; of *recurrent* phenomena, such as rain, snow, hail, Arist.*Mete.*347$^{b}$12, *Pr.*931$^{a}$38. **-εία**, ἡ, = φοίτησις, Theognost.*Can.*25, Suid. (-τία). **-ης**, ου, ὁ, = κῆρυξ, Hsch. **-ησις**, εως, ἡ, *regular* or *repeated going*, mostly in pl., αἱ ἐπὶ τὰς θύρας φ. X.*HG*1.6.7; τῶν εἰς τοὺς γάμους καὶ γενέθλια φοιτήσεων *resortings* to marriages.., Pl.*Lg.*784d. 2. *going to school*, ib.764d (pl.): hence ἐκ φοιτήσεώς τινος of his *school*, Paus.5.17.4. **-ητέον**, *one must resort*, παρά τινα Pl.*Tht.*161e. **-ητήρ**, ῆρος, ὁ, = φοιτητής, Nonn.*D.*4.270: as Adj., = φοιταλέος, φ. Ἔρωτες *in her train*, Coluth.100. **-ητής**, οῦ, ὁ, *one who regularly goes* or *comes*; esp. *disciple, pupil*, Pl.*R.*563a, *Euthd.*295d, *Alc.*1.109d, *Lg.*779d, Phld.*Acad.Ind.*p.17M., *AP*7.122 (D.L.). **-ητός**, ή, όν, *frequenting*: φ. μανία ἐπὶ δεῖπνον *Com.Adesp.*782 (prob. anap.). **-ίζω**, poet. for φοιτάω, Ep.impf. -ίζεσκε *h.Hom.*26.8, cf. Call.*Fr.*9c P., A.R.3.54.

⊛ **φοῖτος**, ὁ, *a repeated going* or *coming*: metaph., *wandering of mind*, σὺν φοίτῳ φρενῶν A.*Th.*661.

**φοιτός**, late spelling of φυτός (q.v.).

⊛ **φόλετρον**, τό, = φόρετρον, *PSI*1.31.16 (ii A.D.), etc.

**φολῐδ-οειδής**, ές, *scaly*, Orib.*Fr.*79. **-όομαι**, Pass., *to be covered with scales*, Philum.*Ven.*18.1, 21.1. **-ώδης**, ες, = φολιδοειδής, v.l. for φολλικώδης in Hp.*Epid.*4.30. **-ωτός**, ή, όν, *clad in scales*, of reptiles, opp. λεπιδωτός (of fishes), Arist.*PA*692$^{b}$11, cf. *HA*490$^{b}$24, al.; also of the signs Scorpio and Pisces, Heph.Astr.1.1; θώραξ φ. a coat of mail *of small metal plates overlapping one another, scale-armour*, Posidipp.26.8, Arr.*Tact.*3.5 (pl.); φ. χιτών Hld.9.15, v.l. for στολιδ- in X.*Cyr.*6.4.2; φ. φιάλη *ornamented with a pattern of scales*, *Inscr.Délos*1414*a*ii 20, cf. 1416*A* i 100 (ii B.C.); παροψίδες, ὀξύβαφα, *BGU*781 i 6, ii 14 (i A.D.); also of the catkins of the filbert, μόρια φ. *imbricated*, Thphr.*HP*3.5.6.

⊛ **φολίς**, ίδος, ἡ, *horny scale*, of reptiles, opp. λεπίς (of fishes), Arist.*HA*490$^{b}$22, *PA*691$^{a}$16, cf. A.R.1.221, Opp.*C.*3.438, Epic.ap.Sch.Nic.*Th.*257; but interchanged with λεπίς, D.S.17.105, etc.; φ. χαλκοῦ Hp.*Vid.Ac.*6. II. *spot on a panther's* or *leopard's skin*, Hld.10.27. III. φ. λιθοκόλλητος *a ceiling in mosaic work*, D.S.18.26. IV. a *bandage*, Heliod.ap.Orib.48.20.11.

**φολκός**, ὁ, dub. sens., prob. *bandy-legged*, epith. of Thersites in Il.2.217; wrongly expld. by Sch. as *squinting*.

**φολλικώδης**, ες, dub. sens. in Hp.*Epid.*4.30 (cf. φολιδώδης), *full of cavities, spongy*, acc. to Gal.19.153; *scabby*, acc. to Erot., who has **φόλλιξ**, ικος, ἡ, in sense of a *scab, leprous sore*.

⊛ **φόλλις**, εως, ὁ, Lat. *follis, bellows*, *AP*9.528 (Pall.). II. *a small coin*, $\frac{1}{288}$ of a *solidus*, *OGI*521.24, al. (Abydos, v/vi A.D.), Procop.*Arc.*25, Suid., Eust.136.13. III. *property-tax*, Zos.2.38, *Cod.Just.*12.2.2.

**φόλυες** κύνες, expld. as πυρροί, with black mouths, Antim.98.

**φολύνει**· μολύνει, καταπίμπλησιν, Hsch.

**φόν-αξ**, ᾱκος, ὁ, *eager for blood*, name of a dog, X.*Cyn.*7.5. **-άω**, Desiderative, *to be athirst for blood, to be murderous*, φονᾷ, φονᾷ νόος ἤδη S.*Ph.*1209 (lyr.); φονώσαισιν..λόγχαις (Boeckh, after Sch., for φονίαισιν) Id.*Ant.*117 (lyr.), cf. Hp.*Virg.*1; ἐοικὼς φονῶντι Ael.*VH*2.44; τῷ ἐξ Ἄρεος φονῶντι ib.3.9; φονῶν τὸ ὄμμα Philostr.Jun.*Im.*9. **-εργάτης** [ᾰ], ου, ὁ, = φονεύς, as Adj., Sch.rec.A.*Th.*122. **-ευμα**, ατος, τό, *that which is destined for slaughter*, of Ion, E.*Ion*1495 (lyr.). ⊛ **-εύς**, ὁ, gen. έως, Ep. ῆος Il.9.632; acc. φονέα (in first foot of trim.) S.*OT*362,721; in E. φονέᾰ, *Hec.*882: nom.pl. φονέες Lesb.Rh.3.8, Att. φονῆς Antipho 4.2.7; acc. φονέας Id.2.3.8, 4.3.1, Lys.12.96, Call. in *PSI*11.1218*a*32, etc.; but contr. φονεῖς Plu.2.162e:—*slayer*, Il. l. c., 18.335, Od.24.434, Hdt.1.45, etc.; δικαιοτάτου δὲ φονῆος Pisand.10; τῷ φονεῖ τἀδελφοῦ τὴν δεξιὰν δέδωκε Arist.*Ath.*18.6.; αὐτόχειρας καὶ φονέας Isoc.4.111; φονέας αὑτῶν *self-murderers*, Lys. l. c.; τοσούτῳ μᾶλλον φονεύς ἐστιν is so much more justly accounted a *murderer*, Antipho 4.3.3; οὐχὶ τὴν ἐμὴν φονέα νομίζων χεῖρα E.*IT.*586; ἀκουσίως τινὸς φ. γενέσθαι Pl.*R.*451a; of the sword on which Ajax had thrown himself, S.*Aj.*1026: as fem., μητέρα φονέα οὖσαν Antipho 1.3 (ὁ φ., even of a woman, ib.20). 2. σοῦ φονέως μεμνημένος you, my *destroyer*, S.*OC*1361. 3. metaph., τῆς ὑμετέρας εὐσεβείας φονῆς Antipho 4.2.7. **-εύσιμος**, η, ον, *that may be slain*, Sch.BT Il.22.13. **-ευτέον**, *one must kill*, Lib.*Or.*46.10. **-ευτής**, οῦ, ὁ, = φονεύς, Lxx 4*Ki.*9.31, *Pr.*22.13. **-ευτικός**, ή, όν, *murderous, deadly*, Sch.Nic.*Th.*1, etc. **-εύτρια**, ἡ, fem. of φονευτής, *murderess*, Sch.E.*Or.*260. ⊛ **-εύω**, *murder, kill*, τινα Hdt.1.35,211, al., A.*Th.*340 (lyr.), S.*OT*716, etc.; c. dupl. acc., [φόνον] φ. τινά Sch.E.*Hec.*335: abs., καὶ τίς φονεύει; S.*Ant.*1174, cf. *El.*34:—Pass., *to be slain*, Pi.*P.*11.17, E.*IA*1317 (lyr.), Th.8.95. 2. of an animal, ἐὰν..ζῷον..τι φονεύσῃ τινά Pl.*Lg.*873e. 3. *stain with blood*, φασγάνῳ δέρην E.*IA*875 (troch.). **-ή**, ἡ, always, exc. in Suid., in pl., *carnage*, esp. on the field of battle, ἀσπαίροντας ἐν ἀργαλέῃσι φονῇσιν Il.10.521; ἐν φοναῖς καλῶς πεσόντ' A.*Ag.*447 (lyr.); ἐν φοναῖς πεπτῶτ' ἄθαπτον S.*Ant.*696; ἔτι ἐν τῇσι φονῇσι ἐόντας Hdt.9.76; κομισθέντα ἐκ τῶν φονῶν Ael.*NA*5.1; also of slain beasts, θηρὶ μαχέσσασθαι ἕλικος βοὸς ἀμφὶ φονῇσιν Il.15.633; ἐν φοναῖς θηροκτόνοις E.*Hel.*154. II. *blood shed by slaying*, θῆκέ τ' Αἴγισθον ἐν φοναῖς laid him weltering *in his blood*, Pi.*P.*11.37, cf. Ael.*NA*1.18,3.21; φονῶν is prob. for φόνων in S.*El.*11, *Tr.*558; so ἑρπετὰ καὶ δάκετα..ὑπ' ἐμᾶς πτέρυγος ἐν φοναῖς ὄλλυται come to a *bloody* end, Ar.*Av.*1070 (lyr., paratrag.); ποίῳ δὲ κἀπελύσατ' ἐν φοναῖς τρόπῳ; what was the manner of her *bloody* end? S.*Ant.*1314; φοναῖς *murderously*, ib.1003 (expld. as Adj. by Sch., cf. φονός). **-ής**, Arc. for φονεύς, *IG*5(2).262.26, 30 (Mantinea, v B.C.). **-ικός**, ή, όν, *inclined to slay, murderous*, γένος -ώτατον Th.7.29, cf. Pl.*Phdr.*252c, D.S.18.33, J.*BJ*2.21.1 (Sup.), Ael.*VH*14.41 (Comp.), Hierocl.*in CA*11p.440 M., etc.; φ. ἀδίκημα *blood*-guiltiness, Lycurg.52; τὸ φ. *a murderous disposition*, Ael.*VH*2.17,6.8; οἱ -ώτατοι (sc. πυρετοί) *most malignant*, Hp.*Judic.*7. Adv. **-κῶς** Demetr.Lac.*Herc.*1014.37, Poll.6.192; πολεμεῖν Polyaen.4.3.30: Comp. -ώτερον J.*BJ*4.9.10; -ωτέρως Lyd.*Ost.*56. II. *of murder* or *homicide*, φ. δίκαι trials *for homicide*, Antipho 4.1.1, Arist.*Pol.*1275$^{b}$10; φ. νόμοι laws *respecting homicide*, D.9.44, 21.43; φ. δικαστήριον Arist.*Pol.*1300$^{b}$24; τὰ φ. *murderous acts, homicides*, Isoc.4.40, Arist.*Pol.*1269$^{a}$1, 1274$^{b}$24. ⊛ **-ιος**, ον, also ος, α, ον A.*Ch.*312 (anap.), S.*Tr.*831 (lyr.), poet. Adj. (cf. φοίνιος), the prose form being φονικός, *bloody*, φ. σταγόνες A.*Ch.*400 (anap.); τραῦμα E.*Rh.*750 (anap.). II. *blood-stained*, χεῖρες A.*Eu.*317 (anap.); φ. πέλεκυς S.*El.*99 (anap.); ὄνυξ E.*Hel.*1089, etc. 2. *murderous, deadly*, δράκων A.*Pers.*82 (lyr.); πληγή Id.*Ch.*312 (anap.); Ἀΐδας S.*OC*1689 (lyr.); ὁρμά Ar.*Av.*345 (lyr.): metaph., φ. ἄλγεα Pi.*Fr.*132; ἄχεα E.*Ph.*1031 (lyr.): γῆρας Id.*HF*649 (lyr., s. v. l.): neut. pl. as Adv., φόνια δερκόμενον Ar.*Ra.*1337 (lyr.). 3. of actions, etc., *murderous*, ἀγών E.*Or.*334 (lyr.), Arist.*Fr.*674 (pl.); ἔργα φ. deeds *of blood*, E.*El.*1178 (lyr.); φ. κατάραι ib.1324 (lyr.); for φονίᾳ νεφέλᾳ, S.*Tr.*831 (lyr.), v. νεφέλη I.2.

**φονο-ειδής**, ές, *blood-coloured*, Zos.Alch.p.216 B. **-εις**, εσσα, εν, *sanguinary*, φάλαγξ *Epigr.Gr.*874*a*8 (Cyzicus). **-κτονέω**, *pollute with murder* or *blood*, Lxx *Nu.*35.33, *Ps.*105(106).38. **-κτονία**, ἡ, *deed of murder*, ib.1*Ma.*1.24. **-κτόνος**, ον, *murdering, slaughtering*, Hsch. s.v. φονίαις. **-λῐβής**, ές, *blood-dripping*, θρόνος A.*Eu.*164 (lyr.); φ. τύχα *murder*, Id.*Ag.*1427 (lyr.). **-ρῠτος**, ον, *blood-reeking*, Id.*Th.*938 (lyr.).

⊛ **φόνος**, ὁ, (θείνω) *murder, slaughter*, τεύξασα πόσει φόνον Od.11.430; τοῖσδεσσι φόνον καὶ κῆρα φυτεύει 2.165; φ. ῥάπτειν 16.379; μερμηρίζειν 2.325; ὁρμαίνειν 4.843; σμικρῇσι φόνον φέρει ὀρνίθεσσι Il.17.757, etc.; φόνον πράσσειν Pi.*N.*3.46; ἀκούσιον φ. ἐξεργάσασθαι Pl.*Lg.*869a; βουλεῦσαί τινι S.*Aj.*1055; ἔθου φόνον Id.*OC*542 (lyr.); ἐκπορίζειν E.*Ion*1114; of arrows, φ. προπέμπειν S.*Ph.*105; τὸν Δωριέος πρὸς Ἐγεσταίων φόνον ἐκπρήξασθαι exact vengeance for the *killing*.., Hdt.7.158; κατὰ ζῴων φόνου καὶ μὴ φόνου ὧδε ἔχει *killing* or not-*killing*, Democr.257; in poet. phrases, φ. συρίζειν, κινύρεσθαι, πνεῖν, A.*Pr.*357 (s.v.l.), *Th.*123 (lyr.), *Ag.*1309; φ. τινός the *murder* of —, Id.*Eu.*580, etc.; φ. Ἑλληνικὸς μέγιστος *slaughter* of Greeks, Hdt.7.170; ὅμαιμος αὐθέντης φ. A.*Eu.*212; πατρῷος S.*El.*955; πολύκερως, ἄρνειος φ., Id.*Aj.*55,309; ἐπὶ φόνῳ πράσσεις φόνον E.*Or.*1579, cf. *HF*1084 (lyr.); γέρων φ. μηκέτ' ἐν δόμοις τέκοι A.*Ch.*805 (lyr.), etc.; ὁ ὑπὸ Θήβης Ἀλεξάνδρου φ. Plu.2.856a; ὁ κατὰ τῶν πολιτῶν φ. D.S.19.8: pl., φόνοι τ' ἀνδροκτασίαι τε Od.11.612 (personified in Hes.*Th.*228); ἔμφυλοι φ. ἀνδρῶν Thgn.51, cf. S.*OC*962. 2. in law, *murder, homicide*, δικάζειν τοὺς βασιλέας αἰτιῶν φόνου Lex Dracontis ap.*IG*1$^{2}$.115.12; φόνου διώκειν τινά Antipho 6.9; δικάζειν δίκας φόνου Id.5.11; παραδοῦναι φόνου δίκην Id.6.42; ἁλῶναι Id.5.59, etc.; φεύγειν Lycurg.133 (poet., παίδων φόνον φεύγουσα fleeing from..E.*Med.*795); ἔνοχοι τῷ φόνῳ Antipho 1.11; φόνου ὑπόδικος D.54.25; φόνου καθαρός, ἁγνός, Pl.*R*.451b, *Lg*.759c: ἀκούσιος φ. D.23.72; φόνων ἀπέχεσθαι Ar.*Ra*.1032 (anap.); αἱ τῶν φ. δίκαι Pl.*Lg*.778d; φόνοι..φόνοις δεόμενοι καθαίρεσθαι ib.870c, al.; λαγχάνονται αἱ τοῦ φ. δίκαι πρὸς [τὸν βασιλέα] Arist.*Ath*.57.2. 3. *death as a punishment*, φ. προκεῖσθαι δημόλευστον S.*Ant*.36. 4. *blood when shed, gore*, ἂμ φόνον, ἂν νέκυας Il.10.298; κέατ' ἐν φόνῳ 24.610; ἐρευγόμενοι φόνον αἵματος 16.162; φ. κέχυται γυναίκων Alc.*Fr*.153 Lobel; φόνον κεύθειν Emp. 100.4; μέλανι ῥαίνων φόνῳ πεδίον Pi.*I*.8(7).55; φόνου κηκίς A.*Ch*. 1012; ἐμοῦσα θρόμβους οὓς ἀφείλκυσας φόνου Id.*Eu*.184; σταγόνες S.*OT*1278; σταλαγμοί E.*Hec*.241; χεῖρα χραίνεσθαι φόνῳ S.*Aj*.43; of a sacrifice, ταυρείου φόνου A.*Th*.44; Ἕλλην οὔ καταστάζει φ. E.*IT*72; rarely in Prose of *blood*, Hp.*Morb*.2.73. 5. *corpse*, πρὶν ἴδω τὸν Ἑλένας φόνον..κείμενον E.*Or*.1357 (lyr.); ἐπὶ φόνῳ χαμαιπετεῖ ματρός ib.1491 (lyr.). 6. *rascal that deserves death, gallows-bird*, a Dorian phrase, *EM*662.4. II. of the agent or instrument of slaughter, φόνον ἔμμεναι ἡρώεσσι to be *a death* to heroes, Il. 16.144, cf. Od.21.24; of poison, *Mim.Oxy*.413.180; ἐν φόνῳ μαχαίρας Lxx *Ex*.17.13, *De*.13.15(16), 20.13; without ἐν, *Nu*.21.24. III. = ἀτρακτυλίς, Thphr.*HP*6.4.6.

**φονός**, ἡ, *murderess*, τὰν Πελίαο φονόν Pi.*P*.4.250 (φόνον codd.). II. φονός, ή, όν, *murderous*, dub. in S.*Ant*.1003 (v. φονή II).

**φονουργός**, όν, *murderous*, Sch.rec.S.*El*.1150.

**φονόω**, *stain with blood*, πεφονωμένον ἔγχος Opp.*C*.4.192.

**-φόντης** = φονεύς, only in compds., e.g. Ἀργει-, βροτο-φόντης, etc.

**φονώδης**, ες, *like blood*, ὀσμὴ φ. a smell *as of blood*, Thphr.*HP*6. 4.6. II. *bloodthirsty*, Lxx 4*Ma*.10.17; βλέπειν φονῶδές τι Alciphr. 3.21. III. Medic., *deadly, malignant*, πυρετός Hp.*Morb*.2.67.

**φοξῖνος**, ὁ, a river-fish, perh. *minnow*, Arist.*HA*567$^{a}$31, 568$^{a}$21, Mnesim.4.33 (anap.).

**φοξίχειλος** [ῐ], ον, *narrowing towards the lip, narrower at the brim than below*, κύλιξ Semon.27.

**φοξός**, ή, όν, *pointed*, φοξὸς ἔην κεφαλήν he was *peaked* in the head, had a *sugar-loaf* head, Il.2.219, cf. Hp.*Epid*.6.1.2, Arist.*Phgn*.812$^{a}$8, *AP*10.8 (Arch.), Sor.1.102, Gal.*UP*9.17; [κύλικες] φοξαὶ τὸ χεῖλος (cf. foreg.) Ath.11.480d.

**φοξότης**, ητος, ἡ, *pointedness, tapering shape* of head, Gal.17(1).822.

⊛**φορά**, Ion. **φορή**, ἡ: (φέρω):—A. as *an act*, I. (from Act.) *carrying*, φορᾶς..φθόνησις οὐ γενήσεται there shall be no refusal *to carry thee*, S.*Tr*.1212; ἐν φορᾷ, i.e. in *their arms*, Id.*Fr*.327; θυρώτοιν φορᾶς payment *for carrying*.., *IG*$4^2$(1).102.305 (Epid., iv B.C.); ψήφου φ. *casting* one's vote, E.*Supp*.484, cf. Pl.*Lg*.949a; ἡ φ. καθάπερ πεττῶν *movement* as of the men in draughts, ib.739a. b. *gestation*, τριετὴς φ. cj. in *IG*$4^2$(1).121.10 (Epid., iv B.C.). 2. *bringing in* of money, *payment*, χρημάτων Th.1.96; δασμοῦ, δασμῶν, Pl.*Lg*. 706b, X.*Cyr*.8.6.16; αἱ ὑπόλοιποι φοραί the remaining *instalments*, Lys.*Fr*.1.4, cf. *Ostr.Bodl*. iii 280 (i A.D.), al. b. φ. ἐργάτου, = *latura*, perh. a workman's *pay*, *Gloss*. (*latura* is also glossed φόρετρον, ibid.; also *onus, sarcina*, ibid.). c. *fare, freight*, πόση τις ἡ φ.; Eup.271, cf. Ar.*Fr*.300. 3. *bringing forth, productiveness*, καρποῦ Thphr.*CP*3.14.5; opp. ἀφορία, Pl.*R*.546a, cf. Arist.*GA*750$^{a}$23; of animals, Ael.*NA*17.40; πτηνῶν *Gp*.1.8.9. II. (from Pass. φέρομαι) *being borne* or *carried along, motion*, of the universe and heavenly bodies, ἡ..θεία τοῦ ὄντος φ. Pl.*Cra*.421b, cf. *Ti*.39b, 81a; ἡ σύμπασα οὐρανοῦ ὁδὸς καὶ φ. Id.*Lg*.897c; ἡ τῶν ἄστρων φ. καὶ ἡλίου Id.*Grg*.451c; ἄστρων φοραί Id.*Smp*.188b; χειρῶν φ. Hp.*Prog*.4; σφαίρας φοραί Pl.*Lg*.898b; ἡ φ. καὶ κίνησις Id.*Cra*.434c, *Tht*.152d; χρόνος..μέτρον φορᾶς Id.*Def*.411b; τύχη φ. ἀδήλου εἰς ἄδηλον ibid.; defined by Arist. as = κίνησις κατὰ τόπον, *Ph*.243$^{a}$8, cf. *GC*319$^{b}$32; κίνησίς ποθέν ποι Id.*EN*1174$^{a}$30; γένεσίς ποθέν ποι Id.*Cael*.311$^{b}$33; φορᾷ ἰέναι Pl.*R*.617b; κυκλεῖσθαι..τὴν αὐτὴν φ. ib.a; μίαν φορὰν κινεῖται Id.*Plt*.269e; τό τάχος τῆς φ. Epicur.*Ep*.1 p. 10 U. 2. *range*, φ. ἀκοντίου Antipho 3.2.5. 3. *rapid motion, rush*, πινέτω κατὰ φορὰν ἡμικοτύλιον let him drink half a cotyle at a *draught*, Hp.*Int*.35; γαστρὸς φοραί Thphr.*Fr*.10.3. 4. of persons, *impulse*, ἡ τοῦ πλήθους φ. Plb.10.4.3; ἄλογος φ. Id.30.2.4; ἀκολουθήσομεν ἀλόγως ταῖς τῶν πολλῶν φ. Epicur.*Nat*.127 G.; πρὸς τὸν νεωτερισμόν Plu.*Galb*.4; παῖς..φορᾶς μεστός Id.*Them*.2; στρατηγὸς μεστὸς φορᾶς Lib.*Or*.49.19: pl., ib.1.2; also, *forceful flow* of narrative, Luc.*Dem.Enc*.7. b. *tendency, line* of thought or action, κατὰ τὰς φ. τῶν Στωϊκῶν on Stoic *lines*, Phld.*Rh*.2.296 S., cf. Id.*Herc*.1251. 19, Luc.*Par*.29. 5. φ. πραγμάτων *force* of circumstances, D.18.271: *forceful quality*, ἡ τοῦ οἴνου [ὑγρότης] φ. ἔχει πολλὴν καὶ δύναμιν Plu.2. 132e; φορᾶς σωματικῆς εἰς ἡμᾶς γιγνομένης, of the *influences* of the stars, Plot.2.3.2; ἄχρις οὗ φ. γένηται, of a *favourable wind*, Plu.*Mar*. 37; *favour*, τοῦ βασιλέως Philostr.*VS*2.32. 6. *time, occasion*, πέντε ἢ ἓξ φορὰς τὸν μῆνα Dsc.*Eup*.2.2 (interpol.), cf. Tz.*H*.13.58.

B. as *a thing, that which is borne*, esp., 1. *load, freight, burden*, μίαν φ. ἐνεγκεῖν Plu.*Ant*.68. 2. *rent, tribute*, X.*Cyr*. 3.1.34: pl., *contributions*, D.21.101; φέροντα σωτηρίας φορὰν πλήρη τῇ πατρίδι Id.25.21; of the *contribution* to an ἔρανος, Antiph.124.9, Hyp.*Ath*.11; of *contributions* in kind, οἴνου φορὴ ἐς τὰ ψυκτήρια *SIG*57.44 (Milet., v B.C.). 3. *that which is brought forth, fruit, produce, crop*, κατανοήσας ἐλαιῶν φορὰν ἐσομένην *a large crop*, Arist. *Pol*.1259$^{a}$11, cf. *HA*553$^{a}$22, $^{b}$23; σίτου φ. καὶ τῶν ἄλλων καρπῶν *SIG* 589.30 (Magn.Mae., ii B.C.); ἡ τοῦ Νείλου φ. τε καὶ αὔξησις *CPHerm*. 6.4 (iii A.D.): metaph., φορὰ προδοτῶν *a large crop* of traitors, D.18. 61, D.S.16.54; ῥητόρων Aeschin.3.234; φ. γάρ τίς ἐστιν ἐν τοῖς γένεσιν ἀνδρῶν *a succession of crops*, Arist.*Rh*.1390$^{b}$25.

**φοράδην** [ᾰ], Dor. **-άδαν**, Adv. *borne along, borne* or *carried in a litter* or the like, as a sick person, E.*Andr*.1166 (anap.), *Rh*.888 (anap.), *IG*$4^2$(1).122.27 (Epid., iv B.C.); φ. ἦλθον οἴκαδε D.54.20; φ. ἀνακομίζεσθαι, ἐκκομίζεσθαι, D.C.56.45, Luc.*DMort*.14.5; ἐν κλινιδίῳ φ. κομισθείς Plu.*Cor*.24. 2. *with rushing motion, violently*, S. *OT*1310 (anap.).

**φοράδιον**, τό, Dim. of φοράς II, *POxy*.922.9 (vi A.D.), *PKlein. Form*.1096 (vi A.D.).

**φορακιώδης**, v. φαρκιδώδης.

**φοράς**, άδος, ἡ, *fruitful*, Thphr.*HP*4.16.2. II. Subst., *brood-mare*, *PHolm*.2.32, 9.11, *PLond*.1821.81, Hsch.

**φορβ-ᾰδικός**, ή, όν, *characteristic of the 'herd'*, ὅσον ἔνεστι τῇ ψυχῇ φ. καὶ ἀγελαῖον καὶ ἀξύνετον λόγου Plu.2.713b. **-αία**, ἡ, late form of φορβειά, Lxx *Jb*.40.20(25), Hsch. **-αῖος**, α, ον, *giving pasture*, ὄρη Call.*Lav.Pall*.50. **-άμων** [ᾱ], ονος, ὁ, ἡ, = φορβάς I, *Hymn.Is*.9. **-αντα**· ἰατρικὰ φάρμακα, Hsch. **-άς**, άδος, ὁ, ἡ (φέρβω) *giving pasture* or *food*, φ. γαῖα *bounteous* earth, S.*Ph*.700 (lyr.); but φ. γῆ land *that nourished* me, Id.*Fr*.300. II. *out at grass, grazing*, φορβάδες ἵπποι, opp. τροφίαι (horses kept in the stable), Arist.*HA*604$^{a}$22; πῶλος ὅπως ἅμα ματέρι φορβάδι E.*Ba*.167 (lyr.); οἷον..πώλους ἐν ἀγέλῃ νεμομένους φορβάδας τοὺς νέους κέκτησθε Pl.*Lg*.666e; αἴξ Nic.*Th*.925; σύες A.R. 2.1024: abs., *mare*, Opp.*C*.1.386, *Hippiatr*.15, Epic. in *BKT*5(1). 112. 2. metaph. of *women who support themselves* by prostitution, Pi.*Fr*.122.15, S.*Fr*.720, cf. Poll.7.203. **-ᾰσία**, ἡ, = φορβειά I, Suid. ⊛**-ειά**, ἡ, (φέρβω), written **φορβεά** *PCair.Zen*.781.16 (iii B.C.), Sor.*Fasc*.14, al.; **φορβέα** cod. Hsch.; also **φορβαία** (q.v.):— *halter by which a horse is tied to the manger*, τῆς ἐπιφατνιδίας φ. X.*Eq*.5.1; περιεζῶσθαι τὴν φ. Arist.*Pol*.1324$^{b}$16; οἱ ἵπποι ἀπὸ φορβειᾶς ἄγονται Str.15.1.52; ἐκ φ. ἕλκειν [ὄνον] Luc.*Asin*.51. II. *mouthband* of leather *put like a halter* round the lips of fifers or pipers, to assist them in regulating the sound, Ar.*V*.582 (anap.), Plu.2.456b: hence φυσᾷ..φορβειᾶς ἄτερ blows the pipes without this check, i.e. too loud, S.*Fr*.768. III. a *bandage*, Heliod.ap. Orib.48.39 tit., Sor.l.c., Paul.Aeg.6.92. ⊛**-ή**, ἡ, *pasture, food*, in Hom. only of horses and asses, *fodder, forage*, Il.5.202, 11.562; of men, καρποὺς ἐς φ. κατατίθεσθαι Hdt.1.202, cf. 4.121, al.; πληρωθέντες φορβῆς καὶ οἴνου Id.1.211, cf. S.*Ph*.43, 162 (anap.); of birds of prey, ὄρνισι φ. παραλίοις γενήσεται Id.*Aj*.1065, cf. Ar.*Av*.348 (lyr.). 2. metaph., *fuel*, *AP*5.238 (Paul.Sil.). **-ια**· φάρμακα, οἱ δὲ **φόρβα**, Hsch. **-ιον**, τό, a plant, *Salvia Horminum*, Gal.12.152; cf. φορμίον. **-ον**· ἀπάνονα, Hsch. **-όν**, τό, = φορβή: pl., φορβά, τά, Orph. *A*.1113; φόρβα Hsch. s.v. φόρβια. **-υτα**· οὖλα (Elean), Id.

**φοργάνη**· ἡ ἀραιότης, Hsch.

**φορεᾱφόρος** or **φορειᾱφόρος**, ὁ, *litter-bearer*, Plu.*Galb*.25, D.L. 5.73; **φοριοφόρος**, *Gloss*.

**φόρεθρον**, v. **φόρετρον**.

**φορ-ειά**, ἡ, = βόρβορος, Hdn.Gr.1.291; cf. Lat. *foria*. **-εῖον**, τό, (φορά, φέρω) *litter, sedan-chair*, Din.1.36, Plb.30.25.18 (pl.), Sor. 1.49, Plu.*Eum*.14, D.L.5.41, etc.; written **φόριον**, Lxx 2*Ma*.3. 27. 2. *beast of burden*, ib.*Ge*.45.17. II. *porter's wages*, Poll.7.133. **-εμα**, ατος, τό, later form for φόρημα, Phot., Suid. s.v. φάκελλος. **-εσις**, εως, ἡ, *wearing of apparel*, Id. s.v. τριβή, Sch.Ar.*Av*.156. **-έσκω**, = φορέω, φέρω, *bring*, [οἷς] κλέος οἶδα φορέσκειν Ramsay *Studies in the Eastern Roman Provinces* p.128. **-ετρίζω**, *load* beasts of burden, *POxy*.1069.16 (iii A.D., prob.); *convey* (written **φολ-**), ib.1589.16 (iv A.D.). ⊛**-ετρον**, τό, *expenses of transport*, *PCair.Zen*.13.2 (iii B.C.), Wilcken *Chr*.30 i 7 (iii/ii B.C.), *Ostr.Bodl*. ii 14 (ii/i B.C.), Poll.7.133, etc.; also **φόρεθρον**, *Gloss*. ⊛**-εύς**, gen. έως, Ep. ῆος, ὁ, *bearer, carrier*, Il.18.566, A.R.1.132. II. *litter-bearer*, Plu.*Art*.22. III. [ἵππος] φ. *pack-horse, sumpter-horse*, Id.*Aem*.19. **-εύω**, = sq., Hsch. ⊛**-έω**, Ep. subj. 3 sg. φορέῃσι Od.5.328, 9.10; Ep. inf. φορῆναι (as if from *φόρημι) Il.2.107, 7.149, Od.17.224; φορήμεναι Il.15.310: impf. ἐφόρεον Od.22.456, 3 sg. ἐφόρει Il.4.137; Ion. φορέεσκον 2.770, 13.372: fut. φορήσω *Scol*.9 (cf. Ar.*Lys*.632), X.*Vect*.4.32; later φορέσω Lxx *Pr*.16.23: aor. ἐφόρησα *IG*$4^2$(1).121.95 (Epid., iv B.C.), Call.*Dian*. 213, Ep. φόρησα Il.19.11, (δια-, ἐκ-) Is.6.43, 42; later ἐφόρεσα Lxx *Si*.11.5, f.l. in Is.4.7, Aristid.*Or*.48(24).80, *Sammelb*.7247.33 (iii/iv A.D.):—Med., fut. φορήσομαι Hsch.; in pass. sense, Plu.2. 398d: aor. ἐφορησάμην (ἐξ-) Is.6.39:—Pass., Aeol. pres. φορήμεθα Alc.18.4: aor. ἐφορήθην (ἐν-) Plu.2.703b: pf. πεφόρημαι Pl.*Ti*.52a; plpf. πεφόρητο Orph.*A*.816:—Frequentat. of φέρω, implying *repeated* or *habitual* action, ἵπποι οἳ φορέεσκον ἀμύμονα Πηλεΐωνα Il.2.770, cf. 10.323; τά τε νῆες φορέουσι Od.2.390; of a slave, ὕδωρ ἐφόρει 10.358, cf. Il.6.457; μέθυ οἰνοχόος φ. Od.9.10; θαλλὸν ἐρίφοισι φ. 17.224; of the wind, *bear to and fro, bear along*, ἄνεμος ἄχνας φορέει Il.5. 499, cf. 21.337, Od.5.328; σώματα..κύμαθ' ἁλὸς..φορέουσι 12.68; τόφρα δέ μ' αἰεὶ κῦμα φ. 6.171; so ἀγγελίας ἐφόρεε *conveyed* messages *habitually, served as a messenger*, Hdt.3.34 (nisi leg. ἐσεφόρεε); φ. θρεπτήρια, of Oedipus *carrying about* food in a wallet, like a beggar, S.*OC*1262; λόγχαν ἔτη ἐφόρησε ἓξ ἐν τᾷ γνάθῳ *IG*$4^2$(1).121.95 (Epid., iv B.C.): abs., ἐγ γαστρὶ ἐφόρει τρία ἔτη *was pregnant*, ib. 14:—Pass., v. infr. II. 2. most commonly of clothes, armour, and the like, *bear constantly, wear*, [σκῆπτρον] ἐν παλάμῃς φ. δικασπόλοι Il. 1.238; μίτρης ἣν ἐφόρει 4.137; θώρηξ χάλκεος, ὃν φορέεσκε 13.372, cf. Od.15.127, Hdt.1.71, etc.; φ. ἐσθήματα S.*El*.269; στολάς Id.*OC* 1357; ζεῦγος ἐμβάδων Ar.*Eq*.872; ἱμάτιον Id.*Pl*.991, Pl.*Tht*.197b; δακτύλιον Ar.*Pl*.883. 3. of features, qualities, etc., of mind or body, *possess, hold, bear*, ἀγλαΐας φ. to be pompous or splendid, Od.17.245; φ. ὄνομα S.*Fr.*658; ἦθος Id.*Ant.*705; δόξαν *Arch.Pap.* 1.220 (ii B.C.); ἕνα γομφίον μόνον φ. Ar.*Pl.*1059; γλῶτταν Pl.Com. 51; ἀπόνοιαν φορεῖς you are mad, *PGrenf.*1.53.15 (iv A.D.); with gen. or adj. added, σκέλεα φ. γεράνου Hdt.2.76; ἰσχυὰς φ. τὰς κεφαλάς Id.3.12, cf. 101; ποδώκη τὸν τρόπον φ. *Trag.Adesp.*519; γένειον διηλιφὲς φ. S.*Fr.*564; ὑπόπτερον δέμας φ. E.*Hel.*619; λῆμα θούριον φ. Ar.*Eq.*757; ῥύγχος φ. ὕειον Anaxil.11; καλάμινα σκέλη φ. Pl. Com.184; ὥσπερ σέλινον οὖλα τὰ σκέλη φ. *Com.Adesp.*208; τὸ στόμ' ὡς κομψὸν φ. Alex.98.21 (troch.). 4. *bear, suffer*, Phld.*Lib.*pp. 59,62O. (dub. l. in both), Plu.2.692d, Opp.*C.*1.298. 5. of Time, *extend, last*, ἃ φορεῖ ἐπὶ ἡμέρας δεκαπέντε dub. sens. in *PFlor.*384.54 (v A.D.). II. Pass., *to be borne along*, ἐν ῥοθίοις A.*Th.* 362 (lyr.); φορούμενος πρὸς οὖδας S.*El.*752; κόνις δ' ἄνω φορεῖθ' ib. 715; ἄνω τε καὶ κάτω φ. E.*Supp.*689; πολλοῖς διαύλοις κυμάτων φ. Id.*Hec.*29, cf. Plu.2.398d; πεφορημένον ἀεί always *in motion*, Pl.*Ti.* 52a: hence, *to be storm-tossed*, ναῒ φορήμεθα σὺν μελαίνᾳ Alc.18.4, cf. Ar.*Pax*144; ποσσὶ φ. Theoc.1.83, cf. Bion 1.23: metaph., δόξαις φορεῖται τοπαζόμενα Pl.*Epin.*976a. 2. *to be carried away*, Th.2.76; simply, *to be shifted*, Dam.*Pr.*293. III. Med., *fetch for oneself, fetch regularly*, E.*El.*309; λευκανίηνδε φορεύμενος *putting* food into *one's* mouth, A.R.2.192. **–ηδόν**, Adv. *bearing like a bundle*, φ. ἄρασθαί τι Luc.*Tim.*21. **–ημα**, ατος, τό, *that which is carried, load*, S.*Ph.*474; φ. φρυγάνων Aen.Tact.29.7; metaph., *burden*, A.*Fr.*392, E.*Fr.*643; ἄσηρον φ. Hp.*Art.*35; οἷον φ. ὁ φόβος X.*Cyr.* 3.1.25, cf. *Hier.*8.10. 2. *that which is worn*, Poll.7.95: hence of ornament or dress, βουβάλια, καρπῶν..φορήματα *worn* upon the wrists, Diph.59; ἡ χλαῖνα ἡρωϊκὸν φ. Ammon.*Diff.*p.140V., cf. Phld.*Piet.*17, D.H.2.72, Plu.*Dem.*30, Luc.*Dem.Enc.*21; σκῆπτρον, βασιλικὸν φ. Corn.*ND*9, etc. 3. of a harp, Paus.9.30.2. 4. = Lat. *ferculum*, as borne in triumphs, Plu.*Sull.*38, *Luc.*37. II. collect. for οἱ φορεῖς, Plb.8.29.7. **–ήμεναι, –ῆναι**, v. φορέω. **–ησις**, εως, ἡ, *wearing*, τῶν πιλωτῶν D.H.2.64; ἱματίου Aeschin.Socr. 41. II. = φορά A.II, *being borne*, D.H.2.49. **–ητέος**, έα, έον, *bearable*, κακά Procop.*Goth.*23. **–ητικός**, ή, όν, *producing motion*, φ. αἰθέριος οὐσία Theo Sm.p.149H. **–ητός**, ή, όν, also ός, όν E. *Hipp.*443, Luc.*Salt.*27: I. *borne, carried*, φορητὰ κυμάτεσσιν Pi.*Fr.* 88.1; φ. ὕδωρ Str.3.2.8; φ. ὑπὸ (v.l. ἐπὶ) δελφίνων Plu.2.163c; of the planets, Poll.4.156. 2. *to be carried, moveable*, οἰκίαι Ph.2. 238; ἱερόν ib.146: metaph., ἄστατος καὶ φ. *constantly moving*, Id. 1.219; [φύσις] μετάβολος καὶ φ. Plu.2.428b; τὸ τῆς φύσεως φ. Hierocl. *in CA*7 p.429M. II. *bearable, endurable*, A.*Pr.*979; Κύπρις γὰρ οὐ φορητὸς E.l.c.; φορητὸς ἡ ᾠδή Luc.l.c., cf. *Tim.*23, Jul.*Gal.* 201e; ἐμβολὴ οὐ φ. *irresistible*, Arr.*Tact.*12.10.

**φορί·** τὸν ὑπὲρ τοῦ ἀγροῦ σῖτον, Hsch. (cf. φορικός).

**φόριγγες**, αἱ, *truffles*, Hsch.

**φορικός**, ή, όν, (φόρος) *rendered as tribute*, σῖτος *PPetr.*2p.62 (iii B.C.); ὄλυρα *PTeb.*823.11 (ii B.C.); neut. pl. φορικά *POxy.*807 (i B.C./ i A.D.).

❀ **φόριμος**, ον, *fruitful*, of trees, *AP*9.414 (Gem.); of land, *PTeb.*5. 97 (ii B.C., prob.), *Cat.Cod.Astr.*5(1).174; opp. ἄφορος, *Sammelb.* 4416.16 (ii A.D.): c. gen., ἀμπέλων φ. *CPHerm.*120ʳiii 19: *profitable*, Hsch. II. ἡ φορίμη, a kind of στυπτηρία, Dsc.*Eup.*1.49, Orib.*Fr.*99.

**φορίνη** [ῐ], ἡ, *skin* or *hide of pachydermatous animals*, esp. of *swine*, Hp.*Acut.*(*Sp.*)50, Ath.9.381c, etc.; of the rhinoceros, Ael. *NA*17.44; of the ox, Eust.1915.13; of the chamaeleon, Ael.*NA*4. 33; of the tortoise's *shell*, dub. in S.*Ichn.*303: also of *human skin*, Antipho Soph.33, Aristomen.10; metaph., φ. παχεῖαν φέρων '*thick-skinned*', Plu.2.57a. II. *fat*, νενημένην χοῖρον πολλῆς φ. Herod. 4.16.

**φόριον, φοριοφόρος**, v. φορεῖον, φορεαφόρος.

**φόρκες**, αἱ, = Lat. *furcae*, Hsch.

**Φορκίδες** [ῐ], ίδων, αἱ, *the daughters of Phorcys*, the three Graiae, A.*Pr.*794; also title of play by A.

**φορκόν·** λευκόν, πολιόν, ῥυσόν, Hsch.

**Φόρκος**, ὁ, = Φόρκυς, Pi.*P.*12.13, S.*Fr.*861, Lyc.477. II. = Ἔρεβος, Phanocl.1.20.

**Φόρκῡς**, ῡνος, ὁ, = sq., Od.1.72, al. (always in gen.), Palaeph.31. II. = Φόρκος II, Euph.94.

**Φόρκῡς**, ῡος, ὁ, *Phorcys*, a sea-god, son of Pontus and Gaia, Hes. *Th.*270.

❀ **φορμαλεία**, ἡ, = Lat. *formula*, *POxy.*1115.12 (iii A.D.); also written **φορμαρία**, *PMasp.*50.11 (vi A.D.), al., and perh. **φρουμαρία**, *POxy.* 43ʳ ii 11, al. (iii A.D.).

**φορμηδόν**, Adv., (φορμός) *like mat-work* or *wattling, cross-wise*, ξύλα..φ. ἀντὶ τοίχων τιθέντες setting up planks *arranged cross-wise*, Th.2.75; φ. ἐπὶ ἁμάξας ἐπιβαλόντες (sc. τοὺς νεκρούς) Id.4.48, cf. Ph.2.530, Aristid.2.312J.

**φορμιγκτάς**, v. φορμικτής.

❀ **φόρμ-ιγξ**, ιγγος, ἡ, *lyre*, freq. in Hom., esp. as the instrument of Apollo, φόρμιγγος περικαλλέος ἣν ἔχ' Ἀπόλλων Il.1.603, cf. 24.63, Od.17.270, Hes.*Sc.*203; of Achilles, φρένα τερπόμενον φόρμιγγι λιγείῃ καλῇ δαιδαλέῃ Il.9.186; with seven strings (after Terpander's time), ἑπτάκτυπος, ἑπτάγλωσσος, Pi.*P.*2.71, *N.*5.24; ἀντιψάλλων ἐλεφαντόδετον φ. Ar.*Av.*219 (anap.). 2. φ. ἄχορδος, metaph. for a *bow*, Arist.Rh.1413ᵃ1. **–ίζω**, *play the* φόρμιγξ, Il.18.[605], Od.1. 155, 4.18, 8.266. II. c. acc., *sing to the lyre of* a thing, Hermesian.7.48. **–ικτήρ**, ῆρος, ὁ, = sq., Nonn.*D.*24.238. **–ικτής**, οῦ, Dor. **–ικτάς**, ὁ, *lyre-player*, of Orpheus, Pi.*P.*4.176 (v.l. -ιγκτάς); of Apollo, Ar.*Ra.*231 (lyr.); of Arion, *AP*9.308 (Bianor). **–ικτός**, ή, όν, *sung to the* φόρμιγξ, καὶ πεζὰ καὶ φ. (sc. μέλη) S.*Fr.*16.

**φορμ-ίον**, τό, Dim. of φορμός, *mat*, Hippon.137. 2. *faggot*, D.L.4.3. II. = φόρβιον (which is v.l.), Paul.Aeg.7.3. **–ίς**, ίδος, ἡ, Dim. of φορμός, *small basket*, Ar.*V.*58, Alex.310; used for fishing, Arist.*HA* 547ᵃ2. **–ίσκιον**, τό, = foreg., Poll.7.173. **–ίσκος**, ὁ, = foreg., Pl.*Ly.*206e, *EM.*798.51.

**φορμο-κοιτέω**, *sleep on a mat*, *Com.Adesp.*1191. **–ρρᾰφέομαι**, Pass., *to be stitched like a mat, to be hampered*, a word of Demosth. ridiculed by Aeschin.3.166. **–ρρᾰφίς**, ίδος, ἡ, *needle for sewing mats with*, Aen.Tact.18.10.

❀ **φορμός**, ὁ, (φέρω) *basket for carrying* corn, etc., Hes.*Op.*482, *IG*1².334.10, *PSI*4.332.13 (iii B.C.); φ. ψάμμου πλήρεες Hdt.8.71; φ. πληρούμενοι ψάμμου Aen.Tact.32.2; φ. ἀχύρων σεσαγμένοι Plb.1.19.13, cf. Poll.7.174; prov., ὁ ἐν Λυκείῳ τὸν φορμὸν δούς 'a friend in need is a friend indeed', Arist.*Rh.*1385ᵃ28. 2. *mat*, Hdt.3.98, Ar.*Pl.* 542 (anap.), Thphr.*HP*2.6.11; φ. σχοίνινος Ar.*Fr.*172. 3. *seaman's cloak of coarse plaited stuff*, Theoc.21.13, Paus.10.29.8. II. *a measure of corn*, Lys.22.5; φ. πυρῶν Ar.*Th.*813 (anap.). III. *sieve*, διὰ φορμοῦ ἐκθλίψας Dsc.1.35.

**φορμοσίκων**, ωνος, ὁ, *obese, corpulent*, Hsch.

**φορμοφορ-έω**, *carry baskets* or *faggots, to be a porter*, D.C.52. 25. ❀ **-ος** (parox.), ὁ, *porter*, Epicur.*Fr.*172: οἱ φ., name of a play by Hermippus.

**φορμύνιος**, ὁ, a kind of *fig*, Androt., Philipp., or Hegem.ap.Ath. 3.75d.

**φορολογ-έω**, *levy tribute from*, πολλὰ μέρη τῆς Σικελίας Plb.1.8.1, cf. D.S.5.32, Str.2.5.8, Plu.*Sull.*24: abs., Poll.4.28, Jul.*Or.*7.224b; c. dat., φορολογήσουσιν αὐτῷ πολλοί Heph.Astr.1.1:—Pass., *to be subject to tribute*, *SIG*344.83 (Teos, Epist.Antigoni), D.S.19. 94. **–ητος**, ον, *tributary*, τινι Lxx*De.*20.11. **–ία**, ἡ, *levying of tribute*, *BGU*1010.3 (iii B.C.), *PTeb.*736.47 (pl., ii B.C.), Lxx 1*Ma.*1.29, al., Ph.2.326; ἐν φορολογίᾳ εἶναι *PRev.Laws*33.20 (iii B.C.). II. *tribute*, *OGI*90.12 (pl., Rosetta, ii B.C.); ἡ τῆς φ. ἐπαύξησις *PTeb.*27.46 (ii B.C.). ❀ **–ος** (parox.), ὁ, *tax-gatherer*, *PPetr.*3 p.304 (iii B.C.), *PSI*4.362.8 (iii B.C.), Lxx*Jb.*3.18, al., Plu.*Pyrrh.*23, *Cat.Cod.Astr.*2.164, Paul.Al.*N.*1; φ. τεττάρων πόλεων Str.14.1.41.

❀ **φόρον**, τό, = Lat. *forum*, Ἀππίου φ. *Act.Ap.*28.15, cf. *PLond.*3. 992.13 (vi A.D.), etc.

**φορός**, όν, (φέρω) *bearing*: I. *bringing on one's way, forwarding*; of a wind, *favourable*, ἄνεμος Plb.1.60.6, 31.15.8; πνεῦμα Str. 6.3.5, D.S.14.55, etc.; so in neut. sense, *tending*, κάτω Arist.*Pr.* 908ᵃ24. 2. metaph., κύβος Luc.*Sat.*4; πρὸς ὑγίειαν φ. *conducive* to health, Str.6.1.12; φορὰ καὶ συνεργὰ πρὸς ἀρετήν Plu.2.5c. II. *productive, fruitful*, γῆ Thphr.*CP*3.20.3; of a woman, Hp.*Mul.*1.40: c. gen., M.Ant.8.15. III. Adv. φορῶς, c. dat., *conformably* to, πλάττουσι ἴδια φ. τῇ κατασκευῇ τῆς δόξης Phld.*Sign.*38; also πρὸς τὴν δόξαν ib.26; τρέπουσιν τὸ σωμάτιον φ. εἰς ἀρρωστίας Id.*Ir.*p.29W.

❀ **φόρος**, ὁ, (φέρω) *that which is brought in by way of payment, tribute*, φόρου ἀπαγωγή Hdt.1.6, 27, cf. *IG*1².65.2, al., Th.1.96, etc.; ξυμμάχους φόρου ὑποτελεῖς subject to pay *tribute*, Id.1.56; φόρον ὑποτελέειν to pay *tribute*, Hdt.1.171, cf. Isoc.12.116; ἀπάγειν Ar.*V.*707 (anap.); φέρειν Id.*Av.*191, X.*An.*5.5.7, *Ath.*2.1; πόλεις ἃς οἱ ἰδιῶται ἐνέγραψαν φ. φέρειν *IG*1².212.88; φ. τάξασθαι to agree to pay *it*, Hdt.3.13; φόρον ταῖς πόλεσι τάξαι to fix their quotas of *tribute*, And.4.11, cf. Isoc.4.120, D.23.209, Aeschin.2.23; φ. δέχεσθαι to receive *it*, Th.1. 96 (of the Ἑλληνοταμίαι), cf. X.*Ath.*3.2; φ. προσῄει *it* came in, And. 3.9; τὸν φ. ἀπὸ τῶν πόλεων τὸν προσιόντα Ar.*V.*657 (anap.): pl., φόροι ἥκουσιν Id.*Ach.*505, cf. *Eq.*313 (troch.): ὁ βασιλικὸς φ., at Sparta, Pl.*Alc.*1.123a. 2. generally, *any payment*, φόρον ἀπέφερον τῷ δήμῳ X.*Smp.*4.32; κατὰ φόρους by *instalments*, Senatus consultum ap.Plb.18.44.7; ἐπιβάλλειν φ. impose a *forced levy*, Plu. *Ant.*24.

**φορο-τελής**, ές, *subject to tribute*, *PFlor.*294.42 (vi A.D.). **–φορέω**, *pay a contribution*, *GDI*1938.21 (Delph., ii B.C.).

**φορτᾰγωγ-έω**, *carry loads* or *burdens*, Longin.43.4. **–ός**, όν, *for carrying loads*, κιβωτοί Aen.Tact.29.4; [ναῦς] φ. a ship *of burden*, Sch.Od.5.250.

**φόρταξ**, ᾱκος, ὁ, *carrier, porter*, *Com.Adesp.*102. 2. *cargo-vessel*, *BGU*1807.3,8 (i B.C.). II. like φορτικός, *a tiresome fool* or *knave*, Numen.ap.Eus.*PE*14.7.

**φορτηγ-έω**, = φορταγωγέω, τοῖσι πλοίοισι Hdt.2.96; of beasts of burden, Luc.*Asin.*33. **–ία**, ἡ, *conveyance of cargo*, opp. ναυκληρία and παράστασις, Arist.*Pol.*1258ᵇ23. **–ικός**, ή, όν, *of* or *for carrying loads*, πλοῖα φ. ships *of burden, merchantmen*, Th.6.88, X.*HG*5.1.21. 2. φ. βρώματα provisions *such as are used in these ships*, i.e. sorry fare, Dionys.Com.2.42. ❀ **–ός**, ὁ, *one who carries cargoes, merchant*, Thgn.679, Simon.178: as Adj., ναυβάτης φ. A.*Fr.* 263; ἄνδρες φ. Metag.4 (hex.); ἄκατοι Critias *Fr.*2.12D.; νῆες Plb. 1.52.6, 5.68.4, etc.; πλοῖα D.S.14.55, 20.85.

**φορτιᾰφόρος**, ὁ, *porter*, *Gloss.*

**φορτ-ίζω**, *load*, φορτίσας τὸν ὄνον Babr.111.3; φορτία φ. τινάς *load* them *with* burdens, *Ev.Luc.*11.46; περισσῇ δαπάνῃ φ. τὰ κοινά Dörner *Erlass des Statthalters von Asia Paullus Fabius Persicus* 16; ὑδατὶς -ίζουσα τὸν ὀφθαλμόν *encumbering*, Paul.Aeg.6.14; αὐχένα φ. Aenigma Sphingis (ap.Sch.E.*Ph.*50):—Med., τὰ μείονα φορτίζεσθαι *ship* the smaller part of one's wealth, Hes.*Op.*690; φορτιούμενος μέλι *to carry away a load of* honey, Macho ap.Ath.13.582f:

metaph., φυτεύειν καὶ φ. Phld.*Vit.*p.33J.—Pass., *to be heavy laden*, πεφορτισμένος *Ev.Matt.*11.28, cf. Luc.*Nav.*45. -ῐκεύομαι, *jest vulgarly*, Sch.Ar.*Ra.*13. -ῐκός, ή, όν: (φόρτος):—prop. *fit for carrying*, πλοῖον φ. a ship *of burden*, D.C.56.27, v.l. in Th.6.88. II. *of the nature of a burden*: metaph. (cf. φόρτος II), *tiresome, wearisome*, τὸ λέγειν..φ. καὶ ἐπαχθές D.5.4; τοῖς συνοῦσι φ. Plu.2.456e, cf. 44a, etc.; φ. ἀκολούθων ὄχλῳ because of the crowd.., Luc.*Nigr.*13; -ωτάτη λειτουργία *most onerous*, *POxy.*904.9 (v A.D.). 2. *coarse, vulgar, common*, ἄνδρες Ar.*Nu.*524; opp. πεπαιδευμένος, Arist.*Pol.* 1342a20; οἱ πολλοὶ καὶ -ώτατοι, opp. οἱ χαρίεντες, Id.*EN* 1095b16; βωμολόχοι καὶ φ. ib.1128a5; φ. καὶ νεόπλουτος Plu.2.708c. b. of things, φ. κωμῳδία a *vulgar, low* comedy, Ar.*V.*66, cf. Pl.*Phdr.*236c; φ. τὸ χωρίον Ar.*Lys.*1218; φ. γέλως *Com.Adesp.*644; δίαιτα -ωτέρα καὶ ἀφιλόσοφος Pl.*Phdr.*256b; ἡδονὴ φ. Id.*R.*581d; φ. καὶ δημηγορικά *base, low* arguments, *ad captandum vulgus*, Id.*Grg.*482e; φ. μὲν καὶ δικανικά, ἀληθῆ δέ Id.*Ap.*32a; τῷ φ. προσχρῆσθαι Id.*Cra.* 435c; -ότερόν τι ἐρήσομαι Id.*Euthd.*286e; φ. ἔπαινος Arist.*EN* 1178b16; ἡ ⟨πρὸς⟩ ἅπαντα μιμουμένη [τέχνη] φορτική art that imitates with a view to any and every man is *vulgar*, Id.*Po.*1462a4; λέγω οὐ τοῦ φ. ἕνεκα I do not say it out of *vulgar arrogance*, Aeschin.1.41; of an inflated rhetorical style, φ. κατασκευή D.H.*Lys.*3; τὸ φ. τῆς λέξεως *vulgarity* of style, Id.*Thuc.*27; τὸ φ. καὶ στρατιωτικόν, of the speeches of Iphicrates, Id.*Lys.*12; τὸ φ. τῶν μέτρων Luc.*JTr.* 14. 3. Adv. -ικῶς *coarsely, vulgarly*, σκοπεῖν Pl.*Tht.*183e, cf. *R.* 367a; φ. ἐπαινεῖν ib.528e; φ. καὶ χύδην λέγειν Isoc.12.24; φ. πολιτεύεσθαι Id.7.53; φ. καὶ σοβαρῶς Plu.2.634c; -ώτερον ἢ φιλοσοφώτερον διαλέγεσθαι to discourse *more like a clown* than one of liberal education, Id.*Sol.*3. -ῐκότης, ητος, ἡ, *vulgarity, bad taste*, τῶν ἀκροατῶν Arist.*Rh.*1395b1, cf. Eust.1081.8, 1469.49. -ῐμος, η, ον, = φορτικός I, πλοῖον Sch.Ar.*Av.*599. ⊛ -ίον, τό, *load, burden, freight*, Sapph.*Supp.*9.13 (pl.), Alc.*Supp.*26.1, Ar.*Pl.*352, *Lys.*312, X.*Mem.* 3.13.6, *An.*7.1.37, al., Lycurg.96, Aq.2*Ki.*15.33; λιβανωτικὰ φ. *OGI* 132.11 (Alexandria, ii B.C.); φέρων ἀνθράκων φ. Ar.*Ach.*214 (lyr.); φ. βαστάζειν Teles p.10H. 2. pl., *wares, merchandise*, Hes.*Op.*643, 693, Hdt.1.1, 2.179, al., Ar.*Ach.*899,910, *V.*1398, *Ra.* 573, Hyp.*Ath.*6. b. esp. of agricultural *produce, crops*, *PRev.Laws* 43.14, al. (iii B.C.), *PTeb.*105.24 (ii B.C.), etc. 3. *of a child in the womb*, X.*Mem.*2.2.5; ἔρωτος f.l. in Anacr.170. 4. metaph., μεῖζον φ. ἢ καθ' αὑτὸν αἱρόμενον taking too heavy a *burden* upon him, D.11.14; μέγα τὸ φ. Antiph.3; οὐκ ἔστιν οὐδὲν βαρύτερον τῶν φορτίων..γυναικός Id.329; οὗτοι τὸ γῆράς ἐστιν..τῶν φ. μέγιστον Anaxandr.53; τὸ φ. μου ἐλαφρόν ἐστιν *Ev.Matt.*11.30; χρυσοῦν φ., of wealth, Secund.*Sent.*9. (Dim. only in form, commonly used for φόρτος in Com. and Prose; wrongly condemned as un-Attic by Moer.p.393P., Thom.Mag.p.16R.) -ίς, ίδος, ἡ, φ. ναῦς ship *of burden, merchantman*, ἔδαφος νηὸς..φ. εὐρείης Od.5.250, cf. 9.323, Luc.*VH*1.11, Aret.*SD*2.13; φ. alone, D.S.16.6, Jul.*Or.*5.159d, etc. -ισμός, ὁ, *carrying of loads*, *Hippiatr.*77.

**φορτοβαστάκτης**, ου, ὁ, *porter*, Sch.Pl.*R.*600c, Suid. s. v. Πρωταγόρας.

⊛ **φόρτος**, ὁ, (φέρω) *load, freight, cargo*, Od.8.163, 14.296, Hes.*Op.* 631, Hdt.1.1, S.*Tr.*537, and later Prose, as *PEnteux.*2.11 (iii B.C.), Plu.*Marc.*14, Luc.*VH*1.34; ἐποιήσαντό με φ., expld. as πεπραγμάτευμαι, προδέδομαι, φόρτος γεγένημαι, Call.*Fr.*4.10P.; φ. ἔρωτος, of Europa on the bull, Batr.78, cf. Nonn.*D.*4.118. 2. metaph., *heavy load* or *burden*, φ. χρείας, κακῶν, E.*Supp.*20, *IT*1306; cf. φορτίον. II. Att., *vulgar stuff, rubbish, balderdash*, Ar.*Pax* 748 (anap.) *Pl.*796. III. *mass of detail*, 'stuff', in semi-colloquial sense, Aret.*CD*1.4.

**φορτο-στόλος**, ον, ἐμπορικοῦ πλοίου φ. *sending off a freighted* merchantman, Man.4.134. -φορέω, *carry a load*, cj. for ποντοπορέω in Plu.*Per.*26.

**φορτόω**, *load*, σφοδρῶς ὄνον Aesop.322b; τί τινι Hld.3.5; δίαιταν ὑπερῴῳ καταγωγίῳ Lyd.*Mag.*2.21:—Pass., *to be burdened*, δάκρυσι πεφορτωμένος τὰς ὄψεις ib.3.73; ζῷα -ωμένα *PAmh.*2.150.39 (vi A.D.).

**Φορύη** [ῠ], ἡ, name of Titan, Emp.123.3 (from φορύνω (?)).

**φορυκαία**· δένδρον ποιόν, Hsch.

**φορυκτός**, ή, όν, (φορύσσω) *stained*, κάλχῃ Lyc.864.

**φορύνω** [ῡ], *defile, spoil*, only impf. Pass., σῖτός τε κρέα τ' ὀπτὰ φορύνετο Od.22.21; λύθρῳ ἐφορύνετο γαῖα Q.S.2.356, cf. 3.604.

**φόρυς**· δακτύλιος ὁ κατὰ τὴν ἕδραν, Hsch.

**φορύσσω**, Act. only in aor. part. and inf., φορύξας, -αι (v.infr.):—Med., aor. ἐφορύξατο Nic.*Th.*203:—Pass., pres. φορύσσεται Opp. *H.*5.269; pf. πεφόρυγμαι (v. infr.):—*defile*, φορύξας αἵματι Od.18.336; ὕδατι φορύξαι *mix up*, Hp.*Mul.*1.74; μέλιτι ἐφθῷ φορύξαντα καὶ φυρήσαντα Id.*Steril.*221, cf. *VM*3:—Pass., πεφορυγμένον ἰῷ Nic.*Th.* 302, cf. Q.S.12.550: c. gen., ἰοῦ Opp.*C.*1.381; λύθροιο φορύσσεται Id.*H.*5.269.

**φορῦτός**, ὁ, *whatever the wind carries along*: hence, *rubbish*, such as collects in a farm-yard or a carpenter's shop, σύες ἐπὶ φορυτῷ μαργαίνουσιν Democr.147; ὅταν μύες περὶ φορυτοῦ μάχωνται Thphr. *Sign.*49, cf. Ar.*Ach.*72, *Com.Adesp.*906; *chips* or *shavings*, Arist. *HA*628b11, Conon 48.8; ξύλων φ. Aen.Tact.37.2; used for packing earthenware to keep it from breaking, Ar.*Ach.*927; of the materials of a bird's nest, Arist.*HA*616a12; βρωμάτων φ. *a mishmash* of all kinds of meat, Alciphr.3.7.

⊛ **φορω**, prob. abbreviation of a name of a vessel, ἐλαίου φορω α' *PCair.Zen.*12.104, cf. 114 (iii B.C.); ἐν φορω ib. 670.8 (iii B.C.).

⊛ **φόσσᾱτον**, τό, = Lat. *fossatum, boundary*, *CIG*5187b9 (Ptolemais in Cyrenaica, Edict. Anastasii), *IGRom.*3.1175 (Syria), Suid. s. v. σέδετον, Zonar.

**φοτεύει**· γεννᾷ, Hsch. (Cypr. for φυτεύει).

**φοῦ**, τό, = ἀγρία νάρδος, Dsc.1.11. II. = φεῦ, Epich.124.

**φουάδδει**· σωμασκεῖ, Hsch.; also **φούαξιρ** (-αέξιερ cod.)· ἡ ἐπὶ τῆς χώρας (fort. 'Ορθίας) σωμασκία τῶν μελλόντων μαστιγοῦσθαι, Id. **φοῦαι**· ἀλώπεκες, Id.

**φουγίων**, ωνος, ὁ, = Lat. *pugio, dagger*, *BGU*40.3.

**φοῦιξ**, = φύσιγξ, Hsch. (Lacon. word).

**φουλβίν**, τό (?), = sq., *PGen.*80.13 (iv A.D.).

⊛ **φουλβῖνον**, τό, = Lat. *pulvinus, cushion*, *POxy.*1290.7 (v A.D.).

⊛ **φουλιᾶτα**, τά, = Lat. *foliata*. a kind of ointment, Gal.6.427,440.

**φουλίδερ**· παρθένων χορός, Hsch.

**φούλλικλον**, τό, *football*, Lat. *folliculus*, Ath.1.14f.

**φ(ο)υλλόμενοι**· τιλλόμενοι (Dorian), Hsch.

**φουμῶσος**, = Lat. *fumosus*, τυρός Ath.3.113d.

⊛ **φοῦνδα**, ἡ, = Lat. *funda, belly-band, Gloss.* 2. *purse*, *PHamb.* 10.34, 38 (ii A.D.).

**φουρνάκιος**, α, ον, *baked in the oven*, Ath.3.113b; so **φουρνίτης** [ῑ], ου, ὁ, Archig.ap.Gal.13.264: but fem. -ῖτις, as epith. of Hecate, is cj. in *Hymn.Mag.*3.2.

**φουρνο-ειδής**, ές, *oven-like*, κάμινος Zos.Alch.p.173B. -πλάστης, ου, ὁ, *potter*, gloss on ἰπνοπλάθης, Tim.*Lex.*

⊛ **φοῦρνος**, ὁ, = Lat. *furnus*, Ath.3.113c, Erot. s.v. ἰπνός.

**φοῦσα**, Boeot. for φῦσα, aor. 2 part. (fem.) of φύω, Corinn.21.

**φοῦσκα**, ἡ, = Lat. *posca, sour wine*, Aët.3.81, Alex.Trall.5.5.

**φόως**, τό, Ep. = φῶς (q. v.): hence **φόωσδε**, *to the light, to the light of day*, Il.2.309, 19.103, etc.

⊛ **φραγέλλ-η**, ἡ, = sq., Sch.Ar.*Ach.*724. ⊛ -ιον, τό, = Lat. *flagellum*, *Ev.Jo.*2.15. II. name of a weight, φ. σιδαρᾶ β' Petersen-Luschan *Reisen in Lykien* No.77a (iv A.D.). -όω, = Lat. *flagellare*, *Ev.Matt.*27.26, *Ev.Marc.*15.15.

**φράγ-μα**, ατος, τό, (φράσσω) *fence, breast-work, screen*, Hdt.8.52, Pl.*Plt.*279d (pl.); *protection*, τοῖς ἕλκεσι Gal.15.343; *boom* placed in a harbour, Aen.Tact.37.8. b. contrivance for catching fish, Str. 17.2.5. 2. generally, *defence, means of defence*, μετώπων φράγματα, of a stag's horns, *AP*6.110 (Leon. or Mnasalc.); of the ink of the sepia, Arist.*PA*679a6; of the eyelids, Id.*deAn.*421b29. -μίτης [ῑ], ου, ὁ, *growing in hedges*, θάμνος Dsc.1.91; κάλαμος ib.85. -μός, ὁ, *fencing in, blocking up*, τῆς ἀκουούσης πηγῆς S.*OT*1387. 2. *intestinal obstruction*, Cael.Aur.*CP*3.17. II. *fence, paling*, X.*Cyn.* 11.4, *AP*9.343 (Arch.) *BGU*1119.32 (i B.C.), *Ev.Matt.*21.33, etc.; *hedge*, Aesop.385; *railing* of the bridge over the Hellespont, Hdt. 7.36: *fortification*, ib.142; of the diaphragm, Hp.*Flat.*10, Arist.*PA* 672b20; of the *shard* of beetles, ib.682b17; of the teeth, Poll.2. 93. 2. metaph., *partition*, *Ep.Eph.*2.14. b. nickname of a man *with a bristly beard*, Luc.*Pseudol.*27.

**φράγνῡμι**, = φράσσω, κελεύθους φράγνῦτε *AP*7.391 (Bass.Loll.); ὀδοὺς φραγνύντες *J.AJ*18.9.1:—Med., Ar.*Fr.*367, Plu.*Phoc.*11, *Caes.* 24, *Sert.*21.

**φρᾰδ-άζω**, (φραδή) *make known*, γᾶν φράδασσε (poet. aor. 1) Pi. *N.*3.26. ⊛ -ατήρ, ῆρος, ὁ, *notary*, *IG*14.211, 212 (Acrae). -άω, = βουλεύομαι, Hdn.Gr.1.439: but φραδάον· ἑρμήνευον, Hsch. -εύω, = φραδάζω, Id. ⊛ -ή, ἡ, poet. Noun, *understanding, knowledge*, τῶν δὲ μελλόντων τετύφλωνται φραδαί Pi.*O.*12.9, cf. Alc.*Supp.* 2.2. II. *hint, warning*, θεόθεν..φραδαῖσιν A.*Ch.*941 (lyr.), cf. E.*Ph.*667 (lyr.); ἀθανάτων φραδῇ Theoc.25.52, cf. *IG*5(2).261.15 (Mantinea, vi B.C.); ἕπου μηνυτῆρος ἀφθέγκτου φραδαῖς, i.e. by the scent, A.*Eu.*245. -ής, ές (or -ύς, ύ), only found in gen. έος, *understanding, wise, shrewd*, φραδέος νόου Il.24.354. Adv. -δῶς, = φραστικῶς, φανερῶς, Hsch. -μοσύνη, ἡ, poet. Noun, *shrewdness, cunning*, in dat. pl. φραδμοσύνῃς *h.Ap.*99, Hes.*Op.*245, *Th.*626, etc.; dat. sg. φραδμοσύνῃ A.R.2.647; cf. φρασμοσύνη. ⊛ -μων, ον, gen. ονος, = φραδής, Il.16.638, Orac.ap.Hdt.3.57, Orph.*Fr.*233.

⊛ **φράζω**, S.*Ph.*25, etc.: poet. impf. φράζον Pi.*N.*1.61: fut. φράσω [ᾰ] A.*Pr.*781, etc.: aor. 1 ἔφρᾰσα *h.Ven.*128, *h.Merc.*442, Hdt.2.150, etc.; poet. φράσα [ᾰ] Od.11.22, A.*Ag.*231 (lyr.); imper. φράσσατε Pi. *P.*4.117: pf. πέφρᾰκα Isoc.5.93, Phld.*Po.*5.23: Ep. aor. πέφρᾰδον, ἐπέφραδον used by Hom. mostly in 3 sg., Il.14.500, al. (in Od.1.273, 8.142, πέφραδε is imper.); opt. πεφράδοι Il.14.335; inf. πεφραδέειν, πεφραδέμεν, Od.19.477, 7.49; 1 sg. ἐπέφραδον only Il.10.127: also aor. 1 part. gen. φράδαντος dub. in *IG*5(2).261.15 (Mantinea, vi B.C.):—Med. and Pass., φράζομαι, Ep. imper. φράζεο, φράζευ, Il.5.440, 9.251; inf. φράζεσθαι Od.1.294: Ep. 3 sg. impf. φράζετο, φραζέσκετο, 11.624, *h.Ap.*346: fut. φράσομαι [ᾰ] Il.15.234, Ep. φράσσομαι Od.16.238: aor. 1 ἐφρᾰσάμην 17.161, Ep. φρᾰσάμην 23.75; 3 sg. and pl. ἐφράσσατο, φράσσαντο, 4.529, Il.15.671; imper. φράσαι Od.24.331, A.*Ch.*113; Ep. 3 sg. subj. φράσσεται Od.24.217; Ep. inf. φράσσασθαι Orac.ap. Hdt.3.57: aor. Pass. ἐφράσθην Od.19.485, Hdt.1.84, E.*Hec.*546: pf. πέφρασμαι (in med. sense) A.*Supp.*438, (in pass. sense) Isoc.15.195; part., προ-πεφραδμένος Hes.*Op.*655.—The aor. Med. is chiefly Ep., also Archil.94, Sol.5.4, 34.1, A.*Ch.*113, E.*Med.*653 (lyr.):—*point out, show* (never *say, tell*, in Hom. acc. to Aristarch.), ἐς χῶρον ὃν φράσε Κίρκη Od.11.22, cf. Il.23.138, Od.15.424; also, *show the way to, show where to find*, ᾗ οἱ Ἀθήνη πέφραδε δῖον ὑφορβόν 14.3, cf. 8.68; σήματ'.., τά οἱ ἔμπεδα πέφραδ' Ὀδυσσεύς *showed*, 19.250; μῦθον πέφραδε πᾶσιν *show, make known* the word to all, 1.273, cf. 8.142; δεῖξε καὶ ἔφρασε *h.Ven.*128; φράσσατέ μοι δόμους *show* me them, Pi.*P.*4.117; ἔφρασε τὴν ἀτραπόν Hdt.7.213; κόποι αὐτόματοι φράζουσι νούσους Hp.*Aph.*

2.5; δμώων δή τινα..μοι φράσον Theoc.25.47; τὸ παράδειγμα ὃ ἂν φράζῃ ὁ ἀρχιτέκτων *IG*2².1668.96: abs., φωνῆσαι μὲν οὐκ εἶχε, τῇ δὲ χειρὶ ἔφραζε Hdt.4.113; ἀντὶ φωνῆς φράζε..χερὶ A.*Ag*.1061. 2. *show forth, tell, declare*, λόγον, ἔπος, ὄνομα, Pi.*O*.2.60, A.*Pers*.173 (troch.), *Supp*.320; φ. τοῖσι ἥκουσι τὰ πρήγματα Hdt.6.100; ἐλοῦ γάρ, ἢ πόνων τὰ λοιπά σοι φράσω σαφηνῶς, ἢ τὸν ἐκλύσοντ' ἐμέ A.*Pr*.781; τι πρός τινα Hdt.1.68, Ar.*Nu*.359 (anap.), etc.: c. dupl. acc., φ. τινά τι Isoc. 15.100; τι Pl.*Phdr*.267b; περί τινος Isoc.15.117 (v. infr.); ἐπί τινος Id.*Ep*.6.8: rarely c. gen., *tell of*, τῆς μητρὸς ἥκω τῆς ἐμῆς φράσων, ἐν οἷς νῦν ἐστι S.*Tr*.1122: folld. by a relat. clause, φ. ὅτι.. Lys.1.23, Pl.*Phdr*.278b, etc.; φ. ὡς δεῖ γεωργεῖν X.*Oec*.16.8; φ. οἷ' ἐπορσύνθη κακά A.*Pers*.267, cf. *Pr*.995, etc.; with double constr., φ. τό τε ὄνομα καὶ ἐν ᾗ κώμῃ οἰκοῦσιν *PRev.Laws* 29.5 (iii B.C.): rarely c. part., πεφραδέειν πόσιν ἔνδον ἐόντα Od.19.477; οὐκ ἔφραζες σῆς προκείμενον νέκυν γυναικός E.*Alc*.1012: later c. acc. et inf., Phld.l.c.; *explain* (opp. λέγω, which means simply *speak, say*), φράσον ἅπερ γ' ἔλεξας *declare, explain* what thou didst say, S.*Ph*.559; φράζε δὴ τί φῄς Id.*OT*655; φράζουσιν ἃ λέγει X.*An*.2.4.18; φράζε λόγῳ S.*Ph*.49, Pl.*Lg*.814c; οὐχ ἁπλῶς εἰπεῖν ἀλλὰ σαφῶς φράσαι περὶ αὐτῶν Isoc.15.117, cf. *Ep*.1.2; σαφῶς φ. τοῖς βουλομένοις συνιέναι Aeschin.1.129; of teachers, Antipho 6.13, Pl.*Tht*.180b; of oracles, Ar.*Eq*.1048, *Pl*.46, Pl.*Lg*.923a, etc.; of letters, Plu.*Cic*.15: abs., τοῦτο φράζει ὅτι this *signifies* that.., X.*Smp*.8.30. b. *cultivate style* or *phrasing*, opp. αὐτὸ τὸ γράφειν, Duris 1 J. 3. c. dat. pers. et inf., *tell* one to do so and so, ἵνα γάρ σφιν ἐπέφραδον ἡγερέεσθαι Il. 10.127; δὴ γάρ μοι ἐπέφραδε..Κίρκη (sc. ἰέναι) Od.10.549; τοῖς ἀνθρώποισι φ. σιγᾶν Ar.*Pax* 98 (anap.); τὰ ὅπλα ὑπολαβεῖν Th.6.58, cf. 3.15. 4. abs., *give counsel, advise, suggest*, δόλος ἦν ὁ φράσας S.*El*.197 (lyr.). II. Med. and Pass., *indicate to oneself*, i.e. *think* or *muse upon, consider, ponder*, Ep., Ion., Trag., but not in Att. Prose; εὔκηλος τὰ φράζεαι ἅσσ' ἐθέλῃσθα Il.1.554; φράζεσθαι βουλήν, βουλάς, 18.313, Od.11.510; ἐνὶ φρεσὶ μῆτιν ἀμείνω Il.9.423; πάντα μετὰ φρεσὶν Hes.*Op*.688; θυμῷ Il.16.646; ἐφράσθη καὶ ἐς θυμὸν ἐβάλετο Hdt.1.84; πρὸς ταῦτα φράζου *bethink thee*, S.*El*.383; ἀμφὶς φ. *to think* differently, Il.2.14: folld. by εἰ c. fut. indic., *consider* whether.., 1.83, Od.10.192. 2. *purpose, plan, contrive*, φ. τινὶ κακά, θάνατον, ὄλεθρον, 2.367, 3.242, 13.373; μέγ' ὄνειαρ 4.444; ἐσθλά Il.12.212; φράσσατο Πατρόκλῳ μέγα ἠρίον 23.126; φράσσεται ὥς κε νέηται *will contrive* how.., Od.1.205; φ. ὅπως ὄχ' ἄριστα γένοιτο 3. 129, cf. S.*Aj*.1041. 3. c. acc. et inf., *think, suppose, believe, imagine* that.., Od.11.624; οὐκ ἐφράζετο δυνατὸς εἶναι Hdt.3. 154. 4. *perceive, observe*, οἷον ἐγὼν οἰωνὸν..ἐφρασάμην Od.17. 161; τὴν (sc. τὴν οὐλήν) ἀπονίζουσα φρασάμην 23.75; with a part., τὸν δὲ φράσατο προσιόντα Il.10.339, cf. 23.453: later c. gen., χειμῶνος Arat.745; πομπᾶς Theoc.2.84: rarely c. part., ψυχὰν Ἀΐδᾳ τελέων οὐ φράζεται *marks* not that he will die, Pi.*I*.1.68. 5. *watch, guard*, [ὀρσοθύρην] Od.22.129. 6. *beware of*, ξύλινον λόχον Orac.ap.Hdt. 3.57: freq. in imper., φράζευ κύνα *cave canem*, Ar.*Eq*.1030 (hex.); φράσσαι κυναλώπεκα μή σε δολώσῃ ib.1067 (hex.); φράζεο δή, μὴ.. μάρψῃ Id.*Pax* 1099 (hex.), cf. Call.*Lav.Pall*.52: c. inf., φράζου μὴ πόρσω φωνεῖν S.*El*.213 (lyr.): abs., φράζου *take care!* A.*Eu*.130. (Perh. cf. Lith. *girdžiù* 'I hear', inf. *girdė́ti*.)

**φρακ-τεύω**, *surround, invest*, *Sammelb*.5111.3 (iii B.C.). **-της**, ου, ὁ, *sluice with gates*, Procop.*Aed*.2.3; = *saeptor*, *Gloss*. **-τικός**, ή, όν, = κατάφρακτος, Ath.5.214a (nisi leg. καταφρακτικός). **-τός**, ή, όν, *fenced, protected*, φολίδεσσι Opp.*H*.1.641; cf. φαρκτός.

**φρανίζω**, = σωφρονίζω, Hsch.

**φράξις**, εως, ἡ, *barricade*, Aen.Tact.2.6. II. *fencing in* of an enclosure, *BCH* 23.566 (Delph.). III. *type of defensive armour*, Afric.*Cest*.p.7 V.

**φράσδω**, Dor. for φράζω.

**φρασίζωον**· διασκεπτόμενον εἰς ζωήν, Hsch.

**φρασίν**, old dat. pl. of φρήν (q.v.).

**φράσις** [ᾰ], εως, ἡ, *speech*, εἰς τὴν Ἑλλάδα φ. cj. in Ael.*VH*9.16. II. *way of speaking, expression*, ἀσαφὴς γὰρ ἦν ἐν τῇ φ. τῶν πραγμάτων Ar. *Ra*.1122; δεινὸς περὶ τὴν φ. Arist.*Fr*.70; τάχος καὶ ὀξύτης τῆς φ. Plu.*Cat.Ma*.12; *style*, φ. ποιητική, τραγική, ἱστορική, Str.1.2.6; τὸν χαρακτῆρα τῆς φ. Sor.*Vit.Hippocr*.13; φ. κυρία, τροπική, D.H.*Thuc*. 22; φ. ἀγκυλωτέρα, φ. ἀσυνήθης, ib.25,54; φ. ὑψηλή Id.*Comp*.18; φ. ἀφελὴς καὶ ἀποίητος Id.*Pomp*.2: pl., Phld.*Rh*.1.161 S.; *expressiveness*, τῶν ὀνομάτων interpol. in D.H.*Pomp*.3; ἡ γενναία φ. noble *diction*, Longin.8.1; opp. εὕρεσις, τάξις, *Stoic*.2.96; ἡ τοῦ λόγου νόησις ἤ τε φ. Longin.30.1. 2. *expression, idiom, phrase*, Ἀττικὴ ἡ φ. Sch. Ar.*Nu*.488. 3. *text*, Asp. *in EN*4.12.

⊕**φρασμοσύνη**, ἡ, Dor. **-σύνα**, = φραδ-, *understanding*, μαντειῶν *IG*1².503.

**φράσσεται**, Ep. aor. 1 subj. of φράζω (q.v.), Od.24.217.

⊕**φράσσω**, Att. **-ττω** X.*Cyn*.2.9, D.21.17, al.: fut. φράξω (δια-) *IG* 2².1668.63, etc.: aor. ἔφραξα, Ep. φράξα Il.12.263, Od.5.256, etc., Att. inf. φάρξαι *IG*1².371.20, part. δια-φάρξας ib.373.251: pf. πέφρᾰκα Ph.2.350, later πέφρᾱγα (περι-) Sch.Hes.*Sc*.298: plpf. ἐμ-πεφράκεσαν *J.AJ* 12.8.5:—Med., v. φράγνυμι; fut. φράξομαι (ἐμ-) Luc.*Tim*.19: aor. ἐφραξάμην, Ep. φρ- Il.15.566:—Pass., fut. φραχθήσομαι (ἐμ-) Gal.5.616; φρᾰγήσομαι 2 *Ep.Cor*.11.10: aor. 1 ἐφράχθην Il.17.268, Pl.*Ti*.84d: aor. 2 ἐφράγην [ᾰ], subj. φραγῇ *Ep.Rom*.3.19, part. φραγεὶς Hero *Spir*.1.19: pf. πέφραγμαι E.*Ph*.733, etc.: plpf. ἐπεφράγμην Luc.*Sat*.11, 3 sg. ἐπέφρακτο Hdt.7.142:—Hom. uses no tense but aor. Act., Pass., and Med. The Att. spellings πεφαργμένος and ἐφάρξαντο are given by Hdn.Gr.2.384, cf. *IG*1². ll. cc., and v. φαρκτός, ναύφαρκτος. [ᾰ by nature, for it does not become η in Ion.]:—*fence in, hedge round*, hence with collat. notion of defence, *secure, fortify*, ῥινοῖσι βοῶν φράξαντες ἐπάλξεις *having fenced* the battlements with shields, Il.12.263; φράξε δέ μιν [τὴν σχεδίην] ῥίπεσσι he *fenced* it with mats, to keep out the water, Od.5.256; ἀρκύστατ' ἂν φράξειεν A.*Ag*.1376; φ. δέμας ὅπλοισι Id.*Pers*.456; ἔρνεσι φ. χεῖρα *fill* them *full* with wreaths of victory, Pi.*I*.1.66:—Med., φράξαντο δὲ νῆας ἕρκεϊ χαλκείῳ they *fenced in their* ships, Il.15.566, cf. A.*Th*.63; φραξάμενοι τὴν ἀκρόπολιν θύρῃσι Hdt.8.51; πύλας..ἐφραξάμεσθα προστάταις A.*Th*.798; but ἐφάρξαντο τὸ τεῖχος they *strengthened* it, Hdt.9. 70: abs., *strengthen one's fortifications*, Th.8.35; φ. πρὸς τὰς διαβάσεις Plu.*Mar*.23; φραξάμενοι *in battle-array*, Batr.166:—Pass., φραχθέντες σάκεσιν *fenced* with shields, Il.17.268, cf. E.*IA*826, etc.; ἡ ἀκρόπολις ῥηχῷ ἐπέφρακτο Hdt.7.142; of the Nile, to be *embanked*, Id.2.99: abs., πεφραγμένοι *fortified, prepared for defence*, Id.5.34, Th.1.82; of a person, *armed*, ἀσπιδίτης καὶ πεφρ. S.*Fr*.426: metaph., ἐλπίδος πεφραγμένος *having the defence of* hope, cj. in Id.*Ant*.235 (cod. Laur. πεπραγμένος, cett. and Sch. δεδραγμένος). II. *put up as a fence*, φράξαντες δόρυ δουρί, σάκος σάκεϊ *joining* spear *close* to spear, shield to shield, Il.13.130; φράξαντες τὰ γέρρα *having put up* the shields *as a close, thick fence*, Hdt.9.61:—Med. πάγας ὑπερκότους ἐφραξάμεσθα cj. in A.*Ag*.823. 2. σχάσασαι τὴν οὐρὰν καὶ φ., of dogs, X.*Cyn*.3. 5. III. *stop up, block*, τὴν ὁδόν Hdt.8.7; τοὺς ἔσπλους Th.4. 13; τὰ παρασκήνια D.21.17:—Pass., ὑπὸ ῥευμάτων φραχθεὶς [ὁ πλεύμων] Pl.l.c.; πεφραγμένων τῶν πόρων Arist.*Pr*.935ᵇ14. 2. metaph., *bar, stop*, τὸ ἡγεμονικόν Ath.4.157d:—Pass., ἵνα πᾶν στόμα φραγῇ *Ep.Rom*.3.19; ἡ καύχησις αὕτη οὐ φραγήσεται εἰς ἐμέ 2 *Ep.Cor*. 11.10.

**φρασ-τέον**, (φράζω) *one must indicate*, Pl.*Ep*.312d. **-τήρ**, ῆρος, ὁ, *teller, expounder*, τινος *of* or *about* a thing, X.*Cyr*.4.5.17; ὁδῶν φ. *guide*, ib.5.4.40, cf. Ph.2.77, Plu.2.243e: φ. ὀδόντες, = γνώμονες, the teeth *that tell* the age, Sch.Ar.*Ra*.421. **-της**, ου, ὁ, = Lat. *eloquens*, *Gloss*. **-τικός**, ή, όν, *indicative, expressive*, τινος Pl.*Def*.414d; τὸ φ. μέρος τοῦ λόγου, opp. ἡ νόησις, Longin.30.1; φ. τόποι *expressive*, Id.32.6; φ. δύναμις M.Ant.1.16, Ael.*VH*3.1; of persons, *eloquent*, D.L.5.65: τὸ φ. *power of speaking*, *Placit*.5.20. 4. **-τύς**, ύος, ἡ, *reflection*, Hsch. **-τωρ**, ορος, ὁ, = φραστήρ, *guide*, A.*Supp*.492.

**φράτ-ηρ** [ᾱ], ὁ, gen. φράτερος (v. sub fin.); Dor. **φρᾱτήρ** Hdn.Gr.1. 47; Ion. **φρήτηρ**, = ἀδελφός, Hsch.:—*member of a* φράτρα: pl., *those of the same* φράτρα, *clansmen*, A.*Eu*.656, *IG*2².1237.9, al., freq. in Is. (v. infr.); σ' ὁ πατὴρ εἰσήγαγ' εἰς τοὺς φ. (which was done when the boy came of age), Ar.*Av*.1669, cf. Lys.30.2; εἰς τοὺς γεννήτας καὶ φ. ἐγγραφεὶς Is.7.43; εἰσαγαγεῖν εἰς τοὺς φ. Id.6.21; οὐκ ἐδέξαντο οἱ φ. ib.22; γαμηλίαν τοῖς φράτερσιν εἰσφέρειν Id.3.79; οὐκ ἔφυσε φράτερας, with a play on φραστῆρας (v. φραστήρ), he has not cut his *citizen-teeth*, is no true citizen, Ar.*Ra*.422, cf. *Av*.765 (troch.); φράτερες τριωβόλου, of the Athenian dicasts, Id.*Eq*.255 (troch.). 2. metaph., of birds, φ. καὶ συγγενής Ael.*NA*8.24. (φράτωρ, ορος (q.v.) is freq. found in codd., but is a later form acc. to Hdn.Gr.1.49, Eust.239.33; cogn. with Skt. *bhrā́tar-*, Lat. *frater*, Goth. *brōþar*, 'brother', etc.) **-ορία**, ἡ, = φράτρα, Sch.Ar.*Av*.766, Suid. ⊕**-ορικός**, ή, όν, = φράτριος, γραμματεῖον D.44.41.

**φράτρα**, ἡ, dat. φράτρῃ *OGI*483.87 (Pergam., ii B.C.), Ion. **φρήτρη**, Dor. **πάτρα** (q.v.), Delph. **πατριά**; Att. **φρατρία**; also **φατρία** and **φάτρα** (v. infr.):—prop. *brotherhood*, but among the Greeks always in polit. sense, cf. Dicaearch.Hist.9: I. in Hom., *tribe, clan*, κρῖν' ἄνδρας..κατὰ φρήτρας, ὡς φρήτρη φρήτρηφιν ἀρήγῃ choose men by *clans*, that *clan* may stand by *clan*, Il.2.362; of the Persian royal *clan* (the Achaemenids), Hdt.1.125. II. later, *political subdivision of the* φυλή, Pl.*Lg*.746d, 785a, Isoc.8.88, Aeschin.2.147; φρατρίαι καὶ φυλαί Arist.*Pol*.1264ᵃ8, cf. 1300ᵃ25, 1309ᵃ12; freq. in Inscrr., φυλῆς καὶ δήμου καὶ φρατρίας ὧν ἂν βούληται ἀπογραψάμενον *IG*1².110.16; προσγραψαμένοις πρὸς φυλὴν καὶ φρατρίαν ἣν ἂν βούλωνται ib.12(5).819.21 (Tenos, ii B.C.); *sub-division of a tribe*, *PHib*. 1.28.10 (iii B.C.); of groups celebrating festivals, e.g. the Carnea at Sparta, Demetr.Sceps.ap.Ath.4.141f; or the Jewish Passover, *J.AJ*3.10.5, *BJ*6.9.3; perh. = σύνοδος I. 2, Pap. in *Harvard Theological Review* 29.40 (i B.C.). 2. used to translate Lat. *curia*, Plu. *Publ*.7; in form **φάτρα**, D.H.2.7, 6.89, al. 3. later, of any *league* or *association*, esp. in bad sense, *conspiracy* (in form **φατρία**), Lib.*Or*.18.141; τῶν πονηρῶν τε καὶ ἀκολάστων φατρίαι ib.17.2. (The form **φάτρα** is found in Arcadia, *IG*5(2).510 (ii B.C.), and at Tenos, ib.12(5).798.23 (iii B.C.); **φατρία** is found at Chios, *Michel* 997.28 (iv B.C.); at Tenos, *IG*12(5).816.16 (iii B.C.); and freq. in codd., e.g. Aeschin. l.c., Arist.*Pol*. ll. cc., cf. Hdn.Gr.1.298, 2.598, Orus ap.*EM*.789.20; cf. φρήτρη, φρητρία.)

**φρᾱτρι-άζω**, *belong to the same* φρατρία, μεθ' ὧν..ἐφρατρίαζε καὶ αὐτὸς D.43.13 (vv.ll. ἐφράτριζε, ἐφατρίαζε). II. *conspire*, Sch. Aeschin.2.77, 189 (in form φατρ-). **-ᾰκός**, ή, όν, *of the curia*, D.H.2.23; φ. ψηφοφορία, = *comitia curiata*, Id.9.41.

⊕**φρᾱτριαρχ-έω**, *to be president of a* φρατρία, *IG*2².1237.11. ⊕**-ος**, ὁ, *president of a* φρατρία, D.57.23, *IG*2².1241.5, al.

**φρᾱτρι-ασμός**, ὁ, *league, combination, conspiracy*, Eust.647.34 (written φατρ-). **-αστής**, οῦ, ὁ, = Lat. *curialis*, D.H.4.43. **-ατικὸς νόμος**, = Lat. *lex curiata*, D.C.37.51, al. **-εύς**, έως, ὁ, = Lat. *curialis*, D.H.2.23.

**φρατρ-ίζω**, = φρατριάζω, Crater.4, *IG*2².1237.37. ⊕**-ικός**, ή, όν, = φρατριακός, ἐκκλησία φ., = Lat. *comitia curiata*, D.H.4.20. ⊕**-ιος**, α, ον, Ion. **φρητρ-**, *of* or *belonging to a* φράτρα, at Athens, epith. of Zeus and Athena, as *tutelary deities of the phratriae*, Pl.*Euthd.*302d; Ζεὺς φ. D.43.14, *IG*2².1237.1, prob. for *φρατόριος in Cratin.Jun.9.5; also at Syros, *IG*12(5).669; Ποτειδὰν ὁ φ. *Schwyzer* 323 *B* 14 (Delph., iv B.C.); οἱ θεοὶ οἱ φρήτριοι *IG*14.759 (Naples), *Röm.Mitt.*27.303 (Aquila). II. **φράτριον**, τό, *a temple of these deities*, or *any shrine used by the* φρατρία, St.Byz. s.v. φρατρία, Poll.3.52 codd. III. φράτριος μήν, ὁ, name of month at Cyme, *IGRom.*4.1302.54 (i B.C./i A.D.).

**φράττω**, Att. for φράσσω (q.v.).

**φράτωρ** [ᾱ], ορος, ὁ, = φράτηρ, *PHib.*1.28.7 (iii B.C.), freq. in codd., v. φράτηρ sub fin.: Ion. **φρήτωρ** *IG*14.759.10, al. (Naples).

**φρε-άντλης**, ου, ὁ, *one who draws from a well*, a pun on the name Cleanthes, D.L.7.168. **-αρ**, Ep. **φρεῖαρ** Nic.*Th.*486, τό, gen. φρέᾱτος (v. sub fin.), contr. φρητός *IGRom.*1.1167 *C*6 (Egypt, i A.D.), Hdn.Gr.1.409; Ep. dat. φρέᾱτι *h.Cer.*99 (s.v.l.), φρητί Call.*Cer.*15; pl. φρέᾱτα, also φρῆτα *PCair.Zen.*499.12 (iii B.C.); Ep. pl. φρείᾱτα (v. infr.):—*an artificial well* (thus distd. from κρήνη, cf. Hdt.4.120, D.14.30; but φ. ἀσφάλτου naphtha-*spring*, Lxx *Ge.*14.10, cf. Hdt.6.119), πᾶσαι κρῆναι καὶ φρείατα μακρὰ νάουσιν Il.21.197; the stem φρεατ- first in *h.Cer.* l.c. 2. later, *tank, cistern, reservoir*, Hdt.1.68, Th.2.48,49, *PHal.*1.98 (iii B.C.), etc.; εἰς φ. καταβαίνειν καὶ κολυμβᾶν Pl.*La.*193c, cf. *Prt.*350a; φ. ὀρώρυκται S.E.*M.*8.129; ποιητὰ φ., v. ποιητός 1: generally, *pit*, φ. διαφθορᾶς Lxx *Ps.*54(55).24. b. perh. *oil-jar*, Ar.*Pl.*810. 3. metaph., εἰς φρέατά τε καὶ πᾶσαν ἀπορίαν ἐμπίπτων Pl.*Tht.*174c; ἐν φρέατι συσχόμενος ib.165b; ἡ περὶ τὸ φ. ὄρχησις, prov. of persons 'on the brink of a volcano', Plu.2.68b; λύκος περὶ φ. χορεύει prov.ap.Hsch., Phot.; πίνειν ἐξ ἀργυροῦ φρέατος, i.e. a large wine-cup, Ath.5.192a, cf. Chamaeleon ap.eund.11.461c. [Att. gen. φρέᾱτος Ar.*Ec.*1004, *Fr.*295, Stratt.57 (troch.), Alex.179, Apollod.Gel.1.] (Orig. φρηϝρ, gen. φρηϝητος, cf. Arm. *albiur* 'well', Goth. and OE. *brunna* 'stream, burn', Lat. *ferveo, defrutum.*)

**φρεᾱτ-ία**, ἡ, *tank, cistern*, X.*HG*3.1.7, Plb.10.28.2. II. *opening* in a raft, Apollod.*Poliorc.*191.3. **-ιαῖος**, α, ον, *belonging to a well* or *tank*, ὕδωρ Hermipp.39, Thphr.*CP*2.6.3; φ. ὕδατα, opp. ῥυτά, Plu.2.954c, cf. Arist.*Mete.*353ᵇ26. **-ιον**, τό, Dim. of φρέαρ, *PSI*4.423.39 (iii B.C.), *PCair.Zen.*745.18 (iii B.C.), Moer.p.193P. **-ιος**, α, ον, = φρεατιαῖος, Ruf.*Fr.*66, *Gp.*2.6.33, Anon.ap. Suid. **-ισμός**, ὁ, *falling into a well*, *Supp.Epigr.*4.573.7 (Notium, ii B.C.).

**φρεᾱτορύκτης**, ου, ὁ, = φρεωρύχος, *EM*799.41, Suid.

**φρεᾱτοτύπᾰνον** [ῠ], τό, *machine for raising water, swipe, water-wheel*, Plb.*Fr.*86 (pl.).

**Φρεαττώ** or **Φρεᾱτώ**, οῦς, ἡ, a court in Peiraeus, where banished men accused of murder were allowed to present themselves for trial, the accused being on board ship, the judges on shore; only dat. (loc.), ἐν Φρεαττοῖ D.23.77,78, Arist.*Pol.*1300ᵇ29:—the nom. is written **Φρεαττύς** in Paus.1.28.11.

**φρεᾱτώδης**, ες, *like a well*, χάσμα Sch.Ar.*Pl.*431.

**φρεῖαρ**, v. φρέαρ.

**φρενᾰπᾰτ-άω**, *deceive*, ἑαυτόν *Ep.Gal.*6.3. **-ης**, ου, ὁ, *soul-deceiver*, *Lyr.Alex.Adesp.*1.18, *Ep.Tit.*1.10, *PLond.*5.1677.22 (vi A.D.).

**φρεναρτίους**· φρενήρεις, Hsch. **φρενεμπάρωτος** [ᾱ, cf. πηρός]· βλαψίφρων, Id.

**φρενήρης**, ες, *sound of mind*, opp. ἐμμανής, Hdt.3.25, cf.30, 35, E.*Heracl.*150, Phld.*Mort.*39, Plu.2.323c, Luc.*Cal.*3, etc.: Sup. -έστατος Harp.Astr. in *Cat.Cod.Astr.*8(3).137.

**φρένιον**, τό, = ἀνεμώνη, prob. in Plin.*HN*21.164.

**φρενῑτ-ιαῖος**, α, ον, = φρενιτικός, f.l. in Hp.*Epid.*3.1.ιαʹ. **-ίασις**, εως, ἡ, = φρενῖτις, Suid. s.v. παρακοπὴ φρενῶν. **-ιάω**, = sq., Plu.*Alex.*75, Alex.Aphr.*Pr.*1.76. **-ίζω**, *be delirious*, D.Chr.66.8, Plu.2.693a, 1128d, S.E.*M.*7.247, Gal.16.493, Alex.Trall.1.13. **-ικός**, ή, όν, *suffering from* φρενῖτις, Hp.*Aph.*4.72; τὰ φ. (sc. νοσήματα) Id.*Epid.*1.6, cf. Arr.*Epict.*2.15.3, Antyll.ap.Orib.9.22.3, Sor.2.1; φ. πυρετός Gal.17(1).890:—φρενη[τικός] prob. in Phld.*Mus.*p.38K., cf. Lat. *phreneticus*. **-ις**, ιδος, ἡ, *inflammation of the brain, phrenitis*, Hp.*Aph.*3.30 (pl.), *Com.Adesp.*344 (pl.), D.Chr.48.12, Luc.*Symp.*20; φλεγμονὴν τοῦ διαφράγματος εἶναι τὴν φ. Diocl.*Fr.*38. **-ισμός**, ὁ, *frenzy*, Plu.*Fr.*25.3 (pl., φρενετ- codd. Stob.).

**φρενοάρας** [ᾰρ], α, ὁ, = φρενήρης, *of sound mind*, B.16.118.

**φρενοβλάβ-εια** [ᾰ], ἡ, *damage of the understanding, madness, folly*, D.H.5.9, Ph.2.49, Luc.*Syr.D.*18, *Cat.Cod.Astr.*2.174. **-έω**, *to be distraught, frantic*, Sch.ABT Il.20.332. **-ής**, ές, (βλάπτω) *deranged, crazy*, Hdt.2.120, Eup.181.7, Luc.*Syr.D.*43, Hierocl. *in CA* 24p.472M., etc. **-ία**, ἡ, poet. -ίη, for φρενοβλάβεια, Man.6.599.

**φρενο-γηθής**, ές, *heart-gladdening*, *AP*9.525.22. **-δαλής**, ές, (δηλέομαι) *ruining the mind*, παραφορά A.*Eu.*330 (lyr.). **-θελγής**, ές, *charming the heart*, Procl.*H.*3.17, Nonn.*D.*1.406. **-θεν** (parox.), Adv. *of one's own mind*, S.*Aj.*182 (lyr.). **-κλοπέω**, *steal the understanding, deceive*, Hsch. **-κλόπος**, ον, *stealing the understanding, deceiving*, Ἔρως *APl.*4.198 (Maec.). **-ληπτος**, ον, *possessed, mad*, *Cat.Cod.Astr.*8(1).264. **-ληστής**, οῦ, ὁ, *robber of the understanding, deceiver*, *AP*12.144 (Mel.). **-μᾰνής**, ές, *distracted, maddened*, A.*Ag.*1140 (lyr.), Aristodem.8.1 **-μόρως**, Adv., (μόρος) *suffering from a calamity to the mind*, νοσοῦντα φ. S.*Aj.*626 (lyr.; -βόρως Dindorf). **-πληγής**, ές, *striking the mind*, i.e. *driving mad, maddening*, A.*Pr.*878 (anap.). **-πληκτος**, ον, *stricken in mind, frenzied*, ib.1054 (anap.). **-πλήξ**, ῆγος, ὁ, ἡ, = foreg., *AP*9.141. **-τέκτων**, ον, gen. ονος, *building with the mind, ingenious*, Ar.*Ra.*820 (lyr.). **-τερπής**, ές, *heart-delighting*, Nonn.*D.*4.135.

**φρεν-όω**, (φρήν) *make wise, instruct, inform*, τινα A.*Pr.*337, S.*Ant.*754, *Tr.*52, E.*Ion* 526 (troch.); φρενώσω δ' οὐκέτ' ἐξ αἰνιγμάτων, i.e. *will teach* plainly, A.*Ag.*1183; poet. Verb, used by X.*Mem.*4.1.5; φ. τινὰ εἴς τι ib.2.6.1:—Pass., Phld.*Lib.*p.52 O.; πεφρενωμένος Luc.*Lex.*19; φρενωθῆναι οὐδὲ πρὸς αὐτῆς τῆς Ἀθηνᾶς Jul.*Or.*7.225b. II. Pass., *to be high-minded, elated*, Lxx 2 *Ma.*11.4, Babr.101.5. III. φ. is prob. a late spelling of φρονῶν (v. φρονέω IV fin.) in the phrase ζῶν καὶ φρενῶν. **-ώλης**, ες, *distraught in mind, frenzied*, A.*Th.*757 (lyr.). **-ωσις**, εως, ἡ, *instruction*, Hsch. **-ωτήριον**, τό, *means of instruction*, Id.

**φρεσσίλῡτος** [ῐ], ον, *mad*, *Stud.Ital.*2(1922).394 (Phalasarna, iv B.C., amulet).

**φρέω**, only in compds. διαφρέω, εἰσφρέω, ἐκφρέω, ἐπεισφρέω, qq.v., exc. aor. imperat. φρές (as if from *φρῆμι) *Com.Adesp.*489.

**φρεωρῠχ-έω**, *dig wells*, Str.16.4.14, Plu.2.776e:—ludicrously, of a gnat, μ' ἐφρεωρύχει *was sinking wells in* me, Ar.*Lys.*1033 (troch.). **-ία**, ἡ, *digging of wells*, J.*AJ*1.18.2. **-ικά**, τά, treatise on *digging of wells* ascribed to Democr., Sch. Basil. in *Gött. Nachr.* 1910.220. **-ος** (parox.), ον, *for digging wells*, σκεύη Plu.2.159c: Subst., ὁ φ. *well-sinker*, Them.*Or.*11.152c.—The forms **φρεορυκτέω**, **-ορύκτης**, only in Suid.

**φρήν**, ἡ, gen. φρενός, pl. φρένες, gen. φρενῶν, dat. φρεσί: older dat. pl. φρασί(ν) *IG*1².971 (vi B.C.), Pi.*N.*3.62, *BMus.Inscr.*909 (Halic., i B.C.): (v. sub fin.): I. *midriff*, κραδία φρένα λακτίζει A.*Pr.*881 (anap.); elsewh. always in pl., ἔνθα φρένες ἔρχαται ἀμφ' ἁδινὸν κῆρ Il.16.481, cf. Hp.*VM*22, *Art.*41; τὰς φρένας διάφραγμα εἰς τὸ μέσον αὐτῶν (sc. τοῦ θώρακος καὶ τοῦ κύτους) τιθέντες Pl.*Ti.*70a; τοῦτο δὲ τὸ διάζωμα καλοῦσί τινες φρένας, ὃ διορίζει τόν τε πλεύμονα καὶ τὴν καρδίαν Arist.*PA*672ᵇ11, cf. *HA*496ᵇ11, 506ᵃ6; also, in Hom., more vaguely, πρὸς στῆθος ὅθι φρένες ἧπαρ ἔχουσι Od.9.301; μένεος φρένες ἀμφὶ μέλαιναι πίμπλαντ' Il.1.103, al.; φρένας..εἰς αὐτὰς τυπείς A.*Pr.*363, cf. *Eu.*159 (lyr.). 2. *heart*, as seat of the passions, e.g. of fear, τρομέοντο δέ οἱ φρένες ἐντός Il.10.10; of joy and grief, φρένα τέρπεσθαι φόρμιγγι 9.186; γάνυται φρένα ποιμήν 13.493; τί σε φρένας ἵκετο πένθος; 1.362; ἄχος πύκασε φρένας 8.124; ἔρως φρένας ἀμφεκάλυψε 3.442; of anger, Od.6.147; of courage, ἕνα φρεσὶ θυμὸν ἔχοντες Il.13.487; ἐς φρένα θυμὸς ἀγέρθη 22.475, cf. 8.202, etc.; of bodily appetites, such as hunger, etc., 11.89: the shades of the dead are without it, ψυχὴ καὶ εἴδωλον, ἀτὰρ φρένες οὐκ ἔνι πάμπαν 23.104 (exc. the shade of Teiresias, Od.10.493): so generally in Poets, φρενὸς ἔνδοθεν ἄλγεα κεῖται Sol.ap.Arist.*Ath.*5.2; κῆλα δαιμόνων θέλγει φρένας Pi.*P.*1.12; φόβος μ' ἔχει φρένας A.*Supp.*379; μαινομένᾳ φρενί Id.*Th.*484 (lyr.); στυγεῖν μιᾷ φρενί Id.*Eu.*986 (lyr.); Διὸς γὰρ δυσπαραίτητοι φ. Id.*Pr.*34; ἐκ φρενός from one's *very heart*, ὁ ἐκ φρενὸς λόγος a *sincere* speech, Id.*Ch.*107; ἐτύμως δακρυχέων ἐκ φρενός Id.*Th.*919 (lyr.); οὐκ ἀπ' ἄκρας φρενός not *superficially and carelessly*, Id.*Ag.*805 (anap.); φρενὸς ἐκ φιλίας ib.1515 (anap.), cf. 546; φῦσαι φρένας to produce *a haughty spirit*, S.*El.*1463. 3. *mind*, as seat of the mental faculties, perception, thought, ἔγνω ᾗσιν ἐνὶ φ. Il.22.296; μή μοι ταῦτα νόει φρεσί 9.600; μετὰ φρεσὶ μερμηρίξαι, βάλλεσθαι, Od.10.438, Il.9.434; ἴδμεν ἐνὶ φρεσίν 2.301; τῷ γὰρ ἐπὶ φρεσὶ θῆκε put in his *mind, suggested* it, 1.55; σφῶϊν δ' ὧδε θεῶν τις ἐνὶ φρεσὶ ποιήσειεν 13.55; ἐν φρεσὶ θέσθε ἕκαστος ib.121, cf. 1.297, etc.; φρένας παραπεῖσαι, πείθειν, 7.120, 16.842; ἐπιγνάμπτει φρένας (v.l. for νόον) ἐσθλῶν 9.514; Διὸς ἐτράπετο φρήν 10.45; ἀνὴρ φρένας ἀφνειός rich (only) *in his imagination*, Hes.*Op.*455; ὀρθᾷ, ἐλευθέρᾳ φρενί, Pi.*O.*8.24, *P.*2.57; φρένες γὰρ αὐτοῦ θυμὸν ᾠακοστρόφουν A.*Pers.*767; ἡ γλῶσσ' ὀμώμοχ', ἡ δὲ φ. ἀνώμοτος E.*Hipp.*612; κατὰ φρένα καὶ κατὰ θυμόν Il.1.193, al.: pl., *wits*, Κύκλωπα περὶ φρένας ἤλυθε οἶνος Od.9.362, cf.454, 18.331; πλήγη φρένας ὡς πάρος εἶχεν Il.13.394; ἐκ γὰρ πλήγη φρένας 16.403; βλάπτε φρένας Ζεὺς ἡμετέρας 15.724; ἐξ... τοι θεοὶ φρένας ὤλεσαν 7.360; φρένας ἄφρων, φρένας ἠλέ or ἠλεέ, 4.104, 15.128, Od.2.243: of losing one's *wits*, φρενῶν ἀφεστάναι, ἐκστῆναι, μεθεστάναι, S.*Ph.*865, E.*Or.*1021, *Ba.*944; τὰς φ. ἐκβάλλειν S.*Ant.*648; ἔξω φρενῶν Pi.*O.*7.47; φρενῶν οὐκ ἔνδον ὢν E.*Heracl.*709; φρενῶν κεκομμένος A.*Ag.*479 (lyr.); κενὸς S.*Ant.*754; τητώμενοι Id.*El.*1326; ἔξεδροι, παράκοποι, E.*Hipp.*935, *Ba.*33; ποῦ ποτ' εἶ φρενῶν; S.*El.*390; φρένες διάστροφοι A.*Pr.*673, S.*Aj.*447; μαργότης φρενῶν Id.*Fr.*846; ἀνακίνησις φρενῶν Id.*OT*727, etc.; of persons in their senses, ἐπήβολος φρενῶν Id.*Ant.*492; ἀνδρὸς νοῦν ἔχοντος καὶ φρένας Ar.*Ra.*535 (lyr.) (so in later Prose, οἱ φρένας ἔχοντες Phld.*Po.*5.19, *Rh.*1.240S.; οἱ τῶν σοφιστῶν τὰς κοινὰς φ. ἔχοντες ib.202S.); also ἔσω φρενῶν λέγειν A.*Ag.*1052; γράφου φρενῶν ἔσω S.*Ph.*1325; τῆς λεπτότητος τῶν φ. Ar.*Nu.*153; φρένες, opp. σῶμα, Hdt.3.134; so αἱ σάρκες αἱ κεναὶ φρενῶν E.*El.*387; attributed to animals, μετὰ φρεσὶ γίγνεται ἀλκή Il.4.245, cf. 16.157, etc.—The word is not common in early Prose, τίς αὐτῶν νόος ἢ φρήν; Heraclit.104; συμφορὰ τῶν φ., i.e. madness, And.2.7; παραλλάττει τῶν φ. Lys.*Fr.*90; καρποῦ μὲν ἀφθονία φρενῶν δὲ ἀφορία X.*Smp.*4.55; νοῦς καὶ φρένες D.18.324, cf. 25.33. 4. *will, purpose*, οὔ τι Διὸς βέομαι φρεσίν Il.15.194; σῆς ἀπεστάτουν φ. S.*Ant.*993, cf.*OC*1182.—In usage there is little or no distinction observable between sg. and pl., but the sg. is not found in Prose (exc. Heraclit. l.c.) or Com. (exc. in paratrag., Ar.*Ra.*886).

**φρηταῖος**, α, ον, = φρεατιαῖος, *PLond.ined.*2086 (iii B.C.).

**φρηταρχ-έω**, = φρατριαρχέω, *IG*14.724 (Naples). **-ος**, ὁ, = φρατρίαρχος, ib. 759 (ibid.).

**φρήτηρ**, v. φράτηρ.

**φρητία**, ἡ, Ion. for φρεατία, Hsch.:—**φρητίον**, τό, *IG*14.217 (pl.).

**φρήτρη**, ἡ, Ion. for φράτρα (q.v.); also **φρητρία**, *IG*14.759 (Naples, φητρ– lapis).

**φρήτριος**, v. φράτριος. **φρήτωρ**, v. φράτωρ.

**φρίζω**, = φρίσσω, *PMag.Osl.*1.262.

**φρῑκ-άζω**, *shudder, shiver*, Poet. *de herb.*71, prob. in Hp.*Coac.* 24. **-ᾰλέος**, α, ον, *shivering with cold*, Hp.*VM*16 (Comp.), *Cat. Cod.Astr.*2.165. II. *dreadful, horrid*, *AP*7.69 (Jul.), 9.300 (Addaeus); σπιλάς ib.7.382 (Phil.), cf. Tryph.195; ἄχθος πόνων Androm. ap.Gal.14.33; *awe-inspiring*, λόγος *Hymn.Is.*12. **-ασμός**, ὁ, *shuddering, shivering*, Lxx 2 *Ma.*3.17. **-η**, ἡ, *shuddering, shivering*, Hp.*Aph.*5.61; a mild form of ῥῖγος, Id.*Morb.*1.24, al.: *cold fit* before fever, Pl.*Phdr.*251a (metaph., Id.*R.*387c), Thphr.*Ign.* 74, Nic.*Th.*721; φρ(ε)ίκη καὶ πυρετός *IG*3.1424.19 (Tab.Defix.), Sor. 1.27: pl., Arist.*Pr.*863ᵇ21. 2. *shivering fear, shuddering*, esp. from religious *awe*, φρίκης αὐτὸν ὑπελθούσης Hdt.6.134; τοίαν φ. παρέχεις μοι S.*OT*1306 (anap.); ὀρθόκερως φ. Id.*Fr.*875, cf. X.*Cyr.*4. 2.15: generally, *shivering fear* of any kind, *horror*, φρίκᾳ τρομερὰν φρένα E.*Ph.*1284 (lyr.); ἐκπληχθεῖσα φρίκᾳ Id.*Tr.*183 (lyr.); φρίκᾳ ματρός Id.*Ion*898 (lyr.); μεγάλην ἐμποιεῖ φ. Phld.*Ir.*p.19 W.; ἀγωνία καὶ φ. Plu.*Mar.*43; φ. καὶ φόβος Id.*Pel.*27; φ. καὶ δέος Jul.*ad Them.* 253b; φρίκῃ καὶ σιωπῇ κατεχόμενον τὸ θέατρον Plu.*Marc.*20. 3. = φρίξ I, ἀκύματος πορθμὸς ἐν φρίκῃ γελᾷ *Trag.Adesp.*336; ἐν γαλήνῃ φρίκης ὑποτρεχούσης Plu.2.921f; τὴν θάλατταν φ. κατέχει Alciphr.1. 10; ἐπ' ἄκρᾳ τῇ φ. τῆς θαλάττης Ael.*NA*16.19. II. *frost, chill*, φ. περὶ τὸν ὄρθρον γέγονε Gell.17.8.7. **-ία**, τά, *aguish shivering*, Dsc.1. 127 (v.l. -ίας), 4.14. **-ίας**, ὁ, *with bristling mane*, name of a horse in Pi.*P.*10.16. **-ῐασις**, εως, ἡ, *shivering*, Sch.Poet. *de herb.*166. **-ιάω**, (φρίξ) like φρικάζω, *shudder, shiver*, esp. from ague, Cass.*Pr.*53.

**φρικνός**, ή, όν, = φρικαλέος, Hsch.

**φρῑκόομαι**, Pass., = φρικάζω, *shudder* or *shiver*, (φρικώσαντα is f.l. for -άσαντα in Hp.*Coac.*24).

**φρῑκοποιός**, όν, *causing a shuddering*, Diph.Siph.ap.Ath.3.74c.

**φρῖκος**, εος, τό, = φρίκη, *shivering*, f.l. in Nic.*Th.*778.

**φρικτέον**, c. inf., *one must shudder* at the thought of.., Porph.*Chr.* 26.

**φρικτοπαλαίμονες** (sc. δαίμονες) dub. sens. in *PMag.Par.*1.1357.

**φρικτός**, ή, όν, (φρίσσω) (misspelt φικτρός *PMag.Osl.*1.261), *to be shuddered at, awful*, θεῆς ἴδες ἱερὰ φρικτῆς Call.*Aet.*3.1.6, cf. Orph.*H.* 14.6, Plu.*Cic.*49, *APl.*4.110 (Philostr.), *AP*9.524.22, Zos.Alch.p.117 B., *PMasp.*97 ii 51 (vi A.D.); [θεοί] prob. in Phld.*D.*1.17: Comp. -ότερος Plu.*Num.*10: Sup. -ότατος Ath.10.440e. Adv. -τῶς Lxx *Wi.*6.5. II. *bristling with spears*, ἀνδρῶν ὄχλος Ezek.*Exag.*197.

**φρῑκ-ώδης**, ες, *attended with shivering*, πυρετὸς φ. a fever *with shivering fits, ague*, Hp.*Epid.*1.2, Sor.1.59; δυσουρία φ. Hp.*Aph.*3. 5; οἱ φ. *those who suffer from such fits*, Id.*Coac.*12, al.; τὸ φ. *roughness, unevenness of the skin*, as in aguish fits, ib.17, cf. Gal.6. 195. II. *that causes shuddering* or *horror, awful, horrible*, ὄψις Ar.*Ra.*1336 (lyr.); τὰ δεινὰ καὶ φ. And.1.29; φρικώδη κλύειν *horrible* to hear, E.*Hipp.*1202; freq. in later Prose, δόξαι φ. Phld.*Mus.* p.50 K.; φ. ἄποψις, θέαμα, Arist.*Mir.*843ᵃ16, Plu.*Marc.*15, Anon.*Oxy.* 416.9, Jul.*Or.*1.31c; τὸ -έστατον τῶν κακῶν ὁ θάνατος Epicur.*Ep.*3 p.61 U.; -έστατος ὅρκος *PStrassb.*48.6 (vi A.D.), etc.: neut. φρικῶδες, as Adv., *horribly*, E.*Hipp.*1216. b. *inspiring religious awe*, Plu. *TG*21 (Sup.), Aristid.1.256 J. Adv. Sup., ἁγιώτατα καὶ φρικωδέστατα ἔχειν, of the terrors of a court of justice, D.23.74. **-ωδία**, ἡ, *horribleness*, Nicom.ap.Phot.*Bibl.*p.143 B. **-ώεις**, εσσα, εν, = φρικώδης, ἄδυτον Aristonous 1.13.

**φρῑμ-αγμός**, ὁ, *snorting*, of any motions of rampant animals, of horses, Lyc.244; of goats, Poll.5.88, D.H.*Comp.*16 (pl.). **-άσσομαι**, Att. **-ττομαι**, *snort and leap*: *wanton*, of goats, Theoc.5.141, cf. *AP*9.558 (Eryc.), Poll.5.88; of high-mettled horses, φριμάξασθαι καὶ χρεμετίσαι Hdt.3.87, cf. *AP*9.281 (Apollonid.); προσιόντος ἐφριμάττετο καὶ ἐπικροτοῦντος ἐφρυάττετο Ael.*NA*6.44 (the distinctions drawn by Poll.5.87 and Ammon.*Diff.*p.138 V. do not hold good). **-άω**, = foreg., Opp.*C.*1.491.

**φρίν**, Locr., = πρίν, *IG*9(1).334.6 (v B.C.).

**φρίνιον**, τό, an unknown utensil, written φρινειν, *PMasp.*6 ii 64 (vi A.D.).

**φρίξ**, ἡ, gen. φρῑκός: (φρίσσω):—*ruffling* of a smooth surface. I. *ripple* caused by a gust of wind sweeping over the smooth sea, ὑπὸ φρικὸς Βορέω Il.23.692; μελαίνῃ φρικὶ καλυφθείς, of Proteus coming to the surface, Od.4.402; Ζεφύροιο ἐχεύατο πόντον ἔπι φρίξ *ripple* spread over the sea from the west wind, Il.7.63; μαλακὴν φρῖκα φέροι Ζέφυρος *AP*7.668 (Leon.); θάλασσα φρικὶ χαρασσομένη ib.10.2 (Antip.Sid.), cf. 14 (Agath.).—Poet. word for Prose φρίκη. II. *bristling up*, as of the hair, κριὸς βαθείῃ φρικὶ μαλλὸν ὀρθώσας Babr. 93.7. 2. *shivering-fit*, Hp.*Morb.*2.68, *POxy.*924.3 (iv A.D.); φρὶξ ἐπέσχε νῶτα καὶ κνήμας Babr.95.59.

**φριξαύχην**, ενος, ὁ, ἡ, *with ruffling neck*, of dolphins, Arion v. 8; κάπρος *Trag.Adesp.*383.

**φριξό-θριξ**, τρῐχος, ὁ, ἡ, *with bristling hair*, Ἰνδοί Ps.-Callisth.3. 8. II. *making the hair stand on end*, *EM*800.32, Suid. **-κόμης**, ου, ὁ, = foreg. I, *APl.*4.291 (Anyte). **-λόφος**, ον, = φριξαύχην, Hsch.

**φριξός**, ή, όν, *standing on end, bristling*, τρίχες Arist.*Phgn.*809ᵇ 25, 812ᵇ28. II. **Φρῖξος**, ὁ, Comic name for *the genius* or *demon of shivering*, *AP*9.617.

**φριξωποβρόνταξ** dub. in *PMag.Lond.*46.19.

**φρίσσω**, Att. **φρίττω** Pl.*R.*387c: fut. φρίξω Gal.13.365: aor. ἔφριξα Il.13.339, etc.: pf. πέφρικα 11.383, etc.; poet. part. πεφρίκοντες Pi.*P.*4.183: plpf. ἐπεφρίκει Plu.2.781e, Alciphr.1.1:—Med., aor. 1 ἐφριξάμην f.l. in Polyaen.4.6.7. [ῑ by nature, hence to be accented φρῖσσον in Hes.*Sc.*171, φρῖξαι S.*El.*1408 (lyr.)]:—*to be rough* or *uneven on the surface, bristle*, φρίσσουσιν ἄρουραι (sc. σταχύεσσι) Il.23.599; φρίξας κάρπιμος στάχυς E.*Supp.*31; of a line of battle, ἔφριξεν μάχη ἐγχείῃσιν Il.13.339; φάλαγγες σάκεσίν τε καὶ ἔγχεσι πεφρικυῖαι 4.282, cf. 7.62; φρίξας εὐλόφῳ σφηκώματι, of the crest of a helmet, S.*Fr.*341; of a tree, φρίσσουσα ζεφύροις Pl.*Eleg.*25; φιάλα χρυσῷ πεφρικυῖα Pi.*I.*6(5).40; χερσὶ δεξιωνύμοις ἔφριξεν αἰθήρ, of a crowd holding up their hands to vote, A.*Supp.*608; of hair, mane, or bristles, *bristle up, stand on end*, μηδ' ὀρθαὶ φρίσσωσιν [τρίχες] Hes.*Op.*540, cf. Arist.*HA*560ᵇ8, *Pr.*888ᵃ38; ἔφριξαν ἔθειραι Theoc. 25.244; of foliage, φύλλα πεφρικότα, opp. κεκλιμένα, Thphr.*HP*3.9. 4: c. acc. of respect, φρίξας εὖ λοφιήν *having set up his bristly mane*, Od.19.446; φ. τρίχας Hes.*Sc.*391; φ. νῶτον, αὐχένας, Il.13.473, Hes.*Sc.*171; χαίταν Ar.*Ra.*822 (lyr.); also πτεροῖσι νῶτα πεφρίκοντες *bristling on* their backs with feathers, Pi.*P.*4.183; λέοντος δέρος χαίτῃ πεφρικός E.*Ph.*1121. 2. ἄσθματι φρίσσων πνοάς *ruckling* in his throat, of one just dying, dub. l. in Pi.*N.*10.74. 3. of the *rippling* surface of smooth water (cf. φρίξ I), φ. θάλασσαι..πνοιῇσι D.P.112, cf. Alciphr.1.1; of breakers, ῥηγμῖνες φ. A.R.4.1575, cf. Ael.*NA*7.33; also of rain, φρίσσοντες ὄμβροι Pi.*P.*4.81, expld. by Sch. as φρίσσειν ποιοῦντες, cf. ὁπόταν..φρίσσων Βορέας ἐπισπέρχῃ Id.*Parth.*2.18. II. freq. of a feeling of *chill, shiver, shudder*: 1. of the effect of cold, *shiver*, Hes.*Op.*512, Hp.*Aff.* 11, Arist.*Pr.*963ᵃ33, 965ᵃ33; χωρὶς τοῦ φρῖξαι unless he *catch a chill*, Gal.10.803; of the teeth, *chatter*, D.H.*Rh.*10.9. 2. of the effect of fear, *shudder*, S.*El.*1408 (lyr.), *Tr.*1044; πέφρικ' ἐγὼ μέν, αὖός εἰμι τῷ δέει Men.*Epit.*480; φ. γαῖα πόντος τε *h.Hom.*27.8; ἄλω δὲ πολλήν..ἔφριξα δινήσαντος I *shuddered* when he swung the vast shield round, A.*Th.*490; οὐ φρίττουσιν (sc. animals) ὡς φρίττουσιν οἱ ἄνθρωποι Phld.*D.*1.12: c. acc., *shudder at* one, οἵ τέ σε πεφρίκασι Il.11.383; πάντες δέ με πεφρίκασιν 24.775, cf. Pi.*O.*7.38, S.*Ant.*997, Ar.*Nu.*1133; τῶν δημοτέων φ. τὸν ἥκιστον Herod.2.30; τοὺς τελώνας πᾶσα νῦν θύρη φρίσσει Id.6.64; πεφρικέναι τὸν θάνατον Phld.*Mort.* 39; φρίττουσι τὴν σύντροφόν τε καὶ φίλην οἱ ἰχθύες θάλατταν Ael.*NA*9. 57: c. acc. et inf., πέφρικα..Ἐρινὺν τελέσαι I *tremble* at the thought of her accomplishing.., A.*Th.*720 (lyr.) (but not c. dat., for ἐρετμοῖσι φρίξουσι they *shall shudder* at the oars is f.l. for φρύξουσι in Orac.ap.Hdt.8.96): c. part., πέφρικα λεύσσων I *shudder at* seeing, A.*Supp.*346; φ. σε δερκομένα Id.*Pr.*540 (lyr.), cf. 695 (lyr.): c. inf., *fear to* do, D.21.135: c. Prep., φ. πρὸς τοὺς πόνους Plu.2.8f; φ. πρὸς τὴν ἀκοὴν τῆς Ῥωμαίων τέχνης Lib.*Or.*24.16; φ. ὑπὲρ ὧν προσήκει παθεῖν D.51.9. 3. *feel a holy thrill* or *awe at*. ἐν ἱερῷ φ. ἅπαντα καὶ προσκυνεῖν Plu.2.26b; τοὺς θεοὺς πέφρικα Jul.*Or.*7.212b, al. 4. *thrill* with passionate joy, ἔφριξ' ἔρωτι S.*Aj.*693, A.*Fr.*387.—Rare in early Prose, exc. in the sense of *shuddering, fearing*, Pl.*R.*387c, *Phdr.*251a, D. ll. cc.

**φροιμιάζομαι, φροιμιαστέον**, v. προοιμιάζομαι, -αστέον.

**φροίμιον**, τό, contr. for προοίμιον (q.v.).

**φρον-έω**, Ep. subj. φρονέῃσι Od.7.75: Ep. impf. φρόνεον Il.17.286, φρονέεσκον A.R.4.1164: fut. -ήσω Ar.*Ec.*630 (anap.), etc.: aor. ἐφρόνησα Hdt.1.60, A.*Eu.*115, etc.: pf. πεφρόνηκα Emp.103.1, Isoc.5.124, D.S.18.66:—Pass., Arist.*Xen.*980ᵃ9; imper. φρονείσθω v.l. for φρονεῖτε in *Ep.Phil.*2.5:—*to be minded*, either of reflection or of purpose: hence, I. *have understanding, be wise, prudent*, rare in Hom., ἄριστοι..μάχεσθαί τε φρονέειν τε best both in battle and *counsel*, Il. 6.79: but freq. in Trag. and Att., [Ζῆνα] τὸν φρονεῖν βροτοὺς ὁδώσαντα A.*Ag.*176 (lyr.); φρονούντως πρὸς φρονοῦντας ἐννέπεις Id.*Supp.* 204, cf. 176; φρονεῖν γὰρ οἱ ταχεῖς οὐκ ἀσφαλεῖς S.*OT*617; φρονεῖν οἶδεν μόνη Id.*Tr.*313; λίαν φ. *to be over-wise*, E.*IA*924; φ. πλέον Pl.*Hp.Mi.*371a; τὸ φρονεῖν *understanding, prudence*, S.*Ant.*1347 (anap.), 1353 (anap.); κράτιστοι φρονεῖν Antipho 2.1.1; καὶ φ. καὶ συμπράττειν X.*Cyr.*5.5.44; εἰδέναι καὶ φ. Pl.*Alc.*1.133c; τὸ φ. καὶ τὸ νοεῖν Id.*Phlb.*11b; λέγειν τε καὶ φ. Id.*Phdr.*266b, cf. Isoc.4.50; τῷ φρονεῖν τε καὶ σωφρονεῖν Pl.*Lg.*712a; τὸ μὴ φρονοῦν, of an infant, A.*Ch.*753; ἐπειδὴ τάχιστα ἤρχετο φ. Is.9.20; ἡ φρονοῦσα ἡλικία Aeschin.1.139: Com. of fish, ἰχθὺς φρονοῦντας *full-grown*, Ephipp.21. 3; ζῷον λογικὸν καὶ φρονοῦν Phld.*Piet.*15: c. acc., φρονῆσαι τὰ κυριώτατα *to be wise* in respect of the most important matters, Id.*Rh.*2. 35 S. 2. with Advbs., εὖ φρονεῖν *think* rightly, περί τινος Hdt.2. 16; *to be sane* (cf. infr. IV), E.*Ba.*851, Ar.*Nu.*817, Lys.19.41, etc.; κέρδιστον εὖ φρονοῦντα μὴ φρονεῖν δοκεῖν A.*Pr.*387; οἱ φρονοῦντες εὖ κρατοῦσι πανταχοῦ S.*Aj.*1252, cf. *El.*394, E.*Or.*99, al. (but εὖ φρ., also, *to be* well *disposed*, v. infr. II. 2); κακῶς, καλῶς φ., Od.18.168, S.*OT*600, *Ant.*557; ὀρθῶς φ. And.2.23; ὀρθῶς φ. πρός τι A.*Pr.* 1000; μῶρα, πλάγια φ., S.*Aj.*594, E.*IA*332 (troch.). 3. *think*, Heraclit.113, Parm.16.3, Emp.108.2, cf. Arist.*de An.*427ᵃ19; ὡς.., ὅτι.., S.*Ant.*49, *OC*872; φρόνει νιν ὡς ἥξοντα Id.*Tr.*289; *mean*, ἄλλα φ. καὶ ἄλλα λέγειν Hdt.9.54; ἕτερα μὲν λέγων, ἕτερα δὲ φρονῶν Din.1.47; ὁ μὴ λέγων ἃ φρονεῖ D.18.282, cf.19.224. 4. *feel by experience, know full well*, σοὶ μὲν δοκεῖν ταῦτ' ἔστ', ἐμοὶ δ' ἄγαν φρονεῖν S.*Aj.*942, cf. *OC*1741 (lyr.); πειρώμενος ὅ τι φρονέοιεν [τὰ μαντήϊα] to test the *knowledge* of the oracles, Hdt.1.46. II. *to be fain* that..,

c. acc. et inf., Il.3.98: c. inf., *to be minded* to do, 9.608, 17.286; without inf., οἱ δ' ἰθὺς φρόνεον [ἰέναι] *were minded to go* right onward, 13.135, cf. 12.124; ᾗ περ δὴ φρονέω [τελέσαι] 9.310; φρονῶν ἔπρασσον *of set purpose*, S.*OC*271: in Prose, *mean*, *intend*, τοῦτο φρονεῖ ἡμῶν ἡ ..ἀγωγή this is what your bringing us here *means*, Th.5.85. 2. freq. with neut. Adj., a. φ. τινί τινα *to have* certain *thoughts for* or *towards* any one, *to be* so and so *minded towards* him, πατρὶ φίλα φρονέων kindly *minded towards* him, Il.4.219, cf. Od.6.313, etc.; κακὰ φρονέουσι..ἀλλήλοισιν Il.22.264; τῷ ὀλοὰ φρονέων 16.701; μαλακὰ φ. ἐσλοῖς Pi.*N*.4.95; πιστά τινι Id.*O*.3.17; φρονοῦντας ἄριστα αὐτοῖς Ar.*Pl*.577 (anap.): with Advbs., εὖ φρονεῖν τισι (cf. supr. I.2) Od.7.74, cf. A.*Ag*.1436, etc.; φρονεῖς εὖ τοῖς ἠγγελμένοις you *rejoice at* them, Id.*Ch*.774; also εἰς ὑμᾶς εὖ φ. And.2.4; τισὶ καλῶς φ. *SIG*527.38 (Crete, iii B.C.); τοιαῦτα περί τινος φ. Isoc.3.60: *to be minded* so and so, *think* or *purpose* such and such things, ἀγαθὰ φ. Il.6.162, Od.1.43; φίλα φ. ib.307; κακά 17.596; τὰ φρονέεις ἅ τ' ἐγώ περ Il.4.361; κρυπτάδια φ. *to have* secret *purposes*, 1.542; ἀταλὰ φ. *to be* gaily *disposed*, 18.567, Hes.*Th*.989; πυκινὰ φ. *have* wise *thoughts*, *be* cunningly *minded*, Od.9.445; ἐφημέρια φ. *think* only of the passing day, 21.85; θεοῖσιν ἶσα φ. Il.5.441; θνητὰ φ. S.*Fr*. 590 (anap.), E.*Alc*.799; ἀθάνατα Pl.*Ti*.90c; οὐ κατ' ἄνθρωπον φ. A.*Th*.425, S.*Aj*.777; ἐπὶ ταῖς εὐτυχίαις ὑπὲρ ἄνθρωπον φ. X.*Cyr*.8.7.3; μηδὲν ὑπὲρ τὴν πήραν φ. Luc.*Tim*.57: also καίρια φ. S.*El*.228 (lyr.); σώφρονα Id.*Fr*.64; οὐ τὰ ἄριστα φ. Th.2.22; ἡ πόλις χεῖρον φ. Isoc.8.126; τυραννικὰ φ. *to have* tyranny *in mind*, Ar.*V*.507 (troch.); ἀρχαϊκὰ φ. *to have* old-fashioned *notions*, Id.*Nu*.821; τὰ τοῦ θεοῦ, τὰ τῆς σαρκὸς φ., *Ev.Matt*.16.23, *Ep.Rom*.8.5; also οὐ παρδάλιος τόσσον μένος ὅσσον Πάνθου υἷες φρονέουσιν the panther's courage is not so great as *is the spirit* of the sons of Panthus, Il.17.23. b. esp. freq. in the phrase μέγα φρονεῖν *to be* high-*minded*, *have* high *thoughts*, *to be* high-*spirited*, Il.11.296, 13.156; of lions and boars, 16.758, 11.325, cf. X.*Cyr*.7.5.62; φρονεῖ γὰρ ὡς γυνὴ μέγα S.*OT*1078, cf. Lys.2.48, Isoc.4.132; in Att., freq. in bad sense, *to be presumptuous*, ἐφ' ἑαυτῷ, ἑαυτοῖς μέγα φ., Th.6.16, X.*HG*7.1.27 (also μεγάλα φ. Ar.*Ach*.988; φ. ἐφ' αὑτῷ τηλικοῦτον ἡλίκον εἰκός..D.21.62): with Comp., μεῖζον φ. *to have* over-high *thoughts*, X.*An*.5.6.8 (but simply *pluck up courage*, ἐπὶ τῷ γεγενημένῳ Id.*HG*3.5.21); φ. μεῖζον ἢ κατ' ἄνδρα S.*Ant*.768; μεῖζον τοῦ δέοντος Isoc.7.7, cf. 6.34: rarely in pl., μείζω τῆς δίκης φ. E.*Heracl*.933; with Sup., οἱ μέγιστον φρονοῦντες Pl.*Phdr*.257e; ἐφ' ἱππικῇ X.*Ages*.2.5; also μάλιστα φ. ἐπί τινι D.28.2; ἐπὶ τοῖς προγόνοις οὐ μεῖον φ. X.*Eq.Mag*.7.3, cf. *Ap*.24; *take pride* in, ἐπὶ παιδεύσει μέγα φρονοῦντες Pl.*Prt*.342d; φ. ἐπὶ τῇ ὥρᾳ θαυμάσιον ὅσον Id.*Smp*.217a; also φ. εἰς ἡμᾶς μέγα E.*Hipp*.6; περὶ τὸ γράφειν λόγους Aeschin.2.125; μέγα φ. ὅτι..X.*Cyr*.2.3.13; μέγα φ. ὡς εὖ ἐρῶν Pl.*Smp*.198d; μέγα φ. μὴ ὑπείξειν *haughty in their resolution* not to.., X.*HG*5.4.45: later φ. alone, = μέγα φ., φρονήσας ἐφ' αὑτῷ Paus.1.12.5; διὰ τὸν πατέρα ἀξιώματι προέχοντα Id.4.1.2: opp. σμικρὸν φ. *to be* poor-*spirited*, S.*Aj*.1120; μικρὸν φ. Isoc.4.151; μικρὸν καὶ ταπεινὸν φ. D.13.25, etc.; ἧσσον, ἔλασσον φ. τινος, E.*Andr*.313, *Ph*.1128; φ. ἔλαττον ἢ πρότερον Isoc.12.47, etc.; οὐ σμικρὸν φ. ἐς τὰς Ἀθήνας E.*Heracl*.386: also μετριώτερον πρὸς ἡμᾶς φ. X.*Cyr*.4.3.7. c. of those who agree in *opinion*, τά τινος φρονεῖν *to be of* another's *mind*, *be on* his *side* or *of* his *party*, Hdt.2.162, etc.; τὰ σὰ φ. Id.7.102; εὖ φ. τὰ σά S.*Aj*.491; φ. τὰ Βρασίδου Ar.*Pax*640 (troch.), cf. D.18.161; also ἶσον ἐμοὶ φρονέουσα *thinking* like me, Il.15.50, cf. S.*Ant*.374 (lyr.); τὠυτὸ or κατὰ τὠυτὸ φ. *to be* like-*minded*, make common cause, Hdt.1.60, 5.3; ἐμοὶ φ. ξυνῳδά Ar.*Av*.635 (lyr.): opp. ἀμφὶς φ. *think* differently, Il.13.345; ἄλλῃ φ. *think* another way, *h.Ap*.469. III. *comprehend*, γιγνώσκω, φρονέω Od.16.136, al.: more freq. c. acc., *to be well aware of*.., τὰ φρονέουσ' ἀνὰ θυμόν, ἃ..2.116; οὐκ ὄπιδα φρονέοντες ἐνὶ φρεσίν *paying* no *heed to* it, 14.82; φ. τὴν ἡμέραν *pay regard to* it, *Ep.Rom*.14.6; *consider*, *ponder*, Il.2.36, 18.4, al. IV. *to be in possession of one's senses*, sts. almost = ζῆν, *to be sensible*, *be alive*, ἐμὲ τὸν δύστηνον ἔτι φρονέοντ' ἐλέησον, for ἔτι ζῶντα, Il.22.59; θανόντι δ', οὐ φρονοῦντι, δειλαία χάρις ἐπέμπετο A.*Ch*.517; ἐν τῷ φ. γὰρ μηδὲν ἥδιστος βίος S.*Aj*.554; μηδὲ ζῆν.., μηδὲ φρονεῖν Pl.*Sph*.249a; but also, *to be in one's senses* or *right wits*, φρονοῦντα, opp. μεμηνότα, S.*Aj*.82, cf. 344; ἔξω ἐλαύνειν τινὰ τοῦ φρονεῖν E.*Ba*.853; φρονεῖς ὀρθὰ κοὐ μαίνῃ Id.*Med*.1129; ἐξεστηκὼς τοῦ φρονεῖν Isoc.5.18; τὰ φαλάγγια τοῦ φ. ἐξίστησι X.*Mem*.1.3.12; οὐκ ἂν παρείμην οἷσι μὴ δοκῶ φρονεῖν S.*OC*1666; ἐγὼ νῦν φρονῶ τότ' οὐ φρονῶν E.*Med*.1329; φρονῶν οὐδὲν φρονεῖς *though in thy wits thou'rt* nothing *wise*, Id.*Ba*.332 (for εὖ φ. v. supr. I.2); δρώντων, φρονούντων, βλεπόντων ὑμῶν Aeschin.3.94: ζῶν καὶ φρονῶν alive and *in his right mind*, freq. in Inscrr., *IGRom*.1.804 (Perinthus), etc.; ζῶν καὶ φρενῶν (sic) *Jahresh*.23 *Beibl*.206 (ibid.), *Rev.Arch*.21(1925).240 (Callatis); νοῶν καὶ φρονῶν *Test.Epict*.1.2, *PPetr*.3 p.4 (iii B.C.). **–ημα**, ατος, τό, *mind*, *spirit*, ἔστ' ἂν Διὸς φ. λωφήσῃ χόλου A.*Pr*.378; Αἰσχύλου φ. ἔχων Telecl.14; with limiting epithets, φ. δύσθεον A.*Ch*.191; ὑπέρτολμον ib.595 (lyr.); ὠμόν Id.*Th*.537; ἐλεύθερον Pl.*Lg*.865d; τυραννικόν Id.*R*.573b, X.*Lac*.15.8: pl., Hdt.9.54. 2. *thought*, *purpose*, *will*, φθέγμα καὶ ἀνεμόεν φ. S.*Ant*.354 (lyr.); ψυχὴ καὶ φ. καὶ γνώμη ib.176, cf. 207; τὸ φ. τῆς σαρκός, τοῦ πνεύματος, *Ep.Rom*.8.6: freq. in pl., καρτεροῖς φρονήμασι with stubborn *thoughts*, A.*Pr*.209; ματαίων..φρονημάτων ἡ γλῶσσ' ἀληθὴς γίγνεται κατήγορος Id.*Th*.438; ἐμπέδοις φ. S.*Ant*.169; τὰ σκλήρ' ἄγαν φ. ib.473; τὰ φ. ἀληθινὰ καὶ πάντῃ μεγάλα ἐκέκτηντο Pl.*Criti*.120e. II. either in good or bad sense, 1. *high spirit*, *resolution*, *pride*, τὸ Ἀθηναίων φ. Hdt.8.144, cf. 9.7.β′; ἀνδρί γε φ. ἔχοντι to a man of *spirit*, Th.2.43; φ. τε καὶ πίστις Arist.*Pol*.1313$^{b}$2; φ. ἔχων ἐλεύθερον ib.1314$^{a}$3; *courage*, opp. δειλία, Jul.*Or*.2.59c (pl.); δουλοῖ τὸ φ. τὸ αἰφνίδιον Th.2.61: c. fut. inf., ἐν φρονήματι ὄντες τῆς Πελοποννήσου ἡγήσεσθαι *aspiring* to be leaders of the P., Id.5.40: freq. in pl., *high thoughts*, *proud designs*, διασείσειν τὰ Ἀθηναίων φ. Hdt.6.109, cf. 3.122, 125, 9.54; οὐ..ξυμφέρει τοῖς ἄρχουσι φ. μεγάλα ἐγγίγνεσθαι τῶν ἀρχομένων Pl.*Smp*.182c, cf. 190b, Isoc.6.89; Ζεύς τοι κολαστὴς τῶν ὑπερκόμπων ἄγαν φ. A.*Pers*.828; τῶν φ. ὁ Ζεὺς κολαστὴς τῶν ἄγαν ὑπερφρόνων E.*Heracl*.387. 2. in bad sense, *presumption*, *arrogance*, φρονήματος πλέως ὁ μῦθός ἐστιν A.*Pr*.953, cf. E.*Heracl*.926 (lyr.), Ar.*V*.1024 (anap.), *Pax*25, Pl.*Plt*.290d, etc.; τὸ τῶν Ἀτρειδῶν φ. Phld.*Rh*.2.217 S., etc.: pl., παυσάμενοι τῶν φ. Isoc.14.37; φ. τυραννικά Plu.*Eum*.13. III. pl., = φρένες, *heart*, *breast*, ἰὸς ἐκ φρονημάτων..πεσών A.*Eu*.478. **–ημᾰτίας**, ου, ὁ, *self-confident*, *high-spirited*, Arist.*Pol*.1313$^{a}$40, Longin.9.4; φ. ἐπὶ τῇ ἱππικῇ X.*Ages*.1.24; of a horse, Poll.1.195. **–ημᾰτίζομαι**, Pass., *to become presumptuous*, Arist.*Pol*.1274$^{a}$13; φρονηματισθέντες ἐκ τῶν ἔργων ib.1341$^{a}$30; πεφρονηματισμένοι διά τι ib.1284$^{b}$2, cf. D.S.5.24; ἐπὶ τοῖς γεγονόσι Plb.21.25.8, D.S.9.2; c. dat., νίκῃ Id.12.48; πλῆθος τῶν –ισμένων ὡς ὁμοίων κατ' ἀρετήν Arist.*Pol*.1306$^{b}$28; φ. ὅτι..*to get a notion* that.., Sch.Theoc.14.48. **–ημᾰτισμός**, ὁ, *presumptuousness*, *arrogance*, Plb(?).*Fr*.235, Them.*Or*.21.251b. **–ημᾰτώδης**, ες, = φρονηματίας, D.C.48.19; φ. καὶ γοργός Philostr.*Her*.2.10; τὸ φ. Id.*VS*1.25.5. **–ησις**, εως, ἡ, *purpose*, *intention*, S.*OT*664 (lyr.); φρόνησιν λαβεῖν λῴω ἡμῖν Id.*Ph*.1078. 2. *thought*, ἰδία φ., opp. λόγος ξυνός, Heraclit.2; φ. ἔχειν Emp.110.10, cf. Arist.*Metaph*.1009$^{b}$18. 3. *sense*, εἴ τις ἄρα τοῖς ἐκεῖ φ. περὶ τῶν ἐνθάδε γιγνομένων Isoc.14.61. 4. *judgement*, κατὰ τὴν ἰδίαν φ. οὐδεὶς εὐτυχεῖ Men.*Mon*.306. 5. *arrogance*, *pride*, E.*Supp*.216; also in good sense, τὸ φῦναι πατρὸς εὐγενοῦς ἄπο ὅσην ἔχει φρόνησιν *just pride*, Id.*Fr*.739. II. *practical wisdom*, *prudence in government and affairs*, Pl.*Smp*.209a, Arist.*EN*1140$^{a}$24, 1141$^{b}$23, Isoc.12.204, 217, Plu.2.97e, etc.; φιλοσοφίας τιμιώτερον ὑπάρχει φ. Epicur.*Ep*.3 p.64 U.: opp. ἀμαθία, Pl.*Smp*.202a; opp. σῶμα, Id.*R*.461a; opp. ῥώμη, Isoc.1.6; φρόνησιν ἀσκεῖν X.*Mem*.1.2.10, Isoc.1.40, cf. 15.209: pl., ἡδοναὶ καὶ φρονήσεις Pl.*Phlb*.63a; ἡλικίαι καὶ φ. Id.*Lg*.665d; also attributed to *sagacious* animals, Arist.*GA*753$^{a}$12, *HA*608$^{a}$15. III. Pythag. name for *three*, *Theol.Ar*.14. **–ητέον**, *one must think*, ἐπί τινι μέγα φ. *one must pride oneself* on..X.*HG*2.4.40; μεῖζον φ. Id.*Ages*.8.4; μεῖον Id.*Ap*.26. **–ητικός**, ή, όν, *concerned with thought*, opp. θυμικός, ἐπιθυμητικός, Nicom.ap.*Theol.Ar*.53.

**φρονίμ-ευμα** [ῐ], ατος, τό, *prudent conduct*, Stob.2.7.11$^{e}$. **–εύομαι**, *to be wise*, *prudent*, Phryn.364. **–ευσις**, εως, ἡ, *exercise of prudence*, *Stoic*.3.25, Sch.Luc.*Bis Acc*.22. **–ος**, ον, also ἡ, όν Plu.2.1070b:—*in one's right mind*, *in one's senses*, S.*Aj*.259 (anap.). II. *showing presence of mind*, ἐν τοῖς δεινοῖς X.*An*.2.6.7; τὸ φ. *presence of mind*, Id.*HG*2.3.56. III. *sensible*, *prudent*, opp. ἄφρων, Gorg.*Fr*.6; ψυχή Pl.*Sph*.247a; opp. ἀνόητος, Isoc.2.14 (Comp.); τὸν φρόνιμον ζητοῦντας..ὥσπερ ἀποδεδρακότα Bato 2.3; ὡς ἂν ὁ φ. ὁρίσειε Arist.*EN*1107$^{a}$1, al.; φ. περί τινος *possessing sagacity* or *discernment* in a thing, X.*Cyr*.1.6.15, 21 (Comp.); περί τι Pl.*Grg*.490b (Comp.), Isoc.12.161 (Comp.); εἴς τι Pl.*Alc*.1.125a; ἐν τῷ σίτῳ φ. καὶ μέτριοι X.*Cyr*.5.2.17. 2. of thoughts, acts, and the like, φ. τι ἐργάσασθαι Ar.*Lys*.42; φιλόπολις ἀρετή, φρόνιμος ib.547 (lyr.). 3. of birds as giving omens, τοὺς ἄνωθεν φρονιμωτάτους οἰωνούς S.*El*.1058 (lyr.). b. *sagacious*, of animals, Pl.*Plt*.263d, Arist.*HA*488$^{b}$15, *PA*648$^{a}$8 (Comp.), 687$^{a}$8 (Sup.), *GA*753$^{a}$11 (Comp.), al. 4. τὸ φ. *practical wisdom*, *prudence*, E.*Fr*.52.9 (lyr.), Pl.*R*.586d, al.; opp. τὸ ἄφρον, Id.*Phdr*.235e; ἰέναι ἐπὶ τὸ φρονιμώτερον X.*Smp*.8.14: pl., ἄπορος ἐπὶ φρόνιμα helpless in point of *wisdom*, S.*OT*692 (lyr.); τὰ –ώτερα ποιεῖν Isoc.15.211. 5. Adv. –μως Ar.*Eq*.1364, *Av*.1333 (lyr.), Pl.*La*.192e, etc.; opp. ἀλόγως, Isoc.3.9; φ. ἔχειν X.*Cyr*.3.3.57; διακεῖσθαι Isoc.8.114: Comp. φρονιμώτερον, διακεῖσθαι τῶν ἄλλων Id.2.10; –ωτέρως Id.13.15: Sup. –ώτατα, λέγειν X.*Ap*.20. **–ότης**, ητος, ἡ, = φρόνησις II, Gal.19.481, *PSI*1.94.2 (ii A.D.). **–ώδης**, ες, = φρονηματώδης, Philostr.*Her*.7 (s. v.l.).

**φρόνις**, εως, ἡ, (φρήν, φρονέω) *prudence*, *wisdom*, περὶ οἶδε δίκας ἠδὲ φρόνιν ἄλλων [Nestor] knows the customs and *wisdom* above other men, Od.3.244; κατὰ φρόνιν ἤγαγε πολλήν he brought back much *wisdom* from Troy, 4.258, cf. Lyc.1456, Opp.*H*.1.653.

**φρονούντως**, Adv. part. pres. Act. of φρονέω, *wisely*, *prudently*, A.*Supp*.204, S.*Ant*.682.

®**φροντ-ίζω**, fut. Att. ιῶ E.*Tr*.1234, Ar.*Nu*.125, X.*Mem*.2.1.24, etc.: aor. ἐφρόντισα A.*Pers*.245 (troch.), etc.: pf. πεφρόντικα E.*Alc*.773, Eup.352, Ar.*Ec*.263, etc.:—Med., fut. φροντιοῦμαι, E.*IT*343 (s.v.l.):—Pass., v. infr. IV: (φροντίς): I. abs., *consider*, *reflect*, *take thought*, φροντίζων εὑρίσκω Hdt.5.24, cf. A.*Pr*.1034, *Supp*.418 (lyr.), Ar.*Nu*.75, al.; ζητεῖν καὶ φ. καὶ βουλεύεσθαι Isoc.9.41; *give heed*, *pay attention*, Pl.*R*.558a. 2. *to be thoughtful* or *anxious*, πεφροντικὸς βλέπεις you look *careworn*, E.*Alc*.773; τίς δ' ἔστιν ὁ..φροντίζων; Phryn.Com.21; τὸ πεφροντικός, as Subst., *care*, *thought*, Plu.2.983b. II. with an object, 1. c. acc. rei, *consider*, *ponder*, ἔχθος ἐμόν Thgn.1247; Σωκράτης..–ίζων τι ἕστηκε Pl.*Smp*.220c; δεινά..τοῖς τεκοῦσι φροντίσαι A.*Pers*.245 (troch.); [ὀνείρατα] Hdt.7.16.β′; *devise*, μηχανήν Id.5.67; τοῦτο φ. ὅκως μὴ λείψομαι Id.7.8.α′ (nisi leg. τοῦτον); ἐκεῖνο δ' οὐ πεφροντίκαμεν, ὅτῳ τρόπῳ..μνημονεύσομεν Ar.*Ec*.263; also directly folld. by a relat. clause, φ. ἥντιν' [ὁδὸν] ἴω προτέρην Thgn.912; φ. πρὸς ἑωυτὸν ὡς δώσει Hdt.8.100; ἐφρόντισ' ᾗ διέφθαρται βίος E.*Hipp*.376; φ. ὅ τι βούλεται ἑαυτὸν καλεῖν D.39.2, cf. X.*Mem*.3.7.6; φ.

τί ποτε τοῦτ' ἔστι Id.*Cyr.*3.3.32; *take thought* that.., *see to it* that, ὅπως..Pl.*Ap.*29e, X.*An.*2.6.8, *PHib.*1.82.10 (iii B.C.); later ἵνα.. ib.43.7 (iii B.C.), Plb.2.8.8; ὡς...*PTeb.*10.6, al. (ii B.C.): c. inf., *Ep.Tit.*3.8, *BGU*8 ii 4 (iii A.D.), etc.: folld. by μή with subj., φ. μὴ ἄριστον ᾖ Hdt.1.155, cf. X.*Mem.*4.2.39, cf. infr. III; οὐδὲν φ. εἰ.. Pl.*Grg.*503a; φ. εἴτε.., εἴτε.. Id.*R.*344e: c. inf., Plu.*Fab.*12: c. part., φροντίζεθ' ὡς μαχούμενοι S.*El.*1370. 2. c. gen., *take thought for, give heed to* a thing, *regard* it, mostly with a neg. expressed or implied. σοὶ δ' ἔμεθεν μὲν ἀπήχθετο φροντίσδην Sapph. 41 (s.v.l.); Περσέων οὐδὲν φ. Hdt.3.97, cf. 100,151, 4.167; γῆ αὐχμοῦ φροντίζουσα οὐδέν Id.4.198; Πενθέως οὐ φροντίσας E.*Ba.*637 (troch.); μηδὲν ὅρκου φροντίσῃς Ar.*Lys.*915; τῶν οἰκετῶν..μηδὲν φ. Lys.7.17; μηδενὸς ἄλλου φ., πλὴν ὅπως..Isoc.15.305; οὐδὲ τῶν νόμων φροντίζουσι Pl.*R.*563d; τὸ παράπαν θεῶν μὴ φ. Id.*Lg.*701c; conversely, τοὺς θεοὺς φ. οὐδὲν τῶν ἀνθρωπίνων ib.888c, cf. Men.*Epit.*552: so with Advbs. implying a neg., σμικρὰ φ. ὄχλου E.*Or.*801 (troch.); ὀλίγον φ. δεσποτῶν Id.*Cyc.*163; σμικρὸν φ. Σωκράτους Pl.*Phd.*91c; also without neg., οὗπερ δεῖ μάλιστα φ. E.*Heracl.*242; τοῦ μὲν ὀνόματος φ., τοῦ δὲ πράγματος ἀμελεῖν And.4.27; σφόδρα σοῦ φ. X.*Mem.*3.11.10; εἰ σοφὸς ἀνὴρ ταφῆς φροντιεῖ Demetr.Lac.*Herc.*1012.26; later, *to be steward* or *bailiff*, τῶν ὑπαρχόντων τινός *BGU*300.4 (ii A.D.): so with Preps., φ. περί τινος *to be concerned* or *anxious* about, σφέων αὐτῶν πέρι Hdt.8.36, cf. X.*Mem.*1.1.12, E.*Hipp.*709; ὑπέρ τινος Pl.*Euthphr.*4d; ὑπὲρ σωτηρίας D.1.2; less freq. in this sense c. acc. only, [Σωκράτης] τἄλλα μὲν πεφρόντικεν Eup.352; ἄλλο οὐδὲν φροντίζειν Pl.*Grg.*501e; ἀλλ' οὐ τὰ βίου..δεῖ φροντίσαι Men.330; ἡ δ' ἐφρόντισ' οὐδὲ ἕν Cratin. 302 (troch.). b. later, *see to, provide for, furnish*, σιτάριον, χρήσιμα, *ZUP*73.5, 69.2 (both ii B.C.); τὰ ἐπιβάλλοντα τῇ ἑορτῇ *BGU*845.18 (ii A.D.); μηδὲν φροντίσας Pherecr.80. c. c. acc. et part., οὐ φροντίζει σκληρῶς σε καθήμενον Ar.*Eq.*783 (anap.). 3. the object is freq. unexpressed, ἐφρόντιζε ἱστορέων, i.e. inquired carefully, Hdt.1.56; οἳ τοὺς φίλους βλάπτοντες οὐ φροντίζετε who though ye do mischief to your friends *reck* not *of* it, E.*Hec.*256; μὴ φροντίσῃς *heed* it not Ar.*V.* 228; οὐ, μὰ Δί', οὐδ' ἐφρόντισα Id.*Ra.*493, cf. 650, *Pl.*215,704; c. part., τοιαῦτα..γιγνόμενα..ὁρῶντες οὐδὲν φροντίζετε And.4.23. III. Med. in signf. II. 1, φροντιζόμενον μή..X.*Hier.*7.10: c. acc., E.*IT*343 (s. v. l.). IV. later in Pass., *to be an object of thought* or *care*, πεφροντισμένος *carefully thought out*; λόγος D.S.15.78, 16.32; λόγοι πεφρ. εὖ Philostr.*VS*1.11; τρέφονται τροφῇ πεφροντισμένῃ Ael.*NA*7. 9; of a ward, ἡ -ομένη ὑπ' ἐμοῦ θυγατριδῆ *BGU*300.16 (ii A.D.). ⊛ -ίς, ίδος, ἡ, (φρονέω) *thought, care, attention* bestowed upon a person or thing, c. gen., φροντίδ' ἔχειν καμάτου Simon.85.10, cf. E.*Med.*1301; παλαισμάτων λάβε φροντίδα take *thought* for them, Pi.*N.*10.22; ἦσαν ἐν φροντίδι ἀλλήλων πέρι Hdt.1.111, cf. 7.205; περὶ ὧν ἐν φ. μεγάλῃ καθίσταται Phld.*Rh.*2.27 S.; ἐκείνοις οὐδὲ εἷς περὶ τούτου λόγος οὐδὲ φ. Pl.*Phd.*101e; φ. ἐποιήσατο τῆς Ἑλλάδος D.S.11.28, cf. 36, Ocell.4. 14; περί τινος ἐποιοῦντο πολλὴν φ. v.l. in D.S.15.28: folld. by a relat. clause, ἐν φ. εἶναι ὅ τι χρὴ ποιεῖν X.*HG*6.5.33, cf. *Cyr.*5. 2.5. 2. abs., *thought, reflection, meditation*, τὰ δ' ἄλλα φροντὶς.. θήσει δικαίως A.*Ag.*912; πολλὰς..ὁδοὺς ἐλθόντα φροντίδος πλάνοις S.*OT*67 (parodied by Henioch.4.5, ἔχον..πολλὰς φροντίδων διεξόδους); ἐν φροντίδι γίγνεσθαι, of a person, X.*Cyr.*6.2.12; but μοι ἐν φροντίδι ἐγένετο [τὸ πρῆγμα] Hdt.2.104; ἐμβῆσαί τινα ἐς φροντίδα to set one *a-thinking*, Id.1.46; φροντίδα..θώμεθα A.*Pers.*142 (anap.); δεῖ βαθείας φ. σωτηρίου Id.*Supp.*407, cf. 417; ποῖ τις φροντίδος ἔλθῃ; S. *OC*170 (anap.): pl., *thoughts*, νόον ὑπὸ γλυκυτάταις ἔθηκε φροντίσιν Pi.*O.*1.19; ἐπὶ φροντίδων ζῆν to live *thoughtfully*, E.*Fr.*684.4: prov., αἱ δεύτεραί πως φ. σοφώτεραι Id.*Hipp.*436. b. esp. of the *speculations* of Socrates and the philosophers, Ar.*Nu.*233, al.; φροντίδ' ἐξήμβλωκας ἐξηυρημένην ib.137; φροντίδα φιλόσοφον ἐγείρειν Id.*Ec.*572. (lyr.) c. *care, anxiety*, Xenoph.8; καί με καρδίαν ἀμύσσει φ. A.*Pers.*161 (troch.); ἐλπὶς ἀμύνει φροντίδ' Id.*Ag.*102 (anap.), cf. 166 (lyr.), *Eu.*453; οὐ φροντὶς Ἱπποκλείδῃ no *matter* to H., Hdt.6. 129. cf. Hermipp.17; παρασχεῖν φροντίδα τινί Ar.*Eq.*612; εἰσέρχεται αὐτῷ δέος καὶ φ. Pl.*R.*330d: pl., *cares, worries*, λύπας καὶ φροντίδας ἐμβέβληκεν Antipho 2.2.2, cf. Isoc.*Ep.*2.11, Epicur.*Ep.*1 p.28 U.; μεστόν ἐστι τὸ ζῆν φροντίδων Men.452. d. *heart's desire*, Pi.*P.* 10.62. e. *hypochondria*, φ. νοῦσος χαλεπή Hp.*Morb.*2.72. II. *power of thought, mind*, τὸ..ἀλώσιμον ἐμᾷ φροντίδι S.*Ph.*863 (lyr.); οὐδ' ἔνι φροντίδος ἔγχος Id.*OT*170 (lyr.); τὸ γὰρ τὴν φ. ἔξω τῶν κακῶν οἰκεῖν γλυκὺ ib.1390; νέα γὰρ φ. οὐκ ἀλγεῖν φιλεῖ E.*Med.* 48. III. *authority*, *PLond.*1.242.8 (iv A.D.); *guardianship*, *PMasp.*26.5 (vi A.D.). 2. *office, function, department*, Lyd.*Mag.* 2.7, al., *Cod.Just.*1.3.38.6 (pl.), Just.*Nov.*8 *Not.*49. 3. *portion of land entrusted* to a person, ἑκάστη φ. τῶν φυτευομένων τόπων *PFlor.*148.12 (iii A.D.), etc. -ισις, εως, ἡ, *care, consideration*, Plot.4.3.4. II. = foreg. III. 1, Just.*Edict.*13.10.2 (pl.). -ισμα, ατος, τό, *that which is thought out, thought, invention*, Ar.*Nu.*155, Luc.*BisAcc.*34, etc.; τὰ φ. *premeditated speeches*, Philostr.*VS*1 *Prooem.*; of a literary *work*, ib.1.18.4, al. II. = φροντίς III. 2, *PLond.*5.1648.12 (iv A.D.), Lyd.*Mag.*1.50, al., *Cod.Just.*12.60.7.9, Just.*Nov.*8*Ed.*1. -ιστέον, *one must take heed*, E.*IT*468; οὐ πάνυ ἡμῖν οὕτω φ. τί ἐροῦσιν οἱ πολλοί Pl.*Cri.*48a: c. gen., μέχρι πόσου φ. [τῶν ἀνθρώπων] Epicur.*Nat.*28.6; οὐ φ. τινός Str.16.4.16. -ιστήριον, τό, *place for meditation, thinking-shop*, ψυχῶν σοφῶν φ., of Socrates' *school*, Ar.*Nu.*94, al.; *monastic community* of Indian sages, Philostr.*VA*3.50, 6.6: generally, *school, study*, Luc.*Ner.*1, Poll.4.41; *lecture-room, auditorium*, Procop.Gaz.*Ep.*114. 2. = Lat. *Curia* (as if from *cura*), D.C.*Fr.*5.8. 3. *law-court*, *PLips.*38.14 (iv A.D.). ⊛ -ιστής, οῦ, ὁ, *deep thinker*, as Socrates is called in derision by Ar.*Nu.*266, cf. 414 (anap.), al.; φ. τῶν μετεώρων, τῶν οὐρανίων, *one who meditates on* supra-terrestrial things, X.*Smp.*6.6, *Mem.*4. 7.6; τὰ..μετέωρα φ. Pl.*Ap.*18b: hence, generally, *philosopher*, X. *Smp.*7.2, cf. Hsch. II. *one who takes care of*, τινων D.S.37.8; *curator*, ἱεροῦ Ἀφροδίτης *IGRom.*1.1167C4 (Egypt, ii A.D.); συναγωγῆς *JHS*28.195 (Side), cf. *BMus.Inscr.*1069 (Fayum, ii A.D.); τῶν δημοσίων πραγμάτων Sch.Ar.*Pl.*908; τῶν ἀρχομένων Poll.1.40: *manager*, κακῷ φ. τὰ καθ' ἑαυτοὺς ἐπιτρέψομεν Porph.*Abst.*1.50; παρύγρων *Cat.Cod.Astr.*8(1).177; without gen., *manager, housekeeper*, Phld.*Oec.*p.51 J.: as transl. of Lat. *procurator*, ὁ φ. Δρούσου *IGRom.*4.219 (Ilium). 2. title of official of a φρατρία, *IG*14. 759.8 (Naples). 3. *bailiff, house-steward*, *Gp.*7.8.1, *BGU*603.2 (ii A.D.), etc. -ιστικός, ή, όν, *of* or *for thinking, thoughtful*, Arist.*Div.Somn.*464ᵃ23; ὑποπίνων δὲ πάνυ φ. (sc. γίγνεται) Antiph. 271; φ. τὴν πρόσοψιν Luc.*Pisc.*12: τὸ λογιστικὸν καὶ φ. the faculty *of* reasoning and *thought*, Plu.2.432c, cf. 966a. II. *considerate, careful*, τὰ θήλεα περὶ τὴν τῶν τέκνων τροφὴν φροντιστικώτερα Arist. *HA*608ᵇ2. Adv. -κῶς X.*Mem.*3.11.10, Ael.*NA*8.25. 2. *nervous, worried*, Gal.10.538. -ίστρια, ἡ, fem. of φροντιστής, *guardian*, υἱωνοῦ *PLond.*3.1164a6 (iii A.D.), cf. *BGU*1662.4 (ii A.D.).

⊛ **φροῦδος**, η, ον, also ος, ον S.*El.*807, E.*IT*154 (lyr.), Plu.2.263a: (contr. from πρὸ ὁδοῦ, as φροίμιον from προοίμιον, φρουρός from *προορός):—*gone away, clean gone* (as Hom. says in full, οἱ δ' ᾤχοντο ἰδὲ πρὸ ὁδοῦ ἐγένοντο, Il.4.382): 1. of persons, *gone, fled, departed*, φ. ἐστι S.*Ant.*15, etc.; φ. ἐξ οἴκων, δόμων ἄπο. E.*Alc.*94 (lyr.), *Andr.*73; σκηνὰς ἐς ἱεράς Id.*Ion*804; βεβᾶσι φ. Id.*IT*1289; οἴχεται φ. Ar.*Ach.*210 (lyr.); c. part., φροῦδοί [εἰσι] διώκοντές σε they are *gone* in pursuit, S.*Ph.*561; φ. ἀναρπασθεὶς Id.*El.*848 (lyr.); φ. ἐξῳκισμένοι Ar.*Pax*197; φ. ἢ πλέων Antipho 5.29; also of the dead, φ. αὐτὸς εἶ θανών S.*El.*1152; Ἀντίλοχος αὐτῷ φ. Id.*Ph.*425, cf. E.*Tr.*41, al.; φ. ἐς Ἅιδην Id.*Med.*1110 (anap., folld. by θάνατος wh. is corrupt). b. *undone, ruined*, ib.722, *Heracl.*703 (anap.), *Or.* 390. 2. of things. *gone, vanished*, φροῦδα τἀπειλήματα S.*OC*660; οὑμοὶ λόγοι πρὸς αἰθέρα φ. E.*Hec.*335; φ. σοι θυσίαι Id.*Tr.*1071 (lyr.); ἐλπίδες Id.*Ion*866 (anap.); τὰ δ' ἐν δόμοις δαπάναισι φ. Id.*HF*592; φρούδη μὲν αὐδή, φροῦδα δ' ἄρθρα they are *gone*, i.e. refuse their office, Id.*Andr.*1078, cf. Ar.*Nu.*718 (anap.).—Rarely found in any case but nom. sg. and pl.: gen. sg. once in S., *Aj.*264.—Trag. word, once in Antipho l.c.; freq. in later Prose, as Luc.*Merc.Cond.*24, Aristid. 1.161 J.: acc. is found in Plu.*Pyrrh.*31, 2.405f.

⊛ **φρουμεντάριος**, ὁ, = Lat. *frumentarius*, *SIG*830.5 (Delph., ii A.D.), Pelekides 86 (Thessalonica, ii A.D.). II. φρουμ⟨εντ⟩αρία, ἡ, *corn-receipt*, *POxy.*43 ii 11 (iii A.D., dub., v. φορμαρία).

**φροῦνος**, ὁ, late form for φρῦνος, *PMag.Osl.*1.235.

⊛ **φρουρά**, Ion. -ρή, ἡ: (v. φρουρός fin.):—*look-out, watch, guard*, as a duty, A.*Ag.*2, Hdt.2.30, *IG*1².3.26, etc.; ἐς φ. δόμων E.*Or.* 1252; φρουρὰν ἐτάξαντ' ἐν δόμοις Id.*Andr.*1099; φρουρὰν ἄζηλον ὀχήσω shall keep unenviable *watch*, A.*Pr.*143 (anap.); ὄμματος φρουρά my *watchful* eye, S.*Tr.*226; φρουρᾶς ἄδων singing *while on guard*, to keep oneself awake or while away the time, Ar.*Nu.*721 (anap.); τοῖς..πιστοτέροις..διετέτακτο ἡ φ. Pl.*Criti.*117d. 2. *a watch of the night*, ἡ νυκτερινὴ φ. Hdn.3.11.6; v.l. in E.*Rh.*5 (anap.). 3. *prison, ward*, Pl.*Phd.*62b, *Grg.*525a. II. of persons set to watch, *guard, garrison*, Hdt.6.26, 7.59, A.*Ag.*301, Th.3.51, *IG*2².28. 14, etc.; esp. of *frontier-posts*, X.*HG*6.5.24, etc.; στρατειῶν καὶ φρουρῶν Lys.16.18; ἐξήλθομεν εἰς Πάνακτον φρουρᾶς προγραφείσης being ordered on *garrison-duty*, D.54.3; τὰ κύκλῳ κατέχειν ἁρμοσταῖς καὶ φρουραῖς Id.18.96; φρουρὰν ὑποδέχεσθαι Id.58.38. 2. at Sparta, *a body of men destined for service*, φρουρὰν φαίνειν proclaim or order out a *levy*, 'call out the *ban*', of the ephors and kings, X.*HG* 3.2.23, 6.4.17; ἐπί τινας ib.4.7.1, etc.; εἰδότες φρουρὰν πεφασμένην ἐφ' ἑαυτούς ib.5.1.29; φ. ἐξάγειν ib.2.4.29.

**φρουραρχ-έω**, *to be commandant of a garrison*, *Inscr.Prien.*19.6 (iii B.C.), 37.66 (ii B.C.), Plu.*Dio*11. -ης, ου, ὁ, = φρούραρχος, Them.*Or.*10.136b (pl.). -ία, ἡ, *office* or *post of* φρούραρχος, X. *Mem.*4.4.17, *Milet.*3No.37d (iii B.C.), Plu.*Phoc.*31. -ος, ὁ, *commander of a watch*, or *commandant of a garrison*, *IG*1².10.13, al., X. *An.*1.1.6, *Cyr.*5.3.17, Pl.*Lg.*760d, Men.*Kol.*60, Aen.Tact.22.20, Plb.21.42.1, *PTeb.*6.13 (ii B.C.), *OGI*111.16 (Egypt, ii B.C.), etc.; οἱ φ. the *guardians*, Pl.*Lg.*843d: metaph., [θεοὶ] ἑκάστῳ τὸν τρόπον συνήρμοσαν φ. Men.*Epit.*554 (spelt **φρούαρχος** Wilcken *Chr.*162 i 11 (ii B.C.), and v.l. in Plb. l.c.). II. *gaoler*, Aristaenet. 1.20.

**φρουρ-έω**, Poet. impf. φρούρουν S.*Tr.*915: fut. -ήσω A.*Pr.*31, etc.: aor. ἐφρούρησα Hdt.2.30, etc.:—Med., fut. -ήσομαι in pass. sense, E.*Ion*603:—Pass., aor. ἐφρουρήθην ib.1390: pf. πεφρούρημαι Hp.*Ep.* 23 (Ps.-Democr.), (δια-) A.*Fr.*265: (φρουρός):—*keep watch* or *guard*, ἐν Ἐλεφαντίνῃ Hdt. l.c., cf. 9.106, *IG*1².99.21, *OGI*38.1 (iii B.C.), etc.; of ships, φ. περὶ Ναύπακτον or ἐν Ναυπάκτῳ, Th.2.80,83; φ. ἐπί τινι *to keep watch* over.., E.*Alc.*35 (anap.); οἱ φρουροῦντες the *guardians*, Pl.*Lg.*763d; συνάπτειν .. φρουροῦντας .. φρουροῦσι ib.758b; prov., ἐν παντὶ..σκορπίος φ. λίθῳ S.*Fr.*37; generally, 'keep a sharp look-out', Id.*Tr.*915. II. trans., *watch, guard*, τὴν χώρην Hdt.3.90; τὴν γέφυραν Id.4.133; τὴν ἀτραπόν Id.7.217; βρέτας A. *Eu.*1024; σὲ δαίμων..φρουρήσας τύχοι S.*OT*1479; τὴν Ποτείδαιαν φ. *garrison* it, Th.3.[17], cf. X.*Cyr.*6.1.17, etc.; φυλακαῖσι φ. σῶμ' Ὀδυσσέως *set* a watch over..E.*Cyc.*690: metaph., φ. πέτραν *keep watch over* it, of Prometheus, A.*Pr.*31; στόμα εὔφημον φρουρεῖν ἀγαθὸν *keep* silence, E.*Ion*98 (anap.); ἡ εἰρήνη τοῦ θεοῦ..φρουρήσει τὰς καρδίας ὑμῶν *Ep.Phil.*4.7:—Pass., *to be watched* or *guarded*, Hdt.7.203, A.*Eu.* 218, S.*OC*1013, E.*Hec.*995, etc.: of the watch kept by besiegers, κύκλῳ φρουρούμενος ὑπὸ πάντων πολεμίων Pl.*R.*579b. b. *hold in subjection*, opp. παραφυλάττειν, Plb.18.4.6. c. Astrol., *occupy*, in Pass., Vett.Val.106.18. d. *bind*, ἁλύσεσι πεφρουρημένος *PMag. Par.*1.3093. 2. *watch for, observe*, φρουρῶν τόδ' ἦμαρ E.*Alc.*27; φ. ὄμμα ἐπὶ σῷ..καιρῷ S.*Ph.*151 (lyr.); φ. χρέος *to be observant of* one's duty, Id.*El.*74. III. Med., *to be on one's guard against, beware of*, c. acc., φρουρούμενος βέλεμνα E.*Andr.*1135:—Act. also in the same sense, ἐφρούρει μηδὲν ἐξαμαρτάνειν Id.*Supp.*900; φ. ὅπως or ὅπως ἄν.., with subj., S.*El.*1402, E.*Hel.*742; φ. μή.., with subj., Id.*El.*1139. -ημα, ατος, τό, poet. Noun: I. *that which is watched* or *guarded*, λείας βουκόλων φρουρήματα the herdsmen's *charge* of spoil, S.*Aj.*54. II. *guard*, A.*Eu.*706; of a single man, Id.*Th.*449; λόγχαι δεσποτῶν φρουρήματα E.*El.*798. III. *watch, ward*, φρούρημα ἔχειν Id.*Ion*511 (troch.). -ησις, εως, ἡ, *watching*, Aq., Sm., Lxx 2*Ki.*5.24. -ητήρ, ῆρος, ὁ, *watcher, guard*, Man.4.47. -ητικός, ή, όν, *fit for watching* or *guarding*, Iamb.*Myst.*3.10, Dam.*Pr.*96,252, Procl.*Inst.*145,154, Lyd.*Mens.*4.67. -ητός, ή, όν, *watched, guarded*, *AP*6.230 (Quint.). -ήτωρ, ορος, ὁ, *guardian*, θεσμῶν ib.9.812. -ικός, ή, όν, *of, for a watch, guard*, or *garrison*, τὸ φ. D.C.56.42. II. φρουρική, ἡ, *guard duty*, *SIG*633.51 (Milet., ii B.C.). -ιον, Dor. φρώριον *Inscr.Cret.*1 xvi 17.15 (Lato, ii B.C.), τό, *fort, citadel*, A.*Eu.*919 (lyr.), *IG*1².93.17, etc.; ἀντὶ τοῦ πόλις εἶναι φρούριον κατέστη Th.7.28: esp. *hill-fort*, as distd. from a fortified town, Id.2.18, 3.18,51, Lys.12.40, X.*Cyr.*1.4.16, etc.; βίον ὡς οἰκτρὸν ἐξαντλοῦσιν οἱ τὰ φ. τηροῦντες Men.74; τὰ φ. καὶ τὰ ὅρια τῆς Ἀττικῆς *IG*2².1028.22. 2. *prison*, of the body, Pl.*Ax.*366a. II. *garrison*, of a place, A.*Pr.*801 (where Sch. also expl. by *thing to be guarded against*); φυλασσόμεσθα φρουρίοισι E.*Or.*760 (troch.); πόλεως φ., of the Areopagites, A.*Eu.*949 (anap.). ❀ -ίς, ίδος, ἡ (sc. ναῦς), *guardship*, *IG*1².22.74, Th.4.13, X.*HG*1.3.17.

**φρουροδόμος**, ον, *guarding the house*, *AP*9.245 (Antiphan.).

❀**φρουρός**, ὁ, *watcher, guard*, *IG*1².11.9, al., 4²(1).40.16 (Epid., v/iv B.C.), E.*Ion*22, *Rh.*506; φρουροὺς ἐγκατέλιπον left *a garrison* in a place, Th.2.6, cf. 4.25; ἐκβάλλειν τοὺς φ. Id.8.108; οἱ φ. οἱ ἐν Ἄνδρῳ *IG*2².123.10; οἱ..ἄριστοι φ. τε καὶ φύλακες..εἰσί Pl.*R.*560b; identified with φύλακες, X.*Cyr.*8.6.1,3; τοὺς φύλακας οἷον φρουρούς Arist.*Pol.*1264ᵃ26. (Contr. from *προορός (cf. οὖρος (B)), as φροίμιον from προοίμιον, φροῦδος from πρὸ ὁδοῦ.)

**φρουρύτης**, ητος, ἡ, *function of a guard*, *PCair.Preis.*15.10 (iv A.D.).

❀**φρύ-αγμα** [ῠ], ατος, τό, *violent snorting*, esp. *neighing* or *whinnying* of a spirited horse (= ἡ τῶν ἵππων καὶ ἡμιόνων διὰ μυκτήρων ἠχή, *EM*801.11), ἱππικὰ φ. A.*Th.*245,475, S.*El.*717; φ. καὶ φύσημα X.*Eq.* 11.12; also of a boar, Opp.*C.*2.457. II. metaph., *wanton behaviour, insolence*, M.Ant.4.48; τὸ ἐπ' ὀφρύσι φ. *AP*12.101 (Mel.); σοβαρὸν φ. ib.5.17 (Rufin.); τὸ φ. αἴρειν Ael.*NA*7.12; φ. πρός τινα Luc.*Cat.*26; φ. ὁμοζύγου πλουσίας Aristaenet.2.12, cf. Philostr.*Im.* 2.2. -αγμᾰτίας, ου, ὁ, *hot-tempered*, of a horse, Hsch. s.v. πεδαωριστής. II. metaph. as Adj., *arrogant, wanton*, βίος Plu. *Ant.*2. -αγμός, ὁ, = φρύαγμα, D.S.19.31; v.l. for φριμ-, D.H. *Comp.*16 (pl.). -αγμοσεμνᾰκος, ον, *wanton and haughty*, ἔχων τρόπους φ., coined to describe Bdelycleon in Ar.*V.*135. -ακτής, οῦ, ὁ, = φρυαγματίας, ἵππος D.L.6.7. -άσσομαι, Att. -άττομαι, prop. of spirited, high-fed horses, *neigh, whinny and prance*, Call. *Lav.Pall.*2, *AP*5.201 (Asclep. or Posidipp.), cf. Thom.Mag.p.381R.; φ. πρὸς τοὺς ἀγῶνας *neigh eagerly* for the race, Plu.*Lyc.*22; also of a cock, Ael.*NA*7.7, cf. infr. II. 2. metaph. of men, *to be wanton, haughty, insolent*, Ph.1.151,297, al., Alciphr.3.27; μὴ γαῦρα φρυάσσου *AP*12.33 (Mel.), cf. Gal.10.180: also c. acc., Ἔρωτες σκῦλα φρυασσόμενοι *APl.*4.215 (Phil.); φ. ἐπί τινι *to be proud* of a thing, D.S.4.74; ἔν τισι *AP*4.3.27 (Agath.). 3. trans., = καταπλήττω, Men. 1081. II. Act. φρυάσσω Lxx *Ps.*2.1 (quoted in *Act.Ap.*4.25); of birds, Cyran.81, cf. *Gloss.*

**φρῠγᾰν-ίζω**, *gather firewood*, Poll.7.142. -ικός, ή, όν, = φρυγανώδης, τὰ φ. Thphr.*HP*1.5.3, 6.6.1; φ. ἔμβλημα *Sammelb.*7361.13 (iii A.D.): Sup., -ώτατα τῇ προσόψει Thphr.*CP*3.7.11. -ιον, τό, Dim. of φρύγανον, Dsc.3.91. -ίς, ίδος, ἡ, = φρύγανον, Eust. 862.32. -ισμός, ὁ, *a gathering of firewood*, ἐπὶ φ. ἐξελθεῖν Th.7.4, cf. 13, Ph.2.167; coupled with λαχανεία, J.*BJ*4.9.8. -ιστήρ, ῆρος, ὁ, *one who gathers firewood*, Polyaen.1.18:—fem. -ίστρια, Ar. *Fr.*887. -ίτης [ῑ], ου, ὁ, *for fuel*, κάλαμος *PCair.Zen.*86.3 (iii B.C.): fem. -ῖτις, ιδος, ὕλη Hld.9.8.

**φρῡγᾰνοειδής**, ές, = φρυγανώδης, Dsc.3.26, 154.

❀**φρύγᾰνον** [ῡ], τό, (φρύγω) *dry stick*; mostly in pl., *firewood*, Hdt. 4.62, Ar.*Av.*642, Th.3.111, X.*An.*4.3.11, *SIG*1027.13 (Cos, iv/iii B.C.), *Act.Ap.*28.3; φρυγάνοις καὶ λίθοις περιφράξαντες Arist.*HA* 603ᵃ9: Com., Φρύγες ἐστὶ καινὸν δρᾶμα τοῦτ' Εὐριπίδου..ᾧ καὶ Σωκράτης τὰ φρύγαν' ὑποτίθησι prob. in Telecl.40: sg. only in collect. sense = τὰ φρύγανα, μαντικῶς τὸ φ. τίθεσθαι Ar.*Pax*1026; τὸ φ. ἐπικαίουσι Plu.2.553c. II. *undershrub*, opp. δένδρα, θάμνος, πόα, defined as τὸ ἀπὸ ῥίζης πολυστέλεχες καὶ πολύκλαδον, Thphr.*HP*1.3.1.

**φρῡγᾰνοφόρος**, ον, *gathering dry sticks*, Lys.*Fr.*257 S.

**φρῡγᾰνώδης**, ες, *of* or *belonging to the class of undershrubs*, Thphr. *HP*6.6.2, Dsc.4.48,150; φ. σπέρματα Porph.ap.Eus.*PE*3.11; τὰ φ. the *class of* φρύγανα, Thphr.*HP*1.3.4: Comp., Dsc.3.155.

**φρύγ-ετρον** [ῠ], τό, (φρύγω) *a vessel for roasting barley*, Polyzel. 6 (troch. (?)): carried by brides in procession, as a symbol of household duties, Lex Solonis ap.Poll.1.246. II. *stick to stir barley while roasting*, Hsch. -εύς, έως, ὁ, = foreg.1, Theopomp.Com. 53. II. *one who roasts*, Poll.7.181. -εύω = φρύγω, ibid. -ία, ἡ, *female roaster*, Hsch. II. = ἀσπληνος, Ps.-Dsc.3.134.

**φρυγιατικόν**, τό, an unknown plant, *Gp.*12.1.2.

**φρῠγιαύλιον**, τό, *music for the flute in the Phrygian mode*, *BGU* 1125.4,30 (i B.C.).

**φρῠγίζω**, *to be like the Phrygians*, τῇ φωνῇ Eudox.ap.St.Byz. s.v. Ἀρμενία; *use Phrygian words*, μεταξὺ Ἑλληνικῶν ὀνομάτων Demetr. *Eloc.*96.

**φρῠγίλος** [ῑ], ὁ, *chaffinch*, Ar.*Av.*763,875 (cf. Lat. *fringilla*).

**φρῠγ-ίνδα** παίζειν, play *with roasted beans*, Poll.9.110,114, Hsch. -ιον, τό, *firewood*, Lxx *Ps.*101(102).4. 2. *drying-place, basking-place*, *EM*561.12. -ιος, α, ον, *dry*, Hsch.

❀**Φρύγιος** [ῠ], α, ον, also ος, ον Luc.*Harm.*1: (Φρύξ):—*Phrygian*, δι' αἴας..Φρυγίας A.*Supp.*548 (lyr.), etc.; δείματα Φ. the terrors *of the Phrygian goddess*, E.*El.*457 (lyr.). 2. Φ. νόμοι, μέλεα, *Phrygian* music, esp. of music played on the flute, said to have been invented by Marsyas, E.*Or.*1426 (lyr.), *Tr.*545 (lyr.); Φ. αὐλοί Id.*Ba.*127 (lyr.): πᾶσα βακχεία..μάλιστα..ἐστὶν ἐν τοῖς αὐλοῖς..' ὁ διθύραμβος ὁμολογουμένως δοκεῖ εἶναι Φ. Arist.*Pol.*1342ᵇ7; τῆς Φρυγίου [ἁρμονίας] τὸ ἔνθεον Luc. l.c.; Φ. διὰ πασῶν εἶδος, τόνος, τρόπος, *Phrygian* scale, Cleonid.*Harm.*9,12, Alyp.*Diat.*7, al. II. Φ. λίθος, an *aluminous* kind of *pumice-stone*, used by dyers, Dsc.5.123.

**Φρῠγιστί**, Adv., of music, *in the Phrygian mode*, Pl.*R.*399a; ἡ Φ. (sc. ἁρμονία) Arist.*Pol.*1290ᵃ21, 1340ᵇ5; τὰ Φ. μέλη ib. 1342ᵇ6.

**φρῠγ-ῖτις**, ἡ, = φρυγία II, Ps.-Dsc.3.134. -μός, ὁ, *drying, roasting*, Hsch. -ω [ῡ], Ar.*Ec.*221, etc. (in late writers also φρύττω, in Pass., Dsc.2.148 (v.l.), Sch.Od.9.388): fut. φρύξω (v. infr.), Dor. -ξῶ Theoc.7.66: aor. ἔφρυξα Cratin.143.2 (hex.), Hp.*Ulc.*11, 12:—Pass., aor. ἐφρύχθην Hom.*Epigr.*14.4, Gal.6.289 (v.l.); ἐφρύγην [ῠ] Hp.*Ulc.*12, *AP*7.293 (Isid.Aeg.), Gal.6.289: pf. πέφρυγμαι Pherecr.159, Th.6.22, Hp.*Acut.*(*Sp.*)47:—*roast* or *parch*, τραγήματα Ar.*Ra.*511, cf. *Ec.*221; φρύξας, ἑψήσας κἀπ' ἀνθρακιᾶς ὀπτήσας Cratin. l.c.; φρύξαντες ἀπέψουσι Hdt.2.94; ἐρετμοῖσι φρύξουσι (Kuhn for φρίξουσι) *they shall cook* with the [wood of the] oars, Orac.ap.Hdt.8. 96:—Pass., φρύγεται τραγήματα Ar.*Ec.*844; πεφρυγμένοι ἐρέβινθοι Pherecr. l.c.; πεφρ. κριθαί *roasted* barley, Th.6.22; κύμινον πεφρ. Sor.1.119. 2. of the sun, *parch*, Theoc.6.16, 12.9; of thirst, ἐφρύγη δίψευς ὕπο *AP* l.c. (The relation to Lat. *frīgo* 'roast', Skt. *bhṛjjáti* 'he roasts', *bhṛṣṭá-* 'roasted', is not clear.)

❀**φρυκτός**, ή, όν, (φρύγω) *roasted*, ὑμᾶς..φρυκτοὺς σκευάσω I'll make *roast meat* of you, Ar.*V.*1331 (lyr.); ἀμύγδαλα φ. Sor.1.123. II. as Subst., φρυκτός, ὁ, *fire-brand, torch*: esp. *signal-fire, beacon*, A.*Ag.*30, 282,292; φρυκτοὶ ἐς τὰς Ἀθήνας πολέμιοι ἤροντο Th.2.94, cf. 3.22, Aen.Tact.7.4, Onos.25.3. 2. φρυκτός (sc. κύαμος), ὁ, *a lot*, because roasted beans were used for drawing lots, Plu.2.492a: also, *a bean for voting*, Poll.8.18. 3. φρυκτοί, οἱ, *small fish for frying, small fry*, Anaxandr.33.11, Alex.155.3; φρυκτά, τά, Hsch. 4. φρυκτή, ἡ, a kind of *resin*, Gal.13.589, Paul.Aeg.3.59.

**φρυκτωρ-έω**, *make fire-signals*, Din.*Fr.*9.5, Onos.25.2:—Pass., ἐφρυκτωρήθησαν νῆες προσπλέουσαι the approach of ships *was signalled by beacon-fires*, Th.3.80. -ία, ἡ, *making signals by beacons*, A.*Ag.*33,490 (pl.), S.*Fr.*432.6; ἔννυχος E.*Rh.*55; καθεστήκασι φρυκτωρίαι ἐν τοῖσι πύργοις Ar.*Av.*1161; τὰ σημεῖα τῆς φ. Th.3.22. II. concrete, = φρυκτός II, v.l. for sq. in Arist.*Mu.*398ᵃ31,32. -ιον, τό, *beacon-tower, signal-station*, ib.398ᵃ31,32, Plu.*Pomp.*24, Hdn.4.2.8. -ός, ὁ, (φρυκτός II, οὖρος (B)), *one who watches on a height to make fire-signals*, A.*Ag.*590, Th.8.102. II. *fire-signal, beacon*, Lyc.345 (proparox., s.v.l.).

❀**φρύνη** [ῡ], ἡ, *toad*, Arist.*HA*530ᵇ34, Timae.156, Ael.*NA*17.12. II. = βατράχιον 2, Cyran.39. III. nickname of several Athenian courtesans, from their complexion, Ar.*Ec.*1101, Macho ap.Ath.13.583b:—so Φρῦνις, ὁ, name of a Com. Poet, Ar.*Nu.*971. (Cf. Skt. *babhrús* 'brown', OHG. *brūn* 'brown', etc.)

**φρῡνικός**, ή, όν, = φρυνοειδής, Asclep.Jun.ap.Gal.13.1023.

**φρύνιον** [ῡ], τό, = ποτίρριον, Dsc.3.15. 2. = βατράχιον 1, Ps.-Dsc.2.175.

**Φρῡνίχειος** [ῐ], α, ον, *of* or *like Phrynichus* (the Com. Poet), τὸ Φ. ἐκλακτίζειν Ar.*V.*1524 (lyr., ubi v. Sch.).

**φρῡνο-ειδής**, ές, *like a toad*, βάτραχος Arist.*Pr.*862ᵃ11. -λόγος, ὁ, *toad-catcher*, or φρυνολόχος, ὁ, (λοχάω) *lying in wait for toads*, a species of hawk, perh. *marsh-harrier*, Id.*HA*620ᵃ21.

**φρῦνος**, ὁ (ἡ, Babr.28.6), = φρύνη, Arist.*HA*609ᵃ24, Nic.*Al.*567, Babr.24.4, *App.Anth.*5.47 (φροῦνον ap. Synes.); cf. φροῦνος. II. a stone, = βατραχίτης, Cyran.39. III. a bird, ibid.

**Φρῡνώνδειος**, ὁ, *a swindler, cheat, rogue* (from Phrynondas, a notorious swindler mentioned by Ar.*Th.*861, Isoc.18.57), Phryn.*PS* p.124 B.

**Φρύξ**, ὁ, gen. Φρῠγός, *a Phrygian*, Il.2.862, al.; as the name of a slave, Ar.*V.*433; Phrygians were a byword for cowardice, δειλότερος λαγὼ Φρυγός prov.ap.Str.1.2.30, cf. Apollod.Com.6.

**φρύξ**, ὁ (?), gen. φρυγός, perh. = φρύγανα, dub. in *Gloss.*

**φρύξις**, εως, ἡ, *burning, parched state, adustion*, Sever.*Clyst.*22, Sch.Orib.iii p.687 D.

**φρύττω**, = φρύγω (q.v.).

**φῦ**, *fie! faugh!* an exclam. of disgust, Ar.*Lys.*295,305, cj. in *Th.* 245. II. Ep. for ἔφυ.

**φῠγᾰγωγός**, όν, (φυγάς) *dragging along fugitives*, f.l. for λαφυραγωγός in Polyaen.8.16.6.

**φύγᾰδε**, Adv., (φυγή) *to flight*, φύγαδε τράπε μώνυχας ἵππους Il.8.157, cf. 257; φύγαδ' αὖτις ὑποστρέψας 11.446; ἄλλοι φ. μνώοντο ἕκαστος 16.697.

**φῠγᾰδ-εία**, ἡ, *exile, banishment*, Plb.6.14.7, Vett.Val.94.1. II. *body of fugitives*, LxxEz.17.21 cod.Alex. **-εῖον**, τό, *place of refuge*, φυγαδεῖα δούλων Lxx2 Es.4.15: written **φυγάδιον** ib.Nu.35.15. **-ευσις**, εως, ἡ, = Lat. *fugitatio*, *Gloss.* **-ευτέον**, *one must banish*, Porph.*VP*22. **-ευτήριον**, τό, *city of refuge*, LxxNu.35.6, Jo.20.2, al. **-ευτικός**, ή, όν, *banishing*, τινος Hld.8.11. II. φ. χρήματα the property *of exiles*, Phot. s. v. μαστῆρες. **-ευτός**, ή, όν, *exiled*, dub. cj. in *Gloss.* ❀**-εύω**, Elean **φυγᾰδείω** *Schwyzer* 424.1 (iv B.C.):—*banish*, X.*HG*2.3.42, 5.4.19; ἐκ τῆς πόλεως D.40.32; δεῦρ' αὐτὸν (sc. Ἔρωτα) ἐφυγάδευσαν ὡς ἡμᾶς κάτω Aristopho11.7: opp. ὀστρακίζω, Arist.*Pol.*1288ᵃ25; metaph., τὸ θῆλυ τοῦ βίου φ. Luc.*Am.*38:—Pass., X.*HG*2.4.14, D.S.14.32, etc.; πεφυγαδευμένοι Plu.*Ant.*15. II. intr., *live in banishment*, *SIG*175.20 (Delph., iv B.C.), *Schwyzer* 424.6 (Elis, iv B.C.), LxxPs.54(55).8: fut. φυγαδεύσομαι *POxy.*1477.15 (iii/iv A.D.), Plb.10.22.1. **-ικός**, ή, όν, *of* or *for an exile*, φ. προθυμία the reckless zeal *of a refugee*, Th.6.92; φ. ἐλπίδες Plu.*Pel.*8; φ. νῆσος Id.2.603b; φ. οἰκίαι *IG*12(9).196.24 (Eretria, iv B.C.); οἱ φυγαδικοί, = οἱ φυγάδες, Plb.22.10.6; τὸ φ. D.H.6.63, D.S.14.32. Adv. -κῶς, ζῶντας Plu.*Tim.*24. **-ις** (parox.), Adv., = φύγαδε, Theognost.*Can.*163, *EM*806.8.

**φῠγᾰδο-δαίμων**, ον, gen. ονος, ἡ (sc. κόρη), a name for *mercury*, Zos.Alch.p.206 B. **-θήρας**, ου, ὁ, *one who hunts after runaways* or *exiles*, Plb.9.29.3, Plu.*Dem.*28, Procl. *in Cra.*p.40 P.

**φῠγ-αίχμης**, ου, Dor. **-μας**, α, ὁ, *fleeing from the spear, unwarlike, cowardly*, A.*Pers.*1025 (lyr.), Call.*Fr.*117. **-ανθρωπεύω**, *shun mankind*, φ. ἐς ἐρημίην Aret.*SD*1.6. **-ανθρωπία**, Ion. **-ίη**, ἡ, *shunning of mankind*, ib.5. **-αρσενία**, poet. **-ίη**, ἡ, *shunning of men*, Man.4.64. **-αρχέω**, *shun rule*, prob. cj. for φιλαρχέω or φυλαρχέω in Arist. *Pol.*1295ᵇ12. **-άς**, άδος, ὁ, ἡ: (φεύγω):—*one who flees* from his country, either voluntarily, *runaway, fugitive*, or by legal sentence, *exile*, Hdt.1.150, 3.138, etc.; ἐξεκηρύχθην φ. S.*OC*430; ἐξελήλαμαι φ. ib.1292; φ. πάσης τῆς χώρας X.*HG*4.1.7; τῆς πατρίδος Pl.*Alc.*2.145b; ἀνθρώπων Plu.*Ant.*69; φ. τῆς τῶν ἐξελασάντων πονηρίας Th.6.92; φ. ἐξ Ἤλιδος, ἐκ Λαρίσης, X.*HG*3.2.29, 6.4.34; φυγάδ' ἀπ' οὐρανοῦ θεόν A.*Supp.*214; φ. ἐξ Ἀθηνῶν ὑπὸ Ἀθηναίων X.*HG*1.5.19; φ. παρ' ὑμῶν *a deserter* from.., Id.*Cyr.*6.3.11; ἔνθεν.. εἰμὶ φ. Id.*An.*5.6.23; τοὺς δὲ φ. ἐντεῦθεν ἐποίησε Lys.13.64, cf. X.*HG*4.1.40; κατάγειν φυγάδας to restore *them*, Hdt.5.31; φ. καθεῖναι, καταδέχεσθαι, X.*HG*2.2.20, 5.2.10: prov., αἱ ἐλπίδες βόσκουσι φυγάδας E.*Ph.*396; αἱ φ. πύλαι D.H.1.46; μηδένα εἶναι.. ὑπερορίαν φυγάδα, is dub. in Pl.*Lg.*855c. II. of an army, *put to flight*, S.*Ant.*108 (lyr.).

**φυγγάνω**, collat. form of φεύγω, A.*Pr.*513, S.*El.*132 (lyr.), Hp. *Int.*12:—the compds. with ἀπο-, δια-, ἐκ-, κατα- occur in Prose.

**φύγδᾰ**, Adv. *in flight*, A.*Eu.*256 (lyr.); **φύγδην**, Nic.*Th.*21.

❀**φύγεθρον**, τό, *a swelling of the glands*, esp. of the groin or armpit, Ruf.ap.Orib.44.21.1, Heliod.ap.Sch. ad l. c. (iii p.687 D.): also spelt **φύγεθλον**, Gal.11.72; Lat. *phygetron*, Cels.5.18.19, 28.10. (Perh. for φλύγ-εθρον, cf. φλυκτίς.)

**φύγεργος** [ῠ], ον, *shunning work*, *EM*199.1.

❀**φῠγή**, ἡ, (φεύγω) *flight* in battle, ἀΐξαντε φυγῇ Od.10.117; οὐδέ τις ἀλκὴ.. οὐδὲ φ. 22.306; ἐς φ. ἐτράποντο Hdt.8.89; ἐς φ. ὁρμᾶσθαι, ὁρμᾶν, E.*Rh.*143, X.*Cyr.*4.2.28; φυγὴν αἱρεῖσθαι, ἀρεῖσθαι, A.*Pers.*481 (sed leg. αἴρονται), E.*Rh.*54; ἰσχυρὰν τὴν φ. τοῖς πολεμίοις.. ἐποίει X.*Cyr.*1.4.22; ἰσχυρὰ φ. ἐγένετο ib.7.1.26; generally, *flight*, *Ev. Matt.*24.20; φ. ἑλέσθαι take *to flight*, *PGnom.*102 (ii A.D.): dat. φυγῇ, used adverbially, *in hasty flight*, φυγᾷ πόδα νωμᾶν S.*OT*468 (lyr.); φυγᾷ ποδὶ ἴχνος ἔφερε E.*Or.*1468 (lyr.); φ. ἐξαλύξωμεν ποδί Id.*El.*218, cf. *Ba.*437, *Hec.*1066 (lyr.); φεύγειν φ., φ. ἀναχωρεῖν, Pl. *Smp.*195b, 221a; φ. φευκτέον Luc.*Ind.*16: pl., ἐν ταῖς φυγαῖς, of the *flight* of the country people of Attica into the city, in the Pelop. war, Ar.*Ec.*243; φεύγουσί τινας οὐκ αἰσχρὰς φ. Pl.*Lg.*706c. 2. *flight* or *escape* from a thing, *avoidance of* it, c. gen., γάμου A.*Supp.*395 (lyr.); νόσων ἀμηχάνων φυγὰς ξυμπέφρασται S.*Ant.*364 (lyr.), cf. *OC*280; λέκτρων φυγαί E.*Hel.*799; ἀγαθῶν φυγάς Pl.*Ti.*69d; τῶν σιτίων Gal.15.180; opp. αἵρεσις, Epicur.*Ep.*3p.62 U., al., cf. S.E.*P.*1.87; τὰς ὀρθὰς αἱρέσεις καὶ φ. Phld.*Herc.*1251.11; opp. δίωξις, Epicur.*Sent.*25. 3. *place of refuge*, D.S.17.78. 4. *slipping* of a bandage, Hp.*Off.*9. II. *banishment, exile*, νῦν μὲν δικάζεις ἐκ πόλεως φυγὴν ἐμοί A.*Ag.*1412, cf. *Ch.*254; ἐκ γῆς S.*OT*659, etc.; ἐνιαυσία ἔκδημος φ. E.*Hipp.*37; τῆς φυγῆς ἧς αὐτοὶ ἔφυγον Lys.13.74; συμφυγεῖν τὴν φ. ταύτην (sc. ὑμῖν) to go into *banishment* with.. Pl.*Ap.*21a; φυγὴν ἐπιβαλὼν ἑωυτῷ imposing *banishment* on oneself Hdt.7.3; φυγῇ ζημιοῦν E.*Or.*900, cf. *IG*1².39.7, Pl.*Grg.*516d; φυγὴν καταγνῶναί τινος And.1.106, Lys.14.38; φυγῆς τιμήσασθαι (sc. δίκην) the penalty *of exile*, Pl.*Ap.*37c, cf. *Cri.*52c; ἐπὶ φόνῳ..φ. Decr.ap. And.1.78 (dub. l.); τῆς πατρίδος φ. ποιήσασθαι Lys.3.42; εὐθύνας.. εἶναι..πλὴν φυγῆς καὶ θανάτου καὶ ἀτιμίας *IG*1.c.73: pl., E.*Hipp.*1043, Pl.*Prt.*325b, etc.; φυγὰς ἐμὰς χθονὸς E.*Med.*400; φυγαὶ καὶ διώξεις Pl.*Lg.*638a. 2. as a collect. Noun, = φυγάδες, *body of exiles* or *refugees*, A.*Supp.*74 (lyr.), Th.8.64, Aeschin.2.143; κατάγειν τὴν φυγήν to recall *them*, X.*HG*5.2.9; pl., συλλέξαι τὰς φυγάς Pl.*Lg.*682e, cf. Plu.*Flam.*12.

**φύγῐμον** [ῠ], τό, *place of refuge, asylum*, τοῖς δούλοις *IG*5(1).1390.80 (Andania, i B.C.).

**φῠγίνδα**, f.l. for φρυγίνδα, Theognost.*Can.*165.

**φῠγο-δέμνιος**, ον, *shunning the marriage-bed*, of Pallas, *AP*6.10 (Antip.). **-δεμνος**, ον, = foreg., Nonn.*D.*2.98, al. **-δῐκέω**, *shirk a trial*, D.40.16, *PPetr.*3p.39 (iii B.C., cf. p.xiii), *PEnteux.*65.4 (iii B.C.), etc. **-δῐκία**, ἡ, *avoidance of a trial*, *Gloss.* **-δῐκος**, ὁ, *one who shirks his trial*, *Sammelb.*5250.4 (ii B.C.). **-λεκτρος**, ον, = φυγοδέμνιος, Orph.*H.*32.8. **-μᾰχέω**, *shun battle* or *fighting*, Plb.3.90.10, al., D.S.17.27, Plu.*Lyc.*16, Onos.11.3; *avoid action*, Id.31.1. **-μᾰχος**, ον, *shunning battle*, Simon.65. **-ξενος**, ον, *shunning strangers, inhospitable*, φ. στρατός Pi.*O.*11(10).17. **-πατρις**, ιδος, ὁ, ἡ, *fugitive from one's country*, *Cat.Cod.Astr.*2.198. **-πολις**, ιδος, ὁ, ἡ, *fleeing from a city*, *EM*328.54. **-πονία**, ἡ, *aversion to work*, Plb.3.79.4, Hierocl.p.50 A. **-πονος**, ον, *shunning work* or *hardship*, Plb.39.1.10. ❀**-πτόλεμος**, ον, poet. for *φυγοπόλεμος, *shunning war, cowardly*, Od.14.213, Q.S.1.740. **-πτολις**, ὁ, ἡ, poet. for φυγόπολις, Max.349.

**φύζ-α** (not φῦζα, Hdn.Gr.1.251), ἡ, expld. as ἡ μετὰ δειλίας φυγή by Aristarch.ap.Apollon.*Lex.* s. v. φόβος:—*headlong flight, rout*, φύζα, φόβου κρυόεντος ἑταίρη Il.9.2, cf. 14.140; ἀνάλκιδα φύζαν ἐνόρσας 15.62; θάνατον καὶ φ. ἑταίρων 17.381; ἐν δὲ Ζεὺς..φύζαν ἐμοῖς ἑτάροισι κακὴν βάλεν Od.14.269. **-ᾰκινός**, ή, όν, *flying, runaway, shy*, ἔλαφοι Il.13.102. **-ᾰλέος**, α, ον, = foreg., *AP*6.237 (Antist.). **-άναι** (inf. of *φύζημι)· φυγεῖν, δειλιάσαι, Hsch. **-ηλός**, ή, όν, = φυζαλέος, Id. **-ω**, late Ion. for φεύγω, Heraclid. ap. Eust.1643.2: part. aor. Pass. φυζηθέντες (as if from φυζάομαι) Nic.*Th.*825.

❀**φυή**, Dor. **φυά**, ἡ, (φύω) *growth, stature*, esp. *fine growth, noble stature*, in Hom., always (as in Hes.) of the human form, and only in acc., θηήσαντο φυὴν καὶ εἶδος ἀγητόν Il.22.370; φυὴν εἰδώην καὶ μήδεα 3.208; most freq. in adv. sense, Νέστορι δίῳ εἶδός τε μέγεθός τε φυήν τ' ἄγχιστα ἐῴκει in shape and in stature and *in size* (or *growth*), 2.58, cf. Od.6.152; οὔ ἑθέν ἐστι χερείων, οὐ δέμας οὐδὲ φυήν, οὔτ' ἂρ φρένας Il.1.115, cf. Od.5.212, 7.210; φυήν γε μὲν οὐ κακός ἐστι 8.134; χρυσέῳ [γένει] οὔτε φυὴν ἐναλίγκιον οὔτε νόημα Hes.*Op.*129, cf. *Sc.*88, B.5.168; later, in gen., οὔτε φυῆς ἐπιδευέες οὔτε νόοιο Theoc.22.160; rare in Trag., τὴν τάλαιναν εὔμορφον φ. A.*Niob.* in *PSI*11.1208.8; φυὰν Γοργόνος ἴσχειν E.*El.*461 (lyr.). 2. after Hom., of animals, plants, or objects, ἐμβάλλων ἐριπλεύρῳ φυᾷ κέντρον Pi.*P.*4.235; κάνθαρος.. Αἰτναῖος φυήν S.*Ichn.*300; also τερπόμεναι ῥοδέῃ φ. of roses, Mosch.2.36; of beans, Luc.*Vit.Auct.*6; of things, ἀνέβη ἡ φ. τοῖς τείχεσιν their *original form* was restored, LxxNe.4.7(1); ἐὰν κατὰ φυὰν διαφθαρῇ τις τῶν λίθων *IG*7.3073.40 (Lebad., ii B.C.). II. poet. for φύσις, *nature, genius*, σοφὸς ὁ πολλὰ εἰδὼς φυᾷ Pi.*O.*2.86; μάρνασθαι φυᾷ Id.*N.*1.25, cf. *I.*7(6).22; φυᾷ τὸ γενναῖον ἐπιπρέπει Id.*P.*8.44; τὸ δὲ φυᾷ κράτιστον ἅπαν Id.*O.*9.100; δεινὸς φυήν Cratin.221. III. *the flower* or *prime of age*, εὐάνθεμος φυά Pi.*O.*1.67. IV. *substance*, ἀναίμων ἐστὶ φυὴ μελέων Opp.*H.*1.639; νεφροὶ τὴν φ. ἀδενώδεες Aret.*SD*2.3. V. μερόπων φυή *the race* of men, *APl.*4.183.7. VI. *produce* of a year, *harvest*, φ. τοῦ ἐνεστῶτος ἔτους *BGU*708.4 (ii A.D.), cf. *PIand.*26.12 (i A.D.), etc.—Poet. and later Prose.

**φύη** or **φυίη**, v. φύω.

**φῡκᾰρίζω**, = φυκόω, τὰς παρειάς Sch.Opp.*H.*1.127.

❀**φῡκάριον**, τό, = φῦκος, Hsch. s. v. ἄφυκα, Zonar.

**φύκης** [ῡ], ου, ὁ, (φῦκος) a fish *living in seaweed*, prob. a species of *wrasse*, *Labrus*, Arist.*HA*567ᵇ20:—the female was **φῡκίς**, ίδος, Mnesim.4.38 (anap.), Arist.*HA*567ᵇ19, 591ᵇ13, Antiph.132.8 (anap.), Anaxandr.41.49 (anap.), Numen.ap.Ath.7.282a: but Alex.110.12,13, distinguishes φυκίς and φύκης.

**φῡκία**, ἡ, = φῦκος, f.l. in Ph.*Bel.*85.25.

**φυκίασις**, εως, ἡ, = *ignia*, *Gloss.* (fort. πυρίασις).

**φῡκίδιον**, τό, Dim. of φυκίς, *AP*5.184 (Ascl.), *PCair.Zen.*66.14 (iii B.C.).

**φῡκιόεις**, εσσα, εν, *full of seaweed, weed-strewn*, θῖν' ἐν φυκιόεντι Il.23.693; ἐπ' αἰόνος..φυκιοέσσας Theoc.11.14, cf. 21.10.

**φῡκίοικος** [ῐ], ὁ, *dweller among sea-wrack*, i.e. Poseidon, Call. *Iamb.*1.263.

❀**φῡκίον** or **φύκιον**, τό, = φῦκος I, Arist.*HA*568ᵃ6, *IG*11(2).145.23, 146*A*67 (Delos, iv B.C.): mostly in pl., Pl.*R.*611d, Arist.*HA*590ᵇ11, Theoc.7.58, etc. 2. a fish, perh. = φύκης, *AP*7.637 (Antip.), Orib.*inc.*13.25. II. = φῦκος II, *orchil* used as *rouge*, φ. ἐντρίβειν Luc.*Hist.Conscr.*8; κομμοῦν τοὺς λόγους οἷον φυκίῳ Them. *Or.*27.336c. b. *rouge-pot*, φ. χρυσοῦν *IG*11(2).161*B*42,101 (Delos, iii B.C.).

**Φύκιος** [ῠ], ὁ, *god of sea-wrack*, epith. of Poseidon at Myconus, *SIG*1024.9 (iii/ii B.C.).

**φῡκιο-φάγος**, ον, *eating seaweed*, of a fish, Arist.*HA*602ᵃ20; cf. φυκοφάγος. **-φόρος**, ον, *bearing seaweed*, ἀκταί Xenocr.ap.Orib.2.58.110. **-χαίτης**, ου, ὁ, *with hair like seaweed*, Hsch. (expld. by ψαφαροχαίτης), *PSI*8.892 (iv (?) A.D.).

**φῡκιόω**, = φυκόω:—Pass., dub. l. in A.*Dict.* in *PSI*11.1209*a*13, cf. Tz.*H.*3.418.

**φῡκίς**, ἡ, v. φύκης.

**φῡκῖτις**, ιδος, ἡ, *a precious stone*, so called from its colour, Plin. *HN*37.180.

**φῡκιώδης**, ες, *covered with seaweed*, λίθοι Sch.Opp.*H.*3.420.

**φῡκο-γείτων**, ονος, ὁ, ἡ, *near the seaweed, dwelling by the sea*, epith. of Priapus, *AP*6.193 (Flacc.). **-θριξ**, τρῐχος, ὁ, ἡ, *shaggy with seaweed*, πέτρη Matro *Conv.*26.

❀**φῦκος**, εος, τό, *seaweed, wrack*, Il.9.7; ὄστρεια..φῦκος ἠμφιεσμένα Alex.110.2; differing from βρύον in size, Arist.*HA*603$^{a}$17, cf. Thphr.*HP*4.6.2: Ep. dat. pl. φύκεσσι Alcm.6: φ. θαλάσσιον οὖλον *orchella-weed*, *Roccella tinctoria*, Dsc.4.99; called φ. πόντιον in Thphr.*HP*4.6.4; φ. θ. πλατύ *peacock's tail*, *Padina mediterranea*, Dsc.l.c.; φ. ὑπόμηκες καὶ ὑποφοινικίζον *Nitrophyllum punctatum*, ibid.; φ. ὅμοιον τῇ ἀγρώστει *mattress grass-weed*, *Zostera marina*, Thphr.*HP*4.6.6; φ. πλατύφυλλον, = πράσον 2, ib.2; φ. τριχόφυλλον ὥσπερ τὸ μάραθον, *Cystoseira foeniculosa*, ib.3. 2. *sedge* or *weed* growing in a lake, Nic.*Al*.576. II. *orchil*, prepared from φῦκος I.1 and used as *rouge* by Greek women, Ar.*Fr*.320.5, Theoc.15.16, *IG*5(1).1390.22 (Andania, i B.C.), Alciphr.1.33. III. = φυκίς, *Gloss.*

**φυκοτύχη**, ἡ, a kind of *plaster*, Aët.15.35, Paul.Aeg.7.17; cf. φικοτύχη.

**φῡκοφάγος** [ᾰ], ον, = φυκιοφάγος, Arist.*Frr*.319,331.

**φῡκόω**, in Med. or Pass., *to be rouged*, φ. τὸ πρόσωπον, Plu.2.142a; φυκούμεναι καὶ μυριζόμεναι ib.693b. II. Pass., *to be stuffed with seaweed*, διφθέραι φυκούμεναι D.S.17.45.

**φύκτῐμος**, = φύξιμος, τὸ ἱερὸν ἄσυλον καὶ φ. εἶμεν *SIG*550.5 (Delph., iii B.C.).

**φυκτός**, ή, όν, older and poet. form of φευκτός, *to be shunned* or *escaped*, *avoidable*, οὐκέτι φυκτὰ πέλωνται Il.16.128, cf. Od.8.299, 14.489.

**φῡκώδης**, ες, *full of seaweed*, τόποι Arist.*HA*602$^{a}$19. II. *of seaweed*, ἀποφορά Dsc.5.118. III. *like seaweed*, Thphr.*HP*4.7.6.

⊛**φύλαγμα** [ῠ], ατος, τό, gloss on ἔρυμα, Sch.Th.6.66; on εἶλαρ, *EM*298.4. 2. *protection*, γῆ αἰώνιον φ. Secund.*Sent*.15, cf. Simp. *in Cat*.373.36. II. *precept*, *commandment*, Lxx*Le*.8.35, 22.9, al., Jul.*Gal*.238c.

**φῡλ-ᾰδόν**, Adv. *by tribes*, Sch.BT Il.12.3. **-άζω**, *form into tribes*, φυλὰς φυλάξαι Rhetra ap.Plu.*Lyc*.6.

**φῠλᾰκ-άρχης**, ου, ὁ, *commandant of the watch*, *PCair.Zen*.6.23 (iii B.C.), *OGI*754.5 (Hieropolis). **-εία**, ἡ, *guard*, *protection*, Poet.*de herb*.181, *Gloss.* **-εῖον**, τό, *post*, *watch-tower*, *fort*, Plb.10.30.6: pl., = Lat. *stationes*, Id.5.75.10, 76.3; **φυλάκιον**, Aen.Tact.20.5 cod.M, App.*Ill*.26, *PRyl*.288 (pl., iii A.D.). 2. *a watch*, *party consisting of four soldiers*, Plb.6.33.7: pl., in form φυλάκια, Id.*Fr*.87 (ap.Suid.). II. in Alex. Greek, *a menstruous cloth*, Dam.*Isid*.52. **-εύς**, έως, ὁ, Ep. for φύλαξ, Ep. pl. φυλακῆες Opp.*C*.4.295. ⊛**-ή**, ἡ, (φύλαξ) *watching* or *guarding*, esp. by night, φυλακῆς μνήσασθε Il.7.371; φυλακὰς ἔχειν keep *watch and ward*, 9.1,471; φ. κατέχειν E.*Tr*.194 (lyr.); φυλακὴ ἔχει αὐτόν *watching* engages him, v.l. in Hes.*Fr*.188.4; φ. νυκτερινή Ar.*V*.2: prov., γυμνῷ φυλακὴν ἐπιτάττειν tell an unarmed man to stand on the defensive, i.e. to give commands that cannot be obeyed, Pherecr.144, cf. Philem.12; περὶ φυλακῆς Εὐβοίας..ἐπιμέλεσθαι *IG*1$^{2}$.39.76; ὅπως ἀφανὴς εἴη ἡ φ. that there might be nothing visible *to watch*, Th.4.67; φυλακὴν [τῶν τειχῶν] ἔρημον καταλιπεῖν Lycurg.17; φυλακὰς φυλάξειν keep *watch and ward*, X.*An*.2.6.10, cf. Pl.*Lg*.758d; τὴν ἐν θαλάττῃ φ. φυλάττειν D.7.14; φ. ποιῆσαι X.*An*.5.7.31; τὴν φ. ποιεῖσθαι Lys.12.16; φυλακὰς ποιήσασθαι X.*An*.6.3.21; ἰσχυρὰς φ. ποιεῖσθαι Id.*Cyr*.1.6.37; φυλακὰς καταστήσασθαι, κατασκευάσασθαι, Ar.*Av*.841, X.*HG*7.2.23. 2. *watch* or *guard*, of persons, Pl.*Prt*.321d (pl.), *Act.Ap*.12.10, etc.; φ. ἑωυτοῦ ποιεύμενός [τινας] Hdt.2.154; φ. τοῦ σώματος a body *guard*, D.23.3; τῶν σωμάτων Din.1.9; φ. περὶ τὸ σῶμα X.*Cyr*.7.5.58, cf. *PHib*.1.59.5 (iii B.C.), etc.; *garrison* of a place or fortress, Hdt.2.30; ἡ ἐν τῇ Ναυπάκτῳ φ., of a squadron of ships, Th.7.17, cf. X.*HG*1.1.22. b. *the rank of* φύλακες, Pl.*R*.415c. 3. *station*, *post*, Il.10.408 (pl.), 416 (pl.), X.*HG*5.4.49; φυλακὰς προλιπών E.*Rh*.18 (anap.); Διὸς φ., Pythag. name for the centre of the universe, Arist.*Cael*.293$^{b}$3. 4. of time, a *watch* of the night, ἐπεὰν τῆς νυκτὸς ᾖ δευτέρη φ. Hdt.9.51; πρώτης φ. ἀρχομένης Wilcken *Chr*.1 ii 18 (iii B.C.); φυλακαῖσι νυκτέροισιν E.*Rh*.765; φ. νυκτερινὰς καὶ ἡμερινὰς καθιστάναι X.*Cyr*.1.6.43: of these there were *three*, acc. to Sch.E.*Rh*.5; but *five* are mentioned in Stesich.55, Simon.219A, E.*Rh*.543 (lyr.); and the Roman division was *four*, *Ev.Matt*.14.25, Suid. 5. *place for keeping* others in, *ward*, *prison*, δημοσία φ. D.S.10.30; εἰς φυλακὴν βληθείς *AP*11.276 (Lucill.); βαλεῖν τινὰ εἰς φ. *Ev.Matt*.18.30, cf. Arr.*Epict*.1.1.24; θέσθαι τινὰ ἐν φυλακῇ Lxx *Ge*.40.3, cf. *Ev.Matt*.14.3; πολιτικὴ φ. the town-*prison*, *POxy*.259.8 (i A.D.). 6. Astrol. = ταπείνωμα, *PMich.* in *Class.Phil*.22.22 (pl.). II. *guarding*, *keeping*, *preserving*, whether for security or custody, ἐν φυλακῇ ἔχειν τινά Hdt.1.24; ἐν φ. ἀδέσμῳ ἔχειν τινά Th.3.34; ἐν φυλακῇσι μεγάλῃσι ἔχεσθαι Hdt.2.99; τὸν Ἰσθμὸν ἔχειν ἐν φ. to keep the Isthmus *guarded* or *occupied*, Id.7.207, cf. 8.40; τὸν ἠνείκαντο γλώσσης χαρακτῆρα τοῦτον ἔχειν ἐν φ. *to preserve* the same character of language, Id.1.57; ἔχειν νόον ἐν φ. Thgn.439; τὰ παρὰ πᾶσιν ἐν πλείστῃ φ., παῖδας καὶ γυναῖκας D.18.215; τὰ κατὰ τὸ στρατόπεδον διὰ φυλακῆς ἔχων Th.7.8; τὸν πλοῦν διὰ φ. ποιησάμενοι Id.8.39; στόματος φυλακᾷ κατασχεῖν φθόγγον prob. in A.*Ag*.236 (lyr.); ἐν φ. σχεθέμεν μεγάλᾳ *be* very *ware of*, Pi.*P*.4.75; φυλακὴν ἔχειν, = φυλάττεσθαι, *keep guard*, *be on the watch*, περί τινα Hdt.1.39; φ. ἔχων εἴ κως δυναίμην..ib.38; φ. ἔχειν μή..Th.2.69; φ. λαμβάνειν μή..Men.*Pk*.20; δεινῶς ἦσαν ἐν φυλακῇσι were straitly on their *guard*, Hdt.3.152, cf. A.*Pers*.592 (lyr.). 2. *custody* of property, Arist.*Pol*.1309$^{b}$6, *EN*1120$^{a}$9. 3. *safeguard*, τὴν μεγίστην φ. ἀνῄρηκε τῆς πόλεως its chief *safeguard*, And.4.19; φ. παρέχειν Isoc.11.13; δημοκρατίας, μοναρχίας φ., Lys.25.28, Arist.*Pol*.1315$^{a}$8. III. (from Med.) *precaution*, πολλῆς φ. ἔργον Pl.*R*.537d; φ. θαυμαστῆς δεομένη Id.*Lg*.906a, al., cf. Th.5.99. 2. c. gen., *precaution against*, εὐλάβεια φ. κακοῦ Pl.*Def*.413d; ὑποψίας φυλακὴν ποιήσασθαι Antipho 2.1.2; φ. τῶν πάντα μολυνόντων Epicur.*Sent.Vat*.80, cf. 73. **-ία**, ἡ, = foreg., *PRyl*.90.13 (iii A.D.); ἱεροῦ *POxy*.1627.12 (iv A.D.). **-ίζω**, *throw into prison*, *Act.Ap*.22.19:—Pass., Lxx *Wi*.18.4. **-ικός**, ή, όν, *watchful*, *careful*, Pl.*R*.375e, 456a, al.; -ώτατοι πόλεως ib.412c; ἡ -κή (sc. τέχνη) ib.428d. 2. *disposed to observe*, δόγματος ib.412e. **-ιον**, v. φυλακεῖον. ⊛**-ίς**, ίδος, fem. of φύλαξ, τούς τε φύλακας καὶ τὰς φυλακίδας (cf. φύλαξ I fin.) ib.457c; φ. νῆες *guard*-ships, D.S.20.16. **-ισσα**, ἡ, = foreg., Lxx *Ca*.1.6. **-ιστής**, οῦ, ὁ, Lat. *phylacistes* in Plaut.*Aul*.3.5.44, *gaoler*, epith. of a *harsh creditor*. 2. = Lat. *cuspator*, Lyd.*Mag*.1.46. **-ῑτεύω**, *serve as* φυλακίτης, *Sammelb*.4309.3 (iii B.C.): c. acc., φ. τὴν τοπαρχίαν *PHib*.1.34.1 (iii B.C.). **-ίτης** [ῑ], ου, ὁ, *police official* in Egypt, *PSI*4.359.8 (iii B.C.), *PTeb*.22.9 (ii B.C.), *OGI*85.4 (iii B.C.), 139.6 (ii B.C.); in Syria, ib.238.2. ⊛**-ῑτικός**, ή, όν, *pertaining to police*, esp. in neut. -ῑτικόν, τό, *tax for maintenance of police*, *PSI*5.509.9 (iii B.C.), *PTeb*.5.15 (ii B.C.), etc. **-ῖτις**, ιδος, ἡ, Pythag. name for *seven*, Nicom.ap.*Theol.Ar*.43. ⊛**-ός**, ὁ (on the accent v. Hdn.Gr.1.150, 2.128), Ep. and Ion. for φύλαξ, Il.24.566, *IG*12(8).356 (Thasos, vi B.C.), Hdt.1.84,89, 2.113, al.; dub. in *OGI*674.12 (Coptos, i A.D.); φ. νεκύων Κέρβερον Theoc.29.38, cf. A.R.1.132; ἥρως πόλεως φ. *Inscr.Prien*.196: as fem., κοῦραι αἱ φυλακοί Call.*Hec*.1.2.12. II. **Φύλακος**, ὁ, as pr. n., Il.6.35, Od.15.231: so Φυλάκη (Il.2.695, etc.), as distd. from φυλακή. ⊛**-τέος**, α, ον, *to be observed*, πρόνοια τοῦ θεοῦ S.*OC*1180; (from Med.) *to be guarded against*, E.*Andr*.63. II. **φυλακτέον**, *one must observe*, *obey*, ἀνάγκην Id.*IT*620; *one must preserve*, τὰ πρεσβεῖα Aristid.1.99 J. 2. (from Med.) *one must guard against*, τι A.*Th*.499; ἡδονήν Arist.*EN*1109$^{b}$7; φ. μή..Pl.*R*.416a; ὅπως μή..X.*Oec*.7.36, cf. Isoc.6.94: c. inf., τοῦτο πράττειν Porph.*Abst*.2.31. **-τήρ**, ῆρος, ὁ, poet. for φύλαξ, in pl., Il.9.66,80, 24.444 **-τηρία**, ἡ, = παννυχίς, Hsch. **-τηριάζω**, in Pass., *to be furnished with an amulet* or *preservative*, *PMag.Par*.1.789, 2627. ⊛**-τήριον**, τό, *guarded post*, *fort*, *castle*, Hdt.5.52: esp. *an outpost communicating with fortifications*, Th.4.31,33,110, X.*Cyr*.7.5.12: pl., *guardrooms*, Arist.*Pol*.1331$^{a}$20. 2. *safeguard*, *security*, Pl.*Lg*.917b: *preservative*, D.6.24; *amulet*, Dsc.5.154, Plu.2.378b, etc.; among the Jews φυλακτήρια were small rolls of parchment with texts from the Law written on them, bound to the forehead by persons praying, *Ev.Matt*.23.5; φ. χρυσᾶ, *symbols* denoting the kingdoms of Upper and Lower Egypt, *OGI*90.45 (Rosetta, ii B.C.); *amulet*, *PMag.Lond*.121.298 (pl.); metaph., τὸ ὄνομά σου ἔχω ἓν φ. ἐν καρδίᾳ *PMag.Leid.W*.18.2. 3. perh. *guard* or *chain*, *PLond.ined*.2199. **-τήριος**, α, ον, *serving as a protection*, τὰ περί τι φ. Pl.*Lg*.842d, **-της**, ου, ὁ, *one who preserves*, τῶν ἰδίων ἐθῶν Ph.2.577 (pl.), sed leg. -τικοί. II. = φυλακτήρ, a magistrate at Cumae, Plu.2.291f. ⊛**-τικός**, ή, όν, *preservative*, opp. ληπτικός, προετικός, Arist.*EN*1120$^{b}$15; ὑγιείας Id.*Top*.106$^{b}$36, cf. *Rh*.1366$^{a}$37; of persons, φ. τῶν ὄντων X.*Mem*.3.4.9; φ. ἐγκλημάτων *cherishing the recollection of* them, Arist.*Rh*.1381$^{b}$4; τὸ φ. Phld.*Oec*.p.34 J., Gal.10.638, Porph.*Antr*.16. Adv. **-κῶς** Arist.*Top*.106$^{b}$37. II. (from Med.) *cautious*, opp. πιστευτικός, Id.*Rh*.1372$^{b}$28. Adv. -κῶς Plb.6.8.3, al.: Comp., -ώτερον χρῆσθαι ταῖς προνομαῖς Id.1.18.1, al. **-τός**, ή, όν, *capable of being preserved*, ὑγίεια Alex.Aphr.*Febr*.22. **-τρον**, τό, = φυλακιτικόν, *POxy*.502.43 (ii A.D.), *PGoodsp.Cair*.10.10 (ii A.D.). ⊛**-τωρ**, ορος, ὁ, ἡ, poet. for φύλαξ, χθὼν ἁ φθιμένοιο φ. *Bull.Soc.Arch.Alex*.7.244 (Egypt, i B.C./i A.D.), cf. Nonn.*D*.2.176.

**φύλαξ** [ῠ], ᾰκος, ὁ, also ἡ (v. infr.): (φυλάσσω):—*watcher*, *guard*, *sentinel*, Hom. (only in Il., always masc. and in pl.), φύλακες ἄνδρες 9.477; ἡγεμόνες φυλάκων ib.85, cf. 10.58; freq. in Trag. and Att. (Hdt. uses φυλακός, exc. in signf. II), φύλακ' ἐπέστησεν βοΐ A.*Supp*.303; νεὼς σῆς φ. S.*Ph*.543; δράκοντα μήλων φ. Id.*Tr*.1100, al.; φ. τοῦ τείχους Th.2.78, cf. *IG*1$^{2}$.44.14, al.; φ. κατὰ τὰς πύλας X.*HG*4.4.8; φύλακα καταστῆσαι Lys.19.31; οἱ φ. the *garrison*, Th.6.100, X.*An*.4.2.5, etc.; φύλακες τοῦ σώματος body-*guards*, Pl.*R*.566b; ὁ τοῦ δεσμωτηρίου φ. Id.*Cri*.43a; τῶν αἰχμαλώτων X.*HG*4.5.6, etc.: λόχοι φύλακες bodies *of reserve*, Id.*An*.6.5.9: as fem., ἔστι κἀμοὶ κλῃς ἐπὶ γλώσσῃ φ. A.*Fr*.316, cf. S.*Aj*.36, *OC*355, E.*Andr*.86: metaph., flames (φλόγες) are called φύλακες Ἡφαίστου κύνες Eub.75.7 (dub. l.); and the hospitable table is φ. φιλίας Timocl.13. II. *guardian*, *keeper*, *protector*, Hes.*Op*.123,253; κτεάνων Pi.*P*.8.58; δωμάτων, χώρας φ., A.*Ag*.914, S.*OT*1418, etc.; παιδός Hdt.1.41; τῆς γυναικός X.*Cyr*.6.3.14; τῆς πολιτείας And.4.16, cf. Pl.*R*.374d, al.; τῆς ἀρχῆς Lys.12.94; τῶν νόμων Pl.*Lg*.966b; τῆς εἰρήνης Isoc.4.175: as fem., E.*Tr*.462, Pl.*Plt*.305c, X.*Mem*.2.1.32; of a divinity, Ἄγγδιστιν..φύλακα καὶ οἰκοδέσποιναν τοῦδε τοῦ οἴκου *SIG*985.51 (Philadelphia, i B.C.): also φ. Ἀργείου δορός a *protector against* it, E.*Ph*.1094; ἐπὶ τοῖς ὠνίοις φύλακας κατεστήσατε, of the ἀγορανόμοι, Lys.22.16. 2. *observer*, τοῦ δόγματος Pl.*R*.413c; τοῦ ἐπιταττομένου X.*Cyn*.12.2. 3. of things, [στήλην] ὥσπερ φ. τῆς δωρεᾶς Plu.*Nic*.3. 4. *chain*, *keeper*, φ. ἀργυροῦς, χαλκοῦς, *IG*7.3498.8 (Orop.), *Inscr.Délos* 1426 *B* ii 45; ὀμφαλὸν καὶ φύλακα περὶ αὐτόν ib.1417 *B* i 93 (ii B.C.). 5. bandage, Gal.19.144. (Cf. Lat. *bubulcus* (Ital. *bifolco*), *subulcus*.)

**Φῠλαξῐθᾰλάσσειος**, ον, *belonging to the Phylaxithalassian tribe* at Alexandria, *POxy*.513.52 (ii A.D.).

**φύλαξις** [ῠ], εως, ἡ, *watching, guarding,* ὕπνου φυλάξεις S.*Fr.*432. 9, cf. Aq.*Is.*26.3. II. *a security,* E.*Hel.*506 (pl.).

⊕**φῡλαρχ-έω,** *to be* or *act as* φύλαρχος, Ar.*Lys.*561 (anap.), X.*Eq.*11. 10, Is.11.41, *Sardis*7 No.56.10 (ii A.D.), f.l. in Arist.*Pol.*1295$^{b}$12 (cf. φυγαρχέω): c. gen., φ. τῆς Ὀλυσίας Is.5.42: c. dat., φ. φυλᾷ Ἰαλυσίᾳ Maiuri *Nuova Silloge* 19 (Rhodes). **-ης,** ου, ὁ, = φύλαρχος, *IG*12 (2).505.4 (Methymna), LXX 2*Ma.*8.32, Ph.1.497, al. ⊕ **-ία,** ἡ, *office of* φύλαρχος, Arist.*Pol.*1322$^{b}$5 (pl.), *Com.Adesp.*25.4 D. (pl.). ⊕ **-ος,** ὁ, *chief officer of a* φυλή, X.*Cyr.*1.2.14, al., *BMus.Inscr.*1005 (Cyzic.), *CIG*3773 (Nicomedia), *Sammelb.*6257 (v/vi A.D.). b. = Lat. *tribunus militum,* D.H.2.7, Plu.*Rom.*20. c. *chief priest* of a tribe among the Jews, LXX 1*Es.*7.8: pl., *elders* of a tribe, ib.*De.*31.28. d. *sheikh,* τῶν Ἀράβων Str.16.1.28, cf. Procop.*Pers.*1.19; Parthian term, = δυνάστης, Arr.*Fr.*171 J. II. as a military term, at Athens, *the commander of the cavalry furnished by each tribe,* Hdt.5.69. III. οἱ φ., an oligarchical council at Epidamnus, Arist.*Pol.*1301$^{b}$22.

**Φυλάσιος** [ᾰ], ὁ, *a man of Phyle* (in Attica), Ar.*Ach.*1028.

⊕**φῠλάσσω,** Att. **-ττω,** Ep. inf. φυλασσέμεναι Il.10.312,419; poet. impf. φύλασσε Pi.*Pae.*6.91: fut. φυλάξω Od.22.195, etc.: aor. ἐφύλαξα, Ep. φύλ- Il.16.686, etc.: pf. πεφύλᾰχα Ath.10.408f, (δια-) X.*Cyr.*8.6.3 (-πεφυλακ- codd.), Din.1.9 (-πεφυλακ- codd.), (παρα-) Pl.*Lg.*632a; πεφύλακα LXX 1*Ki.*25.21, Arg.E.*Med.* (πεφυλακέναι and πεφυκέναι codd.):—Med., fut. -άξομαι A.*Supp.*205, S.*El.*1012, Ar. *Ec.*831, etc.; also in pass. sense, S.*Ph.*48, X.*Oec.*4.9: aor. ἐφυλαξάμην Hdt.7.130 (v.l.), Antipho 3.4.7, etc.:—Pass., fut. -αχθήσομαι D.H.*Rh.*5.6, Gal.1.426: aor. ἐφυλάχθην Luc.*Pisc.*15: pf. πεφύλαγμαι E.*Fr.*472.19 (anap.), cf. infr. c. 1, Lib.*Or.*54.74 (in pass. sense); imper., only in med. sense in early writers, πεφύλαξο Hes. *Op.*797, Orac.ap.Hdt.7.148; part., Il.23.343, etc.

**A.** abs., *keep watch and ward, keep guard,* esp. by night, ἀνίη καὶ τὸ φυλάσσειν πάννυχον ἐγρήσσοντα Od.20.52; οὐδ' ἐθέλουσι νύκτα φυλασσέμεναι Il.10.312, cf. 419,421; εἰ μέν κ' ἐν ποταμῷ δυσκηδέα νύκτα φυλάσσω Od.5.466, cf. 22.195; (Med., v. infr. c); σὺν κυσὶ.. φυλάσσοντας περὶ μῆλα Il.12.303; αὐτοῦ φ. A.*Eu.*243; τὴν μὲν ἡμέραν κατὰ διαδοχὴν φ. τὴν δὲ νύκτα καὶ ξύμπαντες Th.7.28; ἐφύλαττον περὶ τὰ βασίλεια X.*Cyr.*7.5.68; οἱ φυλάττοντες Isoc.10.34; φ. τοῖς Ἀθηναίοις *keep watch* for.., Th.7.53; κατὰ θάλατταν ἐφύλαττεν ὅπως μηδὲν εἰσπλέοι X.*HG*2.4.29; φ. ἕως.. *watch* or *wait* till.., Lys.1.15; φ. πηνίκα.. D.18.308: c. acc. cogn., φυλακὰς φ. X.*An.*2.6.10, *Ev.Luc.* 2.8. 2. *to be on one's guard,* And.1.135.

**B.** trans., *watch, guard, defend,* ἀθανάτων ὅστις σε φυλάσσει Od.15.35, cf. Il.10.417, al.; σύας, μῆλα, Od.17.593, 12.136; τὴν ἑωυτῶν Hdt.8.46; πόλιν φ. A.*Th.*136 (lyr.), *IG*1$^{2}$.108.46; πύλας E. *Andr.*950; σε φυλάττοι Ζεύς Ar.*Eq.*499 (anap.); βρέτας ἧσαι φυλάσσων A.*Eu.*440; φ. τινὰ ἀπὸ τῶν δυσχωριῶν *guard* one from.. X.*Cyr.*1.4. 7 (but τὴν γραῦν φ. ἀπὸ τῶν κεραμίων *keep away* from.., Men.*Sam.* 87): c. acc. et inf., τοὐμὸν φυλάξει σ' ὄνομα μὴ πάσχειν κακῶς S.*OC* 667; ὁ νόμος φ. μὴ ἅπτεσθαι Pl.*Lg.*838b; φ. μηδένα περαιοῦσθαι Th. 7.17; φ. τὸ μηδὲν ἐναντίον γενέσθαι D.18.313: folld. by a relat. clause, φ. ἑαυτὸν ὅπως μὴ ἀδικήσει Pl.*Grg.*480a; φύλαττέ με μὴ παρακρούσωμαί σε Id.*Cra.*393c; φ. τινά, εἰ.. Id.*Smp.*220d:—Pass., *to be watched, kept under guard,* Hdt.3.45, X.*An.*6.4.27. 2. *watch for, lie in wait* or *ambush for,* αὐτὸν ἰόντα λοχήσομαι ἠδὲ φυλάξω ἐν πορθμῷ Ἰθάκης Od.4.670; νόστον φ. Il.2.251; φ. τὸ σύμβολον *look out for* the signal-fire, A.*Ag.*8; τοὺς πολεμίους X.*Lac.* 12.2; φ. τοὺς παράνομα γράφοντας D.58.34; *keep a watch on,* [τινα] Lys.1.6; τοὺς παραβαίνοντας Arist.*Pol.*1289$^{a}$19. b. esp. *watch, wait for, observe* an appointed time or a fixed event, τὴν κυρίην τῶν ἡμερέων Hdt.1.48; φ. τὴν ἡμέραν Antipho 6.37; φυλάξαντες νύκτα *wait for* night, Th.2.3; φυλάσσουσι γραφόμενοι τὸ ἀποβαῖνον Hdt.2.82; τοὺς ἐτησίας D.4.31: with a part. added, δείλην ὀψίην γινομένην φυλάξαντες Hdt.8.9: φ. Ξέρξην.. δεῖπνον προτιθέμενον Id.9.110; ἀριστοποιουμένους φ. τοὺς στρατιώτας D. 23.165: folld. by a relat. clause, φ. ὅ τι χρήσεται.. Hdt.5.12. 3. metaph., *preserve, maintain, cherish,* [χόλον] Il.16.30; αἰδῶ καὶ φιλότητα 24.111; ὅρκια 3.280; φ. ἔπος *observe* a command, 16.686; φ. ῥῆμα Pi.*I.*2.9; τελετάς Id.*O.*3.41; νόμον S.*Tr.*616; τοὺς νόμους Pl. *Plt.*292a, cf. *Grg.*461d, etc.; τὸ σὸν πιστόν S.*OC*626; τὰς συνθήκας Isoc.17.20; τὰ τοῦ γάμου δίκαια *POxy.*905.9 (ii A.D.); λόγον πρός τινα *PFlor.*56.21 (iii A.D., Pass.); φ. σιγήν E.*IA*542; οὐ γὰρ ἀπειλὰς ὑμετέρας ἐφύλαξα I *regarded* not your threats, Call.*Del.*204; φ. σκαιοσύναν *cling to* it, *foster* it, S.*OC*1213 (lyr.); ἄξια ἤθη E.*Ion*736; φ. τῇ μνήμῃ τὰ λεχθέντα Pl.*Lg.*783c; φ. τὸν θυμὸν ib.867a; τὴν τιμωρίαν D.21.40; φ. καὶ ταμιεύειν πάντα τινί Lys.19.40; τὸ μέρος τοῖς θεοῖς X.*An.*5.3.4; τἀγαθά, opp. κτήσασθαι, D.1.23; μᾶλα ἐν κόλποισι Theoc.2.120, cf. 7.64; εἰ μὴ φυλάσσεις μίκρ', ἀπολεῖς τὰ μείζονα Men. *Mon.*172; ἀθάνατον ἔχθραν μὴ φύλαττε ib.4: with a predic. added, φ. τινὰ δεδεμένον Antipho 5.47; ἀδέκαστον φ. τὴν διάνοιαν D.H.*Thuc.* 34; ἀκύμαντον τὸ πέλαγος Luc.*D.Mar.*5.1:—Pass., ὅσος παρ' ὑμῖν ὁ φθόνος φυλάττεται *is fostered* by.., S.*OT*382. 4. *keep* in a place, *continue in,* τόδε δῶμα φυλάσσοις, ἀθάνατός τ' εἴης Od.5.208. 5. *notice, observe,* Ath.l.c. 6. *maintain, hold fast to* a view, τινὰ σπουδαῖον εἶναι Plot.1.4.9. 7. c. acc., *beware of, avoid,* ἅπαντα ταῦτα φυλάττειν κελεύει Gal.18(2).791. 8. φ. μή c. subj., *take care* lest.. E.*IA*145 (anap.), Pl.*Tht.*154d; φ. ἐμὲ καὶ τηρεῖν ὅπως μή.. D.18.276. 9. Med., φυλάξασθε τοῦ ἀγαπᾶν Κύριον *be careful to*.., LXX *Jo.*23.11.

**C.** Med., I. abs., *to be on one's guard, keep watch,* Ar.*Ec.* 769; used by Hom. only in part., νύκτα φυλασσομένοισι Il.10.188; πεφυλαγμένος εἶναι to be *cautious, prudent,* 23.343, cf. X.*HG*7.5.9; φυλαττομένους πορεύεσθαι *with caution,* Id.*Cyr.*5.2.30, cf. *Cyn.*10. 10. 2. c. acc., *keep* a thing *by one, bear* it *in mind* or *memory,* Hes. *Op.*263,561; more fully, ἐν θυμῷ δ' εὖ πάντα φυλάσσεο ib.491; φρεσὶ *h.Ap.*544, cf. Pi.*O.*7.40; τὰ λελεγμένα S.*El.*1012. 3. *guard, keep safe,* καὶ κεφαλὴν πεφύλαξο Orac.ap.Hdt.7.148. 4. c. gen., φυλάσσεσθαι τῶν νεῶν μὴ ξυντρίψωσιν *act cautiously* with regard to the ships, Th.4.11; *beware of,* τῶν εὖ φύλαξαι S.*OC*161 (lyr.); Ἄρκτοι πεφυλαγμέναι ὠκεανοῖο Arat.48; πεφύλαξο παντοίων ἀνέμων Id. 930. II. φυλάσσεσθαί τι or τινα *to beware of, be on one's guard against, avoid* a thing or person, Sapph.27, etc.: ταῦτα Hdt.1. 108, 7.130, cf. Ar.*Ra.*4; τινας A.*Pr.*715,804; τοὺς Ἀτρείδας εἰσορῶν φυλάξομαι S.*Ph.*455; τέττιξ ποιμένας.. πεφυλαγμένος Theoc.16. 95. b. ἐφυλαξάμην διαλέκτους I *put in as a precaution* 'except in dialects', Hdn.Gr.2.932. 2. φ. πρός τι Th.7.69; ἀπό τινος X.*Cyr.*2.3.9, *HG*7.2.10. 3. c. inf., φυλάξομαι δὲ τάσδε μεμνῆσθαι.. ἐφετμάς A.*Supp.*205, cf. Ocell.4.13; φ. μηδὲν ἐξαμαρτεῖν Hdt.1.108, cf. D.25.11; φ. μηδένα βαλεῖν Antipho 3.4.7; but also without μή, ἵνα.. τις ὕστερον φυλάσσηται ἐπὶ γῆν τὴν σὴν στρατεύεσθαι Hdt.7.5; φ. τὸ λυπῆσαι D.18.258; φ. δρᾶσθαι Arist.*HA*611$^{a}$28, cf. D.H.1.70; λέγειν Arist.*Rh.Al.*1441$^{b}$20:—two constructions joined, δισσὰ γὰρ φυλάσσεται [ψυχή], φίλων τε μέμψιν κἀς θεοὺς ἁμαρτάνειν S.*Fr.*472. 4. φ. μή folld. by subj., *take care* lest.., τούτου φυλάσσου μή ποτ' ἀχθεσθῇ κέαρ A.*Pr.*392, cf. *Supp.*498, E.*IT*67, Ar. *Ach.*257, X.*An.*2.2.16, etc.; so φ. ὅπως μή.. Id.*Mem.*1.2.37; ὡς ἐγὼ φυλάξομαι.. μὴ κατουρήσωσί μου Ar.*Ec.*831, cf. X.*Mem.*2.2.14.

**φῡλετ-εύω,** *adopt into a tribe,* ξένους καὶ μετοίκους Arist.*Pol.*1275$^{b}$ 37. **-ης,** ου, ὁ, (φυλή) *one of the same tribe, fellow-tribesman,* Antipho 6.13, And.1.150, Pl.*Lg.*955d, *IG*2$^{2}$.1165.26, 1749.71, *SIG*1023.49 (Cos, iii/ii B.C.); ὦ φυλέτα Ar.*Ach.*568 (lyr.): as Adj., φ. χορός the chorus *of one's tribe,* *IG*2$^{2}$.3114. ⊕ **-ικός,** ή, όν, *of* or *for a* φυλέτης, δικαστήρια, δίκαι, Pl.*Lg.*768c, 915c; φ. φιλίαι Arist.*EN*1161$^{b}$13. Adv. **-κῶς** *like tribesmen,* Id.*SE*164$^{a}$27. 2. = Lat. *tributus,* φ. ἐκκλησία = *comitia tributa,* D.H.7.59; ἡ φ. (sc. ἐκκλησία) App.*BC* 3.30; φ. ἀρχαιρεσίαι D.C.53.23. II. *belonging to a* φυλή, γέαι *BSA*22.212 (Mylasa).

**φῡλή,** ἡ, (φύω) prop., like φῦλον, *a race, tribe*; but acc. to Dicaearch.Hist.9 *a union formed in an organized community* (whether πόλις or ἔθνος): hence, *tribe,* i.e. I. *a body* of men *united* 1. *by supposed ties of blood and descent, clan,* such as the three Dorian *tribes,* Rhetra ap.Plu.*Lyc.*6, Hdt.5.68, St.Byz. s. vv. Ὑλλεῖς, Δυμᾶνες, *IG*4.596 (Argos); of the four Ionic *tribes,* Hdt.5. 69, Arist.*Ath.*8.3, Plu.*Sol.*19, etc.; of the Laconian, Hdt.4.145; of the old Roman, D.H.2.7, etc.; of the Persian, X.*Cyr.*1.2.5 and 12; of the Jewish, LXX *Nu.*1.4, al. (but also of subdivisions of the tribe (σκῆπτρον), ib.1*Ki.*10.20.21), *Ev.Matt.*19.28, etc. 2. *by local habitation,* such as the ten local *tribes* at Athens formed by Cleisthenes, Hdt.5.69, 6.131, *IG*1$^{2}$.10.44, al.; or those formed by Servius at Rome, φ. τοπικαί, opp. γενικαί, D.H.4.14, cf. Plu. *Rom.*20; in Roman Egypt, *BGU*1113.3 (i B.C.), *PFlor.*39.4 (iv A.D.), etc., cf. (in general) Arist.*Pol.*1264$^{a}$8, 1300$^{a}$25, 1309$^{a}$12, Pl. *Lg.*753c, etc. 3. *subdivision of the priests in each Egyptian temple,* *OGI*56.24 (Canopus, iii B.C.), *PAmh.*2.112.7 (ii A.D.), etc. II. *military contingent furnished by a tribe,* among the Athenians, Hdt.6.111, *IG*1$^{2}$.1085; ὁπλιτῶν Th.6.98, cf. 3.90, X.*HG* 4.2.19, Pl.*Lg.*755c,d; ταξίαρχος εἰς τὴν φυλὴν καταστάξας Lys.13. 79. 2. *representatives of a tribe,* on political bodies, φυλῆς πρυτανευούσης, προεδρευούσης, *IG*1.26$^{a}$16, *SIG*589.2 (Magn.Mae., ii B.C.), etc. III. of things, = γένος, *kind, species,* κατὰ φυλὰς διεκρίνομεν τὰ ἔπιπλα X.*Oec.*9.6.

**φυληρις,** = Lat. *cercedula* (i.e. *querquedula*), *Gloss.* (s.v.l.).

**φῡλία,** poet. -ίη, ἡ, a tree mentioned with the olive in Od.5.477 (δοιοὺς.. θάμνους, ἐξ ὁμόθεν πεφυῶτας—ὁ μὲν φυλίης, ὁ δ' ἐλαίης), apptly. (cf. Sch.ad loc., Hsch.) a kind of *wild olive,* but distd. fr. κότινος and said to be Troezenian by Paus.2.32.10 (written φυλλία), cf. Philostr.*Gym.*43, Nonn.*D.*5.474; wrongly identified by Ammon. *Diff.* p.135V. with σχῖνος.

**φύλιος** [ῠ], α, ον, *of a tribe,* θεοί Poll.8.110.

⊕**φυλλ-άζω,** = *frondesco,* *Gloss.* **-άκανθος** [ᾰκ], ον, *with prickly leaves,* Thphr.*HP*1.10.7, 6.1.3. **-άμπελον,** τό, = *pampinus,* *Gloss.* **-αναλογημός,** = *racematio,* ib. **-ανθές,** τό, a plant-name, perh. *Anthemis chia,* cj. in Thphr.*HP*7.8.3, cf. Plin.*HN* 21.99; also **-άνθιον,** τό, Ps.-Democr.Alch.p.42 B. **-άριον,** τό, Dim. of φύλλον, *Inscr.Délos* 1441 *A* ii 67 (ii B.C.), Dsc.1.4, 3.158: metaph., φυλλάρια.. τὰ τεκνία σου M.Ant.10.34. **-άς,** άδος, ἡ, as Adj., *leafy,* λόχμη Nonn.*D.*21.340. II. usu. as Subst., *heap, bed,* or *litter of leaves,* φυλλάδα ἐπιβαλών Hdt.8.24; φ. στιπτή S.*Ph.*33, cf. Bion 1.69, A.R.1.1183, etc. 2. *foliage,* ῥίζης γὰρ οὔσης φ. ἵκετ' A.*Ag.*966; φ. μυριόκαρπος, of a thick grove, S.*OC*676 (lyr.); τεμενία φ. Id.*Tr.*754; φ. Παρνασία E.*Andr.*1100: metaph., φυλλάδος ἤδη κατακαρφομένης A.*Ag.*79 (anap.); also, *leafy branch,* E.*Supp.*32, Ar.*V.*398 (anap.); κλισίαι ἐκ φυλλάδος D.S.19.22, cf. Str.16.4.13, etc.: pl., *Gp.*3.10.6, etc. 3. *salad,* Mnesim.4.31 (anap.), Diphil. 18.4, cf. Poll.6.71. **-εῖν·** ἀδολεσχεῖν, Hsch. **-εῖον,** τό, mostly in pl., *green-stuff, small herbs,* such as mint and parsley, that were given into the bargain, Ar.*Ach.*469; φυλλεῖα ῥαφανίδων radish-*tops,* Id.*Pl.* 544 (anap.). **-ες·** ἀλώπεκες, Hsch. **-ία,** v. φυλία. **-ΐάς·** θρία, Id. **-ΐάω,** *run to leaf* without fruiting, φυλλιῶσαι Arat.333. **-ίζω,** *strip of leaves,* *Gp.*5.2.12 (Pass.). 2. *strip of petals,* interpol. in

Orib.5.33.6. ⊛ **-ικός**, ή, όν, *of a leaf*, βλάστησις Thphr.*HP*3.5.5. 2. *leaf-like*, σφαιρίον ib.3.7.5. II. Φυλλικός (sc. μήν), ὁ, name of a month in Thessaly, *IG*9(2).224.4 (Angeae), 562.5 (Larissa). ⊛ **-ίνης**, ου, ὁ, *where the prize is a wreath of leaves*, ἀγῶνες Poll.3.153, Hsch.: also **φυλλιναίους** ἀγῶνας *EM*802.38. **-ινος**, η, ον, *made of leaves*, τοῖχος Theoc.21.8; στέφανος Luc.*Merc.Cond.*13. **-ιον**, τό, Dim. of φύλλον, Pl.Com.171, Aristid.1.283 J., Poll.6.94: pl., = ἡδύσματα κηπαῖα, Hp.ap.Gal.19.153. 2. perh. a kind of *plate*, φ. ἀργυρᾶ ὀκτώ *PLond.*1.191.11 (ii A.D.). **-ίς**, ίδος, ἡ, = φυλλάς II. 2, *Gp.*7.18.1. 2. = φυλλῖτις, Ps.-Dsc.3.107. II. *salad*, Heraclid. Tar.ap.Ath.3.120d. **-ῖτις**, ιδος, ἡ, *hart's-tongue, Scolopendrium officinale*, Dsc.3.107.

**Φυλλιών**, ῶνος, ὁ, name of month at Iasos, *Rev.Ét.Gr.*6.172.

**φυλλοβολ-έω**, *shed the leaves*, Ar.*Nu.*1007 (anap.), Arist.*GA*783ᵇ10, 784ᵃ12, Thphr.*HP*1.9.6, Call.*Epigr.*44.3. II. *pelt with leaves*, θεάν (sc. Demeter) Philic. in *Stud.Ital.*9.48, cf. Hdn.8.7.2; ῥόδοις, ἴοις, στεφάνοις, Charito 3.8:—Pass., Ph.2.589, Hdn.7.10.8, Sch.E. *Hec.*574. **-ία**, ἡ, *shedding of the leaves*, Thphr.*HP*1.9.6. II. *pelting with leaves or leafy crowns*, as a token of applause bestowed on winners in the games, Eratosth.ap.Sch.E.*Hec.*574. **-ος** (parox.), ον, *shedding leaves*, Thphr.*HP*1.9.3. 2. φυλλόβολα, τά, *fallen leaves*, *IG*2².1362.7.

**φυλλό-κομος**, ον, *thick-leaved*, μῖλαξ Ar.*Av.*215 (anap.); μελία ib.742 (lyr.) **-κόπος**, = *frondator*, Gloss. **-κρίνω**, f.l. for φυλοκρινέω (q.v.). **-λογέω**, *strip the leaves off*, τὴν συκῆν Poll.7.143, cf. *PHamb.*23.27 (vi A.D.), Gloss. **-λογία**, ἡ, *thinning of foliage*, *POxy.*1692.20 (ii A.D.), 1631.13 (pl., iii A.D.). **-λόγος**, ὁ, *leaf-picker, one who thins foliage*, *PLond.*1821.384. **-μᾰνέω**, *run to leaf*, without seeding, Thphr.*HP*8.7.4. **-μᾰνής**, ές, *running to leaf*, Sch. rec. S.*Aj.*143, *EM*474.51.

⊛**φύλλον**, τό, *leaf*; in Ep. and Hdt. always in pl. *leaves*, or collectively *foliage*, φύλλα καὶ ὄζους Il.1.234, al.; φύλλα δ' ἔραζε χέει Hes. *Op.*421; τὰ φ. καταδρέποντες κατήσθιον Hdt.8.115; ὅσσα τε χθὼν ἠρινὰ φ. ἀναπέμπει Pi.*P.*9.46; ψυχὰς ἔδάη..οἷά τε φύλλ' ἄνεμος δονεῖ B.5.65; sg., S.*OC*701 (lyr.), Thphr.*HP.*1.10.6, etc.; οἵη περ φύλλων γενεή, τοίη δὲ καὶ ἀνδρῶν Il.6.146, cf. Mimn.2.1; φύλλων γενεᾷ προσόμοιοι Ar.*Av.*685 (anap.); φύλλοις βάλλειν E.*Hec.*574; πλεκτὰ φύλλα wreathed *leaves*, Id.*Hipp.*807; φύλλον ἐλαίας, poet. for ἐλάα, S.l.c.: metaph. of choral songs, φύλλ' ἀοιδᾶν Pi.*I.*4(3).27; of *leaves* used as *voting-papers*, *IG*12(5).595*A*12 (Ceos, iii/ii B.C.). 2. of flowers, *petal*, [ῥόδον] ἔχον ἑξήκοντα φύλλα Hdt.8.138; ὑακίνθινα φ., λειμώνια φ., Theoc.11.26, 18.39. II. *plant*, in general, φ. ὃν ἐπινηχόμενον τῷ ὕδατι Dsc.1.12, cf. Numen.ap.Ath.9.371b; ἡ κατὰ φύλλον (with or without γεωμετρία) survey according to *plants*, i.e. *crops* grown, *PTeb.*38.3, 78.4 (ii B.C.): ποτίσαι εἰς φύλλον ib.72.362, 105.32 (ii B.C.): esp. of medicinal *herbs*, φ. εἴ τι νώδυνον κάτοιδε S.*Ph.*44; ἠπίοισι φ. ib.698 (lyr.), cf. 649. 2. as a name of definite species: a. = βρυωνία, *dog Mercury, Mercurialis perennis*, Thphr.*HP*9.18.5, Dsc.3.125. b. the leaf-like fruit of silphium, Hp.*Nat.Mul.*72, Thphr.*HP*6.3.1, Polyaen.4.3.32. c. = λευκάκανθα, Dsc.3.19.

**φυλλο-ρόος**, ον, *leaf-shedding*, φθινόπωρον Opp.*C.*1.116. **-ρροέω**, *shed the leaves*, Hp.*Insomn.*90, Pherecr.130.10 (anap., φυλλοροήσει, metri gr.), Arist.*APo.*98ᵃ37, Thphr.*HP*3.13.5, *CP*2.19.2, Dsc.1 *Prooem.*9, 4.143, Plu.2.366e, Pap. in *Hermes* 40.548: metaph., of *becoming bald*, Arist.*GA*783ᵇ17; Com., ἀσπίδας φ. *shed, drop* one's shields, Ar.*Av.*1481 (lyr.). **-ρροια**, ἡ, *falling of the leaves*, Thphr. *HP*3.13.4, *CP*2.19.2. **-σκεπος**, ον, *covered with leaves*, v. φιλόσκεπος. **-στάφῠλον** [ᾰ], τό, = κάππαρις, f.l. for ὀφιοστ- in Ps.-Dsc. 2.173. **-στρωτος**, ον, *made of leafy branches*, χαμεῦναι E.*Rh.*9 (anap.): *leaf-strewn*, heterocl. dat. φυλλοστρῶτι πέδῳ Theoc.*Epigr.*3. **-τόκος**, ον, *producing leaves*, Opp.*C.*1.116. **-τόμος**, ον, *cutting off leaves*, Gloss. **-τρώξ**, ῶγος, ὁ, ἡ, (τρώγω) *nibbling or eating leaves*, Antiph.172.2 (anap.). **-φορέω**, *bear leaves*, Thphr.*CP*3.9.2. **-φόρος**, ον, *bearing leaves*, φ. ἀγῶνες, = φυλλῖναι ἀγῶνες, Pi.*O.*8.76; later in literal sense, Dsc.4.146. **-φυέω**, *put forth leaves*, Gloss. **-χοέω**, *shed leaves*, Plu.2.735b, Phryn.*PS* p.123 B.; φ. κόμην *AP*7.141.6 (Antiphil.). **-χόος**, ον, *shedding the leaves*, φ. μήν the *leaf-shedding month*, Hes.*Fr.*240 (fort. μείς, as in Call.*Hec.*1.1.12), A.R.4.217, cf. Him.*Or.*9.1, Eust.1555.6: pl., Plu.2.734d, 735d.

**φυλλ-όω**, *clothe with leaves*, Hp.*Nat.Puer.*23 (Pass.). **-ώδης**, ες, *like leaves*, Thphr.*HP*1.13.1; σπέρμα Dsc.3.80. 2. *belonging to leaves*, δυνάμεις Thphr.*HP*9.8.1. II. *having petalled flowers*, ib.7.8.3. **-ωμα**, ατος, τό, *foliage*, D.S.3.19 (pl.).

**φῡλοβᾰσῐλ-εύς**, έως, ὁ, *a* βασιλεύς *chosen from each* φυλή to perform sacrifices, *Hesperia* 4.21 (Athens, iv B.C.), Arist.*Ath.*8.3, al., *IG*2².1357, Poll.8.111, 120, Hsch. **-ικά** (sc. χρήματα), τά, *funds at the disposal of the* φυλοβασιλεῖς, *IG*2².1357, *Hesperia* 4.21 (Athens, iv B.C.).

**φῡλοκρῐνέω**, *make distinctions of tribe*, εἰ..φυλοκρινοῖεν οἷς χρεὼν βοηθεῖν Th.6.18; ἐλέγχθη τὸ μὴ φυλοκρινεῖν πρὸς τοὺς ἐξετάζειν τὰ γένη βουλομένους Arist.*Ath.*21.2: hence metaph., *classify*, Luc.*Abd.*4, *Phal.*2.9; also, *distinguish precisely*, ἕκαστον ὁποῖόν ἐστι S.E.*M.*7.183; cf. Phryn.*PS* p.123 B., Poll.8.110, etc. II. *select carefully*, τὸ βουλευτικὸν πᾶν καὶ φ. καὶ διαλέξαι D.C.52.19, cf. Aristid. 1.218 J. (s.v.l.). III. *pick out*, ἀπὸ τῶν φαύλων τοὺς χρηστούς Lib.*Or.*16.51, cf. Porph.*Phil.Hist.Fr.*11; τὰς ἐξ ἡλίου καὶ σελήνης προϊούσας εἰς τὴν γένεσιν ποιήσεις παρατηρητικῶς φ. Procl. *in Cra.* p.74 P. (φιλοκρινέω is freq. f.l.; φυλλοκρίνειν Hsch.)

**φῦλον**, τό, (φύω) *race, tribe*, or *class*, οὔ ποτε φ. ὁμοῖον ἀθανάτων τε θεῶν χαμαὶ ἐρχομένων τ' ἀνθρώπων Il.5.441; γυναικῶν φῦλον Hes.*Th.*1021; θεῶν ἐς φῦλον ib.202, cf. 965, *Op.*199: φῦλον ἀοιδῶν Od.8.481: in Ep. more freq. in pl., φῦλα ἀνθρώπων, θεῶν, Il. 14.361, 15.54; φῦλα γυναικῶν, ἐπικούρων, Γιγάντων, 9.130, 17.220, Od.7.206; ἄγρια φῦλα, μυίας Il.19.30; φῦλα μελισσέων, of a *swarm* of bees, Hes. *Fr.*14.5; in later Poets and Prose usu. in sg. (but pl., φ. ποικίλα θηρῶν Ar.*Av.*777 (lyr.); φῦλα πόντου, of fishes, E.*Fr.*27 (lyr.)), φ. ματαιότατον Pi.*P.*3.21; ἓν φ. ἀνθρώπων S.*Fr.*591.1 (lyr.); τὸ ἄλλο φ. the rest of the *people*, Id.*OT*19; φῦλον ὀρνίθων *the race* of birds, Id.*Ant.*342 (lyr.), cf. Ar.*Av.*231, 253 (both lyr.): πτηνῶν ib.1088 (lyr.); τὸ πτηνὸν φ. Pl.*Sph.*220b; τὸ κηρυκικὸν φ. Id.*Plt.*260d, cf. *Cra.*398e; τὸ φ...οὐ..ῥᾷστον συλλαβεῖν τί ποτ' ἐστίν, ὁ σοφιστής the sophist *tribe*, Id.*Sph.*218c; κατὰ Ὅμηρον καὶ Ἡράκλειτον καὶ πᾶν τὸ τοιοῦτον φ. and all the *tribe* of them, Id.*Tht.*160d; φ. ἀμφορεαφόρων Eup.187; φ. βουλευτικόν, = Lat. *ordo senatorius*, D.C.59.9: metaph., φ. τῶν ἡδονῶν Luc.*Nigr.*16. 2. *sex*, τὸ γυναικεῖον φ. Ar.*Th.*786 (anap.); τὸ θῆλυ, τὸ ἄρρεν, X.*Lac.*1.4. II. *nation*, φῦλα Πελασγῶν Il.2.840; κελαινὸν φ., of the Aethiopians, A.*Pr.*808, cf. *Supp.*544 (lyr.); βάρβαρα φ. E.*IT*887 (lyr.); Σύρους, φῦλον πάμπολυ X.*Cyr.*1.5.2; πολεμικώτατα φ. Plu.*Sull.*29. III. = φυλή II. 1, *clan* or *tribe*, acc. to blood or descent, κρῖν' ἄνδρας κατὰ φῦλα, κατὰ φρήτρας Il.2.362, cf. 363; φῦλον Ἑλένης, φῦλον Ἀρκεισίου, Od.14.68, 181; φ. τρία τριῶν στρατευμάτων E.*Supp.*653.

**φύλοπις** [ῠ], ιδος, acc. ιδα and ιν (v. infr.), ἡ, *battle-cry, din of battle*, freq. in Hom., ἔγειρε δὲ φύλοπιν αἰνήν Il.5.496, cf. 4.65, al.; φυλόπιδα στήσειν πολέμοιο Od.11.314, cf. Hes.*Sc.*114, Il.13.635; πόλεμος καὶ φ. 4.15, 82; νεῖκος φυλόπιδος 20.141.—Ep. word, used once by S.*El.*1072 (lyr.), and in a mock oracle, Ar.*Pax*1076: pl., φυλόπιδας προτέρων ὕμνησαν ἀοιδοί Theoc.16.50.

**φῡλώδης**, ες, *of many races*, πλῆθος νεοσύλλογον καὶ φ. D.S. 34/5.6.

**φῦμα**, ατος, τό, (φύω) *growth*, ἐπανεκλήθη ὡς ἐς φῦμα ζωῆς *beginning of a fresh* life, Aret.*SD*2.13: but usu., II. *that which grows*, Archil.136; freq. of diseased growths, *tumour, tubercle*, etc., Hdt.3.133, Hp.*VM*22, Pl.*Ti.*85c, Thphr.*HP*9.11.1, *Od.*59, *IG*4²(1).123.4 (Epid., iv B.C.), etc.; φῦμα φύειν, φῦμα φύεται, Hp.*Prorrh.* 2.10, 11. [ῡ Archil. l.c.; φῠμάτεσσι only late, Marc.Sid.83.]

**φῡμᾰτ-ίας**, ου, ὁ, *one who has tumours*, φ. σκληρῶν φυμάτων Hp. *Art.*41, cf. Ruf.ap.Orib.7.26.9. **-ιον**, τό, Dim. of φῦμα, Hp.*Mul.*2.133, Ruf.ap.Orib.7.26.15. **-όομαι**, Pass., *have tumours*, Hp.*Epid.*5.59, 7.81. **-ώδης**, ες, *full of tumours*, σκέλεα Id.*Acut.*(*Sp.*)26.

**φῦν, φῦναι**, v. φύω.

**φύξ**, coined as nom. to φύγαδε, *EM*802.46, Eust.1080.17.

**φυξᾰνορία**, ἡ, *aversion to wedlock*, prob. for φυλαξάνοραν (sic) in A. *Supp.*8 (anap.).

**φυξήλιος**, ον, *shunning the sun*, Nic.*Th.*660.

⊛**φύξηλις**, ιος and ιδος, ὁ, ἡ, *cowardly*, φύξηλιν ἐόντα Il.17.143, cf. Nic.*Al.*472, Lyc.943.

**φυξίμηλα** [ῐ] δένδρα, τά, trees *that have grown too large to be hurt by sheep* (μῆλα), A.*Fr.*447, cf. Plu.2.293a.

⊛**φύξῐμος**, ον, (φεύγω) older and poet. form of φεύξιμος, of places, *whither one can flee*, or *where one can take refuge*, ὅθι μοι φάτο φύξιμον εἶναι where she said it was *possible* for me *to escape*, Od.5.359; φ. τόπος Plb.13.6.9; φύξιμον οὐδέν Id.9.29.4; ἱερὸν φ. *an asylum*, Plu.*Rom.*9; φ. λιμήν a harbour *of refuge*, Id.2.823a: cf. φύξιον. II. *which one can escape*; hence, *affording a chance of recovery*, νοῦσος Hp.*Int.*2; *avoidable*, ἦμαρ Max.358. 2. *which one would flee from*, i.e. *loathsome*, ὀδμή Simon.250, Nic.*Th.*54 (s.v.l.). III. c. acc., σ' ἀθανάτων φύξιμος οὐδείς is *able to escape* thee, S.*Ant.*788 (lyr.).

**φύξιον**, τό, f.l. for φύξιμον, *place of refuge*, Plu.*Thes.*36.

⊛**φύξιος**, ον, *of banishment*, οἶτος A.R.4.699. 2. *putting to flight*, epith. of Zeus, Apollod.1.9.1, cf. Lyc.288, Paus.2.21.2, *Supp. Epigr.*7.894.9 (Gerasa, i A.D.); of Apollo, Philostr.*Her.*10.4, Suid.

**φυξίπολις** [ξῐ], εως, ὁ, ἡ, *fleeing the city, banished*, Opp.*H.*1.278.

**φύξις**, εως, ἡ, older and poet. form of φεῦξις, = φυγή, Il.10.311, 447. II. *refuge, escape*, θανάτου Nic.*Th.*588.

⊛**φύος**, τό, = φύτευμα, Hsch. (φυός cod.).

**φύππαξ**, = πύππαξ, Hsch.

**φυράδην**, Adv., a doubtful word (vv. ll. φύρδην, φρούδην), τὸ φ. καὶ ῥύδην οὐκ οἶδα εἰ ἀνεκτά Poll.6.175 (fort. φοράδην).

**φύρακες**· ἐλαφροί, Hsch. (fort. φύζακες· ἐλαφοί).

**φύρ-ᾱμα** [ῡ], ατος, τό, *that which is mixed* or *kneaded, dough*, Mnesim.4.11 (anap.), Arist.*Pr.*929ᵃ25, Lxx *Ex.*8.3 (7.28), 12.34, al., *Ep.Gal.*5.9, *Ep.Rom.*9.21, al.; in brewing, *PTeb.*401.27 (i A.D.); generally, *paste*, κονίας καὶ βολβίτου φ. *Gp.*15.2.8; καλάμου Dsc.1.55; opp. θραῦσμα, Id.3.84: metaph., of the human frame as *a mixture, compound*, Ph.1.184, M.Ant.7.68. 2. generally, *mixture*, σύμμιγμα καὶ φ. ἀέρος καὶ πυρός Plu.2.922a, etc.: in pl., *cements*, ib.811c. ⊛ **-ᾱματικά**, τά, = κονιατικά, *Jahresh.*28.58 (Aphrodisias). ⊛ **-ᾱσις**, εως, Ion. **φύρησις**, ιος, ἡ, *mixing*, Lxx *Ho.*7.4, Aret. *CA*2.3; ἀρωμάτων Dsc.1.58; *mixture*, Gal.6.342. **-ᾱτέον**, *one must mix, knead*, Dsc.5.88. **-ᾱτής**, οῦ, ὁ, *mixer*, i.e. '*cooker*' of accounts, Cic.*Att.*6.9.2, 7.1.9; = Lat. *decoctor, fraudulent debtor*, Gloss.; dub. sens. in *Jahresh.*1 *Beibl.*75 (Ephesus). **-ᾱτός**, ή, όν, *kneaded*, ἄρτος Sor.2.10. **-άω**, 3 pl. φυρῶσι Hdt.2.36: fut. -άσω [ᾱ] A.*Th.*48: aor. ἐφύρᾱσα Pl.*Ti.*73e, Ion. -ησα Hp.*Fist.*10: pf. πεφύρᾱκα Cic.*Att.*6.4.3, 6.5.1:—Med., aor. ἐφυρᾱσάμην Ar.*Nu.*979

(anap.); Ion. -ησάμην Nic.*Th.*932:—**Pass.**, aor. ἐφυράθην [ᾰ] Pl. *Tht.*147c, *APl.*4.191 (Nicaen.); Ion. -ήθην *AP*7.748 (Antip.Sid.): pf. πεφύραμαι, Ion. -ημαι (v. infr.):—lengthd. form of φύρω (but almost limited to the sense of *mixing* flour and similar substances), φ. τὸ σταῖς τοῖσι ποσί Hdt. l. c.; οἴνῳ φυρήσας Hp. l. c., cf. *PHolm.*4.9; εἰς ὕδωρ φ. ib.6.18; φ. μετὰ ὑδραργύρου ib.4.35; μᾶζαν φ. Hp. *Vict.*2.40; οἱ φυρῶντες *bread-kneaders*, X.*HG*7.2.22; γῆν τήνδε φυράσειν φόνῳ *to make* earth *into a* bloody *paste*, A. l. c.; γῆν.. ἐφύρασε καὶ ἔδευσε μυελῷ Pl.*Ti.*73e: Pass., ἄρτος πολλῷ ὕδατι πεφυρημένος Hp.*VM*14; ἰσχυρῶς πεφ. ibid.; οἴνῳ καὶ ἐλαίῳ ἄλφιτα πεφυραμένα (v. l. πεφυρμένα) Th.3.49; γῆ ὑγρῷ φυραθεῖσα πηλὸς ἂν εἴη Pl.*Tht.* 147c. 2. metaph., μαλακὴν φυρασάμενος τὴν φωνὴν πρὸς τὸν ἐραστὴν ἐβάδιζεν *making one's* voice *supple*, i.e. *soft*, towards one's lover, Ar. l. c.; πολέεσσι πεφύρησαι χαλεποῖσι, θυμέ *art confounded by..* Philet.7.1; πεφυρακέναι τὰς ψήφους *to have cooked* the accounts, Cic. ll. cc. -δην, Dor. **φύρδαν** S.*Fr.*210.39 (lyr.), *AP*7.531 (Antip. Thess.):—Adv. *in utter confusion*, A.*Pers.*812; φ. μάχεσθαι X.*Cyr.* 7.1.37; σεσωρεῦσθαι Plb.16.8.9; πάντα εἰκῇ καὶ φ. ἐπράττετο Id.30. 11.6; σύρει φ. drags *headlong*, S. l. c. 2. (φύρω I) *with defilement*, σίδαρον.. φ. μεστὸν ἔχουσα φόνου *AP*l. c.; φ. τείρων φῶτας ἐκβιάζεται Keil-Premerstein *Erster Bericht* p.9.

⊛**φύρκος**, τό, Dor. **φοῦρκος**, = τεῖχος, Hsch., who also has **φύρκορ**· ὀχύρωμα, and **φυρκηλῖται** (-εῖτοι cod.)· τειχήρεις.

**φύρμα**, ατος, τό, *mixture, dung, filth*, Nic.*Al.*485 (pl.), *Th.*723.

**φυρμᾶται**· πτάρνυται, Hsch.

**φυρμός**, ὁ, *mixture, confused mass, disorder*, D.S.18.30, M.Ant. 12.14; φ. καὶ σύγχυσις τῶν κατὰ νόμους δικαίων D.S.36.11; ἀνθρώπων ὁμοῦ καὶ πραγμάτων Ph.*Fr.*33 H.: metaph., 'a pretty kettle of fish', Cic.*Att.*14.5.1.

**φυροῖ**· μολύνει, ῥυποῖ, Hsch.

⊛**φυρός**, ά, όν, = sq., βοῦς *PGen.*48.8 (iv A. D.); perh. cf. Hsch. s. v. φυρτίζεσθαι.

⊛**φυρόχρωμος**, ον, dub. sens. (of the colour of a cow), *PBaden* 19.5 (ii A. D.).

**φύρ-σιμος**, ον, *mixed up*, Nic.*Al.*324. -σις, εως, ἡ, *mixing, kneading*, ἀλεύρου καὶ ὕδατος Sch.D.T.p.215 H.

**φυρτήτης** (leg. -ίτης)· οἶνος, Hsch. **φυρτίζεσθαι**· τὸ παίζειν συνεστραμμένοις φυροῖς τοῖς ἱματίοις, Id. **φυρτός**, ή, όν, *mixed, kneaded up*, Id.

**φύρω** [ῡ], Hes.*Op.*61, Pl.*Phd.*97b: impf. ἔφυρον Il.24.162, A.*Pr.* 450: fut. φύρσω Pi.*Pae.*2.73, Hsch.: aor. subj. φύρσω Od.18.21, inf. φύρσαι A.R.2.59; later ἔφυρα *AP*7.476 (Mel.), Luc.*Prom.*13:—Med., aor. part. φυρσάμενος Nic.*Th.*507:—Pass., fut. πεφύρσομαι Pi.*N.*1.68 codd.; later φυρήσομαι (συμ-) Sch. ad loc.: aor. ἐφύρθην A.*Ag.*732 (lyr.); later aor. 2 ἐφύρην [ῠ] (συναν-) Luc.*Ep.Sat.*28: pf. πέφυρμαι (v. infr.):—*mix* something *dry with* something *wet*, mostly with a sense of *mixing so as to spoil* or *defile*, γαῖαν ὕδει φ. Hes.*Op.*61; esp. of tears or blood, δάκρυσιν εἵματ' ἔφυρον *they wetted, sullied* their garments with tears, Il.24.162: c. gen. pro dat., μή σε.. στῆθος καὶ χείλεα φύρσω αἵματος Od.18.21:—Pass., δάκρυσι πεφυρμένη 17.103, etc.; ὄμμα δακρύοις πεφυρμένοι E.*Or.*1411 (lyr.); πεφυρμένος αἵματι Od.9.397; γῇ αἵματι πεφ. X.*Ages.*2.14; αἵματι δ' οἶκος ἐφύρθη A. l. c. (lyr.); μητρὸς.. ἐν αἵμασι πεφυρμένοι E.*El.*1173; πάντα βορβόρῳ πεφυρμένα Semon.7.3; ἱστίον.. πεφυρμένον πρινὸς ἄνθεϊ *stained, dyed*, Simon.54: dub. in signf. of φυράω, ἐλαίῳ ἄλφιτα πεφυρμένα, v. l. for πεφυραμένα in Th.3.49; τέφρᾳ πεφυρμένη ὄξει, v. l. for πεφυραμένη in *Gp.*5.39.2. 2. of dry things, κόνει φύρουσα.. κάρα E.*Hec.*496; γαίᾳ πεφύρσεσθαι κόμαν *to be doomed to have* one's hair *defiled* with earth, Pi. l. c.; ἄνθος ἔφυρε κόνις *AP*7.476 (Mel.). II. metaph., *jumble together, confound, confuse*, ἔφυρον εἰκῇ πάντα *they mingled* all things up together, did all at random, A.*Pr.*450, cf. Ar.*Ra.*945, Pl.*Phd.*97b; (Med., οὐκ ἂν φύροιο would not *jumble your* arguments, ib.101e); φύρουσι δ' αὐτὰ θεοὶ πάλιν τε καὶ πρόσω ταραγμὸν ἐντιθέντες E.*Hec.*958; ἐν ταῖς ὁμιλίαις φύρειν *to speak confusedly* among themselves, M.Ant.8.51:—Pass., *to be mixed up*, ἐν τῷ αὐτῷ Pl.*Grg.*465c, cf. d; βίοτον ἐκ πεφυρμένου καὶ θηριώδους διεσταθμήσατο from a *confused* and savage state, E.*Supp.* 201. 2. Med., *mix with others, mingle in society*, Pl.*Lg.*950a; φύρεσθαι πρὸς τὸν ἄνθρωπον *associate, have dealings with* him, Id.*Hp. Ma.*291a; φυρομένοισιν ἀεὶ περὶ γαστέρος ὁρμὴν *wallowing* in the lusts of the belly, Opp.*H.*3.440, and cf. μείγνυμι B. 3. *confound*, Pi.*Pae.*2.73 (expld. by Sch. as = ἀποκτενεῖ). 4. Pass., metaph., *to be mutually befouled* by abuse, Plu.2.89d. (Prob. cogn. with πορφύρω.)

**φύς**, Dor. = ὀσφύς, *AB*1096. II. aor. part. of φύω.

**φῦσα**, ης, ἡ, *pair of bellows*, mostly in pl., τὸν δ' εὗρ'.. ἑλισσόμενον περὶ φύσας, sc. Hephaestus, Il.18.372, cf. 409; φύσας ἐσθέντες ἐφύσων Th.4.100; αἱ φ. αἱ ἐν τοῖς χαλκείοις Arist.*Resp.*474ᵃ12; τοῦ χαλκέος δύο φύσας Hdt.1.68: hence ἐν τῇσι φύσῃς in the *smithies* Herod.3.21. 2. *bladder*, Dsc.5.94, *Hippiatr.*33, *Gloss.*; φῦσαν ὑπηνέμιον *AP*9.486 (Pall.); φ. χηνεία *PMag.Lond.*46.382; of the castoreum *pouches* of the beaver, Dsc.2.24. 3. = φαρέτρα, Hsch. 4. = ἀσκός, Id. II. *breath, wind, blast*, ἀγρίαις φύσαισι φυσᾶν S.*Fr.* 768; ἐς τὸν ἀσκὸν φῦσαν ἐνιέναι.. *to inflate*, Hp.*Art.*47, cf. 77. 2. *wind in the body, flatus*, Id.*VM*10,22, *Aph.*4.73; *breaking of wind*, opp. ἐρυγμός, πταρμός, Arist.*Pr.*962ᵃ35: pl., Pl.*R.*405d, Arist.*HA* 604ᵃ12; περὶ φυσῶν, title of work by Hippocrates. 3. of fire, *stream, jet*, φλὸξ φῦσαν ἱεῖσα πυρὸς *h.Merc.*114. 4. *bubble*, φ. ἐπίχρυσοι Luc.*Merc.Cond.*22. III. *crater of a volcano*, Str.1.3.4.11, Oros.6.2.17. IV. *calyx of* φυσαλλίς III, Dsc.*Eup.*1.51. V. name of *a fish* found in the Nile, Str.17.2.4, Ath.7.312b. (Cf. Lith. *pučiù* 'I blow', Lat. *pustula*, etc.; onomatop.; υ may be Egyptian.)

**Φῡσάδ-εια** [ᾰδ], ἡ, name of a fountain in Argos, Call.*Lav.Pall.* 47: hence -ειόθεν, Adv. *from P.*, Antim. in *PMilan.*17.12.

**φυσακτήρ**· ἄρτος ποιός τις ποπανώδης, Hsch.

**φῡσ-ᾰλέος**, α, ον, *windy, full of wind*, Cerc.6.15, Nonn.*D.*43. 405. -αλλίς, ίδος, ἡ, *bladder, bubble*, Luc.*Cont.*19. II. *a wind instrument*, a kind of *pipe*, Ar.*Lys.*1245 (pl.). III. = ἁλικάκκαβος I, Ps.-Dsc.4.71, Paul.Aeg.3.45. IV. *bolus, pill*, Aen. Gaz.*Ep.*20. -ᾰλος, ὁ, a kind of *toad said to puff itself up* even to bursting, and to have poisonous breath, Luc.*Philops.*12, *Dips.* 3. II. a poisonous *fish which puffs itself out*, prob. *Tetrodon*, Ael. *NA*3.18. III. a kind of *whale* (cf. φυσητήρ II. 2), Opp.*H.*1.368, Ael.*NA*9.49.

**φύσανσις** [ῠ], εως, ἡ, '*naturation*', Phlp. *in Ph.*211.8.

**φῡσ-άριον**, τό, Dim. of φῦσα I. 2, Antyll.ap.Orib.10.26.1. -ασμός, ὁ, *blowing*, opp. ἀασμός, Arist.*Pr.*964ᵃ17. -ᾱτήριον, Dor. for φυσητ-.

⊛**φῡσάω**, Ion. pres. part. φυσέων Call.*Iamb.*1.101 (rightly censured by Sch. in *PSI*9.1094.30): (φῦσα): I. abs., *blow, puff* (opp. ἀάζω, Arist.*Pr.*964ᵃ11), of bellows, φῦσαι.. ἐφύσων Il.18.470; of the wind, 23.218; of men, φυσητῆρας ἐσθέντες.. φυσῶσι τοῖσι στόμασι Hdt.4.2, cf. Th.4.100, Call. l. c.; δεινὰ φυσᾷ *snorts* furiously, E.*IA*381 (troch.); metaph. from a flute-player, φυσᾷ γὰρ οὐ σμικροῖσιν αὐλίσκοις S.*Fr.* 768; μέγα φυσᾶν, Lat. *magnum spirare*, E.*IA*125 (anap.); οἱ φυσῶντες ἐφ' ἑαυτοῖς μέγα Men.302; μεγάλα φ. Id.*Epit.*492, Ph.2.85; ἡλίκον ἐφύσα τότε Luc.*Nec.*12; αἱμα φυσῶν Ἄρης *breathing* blood and murder, S.*El.*1385 (lyr.); πολιτικὸν φύσημα φ. *swell* with political pride, Pl. *Alc.*2.145e; abs., παύου φυσῶν Ephipp.5.20 (anap.); οὐκ ἐφύσων οἱ Λάκωνες ὡς ἀπόρθητοί ποτε; Antiph.117 (troch.); τῇ γένῃ φυσῶντες Herod.2.32; φυσῶσα ἐπὶ τῷ γένει D.Chr.58.5. II. trans., *puff* or *blow up, distend*, φ. κύστιν *blow up* a bladder, Ar.*Nu.*405 (anap.); of bag-pipers, Id.*Ach.*863; φ. δίκτυον, prov. of labour in vain, Phryn. *PS*p.121 B.; φ. τὴν γνάθον, of one going to be shaved, Ar.*Th.*221 (but φ. τὰς γνάθους to *puff* them *up*, of pride, D.19.314); *distend*, of disease, *AP*11.13 (Ammian.):—Pass., ἀσκοὶ πεφυσημένοι Sophr. in *PSI*11. 1214d9 (cf. Epich.246); φλέβας φυσωμένας Hdt.4.2; ἡ γαστὴρ ἐπεφυσητό μου Ar.*Pl.*699; πρόβατα ἀποδαρέντα καὶ φυσηθέντα X.*An.*3.5.9; πεφυσημένοι *puffy, swollen*, opp. εὔχροοι, Id.*Lac.*5.8. b. later of a solid *swelling*, e. g. of the tongue, ὅταν φυσηθῇ Aët.8.40; of the male breasts at puberty, φυσῶνται κατὰ ποσόν Paul.Aeg.6.46. 2. metaph., *puff* one *up, make* him *vain*, and so *cheat* him, D.13.12, 59. 38; φ. αὐτὸς ἑαυτόν Aristaenet.1.27:—Pass., *to be puffed up*, ἐπὶ δυνάμει X.*Mem.*1.2.25, cf. D.59.97, Arr.*Epict.*2.16.10; ὑπὸ τῆς τύχης Plu. 2.68f; πεφυσημένοι τὴν ψυχήν D.Chr.30.19. 3. *blow up, kindle*, τὸ πῦρ Pherecr.60, Dionys.Com.2.16; τὸν φανόν Philippid.16: but also, 4. *blow out, extinguish*, τὴν λαμπάδα Ar.*Ra.*1098 (anap.), cf. Thphr.*Ign.*28 (Pass.). 5. *blow out, spurt* or *spout out*, φυσῶντ' ἄνω πρὸς ῥῖνας.. αἷμα S.*Aj.*918. 6. *blow* a wind instrument, φ. κόχλους E. *IT*303; also φυσᾶν abs., Ar.*Av.*859, cf. Epigr.ap.Ath.8.337f; φυσῶντες (Boeot.) Ar.*Ach.*868; χέρ' ἐφύση *blew into..*, Theoc.19.3:—Pass., κόχλου φυσηθέντος Id.22.77. 7. Pass., *to be blown about*, ἀκάνθης πάππος ὡς φυσώμενος S.*Fr.*868; **πέτεται [ὁ πάππος]..**, ὑπὸ τῶν παιδίων φ. Eub.107.22.

**φῡσέχη**, ἡ, word coined from φύσιν ἔχειν or ὀχεῖν, as etymol. of ψυχή, by Pl.*Cra.*400b.

**φυσέων**, v. φυσάω.

**φῡσ-ηλάται**, *folles fabriles*, *Gloss.* -ημα, ατος, τό, *that which is blown* or *produced by blowing*, φ. ἀνεὶς δύσπλητον a hard-drawn *breath*, E.*Ph.*1438; δνοφώδη.. αἰθέρος φυσήματα, of stormy *blasts*, Id. *Tr.*79, cf. *Rh.*440; πόντιον φ. the *roaring* of the sea, Id.*Hipp.* 1211. II. *that which is blown up*, of half-formed shells, Plin. *HN*9.108; δούρειον.. χῆνα τῷ φυσήματι like the Trojan horse (δούρειος ἵππος) *in inflation*, i. e. *stuffed*, Diph.90: *state of inflation*, Luc.*Cont.*19. III. *blowing, puffing, snorting*, of a horse, X.*Eq.*11.12: metaph., *conceit*, πολιτικὸν φ. φυσῶντες Pl.*Alc.*2. 145e; γέμοντες ὄγκου καὶ φ. Plu.2.39d; and, in double sense, of a flute-player, μεῖζον τῆς μητρὸς ἔχων τὸ φ. Hyp.ap.Ath.13.591f; ῥήματα.. ἀποσπῶν γηγενεῖ φυσήματι Ar.*Ra.*825 (lyr.). IV. μέλανος αἵματος φυσήματα black blood *blown from the nostrils*, of newly slaughtered cattle, E.*IA*1114. V. *pine-resin*, Gal.13.475, Aët. 15.3. -ημάτιον, τό, Dim. of foreg., *Gloss.*: metaph. of *petty conceit*, Arr.*Epict.*2.16.10. ⊛ -ησις, εως, ἡ, *blowing upon* or *up*, of coals, Thphr.*HP*5.9.3. -ητέον, *one must blow up*, τὸ πῦρ Ar. *Lys.*293 (lyr.). II. φυσητέος, α, ον, *to be blown up, inflated*, ἀσκός Hp.*Art.*77. -ητήρ, ῆρος, ὁ, *instrument for blowing, blowpipe* or *tube*, φ. ὀστέϊνοι Hdt.4.2, cf. Opp.*H.*4.463. 2. *bellows*, Lxx *Jb.*32.19, Poll.10.147, Gal.2.717. 3. *blow-hole* or *spiracle* of whales, etc., Arist.*HA*566ᵇ3; the *funnel* through which the cuttle-fish squirts its ink, ib.541ᵇ17. II. *one who blows a pipe* or *bellows*, Dsc.5.75 (v. l.), Suid. s. v. ἐξέλιπε. 2. a kind of *whale*, perh. *Biscay whale*, Str.3.2.7. -ητήριον, Dor. **φυσᾱτ-**, τό, *wind-instrument, pipe*, Ar.*Lys.*1242 (pl.); gloss on φυσαλλίδες, Hsch. II. = *spiramentum*, *Gloss.* III. *a furnace with bellows*, opp. αὐτοματάρειον, Olymp.Alch.p.91 B. -ητής, οῦ, ὁ, *blower*, ὑέλοιο Man. 1.79; *bellows blower*, Dsc.5.75. -ητικός, ή, όν, *causing flatulency, flatulent*, Hp.*Mul.*1.75, Arist.*HA*595ᵇ6; φ. τῆς κοιλίας Id.*Pr.* 908ᵇ1. -ητός, ή, όν, *blown, blown out*, ὕελος φυσητή Herod.Med.

ap.Orib.5.30.32. II. **φυσητόν**, τό, *fan for kindling the fire*, *IG*2$^2$.1388.77. **-ήτωρ**, ορος, ὁ, = φυσητήρ, as Adj., ἀσκοί Nonn.*D*.30.70. **-ήφρων**, ονος, ὁ, ἡ, *puffed up in mind*, Hsch. (but the order of the letters requires φυσίφρων).

**φῡσί-ᾱμα** [ῐ], ατος, τό, *breathing hard, blowing*, ῥέγκουσι δ' οὐ πλατοῖσι φυσιάμασιν A.*Eu*.53. **-ασμός**, ὁ, *the sound made in expiration*, Arist.*Pr*.904$^a$2.

**φῡσιάω**, Ep. part. φῡσιόων:—intr., *blow, puff, snort, breathe hard, pant*, ἵπποι φυσιόωντες Il.4.227, 16.506; μόχθοις ἀνδροκμῆσι φυσιᾷ σπλάγχνον A.*Eu*.248; φυσιῶν.. ἐκβάλλει ῥοὴν..φοινίου σταλάγματος S.*Ant*.1238: metaph., μέσφ' ὁ δαίμων οὔρια φυσιάει Cerc.4.49. 2. *hiss*, φυσιόωσα ἔχις Opp.*C*.3.439, cf. 1.262. 3. metaph., *to be puffed up*, Naumach.ap.Stob.4.23.7.

**φῡσίγγη**, ἡ, = φῦσιγξ II, Sch.Ar.*Ach*.525, Suid.

**φῡσιγγιστής**, οῦ, ὁ, = Lat. *plagiaula*, *Gloss*. (dub. l.).

**φῡσιγγόομαι**, Pass., (φῦσιγξ) *to be excited by eating garlic*, prop. of fighting cocks, hence ὀδύναις πεφυσιγγωμένοι *infuriated* by vexations, of the Megarians (who were large growers of garlic), Ar.*Ach*.526.

**Φῡσίγνᾰθος**, ὁ, *Puff-cheek*, name of a frog in Batr.56: hence **φῡσιγναθέω**, = φυσῶ τὰς γνάθους, Tz.*H*.8.tit.201.

**φῡσιγνώμων**, ον, gen. ονος, = φυσιογνώμων, Theoc.*Epigr*.11.1.

❋**φῦσιγξ**, ιγγος, ἡ, *blister* on the heel caused by a burn, Poll.4.198. II. *stalk of garlic*, Hp.*Fist*.3, Thphr.*HP*7.4.12; or (acc. to Sch.Ar.*Ach*.525) *the outer coat of a clove of garlic*. 2. *a particular kind af garlic*, Diocl.*Fr*.120.

**φῡσί-ζοος**, ον, as epith. of earth, prob. *producing* ζέα, αἶα Il.3.243, Od.11.301, Orac.ap.Hdt.1.67; γῆ Il.21.63; but reinterpreted as from ζωή (ζόη), *producing life*, φυσιζόου..γένος Ζηνός prob. in A.*Supp*.584 (lyr., φυσίζοον cod.M); φ. ὕδωρ *AP*9.383.12; ἀήρ Tryph.77, etc. **-ζωος**, ον, *producing life*, Διώνυσος *IGRom*.4.360.15 (Pergam., ii A.D.) (elsewh. as f.l. for foreg.).

**φῡσίκ-ευμα** [ῐ], ατος, τό, *physical explanation*, τῆς ἀστραπῆς Tz.*H*.11.480. **-εύομαι**, *to be* or *speak like a natural philosopher*, Julian. ap.Gal.18(1).255. **-ιλλος**, ὁ, a kind of *bread*, Lacon. word in Ath.4.139a.

**φῡσικλείδιον**, τό, *a spell to open the* φύσις (i.e. pudendum muliebre), *PMag.Osl*.1.283.

**φῠσικός**, ή, όν, *natural, produced* or *caused by nature, inborn, native*, once in X.,*Mem*.3.9.1, not in Pl., freq. in Arist. (τὰ περὶ γένεσιν φ. *Ph*.191$^a$3, al.), and later Prose; opp. διδακτός, X. l.c.; opp. νομικός (conventional), δίκαιον Arist.*EN*1134$^b$19; ἡ φ. χρῆσις, opp. ἡ παρὰ φύσιν, *Ep.Rom*.1.26; of style, *natural, simple*, ἀληθὲς καὶ φ. χρῶμα D.H.*Thuc*.42; τὸ φ., opp. τὸ τεχνικόν, ib.34: φ. υἱός, = ὁ ἐκ πορνείας γεγονώς, opp. γνήσιος, Thom.Mag.p.362 R.; υἱὸς γνήσιος καὶ φ. *PLips*.28.18 (iv A.D.). Adv. **-κῶς** *by nature, naturally*, κινητόν, κινεῖσθαι, Arist.*Ph*.201$^a$24, *Cael*.307$^b$32; ὠχυρωμένη φ. λίμνη D.S.20.55; ἀκατασκεύως καὶ φ. Plb.6.4.7, etc. b. *belonging to the nature* of a plant, *characteristic*, Thphr.*HP*8.4.4, al. 2. *belonging to growth*, *Stoic*.2.205, al. 3. φ. ὀδόντες *milk*-teeth, Nicom.ap.*Theol.Ar*.49. II. *of* or *concerning the order of external nature, natural, physical*, ἡ φ. ἐπιστήμη Arist.*PA*640$^a$2; φ. φιλοσοφία ib.653$^a$9; ἡ φ. Id.*Metaph*.1026$^a$6, etc.; opp. μαθηματική, θεολογική, ib.1064$^b$2; τὰ φ. ib.1026$^a$4; οἱ φ. λόγοι f.l. for οἱ φυσιολόγοι, Id.*EN*1154$^b$7; φ. προτάσεις, opp. ἠθικαί, λογικαί, Id.*Top*.105$^b$21; τὸ φ., τὸ ἠθικόν, τὸ λογικόν, the three branches of philosophy, Zeno *Stoic*.1.15, etc., cf. S.E.*P*.2.13; τὰ πρῶτα καὶ -ώτατα the primal *elements* of things, Plu.2.395d. 2. ὁ φ. *an inquirer into nature, natural philosopher*, Arist.*de An*.403$^a$28, *PA*641$^a$21, *Metaph*.1005$^a$34; περὶ πασῶν [τῶν αἰτιῶν] εἰδέναι τοῦ φ. Id.*Ph*.198$^a$22, cf. *Metaph*.1026$^a$5: esp. of the Ionic and other pre-Socratic philosophers, Id.*Ph*.184$^b$17, 187$^a$12, 205$^a$5, al.: also ὁ φ., of Epicurus, Phylarch.24 J.; ὁ φυσικώτατος, of Thales, Luc.*Ner*.4. b. army *surgeon*, dub. in *IG*1$^2$.950.153. 3. ἡ φ. ἀκρόασις, title of a treatise by Arist.; τὰ φυσικά, a name given to his *physical treatises*, Id.*Ph*.267$^b$21, *Metaph*.1042$^b$8; ἐπιτομὴ φυσικῶν Id.*Pr*. 10tit. 4. Adv. **-κῶς** *according to the laws of nature*, Id.*Ph*.198$^a$23; opp. λογικῶς, ib.204$^b$10: Comp. -ώτερον εἰπεῖν Id.*GC*335$^b$25. III. later, *belonging to occult laws of nature, magical*, φ. φάρμακα *spells* or *amulets*, Alex. Trall.1.15; φυσικοῖς χρῆσθαι *Gp*.2.18.8; φ. θεραπεία ib.2.42.3; φ. δακτύλιοι Sch.Ar.*Pl*.884. Adv. **-κῶς** *Gp*.9.1.5.

**φύσῐμος** [ῠ], ον, *able to produce, productive*, σπέρμα Thphr.*CP*4.4.7, al.; σῖτος ib.4.16.3.

**φῠσιογνωμ-ία**, Ion. **-ίη**, ἡ, perh. = φυσιολογία, cited from Hippocrates by [Gal.]19.530. **-ονέω**, *study the features, judge of* a man's *character thereby*, τινα D.25.98: abs., Arist.*APr*.70$^b$7; φ. ἐκ τῶν γενῶν τῶν ζῴων, κατὰ τὰ ἤθη, Id.*Phgn*.805$^a$20, $^b$1, al.:—Pass., *to be inferred from the features*, ib.806$^a$25. **-ονία**, ἡ, *the science* or *art of judging a man by his features, physiognomy*, Hp.*Epid*.2.5 tit., Arist.*Phgn*.806$^a$19. **-ονικός**, ή, όν, *of* or *for physiognomy*, Hp. *Epid*.2.6 tit.; φ. σοφία S.E.*P*.1.85: **-κή**, ἡ, Philostr.*Gym*.25: **-κόν**, τό, name of a work by Antisthenes, Ath.14.656f; τὰ φ., title of a treatise ascribed to Aristotle. Adv. **-κῶς** Eust.838.19. **-οσύνη**, ἡ, = φυσιογνωμονία, Pall. *in Hp*.2.124 D. **-ων**, ον, gen. ονος, *judging of* a man's *character by* his *features*, Arist.*GA*769$^b$20, *Phgn*.805$^a$18, 806$^a$33, etc.

**φῠσιολογ-έω**, *discourse on nature, investigate natural causes and phenomena*, φ. περὶ πάντων Arist.*Metaph*.988$^b$27, cf. Polystr.p.12 W., D.S.3.62, Plu.2.921d, al.: abs., ὀρθῶς φ. Phld.*Rh*.2.42 S., cf. Plu.2.118d, al., Diog.Oen.3: c. acc., τοὺς ἰχθῦς Philostr.*Gym*.44. II. *explain from natural principles*, Τιμαῖος φ. τὴν ψυχὴν κινεῖν τὸ σῶμα Arist.*de An*.406$^b$26:—Pass., Ph.2.506. **-ημα**, ατος, τό, *scientific proposition*, Epicur.*Ep*.2 p.36 U. **-ητέον**, *one must theorize scientifically*, ibid., S.E.*P*.1.18. **-ία**, ἡ, *inquiring into natural causes and phenomena*, ἡ φ. ἡ περὶ τῶν φυτῶν Arist.*Sens*.442$^b$25; generally, Epicur. *Ep*.1 p.4 U., 2 p.35 U., Metrod.*Herc*.831.8, etc.; φ. καὶ θεολογία, φ. καὶ μαθηματική, D.S.5.40, Str.14.1.7, cf. Cic.*Div*.1.41.90, Ph.1.139, Plu.2.420c, etc.; ἡ Ζήνωνος φ., title of work by Cleanthes: pl., Longin.12.5, etc. **-ικός**, ή, όν, *of* or *for inquiry into nature*, esp. *the nature of man*, Gal.19.351; φ. ἐπιστήμη Hierocl. *in CA*22 p.468 M.; Subst., ὁ φ. Ph.1.139. **-ος** (parox.), ὁ, *one who inquires into natural causes and phenomena*, esp. of the pre-Socratic philosophers, Arist.*Metaph*.986$^b$14, 990$^a$3, *de An*.426$^a$20, *PA*641$^a$7, al.; φ. μᾶλλον ἢ ποιητήν, of Empedocles, Id.*Po*.1447$^b$19; ὁ φ., title of play by Sopater, Ath.3.101a; οἱ ἀρχαῖοι φ., title of work by Chrysippus, D.L.7.187; as Adj., παρρησία φ. cj. in Epicur.*Sent.Vat*.29: Sup., ἀνὴρ -ώτατος τῶν παλαιῶν Phld.*Mus*.p.108 K. Adv. **-γως** M.Ant.10.31.

**φῠσιοποιέω**, *remould as by a second nature*, Democr.33.

**φῠσιόω**, (φύσις) *dispose one naturally*, c. inf., Simp. *in Epict*. p.58 D.:—Pass., πεφυσιωμένος, η, ον, *having become a second nature, inveterate*, Arist.*Cat*.9$^a$2.

**φῡσιόω**, (φῦσα) *puff up*, 1 *Ep.Cor*.8.1 (for Ep. part. φυσιόων v. φυσιάω):—Pass., πρὸς τὰ θέματα πεφυσιωμένος Phld.*Po.Herc*.1676.9, cf. 1 *Ep.Cor*.4.6; ὑπολήψεις πεφ. Phld.*Mus*.p.26 K.

❋**φύσις** [ῠ], ἡ, gen. φύσεως, poet. φύσεος prob. (metri gr.) in E.*Tr*.886, cf. Ar.*V*.1282 (lyr.), 1458 (lyr.), Ion. φύσιος: dual φύσει (v.l. φύση) Pl.*R*.410e, (φύω): I. *origin*, φ. οὐδενός ἐστιν ἁπάντων θνητῶν οὐδὲ..τελευτή Emp.8.1 (cf. Plu.2.1112a); φ. βούλονται λέγειν γένεσιν τὴν περὶ τὰ πρῶτα Pl.*Lg*.892c; ἡ φ. ἡ λεγομένη ὡς γένεσις ὁδός ἐστιν εἰς φύσιν Arist.*Ph*.193$^b$12; φ. λέγεται ἡ τῶν φυομένων γένεσις Id.*Metaph*.1014$^b$16; freq. of persons, *birth*, φύσει νεώτερος S.*OC*1295, cf. *Aj*.1301, etc.; φύσι γεγονότες εὖ Hdt.7.134; φύσει, opp. θέσει (by adoption), D.L.9.25; φύσει Ἀμβρακιώτης, δημοποίητος δὲ Σικυώνιος Ath.4.183d; so ὁ κατὰ φύσιν πατήρ, υἱός, ἀδελφός, Plb. 3.9.6, 3.12.3, 11.2.2; also in acc., ἐκ πατρὸς ταὐτοῦ φύσιν S.*El*.325; ἢ φίλων τις ἢ πρὸς αἵματος φύσιν ib.1125, cf. Isoc.3.42. 2. *growth*, τριχῶν, παιδίου, Hp.*Nat.Puer*.20,29, cf. 27: pl., γενειάσεις καὶ φύσεις κεράτων Plot.4.3.13. II. *the natural form* or *constitution* of a person or thing *as the result of growth* (οἷον ἕκαστόν ἐστι τῆς γενέσεως τελεσθείσης, ταύτην φαμὲν τὴν φ. εἶναι ἑκάστου Arist.*Pol*.1252$^b$33): hence, 1. *nature, constitution*, once in Hom., καί μοι φύσιν αὐτοῦ (sc. τοῦ φαρμάκου) ἔδειξε Od.10.303; φ. τῆς χώρης Hdt.2.5; τῆς Ἀττικῆς X.*Vect*.1.2, cf. *Oec*.16.2, D.18.146, etc.; τῆς τριχός X.*Eq*.5.5; αἵματος, ἀέρος, etc., Arist.*PA*648$^a$21, *Mete*.340$^a$36, etc.: pl., φύσεις ἐγγιγνομένας καρπῶν καὶ δένδρων Isoc.7.74; αἱ φ. καὶ δυνάμεις τῶν πολιτειῶν Id.12.134; ἡ τῶν ἀριθμῶν φ. Pl.*R*.525c; ἡ τῶν πάντων φ. X.*Mem*.1.1.11, etc.; ἡ ἰδία τοῦ πράγματος φ. *IG*2$^2$.1099.28 (Epist.Plotinae). 2. *outward form, appearance*, μέζονας ἢ κατ' ἀνθρώπων φύσιν Hdt.8.38; ἢ νόον ἤτοι φύσιν either in mind or *outward form*, Pi.*N*.6.5; οὐ γὰρ φ. Ὠαριωνείαν ἔλαχεν Id.*I*.4(3).49 (67); μορφῆς δ' οὐχ ὁμόστολος φ. A.*Supp*.496; τὸν δὲ Λάϊον φύσιν τίν' εἶχε φράζε S.*OT*740 (read εἶρπε, taking φ. with ἔχων), cf. *Tr*.379; δρακαίνης φ. ἔχουσαν ἀγρίαν prob. in E.*Ba*.1358; τὴν ἐμὴν ἰδὼν φ. Ar.*V*.1071 (troch.), cf. *Nu*.503; τὴν τοῦ σώματος φ. Isoc.9.75. 3. Medic., *constitution, temperament*, Hp.*Aph*.3.2 (pl.), al.; ἡ φ. καὶ ἡ ἕξις Id.*Acut*.43; φ. φύσιος καὶ ἡλικία ἡλικίης διαφέρει Id.*Fract*.7; φύσιες νούσων ἰητροί Id.*Epid*.6.5.1. b. *natural place* or *position* of a bone or joint, ἀποπηδᾶν ἀπὸ τῆς φ., ἐς τὴν φ. ἄγεσθαι, Id.*Art*.61, 62, al.; ὀστέον μένον ἐν τῇ ἑωυτοῦ φ. Id.*VC*5, al.; φύσιες τῶν ἄρθρων Id.*Nat.Puer*.17. 4. of the mind, one's *nature, character*, ἦθος ἕκαστον, ὅπῃ φ. ἐστὶν ἑκάστῳ Emp.110.5; εὐγενὴς γὰρ ἡ φ. κἀξ εὐγενῶν..ἡ σή S.*Ph*.874; τὴν αὑτοῦ φ. λιπεῖν, δεῖξαι, ib.902,1310; φ. φρενός E.*Med*.103 (anap.); ἡ ἀνθρωπεία φ. Th.1.76; φ. τῆς μορφῆς καὶ τῆς ψυχῆς X.*Cyr*.1.2.2; ὀνόματι μεμπτὸν τὸ νόθον, ἡ φ. δ' ἴση E.*Fr*.168; φ. φιλόσοφος, τυραννική, etc., Pl.*R*.410e, 576a, etc.; δεξιοὶ φύσιν A.*Pr*.489; ἀκμαῖοι φύσιν Id.*Pers*.441; τὸ γὰρ ἀποστῆναι χαλεπὸν φύσεος, ἣν ἔχοι τις Ar.*V*.1458 (lyr.), cf. 1282 (lyr.); Σόλων..ἦν φιλόδημος τὴν φ. Id.*Nu*.1187; ἔνιοι ὄντες ὡς ἀληθῶς τοῦ δήμου τὴν φ. οὐ δημοτικοί εἰσι X.*Ath*.2.19; φύσεως ἰσχύς force *of natural powers*, Th.1.138; φύσεως κακία badness *of natural disposition*, D.20.140; ἀγαθοὶ..γίγνονται διὰ τριῶν, τὰ τρία δὲ ταῦτά ἐστι φ. ἔθος λόγος Arist. *Pol*.1332$^a$40; χρῶ τῇ φύσει, i.e. give rein to your *natural propensities*, Ar.*Nu*.1078, cf. Isoc.7.38; τῇ φ. χρώμενος Plu.*Cor*.18; θείας κοινωνοὶ φ. 2 *Ep.Pet*.1.4: pl., Isoc.4.113, v.l. in E.*Andr*.956; οἱ ἄριστοι τὰς φ. Pl.*R*.526c, cf. 375b, al.: prov., ἔθος, φασί, δευτέρη φ. Jul.*Mis*.353a. b. *instinct* in animals, etc., Democr.278; οὐκ ἐπιστήμῃ οὐδὲ τέχνῃ ἀλλὰ φύσει Herm.ap.Stob.1.41.6; ἐν τοῖς ἄλλοις ζῴοις ἡ αἴσθησις τῇ φ. ἥνωται, ἐν δὲ ἀνθρώποις τῇ νοήσει *Corp.Herm*. 9.1, cf. 12.1. 5. freq. in periphrases, καὶ γὰρ ἂν πέτρου φύσιν σύ γ' ὀργάνειας, i.e. would'st provoke a stone, S.*OT*335; χθονὸς φ. A.*Ag*.633; esp. in Pl., ἡ τοῦ πτεροῦ φ. *Phdr*.251b; ἡ φ. τῶν σωμάτων *Smp*.186b; ἡ φ. τῆς ἀσθενείας its *natural* weakness, *Phd*.87e; ἡ τοῦ μυελοῦ φ. *Ti*.84c; ἡ τοῦ δικαίου φ. *Lg*.862d, al.; ἡ φ., with gen. understood, *Smp*.191a, *Phd*.109e. III. *the regular order of nature*, τύχη..ἀβέβαιος, φ. δὲ αὐτάρκης Democr.176; κατὰ φύσιν Pl.*R*.444d, etc.; τρίχες κατὰ φύσιν πεφυκυῖαι growing *naturally*, Hdt.2.38, cf. Alex.156.7 (troch.); κατὰ φύσιν "νόμος ὁ πάντων βασιλεύς" Pi.*Fr*.169 (cf. Pl.*Grg*.488b); κατὰ φ. ποιεῖν Heraclit.112; opp. παρὰ φύσιν, E.*Ph*.395, Th.6.17, etc.; παρὰ τὴν φ. Anaxipp.1.18; προδότης ἐκ φύσεως a traitor by *nature*, Aeschin.2.165; πρὸ τῆς φ. ἥκειν εἰς θάνατον before the *natural term*, Plu.*Comp.Dem.Cic.*5: freq. in dat. φύσει (ἐν φ. Hp.*Aër.*14) *by nature, naturally*, opp. τύχῃ, τέχνῃ, Pl.*Lg.*889b, cf. *R.*381b; φύσει τοιοῦτος Ar.*Pl.*275, cf. 279, al.; ὁ ἄνθρωπος φ. πολιτικὸν ζῷόν ἐστι Arist.*Pol.*1253a3; ὁ μὴ αὑτοῦ φ. ἀλλ' ἄλλου ἄνθρωπος ὤν, οὗτος φ. δοῦλός ἐστιν ib.1254a15; φ. γὰρ οὐδεὶς δοῦλος ἐγενήθη ποτέ Philem.95.2; opp. νόμῳ (by convention), Philol.9, Archelaus ap.D.L.2.16, Pl.*Grg.*482e, cf. *Prt.*337d, etc.; τὰ μὲν τῶν νόμων ὁμολογηθέντα, οὐ φύντ' ἐστίν, τὰ δὲ τῆς φύσεως φύντα, οὐχ ὁμολογηθέντα Antipho Soph.44*A*i32 (*Vorsokr.*5); ἅπας ὁ τῶν ἀνθρώπων βίος φύσει καὶ νόμοις διοικεῖται D.25.15; τοὺς τῆς φ. οὐκ ἔστι λανθάνειν νόμους Men.*Mon.*492; οὐ σοφίᾳ, ἀλλὰ φύσει τινί Pl.*Ap.*22c; φ. μὴ πεφυκότα τοιαῦτα φωνεῖν S.*Ph.*79, cf. Pl.*Phlb.*14c, etc.; φύσει πάντα πάντες ὁμοίως πεφύκαμεν καὶ βάρβαροι καὶ Ἕλληνες εἶναι Antipho Soph.44*B*ii10 (*Vorsokr.*5); φύσιν ἔχει c. inf., it is *natural*, κῶς φύσιν ἔχει πολλὰς μυριάδας φονεῦσαι (sc. τὸν Ἡρακλέα); Hdt.2.45, cf. Pl.*R.*473a; οὐκ ἔχει φύσιν it is contrary to *nature*, ib.489b; οὔτ' εὔλογον οὔτ' ἔχον ἐστὶ φύσιν D.2.26; τὸ τόλμημα φύσιν οὐκ ἔχει Polem.*Call.*36. IV. in Philosophy: 1. *nature as an originating power*, φ. λέγεται.. ὅθεν ἡ κίνησις ἡ πρώτη ἐν ἑκάστῳ τῶν φύσει ὄντων Arist.*Metaph.*1014b16; ὁ δὲ θεὸς καὶ ἡ φ. οὐδὲν μάτην ποιοῦσιν Id.*Cael.*271a33; ἡ δὲ φ. οὐδὲν ἀλόγως οὐδὲ μάτην ποιεῖ ib.291b13; ἡ μὲν τέχνη ἀρχὴ ἐν ἄλλῳ, ἡ δὲ φ. ἀρχὴ ἐν αὐτῷ Id.*Metaph.*1070a8, cf. *Mete.*381b5, etc.; φ. κρύπτεσθαι φιλεῖ Heraclit.123; ἡ γοητεία τῆς φ. Plot.4.4.44; φ. κοινή, the *principle of growth* in the universe, Cleanth.*Stoic.*1.126; as Stoic t.t., the inner fire which causes preservation and growth in plants and animals, defined as πῦρ τεχνικὸν ὁδῷ βαδίζον εἰς γένεσιν, *Stoic.*1.44, cf. 35, al., S.E.*M.*9.81; *Nature*, personified, χάρις τῇ μακαρίᾳ Φ. Epicur.*Fr.*469; Φ. καὶ Εἱμαρμένη καὶ Ἀνάγκη Phld. *Piet.*12; ἡ κατωφερὴς Φ. *Corp.Herm.*1.14. 2. *elementary substance*, κινδυνεύει ὁ λέγων ταῦτα πῦρ καὶ ὕδωρ καὶ γῆν καὶ ἀέρα πρῶτα ἡγεῖσθαι τῶν πάντων εἶναι καὶ τὴν φ. ὀνομάζειν αὐτὰ ταῦτα Pl.*Lg.*891c, cf. Arist.*Fr.*52 (defined as τὴν πρώτην οὐσίαν.. ὑποβεβλημένην ἅπασι τοῖς γεννητοῖς καὶ φθαρτοῖς σώμασι Gal.15.3); τῶν φύσει ὄντων τὰ στοιχεῖά φασιν εἶναι φύσιν Id.*Metaph.*1014b33; pl., Epicur.*Ep.*1p.6U., al.; ἄτομοι φ. *atoms*, Democr.ap.Diog.Oen.5, Epicur.*Ep.*1p.7U.; ἄφθαρτοι φ. Phld.*Piet.*83. 3. concrete, the *creation*, '*Nature*', ἀθανάτου.. φύσεως κόσμον ἀγήρων E.*Fr.*910 (anap.); περὶ φύσεώς τε καὶ τῶν μετεώρων ἀστρονομικὰ ἄττα διερωτᾶν Pl.*Prt.*315c; περὶ φύσεως, title of works by Xenophanes, Heraclitus, Gorgias, Epicurus, etc.; [σοφία] ἣν δὴ καλοῦσι περὶ φύσεως ἱστορίαν Pl.*Phd.*96a; περὶ φ. ἀφοριζόμενοι διεχώριζον ζῴων τε βίον δένδρων τε φύσιν λαχάνων τε γένη Epicr.11.13 (anap.); so later, ἡ φ. τὸ ὑπὸ ψυχῆς τῆς πάσης ταχθέν Plot.2.2.1; τὰ στοιχεῖα τῆς φ. *Corp.Herm.*1.8; αἱ δύο φ., i.e. heaven and earth, light and darkness, etc., *PMag.Leid.W.*6.42. 4. Pythag. name for *two*, *Theol.Ar.*12. V. as a concrete term, *creature*, freq. in collect. sense, θνητὴ φ. man*kind*, S.*Fr.*590 (anap.), cf. *OT*869 (lyr.); πόντου εἰναλία φ. the *creatures* of the sea, Id. *Ant.*345 (lyr.); ὃ πᾶσα φ. διώκειν πέφυκε Pl.*R.*359c, cf. *Plt.*272c; ἡ τῶν θηλειῶν φ. woman-*kind* (opp. τὸ ἄρρεν φῦλον) X.*Lac.*3.4: also in pl., S.*OT*674, Pl.*R.*588c, *Plt.*306e, X.*Oec.*13.9; in contemptuous sense, αἱ τοιαῦται φ. such *creatures* as these, Isoc.4.113, cf. 20.11, Aeschin.1.191. b. of plants or material *substances*, φ. εὐώδεις καρποφοροῦσαι D.S.2.49; ὑγράν τινα φ. καπνὸν ἀποδιδοῦσαν *Corp.Herm.*1.4. VI. *kind, sort, species*, ταύτην.. ἔχειν βιοτῆς.. φύσιν S.*Ph.*165 (anap.); ἐκλέγονται ἐκ τούτων χρημάτων μίαν φ. τὴν τῶν λευκῶν Pl.*R.*429d; φ. [ἀλωπεκίδων] *species*, X.*Cyn.*3.1; *natural group* or *class* of plants, Thphr.*HP*6.1.1 (pl.). VII. *sex*, θῆλυς φύσα (prob. for οὖσα) κοὐκ ἀνδρὸς φύσιν S.*Tr.*1062, cf. *OC*445, Th.2.45, Pl.*Lg.*770d, 944d: hence, 2. *the characteristic of sex*, = αἰδοῖον, *Tab.Defix.*89a6 (iv B.C.), Nic.*Fr.*107, D.S.32.10, S.E.*M.*1.150, etc.: esp. of the female organ, Hp.*Mul.*2.143, Ant.Lib.41, Artem.5.63, *PMag.Osl.*1.83, 324, Horap. 1.11: pl., τῶν δύο φ., of the testes, Sch.Ar.*Lys.*92, cf. *PMag.Par.*1.318.

**φῠσί-ωμα**, ατος, τό, *natural tendency, bent*, Hipparch. ap.Stob.4.44.81 (pl.). **-ωσις**, εως, ἡ, *natural tendency, character*, [νούσων] Aret.*CD*1.1; φ. καὶ ζωή Porph.*Abst.*1.29.

**φῡσίωσις**, εως, ἡ, *inflation*, [Gal.]14.386 (pl.): metaph., *being puffed up, pride*, 2*Ep.Cor.*12.20 (pl.).

**φύσκη**, ἡ, (φυσάω) *the large intestine*, esp. as *stuffed with pudding, sausage, black-pudding*, gen. φύσκης Ar.*Eq.*364, Pherecr.45; pl. φύσκαι Cratin.164 (troch.); nom. sg. φύσκη Eub.63.6 (anap.), Dor. φύσκα prob. a nickname, 'pot-belly', Sophr.23; acc. φύσκην Philem. 60.2. II. *blister* or *weal on the hand*, Sch.Ar.*V.*1114 (nom. φύσκα). III. *gall-bag* on a plant, Dsc.*Alex.*22.

**φυσκία**, *botellus* (written *botellius*), *Gloss.* (s.v.l.).

**φύσκιον**, τό, Dim. of φύσκη I, *Gloss.*

**φύσκος**, ὁ, = *botellus*, *Gloss.*

⊛**φύσκων** or **φυσκών**, ῶνος, ὁ, *pot-belly*, nickname given to Pittacus, Alc.37B; freq. of Ptolemy VII, J.*AJ*12.4.11, etc. 2. *a throw of the dice*, Poll.7.205.

**φῡσό-βαθρον**, τό, (φῦσα) *frame* or *stand for bellows*, Suid. **-ειδής**, ές, *like a bladder, bladder-shaped*, ᾠά Sch.Nic.*Al.*293.

**φῡσόομαι**, Pass., *to be swollen*, f.l. in Dsc.4.68.

**φύσσ-α, -αλλίς, -αλός, -ητήρ**, etc., incorrect forms for φῦσα, etc.

⊛**φυστή** (sc. μᾶζα), ἡ, Att. name for a kind of *light pastry* or *puff*, Chionid.7, *AP*7.736 (Leon.): in full, φ. μᾶζα Ar.*V.*610 (anap.), Harmod.1, cf. Ath.3.114f (accented φυστῆ by Moer.p.384P.: heterocl. pl. φύστα, τά, *EM*803.1).

**φύστις**, f.l. in A.*Pers.*926 (anap., leg. πάνυ ταρφύς τις, for πάνυ γὰρ φύστις).

**Φυσώ**, οῦς, ἡ, *Growth*, personified, Emp.123.

**φῡσώδης**, ες, (φῦσα) *full of wind, windy*, τὸ φ. Pl.*Cra.*427a: metaph., *bombastic*, Longin.28.1. 2. *flatulent, causing flatulency*, Hp.*Acut.*50, Arist.*HA*522b32, 588a7, Sor.2.85; φ. νοσήματα Arist. *HA*605a23.

**φῠτᾰγωγέω**, *raise a plant*, in Pass., *EM*686.30.

⊛**φῠτᾰλιά** [ῡ metri gr. in Ep.], -ιᾶς, Ion. -ιή, -ιῆς, ἡ, (φυτόν) *planted place*, esp. *orchard* or *vineyard*, opp. corn-land, Il.6.195, 12.314, 20.185, *IG*11(2).161*A*14 (Delos, iii B.C.), Jul.*Or.*3.125a. II. *plant*, ἡ ἰδία φ. (of Athena, i.e. olive) Call.*Lav.Pall.*26; also of the *vine*, *AP*6.44 (Leon.(?)); φ. καλάμου ib.7.714. III. *planting-time*, i.e. the latter part of winter, Hp.*Hebd.*4, Gal.17(1).18. 2. *planting*, φ. καρποῖο A.R.2.1003.

**φῠτᾰλίζω**, = φυτεύω, Hsch.

**φῠτάλιος** [ᾰ], ον, = sq., θεοί Poll.1.24; of Poseidon, Corn.*ND*22; Ζεύς Orph.*H.*15.9. [ῡ metri gr.]

**φῠτάλμιος**, ον, also α, ον Lyc.341: (φύω):—*producing, nourishing, fostering*, epith. of gods, as of Poseidon, *Clara Rhodos* 6/7.386 (Camirus, iii/ii B.C.), Plu.2.158e, *IG*$2^2$.5051, 12(1).905 (Rhodes), etc.; of Zeus, Hsch., cf. *IG*12(5).13 (Ios); of parents, φυτάλμιοι γέροντες A.*Ag.*327; μητρὶ καὶ φ. πατρί S.*Fr.*788; λέκτρα φ. *the marriage* bed, E.*Rh.*920; φ. χθών Lyc. l.c.: τὸ φ. *productive power*, Plu.2.094b. II. *by birth*, ἀλαῶν ὀμμάτων ἆρα καὶ ἦσθα φυτάλμιος; didst thou *bring* blind eyes with thee *to life?* S.*OC*151 (lyr.). (φυτάλμιος is said by *EM*803.4. to be formed by metath. from φυτάλιμος, which is prob. coined *ad hoc*.)

**φῠτ-ᾰρίδιον**, τό, Dim. of sq., dub. in *Gloss.* **-άριον**, τό, Dim. of φυτόν, Ar.Byz.*Epit.*90.19, Ath.5.210c, Sch.Ar.*Av.*663, etc. **-άς**, άδος, ἡ, *plant*, φ. νέα Plu.2.411d. **-εία**, ἡ, *planting*, X.*Oec.*7.20, 19.1, *PSI*4.433.5 (iii B.C.), etc.: pl., X.*Oec.*19.12, Thphr.*HP*2.5.1. 2. *generation, production*, Pl.*Thg.*121c. II. *growth, habit of a plant*, Thphr.*HP*3.8.4. III. *plantation* or simply *a plant*, Moschio ap.Ath.5.207d, *Ev.Matt.*15.13, *OGI*606.7 (Abila, i A.D.). **-ειρον**, τό, = *panucla*, *Gloss.* ⊛**-ευμα**, ατος, τό, *that which is planted, plant*, Pi.*O.*3.18, Pl.*Lg.*761b: metaph., A.*Fr.*99.10, S.*OC*698 (lyr.), cf. Poll.3.12. II. *Montpellier rocket, Reseda Phyteuma*, Dsc.4.128, Plin.*HN*27.125. **-εύσιμος**, ον, *fit for planting* or *for rearing trees*, D.S.1.36. ⊛**-ευσις**, εως, ἡ, = φυτεία, γῆς Arist.*Mu.*399b17 (pl.), cf. Hp.*Hebd.*4, *PHal.*1.81 (iii B.C.), *Gp.*5.6.2, al. **-ευτέον**, *one must plant*, ib.3.3.2: neut. pl. φυτευτέα Poll.1.226. **-ευτήριον**, τό, *layer*, Hp.*Nat.Puer.*23, X.*Oec.*19.13, Thphr.*HP*2.2.4. II. *nursery* or *plantation*, *IG*$1^2$.94.33, $2^2$.2493, D.53.15 (all pl.). **-ευτής**, οῦ, ὁ, = *pastinator*, *Gloss.* **-ευτικός**, ή, όν, *of* or *for planting*, ἡ -κή Poll.7.140; τὰ -κά Porph.ap.Eus.*PE*3.11. **-ευτός**, ή, όν, *planted*, πᾶν τὸ φ. Pl.*R.*510a. ⊛**-εύω**, Od.5.340, etc., Ep. inf. φυτευέμεν Hes.*Op.*812; fut. εύσω X.*Oec.*19.13; aor. ἐφύτευσα Il.6.419, etc.: pf. πεφύτευκα, 3 pl. πεφύτευκαν Lxx *Ez.*19.13:—Med., fut. -ευσόμαι Pi.*P.*4.15: aor. -ευσάμην X.*Mem.*1.1.8:—Pass., fut. -ευθήσομαι *Gp.*5.19.1: aor. ἐφυτεύθην X.*An.*5.3.12, poet. 3 pl. φύτευθεν Pi.*P.*4.69: pf. πεφύτευμαι Hdt.2.138, etc.: (φυτόν). I. c. acc. *of the thing planted, plant* trees, esp. fruit-trees, οὔτε φυτεύουσιν χερσὶν φυτὸν οὔτ' ἀρόωσιν Od.9.108; δένδρεα φ. 18.359, cf. Alc.44, etc.; ἄλσος πεφυτευμένον Hdt. l.c.; συκᾶς Ar.*Fr.*108 (troch.); ὄρχους ἀμπέλους, X.*Oec.*20.3,4; joined with σπείρω, ib.11.16, *Mem.*2.1.13, Pl. *Phdr.*276e; φυτείαν *Ev.Matt.*15.13; ἀρώμεναι ἠδὲ φ. Hes.*Op.*22; φ. ἐν γῇ X.*Oec.*19.2; ἐν ἀφόρῳ ib.20.3; εἰς γῆν Plu.2.986f; φ. ἀπὸ κορύνης *Gp.*10.8.1:—Med., *plant for oneself*, Pi.*P.*4.15, Luc.*Cat.*20:—Pass., δένδρα πεφυτευμένα, opp. to those of spontaneous growth, D.55.13. 2. metaph., *beget, engender*, Hes.*Op.*812, *Sc.*29, Hdt.4.145, Pi.*N.*7.84, etc.; φυτεύων παῖδας E.*Alc.*662, cf. *Or.*11, Ar.*V.*1133, Pl.*Cri.*50d; ὁ φυτεύσας πατήρ S.*OT*793, 1514, E.*IA*1177 (s.v.l.); ὁ φυτεύσας alone, the *father*, S.*Ph.*904, *Tr.*1244; ὁ φ. αὐτόν E.*Andr.*49, etc.: opp. ἡ τεκοῦσα, Lys.11.4 (rarely of the mother, σὲ.. φύτευσεν Αἴθρα Ποσειδᾶνι B.16.59); οἱ φυτεύσαντες the *parents*, S.*OT*1007, *OC*1377; τοὺς τεκόντας καὶ φυτ. Id.*Fr.*64, cf. E.*Supp.*1092: metaph., ὕβρις φυτεύει τύραννον S.*OT*873 (lyr.); Μούσας λέγουσι Ἁρμονίαν φυτεῦσαι E.*Med.*832 (lyr.):—Pass., *to be begotten, spring* from parents, κείνων Pi.*P.*4.144; ἐκ Κρόνου Id.*N.*5.7; τοῦ κακοῦ πότμου φυτευθεὶς S.*OC*1324. 3. generally, *produce, bring about, cause*, mostly of evils, ὅτι τοι κακὰ πολλὰ φυτεύει Od.5.340; πρὶν ἡμῖν πῆμα φυτεῦσαι 4.668 (v.l.); φόνον καὶ κῆρα φ. 2.165, 17.82; once in Il., κακὸν μέγα πᾶσι φ. 15.134; φυτευέ οἱ θάνατον Pi.*N.*4.59; φ. πῆμα S.*Aj.*953; also in good sense, φ. γάμον, δόξαν, Pi.*P.*9.111, *I.*6(5).12; Μίνωϊ τιμάν B.16.68; καδέων ἀνάπαυσιν Id.18.35:—Pass., σὺν θεῷ φυτευθεὶς ὄλβος Pi.*N.*8.17. 4. *implant in*, τοῦθ' ἡμῖν Pl. *Ti.*80e; τι εἴς τι Id.*Phdr.*248d. 5. *set up*, ἄγαλμα ἐν τῷ οἴκῳ Iamb.*VP*18.84. II. less freq. c. acc. *of the ground planted, plant with fruit-trees*, φ. γῆν Th.1.2; χωρίον φ. καὶ γεωργεῖν Is.9.28: abs., Eup.13, Philem.116:—Med., ἀγρόν φ. X.*Mem.*1.1.8:—Pass., γῆ πεφυτευμένη Hdt.4.127, cf. X.*HG*3.2.10; opp. ψιλή, Eup.230, D.20.115; τὰ πεφυτευμένα *PHal.*1.102 (iii B.C.), etc.; γεωργία καὶ ψιλὴ καὶ πεφ. Arist.*Pol.*1259a2.

**φῠτηκομ-έω**, *take care of plants, garden*, Opp.*C.*1.122, Lib.*Decl.*40.67. 2. *produce plants* (i.e. vines), Opp.*C.*4.254. **-ία**, ἡ, *care of vines*, in pl., Id.*H.*1.309, *C.*4.331, Nonn.*D.*47.72. ⊛**-ος** (parox.), ὁ, *gardener, vine-dresser*, Lib.*Decl.*40.72.

**φυτιαῖος**, α, ον, *of plants*, ὄρχοι *IG*$2^2$.2493.27 (iv B.C.).

**φῠτικός**, ή, όν, *of* or *belonging to plants*, τὸ φ. the *vegetative principle*, Arist.*EN*1102ᵇ29; φ. ζωή Porph.*Gaur.*3.2; περὶ φ. αἰτιῶν, title of treatise by Thphr. Adv. -κῶς, ζῆν Porph.*Gaur.*1.1. II. φ. ζῷον, = ζωόφυτον, Arist.*PA*681ᵃ33.

**φύτιος** [ῠ], ον, also α, ον, (φύω) *generative*, epith. of Ἥλιος, Ζεύς, Hsch.; of Leto at Phaestus, Ant.Lib.17: hence as pr. n., Hecat.15J.

**φύτλη**, ἡ, poet. word, *stock, generation, race*, Pi.*O.*9.55, *P.*9.33, Orph.*A.*430, Besant.*Ara*9. II. late word for φύσις, *AP*7.744 (D.L.).

**⊛φύτλον** [ῠ], τό, *plant*, *Epigr.Gr.*1036.4 (Nicomedia).

**φῠτο-βᾰσίλειον** [ῐ], τό, = ζῴνυχον (= κῆμος), Ps.-Dsc.4.133. -ειδῶς, Adv. *after the fashion of plants*, Chrysipp.*Stoic.*3.43. ⊛-εργός, όν, poet. for φυτουργός, D.P.997, *AP*9.4 (Cyllen.).

**φῠτοκομ-έω**, = φυτηκομέω, Eust.1616.31. -ια, ἡ, = φυτηκομία, *Gp.Prooem.*7.

**⊛φῠτόν**, τό, (φύω) *plant* (opp. ζῷον, Diog.Apoll.2, Pl.*Phd.*70d, *R.* 532b, *Lg.*889c), esp. *garden plant* or *tree*, φυτῶν ὄρχατοι Il.14.123; τὸν μὲν ἐγὼ θρέψασα φυτὸν ὣς γουνῷ ἀλωῆς 18.57, cf. Hes.*Op.*571, Pi.*P.* 9.58 (pl.), A.*Eu.*940 (lyr., pl.), E.*Heracl.*281 (pl.), etc.; φυτὰ ἀκροδρύων D.53.15; ἀμπέλων Thphr.*CP*1.12.9; φ. ἔγγεια Pl.*R.*546a; τὰ ἐκ γῆς φ. Id.*Ti.*60a: prov., αὐτίκα καὶ φυτὰ δῆλα ἃ μέλλει κάρπιμ' ἔσεσθαι Lib.*Ep.*32.3. 2. *sucker, slip*, Arist.*Mir.*834ᵃ16. 3. = κυνόγλωσσον, Ps.-Dsc.4.127. II. generally, *creature*, A.*Supp.* 281, etc.; γυναῖκες..ἀθλιώτατον φ. (collective) most miserable *creatures*, E.*Med.*231; εἶτ' οὐ περίεργόν ἐστιν ἄνθρωπος φ.; Alex.141. 1; κακὸν φ. πέφυκεν..γυνή Men.*Mon.*304; also in Pl., ἐμὲ καὶ σὲ καὶ τἆλλα φ. *Sph.*233e; σωμάτων καὶ τῶν ἄλλων φ. Id.*R.*401a. 2. *offspring*, Χαρίτων φυτόν Theoc.28.7; φυτὸν οὐράνιον *plant* rooted in the sky, i.e. man, Pl.*Ti.*90a, cf. *AP*10.45 (Pall.(?)). 3. exceptionally, of iron, κακὸν φ. Call. in *PSI*9.1092.49.

**φῠτόομαι**, Pass., *grow into a vegetative creature*, opp. βρεφοῦσθαι, *Theol.Ar.*6.

**⊛φῠτός**, ή, όν, (φύω) of a wooden statue, *shaped by nature, without art*, Pi.*P.*5.42; πύαλον..φοιτήν (sic) *SIG*1231.8 (Bithynia, iii/iv A.D.). II. *fruitful*, πεδίον Lxx *Ez.*17.5.

**φῠτοσκᾰφία**, poet. -ίη, ἡ, *gardening*, *APl.*4.202.

**φῠτοσκάφος** [ᾰ], ον, *digging round plants*, φ. ἀνήρ *gardener*, Theoc.24.138, cf. 25.27, A.R.1.1172, *AP*6.102 (Phil.). II. proparox. **φῠτόσκᾰφος**, *dug* or *prepared for plants*, γῆ *EM*803.13.

**⊛φῠτοσπορ-ία**, ἡ, *planting of trees*, esp. *of vines*, Man.4.433. ⊛-ος (parox.), ον, *planting*: *generative*, ἀλκή Orph.*Fr.*274: metaph., *begetting*, ὁ φ. *father*, S.*Tr.*359; φυτοσπόροι, οἱ, *ancestors*, hence metaph., *predecessors*, Vett.Val.239.10: c. gen., γένους φ. Ar.Byz.Arg.S.*OT.*

**φῠτοτροφ-έομαι**, Pass., *to be trained*, of vines, Diotog.ap.Stob. 4.1.96. -ία, ἡ, *rearing of plants* or *trees, gardening*, *Gp.*9.5. 11. -ος (parox.), ον, *rearing plants* or *trees*, A.R.3.1403; γῆ *Gp.*5.12.4.

**φῠτουργ-εῖον**, τό, *nursery-garden*, D.S.2.10,13; vulg., φυτούργιον, as in *Gloss.* -έω, *do gardener's work*, Luc.*BisAcc.*1. -ημα, ατος, τό, *care of plants, planting*, Poll.7.140. ⊛-ία, ἡ, *cultivation of plants, gardening*, Thphr.*CP*3.7.5, D.S.20.8 (pl.), Str.11.5.1. 2. *plantation*, Id.3.2.3 (pl.). -ικός, ή, όν, *skilled in gardening*: ἡ -κή (sc. τέχνη), = φυτουργία, *gardening*, Poll.7.140. Adv. -κῶς ib. 141. -ός, όν, *tending plants* or *trees*, φ. δένδρων Secund.*Sent.*16: as Subst., *planter, gardener*, φ. ἱεροὶ Ἀπόλλωνος *SIG*22 (Epist.Darei), cf. *APl.*4.255, Plu.2.2b. II. metaph., *begetting, generating*, πατὴρ φ. A.*Supp.*592 (lyr.); τοῦ φ. πατρός S.*OT*1482; ὁ φ. (without πατήρ) E.*Tr.*481; φυτουργὸς Θέτιδος Id.*IA*949; in later Prose, πατέρα καὶ φ. Jul.*Or.*2.83a. 2. *creator, author*, Pl.*R.*597d.

**φῠτούριον**, τό, = *seminarium*, *Gloss.*; cf. φυτώριον.

**φῠτο-φόρος**, ον, *bearing plants*, γῆ Eust.636.17. -φύλαξ [ῠ], ἄκος, ὁ, *keeper of plants*, *PRein.*54.5 (iii/iv A.D.).

**φύτρα**, ἡ, = φύτλη, φύσις, Hsch.

**φῠτ-ώδης**, ες, *like a plant*, Erot. s.v. ἐκχλοιούμενα (ἐγχ- codd.). -ών, ῶνος, ὁ, *place planted*, esp. *vineyard*, Hdn.*Epim.*146. -ωνῠμος, ον, *named from a plant* or *tree*, *AP*14.34, Ach.Tat.2.14. -ωρ, ορος, ὁ, *father*, Sch.rec.A.*Pr.*233, Hsch.; cj. Dind. for τὸν φύσαντ' in S.*Tr.*1032 (hex.). -ώριον, τό, *nursery*, *Gp.*5.3.1, al.; cf. φυτούριον.

**⊛φύω**, Il.6.148, etc.; Aeol. φυίω fort. leg. in Alc.97: impf. ἔφυον, Ep.3 sg. φύεν Il.14.347: fut. φύσω [ῡ] 1.235, S.*OT*438: aor. ἔφυσα Od.10.393, etc.:—Pass. and Med., 9.109, Pi.*O.*4.28, etc.: fut. φύσομαι A.*Pr.*871, Hp.*Mochl.*42, Pl.*Lg.*831a, etc.: similar in sense are the intr. tenses, pf. πέφῡκα Od.7.114, etc., Ep.3 pl. πεφύασι Il.4.484, Od.7.128; 3 sg. subj. πεφύῃ (ἐμ-) Thgn.396; Ep. part. fem. πεφυυῖα (ἐμ-) Il.1.513, acc. pl. πεφυῶτας Od.5.477; Dor. inf. πεφύκειν Epich.173.3: plpf. ἐπεφύκειν X.*Cyr.*5.1.9, Pl.*Ti.* 69e; Ep. πεφύκειν Il.4.109; Ep. 3 pl. ἐπέφῡκον Hes.*Th.*152, *Op.*149: aor. 2 ἔφῡν (as if from φῦμι) Od.10.397, etc.: Ep. 3 sg. φῦ Il.6.253, etc., 3 pl. ἔφυν (for ἔφῠσαν, which is also 3 pl. of aor. 1) Od.5.481, etc.; subj. φύω or φυῶ E.*Fr.*377.2, Pl.*R.*415c, 597c, Hp.*Carn.*12; 3 sg. opt. φύη Theoc.15.94, (συμ-) Sor.2.89; inf. φῦναι, Ep. φύμεναι Theoc. 25.39, φῦν Parm.8.10; part. φύς Od.18.410, etc., Boeot. fem. φοῦσα Corinn.21: ἔφυσεν, = ἔφυ, dub. in *IG*14.2126.5 (Rome); conversely ἔφυ, = ἔφυσεν, ib.3.1350, *Sammelb.*5883 (Cyrene): later, fut. φυήσω Lxx *Is.*37.31, Pass. φυήσομαι *Gp.*2.37.1, Them.*Or.*21.248c (in Luc. *J.Tr.*19 ἀναφύσεσθαι is restored): aor. 2 Pass. ἐφύην J.*AJ*18.1.1, prob. in *BSA*28.124 (Didyma), (ἀν-) Thphr.*HP*4.16.2; inf. φυῆναι Dsc.2.6, (ἀνα-) D.S.1.7; part. φυείς Hp.*Nat.Puer.*22, *Trag.Adesp.* 529, *PTeb.*787.30 (ii B.C.), *Ev.Luc.*8.6: aor. 1 Pass. συμ-φυθείς Gal. 7.725. [Generally ῠ before a vowel, Ep., Trag. (A.*Th.*535, S.*Fr.* 910.2), etc., ῡ before a consonant; but φύει *Trag.Adesp.*454.2, φύεται S.*Fr.*88.4, *Trag.Adesp.*543 (= Men.565); φύομεν Ar.*Av.*106; ἐφύετο prob. in Ar.*Fr.*680, cf. Nic.*Al.*14, D.P.941, 1013; even in thesi, προσφύονται Nic.*Al.*506, φύουσιν D.P.1031; also in compds.]

A. trans., in pres., fut., and aor. 1 Act.:—*bring forth, produce, put forth*, φύλλα..ὕλη τηλεθόωσα φύει Il.6.148; τοῖσι δ' ὑπὸ χθὼν δῖα φύεν νεοθηλέα ποίην 14.347, cf. 1.235, Od.7.119, etc.; ἄμπελον φύει βροτοῖς E.*Ba.*651; so τρίχες.., ἃς πρὶν ἔφυσεν φάρμακον *made* the hair *grow*, Od.10.393, cf. A.*Th.*535; φ. χεῖρε, πόδε, ὀφθαλμὰ ἀνθρώποις X.*Mem.*2.3.19; of a country, καρπόν τε θωμαστὸν φύειν καὶ ἄνδρας ἀγαθούς Hdt.9.122; ὅσα γῆ φύει Pl.*R.*621a, cf. Anaxag.4. 2. *beget, engender*, E.*Ph.*869, etc.; Ἄτλας..θεῶν μιᾶς ἔφυσε Μαῖαν E. *Ion*3, cf. *Trag.Adesp.*454.2; so of God *creating* man, Antipho 4.1. 2, cf. Plu.2.1065c; ὁ φύσας the *begetter, father* (opp. ὁ φύς the *son*, v. infr. B.I.2), S.*OT*1019, Ar.*V.*1472 (lyr.); ὁ φ. πατήρ E.*Hel.*87; ὁ φ. χἠ τεκοῦσα Id.*Alc.*290; τὴν τεκοῦσαν ἢ τὸν φύσαντα Lys.10.8; of both parents, γονεῦσι οἵ σ' ἔφυσαν S.*OT*436; οἱ φύσαντες E.*Ph.*34, cf. *Fr.* 403.2; φ. τε καὶ γεννᾶν Pl.*Plt.*274a; ὦ γάμοι γάμοι, ἐφύσαθ' ἡμᾶς S.*OT* 1404; ἥδ' ἡμέρα φύσει σε *will bring to light* thy *birth*, ib.438; χρόνος φύει τ' ἄδηλα καὶ φανέντα κρύπτεται Id.*Aj.*647. 3. of individuals in reference to the growth of parts of themselves, φ. πώγωνα, γλῶσσαν, κέρεα, *grow* or *get* a beard, etc., Hdt.8.104, 2.68, 4.29; φ. πτερά Ar. *Av.*106, Pl.*Phdr.*251c; σάρκα Id.*Ti.*74e; φ. τρίχας, πόδας καὶ πτερά, etc., Arist.*HA*518ᵃ33, 554ᵃ29, etc.: for the joke in φύειν φράτερας, v. φράτηρ. 4. metaph., φρένας φῦσαι *get* understanding, S.*OC* 804, *El.*1463 (but also θεοὶ φύουσιν ἀνθρώποις φρένας Id.*Ant.*683): prov., ἁλιεὺς πληγεὶς νοῦν φύσει 'once bit, twice shy', Sch.Pl.*Smp.* 222b; γέροντα τὸν νοῦν σάρκα δ' ἡβῶσαν φύει A.*Th.*622; δόξαν φῦσαι *get* glory or *to form* a high opinion of oneself, Hdt.5.91; θεὸς.. αἰτίαν φύει βροτοῖς A.*Niob.*in *PSI*11.1208.15; αὑτῷ πόνους φῦσαι S. *Ant.*647. II. in pres. seemingly intr., *put forth shoots*, εἰς ἔτος ἄλλο φύοντι Mosch.3.101; δρύες..φύοντι Theoc.7.75, cf. 4.24: so ἀνδρῶν γενεὴ ἡ μὲν φύει ἡ δ' ἀπολήγει one generation *is putting forth scions*, the other is ceasing to do so, Il.6.149; ἐν στήθεσι φύει (fort. φυίει) *grows up, appears*, Alc.97; ῥίζα ἄνω φύουσα ἐν χολῇ Lxx *De.* 29.18.

B. Pass., with intr. tenses of Act., aor. 2, pf. and plpf., *grow, wax, spring up* or *forth*, esp. of the vegetable world, θάμνος ἔφυ ἐλαίης Od.23.190, cf. 5.481; πρασιαὶ παντοῖαι πεφύασιν 7.128; τά γ' ἄσπαρτα φύονται 9.109, cf. Il.4.483, 14.288, 21.352; φύεται αὐτόματα ῥόδα Hdt.8.138, cf. 1.193; ὑπὸ φηγῷ πεφυκυίῃ *growing there*, Id.2.56; πεφυκότα δένδρα trees *growing there*, X.*Cyr.*4.3.5; τὰ φυόμενα καὶ τὰ γιγνόμενα Pl.*Cra.*410d, cf. *Phd.*110d, *Plt.*272a; τοῦ κέρα ἐκ κεφαλῆς ἑκκαιδεκάδωρα πεφύκει from his head *grew* horns sixteen palms long, Il.4.109, cf. Hdt.1.108, 3.133; φύονται πολιαί Pi.*O.*4.28; κεφαλαὶ πεφυκυῖαι θριξί *grown with* hair, D.S.2.50 (s. v. l.); πέφυκε λίθος ἐν αὐτῇ *is produced*, X.*Vect.*1.4: metaph., νόσημα ἐν ὀλιγαρχίᾳ φυόμενον, φυομένη πόλις, Pl.*R.*564b, *Lg.*757d; ὁ σπέρμα παρασχών, οὗτος τῶν φύντων αἴτιος [κακῶν] *of the things produced*, D.18.159; also κατὰ πάντων ἐφύετο *waxed great by* or *upon* their depression, ib.19. —In this sense aor. 2 is rare (v. supr.), exc. in phrases such as ἐν τ' ἄρα οἱ φῦ χειρί (v. ἐμφύω), Od.2.302. 2. of persons, *to be begotten* or *born*, most freq. in aor. 2 and pf., ὁ λωφήσων οὐ πέφυκέ πω A.*Pr.* 27; τίς ἂν εὔξαιτο βροτὸς ὢν ἀσινεῖ δαίμονι φῦναι; Id.*Ag.*1342 (anap.); μὴ φῦναι τὸν ἅπαντα νικᾷ λόγον not *to be born* is best, S.*OC*1224 (lyr.); γονῇ πεφυκὼς..γεραιτέρᾳ ib.1294; οὐχ ὑπὸ θυσιῶν οὐδ' ὑπὸ εὐχῶν φύς Pl.*R.*461a; φύς τε καὶ τραφείς ib.396c; μήπω φῦναι μηδὲ γενέσθαι X.*Cyr.*5.1.7, cf. Pl.*Smp.*197a: construed with gen., πεφυκέναι or φῦναι τινος *to be born* or *descended from* any one, τὸ κοινὸν σπλάγχνον οὗ πεφύκαμεν A.*Th.*1036, cf. S.*OC*1379, etc.; θνατᾶς ἀπὸ ματρὸς ἔφυ Pi.*Fr.*61, cf. S.*OT*1359 (lyr.), *Ant.*562; ἀπ' εὐγενοῦς ῥίζης E.*IT*610; ἀπὸ δρυός Pl.*Ap.*34d, etc.; φ. ἔκ τινος S.*OT* 458, E.*Heracl.*325, Pl.*R.*415c, etc.; ἐκ χώρας τινός Isoc.4.24, etc.; οἱ μετ' ἐκείνου φύντες, opp. οἱ ἐξ ἐκείνου γεγονότες, Is.8.30; ἐκ θεῶν γεγονότι..διὰ βασιλέων πεφυκότι X.*Cyr.*7.2.24. II. in pres., *become*, οὐδεὶς ἐχθρὸς οὔτε φύεται πρὸς χρήμαθ' οἵ τε φύντες..S.*Fr.* 88.4; πιστοὺς φύσει φύεσθαι X.*Cyr.*8.7.13; the pf. and aor. 2 take a pres. sense, *to be* so and so *by nature*, κακός, σοφὸς πέφυκα (-κώς), etc., S.*Ph.*558, 1244, etc.; δρᾶν ἔφυν ἀμήχανος Id.*Ant.*79; φύντ' ἀρετᾷ *born* for virtue, i.e. brave and good *by nature*, Pi.*O.*10(11). 20; so of things, τὸ μὲν εὖ πράσσειν ἀκόρεστον ἔφυ A.*Ag.*1331 (anap.), cf. Pl.*Grg.*479d, etc.; εὐχροώτεροι ὁρῷντο ἢ πεφύκασιν X.*Cyr.*8.1.41, cf. *Oec.*10.2; [τὸ πῦρ] πέφυκε τοιοῦτον Id.*Cyr.*5.1.10; τἄλλα ἕκαστος ἡμῶν, ὅπως ἔτυχε, πέφυκεν D.37.56: with Advs., ἱκανῶς πεφυκότες *of* good *natural ability*, Antipho 2.1.1; δυσκόλως πεφ. Isoc.9.6; οὕτως πεφ. X.*HG*7.1.7; also οἱ καλῶς πεφυκότες S.*El.*989, cf. Lys.2.20; οἱ βέλτιστα φύντες Pl.*R.*431c: then, simply, *to be* so and so, φῦναι Ζηνὶ πιστὸν ἄγγελον A.*Pr.*969; θεοῦ μήτηρ ἔφυς Id.*Pers.*157 (troch.); γυναῖκε..ἔφυμεν S.*Ant.*62; Ἅιδης ὁ παύσων ἔφυ ib.575; ἁπλοῦς ὁ μῦθος τῆς ἀληθείας ἔφυ E.*Ph.*469: c. part., νικᾶν..χρῄζων ἔφυν S.*Ph.* 1052; πρέπων ἔφυς..φωνεῖν Id.*OT*9, cf. 587; τοῦτο ἴδιον ἔφυμεν ἔχοντες Isoc.4.48, cf. 11.41, X.*Smp.*4.54. 2. c. inf., *to be formed* or *disposed by nature* to do so and so, τὰ δεύτερα πέφυκε κρατεῖν Pi.*Fr.*279; πολλῷ γ' ἀμείνων τοὺς πέλας φρενοῦν ἔφυς ἢ σαυτόν A.*Pr.*337; ἔφυν γὰρ οὐδὲν ἐκ τέχνης πράσσειν κακῆς S.*Ph.*88, cf. *Ant.*688; φύσει μὴ πεφυκότα τοιαῦτα φωνεῖν Id.*Ph.*79; πεφύκασι δ' ἅπαντες..ἁμαρτάνειν Th.3.45, cf. 2.64, 3.39, 4.61, etc.; πέφυκε..τρυφὴ ..ἦθος διαφθείρειν Jul.*Or.*1.15c. 3. with Preps., γυνή..ἐπὶ δακρύοις ἔφυ *is by nature prone* to tears, E.*Med.*928 ; ἔρως γὰρ ἀργόν, κἀπὶ τοῖς ἀργοῖς ἔφυ *is inclined* to idleness, Id.*Fr.*322 ; also ἐπί τι Pl.*R.*507e ; εἴς τι Aeschin.3.132 ; most freq. πρός τι, οἱ ἄνθρωποι πρὸς τὸ ἀληθὲς πεφύκασι Arist.*Rh.*1355a16 ; εὖ πρὸς ἀρετὴν πεφυκότες X.*Mem.*4.1.2 ; πρὸς πόλεμον μᾶλλον.. ἢ πρὸς εἰρήνην Pl.*R.*547e ; κάλλιστα φ. πρός τι X.*HG*7.1.3, etc. ; also πρός τινι Id.*Ath.*2.19 (s.v.l., cf. Plb.9.29.10) ; also εὖ πεφ. κατά τι D.37.55. **4.** c. dat., *fall* to one *by nature, be* one's *natural lot,* πᾶσι θνατοῖς ἔφυ μόρος S.*El.* 860 (lyr.) ; χαίρειν πέφυκεν οὐχὶ τοῖς αὐτοῖς ἀεί Id.*Tr.*440 ; ἐφύετο κοινὸς πᾶσι κίνδυνος D.60.18, cf. X.*Cyr.*4.3.19. **5.** impers., *it is natural, it happens naturally,* c. inf., D.14.30, Arist.*Pol.*1261b7, *Po.* 1450a1. **6.** abs., ὡς πέφυκε as *is natural,* X.*Cyn.*6.15, al. ; ᾗ πέφυκεν Pl.*Ti.*81e ; also expressed personally, τοῖς ἁπλῶς, ὡς πεφύκασι, βαδίζουσι D.45.68 : also freq. in part., τὰ φύσει πεφυκότα the order of *nature,* Lys.2.29 ; φύντα, opp. ὁμολογηθέντα, Antipho Soph. 44*A* i 32 (*Vorsokr.*5) ; ἄνθρωπος πεφυκώς man *as he is,* X.*Cyr.*1.1.3. (Cf. Skt. *bhū-* 'to be, become', Lith. *búti* 'to be', Lat. *fui,* Eng. *be,* etc.)

**φῷ,** shortd. dat. of φῶς, E.*Fr.*534.

**φώγᾰνον,** τό, = φρύγετρον in the Κοινή, Poll.10.109.

**φώγω,** imperat. φῶγε Epich.151 ; **φῴζω** Stratt.65, cf. Hp.*Vict.*2. 56 ; also **φωγνύω** (Valck. for φωγύνω) Suid. ; inf. φωγνύναι (as if fr. φώγνυμι) Eust.962.50, *EM*803.32 (so in Pass. 3 sg. φώγνυται Dsc. 1.68, 4.64) : aor. ἔφωξα Hp.*Mul.*1.78, Nic.*Al.*607, but ἔφωσα Hp.*Mul.* 2.113, Dieuch.ap.Orib.4.7.1 :—**Pass.,** aor. ἐφώχθην Dsc.2.97, Aret. *CA*1.10, (προ-) Dsc.2.90 : pf. πέφωγμαι Pherecr.68 ; πέφωσμαι Hp. *Epid.*7.80, *Morb.*2.64, Iatrocl.ap.Ath.14.647c, *Gp.*6.6.2 :—*roast, toast, parch,* ll. cc. ; ἰσχάδες πεφωγμέναι (v.l. πεφρυγμέναι) Pherecr.l.c. (Cf. ONorse *baka,* Engl. *bake.*)

**φωΐς,** ΐδος, ἡ, contr. φῴς, φῳδός, only found in pl. φωΐδες, φῷδες (erroneously written φοῖδες in Arist.*Pr.*967a27), gen. φῴδων (Hdn. Gr.2.342) :—*blister* on the skin, caused by a burn, Hippon.59, Ar. *Pl.*535 (anap.), *Fr.*345, Hp.*Morb.*2.54, Diocl.*Fr.*80.

**Φώκαια,** ἡ, *Phocaea, h.Ap.*35, Hdt.1.80, etc. :—**Φωκαῆθεν,** Adv. *from Ph.,* Luc.*Lex.*7 :—hence **Φωκαιεύς,** Att. **Φωκαεύς,** ὁ, *Phocaean,* Hdt.1.163, Th.1.13, etc. ; also **Φωκαϊκός,** ή, όν, ὀβολὸς *IG*11(2). 161*B*21 (Delos, iii B.C.) ; στατῆρε ib.2².1388*A*42 ; στατῆρες Φωκαεῖς, v. στατήρ :—fem. **Φωκαΐς,** ΐδος, Ael.*VH*12.1, St.Byz. s.v. Φώκαια ; **Φωκαΐδες** ἕκται χρυσίου, of coins, *IG*1².310.105, cf. 2².1382.18 ; Φωκαΐς alone, *IG*11(2).161*A*4, al. (Delos, iii B.C.) : Dim. **Φωκαιΐδιον,** τό, *Inscr.Délos* 1429 *B* i 68 (ii B.C.) ; **Φωκαΐδιον,** ib.1432*Ab* ii 41 (ii B.C.).

**φώκαινα,** ἡ, *porpoise, Delphinus phocaena,* Arist.*HA*566b9, 598b1.

**φωκαρχ-έω,** *hold office of* Φωκάρχης, *IG*9(1).99 (Elatea). **-ης,** ου, ὁ, *one of the chief officials of the Phocian city league,* ib.97,101 (ibid.).

**φώκειος,** α, ον, *of seals,* δέρματα Lyd.*Ost.*45, cf. Cyran.77.

**Φωκεύς,** έως, ὁ, *Phocian,* Ep. gen. pl. Φωκήων Il.2.517, al. ; nom. pl. Φωκέες Hdt.1.146, Φωκῆς S.*El.*1107, 1442, Th.2.9 ; gen. Φωκέων A.*Pers.*485, etc. **II.** **Φωκίς** (sc. γῆ), ίδος, ἡ, *Phocis,* X.*HG*3.5.4, etc. ; as Adj., *Phocian,* γῆ, χθών, S.*OT*733, E.*IA*261 (lyr.) ; ὁδός Id. *Ph.*38 ; γλῶσσα A.*Ch.*564. **III.** Adj. **Φωκικός,** ή, όν, *Phocian,* πόλεμος D.2.7, etc.

**φώκη,** ἡ, *seal,* esp. *Phoca monachus,* φ. νέποδες καλῆς ἁλοσύδνης Od.4.404 ; φ. ζατρεφέες ib.451, cf. Ar.*V.*1035, *Pax* 758 (both anap.) ; ἐσθῆτι χρᾶσθαι φωκέων δέρμασι Hdt.1.202.

**φωκίς,** ίδος, ἡ, a kind of *pear,* Thphr.*CP*2.15.2, Androt.(?) ap. Ath.14.650e. **II.** a kind of *fish,* Gal.1.551 (v.l. φοκίς : φυκίς cj. Helmreich).

**φωκίων,** ονος, ὁ, a kind of *bird,* Hsch. **φῶκος,** ὁ, = φώκαινα, Id.

**φωκτός,** ή, όν, (φώγω) *roasted, broiled,* Nic.*Fr.*68, Dsc.*Eup.*2.39 : **φῶκται,** αἱ, as Subst., of barley-cakes, Luc.*Lex.*3.

**φωλ-άζω,** = φωλεύω, Hsch. **-άς,** άδος, ἡ, *lurking in a hole,* ἀραχναίη, σίλφη, *AP*9.233 (Eryc.), 251 (Even.), etc. : of the bear, *lying torpid in its cave,* Theoc.1.115, *Hymn.Is.*46 ; metaph., of a *shy* maiden (opp. πόρνη), φωλάδα παρθενικήν *AP*11.34 (Phld.) ; ἀγκύρας φωλάδας, of anchors *buried in the sand,* ib.10.2 (Antip.Sid.). **2.** as Subst., a mollusc *that makes holes in stones, Lithodomus,* Ath. 3.88a : Hsch. has φωλαΐδες, from a confusion of φωλάδες and φωλίδες. **II.** *full of holes* or *lurking places,* πέτρη Nonn.*D.*1. 163 ; ὕλη 6.270, 22.116 ; ἔκθορε φωλάδος κοίτης, of a lion, Babr.82. 3. **III.** φωλάς· εἶδος νόσου (i.e. = φωλεία 1), Suid. **-εά,** ἡ, = φωλεός, Arist.*Mir.*835b21 ; incorrectly used for καλιά, Thom.Mag. p.195 R. **-εία,** or **-ία,** ἡ, *life in a hole* or *cave, of the hibernation* of bears, Arist.*HA*600b18, Thphr.*Od.*63 (pl.), Ael.*NA*6.3 ; τὸ πάθος ὃ καλοῦσι φ. Plu.2.971d. **2.** of fishes, Thphr.*Fr.*171.7 (pl.). **-εός,** ὁ, Ep. gen. φωλειοῖο Opp.*H.*2.249, heterocl. pl. φωλεά Nic.*Fr.*83, Ep. dat. φωλειοῖς Id.*Th.*79, Opp.*C.*2.578, al. :—*den, lair,* esp. of *the caves of bears,* in which they hibernate, Plu.2.169e ; of lions, Babr.106.2 ; of molluscs, Arist.*HA*622b4 ; of a serpent, Luc. *Philops.*11 ; of foxes, *Ev.Matt.*8.20, *Ev.Luc.*9.58 ; of animals in general, Sor.2.29 ; of cave-dwellers, Str.11.5.7, cf. Luc.*VH*1.37, etc. **II.** *schoolhouse,* Hsch. **-ευσις,** εως, ἡ, = φωλεία, Ael.*NA* 16.15 (pl.). **-ευτέον,** *one must lie hid, lurk,* Eun.*VS* p.476 B. **-εύω,** *lurk in a hole* or *den,* of lizards, Arist.*HA*503b27 ; of bears, ib.579a26 ; of hedgehogs, ibid.29 ; of πορφύραι, ib.547a15 ; of wasps and hornets, ib.628a8, 629a14 ; of beetles (in dung), ib.552a17 ; of certain birds, ib.542b21 ; of serpents, κνώδαλα φωλεύοντα Theoc.24.85, cf. Nic. *Th.*394 ; of a lion, Babr.92.5 ; of a mouse, Id.108.2 ; τὰ φωλεύοντα *hibernating animals,* Arist.*GA*783b11, Thphr.*HP*1.1.3 ; of suspended animation, Arist.*Fr.*43 ; of disease, *lurk,* ἐν σπλάγχνοισι Aret.*SD*1. 8, cf. 2.1 ; of *hidden* fire, *Stoic.*2.187 ; of the womb, Hp.*Ep.*23. **-έω,** = foreg., Arist.*HA*599a9, al., v.l. in Suid. **-εώδης,** ες, *like a hole,* χειά dub. l. in Plu.2.418a. **-ητήρ,** ῆρος, ὁ, *one who lurks in a hole* or *keeps in one place,* Hsch. **-ητήριον,** τό, *place of secret assembly,* Poll.6.8. **-ία,** ἡ, v. φωλεία. **-ίον,** τό, Dim. of φωλεός, *fox's hole,* Paus.4.18.7. **-ίς,** ίδος, ἡ, a kind of *fish,* Arist.*HA* 621b8.

**φων-άεις,** v. φωνήεις. **-άριον,** τό, Dim. of φωνή, Clearch.Com. 2, *AP*5.131 (Phld.).

**φωνασκ-έω,** *train one's voice, learn to sing* or *declaim,* Pl.*Lg.* 665e, D.18.308, 19.255,336, Ph.2.537 ; οἱ φωνασκοῦντες ἕωθέν τε καὶ νήστεις ὄντες τὰς μελέτας ποιούμενοι Arist.*Pr.*901b1 :—Med., Plu.2. 349a. **-ητής,** οῦ, ὁ, = φωνασκός, *Gloss.* **-ία,** ἡ, *practice of the voice, declamation,* D.18.280, Thphr.*HP*9.9.2 (pl.), Phld.*Acad.Ind.* p.4 M., Sor.1.23 (pl.), Aret.*CD*2.6. **-ικός,** ή, όν, *of* or *for exercising the voice,* φ. ὄργανον a pitch-pipe, Plu.*TG*2 ; οἱ φ. *voice-trainers,* Pall. *in Hp.*2.93 D. Adv. **-κῶς** Arr.*Epict.*1.4.20. **-ός,** ὁ (also ἡ, Sor. 1.22, 2.7), *one who trains the voice, teacher of singing and declamation, IGRom.*4.1432.22 (Smyrna), Arr.*Epict.*1.4.20, Vett.Val.7.28, Alex. Aphr.*Pr.*1.119 ; Lat. *phonascus,* Suet.*Aug.*84, Quint.*Inst.*11.3.19.

**φωναστικοὶ** στίχοι, dub. sens. in Diom.p.498 K.

**φων-έω,** (φωνή) *produce a sound* or *tone* : **I.** prop. of men, *speak loud* or *clearly,* or simply, *speak, give utterance,* Hom. only in aor. (pres. and impf. only in compds.) ; ὣς ἄρα φωνήσας ἀπέβη Il.6. 116, cf. 11.531, al. ; ἔπος φάτο φώνησέν τε Od.4.370 ; φωνήσας προσέφη Il.14.41 ; καί μιν φωνήσας ἔπεα πτερόεντα προσηύδα addressed him *with a loud voice* in winged words, 1.201, cf. 4.284, al. ; φωνοῦντος ἢ ἠχοῦντος ἢ ψοφοῦντος Epicur.*Ep.*1 p.13 U. ; folld. by the words spoken, φώνησε (φώνασε codd.) δ', "εὕδεις, βασιλεῦ" Pi.*O.*13.67 ; χρυσοῖς δὲ φωνεῖ γράμμασιν, "πρήσω πόλιν" A.*Th.*434, cf. *Ag.*1334 (anap.) ; οἱ βουλευταὶ ἐφώνησαν.. the Senators *exclaimed..,* *POxy.* 2110.6 (iv A.D.) ; "βέκος" φ. *utter* the word βέκος, Hdt.2.2 : c. acc. cogn., ὄπα φωνησάσης *having made* her voice *sound,* Od.24.535 ; φ. φάτιν S.*El.*329 : with neut. Adj., φ. μέγιστον ἀνθρώπων *to have the* loudest *voice,* Hdt.4.141, 7.117 ; ὄρθιον φ. Pi.*N.*10.76 ; ἄλλο τι φ. A.*Pr.* 1063 (anap.) ; τάδε φ. Id.*Ch.*314 (anap.) ; μέγα φ. Id.*Eu.*936 (anap.), S.*Ph.*574 ; ἄπυστα φ. Id.*OC*489 ; ὅσια φ. Id.*Ph.*662 ; δεινὸν φ. ib. 1225 ; εὔφημα Id.*Aj.*362,591, E.*IT*687, etc. ; μηδεὶς ἔπος φωνείτω *IG*2².1368.108 ; τὸν ῥηϊδίως φωνεῦντα πᾶν ἔπος Anaxarch.1 : abs., *cry aloud,* as in joy, S.*Tr.*202 ; of a singer, ἀοιδὸς.. αἰόλα φωνέων Theoc.16.44 :—Pass., τὰ φωνηθέντα *sounds* or *words uttered,* Pl.*Sph.* 262c, *Ti.*72a, cf. Longin.39.4. **2.** of animals, *utter their cries,* Arist. *HA*578a32 ; of birds, ib.593a14 ; [τὰ σελάχη] φωνεῖν οὐκ ὀρθῶς ἔχει φάναι, ψοφεῖν δέ ib.535b25 ; ἐφώνησε πέρδιξ Lxx *Je.*17.11 ; of the cock, *crow, Ev.Matt.*26.34, al. **3.** as law-term, *affirm, testify* in court, *Leg.Gort.*1.18, al. (written πωνίω). **4.** of a musical instrument, *sound,* E.*Or.*146 (lyr.) ; of sounds, ἡδὺ φωνεῖν *sound* sweetly, Plu.2. 1021b ; but βροντὴ φ. it *has a voice, is significant,* X.*Ap.*12. **5.** ἄφωνα καὶ φωνοῦντα consonants and *vowels,* E.*Fr.*578 codd. Stob. (fort. ἄφωνα φωνήεντα). **II.** c. acc. pers., *call by name, call,* Αἴαντα φωνῶ I *call* 'Ajax' S.*Aj.*73, cf. *Ph.*229, *Ev.Matt.*27.47, etc. ; *call* by a name, ὑμεῖς φωνεῖτέ με "ὁ διδάσκαλος" *Ev.Jo.*13.13 :—Pass., *to be called,* τὰ ἀρχαῖα ἐκπώματα κισσύβια φωνέεται Nic.*Fr.*1. **2.** φ. τινα c. inf., *command,* σὲ φωνῶ νεκρὸν.. μὴ συγκομίζειν S.*Aj.*1047. **3.** *invite,* τοὺς φίλους *Ev.Luc.*14.12. **4.** c. dat. pers., *call to, cry to,* Ζεῦ ἄνα, σοὶ φωνῶ S.*OC*1485 (lyr.), cf. *OT*1121 ; ἕρποντι φωνεῖς Id.*Aj.* 543. **III.** c. acc. rei, *speak* or *tell of,* προσβολὰς Ἐρινύων A.*Ch.* 283 ; δέδου τέλος.. οἷον οὐδὲ φωνῆσαί τινι ἔξεσθ' *tell* to any one, S.*OC* 1402 ; φ. τὸ Ἐπιχάρμειον *recite* it, Pl.*Ax.*366c. **-ή,** ἡ, *sound, tone,* prop., *the sound of the voice,* whether of men or animals with lungs and throat (ἡ φωνὴ ψόφος τίς ἐστιν ἐμψύχου Arist.*de An.*420b5, cf. 29, *HA*535a27, *PA*664b1) ; opp. φθόγγος (v. φθόγγος II) : **I.** mostly of human beings, *speech, voice, utterance,* φ. ἄρρηκτος Il.2.490 ; ἀτειρέα φ. 17.555 ; φ. δέ οἱ αἰθέρ' ἵκανεν, of Ajax' battle-*cry,* 15.686 ; of the battle-*cry* of an army, Τρώων καὶ Ἀχαιῶν.. φ. δεινὸν ἀϋσάντων 14.400 : pl., of the *cries* of market-people, X.*Cyr.*1.2.3 ; ὁ τόνος τῆς φ. Id.*Cyn.*6.20, D.18.280, Aeschin.3.209 ; ὀξεῖα, βαρυτέρα, λεία, τραχεῖα φ., Pl.*Ti.*67b ; φ. μαλακή Ar.*Nu.*979 (anap.) ; μιαρά, ἀναιδής, Id. *Eq.*218,638 : with Verbs, φωνὴν ῥῆξαι Hdt.1.85, Ar.*Nu.*357 (anap.) ; φ. ἱέναι Hdt.2.2, 4.23, Pl.*Phdr.*259d, etc. ; φ. ἥσει E.*HF*1295 ; προΐεσθαι Aeschin.2.23 ; ἀρθροῦν X.*Mem.*1.4.12 ; διαρθρώσασθαι Pl.*Prt.*322a ; ἐντείνασθαι Aeschin.2.157 ; φ. ἐπαρεῖ D.19.336 ; φωνῇ *with his voice, aloud,* Il.3.161, Pi.*P.*9.29 ; εἶπε τῇ φωνῇ τὰ ἀπόρρητα Lys.6.51 ; διὰ ζώσης φωνῆς Anon.*Geog.Epit.*1 p.488 M. ; μιᾷ φ. *with* one *voice,* Luc. *Nigr.*14 ; ἀπὸ φωνῆς, c. gen., *dictated* by.., Choerob. *in Thd.*1.103 tit., Marin. *in Euc.Dat.*p.234 M., Olymp. *in Grg.*p.1 N., Pall. *in Hp.*2.1 D. : pl., αἱ φ. the *notes of the voice,* Pl.*Grg.*474e ; σχήμασι καὶ φωναῖς Arist. *Rh.*1386a32 : prov., φωνῇ ὁρᾶν, of a blind man, S.*OC*138 (anap.) ; πᾶσαν, τὸ λεγόμενον, φ. ἱέντα, i.e. using every effort, Pl.*Lg.*890d, cf. *Euthd.*293a ; πάσας ἀφιέναι φωνὰς Id.*R.*475a, D.18.195 ; φωνὰς ἀπρεπεῖς προτεντο *PTeb.*802.15 (ii B.C.). **2.** the *cry* of animals, as of swine, dogs, oxen, Od.10.239, 12.86,396 ; of asses, Hdt.4.129 ; of the nightingale, *song,* Od.19.521 ; ἄνθρωπος πολλὰς φωνὰς ἀφίησι, τὰ δὲ ἄλλα μίαν Arist.*Pr.*895a4. **3.** *any articulate sound,* opp. inarticulate noise (ψόφος), φ. κωκυμάτων S.*Ant.*1206 ; ὥσπερ φωνῆς οὔσης κατὰ τὸν ἀέρα πολλάκις καὶ λόγου ἐν τῇ φωνῇ Plot.6.4.12 : στοιχεῖόν ἐστι φ. ἀδιαίρετος Arist.*Po.*1456b22 ; also esp. of *vowel-sound,* opp. to that of consonants, Pl.*Tht.*203b, Arist.*HA*535a32 ; in literary criticism, of *sound,* opp. meaning, Phld.*Po.*5.20 (pl.),

21. 4. of *sounds* made by inanimate objects, mostly Poet., κερκίδος φ. S.*Fr.*595; συρίγγων E.*Tr.*127 (lyr.); αὐλῶν Mnesim.4.56 (anap.); rare in early Prose, ὀργάνων φωναί Pl.*R.*397a; freq. in Lxx, ἡ φ. τῆς σάλπιγγος Lxx*Ex.*20.18; φ. βροντῆς ib. *Ps.*103(104).7; ἡ φ. αὐτοῦ ὡς φ. ὑδάτων πολλῶν *Apoc.*1.15. 5. generally, *sound*, defined as ἀὴρ πεπληγμένος, πληγὴ ἀέρος, Zeno*Stoic.*1.21, Chrysipp.ib.2.43. II. *faculty of speech, discourse*, εἰ φωνὴν λάβοι S.*El.*548; παρέσχε φωνὴν τοῖς ἀφωνήτοις τινά Id.*OC*1283. 2. *language*, Hdt.4.114,117; φ. ἀνθρωπηΐη Id.2.55; ἀγνῶτα φ. βάρβαρον A.*Ag.*1051; φωνὴν ἥσομεν Παρνησίδα Id.*Ch.*563, cf. E.*Or.*1397 (lyr.), Th.6.5, 7.57, X.*Cyn.*2.3, Pl.*Ap.*17d, etc.; τῶν βαρβάρων πρὶν μαθεῖν τὴν φ. Id.*Tht.*163b; κατὰ τὴν Ἀττικὴν τὴν παλαιὰν φ. Id.*Cra.* 398d, cf. 409e. III. *phrase, saying*, τὴν Σιμωνίδου φ. Id.*Prt.* 341b; ἡ τοῦ Σωκράτους φ. Plu.2.106b, cf. 330f, etc.; of *formulae*, στοιχειώματα καὶ φ. Epicur.*Ep.*1p.4U., cf. *Sent.Vat.*41(= Metrod. *Fr.*59); αἱ σκεπτικαὶ φ. S.E.*P.*1.14, cf. Jul.*Or.*5.162b, etc. IV. *report, rumour*, Lxx*Ge.*45.16. b. *message*, *Sammelb.*7252.21 (iii/iv A.D.). V. *loud talk, bragging*, Epicur.*Sent.Vat.* 45. ⊛-ήεις, εσσα, εν, contr. **φωνῆς**, ῆντος Cratin. in *PSI*11.1212.13, cf. Hdn.Gr.2.618; Aeol. and Dor. **φωνάεις** [ᾱ], also in later Prose, as Zeno*Stoic.*1.41, Plu.*Sull.*7, S.E.*M.*1.100, etc.; contr. in pl. **φωνᾶντα**, Pi.*O.*2.85:—*endowed with speech, vocal*, ζῴοισιν ἐοικότα φωνήεσσιν Hes. *Th.*584; τοῦτο γὰρ ἀθάνατον φωνᾶεν ἕρπει Pi.*I.*4(3).40(58), cf. E.*Tr.* 440; βέλη (i.e. ἔπη) φωνᾶντα συνετοῖσι Pi.*O.*2.85; φ. θέατρα Pl.*Lg.* 701a; ὄχλος Plu.l.c.; φ. ζῷα *endowed with speech*, X.*Mem.*2.7.13; opp. ζῷα ψοφητικά, Arist.*HA*488$^a$32; epith. of certain signs of the Zodiac, Vett.Val.10.19, *Cat.Cod.Astr.*1.166; τὸ φωνᾶεν the *power of speech*, Zeno l.c. 2. *musical*, of the lyre, Sapph.45. 3. of a song, *sounding*, Pi.*O.*9.2. 4. *clear*, λόγος B.14.31. 5. τὰ φωνήεντα (φωνάοντα *Mélanges Beyrouth* 15.71 (Syria, gem)) *vowels*, τοῖς ἄλλοις φωνήεσί τε καὶ ἀφώνοις Pl.*Cra.*393e, cf. *IG*2$^2$.2783.4,17, Phld.*Rh.*1.163S., etc.; in full, τὰ φ. γράμματα Aen.Tact.31.30; στοιχεῖα φ. S.E.*M.*1.100. b. *consisting of vowels only*, of a spell, *PMag.Par.*1.2634. -ημα, ατος, τό, *sound made, utterance*, S.*Aj.* 16, *Ph.*1295, *Ichn.*39; of a singer's *voice*, D.C.61.20; of a dog's bark and ass's bray, Gal.18(1).291. 2. *thing spoken, speech, language*, S.*Ph.*234, *OT*324. **-ησις**, εως, ἡ, *sounding, speaking, calling*, Poll.2.111. **-ητήριος**, α, ον, = φωνητικός, φ. ὄργανα organs *of speech*, Str.14.2.28, cf. Poll.2.114; φ. ὄργανον Ph.1.28. **-ητής**, οῦ, ὁ, *clear speaker*, Hsch. s.v. ἠπύτα. **-ητικός**, ή, όν, *vocal*, τὸ φ. the *faculty of speech*, Zeno*Stoic.*1.39, D.L.7.110; τὰ φ. ὄργανα Poll. 2.115, cf. Gal.2.690; φ. δύναμις, [αἴσθησις], Arr.*Epict.*2.23.2, *Theol. Ar.*49. II. *endowed with speech*, ζῷα Corn.*ND*17, Porph.*Abst.*3. 3. **-ητός**, ή, όν, *to be spoken*, ἅ τ' οὐ φωνητὰ πρὸς ἀνδρός *AP*6.210 (Philet.). II. *utterable*, τὸ ἔσχατον φ., opp. τὸ πρῶτον ἀκουστόν, Nicom.*Harm.*2. **-ικός**, ή, όν = φωνητικός, Phld.*Mus.*p.35K.; οἱ φ. *declaimers*, *Cat.Cod.Astr.*8(4).213,214. **-ιον**, τό, Dim. of φωνή, Arist.*Aud.*803$^b$24. **-ίς**, ίδος, ἡ, = foreg., Hdn.Gr.1.94, 2. 859.

**φωνο-βόλος**, ον, *causing to sound*, c. gen., σάλπιγγος Hsch. s.v. σαλπικτής. **-μᾰχέω**, *dispute about words*, Phld.(?)*Herc.*19.24, S.E.*P.*1.195. **-μᾰχία**, ἡ, *dispute about words*, Ptol.*Judic.* 9. **-μῖμος**, ον, *imitating the voice*, Ptol.Heph.ap.Phot.*Bibl.*p.149B.

**φῶνος**, ον, = μεγαλόφωνος, Eup.294 (ap.Sch.Ar.*Av.*42), cf. Theognost.*Can.*66.

**φῶξις**, εως, ἡ, *roasting*, Gal.12.618.

**φώρ**, ὁ, gen. φωρός, dat. pl. φωρσί Ael.*NA*9.45:—*thief*, Hdt.2. 174, etc.; φώρ τινος Pl.*R.*334a; Ἀργεῖοι φῶρες Ar.*Fr.*57; φ. ἄνθρωποι Paus.10.15.5; ἔγνω δὲ φὼρ τε φῶρα καὶ λύκος λύκον prov. in Arist. *EE*1235$^a$9; τὰ τῶν φ. κρεῖττω prov. in Hyp.*Fr.*1: Sup. φώρτατος *most thievish*, Sophr.1. II. a kind of *bee*, prob. *robber-bee*, Arist.*HA*553$^b$9, 625$^a$5. III. φωρῶν λιμήν, a harbour near Athens, a little westward of the Piraeus, used by *smugglers*, D.35. 28,53, Str.9.1.14. (Like Lat. *fur*, from *bher-* (root of φέρω), cf. ἄγειν καὶ φέρειν.)

**φωρ-ά**, Ion. **φωρή**, ἡ, (φώρ) *theft*, *h.Merc.*136 (prob. for φωνῆς), 385, Bion*Fr.*8.6, Nic.*Al.*273; ἱερῶν χρημάτων *SIG*672.16 (Delph., ii B.C.); ἔνοχοι ὄντες φωρᾷ *Sammelb.*4638.17 (ii B.C.); ἐπ' αὐτῇ τῇ φωρᾷ, = ἐπ' αὐτοφώρῳ, Poll.8.69. II. *detection, discovery*, τῆς ἀλλοτριολογίας Phld.*Acad.Ind.*p.67M.; ἀλγεῖν ἐπὶ τῇ φ. D.L.1.96; μεῖζον τῆς φ. τὸ αὐτὸν ἑαυτοῦ κατειπεῖν Ach.Tat.7.11. (φώρης codd. Nic. l.c.; Hsch. has φωρά· κλοπή, but φώρην· τὴν ἔρευναν.) **-ᾱτός**, ή, όν, *that can be detected*, S.E.*P.*1.183. ⊛ **-άω**, fut. άσω [ᾱ] Ar.*Nu.* 499, etc.: (φώρ, φωρά): *search after a thief* or *theft*, *search a house to discover stolen goods*, φωράσων ἔγωγ' εἰσέρχομαι Ar. l. c., cf. *Ra.*1363 (lyr.); φωρᾶν παρά τινι Pl.*Lg.*954a. 2. generally, *detect, discover*, τὰ πλεῖστα φωρῶν αἰσχρὰ φωράσεις S.*Fr.*853; οὐδένα ἂν τις φωράσαι τῶν..καλουμένων δυνατῶν..ῥητόρων ὃς οὐ..Phld.*Rh.*2.247S.: freq. c. part., ἀργύριον πῶς φωράσειεν ἄν τις ἐξαγόμενον; X.*Vect.*4.21; τοῦτο φ. δρῶντας ἡμᾶς Pl.*Ti.*63c; φ. τινὰς ἐπιβουλεύσαντας Arist.*Pol.*1306$^b$30; ψεῦδος ὃν ἐφωράσαμεν Phld.*Mus.*p.55K.: c. acc. et inf., τὸν Ἀχιλλέα ἐρᾶν πεφώρακας Philostr.*Im.*2.7:—Pass., *to be detected*, D.2.10; πεφωραμένος ἐπὶ τοιαύτῃ πράξει Plb.6.56.15; ὁ φωραθεὶς *BGU*1730.8 (i B.C.): mostly c. part., φωραθῆναι τὰ ψευδῆ μεμαρτυρηκώς D.45.19; κλέπτης ὢν φ. Id.22.71, cf. 21.41; εἴ τις φωραθείη φυτεύσας *IG*7.2226.28 (Thisbe, iii A.D.); ἀδύνατος ὢν φ. Th.8.56: also with Adjs., κακὸς (sc. ὤν) ἐφωράθη φίλοις E.*Or.*740 (troch.), cf. Jul.*Or.*2.62a: c. inf., Ἑλληνικὸν εἶναι πεφ. Plu.2.714d. **-ειον**, τό, *penalty for theft*, πεντaπλάσιον τὸ φ. ἐκτίνειν *PLit.Lond.*138 iv 20, cf. 30.

**φωρῐαμός**, ἡ, *chest, trunk, coffer*, esp. for clothes and linen: pl. in Hom., Il.24.228, Od.15.104: sg. in A.R.3.802. (Acc. to Eratosth. 4 from φώρ, φώριος II, *a place for keeping secret.*)

**φωρ-ιάω**, = φωράω, Hsch. **-ίδιος**, α, ον, poet. for φώριος, *stolen*, *AP*9.348 (Leon.Alex.), Max.411, Doroth. in *Cat.Cod.Astr.* 6.104. **-ιον**, τό, (φωρά II) *damning evidence*, J.*AJ*15.3.9, Lib. *Decl.*49.69; τὰ φ. τοῦ ἀδικήματος Them.*Or.*26.314a. ⊛ **-ιος**, ον, (φώρ) *stolen*: τὰ φ. *stolen goods*, *IG*5(2).445.13 (Megalopolis, ii/i B.C.), Luc.*Herm.*38, *Philops.*20, *Tox.*28, Jul.*Or.*2.52c, Chor.p.72B.; ἄγρη Eratosth.4. II. metaph., *secret, clandestine*, εὐνή Theoc. 27.68; λέκτρα, βλέμμα, *AP*5.218 (Paul.Sil.), 220 (Id.).

**φῶρος**, ὁ, *detecter, discoverer*, Hsch., Suid.

**φώρτατος**, Sup. of φώρ (q.v.).

**φώς**, gen. φωτός, ὁ: dual φῶτε, φωτοῖν: pl. φῶτες, φωτῶν, φωσί: poet. Noun (Com., only paratrag., as Ar.*Pax*528, or pseudo-orac., Diph.126.3 (hex.); also in late Prose, *PRyl.*77.34 (ii A.D.)):—*man*, sts. coupled with ἀνήρ, δύο δ' οὔπω φῶτε πεπύσθην, ἀνέρε κυδαλίμω..Il. 17.377; ἀλλότριος φ. 5.214, cf. 11.462, 614, al.; in gen., equivalent to a possessive pronoun, *his*, χρόα φωτός 4.139, al.; in Trag. either of heroes, as A.*Th.*499, S.*Ant.* 107 (lyr.), or of men generally, A. *Pers.*242 (troch.); φῶτ' ἄδικον Id.*Ag.*398 (lyr.); φ. ἀνόσιος, ἀμαυρός, S.*OC*281,1018; ὦ σκῆπτρα φωτός, i.e. ἐμοῦ, ib.1109; joined with other Nouns, φῶτ' Ἀσκληπιοῦ υἱόν Il.4.194, cf. 21.546, Od.21.26; φωτί..δέκτῃ 4.247; φῶτες Αἰγεῖδαι Pi.*P.*5.75; κλωπὸς φωτός E.*Rh.* 709. II. *man*, opp. woman, Od.6.129, S.*Ant.*910, *Tr.*177, etc.; but δύ' οἰκτρὼ φῶτε, of a man and his wife, E.*Hel.*1094; so of lovers, *AP*5.248.5 (Iren.). III. *mortal*, opp. a god, πρὸς δαίμονα φωτὶ μάχεσθαι Il.17.98; φωτῶν ἀλαὸν γένος A.*Pr.*549 (lyr.); φῶτα βρότειον E.*Ba.*542 (lyr.).

**φῶς**, contr. for φάος, *light* (q.v.). **φῴς**, ἡ, pl. φῷδες, contr. from φωΐς (q.v.).

**φώσκω**, *dawn*, Hsch. (mostly in compds. δια-, ἐπι-).

**φώσσω**, = φώγω, φῴζω, Gal.12.618.

**φώσσων** or **φώσων**, ωνος, ὁ, *a coarse linen garment*, used in Egypt, Poll.7.71; ἐν φώσωνι τὴν ἴσην ἔχων μετ' ἐμοῦ διῆγες Cratin.250. 2. *sail, sail-cloth*, Lyc.26, Suid., Eust.1151.12. (Perh. Egyptian.)

**φωσσώνιον** or **φωσώνιον**, τό, Dim. of foreg., *coarse towel*, Luc.*Lex.* 2, *EM*804.24.

**φωστήρ**, ῆρος, ὁ, *that which gives light*, οἱ φ. the *lights of heaven, stars*, Lxx*Ge.*1.14, al., Simp. *in Epict.*p.72D.; οἱ δύο φ., i.e. sun and moon, ibid., cf. Procl.*Hyp.*4.72, etc.; φαίνεσθε ὡς φωστῆρες ἐν κόσμῳ *Ep.Phil.*2.15. 2. *splendour, radiance*, ὁ φ. αὐτῆς ὅμοιος λίθῳ τιμιωτάτῳ *Apoc.*21.11. 3. metaph., of a king, τῷ φ. τῷ ἡμετέρῳ Them.*Or.*16.204c. 4. of the *eyes*, Vett.Val.110.22. II. *opening for light, door* or *window*, Hsch.

**φωσφόρ-εια** (sc. ἱερά), τά, *a festival at which there were torch-processions*, or, *which was sacred to one of the* φωσφόροι θεοί, Plu.2. 1119e, Hsch. **-έω**, *bear* or *bring light*, *BGU*597.33 (poet., i A.D.); *shine*, Nech.ap.Vett. Val.280.2, Ph.1.511, Man.1.65; esp. of the moon or planets, *draw away more than* 15° *from the sun, rise*, Heph. Astr.1.20; οἱ φωσφοροῦντες τόποι the positions *of such risings* in the zodiac, Ptol.*Tetr.*89. 2. trans., *bring into the light*, τὰ ἔμβρυα Olymp. *in Alc.*p.12C. **-ία**, ἡ, Astron., *rising and shining* of the moon or planets *when they have drawn away more than* 15° *from the sun*, Serapio in *Cat.Cod.Astr.*8(4).227, Ptol.*Tetr.*76, Heph.Astr.1. 20. 2. Archit., in pl., *lights* (i.e. windows, etc.) of a building, *PHamb.*15.7 (iii A.D.), etc. ⊛ **-ιον**, τό, *small figure of* ἡ Φωσφόρος as device on a signet-ring, *IG*11(2).203*B*74 (Delos, iii B.C.), al. II. *shrine of* ἡ Φ., *Supp.Epigr.*4.446.17 (Didyma, iii/ii B.C.). III. = foreg. 2, *PStrassb.*9.8 (iv A.D.). ⊛ **-ος** (parox.), ον, poet. **φαοσφόρος** Lyr.Adesp. in *PLit.Lond.*51.5, **φαεσφόρος** Call.*Dian.*204, etc.:—*bringing* or *giving light*, Ἕως E.*Ion*1157; φ. ἀστήρ, of Dionysus at the mysteries, Ar.*Ra.*342 (lyr.); φ. πεῦκαι Id.*Fr.*599; αἴγλη, Ἦμαρ, Orph.*A.*1246, Εὐχή 24. b. Subst., ὁ φ. (sc. ἀστήρ), *the light-bringer*, i.e. *the morning-star*, a name specially given to the planet Venus, Ti.Locr.96e, 97a, Arist.*Mu.*392$^a$27, 399$^a$8, Cic.*ND*2.20.53, Ph.1.504, cf. Alex.Eph.ap.Theon.Sm.p.138H. 2. of the eye, φ. ὄμματα Pl. *Ti.*45b; φ. κόραι, of the Cyclops, E.*Cyc.*611 (lyr.). b. name of an *eye-salve*, Gal.12.747. II. *torch-bearing*, epith. of certain deities, esp. of Hecate, E.*Hel.*569, Ar.*Th.*858, *Fr.*594a; φ. θεά (sc. Ἄρτεμις) E.*IT*21, cf. Call. l.c.; νὴ τὴν Φωσφόρον Ar.*Lys.*443, Antiph. 58.6; of Hephaestus, Orph.*H.*66.3: pl., ἱερεὺς Φωσφόρων *Hesperia* 4.49 (Athens, ii A.D.). III. φωσφόρος, ἡ, *torch-bearer*, title of a priestess, Κλεοπάτρας θεᾶς *PRein.*10.8, etc. (ii B.C.).

**φώσων**, **φωσώνιον**, v. φώσσων, φωσσώνιον.

**φωτᾰγωγ-έω**, *guide with a light, guide*, πρὸς τὴν εὐσέβειαν φ. τινά Lxx 4*M.*17.5. II. *draw down supernatural illumination* by a magical process, Iamb.*Myst.*3.14. **-ία**, ἡ, *magical process of drawing down supernatural illumination*, *PMag.Par.*1.955, Vett. Val.301.22. **-ός**, όν, *enlightening, illuminating*, of the sun, Mich. *in EN*554.29; *bringing to light*, ἀθεμίστων πραγμάτων *PMag.Lond.* 46.190. II. ἡ φ. (sc. θυρίς) *opening for light, window*, Luc.*Symp.* 20, *Dom.*6.

**φωταύγεια**, ἡ, *brightness of light*, Suid., Zonar.; written **-αυγία**, Mich. *in EN*554.30.

**φώταυγος**· ὁ ἥλιος, Zonar.; φωταυγός Suid. (v.l.).

**φωτεινοειδής**, ές, *like light*, Sch.D.T.p.175H., Sch.E.*Hipp.*740.

⊛**φωτεινός**, ή, όν, (φῶς) *shining, bright*, ἥλιος X.*Mem.*4.3.4; σκοτεινὰ καὶ φ. [σώματα] ib.3.10.1, cf. Lxx*Si.*17.31 (Comp.), Plu.2.

1110b, Hierocl. *in CA*26p.478M.; ἀήρ Ath.Med.ap.Orib.9.5.2; οἴκημα Sor.2.10, al. II. metaph., *clear, distinct*, λόγος Plu.2.9b (Comp., s.v.l.); also in moral sense, Hierocl. *in CA*3 p.424 M.; ὅταν ὁ ὀφθαλμός σου ἁπλοῦς ᾖ, καὶ ὅλον τὸ σῶμά σου φ. ἐστιν *Ev.Luc.* 11.34, cf. 36.

**φωτίγγιον**, τό, Dim. of φῶτιγξ, Posidon.2 J., Ael.*NA*6.31.

**φωτιγγιστής**, οῦ, ὁ, *fifer, Gloss.*

⊛ **φῶτιγξ**, ιγγος, ἡ, Plu.2.961e, ὁ Juba ap.Ath.4.175e, cf. Ath.4.182d:—Alexandrian name for a kind of *flute* (πλαγίαυλος) said to be invented by Osiris, ll.cc.

**φωτίζω**, fut. φωτίσω 1*Ep.Cor.*4.5:—I. abs., *shine, give light*, ὁ ἄνθραξ [οὐ δύναται] φωτίζειν ὥσπερ ἡ φλὸξ Thphr.*Ign.*30, cf. Nic.*Fr.*74.66. II. trans., *illuminate*, ὁ ἥλιος φ. τὸν κόσμον D.S.3.48, cf. Plu.2.931b (Pass.):—Pass., τὸ φωτιζόμενον, opp. τὸ φωτίζον, ib.936b: opp. σκοτίζομαι, ib.1120e, cf. Luc.*Luct.*2, Plot.2.3.5; of a planet, *Cat.Cod.Astr.*11(2).110; πεφωτισμέναι ἡμέραι Orph.*Fr.*272. 2. *bring to light, make known*, τὴν ἑκατέρων αἵρεσιν Plb.22.5.10, cf. 28.13.10; τὰ κρυπτὰ τοῦ σκότους 1*Ep.Cor.*l.c., cf. 2*Ep.Ti.*1.10:—Pass., γράμματα ἑαλωκότα καὶ πεφωτισμένα Plb.30.8.1; φωτισθέντος τοῦ θανάτου Id.15.25.8. 3. *enlighten, instruct, teach*, φ. τινάς, πῶς.. Lxx 4*Ki.*17.28; φ. πάντας, τίς ἡ οἰκονομία *Ep.Eph.*3.9. 4. *illuminate with spiritual light*, ὁ ὑπὸ τοῦ θεοῦ πεφωτισμένος *Corp.Herm.*9.3, cf. 13.18 (Pass.). b. in a special sense, *baptize*, in Pass., *Ep.Heb.*6.4, 10.32. 5. *throw light upon, illustrate*, of commentators, Ὅμηρον D.L.1.57.

**φώτιον**· προσφιλές, ἡδύ, Hsch.

**φωτ-ῐσις**, εως, ἡ, *illumination*, Procl. *in Prm.*p.490S. **-ισμα**, ατος, τό, *phase*, of the moon, Eustr. *in EN*31.33. **-ισμός**, ὁ, *illumination, light*, Diocl(?).ap.Gal.19.530, Plu.2.929e, 931b, S.E.*M.*10.224: pl., Dam.*Pr.*23; σελήνης Vett.Val.28.7, Jul.*Or.*5.167d; [ἡμισφαιρίων] ib.4.147b. 2. metaph., *light*, Κύριος φ. μου Lxx*Ps.*26(27).1, cf. 2*Ep.Cor.*4.4,6. ⊛ **-ιστήριον**, τό, *lantern-window, Gloss.* (pl.). **-ιστικός**, ή, όν, *illuminating*, Ascl. *in Metaph.*323.11, Sch.E.*Hipp.*192; φ. δύναμις τοῦ ἡλίου Ammon. *in Int.*133.2, cf. Dam.*Pr.*96; τὸ φ. τοῦ πυρός Eustr. *in EN*117.7. Adv. -κῶς Eust.161.19.

**φωτο-βίας** [ῐ], ου, ὁ, *powerful by light*, *PMag.Par.*1.598. **-βολία**, ἡ, *beam, ray*, Sch.Par.A.R.4.728 (pl.). **-δότης**, ου, ὁ, *giver of light*, Simp. *in Epict.*p.13D.; also **-δώτης**, voc. -δῶτα, *PMag.Par.*1.596. **-ειδής**, ές, *luminous*, Hp.*Cord.*11, Heraclit. (Ἡρακλείδης codd.) ap.*Placit.*4.3.6, Posidon.ap.S.E.*M.*7.93; *flame-like*, Alex. Aphr. *in Sens.*47.15, *de An.*45.15; τὸ φ. Plu.2.382c, cf. Plot.4.4.24, 5.5.7. ⊛ **-θυρίς**, ίδος, ἡ, *window*, *CPR*105.6 (iii A.D.). **-κῑνήτης**, ου, ὁ, voc. -κινῆτα, *mover of light*, *PMag.Par.*1.599. **-κράτωρ** [ᾰ], ορος, ὁ, *lord of light*, ib.595. **-λαμπής**, ές, *blazing with light*, κλίμακες Zos.Alch.p.108B. **-λόγιον**· τυφλόν, νεκρόν, Hsch. **-πλήξ**, πλῆγος, ὁ, ἡ, *smiting with rays of light*, *PMag.Par.*1.2242. **-ποιός**, όν, *making light, enlightening*, Iamb.*Protr.*21.γʹ.

**φωτ-ουλκός**, όν, (ἕλκω) *drawing*, i.e. *admitting, light*, ἄνοιγμα *TAM*2.174C14 (Sidyma). **-ουργός**, όν, *light-giving*, Prisc.Lyd.8.15.

**φωτοφάν-εια** [φᾰ], ἡ, *illumination*, Anon.ap.Suid. s.v. ἐκπλαγεῖς. **-ής**, ές, *brilliant*, Eust.226.6.

⊛ **φωτοφόρος**, gloss on φαεσφόρους, Suid., cf. *EM*786.33.

**φωτώδης**, ες, = φωτοειδής, Hsch. s.v. χιονέα.

**φῶυξ**, v. πῶυξ. **φώψ**, = φάος, φῶς, Hsch.

# X

**X χ**, χεῖ (q.v.), τό, indecl., twenty-second letter of the Gr. alphabet, Pl.*Cra.*414b, *Ti.*36b. As numeral, χʹ = 600, ͵χ = 600,000: but in Inscrr., X stands for χίλιοι, αι, α, = 1000.

**χά**, exclamation representing laughter, *ha! ha!*, *PMag.Leid.W.*4.33.

**χαανaία**, ἡ, *priest's robe*, J.*AJ*3.7.1 (χαναίας codd.): a mistranslation of Aram. *kāhănayyā* 'priests'.

**χαβίτια**, τά, prob. = χαβότια, *PCair.Zen.*680.20 (iii B.C.).

**χαβός**, ή, όν, = καμπύλος, στενός, Hsch.; cf. χαμόν.

**χάβος**, ὁ, = κημός, Sch.Ar.*Eq.*1147.

⊛ **χαβότια**, τά, dub. sens., perh. *honey-pots*, *PSI*4.428.53 (iii B.C.).

⊛ **χαβῶνες**· στέατα ὀπτώμενα ἀπὸ ἀλεύρου, Hsch.

**χάδε, χαδέειν, χαδών**, v. χανδάνω.

**χάδην**, f.l. for χαδέειν, aor. inf. of χανδάνω, Hp.*Genit.*9.

⊛ **χάζω**, *cause to retire*; Act. only in Hsch. and in compd. ἀναχάζω (also παραχάζω, προχάζω Hsch.), and in Ep. redupl. aor. κέκᾰδον, fut. κεκᾰδήσω:—*force to retire from, bereave* or *deprive of*, τοὺς.. θυμοῦ καὶ ψυχῆς κεκαδών Il.11.334; ἀριστῆας κεκαδήσει θυμοῦ καὶ ψυχῆς Od.21.153,170.

B. Med., **χάζομαι**, Il.5.34, etc.; imper. χάζεο, χάζευ, ib.440, Call.*Cer.*54: Ep. impf. χάζετο Il.16.736, 3 du. χαζέσθην A.R.3.1320: fut. χάσομαι, Ep. χάσσομαι Il.13.153: aor. 1 ἐχᾰσάμην, Ep. 3 sg. χάσσατο ib.193, inf. χάσασθαι 12.172; part. χασσάμενος 13.148, etc.: κεκάδοντο (for κεχάδοντο) 3 pl. of redupl. aor. 2 κεκαδόμην, Il.4.497, 15.574:—*give way, draw* or *shrink back, recoil*, freq. in Il. (never in Od.), χάζεο Il.5.440; ὁ δὲ χασσάμενος πελεμίχθη 4.535; οὐδ' ὅ γε πάμπαν χάζετ' 12.407; ἂψ δ' ἑτάρων εἰς ἔθνος ἐχάζετο 3.32, al.; αἰὲν ὀπίσσω χάζοντο 5.702, cf. 18.160, A.R. l.c., Call. l.c., Nonn.*D.*48.618. 2. c. gen., *draw back* or *retire from*, πυλάων χάσσασθαι Il.12.172; χάζοντο κελεύθου 11.504; χάζεσθε μάχης 15.426; μίνυνθα δὲ χάζετο δουρός 11.539; ὁ δὲ χάσσατ' ὀπίσσω νεκρῶν 13.193, cf. 17.357; less freq. with a Prep., χ. ἐκ βελέων 16.122; χάσσονται ὑπ' ἔγχεος 13.153; οὐδὲ δὴν χάζετο φωτός nor in truth *was he* (or *it*, the stone) *far from* the man, i.e. nearly hit him, 16.736. Poet., and mainly Ep., exc. in the compds. ἀνα-, δια-χάζομαι (qq.vv.).—οὐχ ἅζομαι, οὐχ ἅζεται (not οὐ χάζ-), shd. be written in E.*Or.*1116, *Alc.*326, A.*Eu.*389.

**χαίνω**, v. χάσκω.

**χάϊος** [ᾱ], α, ον, *genuine, true, good*, Lacon. word in Ar.*Lys.*91; Comp. χαϊώτερος ib.1157; Ἀναξαγόρου τρόφιμος χαΐου Alex.Aet.7 (Valck. for ἀρχαίου); cf. βαθυχάϊος:—also **χᾱός**, όν, χαοὶ οἱ ἐπάνωθεν *the good men* of olden time, Theoc.7.5, ubi v. Sch., cf. χάσιος.

**χαῖος**, ὁ, or **χαῖον**, τό, *shepherd's staff*, A.R.4.972, Call.*Fr.*125. (Cf. Gaulish *gaiso-* (Lat. *gaesum*, Gr. γαῖσον) 'javelin'.)

**χαιρεκᾰκ-έω**, = ἐπιχαιρεκακέω, Ph.1.314. **-ία**, ἡ, = ἐπιχαιρεκακία, Arist.*MM*1192$^{b}$18 (v.l.), Andronic.Rhod.p.573M. **-ος**, ον, = ἐπιχαιρέκακος, interpol. in Poll.5.128, cf. *EM*808.6.

⊛ **χαιρετ-ίζω**, *say* χαῖρε, *to greet, welcome*, τινα Lxx *To.*7.1, *POxy.*1242ii35 (iii A.D.), D.L.3.98, Lyd.*Mens.*4.158; *salute* a god, *PMag.Par.*1.1053. **-ισμα**, ατος, τό, *greeting, salutation*, Sch.rec.A.*Pers.*935. **-ισμός**, ὁ, *greeting, visit* to a person of rank, Plb.32.15.8; *salutation* addressed to a god, *PMag.Par.*1.1046. **-ιστικός**, ή, όν, Sch.rec.A.*Pers.*l.c.

**χαιρέφυλλον**, τό, *chervil*, *Anthriscus Cerefolium*, only in Lat. form *chaerephy̆lon* (metri grat.) Colum.10.110; *caerefolium* Plin.*HN*19.170.

**χαιρ-ηδών**, όνος, ἡ, *delectation*, Com. word in Ar.*Ach.*4, formed after ἀλγηδών. **-ητικός**, ή, όν, *jovial, hilarious*, Vett.Val.18.29.

**χαιροσύνη**, ἡ, *joy*, *BCH*50.529 (Marathon, ii A.D.), Hsch.

⊛ **χαίρω**, Il.7.191, etc.; 3 pl. imper. χαιρόντων E.*HF*575: impf., Ep. χαῖρον Il.14.156, Ion. χαίρεσκον 18.259: fut. χαιρήσω 20.363, Hdt.1.128, Ar.*Pl.*64, And.1.101, Arr.*An.*5.20.6; Ep. redupl. inf. κεχαρησέμεν Il.15.98; later χᾰρῶ v.l. in *Apoc.*11.10: aor. ἐχαίρησα Plu.*Luc.*25: pf. κεχάρηκα Ar.*V.*764, part. -ηκώς Hdt.3.42, etc., Ep. acc. κεχᾰρηότα, pl. -ότας, Il.7.312, Hes.*Fr.*77:—**Med.** (in same sense), χαίρομαι, noted as a barbarism in Ar.*Pax*291 (v. Sch.), but found in *BCH*36.622 (Perinthus, written χέρ-), Alex.Aphr.*Pr.*1.20, al.: fut. χᾰρήσομαι Ps.-Luc.*Philopatr.*24, (συγ-) Plb.30.18.1, D.S.31.15; Dor. χαρησοῦμαι Pythag.*Ep.*3.7; χᾰροῦμαι Lxx*Za.*4.10, (κατα-) ib.*Pr.*1.26; Ep. κεχᾰρήσομαι Od.23.266: aor. 1 part. χαιρησάμενος *BGU*742ii3 (ii A.D.): Ep. aor. 1 χήρατο Il.14.270; ἐχ- Opp.*C.*1.509, etc.; part. χηράμενος *AP*7.198 (Leon.): Ep. redupl. aor. 2, 3 pl. κεχάροντο Il.16.600 (χάροντο Q.S.6.315); opt. 3 sg. and pl. κεχάροιτο, -οίατο, Od.2.249, Il.1.256:—**Pass.** (in same sense), aor. 2 ἐχάρην [ᾰ] 7.54, etc., Ep. 3 sg. χάρη 5.682, 13.609; subj. χᾰρῇς Pl.*R.*606c; opt. χᾰρείη Il.6.481; inf. χᾰρῆναι Simon.164; part. χᾰρείς Il.10.541, Sapph.118, Pi.*I.*6(5).10, Ar.*Th.*981 (lyr.), etc.; pf. κεχάρημαι *h.Bacch.*7.10, E.*IA*200 (lyr.), Ar.*V.*389 (anap.); part. κεχαρμένος E.*Or.*1122, *Tr.*529 (lyr.), *Cyc.*367 (lyr.): plpf. 3 sg. and pl. κεχάρητο, -ηντο, Hes.*Sc.*65, *h.Cer.*458:—*rejoice, be glad*, Il.3.111, 21.347, etc.; γραῦς ἥδε οἰνοφόρος κεχαρημένη ὧδε κάθηται *IG*12(8).679 (Scyros, ii B.C.): χ. θυμῷ Il.7.191, al.; ἐν θυμῷ 24.491, Od.22.411; φρεσὶν ᾗσι Il.13.609; φρένα 6.481; χ. νόῳ *to rejoice* inwardly, Od.8.78; χαίρει δέ μοι ἦτορ Il.23.647; αὐτὰρ ἐμὸν κῆρ χ. Od.4.260; χ. καὶ γελᾷν S.*El.*1300; ἥδομαι καὶ χαίρομαι κεὐφραίνομαι Ar.*Pax*291; opp. λυπεῖσθαι, A.*Fr.*266.3, S.*Aj.*555, etc.; opp. ἀλγεῖν, Id.*Tr.*1119.—Constr., 1. c. dat. rei, *rejoice at, take pleasure in* a thing, νίκῃ Il.7.312; φήμῃ Od.2.35; δώρῳ Hes.*Op.*358; μόλπᾳ Sapph.*Supp.*25.5, cf. S.*OT*1070, Pl.*Mx.*238d, etc.: c. dat. pers., χαῖρε.. ἀνδρὶ δικαίῳ Od.3.52; with a part. added, χάρη δ' ἄρα οἱ προσιόντι Il.5.682, cf. 24.706, Od.19.463: with Preps., χαίρειν ἐπί τινι S.*Fr.*926, X.*Mem.*2.6.35, *Cyr.*8.4.12, Isoc.2.30, Pl.*Lg.*739d, etc.; πρὸς τοῖς παιδικοῖς Eup.327; with a part. added, ἐπ' ἐξεργασμένοις κακοῖσι χ. E.*Ba.*1040, cf. 1033: rarely ἔν τινι A.*Eu.*996 (lyr.), S.*Tr.*1119: also c. dat. modi, χ. γέλωτι *express one's joy* by laughter, X.*Cyr.*8.1.33. b. of a plant, χαίρει ὑφάμμοις χωρίοις Thphr.*HP*6.5.2; also ἡ κύστις χ. τῇ χολῇ Gal.19.646. 2. rarely c. acc., with a part. added, χαίρω δέ σ' εὐτυχοῦντα E.*Rh.*390; τοὺς γὰρ εὐσεβεῖς θεοὶ θνῄσκοντας οὐ χ. Id.*Hipp.*1340; χαίρω σ' (ἐλθόντα) Id.*Fr.*673 (this usage is said to be Oropian, *EM*808.4). b. with a neut. Adj., ταῦτα λυπεῖσθαι καὶ ταὐτὰ χαίρειν τοῖς πολλοῖς D.18.292: c. acc. cogn., ἁπλῆν χαίρειν ἡδονήν Arist.*EN*1154$^{b}$26; χ. ἀνδραπόδων τινὰ χαράν Plu.2.1091e. 3. c. part., χαίρω.. τὸν μῦθον ἀκούσας *I rejoice at* having heard, *am glad to* hear, Il.19.185, cf. 7.54, 11.73; χαίρουσιν βίοτον νήποινον ἔδοντες Od.14.377, cf. 12.380, Hes.*Op.*55; χαίρω.. κόμπον ἱείς Pi.*N.*8.49; χαίρεις ὁρῶν φῶς, πατέρα δ' οὐ χαίρειν δοκεῖς; E.*Alc.*691; χαίρω φειδόμενος Ar.*Pl.*247; θωπευόμενος χαίρεις Id.*Eq.*1116 (lyr.), cf. Pl.*Smp.*191e, etc. b. c. part. pres., *delight in* doing, *to be wont* to do, χρεώμενοι χαίρουσι Hdt.7.236, cf. S.*Ph.*449, Ar.*V.*764, Pl.*Prt.*318d, 346c, 358a. 4. χαίρειν ὅττι or ὅτι.., Od.14.51, 526, Pi.*N.*5.46; ἐχάρην καὶ ἐθρασυνάμην ὅτι ἔμαθον.. Metrod.*Fr.*42; χ. οὕνεκα.. Od.8.200. II. with negat., esp. with fut., οὐ χαιρήσεις *thou wilt* or *shalt not rejoice*, i.e. *thou shalt* not *go unpunished, shalt repent* it, Ar.*Pl.*64; οὐ χαιρήσετον Id.*Eq.*235; so οὐδέ τιν' οἴω Τρώων χαιρήσειν Il.20.363, cf.15.98, Od.2.249, Ar.*V.*186; ἀλλ' οὐδ' ὣς Κῦρος γε χαιρήσει Hdt.1.128; with an interrog., *σὺ..χαιρήσειν νομίζεις;* Plu.*Alex.*51: rarely with other tenses, *ὅπως ἂν μὴ χαίρωσιν* D.19.299; *οὐκ ἐχαίρησεν* Plu.*Luc.*25: for a similar use of the part., v. infr. IV. 2. **III.** freq. in imper. *χαῖρε*, dual *χαίρετον*, pl. *χαίρετε*, as a form of greeting, **1.** at meeting, *hail, welcome* (esp. in the morning, acc. to D.C.69.18, cf. Luc.*Laps.*), Il.9.197, Od.13.229, etc.; *χαῖρε, ξεῖνε, παρ' ἄμμι φιλήσεαι* 1.123; strengthd., *οὖλέ τε, καὶ μάλα χαῖρε, θεοὶ δέ τοι ὄλβια δοῖεν* 24.402; *χαῖρέ μοι* Il.23.19, cf. S.*OC*1137; repeated, A.*Eu.*996, 1014 (both lyr.), S.*Aj.*91, etc.; *χαῖρ' ὡς μέγιστα, χαῖρε* Id.*Ph.*462; in greeting one's native land, the sun, etc., A.*Ag.*508,22, S.*Ph.*1453 (anap.). **b.** sts. implied in the use of *χαίρω*, *κῆρυξ Ἀχαιῶν, χαῖρε..*Answ. *χαίρω* I *accept the greeting*, A.*Ag.*538; *νῦν πᾶσι χαίρω, νῦν με πᾶς ἀσπάζεται* I *hear the word χαῖρε* from all, S.*OT*596: so in inf., *τὸ χαίρειν* dub. l. in Pl.*Chrm.*164e; *χαίρειν δὲ τὸν κήρυκα προὐννέπω* I bid him *welcome*, S.*Tr.*227; *προσειπών τινα χ. οὐκ ἀντιπροσερρήθη* X.*Mem.*3.13.1; but *χαίρειν τἄλλ' ἐγώ σ' ἐφίεμαι* I bid thee *have thy pleasure*, S.*Aj.*112. **c.** inf. alone at the beginning of letters, *Κῦρος Κυαξάρῃ χαίρειν* (sc. *λέγει*) X.*Cyr.*4.5.27, cf. Theoc.14.1; used by Alexander the Great to Phocion as a mark of respect, Duris 51J. **2.** at leave-taking, *fare-thee-well*, Od.5.205, 13.59, 15.151; *χαῖρε πόλλ' ὠδελφέ* Ar.*Ra.*164; pl., *χαίρετε πολλάκι* Theoc.1.144; freq. put into the mouth of the dying, S.*Aj.*863, *Tr.*921, Pl.*Phd.*116d, etc.: hence in sepulchral inscriptions, *IG*7.203, etc. **b.** hence, imper. *χαιρέτω, χαιρόντων*, *have done with.., away with..*, *εἴτ' ἐγένετο ἄνθρωπος εἴτ' ἐστὶ δαίμων, χαιρέτω* Hdt.4.96; *χαιρέτω βουλεύματα τὰ πρόσθεν* E.*Med.*1044, *χαιρόντων πόνοι* Id.*HF*575; cf. Pl.*Smp.*199a, *Lg.*636d, 886d. **c.** *ἐᾶν χαίρειν τινά* or *τι* *dismiss from one's mind, put away, renounce*, Hdt.6.23, 9.41, Ar.*Pl.*1187, Pl.*Phd.*63e, *Prt.*348a, X.*An.*7.3.23, etc.; *συχνὰ χ. ἐᾶν τινα* Pl.*Phlb.*59b; *ἐλευθερίαν μακρὰ χ. ἐᾶν* Luc.*Apol.*3; *μακρὰ χ. εἰποῦσα* Ael.*VH*12.1; *πόλλα μοι τὰν Πωλυανάκτιδα παῖδα χαίρην* Sapph.86; *τὴν Κύπριν πόλλ' ἐγὼ χαίρειν λέγω* E.*Hipp.*113, cf. 1059, Pl.*Tht.*188a; *χ. κελεύων πολλὰ τοὺς Ἀχαρνέας* Ar.*Ach.*200; *εἰπεῖν χαίρειν τινά* *Ath.Mitt.*56.131 (Milet., Hellenistic), cf. Luc.*Dem.Enc.*50; *χαίρειν προσαγορεύειν* Ar.*Pl.*322 (metaph. in Pl.*Lg.*771a); *χαίρειν προσειπεῖν* Eup.308: less freq. c. dat. pers. (never with *ἐᾶν χ.*), *πολλὰ χαίρειν ξυμφοραῖς καταξιῶ* A.*Ag.*572 (nisi leg. *ξυμφοράς*); *φράσαι..χαίρειν Ἀθηναίοισι* Ar.*Nu.*609 (troch.); *πολλὰ εἰπόντα χ. τῷ ἀληθεῖ* Pl.*Phdr.*272e, cf. *Phd.*64c, *R.*406d, X.*HG*4.1.31 (codd., fort. *ἀλλήλους*), Jul.*ad Them.*255a. **3.** on other occasions, as in comforting, *be of good cheer*, Od.8.408; at meals, 4.60, 18.122; *χαῖρε, γύναι, φιλότητι good luck be* on our union, 11.248; *εὐχωλῇς χαίρετε* 13.358: *χαῖρε ἀοιδῇ* *h.Hom.*9.7. **IV.** part. *χαίρων glad, joyful*, Il.1.446, etc.; *χαίροντα φίλην ἐς πατρίδ' ἔπεμπον εἰς Ἰθάκην* Od.19.461; *χαίροντι φέρειν..χαίρων* 17.83; *λυπούμενοι καὶ χαίροντες* in sorrow and *in joy*, Arist.*Rh.*$1356^{a}$16: also pf. part. *κεχαρηκώς* Hdt.3.27,42, etc. **2.** joined with another Verb, *safe and sound, with impunity*, *χαίροντα ἀπαλλάσσειν* ib.69, cf. 9.106, D.24.153; more freq. with a neg., *οὐ χαίρων to one's cost*, *οὐ χαίροντες γέλωτα ἐμὲ θήσεσθε* Hdt.3.29; *οὔ τι χαίρων ..ἐρεῖς* S.*OT*363, cf. *Ant.*759, *Ph.*1299, E.*Med.*398, Ar.*Ach.*563, Pl.*Grg.*510d; *οὐ γάρ..χαίρων τις..τοὐμὸν ἀλγυνεῖ κέαρ* Eup.90; *οὔτε χαίροντες ἂν ἀπαλλάξαιτε* X.*An.*5.6.32; also *οὔτι χαιρήσων γε σύ* Ar.*V.*186; cf. supr. II. **3.** in the same sense as imper. (supr. III), *σὺ δέ μοι χαίρων ἀφίκοιο fare*-thee-*well*, and may'st thou arrive, Od.15.128, cf. Theoc.2.163; *χαίροισ' ἔρχεο* go thy way *rejoicing*, Sapph.*Supp.*23.7; *ἀλλ' ἑρπέτω χαίρουσα* let her go *with a benison*, S.*Tr.*819; *χαίρων ἴθι fare*-thee-*well*, E.*Alc.*813, *Ph.*921; *χαίρουσα..στεῖχε* Id.*Hipp.*1440. **4.** *τὸ χαῖρον τῆς ψυχῆς* Plu.2.136c, 1089e. **V.** Astrol., of a planet, occupy the position appropriate to another of its own *αἵρεσις*, Serapio in *Cat.Cod.Astr.*8(4).230, Ptol.*Tetr.*51, Vett.Val.63.6, Man.2.348. (Cf. Skt. *háryati* 'take pleasure in', Umbr. *heriest* 'will wish', Lat. *horior.*)

**χαιτ-έεις**, *εσσα, εν*, Old Ionic for *χαιτήεις*, Semon.7.57. ⊛ **–η**, *ἡ*, *loose, flowing hair*, *ξανθὴν ἀπεκείρατο χαίτην* Il.23.141; *τίλλοντό τε χαίτας* Od.10.567, cf. S.*Aj.*634 (lyr.): *χαίταν ἐλαίᾳ..στεφανωσάμενον* B.10.28; pl., of a single person, *χαίτας πεξαμένη* Il.14.175, cf. 10.15, Pi.*N.*1.14, B.16.105, etc.; *χαίτᾱς* (Dor. acc.) *ὑπὲρ κεφαλῆς* Tyrt.1.39 Diehl; used esp. of *back hair*, acc. to Ruf.*Onom.*14. **2.** of a horse's *mane*, *θαλερὴ δ' ἐμιαίνετο χαίτη* Il.17.439, cf. 19.405; *ἀμφὶ δὲ χαῖται ὤμοις ἀΐσσονται* 6.509, cf. X.*Eq.*5.5, 7.1, Plu.*Pel.*22. **3.** after Hom., of a lion's *mane*, E.*Ph.*1121; *ὅσα χαίτην ἔχει, ὥσπερ λέων*, opp. *ὅσα λοφιὰν ἔχει, ὥσπερ ἵππος*, Arist.*HA*$498^{b}$28, cf. *PA*$658^{a}$31: but metaph., *φρίξας λοφιᾶς λασιαύχενα χαίταν*, of Aeschylus, Ar.*Ra.*822 (hex.). **b.** *ὀξυβελεῖς χ.*, of a hedgehog's spines, Emp.83.2. **4.** *crest* of a helmet, Plu.*Alex.*16. **5.** metaph. of trees, *foliage*, Call.*Del.*81: pl., Theoc.6.16, *Anacreont.*17/18.12; also *βύβλος..ἐπ' ἄκρῳ χαίτην ἔχουσα* Str.17.1.15. (Ambraciot word acc. to *AB*1095: not in Prose of human hair; cf. Avest. *gaēsa-* 'curly hair'.) **–ήεις**, Dor. **χαιτάεις**, *εσσα, εν*, *with long flowing hair*, epith. of Apollo, Pi.*P.*9.5, cf. *AP*6.234 (Eryc.). **2.** *with a long mane*, of the horse, Phoc.3, A.R.2.1237; of bears, *shaggy*, Opp.*H.*5.38. **3.** of plants, *thick-leaved*, *καλάμινθος* Nic.*Th.*60; cf. *χαιτέεις*. **–ωμα**, *ατος, τό*, *plume*, *κράνους* A.*Th.*385.

**χάκωμα**, misspelling of *χάλκωμα*, *JHS*32.159 (Pisidia).

**χᾱλά**, *ἡ*, Dor. for *χηλή*.

**χαλαβεῖν**· *θορυβεῖν*, Hsch.; cf. *ἀλαβυτῶ*.

⊛ **χαλάδριον**, *τό*, *mat* or *pallet*, *PTeb.*414.13 (ii A.D.), *POxy.*646 (ii A.D.), etc., cf. *χάλανδρον*; also written **χαλάτριον** *PLond.*5.1714.32 (vi A.D.).

⊛ **χάλαζ-α** [χᾰ], *ης, ἡ*, *hail* (cf. Pl.*Ti.*59e, Arist.*Mu.*$394^{b}$1), *ὄμβρον ..ἠὲ χάλαζαν ἢ νιφετόν* Il.10.6, cf. 15.170, *Apoc.*8.7, etc.: pl., X.*Oec.*5.18, Pl.*Smp.*188b, *R.*397a; *χ. στρογγύλαι hailstones*, Ar.*Nu.*1127 (troch.); *ἀπὸ τῶν χαλαζῶν..ἄπαγε σεαυτόν* Id.*Ra.*852: metaph., *any pelting shower*, *ὀμβρία χ.* S.*OC*1503; *χ. αἵματος* Pi.*I.*7(6).27. **II.** *any small knot like a hailstone*, **1.** *pimple* or *tubercle* in the flesh of swine, Arist.*HA*$603^{b}$18, *Pr.*$963^{b}$34, Androsth.ap.Ath.3.93c. **2.** *small cyst*, such as grows on the eyelid, Gal.19.437, Poll.4.198, etc. **3.** *a knot* or *hard lump*; in an egg, Arist.*HA*$560^{a}$28; in coal, Thphr.*Sign.*25; in ivory, Philostr.*VA*2.13; *λίθοι χαλάζης crystals*, 1*Enoch*14.9,10. (Cf. Sloven. *žled*, Little Russian *oželeda* 'sleet, ice'.) **–αῖος**, *α, ον*, = *χαλαζήεις*, *νιφετός* Nonn.*D.*2.540 (s. v. l.). **II.** (*χάλαζα* II. 3) *knotty*, *φηγός* Orph.*A.*763. **–άω**, *hail*, Luc.*Bis Acc.*2: metaph., *fall thick as hail*, *Com.Adesp.*314. **II.** (*χάλαζα* II. 1) *to have pimples* or *tubercles*, Ar.*Eq.*381; *χαλαζῶσαι* [*ὗες*] Arist.*HA*$603^{b}$21. **–επής**, *ές*, *hurling abuse as thick as hail*, *τάφος*, of Hipponax, *AP*7.405 (Phil.). ⊛ **–ήεις**, Dor. **–άεις**, *εσσα, εν*, *like hail*, *φόνος χ.* blood *thick as hail* (cf. *χάλαζα* I fin.), Pi.*I.*5(4).50; *συρμός* *AP*6.221 (Leon.); *ὀϊστοί* Nonn.*D.*18.232. **II.** *σκορπίος χ.* a scorpion *whose sting causes an icy chill*, Nic.*Th.*13. **–ίας**, *ου, ὁ*, = *χαλάζιος* III, Plin.*HN*37.189. **–ιάω**, *suffer from χάλαζαι* II. 2, Aët.7.83. **–ιον**, *τό*, Dim. of *χάλαζα* II. 2, Cels.7.7.3, Gal.10.1019, Paul.Aeg.3.22. **II.** pl., of *trichinosis*, in pigs, Archig.ap.Aët.13.120. **–ιος**, *ον*, *full of knots* or *clots*, *σπέρμα* Steph. *in Hp.*2.479 D. **II.** epith. of Zeus, *god of hail*, at Cyzicus, *JHS*24.21; of Apollo at Thebes, Procl.ap.Phot.*Bibl.*p.321 B. **III.** Subst., name of a precious stone, *resembling a hailstone*, Orph.*L.*758, cf. *χαλαζίας*.

**χᾰλαζο-βολέω**, *shower hail*, *AP*5.63 (Asclep.). **–βόλος**, *ον*, *showering hail*, *νέφη* Plu.2.499f. **–κοπέω**, *smite with hail*, in Pass., Thphr.*CP*5.8.3, *HP*4.14.1. **–κοπία**, *ἡ*, *damage by hailstorm*, Id.*CP*5.8.2. **–ομαι**, *to be hailed upon*, *Gloss.* **–φύλαξ** [ῠ], *ἄκος, ὁ*, *hail-guard, one who averts hail* by magical rites, Sen.*QN*4.6, Plu.2.700f.

**χᾰλαζ-ώδης**, *ες*, *like hail*, *πάγος ἀέρος* Plu.2.922c. **b.** *granular*, *σπέρματα* Arist.*HA*$582^{a}$30, cf. Ruf.*Anat.*57; *containing granules*, of urinary sediment, Hp.*Coac.*569; of sputum, Aret.*SD*1.12. **2.** *bringing hail*, *ἄνεμοι* Arist.*Mete.*$365^{a}$1, cf. $364^{b}$22, Vett.Val.6.4, *Gp.*1.12.18; *ζῴδιον* (viz. Aries) *Cat.Cod.Astr.*4.152. **II.** (*χάλαζα* II) *pimply*, of the tongue, Hp.*Epid.*4.10; of pigs, *measly*, Arist.*HA*$603^{b}$16. ⊛ **–ωσις**, *εως, ἡ*, *pimpliness*, Gal.14.770.

**χᾰλαίνω**, poet. for *χαλάω* I. 4, *ῥυτὰ χαλαίνοντες* Hes.*Sc.*308.

**χᾰλαίπους**, *ὁ, ἡ*, neut. *πουν*, gen. *ποδος*:—*with loose, trailing feet, halting*, *Ἥφαιστος* Nic.*Th.*458; vv. ll. *χωλοίπους, κυλλόπους*.

**χᾰλαίρῠπος**, *ὁ*, *suds in which clothes have been washed*, Cratin.452, cj. in Polem.Hist.83 (*χαμαὶ ῥυπῶ* codd. Macr.).

**χάλανδρον**· *κράββατον*, Hsch.; cf. *χαλάδριον*.

**χᾱλαργός**, *όν*, Dor. for *χηλαργός*.

**χᾰλᾰρ-ός**, *ά, όν*, *slack, loose*, *δέρματα* Hp.*Aph.*5.71; *ὑποδήματα* Ar.*Th.*263; *ἁλύσεις* Th.2.76; *χαλινός* X.*Eq.*10.3, cf. 7.1; *θῶραξ* ib.12.1; *χ. κοτυληδών loose, supple* joint, Ar.*V.*1495 (anap.); *χ. κνήμη*, opp. *σκληρά*, X.*Eq.*7.6; *χ. ἁρμονίαι loose, languid, effeminate* music, Pl.*R.*398e; *χαλαρωτέραν..ἐποίησε χορδαῖς δώδεκα* (sc. *τὴν μουσικήν*) Pherecr.145.5; *χ. πόροι relaxed, open* pores, Arist.*HA*$514^{a}$32; *τὸ χ.*, = *χαλαρότης*, Anaximen.1. Adv. *–ρῶς* Hp.*Fract.*16; *χ. ἐνηρμόσθαι, δεδέσθαι*, Plb.34.3.5, *Gp.*5.8.4. **–ότης**, *ητος, ἡ*, *slackness, looseness*, X.*Eq.*9.9, 10.13,16, Gal.18(2).87. **–όω**, in Pass., *to be relaxed in tension*, Erot. s. v. *σφυγμοί*.

⊛ **χάλ-ᾰσις** [χᾰ], *εως, ἡ*, *slackening, loosening*, of bandages, Hp.*Fract.*10 (pl.); *τῇ χ. τε καὶ ἀνέσει* Pl.*R.*590b; *relaxation*, *τοῦ ῥοώδους χαλάσεως δεομένου* Gal.*Sect.Intr.*7; *τῶν στεγνῶν* ib.6; but *χ. νόσου remission*, opp. *ἐπίδοσις*, Id.19.190. **2.** *free play* of the parts of a whole, Plot.4.4.45; *τῇ χαλάσει εἰδοποιηθῆναι* Dam.*Pr.*47. **3.** *lowering* by means of pulleys, *κιόνων* *University of Egypt, Faculty of Arts Bulletin* 3(2).58. ⊛ **–ασμα**, *ατος, τό*, *slackened condition, relaxation*, *ἀναπνοὴ καὶ χ.* Plu.2.133d, cf. Luc.*Asin.*9; *lack of elasticity*, Ph.*Bel.*58.8, 65.50; *low tension* of blood-vessels, Orib.7.19.6. **2.** *gap* in the line of battle, Plb.18.30.8; *σύμμετρον ἔχειν χ.* to be packed *not* too *tightly*, Plu.*Aem.*32. **3.** *slit*, Ruf.*Anat.*59, Gal.4.733; *χ. ποιῶν ἐν τῇ ὑποτομῇ* *IG*7.3073.114 (Lebad., ii B.C.). **4.** *baulk* or *footpath* on the edge of arable land, *PLille* 2.16 (iii B.C.), *PGiss.*36.17 (ii B.C.), *PLond.*3.881.21 (ii B.C.), etc. **5.** *dislocation*, *ἄρθρων* Dsc.1.109 (pl.). **6.** *congenital hernia*, Vett.Val.161.19 (pl.). **7.** *free play* (cf. foreg. 2) of a joint, Erot. s. v. *πλοώδης*. **–ασμάτιον**, *τό*, *slight slackening* in a rope, Hero *Aut.*19.3. **–ασμός**, *ὁ*, = *χάλασις*, Dsc.1.109 (pl., v. l.), Herod.Med.ap.Orib.10.8.10, Philum.ap.eund.45.29.2. **–αστέον**, *one must relax*, Herod.Med. in *Rh.Mus.*58.91, Gal.*Sect.Intr.*7. **–αστήρια** (sc. *σχοινία*), *τά*, *ropes for letting down* a portcullis, opp. *ἀνασπαστήρια*, App.*BC*4.78: cf. *σχαστήρια*. **–αστικός**, *ή, όν*, (*χαλάω*) *fit for slackening* or *making supple*, *ἔλαιον σωμάτων χ.* Sch.Il.23.281, cf. Plu.2.658e. **2.** *laxative*, Gal.*Sect.Intr.*7; *ὁ χ. τρόπος τῆς ἐπιμελείας* S.E.*P.*2.240. **–αστόν**, *τό*, *festoon*, Lxx 2 *Ch.*3.5,16; *chain* as ornament, *PSI*2.183.6 (v A.D.). **–αστός**, *ή, όν*, *relaxed*, dub. in *PRyl.*198 *Intr.* (iii A.D.).

**Χᾰλαστραῖος**, *α, ον*, *of, from Chalastra* on the Thermaic Gulf:—

τὸ Χαλαστραῖον (sc. νίτρον) prob. a fine kind of *soda*, found in a lake near that place, used with lye or soap for purposes of cleansing, Pl.*R*.430a, Plu.2.134e (pl.); ῥύμματι καὶ νίτρῳ Χαλαστραίῳ Alciphr. 3.61, cf. Plin.*HN*31.115.—Χαλεστραίου is v.l. in Pl. l.c., Χαλέστρη is found in Hdt.7.123.

**χᾰλᾰτονέω**, *to be loose*, of joints, Dsc.1.112; *get loose*, of a bandage, Heliod.ap.Orib.48.33.5; *relax in tension*, Porph. *in Harm.* p.294 W., Herm. *in Phdr.*p.130 A.

**χαλάτριον**, v. χαλάδριον: hence **χαλατριόομαι**, *to be furnished with mats*, *PLond*.3.1164*h*.7 (iii A.D.).

**χᾰλάω**, A.*Eu*.219, etc., Ep. 3 pl. χαλόωσιν Opp.*H*.2.451; Aeol. 3 pl. χόλαισι Alc.18.9 codd.Heraclit.: fut. χᾰλάσω [λᾰ] Hp.*Aër*.8, *Epid*.7.80: aor. ἐχάλᾰσα A.*Pr*.177 (anap.), Hp.*Epid*.7.23, etc.; Ep. χάλασσα *h.Ap*.6, pl. subj. χαλάσσομεν Alc.*Supp*.23.10; Dor. part. χᾰλάξαις Pi.*P*.1.6; 3 sg. fut. or aor. subj. χαλάξει (dub. sens.) *Berl.Sitzb*.1927.164 (Cyrene):—Med., Ep. aor. χαλάσαντο A.R. 2.1264:—Pass., aor. ἐχαλάσθην, subj. χᾰλασθῇ A.*Pr*.991, Pl. *Phd*.86c: pf. κεχάλασμαι *AP*9.297 (Antip.), App.*Mith*.74, Plot. 4.3.16: plpf. ἐκεχάλαστο Aristid.1.315 J. I. trans., *slacken, loosen*, χ. βιόν, τόξα, *unstring* the bow, *h.Ap*.6, *h.Hom*.27.12; χ. τὰ νεῦρα, opp. συντείνειν, Pl.*Phd* 98d; χ. τὸν πόδα, of a ship, v. πούς II. 2: metaph., τὰ τῆς πολιτείας χ., opp. ἐπιτείνειν, Plu.2.827b:—Pass., opp. ἐπιτείνεσθαι, Pl.*Phd*.86c, 94c; χαλᾶσθαι καὶ διαφθείρεσθαι Id. *Lg*.653c; χαλᾶσθαι ὑπὸ τῆς ἡδονῆς Porph.*Marc*.7. 2. *let down, let fall*, πτέρυγα χαλάξαις Pi.l.c.; χαλάσας ὀλίγον τὸ μέτωπον *having unbent* the brow, Ar.*V*.655 (anap.); μαστοὺς χάλασον, says the Cyclops to his ewe, E.*Cyc*.55 (lyr.); κράβατον, δίκτυα χ., *Ev.Marc*. 2.4, *Ev.Luc*.5.5; τὴν ἱερὰν ἄγκυραν Suid.; *dip* in a liquid, εἰς αἷμα *PMag.Par*.1.2886; *soak*, *PHolm*.14.33:—Med., ἱστὸν χαλάσαντο *lowered* it, A.R.2.1264. 3. *let loose, release*, τινὰ ἐκ δεσμῶν A.*Pr*. 177 (anap.); abs., *let go, slacken one's hold*, μηδαμῇ χάλα ib.58. 4. ἡνίας χ. *slacken* the reins, esp. in metaph. sense, χ. τὰς ἡνίας τοῖς λόγοις Pl.*Prt*.338a, cf. E.*Fr*.409. 5. κλῆθρα χ. *loose* the bars or bolts, i.e. *undo* or *open* the door, S.*Ant*.1187, E.*Hipp*.808; κλῇδας Id.*Med*.1314; χ. τοὺς μοχλοὺς Ar.*Lys*.310; but also πύλας μοχλοῖς χαλᾶτε A.*Ch*.879. 6. *loosen* or *undo* things drawn tightly together, χ. κρεμαστὴν ἀρτάνην S.*OT*1266; χ. πᾶν κάλυμμ' ἀπ' ὀφθαλμῶν Id.*El*.1468; χ. δεσμά E.*Andr*.577; ἀσκόν Id.*Cyc*.161; τὸ στόμα X.*Eq*.6.8:—Pass., τὰ χαλώμενα ὅπλα Hp.*Art*.43; πρὶν ἂν χαλασθῇ δεσμά A.*Pr*.991. 7. of the bowels, etc., ὑγρὰ χ. Hp.*Prorrh*.1. 99, cf. *Coac*.20; ἢν αἱ μῆτραι μὴ χαλάσωσι τὰ ἐπιμήνια Id.*Mul*.1. 61. 8. metaph., τὴν ὀργὴν χ. *let it go*, Ar.*V*.727 (anap.); χ. [τὸν νόον] ἐς ὄψιν τινός Ti.Locr.104c; χ. ἐπιθυμίαν Plu.2.133a; τὸ βαρὺ καὶ ἀμειδές Alciphr.3.3; *remit*, μήτε τῆς προνοίας χαλώσης τὴν.. ὑπεροχήν Procl.*Inst*.122; τὸ ἀεὶ ταῦτα οὕτως ἔχειν ἐχάλασαν *relaxed* the strict *principle* that.. Pl.*Sph*.242e:—Pass., *to be softened*, λίθος εἰς ὑγρότητα κεχαλασμένος Callistr.*Stat*.5; also κεχαλάσθαι εἰς τὸ αὐτεξούσιον *to have free play*, opp. συντετάχθαι, Plot.4.3.16. II. intr., *become slack* or *loose*, opp. συντείνω, Pl.*Phd*.98d; χόλαισιν ἄγκυρραι Alc.18.9 (s. v.l.); ζῶναι χαλῶσι E.*Ba*.935; πύλαι χαλῶσαι *open* gates, X.*Cyr*.7.5.29: metaph. c. gen., *have a remission of*, χαλάσσομεν τὰς θυμοβόρω λύας Alc.*Supp*.23.10; τί χαλᾷ μανιῶν; A.*Pr*.1057 (anap.); (also abs., S.*OC*203 (lyr.), 840); *relax*, φρονήματος χ. E.*Fr*.716; τῆς ὀργῆς Ar.*Av*.383 (troch.); [τὸ ὂν] χαλάσαν τῆς τοῦ ἑνὸς ἁπλότητος Dam.*Pr*.13. 2. c. dat. pers., χ. τινι *give way* or *yield to* any one, *be indulgent to* him, εἰ τοῖσιν.. κτείνουσιν ἀλλήλους χαλᾷς A.*Eu*.219; χάλα τοκεῦσιν E.*Hec*.403; with gen. add., μοι τῆς ἀρχῆς χάλασον Pl.*Men*.86e, cf. Plu.*Lyc*.7: abs., *give way*, εἴκειν ὁδοῦ χαλῶντα τοῖς κακίοσιν E.*Ion*637. 3. abs., *grow slack* or *weak*, ἐπειδὰν αἱ ἐπιθυμίαι παύσωνται κατατείνουσαι καὶ χαλάσωσι Id.*R*.329c; *abate*, χαλάσει ὁ παγετός Hp.*Aër*.8; ὀδύνη Id.*Acut*.16.

**χαλβάνη** [βᾰ], ἡ, the resinous *juice of all-heal, Ferula galbaniflua* (v. πάνακες), Thphr.*HP*9.1.2, 9.7.2, Nic.*Th*.52, Lxx *Ex*.30.34, *Si*.24. 15, Dsc.3.83, Plu.2.1009f. (Hebr. *ḥelbᵉnāh*.)

❋**χαλβᾰνίς**, ίδος, ἡ, *of* or *from* χαλβάνη, ῥίζα Nic.*Th*.938: as Subst., Androm.ap.Gal.14.41.

**χαλβᾰνόεις**, εσσα, εν, *of* or *from* χαλβάνη, ῥίζα Nic.*Al*.555.

**Χαλδ-αΐζω**, *follow the Chaldaean fashion* or *creed*, Ph.1.581, 2. 11. **-αῖος**, ὁ, *Chaldaean*, Hdt.3.155, S.*Fr*.638, etc. II. *astrologer*, Arist.*Fr*.35, Cic.*Div*.1.1.2, Phld.*Rh*.1.42S., Gem.2.5 (since the Chaldaeans were given to astrology, cf. Hdt.1.181, Arr.*An*.7.17.1, etc.):—**Χαλδαία** (sc. γῆ), ἡ, *Chaldaea*, St.Byz., Ptol.*Geog*.5.19:—**Χαλδαϊκός**, ή, όν, *Chaldaean*, γράμματα Ath.12.529f; ἱστορίαι, title of work by Berosus, J.*AJ*10.11.1, cf. *Ap*.1.20; μέθοδος, i.e. astrology, S.E.*M*.5.43 (so -κή alone, ib.45); ἐπιτηδεύματα Dam.ap.Suid. s.v. Χαλδαϊκοῖς: Comp. -ώτερος Id.*Pr*.206. Adv. -κῶς ib.183:—**Χαλδαϊστί**, Adv. *in the Chaldaean language*, Lxx*Da*.2.26, Ph.2. 546.

**χαλειδοφόρος**, v. χαλιδ-.

**χαλεπ-αίνω**, Il.14.399, etc.: fut. -ᾰνῶ Pl.*Tht*.161a, Men.*Sam*.204: aor.1 ἐχαλέπηνα Isoc.4.102, etc.; subj. χαλεπήνῃ Il.16.386; inf. -ῆναι 18.108:—Pass., aor. ἐχαλεπάνθην, v. infr. II: (χαλεπός):—*to be severe, sore, grievous*, μέγα βρέμεται χαλεπαίνων [ἄνεμος] Il.14.399; εἰ καὶ μάλα περ χαλεπαίνοι [ὥρη χειμερίη] Od.5.485. 2. mostly of persons, *to be violent, angry*, ὅτε τις πρότερος χαλεπήνῃ Il.19.183, cf. Ar.*Ra*.1020 (anap.), Th.3.82, 8.92, Pl.*R*.426e, etc.; *display* or *portray anger*, ἀληθινώτατα Arist.*Po*.1455ᵃ31: c. dat., *to be angry with*.., Ζεὺς ὅτε δή ῥ' ἄνδρεσσι κοτεσσάμενος χαλεπήνῃ Il.16.386, cf. Od.5. 147, 16.114, 19.83; χ. τῷ ποταμῷ Hdt.1.189, cf. Pl.*Phd*.116c, X. *An*.1.4.12, etc.; αἱ [κύνες] τοῖς λίθοις, οἷς ἂν βληθῶσι, χαλεπαίνουσι Pl.*R*.469e: folld. by a Prep., χ. ἐπί τινι *to be angry* at a thing, Od. 18.415; πρός τι Th.2.22, 59; πρός τινα X.*Mem*.2.2.1: c. dupl. dat. pers. et rei, χ. τινὶ τοῖς εἰρημένοις *to be angry with* him *for* his words, Id.*An*.5.5.24: rarely, c. gen. causae, ὧν ἐμοὶ χαλεπαίνετε, τούτων τοῖς θεοῖς χάριν εἰδέναι ib.7.6.32; also χ. ὑπέρ τινος Luc.*Ind*.25: folld. by a conjunction, χ. ὅτι.. X.*An*.1.5.14; χαλ. εἰ.. Plu.*Cam*.8, etc. 3. Medic., *to be irritated*, Aret.*SD*2.11. II. Pass., *to be embittered* or *provoked*, χαλεπανθῆναί τινι, ὅτι.. against one, X.*An*.4.6.2, *Cyr*.3.1.38; πρὸς ἀλλήλους ib.5.2.18. III. Pass., *to be judged* or *treated harshly*, ἐλεεῖσθαι.. μᾶλλον εἰκός ἐστί που.. ἢ χαλεπαίνεσθαι Pl.*R*.337a.—Never used in Trag. **-ήρης**, ες, poet. for χαλεπός, ἄεθλον Mimn.11.3. ❋ **-ός**, ή, όν, *difficult* (ὃ ἂν μὴ ῥᾴδιον ᾖ ἀλλὰ διὰ πολλῶν πραγμάτων γίγνηται Pl.*Prt*.341d: opp. ῥᾴδιος, Arist.*Rh*.1363ᵃ24, in various relations): I. in reference to the feelings, *hard to bear, painful, grievous* (so freq. in Hom.), κεραυνός Il.14.417; θύελλα 21.335; ἄνεμοι Od.12.286; πόνος 23.250; ἄλγος, πένθος, 2.193, 6.169; γῆρας Il.8.103; ἄλη Od.10.464; χαλεπώτερος ἄεθλος Hes.*Th*.800; ἄλλα τῶν κατεχόντων πρηγμάτων -ώτερα Hdt.6.40; χ. πνεῦμα A.*Supp*.166 (lyr.); δύα Id.*Th*.228 (lyr.); χαλεπώτατα [πράγματα] S.*Tr*.1273 (anap.); συμφορά E.*Hipp*.768 (lyr.); νόσος, πλάνη, etc., X.*Smp*.4.37, Pl.*Sph*.245e (Comp.), etc.; ἡ ἐσβολὴ αὕτη -ωτάτη τοῖς Ἀθηναίοις ἐγένετο Th.3.26; [θώρακες] δύσφοροι καὶ χ., of ill-fitting cuirasses, X.*Mem*.3.10.13: τὸ χ. τοῦ πνεύματος the *severity* of the wind, Id.*An*.4.5.4; τὰ χ. *hardships*, opp. τὰ τερπνά, Id.*Mem*.2.1.23, etc.; τερπνῶν χαλεπῶν τε κρίσις Pi.*Fr*. 131, cf. Plot.5.9.14: Comp., *more unpleasant*, Jul.*Or*.6.202c. 2. *hard to do* or *deal with, difficult, irksome*, -ώτατον ἔργον ἁπάντων Ar.*Eq*.516 (anap.); cf. Th.3.59 (Sup.), etc.; χαλεπὰ τὰ καλά prov. ap.Pl.*Hp.Ma*.304e, al., attributed to Solon by Sch. ad loc.; χαλεπὸν ὁ βίος X.*Mem*.2.9.1, cf. Pl.*Plt*.299e: c. inf. Act. or Med., χαλεπή τοι ἐγὼ μένος ἀντιφέρεσθαι, = χαλεπόν ἐστί μοι ἀντιφέρεσθαί σοι, Il.21.482; χαλεποὶ δὲ θεοὶ φαίνεσθαι ἐναργεῖς 20.131; χαλεπὸν δέ τ' ὀρύσσειν [τὸ μῶλυ] Od.10.305; χ. προϊδέσθαι καπρός Hes.*Sc*.386; χ. ἔρις ἀνθρώποις ὁμιλεῖν κρεσσόνων Pi.*N*.10.72; χ. προσπολεμεῖν Isoc.4.138, cf. Th.7.51 (Comp.); χ. συγγενέσθαι, εὑρεῖν, γενέσθαι, Pl.*R*.330c, 412b, 502c; χ. πάσχειν Id.*Cri*.49b (Comp.): also c. inf. Pass., χαλεπὸς διαγνωσθῆναι καὶ δειχθῆναι Antipho 2.1.1, cf. Th. 3.94, etc.; χαλεπὸν ληφθῆναι ὁ τόπος Arist.*Ph*.212ᵃ8; χαλεπόν [ἐστι] c. inf., 'tis *hard, difficult* to do, Od.4.651; c. acc. et inf., 'tis *difficult for* one to do.., Il.16.620, Od.20.313: c. dat. et inf., Il.21. 184, Od.11.156. 3. *dangerous*, λιμένες 19.189; θάλασσα Th. 4.24; χ. τὰ παρόντα X.*An*.3.2.2. 4. of ground, *difficult, rugged*, χωρία χ. καὶ πετρώδη Th.4.9; ὁδός Id.5.58, Pl.*R*.328e; χ... καὶ προσάντης.. ὁδός ἐστιν Anaxandr.56; πρόσοδοι X.*An*.5.2.3; πορεία ib.5.6.10; σταθμός ib.4.5.3; χωρίον -ώτατον a place *most difficult to take*, ib.4.8.2. II. of persons, *hard to deal with, cruel, harsh, stern* (opp. πρᾶος, Pl.*R*.493b (Sup.), Arist.*EN*1126ᵃ26), βασιλεύς, δαίμων, Od.2.232, 19.201; χαλεποί τε καὶ ἄγριοι 8.575; -ώτερος *a more bitter enemy*, Th.3.40; -ώτατοι *most difficult to deal with, most dangerous* or *troublesome*, ib.42, cf. 7.21; -ώτεροι πάροικοι Id.3.113; χαλεπόν γε θυγάτηρ κτῆμα Men.18: c. dat. pers., *cruel* or *harsh* towards one, Od.17.388; τοῖς ξυμπροθυμηθεῖσι τὸν ἔκπλουν Th.8.1, etc.; πρὸς τοὺς πολεμίους, τοὺς ἀγνῶτας, Pl.*R*.375c, Arist.*Pol*.1328ᵃ8 (also πρὸς τοὺς δρόμους X.*Cyn*.5.17); ἐπὶ νύμφαις ἀλλοτρίαις Theoc. 22.145. b. of words, χαλεπῷ ἠνίπαπε μύθῳ Il.2.245, etc.; ἐρεθιζέμεν αἰεὶ μύθοισιν χ. Od.17.395; χ. ὀνείδεα, ὁμοκλαί, Il.3.438, Od.17.189; φῆμις 14.239; μῆνις Il.5.178. c. esp. of judges, ἢν τὸ δίκαιον φυλάσσων χ. Hdt.1.100, cf. Pl.*Criti*.107d, And.4.36; also χ. ἀρχή Th.1.77; τιμωρία Pl.*Ap*.39c (Comp.); νόμοι Id.*Hp.Mi*.372a (Comp.), D.21.44, 35.50. d. *savage, fierce*, κύνες X.*An*.5.8.24, *Cyn*.10.23; of bees, Arist.*HA*624ᵇ30 (Comp.); [θηρία] χ. τὰς φύσεις Pl.*Plt*. 274b. 2. *ill-tempered, testy*, χ. ὢν καὶ δύσκολος Ar.*V*.942, cf. Isoc.19.26; ὀργὴν χ. Hdt.3.131; χαλεπῇ τῇ χειρί with a *rough* hand, Ar.*Lys*.1116. 3. of plants, *hurtful to the soil*, Thphr.*HP*8.9. 3 (Sup.).

B. Adv. **-πῶς** *hardly, with difficulty*, διαγνῶναι χ. ἦν ἄνδρα ἕκαστον Il.7.424; χ. δέ σ' ἔολπα τὸ ῥέξειν 20.186; χ. κε φύγοις κακόν Hes.*Op*.684; χ. ὀργὰς μεταβάλλουσιν E.*Med*.121 (anap.); χ. γνῶναι Antipho 3.2.1; τὰ τοῖς ἄλλοις χ. εὑρημένα ῥᾳδίως μανθάνειν Isoc.1.18, cf. 44; οὐ or μὴ χ. without *much ado*, Th.1.2, 7.81, etc. 2. *hardly, scarcely*, δοκέω.. χ. ἂν Ἕλληνας Πέρσῃσι μάχεσθαι Hdt.7.103; χ. παρὰ τοῖς ἐχθροῖς εὑρεθήσεται Lys.29.2; χ. ἂν πείσαιμι Pl.*Phd*. 84d. 3. χ. ἔχει, = χαλεπόν ἐστι, Th.3.53: c. acc. et inf., X.*HG* 7.4.6. 4. *painfully, miserably*, -ώτερον ζῆν Pl.*R*.579d; ἐν τοῖς -ώτατα διῆγον Th.7.71. II. of persons, *angrily, cruelly, harshly*, χ. τιμωρεῖσθαι Id.3.46; ἀποκρίνασθαι Id.5.42, cf. E.*Hipp*.203 (anap.), Ar.*Pl*.60, Pl.*Phdr*.269b; χ. φέρειν τι *take it ill*, Th.2.16, Pl.*R*.330a, etc.; also χ. ἔφερον τῷ πολέμῳ, τοῖς πράγμασιν, X.*HG*5.1.29, *An*. 1.3.3; ἐπὶ τῇ πολιορκίᾳ Id.*HG*7.4.21, cf. D.H.3.50; also χ. φέρειν τινός Th.2.62; also χ. λαμβάνεσθαι τοῦ παιδός Hdt.2.121.δ'; χ. λαμβάνειν περί τινος Th.6.61; of the laws (cf. supr. II. 1 c), χ. προστάττειν Pl.*Lg*.925d. 2. freq. in the phrase χ. ἔχειν *to be angry*, X.*An*.6.4.16, etc.; τινι *with* one, Id.*HG*1.5.16; πρὸς τοὺς λόγους Isoc.3.3, cf. 51; χ. ἔχειν τισὶν ἐπί τινι *with* persons for a thing, D.20.135, cf. Plu.*Cic*.43; χ. διακεῖσθαι πρὸς ἅπαντας Isoc.*Ep*. 7.5; χ. πρὸς φιλοσοφίαν διακεῖσθαι Pl.*R*.500b; χ. πρὸς ἡμᾶς διετέθησαν Isoc.8.79; ἐπί τινι χ. διατεθείς Plu.*Per*.36. b. χ. ἔχειν, also, to be *in a bad way*, χ. ἔχω ὑπὸ τοῦ πότου Pl.*Smp*.176a, cf. *Tht*.142b.—

Beside the regul. Comp. -ώτερον (Th.1.77, 7.50, Pl.*Phd.*94d, etc.) we have -ωτέρως Th.2.50, 8.40, Thphr.*HP*6.7.1: Sup. -ώτατα Th.7.71, 8.95, Pl.*R.*579d, etc. **-ότης**, ητος, ἡ, *difficulty, ruggedness,* τῶν χωρίων Th.4.12,33: metaph. in pl., μεγάλας ἔχουσιν αἱ σύντομοι [ὁδοὶ] χαλεπότητας Jul.*Or.*7.225c. 2. generally, *difficulty,* of understanding, Arist.*APo.*93ᵇ34. II. mostly of persons, *harshness, severity,* opp. ῥᾳστώνη, Pl.*Criti.*107c, *Lg.*902c; ἡ τοῦ σοφιστοῦ χ. Id.*Sph.*254a; τρόπων χ. Id.*Lg.*929d; τῶν πολιτειῶν Isoc.4.142; abs., Th.1.84, Isoc.2.24, etc.; of the Lacedaemonians, Id.12.90; μετὰ χαλεπότητος ἀκροᾶσθαι Id.15.20; of the laws of Draco, Arist.*Pol.*1274ᵇ17: pl., opp. πραότητες, Isoc.5.116. 2. *ill-temper, vice,* of a horse, X.*Eq.*3.10.

**χᾰλεπτύς**, ύος, ἡ, Ion. for foreg., Hsch.

⊛ **χᾰλέπτω**, poet. aor. χάλεψα Dosiad.*Ara*13:—Med. and Pass., v. infr. II:—causal of χαλεπαίνω I. 2, *oppress, crush,* εἴρεσθαι δὲ θεῶν ὅστις σε χαλέπτει Od.4.423; ῥέα δὲ βριάοντα χαλέπτει Hes.*Op.*5; πιέζειν καὶ χ. Plu.2.487b. 2. *wound,* τινὰ ἰῷ Dosiad. l. c. II. *provoke, enrage,* Κύπριδα *AP*5.262 (Agath.):—Med., *to be angry,* χαλεψαμένης Ἀφροδίτης D.P.484, cf. A.R.1.1341; τισι Nic.*Th.*309; χαλέπτεσθαί τινί τινος *with* one *for* a thing, App.*BC*3.43; χαλεψάμενός τινί τινος ib.3.7; τινι alone, 2.29, al.; χαλέπτεο πένθεϊ θυμόν Q.S.3.780:—Pass., χαλεφθείς τινι *enraged at* one, v.l. in Thgn.155; μὴ χαλεφθῇς ἐμοί S.*Ichn.*328 (lyr.); σύγγνωθί μοι καὶ μὴ χαλεφθῇς *Com.Adesp.*281. III. intr. in Act., *to be angry, vexed,* τινι *at* a person or thing, Bion *Fr.*11.2.—Poet. and late Prose.

**Χαλεστραῖον, Χαλέστρη**, v. Χαλαστραῖος.

**χαλία**, ἡ, = ἡσυχία, Hsch. **χαλίδιον**, τό, *tablet,* Id.

**χᾰλῐδοφόρος**, ὁ, (χάλις) *cupbearer,* *IG*5(1).1468, al. (Messene, χαλειδ- lapides).

**χαλικάζω**, v. χαλιμάζω. **χᾰλῐκῖτις**, ιδος, ἡ, dub. in *Ostr. Strassb.*619.2 (ii A. D.).

**χᾰλῐκοκαύστης**, ου, ὁ, *lime-burner,* *Edict.Diocl.*7.4.

**χᾰλίκραιος**, η, ον, = sq., Nic.*Al.*29: irreg. Comp. χαλικρότερος, as if from *χαλικρός, ib.59, 613.

**χᾰλίκρητος**, ον, poet. for ἄκρατος, *unmixed,* μέθυ Archil.78, A.R.1.473; σπονδαί A.ap.Eust.1471.2 (v. Nauck ad A.*Fr.*448); νᾶμα *AP*5.293.6 (Agath.).

**χᾰλῐκ-ώδης**, ες, *in small masses,* Thphr.*Lap.*65. **-ωμα**, ατος, τό, (χάλιξ) in pl., *rubble and mortar, concrete,* Lat. *caementa,* *Gloss.*

**χαλιμ-άζω**, = τὸ περὶ τὰς συνουσίας πείθεσθαι (fort. ἐπτοῆσθαι), Epich.200 (χαλικ- cod. Philem.Gloss.). **-άς**, άδος, ἡ, *a shameless woman,* Hsch.; = πόρνη, Suid. (χαλίμα codd.); of the βάκχαι (χαλωμένας εἰς συνουσίαν), *EM*805.9; also expld. as ἡ ὑπὸ μέθης χαλωμένη, Eust.1471.3; **χαλιμίας** and **χαλίδας** (of the βάκχαι) are vv.ll. in A.*Fr.*448 (ap. Sch.A.R.1.473).

**χᾰλῑνᾰγωγ-έω**, *guide with* or *as with bit and bridle,* γλῶσσαν, σῶμα, *Ep.Jac.*1.26, 3.2, cf. Luc.*Salt.*70, *Tyr.*4; ἄνθρωπον Vett.Val.248.25, cf. Chor.32.139p.376 F.-R., Lib.*Decl.*3 *Intr.*1. **-ία**, ἡ, *guiding as by bit and bridle,* τῶν τῆς νεότητος παθῶν Simp. *in Epict.* p.119 D. **-ός**, όν, *guiding as with bit and bridle.* Νέμεσις Vett.Val.131.6, al.

**χαλῑν-άριον**, τό, Dim. of χαλινός, Arr.*Epict.*4.1.80, *PLond.*5.1657.8 (iv/v A. D.); = *frenum,* *Gloss.*; also gloss on παρήϊον, Sch.D Il.4.142. **-ῖτις**, ιδος, ἡ, *bridling,* epith. of Athena, *who bridled* Pegasus for Bellerophon, Paus.2.4.1, 5.

**χαλῑνο-ποιική** (sc. τέχνη), ἡ, *the art of making bridles,* Arist.*EN*1094ᵃ11 (v.l. -ποιητική, as in Asp. *in EN*4.26). **-ποιός**, ὁ, *bridle-maker,* Them.*Or.*26.329a, *Gloss.*

⊛ **χᾰλῑνός** (Aeol. **χάλιννος** prob. in *Et.Gud.*561.5), ὁ, heterocl. pl. χαλινά A.R.4.1607, Opp.*H.*1.191, Plu.2.613c, Sor.1.100, etc.:—*bit,* once in Hom., ἐν δὲ χαλινοὺς γαμφηλῇς ἔβαλον Il.19.393; χαλινὸν ἐμβαλεῖν γνάθοις E.*Alc.*492; χ. ἐξαιρεῖται X.*Eq.*3.2; of the horse, χ. οὐκ ἐπίσταται φέρειν (metaph. of Cassandra) A.*Ag.*1066; χ. δέχεσθαι, λαμβάνειν, X.*Eq.*3.2, 6.10; λαβεῖν, ἔχειν, Arist.*Rh.*1393ᵇ16,21; τὸν χ. ἐνδακεῖν champ the *bit,* Pl.*Phdr.*254d; of the rider, δοτέον τὸν χ. one must give a horse the *rein,* X.*Eq.*10.12; ὀπίσω σπάσαι, ξυνέχειν ἀνάγκῃ, Pl.*Phdr.*254e, Luc.*DDeor.*25.1; [χ.] εἰς ἄκρον τὸ στόμα καθιέμενος X.*Eq.*6.9.—Expld. of the *bit,* opp. reins (ἡνίαι), by Poll.1.148; so ἡνίας τε... καὶ χ. Pl.*R.*601c; χ. τινα χαλκεῖ ἐκδιδόντα σκευάσαι Id.*Prm.*127a; κατὰ [τὸν κυνόδοντα] ἐμβάλλεται ὁ χ. Arist.*HA*576ᵇ18, cf. A.*Th.*123 (lyr.), S.*OC.*1067 (lyr.); but distd. fr. στόμιον by Hdt.1.215, cf. A.*Th.*207 (lyr.), X.*Eq.*6.9, 10.9, etc.; and may be used generally for *bit and bridle,* Hdt.3.118, 4.64, *IG*1².374.176, *PCair.Zen.*659.11 (iii B. C.). 2. metaph., of *anything which curbs, restrains,* or *compels,* Ἀργοῦς χ., of an anchor, Pi.*P.*4.25; χ. λινόδετοι, = χαλινωτήρια, E.*IT*1043; παρθενίας χ. λύειν, of the virgin zone, Pi.*I.*8(7).48; χαλινοῖς ἐν πετρίνοισιν, of Prometheus' bonds, A.*Pr.*562 (anap.); Διὸς χ., of the will of Zeus, ib.672; χαλινῷ ἀναύδῳ μένει, of forcible constraint, Id.*Ag.*238 (lyr.); πολλῶν χαλινῶν ἔργον οἰάκων θ' ἅμα, i.e. it requires much skill and force to guide, S.*Fr.*869; τῷ δήμῳ χ. ἐμβαλεῖν ὕβρεως *a bridle to curb* their violence, Plu.*Comp.Per.Fab.*1, cf. Luc.*Herm.*82; τῆς γλώττης τὰ χ. Plu.2.613c; ἐπέστω τῷ στόματι χ. Lib.*Ep.*315.4; χ. οὐδεὶς ὀμμάτων Philostr.*VA*6.11. II. generally, *strap, thong,* E.*Cyc.*461 (dual). III. part of the *tackle of a ship,* *IG*2².1610.11,14. IV. *corner of the* horse's *mouth,* where the bit rests, Poll.2.90 (pl.); of the human mouth, Nic.*Al.*117,223, *PUniv.Giss.*44.7, (ii/i B. C.), Heliod. ap.Orib.48.31.4, Sor.1.100, *PSI*9.1016.25 (ii B. C.), Aret.*SA*1.9, Cael.Aur.*TP*1.4, Aët.8.27; but, = ἡ σύνδεσις τῶν γνάθων, Ruf.*Onom.*53, cf. Aët.8.40. 2. *fangs of serpents,* from their shape and position in the mouth, Nic.*Th.*234.

**χᾰλῑνουργός**, ὁ, *bridle-maker,* Lat. *lorarius,* *Gloss.*; abbreviated χαλινου in *Sammelb.*5124.684 (ii A. D.) acc. to Schow.

**χᾰλῑνοφάγος** [φᾱ], ον, *champing the bit,* στόματα Call.*Lav.Pall.*12.

**χᾰλῑν-όω**, *bridle* or *bit* a horse, X.*Cyr.*3.3.27, *An.*3.4.35, *HG*7.2.21:—Pass., Id.*Eq.*5.1, Plb.3.65.6, etc. II. metaph., *curb, bridle, check,* τὴν ναῦν Philostr.*VA*3.23; [φόβον, ἐπιθυμίαν] Epicur.*Fr.*485; τὴν ὀργήν, τὸν θυμόν, Ps.-Phoc.57, Them.*Or.*34 p.454 Dind.; τὸ φιλόφωνον καὶ λάλον Plu.2.967b; τὴν ἀλογίαν Hierocl. *in CA*8 p.431 M.; τὴν ἑαυτῶν ἀπληστίαν Lib.*Or.*47.35:—Pass., *to be bridled, curbed,* τῇ φρουρᾷ καὶ τοῖς ὁμήροις Plu.*Arat.*38; ὑπὸ τοῦ λόγου Philostr.*VA*4.30: abs., *to be tongue-tied,* Hp.*Mul.*1.2. **-ωσις**, εως, ἡ, *bridling,* X.*Eq.*3.11 (pl.), v.l. in Poll.1.184. **-ωτήρια** (sc. ὅπλα), τά, of ships, *mooring-cables,* E.*Hec.*539, Opp.*H.*1.359, Nonn.*D.*3.20.

**χάλιξ** [ᾰ], ῐκος, ὁ and ἡ, *small stone, pebble,* in pl., Arist.*Fr.*213; ἐστρωμένη χάλιξιν ὁδός Luc.*Trag.*226. 2. freq. as collect. in sg., *gravel, rubble,* used in building, Th.1.93, *PCair.Zen.*760 (iii B. C.), *PPetr.*3 p.290 (iii B. C.), Plu.*Cim.*13; τῇ χ. καταμείξαντες τὴν ἀμμοκονίαν, so as to make *concrete,* Str.5.4.6: pl., Ar.*Av.*839; χ. σιδηραῖ dub. sens. in *IG*1².314.44.

⊛ **χάλις** [ᾰ], ιος, ὁ, *neat wine,* Hippon.73, *Docum. ant. dell'Africa Italiana* ii *Cirenaica* 101 (i A. D.), Hsch., Suid., Eust.1471.2. II. = ὁ μεμηνὼς καὶ κεχαλασμένος τὰς φρένας (i. e. = χαλίφρων), Hsch. III. f.l. for σχαλίς, Them.*Or.*23.297a.

**χαλιστόν**· σκαιόν, ἢ ἀγαθὸν καὶ δίκαιον, Hsch.

**χᾰλι-φρονέω**, *to be light-minded,* χαλιφρονέοντα σαοφροσύνης ἐπέβησαν, Od.23.13. **-φροσύνη**, ἡ, *levity, thoughtlessness,* 16.310 (in pl.). **-φρων**, ονος, ὁ, ἡ, (χάλις) *light-minded, thoughtless,* joined with νήπιος, 4.371, 19.530; of Dionysus (cf. χάλις), *AP*9.524.23. II. *of yielding temper, pliable,* χ. νεύματα κούρης Musae. 117.

**χαλκ-άνθεμον**, τό, = χρυσάνθεμον, Ps.-Dsc.4.58. **-ανθές**, τό, = χάλκανθον, Posidon.52J., Str.14.6.5, Dsc.5.79,98, v.l. in Ruf.ap. Orib.7.26.38. ⊛ **-άνθη**, ἡ, v.l. for χάλκανθον in Dsc.3.80. **-ανθίζω**, *resemble* χάλκανθον *in colour,* Ruf.*Fr.*79. II. of water, *to be vitriolic,* Antyll.ap.Orib.10.3.6. **-ανθον**, τό, *solution of blue vitriol (copper sulphate),* used for ink and for shoemaker's blacking, Dsc.3.80, Orph.*A.*960, Plin.*HN*34.123. II. = χρυσάνθεμον, Ps.-Dsc.4.58. **-ανθος**, ὁ and ἡ, = foreg. I, acc. to Gal.12.721, cf. Ruf.ap.Orib.7.26.38 (v.l.). **-άνθρωπος**, ὁ, *copper-man,* alchemical term in Zos.Alch. p.110B. **-ανθώδης**, ες, *vitriolic,* of water, Antyll.ap.Orib.10.3.1, Gal.13.958. **-αρμᾰτος**, ον, *with brazen chariot,* epith. of Ares, Pi.*P.*4.87. **-άς**, άδος, ἡ, = χρυσάνθεμον, Ps.-Dsc.4.58. **-ασπις**, ιδος, ὁ, ἡ, *with brazen shield,* of warriors, Pi.*O.*9.54, B.10.62, Ibyc.3.31 Diehl, E.*HF*795 (lyr.); epith. of Ares, Pi.*I.*7(6).25, E.*IA*764 (lyr.); of Heracles, S.*Ph.*727. II. οἱ χ., a corps in the Maced. army, Plb.2.66.5, al., Plu.*Sull.*16. III. *of one who ran the armed foot-race* (ὁπλιτοδρόμος), Pi.*P.*9.1. **-εγχής**, ές, *with brazen lance,* χαλκεγχέων Τρώων E.*Tr.*143 (lyr.) (χαλκέγχεων in cod.Hsch. is wrongly accented, cf. δολιχεγχής). **-εία**, ἡ, *smith's work,* Hp.*Art.*53; opp. τεκτονική (joiner's work), Pl.*Prt.*324e, cf. *Smp.*197b. II. *smithy, forge,* Hero *Bel.*98.3. **-εῖον**, Ion. **-ήϊον**, τό, = foreg. II, Hdt.1.68, Hp.*Art.*47,77, And.1.40, Pl.*Euthd.*300b. II. = χαλκίον (q. v.): 1. *cauldron, pot,* Hdt.4.81,152 (v.l. χαλκίον), Hp.*Morb.*4.39, Pl.*Prt.*329a codd.: esp. copper in baths, Thphr.*Char.*9.8; χ. ἐρυθρόν *vessel* of pure copper, Hp.*Ulc.*12; χ. μολυβοῦν *POxy.*1648.62 (ii A. D.). 2. *concave metal reflector* in a lamp, X.*Smp.*7.4. 3. *bronze structure,* Paus.2.22.2. III. τὰ χαλκεῖα (sc. ἱερά), at Athens, *a festival at the end of the month Pyanopsion,* Phanod.22, Hyp.*Fr.*90, cf. Poll.7.105; title of play by Menander. ⊛ **-εος**, η, ον, Ep. for χάλκεος, *of copper* or *bronze, brazen,* ἔγχεϊ χαλκείῳ Il.3.380; αἰχμὴ χ. 4.461; κληΐς Od.21.7; αὐγὴ χ. gleam *of brass,* Il. 13.341; χάλκειον γένος, of the Age *of brass,* Hes.*Op.*144; εἰκὼ χαλκείην Maiist.15: once in Trag., χάλκειον κάρα, S.*Fr.*537 (nisi leg. χάλκεον); in late Prose, χάλκειος σφαῖρα S.E.*M.*7.376. II. Subst., χάλκειος, ἡ, *yellow fish thistle, Carlina corymbosa,* Thphr.*HP*6.4.3, Plin.*HN*21.94. III. v. χαλκήϊος. **-είτης**, v. χαλκίτης II. **-ειώδης**, ες, = χαλκοειδής I, φάρμακον prob. l. in Zos. Alch. p.216 B. ⊛ **-έλᾰτος**, ον, poet. for χαλκήλατος, πέλεκυς Pi.*O.*7.36; θάλαμοι *AP*5.216 (Paul.Sil.); σάλπιγξ *Epigr.Gr.*350 (Nicaea); εἰκών ib.944 (Oenoanda). **-εμβολάς**, άδος, poet. fem. of sq., νᾶες E.*IA*1319 (lyr.). **-έμβολος**, ον, *with brazen beak,* D.S.14.59, Plu.*Cim.*13, *Trag.Adesp.*142, Lyr. in *PTeb.*2(a) ii 9; χαλκέμβολοι (abs.), as the name of a special kind of ship, Plu.*Ant.*35. **-ένδῠτος**, ον, *brass-clad,* Sch.E.*Ph.*1130. **-έντερος**, ον, *of brazen bowels,* applied by Suid. to the Grammarian Didymus. **-εντής**, ές, *brass-armed,* πόλεμος Pi.*N.*1.16; στρατιά ib.11.35. **-έντονον**, τό, *torsion-engine with metallic strands,* Ph.*Bel.*56.22.

⊛ **χαλκεό-γομφος**, ον, *brass-riveted,* δῶμα Simon.37.7. **-θῡμος**, ον, = χαλκεοκάρδιος, Polem.*Cyn.*41. **-θώραξ**, Ion. **-θώρηξ**, ηκος, ὁ, ἡ, *with brazen breastplate,* Il.4.448, 8.62; cf. χαλκοθώραξ. **-κάρδιος**, ον, *with heart of brass,* Theoc.13.5. **-κρᾶνος**, ον, *bronze-tipped,* ἰός B.5.74. **-κτῠπος**, ον, *with clang of bronze,* μάχα Id.17.59. **-μήστωρ**, ορος, ὁ, *skilled in arms,* χαλκεομήστορος Ἕκτορος, restored by Burges in E.*Tr.*271 (lyr.) from Hsch. (χαλκεομίστωρ· ἰσχυροφόρος, i. e. χαλκεομήστορος· ἰσχυρόφρονος). **-μίτρας**, Ion. **-ης**, ὁ, = χαλκομίτρας, B.*Scol.Oxy.Fr.*5.8 (and prob. Id.12.109), Q.S.1.274; epith. of the planet Mars, *Cat.Cod.Astr.*1.173. **-νω-**

**τος**, *ον*, *with back of brass*, κύμβαλα Nonn.*D*.10.388. **-πεζος**, *ον*, *brass-footed*, ἕδρη *AP*9.140 (Claudian.).

**χαλκέοπλος**, *ον*, *with arms* or *armour of brass*, Δαναοί E.*Hel.* 693 (lyr.).

⊛ **χάλκεος**, *έα*, Ion. *-έη* (Hom. always *-είη* (v. *χάλκειος*)), *εον* (also *εος*, *εον* Il.18.222 (ὄπα χάλκεον Αἰακίδαο, where Zenod. χαλκέην as disyll.), Hdt. (v. infr.): rarely in Trag., A.*Ch.*686, S.*Fr.*534.3,7 (anap.), E.*Ion* 1; Aeol., Dor. **χάλκιος** Epich.79, Alc.15.3, *SIG* 945.6 (Assos, iv B.C.), *IGRom.*4.1302.35 (Cyme, i B.C./i A.D.), also Boeot., cf. χαλκοῦς; Att. **χαλκοῦς**, *ῆ*, *οῦν* (*IG*1$^2$.313.55, etc., but χαλκέων δέλτων Pl.*Ax.*371a codd.); Ep. also **χάλκειος**, v. χάλκειος: (χαλκός):—*of copper* or *bronze*, *brazen*, οὐδός, δόμος, τεῖχος, Il.8.15, 18.371, Od.10.4; ἄξων, κύκλα, Il.13.30, 5.723; χ. Ἀράων θάλαμοι Antim. in *PMilan.*17.48; χ. καὶ ἀδαμαντίνοις τείχεσι Aeschin.3.84; ὀδός Astyd.9, Ister 30; esp. of arms and armour, ἔγχος, ξίφος, Il.3.317,335; σάκος 7.220; θώρηξ, χιτών, 13.398,440; ἔντεα 18.131, etc.; χαλκέοις ὅπλοις E.*Ph.*1359; also λέβητος χαλκέου A.*Ch.*686, cf. E.*Cyc.*392; χαλκέοισι κάδοις, χαλκέοις δρεπάνοις, S.l.c.; in Trag. mostly contr., χαλκοῖς βάθροισι Id.*OC*1591; χαλκῆς ὕπαι σάλπιγγος Id.*El.* 711; χαλκῆς ἐκ δέλτου Id.*Tr.*683. **b.** of statues, χ. Ζεύς, χ. Ποσειδέων, a *bronze* statue of.., Hdt.9.81; χ. ταῦρος Pi.*P.*1.95; ἡ χαλκῆ Ἀθηνᾶ D.19.272; ἱστάναι τινὰ χαλκοῦν Id.13.21; ἄξιος σταθῆναι χαλκοῦς Arist.*Rh.*1410$^a$33; στήλη ἐφ' ἧ ὁ στρατηγός ἐστιν ὁ χαλκοῦς And.1.38; cf. χαλκῆ. **c.** χ. ἀγών a contest *for a shield of brass*, Pi.*N.*10.22. **2.** metaph., *brazen*, i.e. *hard*, *stout*, *strong*, χάλκεος Ἄρης Il.5.704, etc. (unless *wearing brazen armour*, cf. χάλκεοι ἄνδρες Orac.ap.Hdt.2.152); Χαλκοῦς, nickname of Aristomedes, Din.ap.Did. *in D.*9.57, Philem.1.2 D., Plu.*Dem.*11; χ. στονόεντ' ὅμαδον Pi.*I.*8(7).27; χ. αὐδά Id.*Pae.*2.100; χάλκεον ἦτορ a heart *of brass*, Il.2.490; ὄπα χ. 18.222; χ. ὕπνος, i.e. the sleep of death, 11.241; χαλκέοισι νώτοις, of Atlas, E.*Ion* 1. **3.** χαλκῆ μυῖα, a boy's game, a sort of *blind-man's-buff*, Herod.9a, Poll.9.123. **II.** as Subst., v. χαλκοῦς. [χάλκεοι is disyll. in Hes. *Op.*150.]

**χαλκεό-στερνος**, *ον*, = χαλκοθώραξ, Ἄρης B.5.34. **-τευχής**, *ές*, *armed in brass*, E.*Supp.*999 (lyr.). **-τέχνης**, *ου*, *ὁ*, *worker in metal*, *smith*, *Epigr.Gr.*269 (Aedepsus); of Hephaestus, Q.S.2.440. ⊛ **-φωνος**, *ον*, *with voice of brass*, i.e. *ringing strong and clear*, of Stentor, Il.5.785; of Cerberus, Hes.*Th.*311.

**χαλκέοψ**, *ὁ*, *ἡ*, gen. *οπος*, = foreg., αὐλῶν ὀμφά Pi.*Pae.*3.94.

**χάλκ-ευμα**, *ατος*, *τό*, *anything made of brass*, e.g. *an axe* or *sword*, A.*Ch.*576. **2.** in pl., *brazen bonds*, Id.*Pr.*19. ⊛ **-εύς**, *έως*, *ὁ*: pl. χαλκεῖς, Att. -ῆς Ar.*Av.*490 (anap.), Pl.*R.*370d, Ep. -ῆες (v. infr.): acc. χαλκέας Id.*Smp.*221e, *R.*428d, χαλκεῖς Plu.2.214a:—*coppersmith*, opp. τέκτων (joiner, Pl.*R.*370d), ἣν [ἀσπίδα] χ. ἤλασεν Il.12.295, etc.; μίτρη, τὴν χαλκῆες κάμον ἄνδρες 4.187,216. **2.** generally, *worker in metal*, of a *goldsmith*, Od.3.432; of a *worker in iron*, 9.391; hence later, *blacksmith*, *smith* (χαλκέας τοὺς τὸν σίδηρον ἐργαζομένους Arist.*Po.*1461$^a$29), Hdt.1.68, Ar. l.c., X.*HG*3.4.17; ἀνὴρ χ. Hdt.4.200; χ. χαλκοῦ καὶ σιδήρου Lxx *Ge.*4.22. **II.** *John Dory*, *Zeus faber*, Opp.*H.*1.133, prob. in Arist.*HA*535$^b$18; distd. fr. χαλκίς, Ath.7.328d. **-ευτήριον**, *τό*, = χαλκεῖον, *Gloss.* **-ευτής**, *οῦ*, *ὁ*, = χαλκεύς, χ. ὕμνων *AP*7.34 (Antip. Sid.). **-ευτικός**, *ή*, *όν*, *of* or *for the smith's art*, φῦσα Hp.*Morb.*3.14; ἔργα X.*Vect.*4.6; τὸ χ. πῦρ, opp. τὸ μαγειρικόν, Arist.*Spir.*485$^a$35. **II.** *skilled in metal-working*, X.*Mem.*1.1.7: ἡ -κή (sc. τέχνη) the *smith's art* or *trade*, Id.*Oec.*1.1, Arist.*PA*683$^a$24, *GA*789$^b$10. **-ευτός**, *ή*, *όν*, *wrought of metal*: metaph., στίχος Πιερίδων χ. ἐπ' ἄκμοσιν *AP*7.409 (Antip.). **-εύω**, *make of copper* or *bronze* or (generally) *of metal*, *forge*, δαίδαλα πολλά Il.18.400; ξίφος S.*Aj.*1034, etc.; τὸν χαλκέα αὐτὸν χ. *work* him *on the anvil*, Pl.*Euthd.*301d: metaph., ἀψευδεῖ πρὸς ἄκμονι χάλκευε γλῶσσαν Pi.*P.*1.86: in Med. sense, πέδας χαλκεύεται αὐτῷ Thgn.539; χαλκεύεσθε μηνίσκους φορεῖν Ar.*Av.*1114 (troch.); ἐχαλκεύσατο κράνη..ὁλοσίδηρα Plu.*Cam.*40:—Pass., *to be wrought* or *forged*, ἐξ ἀδάμαντος ἢ σιδάρου κεχάλκευται Pi.*Fr.*123.4; ἀφ' ὁπόσων ταλάντων κεχ. at the cost of.., Luc.*JTr.*11; τῶν κεχαλκευμένων πρὸς ἀπώλειαν ὅπλων D.S.17.58: metaph., ἐπὶ τοῖς δεδεμένοις χαλκεύεται [ταῦτα] these arms *are being forged* against.., Ar.*Eq.*469; also of the victims in Phalaris' bull, Phalar.*Ep.*113. **II.** abs., *to be a smith*, Ar.*Pl.*163,513 (anap.), Th.3.88, Pl.*R.*396a; τὸ χαλκεύειν *the smith's art*, X.*Mem.*4.2.22. ⊛ **-εών**, *ῶνος*, *ὁ*, *forge*, *smithy*, βῆ ῥ' ἴμεν ἐς χαλκεῶνα [where εω must be pronounced as one syll.] Od.8.273, cf. A.R.3.41. **2.** *bar of wrought iron*, Lat. *strictura*, glossed φυσητήρ, χαλκεών (nisi leg. χαλκέων), *Gloss.*

**χάλκη**, v. κάλχη.

**χαλκῆ** (sc. εἰκών), *ἡ*, *bronze statue*, Antig.*Mir.*15, cf. D.L.9.39, 10.9.

⊛ **χαλκηδόνιον**, *τό*, = στίμμι, interpol. in Dsc.5.84.

**χαλκηδών**, *όνος*, *ἡ*, *chalcedony*, *Apoc.*21.19.

**χαλκ-ήϊον**, v. χαλκεῖον. **-ήϊος**, *η*, *ον*, (χαλκεύς) *of* or *for a smith*, ὅπλα Od.3.433; δόμος, i.e. *forge*, 18.328; in form **χαλκεῖος**, θῶκος Hes.*Op.*493.

**χαλκ-ήλᾰτος**, *ον*, (ἐλαύνω) *forged out of brass*, *of beaten brass*, κώδωνες, σάκος, A.*Th.*386,539; πλάστιγξ Id.*Ch.*290; σκάφη Id.*Fr.* 225; ὅπλα S.*Fr.*341; λέβητες ib.378; ἀσπίς E.*Ba.*799, cf. Ar.*Ra.* 929; cf. χαλκέλατος (q.v.). **-ήρης**, *ες*, *furnished* or *fitted with bronze*, of spears and arrows *tipped* or *armed with bronze*, ξυστόν, δόρυ, ὀϊστός, ἰοί, Il.4.469, 5.145, 13.650, Od.1.262; χαλκήρεον (sic) ἔγχος Pancrat. in *POxy.*1085.6; κυνέη, κόρυς, Il.3.316, 15.535; σάκη 17.268; generally, χ. τεύχεα 15.544; χ. στόλος, of a ship's beak, A.*Pers.*408; ναῦς χ. Plu.*Demetr.*42, *Sull.*22.

**χαλκήσιον**, *τό*, = καρχήσιον, Hero *Bel.*88.5.

**χαλκῐαῖος**, *α*, *ον*, *costing one* χαλκοῦς, *PCair.Zen.*19.5 (iii B.C.). **2.** χαλκιαία, *ἡ*, *supplementary tax on sales*, *Sammelb.*5729 (iii B.C.); abbrev. in *Ostr.Bodl.* i 96 (ii B.C.); also written χαλκιεία (q.v.).

**Χαλκῐδ-εύομαι**, *to be parsimonious*, Suid.; cf. **Χαλκιδίζω**. **-εύς**, *έος*, *ὁ*, *inhabitant of Chalcis*, Hdt.5.74, etc.: acc. pl. **Χαλκιδέας** Ar.*Eq.* 238. **II.** expld. by δειλός, Hsch. **-ιακός**, *ή*, *όν*, = **Χαλκιδικός** (quod fort. leg.), Lesb.Gramm.4. **-ίζω**, *imitate the Chalcidians* in παιδεραστία (Hsch.) or parsimony (Eust.279.18), *Com.Adesp.* 1192. ⊛ **-ικός**, *ή*, *όν*, *of* or *from Chalcis* (in Euboea or Thrace), Alc.15, Hdt.7.185, Ar.*Eq.*237. **II.** χαλκιδική, *ἡ*, = χαλκίς II, Dorio ap.Ath.7.328d. **2.** σαύρα χ. = χαλκίς III, σήψ II. 2, Dsc.2. 65, Philum.*Ven.*34. **III.** εἶδος ἀλεκτρυόνος, Hsch. **IV.** *chalcidicum*, = *fori deambulatorium*, *Gloss.*

**χαλκ-ίδιον**, *τό*, Dim. of χαλκίον I, Hermipp.65. **-ιδῖτις**, *ιδος*, *ἡ*, *a penny prostitute*, *Com.Adesp.*1352. **-ιεία**, *ἡ*, = χαλκιαία, *supplementary tax on sales*, *PLond.*3.1200 (ii B.C.). **-ίζω**, *shine like brass*, χ. τὴν χροιάν Sch.Il.14.291; of snakes, χρώματι χ. Philum. *Ven.*32.1; *ring like brass*, φωνὴ χαλκίζουσα Poll.2.117. **II.** *play the game* χαλκισμός, '*spin a copper*', Alex.337, Herod.3.65, Poll.7. 105,206; cf. χαλκίνδα. **-ικός**, *ή*, *όν*, *in copper coin*, *PFrankf.*1.38,91 (iii B.C.). **-ίνᾱος**, *ον*, *dwelling in a brazen temple*, like χαλκίοικος, Hsch. **-ίνδᾰ**, παίζειν to play *the game* χαλκισμός, Id. **-ινος**, *η*, *ον*, *of bronze*, νόμισμα *OGI*339.44 (Sestos, ii B.C.); διάδημα *Ostr.Bodl.* i 262 (ii B.C.); χαλκίνη (sc. δραχμή) *PLond.*2.380 (ii/iii A.D.). **II.** *concerning* or *in bronze coin*, λόγος *PTeb.*119.51 (ii B.C.).

**χαλκίοικος** [ῐ], *ἡ*, *she who dwells in a brazen house* (i.e. Athena, whose name is freq. omitted), at Sparta, from the brazen shrine in which her statue stood, E.*Hel.*228,245 (both lyr.), Ar.*Lys.*1300 (lyr.), Th.1.128,134, Paus.3.17.2, 10.5.11.

⊛ **χαλκίον**, *τό*, *copper vessel*, *cauldron*, *kettle*, *IG*1$^2$.393, Ar.*Ach.*1128, *Fr.*107,330, Eup.108,256, X.*Oec.*8.19; χ. θερμαντήριον, = θερμαντήρ, *IG*2$^2$.1416, 4.39 (Aegina), Gal.13.663. **2.** *cymbal*, τὸ Δωδωναῖον χ., prov. of a *chatterbox*, Men.66, cf. Zen.6.5. **3.** *bowl of the* κότταβος, Poll.6.110. **4.** *copper ticket* given to the dicasts, bearing the name of the court in which they were to serve, D.39. 10. **5.** *piece of copper money*, πονηρὰ χαλκία Ar.*Ra.*724 (troch.); παραλαβὼν τὼ χαλκίω Eub.83; cf. Poll.9.90.—Freq. written χαλκεῖον in codd., but χαλκίον is required by the metre in Com., and corroborated by Inscrr. (v. supr.), and Pap., *PCair.Zen.*630.4 (iii B.C.), *PMich.Zen.*65.2 (iii B.C.), *PSI*6.625.12 (iii B.C.), etc. **II.** prob. Dim. of χάλκη, = κάλχη II, *IG*4$^2$(1).102.242 (Epid., iv B.C.).

**χαλκιοφύλαξ** [ῠ], *ἄκος*, *ὁ*, *boiler-keeper* in a bathing-establishment, *Stoic.*1.10, *PCair.Zen.*799.8 (iii B.C.).

**χαλκίς**, *ίδος*, *ἡ*, an unknown bird (cf. κύμινδις), Il.14.291, cf. Arist.*HA*615$^b$10, Parth.13.4:—Cratin.315 (hex.) parodies Il. l.c., taking χ. in the sense of *a brazen pot*. **2.** = *pica maritima* (i.e. *roller*, *Coracias garrula*), *Gloss.* **II.** a migratory fish, perh. *pilchard* or *sardine*, *Clupea sardina*, Epich.48, al., Arist.*HA*543$^a$2, Numen.ap.Ath.7.328d, Opp.*H.*1.244; also a freshwater fish, Arist. *HA*568$^a$18. **III.** = ζιγνίς, a poisonous *lizard*, *cicigna*, ib.604$^b$23, Plin.*HN*32.30, Aët.13.15; cf. χαλκιδικός II. 2. **IV.** at Lacedaemon, *female slave*, Proxen.8, Eust.1090.57. **V.** as pr. n., Χαλκίς, *ίδος*, *ἡ*, *Chalcis*, name of various cities, Il.2.537, etc.

**χαλκισκάριον**, *τό*, dub. sens. in *PLond.*2.191.8 (ii A.D.).

**χαλκ-ισμός**, *ὁ*, *game played by spinning a copper coin*, which was stopped by the finger before it fell, Poll.9.118, Eust.986.41, 1409. 18. **-ίτης** [ῑ], *ου*, *ὁ*, = sq. I. 2, Gal.1.452 cod.Marc.(ed. Helmreich), 15.32 (prob. l.). **II.** written **-είτης**, = χαλκεύς, *JHS*32.165 (Pisidia); written καχείτης ib.161 (ibid.). **-ῖτις**, *ιδος* (*εως* Gal. 13.375), *ἡ*, *containing copper*, λίθος χ. *copper-ore*, worked in Cyprus, Arist.*HA*552$^b$10; and in Euboea, Plu.2.434a. **2.** a mineral, *rock-alum*, Emp.ap.Gal.15.32 (sed v. foreg.), Dsc.5.99, *POxy.*1088. 19 (i A.D.), Sor.2.41; χ. στυπτηρίη Hp.*Ulc.*14; χ. κυανέη (of doubtful nature) ib.21. **II.** = χρυσάνθεμον, Ps.-Dsc.4.58.

**χαλκο-άρᾱς** [ᾰρ], *α*, *ὁ*, *bronze-armed*, of men, in gen. pl. *-αρᾶν*, Pi.*I.*4(3).63(81); acc. sg. *-άραν* ib.5(4).41. **-βᾰρής**, *ές*, *heavy* or *loaded with bronze*, ἰός Il.15.465, Od.21.423; δόρυ 11. 532: fem. **-βάρεια** (as if from *χαλκόβαρυς), Il.11.96, Od.22.259, 276. **-βᾰτής**, *ές*, (βαίνω) *standing on bronze*, *with brazen base*, or *with floor of bronze*, χαλκοβατὲς δῶ, of the house of Zeus, Od.8.321, Il.1.426, 14.173, etc.; of that of King Alcinoüs, Od.13.4. **-βᾰτος**, *ον*, = foreg., Hsch. **-βόας**, *ου*, *ὁ*, = χαλκεόφωνος, Ἄρης S.*OC*1046 (lyr.). **-γένειος**, *ον*, = sq., *AP*6.236 (Phil.). **-γενυς**, *υ*, *with teeth of bronze*, ἄγκυρα Pi.*P.*4.24. **-γλώχῑς**, *ῖνος*, *ὁ*, *ἡ*, *with point* or *barbs of bronze*, μελίη Il.22.225. **-δαίδᾰλος**, *ον*, *wrought in bronze*, ἀσπίς B.*Fr.*6. **II.** Act., *working in brass*, τέχνα *AP*9. 777 (Phil.). **-δάμᾱς** [δᾰ], *αντος*, *subduing*, i.e. *sharpening bronze*, a word of masc. termin. with fem. Subst., χαλκοδάμαντ' ἀκόναν Pi.*I.*6(5).73. **-δεσμωτήρ** and **-δεσμήτωρ**, expld. by **χαλκόδεσμος** (-δερ- cod.), Hsch. ⊛ **-δετος**, *ον*, *bronze-bound*, σάκη A.*Th.*160 (lyr.); κοτύλαι Id.*Fr.*57.6 (anap.); αὐλαί S.*Ant.*945 (lyr.); ἔμβολα E.*Ph.*114 (lyr.).

**χαλκόδους**, = χαλκώδων, Hdn.*Epim.*208.

**χαλκο-ειδής**, *ές*, *like copper*, *copper-coloured*, Arist.*Col.*793$^a$26; μέλιτται Ael.*NA*17.35; ῥάβδοι D.S.17.90, cf. Dsc.5.99. **II.** epith. of the *cuneiform* bone, χ. ὀστέον, ὀστᾶ, *PLit.Lond.*167.16

(ii/iii A.D.), Gal.14.725. **-ζωνος**, ον, *girt with bronze*, epith. of Heracles, *EM*436.18. **-θερμον**, τό, *hot bath*, *Gloss.* **-θέσιον**, τό, *boiler-room* in baths, *POxy.*2146.5 (iii A.D.), *Stud.Pal.*20.230 (iv A.D.). **-θήκη**, ἡ, a building on the Acropolis of Athens, *IG*2²120, 1469.84. II. *case for bronze vessels*, provided specially for those of value, Ath.6.231d. **-θροος**, ον, *ringing with* or *like bronze*, Nonn.*D.*13.48. **-θώραξ**, ᾱκος, ὁ, ἡ, = χαλκεοθώραξ, Pi.*Pae.*2.1, B.10.123, S.*Aj.*179 (lyr.). ❋ **-κέραυνος**, ον, epith. of the sea, perh. f.l. for χαλκ-αμάρυγος, *gleaming like copper* or *bronze*, A.*Fr.*192.3 (anap.). **-κνήμῑς**, ῖδος, ὁ, ἡ, *bronze-greaved*, Il.7.41. **-κολλητής**, οῦ, ὁ, *copper-welder, coppersmith*, *POxy.*85 ii 4 (pl., iv A.D.). **-κόλλητος**, ον, *welded*, Lat. *ferruminatus*, *Gloss.* **-κορυστής**, οῦ, ὁ, *bronze-armed, equipped with bronze*, Il.5.699, 6.199,398, al.; ὅμιλος Pi.*Pae.*6.108. **-κράς**, ᾶτος, ὁ, ἡ, = foreg., *IG*2².1424a.95, 1425.91; νόμισμα Hsch., Choerob.*in Theod.*1.132, al.; on the accent v. Hdn.Gr.1.51, al. II. *copper-headed*, i.e. *bronze-tipped*, of missiles, Tim.*Pers.*30. **-κρᾱτος**, ον, *mixed with copper*, Polyaen.4.10.2. **-κροδυσταί**, αἱ, a mystic name for the *Nurses of Dionysus*, Plu.2.672b (dub. l.). **-κροτος**, ον, *sounding* or *rattling with bronze*, epith. of Demeter, in allusion to instruments used in her worship, Pi.*I.*7(6).3; χ. ἵπποι horses *that stamp with hoofs of bronze, brazen-hoofed*, Ar.*Eq.*552 (lyr.). II. = χαλκήλατος, φάσγανον E.*Ph.*1577 (lyr.); χαλκόκροτα *bronze utensils*, *POxy.*1657.1 (iii A.D.). III. χαλκοκρότος, ὁ, = Lat. *aerarius*, *Gloss.* (καλκόκροτος cod.). **-κτῠπος**, ον, = foreg.1, καναχά prob. in B.13.16; κύμβαλα, Diog.Ath.1.3. **-κώδων**, ωνος, ὁ, ἡ, *brazen-mouthed*, σάλπιγξ B.17.3. **-λίβᾰνος** [ῐ], ου, ἡ, either *fine brass, brass of Lebanon*, or *yellow frankincense*, *Apoc.*1.15, 2.18. **-λῐθος**, ὁ, *copper ore, copper*, Ps.-Democr.Alch.p.54B. **-λογέω**, *collect* or *exact copper money*, *Rev. Épigr.*1.239 (Naples, ii A.D.), Lyd.*Mag.*3.37, Hsch., *Gloss.* **-λόγος**, ὁ, *collector of money*, *IG*14.759 (Naples), *MAMA*3.514 (Corycus, written χαρκ-), *Gloss.* **-λοφος**, ον, *with bronze crest*, Hsch. (s. v. l.). **-μίτρας**, α, ὁ, *with* μίτρη *of bronze*, Κάστωρ Pi.*N.*10.90 (to be restored for χαλκεομ-):—also **-μιτρος**, ον, Lyc. 997. **-μόλυβδος**, ὁ, *alloy of copper and lead*, Maria ap. Olymp.Alch.p.93B. **-μυια**, ἡ, *a fly of bright metallic hue*, ingredient of an eye-salve, Aët.7.100. **-μωτής**, οῦ, ὁ, *coppersmith*, *PMasp.*143ʳ14 (vi A.D.). **-νωτος**, ον, *bronze-backed*, ἀσπίς, ἰτέα, E.*Tr.*1136,1193. **-πᾰγής**, ές, *made of bronze*, σάλπιγξ *AP*6.46 (Antip.Sid.). **-πάρῃος** [πᾰ], Dor. **-πάρᾱος**, ον, *with cheeks* or *sides of bronze*, epith. of helmets, Il.12.183, 17.294, 20.397, Od.24.523; of a javelin, Pi.*P.*1.44, *N.*7.71; κρέμβαλα *Carm.Pop.*3. **-πεδος**, ον, *with floor of bronze*, ἕδρα θεῶν Pi.*I.*7(6).44. **-πλάστης**, ου, ὁ, *bronze-worker*, Lxx *Wi.*15.9. **-πλευρος**, ον, *with sides of bronze*, τύπωμα χ., of a cinerary urn, S.*El.*54. **-πληθής**, ές, *multitudinous and bronze-clad*, στρατός E.*Supp.*1220. **-πληκτος**, Dor. **-πλακτος**, ον, *smiting with brazen edge*, γένυς, of the battle-axe, S.*El.*484 (lyr.; also expld. as = χαλκήλατος). **-ποιός**, ὁ, *metal-worker*, *Sammelb.*5726. **-πους**, ποδος, ὁ, ἡ, *with feet of bronze*, τρίπους E.*Supp.*1197; ὀδός, *founded on bronze*, S.*OC*57 (expld. by Sch. with ref. to *copper*-mines): in Hom. of horses, to express the solid strength of their hoofs, χαλκόποδ' ἵππω Il.8.41; ταῦροι Pherecyd.112J.; χ. Ἐρινύς, to express her untiring pursuit, S.*El.*491 (lyr.); of Empedocles, *with bronze slippers*, Luc.*DMort.*20.4. **-πρῳρος**, ον, *with prow of bronze*, of ships, Poll.2.102. **-πτερος**, ον, *with wings of metallic hue*, ὄρνις *PSI*6.569.9 (iii B.C.); μυῖα Philum.*Ven.*25.1.

**χαλκ-όπτης**, ου, ὁ, *copper-smelter*, *IG*2.2867 (fort. χαλκο⟨κό⟩πτης); [χαλκ]όπτης dub. in *PCair.Goodsp.*30 xii 30 (ii A.D.).

**χαλκό-πῠλος**, ον, *with gates of brass* or *bronze*, ἱρόν Hdt.1.181; χ. θεά, epith. of Athena, E.*Tr.*1113 (lyr.); ὕδωρ, of Castalia, because issuing *from bronze spouts* in the shape of lions' heads, Pi.*Pae.*6.7. **-πώγων**, ωνος, ὁ, transl. of Lat. *Ahenobarbus*, Plu.*Aem.*25, D.Chr.37.40. ❋ **-πώλης**, ου, ὁ, *dealer in copper* or *bronze*, Critias *Fr.*70 D., Poll.7.196.

**χαλκ-όροφος**, ον, *with roof of bronze*, παρθενεών Nonn.*D.*47.543 (s. v. l.). **-ορῠχεῖον**, τό, f.l. for χαλκωρυχεῖον (q. v.), Thphr.*Lap.*25.

❋ **χαλκός**, Cret. **καυχός** *GDI*5011.4 (iii B.C.), ὁ:—*copper*, χ. ἐρυθρός Il.9.365; with reference to its polished surface, αἶθοψ, ἦνοψ, νῶροψ, φαεινός, 4.495, 16.408, 2.578, 12.151; Τρῶες.. χαλκῷ μαρμαίροντες 13.801; πεδίον.. λάμπετο χαλκῷ 20.156; τῆλε δὲ χ. λάμφ' ὥς τε στεροπή 10.153, cf. 11.65, 19.363; σάκος.. χαλκῷ παμφαῖνον 14.11; and of the ornaments of a house, χαλκοῦ τε στεροπήν Od.4.72; of *copper* as the first metal that men learnt to smelt and work, τῶν δ' ἦν χάλκεα μὲν τεύχεα, χάλκεοι δέ τε οἶκοι, χαλκῷ δ' εἰργάζοντο, μέλας δ' οὐκ ἔσκε σίδηρος Hes.*Op.*151; χ. ἐρυθρός (cf. supr.) Hp.*Ulc.*17, Thphr.*Lap.*57, Callix.1; χ. ἐρυθρὸς καὶ λευκός Thphr.*Od.*71; χ. Κύπριος Posidon.52J., Dsc.1.102, cf. Polyaen.3.10.14; alloyed with tin to form *bronze*, the usual meaning of the word in Hom. (v. infr. II) and freq. in later writers: σίδηρος δὲ καὶ χ. πολέμων ὄργανα Pl.*Lg.*956a, etc.; χ. κεκραμένος D.Chr.28.3. II. in Poets freq. for *anything made of metal*, esp. of arms (hence Pi. calls it πολιός, the proper epith. of iron, *P.*3.48); of offensive arms, ὀξέϊ χαλκῷ, νηλέϊ χ., of a spear, a sword, Il.4.540, 3.292, al.; of a knife, 1.236, al.; of an axe, 13.180, Od.5.244, al.; of a fish-hook, Il.16.408; of defensive arms, as the plates laid on a shield, 20.275; χαλκὸν ζώννυσθαι, of a warrior girding on his armour, 23.130; κεκορυθμένος, αἴθοπι χ. 4.495; ἑδύσετο νώροπα χ. 2.578; of both combined, πλάγχθη δ' ἀπὸ χαλκόφι χαλκός *the spear of bronze* glanced off *the helm of bronze*, 11.351. 2. of vessels, *copper, cauldron, urn*, 18.349, Od.8.426; of a cinerary urn, S.*El.*758; collectively of *bronze plate*, χ. μυρίος, Pi.*N.*10.45; θάλαμον.., ὅθι νητὸς χρυσὸς καὶ χ. ἔκειτο Od.2.338, cf.13.19,21.10,62, Il.2.226; used in payment of ransom, 22.50, cf. 340, Od.5.38. 3. of a *bronze mirror*, A.*Fr.*393, Call.*Lav.Pall.*21, *AP*6.210 (Philet.); used as a burning-glass, Thphr.*Ign.*73. 4. collectively, *copper money*, *IPE*1².24.15 (Olbia, iv B.C.), *Ev.Matt.*10.9, *Ev.Marc.*12.41, cf. ἰσόνομος II; generally, *money*, opp. κύαμοι, *IG*14.423 ii 21 (Tauromenium), cf. *BGU*822.12 (iii A.D.), etc.; χαλκοῦ σπάνις Men.*Mon.*156; χαλκὸν ἔχων πῶς οὐδὲν ἔχεις μάθε *AP* 11.167 (Pollian.). 5. = χάλκωμα, *bronze plate* or *tablet*, τὰν προξενίαν γράψαντας εἰς χαλκὸν ἀνθέμεν *IG*9(1).682 (Corcyra, iv B.C.); οὐετρανοὶ οἱ χωρὶς χαλκῶν, who have not received *bronze copies* of the privileges granted on discharge, *BGU*113.5 (ii A.D.), etc. 6. a weight, ⅛ obol, Gal.19.752. III. χαλκοῦ ἄνθος, particles thrown off by copper when cooling, Hp.*Mul.*1.104, Ph.*Bel.*102.34, Dsc.5.77. b. χαλκοῦ λεπίς, small pieces that scale off under the hammer, ib.78. (Perh. cf. Lith. *geležìs* 'iron'.)

**χαλκο-σάνδᾰλος**, ον, *with sandals of bronze*, Porph.ap.Eus.*PE* 3.11. **-σκελής**, ές, *with legs of bronze*, βοῦς S.*Fr.*336. **-σμάραγδος** [σμᾰ], ἡ, *a green stone with metallic veins*, perhaps *malachite*, Plin.*HN*37.74. **-στερνος**, ον, = χαλκοθώραξ, δυνάμεις Phleg.*Fr.*36.3J. **-στέφᾰνος**, ον, *bronze-crowned*, τέμενος Epigr.ap.D.S. 11.14. **-στομος**, ον, *with mouth of bronze*, χ. κώδων Τυρσηνική, i.e. a trumpet, S.*Aj.*17. II. *with edge* or *point of bronze*, ἔμβολοι A.*Pers.*415, Aristid.*Or.*25(43).4; μέτρον *POxy.*101.40 (ii A.D.). **-τειχής**, ές, *with walls of bronze*, αὐλά B.3.32. ❋ **-τευκτος**, ον, *made of bronze*, κλῇθρα E.*IT*99. **-τήγᾰνον**, τό, *scutra*, *Gloss.* **-τονον**, τό, *torsion-engine with strands of bronze*, Ph.*Bel.*67.43, cf. χαλκέντονον. **-τοξος**, ον, *armed with brazen bow*, Pi.*N.*3.38. **-τόρευτος**, ον, *wrought of bronze*, τρίαινα Orph.*H.*17.2. **-τορέω**, *to work* or *form of bronze*, ἔντεα *APl.*1.15. **-τορος**, ον, *of piercing, sharp bronze*, ξίφη Pi.*P.*4.147. 2. *caused by piercing with bronze*, ὠτειλαί Opp.*H.*5.329 (expld. by **-τρύπητοι** Sch.).

**χαλκοτῠπ-εῖον**, τό, *forge, smithy*, Ph.1.153, Nicom.*Harm.*6. **-έω**, *work in bronze*: τιμαὶ -τυπούμεναι, of honorary statues, *wrought in bronze*, Plu.2.820b. **-ία**, ἡ, *wound by stroke of sword*, Anon.ap. Suid. s.v. χαλκοτύπους (pl.). ❋ **-ική** (sc. τέχνη), ἡ, *art of a χαλκοτύπος*, Pl.*Plt.*288a, Plu.2.1084c. **-ιον**, τό, f.l. for χαλκοτυπεῖον. **-ος** (parox.), ον, *forging* or *working copper*, τέχναι Man.4.570; ἀνὴρ ἐν Κορίνθῳ χ. Plu.2.395c:—Subst., *coppersmith*, χ. καὶ σιδηρεῖς X.*Ages.*1.26. *Vect.*4.6; generally, *smith*, Lycurg.58, D.25.38, *IGRom.*4.1259 (Thyatira), etc.; but distd. from χαλκεύς, X.*HG*3.4.17. 2. = χαλκόκροτος I, μανίη, of the priests of Cybele, *AP*6.51. II. proparox. χαλκότῠπος, ον, Pass., *inflicted with arms of bronze*, ὠτειλαί Il.19.25. 2. *wrought of bronze*, εἰκών *APl.*5.362.

**χαλκουργ-εῖον**, τό, *copper-mine*, Plb.12.1.5 (pl.), Str.3.2.8, 6.1.5. II. *foundry*, Dsc.5.75. **-έω**, *work in bronze*, *Clara Rhodos* 6/7.403 (Camirus, iii B.C.). **-ημα**, ατος, τό, *work of bronze*, J.*AJ* 8.3.5, S.E.*M.*9.75, *BGU*362 i 8 (iii A.D.). II. = χάλκωμα, *Peripl. M.Rubr.*24, *Supp.Epigr.*6.616 (Pisidia). **-ία**, ἡ, *working in bronze*, Poll.7.104. **-ικός**, ή, όν: ἡ -κή (sc. τέχνη) the *coppersmith's art*, Arist.*Pol.*1256ᵃ6. **-ός**, όν, *working copper*, χ. μέταλλα *copper mines*, Dsc.5.91 (nisi leg. -ουργικά): Subst. -γός, ὁ, *miner*, Posidon. 47J.; *worker in bronze*, Luc.*JTr.*33, *BGU*362 x 17 (iii A.D.).

❋ **χαλκοῦς**, ῆ, οῦν, Att. contr. from χάλκεος, q.v. II. Subst. **χαλκοῦς**, ὁ, *copper coin* used at Athens, ⅛ of an obol, Ar.*Ec.*815, 818, D.42.22, Alex.15.2, Philem.64,74, Cerc.17.41, Plu.2.665b, etc.: in pl., *money*, *PCair.Zen.*519 (iii B.C.), etc.

**χαλκο-φάλᾰρος** [φᾰ], ον, *adorned with brass*, δώματα Ar.*Ach.*1072. **-φᾰνής**, ές, *having the appearance of copper*, Dsc.5.74.

**χαλκόφῐ**, Ep. gen. from χαλκός, Il.11.351.

**χαλκο-φόρος**, ον, *producing copper*, *rich in copper*, Eust.1409.8. II. *tipped with copper*, θύρσος Nonn.*D.*14.343. **-φωνος**, ον, = χαλκεόφωνος:—as Subst., ἡ, name of a *metallic-sounding stone*, Plin.*HN*37.154. **-χάρμης**, ου, ὁ, *fighting in armour of bronze*, ξένοι Τρῶες Pi.*P.*5.82; χ. πόλεμος Id.*I.*6 (5).27 (also expld. as (from χάρμα), *delighting in arms*). **-χίτων** [ῐ], ωνος, ὁ, ἡ, *bronze-clad*, Ἀχαιοί Il.1.371, 2.47, etc.; Τρῶες 5.180, al.; Βοιωτοί 15.330; Κρῆτες 13.255; Δαναοὶ πύκα χ. Epigr. ap. Aeschin.3.185. ❋ **-χρους**, ουν, *copper-coloured*, Dsc.2.182. **-χῠτος**, ον, *cast in bronze*, πλευραὶ βοός *AP*9.739 (Jul.).

**χαλκ-όω**, *turn to bronze*, πόρτιν *AP*9.795 (Jul.):—Pass., ib.716 (Anacr.). II. χαλκωθείς *clad in bronze*, Pi.*O.*13.86. **-ύδριον**, τό, Dim. of χαλκός, Zos.Alch.p.216B., Theognost.*Can.*fol.83 (om. Cramer p.126, ante νεανισκύδριον): pl., *small change*, *BGU*1821.12 (i B.C.). **-ώδης**, ες, *like bronze*, χρῶμα Thphr.*Sign* 51; ὄττιες Aret.*SD*2.13. **-ώδων**, οντος, ὁ, ἡ, *bronze-beaked*, στόλοι Hsch. (-όδ- cod., extra ordinem). **-ωμα**, ατος, τό, *anything made of bronze* or *copper, vessel, instrument*, Ar.*V.*1214, *Fr.*436, Lys.19.27, X.*An.*4.1.8, Sophr.30, Nicostr.21.4, *PCair. Zen.*40.1 (iii B.C.), *BGU*993 iii 12 (ii B.C.), Sor.2.29, etc.; ἀσπίδος τὸ χ. the *bronze-work*, opp. τὸ ξύλον, Arist.*Mete.*371ᵃ26, cf. Aen. Tact.37.7; *cauldron*, Plu.*Demetr.*24. 2. *copper plate* or *tablet*, for engraving records on, Plb.3.26.1, 3.33.18, *IG*9(1).685, al. (Corcyra, ii B.C.), 14.612 (Rhegium, i B.C.), 952.22 (Agrigentum, iii B.C.), 953.24 (Melita, iii B.C.); written **χάλχωμα**, *JHS*32.160 (Pisidia). b. generally, *metal plate*, Plb.6.23.14. 3. *beak* of a ship, D.S.20.9, Plu.*Ant.*67, etc. **-ωμᾶς**, ᾶτος, ὁ, = χαλκωματουργός, *PLond.*3.1170$^{v}$.244,257 (iii A.D.). ⊛**-ωμάτιον**, τό, Dim. of χάλκωμα, *Inscr.Délos* 1417*A* i 104 (ii B.C.), Hsch. s.v. πλάτων. **-ωμᾰτουργός**, ὁ, *maker of bronze plates*, *PRyl.*397.3 (iii A.D.). **-ών**, ῶνος, ὁ, cited as a collective noun by Hdn.Gr.1.29. **-ώνητος**, ον, *bought with money*, Hsch., cf. ἀργυρώνητος. **-ῶνυξ**, υχος, ὁ, ἡ, *with brazen hoofs*, ταῦροι Sch.A.R.3.233.

**χαλκωρῠχ-εῖον**, τό, *copper-mine*, Thphr.*Lap.*25, Str.17.2.2, Plu. 2.659c, better written **-ρύχιον**, as in *PPetr.*3 p.320 (iii B.C.), Str. l.c. (v.l.), Plu. l.c. (codd.). **-έω**, *dig* or *mine copper*, Lyc. 484. ⊛ **-ος** (parox.), ον, *digging copper, copper miner*, Tz.ad Lyc. 484.

**χαλκωτήρ**· κέραμός τις, Hsch.

**χαλμαίας**, ὁ, a liquid *measure* used in Egypt, τὸν χαλμαίαν τοῦ ἐλαίου *PSI*5.531 (iii B.C.).

**Χᾰλυβδικός** or **Χᾰλῠβικός** (later, acc. to St. Byz.), ή, όν, *Chalybian*, σίδηρος ὁ Χαλυβικός Arist.*Mir.*$833^{b}22$: **Χαλύβινος** is v.l. in Sch. S.*Tr.*1259 cod.Laur.: ἡ Χ. *the land of the Chalybes*, Hsch. 2. *of steel*, Cratin.247, Lyc.1109; ἄτερ Χαλυβδικοῦ without *Chalybian*, i.e. without *steel*, E.*Heracl.*161; Χ. στόμωμα, v. στόμωμα.

**χᾰλῠβηΐς**, ίδος, poet. fem. of χαλυβδικός, Max.302.

**Χάλυβος**, v. sq. II.

**Χάλυψ** [ᾰ], υβος, ὁ, in pl., *the Chalybes* in Pontus, who were famous for the preparation of steel, οἱ σιδηροτέκτονες Χάλυβες A.*Pr.* 715, cf. Hdt.1.28, X.*An.*5.5.1, Call. in *PSI*9.1092.48 (on another nation of the same name v. Str.12.3.20). II. as Appellat., χάλυψ, *hardened iron, steel*, A.*Pr.*133 (lyr.), S.*Tr.*1260 (anap.), Antip.Sid. in *POxy.*662.52; of a *penknife*, *AP*6.65 (Paul.Sil.); of an *axe*, *APl.* 4.127: as Adj., Nonn.*D.*36.182:—also **Χάλυβος**, ον, Χάλυβος Σκυθῶν ἄποικος, i.e. *steel*, A.*Th.*728 (lyr.); Χαλύβῳ πελέκει E.*Fr.*472.6 (anap.): pl., = Χάλυβες, E.ap.Sch.Il.*Oxy.*1087 i 28; τὸν ἐν Χαλύβοις σίδαρον Id.*Alc.*980 (lyr.).

**χᾰμάδίς** [ᾰδ] (**χᾰμάδι** read in Od.19.599 by Eust.1879.53, cf. χαμάνδις), Adv., Ep. for χαμᾶζε, *to the ground, on the ground*, τὰ μέν τ' ἄνεμος χ. χέει Il.6.147; χ. πέσε 7.16; χ. βάλε ib.190, etc.; once in Trag., A.*Th.*358 (lyr.).

**χᾰμᾱδύτης** [ῠ], ου, ὁ, *earth-creeper*, i.e. *snail*, Hsch.

**χᾰμ-ᾶζε**, Adv., (χαμαί) *to the ground, on the ground*, freq. in Hom., ἐξ ὀχέων σὺν τεύχεσιν ἆλτο χ. Il.3.29, al.; ἀπὸ πύργου βαῖνε χ. stepped *to the ground*, 21.529; [κεραυνὸν] ἧκε χ. 8.134, cf. 14. 497, 20.461; χ. κάππεσεν 15.537; τόξον..θῆκε χ. Od.21.136, cf.22. 340: rare in Trag. and Com., E.*Ba.*633 (troch.), Ar.*Ach.*341, 344 (both troch.); μὴ πέσῃ χ. Id. *V.*1012 (lyr.); χ. προβαίνουσα Babr. 115.13; freq. in later Prose, χ. θυρεοῖς κεκλιμένοις Plu.*Sull.*28; ἔχειν χ. δύ' ὀβολώ Luc.*Lex.*2. (On the exceptional accent cf. Ael. Dion.*Fr.*322, Hdn.Gr.2.951.) ⊛ **-ᾶθεν**, Adv., (χαμαί) *from the ground*, Hdt.2.125, 4.172, Eup.146b, Ar.*V.*249, the Attic form, acc. to A.D.*Adv.*187.7 (who also gives χαμαῖθεν which is found in Plu. 2.296e; χαμάθεν [ᾰ] is v.l. in Hdt.2.125). II. **χαμόθεν** is found in Cratin.296, X.*HG*7.2.7, Stesich.ap.Arist.*Rh.*$1395^{a}2$, Plu. *Alex.*35, Luc.*Ind.*9, and was the colloquial form acc. to A.D.*Adv.* 188.33. ⊛ **-αί**, Adv. *on the ground*, χ. ἧσθαι Od.7.160; τὸν αὖ χ. ἐξενάριξε Il.11.145; χ. ἐρχομένων ἀνθρώπων 5.442, cf. Sapph.94, etc.; χ. τιθεὶς πόδα A.*Ag.*906; αἷμα μητρῷον χ. Id.*Eu.*261 (lyr.), cf. Ar. *Ach.*869, *Eq.*155, *Nu.*231, al.; θέντες χ. Hdt.4.67; χ. καθίζοντες Pl. *Criti.*120b; χ. κείμενος *IG*2$^{2}$.1672.305; of birds, ποιεῖν νεοττιὰν χ., opp. ἐπὶ δένδρου, Arist.*HA*$618^{a}10$. 2. metaph., ἐσλὸν χ. σιγᾷ καλύψαι to bury in silence *underground*, Pi.*N.*9.7; χ. ἐρχόμενοι cleaving to *earth*, Luc.*Herm.*5, *Icar.*6; ὁ χ. βίος Metrod.*Fr.*38. II. = χαμᾶζε, *to earth*, ἐν κονίῃσι χ. πέσεν Il.4.482; χ. βάλον ἐν κονίῃσι 5.588, cf. Od.22.188, Il.4.526; ἐκ δίφροιο χαμαὶ θόρε 8.320; μὴ χ. πεσεῖν *to the ground*, E.*Med.*1170; οὐ χ. πεσεῖται ὅ τι ἂν εἴπῃς Pl. *Euthphr.*14d; ἔπτυσε χ. *Ev.Jo.*9.6; also ἐκβαλεῖν εἰς τὸ χ. *AP*11. 89 (Lucill.). (Cf. Lat. *humus, humi*, Lith. *žẽmė* 'earth'.)

**χᾰμαι-άκτη**, ἡ, *elder, Sambucus Ebulus*, Ps.-Dsc.4.173, Plin. *HN*24.51. **-βάλᾰνος** [βᾰ], ἡ, = ἄπιος (A) II, Dsc.4.175. **-βᾰτος**, ἡ, *blackberry, Rubus ulmifolius*, Thphr.*HP*3.18.4.

**χαμ-αίγειρον**, τό, = βήχιον, Ps.-Dsc.3.112.

**χᾰμαι-γενής**, ές, *earth-born*, epith. of men, *h.Ven.*108, *h.Cer.*352, Hes.*Th.*879, Pi.*P.*4.98; of ants, Nonn.*D.*13.209. **-δάφνη**, ἡ, *periwinkle, Vinca herbacea*, Thphr.*HP*3.18.13, Plin.*HN*21.172. 2. = δάφνη Ἀλεξανδρεία, Dsc.4.147, Plin.*HN*24.132. 3. = δαφνοειδές, Dsc.4.146. **-δῐδάσκᾰλος**, ὁ, *elementary schoolmaster*, *Edict.Diocl.* 7.66, Paul.Al.*O.*2, Sch.Ar.*Ec.*804, Hierocl.*Facet.*61. ⊛**-δῐκαστής**, οῦ, ὁ, = Lat. *judex pedaneus*, Lyd.*Mag.*3.8: hence **-δῐκαστέω**, *fill this office*, *PLips.*64.30 (iv A.D.). **-δρῠάς**, άδος, ἡ, = χαμαίδρυς, Androm.ap.Gal.14.40. **-δρῠΐτης** [ῑ] οἶνος, ὁ, wine *flavoured with germander*, Dsc.5.41. **-δρῦς**, υος, ἡ, *germander, Teucrium Chamaedrys*, Thphr.*HP*9.9.5, Dsc.3.98, Plin.*HN*24.130; gen. sg. written χαμέτρυος *BKT*3 p.32 (v/vi A.D.). 2. = τεύκριον, Ps.-Dsc. 3.97. 3. = σκόρδιον, ib.111; also **-ρωψ** (q.v.). **-εύνη**, ἡ, = χαμεύνη, *PGen.*68.16 (iv A.D.). **-εύνης**, ου, ὁ, *lying, sleeping on the ground*, Σελλοί Il.16.235; λέοντες Emp.127; ἔρως Max.Tyr.24.8:—fem. ⊛**-ευνάς**, άδος, σύες Od.10.243, 14.15; Com., of parasites, Eub.139 (lyr.). **-εύρετος**, ον, *found on the ground*, Anon.ap.Suid. **-ζηλος**, ον (η, ον Hp.*Art.*13):—*seeking the ground, low-growing, dwarf*, χ. φυτά, opp. δένδρα, Arist.*HA*$559^{a}13$; κόνυζα Nic.*Th.*70; οἱ χ. φοίνικες *dwarf-palms* (cf. χαμαιριφής II) Dsc.1.109; καρποὶ καὶ λάχανα Jul.*Or.*5. 175d: generally, τὰ ἐγγὺς ἡμῶν καὶ χ. Them.*Or.*26.327d. b. *sunk down*, ἡ ἐπωμὶς φαίνεται χ. Hp. l.c.; τῇ ἡλικίᾳ χαμαίζηλος Luc.*pro Im.*13. 2. χαμαίζηλος (sc. δίφρος, which is added by Plu.2.150a), ὁ, *low seat, stool*, Hp.*Fract.*37, Pl.*Phd.*89b. b. χ. κρατῆρες *flat* bowls, Polem.Hist.83. 3. Ζεὺς χ., = χθόνιος, Orph.*A.*931; Ποσειδῶν χ. *IG*2$^{2}$.1367. II. metaph., *of low estate, humble*, ψυχή Ph. 1.91, cf. 240, al., Luc.*Somn.*13; τὰ χ. Them.*Or.*15.184d; χ. δικαστής, = *judex pedaneus*, Lyd.*Mag.*2.15. Adv. **-λως** Ph.1.103. III. χαμαίζηλον, τό, = γναφάλιον, Plin.*HN*27.88. 2. = πεντάφυλλον, ib.25.109. **-ζῡμήτης** ἄρτος, ὁ, sine expl., Suid. (leg. -ίτης).

**χᾰμαῖθεν**, v. χαμᾶθεν.

**χᾰμαί-καυλος**, ον, *with creeping stalk*, Thphr.*HP*6.5.2. **-κέρᾰσος**, ὁ, = μιμαίκυλον, Asclep.Myrl.ap.Ath.2.50e. 2. *dwarf cherry, Prunus prostrata*, Plin.*HN*15.104. 3. *May lily, Convallaria majalis*, interpol. in Dsc.*Eup.*1.154 Sprengel (post 145 W.). **-κισσος**, ὁ, *ground-ivy, Glechoma hederacea*, Dsc.4.125, Plin.*HN*24.135. II. = ἰχθυοθήρα, ib.25.116. 2. = κισσός, ib.16.152. **-κλῐνής**, ές, *lying on the ground, lying flat*, κάλαμοι Megasth.13; *creeping*, καυλοί Dsc. 4.71. **-κοιτέω**, *lie on the ground*, Luc.*Syr.D.*55 (v.l. χαμοκοιτέων). **-κοίτης**, ου, ὁ, = χαμαιεύνης, Σελλοί S.*Tr.*1166. **-κοιτία**, ἡ, *a lying* or *sleeping on the ground*, v.l. in Philostr.*Ep.*29 (pl.). **-κοίτιον**, τό, *bed on the ground*, Suid. s.v. στιβάδες. **-κῠπάρισσος** [πᾰ], ἡ, *lavender cotton, Santolina Chamaecyparissus*, Poet. *de herb.*106, Plin.*HN*24.136. **-λεος**, ὁ, poet. for χαμαιλέων II, Nic.*Th.*656. **-λεύκη**, ἡ, = βήχιον, Ps.-Dsc.3.112; also = χαμαίκισσος, ib.4.125. **-λεχής**, ές, *on the ground*, κοῖτα *AP*7.413 (Antip.). **-λέων**, οντος, ὁ, *chameleon, Chamaeleo vulgaris*, Arist. *HA*$503^{a}15$, Plin.*HN*8.120, Lib.*Or.*1.249; used as an image of changefulness, Arist.*EN*$1100^{b}6$, Plu.*Alc.*23. II. name of various plants, so called *from their leaves changing colour*, Thphr. *HP*6.4.3, 9.12.1, 9.14.1; χ. λευκός *pine-thistle, Atractylis gummifera*, Dsc.3.8; χ. μέλας, *Cardopatium corymbosum*, ib.9, Plin. *HN*22.47. **-λίβᾰνος** [ῐ], ὁ, a kind of λίβανος, Aët.1. 129. **-λῠκος**, ὁ, = περιστερεὼν ὕπτιος, Ps.-Dsc.4.60; **-λῠκον**, τό, *PMag.Par.*1.2307. **-μηλᾶτον**, τό, *preparation of camomile*, interpol. in Orib.5.33.7. **-μηλέλαιον**, τό, *camomile-oil*, Alex.Trall.1.10. **-μήλινος**, η, ον, *made of* χαμαίμηλον, Gal. 12.507, interpol. in Dsc.*Eup.*1.120. **-μηλον**, τό, *earth-apple, camomile*, Orph.*A.*921. 2. = ἀνθεμὶς λευκή, Dsc.3.137, Plin.*HN*22. 53. 3. = παρθένιον, Ps.-Dsc.3.138. **-μυρσίνη**, ἡ, = μυρσίνη ἀγριά, Plin.*HN*15.27, 23.165, prob. to be read for sq. **-μύρτη**, ἡ, = foreg., dub. l. in Dsc.4.144. **-πέτεια**, ἡ, *being* χαμαιπετής, Iamb.*Protr.*21.ιϛ'. **-πετέω**, *fall to the ground*, γνώμα χαμαιπετοῖσα thought *that falls to the ground*, Pi.*N.*4.41 (sed leg. χαμαὶ πετοῖσα). **-πετής**, ές, (πίπτω) *falling to the ground*, χ. πίπτει πρὸς οὖδας E.*Ba.*1111 (s.v.l.); φόνος χ. blood *that has fallen on the earth*, Id.*Or.*1491 (lyr.); δόμοι..χαμαιπετεῖς ἔκεισθ' ἀεί ye were lying *prostrate*, A.*Ch.*964 (lyr.); *grovelling*, μηδὲ..χαμαιπετὲς βόαμα προσχάνῃς ἐμοί Id.*Ag.*920; χ. [βέλος], of a *spent* missile, Aen.Tact.32.9; χ. ἐλαῖαι *windfall* olives, Luc.*Lex.*13. 2. *lying* or *sleeping on the ground*, χ. ἀεὶ ὢν καὶ ἄστρωτος Pl.*Smp.*203d. 3. *on the ground*, χ. στιβάς, εὐνή, E.*Tr.*507, *Cyc.*386; δεῖπνον Posidon.5J. 4. of trees, *creeping, dwarf*, Plb.13.10.8. 5. *flying low*, χ. στρουθοί Luc.*Dips.*2. 6. Adv. **-τῶς** *along the ground*, like a goose's flight, Id.*Icar.*10. II. metaph., *falling to the ground*, i.e. *coming to naught*, λόγοι, ἔπος, Pi.*O.*9.12, *P.*6.37. 2. *grovelling, low*, of style, κομιδῇ πεζὸν καὶ χ. Luc.*Hist.Conscr.*16, cf. *Somn.*13. **-πεύκη**, ἡ, *fishbone thistle, Chamaepeuce mutica*, Dsc.4.126, Plin.*HN*24. 136. **-πῐτυς**, υος, ἡ, *ground-pine, Ajuga Chamaepitys*, Nic.*Al.*56, Apollod.ap.Ath.15.681d, Dsc.3.158, Plin.*HN*24.29. 2. *mountain germander, Teucrium montanum*, Dsc. l.c., Plin. l.c. 3. *herb-ivy, Ajuga Iva*, Dsc. and Plin. ll. cc. 4. = ὑπερικόν, Dsc.3.154. 5. = μυρσίνη ἀγρία, Ps.-Dsc.4.144:—hence **χᾰμαιπῐτυΐνος** οἶνος wine *flavoured with one of these plants*, Dsc.5.70. **-πλάτᾰνος** [πλᾰ], ἡ, *dwarf plane*, Plin.*HN*12.13. **-πους**, ὁ, ἡ, **-πουν**, τό, gen. **-ποδος**, *going on foot*, Poll.2.195, 3.40. **-ράφᾰνος** [ρᾰ], ὁ, = ἄπιος (A) II, Paul. Aeg.7.4:—spelt **-ρέφᾰνος** Orib.*Fr.*52, *Hippiatr.*130.184. **-ρεπής**, ές, *creeping on the ground, grovelling*, Gal.12.308. Adv. **-πῶς** Hsch. II. cf. sq. II. ⊛ **-ρῑφής**, ές, (ῥίπτω) *thrown to the ground, mined*, νηόν Inscr. in Ferri *Contributi di Cirene alla storia della religione greca* (Rome, 1923) 5 (ii A.D.), cf. Eust.1279.45. b. = foreg. I, Sch.Gen.Il.5.442; παιδία *EM*781.36. 2. = *collecticius*, *Gloss.* II. φοῖνιξ χ. *dwarf*-palm, *Chamaerops humilis*, Thphr. *HP*2.6.11 (nisi leg. χαμαιρεπής as in Plin.*HN*13.39). **-ρῠτον**, τό, = στρούθιον, Ps.-Dsc.2.163. **-ρωψ**, ἡ, = χαμαίδρυς I, Dsc.3.98 (v.l. χαμαίδρωψ), Paul.Aeg.7.3; acc. sg. *chamaeropem* Plin.*HN*24.130 (elsewh. only nom.). II. *dwarf-palm*, v.l. in Plin.*HN*13. 39. **-στρωσία**, ἡ, *a bed on the ground*, Sch.S.*Ph.*33. **-στρωτος**, ον, *strewed* or *stretched on the ground*, νέκυς Alcmaeonis 2 p.76 K.; χαμαίστρωτα *beds on the floor*, Ph.2.482. **-σύκη** [ῡ], ἡ, *thyme spurge, Euphorbia Chamaesyce*, Dsc.4.169, Plin.*HN*24.134: Adj. **-σύκινος**, η, ον, *Gloss.* II. = ἀστράγαλος VII, Ps.-Dsc.4.61. **-σχῐδής**, ές, *branching from the ground upwards*, πίσος Thphr.*CP*4.14.4.

**χᾰμαιτῠπ-εῖον**, τό, *brothel*, Phld.*Rh.*2.281 S., Ph.2.228, Luc.*DMort.* 10.11, *Nigr.*22, Jul.*Or.*6.186d. **-έω**, *to be a prostitute*, D.Chr.33. 60. **-η**, ἡ, *harlot, strumpet*, Timocl.22.2, Men.879, *Sam.*133, Theopomp.Hist.217 codd.Ath. (χαμαιτύπους codd. Plb.), Phld.*Rh.*1. 236 S., Ph.2.48, Plu.2.5b. **-ής**, ές, *vulgar*, τὸ χ. *vulgarity* of style, D.H.*Thuc.*27. **-ία**, ἡ, *whoredom*, Alciphr.3.64, Man. 4.353. **-ίς**, ίδος, ἡ, = χαμαιτύπη, rejected by Thom.Mag.

p.400 R. **-ος** (parox.), ον, *striking its prey near* or *on the ground*, name of a certain hawk, opp. μετεωροθήρας, Arist.*HA*620ª31. II. χαμαιτύπος πόρνη, = Lat. *scortum*, *Gloss.*; but αἱ χαμαιτύποι is prob. f.l. for αἱ χαμαιτύπαι (corr. Wendland) in Ph.1.345, cf. χαμαιτύπη.

**χᾰμάνδις,** = χαμάδις, Theognost.*Can.*163.

**χᾰμάομαι,** = χασμάομαι, Hsch.

**χᾰμ-ελαία,** ἡ, *spurge-olive, Daphne oleoïdes*, Nic.*Al.*48, Dsc.4.171, Plin.*HN*15.24, 24.133. **II.** = θυμελαία, Dsc.4.172. **-ελαΐτης** [ῑ] οἶνος wine *flavoured with* χαμελαία, Id.5.69. **-ερπής,** ές, *crawling on the ground*, μέροπες *App.Anth.*3.146 (Theon); ζῷον Olymp.Alch. p.102 B., Hsch. **-εταιρίς,** ίδος, ἡ, = χαμαιτύπη, Id., *EM*806.25.

**χάμευν-α** [χᾰ], ἡ, = χαμεύνη, *pallet-bed*, *IG*1².330.5, Nicaenet.6.3, *Eleg.Alex.Adesp.*2.17. ⊛ **-άς,** άδος, ἡ, *on the ground*, εὐναί Lyc.848. **2.** = χαμαιευνάς, *having their lair on the ground*, βοῦς, λέαινα, φώκη, Nonn.*D.*4.348, 6.299, 43.339. **II.** Subst., *lair*, Nic.*Th.*23. **III.** = χαμαιτύπη, Lyc.319. **-έω,** *lie on the ground*, Ph.1.640, Philostr.*VA*6.10, Gal.*Protr.*13. **-η,** ἡ, for χαμαιεύνη, *a bed on the ground*, A.*Ag.*1540 (anap.), S.*Fr.*175, E.*Rh.*852, Theoc.13.33, A.R.4.883, Herod.3.16; χ. φυλλόστρωτος E.*Rh.*9 (anap.). **2.** generally, *bedstead*, Ar.*Av.*816. **-ης,** ου, ὁ, *one who sleeps on the ground*, Hsch. **-ία,** ἡ, *a lying on the ground*, Ph.1.323 (pl.), Gal.17(2).642, Philostr.*VA*3.15, *Gym.*43. **II.** pl., *sleeping-mats*, Poll.6.11. ⊛ **-ιον,** τό, Dim. of χαμεύνη, Pl.*Smp.*220d, Luc.*Asin.*51, Poll.6.9. **-ίς,** ίδος, ἡ, = foreg., Theoc.7.133. **-ος,** ον, *sleeping on the ground*, Hsch.

**χᾰμηλός,** ή, όν, *on the ground, creeping*, λειχήν Nic.*Th.*944; πίτυς χ., = χαμαίπιτυς, ib.841: Comp. -ότερος Id.*Fr.*70.2. **2.** *low*, = χθαμαλός, Str.10.2.12; of a horse's hoofs, *flat*, X.*Eq.*1.3. **3.** *diminutive, trifling*, στιγμῆς εἴ τι -ότερον *AP*7.472.4 (Leon.); χαμηλὰ πνέων one of a *low* spirit, Pi.*P.*11.30.

**χᾰμῖτις** ἄμπελος, ἡ, a vine trained *low on the ground*, *Gp.*3.1.5, Eust.1163.19; without ἄμπελος, Suid.

**χαμνός,** gloss on ἀδευκής, Hsch. (In Mod. Gk. = *thin, watery.*)

**χᾰμόθεν,** v. χαμᾶθεν.

**χᾰμο-κοιτέω,** f.l. for χαμαικ– (q.v.). **-κοιτος·** ὁ εἰς τὴν γῆν κοιμώμενος, Hsch.

**χαμόμυλον** (sic), τό, = χαμαίμηλον, *PLond.*5.1788.12 (vi A.D.).

**χαμόν·** κάμπυλον, Hsch.; cf. χαβός.

⊛ **χαμοσόριον,** τό, *flat tomb*, Heuzey-Daumet, *Mission Archéologique de Macédoine* No.49.

**χᾰμ-ούλκιον,** τό, = *stludio*, *Gloss.*, and **-ουλκίς,** ίδος, ἡ, = *sclodia*, ib. (both perh. Dim. of sq.). **-ουλκός** (sc. μηχανή), ἡ, (ἕλκω) *crane* or *windlass*, *BGU*162 viii 4, Amm.Marc.17.4.14, cf. Poll.7.191. **2.** Lat. = *trahea*, *Gloss.*

⊛ **χάμψα,** ὁ, Egyptian name for κροκόδειλος, Hdt.2.69, cj. in A.*Supp.*878 (lyr.). (Egyptian *msḥ*, Arabic *timsāh*.)

**χάν** [ᾱ], ἁ, Dor. for χήν, *goose*, gen. χᾱνός Epich.152, nom. χάν *IG*4²(1).122.133 (Epid., iv B.C.); acc. pl. χᾶνας Ar.*Ach.*878.

**Χᾰνᾰναῖος,** α, ον, *Canaanite*, Lxx *Ge.*12.6, al.:—as Appellat., *merchant* (of Tyre or Sidon), Id.*Pr.*31.24.

**χᾶνας,** v. χάν.

**χανδά,** = χανδόν, A.D.*Adv.*152.13.

⊛ **χανδάνω,** Hp.*Mul.*1.78, Ep. impf. χάνδανε(ν) Il.23.742, Q.S.12.328: fut. χείσομαι Od.18.17: aor. ἔχᾰδον Il.4.24, Ep. χάδον 11.462, inf. χαδεῖν Nic.*Th.*956, Ep. and Ion. χαδέειν Il.14.34, Hp.*Genit.*9, part. χαδών Nic.*Al.*145: pf. with pres. sense, κέχανδα and plpf. κεχάνδει (κεχόνδει v.l. in Il.24.192, ἐκεχάνδει Hsch.), v. infr.:—Ep. Verb (used once or twice in Ion. Prose, and once in Ar., v. infr.), *take in, hold, contain*, ἓξ δ' ἄρα μέτρα χάνδανεν (sc. κρητήρ) Il.23.742; λέβης τέσσαρα μέτρα κεχανδώς ib.268; οὐκ ἐδυνήσατο πάσας αἰγιαλὸς νῆας χαδέειν 14.34; οἶκος κεχανδὼς πολλὰ καὶ ἐσθλά Od.4.96; ὃς [θάλαμος] γλήνεα πολλὰ κεχάνδει Il.24.192; οὐδὸς ἀμφοτέρους ὅδε χείσεται Od.18.17; Ἥρῃ δ' οὐκ ἔχαδε στῆθος χόλον the breast of Hera *could* not *contain* her rage (v.l. Ἥρη δ'.., Hera *could* not *contain* her anger in her breast), Il.4.24; κρέας ὅσ οἱ χεῖρες ἐχάνδανον as much as his hands *could hold*, Od.17.344; ὅσον χανδάνει χείρ Hp.*Mul.*1.78; [ῥόπαλόν] οἱ ἐχάνδανε χείρ Theoc.13.57, cf. Lyc.317, Arat.697. **2.** in prescriptions, *take*, Nic.*Th.*956, *Al.*58, 145. **II.** metaph., *to be capable, able*, ἤϋσεν ὅσον κεφαλὴ χάδε φωτός Il.11.462; κεκραξόμεσθά γ' ὁπόσον ἡ φάρυξ ἂν ἡμῶν χανδάνῃ δι' ἡμέρας Ar.*Ra.*260; κωκύσασα.. ὅσσον ἐχάνδανε μητρὸς ἀυτή *AP*7.644 (Bianor); ὅσον χάδον, ὅσσον ἔρεξαν Opp.*C.*4.210: c. inf., στόμα χείσεται ἐξονομῆναι τοῦτο prob. for στοναχήσεται in *h.Ven.*252. (Cf. Lat. *pr(a)e-hendo*; root χενδ- in χείσομαι (χενδ-σ-) and κέχονδα (which shd. prob. be restored in Hom.); χα-ν-δ-άνω is formed from ἔχαδον (ἔχn̥δον).)

⊛ **χανδόν,** Adv. *with mouth wide open, greedily, eagerly*, [οἶνον] χ. ἑλεῖν Od.21.294, cf. Call.*Aet.*1.1.11, Nic.*Th.*341, Opp.*C.*4.430 (cj.), etc.; in late Prose χ. ἐκπιεῖν, πιέσθαι, πίνειν, Gal.15.735, Luc.*Merc. Cond.*7, Jul.*Mis.*338c; σπᾶν D.C.71.10; metaph., χ. ἐνεπίμπλαντο εὐχῶν Luc.*Alex.*14; χ. ἐμπιπλάμενος τοῦ ὕπνου Philostr.*Im.*2.22.

**χανδοπότης,** ου, ὁ, *toper*, *AP*11.59 (Maced.).

**χανδός,** ή, όν, *yawning, roomy*, ἐκ χανδῆς ζωροποτῶν κύλικος Epigr. ap.Polem.Hist.79.

**χάννα** or **χάννη,** ἡ, a kind of *sea-perch, Serranus hepatus* or *cabrilla*, Epich.67, Arist.*HA*538ª21, 591ᵇ6, Ael.*NA*4.5; acc. χάνναν Speus.ap.Ath.7.319b; acc. pl. χάνας (sic) *BGU*844.17 (i A.D.):—also **χάννος,** ὁ, Numen.ap.Ath.7.304e; = Lat. *perca*, *Gloss.*

**χάνοι, χανών,** v. χάσκω.

**χάνος** [ᾰ], εος, τό, *mouth*, *Com.Adesp.*1193.

**χᾰνύω** and **χᾰνύσσω,** *speak with mouth wide open*, Hsch.

**χάος** [ᾰ], εος, Att. ους, τό, *chaos*, the first state of the universe, πρώτιστα χ. γένετ', αὐτὰρ ἔπειτα Γαῖ' εὐρύστερνος κτλ. Hes.*Th.*116, cf. Ibyc.28, Epich.170.3, Acus.*Fr.*5 J., Arist.*Metaph.*1091ᵇ6, Ar.*Av.*693 (anap.); χάους.. παῖς καλεῦμαι Simm.*Alae* 7; represented sts. as *infinite space*, S.E.*P.*3.121, cf. Plot.6.8.11; sts. as *unformed matter*, Luc.*Am.*32 (esp., acc. to the Stoics, *water*, Zeno *Stoic.*1.29 (with deriv. fr. χέω)). **2.** *space, the expanse of air*, ἄτρυτον χ. B.5.27, cf. Ar.*Nu.*424 (anap.), 627, *Av.*1218. **b.** τὸ χ. τοῦ ἐφ' ἑκάτερα ἀπείρου αἰῶνος, of *infinite* time, M.Ant.4.3. **3.** *the nether abyss, infinite darkness*, joined with Ἔρεβος, Pl.*Ax.*371e; with ὄρφνη, Q.S.2.614; represented as in the interior of the globe, Plu.2.953a; χάους κύνα, of Cerberus, *APl.*4.91. **b.** generally, *darkness*, A.R.4.1697. **4.** *any vast gulf* or *chasm*, Lxx *Mi.*1.6, *Za.*14.4; of *a pit*, Opp.*C.*4.92; of the *gaping jaws* of the crocodile, ib.3.414, cf. 4.161, *H.*5.52. **5.** Pythag. name for *one*, *Theol.Ar.*6.

**χᾱός,** όν, v. χάϊος.

⊛ **χᾰόω,** *destroy utterly, swallow up*, λέγων χαῶσαι αὐτόν Simp. *in Epict.*p.47 D.:—Pass., ἐν τῇ γῇ χαούμενος Olymp. *in Mete.*143.5.

**χᾰρά,** ἡ: (χαίρω):—*joy, delight*, first in Sapph.*Supp.*1.6, then in Trag. and (less freq.) in Com. and Prose: c. gen., στόματος ἐν πρώτῃ χ., of a hungry man, A.*Fr.*258; c. gen. objecti, *joy in* or *at* a thing, μελέων E.*Alc.*579 (lyr.); πρὸς χαρὰν λόγων in accordance with *joyous* tidings, S.*Tr.*179 (v.l. χάριν); κέρτομος θεοῦ χ. *a joy* sent by some mocking god, E.*Alc.*1125; ἅμα χαρᾷ δακρυούσας X.*HG*7.2.9; χ. ἐπί τινι Pl.*Def.*413e; ἔδωκας ἡμῖν χ. S.*Tr.*201; ἐλάβομεν χ. E.*Ion* 1449 (lyr.); ἐμπλῆσαί τινα χαρᾶς Id.*Ph.*170; χαρά μ' ὑφέρπει A.*Ag.*270; λέγεις μοι χαράν wishest me *joy*, Ar.*Pl.*637 (lyr.); χ. ἐνεργάσασθαι Gorg.*Hel.*8; χαίρειν ἀνδραπόδων τινὰ χαράν Plu.2.1091e, cf. *Ev.Matt.*2.10; ἡδονὴ καὶ τέρψις καὶ χ. Pl.*Phlb.*19; ἀπορέουσι.. χαρᾶς Democr.293, cf. Epicur.*Fr.*2; ζήλου καὶ χαρᾶς καὶ ἐπαίνων ἡ πόλις ἦν μεστή D.18.217; εἴσελθε εἰς τὴν χ. τοῦ Κυρίου σου *Ev.Matt.*25.21: χαρᾷ *with joy*, A.*Ag.*1630, *Ch.*233, etc.; μετὰ χαρᾶς *Com.Adesp.*771, X.*Hier.*1.25, Lxx 1 *Ch.*29.22, al.; μετὰ μεγάλης χ. Plb.21.34.12 (s.v.l.); μετὰ πολλῆς χ. *BGU*1141.3 (i B.C.), cf. 1768.7 (i B.C.); χαρᾶς ὕπο A.*Ag.*541; ὑπὸ χ. X.*Cyn.*6.15; σὺν χαρᾷ S.*El.*934, etc.; opp. λύπη, Sor.1.46, al. **II.** in concrete sense, *a joy*, of persons, χ. μου *Ep.Phil.*4.1, cf. 1 *Ep.Thess.*2.20.

**χᾰράγγελος,** ὁ, = χαρᾶς ἄγγελος, *messenger of joy*, *EM*7.32.

⊛ **χάραγ-μα** [χᾰ], ατος, τό, (χαράσσω) *any mark engraved, imprinted*, or *branded*, χ. ἐχίδνης the serpent's *mark*, i.e. its *bite, sting*, S.*Ph.*267; ἐν ἰσχίοις μὲν ἵπποι πυρὸς χάραγμ' ἔχουσιν *Anacreont.*26 B2; ἔχειν τὸ χ. τοῦ θηρίου *Apoc.*16.2, cf. 13.16; χ. χειρός, i.e. writing, *AP*9.401 (Pall.); χαράγματα παμβασιλῆος, of an imperial *missive*, Epic. in *BKT*5(1).115: abs., *inscription*, *AP*7.220 (Agath.), cf. *PLond.*5.1688.8 (iv A.D.); *stamped document*, *Sammelb.*5275.11 (i A.D.); *brand* on a camel, *PGrenf.*2.50(*a*).5 (ii A.D.); χ. τέχνης *carved work*, *Act.Ap.*17.29; τὸ χ. τοῦ νομίσματος the *impress* on the coin, Plu.*Lys.*16, cf. *Ages.*15, Jul.*Mis.*355d (pl.), etc.; hence, **2.** *stamped money, coin*, *AP*5.29 (Antip.Thess.), *POxy.*144.6 (vi A.D.). **3.** metaph., *mark, stamp, character*, τὸ τῆς μονάδος σημαντικὸν χ. *Theol.Ar.*6. **4.** *endorsement*, *Arch.Pap.*1.85. **-μή,** ἡ, *loaf*, σιλιγνίων χ. *PKlein.Form.*986 (v/vi A.D.); written σιλικνίων χαρακμή ib.985 (v/vi A.D.). **2.** *water-channel*, *Gloss.* **-μός,** ὁ, *incision, notch*, Thphr.*HP*3.11.3, 3.13.5. **II.** *stamped document*, *PRyl.*160(*a*).10 (i A.D.).

**χάρᾰδος** [χᾰ], εος, τό, Dor. for sq., *Tab.Heracl.*1.60.

**χᾰράδρ-α,** Ion. χαράδρη, ἡ, *mountain-stream, torrent, which cuts itself* (χαράσσει) a way down the mountain-side, κλειτῦς τότ' ἀποτμήγουσι χαράδραι Il.16.390, cf. D.P.1077; οἴνῳ.. ἅπασ' ἔρρει χ. Teleclid.1.4 (anap.); χ. χειμερίη A.R.4.460; χ. χειμάρρους καὶ βαθεῖα Plb.10.30.2; φωνὴ χαράδρας ὄλεθρον τετοκυίας (of a loud, harsh voice), Ar.*V.*1034 (anap.); χ. κατελήλυθεν, of a *torrent of words*, Pherecr.51. **II.** *the bed of such a stream, gully, ravine*, κοίλης ἔντοσθε χαράδρης Il.4.454; cf. Hdt.9.102, Th.3.98, 107, X.*An.*3.4.1, D.55.5; χ. κρημνώδης Th.7.78; ἡ Νεμεὰς χ. Aeschin.2.168, cf. X.*HG*4.2.15. **2.** metaph. of *wounds* produced by scourging, Lib.*Or.*57.16. **3.** prov., Οἰνώνη (fort. Οἰνόη) τὴν χ. of those who bring misfortune on themselves, interpol. in Str.8.6.16. **-αῖος,** α, ον, *of* or *from a* χαράδρα, ἰλύς *APl.*4.230 (Leon.); πηγή, ῥέεθρον, Nonn.*D.*15.191, 2.444. **2.** *jagged*, αἰχμή, βέλεμνα, ib.28.210, 35.4; παρειαὶ *furrowed*, ib.2.641. **-ειον,** τό, poet. for χαράδρα, Nic.*Th.*389. **-εών,** ῶνος, ὁ, *ground broken up by gullies*, Hdn.*Epim.*199. **-ήεις,** εσσα, εν, = *full of gullies*, Πυθώ Nonn.*D.*9.251. **2.** = χαραδραῖος 2, κενεών ib.48.34; βέλεμνον ib.17.202, al. **-ιον,** τό, Dim. of χαράδρα, Str.16.4.13. **-ιός,** ὁ, a bird, prob. the *thick-knee* or *Norfolk plover, Charadrius oedicnemus*, Ar.*Av.*266, 1141, Hp.*Int.*37, Arist.*HA*593ᵇ15, 615ª1, Lxx *Le.*11.19, *De.*14.17(18); it was very greedy, hence prov. χαραδριοῦ βίον ζῆν, of a glutton, Pl.*Grg.*494b; the sight of it was held to be a cure for the jaundice, cf. Hippon.52, Plu.2.681c, Ael.*NA*17.13. **-όομαι,** Pass., *to be broken into clefts by mountain-streams, to be full of gullies*, χώρη κεχαραδρωμένη Hdt.2.25; ὡς ἂν χαραδρωθείη ὁ χῶρος Id.7.176: metaph., οἱ πόροι χαραδροῦνται the pores *are widened into large channels*, Hp.*Flat.*10. ⊛ **-ος,** ὁ, = χαράδρα, Plu.*Agis* 8, *IG*7.3170 (Orchom. Boeot.), *SIG*826 *E* 23 (Delph., ii B.C.): as pr. n. of many *torrents* in Greece, Th.5.60, Paus.2.25.2, 7.22.11, etc. **-ώδης**, ες, *full of gullies*, τόποι Dsc.4.57. **2.** *of a torrent*, τὰ χ. ὕδατα Str.14.1.43.

❋ **χᾰρᾰκ-ίας**, ου, ὁ, (χάραξ) *of* or *fit for a stake, pale*, or *palisade*, a species of κάλαμος, Thphr.*HP*4.11.1, Plin.*HN*16.168. **II.** a kind of τιθύμαλλος ἄρρην, *wood spurge, Euphorbia Sibthorpii*, Dsc.4.164, Plin.*HN*26.62 (χαράκης is f.l. in Hsch.). **III.** a fish, *Gp.*20.7.1. **-ίζω**, *fence with stakes driven in cross-wise*: metaph. of a fly, χ. τοῖς προσθίοις σκέλεσι *dress itself by crossing* the forelegs, Arist.*PA*683ᵃ30. **-ιον**, τό, Dim. of χάραξ, in pl., = ὑποστηρίγματα, Hsch. **2.** χαράκιν (sic), = Lat. *tessera, Gloss.* **-ίδες**, = *terriclae*, ib. ❋ **-ισμός**, ὁ, *palisading, fencing*, Pherecr.130.2 (anap.), *JHS*33.338 (Maced., iii A. D.). ❋ **-ίτης** [ῑ], ου, ὁ, *living behind a fence*: metaph., *cloisterling*, βιβλιακοὶ χ. Timo 12.2. **2.** χ. τιθυμαλίς, = χαρακίας II, Afric.*Cest.*p.81 V., Aët.1.397.

❋ **χᾰρᾰκο-βολία**, ἡ, *forming a palisade*, Lxx *Ez.*17.17. **-λογέω**, *collect stakes*, *BGU*1534.2 (iii B.C.). **-ποιέομαι**, *form a palisade, fortify a camp*, App.*BC*5.110. **-ποιία**, ἡ, *making of a vallum*, Plb.6.34.1.

**χᾰρᾰκόω**, *fence by a palisade, fortify*, Ἐλάτειαν Aeschin.3.140; χ. καὶ ταφρεύειν πόλιν D.S.23.18, cf. Plu.*Cleom.*20; metaph., χ. τὸν πλοῦτον Philostr.*VA*7.23: c. dat. modi, τὸ στόμα ὀδοῦσι Herm.ap. Stob.1.49.69; τὼ πόδε σκύτεσιν Max.Tyr.36.2:—Pass., ὄστρακον κεχαρακωμένον ταῖς ἀκάνθαις, of the echinus, Arist.*PA*679ᵇ29; metaph., μᾶζα κεχαρακωμένη ἀχύροις Antiph.226.1: f.l. for ἐκαρώθη in Ant.Lib.12.4. **2.** abs., χ. ἐπὶ Ἱερουσαλὴμ *raise a barricade against* it, *besiege* it, Lxx *Je.*39(32).2. **II.** *prop vines with stakes*, [ἄμπελον] *PCair.Zen.*229 (iii B.C.), cf. *Gp.*5.27.1; βλαστόν *PSI*6.624.14 (iii B.C.).

❋ **χᾰρακτήρ**, ῆρος, ὁ, (χαράσσω) *engraver*, Euryph.ap.Stob.4.39.27; *one who mints coins*, *IPE*1²16*A* 14 (Olbia, iii B.C.). **2.** *graving tool*, Daimachus 4 J. (pl.) ap.St.Byz. s.v. Λακεδαίμων. **3.** *die, stamp*, *IG*2².1013.64, 1408.11, 1424ᵃ120, 280, 1469.107; in a simile, Arist.*GA*781ᵃ28. **4.** *branding-iron*, *Clara Rhodos* 2.171 (ii B.C.). **II.** *mark engraved, impress, stamp* on coins and seals, ἀργύρου λαμπρὸς χ. E.*El.*559, cf. Pl.*Plt.*289b, Arist.*Pol.*1257ᵃ40; *coin type, standard*, ἦν δ' ὁ ἀρχαῖος χ. δίδραχμον Id.*Ath.*10.2, cf. *OGI*339.45 (Sestos, ii B.C.), D.S.17.66; Κότυος χ. Head *Hist.Num.*²285 (Thrace, i B.C.): hence, in pl., = χάραγμα I.2, *PFlor.*61.21 (i A.D.): metaph., οἷς ἡ ἀρετὴ εὐδοξίας χαρακτῆρα τοῖς ἔργοις ἐπέβαλεν set a *stamp* upon them, Isoc.1.8; Κύπριος (s. v.l.) χαρακτὴρ .. ἐν γυναικείοις τύποις εἰκὼς πέπληκται A.*Supp.*282. **2.** esp. of *figures* or *letters*, οἱ τῶν γραμμάτων χ. Plu.2.214f; ὁ τύπος τῶν χ. ib.577f, cf. 1120f, D.S.3.67; of the *letters* used by Hp. in *Epid.*3.1, Zeno and Apollonius ap.Gal.17(1).618, cf. 524 sq.; of a single *letter* of the alphabet, Jul.*Or.*2.72a; ξυλήφια βραχέα ἔχοντα χαρακτῆρα Plb.6.35.7; *brand* on a camel, *PGen.*29.8 (ii A.D.); of *symbols* in a prescription, Gal.13.995; of magical *symbols* (such as the seven vowels), τῶν χ. ἡ ἀπόρρητος φύσις Jul.*Or.*7.216c, cf. Iamb.*Myst.*3.13, Sallust.15; of hieroglyphs, opp. γράμματα, Luc.*Herm.*44. **3.** metaph., *distinctive mark* or *token impressed* (as it were) *on* a person or thing, by which it is known from others, *characteristic, character*, χ. γλώσσης, of a particular dialect, Hdt.1.57,142; χ. αὐτὸς ἐν γλώσσῃ S.*Fr.*176; χ. ἡμεδαπὸς τῶν ῥημάτων Ar.*Pax*220; ὁ Ἑλληνικὸς χ. Greek *idiom*, D.H.*Pomp.*3: freq. of persons, *feature*, ὁ χ. τοῦ προσώπου Hdt.1.116; εἰληφέναι χαρακτῆρα ἑκατέρου τοῦ εἴδους Pl.*Phdr.*263b; οἱ τῆς ὄψεως χ. D.S.1.91; ἀνδρῶν οὐδεὶς χ. ἐμπέφυκε σώματι E.*Med.*519; δεινὸς χ. κἀπίσημος .. ἐσθλῶν γενέσθαι Id.*Hec.*379; φανερὸς χ. ἀρετᾶς Id.*HF*659 (lyr.); ἠθικοὶ χ., title of work by Thphr.: pl., οἱ χ. the *features* of the face, J.*AJ*13.12.1, cf. *OGI*508.13 (Ephesus, ii A.D.); χ. μορφῆς ἐμῆς ib.383.60 (Nemrud Dagh, i B.C., sg.); [τοῦ ἐμβρύου] Sor.1.33 (pl.): hence, **4.** *type* or *character* (regarded as shared with others) of a thing or person, rarely of an *individual nature*, ἀνδρὸς χ. ἐκ λόγου γνωρίζεται Men.72; χ. μοχθηρότατον παραπλάττεσθαι Phld.*Rh.*1.6S.; τὸν χ. τὸν Διογένους Arr.*Epict.*3.22.80; τίνα ἔχει χ. τὰ δόγματα; ib.4.5.17; of nations, Plb.18.34.7. **5.** *style*, freq. in Rhet., ὁ Δημοσθένους χ. D.H.*Dem.*9, cf. *Pomp.*1, Cic.*QF*2.15(16).5; χ. δικανικός Phld.*Rh.*2.137S.; χ. *optimi* the ideal *type*, Cic.*Orat.*11.36, cf.39.134; χ. ἰσχνός, μεγαλοπρεπής, γλαφυρός, δεινός Demetr.*Eloc.*36, cf. D.H.*Dem.*33; χ. λέξεως Id.*Lys.*11; χ. Ἀσιανός Str.13.1.66. **6.** *impress, image*, τῆς ὑποστάσεως [τοῦ θεοῦ] *Ep.Heb.*1.3; πάθους, ἀρετῆς, Longin.22.1, Eun.*Hist.*p.243 D.: abs., οἱ Σεβάστειοι χ. the imperial *seal*, i.e. the emperor himself, *IG*5(2).268.24 (Mantinea, i B.C.). **7.** Gramm., *typical form*, A.D.*Synt.*20.10, 103.23.

**χαρακτηρ-ιάζω**, *mint, coin*, *IGRom.*4.960 (Samos, i A.D.). **II.** = sq. 2, *Gloss.* ❋ **-ίζω**, fut. -ίσω Phld.*D.*3.14: pf. κεχαρακτήρικα Aristeas 153:—*engrave, inscribe*, Manetho ap.Syncell.1 p.72 D. (Pass.); *form, stamp*, τὸ κηρύκειον ἐκ τοῦ Βαβυλωνίου χρυσοῦ -ίζεσθαι πέφυκεν Aristaenet.2.1: metaph., ἐκ θεῶν -ίζεσθαι *to be made in the image* of gods, Men.Prot.p.16 D. **2.** *designate by a characteristic mark, characterize*, Ph.1.151, Gal.8.188, Plot.1.8.3, Sch.E.*Hec.*379; μειζόνως χ. τὸν Δία Max.Tyr.17.3: abs., περί τινων Hermog.*Id.*2.10:—Pass., *to be characterized*, Phld.*Herc.*1457.11; χ. κατὰ διαφοράν *Stoic.*2.132, cf. Iamb.*Comm.Math.*4. **3.** *emphasize*, c. acc. et inf., Aristeas l.c.; *indicate, expound*, τι Phld.*D.*3.14. **-ικός**, = χαρακτηριστικός (q.v.). **-ισμα**, ατος, τό, = χαρακτήρ II.5, in pl., ποιητῶν Tz.*Proll. Hes.*, *Proll.Lyc.* **-ισμός**, ὁ, *characterization*, Tryph.*Trop.*2.6, Plb. Rh.p.108S., Sch.E.*Hec.*379. **-ιστέον**, *one must characterize*, Hermog.*Id.*2.10, Eust.1388.26. **II.** *one must endow with distinctive character*, Iamb.*Myst.*3.27, Dam.*Pr.*102. **-ιστικός**, ή, όν, *characteristic*, τῆς Λυσίου λέξεως D.H.*Lys.*11 (Sup.); λόγου Δημοσθενικοῦ μηνύματα χ. Id.*Dem.*34, al.; τοῦ ἀγαθοῦ, τῆς ὕλης, S.E.*P.*3.173, Dam.*Pr.*36; τοῦ ἁπλῶς βαρέος, κούφου, Simp. *in Cael.*713.24; τὸ χ. A.D.*Synt.*103.17, cf. Choerob. *in Theod* 2.31 H. Adv. -κῶς Eust. 1167.59.—The form **χαρακτηρικός** is found in Phld.*Po.Herc.*1676.7, in codd. of D.H.*Dem.*39, 51, and is v.l. in Id.*Lys.* l.c. Adv. χαρακτηρικῶς Phld.*Rh.*2.297S.

**χᾰράκ-της**, ου, ὁ, *stamper, coiner*, Man.6.388. **-τός**, ή, όν, *notched, toothed*, πρίων, ῥῖναι, ξοΐς, Hp.*VC*21, *AP*6.205 (Leon.), *IG*7.3073.104 (Lebad., ii B.C.); κνηστῆρι χαρακτῷ (v.l. χαράκτρῳ) Nic.*Al.*308; χαρκᵃ σκάφιν perh. written for χαρακτὸν (*engraved*) σκάφιον in *PLond.*2.193ᵛ11, al. (ii A.D.). **-ωμα**, ατος, τό, *palisaded enclosure, entrenched camp*, X.*HG*5.4.38, 6.2.23; χαρακώματα πρὸ τῆς πόλεως βαλέσθαι Plu.*Cat.Mi.*58. **II.** *palisade*, X.*An.*5.2.26; χ. καὶ τείχη καὶ τάφροι D.6.23: metaph., of the eyelashes, Arist.*PA*658ᵇ18. **2.** = Lat. *vallum*, Plb.9.3.2; χ. διπλᾶ Id.10.31.8. ❋ **-ών**, ῶνος, ὁ, perh. *vineyard containing staked vines*, *PRyl.*427 *Fr.*19 (ii/iii A.D.), Hdn.Gr.1.30. **-ωσις**, εως, ἡ, *palisading, fortifying*, Lycurg.44, Ph.*Bel.*85.48 (pl.), Plu.*Mar.*7. **2.** *palisade*, Lxx *De.*20.20. **II.** *propping of vines*, *PSI*6.595.3 (iii B.C.), *Gp.*5.27 tit.

**χαραμβαλιαστύς**· γέλως ὁ μετὰ παιδιᾶς, Hsch. (post χρῆν); leg. **κραμ-**, q.v.

**χαραμός**· ἡ τῆς γῆς διάστασις, οἷον χηραμός (χιρ- cod.), Hsch.

**χάραξ** [χᾰ], ἄκος, ὁ, also ἡ, (χαράσσω) *pointed stake*: esp., **I.** *vine-prop, pole*, Ar.*Ach.*986, *V.*1201, *Pax*1263, Th.3.70, *BGU*1122.17 (i B.C.): prov. ἐξηπάτησεν ἡ χ. τὴν ἄμπελον, of those who trust in a 'broken reed', Ar.*V.*1291. **II.** *pale*, used in fortifying the entrenchments of a camp, Id.*Ach.*1178, D.21.167; = Lat. *vallus*, Plb.1.29.3, 18.18.1: **2.** collectively, = χαράκωμα, *palisaded camp*, Theophil.Com.9, *SIG*363.1 (Ephesus, iii B.C.). Men.77, Plu.*Caes.*17 (pl.), Jul.*Or.*2.60b; τὰν ἐκτὸς τοῦ χ. χώραν *IG*4²(1).76.21 (Epid., ii B.C.); *palisade*, χάρακα βαλέσθαι πρὸς τῇ πόλει (v.l. χαράκωμα) D.18.87; = Lat. *vallum*, Plb.1.80.11, 3.45.5, al., *Ev. Luc.*19.43; χάρακα τίθεσθαι form *an entrenched camp*, D.H.6.29; χ. βαλέσθαι Plu.*Aem.*17, cf. *Marc.*18, etc.; βάλλειν Id.*Sull.*28; ἀποταφρεύειν, περιταφρεύειν, ib.21, *Luc.*31; διασπᾶν Id.*Ant.*18; χ. σεσιδηρωμένος καὶ ἁλύσεσι δεδεμένος D.S.19.83; χ. κύκλῳ τῆς νεὼς Moschio ap.Ath.5.208d. **III.** *cutting, slip*, esp. of an olive, Thphr.*HP*2.1.2, *CP*5.1.[4], *Gp.*9.11.5; of other plants, Thphr.*CP* 1.12.9. **2.** collectively, = ἀκανθώδη φυτά, Hsch. **IV.** a seafish, one of the *breams*, *Sargus*, Diph.Siph.ap.Ath 8.355e, Opp.*H.*1.173; also a fish of the Red Sea, Ael.*NA*12.25. **V.** name of a *bandage*, Heliod.ap.Orib.48.31 tit., Sor *Fasc.*17, Gal.18(1).777. (Phryn.43 gives ἡ χ. in signf. I, and in *PS*p.125B. gives ὁ χ. in signf. II, cf. Poll.1.162; but this distinction is not observed by later writers.)

**χᾰραξίποντος** [ῐ], ον, *ploughing the sea*, ναΐα κλαΐς χ. Simon.23.

**χάραξις** [χᾰ], εως, ἡ, *incision, mark*, Sch.Ar.*Nu.*23 (pl.); ἡ χ. τοῦ ἀρότρου Theognost.*Can.*38; τῶν τροχῶν Hsch. s.v. ἁματροχιάς; τοῦ τροχοῦ, = Lat. *orbita*, *Gloss.* **2.** *erasure*, *PLips.*10 ii 4 (iii A.D.). **3.** metaph. of acute pain, ὑπὸ βηχὸς ἴσχει τραχύτητας καὶ χ. Plu.2.698c. **II.** *coining, minting*, τοῦ λεπτοῦ χαλκοῦ *OGI*485.12 (Magn.Mae.).

❋ **χᾰράσσω**, Att. **-ττω**, *make pointed, sharpen, whet*, ἅρπας, ὀδόντας, Hes.*Op.*573, *Sc.*235, cf. Plu.2.350d; καθάπερ βέλη τὰ πράγματα ib. 825f; χαρασσόμενος σίδηρος Hes.*Op.*387. **2.** *furnish with notches* or *teeth*, like a saw, τὰ σιδήρια Arist.*Aud.*803ᵃ3:—Pass., of certain birds, ἔχουσι..τὰ ἄκρα τοῦ ῥύγχους κεχαραγμένα Id.*PA*662ᵇ16; φύλλα κεχαραγμένα *serrated* leaves, Dsc.4.173, cf. Thphr.*HP*3.10.5; σκύταλον κεχ. ὄζοις *jagged* or *rugged* with.., Theoc.17.31. **3.** metaph., *whet, stimulate*, ἔρως ψυχὰς χ. S.*Fr.*684 codd. Stob. (ταράσσει E.*Fr.*431 codd. Clem.Al.); τὸ φιλόνικον Plu.2.92a, cf. 825f:—Pass., κεχαραγμένος τινί *exasperated at..*, Hdt.7.1; κείνῳ τόδε μὴ χαράσσου *be not angry at him for this*, E.*Med.*157 (lyr.); τῇ παρρησίᾳ χαραχθείς Plu.2.74e. **II.** *cut into furrows, scratch*, στρωμνὰ δὲ χαράσσοισ' ἅπαν νῶτον κεντεῖ Pi.*P.*1.28; κῦμα χ. Orph.*A.*372; ἀρότρῳ..χ. χέρσον *AP*6.238 (Apollonid.); ὕδωρ ἐρετμοῖς Nonn.*D.*3.46, cf. 41.114 (Pass.); τῷ θερμῷ χαράσσοντι τὴν ἐπιφάνειαν Plu.2.651e:—Pass., νῶτον χαραχθείς *wounded*, E.*Rh.*73; κέκοπται καὶ χαράσσεται πέδον A.*Pers.*683; θάλασσα φρικὶ χαρασσομένη *AP*10.2 (Antip. Sid.), cf. 10.14 (Agath.); τόπος κεχαραγμένος ὑπὸ ὄμβρου, gloss on ῥωχμός, Sch.Gen.Il.23.420. **2.** *smite*, Lxx 3 *Ki.*15.27. **3.** *stamp, seal*, *PRyl.*160.6 (i A.D.), etc. **4.** *brand*, *BGU*100.3 (Pass., ii A.D.), etc. **III.** *engrave, carve*, ἐν νομίσματι [Βάττον] χ. (i.e. *stamp* his portrait) Arist.*Fr.*528; οὔρεα καὶ πόντον ὑπὲρ τύμβοιο *AP*7.237 (Alph.); στάλαν ib.547 (Leon.Alex.); *inscribe*, δόγματα..εἰς στήλην *SIG*795*B* 27 (Delph., i A.D.); γράμμα..τοίχοισι χαράξω Theoc.23.46, cf. *AP*12.130; ἐν τύμβῳ γράμμ' ἐχάραξε τόδε Erinn.5.8; τὸν Τροίης πόλεμον σελίδεσσι χ. *APl.*4.293; γραφίδεσσι..χάραξα..ἱερὸν λόγον *Hymn.Is.*11; [νόμους] εἰς πίνακας χ. D.S.12.26; ὁ γραμματεὺς τοῦ δήμου τὸ β' ἐχάραξα *B.Mus.Inscr.*481*.430 (Ephesus); simply, *write*, γράμματα *PMasp.*2 ii 2 (vi A.D.), *sketch, draw*, μορφὴν χαράξαι *AP*11.412 (Antioch.), cf. *Anacreont.*55.5; of the down *marking* the cheek, *APl.*5.344:—so in Med., ἴουλος ἄχνοα χιονέης ἐχαράσσετο κύκλα παρειῆς Nonn.*D.*10.180:—Pass., ib.5.404; [ὄμμα] ἠλεμάτοις ἀκτῖσι χαράσσεται, of lines *drawn* with antimony, *AP*9.139 (Claudian.)· ἐπὶ τοῦ νομίσματος κεχαράχθαι πέλεκυν Arist.Fr.593; στήλας γράμμασι κεχαραγμένας D.S.3.44; στῆλαι χαράσσονται IG14.297 (Panormus); τοῖχος ἅπας ἐχαράσσετο Luc.Am.16; τὸ χαραχθὲν νόμισμα *stamped* money, *coin*, Plb.10.27.13; χρῆσθαι τῷ..μέτρῳ κεχαραγμένῳ τῷ χαρακτῆρι IG2$^2$.1013.64; also of the letters *engraved*, Peripl.M.Eux.2: metaph., λέξις κεχαραγμένη *with a stamp*, i.e. character of its own, Diocl.Magn.Stoic.3.213; τὴν μὲν (sc. τὴν σοφιστικὴν) ἰδιώματι κεχαράχθαι φήσομεν Phld.Rh.1.77S. (Perh. a Semitic loan-word, cf. Hebr. *ḥāraš* 'engrave'; or cogn. with Lith. *žerti* 'rake, scrape'.)

**χᾰρῆναι, χᾰρήσομαι,** v. χαίρω.

**χαρία·** βουνός, Hsch.; also **χάρεια** in Hdn.Gr.2.603, Suid.

**χᾰρῐ-δότης,** written for sq., in codd. of Plu. ll. cc., Jul. l.c. and Or.4.148d.

**χᾰρῐ-δώτης,** ου, ὁ, *joy-giver*, epith. of Hermes, h.Hom.18.12, Plu.2.303d; of Dionysus, Id.Ant.24,2.613e, Jul.Caes.308d; of Zeus, Plu.2.1048c; Dor. **-δώτας,** of Dionysus, Africa Italiana 2.144 (Cyrene):—fem. **-δῶτις,** ιδος, Orph.H.55.9.

⊛**χᾰρίεις,** χαρίεσσα (Boeot. χαρίϝεττα Mon.Piot2.138 (statuette from Thebes, vii/vi B.C.), χαρίεν (for χάριεν, v. infr. IV): gen. χαρίεντος, dat. -εντι: voc. χαρίει, χαρίεν, acc. to Theodos.Can.1.11, 209H.: (χάρις):—*graceful, beautiful*: **I.** in Hom. freq. of the works of men, [πέπλος] χαριέστατος Il.6.90,271; εἵματα 5.905; ἔργα Od.10.223; φᾶρος 5.231; also, *gracious*, ἀμοιβή 3.58; ἀοιδή 24.197; τέλος χαριέστερον 9.5; δῶρα χ. *acceptable* gifts, Il.8.204, Ar.Pl.849; οὐ πάντεσσι θεοὶ χαρίεντα διδοῦσιν Od.8.167; εἴ ποτέ τοι χαρίεντ' ἐπὶ νηὸν ἔρεψα Il.1.39; of the parts of a person, χ. μέτωπον, πρόσωπον, κάρη, 16.798, 18.24, 22.403; μέλεα Archil.12; of a youth, πρῶτον ὑπηνήτῃ, τοῦπερ χαριεστάτη ἥβη Il.24.348 (also -έστατος ἥβη Od.10.279); of persons first in Hes.Th.247; χαρίεσσα δέμας ib.260; ὦ κάλα, ὦ χαρίεσσα Sapph.η̄5 App.p.48 Lobel, cf. Alc.46; φυὴν χαριέστερος Tyrt.12.5; σοὶ χάριεν μὲν εἶδος Sapph.η̄9 App.p.49 Lobel; once in Trag., σὰν χαρίεσσαν ὥραν E.Fr.453.6 (lyr.); also χαρίεσσα χελιδοῖ Anacr.67: later ζῷα ὀφθῆναι χαρίεντα Luc.Prom.Es3. **II.** in Att., freq. of persons, in relation to qualities of mind, *elegant, accomplished*, χ. ἦσαν οἱ Λακωνικοί Ar.Lys.1226; οἱ χαριέστατοι *men of taste*, Isoc.12.8, Arist.Metaph.1060$^a$25, cf. Pl.R.605b (Comp.); οἱ χ. Arist.Pol.1297$^b$9, Phld.Mort.31; opp. οἱ πολλοὶ καὶ φορτικώτατοι, Arist.EN1095$^b$22, cf. Pol.1267$^a$1; τὰ τῶν χ. σκώμματα the *wits*, Pl.R.452b; χ. καὶ νοῦν ἔχοντες Arist.Pol.1320$^b$7; χαριέστατος τὴν μουσικήν *accomplished* in.., Pl.La.180d; περὶ φιλοσοφίαν Id.Ep.363c; χ. ποιητής Id.Lg.680c; τῶν ἰατρῶν οἱ χ. Arist.EN1102$^a$21; στρατηγοί D.S.12.33 (Sup.); γεωργός, παιδαγωγός, etc., Plu.2.92b, Cat.Mi.1, etc. **2.** of things, *graceful, elegant*, μέλος, πόνος, Pi.P.5.107, N.3.12, cf. Ar.Pl.145; φιλοσοφία ἐστὶν χαρίεν Pl.Grg.484c, cf. Sph.234b (Comp.); χαρίεντα μὲν γὰρ ᾄδω, χ. δ' οἶδα λέξαι Anacr.45; λόγον λέξαι χαρίεντα Ar.V.1400; βοήθειαι χαριέσταται πρός τι Pl.R.602d; ἐνθύμημα χ. *clever, smart*, X.An.3.5.12; τὸ ἀστεῖον καὶ χ. Luc.VH1.2; χαρίεντα..ἐσοφίσω καὶ σοφά Ar.Av.1401; ironical, χαρίεντα πάθοιμ' ἄν I should be *nicely* off, Id.Ec.794; χαρίεν [ἐστὶ] εἰδέναι *it is well* to know, Hp.Art.34; χ. οὖν..λαλεῖν Ar.Ra.1491 (lyr.); δοκεῖ χαριέστερον εἶναι..λέγειν Pl.Prt.320c; also χαρίεν γάρ, εἰ.. it would be *a pretty thing*, if..! X.Cyr.1.4.13, Luc.JTr.26. **3.** rarely of natural objects, θεῶν χ. ἐναύλους Hes.Th.129; χαρίεντα τὰ ὑδάτια φαίνεται Pl.Phdr.229b; πηγὴ χαριεστάτη ib.230b; τὴν Ἰνδῶν λίθον χ. Jul.Or.2.51a. **4.** name of a plant, χαρίεν τὸ ἐπονομαζόμενον, τούτου ῥίζαν πρόσθες Hp.Mul.1.78. **III.** Adv. χαριέντως *gracefully, elegantly, cleverly*; πάνυ χ. ἀποδεδεῖχθαι Pl.Phd.87a, cf. Plt.300b; χ. ἔχων τὸ σῶμα *in fine condition*, Id.Phd.80c; δείπνου χ. πεπρυτανευμένου Alex.110.4; χ. εἰπεῖν Pl.R.331a: Comp., ἀνθηρότερον καὶ -έστερον τῶν ἄλλων λέγειν Isoc.13.18; οἱ -εστέρως λέγοντες Arist.Metaph.1075$^a$26. **2.** *kindly, courteously*, Isoc.5.22. **3.** *with good intention*, χ. μέν, ἀπειροτέρως δὲ ἐπαινεῖν Id.12.37. **IV.** the neut., as Adv., was written proparox. χάριεν in Att., acc. to Hdn.Gr.1.350, A.D.Adv.160.22, etc., but no example is quoted; neut. as Adj. is proparox. acc. to Suid.

**χᾰριεντ-ίζομαι,** *to be witty, jest*, Ar.Fr.166, Pl.R.436d; σπουδῇ χ. *to jest* in earnest, Id.Ap.24c; χ. ἐν οὐ χαρίεντι καιρῷ D.H.Lys.14, cf. 13.—Late in Act., Procop.Arc.9. **2.** χ. ἐξ ἀναφορᾶς *make a charming use of*.. Demetr.Eloc.141. **-ισμα,** ατος, τό, *witty saying, bon mot*, in pl., Ph.2.570, Sch.Ar.Ach.380. **-ισμός,** ὁ, *wit*, Pl.Tht.168d; χ. καὶ εὐτραπελία Id.R.563a; opp. σπουδή, Plu.2.11e; χ. ἐν σπουδῇ γενόμενος D.H.Isoc.12; including a vein of irony, coupled with δριμύτης, Hermog.Id.2.5. **-ότης,** ητος, ἡ, *gracefulness of manner, playfulness*, Plu.2.441b (pl.).

**χᾰρῐεργός,** όν, prob. *elegantly working, artistic*, epith. of Athena, as protectress of artificers, AP6.205 (Leon.).

⊛**χᾰρίζω,** fut. χαριῶ Phld.Rh.1.381S., Gloss.: aor. imper. χάρισον PMag.Lond.122.17:—usu. Med. **χαρίζομαι,** fut. -ιοῦμαι Th.3.40, 8.65; χαριῇ (v.l. -εῖ) also in Hdt.1.90; Cret. χαριξίομαι GDI5176.16 (found at Teos); also χαρίξομαι ib.5178.17 (ibid.); χαρίηνται is a false Aeol. form in Milet.3 No.152.56; later χαρίσομαι Ep.Rom.8.32, Luc.DDeor.22.4: aor. ἐχαρισάμην Hdt.1.91, etc.; opt. χαρίσαιτο Il.6.49; Aeol. imper. χάρισσαι Sapph.Supp.16.4; Cret. inf. χαρίξασθαι GDI5163b8 (Mylasa):—Pass. forms, fut. χαρισθήσομαι in pass. sense, Ep.Philem.22: aor. ἐχαρίσθην in pass. sense, Act.Ap.3.14, 1 Ep.Cor.2.12: pf. κεχάρισμαι in act. sense, κεχάρισαι Ar.Ec.1045, -ισται Id.Eq.54; also in pass. sense, imper. -ίσθω Pl.Phdr.250c: plpf. ἐκεχάριστο Hdt.8.5, Ep. κεχάριστο Od.6.23:—*say or do something agreeable* to a person, *show* him *favour* or *kindness, oblige, gratify*, c. dat. pers., freq. in part., χαριζομένη πόσεϊ ᾧ Il.5.71, cf. 11.23, 15.449, Od.8.538, 13.265; once in Hes., ποίησε..χαριζόμενος Διί Th.580; πᾶσι χαριζοίμην ἄν Hdt.6.130, cf. Th.3.40; τοῖς θεοῖς X.Mem.4.3.16; Καλλίᾳ χαριζόμενος *to oblige, humour* him, Pl.Prt.362a, cf. Men.75b, Ar.Eq.1368; of a judge, give a *partial* verdict, χ. οἷς ἂν δοκῇ αὐτῷ Pl.Ap.35c; also χ. τῷ ἵππῳ X.Eq.10.12: abs., *make oneself agreeable, comply*, opp. ἀντία φάσθαι, once in A., Pers.700 (lyr.); οἱ ὑπὲρ καιρὸν χαριζόμενοι And.4.7: c. acc. cogn., χάριτας χ. E.Fr.360.1, Isoc.1.31, D.18.239; χ. τι καὶ αὐτός Th.3.42; with part. added, χαρίζετο ἱερὰ ῥέζων Od.1.61, cf. Hdt.1.90, Ar.Ec.1045, Pl.R.338a, 426c, etc.: more freq. c. dat. modi, μήτε τί μοι ψεύδεσσι χαρίζεο *do* not *court favour* by lies, Od.14.387; χαριζόμενος φιλότητι 10.43, etc.; λόγῳ θωπεῦσαι καὶ ἔργῳ χ. Pl.Tht.173a codd.; opp. τὰ βέλτιστα λέγειν, D.9.2, cf. Plu.2.66a. **2.** *gratify* or *indulge* a humour or passion, once in S., θυμῷ χαρίζεσθαι κενά El.331, cf. Antipho4.3.2, X.An.7.1.25; ὀργῇ E.Fr.31; γλώσσῃ Id.Or.1514 (troch.); ἔρωτι Pi.Fr.127; τῇ ἐπιθυμίᾳ Pl.R.561c: τῷ σώματι X.Mem.1.2.23; τῇ γαστρί ib.2.1.2, Cyr.4.2.39; τῇ ἡδονῇ ib.4.3.2. **3.** in erotic sense, *grant favours* to a man, Ar.Ec.629 (anap.), Pl.Smp.182a, Phdr.231c, 256a, X.Mem.3.11.12, etc.: hence of Comedy, ὀλίγοις χαρίσασθαι Ar.Eq.517 (anap.): c. acc. cogn., χ. θήλειαν ἀπόλαυσιν Luc.Am.27. **II.** c. acc. rei, *give graciously* or *cheerfully*, δῶρα Od.24.283; ἄποινα Il.6.49, 10.380; χαρίζεσθαί τινί τι Hdt.1.91, Ar.Ach.437, Eq.54, X.Cyr.1.4.9, etc.; πωλεῖν καὶ χ. καὶ τέκνοις μεταδιδόναι PGrenf.1.60.45 (vi A.D.); so c. acc. pers., χαρίζομαί σε τοῖς ὄχλοις PFlor.61.61 (i A.D.): with a strong oxymoron, ξείνια δυσμενέσιν λυγρὰ χ. Archil.7: c. inf. with Art., χ. τὸ ποθεῖν Plu.2.609a; τὸ ζῆν Lxx 2 Ma.3.33; without the Art., πολλοῖς ἐχαρίσατο βλέπειν (v.l. τὸ β.) Ev.Luc.7.21; χάρισαι [αὐτοῖς] μένειν *allow* them to remain, Luc.Am.19, cf. AP5.236 (Agath.); so ἆρ' ἄν τί μοι χαρίσαιο τοιόνδε—μή μου καταγελᾶν; Pl.Hp.Mi.364c. **b.** χ. τὴν δέησιν *grant* the request, Luc.Bis Acc.14. **c.** Pass., c. acc., *to be favoured with*, ἀνάγκᾳ πνεῦμα χαριζόμενος Epigr.Gr.204.18 (Cnidus). **2.** c. gen. partit., *give freely of* a thing, ἀλλοτρίων χ. Od.17.452; ταμίη..χαριζομένη παρεόντων *giving freely of* such things as were ready, 1.140, etc.; παντοίων ἀγαθῶν γαστρὶ χαριζόμενοι Thgn.1000; γλώσσης μαψιδίοιο χ. παρεοῦσι Theoc.25.188; προικὸς χαρίζεσθαι, of his bounty, Od.13.15. **3.** c. acc. pers., *give up as a favour*, τῇ μητρὶ χ. Ὀκτάβιον, by dropping a law aimed at him, Plu.CG4; but also, by unjust condemnation, Act.Ap.25.11,16; also τῷ θεῷ με ἐχαρίσω, of a *dedication* ceremony, PBremen49.14 (ii A.D.). **4.** *forgive*, τὴν ἀδικίαν τινί 2 Ep.Cor.12.13, cf. Ep.Col.2.13: abs., 2 Ep.Cor.2.7, etc. **III.** Pass., esp. in pf. and plpf., κεχάριστο θυμῷ *was dear* to her heart, Od.6.23; τοῖσι Εὐβοεῦσι ἐκεχάριστο the *pleasure* of the Euboeans *was done*, Hdt.8.5; ταῦτα μὲν οὖν μνήμῃ κεχαρίσθω *let a tribute be paid*.. Pl.Phdr.250c; cf. χάρις A.V. **2.** mostly part. pf. κεχαρισμένος, η, ον, as Adj., *acceptable, welcome*, ἐμῷ κεχαρισμένε θυμῷ Il.5.243,826, etc.; κεχαρισμένα δῶρα θεοῖσι δίδωσι, 20.298, cf. Od.16.184, 19.397; κεχαρισμένα θεῖναί τινι to do *things pleasing* to one, Il.24.661; ἀνὴρ κεχαρισμένα εἰδώς Od.8.584; θεοῖς κεχαρισμένα ποιεῖν Lys.6.33; κεχ. τοῖς θεοῖς λέγειν τε καὶ πράττειν, Pl.Euthphr.14b, cf. Phdr.273e; δοίη ᾧ κ' ἐθέλοι καί οἱ κεχαρισμένος ἔλθοι Od.2.54, cf. Hdt.1.87, 3.119, X.Mem.1.2.10, etc.; κεχαρισμένα θύρσῳ E.HF892 (lyr.); κεχαρ. χοιρίδιον Ar.Pax386 (lyr.); πᾶσιν κεχαρισμένος Pl.Sph.218a; λόγος κεχ. D.14.1; σιτίον ἢ ποτόν X.Mem.2.1.24; ἐν τοῖς μὴ κεχαρισμένοις..πρὸς τὴν αἴσθησιν Arist.PA645$^a$7; cf. κεχαρισμένως. **3.** later, Comp. κεχαρισμενώτερος Ael.NA12.7; Sup. -ώτατος Alciphr.3.65.—Rare in Trag., but freq. in Att. Prose.

**χᾰρῐλαμπέτις,** ιδος, ἡ, *graciously shining*, epith. of the moon, Antioch.Astr. in Cat.Cod.Astr.1.111.

**χάριν,** v. χάρις A.VI.1.

⊛**χάρις** [ᾰ], ἡ, gen. χάρῐτος: acc. χάριν [ῑ in arsi, Il.5.874], etc.; also χάριτα Hdt.6.41, 9.107, E.El.61, Hel.1378, X.HG3.5.16, Phylarch.24J., PGen.47.17 (iv A.D.), etc. (un-Attic, acc. to Moer.p.414P.): χάριταν Gloss.: pl. χάριτες; dat. χάρισι, χαρίτεσσι, Od.6.237, Il.17.51, Pi.O.7.93: (χαίρω):—*grace*: **I.** in objective sense, *outward grace* or *favour, beauty*, prop. of persons or their portraits, θεσπεσίην δ' ἄρα τῷ γε χάριν κατεχεύατ' Ἀθήνη Od.2.12, etc.; χάριν ἀμφιχέαι κεφαλῇ Hes.Op.65; εὐμόρφων δὲ κολοσσῶν ἔχθεται χ. ἀνδρί A.Ag.417 (lyr.): pl., *graces*, κάλλεϊ καὶ χάρισι στίλβων Od.6.237; ὅσσοις χάριτας Ἀφροδίτης ἔχων E.Ba.236; μετὰ χαρίτων *gracefully*, Th.2.41: less freq. of things, χ. δ' ἀπελάμπετο πολλή, of ear-rings, Il.14.183; of works, ἔργοισι χάριν καὶ κῦδος ὀπάζει Od.15.320; of words, οὔ οἱ χ. ἀμφιπεριστέφεται ἐπέεσσιν 8.175; πλείστη δὲ χ. κατὰ μέτρον ἰούσης [γλώσσης] Hes.Op.720; ταὶ Διωνύσου σὺν βοηλάτᾳ χάριτες διθυράμβῳ Pi.O.13.19; ἡ τῶν λόγων χ. D.4.38, cf. D.H.Comp.23; μῦθοι πληθόμενοι χαρίτων AP9.186 (Antip.Thess.). **2.** *glory*, Φερενίκου χ. Pi.O.1.18, cf. 8.57,80. **II.** in subjective sense, *grace* or *favour felt*, whether on the part of the doer or the receiver (both senses appear in such phrases as ὅτ'..ἡ χάρις χάριν φέροι S.OC779; χάρις χάριν γάρ ἐστιν ἡ τίκτουσ' ἀεί Id.Aj.522, cf. E.Hel.1234, Arist.Rh.1385$^a$16): **1.** on the part of the doer, *grace, kindness, goodwill*, τινος *for* or *towards* one, Hes.Op.190; τῶν Μεσσηνίων χάριτι πεισθείς Th.3.95; οὐ χάριτι τῇ ἐμῇ not for any *kind feeling towards* me, Antipho5.41: abs., εἰ δέ τις μείζων χ. A.Supp.960; τῆς παλαιᾶς χ. ἐκβεβλημένη S.Aj.808; ἢ μεγάλα χ. δώρῳ σὺν ὀλίγῳ Theoc.28.24; χ. εὑρεῖν ἐναντίον τοῦ θεοῦ Lxx *Ge.*6.8, al.; χάριν ἔχειν πρὸς τὸν δῆμον Plu.*Dem.*7; *partiality, favour*, μήτε ἔλεον μήτε συγγνώμην μήτε χ. μηδεμίαν περὶ πλείονος ποιήσασθαι τῶν νόμων Lys.14.40; οὐ συμφωνοῦσιν ὀργαὶ καὶ χάριτες μακαριότητι Epicur.*Ep.*1p.28 U., cf. Pl.*Lg.*740c. 2. more freq. on the part of the receiver, *sense of favour* received, *thankfulness, gratitude*, χάριν καὶ κῦδος ἄροιο Il.4.95; ἀρέομαι πὰρ Σαλαμῖνος Ἀθαναίων χ. Pi.*P.*1.76; τινος *for* a thing, οὐδέ τίς ἐστι χάρις μετόπισθ' εὐεργέων Od.4.695, cf. 22.319; ἀντὶ πόνων χ. Th.4.86: less freq. c. inf., οὐκ ἄρα τις χάρις ἦεν μάρνασθαι one has, it seems, no *thanks for* fighting, Il.9.316, 17.147; οἵ οἱ ἀπεμνήσαντο χ. εὐεργεσιάων Hes.*Th.*503, cf. Th.1.137; χάριν φέρειν τινί Pi.*O.*10(11).17; χ. τροφεῦσιν ἀμείβων A.*Ag.*728 (lyr.); φιλότητος ἀμειβόμεναι χ. S.*El.*134 (lyr.); χάριν εἰδέναι τινί to acknowledge *a sense of favour, feel grateful*, once in Hom., ἐγὼ δέ κέ τοι ἰδέω χ. ἤματα πάντα Il.14.235; freq. in Prose, Hdt.3.21, Lys.2.23, Isoc.4.175, etc.; τούτων *for* a thing, X.*Cyr.*1.6.11, etc.; τοῖς διαπεπραγμένοις Plu.*Alex.*62; μοι χ. οἶδεν ἐπὶ τούτοις Luc.*Bis Acc.*17; χ. προσειδέναι Pl.*Ap.*20a; ἀποδιδόναι Id.*R.*338a; τινὰ ἀποστερῆσαι χάριτος Id.*Hp.Mi.*372c; later χ. γνῶναι Philostr.*VA*2.17; πολλὴν γνοῦσα χ. X.Eph.3.5; χ. ἐπίσταμαι πᾶσι Charito 3.4, cf. 8.5, Poll.5.142, Jul.*Or.*8.246c; also τῶν παροιχομένων ἔχειν σφι μεγάλην χ. Hdt.7.120, cf. 1.71, E.*Heracl.*767 (lyr.), *IT*847 (lyr.), Lys.16.1, Hyp.*Ath.*5: c. part., χ. ἔχειν σωθέντες X.*An.*2.5.14; also χάριτας ἔχων πατρὸς owing him a debt of *gratitude*, E.*Or.*244: but ἀσπασμάτων χάριν τίν' ἕξει; what *thanks* will she have *for*..? Id.*Hec.*830; χ. ἂν ἐν τούτῳ μείζω ἔτι ἔσχεν Th.8.87; χ. ὀφείλειν to owe *gratitude*, be beholden, τοῖς θεοῖς S.*Ant.*331, cf. X.*Cyr.*3.2.30; προσοφείλειν D.3.31; χ. οὐδεμία ἐφαίνετο πρὸς Ἀθηναίων Hdt.5.90; χάριν ἀθάνατον καταθέσθαι to lay up a store of undying *gratitude*, Id.7.178, cf. 6.41; τῇ πόλει χ. καταθέσθαι Antipho 5.61, cf. Th.1.33; χάριν λαβεῖν τινος receive *thanks from* one, S.*OT*1004, etc.; ἀπολαβεῖν παρά τινων Lys.20.31; τινος *for* a thing, X.*Mem.*2.2.5, Aeschin.2.4; διπλῆν ἐξ ἐμοῦ κτήσει χάριν S.*Ph.*1370; κἀπ' ἐμοῦ κτήσει χ. Id.*Tr.*471; κομίσασθαι χ. Th.3.58; χάριτος τυχεῖν Lycurg.135; ἀπέχειν χάριτας Call.*Epigr.*51.4, etc.; τοῖς θεοῖς χάρις (sc. ἐστί) ὅτι.., *thank* the gods that.., X.*An.*3.3.14, *Cyr.*7.5.72; χ. τινί τινος Luc.*Tim.*36; τινὶ ὑπέρ τινος Plu.2.1122a. 3. *favour, influence*, opp. force, χάριτι τὸ πλέον ἢ φόβῳ Th.1.9; χ. καὶ δεήσει, opp. ἀπειλῇ, Plu.*Sull.*38. 4. *love-charm, philtre*, Luc.*Alex.*5, *Merc.Cond.*40. III. in concrete sense, *a favour* done or returned, *boon*, χάριν φέρειν τινί confer *a favour* on one, do a thing *to oblige* him, Il.5.211,874, 9.613, Od.5.307, E.*IT*14, *Or.*239, And.2.24 (so in Med., of the recipient, ib.9); ἄλλοις χ. φέροντες Th.3.54; χάριν θέσθαι or τίθεσθαί τινι, Hdt.9.60,107, A.*Pr.*782, E.*Hec.*1211, etc.; προσθέσθαι S.*OC*767; χ. ὑπουργῆσαί τινι A.*Pr.*635; παρασχεῖν S.*OC*1183; πράσσειν E.*Ion*36, 896 (lyr.); δράσας Th.2.40; ἀνύσαι prob. in S.*Tr.*995 (anap.); νέμειν Id.*Aj.*1371; χ. δοῦναί τινι A.*Pr.*821, S.*OC*1489 (but χ. δοῦναι, = χαρίζεσθαι (I.2), *indulge, humour*, ὀργῇ ib.855; γαστρί Cratin.317); χ. χαρίζεσθαι, v. χαρίζομαι I.1: χ. ἀνθυπουργεῖν return *a favour*, S.*Fr.*339; τίνειν A.*Pr.*985, *Ag.*821; χάριτας πατρῴας ἐκτίνων E.*Or.*453, cf. Pl.*Mx.*242c, etc.; χ. ἀποδιδόναι τινί Lys.12.60, 28.17; ἀντί τινος X.*Ages.*2.29; ὑπέρ τινος Isoc.4.56; τῶν ἔργων τὰς χάριτας ἀποδ. τινί Lys.31.24; χάριτας ἀντιδιδόναι Th.3.63; opp. χάριν ἀπαιτεῖν to ask the repayment of *a boon*, E.*Hec.*276, cf. Lys.18.23, D.20.156; χάριτας ἀπ. Lycurg.139; χάριν ἐξαιτεῖσθαι S.*OC*586; χ. ἀποστερεῖν withhold *a return* for what one has received, Pl.*Grg.*520c; τὰς αὑτοῦ εἰς τοὺς φίλους χ. the *favours* one has done them, Id.*Lg.*729d; χ. ἄχαρις *a* thankless *favour*, one which receives, or deserves, no thanks, A.*Pr.*545 (lyr.); χ. ἀχάριτος Id.*Ch.*42 (lyr.), E.*Ph.*1757 (lyr.). b. *grant* made in legal form, *POxy.*273.14 (i A.D.), *PGrenf.*2.70.5 (iii A.D.), etc.; αἱ τῶν Σεβαστῶν χ. imperial *grants*, *OGI*669.44 (Egypt, i A.D.). 2. esp. in erotic sense, of *favours granted* (v. χαρίζομαι I. 3), ἀλόχου χάριν ἰδεῖν Il.11.243, cf. A.*Ag.*1206: more freq. in pl., X.*Hier.*1.34, 7.6, etc.; βίᾳ δ' ἔπραξας χάριτας ἢ πείσας κόρην; *Trag.Adesp.*402; in full, χάριτες ἀφροδισίων ἐρώτων Pi.*Fr.*128, cf. Pl.*Phdr.*254a, al. IV. *gratification, delight*, τινος in or *from* a thing, συμποσίου Pi.*O.*7.5; νίκας Id.*O.*10(11).78; ὕπνου χ. E.*Or.*159 (lyr.); even χ. γόων Id.*Supp.*79 (lyr.); also concrete, of things, *a delight*, Pi.*I.*2.19 (pl.); τὰν βοτρυώδη Διονύσου χ. οἴνας E.*Ba.*535 (lyr.), cf. Ar.*Nu.*311 (lyr.), Jul.*Or.*3.125b; ἔνοπτρα, παρθένων χάριτας E.*Tr.*1108 (lyr.): abs., Ἔρως.. εἰσάγων γλυκεῖαν χ. Id.*Hipp.*527 (lyr.); opp. λύπη, S.*El.*821, E.*Hel.*655 (lyr.); opp. πόνος, S.*OC*232 (lyr.); θανεῖν πολλὴ χάρις A.*Ag.*550, cf. 1304; βίου χ. μεθεῖσα E.*Med.*227; οὐδεμίαν ἔχω τῷ βίῳ χάριν Ar.*Lys.*865; τοῖς δὲ σιτίοις χ. οὐδεμίαν οἶδ' ἐσθίων ib.869; less freq. in Prose, χ. καὶ ἡδονή Pl.*Grg.*462c, cf. D.20.26; τοσαύτην ἔχει χ. Isoc.9.10. V. δαιμόνων χάρις *homage due* to them, their *worship, majesty*, A.*Ag.*182 (lyr.); ἀθίκτων χ. ib.371 (lyr.); ὅρκων E.*Med.*439 (lyr.). 2. *thank-offering*, εὐκταία χ. τινός, opp. a common gift, A.*Ag.*1387, cf. X.*Hier.*8.4; ἔπεμψε χαίτην κουρίμην χ. πατρὸς A.*Ch.*180, cf. 517; τιμὴ καὶ γέρα καὶ χ. Pl.*Euthphr.*15a, cf. *La.*187a. VI. Special usages: 1. acc. sg. as Adv., χ. τινός *in* any one's *favour, for his pleasure, for his sake*, χ. Ἕκτορος Il.15.744; ψεύδεσθαι γλώσσης χ. *for* one's tongue's *pleasure*, i.e. *for* talking's *sake*, Hes.*Op.*709, cf. A.*Ch.*266; rarely with Art., τὴν Ἀθηναίων χάριν ἐστρατεύοντο Hdt.5.99. b. as Prep., sts. before its case (once in Pi., *P.*2.70; χάριν πλησμονῆς Pl.*Phdr.*241c; χ. φιλίας Epicur.*Sent.Vat.*28; χ. τίνος; Lxx 2*Ch.*7.21, cf. *POxy.*743.29 (i B.C.), etc.), but mostly after, *for the sake of, on behalf of, on account of*, κακά νιν ἕλοιτο μοῖρα δυσπότμου χάριν χλιδᾶς S.*OT*888 (lyr.); τοῦ χάριν; *for* what *reason?* Ar.*Pl.*53; συγχωρῶ τοῦ λόγου χ. Pl.*R.*475a; so ἐμὴν χάριν, χάριν σήν, *for* my, thy *pleasure* or *sake*, A.*Pers.*1046 (lyr.), E.*HF*1238, etc.; κεῖνόν τε καὶ σὴν ἐξ ἴσου κοινὴν χ. S.*Tr.*485: less freq. with the Art., τὴν σὴν δ' ἥκω χ. Id.*Ph.*1413 (anap.); σοῦ τε τήν τ' ἐμὴν χ. E.*Ph.*762:—pleon., τίνος χάριν ἕνεκα; Pl.*Lg.*701d; also χάριν τινός *as far as regards.., as to..*, ἔπους σμικροῦ χ. S.*OC*443; δακρύων χάριν *if* tears *would serve*, Id.*Fr.*557.6; χ. θανάτου πόλιν ἀτείχιστον οἰκοῦμεν Epicur.*Sent.Vat.*31; also, *about*, ἔπεμψεν ἐπὶ τὴν πενθεράν σου χ. τοῦ κτήματος *about* the farm, *PFay.*126.5 (ii/iii A.D.).—Orig. an acc. in apposition with the sentence, as in Il.15.744, etc., *being a favour, since it is (was) a favour*, as is evident in κακῆς γυναικὸς χάριν ἄχαριν ἀπώλετο E.*IT*566; τινὸς νίκας ἀκάρπωτον χ. S.*Aj.*176 (lyr.). 2. with Preps.: a. εἰς χάριν *to do a pleasure*, οὐδὲν ἐς χ. πράσσων Id.*OT*1353 (lyr.); ἐς χ. τίθεσθαί τι Plu.*Mar.*46; μηδὲ κρίσιν εἰς χ. ἕλκε Ps.-Phoc.9 (but ἐς τὴν τῶν ξυμμάχων χ. in such a way as to earn *thanks*.. Th.3.37); also κατὰ χάριν Pl.*Lg.*740c; χάριτος ἕνεκα ib.771d. b. πράσσειν τί τινι πρὸς χάριν S.*OC*1776 (anap.); δρᾶσαι E.*Hel.*1281; τοῖσι πολλοῖς πρὸς χάριν λέγειν τι Id.*Hec.*257, cf. X.*Mem.*4.4.4, *HG*6.3.7, Isoc.2.18, D.8.1 (but πρὸς χ. βορᾶς *for the sake* of it, S.*Ant.*30); πρὸς χ., opp. κλαίων, Id.*OT*1152:—but πρὸς χ. εὐσεβίας, just like χάριν, Pi.*O.*8.8; τίνος νόμου ταῦτα πρὸς χ. λέγω; S.*Ant.*908; πρὸς ἰσχύος χ. E.*Med.*538; πρὸς χ. alone, *as a favour, freely*, πρὸς χ. τε κοὐ βίᾳ S.*Fr.*28; but κορέσαι στόμα πρὸς χ. *to* their *heart's content*, Id.*Ph.*1156 (lyr.). c. ἐν χάριτι κρίνειν τινά to decide *from partiality* to one, Theoc.5.69; but also, *for* one's *gratification, pleasure*, ἐν χάριτι διδόναι or ποιεῖν τινί τι, X.*Oec.*8.10, Pl.*Phd.*115b: παραλαμβάνειν ἐν χάρισιν *gratefully*, Id.*Lg.*796b. d. διὰ χαρίτων εἶναι or γίγνεσθαι [τινι] to be *pleasing* to one, X.*Hier.*9.1,2. e. ἐθελοντὶ καὶ μετὰ χάριτος *of pure good will*, Plb.2.22.5, etc.; ἐθελούσιοι καὶ χάριτος ἕνεκα ἐξιόντες X.*Cyr.*4.2.11. VII. metaph. of *the cypress*, *Gp.*11.4.1; of some kind of *myrtle*, Sch.Il.17.51; of *salt*, ὅτι τὸ ἀναγκαῖον ἡδὺ ποιοῦσιν (sc. ἅλες) Plu.2.685a.

B. Χάρις, ἡ, as a mythological pr. n. declined like χάρις, save that the acc. is generally Χάριτα (exc. *AP*5.148 (Mel.), Luc.*DDeor.*15.1, Paus.9.35.4): poet. dat. pl. Χαρίτεσσι Il.17.51, Pi.*N.*9.54; Χάρισσιν ib.5.54:—*Charis*, wife of Hephaestus, Il.18.382; mostly in pl. Χάριτες, αἱ, *the Graces*, 14.267,275, Od.6.18, Pi.*O.*2.50, etc.; three in number, Hes.*Th.*907, etc. (τέσσαρες αἱ Χ., as a compliment, Call.*Epigr.*52.1); attendants of Aphrodite, Il.5.338, Hes.*Op.*73, *h.Ven.*61, Paus.6.24.7; coupled with Μοῦσαι, Hes.*Th.*64; κόμαι Χαρίτεσσιν ὁμοῖαι, i.e. like that of the *Graces*, Il.17.51; worshipped at Orchomenus in Boeotia, Ἐτεόκλειοι Χάριτες θεαί Theoc.16.104, cf. Sch. ad loc., Str.9.2.40, Paus.9.35.3, 9.38.1: but at Lacedaemon and Athens only two were orig. worshipped, Id.3.18.6, 9.35.2; Χαρίτων ἱερὸν ἐμποδὼν ποιοῦνται Arist.*EN*$1133^{a}3$; θύειν ταῖς Χ. Plu.2.141f; in adjurations, πρὸς τῶν Χαρίτων Pl.*Tht.*152c; νὴ τὰς Χ. Luc.*Hist.Conscr.*26; ὦ φίλαι Χ. Plu.2.710d.—Rarely in sg., Χ. ζωθάλμιος Pi.*O.*7.11; Χάριτος ἡδίστης θεῶν Antiph.228.4.

**χᾰρ-ίσιος** [ῐ], α, ον, *of thanksgiving*, ἕδνον Call.*Fr.*193. 2. *free*, χαρίσια *free gifts*, Dam.*Isid.*216. 3. χαρισία βοτάνη *love-plant*, used as a philtre, Arist.*Mir.*$846^{b}7$, Ps.-Plu.*Fluv.*17.4. II. χ. πλακοῦς, a sort of cake, Ar.*Fr.*202; πέττουσα τὸν χ. (sc. πλακοῦντα) Eub.2, cf. Ath.15.668c. III. τὰ Χαρίσια (sc. ἱερά), = Χαριτήσια, Eust.1843.24. **-ισμα**, ατος, τό, *grace, favour*, θεοῦ Ph.1.102, cf. *Fr.*84 H.; esp. in *NT*, *gift of God's grace*, 1*Ep.Cor.*12.4, al.: opp. ὀψώνια, *Ep.Rom.*6.23; later, generally, *favour bestowed*, *BGU*1044.4 (pl., iv A.D.). ✱**-ισμός**, ὁ, *bestowing of favours, gratifying*, Sopat. in Rh.8.70 W. **-ιστεῖον**, τό, *thank-offering*, *IG*12(3).416, 420 (Thera): pl., *SIG*1146.3 (Cnidus):—in form **χαριστήιον**, *Schwyzer* 192 (Crete). II. *charistia, = dies festus inter cognatos*, *Gloss.* ✱**-ιστέον**, *one must humour*, τινι Pl.*Phdr.*227c. II. *one must give freely*, opp. ἀνταποδοτέον, Arist.*EN*$1164^{b}32$; οὐ πάντα πᾶσιν χ. Ph.1.253. ✱**-ιστήριος**, ον, *of* or *for thanksgiving*, θυσία D.H.1.88: so in pl., Id.10.17,54, *IGRom.*4.566.19 (Aezani, ii A.D.); ἀπαρχαί Ph.2.236; ἀμοιβαί D.H.1.6; ὕμνος Jul.*Or.*4.158a: c. gen., θυσία χ. ὑδάτων D.H.1.55, cf. Plu.*Lyc.*11. II. Subst., χαριστήριον, τό, *thank-offering*, *IG*$2^2$.3003,4798, 7.3100 (Lebad.), Plu.*Caes.*57, Ath.15.672a, etc.: freq. in pl. χαριστήρια, τά, *thank-offerings*, χ. τοῖς θεοῖς ἀποτελεῖν X.*Cyr.*4.1.2; ὀφειλήσειν ib.7.2.28; προσφέρειν, θῦσαι, D.S.5.31, 20.76: c. gen., θύειν τοῖς θεοῖς χ. τῶν εὐτυχημάτων Plb.21.2.2; χ. τροφῶν ἀποδιδόναι Luc.*Patr.Enc.*7; τῇ Ἑκάτῃ χ. τῆς νίκης ἑορτάζειν Plu.2.862a; χ. ἐλευθερίας, in memory of the liberation by Thrasybulus on 12th Boëdromion, ib.349f, cf. Neanth.9 J., *OGI*654.8 (Egypt, i B.C.); = Lat. *supplicatio*, Plu.*Cam.*7. **-ιστικός**, ή, όν, *giving freely, bounteous*, φιλοτιμία Aristeas 227: of persons, Democr.96, Corn.*ND*15 (Comp.), Plu.2.632c, Ptol.*Tetr.*67, etc.; μεγαλόθυμος καὶ χ. Phld.*Herc.*1457.5; τὸ χ. *bounteousness*, τοῦ θεοῦ Ph.1.108, cf. Plu.2.332d. Adv. -κῶς Corn. l. c. ✱**-ιστίων**, ωνος, ὁ, *an instrument* of Archimedes *for weighing*, Simp. *in Ph.*1110.4; = Lat. *campana*, *Gloss.*; or *for lifting*, Tz.*H.*2.130. **-ιστωνία**, ἡ, *buying of favour*, Anon. Epicureus in *POxy.*215 ii 10.

**χαρίτερπνος** [ῐ], η, ον, *delightsome*, *Epic.Alex.Adesp.*9 iii 5.

✱**χαρῑτήσιον**, τό, *thank-offering*, καλὰς χ. ἄγρας Antip.Sid. in *Oxy.*662.53, cf. *Supp.Epigr.*8.464 (Egypt). II. *spell for winning* *favour*, *PMag.Par.*1.2227, *PMag.Leid.W.*8.28 (both pl.), *PMag.Osl.* 1.35, Cyran.121, *Gloss.* III. **Χαριτήσια** (sc. ἱερά), τά, *feast of the Charites*, *IG*7.3195.2 (Orchom.Boeot., **-είσια** lapis). IV. ἱερὸν Χ. temple *of the* Χάριτες, *PLond.*2.353.8 (iii A.D.).

**χαριτία**, ἡ, *jest, joke*, X.*Cyr.*2.2.13.

® **χαρίτινος**, η, ον, dub. sens., [ξύλ]α *PBerl.Leihg.*9.1 (iii A.D.).

**χαρίτιον**, in form **χαρίτιν**, τό, = Lat. *fimirium* or *fimarium*, *Gloss.* (in section headed ὅσα ἐν τῷ θεάτρῳ).

**χᾰρῐτο-βλέφᾰρος**, ον, *with eyelids* or *eyes like the Charites*, ὄμματα *IG*3.1376; Com., μᾶζα χ. Eub.112.4 (lyr.); of a person, *MAMA*4.133 (Metropolis, ii A.D.); applied to Demetrius of Phalerum, Hsch. Mil.*Fr.*7.17M. 2. Subst., a plant, used in philtres, Plin.*HN* 13.142. **-γλωσσέω**, Att. **-ττέω**, *speak to please*, A.*Pr.*296 (anap.), Ath.4.164b, Sch.E.*Or.*1514 (v.l. χαριτογλώττιζεις). **-δότης**, ὁ, = χαριδώτης, of Dionysus, Plu.2.158e; of Hermes, cj. for χαριδότης in Jul.*Or.*4.148d. **-δώτειρα**, ἡ, *bestower of favour*, epith. of Isis, *POxy.*1380.10 (ii A.D.). **-εις**, εσσα, εν, = χαρίεις, Anacr.ap.Hdn. Gr.2.921: neut. χαριτοῦν ἦθος cj. in Anacr.44. **-μορφος**, *endued with grace of form*, epith. of Isis, *POxy.*1380.59 (ii A.D.). **-ποιέω**, *make graceful*, Sch.Il.17.600. **-πωλις**, ιδος, ἡ, *she who sells her favours*, *Tab.Defix.*68*a*.6.

**χάρῐτος** [ᾰ], η, ον, *acceptable*, *SIG*741.13 (Nysa, i B.C., Epist. proconsulis).

**χᾰρῐτόφωνος**, ον, *with gracious voice*, Philox.8.

**χαρῐτ-όω**, *show grace to* any one, τῆς χάριτος ἧς ἐχαρίτωσεν ἡμᾶς *Ep.Eph.*1.6:—Med. χαριτώσομαι I *will bestow favour* upon thee, *BGU* 1026 xxiii 24 (iv A.D.):—Pass., *to have grace shown one, to be highly favoured*, Lxx *Si.*18.17, *Ev.Luc.*1.28; πρὸς πάντας ἀνθρώπους Aristeas 225, cf. Heph.Astr.1.1; ὄμμα στροφαῖς -ούμενον prob. in Lib.*Descr.*30.12. **-ώνῠμος**, ον, *of gracious import*, ἀγγελία B.2.2. ® **-ώπης**, ου, ὁ, (ὤψ) *graceful of aspect*, Orph.*H.*17.5: fem. χαριτῶπις, ιδος, *IG*3.1376. **-ώσιος**, α, ον, = χαριτήσιος, Ibyc.51 (Rhegine, acc. to Sch.D.T.p. 542 H.).

**χαρκ-εύς**, έως, ὁ, written for χαλκεύς, *MAMA* 3.329 (Corycus). **-ολόγος**, ὁ, written for χαλκολόγος, *money-collector*, ib.514 (ibid.). **-ωματᾶς**, ᾶδος, ὁ, = χαλκωματουργός, *Schwyzer App.II.* 5.2 (Lydia).

**χάρμα**, ατος, τό, (χαίρω): I. in concrete sense, *source of joy, delight*, χ. γενέσθαι or ἔσσεσθαί τινι, Il.17.636, 23.342; χ. φίλοις Thgn.692; χ. μεῖζον ἐλπίδος κλύειν A.*Ag.*266, cf. S.*Fr.*636.1; μᾶζαν, ἥν..Δηὼ βροτοῖσι χ. δωρεῖται Antiph.1; of victory in the games, ἄπονον ἔλαβον χ. Pi.*O.*10(11).22; καλλίνικον χ. Id.*I.*5(4).54: freq. in pl., Od.6.185; μὴ γείτοσι χάρματα γήμῃς Hes.*Op.*701, cf. Max.87 (sg.); χάρματ' Ἐρινύος, χάρματα θηρῶν, E.*Ph.*1503, *Supp.*282 (both lyr.); χάρματ' ἄλλοις ἔθηκεν, ἐμβαλεῖν χ. ἀνθρώποισι, Pi.*O.*2.99, 7.44; ἀντιδιδόναι A.*Eu.*984 (lyr.). 2. *source of malignant joy*, Il.3.51, 6.82, al.; λυπρά, χάρματα δ' ἐχθροῖς A.*Pers.*1034 (lyr.). II. in abstract sense, *joy, delight*, τὴν δ' ἅμα χ. καὶ ἄλγος ἕλε φρένα Od.19.471, cf. *h.Cer.*371, Hes.*Sc.*400.—Poet. and late Prose, Plu.*Mar.*46.

**χάρμη** (A), ἡ, prop. *joy of battle, lust of battle*, χάρμῃ γηθόσυνοι τήν σφιν θεὸς ἔμβαλε θυμῷ Il.13.82; once in Od., μνησώμεθα χάρμης 22.73, cf. Il.4.222, 8.252, al.; opp. λήθετο χάρμης 12.203, 393, etc.: pl., δύο χάρμαι two *battle-joys*, i.e. *victories*, Pi.*O.*9.86; *successes*, opp. κακά, Ps.-Phoc.118: but, II. *battle*, προκαλέσσατο χάρμῃ Il.7.218; ἔλθοι τεθνηώς, καί μιν ἐρυσαίμεθα χάρμης 17.161; εἰδότε χάρμης 5.608; μηδ' εἴκετε χάρμης Ἀργείοις 4.509; παῦσαί τινα χάρμης 12.389; ἐρωήσουσι δὲ χάρμης 14.101.

**χάρμη** (B), ἡ, = ἐπιδορατίς, Stesich.94, Ibyc.62, Pi.*Dith.*3.13. (Cf. Polish *grot* 'arrow-point', Welsh *garth* 'promontory', Gr. χαρία, χοιράς.)

**χάρμη** (C), ἡ, or **χάρμης**, ὁ, name of an antidote sold by one Χάρμης, Damocr.ap.Gal.14.126 (found in acc. sg. χάρμην).

**Χαρμίδεια**, τά, *games* celebrated *in honour of Charmides* at Antioch on Maeander, *Rev.Phil.*55.133.

**χαρμοδότειρα**, ἡ, *giving delights*, ὄμφαξ prob. in *Hymn.Is.*169.

**χαρμονή**, ἡ, = χάρμα 1, *joy, delight*, esp. in pl., τέρψιν παλαιᾶν χαρμονᾶν E.*Ph.*317 (lyr.), cf. *Ion* 1379, *HF*384 (lyr.), 742 (lyr.). II. = χάρμα II, *joy, delight*, S.*Aj.*559; also found in Prose, [βίον] ἄλυπόν τε καὶ ἄνευ χαρμονῶν Pl.*Phlb.*43c; ὑπὸ τῆς χαρμονῆς X.*Cyr.*1.4.22, cf. Lxx *Jb.*3.7, al., Plu.2.1098c, Jul.*Or.*2.56a.

**χαρμονικός**, ή, όν, *pleasant*, paraphrase of θυμήρης, Procl.*Par.Ptol.* 274.

**χαρμοσύνη**, ἡ, *joyfulness, delight*, Lxx 1*Ki.*18.6, *Je.*40(33).11, Plu.2.1102a, Orph.*H.*60.4. II. *day of rejoicing*, ἑορταὶ καὶ χ. Lxx *Ju.*8.6.

**χαρμόσυνος**, η, ον, *joyful, glad*, χαρμόσυνα ποιέειν hold a *festival of thanksgiving*, Hdt.3.27, cf. Plu.2.362d, Sch.E.*Hec.*916; χαρμόσυνα ἐκφωνεῖν Onos.23 tit.

**χαρμόφρων**, ονος, ὁ, ἡ, (φρήν) *heart-delighting*, or *of joyous heart*, epith. of Hermes, *h.Merc.*127.

**χᾰροποι-έω**, *make joyful, delight*, Sm.*Ps.*20(21).7, *Gloss.* **-ημα**, ατος, τό, *joy caused to any one*, = ἀγαλλίαμα, Zonar. **-ός**, όν, *gladdening*, Procl.*Par.Ptol.*16, Hsch. s.v. εὐρίζων ἀγαλλιάματι, f.l. for χαροποί in Lxx *Ge.*49.12.

**χᾰροπός**, ή, όν, also ός, όν Arat.1152, epith. of dub. sense, perh. *fierce*, λέοντες Od.11.611, *h.Merc.*569, *IG*$4^2$(1).131.12 (Epid.); λέων Hes.*Th.*321; κύνες *h.Merc.*194; κύνα, of Hecuba, *Lyr.Adesp.* 101; θῆρες S.*Ph.*1146 (lyr.); χαροποῖσι πιθήκοις (παρὰ προσδοκίαν for λέουσι, in an oracle alluding to the Spartans) Ar.*Pax* 1065 (hex.); of serpents, *AP*10.22 (Bianor); *grim*, Ἄρης *IG*9(1).868.1 (Corc., vii/vi B.C., nisi leg. Χάροπος, gen. of Χάροψ); γένεια, of bears, Nonn.*D.*5.363; κεραίαι, of a bull, ib.40.52; γενειάδες, of dogs, ib.307. Adv. -πῶς Sch.Opp.*C.*3.510. 2. of eyes, *flashing, bright*, βλέποντος χαροποῖς τοῖς ὀφθαλμοῖς ὑπὸ τὴν κόρυν οἷον οἱ λέοντες ἐν ἀναβολῇ τοῦ ὁρμῆσαι Philostr.*Her.*$12^a$.1; τὸ χ. αὐτοῦ καὶ γοργόν Id.*Im.*1.23; χ. βλέμματος ἀστεροπαί *AP*5.152 (Asclep.), cf. 155 (Mel.); ὄμματά μοι γλαυκᾶς χαροπώτερα πολλὸν Ἀθάνας Theoc.20.25; ὄμμα χ., typical of a brave man, Arist.*Phgn.*$807^b$1; of persons, *flashing-eyed*, φοβερὰ καὶ χαροπὴ καὶ δεινῶς ἀνδρική (sc. ἡ Ἀθηνᾶ) Luc.*DDeor.*19.1: neut. as Adv., χαροπὸν βλέπειν Philostr.*Im.*1.28; χαροπὸν στράπτουσιν ὀπωπαί (of the hare) Opp.*C.*3.510 (regul. Adv. -πῶς Sch. ad loc.). b. *glassy, glazed, dull*, of the eyes of wine-drinkers, Al.*Ge.*49.12 (χαροποιοὶ..ὑπὲρ οἶνον, v.l. ἀπὸ οἴνου, Lxx l.c., s.v.l.), Sm.*Pr.*23.29 (πελιοὶ Lxx l.c.). 3. of one of the chief eye-colours in men and animals, perh. *bluish-grey*, distd. fr. μέλας, γλαυκός, and αἰγωπός, Arist.*HA*$492^a$3, *GA*$779^b$14; τὰ χ. ἢ μέλανα ὄμματα Luc.*DMort.*1.3; of persons, *bluish-grey-eyed* *PPetr.*1 p. 54, al. (iii B.C.), Theoc.12.35, cf. Philostr.*Im.*2.5, al.; of horses, Opp.*C.*1.310, 4.113; of dogs, X.*Cyn.*3.3, Arr.*Cyn.*5.1 (prob.), *Gp.*19.2.1; of rams, ib.18.1.3; of παρδάλεις, Eust.1703.29; opp. μελανόφθαλμος, S.E.*M.*7.198; persons with this eye-colour are φθινώδεες acc. to Hp.*Epid.*3.14 (where Gal.17(1).726 thinks Hp. ought to have mentioned a different colour, γλαυκός). Adv. Comp. -ώτερον, μελαίνεσθαι (of the eyes) Hld.2.35. 4. of the sea, *bluish-grey, grey*, χαροποῖο θαλάσσης Orph.*Fr.*245.21, cf. *A.*272, [S.]*Fr.*1126.3, *AP*12.53 (Mel.), 9.36 (Secund.), *Anacreont.* 53.30, Nonn.*D.*4.187, al.; of the dawn, χ. ἠώς A.R.1.1280; of the moon, Arat.1152, Q.S.10.337; πρὸς ἕω λαμβάνει [ἡ σελήνη] χρόαν κυανοειδῆ καὶ χαροπήν Plu.2.934d; of certain stars, χ. καὶ ἀναλδέες εἱλίσσονται Arat.394, cf. 594. 5. metaph., *grey*, ὑπὸ σὸν (sc. τῆς Νεμέσεως) τροχὸν ἄστατον ἀστιβῆ χαροπὰ μερόπων στρέφεται Τύχα Mesom.*Nem.*8.

**χᾰροπ-ότης**, ητος, ἡ, *brightness of eye*, *Stoic.*3.33, Archyt.ap.Simp. *in Cat.*93.2, *EM*807.30. 2. *light-blue colour*, of the eyes of the Germans, Plu.*Mar.*11; also αἰθέριος χ., of sky-*blue*, Id.2.352d. 3. *brightness*, Simp. *in Cat.*298.15. **-όφθαλμος**, ον, *bright-eyed*, Phlp. *in GA*212.9.

**χάροψ**, οπος, ὁ, ἡ, poet. for χαροπός, *bright-eyed*, γλαῦκος Opp.*C.* 3.114.

**χαρτ-αρέα**, ἡ, = χαρτηρά, *tax on papyrus*, *Abh.Berl.Akad.*1932(5).46 (Pergam.). ® **-άριον**, τό, Dim. of χάρτης, *small piece of papyrus*, *AP*12.208 (Strat.), *BGU*466.12 (ii/iii A.D.), *PMed.* in *PSI*10.1180.50 (ii A.D.), etc. **-ηρά**, ἡ, *tax on papyrus*, *PTeb.*140 (i B.C.), *Sammelb.*5636 (Iconium, ii A.D.). II. *expenditure on papyrus*, *BGU*277 ii 11 (ii A.D.). **-ηρία**, ἡ, = sq., Lxx 3*Ma.*4.20. ® **-ης**, ου, ὁ, = foreg., *papyrus*, or a *roll* made thereof, χ. δύο *IG*$1^2$.374.279; τὰ γραμματεῖα τούς τε χ. ἐκφέρων Pl.Com.194, cf. Lxx *Is.*8.1 cod.Alex., *PCair.Zen.*687.4 (iii B.C.), *Inscr.Délos* 442*A*182 (ii B.C.), *PTeb.*112.61 (ii B.C.), Dsc.1.86, Ceb.4, etc., *AP*9.174 (Pall.), 401 (Id.); ὥσπερ χάρτην εὐεργὸν εἰς ἀπογραφήν (of the soul at birth) *Stoic.*2.28; χάρται βυβλίων Theopomp.Hist.283; χ. βασιλικοί, of the finest papyrus, Hero *Aut.*26.3; χ. κεκαυμένος used in Medicine, Gal. 10.382, 13.315; also χάρτου σποδιά Lycus ap.Orib.8.25.15; τὸ διὰ χάρτου μέλαν Sor.2.41. 2. metaph., *any leaf* or *thin plate*, χ. μολύβδινοι *sheets* of lead, Lysim. ap. J.*Ap.*1.34. ® **-ιᾱτικά**, τά, = Lat. *chartiatica*, *money for paper*, *CIG*5187*c*21 (Ptolemais, vi A.D.). **-ίδιον** [ῐδ], τό, = sq., Ph.2.3, al., Alciphr.1.26, *Sammelb.* 5224.3 (-ειδ-).

® **χαρτίον**, τό, Dim. of χάρτης, *IG*$4^2$(1).103.159 (Epid., iv B.C.), Lxx *Je.*43(36).2, *PGrenf.*2.38.5 (i B.C.), Plu.2.60a, Gal.7.493, D.L. 7.174, D.C.46.36.

® **χάρτισμα**, ατος, τό, dub. sens. in *PStrassb.*35.18 (v A.D.).

**χαρτο-γράφος** [γρᾰ], ὁ, = Lat. *chartularius*, *Gloss.* **-θήκη**, ἡ, = Lat. *scrinium*, ib. **-πηρον**, τό, *repository of papers*, ib. **-ποιός**, ὁ, *paper-maker*, dub. in *PTeb.*112.62 (ii B.C.): v. χαρτοπώλης. **-πράτης** [πρᾱ], ου, ὁ, *dealer in papyrus*, *Cod.Just.*11.18 tit. **-πώλης**, ου, ὁ, = foreg., *Gloss.*, prob. in *PTeb.*112.62 (ii B.C.).

® **χαρτός**, ή, όν, (χαίρω) *causing delight, welcome*, χαρτὸν εἴ τι καὶ φέρεις S.*Tr.*228; χαίροις ἄν, εἴ σοι χαρτὰ τυγχάνει τάδε Id.*El.*1457; εἴτε ἡδὺ εἴτε τερπνὸν λέγεις εἴτε χ. Pl.*Prt.*358a: χαρτά *delights*, opp. κακά, χαρτοῖσιν χαῖρε Archil.66.6; χαρτὰ πάσχω E.*Ph.*618 (troch.); τὸ χ. Chrysipp.*Stoic.*3.9, Epicur.*Fr.*423, S.E.*M.*11.85, etc. 2. of persons, εἰ χ. ἀνέλθοι *AP*12.24 (Tull.Laur.). Adv. -τῶς, χ. ἐμοὶ λέγειν Sch.*S.Aj.*112.

**χαρτοτόμος**, ον, *paper-cutting*, *Gloss.* 2. Pass., χαρτότομος, ον, *cut in* or *from paper*, Sch.Il.15.389.

® **χαρτουλάριος**, ὁ, *chartularius, keeper of archives*, *PKlein.Form.* 1024 (v/vi A.D.), *Sammelb.*5656.4 (vi A.D.), *Cod.Just.*1.2.24.8, al., Lyd.*Mag.*3.20.

**χαρτο-φῠλάκιον** [ᾰκ], τό, *case for storing papers*, Suid., *Gloss.* **-φύλαξ** [ῠ], ᾰκος, ὁ, = χαρτουλάριος, Lyd.*Mag.*3.19, Choerob. *in Theod.*1.287H., Suid. s.v. Γεώργιος.

**χαρτῠφάντης**, ου, ὁ, *papyrus-weaver*, i.e. maker of papyrus sheets, *MAMA*3.310, 361 (Corycus).

® **Χάρυβδις** [ᾰ], εως, Ion. ιος, ἡ, *Charybdis*, a whirlpool on the coast of Sicily, opposite Scylla, Od.12.104, E.*Tr.*436, Th.4.24, Str.6.2.

3. **2.** generally, *whirlpool, gulf*, πάντα μίαν ἱκνεῖται χ. Simon.38, cf. E.*Supp*.500, Str.6.2.9. **3.** metaph. of a rapacious person, χ. ἁρπαγῆς Ar.*Eq*.248 (troch.).

* **χάρων** [ᾰ], ωνος, ὁ, ἡ, poet. for χαροπός, Μήνης παῖδα χάρωνα, of the Nemean lion, Euph.84.4; so as Subst. (said to be Maced.), χάρωνος ὠμηστοῦ δορά Lyc.455, cf. Hsch., etc.; also of *the eagle*, Lyc.260; of the Cyclops, Id.660. **II.** as pr. n., *Charon*, the ferryman of the Styx, E.*Alc*.254 (lyr.), 361, al.; voc. ὦ Χάρον Cratin.324c (v.l. Χάρων); but χαῖρ' ὦ Χάρων (with a pun) Ar.*Ra*.184.

**Χᾰρών-ιος** (later -**ειος**), ον, *of* or *belonging to Charon*: hence, **1.** Χ. θύρα the gate *through which criminals were led to execution*, Zen. 6.41, Suid.; also Χαρώνιον, τό, Poll.8.102, Hsch. **2.** Χ. κλίμακες, a staircase in the theatre, leading up to the stage as if from the underworld, by which ghosts entered, Poll.4.132. **3.** χαρώνια, τά, *caverns filled with mephitic vapours*, being looked on as entrances to the nether world, Str.12.8.17; sg., Id.14.1.11,44: **χαρωνῆϊα**, prob. in Aret.*SA*1.7; in full, χαρώνεια βάραθρα Gal.17(1).10; χ. χωρία Id.15.117. **-ῖται**, οἱ, used to translate the Lat. *Orcini*, *Senators from the nether world*, viz. those who were created after the death of Caesar, professedly on the authority of papers left behind by him, Plu.*Ant*.15.

**χᾰρωπός**, όν, late form for χαροπός, Man.5.230, *Gloss*., f.l. in Arr.*Cyn*.4,5.

* **χάσιος**· ἀγαθός, χρηστός, Hsch.

**χάσις**, εως, ἡ, *chasm, separation*, Hsch.

**χασκάζω**, Frequentat. of χάσκω, χ. τὸν κωλακρέτην *keep gaping at* or *after* him, Ar.*V*.695 (anap.).

**χάσκᾰνον**, τό, = ξάνθιον, Dsc.4.136.

* **χάσκαξ**, ᾰκος, ὁ, *gaper, gaby*, Eust.1909.54.

* **χάσκω**, Anacr.14.8, Ar.*V*.1493 (anap.); subj. χάσκῃς Id.*Eq*.1032 (hex.); inf. χάσκειν X.*Eq*.10.7, (ἐγ-) Ar.*V*.721; part. χάσκων Sol. 13.36, Hp.*Art*.30, f.l. in Ar.*Eq*.1018 (hex.), (ἀνα-) Id.*Av*.502 (anap.): Ion. fem. χασκευσα Herod.4.42 Pap. (also Med. χασκόμενοι Cass.*Pr*. 20): pres. **χαίνω** only in late writers, Phld.*Rh*.2.189 S., Antig.*Mir*. 128, *AP*9.797 (Jul.), 11.242 (Nicarch.), Gal.7.686, *Gp*.10.30tit., etc., (ἐπι-) Luc.*DMort*.6.3, (περι-) Ael.*NA*3.20: fut. χᾰνοῦμαι (ἐγ-) Ar.*Eq*. 1313 (troch.), (ἀνα-) Hp.*Steril*.217, *Superf*.29, etc.: aor. 2 ἔχᾰνον Il.4. 182, al., Hp.*Art*.30, S.*Aj*.1227, Ar.*V*.342 (lyr.), etc.; aor. 1 ἔχᾶνα Aesop.223: pf. κέχηνα Il.16.409, Hp.*Coac*.487, etc.; Dor. 3 pl. κεχάναντι Sophr.25 (Hdn.Gr.2.793 cites κεχήνετε from Ar.*Ach*.133, and A.D.*Adv*.197.31 has κέχαγκα): plpf. ἐκεχήνεσαν Ar.*Eq*.651; early Att. 'κεχήνη Id.*Ach*.10.—Used by Hom. only in aor. 2 χάνοι, χανών, and pf. part. κεχηνώς:—*yawn, gape*, τότε μοι χάνοι εὐρεῖα χθών then *may* earth *yawn* for me, i.e. to swallow me, Il.4.182, 8.150, cf. 17. 417; esp. of *opening the mouth wide*, [αἷμα] ἀνὰ στόμα καὶ κατὰ ῥῖνας πρῆσε χανών 16.350; ἕλκ' ἐκ δίφροιο κεχηνότα ib.409; ἐάλη τε χανών, of a lion, 20.168; πρὸς κῦμα χανὼν ἀπὸ θυμὸν ὀλέσσαι, of one drowning, Od.12.350: c. acc., στόμα χάσκων *AP*11.418 (Trajan); of a wound, v.l. in S.*Fr*.508; of shellfish, αἵ γα μὰν κόγχαι..κεχάναντι πᾶσαι Sophr. l.c.; ἐπεὰν ὁ κροκόδειλος..χάνῃ..πρὸς τὸν ζέφυρον Hdt.2.68; of a goose, πλατυγίζοντα καὶ κεχηνότα Eub.115; of fruit, *burst with ripeness*, M.Ant.3.2, *Gp*.l.c. **2.** after Hom., *gape* in eager expectation, χάσκοντες κούφαις ἐλπίσι τερπόμεθα Sol. l.c.: freq. in Com., ὅτε δὴ 'κεχήνη προσδοκῶν τὸν Αἰσχύλον when *I was all agape*, Ar.*Ach*.10; λύκος ἔχανεν the wolf *opened his mouth* (for nothing), prov. of disappointed hopes, Id.*Fr*.337, cf. Eub.15.11, Euphro 1.30: with Preps., πρὸς ταῦτα κεχηνὼς Ar.*Nu*.996 (anap.); πρὸς ἄλλην τινὰ χάσκει Anacr. l.c., cf. Ar.*Eq*.651,804 (anap.), Porph.*Marc*.9, etc.; ἔς τι (sc. νόμισμα) Philostr.*VA*2.7; ἄνω κεχηνώς, of a stargazer, Ar.*Nu*.172, cf. *Av*.51, Pl.*R*.529b; ὧδε χὧδε χ. Herod.4.42; κεχηνότες *gaping fools*, Ar.*Ra*.990 (lyr.), cf. *Eq*.261 (troch.), *V*.617 (anap.), and v. Κεχηναῖοι. **3.** *yawn* from weariness, ennui, or inattention, Id.*Ach*.30; ὅταν σύ που ἄλλοσε χάσκῃς Id.*Eq*.1032 (hex.), cf. *Lys*.426; χάσκεις αὐτός; *are you yawning? paying no attention?* Mnesim.4.22 (anap.). **4.** metaph., ἀναπληροῦν τὸ κεχηνὸς τῆς ἑρμηνείας fill the *lacuna*, A.D.*Synt*.266.22. **II.** less freq., *speak with open mouth, utter*, c. acc., σὲ δὴ τὰ δεινὰ ῥήματ'..καθ' ἡμῶν..χανεῖν; S.*Aj*.1227; τοῦτ' ἐτόλμησεν χανεῖν; Ar.*V*.342 (lyr.); οἴζυρόν τι χανοῦσα Call.*Ap*.24. **III.** in Paus.6.21.13, if the text be correct, it must be trans., χανεῖν..τὴν γῆν..τὸ ἅρμα *opened and swallowed* the chariot.—Not in A. (exc. in compd. προσ-, q.v.) or E.; rare in early Prose, exc. Hp.; once in Hdt. (v. supr. I. 1).

**χασκωρέω**, = χασκάζω, Hsch.

* **χάσμα**, ατος, τό, (χαίνω) *yawning chasm, gulf*, χ. μέγα, of Tartarus, Hes.*Th*.740; Ταρτάρου..ἄβυσσα χ. E.*Ph*.1605; χ. γῆς Hdt. 7.30; τὰ χ. τῆς γῆς Pl.*Phd*.111e; χθονός, πέτρας, E.*Ion* 281, *IT*626; σεισμοὶ καὶ χάσματα Jul.Laod. in *Cat.Cod.Astr*.1.134. **II.** *open, gaping mouth*, χ. θηρός E.*HF*363 (lyr.); as forming a helmet, Id. *Rh*.209; of a *yawning gulf*, Χάρυβδις..ἅρμα περιβαλοῦσα χάσματι Id.*Supp*.501; Σκύλλης χάσμασιν *AP*11.379 (Agath.); χ. φάρυγος, of a lion, ib.6.218 (Alc.); χ. ὀδόντων *Anacreont*.24.4, etc. **III.** generally, *any wide opening*, θυρέτρων χ. ἀχανές Parm.1.18; also, *expanse*, of the sky and sea, χ. πελάγεος τὸ δὴ Αἰγαῖον καλέεται Hdt. 4.85; τὸ χ. τοῦ οὐρανοῦ Pl.*R*.614d.

**χασμᾰθυπουργός**, ὁ, *servant in the chasm*, *PMag.Lond*.121.353 (pl.).

**χασμ-άομαι**, *yawn, gape*, ὁπόταν χασμᾷ when *you are gaping*, Ar.*Eq*.824 (anap.), cf. Hp.*Mochl*.4, Arist.*GA*719$^{a}$19, Porph.*Abst*.1. 28, etc.; οἱ τοὺς χασμωμένους ὁρῶντες Pl.*Chrm*.169c; ἰλιγγιᾶν καὶ χ. Id.*Grg*.486b, 527a; of a door, τῆς θύρας χασμωμένης Alex.257. **II.** οἱ χασμώμενοι, = οἱ κεχηνότες, *gabies*, Porph.*Chr*.49. **-ᾰτίας**, ου, ὁ, a kind of earthquake, *which causes fissures in the earth*, Arist.*Mu*.396$^{a}$4 (v.l. ἰζηματίαι), Posidon.ap.D.L.7.154, Heraclit. *All*.38. **-άτιον**, τό, *small aperture, vent*, Hero *Spir*.2.34; χαλκᾶ λεόντων χ., of the *spouts* of a fountain, Sch.Pi.*Pae*.6.7. **-έομαι**, = χασμάομαι, εἰς ταύταν χασμεύμενος Theoc.4.53. **-η**, ἡ, *yawning, gaping*, Hp.*Aph*.7.56; esp. from drowsiness, Id.*VM*10, Pl.*R*.503d, etc.: pl., Hp.*Art*.30, Plu.2.45d. **2.** *object of idle gaping, gazing-stock*, Antip.*Stoic*.3.254. **-ημα**, ατος, τό, *a wide yawn* or *gape*, Ar.*Av*.61. **-ησις**, εως, ἡ, = χάσμη, Hsch. s.v. ἀλυχήν, *EM* 495.47, *Gloss*. **II.** = χασμωδία, Eust.12.4.

**χασμωδ-έω**, *write verses that have hiatus*, Eust.11.42. **-ης**, ες, *always yawning*, D.L.4.32; τὸ χ. *listlessness*, Plu.2.92d. **II.** τὸ χ. τῶν φωνηέντων *hiatus*, A.D.*Pron*.50.11. **-ία**, ἡ, *hiatus* in verse, Eust.11.33, 12.8, Sch.Ar.*Pl*.696.

**χαστηρία**, f.l. for σχαστ- in Hsch.

**χᾰτεύω**, = sq., Hsch.

**χᾰτέω**, Ep. Verb, used by Hom. only in pres.: later, impf. χατέεσκε Nonn.*D*.4.56. **I.** c. inf., *crave, need*, οὐδέ τις ἡμῖν δόρπου μνῆστις ἔην, μάλα περ χατέουσιν ἑλέσθαι Od.13.280; δμῶες χατέουσιν ἄντια δεσποίνης φάσθαι 15.376: abs., χατέοντί περ ἔμπης Il.15.399, cf. 9.518; μάλα περ χατέουσα Od.2.249. **II.** c. gen., *want, have need of*, πάντες δὲ θεῶν χατέουσ' ἄνθρωποι 3.48; μάλα περ χατέοντες ἀρωγῆς Epic.*Oxy*.422, cf. *AP*5.301.20 (Agath.), 7.583 (Id.), etc. **III.** rarely c. acc. οἷά τε πολλὰ ἄνθρωποι χ. A.R.4.1557.

**χᾰτίζω**, = foreg., only in pres., *have need of, crave*: c. gen. rei, νόστοιο χατίζων Od.8.156, 11.350, cf. Il.2.225: c. gen. pers., Θέτις νύ τι σεῖο χ. 18.392; ἑρμηνέων χ. Pi.*O*.2.86; οὐ σοῦ χατίζων E. *Heracl*.465: abs., οὐδὲ χατίζων nor *in want* [of anything], Od.22. 351, Il.17.221; χατίζων *in want, needy*, Hes.*Op*.394. **2.** *lack, be without*, ἔργοιο χ. i.e. to be idle, ib.21; ἅσσα χατίζει μάλιστα κατὰ ταῦτα a diet most *defective* in these elements, Hp.*Morb*.4.39.

**χατίς**· ἐπιθυμία, χρῆσις, Hsch. (perh. χᾶτις, Dor. for χῆτις).

**χατος**, ὁ, = Lat. *maritus*, *Gloss*. (dub.).

**χαυλίξυν**· ἀλαζόνα, Hsch.

**χαυλιόδους**, όδοντος, ὁ, ἡ, neut. -όδουν Arist.*PA*661$^{b}$23. **I.** of animals, *with outstanding teeth* or *tusks*, κάπρος χ. (where most codd. χαυλιόδων, contr. to the rule of Hdn.*Epim*.208, that the correct forms are χαυλιόδους and χαυλιώδων), Hes.*Sc*.387, cf. Arist. l.c., 663$^{a}$7; χ. γένεθλα Opp.*C*.3.6. **II.** Subst., of projecting teeth, *tusks, tushes*, ἔχει [ὁ κροκόδειλος] ὀδόντας μεγάλους καὶ χαυλιόδοντας Hdt.2.68; τετράπουν χαυλιόδοντας φαῖνον, of the hippopotamus, Id.2.71, cf. D.S.1.35; opp. καρχαρόδους, Arist.*HA*501$^{a}$ 15, *PA*661$^{b}$18, cf. *HA*538$^{b}$21.

**χαῦναξ**, ᾰκος, ὁ, *braggart, impostor*, Hsch. **χαυνιάζω**, *cheat*, Id.

**χαυνό-γειον**, τό, *friable earth*, *PTeb*.342.27 (ii A.D.). **-λόγος** and **-ποιός**, = χαῦναξ, Hsch. **-πολίτης** [ῑ], ου, ὁ, *gaping fool*, who *swallows open-mouthed* all that is told him (cf. Κεχηναῖοι), Ar.*Ach*. 635 (pl., anap.). * **-πρωκτος**, ον, *wide-breeched*, ib.104.

**χαῦνος**, η, ον, but ος, ον Pl.*Lg*.728e, Arist.*Pr*.934$^{b}$11:—of tissues, *porous, spongy*, Hp.*Aph*.5.67; χ. ὀστέα, such as the collar-bone, Id.*Art*.14; *loose*, συστροφή Pl.*Plt*.282e; μαστοί Sor.1.88; ἅλες χ. καὶ λεπτοὶ ὥσπερ χιών Arist.*Mete*.359$^{a}$32; γῆ, opp. στερρός, Id.*Pr*. l.c., cf. Ephor.65(*e*) J.; *loose-grained*, of timber, Thphr.*HP*3.4.3, 5.3.3; also of the fruit of the medlar, *spongy*, ib.3.12.5; -ότατος πυρετός, = ῥοώδης (A) II.a, Erot. s.v. σπόγγοι; τὸ χ. D.S.3.14. Adv. -νως, of garments hanging *loosely*, Hdn.4.15.3; of bandaging, Pall. *in Hp. Fract*.12.285 C. **II.** metaph., *empty, frivolous*, νόος Sol.11.6; πραπὶς Pi.*P*.2.61; κενεᾶν ἐλπίδων χαῦνον τέλος Id.*N*.8.45; χαῦνα μὲν τότ' ἐφράσαντο Sol.34; χαύνους τὰς ψυχὰς καὶ θρασείας ποιεῖ *conceited*, Pl.*Lg*.728e; ὁ μεγάλων ἑαυτὸν ἀξιῶν, ἀνάξιος ὤν, χαῦνος Arist.*EN* 1123$^{b}$9: Comp., οἱ -ότεροι τεχνῖται Phld.*Rh*.1.376 S. Adv. -νως *sluggishly*, Eustr. *in EN*379.15. **2.** *of vast extension*, ὄνομα Ar. *Av*.819. Adv. χαύνως *frivolously*, Simp. *in Epict*.p.121 D. (Cf. χάος.)

**χαυνόσομφος**, ον, *loose and flaccid*, Erot. s.v. σκηρόν.

* **χαυνότης**, ητος, ἡ, *porousness, sponginess*, τῆς γῆς interpol. in X.*Oec*.19.11; τάφρου Plu.*Pyrrh*.28; of snow, Id.2.649c; of foam, ib.99b. **2.** *looseness* of a bandage, Gal(?). ap.Orib.46.1.15. **II.** metaph., *empty conceit, vanity*, ἀνοήτου ψυχῆς Pl.*Tht*.175b; opp. μεγαλοψυχία, Arist.*EN*1107$^{b}$23.

**χαυνόφρων**, φρονος, ὁ, ἡ, = χαλίφρων, Sch.Od.4.371.

**χαυν-όω**, *make flaccid, relax*:—Pass., *to become so*, Heliod. ap.Orib.46.22.1, Ael.*NA*12.17; ἡ γῆ χ. εἰς ῥαγάδας *Gp*.5.2. 2. **b.** Pass., of inflammation, *subside*, Alex.Trall.3.3. **2.** χαυνοῦσα (codd.Ath.) is f.l. for χανοῦσα, *opening the mouth in kissing*, in Ephipp.6.5. **II.** metaph., *puff up, fill with conceit*, E.*Andr*.931, Pl.*Ly*.210e:—Pass., *become vain*, Arist.*VV*1251$^{b}$18, Plb.6.57.7; ταῖς πράξεσι Phld.*Hom*.p.55 O.; ἐπὶ τούτοις Plu.*Caes*. 29; ὁ νοῦς ἐχαυνώθη Babr.95.36; κόραξ ἐπαίνῳ καρδίην ἐχαυνώθη Id.77.8; ὑπὸ τῆς δυνάμεως D.C.*Fr*.49.3. **2.** *relax, weaken*, εἰρήνη χ. τὴν πολιτείαν Lyd.*Mag*.3.51:—Pass., of character, Heliod. *in EN*149.13. **-ωμα**, ατος, τό, *loosened earth*, Plu.*Sert*.17. * **-ωσις**, εως, ἡ, *making slack* or *loose*, opp. στέγνωσις, S.E.*P*.1.238. **2.** *void space* or *interval*, *Gp*.10.75.17. **II.** metaph., *making confused, mystification*, χ. ἀναπειστηρία Ar.*Nu*.875 (ubi v. Sch.). **2.** *puffing up*, χαύνωσιν ἐργάζεσθαι Phld.*Rh*.1.219 S.: pl., Iamb.*VP*15.

64. 3. *relaxation*, *relief*, Alex.Trall.4.1. **-ωτικός**, ή, όν, *apt to make loose* or *flabby*, σαρκός Plu.2.771b.

⊛ **χαυών**, a kind of *cake*, in Lxx to represent Hebr. *kavvân*, Lxx *Je.*7.18, 51(44).19, cf. *EM*807.43, Suid., etc.:—wrongly written **χαυνών** in Hsch.

**χάω**, contr. χῶ, = χωρῶ, coined as etym. of χάος by Simp. *in Ph.* 620.14.

**χᾰώδης**, ες, *like chaos*, Dam.*Pr.*107.

**χεδρία**, ἡ, = sq., *PLond.*5.1833.5 (iv A.D.), *PMasp.*143.4 (vi A.D.): hence **χεδριοφόρος**, ὁ, *hawker of* χεδρίαι, ib.143$^{v}$6 (vi A.D.).

**χεδροπά**, τά, *leguminous fruits, pulse*, Hp.*Nat.Puer.*12, Arist. *Mete.*389$^{a}$15, *GA*750$^{a}$24, Thphr.*HP*8.2.2, *CP*4.7.2, al.; gen. χεδρόπων or χεδροπῶν, Arist.*PA*653$^{a}$24, *GA*752$^{a}$21.—Acc. sg. χέδροπα occurs in Python1.12 (prob.), Porph.*Abst.*2.6, and nom. **χέδροψ** Hsch., and τοὺς καρποὺς τοὺς χέδροπας (v.l. χεδροπούς) is found in Arist.*HA*594$^{b}$7: but the accent seems to point to sg. χεδροπός. (Perh. a compd. of χείρ, δρέπω, as if χερ-δροπά, *plucked by the hand*, cf. χειροδρόποι δ' ἵνα φῶτες ἄτερ δρεπάνοιο λέγονται ὄσπρια, χέδροπά τ' ἄλλα Nic.*Th.*752.)

**χεδροπώδης**, ες, *like* χεδροπά, φύσις Phanias ap.Ath.9.406c.

**χέεια**, ἡ, Ep. for χειά, cj. in Nic.*Th.*79.

**χεζᾰνάγκη**, ἡ, *purgative plaster*, Aët.3.135, Paul.Aeg.7.9.

**χεζητιάω**, Desiderat. of χέζω, *want to ease oneself*, Ar.*Nu.*1387, *Ra.*8, al.

**χέζω**, fut. χεσοῦμαι Ar.*V.*941, *Pax*1235; also κατα-χέσομαι Id.*Fr.*152: aor. 1 ἔχεσα Id.*Ec.*320,808, (ἐγ-) ib.347, (κατ-) *Nu.* 174: aor. 2 ἔχεσον (κατ-) Alc.Com.4 (cf. Hdn.Gr.2.801); inf. χεσεῖν Ar.*Th.*570, *AP*7.683 (Pall.): pf. κέχοδα (only in compds. ἐγ-, ἐπι-χέζω): Pass., κέχεσμαι (v. infr.):—*ease oneself*, Ar. ll. cc., etc.: prov., εἰ μηδὲ χέσαι γε..σχολὴ γενήσεται Stratt.51; οὐκ ἔχεις ὅ[ποι χέσῃς] ὑπὸ τῶν ἀγαθῶν cj. in Men.530.9, cf. *Com.Adesp.* 491; ἐλευθέρα Κόρκυρα· χέζ' ὅπου θέλεις Str.7*Fr.*8: c. acc., χ. σησαμίδας Eup.163 (lyr.):—Med. (for the sake of the pun), χέσαιτο γὰρ εἰ μαχέσαιτο Ar.*Eq.*1057 (hex.):—Pass., πέλεθος ἀρτίως κεχεσμένος dung just *dropped*, Id.*Ach.*1170. (Cf. Skt. *hádati* (same sense).)

⊛ **χεῖ**, τό, name of the letter χ, *IG*2$^{2}$.1491.33, Pl.*Ti.*36b, Hellad.ap. Phot.*Bibl.*p.530B.; later written **χῖ**, v. l. in Hp.*VC*1.

**χειά**, Ion. **χειή**, ἡ, *hole*, esp. of serpents, Il.22.93,95, Plu.2.169e, Orph.*L.*473; ἥβαν οὐχ ὑπὸ χειᾷ δάμασεν he buried not his youth in *a hole*, Pi.*I.*8(7).77: pl., *Schwyzer*194.5 (Crete).

**χειλ-άριον** [ᾰ], τό, Dim. of χεῖλος, *small lip*, *Gloss.* **-ᾶς**, *labrosus*, ib.

**χειλίαρχος**, = χιλ- *Sammelb.*4018.3, etc.

**χειλο-λάβος** [ᾰ], ὁ, surgical *bandage for the lips*, Gal.*Fasc.*69,71 tit. (12.489 Chart.). **-ποτέω**, *drink with the lips*, *sip*, *AP*7.223 (Thyill.).

**χειλός**, ὁ, with its derivs., v. χιλός.

⊛ **χεῖλος** (Dor. **χῆλος** Cerc.1.5, Aeol. **χέλλος** Choerob. in *An.Ox.* 2.278), εος, τό: pl., gen. χειλῶν Arist.*HA*492$^{b}$26; χειλέων Herod. 3.4, Lxx*Pr.*12.13, al., Plu.*Cat.Ma.*12, v.l. in D.H.*Comp.*14: poet. dat. χείλεσσι (v. infr.):—*lip*, Hom., etc.: prov., ἐγέλασσε χείλεσιν laughed *with the lips only*, Il.15.102; χείλεα μέν τ' ἐδίην', ὑπερῴην δ' οὐκ ἐδίηνε wetted *the lips*, but not the palate, i.e. drank sparingly, 22.495; νέκταρ ἐν χείλεσσι στάξοισι Pi.*P.*9.63; πειθώ τις ἐπεκάθιζεν ἐπὶ τοῖς χ., of Pericles, Eup.94.5; χείλεσιν διδοὺς ὀδόντας E.*Ba.*621 (troch.); χείλεσιν ἀμφιλάλοις, of incessant talk, Ar.*Ra.* 678 (lyr.); δάκνων τὰ χ., of one in a difficulty, Eub.53.6; ἄχρις ἡ ψυχὴ..ἐπὶ χειλέων λειφθῇ Herod. l.c.; ἐπὶ τοῖς χείλεσι τὰς ψυχὰς ἔχοντες 'with their hearts in their mouths', D.Chr.32.50; ἀπὸ χειλέων, opp. ἀπὸ καρδίας, Plu. l.c.; ἀπ' ἄκρου χ. φιλοσοφεῖν *on the surface only*, Luc.*Apol.*6; ἐπ' ἄκρου τοῦ χ. on the tip of one's *tongue*, Id.*Ind.*26; προσαρμόσαι τὰ χ. (sc. τῇ κύλικι) Id.*DDeor.*5. 2; προσαρμόζειν τὰ χ., χείλη προσεγγίσαι χείλεσιν, of persons kissing, Id.*DMeretr.*5.3, *Am.*53; χείλεσιν διερρυηκόσιν with gaping *lips*, Ar.*Nu.*873; ἐν τοῖς χ. τιμᾶν Lxx *Is.*29.13; ἐν χ. ἑτέρων λαλεῖν, i.e. in strange *speech*, 1*Ep.Cor.*14.21; χ. ἓν πάντων Lxx*Ge.*11. 6, cf. *Pr.*10.19. 2. of horses, X.*Eq.*6.8: of birds, *bill*, *beak*, E.*Ion*1199, Opp.*H.*3.247, *AP*9.333 (Mnasalc.). II. metaph. of things, *edge*, *brink*, *rim*, of a bowl, χρυσῷ δ' ἐπὶ χείλεα κεκράανται Od.4.616, cf. 132; Ἐλπὶς..ἔμιμνε πίθου ὑπὸ χείλεσιν Hes.*Op.*97, cf. Hdt.3.123, Ar.*Ach.*459; of a ditch, Il.12.52, Hdt.1.179, Th.3.23; of the ocean, Mimn.11.7, cf. Lxx*Ge.*22.17; τῶν τῆς γῆς τροχῶν Pl. *Criti.*115e; of rivers, lakes, Hdt.2.70,94, Arist.*HA*570$^{a}$22; of the whorls, Pl.*R.*616d,e; αὐλαίας, τείχους, Lxx*Ex.*26.4, Plb.10.44.11; of the womb, Arist.*HA*583$^{a}$16; of a wound, Gal.11.127.

**χειλοτένων**, οντος, ὁ, epith. of crabs, Batr.297.

**χειλοφύλαξ** [ῠ], ᾰκος, ὁ, *bandage for the lips*, Heliod.ap.Orib.48.35.

**χείλωμα**, ατος, τό, *lip*, *rim*, Aq.*Ex.*37(38).2.

**χεῖμα**, ατος, τό, *winter weather*, *cold*, *frost*, Od.14.487: then, *winter* as a season of the year, χείματος ὥρη Hes.*Op.*450; οὔποτε καρπὸς ἀπολείπει χείματος οὐδὲ θέρευς Od.7.118, cf. Alcm.76; φέροντας χ. καὶ θέρος βροτοῖς, of the stars, A.*Ag.*5; οὔτε χείματος τέκμαρ οὔτ' ἀνθεμώδους ἦρος Id.*Pr.*454; χεῖμα in acc., during *winter*, Od.11.190, Hes.*Op.*640; χείματι S.*Ph.*293. II. *storm*, χ. πῦρ τε δάϊον Alcm. 79, cf. *Lyr.Adesp.*100, A.*Ag.*199 (lyr.), 627, E.*Andr.*748, al.; κάλλιστον ἦμαρ εἰσιδεῖν ἐκ χείματος A.*Ag.*900.—Poet. form of χειμών, used also in Pl.*Ax.*371d. (Cf. Skt. *héman* 'in winter', Lith. *žiemà* 'winter', etc.)

**χειμᾰδ-εύω**, = χειμάζω, Str.4.6.7, Onos 9.1. **-ίζω**, = foreg., dub. l. in J.*AJ*18.1.3 (fut. part. -ιοῦσαν). **-ιον**, τό, *winter dwelling*, *winter quarters*, χειμαδίῳ χρῆσθαι Λήμνῳ D.4.32, cf. Str. 11.13.1, Hld.5.18: esp. in pl., χειμάδια πήγνυσθαι to fix one's *winter quarters*, Plu.*Sert.*6, cf. *Luc.*3, *Eum.*15, Jul.*Ep.*98.—Adj. **χειμάδιος**, α, ον, is cited in Poll.1.62, Suid.; ἡ χειμαδία (sc. ὥρα) *Et.Gud.*563.53.

**χειμ-άζω** (fut. -άσω Thphr.*Sign.*38):—trans., *expose to the winter cold*: found only in Pass., *to be exposed thereto*, Hp.*Vict.*3.68; *pass the winter*, S.*Fr.*503; ὅπως χειμασθῇ καὶ ἡλιωθῇ ἡ γῆ Thphr.*CP*3.20.7; of trees, *live through the winter*, χειμασθέντα [δένδρα] Id.*HP*4.14.1; χειμασθῆναι χειμῶσι ὡραίοις καὶ καλοῖς Id.*CP*2.1.2. 2. intr., *pass the winter*, Ar.*Av.*1097 (lyr.), X.*Oec.*5.9, Isoc.7.54, etc.: of armies, *go into winter quarters*, Hdt.8.133, X.*HG*1.2.15, 3.2.1, Plb.27.18. 1, etc. II. *raise a storm* or *tempest*, θεοῦ τοιαῦτα χειμάζοντος S.*OC*1504; ὅταν χειμάζῃ ὁ θεὸς ἐν τῇ θαλάττῃ X.*Oec.*8.16, cf. *IG*7. 4255.5 (Orop.); χειμάσει [ἡ νεφέλη] ἐφ' ἡμᾶς Plu.2.195d: impers., ἐχείμαζε ἡμέρας τρεῖς *the storm continued*, Hdt.7.191; χειμάσει *there will be stormy weather*, Thphr.*Sign.* l. c. III. c. acc., *drive forth* or *away*, of a storm, ἔξω χ. [τοὺς μύας] Id.*Fr.*174.7:—Pass., *to be driven by a storm*, *overtaken by it*, Th.2.25, 3.69, al.; χειμασθεὶς ἀνέμῳ Id.8.99; ἐν θαλάττῃ χειμαζομένου πλοίου Pl.*Ion*540b, etc. 2. metaph., *toss like a storm*, *distress*, τόδ' αἷμα χ. πόλιν S.*OT*101; τὴν σάρκα τὸ παρὸν μόνον χειμάζειν Epicur.*Fr.*452: also, *annoy*, *vex*, S.*Ichn.*331, Men.208, Phld.*Lib.*p.61 O., *POsl.*48.8 (i A.D.); σφὴξ τοῖς κέντροις πλήσσων ἐχείμαζε Aesop.393:—Pass., *to be tempest-tossed*, *distressed*, esp. of the state considered as a ship, E.*Supp.*269, Ar.*Ra.*361; δόμων ὄλβος χειμάζεται E.*Ion*966; also of single persons, κατὰ θάλασσαν χειμασθεῖσαι (as example of a ψυχικὸν πάθος) Sor.3.84; *suffer grievously*, A.*Pr.*563 (anap.), 838, S.*Ph.*1460 (anap.), Gorg.*Pal.*11, Pl.*Plt.*273d; ἰσχὺς ἐν νόσῳ χειμάζεται S.*Ichn.* 267; ταῖς σαῖς ἀπειλαῖς αἷς ἐχειμάσθην Id.*Ant.*391; ἄλλῃ δ' ἐν τύχῃ χ. E.*Hipp.*315; χειμαζόμεθα..ὑπ' ἀπορίας ἐν τοῖς νῦν λόγοις Pl.*Phlb.* 29b, cf. *La.*194c; ὑπό τινων *PSI*4.349.4 (iii B.C.); ἐν στρατείαις ἢ νόσοις ἢ ἐν θαλάττῃ χ. Pl.*Tht.*170a; of feverish patients, χειμάζονται μάλιστα πεμπταῖοι Hp.*Prog.*24. **-αίνω**, aor. 1 ἐχείμηνα (v. infr.), *drive by a storm*:—Pass., *to be driven by a storm*, *be tempest-tossed*, Hdt.8.118: metaph., φόβῳ κεχείμανται φρένες Pi.*P.*9.32. 2. metaph., *disturb as by a storm*, χειμαίνει ὁ χειμαζόμενος he who is himself in distress *brings others into a like state*, Arist.*Po.*1455$^{a}$31; χειμαίνει δ' ὁ βαρὺς πνεύσας Πόθος *AP*12.157 (Mel.). II. intr., *to be stormy*, θάλασσα..ἄγρια χειμήνασα ib.7.652 (Leon.) 2. impers., χειμαίνοντος *when it is winter*, Theoc.9.20. **-άμῡνα** [ᾰμ], ἡ, *defence against winter*, *thick winter cloak*, A.*Fr.*449, S.*Fr.*1112, Ael.Dion.*Fr.*445.

**χείμᾰρος**, ὁ, *plug in a ship's bottom*, drawn out when the ship was brought on land, to let out the bilge-water, Hes.*Op.*626.

⊛ **χειμάρροος**, ον, contr. **-ρρους**, ουν, and shortened **χείμαρρος**, ον: (χεῖμα, ῥέω):—*winter-flowing*, *swollen by rain and melted snow*, of mountain-streams, I. joined with ποταμός, ὅν τε [the stone] ποταμὸς χειμάρροος ὤσῃ Il.13.138; ὡς δ' ὁπότε πλήθων ποταμὸς πεδίονδε κάτεισιν χειμάρρους κατ' ὄρεσφιν 11.493: freq. in contracted forms, ποταμῷ πλήθοντι ἐοικὼς χειμάρρῳ 5.88; ὡς δ' ὅτε χείμαρροι ποταμοὶ κατ' ὄρεσφι ῥέοντες 4.452; χειμάρρῳ ποταμῷ ἴκελος Hdt.3.81, cf. Thgn.348; παρὰ ῥείθροισι χειμάρροις S.*Ant.*712; φάραγγες ὕδατι χειμάρρῳ ῥέουσαι E.*Tr.*449 (troch.); διὰ χειμάρρου νάπης Id.*Ba.*1093; χαράδρα χ. Plb.10.30.2. 2. πλεκτάνη χειμάρροος seems to be *rushing*, *furious* lightning A.*Fr.*281. II. Subst., *torrent*, Pl. *Lg.*736b, X.*HG*4.4.7; ὥσπερ χειμάρρους ἂν εἰς τὴν πόλιν εἰσέπεσε D.18.153. 2. simply, *river*, Lxx*Nu.*34.5. 3. *drain*, *gutter*, οἱ ἐκ τῶν οἰκιῶν χ. D.55.19. 4. *valley*, *watercourse*, Lxx 4*Ki.*3.16. (Plur. accented χείμαρροι by Ptol.Ascal., χειμάρροι by Nicias, Eust. 496.37; later nom. χείμαρρος Paus.9.33.7, 10.37.3, acc. χείμαρρον Lxx l.c. cod.Alex., *Ps.*123(124).4, Paus.1.35.7.)

**χειμαρρώδης**, ες, *like a torrent*, Str.9.1.24, 13.1.70.

**χειμ-άς**, άδος, ἡ (sc. ὥρα), *winter season*, Hsch. 2. (sc. ἐσθής) *winter garment*, Id. **-ᾰσία**, Ion. **-ίη**, ἡ, *passing the winter*, *wintering*, φοιτῶσι ἐς χ. ἐς τοὺς τόπους τούτους Hdt.2.22. 2. *winter quarters*, Plb.2.54.14, al., D.S.19.37, App.*BC*2.52, *Dura*$^{6}$434 (iii A.D.). II. = χειμών, *storm*, Arist.*Pr.*940$^{b}$15 (pl.), Thphr.*Vent.* 50 (pl.), Hsch. **-ᾰσις**, εως, ἡ, *tempestivitas*, *Gloss.* **-ασκέω**, *exercise oneself in winter*, of soldiers, Plb.3.70.4, Arr.*Epict.*1.2. 32. **-αστρον**, τό, *winter clothing*, Ar.*Fr.*888. **-ᾰτικός**, ή, όν, late form for χειμέριος, Sch.Opp.*H.*3.459. ⊛ **-άω** and (dub.) **χειμέω**, = ῥιγέω, Hsch.

**χειμέθλη**, v. χιμέτλη.

**χειμερ-ίζω**, = χειμάζω I. 2, *pass the winter*, *winter*, περὶ Μίλητον Hdt.6.31; περὶ Θεσσαλίην 8.126; ἐνθαῦτα 7.37; ἐν Κύμῃ, αὐτοῦ, 8. 130; also in later Prose, D.H.15.10; μετὰ τῶν λόγων Them.*Or.*10. 130a. II. *to be stormy*, Thphr.*Sign.*42. **-ῐνός**, ή, όν, *of* or *in winter*, opp. θερινός, χ. τροπαί Democr.14, etc.; χ. μῆνες Th.6. 21; πρὸς ἥλιον τὸν χ. Hdt.1.193, cf. X.*Mem.*3.8.9; χ. ἀνατολὴ τοῦ ἡλίου καὶ δυσμαὶ αἱ χ. Hp.*Aër.*3, cf. Arist.*Mete.*364$^{b}$3; ὄμβροι Plb. 9.43.5; συσσίτια χ. Pl.*Criti.*112b; δεξαμεναί ib.117b; πυρετός Hp. *Acut.*(*Sp.*)24; νόσοι Gal.17(1).734; ἀργυρώματα Ath.6.230d; μάχη D.18.216; [τινὰ τῶν ζῴων] ἀποβάλλει τὰς χ. τρίχας their *winter coat*, Arist.*Pr.*893$^{a}$5; χ. ὄνειρος a *winter night's* dream, Luc.*Somn.* 17; also τὴν χ. (sc. ὥρην) the *winter season*, Hdt.1.202, cf. Thphr.*CP* 4.8.1, D.S.1.11; τὰν χ. (sc. ἑξάμηνον) ἄρχειν *SIG*$^{2}$940.3 (Cos); τὰ χ.

Pl.*Lg*.683c, 915d. 2. *stormy*, χωρίον Th.2.70; τὸ χ., opp. τὸ εὐδιεινόν, Thphr.*Vent*.1. 3. χ. σημεῖον sign *of a* coming *storm*, Arist.*Pr*.941$^a$2, Thphr.*Sign*.11. **-ιος**, α, ον, Il.2.294, Pi.*O*.6.100; also ος, ον S.*Ph*.1194 (lyr.), Th.3.22:—*wintry, stormy*, ἄελλαι Il.l.c.; νιφάδες 3.222: ὕδωρ 23.420; ὄμβρος Hes.*Sc*.478, Pi.*P*.6.10, E.*Hel*.1481 (lyr., nowhere else in E., never in A.); νότος S.*Ant*.335 (lyr.); ἄνεμοι Democr.14; ὥρη χειμερίη the *wintry* or *stormy* season, Od.5.485, Hes.*Op*.494; ἦμαρ χ. Il.12.279, Hes.*Op*.524, 565 (pl.); νύξ Emp.84.2, Pi.*O*.6.100; νὺξ χ. ὕδατι καὶ ἀνέμῳ Th.l.c.; χ. πῦρ Pi.*P*.4.266; οἱ χειμεριώτατοι μῆνες the *most wintry* months, Hdt.2.68; τὰς χειμεριωτάτας [ἡμέρας] Arist.*HA*599$^a$24; so χ. κατὰ μῆνα Simon.12; ἦρ χ. a *stormy, cold* spring, Hp.*Aër*.10; ἀκτὰ κυματοπλὴξ χειμερίᾳ a shore stricken by the *wintry* waves, S.*OC*1241 (lyr.); neut. pl. as Adv., χειμέρια βροντᾷ Ar.*Fr*.46; ἐν χειμερίοις in *cold places*, opp. to ἐν ἀλεεινοῖς, Arist.*HA*613$^b$2; ἐὰν ἴδωσι.. χειμέρια *stormy weather*, ib.614$^b$21; χ. αἱ σύνοδοι τῶν μηνῶν μᾶλλον ἢ αἱ μεσότητες Id.*GA*738$^a$21. Adv. -ίως *in wintry fashion*, Hp.*Epid*.4.7. 2. metaph., χ. λύπα *raging* pain, S.*Ph*.1194 (lyr.); χ. τὰ πράγματα, punningly, Ar.*Ach*.1141.—Correct writers use χειμέριος = *wintry, stormy*, χειμερινός (opp. θερινός) = *in winter-time, in the winter season*, but later authors neglected this distinction, χειμερίῃσι (sc. ὥραις) Nic.*Al*.623; χειμέριοι τροπαί App.*BC*2.48, 52. **-ιώδης**, ες, *stormy*, χειμών Gp.1.12.23. **-ος**, ον, poet. for χειμέριος, Arat.797, 1084.

**χείμετλον**, v. χίμετλον.

**χειμῐ-έω**, *to be chilled*, χειμιοῦσα σάρξ Hp.*Loc.Hom*.29. **-η**, ἡ, Ion. for χεῖμα, *winter cold, chilly weather*, ib.10.

**χειμο-θνής**, ῆτος, ὁ, ἡ, (θνῄσκω) *frozen to death*, Luc.*Lex*.14. **-σπορέομαι**, Pass., *to be sown in winter*, Thphr.*CP*4.11.3. **-σπορος**, ον, *sown in winter*, ib.4.11.1. **-φῠγέω**, *avoid the winter* or *wintry weather*, Str.1.2.28.

**χειμών**, ῶνος, ὁ, (χεῖμα) *winter*, χειμῶνος δυσθαλπέος ὅς ῥά τε ἔργων ἀνθρώπους ἀνέπαυσεν Il.17.549; χειμῶνι *in winter*, 21.283; ἐν χειμῶνι Pi.*I*.2.42, A.*Ag*.969, X.*Mem*.4.3.8; ἐν τῷ χ. Id.*Cyr*.8.8.17; χειμῶνος ὥρᾳ And.1.137; also χειμῶνος *in winter-time*, X.*Mem*.3.8.9, Pl.*R*.415e; χ. μέσου *in* mid-*winter*, Ar.*Fr*.569.1; τοῦ χ. *in the course of the winter*, Th.7.31; τοῦ αὐτοῦ χ. Id.8.30; διὰ χειμῶνος, διὰ τοῦ χ., Pl.*Ti*.74c, X.*HG*3.2.9; χειμῶνα *during winter*, S.*OT*1138 (v.l. χειμῶνι); τὸν χ. *during* the *winter*, Hdt.3.117, X.*HG*1.4.1; τὸν δεινὸν χ. Id.*An*.7.6.9; τὸν χ. ὅλον Ar.*Fr*.345; ὁ ἀμφὶ τὸν χ. χρόνος X.*Cyr*.8.6.22; ὄρος ἄβατον ὑπὸ χειμῶνος in consequence of *the cold weather*, Hdt.8.138, cf. Th.2.101: pl., νιφοστιβεῖς χειμῶνες S.*Aj*.671; opp. καύματα, Pl.*Lg*.829b; ἀμυντικὴ χειμώνων Id.*Plt*.280e. 2. *the wintry quarter* of the heavens, *the north*, Βορέης καὶ χ. Hdt.2.26. II. *wintry, stormy weather*: generally, *storm*, ἐπεὶ οὖν χειμῶνα φύγον καὶ ἀθέσφατον ὄμβρον Il.3.4; οὐ νιφετὸς οὔτ' ἂρ χ. πολὺς οὔτε ποτ' ὄμβρος Od.4.566; ὅτε τις χ. ἔκπαγλος ὄροιτο 14.522; ὀπωρινὸν ὄμβρον καὶ χειμῶν' ἐπιόντα Hes.*Op*.675, cf. Alc.18, Sapph.*Supp*.11.6, etc.; Γαιάοχος εὐδίαν ὑπάσσεν ἐκ χειμῶνος Pi.*I*.7 (6).39; θεὸς χειμῶν' ὦρσε A.*Pers*.496, cf. *Ag*.649,656, S.*Aj*.1145, etc.; χ. ὀρνιθίας Ar.*Ach*.876; χ. κατερράγη Hdt.1.87; ἐπέπεσέ σφι χ. τε μέγας καὶ πολλὸς ἄνεμος Id.7.188, cf. Pl.*Prt*.344d; ἐπιγενόμενος χ. Hdt.7.34, Th.4.6; χειμῶνι χρησάμενοι Antipho 5.21; χ. νοτερός *a storm* of rain, Th.3.21; ἐν εὐδίᾳ χειμῶνα ποιεῖν X.*HG*2.4.14: pl., ὑπὸ τῶν χ. because of the *winter-storms*, Hdt.4.62; ἔν γε χειμῶσιν καὶ ἐν εὐδίαις Pl.*Lg*.961e, cf. 919a. 2. metaph., θεόσσυτος χ. *storm of calamity* sent by the gods, A.*Pr*.643; χ. καὶ κακῶν τρικυμία ib.1015, cf. *Ch*.202 (pl.), 1066 (anap.); δορὸς.. ἐν χειμῶνι in the *storm* of battle, S.*Ant*.670; θολερῷ.. χ. νοσήσας, of the madness of Ajax, Id.*Aj*.207 (anap.); χ. γήρως βαρύς, of life's *winter*, *AP*10.100 (Antiphan.); of a person, χ. ὁ μειρακίσκος ἐστὶ τοῖς φίλοις Alex.178.7, cf. 46.4; χ. κατ' οἴκους.. κακὴ γυνή Men.*Mon*.540: rare in Prose, of battle, Onos.32.10; of mental and moral *trouble*, Epicur.*Ep*.3p.62U., Polystr.p.19W.; χ. τοῦ κλύδωνος χαλεπώτερος, of pirates, Them.*Or*.23.286a: pl., χειμῶνας ἔχειν to have *trouble* (in cutting teeth), Hp.*Dent*.12.

❋ **χειμωνικός**, ή, όν, *for winter use*, ἱμάτια *POxy*.1901.37 (vi A.D.). II. *wintry*, καιρός Sch.Opp.*H*.1.601: Comp. -ώτερος *Cat.Cod.Astr*.1.144.

❋ **χειμωνόθεν**, Adv. *in a storm*, Arat.995.

**χειμωνοτύπος** [ῠ], ον, *buffeting stormily*, λαῖλαψ A.*Supp*.34 (anap.).

❋ **χείρ**, ἡ, χειρός, χειρί, χεῖρα, dual χεῖρε, χεροῖν, pl. χεῖρες, χερῶν, χεῖρας, penult. being regularly short, when the ult. is long; dat. pl. regularly χερσί (χειρσί occurs in cod.Vat. of Lxx, as *Jd*.7.19, 1*Ch*.5.10, and late Inscrr. as *CIG*2811*b*.10 (Aphrodisias), 2942*c* (Tralles): but Poets used the penult. long or short in all cases, as the verse required, χερός, χερί, χέρα, χέρε, χέρες, χέρας (of which Hom. uses only χερί; χέρα *h.Pan*.40); gen. dual χειροῖν S.*El*.206 (lyr.), 1394 (lyr.), *IG*2$^2$.1498.76; gen. pl. χειρῶν ib.31, common in Prose.—Poet. forms, dat. pl. χείρεσι(ν) once in Hom., Il.20.468, also Q.S.2.401, 5.469 (v.l.); χείρεσσι Il.12.382, Pi.*O*.10(11).62, S.*Ant*.976 (lyr.), 1297 (lyr.), and once in trim., E.*Alc*.756; χέρεσσι(ν) Hes.*Th*.519, 747, B.17.49; χερέεσσιν *AJA*36.460 (Galatia):—Dor. nom. **χέρς** Timocr.9; **χήρ** Sophr. in *PSI*11.1214*a*3 (also, = δίψακος, Ps.-Dsc.3.11); gen. χηρός Alcm.32, *IG*4$^2$(1).121.22 (Epid., iv B.C.); acc. pl. χῆρας ib.96, Aeol. χέρρας Alc.*Supp*.4.21, Theoc.28.9.—On the accent and declension of these forms, v. Hdn.Gr.2.277,748:—*the hand*, whether *closed*, παχεῖα Il.3.376; βαρεῖα 11.235, al.; or *open, flat*, χερσὶ καταπρηνέσσι, χειρὶ καταπρηνεῖ, 15.114, Od.13.164, al.; εἰς τὴν χ. ἐγχεάμενοί τι X.*Cyr*.1.3.9: freq. in pl. where *a single hand* is meant, Il.23.384, etc.; reversely, sg. where more than one *hand* is spoken of, e.g. Od.3.37, etc.; dual joined with pl., ἄμφω χεῖρας 8.135; χεῖρε ἀμφοτέρας Il.21.115. 2. *hand and arm, arm* (cf. Ruf.*Onom*.11,82, Gal.2.347), πῆχυν χειρὸς δεξιτερῆς Il.21.166; κατὰ χεῖρα μέσην ἀγκῶνος ἔνερθε 11.252; χεῖρες ἀπ' ὤμων ἀΐσσοντο Hes.*Th*.150; χ. εἰς ὤμους γυμναί Longus 1.4; ἐν χερσὶ γυναικῶν πεσέειν into *the arms*, Il.6.81, etc.: hence, words are added to denote the *hand* as distinct from the *arm*, ἄκρην οὔτασε χεῖρα 5.336; περὶ ἄκραις ταῖς χ. χειρῖδας ἔχουσι X.*Cyr*.8.8.17, cf. Pl.*Prt*.352a. 3. of the *hand* or *paw* of animals, ὅσα [ζῷα] χεῖρας ἔχει X.*Mem*.1.4.14; πορεύεσθαι ἐπὶ χειρῶν go on *all fours*, Lxx *Le*.11.27; so of monkeys, Arist.*HA*502$^b$3; of the *fore-paws* of the hyena, Id.*Fr*.369; of the bear, Plu.2.919a. II. Special usages: 1. to denote position, ποτέρας τῆς χερός; on which *hand?* E.*Cyc*.681; ἐπὶ δεξιὰ χειρός Pi.*P*.6.19; ἐπ' ἀριστερὰ χειρός Od.5.277; χειρὸς εἰς τὰ δεξιὰ S.*Fr*.598; λαιᾶς χειρός A.*Pr*.714 (but χείρ is often omitted with δεξιά, ἀριστερά, as we say *the right, the left*). 2. freq. in dat. of all numbers with Verbs which imply the use of hands, λάβε χειρί, χερσὶν ἑλέσθαι, Il.5.302, 10.501; χερσὶν ἀσπάζεσθαι Od.3.35; προκαλίζεσθαι 18.20; χειρί, χεροῖν ψαῦσαι, S.*OT*1510,1466: sts. this dat. is added pleon. by way of emphasis, ὄνυξι συλλαβὼν χερί Id.*Aj*.310. 3. gen., *by the hand*, χειρὸς ἔχειν τινά Il.4.154; χειρὸς ἑλών 1.323, etc.; γέροντα δὲ χειρὸς ἀνίστη he raised him *by the hand*, 24.515, cf. Od.14.319; χειρὸς ἑλὼν Pi.*P*.9.122; τινὰ χειρὸς ἕλκειν Id.*N*.11.32; ἀνέλκειν τινὰ τῆς χ. Ar.*V*.569 (anap.). 4. the acc. is used when one takes the *hand* of a person, χεῖρα γέροντος ἑλών Il.24.361; χεῖρ' ἕλε δεξιτερήν Od.1.121; χεῖράς τ' ἀλλήλων λαβέτην, in pledge of good faith, Il.6.233; so ἔμβαλλε χ. δεξιὰν πρώτιστά μοι S.*Tr*.1181; also ἔμβαλλε χειρὸς πίστιν Id.*Ph*.813, cf. *OC*1632. 5. other uses of the acc.: a. in prayer or entreaty, χεῖρας ἀνασχεῖν [θεοῖς] Il.3.275, etc.; ποτὶ γούνασι χεῖρας βάλλειν Od.6.310; ἀμφὶ.. Ἄρητης βάλε γούνασι χεῖρας Ὀδυσσεύς 7.142; ἀμφὶ δὲ χεῖρας δειρῇ βάλλ' Ὀδυσῆϊ 23.207; ἀμφί τινι χεῖρε β. 21.223; περίβαλε δὲ χέρας Ar.*Th*.914, cf. A.*Ag*.1559 (anap.); χεῖρας προΐσχεσθαι Th.3.58, 66; so also χεῖρας ἀείρων Od.11.423, cf. Il.7.130 (tm.); χ. ἀνατείνειν (v. ἀνατείνω I. 1). b. τὰς χεῖρας αἴρειν to hold up *hands* in token of assent or choice, of persons voting, Ar.*Ec*.264; τὴν χ. αἴρειν And.3.41; ὅτῳ δοκεῖ ταῦτα, ἀράτω τὴν χ. X.*An*.5.6.33, cf. 7.3.6; ἀνατεινάτω τὴν χ. ib.3.2.9, 33; χεῖρας ὀρεγνύς Il.22.37; χεῖρ' ὀρέγων εἰς οὐρανόν 15.371; χεῖρας ὀ. τινί Od.12.257; πρός τινα Pi.*P*.4.240; ποτὶ στόμα χεῖρ' ὀρέγεσθαι Il.24.506 (but χεῖρά τισι ὀ. to reach them *one's hand* in help, X.*HG*5.2.17); also χεῖρε ἑτάροισι πετάσσας Il.4.523, etc.; πιτνὰς εἰς ἐμὲ χεῖρας Od.11.392 (but χεῖρε πετάσσας abs., of one swimming, etc., 5.374, al.). c. [Ἰλίου] χεῖρα ἑὴν ὑπερέσχε held the *hand* over I. as a protector, Il.9.420, etc.: less freq. τισι, 4.249, cf. 5.433; χεῖρά θ' ὕπερθεν ἔχεις *IG*14.1003.10 (Rome). d. in hostile sense, χεῖρας or χεῖρα ἐπιφέρειν τινί, Il.1.89, 19.261, al.; χεῖρας ἐφιέναι τινί 1.567, Od.1.254, al.; χεῖρας ἐπιβάλλειν τισί Plb.3.2.8, etc.; χέρα τινὶ προσενεγκεῖν Pi.*P*.9.36; χεῖρας ἐπί τινι ἰάλλειν, v. ἰάλλω I.1. e. χεῖρας ἀπέχειν keep *hands* off, λοιμοῖο βαρείας χεῖρας ἀφέξει Il.1.97 codd.; κερτομίας δέ τοι.. καὶ χεῖρας ἀφέξω.. μνηστήρων Od.20.263; ἀθανάτων ἀπέχειν χέρας A.*Eu*.350 (lyr.); τὼ χεῖρε ἀπέχεται Pl.*Smp*.213d; παύειν χεῖράς τινος Il.21.294. f. χεῖρας ἐπιτιθέναι τινί, in token of consecration, 1*Ep.Ti*.5.22, etc. 6. with Preps.: a. ἀνὰ χεῖρας ἔχειν τινάς to be intimate with.., Plb.21.6.5; αἱ ἀνὰ χεῖρά τινων ὁμιλίαι S.E.*M*.1.64; τὰ ἀνὰ χεῖρα πράγματα the matters *in hand*, Plu.2.614b, etc. (also οἱ ἀνὰ χ. χρόνοι the *current* period, *PRyl*.88.21 (ii A.D.)); τὰ ἀνὰ χ. what comes his way, Ps.-Ptol.*Centil*.18; ἀνὰ χ. τῆς πύλης *hard by*.., Lxx 2*Ki*.15.2. b. ἀπὸ χειρὸς λογίσασθαι to reckon *off-hand, roughly*, Ar.*V*.656 (anap.), cf. Luc.*Hist.Conscr*.29: but πότισον τὴν γῆν ἀπὸ χειρός by *hand*, *PCair.Zen*.155 (iii B.C.). c. διὰ χερῶν ἔχειν, λαβεῖν, literally, to have or take *between* the *hands*, A.*Supp*.193, S.*Ant*.916; διὰ χειρὸς ἔχειν to hold *in the hand*, ib.1258 (anap.), Ar.*V*.597 (anap.); to have *in hand*, i.e. *under control*, Th.2.76; διὰ χειρῶν ἔχειν τὴν πολιτείαν Arist.*Pol*.1308$^a$27; τὰ τῶν ξυμμάχων keep *under control*, Th.2.13: later, to have a work *in hand*, be engaged in it, Phld.*Acad.Ind*.p.69M. (χερός), D.H.*Isoc*.4; τὰ ὅπλα Plu.*Cor*.2, etc. (also διὰ χ. by direct payment, opp. διὰ τῆς τραπέζης by banker's order, *BGU*1156.8 (i B.C.), etc.; cf. διὰ χ. ἔσπευδε τὴν πρᾶσιν Charito 1.12); of arms, διὰ χειρὸς εἶναι Luc.*Anach*.35; διὰ χ. ἔχειν, c. part., to be *continually* doing, Plu.2.767c; διὰ χειρός τινος ποιεῖν τι Lxx *Jo*.17.4, al., cf. *Act.Ap*.7.25, al. d. ἐς χεῖρας λαβεῖν τι literally, S.*El*.1120, etc.; to take a matter *in hand*, undertake it, πρᾶγμ' ἐς χέρας λαβόντ' E.*Hec*.1242; ἄγεσθαί τι ἐς χεῖρας Hdt.1.126, 4.79, etc.; δοῦναί τινι ἐς χέρας, εἰς χεῖρα, S.*El*.1348, X.*Cyr*.8.8.22; καταστῆσαι εἰς τὰς χ. τινος Aeschin.2.28; of persons, ἵκεο χεῖρας ἐς ἁμάς thou hast fallen into our *hands*, Il.10.448 (in Hom. also simply ὅ τι χεῖρας ἵκοιτο Od.12.331, cf. 24.172); so εἰς χεῖρας ἐλθεῖν τινι X.*Cyr*.7.4.10, cf. 2.4.15: generally, to have to do with any one, *converse* with him, Id.*An*.1.2.26 (so ἐς χεῖρα γῇ ξυνῆψαν E.*Heracl*.429): most freq. ἐς χεῖρας ἐλθεῖν τισι to come to *blows* or *close quarters* with.., A.*Th*.680; ἀλλήλοις Th.7.44: abs., εἰς χ. ἐλθεῖν Id.4.96; ἐς χ. ἰέναι Id.2.3, 4.72, cf. *PTeb*.765.6 (ii B.C.); συνιέναι X.*Cyr*.8.8.22; also ἐς χειρῶν νόμον (fort. νομόν) ἀπικέσθαι Hdt.9.48; ἐν χειρῶν νόμῳ (fort. νομῷ) ἀπόλλυσθαι Id.8.89, cf. Aeschin.1.5, *SIG*167.37 (Mylasa, iv B.C.), Heraclid.*Pol*.25, Plb.1.34.5, 5.111.6; ἐν χειρὸς νόμῳ

Arist.*Pol.*$1285^{a}10$, D.H.6.26; ἐν χειρῶν νομαῖς *SIG* 700.29 (Lete, ii B.C.), v.l. in Lxx 3 *Ma.*1.5; ἐν χεροῖν δίκῃ cj. in E.*Ba.*738; εἰς χεῖρας συμμεῖξαι τοῖς ἐν χειρονομίαις X.*Cyr.*2.1.11; also εἰς χεῖρας δέχεσθαί τινας to await their charge, Id.*An.*4.3.31; ἐς χ. ὑπομεῖναί τινας Th. 5.72. **e.** ἐκ χειρός by *hand of man*, S.*Aj.*27: from *near at hand, at close range*, ἐκ χειρὸς βάλλειν X.*An.*3.3.15; ἀμύνασθαι ib.5.4.25; μάχεσθαι Id.*HG*7.2.14, cf. D.S.19.6; πληγὰς ἐκ χ. ἀναδέξασθαι Plu. *Tim.*4; οὐ μὴ σωθῇ ἐκ χ. σιδήρου Lxx *Jb.*20.24; ἡ ἐκ χ. δίκη *lynch law*, D.H.4.37; ἡ ἐκ χ. βία Plb.9.4.6: metaph., ἡ ἐκ χ. θεωρία *close-range* reading, D.H.*Isoc.*2; so of time, *out of hand, off-hand, forthwith*, Plb.5.41.7, al. **f.** δέπας μητρὶ ἐν χειρὶ τίθει Il.1.585, cf. Od.13. 57, 15.120, al. (always so of a cup, hence ἐν χερσὶ τίθει δέπας, though found in most codd., was condemned by the critics in Il. l.c., Od.3.51, 15.130); πρεσβήϊον ἐν χερὶ θήσω Il.8.289; τόξον, ἔγχος ἔχων ἐν χειρί, 15.443, 17.604; σκῆπτρον δέ οἱ ἔμβαλε χειρί Od.2.37; but ἐν.. χειρὶ σκῆπτρον ἔθηκεν Il.23.568; of a gift, ἐν χερσὶ τίθει 1.441, 446; ἐν ταῖς χ. ἔχειν, literally, Pl.*R.*432d; τὰ ὅπλ' ἐν ταῖς χ. ἔχων D.9.8, etc. (metaph., ἔτι μεμνημένων ὑμῶν καὶ μόνον οὐκ ἐν ταῖς χερσὶν ἕκαστ' ἐχόντων Id.18.226); but ἐν χερσὶν ἔχειν also, to have *in hand, be engaged in*, τὸν γάμον Hdt.1.35; ἑορτήν Plu.*Alex.*13; τὴν περὶ Δημοσθένους πραγματείαν D.H.*Thuc.*1; ἐν χειρί τινα δίκην ἔχων Pl.*Tht.* 172e; ὁ ἐν χερσὶ πόλεμος the war *in hand*, D.H.8.87; περιτειχισμὸς ἐν χερσὶν ὤν ib.21; ἡ ἐν χ. ζήτησις S.E.*M.*11.208, etc.; freq. of fighting, ἐν χερσί *hand to hand*, ἐν χ. ἦν ἡ μάχη Th.4.43; ἐν χ. ἀποκτεῖναι Id.3.66, cf. 4.57,96, etc.; ἐν χ. γίγνεσθαι τοῖς ἐναντίοις Id.5.72; ἐν χ. εἶναί τινος X.*HG*4.6.11; δίκη ἐν χερσί Hes.*Op.*192; ὁ ψόφος τῶν ὅπλων καὶ τῶν ἵππων ὁ φρυαγμὸς ἐν χερσὶν ἐδόκει εἶναι D.S.19.31; ἡ ἐν χερσὶν [δυστυχία] Plu.*Cleom.*22: also in dual, τὰν χεροῖν S.*Ant.*1345 (lyr.); ἐν χειρί τινος *by the hand* of.., Lxx *Jo.*21. 2, al.; ἐν χ. ἀγγέλου *Act.Ap.*7.35 (v.l.). **g.** ἐπὶ χειρὸς ἔχειν *on* or *in* one's *hand*, Thgn.490; ἐπὶ χεῖράς τινων ἐκφέρουσι put into their *hands*, Plu.2.815b; also ἐπὶ χεῖρά τινος *next* to, Lxx *Ne.*3.4. **h.** κατὰ χειρός, of washing the hands before meals, ὕδωρ κατὰ χειρός (sc. φερέτω τις), Ar.*V.*1216, cf. *Av.*464 (anap.), *Fr.*502 (lyr.), Philox. 1, Ath.9.408e; (without ὕδωρ) κατὰ χ. ἐδόθη Alex.261.2, cf. Arched. 2.3: prov. of that which is easily come by, Telecl.1.2 (anap.); πάντα μοι κατὰ χ. ἦν τὰ πράγματα *at hand*, Pherecr.146.5; also κατὰ χειρῶν δοῦναι, χέειν, λαβεῖν, Philyll.3, Antiph.287 (v.l.), Men.470 (troch.), cf. Phot.s.v. κατὰ χειρὸς ὕδωρ: κατὰ χεῖρα in *deed* or *act*, κατὰ χ. γενναιότατοι D.H.7.6; opp. συνέσει, Plu.*Phil.*7; κατὰ χεῖρά σου according to thy *will*, Lxx *Si.*25.26: but κατὰ χεῖρας [τῆς σοφίας] by her *side*, ib.14. 25. **i.** μετὰ χερσὶν ἔχειν *between*, i.e. *in, the hands*, Il.11.4, 15.717; [ἄλεισον] μετὰ χ. ἐνώμα Od.22.10: μετὰ χεῖρας ἔχειν to have *in hand*, be engaged in, Hdt.7.16.β', Th.1.138. **k.** λάβε παρὰ χεῖρα take *in hand*, Lxx *To.*11.4; but τὸ πὰρ χειρός the work *in hand*, B.13. 10. **l.** πρὸ χειρῶν *close before one*, S.*Ant.*1279, E.*Tr.*1207 (s.v.l.), *Rh.*274; πρὸ χειρὸς εἶναι cj. in Pl.Com.69.5. **m.** πρὸς χειρός τινος by his *hand*, A.*Supp.*66 (lyr.), etc.; πρὸς ἐμὴν χεῖρα at the signs *given by* my *hand*, S.*Ph.*148 (anap.); πρὸς χεῖρα ὑποβορβορύζοντες on *pressure*, Hp.*Epid.*4.7. **n.** ὑπὸ χερσὶ ἁλοῦσα *under*, i.e. *by*, another's *hands*, Il.2.374, etc.; ὑπὸ χεῖρα ποιεῖσθαι to bring *under one's power*, X.*Ages.*1.22; οἱ ὑπὸ χ. persons *in one's power*, D.6.34; ὑπὸ τὴν χ. ἐλθεῖν to come *into one's hand*, Luc.*Herm.*57, etc.; ὑπὸ χ. in *hand*, i.e. in *stock*, Arist.*Mete.*$369^{b}33$; but also, *at hand*, i.e. *at once*, Plu.2.548e; τὰ ὑπὸ χ. ib.56b, Dsc.1.35; ὁ ὑπὸ χ. the attendant, Dsc.5.75; παρέργως καὶ ὑπὸ χ. *extempore*, Plu.*Arat.*3, etc.; also καθύπο χεῖρα κινῶν [τὰς οὐσίας], in Alchemy, Ps.-Democr. p.51B. **III.** *the hand* often receives the attributes of *the person using it*, χ. μεγάλη, of Zeus, Il.15.695 (χ. παγκρατής, of God, Secund.*Sent.*3; χ. ὑπερμήκης, of the 'long *arm*' of the king, Hdt.8. 140.β'); θοὴ χ., of one throwing, Il.12.306; ἀφνειά Pi.*O.*7.1, cf. S.*El.* 458; εὐσεβεστέρα, εὐφιλής, A.*Ch.*141, *Ag.*34; κάρβανος ib.1061; γεραιά E.*Hec.*143 (anap.); πονηρά Id.*Ion*1316, etc.: to denote wealth or poverty, πλειοτέρῃ σὺν χ. Od.11.359; κενεὰς σὺν χ. ἔχοντες 10.42, cf. E.*Hel.*1280, etc. **2.** it is represented as acting of itself, χεῖρες μαιμῶσιν Il.13.77, cf. S.*Aj.*50; χεὶρ δρᾷ τὸ δράσιμον A.*Th.*554; δήμου κρατοῦσα χ. Id.*Supp.*604 (dub. l.): prov., ἁ δὲ χ. τὰν χ. νίζει Epich.273; or simply, ἁ χ. τὰν χ. *AP*5.207 (Mel.). **3.** pl., in theurgy, name for spiritual *powers*, αἱ δημιουργικαὶ [τοῦ Ἀπόλλωνος] δυνάμεις ἃς θεουργῶν παῖδες χεῖρας ἀποκαλοῦσιν Procl. *in Cra.* p.101P., cf. eund. *in R.*2.252K. **IV.** to denote *act* or *deed*, opp. mere words, in pl., ἔπεσιν καὶ χερσὶν ἀρήξειν Il.1.77; μνῆμ' Ἑλένης χειρῶν of her *handiwork*, her *art*, Od.15.126 (so in sg., δώρημ' ἐκείνῳ τἀνδρὶ τῆς ἐμῆς χ. S.*Tr.*603); χερσὶν ἢ λόγῳ Id.*OT*883 (lyr.), cf. *OC*1297, etc.; τῇ χειρὶ χρᾶσθαι to use one's *hands*, i.e. be active, stirring, opp. ἀργὸς ἐπεστάναι, Hdt.3.78, cf. 9.72; τὰς χ. προσφέρειν to apply *force*, X.*Mem.*2.6.31: sg., βούλευμα μὲν τὸ Δῖον, Ἡφαίστου δὲ χείρ A.*Pr.*619; μιᾷ χειρί single-*handed*, D.21.219; χειρὶ καὶ ποδὶ καὶ πάσῃ δυνάμει Aeschin.3.109, cf. 2.115; χερσίν τε ποσίν τε Il.20.360, cf. Pi.*O.*10(11).62, esp. of using the hands in a fight, cf. supr. II.6d, e, f; of deeds of violence, πρὶν χειρῶν γεύσασθαι before we try *force*, Od.20.181; ἀδίκων χ. ἄρχειν to give the first *blow*, X.*Cyr.*1.5.13, Antipho 4.2.1, Lys.4.11, etc.; ἀμυνόμενος ἄρχοντα χειρῶν Pl.*Lg.*869d: generally, χεῖρες *violent measures, force*, ἐπίσχετε θυμὸν ἐνιπῆς καὶ χειρῶν Od.20.267; ὑπόδικος χερῶν A.*Eu.*260 (lyr.); χερσὶ πεποιθώς Il.16.624, etc.; ἐν χειρῶν νόμῳ v. supr. II. 6d; ὅπως θανάτοιο βαρείας χ. ἀλάλκοι, v.l. for κῆρας, Il.21.548. **V.** *a number, band, body* of men, esp. of soldiers, χεὶρ μεγάλη Hdt.7.157; in dat., οὐ σὺν μεγάλῃ χ. Id.5.72; πολλῇ χ. 1.174, Th.3.96, E.*Heracl.* 337; pleon., χ. μεγάλη πλήθεος Hdt.7.20; δεδωμάτωμαι δ' οὐδ' ἐγὼ σμικρᾷ χερί A.*Supp.*958; οἰκεία χείρ, for χεὶρ οἰκετῶν, E.*El.*629; σὺν πλήθει χερῶν S.*OT*123. **VI.** *handwriting*, τὴν ἑαυτοῦ χεῖρα ἀρνήσασθαι Hyp.*Lyc.Fr.*5, cf. *IG*9(1).189 (Phocis); τῇ ἐμῇ χ. Παύλου 1 *Ep. Cor.*16.21, *Ep.Col.*4.18: *copy, counterpart* of a document, *SIG*712.31 (Crete, ii B.C.); *deed, instrument*, ἡ χ. ἥδε κυρία ἔστω *PRein.*28.18 (ii B.C.), cf. *PCair.Zen.*477 (iii B.C.), etc. **b.** *handiwork* of an artist or workman, γλαφυρὰ χ. Theoc.*Epigr.*8.5, etc.; αἱ Ἐφεσίου χεῖρες Herod.4.72, cf. 6.66; σοφαὶ χέρες *APl.*4.262; τὰς Φειδίου χ. Lib.*Or.* 30.22. **VII.** of any implement resembling a hand: **1.** a kind of *gauntlet*, X.*Eq.*12.5, Poll.1.135 (pl.). **2.** χ. σιδηρᾶ *grappling*-iron, Th.4.25, 7.62; also of an *anchor*, *AP*6.38 (Phil.). **3.** *axle-tree*, Lxx 3 *Ki.* 7.18(32). **4.** in Lxx, *pillar* or *cairn*, as it were *a finger pointing to heaven*, χεὶρ Ἀβεσσαλώμ Lxx 2 *Ki.*18.18; also ἀνέστακεν αὐτῷ χεῖρα, i.e. *trophy*, ib.1 *Ki.*15.12. **5.** χεῖρες ἐλάτιναι, of oars, Tim.*Pers.*7. **6.** *catch* of a trigger, Hero *Aut.*13.9; χ. κατάγουσα τὴν τοξῖτιν Ph.*Bel.* 68.4, cf. Hero *Bel.*78.2. **7.** instrument of torture, Lxx 4 *Ma.*8. 13. **VIII.** *handful*, κορώνῃ χεῖρα πρόσδοτε κριθέων Phoen. 2.1. **IX.** *ointment* containing *five* ingredients, Orib.*Fr.*89, Alex. Trall.7.1. (Cf. Arm. *jeṙn* (*dzeṙn*), Alb. *dore*, Tocharian (A-dialect) *tsar*, (B-dialect) *ṣar*, all = *hand.*)

⊛ **χειράγρ-α,** ἡ, *gout in the hand*, Asclep.ap.Gal.13.1026, Ptol.*Tetr.* 153 (pl.). ⊛ **-ικός,** ή, όν, *suffering from* χειράγρα, cj. in Aët.2. 25. **-ος,** = foreg., *Gloss.*

**χειρᾰγωγ-έω,** *lead by the hand*, τινα Lxx *Jd.*16.26 cod. A, Muson.*Fr.*$15^{A}$ p.79H., *Act.Ap.*9.8, Plu.*Cleom.*38: generally, *guide, direct*, φρυκτώρια ἐς ἀσφαλεῖς καταγωγὰς τὰς ναῦς χ. Hdn.4.2.8; χ. τούτῳ τὴν ἔξοδον will *guide* his exit, Procop.Gaz.p.158B.: metaph., χ. τὴν εὕρεσιν μνήμῃ Plu.2.48b; τὴν ψυχὴν ἐπί τι Max.Tyr.10.6; also '*lead by the nose*', *cajole*, Posidon.36J.: abs., Luc.*Tim.*32, Porph. *Chr.*30:—Pass., Lxx *To.*11.16 cod. ℵ, ὑπ' αὐτῶν τῶν πραγμάτων *PPetr.* 3 p.22 (iii B.C.), cf. D.S.13.20; ἐπί τι Hdn.7.1.2. **-ημα,** ατος, τό, *leading by the hand*, Sch.E.*Ph.*848. **-ία,** ἡ, = foreg., *BGU*1768.11 (i B.C.), Longus 4.12, Sch.E.*Or.*883, Suid.: metaph., πρὸς τὴν χ. τῆς κράσεως in order to *induce* mixture, Max.Tyr.15.4. **-ῐμος,** ον, *liable to seizure*, *PLond.*2.220 ii 21 (ii B.C.). **-ός,** όν, *leading, guiding*, χ. ἀρχή *Supp.Epigr.*8.464 (Egypt). **2.** Subst., *leader, guide*, ἔχει.. χ. τὸν πλοῦτον ὁ γέρων Philem.127; cf. *Act.Ap.*13.11, Plu.2. 794d: τοῦ βίου τυφλὴ χ. (of Τύχη), ib.98b; θεοῖς ἕπεσθαι χειραγωγοῖς ἡγούμενοι Lib.*Or.*61.4.

**χειρ-αλγός,** ὁ, *suffering from gout in the hand*, Petr.Patr. in Boissevain D.C. iii p.744 No.166. **-ᾰλειπτέω,** *anoint the arms* for wrestling, *practise wrestling*, D.S.26.3. **-άλῠσις** [ᾰ], εως, ἡ, *manacle, handcuff*, Sm.*Je.*40(47).1:—hence Dim. **-ᾰλῠσίδιον,** τό, *Gloss.* **-άμαξα** [ᾰμ], ἡ, *bath-chair*, Herod.Med.ap.Orib.6.25. 2, Paul.Aeg.3.18. **-ᾰμάξιον,** τό, Dim. of foreg., Petron.28; child's *go-cart*, Sor.1.117.

**χειραμός,** = χηραμός, *EM*810.25, perh. to be read in Lyc.181.

**χειραπτ-άζω,** *touch with the hand, take in hand, handle*, Hdt.2. 90. ⊛ **-έω,** = foreg., Orib.*Fr.*19.

**χειράς,** άδος, ἡ, (χείρ) *chap, crack*, prop. in the hands, but also in the feet, χειράδες χειρῶν, ποδῶν, *chapped* hands or feet, D.L.1. 81; also χιράς Suid., Eust.194.40. **II.** *heap of stones*, etc., Hsch.

**χειρ-αφεσία,** ἡ, = *emancipatio*; **-αφετέω,** = *emancipare*; and **-άφετος,** = *emancipatus*, *Gloss.* **-αψία,** ἡ, (ἅπτω A) *violence offered, rough handling*, *Sammelb.*6152.13 (i B.C.). **2.** *hand to hand fight, close combat*, χειραψίαι καὶ πεζῶν καὶ ἱππέων Anon.ap.Suid. **II.** as a term of wrestling, *clasping of one's antagonist* so as to throw him (cf. ἅμμα I.5), Plu.2.234d. **III.** *gentle friction, massage*, Cael.Aur. *TP*1.4; *gentle treatment*, in operations, Heliod.ap.Orib.50.47. 1. **-εκμᾰγεῖον,** τό, = χειρόμακτρον, Sotacus ap.Apollon.*Mir.*36, *Gloss.* **-εργάτης** [ᾰ], ου, ὁ, *one who works by hand*, Tz.*H.*10. 779. **-ητής,** οῦ, ὁ, *manual labourer*, *BGU*9 iii 19 (iii A.D.). **-ιάω,** *have chaps in the hand*, Poll.2.152.

⊛ **χειρίδ-ιον,** τό, *glove for rubbing* the body, Antyll.ap.Orib.6.18.5; χειριδίων v.l. for χειρίδων in Gal.6.230. **-όομαι,** Pass., *to be furnished with hands*, Nicostr.ap.Simp. *in Cat.*369.11. **II.** *to be furnished with sleeves*, *Gloss.* **-ωτός,** όν, *sleeved*, κιθών as worn by Asiatics, Hdt.7.61, cf. *PTeb.*46.34 (ii B.C.), Philostr.*Im.*1.28, Hdn.5. 3.6; of the Gallic χιτὼν σχιστός, Str.4.4.3. **II.** *having hands*, Suid.

⊛ **χειρ-ίζω,** Dor. fut. χειριξοῦντι *Rev.Arch.*1925(22).62 (Callatis), part. χειριξοῦντας *IG*9(1).694.44 (Corc., ii B.C.): pf. κεχείρικα *PTeb.* 76.3 (ii B.C.):—*handle, manipulate*, of a surgeon, Sor.*Vit.Hippocr.* 12:—Pass., Hp.*Off.*3, al., Sor.*Fasc.*7. **II.** *manage, administer*, esp. of public funds, Plb.1.20.4, 1.75.1, al.; πρόσοδον *PTeb.* l.c.; χρήματα *Tab.Defix.*96.17 (iii B.C.); ἀργύριον *IG* l.c.; τὴν ζυτηράν Wilcken *Chr.*272.11 (ii A.D.). **2.** generally, *handle*, λόγους S.E.*M.*7.443; *control, manage*, ὀργὰς καὶ πάθη Phld.*Rh.*2.263S. **3.** Med., *nominate, appoint*, *POxy.*59.14 (iii A.D.):—Pass., ib.1029.5 (ii A.D.): metaph., γενέσει χειρισθεὶς ἀπέθανες *as appointed* by your nativity, *Supp.Epigr.*7.904 (Gerasa). ⊛ **-ικός,** ή, όν, *manual*, ἔργα *POxy.*1692. 5 (ii A.D.). **-ιξις,** ιος, ἡ, = χειρισμός I, Hp.*Fract.*7. **II.** *administration*, τοῦ ἀργυρίου *IG*9(1).694.66 (Corc., ii B.C.). **-ιος,** α, ον, = ὑποχείριος, *in the hands, under control*, E.*Andr.*411; mostly with a Verb, χειρίαν ἀφείς τινι having left me *in the power of, captive to*, another, S.*Aj.*495; ἐλάβετε.. Ἑλένην χειρίαν; did you get her *into your power?* E.*Cyc.*177; χ. ἁλοῦσα Id.*Ion* 1257 (troch.). **-ῐπέδα,** Boeot. = χειροπέδη, *IG*7.2420.27 (Thebes, iii B.C.). **-ίς,** ῖδος, ἡ, *a covering for the hand, glove*, Od.24.230, X.*Cyr.*8.8.17, Clearch.

14. 2. *covering for the arm, loose sleeve*, such as the Persians wore, ἐπικατήμενος χειρίδι πλέῃ (χειρὶ διπλῇ codd.) ἀργυρίου Hdt.6.72, cf. X. *HG*2.1.8, *Cyr*.8.3.14, *PLips*.40 iii 23 (iv A.D.); used also by the Gauls, Plu.*Oth*.6; by tragedians, Luc.*JTr*.41. 3. = χειρίδιον, Agathin.ap. Orib.10.7.18, Gal.6.187. (On the accent v. Hdn.Gr.2.437; χειρῖδας Od. l.c.) **-ισμα**, ατος, τό, *part handled* or *operated upon*, Hp. *Art*.11. II. *treatment*, ib.14,42. ⊛ **-ισμογράφος** [ᾰ], ὁ, *inventory-keeper, registrar*, *PLips*.102 i 9 (iv A.D.), *Stud.Pal*.20.81.4 (iv A.D.). **-ισμός**, ὁ, *handling, manipulation, treatment*, esp. in surgery, Hp.*Off*.3, Paul.Aeg.6.122. 2. *management, handling*, τῆς τύχης *by* fortune, Plb.1.4.1; τῶν πραγμάτων *of* business, 5.26. 4; ὁ κατὰ μέρος χ. 2.35.3; ὁ χ. τῆς χάριτος *exercise*, 31.28.11; τῶν δογμάτων *execution*, 6.12.3: abs., 1.28.4; of literary or rhetorical *treatment*, D.S.5.1, Phld.*Rh*.1.371 S. 3. esp. of *financial administration*, *Schwyzer*631.11 (Milet., ii B.C.), *Rev.Arch*.1925(22).62 (Callatis), *POxy*.2125.3 (iii A.D.); *department*, *PTeb*.758.14 (ii B.C.), Wilcken *Chr*.432.13 (ii A.D.), 170.27 (iii A.D.). 4. pl., *administrative posts*, Vett.Val.39.12. 5. *inventory, register* of property, Wilcken *Chr*.71.11 (pl.), 91.14 (both ii A.D.). b. *guild, corporation*, τῶν κυβερνητῶν *PGiss*.11.11 (ii A.D.), cf. *PPetr*.3 p.206, al. (iii B.C., abbrev.).

**χειρίσοφος**, f.l. for χειρόσοφος.

**χειρ-ιστέον**, *one must manage* or *conduct*, τὸν πόλεμον D.S.17. 16. II. χειριστέος, α, ον, *to be operated upon*, Hp.*Mochl*. 40. **-ιστεύω**, *act as administrator*, *TAM*2.539 (Arsada, Lycia). ⊛ **-ιστής**, οῦ, ὁ, *manager, administrator*, *PHib*.1.74 (iii B.C.), *PCair.Zen*.737.15 (iii B.C.), Plb.3.4.13, 98.8, al., *Cat.Cod.Astr*.2.193; ἀλλοτρίων Vett.Val.10.14, al.; οἱ διὰ τῶν οἰκονόμων χ., Ἑλληνικά 7. 179 (Chalcis, iii B.C.). **-ιστικόν**, τό, *salary of* χειριστής, *PTeb*. 121.49 (i B.C.). II. *ledger*, *POxy*.1257.10 (iii A.D.), etc. 2. Adj. **-κός**, ή, όν, *entered in a list*, κατ' ἄνδρα χ. πυρός ib.1444.4 (iii A.D.), 1526.4 (iii A.D.). **-ιστος**, η, ον, irreg. Sup. of χείρων (v. χείρων B).

**χειρο-άλῠσις** [ᾰ], εως, ἡ, = χειράλυσις, *Gloss*. **-άναξ**, etym. of χειρῶναξ, *EM*811.8. **-βαλλίστρα**, ἡ, *hand-sling*, = Lat. *falarica*, *Gloss*.; title of work wrongly ascribed to Hero. **-βάναυσος** [βᾰ], ον, = βάναυσος, Poll.7.7. **-βᾰρής**, ές, *heavy in the hand*, Philetaer.10 (lyr.). **-βῐος**, ον, *living by handiwork*, *PEnteux*.82. 7 (iii B.C.), Suid. **-βλημα**, ατος, τό, and **-βλητον**, τό, glossed by δράγματα, Hsch. **-βλῐμάομαι**, = ψηλαφάω, Luc.*Pseudol*.24 (-βλημ- cod.). **-βολέω**, *throw the arms about*, Id.*Lex*.5. **-βολον**, τό, *handful, bundle*, Tz.ad Lyc.34 (χερο- cod.). ⊛ **-βοσκός**, όν, *supporting oneself by manual work*, Poll.7.7, Hsch. **-βρώς**, ῶτος, ὁ, ἡ, *gnawing the arms*, δεσμός Stesich.4. **-γάστωρ**, ορος, ὁ, ἡ, *one who fills his belly with his hands*, i.e. *lives by handiwork*, Hecat.367 J.: Χειρογάστορες, name of play by Nicopho. **-γονία**, ἡ, *Hand-production*, a name of Persephone, Hsch. (fort. -γένεια).

**χειρογρᾰφ-έω**, *report in writing*, *PTeb*.72.465 (ii B.C.). 2. *give a guarantee by note of hand*, περί τινος ib.48.5 (ii B.C.): c. inf. fut., ib.66.59 (ii B.C.): but, 3. esp. χ. τὸν βασιλικὸν ὅρκον *subscribe to* the royal oath, *make an* attested *declaration*, *PRev.Laws* 27.5, al. (iii B.C.), etc. ⊛ **-ία**, ἡ, *report in writing*, *PTeb*.64(*a*).54 (ii B.C.). 2. *declaration* attested by oath, *written testimony*, χ. ὅρκου βασιλικοῦ ib.27.32 (ii B.C.); κατὰ νόμους χειρογραφίας *PRev. Laws* 37.13 (iii B.C.); παραβεβηκότος τὰ τῆς χ. *PAmh*.2.35.31 (ii B.C.). **-ος**, ον, *written with the hand, holograph, manuscript*, σύμβολον, ἀσφάλ⟨ε⟩ια, *PFay*.303 (ii A.D.), *PGrenf*.2.75.13 (iv A.D.): hence **χειρόγρᾰφον**, τό, *manuscript note*, *IG*2².1013.52, Plb.30.8.4, Lxx *To*.5.3, D.H.5.8, Artem.3.40; τὸ καθ' ἡμῶν χ. *Ep.Col*.2.14. 2. *note of hand, bond*, *PRein*.7.22 (ii B.C.), Plu.2.829a, etc.; also **χειρόγρᾰφος**, ὁ, *CIG*4629 (Syria). II. parox., χειρογράφος [ᾰ], ὁ, *clerk, amanuensis*, *PTeb*.209 (i B.C.).

**χειρο-δάϊκτος** [ᾰ], ον, *slain by hand*, σφάγια S.*Aj*.219 (anap.). **-δεικτος**, ον, *manifest*, Id.*OT*901 (lyr.). **-δεσμος**, ὁ, *handcuff, manacle*, *Gloss*. **-δίκαιος** [ῐ], ον, = sq., Suid. **-δίκης** [ῐ], ου, ὁ, *one who asserts his right by hand, uses the right of might*, Hes. *Op*.[189]. **-δόσιον**, τό, *wages, hire*, *Gloss*. **-δοτέω**, *give with the hand*, χειροδοτεῖ τρόπον ἀλείπτου καὶ πρὸς τὰ γυμνάσια καλεῖ Ph.1.640 codd. (χειροδετεῖ *binds his hands with the cestus*, cj. Wyttenbach; συγκροτεῖ cj. Mangey). **-δοτος**, ον, *given by hand*, χ. δάνεισμα money *lent without written acknowledgement*, Poll. 2.152. II. χ. παράφερνα *movable goods*, *Arch.Pap*.4.130 ii 30. III. *furnished with hands*, Porph. *in Cat*.123.11. **-δράκων** [ᾰ], οντος, ὁ, ἡ, *with serpent hands* or *arms*, E.*El*.1345 (anap.). **-δρόπος**, ον, *plucking with the hands*, Nic.*Th*.752. **-έρκτης**· χειρουργός, Hsch. **-ήθεια**, ἡ, *domestication*, Arist.*Phgn*.809ᵃ33, *Gp*.16. 1.11. **-ήθης**, ες, *accustomed to the hand, manageable*, commonly of animals, *tame*, κροκόδειλος Hdt.2.69; θεός τις χ., as Cambyses sneeringly calls Apis, Id.3.28; χ. πῶλος X.*Eq*.2.3; λέων D.S.1.48, etc.: c. dat., *used to*, ἐγχέλεις ἀνθρώποις χ. Plu.2.976a; [θηρία] χ. γιγνόμενα τοῖς πόνοις, i.e. by training, ib.2f. 2. of persons, *civilized*, Str.11.2.4; *amenable*, c. dat., μοι χ. ἦν καὶ ἐτιθασ(σ)εύετο (fort. ἐτετιθάσευτο) had become *submissive* to me, of a person, X. *Oec*.7.10; τιθασεύουσι χειροήθεις ἑαυτοῖς ποιοῦντες D.3.31; τῷ δήμῳ Plu.*Per*.15; τοῖς [ἐν φιλοσοφίᾳ λεγομένοις] παρέχουσιν ἑαυτοὺς χ. Id.2. 14e; χ. ὕβρει *used* to it, Luc.*Merc.Cond*.35: Comp., ἡδονῇ -έστερος Jul.*Caes*.318a. 3. of things, *manageable, tolerable*, τῇ διανοίᾳ χ. διὰ τῆς ὄψεως Plu.*Mar*.16; τὰ ὅπλα τοῖς σώμασιν ἐγίνετο χ. Id.*Phil*.9, cf. 2.47b; αὐτῷ χ. καταστησάτω τὸ παθηματικὸν τῆς ψυχῆς μόριον Jul. *Or*.6.199c. **-θεσία**, ἡ, *application by hand*, of an instrument, Artemo Hist.ap.Ath.14.637c. **-κμητος**, ον, *wrought by hand*, παραδείγματα Ti.Locr.99.4, cf. Arist.*Cael*.287ᵇ16, *Mete*.381ᵃ30; οἰκήματα Str.2.5.10; χ. ὕδατα, = φρεατιαῖα, of *artificial* reservoirs, Arist.*Mete*. 353ᵇ25; χ. θεός Heraclit.*Ep*.4.2; neut. pl. as title of work by [Democr.], *Fr*.300 (variously corrupted). **-κοπέω**, *cut off the hand of*, τινας D.S.25.3, cf. 33.14, App.*Hisp*.68:—Pass., *have one's hand or hands cut off*, Str.15.1.54, Plu.2.305c. **-κόπος**, ον, *cutting off the hands*, Macr.*Exc*.p.601 K. **-κρᾰσία**, ἡ, = χειροκρατία, Phld.*Ir*. p.32 W., D.H.6.65, 8.72, D.S.36.6, Plu.2.332c. **-κρᾰτέω**, *grasp by the hand* (or *violently*), *PMag.Berol*.1.82. **-κρᾰτησία**, ἡ, *seizure by violence*, Nech.ap.Heph.Astr.1.21, *Cat.Cod.Astr*.7.135 (both pl.). **-κρᾰτία**, ἡ, *right of might, government by force*, Plb.6.9.7, D.S.36.11, App.*BC*1.17. **-κρᾰτικός**, ή, όν, *using the right of might*, ὁ θηριώδης [τρόπος τῆς πολιτείας] καὶ χ. Plb.6.10.4. **-κρίτης** [ῐ], ου, ὁ, *counter of votes, teller*, *BCH*58.319 (Mylasa), *Wiener Sitzb*. 132(2).12 (ibid.), *Inscr.Magn*.110ᵃ1. **-κτῠπος**, ον, *stricken by the hand*; v. χοροιτύπος I. **-λάβη** [ᾰ], ἡ, *handle*, Ph.*Bel*.76.23, *Inscr.Délos* 1441 *A* ii 53 (ii B.C.). **-λᾰβίς**, ίδος, ἡ, = foreg., Hero *Spir*. 1.5: esp. *plough-handle*, Poll.1.252. **-λογέω**, *gather by hand*, Gp.10.21.6 (Pass.). **-λυχνία**, ἡ, *lantern*, *PGrenf*.2.111.25 (v/vi A.D.). **-μακτρον**, τό, *cloth for wiping the hands, towel, napkin*, Hdt.4.64, Ar.*Fr*.502, X.*Cyr*.1.3.5, *PCair.Zen*. 77.8, al. (iii B.C.): the Scythians used scalps as χειρόμακτρα, Hdt. l.c.: hence Σκυθιστὶ χ. ἐκκεκαρμένος S.*Fr*.473. II. *head-cloth*, used by women, Sapph.44, Hecat.358 J., and perhaps so in Hdt.2.122, χ. χρύσεον. [Written χειρώμακτρον *PRev.Laws* 94.4 (iii B.C.), *PEnteux*.38.3,9 (iii B.C.), but χειρόμακτρον *PCair.Zen*. ll. cc. (iii B.C.): -ω- might be due to 'contamination' with the root of ὀμόργ-νυμι.] **-μαντις**, εως, ὁ, *diviner by palmistry, fortune-teller*, Poll.2.152. **-μάππιον**, τό (cf. Lat. *mappa*), *towel*, *Sammelb*.7033. 43 (v A.D.). **-μάχα** [μᾰ], ἡ (sc. ἑταιρεία), *the working-class faction* at Miletus, opp. ἡ πλουτίς, Plu.2.298c, cf. Eust.1425.64. **-μᾰχέω**, *fight with the hands*, sens. obsc., *AP*12.22 (Scyth.). **-μᾰχία**, ἡ, *manual labour*, Eust.1716.3. **-μήριον**, τό, gloss on ῥυκάνη, Hsch. **-μύλη** [ῠ], ἡ, *hand-mill*, X.*Cyr*.6.2.31. **-μύλιον** [ῠ], τό, Dim. of foreg., Dsc.5.88, *PMag.Par*.1.3089. **-μῠλον**, τό, = χειρομύλη, Cass.Fel.40, *Gloss*.; also **-μῠλος**, ὁ, ib., *Edict.Diocl*.15. 55. **-νῖβον**, τό, = sq., Epich.79 (pl.). ⊛ **-νιπτρον**, τό, *basin for washing the hands*, Eup.118.1, prob. in *IG*2².1416.7. 2. *water for washing the hands*, Poll.2.150, *EM*810.50. II. *hand-washing*, Dsc.1.7.

⊛ **χειρονομ-έω**, *gesticulate* with the hands, X.*Smp*.2.19, D.C.36.30, τοῖσι σκέλεσι ἐχειρονόμησε, of one standing on his head, Hdt.6.129; χειρονομοῦντα *volanti cultello, flourishing* the knife, of an expert carver, Juv.5.121. II. *practise shadow-boxing*, Thrasym.*Fr*.4, Pl.*Lg*. 830c, Plu.2.747b. **-ησείω**, Desiderat., *wish to gesticulate*, Cratin. 453. **-ία**, ἡ, *shadow-boxing*, Hp.*Vict*.2.64, Antyll.ap.Orib.6.30.1, Gal.6.324 (pl.), etc. II. *pantomimic movement, gesticulation*, Ath. 14.631c, Plu.2.997c, Luc.*Salt*.78, Plot.5.9.11. III. ἐν χειρονομίαις, = ἐν χειρῶν νόμῳ (v. χείρ II.6d), Lxx 3 *Ma*.1.5 (v.l. ἐν χειρῶν νομαῖς). ⊛ **-ος** (parox.), ὁ, *one who moves the hands in pantomimic gestures, posture-master*, Hsch.

**χειρόνως**, Adv. of χείρων, *worse, for the worse*, J.*AJ*17.9.5, Procop. *Arc*.6, Pall. *in Hp.Fract*.12.281 C., Suid. s.v. Ἄβελ.

**χειρο-πέδη**, ἡ, *handcuff*, *IG*2².1424 *a* 274, *PCair.Zen*.782(*a*).13 (iii B.C.), Lxx *Ps*.149(150).8, *Si*.21.19, al., D.S.20.13, Poll.2.152, etc. **-πεδον**, τό, = foreg., *Gloss*. **-πληθής**, ές, *filling the hand, as large as can be held in the hand*, λίθοι X.*An*.3.3.17; κορύνη Theoc. 25.63; ἀγκάλισμα Luc.*Am*.14; χ. μέγεθος *handful*, Thphr.*HP*4.2. 7; so χ. δέσμη Dsc.1.8, etc.; neut., ἀλφίτων χειροπληθές *Gp*.14.17. 2. Adv. **-θῶς** *by handfuls*, Sch.Luc.*Tim*.20. **-πληθιαῖος**, α, ον, = foreg., Thphr.*HP*9.4.10, D.S.3.23,28. **-πόδης**, ου, ὁ, *with chapped feet*, Alc.37 B. **-ποιέομαι**, Med., *perpetrate with one's own hand*, αὐτὴ πρὸς αὑτῆς χειροποιεῖται τάδε S.*Tr*.891. **-ποίητος**, ον, *made by hand, artificial*, opp. αὐτοφυής (natural), σκῆπτρον Hdt. 1.195; λίμνη 2.149; ἔργον Pl.*Criti*.118c; ὁδός X.*An*.4.3.5; τείχη J.*BJ*4.10.5; γήλοφος, τέλμα, Jul.*Or*.2.63b, 65c: freq. in Lxx of idols, *Is*.2.18, al.; φλὸξ χ. a fire *intentionally kindled*, opp. ἀπὸ ταὐτομάτου, Th.2.77; so λιμός, opp. αὐτόματος, Procop.*Arc*.26; ἀνάγκη, τέχνη, Id.*Goth*.4.26,22. Adv. **-τως** Plb.10.10.12: χ. ὠχύρωτο, opp. φύσει, J.*BJ*7.8.3. **-πόνια** (sc. ἱερά), τά, *holiday of workmen and artisans*, Hsch (-πονία cod.). **-πους**, ὁ, ἡ, **-πουν**, τό, gen. **-ποδος**, = χειροπόδης, Poll.2.152. **-σίδήριον**, τό, *grapnel, grappling-hook*, ibid. (v.l.). **-σκοπία**, ἡ, *vote by show of hands*, *Revue de l'histoire des religions* 63.331 (Tyre). **-σκοπικός**, ή, όν, *based on palmistry*, οἰώνισμα Suid. s.v. Ἕλενος. **-σκόπος**, ὁ, *inspecting the hand*, = χειρόμαντις, Artem.2.69. II. *counter of hands*, i.e. *teller of votes*, *IG*9(1).109.8 (Elatea), *Bull. Soc. royale des lettres de Lund* 1928/9 iv 43 (Cardamyle, i A.D.), Tim.*Lex*., Suid. **-σοφος**, ον, *skilled with the hands*, esp. *gesticulating well*, Luc.*Rh.Pr*.17, *Lex*. 14, Lesbon.ap.eund.*Salt*.69:—χειρίσοφος is a f.l. **-στρόφιον**, τό, *instrument of torture for twisting the hands or arms*, Hdn.*Epim*. 150. **-τένων**, οντος, ὁ, ἡ, *with outstretched arms*, of the crab, f.l. for χειλο- Batr.297.

**χειρότερος**, η, ον, Ep. for χείρων, Il.15.513, 20.436, Hes.*Op*.127, Parm.8.24, etc.

**χειροτεχν-έω**, *to be a* χειροτέχνης, Hp.*Ep*.17, Poll.7.6. **-ημα**, ατος, τό, *work of art*, Babr.30.4 (cj.), Poll.7.7, Lib.*Or*.11.254. **-ης**, ου, ὁ, *handicraftsman, artisan*, Hdt.2.167, Ar.*Pl*.533 (anap.), 617 (anap.), Th.6.72, Pl.*R*.597a, *PBremen*48.27 (ii A.D.), etc.; opp. ἀρχιτέκτων, Arist.*Metaph*.981ᵃ31; of slaves who brought in income to their owner, X.*Mem*.3.11.4; φαύλους καὶ χ. Pl.*R*.405a; opp. φιλόσοφοι, X.*Vect*.5.4; opp. πολιτικοί, Plb.10.17.6; τίς ὁ χ. ἰατορίας..; who is the *expert* in surgery..? S.*Tr*.1000 (anap.), cf. Hp.*VM*7; πολέμου χ. Plu.*Comp.Lyc.Num*.2. **-ία**, ἡ, *handicraft*, βαναυσία καὶ χ. Pl.*R*. 590c: pl., γεωργιῶν ἀπέχεσθαι..καὶ χ. ib.547d; αἱ περὶ χειροτεχνίας ἐπιστῆμαι Id.*Plt*.304b. **-ικός**, ή, όν, *skilful*, Ar.*V*.1276 (Sup.). 2. *of handicraftsmen* or *artisans*, συμβόλαια Pl.*R*.425d: ἡ -κή (sc. τέχνη), = χειροτεχνία, Id.*Plt*.259c: pl., Id.*Phlb*.55d. Adv. -κῶς Poll.2.148. **-ιον**, τό, *tax on handicraft*, *SIG*481*B*3, *BCH*59.9 (both Delph., iii B.C.). **-ίτης** [ῑ], ου, ὁ, = χειροτέχνης, Sch.rec.A.*Pr*.893.

**χειρό-τμημα**, ατος, τό, in pl., f.l. for χειρόκμητα in Zos.Alch. pp.209,239 B. **-τμητος**, ον, *cut by hand*, πόντος Ph.1.674 (sed leg. -κμητος); v.l. in Str.1.3.18.

® **χειροτον-έω**, *stretch out the hand*, for the purpose of giving one's vote in the assembly, περὶ τῶν ἀνδρῶν Plu.*Phoc*.34; μὴ χ. *vote against* the motion, Luc.*Deor.Conc*.9:—but mostly, II. c. acc. pers., *elect*, prop. *by show of hands*, Ar.*Ach*.598, *Av*.1571, etc.; εἰς τὴν ἀγορὰν χ. τοὺς ταξιάρχους.., οὐκ ἐπὶ τὸν πόλεμον D.4.26; c. dupl. acc., στρατηγὸν χ. τινά X.*HG*6.2.11, cf. Isoc.8.50:—Pass., *to be elected*, Ar.*Ach*.607; ἐπὶ τοῦτ' ἐχειροτονήθησαν, ἵνα.. Lys.28.14; χ. ἔκ τινων Pl.*Lg*.763e; χ. ἐπὶ τῆς διοικήσεως Decr.ap.D.18.115: c. acc. cogn., χ. τὴν ἀρχὴν τὴν ἐπὶ τῷ θεωρικῷ Aeschin.3.24, cf. Ar.*Ec*. 517 (anap.); χειροτονηθεὶς ἢ λαχὼν Pl.*Plt*.300a, cf. Aeschin.1. 106. b. later, generally, *appoint*, Ph.2.112; of the Jewish High Priest, J.*AJ*13.2.2; τὸν ὑπὸ τοῦ θεοῦ κεχειροτονημένον βασιλέα ib.6.13.9, cf. 7.9.3; *appoint to an office* in the Church, πρεσβυτέρους *Act.Ap*.14.23, cf. 2*Ep.Cor*.8.19 (Pass.). 2. c. acc. rei, *vote for* a thing, Ar.*Ec*.297 (lyr.), 797, Isoc.7.84; γνώμας D.18.248: c. inf., ὁ δῆμος ἐχειροτόνησεν ἐξεῖναι..πέμπειν *voted* to send, Aeschin. 2.13, cf. *IG*1².57.29, 63.4:—Pass., κεχειροτόνηται ὕβρις τὸ πρᾶγμ' εἶναι *it is voted, ruled* to be.., D.21.216. III. *span with the hand*, τὸ αἰδοῖον Artem.1.78 (ap.Suid.; χειροκοπεῖν codd.). **-ητέον**, *one must vote*, Ar.*Ec*.266. II. *one must appoint*, τινὰ ἐπιμελητὴν Ph.2.57. ® **-ητής**, οῦ, ὁ, = Lat. *creator*, *Gloss*. **-ητός**, ή, όν, *elected by show of hands*, Aeschin.3.25, Arist.*Ath*.54.3; ἀρχὴ χ. an *elective* magistracy, opp. κληρωτή, Aeschin.1.19,113, 3.14, Arist.*Rh. Al*.1424ᵃ14. ® **-ία**, ἡ, *extension of the hand*, Lxx *Is*.58.9. II. *voting by show of hands*, Th.3.49; χειροτονίαν μνηστεύειν to court or seek *election*, Isoc.8.15; χ. τοῦ δήμου *election* by the people, Din.1.114, *S.Pelekides* 76 (Thessalonica). 2. generally, *election, appointment*, Ph.2.93, etc. 3. *a vote*, in pl., Pl.*Lg*.659b, Aeschin. 3.3; collectively, *votes*, οἷς ἂν ἡ πλείστη χ. γίγνηται Pl.*Lg*.755d, cf. 756b. **-ος**, ον, *stretching out the hands*, χ. λιταί *offered with outstretched hands*, A.*Th*.172 (lyr.).

**χειρο-τρῐβέω**, *rub with the hands, rub*, Heliod.ap.Orib.49.3.9, *Hippiatr*.10, Sch.D.3.31:—**χειρο-τρίβω** (sens. obsc.) is f.l. in *EM* 100.15. **-τρῐβία**, Ion. -ίη, ἡ, *surgical* or *medical treatment*, χειροτριβίης ἀτρεμαιότης Hp.*Praec*.13. II. *rubbing, handling*, *Hippiatr*. 33. **-τῠπής**, ές, *struck by the hands*, κροτάλων χειροτυπὴς πάταγος *AP*5.174 (Mel.).

**χειρουργ-έω**, *do with the hand, execute*, διακονήσασα καὶ χειρουργήσασα Antipho 1.20; esp. of *acts of violence*, νεανίσκοι, οἷς ἐχρῶντο εἴ τί που δέοι χειρουργεῖν Th.8.69, cf. Aeschin.2.117. 2. *make by hand, build*, οἰκοδομίαν Ael.*NA*3.24:—Pass., πολλὰ γυμνάσια ἐκεχειρούργητο Pl.*Criti*.117c. b. *use as material, work in*, ἐλέφαντα cj. in Ael.*NA*17.32. 3. *practise* an art, esp. of music, ᾄδοντές τε καὶ χειρουργοῦντες Arist.*Pol*.1340ᵇ20, cf. 1342ᵃ3, Iamb.*Comm.Math*.26; *produce by art*, of hatching eggs by artificial means, D.S.1.74:—Pass., *to be highly cultivated*, of vines, ὑπὸ τῆς ἀνθρωπίνης ἐμπειρίας Id.3.62; *to be dressed*, of meats, Megasth.28. 4. of surgeons, *operate*, Hp.*Flat*.1, Plu.2.71a, Gal.2.228: c. acc., *operate upon*, Sor. 1.4, Artem.4.2:—Pass., ὁ χειρουργηθεὶς ἄνθρωπος Gal.10.943. 5. sens. obsc., D.L.6.46. **-ημα**, ατος, τό, *handiwork*, a word used by Gorgias, Pl.*Grg*.450b, ubi v. Sch. II. *manufactured article*, D.H.*Pomp*.1.7 **-ητέον**, *one must perform an operation*, Antyll. ap.Orib.4.4.7. **-ητέος**, α, ον, *to be operated on*, Paul.Aeg.6. 21. **-ία**, Ion. -ίη, ἡ, *working by hand, practice of a handicraft* or *art, skill herein*, Ar.*Lys*.673, etc.; opp. γνώμη and γνῶσις (theory), Hp. *Morb*.1.6, Pl.*Plt*.259e; opp. ξύνεσις, Id.*Amat*.135b. II. *a handicraft* or *art*, Id.*Plt*.258d, 277c; τῶν ζῳγράφων..ἡ καλὴ χ. Anaxandr. 33.1: pl., περὶ τέχνας ἤ χειρουργίας τινάς Pl.*Smp*.203a, cf. *Grg*. 450b. 2. esp. *the art* or *practice of surgery*, opp. the administration of medicine, χειρουργίῃ χρῆσθαι perform *an operation*, Hp.*Prog*. [23]; χειρουργίην ἐν γραφῇ διηγεῖσθαι *the mode of operation*, Id.*Art*. 33, cf. D.S.5.74, Ph.1.253, Dsc.5.15, Ruf.ap.Orib.8.24.7, Sor.1.12, etc. ® **-ικός**, ή, όν, *of technical dexterity*, ἡ χ. ἐπιστήμη Arist.*Pol*. 1341ᵇ1; τὰ μὴ χ. (sc. τῶν τεχνῶν) Phld.*Po*.5.2; χ. μέρος τῆς μουσικῆς the *practical* part of music, i.e. *execution*, Plu.2.1135d. 2. *of* or *for surgery*, ἡ -κή (sc. τέχνη) *surgery*, D.L.3.85. Adv. -κῶς Poll.2.148. II. *worked by hand*, τόξα Hero *Bel*.75.5. **-ός**, όν, *working* or *doing by hand*, Plu.2.564e: *practising a handicraft* or *art*, περὶ γραφικὴν Ael.*NA*17.9; οἱ χ. *artificers, artists*, Id.*VH*14.47, etc.; also χ. τέχναι Lib.*Or*.25.36. II. χειρουργός, ὁ, *surgeon*, Plu.2.486c, Ptol.*Tetr*.180, Gal.10.455, Artem.4.2, *AP*11.280 (Pall.).

**χειρό-χρηστοι** λόγοι *handbooks, manuals*, Iamb.*VP*29.161 (s.v.l.). **-χωλος**, ον, *maimed in the hand*, Hippon.139.

**χειρ-όω**, (χείρων) *worst, master, subdue*, τινὰ πρὸς βίαν χειροῦν Ar.*V*. 443 (troch.); χ. τὸν ἐλέφαντα Ael.*NA*17.32 (s.v.l.). II. mostly in Med., fut. -ώσομαι S.*Ph*.92, Th.1.122, etc.: aor. ἐχειρωσάμην Hdt.1.211, Th.3.11, etc.: pf. κεχείρωμαι Luc.*Salt*.79, D.C.50.24 (Pass., v. III):—both of countries or nations, and of single persons, *conquer, overpower, subdue*, ὡς ἐχειρώσαντο τοὺς ἐναντίους Hdt. l.c., cf. 2.70, al., E.*IT*330,359, *HF*570; τόξοις χειροῦσθαι A.*Ch*. 694; οὐ γὰρ ἡμᾶς..πρὸς βίαν χειρώσεται S. l.c.; βίᾳ χ. τοὺς ἐναντίους X.*Ages*.1.20; χ. τινὰ σφίσι Th.4.28: sts. with collat. notion of *killing*, X.*Cyr*.7.5.30, Isoc.10.25; also, of *taking prisoner*, E.*Tr*. 861, X.*HG*2.4.26; τήνδ' ἐχειρούμην ἄγραν *became master of* this booty, S.*OC*950. 2. without any sense of violence, χ. τινὰ λόγοις Pl.*Sph*.219c, cf. X.*Mem*.3.7.8; χ. θρέμματα *tame* them, Pl. *Sph*.222a; ἡ ὄρχησις κεχείρωται τοὺς ἀνθρώπους Luc. l.c.; δι' ἡδονῆς Plu.2.139a; διὰ τῆς κολακείας Ael.*VH*14.48, etc. III. Pass., *to be mastered, conquered, subdued*, πρὸς βίαν χειρούμενον Τυφῶνα A.*Pr*.355, cf. S.*Tr*.279, E.*El*.1168: fut. χειρωθήσομαι D.11.5: aor. ἐχειρώθην Hdt.3.120,145, al.; χειρωθεὶς βίᾳ S.*OC*903, cf. *Tr*.1057; χειρωθῆναι σφίσιν Th.8.71: pf. κεχείρωμαι Id.5.96; κεχειρωμένας ἄγεσθαι to be led *captive*, A.*Th*.326 (lyr.); αἰχμαλώτους κεχ. Pl.*Lg*. 919a. **-ωμα**, ατος, τό, *that which is subdued, a conquest*, δούλης θανούσης, εὐμαροῦς χειρώματος A.*Ag*.1326. 2. *deed of violence*, ἄφαντος ἔρρει θανασίμῳ χ. S.*OT*560. II. *a work wrought by the hand*, τυμβοχόα χ., of earth thrown up (v. τυμβοχόος), A.*Th*. 1027.

**χείρων**, ὁ, ἡ, neut. χεῖρον, gen. -ονος, acc. -ονα: nom. and acc. pl. χείρονες, -ας, χείρονα, contr. in Att. Prose χείρους, χείρω; dat. χείροσι, poet. χειρόνεσσι Pi.*N*.8.22:—(for Ep. form χερείων, poet. χειρότερος, χερειότερος, v. sub vocc.):—irreg. Comp. of κακός: (χείρων from *χερ-γων, cf. χερείων): I. of persons, *meaner, inferior*, either in bodily strength and bravery, or in rank, opp. ἀρείων, Il.10.238, Od.20.133; σὺ μὲν ἐσθλὸς ἐγὼ δὲ σέθεν πολὺ χείρων Il.20.434; τοῦ γένετ' ἐκ πατρὸς πολὺ χείρονος υἱὸς ἀμείνων 15.641, cf. Od.20.82; ἢ πολὺ χείρονες ἄνδρες ἀμύμονος ἀνδρὸς ἄκοιτιν μνῶνται 21. 325; opp. κρείσσων, Pi.*I*.4(3).34(52); τὸν ὄλβιον τόν τε χ. E.*Ba*.422 (lyr.); τὰ χείρονα S.*Fr*.192, E.*Supp*.196. 2. later in moral sense, *worse than others*, sts. almost like a positive, *knave*, opp. ἀγαθός, S.*Ph*.456, cf. Th.3.9, Lys.16.3; οἱ πένητες καὶ οἱ δημόται καὶ οἱ χ. X.*Ath*.1.4, cf. 3.10; οἱ χ., opp. οἱ ἀγαθοί, Pl.*R*.460c, etc. b. χ. βίος, opp. ἀμείνων, ib.618d; γνώμη X.*Cyr*.8.8.7. 3. *worse* in quality, *inferior*, of horses, Il.23.572: *inferior, less skilful*, ἰητροί Hp.*Acut*.6; ζωγράφοι, δημιουργοί, etc., Pl.*Cra*.429a, *R*.421e, etc.: χ. εἰς σοφίαν, εἰς τὴν ἀρετήν, Id.*Tht*.162c, *R*.335b; πρὸς ἀλήθειαν Luc. *JTr*.48; c. acc., χ. τὰ πολεμικά X.*Cyr*.8.8.20; χ. τὴν ψυχήν, τὴν διάνοιαν, Aeschin.3.46, Isoc.11.43; τὰ ἄλλα μηδὲν χ. Id.4.105; c. inf., χ. ἡμῶν ταῦτα ποιεῖν X.*Cyr*.2.1.16; οὐδὲν χείρους ἔσεσθε..ἀκηκοότες you will be none *the worse* for having heard.., D.24.139; *less kind*, μὴ χ. περὶ ἡμᾶς αὐτοὺς εἶναι..τῶν ὑπαρχόντων Id.2.2. II. of things, *inferior* in quality, ἄεθλον Il.23.413; ὑποδήματα X.*Oec*. 13.10; ὄνομα Pl.*Cra*.429b. 2. *worse, harder, more severe*, νόσος E.*Andr*.220; μοῖρα Pl.*Phdr*.248e; τιμωρία *Ep.Hebr*.10.29. III. neut., 1. as a Subst., τὸ χ. *inferiority*, Polem.*Call*.27; but mostly in phrases with Preps., ἐπὶ τὸ χ. τρέπεσθαι, κλῖναι, fall off, get *worse*, X.*Cyr*.8.8.2, *Mem*.3.5.13; ἐπὶ τὸ χ. μεταβάλλει ἑαυτόν Pl.*R*. 381b; ἀλλοιοῦσθαι ἐπὶ τὸ χ., opp. ἐπὶ τὸ βέλτιον, Thphr.*CP*6.3.3; also πάντα ὑποπτεύοντες ἐπὶ τὸ χ. putting the *worst* construction on.. D.H.6.85; λαμβάνειν τι ἐπὶ τὸ χ. J.*AJ*16.7.4; also πρὸς τὸ χ. μεταβάλλειν D.S.20.57; κατὰ τὸ χ. Pl.*Lg*.720e; in the *lower* sense, opp. κατὰ τὸ κρεῖττον, Dam.*Pr*.7: less freq. in pl., ἐπὶ τὰ χείρω ἰέναι X. *Mem*.3.9.9; τὰ χ. προαιρεῖσθαι Isoc.8.110. 2. as a predicate, ἀλλὰ σοὶ αὐτῷ χ. (sc. ἐστί or ἔσται) Od.15.515, cf. X.*An*.7.6.4; with a neg., οὐ χ. [ἐστι] c. inf., we may *as well*, Pl.*Phd*.105a, Arist. *EN*1127ᵃ14; simply οὐ χεῖρον, in an answer, it is *as well*, Ar.*Eq*. 37; λάβ', ὡγάθ'· οὐδὲν χ. Clearch.Com.4. 3. as Adv., *worse*, χ. βουλεύσασθαι Th.3.46, cf. 6.89; χ. πρᾶξαι Id.7.67; βιῶναι, ζῆν, Pl. *R*.344e, 519d. b. *in inferior degree, less*, ἀγαπᾶν Id.*Lg*.928a; φυλακὰς χ. φυλαττομένας X.*HG*6.2.17, etc.

B. Sup. **χείριστος**, η, ον, *worst*, Pl.*Plt*.303a, etc.; ὁ χ., opp. ὁ βέλτιστος, Lys.1.2; esp. οἱ χ. *men of lowest degree*, X.*Mem*.1.2.32. Adv. χείριστα Arist.*PA*687ᵇ24, *Metaph*.1083ᵇ2 (dub. l.); also -τως Lxx 2*Ma*.7.39.

**Χείρων**, ωνος, ὁ, Aeol. **Χέρρων** Alc.*Supp*.8.9, Dor. and Thess. **Χίρων** [ῑ] *IG*12(3).360 (Thera), *Supp.Epigr*.1.248.6 (Thessaly, iv B.C.):—*Cheiron*, one of the Centaurs, δικαιότατος Κενταύρων Il.11.832; son of Cronus and Philyra, Hes.*Th*.1001, etc.: teacher of Achilles, Il. l.c., 16.143, 19.390; of Asclepius and Jason, Pi.*N*.3.53; worshipped as the father of the Art of Medicine, Plu.2.647a: Χείρωνος ὑποθῆκαι, title of a poem ascribed to Hes., Quint.*Inst*.1.1.15, Sch. Pi.*P*.6.16. II. Χείρωνος ῥίζα, = πάνακες τὸ Χειρώνειον (v. Χειρώνειος II), Nic.*Th*.500.

**χειρων-ακτέω**, *practise handicraft*, Eustr. *in EN*7.6, Sch.Il.7.435. **-άκτης**, ου, ὁ, = χειρῶναξ, Zonar.: -ακτέων (gen. pl.) is f.l. in Hp. *Acut*.44. **-ακτικός**, ή, όν, *of* or *for handicrafts, mechanical*, χ. καὶ βάναυσοι Pl.*Ax*.368b, cf. Gal.*Protr*.14; χ. γένος D.Chr.12.69; χ. τέχνη Gal.17(1).521; χ. ἐργασία Sch.B Il.18.468. **-αξ** (properisp.), ακτος, ὁ, *one who is master of his hands* (ἄναξ τῶν χειρῶν), i.e. *handicraftsman*, Hdt.1.93, 2.141, Hp.*Acut*.8, *Art*.53, D.H.6.51, Plu.2.802a, etc. b. as Adj., πᾶς ὁ χ. λεώς S.*Fr*.844. II. generally, *one who handles, deals in* a thing, τῶνδε χειρώνακτες...λόγων, i.e.

soothsayers, E.Fr.795.3. -αξία, Ion. -ίη, ἡ, handiwork, handicraft, Hdt.2.167(pl.), A.Pr.45, Ch.761 (pl.), D.Chr.12.82. II. = sq., PGrenf.2.60.4 (ii A.D.). -άξιον, τό, a tax paid by handicraftsmen, Arist.Oec.1346$^a$4, PPetr.3p.307 (iii B.C.); PTeb.287.10 (ii A.D.), etc.: pl., POxy.1647.44 (ii A.D.); χ. γερδίων ib.285.6 (i A.D.).

Χειρώνειος, ον, of or from Cheiron, Χ. ἕλκος a sore like Cheiron's or needing his aid, a malignant sore, Zen.6.46, Gal.10.1006, Alex.Aphr.Pr.1.92, Hierocl.in CA14p.451 M. II. πάνακες Χειρώνειον, elecampane, Inula Helenium, Thphr.HP9.11.1, Plin.HN 25.32. 2. Cheiron's all-heal, Hypericum olympicum, Dsc.3.50. III. Χ. ῥίζα, = ἄμπελος ἀγρία, bryony, Gal.14.186.

Χειρωνιάς, άδος, ἡ, = κενταύρειον τὸ μέγα, Ps.-Dsc.3.6: Χειρώνιος ἄμπελος, = ἄμπελος μέλαινα, Dsc.4.183; Χειρώνιον, = γεντιανή, Ps.-Dsc.3.3.

Χειρωνίς (sc. βίβλος), ίδος, ἡ, a book on surgery, AP7.158 (pl.).

χείρ-ωσις, εως, ἡ, subduing, Pl.Ep.332b, J.AJ18.9.3, D.C.53.7. -ωτικός, ή, όν, apt at conquering or subduing, Pl.Sph.219d: ἡ -κή (sc. τέχνη) the art of subduing, ib.221b. -ωτός, ή, όν, to be subdued, tameable, Hsch. II. furnished with hands, Simp. in Cat. 197.15.

χείσομαι, v. χανδάνω II.

χείω, Ep. for χέω, pour, Hes.Th.83.

✱χέλειον, τό, crab's shell, Nic.Al.561, Hsch. (χέλιον cod.); tortoise-shell, chelium testudinum, Plin.HN6.173, cf. 9.38. II. perh. = χηλή I. 3, of Cancer, Euph. in Philol.90.137 (pl.), Arat.494.

χελεύς, έως, ὁ, = χέλυς, Hsch.

χελῑδ-όνειος, ον, v. χελιδόνιος. -όνεως, ω, ἡ, tree which bore the figs called χελιδόνια, Anon. (Androt., Phil., or Hegem.) ap.Ath. 3.75d, Choerob. in Theod.1.253 H. (v.l. χελιδώνεως). -ονία, ἡ, swallow's nest, prob. in Arist.HA626$^a$12. -ονιαῖος, α, ον, = χελιδόνιος II, ὄνος Sammelb.6001.5 (ii A.D.); ἰχθῦς PLond.1.130.104 (i/ii A.D., horoscope); ἱ[ππάδα] PThead.4.6 (iv A.D.); = badius, Gloss.; αἱ χελιδονιαῖαι ἀσπίδες prob. for χελιδοναῖαι in Aët. 13.22. -ονίας, ου, ὁ, a kind of tunny-fish, Diph.Siph.ap. Ath.8.356f. 2. χ. ἰχθῦς the more northerly fish of the constellation Pisces, Theon ad Arat.242. II. the spring wind, because the swallows come with it, Thphr.HP7.15.1, Plin.HN2.122. -ονῑδεύς, έως, ὁ, young swallow, Eust.753.56. -ονίζω, twitter like a swallow: hence, = βαρβαρίζω (cf. χελιδών I), A.Fr. 450. II. sing the swallow-song, Thgn.Hist.ap.Ath.8.360c, Eust.1914.43. -όνιον, τό, celandine, Chelidonium majus, Thphr.HP7.15.1, Ath.15.684e; χ. τὸ μέγα Dsc.2.180. 2. = ἄμπελος λευκή, Id.4.182. 3. χ. τὸ μικρόν pilewort, Ranunculus Ficaria, Id.2.181. II. young swallow, Gal.14.386. ✱-όνιος or -όνειος, α, ον, also ος, ον Poll.6.81:—of the swallow, μέλος Suid.; χ. τεῖχος built by swallows, Thrasyll.ap.Ps.-Plu.Fluv.16.2. II. like the swallow, esp. coloured like the swallow's throat, reddish-brown, russet, ἰσχάδες χελιδόνιαι russet-coloured figs, Philem.Gloss.ap.Ath. 14.652f., cf. Dsc.5.32, Poll. l. c.; χ. πυρός Dsc.Eup.1.228; χελιδόνια (sc. σῦκα) Ar.Fr.569.4 (χελιδόνεια Epigen.1.2). 2. χελιδονία, ἡ, a kind of gem, Plin.HN37.155; lapis chelidonius ib.11.203. 3. χ. ἀσπίς, a kind of asp, Philum.Ven.16.1, Gal. 14.235, cf. χελιδονιαῖος. 4. δασύπους χελιδόνειος, of the common hare, Diph.1. 5. χελιδονεία κύλιξ, name of a kind of cup, IG11(2).154B7 (pl., Delos, iii B.C.), cf. 145.46 (ib., iv. B.C.), Inscr.Délos385$^a$53 (ii B.C.). 6. χελιδόνιον, τό, an eye-salve, CIL13.10021.93. -ονίς, ίδος, ἡ, poet. for χελιδών, AP6.160 (Antip.Sid.): metaph. of a poetess, IG14.1892 (Rome). ✱-ονισμός, ὁ, singing of the swallow-song, which the Rhodian boys went about singing at the return of the swallows in the month Boëdromion; such a song is preserved by Ath.8.360c. -ονισταί, οἱ, singers of the swallow-song, Hsch. ✱-ών, όνος, ἡ (even of the male, S.E.M.1.151); but masc., metaph. of men, Ion Trag.33, cf. Hdn.Gr.1.25: voc. χελιδοῖ, as if from a nom. χελιδώ, Anacr.67, Simon.74, Ar.Av.1411 (anap.), AP9.70 (Mnasalc., with v.l. χελιδόν, as in Anacreont.9.2 cod.):—swallow, Od.21.411, 22.240, Hes.Op.568, Hdt.2.22, Democr.14, etc.: πέδοικος χ. A.Fr.53, cf. Ar.Av.714 (anap): prov., μία χ. ἔαρ οὐ ποιεῖ Cratin.33 (cf. Arist.EN1098$^a$18); δεῖσθαι δ' ἔοικεν οὐκ ὀλίγων χ. Ar.Av.1417, cf. 1681; χ. λευκή, of a rare event, Thphr.Sign.39; the twittering of the swallow was prov. used of barbarous tongues by the Greeks, εἴπερ ἐστὶ μὴ χελιδόνος δίκην ἀγνῶτα φωνὴν βάρβαρον κεκτημένη A.Ag.1050: hence ὁ χ., = ὁ βάρβαρος, Ion l. c.; Θρῃκία χ. ἐπὶ βάρβαρον ἑζομένη πέταλον Ar.Ra.681 (lyr.); χελιδόνων μουσεῖα bowers that ring with poetasters' twitterings, ib.93 (parodied from ἀηδόνων μουσεῖα in E., v. Fr.88). 2. metaph. of letters, τῶν σῶν χ. αἱ ἡμέτεραι πλείους Lib.Ep.46.2. II. flying-fish, Dactylopterus volitans, hirondelle de mer, Ephipp.12.5 (anap.), Speus.ap.Ath.7.324f; χ. θαλάττιαι Arist.HA535$^b$27. III. frog in the hollow of a horse's foot (expld. by Hsch. τὸ κοῖλον τῆς ὁπλῆς), so called from its being forked like the swallow's tail, X.Eq. 1.3, 4.5, 6.2, Poll.1.188. 2. the like part of a dog's foot, Suid. 3. = λειχήν 4, Cael.Aur.TP1.138 (pl.); a growth on the knee in horses, Sch.Nic.Th.945. 4. hollow above the bend of the elbow, Hsch. 5. pudenda muliebria (with play on Ar.Lys.770 (hex.)), Suid., cf. Juv.6.365(6). 6. a kind of ship, Suid. 7. a Peloponnesian silver coin, Id. (Χελιδϝών as pr. n., IG9$^2$(1).86 (Corinthian, found at Thermon); cf. Assyr. hinundu, Lat. hirundo.)

χελίσκιον, τό, slight cough, Hp.ap.Gal.19.154.

χέλισκον, τό, = τρύβλιον, a dish, Hp.ap.Erot.

✱χελιχελώνη, ἡ, a girls' game, in which a ring was formed round a player called χελώνη, Poll.9.125, Eust.1914.54. The χελι- seems to be merely an iteration of the first syll. in χελώνη; cf. Carm.Pop. 21 (written χέλει χ. Eust. l. c.).

χελλαρίης, ου, ὁ, a sea-fish, = ὀνίσκος, Dorio ap. Ath.3.118c.

χελληστυάρχ-ας, α, ὁ, president of a χελληστύς, IG12(2).498, al. (Methymna). -εω, hold such office, ib.515 (ibid.).

χελληστύς, ύος, ἡ, = χιλιαστύς, at Methymna, IG12(2).498, al.

χέλλιοι, οἱ, Aeol. for χίλιοι, Hdn.Gr.2.604; cf. διςχέλιοι. χέλλος, τό, Aeol. for χεῖλος, ib.603. χελλύσσω, v. χελύσσομαι.

χελλών or χελών, ῶνος, ὁ, a kind of mullet, Mugil chelo, Arist. HA543$^b$15, 570$^b$2, 591$^a$23, Fr.318, Hices.ap.Ath.7.306e; χελλών (χελμών cod.)· ἰχθῦς ποιός, Hsch.

χελύδριον, τό, Dim. of sq., cj. for χένδριον in Gloss.

χέλυδρος, ὁ, amphibious serpent, Nic.Th.411. 2. a kind of tortoise, Sch.Lyc.340.

χελύκλονος, ον, resounding with tortoise-shell, φόρμιγξ Orph.A. 383 codd. (χελυκλόνου with Ἑρμάωνος Abel).

χέλυμνα, ἡ, = χελώνη, dub. in Babr.115.5.

χελῡνάζω, = χλευάζω, φλυαρέω, Hsch.

χελύνειον [ῡ], τό, (leg. χελύνιον) Dim. of sq. 2, Hp.Ep.23 codd.

✱χελύνη [ῡ], ἡ, = χεῖλος lip, ὑπ' ὀργῆς χελύνην ἐσθίειν Ar.V.1083 (troch.), Com.Vet.ap.Poll.2.89; Ion. gen. pl. χελυνέων Hsch. 2. jaw, Ael.NA16.12. II. = χελώνη I. 2, Nic.Al.555, 558 cod. Π, cj. in Olymp.in Mete.116.13.

✱χελύνιον [ῡ], τό, Dim. (in form only) of foreg. I. 1, lip, Mitteil. aus d. Papyrussamml. d. Nationalbibl. in Wien 1 (1932).160, Hippiatr. 1. 2. Dim. (in form only) of foreg. I. 2, jaw, Hp.Ep.23 (-ειον codd.), Hipparch.2.3.35, J.AJ4.4.4, Hippiatr.34. 3. cranium, Hipparch.3.2.8. II. = χελώνιον I. 1, Hsch.: pl., f.l. for χελώνια II, LxxDe.34.7 cod.Alex.

χελύννα, ἁ, Aeol. for χελώνη II. 2, Sapph.Oxy.1787 Fr.1 + 2.11, Erinn. in PSI9.1090.42 + 2 (p. xii), 1090.65.

χελῡνοίδης, ου, ὁ, with swollen lips, Com.Adesp.1194, Eust.1684.29.

χελῠοσσόος, ον, (χέλυς) stirring, sounding the lyre, Alex.Eph.ap. Theon.Sm.p.139H., Cat.Cod.Astr.1.173.

χέλυς, υος, ἡ, tortoise, h.Merc.33. 2. lyre (since Hermes made the first lyre by stretching strings on a tortoise's shell, which acted as a sounding-board), ib.25,153, Sapph.45, A.Fr.314; καθ' ἑπτάτονον ὀρείαν χ. E.Alc.448 (lyr.), cf. HF683 (lyr.). 3. the constellation Lyra, Arat.268. II. arched breast, chest, from its likeness of shape to the back of a tortoise, Hp.Anat.1, E.El. 837; cf. χελώνιον II. [ῠ in nom. and acc. sg., h.Merc.33,153; later ῡ, Call.Ap.16, Arat.268, Opp.H.5.404.] (Cf. OSlav. žely 'tortoise'.)

χέλυσμα, ατος, τό, sheathing like the shell of a tortoise, to protect the lower part of a ship during haulage, Thphr.HP5.7.2.

χελύσσομαι, Ep. χελλύσσομαι, expectorate, (χέλυς II) Nic.Al. 81, Moer.p.102 P.:—Hsch. cites χελούειν, = βήσσειν (Lacon. or Boeot.). II. Act. χελλύσσω, metaph. of a swimmer, spit out, i.e. the waves, Lyc.727, cf. Sch.ad loc.

χελῦτις, ἡ, a name of Artemis at Sparta, Clem.Al.Protr.2.38.5 (said to be from χελύσσω, = βήσσω).

χελών, ῶνος, ὁ, v. χελλών.

χελων-άριον, τό, Dim. of χελώνη, inferior tortoise-shell, Peripl. M.Rubr.10. 2. tail-piece, of the stand of a torsion-engine, Hero Bel.84.8.

χελώνειον, τό, v.l. for χελώνιον in Ael.NA7.16. II. = κυκλάμινος, Ps.-Dsc.2.164 (sed leg. χελ⟨ιδ⟩όνιον).

✱χελών-η, ἡ, tortoise, h.Merc.42,48, Orac.ap.Hdt.1.47,48; χ. χερσαία (cf. infr. 2) Arist.PA671$^a$28: prov. of insensibility, ἰὼ χελῶναι μακάριαι τοῦ δέρματος Ar.V.1292, cf. 429 (lyr.), S.Fr.279, Luc.Vit.Auct.9; of slowness, Plu.2.1082e, Lib.Ep.74.1, etc. 2. ποντιὰς χ. turtle, Crates Com.29; χ. θαλασσία Arist. l. c., cf. 540$^a$29, Ael.VH1.6, Paus. 1.44.8. II. tortoise-shell, Ph.2.478. 2. sounding-board of lyre, Plu.2.1030b. III. pent-house or shed for protecting beseigers, χ. ξυλίνη X.HG3.1.7, cf. Aen.Tact.32.11; χ. χωστρίς, used to protect sappers and miners, Plb.9.41.1, 10.31.8, Onos.42.3; κριοφόρος, to cover the battering-ram, D.S.20.48, etc., cf. App.Mith.31. b. = Lat. testudo, overlapping shields, D.C.49.30. 2. a kind of frame or cradle, on which heavy weights were moved by means of rollers underneath, Hero Mech. 3.1 (vol. ii p. 294 Schmidt). 3. footstool, Polem.Hist.44, Hsch., Suid. 4. coin bearing the impress of a tortoise, first coined at Aegina, Poll.9.74, Hsch. 5. pl., hillocks, LxxHo.12.11. 6. tomb with arched roof, JHS10.82 (Patara). 7. a kind of bandage, Heliod.ap.Orib.48.66 tit., Sor.Fasc.56. 8. part of a surgical machine, from its slow uniform motion, Orib. 49.4.45. 9. = χελώνιον III, IG11(2).159A 26,60 (Delos, iii B.C.). -ία and -ῖτις, ιδος, ἡ, tortoise-stone, name of a gem, Plin.HN37.155. -ιάς, άδος, ἡ, a kind of beetle, κανθαρίς Hsch. -ινος, η, ον, made of tortoise-shell, Edict.Diocl.16.6. -ιον, τό, tortoise-shell, Arist. PA671$^a$32, Resp.479$^a$6 (v.l. χελωνιδίων), Ael.NA7.16. 2. crab's shell, Plu.2.400a, Suid. s. v. Τενέδιος. II. arched part of the back, Poll.2.177: pl., muscles of the back, prob. for χελύνια in Lxx De.34.7. III. part of a lock, IG11(2).287A 46 (Delos, iii B.C.), Inscr.Délos 316.72 (iii B.C.), PTeb.46.17 (ii B.C.), BGU1028.20,26 (ii A.D.), *POxy*.113.4 (ii A.D.), Theognost.*Can*.124, Sch.Od.21.47. 2. *arch* or *bow* for releasing the string of the stomach-bow, Hero *Bel*.77.11. 3. *knob* against which the butt-ends of the arms of a torsion-engine rest, ib.93.7. 4. prob. part of an irrigation machine, *PLond*.3.1177.179 (ii A.D.); part of a crane in which the axle turns, Vitr.10.2.2, al. **-ίς**, ίδος, ἡ, = χέλυς I.2, *lyre*, Posidon. 10 J. II. = χελώνη III. 3, *footstool*, Att. and Coan word acc. to S.E.*M*.1.246. III. *threshold*, Lxx *Ju*.14.15, Hsch.

**χελωνοειδής**, ές, *like a tortoise*, Eust.869.24.

**χελωνός**, ὁ, *turtle*, Hsch. (Lobeck for χελῶνος).

**χελωνοφάγος** [ᾰ], ον, *eating tortoises*, name of an eagle or *Lämmergeier*, Hsch. II. *turtle-eaters*, pr. n. of a people on the Arabian Gulf, Str.16.4.14, D.S.3.21, etc.; on the Indian Ocean and Persian Gulf, Plin.*HN* 6.109, cf. 9.38, etc.

**χελώτρα**, ἡ, *stillicidium*, *Gloss*.

**χέννιον**, τό, *quail* (Egyptian *chennu*), salted and eaten by the Egyptians, *PSI*4.428.21, 7.862.11 (iii B.C.), Hipparch.Epic.ap.Ath. 9.393c, *AP*9.377 (Pall.), *PLond*.2.239.12 (iv A.D.). II. a kind of *fish*, Hsch.

**χενόσιρις**, ὁ, Egyptian name of *ivy*, Plu.2.365e.

**χέραβος**· χάσμα γῆς, Hsch.

⊛ **χέρᾰδος**, εος, τό, *silt, gravel, and rubbish*, brought down by torrents, ἅλις χέραδος περιχεύας Il.21.319; μὴ κίνη χέραδος Sapph. 114, cf. Alc.105 Lobel, Pi.*P*.6.13, A.R.1.1123; χεράδες (pl.) is given by Hsch., χεράδας is f.l. in Sapph. l.c. (ap.*EM*808.39), and so χεράδι (for χεράδει) in Pi. l.c., and χεράδος (for χέραδος) in A.R. l.c.; χέραδος is confirmed by Sch.Il. l.c., Apollon.*Lex*., *EM*808.40.

**χεράριος**, ὁ, a public officer at Ilium, perh. (from χείρ) = χειρονόμος (q.v.), *CIG*3620, 3621.

**χερδαμός**· λίθος πληρῶν τὴν χεῖρα, Hsch. (i.e. χερμάδιος).

**χέρεια**, v. χερείων.

**χερειότερος**, η, ον, Ep. Comp. for sq., Il.2.248, 12.270, *AP*7.371 (Crin.), Q.S.5.555.

**χερείων**, ὁ, ἡ, gen. ονος, nom. pl. χερείους A.R.2.1220:—Ep. for χείρων, *meaner, inferior*, in rank, worth, or wealth, κεῖνος δὲ χερείονος ἐκ θεοῦ ἐστιν Il.20.106, cf. Od.20.45; τὰ χερείονα νικᾷ Il.1.576; χερειονά περ καταπεφνών 17.539; in body or mind, ἐπεὶ οὔ ἑθέν ἐστι χ., οὐ δέμας οὐδὲ φυήν, οὔτ' ἂρ φρένας οὔτε τι ἔργα 1.114, cf. Od. 5.211; rare in Prose, ἄρχεσθαι ὑπὸ χερείονος Democr.49; opp. κάρρων, Aesar. ap. Stob.1.49.27. 2. of things, οὔ τι χέρειον ἐν ὥρῃ δεῖπνον ἑλέσθαι 'tis not *the worse part*, 'twere not *amiss*, Od.17.176, cf. 23.262. II. irreg. forms, dat. χέρηϊ, acc. χέρεια, nom. pl. χέρηες, acc. neut. χέρεια, all used in compar. sense, κρείσσων γὰρ βασιλεύς, ὅτε χώσεται ἀνδρὶ χέρηϊ with a man *of meaner rank*, Il.1.80; οἷά τε τοῖς ἀγαθοῖσι παραδρώωσι χέρηες Od.15.324; ἐσθλά τε καὶ τὰ χέρεια 18.229, 20.310; ἐσθλὰ μὲν ἐσθλὸς ἔδυνε, χέρεια δὲ χείρονι δόσκον, where ἐσθλὰ ἐσθλός and χέρεια χείρονι are evidently correlative, Il.14.382; c. gen., υἱὸν.. εἷο χέρεια μάχῃ, ἀγορῇ δὲ ἀμείνω 4.400; οὔ τι χέρεια πατρός Od.14.176.—χέρεια was written by Aristarch. in Od.14.176, where codd. have χερείω (χέρῃα Eust.488.38).

**χέρεσσι**, Ep. dat. pl. of χείρ, Hes.*Th*.519.

**χερϊάρης** [ᾰ], ου, ὁ, *skilled in fitting with the hand, dexterous*, τέκτονες Pi.*P*.5.35.

**χέριον**, τό, Dim. of χείρ, Sor.1.84, Paul.Aeg.6.74. 2. *small handle*, Hero *Aut*.24.3.

**χερϊφυρής**, ές, *mixed* or *kneaded by hand*, *AP*6.251 (Phil.).

**χέρμα**, ατος, τό, = χάλιξ, Hsch.; of the upper stone in an olive-press, Q.S.14.263 (s. v.l.).

**χερμ-άδιον** [ᾰ], τό, *large stone, boulder*, such as were used for missiles by the heroes of the Il., ὀκριόεν 4.518; μεγάλα 11.265, cf. 14.410; ὁ δὲ χερμάδιον λάβε χειρὶ.., μέγα ἔργον, ὃ οὐ δύο γ' ἄνδρε φέροιεν 5.302, 20.285; twice in Od., ἀνδραχθέσι χερμαδίοισι βάλλον, of the Laestrygones, 10.121, cf. 21.371. II. = χερμάς I, Aen. Tact.38.6.—Not a Dim. of χερμάς, but neut. of an Adj. **χερμάδιος**, ον, *of the shape* or *size of a* χερμάς, μολύβδαιναι χερμάδιοι leaden balls *for arm-exercises*, Luc.*Lex*.5. **-άζω**, *clear a field of stones*, Hsch. s. v. ἐχερμάζομεν. **-άς**, άδος, ἡ, *large pebble* or *stone*, esp. for throwing or slinging, *sling-stone*, τηλεβόλος Pi.*P*.3.49; ὀκριόεσσα A.*Th*.300 (lyr.); κραταίβολος E.*Ba*.1096: of *pebbles* on the sea-beach, A.R.2.695 (cf. στία), *AP*7.693 (Apollonid.); also in later Prose, D.H.9.21, al. II. in later Poets, *large block of stone*, Lyc.20,616, *AP*7.371 (Crin.). **-αστήρ**, ῆρος, ὁ, *slinger*, ῥινὸς χ. the leather *of a sling*, out of which the stone was thrown, ib.172 (Antip.Sid.), cf. Suid. **-άτης** [ᾱ], ου, ὁ, *slinger*, D.H.20. 1. **-ατιστής**· λίθος χειροπληθής, καὶ δίσκος βακχεῖος, Hsch.

**χέρνα**, ἡ, *poverty*, Hsch.; also **χέρνη**, ἡ, Sch.Orib.*inc*.22(6).13.

⊛ **Χέρνᾱσος**, prob. = Χερρόνησος, Χερσόνησος, ἐγ Χερνάσοις *Docum. ant. dell' Africa Italiana* ii *Cirenaica* 94.

**χερν-ής**, ῆτος, Dor. **χερνάς**, ᾶτος, ὁ, *poor, needy*, ἐν χερνῆσι δόμοις E.*El*.207 (lyr.); χερνῆτα βίον *AP*6.39 (Arch.); with fem. Subst., γυνὴ χ. Gal.ap.Orib.*inc*.22(6).13; χέρνης Hsch., but χερνής Hdn. Gr.1.64; fem. **χερνῆσσα** ib.1.250. (Acc. to Hsch. from χέρνα, *poverty*: but acc. to Arist.*Pol*.1277$^{a}$38 ὁ ζῶν ἀπὸ τῶν χειρῶν.) **-ήτης**, ου, ὁ, = χερνής, A.*Pr*.893 (lyr.), D.H.7.11, S.E.*M*.2.105, Ael.*Fr*.342; ἀνδρὸς χερνήτεω Simon.124A. **-ητικός**, ή, όν, *of* or *for a day-labourer*: τὸ χ. the *proletariate*, Arist.*Pol*.1291$^{b}$25. **-ῆτις**, ιδος, fem. of χερνήτης, *a woman that spins for daily hire*, γυνὴ χ. Il.12. 433, Parth.27.1, Cels.ap.Orig.*Cels*.1.28; γρηῦς χ. *AP*6.203 (Lacon. or Phil.): abs., ib.9.276 (Crin.), cf. Ael.*Fr*.343. **-ήτωρ**, ορος, ὁ, poet. for χερνήτης, Man.4.114.

**χερνῐβ-εῖον**, τό, *vessel for water to wash the hands, basin*, τὸ χ. πρῶτον, ἡ πομπὴ σαφής Antiph.66, cf. *IG*2$^{2}$.1400.41, al., *Michel* 832. 46 (pl., Samos, iv B.C.). **-ιον**, τό, Dim. of sq., Ar.*Fr*.316, And. 4.29 (cf. Ath.9.408c, wrongly citing Lys.). II. *chamber-pot*, Hp.*Epid*.7.83. **-ον**, τό, = χερνιβεῖον, Il.24.304, *IG*11(2).144*A* 32 (Delos, iv B.C.), cf. Hdn.Gr.1.378: pl. χέρνιβα Philostr.*Im*.2.23.

⊛ **χερνῐβόξεστον**, τό, *wash-basin*, *Stud.Pal*.20.151.10 (vi A.D.), prob. in *Gloss*.

**χέρνιμμα**, ατος, τό, *washing of the hands*, Philonid.14.

**χερνίπτομαι**, fut. -ψομαι E.*IT*622: Med.: (χείρ, νίζω):—*wash one's hands with holy water*, esp. before sacrifice, χερνίψαντο δ' ἔπειτα Il.1.449; αὐτός γε χερνίπτου Ar.*Pax* 961; ἐχερνίψατο ἐκ τῆς ἱερᾶς χέρνιβος Lys.6.52. 2. *sprinkle with holy water, purify* or *dedicate thereby*, χαίτην E. l.c. II. Act. χερνίπτω, *sacrifice*, only Lyc.184:—aor. Pass. χερνιφθείς *dedicated*, *AP*6.156 (Theodorid.).

**χερνίτης** [ῑ], ου, ὁ, *a kind of white marble*, Thphr.*Lap*.6, Plin.*HN* 36.132.

⊛ **χέρνιψ**, ἡ, used by Hom. (only in Od., v. infr.) always in acc. χέρνιβα; later in nom., A.*Eu*.656; gen. χέρνιβος S.*Fr*.1127.7, Ar. *Lys*.1129, Lys.6.52, D.20.158; dat. χέρνιβι Ar.*Av*.897 (lyr.), Th.4. 97; pl., freq. in Trag. (v. infr. 2); poet. dat. χερνίβεσσιν Simon.44: (χείρ, νίζω):—*water for washing the hands*, before meals, Od.1.136, 3.440, 4.52, etc.: esp. of holy water used before sacrifices, 3.445, Ar.*Av*.850, *Lys*.1129; ὕδωρ, ὃ ἦν ἄψαυστον σφίσι, πλὴν πρὸς τὰ ἱερὰ χέρνιβι χρῆσθαι Th. l.c.. εἴργεσθαι χέρνιβος D. l.c. 2. freq. in pl. χέρνιβες, *purifications with holy water*, Simon.45, E.*Or*.1602 *Ph*.662 (lyr.), etc.; χέρνιβας νέμειν allow *the use of holy water*, S.*OT*240; κοινωνὸς χερνίβων a partaker *therein*, i.e. an inmate of the same house or companion at table, A.*Ag*.1037; εἰς ἱέρ' εἰσιόντα καὶ χερνίβων καὶ κανῶν ἁψόμενον D.22.78, cf. E.*IA*675, 1479 (lyr.), *IT*58, 244, 335; προχύτας χέρνιβάς τ' ἐνάρξεται Id.*IA* 955; used before entering the house after a funeral, Id.*Alc*.100 (lyr., sg.). 3. rarely of *libations* to the dead, A.*Ch*.129. (On the accent v. Hdn.Gr.1.246.)

**χερο-κένως**, Adv. *with empty hands*, Lxx 1 *Ch*.12.33. **-μυσής**, ές, *defiling the hand*, φόνος A.*Ch*.73 (lyr.). ⊛ **-νησος**, ἡ, poet. for χερσόνησος, A.R.1.925, *IG*12(5).1076.98 (Ceos), D.H.*Comp*. 25. ⊛ **-νιπτρον**, τό, = χειρόνιπτρον, Eust.1351.53. **-πληθής**, ές, poet. for χειροπληθής, Nic.*Th*.94. **-πληκτος**, ον, *struck by the hand*, χερόπληκτοι.. δοῦποι the sound *of beating with the hand*, S.*Aj*. 632 (lyr., leg. -πλακτοι).

**χερρόνησος**, ἡ, Att. for χερσόνησος, also *OGI*330.4 (Thyatira, ii B.C.): for all words formed from it, v. χερσ-; for **χέρρος**, v. χέρσος.

**χερσ-άβροχος**, ἡ (sc. γῆ), *uninundated land*, *PRyl*.207(*a*).30 (ii A.D.) ⊛ **-αῖος**, α, ον, also ος, ον Lyc.534: (χέρσος):—*from* or *of dry land, living* or *found thereon*, ὄρνιθες χ., opp. λιμναῖοι, Hdt.7.119; κροκόδειλοι Id.4.192; ζῷα χ., opp. θαλάσσια, πετεινά, Id.2.123, cf. Pl. *Ti*.40a; χελώνη χ., opp. θαλασσία, v. χελώνη; μύες χ., Arist.*Mir*. 842$^{b}$7; ὄφεις, opp. θαλάττιαι, Id.*HA*505$^{b}$9; ἡ χ. (sc. θήρα) *hunting of land-animals*, opp. fishing, Pl.*Sph*.223b, cf. *AP*9.14 (Antiphil.); of *landsmen*, opp. seamen, E.*Andr*.457, Th.7.67; χ. παρασκευή, opp. ναυτική, Ascl.*Tact*.1.1; χ. πόλις *an inland* city, opp. seaport (ἐπιθαλαττίδιος), Pl.*Lg*.704b; ὁδοὶ χ., opp. voyages, *AP*11.42 (Crin.), cf. 4.3$^{b}$.46 (Agath.): *travelling by land*, βραδὺς καὶ χ. Ἔρως Plu.2.750b; κῦμα στρατοῦ, opp. a fleet, A.*Th*.64: neut. pl. as Adv., Arat. 919. II. ἡ χερσαῖος, as Subst., = χερσόνησος, Lyc.534. **-άλμη**, ἡ, *barren land covered with a crust of salt*, *PHamb*.12.9 (iii A.D.). **-αμμος**, ἡ, *sandy waste*, *POxy*.988 (iii A.D.). **-άμπελος**, ἡ (sc. χώρα), *dry vineland*, ib.506.25 (ii A.D.), 729.30 (ii A.D.). **-άνιππος**, ὁ, *unmounted desert-guard*, *PSI*4.399 (iii B.C.). **-άρᾰκος** [ᾰρ], ἡ (sc. γῆ), *inferior land planted with* ἄρακος, *PHib*.1.130 (iii B.C.). **-άσπορος**, ἡ (sc. γῆ), *land not worth sowing*, *PCair. Preis*.47.9 (iv A.D.). **-εία**, ἡ, *uncultivated state*, Hsch.; written χερσία, *CPR*233.7 (iv A.D.). **-εύω**, intr., *abide on dry land, live* or *lie thereon*, S.*Fr*.321, E.*Fr*.636, Plu.2.982b. 2. *to be dry land*, opp. ἔνυδρος εἶναι, Arist.*Mete*.352$^{a}$23. b. *lie waste* or *barren*, X.*Oec*. 5.17, 16.5. II. Pass., *to be left as dry land*, opp. πλωτὰ εἶναι, Arist.*Mete*.353$^{a}$25 (v. l. -εύει). III. *make* or *leave barren*, *PTeb*.61 (*b*).114, 74.29 (ii B.C.):—Pass., *to be made, become barren*, Plu.2.2d, Epist.Philipp. in *IG*9(2).517.30 (Larissa, iii B.C.), *PTeb*.61(*b*).144, 202, al. (ii B.C.), *BGU*1120.31 (i B.C.), etc. **-έφιππος**, ὁ, *mounted desert-guard*, *PTeb*.62.34 (ii B.C.). **-ία**, v. χερσεία. **-ῖνος**, η, ον, = χερσαῖος, of tortoises, Plin.*HN*9.38. **-ίτης** [ῑ], ου, ὁ, perh. *cultivator of waste land*, *PPetr*.2 p.110 (iii B.C.).

**χερσό-βιος**, ον, *living on dry land*, opp. λιμνόβιος, Philum.*Ven*. 36.1. **-θεν**, Adv. *from dry land*, opp. sea, E.*Heracl*.429, *Hel*. 1269. II. *from the ground*, opp. water, Pi.*O*.2.73. **-θί**, Adv. *on dry land*, *AP*9.105. **-θρύϊον** [ῠ], τό, (θρύον) *land overgrown with rushes*, *Ostr*.1224. **-θρῦϊτις**, ιδος, ἡ (sc. γῆ), = foreg., *POxy*.1347 (iii A.D.).

**χερσοκοπ-έω**, *break up unirrigated land*, *PTeb*.105.18 (ii B.C.). **-ία**, ἡ, *breaking up of unirrigated land*, ib.20. **-ος** (parox.), ὁ, *worker on unirrigated land*, *BGU*1527.1 (iii B.C.).

**χέρσονδε**, Adv. *to* or *on dry land*, Il.21.238, *h.Ap*.28, Alcm.6, Theoc.16.61.

**χερσονησ-ίζω**, later Att. **χερρ-**, *form a peninsula*, Plb.1.73.4,

10.10.5: **χερρονησιάζω** is read in Str.11.14.6 and is v.l. Id.2.5.29, 11.1.5. **-ιος,** later **χερρ-,** *α, ον, peninsular,* Hsch. II. *of the Thracian Chersonese,* E.*Hec.*8,33, al. III. Χερσονήσια, τά, festival at Delos, *Inscr.Délos* 353*B* 45, 366*A* 132 (iii B.C.). 2. **χερσονήσιον,** *τό, revenue from the* χερσόνησος (a domain of the Delian temple), ib.354.22, al. (iii B.C.). **-ίτης** [ῑ], later **χερρ-,** *ου, ὁ, dweller in the Thracian Chersonese,* X.*HG*1.3.10, 3.2.8, D.5.25. **-οειδής,** later **χερρ-,** *ές, peninsular,* Hdt.7.22, Str.9.1.9; *σκόπελος,* of Circeii, D.H.4.63. **-ος,** *ἡ,* later **χερρόνησος,** poet. **χερόνησος** (q.v.), Dor. **χερσόνᾱσος** *SIG* 709.52 (ii B.C.), **χέρνασος** (q.v.):—*peninsula,* Hdt. 4.12, Th.6.97, Str.16.2.10, Plu.*Pyrrh.*6, etc. 2. *island with a bridge to it,* Paus.5.24.1. II. as pr. n., of various peninsulas, esp. 1. *the Chersonese,* i.e. the peninsula of Thrace that runs along the Hellespont, Hdt.6.33. 2. the *Tauric Chersonese* or *Crimea,* Id.4.99, etc. 3. the peninsula between Epidaurus and Troezen, Th.4.42. **-ώδης,** *ες,* later **χερρ-,** = χερσονησοειδής, Str.14.6.3.

⊛ **χερσονομή,** *ἡ,* in pl., *waste land used as pasture, PTeb.*74.22 (ii B.C., prob.), *Sammelb.*5172.5.

⊛ **χέρσος,** later Att. **χέρρος,** *ἡ, dry land,* opp. water, ἐπὶ χέρσου, opp. ἐν πόντῳ, Od.10.459, cf. 15.495; κύματα μακρὰ κυλινδόμενα προτὶ χέρσον 9.147; λάϊγγας ποτὶ χ. ἀποπλύνεσκε θάλασσα 6.95; κῦμα..βοάᾳ ποτὶ χ. Il.14.394; κῦμα..χέρσῳ ῥηγνύμενον μεγάλα βρέμει 4.425; χέρσον ἱκέσθαι Od.9.486, 542; ἐπὶ χέρσω Sapph.*Supp.*9.10; κατὰ χέρσον A.*Pers.*873 (lyr.), E.*IT*884 (lyr.); χέρσῳ *on* or *by land,* A.*Pers.*977 (lyr.), *Ag.*558, E.*Hel.* 1066: prov., ἐν πόντῳ νᾶες, ἐν χέρσῳ πόλεμοι Pi.*O.*12.4, cf. *N.*1.62; πολλὰ..ἐκ θαλάσσης, πολλὰ δ' ἐκ χέρσου κακὰ γίγνεται A.*Pers.*707 (troch.); πάνδοκον εἰς ἀφανῆ τε χ., of the realm of Hades, Id.*Th.*860 (lyr.).—In Hom. the gender cannot be determined, fem. Pi.*Fr.*75.17 (dub. l.), A.*Supp.*31 (anap.), Thphr.*CP*3.13.3, D.S.3.15, etc.: pl., ἐν ταῖς χέρσοις on *barren soils,* Thphr.*HP*8.6.4. II. after Hom. as Adj., χέρσος, ον, *dry, firm,* of land, Hdt.2.99; Εὐρώπαν ποτὶ χέρσον to *the mainland* of Europe, Pi. *N.*4.70; ἐν κονίᾳ χέρσῳ, opp. πόντῳ, ib.9.43. 2. *dry, hard, barren,* τῆς χώρης ἐούσης χ. Hdt.4.123; στύφλος δὲ γῆ καὶ χ. S.*Ant.*251; παραδοῦναι [τὴν γῆν] χέρρον, i.e. ψιλήν, *without a crop* on it, *IG*2$^{2}$. 2492.16; χ. καὶ ἄκανθα ἔσται ἡ γῆ Lxx *Is.*7.24; χέρσα *waste places,* A.*Fr.*189; χ. λιμήν a harbour *left dry, AP*9.427 (Barb.): freq. in Pap., *PAmh.*2.31.12 (ii B.C.), etc. 3. metaph., *barren,* of women, χέρσους φθαρῆναι κἀγάμους S.*OT*1502. b. c. gen., *barren of,* πυρὰ χέρσος ἀγλαϊσμάτων E.*El.*325. (Cf. Skt. *hárṣate* 'become stiff, bristle', Avest. *zarštva-* 'stone', Lat. *horreo.*)

**χερσ-όω,** *make into dry land,* Tz.*H.*2.27; *make dry and barren, BGU*195.19 (ii A.D.):—Pass., *to be left dry and barren,* γῆ κεχερσωμένη Plu.2.10d, Lxx *Pr.*24.46 (31), *PTeb.*5.94 (ii B.C.), cf. *IGRom.*4. 147 (Cyzicus). **-υδρος,** *ὁ, an amphibious serpent,* Nic.*Th.*359, Androm.ap.Gal.14.34, Philum.*Ven.*24.1. **-ώδης,** *ες, barren,* of land, *PLond.*5.1674.30 (vi A.D.); = *dumosus, Gloss.*

**χερύδριον,** *τό,* Dim. of χείρ, *little hand* or *arm,* Mosch.1.13.

**χεσᾶς,** *ᾶντος, ὁ,* = χεζητιῶν, Poll.5.91, Sch.Ar.*Av.*791, Suid.

**χεσείω,** Desiderat. of χέζω, Ar.*Eq.*888, *Nu.*295 (anap.).

**χεσῐφωνέω,** *use filthy language,* prob. for χθεσι- in Hsch., Suid.

**χέσμα,** *ατος, τό, excrement,* Heras ap.Gal.12.939,942, *Gloss.*

**χεῦα, χεῦαν, χεῦε,** v. χέω.

**χεῦμα,** *ατος, τό,* (χέω) *that which is poured, stream,* χ. κασσιτέροιο *stream of molten* tin, Il.23.561; χ. θαλάσσης A.*Fr.*192.2 (anap.); πόντου E.*Fr.*316.2, *Trag.Adesp.*157; ποτάμιον χ. ὑδάτων E.*Hel.*1304 (lyr.); χ. Ἐρασίνου A.*Supp.*1020 (lyr.), cf. *Eu.*293; χ. ἀκήρατον pure *spring water,* S.*OC*471; even σταθερὸν χ. standing *water,* A.*Fr.*276; also ἄνεμός ἐστιν ἠέρος ῥεῦμα καὶ χ. Hp.*Flat.*3: pl., *streams,* Σκαμάνδρου Pi.*N.*9.39, cf. A.*Supp.*1028 (lyr.), E.*Ph.*793 (lyr.). 2. generally, χ. νιφετοῖο *fall* of snow, Nonn.*D.*3.213, cf. 210. 3. metaph., *stream, flow,* εὔμουσα χ. *AP*9.661 (Jul.Aeg.): of language, Longin.13.1. II. pl., *cast vessels, bowls,* χεύματα ἀργύρεα κυκλοτερέα Hdt.1.51, cf. Poll.10.82.

**χεύω,** v. sq.

⊛ **χέω,** used in the simple form mostly by Poets, but v. ἐγ-, κατα-, συγ-χέω; -εει is not contr. by Ep., v. Il.6.147, 9.15, Hes.*Op.*421; but in Trag. and Att. always so, ἐκ-χεῖ, συγ-χεῖς, κατα-χεῖν, S.*El.* 1291, E.*IA*37 (anap.), Ar.*Eq.*1091 (hex.); for -εε no rule is observed, impf. χέε Il.23.220; but σύγ-χει 9.612, 13.808, χεῖσθαι Od.10.518; κατ-έχεε Ar.*Nu.*74, D.45.74; ἐν-έχει, ἐν-έχεις, ἐξ-έχει, Antipho 1.19, Ar.*Pl.*1021, A.*Ag.*1029 (lyr.):— -έῃ, -έο, -έου, -έω seem never to have been contracted, exc. ἐγχεῦντα Theoc.10.53:—fut. χέω (ἐκ-χεῶ acc. to Choerob. *in Theod.*2.168 H., but this is Hellenistic, Lxx *Je.*6.11, al., ἐκ-χεεῖς ib.*Ex.*4.9, ἐκ-χεεῖ ib.*Le.*4.18,25, ἐκ-χεεῖτε ib.*De.*12.16,24, ἐκ-χεοῦσι ib.*Le.*4.12, προσ-χεεῖς ib.*Ex.* 29.16, al., and the Med. χεόμενος (v. infr.) points to Att. χέω), συγ- E.*Fr.*384, ἐπι-χεῖς Ar.*Pax*169 (anap.); παρα-χέων Pl.Com. 69.3; Ep. fut. χεύω Od.2.222 (χρειώ Aristarch., whence χείω Porson): aor. ἔχεα Il.18.347, Pi.*I.*8(7).64, etc.; Ep. ἔχευα Il.3.270, 4.269, χεῦα 14.436, Od.4.584, etc.; Ep. aor. 1 subj. χεύομεν Il.7.336 (late ἔχευσα *AP*14.124 (Metrod.)): pf. κέχῠκα, (ἐκ-) Men.915, *APl.*4. 242 (Eryc.):—Med., fut. Att. χεόμενος Is.6.51: aor. ἐχεάμην Hdt.7. 43, A.*Pers.*220 (troch.), S.*OC*477, Ar.*V.*1020 (anap.); Ep. ἐχευάμην, χευάμην, Il.5.314, 18.24, etc.; Ep. subj. χεύεται (περι-) Od.6.232 (perh. indic.):—Pass., fut. χῠθήσομαι (συγ-) D.23.62, cf. J.*AJ*8. 8.5: later χεθήσομαι, (ἐκ-) Arr.*Epict.*4.10.26:—aor. 1 ἐχύθην [ῠ] Od.19.590, etc.: later ἐχέθην, not in Inscrr. or Pap., f.l. in Ph.1. 455, Euc.*Catoptr.Prooem.* (vii p. 286 H., ἐγ-, ἐκ-), etc.: also Ep. aor. χύτο [ῠ] Il.23.385, Od.7.143; ἐξ-έχῠτο 19.470; ἔχυντο, χύντο, 10.415, Il.4.526; part. χύμενος, η, ον, 19.284, Od.8.527, and Trag. in lyr., A.*Ch.*401, *Eu.*263, E.*Heracl.*76: pf. κέχῠμαι Il.5.141, Sapph. *Supp.*25.12, Pi.*I.*1.4, etc.: plpf. Ep. κέχῠτο Il.5.696, etc.—Ep. pres. **χείω,** Hes.*Th.*83; later Ep. pres. **χεύω** both in the simple Verb and compds., Nic.*Al.*381, *Lyr.Alex.Adesp.*35.19 (fort. Mesom.), Nonn. D.18.344, Opp.*C.*2.127:—Med., χεύομαι A.R.2.926: in later Prose pres. **χύνω** (q.v.); χῦσαι is f.l. for λῦσαι in codd. dett. of Tryph. 205.—Rare in Prose, exc. in compds. and in Med.

Radic. sense, *pour*: I. prop. of liquids, *pour out, let flow,* κρήνη κατ' αἰγίλιπος πέτρης χέει ὕδωρ Il.9.15; βασιλεῦσιν ὕδωρ ἐπὶ χεῖρας ἔχευαν 3.270, cf. Od.1.146, etc.; οἶνον χαμάδις χέε Il.23.220; κατὰ στόματος νέκταρ Theoc.7.82: χέει ὕδωρ, of Zeus, i.e. makes it rain, Il.16.385; ὅταν βορέας χιόνα..χέῃ E.*Cyc.*328: abs., χέει it *snows,* Il.12.281 (νειφέμεν is in l. 280): freq. of drink-offerings, χέουσα χοάς A.*Ch.*87:—Med., χοὴν χεῖσθαι νεκύεσσι Od.10.518; χοὴν χεόμην νεκύεσσι 11.26; χοὰς χέασθαι Hdt.7.43, etc.: abs., Is.6.51,65:—Pass., κέχυται Il.12.284; κρῆναι χέονται they *gush forth,* E.*Hipp.*748 (lyr.); ποτοῦ χυθέντος ἐς γῆν S.*Tr.*704; χέεσθαι βουτύρῳ, γάλακτι *to flow with..,* Lxx *Jb.*29.6. 2. χ. δάκρυα *shed* tears, δάκρυα θερμὰ χέοντες Il.7.426, cf. 16.3, E.*Tr.*38; ἀπ' ὀφθαλμῶν Id.*Cyc.*405:—Med., ὅσα σώματα χεῖται Pl.*Ti.*83e:—Pass., of tears, *flow,* δάκρυα θερμὰ χέοντο Od.4.523; ἀπ' ὀφθαλμῶν χύτο δάκρυα Il.23.385; of blood, *to be shed, drip,* φονίας σταγόνας χυμένας ἐς πέδον A.*Ch.*401 (anap.), cf. *Eu.*263 (lyr.). 3. *smelt* metal, Lxx *Ma.*3.3. b. *cast,* of bronze statues, *SIG* 3*g* (Susa, from Didyma, vi (?) B.C.). 4. Pass., *become liquid, melt, dissolve,* τὰ κεχυμένα, opp. τὰ συνεστῶτα, Pl.*Ti.*66c; of the ground in spring, X.*Oec.*16.12, Thphr.*CP*3.4.4; κεχυμένοι ὀφθαλμοί perh. *moist, languishing* eyes, Heph.Astr.1.1. II. of solids, *shed, scatter,* φύλλα ἄνεμος χαμάδις χέει Il.6.147; κῦμα φῦκος ἔχευεν 9.7; πτερὰ ἔραζε Od. 15.527; ἐν.. ἄλφιτα χ. δοροῖσιν *pour* into.., 2.354; [κρέα] εἰν ἐλεοῖσιν Il.9.215; κόνιν κὰκ κεφαλῆς 18.24, Od.24.317; καλάμην χθονί, of a mower or reaper, Il.19.222:—Pass., ἐν νάσῳ κέχυται σπέρμα Pi.*P.* 4.42; πάγου χυθέντος when the frost *was on the ground,* S. *Ph.*293; κέχυται νόσος *has spread through* his frame, Id.*Tr.*853 (lyr.). 2. *throw up* earth, so as to form a mound, σῆμ' ἔχεαν Il.24.799; χεύαντες δὲ τὸ σῆμα ib.801, cf. Od.1.291; τύμβον χ. Il.7.336, etc.; θανόντι χυτὴν ἐπὶ γαῖαν ἔχευαν Od.3.258, cf. Il.23. 256. 3. χ. δούρατα *shower* spears, 5.618:—Med., βέλεα χέοντο they *showered their* darts, 8.159. 4. *let fall, drop,* κατὰ δ' ἡνία χεῦεν ἔραζε 17.619; εἴδατα ἔραζε Od.22.20; ἀπὸ κρατὸς χέε (v.l. for βάλε) δέσματα Il.22.468; κρόκου βαφὰς ἐς πέδον χέουσα A.*Ag.*239 (lyr.) (but καρπὸν χ., of trees, not *to shed* their fruit, but *to let* it *hang down* in profusion, Od.11.588):—Pass., πλόκαμος γένυν παρ' αὐτὴν κεχυμένος *streaming down, falling,* E.*Ba.*456. 5. in Pass., *to be heaped up, massed together,* [ἰχθύες] ἐπὶ ψαμάθοισι κέχυνται Od. 22.387, cf. 389; of dead geese, 19.539; of dung, 17.298, Il.23.775; also σωρὸν σίτου κεχυμένον Hdt.1.22. 6. Pass., of living beings, *stream in a dense throng,* Il.16.267, etc.; δακρυόεντες ἔχυντο Od.10. 415, etc.: of sheep, Il.5.141. 7. of persons, ἀμφ' αὐτῷ χυμένη *throwing herself* around him, 19.284, Od.8.527:—Med., ἀμφὶ φίλον υἱὸν ἐχεύατο πήχεε Il.5.314:—Pass., of things, ἀμφὶ δὲ δεσμοὶ τεχνήεντες ἔχυντο Od.8.297. 8. pf. Pass. κέχυμαι, *to be wholly engaged* or *absorbed in,* Δᾶλος, ἐν ᾇ κέχυμαι Pi.*I.*1.4; κεχυμένος ἐς τἀφροδίσια, Lat. *effusus in Venerem,* Luc.*Sacr.*5; πρὸς ἡδονήν Alciphr.1. 6. III. of impalpable things: 1. of the voice, φωνήν, αὐδὴν χ., Od.19.521, Hes.*Sc.*396, cf. *Th.*83; ἐπὶ θρῆνον ἔχεαν Pi.*I.* 8(7).64; Ἑλλάδος φθόγγον χέουσα A.*Th.*73, cf. *Supp.*632 (lyr.), *Fr.*36 (lyr.); of wind instruments, πνεῦμα χέων ἐν αὐλοῖς Simon. 148.8, cf. *APl.*4.226 (Alc.):—Med., κωμῳδικὰ πολλὰ χέασθαι Ar.*V.* 1020 (anap.):—but in Pass., κεχυμένα ᾄσματα *non-rhythmical* melodies, Aristid.Quint.1.13. b. κὰκ κεφαλῆς χεῦεν πολὺ κάλλος Od.23.156; δόλον περὶ δέμνια χεῦεν 8.282. 2. of things that obscure the sight, κατ' ὀφθαλμῶν χέεν ἀχλύν *shed* a dark cloud over the eyes, Il.20.321; πολλὴν ἠέρα χεῦε *shed* a mist abroad, Od.7.15, etc. (so εὔκρατος ἀὴρ χεῖται Pl.*Ax.*371d); τῷ δ' ὕπνον ἀπήμονά τε λιαρόν τε χεύῃ ἐπὶ βλεφάροισιν Il.14.165, cf. Od.2.395, etc.:—Pass., ἀμφὶ δέ οἱ θάνατος χύτο *was shed* around him, Il.13.544; κατ' ὀφθαλμῶν κέχυτ' ἀχλύς 5.696; νύξ Hes.*Th.*727 (but πάλιν χύτο ἀήρ the mist *dissolved* or *vanished,* Od.7.143); οὔ κέ μοι ὕπνος ἐπὶ βλεφάροισι χυθείη 19.590; ἐχεύατο πόντον ἔπι φρίξ (Med. in pass. sense) Il.7.63. 3. aor. Pass., ἐχύθη οἱ θυμός his mind *overflowed with joy,* A.R.3.1009. 4. Pass., *to be dissipated, diffused,* Plot. 1.4.10; οὐδὲν τοῦ χεῖσθαι δεηθέν Id.6.5.3; *to be rarefied,* opp. πιλεῖσθαι, Gal.15.28. (Cf. Skt. *juhóti* 'pour (sacrificial offerings)', part. *hutás* (= χυτός), Lat. *fundo,* Goth. *giutan* 'pour'.)

**χῆ·** ἔθος, ἀπορία, Hsch.

**χηλαμός,** late form of χηραμός, Eust.1248.53.

**χηλαργός,** Dor. **χᾱλ-,** *όν,* (χηλή) *with fleet hoofs,* χ. ἅμιλλαι the racing *of fleet horses,* S.*El.*861 (lyr.).

**χηλ-ᾶς,** *ὁ,* = ῥάπτης, πλέκτης, Hsch. **-ευμα,** *ατος, τό, awl,* S.*Fr.* 486, Poll.7.83, 10.141, Hsch. **-ευτός,** *ή, όν, netted, plaited,* κράνεα Hdt.7.89, cf. Poll.7.83. **-εύω,** (χηλή III. 5) *net, plait,* Eup.388, Hsch. II. Pass., κεχήλευμαι πόδας I *have my* feet *stitched together, Trag.Adesp.*220. ⊛ **-ή,** Dor. **χᾱλά,** *ἡ, horse's hoof,* Hes.*Sc.*62, E.*Ph.* 42, *Ion*1242 (lyr.), cf. χηλαργός. 2. of oxen and the like, *cloven hoof,* χηλαὶ ποδῶν Id.*Ba.*619 (troch.), cf. A.R.2.667; τὰ δὲ δισχιδῆ καὶ ἀντὶ τῶν ὀνύχων χηλὰς ἔχει Arist.*HA*499$^{b}$9, cf. *PA*655$^{b}$4, 663$^{a}$29; of

Chimaera, E.*El.*474 (lyr.). **3.** crab's *claw*, Arist.*HA* 527$^{b}$5, *PA* 684$^{a}$27; *ὅ τι ἂν λάβῃ, προσάγεται πρὸς τὸ στόμα τῇ δικρόᾳ χηλῇ καθάπερ οἱ καρκίνοι* Id.*HA* 590$^{b}$25: hence, **b.** Astron., Χηλαί, αἱ, the *claws* of the Scorpion, i.e. the constellation *Libra*, Arat.89, 232, al., Ptol.*Tetr.*24, etc. **4.** poet. pl., *talons* of a bird, A.*Pers.* 208, S.*Ant.*1003, E.*Ion* 1208; of the Sphinx, Id.*Ph.*808 (lyr.), 1025 (lyr.); of a wolf's *claws*, Theoc.*Epigr.*6.4, cf. E.*Hec.*90 (lyr., expld. by Hsch. = *γνάθος*). **II.** *breakwater*, formed of stones laid at the base of a sea-wall, mostly in pl., Th.1.63 (ubi v. Sch.), 7.53, X.*An.*7.1.17; *αἱ χ. τοῦ λιμένος* D.S.13.78, cf. D.C.74.10; sg., D.S. 3.44; *ἐπαιγιαλῖτις χ.* *AP* 10.8 (Arch.). **2.** *spur of a mountain* or *ridge of rocks* answering a like purpose, *χ. γὰρ τοῦ Πειραιῶς ἡ Ἠετιώνεια* Th.8.90, cf. Plu.*Sol.*9, Anon.ap.Suid. s.v. *χ. ὄρους*. **III.** of various *cloven* or *hooked implements*: **1.** in surgery, *forked probe*, Hp.*Morb.* 2.33. **2.** *notch* of an arrow, Hero *Bel.*111.1, Hsch. s.v. *γλυφίδες*; but also (pl.) the *claws* composing the hook (*χείρ*), Hero ib.2; also the *claws* or *arms* of the *σκορπίος* v, Vitr.10.10.4, 10.11.7. **3.** *rims of the eyelids*, Ruf.*Onom.*20. **4.** *crack* in the heels or other parts, Poll.4.198. **5.** *net, plait*, Hsch. s.v. *χηλευτὰ κράνη*. **-ινος,** *η, ον,* = *χηλευτός, ἄγγος* Anacr.37.

**χηλοδευσεῖν·** *ἀδολεσχεῖν, οἱ δὲ τρίβειν*, Hsch.

**χηλός,** *ἡ*, *large chest, coffer*, *χηλοῦ δ' ἀπὸ πῶμ' ἀνέῳγε καλῆς δαιδαλέης* Il.16.221; *ἐϋξέστῃ ἐνὶ χηλῷ* Od.13.10, etc.; *κενεᾶς ἐν πυθμένι χηλοῦ* Theoc.16.10. **II.** *coffin*, *IG* 12(8).600.6 (Thasos).

**χηλ-όω,** *notch arrows*, Ph.*Bel.*77.8:—Pass., of a hook, *to be equipped with claws*, Hero *Bel.*111.1. ⊛**-ωμα,** *ατος, τό*, *notch*, Hp.ap. Gal.19.155, Eratosth.*Cat.*29. **-ώτιον,** *τό*, *netting-needle*, Hsch.

**χῆμαι,** gloss on *γλίσχραι*, Hsch.

**χημ-εία, -ευτικός,** v. *χυμ-εία, -ευτικός*.

**χήμη,** *ἡ*, (*χάσκω*) *yawning, gaping*, Hsch. **II.** *clam*, Philyll. 13, Arist.*HA* 547$^{b}$13, Ael.*NA* 15.12; *χ. τραχεῖαι, λεῖαι*, *PCair.Zen.* 82.12 (iii B.C.), cf. Xenocr.*Aq.*31. **2.** *measure*, Hp.*Mul.*1.75, 78: there were larger and smaller kinds, Cleopatra ap.Gal.19.769.

**Χημία,** *ἡ*, *Black-land, Chemmi*, Egyptian name for Egypt, Plu. 2.364c. (Egypt. *Kmt*, Copt. **ⲕⲏⲙⲉ, ϫⲏⲙⲓ** 'Egypt'.)

**χημίον,** *τό*, Dim. of *χήμη*, Gal.6.734, Orib.3.28.1.

**χήμωσις,** *εως, ἡ*, *an affection of the eyes*, when the cornea swells *like a cockle-shell* (*χήμη*) so as to impede sight, Gal.19.436, Demosth. Ophth.ap.Orib.*Syn.*8.42, Paul.Aeg.3.22.

**χήν,** *ὁ* and *ἡ*, Dor. **χάν** (q.v.), gen. *χηνός*: Ion. gen. pl. *χηνῶν* (not *χηνέων*) Hdt.2.45; irreg. acc. pl. *χένας* *AP* 7.546:—*wild goose, Anser cinereus*, *χηνῶν ἢ γεράνων ἢ κύκνων* Il.2.460; *χ. πλατυγίζων καὶ κεχηνώς* Eub.115, cf. Arist.*HA* 593$^{b}$22; *εἰ μὴ σὺ χηνὸς ἧπαρ ἢ ψυχὴν ἔχεις* Eub.101. **2.** *tame goose*, *χῆν' ἥρπαξ' ἀτιταλλομένην ἐνὶ οἴκῳ* Od.15.174, cf. 161; *χῆνές μοι κατὰ οἶκον ἐείκοσι πυρὸν ἔδουσιν* 19.536; *χ. τιθασός* S.*Fr.*866; *ὥσπερ χῆνα σιτευτὸν..ἔτρεφέ με* Epigen.2; *γάλακτι χηνός*, of an unknown luxury, Eub.90.5; *ἥπατα χηνῶν* Plu.2.965a. **3.** *νὴ* or *μὰ τὸν χῆνα* was Socrates' oath, Ar.*Av.*521 (anap., ubi v. Sch.), Cratin.231, Zen.5.81. (Cf. Skt. *haṃsás*, Lith. *žąsìs*, OHG. *gans*, all = *goose*.)

⊛ **χηνάγριον,** *τό*, *young wild goose*, *POxy.*1923.22 (v/vi A.D.). **2.** a woman's ornament, *PLond.ined.*2199 (iv A.D.).

**χηνάλοπες,** = *χηναλώπεκες*, Hsch.

**χηνᾰλωπ-έκειος,** *α, ον*, *of the χηναλώπηξ*, *ᾠά* *PLond.ined.*2098 (iii B.C., written *-εα*), *PCair.Zen.*562.17 (iii B.C.), Epaenet. and Heraclid.Syrac.ap.Ath.2.58b. **-εκιδεύς,** *έως, ὁ*, *young of the χ.*, Ael.*NA* 7.47. **-ηξ,** *εκος, ὁ* (*ἡ* Herod.4.31. v.l. in Ael.*NA* 5.30), *Egyptian goose, Chenalopex aegyptiaca*, Hdt.2.72, Ar.*Av.*1295, Arist.*HA* 593$^{b}$22, Herod.4.31.

**χην-αμύχη,** *ἡ*, = *νυκτήγρετον*, Plin.*HN* 21.62. **-άριον,** *τό*, Dim. of *χήν*, Cyran.100, Hdn.*Epim.*150, *Et.Gud.*563. **-ειος,** *α, ον*, Ion. **χήνεος,** *η, ον* (also *PCair.Zen.*130.26 (iii B.C.)): (*χήν*):—*of* or *belonging to a goose*, *κρεῶν βοέων καὶ χηνέων πλῆθος* Hdt. 2.37; *ᾠόν* Arist.*HA* 558$^{a}$22, cf. *PCair.Zen.* l.c.; *χήνεια* (sc. *κρέα*) Menipp.ap.Ath.14.664e; *στέαρ* Dsc.1.68.3, Sor.1.50; *χήνεια ἥπατα*, a Greek dainty, *foie gras*, Ath.9.384c (*ἀρνεία* shd. be read in E.*Fr.*467). **-έρως,** *ωτος, ἡ*, a small kind of *goose*, Plin.*HN* 10.56. **-ημα,** *ατος, τό*, *wide gape, mocking laugh*, Hsch.; also aor. **χηνῆσαι·** *καταμωκήσασθαι*, from *χηνάω* or *-έω*. ⊛**-ιάζω,** *cackle like a goose*, of a bad flute-player, Diph.77. **-ῐδεύς,** *έως, ὁ*, *gosling*, Ael.*NA* 7.47, Eust.753.56. **-ίζω,** = *χηνιάζω*, Ath.14. 657e. **-ίον,** *τό*, *gosling*, *BGU* 1501 (Ptolemaic). **-ίσκος,** *ὁ*, Dim. of *χήν*, Eub.15.3. **II.** *top of a ship's stern post in the form of a goose's head and neck*, Ptol.*Alm.*8.1, Luc.*VH* 2.41, *Nav.*5, *JTr.*47, Artem.2.23, Eust.667.16. **2.** ornament on a bowl, *Inscr.Délos* 372 *B* 72 (iii/ii B.C.); part of a machine, Orib.49.4.28.

**χηνο-βοσία,** *ἡ*, *keeping* or *feeding of geese*, Att. acc. to Moer. p.403 P.: pl., Poll.9.16 (misquoting Plato, v. *χηνοβωτία*). **-βοσκικός,** *ή, όν*, *of a gooseherd*, *κλῆρος* Pap. in *Atti del IV Congresso Internazionale di Papirologia* p.70 (Ptolemaic). **-βόσκιον,** *τό*, *place for feeding geese, goose-pen*, *Gp.*14.22.1; written *chenoboscion*, Varro *RR* 3.10.1, Colum.8.14.1; as place-name, *PGrenf.*1.42.14 (ii B.C.), Mitteis *Chr.*87.38 (ii A.D.). **-βοσκός,** *ὁ*, *gooseherd*, Cratin.46, *PTeb.*701.290 (iii B.C.), *Ostr.Bodl.* i 304 (ii B.C.), *Sammelb.*6254 (ii B.C.), D.S.1.74; *βασιλικοὶ χ.* *PPetr.*2 p.25 (iii B.C.). **-βωτία,** *ἡ*, = *χηνοβοσία*, Pl.*Plt.*264c (pl.). **-μεγέθης,** *ες*, *as large as a goose*, Str.15.1.57. **-τροφεῖον,** *τό*, = *χηνοβόσκιον*, Colum.8.1.3 (v.l. **-τρόφιον**). **-τρόφος,** *ον*, = *χηνοβοσκός*, *Sammelb.*5380, *EM* 811.1: misspelt *-τρόπος* *Ostr.*304 (ii A.D.).

**χην-ύστρα,** *ἡ*, = *χάσμη*, Hsch.; also, = *τὸ στραγγεύεσθαι*, Id. **-υστράομαι,** *yawn*, Id. **-υστ⟨ρ⟩εῖς·** *βοᾷς*, Id.

**χηνώδης,** *ες*, *like a goose*, S.E.*M.*7.329.

**χήρ,** *ὁ*, gen. *χηρός*, *hedgehog*, Hsch. (Cf. Lat. *ēr*.)

**χήρ-α,** Ion. **χήρη,** *ἡ*, *widow*, *χῆραι γυναῖκες* Il.2.289; *μήτηρ χ.* 22. 499; *μὴ παῖδ' ὀρφανικὸν θήῃς χ. τε γυναῖκα* 6.432; *λείπειν τινὰ χ. ἐν μεγάροισιν* 22.484, 24.725, cf. S.*Aj.*653, E.*Andr.*348, *Tr.*380; *χήρας δὲ γυναῖκας ἐποίησαν* Lys.2.71; as a name of Hera, Paus.8.22.2 (*χῆραι· αἱ μὴ ἔχουσαι ἄνδρας*, Hsch.; *ἡ μονωθεῖσα ἀπ' ἀνδρὸς χ.* Poll.3.47). **2.** Com., of a dish, *widowed*, i.e. *without sauce*, Sotad.Com.1.26. **3.** later masc. **χῆρος,** *widower*, Arist.*HA* 612$^{b}$34 (of birds), Call.*Epigr.* 17, Gramm. post Hdn.*Epim.*286. **II.** **χῆρος,** *α, ον*, Adj., metaph., *bereaved*, *χῆρα μέλαθρα* E.*Alc.*862 (anap.); *μάνδραι* Call.*Cer.*106; *βίος* *Epigr.Gr.*406.13 (Iconium); *εὐνή* *IG* 14.1389 i 12; *δόμος* Call.*Epigr.* 22; *δρυμοὶ χ.* *bereft* of men, *AP* 9.84 (Antiphan.): c. gen., Il.6.408; *φάρσος..στελεοῦ χῆρον ἐλαϊνέου* *AP* 6.297 (Phanias), cf. Vett.Val. 117.6; *χήρους γυναικῶν οἰκεῖν* Str.7.3.4; *τὰ χῆρα φρονήσεως* Ph.1. 601; *ναῦς ὕδατος χ.* Ael.*NA* 13.28. (Cf. *χωρίς, χατίζω*, Skt. *jáhāti* 'abandon, renounce'.) **-αίνω,** *to be parted from one's husband*, Herod.1.21. **-αιότης,** *ητος, ἡ*, *widowhood*, *PMasp.*5.23, al. (vi A.D.).

**χηράμβη,** *ἡ*, a kind of *scallop*, Archil.198, Sophr.44.

**χηραμβής·** *χηρῶν οἴκημα*, Hsch. (nisi leg. *-άμβη*, cf. *χηράμβας* (sine expl.) Suid.).

**χηρᾰμίς,** v.l. for *χηραμύς*, Hp.*Morb.*3.15, 16.

**χηρᾰμοδύτης,** *ου, ὁ*, *one who creeps into holes*, *AP* 7.295 (Leon.) (ῡ metri gr., nisi leg. **-δύπτης**).

**χηρᾰμόθεν,** Adv. *from* or *out of holes*, Orph.*L.*707.

⊛ **χηρᾰμός,** *hole, cleft, hollow*, *κοίλην εἰσέπτατο πέτρην, χηραμόν*, of a rock pigeon, Il.21.495, cf. Arist.*HA* 614$^{b}$35, Hld.8.16; *χ. [σφηκῶν]* Lyc.181; of a mouse's *hole*, Babr.107.13; of a *hollow* in the hilt of a sword, Ach.Tat.3.20, 21; of a shell, Id.2.11; of the *hollows* on the sides of the tongue, Poll.2.107.—The gend. is undetermined in Hom.; fem., A.R.4.1452, prob. in Arist. l.c.; masc., Ael.*NA* 3.26, Philostr.*VA* 2.14: heterocl. pl. *χηραμά, τά*, Nic.*Th.*55, 149, Q.S.9. 382; cf. *χηλαμός, χαραμός, χειραμός*.

**χηρᾰμύς,** *ύδος, ἡ*, *scallop-shell*, used as a measure, Xanth.3 (pl.), Hp.*Mul.*1.34, Str.17.3.11. **II.** = foreg., Hsch. (pl.).

**χηρᾰμών,** *όνος, ὁ*, = *χηραμός*, dat. pl. *χηραμόνεσσιν* Orph.*A.*1266.

**χήρατο, χήραντο,** v. *χαίρω*.

**χηρ-εία,** *ἡ*, *widowhood*, Th.2.45, Lxx *Mi.*1.16, Sor.1.31, etc.: pl., *χηρείαις τὸν ἅπαντα χρόνον μείνασα* *IG* 14.1960.5. **II.** metaph., *want*, *διὰ χηρείαν ἐπιστήμης* Ph.1.358; *νόθῳ κόσμῳ χηρείᾳ γνησίου* Id.2.492. ⊛**-ειος,** *α, ον*, *widowed*, *λέκτρα* *AP* 9.192 (Antiphil.): Ion. **χηρήϊος,** *οἶκος* Antim.99. ⊛**-ευσις,** *ἡ*, = *χηρεία* I, Lxx *Ge.*38. 14, *Ju.*8.5. **II.** *separation from a husband*, *Leg.Gort.*3.45. ⊛**-εύω,** intr., *to be without, lack*, c. gen., *νῆσος ἀνδρῶν χ.* Od.9.124, cf. Plu. *Pomp.*28, Ael.*NA* 4.59: *γῆ χ. τῶν ἐκπονούντων* Alciphr.3.25; *ὁλκὰς τῶν ἐμπλεόντων χηρεύουσα* Hld.1.1; *τῶν τῆς Ἀφροδίτης ὀργίων χ.* Ach. Tat.4.1; *οὐδέποτε χ. τῶν ὄντων τινὸς ὁ κόσμος* Herm.ap.Stob.1.41.6; *χ. ἀπό τινος* Steph. *in Hp.*1.219 D. **2.** abs. of a woman, *to be widowed, live in widowhood*, Is.6.51, D.30.11, 33; of birds, Arist. *Fr.*347; also of men, *to be a widower*, Plu.*Cat.Ma.*24:—Med., *χηρεύσῃ λέχος* E.*Alc.*1089. **3.** *live in solitude*, of a fugitive, S.*OT* 479 (anap.). **II.** trans., *bereave*, E.*Cyc.*440; *πεσὼν χηρεύσει σύνοικον* Aphth.*Prog.*13. **-ικός,** *ή, όν*, *of* or *for a widow*, Tz.*H.*13. 591. **-ος,** v. *χήρα*. **-οσύνη,** *ἡ*, *bereavement, widowhood*, *Epigr. Gr.*370 (Cotiaeum), 574; *χ. πόσιος* A.R.4.1064: pl., Man.3.82. **-όω,** *make desolate*, *χήρωσε δ' ἀγυιάς* Il.5.642: esp. *make* a woman *a widow*, *χήρωσας δὲ γυναῖκα* 17.36; *Πριάμου γαῖ' ἐχήρωσ' Ἑλλάδα* E.*Cyc.*304:—Med., *ἐχηρώσαντο πόληα* Q.S.9.351. **2.** c. gen., *bereave*, *με.. ἠελίου χήρωσεν* *AP* 7.172 (Antip.Sid.); *πνοιῆς* ib.287 (Antip.):—Pass., *τῶν..αὐτοῦ χηρώσει* (2 sg.) *πολλῶν* (v.l. *κτεάνων*) Thgn.956; *πολλῶν ἂν ἀνδρῶν ἥδ' ἐχηρώθη πόλις* *would have been bereft of..*, Sol. 37; *Ἄργος ἀνδρῶν ἐχηρώθη* Hdt.6.83. **3.** c. acc., *forsake, deprive of one's presence*, *ἀελίου χήρωσεν αὐγάς* Arist.*Fr.*675.13 (nisi leg. *αὐγᾶς*). **4.** c. acc., *take away*, *πᾶσαν ἐρωήν* Opp.*C.*4.421. **II.** intr., *to be bereft of..*: abs., *live in widowhood*, f.l. for *χηρεύω* in Plu. 2.749d. **-ωσις,** *εως, ἡ*, *being bereaved*, c. gen., Sch.Il.1.13, cf. *Gloss.* **-ωσταί,** *ῶν, οἱ*, *far-off kinsmen*, who seize and divide among themselves the property of one who dies without heirs (*χῆρος*), *χηρωσταὶ δὲ διὰ κτῆσιν δατέοντο* Il.5.158, cf. Hes.*Th.*607 (v. Sch. ad loc.), Q.S.8.299, Hsch., = *οἱ μακρόθεν* (or *πόρρωθεν*) *συγγενεῖς* (also expld. = *ὀρφανιστής*, *one who acts as a guardian to widows and orphans*, Eust.533.30). (Compd. of *χηρο-* 'abandoned' and *-ωστᾱ-* from *-ω-δ-τᾱ-*, nomen agentis of *ω-δ-*, cf. Skt. *ā́ dā-* 'receive'; and Lat. *hērēd-* (*ĝhēro* + *ē-d-*).)

**χητ-εία,** *ἡ*, *want, need*, Hsch. **-ειος,** *α, ον*, *in want, bereaved*, v.l. for *Κήτειοι* in Od.11.521 acc. to Eust.1697.27. **-ίζω,** = *χατίζω*, *EM* 811.45. ⊛**-ος,** *τό* (only used in dat.), *want, lack*, c. gen. pers., *χήτεϊ τοιοῦδ' ἀνδρός* *from need* of such a man, Il.6.463; *χήτεϊ τοιοῦδ' υἷος* 19.324; *χήτει ἐνευναίων* Od.16.35; *χήτεϊ λαῶν* *h.Ap.* 78; *χήτεϊ συμμάχων* Hdt.9.11; *χήτει πρίνης* Eup.360; *χήτει οἰκείων* Pl.*Phdr.*239d (referred to *χῆτις* by Tim.*Lex.*); *χ. γνησίου κάλλους* Ph.2.266; *ὀστῶν χ.* Poll.2.166; *χ. [κόσμου], παραδείγματος*, Them. *Or.*24.306b, 4.62d; *χ. χαλινοῦ καὶ ἡνιόχου* Jul.*Or.*2.50b; *χήτεϊ.. νοήματος* Orph.*L.*76. (Cogn. with *χῆρος*.) **-οσύνη,** *ἡ*, *desolation, loneliness*, *AP* 9.408 (Antip.).

**χθᾰμᾰλοπτήτης,** *ου, ὁ*, *flying near the ground*, epithet of a kind of hawk, Arist.*HA* 620$^{a}$21.

**χθᾰμᾰλός**, ή, όν, *near the ground, on the ground, low*, εὐναί Od.11.194; σκόπελος -ώτερος 12.101; τεῖχος -ώτατον Il.13.683, cf. Plu. *Arat.*18; οἰκοδομεῖν -ώτερα τὰ πρὸς ἄρκτον X.*Mem.*3.8.9; χ. Αἴγυπτος Theoc.17.79; λόφοι -ώτεροι Plb.10.10.7; χ. δένδρα Plu.2.320c; τὰ χ. ib.103e; τὴν πόλιν ἐν τῷ χ. κεῖσθαι D.Chr.6.2; also of the sea, κῦμα χ. Hld.5.1, cf. Ach.Tat.3.2. II. of Ithaca, αὐτὴ δὲ χθαμαλὴ πανυπερτάτη εἰν ἁλὶ κεῖται πρὸς ζόφον dub. sens. in Od.9.25, cf. 10. 196, Str.10.2.12. III. metaph. of persons *of humble station*, χ. καὶ μικροπρεπεῖς Them.*Or.*9.126a, 34p.469 Dind. (Comp.); also δικαιοσύνη Id.*Or.*8.118d (Comp.). 2. *sitting in a lower place*, Hld.10. 6. 3. *pedestrian*, ἀνειμένη καὶ χ. Δωρίς Proll.Theoc.p.5 Wendel.

**χθᾰμᾰλότης**, ητος, ἡ, *lowness, flatness*, Theon Sm.p.124 H., Dexipp.p.184 D., Eust.833.35.

**χθᾰμᾰλόω**, *level*, J.*BJ*3.6.2.

**χθές**, Adv. (lengthd. ἐχθές (q.v.); where the word occurs in *NT*, *Ev.Jo.*4.52, *Act.Ap.*7.28, *Ep.Hebr.*13.8, codd. vary betw. ἐχθές and χθές; χθές is not found in Ptolemaic papyri, but in *PLond.*2.161. 8 (iii A.D.)):—*yesterday*, *h.Merc.*273, Th.3.113, Pl.*R.*327a, *Smp.*174a, etc.: freq. placed between Art. and Subst., ἡ χ. ὁμολογία, οἱ χ. λόγοι, Pl.*Sph.*216a, *Ti.*26e; τῇ χ. ἡμέρᾳ Plu.2.773e; χ. μὲν.., τὰ νῦν δὲ.. Pl.*Ti.*17a: freq. πρῴην τε καὶ χ., χ. καὶ πρῴην, v. πρῴην II; χ. καὶ τρίτην ἡμέραν v.l. in X.*Cyr.*6.3.11, cf. Lxx *Ge.*31.2. (Cf. Skt. *hyás* 'yesterday', Lat. *heri*, *hesternus*, OHG. *gestaron* 'yesterday', etc.)

⊛ **χθεσῖνός**, ή, όν, = χθιζός, κραιπάλη Luc.*Laps.*1 (wrongly given as Att. by Phryn.295, *PS* p.127 B.).

**χθεσιφωνῶν**· κακολογῶν, Hsch., Suid.

**χθιζ-ά**, v. χθιζός. **-ῖνός**, ή, όν, = χθιζός, twice restored metri gr. for χθεσινός in Ar. (both lyr.), διὰ τὸν χ. ἄνθρωπον *V.*281; τὸ σκόροδον τὸ χ. *Ra.*987, cf. Gal.6.88, Alciphr.3.61. ⊛ **-ός**, ή, όν, (χθές) *of yesterday*, τὸ χ. χρεῖος their *yesterday's* debt, Il.13. 745; ὁ χ. πόνος *yesterday's* labour, Hdt.1.126; ἡ χ. μέθη Plu.2.13e; αἱ χ. ἀβελτερίαι ib.75e, cf. Sor.1.40, etc.: freq. in adverb. sense, with Verbs, χθιζὸς ἔβη he went *yesterday*, Il.1.424; χ. ἤλυθες Od. 2.262; χ. ἐεικοστῷ φύγον ἤματι 6.170; ὅσσα.. χ. ὑπέσχετο Il.19.141; χ. ἐμυθεόμην Od.12.451; ἴδον Μέντορα χ. 4.656; αἲ γάρ.. τοῖος ἐών τοι χ... ἐφεστάμεναι would I had stood by thee *yesterday!* 24.379: neut. χθιζόν as Adv., = χθές, Il.19.195; neut. pl. χθιζά, v. πρωιζός.

**χθίσδος**, = χθιζός, *Epigr.Gr.*989 (Balbilla).

**χθόα**· σῶμα, Hsch. **χθόϊνος**· χθόνιος, Id.

**Χθόν-εια**, τά, *festival of the* χθόνιαι θεαί (Demeter and Persephone), *IG*4.679.17 (Hermione).

**χθονήρης**, ες, = χθόνιος, Hsch.

⊛ **χθόνιος**, α, ον, also ος, ον S.*OC*1727 (lyr.), E.*Hipp.*1201, *Hel.*345 (lyr.): (χθών):—*in, under*, or *beneath the earth*, θεός, δαίμων, Hes.*Th.* 767, A.*Th.*522 (lyr.); Ἄϊδα στόμα, of the cavern at Taenarus, Pi.*P.*4. 43, cf. S.*OC*1727 (lyr.); χ. λίμνη E.*Alc.*902 (anap.); Ζεὺς χ., of Hades or Pluto, Hes.*Op.*465; κτύπησε Ζεὺς χ., of noise from beneath the earth, S.*OC*1606; βροντήματα χ. A.*Pr.*994; ἠχὼ χ. ὡς βροντὴ Διός E.*Hipp.* l.c., cf. Ar.*Av.*1750 (lyr.); χ. θεοί gods *of the nether world*, opp. ὕπατοι, A.*Ag.*89 (anap.), etc.; χ. δαίμονες Id.*Pers.*628 (anap.); χθόνιοι alone, μάνις χθονίων Pi.*P.*4.159, cf. A.*Pers.*641 (lyr.), *Ch.* 399 (lyr.), al., Pl.*Lg.*828c, 959d (but Ion. χθονίη, ἡ, earlier name of Γῆ, Pherecyd.Syr.1, cf. Dam.*Pr.*124[bis]; χ. θεαί, i.e. Demeter and Persephone, Hdt.6.134, 7.153; of the Erinyes, S.*OC*1568 (lyr.); χ. Ἅιδας, Ἅιδης, E.*Alc.*237 (lyr.), *Andr.*544 (anap.); χ. Ἑρμῆς, as conductor of the dead, A.*Ch.*1, S.*El.*111 (anap.), *Aj.*832, Ar.*Ra.* 1145, Plu.*Arist.*21; χ. πορεία, opp. οὐρανία, Pl.*R.*619e; χθονίᾳ φρενί, of the dead, Pi.*P.*5.101; χ. Ἑκάτη Ar.*Fr.*500 (anap.); χάρις ἡ χ. grace *with the gods below*, S.*OC*1752 (lyr.); χ. φάμα rumour *that is heard in the world below*, Id.*El.*1066 (lyr.). II. *sprung from the earth*, Τιτῆνες Hes.*Th.*697; of Echion, one of the Theban γηγενεῖς, E.*Ba.*541 (lyr.), cf. Paus.9.5.3, etc.; but also of mankind, ὁ χ. ἄνθρωπος, opp. ὁ ἐν οὐρανῷ.. λαχὼν τὴν ὑπόστασιν, Procl. *in Prm.*p. 765 S. Adv. χθονίως *in an earthly manner*, opp. οὐρανίως, Id.*Sacr.* p.148 B. 2. *in* or *of the country*, θεοί, ἡρῷσσαι, E.*Hec.*79 (anap.), A.R.4.1322; *native*, Ἄρεος.. πάγον.. ξυνῄδη χθόνιον ὄντα S.*OC*948; γενεᾶς χθονίων ἀπ' Ἐρεχθειδᾶν Id.*Aj.*202 (anap.). III. of things, *of the earth*, χ. κόνις (sed leg. γαία, Hsch.), A.*Th.*736 (codd., lyr.); opp. ἀέριος, E.*Fr.*27.4 (lyr.); πρηστήρ Arist.*Mu.*395[a]10.—Poet. word, used once or twice in Pl. and in late Prose (v. supr.).

**χθονο-παις**, ὁ, ἡ, *earth-born, child of earth*, Ὥρα Hsch. **-πλαστος**, ον, *formed of earth*, Suid. **-ρῖφής**, ές, (ῥίπτω) *flung on the ground*, *PMag.Par.*1.196. **-στῖβής**, ές, *treading the earth*, opp. οὐράνιος, S.*OT*301. **-τρεφής**, ές, *bred from earth*, ἐδανὸν A.*Ag.*1407 (lyr.).

**χθύπτης**, ου, ὁ, epith. of τυρός, Thespis 4 (anap., θύπτην cj. Salmasius, cf. θύπτης).

**χθών**, ἡ, gen. χθονός, *earth*, esp. *the surface of it* (rarely *soil*, χθονὸς τρίμοιρον χλαῖναν A.*Ag.*872): poet. word (Com. only in lyr. or paratrag.), very rare in Prose, Lxx 3 *Ki.*14.15 (cod. Alex.), *Supp.Epigr.* 2.520 (Rome); seldom with Art. (only when an Adj. is added, v. infr. II); ἀπὸ χ. ὑψόσ' ἀερθείς Od.8.375, cf. 10.149, Il.14.349; ἐξ ἵππων ἀποβάντες ἐπὶ χθόνα 8.492, cf. 11.619; ἐπὶ χθονὶ κεῖτο τανυσθείς 20.483; κατέθηκεν ἐπὶ χθονί 6.473, cf. 3.89; χθονὶ φύλλα πελάσσαι 13.180; ἐπὶ χ., opp. οὐρανῷ, 4.443; ζῶντος καὶ ἐπὶ χθονὶ δερκομένοιο 1.88; ἐπὶ χ. σῖτον ἔδοντες Od.8.222, etc.; τοὶ ἐπὶ χ. ναιετάουσι 6.153; ἄριστον ἄνδρα τῶν ἐπὶ χ. S.*Tr.*811; χθόνα δύμεναι to go beneath *the earth*, i.e. to die, Il.6.411, Hes.*Sc.*151; ἐτέθαπτο ὑπὸ χθονός Od.11.52: κεκευθὼς ὑπὸ χθονὸς buried, A.*Th.*588; κατὰ χθονὸς κρύψαι τινά S.*Ant.*24, cf. *OC*1546 (Pass.); χθονὶ γυῖα καλύψαιμι Pi.*N.*8.38; κοῦφα σοι χ. ἐπάνωθε πέσοι E.*Alc.*463 (lyr.); opp. θάλασσα, A.*Ag.*576; ὑπὸ χθονός, of *the nether world*, Τάρταρον..., ἧχι βάθιστον ὑπὸ χ. ἐστι βέρεθρον Il.8.14; κάτω μελαίνας χ. Alc.*Supp.*7.10, cf. A.*Eu.*72; οἱ ὑπὸ χ. φίλοι, i.e. those *in the shades below*, Id.*Ch.*833 (lyr.), cf. S.*Ant.*65; ὦ κατὰ χθονὸς θεαί, i.e. the Erinyes, A.*Eu.*115; εἰς τοὺς ἔνερθε καὶ κάτω χ. τόπους ib. 1023. 2. *earth*, i.e. *the world*, Id.*Pr.*139 (anap.), *Ag.*528; ἐπ' ἔσχατα χθονὸς S.*Fr.*956. 3. *Earth*, as a goddess, A.*Pr.*207, *Eu.*6. II. *land, country*, once in Hom., εἴσατο δὲ χ., of Ithaca, Od. 13.352; πολύμηλος χ., of Libya, Pi.*P.*9.7; εὔκαρπος χ., of Sicily, Id.*N.*1.14; freq. in Trag., freq. without Art., χ. Ἀσιᾶτις, Φωκέων, A.*Pers.*61 (anap.), 485; with Art., πᾶσαν τὴν Μυκηναίων χθόνα S.*El.*423; τῆς περιρρύτου χ. Λήμνου Id.*Ph.*1; τὴν Κορινθίαν χ. Id. *OT*795; τὴν ἐμὴν χ. Id.*Aj.*846; τῆς Ἀθηναίων χ. (paratrag.) Ephipp. 14.13; even of a *city*, τῆσδε δημοῦχοι χ. S.*OC*1348; νόμους χθονός Id.*Ant.*368 (lyr.), cf. *OT*736, 939; Com., ὦ πόλι φίλη Κέκροπος,.. οὖθαρ ἀγαθῆς χθονός Ar.*Fr.*110 (lyr.); ξένης ἀπὸ χ. Eup.71 (paratrag.). (Cf. Skt. loc. *kṣámi* 'on the ground', Hittite *tegan* 'ground', Tocharian *tkan-* 'place', Ir. *dū* 'place' (acc. *don*, dat. *dun*).)

**χθωρόδλαψον**, τό, said to be a *Syrian article of food*, Ath.3.126a.

**χῖ**, v.l. for χεῖ, Hp.*VC*1.

**Χῖάζω**, *play the Chian*: esp. *imitate the Chian musician* Democritus, Ar.*Fr.*912 (anap.), Poll.4.65. II. χιάζω, *mark with two lines crossing like a* X:—Pass., ζῷα δυσὶ γραμμαῖς κεχιασμένα D.S.2.58: esp. of words or lines in which the critic wishes to point out something remarkable, τὸ δὲ τοιοῦτον κεχίασται Sch.S.*Ph.*201; χιάζεται ὁ στίχος (in allusion to the word Ἑλένη) Sch.E.*Or.*81, etc.; absurdly expld. by Eust.1462.41. 2. Rhet., *arrange four clauses crosswise*, Hermog.*Inv.*4.3, Porph. *in Cat.*79.6. 3. *make a cruciform incision*, Antyll.ap.Orib.44.20.31 (χιεζοῦμεν codd.). 4. *cross out, cancel* a document, *PFlor.*61.65 (i A.D.), *POxy.*1282.34 (i A.D.), etc.

**Χῖαι**, αἱ (sc. κρηπῖδες), a kind of *men's shoes*, Hp.*Art.*62, Hsch.: cj. for λεῖαι in Herod.7.57.

**χῖακά**, τά, a class of *eye-salves*, Dem.Ophth.ap.Aët.7.112; also χιακόν, τό, a styptic, Orib.*Fr.*86.

**Χῖάς**, άδος, ἡ, = Χῖος II, Poll.9.100.

⊛ **χῖ-ασμα** [ῑ], ατος, τό, *cross-piece of wood*, Bito 54.3 (pl.). 2. *cross-bandage*, Sor.*Fasc.*22 (in form χίεσμα), Gal.18(1).787. **-ασμός**, ὁ, *placing crosswise, diagonal arrangement*, esp. of the clauses of a period, so that the 1st corresponds with the 4th, and the 2nd with the 3rd, Hermog.*Inv.*4.3; κατὰ χιασμόν Sch.Isoc.12.47. 2. *cruciform incision*, Antyll.ap.Orib.44.20.32 (-εσμός codd., and so of a noose, Heraclasap.eund.48.9.2; of a bandage, Heliod.ap.eund. 48.65 tit.). 3. *decussation*, σκιῶν Cleom.1.9, cf. Nicom.*Ar.*1.19 (pl.); of nerves, Aret.*SD*1.7. 4. *cancellation* of a document, *PMasp.*151.292 (vi A.D.). **-αστέον**, *one must cut a bandage in the form of a* X, Sor.1.56. **-αστί**, Adv. *like the Chians*, τίλλειν Eust.1462.34, Hsch. II. *crosswise, diagonally*, χ. τῶν εὐθειῶν κειμένων Procl. *in Euc.*p.357 F. **-αστός**, ή, όν, *arranged diagonally*, λίθοι Ph.*Bel.*94.45; of a noose (in form χιεστός) Heraclasap.Orib. 48.3 tit.; of a bandage, Sor.*Fasc.*7 (in form χιεστός), Gal.18(1). 819. Adv. -τῶς of an incision, *PSI*10.1180.47 (ii A.D.). 2. *in the shape of a* X, σημεῖον Eust.599.35. II. esp. in Rhet. (cf. χιάζω), χ. περίοδος Sch.Isoc.6.42, cf. Sch.Il.16.564, Porph. *in Cat.* 78.36.

**χιδά**· φρικτή, Hsch. **χίδαδον**· τὸ παιδίον, Id. (leg. **χίδαλον**· ἀντὶ τοῦ ⟨κίδαλον⟩· τὸ αἰδοῖον). **χίδαι**· ἀντὶ τοῦ ⟨..⟩ (Cret.), Id. **χιδαλέον**· τυφλόν, ἄγαμον, πεφρικός, Id. **χιδᾶν**· χ⟨ε⟩ιμάζεσθαι, δειλιᾶν, Id. **χίδηλος**, etym. of κίβδηλος, Eust.1462.43.

**χιδρίας** πυρός, ὁ, *unripe* wheat, Ar.*Fr.*889.

⊛ **χῖδρον**, τό, mostly in pl. **χῖδρα**, τά, *unripe wheaten-groats*, rubbed from the ear in the hands, Ar.*Eq.*806 (anap.), *Pax* 595 (troch.) (cf. Sch.ad locc., Suid.), *PCair.Zen.*129.13 (iii B.C.), Alex.Trall.1.13, 2.1, al.; νέα πεφρυγμένα χ. Lxx *Le.*2.14, cf. 23.14: sg., Alcm.75; **χίδρα**, ἡ, is corrupt in Hsch.; **χέδρα** is v.l. in Ph.1.180.

**χιδροπώλης**, ου, ὁ, *dealer in* χῖδρα, Poll.7.199.

**χίδρυ**· ὄνομα δειλόν, Hsch.

**χῖ-εζέω**, -εσμα, -εσμός, -εστός, vv.ll. for χιάζω, χιασμός, etc. (qq. vv.).

**χίθος**, = *cilicia*, Gloss. (also written λίθος and ζύθος, ib.).

**χῐθωνίσκος**, ὁ, = χιτων-, *IG*2[2].1514.7.

**χιλάαγρα**· ζῳφύφιόν τι, Hsch.

⊛ **χῑλ-εύω**, *supply with fodder*, ὑποζύγια Thphr.*CP*2.17.6. II. *feed on, graze*, c. acc. loci, Nic.*Th.*635. **-ή**, ἡ, = χιλός, Gal.*Consuet.*2, Suid. **-ήγονος**, ον, *grown as fodder for cattle*, Nic.*Al.*424.

**χῑλιάγωνος** [ᾰ], ον, *with a thousand angles*, Archim.*Aren.*1.10, al.

**χῑλι-άζω**, *to be a thousand years old*, Tz.*H.*9.656. **-άκις**, Adv. *a thousand times*, Gloss. **-ανδρος**, ον, *containing a thousand men*, πόλις Pl.*Plt.*292e. **-άριθμος** [ᾰ], ον, *numbering* 1,000 *men*, in phrase -αρίθμου ἡγήτωρ στρατιῆς = Lat. *tribunus militum*, *JRS* 2.90 (Antioch.Pisid.). **-άροτρος** [ᾰρ], ον, *containing a thousand plough-gates*, τέμενος Sch.BT Il.13.703.

**χῑλιαρχ-έω**, impf. ἐχιλιάρχει, aor. ἐχιλιάρχησα, Plu.*Cat.Mi.*8, *Flam.* 20: pf. part. κεχιλιαρχηκώς D.C.67.11:—*to be a* χιλίαρχος, Luc. *DMeretr.*9.4: esp. at Rome, *to be a tribunus militum*, *IG*14.282

(i B.C.), J.*BJ*3.4.1, Plu. ll. cc., App.*Pun.*112, etc. **-ης,** ου, ὁ, = χιλίαρχος I, Hdt.7.81. **2.** *commander of a* χιλιαρχία II, Ascl.*Tact.*2.10, Ael.*Tact.*9.6. **II.** = Lat. *tribunus militum*, J.*AJ*19.1.13, App.*BC* 2.102, Hdn.6.9.6 (less common than χιλίαρχος). ⊛ **-ία,** ἡ, *office* or *post* of χιλίαρχος, X.*Cyr.*4.1.4. **2.** office of *tribunus militum* Plu. *Cam.*38, al., D.C.59.29; ἀπὸ τριῶν χ., = Lat. *tribus militiis*, *IGRom.* 4.1204 (Thyatira). **II.** *unit under the command of a* χιλίαρχος, *corps of* 1024 *men*, Ascl.*Tact.*2.10, Ael.*Tact.*9.6, Arr.*Tact.*10.5. **2.** = χιλιάς, Lxx *Nu.*31.48, 1 *Ma.*5.13. **3.** Persian military district, *AJA* 16.13 (Sardis, iv/iii B.C.). **III.** = χιλιετηρίς, applied to work by Asinius Quadratus, St.Byz. s. v. Ὀξύβιοι (cf. χιλιάς II). **-ικός,** ή, όν, *of a tribunus militum*, ἡγεμονία D.S.19.3. **-ος,** ὁ, *captain over a thousand*, A.*Pers.*304: esp. *commandant* of a garrison, X.*Cyr.*8.1.14, *Oec.*4.7. **II.** = χιλιάρχης II, Plb.6.19.1, al., D.H.2.14, *Inscr.Magn.*157b (i A.D.), etc. (the usual form in this sense). **2.** title of Persian court official, Plu.*Art.*5, Ael. *VH*1.21; also in Macedonia, D.S.18.48.

**χῑλι-άς,** άδος, ἡ: gen. pl. χιλιάδων Hdt.2.28 (χιλιαδέων v. l. in 7.28):—*a thousand*, Id.6.58, 7.28, A.*Pers.*341; χ. τέτορες Simon. 91; c. gen., πολλὰς χιλιάδας ταλάντων Hdt.2.96, cf. 28; ἐννέα χιλιάδας ἐτῶν Pl.*Phdr.*257a. **2.** generally, *large number*, Theoc.16.91, Luc.*Herm.*56; πολλαὶ χ., of lines of poetry, Call.*Aet.Oxy.*2079.4. **3.** Χιλιάδες, αἱ, title of poem by Euph., Ath.10.436f, etc. **II.** = χιλιετηρίς, Alex.Aetol.4.4; Ῥωμαϊκὴ χ., title of work by Asinius Quadratus, St.Byz. s. v. Ἄνθιον (cf. χιλιαρχία III, χιλιετηρίς). ⊛ **-αστήρ,** ῆρος, ὁ, *member of a* χιλιαστύς, *SIG*1043.5 (Samos, iii B.C.). **-αστύς,** ύος, ἡ, a division of the people at Ephesus, ib.353.9 (iv B.C.); at Samos, ib.312.30 (iv B.C.); at Cos, ib.1025.17 (iv/iii B.C.); cf. χελληστύς.

**χῑλῐετ-ηρίς,** ίδος, ἡ, *a period of a thousand years*, title of a work by Asinius Quadratus, Suid. s. v. Κοδρᾶτος (cf. χιλιαρχία III, χιλιάς II). **2.** *festival held after an interval of a thousand years*, Hierocl.*Facet.* 62. **-ης,** ου, ὁ, or **-ετής,** ές, ὁ, ἡ:—*lasting a thousand years*, περίοδος, πορεία, Pl.*Phdr.*249a, *R.*621d; βίος Arist.*GA*745$^{a}$34: fem. acc. -ετιν v.l. in Pl.*R.*615a. **II.** χειλιέτης ἀγών, celebration of the *thousandth anniversary* of the founding of Rome, *IG*2$^{2}$.3169.14 (iii A.D.).

**χῑλιοδύνᾰμος** [ῠ], = πολεμώνιον, Dsc.4.8 (v. l. -δύναμις, as in Gal. 12.106); Lat. *-dynamias* Plin.*HN*25.64.

⊛ **χίλιοι** [χῑ], αι, α: gen. pl. fem. χιλιῶν, irreg. in Att. acc. to Hdn. Gr.1.426 (prob. only when χίλιαι was used as a fem. Subst. (v. infr. 3)); dat. pl. fem. (orig. loc.) χιλίᾱσιν *IG*1$^{2}$.10.18; χιλίαισι ib.76.20, 94.10; later χιλίαις: dialect forms, Locr. **χίλιοι** (as in Att., v. supr.) *IG*9(1).334.39 (Oeanthea, v B.C.); Dor. **χήλιοι** (written **χέλ-**) ib. 5(1).1.23 (Sparta, v B.C.), Lesb., Thess. **χέλλιοι** *EM*817.1 (cf. χελληστύς), *IG*9(2).1229.29 (Phalanna, ii B.C.); Ion. **χείλιοι** *Schwyzer* 688*C*15 (Chios, v B.C.), which shd. prob. be restored in Hom., cf. δεκάχ(ε)ιλοι:—*a thousand*, Hom. only in neut., χ. μέτρα, πυρά, Il.7.471, 8.562; πρῶθ' ἑκατὸν βοῦς δῶκεν, ἔπειτα δὲ χίλι' ὑπέστη (sc. πρόβατα), αἶγας ὁμοῦ καὶ ὄϊς 11.244: usu. agreeing with its Subst., Hes.*Th.* 364, etc.; but sts. as Subst. folld. by gen., χίλιοι Μακεδόνων Th.2.80: to express the addition of a smaller number, that number may either precede or follow, διακόσιοι καὶ χ. Isoc.4.87, 93, Pl.*Criti.*119b: but χ. καὶ πεντακόσιοι Aeschin.2.77; later καί is freq. omitted, Plb.3.33.10, Lxx *Da.*12.11, *Apoc.*11.3; with Preps. χ. ἐπὶ μυρίοις Pl.*Lg.*895a; τέτταρας πρὸς τοῖς χ. Luc.*Cat.*4; οἱ χ. λογάδες (at Argos) *the Thousand*, Th.5.67, cf. D.S.12.80. **2.** sg. with collect. nouns, χιλίη ἵππος *a thousand* horse, Hdt.5.63, 7.41; τὴν ἵππον τὴν χιλίην Id.8.113; so ἵππον ἔχω εἰς χιλίαν X.*Cyr.*4.6.2; also χιλία ὁλοκαύτωσις burnt-offering *of 1000 cattle*, Lxx 3 *Ki.*3.4. **3.** χίλιαι (sc. δραχμαί) as Subst., *a thousand drachmae*, περὶ χιλιῶν κινδυνεύειν D.22.21; ἐν χιλίαις ὁ κίνδυνος ib.26 (χ. δραχμαί in full, Pl.*Ap.*36b). (Cf. Skt. *sahásram* 'a thousand' (with prefix *sa-* = *sm̥-*); I.-E. *ĝheslo-*, *ĝheslio-*.)

**χῑλιο-καιπεντηκονταπλᾰσίων,** ον, gen. -ονος, *1050 times as much*, Cleom.2.1. **-κράτωρ,** ορος [ᾰ], ὁ, = χιλίαρχος, Tz.*H.*3.719.

**χῑλιοκτᾰκοσιογδοηκονταπλᾰσίων,** ον, gen. -ονος, *eighteen hundred and eighty times as great*, Hipparch.ap.Theon.Sm.p.197 H.

**χῑλιόκωμος,** ον, *with a thousand villages*, πεδίον Str.12.3.39.

**χῑλιόμβη,** ἡ, *sacrifice of a thousand victims* (formed like ἑκατόμβη), Jul.*Or.*7.214a, Eust.1454.26, etc.

**χῑλιό-ναυς,** εως, ὁ, ἡ, *of a thousand ships*, στρατός E.*Or.*352 (anap.); ὁ χ. Ἑλλάδος Ἄρης Id.*Andr.*106 (eleg.); ἐλάταις χιλιόναυσιν, = χιλίαις ναυσί, Id.*IA*174 (lyr.); also in later Prose, χ. στόλος Str. 13.1.27. **-ναύτης,** ου, Dor. **-ναύτας,** α, ὁ, ἡ, *with* or *of a thousand ships*, στόλος Ἀργείων A.*Ag.*45 (anap.); σὺν κώπᾳ χιλιοναύτᾳ Ἀτρεΐδα prob. in E.*IT*141 (lyr.).

**χῑλιό-ομαι,** Pass., *to be fined a thousand drachmae*, Lycurg.*Frr.* 11, 60, *EM*404.43. **-πᾰλαι,** Adv. *long long ago*, Com. word, Ar.*Eq.*1155. **-πηχυς,** υ, *of 1000 cubits*, Plot.2.9.9. **-πλάσιος** [ᾰ], α, ον, = sq., only Adv. -ίως Lxx *De.*1.11. ⊛ **-πλᾰσίων,** ον, gen. -ονος, = foreg., Sm.2 *Ki.*18.3.

**χίλιος,** v. χίλιοι.

**χῑλιοστ-ός,** ή, όν, *thousandth*, X.*Cyr.*2.3.6, Pl.*Phdr.*249b, *R.*615c, etc.: ἡ χ. *tax of 1000th*, *PEleph.*14.12 (iii B.C.), Hsch. **-ύς,** ύος, ἡ, *body of a thousand*, X.*Cyr.*2.4.3, 6.3.13, 31.

**χῑλιο-τάλαντος** [τᾰ], ον, *weighing* or *worth a thousand talents*, ναοί, μύδροι, Plu.*Per.*12, 2.924a; ὀφρῦς ἔχον χ., Com. phrase, Alex. 116.7. **-φόρος,** ον, *carrying a thousand*, πλοῖον χ. vessel *of a thousand* ἀμφορεῖς, D.C.56.27. **-φυλλος,** ὁ, = πολύγονον ἄρρεν, Ps.-Dsc.4.4. **2.** = Ἀχίλλειος, ib.36. **II.** v. στρατιώτης II. **-χρῡσος,** ὁ, name of a compound plaster, Alex.Trall.12 p.561 P.

**χῑλίωρος,** ον, (ὥρα) *of a thousand years*, χρόνος Lyc.1153.

**χῑλοποι-έομαι,** late spelling for χυλο-, *digest*, Phlp.*in APo.*417.15: hence **-ησις,** εως, ἡ, *digestion*, Sophon.*in de An.*61.28.

⊛ **χῑλ-ός** (**χειλός,** Ael.Dion.*Fr.*323 (cf. 397)), ὁ (ἡ Babr.46.3), *green fodder for cattle*, esp. for horses and beasts of burden, *forage*, *provender*, Hdt.4.140, X.*An.*1.9.27; τὰ δὲ κτήνη πάντα χιλῷ ἔνδον ἐτρέφοντο ib.4.5.25; of soldiers, λαμβάνειν χιλόν *forage*, Id.*Cyr.*6.3.5; πρὸς χ. διατελέσαι (sc. τὴν ὁδόν) complete a stage for *forage*, Id. *An.*1.5.7; ἵπποις χ. ἐμβαλεῖν, παραβάλλεσθαι (Pass.), Plu.*Eum.*9, 2.678a; ξηρὸς χ. *hay*, X.*An.*4.5.33. **2.** later, *pasturage*, Babr. l.c. **-όω,** *fodder*, διὰ τὸν φόβον..ἐχίλου τοὺς ἵππους, i.e. did not suffer them to graze, X.*An.*7.2.21:—Pass., *to be stall-fed*, Hsch. ⊛ **-ωμα,** ατος, τό, *fodder*, Agatharch.61. **II.** f.l. for κένωμα, A.*Fr.*275.

**Χῑλώνειος,** α, ον, *of* or *from* Χίλων, τὸ Χ. the *saying of Chilon* (i.e. μηδὲν ἄγαν), Arist.*Rh.*1389$^{b}$3.

**χῑλωτήρ,** ῆρος, ὁ, *nose-bag for cattle* or *horses*, *UPZ*76.3 (ii B.C.), *PLond.*2.402.24 (ii B.C.), Poll.1.185, Hsch.

**χίμαιρ-α** [ῐ], ἡ, *she-goat*, Il.6.181, Hes.*Th.*322, *PCair.Zen.*576.3 (iii B.C.); sacrificed before battle to Ἄρτεμις Ἀγροτέρα, A.*Ag.*232 (lyr.), X.*An.*3.2.12, *HG*4.2.20, *Lac.*13.8; θαλλὸν χιμαίραις προσφέρων S.*Fr.*502; *a young she-goat* (cf. χίμαρος), Arist.*HA*523$^{a}$1; χ. ἐξ αἰγῶν *kid*, Lxx *Le.*4.28, 29. **II.** Χίμαιρα, ἡ, *Chimaera*, a fire-breathing monster, Il.6.179, cf. 16.328; Hes.*Th.*319, etc.; χ. πύρπνοος Anaxil.22.3 (troch.), Epinic.2.10. **2.** expld. as mythical for a volcano in Lycia, Str.14.3.5. **-άς,** άδος, ἡ, = foreg. I, *Schwyzer* 644.16 (Aegae). **-ειος,** α, ον, *of a goat*, θράσος Hdn.*Epim.*149. **-ίς,** ίδος, ἡ, *kid*, Alciphr.*Fr.*6.10.

**χῐμαιρο-βάτης** [ᾰ], ου, Dor. **-τας,** ὁ, *goat-mounter*, or *goat-footed*, of Pan, *AP*6.35 (Leon.). **-θύτης** [ῠ], ου, ὁ, *goat-sacrificer*, ib. 300 (Id.). **-φόνος,** ον, *goat-slaying*, ib.9.774 (Glauc.). **-φύλαξ** [ῠ], ακος, ὁ, *goatherd*, A.D.*Adv.*188.27.

**χῐμάρα** [ᾰρ], ἡ, = χίμαιρα I, *AP*9.317.

**χῐμάραρχος** [μᾰ], ὁ, *goat-leader*, τράγος χ. the he-goat *that leads the flock*, *AP*9.744 (Leon.).

**χῐμᾰροκτόνος,** ον, = χιμαιροφόνος, Opp.*C.*1.233.

⊛ **χίμᾰρος** [ῐ], ὁ, *he-goat*, Ar.*Eq.*661, *Schwyzer* 784$^{a}$1 (Tenos, iv B.C.), Theoc.*Epigr.*4.15, *AP*6.190.10 (Gaet.): a young he-goat, older than ἔριφος, Ar.Byz.ap.Eust.1625.33; χ. ἐξ αἰγῶν *kid*, Lxx *Le.*4.23; χ. ἐρυθρός *Berl.Sitzb.*1927.156 (Cyrene). **II.** fem. = χίμαιρα, Theoc.1.6, *Epigr.*6.3, *AP*6.157 (Theodorid.), 9.403 (Maec.). (Cogn. with χεῖμα, χειμών, lit. 'one winter old', cf. Lat. *bīmus* (fr. **bi-himus*, cf. Skt. *himás* 'winter').)

**χῐμᾰροσφακτήρ,** ῆρος, ὁ, *goat-slayer*, λύκος *AP*9.558 (Eryc.).

**χίμεθλον** [ῐ], τό, = χιμέτλον, Parod. Epic.ap.Arist.*Rh.*1412$^{a}$31; v.l. in Dsc.2.42.

**χῐμέτλ-η,** ἡ, = χίμετλον, Dsc.1.128, 2.42. **-ιάω,** *have chilblains*, ib.37. **-ον,** τό, *chilblain*, mostly in pl., Hippon.19.4, Ar.*V.*1167, Nic.*Th.*682, Lyc.1290: sg., Poll.2.198. (Cogn. with χεῖμα; misspelt χείμεθλον, χείμετλον in *Gloss.*)

**Χῑογενής,** ές, *of Chian growth*, of wine, *AP*11.44 (Phld.).

**χῑοειδής,** ές, *in form of a* Χ, Sor.2.41 (cj.); ἐπίδεσμος Paul.Aeg. 6.66. Adv. -δῶς Sophon.*in de An.*19.34.

**χῖον,** τό, *a Chian wine-jar*, Macho ap.Ath.13.579e. **II.** a measure, *PCair.Zen.*12.17, al. (iii B.C.).

**χῐόν-εος,** α, ον, (χιών) *snowy*, *snow-white*, χιτῶνες Asius 13.3; σάρξ Bion 1.10; στήθεα *Scol.Anon.*26 (Diehl *Anthologia Lyrica* (ed. 1) ii 188). **2.** *of* or *from snow*, ὕδατα *Lyr.Alex.Adesp.*37.12; νιφάδες *AP*9.244 (Apollonid.); κρύσταλλος ib.753 (Claudian.). [ῐ by nature, but ῑ metri gr. in hexam.] **-ίζω,** *snow upon*, *cover with snow*: impers., εἰ ἐχιόνιζε..τὴν χώρην [sc. ὁ θεός] Hdt.2.22: abs., εἰ ἐχιόνιζε if *it snowed*, ibid.:—Pass., *to be covered with snow*, D.S.1.39, Sm.*Ps.*67(68).15, Dsc.4.61, D.L.6.23 (v. l. κεχιονωμένους), Sch. A.R.4.269. **II.** *turn into snow*, in Pass., *PMag.*13.299 Preisendanz; *make snow-white*, Hsch. **-ικός,** ή, όν, *of snow*, σημεῖον Thphr.*Sign.*42. **II.** *crystalline*, ἐδάφη 1 *Enoch* 14.10. **-ῖνος,** η, ον, *snow-white*, τῇ χροιᾷ Ptol.Euerg.10 J. **-ιον,** τό, a kind of *eye-salve*, Alex.Trall.2.1. **-ισμός,** ὁ, *snowing*, Apollon.*Lex.* s. v. νιφάδεσσι, Hsch. s. v. νιφετός.

**χῐονό-βᾰτος,** ον, f.l. for -βλητος, ὄρεα Arr.*Ind.*6.7. **-βλέφᾰρος,** ον, *with eye of dazzling white*, Ἀώς Mesom.*Sol.*7. **-βλητος,** ον, *snow-beaten*, Ὀλύμπου κορυφαί Ar.*Nu.*270 (anap.). **-βολέομαι,** Pass., *to be covered with snow*, Str.15.2.10, D.S.5.39, 17.82, 18.25, Ath. Med.ap.Orib.1.2.6. **-βόλος,** ον, *snowy*, χ. ὥρα Plu.2.182e. **II.** χιονόβολος, ον, *snow-covered*, ὄρη Str.9.2.25; cf. χιονόβλητος. **-βοσκος,** ον, *nourished by snows*, λειμών A.*Supp.*559 (lyr.). **-εις,** εσσα, εν, poet. for χιόνεος, Nic.*Al.*512. [ῑ metri gr.] **-θρέμμων,** ον, gen. -ονος, *fostering snow*, *snow-clad*, σκοπιαί E.*Hel.*1323 (lyr.). **-κτῠπος,** ον, *snow-beaten*, of a mountain, S.*Aj.*696 (lyr.). **-μελι,** ιτος, τό, *snow-honey*, a cooling remedy, *Gp.*8.28.3. ⊛ **-ομαι,** Pass., v. χιονίζω. **II.** *become snow-white*, Lxx *Ps.*67(68).15. **-πεζα,** ἡ, *with snow-white feet*, Nonn.*D.*22.136. [ῑ metri gr.] **-τρόφος,** ον, = χιονοθρέμμων, Ἀρτέμιδος -τρόφον ὄμμα Κιθαιρών E.*Ph.*802 (hex.). **-χροος,** ον, heterocl. acc. pl. -χροας, *snow-white*, μᾶζαι Philox.2.6. **-χρως,** ωτος, ὁ, ἡ, *snow-white*, of a swan, E.*Hel.*215 (lyr.).

**χῐον-ώδης,** ες, *snowy*, Hp.*Epid.*3.2, E.*Hec.*81 (anap.), A.R.1.826,

Nic.*Al*.150, Call.*Fr*.1.53P.; βόλβα *AP*11.410 (Luc.); αἶγες Orac. ap.D.S.7.16. **-ωπός**, όν, *snow-white, fair*, Nonn.*D*.17.43.

**Χίος** [ῐ], ἡ, *Chios*, Od.3.170, Hdt.1.142, etc.: sts. with Art., Th. 8.15,28,38,99,101. [Χῖον ἐς ἀμφιρύτην is dub. in Simon.[119]; but Χῖος is found *IG*2.3412.]

❀ **Χῖος**, α, ον, (contr. from Χίιος) *of* or *from Chios*, Χῖαι [κρηπῖδες] Hp.*Art*.62, cf. Aristomen.11, etc.; σύκινα *PCair.Zen*.33.12 (iii B.C.); Χ. ἀοιδός, i.e. *Homer*, Theoc.7.47; Χ. ἄνθρωπος D.35.52: prov., Χῖος δεσπότην ὠνήσατο 'caught a Tartar', Eup.269. **b.** esp. οἶνος Χ. Ar.*Ec*.1139: freq. without οἶνος, Id.*Fr*.216.3, etc.; ἐν ἀκρήτῳ Χίῳ *AP*7.422 (Leon.). **2.** as Subst., Χῖοι or οἱ Χῖοι *the Chians*; without Art., Hdt.1.142, Th.1.19, 3.32, etc.; with Art., Id.8.15,22, etc. **II.** ὁ Χῖος (sc. βόλος), = κύων VI, the worst throw of the dice (cf. χιάς), i.e. the external face of the ἀστράγαλος (Ruf.*Oss*. 38), with the *ace-dot*, opp. Κῷος (q.v.), Χῖος παραστὰς Κῷον οὐκ ἐᾷ λέγειν Stratt.23, cf. Arist.*Cael*.292ᵃ29, *AP*7.422 (Leon.), Poll. 7.204,205, Zen.4.74: hence prov., Χῖος πρὸς Κῷον ibid. (in Arist. *HA*499ᵇ29 χῖα is cj. for ἰσχία, κῷα for κῶλα). **2.** οὐ Χῖος ἀλλὰ Κεῖος, v. Κέως. **III.** Χία, ἡ, = μαστίχη, *Gloss*.

**Χιουργής**, ές, *of Chian work*, Critias 35; Χιουργές, τό (sc. ποτήριον), *IG*11(2).110.27 (Delos, iii B.C.): pl., ib.111,112.

**χῐόω**, (χῖ) *mark with a* Χ *or cross*, Tz.*H*.5.164. **2.** *write* or *mark crosswise*, κύκλος ἐπ' εὐθείας χιούμενος Lyd.*Mens*.3.4: pf. inf. κεχιῶσθαι Eun.*Hist*.p.272D.

**χῑρᾰλέος**, α, ον, *with chapped hands* or *feet*, Hsch.

**χίραμα**, ατος, τό, a disease in horses' feet, *Hippiatr*.52.

**χῑράς**, = χειράς, Suid.

**χιτάναλλον**, v. κιττάναλον.

❀ **χῐτών**, in Ion.Prose **κιθών**, ῶνος, ὁ (also prob. in *Sammelb*.4291), Dor. **κιτών** (q.v.):—*garment worn next the skin, tunic*. **I.** in early times, only of *a man's tunic* (the woman's being πέπλος, Sch.BT Il.2. 42), χιτῶνα περὶ χροῒ δῦνεν Od.15.60; κιθῶνας ὑποδύνειν τοῖσι εἵμασι Hdt.1.155: sts. with a girdle, Od.14.72; τερμιόεις 19.242, Hes.*Op*. 537; μαλακός, ἐΰννητος, Od.1.437, Il.24.580; [χ.] λαμπρὸς.. ἠέλιος ὥς Od.19.234; χλαῖνάν τε χιτῶνά τε 14.132,154; οἱ δ' ἀροτῆρες ἤρεικον χθόνα δῖαν ἐπιστολάδην δὲ χιτῶνας ἐστάλατ' Hes.*Sc*.287. **2.** later worn also by women, ἅμα κιθῶνι ἐκδυομένῳ συνεκδύεται καὶ τὴν αἰδῶ γυνή Hdt.1.8; σύροισα χιτῶνα Theoc.2.73; the Ionian sleeved χ. was distd. fr. the Dorian, fastened with περόναι, μετέβαλον [αἱ τῶν Ἀθηναίων γυναῖκες] ἐς τὸν λίνεον κ. ἵνα δὴ περόνῃσι μὴ χρέωνται Hdt. 5.87; οἱ πρεσβύτεροι [τῶν Ἀθηναίων] οὐ πολὺς χρόνος ἐπειδὴ χιτῶνας λινοῦς ἐπαύσαντο φοροῦντες Th.1.6, cf. Eust.954.50; χ. ποδήρης, ὀρθοστάδιος, σταρός (v. sub vocc.); κιθὼν ποδηνεκής, worn by Babylonians, Hdt.1.195; κιθῶνες λίνεοι περὶ τὰ σκέλεα θυσανωτοί, worn by Egyptians, Id.2.81; κιθῶνες εἰρίνεοι, worn by Cilicians, Id.7.91; dub. in E.*IT*288 (pl.). **II.** *coat of mail*, prob. of leather covered with scales or rings, στρεπτὸς χ. Il.5.113; χ. χάλκεος 13.439; κιθῶνες χειριδωτοὶ λεπίδος σιδηρέης *coats* of iron scales with sleeves, Hdt.7.61 (s.v.l.): but distd. fr. θώρηξ Id.9.22, cf. X.*Cyr*.6.4.1. **III.** *part of a shoe that coats the foot, upper*, ib.8.2.5 (pl.), Arist.*Rh*.1392ᵃ 31. **IV.** metaph., *any coat, case*, or *covering*, λάϊνος χιτών (v. λάϊνος); τειχέων κιθῶνες, i.e. walls, Hdt.7.139; in Anatomy, *coat, membrane*, τὸν ἀμφὶ τὴν ὄψιν χ. Hp.*VM*19, cf. *Aph*.7.45, Epicur. *Nat*.2.993.1; ὁ.. χ. τῆς καρδίας Arist.*Resp*.480ᵃ4; χ. ὑμενώδης, ἀραχνιώδης, Id.*PA*679ᵃ1, *HA*557ᵇ16; τοῦ ᾠοῦ οἱ χ. οἱ περιέχοντες ib. 561ᵃ14; of foetal *membranes*, Sor.1.7,58, al.; τριγλοφόροι χιτῶνες, of fishing-nets, *AP*6.11 (Satyr.); χιτῶνες ἀραχνίων spiders' *webs*, Hp.*Int*.3: pl., *pods* or *coats* of seeds, bulbous roots, etc., Thphr. *HP*1.12.3, 8.4.1, *CP*1.4.1, al. **2.** *vesture*, [φύσις] σαρκῶν ἀλλογνῶτι περιστέλλουσα (sc. ψυχάς) χιτῶνι Emp.126; σῶμα χ. ψυχῆς *IG*14.2241: pl., προσθέσει χιτώνων ἐνυλοτέρων, of the soul, Procl. *Inst*.209. (Accad. *kitinnu* 'linen garment', Hebr. *kĕtōnet* 'tunic'; χεθὼν γὰρ τὸ λίνον ἡμεῖς καλοῦμεν J.*AJ*3.7.2.)

**χῐτων-άριον**, τό, Dim. of χιτών, *woman's frock*, Men.727, *PCair. Zen*.469 (iii B.C.); of men's wear, *AP*11.154 (Lucill.), Arr.*Epict*. 1.25.21; of a baby's *frock*, Sor.1.111. **-η**, ἡ, a name of Artemis, represented as a huntress in a short Dorian χιτών, Call.*Jov*.77, *Dian*. 225; **χιτωνέα** Ἄ., at Syracuse, Epich.127, Ath.14.629e; **Κιθώνη**, at Miletus, *Milet*.1(7) No.202. **-ία**, ἡ, *dress*, Melamp.*Naev*.p.508 Franz. **-ιον**, τό, Dim. of χιτών, prop. *woman's frock* or *shift*, Ar.*Ra*.414 (lyr.), *Pl*.984, *Lys*.48,150, *Fr*.325; τὸ γυναικεῖον τοδὶ χ. ib.632, cf. *IG*1².386.23,387.34, 2².1514.51, 1517.125, al., *PCair. Zen*.776.8 (iii B.C.); also of men's wear, Luc.*Merc.Cond*.37: prov., [οὐ πρέπει] γαλῇ χ. Stratt.71. **-ισκάριον**, τό, Dim. of χιτωνίσκος, Eust.1166.51. ❀ **-ίσκιον**, τό, Dim. of sq., *IG*2².1514.28. **-ίσκος**, ὁ (**κιθωνίσκος** ib.1523.18), Dim. of χιτών, *short frock* (ὑπὲρ γονάτων X.*An*.5.4.13), worn by men, Ar.*Av*.946, Lys.10.10, Phld.*Ir*.p. 39 W., etc.; with a girdle, Pl.*Hp.Mi*.368c; ὥστε με.. θοἰμάτιον προέσθαι καὶ μικροῦ γυμνὸν ἐν τῷ χ. γενέσθαι D.21.216, cf. Pl.*Hp.Mi*. 368c: less freq. of women, *shift*, D.19.197, *IG*2².1514.12, al.; σχιστὸς χ. Apollod.Com.12. **II.** *coat* of an abscess, Archig.ap. Aët.8.76.

**χῐωδῶς**, Adv. = χιοειδῶς, Pall. *in Hp.Fract*.12.285C.

**χιών**, όνος, ἡ: (v. sub fin.):—*snow*, in Hom. mostly of *fallen snow*, Il.10.7, 22.152; ὡς δὲ χ. κατατήκετ' ἐν.. ὄρεσσιν Od.19.205; ὕπερθε χ. γένετ' ἠΰτε πάχνη 14.476; τὸν Νεῖλον ῥέειν ἀπὸ τηκομένης χιόνος Hdt.2.22; ἐπὶ χιόνι πεσούσῃ ibid., cf. 4.50; Ἰδαία χ. A.*Ag*.564; ἥλιος.. τήκει πετραίαν χιόνα Id.*Fr*.300.5; καί νιν.. χιὼν οὐδαμὰ λείπει S.*Ant*.830 (lyr.); also of *falling snow*, ὥς τε νιφάδες χιόνος πίπτωσι θαμειαί thick fall the *snow*-flakes, Il.12.278; χ. πίπτουσα Hdt.4.31; κατένειψε χιόνι τὴν Θρᾴκην Ar.*Ach*.138; ὅταν βορέας χιόνα χέῃ E.*Cyc*. 329, cf. *Ba*.662; ἐπιπίπτει χ. X.*An*.4.4.11; χιόνες πολλαὶ γίνονται Thphr.*Sign*.24: [χ.] σφοδρὰ καὶ ἀθρόα καταφερομένη νιφετὸς ὀνόμασται Arist.*Mu*.394ᵃ36. **II.** *snow-water, ice-cold water*, Θρῄκην χιόνι.. κατάρρυτον E.*Andr*.215; χ. ποταμία Id.*Tr*.1067 (lyr.); used to cool wine, εἰ χιών ἐστ' ὠνία Euthycl.1; οἶνον πιεῖν.. χιόνι μεμιγμένον Stratt.57; χιόνα πίνειν Alex.141.10; τοῦ θέρους χιόνα.. ζητεῖς X. *Mem*.2.1.30; ἡδὺ θέρους.. χιὼν ποτόν *AP*5.168 (Ascl.): rare in pl., Arist.*Mu*.394ᵃ16. [ῐ by nature, ῑ Ep. metri gr.] (Cf. Skt. *himás* 'cold, winter', Lat. *hiems*, Avest. *zyam-* 'winter', etc.)

**χλαβός**, ή, όν, *well-fed*, Hsch.; cf. χλαμυρός.

***χλάδω**, *exult loudly*, assumed as pres. of κέχλᾱδα, wh. occurs thrice in Pi., καλλίνικος.. κεχλαδώς, of a triumphal hymn, *O*.9.2; κεχλάδοντας ἥβᾳ, of two young heroes, *P*.4.179; κέχλαδεν κρόταλα *Dith.Oxy*.2.10; Hsch. has κεχλῆδέναι· ψοφεῖν.

❀ **χλαῖνα**, ης, ἡ, *upper-garment, cloak, wrapper*, worn loose over the χιτών, Hom. (v. infr.), Alc.*Supp*.9.3, Sapph.*Supp*.22.9, etc.: in Hom. worn only by men, ἀνεμοσκεπής, ἀλεξάνεμος, Il.16.224, Od. 14.529; πυκνὴ καὶ μεγάλη ib.520; οὔλη 4.50, al.; ἀμφὶ δ' ἄρα χλαῖναν περονήσατο φοινικόεσσαν διπλῆν ἐκταδίην Il.10.133; ἀπ' ὤμοιϊν χ. θέτο Od.21.118; βῆ δὲ θέειν, ἀπὸ δὲ χ. βάλε Il.2.183, cf. Od.14. 500; given as a prize, Hdt.2.91; as ransom, Il.24.230; αἱ Πελληνικαὶ χ. ἃς καὶ ἆθλα ἐτίθεσαν ἐν τοῖς ἀγῶσι Str.8.7.5; also used as a *blanket* or *covering* in sleep, Od.4.299, 20.4; δέμνια καὶ χλαῖναι καὶ ῥήγεα 11.189; χλαῖναι καὶ ῥήγεα.. ἐνεύδειν 3.349; of husband and wife, μίμνομεν μιᾶς ὑπὸ χλαίνης S.*Tr*.540, cf. E.*Fr*.603.4, Theoc.18.19, *AP*5.164 (Mel.), 168 (Ascl.): metaph., χθονὸς χλαῖνα, i.e. earth thrown over a body *like a cloak* or *blanket*, A.*Ag*.872: prov., ἢ μήτε χ. μήτε σισύρα συμφέρει content neither with *cloak* nor rug, i.e. never satisfied, Ar.*Ra*.1459 (the σισύρα being coarser, cf. χλαῖναν μαλακήν, σισύραν Id.*V*.738 (anap.)); but also χ. δέ σοι λαβὼν παχεῖαν ἐπιβαλῶ Λακωνικήν Theopomp.Com.10; χ. πωλεῖν, when spring comes, Ar.*Av*.715 (anap.), cf. χλαῖνα· χλανίς, ἢ ἱμάτιον χειμερινόν, Hsch.: prov., ἐν τῷ θέρει τὴν χ. κατατρίβων, of reckless improvidence, Metrod.*Fr*.55: τράγου χ. μελέα, of a goatskin *cloak*, E.*Cyc*.80 (lyr.).

**χλαινηφόρος**, ον, *wearing a* χλαῖνα, Epic. in *BKT*5(1).115.

**χλαιν-ίζω**, *clothe with a* χλαῖνα, Hdn.*Epim*.149. **-ίον**, τό, Dim. of χλαῖνα, *AP*12.40. **-ιστής**, οῦ, ὁ, *one who clothes with a* χλαῖνα, Hdn.*Epim*.149.

**χλαινοθήρας**, ου, ὁ, = λωποδύτης, Eust.1863.59.

**χλαιν-όω**, *cover with a cloak*, φάρεϊ *AP*9.293 (Phil.): generally, *clothe*, εἵμασι Nonn.*D*.1.373. **-ωμα**, ατος, τό, *clothing*, χ. λέοντος the lion's skin *cloak*, *APl*.4.104 (Phil.).

❀ **χλᾰμῠδηφόρος**, ὁ, *one who wears a* χλαμύς, epith. of ephebi, Theoc.15.6, *IGRom*.4.360.25 (Pergam., ii A.D.).

**χλᾰμύδ-ιον** [ῠ], τό, Dim. of χλαμύς, Men.442 (troch.), *PCair.Zen*. 609.4 (iii B.C.), D.S.19.9, Plu.*Rom*.8, etc.; worn by ἔφηβοι, πρὶν ἐγγραφῆναι καὶ λαβεῖν τὸ χ. Antidot.2.2, cf. Teles p.42 H. **2.** *shabby cloak*, Plu.*Phoc*.29, *Demetr*.9, etc. **-ίσκη**, ἡ, in Boeot. form **χλᾰμουδίσκα**, = foreg. 1, *Schwyzer* 462 *B* 36 (Tanagra, iii B.C.).

**χλᾰμῠδο-ειδής**, ές, *like a* χλαμύς *in shape*, Str.2.5.9,14. **-ποιία**, ἡ, *making of* χλαμύδες, Poll.7.33,159, v.l. in X.*Mem*.2.7.6.

**χλᾰμῠδουργ-ία**, ἡ, = foreg., X.*Mem*.2.7.6. **-ός**, ὁ, *maker of* χλαμύδες, Poll.7.159.

❀ **χλᾰμῠδοφορέω**, *wear a* χλαμύς, = Θετταλίζειν, Poll.7.46.

**χλᾰμῠδόομαι**, Pass., *to be clad in a chlamys*, μειράκιον.. κεχλαμυδωμένον Nicostr.32.

**χλαμυρίς**, = βρόμος (B), Hsch.

**χλαμυρός**, ά, όν, *luxurious*, Hsch.; cf. χλαβός.

**χλᾰμύς** [ῠ], ύδος, ἡ: acc. χλαμύδα, also χλάμυν Sapph.64:—*short mantle*, worn prop. by horsemen, X.*An*.7.4.4; borrowed with the πέτασος from Thessaly, Philem.34, Poll.10.124; but said to be Macedonian, Arist.*Fr*.500, Phylarch.62 J.; worn by ἔφηβοι, Philem. l.c., cf. *AP*6.282 (Theod.); μάτηρ σε.. δῶρον ἐς Ἀΐδαν ὀκτωκαιδεκέταν ἐστόλισεν χλαμύδι ib.7.468 (Mel.); χλαμύδεσσ' ἀμφεμμένοι, of ephebi, *IGRom*.4.360.35 (Pergam., ii A.D.); ἐκ χλαμύδος, = ἐξ ἐφήβου, Plu.2.752f, cf. 754f; ἐκ χλαμύδος.. ᾤχετ' ἐς Ἀΐδα *IG*12(7).447.6 (Amorgos); worn by Hermes, Luc.*Tim*.30; also by Eros, Sapph. l.c. (v. Poll.10.124), Philostr.*Im*.1.6, cf. *AP*12.78 (Mel.). **2.** generally, *military cloak*, of foot-soldiers, Antiph.16, Men.331, Plu.*Phil*.11, etc.; of heralds, Ar.*Lys*.987. **3.** of *the general's cloak*, Phld.*Vit*.p.27 J., Plu.*Per*.35, *Lys*.13, etc.; worn by kings, Id.*Demetr*.42, etc.; by tragic kings and heroes, Luc.*JTr*.41; by Σειληνοί in a procession, Callix.2: = Lat. *paludamentum*, D.C.59. 17, 60.17, al., Hdn.4.7.3, *Cod.Theod*.14.10.1. **4.** a civilian's *mantle*, *PCair.Zen*.263.2, al. (iii B.C.), *PLond*.2.402 ii 16 (ii B.C.), X.Eph.1.8 cod., *POxy*.1288.24 (iv A.D.). (For its shape cf. Plu. *Alex*.26.)

❀ **χλᾰνίδ-ιον** [ῐδ], τό, Dim. of χλανίς, mostly of *a woman's mantle*, Hdt.1.195, Chaerem.14.9, *Trag.Adesp*.7, E.*Supp*.110, Ar.*Lys*.1190 (lyr.): pl., of *blankets, bedclothes*, E.*Or*.42: later, = Lat. *paludamentum*, Jul. *ad Ath*.277a; contemptuously addressed to Cicero, τὰ λεπτά σου χ. D.C.46.18:—also **χλάνδιον**, *Michel* 832.30 (Samos, iv B.C.), *GDI*5633.13 (near Teos). **-ίσκα**, ἁ, Boeot., = foreg., *Schwyzer* 462 *B*33 (Tanagra, iii B.C.). **-ίσκιον**, τό, = χλανίδιον, Aristaenet.1.11 (nisi leg. χλανισκίδιον).

**χλᾰνίδο-ποιία**, ἡ, *trade of a* χλανιδοποιός, X.*Mem*.2.7.6. **-ποιός**, ὁ, *maker of* χλανίδες, Poll.7.159.

**χλᾰνῐδ-ουργία**, ἡ, = χλανιδοποιία, Poll.7.34.

**χλᾰνίς**, ίδος, ἡ, *upper-garment of wool*, finer than χλαῖνα (but gloss on χλαῖνα, Hsch.), worn by women as well as men, Simon.37.12, Hdt.3.139, 140, Phld.*Vit.*p.21 J., etc.; used by old people, Ar.*Ec.* 848, Antiph.33.3; Μιλησία χ., i.e. of fine wool, Plu.*Alc.*23, 2.583e; χλανίδα φορεῖν, as a mark of effeminacy, D.36.45, cf. 21.133; παρθενικαί.. χλανίσιν μαλακαῖς κατάθρυπτοι Eub.108 (hex.), cf. *Com.Adesp.*338; σεμνὸς σεμνῶς χλανίδ' ἕλκων Ephipp.19 (anap.), cf. Anaxil.18.2 (anap.); opp. the τρίβων of the philosophers, Teles p.40 H., cf. p.53 H.; worn on festive occasions, γαμικὴ χ. *a wedding mantle*, Ar.*Av.*1693; χ. λευκή Id.*Fr.*491; used as a *blanket*, *AP*5.172 (Mel.), Plu.2.989f. 2. later, = χλαμύς 3, Lat. *paludamentum*, Jul.*ad Ath.*274c, 278d.

**χλᾰνίσκιον**, τό, Dim. of foreg., Ar.*Ach.*519, Aeschin.1.131; ὑπὸ τοὐμὸν κοιμωμένη χ. Alciphr.1.38.

**χλᾰνισκίδιον**, τό, = foreg., Ar.*Pax* 1002 (anap.).

**χλανίτιδες**, αἱ, *necklaces*, Hsch. **χλάνος**· τὸ περὶ τοὺς τραχήλους δάσος, Id.

**χλᾰρός**, ά, όν, only Pi.*P.*9.38 χλαρὸν (v.l. χλιαρόν) γελάσσαις to laugh *exultingly, gaily* (fort. χλοαρόν); but Hsch. has χλαρόν· κόχλαξ; also, = ῥυπαρόν, λεπτόν, τρυχαλέον, ὠχρόν, and = ἐλαιηρὸς κώθων, Id.

**χλεμερός**, ά, όν, *warm*; and **χλεμυρός**, ά, όν, *fresh-growing*, Hsch.

**χλέος**, ὁ, = χλῆδος, *IG*5(2).4.19 (Tegea, iv B.C.).

**χλευ-άζω**, (χλεύη) *jest, scoff*, ἐπισκώπτων καὶ παίζων καὶ χ. Ar.*Ra.* 376 (lyr.); τοῖς καταγελῶσι καὶ χ. καὶ σκώπτουσι Arist.*Rh.*1379a29, cf. Plb.4.3.13, Cerc.18 ii 5, Phld.*Lib.* p.29 O., etc. 2. c. acc., *scoff, jeer at, treat scornfully*, τινα Pl.*Erx.*397d, D.7.7, 19.23, 47.34, D.C.*Fr.*109.16; ἐμαυτὴν.. λέληθα χλευάζουσ' Men.*Epit.*215; c. acc. rei, Plu.*Rom.*10, etc.:—Med., Id.*Brut.*45:—Pass., Epicr.11.31 (anap.), Arist.*Pr.*952b22, Plu.*Sert.*13, 25, 2.504f. **-αξ**, ᾶκος, ὁ, Com. for χλευαστής, Poll.9.149. **-ᾰσία**, ἡ, *mockery, scoffing*, D.24.16, Arist.*Top.*144a6, D.C.39.19, al. **-ασμα**, ατος, τό, *mockery*, Lxx *Jb.*12.4, Sch.B *Il.*14.459. **-ασμός**, ὁ, = χλευασία, D.18.85, Plb.18.6.5, Phld.*Herc.*1457.9 (pl.), etc.; μετὰ χλευασμοῦ Plb.8.6.5; ἐπὶ χλευασμῷ Plu.2.277c; as a figure of speech, *irony*, Anon.*Fig.* p.213 S. 2. *mockery*, χ. εἶναι τὸ χρῆμα ἡγούμενος Plu.*Pomp.*36; *piece of impertinence*, Id.*Arat.*39. **-αστής**, οῦ, ὁ, *mocker, scoffer*, Arist.*Rh.*1380a29, Procl.*Par.Ptol.*230, Poll.9.149, etc.: c. gen., M.Ant.6.47. **-αστικός**, ή, όν, *derisory*, σκῶμμα Ph.2.552. Adv. -κῶς Satyr.*Vit.Eur.Fr.*39 xvii 9, Poll.6.200.

**χλευδόν**· χύδην, σωρηδόν, πληθύοντα, Hsch.

⊕ **χλεύη**, ἡ, *joke, jest*, *h.Cer.*202 (pl.); χλεύην ποιεῖσθαί or τίθεσθαί τινα (or τι) make *a jest* of.., Aeschrio 8, Ph.2.111; πρᾶγμα χλεύης ἄξιον Luc.*Par.*40, cf. Hdn.7.8.4. (Cf. ONorse *glý*, OE. *gléo* 'glee'.)

**χλήδης**, ου, ὁ, *eunuch*, Hsch.

⊕ **χλῆδος**, ὁ, *slime, mud, the rubbish carried down by a flood* or *swept out of a house*, A.*Fr.*16, D.55.22, 27: metaph., ἀργυρίου χλῆδον λαβών Crates Com.28 (on the accent v. Hdn.Gr.1.142; χλίδος Suid.).

**χλιά**, ἡ, *warmth*, D.S.34/5.15. **χλιάζω**, *warm*, Sch.Nic.*Al.*206.

⊕ **χλιαίνω**, fut. -ᾰνῶ Ar.*Lys.*386: pf. κεχλίαγκα Hsch.: Ion. aor. 1 ἐχλίηνα Hermesian.7.89: inf. χλιῆναι *AP*9.244 (Apollonid.):—Pass., aor. ἐχλιάνθην, Luc.*Am.*40, etc.: (χλίω):—*warm*, σεαυτόν Ar. l.c., cf. S.*Eleg.*4; κατὰ μικρὸν χ. τινά Arist.*Pr.*888b40; χ. ἵν' ἡ ὀδύνη ἔχῃ *foment* the painful place, Hp.*Aff.*10; προσπτήσαντα χ. πάλιν *warm up* meat, Alex.149.11; opp. ὀπτᾶν, Arist.*Pr.*929b31:—Pass., *warm oneself, grow warm*, dub. in Ar.*Ec.*64 (leg. ἐχραινόμην); κέρατα χλιαινόμενα τῷ κηρῷ *smeared with hot* wax, Arist.*HA*595b12; οἶνος κεχλιασμένος Sor.2.87; of persons affected by fever, Hp.*Coac.* 154; esp. *to be warmed by contact*, χρωτὶ *AP*5.164, al. (Mel.): also metaph. of passion, εἰδώλοις κάλλευς κωφὰ χ. ib.12.125 (Id.). [ῑ in Ar.*Lys.*, Alex., Hermesian., Apollonid.; ῐ in S.*Eleg.*, Ar.*Ec.* l.c. (sed v. supr.), Mel.]

⊕ **χλιᾰρός**, ά, όν, also ός, όν Nic.*Al.*360; Ion. **χλιερός** (also in Alcm. 33.5, Sor.1.52; misspelt χλιεριον in *PHolm.*16.27), ή, όν: (χλίω):—*warm*, Epich.[290]; ὕδωρ Hdt.4.181, Diocl.*Fr.*139, Sor.1.82; of food, Magnes 1, Cratin.125 (troch.), 143 (hex.), Ar.*Ach.*975 (lyr.); τὸ σῶμα ἡμῶν ἀτμίδα τινὰ χ. ἀφίησιν Arist.*Pr.*884b17; τὸ χ. τὸ ἐν γλώσσῃ *Placit.*4.18.1. Adv. χλιηρῶς (v.l. -ρῷ) Hp.*Fist.*9; καταπλάσσειν χλιηρόν ibid. 2. of persons, *lukewarm*, *Apoc.*3.16. [ῑ in Com. ll. cc.; but ῐ in Epich. l.c., Alcm. l.c.]

**χλιᾰρότης**, ητος, ἡ, *warmth*, Procl.*Par.Ptol.*53.

**χλιᾰροψύχιον** [ῡ], τό, *tepid bath*, *Gloss.*

**χλί-ασμα**, ατος, τό, *fomentation*, in pl., Hp.*Acut.*(*Sp.*)33, *Mul.*1.35, Sor.2.28. ⊕ **-άω**, *to be warm*, in Ep. part., χλιόωντι ποτῷ Nic.*Al.*110 (v.l. χλιόεντι); κρίμνον χλιάον Id.*Fr.*68.8 (sed leg. χλιαρόν); ἀτὰρ ἦγὸς ἀφάσσων στέρνα πόθῳ χλιάοι dub. sens. in *Hesperia* 5.95 (Athens, iii A.D.).

⊕ **χλίβιον**, τό, an Egyptian measure, σκόρδων, ταρίχου, *Aegyptus* 9.268 (ii A.D.).

**χλῐδ-αίνομαι**, Pass., *to be luxurious*, ἁβρότητι χλιδαίνεσθαι *revel* in luxury, lead a voluptuous, sensual life, X.*Smp.*8.8. **-ᾰνός**, ή, όν, Aeol. **χλίδᾰνος** [ῐ], α, ον, *luxurious, delicate, voluptuous*, Sapph.*Supp.*21.8; χλιδανῆς ἥβης τέρψιν A.*Pers.*544 (anap.); ἑταίρα E.*Cyc.* 500 (lyr.); of Alcibiades, Plu.*Alc.*23; cf. χλιδή sub fin. **-ᾰνόσφῠρος**, ον, *with delicate ankles*, Anacreont.41.7. **-άω**, poet. Verb, *to be soft* or *delicate*, χλιδῶσα μολπά Pi.*O.*10(11).84; χλιδῶν πλόκαμος A.*Fr.*313: but mostly in bad sense, *live delicately* or *luxuriously*, Ar.*Lys.*640 (troch.); rare in Prose, χ. κατὰ τὴν δίαιταν Arr.*An.*5.4.4: c. dat., *revel in*, τοῖς παροῦσι πράγμασι A.*Pr.*971; πλούτῳ E.*Fr.* 986; πώγωνι S.*Ichn.*358; χ. ἐπί τινι *to pride oneself* upon a thing, δῶρ' ἐφ' οἷσι νῦν χλιδᾷς Id.*El.*360: abs., *show insolence*, A.*Supp.*833 (lyr., s. v.l.). **-ή**, ἡ, *delicacy, luxury, effeminacy*, ἐπὶ πλεῖστον χλιδῆς ἀπίκετο Hdt.6.127; ἄγαλμα τῆς ὑπερπλούτου χ. A.*Pr.*466; εὐνῆς παροψώνημα τῆς ἐμῆς χ. Id.*Ag.*1447; οἶκος ὀγκωθεὶς χλιδῇ S.*Fr.*942; τρυφή, ἁβρότης, χ. Pl.*Smp.*197d; ἐν χλιδῇ τεθράμμεθα X.*Cyr.*4.5.54. 2. *wantonness, insolence*, μή τοι χλιδῇ δοκεῖτε μηδ' αὐθαδίᾳ σιγᾶν με A.*Pr.*436; δυσπότμου χάριν χ. S.*OT*888 (lyr.). 3. concrete, of *luxuries, fine raiment, costly ornaments*, etc., E.*Ion* 26; μυρίων πέπλων χλιδή Id.*Rh.*960: pl., χλιδὰς πόντος ἥρπασε Id.*Hel.* 424; of *personal charms*, παρθένων χλιδαῖσιν εὐμόρφοις A.*Supp.* 1003; καράτομοι χλιδαὶ *luxuriant hair* cut from the head, S.*El.*52; ζῶμα.. οὐ χλιδαῖς ἠσκημένον *luxuriously, richly*, ib.452; κόμας ἐμάς.. παρθένιον χλιδάν a maiden's *pride*, E.*Ph.*224 (lyr.):—Mostly poet. [ῑ only late, Ps.-Phoc.212 (sed leg. χλιδαναῖς).] (Cf. χλοιδᾶν, ONorse *glita, glitra* 'glitter', Goth. *glitmunjan* 'shine bright' (of clothes).) **-ημα**, ατος, τό, = χλιδή, E.*IA*74. **-ῐάω**, Desiderat., *wish to be luxurious*, cj. Lobeck (*Path.El.*1.157) for κιχλιδιάω in *Com. Adesp.*1038. **-ος**, εος, τό, = χλίδημα, Ion Trag.3. 2. v. χλῆδος. II. χλιδός· σακκοπάθνιον, Hsch. ⊕ **-ων**, ωνος, ὁ, *ornament, bracelet*, or *anklet*, Asius *Fr.Ep.*13.6 K., Ar.*Fr.*320.11, Polyzel.11, *IG*$2^2$.1388.85, 1417.9: pl., D.S.18.27, Plu.2.145a (prob. l.), Lxx *Nu.*31.50, al. (on the accent v. Hdn.Gr.2.729). ⊕ **-ώνιον**, τό, Dim. of foreg., *IG*$2^2$.1445.46.

**χλιδωνόπους**, ὁ, ἡ, gen. -ποδος, *with ornaments on the feet*, Hsch.

**χλίδωσις**, εως, ἡ, *ornamentation*, f.l. for χλίδωσι (cf. χλίδων), Plu.2.145a.

**χλῐεροθαλπής**, ές, *lukewarm*, Philox.2.40.

**χλῐερός**, ή, όν, Ion. for χλιαρός: also Adv. **χλιηρῶς**, Hp.*Mul.*1.78; cf. χλιαρός.

***χλίζω**, only pf. part. κεχλιδότα· ἀνθοῦντα, Hsch.

**χλῐόεις**, εσσα, εν, = χλιαρός, v.l. for χλιόωντι in Nic.*Al.*110.

**χλιόομαι**, Pass., = σχίζομαι, Hsch.

**χλίω** [ῑ], *luxuriate, revel*, ἐν τοῖσι σοῖς πόνοισι χλίουσιν μέγα A.*Ch.* 137; ὅμιλον.. πέπλοισι βαρβάροισι.. χλίοντα Id.*Supp.*236.

**χλῐώδης**, ες, *slightly hot*, πυρετός Herod.Med.ap.Orib.6.20.23.

**χλο-άζω**, (χλόη) *to be bright green*, Arist.*Mir.*846b13: esp. of plants, Corn.*ND*28, Plu.2.517d, *Gp.*11.18.8; τὸ χλοάζον πᾶν Ael.*VH*3.1. II. *sprout, bud*, Nic.*Th.*576; σπέρμα παρ' ἀτραπιτοῖσι χλοάζον ib.917. III. Med., *feed on grass*, *Hippiatr.*97. IV. metaph., ἄρτι χλοαζούσας αὐλητρίδας *budding*, cj. for χνο- in Metag.4.3 (hex.). **-ανθέω**, *bud, sprout*, Hsch. **-ανθής**, ές, *budding, sprouting*, πράσιον Nic.*Th.*550. 2. *pale*, Philum.*Ven.* 16.5, Dsc.*Ther.*17. **-ᾰνός**, ή, όν, *greenish*, Lyd.*Mens.*1.12. II. f.l. for χοάνοις, Hsch. **-αρός**, = χλωρός, cj. in Pi.*P.*9.38; cf. χλαρός. **-ασμα**, ατος, τό, f.l. for χλώρασμα, Gal.17(1).929. **-αυγής**, ές, *with a greenish lustre*, Luc.*Dom.*11. **-άω**, = χλοάζω I or II, Eup.105, Nic.*Th.*30, al., *AP*5.291 (Agath.); πρὶν χλοῆσαι τὴν γῆν Ph.1.30, cf. Jul.*Caes.*329d. II. *grow pale*, Nonn.*D.*8.207, al. **-δη**· ἔκλυσις καὶ μαλακία, Hsch. **-ερός**, ά, όν, *verdant*, ὄζος Hes.*Sc.*393; χλοεραῖς λείμακος ἡδοναῖς E.*Ba.* 866 (lyr.); χ. στάδια, ῥέεθρα, Id.*Ion* 497 (lyr.), *Ph.*660 (lyr.); χ. ὑλώδη πάγον S.*Ichn.*215; χ. μέλεα Theocr.27.67. **-εροτρόφος**, ον, *producing green grass*, πεδίον E.*Ph.*826 (lyr.). **-εύνης**, v. χλούνης I. 4.

**χλόη**, ἡ, Ion. **χλοίη** Hp.*Acut.*64, cf. infr. II, also *PTeb.*112.46 (ii B.C.), Babr.181; Dor. **χλόα**, ας (E. in lyr., *Hipp.*1139, *IA* 1058, al.):—*the first green shoot of plants* in spring, ναὶ μὰ μήκωνος χλόην Archil.108; esp. *young green corn* or *grass*, Hdt.4.34, E.*Hipp.* l.c., *IA* 422, etc.; χλόην νέμεσθαι Id.*Ba.*735; ποτὰ τὰ ἀπὸ χλοίης Hp. l.c.; opp. καρποί, Pl.*Ti.*80d; χλόης γενομένης ἀπὸ τοῦ σπέρματος, of the corn when it first springs up, X.*Oec.*17.10; ἐν τῇ χ., opp. ἐν τοῖς σπέρμασιν, Thphr.*CP*4.4.7, cf. *HP*8.2.4; πιαίνονται βόες χλόῃ κυάμων Arist.*HA*595b7. 2. poet., *young verdure* of trees, *foliage*, χ. ἀμπέλου E.*Ba.*12, cf. *Supp.*258, *Ion* 1435, *Hel.*180 (lyr.), 1360 (lyr.). 3. *juice* of green shoots, χ. ἐλαίας *IG*7.3073.162 (Lebad. ii B.C.). [ο̆]: but σατυρίου χλόῃ is prob. f.l. for σαύρου χολῇ in *Gp.*10.21.12. 4. *vegetables, herbs, greens*, Antiph.1.5, Sotad.Com.1.9, al. II. epith. of Demeter, *Verdant*, from the young corn, worshipped in Attica, *IG*$2^2$.1356.16, Semus 19, Paus.1.22.3; at Myconos, etc., *SIG*1024.11 (Myconos, iii/ii B.C.), Corn.*ND*28; Δήμητρος Χλοίης ἱερόν *IG*$2^2$.5006.4; also Χλόη alone, ib.1358.49, Ar.*Lys.*835. (Perh. cogn. with Lith. *žélti* 'to be green, grow', Lat. *holus*.)

**χλοη-βᾰφος**, ον, *dyed green*, f.l. for χολήβαφος (q.v.). **-κομέω**, *have green shoots*, *AP*9.750 (Arch.).

**χλοήρης**, ες, = χλοερός, χλωρός, μῖλαξ prob. in E.*Ba.*107 (lyr.); **χλοηρός**, Hp.ap.Gal.19.155.

**χλοη-τόκος**, ον, *producing young shoots*, Luc.*Trag.*45. **-φᾰγέω**, *to be herbivorous*, Ph.2.340. **-φᾰγία**, ἡ, *eating of grass*, ib.289. **-φάγος** [ᾰ], ον, *herbivorous*, ζῷα ib.238. **-φορέω**, *put out young shoots*, Thphr.*HP*8.6.5, Ph.1.358. **-φόρος**, ον, *bearing green grass* or *leaves*, γύαι, ἔνεα, E.*Ph.*647 (lyr.), 653 (lyr.); γῆ Ph.2.494, al.

⊕ **χλόϊα**, τά, *festival of Demeter* Χλόη and Κόρη at Eleusis, *IG*$2^2$.949.7, 35, cf. χλοιά (sic)· ἑορτὴ ἀπὸ τῶν καρπῶν (κάλπων cod.), Hsch.

**χλοιδᾶν**· διέλκεσθαι καὶ τρυφᾶν, Hsch.; also **χλοιδῶσι**· θρύπτονται, Id., and **χλοιδέσκουσαι**· γαστρίζουσαι, Id. (Cf. χλιδή, χλιδάω.)

**χλοιόομαι**, Pass., = χλωραίνομαι, Hp.ap.Gal.19.155, Gal.17(1).343.

**χλοό-καρπος**, ον, *producing green fruits*, epith. of Demeter, Orph. *H*.40.5. **-μορφος**, ον, *like grass, greenish*, ib.84.6.

⊛ **χλόος**, ὁ, *greenish-yellow* or *light green colour*: hence, *pallor*, χ. εἷλε παρειάς A.R.2.1216, cf. 3.298, Nic.*Al*.570, 579; δειελινὴν τήν δ' εἷλε κακὸς χ. Call.*Aet*.3.1.12; contr. **χλοῦς** Hp.ap.Gal.19.155.

**χλοσσός**, ὁ, Ion. for ἰχθύς, Hsch.

**χλουβοκεραμεύς**, έως, ὁ, perh. *maker of ovens* or *kilns*, *POxy*.1913.21 (vi A.D.).

**χλούδειν**, v. χλούνης II.3.

**χλουία**, ἡ, dub. sens. in *PHarris* 79 (iii A.D.).

**χλουνάζειν**· κινύρεσθαι, Hsch.

**χλούνειος**, α, ον, *of the wild boar*, Zonar.: neut. Χλούνειον, τό, place-name, Hdn.Gr.2.459.

**χλούνης**, ου, ὁ, Ep. epith. of the wild boar, χ. σῦς ἄγριος Il.9.539; χλοῦναι σύες Hes.*Sc*.177; συῶν ἀγέλαι χλούνων ib.168; χ. κάπρος Call.*Dian*.150. II. χλούνης alone, as Subst., = κάπρος, *wild boar*, Opp.*H*.1.12: hence ἤνυσε.. χλούνηνδε reached the *wild boar's lair* Nic.*Fr*.74.6. The word was variously interpreted: 1. = τομίας, *castrated* (because larger and more vicious), Arist.*HA*578ᵇ1, etc.: hence χ. τε καὶ γύνανδρος ἀνήρ, ὁ χ. τε καὶ γύννις, Ael.*Fr*.10. 2. = μονιός, *solitary*, κατά τε χαλεπότητα καὶ ἀλκήν Ar.Byz.ap.Eust. 772.59. 3. = ἀφριστής, *foaming* at the mouth, from Dor. *χλούδειν, = ἀφρίζειν, Sch.B Il.9.539. 4. = χλοεύνης, ὁ ἐν τῇ χλόῃ εὐναζόμενος, *couching in the grass* or *greenwood*, Apollon.*Lex*., *AB*1260, *EM*812.46. III. *robber*, cf. χλοῦναι· λωποδύται οἱ τῇ χλόῃ εὐναζόμενοι, Hsch.; thus ἄνδρα δ' ἑσπέρης καθεύδοντα ἀπ' ὧν ἔδυσε.. χλούνης Hippon.61; ἢ φῶρας ἀναιδέας ἤ τινα χλούνην Alex.Aet.5.7; so perh. μακροσκελὴς μὲν ἆρα μὴ χ. τις ᾖ; A.*Fr*.62.

**χλοῦνις**, ἡ, *virility*, σπέρματός τ' ἀποφθοραὶ (Musgrave ἀποφθορᾷ) παίδων κακοῦται χ. A.*Eu*.188.

**χλουνός**, ὁ, = χρυσός, Hsch.

**χλοῦς**, v. χλόος.

**χλοώδης**, ες, *grass-green, greenish-yellow, pale*, Hp.*Epid*.4.13, Pl. *Ti*.83b, Thphr.*HP*3.18.8, 7.9.2, *Gp*.10.74.1.

**χλυρών**, = *sanium*, *Gloss*. (dub.).

**χλωρ-άζω**, *eat green provender*, Gal.17(1).929. **-αθέω**, *gleam green* (formed on the analogy of λευκαθέω), cj. in Theoc.25.158, *IG*14.1389 ii 24 (v. θέω (B): but these poets may have meant χλωρὰ θεούσῃ (-αν), misunderstanding λευκαθεόντων in Hes.*Sc*.146). **-αίνομαι**, Pass., *become pale*, aor. part. Pass. -ανθείς S.*Fr*.1114; -αίνεσθαι as expl. of (ἐκ-)χλοιοῦσθαι, Gal.17(1).343:—Act. in *Gloss*. **-άκοπον** [ᾰ], τό, *a green plaster for the relief of pain* (cf. ἄκοπος II. 2), Heras ap.Gal.13.1046. **-ασμα**, ατος, τό, = χλωρότης, Hp. *Epid*.6.2.6. **-αύχην**, ενος, ὁ, ἡ, *fresh-throated*, of the nightingale, Simon.73; *with the bloom of youth on her neck*, of Deïanira, B.5.172. **-άω** or **-έω**, = χλωριάω, f.l. in Jul.*Caes*.329d. **-εύς**, έως, ὁ, an unknown *bird*, Arist.*HA*609ᵃ7, Plin.*HN*10.203, Ael.*NA* 5.48. **-ηΐς**, ΐδος, pecul. poet. fem. of χλωρός, *of the greenwood*, or (less prob.) *pale green*, epith. of the nightingale, χλωρηῒς ἀηδών Od.19.518. **-ίασις**, εως, ἡ, *a greenish colour, paleness*, Hsch. s. v. χλόος. **-ιάω**, *to be greenish, to be pale*, Hp.*Epid*.4.35, Longus 4.31. **-ίζω**, *to be greenish* or *pale*, Lxx *Le*.13.49, 14.37; λίθος -ίζων Herm.Trism. in *Rev.Phil*.32.258, cf. Aët.4.9. ⊛ **-ικός**, ή, όν, perh. f.l. for χωρικός, ἀρτεμισία *PMag.Par*.1.914. **-ίς**, ίδος, ἡ, *greenfinch*, *Fringilla chloris*, Arist.*HA*592ᵇ17, 615ᵇ32, Nic.*Fr*.54, Ael.*NA*4.47. II. a kind of *grape*, *Gp*.5.2.4. **-ῖτις** (sc. λίθος), ιδος, ἡ, *grass-green stone*, Plin.*HN*37.156. **-ίων**, ωνος, ὁ, *golden oriole*, *Oriolus galbula*, Arist.*HA*616ᵇ11, 617ᵃ28, Plin.*HN*10.87.

**χλωρο-βοτάνη** [ᾰ], ἡ, v.l. for χλωρὰ β., Lxx 4*Ki*.19.26 cod.Alex. **-ειδής**, ές, *of a greenish appearance*, Thphr.*Lap*.33 (Comp.). **-κομος**, ον, *green-leaved*, στέφανος δάφνας E.*IA*759 (lyr.). **-κυρτίς**, ίδος, ἡ, a kind of *prawn* (καρίς), Hsch. **-μέλᾱς**, μέλαινα, μέλᾰν, *dark green*, Gal.17(2).66. **-ποιός**, όν, *making green* or *pale*, S.E. *M*.6.49, Hsch. s.v. χλωρὸν δέος, etc. **-πτῖλος**, ον, *with green feathers*, πελειάδες Ael.*NA*16.2.

⊛ **χλωρός**, ά, όν, *greenish-yellow, pale green*, χλωραὶ ῥῶπες Od.16.47; ὕρος.. χλωρόν *h.Ap*.223; χλωραὶ ἐλάται Pi.*Fr*.167, E.*Ba*.38; χλωραῖς ὑπὸ βάσσαις S.*OC*673 (lyr.); χλωρὰν ἀν' ὕλην E.*Hipp*.17; δόνακι χλωρὸν Εὐρώταν Id.*Hel*.349 (lyr.), cf. S.*Ant*.1132 (lyr.); also in Prose, σίτου ἔτι χ. ὄντος Th.4.6; τὰ φυόμενα χ. τὸ πρῶτον εἶναι Thphr.*Sens*. 78; ἡ χ. the *green plaster*, Androm.ap.Gal.13.470; χλωρὸς λίθος, = σμάραγδος, *PHolm*.5.10; of sea-water, Poet.ap.Plu.2.767f (cf. E.*Fr*. 1084); of other water, *AP*9.669.3 (Marian.): χλωρά, ἡ, *green paint*, as a stage-property to represent a river in scenery, Pap. in *Eos* 32. 30 (v/vi A.D.). 2. *yellow*, μέλι χ. Il.11.631, Od.10.234; ἀμφὶ χλωρὰν ψάμαθον on the *yellow* sand, S.*Aj*.1064; φοῦ τὸ χ. *yolk* of egg, Zopyr.ap.Orib.14.61.1. II. generally, *pale, pallid*, χλωρὸς ἀδάμας Hes.*Sc*.231: most freq., 2. of persons, *pale*, χλωρὸς ὑπαὶ δείους Il.10.376, 15.4; χ. 'Αχλὺς (personified) Hes.*Sc*.265; χλωροτέρα.. ποίας ἔμμι Sapph.2.14; hence as an epith. of fear, χλωρὸν δέος Il.7.479, Od.11.43, etc.; χλωρῷ δείματι A.*Supp*.566 (lyr.), cf. E.*Supp*.599 (lyr.): in Medic. writers, *yellow, bilious-looking*, ὀφθαλμοὶ -ότεροι v.l. in Hp.*VM*10; χρῶμα χ. ἴσχειν Id.*Prog*. 24; σῶμα.. οὔτε χ. ἀλλ' ὑπέρυθρον Th.2.49; also χ. πτύελος, οὖρον, Hp.*Prog*.14, *VM*10 (Comp.). III. without regard to colour, *green*, i.e. *fresh*, opp. dry, esp. of wood, ῥόπαλον.. χλωρὸν ἐλαΐνεον of *green* olive-wood, Od.9.320, cf. 379; opp. αὖος, Hes.*Op*.743; τὰ σφόδρα χ. ἄκαυστα Arist.*Mete*.387ᵃ22; χ. ξύλα ib.374ᵃ5, al.; of various things, χλωραὶ ἐέρσαι Pi.*N*.8.40; τυρὸς χ. *fresh* cheese, Ar.*Ra*.559, Lys.23.6; of fish, *fresh, not salted*, Ath.7.309b; of fruit, *fresh picked*, *IG*2².1013.23, Dsc.1.113. 2. metaph., *fresh, blooming*, χλωρόν τε καὶ βλέποντα Trag.ap.Hsch. (perh. to be read in A.*Ag*.677 for καὶ ζῶντα καὶ β.); λειμὼν ἄνθεσι (sed fort. ἔρνεσι) θάλλων χλωροῖς E.*IA*1297 (lyr.); χλωρὸν γόνυ Theoc.14.70; χ. αἷμα *fresh, living*, S.*Tr*.1055, E.*Hec*.127 (anap.); χ. δάκρυ *fresh, bursting* tear, E.*Med*.906, cf. 922, *Hel*.1189; χλωρὰ δακρύων ἄχνα S.*Tr*.847 (lyr.); οἴνου χλωραὶ σταγόνες *sparkling*, E.*Cyc*.67 (lyr.). 3. metaph., *unripe*, χ. καὶ ἄναιμα πράγματα Gorg.*Fr*.16. (Not contr. fr. χλοερός but cogn. with it and χλόη.)

**χλωρο-σαῦρα**, ἡ, *green lizard*, Sch.rec.Theoc.2.58, 7.22. **-στρουθίον**, τό, = *galucis*, *Gloss*. (dub.).

⊛ **χλωρότης**, ητος, ἡ, *greenness*, ὕλης Plu.*Flam*.3; *yellowness*, χρυσίου Lxx *Ps*.67(68).14; *freshness*, Sch.Opp.*H*.2.495. II. *pale colour*, of gold mixed with silver, Plu.2.952c; *pallor*, νοσώδης χ. ib.395c.

**χλωρό-τομος**, ον, *freshly cut*, δάφνα Aristonous 1.10. **-τῦρα**, τά, *green cheese*, dub. in *Gloss*. **-φᾰγέω**, *eat green food*, *Hippiatr*. 10. **-φάγος** [ᾰ], ον, *eating green food*, Hp.*Vict*.2.49. **-φυλλακία**, ἡ, = *viridiarium*, *Gloss*.

**χνάσμι**, τό, given as instance of a neuter Subst. in Theognost. *Can*.120.

**χναῦμα**, ατος, τό, *slice, tit-bit*, Mnesim.4.12 (anap., Meineke for χναύω), cf. Poll.6.62, Hsch.; πᾶν χ. 'every scrap', = πᾶν πρᾶγμα, Zen.5.73; **χναυμάτιον**, τό, Dim. of foreg., Ar.*Fr*.224 (anap.), Teleclid.1.14 (anap.), Ath.9.381b.

**χναυρός**, ά, όν, *dainty*, πλευρὰ δελφάκει'.. χναυρότατα Pherecr. 108.17.

**χναυστικός**, ὁ, *one of a sweet tooth*, Posidipp.1.7.

**χναύω**, *nibble*, c. acc., Epich.164, E.*Cyc*.358 (lyr.), Eub.150.6, Ephipp.8.4.

**χνιαρωτέρα**· χνοω⟨δεσ⟩τέρα, Hsch. **χνίει**· ψακάζει, θρύπτει, Id.

**χνοάζω**, prop. of youths, *get the first down*, Him.*Or*.7.3; also of girls, αὐλητρίδες ἄρτι χνοάζουσαι Metag.4.3 (hex.); cf. χλοάζω IV. II. χνοάζων ἄρτι λευκανθὲς κάρα just *sprinkling* his hair with white, S.*OT*742.

⊛ **χνοάω**, commoner form of foreg., of a girl's cheeks, μᾶλα τεὰ.. χνοάοντα Theoc.27.50: more freq. of youths, τὴν παρειὰν χνοῶν Luc. *Bacch*.2; c. acc. cogn., χνοάοντα ἰούλους A.R.2.779, cf. Opp.*C*.4.347; of the down itself, χνοάοντες ἴουλοι *the bloom of the first down*, A.R. 2.43; ἔτι χνοάοντος ἰούλου δευόμενος *IG*14.1362.1 (Rome); of fruit, σίκυον χνοάοντα a gourd *with the bloom on it*, v.l. for χλοάοντα (ap. Sch.Ar., Suid.) in *AP*6.102 (Phil.): metaph., *fresh*, χνοάωσαν χάριν ὄμβρου Tryph.343.

**χνόη**, Ion. **χνοίη**, *axle-box, nave*, ἄξων ἐν χνοίῃσιν Parm.1.6; prob. in Emp.46; ἔλακον ἀξόνων βριθομένων χνόαι A.*Th*.153 (lyr); ἔθραυσε δ' ἄξονος μέσας χνόας S.*El*.745, cf. 717; ἀντύγων χνόας E.*Rh*.118. 2. metaph., χνόαι ποδῶν *the joints* on which the feet play, as the wheels on the axle, A.*Th*.371.

**χνοΐζω**, *to be downy*, νεογνὰ γενειάσι χρῶτα χνοΐζων *Inscr.Cret*.1 xxii 59 (Olus, ii A.D.):—also Pass., Gal.14.778.

**χνόϊος**, α, ον, *downy*, παρειή *Anacreont*.16.18.

⊛ **χνόος**, ὁ (ἡ E.*Fr*.1106), Att.contr. **χνοῦς**, gen. χνοῦ: heterocl. gen. χνοός Choerob. *in Theod*.1.234H.; dat. χνοΐ Thphr.*CP*6.10.7, Gal.13.850:—ἁλὸς χ. *incrustation* from salt water, ἐκ κεφαλῆς ἔσμηχεν ἁλὸς χνόον, Od.6.226; *wool pulled* for stuffing cushions, *flock*, f.l. for μνοῦς in Hp.*Mul*.1.61; used in applying a powder, Gal. l.c.; *chaff*, Lxx *Ps*.1.4: *powder*, prov., [ὄνος] εἰς ἄχυρα καὶ χνοῦν Ar.*Fr*.76; *dust* of the earth, Lxx 2*Ki*.22.43, 2*Ch*.1.9; ὡς δοκεῖν τοῦ καλουμένου χνοῦ μεστοὺς εἶναι (sc. τοὺς ὀφθαλμούς) Gal.16.552. II. *fine down* on a flower or in the seed-vessel, Thphr.*HP*2.8.4, D.S.2.59: *bloom* on fruit, ἐν Καρίᾳ φασὶν ἀπιόν τιν' ἔχειν χνοῦν ἁλμώδη Thphr.*CP*6.10.7; μάλων χνοῦς ἐπικαρπίδιος *AP*9.226 (Zon.); *the first down on the chin* or *cheeks*, χνοῦς ὥσπερ μήλοισιν ἐπήνθει Ar.*Nu*.978 (anap.); κοῦρος ἔτ' ἀρτιγένειον ἔχων χνόον *AP*9.219 (Diod.); θηλείαις οὐδ' ὅσσον ἐπὶ χνόος ἦλθε παρειαῖς Call.*Ap*.37; ἐντίκτει τι χνοῦ ἀνάπλεων Arist.*HA*605ᵇ15: pl., D.H.*Dem*.51. 2. metaph., *bloom* or *film* of archaism in writing, ὃ τε πίνος αὐτῇ (i.e. in Plato's style) [καὶ χ.] ὁ τῆς ἀρχαιότητος.. ἐπιτρέχει interpol. in D.H.*Dem*.5; ἐπανθεῖ τις.. χνοῦς ἀρχαιοπινής ib.38, cf. Plu.2.79d; οἱονεὶ τῆς γονίμου φύσεως χ., of χλόη, Porph.*Abst*.2.5. (Cf. χνιαρωτέρα, χνίει.)

**χνοώδης**, ες, *like fine powder, downy*, Hp.*Ulc*.17, Thphr.*HP*1.10.3, Dsc.4.68; μηλέαι prob. in Androt.*Georg*.ap.Ath.3.82c (χνοωδίας codd.); of salt, Sor.1.82; of arsenic, Olymp.Alch.p.75B.: Comp., Dsc.2.175, Anon.ap.Suid.: Sup., Gal.6.283, Sch.E.*Or*.115. Adv. -δῶς Gal.11.405. II. ἀὴρ χ., *soft*, 'muggy', opp. λαμπρός, v.l. for νοτώδης Hp.*Aër*.15.

**χοαῖος**, α, ον, *holding a* χοῦς (A), σκύφος Hippoloch.ap.Ath.4.129e; σταμνία Anon.ap.Suid. (χοίδια codd.).

⊛ **χοᾰν-εύω**, contr. **χωνεύω**, (χόανος) *cast in a mould*, χοανεύει Ar. *Th*.57, cf. 62 (both anap.): c. acc., *cast, form by casting*, χωνεύσεις.. βάσεις χαλκᾶς Lxx *Ex*.26.37, cf. 2 *Ch*.4.3, al.:—Med., διέχεαν χαλκὸν πρῶτοι καὶ ἀγάλματα ἐχωνεύσαντο 'Ροῖκος κτλ. Paus.8.14.8. II. *smelt* or *cast* metal, Lxx 2 *Ch*.34.17:—Pass., χωνευθείς

Plb.34.9.11, D.S.5.35; ὑπὸ τοῦ πυρὸς κεχωνευμένος Id.16.45; κεχ. ἀργύριον Plu.*Luc.*37. III. metaph., *get together*, ἀργύριον Lxx 4 *Ki.*22.9. IV. v. χωνεύω II. **–η**, contr. **χώνη**, *funnel*, δίκην δὲ χοάνης (fort. ἀκοῇ δὲ χοάνην) ὦτα διετετρήνατο Ar.*Th.*18, cf. Ph.1.245; κύλικας ἀντλεῖν διὰ χώνης Pherecr.108.31; καταχεῖν ὥσπερ διὰ χώνης Pl.*R.*411a; as a name of the throat, Alex.Aphr.*Pr.*2.3; as nickname of a great drinker, Ath.10.436e. 2. Medic., *funnel-shaped hollow in the brain*, also called ληνός, πύελος, Herophil.ap. Theophil.*Corp.Fabr.*4.5.5. 3. *hollow* behind the eye, cj. in Emp. 84.9 (pl.). II. = χόανος, *melting-pot*, Posidon.48J., Dsc.5.75, *AP*9.528 (Pall.).—The form χοάνη is said by Moer.p.401 P. to be Att. (cf. *IG*1$^{2}$313.127, 314.144), χώνη Hellenic. **–ος**, ὁ, (χέω) *hollow in which metal was placed for melting*, *melting-pot*, from which it was run into the mould, φῦσαι δ' ἐν χοάνοισιν..ἐφύσων Il.18.470; κασσίτερος..ἐν εὐτρήτοις χοάνοισιν θαλφθείς Hes.*Th.*863, cf. Emp.96.1, Hp.*Cord.*8, A.R.3.1299. 2. poet. for λίγδος II, *mould for casting* metal in, Anacr.116. II. = χοάνη I, *funnel*, Hp.*Cord.*2 (χῶνος, as in *PLeid.X.*29B., Hsch.).

**χοάρβηνα·** τὰ γράμματα, Hsch. **χοᾶσθαι·** καυχᾶσθαι, Id.

**Χοασπῖτις** [ῑ], ιδος, ἡ (sc. λίθος), a precious stone *found in the Choaspes*, Plin.*HN*37.156.

**χοάσσομαι·** ἐπίξομαι, Hsch.

**χοαχύτης**, ου, ὁ, *keeper of mummies*, ecclesiastical title in Egypt, *UPZ*157.34 (iii B.C.), *PLond.*1.3.3 (ii B.C.).

**χόδᾰνος**, ὁ, = ἕδρα, Hsch. (cf. χέζω).

⊛ **χοδέαντες**, = χοδιτεύοντες, Sophr. in *PSI*11.1214*d*.5.

**χοδιτεύειν·** ἀποπατεῖν, Hsch.

**χοεῖον**, τό, = παχὺ ἔντερον (i.e. f.l. for χόριον), Suid.

**χόες, χοεύς**, v. χοῦς (A).

**χοεύω**, = χώννυμι, *IG*4.823.36 (Troezen).

**χοή**, ἡ, (χέω) *pouring out* of liquid, *drink-offering*, esp. made to the dead or over their graves (opp. λοιβή, σπονδή made to the gods), χοὴν χεῖσθαι νεκύεσσιν (where it is mixed with milk), of honey, wine, and water, poured out in succession, Od.10.518, cf. 11.26, Arist.*Mu.*400$^{b}$22: freq. in Trag., always in pl. (as also Hdt.7.43), χέουσα κηδείους χοάς A.*Ch.*87; χοὰς φέρειν τινί Id.*Pers.*609, *Ch.*15, etc.; χ. γῇ τε καὶ φθιτοῖς χέασθαι Id.*Pers.*219 (troch.), cf. S.*OC*477; κεχυμένων χοᾶν A.*Ch.*156 (lyr.); σπεῖσαι, κατασπείσειν, ἐπισπένδειν, E.*Or.*1322,1187, A.*Ch.*149; πέμπειν Id. *Pers.*624 (anap.); δοῦναι S.*Ant.*902, etc.; πατρὶ τυμβεῦσαι χ. Id.*El.* 406; αἴρειν, στάξαι, E.*Hec.*529, *Heracl.*1040; χοαῖσι στέφειν τὸν νέκυν S.*Ant.*431; ἱλάσκεσθαι γῆν X.*Cyr.*3.3.22. 2. rarely of *libations* in general, S.*OC*469,1599. II. generally, *stream*, Ἀχέροντος ἄρσενας χοάς Id.*Fr.*523.—Mostly poet.

**χοήρης**, ες, *fitted for the Pitcher-feast* at Athens (v. χοῦς A. III), ἄγγος E.*IT*960.

**χοηφόρος**, ον, *offering* χοαί *to the dead*; **Χοηφόροι**, a Tragedy by A., in which the Chorus pours χοαί to the shade of Agamemnon.

⊛ **χοΐδιον**, τό, f.l. in Suid.; cf. χοαῖος.

**χοϊεῖος**, α, ον, *holding one* χοῦς, *PCair.Zen.*61.3, *PSI*5.535.15 (both iii B.C.).

**χοϊκός**, ή, όν, (χοῦς B) *of earth* or *clay*, 1*Ep.Cor.*15.47; κόνις Ph. 2.673. II. *of the age to take part in the festival of* χόες, *IG*3.1342.

**χοινίκ-η** [ῐ], ἡ, = τοῦ τροχοῦ ἐν ᾧ στρέφεται ὁ ἄξων, Hsch. (s.v.l.; cf. χοινικίς I). **–ιαῖος**, α, ον, *made from a choenix-measure* of flour, πόπανον *IG*2$^{2}$.1367.3, al.; ἐλατήρ ib.1237.7. **–ιον**, τό, Dim. (in form) of χοῖνιξ I, Phld.*Ind.Sto.*5. II. Dim. of χοῖνιξ II, Them.*Or.*21.248d. III. = sq. II, Gal.14.783. **–ίς**, ίδος, ἡ, *nave* of a wheel, Id.18(2).479, Sch.E.*Hipp.*1234, Sch.Il.2. 104. II. a kind of *trepan*, Cels.8.3.1 (acc. written –εικίδα), Gal. 10.448, 19.126. III. *ring* forming the stand for a crown, D.22. 72, 24.180. IV. = χοῖνιξ II, App.*BC*4.30. V. *cave in a rocky shore*, Str.12.3.11. VI. *box* or *socket for the hinge of a door*, *IG*2$^{2}$. 1672.201, 11(2).165.11, 287*A*102, al. (Delos, iii B.C.). VII. *axle-box*, Hero *Aut.*11.2, Wilcken *Chr.*176.8 (i A.D.), cf. Hsch. s.v. χνόαι. VIII. in torsion-engines, *box* or *hub* containing strands of gut, Ph.*Bel.*63.7, 60.3, Hero *Bel.*96.5. IX. = χνόη 2, *Hippiatr.* 96.2,117.

**χοινῑκομέτρης**, ου, ὁ, *one who measures with a* χοῖνιξ, *as a slave's daily allowance*, Ath.6.272c.

**χοῖνιξ**, ῐκος, ἡ, *choenix*, a dry measure, esp. for corn, Hdt.1.192, etc.; the *choenix* of corn was one man's daily allowance, Id.7.187; ἡ γὰρ χ. ἡμερησία τροφή D.L.8.18; given to slaves, Th.4.16; hence, ὅς κεν ἐμῆς γε χοίνικος ἅπτηται, i.e. whoever eats of my *bread*, Od. 19.28: prov., ἐπὶ χοίνικος καθέζεσθαι, i.e. sit idle, live in idleness, Pythag. ap. Arist.*Fr.*197, cf. Plu.2.703f, Ath.10.452e, Ael.*VH*1.26; οὐδὲ τὴν χ. ἔτι λήψει (of gold) Luc.*Nav.*27; χ. Ἀττική ($\frac{1}{48}$ of the μέδιμνος = 4 κοτύλαι) X.*An.*1.5.6; in Pap. usu. abbreviated χ, as in *PCair.Zen.*645.11 (iii B.C.), *POxy.*1044.3 (ii A.D.), etc. II. from the likeness of shape, a kind of *stocks* for fastening the legs, Ar.*Pl.* 276, D.18.129. III. = χοινικίς VI, *PCair.Zen.*782*a*.7 (iii B.C.), prob. in *Supp.Epigr.*4.447.48 (Didyma, ii B.C.).

**χοίρα**, ἡ, fem. of χοῖρος, *sow*, Orph.*Fr.*49.41,117.

**χοιράγχη**, ἡ, = ὑάγχη, Sophr.98.

**χοιρᾰδικός**, ή, όν, *suffering from* χοιράδες (II), Aët.12.49. II. *like* χοιράδες (II), Hdn.*Epim.*153. III. χοιραδικόν, τό, name of a remedy, Orib.*Fr.*91 tit.

**χοιρᾰδ-όλεθρον**, τό, = ξάνθιον, Dsc.4.136. **–ώδης**, ες, (χοιράς I) *rocky*, Str.3.1.9. II. (χοιράς II) *scrofulous*, φύματα Plu.2.664f.

**χοιρ-άς**, άδος, ἡ, *like a hog* or *a hog's back*, χ. πέτρα *low* rock rising just above the sea *like a hog's back*, Pi.*P.*10.52, cf. *AP*9.289 (Bass.) 2. Subst., χ. ἀμυδρά sunken *rock*, Archil.128, cf. Thgn. 576; opp. σκόπελοι ὀξέες, Hdt.2.29; ἀκταὶ..χοιράδες τε A.*Pers.*421; χ. Δηλία the Delian *rock*, i.e. *the rocky isle* of Delos, Id.*Eu.*9; Δήλιοι χ. E.*Tr.*89; χ. Σηπιάς Id.*Andr.*1265; χοιράδες, of the Symplegades, Theoc.13.23; αἱ χ. νῆσοι, off Tarentum, Th.7.33. II. in pl., *scrofulous swellings in the glands of the neck*, etc., Hp.*Aph.*3.26, *AP*11.333 (Callicter), Plu.*Cic.*9,26. III. *sow*, *PMag.Osl.*1. 107. **–άφιος**, ὁ, *farrow*, *PFlor.*148.4,7 (iii A.D.). **–ειος**, α, ον, Ep. **χοίρεος**, η, ον:—*of a swine*, κρέα χοίρεια Ar.*Ra.*338, X.*An.*4.5. 31; κόπρος Arist.*Fr.*277; κόπρον χυρίαν (sic) *PHolm.*25.16. II. χοίρεα (sc. κρέα) *pig's*-flesh, Od.14.81; χοίρειον φαγεῖν S.E.*P.*3. 223, cf. Hp.*Epid.*6.4.4. **–έμπορος**, ὁ, *pig-dealer*, *Sardis* 7(1). 159 (iii A.D.), *PGiss.*40 ii 18 (iii A.D.); restd. in *PCair.Zen.*331. 10 (iii B.C.). **–εών**, ῶνος, ὁ, *pig-sty*, Tz.*H.*11.429. **–ῐδιέμπορος**, ὁ, *pig-dealer*, *PFay.*108 (ii A.D.). **–ίδιον** [ῐ], τό, Dim. of χοῖρος, Ar.*Ach.*521,806, Pl.*Euthd.*298d, *PCair.Zen.*478 (iii B.C.), Plu.*Phoc.*28, D.C.78.25; without dimin. sense, γάλα χοιριδίου *PMag. Leid.V.*13.16. **–ίζω**, 'behave like a pig', Sch.Pl.*Tht.*166c. **–ίημα**, ατος, τό, = χοιρίδιον, Hsch. **–ικός**, ή, όν, late form for χοίρειος, condemned by *EM*775.33. **–ίνας** [ῐ] (sc. πλακοῦς), ὁ, a kind of *cake*, Philox.3.14, Iatrocl.ap.Ath.14.647b. **–ίνη** [ῑ], ἡ, *small sea-mussel*, used by the Athenian dicasts in voting, Ar.*Eq.*1332, *V.*333, 349 (all anap.), Poll.8.16; wrongly expld. by Suid., of *hog's bristles.* **–ῐνος**, η, ον, = χοίρειος, *of hog's skin*, ἀσπίς Luc.*Hist.Conscr.*23. **–ίον**, τό, Dim. of χοῖρος, *pigling*, *porker*, Ar.*Ach.*740. II. Dim. of χοῖρος I.2, Id.*V.*1353. ⊛ **–ίσκος**, ὁ, Dim. of χοῖρος, Luc.*DMeretr.*7.3.

**χοιρο-βοσκός**, ὁ, *swineherd*, Sch.D Il.21.282, *Gloss.* **–γρύλλιος**, ὁ, = Heb. *shâphân*, *Hyrax syriacus*, *coney*, Lxx *Le.*11.6, *De.*14.7, *Ps.* 103(104).18, *Pr.*24.61(30.26); also **–γρυλλος**, *PMag.Leid.V.*12.28, *Gloss.*; wrongly expld. by Hsch. (who makes it neut.) and Suid. as ἀκανθόχοιρος, ὕστριξ, ἐχῖνος χερσαῖος. **–δέλφαξ**, ᾰκος, ὁ, ἡ, *very young pig*, *PCair.Zen.*274 (iii B.C.), *Sammelb.*7469.5 (ii A.D.). **–θλιψ**, ῑβος, ὁ, ἡ, sens.obsc. (χοῖρος I.2), Ar.*V.*1364. **–κᾰλᾰμίς**, = καλαμάγρωστις, Ps.-Dsc.4.30. **–κομεῖον**, τό, *pen for keeping swine in*, Ar.*V.*844, Hsch., Suid. II. (χοῖρος I.2) *bandage used by females*, Ar.*Lys.*1073. **–κτονεῖον**, τό, = *porcinarium*, *Gloss.* **–κτόνος**, ον, *slaying swine*, Sch.Ar.*Pax* 373. II. proparox., καθαρμοὶ χοιρόκτονοι purification *by the sacrifice of swine*, A.*Eu.*283; αἷμα χ. blood *of a slain swine*, Id.*Fr.*327. **–μάγειρος** [ᾰ], ὁ, *pork-butcher*, *PSI*3.202.3 (iv A.D.), *PKlein.Form.*1052 (vi A.D.), etc. **–πίθηκος** [ῐ], ὁ, *ape with a hog's snout*, perh. *baboon*, Arist.*HA*503$^{a}$19, *IG*14. 1302 (Praeneste). **–πωλέω**, (χοῖρος I.2) *to be a prostitute*, Suid. s.v. χοῖρος. **–πώλης**, ου, Dor. **–ας**, α, ὁ, *pig-dealer*, Ar.*Ach.*818, *Fr.*578.

⊛ **χοῖρος**, ὁ (ἡ Hippon.40, S.*Fr.*230, Ar.*Ach.*764):—*young pig*, *porker* (younger than δέλφαξ, Ar.Byz.ap.Ath.9.375, Cratin.3a), Od. 14.73, Alc.*Supp.*24.2, Hdt.2.48, A.*Fr.*309, Ar.*Ach.*781, etc.; offered as one of the smaller sacrifices, Pl.*R.*378a, X.*An.*7.8.5, D.54.39, Henioch.2. b. generally, = ὗς, σῦς, *swine*, ἤδη δέλφακες, χοῖροι δὲ τοῖσιν ἄλλοις Cratin. l.c., cf. Mnesim.4.47 (anap.), Plu.*Cic.*7, *Ev.Matt.* 8.30. 2. *pudenda muliebria*, freq. in Com. poets, who are always punning on the word and its compds., Ar.*Ach.*773 sq., etc.; said to be a Corinthian usage, Suid. II. a fish of the Nile, Str.17.2.4, Ath.7.312a, *Gp.*20.7.1,13 tit. (Perh. for *ĝhoryo-* 'grey', cf. Norse *griss* 'sucking-pig', OHG *grīs* 'grey', or cf. Alb. *derr̄* 'pig'.)

**χοιρό-σᾰκον**, τό, = χοιροκομεῖον II, Hsch. **–σπέλεθος**, ὁ, = ὀνόκλεια, Paul.Aeg.7.17. ⊛ **–σφᾰγεῖον**, τό, *place where swine are slaughtered*, *Gloss.* **–σφᾰγία**, ἡ, *slaughter of swine*, Lyd.*Mens.* 4.158. **–σφάγος** [ᾰ], ον, *sacrificing swine*, Hsch. **–τροφεῖον**, τό, *pig-sty*, Eup.453, Phryn.Com.43. II. = χοιροκομεῖον II, Hsch. **–φορβεῖον**, τό, gloss on συβόσιον, Sch.D Il.11.678, Suid. **–φορέω**, *carry a young pig*, of the priests in the lustral processions at Athens, prob.l. in Ister 32. **–φόρημα**, ατος, τό, *young pig*, Hsch. **–ψάλας**, ὁ, Dor. for –ης, = χοιρόθλιψ, epith. of Dionysus, Polem.Hist.72.

**χοιρ-ώδης**, ες, *swinish*, Leonid.ap.Aët.16.44, Hdn.*Epim.*153. **–ωδία**, ἡ, *swinishness*, Sch.Ar.*Eq.*980. **–ώνια**, τά, misspelling of χειρώνεια (sc. ἕλκη), Cyran.34, cf. 9.

⊛ **χοΐσκος**, ὁ, Dim. of χοῦς, *Inscr.Délos* 1426*A* i 15 (ii B.C.).

**χολ-ᾰγωγός**, όν, *carrying off bile*, πόροι Gal.*UP*5.3; φάρμακα Id. 17(2).658. **–άδια·** τὸ σχολάζειν, Hsch. **–αίνω**, = χολάω, v.l. in Aesop.184 (ii p.263 Chambry). **–αῖος**, α, ον, *biliary*, ἧπαρ Suid.

**χόλαισι**, v. χαλάω.

**Χολαργεύς**, έως, ὁ, *a member of the* Attic *deme Cholargos*, Ar. *Ach.*855, etc.

**χολ-άς**, άδος, ἡ, commonly in pl. χολάδες, *bowels*, *guts*, Il.4.526, *h.Merc.*123, Antim.45; made into strings for lyre, etc., *AP*11.352.12 (Agath.): in Com., also **χολλάδες**, Pherecr.246, Men.23. II. in sg., *gut-cavity*, common to the ὑποχόνδριον and λαγών, Arist.*HA* 493$^{a}$21. (Cf. χόλ-ιξ, Slav. *želudŭkŭ* 'stomach'; not cogn. with χολή as implied by Aret.*SD*2.9.) **–άω**, (χολή) *to be full of black bile*, *to be melancholy mad*, ἀνδράσιν πείθει χολῶσιν Ar.*Nu.*833, cf. Epicr.5.7, Strato 1.7, Men.*Epit.*176. II. = χολόομαι, *to be angry*, *rage*, Antiph.334, D.L.9.66, v.l. in Mosch.1.10, Lxx 3*Ma.*3.1; Ep. part. χολόων Nic.*Th.*140. ⊛ **–έδρα**, ἡ, *groove*, Eratosth.ap.Eutoc. *in Archim.*p.94 H. (pl.). 2. *gutter*, *drain-pipe*, Ph.*Bel.*98.9,

Apollod.*Poliorc.*182.7, Horap.1.21; written χολέρα, Hsch. **-εμεσία, -εμετέω,** worse forms for χοληµ-, Gal.8.179, 13.185.

**χολέρ-α,** Ion. **-ρη,** ἡ, *cholera*, a disease in which the humours of the body (χολή, χολαί) are violently discharged by vomiting and stool, Hp.*Coac.*117, *Acut.*(*Sp.*) 49, al., Aret.*SA*2.5; but, 2. ξηρὴ χολέρη obstinate *obstruction*, Hp.*Acut.*(*Sp.*).48. (Fr. χολή acc. to Cels.4.18(11), but fr. χολάς, Alex.Trall.8.1.) 2. *nausea*, ἔσται ὑμῖν εἰς χολέραν Lxx *Nu.*11.20. II. = χολέδρα, Hsch. **-ιάω,** *suffer from cholera*, Dsc.1.115, Plu.2.974b, Gal.14.273. **-ικός,** ή, όν, *of* or *like cholera*, [πάθεα] Hp.*Epid.*7.82, cf. S.E.*P.*1.131. 2. of persons, *suffering from cholera*, Dsc.4.4, Gal.6.564, Plu.2.831b. 3. χολερικῇ ληφθῆναι to be attacked by *cholera*, D.L.6.76. 4. *liable to produce cholera*, Xenocr.ap.Orib.2.58.84. **-ώδης,** ες, *of the nature of cholera*, τρόπος Hp.*Coac.*524. 2. *liable to cause cholera*, of pork, Id.*Acut.*(*Sp.*)50, cf. Xenocr.ap.Orib.2.58.79.

⊛ **χολή,** ἡ, *gall*, *bile*, Archil.131, A.*Ch.*184, E.*Fr.*682, Th.2.49, etc.; χ. μέλαινα black, i.e. diseased, *bile*, Hp.*Aph.*4.23, Pl.*Ti.*83c (but, = μελαγχολία, Men.*Epit.*459); ξανθὴ χ. Hp.*VM*19; πυρρά Gal.15.658; χολὴν ἐμεῖν, βῆξαι, Nicopho 12, Herod.3.70 (prob. l.): prov., πικρῷ πικρὰν κλύζουσι φαρμάκῳ χολήν S.*Fr.*854; πικρότερ' αὐτῆς τῆς χ. Alex.16.12; χολῇ ἀλείφειν, prov. of *giving one a disgust for a thing*, from the custom of mothers putting gall to the nipple when the child was to be weaned, Diph.74. 2. pl. χολαί, *gall-bladder*, S.*Ant.*1010; called δοχαὶ χολῆς, E.*El.*828; also in sg., A.*Pr.*495; χολὴν τῶν ζῴων τὰ μὲν ἔχει τὰ δ' οὐκ ἔχει Arist.*HA*506$^a$20, cf. *PA* 677$^b$11. 3. metaph. (mostly in Poets) like χόλος (q.v.), *bile*, *gall*, i.e. *bitter anger*, *wrath*, Ar.*Pax*66; ἢ γυναιξὶν οὐκ οἴει χολὴν ἐνεῖναι; Id.*Lys.*465; οὐδεὶς χολὴν οὐδ' ὀργὴν ἔχων φανήσεται D.25.27; πάνυ ἐστ' ἤδη χ. stirs my *bile*, makes me sick, Ar.*Ra.*4; ἐπιζεῖ χ. *the bile* boils over, Id.*Th.*468; χολὴν κινεῖν Id.*V.*403, cf. Pherecr.69. II. *ink of the cuttle-fish*, Nic.*Al.*473, *Th.*561. III. in Lxx = Hebr. *rôsh*, a poisonous plant, variously called *hemlock* or *poppy*, *Ps.*68(69).22, *Je.*8.14. IV. serpent's *venom*, χ. ἀσπίδος ib.*Jb.*20.14; of the hydra's *venom*, Apollod.2.5.2, D.S.4.11. V. *bitter drink*, *Ev.Matt.*27.34. (With χολή, χόλος, cf. Lat. *fel*, ONorse *gall*, etc., 'bile, gall':— prob. the name is derived from the colour of bile, and is cogn. with Lat. (*h*)*olus*, *helvus*, Germ. *gelb* 'yellow', perh. also χλόη.)

**χολήβᾰφος,** ον, *bile-coloured*, of persons, Aret.*SD*1.13 (vulg. χλοήβαφος).

**χοληγός,** όν, *carrying off bile*, φάρμακον Hp.*Loc.Hom.*27,28 (χοληγαγικός and -ηγαγός codd.).

**χοληδόχος,** ον, *containing bile*, κύστις χ. *gall-bladder*, Alex.Aphr.*Pr.*1.40; ἡ χ. (without κύστις) Gal.*UP*4.12; τὸ χ. ἀγγεῖον ib.5.2.

**χοληµ-εσία,** ἡ, *vomiting of bile*, Poll.2.214, Plu.2.692f; cf. χολεμεσία. **-ετέω,** *vomit bile*, Orib.5.31.4; cf. χολεμετέω.

**χολ-ίκιον,** το, Dim. of χόλιξ, Thphr.*Char.*9.4, Poll.6.52. **-ικός,** ή, όν, (χολή) *bilious*, Plu.2.101c, *Gloss.* **-ιξ,** ῐκος, ἡ, later ὁ (Phryn.283, Id.*PS* p.125 B.):—mostly in pl. χόλικες, = χολάδες, *guts* or *bowels* of oxen, χόλικες βοός Pherecr.108.15, Eub.63.4 (anap.); without βοός, Ar.*Ra.*576, *Fr.*82 (anap.); χόλικες ἑφθαί Id.*Pax*717: sg., Id.*Eq.*1179, *Milet.*6.21 (v B.C.); Com. κρόκης χόλιξ wool-*sausages*, cf. κρόκη I.3. (Cf. χολάς.)

**χόλιον,** τό, Dim. of χολή, M.Ant.6.57.

**χόλιος,** α, ον, *angry*, c. dat., *AP*9.165 (Pall.).

**χολλάς,** v. χολάς.

**Χολλείδης,** ου, ὁ, *a member of the deme Cholleidae* in Attica, Ar.*Ach.*406, Lys.13.58, *IG*2$^2$.2382.14 (iv B.C.), etc.: also written **-ηΐδης** ib.1742.39, **-ήδης** ib.159 (iv B.C.).

⊛ **χολο-βᾰφής,** ές, = sq., Marcellin. in Sch.Hermog.Rh.4.148W.
⊛ **-βάφῐνος** [ᾰ], η, ον, *dyed bile-colour*, *yellow-coloured*, Arist.*SE*164$^b$24, Poll.2.214. **-βᾰφος,** ον, = foreg., Aret.*SA*2.4. **-δεκτικός,** ή, όν, = *irascibilis*, *Gloss.* **-δόχος,** ον, = χοληδόχος, Gal.2.579. **-ειδής,** ές, = χολώδης, Nic.*Th.*435; αἷμα Aret.*SD*1.15. **-εις,** εσσα, εν, *of bile* or *gall*, *full thereof*, Nic.*Th.*253; ἀκόνιτον, ποτόν, Id.*Al.*12,17, cf. Opp.*C.*1.381.

**χολοί-βᾰφος,** ον, poet. for χολοβαφής, Nic.*Th.*444. **-βόρος,** ον, *eating like bile*, ἰός ib.593.

**χολοποιός,** όν, *producing bile*, θέρος Hp.*Hum.*14, cf. S.E.*M.*9.96, etc. II. χ., τό, = ἀβρότονον, Ps.-Dsc.3.24.

⊛ **χόλ-ος,** ὁ, rarely in physical sense (= later χολή), *gall*, *bile*, χόλῳ ἄρα σ' ἔτρεφε μήτηρ Il.16.203. II. generally, metaph., *gall*, *bitter anger*, *wrath*, οὐκ Ἀχιλῆϊ χ. φρεσίν Il.2.241; φρενῶν χ. E.*Med.*1266 (lyr.); χ. καὶ μῆνις Il.15.122; χ. λάβε τινά 1.387, etc.; χ. ἔδυ τινά 9.553; χ. δάμασσέ τινα 18.119; χ. ᾕρει τινά 4.23; χ. ἔμπεσε θυμῷ 9.436, etc.; χ. ἔχει θυμόν ib.675; ὅτε χ. ἵκοι τινά ib.525; οἰδάνεται κραδίη χόλῳ ib.646; χόλον πέσσειν, καταπέσσειν (v. sub vocc.); σβέσσαι χ. ib.678; παῦσαι 1.192, etc.; ἐᾶν 9.260; μεθέμεν 1.283; ἐξακέσασθαι 4.36, Od.3.145; ἐκ χόλου μεταστρέψαι ἦτορ Il.10.107; χόλοιο μεταλήγειν (v. sub voc.); λήγειν Hes.*Th.*221; χόλου παύθη ib.533; ἐκ δὲ χόλω τῶδε λαθοίμεθα Alc.*Supp.*23.9; λωφῆσαι A.*Pr.*378; πόσει πάρες χόλον E.*IA*1609; opp. ἐν θυμῷ βάλλεσθαί τινι χόλον Il.14.50; χ. ἔνθεο θυμῷ 6.326; χ. ἐνέχειν τινί Hdt.1.118, 6.119, 8.27; ἔχειν τινί E.*Hec.*1118; ὄρσαι Pi.*P.*11.23; κινεῖν E.*Med.*99 (anap.); Τυφὼς ἐξαναζέσει χ. A.*Pr.*372; χόλου ἄρξασθαι ib.201: c. gen. subj., a person's *rage*, χ. Ἥρης, Ἀθηναίης, Il.18.119 (v. supr.), Od.3.145 (v. supr.): also c. gen. obj., *anger towards* or *because of* a person, Il.6.335, 15.138; or *anger for*, *because of* a thing, τίνος χόλον κατ' αὐτῶν ἐγκαλῶν ἐλήλυθας; S.*Ph.*328; ὧν ἔχων χ. Id.*Tr.*269: also ὄφρα ἑ.. χόλου.. ἀθανάτοις παύσειεν *h.Cer.*350, cf. 410, E.*HF*840. 2. *bitterness*, ἔριδος χ. Sol.4.39. 3. *cause of anger*, *AP*11.381 (Pall.).—In Prose used only by Hdt. and late writers, as Luc.*Am.*2. (On the Root, v. χολή.) **-όω,** inf. fut. χολωσέμεν Il.1.78: aor.1 ἐχόλωσα 18.111, Od.8.205, 18.20, S.*Tr.*1035 (hex.):—*anger*, *provoke*, c. acc. pers., Hom. ll. cc.; ἐχόλωσε δέ μιν φίλον ἦτορ Hes.*Th.*568; χ. τινά τινι *to anger* one *by* a thing, S. l. c. II. Med. and Pass. **χολόομαι** (contr. χολοῦμαι even in Hom.Il.8.407); 3 sg. opt. χολῷτο Thgn.325 (s.v.l.): fut. χολώσομαι E.*Tr.*735; but in Hom. mostly κεχολώσομαι Il.5.421, al.: aor. Med. and Pass. ἐχολωσάμην (χολώσεαι in Il.14.310 may be either fut. ind. or aor. subj.), ἐχολώθην; Ep. χολώθην Hom. (v. infr.), etc.: pf. κεχόλωμαι, mostly in part. κεχολωμένος, v. infr.: plpf. 2 and 3 sg. κεχόλωσο, -ωτο, Il.16.585, 21.146; Ep. 3 pl. κεχολώατο Od.14.282, 16.425:—*to be angered* or *provoked to anger*, κεχολῶσθαι ἐνὶ φρεσίν Il.16.61; θυμῷ κεχολωμένος 1.217, etc.; θυμὸν.. χολώθη 4.494; περὶ κῆρι.. ἐχολώθη 13.206; κεχόλωσο κῆρ 16.585; χολώσατο κηρόθι μᾶλλον 21.136, Od.9.480: c. dat. pers., Ἥρῃ δ' οὔτι τόσον νεμεσίζομαι οὐδὲ χολοῦμαι Il.8.407, cf. 421; βασιλῆϊ χολωθείς 1.9, etc.: but also c. gen., *to be angry for* or *because of* a person or thing, 11.703, 13.660, Od.1.69, al.; ὅπλων χολωθείς Pi.*N.*7.25: with a Prep., κεχολωμένη εἵνεκα νίκης Od.11.544; ἀμφ' ἀστραγάλοισι, ἀμφὶ βουσίν, Il.23.88, Pi.*N.*10.60; ἐξ ἀρέων Il.9.566; ἐπὶ παιδί Batr.109: rare in Trag., χολώσεται E.*Tr.*735; χολωθείς S.*Ph.*374; αὐτῷ χ. Id.*Ant.*1235; οὗ δὴ χ. E.*Alc.*5 (also in later Prose, D.S.3.67); κεχολωμένος Hdt.8.31, Plu.*Fab.*22, al., *SIG*1241 (Lyttus, iii A.D.). III. Pass., *to be turned into bile*, τὸ οὖρον.. οὐ χολοῦται Steph.*in Hp.*1.163 D. **-ώδης,** ες, = χολοειδής, *like bile* or *gall*, *bilious*, ἐκκρίσιες, ἔμεσμα, Hp.*Aph.*2.15, *Epid.*6.4.4.; χυμοί Pl.*Ti.*86e; ὑγρότης Arist.*HA*506$^b$3; χλωραὶ γλῶσσαι χολώδεες *caused by biliousness*, Hp.*Epid.*6.5.8; χολώδεις *bilious persons*, Arist.*Metaph.*981$^a$12, Ruf.ap.Orib.7.26.12. Gal.15.568. 2. *bile-coloured*, χρώματα Pl.*Ti.*71b, 83b; οἷς ἂν ἐπὶ τὸ χολωδέστερον ἡ χρόα μεταβάλῃ Gal.17(2).270. II. *bilious*, *angry*, χ. τι ὑποβλέπειν Luc.*Vit.Auct.*7, cf. Philostr.*Im.*2.12. **-ώομαι,** = χολόομαι, Nonn.*D.*5.447, part. χολωόμενος ib.437, *APl.*4.128. **-ωτός,** ή, όν, *angry*, *wrathful*, χολωτοῖσιν ἐπέεσσιν Il.4.241, Od.22.26, etc. II. literally, *bilious*, Luc.*Lex.*20 (sed leg. χολώντων).

**χονδρ-άκανθος** [ᾰκ], ον, *with cartilaginous skeleton*, epith. of the σελάχη, Arist.*HA*516$^b$15, *PA*655$^a$23. **-εύω,** *make groats*, Hsch.:—corrupt in Anaxipp.1.26. **-ιάω,** of women's breasts, *swell with clots of milk*, Dsc.2.107. **-ίλη** [ῑ], ἡ, *gum succory*, *Chondrilla juncea*, ib.133, Gal.6.622, al., Hsch. (χονδρίλλη v.l. in Dsc. l. c.; χόνδρυλλα cj. in Thphr.*HP*7.7.1, 7.11.4, cf. Plin.*HN*21.105); ἕτερον εἶδος χονδρίλης, *Chondrilla ramosissima*, Dsc. l. c. **-ῖνος,** η, ον, = χονδρίτης, ἄρτος Archestr.*Fr.*4.13. **-ίον,** τό, Dim. of χόνδρος, Hp.*Art.*45 (pl.); expld. by πίναξ, κέραμος, Hsch. **-ίς,** ίδος, ἡ, = ψευδοδίκταμνος, Plin.*HN*25.93, 26.49. **-ίτης** [ῑ], ου, ὁ, *made of groats* or *coarse meal*, ἄρτος Trypho ap.Ath.3.109c, Philistio ap.Ath.3.115d, Lxx *Ge.*40.16. **-ιωτός,** ή, όν, epith. of κάναστρον, dub. in *Supp.Epigr.*1.414.6 (cf. p.139) (Gort., v/iv B.C.).

**χονδρο-βολία,** ἡ, *tessellated work*, χονδροβολίας ἔδαφος *Gloss.* **-κοπεῖον,** τό, *mill for making groats* or *coarse meal*, Poll.3.78, 7.19; **χονδροκόπια** (sic)· μυλὼν ὅπου ὁ χόνδρος κόπτεται, Hsch. **-νευρώδης,** ες, *neuro-cartilaginous*, *of a substance between cartilage and sinew*, δεσμός Hp.*Mochl.*1. **-ποιητικός,** ή, όν, *of making cartilage*, δύναμις Gal.*Nat.Fac.*1.6. **-πτῐσάνη** [ᾰ], ἡ, *gruel of groats* as a drink for sick persons, Paul.Aeg.1.72.

**χόνδρος,** ὁ, *granule* or *lump* of salt, ἁλὸς χόνδρους Hp.*Ulc.*17, cf. Sophr. in *PSI*11.1214*a*.3: pl., *PLit.Lond.*167.18 (ii/iii A.D.); ἁλὸς τρύφεα κατὰ χόνδρους μεγάλους Hdt.4.181; οἰκία ἐκ τῶν ἁλίνων χ. οἰκοδομέαται ib.185:—χόνδρος abs., *salt*, χ. ἐποψίδιος *AP*7.736 (Leon.); also of the *gum* of frankincense, Thphr.*HP*9.4.10; λιβανωτοῦ χ. Luc.*Sat.*16, cf. *Asin.*12; χ. λιβάνου Dsc.1.68.7. 2. *groats of wheat* or *spelt* (esp. the latter, Dsc.2.96, *Gp.*3.7); σασαμίδας χόνδρον τε καὶ ἐγκρίδας Stesich.2; χόνδρον ἕψων Ar.*Fr.*203, cf. 412 (anap.); χ. γάλακι κατανενιμμένος Pherecr.108.18; ἐκ δ' Ἰταλίας χ. καὶ πλευρὰ βόεια Hermipp.63.6 (hex.); χ. Μεγαρικός, Θετταλικός, Antiph.34.2,3, Alex.191; ὁ χ. πλεῖον ὕδωρ δέχεται ἢ οἱ πυροὶ ἐξ ὧν ὁ τοιοῦτος ἐγένετο χ. Arist.*Pr.*929$^b$1, cf. Thphr.*CP*4.16.2, Plb.12.2.5; χόνδρου πτισάνη Gal.6.496: hence, *gruel*, *porridge*, Thphr.*HP*4.4.9, Orac.ap.Hierocl. *in CA* 1 p.421 M.: prov., of an old man, χόνδρον λείχειν Ar.*V.*737 (anap.). II. *gristle*, *cartilage*, Hp.*Aph.*6.19, Arist.*HA*516$^b$31, *PA*655$^a$37: esp. *the cartilage of the breast*, which unites the false ribs at the termination of the breast-bone, Hp.*Epid.*7.3, cf. *Prorrh.*2.7, Nic.*Al.*123; and v. ξιφοειδής; also, *the cartilage* of the ear, Arist.*HA*492$^a$16; of the nose, Poll.2.79; of the windpipe (i.e. *uvula*), ib.99; ὠλενίτης χ. the shoulder-*blade*, Lyc.155; also of *the young horns* of deer, Ael.*NA*6.5.

**χονδρός,** ά, όν, *granular*, *coarse*, ἄλευρα χονδρότερα Hp.*Mul.*2.193; ἄλφιτον ἀραιὸν καὶ χονδρόν Arist.*Pr.*927$^b$35: mostly of *coarse* salt, ἅλες οὐ χονδροί, ἀλλὰ χαῦνοι καὶ λεπτοὶ ὥσπερ χιών Id.*Mete.*359$^a$32; χᾶλα λήψεται χονδρόν Phoen.2.5; χονδροὺς ἅλας (cod.Rav. χονδρὰς ἅλας) is prob. in Ar.*Ach.*521 (v.l. χόνδρους ἁλός): χονδρός Adj., χόνδρος Subst. are distd. by Hdn.Gr.1.203, 2.716; Comp. and Sup. -ότερος, -ότατος, Choerob. *in Theod.*2.76 H. II. later, generally, *coarse*, τρίχες Ps.-Callisth.2.33; οὐηλάρια μικρὰ χοντρὰ (sic) δύο *Sammelb.*7033.39 (v A.D.); χονδρός, = *grossus*, *Gloss.* (χόνδρος and χονδρός dissim. fr. *χρονδ-ρο-, cogn. with Engl. *grind*.)

⊛ **χονδρο-σύνδεσμος,** ὁ, *cartilaginous connexion*, Gal.1.569. **-τῠ-**

πος, ον, *formed of cartilage*, Arist.*HA*617ᵇ2. **-φυής**, ές, *cartilaginous*, Matro *Conv*.27.

**χόνδρυλλα**, v. χονδρίλη.

**χονδρ-ώδης**, ες, *like groats, granular*, f.l. in Hp.*Nat.Mul*.105 (leg. χονδροτέρα). II. *like gristle, cartilaginous*, Id.*Mochl*.1, Arist.*HA*493ᵃ7, 524ᵇ27 (Comp.), *PA*654ᵇ25, Aret.*SD*1.9, al.; opp. νευρώδης, ὀστώδης, Arist.*HA*500ᵇ20; χονδρώδη, τά, *the swimmerets* of crayfish, ib.549ᵃ25. **-ωσις**, εως, ἡ, an affection of the breasts, Sor.1.76.

**χόννος**, ὁ, Cretan word for *a copper cup*, Hermonax ap.Ath.11.502b, Eust.1153.42 (**χόνος** Hsch.): pl., perh. name of a festival (cf. χόες, χύτροι), *Supp.Epigr*.1.414.11 (Gort., v/iv B.C.).

**χοο-πλάστης**, ου, ὁ, (χοῦς B) *one who forms of earth*, *PMag.Par*.1.3047. **-ποίησις**, εως, ἡ, *treatment by fusion*, Anon.Alch. in *Gött. Nachr*.1919.25; written **χοωποίησις**, Zos.Alch.p.210B. **-πότης**, ου, ὁ, *one who drinks whole* χόες, of Dionysus, Possis 1.

**χοός**, v. χοῦς (A) and (B).

**χοότης**, ητος, ἡ, *earthy nature* (cf. χοϊκός 1), Anon.Alch. in *Gött. Nachr*.1919.16.

**χοοφορ-έω**, *carry earth*, *CPHerm*.127 *Fr*.12 *B*8 (iii A.D.). ✻ **-ία**, ἡ, *carriage of earth*, ib.*Fr*.3*B*3; cf. χωφορέω, -ία.

**χορᾱγ-εῖον**, -ιον, -ός, Dor. for χορηγ-. **χορᾱγέτας**, α, ὁ, Dor. for χορηγέτης.

✻**χοραυλ-έω**, *accompany the chorus on the flute*, Str.17.1.11. **-ης**, ου, ὁ, *one who accompanies a chorus on the flute*, *AP*11.11 (Lucill.), Plu.*Ant*.24: freq. in Inscrr., as *IG*7.1773 (Thespiae), *CIG*1719 (Delph.), etc.

**χορδ-άριον** [ᾰ], τό, Dim. of χορδή, Alex.132 (lyr.). **-αψός**, ὁ (on the accent v. Hdn.Gr.1.227), *a disease in the great guts*, the same as εἰλεός in the small ones, Hp.*Coac*.502; but the meanings are reversed by Diocl.(*Fr*.73) ap.Cels.4.20.1; an aggravated form of εἰλεός acc. to Aret.*SA*2.6, but not distd. fr. it by Gal.8.388 (fr. χορδή, ἕψω, acc. to Aret. l. c.). **-ευμα**, ατος, τό, *sausage, black-pudding*, Ar.*Eq*.315. **-εύω**, *make into sausages*: metaph., χ. τὰ πράγματα *make mince-meat of* state-affairs, ib.214. **-ή**, ἡ, pl., *guts, tripe*, Batr.222, Pherecr.130.9 (anap.), Ar.*Fr*.687 (anap.), 461 (sg). II. *that which is made from guts*: 1. *string of gut*, τὰ ὑποχόνδρια τελαμῶσι καὶ χορδαῖς διασφίγγει Sor.2.29; in a loom, Arist.*GA*787ᵇ23: esp. *string* of a lyre or harp (not in A. or S., once in E., v. infr.), Od.21.407, *h.Merc*.51, etc.; ἐν Αἰολίδεσσι χ. Pi.*P*.2.69, cf. E.*Hipp*.1135 (lyr.); χορδὰς ἐπιτείνειν, opp. ἀνιέναι, Pl.*Ly*.209b; ἐν τῇ ἐπιτάσει καὶ ἀνέσει τῶν χ. Id.*R*.349e; ὀξυτάτην καὶ βαρυτάτην χορδὴν ποιεῖν Id.*Phdr*.268e; τὰς χ. ἀλλήλαις συνιστάντα Id.*R*.412a: metaph., κινοῦσα χ. τὰς ἀκινήτους φρενῶν *Trag.Adesp*.361. b. musical *note*, Pl.*Phlb*.56a. 2. *sausage* or *black-pudding*, χορδῆς τόμος Cratin.192, cf. Ar.*Ach*.1119, *Nu*.455 (anap.): he puns on the two senses in *Ra*.339. (Cf. Skt. *hirā́* 'vein', *hiras* 'strip, band, fillet', Albanian *zorë* 'entrails', Lat. *haru-spex*, ONorse *gǫrn* 'entrails', *garn* 'yarn'.) **-ίον**, τό, = foreg. 1, *SIG*1002.10 (Milet., v/iv B.C.).

**χορδο-λογέω**, *touch the strings* before playing, Plu.2.87f. **-ποιός**, ὁ, *maker of strings* for musical instruments, Poll.7.154, who also has **-ποιία**, ἡ, *the art* or *trade of such a person*, Adj. **-ποιικός**, ή, όν, *fit for such work*, and Adv. **-κῶς** ibid. **-πώλης**, ου, ὁ, *dealer in musical strings*, Critias 67 D. **-στροφία**, ἡ, *twisting of strings* for a musical instrument, Ael.*NA*17.6 (pl.). **-στρόφος**, ὁ, *twister of strings*, D.Chr.8.4, Ptol.*Tetr*.180 (misprinted χονδρο-, cf. Procl.*Par.Ptol*.250). **-τόνιον**, τό, = sq., Artemon Hist. 12 (pl.). **-τόνον**, τό, *tail-piece for keeping the strings taut*, Arist.*Aud*.803ᵃ41, Poll.4.62, Nicom.*Harm*.6. II. Adj. proparox. χορδότονος, ον, Pass., *stretched with strings*, λύρα S.*Fr*.244 (lyr.).

**χορ-εία**, ἡ, *dance*, esp. *choral dance with music*, E.*Ph*.1265 (pl., nowhere else in Trag., exc. Chaerem.14.3), Ar.*Ra*.336 (lyr.); ῥυθμὸν χορείας ὕπαγε Id.*Th*.956 (lyr.); εὔκυκλος χ. ib.968 (troch.); χ... ὀρχησίς τε καὶ ᾠδὴ τὸ σύνολόν ἐστιν Pl.*Lg*.654b; ὅλη..χ. ὅλη παίδευσις ἦν ἡμῖν ib.672e; μιμήματα τρόπων ἐστὶ τὰ περὶ τὰς χ. ib.655d; θυσίαι τε καὶ χ. ib.772b; ἐπάρχεσθαι..τοὺς χοροὺς χορείας τῷ Διονύσῳ dub. in *IG*12(9).192.11 (Eretria). 2. of any *circling motion*, as of the stars, χ. καλλίστην χορεύοντα Pl.*Epin*.982e, cf. Arist.*Fr*.11 (pl.), Luc.*Salt*.17; πλανήτων τε καὶ ἀπλανῶν χορείας Ph.1.16. II. *dance-tune*, ἄκουε τὰν ἐμὰν Δώριον χ. Pratin.Lyr.1.17, cf. Ar.*Ra*.247 (lyr.). **-εῖον**, τό, *dancing-place*, Zonar.; = βωμός τις, Hsch.: of a place of torture, Lxx 4 *Ma*.15.20. 2. = αὔλημα, Hsch.; = διδασκαλεῖον, Id. (sed leg. χορ⟨ηγ⟩εῖον). ✻ **-εῖος**, α, ον, *of* or *belonging to a chorus* or *dance*, ἀοιδή A.R.2.714, cf. Ael.*NA*2.11; epith. of Dionysus, Plu.2.680b; of Antinous, *IG*2².1105 *A b*10, *A c*3; χορεῖοι (sc. ἀγῶνες) *CIG*5328 (Teuchira). II. in metre, χορεῖος, ὁ, = τροχαῖος, Cic.*de Or*.3.50.193, Plu.2.1141b. 2. = τρίβραχυς, D.H.*Comp*.17,18, Aristid.Quint.1.22. III. pl. χορεῖα, τά, *thank-offerings for victory of a chorus*, *IG*11(2).161 *B*13 (Delos, iii B.C.), *BCH*35.260 (ibid.), *Inscr.Délos* 442 *A* 189 (ii B.C.). 2. *fee for right of attendance* at rites of ὑμνῳδοί, *IGRom*.4.353*D*21 (Pergam., ii A.D.). **-ευμα**, ατος, τό, *choral dance*, Pratin.Lyr.1.1 (pl.), E.*Ph*.655 (lyr.), *Ion* 1474 (lyr., pl.), *El*.875 (lyr.); τὰ τῆς κακίας χ. *dances representing*.., Pl.*Lg*.655c. **-ευσις**, εως, ἡ, *dancing*, Pi.*Pae*.6.9, Suid. s.v. χορεῖον. **-ευτέον**, *one must dance*, E.*Ba*.324. **-ευτής**, οῦ, ὁ, *choral dancer*, Pi.*P*.12.27, Ar.*Ach*.443, Pl.*R*.373b, etc.; τῶν χ. ἐξάγειν τινά And.4.20; τὰ ἐπινίκια ἔθυεν αὐτός τε καὶ οἱ χ. Pl.*Smp*.173a: metaph., [θεοῦ] χ. *the devoted follower* of a god, Id.*Phdr*.252d; of a philosopher, οἱ Πυθαγόρου καὶ Πλάτωνος καὶ Ἀριστοτέλους χ. Jul.*Or*.6.197d: generally, *pupil*, Lib.*Or*.54.38. II. epith. of Pan, Pi.*Fr*.99; of Dionysus, Orph. Εὐχή 9. 2. used of dolphins, from their movements, *Anacreont*.55.24; of cicadae, Ael.*NA*1.20. **-ευτικός**, ή, όν, *of* or *for the dance*, ib.2.11, Luc.*Salt*.10. ✻**-εύω**, fut. -σω E.*Ba*.195, etc.: aor. ἐχόρευσα Id.*Cyc*.156, etc.: pf. κεχόρευκα Pl.*Lg*.654b:—Med., in same sense, E.*Ion* 1084 (lyr.): fut. -εύσομαι A.*Ag*.31: aor. ἐχορευσάμην Ar.*Th*.103 (lyr.), (ἐξ-) E.*Hel*.381 (lyr.):—Pass., aor. ἐχορεύθην, pf. κεχόρευμαι, v. infr. II:—*dance a round* or *choral dance*, Pi.*Fr*.116, Epich.109, S.*Aj*.701 (lyr.), etc.; esp. of the Dionysiac chorus or dance, E.*Cyc*.156, *Ba*.21,184,207, etc.: hence, *take part in the chorus*, regarded as a matter of religion, εἰ γὰρ αἱ τοιαίδε πράξεις τίμιαι, τί δεῖ με χορεύειν; S.*OT*896 (lyr.); *to be one of a chorus*, Ar.*Ra*.390 (lyr.), interpol. in D.18.265; considered as a high honour by Athenian citizens, Id.39.16,23; τὸ παλαιὸν οἱ ἐλεύθεροι ἐχόρευον Arist.*Pr*.918ᵇ21; not allowed to foreigners, Plu.*Phoc*.30: c. dat. pers., *dance to* him, *in* his *honour*, Βακχίῳ E.*Ba*.195, cf. X.*Eq.Mag*.3.2; περί τινα Pl.*Euthd*.277e; ἀμφὶ σὰν κιθάραν E.*Alc*.582 (lyr.); ἐπὶ Κυρβάντεσι perh. in their train, S.*Fr*.862 (lyr.). 2. generally, *dance*, esp. from joy, χ. ὑφ' ἡδονῆς Ar.*Pl*.288, cf. 761; αὐτὼ τὼ σκέλει χορεύετον Id.*Pax* 325 (troch.); ἀνὴρ χορεύει, καὶ τὰ τοῦ θεοῦ καλά Phryn.Com.9; χ. καὶ ἐν εὐπαθείῃσι εἶναι Hdt.1.191. 3. metaph., *practise dancing in the chorus*, hence *practise* a thing, *be versed* in it, ἔν τινι Pl.*Tht*.173c, cf. *Lg*.654b. 4. of any *circling motion*, as of the heavenly bodies, ἀνεχόρευσεν αἰθήρ, χορεύει δὲ Σελάνα E.*Ion* 1080 (lyr.), cf. *Ba*.114 (lyr.); so of a cup, δέπας μεστόν, κύκλῳ χορεῦον Antiph.237.3. II. c. acc. cogn., χορείας χ. Pl.*Lg*.942d, *Epin*.982e; φροίμιον χορεύσομαι I *will dance* a prelude, A.*Ag*.31; χ. γάμους *to celebrate* them, E.*IA* 1057 (lyr.); ὄργια Μουσῶν Ar.*Ra*.356 (anap.); ἀγῶνας Plb.4.20.9:—Pass., κεχόρευται ἡμῖν (sings the Chorus) our *part is played*, Ar.*Nu*.1510 (anap.); τὰ χορευθέντα *things represented in mimic dance*, Pl.*Lg*.655d. 2. trans., *celebrate in choral dance*, Φοῖβον Pi.*I*.1.7, cf. S.*Ant*.1153 (lyr.), E.*HF* 871 (troch.); so Med., Id.*Ion* 1084 (lyr.):—Pass., *to be celebrated in choral dance*, πρὸς ἡμῶν S.*OT* 1093 (lyr.), cf. E.*Ion* 463 (lyr.). 3. Pass., also, *to be filled with dances* in honour of, c. dat., ἄστεα διφρηλάτᾳ πάντα δι' ἀνακτόρων Ἴσιδι χορεύεται *Lyr.Alex.Adesp*.36.19. III. Causal, *set one dancing, rouse to the dance*, τινα E.*HF*686 (lyr.); πόδα χορεύσας, of spreading ivy, *AP*11.33 (Phil.); ὁ δ' αὐλὸς ὕστερον χορευέτω Pratin.Lyr.1.7:—metaph. in Pass., μανίαισιν Λύσσας χορευθέντ' ἀναύλοις E.*HF*879 (lyr.).

**χορηγ-εῖον**, τό, = χορήγιον, *the school in which a chorus was trained* for public performance, Phryn.*PS*p.126 B. 2. generally, *school*, Epich.13,104. II. *treasury, revenue*, τὸ Διονυσίου χ. Aristox. *Fr.Hist*.15. **-έτης**, ου, ὁ, = χορηγός 1, Iamb.*VP*30.186: Dor. **χορᾱγέτας** *IG*4²(1).133.7 (Epid., hymn). **-έω**, Boeot. and Dor. **-ᾱγέω**, *IG*7.3210 (Orchom.), 12(1).383 (Rhodes), etc.:—*lead a chorus*, χορῷ Simon.147, Pl.*Grg*.482b (cf. signf. II): c. gen., χ. ἡμῶν Id.*Lg*.654a: hence metaph., *take the lead in* a matter, c. gen., τούτου τοῦ λόγου Id.*Tht*.179d. II. of the χορηγός, *defray the cost of bringing out a chorus* at the public festivals, abs., χορηγεῖν, τριηραρχεῖν, εἰσφέρειν D.18.257; ἐχόρευες, ἐγὼ δ' ἐχορήγουν interpol. ib.265; χ. λαμπρῶς Antipho 2.2.12, etc.; κάλλιον Isoc.19.36: freq. in Inscrr., Θεμιστοκλῆς ἐχορήγει· Φρύνιχος ἐδίδασκεν· Ἀδείμαντος ἦρχεν ap.Plu.*Them*.5, cf. *IG*1².770, etc.; also ὁ δῆμος ἐχορήγει *IG*2².3079, al.: c. acc. cogn., χορηγίας χ. Antipho 5.77, Lys.12.20; [τῇ φυλῇ] Luc.*Dem.Enc*.45; χ. Ἀθηναίων Plu.2.724b: freq. with a word to denote the occasion, Λήναια χορηγῶν Ar.*Ach*.1155 (lyr.); χ. παισὶν Διονύσια D.21.64; εἰς Ἀπολλώνια *IG*11(2).106.1 (Delos, iii B.C.); ἀνδράσι χ. ἐς Διονύσια Lys.21.2; χ. κωμῳδοῖς, πυρριχισταῖς, ib.4; τραγῳδοῖς Is.6.60; κωμῳδοῖς *IG*2².3090 (less freq. with the Art. added, χ. τὰ Διονύσια τοῖς τραγῳδοῖς Arist.*Fr*.630); also Παναθηναίοις χ. D.21.156:—Pass., *to have choragi found for one*, χορηγοῦσιν μὲν οἱ πλούσιοι, χορηγεῖται δὲ ὁ δῆμος X.*Ath*.1.13; ἄριστα χορηγοῦνται οἱ παῖδες *are well found by their choragus*, Antipho 6.13. 2. metaph., *minister to*, χ. ταῖς σεαυτοῦ ἡδοναῖς Aeschin.3.240; ταῖς ἐπιθυμίαις Luc.*Par*.12; πρὸς ἔπαινον Lib.*Or*.18.7; πρὸς μῆκος λόγου ib.13.26. 3. metaph. also, a. c. acc. pers., *furnish abundantly* with a thing, esp. *with supplies for war*, χ. τὸ στρατόπεδον τοῖς ἐπιτηδείοις Plb.3.68.8, cf. 49.11, 52.7, etc.; χρήμασι πρός τι Id.5.42.7:—Pass., *to be well supplied*, τοῖς ἐκτὸς ἀγαθοῖς κεχορηγημένος Arist.*EN*1101ᵃ15, cf. 1179ᵃ11: abs., κάλλιστα κεχορηγημένος best *furnished*, Id.*Pol*.1288ᵇ14; κεχ. ἐπὶ τοσοῦτον ὥστε..ib.1323ᵇ41; ἀρετὴ κεχορηγημένη ib.1289ᵃ33: generally, ἐμβαμματίοις κεχ., of fish, Anaxipp.1.35; πολλαῖς ἀφορμαῖς κεχ. πρός τι Plb.4.77.2; διαφόρῳ φύσει, συνέσει, D.S.1.15, 2.6, D.H.*Vett.Cens*.5.6; κεχ. ὑπὸ τῆς φύσεως ἀγχινοίᾳ D.S.26.2. b. c. acc. rei (with or without dat. pers.), *supply, furnish*, τοὺς Ἴβηρας οὓς χορηγεῖς μοι, i.e. the archers, Ar.*Fr*.551; χρήματα ἡμῖν D.11.6; τὰς τροφάς D.S.2.35; σπόρον 2 *Ep.Cor*.9.10; ἐξ ἰσχύος ἧς χ. ὁ θεός 1 *Ep.Pet*.4.11; πάθη τὰ χορηγοῦντα βοήθειαν *affording*, i.e. admitting, a cure, Ptol.*Tetr*.13: c. dat. pers. only, τῷ βασιλεῖ Lxx 3 *Ki*.4.7:—Med. in act. sense, χορηγούμενός σοι τὸν φόρον *BGU*920.29 (ii A.D.):—Pass., τῶν ἐκ μιᾶς δαπάνης χορηγηθέντων (sc. δείπνων) Arist.*Pol*.1281ᵇ3. **-ημα**, ατος, τό, *expenditure on* χοροί, *Inscr.Délos* 399*A* 51 al. (pl., ii B.C.). 2. generally, *means of providing for*, τινος Plu.*Oth*.9. **-ησις**, εως, ἡ, *expenditure*, *BGU*1208.18 (i B.C.); *supply*, ξύλων *Stud.Pal*.22.177.19 (ii A.D.). ✻ **-ία**, ἡ, *office* or λῃτουργία of a χορηγός, *defraying of the cost of the public choruses*, Antipho 2. 3.8 (pl.), 5.77 (pl.), Th.6.16 (pl.), etc.: used generally of λητουργίαι other than the τριηραρχία, Lys.19.57 (pl.), D.20.19 (pl.), Lex ap. eund. 18.106. 2. generally, *expense*, Democr.282. II. generally, *abundance of external means, fortune*, ἡ ἐκτὸς χ. Arist.*EN*1178a24, cf. *Pol.*1255a14, al.; πολιτικὴ χ. *things necessary to furnish* or *constitute* a state, ib.1326a5: pl., βασιλικαὶ χ. Jul.*Ep.*89b; πρόγονοι καὶ χ. καὶ δόξα *great fortunes*, Lib.*Or.*33.20. 2. metaph., in later historians, of *supplies for war*, τῶν ἀναγκαίων, τῶν ἐπιτηδείων, Plb. 1.18.9, 4.71.10, etc.: pl., Id.1.16.6, etc. b. generally, *supplies* for a banquet, Plu.2.692b. c. *extraneous, adventitious aids*, Arist. *Po.*1453b8. d. *abundance*, τῶν εὐτυχημάτων Id.*Pol.*1333b17; ὕλης Luc.*Anach.*35; ὕδατος Hdn.8.2.6; τῶν πηγῶν Lib.*Or.*61.18; πᾶσα χ. τῆς νόσου all *that feeds* the disease, Philostr.*Im.*2.23. e. *subvention, assistance*, Ph.*Bel.*50.39. III. f.l. for χορεία, Pl.*Euthd.* 277d. **-ικός**, ή, όν, *of* or *for a* χορηγός, χ. ἀγῶνες rivalry *in bringing out choruses*, X.*Hier.*9.11; χ. τρίποδες tripods *dedicated to a god by victorious choruses*, Plu.*Aristid.*1, *Nic.*3; χ. ἀργύριον *IG*11(2).161*A*27, 39 (Delos, iii B.C.); τὸ χ. alone, *Inscr.Délos*453*A*24 (ii B.C.). **-ιον**, τό, = χορηγεῖον I, D.19.200, Poll.4.106. II. pl., *supplies* for an army, Plb.1.17.5, al.: generally, *maintenance*, *PRyl.*181.7 (iii A.D.). III. (in Dor. form **χοράγιον**) *stage-building* in a theatre, *BGU*1028.21 (ii A.D.). **-ίς**, ίδος, ἡ, *woman-choragus*, title of a Comedy by Alexis. **-ός**, ὁ (also ἡ), Dor. **χορᾱγός** Alcm.23.44, Ar.*Lys.*1315 (lyr.): (χορός, ἡγέομαι):—*chorus-leader*, like the later κορυφαῖος, θεοὺς συγχορευτάς τε καὶ χορηγοὺς ἡμῖν δεδωκέναι τόν τε Ἀπόλλωνα καὶ τὰς Μούσας Pl.*Lg.*665a: generally, *leader of a train* or *band*, πῦρ πνεόντων χ. ἄστρων, of Dionysus, S.*Ant.*1147 (lyr.); χ. δελφίνων E.*Hel.* 1454 (lyr.). II. at Athens and elsewhere, *one who defrays the costs for producing a chorus*, χορηγῶν ἀποδεικνυμένων ἑκατέρῃ τῶν δαιμόνων δέκα ἀνδρῶν Hdt.5.83; χορηγὸν καταστῆσαί τινα *IG*2².141. 34; χ. κατεστάθην εἰς Θαργήλια Antipho 6.11; καταστὰς χ. τραγῳδοῖς Lys.21.1, cf. 3; supplied by the φυλαί in turn, D.20.130, cf. Aeschin. 1.11; χ. αἱρεθείς, ἱμάτια χρυσᾶ παρασχὼν τῷ χορῷ, ῥάκος φορεῖ Antiph. 204.5 (troch.); used of a woman, *Milet.*1(7).No.265: generally, of liturgies other than the trierarchy, εἰσποιεῖ χορηγοὺς εἰς ἐκείνας τὰς λητουργίας D.20.19. 2. metaph., *one who defrays the costs* for any purpose, χ. ἔχοντες Φίλιππον Id.9.60; Φιλίππῳ χ. χρώμενος Id.19.216; χ. τὸν πατέρα ἔχειν εἴς τι Id.40.51; λήψεται χ. τῇ ἑαυτοῦ βδελυρίᾳ Aeschin.1.54, cf. 2.79; οἱονεὶ χ. καὶ μισθοδότης Plb.2.44.3, cf. 8.7.2; τῆς φύσεως αὐτῶν ὁ θεὸς χ. Iamb.*Bab.*p.51 Hinck. 3. Astrol., of planets, *patron* of a profession or trade, Paul.Al.*P.*2. 4. Medic., *supply-veins*, Orib.45.18.23. b. a dressing, Id.46.19.6.

**χορῐαμβ-ικός**, ή, όν, *choriambic*, μέτρον Heph.9.1, cf. Aristid. Quint.1.26, etc. **-ος**, ὁ, in metre, *choriambus*, i.e. foot of four syllables (–⏑⏑–), consisting of a *chorius* (–⏑) and *iambus* (⏑–), Heph.3.3, Aristid.Quint.1.22.

**χορικός**, ή, όν, *of* or *for a choral dance*, ἡ χ. μοῦσα Pl.*Lg.*670a; αἱ ᾠδαὶ αἱ χ. the *choral songs* in Tragedy and Comedy, Arist.*Pr.*918b14; χ. μέλη Id.*Po.*1452b21; χορικά (sc. μέλη) Ar.*Eq.*589 (lyr.); χορικόν, τό, *choral part* of a drama, Arist.*Po.*1452b22; οἱ χ. (sc. αὐλοί) Poll.4.81. Adv. -κῶς Ael.*NA*2.11.

**χορῐοειδής**, ές, *like the afterbirth*, ὑμήν Arist.*HA*561b32, etc. II. χ. χιτών *choroid* coat of the eye, Ruf.*Onom.*153, Gal.*UP*10.2; χ. μῆνιγξ, of the brain, the *pia mater*, ib.8.9, Herophil.ap.Ruf.*Onom.* 149; so of the *ventricles* of the brain, ibid.; χ. πλέγματα (called συστρέμματα by Herophil.) in the brain, Gal.2.719.—Sts. wrongly written χοροειδής in codd., as in Arist.*GA*753b22, etc. Adv. -δῶς Steph. *in Hp.*2.373 D.

**χόρῐον**, τό, *membrane that encloses the foetus* in the womb, *afterbirth*, Hp.*Nat.Puer.*16, Arist.*HA*562a6, Dsc.3.150, Gal.*UP*15.4, Ruf.*Onom.*230, Porph.*Marc.*32, etc.; certain animals are said to eat it, Arist.*HA*611a18, Thphr.*Fr.*175; cf. ἀμνίον 1.2. 2. *membrane round the inside of the egg*, Arist.*GA*754a1. II. *any intestinal membrane*: hence in pl. χόρια, τά, *a dish made by stuffing it with honey and milk, haggis*, Cratin.326, Ar.*Fr.*569.4, Alex.172.17, Theoc.9.19, ubi v. Sch.—It is uncertain to which of these senses is to be referred the prov. χαλεπὸν χορίῳ κύνα γεῦσαι 'don't let a dog taste blood', Theoc.10.11.

**χόριος**, ὁ, = χορεῖος II, *AP*14.15. II. in Tactics, a form of ἐξελιγμός, Ael.*Tact.*27.1, 28.3, Arr.*Tact.*23.1, 24.3.

⊕**χορῖτ-εία**, ἡ, = χορεία, *IG*5(1).1390.73 (Andania, i B.C.). **-ις**, ιδος, ἡ, *dancing-girl*, Call.*Dian.*13, *Del.*306, Nonn.*D.*1.504, 46.158, etc.; χορίτιδες (sic) ἐννέα Μοῦσαι Dioscorus in *PLit.Lond.*100*D*4.

**χοροβᾰτέω**, *dance in a chorus*, Suid.:—**βᾰτία**, ἡ, *dancing in a chorus*, Hdn.*Epim.*152.

**χορόδανον**, τό, = σφονδύλιον, Ps.-Dsc.3.76 (nisi leg. χοιρ-).

**χοροδῐδασκᾰλ-ία**, ἡ, *office of* χοροδιδάσκαλος, Pl.*Alc.*1.125e. **-ικός**, ή, όν, *of* or *for the* χοροδιδάσκαλος, [ἀρετή] ibid. **-ος**, ὁ, *trainer of the chorus*, Ar.*Ec.*809, Pl.*Lg.*812e, 655a, *SIG*450.5 (Delph., iii B.C.), etc.

**χοροειδής**, f.l. for χοριοειδής.

**χοροήθης**, ες, *accustomed to the choral dance*, νύμφαι *h.Pan.*3.

**χοροι-θᾰλής**, ές, *flourishing in the dance*, κοῦραι *AP*6.287 (Antip.). **-μᾰνής**, ές, Ep. for χορομανής, Orph.*H.*52.7, *Fr.*282, Max.496. **-μᾰνία**, poet. **-ίη**, ἡ, *furious dancing*, *APl.*4.289.

**χοροιτῠπ-έω**, *beat the ground in the dance*, Opp.*H.*1.472, *C.*4. 342. ⊕**-ία**, Ep. -ίη, ἡ, *choral dancing*, χοροιτυπίῃσιν ἄριστοι Il.24. 261; later in sg., *AP*7.448 (Leon.), 9.82 (Antip.Thess.): metaph., ib. 12.253 (Strat.). **-ος** (parox.), ον, Ep. for χορο-τύπος, *beating the ground in the choral dance*, generally, *dancing*, Pi.*Fr.*156, Opp.*H.*3. 250, Nonn.*D.*9.202, al.; cj. for χειροκτύπῳ in Telest.1.5. II. proparox. χοροίτυπος, ον, Pass., *played for* or *to the choral dance*, χέλυς *h.Merc.*31. 2. *danced over*, ἄλσος Nonn.*D.*13.95.

**χοροκάλη**, ἡ, prob. an error for χορῷ κ. (Il.16.180), Hsch.

**χοροκῐθᾰρ-εύς**, έως, ὁ, *one who plays the cithara to a chorus*, *CIG* 2758*f*, al. (Aphrodisias); dat. sg. written χοροκιθαρι (sic) *IG*14. 611 (Sardinia). **-ίζω**, *play the cithara to a chorus*, Macr.*Exc.* p.600 K. **-ιστής**, οῦ, ὁ, = χοροκιθαρεύς, Suet.*Dom.*4.

**χορο-κτόνος**, ον, *choir-destroying*, Strattis 15. **-λέκτης**, ου, ὁ, *conductor of a chorus*, Hecat.Abd.ap.Ael.*NA*11.1, cf. 15.5, Poll.4. 106. **-μᾰνής**, ές, *mad after dancing*, τρόπος Ar.*Th.*961 (lyr.); cf. χοροιμανής.

**χορόνδε**, Adv. *to the festive dance*, Il.3.393.

**χορό-νῖκος**, ον, *victorious with the chorus*, Alex.19 (perh. a pr. n.). **-παίγμων**, ον, gen. ονος, *sporting in the choral dance, dancing merrily*, Orph.*H.*24.2. **-παίκτης**, ου, ὁ, = foreg., *AP*6. 108 (Myrin.). **-πλεκής**, ές, *weaving*, i.e. *mixing in the dance*, Nonn.*D.*6.49, 14.33, al. **-ποιία**, ἡ, *institution, arrangement of a chorus*, Poll.4.106. **-ποιός**, όν, *instituting* or *arranging a chorus*, X.*Ages.*2.17, *IG*14.82* (prob. a forgery). II. in Poets, *leading the dance*, ὦ θεῶν χοροποί' ἄναξ, of Pan, S.*Aj.*698 (lyr.); Χάριτες E.*Ph.*788 (lyr.); ἥβα Ar.*Ra.*353 (lyr.); θυσίαι E.*Hec.*917 (lyr.); χαροποιός is found in codd. of E.*Ph.* l.c. and v.l. in E.*Hec.* l.c.

**χορός**, ὁ, *dance*, αἰεὶ δ' ἡμῖν δαίς τε φίλη κίθαρίς τε χοροί τε Od.8. 248; μετὰ μελπομένῃσιν ἐν χορῷ Ἀρτέμιδος Il.16.183; τοὶ δ' ἄνδρες ἐν ἀγλαΐῃς τε χοροῖς τε τέρψιν ἔχον Hes.*Sc.*272, cf. 277; εἰς χ. ἐλθέμεν Il.15.508, cf. Od.18.194; οὐδέ κε φαίης ἀνδρὶ μαχεσσάμενον τόν γ' ἐλθεῖν, ἀλλὰ χορόνδε ἔρχεσθ' ἠὲ χοροῖο νέον λήγοντα καθίζειν Il.3.393, 394; χορῷ καλὴ Πολυμήλη 16.180: later of the *dance* as a public religious ceremony, Διόνυσον τιμῶσας χοροῖς E.*Ba.* 220; φυλῆς Ἀκαμαντίδος ἐν χοροῖσιν Simon.148, cf. Hdt.2.48, Isoc.9.1; χοροὺς ἀνῆγον αἱ πόλεις (sc. εἰς τὴν Δῆλον) Th.3.104; πεντήκοντ' ἀνδρῶν χ. Simon.147, cf. Sch.Aeschin.1.10; κύκλιος χ. (v. κύκλιος); θυσίῃσί σφεα (sc. Δαμίην καὶ Αὐξησίην) καὶ χοροῖσι γυναικηίοισι κερτόμοισι ἱλάσκοντο Hdt.5.83; ἵστασαν χοροὺς παρθένων τε καὶ ἠϊθέων Id.3.48; παιδικὸς χ. Is.7.40, etc.; χ. ἀνδρικός X.*HG*6.4.16, cf. Pl.*Lg.*665b; τραγικοὶ χοροί, at Sicyon, Hdt.5.67: hence of the *chorus* in the Attic drama, οἱ χ. τῶν τραγῳδῶν Ar.*Av.*787, cf. *Pax* 807 (lyr.); χ. τραγικός, κωμικός, Arist.*Pol.*1276b4; also χ. τρυγικός, τρυγῳδικός, Ar.*Ach.*628 (anap.), 886; arranged in six rows, Cratin. 173; ὃς οὐκ ἔδωκ' αἰτοῦντι Σοφοκλέει χορόν (of the archon to whom the poet applied) Id.15; χ. αἰτεῖν Ar.*Eq.*513 (anap.); διδόναι Pl.*R.*383c, etc.; χορὸν λαβεῖν, ἔχειν, Ar.*Ra.*94, *Pax* 803, 807 (lyr.); χ. συλλέξαι, χοροὺς ἀθροίζειν (i.e. from the tribe), Antipho 6.11, X.*Hier.*9.4; [χοροὺς] διδάσκειν ibid.; χορὸν εἰσάγειν Ar.*Ach.*11: general phrases, χοροὺς ἱστάναι Hdt.3.48 (v. supr.), S.*El.*280; ἔστασεν Pi.*P.*9.114; ἱερὸν χ. ἵστατε Νύμφαις Ar.*Nu.*271 (anap.), cf. *Av.*220 (anap.); ἅψαι A.*Eu.*307 (anap.); χορῶν κατάστασις Id.*Ag.*23, cf. Ar.*Th.*958; τοῖς χ. νικᾶν X.*Mem.*3.4.3; χοροῦ προεστάναι ibid.; χορῷ χορηγεῖν Pl.*Grg.* 482b, etc. II. *choir, band of dancers and singers*, *h.Ven.*118, Pi.*N.*5. 23, *Fr.*199; συμφωνία καὶ χοροί *Ev.Luc.*15.25. 2. generally, *choir, troop*, ἰχθύων S.*Fr.*762; μελιττῶν Ael.*NA*5.13; χ. καλλίμορφος τέκνων E.*HF*925, cf. Pl.*Prt.*315b, *Tht.*173b, etc.; of things, ἄστρων αἰθέριοι χ. E.*El.*467 (lyr.), cf. Mesom.*Sol.*17; χ. σκευῶν *row* of dishes, X.*Oec.*8.20; χ. δονάκων *row* of reeds, i.e. Pan's pipe, Coluth.124; χ. ὀδόντων *a row* of teeth, Gal.*UP*11.8 (hence οἱ πρόσθιοι χοροί, for the front teeth, Ar.*Ra.*548); τὴν σοφίαν ποῦ χοροῦ τάξομεν; in what *class* shall we place it? Pl.*Euthd.*279c, cf. Chor.12.28 p.160 F.-R. III. *place for dancing*, ἐν δὲ χ. ποίκιλλε.. Ἀμφιγυήεις Il. 18.590; λείηναν δὲ χ. Od.8.260, cf. 264; ὅθι τ' Ἠοῦς ἠριγενείης οἰκία καὶ χοροί εἰσι 12.4; Νυμφέων καλοὶ χ. ἠδὲ θόωκοι ib.318; at Sparta the ἀγορά was called χορός, Paus.3.11.9; so perh. in Crete, *Supp. Epigr.*2.509.6 (Eltynia, prob. v B.C.): v. infr. (Acc. to Hsch. χορός = κύκλος, στέφανος, and therefore prop. denotes *a ring-dance*.)

**χορο-στάδες**, ἑορταί feasts *celebrated with choral dances*, Call. *Fr.*66a (cf. Sch.Th.*Oxy.*853 x10). **-στᾰσία**, poet. **-ίη**, ἡ, *institution of choruses*: generally, *chorus, dance*, *AP*.7.613.6 (Diog.), 9.603 (Antip.): pl., Call.*Lav.Pall.*66, *IG*14.1389 i 58. ⊕**-στᾰτέω**, *lead a chorus* or *as in a chorus*, Hsch., f.l. in Ph.2.266. **-στάτης** [ᾰ], Dor. **-στάτας**, ου, ὁ, *leader of a chorus*, *IG*12(2).645.36 (Nesus, iv B.C.), Him.*Or.*9.3, Jul.*Ep.*186:—fem. **-στάτις**, ἡ, Alcm.23. 84. **-στᾰτικός**, ή, όν, *of instituting choruses*: ἡ χ. (sc. τέχνη) Men. Rh.p.360S. **-τερπής**, ές, *delighting in the dance*, Nonn.*D.*14. 249. **-ψάλτρια**, ἡ, *female harpist who accompanied a chorus*, *SIG*689. 3 (Delph., ii B.C.), *BCH*53.34 (ib., i B.C.), *Michel*910.24 (Iasus, ii B.C.).

**χορτ-άζω**, *feed, fatten*, prop. of cattle (Ael.Dion.*Fr.*326), χ. ἕλικας βόας ἔνδον ἐόντας Hes.*Op.*452; χορτάσω τὸν κάνθαρον (the beetle being comically treated as a horse), Ar.*Pax* 176; τούτοισι (sc. σιτίοις)..τοῦτον χορτάσω ib.139; c. acc. rei, Pl.*R.*372d:—Pass., *eat their fill*, of cattle, ib.586a; τινος of a thing, Thphr.*CP*4.9.1. II. of persons, *feed*, βολβοῖς ἐμαυτὸν χορτάσω Eub.7.5; ἡ θυγάτηρ τὴν μητέρα οὐκ ἐχόρτασεν οὔτε ἡ μήτηρ τὴν θυγατέρα *Supp.Epigr.*6.187 (Phrygia): c. gen., *fill full of..*, θεράπευε καὶ χόρταζε τῶν μονῳδιῶν (metaph.) Ar.*Fr.*154:—Pass., c. acc., χορταζόμενοι γάλα λευκόν Cratin.142 (hex.): c. dat., χ. ἅπασιν ἀγαθοῖς Amphis 28: c. gen., στεμφύλων Arist.*Fr.*107: metaph., λύπης Ps.-Callisth.2.22; ζωῆς Lxx *To.*12.9; ἔν τινι *Ps.*16(17).15: abs., *feast*, κεχόρτασμαι..οὐ κακῶς

Eub.30.1, cf. Araros 21, Nicostr.20, Men.465, *Ev.Marc.*7.27, Arr. *Epict.*1.9.19.

**χορταιό-βᾱμος**, ὁ, epith. of Silenus (cf. sq. 1), Hsch.; also **-βάμων** [ᾰ], ον, gen. *ονος*, *Trag.Adesp.*601.

**χορτ-αῖος**, *α*, *ον*, *of* or *for a farmyard* (v. χόρτος I):—χιτὼν χ. *a shaggy coat of skins* worn by the actor who played Silenus, expld. by μαλλωτός, D.H.7.72, cf. Ael.*VH*3.40: generally, *rough coarse coat*, Ar.*Fr.*707a, Hsch. II. χορταία, ἡ (sc. γῆ), *pasture*-land *POxy.*2113.19 (iv A.D., written κορτ-). **-άρᾰκος** [ᾰρ], ἡ, *mixture of ἄρακος and hay*, as fodder, *PLond.*3.1171.38 (i B.C.), *PTeb.*423.6 (iii A.D.). II. Adj. fem. -αράκη (sc. γῆ) *PHib.*1.75.6 (iii B.C.). ⊛ **-άριον**, τό, *coarse grass*, such as grows in bogs, Dsc.5.119 (pl.). **-ᾰσία**, ἡ, *being fed*, *fullness*, κοιλίας Lxx *Pr.*24.15; εἰς χορτασίαν *Sammelb.*6949.17 (Axum, iv A.D.). 2. *being fed*, *AP*11.313 (Lucill.). ⊛ **-ασμα**, ατος, τό, mostly in pl., *fodder*, *forage*, for cattle, Plb.9.4.3, D.S.20.42, Phylarch.36 J., Lxx *Ge.*24.25,32, al. 2. *food* for men, *Act.Ap.*7.11 (pl.). **-ασμός**, ὁ, = χορτασία, Anaxandr.76, Simp. *in Epict.* p.69 D. **-αστικός**, ή, όν, (χορτάζω) *good for feeding*, *nutritious*, Hsch. s.v. καπανικώτερα (Comp.). **-αστός**, ή, όν, = *satiabilis*, *Gloss.* ⊛ **-άχῠρον** [ᾰ], τό, *chopped hay*, *PSI*7.820.5 (iv A.D.); written **χορτοάχυρον**, *POxy.*1862.25 (vii A.D.). **-έγχερσος**, ἡ, *meadow-land*, *grass-land*, *PAmh.*2.94.6 (iii A.D.). **-ηγέω**, *carry hay*, *BGU*1502.1 (iii B.C.), *PFlor.*322.39 (iii A.D.). **-ηγία**, ἡ, *hay-harvest*, ib.198.2 (iii A.D.). ⊛ **-ηγός**, ον, *hay-carrying*, πλοῖα *PCair.Zen.*191.7 (iii B.C.). **-ικός**, ή, όν, *of* or *for hay*, γενήματα *PPetr.*2 p.121 (iii B.C.); φόρος *CPR*40.23 (iii A.D.), etc.; τὰ χ. Ptol.*Tetr.*81.

**χορτίον**, τό, Dim. of χόρτος I, χ. αὐλᾶς Erinn. in *PSI*9.1090 (p. xii).

**χορτο-άχῠρον**, v. χορτάχυρον. **-βολον**, τό, (βάλλω) *place for throwing grass* or *hay into*, *hay-loft*, *PPetr.*3 p.139 (iii B.C.). **-βολών**, ῶνος, ὁ, = foreg., *Gloss.* **-βωλος**, = *caespes*, ib. **-δρέπᾰνον**, τό, *scythe*, ib. **-θήκη**, ἡ, *hay-loft*, *barn*, *BGU*1832.12 (i B.C.), *PRyl.*129.11 (i A.D.), etc. ⊛ **-κοπή**, ἡ, *hay-making*, *PTeb.*337.21 (ii/iii A.D.). **-κοπία**, ἡ, = *fenaria*, *Gloss.* **-κοπικός**, ή, όν, *for cutting hay*: -κοπικόν, τό, *scythe*, *PRyl.*138.21 (i A.D.). ⊛ **-κόπιον**, τό, *meadow*, *BSA*22.197 (Olymus), Dsc.2.147, 3.18, *Gp.*3.6.7. **-κόπος**, ον, *mowing hay*, δρέπανα *PCair.Zen.*782(*a*).123 (iii B.C.). 2. -κόπον, τό, *scythe for mowing hay*, *PRyl.*393$^v$10 (ii/iii A.D.). 3. -κόπος, ὁ, *mower*, *reaper*, *PGoodsp.Cair.*30 XX 12 (ii A.D.), *Gloss.* **-λογέω**, *collect fodder*, *forage*, App.*Hisp.*65. **-λογία**, ἡ, *collecting of fodder*, *foraging*, Plb.18.22.1, 21.39.12 (pl.), App.*BC*1.109, al. **-λόγος**, ον, *collecting fodder*, οἱ χ. *foragers*, Str.15.1.52. **-μᾰνέω**, *run to grass*, *grow rank*, Lxx *Pr.*24.46(31). **-νομή**, ἡ, *green crops grown for fodder*, *PTeb.*61(*a*).192, al. (ii B.C.), *POxy.*918 xi 10 (ii A.D.). **-παραλήμπτης**, ου, ὁ, *receiver of hay*, ib.1911.179 (vi A.D.). **-πάτητος** [ᾰ], ον: neut., *threshed straw*, ἐσθίουσι χ. μικτὸν ἀχύρῳ ἐπὶ τῆς ἅλω ib.1734.4, al. (ii/iii A.D.). **-πηγεῖον**, τό, dub. sens., *IG*9(2).522.6 (Larissa, iii/ii B.C.). **-πηγία**, ἡ, dub., ib.7. **-πλινθον**, τό, and **-πλινθος**, ἡ, *square of turf*, *sod*, *Gloss.* **-πράτης** [ᾱ], ου, ὁ, *hay-dealer*, *Stud.Pal.*10.251.9 (vi A.D.). **-πώλης**, ου, ὁ, = foreg., *PLond.*3.1177.254 (ii A.D.).

⊛ **χόρτος**, ὁ, prop. *enclosed place* (v. sub fin.), but always with collat. notion of *a feeding-place*: in Il., *farmyard*, in which the cattle were kept, αὐλῆς ἐν χόρτῳ 11.774; αὐλῆς ἐν χόρτοισι 24.640. 2. generally, *any feeding-ground*, *pasturage*, freq. in pl., χόρτοι λέοντος, of Nemea, Pi.*O.*13.44; χόρτοι εὔδενδροι E.*IT*134 (lyr.); χόρτος οὐρανοῦ *the expanse* of heaven, Poet.ap.Hsch. II. *fodder*, *provender*, esp. for horses and cattle, Hdt.5.16 (of fish); θηρῶν ὀρείων χόρτον, οὐχ ἵππων λέγεις E.*Alc.*495; *grass*, Hes.*Op.*606, E.*Rh.*771, 1*Ep.Cor.*3.12; χ. κοῦφος *hay*, X.*An.*1.5.10; χ. ἐβλάστησεν, ἐξηράνθη, *Ev.Matt.*13.26, 1*Ep.Pet.*1.24; ἄνθος χόρτου *Ep.Jac.*1.10: opp. σῖτος (food for man), Hdt.9.41, X.*Cyr.*8.6.12; χόρτον ἔχει ἐπὶ τοῦ κέρατος as translation of the Lat. proverb, *foenum habet in cornu*, of a dangerous ox, Plu.*Crass.*7. b. *green crop*, [γῆ] ἐσπαρμένη χόρτῳ *PTeb.*27.72 (ii B.C.), al. 2. Poet., *food* generally, δούλιος χ. Hippon.35.6, cf. E.*Cyc.*507 (lyr.), Crates Theb.10; cf. χορτάζω. (Cf. Lat. *hortus*, Welsh *garth* 'fold, enclosure', Irish *gort* 'crop', 'field'.)

**χορτό-σπερμον**, τό, *grass-seed*, *PLond.*3.1171.55 (i A.D.), *POxy.*533.7 (ii/iii A.D.), *Gloss.* **-σπορέω**, *sow fodder-crops*, *PCair.Zen.*497 (iii B.C.): irreg. fut. Pass. χορτοσπαρήσομαι (sic) ib.723 (iii B.C.). **-σπορία**, *sowing for fodder*, *POsl.*32.11 (i A.D.). **-στᾰσία**, ἡ, pl., = *stationes*, *Gloss.* **-στρωμα**, ατος, τό, *litter of grass* or *hay*, ib.; **-στρωτοι** στιβάδες ib. **-τηλις**, ιδος, ἡ, *mixture of hay and* τῆλις, *PLond.*1.131.606 (i A.D.). **-τομία**, ἡ, *a cutting of grass for hay*, *Gloss.* **-τόμος**, ον, *for cutting hay*, δρέπανα *PCair.Zen.*782(*a*).125 (iii B.C.). **-φᾰγέω**, *eat hay*, *PTeb.*703.68 (iii B.C.). **-φάγος** [ᾰ], ον, *eating grass*, *EM*215.57. **-φόρος**, ον, *carrying fodder*, Str.15.1.42; χ. ἅμαξα Polyaen.3.15. II. *producing grass*, *PSI*6.579.6 (iii B.C.), *Gp.*3.11.7. **-φύλαξ** [ῠ], ᾰκος, ὁ, *guard of hay*, *PCair.Zen.*368.24 (iii B.C.).

**χορτώδης**, ες, *of grass*, *like grass*, τροφή Lxx 2 *Ma.*5.27, cf. Dsc.4.69; τὴν ὑποστάθμην, τοῦτ' ἔστι τὰ χ. Aët.12.55; τόποι *grassy*, *Hippiatr.*117.

**χορῳδ-έω**, (ᾠδή) *sing in* or *to a chorus*, D.C.61.19. **-ία**, ἡ, *choral song*, opp. μονῳδία, Pl.*Lg.*764e.

**χορωνός**, ὁ, = κορώνη (II. 6), *crown*, Simon.174 (ap.Ath.15.680d).

**χορωφελήτης**, ου, Dor. **-τας**, ὁ, *helping* or *cheering the chorus*, κρότος Ar.*Lys.*1319 (lyr., Herm. for χορωφελέτας).

⊛ **χοῦς** (A), ὁ, also ἡ Anaxandr.41.13 (anap.), Nic.*Th.*103: (χέω):—a measure of capacity, = 12 κοτύλαι: nom. sg. χοῦς Anaxandr.71, Alex.15.19, Men.*Her.Fr.*5, *IG*11(2).219*A*40 (Delos, iii B.C.); gen. χοός Ar.*Th.*347 (cod. R and Suid., fort χοῶς), *Tab.Heracl.*2.36,57, *IG*2$^2$.1013.55; χοῦ (in signf. II) ib.1252.11, *Ath.Mitt.*30.146 (Mysia); dat. χοΐ Anaxandr.41.13, D.*Prooem.*53, *PFrankf.*1.19, al. (iii B.C.) (also Dor., *Tab.Heracl.*1.103); χῷ (in signf. II) *Ath.Mitt.*30.145; acc. χοῦν Dsc.5.7, Ael.*NA*16.12, *IG*2$^2$.1366.23, *PHolm.*16.10; written χον (in signf. II), *SIG*57.21 (Milet., v B.C.); χόα Choerob. *in Theod.*1.238H.; nom. pl. χόες Pl.*Tht.*173e, *IG*2$^2$.1672.200, *Inscr. Délos* 396 *A* 67 (iii B.C.), Gal.18(2).258; contr. χοῦς *AP*5.182 (Posidipp.); gen. pl. χῶν *IG*12(5).593*A*9 (Ceos, v B.C.), χοῶν *SIG*647.27 (Stiris, ii B.C.); acc. χοῦς *Tab.Heracl.*1.103, *PMich.Zen.*94.4 (iii B.C.); χόας Hero *Mens.*19, *Geom.*23.63, Aristid.1.18J., Lib.*Or.*11.126, *Gp.*8.20.1, al. (χοας unaccented, *SIG*953.18 (Cnidus, ii B.C.)):—also nom. sg. **χοεύς** Hp.*Epid.*7.10, *IG*11(2).219*A*8 (Delos, iii B.C.); gen. χοῶς Ar.*Pax*537 (χοός ap. Suid.); χοέως Gal.12.932, S.E.*M.*9.320; dat. χοέϊ or χοεῖ Hp.*Salubr.*5, *Morb.*3.17 cod. θ, *PHib.*1.90.11 (iii B.C.), Choerob. *in Theod.* 1.238H.; acc. χοᾶ Ar.*Eq.*355, *Ach.*1202 (lyr.), Men.915 (contr. fr. χοέα, as correctly expld. by Hdn.Gr.2.13 and Choerob. l.c.; found at end of a verse in Ar.*Eq.*95,113, *Ach.*1133, Eub.80.4, Men. l.c.); χοέα Hp.*Morb.*3.17, Dsc.5.72,73, *Gp.*2.6.42, Gal.12.931: nom. pl. χοεῖς *IG*11(2).237.3 (Delos, iii B.C.), *Inscr.Délos* 440 *A* 20, 62 (ii B.C.), *Ostr.Bodl.*i 343 (ii B.C.); written χοιεῖς *PCair.Zen.*160.3 (iii B.C.); acc. χοᾶς Ar.*Ec.*44, *Th.*746 (cod. R, cf. Suid.), Arist.*HA*627$^b$4; later χοέας Ph.*Bel.*90.26; χοεῖς Lxx 3 *Ki.*7.24(38), Dsc.5.7,63,68, *PHolm.*16.11,17; dat. χοεῦσιν Arist.*GC*328$^a$27; χόεσι or χοέσι (perh. formed like δρομέσι) Wilcken *Chr.*176.7 (i A.D.): the unaccented forms χοα, χοας, χοων, *PCair.Zen.*516.21,16,19 (iii B.C.), prob. belong to χοεύς: prov., of attempts to measure the immeasurable, οἱ τῆς θαλάττης λεγόμενοι χόες Pl.*Tht.*173d; ὥσπερανεί τις ἐξαριθμεῖσθαι βούλοιτο τοὺς χόας τῆς θαλάττης Aristid. l.c. II. = συμβολή IV, ἡ πόλις διδοῖ..χο͂ν (v. supr.) τὸμ παλαιὸν ὀρτῆς ἑκάστης *SIG*57.21 (Milet., v B.C.); εἶναι αὐτοῖς ἀτέλειαν τοῦ χοῦ *IG*2$^2$.1252.11; Argive acc. sg. χῶν Hegesand.31. 2. name of a society or club, ἄρξαντα χοῦ *Ath.Mitt.*30.146 (Mysia); Διῒ Ὑψίστῳ καὶ τῷ χῷ ib.145 (ibid.). III. Χόες, οἱ, *the Pitcher-feast*, a name given to the second day of the Anthesteria, Call.*Aet.*1.1.2; gen. Χοῶν Eubulid.1, Timae.128; dat. τοῖς Χουσί Ar.*Ach.*1211, Ath.7.276c; acc. τοὺς Χοᾶς Ar.*Ach.*961; τοὺς Χοᾶς ἄγειν D.39.16, cf. Phanod.13; τοὺς Χοῦς *IG*3.1342.

**χοῦς** (B), ὁ, also ἡ Str.10.2.19, 12.8.17, 16.1.9: (χέω):—*soil excavated* or *heaped up*, ὁ χ. ὁ ἐξορυχθείς Hdt.2.150; τὸν αἰεὶ ἐξορυσσόμενον χοῦν Id.7.23, cf. 1.185, 8.28, Pherecr.121 (anap.), Th.2.76, 4.90, *IG*2$^2$.380.26, etc.: gen. χοῦ Arr.*An.*2.27.4, *POxy.*1631.28 (iii A.D.) (uncontr. χόου *IG*9(1).691.6 (Corcyra)); also (from confusion with χοῦς A) gen. χοός Lxx *Ec.*3.20, *PTeb.*342.27 (ii A.D.), *PBremen*14.13; dat. χοΐ *IG*12(3), 248.10 (Anaphe, ii B.C.), Hsch. 2. = κονιορτός, *dust*, Lxx 3 *Ki.*18.38, al., *Ev.Marc.*6.11. 3. χοῦς θανάτου *the grave*, Lxx *Ps.*21(22).16, cf. Hsch., Suid.

**χόω**, 3 sg. χοῖ (προσ-) Th.2.102, 3 pl. χοῦσι Hdt.4.71; inf. χοῦν Id.2.137; part. χῶν Id.1.162: impf. ἔχουν Th.2.75, etc.: later **χώννυμι**, **-ύω** (qq. v.): fut. χώσω S.*Ant.*81, etc.: aor. ἔχωσα Hdt.2.140, *PTeb.*799.16 (ii B.C.), etc. (Cret. 3 pl. ἔχουσαν *GDI*5056.6 (Istron)): pf. κέχωκα (ἀνα-) D.55.28:—**Med.**, aor. ἐχωσάμην Luc.*DDeor.*14.2, Philostr.*VA*4.10:—Pass., fut. χωσθήσομαι E.*IA*1442, (ἐγ-) Plb.4.40.4: aor. ἐχώσθην (v. infr.); also ἐχώθην (συν-) *IG*4.823.30 (Troezen, iv B.C.): pf. κέχωσμαι Pl.Com.183, Th.2.102, (ἐκ-, συγ-) Hdt.2.138, 8.144:—*throw* or *heap up*, of earth, χοῦσι χῶμα μέγα Id.4.71; χώματα χοῦν Id.2.137, Pl.*Lg.*958e; χώματα χῶν πρὸς τὰ τείχεα *throwing up* banks against.., Hdt.1.162; χῶμα ἔχουν πρὸς τὴν πόλιν Th.2.75; νῆσον χώσας σποδῷ *having formed* an island *with heaped up* ashes, Hdt.2.140; esp. of a sepulchral mound, χῶσαι τάφον Id.9.85, S.*Ant.*81; τύμβον ib.1204, E.*IT*702, *IA*1442 (Pass.); μνῆμα X.*Cyr.*7.3.11; πολυάνδρια (cf. -άνδριος II. 2), Plu.*Eum.*9. 2. *block up by throwing earth in*, λιμένας D.25.84, cf. Aeschin.3.109 (s. v.l.); χ. φορμοῖς τὰς τάφρους Plb.1.19.13:—Pass., *to be filled with earth*, esp. of bays in the sea, *to be silted up*, πορθμοῦ χωσθέντος Emp.100.17; τί μιν (sc. τὸν κόλπον) κωλύει..χωσθῆναι; Hdt.2.11; but of cities, *to be raised on mounds*, ib.137. 3. less freq., *cover with earth*, *bury*, χῶσαί τινα τάφῳ E.*Or.*1585, cf. Pl.*Lg.*947e, *IG*5(1).1249.17 (Laconia), cf. χώννυμι fin. 4 [ὁ τρωγλοδύτης] ταριχεύεται καλῶς.. χωσθεὶς εἰς ἅλας *covered over* with salt, Aët.11.11.

**χοωποίησις**, v. χοοποίησις.

**χραδαμύλα**· ὁ κοχλίας (Tarent.), Hsch. (ἀχραδάμυλλα cod.).

**χραίνω**, A.*Th.*61, etc., fut. χρᾰνῶ E.*Hec.*366: aor. ἔχρᾱνα A.*Eu.*170 (lyr.); subj. χράνῃ Id.*Fr.*327; inf. χρᾶναι Poll.7.129, Porph.*Chr.*49:—*touch slightly*, ὀλιγάκις ἄστυ κἀγορᾶς χραίνων κύκλον, i.e. keeping aloof from it, E.*Or.*919; χ. οὐραίοισιν εὐδίαν ἁλός, of fishes, Achae.27.3: hence, *smear*, *paint*, χ. ἢ ἀποχραίνειν Pl.*Lg.*769a, cf. Poll. l.c., Max.Tyr.40.2: *besmear*, *anoint*, τινι Nic.*Al.*246:—Pass., χραινομένην μέλιτι *AP*7.622 (Antiphil.). 2. *stain*, βωμὸν αἵματι μήλων B.10.111; πεδία δ' ἀργηστὴς ἀφρὸς χραίνει σταλαγμοῖς A.*Th.*61, cf. *Fr.*327; *defile*, μιάσματι μυχὸν ἔχρανας Id.*Eu.*170 (lyr.); esp. of moral pollution, λέχη δὲ τοῦ θανόντος ἐν χεροῖν ἐμαῖν χραίνω S.*OT*822, cf. E.*Hipp.*1266, *Hec.*366; ὄμμα χ. θανασίμοισιν ἐκπνοαῖς Id.*Hipp.*1438; οὔτε φόνῳ τοὺς τῶν θεῶν βωμοὺς χραίνειν δεῖ Porph.*Abst.*2.28; of words, θεῶν ὀνόματα μὴ χ. ῥᾳδίως

Pl.*Lg*.917b:—Med., χεῖρα χραίνεσθαι φόνῳ S.*Aj*.43:—Pass., αἱμάτων μιάσμασι χρανθεῖσα γαῖα A.*Supp*.266; καπνῷ χραίνεται πόλισμα Id. *Th*.342 (lyr.), cf. S.*OC*368; τὰ ὄμματα μὴ κεχράνθαι τοῖς ἀσεβήμασι Jul.*Or*.7.205a; ὄψιν τε καὶ ἀκοὴν ἐχράνθημεν Hld.10.9.

⊕ **χραισμ-έω**, Ep. Verb (not in Od. or Hes.), pres. only in Nic.*Th*. 914: fut. 3 sg. χραισμήσει Il.20.296, Ep. inf. -ησέμεν 21.316: aor. 1 Ep. 3 sg. χραίσμησε 16.837; inf. χραισμῆσαι 11.120: used by Hom. most freq. in aor. 2, 3 sg. ἔχραισμε 14.66, Ep. χραῖσμε 5.53, 7.144; subj. 3 sg. χραίσμῃ, χραίσμῃσι, 1.28, 11.387; 3 pl. χραίσμωσι 1.566; inf. χραισμεῖν ib.242, al.:—prop. *ward off* something destructive *from one*, c. acc. rei et dat. pers., οὐ κορύνη οἱ ὄλεθρον χραῖσμε σιδηρείη Il.7.144; οὐδέ τί οἱ χραισμήσει λυγρὸν ὄλεθρον 20. 296; τοῖς οὔ τις δύνατο χραισμῆσαι ὄλεθρον Τρώων 11.120: once c. acc. pers. (supplied), μή νύ τοι οὐ χραίσμωσιν [με] ἆσσον ἰόνθ' *keep* [me] *off* from you, 1.566. 2. more freq. c. dat. pers. only, *defend, succour* (though the notion of *warding off injury* is always implied), freq. in Il., 1.28, 5.53, al.: c. neut. Adj., χραισμεῖν τι *assist, avail* at all, 1.242, 21.193, al.; abs., 14.66, 15.652.—Hom. uses χραισμεῖν with negs. expressed or implied (in Il.21.193, εἰ δύναταί τι χραισμεῖν is ironical for οὔτι χ. δύναται), cf. 15.32. In positive clauses first in A.R.2.249, al.; imper. χραίσμετε Id.2.218. (Said by Sch.A.R.2. 218 to belong to the dialect of the Clitorians in Arcadia.) **-η**, ἡ, *help, succour*, Nic.*Th*.583: pl., ib.852. **-ήεις**, εσσα, εν, *serviceable*, ib.576. **-ῄον**, τό, *means of help, remedy*, Marc.Sid.42. ⊕ **-ημα**, ατος, τό, = foreg., v.l. in Nonn.*D*.33.369. ⊕ **-ησις**, εως, ἡ, = foreg., Nic.*Th*.926, *Epigr.Gr*. (add.) 903*a*.3 (Hypaepa). **-ήτωρ**, ορος, ὁ, *protector*, prob. in Nonn.*D*.33.369.

**χραντός**, ή, όν, (χραίνω) *stained, defiled*, Gloss.

**χράομαι**, v. χράω (B) C.

**χραῦσις**, εως, ἡ, *anchor with one hook, grapnel*, Hsch.

**χραυτίζω**, in impf. ἐχραύτιζεν, = ἴξευεν, Hsch.

⊕***χραύω** (this pres. implied by impf. ἐνέχραυε, v. ἐγχραύω), *scrape, graze, wound slightly*, ὅν ῥά τε ποιμὴν.. χραύσῃ Il.5.138; ἵνα χραύσαντα δαΐξῃ Q.S.11.76; ἔχραυσεν, glossed by ἐπέτυχεν, Hsch. II. Med. c. gen., of lands, *touch, be adjacent to*, χραυόμενον *Inscr.Cypr*.135.9H.; also **χραυζόμενον** ib.18.

**χράω** (A), used in Ep. only in aor. 2, *fall upon, attack, assail*, c. dat. pers., στυγερὸς δέ οἱ ἔχραε δαίμων Od.5.396; τίς τοι κακὸς ἔχραε δαίμων; 10.64; so ἠϊθέοις οὐκ ἔστι τόσος πόνος, ὁππόσος ἡμῖν ..ἔχραε *AP*5.296 (Agath.): cf. ἐπιχράω (B). II. c. acc. rei, *inflict* upon a person, κακὸν δέ οἱ ἔχραε κοῖτον Nic.*Th*.315. III. c. inf., *conceive a desire* to.., τίπτε σὸς υἱὸς ἐμὸν ῥόον ἔχραε κήδειν ἐξ ἄλλων; why *did he want* (or *needed he*) to vex my stream of all others? Il.21.369; μνηστῆρες.., οἳ τόδε δῶμα ἐχράετ' ἐσθιέμεν καὶ πινέμεν ye suitors.., who *have become so eager* to.., Od.21.69. (For signfs. I, II, cf. ζαχρηής; for III perh. cf. χρή, κέχρημαι (χράω (B) C), χρῆ, χρῆς.)

⊕ **χράω** (B). A. Forms: contr. χρῇ S.*El*.35, Ion. χρᾷ Hdt.1.62 (also Luc.*DMort*.3.2); inf. χρᾶν Hdt.8.135 (also Luc.*Alex*.19); Ion. part. χρέων *h.Ap*.253, fem. χρέωσα Hdt.7.111; Ep. χρείων Od.8.79, *h.Ap*. 396: impf. ἔχραον Pi.*O*.7.92 (v.l. ἔχρεον), A.R.2.454; 3 sg. ἔχρη Tyrt.3.3, Hermesian.7.89, (ἐξ-) S.*OC*87: fut. χρήσω *h.Ap*.132, Hdt.1.19, A.*Ag*.1083: aor. ἔχρησα Hdt.4.156, etc.:—**Pass.**, aor. ἐχρήσθην Id.1.49, etc.: pf. κέχρησμαι (v.l. κέχρημαι) Id.4.164, 7.141: plpf. ἐκέχρηστο (v.l. ἐκέχρητο) Id.2.147,151, 3.64, etc.:—**Med.**, χρῶμαι Th.1.126, etc., Ion. χρέομαι Hdt., inf. χρέεσθαι 1.157 (χρᾶσθαι ib.172); part. χρεώμενος 4.151: impf. 3 pl. ἐχρέωντο (v.l. ἐχρέοντο) 4.157, 5.82: fut. χρήσομαι Od.10.492, etc. I. in Act. of the gods and their oracles, *proclaim*, abs., χρείων μυθήσατο Φοῖβος 8.79: χρείων ἐκ δάφνης γυάλων ὕπο Παρνησοῖο *h.Ap*.396: c. acc. rei, χρήσω ἀνθρώποισι Διὸς βουλήν ib.132, cf. Thgn.807, Pi.l.c., Plot.2. 9.9; ἡ Πυθίη οἱ χρᾷ τάδε Hdt.1.55, cf. 4.155; χρῆσε οἰκιστῆρα Βάττον *proclaimed* him the colonizer, Pi.*P*.4.6; also in Trag., ὁ χρήσας A. *Eu*.798; χρήσειν ἔοικεν ἀμφὶ τῶν αὑτῆς κακῶν Id.*Ag*.1083; χρῇ μοι τοιαῦθ' ὁ Φοῖβος S.*El*.35; σοὶ δ' οὐκ ἔχρησεν οὐδέν E.*Hec*.1268; χ. φόνον Id.*El*.1267: also c. acc. cogn., χ. χρησμὸν Id.*Ph*.409; ὑμνῳδίαν Id.*Ion*681 (lyr.): c. inf., *warn* or *direct by oracle*, ἔχρησας ὥστε τὸν ξένον μητροκτονεῖν A.*Eu*.202; without ὥστε, ib.203; χρήσαντ' ἐμοὶ.. ἐκτὸς αἰτίας κακῆς εἶναι *that* I should be.., Id.*Ch*.1030; c. inf. aor., Ar. *V*.159: rare in Att. Prose, τάδε ὁ Ἀπόλλων ἔχρησεν *IG*1$^2$.80.10; τὸν Ἀπόλλω ταύτην τὴν γῆν χρῆσαι οἰκεῖν Th.2.102; τοῦ θεοῦ χρήσαντος Id.5.32, cf. Lycurg.99; ἔχρησεν ὁ θεός *SIG*1044.5 (Halic., iv/iii B.C.); ὁ θεὸς ἔχρησε *IG*4$^2$(1).122.78 (Epid., iv B.C.). II. Pass., *to be declared, proclaimed* by an oracle, τίς οὖν ἐχρήσθη; E.*Ion*792; mostly of the *oracle delivered*, τὰ ἐκ Δελφῶν οὕτω τῷ Κροίσῳ ἐχρήσθη Hdt.1.49; τὰ χρηστήρια ταὐτὰ σφι ἐχρήσθη Id.9.94; ἠπίως χρησθῆναι Id.7.143; τὸ χρησθέν, τὰ χρησθέντα, the *response*, Id.1.63, 7.178; ἐν Πυθῶνι χρησθὲν παλαίφατον Pi.*O*.2.39; πεύθου τὰ χρησθέντ' S.*OT* 604; χρησθὲν αὐτῷ ἐν Νεμέᾳ τοῦτο παθεῖν *since it was foretold* him *by an oracle* that..Th.3.96; ἃ τοὐδ' ἐχρήσθη σώματος which *were declared* about it, S.*OC*355; τὸν κεχρησμένον θάνατον Hdt.4.164 (-χρημ- codd.); τοῦ κακοῦ τοῦ κεχρησμένου Id.7.141 (v.l. -χρημ-): impers., c. inf., καί σφι ἐχρήσθη ἀνέμοισι εὔχεσθαι ib.178: c. acc. et inf., ἐκέχρηστό σφι..τοῦτον βασιλεύσειν Id.2.147; c. inf. aor., Id.7. 220. III. Med., of the person to whom the response is given, *consult a god* or *oracle*, c. dat., ψυχῇ χρησόμενος Θηβαίου Τειρεσίαο Od.10.492,565; χ. θεῷ, χρηστηρίοισι, μαντηΐῳ, Hdt.1.47,53,157; τῷ θεῷ Aeschin.3.124; χ. μάντεσι Μούσαις Ar.*Av*.724 (anap.), cf. Pl. *Lg*.686a; ὅσοι μαντικὴν νομίζοντες οἰωνοῖς χρῶνται X.*Mem*.1.1.3; χ. χρηστηρίῳ εἰ..*inquire at* the oracle whether.., Hdt.3.57: abs., ὑπέρβη λάϊνον οὐδὸν χρησόμενος Od.8.81, cf. *h.Ap*.252,292; ἀπέστειλε ἄλλους χρησομένους Hdt.1.46; οἱ χρώμενοι the *consulters*, E.*Ph*.957; χρωμένῳ ἐν Δελφοῖς Th.1.126; also χ. περὶ τοῦ πολέμου Hdt.7.220, cf. 1.85, 4.150,155, etc.; κεχρημένος *having inquired of an oracle*, Arist.*Rh*.1398$^b$33: c. inf., σωφρονεῖν κεχρημένον *being divinely warned* to be temperate, A.*Pers*.829, cf. Marcellin.*Vit.Thuc*.6: later simply, *receive a divine revelation*, Plot.5.3.14.—Hom. has the word in this sense only in Od.: the Act. only in pres. part. χρείων (fut. χρήσω *h.Ap*.132): the Med. only in part. fut. χρησόμενος.

B. *furnish with* a thing, in which sense the pres. was **κίχρημι**, D.53.12, Plu.*Pomp*.29; Cret. 3 sg. κίγχρητι *Inscr.Cret*.1 xxiii 3 (Phaestus, ii B.C.); Delph. 3 sg. pres. subj. κιχρῇ *Schwyzer*324.17 (iv B.C.): aor. χρέη ib.13; pres. part. κιχρέντε ib.adn. (rarely **χρηννύναι, χρηννύω**, Thphr.*Char*.5.10, 10.13: Med., χρηννυόμεθα *PCair.Zen*. 304.4 (iii B.C.)): fut. χρήσω Hdt.3.58: aor. ἔχρησα ibid., 6.89, Ar. *Th*.219, X.*Mem*.3.11.18, Lys.19.24, *IG*1$^2$.108.16, etc. (3 sg. written ἔκχρησεν *IG*12(3).1350.4 (Thera)); imper. χρῆσον Ar.*Ra*.1159, Pl. Com.205: pf. κέχρηκα Men.461,598, Plb.29.21.6 (= D.S.31.10): plpf. ἐκεχρήκει App.*BC*2.29:—**Pass.**, pf. κέχρημαι (δια-) D.27.11:—**Med.**, pres. κίχραμαι Plu.2.534b; inf. κίχρασθαι Thphr.*Char*.30.20: impf. ἐκιχράμην *AP*9.584.10: aor. ἐχρησάμην, imper. χρῆσαι E.*El*.191 (lyr.), etc.:—*furnish the use of* a thing, i.e. *lend*, usu. in a friendly way, δανείζω being the word applied to usurers (but χ. = δανείζω in Antipho Soph.54), ll. cc.; οὐ δεδωκώς, ἀλλὰ χρήσας Arist.*EN*1162$^b$ 33, cf. Lxx*Ex*.11.3; ἡ πειρατικὴ δύναμις χρήσασα ταῖς βασιλικαῖς ὑπηρεσίαις ἑαυτήν Plu.*Pomp*.24; χ. τὴν ἑαυτοῦ σχολήν τισι Id.*Phil*. 13; χ. τὰν χέρα, in the formula of manumission, *IG*9(1).189,194 (Tithora):—Med., *borrow*, τι E.*El*.191 (lyr.), Thphr.*Char*.30.20: abs., χρησαμένη γὰρ ἔνησα καὶ οὐκ ἔχω ἀνταποδοῦναι Batr.186; πόδας χρήσας, ὄμματα χρησάμενος having *lent* feet and *borrowed* eyes, of a blind man carrying a lame one, *AP*9.13 (Pl.Jun.), cf. Pl.*Dem*. 384b,c. II. = χρηματίζω III, τοῦ χρέοντος γραμματέως *CIG*2562. 18 (s. v. l., Hierapytna).

C. Med. **χράομαι**, Att. **χρῶμαι**, χρῇ prob. in Pl.*Hp.Mi*.369a, χρῆται Ar.*V*.1028 (anap.), etc. (also Trag., A.*Ag*.953), χρώμεθα, χρῆσθε, χρῶνται, And.4.6, Pl.*La*.194c, Th.1.70, etc.; Dor. **χρέομαι** Sophr.126; Ion. χρᾶται Hdt.1.132, al. (so in later Prose, Iamb. *in Nic*.p.28P.); χρέεται v.l. in Hdt.4.50; χρέονται Hp.*Aër*.1; χρέωνται Hdt.1.34, 4.108, al.; χρείωνται Heraclit.104; opt. χρῴμην, χρῷο Pl. *Cri*.45b, χρῷτο Gorg.*Fr*.20, etc.; Ion. χρέοιτο Hp.*Acut*.56; imper. χρῶ Democr.270, Ar.*Th*.212, Isoc.1.34, Ion. χρέο Hp.*Steril*.230, Hdt. 1.155 (v.l. χρέω, as in Hp.*Acut*.(*Sp*.)62); 3 sg. Dor. χρείσθω *SIG* 1009.7 (Chalcedon, iii/ii B.C.); 2 pl. χρῆσθε And.1.11; 3 pl. χρήσθων Ar.*Nu*.439 (s. v. l.; v. infr. III. 4b), Th.5.18; χράσθων *IG*1$^2$.122.5; Dor. χρόνσθω *Mnemos*.57.208 (Argos, vi B.C.); inf. Att. and Ion. χρῆσθαι *IG*1$^2$.57.19, Ar.*Av*.1040, Lys.25.20, *SIG*57.5 (Milet., v B.C.), *IG*12(5).593*A*12 (Ceos, v B.C.); Ion. and Hellenistic χρᾶσθαι Hdt. 2.15, 3.20, al., *IG*12(5).606.9 (Ceos, iv/iii B.C.), *SIG*344.50 (Teos, iv B.C.), 1106.80 (Cos, iv/iii B.C.), *PCair.Zen*.299.10 (iii B.C.), *OGI*214. 19 (Didyma, iii B.C.), *IG*2$^2$.1325.24 (both forms in Phld.*Rh*.1.66S. and Ph.*Bel*., χρῆσθαι 57.35, al., χρᾶσθαι 53.49, al.), Ion. χρέεσθαι as v.l. for χρῆσθαι Hdt.1.21, 187, al. (χρῆσθαι ib.153 codd.), so in Arc., *IG*5 (2).514.14 (Lycosura, ii B.C.), Elean χρηῆσται *Inscr.Olymp*.1.3 (vii/vi B.C.), Boeot. χρειεῖσθη *IG*7.3169 (Orchom., iii B.C.); Locr. and Lacon. χρῆσται *IG*9(1).334.19,23 (Oeanthea, v B.C.), 5(1).1317.8 (Thalamae, iv/iii B.C.); part. Att. χρώμενος A.*Eu*.655, *IG*1$^2$.81.6, etc.; Ep. and Ion. χρεώμενος Il.23.834 (as a dactyl), Hdt.2.108, Hp.*Acut*.18, Dor. χρείμενος *SIG*395.4, 438.11 (both Delph., iii B.C.), *Berl.Sitzb*.1927. 156 (Cyrene), χρήμενος *Riv.Fil*.58.472 (Gortyn, ii B.C.), χρεύμενος *SIG*1166.3 (Dodona): impf. Att. ἐχρώμην Antipho 5.63, ἐχρῶ Ar.*Ra*. 111, And.1.49, ἐχρῆτο Th.1.130, etc.; pl., ἐχρώμεθα Lys.*Fr*.29, ἐχρῶντο Antipho 6.28, etc.; Ion. ἐχρᾶτο Hdt.2.173 (v.l. -ῆτο), 3.3, 129, al. (also found in Anaxipp.1.9 codd.Ath.), ἐχρέωντο Hdt.2.108, al.: but ἐχρῆτο 3.41 codd., Herod.6.55, (προσ-) Hp.*Epid*.3.17.α': fut. χρήσομαι S.*Ph*.1133 (lyr.), etc.; also **κεχρήσομαι** Theoc.16.73: aor. ἐχρησάμην S.*OT*117, Th.5.7, al.: pf. κέχρημαι (v. infr. I): aor. ἐχρήσθην in pass. sense (v. infr. VII):—in pf. κέχρημαι (with pres. sense) c. gen., *desire, yearn after*, the usual sense in Ep., οὔτ' εὐνῆς πρόφασιν κεχρημένος (sc. αὐτῆς) οὔτε τευ ἄλλου Il.19.262; νόστου κεχρημένον ἠδὲ γυναικός Od.1.13; κομιδῆς κεχρημένοι ἄνδρες 14.124, cf. 17.421, 20.378, 22.50; μαντοσυνέων κεχρημένοι Emp.112.10. 2. *to be in want of, lack*, τοῦ κεχρημένοι; S.*Ph*.1264, cf. E.*IA*382 (troch.); [βορᾶς] κεχρημένοι Id.*Cyc*.98; οὐ πόνων κεχρήμεθα Id.*Med*.334; τίνος κέχρησθε, γυναῖκες; Theoc.26.18: fut., ὃς ἐμεῦ κεχρήσετ' ἀοιδοῦ Id. 16.73; χρησόμεθα εἰς τὰ ἔργα καὶ ὁδοῦ..καὶ ὕδατος we *shall need*.., *SIG*1182.12 (Ephes., iii B.C.): freq. abs. in part. κεχρημένος, *lacking, needy*, Od.14.155, 17.347, Hes.*Op*.317,500, E.*Supp*.327, Pl.*Lg*. 717c: but κεχρηόσι δαίτης is f.l. for κεχαρηόσι in Nic.*Fr*.70.18. 3. pf. and plpf. κέχρημαι, κεχρήμην, in pres. and impf. sense, c. dat., *enjoy, have*, φρεσὶ γὰρ κέχρητ' ἀγαθῇσι(ν) Od.3.266, 14.421, 16.398; αὕτη (sc. ἡ χώρη) ὕδασι κάλλιστα κέχρηται Hp.*Aër*.12; ἡ καταδεεστέροις τούτοις (sc. τοῖς εἴδεσι) κεχρημένη τραγῳδία Arist.*Po*.1450$^a$32, cf. $^a$13, $^b$33; ἄλλαις, μικραῖς διαφοραῖς, Id.*Metaph*.1042$^b$31, *Phgn*.809$^a$8; ὑγροτέραις σαρξὶ ib.$^b$11; θριξὶ ξανθαῖς ib.25; καθαρωτάτῳ..αἵματι Id. *Resp*.477$^a$21; τῶν..πλαγίαις ταῖς ῥάβδοις κεχρημένων (sc. ἰχθύων) Id. *Fr*.295; εὐγενείᾳ κεχρημένος *IG*4$^2$(1).83.10 (Epid., i A.D.); σφαιρικῷ ὄγκῳ *PLit.Lond*.167.25 (ii/iii A.D.), cf. κεχρημένως (Addenda); so in pres., χρῶνται δειλαῖς φρεσί, δαίμονι δ' ἐσθλῷ Thgn.161; μέρη τραγῳδίας, οἷς ὡς εἴδεσι δεῖ χρῆσθαι, πρότερον εἴπομεν Arist.*Po.*1452ᵇ14, cf. 1458ᵇ14. II. *use*, pres. once in Hom., abs., ἕξει μιν καὶ πέντε περιπλομένους ἐνιαυτοὺς χρεώμενος Il.23.834: later mostly c. dat. (for acc. v. infr. VI), ἀκμαζούσῃ τῇ ῥώμῃ τῶν χειρῶν χρώμενος Antipho 4.3.3; ἐσθῆτι τοιῇδε χρέωνται Hdt.1.195, cf. 202, Ar.*Ra.* 1061 (anap.); διφασίοισι γράμμασι χ. Hdt.2.36; τοῖσι οὐνόμασι τῶν θεῶν ib.52; πλατυτέροισι ἐχρέωντο τοῖσι πόμασι, ἐκ φρεάτων χρεώμενοι ib. 108; τοῖσι ἐποποιοῖσι χρεώμενον λέγειν ib.120; ὅστις ἐμπύρῳ χρῆται τέχνῃ *consults* burnt offerings, E.*Ph.*954; χ. ἀργυρίῳ *make use of* money, Pl.*R.*333b; ἀργύρῳ Ar.*Ec.*822; χ. ἵπποις *manage* them, X.*Smp.*2.10; χ. ἰχθύσι *use* for food, Plu.2.668f; οἴνῳ χ. ἐπὶ πλέον ib.715d; χ. ναυτιλίῃσι, θαλάσσῃ, Hdt.2.43, Th.1.3; ὠνῇ καὶ πρήσι Hdt.1.153; δρασμῷ Aeschin.3.21; τέχναις X.*Mem.*3.10.1, *Oec.*4.4; τῇ τέχνῃ *POxy.*1029.25 (ii A.D.); χρώμενοι τῇ πόλει *taking a part in* politics, E.*Ion* 602; ἐκκλησίαισιν ἦν ὅτ' οὐκ ἐχρώμεθα Ar.*Ec.*183; ἄλλον τρόπον τῇ πολιτείᾳ κέχρημαι, = πεπολίτευμαι, Hyp.*Eux.*28; φωνὴν δυναμένην ὄχλῳ χρῆσθαι Isoc.5.81; τῇ τραπέζῃ τῇ τοῦ πατρὸς ἐχρῆτο he *had dealings with* my father's bank, D.52.3; χ. τοῖς πράγμασι καὶ τοῖς καιροῖς *administer* them, Isoc.6.50. III. *experience, suffer, be subject to*, esp. external events or conditions, δάμαρτος Ἱππολύτας Ἀκάστου δολίαις τέχναισι χρησάμενος *having experienced*, Pi.*N.*4.58; κείμεθ' ἀγηράντῳ χρώμενοι εὐλογίῃ Simon.100.4; νιφετῷ Hdt.4.50; στίβῃ καὶ νιφετῷ Call.*Epigr.*33.3; χειμῶνι Antipho 5.21, D.18.194; λαίλαπι *AP*7.503 (Leon.); στυγεροῖς πνεύμασι Epigr.ap.D.S.13.41 (iv B.C.); ἀνάγκῃ Antipho 5.22; οἰκεῖα πράγματ' εἰσάγων, οἷς χρώμεθ', οἷς σύνεσμεν Ar.*Ra.*959; γυναικῶν τῶν τοῖς τόκοις χρωμένων πλείοσιν Arist.*HA*582ᵃ24; ἀπεψίαις χ. *IG*4²(1).126.4 (Epid., ii A.D.); ἑκὼν.. οὐδεὶς δουλίῳ χρῆται ζυγῷ A.*Ag.*953; νόμοισι χ. *live under* laws, Hdt. 1.173, 216, cf. *IG*9(1).334.19 (Locr., V B.C.); νόμοις τοῖς ἰδίοις *Riv.Fil.*58.472 (Gortyn, iii B.C.); ἀνομίᾳ X.*Mem.*1.2.24; γαλανείᾳ χρησάμενοι μανιάδων οἴστρων E.*IA*546 (lyr.); χ. εὐμαρείᾳ *to be at* ease, S.*Tr.*193 (but, *ease* oneself, Hdt.2.35); συντυχίῃ χ. Id.5.41; τύχῃ E.*Heracl.*714, And.1.67, 120; πολλῇ εὐτυχίᾳ Pl.*Men.*72a; πολλῇ τῇ νίκῃ χρῆται, = παρὰ πολὺ νικᾷ, And.4.31; συμφορῇ κεχρημένος Hdt.1.42, cf. E.*Med.*347; τοιούτῳ μόρῳ ἐχρήσατο ὁ παῖς Hdt. 1.117; θείῃ πομπῇ χρεώμενος divinely sent, ib.62; of mental conditions present in the subject, τῷ χόλῳ χρέομαι I *feel* anger, Sophr. 126; λογισάμενος ἣν εὑρίσκῃ πλέω τε καὶ μέζω τὰ ἀδικήματα ἐόντα τῶν ὑποργημάτων, οὕτω τῷ θυμῷ χρᾶται Hdt.1.137; μὴ πάντα θυμῷ χρέο ib.155; ὀργῇ χρωμένη S.*OT*1241; ὀργῇ μεγάλῃ μοι ἐχρήσω Lxx *Jb.*10.17, cf. 19.11, al.; ἀγνωμοσύνῃ χρησάμενοι ἀπέστησαν they stiffened their necks and.. Hdt.5.83; οἴησις γάρ, καὶ μάλιστα ἐν ἰητρικῇ, αἰτίην μὲν τοῖσι κεχρημένοισιν, ὄλεθρον δὲ τοῖσι χρεωμένοισι ἐπιφέρει vanity brings blame on its *possessor* (or *victim*) and ruin on those who *consult* him, Hp.*Decent.*4; πολλῇ ἀνοίᾳ χρώμενος Antipho 3.3.2; ἀμαθίᾳ πλέονι.. χρῆσθε Th.1.68; ταῖς ἐπιθυμίαις μείζοσιν ἢ κατὰ τὴν ὑπάρχουσαν οὐσίαν ἐχρῆτο Id.6.15; φθόνῳ καὶ διαβολῇ χ. Pl.*Ap.*18d; οὐ τῇ ἑαυτοῦ ἁμαρτίᾳ, ἀλλὰ τῇ τοῦ πατάξαντος χρησάμενος ἀπέθανεν Antipho 4.3.4; τοῖς ἁμαρτήμασι παραπλησίοις ἐχρήσαντο Isoc.8.104; μή τι ἄρα τῇ ἐλαφρίᾳ ἐχρησάμην; 2 *Ep.Cor.*1.17. 2. with verbal nouns, periphr. for the verb derived from the noun, ἀληθεῖ λόγῳ χ. *use* true speech, i.e. speak the truth, Hdt.1.14; ἀληθείῃ χ. ib.116, 7.101; βοῇ χ. *set up* a cry, Id.4.134; τοιούτῳ πράγματι οὐ κέχρησαι, = οὐδὲν τοιοῦτο ἔπραξας, Hyp.*Eux.*11; δαψιλεῖ τῷ ποτῷ (fort. πότῳ) χρησαμένους Hdt.2.121.δ'; ἐσόδῳ χρέο πυκνῶς *visit* often, Hp.*Decent.*13; ἡ σελήνη.. διὰ παντὸς τῇ ἴσῃ παραυξήσει καὶ μειώσει χρῆται Gem.18.16. 3. c. dupl. dat., *use as* so and so, τοῖς ἀγαθοῖσιν.. χ. πρὸς τὰ κακὰ ἀλκῇ Democr.173; μιᾷ πόλει ταύτῃ χ. Th.2.15; χ. τῷ σίτῳ ὄψῳ ἢ τῷ ὄψῳ σίτῳ X.*Mem.*3.14.4. 4. χ. τισιν ἔς τι *use* for an end or purpose, Hdt.1.34; πρός τι X.*Oec.*11. 13; ἐπί τι Id.*Mem.*1.2.9; ἀμφί or περί τι, Id.*Oec.*9.6, *An.*3.5.10; with neut. Adj. or Pron. as Adv., τάδε [τῷ ἀμφιβλήστρῳ] χ. *makes* the following *use* of the net, Hdt.2.95; χρέωνται οὐδὲν ἐλαίῳ Id.1. 193; χρυσῷ καὶ χαλκῷ τὰ πάντα χρέωνται ib.215; λογισμῷ ἐλάχιστα χ., πλεῖστα ἀρετῇ χ., Th.2.11, 5.105; τί χρήσεται ποτ' αὐτῷ; what *use will he make* of him? Ar.*Ach.*935, cf. X.*An.*1.3.18; χ. τἀνδρὶ τοῖς τ' ἐμοῖς λόγοις S.*Tr.*60; ἠπορούμην ὅ τι χρησαίμην τῇ τούτου παρανομίᾳ Lys.3.10. b. *treat, deal with*, παραδίδωμι χρᾶσθαι αὐτῷ τοῦτο ὅ τι σὺ βούλεαι Hdt.1.210, cf. Ar.*Nu.*439 (anap.; fort. delendum χρήσθων), Isoc.12.107; εἰ τύχοι (sc. γυνὴ) μὴ ἐπιτηδεία γενομένη, τί χρὴ τῇ συμφορᾷ χρῆσθαι; Antipho Soph.49; ἀπορέων ὅ τι χρήσηται τῷ παρεόντι πρήγματι not knowing what *to make of* it, Hdt.7.213; ἠπόρει ὅτι χρήσαιτο Pl.*Prt.*321c; οὐκ ἂν ἔχοις ὅτι χρῷο σαυτῷ Id.*Cri.*45b; in elliptical phrases, τί οὖν χρησώμεθα; Id. *Ly.*213c; Θηβαίους ἔχοντες.. τί χρήσεσθε; D.8.74: c. dat. et acc. cogn., χρωμένους τῷ κτείναντι χρείαν ἣν ἂν ἐθέλωσι Pl.*Lg.*868b, cf. 785b, *Clit.*407e. IV. of persons, χρῆσθαί τινι ὡς.. *treat* him as.., χ. τινὶ ὡς ἀνδρὶ ψεύστῃ Hdt.7.209; χ. [τισὶν] ὡς πολεμίοις, ὡς φίλοις καὶ πιστοῖς, *treat* as friends or enemies, *regard* them as such, Th.1.53, X.*Cyr.*4.2.8; so φιλικώτερον χρῆσθαί τισι Id.*Mem.*4.3.12; ὑβριστικῶς χ. τισί D.56.12; also without ὡς, ἔμοιγε χρώμενος διδασκάλῳ A.*Pr.*324, cf. Heraclit.104; ὥς γ' ἐμοὶ χρῆσθαι κριτῇ E.*Alc.* 801; οὐ σφόδρα ἐχρώμην Λυκίνῳ φίλῳ Antipho 5.63; πλείστοις καὶ δεινοτάτοις ἐχθροῖς χ. And.4.2; ἀσθενέσι χ. πολεμίοις X.*Cyr.*3.2.4. b. χρῆσθαί τινι (without φίλῳ) *to be intimate with* a man, X.*Hier.*5.2, *Mem.*4.8.11; χρῆσθαι καὶ συνεῖναί τισι And.1.49; ἀνάγκη, ὃς ἂν γένηται (sc. παῖς, son), τούτῳ χρῆσθαι one must *put up with* the son that is born, Democr.277: ἰητρῷ μὴ χρωμένους not *consulting* a doctor, Hp.*de Arte* 5 (so c. dat. et acc., ἐσιέναι παρὰ βασιλέα μηδένα, δι' ἀγγέλων δὲ πάντα χρᾶσθαι (sc. αὐτῷ) *deal with* him in everything by messengers, Hdt.1.99); so Πλάτωνι, Ξενοφῶντι, χ. *use, study* their writings, Plu.2.79d: abs., οἱ χρώμενοι *friends*, X.*Ages.*11.13, *Mem.*2.6.5, Isoc.6.44. 2. esp. of sexual intercourse, γυναιξὶ ἐχρᾶτο Hdt.2.181, cf. X.*Mem.*1.2.29, 2.1.30, Is.3.10, D.59.67. 3. χρῆσθαι ἑαυτῷ *make use of* oneself or one's powers, with a part., οὐδ' ὑγιαίνοντι χρώμενος ἑαυτῷ Plu.*Nic.*17; αὐτῷ νήφοντι χ. Id.*Eum.*16: so with an Adv., χ. ἑαυτῷ πρὸς τοὺς κινδύνους ἀφειδῶς Id.*Alex.*45; παρέχειν ἑαυτὸν ταῖς ἀρχαῖς χρῆσθαι place oneself at the *disposal* of another, X.*Cyr.*1.2.13, cf. 8.1.5. V. abs., or with Adv., χρῶνται Πέρσαι οὕτω so the Persians *are wont to do*, such *is* their *custom*, ib.4.3.23. VI. in later Gk. (τῷ μεγαλόφρονι shd. be read for τὸ μεγαλόφρον in X.*Ages.*11.11) c. acc. rei, χ. τὰ ἀπὸ λιμένων.. εἰς διοίκησιν τῆς πόλεως Arist.*Oec.*1350ᵃ7; [θησαυρὸν] χρησάμενοι (v.l. κτησάμενοι) Lxx *Wi.*7.14; οἱ χρώμενοι τὸν κόσμον ὡς μὴ καταχρώμενοι 1 *Ep.Cor.*7.31; ἄνηθον μετ' ἐλαίου χρήσασθαι *IG*4²(1).126.27 (Epid., ii A.D.); ὕδωρ χρῶ *PTeb.*273.28 (ii/iii A.D.):—for Hdt.1.99, v. supr. IV. 1 b. VII. Pass., *to be used*, esp. in aor., αἱ δὲ (sc. αἱ νέες) οὐκ ἐχρήσθησαν Hdt.7.144; τέως ἂν χρησθῇ so long as *it be in use*, D.21.16; [σιδήρου τοῦ] χρησθέντος εἰς τύλους *Supp. Epigr.*4.447.48 (Didyma, ii B.C.); Hsch. also has χρησθήσεται· χρησιμεύσει:—v. supr. A. II.

D. for χρή, v. sub voc. (Origin and historical order of the forms and senses not clear: χρή and χρῄζω are cogn.)

**χρέα**, v. χρεία, χρέος.

**χρε-ᾰγωγός**, ὁ, *one who carries a debtor to prison*, Hsch. **-άρπαξ**, ἄγος, ὁ, *one who grasps at money*, Man.4.330.

**χρέεσθαι**, v. χράω (B) A init.

⊛ **χρεία** (written χρέα *PCair.Zen.*25.2, 148 (iii B.C.)), Ion. **χρείη** Call. in *PSI*11.1216.43, ἡ: (χράομαι, κέχρημαι):—*need, want*, χρείας ὕπο A.*Th.*287; ἵν' ἕσταμεν χρείας considering in what great *need* we are, S.*OT*1443; χρείᾳ πολεμεῖν to war with *necessity*, Id.*OC* 191 (anap.): c. gen., *want of*.., φαρμάκων χρείᾳ κατεσκέλλοντο A.*Pr.* 481; ἐν χρείᾳ τύχης Id.*Th.*506; ἐν χρείᾳ δορὸς in the *need* or *stress* of war, S.*Aj.*963; φορβῆς χρείᾳ Id.*Ph.*162 (anap.), cf. 1004: ἵππων ἡμῖν χρεία μὲν οὔτε τις πολλῶν οὔτε πολλή [ἐστιν] Pl.*Lg.*834b; ἦ μὴν ἔτ' ἐμοῦ χρείαν ἕξει will have *need* of my help, A.*Pr.*170 (anap.), cf. Call.l.c.; ἀφίκοντο εἰς χρείαν τῆς πόλεως came to feel *the need* of its assistance, Pl.*Mx.*244d; ἰατρῶν ἐν χρείαις ἐσόμεθα, ἐν χρείᾳ ἡγεμόνος εἶναι, Pl.*R.*373d, 566e; ὅτου σε χ. ἔχει S.*Ph.*646; so τίς χ. σ' ἐμοῦ [ἔχει]; E.*Hec.*976, cf. χρεώ I.2: χρείαν ἔχω, c. inf., *Ev.Matt.*3.14 (folld. by ἵνα, *Ev.Jo.*2.25); signfs. I.1 and III in the same sentence, οὐχ οὕτως χ. ἔχομεν τῆς χ. παρὰ τῶν φίλων ὡς.. Epicur.*Sent.Vat.*34: prov., χ. διδάσκει, κἂν βραδύς τις ᾖ, σοφόν '*necessity* is the mother of invention', E.*Fr.*715, cf. *El.*376, Men.263: pl., αἱ χρεῖαι τολμᾶν βιάζονται Antipho 3.2.1; αἱ τοῦ σώματος χ. X. *Mem.*3.12.5; πρώτη γε καὶ μεγίστη τῶν χ. ἡ τῆς τροφῆς παρασκευή Pl.*R.*369d; αἱ ἀναγκαῖαι χ. D.23.148, cf. 45.67 (sg.); πολεμικαὶ χ. Arist. *Pol.*1328ᵇ11. 2. *want, poverty*, S.*Ph.*175 (lyr.), E.*Hel.*420, etc.; διὰ τὴν χ. καὶ τὴν πενίαν Ar.*Pl.*534 (anap.). 3. *a request of necessity*, opp. ἀξίωσις (a claim of merit), Th.1.37, cf. 33: generally, *request*, τὴν πρίν γε χ. ἠνύσασθ' ἐμοῦ πάρα A.*Pr.*700; κἀγὼ.. τοιάνδε σου χ. ἔχω make such *a request* of or to thee, Id.*Ch.*481. II. *business*, ὡς πρὸς τί χρείας; for what *purpose*? S.*OT*1174, cf. 1435; χρῆσθαί τινι χρείαν ἣν ἂν ἐθέλωσι Pl.*Lg.*868b; δοῦναι ἑαυτὸν εἰς τὴν χ. Plb.8.16.11. b. esp. *military* or *naval service*, ἡ πολεμικὴ χ. καὶ ἡ εἰρηνική the *employments* of war and of peace, Arist.*Pol.*1254ᵇ32; αἱ κατὰ θάλατταν [χ.], ἡ ἐν τῇ γῇ χ., Plb.6.52.1, 31.21.3; οἱ ἐπὶ τῶν χ. Aristeas 110, Lxx 1 *Ma.*12.45; οἱ πρὸς ταῖς χ. *Ju.*12.10; οἱ ἐπὶ χρειῶν τεταγμένοι *BGU*543.1 (i B.C.); in military sense, *action, engagement*, αἱ κατὰ μέρος χ. Plb.1.84.7, al. c. generally, *business, employment, function*, Id.3.45.2, etc.; ἡ ἐγκεχειρισμένη χ. the *duty* assigned, *PTeb.*741.11 (ii B.C.); οὓς καταστήσομεν ἐπὶ τῆς χ. ταύτης *Act.Ap.*6.3; χ. πολιτικαί Plu.*Mar.* 32, etc. d. *a business, affair, matter*, like χρέος, Plb.2.49.9, al.; τὴν ὑπὲρ τούτων χ. the *study* of these things, Epicur.*Ep.*1 p. 29 U. e. χ. ἀναγκαία *need* of nature, D.S.4.33; τροφῆς χ. Ph.2. 472. III. *use*, 1. as a property, *use, advantage, service*, χρείης εἵνεκα μηδεμιῆς Thgn.62; τῆς χ. τοῦ παιδὸς ἀποστερηθῆναι Antipho 3.3.4; ἡ χ. τῆς ῥητορικῆς Pl.*Grg.*480a; πωλοῦντες τὴν τῆς ἰσχύος χ. Id. *R.*371e; χρείαν ἔχειν τοῖς ἀνθρώποις to be *of service* to mankind, Id. *Smp.*204c; τὰ οὐδὲν εἰς χρείαν things of no *use* or *service*, D.*Prooem.* 56.3; χρείαν ἔχει εἴς τι is *of service* towards.., Sosip.1.41; for S.*OT* 725, v. ἐρευνάω I: pl., χρεῖαι.. φίλων ἀνδρῶν *services rendered* by them, Pi.*N.*8.42; χρείας παρέχεσθαι render *services*, Decr.ap.D.18. 84, *IG*2².654.15, cf. Plb.1.16.8 (sg.); ἵνα σοι τὰς χ. παρέσχωμαι (sic) *PCair.Zen.*498 (iii B.C.); μεγάλην παρεῖχε χ. τοῖς κοινοῖς πράγμασιν Plb.3.97.4; παρέχειν χ. to be *serviceable, useful*, Aristo *Stoic.*1.79; ἑξήκοντα καὶ τριακόσια χρειῶν γένη παρέχον δένδρον Plu.2.724e; χ. ναυτικαί *equipments*, Ael.*VH*2.10. 2. as an action, *using, use*, κτῆσις καὶ χ. X.*Mem.*2.4.1, Pl.*R.*451c; ἐν χρείᾳ εἶναι in *use*, Id. *Phd.*87c; κατὰ τὴν χ. for *use*, Id.*R.*330c; πρὸς τὴν ἀνθρωπίνην χ. X.*Mem.*4.2.25; ἡ χ. τῶν λόγων the *employment* of words, Pl.*Sph.* 239d, cf. *Plt.*272d: pl., λάμπει γὰρ ἐν χρείαισιν ὥσπερ.. χαλκός is made bright by *constant use*, S.*Fr.*864. IV. of persons, *familiarity, intimacy*, τινος *with* one, Antipho 5.63: generally, *any relation of business* or *intercourse*, ἐν χρείᾳ τινὶ τῇ πρὸς ἀλλήλους Pl.*R.*372a; ἡ πρὸς ἀλλήλους χ. Arist.*Rh.*1376ᵇ13; [Νικόμαχος] συνεβίω Ἀμύντᾳ.. ἰατροῦ καὶ φίλου χρείᾳ *in the relationship, capacity*, D.L.5.1. V.

Rhet., *pregnant sentence, maxim*, freq. illustrated by an anecdote, Sen.*Ep.*33.7, Hermog.*Prog.*3, Aphthon.*Prog.*3, Theon *Prog.*5, etc.: pl., title of works by Zeno (D.L.6.91), Aristipp., etc.; by Macho, a collection of sayings of courtesans, Ath.13.577d; ἡ τοῦ Κλεομένους χ. Plu.2.218a; χρεῖαι καὶ ἱστορίαι ib.78f.

⊛ **χρειᾰκός**, ή, όν, *serving*, χρειακοὶ *crew* of a boat, opp. κυβερνῆται, *Peripl.MRubr.*16; **χρεακοί** (in more general sense) *BGU*14 ii 9 (iii A.D.).

**χρεῖος**, τό, Ep. for χρέος, q.v.

**χρεῖος**, ον, (χρή) *needing, in want of*, νῦν γὰρ εἶ χ. φίλων E.*HF* 1337; πάντων..χρεῖοι ib.51: abs., *needy, poor*, χρεῖος εἶ, ξένη, φυγάς A.*Supp.*202; χ. ὢν οὐδὲν σθένει E.*Fr.*142; also in later Prose, ἄνθρωποι χ. τροφῆς D.Chr.32.9; λουτροῦ χρεῖός ἐστιν Luc.*Am.*42, cf. Ph.2.98, etc., v. Moeris p.415 P., Thom.Mag. p.400R. II. *useful*, ἀνὴρ εἰς οὐδὲν χ. Anon.ap.Eust.218.8; χρεῖον οὐκ ἔχων ἀγωγῆς τοῦτον τὸν τρόπον holding this form of education *unnecessary*, Phld. *Acad.Ind.*p.79M.; ἐὰν..χρ[ῖ]ον ἔχῃς (sc. ἔλαιον) dub. in *POxy.* 1665.16 (iii A.D.).

**χρειοφελέτης**, ου, ὁ, Ion. for χρεωφειλέτης, Hp.*Ep.*17.

**χρει-όω**, *have force, avail*, πρός τι S.E.*M.*7.436. **-ώ**, v. χρεώ. **-ώδης**, ες, *needful*, Phld.*D.*3*Fr.*87, Ph.2.23, J.*BJ*5.5.8, Ruf.ap.Orib.8.24.7, Ael.*Tact.*34.1; τισι Crantor ap.S.E.*M*11.53, Plu.2.724e; τὸ χ. *necessity*, Luc.*Am.*38; τὸ ἀναγκαῖον καὶ χ. Plu.2. 1118b; ἐν πᾶσιν τοῖς χριώδεσιν (sic) τῆς πατρίδος *IG*4.716.13 (Hermione); χ. ἀπόφθεγμα, = χρεία v, D.L.4.47: Comp. and Sup., -έστερος, -έστατος, Ael.*Tact.*1.7: Comp., Hld.6.11: Sup., Ps.-Luc. *Philopatr.*19. II. *in need of*, τἆλλα ὧν ὁ ἀνθρώπινος βίος χρειώδης Ph.ap.Eus.*PE*8.11: abs., of parts of the body, *needy*, opp. ἐνεργά (productive), Mnesith.ap.Steph. *in Gal.*1.241D.; *deficient*, τὸ χ. *Corp. Herm.*18.6.

**χρείων**, Ep. part. of χράω (B) A. **χρειών**, v. χρεών. **χρείως**· δέησις, Hsch.

**χρεμέδα**· ἠχῇ ὡς Καλλίμαχος, Hsch. (χρεμετῇ· ἠχεῖ Salm., χρεμέδα· ἠχή Bentl., χρεμεδά (Advb.)· ἠχητικῶς cj. Schneid.Call.*Fr.* 352.)

**χρεμέθω**, = sq., 3 pl. χρεμέθουσι, and subj. -ωσι, Opp.*C.*1.224,163; part. -ων ib.263, *AP*9.295 (Bianor).

**χρεμετ-ίζω**, *neigh, whinny*, of horses, Il.12.51, Hdt.3.86,87, Pl. *R.*396b, *Phdr.*254d, Jul.*Mis.*366a: metaph. of lewd men, χ. ἐπὶ γυναῖκα Lxx *Je.*5.8.—In Hes.*Sc.*348 we have a shorter form of 3 pl. aor.1, χρέμισαν, as if from **χρεμίζω**. (Cf. χρόμη, χρόμαδος, OE. *gremettan, grymettan* 'to roar', OSlav. *vŭz-grĭmĕti* 'to thunder'.) **-ισμα**, ατος, τό, *neighing, whinnying*, Iamb.*Bab.*p.50H. (pl.): metaph., χ. γάμου προκέλευθον ἱεῖσα *AP*5.244 (Maced.). **-ισμός**, ὁ, = foreg., Ar.*Eq.*553 (lyr.), Lxx *Am.*6.7: pl., D.H.*Comp.*16, *Placit.*4.19.1:—hence, 2. of any loud noise, *thunder*, Th.*Jb.*39.19. **-ιστικός**, ή, όν, *fond of neighing, able to neigh*, ζῷον Ph.1.310, S.E.*P.*2.211, Plu.2.877b, cf. Alex.Aphr.*in Top.*235.24.

**χρέμης**, ητος, ὁ, a fish, prob. = χρόμις, Opp.*H.*1.112, Ael.*NA* 15.11.

**χρεμίζω**, v. χρεμετίζω. **χρεμίς**· χρεμετίς, Hsch.

**χρέμμα**, ατος, τό, *spittle, expectoration*, D.L.2.67 (sed leg. κράματι).

**χρέμπτομαι**, aor. ἐχρεμψάμην Luc. (v. infr.), Jul.*Or.*7.205c:—*clear one's throat, hawk and spit, cough*, E.*Cyc.*626; esp. before making a speech, Ar.*Th.*381; χ. ὡς πτύσων Gal.*Protr.*8: c. acc., αἱματῶδες χ. *spit* blood, Hp.*Epid.*5.14; μῆλα χ. Eup.163 (lyr.); πλατὺ χρεμψάμενος Luc.*Cat.*12, cf. *Pr.Im.*20:—Pass., πράσα..χρέμπτεται *are expectorant*, Ruf.ap.Orib.*inc.*4.28. (Akin to χρεμετίζω.)

**χρέμυς**, υος, ὁ, a fish, = ὀνίσκος, Hsch.; cj. for **κρέμυς**, Arist.*Fr.* 294:—cf. χρόμις.

**χρέμψ**, a kind of *fish*, prob. = χρόμις, Arist.*HA*534a8 (v.l. χρέψ).

**χρεμψῐθέατρος**, ον, = ἐν τῷ θεάτρῳ χρεμπτόμενος, *Com.Adesp.* 1198.

**χρεο-δοσία**, ἡ, *payment of a debt*, Aq.*De.*24.13, Hdn.*Epim.*207. **-δοτέω**, *pay debts*, Hdn. ibid.

**χρεοκ-, χρεολ-**, etc., later forms in compos. for χρεω-, acc. to Lob.*Phryn.*390; but Hdn.Epim.207 prefers the short vowel.

**χρεόν**, v. χρεών.

⊛ **χρεονόμος**, ὁ, dub. sens., title of an official, *BSA*26.166 (Sparta, ii A.D.).

**χρέος**, τό, Ep. **χρεῖος** Hom. (who also uses χρέος, but only in Od., v. infr. I.1): Att. **χρέως** Phryn.370, Moeris p.403 P., Choerob.*in Theod.*1.360H. (and this form appears in codd. of D.25.69, 33.24, 38. 14, 40.37, 42.5; but χρέος in Pl.*Plt.*267a, *Lg.*958b): gen. χρείους E.*IA*373 (troch., s.v.l.), χρέους Lys.17.5 codd., χρέως D.49.18 (and so Choerob. l.c.); no dat. occurs in Ep. forms:—pl., nom. and acc. χρέᾰ Hes.*Op.*647, χρέᾱ Ar.*Nu.*39, 443 (anap.), cf. Isoc.21.13, Pl.*Lg.* 684e, etc.; Arc. χρήατα (but *Schwyzer* [665] χρῆα τά) *IG*5(2).343.20, 27 (Orchom., iv B.C.); gen. χρεῶν Ar.*Nu.*13,117, Pl.*R.*566a, etc.; Ep. χρειῶν Hes.*Op.*404 (χρεέων cj. Rzach); Ep. dat. χρέεσι Man. 4.135; χρήεσσι A.R.3.1198: (χράομαι, χρή): I. *that which one needs must pay, obligation, debt*, Ἄρης..χρέος καὶ δεσμὸν ἀλύξας Od. 8.353, cf. 355; χρεῖος ἀποστήσασθαι, i.e. pay *it* in full, Il.13.746: esp. *of the obligation to restore or pay for 'lifted' cattle and plunder*, so the heralds of the Pylians summoned to share in booty all οἷσι χρεῖος ὀφείλετ'..πολέσιν γὰρ Ἐπειοὶ χρεῖος ὄφειλον (where Sch. A, τὰ περιελασθέντα ἐκ τῆς Πύλου ὑπὸ τῶν Ἐπειῶν θρέμματα χρέως καλεῖ) Il. 11.686, cf. Od.3.367, 21.17; later simply, *debt*, αὐτὸς ἔτεισε..χρέος Thgn.205; ἀρᾶς τίνει χ. pays *the debt demanded by* the curse, A.*Ag.* 457 (lyr.); μή τι πέρα χρέος..πόλει προσάψῃς *debt*, i.e. *guilt*, S.*OC*235 (lyr.); χ. πράσσειν τινά exact payment of a *debt* from one, Pi.*O.*3.7; ἐμὸν καταισχύνει χ. dishonoured my *debt*, i.e. dishonoured me *for not paying my debt, for not keeping my promise*, ib.10(11).8; τεὸν χ. *the debt due* to thee, Id.*P.*8.33: in Com. and Prose, χ. ἀποδιδόναι repay a *debt*, Hdt.2.136 (where also we have χ. διδόναι to give a *loan*, and χ. λαμβάνειν to receive a *loan*), cf. Ar.*Nu.*117, Pl.*Plt.*267a; ἔχω χ. ὡς εἰπεῖν οὐδὲν ἀνδρὸς Ἕλληνος I know of nothing *that I owe* to any man of Greece, Hdt.3.140; χ. ἀπαιτεῖν Plu.*Oth.*2; τὰ ὑπάρχοντα τῶν χ. ἀνεῖσθαι Id.*Sol.*15; τὸ ἐπὶ τὴν τράπεζαν χρέως (sc. ὀφειλόμενον) D.33.24; ὦ καλὸν εἰς ἄλοχον θέμενος χ., like χάριν θέσθαι (v. τίθημι A. II.7 fin.), Epigr. in *Arch.Pap.*1.220 (Ptolemaic); ἔχειν εἴς τι χ. Plu.*Caes.*48: pl., *debts*, Hes.*Op.*647, Ar.*Nu.*13, etc.; χρειῶν λύσις Hes.*Op.*404; χρέα ἀπολαβεῖν And.3.15; χρέα ἐπὶ τόκοις ὀφειλόμενα Is.11.42; τὴν οὐσίαν ἅπασαν χρέα κατέλιπον left all the property *in outstanding debts*, D.38.7; εἰσπραχθέντα χρέα ibid.; ἐκπληρῶσαι τὸ χ. ἅπαν pay *it*, Pl.*Lg.*958b; τὸ χ. διαλυέτω *SIG*306. 46 (Tegea, iv B.C.), cf. Plu.*Luc.*20 (Pass.); πρὸς τὰ χ. ἀπάγεσθαι Plb.38.11.10, D.H.4.9:—cf. ἀποκοπή. 2. metaph., *the debt that all must pay, fate, death*, οὐκ ἔστι τὸ χ. φυγεῖν Alciphr.1.25; τὸ τῆς ψυχῆς ἀπαιτηθεὶς χ. Lxx *Wi.*15.8; also ἂν μή τις θᾶττον ὡς χ. ἀποδιδῷ τὸ ζῆν Pl.*Ax.*367b; ὁπότε εἰς τὸν ἀέρα ἀναδράμῃ τὸ χ. (sc. ἡ ψυχή, regarded as lent to the body) Vett.Val.330.33. II. in Poets, *business, affair, matter*, ἐὸν αὐτοῦ χρεῖος ἐελδόμενος Od.1.409, cf. 2.45; χρέος πᾶν ἐπικραίνεις, of Pelasgos, A.*Supp.*374 (lyr.); *purpose, object*, εἰ μὲν γὰρ ὑμῖν μὴ τόδ' ἐκπράξω χρέος ib.472, cf. S.*OT* 156 (lyr.); πᾶν ὃ θέλεις..χ. ἐκτετέλεσται Theoc.25.53: c. gen., σὸν οὐκ ἔλασσον ἢ κείνης χ. your *affair*, E.*Hec.*892. 2. almost = χρῆμα, *thing*, τί χρέος; = τί χρῆμα; A.*Ag.*85 (anap.), E.*Heracl.*95 (lyr.), cf. S.*OC*251 (lyr.); ἐφ' ὅ τι χ. ἐμόλετε E.*Or.*150 (lyr); τί χ. ἔβα δῶμα; Id.*Fr.*1011 (lyr.); τί καινὸν ἦλθε δώμασιν χ.; Id.*HF*530, cf. Ar. *Nu.*30 (with play on signf. I), Theoc.24.66. 3. ἐλάφους, μέγα τι χ. (cf. χρῆμα II.3) Call.*Dian.*100. III. in Od.11.479, ἦλθον Τειρεσίαο κατὰ χρέος seems to be = Τειρεσίᾳ χρησόμενος (10.492) *to consult* him. 2. elsewh. κατὰ χρέος means according to *what is needful*, in *due* fashion, *h.Merc.*138, A.R.3.189, Arat.343. IV. *duty, task, charge, office*, ἦλθε τωὔτ' ἐπὶ χρέος Pi.*O.*1.45, cf. 7.40; οἷς τόδ' ἦν χρέος A.*Pers.*777, cf. *Th.*20; τὸ σὸν μελέσθω..φρουρῆσαι χρέος S.*El.*74, cf. E.*Or.*1253 (lyr.), *IT*883 (lyr.). V. τὸ συνδρῶν χ. the *circumstance* of being an accomplice, E.*Andr.*337. VI. *anything useful* or *serviceable*, χρεῶν χρῄζοντι μετάδοσιν ποιήσασθαι Hp.*Jusj.*; δέκα στατῆρανς καταστασεῖ, τῶ δὲ χρήιος (= χρέους) διπλεῖ ὅτι κ' ὁ δικαστὰς ὀμόσει συνεσσάκσαι *Leg.Gort.*3.14, cf. 11, *GDI*5100.11 (Malla). 2. *value, validity*, μηδὲν ἐς χρῆος (or χρέος) ἤμην τὰν δόσιν the gift shall be of no *value*, i.e. invalid, *Leg.Gort.*10.24, cf. 31. VII. παρὰ χρέος, = παραχρῆμα, Call.*Aet.Oxy.*2080.14 (παραχρῆμ' ap.Stob.), Nic.*Al.*614 (prob. orig. = signf. VIII). VIII. = χρεία, χρεώ, *need*, τί δ', ὦ τάλας, σε τοῦδ' ἔχει πλέκους χρέος; Answ. χ. μὲν οὐδέν, βούλομαι δ' ὅμως λαβεῖν Ar.*Ach.*454, cf. Bion *Fr.*2.2.

**χρε-οφελέτης**, v. χρεωφ-; **χρε-οφείλης** dub. in A.D.*Pron.*5.7.

⊛ **χρεο-φῠλάκιον**, τό, v. χρεωφ-. **χρέψ**, v. χρέμψ.

**χρεώ**, Ep. **χρειώ**, gen. οῦς, ἡ, less freq. neut., Il.10.142, Od.2. 28, 5.189 (where τόσον agrees with χ.), 4.312, Il.10.85, 11.606, perh. 9.197, 608, 21.322, 23.308, Od.4.707; τὸ χ. *Inscr.Prien.*99, al. (ii/i B.C.): (χρή, χρεία):—*want, need*; ἦ τι μάλα χρεώ of a truth there is much *need*, Il.9.197; χρειοῖ ἀναγκαίῃ by dire *necessity*, 8.57; ἀναγκαίης ὑπὸ χρειοῦς φεύγοντες Sol.[36.9] ap.Arist.*Ath.*12.4: c. gen., ἵν' οὐ χρεὼ πείσματός ἐστιν where there is no *need of* a cable, Od.9.136; χρειὼ ἱκάνεται *want, necessity* arises, Il.10.118, cf. 142, Od.6.136; εἴ ποτε δὴ αὖτε χρειὼ ἐμεῖο γένηται Il.1.341; χρειὼ βεβίηκεν Ἀχαιούς 10. 172; τίπτε δέ σε χρειὼ δεῦρ' ἤγαγε; ..δήμιον ἢ ἴδιον; Od.4.312; ὅτε με χρειὼ τόσον ἵκοι if so great a *need* should come upon me, 5.189; τίνα χρειὼ τόσον ἵκει; 2.28; also ἐμὲ δὲ χρεὼ γίγνεται αὐτῆς (sc. τῆς νηός, χρεὼ γίγνεται being = χρή I.2) 4.634; even οὐδέ τί μιν χρεὼ ἔσται τυμβοχόης Il.21.322. 2. used by Hom. ellipt., χρεώ c. acc. pers., τίπτε δέ σε χρεώ (sc. ἱκάνει); Od.1.225, Il. 10.85: folld. by a gen., οὔ τί με ταύτης χρεὼ τιμῆς *need of* it touches me not, 9.608; χρεὼ βουλῆς ἐμὲ καὶ σέ 10.43, cf. 9.75; τί δέ σε χρεὼ ἐμεῖο; 11.606: also c. inf., τὸν δὲ μάλα χρεὼ ἑστάμεναι κρατερῶς he *needs* must stand firm, ib.409; οὐδέ τί μιν χρεὼ νηῶν ἐπιβαινέμεν Od.4.707, cf. Il.18.406, Od.15.201, A.R.1.649. II. = χρεών, *necessity, destiny, fate*, A.R.1.440; ἡ εἰς τὸ χ. μετάστασις *Inscr.Prien.*99, al. (ii/i B.C.). 2. *oracle, prophecy*, χρειὼ θεσπίζων μεταμώνιον A.R.1.491. III. = χρέος or χρῆμα, *affair, object*, Id.4.191; simply, *thing*, Id.3.33.—The word is mostly Ep.—Hom. uses both forms χρεώ and χρειώ: but in the ellipt. phrase, mentioned I.2, he always has χρεώ, as monosyll.:—in Il.11.606 χρεώ before a vowel is used short:—χρεώ is disyll. in Parm.1.28.

**χρεωκοπ-έω**, *cut down a debt, defraud one's creditors*, Plu.2.829c, Str.8.3.29, Ph.1.345: metaph., πολλῶν θανάτων ὀφειλήματα D.S.38/9. 8 χ. τὸν λόγον Plu.2.764a; *withhold fraudulently*, μέρος ἥμισυ ib. 968d; *minimize*, τι τῆς διδασκαλίας S.E.*M.*6.6; *cut down*, Vett.Val.137. 13, al.:—Pass., *to be cheated* or *defrauded*, Plu.2.829c, Phalar.*Ep.*81. 2; *to be disappointed*, Herm.ap.Stob.1.49.44. (It is uncertain whether χρεοκ- or χρεωκ- should be read: v. χρεοκ-.) **-ία**, ἡ, *cancelling of debts*, D.H.5.67, D.S.29.33. **-ίδης**, ου, ὁ, *one who cancels his debts, an insolvent*: esp. said of those friends of Solon at Athens, who took advantage of his σεισάχθεια, Plu.*Sol.*15 **-ος** (parox.), ὁ, = *creditor, decoctor*, *Gloss.* (χρεο-).

**χρεωλῡτ-έω** or **χρεολ-** (so *Supp.Epigr.*3.436 (Thermum, iii (?) B.C.)), *discharge a debt*, Plu.*Alc.*5; χ. τὸν μισθὸν *pay* wages *that are due*, J.*AJ*18.8.9. **-ησις**, εως, ἡ, *payment, discharge*, *BGU*362 ix 9 (iii A.D., χρεολ-).

**χρεώμενος**, Ion. part. of χράομαι, Il.23.834.

⊛ **χρεών**, Ion. **χρεόν** (the form best attested in Parm.8.45 and Hdt.); also **χρειών**, Democr.55, τό: gen. τοῦ χρεών E.*Hipp.*1256, *HF*21, but little used save in nom. and acc.:—*that which must be*, κατὰ τὸ χ. Anaximand.1 (Diels *Vorsokr.*[5]); τὴν μοῖραν εἰς τὸ μὴ χ. παραστρέφων E.*Fr.*491.3; χ. τοῦ χρησμοῦ Plu.*Nic.*14. **II.** *necessity, fate*, ἡ τε ἡλικία καὶ τὸ χ. Pl.*Phdr.*255a; μοίρας τοῦ χρεών τ' ἀπαλλαγή E.*Hipp.*1256; εἰς τὸ χ. ἰέναι Pl.*Ax.*364c; ἀπελθεῖν εἰς τὸ χ., εἰς τὸ χ. ἀπαλλάσσεσθαι, Str.1.3.21, J.*AJ*7.15.1; οἱ τὴν εἰς τὸ χ. πορευόμενοι (cj. for ποιούμενοι), v.l. τῶν εἰς τὸ χ. ὁδευόντων, Plu.2.113c; τό τοι χρεὼν οὐκ ἔστι μὴ χρεὼν ποιεῖν *Trag.Adesp.*368; ὅ τι γὰρ μὴ χ. οὔτοι χ. παθεῖν E.*Ba.*515; ['Αλέξανδρον] τὸ χ. ἐν Βαβυλῶνι κατέλαβε Jul.*Or.*3.107c. **2.** mostly in the phrase χρεών (sc. ἐστί), like χρή, it is *necessary*, c. inf., Thgn.564, A.*Ag.*922, S.*OT*633, Democr. l. c., etc.: c. acc. et inf., Pi.*P.*2.52, Hdt.1.41,57, 2.133, A.*Pr.*772,970, al., S.*Ph.*1439, Ar.*Eq.*138, Th.5.49; τὸ χ. γενέσθαι Hdt.7.17. **3.** sts. as a neut. part. (like ἐξόν, etc.), *it being necessary, since it was necessary*, Id.5.50. **III.** less freq., *that which is expedient* or *right*, ὅρκον δ' οὔτ' ἄδικον χ. ἔμμεναι οὔτε δίκαιον Choeril.7; ἔννεπε τί σοι χρεὼν ὑπουργεῖν S.*Ph.*143 (lyr.); μητέρ' εἰ χ. ταύτην προσαυδᾶν Id.*El.*273, cf. 983, Ar.*Nu.*1446 (lyr.), etc.; with the Art., ἔκανες ὃν οὐ χρῆν, καὶ τὸ μὴ χ. πάθε A.*Ch.*930: abs. in part., ὑμεῖς ἂν οὐ χ. ἄρχοιτε ye would rule un*rightfully*, Th.3.40.—In Trag. χρεών (= χρή) appears without ἐστί or ἦν; in Ar. and Prose the verb is more commonly added, but not in Ar.*Nu.* l. c., Pl.*Sph.*220d, *Criti.*107b, al. **IV.** as Adj., τῷ χ. πόσει E.*Fr.*501. (Not in Hom. or Hes., Od.15.201 being f.l. for χρεώ.) [In Poets χρεών is sts. monosyll., as in Choeril. l. c., Parm.4.5, al.; outside of hexameters prob. always disyll., since χρή can be restored in E.*IT*1486, *Fr.*733.3.] (From χρεώ, with addition of ν from the synonym δέον; when used as part. abs., as in Sol.*Fr.*34.6, Th.3.40, from χρεὼ ὄν.)

**χρέως**, τό, Att. for χρέος I (q. v.).

**χρεωσ-τέω**, *to be in debt*, Asp.*in EN*186.27: c. inf., χρεωστῶ τὴν ἐξέτασιν ποιήσασθαι Sever.*Clyst.*33:—Med., *have a claim to*, τι Hld.7.8; *have a debt owing to one*, Id.5.31:—Pass., *to be owed, owing*, *Sammelb.*4422.4, Sch.D Il.11.685. **-τημα**, ατος, τό, *debt*, Hsch., Phot. s.v. ὄφλημα. **-της**, ου, ὁ, *debtor*, Ph.1.634, al., J.*AJ*3.12.3, Plu.2.101c, *SIG*833.9 (Epist.Hadriani), Luc.*Abd.*15, *CIG*2817.14 (Aphrodisias). **-τησις**, εως, ἡ, gloss on ὄφλησις, Hsch. **-τία**, ἡ, *indebtedness*, Vett.Val.37.26, al. **-τικῶς**, Adv. *as a debt*, Eust.56.35.

**χρεωφειλ-έτης**, ου, ὁ, *debtor*, Aen.Tact.5.2, D.S.32.26, *Ev.Luc.*7.41: c. gen. pers., ib.16.5, Cic.*Att.*7.8.5: c. gen. rei, Plu.*Caes.*5: metaph., opp. εὐεργέτης, Id.*Galb.*8. (Spelt χρεοφιλ- in *SIG*742.53 (Ephes., i B.C.), cf. Lxx *Jb.*31.37.) **-ημα**, ατος, τό, *debt*, Poll.8.141.

**χρεω-φῠλᾰκέω**, *to be a* χρεωφύλαξ, *CIG*3831a[9], a[4]13 (Aezani, χρεοφ-), *IGRom.*4.580 (χρεω[φ]-), 585 (ibid.), 657 (Acmonia), 801 (Apamea), 820 (Hierapolis). **-φῠλᾰκία**, ἡ, *office of* χρεωφύλαξ, *CIG*3847b11 (Nacolea, χρεοφ-), *IGRom.*4.555.11 (Ancyra, χρεοφ-). ⊛ **-φῠλᾰκικός**, ή, όν, *of the* χρεωφύλαξ, *Supp.Epigr.*7.41 (Babylonia, χρεοφ-). ⊛ **-φῠλάκιον** [ᾰ], or **χρεοφ-**, τό, *the office in which the register of public debtors is kept*, *Supp.Epigr.*7.15.17 (Susa, ii B.C.), *GDI*5149.33 (Cretan, ii B.C., found at Delos), *CIG*2826.38, 2827.13, 2829.15, al. (Aphrodisias), *Rev.Et.Gr.*19.247,259,262, al. (ibid.).

⊛ **χρεω-φύλαξ** [ῠ], ᾰκος, ὁ, *keeper of the register of public debtors*, *IG*12(7).3,36 (Amorgos, iv B.C., χρεωφ-), *GDI*3706 vi 37, vii 41 (Cos, χρεοφ-), *BSA*26.166 (Sparta, ii A.D., χρεοφ-), *CIG*3429 (Philadelphia, χρεοφ-), *IG*9(1).375 (Naupactus, χρεοφ-). **-φυλάσσω**, in aor. part. χρεοφυλάξαντα, = -φυλακήσαντα, *IGRom.*4.1638 (Philadelphia). (In this group of words χρεωφ- is found only in χρεωφυλακέω *IGRom.*4.580, χρεωφυλάκιον *GDI* l. c., *CIG*2826.38, 2843.9, χρεωφύλαξ *IG* l. c.)

⊛ **χρή**, impers., Il.1.216, etc.; Aeol. **χρῆ** Alc.20,35,46; other forms are contractions (crases) of χρή (prob. orig. a neut. Subst.) with forms of εἰμί (*sum*): fut. χρῆσται S.*OC*504, *Fr.*599, Pherecr.103, Ar.*Fr.*362, Phryn.Com.34 (on this form, for which codd. generally have χρῆται or χρῆσθαι, v. Sch.S.*OC* l. c.): subj. χρῇ S.*Ph.*999, E.*Alc.*49, Ar.*Lys.*133; opt. χρείη A.*Pr.*215, S.*Tr.*162, Lys.12.44, Pl.*Euthphr.*4c; inf. χρῆναι Democr.276, Ar.*Ec.*210, Antipho 5.84, etc.; also χρῆν (v. infr. III); part. neut. pl. χρηεόντα (or χρὴ ἐόντα) Democr.174: impf. ἐχρῆν Pi.*N.*7.44, A.*Ch.*907, S.*Fr.*107.6 (only here in S., χρῆν l. 5), Ar.*Ra.*152, al., Antipho 1.1, And.1.114, Lys.3.22, al., Th.6.57, Pl.*Prt.*335c, D.4.3, al., etc.: freq. also without the augm., χρῆν Pi.*Fr.*123.1, S.*El.*529, 579, *Tr.*1133, Ar.*Eq.*535 (anap.), al., Lys.8.6, al., Th.3.63, D.15.33, al., etc.; both forms in Ar.*Ach.*540, ἐρεῖ τις, "οὐ χρῆν"· ἀλλὰ τί ἐχρῆν εἴπατε: fut. χρήσει Hdt.7.8:—*it is necessary*: c. inf. praes. aut aor., *it must needs, one must* or *ought* to do (like δεῖ, which is only once used in Hom.), νῦν δὲ χ. τετλάμεν ἔμπης Od.3.209; τὸν νῦν χ. κομέειν 6.207, cf. Il.1.216, 4.57, etc.; σήμαιν' ὅ τι χ. σοι συμπράσσειν A.*Pr.*297 (anap.); ὅ τι χ. πάσχειν ἐθέλω ib.1067; ὅ τι χρείη ποιεῖν Pl.*Euthphr.*4c, cf. 9a; τούτου θανεῖν χρῆν αὐτὸν οὕνεκ' ἐκ σέθεν; S.*El.*579; χρὴ τὸ λέγειν Parm.6.1: more freq. c. acc. pers. et inf., *one must*, ἐμὲ δὲ χ. γήραϊ πείθεσθαι Il.23.644; τῷ σε χ. πολέμοιο.. παῦσαι 7.331; οὐδέ τί σε χ. νηλεὲς ἦτορ ἔχειν 9.496; τί χ. με.. στέγειν ἢ τί λέγειν; S.*Ph.*135 (lyr.): χρῆν γὰρ Κανδαύλῃ γενέσθαι κακῶς (where γενέσθαι is inf. of an impers. verb) Hdt.1.8.—Sts. the inf. must be supplied from the context, esp. in Hom. in phrases like τίπτε μάχης ἀποπαύεαι; οὐδέ τί σε χρή (sc. ἀποπαύεσθαι) Il.16.721, cf. 19.420; ὅθι χ. πεζὸν ἐόντα (sc. μάρνασθαι) Od.9.50; so in Trag. and Att., πορθεῖν ἃ μὴ χ. (sc. πορθεῖν) A.*Ag.*342; φύς τ' ἀφ' ὧν οὐ χρῆν (sc. φῦναι), ξύν οἷς τ' οὐ χρῆν (sc. ὁμιλεῖν) ὁμιλῶν S.*OT*1184; ἔκανες ὃν οὐ χρῆν (sc. κτεῖναι) A.*Ch.*930; ἐπιπλεύσειέ τις ὡς χ. (sc. ἐπιπλεῦσαι) Th.2.89; θύσαντες οἷς χ. (sc. θῦσαι) Pl.*R.*415e; ἀκαιρότερον ὄντα ἢ χ. Id.*Plt.*307e; λαλεῖν μετὰ ἀφελείας ἔνθα χ. Longin.34.2.; so ὡς χ. A.*Ag.*1556 (anap.), etc.—The impf. freq. expresses something that ought to have been, but is not, ἐνθάδ' οὐ παραστατεῖ, ὡς χρῆν, Ὀρέστης ib.879, cf. S.*Tr.*1133; and sts. stands for χρή, χρῆν τι λέγειν ὑμᾶς σοφὸν ᾧ νικήσετε Ar.*Pl.*487 (anap.), cf. 432: abs., ἐρεῖ τις, "οὐ χρῆν"· ἀλλὰ τί ἐχρῆν εἴπατε Id.*Ach.*540. **2.** in Hom. without inf., c. acc. pers. et gen. rei, οὐδέ τί σε χρὴ ἀφροσύνης thou *hast* no *need of* imprudence, i. e. it does not *befit* thee, Il.7.109; οὐ μέν σε χ. ἔτ' αἰδοῦς Od.3.14; τί με χ. μητέρος αἴνου; 21.110; μυθήσεαι ὅττεό (i.e. ὅτου) σε χ. 1.124; τέο σε χ.; 4.463: τί χρὴ φίλων is found in most codd. of E.*Or.*667 (δεῖ cod. V). **3.** c. dat. pers. pro acc. is not found; in Il.5.490, A.*Pr.*3, the dat. belongs to the inf. μέλειν; in S.*Ant.*736 Dobree restored με for γε; in E.*Med.*886 ἦ depends on μετεῖναι; in *Ion*1316 Dobree read τοὺς δέ γ' ἐνδίκους, and in Lys.28.10 δικαίους.. ὀφελομένους was restored by Cobet. **II.** sts. in a less strong sense, πῶς τοῦτο περᾶσαι χρή; how *is one to* get through this? Theoc.15.45; τί ἐχρῆν με ποιεῖν; what *was I to* do? D.18.28; ἐν οὐδὲν κατέστη ἴαμα ὅτι χρῆν προσφερόντας ὠφελεῖν there was no one remedy by the application of which one *could* (or *was bound to*) help them, Th.2.51, cf. 1.91. **III.** τὸ χρῆν (inf.) *fate, destiny*, E.*Hec.*260 (s. v.l., τὸ χρὴ Nauck); τὸ χρὴ Id.*HF.*828; cj. for τὸ χρεών (monosyll.) in Id.*Fr.*733.3, *IT*1486.

**χρῇ, χρῇς**, 3 and 2 pers. sg. pres. indic. of a defect. verb, expld. by Hsch. and Sch.S.*Ant.*887 by θέλει χρῄζει, θέλεις χρῄζεις and found in the following passages: εἴτε χρῇ θανεῖν whether she *desires* to die, S.*Ant.*887 (χρή codd., cf. Sch. ad loc.); σοὶ δὲ δρᾶν ἔξεσθ' ἃ χρῇς Id.*Aj.*1373 (χρή codd.); εἴτε χρῇς (sc. κηρύσσειν με) Id.*El.*606 (χρή codd.); πρὸς ταῦθ' ὅ τι χρῇ καὶ παλαμάσθων E.*Fr.*918 (anap., χρή codd.); πάρα δ' ἄλλ' ὅ τι χρῇς Cratin.127, cf. Eup.4 (prob. l.); οὐ χρῇσθα (sc. φωνεῖν); Ar.*Ach.*778 (Megarian). (Cogn. with χρή, κέχρημαι 'I yearn after', χρῄζω.)

**χρηέομαι**, in some dialects, = χρῶμαι, v. χράω (B) c.

**χρήεσσι**, v. χρέος.

⊛ **χρῄζω**, Thgn.958, A.*Pr.*376, Ar.*Nu.*891 (anap.), Th.3.109, etc.; in Att. hardly found exc. in pres. and impf. (but v. infr. II): Ep. and Ion. **χρηΐζω**, as always in Hom., and Hdt.1.41, 5.19, 30, 9.87; written **χρηιίζω**, *SIG*57.41 (Milet., v B.C.); also **χρεΐζω**, Herod.7.64; Dor. **χρῄζω** *SIG*56.23 (Argos, v B.C.); also **χρῄζω** ib.1006.3 (Cos, iii B.C.); **χρείζω** ib.953.27 (Calymna, ii B.C.): Sicil. Dor. **χρῄσδω** Theoc.8.11; Megar.Dor. **χρῄδδω** Ar.*Ach.*734: fut. χρῄσω Ti.Locr.99a, Ion. χρηΐσω Hdt.7.38: aor. Ion. χρηΐσαι prob. Id.5.65; part. χρηΐσας ib.20, 7.38: (χρή):—*want, lack, have need of*, c. gen., χρηΐζοντα.. ἰητῆρος Il.11.835; εἴρετο.. ὅττευ χρηΐζων ἱκόμην Od.17.121, cf. 558; οὐδ' ἐμοῦ διδασκάλου χρῄζεις A.*Pr.*376; δύο χρῄσει [μεσοτάτων] Ti.Locr. l. c.: abs. in part. χρηΐζων *needy, poor*, Od.11.340, Hes.*Op.*351. **2.** *desire, long for, crave*, χρηΐζειν ἀπεόντος ib.367; τοῦτον ὧν δοκέω.. ποιήσειν ὧν ἂν χρηΐζωμεν Hdt.5.30; χρημάτων χ. Id.9.87; βορᾶς A.*Ch.*530; τοῦ μακροῦ χ. βίου Soph.*Aj.*473: rarely c. acc., πᾶν μᾶλλον δοκέων μιν χρηΐσειν ἢ τὸ ἐδεήθη Hdt.7.38; ὥστ' ἄλλα χρῄζειν S.*OT*595, cf. E.*Supp.*123; an inf. may freq. be supplied, φράζε.. ὅ τι χρῄζεις (sc. φράζειν) Ar.*Nu.*359, cf. 453 (both anap.); ἴθ' ὅποι χρῄζεις (sc. ἰέναι) ib.891 (anap.), cf. *Th.*751, A.*Pr.*928, S.*OT*365; τί δῆτα χρῄζεις; ib.622, *OC*643. **b.** c. acc. pers. et inf., *ask* or *desire* that one should do a thing, Hdt.1.41, 112, 152, al.; so c. gen. pers. et inf., *desire of* one to do, Id.5.19,65, 9.55; in Trag., c. inf. only, *desire* to do a thing, A.*Pr.*235, 285, al., S.*OT*91, E.*Hec.*347, etc.: rare in Prose, Th.3.109, X.*Cyr.*1.6.15. **c.** c. dupl. gen. pers. et rei, τῶνδε ἐγὼ ὑμέων χρηΐζων συνέλεξα Hdt.7.53. **d.** χρῄζειν παρά τινος c. inf., Ps.-Hdt.*Vit.Hom.*13. **3.** part. χρῄζων is used abs. for εἰ χρῄζει, *if one will, if one chooses*, Thgn.958, A.*Ch.*340 (anap.); ἄλλα φανεῖ χρῄζων (sc. Ἑρμῆς) *if propitious*, ib. [815] (lyr.); ἢν τὸν θεὸν χρῄζοντ' ἔχῃ E.*Supp.*597; ποταγγελλέτω ὁ χρῄζων, = ὁ βουλόμενος, *IG*12(1).677.34 (Ialysus); also τὸ χρῇζον *your solicitation*, E.*IA*1017. **II.** Pass., χρησθείς is f.l. in S.*Ant.*24.

**χρῄζω**, = χράω (B) A. 1, *deliver an oracle, foretell*, only in E.*Hel.*516 (lyr.; leg. χρήσασ').

**χρῆτα**· πενία, ἡ χρήματα, Hsch. **II.** χρῆïα, Cret., = χρήματα, *SIG*527.84 (Dreros, iii B.C.), cf. Hsch.

**χρητίζω**, Ion. for χρῄζω.

**χρηΐσκομαι**, *need*, τῷ ὕδατι Hdt.3.117.

⊛ **χρῆμα**, ατος, τό, (χράομαι):—*need*, in the phrase παρὰ χ. or παραχρῆμα (q. v.); *a thing that one needs* or *uses*, cf. X.*Oec.*1.9 sq. (pl.): hence in pl., *goods, property* (χρήματα λέγομεν πάντα ὅσων ἡ ἀξία νομίσματι μετρεῖται Arist.*EN*1119b26), Od.2.78, 203, al. (never in Il.), Hes.*Op.*320, 407, etc.; of temple-*treasures, heirlooms*, etc., *Mnemos.*57.208 (Argos, vi B.C.); τὰ ἱρὰ χ. τῆς Ἀθηναίης Hdt.2.28, cf. 9.81; θησαυρούς.. ἄλλα τε χρύσεα ἄφατα χ. Id.7.190; πολλῶν χ. ἐξαίρετον ἄνθος A.*Ag.*954; πειρῶ τὸν πλοῦτον χρήματα καὶ κτήματα κατασκευάζειν· ἔστι δὲ χ. μὲν τοῖς ἀπολαύειν ἐπισταμένοις, κ. δὲ τοῖς κτᾶσθαι δυναμένοις Isoc.1.28; τοῖς σκεύεσι καὶ τοῖς χρήμασιν ἀποθήκη Th.6.97; πρόβατα καὶ ἄλλα χ. X.*An*.5.2.4; τὰ ἀνδράποδα..καὶ χρήματα τὰ πλεῖστα ἀπέδρα αὐτούς ib.7.8.12: prov., χρήματα ψυχὴ πέλεται..βροτοῖσι a man's *money* is his life, Hes.*Op*.686; χρήματ' ἀνηρ '*money* makes the man', Alc.49, Pi.*I*.2.11; ἐν χρήμασιν οἰκεῖ πατρῴοις A.*Eu*.757, cf. *Ch*.135; also χρημάτων πένητες E.*El*.37; τὰ χρήματ' ἐνεχυράζομαι Ar.*Nu*.241; χρήματα πορίζειν Id.*Ec*.236; ἄτιμοι ἦσαν τὰ σώματα, τὰ δὲ χ. εἶχον And.1.74; χρημάτων ἥσσων Democr.50; χρημάτων κρείσσων Th.2.60; χρήμασι νικώμενος ibid.; χρημάτων ἀδωρότατος ib. 65; ἐλπίδα χρήμασιν ὠνητήν Id.3.40; μήτε χρημάτων φειδομένους μήτε πόνων Pl.*Phd*.78a; ζημιοῦσθαι χρήμασιν Id.*Lg*.721b; even of debts, διαλῦσαι τὰ χ. D.20.12; δεθέντ' ἐπὶ χρήμασιν ἐν τῷ δεσμωτηρίῳ Id. 24.168.—Acc. to Poll.9.87 the Ion. used also the sg. in this sense, and so we find, ἐπὶ κόσῳ ἂν χρήματι..; for how much *money*..? Answ. ἐπ' οὐδενί, Hdt.3.38; ταύτην (sc. τὴν χλανίδα) πωλέω μὲν οὐδενὸς χ. δίδωμι δὲ ἄλλως ib.139; also in Thgn.197, χ. δ' ὃ μὲν Διόθεν καὶ σὺν δίκῃ ἀνδρὶ γένηται; in Att., οὐδενὸς ἂν χ. δεξάμενοι at no *price*, And.2.4; and in later Prose, *fund, sum of money*, *Arch. f. Religionswiss*.10.211 (Cos, ii B.C.); τὸ πλῆθος τοῦ χ. D.S.13. 106, cf. *Act.Ap*.4.37, Luc.*VH*1.20; χρήματα *merchandise*, Heraclit. 90, X.*HG*1.6.37, Th.3.74; *property, substance*, *Berl.Sitzb*.1927.161 (Cyrene). **II.** generally, *thing, matter, affair*, esp. in Ep. and Ion., *h.Merc*.332, Hes.*Op*.344,402; χρημάτων ἄελπτον οὐδέν Archil. 74; πάντων χ. δικαιότατον Mimn.8; πρῶτον χρημάτων πάντων Hdt.7.145; ἀντὶ πάντων χ. on every *account*, And.2.21; δεινότατον ἁπάντων χρημάτων ib.1; πᾶν χ. ἐκίνεε 'left no stone unturned', Hdt.5.96; τεκμαίρει χρῆμ' ἕκαστον 'deeds show the man', Pi.*O*.6. 74; πάντων χ. μέτρον ἄνθρωπος Protag.1; περαίνεται τὸ χ. the *issue* is being decided, Plu.*Caes*.47: pl., simply, *things*, ὁμοῦ πάντα χ. ἦν Anaxag.1, cf. Pl.*Cra*.440a, *Euthd*.294d, Plot.4.2.1. **2.** χρῆμα is freq. expressed where it might be omitted, δεινὸν χ. ἐποιεῦντο Hdt.8.16; οἷόν τι χ. ποιήσειε ib.138; ἐς ἀφανὲς χ. ἀποστέλλειν ἀποικίην to send out a colony without any certain *destination*, Id.4.150; freq. in Trag., τί χρῆμα; = τί; *what?* τί χ. λεύσσω; A.*Pr*.300, *Ch*.10; or *why?* E.*Alc*.512; so in gen., τοῦ χ. (sc. ἕνεκα); Ar.*Nu*.1223; τί χ. δρᾷς; S.*Aj*.288, cf. *Ph*.1231; τί χ. πάσχει; E. *Hipp*.909; τί δ' ἐστὶ χρῆμα; what is *the matter?* A.*Ch*.885; πικρόν τί μοι δοκεῖ χ. εἶναι Pl.*Grg*.485b; ἡδύ Id.*Tht*.209e, al.; μάλιστα χρημάτων most *of anything*, i.e. *certainly*, Anon.*Oxy*.1611.68 (iii A.D.); cf. χρέος II.2. **3.** used in periphrases to express something strange or extraordinary of its kind, ὑὸς χ. μέγα a huge *monster* of a boar, Hdt.1.36; ἦν τοῦ χειμῶνος χ. ἀφόρητον Id.7.188; τὸ χ. τῶν νυκτῶν ὅσον what a *business* the nights are! Ar.*Nu*.2; λιπαρὸν τὸ χ. τῆς πόλεως what a grand city! Id.*Av*.826, cf. *Lys*.83; κλέπτον τὸ χ. τἀνδρός a thievish *sort* of fellow, Id.*V*.933; τὸ χ. τοῦ νοσήματος Id. *Lys*.1085; μακάριον..λέγεις τυράννου χ. your tyrant-*creature*, Pl.*R*. 567e; χ. θαυμαστὸν γυναικός Plu.*Ant*.31: without a gen., ἔλαφον, καλόν τι χ. καὶ μέγα X.*Cyr*.1.4.8; σοφόν τοι χρῆμ' ἄνθρωπος truly a clever *creature* is he! Theoc.15.83; κοῦφον χ. ποιητής ἐστιν καὶ πτηνὸν καὶ ἱερόν, of the poet, Pl.*Ion* 534b; χ. καλόν τι such a fine *thing!* Theoc.15.23; also in a periphrastic use, οὐδὲν χ. τοῦ ἀγκῶνος κάμψαι δύνανται cannot bend the elbow *at all*, Hp.*Fract*.42. **b.** so, to express a great number or mass, as we say, *a deal, a heap of*.., πολλόν τι χ. τῶν τέκνων, χ. πολλὸν ἀρδίων, νεῶν, Hdt.3.109, 4.81, 6.43; χ. πολλόν τι χρυσοῦ Id.3.130; σμικρὸν τὸ χ. τοῦ βίου E. *Supp*.953; ὅσον τὸ χ. παρνόπων what a *lot* of locusts! Ar.*Ach*.150; ὅσον τὸ χ. τοῦ πλακοῦντος Id.*Eq*.1219; πολὺ χ. τεμαχῶν Id.*Pl*.894; τὸ χ. τῶν κόπων ὅσον what a *lot* of them! Id.*Ra*.1278; τῶν λαμπάδων ὅσον τὸ χ. Id.*Th*.281; also of persons, χ. θηλειῶν woman*kind*, E.*Ph*. 198; σφενδονητῶν πάμπολύ τι χ. X.*Cyr*.2.1.5; μέγα χ. Λακαινᾶν Theoc.18.4: without a gen., ὅσον τὸ χ. ἐπὶ δεῖπνον ἦλθε what a *crowd*..! Ar.*Pax*1192. **III.** (χράω (B) A) *oracle*, Emp.115.1.

**χρημᾰτ-ᾰγωγός**, ὁ, *money-carrier*, *PHib*.1.110.52, al. (iii B.C.). **-ίζω**, fut. -ίσω *Ep.Rom*.7.3, Att. -ιῶ Lycurg.37: pf. κεχρημάτικα Din.1.103, *OGI*106.7 (Egypt, ii B.C.): (χρῆμα):—Prose Verb, *negotiate, have dealings*, esp. in money matters (in this sense mostly Med. (v. infr. II)), Th.1.87, 5.61, Plb.5.81.5; χ. τι Th.6.62, Isoc.4.157, Plu. *Them*.18. **2.** of public assemblies, *deliberate*, περὶ Εὐριπίδου ὅ τι χρὴ παθεῖν Ar.*Th*.377, cf. Arist.*Pol*.1298$^{b}$29, *Rh*.1359$^{b}$3, Lex ap.D.21.8; τὰ λοιπὰ τῶν δημοσίων Plu.*Tim*.38; περὶ ὧν ἂν ἅπαξ γνῷ τὸ δικαστήριον, πάλιν χρηματίσαι D.24.55; of presiding officers, *conduct business*, Decr.ap.D.18.75, cf. Aeschin.1.23; of the βουλή, D.18.169; ὅσα δεῖ χρηματίσαι τὴν βουλήν Arist.*Ath*.43.3. **b.** c. dat., *transact business with*, τῇ βουλῇ, τῷ δήμῳ, X.*Ath*.3.1; *negotiate with*, πόλεσι περὶ φιλίας Th.5.5: abs., ib.61; ἰδίᾳ χ., of intriguing persons, D.19.278; χ. ὑπὲρ δημοσίων καὶ κοινῶν πραγμάτων Ael.*VH*3.4:—Med., X.*Ath*. 3.3. **3.** *give audience to*, πρεσβευταῖς Plb.3.66.6, cf. Jul.*Or*.1. 13a. **4.** of an oracle, *give a response* to those who consult it, Lxx *Je*.33(26).2, al., D.S.15.10, *JAJ*11.8.4, Plu.2.435c, Porph. *Abst*.2.48; δι' ὕδατος Iamb.*Myst*.3.11; of gods, *give ear to*, χ. τοῖς εὐχομένοις Luc.*Pseudol*.8:—Pass., *receive an answer, warning*, in *NT* of *divine warnings* or *revelations*, *Ev.Matt*.2.12, etc.; ὑπ' ἀγγέλου *Act.Ap*.10.22; ἦν αὐτῷ κεχρηματισμένον *a warning had been given* him, *Ev.Luc*.2.26; χ. ὑπὸ δαιμονίων καὶ φαντασίας εἰδώλων Vett.Val.67.5. **5.** *issue* ordinances, etc., χ. ἀπορρήσεις Ph.2.438; *administer justice*, ἐν τῷ Προσωπίτῃ *OGI* l.c.; ταῖς πόλεσι App.*Hisp*.98. **b.** *issue orders* for payment, *pay*, ἀπὸ τῆς..τραπέζης *PGrenf*.2.23.4 (ii B.C.); τινι *Ostr.Bodl*.i 248 (ii B.C.); λόγον χ. ἐς τὰ δαμόσια γράμματα *furnish* an account.., *Arch.f.Religionswiss*.10.211 (Cos, ii B.C.):—Pass., ἐχρηματίσθη πολλὰ διάφορα he *was furnished with* large sums, Aristeas 9. **6.** *take cognizance of, decide upon* petitions, [ἔντευξιν] χ. *PEnteux*.75.9 (iii B.C.), *PFay*. 12.28 (ii B.C.); ἔντευξις κεχρηματισμένη *PPetr*.2 p.3 (iii B.C.). **7.** generally, *have dealings with, stand in any relation to* a person, οὐδὲν αὐτῷ (sic legendum videtur) πρὸς γένος ἐχρημάτιζεν Ctes.*Fr*. 29.2: hence even μόλις ταῖς ἀναγκαίαις [ὀρέξεσι] χ. *to be influenced, affected* by them, Plu.2.125b. **8.** Astrol., *operate*, of influences, Vett.Val.5.7. **II.** Med., χρηματίζομαι: fut. Att. -ιοῦμαι Lys.29. 14, etc.: pf. κεχρημάτισμαι Din.1.15:—*negotiate* or *transact business for oneself* or *to one's own profit, make money*, οἰόμενοι χρηματιεῖσθαι μᾶλλον ἢ μαχεῖσθαι Th.7.13; χρηματιούμενος ἀλλ' οὐ πρὸς ὑμᾶς φιλοτιμησόμενος Lys. l.c.; οἱ χρηματισάμενοι Pl.*R*.330c; ἄλλῳ χ. καὶ οὐχ αὑτῷ Id.*Grg*.452e; esp. by base arts, ἐξ αὐτῆς τῆς πόλεως Din. l.c., cf. Is.9.25; χ. ἀπό τινος *to make money* of or from a thing, Pl. *Sph*.225e; ἀπὸ τῶν κοινῶν Arist.*Pol*.1286$^{b}$14; ἀπὸ γεωμετρίας Iamb. *Comm.Math*.25; ἔκ τινος Lys.25.3; ἐκ φιλοσοφίας Isoc.11.1; also c. acc. cogn., χ. τὸν ἐκ γῆς χρηματισμόν Id.*Lg*.949e, cf. *Grg*.467d; χρήματα X.*Cyr*.3.3.5. **2.** generally, *transact business, have dealings with*.., τινι Hdt.3.118, 7.163. **3.** c. acc. rei, χ. τὸ νόμισμα *traffic in* money, like a money-lender or banker, Arist.*Pol*.1257$^{b}$34; but c. acc. pers., χ. τινας *make money out of* any one, i.e. *get* it *from* them *by extortion*, Plb.32.5.13; so χ. παρὰ τῶν νεωτέρων Isoc.10.6. **III.** in later writers, from Plb. downwards, the Act. χρηματίζω takes some special senses: **1.** *to take and bear a title* or *name, to be called* or *styled* so and so, χρηματίζειν βασιλεύς Plb.5.57.2, 30.2.4, cf. Aristeas 298; Πτολεμαῖος..νέος Διόνυσος χ. D.S.1.44; ἐχρημάτιζε Χαλκηδόνιος, Κρητικός, Str.13.1.55, App.*Sic*.6; νέα Ἶσις ἐχρημάτιζε Plu.*Ant*.54; μὴ πατρόθεν, ἀλλ' ἀπὸ μητέρων χ. *to call themselves* not after their fathers, but after their mothers, Id.2.248d; χ. ἀπὸ τοῦ δήμου Harp. s.v. δημοτευόμενος; χ. τοὺς μαθητὰς Χριστιανούς *Act.Ap*. 11.26; τιμῆς καὶ πίστεως χ. ἄξιοι *to be deemed*.., App.*BC*2.111. **2.** generally, *to be called*, μοιχαλίς *Ep.Rom*.7.3: μήτηρ Ph.1.440; καὶ ὡς χ. 'and so forth' (omitting some of the writer's names), *POxy*.100.1 (ii A.D.), etc.; also c. dat., ἀεὶ -ίζων τῷ προκειμένῳ ὀνοματίῳ ib.2131.8 (iii A.D.). **3.** *change* or *be changed*, εἴς τι *Gp*.12.1.9. **-ικός**, ή, όν, (χρήματα) *of* or *in money*, χ. ζημία a *money* fine, J.*AJ*11.5.1, Plu.*Dem*. 27; χ. συμβόλαια *money* contracts, Id.*Lyc*.13; οἱ χ. the *moneyed men*, Id.*Sol*.14; χ. πενία Id.2.524e; δίκη *POxy*.237 viii 13 (ii A.D.); δόσις *BGU*473.9 (ii/iii A.D.). Adv. -κῶς, *civiliter*, *Gloss*. ❀ **-ῐσις**, εως, ἡ, = sq. II, X.*Oec*.11.11, 20.22, Ael.*Fr*.186. **II.** Astrol., *operation, activity*, Vett.Val.289.31. ❀ **-ισμός**, ὁ, *negotiation, giving audience to ambassadors*, Plb.28.16.10 (pl.); ἐποιεῖτο τὸν χ. καὶ τοὺς λόγους ib.16. 4, cf. Vett.Val.63.20 (pl.). **2.** *decree* or *ordinance*, made by a sovereign or some public authority, D.S.1.64,70 (but χ. στρατηγῶν *business* introduced by the generals, Decr.Del.ap.J.*AJ*14.10.14); *decision* on a case or petition, *UPZ*25.2 (ii B.C.), *OGI*139.18 (pl., Philae, ii B.C.), etc. **3.** *administration of justice by* χρηματισταί, *PCair.Zen*.513 (iii B.C.). **4.** any *public instrument* or *document*, D.S.14.13, *Supp. Epigr*.3.367.34 (Lebad., ii B.C.), Lxx 2 *Ma*.11.17; *public records*, *PEnteux*.22.9 (iii B.C.), *PPar*.65.15 (ii B.C.), *Chron.Lind*.A.7 (pl.), *Supp.Epigr*.3.674.32 (Rhodes, ii B.C.). **b.** generally, *deed, legal instrument*, *Arch.Pap*.4.130 iii 41 (ii A.D.), etc.; δημόσιος χ. notarial *instrument*, Mitteis *Chr*.200.9 (iii A.D.), etc.: pl., ib.192.35 (Edict of Mettius Rufus, i A.D.); τῶν δούλων τοὺς χ. the *title-deeds* referring to the slaves, *PUniv.Giss*.20.8 (ii A.D.). **5.** *oracular response, divine injunction* or *warning*, Lxx 2 *Ma*.2.4, *Ep.Rom*.11.4, Artem.1.2, Vett.Val.1.7, *PMag.Par*.1.2206. **II.** (from Med.) *doing business for one's own gain, money-making*, freq. in Pl., ἀμελήσας χρηματισμοῦ καὶ οἰκονομίας *Ap*.36b; ἰάτρευσις καὶ ὁ ἄλλος χ. *R*. 357c; χ. διὰ βαναυσίας καὶ τόκων *Lg*.743d; ὁ ἐκ γῆς χ. ib. 949e: pl., *R*.465c, *Lg*.741e, Isoc.3.50; χρηματισμός, οὐ λῃτουργία γέγονεν ἡ τριηραρχία D.21.167. **III.** later, *appellation, title, designation*, *SIG*739.2 (Delph., i B.C.), D.L.1.48 (pl.); *use of a name* or *designation*, *Arch.Pap*.4.122 v 7 (ii A.D.); simply, *name*, Dosith.p. 382 K. **IV.** 'affair', χ. εὔχρηστος (of σπάργανα) Sor.1.111 (sed leg. σχημ-). **-ιστέον**, *one must make money*, X.*Lac*.7.3. **-ιστήριον**, τό, *place for transacting business, council-chamber*, D.S.1.1; *seat of judgement*, Lxx 1 *Es*.3.14(15); τῆς Μακεδονίας Str.7 *Fr*.20; *place of business*, Plu.*Caes*.67. **II.** *oracle, sanctuary*, of the Holy of Holies, Aq., Sm.3 *Ki*.6.5. ❀ **-ιστής**, οῦ, ὁ, *money-getter, trafficker*, Pl.*Grg*. 452a, *R*.330b, Onos.1.20, etc.; joined with δημιουργός, Pl.*R*.434a; δεινὸς χ. X.*Oec*.2.18: metaph., πρᾳότητος χ. Philostr.*VS*2.17. **2.** as Adj., ὁ χ. [βίος] Arist.*EN*1096$^{a}$5 (s.v.l.). **II.** in Egypt, *circuit-judge*, *PCair.Zen*.513 (iii B.C.), *PRev.Laws*15.4 (iii B.C.), *OGI* 106.6 (ii B.C.), Aristeas 111, etc.; οἱ ἐπὶ τῶν τόπων χ. *PFay*.11.25 (ii B.C.), cf. *UPZ*162 ii 5 (ii B.C.), etc. **-ιστικός**, ή, όν, *of* or *for traffic* and *money-making*, ὁ χ. *a man of business*, Pl.*R*.581d; opp. ἀναλωτικός, ib.558d; opp. στρατιωτικός, οἰκήσεις ib.415e; opp. στρατηγικός, διατριβαί Plu.*Crass*.17; χ. οἰωνός an omen *portending gain*, X.*An*.6.1.23; τὸ χ. the *commercial class*, opp. τὸ πολεμικόν, etc., Arist.*Pol*.1291$^{b}$21; ἡ -κή (sc. τέχνη) the *art of money-making*, Pl. *Grg*.477e, *Euthd*.307a, al.; on its varieties, v. Arist.*Pol*.1256$^{b}$41. **II.** *belonging to* or *fitted for the dispatch of public business*, χ. σκηνή, πυλών, a tent, hall *for holding conferences, giving audience*, Plb.5.81. 5, 15.31.2. **2.** *notarial*, τράπεζα *PLond*.3.1164*d*.4 (iii A.D.). **III.** *oracular, prophetic*, ψυχή Porph.*Abst*.4.10. **IV.** Astrol., *effective, operative*, τόποι Vett.Val.29.18, Antioch.Astr. in *Cat.Cod.Astr*. 8(3).107; of stars, Iamb.*Myst*.3.30. **-ίτης** [ῑ], ου, ὁ, ἀγών contest *for a money-prize*, *Marm.Par*.53, cf. Sch.Pi.*O*.8.101.

**χρημᾰτο-δαίτης**, ου, Dor. **-τας**, ὁ, *divider of wealth*, κτεάνων χ. A.*Th*.729 (lyr.). **-ποιός**, όν, *money-making, money-getting*, Ar. *Ec*.442; τέχνη X.*Oec*.20.15.

**χρημᾰτουργία**, ἡ, Astrol., *operation, activity*, τῶν ἀστέρων Rhetor. in *Cat.Cod.Astr*.8(4).214.

**χρημᾰτο-φθορικός**, ή, όν, *fitted for wasting money, spendthrift*, opp. χρηματιστικός, Pl.*Sph*.225d. **-φῠλάκιον** [ᾰκ], τό, *treasury*, Str.12.2.6. ⊛ **-φύλαξ** [ῠ], ᾰκος, ὁ, = Lat. *praefectus aerarii*, Vett.Val.38.34.

**χρήμη**, ἡ, Ion. for χρεία I, Archil.56.5, Ps.-Hdt.*Vit.Hom*.13,14, dub. in Call. in *PSI*11.1216.19; ὅτεῳ χρήμη τεά ἐστι παῖδα ποιήσασθαι cj. in Democr.277.

**χρημοσύνη**, ἡ, *need, want, lack*, Thgn.389,394, al., dub. cj. in *Trag.Adesp*.509 (lyr.).

**χρῆν**, v. χρή. **χρήννυμι** and **-ύω**, v. χράω (B) B.

**χρῆος**, τό, Dor. for χρέος. **χρῇς, χρῆσθα**, v. χρῇ. **χρῄσδω**, Dor. for χρῄζω.

**χρησῐμ-εύω**, *to be useful* or *serviceable*, τοῖς ἐπιλήπτοις Thphr. *Fr*.175, cf. Phld.*Rh*.1.221, al., Luc.*DMort*.10.9; τῇ πατρίδι *IGRom*.4.1228 (Thyatira); πρός τι D.S.1.81, Dsc.2.149; εἴς τι Epicur.*Fr*.458, Gal.19.396, Iamb. *in Nic*.p.12 P.: abs., Lxx *Wi*.4.3, Muson.*Fr*.18 A p.95 H., Alex.Aphr. *in Top*.430.2: sens.obsc., D.L.6.91:—rejected by the Atticists, cf. Phryn.367. **-ολογέω**, *speak for edification*, prob. in Phld.*Po*.5.13. **-ολογία**, ἡ, *edification*, ibid. ⊛ **-ος**, η, ον, also ος, ον X.*Mem*.3.8.8, Pl.*Grg*.480b, *R*.333b: (χράομαι):—*useful, serviceable*, first in Thgn.406; εἰς ἀνάγκαν, ἔνθ' οὐ ποδὶ χρησίμῳ χρῆται S.*OT*878 (lyr.); τὸ χ. φρενῶν the *excellence* of.., E.*Ph*.1740 (lyr.); τὸ αὐτίκα χ. Th.3.56; ἡ διὰ τὸ χ. φιλία Arist.*EN*1159ᵇ13; τὰ χ. Men.*Mon* 579; χ. εἴς τι *useful* for something, Hdt.4.109, Ar.*Pl*.493 (anap.), Pl.*R*. l.c.; ἐπί τι Id.*Grg*. l.c.; πρός τι E.*Hipp*.482 (Comp.); ἰδίᾳ ἑκάστῳ χ. καὶ ὑπὲρ τοῦ κοινοῦ ὠφέλιμα X.*Cyr*.6.2.34; τοῦτ' οὖν τί ἐστι χρήσιμον; Ar.*Nu*.202; χρήσιμόν ἐστι, c. inf., Id.*Av*.382 (troch.). 2. of persons, *serviceable, useful*, S.*Aj*.410, D.20.7, etc.; Comp. -ώτερος Pl.*Lg*.819c: esp., like χρηστός, *a good and useful citizen*, χ. πόλει E.*Or*.910; χ. πολίτης Eup.118; χ. τινι Is.*Fr*.16.1; ἐπί τι D.25.31; τοὺς εὐπόρους δεῖ χ. αὑτοὺς παρέχειν τοῖς πολίταις to show themselves *useful, serviceable* to the state, Id.42.22, cf. E.*Supp*.887, Is.*Fr*.10.1 (Comp.); τοῖς σώμασι -ώτεροι more *able*-bodied, X.*Lac*.5.9; opp. ἀργαλέος τὴν ὄψιν, Aeschin.1.61. 3. *used, made use of*, τέμενος -ώτατον a *much-frequented* sanctuary, dub. in Hdt.2.178. 4. χρησίμη διαθήκη an *available* (i.e. *authentic*) will, Is.6.30. 5. νομίσματα οὐ χρήσιμα ἔξω money *that will not pass* abroad, X.*Vect*.3.2. II. Adv., -μως ἔχειν to be *serviceable*, Th.3.44, X.*Cyr*.8.5.9; χ. τινὶ σωθῆναι *with advantage* to him, Th.5.91, cf. J.*BJ*6.2.9; τὰ -μως λεγόμενα Plu.2.36d. ⊛ **-οτης**, ητος, ἡ, *usefulness*, Gloss.

⊛ **χρῆσις**, εως, ἡ, (χράομαι) *employment, use* made of a thing, ἀνέμων Pi.*O*.11(10).2; χρημάτων Democr.282; οἰκίας Pl.*Erx*.394d, cf. *SIG*987.33 (Chios, iv B.C.); τὴν κατ' ἀξίαν χ. ποιοῦνται ἑκάστῳ (fort. leg. ἑκάστου) Iamb.*Protr*.5; *use, practice*, Hp.*VM*4; in pl., *uses, advantages*, Pi.*N*.1.30; αἱ ἐς τὰ πολεμικὰ χ. the *uses* of war, X.*Cyr*.8.5.7; αἱ πολιτικαὶ χ. Arist.*Pol*.1267ᵃ23; opp. κτῆσις, Pl.*Mx*.238b, Arist.*EN*1098ᵇ32, Cic.*Fam*.7.29.1; opp. πώλησις, X.*Oec*.3.9. 2. *usefulness*, Th.7.5; opp. ἀχρηστία, Pl.*R*.333d; ἐς χρῆσιν κρατύνεσθαι *so as to become useful*, Hp.*Art*.27; ἔχειν χρῆσιν to be *useful*, D.11.8. 3. *intimacy, acquaintance*, ἡ οἰκειότης καὶ ἡ χ. [τῆς πόλεως] Isoc.*Ep*.2.14; ἡ χ. ἡ πρὸς ἀλλήλους Arist.*Pol*.1280ᵃ36; αἱ οἶκοι χρήσεις Isoc.19.11; ἡ τῶν ἀφροδισίων χ. Pl.*Lg*.841a, Arist.*HA*581ᵇ13, cf. *Pol*.1262ᵃ34 (pl.), *Ep.Rom*.1.26; τὰ ἐν χρήσει *familiar* objects, Plot.4.4.37. 4. Gramm., *usage*, of words, ἡ ἐξαλλαγὴ τῆς συνήθους χ. D.H.*Amm*.2.3; ἀναστρέφων τὰς χ. ib.2, cf. A.D.*Synt*.119.24, al.; ἡ Πλάτωνος χ. Id.*Pron*.72.18; in concrete sense, *example* of a word or use, πυκνῶς αἱ χ. παρὰ Αἰολεῦσιν ib.66.3; *passage* cited, f.l. for κρίσει in D.H.*Rh*.4.3; indicated by the symbol ⳨, Anon.*Oxy*.1611.56 (iii A.D.); ⳨ Ἀριστοφάνους (referring to *Av*.1181) *An.Ox*.2.452. II. (χράω (B) A), *oracular response*, ἀπὸ κείνου χρήσιος at his *bidding*, Pi.*O*.13.76. III. (χράω (B) B), *lending, loan*, Arist.*EN*1131ᵃ4, Plb.31.23.4, Ps.-Phoc.106.

**χρησμ-ᾰγόρης**, ου, ὁ, *utterer of oracles*, of Apollo, *AP*9.525.23. **-ηγορέω**, *utter oracles*, Luc.*Syr.D*.10. **-ηγόρος**, ον, *uttering oracles*, ἄδυτον *Rev.Phil*.46.114 (Yazili Kaya); Σίβυλλα *IGRom*.4.1540 (Erythrae).

**χρησμο-γράφιον** [ᾰ], τό, *office where oracles are recorded*, *Rev.Phil*.44.249,251 (Didyma, ii B.C.). **-δοσία**, ἡ, *a giving of oracles*, Vett.Val.184.6 (pl.).

⊛ **χρησμοδοτ-έω**, *give oracles*, Poll.1.17:—Pass., *receive an oracular response*, *CIG*4539 (Palestine); aor. inf. written -ισθῆναι (as if from -ίζω) Ps.-Callisth.3.17 cod.Leid. **-ημα**, ατος, τό, *oracular response*, Suid. **-ης**, ου, ὁ, *one who gives oracles, prophet, soothsayer*, Poll.1.14, Vett.Val.112.10.

**χρησμο-λᾰλος** [ᾰ], ον, = χρησμολόγος, τρίποδες Orac. in *App.Anth*.6.82.10. **-λέσχης**, ου, ὁ, = foreg., Lyc.1419.

**χρησμολογ-έω**, *utter oracles*, Ar.*Av*.964,991, D.S.16.26; εἰρήνην χ. *to prophesy* peace, Lxx *Je*.45(38).4. **-ία**, ἡ, *an uttering of oracles*, D.S.16.26, Poll.1.18. **-ική** (sc. τέχνη), ἡ, *the art of divination*, ib.19. **-ιον**, τό, *divination*, ib.18. ⊛ **-ος** (parox.), ον, *uttering oracles*, χ. ἀνήρ *soothsayer, diviner*, Hdt.1.62, 8.96; of Musaeus, S.*Fr*.1116. II. *expounder of oracles*, Hdt.7.142,143; and in 7.6, of Onomacritus, *collector of oracles, oracle-monger*, cf. Ar.*Av*.960, *Pax*1047, Th.2.8,21.

**χρησμολύτης** [ῠ], ου, ὁ, *expounder of oracles*, Tz. ad Lyc.494.

**χρησμο-πευστέω**, *consult an oracle*, *An.Bachm*.1.418 (ubi male -πνευστοῦντι). **-ποιός**, όν, *making oracles in verse*, Luc.*Alex*.23.

**χρησμός**, ὁ, (χράω (B) A) *oracular response, oracle*, Pi.*P*.4.60, *SIG*1044.49 (Halic., iv/iii B.C.), etc.; χ. ἀσήμους δυσκρίτως τ' εἰρημένους A.*Pr*.662; ἔχρησ' Ἀδράστῳ Λοξίας χρησμόν E.*Ph*.409; σφι χρησμὸν ἔφαινε delivered *an oracle* to them, Hdt.1.159; ᾄδειν Th.2.21 (cf. χρησμῳδός); εὔτεκνοι χ. promising happy progeny, E.*Ion*424; χ. ἔμμετρος Plu.2.396c; καταλογάδην τοὺς χ. λέγειν ib.397d; χρησμὸς.. περαίνεται is fulfilled, E.*Ph*.1703; χρησμοῦ ὄντος.. τὴν πόλιν διαφθαρῆναι Pl.*R*.415c; ὥσπερ χρησμοὺς γράψαντες, i.e. with all solemnity, Lycurg.92, cf. Isoc.4.171.

**χρησμοσύνη**, ἡ, *need, want, poverty*, Tyrt.10.8, A.R.2.473, Plot.1.8.5. 2. in mystical sense, opp. κόρος and corresponding to διακόσμησις, Heraclit.65, cf. Ph.1.89, 2.242, Plu.2.389c. II. *importunity*, τῆς χ. μετίεσαν Hdt.9.33. III. *service*, A.R.1.837.

**χρησμο-φόρος**, ον, *bringing oracles*, Paus.4.9.3. **-φύλαξ** [ῠ], ᾰκος, ὁ, *keeper of oracles*, Luc.*Alex*.23.

**χρησμῳδ-έω**, *deliver oracles, prophesy*, Hdt.7.6, Ar.*Eq*.818 (anap.), Pl.*Cra*.396d; τι X.*Ap*.30; τισι Pl.*Ap*.39c; τὰ συμφέροντα Epicur.*Sent.Vat*.29; χ. ἐμμέτρως Plu.2.623c:—Pass., κεχρησμῳδήσθω Pl.*Lg*.712a; τὰ κεχρησμῳδημένα Id.*Ep*.323c. II. Pass., *to be inspired, receive a divine revelation*, Ph.2.384. **-ημα**, ατος, τό, *oracular response*, Hsch., Eust.1426.62.

**χρησμῴδης**, ες, *oracular*, Philostr.*Her*.10.4; σοφία Id.*VA*6.11.

**χρησμῳδ-ία**, ἡ, *answer of an oracle, prophecy*, prop. *chanted* or *in verse*, A.*Pr*.775, Plu.2.402d: pl., Pl.*Prt*.316d. **-ικός**, ή, όν, *oracular*, Luc.*Alex*.22. Adv. -κῶς Eust.45.39. **-όληρος**, ὁ, *oracular nonsense*, cj. for χρησμοδέληρος in Pl.Com.13 D. **-ός**, όν, (ᾠδή) prop. *chanting oracles*, or *delivering them in verse*; then, generally, *prophesying, prophetic*, χ. παρθένος, of the Sphinx, S.*OT*1200 (lyr.); epith. of Apollo, *Epigr.Gr*.1023.2 (Nubia). 2. *oracular*, φάτις S.*Fr*.573. II. as Subst., *soothsayer, oracle-monger*, Pl.*Ap*.22c, *Ion*534d, al.

**χρῆσται, χρὴ 'σται**, or **χρῆ 'σται**, v. χρή.

**χρηστέον**, (χράομαι) *one must use*, c. dat. rei, Hp.*Art*.77, Pl.*Sph*.267e; ὅπῃ καὶ ὅπως χ. τινὶ X.*Mem*.3.1.11; πῶς χ. εἴη περί τινος D.S.18.64; πῶς χ. προτρέποντα = πῶς δεῖ τινα χρῆσθαι, Arist.*Rh*.1375ᵃ26 cf. Plb.5.98.9, Phld.*Mort*.19, Porph.*Abst*.2.44, etc.

⊛ **χρηστεύομαι**, *to be kind* or *merciful*, 1 *Ep.Cor*.13.4.

**χρηστήρ**, ῆρος, ὁ, = χρήστης I, Choerob. *in Theod*.1.262 H., al.

**χρηστηριάζω**, *give oracles, prophesy*, τισι Ephor.31(b) J.; χ. τάδε πρὸς τὴν ἐρώτησιν *SIG*557.6 (Magn.Mae., iii B.C.). II. mostly in Med. (fut. -άσομαι Theopomp.Hist.314), *consult an oracle*, Hdt.1.55; χρηστηριάζεσθαι ἐν Δελφοῖσι ἐπί τινι ib.66; χ. θεῷ *consult* a god, Id.7.178; ἱροῖσι χ. *by means of* victims, Id.8.134; αἰεὶ μάλιστα χ. D.S.16.26; περί τινος respecting something, Hdt.2.52; χ. εἰ.. *to ask the oracle* whether.., Id.5.67; εἰς ἥντινα παρέσονται χώραν Ant.Lib.8.2:—aor. Pass., τῶν βουλομένων -ασθῆναι *IG*9(2).1109.34 (Thessaly, ii/i B.C.).

**χρηστήριον**, τό, *an oracle*, i.e., I. *the seat of an oracle*, such as Delphi, *h.Ap*.81,214, Hes.*Fr*.134.6, Hdt.1.47, al., E.*Med*.667, etc.; τὸ ἐν Δελφοῖσι χ. Hdt.1.13, cf. X.*Cyr*.7.2.15; χρᾶσθαι χρηστηρίοισι Hdt.1.47,53, al.: distd. fr. the νηός, Id.6.19: sts. in pl. for sg., A.*Th*.748, *Eu*.194. 2. *oracular response*, Hdt.1.63,69, al., Th.1.25, 2.54: pl., A.*Ag*.964, S.*OC*604,1331, E.*Ion*532 (troch.). II. *an offering for the oracle*, made by those consulting it: generally, *sacrificial victim*, χ. θέσθαι Pi.*O*.6.70; χ. παρέχειν *IG*2².1126.33; χρηστήρια θεοῖσιν ἔρδειν A.*Th*.230, cf. *Supp*.450; χ. πέπτωκε E.*Ion* 419: metaph., *victim, sacrifice*, σφάγια.. κείνου χρηστήρια τἀνδρός S.*Aj*.220 (anap.).

**χρηστήριος**, α, ον, also ος, ον A.*Eu*.241: (χράω (B) A): *oracular, prophetic*, ἐφετμαί l.c.; ὄρνιθες Id.*Th*.26; χρηστηρίαν ἐσθῆτα Id.*Ag*.1270; τρίπους χ. E.*Ion*1320; τοὔνομα Id.*Hel*.822; also Ἄπολλον χρηστήριε *author of oracles*, Hdt.6.80, cf. *OGI*312 (Aegae, ii B.C.). II. (χράομαι) = χρηστικός, *fitted* or *designed for use, useful*, χρηστήρια σκεύη *household* utensils or furniture, Pl.Com.27 (τὰ πρὸς θεωρίαν ἢ θυσίαν σ. Poll.10.11); without σκεύη, *Mnemos*.57.208 (Argos, vi B.C.), *OGI*326.30 (Teos, ii B.C.); ὅσα σκύτινα τῶν ὅπλων καὶ τῶν χ. Str.13.1.48, cf. 15.2.6, Nic.Dam.106 J.; τὸν περίβολον καὶ τὰ ἐν αὐτῷ χ. *Expl.Arch.de Délos* 11.291, cf. 120, Durrbach *Choix d'inscr.de Délos* 119 (ii B.C.); τὰ δώματα καὶ τὰ χ. τῶν ὑδάτων *Supp.Epigr*.8.170 (Palestine), cf. *PCair.Zen*.764.37 (iii B.C.).

**χρηστηριώδης**, ες, *oracular, divine*, μαντικὴ χ., opp. ἀνθρωπίνη, Philostr.*VS*1 *Prooem*.

⊛ **χρήστ-ης** (written **χρείστης** *SIG*364.40 (Ephes., iii B.C.)), ου, ὁ: gen. pl. χρήστων (not χρηστῶν, to distinguish it from the gen. pl. of χρηστός, Hdn.Gr.1.425): (χράω (B) A):—*one who gives* or *expounds oracles, prophet, soothsayer*, Hsch., prob. in *Milet*.7p.50 (Didyma, i B.C.). II. (κίχρημι) *creditor, usurer*, Ps.-Phoc.83, Ar.*Nu*.240,434 (anap.), Lys.32.29, Lycurg.22, etc. 2. (χράομαι, κίχραμαι) *debtor*, Phoc.16, D.30.12, 32.12, *IPE*1².32 *B*84 (Olbia, iii B.C.), cf. Harp. s.v.: c. gen., κακοῦ ἀνδρὸς Phoc. l.c.; χρημάτων D.36.6. **-ικός**, ή, όν, (χράομαι) of persons, *knowing how to use, understanding the use of* a thing, τῶν ὑπαρχόντων Arist.*Oec*.1344ᵇ26; δεσποτικὴ ἐπιστήμη ἡ χ. δούλων Id.*Pol*.1255ᵇ31: abs., δύναμις χ., opp. ὑπηρετική, Procl. *in Prm*.p.735 S.: also c. dat. (like the Verb), M.Ant.7.55. 2. of things, *useful, serviceable*, σώματος ἕξις Plu.

Cat.Ma.1: Sup., μέλι -ώτατον Id.2.32e. Adv. -κῶς ib.80b: Comp. -ώτερον Arr.Epict.2.9.19.

**χρηστο-γρᾰφία**, ἡ, good or beautiful painting, Plu.Arat.13. **-ήθεια**, ἡ, goodness of heart, Lxx Si.37.11, Demetr.Eloc.244. **-ήθης**, ες, good-natured, well-disposed, Arist.Rh.1395$^{b}$17, Ptol.Tetr.163, al.

**χρηστ-οινέω**, produce good wine, Str.14.1.15.

**χρηστο-καρπία**, ἡ, the bearing of good fruits, Str.6.4.1. **-καρπος**, ον, having, bearing good fruits, ib.3.6. **-λογέομαι**, Pass., to be used in a favourable sense, Eust.766.29. **-λογία**, ἡ, fair speaking, in bad sense, Ep.Rom.16.18. **-λόγος**, ον, giving fair words, speaking plausibly, Hist.Aug.Pertinax 13.5. **-μάθεια** [ᾰ], ἡ, desire of learning, Longin.44.1. II. book containing a summary of useful knowledge or select passages, e.g. the χ. γραμματική of Procl. and the χρηστομάθειαι of Hellad., cf. Sor.1.2, al.; so in pl. of the epitome of Strabo; also περὶ -μαθίας (sic) EM227.53, Orus in EM685.57. **-μᾰθέω**, to be desirous of learning, Longin.2.3.⊛ **-μᾰθής**, ὁ, ἡ, an adept in polite learning, Cic.Att.1.6.2. Adv. -θῶς, εἴρηται Phld.Mus.p.83 K. **-μουσέω**, to be devoted to good music, Ath.14.633b.

⊛ **χρηστός**, ή, όν, (χράομαι) of things, like χρήσιμος, useful, good of its kind, serviceable, [τόξα] χρηστὰ οὐδέν Hdt 3.78; [ἀτραπὸς] οὐδὲν χ. τισι Id.7.215; χ. ἐπίπλοα Id.1.94; [γῆ] E.Hec.594; οἰκίη, opp. μοχθηρά, Pl.Grg.504a; ἡ χ. μέλιττα, opp. οἱ κηφῆνες, Arist.HA 624$^{b}$23: freq. of wholesome food, μελίτωμα Batr.39; ποτόν, σῖτος, Pl.R.438a; περὶ τὸ σῶμα Pl.Prt.313d: c. gen., for a thing, νεύρων for the sinews, Ael.NA14.21; ῥάφανος Alex.15.8; ὄψον Antiph.242, etc. (but pleasant to taste, nice, Thphr.Char.2.10): generally, πολιτεία Isoc.12.135; βίος Aeschin.1.179; of victims and omens, auspicious, ἱρά, σφάγια, Hdt.5.44, 9.61,62; τελευτὴ χ. a happy end or issue, Id.7.157; εἰ..τοῦτό γε δοκέει ὑμῖν εἶναι χρηστόν Id.5.92.α': pl., τὰ χ., as Subst., benefits, kindnesses, Id.1.41, 42; χρηστὰ φέρειν Id.4.139; χρηστόν τι συμβουλεύειν, χρηστὰ ἐπιτηδεύειν, Ar.Nu.793, Antipho 3.3.9; χρηστὰ λέγειν, πράττειν, etc., Men. 725,787, etc.: but τὰ χ. also, happy event, ἐκτελοῖτο δὴ τὰ χ. A.Pers. 228 (troch.); prosperity, success, τὰ χ. δ' αὔθ' ἕκαστ' ἔχει φίλους E.Hec.1227. 2. in moral sense, opp. κακός, Eup. in PSI11. 1213.2; opp. πονηρός, Pl.Prt.313d; τὸ χ., opp. τὸ αἰσχρόν, S.Ph. 476; χρηστός, opp. λυπρός, E.Med.601: but λῦπαι χρησταί if working for good, Pl.Grg.499e. 3. good for its purpose, effective (even for evil), τραῦμα, δῆγμα, Luc.Symp.44, Alex.55. 4. Gramm., in use, current, ποιηταῖς χρηστά Eust.215.8. II. of persons, good, esp. in war, valiant, true, Hdt.5.109, 6.13, S.Ph.437, etc.: generally, good, honest, worthy, Id.OT610; οἰκέται X.Oec.9.5; of women, ἐρεῖ τις ὡς Κλυταιμνήστρα κακή· Ἄλκηστιν ἀντέθηκα χρηστήν Eub. 117.11, cf. Men.Mon.634; of good citizens, useful, deserving, D.20. 7: c. acc. cogn., ἃ χρηστοὶ ἐγένεσθε Th.3.64; χ. περὶ τὴν πόλιν γεγενημένος Lys.14.31; χ. καὶ φιλόπολις Ar.Pl.900; collectively, ὀλίγον τὸ χ. Id.Ra.783; but also ironically, ὁ χ. οὑτοσί Id.Nu. 8; οἱ χ. πρέσβεις οὗτοι D.18.30, cf. 89; ἐκλελάκτικεν ὁ χ. ἡμῖν μοιχός Men.16. b. freq. on Epitaphs, IG3.3149,3155, al. c. c. inf., ὅσοι προβατεύειν χ. Him.Or.14.32. 2. οἱ χρηστοί, like οἱ ἀγαθοί, those of good family, X.Ath.1.4,6. 3. of the gods, propitious, merciful, bestowing health or wealth, θεῶν χρηστῶν ἥκειν εὖ Hdt.8.111, cf. M.Ant.9.11. 4. of men, good, kindly, δούλῳ..χ. γενόμενός ἐστι δεσπότης πατρίς Antiph.265; ὡς ἡδὺ δούλῳ δεσπότου χρηστοῦ τυχεῖν Men.Mon.556, cf. Philem.227; ὁ χ., ὡς ἔοικε, καὶ χρηστοὺς ποιεῖ Men.203b, cf. Plu.Phoc.10; χ. περί τινα D.59.2; ἐπί τινας Ev.Luc.6.35; εἰς ἀλλήλους Ep.Eph.4.32. b. sts. simple, silly, like εὐήθης, χρηστὸς εἶ ὅτι ἡγῇ.., you're a nice fellow, to think that.., Pl.Phdr.264b, cf. Tht.161a; ὦ χρηστέ D.18.318. 5. of a man, strong, able in body for sexual intercourse, = γυναικὶ χρῆσθαι δυνάμενος, Hp.Genit.2. 6. of the dead, whence χρηστὸν ποιεῖν = ἀποκτιννύναι, in a treaty between the Spartans and Tegea, Arist.Fr. 592. III. Adv. -τῶς well, properly, Hdt.4.117, Hp.Art.32; χ. ἔχειν Ar.Ec.219; σκευάσαι χ. τοὔψον Alex.149.6: ironically, χ. τὴν πατρίδα ἐπετρόπευσας Hdt.3.36.

**χρηστότης**, ητος, ἡ, goodness, honesty, uprightness, χρηστότητα ἀσκεῖν E.Supp.872; μέγιστον ἀγαθόν ἐστι μετὰ νοῦ χ. Men.788, cf. 472.1; χρηστότητος εἵνεκα as a reward for honesty, Aristopho 14.4 (troch.), Timocl.8.17; ποιεῖν χ. Lxx Ps.13(14).3; ἀκολουθεῖ τῇ ἀρετῇ χ. Arist.VV1251$^{b}$33; ἡ σὴ χ., as a honorific address, PGiss.7.15 (ii A.D.), PLond.2.411.6 (iv A.D.), etc. II. goodness of heart, kindness, Is.2.7 (but in depreciatory sense, soft-heartedness, Men. 579); εὔνοιαν καὶ χ. παρέσχητο Hdn.2.9.9; χ. καὶ φιλοστοργία, φιλανθρωπία καὶ χ., Plu.Agis 17, Comp.Dem.Cic.3, cf. Luc.Tim.8, D.C. 73.5; ἡ χ. καὶ ἡ φιλανθρωπία τοῦ θεοῦ Ep.Tit.3.4, cf. Ep.Rom.11.22, al.; χ. ἐφ' ἡμᾶς Ep.Eph.2.7; ποιεῖν χρηστότητα to show kindness, Lxx Ps.118(119).65; πολλὰ τῇ χ...κτῶνται Phld.Rh.1.262S. 2. simplicity, silly good nature, ἤθους ἀπλαστία μετ' ἀλογιστίας, Pl.Def. 412e.

**χρηστουργία**, ἡ, good deed, service, Iamb(?).ap.Suid. (Berl.Sitz. 1875 p.4).

**χρηστο-φῐλία**, ἡ, the friendship of good men, Arist.Rh.1361$^{b}$ 35. **-φιλος**, ον, possessed of good friends, ib.38. II. trusty friend, opp. κακόφιλος, Rhetor. in Cat.Cod.Astr.8(4).146. **-φωνία**, ἡ, goodness of voice, Antyll.ap.Orib.6.10.7.

**χρήστωρ**, ορος, ὁ, = μάντις, Hsch.

**χρητήρ**, ῆρος, ὁ, perh. = χρηστήριον (v. χρηστήριος II), PGrenf.1.21. 10 (ii B.C., pl.).

**χρῖ**· χρίει, Hsch. **χρία**· μυρμήκων κοίτη, Id.

**χρῖμα**, ατος, τό, = χρῖσμα, unguent, oil, Xenoph.3.6 (pl.), A.Ag.94 (anap.), Achae.5.2, X.An.4.4.13 (χρίσμα vel χρῆμα codd.), Call.Lav. Pall.16 (pl.), Iamb.1.241, 272, POxy.529.4 (ii A.D.).

**χρίμπτω**, bring near; Act. in Hom. only in compd. ἐγχρίμπτω (q.v.); πόδας χρίμπτουσα ῥαχίαισι keeping one's steps close along the shore, A.Pr.713; ὑπ' ἐσχάτην στήλην ἔχριμπτ' ἀεὶ σύριγγα kept the axle close to the post, S.El.721:—Med., πόδα χριμπτόμενος εἰναλίῳ κώπᾳ E.Hel.526 (lyr.); χρίμψασθαι ποτὶ πλευρὰ κάρη Theoc.25. 144:—more freq. in Pass., touch the surface of a body, graze, scratch, χριμφθεὶς πέλας grazing near, close even to touching, Od.10.516; ἐκ γενύων χριμφθεὶς γόος the wail or cry forcing its way to the ear from the clenched jaws, Pi.P.12.21: generally, draw near, approach, c. dat., δόμοισι τοῖσδε χρίμπτεσθαι A.Eu.185; τείχεσι χριμπτομένα E.Ph.809 (lyr.); δόμοις ib.99; ἐχριμπτόμην Κύκλωπι Id.Cyc. 406: τόπους εἰς τούσδε Critias 16.4 D.: also in aor. 1 Med., ἀμάθοισιν ἐχρίμψατο νηῦς h.Ap.439; ὅτεῳ χριμψαίατο λύθρον Euph.50: c. gen., νεκροθήκης οὐ χριμπτόμενος E.Fr.472.18 (anap.). II. intr. in Act., αὐδῶ μὴ χρίμπτειν θριγκοῖς Id.Ion156 (lyr.); λίσσου, γούνασι δεσπότου χρίμπτων Id.Andr.530 (lyr.): abs., χρίμψε κιών A.R.3. 1286.

**χρίσῐμος** [ῐ], η, ον, used for anointing, Sch.Ar.Pl.529.

**χρῖσις**, εως, ἡ, (χρίω) smearing, ἡ τοῦ ἐλαίου εἰς ἱμάτιον χ. Arist. Pr.966$^{b}$35; τῶν ἀγγείων Dsc.1.58 (χρῆσιν codd.); [τῆς κεφαλῆς], = ἄλειψις, Diocl.Fr.141. 2. anointing, PPetr.2 p.72 (iii B.C.), Lxx Ex.29.21, al.; φαρμάκων J.AJ2.14.3 (pl.) II. colouring, varnish, wash, Muson.Fr.19 p.108 H. (pl.), Ael.NA6.41; colour-washing, τῶν σκαναμάτων IG4$^{2}$(1).109 i 128 (Epid., iii B.C.), cf. Supp.Epigr.4.270 (Panamara, i (?) B.C.).

⊛ **χρῖσμα**, ατος, τό, (χρίω) later form for χρῖμα (q.v.), found in codd. of X.Smp.2.4, An.4.4.13, Thphr.Od.8,15, Sor.1.4, Gal.6. 402, etc. II. anointing, unction, Lxx Ex.29.7, 35.15, Gal.10. 892. 2. in NT of spiritual grace, χρῖσμα ἔχετε ἀπὸ τοῦ ἁγίου 1Ep.Jo.2.20, cf. 27. III. coating of wall, plaster, D.S.2.9, Luc. Hist.Conscr.62. (The usual accent χρίσμα is wrong, cf. χρῖμα.)

**χρισ-τέον**, (χρίω) one must anoint, smear, Orib.Fr.74, Syn.1.20, Gp.16.4.1. **-τήριον**, τό, unguent, a bottle of ointments, Suid. **-της**, ου, ὁ, white-washer, Hsch. s.v. κονιαταί. II. stucco-maker, Steph. in Hp.2.397 D.

**Χριστιᾰνικός**, ή, όν, Christian, Porph.Chr.88.

**Χριστιᾱνός**, ὁ, Christian, Act.Ap.11.26, 26.28, 1Ep.Pet.4.16, etc. Adv. -νῶς, ζῆν Porph.ap.Eus.HE6.19.

**χριστός**, ή, όν, (χρίω) to be rubbed on, used as ointment or salve, opp. πιστός, A.Pr.480, cf. E.Hipp.516, Triclin. ad Theoc.11.1; τὸ ἔλαιον τὸ χ. anointing oil, Lxx Le.21.10. II. of persons, anointed, ὁ ἱερεὺς ὁ χ. ib.4.5,16, 6.22: pl., ib.2Ma.1.10. 2. esp. of the Kings of Israel, ὁ χ. Κυρίου ib.1Ki.24.7, cf. Ps.17 (18).51; also τῷ χ. μου Κύρῳ Is.45.1; pl., of the patriarchs, Ps.104 (105).15. 3. in NT, ὁ χ. the Messiah, Ev.Matt.2.4, etc.; ὁ χ. Κυρίου Ev.Luc.2. 26; then used as pr. n. of Jesus, Ἰησοῦς Χ. Ev.Matt.1.1, etc.; Ἰησοῦς ὁ λεγόμενος Χ. ib.16.

⊛ **χρίω**, Ep. impf. χρῖον Od.4.252, also χρίεσκε A.R.4.871: fut. χρίσω E.Med.789: aor. ἔχρῖσα Od.10.364, etc., Ep. χρῖσα Il.16. 680, Od.4.49: pf. κέχρῐκα Lxx 1Ki.10.1, al.:—Med., fut. χρίσομαι Od.6.220: aor. part. χρῑσάμενος ib.96, Hes.Op.523, etc.:—Pass., fut. χρισθήσομαι Lxx Ex.30.32: aor. ἐχρίσθην A.Pr.675, Achae.10: pf. κέχρῐμαι Hdt.4.189,195, Magnes 3, etc., later κέχρισμαι Lxx 2Ki. 5.17: plpf. ἐκέχριστο f.l. in X.Cyr.7.1.2; 3 pl. ἐκέχριντο Callix.2. [Even in pres. and impf. ι is long. Od.21.179 (ἐπι-χρῖοντες), Il.23.186, S.Tr.675, etc.; χρῐει only in late Poets, as AP6.275 (Noss.): in fut. and all other tenses ῑ without exception, whence the proper accent. is χρῖσαι, κεχρῖσθαι, χρῖσμα, etc.:—touch the surface of a body slightly, esp. of the human body, graze, hence, I. rub, anoint with scented unguents or oil, as was done after bathing, freq. in Hom., λόεον καὶ χρῖον ἐλαίῳ Od.4.252; ἔχρισεν λίπ' ἐλαίῳ 3.466; λοέσσαι τε χρῖσαί τε 19.320; of a dead body, χρῖεν ἐλαίῳ Il.23.186; anoint a suppliant, Berl.Sitzb.1927.170 (Cyrene); πέπλον χ. rub or infect with poison, S.Tr.675, cf. 689,832 (lyr.): metaph., ἱμέρῳ χρίσασ' οἰστόν E.Med.634 (lyr.); οὐ μέλανι, ἀλλὰ θανάτῳ χ. τὸν κάλαμον Plu.2. 841e:—Med., anoint oneself, Od.6.96; κάλλεϊ ἀμβροσίῳ οἵῳ..Κυθέρεια χρίεται 18.194, cf. Hes.Op.523; ἐλαίῳ Gal.6.417; ἐκ φαρμάκου Luc. Asin.13: c. acc. rei, ἰοὺς χρίεσθαι anoint (i.e. poison) one's arrows, Od.1.262:—Pass, χρίεσθαι ὑπὸ τοῦ ἡλίου Hdt.3.124; βακκάριδι κεχριμένος Magnes l.c.; συκαμίνῳ τὰς γνάθους κεχριμέναι Eub.98.3: metaph., Σοφοκλέους τοῦ μέλιτι κεχριμένου Ar.Fr.581. 2. in Lxx, anoint in token of consecration, χ. τινὰ εἰς βασιλέα 4Ki.9.3; εἰς ἄρχοντα 1Ki.10.1; εἰς προφήτην 3Ki.19.16; also χ. τινὰ τοῦ βασιλεύειν Jd.9.15: c. dupl. acc., χ. τινὰ ἔλαιον Ep.Heb.1.9. II. wash with colour, coat, αἰγέαι κεχριμέναι ἐρευθεδάνῳ Hdt.4.189; πίσσῃ ib.195, cf. Inscr.Délos442A 188 (ii B.C.); ἀσφάλτῳ X.Cyr.7.5. 22 (Pass.); στοάν Supp.Epigr.4.268 (Panamara, ii A.D.):—Med., τὸ σῶμα μίλτῳ χρίονται smear their bodies, Hdt.4.191. III. wound on the surface, puncture, prick, sting, of the gadfly in A.Pr.566,597, 880 (all lyr.):—Pass., ὀξυστόμῳ μύωπι χρισθείς' ib.675.

**χρόα**, ἡ, v. χροιά. **χρόα**, χροΐ, v. χρώς.

**χροάζω**, colour, οὖρα, διαχώρημα, Ruf.Fr.79.

**χροανθές**· εὐφεγγές, Hsch.

⊛ **χροιά**, Ep. and Ion. χροιή, Il.14.164, Thgn.1017 (in Call.Lav. Pall.28 χροϊά (χροίην codd.)), Att. χροιά and χρόα, the latter always in Pl. (v. infr.), also in Phld.*D.*3.9, *Sign.*5, al. (v. χρώς):—*skin*, esp. of the human body, hence *the body* itself, παραδραθέειν φιλότητι ἠ χροιῇ Il. l. c.; κατὰ χροιὴν ῥέει ἱδρώς Thgn. l. c.; ὄζειν..τῆς χρόας ἔφασκεν ἡδύ μου Ar.*Pl.*1020; τὰ ἐξανθεῦντα ἐς τὴν χροιὴν (*skin, surface*) ἢ χροιῇ (*colour*, signf. II) ἢ οἰδήμασι Hp.*deArte*9: cf. χρώς. **2.** metaph., 'skin', i.e. *surface*, Pythagorean term, Arist.*Sens.*439ᵃ31, *Placit.*1.15.2, *Theol.Ar.*18 (pl.); χ. ἐπίπεδος ib.10; so perh. in Epicur.*Fr.*81, Phld.*Sign.*5, al. **3.** *appearance* to the eye, of heavenly bodies, Id.*D.*3.9. **II.** *superficial appearance* of a thing, its *colour*, Thgn.451, A.*Pr.*493, E.*Cyc.*517 (lyr.); παντοδάπαισι μεμειχμένα χροίαισιν Sapph.20, cf. Numen.ap.Ath.7.282a; τοιοῦτον (sc. ἐρυθρόν) εἶναι τῇ χροιᾷ τὸ μέλι Porph.*Antr.*16; ἔστιν..χρόα ἀπορροὴ σχημάτων ὄψει σύμμετρος καὶ αἰσθητός Pl.*Men.*76d; νόμῳ χροιή..ἐτεῇ δ' ἄτομα καὶ κενόν Democr.125, cf. Anaxag.4, Arist.*Sens.*440ᵃ8; ἐκ τριῶν τὰς χρόας ἅπασας μεμεγμένας, τοῦ φωτός, καὶ δι' ὧν φαίνεται τὸ φῶς, καὶ τῶν ὑποκειμένων χρωμάτων Id.*Col.*793ᵇ33. **2.** esp. *colour of the skin, complexion*, χροιῆς ἄνθος ἀμειβομένης Sol.27.6; χροιᾶς ἀμείψεις ἄνθος A.*Pr.*23; χροιὰν ἀλλάξασα E.*Med.*1168; λευκὴν χ. ἐκ παρασκευῆς ἔχεις Id.*Ba.*457, cf. Ar.*Nu.*1012 (anap.); χρόᾳ ἀδήλῳ τῶν δεδραμένων πέρι *with colour* that gives no hint of what has passed, E.*Or.*1318; χρόαν..τὴν σὴν ἥλιος..αἰγυπτιώσει Pl.Com.(?).p.615K. (post *Fr.*55); χρόας κάλλος Pl.*Smp.*196a; ἐρίζοι καὶ γάλακι χροιήν Call.*Hec.*1.4.3. **III.** in Music, *nuance* of a scale, Plu.2.1143e.—On the accent, v. Hdn.Gr.1.301, al.

❀ **χρο-ΐζω**, = χρῴζω, *touch the surface* of a body, and generally, *touch*, Ἥβας χροΐζει λέχος E.*Heracl.*915 (lyr.), cf. Pi.*Fr.*139.6 (Med.):—Med., *touch another's skin with one's own, lie with*, τινι, of a woman, Theocr.10.18 (in Dor. fut. χροϊξεῖται). **II.** *colour, stain*, χ. ἐπ' ὀλίγον ἀγχούσῃ Dsc.2.80; poet. aor. Pass. χροισθεῖσαι Nic.*Fr.*74.26, cf. Gal.17(2).275. **-ϊσις**, εως, ἡ, *coloratus*, Gloss. **-ϊσμός**, ὁ, *coloratura*, ib.

**χρόμᾰδος**, ὁ, *crashing sound*, χ. γενύων, in a pugilistic contest, Il.23.688. (From the same Root as χρεμ-ετίζω, χρέμ-πτομαι.)

**χρόμη**, ἡ, and **χρόμος**, ὁ, = foreg.: also *the neighing* of horses, Hsch.

**χρόμις**, ιος, ὁ (ἡ in Ael.*NA*9.7), a sea-*fish* like σκίαινα, perh. *Umbrina cirrhosa*, Anan.5.1 (χρόμιος), Epich.58 (χρόμιος or -ίας codd.Ath.), Arist.*HA*534ᵃ9 (v.l. χρέμις), Numen.ap.Ath.7.295b; cf. χρέμυς.

**χρον-ίζω**, (χρόνος): **I.** intr., *spend time*, περὶ Αἴγυπτον Hdt.3.61. **2.** *last, continue*, τὸ μὲν καλῶς ἔχον ὅπως χρονίζον εὖ μενεῖ βουλευτέον A.*Ag.*847; ἐν τῇ ὑστέρᾳ Arist.*HA*523ᵃ23; χρονίζωσι ib.537ᵃ7; οὐ χ. τὸ ἀλγοῦν συνεχῶς ἐν τῇ σαρκί Epicur.*Sent.*4, cf. Diog.Oen.58. **3.** χ. δρῶν *persevere* in doing, Pl.*Phdr.*255b. **4.** *take time, tarry, linger*, A.*Ag.*1356, *Ch.*64 (lyr.), Th.6.49, 8.16; κεχρονικότες, opp. ὑπόγυιοι τῇ ὀργῇ ὄντες, Arist.*Rh.*1380ᵇ5; κεχρονικὼς ἐν Ῥώμῃ Plb.33.16.6; χρονίσαι κατὰ τὸ βαλανεῖον Gal.6.417; ἡ ναῦς καὶ τὸν χρόνον τοῦτον ὃν ἐπιστέλλω σοι χρονίζει Hp.*Ep.*14: c. inf., *delay* to do, χ. καταβῆναι Lxx *Ex.*32.1 (also χ. τοῦ ποιῆσαί τι ib.*Ge.*34.19), *Ev.Luc.*12.45. **5.** of ailments, *to be* or *become chronic*, Hp.*Aph.*3.28. **6.** of wine, *to be* or *become old, to have age*, Ath.1.33a. **II.** Pass., *to be prolonged* or *delayed*, τῶνδε πίστις οὐκ ὄκνῳ χρονίζεται A.*Th.*54, cf. *Ch.*957 (lyr.); πολέμου χρονισθέντος And.3.27; [τὴν εὔνοιαν] χρονιζομένην..φιλίαν γενέσθαι Arist.*EN*1167ᵃ11; χ. ἐν τῷ σώματι *continue*, Id.*Pr.*907ᵇ22; τὰ κεχρονισμένα νοσήματα Gal.18(2).31. **2.** *grow up*, χρονισθεὶς δ' ἀπέδειξεν ἔθος A.*Ag.*727 (lyr.). **3.** *to be located in time, made temporal*, Simp. *in Ph.*716.11, Dam.*Pr.*405. **-ικός**, ή, όν, *of* or *concerning time, temporal*, opp. τοπικός, Plot.3.7.9; χ. ποίησις creation *in time*, Jul.*Or.*4.146b. Adv. -κῶς ib.145d, Prisc.Lyd.36.2, Dam.*Pr.*404. **II.** *chronological*, κανόνες Plu.*Sol.*27: τὰ χ. (sc. βιβλία) *annals* or *chronology*, Id.*Them.*27; αἱ χρονικαί (sc. γραφαί) D.H.1.8; χ. σύνταξις D.S.13.103. **III.** Gramm., χ. ἐπιρρήματα adverbs *of time*, A.D.*Pron.*15.24, cf. Sch.Il.*Oxy.*2211 5; *temporal*, i.e. quantitative, παράγγελμα A.D.*Pron.*58.22; of the *temporal* augment, χ. αὐξήσεις Eust.72.45. Adv. -κῶς *in respect of time*, διαφέρειν A.D.*Synt.*209.23. **-ιόομαι**, Pass., *become chronic*, οἷσι ἂν χρονιωθῇ Hp.*Art.*50. ❀ **-ιος**, α, ον, also ος, ον E.*Ion*470 (lyr.), *Andr.*84, Th.6.31:—*after a long time, late*, ἐλθὼν χρόνιος Od.17.112; χρονία μὲν ἥκεις Cratin.222, cf. Ar.*Th.*912; χ. φανείς S.*Ph.*1446 (anap.); χρόνιος (v.l. χρόνιον) εἰσιδὼν φίλον E.*Or.*475; τροπαία χρονία A.*Th.*706 (lyr.); χρόνιοι ξυνιόντες Th.1.141. Adv. -ίως *after a long time*, *Sammelb.*4314.2 (iii B.C.). **b.** *long-delaying, tardy*, Δίκα E.*Fr.*223 (lyr.); χ. τὰ τῶν θεῶν Id.*Ion*1615 (troch.). **2.** *for a long time, a long while*, χρόνιόν τινα ἐκβεβληκότες, ἤλαυνε, S.*Ph.*600, *OC*441; μή..χρόνιοι μέλλετε πράσσειν Id.*Ph.*1449 (anap.); χρόνιος ὤν, ἀπών, E.*Or.*485, *IA*1099; χρόνιός εἰμ' ἀπ' ἀνθρώπων βορᾶς Id.*Cyc.*249. **3.** *long-continued*, ἀρετὰ χρονία τελέθει Pi.*P.*3.115; ἅπλοιαι A.*Ag.*149 (lyr.); χρόνια λέκτρ' ἔχων having been long married, E.*Ph.*14; χ. ἐτῶν ἐνιαυτοί Ar.*Ra.*347 (lyr.); στόλος..χ. ἐσόμενος, χρόνιος στρατεία, Th.6.31; δεσμὰ χ. Pl.*Lg.*855b; of plants, *perennial*, opp. ἐπέτειος, Thphr.*HP*1.1.9. **4.** of ailments, *chronic*, νοσήματα Hp.*Aph.*2.39, *Coac.*203; [πόνοι] Epicur.*Fr.*447; νόσοι D.H.1.37, Gal.6.356; ἰσχιάς Dsc.1.10; [βῆχες] Paul.Aeg.3.28 (Comp.). Adv. -ίως Philum.ap.Orib.8.45 tit.: Comp. -ιωτέρως Hp.*Coac.*197. **5.** Astrol., χ. ζῴδια, f.l. for Κρονικά, *Cat.Cod.Astr.*1.133. **II.** Adv. -ίως Arist.*GC*328ᵃ35, Thphr.*Sud.*22; neut. pl. χρόνια as Adv., E.*Or.*152 (lyr.): Comp. -ώτερον Pi.*N.*4.6.—Rare in Prose, and only (as it seems) in signf. I. 3 and 5. **-ιότης**, ητος, ἡ, *long duration*, Thphr.*HP*9.14.2, Sor.2.28, *Theol.Ar.*23. **-ίσκος**, ὁ, Dim. of χρόνος, *a short time*, Lxx 2*Ma.*11.1; dub. cj. for Κρονίσκοι in Gal.*Libr.Propr.*12. **-ισμός**, ὁ, *tarrying* in a place, Plb.1.56.3. **II.** *delaying, coming late*, D.H.6.52. **III.** *a becoming chronic*, Sor.2.84, Orib.*Fr.*55. **-ιστέον**, *one must spend time*, ἔν τινι Arist.*Rh.*1417ᵇ30. **-ιστός**, ή, όν, *tarrying, tardy*, δίκης τέλος Orac.ap.Ael.*VH*3.43.

**χρονογρᾰφ-έω**, *compile annals*, Tz.*H.*12.718. ❀ **-ία**, ἡ, *chronological record, annals*, Plb.5.33.5 (pl.); αἱ χ. καὶ ἡ Ἀτθίς *Anon.Argentinensis* p.77 Keil. **II.** Astrol., description of χρονοκρατορίαι, Nech.ap.Vett.Val.278.24, Paul.Al.*S.*1. **III.** Astron., *method of reckoning*, Ptol.*Phas.* p.10 H. **-ος** (parox.), ὁ, *chronicler, annalist*, Str.1.2.9 (pl.), Luc.*Alex.*6 (v.l. χορο-), Agath.4.30.

**χρονοκρᾰτ-έω**, Astrol., *to be dominant for a specified period*, Vett.Val.186.4; also **-ορέω**, ib.276.10: hence ❀ **-ορία**, ἡ, ib.165.11. ❀ **-ωρ**, ορος, ὁ, *heavenly body dominant for a specified period*, Ptol.*Tetr.*209.

**χρονολάβον** [ᾰ], τό, *instrument for measuring time*, Procl.*Hyp.*4.71 (pl.); ἐξ ὑδρολογίου -ου ib.79.

❀ **χρόνος**, ὁ, *time*, Hom. (v. infr.), etc.: dist. fr. καιρός, D.59.35, cf. Ammon.*Diff.*p.79 V.; τῶν δὲ πεπραγμένων ἀποίητον οὐδ' ἂν χ. δύναιτο θέμεν τέλος P.*O.*2.17; μυρίος χ. Id.*I.*5(4).28, S.*OC*618; μακρὸς κἀναρίθμητος χ. Id.*Aj.*646; ὁ πᾶς χ. Pi.*P.*1.46, cf. A.*Eu.*484; πρόπας χ. ib.898; ἐς τὸ πᾶν χρόνου ib.670; but in Prose, τοῦ χ. τὸν πλεῖστον Th.1.30, cf. Isoc.9.41; τὸν πρῶτον τοῦ χ. X.*Lac.*1.5; τὸν δι' αἰῶνος χ. A.*Ag.*554; χρόνου πολλοῦ δέονται take *a long time*, X.*Smp.*2.4, etc.; ὥστε τι τῷ χ. Antipho 5.86. **b.** *time* in the abstract, ἀμερὴς χ. Timo 76; τριμερὴς S.E.*M.*10.197, cf. Plu.2.153b; defined by Zeno *Stoic.*1.26, Apollod. ib.3.260. **2.** *a definite time, period*, δεκέτης, τρίμηνος, S.*Ph.*715 (lyr.), *Tr.*164; χ. βίου, ἥβης χ., E.*Alc.*670, *El.*20; πολὺν ἀριθμὸν χρόνου γεγονότες Aeschin.1.49: pl., of points or periods of time, τοῖς χ. ἀκριβῶς with *chronological* accuracy, Th.1.97; τοῖς χ. by the *dates*, Isoc.11.36; μετενεγκόντα τοὺς χ. altering the *dates*, D.18.225; μακρῶν καὶ πολλῶν χρόνων Pl.*Lg.*798b; τεσσαράκοντα χρόνους ἐνιαυτῶν *IG*5(1).728.7 (Sparta), cf. 14.1747.3 (Rome); χρόνων μῆκος (dub., leg. χρόνου) Chor.35.51 p.403 F.-R. **b.** *date, term* of payment due, *Leg.Gort.*1.10, al. **c.** *year*, Ἑλληνικά 1.233 (Rhamnus, i B.C.), *PLond.*2.417.14 (iv A.D.), *App.Anth.*6.154.1 (leg. εἰς ἔτι), Ps.-Ptol.*Centil.*24, cf. *EM* 254.13. **d.** *equatorial degree*, Ptol.*Tetr.*44, Paul.Al.*A.*2, al., *Cat.Cod.Astr.*5(1).240. **3.** Special phrases: **a.** acc., χρόνον *for a while, for a long* or *short time*, Od.4.599, 6.295, Hdt.1.175, 7.223, etc.; πολὺν χρόνον *for a* long *time*, Od.11.161; δηρὸν χ. Il.14.206; οὐκ ὀλίγον χ. 19.157; τοῦτον τὸν χ. Hdt.1.75; ἐς τὸν αἰὲν χ. for ever, E.*Or.*207 (lyr.); οὐ πολὺς χ. ἐξ οὗ..Pl.R.452c; παλαιὸς ἀφ' οὗ χρόνος S.*Aj.*600 (lyr.); ἦν χρόνος ἐν ᾧ.., or ὅτε.., Linus ap.D.L.*Prooem.*4, Critias 25.1 D.; ἕνα χ. *once for all*, Il.15.511. **b.** gen., χρόνου περιιόντος as *time* came round, Hdt.4.155; so χ. ἐπιγενομένου, διεξελθόντος, προβαίνοντος, Id.1.28, 2.52, 3.53; χρόνου γενομένου after *a time*, D.S.20.109; ὀλίγου χρόνου *in a* short *time*, Hdt.3.134; πολλοῦ..οὐχ ἑόρακά πω χρόνου Ar.*Pl.*98; οὐ μακροῦ χ., τοῦ λοιποῦ χ., S.*El.*478 (lyr.), 817; βαιοῦ κοὐχὶ μυρίου χ. Id.*OC*397; ποίου χρόνου; A.*Ag.*278; πόσου χ.; after how *long?* Ar.*Ach.*83. **c.** dat., χρόνῳ *in process of time*, Xenoph.18, Hdt.1.80, 176, al.: freq. in Trag., as A.*Ag.*126, 463, *Ch.*650 (all lyr.); also χρόνῳ κοτέ Hdt.9.62; τῷ χ. ποτέ Ar.*Nu.*865; χρόνῳ, χρόνοις ὕστερον, *long* after, Th.1.8, Lys.3.39; οὐ χρόνῳ *immediately*, Ps.-Democr.Alch.p.49 B.: also c. Art., τῷ χ. Ar.*Nu.*66, 1242. **d.** ὁ ἄλλος χ., in Att., of *past time*, D.20.16, ὁ λοιπὸς χ., of *future*, v. λοιπός 3; so χ. ἐφέρπων, ἐπαντέλλων, μέλλων, Pi.*O.*6.97, 8.28, 10(11).7; also κατὰ χ. ἱκνούμενον or κατὰ χ. ⟨τὸν⟩ ἱ. at a later (or the fitting) *time*, Ant.Lib.27.4 (cf. ἱκνέομαι II. 2). **4.** with Preps.:—ἀνὰ χρόνον in course of *time*, after *a time*, Hdt.1.173, 2.151, 5.27, al. **b.** ἀφ' οὗ χρόνου from such *time* as.., X.*Cyr.*1.2.13. **c.** διὰ χρόνου after *a time*, after *an interval*, S.*Ph.*758, Ar.*Lys.*904, *Pl.*1055, Th.2.94; διὰ χρόνου πολλοῦ Hdt.3.27; διὰ π. χ. Ar.*V.*1476; διὰ μακρῶν χρόνων Pl.*Ti.*22d: but χρόνος..διὰ χρόνου προὔβαινέ μοι means *one space of time* after *another*, day after day, S.*Ph.*285. **d.** ἐκ πολλοῦ τευ χ. a long *time* since, long *ago*, Hdt.2.58. **e.** ἐν χρόνῳ, like χρόνῳ, *in course of time, at length*, A.*Eu.*1000 (lyr.); *for a long time*, Pl.*Phdr.*278d; ἐν πολλῷ χρόνῳ ib.228a; ἐν χρόνοισι perh. *formerly*, [Emp.]*Sphaer.*108 (leg. Κάρπιμος). **f.** ἐντὸς χρόνου within *a certain time*, Hdt.8.104. **g.** ἐπὶ χρόνον for *a time*, for *a while*, Il.2.299, Od.14.193, Hdt.1.116; πολλὸν ἐπὶ χρόνον χ. Od.12.407; χρόνον ἐπὶ μακρὸν Hdt.1.81; παυρίδιον or παῦρον ἐπὶ χ., Hes.*Op.*133, 326. **h.** ἐς χρόνον *hereafter*, Hdt.3.72, 9.89. **i.** μετὰ χρόνον after *a time*, Id.2.52, etc.; μέχρι τοῦ αὐτοῦ χ. up to the same *time*, Th.1.13. **k.** πρὸ τοῦ καθήκοντος χ. Aeschin.3.126; so τοῦ χρόνου πρόσθεν S.*Ant.*461. **l.** σὺν (ξὺν) χρόνῳ, like χρόνῳ or διὰ χρόνου, A.*Ag.*1378, *Eu.*555 (lyr.). **m.** ὑπὸ χρόνου by *lapse of time*, Th.1.21: but ὑπὸ αὐτὸν τὸν χ. *about* the same *time*, Hdt.7.165, cf. Th.1.100 (pl.). **II.** *lifetime, age*, ὁ μακρὸς ἀνθρώπων χρόνος S.*Ph.*306; χρόνῳ παλαιοί Id.*OC*112; χρόνῳ μείων ib.374; τοσόσδε τῷ χ. so far gone *in years*, Pl.*Ax.*365b; χρόνῳ βραδύς S.*OC*875. **III.** *season* or *portion of the year*, περιγράψαι τοῦ ἔτους χρόνον X.*Mem.*1.4.12. **IV.** *delay*, οὐδ' ἐποίησαν (fort. ἐνεποίησαν) χ. οὐδένα D.19.163; χρόνον δ' αἱ νύκτες ἔχοντι *linger*, Theoc.21.25; χρόνους ἐμποιεῖν to interpose *delays*, D.23.93. **V.** Gramm., **1.** *tense* of a verb, D.H.*Th.*24, A.D.*Adv.*123.17, D.T.638.3. 2. *time* or *quantity* of a syllable, Longin.39.4, A.D.*Synt.*130.4, al.: βραχὺς χ. a short syllable, ib.309.23; of the augment, ib.237.10. 3. in Rhythmic and Music, *time*, διαιρεῖται ὁ χ. ὑπὸ τῶν ῥυθμιζομένων Aristox.*Rhyth.*p.79 W., etc.; ὁ πρῶτος [χ.] *time-unit*, ibid., Aristid. Quint.1.14, etc.; χρόνος κενός ib.18: freq. in pl., λέξις εἰς χρόνους τεθεῖσα διαφέροντας Aristox.*Rhyth.* p.77 W., cf. Anon.Rhythm.*Oxy.* 9ii6; [μέτρα] προχωρεῖ ἕως λʹ χρόνων Aristid.Quint.1.23.

**χρονοτρῐβέω**, *waste time, loiter*, Arist.*Rh.*1406ᵃ37, Leonid.ap.Plu. 2.225b, *Act.Ap.*20.16, Men.Prot.p.21 D.:—Med., *UPZ*39.29 (ii B.C.). 2. c. acc., χ. τὸν πόλεμον *protract* the war, Plu.*Cat.Mi.* 53, Eun.*Hist.*p.242 D.

**χρονουλκέω**, (ἕλκω) = χρονοτριβέω, gloss on μοργυλλεῖ, Hsch.

**χρονόω**, *make temporal*, [ἡ ψυχὴ] ἑαυτὴν ἐχρόνωσε Plot.3.7.11.

**χροός**, v. χρώς.

**χροτιή**, ἡ, late poet. form for χρώς, *AP*15.35 (Theoph.).

**χρούστη**, ἡ, = Lat. *crusta*, *Ann.Épigr.*1905 No.172 (Thessalonica).

**χρῡσ-άετος** [ᾰ], ὁ, *golden eagle*, Ael.*NA*2.39. **-αιγις**, ιδος, ἡ, *with golden aegis*, epith. of Athena, B.*Fr.*11, cf. *IG*12(5).611 (Ceos). (Oxyt. in codd., but proparox. acc. to the rule given in *EM*518. 54.) **-αΐζω**, *adorn with gold*, Hsch. (Pass.). **-αϊκόν**, τό, name of a coin, dub. l. in *Inscr.Délos* 1442 *B*51 (ii B.C.).

**χρῡσ-άκτιν**, ῑνος, ὁ, ἡ, *with golden rays* or *beams*, Hdn.Gr.1.18; in *EM*518.39, **-άκτις**.

**χρυσαλάκατος**, ον, Dor. for χρυσηλ- (q.v.).

⊛ **χρῡσαλλίς**, ίδος, ἡ, *chrysalis*, Arist.*HA*551ᵃ19, *GA*758ᵇ31, Thphr.*HP*2.4.4, etc. II. old name for a *cockchafer*, Eust.1329.29.

**χρύσ-αμμος** [ῠ], ἡ, *golden sand*, Olymp.Alch.p.98 B.; = *balluca*, *Gloss.* **-ᾰμοιβός**, ὁ, expld. by Hsch. as = ἀργυρογνώμων: metaph., ὁ χ. Ἄρης σωμάτων *he who traffics in* men's bodies, or *who ransoms* the dead *by gold*, A.*Ag.*437 (lyr.). ⊛ **-άμπυξ**, ῠκος, ὁ, ἡ, *with fillet* or *frontlet of gold*, epith. of horses, Il.5.358,363, al. (never in Od.); Ὧραι *h.Hom.*6.5,12; Μοῦσαι Hes.*Th.*916, cf. Pi.*P.*3.89; Λάχεσις Id.*O.*7.64; Οὐρανία B.5.13; also χ. χαλινός Pi.*O.*13. 65. **-ανθεμίς**, ίδος, ἡ, = sq. 4, Ps.-Dsc.4.58. ⊛ **-άνθεμον**, τό, = ἑλίχρυσον, Dsc.4.57 (also **χρυσάνθεμος**, ἡ, Cyran.44, *Gloss.*). 2. = βατράχιον I, *garden ranunculus*, *Ranunculus asiaticus*, *Gp.*2.6. 30. 3. = χρυσοκόμη, Ps.-Dsc.4.55. 4. = χάλκας, ib.58. ⊛ **-ανθής**, ές, *with flower of gold*, ἔρνος *Trag.Adesp.* in *Gött.Nachr.*1922 p.27; κρόκος *AP*12.256 (Mel.). II. χρυσανθές, τό, = ἑλίχρυσον, Nic.*Fr.* 74.69. 2. *yellow dye*, *PHolm.*22.2. ⊛ **-άνθινα**, τά, games celebrated at Sardis, *IG*2².3169.23 (iii A.D.). **-άνθρωπος**, ὁ, '*gold-man*', symbol in Alchemy, Zos.Alch.p.207 B.; cf. μολυβδάνθρωπος.

**χρυσάνιος**, Dor. for χρυσήνιος (q.v.).

**χρῡσ-ανταυγής**, ές, *reflecting golden light*, πέταλα E.*Ion* 890 (lyr.). **-άντινος**, η, ον, written for -άνθινος, *gold-coloured*, γαυνάκης *Stud.Pal.*20.67.12 (ii/iii A.D.): Lat. *crissantinum*, = *phlomi flores*, *Gloss.*

**χρυσάορος** [ᾱ], ον, (ἄορ) = χρυσάωρ, *with sword of gold*, epith. of Apollo, Il.5.509, 15.256, Pi.*P.*5.104; also of Demeter, *h.Cer.*4; of Artemis, Orac.ap.Hdt.8.77; of Orpheus, Pi.*Fr.*139.9; so **χρυσᾱορεύς**, έως, of Zeus at Stratonicea, Str.14.2.25, cf. *OGI*234.24 (Delph., iii B.C.); also **χρυσᾱόριος**, *CIG*2720,2721 (Stratonicea): hence

⊛ **Χρῡσᾱορεῖς**, οἱ, of a league formed by his worshippers, τὸ Χρυσαορέων ἔθνος *OGI* l.c. 12, cf. 111.8 (Egypt, ii B.C.); called τὸ χρῡσᾱορικὸν σύστημα, Str. l.c.; cf. St.Byz. s. v. Χρῡσᾱορίς.

**χρῡσ-αργύριον** [ῠ], τό, = *pecunia auri*, *Gloss.* **-άργῠρος**, ὁ, *alloy of gold and silver*, Maria ap.Zos.Alch.p.169 B. 2. *tribute of gold and silver*, Zos.2.38, *PLips.*64.30 (iv. A.D.). **-άρμᾰτος**, ον, *with* or *in car of gold*, Ἀθάνα B.12.194; Μήνα Pi.*O.*3.19; also of heroes, Id.*P.*5.9, *I.*6(5).19. II. οἱ χ., of a body of the Macedonian royal guard, Poll.1.175. **-ασπις**, ῐδος, ὁ, ἡ, *with shield of gold*, Ἄρης B.19.11; Θήβα Pi.*I.*1.1; Παλλάς E.*Ph.*1372; οἱ χ., a corps in the Macedonian army, Poll.1.175. ⊛ **-αστράγᾰλος** [ᾰγ], φιάλα *golden* goblet *with bottom shaped like a knuckle-bone*, Sapph.170 (pl.). **-αττικὸς** οἶνος, *golden Attic* wine, *Edict.Diocl.*2.14, Alex. Trall.1.17, al.; **-κόν**, τό, Paul.Aeg.3.50.

**χρῡσαύγ-εια**, ἡ, *golden lustre*, Eust.695.4. **-έω**, *shine like gold*, Lxx *Jb.*37.22. **-ής**, ές, *gold-gleaming*, κρόκος S.*OC*685 (lyr.); δόμος Ar.*Av.*1710, cf. *Cat.Cod.Astr.*2.82; τὸ τῆς δειρῆς χ., of a peacock, Lib.*Descr.*24.6: metaph., φρόνησις Ph.1.57: neut. as Adv., χρυσαυγὲς μειδιᾶν Him.*Or.*13.7. **-ίζω**, = χρυσαυγέω, Lib.*Descr.* 30.13.

⊛ **χρῡσάφιον** [ᾰ], τό, Dim. of χρυσός, Hdn.Gr.1.368, Eust.492.36.

**χρῡσᾰφος**, ὁ, *a kind of fish*, perh. *gilt head*, Marc.Sid.12.

**χρῡσ-άωρ** [ᾰ], ορος, ὁ, ἡ, (ἄορ) = χρυσάορος (q.v.), *h.Ap.*123, Hes. *Op.*771, Pi.*P.*5.104. **-εγχής**, ές, *with spear of gold*, Orph.*H.*52.11 codd. (θυρσεγχής Herm.).

⊛ **χρῡσεῖον**, τό, *gold-mine*, Plb.34.10.10: pl. χρυσεῖα *gold-mines*, X. *HG*4.8.37, Plb.3.57.3, etc.: gen. pl. written χρυσέων, *PSI*6.601.10 (iii B.C.).

**χρύσειος** [ῠ], η, ον, Ep. for χρύσεος (q.v.).

**χρῡσ-εκλέκτης**, ου, ὁ, *one who picks gold-dust from river-sand*, *gold-washer*, Lat. *aurilegulus*, *Gloss.* **-ελεφαντήλεκτρος**, ον, *of gold, ivory, and electrum*, *overlaid therewith*, ἀσπίς Epigr.ap.Plu. *Tim.*31. **-ελεφάντῐνος**, η, ον, *of gold and ivory*, *overlaid therewith*, Philoch.97, Sch.Ar.*Eq.*1166. **-έμβολος**, ον, *with beak of gold*, of a ship, App.*Praef.*10. ⊛ **-έμπαικτος**, ον, *inlaid with gold*, *BGU*781 iv 1 (i A.D.). **-ένδετος**, ον, *gold-inlaid*, σπάθη Philem.70; cf. Mart.2.43, 6.94. II. *set in gold*, σφραγίς *IG*11(2) 161 *B*49, 203 *B*67 (Delos, iii B.C.); σμάραγδος Plu.*Luc.*3.

**χρῡσεο-βόστρῡχος**, ον, *with golden tresses*, Διὸς ἔρνος E.*Ph.*191 (lyr.), Philox.8. **-δμητος**, ον, *built* or *formed of gold*, A.*Ch.* 617 (lyr., but Herm. χρυσεοκμήτοισι, *gold-wrought*).

**χρῡσε-όδους**, όδοντος, ὁ, ἡ, *gold-pronged*, τρίαινα Lyr. in *Mitteil. aus d. Papyrussamml. d. Nationalbibliothek in Wien* 1(1932).138.

**χρῡσεό-κμητος**, ον, v. χρυσεόδμητος. **-κόλλητος**, ον, = χρυσοκόλλητος, Paul.Sil.*Ambo* 159. **-κόμης**, ου, Dor. **-κόμας**, α, ὁ, = χρυσοκόμης, Simon.26 B, *Pae.Delph.*3. ⊛ **-κυκλος**, ον, *with disk of gold*, φέγγος, of the sun, E.*Ph.*176 (lyr.). **-μαλλος**, ον, = χρυσόμαλλος, ποίμνα, δέρος, Id.*El.*724 (lyr.), *Hyps.Fr.*3(1) ii 22 (lyr.), cf. Orph.*A.*1018. **-μίτρης**, ου, ὁ, = χρυσομίτρης, *AP*9.524.23:—fem. **-μίτρα**, Melinno ap.Stob.3.7.12. **-νωτος**, ον, = χρυσόνωτος, ἀσπίς E.*Fr.*159 (lyr.). **-πήληξ**, ηκος, ὁ, ἡ, = χρυσοπήληξ, *h.Mart.*1, Call.*Lav.Pall.*43. **-πήνητος**, ον, *with woof of gold*, *gold-inwoven*, φάρεα E.*Or.*840 (lyr.); χ. γραφίς a line or thread *of gold inwrought*, *AP*5.275.2 (Agath.). **-πλοκος**, ον, *inwoven with gold*, ταινίαι B.16.106. **-ρῠτος**, ον, *flowing with gold*, ὄλβος *Supp.Epigr.* 7.14.23 (Susa, Hymn to Apollo, i A.D.).

⊛ **χρύσεος**, η, ον, also ος, ον in *AP*5.30 (Antip.Thess.), Att. contr. **χρυσοῦς**, ῆ, οῦν *IG*1².358.4, etc.; Ep. **χρύσειος**, η, ον: Hom. and Hes. use both χρύσεος and -ειος, χρυσῇ is dub. in Il.5.425; Lyr. used χρύσεος, α, ον, and this form sts. occurs in Trag. dialogue and even in Prose, as X.*Ages.*5.5 codd., Plu.*Luc.*37, Apollod.2.5.10, Ant.Lib.36. 1; Aeol. **χρύσιος** Sapph.1.8, al. (but χρύσεα Theoc.29.37); Boeot. **χρούσιος** *SIG*337.8 (iv B.C.): (χρυσός):—*golden*, freq. in Ep., esp. of what belonged to gods, χρυσέῳ ἐν δαπέδῳ, χρυσέοις δεπάεσσι, χρύσειον ἐπὶ θρόνον, etc., Il.4.2,3, 8.442, al.; χ. τάλαντα the *golden* scales of Zeus, 22.209; χ. ἴτύς, ζυγόν, of Hera's chariot, 5.724,730; ἱμάσθλη χ., of Zeus and Poseidon, 8.44 = 13.26; ζώνη χ., of Calypso and Circe, Od.5.232 = 10.545, etc.; δόμος Sapph. l.c.; of possessions of mortals, Il.4.133, 5.425, al.: sts. *enriched* or *adorned with gold*, χ. σκῆπτρον 1.15, cf. 246; μάχαιρα 18.598; θύραι Od.7.88; κλῖναι, κρητῆρες, Hdt.9.82,80; ἕστηκε.. Ἀλέξανδρος ὁ χ., of a statue, Id.8. 121; χρυσοῦς στάθητι Luc.*Pseudol.*15. 2. χρύσεια μέταλλα *gold-mines*, Th.4.105 (the only instance of χρύσειος in Att., cf. χρυσεῖον). 3. χρυσοῦς (sc. στατήρ), ὁ, *a gold coin*, = στατήρ, *IG*7. 303.98, al. (Oropus, iii B.C.), *IPE*1².32 *A* 13 (Olbia, iii B.C.), Lxx *Ge.* 24.22, Plu.*Per.*25 (in Pap., not a coin, but the equivalent of 20 silver drachmae, *PCair.Zen.*28.11 (iii B.C.), etc.); χρυσοῖ ἐπίσημοι Plb.4.56. 3, cf. Poll.9.53,59, Hsch. 4. χρύσεον, τό, *gold plaque*, *SIG*1122.7 (Selinus, v B.C.). II. *gold-coloured*, *golden-yellow*, ἔθειραι Il.8.42, 13. 24; χ. νέφη ib.523, etc.; ἀέρος κόμαι Pi.*Pae.*6.137; τῶν ᾠῶν τὰ χρυσᾶ the *yolks* of eggs, Ath.9.376d. III. metaph., *golden*, χρυσέη Ἀφροδίτη Il.3.64, Od.8.337; Μοῖσα Pi.*I.*8(7).5; σθένος ἀελίου χ. Id.*P.*4.144; ὦ χ. θύγατερ Διός S.*OT*188 (lyr.); Ἐλπίς ib.158 (lyr.); τιμή Id.*Ant.* 699; ὦ χρυσοῖ θεοί Ar.*Ra.*483; χ. ὑγίεια Pi.*P.*3.73; λογισμοῦ ἀγωγή Pl.*Lg.*645a; ἦθος Antiph.212.5; τὸ χ. ὀρνίθων γένος Id.175; χ. γένος ἀνθρώπων, of the *Golden* Age, Hes.*Op.*109, cf. Pl.*R.*468e, *Phdr.* 235e, *Cra.*397e. b. sts. used ironically, ἐγὼ δὲ ὁ χ. but I, *fine fellow that I am*.., Luc.*Laps.*1; Πλάτωνα χρυσοῦν (sc. Ἐπίκουρος ἐκάλει) D.L.10.8, cf. Menodot.ap.Gal.*Subf.Emp.*63. 2. *wealthy*, Palaeph. 31.4 (s. v. l.). [χρῡσέη, χρῡσέην, χρῡσέου, χρῡσέῳ, etc., in Hom. must be pronounced as disyll., as is fully proved by such passages as Il.1.15,374: but Lyric Poets sts. used ῠ in χρύσεος, Pi.*P.*3.73, 4.4,144, al., B.9.6, 15.2; so also Trag., but only in Lyr., not in Iambics or Anapaestics, S.*OT*157,188, *Ant.*103, E.*Med.*632,978, *IA* 1051, *IT*1253, *Tr.*856, *Ba.*372, *Heracl.*916, *HF*351,396, *El.*192; sts. also Epigrammatists, *AP*6.292.2 (Hedyl.), 7.233.1 (Apollonid.), 13. 18.4 (Parmeno), *APl.*4.96.8.]

**χρῡσεο-σάμβᾰλος**, ον, v. l. for sq. in cod. H (Jerusalem palimpsest) of E.*Or.*1468 (lyr.), cf. *Hermes* 64.424. **-σάνδᾰλος**, ον, *with sandals of gold*, ἴχνος χ. the step *of golden sandals*, E. l.c., *IA*1042 (lyr.). **-σκαπτρος**, Dor. for *-σκηπτρος, ὁ, *with golden sceptre*, epith. of Zeus, B.8.100. **-στέφᾰνος**, ον, f.l. for χρυσοστέφανος (q.v.). **-στολμος**, ον, *decked with gold*, δόμοι A.*Pers.*159 (troch.). **-στολος**, ον, = foreg., πέπλων χ. φάρος E.*HF*414 (lyr.). **-ταρσος**, ον, *with golden feet* or *wings*, αὖραι Orph.*A.* 340. **-τευκτος**, ον, = χρυσότευκτος (q.v.), Id.*H.*55.18. **-φεγγής**, ές, *with golden lustre*, Id.*Fr.*236.4.

**χρῡσ-εργής**, ές, *made of* or *with gold*, ἱμάτιον Tz.*H.*3.980. **-εργός**, όν, *making* or *producing gold*, Lyc.1352. **-εντική** (sc. τέχνη), ἡ, *goldsmith's art*, Eustr. in *EN*296.10. **-εψητής**, οῦ, ὁ, (ἕψω) *gold-melter*, Lat. *auricoctor*, *Gloss.* **-ήγορος**, ον, *of golden eloquence*, Epigr.ap.Geel *Catal.Mss.Lugd.Bat.*p.18 No.54. **-ηλάκᾰτος** [ᾰκ], Dor. **χρῡσᾱλ-**, ον, *with distaff of gold*, not (as Sch.) *with arrow of gold*, epith. of Artemis in Il.20.70, al., cf. B.10.38, S.*Tr.*637 (lyr.); of Amphitrite, the Nereids, and Leto, Pi.*O.*6.104, *N.*5.36, 6.36; of the Χάριτες, B.8.1. ⊛ **-ήλᾰτος**, ον, (ἐλαύνω III. 1) *of beaten gold*, A.*Th.*644, S.*OT*1268, E.*Ph.*62, Ar.*Pl.*9, Plu.*Demetr.*53; ἄνδρες Luc. *Sat.*8; Παρία πέτρα E.ap.Satyr.*Vit.Eur.Oxy.*1176*Fr.*38 ii 24. **-ήλεκτρος**, ὁ and ἡ, *gold-electrum*, *gold-amber*, Plin.*HN*37.127, Aët. 2.35. ⊛ **-ήνιος**, ον, (ἡνία) *with reins of gold*, epith. of Ares, Od.8. 285; of Artemis, Il.6.205; of Demeter, Pi.*Fr.*37; Dor. **χρυσάνιος** [ᾱ], of Aphrodite, S.*OC*693 (lyr.). **-ήρης**, ες, *furnished* or *decked with gold*, *golden*, οἶκοι E.*Ion* 157 (lyr.); Ἄρκτος στρέφουσ' οὐραῖα χρυσήρη πόλῳ ib.1154; ναῶν θριγκοί Id.*IT*129 (lyr.).

**χρῡσιαῖος**, α, ον, *priced in gold coin*, δεῖξεις D.L.4.38.

**χρῡσῐδάριον**, τό, = sq., Ar.*Fr.*90.

**χρῡσίδιον** [σῐ], τό, Dim. of χρυσίον, *a small piece of gold*, used in contempt, ἀργυρίδιον καὶ χ. τὸν πλοῦτον ἀποκαλοῦντες Isoc.13.4, cf. D.27.15; *a small sum of money*, Plu.*Cleom.*38. 2. Dim. of χρυσίς I, *IG*1².369.10 (pl.).

⊕ **χρῡσίζω**, *to be golden* or *like gold*, Dsc.1.15, Crito ap.Gal.12.446, Ps.-Callisth.3.21, Hdn.5.6.8, Ath.7.322a; τὸ χρυσίζον τοῦ ᾠοῦ the *yolk*, *Gp.*14.7.5. II. *abound in gold*, Arist.*Mir.*833ᵇ8.

**χρῡσικός**, ή, όν, *made in cash*: χρυσικά, τά, *cash* payments, *POxy.*136.13 (vi A.D.); χ. στέφανοι *PTeb.*60.102 (ii B.C.), al. II. = χρύσεος I. 2, μέταλλα Eupolem.ap.Alex.Polyh.*Fr.*18M.

⊕ **χρύσῐνος** [ῠ], η, ον, late form of χρύσεος, λυχνεῖα χ. Cumont *Fouilles de Doura-Europos* 372 No.13: as Subst., χρύσινος, ὁ, = χρυσοῦς I. 3, Alciphr.3.3, al., *IG*7.26 (Megara, v/vi A.D.), Lyd.*Mag.*3.27, al., Olymp.Hist.p.462D.

**χρῡσίον**, τό, Dim. of χρυσός, *a piece of gold*, generally, *gold*, Hdt.3.95,97, Pl.*Euthd.*288e, *R.*336e, al. 2. *anything made of gold, gold plate, ornaments of gold*, etc., ἄσημον Th.2.13: pl., D.27.10, 48.55, Men.*Sam.*167, 1 *Ep.Pet.*3.3, Plu.*Tim.*15. 3. esp. *gold coin, money*, E.*Cyc.*161; οὔτ' ἀργύριον οὔτε χρυσίον Ar.*Eq.*472, cf. *Pl.*808, *Ra.*720 (troch.), etc.; χ. Ἀττικόν *IG*2².1687.16; λῆρος πάντα πρὸς τὸ χ. Antiph.232.1; ἐγὼ δ' ὑπέλαβον χρησίμους εἶναι θεοὺς τἀργύριον καὶ τὸ χ. Men.537.4: but στατῆρας χρυσίου Eup.112; χρυσία *pieces of gold*, Pl.*R.*336e. 4. *gold thread*, Hp.*Art.*32. II. as a term of endearment, *my little treasure!* Ar.*Lys.*930, cf. *AP*11.232 (Callias Arg.). 2. = τὸ τῶν παιδίων αἰδοῖον, Hsch.

**χρῡσιοπλύσιον**, τό, f.l. for χρυσοπλ- (q.v.).

**Χρῡσίππειος**, ον, *of, belonging to Chrysippus*, διαλεκτική D.L.7.180; τὰ Χ. his writings, Arr.*Epict.*2.16.34. II. *Chrysippius*, a plant named from its discoverer, Plin.*HN*26.93.

**χρῡσίς**, ίδος, ἡ, *a vessel of gold, piece of gold plate*, Hermipp.37 (troch.), Pherecr.128, Ar.*Ach.*74, *Pax*425, *IG*1².268.111, al.; χρυσίδων βότρυες Lib.*Ep.*22.3; an Att. word, Ath.11.502a. II. *gold-broidered dress*, Luc.*Nigr.*11: pl., *gold-embroidered shoes*, Id.*DDeor.*2.2.

**χρῡσίσκηπτρον**, τό, = χαμαιλέων λευκός, Ps.-Dsc.3.8.

⊕ **χρῡσίτης** [ῑ], ου, ὁ, mostly in fem. **χρυσῖτις**, ιδος, *like gold, containing gold*, ψάμμος χρυσῖτις Hdt.3.102, Str.3.2.8; λίθος *IG*2².1424*a*.254; χ. σποδός a *yellow* powder used for the eyes, Hp.*Mul.*1.103; χ. γῆ Gal.12.184; χρυσῖτις alone, a form of λιθάργυρος, Dsc.5.87. II. ἡ χ. *gold-dust* or *ore*, Plu.2.526b. 2. *touchstone, lapis Lydius*, Poll.7.102. 3. = χρυσοκόμη, Dsc.4.55.

**χρῡσο-βάλᾰνος** [βᾰ], ἡ, = βάλανος μυρεψική, Gal.13.147,155. **-βᾰφής**, ές, *gold-embroidered*, Plu.*Demetr.*41; χ. ἄνακτες Simm.25.4. **-βέλεμνος**, ον, *with shafts, arrows of gold*, *AP*9.623 (Cyrus), Orac.ap.Lyd.*Mens.*3.10. **-βήρυλλος**, ὁ, *beryl with a tinge of gold colour*, Plin.*HN*37.76. **-βόστρῠχος**, ον, in Alchemy, *golden-tressed*, Olymp.Alch.p.95B. **-βωλος**, ον, *with soil of gold*, i.e. *containing gold*, γῆς λέπας E.*Rh.*921. **-γεως**, ων, (γῆ) *with soil of gold*: τὸ χρυσόγεων the *land of gold-ore*, Philostr.*VA*6.1:— **χρῡσόγειος**, ον, Suid. **-γλῠφος**, ον, gloss on χρυσοτόρευτος, Hsch., Suid. **-γλωσσος**, ον, *golden-tongued*, Tz.*H.*10.234. **-γονον**, τό, *black turnip, Bongardia Chrysogonum*, Dsc.4.56. **-γονος**, ον, *born* or *begotten of gold*, γενεά, i.e. the Persians, because (by the legend) they were descended from Perseus, who was begotten of Zeus in the form of a shower of gold, A.*Pers.*79 (lyr., Sch., -νόμου cod.M); of Perseus, Orph.*L.*551. **-γρᾰφής**, ές, *gold-embroidered*, ἐμβάδες Callix.2. **-γρᾰφία**, ἡ, *a writing with letters of gold*, Aristeas 176, *PMag.Leid.X.*34 B. **-δαίδαλτος**, ον, *decked with rich work of gold*, Ar.*Ec.*972 (lyr.), E.*IA*219 (lyr.). **-δακτύλιος** [ῠ], ον, *with ring of gold*, ἀνήρ *Ep.Jac.*2.2. 2. gloss on χρυσοκόλλητος, χ. σφραγίς *set in a gold ring*, Hsch. **-δέκτης**, ου, ὁ, *receiver of gold*, Epic.in *BKT*5(1)p.120 (vi A.D.).

**χρῡσό-δετος**, ον, also α, ον Alc.33: (δέω (A)):—*bound with gold, set in gold*, σφρηγίς Hdt.3.41. 2. *overlaid* or *enriched with gold*, ἐλεφαντίναν λάβαν τῶ ξίφεος χρυσοδέταν Alc. l.c.; χ. κέρας, of a lyre, S.*Fr.*244 (lyr.); χ. ἕρκεσι γυναικῶν, of the *golden* necklace with which Eriphyle was bribed, Id.*El.*838 (lyr.); περόναι χ. E.*Ph.*805 (lyr.): metaph., χ. σώματος ἀλκὴν *in golden armour*, Id.*Rh.*382 (anap.). **-δίνας** [ῑ], α, ὁ, *with golden eddies*, Πακτωλός B.3.44. ⊕ **-έθειρ**, ρος, ὁ, ἡ, *with golden hair*, Archil.121; voc. χρυσοέθειρε *IG*12(5).893.3 (Tenos, restored); fem. -έθειρα in Max.95. **-ειδής**, ές, *like gold*, γῆ Pl.*Phd.*110c; χρῶμα X.*Cyr.*7.1.2, cf. Thphr.*HP*6.3.5; μέλι Arist.*HA*627ᵃ2; κόμη Plu.2.771b; of a kind of jaundice, Hp.ap.Herod.Med(?). in *Rh.Mus.*49.554. **-είμων**, ον, gen. ονος, *with robe of gold*, ἄγαλμα *IG*4.558.14 (Argos, ii B.C.), cf. Eust.693.48. **-έλικτος**, ον, *twined with gold*, Paul.Sil.*Ambo*255. **-ζῠγος**, ον, *with yoke of gold*, *h.Hom.*31.15, X.*Cyr.*8.3.12. **-ζύμιον** [ζῠ], or **-ζώμιον**, τό, in Alchemy, *ferment of gold*, Zos.Alch. pp.160B. (-ζύμ-), 247B. (-ζώμ-). ⊕ **-ζωνος**, ον, *with girdle of gold*, Hes.*Fr.*278.4. **-ηλος**, ον, *with nails* or *studs of gold*, Eust.95.6. **-θριξ**, τρῐχος, ὁ, ἡ, *golden-veined*, λᾶε Orph.*L.*292. **-θρονος**, ον, *with throne of gold*, epith. of Hera, Artemis and Eos, Il.1.611, al.; of Cyrene, Pi.*P.*4.260; of Isis, *Hymn.Is.*7:—poet. word (v. Ar.*Av.*950 (lyr.)), used by Jul.*Caes.*307d. **-θώραξ**, ᾱκος, ὁ, ἡ, *with breastplate of gold*, Iamb. post Polem.p.49 Hinck, Tz.*H.*1.993. **-καλλίας**, ου, ὁ, = ἀνθεμίς, cj. in Dsc.3.137. 2. = παρθένιον, cj. in Ps.-Dsc.3.138. **-κάνθᾰρος**, ὁ, *chafer* (cf. χρυσομηλολόνθιον), Sch.Ar.*Nu.*761; -κάνθαροι, = Lat. *bulli* (dub. sens.), *Gloss.*; also **-κανθαρίς**, Jo.Sic. in *AB*1432. **-κανθος**, in Lat. form. *crisocantes* (or *-is*), expld. as *peristola* or *periscola*, *Gloss.* **-κάρηνος** [ᾰ], ον, Dor. **-ᾱνος**, *with head of gold*, E.*HF*375 (lyr.). ⊕ **-καρπος**, ον, *with golden fruit*: as Subst., *ivy*, = κισσός, Ps.-Dsc.2.179, Plin.*HN*16.147. ⊕ **-κέλευθος**, ον, *travelling on a golden path*, *PMag.Berol.*2.91.

**χρῡσόκερως**, ωτος, ὁ, ἡ, and **-ρως**, ων, gen. -ω (also Dor. acc. in *SIG*398.24 (Cos, iii B.C.)):—*with horns of gold*, ἔλαφος Pi.*O.*3.29, E.*Hel.*382 (lyr., Elmsl. χρυσοκέρατα); as epith. of Pan, Cratin.321 (lyr.); of the moon, *AP*5.15 (Marc.Arg.). II. *with gilded horns*, like a victim ready to be sacrificed, τρίττοιαν βόαρχον -κερων *IG*1².76.37, cf. Aeschin.3.164, Pl.*Alc.*2.149c, *SIG* l.c., Porph.*Abst.*2.15.

**χρῡσο-κέφᾰλος**, ον, *with golden head*, epith. of a fish, Phryn.Com.50. **-κίθᾰρις** [κῐ], *with golden lyre*, prob. in Tim.*Pers.*215 (χρυσεο- Pap.), cf. Hsch. s.v. χρυσάωρ; also **-κίθᾰρος**, Suid. s.v. χρυσάορον. **-κίτρινος**, η, ον, *of a pale golden hue*, Porph. *in Ptol.*199. **-κλυστος**, ον, *washed with gold*, i.e. *gilded*, θηρικλείων -κλύστων ζεῦγος Ister 38; φιάλη *IG*11(2).161 *B*13 (Delos, iii B.C.); ποτήριον Phleg.*Fr.*36.1 J., cf. Nicom.Com.4 (-κλαῦστα (sic) codd.Ath.). **-κογχύλιον** [χῠ], τό, *a gold shell*, i.e. *rolled gold*, Ps.-Democr.p.44 B. **-κοκκος**, ον, *with gold seeds* or *grains*, Ps.-Apul.*Herb.*130. ⊕ **-κόλλα**, ἡ, *gold-solder, malachite, basic copper carbonate*, Arist.*Mir.*834ᵇ20, Thphr.*Lap.*26,40, Dsc.5.74,89, Plin.*HN*33.86. II. *a dish of linseed and honey*, Alcm.74 B. **-κολλος**, ον, *soldered* or *inlaid with gold*, ἐκπώματα S.*Fr.*378; κώπη E.*Fr.*587; also **-κόλλητος** δίφρος Id.*Ph.*2, cf. Antiph.106.2,237, Luc.*Ind.*29; ἅρματα Jul.*Or.*2.50d; cf. χρυσοδακτύλιος.

**χρῡσοκομ-έω**, *have golden hair*, Philostr.*Ep.*55. **-η**, ἡ, *immortelle, Helichrysum orientale*, Dsc.4.55, Plin.*HN*21.50, 148. **-ης**, ου, Dor. **-κόμας**, α, ὁ, *golden-haired*, epith. of Dionysus, Hes.*Th.*947; of Eros, Anacr.14, E.*IA*548 (lyr.); of Apollo, Tyrt.3.4, B.4.2, E.*Supp.*975 (lyr.), Ar.*Av.*217 (anap.); ὁ Χ., abs. for Apollo, Pi.*O.*6.41, 7.32, E.*Tr.*254 (lyr.). II. *with golden ornaments in the hair*, Luc.*Gall.*13. ⊕ **-ος**, ον, *golden-haired*, *AP*6.264 (Mnasalc.); of the plumage of birds, χ. πτέρα Hdt.2.73.

**χρῡσο-κόραλλος**, ἡ, '*gold-coral*', name of several metals, Ps.-Democr.p.44 B. **-κόρυμβος**, ον, *with golden clusters*, κισσός Dsc.*Eup.*1.69. **-κοσμήτης**, ου, ὁ, *decorator with gold*, Vett.Val.3.24, Rhetor. in *Cat.Cod.Astr.*8(4).136 (v.l.). **-κρότᾰλος**, ον, *tinkling with gold*, σπατάλη cj. in *AP*5.270 (Maced.). **-λᾰβής**, ές, *with haft of gold*, ἐγχειρίδιον Men.20. ⊕ **-λαμπίς**, ίδος, ἡ, *glow-worm*, Phryn.*PS* p.126 B. II. a precious stone, Plin.*HN*37.156. **-λάχᾰνον** [λᾰ], τό, = ἀνδράφαξυς, Ps.-Dsc.2.119, *Gp.*12.1.1, Lyd.*Mens.*4.42. ⊕ **-λῐθος**, ὁ, *topaz*, LXX *Ex.*28.20, 36.20 (39.13), D.S.2.52, *Apoc.*21.20, Plin.*HN*37.126, Orph.*L.*298,300, *PLond.*3.928.15 (iii A.D.). **-λῐνον**, τό, *gold thread, gold wire*, Paul.Aeg.6.92. **-λοβος**, ον, *decked with gold ear-rings*, οὔατα, as Pors. in Epigr.ap.Ath.8.343f (Juba), for χρυσοβόλοις. **-λογέω**, *speak of gold*, Luc.*Gall.*6. **-λόγος**, ον, *gathering gold*, *Gloss.* **-λογχος**, ον, *with spear of gold*, Παλλάς E.*Ion*9, cf. Ar.*Th.*318 (lyr.).

**χρύσολον**, τό, dub. sens. in Zos.Alch.p.247 B. (s. v.l.).

**χρῡσο-λοπος**, ον, *with golden scales*, gloss. on sq., Hsch. **-λοφος**, ον, *with golden crest*, B.*Scol.Oxy.*2081(*e*)*Fr.*5.7; δράκοντες Hsch.; fem. χρυσολόφα in Ar.*Lys.*344 (lyr.) as epith. of Athena. ⊕ **-λύρης** [λῠ], ου, Dor. **-λύρας**, α, ὁ, *with lyre of gold*, of Apollo, Pi.*Pae.*5.41, Ar.*Th.*315 (lyr.). *Supp.Epigr.*4.467.20 (Branchidae, iii A.D.), Orph.*H.*34.3 (voc. -λύρη); of Orpheus, Arist.*Pepl.*48, *AP*7.617. ⊕ **-μαλλος**, ον, *with golden wool* or *fleece*, κῶας Pherecyd.105 J.; ἀρνὸς τέρας E.*Or.*998 (lyr.): metaph., πρόβατον χ., of a rich fool, Diog.ap.D.L.6.47. ⊕ **-μᾰνής**, ές, *mad after gold*, σπατάλη *AP*5.301.2 (Agath.): hence **-μᾰνέω**, Suid.; **-μᾰνία**, ἡ, Tz.*H.*3.301 (pl.). **-μηλολόνθιον**, τό, Dim. as if from *χρυσομηλολόνθη, *a little golden beetle* or *cockchafer*, as a term of endearment, Ar.*V.*1341. **-μηλον**, τό, = κυδώνιον, Plin.*HN*15.37, Alex.Trall.1.16. **-μήτρις**, ιδος, ἡ, *goldfinch, Fringilla carduelis*, Arist.*HA*592ᵇ30. **-μίτρης**, ου, Dor. **-μίτρας**, α, ὁ, *with girdle* or *headband of gold*, epith. of Dionysus, S.*OT*209 (lyr.); pecul. fem. -μίτρη, of Phoebe, Opp.*C.*2.2. 2. *gold-bound*, πίνακες Hippoloch.ap.Ath.4.130b. **-μορφος**, ον, *in the likeness of gold*, of Zeus descending to Danaë, S.*Fr.*[1127.2].

**χρῡσ-όμφᾰλος**, ον, *with golden* or *gilded boss*, φιάλη ἀργυρᾶ χ. *IG*1².313.65, 314.72, 2².1544.29, cf. *Chron.Lind.*B.48, Poll.6.98.

**χρῡσό-νημα**, ατος, τό, *gold thread, gold wire*, Paul.Aeg.6.92. **-νήστρια**, ἡ, fem. of sq., Lat. *aurinetrix*, *Gloss.* **-νήτης**, ου, ὁ, *spinner of gold thread*, Vett.Val.3.24 (pl.). ⊕ **-νομος**, ον, *feeding in gold, very rich*, v.l. for χρυσόγονος (q.v.). 2. perh. = χρυσοῦς, ποτήρια *PBaden* 54.4 (v A.D.). II. parox. -νόμος, ὁ, *distributor of gold*, χ. τῶν λαμπαδιστῶν *SIG*1068.11 (Patmos, iii/ii B.C.). **-νωτος**, ον, *with golden back* or *surface*; χ. ἡνία a rein *studded with gold*, S.*Aj.*847. **-ξῐφος**, ον, *with sword of gold*, gloss on χρυσάορος, Cyr., *Lex.Havn.* in Schmidt Hsch. s.v. χρυσάορον. **-ξῠλον**, τό, *gold-wood*, = θάψος, Sch.Ar.*V.*1404; = σκυθάριον, Sch.Theoc.2.88. **-πᾰγής**, ές, *built of gold*, δώματα *IG*4.620.14 (Argos). **-πάρῠφος**, ον, *with border* or *hem of gold*, Plu.*Demetr.*41. ⊕ **-παστος**, ον, also α, ον Alc.*Fr.*90 Lobel: (πάσσω):—*shot with gold*, κυνία l.c.; χ. τιήρης a turban *of gold tissue*, Hdt.8.120; τὰ χ. ἔσθλα (Wilamowitz for ἐσθλά) A.*Ag.*776 (lyr.); χ. κόσμος D.50.34; ταῖς ξυστίσιν ταῖς χ. Eub.134; μίτρα Duris 14J.; ἐσθής Luc.*Ind.*8; opp. χρυσήλατος, Iamb.post Polem.p.50 Hinck. **-πατρος**, ον, *sprung of a golden father*, epith. of Perseus (cf. χρυσόγονος), Lyc.838: also

**-πάτωρ** [ᾰ], ορος, ὁ, Nonn.*D*.47.471. **-πέδῖλος**, ον, *gold-sandalled*, epith. of Hera, Od.11.604, Hes.*Th*.454; of Eos, Sapph.18. **-πε-πλος**, ον, *with robe of gold*, κούρα Anacr.76; Μναμοσύνα Pi.*I*.6(5).75; Ἥρη B.18.22. **-πέτᾰλος**, ον, *covered with gold plaques*, Lat. *bracteolatus*, χιτών Lyd.*Mag*.2.4. **-πήληξ**, ηκος, ὁ, ἡ, *with helm of gold*, of Ares, A.*Th*.106 (lyr.); χ. στάχυς σπαρτῶν, of the Sparti at Thebes, E.*Ph*.939. **-πήνιτος** (leg. -ητος), ον, *brocaded with gold*, χιτών Cyr. **-πηχυς**, Dor. **-πᾶχυς**, υ, *with golden arms*, Ἀώς B.5.40. **-πλευρος**, ὁ, = σάλπη, *Gloss.* **-πλόκᾰμος**, ον, *golden-haired*, *h.Ap*.205, Tim.*Pers*.138.

**χρύσ-οπλος** [ῠ], ον, *with golden armour*, Tz.*H*.10.435.

**χρῡσο-πλύσιον** [ῠ], τό, *gold-wash*, *placer*, where gold is washed from the river-sand, Str.3.2.8 (pl.); wrongly **χρυσιοπλ-**, Id.5.1.8. **-ποιία**, ἡ, *the making of gold*, Syn.Alch.p.61 B, Zos.Alch.p.220 B. **-ποίκῖλος**, ον, *gold-embroidered*, Callix.2. **-ποίκιλτος**, ον, = foreg., *IG*11(2).287*B*72 (Delos, iii B.C.), *Inscr.Délos* 380.63 (ii B.C.), D.S.18.26. ⊛ **-ποιός**, ὁ, *goldsmith*, Luc.*Cont*.12. **-ποκος**, ον, *with fleece of gold*, Nonn.*D*.10.102. **-πολις**, εως, ἡ, *golden city*, of Hierapolis, *Epigr.Gr*.1074. II. name of a fabulous plant, Aristaenet.1.10, Ps.-Plu.*Fluv*.7.4. **-πους**, ὁ, ἡ, neut. -πουν, gen. -ποδος, *gold-footed*, φορεῖα Plb.30.25.18; κλίνη Heraclid.Cum. 2. **-πράσιος** [ᾰ] λίθος, ὁ, = sq., *PHolm*.11.10; -ίου (perh. neut.) ποίησις ib.5. **-πρᾰσος**, ὁ, *chrysoprase*, a precious stone *of golden-green colour*, *Apoc*.21.20, cf. Plin.*HN*37.113. **-πρεπώδης**, ες, *looking like gold*, Tz.*H*.5.389 (Comp.). **-πρόσωπος**, ον, *golden-faced*, epith. of the sun, *PMag.Par*.2.133. **-πρυμνος**, ον, *with gilded poop*, Plu.*Ant*.26, App.*Praef*.10. **-πρῳρος**, ον, *with gilded prow*, ἀκάτιον Philostr.*Im*.1.12.

**χρύσοπτα**, τά, = αἱ αἰθάλαι αἱ ξανθαί acc. to *Gloss*.ap.Steph.*Thes.* et Ducange; χ. πάντα ποιεῖ (sc. ὁ ἐτήσιος λίθος) Maria ap.Olymp. Alch.p.93 B., cf. Zos.Alch.p.120 B.

⊛ **χρῡσο-πτερος**, ον, *with wings of gold*, of Iris, Il.8.398, 11.185, *h.Cer*.314; Ἔρως Ar.*Av*.1738 (lyr.); παῖδες Ἀφροδίτης Aristaenet.2.10. II. χρυσόπτερον, τό, a gem similar to χρυσόπρασος, Xenocr. *Lap*.90, Plin.*HN*37.109. 2. a bird, Cyran.44. ⊛ **-πτέρῠγος**, ον, = foreg., Μοῦσαι Him.*Or*.14.37. **-πώλης**, ου, ὁ, *dealer in gold*, Sch.Ar.*Pl*.884. **-ραγές**· χρυσοβαφές, Hsch. (cf. ῥέζω (B), ῥο-γεύς). **-ρᾰνίς**, ίδος, ἡ, *golden ewer*, Id. **-ρᾰπις**, ὁ, poet. for χρυσόρραπις, Pi.*P*.4.178.

⊛ **χρῡσορόης**, ου, ὁ, poet. for χρυσορρόης, Τμῶλος E.*Ba*.154 (lyr.): of Zeus descending in gold, Hedyl.ap.Ath.8.345a.

⊛ **χρῡσ-όροφος**, ον, *with golden roof* or *ceiling*, Philox.14, Ph.1.666, Luc.*Cyn*.9; also **-ώροφος**, σκηνή Plu.2.329d.

**χρῡσό-ρραβδος**, ον, *with golden wand*, Hdn.*Epim*.154 (with single ρ). **-ρρᾰγής**, ές, (ῥήγνυμι) ἔρνος *a golden* branch *plucked off*, Poet.ap.Hsch. **-ρρᾰπις**, ιδος, ὁ, ἡ, *with wand of gold*, epith. of Hermes, Od.5.87, 10.277, *h.Merc*.539; cf. χρυσόραπις.

**χρυσορρήμων**, ον, gen. ονος, *of golden speech*, Cyr. **-ρρόης**, ου, Dor. -ρρόας, ὁ, *streaming with gold*, Νεῖλος *Supp.Epigr*.8.549.17 (Egypt, Hymn to Isis), Ath.5.203c; cf. χρυσορόης. **-ρρῠτος**, ον, *gold-streaming*, A.*Pr*.805; νάματα *Supp.Epigr*.4.467.2 (Didyma, iii A.D.); cf. χρυσόρυτος.

**χρῡσ-ορύκτης**, ου, ὁ, *gold-digger*, *Gloss.*

**χρῡσόρῠτος**, ον, = χρυσόρρυτος, γοναί, of Perseus the son of Danaë, S.*Ant*.950 (lyr.).

⊛ **χρῡσός**, ὁ, *gold*, τιμῆς Il.18.475, etc.; coupled with other precious things, e.g. χαλκός, σίδηρος, 6.48; ἐσθής, Od.5.38; χρυσὸν κέρασιν περιχεύας (of a victim) Il.10.294 = Od.3.384, cf. 437; ὡς δ' ὅτε τις χρυσὸν περιχεύεται ἀργύρῳ 6.232; χ. δαμασίφρων Pi.*O*.13.78; κοῖλος ἄργυρος καὶ χ. silver and *gold* plate, Theopomp.Hist. 283a, cf. Luc.*Nav*.20; λευκὸς χ. white *gold*, i.e. gold alloyed with silver, opp. χ. ἄπεφθος refined *gold*, Hdt.1.50; χ. ἑψόμενος Pi.*N*.4.82; χρυσὸν καθαίρειν Pl.*Plt*.303d; βασανίζειν ἐν πυρί Id.*R*.413e. 2. *gold*, to express anything made of gold, e.g. *golden* armour or raiment, χρυσὸν.. ἔδυνε περὶ χροΐ, of Zeus, Il.8.43; of Poseidon, 13.25; τὸ ἐμὸν σῶμα μήτε ἐν χ. θῆτε.. X.*Cyr*.8.7.25; ἀραρότως σύνδεσμα χρυσὸς (a gold crown) εἶχε E.*Med*.1193; ἐν χρυσῷ πίνειν Luc.*Merc. Cond*.26. 3. freq. used by Poets to denote *anything dear* or *precious*, ταῦτα μὲν.. κρείσσονα χρυσοῦ.. φωνεῖς A.*Ch*.372 (anap.); ὁ χ. ἥσσον κτῆμα τοῦ κλάειν ἂν ἦν S.*Fr*.557; ὡς χρυσὸς αὐτῷ τἀμὰ.. κακὰ δόξει ποτ' εἶναι E.*Tr*.432, cf. D.H.*Rh*.9.4; cf. Pi.*O*.1.1, 3.42, Plu.*Sert*. 5: metaph. also, χρυσὸς ἐπῶν golden words, Ar.*Pl*.268; χρυσῷ πάττειν τινά Id.*Nu*.912 (anap.); ὕσαι χρυσόν τινι Pi.*O*.7.50. [ῡ in χρυσός and all derivs., though Lyric Poets sts. made υ short in the Adj. χρύσεος (q.v.); once we have χρῠσός, Pi.*N*.7.78.] (Borrowed from Semitic, cf. Hebr. *chārūts*, Assyr. *ḫurāšu* 'gold', Aram. *hara* 'yellow'.)

**χρῡσο-σανδᾰλαιμοποτιχθονία**, ἡ, *goddess of the lower world wearing golden sandals and drinking blood*, epith. of Hecate, Tab. Defix. in *Rh.Mus*.55.250 (-ατμο- lapis). **-σάνδᾰλος**, ον, *golden-sandalled*, Porph.ap.Eus.*PE*3.11. **-σάπφειρος**, ἡ, *gold-sapphire*, Alex.Trall.2.1. **-σημος**, ον, *embroidered with gold*, χιτών, of the Roman *tunica palmata*, D.H.3.61, cf. Alex.Aphr. *in Top*.262.1. **-σπερμον**, τό, = ἀείζωον τὸ μέγα, Ps.-Dsc.4.88 (χρυσί- codd.). 2. = χρυσόγονον, ib.56, *PMag.Leid.V*.13.30. **-σπόρος**, ον, *sowing gold*, Nonn.*D*.10.145. **-σταθμος**, ον, *worth its weight in gold*, ἰχθύων ποικιλία Lyd.*Mag*.3.62. **-στεγος**, ον, *with roof of gold*, Him.*Or*.18.3. **-στέπτωρ**, ορος, ὁ, ἡ, = sq., Man.4.39. **-στέ-φᾰνος**, ον, *gold-crowned*, Φοίβη Hes.*Th*.136; κόρα E.*Ion* 1085 (lyr., χρυσεο- codd.); epith. of Hebe, Hes.*Th*.17, Pi.*O*.6.57; of Aphrodite, *h.Hom*.6.1, Sapph 9; χ. ἄεθλα *in which the prize was a crown of gold*, Pi.*O*.8.1. **-στεφής**, ές, = foreg., γέρας meed *of a golden crown*, S. *Ichn*.45. cf. *PMag.Par*.1.2271; *winner of a golden crown*. *PLond*.3.1243.4 (iii A.D.). **-στήμων**, ον, gen. ονος, *woven with gold*, χιτῶνες Lyd.*Mag*.3.64. **-στομος**, ον, *of golden mouth*, i.e. *dropping words of gold*, epith. of orators, as Dio Chrysostom, Men.Rh.p.390 S., cf. Suid. s.v. Ἰωάννης Ἀντιοχεύς. **-στροφος**, ον, *made of twisted gold*, ἀγκύλαι S.*OT*203 (lyr.). **-σωρος**, ον, *with heaps of gold*, Tz.*H*.12.332. **-τέκτων**, ονος, ὁ, *goldsmith*, *AP*6.92 (Phil.), Luc.*Lex*.9.

**χρῡσότερος**, α, ον, a Comp. formed from χρυσός (3), *more golden*, χρύσω χρυσοτέρα Sapph.122; αὐτῆς χρυσοτέρη Κύπριδος *IG*14.1892.

**χρῡσό-τευκτος**, ον, *wrought of gold*, A.*Th*.660, *Fr*.184, E.*Ph*.220 (lyr.), Eub.20.4. dub. in E.*Med*.984 (lyr., fort. legit Sch.). **-τευ-χής**, ές, *with golden armour*, Id.*Rh*.340. **-τόκος**, ον, *laying golden eggs*, ὄρνις Aesop.343. **-τοξος**, ον, *with bow of gold*, of Apollo, Pi.*O*.14.10, Isyll.48. **-τόρευτος**, ον, *embossed with gold*, Lxx *Ex*.25.17(18); also **-τόρνευτος**, κρατήρ Ps.-Callisth.3.28. **-τρῐαίνης**, ου, ὁ, = sq., cj. in Arion l.2. **-τρίαινος** [ῐ], ον, *with trident of gold*, of Poseidon, Arion l. 2, Ar.*Eq*.559 (lyr.), *IG*1².706.

⊛ **χρῡσότῠπος**, ον, *wrought of gold*, κρᾶνος E.*El*.470 (lyr.); φιάλη Critias 2.8 D.

**χρῡσ-ούᾰτος**, ον, *with ears* or *handles of gold*, τρίπους Hom.*Fr*.17.

**χρῡσοῡποδέκτης**, ου, ὁ, = χρυσυποδέκτης, *PFlor*.11.5 (vi A.D.).

**χρῡσουργ-εῖον**, τό, *gold-mine*, Str.4.6.7. **-έω**, *to be a χρυσ-ουργός*, Poll.7.97. ⊛ **-ός**, ὁ, *goldsmith*, Lxx *Wi*.15.9, Poll. l. c.

**χρῡσοῦς**, ῆ, οῦν, Att. contr. for χρύσεος (q.v.).

**χρῡσο-ϋφής** [ῠ], ές, *interwoven with gold*, χιτῶνες Callix.2, Hdn. 5.3.6, cf. Chares 4 J.; τήβεννα Ptol.Euerg.3 J.; μίτραι D.S.5.46. **-φάεννος** [ᾰ], ον, = sq., πτέρυγες Anacr.25. ⊛ **-φᾰής**, ές, Boeot. χρουσο- Corinn.*Supp*.1.20:—*gold-shining*, κάλπιδες l. c.; Ἅλιος E.*Hec*.636 (lyr.); Ἔρως Id.*Hipp*.1275 (lyr.); στέφανος Epigr. ap.Plu.*Flam*.12; also χρυσοφάη θεράπαιναν Ἀφροδίτας Sapph. 57 A. **-φάλᾰρος** [φᾰ], ον, *with trappings of gold*, E.*Tr*.520 (lyr., cj. for χρυσεο-), Plb.30.25.6, D.S.31.18, App.*Pun*.32. **-φᾰνής**, ές, *shining like gold*, Dsc.5.100, Corn.*ND*17: hence Subst. **-φάνεια**, ἡ, Eust.991.22. **-φαντος**, ον, = χρυσοφανής, πλοῦτος S.*Ichn*. 156. **-φάσγᾰνος**, ον, *with sword of gold*, Sch.D Il.5.509. **-φεγ-γής**, ές, *gold-beaming*, σέλας A.*Ag*.288.

**χρῡσοφορ-έω**, *wear golden ornaments* or *apparel*, Hdt.1.82, Euph. 38, Sotad.9.4, Arist.*Oec*.1349ᵃ24, Chor.32.70 p.360 F.-R.; διά τινα ἀρχὴν ἢ ἱερωσύνην Artem.2.9, cf. 1.77; esp. of priests, δεδόχθαι τοὺς ἱερεῖς -φορεῖν τοῖς θεοῖς *SIG*704*E*31 (Delph., ii B.C.); οἱ -φοροῦντες τῇ θεῷ ἱερεῖς *BMus.Inscr*.4.481*.437 (Ephes., ii A.D.); also [ἰχθὺς] χρυ-σοφορέων *wearing a gold ornament*, Luc.*Syr.D*.45; *wear a gold ring*, App.*Pun*.104. II. *pay gold as a tax*, D.S.4.83. III. *carry gold*, of streams, App.*Mith*.103. **-ητός**, ή, όν, *borne about by gold*, Man.5.309. **-ία**, ἡ, *wearing of golden ornaments*, Str.17.3.7: pl., D.Chr.2.51, Vett.Val.3.17. 2. *right to wear gold ornaments*, *SIG*704*H*26 (Delph., ii B.C.); χ. μετὰ πορφύρας *IG*4.606.16 (Argos). 3. esp. = Lat. *jus anuli aurei*, *IG*5(1).1432.37 (Messene, i B.C./i A.D., cf. l.12), 2².4193.14 (i A.D.).

⊛ **χρῡσοφόρος**, ον, *wearing gold*, *golden ornaments* or *apparel*, Μῆδοι Simon.90; παρθένοι Lycophronid.1, cf. Hdt.4.104; δειρή E.*Hec*. 152 (anap.). b. epith. of Ὁμόνοια, *BMus.Inscr*.4.481*.471 (Ephes., ii A.D.). 2. as a priestly title (cf. χρυσοφορέω 1), συνέδριον χρυσο-φόρων *Ephes*.2 No.83c; χ. στρατηγός *BCH*28.81 (Tralles); χ. alone, *CIG*2929 (ibid.). 3. *carrying gold*, ἡμίονος App.*Mith*.82. 4. *producing gold*, περὶ χ. γῆς, title of work by Teucer Cyzic.ap. Suid. s.v. Τεῦκρος. II. χρυσοφόρον, τό, = ἤλεκτρον 1, Dsc.1.83.

**χρῡσ-οφρῦς** [χρῡ], υος, ὁ, a sea-fish *with a golden spot over each eye*, *gilt-head*, *Sparus aurata*, Epich.51, Eup.150, Archipp.18, Arist. *HA*598ᵃ10, *PSI*7.862.6 (iii B.C.), Ptol.Euerg.1 J.; written **χρύσο-φος** in Cyran.44, *Gloss.*

**χρῡσο-φύλαξ** [ῠ], ᾰκος, ὁ, *gold-keeper*, of gryphons, Hdt.4.13, 27; σωρευτὰς χρημάτων καὶ χ. Rhetor. in *Cat.Cod.Astr*.8(4).150; *treasurer*, θεοῦ E.*Ion* 54. 2. *keeping money*, θύλακος Plu.*Arist*.24. **-χαίτης**, ου, poet. **-χαίτᾱ**, ὁ, *golden-haired*, of Apollo, Pi.*P*.2.16; Dor. nom. **-τᾱς**, Limen.4; of Eros, *Anacreont*.41.12. **-χάλῑνος** [ᾰ], ον, *with gold-studded bridle*, ἵπποι Hdt.9.20, X.*Cyr*.1.3.3, etc.; χ. πάταγον ψαλίων Ar.*Pax* 155 (anap.). **-χαλκος**, ὁ, = *aurochalcum* (sic), *Gloss.* **-χειρ**, χειρος, ὁ, ἡ, *with gold on the hands*, i.e. *with gold rings*, Luc.*Tim*.20. **-χελυς**, υ, *with golden lyre*, Παιάν *Epigr.Gr*.1023 (Nubia). **-χίτων** [ῑ], ωνος, ὁ, ἡ, *in coat of gold*, *gold-robed*, Θῆβα Pi.*Fr*.195; Λυδοί Pisand.ap.Lyd.*Mag*.3.64; *with rind of gold*, ἐλάη *AP*6.102 (Phil.).

**χρῡσοχο-εῖον**, τό, *the shop of a* χρυσοχόος, Test.ap.D.21.22, Plb. 26.1.2, Zeno *Stoic*.1.58. **-έω**, *follow the trade of goldsmith*, Ar. *Pl*.164, X.*Oec*.18.9. II. *smelt ore in order to extract gold* from it: hence prov. of those who *fail in any speculation*, as the Athenians in their attempts to extract gold from their silver-ores, Pl.*R*.450b, cf. Din.*Fr*.6.13, Harp. **-ης**, ου, Dor. **-ᾱς**, α, ὁ, = χρυσοχόος, *Dialex*.7.3 (in acc. pl. -ας). **-ῐκός**, ή, όν, *of* or *for a goldsmith* or *gold-smelter*, τὸ χ. πῦρ Arist.*Spir*.485ᵃ34; ἐργάζεσθαι χ. τέχνην follow the trade *of a goldsmith*, Test.ap.D.21.22, cf. Poll.7.102; ἄχυρα χ. *goldsmith's* dross, *PHolm*.5.7, cf. *PLeid.X*.33 B. 2. **-κή**, ἡ, *tax paid by goldsmiths*, *PPetr*.2 p.141 (iii B.C.). ⊛ **-ος** (parox.), ὁ, (χέω) *one who melts* or *casts gold*; of *one who gilds the horns* of a sacrificial victim, Od.3.425. 2. *goldsmith*, Ar.*Lys*.408, D.21.16,

Plu.2.658d; usually uncontracted in Att., *IG*1$^2$.374.103, 2$^2$.1558.56, but **-χοῦς** ib.1$^2$.347.40, and so later, *PStrassb.*92.4 (iii B.C.), Baillet *Inscr.Gr. et Lat.des tombeaux des rois* 1076, *Ostr.Bodl.* i 304 (ii B.C.).
⊛ **χρῡσό-χροος**, ον, heterocl. acc. -χρόα, *gold-coloured*, *AP*9.525. **-ψέλια**, τά, = περισκελίδες, *Gloss.* (*crisobsella* cod.).

**χρῡσόω**, fut. -ώσω Lxx *Ex.*26.37:—*make golden, gild*, *IG*1$^2$.374.29, D.S.1.23, Luc.*Ind.*15, *Dialex.*2.13, *IGRom.*4.1431.16 (Smyrna), Aët.1.106; χρυσίῳ χ. τι Lxx l.c., al.:—Pass., χ. παχέϊ κάρτα χρυσῷ Hdt.2.132; Παλλαδίων χρυσουμένων Ar.*Ach.*547; τῶν.. κρανίων κεχρυσωμένων Pl.*Euthd.*299e; perh. of *gilding* the horns of victims, *Supp.Epigr.*6.629,630 (Pisidia).

**Χρυστουμῖνος**, ἡ (sc. ἄπιος A), = *Crustuminus, Crustumerian pear* (cf. Plin.*HN*23.115), *PLond.*3.964.17 (iii A.D.).
⊛ **χρῡσ-υποδέκτης**, ου, ὁ, *receiver* or *collector of* taxes in *gold*, *Stud.Pal.* 8.1111.5 (vi A.D.), *Gloss.*, etc.; in papyri also **χρυσουποδέκτης**, e.g. *PFlor.*11.5 (vi A.D.). **-ωμα**, ατος, τό, *that which is made of gold, wrought gold*, E.*Ion* 1030,1430; χρυσώματα *gold plate*, Lys.*Fr.*56, *OGI*214.26 (Didyma, iii B.C.), Plb.30.25.16. **-ωμᾰτοθήκη**, ἡ, *plate-chest*, Callix.2. **-ών**, ῶνος, ὁ, *treasure*, *PLips.*102.7 (iv A.D.). **-ωνέω**, *buy* or *change gold*, Isoc.17.40, *IG*2$^2$.1493(*Phil. Wochenschr.*48.783). **-ώνης**, ου, ὁ, *financial officer* in Egypt, *PBremen* 83 iii 4 (iv A.D.), *PLips.*62 i 2, al. (iv A.D.), etc. **-ώνητος**, ον, *bought for gold*, of slaves, Callistr.Hist.10. ⊛ **-ῶπις**, ιδος, ἡ, pecul. fem. of sq., of Leto, Ar.*Th.*321 (lyr.); of fish, χρυσώπιδες ἰχθύες ἐλλοί Titanomach.*Fr.*4 (with masc. Subst.). **-ωπός**, όν, (ὤψ) *with golden eyes* or *face, beaming like gold*, of the sun, E.*El.*740 (lyr.), cf. Corn.*ND*32; αἰθήρ S.*Fr.*[1128]. 2. *gold-coloured*, Plu.*Sull.*6; μάργαρος Ael.*NA*15.8 (Comp.). II. a fish, = χρύσοφρυς, Plu.2.977f.
⊛ **χρῡσώρυφος**, ον, perh. an error for χρυσωρύχος, ἔργα, i.e. *gold-mines*, *IGRom.*4.608 (Phrygia).

**χρῡσωρῠχ-εῖον**, τό, *gold-mine*, Str.3.2.8; also **-ιον**, τό, Agatharch.24. 2. *book on gold-mining*, Olymp.Alch.p.87B. **-έω**, *mine for gold*, Ael.*NA*4.27 codd. (χρυσοχοεῖν Gesner). **-ίτης** [ῑ], ου, ὁ, *gold-extractor, alchemist*, Ὧρος ὁ χ. Olymp.Alch.p.103B. ⊛ **-ος** (parox.), ον, (ὀρύσσω) *digging for gold*, μύρμηκες Str.2.1.9; ἔργα *Supp. Epigr.*6.166 (Phrygia, iv A.D.): as Subst., *gold-miner*, Zos.Alch. p.240B.; cf. χρυσώρυφος.
⊛ **χρύσ-ωσις** [ῡ], εως, ἡ, *gilding*, Callix.1, Plu.*Publ.*15, *Nic.*3, *PLeid. X.*49B., Aët.1.106. **-ωτής**, οῦ, ὁ, *gilder*, *IG*2$^2$.1635.37, Plu.2.348e. **-ωτός**, ή, όν, *gilt*, Phalaec.ap.Ath.10.440d, restd. in *IG*1$^2$.359.3. **-ώτρια**, ἡ, *female gilder*, *Tab.Defix.*69.4 (iii B.C.). **-ώψ**, ῶπος, ὁ, ἡ, *gold-coloured, shining like gold*, θύρσος E.*Ba.*553 (lyr.).

**Χρυτταῖος**, ὁ (sc. μήν), name of month at Lamia in Thessaly, *IG*9(2).71.5, al. (ii B.C.).

**χρῷ**, heterocl. dat. of χρώς (q.v.).
⊛ **χρῴζω**, E.*Ph.*1625, Alex.141.9, Arist.*Mir.*834$^a$8, later **χρώννῡμι**, **-ύω** (qq.v.): fut. χρώσω Hsch.: aor. ἔχρωσα Arist.*Mete.*371$^a$24, Luc. *Im.*7, etc.: pf. κέχρωκα (ἐπι-) Plu.2.395d:—Pass., fut. χρωσθήσομαι Gal.1.278, 9.394: aor. ἐχρώσθην Pl.*Tht.*156e, etc.: pf. κέχρωσμαι Hp.*Epid.*7.17, E.*Med.*497, etc.: plpf. ἐκέχρωστο Alciphr. *Fr.*6.17:—= χροΐζω, *touch the surface of a body*, and generally, *touch*, γόνατα μὴ χρῴζειν ἐμά E.*Ph.*1625. 2. *tinge, stain*, ἔχρωσε μέν, ἔκαυσε δ' οὔ Arist.*Mete.*371$^a$24, etc.; τὸ καλὸν χρῶμα δευσοποιῷ χρῴζομεν Alex.l.c.; πόσον αἷμα τὴν γῆν ἔχρωσεν; Lib.*Or.*42.41; εὖ χ. *gives* a good *complexion*, Orib.*Syn.*5.23:—Pass., Arist.*Col.*793$^b$23, *Mete.*375$^a$6, Zos.Alch.p.171B.; ὑπὸ τοῦ ἡλίου Luc.*Anach.*25; κεστρεὺς χρωσθείς *browned* in frying, Antiph.217.11; ὑπόξανθος τοῖς φύλλοις ἐκέχρωστο αὐγή Alciphr.l.c.; of the moon, χρωσθεῖσα φύσιν πολυκαμπέα Alex.Eph.ap.Theon.Sm.p.140H.; of the tongue, Gal.9.394; τὰ μέλανα (sc. διαχωρήματα) ὑπὸ μελαίνης χολῆς.. χρῴζεται Id.18(2).142. 3. *taint, defile*, αἵματι παλάμαν *APl.*4.138, cf. Porph.*Antr.*11:—Pass., metaph., μάτην κεχρώσμεθα κακοῦ πρὸς ἀνδρός E.*Med.*497; of air, *to be infected*, μιάσμασιν Hp.*Flat.*6. 4. metaph. of an author, *paint*, ἔχρωσα.. κατηφεῖ χρώματι τὰ νάματα Him.*Ecl.*12.7.
⊛ **χρῶμα**, ατος, τό, (χρώννυμι) *skin*, esp. of the human body, κάθαρσις διὰ τοῦ χρώματος Hp.*Insomn.*89 (sed χρωτός recte cod. θ). II. *colour*, esp. of the skin or body, *complexion*, Hdt.2.32, 3.101, Hp. *Aph.*4.40, etc.; χρῶμα ἀλλάξαι E.*Ph.*1246, cf. Men.*Epit.*466; μεθιστάναι τοῦ χρώματος Ar.*Eq.*399 (lyr.); τὸ χ. διακεκναισμένος Id.*Nu.* 120; παντοδαπὰ ἠφίει χρώματα changed *colour* continually, Pl.*Ly.* 222b; χ. διαμένον an unchanging *colour* (of the face), Nicol.Com.1.28; so of animals, X.*Cyn.*4.7. 2. generally, *colour*, Gorg.ap.S.E.*M.* 7.85; defined by Zeno *Stoic.*1.26; χρώματα βάπτειν use *pigments* for dyeing, Pl.*R.*429e; ἐκ τῶν χρωμάτων καὶ σχημάτων θεωρεῖν, i.e. look to *the outside* only, ib.601a; διὰ τῶν χ. ἀπεικάζειν X.*Mem.*3.10.1; χρώμασι καὶ σχήμασι μιμεῖσθαι Arist.*Po.*1447$^a$18; περὶ χρωμάτων, title of treatise by Arist.; ἐναλείφειν τοῖς χ. Id.*GA*743$^b$24; χρωμάτων κρᾶσις Luc.*Zeux.*5; χρώματος ἔντριψις, of cosmetics, X. *Cyr.*1.3.2; τοῖς ἐγχρίστοις εἰς τοὺς ὀφθαλμοὺς χρώμασιν Arist.*GA* 747$^a$10; of medicines, φάρμακα χρώμασι καὶ ὀσμαῖς πεποικιλμένα Pl. *Cra.*394a. III. *turmeric, Curcuma longa*, used in dyeing, Thphr.*Od.*31. IV. *complexion, character of style* in writing, χρώματα [λέξεως] (of τὸ στριφνόν, τὸ πυκνόν, etc.) D.H.*Amm.*2.2; ποιητικῆς χρώματα Phld.*Mus.*p.84K., cf. Hermog.*Id.*1.12. 2. metaph. in pl., *ornaments, embellishments*, ἀλλοτρίοις χ. καὶ κόσμοις Pl.*Phdr.*239d, cf. *Grg.*465b; also of style or language, D.H.*Comp.* 20; of Music, γυμνωθέντα.. τῶν τῆς μουσικῆς χρωμάτων τὰ τῶν ποιητῶν Pl.*R.*601b. 3. in Music, a *modification* of the simplest music: τὰ μέλη μεταβολαῖς καὶ χρώμασιν ὡς εὖ κέκραται Antiph.209. 4; χρώματα εὔχροα ἐκιθάρισε Philoch.66: but esp. b. *chromatic* scale or music, οὔτε χρῶμα δειλοὺς οὔτε ἁρμονία ἀνδρείους ποιεῖ Anon. in *PHib.*1.13.22, cf. Cleonid.*Harm.*3, Bacch.*Harm.*23, etc.: χ. μαλακόν, ἡμιόλιον, τονιαῖον, Cleonid.*Harm.*7. 4. Rhet., *complexion, colourable pretence*, Hermog.*Stat.*1, 3(pl.), Arg.D.19 §12. V. of the factions in the Circus at Constantinople, Agath.5.14,21. VI. Astrol., = χρόα I.3, *complexion* of heavenly bodies, Phld.*D.*3.9, Vett. Val.107.26.

**χρωμᾰτ-ίζω**, *colour, tinge*, Arist.*PA*664$^b$16, *GA*747$^a$10, Thphr. *Od.*31; τί τινι Alex.188.4:—Pass., *to be of such and such a colour*, Hp.*Coac.*380; χ. παντοδαπὰς χρόας Arist.*Mete.*342$^b$4. 2. metaph. in literary criticism, χ. τῇ πρεπούσῃ ὑποκρίσει (of Demosthenes) D.H.*Dem.*22, cf. Phld.*Po.*2.43. **-ικός**, ή, όν, *of, relating to colour*:—but only found, II. metaph., in Rhet., *offering a colourable pretext* (χρῶμα IV. 4), τὸ χ., as name of a form of rebuttal, Aps.p.273H. (v.l. χρωμάτιον). 2. in Music, *chromatic* (cf. χρῶμα IV. 3), μελῳδία D.H.*Comp.*19; μέλος, opp. διάτονον, ἐναρμόνιον, Alciphr.1.18, cf. Aristox (?).*Oxy.*667.1; τὸ -κὸν [γένος] the *chromatic genus*, Plu.2.744c, cf. Phld.*Mus.*p.63K., Ph.1.321. ⊛ **-ῖνος**, η, ον, *coloured*, ἀβόλλαι, λάκκος, *Peripl.M.Rubr.*6, cf. Sotion p. 183W. **-ιον**, τό, *pigment, paint*, *AP*.11.423 (pl., Hellad.). II. v. χρωματικός II.1. **-ισμός**, ὁ, *colouring, dyeing*, μύρων Dsc.1.71 (pl.), Sch.Ar.*Nu.*516.

**χρωμᾰτο-ποιία**, ἡ, *laying on of colour* or *paint*, Philostr.*Ep.*40. **-πώλης**, ου, ὁ, *dealer in colours*, *Gloss.*

**χρωμᾰτουργ-ία**, ἡ, *dyeing*, *Cat.Cod.Astr.*2.177. **-ός**, ὁ, *dyer*, Rhetor. ib.8(4).137.

**χρωμοκρᾱσία**, ἡ, *mixture of colours, changing of complexion*, Ptol. *Tetr.*182 (pl., = αἰσχημοσύναι acc. to Sch. ad loc.(152)).

**χρώννῡμι**, = χρῴζω (i.e. *apply* χρῶμα IV.2), τῇ λέξει Luc.*Hist.Conscr.* 48:—Pass., Steph.*in Hp.*1.165; **χρωννύω**, = χρῴζω, Alex.Aphr.*in de An.*45.16, Lib.*Decl.*7.7.
⊛ **χρώς**, ὁ, gen. χρωτός, dat. χρωτί, acc. χρῶτα (Att. χρώ only in Choerob.*in Theod.*1.248H.): Ep. and Ion. gen. χροός, dat. χροΐ, acc. χρόα (also in Lesbian, Sapph.*Supp.*10.6, al.), as always in Hom. and Hes., exc. gen. χρωτός in Il.10.575, acc. χρῶτα Od.18.172, 179, Hes. *Op.*556; Emp. uses χρωτός, 76.3 (but χροΐ 100.17); Pi. uses χρωτί, χρῶτα, *P.*1.55, *I.*4(3).23(41); these forms are freq. in Trag., but Ion. dat. χροΐ occurs in S.*Tr.*605, and χροός, χροΐ, χρόα are freq. in E., *Hec.* 548, *Med.*1175, *Ph.*264, al.:—dat. χρῷ occurs in the phrase ἐν χρῷ, v. infr. I.2 and in Sapph.2.10.—Rare in Com. and Att. Prose. I. of the human body, *skin* or *flesh*, οὔ σφι λίθος χρὼς οὐδὲ σίδηρος Il.4.510; καὶ γάρ θην τούτῳ τρωτὸς χρώς 21.568; χρῶτ' ἀπονιψαμένη Od.18.172; ἀκρότατον δ' ἄρ' ὀϊστὸς ἐπέγραψε χρόα Il.4.139; ταμέειν χρόα νηλέϊ χαλκῷ 13.501; λιλαιομένη χροὸς ἆσαι, of a spear, 21.168; κακὰ χροΐ εἵματ' ἔχοντα Od.14.506; χρῷ πῦρ ὑπαδεδρόμακεν Sapph.2. 10; μύροις χρῶτα λιπαίνων Anaxil.18.1 (anap.): esp. *flesh*, opp. bone, φθινύθει δ' ἀμφ' ὀστεόφι χρώς Od.16.145; οὐδέ τί οἱ χρὼς σήπεται Il.24.414, cf. 19.33 (which usage is said by Gal. to have been Ionic, 18(2).435, with reference to Hp.*Fract.*9); τὸ δέρμα τοῦ χρωτός Lxx *Le.*13.11, etc.; τοῦ χρωτὸς ἥδιστον ἀπέπνει Aristox.*Fr.Hist.*84: generally, *one's body, frame*, Pi.*P.*1.55, A.*Fr.*192.6 (anap.); χριμφθῆναι χροΐ Id.*Supp.*790 (lyr.); στεῖλαί νυν ἀμφὶ χρωτὶ.. πέπλους E. *Ba.*821, cf. S.*Tr.*605: pl., διὰ τί.. οἱ χρῶτες ὄζουσι; Arist.*Pr.*877$^b$21; also κατεδήσαντο.. τοὺς ὑγιεῖς χρῶτας, ὡς τραυματίαι D.H.9.50. 2. ἐν χροΐ, or ἐν χρῷ, *close to the skin*, ἐν χροΐ κείρειν to shave *close*, Hdt.4.175; ἐν χρῷ κεκαρμένοι X.*HG*1.7.8; ἐν χρῷ κουριῶντας Pherecr. 30:—metaph., *to the quick*, ξυρεῖ γὰρ ἐν χρῷ τοῦτο S.*Aj.*786; ἐν χρῷ παραπλεῖν sail past *so as to shave* or *graze*, Th.2.84; τὴν μάχην συνάψαι ἐν χρῷ to fight *at close quarters*, Plu.*Thes.*27; ἡ ἐν χρῷ συνουσία *close* acquaintance, Luc.*Ind.*3: c. gen., ἐν χρῷ τινος *close to, hard by* a person or thing, τοῦ θώρακος (v.l. σώματος) Plu.2.345a; τῆς γῆς ib. 925b, Luc.*Herm.*5: abs., ἐν χρῷ *near at hand*, Id.*Hist.Conscr.*24, al.; cf. *EM*313.53, Hsch. II. *the colour of the skin, complexion*, μελαίνετο δὲ χρόα καλόν Il.5.354; τρέπεται χ. his *colour* changes, i.e. he turns pale, 13.279, cf. 17.733; ὠχρήσαντα χρόα Od.11.529; χρόα.. ἀμείβειν Parm.8.41; μεθίστη χρωτὸς.. φύσιν E. *Alc.*174; μεταλλακτῆρα πουλύπουν χροός Ion Trag.36; τί χρὼς τέτραπται; (paratrag.) Ar.*Lys.*127; φεῦγε δ' ἀπὸ χρώς Theocr.23.13; rare in Att. Prose, ἐπὶ τῷ χρωτὶ μέγα φρονεῖν X.*Smp.*4.54, cf. *Oec.*10. 5: in Ion. Prose, of the *colour* of a finger, χροΐ δῆλα Pherecyd.Syr. ap.D.L.1.118 (v.l. χρωΐ, cf. *Vorsokr.*$^5$i.44). 2. generally, *colour*, ἀμείβων χρῶτα πορφυρᾷ βαφῇ A.*Pers.*317; τὸν χρῶτα [μεταβάλλει] ὁ χαμαιλέων Arist.*Mir.*832$^b$14; χρὼς αἵματος Orph.*L.*660.

**χρῶσις**, εως, ἡ, *colouring, tinting*, Dsc.5.112, Poll.7.169, *PLeid. X.*15B.; χ. λαμβάνειν Epicur.*Ep.*2p.51U.

**χρωστήρ**, ῆρος, ὁ, *that which colours* or *dyes*: χ. μόλυβος a *lead-pencil*, *AP*6.68 (Jul.).

**χρωτίδιον**, τό, Dim. of χρώς, Cratin.302 (troch.).
⊛ **χρωτίζω**, *colour*, χ. τὸν οἶνον *give* it *colour and flavour*, Plu.2. 693c:—Med., χ. τὴν φύσιν τινί *tinge one's* nature with.., Ar.*Nu.* 516 (lyr.).

**χῠδαΐζομαι**, (χυδαῖος II) Pass., metaph., *to be used in vulgar language*, Eust.421.19.

**χῠδαιολογία**, ἡ, *vulgar language, coarseness*, Phot.*Bibl.*p.56.
⊛ **χῠδαῖος**, ον, (χέω) *poured out in streams, abundant*, Lxx *Ex.*1.7; στέφανοι, i.e. χύδην πεπλεγμένοι, Ath.15.686a. Adv. -ως *pell-mell*, Herm.ap.Stob.1.49.68. II. *common, ordinary*, φοίνικες Dsc.5.31, cf.

Plin.*HN*13.46; λίθος Plu.2.85f; ἔλαιον *Hippiatr.*69. **b.** of persons, χ. πλῆθος Str.1.2.8; ὁ χ. Porph.*Abst.*4.18; οἱ χ. Str.3.1.5, Ph.Bybl. 5, Porph.*Chr.*63; opp. οἱ σοφοί, Phld.*Po.*5.23, cf. *Rh.*2.157S., al.: Comp. οἱ χυδαιότεροι (misspelt χυδεώτεροι) Sch.E.*Hipp.*948. **2.** metaph., *common, vulgar, coarse*, λαλιά Plb.14.7.8; χυδαῖα καὶ φαῦλα Phld.*Mus.*p.95 K.

**χυδαιότης**, ητος, ἡ, *vulgarity*, Jul.*Gal.*43b, 238b.

**χῠδαιόω**, *make vulgar, debase*, in Pass., Aq.*Is.*33.9.

**χῠδαϊστί**, Adv. *in common speech*, Eust.50.14.

**χῠδᾰνός**, ή, όν, = χυτός I.2, χ. γαῖα *IG*7.580 (Tanagra).

⊛ **χύδην** [ῠ], Dor. **χύδαν** Call.*Fr.*1.11 P., Adv., (χέω) *as if poured out, in floods* or *heaps*: hence, **I.** *without order* or *system, promiscuously, indiscriminately*, καταπάττειν χ. *wholesale* (opp. κοτυλίζειν, to sell by retail), Pherecr.168; χ. βεβλῆσθαι Pl.*Phdr.*264b; στεφάνων χ. πεπλεγμένων Alex.52; πάντα χ. ἔστω *AP*10.100 (Antiphan.); τὰ χ. μαθήματα.. ἐν τῇ παιδείᾳ γενόμενα Pl.*R.*537c; φορτικῶς καὶ χ. ὅ τι ἂν ἐπέλθῃ λέγουσιν Isoc.12.24, cf. *Ep.*9.5; νομίμων χ. ὡς εἰπεῖν κειμένων Arist.*Pol.*1324$^b$5; ἐναλείφειν τοῖς καλλίστοις φαρμάκοις χ. Id.*Po.*1450$^b$2. **II.** *in unfettered language*, i.e. *in prose*, opp. ἐν ποιήμασι, Pl.*Lg.*811d; τὰ χ., opp. τὰ μέτρα, Arist. *Rh.*1409$^b$7. **III.** *abundantly*, *AP*9.316 (Leon.), Hp.*Ep.*3; [ἃ] χύδαν.. λύπα *overflowing* grief, Call. l.c.; *spreading*, of poison, *AP*9.233 (Eryc.).

**χυθρίδιον, χυθρίς**, v. χυτρίδιον, χυτρίς.

**χῡλ-άριον**, τό, Dim. of χυλός, *a little juice*, Damocr.ap.Gal.14.96; ὁ Φάλερνος χ. σταφυλίου M.Ant.6.13. **-ιάζω**, = sq., Aët.5.139, 7.90 (Ald.). **-ίζω**, *extract the juice* from a plant *by infusion* or *decoction*, Dsc.*Praef.*9:—Pass., σπέρμα χυλισθέν Thphr.*HP*9.9.4, cf. Dsc.2. 182, etc. **-ισμα**, ατος, τό, *the extracted juice of plants*, Thphr. *HP*9.8.3, Dsc.3.19, *Eup.*1.35, Zopyr.ap.Orib.14.64.3, Archig.ap. Gal.12.855. **-ισμός**, ὁ, *extraction of the juice of plants*, Thphr. *HP*9.8.3. **-ιστά**, τά, cj. for *quinista* (= *confectio in dynamidia*) in *Gloss.*

**χῡλοειδής**, ές, *like juice*, S.E.*M.*7.119.

**χῡλοποι-έω**, *make into* χυλός I.3, Ps.-Hp. *de hom. fabr.*p.285 Ermerins, Alex.Trall.9.2, Paul.Aeg.3.46: hence Subst. **-ησις**, εως, ἡ, Olymp. *in Mete.*284.24, Steph. *in Hp.*1.154 D.

**χῡλ-ός**, ὁ, (χέω) *juice* in general, opp. ὕδωρ, Ocell.2.3, cf. Iamb. *in Nic.*p.81 P.; in various uses: **I.** *juice of plants*, χυλῶν στακτῶν εἴτε ἀνθῶν ἢ καρπῶν Pl.*Criti.*115a, cf. Arist.*HA*596$^b$15, *Col.* 796$^a$23, *Aud.*802$^a$15, Thphr.*HP*6.4.6, Lxx 4*Ma.*6.25. **b.** *decoction*, Dsc.*Eup.*1.55; but distd. fr. ἀφέψημα, Id.1.105. **2.** of *animal juices*, Hp.*Alim.*11,14, Arist.*Col.*794$^a$21. **3.** *juice produced by the digestion of food, chyle*, Gal.*UP*4.3. **4.** *barley-water, gruel*, having the barley or groats strained off, whereas πτισάνη was taken unstrained, πτισάνης χ. Hp.*Acut.*6, cf. Cratin.297 (lyr.), Ephipp.13. 6 (anap.): pl., Anaxipp.1.46. **II.** = χυμός II, *flavour, taste*, Gorg. ap.S.E.*M.*7.85, v.l. in Arist.*EN*1118$^a$28; αἱ διὰ χυλῶν ἡδοναί Epicur. *Fr.*67, cf. *Ep.*3.p.63 U., Diocl.*Fr.*112, Phld.*Mus.*p.103 K.; κατ' ὀσμὴν καὶ χρόαν καὶ χυλόν Id.*Sign.*27: metaph., χ. στωμυλμάτων, φιλίας, Ar.*Ra.*943, *Pax* 997 (anap.). (Gal.11.450 distinguishes χυλός *juice* fr. χυμός *flavour*, attributing this usage to Aristotle and later writers, whereas earlier authors used χυμός in both senses: the Mss. vary.) **-όω**, *convert into juice, make a decoction* or *infusion of* a thing, τι Hp.*Mul.*2.209:—Pass., *to be converted into juice* or *chyle*, Ti.Locr.101a; κεχυλωμένη τροφή Gal.14.718, cf. *Nat.Fac.*3.4: *have the juice extracted*, ῥίζαι χυλωθεῖσαι Dsc.2.181. **b.** *to be moistened*, Eust. 1552.33. **II.** *extract the juice of*, μῆλα *Gp.*8.27.2. **-ώδης**, ες, contr. for χυλοειδής, Simp. *in Ph.*23.26, [Gal.]14.515, *Gp.*2.22.2. **-ωμα**, ατος, τό, dub. sens. in *IG*2$^2$.1672.200. **-ωσις**, εως, ἡ, *converting into juice* or *chyle*, χ. τῆς τροφῆς Plu.2.700b, cf. Gal.*Nat.Fac.*3.4, Thphr.*HP*7.5.1. **2.** *thickening of a juice by decoction*, Dsc.2.86, 109. **-ωτός**, ή, όν, *converted into a 'humour'*, *Anon.Lond.* 39.12.

⊛ **χύμα** [ῠ], ατος, τό, *that which is poured out* or *flows, fluid*, Arist. *HA*550$^b$27, D.S.17.75; even χ. νιφάδος Alciphr.1.23; χ. τέσσαρα, viz. the hot, cold, moist, and dry, Ptol.*Tetr.*19. **2.** *ingot, bar*, *IG*7. 303.104 (Orop., iii B.C.); χ. χρυσοῦν *Inscr.Délos* 442 *B* 6 (ii B.C.), [χρυσίου] ib.1432 *Ab* i 17 (Delos, ii B.C., pl.), cf. Agatharch.28. **3.** metaph., *confused mass*, τῶν ἀριθμῶν Lxx 2*Ma.*2.24; *aggregate*, *Theol.Ar.*34; *crowd*, πρεσβυτέρων καὶ νεωτέρων Aristeas 14. **4.** αὐτὰ τὰ χ. τῶν σφαιρῶν *materials, constituents*, Phlp. *in Mete.*26.8; τοῦ χ. αὐτοῦ τῶν σφαιρῶν ἡ οὐσία ib.4.2. **5.** χ. καρδίας *largeness* of heart, Lxx 3*Ki.*4.25(5.9). [On accent and quantity v. Hdn.Gr.2.15.]

**χῠμάτιον** [ᾰ], τό, Dim. of χύμα 2, *Inscr.Délos* 396 *B* 74, 1409 *Ba* i 101 (ii B.C.). **2.** χ. στύρακος, *lump* of styrax, Aët.16.136(146).

**χῠμ-εία**, ἡ, the *art of alloying metals, alchemy*, Zos.Alch.ap. Syncell.p.24 Dindorf (written χημεία, but *khumia* in the Syriac version, Diels *Antike Technik* p.109), Olymp.Alch.p.94 B. (χυμεία), Joann.Antioch.*Fr.*15.3 (*FHG* iv p.548 (χημ-), and so Suid. s.v. δέρας, but (χειμ-) in Anon.*Incred.*3 cod.), *Fr.*165 (*FHG* iv p.601, χημία cod.P, χημεία Suid. s.v. Διοκλητιανός (vv.ll. χειμεία, μοιχεία), Id. s.v. χημεία (v.l. χειμ-)). (Named from its supposed inventor Χύμης (v.l. Χημ- Χειμ-) acc. to Zos.Alch. l.c., cf. eund.pp.169, 172 B. (Χυμ-), Olymp.Alch.p.84 B. (Χημ-); more prob. from χύμα, cf. Diels l.c.) **-ευσις**, εως, ἡ, *alloy*, *EM*630.52, Eust.828.16, Tz.ad Hes.*Sc.*122. **-ευτικός**, ή, όν, *concerning alchemy*, βίβλος Zos.Alch.p.220 B. (χυμ-), Olymp.Alch.p.80 B. (χημ-); [βιβλία] Suid. s.v. Ζώσιμος (χειμ-).

**χῡμ-ίζω**, *make savoury, season*: metaph., χ. ἁρμονίαν *soften* rough music, Ar.*Th.*162. **-ίον**, τό, Dim. of χυμός, Sotad.Com.1.19.

⊛ **χῡμ-ός**, ὁ, (χέω) used much like χυλός, though sts. distd. fr. it (v. χυλός). **I.** *juice* of plants, Hp.*Epid.*6.6.3 (cf. Gal.17 (2).327), Pl.*Ti.*60a,b (pl.), Arist.*HA*554$^a$13 (pl.), 596$^b$17, Thphr. *HP*9.1.1, al. **2.** *animal juices*, 'humours', Hp.*VM*18, Arist.*HA* 556$^b$22, *PA*676$^a$16; *juice* in a wider sense covering I.1 and 2, Id.*Mete.* 380$^b$2 (pl.), 32: freq. in later writers, Gal.15.62, 16.497, Porph.*Abst.* 2.45, etc.; ἡμίπεπτοι χ. Gal.6.258; πέψαι τοὺς χ. ib.253. **3.** χυμός· σίελος, Hsch. (αἱ τῶν χυμῶν κενώσεις include πτύσματα in Gal.16. 644). **II.** *flavour*, ἅμα τῇ γεύσει ὁ χ. Arist.*Ph.*245$^a$9, cf. *Mete.* 356$^a$13 (pl.), *de An.*414$^b$11: but not of the *action of causing taste*, ἡ τοῦ χ. [ἐνέργεια] ἀνώνυμος ib.426$^a$15; ἰχθῦν.., ἔχοντα τοὺς χ. ἐν αὑτῷ Arched.2.9; opp. ὀσμαί, χρόαι, Plu.2.646b (and so interchangeable with χυλός II (q.v.), Diocl.*Fr.*138): several varieties distd. by Thphr. *CP*6.4.1, cf. Plu.2.913b. **-όω**, *impart a taste* or *flavour*, Suid. s.v. ἄγευστος. **II.** Pass., *to be converted into* χυμός I.2, Gal.9. 595. **-ώδης**, ες, *like juice, juicy*, Sch.Nic.*Th.*733. **-ωσις**, εως, ἡ, a stage of πέψις, almost = χύλωσις, ἀποτυχία χυλοποιήσεως καὶ χυμώσεως καὶ τῆς πέψεως Steph. *in Hp.*1.154 D.

**χύνω**, later form for χέω, found in compds.; ἐκχύνειν condemned by Luc.*Pseudol.*29; also **χύννω**, *Gloss.*

**χυρβιάζω**· σκιρτῶ, Hsch. **χύρρα**, a call used by swineherds, Id. **χυρράβιος**, ὁ, *swine-collar*, Id.: but **χύρραβος**, ὁ, a bird, Id.

**χυρρεῖον**, τό, = χυρράβιος, Hdn.Gr.1.372.

**χύσις** [ῠ], εως, ἡ, (χέω) *shedding, pouring out* or *forth*, αἱμάτων Thphr.*Fr.*174.6 (pl.): metaph., *squandering*, οὐσίας Alciphr.1.21. **2.** *diffusion*, e.g. of nutriment, Gal.6.87; opp. πίλησις, Id.*Nat.Fac.*1.3 (pl.); coupled with ἀνάλυσις, διάλυσις, Chrysipp.*Stoic.*2.136, cf. 188. **3.** *melting*, κηροῦ S.E.*P.*3.14; *casting, fusing*, Str.16.2. 25. **4.** *dispersion*, ἐν τῇ χ. τοῦ ἑνὸς πλῆθος γίγνεται Plot.6. 6.1. **II.** *liquid poured forth, flood, stream*, ἐκχέασα γάποτον χ., of a libation, A.*Ch.*97; πόντου χ. Opp.*H.*5.78; ὕδατος Arat.393, A.R.4.1416: metaph., χρονίη χ. *lapse* of time, *AP*9.153 (Agath.). **2.** of dry things, *heap*, φύλλων χ. Od.5.483, 19.443; νότος.. χύσιν κατεχεύατο φύλλων Call.*Hec.*1.1.11, cf. *AP*9.282 (Antip.Thess.); καλάμης Nic.*Th.*297. **3.** metaph. of *fluency* or *copiousness* of speech, ascribed to Cicero in contrast to the ὕψος ἀπότομον of Demosthenes, ὁ Κικέρων ἐν χύσει Longin.12.4; ἡ χ. τῶν λέξεων Phld.*Po.Herc.* 1676.6. **4.** *quantity, abundance*, σαρκῶν *AP*5.36 (Rufin.); χ. φαυλότητος *a great deal* of badness, Porph.*Abst.*3.2.

**χυσταία**, ἡ, dub. sens. in *Sammelb.*4425 iv 7 (ii A.D.).

**χύστος**, τό, name of an ingredient of a purple dye, χ. θαλάσσιον σὺν φύκει καὶ ὄξει ἕψον *PHolm.*23.2; gen. sg. written **κύσθους** θαλασσείου ib.22.42.

**χῠτήρ**, ῆρος, ὁ, = *fusorium*, *Gloss.*

**χύτης** [ῠ], ου, ὁ, *metal-caster*, *Gloss.*

**χῠτικός**, ή, όν, (χέω) *having a dissolving power*, Arist.*Pr.*863$^a$6, Gal.11.711.

**χυτλ-άζω**, *anoint* one *after bathing*, Hp.ap.Erot. (Pass.), cf. Gal. 19.155; cf. χύτλον 2. **2.** metaph., *throw carelessly down*, τὰ γόνατ' ἔκτεινε καὶ γυμναστικῶς χύτλασον σεαυτὸν ἐν τοῖς στρώμασιν Ar.*V.* 1213, ubi v. Sch. ⊛ **-ον**, τό, (χέω) *anything that can be poured, liquid, fluid*; esp., **1.** in pl., χύτλα, *water for washing, the bath*, Lyc.1099, Euph.9.7; but also, *libations* to the dead, *Berl.Sitzb.* 1927.161 (Cyrene), A.R.1.1075, 2.927, Orph.*A.*32. **2.** *a mixture of water and oil*, elsewh. ὑδρέλαιον, rubbed in after bathing, Erot. s.v. χυτλάζηται. **3.** *running water, stream*, Lyc.701. **-όω**, *wash, bathe*, γυῖα χυτλῶσαι Id.322:—also in Med., A.R.4.1311: mostly, **II.** Med., *anoint oneself after bathing*, Od.6.80: Medic., χυτλώσασθαι *to rub oneself with a mixture of water and oil* (cf. χύτλον 2), Gal.11.532. **2.** c. acc., *wash off from oneself, wash off*, ᾧ κε (sc. τῷ ῥόῳ) τόκοιο λύματα χυτλώσαιτο Call.*Jov.*17.

**χῠτός**, ή, όν, (χέω) *poured, shed*, αἷμα χυτόν blood *shed*, A.*Eu.* 682. **2.** of dry things, *heaped up*, Hom., only in phrase χυτὴ γαῖα *a mound* of earth, esp. a sepulchral mound, like χῶμα, Il.6.464, 14.114, Od.3.258; so χυτῇ θινί Opp.*H.*2.635; χυτὰ κόνις *IG*14.1721.5 (Rome), cf. 12(8).38.4 (Lemnos); also χυτή alone (sc. γαῖα) *Epigr. Gr.*1034.25 (Callipolis). **b.** Subst., χυτός, ὁ, = χῶμα, *mound, bank, dyke*, Hdt.7.37. **3.** χ. λιμήν *protected by a mole* or *mound*, A.R.1. 987, ubi v. Sch. **II.** *cast, melted*, ἀρτήματα λίθινα χυτά Hdt.2.69; ἐν σκύφῳ χυτῆς λίθου Epin.1.8; χ. ἄργυρος, πίσσα, Thphr.*Lap.*60, Nic.*Al.*116; χαλκός Orib.49.3.8; τὰ χυτά things *fused* or *welded together*, Iamb. *in Nic.*p.81 P. **2.** *that can be liquefied, fusible*, Pl.*Ti.*58d, 61c; opp. ἐλατός, Arist.*Mete.*378$^a$27. **III.** generally, *liquid, fluid, flowing*, νέκταρ Pi.*O.*7.7; θάλασσα *AP*6.66 (Paul.Sil.): poet. also of the hair, *flowing, streaming*, Nic.*Th.*503; χ. ἔρνος a *luxuriant* shoot or sprout, ib.391. **IV.** *in shoals*, χυτοὶ ἰχθύες, of fish caught in nets, Arist.*HA*543$^a$1. **V.** χυτή, ἡ, *case* or *jacket* enclosing a wooden model of an engine, Hero*Bel.*96.10.

⊛ **χύτρ-α**, ἡ, Ion. **κύθρη** Herod.*Fr.*3 Bgk., later Gr. **κύθρα** *PTeb.* 112.42, al. (ii B.C.), Choerob. *in Theod.*2.146 H.; Sicil. (acc. to Greg. Cor.p.341 S.) **κύτρα** (but **κύθρα** is Dor. acc. to Choerob. *in Theod.*2. 423 H., and **χύτρα** is found in Epich.33): (χέω):—*earthen pot, pipkin*, Ar.*Ach.*284 (troch.), *Av.*43, al., X.*HG*4.5.4, Antiph.70, Thphr. *Char.*10.5, etc.; χύτρας ἴχνος ἀπὸ σποδοῦ ἀφάνιζε Pythag.ap.Iamb. *Protr.*21.λδ'; χύτραι δίωτοι Pl.*Hp.Ma.*288d; τοὐπίθημα τῆς χ. ἀφελών Hegesipp.1.13; children were exposed in pots, τὸ δ' εἰσέφερε γραῦς ἐν χύτρᾳ τὸ παιδίον Ar.*Th.*505; cf. χυτρίζω. **2.** χύτραις ἱδρύειν set up, consecrate an altar or statue with *pots* of pulse, τὰς χ. αἷς τὸν θεὸν (sc. Πλοῦτον) ἱδρυσόμεθα Id.*Pl.*1197, cf. Sch. ad loc.; Ζηνὸς ἑρκείου χύτρας, μεθ' ὧν ὁ βωμὸς..ἱδρύθη Id.*Fr.*245; τί δ' ἄλλο γ' ἢ ταύτην (sc. Εἰρήνην) χύτραις ἱδρυτέον; Answ. χύτραισιν, ὥσπερ μεμφόμενον Ἑρμήδιον; Id.*Pax*923, cf. Sch. **3.** αἱ χύτραι the *pottery-market*, Id.*Lys.*557 (anap.), Poll.7.163. **4.** prov., χύτραις λημᾶν to have swellings as big as *pipkins* in the corners of the eye (cf. λημᾶν κολοκύνταις), Luc.*Ind.*23, Diogenian.5.63, Hsch. **5.** name given to black figs by Mariandyni, Pherecr.68.4. **II.** *a kiss in which one held the other by the ears as by handles* (cf. Pl. l. c.), λαβοῦσα τῶν ὤτων φίλησον τὴν χύτραν Eunic.1. **-αῖος,** α, ον, = χυτρεοῦς, Ar.*Fr.*472 codd.Poll. (sed leg. χυτρεᾶν). **-ειος,** α, ον, = χυτρεοῦς, χ. πάταγος Id.*Lys.*329 (lyr.). **II.** τὰ χυτρεῖα *earthenware, pottery*, Choerob. in *An.Ox.*2.278. **-εοῦς,** οῦν, *of earthenware*, Ar.*Nu.*1474. **-εύς,** έως, ὁ, *potter*, Pl.*R.*421d, *Tht.*147a, Eustr. *in APo.*158.13. **-εψός,** ὁ, *boiler of pots*, Parmenio ap.Ath.13.608a. **-ίδιον** [ῐ], τό, Dim. of χυτρίς, *a small pot, cup*, Hp.*Ulc.*17, Ar.*Ach.*463, 1175, Alex.244.2, *Inscr.Délos* 1403 *A b* i 84 (ii B.C.); also **χυθρίδιον,** Aët.11.11; Ion. **κυθρίδιον,** Epicur.*Fr.*182, Olymp.Alch. p.75 B. **-ίζω,** *put in a pot*: esp. *expose a child in a pot*, A.*Fr.*122, S.*Fr.*532, Pherecr.247. **-ικός,** ή, όν, = χύτρινος, κέραμος *Tab. Defix.Praef.*p. ii (iv B.C.). (Perh. χ. κέραμος = χύτραι, cf. χύτρα 1. 3.) **-ίνδα παίζειν,** *a game* described by Poll.9.110, Hsch. **-ῐνος,** η, ον, Ion. later **κύθρ-** Apollod.*Poliorc.*152.12, *of earthenware*: Subst. ὁ χ., = χύτρα, Hp.*Mul.*2.133; κ. ὀστράκινοι Apollod. l.c. **2.** χύτρινοι ἀγῶνες games at the festival οἱ χύτροι (v. χύτρος II. 2), Philoch. 137. **-ῖνος,** ὁ, *deep hole* from which water springs, Hsch.; of a hot spring or geyser in Cos, Antig.*Mir.*160; *deep hole*, in a river, *Peripl.M.Rubr.*44, in form **κυθρῖνος.** **2.** *niche for a nest* in a dove-cot, in form **κυθρ-,** *Gp.*14.6.2. **-ίον,** τό, f.l. for χυτρίδιον, Ar.*Ach.*1175. **II.** = κρανίον, Hsch. **-ίς,** ἡ, Dim. (in form only) of χύτρα or χύτρος, gen. ίδος or ῖδος (dual χυτρῖδε Bato 3.2), Hdt. 5.88, *IG*11(2).110.25 (Delos, iii B.C.), al., Erasistr. ap. Gal.11.215, Apollon.ap.eund.12.651; also **χυθρίς,** *IG*7.3498.13,44 (Orop.). **-ίσκη,** Dim. of χύτρα, *PHolm.*6.28. **-ισμός,** ὁ, *exposure of a child in a pot*, Hsch. **-ίτης** [ῑ], ου, ὁ, = πυός, Sch.Ar.*Pax* 1150.

⊛ **χυτρό-γαυλος,** ὁ, *a kind of pot*, prob. like *a bucket*, *IG*11(2).154*A* 71 (Delos, iii B.C.), Lxx 3 *Ki.*7.24(38), *PSI*4.428.62 (iii B.C.), Poll.6. 89: **κυθρόγαυλος** is v.l. in J.*AJ*8.3.6:—Dim. **-γαύλιον,** τό, *IG*11(2). 154*A* 72 (Delos, iii B.C.). **-ειδής,** ές, *like a pot*, Sch.Theoc.5. 58. **-πλάθος** [ᾰ], ὁ, *potter*, Poll.7.163, Phryn.*PS* p.125 B. **-πους,** ποδος, ὁ, *stand for a pot*, Alciphr.3.5, Sch.Ar.*Pax* 893 (gloss on λάσανα); also **κυθρόπους** *PMag.Lond.*46.269, Zos.Alch.p.222 B. **2.** *pot* or *cauldron*, χυτρόποδες Hes.*Op.*748, Lxx *Le.*11.35; χ. κέραμοι *App.Anth.*5.29.5 (Juba). **3.** = τορύνη, Sch.Ar.*Ra* 509:—Dim. **-πόδιον,** τό, Hippon.25. **-πώλης,** ου, ὁ, *pot-seller*, Critias 70 D.: fem. **-πωλις,** ιδος, as epith. of Aegina, *Com.Adesp.*669 (χυτρόπολιν Meineke). **-πώλιον,** or **-εῖον,** τό, *pottery-market*, Poll.7.163, Sch.Ar.*Av.*13: pl., = Lat. *ollaria*, Agath.2.20.

⊛ **χύτρος,** ὁ, Ion. **κύθρος** *EM*543.38, (χέω) = χύτρα, Diph.41, Nic. *Al.*136, *PHolm.*19.12. **2.** pl., of *deep holes* in Lake Copais, Thphr.*HP*4.11.8. **II.** οἱ Χύτροι, name of *the hot springs* at Thermopylae, Hdt.7.176, *Delph.*3(5).22.53 (iv B.C.). **2.** *pot-feast*, the 3rd day of the Anthesteria at Athens, Ar.*Ach.*1076, *Ra.*218 (lyr.).

**χυτρο-τομέω,** *make a fool of*, τινα dub. in Arg.Ar.*Lys.* **-φόρος,** ον, *bearing a pot* or *pots*, Sch.Ar.*Av.*448.

**χυτρώδης,** ες, *pot-shaped*, S.*Ichn.*295.

**χωλ-αίνω,** fut. -ᾰνῶ, Lxx 3 *Ki.*18.21: aor. ἐχώλᾱνα ib.*Ps.*17(18). 46:—*to be* or *go lame*, Pl.*Lg.*795b, *Hp.Mi.*374c, *POxy.*465.39 (ii A.D.), etc. **II.** trans., *make lame*, Sch.T Il.8.402:—Pass., ἐχωλάνθη Lxx 2 *Ki.*4.4. **-ανσις,** εως, ἡ, *lameness*, Epict.*Ench.*9: metaph., in metric, of *a halting line*, Eust.400.3. **-ασμα,** ατος, τό, *lameness*, *Hippiatr.*2 (pl.). **-άω,** = χωλεύω I, dub. in Them.*Or.*22. 282b. **-εία,** ἡ, *lameness*, Pl.*Hp.Mi.*374d, Luc.*Vit.Auct.*21, Plot. 5.9.10. **-ευμα,** ατος, τό, *a lameness*, Hp.*Art.*60 (pl.). **-εύω,** *to be* or *become lame, halt, limp*, Il.18.411,417, 20.37, X.*HG*3.3.3, Porph.ap.Eus.*PE*3.11. **2.** metaph., *to be maimed*, i.e. *defective, imperfect*, χωλεύει ἡ ζωὴ τῷ φαύλῳ Plot.1.7.3; ἂν [ἡ πόλις] τούτῳ χωλεύῃ τῷ μέρει Lib.*Or.*47.10, cf. 59.33, Max.Tyr.20.6, Them.*Or.*6. 75d; ὁ νόμος ἐχώλευεν Palaeph.50; κατὰ τὴν ἰατρικήν Gal.15. 396. **II.** trans., *make lame*, Hp.*Mul.*1.4, S.E.*P.*3.217:—Pass., *to be* or *become lame*, Luc.*Sacr.*6; and, generally, *to be maimed* or *imperfect*, Pl.*Phdr.*248b.

**χωλ-ῐαμβοποιέω,** *compose choliambics*, Eust.1684.51. **-ίαμβος** [ῐ], ὁ, *a lame* or *halting iambic*, i.e. one that has a spondee for an iambus in the last place, said to have been invented by Hipponax, Demetr.*Eloc.*251, Sch.Heph.p.101 C.

**χώλοθρον·** ἡ κοιλασία, Hsch.

**χωλο-κράββατον,** τό, = σκιμπόδιον, Suid. s.v. σκίμπους; also **-κραβάτιον** Sch.Ar.*Nu.*254.

**χωλόομαι,** Pass., *to become lame*, Hp.*Aph.*6.60: generally, *to be maimed, damaged*, Id.*Morb.*1.3, Ruf.ap.Orib.5.7.6.

**χωλο-ποιός,** όν, *making lame*, of Euripides, as being fond of *introducing lame men* upon the stage, Ar.*Ra.*846. **-πους,** ὁ, ἡ, gen. -ποδος, *lame-footed*, Man.4.118.

⊛ **χωλός,** ή, όν, *lame* in the feet, *halting, limping*, c. acc., χωλὸς δ' ἕτερον πόδα Il.2.217, cf. 9.503, Od.8.308, Hdt.5.92.β', S.*Ph.*486, 1032; χ. καὶ οὐκ ἀρτίπους Hdt.4.161; χ. τὼ σκέλει Ar.*Th.*24; also c. dat., σκέλει χωλός Plu.2.739b; χωλὸς ἀμφοτέροις Luc.*Tim.*20: later also of the hand, like κυλλός, χωλὸς τὴν χεῖρα Eup.343; χεῖρα χωλὴν ἔξειν Hp.*Prorrh.*2.1, cf. Pl.*Lg.*794e: of animals, X.*Eq.*1.5, etc. **II.** metaph., *defective*, φύσις Pl.*Phd.*71e; *one-sided*, Id. *R.*535d; βασιλεία Orac.ap.X.*HG*3.3.3. **2.** of metre, esp. of the χωλίαμβος (q.v.), *halting*, μέτρον Heph.5.4, Demetr.*Eloc.*301; also of a trochaic metre, Aristid.Quint.1.25. **3.** ἀείδειν χωλά, of a '*lame* tale', Herod.1.71.

**χωλ-ότης,** ητος, ἡ, *lameness*, σκέλους Plu.2.963c, Jul.*Or.*6.201b: pl., Plu.2.35c: metaph., *lameness* or *deformity*, of metres, Ath.14. 632e. ⊛ **-όω,** *maim*, Did. ad D.11.22.

⊛ **χώλ-ωμα,** ατος, τό, *lameness*, Hp.*Art.*62 (pl.). 64, Gal.18(1). 678. ⊛ **-ωσις,** εως, ἡ, *being made lame, lameness*, Hp.*Art.*66, Ptol. *Tetr.*151 (pl.), Vett.Val.109.36.

⊛ **χῶμα,** ατος, τό, (χόω, χώννυμι) *earth thrown up, bank, mound,* thrown up against the walls of cities to take them, αἴρεε τὰς πόλιας χώμασι Hdt.1.162; χ. ἔχουν πρὸς τὴν πόλιν Th.2.75, cf. Lxx *Ez.*21. 22(27), *Hb.*1.10, *OGI*90.24 (Rosetta, ii B.C., pl.). **2.** *dyke* to hinder a river from overflowing, Hdt.1.184: freq. in Pap., *PPetr.*3 pp.125,341 (iii B.C.), etc.; βασιλικὸν χ. Wilcken *Chr.*11 *A* 8 (ii B.C.); δημόσιον χ. *POxy.*290.34 (i A.D.). **3.** *dam*, Hdt.7.130. **4.** *mole* or *pier*, carried out into the sea, *jetty*, Id.8.97, D.50.6, Arg.Id. 51, *IG*11(2).199*A* 33 (Delos, iii B.C.), etc. **5.** *promontory, spit of sand*, A.*Supp.*870 (lyr.). **II.** *sepulchral mound*, Hdt.1.93, 9.85, A.*Ch.*723 (anap.), S.*Ant.*1216, etc.; τάφων χώματα γαίας E.*Supp.* 53 (lyr.); χῶμα μὴ χοῦν ὑψηλότερον πέντε ἀνδρῶν ἔργον Pl.*Lg.* 958e. **III.** *mass of soil* in which roots are found, cj. in Thphr. *HP*2.5.2. **IV.** *heap of rubbish, ruin*, Lxx *Jo.*8.28, *Is.*25.2, Lib. *Or.*61.13. **V.** τὸ χ. τῆς γῆς the *dust* of the earth, Lxx *Ex.*8.16.

⊛ **χωμᾰτ-εκβολεύς,** έως, ὁ, = ἐκβολεύς, Pap. in *Wiener Denkschr.* 47(4).55 (iii A.D.). **-εκβολία,** ἡ, *supervision of dykes*, *PRyl.*90. 17 (iii A.D.). **-επείκτης,** ου, ὁ, *supervisor of dyke-building*, *POxy.* 1469.20 (iii A.D.), etc.: written **-επέκτης** in Hsch., **-επίκτης** in Cyr. ⊛ **-επιμελητής,** οῦ, ὁ, *overseer of dykes*, *BGU*12.11 (ii A.D.), etc. **-επιστάτης** [ᾰ], ου, ὁ, *overseer of dykes*, *PPrinceton* 72.14 (iii A.D.). **-εργολάβος** [ᾰ], ὁ, *contractor for construction of dykes*, *PFay.*214 (i A.D.). **-ίας,** ου, ὁ, *piling up earth*, of earthquakes, f.l. in Arist.*Mu.*396ᵃ4 (ap Stob.); of rivers, cj. for γωματίαι in Poll. 3.103. **-ιζω,** *fortify with mounds*, Lxx *Jo.*11.13 (Pass.). **II.** *embank with dykes*, *Sammelb.*7376.13 (i A.D.):—Pass., γῆ κεχωματισμένη *PTeb.*105.26 (ii B.C.). **-ικός,** ή, όν, *connected with dykes*, ἔργα ib.13.6 (ii B.C.), Wilcken *Chr.*388.3 (ii A.D.); without ἔργα, ib.385.19 (iii B.C.), *PSI*5.488.20 (iii B.C.). **II.** χωματικόν, τό, *tax for maintenance of dykes*, ib.4.344.14,388.1 (iii B.C.), *PHib.*1.45.23, al. (iii B.C.), *Ostr.Bodl.*i 31 (iii B.C.), iii 79 (i A.D.): pl., *PPetr.*3 p.162 (iii B.C.), *BGU*1198 (i B.C.), *POxy.*288.20 (i A.D.). **-ιον,** τό, Dim. of χῶμα, *PSI*4.403.21 (iii B.C.), D.H.1. 64. **-ισμός,** ὁ, *construction of dykes*, in pl., *PTeb.*106.21 (ii B.C.), *PAmh.*2.91.10 (ii A.D.), etc.

**χωμᾰτο-γρᾰφία,** ἡ, *plan* or *register of dykes*, *PTeb.*237 (ii B.C.). ⊛ **-φύλαξ** [ῠ], ᾰκος, ὁ, *dyke-warden*, *PPetr.*3 p.134, *PSI*4.421 (iii B.C.).

⊛ **χων-εία,** ἡ, *melting and casting of metal*, Plb.34.10.12, D.S.5. 13. **-εῖον,** τό, *funnel*, Archig.ap.Gal.12.822, Alex.Aphr.*Pr.*2. 3. **2.** = χωνευτήριον, interpol. in Suid. **-ευμα,** ατος, τό, *molten-work, molten image*, Lxx *De.*9.12, al., *PLeid.X.*21 B. **-ευσις,** εως, ἡ, = χωνεία, *PLond.ined.*2325 (iii B.C.), Lxx 2 *Ch.*4.3, Maria ap.Zos.Alch.p.149 B. ⊛ **-ευτήρ,** ῆρος, ὁ, = χόανον, Sch.Hes. *Th.*863. **-ευτήριον,** τό, *smelting-furnace*, Lxx 3 *Ki.*8.51, al.; cf. χωνεῖον. **-ευτής,** οῦ, ὁ, *smelter, metal-caster*, ib.*Jd.*17.4 (cod. Alex.); *Musée du Caire, Greek Inscriptions* 9330 (ii/iii A.D.), Ptol.*Tetr.* 179. ⊛ **-ευτός,** ή, όν, *formed of cast metal, molten*, Lxx 3 *Ki.*7.19 (33), al.

**χωνεύω,** contr. fr. χοανεύω (q.v.). **II.** *coat* jars *with pitch*, τοὺς χωνεύοντας κεραμεῖς *PSI*4.441.3, cf. 15 (iii B.C.); κεχωνευκώς *PCair.Zen.*741.26 (iii B.C.): but pf. part. Pass. κεχωνημένα ib.742. 4 (iii B.C.) (χωνεύω and κωνάω became assimilated; cf. ἀχώνευτος and ἀχώνητος (Addenda)).

**χώνη,** ἡ, contr. fr. χοάνη (q.v.).

**χωνίον,** τό, Dim. of χώνη or χῶνος, *crucible*, interpol. in Suid. s.v. χωνεῖον.

**χώννῡμι,** later form of χόω, Arr.*An.*2.18.3, etc.; also **χωννύω** Plb.1.47.3: impf. ἐχώννυον D.S.14.49, etc.; 3 pl. ἐχώννυσαν D.C.66. 4:—Pass., inf. χώννυσθαι Plb.4.40.4, etc.; subj. χωννύηται *PSI*5. 486.5 (iii B.C.); ἐχωννύμεθα *we were covered with a heap of earth*, i.e. *had a sepulchral mound raised over us* (cf. χόω fin.), *AP*7.136 (Antip.), 137.

**χῶνον,** τό, **χῶνος,** ὁ, contr. for χόανον, χόανος, = χώνη, χοάνη.

**χῶνος·** βουνός, Hsch.

**χώομαι,** Ep. imper. χώεο, v. infr.: Ep. impf. χώετο Il.21.306: fut. χώσομαι, 3 sg. χώσεται, Lyc.362: aor. ἐχωσάμην, v. infr.: Ep. aor. subj. χώσεται Il.1.80:—Ep. Verb, *to be angry*, freq. in Hom. (esp. Il.), 21.519, al., Hes.*Th.*533: with the addition of θυμόν Il.16.616; κῆρ 1.44; κηρόθι Od.5.284; φρεσὶν ᾗσι Il.19.127; χ. θυμῷ *h.Cer.*330; χ. φρένας ἀμφί Hes.*Th.*554.—Construction: **1.** c. dat. pers., *to be angry at* one, ὅτε χώσεται ἀνδρὶ χέρηϊ Il.1.80, al. **2.** c. gen. pers. vel rei, χωόμενον κατὰ θυμὸν..γυναικός *about* or *because of* her, ib.429, cf. 2.689; χώσατο δ' αἰνῶς ἀμφότερον νίκης τε καὶ ἔγχεος 13.165, etc. **3.** c. acc. rei, only in the phrase μή μοι τόδε χώεο *be* not *angry with* me *for* this, Od.5.215; μὴ νύν μοι τόδε χώεο 23.213. **4.** folld. by ὅττι, χώσατο δ' Ἕκτωρ, ὅττι ῥά οἱ βέλος ὠκὺ ἐτώσιον ἔκφυγε χειρός Il.14.406, 22.291. 5. with a Prep., περὶ βουσί(ν) Hes.*Sc.*12, *h.Merc.*236.

⊛ **χώρα**, Ion. **χώρη**, ἡ, = χῶρος, *space* or *room in which a thing is*, defined as *partly occupied space*, distd. fr. κενόν and τόπος, Zeno *Stoic.* 1.26 (cf.2.163), S.E.*P.*3.124; ποταγορεύοντι τὰν ὕλαν τόπον καὶ χώραν Ti.Locr.94b (in ὁ τόπος τῆς χ. Pl.*Lg.*705c χώρα = *country* (cf. II.1); so χώρας ἐν τόποις Λιβυστικοῖς A.*Eu.*292); οὐδέ τι πολλὴ χώρη μεσσηγύς Il.23.521; νόμισμα.. χώρας μεγάλης δέοιτ' ἄν X.*Lac.*7.5; χώραν τινὶ καταλιπεῖν leave *room* for it, Plu.2.123f, etc. 2. generally, *place, spot*, στρέψεσθ' ἐκ χώρης ὅθι.. Il.6.516, cf. Od.16.352; ὀλίγῃ ἐνὶ χ. Il. 17.394; χώραν ἐκ χώρας μεταβάλλειν move from *place* to *place*, Pl.*Tht.* 181c; *field* in a ceiling, *IG*4²(1).103.193, 106ii 139 (Epid., iv B.C.); ἡ πρώτη χ. the first *field* (on the chest of Cypselus), Paus.5.17.6; *socket* or *cavity* of a joint, Hp.*Art.*79, 80; of the eye, *IG*4²(1).121. 76 (Epid., iv B.C.); as euphemism for the *genital organs*, *Hippiatr.* 33, 71. 3. *the position, proper place* of a person or thing, ἐνὶ χώρῃ ἕζεται Il.23.349: esp. a soldier's *post*, Ἄρης οὐκ ἐνὶ χώρᾳ is not at his *post* (or perh. in the *land*, cf. Ar.*Lys.*524) A.*Ag.*78 (anap.); χώραν λιπεῖν, προλείπειν, Th.4.126, 2.87; μισθοφορεῖν κενάς χ. draw pay for unfilled *vacancies*, Aeschin.3.146; ἐπιγράψαι αὐτῷ τὴν χ. *UPZ*14. 88 (ii B.C.): later τὴν χ. τινὸς ἀποπληρῶσαι, ποιῆσαι, fill a person's *place*, *POxy.*136.15 (vi A.D.), *PMasp.*32.11 (vi A.D.): χώραν λαβεῖν take a *position*, find *one's place*, ἕως ἂν χώραν λάβῃ [τὰ πράγματα] till they are brought into *position*, into *order*, X.*Cyr.*4.5.37; οὐ διδοὺς ἑτέρῳ τόπον οὐδὲ χώραν διακονίας Plu.2.62d; οὐκ ἂν ἔχοι χώραν νοήσεως ἥντινοῦν τὸ ἀγαθόν the Good cannot have any *possibility* of thinking, Plot.5.6.6; σοὶ ἀστρονομεῖν χ. your *province* is astronomy, Philostr. *VA*5.15; ἐν τοῖς ἀτέχνοις χώραν ἔχει τὸ αὐτόματον Eun.*Hist.*p.225 D.: freq. in the phrase ὥρα καὶ χ., time and *place*, ἐν ὁποίᾳ ἀξία φυτευθῆναι καὶ ὥρᾳ καὶ χώρᾳ Pl.*Hipparch.*225c; ἐν ἄλλῃ ὥρῃ καὶ χώρῃ Hp.*Hum.* 14; πρὸς ὥρας καὶ χώρας καὶ διαίτας ib.16, *Aph.*3.3; ἥ τε τοῦ ἔτους ὥρα καὶ χ. καὶ φύσις τοῦ θεραπευομένου σώματος Gal.18(2).399, cf. Alex.Trall.1.10, Steph. *in Hp.*1.161, 180 D. b. in metric, *position* of a foot in a verse, τὸ δακτυλικὸν δέχεται δακτύλους καὶ σπονδείους κατὰ πᾶσαν χ. Heph.7.1, cf. 8.1; αἱ περιτταὶ χ. Id.5.1, 6.1. 4. metaph., *station, place, position*, ἐν χώρᾳ τινὸς εἶναι to be in his *position*, be counted the same as he is, ἐν ἀνδραπόδων or μισθοφόρου χώρᾳ εἶναι to be in the *position* of slaves or mercenaries, to pass or rank as such, X.*An.*5.6.13, *Cyr.*2.1.18; ἐν οὐδεμιᾷ χ. εἶναι to have no *place* or *rank*, be in no *esteem*, Id.*An.*5.7.28; οὐ μέλλει χώρη μηδεμίαν θέμεναι Thgn.152; τούτων τοι χώρη.. ὀλίγη τελέθει Id.822; τὰς μεγίστας χ. ἔχειν Plb.1.43.1. 5. in senses 3 and 4 freq. with a Prep., ἐκ χώρας ὁρμᾶν, opp. πορευόμενος μάχεσθαι, X.*An.*3.4.33; εἰς τὰς ἑαυτῶν χ. πάρεισι are at their *posts*, Id.*Cyr.*1.2.4, cf. Theoc. 15.57; εἰς τὰς τῶν λοχαγῶν χ. καταστήσεσθαι X.*Cyr.*2.1.23; ἐν χώρᾳ in *one's place*, at *one's post*, ἐν ταῖς χ. γενέσθαι Id.*An.*4.8.15; ἐν χώρᾳ πίπτειν, ἀποθνήσκειν, die at *one's post*, Id.*HG*4.2.20, 8.39; ἐπὶ χώρας ἔσσαι set it in *its place*, Pi.*P.*4.273; also μένειν ἐπὶ χώρας, = μένειν κατὰ χώραν, remain in *force*, *OGI*90.16 (Rosetta, ii B.C.), *BGU*183. 9 (i A.D.); κατὰ χώρην εἶναι be in *one's place*, Hdt.4.135; [φόροι] κατὰ χώρην διατελέουσι ἔχοντες Id.6.42, cf. Ar.*Pl.*367, *Ra.*793; κατὰ χ. μένειν Hdt.7.95, 8.108, Ar.*Eq.*1354, Th.4.26; ἤλπιζον.. οὐ μενεῖν κατὰ χ. τὰ πράγματα ib.76; μένει τὸ ὅρκιον κατὰ χ. *as it was, undisturbed*, Hdt.4.201; ἐᾶν κατὰ χ. τὴν πόλιν leave in *its place*, leave *as it was*, X.*HG*6.5.6, cf. Hdt.1.17; κατὰ χώραν μένειν τοὺς ἄλλους [νόμους] ἐᾶν D.24.5; κατὰ χ. ἀπιέναι retire in their old *order*, X. *An.*6.4.11. II. *land*, viz., 1. *a land, country*, ἅς τινας ἵκεο χώρας ἀνθρώπων Od.8.573; ἡ χ. ἡ Ἀττική Hdt.9.13; ἐμπορεύεσθαι εἰς τὴν χ. *IG*1².57.21, cf. 63.22, al.: freq. in Trag., Ἑλλάδα χώραν A.*Pers.*271 (lyr.); Εὐβοΐδα χ. S.*Tr.*74, etc.; *territory*, ὁ τύραννος ἢ πόλεως ἢ χ. πολλῆς [ἐπιθυμεῖ] X.*Hier.*4.7: pl., *OGI*54.11 (Adule, iii B.C.), etc. 2. *landed estate*, X.*Cyr.*8.4.28, 8.6.4. b. *country town*, τοὺς κήρυκας διαπέμψαντες ἐς τὰς χ. *Schwyzer* 688 *B*8 (Chios, v B.C.). 3. *the country*, opp. to the town, ἡ πόλις καὶ ἡ χ. Lycurg. 1; τὰ ἐκ τῆς χώρας Th.2.5, X.*Mem.*3.6.11; ὁ ἐκ τῆς χ. γιγνόμενος σῖτος ib.13; οἱ ἐν τῇ χ. ἐργάται Id.*Hier.*10.5; ἐν τῇ χώρᾳ κοιταῖον γίγνεσθαι, opp. ἐν ἄστει, Decr.ap.D.18.37; ἁ κοινὰ χ. (of two cities) *IG*4²(1).77.2 (Epid., ii B.C.): esp. of Egypt as opp. Alexandria, *OGI*56.5 (Canopus, iii B.C.), *PHib.*1.27.167 (iii B.C.), etc. (but in *PTeb.*5.98 (ii B.C.) ἐν τῇ Ἀλεξα(νδρέων) χ. means 'in Alexandria'); ἡ ἄνω χ. καὶ ἡ κάτω, Upper and Lower Egypt, *OGI*90.46 (Rosetta, ii B.C.), cf. Wilcken *Chr.*109.9 (iii B.C.).—χῶρος is another form: in signf. II χώρα alone is used in Att.; whereas in signf. I χῶρος is common, exc. in the special sense of *one's proper place* or *post* (χῶρος and χώρα perh. cogn. with χῆρος, χῆτος).

**χωρ-άζω**, Dor. I. aor. imper. χωραξάντω *IG*5(1).1390.37 (Andania, i B.C.):—*set up*, ὑδρἀνας l.c.; of an inscription, χ. ἰν τὸς νόμος ... τὰν ἐκεχειρίαν *SIG*559.47 (Magn. Mae., from Megalopolis, iii B.C.). **-αρχία**, ἡ, *district under a governor*, *S.Pelekides* 74 (Thessalonica). **-άσμιος**, α, ον, dub. sens., χωράσμιαι ἐλέαι ( = ἐλαῖαι) *Supp.Epigr.*6.673.3 (Pamphylia, ii A.D.) (but χ' ὡρασμέναι ἐλέαι '600 *mature* olive plants' (fr. ὡράζω, = ὡραΐζω) acc. to Keil's reading). **-αυλος**, ον, (αὐλή) *dwelling in the country*, Suid. **-αφιαῖος**, α, ον, *belonging to a small farm*, Hdn.*Epim.*152. ⊛**-άφιον** [ᾰ], τό, Dim. of χώρα, *small farm*, Thphr.*Fr.*171.7; gloss on βλάστημα, Sch.E.*Hec.*1204. ⊛ **-επίσκοπος**, ὁ, *country-bishop*, i.e. *coadjutor* or *suffragan-bishop*, *Supp.Epigr.*8.21.3 (Palestine, vi A.D.), etc. ⊛**-έω**, Anacr.108, etc.; fut. χωρήσω Il.16.629, Hdt.5.89, 8.68.β', Hp.*Nat.Puer.*18, and in later Prose, as D.H.4.9, Luc.*DDeor.* 20.15, etc.; Att. only in Th.1.82 (exc. in compds., ἀνα-χωρήσω Id. 7.72, ἀπο- X.*Eq.Mag.*6.2, προ- Th.3.4, προσ- Id.2.2, συγ- Id.1.140, etc.); elsewh. in Trag. and Att. always in med. form, χωρήσομαι, A.*Th.*476, S.*El.*404, Th.2.20, etc., and freq. in compds.: aor. ἐχώρησα, Ep. χώρησα, Il.15.655, *h.Cer.*430, Th.4.120, etc.: pf. κεχώρηκα Hdt.1.120, 122, Th.1.122, Hp.*Acut.*19, etc.:—**Pass.**, fut. χωρηθήσομαι (συγ-) Plb.15.17.5: aor. ἐχωρήθην (συν-) X.*HG* 3.2.31, D.38.4: pf. κεχώρηται (παρα-) D.H.11.52, (συγ-) Pl. *Phlb.*15a: (χῶρος):—*make room for another, give way, withdraw*, ἐχώρησαν πάλιν αὖτις Il.17.533; γαῖα ἔνερθε χώρησεν the earth *gave way* from beneath, i.e. opened, *h.Cer.* l.c.; χ. πρύμναν, = κρούεσθαι πρύμναν, *put back, retire*, E.*Andr.*1120; χωρεῖτε *begone!* A.*Eu.*196, cf. E.*Or.*1678, *Med.*820, etc.—The uncompounded word does not occur in Od. and only fut. and aor. in Il.—Construction: 1. c. gen. rei vel loci, χώρησεν τυτθὸν ἐπάλξιος Il.12.406; νεῶν ἐχώρησαν 15.655; νεκροῦ χωρήσουσι 16.629; also νηῶν ἄπο.. ἐχώρησαν προτὶ Ἴλιον 13.724; ἀπὸ κρατερῆς ὑσμίνης χωρήσαντες 18.244; ἔξω τῶνδε δωμάτων χωρεῖτε A.*Eu.*180; ἐκ πυλῶν Id.*Th.*476; ἐκ προαστίου S.*El.* 1432. 2. c. dat. pers., *give way to* one, *make way for* him, *retire before* him, οὐδ' ἂν Ἀχιλλῆϊ χωρήσειεν Il.13.324, cf. 17.101. II. after Hom., *go forward, advance*, τὸ πῦρ.. πρόσω κεχώρηκεν Call. in *PSI*11. 1216.34; simply, *go* or *come*, Hdt.1.10, etc.; *go on one's journey, travel*, S.*OT*750; χ. ἐπ' ἀδελφεοῦ βίαν Pi.*N.*10.73, etc.; ἐς ναῦν A.*Pers.* 379; χ. πρὸς ἔργον *come* to action, S.*Aj.*116, Ar.*Ra.*884; χ. πρὸς ἧπαρ *go* to one's heart, S.*Aj.*938; χωρῶν ἀπειλεῖ νῦν *go and* threaten, Id.*OC*1038; διὰ φόνου χ. E.*Andr.*176; τὰ τοξεύματα ἐχώρει διὰ τῶν ἀσπίδων, of weapons, X.*An.*4.2.28; τὸ ὕδωρ κατὰ τὰς τάφρους ἐχώρει it *went off* by.., Id.*Cyr.*7.5.16; ἄνω ποταμῶν χωροῦσι παγαί E.*Med.* 410 (lyr.), cf. X.*HG*2.4.10; χώρει κάτω *go* downwards, i.e. beginning from the upper parts of the body, A.*Pr.*74; διὰ στόμα χωροῦντα.. ἀφρόν E.*Med.*1174; χ. κύκλῳ [ὁ ποταμός] Pl.*Phd.*113b; ὁμόσε χ. τισί to join battle, Th.6.101, Ar.*Lys.*451, cf. ὁμόσε I. 2; χ. ὁμόσε τοῖς λόγοις E.*Or.*921; χ. δειπνήσων Ar.*Fr.*272; πρὸς τὸ ἱερὸν χωρῆσαι δρόμῳ Th.1.134; χωροῖς ἂν εἴσω S.*El.*1491, *Ph.*674; χώρει, ξέν', ἔξω Id.*OC*824: of Time, νὺξ ἐχώρει the night *was passing, near an end*, A.*Pers.*384; βιοστερὴς χ. *wander about*, S.*OC*747: Medic., of excretions, τὰ χωρέοντα μὴ τῷ πλήθει τεκμαίρεσθαι, ἀλλ' ὡς ἂν χωρέῃ οἷα δεῖ Hp.*Aph.*1.23; also of the menses, Id.*Mul.*1.2: c. acc. loci, Κεκροπίαν χθόνα χ. E.*Ion*1572. b. *to be in motion* or *flux*, πάντα χωρεῖ Heraclit.ap.Pl.*Cra.*402a, cf. Hp.*Vict.*1.5. 2. *go forward, make progress*, τοὔργον οὐ χωρεῖ πρόσω A.*Dict.* in *PSI*11.1209.16; πῶς οὖν οὐ χωρεῖ τοὔργον; Ar.*Pax*472 (lyr.); χωρεῖ.. τὸ πρᾶγμα ib. 509; τόκοι χωροῦσιν Id.*Nu.*18; χωρεῖ τὸ κακόν Id.*V.*1483, *Nu.*907 (both anap.). 3. *come to an issue, turn out* in a certain manner, παρὰ σμικρὰ.. κεχώρηκε *have come* to little, of the event of oracles, Hdt.1.120; εὐτυχέως χ. Id.3.39; κακῶς χ. *turn out* ill, Pl.*Lg.*684e; δόξα δ' ἐχώρει δίχα E.*Hec.*117 (anap.), cf. *Hel.*759: freq. abs., *advance, succeed*, Hdt.3.42, 5.89; πάντα διὰ πράξεων καὶ.. ἀγώνων κεχωρηκότα.. Ῥωμαίοις Onos.*Praef.*8; τὰ πράγματα χωρεῖ κατὰ λόγον Plb. 28.17.12; ὁ λόγος ὁ ἐμὸς οὐ χωρεῖ ἐν ὑμῖν *Ev.Jo.*8.37 (unless in signf. III. infr.); also, *to be possible*, οὐ γάρ οἱ χωρεῖ περιβαλεῖν κτλ. Ael. *VH*1.3 (sed leg. ἐγχωρεῖ). 4. *to be spread abroad*, ἡ φάτις κεχώρηκε a report *spread*, Hdt.1.122; διὰ πάντων οὕτως ἐχώρει "τίς ἕψεται;" X.*Cyr.*3.3.62; κλαυθμὸς διὰ πάντων ἐχώρει Plu.*Rom.*19; ὄνομα δόξῃ διὰ πάντων ἀνθρώπων κεχωρηκός a name *spread abroad*, ib.1. 5. of money, *to be spent*, τὰς μὲν δαπάνας χωρεῖν ἐντελεῖς ἐκ τῶν οἴκων, τὰ δὲ ἔργα μὴ τελεῖσθαι λυσιτελούντως πρὸς τὴν δαπάνην X.*Oec.*20.21; τὰ προσγεινόμενα χωρήσει εἰς ἃ ἂν ὁ δῆμος θελήσῃ *IG*5(1).18*B*6 (Sparta), cf. 1432.4 (Messene, i B.C./i A.D.). III. trans., *have room for* a thing, *hold, contain*, freq. of measures, κρητὴρ χωρέων ἀμφορέας ἑξακοσίους Hdt.1.51, cf. 192, 4.61, Ar.*Nu.* 1238, Pl.*Smp.*214a; οὐκ ἐχώρησεν αὐτοὺς ἡ πόλις Th.2.17, cf. D.21. 200, Aeschin.3.164, E.*Hipp.*941; οὐκ ἐχώρει αὐτοὺς ἡ γῆ κατοικεῖν ἅμα Lxx *Ge.*13.6; ποτήρια.. οὐχὶ χωροῦντ' οὐδὲ κόγχην Pherecr. 143.3 (troch.); κοτύλας χ. δέκα Men.*Kol.Fr.*2, cf. Diph.96, etc.; χωρήσατε ἡμᾶς *take* us *into your hearts!* 2 *Ep.Cor.*7.2; οὐ πάντες χωροῦσι τὸν λόγον τοῦτον *find room for*.., *Ev.Matt.*19.11 (so perh. intr., *Ev.Jo.*8.37, v. supr. II. 3); *to be capable of*, τὸ Κάτωνος φρόνημα Plu.*Cat.Mi.*64: c. inf., *to be capable* of doing, οὐ χωρεῖ μεγάλην διδαχὴν ἀδίδακτος ἀκούειν (v.l. for ἀκουή) Ps.-Phoc.89; δωρεὰν ὅσην οὐκ ἐχωρήσατε αἰτεῖσθαι *IG*7.2713.11 (Acraeph., Oratio Neronis). 2. impers., ὅταν μηκέτι χωρῇ αὐταῖς ἐργαζομέναις [ταῖς μελίτταις] when *there is* no more *room* for them, Arist.*HA*626ᵇ11. **-ημα**, ατος, τό, *space, room*, *Gp.*4.1.16, *PMag.Par.*1.1087, Secund.*Sent.*15; *cavity*, τὸ τοῦ ἀναδέσμου χ. Heliod.ap.Orib.48.50.3: *receptacle*, c. gen., χ. ἡ ψυχὴ ἢ θεῶν ἢ δαιμόνων Porph.*Marc.*21, cf. 19; χόριον τὸ χ. τοῦ ἐμβρύου Gal.19.454. **-ημάτιον**, τό, Dim. of foreg., Ps.-Callisth.1.6. **-ησις**, εως, ἡ, *a going, proceeding*, ἡ ὁμόσε χ., = τὸ ὁμόσε χωρεῖν (v. χωρέω II. 1), Hld.6.5. II. Math., *progression*, ἡ ἐπ' ἄπειρον χ. *Theol.Ar.*34 (v.l. προχ-). III. = *capacitas*, *Gloss.* **-ητέον**, *one must go on, proceed*, D.H.1.56, Herod.Med. in *Rh.Mus.*58.106, Iamb. *in Nic.*p.35 P.: pl., ὅπῃ αὐτοῖς χωρητέα εἴη Procop.*Vand.*1.19. ⊛ **-ητικός**, ή, όν, *able to contain*, ὑγρότητος Sch.Ptol.19. 2. *capable of*, ἄνθρωπος ζῷον λογισμοῦ χ. Ael.*NA*2. 11, cf. S.E.*P.*3.121. Adv. **-κῶς** Suid. s.v. χανδόν.

**χωρί**, = χωρίς, χ. διατμήγουσι Call.*Fr.*48, cf. *Test.Epict.*5.7: c. gen., *excluding*, *Schwyzer* 197.38 (Itanos, iii B.C.).

**χωριάζεσθαι**· λέγειν, Hsch. **χωρῐᾱμός**· κίστη Id. (perh. for φωριαμός).

⊛ **χωρίδιον**, τό, Dim. of χωρίον 3, Lys.19.28, Plu.Cat.Ma.2; written **χωρείδιον** IG7.2808.8 (Hyettus, iii A.D.) [ῐ in Com.ap.POxy.1803.23].

**χωρ-ίζω**, pf. Pass. κεχώρισμαι, 3 pl. Ion. κεχωρίδαται Hdt.1.140, 151, al.: (χωρίς). I. in local sense, separate, divide, χ. ἀλλήλων λόχους E.Ph.108; exclude, τὴν πτέρνην Hp.Fract.11, etc.: τί τινος, freq. in Pl., χ. τὴν ψυχὴν τοῦ σώματος R.609d, cf. Phlb.55e; ἀπὸ τοῦ σώματος τὴν ψ. Phd.67c, cf. Plt.268c, etc.; πάντα κατὰ φυλάς X.Oec.9.8; with inf. added, [τὴν τάξιν] ἐπὶ τῷ μέσῳ ἐχώρισεν ἕπεσθαι Id.An.6.5.11; οἱ χωρίζοντες the Separators, a name given to those Grammarians (Xenon and Hellanicus acc. to Procl.Chr.p.102 Allen) who ascribed the Iliad and Odyssey to different authors, Sch.A Il.2.356,649, 11.692, 21.416:—Pass., to be separated, severed, or divided, Hdt.1.151, 3.12, al.; τινος E.IT1002, Pl.Ti.31b; σοφὸν..πάντων κεχωρισμένον Heraclit.108. II. separate in thought, distinguish, ἡδύ τε καὶ δίκαιον Pl.Lg.663a; ἀπὸ τῶν ὠφελίμων τὰ καθ' αὑτά Arist.EN1096b14; χ. καὶ διασπᾶν Id.PA642b18; esp. in Logic, τὸν ἴδιον τῆς οὐσίας ἑκάστου λόγον ταῖς..οἰκείαις διαφοραῖς χ. Id.Top.108b6, cf. 132a13:—Pass., to be different, κεχωρίδαται πολλὸν τῶν..ἄλλων ἀνθρώπων Hdt.1.140: less freq. c. dat., κεχώρισται οὗτος ὁ χειμὼν..τοῖσι ἐν ἄλλοισι χωρίοισι γινομένοισι χειμῶσι Id.4.28; ἀπ' ἀλλήλων Isoc.14.49; νόμοι κεχωρισμένοι τῶν ἄλλων ἀνθρώπων laws apart from others, far different, Hdt.1.172, cf. Plb.31.23.11; γνῶμαι κεχωρισμέναι Hdt.4.11; opp. συγκεχυμένος, Pl.R.524c; κεχώρισται πλεῖστον τό τ' εἶναι καὶ τὸ τοῦτον φάσκειν D.45.26. III. Pass., κεχωρισμένη ἀπὸ τοῦ ἀνδρός divorced, Plb.31.26.6; θᾶσσον..οἰστοῦ..χωρίζεται, of a wife, E.Fr.1063.13. IV. later in Pass., depart, go away, Plb.3.94.9, D.S.19.65, Heraclit.Incred.8; ἐκ θρόνων Ezek.Exag.76. **-ικός**, ή, όν, (χώρα) rustic, rural, Vett.Val.7.8; ἐργάται POxy.141.5 (vi A.D.), cf. Poll.9.13; in Egypt, λειτουργίαι χ., of services rendered in the χώρα, i.e. outside Alexandria (cf. χώρα II.3), OGI669.34 (i A.D.); χ. βιβλιοθήκη PFlor.46.1 (ii A.D.). 2. indigenous, κάλαμος PMag.Par.1.63; ἀρτεμισία cj. for χλωρ- (q.v.) ib.914; φῦκος PHolm.21.45. ⊛ **-ίον**, τό, Dim. (only in form, cf. χ. μέγιστον Th.2.19) of χῶρος and χώρα: 1. place, spot, district, very freq. in Prose from Hdt. downwards, e.g. 2.8,10,29, Th.2.54; also in Com., as Ar.Nu.209, etc.; never in Trag.: ἐκ τοῦ αὐτοῦ χ. from the same spot, Hdt.1.11; χ. ἔρημον, χ. χαλεπὰ καὶ πετρώδη, Th.4.9; χ. ἱππάσιμα X.Cyr.1.4.14: pl., sites, οἰκίσαι χωρία Th.1.12. 2. town, ib.100, etc.; χωρίων κατάληψις Pl.Grg.455b, cf. Lys.28.7, etc. 3. landed property, estate, Th.1.106, Pl.Lg.844b, Lys.7.4, IG1².325.10; used with ἀγρός, X.HG2.4.1, etc. 4. place of business, office, D.45.33. 5. space, room, Th.1.63, etc.; esp. in Geom., space enclosed by lines, area, figure, Pl.Men.82b sq., Ar.Nu.152, Euc.Dat.55, Papp.240.17: esp. rectangle, Archim.Con.Sph.2, al. 6. passage in a book, Hdt.2.117 (unless interpol.), Luc.Hist.Conscr.12, Ath.15.672a, Simp.in Cael.126.4. b. subject, Th.1.97: pl., topics, Lycurg.31. 7. Medic., part of the body, Hp.Fract.2, cf. Aph.1.21 (pl.); τὸ χ. τὸ ἐπὶ τοῦ ἥπατος periphr. for the gall-bladder, Id.Morb.4.36.

**χωρίς**, Adv., also **χωρί**, q.v.: (v. χῆρος):—separately, apart, once in Il., 7.470; χ. μὲν πρόγονοι, χ. δὲ μέτασσαι, χ. δ' αὖθ' ἕρσαι Od.9.221, cf. 4.130, Sapph.Supp.20a.16, IG1².108.32, al.; χ. ἡ τιμὴ θεῶν A.Ag.637; κεῖται χ. ὁ νεκρός Hdt.4.62; χ. περὶ αὐτῶν ἑκάστου οἱ νόμοι κεῖνται Antipho 5.10; χίλια τάλαντα..χ. θέσθαι set them apart, in reserve, Th.2.24; χ. οἰκεῖν live apart, have an independent establishment, D.4.36, 47.72; χ. γενόμενοι being separated, X.Cyr.4.1.18; χ. ἀπ' ἀλλήλων Parm.8.56, Pl.Phd.98c; μή με χ. αἰτιῶ without evidence, S.OT608; χ. ποιῆσαι distinguish, Isoc.15.68; χ. βλέπειν look two ways, squint, Timocl.27.6; opp. κοινῇ, Isoc.12.160; opp. κοινόν, E.Hec.860; χ. δέ..and separately, and besides, Th.2.13; separately, Lys.22.16, Plu.Arist.20; λέγειν χ. περὶ ἑκάστου Lex ap.Aeschin.1.35; χ. καὶ ἐν μέρει Id.3.2; περὶ τὸ ἓν καὶ χ. about the one and without [the one] Arist.Ph.203a14; otherwise, χ. δὲ μηδαμῶς Pl.Lg.950c; χ. ἢ ὁκόσοι except so many as.., Hdt.2.77; χωρὶς ἢ ὅσα D.C.53.21; χωρὶς ἢ ὅτι Hdt.1.94, 4.61,82; also χ. εἰ μή (condemned by Ps.-Hdn. post Moer.p.462 P.), Plu.2.698f, A.D.Pron.91.8, al.; χ. πλήν Paus.1.34.4. 2. metaph., of different nature, kind, or quality, Semon.7.1; χ. τό τ' εἶναι καὶ τὸ μὴ νομίζεται E.Alc.528; χ. τό τ' εἰπεῖν πολλὰ καὶ τὰ καίρια S.OC808; χ. φημὶ εἶναι τὸ συνεῖναί τε ἀλλήλοις διαλεγομένους καὶ τὸ δημηγορεῖν Pl.Prt.336b. II. as Prep. c. gen., without, A.Ag.926, etc.; without the help or will of, χ. Ζηνὸς S.Tr.1002 (lyr.): after its case, πόνου χ. Id.El.945, cf. Theon.Sm.p.1H. 2. separate from, apart from, χ. ἀθανάτων Pi.O.9.41; χ. ἀνθρώπων στίβου S.Ph.487; χωρὶς ᾤκισται θεῶν E.Hec.2; χ. ὀμμάτων ἐμῶν Id.Or.272; ἡ ψυχὴ χ. τοῦ σώματος Pl.Phd.67a, etc. 3. independently of, without reckoning, Hdt.1.93,106, 6.58; χ. τε γένους οὐκ ἔστιν ὅτῳ μείζονα μοῖραν νείμαιμ' ἢ σοί A.Pr.293 (anap.); χ. δὲ τῆς δόξης οὐδὲ δίκαιόν μοι δοκεῖ..Pl.Ap.35b. 4. differently from, otherwise than, χ. μυρηρῶν τευχέων πνέων A.Fr.180.5; χ. δήπου σοφία ἐστὶν ἀνδρείας Pl.La.195a, cf. D.19.13.

**χωρ-ίσιμος** [ῐσ], η, ον, separate (?), PFlor.64.9, al. (iv A.D.); written **χωρήσιμος** PLond.5.1653.47 (iv A.D.). **-ισις**, εως, ἡ, separation, Plot.1.3.3, Hsch. s.v. χάσις (χώρησις cod.). **-ισμα**, ατος, τό, a separated space, Sch.B Il.5.137. ⊛ **-ισμός**, ὁ, separation, λύσις καὶ χ. ψυχῆς ἀπὸ σώματος Pl.Phd.67d; χ. δέχεσθαι, opp. συνεζεῦχθαι, Arist.EN1175a20. 2. secretion of sap, Thphr.CP6.7.3. 3. abstraction, Plot.4.7.8. II. (from Pass.) a being separated, parting, departure, Plb.5.16.6, D.S.17.10; τὸν χ. ποιήσασθαι Id.2.60; seclusion, LxxLe.12.2, 18.19; ὁ ἀπὸ θεοῦ χ. Hierocl. in CA24p.472M. **-ιστέον**, one must separate, τι ἀπό τινος Pl.Plt.303d; also τι τινός, τῆς ὀχείας τοὺς κριούς Gp.18.3.1, cf. Iamb.Protr.21.κγ'. 2. χωριστέος, α, ον, to be separated, A.D.Pron.52.23. **-ιστής**, οῦ, ὁ, one who separates, Gloss. **-ιστικός**, ή, όν, separative, only in Adv. -κῶς, Gal.19.466. ⊛ **-ιστός**, ή, όν, separable, physically or logically, λόγῳ ἢ τόπῳ Arist.de An.413b14; μεγέθει ib.432a20; τῇ νοήσει Id.Ph.193b34; κατὰ τὸν λόγον χ. Id.Metaph.1025b28; of the Platonic ideas, ib.1086b9, cf. EN1096b33; χ. κτῆμα alienable property, of slaves, Id.Pol.1254a17. II. existing separately, abstract, οὐθὲν..χωριστόν ἐστι παρὰ τὴν οὐσίαν Id.Ph.185a31, cf. Metaph.1028a34, 1029a28; χ. ποσόν abstract quantity, Plot.6.3.11; χ. δημιουργία Jul.Or.4.144b, cf. 7.217d. Adv. -τῶς Iamb.Myst.1.9, al., Id.ap.Stob.1.5.18. ⊛ **-ίτης** [ῑ], ου, ὁ, countryman, rustic, boor, S.Fr.21, X.HG3.2.31, AP7.657 (Leon.), Muson.Fr.11p.60H.:—fem. **-ῖτις**, -ιδος, a country girl, Luc.DDeor.20.13. 2. one dwelling in a place or country, inhabitant, A.Eu.1035 (lyr.); χ. δράκων Id.Fr.123, cf. S.Fr.226. 3. inhabitant of a country town (χῶρος II.4), οἱ χ. οἱ Ζελειτῶν, opp. οἱ κωμῆται οἱ Συκηνῶν, LW1534 (Smyrna). **-ιτικός**, ή, όν, of country-folk, rustic, πλῆθος Plu.Per.34; χ. ἀνήρ countryman, Ael.VH9.27. Adv. -κῶς in rustic fashion, opp. ἐν χλιδῇ, X.Cyr.4.5.54, cf. Muson.Fr.11p.59H.

**χωροβᾰτ-έω**, measure by paces, survey, τὴν γῆν LxxJo.18.8, cf. PCair.Zen.329.11 (iii B.C.). 2. use a level, Hero Dioptr.12. **-ης** [ᾰ], ου, ὁ, instrument used by surveyors, level, Vitr.8.5.1 II. land-surveyor, MAMA3.694 (Corycus, spelt χορο-).

**χωρογρᾰφ-έω**, describe countries, χ. τὴν Εὐρώπην Str.2.4.1. 2. mark out boundaries, Ostr.Strassb.664,669. 3. design, lay out, plan, τὸ μῆκος τῆς πόλεως Ps.-Callisth.1.31. 4. serve as metator in the Roman army, IGRom.1.1365 (Egypt, i A.D.). 5. generally, demarcate, of a snake's teeth, Sch.Nic.Th.234 (Pass.). **-ία**, ἡ, description of a country or countries, Plb.34.1.5, Str.8.3.17; title of works by Varro, Cicero, etc., cf. Ptol.Geog.Praef.1: pl., plans or maps, SIG685.71 (Magn. Mae., ii B.C.), Vitr.8.2.6. II. Astrol., assignment of countries to their tutelary sign or planet, Vett.Val.360.24. **-ικός**, ή, όν, of or for the description of countries, πίναξ Str.2.5.17. **-ος** (parox.), ον, describing countries, opp. to the more special term τοπογράφος (describing the single places), as well as to the still more general term γεωγράφος, Str.1.1.16.

**χωροθεσία**, ἡ, geographical situation, Ps.-Plu.Fluv.5.1.

**χωρομετρ-έω**, survey a country, Str.13.4.12. **-ης**, ου, ὁ, land-surveyor, IG5(1).1431.40 (Messene, i A.D.); rendering of Lat. metator, Lyd.Mag.1.46. **-ία**, ἡ, land-surveying, Str.16.2.24.

**χωρονομικός**, ή, όν, (νέμω) of or for the distribution of land, νόμος χ., = Lat. lex agraria, D.H.10.36.

⊛ **χῶρος**, ὁ, like χώρα I, a definite space, piece of ground, place, χῶρον μὲν πρῶτον διεμέτρεον Il.3.315; διαμετρητῷ ἐνὶ χώρῳ ib.344; νεκύων διεφαίνετο χῶρος a space clear of the dead, i.e. not filled by them, 8.491; χ. ὑλήεις, ἐρῆμος, οἰοπόλος, ψαμαθώδης, Od.14.2, Il.10.520, 13.473, h.Merc.75; πίων Hes.Op.390; εὐαής ib.599; καταστύφελος Id.Th.806; ἀσυνήθης Emp.118; region, ἀτερπὴς χ., of the lower world, Od.11.94, cf. Emp.121; so εὐσεβῶν χ. Lycurg.96, Pl.Ax.371c, cf. IG12(7).115.20 (Amorgos); χ. ἀσεβῶν Pl.Ax.371e, Luc.Nec.12; ὁ περίγειος χ. the region of this world, τὸν π. καταλελοιπότες χῶρον μετεωροπολεῖν ἐγνώκασιν Ph.1.196; δένδρε' ἔθαλλεν χ. Pi.O.3.23: pl., Hdt.2.178; Βρόμιος δ' ἔχει τὸν χ. A.Eu.24; θηρῶν οὓς ὅδ' ἔχει χῶρος S.Ph.1148 (lyr.); Μακραὶ δὲ χῶρός ἐστ' ἐκεῖ κεκλημένος E.Ion 283; πόδες δέ οἱ οὐχ ἑνὶ χώρῳ Call.Del.192. 2. space, compass, ποιῆσαι ἐν βραχεῖ χώρῳ τὴν δύναμιν Plb.11.1.3. II. land, country, Hdt.4.30; ὁ Λιβυκὸς χ. v.l. in Id.2.19; τοῦ Ἀταρνέος ἐστὶ χ. Id.1.160; τῆς Ἀραβίης 2.75: pl., lands, τῶν Θηβαίων ἔκειρε τοὺς χ. Id.9.15, cf. S.OT1126: metaph., τὸ γὰρ νεάζον ἐν τοιοῖσδε βόσκεται χ. Id.Tr.145; χ...οὗτος (leg. αὐτός) ἀνθρώπου φρενῶν Id.Fr.910. 2. landed property, estate, Axiop.5, X.Cyr.7.4.6. 3. the country, opp. the town, ἐν τῷ χ. καὶ ἐν τῷ ἄστει Id.Oec.5.4, cf. 11.18; σπείρω τ' ἄρουραν..Βερέκυντα χ. A.Fr.158. 4. country town, IG12(9).189.26 (Eretria, iv B.C., pl.); ὁ χ. ὁ Μοττιανῶν κτλ. LW1745 (Gergis).—Rare in pure Att. Prose (Th.2.20, 7.78, f.l. in Antipho 3.2.8), but common in X.

**χῶρος**, ὁ, north-west wind, Lat. corus, Act.Ap.27.12.

**χωροφῐλ-έω**, = φιλοχωρέω (cf. D.H.Comp.6), cling to a place or spot, haunt it, Thales ap.D.L.1.44; ἐν Αἴνῳ Antipho 5.78. **-ία**, ἡ, love of a place or country, variant in Philostr.Ep.28.

**χωροφύλαξ** [ῠ], ᾰκος, ὁ, guard or watcher of a country or place, Gloss., dub. in CIG5040 (Nubia).

**χωρυτός**, ὁ, collat. form of γωρυτός, Hsch. s.h.v.

⊛ **χῶς**, Dor. for χοῦς (q.v.).

**χῶσις**, εως, ἡ, heaping up, esp. of earth, raising a mound or bank, esp. against a city, Th.2.76. 2. filling up, blocking by earth thrown in, χ. τῶν λιμένων Id.3.2; τάφρου D.H.5.41. 3. embanking, τοῦ θεάτρου IG9(2).522.26 (Larissa, iii/ii B.C.).

**χῶσμα**, ατος, τό, late form for χῶμα, D.S.24.3 cod.

**χωστέον**, one must fill up, τὴν φάραγγα Arr.An.4.21.2; one must pile up, λουτῆρα Gp.14.6.4.

**χωστός**, ή, όν, made by earth thrown up, ἐν χωστοῖς τάφοις κεῖνται E.Rh.414; στενὴ καὶ χωστὴ πάροδος Plb.4.61.7. II. of persons, buried, Tz.H.9.330.

**χωστρίς**, ίδος, ἡ, (χώννυμι) χελώνη χ. a shed to protect besiegers in *filling up the ditch of a town*, Plb.9.41.1, D.H.9.68(pl.), Onos.42.3, Ath.Mech.18.8, al.; without χελώνη, Ph.*Bel.*97.28, Did.ad D.11.22; χωστρίδες distd. fr. χελῶναι, D.S.24.1; opp. χελῶναι κριοφόροι, Id. 20.91.

**χῶν**, prob. Egypt. name of an unguent, νέον χῶν (unless it is one word νεονχων), *PPetr.*2 p.114 (iii B.C.); not found in Egyptian sources.

**χωφορ-έω**, *cart earth*, *PLond.*1.131$^{r}$36, al. (i A.D.), *POxy.*1631.15 (iii A.D.). ❀ **-ιον**, τό, *load of earth*, *PLond.* l. c. 138 (i A.D.), *POxy.* 1577.4 (iii A.D.).

# Ψ

**Ψ ψ**, ψεῖ (q.v.), τό, indecl., twenty-third letter of the Ionic alphabet, Pl.*Cra.*427a, Callias ap.Ath.10.453d: not used in the Attic alphabet: in the Western Gr. alphabets it represents the sound χ (*kh*): with the value *ps* it is found in *SIG*1 (Nubia, vi B.C.), etc.: as a numeral, ψʹ = 700, but ͵ψ = 700,000.

ψ repeated, as exclamation, S.*Ichn.*170.

❀ **ψάγδᾱν**, ᾱνος, or σάγδας, ὁ, an Egyptian *unguent*; the following forms are found: Αἰγυπτίῳ ψάγδανι τρὶς λελουμένη Eub.102; φέρ' ἴδω, τί σοι δῶ τῶν μύρων; ψάγδαν φιλεῖς; Ar.*Fr.*206; σάγδαν ἐρυγγάνοντα Eup.198; βακκαρίς τε καὶ σάγδας ὁμοῦ Epil.1: ψάδᾳ (sic codd.) is cited by Erot. fr. Hp. (not found in codd. Hp.), and fr. Eup. (*Fr.*198 ?): nom. ψαγδης (unaccented) Ath.15.690e, cf. **ψαγδῆς**, Hsch. (Egypt. *sgnn* with or without prefixed masc. Art. *p3*).

**ψάγιος** [ᾰ], α, ον, *oblique, askew*, metaph., *mal à propos, blundering*, εἰ πὰρ μέλος ἔρχομαι ψάγιον (sic codd. vett.) δᾶρον ἐννέπων Pi.*N.*7. 69: **ψάγιον**· πλάγιον, λοξόν, ἐπικεκλιμένον, Hsch.; **ψάδιον**· κάταντες, Id.

**ψάδδα**· ἡ κινάβαρις, Id. **ψαδυρός**, v. ψαθυρός. **ψαέναι**· φθάσαι, κτίσαι, Id.

**ψᾰθάλλω**, *scratch, rub*, σὺ δὲ τὴν κεφαλὴν ψάθαλλέ μου *scratch* my head, Hermipp.78, cf. Pl.Com.59.

**ψαθαρός**, v. ψαθυρός.

**ψάθεα**· ψωμία, Hsch. (ψαθέα cod.).

**ψᾰθοπλόκος**, ὁ, = ψιαθοπλόκος, *Sammelb.*5124.332 (ii A.D.).

**ψᾰθύριον** [ῠ], τό, = ψώθιον, Ath.14.646c.

**ψαθύρματα**· ἀποκόμματα, Hsch.

**ψᾰθῠρόομαι**, Pass., *crumble away*, Aq.*Jo.*9.5(11), *Ps.*101(102).4.

**ψᾰθῠρός**, όν, *friable, crumbling*, of the roe in fish, Arist.*HA*510$^{b}$26; ἰχθῦς.. τοὺς σαρκώδεις καὶ ψ. Diocl.*Fr.*141; opp. γλίσχρος, Arist. *Mete.*387$^{a}$15; of bread, Gal.6.523; of cheese, opp. κολλώδης, ib.698 (Comp.); of meat, Ruf.ap.Orib.4.2.8 (Comp.); τὸ ὕδωρ ψ. Arist. *Sens.*441$^{a}$25; of air, Id.*de An.*419$^{b}$35; of earth, Thphr.*CP*2.4.11, Nic.*Al.*145; γῆ -ωτέρα *Gp.*3.3.10; of the texture of some bulbs, Thphr.*HP*7.9.4; of leaves in a salad, Hp.*Liqu.*5 (Comp.); also **ψαδυρόν**· ἀσθενές, μαδαρόν, ψαθυρόν, Hsch. (the form is Att. acc. to Gal.16.760), and **ψαθαρά**· εὔθλαστα, etc., Hsch.; cf. ψαφαρός.

**ψᾰθῠρότης**, ητος, ἡ, *looseness of consistency*, Arist.*HA*524$^{b}$26, *Pr.* 928$^{a}$10, Gal.6.799.

**ψαιδρά**· ἀραιότριχα, Hsch.: **ψαιδρόν**· φαιδρόν, .., Id. (Cypr. acc. to *Et.Gud.*572.53). **ψαιθόν**· ὑποφοινίσσον, Hsch. **ψαικάζει**· ῥα(ί)νει, Id. (ψακ- poscit ordo). **ψαίκαλον**· ἔμβρυον, βρέφος, Id. (leg. ψακ-). **ψαικαλοῦχον**· ἔμβρυον, Id. **ψαῖμα**· ὀλίγον Id.; cf. ψαῖσμα. **ψαινούζειν**· διὰ ῥ.πισμοῦ καταψύχειν. γὰρ δὲ καὶ δραπισμοῦ, Id. (Fort. ψαινυθίζειν· διὰ ῥιπισμοῦ κ., γρ(άφεται) δὲ καὶ διὰ πρισμοῦ καταψήχειν.)

**ψαινύθιος**, ον, *false, vain*, Hsch.:—Lyc.1420 has **ψαίνυνθα** θεσπίζειν prophesy *falsely* (formed like μίνυνθα).

**ψαινύντες**· ψωμίζοντες, Hsch. **ψαίννον**· ἀχρεῖον, Id. **ψαινύροιτο**· διεσείσατο, Id. **ψαίνυσμα**· ὀλίγον, Id.; cf. ψαῖσμα. **ψαινύσσειν**· ῥ(ι)πίζειν, Id.

**ψαίρω**, only pres., and not in Att. Prose: (v. ψάω): I. trans., *graze, brush lightly, touch gently*, οἶμον αἰθέρος ψαίρει πτεροῖς.. οἰωνός *is ready to skim* the path of ether, A.*Pr.*396; *rub, scrape gently* in washing, Eun.*VS*p.486 B. II. intr., *move lightly* or *quiver, flutter, palpitate*, of an irregular pulse and the like, Hp.*Mul.*2.120: hence, *rustle, murmur*, of the *rustling* of leaves in the breeze, Luc. *Trag.*315; of stars, *twinkle*, Nic.*Th.*123. 2. ψαίρειν λέγομεν τὸ ἱστίον ὅταν ἐλαφρῶς διαπνέηται Hsch. s. v. διαψαίρουσι.

**ψαῖσμα**· σῖτον ὀλίγον, Hsch., cf. ψαῖμα, ψαίνυσμα.

**ψαιστ-ίον**, Dim. of ψαιστόν, *AP*5.16 (Gaet.), dub. in *IG*5(1).1447 (Messene, iii/ii B.C.). ❀ **-ός**, ή, όν, (ψαίω) *ground*, ψ. μᾶζα a cake *of ground barley* mixed with honey and oil, Hp.*Int.*20; ψαιστόν, τό (sc. πέμμα or πόπανον), a *cake of this kind*, used at sacrifices, Ar.*Pl.* 138, 1115, Antiph.206.3, *Com.Adesp.*372, Thphr.ap.Porph.*Abst.*2. 15, *SIG*1038.18 (Eleusis, iv/iii B.C.), Herod.4.92, *AP*6.190 (Gaet.), 191 (Corn. Long.): perh. to be written **ψᾳστός**, cf. ψᾷστον· σὺν τῷ ῑ, ἐκτείνουσι τὸ ᾱ, ὡς Εὐφρόνιος, *Lex.Mess.*p.411: v. ψαστής. **-ώδης**, ες, *like a ψαιστόν*, *AB*313.

**ψαίστωρ**, ορος, ὁ, *one that wipes off*, σπόγγος *AP*6.205 (Phan.).

**ψαίω**, = ψάω (q.v.), *rub away, grind down*, in aor. 1 Med., Thphr. ap.Porph.*Abst.*2.6:—aor. Pass., ibid.

**ψᾰκάδιον**, later **ψεκάδιον**, τό, Dim. of ψακάς, *drizzle*, Polioch.2.5, Thphr.*CP*2.9.3.

**ψᾰκάδ-ισσα** [ᾰδ], ἡ, *spotted, dappled*, of a mare, prob. in *PPetr.* 2 p.115 (ii B.C.). **-ισχίοις** (dat. pl.), *with dappled haunches* (?), of horses, ibid.

**ψᾰκάζω**, later **ψεκάζω**, (ψακάς):—*rain in small drops, drizzle, drip*, Ar.*Nu.*580: impers., ψακάζει *it drizzles*, ψακαζέτω ἄρτοισι *let it rain* loaves, Nicoph.13:—Med., εἰκάζουσι.. λύχνῳ ψακαζομένῳ μύωπα they liken a short-sighted person to a *sputtering* (i.e. dying) lamp, prob. in Arist.*Rh.*1413$^{a}$4 (cf. Anon. *in Rh.*217.3; εἰς μύωπα codd., εἰς secl. Buhle):—Pass., ψεκασθέντα *moistened with slight rain*, Thphr.*CP*6.19.5.

**ψᾰκᾰλον** [ᾰ], τό, *new-born animal*, Ar.Byz.ap.Eust.1625.48; **ψάκαλος**, ὁ, Id.ap.Ael.*NA*7.47: **ψαίκαλον** in cod. Hsch. (From ψακάς; for the sense cf. δρόσος, ἕρση.)

**ψᾰκᾰλοῦχος**, ον, (ἔχω) *having young*, μητέρες ψ. mothers *with their young*, S.*Fr.*793 (anap.); cf. ψαικαλοῦχον.

**ψᾰκάς**, Ion. and later (cf. Moer.p.419 P.) **ψεκάς**, άδος, ἡ:—*drop of rain*, ὅταν μὲν κατὰ μικρὰ φέρηται, ψακάδες, ὅταν δὲ κατὰ μείζω μόρια, ὑετὸς καλεῖται Arist.*Mete.*347$^{a}$11, cf. 348$^{a}$7, al.; *particle*, ib.373$^{b}$16: mostly collect., *drizzle*, ψακὰς δὲ λήγει, i.e. heavy rain (ὄμβρος) is coming, A.*Ag.*1534 (lyr.); opp. ὑετοί, X.*Cyn.*5.4 (pl.); ὕσθησαν αἱ Θῆβαι ψακάδι Hdt.3.10: generally, *rain*, ὑπὸ στέγῃ πυκνῆς ἀκοῦσαι ψακάδος S.*Fr.*636, cf. E.*Hel.*2, Ar.*Th.*856; so **ψεκάς** Hp.*Epid.*2.3.1: ψεκάδες *showers*, Gal.17(1).37; also φοίνισσα ψακάς *a shower* of blood, Simon.106; βάλλει μ' ἐρεμνῇ ψακάδι φοινίας δρόσου A.*Ag.*1390; Βρομίου ψακάδεσσι, i.e. *drops* of wine, Critias 1.10. 2. Comic name for *a sputterer*, Ar.*Ach.*1150 (lyr.), cf. Suid. s.v. II. metaph. of solids, ἀργυρίου μηδὲ ψακάς not a *drop* of money, Ar.*Pax* 121; [ψάμμου] ψεκὰς *grains* of sand, *AP*12.145. (ψακάς prob. by assimilation from ψεκάς.)

**ψᾰκαστός**, ή, όν, *dripping*, μύρον Ephipp.26.

**ψάκελον**· μέγα, Hsch. (cod. μέσα), Suid.

**ψάκιον** [ᾰ], τό, Dim. of ψακάς, *small piece* or *drop*, Hsch. **ψάκτα**, ἡ, a kind of *cake*, Id. **ψακτήρ**, ῆρος, ὁ, = ψήκτρα, Id. (perh. for *ψηκτήρ).

**ψαλάθριον**, dub. l. in *AP*7.472.11 (Leon.).

**ψᾰλάκανθα** [ᾰκ], ἡ, name of a fabulous plant, Eub.28 (hex.), Ptol. Heph.ap.Phot.*Bibl.*p.150 B. (Ptol.Cyther., Suid.).

**ψαλάκιος**, ὁ, perh. an occupational name, dub. in *PLond.*3.604. 40 (i A.D.).

**ψᾰλακτός**, ή, όν, *to be touched*, dub. in Hsch.; cf. ἀψάλακτος.

❀ **ψᾰλάσσω**, later Att. -ττω, like ψάλλω, ψαθάλλω, *touch lightly*, Ael.*NA*3.18; ψ. κτύπον νευρᾶς make a string sound *by touching* it, Lyc.139:—aor. 1 Med. in Hsch.

**ψᾰλίδιον** [ῐδ], τό, *pair of scissors*, *POxy.*1289.5,6 (v A.D.). 2. as pr. name, *Scissors*, nickname of Alexander Logotheta, because he *clipped* the coins, Procop.*Arc.*26, *Goth.*3.1.

**ψᾰλῐδο-ειδής**, ές, (ψαλίς II) *like a vault* or *arch*, Ph.*Bel.*81.35, Gal.*UP*8.11. **-στομος**, ον, *nipper-mouthed*, Com. epith. of crabs, Batr.295.

**ψᾰλῐδ-όω**, (ψαλίς II) *vault, arch*, Bito 54.7 (Pass.). **-ωμα**, ατος, τό, *vault*, *CIG*4385 (Isauria, ii A.D.); ψ. καμαρωτά Str.16.1.5, cf. *Gloss.* **-ωτός**, ή, όν, *arched, vaulted*, ἱππαφέσεις D.H.3. 68.

**ψᾰλ-ίζω**, fut. -ίξω *Anacreont.*9.4: (ψαλίς):—*clip with scissors*, l. c., Archig.ap.Orib.8.2.10, Antyll.ap.eund.7.21.6; τὸν μαλλὸν ἐψάλιζεν Babr.51.4, cf. Aesop.382$^{b}$: ψαλίξαι· κεῖραι, Hsch. **-ιον**, τό, part of the bridle, *curb-chain*, ῥυταγωγέα.. ἐκ τοῦ ψ. ἠρτημένον X.*Eq.* 7.1; τὸ περὶ γένειον διειρόμενον, ψάλιον Poll.1.148; = κρίκος τοῦ χαλινοῦ, Sch.E.*Ph.*792: freq. in pl., because *the curb-chain* was formed of links, which rattled as the horse moved, χρυσοχάλινον πάταγον ψαλίων Ar.*Pax*155 (anap.); ψαλίων κρότον καὶ χαλινοῦ κτύπον Ael. *NA*6.10; ψαλίοις ἐδάμασε πώλους E.*HF*381 (lyr.): metaph., οἷον ψ. αὐτῇ [τῇ βασιλείᾳ] ἐνέβαλε τὴν τῶν Ἐφόρων δύναμιν Pl.*Lg.*692a. 2. generally, *chain, bond*, A.*Pr.*54 (pl.): metaph., μέγα δ' ἀφῃρέθη ψ. οἰκετῶν Id.*Ch.*962 (lyr.). 3. βορινοῦ καὶ νοτινοῦ ψαλίου (or Ψαλίου) the N. and S. *ring* (or *Ring*), in description of an estate, *POxy.* 1632.12 (iv A.D.). 4. a horse's *jaw*, *Hippiatr.*28 (cf. ψέλιον, ψάλλιον).

❀ **ψᾰλ-ίς**, ίδος, ἡ, *a pair of scissors*, among the toilette articles of a lady, Ar.*Fr.*320.1, S.*Fr.*413 (nisi leg. ψέλια), *PTeb.*331.13 (ii A.D.); δρεπάνοισι καὶ οὐ ψαλίδεσσι καρῆναι *AP*11.368 (Jul.Antecessor). b. *razor*, expld. by μιᾷ μαχαίρᾳ (v. μάχαιρα), Poll.2.32, 10.140. II. *sewer, drain*, στενὴν δ' ἔδυμεν ψαλίδα S.*Fr.*367; *vault, crypt*, ψαλίδα προμήκη λίθων ποτίμων Pl.*Lg.*947d; *barrel-vault*, *Supp.Epigr.*2.582 (Ionia, iii/ii B.C.), *Explor.Arch. de Délos* 11.262, Ph.*Bel.*80.46 (pl.), Hero *Stereom.*2.28; ἀνήγειρεν τὴν ψ. ταύτην *Supp.Epigr.*2.755 (Syria, ii A.D.); Gal. compares the *fornix* (ψαλιδοειδές) of the brain to a ψ. οἰκοδομήματος σφαιροειδοῦς, 2.725; similarly the *arch* of the foot, *UP* 3.8; having keystones (ὀμφαλοί), Arist.*Mu.*399$^{b}$30; and being curved (καμφθεῖσα), Str.17.1.42 (dub.), D.S.2.9; expld. by καμάρα and ἁψίς, Sch.Pl. l. c., Suid.; as entrance and exit of a theatre, *LW*1586 (Aphrodisias, written **ψελίς**). III. αἱ ψ. τῶν στύλων prob. the *rounded mouldings* between the capital and the column, Lxx *Ex.*27.10,11; so perh. **ψαλλίδες** in *BGU*1028.9 (ii A.D.). 2. pl., *rings* for the staves of the altar of incense, Lxx *Ex.*30.4; *iron bands* for strengthening an engine, Ph.*Bel.*57.33. IV. = ταχεῖα κίνησις, Sch.Pl.*Lg.*947d. **-ισμός**, ὁ, *clipping*, Archig.ap.Orib.8.2.

5. **-ιστέον**, *one must clip*, Antyll.ap.Orib.45.24.10. **-ιστός**, ή, όν, *clipped*, Hierocl.p.54A., Antyll.ap.Orib.8.5.1, Aët.3.129.

⊛ **ψαλίττεται**· ἀμιλλᾶται, Hsch.

**ψαλληγενής**, ές, (ψάλλω) *sprung from harp-playing*, Com. epith. of Archytas, strictly a parody of Homer's μοιρηγενής, Bion ap. D.L.4.52.

**ψάλλιον**, τό, = ψάλιον, prob. *chain*, *PLond*.3.1177.234 (ii A.D.).

**ψαλλίς**, v. ψαλίς III.

**ψαλλός**· ὕλη, Hsch.

⊛ **ψάλλω**, fut. ψαλῶ Lxx*Jd*.5.3, 1*Ep.Cor*.14.15: aor. ἔψηλα Pl.*Ly*. 209b, etc., and in Lxx ἔψαλα *Ps*.9.12, al.:—*pluck, pull, twitch*, ψ. ἔθειραν *pluck* the hair, A.*Pers*.1062: esp. of the bow-string, τόξων χερὶ ψάλλουσι νευράς *twang* them, E.*Ba*.784; κενὸν κρότον Lyc.1453; ἐκ κέραος ψ. βέλος *send* a shaft *twanging* from the bow, *APl*.4.211 (Stat. Flacc.); so μιλτοχαρὴς σχοῖνος ψαλλομένη a carpenter's red line, which *is twitched* and then suddenly let go, so as to leave a mark, *AP*6.103 (Phil.): metaph., γυναῖκας ἐξ ἀνδρῶν ψόγος ψάλλει, κενὸν τόξευμα E.*Fr*.499. II. mostly of the strings of musical instruments, *play* a stringed instrument *with the fingers*, and not with the plectron, ψῆλαι καὶ κρούειν τῷ πλήκτρῳ Pl. l. c., et ibi Sch.; ἐάν τις ψήλας τὴν νήτην ἐπιλάβῃ Arist.*Pr*.919ᵇ15; μουσικώτατος ὢν κατὰ χεῖρα δίχα πλήκτρου ἔψαλλε Ath.4.183d; opp. κιθαρίζω, Hdt.1. 155, *SIG*578.18 (Teos, ii B.C.); πρὶν μέν σ' ἑπτάτονον ψάλλον (sc. τὴν λύραν) Ion Eleg.3.3: abs., Hdt. l. c., Ar.*Eq*.522, Hippias (?) in *PHib*.1.13.24; κόραις Men.*Epit*.260; ψάλλειν [οὐκ ἔνι] ἄνευ λύρας Luc.*Par*.17:—Prov., ῥᾷον ἢ τις ἂν χορδὴν ψήλειε 'as easy as falling off a log', Aristid.*Or*.26(14).31. 2. later, *sing to a harp*, Lxx *Ps*.7.18, 9.12, al.; τῇ καρδίᾳ *Ep.Eph*.5.19; τῷ πνεύματι 1*Ep.Cor*. l. c. 3. Pass., of the instrument, *to be struck* or *played*, ψαλλομένη χορδή Arist.*Pr*.919ᵇ2; also of persons, *to be played to on the harp*, Macho ap.Ath.8.348f.

**ψάλ-μα**, ατος, τό, *tune played on a stringed instrument*, *AP*11.34 (Phld.), Max.Tyr.37.4. **-μίζω**, *sing psalms*, and **-μιστής**, οῦ, ὁ, *psalmist*, *Gloss*. **-μός**, ὁ, *twitching* or *twanging* with the fingers, ψαλμοὶ τόξων E.*Ion*173 (lyr.); τοξήρει ψαλμῷ [τοξεύσας] Id. *HF*1064 (lyr.). II. mostly of musical strings, πηκτίδων ψαλμοῖς κρέκον ὕμνον Telest.5, cf. Diog.Trag.1.9, Aret.*CA*1.1. 2. *the sound of the cithara* or *harp*, Pi.*Fr*.125, cf. Phryn.Trag.11; ψαλμὸς δ' ἀλαλάζει A.*Fr*.57.7 (anap.); there were contests in τὸ ψάλλειν, *Michel*898.10 (Chios, ii B.C.), 913.6 (Teos, ii B.C.). 3. later, *song sung to the harp, psalm*, Lxx 2*Ki*.23.1, al., *Ep.Eph*.5.19; βίβλος ψαλμῶν *Ev.Luc*.20.42.

**ψαλμοχᾰρής**, ές, *delighting in harp-playing*, of Apollo, *AP*9.525.24.

**ψαλμῳδ-ία**, *singing to the harp*, Aristid.2.310J. **-ός**, ὁ, *psalmist*, Lxx*Si*.47.9 cod.Sin., 50.18.

**ψάλ-σις**, εως, ἡ, = ψαλμός, Philostr.*VA*6.10. ⊛ **-τήριον**, τό, *stringed instrument, psaltery, harp*, τρίγωνα ψ. Arist.*Pr*.919ᵇ12, cf. Hippias (?) in *PHib*.1.13.31, Apollod.ap.Ath.14.636f, Thphr.*HP*5. 7.6, Lxx*Ge*.4.21, al., Jul.*Or*.2.49c. ⊛ **-της**, ου, ὁ, *harper*, Men.495, Hippias (?) in *PHib*.1.13.7,25, Macho ap.Ath.8.348f, Lxx 1*Es*.5.42, Plu.2.67f, 223f, cf. κιθαριστὴς ἢ ψ. *SIG*578.15 (Teos, ii B.C.); epith. of Apollo, *AP*9.525.24. [Oxyt. in Att., parox. in Hellenistic Gr., Choerob. *in Theod*.1.187H.] **-τιγξ**, ιγγος, ἡ, = κιθάρα, Hsch., Suid. **-τικός**, ή, όν, *of* or *for harp playing*, ψ. ὄργανον a stringed instrument, Ath.14.634f (of the μάγαδις); ἄνδρα ψαλτικὴν ἀγαθόν a good *harpist*, Ael.ap.Ar.Byz.*Epit*.84.8. **-τός**, ή, όν, *sung to the harp, sung of*, Lxx*Ps*.118(119).54. **-τρια**, ἡ, *female harper*, Pl.*Prt*. 347d, Ion Trag.22, Arist.*Ath*.50.2, Men.319.4, Plu.*Caes*.10, al.

**ψαλτῳδ-έω**, *sing to the harp*, Lxx 2 *Ch*.5.13. **-ός**, όν, = ψαλμῳδός, ib.1*Ch*.9.33, 2*Ch*.5.12, al., v.l. ib.*Si*.47.9.

**ψαλύγων**· ἔνιοι ψάλυγας τὰς λεγομένας ψυχάς, ἄμεινον. καὶ τοὺς ἀσθενεῖς σπινθῆρας, Hsch. (cf. φεψάλυξ).

**ψᾰμᾰθ-ηΐς**, ΐδος, ἡ, *sandy*, Nic.*Th*.887. **-ία**, ἡ, *sandy seashore*, Hsch. **-ίς**, ῖδος, ἡ, a sea-fish, elsewh. ὗς, Numen.ap.Ath. 7.327a. **-ος**, ἡ (poet., also in a Homeric paraphrase, Plu.2.393e), *sand of the sea-shore*, ἔρειπε δὲ τεῖχος Ἀχαιῶν.., ὡς ὅτε τις ψάμαθον πάϊς ἄγχι θαλάσσης..συνέχευε Il.15.362; ψαμάθῳ εἰλυμένα πολλῇ Od. 14.136; ἀμφὶ χλωρὰν ψ. S.*Aj*.1064; παρακτία ψ. E.*IA*165 (lyr.), cf. 1054 (lyr.); παρὰ ψ. καὶ θῖν' ἁλός Ar.*V*.1520 (lyr.): freq. in pl., νῆα ..ἐπ' ἠπείροιο ἔρυσσαν ὑψοῦ ἐπὶ ψαμάθοις Il.1.486; ἐπὶ ψαμάθοις ἁλίῃσι Od.3.38, cf. 4.438; of *river-sand*, Il.21.202,319. 2. prov. of a countless multitude, ὅσα ψ. τε κόνις τε ib.9.385: pl., *grains of sand*, φύλλοισιν ἐοικότες ἢ ψαμάθοισιν 2.800; ὁπόσαι ἐν θαλάσσᾳ καὶ ποταμοῖς ψάμαθοι κλονέονται Pi.*P*.9.47. (Perh. formed by combining ψάμμος and ἄμαθος; similarly ἄμμος (ἄμμος) by combining ἄμαθος and ψάμμος; ἄμαθος is cogn. with Engl. *sand*.) **-ώδης**, ες, *sandy*, χῶρος *h.Merc*. 75, al., cf. A.R.4.1376, etc.

**ψάμμα**, ατος, τό, in pl. ψάμματα· σπαράγματα, Hsch.

**ψαμμαῖος**, α, ον, *sandy*, *Inscr.Prien*.326.2.

**ψαμμᾰκόσιοι**, αι, α, *sand-hundred*, Com. word formed from ψάμμος after the analogy of διακόσιοι, τριακόσιοι, etc., to denote a countless multitude, ψ. θεαταί Eup.286 (ψαμμοκ- v.l. ap.Suid.), cf. Ath. 15.671a; also ὀνόματα ψ. *grandiloquent* terms, Id.6.230d.—So the exaggerated form **ψαμμᾰκοσιογάργᾰροι**, αι, α, Ar.*Ach*.3 (v.l. ψαμμοκ-): cf. γάργαρα.

**ψαμμᾰτίζω**, = ψωμίζω, Hsch.

⊛ **ψάμμη**, ἡ, rarer form of ψάμμος, Hdt.4.181 (v.l. ψάμμος), who elsewh. always has the common form: Dor. **ψάμμα** A.*Pr*.573 (lyr.), Ar.*Lys*.1261 (lyr.).

**ψάμμητον**, τό, a kind of *cake*, Harp. s. v. Ἑκάτης νῆσος.

**ψαμμ-ιαῖος**, α, ον, *of the size of a grain of sand*, μέγεθος Olymp. *in Phd*.p.31 N. **-ίας** ἀκάτα corrupt in A.*Ag*.985 (lyr.). **-ῖνος**, η, ον, *of sand, sandy*, Hdt.2.99, Philostr.*Her*.3.4. **-ίον**, τό, Dim., *grain of sand*: in pl., of *gravel* in urine, Ruf.*Ren.Ves*.3.6,11, Aret.*SD*2.3, Alex.Aphr.*Pr*.1.110. **-ισμός**, ὁ, *burying in sand*, Paul.Aeg.3.78.19 (pl.). **-ίτης** [ῑ], ου, ὁ, *from sand*, δόρπος *AP*9.551 (Antiphil.). 2. (sc. ἀριθμός) name of a treatise (*Arenarius*) by Archimedes. II. ὗς **ψαμμῖτις** *sand-*eel, Archestr.*Fr*.22.2.

**ψαμμό-γεως**, ων, *with a sandy soil*, Hdn.*Epim*.208. **-δύτης** [ῠ], ου, ὁ, like ἀμμοδύτης, *sand-diver*; name of *a fish that buries itself in the sand*, elsewh. καλλιώνυμος, Hsch. II. name for a *mole*, Cyran.78. **-ειδής**, ές, *like sand, sandy*, Hp.*Nat.Hom*.14.

**ψαμμοκόσιοι**, v.l. for ψαμμακόσιοι (q. v.), which is to be preferred.

⊛ **ψάμμος**, ἡ, but in Archim.*Aren*.1.1, al., always ὁ:—*sand*, used by Hom. for ψάμαθος only in Od.12.243, later very freq., Hdt.8.71, etc.: pl., *grains of sand*, αἱ ἀπ' ἀλλήλων ἐσκεδασμέναι ψάμμοι S.E.*P*.1.130: prov., ψάμμος ἀριθμὸν περιπέφευγεν Pi.*O*.2.98; οἶδα δ' ἐγὼ ψάμμου τ' ἀριθμόν Orac.ap.Hdt.1.47; ἐκ ψάμμου σχοινίον πλέκειν, of labour in vain, Aristid.2.309 J.; of something worthless, Lxx*Wi*.7.9, D. Chr.77/8.30; ψάμμου ἄξιον Oenom.ap.Eus.*PE*5.21. 2. metallic ore used by alchemists, in pl., Olymp.Alch.p.106 B., Zos.Alch. p.239 B. II. ἡ ψ. the *sandy desert* of Libya, the *sand*, Hdt.3. 25, 4.173; πλείστης ψάμμου *OGI*666.27 (Egypt, i A.D.). (Prob. *ψαφ-μος, cf. ψαφαρός, ψῆφος, Lat. *sabulum*.)

**ψαμμ-ουργία**, ἡ, and **-ουργική**, ἡ, *art of extracting gold from sand*, Zos.Alch.p.241 B. **-ώδης**, ες, *sandy*, Hdt.2.32, Aen.Tact. 8.2: τὰ ψ. *sandy sediment* in the urine, *gravel*, Hp.*Aph*.4.79, Gal. 6.571; called ψ. ὑποστάσεις by Id.17(1).836. **-ωτός**, ή, όν, *of plaster* or *stucco*, κόσμος τοίχου Lxx*Si*.22.17.

**ψανισμός**· ναυτιασμός, Hsch.

**ψᾱνός**, = ψηνός (q. v.).

**ψάπιγμα**, v. ψήφισμα.

**ψάρ**, ὁ, gen. ψᾱρός: pl. ψᾶρες: Ion. **ψήρ**, ψηρός, ψῆρες:—*starling, Sturnus vulgaris*, ὥς τε ψαρῶν νέφος..ἠὲ κολοιῶν Il.17.755; ἴρηκι ἐοικὼς ὠκέϊ, ὅς τ' ἐφόβησε κολοιούς τε ψῆράς τε 16.583; ψῆρες, dat. ψήρεσι, Q.S.8.387, 11.218; ψᾶρες Antiph.302 (anap.), *AP*9.373, Gal.6.567; Plu.2.972f mentions their being taught to speak, cf. Gell.13.21 (20).25.

**ψᾶρις**· γένος στρουθοῦ, Hsch.; also εἶδος νεὼς τριήρους, Id. **ψαρίχοι** (-ίγχοι cod.)· ψᾶροι, Id.

**ψᾱρομᾰχία**, ἡ, *battle of the starlings*, Suid. s. v. Ὅμηρος.

⊛ **ψάρος** or **ψᾶρος**, ὁ, = ψάρ, Arist.*HA*617ᵇ26; gen. pl. ψάρων Gal. 6.435.

**ψᾱρός** (A), ά, όν, (ψάρ) *like a starling*, i. e. *speckled, dappled*, ψ. ἵππος a *dapple-grey* horse, Ar.*Nu*.1225, Lxx*Za*.1.8; Arist.*HA*632ᵇ19 distinguishes it fr. ποικίλος, which implies that the spots are more distinctly marked:—Comp. ψαρότερος Ael.*NA*12.28, Aët.11.11.

**ψαρός** (B), ά, όν, neut. ψαρόν, τό, name of a siccative powder, Paul.Aeg.7.13.11; perh. cf. ψηρός.

**ψαστής**· τὰ ψαιστὰ ῥόδα, Hsch. (Perh. ψάστ' ἧς (i. e. ψαιστὰ ἦν ?), Ῥόδιοι.) **ψᾶστον**, v. ψαιστόν. **ψατᾶσθαι**· προκαταλαμβάνειν, Id.: **ψατῆσαι**· προειπεῖν, Id. (Prob. cogn. with φθάνω.) **ψαυγές**· θορυβῶδες, Id.

⊛ **ψαυκροπόδης**, ὁ, and **ψαυκρόποδα** (acc. sg. masc.), *swift-footed*, epith. of the horse Arion, *EM*817.45, Hsch.

⊛ **ψαυκρός**, ά, όν, in neut. ψαυκρὸν γόνυ· κοῦφον, ἀπὸ τοῦ ἄκρως ψαύειν, Hsch.; also **ψαυκρός**· καλλωπιστής, ταχύς, ἐλαφρός, ἀραιός, Id.: cf. σαυκρός.

**ψαῦος**, sine expl., Alcm.ap.Sch.A Il.12.137.

**ψαύριος** or **ψαυρός**, ὁ, acc. to Hsch. = κονιορτός, φορυτός.

⊛ **ψαῦσις**, εως, ἡ, *touching, contact*, Democr.11, Plu.2.683c, Sor. *Fract*.13, Gal.18(2).786:—esp. of lovers, *caress*, φιλήματων καὶ ψαύσεως Plu.*Alc*.4, cf. 2.768b.

**ψαῦσμα**, ατος, τό, *touch, caress*, X.Eph.3.2.

**ψαυστέον**, *one must touch*, Antyll.ap.Orib.10.23.23.

**ψαυστός**, ή, όν, *touched*, ἄγαλμα οὐδὲ ψ. χειρὸς ἀνθρωπίνης, i. e. not *made* by mortal hand, Hdn.1.11.1.

⊛ **ψαύω**, Ep. impf. ψαῦον Il.13.132; ψαύεσκον (ἐπι-) Orph.*L*.126: fut. ψαύσω A.*Ch*.182, etc.: aor. ἔψαυσα Pi.*N*.5.42, etc.: pf. ἔψαυκα (παρ-) S.E.*M*.7.116:—**Pass.**, aor. ἐψαύσθην Dsc.2.14: pf. ἔψαυσμαι (παρ-) Hp.*Morb*.4.44:—*touch*, τινος Il.23.519,806, Hdt.2.47, etc.; ἁπτόμενοι καὶ ψ. ἀλλήλων *in close contact*, Plu.*Pyrrh*.12: metaph., μὴ ψαύειν ἀδικίας ὃν τρόπον οὐδὲ πυρός Phld.*Rh*.2.155S.: c. dat. instr., ψαῦον..κόρυθες..φάλοισι the helmets *touched with* their φάλοι, Il.13.132, 16.216; τῇ κεφαλῇ τοῦ οὐρανοῦ ψ. Hdt.3.30; χεροῖν..ἔψαυσα πηγῆς A.*Pers*.202; εἰ τῆσδε χώρας μήποτε ψαύσει ποδί Id.*Ch*.182: but the dat. is used for the gen. in Pi.*P*.9.120, Herod.4.75, Q.S.8.349 (cf. θιγγάνω II.3, προσψαύω):—ψαύω never takes acc. exc. in αἵματι ψαῦσαι θύρας Ezek.*Exag*.158: in S.*Ant*. 857, ἔψαυσας ἀλγεινοτάτας ἐμοὶ μερίμνας, πατρὸς τριπόλιστον οἶκτον (v.l. οἶτον), μερίμνας is gen. sg. and οἶκτον or οἶτον is acc. depending on ἔψαυσας..μερίμνας, = ἐποίησάς με μεριμνᾶν; and ib.961, κεῖνος ἐπέγνω μανίαις ψαύων τὸν θεὸν ἐν κερτομίοις γλώσσαις, the construction is ἐπέγνω τὸν θεόν, ψαύων (sc. αὐτοῦ) he learned to know the god, *assailing* (him): later writers used the Pass. as if the Act. had a trans. sense, Dsc. l. c., Plu.2.951d. 2. *touch lightly*, a way of feeling the pulse, opp. θλίβω, Gal.8.808: metaph., *touch upon* a subject, *notice it slightly*, Plb.1.13.8:—Med., c. acc. rei, *touch* *lightly upon* a subject, Gal.18(1).331. 3. *touch as an enemy, lay hands upon*, τινος E.*IA*1559: abs., κλάδοις ἄν, εἰ ψαύσειας A.*Supp.* 925, cf. S.*OC*856. 4. *touch, affect*, οὐ γὰρ ἄκρας καρδίας ἔψαυσέ μου E.*Hec.*242. 5. *reach, gain*, ὕμνων Pi.*N.*5.42; ψ. Ἀφροδίτας Id.*O.* 6.35: abs., *hit the mark*, *AP*7.428.11 (Mel.). 6. Math., ἐπίπεδα ψαύοντα *tangent* planes, Archim.*Con.Sph.*17. II. rarely in Pass., *to be touched*, of the star-fish, ἐνδίδωσι τὸ σῶμα καὶ περιορᾷ ψαυόμενον ὑπὸ τῶν παρατρεχόντων Plu.2.978b, cf. 951d (if the comma be placed before, not after, οὐσίας); ὅσοι ὑπὸ τῶν Ἀμινναίων (sc. οἴνων) ψαύονται κεφαλῆς those who *are affected* in the head., Dsc. 5.19.—The word is very rare in early Prose, Antipho 3.3.5, X. *Mem.*1.4.12: freq. later, Plb.1.13.8, al., Plu.2.589f, al.

**ψάφα**· κνέφας, Hsch.

**ψᾶφαξ**, ακος, Aeol. for ψῆφος, Greg.Cor.p.623 S.

**ψᾰφᾰρ-ία**, ἡ, *dust, dirt*, Dsc.1.97 (v.l. ψαθ-). **-ίτης** [ῑ], ου, ὁ, = ψαφαρός, ῥύπος *AP*12.192 (Strat.).

**ψᾰφᾰρόθριξ**, τρῐχος, ὁ, ἡ, *with dry, rough hair* or *coat*, μῆλα *h. Pan.*32.

**ψᾰφᾰρ-ός**, ά, όν, Ion. **ψαφερός**, ή, όν, Hp. (v. infr.):—*friable, powdery, crumbling*, σποδός A.*Th.*323 (lyr.), cf. Euph.50; κόνις *AP* 7.315 (Zenod. or Rhian.); ψαφαρόν, = ἁπαλόν, perh. of a fine powder, Pl.Com.118: freq. of soil, *sandy*, λεπτόγεως καὶ ψ. χώρα Thphr. *HP*8.2.11; opp. ἀγαθή, ib.8.9.1 (Comp.); ἡ ψαφαρή the *sandy* shore, opp. ἅλς, *AP*12.145; ἐνὶ ψαφαρῇ Σαλαμῖνι Euph.30. 2. *of loose texture*, of the glands, the brain, Hp.*Gland.*1,10, Sor.1.12 (ψαθ- cod.), al. 3. of semi-liquids, *thin, watery*, διαχώρημα Hp.*Coac.*596; νάρδος *AP*6.231 (Phil.); πόλτος ψαφαρώτατος Sor.1.51 (ψαθ- cod.). 4. of wine, *rough, dry*, joined with ἀλιπής, Gal.ap.Ath.1.26d, cf. ψαθυρός. 5. metaph. of a serpent, χροιῇ ψ. *dry, dusty-looking*, Nic. *Th.*262.—Cf. ψαθυρός fin. **-όομαι**, *become disintegrated*, Olymp. Alch.p.94 B.

**ψᾰφᾰρο-χαίτης**, ου, ὁ, gloss on φυκιοχαίτης, *PSI*8.892 (iv A.D.), restd. fr. Hsch. s.v. φυκιοχαίτης. **-χροος**, ον, contr. **-χρους**, ουν, *rough on the surface, squalid*, κάρα E.*Rh.*716 (lyr.).

**ψᾰφερός**, ή, όν, Ion. for ψαφαρός (q.v.). **ψάφιγμα**, v. ψήφισμα.

**ψᾰφιγξ**, ιγγος, ἡ, Aeol. for ψῆφος, κρύπτᾳ ψάφιγγι *IG*12(2).526a. 16 (Eresus, iv B.C.), cf. *EM*554.52.

**ψάφιξις**, v. ψήφισις. **ψᾶφος**, ἡ, Dor. for ψῆφος.

**ψάω** [ᾱ, but always contracted], ψῇ S.*Tr.*678, inf. ψῆν (περι-) Ar.*Eq.*909: impf. contr. 3 sg. prob. ἀπέψη (v. ἀποψάω): fut. ψήσω (ἀπο-) Id.*Lys.*1035: aor. ἔψησα Hippon.12 Diehl, A.R.3.831, (κατ-, περι-) Pl.*Phd.*89b, Ar.*Pl.*730:—Med., freq. in compos. with ἀπό:— Pass., aor. ἐψήθην (συν-) Lxx *Je.*31(48).33 (v.l. -ψήσθ-); ἐψήσθην (ἀν-) *BGU*530.17 (i A.D.): pf. ἔψησμαι (παρ-) Poll.4.152. Later authors sts. use the contr. by ᾱ instead of η, inf. ἀνα-ψᾶν Dsc.4.64:— *rub, wipe*, τίς ὀμφαλητόμος σε.. ἔψησε κἀπέλουσεν; Hippon. l.c.; *polish*, *PHolm.*3.19; *rub smooth*, αὐσταλέας δ' ἔψησε παρηΐδας A.R. l.c.; of solderers, *PLond.*3.1177.285 (ii A.D.). II. intr., *crumble away, vanish, disappear*, S.*Tr.*678 (s.v.l.). (ψάω, ψαίω, ψαύω, ψαίρω, ψήχω, ψώχω, and perh. ψίω, ψωμός, seem to be different enlargements of ψ-, which corresponds to *ps-* in Skt. *psā́ti*, *bhes-* in Skt. *babhasti* 'crush, chew, devour', *bhasman* 'ashes'.)

**ψε**, v. σφεῖς A. II. **ψεαυτόνς**, v. σφεῖς A. II.

**ψέγος**· τάφος, Hsch.: cf. ἐπιψέγω.

**ψέγω** (A), S.*OT*338, etc.: fut. ψέξω Pl.*Grg.*518d: aor. ἔψεξα Thgn.611, S.*Aj.*1130, Pl.*Lg.*634c, etc.:—Pass., pf. ἔψεγμαι Hp. *Acut.*51:—*blame, censure*, τινα Thgn. l.c., A.*Ag.*186 (lyr.), 1403; τι S.*OC*977, etc.; λόγον δοῦναι.. περὶ ὧν ψέγουσι Pl.*Tht.*177b; διά τι Id.*Prt.*346c; ἐπί τινι X.*HG*6.5.49: c. acc. rei, τὸ.. διδάσκειν Id.*Eq.* 6.5: c. dupl. acc., τίς ποτ' ἐστὶν ὅν γ' ἐγὼ ψέξαιμί τι; S.*OC*1172; ἃ ψέγομεν τὸν Ἔρωτα Pl.*Phdr.*243d; ταὐτὰ ψέγων καὶ ἐπαινῶν Id.*Grg.* 510c, cf. *Lg.*634c; ψ. τινὰ ὅτι.., εἰ.., Isoc.*Ep.*2.15, X.*HG*6.5.51; τινα c. inf., Pl.*R.*404d: c. acc. cogn., ψ. ψόγους Id.*Grg.*483c:—Pass., ἡ ἐπιείκεια οὐ ψέγεται *there is no objection to it, we find no fault with* it, Th.5.86; ψέγεται ὡς τοιοῦτον ὄν Pl.*R.*358a; ψεγ[όμενα], of damaged goods, prob. in *Supp.Epigr.*7.417.18 (Dura, iii A.D.).

**ψέγω** (B), in compd. ἐπιψέγω (q.v.), cf. ψέγος.

**ψέδειν**· ἐντρέπειν, φροντίζειν, Hsch. (fort. ψέφειν).

**ψεδνό-θριξ**, τριχος, ὁ, ἡ, *sparse-haired, bald*, Tz.*H.*7.891. **-κάρηνος** [ᾰ], ον, *bald-headed*, Orph.*L.*253. **-ομαι**, Pass., *become bald*, S.E.*M.*1.255.

**ψεδνός**, ή, όν, *thin, spare, scanty*, λάχνη Il.2.219; χαῖται *AP*9. 430 (Crin.); κόμαι Aret.*SD*2.13: later of a person, *bald-headed*, Luc.*DMort.*25.1: generally, *bare, naked*, χωρία Aristid.*Or.*36(48). 67 (Comp.):—v.l. for ψυδρός or ψυδνός in Thgn.122.

**ψεδνότης**, ητος, ἡ, *baldness*, Adam.2.37.

**ψεδόναι**· λόγοι, Hsch.

**ψεδῡρός**, = ψίθυρος, A.*Supp.*1042 (lyr.), Hsch.

**ψεδών**, όν, = ψίθυρος, Hsch.: cf. ψιδόνες, ψυθῶνες.

**ψεῖ**, τό, name of the letter ψ, Hellad.ap.Phot.*Bibl.*p.530 B.

**ψειαί**, v. ψίαι, ψόα.

**ψεινάζει**· ἀπορρεῖ Hsch. (cf. ψινάζει). **ψείρει**· φθείρει, Id.

**ψείω**, = τὸ ἐλαττοῦν τὴν οὐσίαν οὑτινοσοῦν ὑποκειμένου acc. to Hdn. Gr.ap.Orion.*Lex.*col.168: but ψιάω is thus glossed in *An.Ox.*1.401.

**ψεκάδιον** [ᾰ], **ψεκάζω**, **ψεκάς**, later forms for ψακ-, q.v.

**ψεκ-τέον**, (ψέγω) *one must blame*, τι Plu.2.27b. 2. ψεκτέος, α, ον, *to be blamed*, S.E.*M.*2.105. **-της**, ου, ὁ, *censurer, faultfinder*, Hp.*Acut.*6, Pl.*R.*589c, *Lg.*639c. **-τικός**, ή, όν, *censorious*, Arist.*Rh.Al.*1421ᵇ9, Poll.5.117; τὸ -κόν *Stoic.*2.62. Adv. -κῶς Poll.5.118. **-τός**, ή, όν, *blameworthy*, opp. ἐπαινετός, Pl. *Cra.*416c, Arist.*EN*1108ᵃ16, Plb.3.4.1, etc. Adv. -τῶς Poll.4.26 (s.v.l.).

* **ψέλιον**, later sts. **ψέλλιον** (v.l. in X.*Cyr.*1.3.2, never in Hdt.), *POsl.*46.8 (iii A.D.), *Supp.Epigr.*7.428 (Dura, iii A.D.), in Inscrr. **ψίλιον**, **ψίλλιον** (qq.v.), τό:—*armlet* or *anklet*, ψέλιον περὶ ἑκατέρῃ τῶν κνημέων Hdt.4.168; mostly in pl. ψέλια, a favourite ornament of the Persians, Id.3.20, 22, 9.80, X.*An.*1.2.27, *Cyr.*1.3.2; worn by women in Egypt, *BGU*1101.8 (i B.C.), *POxy.*259.11 (i A.D.), etc., and in Greece, Plu.2.142c. 2. an iron implement, perh. agricultural, *PCair.Zen.*782 (*a*).42 (iii B.C.); ψελίου καὶ δρεπάνου *PPetr.*2 p.113 (iii B.C.). II. οἱ Δωριεῖς ψέλλιον καλοῦσι τὸ ἄκρον· ὅθεν καὶ ἡμεῖς τὴν ἐπ' ἄκρων χειλέων λεγομένην προσῳδίαν ψιλὴν ἐκαλέσαμεν, ὥς φησι Τρύφων Ammon.*Diff.*p.143 V. (ψέλιον is distd. from ψάλιον by Ammon.*Diff.*p.142 V., Ptol.Asc.p.396 H., but is the later form of ψάλιον acc. to Moer.p.420 P., Sch.E.*Ph.*792 (ἔστι δὲ ψέλιον ὁ κρίκος τοῦ χαλινοῦ, ἢ ἁπλῶς ὁ κρίκος) and this may be the meaning in *PCair. Zen.* l.c.)

**ψελιοποιός**, ὁ, *armlet-maker*, *Gloss.* (ψελοπ- cod.).

* **ψελιοφόρος**, ον, *wearing bracelets*, Hdt.8.113.

**ψελιόω**, *twine, wreathe*, ψ. αὐχένα στεφάνοις *AP*7.234 (Phil.). 2. Med., *put on an armlet*, ψελιουμένη subject of statue by Praxiteles, Plin.*HN*34.70.

**ψελίς**, v. ψαλίς.

**ψελλίζω**, (ψελλός) *falter in speech, speak inarticulately*, like a child, ψ. καὶ τραυλίζουσι Arist.*HA*536ᵇ8:—so in Med., Pl.*Grg.*485b,c; ψελλίζονται καὶ τραυλίζουσι (-ονται Bonitz), τοῦτο δ' ἐστὶν ἔνδεια τῶν γραμμάτων Arist.*PA*660ᵃ26; ψελλιζόμενος τὴν Ἑλλάδα φωνήν Hld.8.15: metaph., of Empedocles and the early philosophers, *speak indistinctly*, ἃ ψελλίζεται λέγων Ἐμπεδοκλῆς Arist.*Metaph.*985ᵃ5; ψελλιζομένῃ ἔοικεν ἡ πρώτη φιλοσοφία περὶ πάντων ib.993ᵃ15; of metals, *hesitate* to alloy, Id.*GC*328ᵇ9:—Act. is later in this sense, used of Aristotle, Phld.*Rh.*2.51 S. 2. metaph., ψελλιζόμενος ἐς τὰ πολεμικά, of a boy soldier, Philostr.*Her.*19.2.

**ψελλινία**, ἡ, perh. = ψέλιον, *necklace* or *armlet*, *PPar.*9.14 (ii B.C., pl.).

**ψέλλιον**, v. ψέλιον.

**ψέλλισ-μα**, ατος, τό, *inarticulate speech*, of a child's attempts at talking, Him.*Or.*23.21; of a nurse's 'baby-talk', Sor.1.109 (pl.). **-μός**, ὁ, *stammering*, ψελλισμοὶ γλώσσης Plu.2.650e. II. metaph., *indistinctness*, ib.1066d, ποδάγρας ψ. *unpronounced* (i.e. *suppressed*) gout, Plu.*Sull.*26. **-τής**, οῦ, ὁ, *stammerer*, *Gloss.* II. of horses who injure their hoofs in the stable, ψελλισταὶ οἱ λεγόμενοι *Hippiatr.*10 (v.l. ψυλλισταί, κονδυλισταί).

* **ψελλός**, ή, όν, *faltering in speech*, like a child; distd. fr. τραυλός (lisping), Arist.*HA*492ᵇ32, *Pr.*902ᵇ22; τὸ ψ. prob. in Phld.*Rh.*2. 206 S.; ἡ ψελλὴ "οὐ πιττεύω" (i.e. πιστεύω) Suid., *App.Prov.*3. 17. II. Pass. of words, *inarticulate, obscure, unintelligible*, A.*Pr.* 816; ψελλόν ἐστι καὶ καλεῖ τὴν ἄρκτον ἄρτον *Com.Adesp.*393.

**ψελλότης**, ητος, ἡ, *imperfect pronunciation*, distd. fr. τραυλότης by Arist.*Pr.*902ᵇ24; ψ. γλώσσης ἰδία νόσος Plu.2.963c.

**ψεμμή**, ἡ, a weight, = ⅓ of a γράμμα 11.5, Hero *Geom.*23.61.

**ψέξις**, εως, ἡ, *blame*, *Gloss.*

**ψέτ**, dub. sens., ἰς τὸ ψέτ, item in household accounts, *PGoodsp. Cair.*30 xxx 4, al. (ii A.D.).

**ψευδαγγελ-έω**, *to be a false messenger* (and *false angel*), Ph.1.273; cf. sq. **-ής**, ές, = ψευδάγγελος, ψευδαγγελὴς εἶν' Ar.*Av.*1340 codd. (ψευδαγγελήσειν Bentl.). **-ία**, ἡ, *false report*, X.*Eq.Mag.*5.8, D.C.49.28. **-ος**, ον, *bringing a false report, lying messenger*, Il. 15.159; Ὀδυσσεὺς ὁ ψ., title of play, Arist.*Po.*1455ᵃ14.

**ψευδ-αγνοέω**, *pretend ignorance falsely, dissemble*, D.C.44.38. **-άγχουσα**, ἡ, *bastard* ἄγχουσα, Plin.*HN*22.50.

**ψευδ-άδελφος** [ᾰ], ὁ, *false brother, pretended Christian*, 2 *Ep.Cor.* 11.26, *Ep.Gal.*2.4, *Gloss.* **-αιολικός**, ή, όν, *in false Aeolic*, of dialect, Choerob.*in Theod.*1.262 H. **-ᾰλαζών**, όνος, ὁ, ἡ, *lying braggart*: as Adj., ψ. λόγοι *Com.Adesp.*294.

**Ψευδ-ᾰλέξανδρος**, ὁ, *sham-Alexander, an impostor pretending to the name*, J.*AJ*17.12.2, Luc.*Ind.*20.

**ψευδάλεος**, α, ον, *false, counterfeit*, Nonn.*D.*8.325: so **ψευδάλμιον**· ψευδές, Hsch.

**ψευδᾰμάμαξυς** [ᾰμ], υος, ὁ, *bastard vine*, Ar.*V.*326 (anap.).

**Ψευδαντωνῖνος**, ὁ, *pseudo-Antoninus*, D.C.78.32.

**ψευδ-άνωρ** [ᾰ], ορος, ὁ, *sham man*, epith. of Dionysus, Polyaen. 4.1. **-απόστολος**, ὁ, *false ambassador* or *apostle*, 2 *Ep.Cor.*11. 13. **-άργῠρος**, ὁ, *false silver*, i.e. perh. *zinc*, Str.13.1.56. **-ἀριθμός** [ᾰ], ὁ, *false number*, Sch.Pl.*Tht.*191b.

**ψευδάριον**, τό, *fallacy*, in pl. title of work by Euclid, Procl. *in Euc.*p.70 F., cf. p.59 F.

**Ψευδᾰριστοφάνειος** [φᾶ], ὁ, *a pretended follower of Aristophanes*, Ath.1.5b.

**Ψευδαρτάβας** [ᾰβ], Comic name of a mock-Persian in Ar.*Ach.*91, 99 (*False-measure*, cf. ἀρτάβη).

**ψευδ-ατράφαξυς** [ᾰφ], υος, ἡ, *false orach*, Com. name of a plant in Ar.*Eq.*630; cf. ψευδαμάμαξυς. **-αττικός**, ή, όν, *false Attic*, Luc. *Sol.*7, Phryn.48. **-αυτομολία**, ἡ, *sham desertion*, Polyaen. 3.9.32. **-αυτόμολος**, ὁ, ἡ, *sham deserter*, X.*Eq.Mag.*4.7.

**ψευδεγγρᾰφ-ῆς** γραφή, ἡ, an action brought by a citizen *to show that he has been wrongly entered in a list of debtors*, an action *for false entry*, Arist.*Ath.*59.3, cf. Lycurg.*Fr.*12; Ἀναψυκτίδου διώξαντος ψευδεγγραφὴν ὤφλεν κτλ. *IG*11(2).146*B*29 (Delos, iv B.C.), cf. *Inscr. Délos* 399*A*98 (ii B.C.). **-ος**, ον, *falsely entered, bogus, Senatus consultum* Cic.*Att.*15.26.1.

**ψευδ-ενέδρα**, ἡ, *feigned ambuscade*, X.*An.*5.2.28, *Eq.Mag.*5.8. **-ενεχῠρᾰσία**, ἡ, *false* (i.e. *forbidden*) *seizure of security*, prob. in *PHal.*1.241 (iii B.C.).

**ψευδεπέω**, = ψευδοεπέω, ψευδολογέω, Hsch.

**ψευδεπί-γρᾰφος**, ον, *with false superscription* or *title, not genuine*, D.H.*Dem.*57, *Inscr.Prien.*37.123 (ii B.C.); φιλόσοφος Plu.2.479e; τρόπος *superficial*, Plb.23.5.5. **-εικής**, ές, *pretending to be good*, Heph.Astr.2.2 (in *Cat.Cod.Astr.*8(2).58). **-τροπος**, ὁ, *a false, illegal guardian*, Plb.15.25.1.

**Ψευδεπιχάρμειος**, ον, *falsely ascribed to Epicharmus*, Ath.14.648d.

**ψευδέφοδος**, ἡ, *feigned attack*, Polyaen.3.9.32.

**ψευδηγορ-έω**, *speak falsely*, A.*Pr.*1032, E.*Fr.*396, Philem.102.5; ὅσσα..-έουσιν ἀοιδοί Opp.*C.*4.319; τὰ ἄλλα..ἐψευδηγόρηται *PMag. Leid.V.*10.8. **-ία**, ἡ, *false discourse, lying*, Alciphr.1.18. **-ος** (parox.), ον, *speaking falsely, lying*, Lyc.1455.

**ψευδηλογέω**, = ψευδολογέω, dub. in Luc.*Ocyp.*63:—**ψευδηλόγος**, ον, = ψευδολόγος, gloss on ψευδηγόρος, *Lex.* in *An.Bachm.*1.419, v.l. in Suid. s.v. ψευδηγόρος.

**ψευδήμων**, ον, gen. ονος, poet. for ψευδής, Nonn.*D.*8.39, *AP*15.1.

**Ψευδηρακλῆς**, έους, ὁ, *sham-Hercules*, name of a Comedy by Menander, Plu.2.59c, Ath.4.172a.

**ψευδήριον**, τό, = κενήριον, *cenotaph*, Lyc.1048,1181.

※**ψευδής**, ές (the neut. sg. ψευδές is not found in early writers, ψεῦδος being used instead, cf. ψεῦδος III; it is found in later Gr., *OGI*669.54 (Egypt, i A.D.), Palaeph.6, al., Gal.18(2).782); gen. sg. ψευδοῦς Id.15.168; old Att. acc. pl. ψευδᾶς *IG*1[2].700: (ψεύδομαι):—*lying, false, untrue*, of things, opp. ἀληθής, ψ. λόγοι Hes.*Th.*229; μῦθοι A.*Pr.*685, E.*Hipp.*1288 (anap.); τρέπεσθαι ἐπὶ ψευδέα ὁδόν to betake oneself to *false*hood, Hdt.1.117; ψ. κατηγορία, αἰτίαι, *false* charges, Aeschin.2.183, Isoc.15.138, Plb.5.41.3; λόγοι S.*OT*526; λόγος Pl.*Sph.*240e, *Cra.*385b: ψ. λόγοι are also *fallacies*, in Logic, Arist.*Top.*162$^b$3 sqq.; ἥδε ἡ ψ. οὐσία this *unreal* Being (sc. the world of sense), Plot.5.8.9: irreg. Sup. ψευδίστατος, εἴδη Ael.*VH*14.37. 2. of persons, *lying, false*, and as Subst., *liar*, οὐ γὰρ ἐπὶ ψευδέσσι πατὴρ Ζεὺς ἔσσετ' ἀρωγός Il.4.235 (only here in Hom.; perh. ψευδέσσι from ψεῦδος is the true accent; so Hermappias ap.Hdn.Gr.2.45 against Aristarch. and Ptol.Asc. ibid.); τοὺς θεοὺς ψευδεῖς τίθης S.*Ph.*992, cf. *Ant.*657; ψ. ἔφυς E.*Or.*1608; ψ. φανήσεσθαι to be detected *in falsehood*, Th.4.27, cf. Pl.*Tht.*148b; Κριτίαν ψευδῆ ἐπιδείξω Id.*Chrm.*158d: irreg. Sup. ψευδίστατος *arrant liar*, *EM* 110.29, cf. Eust.1441.25. 3. τὰ ψευδῆ *falsehoods, lies*, οὐ ψευδῆ λέγω A.*Ag.*625, cf. Antipho 1.10, etc.; οὐκ ἔσθ' ὅπως λέξαιμι τὰ ψευδῆ καλά A.*Ag.*620; τινὰς ψ. διαβάλλειν Ar.*Eq.*64; ψευδῶν συγκολλητής Id.*Nu.*446 (anap.). 4. ψευδέων ἀγορή, in Hp.*Epid.*3.1.η', ιβ', said to be a name of *the monkey-market*, perhaps as being *villanous counterfeits of humanity*. II. Pass., *beguiled, deceived*, E.*IA*852. III. Adv. ψευδῶς *falsely*, λέγειν Id.*IT*1309 codd.; προσποιήσασθαι Th.1.137; *mistakenly*, ψ. δοξάζειν Pl.*Phlb.*40d; ψ. γενέσθαι τὸν φόβον *groundlessly*, Plb.5.110.7.

**Ψευδησιόδειος**, ον, *falsely ascribed to Hesiod*, Cic.*Att.*7.18.4.

**ψευδῐερεύς**, έως, ὁ, *false priest*, J.*AJ*9.6.6, al.

**ψεῦδις**, ιος, ὁ, ἡ, poet. word, = ψευδής, Pi.*N.*7.49.

**ψευδῐσόδομος**, ον, *built of equal blocks, but in courses of unequal size*, Vitr.2.8.5.

**ψευδο-βοήθεια**, ἡ, *pretended help*, X.*Eq.Mag.*5.8, Polyaen.3.9.32. **-βούνιον**, τό, *Cretan pimpinell, Pimpinella cretica*, Dsc.4.124, Plin.*HN*24.153. **-γαυρόομαι**, *to be elated on unreal grounds*, Tz.*H.*4.720. **-γλωττέω**, = ψευδολογέω, Phryn.*PS*p.127 B.

**ψευδογρᾰφ-έω**, Geom., *give a fallacious proof*, Arist.*Top.*101$^a$10:—Pass., ib.132$^a$33, 160$^b$36. 2. *write false accounts* or *statements*, *PEnteux.*63.18 (iii B.C.), Plb.12.7.6, 16.14.8, *PTeb.*78.17 (ii B.C.). **-ημα**, ατος, τό, *false diagram, fallacious proof*, Arist.*SE* 171$^b$12 (pl.), Alex.Aphr. *in Top.*22.20, *in SE*76.23. ※**-ία**, ἡ, = foreg., in pl., Ps.-Archyt.ap.Stob.1.41.5, Quint.*Inst.*1.10.39. 2. *false account*, Ath.5.216b. **-ος** (parox.), ὁ, *a drawer of false diagrams*, Arist.*SE*171$^b$35, al. 2. *writer of falsehoods*, Thom.Mag. p.224 R.: = *falsarius*, *Gloss.*

**ψευδό-δειπνον**, τό, *false, unreal repast*, A.*Fr.*258 (pl.). **-διαλεκτικός**, ή, όν, *pretending to skill in dialectics*, Gal.8.629. **-δῐδάσκᾰλος**, ὁ, *false teacher*, 2*Ep.Petr.*2.1. **-δίθῠροι** θύραι *sham double doors*, *PMich.Zen.*38.33 (iii B.C.). **-δίκταμνον**, τό, *false dittany*, *Ballota acetabulosa*, Hp.*Nat.Mul.*32, Thphr.*HP*9.16.2, Dsc.3.32. **-δίπτερος**, ον, *false dipteral*, of a temple in which there is only one row of columns along the sides, though there is space left for two, Vitr.3.2.1.

※**ψευδοδοξ-έω**, *entertain a false opinion* or *notion*, Epicur.*Fr.*253, Plb.10.2.3, 16.12.11, Phld.*Ir.*p.76 W., Ph.1.363, J.*AJ*9.4.3. **-ία**, ἡ, *false opinion* or *notion*, Polystr.p.14 W., Phld.*D.*1.14 (pl.), Str.14.5.28, Plu.2.716b, Hierocl. *in CA*12p.446 M., etc. **-ος**, ον, *holding a false opinion* or *notion, labouring under a delusion*, Gal.19.484.

**ψευδο-ενέδρα**, ἡ, = ψευδενέδρα, Polyaen.3.9.32. **-επέω**, *speak falsely*, Jul.*Gal.*351c. **-θῠρίς**, ίδος, ἡ, *secret door*, Lxx *Bel* 15; Dim. **-θύριον** [ῠ], τό, ib.21. **-θῠρον**, τό, *false* (i.e. *secret*) *door*, Cic.*Verr.*2.2.20, al., *Gloss.* **-ῐστορέω**, *narrate falsely*, Eust.363.28. **-κάρπᾰσος**, ὁ, = κάχρυ, Ps.-Dsc.3.74. **-κασσία**, ἡ, *spurious cassia*, Str.16.4.14, Dsc.1.13, Gal.14.258.

**ψευδοκατηγορ-έω**, *accuse falsely*, *Cod.Just.*1.4.34.17. **-ία**, *false accusation*, Man.4.332, Vett.Val.231.1, Heph.Astr.2.28 (*Cat. Cod.Astr.*8(2).94). **-ος**, ὁ, *false accuser, slanderer*, Hsch. s.v. ἀνάδικοι, *Cat.Cod.Astr.*7.112.

**ψευδο-κῆρυξ**, ῡκος, ὁ, *false, lying herald*, S.*Ph.*1306. **-κιννάμωμον** [ᾰ], τό, *spurious cinnamon*, Dsc.1.14 (-κινά-), Gal.12.26.

**ψευδοκλητ-εία**, ἡ, (κλητεύω) *the offence of falsely subscribing one's name as witness to a summons* (κλητήρ), γραφὴ ψευδοκλητείας a prosecution *for such false subscription*, D.53.17, Arist.*Ath.*59.3; βαδίζειν ἐπί τινα τῆς ψευδοκλητείας D.53.15; ψευδοκλητείας τρὶς ὀφλεῖν And.1.74.—This is the form found in Arist. l.c. (Pap.), in the best codd. of D. and in Poll.8.40,44; **ψευδοκλητία** is found in codd. of And. and as v.l. in D.; **ψευδοκλησία** in Harp. (with vv.ll. -κλητία, -κληστία, -κλησις), Suid. **-ήρ**, ῆρος, ὁ, *one who falsely subscribes his name as witness to a summons*, Theopomp.Hist.267.

**ψευδο-κορα**, dub. (perh. incomplete) in *Ostr.Bodl.*iii 295 (i A.D.). **-κόρη**, ἡ, *a pretended maid*, Poll.4.151. **-κύπειρος** (v.l. -κύπερος) [ῠ], ὁ, *bastard* κύπειρος, Dsc.5.75.15; *pseudocypirus* Plin.*HN*17.95. **-κύων** [ῠ], κυνός, ὁ, *sham Cynic*, Plu.*Brut.*34. **-λήρημα**, ατος, τό, *silly falsehood*, Tz.*H.*10.868. **-λῃστής**, οῦ, ὁ, *sham robber*, name of a Comedy by Timocles. **-λιτρος**, ον, Att. for ψευδόνιτρος: ψ. κονία lye or soap *made from adulterated soda*, Ar.*Ra.*711 (lyr.).

**ψευδολογ-έω**, *speak falsely, spread false reports*, Isoc.10.8, Aeschin.2.119, etc.; *give a wrong account*, Phld.*Sign.*21. **-ημα**, ατος, τό, *false statement, lie*, Sch.Par.A.R.4.57. **-ία**, ἡ, *falsehood*, Isoc.12.1, D.35.32, etc.: pl., Isoc.12.78, Thphr.*Char.*8.15. **-ικός**, ή, όν, *lying, false*, *Proll.Hermog.* in *Prolegomenon Sylloge* p.282 Rabe. **-ιστής**, οῦ, ὁ, = sq., name of a treatise by Lucian. **-ος** (parox.), ον, *speaking falsely, lying*, Ar.*Ra.*1521 (anap.); ὁ ψ. Plb.31.22.9, cf. Phld.*Po.*5.14, Gal.*Anim.Pass.*2.2, etc.; σοφίης *AP* 9.80 (Leon.).

**ψεύδομαι**, v. ψεύδω B.

**ψευδόμαντις**, εως, ὁ, ἡ, *false prophet*, Hdt.4.69, A.*Ag.*1195, S.*OC* 1097, E.*Or.*1667, etc.

**Ψευδομάριος** [ᾰ], *false Marius*, App.*BC*3.2.

**ψευδομάρτῠρ-α**, τά, = ψευδομαρτύρια, *IG*5(2).357.5,6 (Stymphalus, iii B.C.). **-έω**, *to be a false witness, bear false witness*, Critias 61, Pl.*R.*575b, X.*Mem.*4.4.11, Arist.*Rh.*1375$^a$12; κατά τινος Lxx *Ex.* 20.16, *Ev.Marc.*14.56. **-ία**, ἡ, *false witness*, D.41.16 codd.; ψευδομαρτυρίαν καταγνῶναί τινος Is.12.6 codd.: ἐν ψευδομαρτυρίαις D.57.53 codd.: but mostly in gen. pl., ψευδομαρτυριῶν διάκρισις Pl. *Lg.*937b; -ιῶν δίκη Is.3.6; κρίσεις Arist.*Pol.*1263$^b$21; -ιῶν ἑλεῖν τινα to convict, and ἁλῶναι to be convicted, of *perjury*, Is.5.15, And.1.7, Lys.10.25, Aeschin.1.85; ὀφλεῖν And.1.74; -ιῶν ἐπισκήψασθαί τινι make allegation of *perjury* against one, D.29.7; etc. (This form is perh. always corrupt in codd. of classical authors; -ίων (gen. pl. neut., cf. sq.) shd. prob. be read for -ιῶν, and may be restored for -ίαν in D.41.16, Is.12.6; so -ίοις for -ίαις in D.57.53: των ψευδομαρτυριων is unaccented in Pap. of Hyp.*Phil.*12: ψευδομαρτυρια[ν is an uncertain restoration in *IG*5(2).357.3 (Stymphalus, iii B.C.)); but the fem. form existed later, *Ev.Matt.*15.19, 26.59.) **-ίου δίκη**, an action *for false witness* or *perjury*, Cratin.454, *PHal.*1.24,41,49, al. (iii B.C.); in dat. pl., ἔνοχος τοῖς ψευδομαρτυρίοις Pl.*Tht.*148b; acc. pl. τὰ -μαρτύρια Arist.*Ath.*59.6.

**ψευδομάρτυς**, ῠρος, ὁ, *false witness*, pl. in Gorg.*Pal.*23, Pl.*Grg.* 472b, Critias 61: sg., *IG*5(2).357.4 (Stymphalus, iii B.C.): ψευδομάρτυρες τοῦ θεοῦ *false witnesses* about God, 1*Ep.Cor.*15.15; as Adj., τὰν δίκαν τὰν ψευδομάρτυρα the action *for false witness*, *IG* l.c. l. 8; ψ. τιμαί honours *attesting no real* merit, Plu.2.821f.

**ψευδόμενος**, ὁ, v. ψεύδω B. IV.

**ψευδόναρδος**, ἡ, *lavender spike, Lavandula spica*, Plin.*HN*12.43.

**ψευδ-όνειρος**, ον, *dreaming a false dream*, Charito 3.7.

**Ψευδονέρων**, ωνος, ὁ, *a false Nero*, Luc.*Ind.*20.

**ψευδό-νιτρος**, ον, Att. ψευδόλιτρος (q.v.). **-νύμφευτοι** γάμοι, *a false, feigned marriage*, E.*Hel.*883. **-πᾰθές**, τό, = σταφὶς ἀγρία, Ps.-Dsc.4.152. **-παιδεία**, ἡ, *false, sham education*, Cebes 11, Gal. 6.633. **-παν**, ᾶνος, ὁ, *false Pan*, Jul.*Or.*7.234d. **-πᾰνικά**, ῶν, τά, *pretended panic, terror*, Polyaen.3.9.32. **-παρήχησις**, εως, ἡ, *use of words of similar sound but different meanings*, Eust.29.40. **-πάρθενος**, ἡ, *pretended maid* or *virgin*, Hdt.4.180; as Adj., ψ. ἑταίρα Ach.Tat.8.3. **-πατον**, τό, *false pavement* or *floor*, *Cod.Just.*8.10.12.3a. **-πάτωρ** [ᾰ], ορος, ὁ, *false, unnatural father*, Call.*Cer.*99. **-περίπτερος**, ον, *with false peristyle*, of a temple in which the columns on the sides are attached to the walls instead of standing free, Vitr.4.8.6. **-πῖθος**, ὁ, *false* πίθος, i.e. of a different capacity from the official πίθος, *BCH*50.214 (Thasos, v B.C.). **-πλάνης** [ᾰ], ητος, ὁ, and **-πλᾰνήτης**, ου, ὁ, prob. *lying vagrant*, Eust.1762.2, 1742.23, of Odysseus. **-πλάστης**, ου, ὁ, *forger of lies*, Sch.Ar.*Nu.*445. **-πλουτος**, ον, *feigned to be rich*, Sch.Ar.*V.*457. **-ποιέω**, *misrepresent*, τὰ εὐεργετήματα.. τῶν ἄλλων ἐπειρᾶτο ψευδοποιεῖν καὶ ταπεινοῦν Plb.30.4.13. II. *give the lie to, expose as false*, τὰς ἀποφάσεις τῶν ποιητῶν Id.12.25.4, cf. 12.25$^c$.3, S.E.*M.*8.24; folld. by acc. et inf., *stigmatize as false* the doctrine that.., Phld.*Rh.*2.87 S. III. Pass., *to be deceived* or *mistaken, err*, αἴσθησις -εῖται *Placit.*4.9.5. **-πολίχνιον**, τό, *pretended little town*, J.*BJ*4.9.9. **-πόρφῠρον**, τό, *sham purple garment*, *POxy.* 1051.15 (iii A.D.). **-πρεσβευτής**, οῦ, ὁ, *false ambassador*, Sch.S.*Ph.*1306. **-προδοσία**, ἡ, *pretended treachery*, Polyaen.3.9.32. **-προδότης**, ου, ὁ, *pretended traitor*, Id.6.38.7. **-προφή-**

**της**, ου, ὁ, *false, lying prophet*, J.*AJ*9.6.6, al., 2 *Ep.Pet.*2.1, Ph.2.343, etc. **-πτωμα**, ατος, τό, a technical term of wrestlers, *sham* or *unfair fall* from which one starts up again and renews the contest, Plu.*Comp.Pel.Marc.*1, Sch.Ar.*Eq.*568, Macar.8.88. **-πτωχος**, ὁ, *pretended beggar*, Eust.1761.54. **-πῦρα**, ων, τά, *false watch-fires*, Suid., Macar.8.86. **-ραψῳδός**, ὁ, *false rhapsodist*, Hsch., as gloss on ψευδοραβδοθίαι (sic).

**ψευδορκ-έω**, *swear falsely*, Ar.*Ec.*603 (anap.); distd. fr. ἐπιορκεῖν by Chrysipp.*Stoic.*2.63. **-ία**, ἡ, *perjury*, Ph.2.196. **-ιος**, ον, *perjured, forsworn*, Hdt.1.165. **-ος**, ον, = foreg., E.*Med.*1392 (anap.), Ps.-Phoc.17: Sup., Ph.1.412.

**ψευδορρήμων**, ον, gen. ονος, τὰ ψ. *false locutions*, perh. *made-up words*, Phld.*Po.*2.41.

⊛**ψεῦδος**, εος, τό, Ep. dat. pl. ψεύδεσσι, v. ψευδής I. 2: (ψεύδω):—*falsehood, lie*, ψεύδεα.. ἐτύμοισιν ὁμοῖα Od.19.203, Hes.*Th.*27; ψεῦδός κεν φαῖμεν Il.2.81; ψεῦδος δ' οὐκ ἐρέει Od.3.20; εἴ τε ψεῦδος ὑπόσχεσις εἴ τε καὶ οὐκί whether the promise be a *lie* or no, Il.2.349; οὔτι ψεῦδος ἐμὰς ἄτας κατέλεξας 9.115; ψεύδεσσιν θέλγειν τινά 21.276, cf. 23.576, Od.14.387; οὐ ψευδεῖ τέγξω λόγον Pi.*O.*4.19; ψ. ποικίλα, αἰόλον ψ., Id.*O.*1.29, *N.*8.25; ψ. γλυκύ a sweet *deceit*, Id.*P.*2.37; ψεῦδος οὐδὲν ὧν λέγω S.*El.*1220; οὐδὲν ἕρπει ψ. εἰς γῆρας χρόνου Id.*Fr.*62; εἴ τι ψεῦδος εἴρηκα Antipho 3.4.2; ψ. ἐπιφέρειν Aeschin.3.41: ψ. λέγειν distd. fr. ψεύδεσθαι, *Stoic.*2.42. 2. in Logic, *false conclusion, fallacy*, συλλογισμὸς τοῦ ψεύδους Arist.*APr.*61$^{b}$3; συμβαίνει ψ. ib.37$^{a}$36:—in *NT* of what is opposed to religious truth, *false doctrine*, *Ep.Rom.*1.25; ποιῶν βδέλυγμα καὶ ψ., i.e. doing what is repugnant to the true faith, *Apoc.*21.27; of false anatomical doctrine, τὸ οἴεσθαι.. ψ. ἐστι Sor.1.17. II. in Theoc.12.24 ψεύδεα are *spots, pimples* on the nose; supposed to be characteristic of liars, cf. Sch. ad loc.; cf. ψυδράκιον. 2. *white spots* on the finger-nails, Alex.Aphr.*Pr.Anecd.*2.58. III. In Pl. ψεῦδος is freq. opp. ἀληθές, *Grg.*505e, *R.*382d, *Euthd.*272b, al.; so almost like an Adj. (cf. ψευδής init.), ὄνομα ψεῦδος καὶ ἀληθὲς λέγειν *Cra.*385c; παράδοξόν τε καὶ ψεῦδος ὄνομα *Plt.*281b: cf. E.*Heracl.*462 codd.

⊛**ψευδο-σέληνον**, τό, *false moonlight, absence of the moon*, Hsch., Suid. **-σέλῖνον**, τό, = πεντέφυλλον, Dsc.4.42.

**ψευδοσοφ-ία**, ἡ, *false wisdom*, and **ψευδόσοφος**, ον, *falsely wise*, Philostr.*VA*8.7. ⊛**-ιστής**, οῦ, ὁ, *sham-sophist*, name of a treatise by Lucian.

**Ψευδοστιγμᾰτίας**, ου, ὁ, *a false* or *pretended* στιγματίας, name of a play by Nicostr.Com.

**ψευδόστομ-α**, ατος, τό, *the false* or *blind mouth of a river*, Str.17.1.18 (pl.). **-έω**, *speak falsely*, S.*OC*1127, Luc.*Ocyp.*8. **-ος**, ον, *having false* or *blind mouths*, name of a river in India, Ptol.*Geog.*7.1.8, al.; ψ. στόμα = ψευδόστομα, ib.4.5.5, 3.10.2, al.: hence τὸ Ψ. as pr. n., D.S.20.75.

**ψευδο-συγγρᾰφεύς**, έως, ὁ, *a false writer*, Tz. in *An.Ox.*3.332, and **-συγγρᾰφέω**, *write falsely*, Id.*H.*8.185. **-σφήξ**, ηκος, ὁ, *false wasp*, a solitary kind, Plin.*HN*30.98. **-τάφιον** [ᾰ], τό, = κενοτάφιον, Philostr.*VA*8.31. **-τεχνία**, ἡ, *false, spurious art*, Sch. Aphthon. in Rh.2.623 W., Serv.Dan.ad Verg.*Aen.*1.464. **-τρισκαιδέκᾰτος**, η, ον, *falsely reckoned the thirteenth*, Tz.*H.*2.505.

**ψευδουργός**, ὁ, *one who practices deceitful arts*, Pl.*Sph.*241b.

**ψευδο-φαής**, ές, *shining with false*, i.e. *borrowed, light*, of the moon, D.L.2.1. **-φᾰνής**, ές, = foreg., *Placit.*2.30.4. **-φημος**, ον, *falsely uttered*, S.*OC*1517.

**Ψευδοφίλιππος** [φῐ], ὁ, *a false Philip*, Luc.*Ind.*20.

**ψευδόχριστος**, ὁ, in pl., *false Christs*, *Ev.Matt.*24.24.

**ψευδόχρῡσος**, ὁ, *a false chrysolite*, D.S.2.52 (ψευδοχρυσολίθους cj. Salmasius).

**ψευδόχρῡσος**, ον, *of mock gold*, Plu.2.50a.

**ψευδ-υποβολιμαῖος**, α, ον, *falsely held to be supposititious*; ὁ Ψευδυπ. name of plays by Crobylus and Cratin.Jun.

⊛**ψεύδω**, S.*Ant.*389, etc.: fut. ψεύσω Id.*OC*628, X.*Cyr.*1.5.13: aor. ἔψευσα A.*Pers.*472, Plb.18.11.11, etc.:—**Pass.**, fut. ψευσθήσομαι S.*Tr.*712, Gal.15.143: aor. ἐψεύσθην Hdt.1.141, etc.: pf. ἔψευσμαι (v. infr.); imper. ἐψεύσθω Aeschin.1.162:—*cheat by lies, beguile*, τινα S.*OC*628, etc.:—Pass., *to be cheated, deceived*, A.*Ch.*759, etc.; εἰ μὴ πολύ γε ἔψευσμαι unless *I am* much *deceived*, Antipho 3.2.1. 2. c. gen., *cheat, balk, disappoint* one *of* a thing, ψεύσει σ' ὁδοῦ τῆσδ' ἐλπίς E.*Hec.*1031; ἔψευσας φρενῶν Πέρσας A.*Pers.*472; μὴ ψεῦσον ὦ Ζεῦ τῆς ἐπιούσης ἐλπίδος Ar.*Th.*870; πιστεύω.. μή ψεύσειν με.. τὰς ἐλπίδας X.*Cyr.*1.5.13; πόλλ' ἐλπίδες ψεύδουσι καὶ λόγοι βροτούς E.*Fr.*650:—Pass., *to be cheated, balked, disappointed*, τινος *of* a thing, ψευσθῆναι ἐλπίδος, γάμου, Hdt.1.141, 5.47; ἑτάρων S.*Aj.*178 (lyr.); δείπνου Ar.*Nu.*618 (troch.); ψευσθέντες τῶν σκοπῶν *disappointed of receiving tidings* from the scouts, Th.8.103. 3. in Pass., also, *to be deceived, mistaken in* or *about* a thing, ἐψευσμένοι γνώμης *deceived* in their judgement, *mistaken* in opinion, Hdt.8.40, cf. S.*Tr.*712 (also ψευσθῆναι γνώμῃ Hdt.7.9.γ'); ἐψευσμένοι τῆς Ἀθηναίων δυνάμεως *deceived* or *mistaken in their notions of* the Athenian power, Th.4.108; πολλῶν ἐψεύσθητε τῆς οὐσίας you have often *had a mistaken idea of* a man's wealth, Lys.19.45; τούτου οὐκ ἐψεύσθην Pl.*Ap.*22d; ἐψεῦσθαι τῆς ἀληθείας Id.*R.*413a; τῆς ὥρας And.1.38; ἐψευσμένοι τῶν ὄντων Pl.*Tht.*195a; ἐψεῦσθαι ἑαυτῶν, opp. εἰδέναι ἑαυτούς, X.*Mem.*4.2.26; also ψευσθῆναι ἔν τισι Hdt.9.48; περί τινος X.*An.*2.6.28, Pl.*Prt.*358c: also c. acc., ἐψεύσθη τοῦτο X.*An.*1.8.11, etc.; αὐτοὺς ἐψευσμένη ἡ Ἑλλάς *deceived in its estimate of* them, Th.6.17 (where αὐτοὺς is prob. corrupt, and shd. perh. be omitted): c. acc. cogn., εὐτυχέστατον ψεῦσμα ἐψευσμένος most happily *deceived* or *mistaken*, Pl.*Men.*71d: more rarely in Act., καί μ' ἔψευσας ἐλπίδος πολύ thou hast much *belied* my expectation, i.e. turned out better than I feared, S.*Aj.*1382. 4. of statements, *to be untrue*, ἡ τρίτη τῶν ὁδῶν μάλιστα ἔψευσται the third mode of explanation *is* most *untrue*, most *mistaken*, Hdt.2.22. II. c. acc. rei, like ψευδοποιέω II, *represent* a thing *as a lie, falsify*, ψεύδοντες οὐδὲν σῆμα τῶν προκειμένων S.*OC*1512 (prob. for σημάτων); ψεύδει ἡ 'πίνοια τὴν γνώμην afterthought *gives* opinion *the lie*, Id.*Ant.*389:—Pass., ἢν τάδε ψευσθῇ λέγων if his word *prove* (lit. *be proved*) *false*, Id.*Ph.*1342; ἡ ψευσθεῖσα ὑπόσχεσις the promise *broken*, Th.3.66; πάντα πρὸς ὑμᾶς ἔψευσται *have been falsely reported*, D.52.23; in E.*Andr.*346 for ἀλλὰ ψεύσεται *it will be falsely said*, Porson's correction ἐψεύσεται is probable (πεύσεται Kiehl).

**B.** earlier and more common **ψεύδομαι**, imper. ψεύδεο Il.4.404 (the Act. is very rare in Att. Prose): fut. ψεύσομαι Hom., Pi., Att.: aor. ἐψευσάμην, v. infr.: fut. 2 ἐψεύσομαι (*will have made a false statement*) Gal.15.137 (s. v.l.): pf. ἔψευσμαι X.*An.*1.3.10. I. abs., *lie, speak false, play false*, ψεύσομαι ἢ ἔτυμον ἐρέω; Il.10.534, Od.4.140; οὐκ οἶδα ψεύδεσθαι *h.Merc.*369; οὐ ψεύσομ' ἀμφὶ Κορίνθῳ Pi.*O.*13.52; περί τινος Pl.*Prt.*347a; ψ. κατά τινος, opp. λέγειν τἀληθῆ κατά τινος, Id.*Euthd.*284a, Lys.22.7; ψ. πρός τινα X.*An.*1.3.5; ψ. τινι *Act.Ap.*5.4 and εἴς τινα *Ep.Col.*3.9. 2. c. inf., *say falsely, pretend* that.., Plu.2.506d. 3. c. acc. rei, *say that which is untrue*, whether intentionally or not, τοῦτό γ' οὐκ ἐψεύσατο Ar.*Ec.*445; οὐδὲν αὐτῶν ψεύδεται Id.*Ach.*561; κἂν λάβῃς ἐψευσμένον, φάσκειν ἔμ' ἤδη μαντικῇ μηδὲν φρονεῖν S.*OT*461; ἐάν τι μὴ ἀληθὲς λέγω.., εἰπὲ ὅτι τοῦτο ψεύδομαι· ἑκὼν γὰρ εἶναι οὐδὲν ψεύσομαι Pl.*Smp.*214e, cf. X.*Mem.*4.2.19; περὶ ὧν ἐψεύσατο διδάσκειν ὑμᾶς Lys.3.21. 4. *to be false* or *faithless, to be perjured* or *forsworn*, Hes.*Op.*283. 5. ὁ ψευδόμενος, the *Liar*, name of a fallacy or logical puzzle invented by Eubulides, a disciple of Euclides of Megara, Thphr.ap.D.L.2.108, cf. Chrysipp. *Stoic.*2.92 (ψευδόμενος is an interpolation in ὁ σοφιστικὸς λόγος ψ. Arist.*EN*1146$^{a}$22). II. like Act. II, *belie, falsify*, ὅρκια ψεύσασθαι *break* them, Il.7.352; so συνθήκας ψ. X.*Ages.*1.12; γάμους E.*Ba.*31,245; so in plpf., ἔψευστο τὴν ξυμμαχίαν Th.5.83; so also οὐκ ἐψεύσαντο τὰς ἀπειλάς *they did* not *belie*, i.e. they made good, their threats, Hdt.6.32; τὰ χρήματα.. ἐψευσμένοι ἦσαν *had broken their word* about the money, X.*An.*5.6.35. III. like Act. I, *deceive by lies, cheat*, Λοξίαν ἐψευσάμην A.*Ag.*1208, cf. X.*HG*3.1.25; also ψ. τινά τι *deceive* one *in* a thing, S.*OC*1145, E.*Alc.*808; ἅπερ αὐτὸν οὐ ψεύσομαι and therein I *will* not *disappoint* him (ironical), i.e. I will carry out my threat, And.1.123; τῶν ἔργων ὧν ἂν τὸν ἐκδόντα ψεύσηται (ὧν being in gen. by attraction) Pl.*Lg.*921a. IV. of combinations of words, *make a false statement*, Arist.*Int.*16$^{a}$3.

**ψευδ-ωμότης**, ου, ὁ, *false swearer*, Lyc.523. **-ώμοτος**, ον, *falsely sworn, forsworn*, ὅρκος Id.932. **-ώνῠμος**, ον, *under a false name, falsely called*, Ὑβριστὴν ποταμὸν οὐ ψευδώνυμον A.*Pr.*717; πανδίκως ψ. Id.*Th.*670; οὔνομα δ' Εὐτυχίδης· ψευδώνυμον ἀλλά με δαίμων θῆκεν ἀφαρπάξας *IG*3.1308; ψ. θεοί Ph.2.161, cf. 2.599; ψ. γνῶσις 1 *Ep.Ti.*6.21; φιλόσοφος ψευδεπίγραφος καὶ ψ. Plu.2.479e; opp. ἀληθής, τὸ μεριστὸν ψ. Dam.*Pr.*399. Adv. **-μως** *by a false name*, ψ. σε δαίμονες Προμηθέα καλοῦσιν A.*Pr.*85, cf. Them.*Or.*2.30a.

**ψευσίστυξ**, ῠγος, ὁ, ἡ, *hating falsehood*, epith of Apollo, *AP*9.525.24.

⊛**ψεῦσ-μα**, ατος, τό, *lie, untruth, fraud*, εὐτυχέστατον ψεῦσμα ἐψευσμένος Pl.*Men.*71d, cf. Luc.*Tim.*55, Plu.*Art.*13. II. τοὺς ἐπὶ τῆς ῥινὸς φυομένους ἰόνθους Σικελιῶται ψεύσματα ἔλεγον Sch.Theoc. 12.24, cf. Kaibel *CGF* p.218. **-τάζω**, = ψεύδομαι, *lie*, Tz.*H.*9.434. **-τέω**, *to be a liar*, Il.19.107. **-τήρ**, ῆρος, ὁ, = sq., Man. 4.119. **-της**, ου, ὁ, (ψεύδω) *liar, cheat*, Il.24.261; ἀνὴρ ψ. Hdt. 7.209, cf. Lxx *Si.*15.8: c. gen. rei, ὧν.. ψεῦσται φανούμεθα wherein we shall be found to be *liars*, S.*Ant.*1195, cf. Arist.*EN*1127$^{b}$16, *AP*12.70 (Mel.), Phld.*Herc.*1457.12. 2. Adj., = ψευδής, *lying, false*, ψ. λόγος Pi.*N.*5.29; ψεύστης δ' οὗτος ἔπεστι λίθος, of a cenotaph, *AP*7.273 (Leon.); τὸν ψεύσταν δέ με τύμβον.. θέντο· τί θαῦμα; Κρῆτες ὅπου ψεῦσται, καὶ Διός ἐστι τάφος ib.275 (Gaet.), alluding to Κρῆτες ἀεὶ ψεῦσται, Epimenid.1, which is cited by Call.*Jov.*8, *Ep.Tit.*1.12. **-τία**, ἡ, = *fallacia*, dub. in *Gloss.* **-τικός**, ή, όν, *mendacious*, Vett.Val.17.31.

**ψεῦστις**, ιδος, ἡ, fem. of ψεύστης, νύξ *Epigr.Gr.*418 (Cyrene).

**ψεφ-αίαις**· σκοτειναῖς, and **ψεφαῖον**· λυπρόν, σκοτεινόν, Hsch. **-ᾰρός**, ά, όν, *gloomy, cloudy*, Hp.ap.Gal.19.156 (v.l. for ὑποψ- in Hp.*Prorrh.*1.116). **-ας**, ἄος, τό, *gloom, darkness*, Pi.*Fr.*324. **-αυγοῦς**· σκοτεινῆς, Hsch. **-ηνός**, ή, όν, *dark, obscure*, metaph. of a person, Pi.*N.*3.41 codd. (-εινός Bgk., -εννός Pors.).

**ψεφοειδής**, ές, gloss on ψεφαρός, Gal.19.156.

**ψέφος**, εος, τό, *darkness*, cj. Lobeck in Alc.112 (ψόφου, σκότου codd.), cf. Gal.19.156; = καπνός, Hsch.

**ψέφω**, in 3 sg. ψέφει· δέδοικεν, ἐντρέπει, λυπεῖ, φροντίζει, Hsch.: cf. μετα-ψέφω; also prob. ἐπί-σσοφος.

**ψέω**, = ψάω, *EM*818.2. **ψῆ**, v. ψάω.

**ψῆγ-μα**, ατος, τό, (ψήχω) *that which is rubbed* or *scraped off, shavings, scrapings, chips*, ψ. χρυσοῦ gold-*dust*, Hdt.4.195; so without χρυσοῦ, Id.1.93, 3.94 sq.; ψ. χρυσότευκτον Eub.20; ψ. ἀργυρᾶ *Inscr.Délos* 442*B*89 (ii B.C.); πυρωθὲν ψ., of dust and ashes, A.*Ag.*442 (lyr.); of wood, τὰ τῶν αἰγείρων ψ. Philostr.*Im.*1.11; ἥλων ψ., = χαλκοῦ ἄνθος, Dsc.5.77; μὴ διαλύεσθαι μέχρι ἐλαχίστου ψήγματος (of gum)

Id.3.22; of *motes* in a sunbeam, Arist.*Cael.*313$^a$20, cf. 304$^a$21, Plu.2.722a, and v. τίλα II. **-μάτιον**, τό, Dim. of foreg., *Inscr.Délos*1429*B* ii 17 (ii B.C.), *Placit.*1.13.2.

**ψηκεδών**, όνος, ἡ, (ψάω, ψήχω) = κονιορτός, Hsch.

**ψηκτὸς** μόδιος, *filled only level with the brim*, i.e. not heaped up (κορυστός), *Gloss.*

⊕**ψήκτρ-α**, ἡ, (ψήχω) *curry-comb* for horses, S.*Fr.*475, E.*Hipp.*1174, Ar.*Fr.*62, *AP*6.233 (Maec.), 246 (Phld. or Marc.Arg.), *PSI* 4.430.5 (iii B.C.), etc. In Hsch. also **ψακτήρ** and (as glosses on ξύστρα) **ψηκτρίς** and **ψηκτρία** (fort. ψήκτρια). **-ίζω**, *scrape down, rub down*, Sch.E.*Hipp.*110. **-ίον**, τό, Dim. of ψήκτρα, *Gloss.* (in form ψηκτριν).

**ψηλᾰφ-άω**, mostly used in pres.: fut. -ήσω Lxx *Za.*9.13: aor. ἐψηλάφησα ib.*Ge.*27.22:—Pass., fut. ψηλαφηθήσομαι ib.*Na.*3.1: aor. ἐψηλαφήθην S.E.*M.*8.108, Plu.2.599c:—*feel* or *grope about* to find a thing, like a blind man or hoodman-blind, χερσὶ ψηλαφόων (Ep. for -άων), of the Cyclops when blinded, Od.9.416; ψηλαφῶν οὐκ ἐδυνάμην εὑρεῖν [τὸ ἱμάτιον] Ar.*Ec.*315; ψηλαφῶντες.. ὥσπερ ἐν σκότει Pl.*Phd.*99b: metaph., ψ. περί τινων Phld.*D.*1.14. 2. c. acc. rei, *feel about for, grope* or *search after*, ἐψηλαφῶμεν ἐν σκότῳ τὰ πράγματα Ar.*Pax*691; εἰ.. ψηλαφήσειαν αὐτὸν (sc. τὸν θεὸν) καὶ εὕροιεν *Act.Ap.*17.27. II. *feel, touch, handle, stroke*, Poll.1.183; μή ποτε ψηλαφήσῃ με ὁ πατήρ, of Isaac and Jacob, Lxx *Ge.*27.12, cf. *Ev.Luc.*24.39; ψ. καὶ τρίβειν τοῖς δακτύλοις Arist.*HA*571$^a$33; esp. in Medic., of uterine examination, Hp.*Mul.*1.40, al.:—Pass., ὧν ψηλαφωμένων ὁ ἵππος.. ἥδεται X.*Eq.*2.4; [ὄρνιθες] τῇ χειρὶ ψηλαφώμεναι Arist.*HA*560$^a$9. III. metaph., *test, examine*, τὸν ὗν Plb.8.29.8; τὸν οἶνον *Gp.*7.5.1; πᾶσαν ἐπίνοιαν Plb.8.16.4; τὰς ἀλλήλων νοήσεις οἷον ὑπὸ σκότῳ διὰ φωνῆς ψ. Plu.2.589b; εἴδωλον [τοῦ καλοῦ] διώκοντες καὶ ψ. ib.766a:—Pass., S.E. l.c., τὰ ψηλαφηθέντα ὑπ' Ἀντιόχου the *attempts made* by.., J.*AJ*13.9.2. **-ημα**, ατος, τό, *touch*, Ph.1.597; *caress*, X.*Smp.*8.23. **-ησις**, εως, ἡ, *feeling, touching, palpation*, Hp.*Steril.*213, al., Epicur.*Fr.*21 (pl.), Lxx *Wi.*15.15, Plu.*Aem.*14; *tickling*, αἱ τῶν μασχαλῶν ψ. Plu.2.125c, cf. 547b (pl.). **-ητέον**, *one must feel, handle*, Archig.ap.Aët.6.3. **-ητής**, οῦ, ὁ, *one who feels, a searcher*, Sch.Opp.*H.*2.435. **-ητικῶς**, Adv., *by way of feeling*, Eust.1717.16. **-ητός**, ή, όν, *that can be felt*, σκότος Lxx *Ex.*10.21 (so ψηλαφῆσαι σκότος ib.*Jb.*12.25). **-ία**, Ion. -ίη, ἡ, = ψηλάφησις, *touching*, Hp.*Decent.*8, Phld.*D.*1.13, Aret.*CA*1.1, Ruf.ap.Orib.*inc.*2.30; *handling*, οὐ πολλῆς ψ. δεῖσθαι Ph.*Bel.*56.33. **-ίζω**, = ψηλαφάω, Anaxil.44. **-ίνδᾰ** παίζειν, play *blind-man's-buff*, Phryn.*PS*p.128 B (-ίνδρα cod.). **-ώδης**, ες, *like one feeling* or *groping in the dark*, of the gestures of delirious persons, Hp.*Prorrh.*1.109.

**ψήληκες**· τῶν ἀλεκτρυόνων οἱ νοθογένναι, Hsch. (ψήλικες cod.), Suid.

**ψημύθιον, ψημυθιόω**, v. ψιμύθιον, ψιμυθιόω.

**ψήν**, ὁ, gen. ψηνός, *gall-insect, Cynips psenes*, which lives in the fruit of the wild fig and male palm, Hdt.1.193, Ar.*Av.*590 (anap.), Arist.*HA*557$^b$26, Thphr.*HP*2.8.1. 2. *fruit of the male palm*, Poll.1.244.

**ψηνίζω**, = ἐρινάζω, ὀλυνθάζω:—hence, sens. obsc., οὐδεὶς κομήτης ὅστις οὐ ψηνίζεται *Com.Adesp.*12. II. *to Psenize*, alluding to the Ψῆνες, a Comedy by Magnes so called, Ar.*Eq.*523 (anap.).

**ψηνός**, ὁ, = ψεδνός, *bald headed*, Semon.40: cf. **ψανός**· ψεδνός, Hsch. (prob. ᾱ and Dor., Aeol., or Arc.-Cypr.).

**ψηνύξαι**· ξύσαι, σοβῆσαι, Suid.

**ψῆξις**, εως, ἡ, (ψήχω) *rubbing down, currying*, of horses, X.*Eq.*5.3,10.

**ψήρ**, ὁ, gen. ψηρός, Ion. for ψάρ (q. v.).

**ψηροπῡρίτας** [ῑ] ἄρτος, = αὐτόπυρος, Hsch.

**ψηρός**, ά, όν, = ξηρός, Suid.; cf. μεσ⟨σ⟩όψηρον, and perh. ψαρός (B).

**ψησσίον**, τό, Dim. of ψῆσσα (v. ψῆττα), Zonar.

**ψῆττα**, ἡ, a kind of *flat-fish*, prob. *turbot, Rhombus maximus*, Ar.*Lys.*115,131, Pl.*Smp.*191d, Antiph.132.7 (anap.), Ath.7.329e, Luc.*Pisc.*49, Alciphr.1.7; ψ. χονδροφυὴς perh. *a skate*, Matro *Conv.*27. II. a nickname for *a glutton*, Pl.Com.106. (The form **ψῆσσα** Alex.Trall.1.15, al., Zonar.; **ψησία** (s. v. l.) Suid.)

**ψηττάριον** [ᾰ], τό, Dim. of ψῆττα, Anaxandr.27 (anap., ψιτταδίοις cod.A Ath., corr. Lobeck).

**ψηττο-ειδής**, ές, *like a flat-fish*, Arist.*IA*714$^b$6. **-ποδες**, οἱ, *turbot-footed*, name of a fabulous people in Luc.*VH*1.35.

**ψηφάς**, άδος, ὁ, *juggler*, *Cat.Cod.Astr.*7.118, 8(3).110, 8(4).217.

**ψηφη-φορέω, -φορία**, later forms of ψηφοφ-.

**ψηφίδιον**, τό, *a little pebble*, Iamb.*Myst.*3.17 (v.l. ψηφίδων gen. pl.).

**ψηφῑδοφόρος**, ον, = ψηφοφόρος, Hdt.6.109.

**ψηφῑδώδης**, ες, *pebbly, stony*, γῆ *Gp.*2.6.41, al.

⊕**ψηφ-ίζω**, fut. Att. -ιῶ (ἐπι-) Aeschin.2.84: aor. ἐψήφισα Plu.2.141c, (ἐπι-) Th.2.24: pf. ἐψήφικα (ἐπ-) X.*An.*5.6.35, (κατ-) D.H.5.8:—Med., v. infr. II:—Pass., v. infr. III:—*count, reckon*, prop. *with pebbles* (ψῆφοι), Plb.5.26.13, *AP*11.168 (Antiphan.), 171 (Lucill.); ψ. δακτύλοις Plu. l.c. 2. ἐὰν ψηφίσῃς τὸ ἓν ἐν γράμμασιν, i.e. if you *add up the numerical values* of the letters in the word ἕν, *Theol.Ar.*64. II. more freq. in Med. **ψηφίζομαι**: fut. Att. ψηφιοῦμαι Ar.*V.*769, Th.7.48, Pl.*Smp.*177d, etc. (ψηφίσομαι is f.l. where found, e.g. in Lys.12.44, 14.47, (κατα-) Antipho 1.12, 6.10, (ἀπο-) ibid.): aor. ἐψηφισάμην Hdt.5.97, Th.7.48, etc.: pf. ἐψήφισμαι in med. sense, Ar.*V.*591 (anap.), Th.1.120, etc.:—prop., *cast one's vote with a pebble*: 1. abs., εἰς ὑδρίαν ψ. X.*HG*1.7.9, cf. Ar.*V.*755 (anap.): generally, *vote*, ψήφῳ ψηφίζεσθαι μὴ φεύγειν Hdt.9.55; τοῖς νόμοις ψηφίσασθαι *vote in support of* the laws, D.21.188; ἐναντία ψ. τινι Pl.*Smp.*177d. 2. c. acc., *vote for, carry by vote*, τὸν πόλεμον Th.1.86; ψηφίσασθαί τινι τὸν πλοῦν *vote* him the voyage, Id.4.29; ψ. παρασκευήν Id.6.25, cf. Ar.*Lys.*951; ἐπιβολὴν ψ. Id.*V.*769; δίκην Is.3.7; ἄδειαν And.1.12; διαδίκασμα ψ. τινι Lys.17.10; κλῆρόν τινι ψ. *to adjudge* it to.., D.43.6: c. dupl. acc., ψ. τινα θεόν *vote* him a god, Plu.2.187e. 3. c. inf., *vote, resolve to do* something, c. inf. pres., ψ. μένειν Hdt.7.207, cf. 9.55 (supr. cit.); ψ. τι δρᾶν A.*Ag.*1353: c. inf. aor., ψ. νέας ἀποστεῖλαι Hdt.5.97, cf. Ar.*V.*591 (anap.), Pl.*Grg.*516e: c. inf. fut., ψ. πάντας ἀποσφάξειν (better ἀποσφάξαι as cod. P) D.S.12.72: c. acc. et inf., *vote that*.., ψ. τὰς σπονδὰς λελύσθαι Th.1.88; ψ. ὥστε μὴ ἴσον ἕκαστον τυγχάνειν X.*Cyr.*2.2.20; ψ. ὅπως τις ἄρχοι μόνος Plu.*Pomp.*54. 4. ψ. περί, ὑπέρ τινος, Pl.*Dem.*382d, Aeschin.1.154. III. Act. is used in signf. *decide by vote*, δίκην κατ' ἄλλου.. ἐψήφισαν S.*Aj.*449, and is also found in *IGRom.*4.293 *a* ii 57 (Pergam., ii B.C.); ψηφίζομεν is dub. in Hdn.2.3.4 (ἐπευφημίζομεν Schwartz):—Pass., aor. ψηφισθῆναι *be voted*, τοῖς στρατηγοῖς εἴ του προσδέοιντο ψηφισθῆναι ἐς τὸν ἔκπλουν Th.6.8; τὸ ψήφισμα ἐψηφίσθη Lys.13.29; τὰ ψηφισθέντα πλοῖα X.*HG*1.2.1: fut., τὰ ψηφισθησόμενα Isoc.6.92: pf., ἐψηφισμένοι θανεῖν *condemned by vote*, E.*Heracl.*141; τοῖς ἰχθυοπώλαις ἐστὶν ἐψηφισμένον.. στῆσαι Alex.56. **-ικός**, ή, όν, *involving calculations*, Vett.Val.191.30, al. **-ῖνος**, ον, perh. *made of marble*, λίθινος ἢ ψ. μυροθήκη as expl. of ἀλάβαστρον, *AB*374: ἀλάβαστρον· μυροθήκη λίθος ψήφινος, Hsch. (λίθινος ἢ ψ. Cyr.): ἀπὸ Ἁρποκράτου ψηφίνου from a *marble* (statue of) Harpocrates, *PMag.Par.*1.1074. ⊕**-ίον**, τό, Dim. of ψῆφος, *small pebble, gravel*, Aq.*Am.*9.9; *pellet*, μέλιτος Orib.*Fr.*35 (pl.). ⊕**-ίς**, ῖδος (cf. Hdn.Gr.2.186), ἡ, Dim. of ψῆφος, *small pebble*, Il.21.260, Lex Solonis ap.Sch.Gen.Il. l.c., Democr.164, Luc.*DMar.*3.2. 2. *pebble for reckoning*, *AP*11.365 (Agath.). 3. *tessellated work*, Chor.p.86 B. II. *gem* or *amulet* worn in a ring, Longus 4.17, Alex.Trall.11.1. **-ισις**, εως, ἡ, *voting*, only in Locr. acc. sg. **ψάφιξιν** [ᾰ], *IG*9(1).334.45 (Oeanthea, v B.C.). ⊕**-ισμα**, ατος, τό, Dor. **ψάφιγμα** [ψᾰ] *Inscr.Cret.*1.v 20 *A* 17 (Arcades, ii B.C.); written [ψ]άπιγμα *Supp.Epigr.*4.171.53 (Tymnus, v/iv B.C.):—*proposal passed by a majority of votes*: esp. *measure passed by a popular assembly, decree, act*, A.*Supp.*601 (pl.), Ar.*Ach.*536, al.: c. gen. suasoris, *the decree proposed by* him, τὸ Καννωνοῦ ψ. Id.*Ec.*1090, cf. And.1.27: but τὸ Μεγαρέων ψ. the *decree concerning* them, Th.1.140 (more freq. τὸ περὶ M. ψ. ib.139, cf. X.*HG*2.1.32); also τὸ ψ. τὸ διὰ τὰς λαικαστρίας Ar.*Ach.*536; ἐγένετο ψ. μὴ ἐξεῖναι.. X.*HG*2.2.15; ψ. γράφειν bring in a *decree*, Ar.*Nu.*1429; ψ. ἐπιψηφίζειν put *it* to the vote, Aeschin.2.84; ψ. νικᾶν carry *it*, Id.3.68; ψ. καθαιρεῖν rescind *it*, Th.1.140; ἐξαλεῖψαι, ἀφελέσθαι, And.1.76, 2.24: prop. concerned with special circumstances (οὐδὲν ἐνδέχεται ψ. εἶναι καθόλου Arist.*Pol.*1292$^a$37); opp. νόμος (general law, statute), νόμους καὶ ψηφίσματα Pl.*Tht.*173d; ὅταν τὰ ψ. κύρια ᾖ ἀλλὰ μὴ ὁ νόμος Arist.*Pol.*1292$^a$6; περὶ ἐνίων ἀδύνατον θέσθαι νόμον, ὥστε ψηφίσματος δεῖ Id.*EN*1137$^b$29; ψηφισμάτων οὐδ' ὁτιοῦν διαφέρουσιν οἱ νόμοι, ἀλλὰ νεώτεροι οἱ νόμοι, καθ' οὓς τὰ ψ. δεῖ γράφεσθαι, τῶν ψ. αὐτῶν D.20.92. II. generally, *decree, law*, θεῶν ψ. παλαιόν Emp.115, cf. Ar.*V.*378 (lyr.), Lexap.And.1.96, Lxx *Es.*3.7, al.

**ψηφισμᾰτο-πώλης**, ου, ὁ, *one who drives a traffic in* ψηφίσματα, Ar.*Av.*1037; also **-γράφος** [ᾰ], ὁ, Arg.Ar.*Av.*

**ψηφισ-μᾰτώδης**, ες, *of the nature of a* ψήφισμα, Arist.*EN*1134$^b$24. **-μός**, ὁ, *the use of pebbles* (in casting lots), διὰ ψηφισμοῦ ᾑρημένος as gloss on ἀπὸ τοῦ κυάμου, Sch.Th.8.69. **-τέον**, *one must calculate*, Vett.Val.33.31. **-τής**, οῦ, ὁ, *calculator*, *Cat.Cod.Astr.*2.178 (pl.).

**ψηφο-βόλον**, τό, *dice-box*, Suid. s.v. τάβλα. **-ειδής**, ές, *pebbly*, Thphr.*Lap.*47. ⊕**-θεσμία**, ἡ, *laying of a mosaic pavement*, *Inscr. gr. et lat. de la Syrie* 1.168 (Nicopolis, ii/iii A.D.). ⊕**-θέτης**, ου, ὁ, *maker of tessellated pavements*, *Gloss.*; written **ψηφοδ[έ]τας** in *Epigr.Gr.*532 (Perinthus):—hence **-θετέω**, *make such work*, *JRS* 18.171 (Gerasa), *Gloss.*; and **-θέτημα**, ατος, τό, *the work itself*, ib. **-θήκη**, ἡ, *box for counters* or *ballots*, Sch.Ar.*Th.*1040. **-κλέπτης**, ου, ὁ, = ψηφοπαίκτης, Ath.1.19b, cf. Eust.1601.50. **-λογεῖον**, τό, *account-board*, Ar.*Fr.*348. ⊕**-λογέω**, = ψηφοθετέω, Lxx *To.*13.17 (Pass.):—hence **-λόγημα**, ατος, τό, Hero *Stereom.*2.35, Lyd.*Mag.*3.65 (pl.), *Expl. Arch. de Délos* 11.261 (pl.); **-λογία**, ἡ, **-λογητός**, όν, *Gloss.* ⊕**-λογικός**, ή, όν, *juggling*, Suid., f.l. in *EM*535.1. **-λόγος**, ον, *playing juggling tricks, juggler*, Suid. **-παικτέω**, *play juggling tricks*, Artem.3.55. 2. ψ. τὸ δίκαιον *juggle away* right, Lys.*Fr.*17. **-παίκτης**, ου, ὁ, (παίζω) *one who juggles with pebbles*, Eudox.Com.1, S.E.*P.*2.250. **-παιξία**, ἡ, *juggling, legerdemain, sleight-of-hand*, *Gloss.* **-περιβομβήτρια**, ἡ, *jar of pebbles* used as a rattle (?), dub. sens. in Eub.56. **-ποιός**, όν, (ψῆφος II. 5) *making votes* or *tampering with them*, κλέπτης γὰρ αὐτοῦ ψηφοποιὸς εὑρέθης S.*Aj.*1135.

⊕**ψῆφος**, Dor. **ψᾶφος**, Aeol. **ψᾶφαξ**, ἡ, gen. pl. ψηφάων Man.4.448: (ψάω):—*a small round worn stone, pebble*, ψᾶφος ἑλισσομένα Pi.*O.*10(11).9; οὐκ ἂν εἰδείην λέγειν ποντιᾶν ψάφων ἀριθμόν ib.13.46; ψήφῳ μούνῃ διατετρανέεις, opp. μόγις ἂν λίθῳ παίσας διαρρήξειας, Hdt.3.12; ψ. ἄμμου a *grain* of sand, Lxx *Si.*18.10. 2. *precious stone, gem*, Philostr.*VA*3.27; esp. worn in a ring, Luc.*DMeretr.*9. II. acc. to the various uses made of such pebbles: 1. *pebble used for reckoning, counter*, λογίζεσθαι ψήφοις calculate or reckon by *abacus, cipher*, Hdt.2.36, etc.: hence to reckon *exactly* or *accurately*, opp. ἀπὸ χειρὸς λ., Ar.*V.*656 (anap.); οὐ τιθεὶς ψήφους D.18.229; ἐν ψήφῳ λέγειν A.*Ag.*570; ἐν ψήφου λόγῳ θέσθαι E.*Rh.* 309: metaph., ταῖς τοῦ συμφέροντος ψήφοις μετρεῖν τὰς ἔχθρας καὶ τὰς φιλίας Plb.2.47.5: hence ψῆφος itself for a *cipher, number*, ποτ ἄρτιον (sc. ἀριθμὸν) ποτθέμειν..ψᾶφον Epich.170: pl., *accounts*, καθαραὶ ψ., where there is an exact balance, D.18.227; οἱ περὶ τὰς ψ. *calculators*, Alciphr.1.26; ψήφων ἄπειρος Plu.2.812e; δακτυλικὴ ψ. *reckoning* on the fingers, *AP*11.290 (Pall.); of astrological *calculations*, Vett.Val.10.15, al. b. in Magic, κατέχων τὴν ψ. (i.e. the object on which the *number* is written) λέγε..*PMag.Par.*1.1048, cf. 937. 2. *pebble used for a draughts-* or *chess-man*, Pl.*R.*487c; κύβος ἐν παιδιῇ ψήφων Plu.2.427f. b. *pebble* used by jugglers, ψηφάων παίκται Man.4.448. 3. *pebble used in divination*, ἡ διὰ ψήφων μαντική Apollod.3.10.2. 4. *cube* used in mosaic pavements, Gal.*Protr.*8. 5. *pebble used in voting*, ψήφῳ ψηφίζεσθαι Hdt.9.55; ἐὰν μὴ τῇ ψ...ψηφίσωνται κρύβδην ψηφιζόμενοι D.59.89: hence, *the vote* itself, ψῆφον φέρειν give *one's vote*, ἐν καρδίᾳ ψ. φέροντες A.*Eu.*680, cf. And.1.2, D.57.61, etc.; ὑπέρ τινος Lycurg.7; περί τινος Id.11, etc.; ψήφου φορά E.*Supp.*484; ψῆφον τίθεσθαι, = ψηφίζεσθαι, Hdt.8.123, cf. 6.57; εἰς τεῦχος..ψήφους ἔθεντο A.*Ag.*816; c. inf., Hdt.3.73; ψ. προσθέσθαι Th.1.40; ψήφῳ διαιρεῖν to determine *by vote*, A.*Eu.*630; ψήφῳ κρίνειν, Th.1.87, etc.; μεταλαβὼν τὸ πέμπτον μέρος τῶν ψ. Pl.*Ap.*36b, cf. Lex ap.D.21.47: in collect. sense, ἐχρῆν..ψ. περὶ αὐτοῦ γενέσθαι *a vote* is taken, Antipho 5.47; ἡ καθαιροῦσα ψ. Lys.13.37; ἡ σῴζουσα ψ. D.19.66; οἷς ἂν πλείστη γένηται ψ. a majority *of votes*, Pl.*Lg.*759d: τὴν ψῆφον ἐπάγειν to put *the vote* or *question*, of the president, Th.1.119,125; ψῆφον δοῦναι περί τινος *IG*2².222.24, cf. D.21.188; ψ. ἀναδοὺς περί τινος App.*BC*1.100; so ψ. περὶ ἡμῶν ὑπὲρ ἀνδραποδισμοῦ προτεθεῖσαν D.19.65; διένεμον (vv. ll. διενέμοντο, ἔφερον) τὰς ψ. were casting their *votes*, Hdt.8.123; ὑπὸ ψήφου μιᾶς with one *accord*, Ar.*Lys.*270; ψ. φανερά open *voting*, ψ. φανερὰν διενεγκεῖν Th.4.74; τὴν ψ. οὐκ εἰς καδίσκους ἀλλὰ φανερὰν ἐπὶ τὰς τραπέζας τίθεσθαι Lys.13.37, cf. Pl.*Lg.*767d, 855d; opp. ψ. ἀφανὴς *voting* by ballot, Aeschin.3.233; κρύβδην τὴν ψ. φέρειν Arist.*Rh.Al.*1433$^a$23, cf. 1424$^b$2, *Ath.*69.1. b. *that which is carried by vote, a vote*, ψ. καταγνώσεως *a vote* of condemnation, Th.3.82; ψῆφος αὐτῷ ἐπῆκτο περὶ φυγῆς *a vote* of banishment was moved for against him, X.*An.*7.7.57, cf. A.*Th.*198; ψῆφῳ πόλεως γνωσθεῖσαι Id.*Supp.*7 (anap.):—hence, c. *any resolve* or *decree*, ψ. τυράννων S.*Ant.*60; λιθίνα ψᾶφος *a decree* written on stone, Pi.*O.*7.87; διδοῖ ψᾶφον περ' αὐτᾶς [the oak] gives *judgement* of itself, Id.*P.*4.265; ψ. φλεγυρὰ βροτῶν, i.e. *public opinion*, Cratin.57 (lyr.); τίν' ἂν ψῆφον θεῖο; what *judgement*..? Pl.*Prt.*330c, cf. *R.*450a; ἡ ἐμὴ ψ. Id.*Phlb.* 57a. d. Ἀθηνᾶς ψ., *calculus Minervae*, prov. phrase to express *acquittal*, when the votes were even, Philostr.*VS*2.3. e. ψ. is sts. omitted, κἂν ἴσαι γένωνται Ar.*Ra.*685 (lyr.); πάσαις κρατεῖν Luc.*Bis Acc.*18, cf. 22. f. Διὸς ψῆφος (ψῆφοι Hsch.), prov. ἐπὶ τῶν ἱερῶν καὶ ἀθίκτων, of the scene of contest betw. Athena and Poseidon, Suid., etc. g. Κόννου ψ., *negligible quantity, cipher*, Ar.*V.*675 (anap.), cf. Κοννᾶς. 6. *place of voting, tribunal*, E.*IT*945, *El.* 1263. 7. metaph., *influence*, πόλις μεγάλην ψ. ἔχουσα Lib.*Or.*18.13.

**ψηφοφορ-έω**, *give one's vote, vote*, D.H.4.20, Luc.*Tim.*36, S.E.*M.*2.40; *determine by vote*, ὅστις ἡγήσεται Phld.*Acad.Ind.* p.38 M. II. *elect by vote*, ψ. ὑπάτους D.H.10.56:—Pass., Id.9. 43:—sts. written **ψηφηφ-**, v.l. in Id.4.20. **-ία**, ἡ, Dor. **ψᾱφο-**, *vote by ballot*, Arist.*Pol.*1268$^a$2; opp. χειροτονία, Id.*Rh.Al.* 1446$^b$22: generally, *voting*, *Foed.Delph.Pell.*1 A 12, Phld.*Rh.*2. 189 S., D.H.4.20, 7.59, Plu.*Cor.*20, etc.; αἱ ὑπατικαὶ ψ. *voting* at the consular comitia, Id.*Marc.*4. 2. *judgement, decree*, θεοῦ J.*AJ.* 4.2.4. 3. Astron., *calculation*, Ptol.*Alm.*4.9(pl.), Procl.*Hyp.*1.27, etc.:—sts. written **ψηφηφορία**, as in Arist.*Rh.Al.* l.c. **-ος** (parox.), ον, *voting*, ἐκκλησία D.H.7.59; = *suffragator, Gloss.*

⊛**ψηφ-όω**, *adorn with gems*, τοὺς πόδας Lyd.*Mag.*1.4, cf. *Mens.*1. 26. II. *work in mosaic*, *Supp.Epigr.*7.993 (Arabia, Pass.); *adorn with mosaics*, τὸ θυσιαστήριον Ἀρχ.Δελτ.12.27 (Lesbos). **-ων**, ωνος, ὁ, *ready reckoner*, Man.5.277 (dub.; v.l. ψηφῶν). ⊛ **-ωσις**, εως, ἡ, = ψηφολογία, ψηφολόγημα, *Gloss.* **-ωτός**, ή, όν, *inlaid with ψῆφοι, tessellated*, Keil-Premerstein *Dritter Bericht* No.117 (Tire, i A.D.), *Gloss.*

⊛**ψηχρός**, ά, όν, (ψήχω) *ground fine*, Hsch., Suid.

⊛**ψήχω**, Ar.*Fr.*42, etc.: fut. ψήξω X.*Eq.*4.4:—Pass., aor. ἐψήχθην (κατ-) Nic.*Th.*53, etc.; pf. ἔψηγμαι (κατ-) S.*Tr.*698:—*rub down, curry* a horse, Ar. l.c., X.*Eq.*4.5, 5.1, etc. 2. *stroke*, ψήχων δέρην μέτωπά τ' E.*Hel.*1567; φαρμάκῳ ἔψηχεν θηρὸς κάρη A.R.4. 164. 3. *scratch*, dub. in Jul.*Caes.*310a. II. *rub down, wear away*, ψ. πέτρην χρόνος *AP*7.225:—Pass., ψήχεται [ἡ πέτρα] διὰ τὴν πληγὴν τῶν κυμάτων Arist.*Pr.*935$^a$13; metaph., of remembrance, *to be worn away*, Id.*Mem.*450$^b$3. III. metaph., *scribble*, ἄδικα βιβλία Call.*Fr.*86.

⊛**ψῐά**, ἡ, = χαρά, γελοίασμα, παίγνια, Hsch: hence **ψιάζω**, Dor. **ψιάδδω**, *play, sport*, τοὶ δὴ παρ' Εὐρώταν ψιάδδοντι Ar.*Lys.*1302 (lyr.); ψιάδδειν· παίζειν, Hsch. (Prob. shortd. forms of ἑψία, ἑψιάομαι, qq. v.)

**ψιάζω**, (ψιάς), = ψακάζω, Hsch.

**ψῐᾰθ-ηδόν**, Adv. *like rush-mats*, to expl. φορμηδόν, Sch.Th.2.75, Suid. **-ίζομαι**, *lie on a mat*, Hierocl.*Facet.*107. ⊛ **-ιον**, τό, Dim. of ψίαθος, Philem.26, interpol. in Dsc.5.88: perh. *rush-basket*, ψιέθιν (sic) ψωμίων ά *POxy.*1923.7 (v/vi A.D.): τὰ αἱρούμ(τα) ὑμῖν ψιάθια (ψαίθια Pap.) εἰς τὸν καταγγισμὸν τοῦ ἄνθρακος *PBaden*29. 7 (v A.D.).

⊛**ψῐᾰθοπλόκος**, ὁ, *a plaiter of mats*, *PSI*10.1132.8 (i A.D.), Greg. Cor.p.551 S., *Lex.Herodot.*ap.Stein *Herodotus* ii p.458, Suid. s.v. σχοίνου συμβολεῖς: written **ψαθοπλόκος** in *Sammelb.*5124.332 (Tebtunis, ii A.D.):—also **-ποιός**, ὁ, *Gloss.*

⊛**ψίᾰθ-ος** [ῐ], ἡ (also ὁ, read by Callistr. in Ar.*Ra.*567, cf. Sch. ad loc. (575)), also **ψίεθος**, Antig.*Mir.*97, *Ostr.Bodl.* iii 228 (i A.D.), etc. (condemned by Phryn.281):—*a rush-mat*, used for sleeping on, *Hesperia* 5.382 (Athens, v B.C.), Ar.*Ra.*567, *Lys.*921, Arist.*HA*559$^b$3, Thphr. *HP*4.8.4, 9.4.4; ἐκ τῆς αὐτῆς ψ. γεγονώς, prov. of persons in like condition, *bedfellow*, *Com.Adesp.*789 (anap. (?)); Dor. pl. acc. ψιάθως Ar.*Ach.*874. II. *blind*, Apollod.*Poliorc.*169.6. III. perh. *sack*, χόρτου πλήρης Sor.1.83; used for carriage of wool or stone, *PCair.Zen.*430, 518 (iii B.C.). **-ώδης**, ες, *like a mat*, Eust. 1344.45, Sch.Ar.*Ach.*72, etc.

**ψίαι**· ἀλώπεκες, Hsch. (cf. ψύα); also **ψειαί**· ἀλώπεκες, ψῆφοι, Id. **ψῐαίνω**, aor. inf. ψιῆναι· ψίξαι, Id., Suid. (ψέξαι codd.); cf. σιαίνω. **ψῐᾰρός**, ά, όν, = εὐώδης, Hsch.

**ψῐάς**, άδος, ἡ, = ψακάς, *drop*, αἱματοέσσας δὲ ψιάδας κατέχευεν ἔραζε (sc. Ζεύς) Il.16.459, cf. Hes.*Sc.*384: also **ψίαξ**, ακος, (pl.), Hsch.; cf. ψίδες.

**ψιάω**, v. ψείω. **ψιβδεῖ**· ὑποπνεῖ, βδεῖ, Hsch. **ψίγναι**, αἱ, = τρίχες, Id. **ψίδες**· ψιάδες, ψακάδες, Id.

**ψίδιον**, τό, pl. ψίδια, prob. engraver's error for ψίλια, *IG*11(2). 161 *B* 19, 287 *B* 21 (Delos, iii B.C.): v. ψίλιον.

**ψιδόνες**· διάβολοι, ψίθυροι, Hsch.; cf. ψυθῶνες.

**ψίεθος**, v. ψίαθος. **ψίεντα** and **ψίεσσα**, v. ψίης.

**ψίζομαι**, *weep*, ἄ με ψισδομένα κατελίμπανεν Sapph.*Supp.*23. 2; ψιζομένη· κλαίουσα, Hsch.; ἔψιδεν· ἔκλαυσεν, Id.; cf. ψίνδεσθαι.

**ψίζω** or **ψίω**: from the former we have fut. ψιῶ (ἐπι-ψιεῖ) Hsch., pf. Pass. ἔψισμαι (v. infr.): from the latter, aor. ἔψῑσα, fut. Med. ψίσομαι [ῑ], v. infr., cf. ἐμψίω:—*feed on pap*, = ψωμίζω (Eust.1631. 43, Phot., etc.), or = ποτίζω (Orion *Lex.*col.168); λευκῷ σ' ἔψισα γάλακτι (Meineke for ἔψησα) Euph.92:—Med., *chew*, ψίσεται πύρνον γνάθῳ Lyc.639:—Pass., *to be fed*, ἐξ ὑμέων ἐψισμένον (sc. βρέφος) *AP*9.302 (Antip.).

**ψίης**· μακάριος, εὐδαίμων, also **ψίεσσα**· εὐδαίμων, μακαρία, and **ψίεντα**· τὰ αὐτά, Hsch. (Ion. forms [ψιῆς, etc.] from *ψιήεις [*ψιή = ψιά].) **ψιθήν**· τὴν ἀπώλειαν, Id.

**ψίθιος** [ῐ], α, ον, Adj., name of a kind of grape, σταφυλή Dsc. 5.5, cf. Verg.*G.*2.93, 4.269, Stat.*Silv.*4.9.38; ἐκ ψιθίης ἐλίνοιο Nic. *Al.*181: hence was made ψίθιος οἶνος Eub.138 (anap.), cf. Anaxandrid.71, Plin.*HN*14.80:—also spelt **ψύθιος**, σταφυλὰ ψ. *Docum. ined. dell' Africa Italiana* 1.86, al. (Cyrene, iv B.C.), v.l. in Eub. and Anaxandr. ll. cc.

**ψίθῠρ** [ῐ], ῠρος, ὁ, = ψίθυρος, a form actually found acc. to *EM*506. 31, cf. Sch.Theoc.1.1.

**ψῐθύρα** [ῠ], ἡ, a Libyan (esp. Trog(l)odyte) musical instrument, identified by some with the ἄσκαρος, Poll.4.60; ψιθυρᾶν μάλ' αἰολᾶν S.*Inach.* in *PTeb.*692 iii 1 (lyr.).

**ψῐθῠρ-ίζω**, Dor. **-ίσδω**: (ψίθυρος):—*whisper*, Pl.*Grg.*485e; πρός τινα Id.*Euthd.*276d, Duris 69 J.; ἀλλήλοις Theoc.27.68. 2. *whisper what one dares not speak out, whisper slanders*, κατά τινος Alciphr.3.58, Lxx *Ps.*40(41).7; ψ. καὶ διαβάλλειν Them.*Or.*21. 262c:—Pass., τὸ ψιθυριζόμενον ὄνομα Plu.*Alc.*23. 3. metaph. of trees, *whisper* (i.e. *rustle*), ὁπόταν πλάτανος πτελέᾳ ψιθυρίζῃ Ar. *Nu.*1008 (anap.); also of swallows, *twitter*, Poll.5.90. **-ισμα**, ατος, τό, *whispering*, ψ. τὸ ναυτικὸν *AP*9.546 (Antiphil.); δόλια ψ. ib. 3.3 (Inscr.Cyzic.). 2. any *low whispering noise*, as of trees *rustling*, Theoc.1.1. **-ίς**, v. ψύθιος. **-ισμός**, ὁ, *whispering*, Phld.*Ir.*p.55 W., Luc.*Am.*15; πρός τινα Plu.2.45d, etc. 2. *slandering*, ib.143f, 2 *Ep. Cor.*12.20 (pl.). 3. *whistle* of a snake-charmer, Lxx *Ec.*10.11. 4. *crepitation*, Dsc.5.159. **-ιστής**, οῦ, ὁ, *whisperer*, at Athens as epith. of Hermes, D.59.39; of Ἔρως, *AB*317: perh. cf. *Mercurius Susurrio*, *CIL*13.12005 (Aachen). 2. *slanderer*, *Ep.Rom.*1. 30. **-ιστικός**, ή, όν, *slanderous*, τὸ ψ. *Cat.Cod.Astr.*8(2).33. **-ος**, ον, *whispering, slanderous*, λόγοι S.*Aj.*148 (anap.): as epith. of Aphrodite, Paus.Gr.*Fr.*330: as Subst., ψίθυρος, ὁ, = ψιθυριστής, *whisperer, slanderer*, Pi.*P.*2.75, Ar.*Fr.*167 (anap.), Lxx *Si.*5.14, Plu.2.727d. Adv. **-ρως** App.*Hann.*46. 2. *twittering*, of birds, *AP*12.136; so of music, ψίθυρον εὐήθη νόμον Ar.*Fr.*671.

**ψῑλᾱγία**, ἡ, *a body of* 250 ψιλοί, Arr.*Tact.*14.4.

**ψῑλᾰγνάφος**, ὁ, (ψιλός II. 1 b) *carpet-cleaner* (?), Keil-Premerstein *Dritter Bericht* No.15.

**ψίλακερ**· τὸ ἡγεῖσθαι χοροῦ, Hsch.

**ψίλαξ** (A) [ῐ], ακος, ὁ, = ψιλός, Ar.*Fr.*891.

**ψίλαξ** (B), ακος, ὁ, epith. of Dionysus at Amyclae, Paus.3.19.6; he explains it as *winged* (from ψίλον Dor. for πτίλον), which suggests that it has ῐ.

**ψιλεύς**, έως, ὁ, in pl. ψιλεῖς· οἱ ὕστατοι χορεύοντες, Hsch.; ἐπ' ἄκρου χοροῦ ἱστάμενος, Suid.

**ψιλήπλευρα**, = *ofellas iuscellatas, Gloss.*; cf. ψιλόπλευρον.

⊛**ψῑλ-ῆται**, οἱ, = οἱ ψιλοί, *the light troops*, Eust.1222.53; also **ψιλής**, ῆτος, ὁ, A.*Fr.*451. **-ίζομαι**, later form for ψιλόομαι, D.C.63.9, al.; cf. *Lex.Rhet.*ap.Eust.907.38. **-ικός**, ή, όν, *of* or *for a light-armed soldier*: τὰ ψ., = οἱ ψιλοί, the *light troops*, D.S.15.32, cf. Luc.*Zeux.* 8.

**ψιλινοποιός**, ὁ, *maker of* ψίλινοι στέφανοι, *IG*5(1).208, 209 (Sparta).

**ψίλινος**, η, ον: στέφανοι ψ. a chaplet of *palm-branches*, used at

Sparta by the leaders of the choruses in the γυμνοπαιδίαι, Sosib.5: cf. ψιλίον·..εἶδος ἄνθους, Hsch.

**ψιλίοις**· πλαγίοις, ὑπτίοις, Hsch. (cf. ψάγιος).

⊛ **ψίλιον**, τό, = ψέλιον, *armlet*, *IG*11(2).161 *B* 26, 162 *B* 15, 199 *B* 57, 203 *B* 82 (Delos, iii B.C.), *Inscr.Délos* 296 *B* 37 (iii B.C.); ψιλίον (sic)·..ψέλλιον, Hsch.; also **ψίλλιον** *IG*11(2).203 *A* 4 (iii B.C.): v. ψίδιον.

**ψιλοβάφος** [ᾰ], ὁ, = *plumarius* (*feather-dyer*, from ψίλον?, v. Ψίλαξ (B)), *Gloss.*

**ψῑλο-γρᾰφέω**, *write with a single vowel*, not a diphthong, Tz.*H.* 5.696. **-δαπις**, v. ψιλόταπις. **-κέρᾰμος**, ὁ, or -ον, τό, perh. *glazed tiles*, κεραμῶσαι τῆς στοᾶς μεταστύλια ἐξ ψιλοκεράμῳ *Inscr. Délos* 366 *A* 33, cf. 462 *A* 19 (ii B.C.), but -κέρᾰμον = *suggrunda* (i.e. *eaves*), *Gloss.* **-κερως**, ων, *deprived of its horn*, Tz.*H.*5.412. **-κῐθᾰριστής**, οῦ, ὁ, = ψιλὸς κιθαριστής (which is found in Philoch.66 (pl.)), *one who plays the κιθάρα without singing to it*, *instrumental performer*, Chares 4J., cf. Ath.10.452f, Suet.*Dom.*4; also **-κῐθᾰρεύς**, έως, ὁ, *CIG*2759 (Aphrodisias):—and **-κῐθᾰριστική** (sc. τέχνη), ἡ, = ψιλὴ κιθάρισις, Philoch. l.c.:—cf. ψιλός IV.3. **-κορρέω**, *to be bald-headed*, Diog.*Ep.*19. **-κόρσης**, ου, ὁ, *bald-headed*, Call.*Iamb.* 1.100 (cf. Sch.Call. in *PSI*9.1094.29), Hdn.4.8.5. **-κουρος**, ον, *smooth-shaved*, gloss on ψιλοκόρσης (v. foreg.), Sch.Call. l.c. (ψειλ-), condemned by Phryn.41, who recommends ἐν χρῷ κουρίας. **-κρᾱνος**, ον, *bald-headed*, Tz.ad Hes.*Op.*374. **-μετρία**, ἡ, *verse not accompanied by music*, Arist.*Po.*1448$^{a}$11 (cf. ψιλός IV.2). II. *prose composition*, Them.*Or.*26.319a.

**ψίλον**, τό, Dor. for πτίλον, v. Ψίλαξ (B).

**ψῑλό-πλευρον**, τό, = *armus, ofella, ofla*, *Gloss.* **-ποιεω**, *write with a smooth breathing*, Theodoretus περὶ πνευμάτων in cod. Barocc. 68 (Epit. of Hdn.Gr.καθολικὴ προσῳδία, Bk.xx).

**ψῑλός**, ή, όν, I. of land, *bare*, ψ. ἄροσις *open* cornland, Il.9.580; πεδίον μέγα τε καὶ ψ. Hdt.1.80; ὁ λόφος..δασὺς ἴδησί ἐστι, ἐούσης τῆς ἄλλης Λιβύης ψ. Id.4.175; ἀπὸ ψ. τῆς γῆς Pl.*Criti.* 111d, cf. X.*An.*1.5.5, etc.: in full, [γῆ] ψ. δενδρέων Hdt.4.19,21; ἄδενδρα καὶ ψ., of the Alps, Plb.3.55.9; τὰ ψ. (sc. χωρία), opp. τὰ ὑλώδη, X.*Cyn.*5.7; τόποι ψ. ib.4.6; ψ. γεωργία the tillage of land *for corn and the like*, opp. γ. πεφυτευμένη (the tillage of it *for vines, olives*, etc.), Arist.*Pol.*1258$^{b}$18, Thphr.*CP*3.20.1; so γῆ ψ. Eup. 230, D.20.115, *Tab.Heracl.*1.175, 2.33; ἐλαῖαι, ὧν νῦν τὰ πολλὰ ἐκκέκοπται καὶ ἡ γῆ ψ. γεγένηται Lys.7.7. II. of animals, *stripped of hair* or *feathers*, *smooth* (cf. λεῖος I.3), δέρμα..ἐλάφοιο Od.13.437; σάρξ Hp.*Aër.*19; ἡμίκραιραν ψ. ἔχων with half the head *shaved*, Ar. *Th.*227; ψ. γνάθοι ib.583; τὴν ὀσφὺν κομιδῇ ψ. Pherecr.23.4 (anap.); used of dogs *with a short, smooth coat* of hair, X.*Cyn.*3.2; τὴν δίποδα ἀγέλην τῷ ψ. καὶ τῷ πτεροφυεῖ τέμνειν Pl.*Plt.*266e; ἄνθρωπος -ότατον κατὰ τὸ σῶμα τῶν ζῴων πάντων ἐστί Arist.*GA*745$^{b}$16; so ἶβις ψ. τὴν κεφαλήν *without feathers*, *bald* on the head, Hdt.2.76; *hairless*, of the foetus of a hare, Id.3.108; ψ. τὰ περὶ τὴν κεφαλήν, of the ostrich, Arist.*PA*697$^{b}$18. b. ψιλαὶ Περσικαί Persian *carpets*, Callix.2; such a carpet is called ψιλή alone, *PSI*7.858.2 (iii B.C., pl.), LXX *Jo.*7.21; ψιλὴ πολύμιτος, *Babylonicum*, *Gloss.*; ψιλή = *aulaeum, tapeta*, ib.; cf. ψιλόταπις. 2. generally, *bare, uncovered*, ψ. ὡς δρᾷ νέκυν, i.e. without any earth over it, S.*Ant.*426; of a horse which has thrown its rider, *AP*13.18 (Parmeno). b. c. gen., *bare of, separated from*, ψ. σώματος οὖσα [ἡ ψυχή] Pl.*Lg.*899a; τέχναι ψ. τῶν πράξεων Id.*Plt.*258d; ψ. ὅπλων Id.*Lg.*834c; ἱππέων X.*Cyr.*5.3.57; θηρία μεμονωμένα καὶ ψ. τῶν Ἰνδῶν Plb.11.1.12. c. *stripped of appendages, naked*, ψ. [τρόπις] the *bare* keel with the planks torn from it, Od.12.421; ψ. μάχαιραι swords *alone, without other arms*, etc., X.*Cyr.*4.5.58; θάλαττα ψ. *blank* sea, Aristid.*Or.*25(43). 50. III. freq. in Prose, as a military term, of *soldiers without heavy armour, light troops*, such as archers and slingers, opp. ὁπλῖται, first in Hdt.7.158, al., freq. in Th., e.g. ὁπλίζει τὸν δῆμον, πρότερον ψ. ὄντα 3.27, cf. Arr.*Tact.*3.3; ὁ ψ. ὅμιλος Th.4.125; so ψιλοί or τὸ ψιλόν, opp. τὸ ὁπλιτικόν, X.*HG*4.2.17, Arist.*Pol.*1321$^{a}$7; ψιλός, opp. ὡπλισμένος, S.*Aj.*1123: coupled with ἄσκευος, Id.*OC*1029; ψιλὸς στρατεύσομαι Ar.*Th.*232; ψ. δύναμις Arist.*Pol.*1321$^{a}$13; αἱ κοῦφαι καὶ αἱ ψ. ἐργασίαι work *that belongs to unarmed soldiers*, ib.1321$^{a}$25; ψ. χερσὶν πρὸς καθωπλισμένους Ael.*VH*6.2: but ψ. ἔχων τὴν κεφαλήν *bare*-headed, *without helmet*, X.*An.*1.8.6; ψ. ἵππος a horse *without housings*, Id.*Eq.*7.5: *unarmed, defenceless*, S.*Ph.*953. IV. λόγος ψ. *bare* language, i.e. *prose*, opp. to poetry which is clothed in the garb of metre, Pl.*Mx.*239c, Phld.*Mus.*p.97 K.; more freq. in pl., ψ. λόγοι Pl.*Lg.*669d; opp. τὰ μέτρα, Arist.*Rh.*1404$^{b}$14,33: but in D.27.54 ψ. λόγος is a *mere* speech, a speech *unsupported by evidence*; and in Pl.*Tht.*165a ψιλοὶ λόγοι are *mere forms* of argumentation, dialectical abstractions (so ψιλῶς λέγειν speak *nakedly, without alleging proofs*, Id.*Phdr.*262c, cf. *Lg.*811e); τὰς πράξεις αὐτὰς ψιλὰς φράζοντες Arist.*Rh.Al.*1438$^{b}$27. 2. ποίησις ψ. *mere* poetry, *without music*, i.e. *Epic* poetry, opp. *Lyric* (ἡ ἐν ᾠδῇ), Pl.*Phdr.*278c; so ἄνευ ὀργάνων ψ. λόγοι Id.*Smp.*215c, cf. Arist.*Po.*1447$^{a}$29; ψ. τῷ στόματι, opp. μετ' ὀργάνων, as a kind of μουσική, Pl.*Plt.*268b; λύρας φθόγγοι..ψιλοὶ καὶ ἀμεικτότεροι τῇ φωνῇ Arist.*Pr.*922$^{a}$16; ἡ ψ. φωνή the *ordinary* sound of the voice, opp. singing (ἡ ᾠδική), D.H. *Comp.*11. 3. ψ. μουσική *instrumental* music *unaccompanied by the voice*, opp. ἡ μετὰ μελῳδίας, Arist.*Pol.*1339$^{b}$20; ψιλῷ μέλει διαγωνίζεσθαι πρὸς ᾠδὴν καὶ κιθάραν, of Marsyas, Plu.2.713d, cf. Phld.*Mus.* p.100K.; so ψ. κιθαρισις καὶ αὔλησις Pl.*Lg.*669e; ψιλὸς αὐλητής one who plays *unaccompanied* on the flute (cf. ψιλοκιθαριστής), Phryn. 145. V. *mere, simple* (cf. supr. IV. 1), ἀριθμητικὴ ψιλή, opp. geometry and the like, Pl.*Plt.*299e; ὕδωρ ψ., opp. σὺν οἴνῳ, Hp.*Int.*35; ψ. ἀναίρεσις *mere* removal, Phld.*Sign.*12; ψ. ἄνδρες, i.e. men *without women*, Antip.*Stoic.*3.254:—Oedipus calls Antigone his ψιλὸν ὄμμα, as being *the one poor* eye left him, S.*OC*866. Adv. ψιλῶς *merely, only*, Plu.*Per.*15; ἕνεκα τοῦ ψ. εἰπεῖν for the purpose of *merely* saying, Sch. Il.*Oxy.*1086.65; ψ. ὀνομάζειν call by the *bare* name (without epithet), Phld.*Vit.*p.39 J. VI. Gramm. of vowels, ψ. ἦχος *without the spiritus asper*, Demetr.*Eloc.*73; ψ. πνεῦμα A.D.*Adv.*148.9, D.T.*Supp.* 674.15; ψιλῶς λέγεσθαι A.D.*Pron.*57.3. b. of the letters ε and υ *written simply*, not as αι and οι, which represented the sounds in late Gr., μαθόντες τὰ διὰ τοῦ διφθόγγου αι τυχὸν ἅπαντα, ἐδιδάχθημεν τὰ ἄλλα πάντα ψιλὰ γράφεσθαι Hdn.*Epim.*162, cf. *An.Ox.*1.124: hence ἐψιλόν as name of the letter ε and ὑψιλόν as name of υ, which are first found in Anon. post *Et.Gud.*679.6, 678.55, and Chrysoloras: ἒ ψιλόν is f.l. in D.T.631.5: but in πᾶσα λέξις ἀπὸ τῆς κε συλλαβῆς ἀρχομένη διὰ τοῦ ε ψιλοῦ γράφεται..πλὴν τοῦ καί, κτλ. Hdn.*Epim.*62, ε ψ. is not yet merely the name of the letter: for ὑψιλόν v. sub ὗ, cf. Sch. Heph.p.93C. 2. of mute consonants, the *litterae tenues*, π κ τ, opp. φ χ θ, ὅσαι γίγνονται χωρὶς τῆς τοῦ πνεύματος ἐκβολῆς, Arist. *Aud.*804$^{b}$10, cf. D.H.*Comp.*14, D.T.631.21; ψιλῶς καλεῖν pronounce *with a littera tenuis* for an aspirate, e.g. ῥάπυς for ῥάφυς, ἀσπάραγος for ἀσφάραγος, Ath.9.369b, cf. Eust.81.5, Tz.*H.*11.58.

**ψῑλό-τᾰπις**, ιδος, ἡ, *a smooth carpet, a carpet without pile*, *PCair. Zen.*48.2 (iii B.C.); opp. ἀμφίταπις, Lycon ap.D.L.5.72, cf. Cephisodor.ap.Ath.12.548e, Clearch.25; written **ψιλόδαπις** in Paus.Gr. *Fr.*304; cf. ψιλός II.1. ⊛ **-της**, ητος, ἡ, *bareness*, τῆς γῆς Hp.*Aër.* 19, cf. Plu.*Fab.*11. 2. *baldness*, Id.*Galb.*27: pl., Artem.1.21. 3. *smoothness*, of a woman's body, Plu.2.651a; opp. τραχύτης, ib. 979a; opp. δασύτης, Arist.*HA*499$^{a}$11. II. *tenuity* (cf. ψιλός VI. 2), opp. δασύτης, Id.*Po.*1456$^{b}$32, D.H.*Comp.*14. 2. *the spiritus lenis*, Plb.10.47.10 (pl.). **-φῠτος**, ον, *bare of plants*, ἐν ψιλοφύτῳ in the *open country*, *PAvrom.*2 *A* 6, 2 *B* 7 (i B.C.).

**ψῑλ-όω**, *strip bare*, mostly of hair, ψ. τὴν κεφαλήν τινος Hdt.4.26; ψιλοῦν τὰ δέρματα Thphr.*HP*9.20.3; ψ. τὰ δένδρα *strip* them *bare*, ib.4. 14.9:—Pass., *become bald*, ψιλοῦτο δὲ καλὰ κάρηνα Hes.*Fr.*29; χελιδόνες..ἐψιλωμέναι *bare of feathers*, Arist.*HA*600$^{a}$16. II. c. gen., *strip bare of*, σαρκῶν ἐπωμίδα Hp.*Art.*1:—Pass., ὀστέων κατήγματα ἐψιλωμένα Id.*Aph.*5.22, cf. *Art.*69, Arist.*HA*519$^{b}$5. 2. *strip, rob, deprive of* a thing, ψ. [τινὰ] τὰ πλεῖστα τῆς δυνάμιος Hdt.2.151; τινὰ χρημάτων Alciphr.1.18: abs. in same sense, X.*Cyr.*4.5.12:—Pass., ἐλπίδος ὁ καιρὸς ἐψιλώθη Phld.*Herc.*1232 p.67V. 3. generally, *leave naked, unarmed*, or *defenceless*, Th.3.109. 4. Pass., *to be laid bare*, of roots, X.*Oec.*17.12 sq.; ψιλωθέντα κέρατα *exposed, unprotected*, Plb.3.73.7; τὸ ψιλούμενον στεγαστέον X.*Eq.*12.7. 5. *strip off, pull out*, τρίχας Dsc.2.179:—Pass., of things, *to be stripped off* something, τὰ κρέα ἐψιλωμένα τῶν ὀστέων Hdt.4.61; cf. ψίλωμα. III., Gramm., *write* or *pronounce with the spiritus lenis* or *a littera tenuis*, opp. δασύνω, Phld.*Rh.*1.155 S., cf. *EM*780.31 (Pass.), D.T.*Supp.*675.11, A.D.*Synt.*39.1, *Pron.*57.2, Eust.515.38, Tz.*H.* 11.53. **-ωθρον**, τό, *depilatory*, Thphr.*HP*9.20.3, Menemach. ap.Orib.10.14.1, Crito ap.Gal.12.447; used of the plant ἄμπελος λευκή, Nic.*Th.*902, Dsc.4.182 (since the root was used as a depilatory, Thphr. l.c.); also **ψιλώθριον** Hp.*Fist.*9. **-ωμα**, ατος, τό, *bone laid bare of flesh*, ἀφικέσθαι ἐς ὀστέων ψιλώματα Hp.*Art.*69, cf. *Epid.*3.4. **-ωσις**, εως, ἡ, *stripping bare of flesh*, ὀστέου Hp. *Aph.*7.19; *of hair*, Clearch.9; ψ. τῆς κεφαλῆς *shaving*, Archig.ap. Gal.8.150; *of leaves*, Plu.2.646d; χρημάτων J.*AJ*17.11.2. II. Gramm., *writing* or *pronouncing with the spiritus lenis*, or *an unaspirated consonant*, Eust.515.37. **-ωτέον**, *one must write* or *pronounce with the spiritus lenis*, Sch.Il.1.335, etc. **-ωτής**, οῦ, ὁ, *one who writes* or *pronounces with the spiritus lenis*, or *litterae tenues*, Tz.*H.*11.52. **-ωτικός**, ή, όν, *stripping, making hairless*, πάθος ψ. τοῦ γενείου *EM*74.50; φάρμακα Gal.12.451. II. Gramm., *fond of the spiritus lenis*, οἱ Ἴωνες Eust.515.38.

**ψιλωτόν**, τό, = *quinquefolia*, *Gloss.* (perh. the *feathered* plant, fr. ψίλον).

**ψίμαρον**· εὐδιαῖον, Hsch., Suid. (Leg. χίμαρον, cf. Hsch. s.v. εὐδιαῖον.)

**ψιμίθιον**, v. ψιμύθιον.

**ψιμυθ-ίζω**, = ψιμυθιόω, *paint with white lead*, Zonar. ⊛ **-ιον** (v. infr.), τό, = ψίμυθος, *white lead*, used as a pigment, esp. to whiten the skin of the face, Ar.*Ec.*878,929, Amips.3, *Dialex.*2.6, etc.; even for the hair, Pl.*Ly.*217d; ἐντετριμμένην ψιμυθίῳ X.*Oec.*10.2; περιπεπλασμένη ψιμυθίοις.., ἀνάπλεῳ ψιμυθίου, Eub.98, cf. Ar.*Ec.*1072; τῷ ψ. κεχρισμένος Jul.*Or.*7.233b; also used in salves, *Gp.*17.7.2, 18.15.3: for its preparation, v. Thphr.*Lap.*56. (Written **ψιμίθιον** in *PCair.Zen.*763.19, 789.11,12 (iii B.C.), *IG*5(1).1390.22 (Andania, i B.C.), *POxy.*1088.4 (i A.D.), *PLond.*3.928.21, *PMed.Strassb.*p.4 (ii A.D.), and as v.l. in Dsc.5.88, etc.; **ψιμμύθιον** Jul. l.c., v.l. in *Gp.* ll. cc.; **ψιμμίθιον** as v.l. in Dsc. l.c.: Aeol. **ψημύθιον**, acc. to Choerob. *in Theod.*1.201 H., Id. in *An.Ox.*2.241 (Ion. acc. to *EM*103. 25): v. ψιμυθιόω.) [ῡ, Ar. ll.cc., etc.; ψῐ- indeterminate in these passages; ψῐμῠθίου in a hexam. (Nic.*Al.*75) might be due to metrical lengthening of ψῐ-: cf. ψίμυθος.]

**ψιμυθιοφᾰνής**, ές, *looking like white lead*, Dsc.5.82 (vv. ll. ψιμμιθιοφανής, μὴ θειοφανής, etc.).

**ψιμυθι-όω**, *paint with white lead*, τὸ πρόσωπον Plu.*Alc.*39:—Pass., τὸ πρόσωπον ἐψιμυθιῶσθαι Lys.1.14, cf. 17, Ath.12.528f: Achaean **ψημυθιόω**, abs. in Pass., ψημυθιοῦσθαι *Schwyzer*429 (Dyme, post iii B.C.): pf. Pass. ἐψημυθιῶσθαι Phot. **-ιστής**, οῦ, ὁ, *one who paints with white lead* or *cosmetics*, *Gloss.*

⊛ **ψιμυθοειδής**, ές, *like white lead*, *Gp.*7.15.18.

**ψίμυθ-ος**, ὁ, radic. form of ψιμύθιον, *IG*11(2).145.9 (Delos, 301 B.C.): scanned ψῐμῠ- in *AP*11.374 (Maced.), 408 (Lucian.). **-όω**, = ψιμυθιόω, Thom.Mag.p.128 R.

**ψίν**, Dor. for σφίν, v. σφεῖς.

**ψινάζει**· ἀπορρεῖ τὰ ἀσθενῆ τοῦ καρποῦ, φυλλορροεῖ, Hsch. (ψειvάζει Id.). **ψίναθος**· ἀγρία αἴξ, Id. **ψινάς**, = φθινάς, in pl. ψινάδες· αἱ ῥυάδες ἄμπελοι, Id.: cf. ψίνω. **ψίνδεσθαι**· κλαίειν, Id. (Cf. ψίζομαι and ἔψιδεν Id.) **ψίνθος**· τέρψις, Id. **ψινύθιον**· φαῦλον, Id.

**ψίνω**, Cretan for φθίνω, *IG*12(5).867; part. ψίμενος *Philol.*50.578:—Med. ψίνομαι, *shed the fruit before ripening*, of the vine, Thphr.*HP*4.14.6: cf. ἐψίσθη· ἀπέθανε, Hsch.: v. ψείω.

**ψίξ**, ὁ and ἡ, gen. ψῖχός, nom. pl. ψῖχες:—*crumb*, *morsel*, *bit*, esp. of bread, Plu.2.77f, Aret.*CD*2.12, *CA*2.11, Alex.Aphr.*Pr.*1.40.—Hsch. has also the plurals ψίχαι, ψίχηνα (s. v.l.); cf. ψιχίον.

**ψίσδομαι**, v. ψίζομαι.

**ψίσις**· ἀπώλεια, Hsch. (Dialectic form of φθίσις, cf. ψίνομαι.)

**ψίττᾰ**, = σίττα (q. v.), Sch.Theoc.4.45; = ταχέως, εὐθέως, Hsch. (cf. ψύττα); used in a game, Poll.9.122,127, Eust.855.25, al. (φίττα in codd. Poll., Eust., is f.l.).

**ψιττάζω**, *call* ψίττα, Paus.Gr.*Fr.*331, Hsch.

**ψιττάκη**, ἡ, v. ψιττακός.

**ψιττάκιον**, τό, v. πιστάκιον. 2. an eye-salve, Gal.12.764, Alex. Trall.3.7. II. pl., a kind of woman's shoes, Herod.7.58 (ψιντακαια Pap.), Hsch., *EM* (cod. V post 819.6); ψιττακίαν Suid.: cf. φιττάκια, φιττακίδες.

**ψιττᾰκός**, ὁ, *parrot*, Call.*Iamb.*1.167, *PMag.Par.*2.508 (202) Preisendanz, Plu.2.972f, Callix.3, D.S.2.53, etc.; also **ψιττάκη**, ἡ, Arist.*HA*597$^{b}$27:—also **βίττακος**, **σιττακός**, qq. v. II. an eye-salve, Gal.12.745.—On the accent, v. Hdn.Gr.1.150. (Loan-word.)

**ψιττία**· ψωμία, Ἀττικοί, Hsch. **ψιφά**· ἔψιτὰ λεπτά, Id. **ψιφαῖον**· ἱστίον, ὅτε δὲ ψίαθος, ἢ μικρὸν ὀρνιθάριον, Id.

**ψῖχ-άρπαξ**, ἄγος, ὁ, (ψίξ) *Crumb-filcher*, name of a mouse in Batr.105. **-ίδιον**, τό, = sq., *EM*168.1. **-ίον**, τό, Dim. of ψίξ, *crumb*, *Ev.Matt.*15.27. 2. of stomachic residue after emesis, Archig.ap.Orib.8.23.5. **-ιώδης**, ες, *like a crumb*, *minute*, ψωμοί Eust.1817.44.

**ψῖχολογέω**, (ψίξ) *pick up crumbs*, *Gloss.*

**ψίω**, v. ψίζω.

**ψό**, a shepherd's call, S.*Fr.*521, cf. Ael.Dion.*Fr.*337. II. an exclamation of disgust or contempt, *pshaw!* Phot.; dub. in A.*Fr.*82, Ar.*Fr.*892/3.

**ψόα** or **ψύα**, ἡ, more freq. in pl. ψόαι or ψύαι, *muscles of the loins* (cf. ἀλώπηξ IV), Hp.*Art.*45 (ψύας codd.*MV*), *Nat.Hom.*11 (ψόας), cf. *Oss.*18 (ψύαν), *Morb.Sacr.*3 (ψύην), and Lxx *Le.*3.9, 2 *Ki.*2.23, *Ps.*37(38).8, al.; ψύαι Euphro 7, Clearch.72, Aret.*CD*2.3 (but ψόαι Id.*SD*2.3); acc. pl. ψοιάς (v.l. ψύας, ψυάς) Polybus ap.Arist.*HA*512$^{b}$21: ψόα Lxx *Le.* l.c. and three times in cod. Vat. of 2 *Ki.* (cod.Alex. ψοία); ψύαι *Ps.* l.c. (corrupted to ψυχή): acc. pl. ψόας in Bilabel Ὀψαρτ. p.11:—Hsch. has ψίαι, ψειαί, and ψυῖαι, also φοῦαι and φύλλες: the word in all its spellings is declared un-Attic by Phryn.269, Phot.; the form ψύη was recognized by Irenaeus ap.Orion.col.168. [ῠ in ψύαι, Euphro l.c.; but ῡ in an Epic Fragm. in Ath.9.399a, ψύας ἔγχεῖ νύξε, where perh. ψοίας shd. be written.]

**ψόγ-ειος**, and neut. pl. ψόγεια, *blameworthy*, εἰ δίφθογγος καὶ προπαροξύνεται, Choerob. in *An.Ox.*2.279, cf. Hsch. **-ερός**, ά, όν, (ψόγος) *fond of blaming*, *censorious*, *libellous*, of Archilochus, Pi.*P.*2.55, Plu.*Comp.Cim.Luc.*1 (Sup.). Adv. **-ρῶς** *by way of blame*, Eust.827.29. II. *blamable*, Hsch. **-έω** or **-ίζω**, = ψέγω, aor. ψογῆσαι, ἐψόγησεν (v.l. -ίσαι, -ισεν), Lxx 1 *Ma.*11.5,11: fut. Pass. ψογηθήσονται Vett.Val.119.25; ψογισθήσεται Id.120.37. **-ιστής**, οῦ, ὁ, *fault-finder*, Rhetor. in *Cat.Cod.Astr.*8(4).196.

**ψόγξαι**· ἀκοῦσαι, Hsch.

**ψόγος**, ὁ, (ψέγω) *blamable fault*, *blemish*, *flaw*, ἄνευ ψόγου τετυγμένος Simon.5.2. II. *blame*, *censure*, ὀνείδεα καὶ ψ. Xenoph.11.2; σκοτεινὸς ψ. Pi.*N.*7.61; μὴ τὸν ἀνθρώπειον αἰδεσθῇς ψόγον A.*Ag.*937, cf. E.*Ph.*94: pl., ἐπὶ ψόγοισι δεννάσεις ἐμέ S.*Ant.*759; οὐ φιλῶ ψόγους κλύειν cj. for ψόφους in E.*Ion*630; also in Com. and Prose, Ar.*Th.*146,895, etc.; τοῖς πέλας ψ. ἐπενεγκεῖν Th.1.70, cf. 2.45; ψ. φέρειν Pl.*Smp.*182a; ψ. ἔχειν *to be blamed*, Id.*Lg.*823b; ψ. ἀμουσίας ὑφέξοντα Id.*R.*403c: pl., ἐγκώμιά τε καὶ ψόγους ποιεῖν ἀλλήλοις *lampoons*, Id.*Lg.*829c, cf. *Grg.*483c, al., Arist.*Po.*1448$^{b}$27; τὸ.. κάλλος καὶ ψ. πολλῶν γέμει Men.703:—c. dat., ἄλγος σοί, ψ. δὲ σῷ πατρί E.*Hel.*987.

**ψοθάλλω**, = ψοφέω, Hsch. **ψόθιον**· αἰθαλῶδες, Id.; cf. ψόθος.

**ψοθοιὸς** ὁ ἀκάθαρτος Theognost.*Can.*53 (given as oxyt.); πλέω γράσου καὶ ψοθοίου (here = ἀκαθαρσία and not oxyt.) καὶ ῥύπου γε καὶ ψόθου cited by Phot. perh. fr. Ar. (v. ad *Fr.*892/3) and A. (cf. *Fr.*82).

**ψοθόκη**, = ἀκαθαρσία, Hdn.Gr.1.315.

**ψόθος**, ὁ, = ἀκαθαρσία, Phryn.Com.95 (fr. Hsch. (where also = ψώρα and θόρυβος), Phot., Suid.); = ψόφος acc. to Theognost.*Can.*54.

**ψοθώα**, ἡ, = ψώρα, Theognost.*Can.*106. **ψόθωρ**· αὐχμηρόν, Hsch. (s. v.l.). **ψοία**, v. ψόα. **ψοίθης**, ὁ, ου, = ἀλαζών, Theognost. *Can.*26.

**ψοιθός**, ή, όν, of an animal, prob. *ash-coloured* (cf. sq.), *BCH*29.430 (Delos, iv B.C.).

**ψοῖθος**, ὁ, = σποδός, Theognost.*Can.*26, *EM* (cod. V post 819.7), Phot., Suid.

**ψοίτης** [ῑ] μυελός, ὁ, (ψόα) *lumbar* portion of the spinal cord, Gal.8.328.

**ψολό-εις**, εσσα, εν, also εις, εν Nic. (v. infr.): (ψόλος):—*sooty*, *smoky*, mostly as epith. of κεραυνός, *lurid*, Od.23.330, 24.539, Hes.*Th.*515; opp. ἀργής (vivid), Arist.*Mete.*371$^{a}$21, *Mu.*395$^{a}$26; also of a serpent, opp. αἰθός, χροιῇ ψολόεις Nic.*Th.*288, cf. 129 (where ψολόεις is fem.), Opp.*C.*3.439; Αἴτνη ψολόεσσα Euph.51.11. II. **Ψολόεις**, οἱ, the male mourners in a ritual at the Boeotian Orchomenos, Plu.2.299e: prob. so called because δυσειματοῦντες, cf. Plu. l. c. **-κομπία**, ἡ, *thunderous talk*, i. e. *empty noise*, Ar.*Eq.*696 (pl.).

**ψόλος**, ὁ, *soot*, *smoke*, ἐπιβωμίῳ ψόλῳ A.*Fr.*24:—in Hsch. also = φλόξ.

⊛ **ψόμμος**· ἀκαθαρσία, καπνός, Hsch.

⊛ **ψόρος**, ὁ, an unknown fish, Numen.ap.Ath.7.313e; also **ψύρος**, Speus. ibid.

**ψούδια** (ψοδία cod.)· ψευδῆ, Λάκωνες δὲ τὸν στόμαχον, Hsch.: **ψουδία**· ψευδῆ, Κρῆτες, Suid. (unaccented in cod. Phot.).

**ψόφ-αξ**, ὁ, *noisy fellow*, Λεωνίδης ψ. (or Ψ.?) κληθεὶς *CIG*(add.) 3827s (Cotiaeum). **-εύω**, v. ψοφέω IV. **-έω**, pf. ἐψόφηκα Men.*Sam.*324, etc.:—*sound*, *make a noise* (opp. φωνέω, Arist.*de An.*420$^{b}$30, *HA*535$^{b}$3), E.*Or.*137; ψοφεῖ ἀρβύλη Id.*Ba.*638 (troch.); πύλαι ψοφοῦσι Id.*HF*78 (v. infr. II); ψοφεῖ λάλον τι, like a cracked pot, Ar.*Ach.*933 (lyr.); ἐψόφησεν ἄμπελος Id.*Pax*612 (troch.); ἐψόφει... οὐκ οἶδ' ἅττα ib.1152 (troch.); ὥσπερ κύμβαλον ψοφεῖ πρὸς τῷ δαπέδῳ ἡ κοίλη ὁπλή X.*Eq.*1.3; ποταμοὶ ψοφοῦντες Pl.*R.*396b; of a bell, Str.14.2.21: c. acc. cogn., [ἡ χαλκὶς] ψοφεῖ οἷον συριγμόν Arist.*HA*535$^{b}$19; ψ. ψόφον ib.$^{b}$13. 2. esp. of *an empty noise*, παντα γάρ τοι τῷ φοβουμένῳ ψοφεῖ S.*Fr.*61; κόμποι ψοφοῦσιν Alex.25.9; μέγα ψοφέουσαν ἀοιδήν Call.*Aet Oxy.*2079.19 (cf. *Fr.*165). II. c. acc., ψοφεῖν τὰς θύρας *knock at* the door inside to show that one is coming out (opp. κόπτειν or κρούειν *knock at the outside*), τὴν θύραν ψοφεῖ τις ἐξιών Men.*Pk.*126, cf. *Epit.*454; ἐψόφηκε προϊὼν τὴν θύραν Id.*Sam.*324, cf. Luc.*Sol.*9; but the two words are sts. used indiscriminately, cf. Plu.*Publ.*20; also of the door (intr.), τί αἱ θύραι νύκτωρ ψοφοῖεν why they *were heard to open*, Lys.1.14, cf. 17, Men.*Sam.*222; ἐψόφηκεν ἡ θ. *Com.Adesp.*21.1 D.; ἐψόφηκε ῥόπαλον *CIG*5149b (Cyrene). 2. *rattle* a chain, Herod.7.11. III. intr., κλαίοντες αὐτῇ δειλίᾳ ψοφήσετε perh. = *you will perish*, *come to a bad end*, S.*Ichn.*162: cf. διαφωνέω 3b. IV. = μαστιγόω, ἐξουσίαν ἐχέτω.. ἐπιτειμέων τρόπ[ῳ ᾧ κα θέλῃ καὶ ψο]φέων καὶ διδέ[ων] καὶ πωλέων *Supp.Epigr.*2.307 (Delph.); ἐπιτιμέουσα καὶ ψοφευσασα (sic lapis; leg. ψοφεῦσα) καὶ διδέουσα κτλ. *Delph.*3(2).131 (i B.C.); cf. μαστιγοῦσαι replacing ψοφέουσαι in the same formula, *GDI*2324 (Delph.). **-ημα**, ατος, τό, *noise*: pl., *bombast*, S.*Inach.* in *PTeb.*692 ii 7. **-ησις**, εως, ἡ, *making a noise*, *sounding*, ἰκρίων Cratin.323 (lyr.), cf. Arist. *de An.*426$^{a}$1. **-ητικός**, ή, όν, *able to make a noise*, of animals, opp. both to τὰ ἄφωνα and to τὰ φωνήεντα, Id.*HA*488$^{a}$31; τὸ ψ. *a thing capable of producing sound*, opp. τὸ ὁρατόν, Id. *de An.*423$^{b}$5, cf. 420$^{a}$3.

**ψοφο-δέεια**, ἡ, *fear at every noise*, *Stoic.*3.99. **-δεής**, ές, (δέος) *frightened at every noise*, *shy*, *timid*, esp. of animals, Plu.*Cam.*27; [ἵπποι] ψ. καὶ εὐπτόητοι Id.2.642a; of men, Pl.*Phdr.*257d, D.H.11.22, cf. *PGrenf.*2.7(*a*).2 (iii B.C.); name of a play of Menander: τὸ ἐν τῇ πολιτείᾳ ψ. *timidity*, Plu.*Nic.*2. Adv. **-εῶς** Id.2.47b, Luc.*Pr. Im.*7,28, Herod.Med.ap.Orib.10.11.2, Jul.*ad Ath.*277c. ⊛ **-ειδής**, ές, *noise-like*, φωνήεντα D.H.*Comp.*16. Adv. **-δῶς** f.l. for ψοφοδεῶς, Hsch. **-μήδης**, ες, *meditating noise*, *noisy*, *uproarious*, epith. of Dionysus, *AP*9.524.24.

**ψόφ-ος**, ὁ, *noise* (prop. of one thing striking against another, Arist. *de An.*420$^{a}$21; or of insects, which produce a sound, but not by the larynx, Id.*HA*535$^{a}$28; opp. φωνή, Id. *de An.*420$^{b}$29, *HA*535$^{b}$31, al.; ψόφος μόνον [τὸ σῖγμα] Pl.*Tht.*203b, cf. *Lg.*669d, Aristox. ap. D.H.*Comp.*14); first in *h.Merc.*285, ἄτερ ψόφου; γλώσσης ψ. E.*HF*229; φιλημάτων S.*Fr.*537; ψόφοι ἀνέμων Pl.*R.*397a; of rolling stones, X.*An.*4.2.4; of footsteps, ψόφῳ τῷ ἐκ τοῦ προσιέναι αὐτοὺς ἀντιπαταγοῦντος τοῦ ἀνέμου Th.3.22, cf. Hdt.7.218; of *knocking* at a door, Ar.*Ra.*604 (lyr.), Pl.*Smp.*212c; cf. ψοφέω II; *crash* of a falling building, Th.4.115; also of musical instruments, λωτοῦ, κιθάρας, E.*Ba.*687, *Cyc.*443; of a trumpet, Paus.2.21.3. 2. *mere sound*, *noise*, τοῦ σοῦ ψ. οὐκ ἂν στραφείην your *noise* will never turn me, S.*Aj.*1116; κενὸς ψ. E.*Rh.*565; εὐδοξία ψόφος ἐστὶ μαινομένων ἀνθρώπων Diog. ap.Arr.*Epict.*1.24.6; ψόφοι *mere sounds*, of high-sounding words or names, ὁ μὴ φρονῶν.. ψόφοις ἁλίσκεται Men.737, cf. Alciphr.2.3, Luc.*DMeretr.*15.3, Arr.*Epict.*2.6.19; ψόφου πλέως, of Aeschylus, Ar.*Nu.*1367; ὁ ψ. τῶν ῥημάτων, of his language, Id.*Ra.*492. **-ώδης**, ες, *noisy*, Hp.*Epid.*1.23; *full of sound*, οἱ διθυραμβοποιοί Arist.*Rh.*1406$^{b}$2.

**ψύα**, v. ψόα.

**ψῠᾰδικός**, ή, όν, *suffering from lumbago*, Orib.*Fr.*73: Lat. *psiadicus* (i. e. ψοιαδικός for ψυαδικός) Cass.Fel.53. **ψῠάδιν**, = *lumbus*, *Gloss.*

**ψῠαλγικοί**, = *psialegici*, *Gloss.* (*lumborum dolores*).

**ψῡγ-εῖον**, τό, (ψύχω) *cooler*, Hsch.; pl. prob. in *IG*2$^{2}$.1695.21 (iii B.C.). **-εύς**, έως, ὁ, *cooler*, = ψυκτήρ I, Alex.64, Euphro 3.

**ψῦγμα**, ατος, τό, *a means of cooling*, *anything that cools*: hence, I. *a cooling lotion*, Hp.*Morb.*2.16 (pl.); *a cooling medicine*, Id.*Aff.*11. 2. *fan*, Clearch.25 (cj. Casaubon: ψῆγμα codd.Ath., Kaibel). II. *breath drawn*, *inhalation*, D.H.*Comp.*20. III.

*cold, chilling behaviour*, J.*BJ* 1.24.2. **IV.** *chink, fissure*, Longin. 10.7 codd.

**ψυγμοκατάρρους**, ὁ, *chill, catarrh*, Cyran.60.

⊛ **ψυγμός**, ὁ, *chilliness, dampness*, Porph.*Abst.*1.28, Vett.Val.127.5(pl.). **2.** *cold fit of an ague*, or *rigor* caused by poison, Ruf.ap.Orib. 8.24.17, Dsc.5.11, Gal.11.519, Poll.4.186; cf. ψυχμός. **II.** *drying-place*, σαγηνῶν Lxx *Ez.*26.5,14: ψ. ἁλιέων Pap. in *Hermes* 40.548; also ψ. γναφέων *PTeb.*86.45,51 (ii B.C.); εἰς ψυγμὸν ἐργάταις *PSI* 4.332.27 (iii B.C.); τῷ συμψήσαντι τὸν ψυγμὸν *PPetr.*2p.110(iii B.C.); ἐφ' ὃν ἔχομεν ἐν τῷ ψυγμῷ σὺν τῷ ἀχύρῳ κνῆκον *PRyl.*69.9 (i B.C.). **III.** *refreshment*, ἔψυξαν ἑαυτοὺς ψυγμοὺς Lxx *Nu.*11.32.

**ψυγός**, ὁ, = ταρσός, Sch.Od.9.219.

**ψύγω**, = ψύχω, *dry*, Dsc.1.26, al., *Gp.*9.33.2, 11.26.3, *EM*366.47.

**ψύδα**· δυσῳδία, Theognost.*Can.*26.

**ψύδος**, coined as etym. of ψύθος, *EM*819.13: ψύδη v.l. for ψύθη, A.*Ag.*999 (lyr.).

**ψυδνός**, ή, όν, v.l. for ψυδρός in Thgn.122. **II.** ψυδνή· χέρσος· ἀραιά, ὀλίγη, Hsch.: misspelt ψυάνη· ἀρεά, ὀλίγη, Theognost.*Can.* 26. (With ψυδνός (s.v.l.) cf. κυδνός; for the sense cf. ψύθιος.)

**ψυδρ-άκιον** [ᾰ], τό, *pimple*, τὰ ἐν κεφαλῇ Dsc.5.109, cf. Damocr. ap.Gal.13.945; on the eyelid, *stye*, Cyran.35; on the nose, said to be caused by telling a lie, Sch.Theoc.12.24; cf. ψεῦσμα II. **-ακόω**, *form into blisters*, Crito ap.Gal.13.874. **-αξ**, ἄκος, ἡ, οἱ Ἴωνες ψύδρακας λέγουσι τὰς ποικίλας· ὅθεν καὶ ἡμεῖς ψύδρακας καλοῦμεν τὰ ἐπὶ τοῦ σώματος ἐξανθήματα *EM*819.10.

⊛ **Ψυδρεύς**, έως, ὁ, name of a month at Corcyra, *IG*9(1).682 (iv B.C.).

⊛ **ψυδρός**, ά, όν, = ψευδής, *lying, untrue*, Thgn.122 cod.A (v.l. ψυδνός), Lyc.235,1219.

**ψυθ[..** incomplete word in *IG*1².327.

**ψυθιζομένων**· γογγυζόντων, Hsch. **ψύθιον**· ὀλιγοχρόνιον, Id. **ψύθιος**· ἀραιά, ὀλίγη, ψιθυρίς, Id. **II.** = ψίθιος (q.v.). **ψυθιστάς**· ψιθυριστάς, Id.

**ψύθος** [ῡ], εος, τό, poet. collat. form for ψεῦδος, *lie, untruth*, A.*Ag.* 478 (lyr.), 999 (lyr., pl.), 1089 (pl.):—in Call.*Fr.*184, οὐ ψύθος οὔνομ' ἔχουσα, ψ. is a Subst. in appos. with οὔνομα.

**ψυθῶνες**· διάβολοι, Hsch.: cf. ψιδόνες. **ψυῖαι**, v. ψόα. **ψυκτά**· ἡ μὴ πολλῷ ὕδατι πεφυρμένη μᾶζα, Id.

**ψυκ-τέον**, *one must cool*, Gal.1.284; Adj. **-τέος**, Hp.*Liqu.*2. **-τήρ**, ῆρος, ὁ, *wine-cooler*, E.*Fr.*726, Pl.*Smp.*213e, *IG*2².1638.62, al., Stratt.59 (anap.), *IG*7.3498.29 (Orop.), Callix.2, J.*AJ*11.1.3, App. *Mith.*115, Ath.11.502c; ψ. ἀργυροῦς μέγας δίωτος *OGI*214.56 (Branchidae, iii B.C.); ψυκτῆρά τις προὔπινεν αὐτοῖς Men.510, cf. Antiph.114, Alex.9.12; ψυκτῆρες γάλακτος Philostr.*Im.*1.31, cf. Poll.10.74. **II.** ψυκτῆρες, οἱ, *cool shady places for recreation*, Nic.Thyat.ap.Ath.11. 503c (ψυκτήρια Casaubon). **III.** ψυκτῆρες, = ταρσοί, Sch.Od.9. 219. **-τηρίας**, ου, ὁ, = foreg.I, Euphro 3. **-τηρίδιον** [ῐ], τό, = ψυκτήριον I, Alex.2.7, *Inscr.Délos* 1432 *Ab* ii 67 (ii B.C.). **-τήριον**, τό, Dim. of ψυκτήρ I, Nicostr.Com.9, Callix.2, *IG*2².1543 (Eleusis, iv B.C.), *Inscr.Délos* 461 *Ba* 56 (ii B.C.). **II.** ψυκτήρ II, *a cool shady place*, Hes.*Fr.*190, A.*Fr.*146, E.*Fr.*782. **-τήριος**, α, ον, *cooling*, ψ. πτερά, i.e. fans, Achae.10, cf. Hp.*Loc.Hom.*27. **-τηρίσκος**, ὁ, *small wine-cooler*, *PCair.Zen.*38.7 (iii B.C.). **-τικός**, ή, όν, = ψυκτήριος, *cooling*, τὰ ψ. *refrigerants*, Hp.*Aph.*7.37; ψ. δύναμις, opp. θερμαντική, Epicur.*Fr.*60; ψ. φασὶν εἶναι τὸν οἶνον ib.59, cf. Plu. 2.652f, 691b (Sup.), etc. **II.** *bringing difficulty* (cf. ψῦξις III), *embarrassing*, ὁ χρόνος ἔσται -κὸς εἰς πάντα Heph.Astr.2.29. **-τρα**, ἡ, *drying-place*, ψ. τὰς πρὸς τοῖς νεωρίοις *IG*2².1035.43 (i B.C.), cf. ψυγμός II; but others take it as = ψυκτήριον II. **2.** *tray for drying figs on*, Hsch. s.v. τρασιά.

⊛ **ψύλλα**, ης, ἡ, *flea*, Ar.*Nu.*145, al., X.*Smp.*6.8, Arist.*HA*556ᵇ22, etc.; also **ψύλλος**, ὁ, Epich.199, Arist.*HA*537ᵃ6 (v.l. ψύλας), rejected by Phryn.308 in favour of ψύλλα; also **ψύλλαξ**, ἡ, Hsch. **II.** *a venomous spider*, perhaps *Lathrodectes* or *malmignatte*, Arist.*HA* 622ᵇ31. **2.** an insect attacking ῥαφανίς and ἐρέβινθος, Thphr. *HP*7.5.4, 8.10.1. **3.** = πιθήκη, ὑπόδρομος Ael.*NA*6.26. (Lith. *blusà*, OSlav. *blŭcha* 'louse', Skt. *plusis* (a noxious insect), Arm. *lu* (prob. fr. **pluso-*), Lat. *pūl-ex* (prob. fr. **pusl-ex*): there seem to be four primitive forms, *bhlus-*, *plus-*, *pusl-*, and *psul-*.)

**ψύλλειον**, τό, = ψύλλιον, Orph.*A.*961.

**ψύλλερις**, ἡ, = ψύλλιον, Ps.-Dsc.4.69.

**ψυλλία**, ἡ, dub. in Ptol.*Tetr.*181.

**ψυλλίζω**, *catch fleas*, Suid.

⊛ **ψύλλιον** or **ψυλλίον**, τό, *flea-wort, Plantago Psyllium*, Dsc.4.69, Luc.*Trag.*157.

**ψυλλιστής**, v. ψελλιστής.

**ψύλλο**, barbarism for ψύλλα in Ar.*Th.*1180.

**ψυλλόβρωτος**, ον, *eaten of fleas* (or perh. *red spiders*), λάχανα *Gp.*12.7.1.

**ψύλλος**, ὁ, = ψύλλα (q.v.). **2.** ψ. θαλάσσιος, sea-*flea*, Cyran. 45,78. **II.** = τὸ παχὺ τὸ συνέχον τὸ τοῦ κάπρου αἰδοῖον, Hsch.

**ψυλλοτοξότης**, ου, ὁ, *flea-archer, flea-skirmisher*, Comic word in Luc.*VH*1.13.

**ψύλων**, v.l. for τίλων (q.v.).

**ψῦξις**, εως, ἡ, *a cooling, chilling*; χιόνος ἢ ἄλλης ψύξιος *means of cooling*, v.l. in Hp.*VM*16. **2.** *a being* or *becoming cold*, ψ. νεηνικωτάτη ib.16; αἵματος ἐν ψύξει ὄντος Pl.*Ti.*85d: pl., opp. καύσεις, Id.*Tht.*156b; opp. θερμότητες, *Lg.*897a, Arist.*GA*777ᵇ27. **II.** = πνοή, Hsch. **III.** metaph., ψύξεις πράξεων *difficulty, embarrassment*, Vett.Val.191.4, cf. 42.18; ψ. πραγμάτων Heph.Astr.2.31.

**Ψύρα** [ῠ], τά, *Psyra*, a barren islet near Chios, taken as the type of what is insignificant: prov., Ψύρα τὸν Διόνυσον ἄγοντες (*saying 'a fig for Dionysus!'*), of persons who drink no wine, Cratin.352; Ψύρα τε τὴν Σπάρτην ἄγεις Id.112; also called **Ψῦρίη**, ἡ, Od.3.171: **ψύριος**· ἀκάθαρτος Hsch.: **ψῦρὶς** γῆ *barren* land, like that of Psyra, Id.

**ψύρος**, ὁ, = ψόρος (q.v.).

**ψύττᾰ**, = ψίττα, σίττα, E.*Cyc.*49 (lyr.). **II.** = ταχέως, esp. in the phrase ψ. κατατείνας, τείνασαι, Luc.*Lex.*3, *Ep.Sat.*35, cf. *AP* 11.351 (Pall.), prob. in Alciphr.3.24; cf. Hsch.

**ψύτταρον**· σκαφίον, Hsch.

**ψύττω**, = πτύω, *spit*, and **ψυττόν**, τό, *spittle*, Hsch.

⊛ **ψῡχᾰγωγ-έω**, (ψυχαγωγός) *lead departed souls to the nether world*, esp. of Hermes, Luc.*DDeor.*7.4, 24.1. **II.** *evoke* or *conjure up the dead* by sacrifice; hence metaph., *lead* or *attract the souls of the living, win over, persuade, allure*, ψ. μὲν πολλοὺς τῶν ζώντων, τοὺς δὲ τεθνεῶτας φάσκοντες ψυχαγωγεῖν Pl.*Lg.*909b; ψ. διὰ τῆς ὄψεως τοὺς ἀνθρώπους X.*Mem.*3.10.6; διὰ τῆς μελῳδίας D.S.4.4; of speakers, ψ. τοὺς ἀκούοντας Phld.*Rh.*1.148 S.; τὰ μέγιστα, οἷς ψυχαγωγεῖ ἡ τραγῳδία Arist.*Po.*1450ᵃ33:—Pass., ἐκ τῆς μουσικῆς ψ. Ael. *VH*2.39; ὑπό τινων D.S.2.53. **2.** in bad sense, *lead away, inveigle, delude*, ψ. τοὺς ἀκροωμένους Isoc.2.49, cf. 9.10; τινὰς λόγοις ψ. Lycurg.33; ψ. τινα ὥστε.., c. inf., Plb.13.8.3:—Pass., ὑπὸ εἰδώλων καὶ φαντασμάτων Pl.*Ti.*71a; κολακείαις, θεραπείᾳ ψ., D.44.63, 59.55; ὁ νοῦς..πρὸς ἀλλοτρίῳ ψυχαγωγηθεὶς πάθει *beguiled* by contemplating another's sufferings, Timocl.6.6:—with a play upon these senses, λίμνη τις.., οὗ ψυχαγωγεῖ Σωκράτης where Socrates *evokes* (*beguiles*) *souls*, Ar.*Av.*1555 (lyr.). **III.** = τὸ ἐξαπατῶντα πιπράσκειν, *AB* 116. **-ή**, ἡ, = *oblectamentum*, *Cod.Just.*8.10.12.6b. **-ία**, ἡ, *evocation of souls from the nether world*, Philostr.*Her.*18.3, Eust.1614. 59. **II.** metaph., *winning of men's souls, persuasion*, whence Rhetoric is called a ψυχαγωγία by Pl.*Phdr.*261a, cf. 271c, *Com. Adesp.*199, Phld.*Rh.*1.148 S.; also of poetry, Id.*Po.*2.61, al.: generally, *gratification, pastime*, Plb.31.29.5, D.S.1.91, Aristeas 78, Lxx 2*Ma.*2.25, J.*AJ*15.7.7, Luc.*Nigr.*18; *amusement*, Sor.1.117 (pl.); opp. διδασκαλία, as the aim of a poet, Eratosth.ap.Str.1.1.10: pl., μουσικαὶ ψ. Phld.*Mus.*p.86 K., cf. Aristid.*Or.*29(40).21. **III.** (ψυχρός, ψῦχος) *cooling treatment* in acute fever, Philum.ap.Aët.5. 78 (but, *animi oblectamenta procurentur*, in Lat. version): in heart disease, Paul.Aeg.3.34. **-ικός**, ή, όν, *attractive, persuasive*, ἔστι δὲ..-κώτατον ἡ τραγῳδία Pl.*Min.*321a; ψυχαγωγικὸν ἡ ὄψις, ἀτεχνότατον δέ Arist.*Po.*1450ᵇ17. **-ιον**, τό, = ψυχομαντεῖον, *a place where departed souls are conjured up*, *EM*819.25. **II.** *air-hole, ventilator in the shafts of mines*, Thphr.*Ign.*24 (v.l. -εῖον). **III.** *reservoir, reserve water-tank*, *AB*317. **-ός**, όν, *leading departed souls to the nether world*, epith. of Hermes, Hsch. **II.** *conjuring up the dead* to question them, ψ. γόοι A.*Pers.*687:—Subst., *necromancer*, E.*Alc.*1128, Plu.2.560f; Ψ., οἱ, name of a play by Aeschylus. **III.** *kidnapper*, Alexandrian word acc. to Phryn.*PS*p.127 B.

**ψῡχ-άζω**, *refresh oneself in the shade*, Alciphr.3.12, Ael.*NA*5.21, Procop.Gaz.p.175 B. **-αῖος**, α, ον, *of the soul*, σπινθήρ Orac. Chald.ap.Lyd.*Mens.*1.11; φύσεις Simp. *in Ph.*780.14. **-απάτης**, [πᾰ], ου, ὁ, *beguiling the soul*, οἶνος Eratosth.36.5; ὄνειρος *AP*5.165 (Mel.); στέφανος *AP*12.256 (Id.), etc.; v. ψυχροπότης. ⊛**-άριον** [ᾰ], τό, Dim. of ψυχή, Pl.*R.*519a, *Tht.*195a, M.Ant.9.34, al., Jul.*Or.*7.206d, Herm. *in Phdr.* p.192 A.; ψ. εἶ βαστάζον νεκρόν Epictet.ap.M.Ant.4. 41. **-ασμός**, ὁ, sine expl., prob. *refreshment*, Hdn.*Epim.*155. **-αστής**, οῦ, ὁ, *one who cools himself in the shade*: Ψυχασταί, οἱ, a play of Strattis. **-εινός**, ή, όν, *cooling, fresh*, Hp.*Epid.*1.1; opp. ἀλεεινός, X.*Cyn.*10.6, *Oec.*9.3,4, Id.*Mem.*3.8.9. (In codd. as of Hp. l.c. (cod. A), Thphr.*CP*3.23.4 (codd. exc. Urb.), wrongly ψυχινός; ψυχεινός confirmed by Choerob. in *An.Ox.*2.279: Comp. -εινότερα (v.l. -ινώτερα) Arist.*Pr.*965ᵃ1.) **-εῖον**, τό, *place for cooling* water, Semus 4. **-εμπορικός**, ή, όν, *of* or *for a trafficker in souls*:—ἡ -κή (sc. τέχνη) *traffic in mental wares*, Pl.*Sph.*224b. **-έμπορος**, ον, *trafficking in lives* or *men*, Hsch. ⊛**-ή**, ἡ, *life*, λύθη ψ. τε μένος τε Il.5.296, etc.; ψ. τε καὶ αἰών 16.453, cf. Od.9.523; θυμοῦ καὶ ψ. Il.11.334, Od.21.154; λαυκανίην, ἵνα τε ψυχῆς ὤκιστος ὄλεθρος Il.22.325; ψυχὰς παρθέμενοι at hazard of their *lives*, Od.3.74, 9.255; αἰεὶ ἐμὴν ψ. παραβαλλόμενος Il.9.322; λίσσομ' ὑπὲρ ψ. καὶ γούνων by your *life*, 22.338; so ἀντὶ ψ. S.*OC*1326: but περὶ ψ. to save their *life*, Od.9.423; περί τε ψυχέων ἐμάχοντο 22.245; περὶ ψ. θέον Ἕκτορος Il.22.161; τρέχων περὶ τῆς ψ. Hdt.9.37; τῆς ἐμῆς περὶ ψ. A.*Eu.*115, cf. E.*Hel.*946, *Heracl.*984; περὶ ψ. κινδυνεύων Antipho 2.1.4, cf. Th. 8.50; ἀγὼν..σῆς ψ. πέρι S.*El.*1492, cf. E.*Ph.*1330, *Or.*847, X.*Cyr.*3. 3.44; τὸν περὶ ψ. δρόμον δραμεῖν Ar.*V.*375 (lyr.); ἀγωνίζεσθαι περὶ τῆς ψ. X.*Eq.Mag.*1.19; ὃ ἂν θέλῃ, ψυχῆς ὠνεῖται [θυμός] in exchange for *life*, Heraclit.85; τῆς ψ. πρίασθαί τι X.*Cyr.*3.1.36; τί γὰρ δοῖ ἄνθρωπος ἀντάλλαγμα τῆς ψ. αὐτοῦ; *Ev.Marc.*8.37. In early poets: ψυχὰν ἀποπνεῖν Simon.52; ψυχὰς ἔχοντες κυμάτων ἐν ἀγκάλαις Archil.23; ψυχέων φειδόμενοι Tyrt.10.14; φειδωλὴν ψ. θέμενος Sol.13.46; ψυχῆς εἵνεκα καὶ βιότου Thgn.730; ψυχὰν Ἀΐδᾳ τελέων Pi.*I.*1.68; ψυχὰς βαλὸν Id.*O.*8.39; χαλκῷ ἀπὸ ψυχὴν ἀρύσας Emp.138; τοὐμὸν ἐκπίνουσ' ἀεὶ ψυχῆς ἄκρατον αἷμα S.*El.*786; τῆς ἐμῆς ψ. γεγώς ib.775; τὴν ψ. ἐκπίνουσιν Ar.*Nu.*712 (anap.); ψ. ἀφήσω E.*Or.*1171; ψ. σέθεν ἔκτεινε Id.*Tr.*1214; ψ. παραιτέεσθαι Hdt.1.24; ποινὴν τῆς Αἰσώπου ψ. satisfaction for the *life* of A., Id.2.134; ψυχῆς ἀποστερῆσαί τινα Antipho 4.1.6, cf. Th.1.136, etc.; τὴν ψ. ἢ τὴν οὐσίαν ἢ τὴν ἐπιτιμίαν τινὸς ἀφελόμενος Aeschin.2.88; τὸ τῆς ψ. ἀπαιτηθεὶς χρέος Lxx *Wi.*15.

8, cf. *Ev.Luc.*12.20; ζητοῦσι τὴν ψ. μου Lxx 3*Ki.*19.10, cf. *Ev.Matt.* 2.20; τὴν ψ. αὐτοῦ τίθησιν ὑπὲρ τῶν προβάτων *Ev.Jo.*10.11, etc.; δεῖρον ἄχρις ἡ ψ...ἐπὶ χειλέων λειφθῇ within an inch of his *life*, Herod.3.3:—the phrase ἐν τῇ χειρὶ τὴν ψ. ἔχοντα taking his *life* in his hands, is prob. f.l. in Xenarch.4.20; ἡ ψ. μου ἐν ταῖς χερσί [σου] διὰ πάντος Lxx *Ps.*118(119).109, cf. 1*Ki.*19.5, 28.21, al.; of *life* in animals, Od.14.426, Hes.*Sc.*173, Pi.*N.*1.47, etc.; τὰ ἄλλα ζῷα, ὅσα ψ. ἔχει Anaxag.4, cf. 12; πάντων τῶν ζῴων ἡ ψ. τὸ αὐτό, ἀήρ Diog. Apoll.5 (cf. infr. IV. 1); ἡ φύσις τοιαύτη πάντων ὅσσα ψ. ἔχει Democrit.278; ἐπῴζει καὶ ποιεῖ ψ. ἔχειν (of incubation) Epich.172; [ἑρπετὸν] ὃ ἔχει ἐν ἑαυτῷ ψ. ζωῆς Lxx *Ge.*1.30; ἡ ψ. πάσης σαρκὸς αἷμα αὐτοῦ ἐστιν ib.*Le.*17.11, cf. *De.*12.23. 2. metaph. of things *dear as life*, χρήματα γὰρ ψ.... βροτοῖσι Hes.*Op.*686; πᾶσι δ' ἀνθρώποις ἄρ' ἦν ψ. τέκν' E.*Andr.*419; τἀργύριόν ἐστιν αἷμα καὶ ψ. βροτοῖς Timocl.35; so as an endearing name, Hld.1.8, al.; ζωὴ καὶ ψ. Juv.6.195; ψ. μου Mart.10.68. II. in Hom., *departed spirit, ghost* (ὑποτίθεται [Ὅμηρος] τὰς ψ. τοῖς εἰδώλοις τοῖς ἐν τοῖς κατόπτροις φαινομένοις ὁμοίας..ἃ καθάπαξ ἡμῖν ἐξείκασται καὶ τὰς κινήσεις μιμεῖται, στερεμνιώδη δὲ ὑπόστασιν οὐδεμίαν ἔχει εἰς ἀντίληψιν καὶ ἁφήν Apollod. Hist.*Fr.*102(a) J.); ψ. Πατροκλῆος..πάντ' αὐτῷ..ἐϊκυῖα Il.23.65: freq. in Od.11, ψ. Ἀγαμέμνονος, Ἀχιλῆος, etc., 387,467, al.; ψ. καὶ εἴδωλον Il.23.104, cf. 72, Od.24.14; ψ. κατὰ χθονὸς ᾤχετο τετριγυῖα Il.23.100; ψυχὰς ἡρώων, opp. αὐτούς, 1.3, cf. Hes.*Sc.*151; ψυχαὶ δ' Ἄϊδόσδε κατῆλθον Il.7.330; ψ. δὲ κατ' οὐταμένην ὠτειλὴν ἔσσυτ' ἐπειγομένη 14.518; sts. hardly dist. from signf. I, ἅμα ψ. τε καὶ ἔγχεος ἐξέρυσ' αἰχμήν 16.505; in swoons it leaves the body, τὸν δὲ λίπε ψ. 5.696; so in later writers (seldom in Trag.), σὺν Ἀγαμεμνονίᾳ ψυχᾷ Pi.*P.*11.21; ἐὰν ψυχὰν κομίξαι ib.4.159, cf. *N.*8.44; αἱ ψ. ὀσμῶνται καθ' Ἅιδην Heraclit.98; πέμψατ' ἔνερθεν ψυχὴν ἐς φῶς A.*Pers.*630 (anap.); ποτωμένην ψ. ὑπὲρ σοῦ E.*Or.*676, cf. *Fr.* 912.9 (anap.); τὰς τῶν κεκμηκότων ψ., αἷς ἐστιν ἐν τῇ φύσει τῶν αὑτῶν ἐκγόνων κήδεσθαι Pl.*Lg.*927b; ψ. σοφαί, perh. 'wise *ghosts*', Ar.*Nu.* 94; δὶς ἀποθανουμένη ψ. Anon.ap.Plu.2.236d. III. the immaterial and immortal *soul*, first in Pindar, ἐς τὸν ὕπερθεν ἅλιον κείνων.. ἀνδιδοῖ [Φερσεφόνα] ψυχὰς πάλιν *Fr.*133, cf. Pl.*Men.*81b; εἰπόντες ὡς ἀνθρώπου ψ. ἀθάνατός ἐστι Hdt.2.123; ἀγένητόν τε καὶ ἀθάνατον ψ. Pl.*Phdr.*246a, cf. *Phd.*70c, al.; ἀθάνατος ἡμῶν ἡ ψ. καὶ οὐδέποτε ἀπόλλυται Id.*R.*608d; ἁ ψ. τῷ σώματι συνέζευκται καὶ καθάπερ ἐν σάματι τέθαπται Philol.14, cf. Pl.*Cra.*400c: hence freq. opp. σῶμα, ψ. καὶ σῶμα X.*Mem.*1.3.5, cf. *An.*3.2.20; ψ. ἢ σῶμα ἢ συναμφότερον, τὸ ὅλον τοῦτο Pl.*Alc.*1.130a; εἰς θηρίου βίον ἀνθρωπίνη ψ. ἀφικνεῖται καὶ ἐκ θηρίου..πάλιν εἰς ἄνθρωπον Id.*Phdr.*249b; κατὰ τοὺς Πυθαγορικοὺς μύθους τὴν τυχοῦσαν ψ. εἰς τὸ τυχὸν ἐνδύεσθαι σῶμα Arist.*de An.* 407$^b$22; οὐδὲ τοῦτο ἐπείσθην, ὡς ἡ ψ., ἕως μὲν ἂν ἐν θνητῷ σώματι ᾖ, ζῇ, ὅταν δὲ τούτου ἀπαλλαγῇ, τέθνηκεν X.*Cyr.*8.7.19; ἀνθρώπου γε ψ., ἣ τοῦ θείου μετέχει,..ὁρᾶται δ' οὐδ' αὐτή Id.*Mem.*4.3.14, cf. *Cyr.* 8.7.17; αἰθὴρ μὲμ ψυχὰς ὑπεδέξατο, σώ[ματα δὲ χθών] *IG*1$^2$.945 (V B.C.); ὁπόταμ ψ. προλίπῃ φάος ἀελίοιο Orph.*Fr.*32*f*.1; ἡμεῖς ἐσμεν ψ., ζῷον ἀθάνατον ἐν θνητῷ καθειργμένον φρουρίῳ Pl.*Ax.* 365e. IV. the *conscious self* or *personality* as centre of emotions, desires, and affections, χερσὶ καὶ ψυχᾷ δυνατοί Pi.*N.*9.39; μορφὰν βραχύς, ψυχὰν δ' ἄκαμπτος Id.*I.*4(3).53(71); ἐνίους τῶν καλῶν τὰς μορφὰς μοχθηροὺς ὄντας τὰς ψ. X.*Oec.*6.16; θνητοῦ σώματος ἔτυχες, πειρῶ τῆς ψ. ἀθάνατον μνήμην καταλιπεῖν Isoc.2.37; opp. material blessings, κτεάνων ψ. ἔχοντες κρέσσονας Pi.*N.*9.32; μήτε σωμάτων ἐπιμελεῖσθαι μήτε χρημάτων..οὕτω σφόδρα ὡς τῆς ψ. ὅπως ὡς ἀρίστη ἔσται Pl.*Ap.* 30b, cf. 29e: hence regarded in abstraction, τὸ παρεχόμενον ἡμῶν ἕκαστον τοῦτ' εἶναι μηδὲν ἀλλ' ἢ τὴν ψ., τὸ δὲ σῶμα ἰνδαλλόμενον ἡμῶν ἑκάστοις ἕπεσθαι Pl.*Lg.*959a; ἡ ψ. ἐστιν ἄνθρωπος Id.*Alc.*1. 130c; οὐδὲ νῦν τήν γ' ἐμὴν ψ. ἑωρᾶτε X.*Cyr.*8.7.17, cf. supr. III: sts., therefore, distd. from oneself, ψ. γὰρ ηὔδα πολλά μοι μυθουμένη S.*Ant.*227; ἡ ψ. μου πεπότηται Ar.*Nu.*319 (anap.); τί ποτ' ἔστι μαθεῖν ἔραται ψ. E.*Hipp.*173 (anap.); ἄλλο τι βουλομένη ἑκατέρου ἡ ψ. δήλη ἐστίν Pl.*Smp.*192c; οἴμοι ψυχή woe is *me!* Lxx *Mi.*7.1; καὶ ἐρῶ τῇ ψ. μου, "ψυχή, ἔχεις πολλὰ ἀγαθά" *Ev.Luc.*12.19; in periphrases, ψ. Ὀρέστου, = Ὀρέστης, S.*El.*1127, al.: but τὴν Φιλοκτήτου ψ. ἐκκλέψεις his *wits*, Id *Ph.*55; ἡ δ' ἐμὴ ψ. τέθνηκεν Id.*Ant.*559, cf. *OC*999; so ψυχαί abs., = ἄνθρωποι, ψ. ὀλέσασα A.*Ag.*1457 (lyr.); ψ. πολλαὶ ἔθανον many *souls* perished, Ar.*Th.*864; πᾶσαι αἱ ψ., υἱοὶ καὶ αἱ θυγατέρες λʹ γʹ Lxx *Ge.*46.15, cf. *Ex.*12.4, al.; [κιβωτὸς] εἰς ἣν ὀλίγοι, τοῦτ' ἔστιν ὀκτὼ ψ., διεσώθησαν 1*Ep.Pet.*3.20. In apostrophe, μή, φίλα ψ. Pi.*P.*3.61; ὦ μελέα ψ. S.*Ph.*712 (lyr.); ὦ ἀγαθὴ καὶ πιστὴ ψ. X.*Cyr.*7.3.8; in referring to persons, ὅταν μεγάλη ψ. φυῇ Pl.*R.* 496b (cf. μεγαλόψυχος); καλεῖται γοῦν ἡ ψ. Κρινοκοράκα the *creature*, Thphr.*Char.*28.2; πάσῃ ψ. τετελευτηκυίᾳ Lxx *Nu.*6.6,11; πᾶσα ψ. ὑποτασσέσθω *Ep.Rom.*13.1, etc.: generally, *being*, ψυχὴ ζῶσα living *creature*, Lxx *Ge.*1.24, cf. 20 (pl.). 2. of various aspects of the *self*, ἐν πολέμοιο μάχαις τλάμονι ψ. παρέμειν' enduring *heart*, Pi.*P.*1.48; διεπειρᾶτο αὐτοῦ τῆς ψ. Hdt.3.14, ἦν γάρ..ψυχὴν οὐκ ἄκρος poor-*spirited*, Id.5.124; ψυχὴν ἄριστε πάντων Ar.*Eq.*457; καρτερὰν ψ. λαβεῖν Id.*Ach.*393; κράτιστοι ἂν τὴν ψ. κριθεῖεν Th.2.40; τοῖς σώμασι δύνανται τὰς δὲ ψ. οὐκ ἔχουσιν Lys.10.29; ὁ γὰρ' λόγχην ἀκονῶν καὶ τὴν ψ. τι παρακονᾷ X.*Cyr.*6.2.33, cf. *Oec.*21.3. 3. of the emotional self, ὑπείργασμαι μὲν εὖ ψυχὴν ἔρωτι E.*Hipp.*505, cf. 527 (lyr.); πάνυ μου ἡ ψ. ἐπεθύμει X.*Oec.*6.14; τίνα ποτὲ ψ. ἔχων; Lys.32.12; τίν' οἴεσθ' αὐτὴν ψ. ἕξειν, ὅταν ἐμὲ ἴδῃ; how will she *feel?* D.28.21; μία ψ., prov. of friends, Arist.*EN*1168$^b$7; ψ. μία ἥστην prob. in Phryn. *PS* p.128 B.; of appetite, ψυχῇ διδόντες ἡδονήν A.*Pers.*841 (s.v.l.), cf. Epich.297, Theocr.16.24; λίχνῳ δὲ ὄντι τὴν ψ. Pl.*R.*579b; τῷ δὲ ἡ ψ. σῖτον μὲν οὐ προσίετο, διψῆν δ' ἐδόκει X.*Cyr.*8.7.4. 4. of the moral and intellectual *self*, ἀπὸ πάμπαν ἀδίκων ἔχειν ψ. Pi.*O.* 2.70; ψ. τε καὶ φρόνημα καὶ γνώμην S.*Ant.*176; ἀρκεῖν...κἀντὶ μυρίων μίαν ψ. τάδ' ἐκτίνουσαν, ἢν εὔνους παρῇ Id.*OC*499; ψ. γὰρ εὔνους καὶ φρονοῦσα τοὔνδικον Id.*Fr.*101; ἡ κακὴ σὴ ψ. Id.*Ph.*1014; ψυχῆς κατήγορος κακῆς X.*Oec.*20.15, cf. Pl.*R.*353e; ἡ βουλεύσασα ψ. Antipho 4.1.7, cf. Pl.*Lg.*873a; τὸ σῶμα ἀπειρηκὸς ἡ ψ. συνεξέσωσεν..διὰ τὸ μὴ ξυνειδέναι ἑαυτῇ the *mind* conscious of innocence, Antipho 5. 93; τὸ ἐπιμελεῖσθαι καὶ ἄρχειν καὶ βουλεύεσθαι..ἔσθ' ὅτῳ ἄλλῳ ἢ ψυχῇ δικαίως ἂν ἀποδοῖμεν; Pl.*R.*353d; τὴν τῆς ψ. ἐπιμέλειαν X.*Mem.* 1.2.4, Isoc.15.304; τὰ ἐν τῇ ψ. διὰ τὴν παιδείαν ἐγγιγνόμενα ib.290; τῆς ψ. ἐξελθούσης, ἐν ᾗ μόνῃ γίγνεται φρόνησις X.*Mem.*1.2.53; νοῦς τε καὶ ψ. Pl.*Cra.*400a, cf. *Phdr.*247c, al.; ἐμπαίει τί μοι ψυχῇ σύνηθες ὄμμα S.*El.*903; ἰδὼν μὲν γνούς τε σῇ ψ., τέκνον E.*Tr.*1171. Phrases:— ἐκ τῆς ψ. φίλος X.*An.*7.7.43; ἀπὸ τῆς ψ. φιλεῖν with all the *heart*, Thphr. *Char.*17.3; βόσκοιτ' ἐκ ψυχᾶς τὰς ἀμνάδας Theoc.8.35; ὅλῃ τῇ ψ. κεχαρίσθαι τινί X.*Mem.*3.11.10; οὐκ ἐᾷ ἡμᾶς οὐδὲ ψυχῆς λαχεῖν he won't let us call our *soul* our own, Phryn.*PS* p.128 B. 5. of animals, ψ. μεγαλόφρων, of a horse, X.*Eq.*11.1; θηρίων ψ. ἡμεροῦμεν Isoc.2.12; ψ. χηνός, ὀρτυγίου, Eub.101, Antiph.5. 6. of inanimate things, πᾶσα πολιτεία ψ. πόλεώς ἐστιν Isoc.12.138, cf. 7.14; ἡ τῶνδε τῶν ἀνδρῶν ἀρετὴ τῆς Ἑλλάδος ἦν ψ. D.60.23; οἷον ψ. ὁ μῦθος τῆς τραγῳδίας Arist.*Po.*1450$^a$38; also of the *spirit* of an author, D.H.*Lys.*11. V. Philosophical uses: 1. In the early physicists, of the primary substance, the source of *life and consciousness*, ὁρίζονται πάντες (sc. οἱ πρότεροι) τὴν ψ. τρισίν, κινήσει, αἰσθήσει, τῷ ἀσωμάτῳ Arist.*deAn.* 405$^b$11; τὸν λίθον ἔφη [Θαλῆς] ψ. ἔχειν ὅτι τὸν σίδηρον κινεῖ, of the magnet, ib.405$^a$20; ψυχῇσιν θάνατος ὕδωρ γενέσθαι, ὕδατι δὲ θάνατος γῆν γενέσθαι, ἐκ γῆς δὲ ὕδωρ γίνεται, ἐξ ὕδατος δὲ ψ. (sc. πῦρ) Heraclit. 36; ἡ ψ. πνεῦμα Xenoph.ap.D.L.9.19; καρδία ψυχῆς καὶ αἰσθήσιος [ἀρχά] Philol.13; τοῦτο [ἀὴρ] αὐτοῖς καὶ ψ. ἐστι καὶ νόησις Diog. Apoll.4; τὴν τῶν ἄλλων ἁπάντων φύσιν οὐ πιστεύεις Ἀναξαγόρᾳ νοῦν καὶ ψ. εἶναι τὴν διακοσμοῦσαν; Pl.*Cra.*400a, cf. Arist.*de An.*404$^a$25; Δημόκριτος πῦρ τι καὶ θερμόν φησιν αὐτὴν (sc. ψυχὴν) εἶναι ib.404$^a$1, cf. *Resp.*472$^a$4. 2. the *spirit* of the universe, ψ. εἰς τὸ μέσον [τοῦ κόσμου] θεὶς Pl.*Ti.*34b, cf. 30b; τὴν τοῦ παντὸς δῆλον ὅτι τοιαύτην εἶναι βούλεται [ὁ Τίμαιος] οἷόν ποτ' ἐστὶν ὁ καλούμενος νοῦς Arist.*de An.*407$^a$3; ἐν τῷ ὅλῳ τινὲς [τὴν ψ.] μεμεῖχθαί φασιν, ὅθεν ἴσως καὶ Θαλῆς ᾠήθη πάντα πλήρη θεῶν εἶναι ib.411$^a$8; ὁ κόσμος ψ. ἐστὶν ἑαυτοῦ καὶ ἡγεμονικόν Chrysipp.*Stoic.*2.186; ψ. [κόσμου] Plu.2.1013e, cf. M.Ant.4.40; ψ. ἐλθοῦσα εἰς σῶμα οὐρανοῦ Plot.5.1.2; τόδε τὸ πᾶν ψ. μίαν ἔχον εἰς πάντα αὐτοῦ μέρη Id.4.4.32; περὶ ψυχᾶς κόσμου καὶ φύσιος, title of work by Ti.Locr. 3. In Pl. the immaterial principle of movement and life, ὅταν παρῇ [ψυχὴ] τῷ σώματι, αἴτιόν ἐστι τοῦ ζῆν αὐτῷ Pl.*Cra.*399d, cf. *Def.*411c; [ψυχῆς λόγον ἔχομεν] τὴν δυναμένην αὐτὴν αὑτὴν κινεῖν κίνησιν Id.*Lg.*896a; μεταβολῆς τε καὶ κινήσεως ἁπάσης αἰτία [ἡ ψ.] ἅπασιν ib.b, cf. 892c; its presence is requisite for thought, σοφία καὶ νοῦς ἄνευ ψ. οὐκ ἄν γενοίσθην Id.*Phlb.*30c, cf. *Ti.* 30b, *Sph.*249a; defined by Arist. as οὐσία ὡς εἶδος σώματος φυσικοῦ δυνάμει ζωὴν ἔχοντος *de An.*412$^a$20; ἐντελέχεια ἡ πρώτη σώματος φυσικοῦ ὀργανικοῦ ib.412$^b$5; the tripartite division of ψ., οἱ δὲ περὶ Πλάτωνα καὶ Ἀρχύτας καὶ οἱ λοιποὶ Πυθαγόρειοι τὴν ψ. τριμερῆ ἀποφαίνονται, διαιροῦντες εἰς λογισμὸν καὶ θυμὸν καὶ ἐπιθυμίαν Iamb.ap.Stob.1.49.34, cf. Pl.*R.*439e sqq.; in Arist. ἡ ψ. τούτοις ὥρισται, θρεπτικῷ, αἰσθητικῷ, διανοητικῷ, κινήσει· πότερον δὲ τούτων ἕκαστόν ἐστι ψ. ἢ ψυχῆς μόριον; *de An.*413$^b$11, cf. *PA*641$^b$4; ἡ θρεπτικὴ ψ. Id.*de An.*434$^a$22, al.; in the Stoics and Epicureans, σῶμα ἡ ψ. Zeno and Chrysipp. *Stoic.*1.38; of the *scala naturae*, τὰ μὲν ἕξει διοικεῖται, τὰ δὲ φύσει, τὰ δ' ἀλόγῳ ψ., τὰ δὲ καὶ λόγον ἐχούσῃ καὶ διάνοιαν *Stoic.*2.150, cf. M.Ant.6.14; ἡ ψ. σῶμά ἐστι λεπτομερές..προσεμφερέστατον πνεύματι θερμοῦ τινα κρᾶσιν ἔχοντι Epicur.*Ep.*1 p.19 U.; τέλος..τὸ μήτε ἀλγεῖν κατὰ σῶμα μήτε ταράττεσθαι κατὰ ψ. Id.*Ep.*3 p.64 U.; in the Neo-Platonists characterized by discursive thinking, τοὺς λογισμοὺς ψυχῆς εἶναι ἐνεργήματα Plot.1.1.7; related to νοῦς as image to archetype, εἰκών τίς ἐστι νοῦ [ψ.] Id.5.1.3; present in entirety in every part, πάρεστι πᾶσα πανταχοῦ ψ. Id.5.1.2, cf. 4.7.5; φύσις ψ. οὖσα, γέννημα ψυχῆς προτέρας Id.3.8.4; animal and vegetable bodies possess οἷον σκιὰν ψυχῆς Id.4.4.18; πᾶν σῶμα..ψυχῆς μετουσίᾳ κινεῖται ἐξ ἑαυτοῦ καὶ ζῇ διὰ ψ. Procl.*Inst.*20. VI. *butterfly* or *moth*, Arist.*HA*551$^a$14, Thphr.*HP*2.4.4, Plu.2.636c. 2. τριπόλιον, Ps.-Dsc.4.132. VII. *Psyche*, in the allegory of Psyche and Eros, Apul.*Metam.* bks. 4–6, Aristophontes ap. Fulg.*Myth.*3.6. (See ancient speculations on the derivation, Pl.*Cra.*399d–400a, Arist.*de An.*405$^b$29, Chrysipp.*Stoic.*2.222; Hom. usage gives little support to the derivation from ψύχω 'blow, breathe'; τὸν δὲ λίπε ψ. Il.5. 696 means 'his *spirit* left his body', and so λειποψυχέω means 'swoon', not 'become breathless'; ἀπὸ δὲ ψ. ἐκάπυσσε Il.22.467 means 'she gasped out her *spirit*', viz. 'swooned'; the resemblance of ἄμπνυτο 'recovered consciousness' to ἀμπνέω 'recover breath' is deceptive, v. ἄμπνυτο, ἔμπνυτο: when concrete the Homeric ψ. is rather *warm blood* than *breath*, cf. Il.14.518, 16.505, where the ψ. escapes through a wound; cf. ψυχοπότης, ψυχορροφέω, and S.*El.*786, Ar.*Nu.*712 (v. supr. I).) **–ήϊος**, η, ον, *having a* ψυχή, *alive, living*, Pythag.ap.Luc.*Vit.Auct.*6 (v.l. ἐμψ.).

**ψυχθρός**, v. ψυχρός.

**ψῡχί-διον**, τό, Dim. of ψυχή, *little soul*, Luc.*Nav.*26, D.C.77. 16. **–ζομαι**, Pass., *grow cold, freeze*, Gloss. **–κός**, ή, όν, *of the soul* or *life, spiritual*, opp. σωματικός, ἡδοναί Arist.*EN*1117$^b$28; ὁρμαί Plb.8.10.9; πνεῦμα ψ. the spirit, or breath *of life*, Plu.2.1084e, etc.; νόσος ib.524d. Adv. **-κῶς** Ph.1.81; opp. σωματικῶς, νοερῶς, Procl.*Inst.*139; also, *heartily, from the heart*, Lxx 2 *Ma.*4.37, 14.24. 2. *of the animal life, animal*, ὁ ψ. ἄνθρωπος the *natural* man, opp. ὁ πνευματικός, 1 *Ep.Cor.*2.14, cf. *Ep.Jud.*19, Phot. s. v. 3. *brave*, Alex.338. II. *for the soul* or *spirit* of one deceased, ψ. δῶρα διδούς, sc. to Hermes, *Epigr.Gr.*815.4 (Crete). III. *cooling*, Vett.Val.6.27 (s. v. l.). **-νός**, ή, όν, v. ψυχεινός.

**ψῡχ-ίον**, τό, = ψυχάριον, *IG*14.2068. **-μός**, ὁ, later form for ψυγμός, Man.2.443 (signf. I. 2).

**ψῡχογον-ία**, ἡ, *the generation of the soul*, Plu.2.415e, al., Herm. *in Phdr.*p.128 A. (in reference to Plato's *Timaeus*). ⊛ **-ικός**, ή, όν, *of* or *for* ψυχογονία, ὁ ἐξ ἀριθμὸς ψ. ἐστιν Lyd.*Mens.*2.11, cf. *Theol. Ar.*40. **-ιμος**, ον, *producing life* or *spirit*, στοιχεῖα Ph.2.96 (Sup.). **-ος** (parox.), ον, = foreg., *Corp.Herm.*13.12.

**ψῡχο-δᾰϊκτής**, οῦ, ὁ, *destroying* or *killing the soul*, epith. of Dionysus, *AP*9.524.24. **-δοσία**, ἡ, *giving of souls*, *Tab.Defix. Aud.*242.12 (Carthage, iii A.D.). **-δοτήρ**, ῆρος, ὁ, *giver of the soul* or *life*, epith. of Apollo, *AP*9.525.24. **-ειδής**, ές, *of the nature of soul, spiritual*, Ph.1.15, 2.17, *Theol.Ar.*39.

**ψῡχο-κρᾰτητικός**, ή, όν, *getting the soul*, τοῦ -κοῦ, ὅς ἐστιν ἕβδομος (sc. ἐνιαυτός) Lyd.*Mens.*3.9.

**ψῡχ-όλεθρος**, ὁ, *the death of the soul*, Hdn.*Epim.*203. ⊛ **-ολέτης**, ου, ὁ, *soul-destroyer*, ib.211.

⊛ **ψῡχο-λῐπής**, ές, *lifeless*, βρέφος Max.227; δύναμις *APl.*4.266. **-μαντεία**, ἡ, *necromancy*, Aen.Gaz.*Thphr.*p.61 B. ⊛ **-μαντεῖον**, τό, *place where the dead are conjured up*, Plu.2.109c. **-μαντις**, εως, ὁ, *necromancer*, Hsch. s. v. θυμόμαντις. **-μᾰχέω**, *fight to the last gasp, fight desperately*, Plb.1.58.7, 6.52.7, 10.39.7, App.*BC*5.37. 2. *suffer anguish*, *Lyr.Alex.Adesp.*4.21. **-μᾰχία**, ἡ, *desperate fighting*, Plb.1.59.6. **-πλᾰνής**, ές, *making the soul wander*, epith. of Dionysus, *AP*9.524.24. **-ποιία**, ἡ, *the making of souls*, Herm.ap.Stob.1.49.68. **-ποιός**, όν, *making souls*, χεῖρες ib.1.49.44, cf. *Theol.Ar.*34. II. (ψῦχος) *chilling*, Vett.Val.6.28. **-πομπεῖον**, τό, *a place where departed souls are conjured up*, Plu.2.560e. **-πομπός**, ὁ, *conductor* or *guide of souls*, of Charon, E.*Alc.*361; of Hermes, D.S.1.96, Plu.2.758b. II. as Adj., ψ. δυνάμεις Porph.*Antr.*8. **-πονία**, ἡ, *anguish of soul*, Heph. Astr.2.28 (pl.). **-πότης**, ου, ὁ, *drinking the life*, i.e. *the blood*, Hsch. s.v. εἰαροπότης.

**ψυχορόφους**· τὰς τὴν ψυχὴν ἐκπινούσας, Hsch.: cf. ψυχορροφέω.

⊛ **ψῡχορρᾰγ-έω**, *let the soul break loose*, i.e. *lie at the last gasp*, E.*Alc.*20, *HF*324, A.R.2.833, Plu.*Crass.*27, Hld.9.21. **-ής**, ές, *letting the soul break loose*, hence *lying at the last gasp*, γυναῖκες ἐν τόκοις ψυχορραγεῖς E.*IT*1466. **-ία**, ἡ, *death-struggle*, Olymp. *in Phd.*p.142 N.

**ψῡχορροφέω**, (ψυχή) *suck out the life*, Phryn.*PS*p.128 B.; cf. ψυχορόφους. II. (ψῦχος) *drink cold water*, Pl.Com.259.

**ψῦχος**, εος, τό, (ψύχω II) *cold*, Emp.65.2; opp. θάλπος, Hp.*Aph.*3.4; opp. ἀλέα, Arist.*HA*$598^{a}$1; opp. καύματα, Id.*Mete.*$362^{b}$17; ἐν ψύχει *in winter-time*, S.*Ph.*17; ἐν τῷ ψ. καθηῦδον Pl.*Smp.*220d; ψ., = ῥῖγος, Hermipp.97: pl. ψύχεα *frosts, cold weather*, Hdt.4.28,129, 5.10; ψύχη X.*Oec.*5.4, *Cyn.*5.9; ἐν τοῖς σφόδρα ψ. καὶ ἐν ταῖς σφόδρα ἀλέαις Arist.*HA*$599^{a}$19, cf. *Mete.*$379^{a}$26; sg., Hp.*VM*16. 2. once in Hom., *coolness*, ψύχεος ἱμείρων Od.10.555: metaph., ψ. ἐν δόμοις πέλει A.*Ag.*971.

**ψῡχοσσόος**, ον, *saving the soul*, *AP*9.197 (Marin.Neap.), 15.12 (Leo Phil.).

⊛ **ψῡχο-στᾰσία**, ἡ, *weighing of lives*: the title of a tragedy of A., in which Thetis and Eos *weighed the lives* of Achilles and Memnon against one another, and the latter was found lighter, Plu.2.17a. **-στόλος**, ον, *escorting souls*, of Hermes, Tryph.572. **-τᾰκής**, ές, *melting the soul* or *heart*, στόματος πρόθυρα (i.e. χείλη) *AP*5.55 (Diosc.); δάκρυα *APl.*4.198 (Maec.). **-τᾰμίας**, ου, ὁ, *keeper of souls*, Herm.ap.Stob.1.49.69. ⊛ **-τροφον**, τό, = κέστρον, Dsc.4.1. **-τρόφος**, ον, *sustaining life* or *soul*, αὖραι Orph.*H.*16.3.

**ψῡχουλκ-έομαι**, *to be at the last gasp*, Lxx 3 *Ma.*5.25. **-ός**, όν, *attracting souls*, αἷμα (in Hom.Od.11) Procl.*in R.*2.111 K.; *drawing the soul* out of the body, ῥάβδος Clearch.ib.2.122 K. II. = ἑλξίνη, Ps.-Dsc.4.39.

**ψῡχοφθόρος**, ον, *destructive of life, deadly*, Orph.*H.*68.6. 2. *soul-destroying*, πάθη Ph.*Fr.*103 H., cf. *Cod.Just.*1.1.5.3.

**ψῡχόω**, (ψυχή) *give soul to*, λίθον *APl.*4.159; σῶμα Ph.1.33, cf. Nonn.*D.*25.542; ψυχοῦν τὸν λόγον, of νοήματα, *animate, make alive*, Ph.1.693, cf. Plot.4.4.22, Procl.*Inst.*196:—Pass., Ph.1.263, al., Plot.2.3.9. 2. *give a psychical* (opp. physical) *character* to physical sensations, Id.4.4.28. II. (ψῦχος) Pass., *to be made cold, become cold*, Hp.*Steril.*213, f.l. in Plu.2.1052f (ψυχόμενον Bernardakis).

**ψύχρ-α**, ἡ, *cold*, Sch.BT Od.5.467. **-αίνω**, *make cool* or *cold, cool*, in Pass., Plu.*Fr.inc.*149, Alex.Trall.1.14, Procl.*in Prm.* p.571 S.: metaph., φιλίας ταχὺ -αινομένας Id.*Par.Ptol.*270. **-αντικός**, ή, όν, *for cooling*, σκεῦος -κόν, i.e. ψυκτήρ, Hdn.*Epim.*155. **-ᾰσία**, ἡ, *a making cold*, Epicur.*Ep.*2 p.49 U., *Fr.*59. **-ευμα**, ατος, τό, *a frigid discourse*, Gal.9.935. **-εύομαι**, *furnish example of bad taste*, Hermog.*Id.*1.6. **-ηλᾰτέω**, *hammer* metal *while it is cold*, σίδηρον..-ήσας ποίησον δακτύλιον *PMag.Par.*1.2131. **-ήλᾰτος**, ον, (ἐλαύνω III. 1) *cold-forged*, of iron implements, Plu.2.434a, Asclep. Myrl.ap.Ath.11.501b, Ath.Mech.17.2, Plu.*Brut.*1: γράψας ψυχρηλάτω (sic) τινὸς τὸ ὄνομα *PMag.Par.*1.1848. **-ία**, ἡ, *chilliness*; metaph. of rhetoric, *frigidity*, Chrysipp.*Stoic.*3.50, cf. Plu.*Alex.*3. **-ίζω**, *cool*, Gal.6.811 (Pass.). **-ιστός**, ή, όν, *cooled*, *Gloss.*

⊛ **ψυχρο-βᾰφής**, ές, *dipped in cold water*, Luc.*Lex.*5. II. *imparted by a cold tincture*, of colours and scents, ψ. ἄνθη Thphr.*Od.*22. **-γρᾰφέω**, *write frigidly*, Eust.1207.6. **-δοσία**, ἡ, *administration of cooling drinks*, Herod.Med.ap.Aët.5.129. **-δόχος**, ον, *receiving what is cold*, οἶκος ψ. *cold-bath* room, Luc.*Hipp.*7. **-καυτήρ**, ῆρος, ὁ, *a caustic*, Paul.Aeg.6.58, 87. **-κοίλιος**, ον, *having a cold stomach*, (Saturn makes) *-ίους*, i.e. he diminishes the innate digestive heat, Ptol.*Tetr.*151. **-κόμψευμα**, ατος, τό, *a frigid conceit*, *Com.Adesp.*1199 (-ψώματα cod. Hsch.).

**ψυχρολογ-έω**, *talk nonsense*, Luc.*Pseudol.*27; *use silly arguments*, Jul.*Gal.*347b. **-ία**, ἡ, *nonsense*, Luc.*DMort.*16.5, Arr.*Epict.*4.3.2, Gal.8.589. **-ος** (parox.), ον, *talking nonsense, idiotic*, Sch.E.*Hec.*356, Hsch.

**ψυχρο-λουσία**, ἡ, *a bathing in cold water*, Hp.*Mul.*2.110, Thphr. *Sud.*16: pl., D.C.53.30, Sor.1.56. **-λούσιον**, τό, = *frigidarium*, *Supp.Epigr.*4.241 (Caria). **-λουτέω**, *bathe in cold water*, Ar.*Fr.*237, Hp.*Morb.*2.66, Plu.*Alc.*23, Herod.Med.ap.Orib.10.39.6, Agathin.ap.eund.10.7.6:—in codd. freq. written -λουτρέω, q. v. **-λούτης**, ου, ὁ, *bather in cold water*, Lat. *psychroluta* Seneca *Ep.*53.3. **-λουτητέον**, *one must take cold baths*, Agathin.ap.Orib.10.7.6. **-λουτρέω**, *bathe in cold water*, Arist.*Pr.*$862^{b}$36, Str.3.3.6, Arr. *Epict.*1.1.29. **-μῐγής**, ές, *mixed with cold*, *Placit.*2.30.2. **-μῡθουργία**, ἡ, *frigid story*, Tz.*H.*2.740. **-πᾰγής**, v. ψυχροσταγής.

**ψυχρόομαι**, Pass., *to be chilly, uninteresting*, *AP*12.7 (Strat.).

**ψυχρο-ποιός**, όν, *making cold, chilling*, Sch.Il.5.75, *EM*541.54, Olymp.*in Mete.*199.4, cf. ψυχοποιός II. **-ποσία**, ἡ, *a drinking of cold water*, Aret.*SA*2.6, Plu.2.692d, etc.: in pl., D.C.53.30. ⊛ **-ποτέω**, *drink cold water*, Plu.2.60a, Antyll.ap.Orib.5.2.29. **-πότης**, ου, ὁ, *cold-water drinker*, Plu.2.69cb, cj. for ψυχαπάτης in *AP*12.81 (Mel.).

⊛ **ψῡχρός**, ά, όν, *cold*, χάλαζα, νιφάδες, χιών, Il.15.171, 19.358, 22.152; ψ. χαλκός (as we say '*cold* steel') 5.75: freq. of water, ψ. ὕδωρ Od.9.392, Th.2.49; ψυχρόν (without ὕδωρ) Thgn.263; λοῦνται ψυχρῷ Hdt.2.37; ἀναγαργαρίζεσθαι ψυχρῷ *IG*$4^{2}$(1).126.30 (Epid., ii A.D.) (but τὸ ψυχρὸν also = ψῦχος, *cold*, Hdt.1.142); ψ. ὥστε λούσασθαι X.*Mem.*3.13.3: of the air, αὔρη ψ. Od.5.469; αἰθήρ Pi.*O.*13.88 (s. v. l.); νύκτες Th.7.87; κυνὸς ψυχρὰ δύσις S.*Fr.*432.11; ψ. βίος life *in the cold*, Ar.*Pl.*263: esp. of dead things, νέκυς (opp. θερμὸν αἷμα) S.*OC*622; of *cold* meats, Alex.173.4, etc.; of a snake, Theoc.15.58: Comp. -ότερος Hdt.2.22, Pl.*Phlb.*24b: Sup. -ότατος D.S.1.41. II. metaph., 1. *ineffectual, vain*, ἐπικουρίη ψ. Hdt.6.108; ἐπαρθεὶς ψυχρῇ νίκῃ Id.9.49; ψ. παραγκάλισμα S.*Ant.*650; θερμὴν ἐπὶ ψυχροῖσι καρδίαν ἔχεις a hot spirit in *a cold business*, ib.88. 2. of feelings, ψ. τέρψις, ἐλπίς, E.*Alc.*353, *IA*1014. 3. of persons, *cold-hearted, heartless, indifferent*, X.*Cyr.*8.4.22,23; ψ. καὶ μελαγχολικοί Arist.*MM* $1203^{b}$1; ἐκ σιδάρου κεχάλκευται μέλαιναν καρδίαν ψυχρᾷ φλογί Pi.*Fr.*123.5; οὔτε ψ. εἶ οὔτε ζεστός *Apoc.*3.15. 4. of *flat, lifeless, insipid* productions, τὸν Παλαμήδην (the play so named) ψυχρὸν ὄντ' αἰσχύνεται Ar.*Th.*848; σκῶμμα..σφόδρα ψ. Eup.244; ψ. καὶ ἀηδὴς [Μοῦσα] Pl.*Lg.*802d; ἕωλα καὶ ψ. D.21.112; πρᾶγμα..φρέατος..ψυχρότερον 'Αραρότος Alex.179, cf. Arist.*Rh.*$1405^{b}$34, Demetr.*Eloc.*114, etc.: hence jokes in Ar.*Ach.*138–140, Macho ap.Ath.13.580a; also of authors themselves, γίνεται ψυχρός D.H.*Isoc.*3. Adv., ὁ δ' αὖ Θέογνις ψυχρὸς ὢν ψυχρῶς ποιεῖ Ar.*Th.*170; σκώψαντι ψ. ἐπιγελάσαι to laugh at a *feeble* joke, Thphr.*Char.*2.4; τοὺς γοῦν ψυχροὺς ψ. λέγουσι διαλέγεσθαι Pl.*Euthd.*284e. 5. *silly*, γραϊδίοις ψυχροῖς ὁμιλοῦντες Jul.*Ep.*89b. [Written ψυχθρός *IG*12(5).1104 (Syros, ii A.D.); cf. conversely μάκρα for μάκτρα (ψυχρός orig. 'cooled by blowing' from ψύχω 'blow').]

**ψυχρό-σαρκος**, ον, *with cold flesh*, Hp.*Epid.*6.4.19. **-στᾰγής**, ές, *congealed*, ὡς ἀπὸ κρυστάλλου ψ. Aret.*SD*2.7 (-παγής Hude, -στάγδης codd.). **-της**, ητος, ἡ, *coldness, cold*, opp. θερμότης, Hp.*VM*16, Pl.*R.*437e; ἡ τοῦ περιέχοντος ψ. καὶ στυγνότης Plb.4.21.1: pl. ψυχρότητες *chills, frosts*, Plu.2.701b. II. metaph. of persons, *want of feeling, bad taste*, D.18.256: *sluggishness*, Plu.*Fab.*17. 2. of exaggerated, glittering phrases and the like, *frigidity*, Longin.3.4, Agatharch.21, Demetr.*Eloc.*6, al. **-ῡδρία**, ἡ, *watering with cold water*, Thphr.*CP*2.14.2. **-φαντάσματα**, gloss on ψυχροκομψώματα (sic), Hsch. **-φόβος**, ον, *dreading cold water*, Gal.10.627. ⊛ **-φόρον**, τό, = *frigidarium*, *Gloss.*: **ψυχροφόρος** σωλήν a (leaden) *water-pipe*, *PMag.Lond.*121.397: -φόρον πέταλον lead tablet *made out of a water-pipe*, *Tab.Defix.Aud.*155 *A* 28, *B* 23 (Rome, iv/v A.D.).

**ψύχω**, Hdt.3.104, etc.: fut. ψύξω Alex.25.10, Arist.*PA*$653^{b}$4: aor. ἔψυξα Il.20.440, Hp.*Flat.*7: pf. ἔψῡχα Ps.-Hdn.Gr. in *An. Ox.*3.256; but ἔψῠχα Choerob. *in Theod.*2.73 H.:—Pass., fut. ψυχθήσομαι Hp.*Acut.*(*Sp.*)15: fut. 2 ψῠγήσομαι *Ev.Matt.*24.12 (v.l. ψῠχήσομαι), Gal.11.388: aor. ἐψύχθην Hp.*Epid.*5.19, Pl.*Ti.*60d, 76c, X.*HG*7.1.19, cf. ἀναψύχω: aor. 2 ἐψύχην [ῠ] Ar.*Nu.*151, (ἀπ-) A.*Fr.*104, Pl.*Phdr.*242a; κατα-ψῠχῆναι *Inscr.Magn.*103.55 (ii B.C.): later ἐψύγην Dsc.1.55, Gal.7.748, (δια-) *PSI*6.603.11 (iii B.C.), cf. Moer.p.421 P.: pf. ἔψυγμαι Hp.*Vict.*1.33, Pl.*Criti.*120b, Alex.124.15:—*breathe, blow*, 'Αθήνη..ἦκα μάλα ψύξασα Il.20.440. II. *make cool* or *cold* (not necessarily by blowing), ἀπιὼν ἐπὶ μᾶλλον ψύχει (sc. ὁ ἥλιος) Hdt.3.104, cf. Hp.*VM*16 (v.l. for διέψυξε); opp. θερμαίνω, Pl.*Phdr.*268b; θερμὸν ψύχεται Heraclit.126; ψῦξον τὸν οἶνον Diph.56, cf. Isoc.15.287:—Pass., *grow cool* or *cold*, Hdt.4.181, Ar.*Nu.*151, Pl.*Phd.*71b, Arist.*Pr.*$931^{a}$1; οἶνον.. ψυχόμενον ἐν τῷ φρέατι Stratt.57; of fire, *to be put out*, Pl.*Criti.*120b:

metaph., ψυγήσεται ἡ ἀγάπη *will grow cold*, *Ev.Matt.* l. c. 2. *cool, refresh*, θάλπουσα καὶ ψύχουσα, of a nurse tending a child, *Trag.Adesp.* 7.2: intr. in Act., *seek the cool air*, Nic.*Th.*473, Lxx 4*Ki.*19.24. 3. *chill, torment*, ἀμφάκει κέντρῳ ψύχειν ψυχὰν ἐμάν (Meineke cj. ψήχειν) A.*Pr.*693 (lyr.); of death, ψύξει σε δαίμων τῷ πεπρωμένῳ χρόνῳ Alex.25.10; ἀπαράμονοι καὶ ψύχοντες τὰς πρώτας πράξεις Vett.Val.44.28; τοὺς γάμους Id.116.7:—Pass., ψύχετ' ἀμηχανίῃ A.R.4.1527. 4. metaph. in Pass., *to be frigid*, Longin.27.1. III. *dry, make dry*, δάκρυα δ' οὐ ψύχει γενέτης ἐμός *IG*3.1335.13; ψ. τι πρὸς τὸν ἥλιον Lxx *Je.*8.2: *air*, ἱμάτια Arr.*Epict.*1.18.13:—Pass., X.*Cyn.*5.3; οὗ τὰ σῦκα ψύχεται, gloss on τρασιά, Phot.: in Hom. generally of *drying* in the wind, opp. τερσήμεναι of *drying* in the sun, Sch.Il.11.621. (Fr. signf. I comes ψυχή perhaps, but v. ψυχή: signf. II (and with it ψῦχος, ψυχρός, etc.) comes fr. signf. I: also signf. III fr. signf. I.) [ῡ always, exc. in aor. 2 Pass., v. Ar.*Nu.*151.]

⊕ **ψύχ-ωσις** [ῡ], εως, ἡ, *a giving soul* or *life to, animating, quickening*, Ph.1.15, *Theol.Ar.*48, M.Ant.12.24:—also, *the principle of life*, Philol.ap.*Theol.Ar.*55. **-ωφελής**, ές, *profiting the soul* or *spirit*, Suid.:—Subst. **-ωφέλεια**, ἡ, Id.

**ψχέντ**, Egyptian word for a royal head-dress, *OGI*90.44 (Rosetta, ii B.C.).

**ψώα**, ἡ, *rottenness, putrid stench*, A.R.*Fr.*5: but **ψῶα**· μέρος περὶ τὸν ὦμον, Hdn.*Epim.*155. **ψωδαρέον**· αὐχμηρόν, Hsch. (ψωραλέον Ruhnk.).

**ψώδη**· γλῶττα, Hsch.

**ψῶζα**, ἡ, apptly. = ψώρα, Eup.191 (anap.).

**ψωθίον**, τό, (ψώω) *small crumb, morsel*, Pherecr.81 (acc. to Ath. 14.646c):—also **ψωθία**, ἡ, *blister on under-surface of loaf*, Poll.7.23; hence of coin used in Hades, Pherecr. l. c. (acc. to Poll.9.83).

**ψωΐα**, ἡ, = ψώα, Hsch. **ψώϊζος**· ἄφοδος ὑγρὰ ἢ ὄνθος, δυσωδία, κτλ., Id. **ψώκτης**, ου, ὁ, = *quadratarius*, *Gloss.* **ψωκτός**, ή, όν, (ψώω) dub. in Hsch., ψωκτόν· τράπεζαν.

**ψωλή**, Dor. **ψωλά**, ἡ, prop. fem. of ψωλός, *membrum virile praeputio retracto*, Ar.*Lys.*143, *Av.*560 (anap.), *Supp.Epigr.*3.596 (Panticapaeum, v B.C.).

**ψωλήκυσθος**· οὐδενὸς ἄξιος, Hsch.

**ψωλός**, ὁ, *with the prepuce drawn back*, Ar.*Av.*507 (anap.) (ubi v. Sch.), *Eq.*964, *Pl.*267, Diph.39.

**ψώλων**, ωνος, ὁ, = foreg., Hsch. s.v. πόσθων.

**ψωμάριον**, τό, *fragment*, Zos.Alch.p.221 B.

**ψώμηξ**, ηκος, ὁ, *a grub that eats the roots of corn*, Hsch. (pl.).

**ψῶμιγξ**· σφήκωμα, Id.

**ψωμ-ίζω**, fut. Att. -ιῶ Lxx *Nu.*11.4:—*feed by putting little bits into the mouth*, as nurses do to children, Ar.*Th.*692, *Lys.*19, Hp.*Morb.* 4.54; or sick people, Id.*Epid.*7.3; ψ. τινά τι Lxx l. c.:—Pass., ἐπίσταμαι γὰρ.., οἷς ψωμίζεται with what *tit-bits he is fed*, Ar.*Eq.* 715. II. *give* food *by hand*, σῖτον οὐδ' ἐάν τις ψωμίζῃ δύνανται καταπιεῖν Arist.*HA*592ᵃ30; *bestow for food*, ψ. πάντα τὰ ὑπάρχοντα 1*Ep.Cor.*13.3. 2. *bait*, ἄγκιστρον *PFay.*2 iii 14 (*Lyr.Adesp.*). ⊕ **-ίον**, τό, Dim. of ψωμός, of a bun for a crocodile, *PTeb.*33.14 (ii B.C.), cf. D.L.6.37, *Ev.Jo.*13.26, M.Ant.7.3. **-ίς**, ίδος, ἡ, = ψωμίον, *morsel*, Arist.*Fr.*348. **-ισμα**, ατος, τό, *morsel*, Democrat.ap.Arist.*Rh.* 1407ᵃ7, Plu.*Rom.*2 (pl.), dub. l. in *POxy.*1088.39. **-ισμός**, ὁ, *feeding with morsels*, Sor.1.115 (pl.).

**ψωμό-δουλος**, ὁ, *a slave to morsels of food*, Hsch. s. v. ἐνθεσίδουλος. **-κόλαξ**, ᾰκος, ὁ, *flatterer for morsels of bread, parasite*, Ar.*Fr.*167 (anap.), Philem.8, Sannyr.10:—hence **-κολᾰκεύω**, Philippid.8. **-κόλᾰφος**, ὁ, *one who takes cuffs for the sake of morsels of bread, low parasite*, Diph.49.

**ψωμ-όλεθρος**, ὁ, *bread-pest*, Com. name for a parasite, Suid., Hdn.*Epim.*203:—also **ψωμολεθρία**, ἡ, Zonar.

⊕ **ψωμός**, ὁ, (ψώω) *morsel, bit*, ψ. ἀνδρόμεοι *gobbets* of man's flesh, Od.9.374, cf. Amips.19.2 (anap.), X.*Mem.*3.14.5, Pericles ap. Arist. *Rh.*1407ᵃ2, Plb.30.26.6; ψ. ἄρτου Lxx *Jd.*19.5, al. (ψ. alone, *Ru.*2. 14).

⊕ **ψώρ-α**, Ion. **ψώρη**, ἡ, (ψάω, ψώω) *itch, mange, scurvy*, of men and beasts, Hdt.4.90, Pl.*Phlb.*46a, Hermipp.63.7 (hex.), Phryn.Com.26 (dub.); ἵππων Plb.3.88.1; βοσκημάτων Thphr.*HP*9.9.4; τοὺς ὀφθαλμοὺς ἐν ψώρᾳ συνεχομένους Phld.*Rh.*2.143 S.; called by Suid. κνησμονή (fr. κνάω to scratch): pl., Pap. in *Stud.Ital.*12(1935).94 (iii A.D.); ψώρα ἀγρία, of a malignant kind, Lxx *Le.*21.20. 2. metaph., ψ. περὶ τὰς αἱρέσεις Gal.8.148. II. *a disease of trees, scab, Cladosporium herbarum*, esp. of fig-trees, when they are overgrown with moss, Thphr.*HP*4.14.3, etc.; also of the olive, Hp.*Nat.Mul.*79, *Mul.*2. 117; cf. λειχήν. III. *a moth*, = φάλαινα, Sch.Nic.*Th.*760. **-αγριάω**, *have malignant itch*, Lxx *Le.*22.22. **-ᾰλέος**, α, ον, *itchy, scabby, mangy*, ζῷα X.*Cyr.*1.4.11; βόες Longus 3.29. ⊕ **-ανθεμίς**, ίδος, ἡ, = λιβανωτίς, Ps.-Apul.*Herb.*80. **-άριος**, α, ον, = ψωραλέος, *Gloss.* ⊕ **-άω**, = ψωριάω, Pl.*Grg.*494c: ψωρᾶν Ἀττικοί, ψωριᾶν Ἕλληνες prob. in Moer. p.419P. **-ίᾰσις**, εως, ἡ, = ψώρα, in pl., Dsc.1.100, 3.5. **-ιάω**, *to have the itch, scab*, or *mange*, Hp.*Aph.*4.77, Plu.2. 126b; ψ. τὴν κύστιν Dsc.3.151, v.l. for ψωράω in Pl.*Grg.*494c; of dogs, *Gp.*19.3.2. II. of trees, *to be scabby, cankered*, esp. of the fig, Thphr.*CP*5.9.10, *HP*4.14.3, etc.; of κύμινον, ib.8.10. 1. **-ικός**, ή, όν, *of* or *belonging to the itch, scab*, or *mange*, ἐξανθήματα Plu.2.671a. II. ψωρικόν, τό (sc. φάρμακον, σμῆγμα), *itch-salve*, Dsc.5.99, Orib.14.24.5. 2. ψωρικά, τά (sc. νοσήματα), *cutaneous complaints*, Plu.2.732a. **-ίτης** [ῑ] λίθος, ὁ, = πῶρος I, Cyran.46.

**ψωροπέταλοι**· ἰχθύες εὐτελεῖς, Hsch.

⊕ **ψωρός**, ά, όν, *itchy, scabby, mangy*, ὁπλή Herod.7.117, cf. Lysim. ap.J.*Ap.*1.34: generally, *rough*, Dsc.5.121. II. **ψῶρος**· παιδεραστής, Hsch. III. ψῶρ' ἔχε Συρακόσιον is corrupt in Phryn. Com.26.

**ψωρ-οφθαλμία**, ἡ, *a disease of the eyes, excessive dryness attended with itching*, *PMed.Strassb.*p.6, Gal.14.766: pl., Dsc.1.68.5:—hence **-οφθαλμιάω**, Gal.12.799; and **-όφθαλμος**, ον, *a sufferer from blepharitis*, Id.12.798. **-ώδης**, ες, *of the nature of the itch, scabby*, Dsc.1.13, Ruf.ap.Orib.8.24.35, Antyll.ap.Orib.8.14.1, Gal.12.717, Lyd.*Ost.*33; ψ. ὀφθαλμοί *PSI*10.1180.99 (iii A.D.). **-ωσις**, εως, ἡ, = ψώρα, Lyd.*Ost.*35.

**ψῶσαι**· θάλψαι, Hsch.; perh. Cypr. for φῶσαι, φῶξαι.

**ψώσματα**· παρὰ Ἀριστωνύμῳ (*Fr.*9) πέπαικται ἡ λέξις τῇ Βοιωτῶν διαλέκτῳ, Hsch.

**ψωχὸς γῆ**· ψαμμώδης, Hsch. (sine accentu, cod. Phot.).

⊕ **ψώχω**, (ψώω) *rub small*, ψ. τοὺς στάχυας ταῖς χερσί *Ev.Luc.*6.1, cf. Dsc.5.159 (Pass.):—Med., Nic.*Th.*629, cf. κατα-σώχω.

***ψώω**, *rub, grind*, etc., only found in Gramm., as etym. of ψώχω, ψωχός, ψωμός, ψώρα, etc.

# Ω

**Ω**, ὦ, τό, twenty-fourth and last letter of the Ionic alphabet, ἀπὸ ἄλφα ἕως .ω. *Gloss.*iii 283 (ix A.D.); thence used as a symbol of *the end, the last*, ἐγώ εἰμι τὸ ἄλφα καὶ τὸ ὦ (not τὸ ὦ μέγα) *Apoc.*1.8, al.:—as a numeral ω' = 800, but ͵ω = 800,000. The epichoric Att. and other alphabets of the Inscrr. had used ο indifferently to represent the sounds of the later ο and ω: Ω is a differentiated form of ο, and, though usu. = ω, was used in the Ionic islands of Paros, Thasos, and Siphnos with the value ο, while O or Θ represented the sound ω. The name of the letter was τὸ ὦ (perispom. acc. to Hellad.ap.Phot.p.530 B.), cf. Achae.33.3, Pl.*Phdr.*244d, *Cra.* 420b, *Tht.*203c: after the loss of the distinction betw. long and short vowels, ο and ω had the same pronunciation; they begin to be confused in Papyri of iii B.C. (οἰκωνόμου *PRev.Laws*50.22 (iii B.C.)), but the name ω μέγα appears first in later Greek, Theognost.*Can.* 13; κατὰ σχῆμα διπλοῦ ω̄ ἤτοι μεγάλου Eust.869.26; οἱ δὲ περὶ Ἀρίσταρχον αὐτὸ τὸ ποτήριον ω̄ μέγα εἶναί φασιν, ὁποῖον ἴσως τὸ κατὰ δύο ῡ ἐσχηματισμένον Id.869.29; ἐν τῷ ω̄ μεγάλῳ under *omega* (in a lexicon), Id.1828.49; διὰ τοῦ ω̄ μεγάλου Hdn.*Epim.*208.

⊕ **ὦ** and **ὤ**, an exclamation, expressing surprise, joy, or pain, *O! oh!* with nom., ὦ τάλας ἐγώ S.*Aj.*981, etc.; ὢ ἔθενος, ὢ χρυσός Theoc.15.123: also c. gen., ὢ τῆς ἀναισχυντίας Luc.*Pisc.*5; with interrog., ὤ, τί λέγεις; Pl.*Prt.*309d; in the middle of a sentence, E.*Hipp.*362 (lyr.), al. II. with voc., a mode of address, whether at the beginning of a sentence or in a parenthesis, ὦ Ἀχιλεῦ Il.1.74, etc., esp. in dialogue and Oratt., ἐβουλόμην, ὦ ἄνδρες, τὴν δύναμιν κτλ. Antipho.5.1; in invocations of the gods, ὦ Ζεῦ τε καὶ Γῆ καὶ πολισσοῦχοι θεοί A.*Th.*69, etc.; with imper., ὦ χαῖρε Id.*Ag.*22, S.*Aj.* 91; ὦ πρὸς θεῶν ὕπεικε ib.371, cf. D.21.98: sts. following the Verb, E.*Tr.*335 (lyr.); in different number from the voc., προσέλθετ', ὦ παῖ, πατρί S.*OC*1104, cf. 1112, Sch.Ar.*Pl.*66. 2. with nom. instead of voc., ὦ δῖος αἰθήρ, ὦ φίλος, A.*Pr.*88, 545; ὦ γενναῖος Pl. *Phdr.*227c; ὦ οὗτος Αἴας S.*Aj.*89; ὦ οὗτος οὗτος Οἰδίπους Id.*OC* 1627; also οὗτος, ὦ σέ τοι (sc. καλῶ) Ar.*Av.*274. 3. with both together, φίλος ὦ Μενέλαε Il.4.189; ὦ τλάμων πάτερ S.*Aj.*641 (lyr., τλᾶμον codd. rec., edd.). 4. with the latter of two nouns, Ἀγάμεμνον, ὦ Μενέλαε Id.*Ph.*794.—In the first sense usu. written ὤ, in the second ὦ: [τὸ ὢ] ἡνίκα θαυμαστικὸν λαμβάνεται βαρύνεται, καὶ χωρεῖ εἰς ἐπιρρηματικὴν σύνταξιν, οἷον ὢ Ἡρακλῆς *EM*79.13: Thom.Mag. p.408 R. prescribes ὢ with the gen., but ὦ with the voc., e.g. ὦ Ἡράκλεις, where the whole expression, and not merely the ὤ (ὦ), expresses surprise (but A.D.*Adv.*127.24 seems to imply ὦ in both senses); ὤ as an exclam. is found in forms like ὤ μοι, ὤ μοι ἐγώ, ὢ πρὸς τῶν θεῶν D. l. c.: but ὢ πόποι δυσὶ τόνοις χρῆται Hdn.Gr.1. 503, so that ὦ πόποι is improbable, cf. Theognost.*Can.*158 (as emended by Lehrs *Aristarch.*³p.119); ᾤμοι and ὤμοι are both recognized by *EM*822.33, cf. *Lex.Mess.*p.413; ωιμ' Sapph.*Supp.*23.4; in E., when it stands in the middle of a sentence, it shd. be written ὤ. *Hipp.*362, al.: sts. doubled, ὢ ὢ κακά A.*Ag.*1214; ἰὼ ὢ ὤ S.*OC* 224 (v.l. ὢ ὢ ὤ); written ὠώ in Pap. of S.*Ichn.*61; tripled, ὢ ὢ ὤ A.*Pers.*985 (lyr., prob.). To those who (like D.T.640.11, cf. Sch. D.T.p.257 H.) took ὦ for the voc. of the Art. ὁ, A.D.*Synt.*45.22–53 replies at length.

⊕ **ὧ**, Dor. for ὡς, A.D.*Pron.*48.27, *Synt.*156.22, al. II. Dor. for ὅθεν, *Leg.Gort.*10.36, *SIG*47.21 (Locris, v B.C.), Theoc.3.11, al.; ὢ τοὶ λίθοι.. (*from which* the stones..) shd. be read in *IG*4.823.66, cf. 33 (Troezen, iv B.C.): formed like Dor. ϝοίκω = οἴκοθεν.

**ὧ**, Dor. for ὧδε, *hither*, φέρ' ὧ τὰν σκύλακα Sophr. in *Stud.Ital.* 10.123.

⊕ **ᾦα** (A), ἡ, = μηλωτή, *sheepskin*, Hermipp.57 (anap.), cf. Poll.10. 181, Hsch.; στέγασμα, εἴ τι βόλεστε, ἀποπέμψαι ἢ ὤας ἢ διφθέρας ὡς εὐτελεστάτας καὶ μὴ σισυρωτάς *SIG*1259 (Athens, iv B.C.). 2. *garment of this material*, a sort of *drawers* or *apron*, used by bathers, περιζωσάμενος ᾤαν λουτρίδα, κατάδεσμον ἥβης Theopomp.Com.37;

ᾠαν λούμενος (Bentl. for λουμένῳ) προζώννυται Pherecr.62; worn at certain sacred rites, Hermipp.53 (anap.). **II.** = ὄα (B).1, *border* or *fringe of a garment*, = τὸ κράσπεδον τοῦ ἱματίου, Ar.ap.*Lex.Mess.* p.411 (σὺν τῷ ι, but Phot. and Eust. cite (*Fr.*228) the same play for ὀαὶ τῶν ἱματίων); τὴν ᾠαν τοῦ ἐνδύματος Lxx *Ps.*132(133).2, cf. Gal.18(1).776, dub. cj. in Aen.Tact.31.23 (bis); ᾠαν ἔχον κύκλῳ τοῦ περιστομίου, ἔργον ὑφάντου, ἵνα μὴ ῥαγῇ Lxx *Ex.*28.28, cf. 36.31; Eust. speaks of the χρυσῆ ᾠα of Odysseus, 1828.53. **2.** generally, *edge*, ἐς τὰν ἄνω ὠίαν τᾶς πέτρας *GDI*5075.59 (Crete); ἡ ὤα τοῦ ἄντρου τῆς μεγάλης πέτρας ἦν τὸ μεσαίτατον Longus 1.4; τὰν βωίαν (i.e. ϝωίαν) Ὀρυκόππαν *GDI*5024*A*24 (Crete); στεφάνυσι [δέ] ἑκατ' ὤιαν ἐκόσμιον *summit*, dub. in Corinn.*Supp.*1.26.—Gramm. vary in spelling, ὄα Poll.7.62, Hdn.Gr.2.271; ὄα and ᾠα Hsch.; ᾦα Theognost.*Can.*106; ὦα Eust. (v. supr.), quoting Ael.Dion.*Fr.*266 (whose lexicon gave both ὄα and ᾦα) and an anonymous lexicon which gave ὀαὶ ἱματίων (ὀξυτόνως καὶ συνεσταλμένως, = Ar.*Fr.*228): *SIG*1259 (v. supr.) is by a half-educated writer: Eust. considers ᾠα to be contr. from οἰέη or ὀΐα, 877.53, 1828.51.

**ὤα** (B), v. ὠβά, cf. οἴη (A).

**ὠαιαί**, exclam. of pain, A.D.*Adv.*127.31; also ᾠαι Aeol. for ὠαιαί ib.128.2, cf. Theoc.30.1, *Lex.Mess.*p.412 (σὺν τῷ ι).

**ᾠάριον** [ᾰ], τό, Dim. of ᾠόν, *small egg*, Ephipp.24, Anaxandr.77, *BGU*781$^{v}$6: ὠάρια σιδηρᾶ Hsch. s.v. κυάθους.

**Ὠᾰρίων, Ὠᾰριώνειος**, v. sub Ὠρίων.

**ὦας**, τό, Dor. for οὖας, οὖς, *ear*, Sophr. in *Stud.Ital.*10.123, cf. Hdn.Gr.2.921; **ὤατα** and **ὤασιν** are cited by Hsch.:—hence seems to be formed the fut. **ὠᾰτωθήσω**, = ἀκούσομαι, Id., Phot.; **ὠατοθησῶ** Suid.; Dor. word, acc. to Phot. and Suid.

**ὤατον**, τό, *vat, tub*, Hero *Stereom.*2.21.

**ὠβ-ά**, ἡ, in Laconia, a local division of the Spartan people, *IG*5(1).26.11 (ii/i B.C.), 27.18; οἱ νικάσαντες τὰς ὠβάς ib.675, al.; ὠ. Λιμναέων ib.688; ὠβὰς ὠβάξαι Plu.*Lyc.*6:—cf. οὐαί· φυλαί, Hsch. (οὐᾷ (dat.) shd. perh. be read in an Inscr. from Orcistus, cf. *JHS* 57.247 (iii A.D.)) (prob. Cypr. or Thess.); ὤας· τὰς κώμας, Hsch. (β represents the digamma, cf. **ὠγή**· κώμη, Id.) **-άζω**, *divide the people into* ὠβαί, v. foreg.

**ὠβάλλετο**· διωθεῖτο, Hsch. **ὠβάτας**· τοὺς φυλέτας, Id. (ὠβάτους cod.); cf. ὠβά.

**ὤβεον**, τό, (i.e. ὤϝεον) *egg*, and **ὠβεοκόπτης**, ου, ὁ, *egg-breaker*, name of a species of snake, Hsch.

**ὦβος**, ὁ, dub. sens. in δὴς [i.e. δὶς] δεκάδας δ' ἐτέων πλήσας κεῖμαι τῶδ' ὑπὸ ὤβῳ Keil-Premerstein *Zweiter Bericht* No.145 (near Thyatira, ca. i B.C.); cf. ὦβοι· τόποι μεγαλομερεῖς, Hsch. (sed leg. ὠβαί).

**ὤβρατο**· εἵμαρτο, Hsch. (Perh. cf. ὁμείρομαι.)

**ὤγᾰνον**, τό, = κνημίς II, *AB*318, Hsch.

**Ωγενος**, ὁ, = Ὠκεανός, Lyc.231, St.Byz., etc.; **Ὠγηνός** Pherecyd. Syr.*Fr.*2 D.; **Ὠγήν**, ῆνος, Hsch.:—hence **Ὠγενίδαι** = Ὠκεανίδαι, Id.; and **ὠγένιος**, α, ον, = ἀρχαῖος, ὠ. Στυγὸς ὕδωρ Parth.*Fr.*7, cf. ὠγένιον· παλαιόν, Hsch.

**ὠγή**, v. ὠβά; also expld. by φάλαγγος τὸ ἔσχατον, καὶ τὸ ἄκρον (i.e. ᾠα), Hsch.

**ὠγμός**, ὁ, (ὤζω) *a crying oh!* Hsch., cf. A.*Eu.*123,126.

**Ὠγῠγία**, ἡ, *Ogygia*, a mythical island in the Mediterranean, the abode of Calypso, Od.1.85 (written **Ὠγυλίη** by Antim., Sch. l.c.). **II.** epith.(?) of *Egypt*, Eust.ad D.P.239. **III.** of *Attica* and *Boeotia*, St.Byz. **IV.** an island west of Britain in which Kronos was imprisoned, Plu.2.941a.

⊛ **Ὠγύγιος** [ῠ], α, ον, A.*Th.*321 (lyr.), but in Trag. mostly ος, ον:—*Ogygian, of* or *from Ogyges*, a mythical king of Attica: hence generally, *primeval, primal*, Στυγὸς ὕδωρ Hes.*Th.*806; ὠ. πῦρ Emp. 84.7; Φλιοῦντος ὑπ' ὠγυγίοις ὄρεσιν Pi.*N.*6.44 (ὠγυγίοι' Bgk.); τὰς ὠ. Θήβας A.*Pers.*37 (anap.), cf. S.*OC*1770 (anap.); τὰς ὠ. Ἀθάνας A.*Pers.*975 (lyr.), cf. *Th.*l.c.; γᾶς ὑπο κεύθεσιν ὠ. Id.*Eu.*1036 (lyr.); σὲ..τόδ' ἐλήλυθεν πᾶν κράτος ὠγύγιον *from earliest ages*, S.*Ph.*142 (lyr.). **2.** *gigantic*, Hld.10.25.

**ᾠδάριον** [ᾰ], τό, Dim. of ᾠδή, Arr.*Epict.*3.23.21, Longin.41.2, Petron.53.

⊛ **ὧδε**, Att. also **ὡδί** (q.v.), demonstr. Adv. of ὅδε: **I.** of Manner, *in this wise, thus*, sts. *so very, so exceedingly*, freq. from Hom. downwards: in Hom. usu. before the Verb, but after it in Il.1.181,574, 10.91, 18.392; Pl. and X. mostly place it after the Verb:—in construction ὧδε is answered by ὡς, *so...*, as.., Il.3.300, Od.19.312: answering ὥς περ, Il.6.478, cf. S.*OT*276, etc.: folld. by a relat., τίς ὧδε τλησικάρδιος, ὅτῳ..; A.*Pr.*160 (lyr.); by εἰ, δοκῶ μοι ὧδε ἂν μᾶλλον πιθέσθαι σοι, εἴ μοι δείξειας.. Pl.*Cra.*391a; εἰ φρονῶν ἔπρασσον, οὐδ' ἂν ὧδ' ἐγιγνόμην κακός S.*OC*272: c. part., δύαις τε καμφθεὶς ὧδε δεσμὰ φυγγάνω A.*Pr.*513: ὧδέ πως is freq. in Att., Pl.*R.*393d, X.*Mem.* 2.1.21, etc.; also in later Prose, Luc.*Herm.*32, etc. **2.** of a State or Condition, *as it is*, πρόμολ' ὧ. come forth *just as thou art*, Il.18.392, cf. Od.1.182, 2.28 (rightly so taken by Aristarch.ap.Sch.A Il.2.271, cf. Sch.A Il.18.392: v. infr. II); στρεύγεσθαι ὧδ' αὔτως Il.15.513, cf. 10.91. **3.** of something following, *thus, as follows*, esp. to introduce quoted words, Il.1.181 (where it follows the verb), Od.2.111, Hes. *Op.*203, etc.; ὧδ' ἠμείψατο S.*Ph.*378: sts. referring to what goes before, Hdt.5.2. **4.** pleon., τόσον ὧδ' ἐβόησας Od.9.403; ὧδε..τῇδε S.*El.*1301. **5.** c. gen., γένους μὲν ἥκεις ὧ. τοῖσδε (where ἥκεις = προσήκεις) E.*Heracl.*213. **II.** of Place, *hither*, cf. ὅδε I: Aristarch. denied this usage in Hom. altogether (cf. Sch.A Il.2.271, Apollon.*Lex.* s.v. ὧδε, A.D.*Adv.*178.25, Eust.792.2, al.); and most of the passages taken in this sense may be referred to signf. I.1 or 2, *just as you see*, v. supr. I.2: but *hither* seems prob. in Od.17.544, Il.12.346, 10.537: examples of ὧδε, *hither*, are found in Trag. (esp. in S., as *OT*7,144,298, *OC*182 (lyr.), 841 (lyr.), 1206,1547, *Tr.*402); also in Com., as ἴτω τις ὧ. Ar.*Av.*229 (lyr.); and later, as Herod.1.49; χιλίας ὧ. καὶ χιλίας ὧδ' ἐμβαλεῖν Id.5.48; ὧ. χὦδε χασκεύσῃ Id.4.42; ὧδε καὶ ὧδε *this way* and *that*, *AP*5.128 (Autom.): προσάγαγε ὧ. τὸν υἱόν σου *Ev.Luc.*9.41. **2.** *here*, Herod.2.98; εἰσὶν ὧ. πρὸς ἡμᾶς they are *here* with us, *Ev.Marc.*6.3; ὧ. κἀκεῖ Plu. 2.34a, cf. *Ev.Marc.*13.21: τηνεῖ δρύες, ὧδε (v.l. ἠδὲ) κύπειρος Theoc. 1.106, cf. 120,121: so Cratin.54 (anap.) acc. to Phot. (but v. Kock).

**ὥδεθεν**, Adv. *from this neighbourhood*, ὀνηλάτας μισθώσασθαι *PCair.Zen.*164.2 (iii B.C.).

**Ὠιδεῖον**, τό, *the Odeum*, a public building at Athens built by Pericles *for musical performances* (ᾠδαί), having an orchestra, And. 1.38, *IG*2$^{2}$.1688.3, Eup.18 D.; and other apparatus of a theatre, Paus. 1.8.6, 1.14.1; used as a law-court, Ar.*V.*1109 (troch., cf. Sch.), D.59. 52; for philos. disputations, Alex.25.2, D.L.7.184, Plu.2.605a; for soldiers' quarters, X.*HG*2.4.9,24; as a place for distributing corn, D.34.37: it seems to have been circular, with a peaked roof, whence the line of Cratin.71, ὁ σχινοκέφαλος Ζεὺς ὁδὶ προσέρχεται ὁ Περικλέης, τᾠδεῖον ἐπὶ τοῦ κρανίου ἔχων, cf. Plu.*Per.*13, Thphr. *Char.*3.4: rebuilt, after having been burnt, by Ariobarzanes, App. *Mith.*38. **2.** of other *music-halls*, as that at Athens, built by Herodes Atticus, Paus.7.20.6; at Corinth, Id.2.3.6; at Patrae, Id.7. 20.6; at Patara, *Epigr.Gr.*412; at Samos, *GDI*5702.41 (iv B.C.); at Rome, built by Hadrian, D.C.69.4; θεατροειδὲς ᾠ. *CIG*4614 (Palestine).

**ᾠδή**, ἡ, contr. for ἀοιδή, *song, lay, ode*, *h.Ap.*20, *h.Cer.*494; in Trag. (exc. that A. uses only ἀοιδή (q.v.)), of dirges, πολλὰς θρήνων ᾠδάς S.*El.*88 (anap.); ὀξυτόνους ᾠ. θρηνήσει Id.*Aj.*631 (lyr.); ᾠδὰ ἐπικήδειος E.*Tr.*514 (lyr.); but also of *joyful songs, songs of praise*, καλλίνικος Id.*El.*865 (lyr.); ἴακχος Id.*Cyc.*69 (lyr.); λύπας πολυχόρδοις ᾠ. παύειν Id.*Med.*197 (anap.); ᾠδὰς ὑστέροισι θήσετε Id.*Supp.*1225; χαίροντες ᾠδῆς..μέλεσιν Ar.*Ra.*244 (lyr.); ὑμεναίοις καὶ νυμφιδίοισι δέχεσθ' ᾠ. Id.*Av.*1729 (lyr.): freq. in Pl., ᾠ. κιθαρῳδική *Lg.*722d; κιθαρίζειν πρὸς τὴν ᾠ. *Alc.*1.108a; ᾠδαὶ καὶ ἡ ἄλλη ποίησις *lyric poetry* and.., *Phdr.*245a; ἐν ταῖς ᾠδαῖς καὶ μέλεσιν *R.*399c, cf. 398c; opp. λέξις, *Lg.*816d; ἐν ᾠδαῖς καὶ μύθοις καὶ λόγοις ib.664a; of poems such as those of Stesichorus on Helen, Isoc.10.64; of the various songs associated with particular employments or conditions, Clearch.37, cf. Eust.1164.10, 1236.60. **2.** = ἐπῳδός, *magic song, spell*, Longus 2.7. **3.** meton. for χορδή, Τέρπανδρος..δέκα ζεῦξε Μοῦσαν ἐν ᾠδαῖς Tim.*Pers.*238. **II.** *singing*, Plu.*Crass.*33, etc.; of birds, Arist.*HA*613$^{b}$24.

**ὡδί** [ῑ], Att. strengthd. form of ὧδε, ὠ. κεχηνώς Ar.*Pax*57, cf. *Nu.*690, Pl.*Prt.*353c, *Grg.*477c, al., Plot.6.4.8; never in Trag.

**ᾠδικός**, ή, όν, *musical*, as Subst., *musician*, Ar.*Fr.*8 D., Arist.*EE* 1238$^{a}$36, etc.; opp. ῥητορικός, Plu.2.622a; opp. ὀρχηστικός, Theopomp.Hist.111(*a*); of animals, opp. ἄνῳδος, Arist.*HA*488$^{a}$34; ᾠδικώτερος κύκνων Luc.*Tim.*47, cf. *DMar.*1.5 (Comp.), *Electr.*4; ὄρνιθες τῶν ᾠδικῶν Ael.*VH*14.30. Adv. **-κῶς** Ar.*V.*1239, Pl.Com.8 D.: Comp. **-ώτερον** Luc.*Sat.*4.

**ὠδίν**, ἡ, v. ὠδίς.

⊛ **ὠδῑνολύτης** [ῠ], ου, ὁ, *setting free from pain*, name of a kind of shell-fish, Plin.*HN*32.6.

⊛ **ὠδίνω** [ῑ], used by early writers only in pres.: fut. ὠδῑνήσω Lxx *Hb.*3.10: aor. ὤδῑνα *AP*7.561 (Jul.Aeg.), Opp.*C.*1.5, Jul.*Or.*2.56d; ὠδίνησα Lxx *Ps.*7.15:—so aor. Med. and Pass., ὠδινησάμην, -ήθην, Aq.*Ps.*113(114).7, *Pr.*8.25:—*to have the pains of childbirth, be in travail*, ὡς δ' ὅταν ὠδίνουσαν ἔχῃ βέλος ὀξὺ γυναῖκα Il.11.269; ὠδίνειν τρομέω· χαλεπὸν βέλος Εἰλειθυίας Theoc.27.29, cf. Ar.*Th.*502, *Ec.*529, Hp.*Epid.*5.25, Pl.*R.*395e, etc. **2.** c. acc., *to be in travail of* a child, *bring forth*, E.*IA*1234, Lxx *Ca.*8.5: of animals, ὠ. νεοττούς Ael.*NA* 2.46: prov., ὤδινεν ὄρος Luc.*Hist.Conscr.*23. **II.** metaph. of any great pain, *to be in travail* or *anguish*, of the Cyclops, στενάχων τε καὶ ὠδίνων ὀδύνῃσι Od.9.415; Κύπριδι *AP*7.30 (Antip.Sid.); *labour painfully*, ὠδίνουσι μέλισσαι ib.9.363.22 (Mel. (?)); of the mind, *to be in the throes* or *agonies of thought*, Pl.*Tht.*148e, al.; κυοῦμέν τε καὶ ὠ. περὶ ἐπιστήμης ib.210b; ὑπὲρ δισσῶν μίαν ὠδίνειν ψυχήν E.*Hipp.* 258 (anap.); ὥστε μ' ὠδίνειν τί φῄς what you mean, S.*Aj.*794, cf. E.*Heracl.*644; ὠδίνειν εἴς τι *to long painfully* for a thing, Hld.5. 32: c. inf., Id.2.21, Him.*Ecl.*13.38, *Or.*4.1: c. acc., Hld.10.31; ἔξοδον Chor.42.20 p.517 F.-R. **b.** *worry, fuss*, ὠδίνοντα μήποτε λήγειν περὶ τοῦ σώματος Pl.*R.*407c. **2.** c. acc., *to be in travail with*, συμφορᾶς βάρος S.*Tr.*325; τὴν καύχησιν τὴν σοφιστικήν Epicur.*Fr.* 93, cf. *AP*9.578 (Leo Phil.) (where ὧν is in the case of the anteced. by attraction). **3.** Causal, *cause to quiver*, as in travail, φωνὴ βροντῆς ὠδίνησε γῆν Lxx *Si.*43.17(18) cod.Alex.

⊛ **ὠδίς** (A.*Ch.*211, Pl.*Ep.*313a), ῖνος, ἡ: Ep. dat. pl. ὠδίνεσσι *h.Ap.* 92, Theoc.17.61, etc.: later nom. **ὠδίν** Lxx *Is.*37.3, 1*Ep.Thess.*5.3:—mostly in pl., *pangs* or *throes of childbirth*, πικρὰς ὠδῖνας ἔχουσαι Il. 11.271; τέκε..ἐν μόναις ὠδῖσιν..διδύμων σθένος υἱῶν at a single *birth*, Pi.*P.*9.85; πόνους ἐνεγκοῦσ' ἐν ὠδῖσι E.*Supp.*920 (lyr.); ἐν ὠδίνων λοχίαις ἀνάγκαισι Id.*Ba.*89 (lyr.), cf. *Ion* 452 (lyr.); αἱ δι' ὠδίνων γοναί Id.*Ph.*355: also in sg., Pi.*O.*6.43, *N.*1.36, S.*OC*533 (lyr.); γυνὴ φεύγει πικρὰν ὠδῖνα παίδων Id.*Fr.*932. **2.** in sg. also, *that which is born amid throes, child*, παῖδα, φιλτάτην ἐμοὶ ὠδῖνα A.*Ag.*

1418, cf. Pi.*O.*6.31, E.*Ion* 45; θαλλὸν ἱερὸν ἐλαίας, Λατοῦς ὠδῖνα (fort. ὠδῖνι) φίλαν Id.*IT*1102 (lyr.); ἄπτερον ὠδῖνα τέκνων, of young birds, Id.*HF*1040: pl., *children*, *AP*7.549 (Leon.Alex.); ὀρταλίχων ἁπαλὴ ὠδίς, of eggs, Nic.*Al.*165; τοῦ ᾠοῦ ἐν ὠδῖνι ὄντος Arist.*HA*560b22; ὠ. Θαλάσσας, of Aphrodite, *AP*9.386; ὠδὶς μελίσσης, of honey, Nonn.*D.*5.228, al. II. metaph., *travail, anguish*, A.*Ch.*211, *Supp.*770 (both sg.): also in pl., of love, ἐμοὶ πικρὰς ὠδῖνας αὐτοῦ προσβαλὼν ἀποίχεται S.*Tr.*42, cf. Pl.*R.*574a, *Phdr.*251e: freq. in Lxx, *Ex.*15.14, al., *Ev.Matt.*24.8. 2. *fruit of* the mind's *travail*, τῆς ἐμῆς ὠ. Luc.*Dem.Enc.*25; λόγων ὠδῖνες Him. *Or.*18.3; ἐπέων Tryph.117. 3. ὠδῖνες θανάτου, ᾅδου, the *bonds* of death, Lxx 2*Ki.*22.6, *Ps.*17(18).5,6 (due to confusion of Heb. *ḥēbel* 'pang' with *ḥěbel* 'cord'), cf. *Act.Ap.*2.24.

**ὠδόν**· οὐδόν, Hsch. (-ῶν..-ῶν cod.: Dor. form of ὀδ[ϝ]ός; cf. οὐδός).

**ᾠδοποιός**, όν, *making songs* or *odes*, Theoc.*Epigr.*17.4.

**ᾠδός**, ὁ (and in Paus.10.5.12, ἡ), contr. for ἀοιδός, *singer*, χρησμῶν E.*Heracl.*488, cf. Phld.*Mus.*p.20 K., etc.; μετὰ Λέσβιον ᾠδόν, prov. of a second-rate musician, Cratin.243, cf. Arist.*Fr.*545; οἱ τοῦ Διονύσου ᾠ. Pl.*Lg.*812b; χορούς τινας..ᾠδούς ib.800e; of cicadae, οἱ ὑπὲρ κεφαλῆς ᾠ. Id.*Phdr.*262d, cf. *AP*6.54 (Paul.Sil.); τὸν ἀλεκτρυόνα τὸν ᾠδὸν ἀποπνίξασά μου Pl.Com.14 D.; ὑπὸ τὸν ᾠδὸν ὄρνιθα about cockcrow, Poll.1.71. II. *the cup passed round when a scolion was sung*, Antiph.85.2, cf. Trypho ap.Ath.11.503d.

**ὠδόσα**· ἐκ τοῦ ὧδε μέρους, Hsch.

**ὠδύσίη** and **ὤδυσις**, εως, ἡ, *anger, wrath*, Hsch.; cf. *ὀδύσσομαι.

**ὠδώδει**, poet. for ὀδώδει, 3 sg. plpf. of ὄζω. **ᾠειδής**, f.l. for φοειδής, D.S.32.10.

**ᾤεον**, τό, v. ᾠόν.

**ὤζω**, *cry oh!* A.*Eu.*124, Ar.*V.*1526 (lyr.). (Fr. ὤ, as οἴζω fr. οἴ.)

**ὠή**, a cry or call, *holla!* A.*Eu.*94, E.*Cyc.*51 (lyr.), al., and once in Prose, X.*Cyn.*6.19.

❀ **ὠθ-έω**, Att. impf. ἐώθουν Ar.*Pax*637 (troch.), D.9.65, (ἐξ-) Th. 7.52, etc., and ἐώθει even in *h.Merc.*305; Ion. and Ep. 3 sg. ὤθει Il.21.241; Ion. ὤθεσκε Od.11.596: but ὤθει E.*IT*1395 is f.l. for ὠθεῖ (Kirchhoff): fut. ὠθήσω Id.*Cyc.*592, Ar.*Ec.*300 (lyr.), (ἐξ-) S.*Aj.*1248; but ὤσω E.*Med.*379, *Andr.*344, and always in Prose; ἀπ-ώσω Od.15.280, Ep. inf. ἀπ-ωσέμεν Il.13.367: Att. aor. ἔωσα Pl.*Ti.*60c, etc., (ἐξ-) S.*OC*1296,1330, etc.; Ion. and Ep. ὦσα Il.1. 220, Hdt.7.167, Ep. ὤσασκε Od.11.599; but ἔωσα Il.16.410, (ἀπ-) Od.9.81; later ὤθησα Ael.*NA*13.17, etc.: pf. ἔωκα (ἐξ-) Plu.2. 48c: plpf. ἐῴκει (ἐξ-) Id.*Brut.*42:—Med., fut. ὤσομαι (ἀπ-) S.*El.*944, etc., (δι-) A.*Fr.*199.9, etc.:—Att. aor. ἐωσάμην Th.4.43, Ar.*V.*1085 (troch., with vv.ll.); Ion. and Ep. ὠσάμην Il.16.592, Hdt.9.25, v.l. in Ar.*V.* l.c.:—Pass., fut. ὠσθήσομαι E.*Med.*335 (v.l. ὠθήσομαι), (ἐξ-) D.24.61: Att. aor. ἐώσθην (ἐξ-) X.*HG*2.4.34, etc.; later ὤσθην (ἐξ-) Arr.*An.*4.25.3, Plot.4.4.45: Att. pf. ἔωσμαι X.*Cyr.*7. 1.36, (ἀπ-, περι-) Th.2.39, 3.57; Ion. part. ἀπωσμένος Hdt.5.69:—*thrust, push*, I. mostly of human force, as of Sisyphus, σκηριπτόμενος χερσίν τε ποσίν τε λᾶαν ἄνω ὤθεσκε ποτὶ λόφον *he kept pushing it*.., Od.11.596, cf. 599; ἀπὸ εἷο τράπεζαν ὦσε ποδὶ πλήξας 22.20; [ἔγχος] ὑπὲκ δίφροιο *pushed* it away from.., Il.5.854; ἂψ ἐς κουλεὸν ὦσε ξίφος 1.220; τοῖσι δ' ἀπ' ὀφθαλμῶν νέφος ἀχλύος ὦσεν Ἀθήνη 15.668; τὸν δὲ Ζεὺς ὦσεν ὄπισθε χειρί ib.694, cf. 13.193; ὦσαί [τινα] ἀφ' ἵππων 5.19; ἀφ' ἵππων χαμᾶζε ib.835, etc.; so ὦσαι ἑωυτὸν ἐς τὸ πῦρ *rush* into the fire, Hdt.7.167; ὠ. τινα ἐπὶ κεφαλήν *throw* him headlong down, Pl.*R.*553b (Pass., ὠθέεσθαι ἐπὶ κ. Hdt.7.136); ὠ. τινα ἐπὶ τράχηλον Luc.*DMort.*27.1; πετρῶν ὦσαι κάτω E.*Cyc.* 448, cf. Pl.*Phdr.*229c; εἰς λιθοτομίας D.53.17: freq. of weapons, ὠ. ξίφος δι' ἀμφοτέρων *thrust* it through both, Hdt.3.78; τεκούσης ἐς σφαγὰς ὦσαι ξίφος E.*Or.*291; διὰ μέσου αὐχένος ὠθεῖ σίδηρον Id.*Ph.* 1458; φάσγανον δι' ἥπατος Id.*Med.*379; ξίφος πρὸς ἧπαρ Id.*Hel.*983; δαλοῦ κώπην ἔσω βλεφάρων Id.*Cyc.*485 (anap.), cf. 636; ἐκ μηροῦ δόρυ ὦσε θύραζε *forced* it out from the thigh, Il.5.694; τὸ ἱμάτιον ὦσαι εἰς τὸ στόμα *stuff* it into his mouth, Thphr.*Char.*2.4: τὴν θύραν ὠθεῖ *forces* the door, Ar.*V.*152, cf. Lys.1.24; πύλας E.*Or.*1562: sts. of other than human force, as of a stream, ὦσε δὲ νεκρούς Il.21.235, cf. 241; of the wind, Νότος μέγα κῦμα ποτὶ..ῥίον ὠθεῖ Od.3.295; [ὁ ποταμὸς] ὠθεῖ κῦμα Metagen.6.3; ὠ. κολόκυμα Ar.*Eq.*692: metaph., ἃ δ' ἀτέρα τὰν ἀτέραν κύλιξ ὠθήτω Alc.41. 2. *force back* in battle, Il.8.336, 13.193, etc.; ἄνδρας προτὶ ἄστυ 16.45; v. infr. II. 3. *thrust out, banish*, ὠ. ἅπαντας τὸν ἀσεβῆ S.*OT*1382; ἔξω δόμων τε καὶ πάτρας ὠθεῖν τινα A.*Pr.*665; ἀπ' οἴκων S.*OT*241; ἐκ δόμων E.*Andr.*344; ἔξω τινὰ φυγάδα Pl.*R.*560d; σπονδῶν ἄπο, ἀπὸ τῶν ἱερῶν, E.*Ba.*46, Aeschin. 2.86; ὠ. τινας ἀθάπτους S.*Aj.*1307:—Pass., ὠθούμεθ' ἔξω Id.*Fr.*583. 7. 4. metaph., ὠ. τὰ πρήγματα *push* matters *on, hurry* them, Hdt.3.81; ἐπιθυμία ὠθεῖ ἐπὶ τὰς ἀπολαύσεις Arist.*VV*1250a24. 5. abs., ὦσα παρέξ *pushed off* from land, Od.9.488; ὠθεῖ βιαίως E.*Tr.* 356, cf. X.*HG*7.4.31; τὸ ὠθοῦν the *motive power*, Pl.*Cra.*401d. II. Med., mostly in aor., *thrust* or *push away from oneself, force back*, esp. in battle, freq. in Il., ὄφρα τάχιστα ὤσαιτ' Ἀργείους 5.691; τείχεος ἂψ ὤσασθαι 12.420; ὤσασθαι προτὶ Ἴλιον, προτὶ ἄστυ, 8.295, 16.655; τὴν ἵππον ὤσαντο Hdt.9.25, cf. 3.72, 6.37; ὤσασθαί τινας κατὰ βραχὺ Th.4.96; ὠσαμένω τὸ εὐώνυμον κέρας Id.6.70, etc.; once in Trag., E.*IT*326: of a horse, *throw* its rider, Thgn.260 (s.v.l.). 2. intrans., *push, press forward*, Th.4.11,35, Plu.*Ages.*32; ὠθεῖσθαι εἰς τὸ πρόσθεν X.*HG*7.1.31; πρὸς τὴν πληγὴν ὁμόσε ὠθεῖσθαι Pl.*Euthd.* 294d; εἰς χεῖρας ὠθεῖσθαι τοῖς ἐναντίοις Plu.*Thes.*5. III. Pass., *to be thrust, pushed*, or *forced, rush* or *fall violently*, ἐπὶ κεφαλὴν Hdt. (v. supr. I.1); πρὸς βίαν E.*Hec.*406; βίᾳ Id.*Med.*335, etc.; ἱδρῶτες ταχέως ὠθούμενοι Hp.*Aph.*7.85. 2. Med., *crowd, throng, jostle*, X.*Cyr.*3.3.64; ὠ. ὥσπερ ὕες Theoc.15.73, cf. Arist.*HA*572b25: impers. in Pass., ἐπὶ μέζον ὠθεῖται *the crush gets* worse, Herod.4. 54. **-ησις**, εως, ἡ, = ὠθισμός, Alex.Aphr.*Pr.*1.90.

**ὠθιακὰ** χρώματα, dub. sens. in Zos.Alch.p.245 B. (fort. ὠθυντικά).

❀ **ὠθ-ίζω**, = ὠθέω, *thrust, push*, or *push on*, Them.*Or.*24.304a. II. Med., *push against one another, jostle, struggle*, Luc.*Pisc.*42; εἰς τὴν προεδρίαν, πρὸς τὸ ἀδύνατον, Aristid.2.95 J., 1.388 J.: metaph., *wrangle*, Hdt.3.76. **-ισμός**, ὁ, *thrusting, pushing*, ἀσπίδων of shield against shield, Th.4.96. II. *jostling, struggling*, of combatants in a mêlée, Περσέων τε καὶ Λακεδαιμονίων ὠ. ἐγένετο πολλός Hdt.7.225; ἀπικέσθαι ἐς ὠ. to come to *close quarters*, Id.9. 62; ὠ. ἀμφὶ τὰ θύρετρα X.*An.*5.2.17; ὁ περὶ τὰς πύλας ὠ. καὶ πνιγμός Plb.4.58.9, cf. Anaxandr.33.7: metaph., ὠ. λόγων *dispute, altercation*, Hdt.8.78, 9.26.

**ὠΐα** or **ᾤα**, ἡ, v. ᾠά. **ὠΐδας**· τὰς μημ..οἰκίδας, Hsch.: also **ὠΐδας**· οὐδός, Id. (leg. ὠδός, Dor. for ὀδ[ϝ]ός, οὐδός). **ᾠέτο**, v. οἴομαι. **ᾠΐζω**, (ᾤιον, ᾠόν) *to sit on eggs, brood*, Id. (Fort. ᾠίζω [i.e. ᾠζω], cf. ἐπῴζω.) **ᾤξεν**, v. οἴγνυμι. **ᾤιον**, τό, v. ᾠόν. **ὤϊσχα**· ὑπήνεμα, and **ὠηρίχθαι**· ὑπήνεμοι, ὥριμοι, Id.

**ὦκα**, poet. Adv. of ὠκύς, *quickly, swiftly*, Il.1.402, 5.88, Od.6.317, etc.; strengthd., μάλ' ὦ. Il.2.52, Od.2.8, etc.; ὦ. μάλ' Il.17.190, al. 2. of Time, ὦ. δ' ἔπειτα *immediately*, Od.17.329, Il.18.527, al.:—Cleitorian (Arc.) word acc. to *AB*1096.

**ὠκᾰλέον**· ταχύ, ὀξύ, Hsch.

**Ὠκεάν-ειος** [ᾰ], ον, *of Ocean*, Gal.19.189, Porph.*Chr.*69, Sch. rec. A.*Pr.*300, Sch.E.*Hipp.*121, etc. (sts. incorrectly written ὠκεάνιος). **-ηΐας**, άδος, ἡ, Ep. fem. of Ὠκεάνειος, Nonn.*D.*32.53. ❀ **-ης**, ου, ὁ, an old name of *the Nile*, acc. to D.S.1.19; in 1.12 interpreted τροφὴ μήτηρ. **-ίνη** [ῑ], ἡ, *daughter of Ocean, Ocean nymph*, Hes. *Th.*364,389, etc. **-ίς**, ίδος, ἡ, = ὠκεανῖτις II, αὖραι Pi.*O.*2.71; νῆσος Phld.*Rh.*1.179 S. II. pl., Ὠ. Νύμφαι *Ocean* nymphs, Call. *Fr.*24a, Arg.A.*Pr.* **-ῖτις**, ιδος, ἡ, *daughter of Ocean*, Virg.*G.*4. 341. II. Adj. *of, in, from the Ocean*, Θούλη *AP*4.3b.8 (Agath.); ὠ. θάλασσα, = ὠκεανός II, D.H.1.3. 2. ἡ Ὠκ. (sc. γῆ) the *shore of Ocean*, Str.1.2.28.

**Ὠκεᾰνόβρῠτος**, ον, *copious as ocean*, γλῶσσα Olymp.Alch. p.83 B.

**Ὠκεᾰνόνδε**, Adv. *to Ocean*, *h.Merc.*68, *h.Hom.*31.16.

❀ **Ὠκεᾰνός**, οῦ, ὁ, *Oceanus*, son of Uranus and Gaia, Hes.*Th.* 133: wedded to Tethys, father of Thetis, Il.14.302, 18.399; and of all the Oceanids, Hes.*Th.*337 sqq., A.*Pr.*140 (anap.); god of the primeval water, and source of all smaller waters, Il.21.195 sqq., Hes.*Th.*368; Ὠκεανὸν θεῶν γένεσιν Il.14.201; ποταμοῖο ῥέεθρα Ὠκεανοῦ, ὅσπερ γένεσις πάντεσσι τέτυκται ib.246; conceived as a *great River* which compasses the earth's disc, returning into itself, ἀψόρροος Il.18.399, Od.20.65; represented as encircling the shield of Achilles, Il.18.607, cf. Hes.*Sc.*314; Ὠκεάνω γᾶς τ' ἀπὸ περράτων Alc.84; Ὠ. ἀκαλαρρείτης, βαθύρροος, βαθυρρείτης, Il.7.422, 21.195; ῥόος Ὠκεανοῖο, ῥοαὶ Ὠ., 16.151, 3.5 (so Ὠ., παγαί Pi.*Fr.*30.2; Ἴναχε νᾶτορ, παῖ τοῦ κρηνῶν πατρὸς Ὠκεανοῦ S.*Fr.*270 (anap.)); criticized by Hdt. οὐ τινα ἔγωγε οἶδα ποταμὸν Ὠ. ἐόντα 2.23, cf. 4.8, Str.1.1.7: but Ὠκεανὸς ὃν ταυρόκρανος ἀγκάλαις ἑλίσσων κυκλοῖ χθόνα E.*Or.*1377 (lyr.). II. later the name of *the great Outward Sea*, opp. to the Inward or Mediterranean (θάλασσα, πόντος), Hdt. ll. cc., Pi.*P.*4.26,251; τὴν Εὐρώπην καὶ τὴν Ἀσίαν καὶ τὴν Λιβύην νήσους εἶναι ἃς περιρρεῖν κύκλῳ τὸν Ὠκεανόν Theopomp.Hist.*Fr.*74(*a*), cf. Arist.*Mu.*393a17; Ὠ. ὁ βόρειος, ὁ ἑσπέριος, ὁ κατὰ μεσημβρίαν, Plu.*Mar.*11, *Ant.*61, D.S.17.96; Πρεττανικός, Γερμανικός, Καντάβριος, etc., Ptol.*Geog.*2.3.3, 2.3.4, 2. 6.3, al. III. metaph., ὠ. χρημάτων *oceans* of wealth, Lyd. *Mag.*3.62 (pl.); πραγμάτων ib.2.7. IV. ὠκεανέ *bravo!* in acclamations, *POxy.*41.4 (iii/iv A.D., ωκαιαναι and ωκαανai Pap.: an exaggeration of Νεῖλος similarly used, Jo.Chrys. περὶ κενοδοξίας cap.8 Schulte). V. Pythag. name for 9, *Theol.Ar.*57.

**ὠκήεις**, εσσα, εν, later poet. form of ὠκύς, τέρετρα *AP*6.205 (Leon.).

**ὠκίμινος** [ῐμ], η, ον, made of ὤκιμον, Dsc.1.49.

**ὠκῐμοειδής**, ές, *like* ὤκιμον, neut. as Adv., ὠκιμοειδὲς ὄδωδε Nic. *Al.*280. II. ὠκιμοειδές, τό, *catchfly, Silene gallica*, Dsc.4.28, Gal.12.158. 2. = χαμαιλέων μέλας, Dsc.3.9. 3. = κλινοπόδιον, ib.95. 4. = ἔρινος, *Campanula Erinos, small rampion*, Ps.-Dsc.4. 141.

**ὤκῐμ-ον**, τό, *basil, Ocimum Basilicum*, Stratt.66.5 (lyr., pl.), Eub.54, Thphr.*HP*1.6.6, al., Dsc.2.141, Gal.6.640, etc. **-ώδης**, ες, = ὠκιμοειδής I, *like basil*, φύλλον Thphr.*HP*7.7.2.

**ὤκῐνον**, τό, a fodder-plant, perhaps *clover* (= ὠκύθοος II), Lat. *ocinum*, Cato *RR*27,33 (cf. Plin.*HN*17.198), Varro *RR*1.31.

**ὠκίς**, ίδος, ἡ, = ἐνώτιον, *ear-ring*, Hsch.

**ὤκιστος**, old Sup. of ὠκύς (q. v.).

**ὠκύ-ᾰλος** [ῠ], ον, perh. *sea-swift, speeding o'er the sea*, epith. of a ship, Il.15.705, Od.12.182, 15.473, S.*Aj.*710 (lyr.), Mosch.2.60. 2. later, generally, *swift, violent*, ῥιπή Opp.*H.*2.535, cf. Pi.*Parth.*2.19. (It is doubtful whether -αλος comes from ἅλς; see opinions of D.H. and Hdn.Gr.ap.Sch.Il. l. c.) **-βόαι**· ταχυμάχαι, Hsch.; but ὦκα βοᾶς ἀκοὰν μεθέπων is correct in *AP*15.27 (Simm.*Ov.*). **-βόλος**, ον, *quick-shooting, quick-striking*, τόξα S.*Ph.*710 (lyr.); ἰοί *AP*6. 118 (Antip.); χεῖρες *APl.*4.195 (Satyr.); of the μελανάετος, Arist. *HA*618b29. **-γένεθλος**, ον, *quickly born* or *gendered*, εἰς τόκον ὠκυγένεθλον Jo.Gaz.*Ecphr.*2.59. **–δήκτωρ,** ορος, ὁ, *sharp-biting,* ῥίνη *AP*6.92 (Phil.). **–δίδακτος** [ῐ], ον, *quickly taught,* οἰωνός ib. 9.562 (Crin.). **–δίνητος** [ῑ], Dor. **–ᾱτος,** ον, *quick-whirling,* ἅμιλλαι Pi.*I*.5(4).6.

**ὠκυδρόμ-ας,** ου, ὁ, = ὠκύδρομος, Epigr.ap.Paus.6.13.10. **–έω,** *run swiftly,* Ph.1.560; πρὸς ἀρετήν ib.459. **–ος,** ον, *swift-running,* ἄελλαι E.*Ba.*872 (lyr.); σκύλακες Arion 1.8; [Ἐρινύες] ὠ. ὥστε νόημα Orph.*H.*69.9; νέων ὠ. ἥβη *Historia* 6.595 (Gortyn, ii B.C.): Sup. –ώτατος Ph.1.143,648, al.: Comp. –ώτερα 1.569.

**ὠκῠ-επής,** ές, *quick-speaking,* of Apollo, *AP*9.525.25. **–θοος,** α, ον, *swift-running,* Νύμφαι E.*Supp.*993 (dub. l., lyr.). **II.** *quick-growing,* τριπέτηλον Call.*Dian.*165; = τρίφυλλος, *clover,* Hsch. **–κέλευθος,** ον, *completing life's journey quickly, Supp.Epigr.*7.329 (Caesarea Philippi). **–λόχεια,** ἡ, *giving a quick birth,* of Artemis, Orph. *H.*2.4, 36.8; of Φύσις, ib.10.19. **–μάχος** [ᾰ], ον, *quick to fight, AP*6.132 (Nossis). **–μοιρος,** ον, = ὠκύμορος, *Epigr.Gr.*246.1 (Bithynia). **–μολος,** ον, *quick-going,* Suid. **–μορος,** ον, *quickly dying, dying early,* of Achilles, Il.1.417, 18.95,458; ὠκυμορώτατος ἄλλων 1.505; of the suitors, Od.1.266, al.; of φιτρός of Meleager, B.5.141; in Epitaphs, *Epigr.Gr.*527 (Beroea), 540 (Thrace), al.; so in later Prose, Ph.2.45; of flowers, Philostr.*Ep.*4: of things, *transient,* J.*AJ*11.3.6, Ph.1.478: neut. pl. as Adv., *Supp.Epigr.*6.501 (Isaura). **II.** Act., *bringing a quick* or *early death,* ἰοί Il.15.441, Od.22.75; φαρμάκων δυνάμεις Plu.*Ant.*71; κώνειον –ώτατον Id. *Dio* 58. **–νοος,** ον, *quickly marking,* Opp.*C.*1.37.

**ὠκύνω,** = ταχύνω, ὀξύνω, Hsch.

**ὠκῠ-πέδῑλος,** ον, *with swift sandals, swift-footed,* Nonn.*D.*8.220. **–πέτης,** ου, ὁ, *swift-flying, swift-running,* ἵππω ὠκυπέτα Il.8.42, 13.24; ἴρηξ Hes.*Op.*212: metaph., ὠ. μόρος S.*Tr.*1042 (lyr.):—also fem. Ὠκυπέτη, name of a Harpy, Hes.*Th.*267; and **ὠκυπέτεια** χελιδών, of a fish (cf. χελιδών II), Marc.Sid.17. **–πλᾰνος,** ον, *quick-wandering,* ὠ. πτερύγων ῥιπαῖς E.*Fr.*594.4 (anap., = Critias 18.4 D.). ❀ **–πλοος,** ον, *quick-sailing,* Hsch. s.v. ὁ ὠκύκλοος, Suid. **–πόδης,** ου, ὁ, poet. for ὠκύπους, δρόμος *AP*5.222 (Maced.); λαγωός 9.371: in Dor. form, **ὠκυπόδας** Ἄδραστος *E.Hyps.Fr.*1 ii 34 (lyr.). **–ποινος,** ον, *quickly avenged,* παρβασία A.*Th.*743 (lyr.). **–πομπος,** ον, *conveying rapidly,* of ships, δόρυ B.16.90; ναῦς E.*IT*1137 (lyr.); πλᾶται ib.1427. **–πορέω,** *move quickly,* Str.8.3.29; of a ship, *Epigr.Gr.*981.10 (Philae). **–πορος,** ον, *quick-going,* in Hom. always epith. of ships, Il.1.421,488, al., cf. Choeril.6; of streams, *swift-flowing,* πόρθμευμ' ἀχέων A.*Ag.*1557 (anap.); κυμάτων ῥιπαί Pi.*P.*4.194: later, ὀϊστοί *AP*5.85 (Claudian.); of a person, ὠκύπορος μετανίσσεται E.*Hyps.Fr.*1 iii 37 (lyr.). **–πος** (parox.), ον, poet. form of sq., of Apollo, *AP*9.525.25. **–πους,** ὁ, ἡ, πουν, τό: acc. masc. ὠκύπουν E.*Hel.*243 (lyr.): Ep. dat. pl. –πόδεσσι Il.2.383, etc.:—*swift-footed,* in Hom. always epith. of horses, Il. l. c., al., and so in Pi.*Parth.*2.44; of the hare, Hes.*Sc.*302; ἔλαφοι S.*OC*1093 (lyr.); ἱππικῶν.. ὠκύπουν ἀγών Id.*El.*699; κύνες E.*Hipp.*1129 (lyr.); of Hermes, Id.*Hel.* l.c. **–πτερος,** ον, *swift-winged,* ἴρηξ Il.13.62: metaph. of ships (πτερά being *the sails*), A.*Supp.*734. **II.** ὠκύπτερα, τά, *the long quill-feathers in a wing,* Ar.*Av.*803, Stratt.27, A.R.2.1255, Babr.99(100).4, Plu.*CG*1. **–ῥέεθρος,** ον, = ὠκύροος, Nonn.*D.*26.362. **–ῥόης,** Dor. **–ῥόας,** ὁ, = sq., E.*Ba.*568 (lyr.), *AP*9.219 (Diod.Sard.), A.R.2.349,650. **–ῥοος,** ον, poet. Adj. *swift-flowing,* ποταμός Il.5.598, 7.133:—fem. Ὠκυρόη, ἡ, an Oceanid, *h.Cer.* 420, Hes.*Th.*360.

❀ **ὠκύς** [ῠ], ὠκεῖα, ὠκύ, gen. έος, είας, έος: Ep. and Ion. fem. ὠκέᾰ, as always in Il., 2.786, al. (in the formula ὠκέα Ἶρις), cf. Hes.*Th.* 780; in Od., only in 12.374 (v.l. ὠκύς): fem. pl. ὠκεῖαι Od.7.36; Ep. gen. ὠκειάων 9.101, Il.4.500, etc.; fem. ὠκύς Jo.Gaz.*Ecphr.*1.240, v.l. (ἐν πολλοῖς Sch.) in Od.12.374:—*quick, swift, fleet,* κιχάνει τοι βραδὺς ὠκύν Od.8.329; mostly of persons, freq. with πόδας added, specially of Achilles, Il.1.58, etc.; also ὠκὺς Ἀχ., without πόδας, 21.211, 22.188; so ὠκέα, of Iris, 2.786, al. (ὦκα δὲ Ἶ. shd. be read for ὠκέα δ' Ἶρις, 23.198); of animals, [ἴρηξ] ὤκιστος πετεηνῶν 15.238, cf. 21.253; ἵπποι 8.88; ἔλαφοι Od.6.104; also of things, esp. of ships, Il.8.197, Od.7.36; of arrows, Il.15.106,112, al.; ὠ. πτέρυξ Pi.*P.*1.6; αἰετός Id.*N.*3.80; ἴτ' ἄσσον ὠκεῖς S.*Ant.*1215, cf. E.*Ba.* 452, etc.; ὠκὺς Ἄρης Id.*Andr.*106 (eleg.), cf. Od.8.331 (Sup.); of the sun, ὠ. ἠέλιος Mimn.11.5, *AP*7.466 (Leon.): also ὠκὺ νόημα *h. Merc.*43, cf. Od.7.36; θνατῶν φρένες ὠκύτεραι Pi.*P.*4.139; πρᾶξις, γάμος, ib.9.67,114 (Sup.); ὠκεῖαι χάριτες γλυκερώτεραι *AP*10.30: τὸ ὠκύ *quickness, sharpness,* E.*Fr.*1032; ὤκιστος τῇ ἀκοῇ Ael.*NA*6.63. **2.** of sound, *shrill,* ἀοιδαί, of the creaking of door-hinges, A.R.4.42. **II.** Adv. **–έως** Pi.*P.*3.58, *N.*10.64, *Parth.*2.6, Luc.*Salt.*19; cf. ὦκα: once neut. ὠκύ as Adv., ὣς ἔπεσ' Ἕκτορος ὠκὺ χαμαὶ μένος Il.14.418 (v.l. ὦκα, v. Sch.). **III.** degrees of Comparison, regul. Sup. ὠκύτατος Od.8.331, Pi.*P.*9.114: irreg. Sup., ὤκιστος πετεηνῶν Il. 15.238, 21.253; ὤκιστος ὄλεθρος 22.325; [καιρός] A.*Th.*65. Adv. ὤκιστα Od.22.77,133, A.R.4.242.—The word is mostly Ep., being used once by A. and once by S., but more freq. in E.; also in late Prose, as Aret.*SA*2.3 (Comp.), Ael. l.c., Luc.*Herm.*77.

**ὠκύσημον** (–σιμον cod.)· ταχέως φανερόν, Hsch.

**ὠκῠ-σκοπος,** ον, *quick-aiming,* of Apollo, *AP*9.525.25. **–στολος,** ον, *journeying swiftly, JRS*16.90 No.222 (Phrygia).

**ὠκύτης,** ητος, Dor. **–τας,** ἡ, *swiftness, fleetness,* Pi.*P.*11.50, E.*Ba.*1090, Pl.*Ax.*364c, Arr.*An.*1.1.13, Hippodam.ap.Stob.4.39.26; ὠ. ψυχῆς Onos.1.7.

**ὠκῠ-τοκεύς,** v. sub ὠκυτόκιον fin. **–τοκία,** ἡ, *speedy delivery,* cj. for ὀξυτοκία in Rhetor. in *Cat.Cod.Astr.*8(4).133. ❀ **–τόκιος,** ον, *promoting a quick birth,* Dsc.4.14, 5.154: λίθος Cyran.46. **II.** ὠκυτόκιον (sc. φάρμακον), τό, *a medicine for this purpose,* Hp.*Mul.*1.77, *Steril.*224, Ar.*Th.*504, Thphr.*HP*9.9.3, *Berl.Sitzb.*1934.1046 (pl.):—in Ar. the Rav.Ms. gives ὠκυτόκει'; τὸ ὠκυτόκειον προπαροξύνεται Hdn.Gr.1.376; ὠκυτόκειον, ει δίφθογγος· καὶ γὰρ **ὠκυτοκεύς,** Choerob. in *An.Ox.*2.280; ὠκυτόκια is cited from Ar. by Poll.2.7, cf. 4.208. **–τόκος,** ον, *causing quick and easy birth,* σελήνη (i.e. Artemis), Tim.*Fr.*28. **2.** of a river, ὠ. πεδίων ἐπινίσεται *giving quick increase,* S.*OC*689 (lyr.). **II.** ὠκύτοκον, τό, *quick birth, easy delivery,* Hdt.4.35. **–φόνος,** ον, *quickly fatal,* of diseases, prob. in Aret.*SA*2.3.

**ὦλαξ,** ακος, ἡ, Dor. for αὖλαξ, *EM*625.37.

**ὠλεκρᾱν-ίζω,** *thrust with the elbow, Com.Adesp.*1093 ap.Poll.2.140: but **ὀλεκρανίζεσθαι** Phryn. *PS*p.97 B.; cf. sq. **–ον,** τό, for ὠλενόκρανον, = ὠλένης κρανίον (Ἀριστοφάνης ὀλέκρανα λέγει τὰ τῶν ὠλενῶν κρανία Suid. s.v. ὀλέκρανον), *point of the elbow,* Arist.*HA*493[b]27 (v.l. ὀλέκρανον), al.; Hp. used ἀγκών for ὠλέκρανον, acc. to Gal. *UP*2.2,14: but ὀλεκρ. is found in Hp.*Epid.*7.61. [ὀλέκρανον is required by the metre in Ar.*Pax* 443; τὸ ὠλέκρανον διὰ τοῦ ω προφέρουσιν, ἡ δὲ συνήθεια διὰ τοῦ ο Hellad.ap.Phot.p.533 B.; Phot. has ὠλ–, but places it after ὀλέκει.]

❀ **ὠλέν-η,** ἡ, *elbow,* or rather *the arm from the elbow downwards* (cf. ὦμος 1.1), *h.Merc.*388, A.*Pr.*60, S.*Tr.*926, etc.; περίβαλλ' ὠλένας Ar.*Ra.*1322 (lyr.): freq. in E., ὠλέναις, ἐν ὠλέναισιν φέρειν, *HF* 1381, *Ba.*1238; μεταίρειν ἐν ὠλέναις *IT*1158; ὠλέναις λαβεῖν *Ba.* 1125 codd.; ἀπ' ὠλένης βαλεῖν *Ph.*1375; φίλην ὀρέγετ' ὠλένην; *Med.*902; περὶ ὠλένας δέρᾳ βαλεῖν *Ph.*165 (lyr., cf. 307, 311); εἰς ὠλένας τινὸς δοῦναί τι *Tr.*1142; ὠ. ἄκραι the hands, *IT*283; ἴσας δέ μοι ψήφους διηρίθμησε Παλλὰς ὠλένῃ is dub. l. ib.966: in later Prose, Luc.*DDeor.*20.10, al. (of the *wing-bone* of a bird, Id.*Icar.*3): Cleitorian (Arc.) word acc. to *AB*1096. **2.** στεφάναι is glossed by αἱ τῶν βωμῶν ὠλέναι, Hsch. **3.** *mat, mattress,* gloss on Lat. *torus* (which has these and other senses), *Gloss.*: cf. ὠλήν, ὠλενοστρόφος. (Lat. *ulna,* OHG. *elina,* OE. *eln, el-bogi,* 'ell, elbow'; Goth. *aleina*; also Skt. *aratnis,* OSlav. *lakŭtĭ,* Lith. *uolekùs* (all = *elbow* and *ell*); cf. ὠλλόν and ἄλαξ.) **–ιος,** α, ον, *in the elbow* or *arm,* αἲξ ὠ. the star Capella *in the elbow* of Auriga, Arat.164, v. Sch.; misinterpreted as Ὠλένιος (cf. Ὤλενος), Str.8.7.5. **II.** v. Ὤλενος. **–ίς,** ίδος, ἡ, *mat* or *bundle,* Poll.10.170. **–ίτης** [ῑ], ου, ὁ, *of the arm,* Lyc. 155.

**Ὤλενος,** ἡ, *Olenos,* a city of Achaia, Il.2.639: prob. named from its lying *in the bend* (ὠλένη) of a hill, hence Adj. **Ὠλένιος,** α, ον, *Achaean, AP*7.723.

**ὠλενοστρόφος,** ὁ, *mat-maker, PPetr.*3 p.173 (iii B.C.), *BGU*1528 (iii B.C.); *toranus* (leg. *torarius*) = ωλενος· τροφος, *Gloss.*: cf. ὠλένη 3 and ὠλήν.

**ὠλεσί-βωλος** [ῐ], ον, *clod-crushing,* σφῦρα *AP*6.104 (Phil.), 297 (Phanias). **–καρπος,** ον, *losing its fruit,* ἰτέαι ὠ., because they shed their fruits before ripening, Od.10.510, cf. Thphr.*HP*3.1.3; [ἐρινεός] Id.*CP*2.9.14: metaph., ὠ. τύμπανον the kettledrum in the mysteries of Cybele, *because the priests who beat it were eunuchs,* Opp.*C.*3.283: dub. sens. in Cerc.6.14. **–οικος,** ον, *destroying the house,* τὰν ὠ. θεόν (sc. Ἐρινύν) A.*Th.*720 (lyr.); ἀνάστασιν ὠλεσίοικον Orph.*Fr.*285.26; ἁρπαγαὶ ὠ. ib.58; written ὀλεσ– in Lib. *Decl.*26.32 codd. **II.** *squandering one's substance, Com.Adesp.* 1200. **–τεκνος,** ον, *child-murdering,* Nonn.*D.*44.91.

**ὠλήν,** ένος, ὁ, collat. form of ὠλένη, = βραχίων, Suid. s.vv. ὠλένη (where gen. ὠλῆνος) and ὠλήν: esp. in sense *mat* (cf. ὠλένη 3), ἐὰν ἐκ τῆς καλάμης ὠλένας ποιήσας κύκλῳ περὶ τοὺς σιροὺς περιτείνῃς αὐτούς Ph.*Bel.*88.4 (cf. ὄλινοι· κριθῆς δεσμοί, Hsch.): ὠλένων δορωσίμων mentioned in brick-building accounts, *PPetr.*3 p.139 (iii. B.C.); also fem., τὰς ὠλένας τοῦ ἐλαιουργίου διπλᾶς ποίησον *PFay.*110.29 (i A.D.), cf. *Jahresh.*26 *Beibl.*54 (Ephes., i A.D., ὀλένας lapis): they were straw mats used to bind together layers of bricks, καλαμίδας τὰς νῦν λεγομένας ὠλένας, ἐπεὶ ἀπὸ καλάμων γίνονται, ἢ τοὺς θηλυκοὺς καλάμους τοὺς πρὸς σύνδεσμον τῶν πλινθίνων καταστρωμάτων τῆς οἰκοδομίας (*AB* 269, cf. *EM*485.30): ὠλένες in pl. = *matting* for a roof, Hsch. s.v. κόνυζα (ὠλένων cod., rightly).

**ὤλης,** ες, *destroyed,* ὤλη καὶ πανώλη γένοιτο αὐτοῦ τὸ γένος τε καὶ αὐτός *Ath.Mitt.*15.154 (Iasos); ὤλη πανώλη γένοιτο Keil-Premerstein, *Zweiter Bericht* No.157 (near Thyatira, ii A.D.); μηδὲ γῆ καρποφορήσοιτο αὐτῷ..ἀλλὰ ὠληπανώλη (sic) *BMus.Inscr.*918.5 (Halic., ii or iii A.D.).

**ὠλίγγη,** ἡ, variously expld. in *EM*821.43, *AB*318, **1.** = ἀκαριαῖον, ἐλάχιστον. **2.** Att. for *doze* (ἐπὶ τοῦ νυστάξαι). **3.** *wrinkles beside the eyes,* '*crow's feet*'; this last sense is given by Poll. 2.67 (where vv. ll. οὐλιγγας, ὠλίγκας, ἕλιγγας, ὤριγγας) as found in poets, and the remark τὴν δὲ ὠλίγγην (v.l. ὠλλ–) δηλοῦν καὶ πνοὴν καὶ σκιὰν καὶ ἀκαρὲς πνεῦμα (*EM* and *AB* ll. cc.) may refer to the same poet. passage. Hsch. cites **ὠλιγγία** in all three senses, also **ὠλιγγιάω,** = νυστάζω, and **ὠλιγγήῖος,** α, ον, = ὀλίγος.

**ὠλίγγιον,** glossed by ὀλίγον, *EM*821.46, *AB*318.

**ὠλίσθησα, ὤλισθον,** v. ὀλισθάνω.

**ὠλῑτήμερος,** ον, in Hsch., Ion. crasis for ὁ ἀλιτήμερος.

**ὦλκα, ὦλκας,** only in acc. sg. and pl., = ἄλοξ, αὖλαξ, *furrow,* Il. 13.707, Od.18.375, Mosch.2.81, A.R.3.1054, 1333. (κατὰ ὦλκα Il. l. c. has perh. replaced κατ' *ἄϝολκα which may have been an old Aeol. form (ἀϝ͂ϝκα).)

**ὦλλοι,** Ion. crasis for *οἱ ἄλλοι*, Hdt.1.48: read by Zenod. in Il.2.1.

**ὦλλόν·** τὴν τοῦ βραχίονος καμπήν, κτλ., Hsch. **ὠλυγίων·** σκοτεινῶν, κακῶν, μακρῶν, ὀξέων, μεγάλων, Id.

**ὠμάδιος** [ᾰ], ὁ, (ὠμός) as epith. of Dionysus, = ὠμηστής, because he had *human sacrifices* at Chios and Tenedos, Orph.*H.*30.5, Euelp. ap.Porph.*Abst.*2.55; ὠ. χοροί dances in his honour, *IG*14.2138. **2.** *raw*, κρέα Epic. in *Arch.Pap.*7 p.4. **II.** (ὦμος) *passing over the shoulder*, νεβρίς, τελαμών, Nonn.*D.*1.34, 13.308, cf. Hsch.

**ὠμᾰδίς, ὠμᾰδόν,** Adv. *on the shoulder, on the shoulders*, Hsch.

**ὠμαλγία,** ἡ, *pain in the shoulder*, Orib.*Fr.*70(pl.).

**ὠμαλθής,** ές, (ὠμός, ἀλθαίνω) ἕλκος ὠ. a wound *scarred over too soon, without healing properly*, Hsch.

⊛ **ὠμαλία,** ἡ, *flat rate, average*, ἐγδίδομεν..τὰς μὲν στήλας..πρὸς λίθον ἐφ' ὠμαλίαν ὅ τι ἂν εὕρωσιν *IG*7.3073.7 (Lebad., ii B.C.); συντελέσει διάχωμα μῆκος ἐφ' ὠμαλίαν ε̄, πλάτος κάτω ξ̄ ἄνω μ̄, ὥστ' εἶναι ἐφ' ὠμαλίαν ν̄ *PPetr.*3 p.125 (iii B.C.). (Formed fr. ἀν-ωμαλία, cf. ὁμαλός.)

**ὠμαμπέλῖνος,** η, ον, *of the colour of the fresh vine-leaf*, opp. ξηραμπέλινος, *Peripl.M.Rubr.*65.

**ὠμαχθής,** ές, *heavy to the shoulders*, πήρη *AP*6.104 (Phil.).

**ὦμβροι,** = οἱ πονηροί, Hsch. (ὄμβρει cod.).

**ὠμήλετον·** ἐρηριγμένον, Hsch.: cf. sq.

**ὠμήλῠσις,** εως, ἡ, *bruised meal of raw corn*, esp. barley or wheat (hence with κριθίνη or πυρίνη added), used for poultices, Hp.*Morb.* 2.31, *Nat.Mul.*27, Gal.10.282, 19.156; applied without water, Id.12.863; written divisim, μετὰ ὠμῆς λύσεως Dsc.3.24, Archig.ap. Gal.12.675, *Gp.*14.7.7. (Compd. of ὠμός and *ἄλυσις 'grinding', cf. ἄλεσις, ἀλέω, ἄλευρον, and foreg.; also perh. OE. *ealu* 'ale':—the form ὠμῆς λύσεως by popular etymology: εἰρῆσθαι δὲ ὅτι οὐ φρυγόμενον ἀλήθεται *AB*318.)

**ὠμησ-τήρ,** ῆρος, ὁ, = sq., Opp.*H.*5.324. ⊛ **-τής,** οῦ, Dor. **-τάς,** ὁ, (ὠμός, ἔδω) *eating raw flesh*, οἰωνοί Il.11.454; κύνες 22.67, S.*Ant.*697; ἰχθύες Il.24.82; Κέρβερος Hes.*Th.*311; λέων B.12.46, Orac.ap.Hdt. 5.92.β'; ἀνήρ A.*Ag.*827 (as a noun, of a lion, *AP*6.237 (Antist.)); αἰετός A.R.2.1259; ὄφις (sc. Ἔχιδνα) ὠμηστής Hes.*Th.*300; epith. of Dionysus, = ὠμάδιος 1, *AP*9.524.25, cf. Plu.2.462b (of ἄκρατος). Adv. **-τί** Zonar. **2.** *savage, brutal*, ὠ. καὶ ἄπιστος ἀνήρ Il.24.207, cf.Plu. *Ant.*24. (Aristarch. pronounced it ὠμησταί like ἀθληταί; Tyrannio ὠμῆσται like κομῆται, Sch.Il.22.67.)

⊛ **ὠμία,** ἡ, (ὦμος) *shoulder*, i.e. (apptly.) *angle*, of a building, Lxx 3*Ki.*6.13(8), 7.17(30), al., cf. *PVat.*11ʳ v 16 (ii A.D.).

**ὠμιαία** φλέψ, the *humero-cephalic vein*, Gal.18(1).386, al. **II.** neut. pl. **ὠμιαῖα,** νεῦρα *shoulder*-muscles, Arist.*HA*515ᵇ10, cf. Hld. 10.27.

**ὠμίας,** ου, ὁ, *a broad-shouldered person*, Poll.3.149, Hsch.

**ὠμίᾰσις,** εως, ἡ, *shouldering*, an allegorization of the name Shechem, Ph.1.92,471.

**ὠμίδιος,** α, ον, cited as radical of ἐπωμίδιος, Theognost.*Can.*54.

**ὠμίζομαι,** Med., *take on one's shoulders*, Suid. (v.l. ὠμησάμενος), Zonar.

**ὦμιλλα,** ἡ, *a game* in which nuts, etc., were thrown into a ring (εἰς ὤμιλλαν Poll.9.102): hence metaph. of a *party, circle*, εἰς ὦ. ἀριστήσομεν Eup.250; εἴσειμ' εἰς ὦ. Id.288.

**ὤμιον,** Dim. of ὦμος, *AP*11.157 (Ammian.); dub. l. in Lxx*Jb.*18. 13.

**ὠμιστής,** οῦ, ὁ, (ὠμίζομαι) *porter*, Hdn.*Epim.*100 (ὠμισθής).

⊛ **ὠμο-βόειος,** α, ον, Ion. **-βόεος,** or **-βόῖνος,** *of raw, untanned ox-hide*, ἀσπίδας ὠμοβοΐνας Hdt.7.76,79; γέρρα δασειῶν βοῶν ὠμοβόεια (v.l. -βόινα) X.*An.*4.7.22; δερμάτων ὠμοβοείων (v.l. βοΐνων) ib.26; σάλπιγξιν ὠμοβοΐναις ib.7.3.32 codd.:—ἡ ὠμοβοέη (sc. δορά), *a raw ox-hide* (cf. λεοντέη, etc.), Hdt.3.9, 4.65: in later writers usu. in form **-βόϊνος,** Str.15.1.42, D.S.3.8, etc.: acc. pl. ὠμοβοεῖς in *AP*6.21.4 is formed by a false analogy, as if fr. ὠμοβοεύς. **II.** ὠμοβοείου μοι παραθεὶς τόμον.., καὶ τρία μοι κεράσας ὠμοβοειότερα.. having set before me a slice *of raw beef*, and mixed me three cups *yet more raw than beef*, *AP*11.137 (Lucill.). **-βόϊος,** ον, *made from untanned ox-hide*, κόλλαν ὠμοβόϊον *Supp.Epigr.*3.147 (Eleusis, iii B.C.). **-βορεύς,** έως, ὁ, = sq., Nic.*Th.*739. ⊛ **-βόρος,** ον, = sq., A.R.1.636, Ael.*NA*15.11, Ph.1.670; βλέπειν ὠμοβόρον v.l. in Alciphr.3.21. **-βρώς,** ῶτος, ὁ, ἡ, *eating raw flesh*, E.*Tr.* 436, *HF*889 (lyr.), Tim.*Pers.*150, prob. in S.*Fr.*799.5. **-βρωτος,** ον, *eaten raw*, Nic.*Al.*428. **-βύρσῖνος,** η, ον, *made of raw leather*, ἀσπίδες Str.16.4.17; σάκη Sch.D Il.5.453: (hence corrupted **-βύρσια,** τά, *EM*558.42, Zonar. s.v. λαιψήϊα):—also **-βυρσος,** ον, θώρακες Plu.*Crass.*25. ⊛ **-γέρων,** οντος, ὁ, ἡ, *a fresh, active old man*, Il.23.791, Megasth.ap.Arr.*Ind.*9.7(pl.), *AP*7.363.9, Gal.6. 379, cf. Hsch. **II.** *one untimely old*, as expl. of the Ep. ὠμὸν γῆρας (v. ὠμός II. 3), *EM*821.48: so as Adj., βόστρυχος ὠ. *AP*5.263 (Paul.Sil.). **-γραυς,** ἡ, fem. of foreg., Men.979. **-δαΐκτον·** ὠμοσπάρακτον, Hsch. **-δακής,** ές, *fiercely gnawing*, ἵμερος A.*Th.* 692 (lyr.).

**Ὠμόδᾰμος,** ὁ, *Fierce Conqueror*, alleg. name of a demon, Hom. *Epigr.*14.10.

**ὠμο-δέψητος,** ον, *raw-tanned*, Suid. s. v. Σεμίραμις. **-δροπος,** ον, *plucked unripe*, νόμιμα ὠ., prop. the right *of plucking the fresh fruit*, metaph. for the rights *of the marriage-bed*, the *husband's* rights, A.*Th.*333 (lyr.).

**ὠμοθάλεκτα·** ὠμά, Hsch.

**ὠμο-θετέω,** in sacrificing, *place the raw pieces* duly on the altar, Il.1.461, 2.424, Od.3.458:—Med., ὠμοθετεῖτο, πάντων ἀρχόμενος μελέων, ἐς πίονα δημόν 14.427: later, generally, *sacrifice*, ἀρνειόν A.R.3.1033 (Act.). (Fr. ὠμός, *raw*. Eust., however, says (134.35) that some derived it fr. ὦμος *shoulder*, and expld. it accordingly.) **-θριξ,** τρῐχος, ὁ, ἡ, *fierce-crested*, χέλυδρος (of Antenor) Lyc. 340. **-θῡμος,** ον, *savage-hearted*, S.*Aj.*885 (lyr.), Ph.2.15, al.

**ὦμοι,** v. ὤ.

**ὠμ-οίδης,** ου, ὁ, (οἰδέω) *with swollen* or *high shoulders*, Eust.1684. 28.

**ὠμο-κοτύλη** [ῠ], ἡ, *shoulder-joint*, Poll.2.137. **-κράτης,** ές, *of rude untamed might*, of Ajax, S.*Aj.*205 (anap.); also expld. as *strong-shouldered*, v. Sch. ad loc. **-κῡδιάω,** *to be proud of broad shoulders*, *Com.Adesp.*1201. ⊛ **-λῖνον,** τό, *raw flax*, A.*Fr.*206; used for *lint*, Hp.*Morb.*2.60, *Int.*23, al.; gloss on σχίδια, Hsch. (pl.). **II.** *coarse linen towel* or *napkin*, Cratin.9 (lyr., pl.), Plu. 2.509a. **-λῖνος,** ον, *made of raw flax*, Hp.*Mul.*2.157.

**ὡμολογημένως,** Adv. part. pf. Pass. of ὁμολογέω, *confessedly, without contradiction*, D.S.15.10, Poll.6.208, Phalar.*Ep.*119.3; cf. ὁμολογουμένως.

**ὠμοπλάτη** [ᾰ], ἡ, (ὦμος) *shoulder-blade*, freq. in pl. ὠμοπλάται Arist.*HA*493ᵇ12, al.: sg. in Hp.*Art.*1, Diog.Apoll.6; also of animals, as of the horse, X.*Eq.*1.7; of the dog, hare, boar, Id.*Cyn.*4.1, 5.10: sg., ib.10.16, *Eq.*6.2, Arist.*HA*498ᵃ33, 512ᵃ28, *PA*693ᵇ1, *SIG*1017.8 (Sinope, iii B.C.); σὺν ὠμοπλάτᾳ μέγαν ὦμον Theoc.26. 22.

**ὠμοργής,** ές, = σκληρὸς καὶ χαλεπός, *EM*822.12, *AB*318: also **ὠμοργός,** όν, ibid., cf. Hsch.

⊛ **ὦμος,** ὁ: (v. sub fin.):—*the shoulder with the upper arm* (ὠλένη being *the lower*), ξίφεϊ κληῗδα παρ' ὦμον πλῆξ', ἀπὸ δ' αὐχένος ὦμον ἐέργαθεν ἠδ' ἀπὸ νώτου Il.5.146, cf. 8.325, Hdt.4.62; μεταφρένῳ ἐν δόρυ πῆξεν ὤμων μεσσηγύς Il.5.41; τεύχε' ἀπ' ὤμων συλήσειν 15.544; ὦμος στιβαρός, ὦμοι ἴφθιμοι, 5.400, 18.204; εὐρέες 3.210; κυρτώ 2. 217; ἀμφ' ὤμοισιν ἔχει σάκος 11.527, cf. S.*Fr.*453; ἐπ' ὤμου.. φέρειν Od.10.170, cf. Isoc.19.39; ἀρεῖτ' ἐπ' ὤμου Herod.3.61; κατ' ὤμου δεῖρον ib.3; ἐπ' ὤμων πατέρ' ἔχων S.*Fr.*373; τὰ ὦτα ἐπὶ τῶν ὤμων ἔχειν Pl.*R.*613c; ὤμοισι φόρησεν Il.19.11; ἑλὼν..σάκος ὤμῳ 15.474; ὤμῳ or ὤμοισιν ἔχειν, 14.376, 1.45, al.; ὤμοις or ἐπ' ὤμοις φέρειν, S.*Fr.*454, *Tr* 564; ἔχειν ἀνὰ φαιδίμῳ ὤμῳ Od.11.128, 23.275; λαβὼν.. ὦμον εἰς ἀριστερόν E.*IT*1381; ἐπ' ὤμοις θεῖναι Id. *Ba.*755; κίον' οὐρανοῦ..ὤμοις ἐρείδων A.*Pr.*350; ὤμοισι τοῖσι ἐμοῖσι 'by the strength of mine *arms*', Hdt.2.106; ἀποστρέψαι τὸν ὦ. to dislocate *it*, Ar.*Eq.*263 (troch.); ὁ δ' ὦμος..πιέζεται Id.*Ra.*30; τὸν ὦμον θλίβομαι Id.*Fr.*323: pl. for sg., ὤμοις ἀριστεροῖσιν ἀνακλάσας δέρην E.*Or.*1471. **b.** *the shoulder* is sts. more exactly specified as πρυμνότατος or πρυμνὸς ὦμος, Od.17.462,504; νείατος ὦ. Il.15. 341, 17.310; sts. opp. χείρ (the arm), χεῖρες ὤμων..ἐπαΐσσονται 23.628; τῶν ἑκατὸν μὲν χεῖρες ἀπ' ὤμων ἀΐσσοντο Hes.*Th.*150; τοὺς ὤμους ἀποταμόντες σὺν τῇσι χερσί (arms) Hdt.4.62; ἀποταμόντα ἐν τῷ ὤμῳ τὴν χεῖρα Id.2.121.ε', cf. E.*Ba.*1127, Arist.*HA*493ᵇ26. **2.** also of animals, as of a horse, Il.6.510, 15.267, X.*Eq.*8.6; of a lion, Hes.*Sc.*430; of a dog, X.*Cyn.*4.1; of crabs, Batr.296; of birds, Plu.2.983b; of ants, *Gp.*13.10.14. **3.** *the shoulder*, in a dress, ἐπὶ τῶν ὤμων τῆς ἐπωμίδος Lxx*Ex.*28.12, cf. 25(29); ἐπὶ τῷ ὤμῳ τοῦ χιτῶνος ὑποθέντες Aen.Tact.31.23 codd. (ἐπὶ τῇ ᾤᾳ cj. Haupt). **II.** metaph. *of the parts below the top* or *head* of anything, esp. of *the fork of a vine* (cf. ὠμοχάραξ), *Gp.*4.12.4; of the womb, Heroph.ap. Gal.4.596, cf. Ruf.*Onom.*195. (Cf. Lat. *umerus* (fr. **omesos*), Goth. *ams* (stem *amsa-*), Skt. *áṃsas*, also Aeol. ἐπ-ομμάδιος, and (non-Greek) ἀμέσω Hsch.)

⊛ **ὠμός,** ή, όν: (v. sub fin.):—*raw, crude* (cf. Arist.*Mete.*380ᵇ 5): **I.** prop. of flesh, *raw, uncooked*, Il.22.347, al.; opp. ὀπταλέος, Od.12.396; ὠμὸν καταφαγεῖν τινα or ὠμοῦ ἐσθίειν τινός to eat one *raw*, prov. of savage cruelty, X.*An.*4.8.14, *HG*3.3.6; so ὠμὸν βεβρώθοις Πρίαμον Il.4.35, cf. Od.18.87, etc. **2.** of eggs, Thphr. *Vert.*2; of vegetables, μύκητας ὠμοὺς..φαγεῖν Antiph.188; κριθαί Luc.*Asin.*17; cf. ὠμήλυσις. **3.** of water, *crude*, opp. ἀπεφθος, Alex.198; also of milk, Arist.*Mete.*380ᵇ8. **4.** of fruit, *uncooked by the sun, unripe*, opp. πέπων, Ar.*Eq.*260 (troch.), cf. X.*Oec.*19.19 (Comp.), Arist.*Mete.*380ᵇ7. **5.** of pitch, opp. ἑφθή, *Gp.*6.5.5, cf. Plb.5.89.6; of pottery, *unbaked*, χύτραι Dsc.1.68, *Gp.*10.21.1; κέραμος ὠμός Arist.*Mete.*380ᵇ8, cf. *GA*743ᵃ9: even of soil which needs to be exposed to the sun, ὡς ἡ ὠμὴ αὐτῆς ὀπτῷτο X.*Oec.*16.15. **6.** of food, *undigested*, Anon.Lond.25.7, al., Plu.2.131c, 133d; of a person, *suffering from indigestion*, Philostr.*Gym.*54; also οὖρα, ὑποχωρήσεις, κατάρροι, Arist.*Mete.*380ᵇ5. **II.** metaph., *savage, fierce, cruel*, [δεσπόται] ὠμοί τε δούλοις A.*Ag.*1045; ὠ. φρόνημα Id. *Th.*536; ὠμῇ ξὺν ὀργῇ Id.*Supp.*187; δαίμων S.*OT*828; τὰ..'Αγαμέμνονος κλύεις ὠμὰ καὶ πάντολμ' E.*IA*913 (troch.); ὠμὸς ἔς τινα Id.*Hipp.*1264; and so in Prose, ὠμὸν τὸ βούλευμα..ἐγνῶσθαι Th. 3.36; οὕτως ὠμὴ ⟨ἡ⟩ στάσις προὐχώρησε ib.82; θηρευταὶ ὠμοὶ καὶ ἄνομοι Pl.*Lg.*823e; ὠμὴ ψυχή ib.718d; χαλεπὸς καὶ ὠ. X.*An.*2.6.12; τὸν οὕτως ὠμόν, τὸν οὕτως ἀγνώμονα D.21.97; ὠμοὶ χρόνοι *hard* times, *IG*3.1372 (metr.). Adv., ὠμῶς καὶ ἀπαραιτήτως Th.3.[84], cf. X. *Vect.*5.6; ὠ. καὶ σχετλίως ἔχειν Isoc.19.31; ὠ. καὶ πικρῶς D.29.2; ὠ. ἀποκτείνειν Lys.13.63 codd. (ὁμοίως Lipsius): Sup., ὠμότατα διακεῖσθαι πρός τινα Isoc.9.49. **2.** *harsh, rough, cruel*, νόμοι S.*Aj.*548; δηλοῖ τὸ γέννημ' ὠμὸν ἐξ ὠμοῦ πατρὸς Id.*Ant.*471; πῶς ἂν ὠμότερος συκοφάντης γένοιτ'; *a more coarse, more unmitigated* sycophant,

D.18.212. Adv. ὠμῶς *rudely, coarsely*, παρελθεῖν ὠ. καὶ ἀναιδῶς ib. 285. 3. (from I. 4) ὠμὸν γῆρας an *unripe, premature* old age, Od. 15.357, Hes.*Op.*705 (but ὠμότατον καὶ ἀγριώτατον γῆρας in signf. II. 1, Plu.*Mar.*2), cf. ὠμογέρων : ὠμὸς τόκος an *untimely* birth, Philostr. *VS*2.1.8. (Cf. Skt. *āmás* 'raw, uncooked'.)

**ὠμο-σῑτία**, ἡ, *feeding on raw flesh*, Str.15.2.10. **-σῖτος**, ον, *eating raw meat*, of the Sphinx, *eating men raw*, A.*Th.*541 ; χαλαί (also of the Sphinx) E.*Ph.*1025 (lyr.); σκύλακες Id.*Ba.*338. II. Pass., *eaten raw*, Lyc.654. **-σπάρακτος** [ᾰρ], ον, *torn in pieces raw*, Ar.*Eq.*345. ❋ **-τάρῑχος** [ᾰ], ὁ, prob. *pickled flesh of the tunny's shoulder*, Nicostr.Com.1, Alex.15.4, Matro *Conv.*17, Dsc.2.31 :— also **-τάρῑχον**, τό, Diph.Siph.ap.Ath.3.121b.

**ὠμότης**, ητος, ἡ, *rawness, crudeness*, opp. πέπανσις Arist.*Mete.* 380b4. 2. *indigestion, crudity*, Thphr.*Lass.*4, D.S.10.7: pl., ὠμότησιν ἁλίσκεται Plu.2.661b, cf. Dsc.3.1. II. metaph., *savagery, fierceness, cruelty*, S.*Inach.* in *PTeb.*692 iv 15, E.*Ion*47, X.*Cyr.*4.5.19, Isoc.4.112, 11.32, D.21.109, etc.; ἴσον λεαίνης καὶ γυναικὸς ὠ. Men. *Mon.*267 ; εἴς τινας Lxx 2 *Ma.*12.5 ; ὠ. κατά τινος Luc.*Phal.*1.6 : pl., Id.*VH*1.3, J.*BJ*7.8.1.

**ὠμοτοκ-έω**, *bring forth untimely, miscarry*, Lxx *Jb.*21.10 ; ὠμοτοκοῦσαί τε.. καὶ νεκρὰ τίκτουσαι D.H.9.40. **-ία**, ἡ, *premature childbirth*, Ptol.*Tetr.*149, Sor.2.47. **-ος** (parox.), ον, *bringing forth immature offspring*, λέαινα Call.*Cer.*53 ; ὠμοτόκους ὠδῖνας ἀπηρείσαντο λέαιναι Id.*Del.*120 (referring to the shapelessness of the lion cub at birth) : metaph. of a vine, *AP*9.561 (Phil.).

**ὠμο-τομέω**, *cut* an abscess *before it is ripe* or *fully purulent*, Paul. Aeg.6.34 :—hence **-τομητέον**, Archig.ap.Gal.12.677. **-τρῐβής**, ές, *pressed raw*, ὠ. ἔλαιον oil *from unripe olives*, preferred for many purposes, Thphr.*Od.*15, Dsc.1.30. **-ϋπνος**, ον, *with one's sleep not slept out*, ὠ. ἀνιστάναι τινά Eup.305 ; ἀναπηδῆσαι ὠ. Philostr. *VA*8.31.

**ὠμοφᾰγ-έω**, *eat raw flesh*, Str.15.2.2, Arr.*Ind.*28.1, Porph.*Abst.* 1.13, *Gp.*19.2.13. **-ία**, ἡ, *eating of raw flesh*, Plu.2.417c (pl.). **-ιον**, τό, *a victim eaten raw*, *Milet.*6.22 (iii B.C.). **-ος** (parox.), ον, *eating raw flesh, carnivorous*, of savage beasts, λέοντες, θῶες, λύκοι, Il.5.782, 11.479, 16.157 ; θῆρες *h.Ven.*124 ; of the Centaurs, Thgn. 542 ; of savage men, Th.3.94, Str.15.1.57, Porph.*Abst.*1.13 ; of certain daemons, ὠμοφάγοι χθόνιοι *PMag.Par.*1.1444 ; τὰ ὠ. *carnivores*, Hp.*Vict.*2.49 cod.M, Arist.*HA*608b25, *PA*694a1 ; ὠ. χάρις (cf. ἀνδροβρώς) E.*Ba.*139 (lyr.). II. rarely proparox. ὠμόφᾰγος, ον, Pass., *eaten raw*, of sacrifices offered to Dionysus, E.*Fr.*472.12 (anap., τάς τ' ὠμοφάγους δαῖτας τελέσας codd. perh. rightly, cf. ὠμοφάγιον).

**ὠμο-φόριον**, τό, = *palliolum*, *Gloss.* **-φόρος**, ὁ, (ὦμος) *porter*, *AJA*42.56 (Tarsus, iii A.D.).

**ὠμό-φρων**, ονος, ὁ, ἡ, (φρήν) *savage-minded*, λύκος A.*Ch.*421 (lyr.); of persons, S.*Aj.*930 (lyr.), *Tr.*975 (anap.), *Ph.*194 (anap.), E.*El.* 27, Lxx 4 *Ma.*9.15, etc. : metaph., ὠ. σίδαρος A.*Th.*730 (lyr.). Adv. ὠμοφρόνως Id.*Pers.*911 (anap.), cj. in J.*Vit.*35. **-χάραξ** [ᾰ], ᾰκος, ὁ or ἡ, *a prop for the forks of vines* (v. ὦμος II), *Gp.*5.22.4. **-χειρούργητος**, ον, *premature*, of a surgical operation, ὠ. ποιῆσαι τὴν χειρουργίαν Steph.*in Hp.*1.180d.

**ὠμφύνω**, f.l. for ὀμφύνω in Hsch. **ὦν**, Ion. and Dor. for οὖν. **ὦνα, ὦναξ**, poet. contr. for ὦ ἄνα, ὦ ἄναξ. **ὠνάμην, ὤνατο**, aor. Med. of ὄνομαι. II. also of ὀνίνημι (q.v.). **ὠνάρχος**· δήμψος, Hsch.

**ὠνᾱτάς**, ᾶ, ὁ, Dor. for ὠνητής, *GDI*2146.8 (Delph., ii B.C.).

❋ **ὠνέομαι**, Hes.*Op.*341, etc. : fut. -ήσομαι E.*Hec.*360, Ar.*Ach.*815, *Pax*1261, Lys.22.22, Dor. ὠνασοῦμαι (v. infr.) :—in Att. usu. with the syllabic augment, ἐωνούμην Eup.184, And.1.134, ἀντ-εωνεῖτο X. *Oec.*20.26, etc. : but ὠνέετο Hdt.3.139, ὠνέοντο Id.1.69, ὠνούμην Lys. 7.4 codd., ἀντ-ωνεῖτο And.1.134, ἐξ-ωνεῖτο Aeschin.3.91 : aor. 1 ἐωνησάμην Plu.*Cic.*3 ; ὠνησάμην Hp.*Ep.*17, Plu.*Nic.*10, Luc.*Herm.*81 ; part. ὠνησάμενος Plb.4.50.3, D.H.7.20 : ὠνήσασθαι not in Attic inscrr. earlier than *IG*2².1035.8 (i B.C.), ἐπριάμην being used in Att. ; ὠνησάμην in the prov. Χῖος δεσπότην ὠνήσατο Eup.269 : pf. ἐώνημαι in act. sense, Ar.*Pl.*7, Lys.7.2 (so plpf. ἐώνητο D.37.5) ; also as Pass. (v. infr. II) : aor. in pass. sense (v. infr. II) ἐωνήθην ; fut. in pass. sense ἀπ-ωνηθήσεται Theopomp.Com.84 : this verb is usu. replaced in later Gr. by ἀγοράζω :—*buy, purchase*, opp. πωλέω, πιπράσκω ; πῶ τις ὦν ὄνον ὠνασεῖται ; Sophr.125 ; but in pres. and impf. (which are the tenses most in use), *offer to buy, bargain* or *bid* for a thing, ὄφρ' ἄλλων ὠνῇ κλῆρον Hes.*Op.*341 ; ὠνέεσθαι τῶν φορτίων *wished to buy* some of their wares, *began to bargain* for them, Hdt. 1.1 ; Κροῖσός σφι ὠνεομένοισι ἔδωκε gave it them *when they offered to buy*, ib.69 ; τὰς νήσους οὐκ ἐβούλοντο ὠνευμένοισι πωλέειν ib.165, cf. 3.139, 6.121 ; ὀκτὼ λάβοις ἄν (sc. ὀβολούς); Answ. εἴπερ ὠνεῖ τὸν ἕτερον if *you are willing to buy* the other fish, Alex.16.10, cf. 78.7 ; ὠνεῖσθαι καὶ πωλεῖν πρὸς ἀλλήλους Pl.*Lg.*741b ; ὠ. τὰς γυναῖκας παρὰ τῶν γονέων Hdt.5.6, cf. Pl.*Prt.*313d,e, D.9.48 ; ἀπό τινος Ach.Tat. 5.17 : c. dat. pers., *buy from*.., Ar.*Ach.*815, *Pax*1261 ; also ὠ. ἐκ Κορίνθου *buy goods* from Corinth, X.*HG*7.2.17 : ὠ. ἐξ ἀγορᾶς Id.*An.* 3.2.21 ; metaph., καιρόν, σπονδάς ὠ., Plu.*Sert.*6, Hdn.6.7.9 ; ὠ. μὴ ἀδικεῖσθαι τοὺς ἐμπόρους D.8.25 ; c. gen. pretii, *buy for* so much, Hdt. 5.6, cf. E.*Hec.*360, X.*An.*7.6.24 ; ψυχῆς *at the price of* life, Heraclit. 85 : also c. dat., *buy with*.., τάχιστα τοῖσι φιλτάτοις ὠνούμεθα E.*IA* 1170 : abs., X.*Mem.*2.10.4, *Ages.*1.18 : esp. in partic., ὠνουμένους ἔξειν τὰ ἐπιτήδεια *by purchase*, Id.*An.*2.3.27, cf. 5.5.14, etc. ; also ὁ ὠνούμενος the *buyer, purchaser*, δρῶντος τοῦ ὠνουμένου Id.*Eq.*3.2, cf. Plu. *Cat.Mi.*36 ; ὁ ἐωνημένος the *owner by purchase* (of a slave), Ar.*Pl.*7 ; ὁ ὠνησάμενος Plu.2.242d ; ὁ ὠνησόμενος the *intending purchaser*, Din. 3.10 : metaph., χάριτας πονηρὰς ὠ. E.*Hel.*902 ; ὅσα ἄνθρωποι ἄθλων ὠνοῦνται X.*Hier.*9.11 ; εὔνοιαν παρά τινος D.12.20 ; ὠ. τὰς αὐτῶν ψυχὰς παρὰ τῶν ἐχθρῶν Lys.28.9 :—in A.*Supp.*337 Robortello restored ὤνοιτο. 2. *bid for, purchase the farming of public taxes* or *properties*, λ' ταλάντων And.1.134, Lys.7.2 (in part. pf. Pass. with trans. sense) ; τέλη παρὰ τῆς πόλεως X.*Vect.*4.19, etc. ; ὠ. μέταλλα D.19.293 ; τὸν ἐωνημένον τὴν ἰλὺν ἐκκομίσασθαι *IG*1².94.20, cf. ὠνή II. 3. *buy off, avert by giving hush-money*, ὠ. τὸν κίνδυνον D.38.20 ; τὰ ἐγκλήματα ib.8 ; ταλάντου τὸ πλημμέλημα (i.e. its penalty) παρά τινος Luc.*Herm.*81. 4. ὠ. τινα *to buy* a person, of one who bribes, D.18.247 ; ὠνεῖται καὶ διαφθείρει τινάς Id.9.45, cf. Plu.*Phil.*15. II. sts. used as Pass., dub. in pres. since [ὠνούμενά τε καὶ πιπρασκόμενα] is interpol. in Pl.*Phd.*69b ; occasionally in pf., part. ἐωνημένος Id.*R.* 563b, Is.11.42, D.19.209 (but indic. ἐώνηνται Anon.ap.Arist.*Rh.* 1410a19 is Act. in sense) : plpf. ἐώνητο Ar.*Pax*1182 (troch.) ; also in aor. ἐωνήθην X.*Mem.*2.7.12, ὠνηθῇ Id.*Vect.*4.19 ; part. ὠνηθεὶς Is.6. 19, Pl.*Sph.*224a, *Lg.*850a. III. Act. pf. part. ἐωνηκώς, = ἐωνημένος, Lys.*Fr.*135 S. : aor. ὠνῆσαι· ἀγοράσαι, Zonar. : pres. ὠνεῖν· πωλεῖν, ἀπολαύειν, Hsch. : the sense πωλεῖν is Cretan, ὠνῆν τὰ χρήματα they shall *sell* the property, *Leg.Gort.*5.47 ; αἰ δέ τις..τὸ νόμισμα μὴ λείοι δέκεσθαι ἢ καρπῶ ὠνίοι if any one refuses the currency or *sells* for produce, *SIG*525.8 (Crete, iii B.C.).

**ὠν-ή**, Aeol. ὄννα *IG*11(2).1064 (ii B.C.), ἡ, (cf. ὦνος) *buying, purchasing*, ὠ. καὶ πρῆσις *buying* and selling, Hdt.1.153, cf. Hyp.*Ath.*5, S. *Fr.*909, Pl.*R.*371d, *Sph.*223d ; ὠνὴν ποιεῖσθαί τινος D.33.8, cf. Pl.*Lg.* 849b ; δι' ὠνῆς Plu.2.753d ; διὰ τὴν ὠ. Luc.*Ind.*16 ; ἐν τῇ τῶν σιτίων ὠ. Pl.*Prt.*314a. 2. *purchase, bargain*, E.*Cyc.*150. II. *contract for the farming of taxes* or other sources of revenue, ὠνὰς πρίασθαι ἐκ τοῦ δημοσίου And.1.73, cf. 92, Plu.*Alc.*5 ; τοὶ πριάμενοι τὰν ὠνὰν σίτου, οἴνου, τετραπόδων, *SIG*1000.4,5,6 (Cos, i B.C.) ; τρὶς ἀναπραθείσης τῆς ὠ. *IPE*1².32 A 53 (Olbia, iii B.C.) ; ὠνὰς *omnium venditas*, of the proceeds of local taxes, Cic.*Att.*5.16.2. 2. in Dor. Inscrr. (also in Arg.D.37 (pl.)), *deed of sale, contract*, ἁ ὠνὰ παρὰ Ξενοκράτη Δελφόν *GDI*1715, al. (Delph., ii B.C.) ; ὠνὰν τὰν ἐν τῷ ἱαρῷ ἀναγεγραμμέναν ib.1764 (ibid., ii B.C.) ; τᾶς ὠ. τὸ ἀντίγραφον *IG*9(1).331.5 (Chaleion, ii B.C.). III. *purchase-money, price*, εἰς..τῶν ὅπλων τὴν ὠ. παρέσχε τρισμυρίας δραχμάς Lys.19.43 ; ἐπέθηκε τῇ ὠ. τάλαντον Plu.*Alc.* 5. **-ημα**, ατος, τό, *a purchase*, *IG*1².374.190, al., 2².1172.24. **-ησείω**, Desiderat. of ὠνέομαι, *wish to buy*, D.C.47.14. **-ησις**, εως, ἡ, *buying*, Decr.Att.ap.Poll.7.15, prob. in *CIG*3597b (Ilium). **-ητέος**, α, ον, *to be bought*, Pl.*Lg.*849c, Amphis 1.4. 2. ὠνητέον, *one must buy*, Luc.*Herm.*58. **-ητής**, οῦ, ὁ, *buyer, purchaser*, X.*Oec.* 2.3, Thphr.*Char.*12.8, Is.*Fr.*173, Plu.*Cat.Mi.*36, etc. ; τινος of something, Pl.*Erx.*394e, Aeschin.1.108, Plu.*Ages* 9 ; ὠνητὴν λαβεῖν to find *a purchaser*, Antiph.161.7. 2. *contractor*, *IG*2².1596.3 ; *lessee* of mines, ib.1587.4, al. **-ητιάω**, = ὠνησείω, Thphr.*Char.*23.7, D.C.73.11, Poll.3.80. ❋ **-ητικός**, ή, όν, *inclined to buy* : Adv. -κῶς, ἔχειν Ph.2.465, al. **-ητός**, ή, όν, also ός, όν, E.*Hel.*816 :—*bought*, of slaves, ἐμὲ δ' ὠνητὴ τέκε μήτηρ Od.14.202 ; δοῦλος οὐκ ὠνητὸς ἀλλ' οἴκοι τραφείς S.*OT*1123, cf. E.*Hec.*365, Pl.*Lg.*841d, etc. ; opp. μίσθιος, Plu.*Lyc.*16 : but ὠνητὴ δύναμις a *mercenary* force, opp. οἰκεία, Th.1.121 ; ὠν. σῖτος, opp. δωρητός, Plu.*Cor.*16. II. *to be bought, that may be bought*, ἐλπίς E.*Hel.*816 ; λόγοι Id.*Fr.*978 ; βασιλεῖαι Pl.*R.*544d ; ἀρχαί Arist.*Pol.*1273a36 ; φιλίη *APl.*4.80 (Agath.) : c. gen. pretii, δόξα χρημάτων οὐκ ὠνητή not *to be bought for* money, Isoc.2.32 : but ἐλπὶς χρήμασιν ὠνητή *with* money, Th. 3.40. **-ήτωρ**, ορος, ὁ, later form of ὠνητής, ὀπωρῶν ὠνήτωρ οἱ ἀγοραῖοι, σὺ δὲ ὀπωρώνης λέγε Thom.Mag.p.258 R. **-ιακός**, ή, όν, of or *for a sale*, ἀσφάλεια (deed of sale) *PGrenf.*1.60.17 (vi A.D.), cf. Just.*Nov.*120.6.2. **-ιος**, α, ον, Aeschin.3.160 ; also ος, ον Luc.*Nigr.*25, Plu.*Cat.Mi.*21 :—*to be bought, for sale*, Epich. 71 ; πῶς ὁ σῖτος ὤ.; how's corn *selling?* Ar.*Ach.*758, cf. *Eq.* 480 : c. gen. pretii, αἵματος ἡ ἀρετὴ ὤ. Aeschin. l.c. ; τῆς οὐσίας γὰρ εἰσιν..ὤνιοι (sc. ἰχθύες) Alex.76.7 ; θανάτου γάρ ἐστιν ὤνιον Men.366, cf. Phld.*Mus.*p.67 K. ; οὐ γὰρ ἀργίας ὤνιον ἡ ὑγίεια Plu.2. 135b ; ἐς ὤνιον ἐλθεῖν come to *market*, Thgn.127 (dub. cj., ὥριον codd.) ; ὤνιον εἶναι to be *on sale*, Pl.*Lg.*848a ; οὐ δ' οἶνος ὤνιος Is.6. 20 ; οὗ τὰ βιβλί' ὤνια Eup.304 ; εἰς Ῥώμην ὤνιος ἤχθη Plu.*Crass.* 8 ; οἰκέτας ὠνίους ἐξάγειν Id.2.680e ; Ἀττικὰς ἰσχάδας ὠνίους κομισθείσας *commercially imported* Attic figs, ib.173c ; ὥστε ὀρόβους ὄντας ὠνίους, prov. of great distress, D.22.15 ; τὰ ὤ. *goods for sale, market-wares*, X.*Cyr.*1.2.3, Lys.22.16, D.8.67 ; τὴν ἀγορὰν τῶν ὠνίων *SIG* 799.22 (Cyzicus, i A.D.), cf. Wilcken *Chr.*41 iii 31 (iii A.D.). 2. of a *venal* magistrate, τοῦ στρατηγοῦ ὠνίου ὄντος Din.1.20 ; διὰ τὴν ἀπορίαν ὤνιοι Arist.*Pol.*1270b10 ; so ἀρχαιρεσίαι ὤ. Plu.*Cat.Mi.* 21.

**ὤννυ**· οὕτως, Hsch. (Perh. Arc. or Cypr., fr. ὦς-νυ, cf. Arc. ταίνυ fr. ταίς-νυ, = ταῖσδε, *Schwyzer*657.30 (iv B.C.)).

**ὠνομάδαται**, 3 pl. pf. Pass. of ὀνομάζω, D.C.37.16.

**ὠνομασμένως**, Adv. part. pf. Pass. of ὀνομάζω, *by giving names*, Arist.*Rh.*1405a36.

**ὦνος**, ὁ, *price paid* for a thing, ὁ δ' ἄξιον ὦνον ἔδωκε Od.15.388, cf. Il.21.41 ; ἄσπετον ὦνον ἕλοιτο Od.14.297 ; ὁ δ' ὑμῖν μυρίον ὦνον ἄλφοι 15.452 ; the person or thing bought being in gen., Λυκάονος ὦνον ἔδωκε *for* Lycaon, Il.23.746, cf. Theoc.1.58, *Inscr.Délos* 502 A 17 (iii B.C.). II. *purchase*, ἐπείγετε δ' ὦνον ὁδαίων Od.15.445. III. *articles of traffic*, ὦνον ἀμείβονται βιοτήσιον A.R.2.1006, cf. D.P.

1106. (Cf. Skt. *vasnás* 'price bid', *vasnám* 'wage', Lat. *vēnum* (fr. **vĕsnom*, this fr. **vŏsnom*); ὦνος and ὠνή from **wŏsnos*, **wŏsnā*, cf. Aeol. ὄννα.)

**ὠνοφύλαξ** [ῠ], ακος, ὁ, cj. for οἰνοφύλαξ in *Milet.*3 p.177 No.33*e* (Vollgraff *Mnemos.*47.71).

**ᾦξε**, v. οἴγω.

**ᾠο-βρᾰχής**, ές, *soaked in white of egg*, Leonid.ap.Aët.6.1, Heliod. ap.Orib.48.33.1. **-γάλα**, ακτος, τό, *eggs mixed with milk*, Paul. Aeg.3.42,6.8, Aët.9.42, etc. **-γενής**, ές, *born of an egg*, Orph. *H.*6.2. **-γονέω**, *lay eggs*, *Gp.*14.1.4. **-γονία**, ἡ, *laying of eggs*, Philostr.*VA*2.14. **-ειδής**, ές, *egg-shaped, ovoid*, Arist.*HA*539$^b$12, 555$^b$24, *GA*733$^a$31, Eudox.*Ars*19.14; cf. ᾠώδης. II. τὸ ᾠ., = τὸ ὑδατοειδές, the *aqueous humour* of the eye, Gal.19.358, Aët.7. 1. **-θεσία**, ἡ, *row of eggs*, i.e. *ovate border*, Aristeas 62. **-θῠτικά**, τά, = ᾠοσκοπικά, Suid. s.v. Ὀρφεύς, prob. in Zos.Alch.p. 245 B.

⊛ **ὠιοί**, v. ὠαιαί. **ᾠοίφιον**, = ᾠύφιον, q.v.

⊛ **ᾠόν**, τό, old poet. forms **ὤεον, ᾤιον**, v. sub fin. :—*egg*, τίκτει ᾠὰ ἐν γῇ καὶ ἐκλέπει [ὁ κροκόδειλος] Hdt.2.68; ᾠὰ χήνεια Eriph. 7; of all birds, Arist.*HA*559$^a$15; but mostly of *hens' eggs*, Ar. *Lys.*856, *Fr.*185, etc.; [ᾠοῦ] τὸ λευκόν, τὸ ὠχρόν, Arist.*HA*559$^a$ 18; τὸ πυρρόν, τὸ χρυσοῦν, Hp.*Mul.*2.171, Ath.9.376d; ᾠὰ ἡμιπαγέα half-boiled *eggs*, Hp.*Acut.*(*Sp.*)53; ἑφθά, ὠμά, Thphr.*Vert.* 2; ᾠὸν ῥοφεῖν Nicom.Com.3; καταπίνειν Antiph.140.5; ᾠὰ κολάπτειν Anaxil.18.4 (anap.); ᾠὰ γόνιμα fertile *eggs*, opp. ὑπηνέμια, ἄγονα, Arist.*GA*730$^a$6,20; also ᾠὰ πλήρη Id.*Mete.*359$^a$14; ᾠὸν τέλειον, opp. ἀτελές, Id.*GA*718$^b$23,24; ᾠὸν ἀνεμιαῖον, ζεφύριον, wind-*egg*, Arar.6, Arist.*HA*560$^a$6; σμύρνης ᾠ. *lump*, Hdt.2.73; ὁ Χρόνος ἐγέννησεν ᾠόν Orph.*Fr.*54, al., cf. Epimenid.5: metaph., ᾠὸν ἅπας γέγονεν he has become *bald as an egg*, *AP*11.398 (Nicias). 2. of the *eggs* or *spawn* of fish, Hdt.2.93; τὰ ᾠὰ ἀφιᾶσι Arist.*HA*567$^b$22, cf. 525$^a$7; of serpents, ib.558$^a$26; of tortoises, ib.558$^a$4. 3. of plants, *seed*, Id. *GA*731$^a$6; cf. ᾠοτοκέω 2. 4. *cupping-glass*, τὰ ἰατρικὰ ᾠὰ ὑέλινα ὄντα καὶ σύστομα Hero *Spir.*1*Prooem.*: *egg-shaped cup*, Dinon 14. The word has the foll. forms: Att. ᾠόν (–⏑), confirmed by Inscrr. ᾠιῶν *IG*11(2).224 *A*11,12 (Delos, iii B.C.), Papyri (ᾠιὰ χήνεα *PCair.Zen.* 130.26 (iii B.C.)), and later Mss.; Aeol. ὤιον, gen. ὤίω (–⏑⏑̱), Sapph.56,112; ὤεον Ibyc.16, Semon.11, Call.*Ep.*6.10, Nic.*Th.*192, Arat.956; ὤβεον is Argive acc. to Hsch. (i.e. ὤϝεον); ᾠόν oxyt. acc. to Theognost.*Can.*130; ὤεον proparox., ib.121. The form ὠόν, which Lat. *ovum* would lead us to expect, is found only in late texts (Lxx *De.*22.6, *Ev.Luc.*11.12, etc.) and is due to loss of the ι in ii B.C.; cogn. with Lat. *ovum*, OHG *ei*, ONorse *egg* (prim. Germanic *aiǯa*–), whence Engl. *egg*.

**ᾦον**, τό, = ὑπερῷον, Laced. word, Clearch.41, Sch.T Il.16.184.

**ᾠόπ**, also ὠὸπ ὄπ, a cry of the κελευστής to give the time to the rowers, Ar.*Ra.*180,208, cf.*Av.*1395 and Sch.

**ᾠό-πωλις**, ιδος, ἡ, *egg-dealer, egg-wife*, Sch.Ar.*Pl.*427. ⊛**-σκοπία**, ἡ, *inspection of eggs, divination from them*, Suid. s.v. Ἑρμαγόρας:—⊛**σκοπικά**, τά, *a treatise thereon*, attributed to Orph., Id. s.v. Ὀρφεύς. **-σκύφιον** [ῠ], τό, *egg-shaped cup* with a double bottom, Asclep.Myrl.ap.Ath.11.503e, cf. 488f.

**ᾠοτοκ-εύς**, έως, ὁ, poet. for ᾠοτόκος, Opp.*H.*1.750. **-έω**, *lay eggs*, Arist.*HA*566$^b$1, etc.; opp. σκωληκοτοκέω and ζωοτοκέω, Id. *Pol.*1256$^b$13, *GA*732$^a$28, al.; τὰ ᾠοτοκοῦντα *oviparous* animals, ib. 749$^a$17:—Pass., *to be produced as eggs*, τὰ ᾠοτοκούμενα ib.746$^a$ 27. 2. of plants, *produce seed*, Emp.79. **-ία**, ἡ, *laying of eggs*, Arist.*HA*538$^a$7, *GA*728$^b$7; πρὸ τῆς ᾠ. before *they lay their eggs*, Plu.2.637f: pl., Hld.9.22, *Gp.*14.7.9. **-ος** (parox.), ον, *oviparous*, Arist.*GA*719$^a$6, al.; of fish, Id.*HA*539$^a$12, al.; ὄφιες Nic.*Th.*136; ἀγέλη ᾠ. *poultry*, *AP*9.286 (Marc.Arg.); τὰ ᾠ., opp. τὰ ζωοτόκα, Arist.*HA*489$^a$34.

**ᾠο-φᾰγέω**, *eat eggs*, *Gp.*14.7.5. **-φορέω**, = ᾠοτοκέω, *EM*404. 36. **-φόρος**, ον, *bearing eggs* or *roe*, ἰχθύες Arist.*HA*621$^b$20; ὠδῖνες ᾠ. the pains *of egg-laying*, Opp.*H.*1.478. 3. of plants. **-φῠλᾰκέω**, *guard their eggs*, of the males of some fish, esp. the *Silurus*, Arist. *HA*568$^b$13, 621$^a$23, al.

**ὠπάζομαι**, *gaze at*, Hsch.: also a fut. ὠπήσεσθαι Id.: aor. ὠπήσασθαι Opp.*C.*3.160; –ήσαντο ib.4.82; –ήσωνται ib.3.404.—A part. Act. ὠπῶντες in *EM*332.9, as etym. of ἑλίκ-ωπες.

**ὦπερ**, Dor. for ὅθενπερ, *whence*, Theoc.3.26.

**ὠπή**, ἡ, (ὄπωπα) *view, sight*, ἀντήσειεν ἐς ὠπήν A.R.3.821, cf. 908. 2. *look, aspect*, Nic.*Al.*377, *Th.*657.

**ὤπιον**, τό, Dim. of ὤψ, = ὀφρύδιον, Hsch.

⊛ **Ὦπις**, ἡ, = Οὖπις, title of Artemis, Pl.*Ax.*371a, Alex.Aet.4.5, cf. Hdt.4.35. **ὠπισταί**, gloss on σκερολίγγες, Hsch. **ὠπλή**, ἡ, *blow of the hand*, Id. (dub.). **ὦπται**, v. ὁράω. ***ὤρ**, ἡ, dat. pl. ὤρεσσιν contr. for ὀάρεσσιν (v. ὄαρ), Il.5.486. II. **ὦρες**, οἱ, *strong towers*, Hsch.

**ὤρα** (A), Ion. **ὤρη**, ἡ: (v. sub fin.):—*care, concern*, mostly c. gen. and usu. joined with some word expressing or implying negation, ὤρη γάρ τ' ὀλίγη πέλεται νεικέων little *heed* is there *for* strifes, Hes.*Op.*30; ἀνδρὸς ἀλωμένου οὐδεμί' ὤρη Tyrt.10.11; μηδεμίαν ὤρην ἔχειν ἁρπασθεισέων [γυναικῶν] Hdt.1.4, cf. 3.155, Alciphr. 1.27; ὤρην ἐποιήσαντο οὐδεμίαν Hdt.9.8, cf. Herod.4.43; ἤδη γὰρ ἔσχες ἐλπίδ' ὡς ἐμοῦ θεοὺς ὤραν τιν' ἕξειν; S.*OC*386; ἔχω δέ τοι οὐδ' ὅσον ὤραν χείματος Theoc.9.20; περὶ τῶν..πλευρῶν οὐδεμίαν ὤ. ἔχεις Pl.Com.2; ὑπὲρ τούτων οὐδ' ὀλίγην ἔθεντο ὤ. Ael.*NA*1.59; τὰ θεῖα ἐν μηδεμιᾷ ὤ. τίθεσθαι Id.*Fr.*106; without a neg., εἰ πατρὸς νέμοι τιν' ὤραν S.*Tr.*57; εἰ δεῖ τῆς τῶν Αἰγυπτίων σοφίας..ὤραν τίθεσθαι Ael.*NA* 12.7. Poet. word, used in Ion. and late Prose. (Hence ὀλιγ-ωρία, cf. Hes.*Op.* l.c.: prob. fr. *ϝώρα, 'watching', cf. βῶροι (i.e. ϝῶροι)· ὀφθαλμοί, Hsch., and ὁράω; cf. οὖρος (B).)

**ὤρα** or **ὥρα** (B), only in Ion. form **ὤρη**, or **ὥρη**, some part of a sacrificial victim, λάψεται γλῶσσαν, ὀσφῦν δασέαν, ὤρην *SIG*1037.2 (Milet., iv/iii B.C.); τοὺς Ἴωνας λέγειν φασὶ τὴν κωλῆν ὤρην καὶ ὡραίαν Sch. HQ Od.12.89: but distd. fr. κωλῆ, λάψεται..κωλῆν ἀντὶ τῆς ὤρης *SIG* l.c. 5; cf. ἄωρος (B). (Perh. cogn. with Lat. *sūra*.)

⊛ **ὥρα** (C), Ion. **ὥρη**, ἡ: Ep. gen. pl. ὡράων, Ion. ὡρέων: loc. pl. ὥρασι, q.v.

A. *any period*, fixed by natural laws and revolutions, whether of the year, month, or day (the sense 'day' is implied in the compd. ἑπτάωρος, q.v.), νυκτός τε ὥραν καὶ μηνὸς καὶ ἐνιαυτοῦ X.*Mem.* 4.7.4, cf. E.*Alc.*449 (lyr.), Pl.*R.*527d; τοῦ γνώμονος ἡ σκιὰ ἐπιοῦσα ἐπὶ τὰς γραμμὰς σημαίνει τὰς ὥρας τοῦ ἐνιαυτοῦ καὶ τῆς ἡμέρας *IG*12(8). 240 (Samothrace): but specially, I. in Hom., *part of the year, season*; mostly in pl., the *seasons*, ὅτε τέτρατον ἦλθεν ἔτος καὶ ἐπήλυθον ὧραι Od.2.107, 19.152; ἀλλ' ὅτε δὴ μῆνές τε καὶ ἡμέραι ἐξετελεῦντο, ἂψ περιτελλομένου ἔτεος, καὶ ἐπήλυθον ὧραι 11.295, 14.294; ἀλλ' ὅτε δή ῥ' ἐνιαυτὸς ἔην, περὶ δ' ἔτραπον ὧραι 10.469, cf. Hes.*Th.* 58; Διὸς ὧραι Od.24.344, cf. Pi.*O.*4.2; ὁ κύκλος τῶν ὡρέων ἐς τὠυτὸ περιιών Hdt.2.4, cf. 1.32; δυώδεκα μέρεα δασαμένους τῶν ὡρέων ἐς [τὸν ἐνιαυτόν] Id.2.4; οὐ μεταλλάσσουσι αἱ ὧραι ib.77; περιτελλομέναις ὥραις S.*OT*156 (lyr.); πάσαις ὥραις at all *seasons*, Id.*Fr.*592.6 (lyr.), Ar.*Av.*696 (anap.); ὧραι ἐτῶν καὶ ἐνιαυτῶν Pl.*Lg.*906c, cf. *Smp.*188a, etc.; τῆς..ὥρας τοῦ ἐνιαυτοῦ ταύτης οὔσης, ἐν ᾗ ἀσθενοῦσιν ἄνθρωποι μάλιστα Th.7.47; χαλεπὴ ὥ. *a bad season*, Pl.*Prt.*344d; ἁ δ' ὥρα χαλέπα Alc.39; ἡ ὥ. αὕτη this *season*, X.*Cyn.*7.1, cf. 5.6; κατὰ τὰς ὥρας according to the *seasons*, Arist.*GA*786$^a$31; οἱ περὶ τὴν ὥραν χρόνοι Id.*Pol.*1335$^a$37.—Hom. and Hes. distinguish three seasons, and express each by the sg. ὥρη, with a word added to specify each: a. *spring*, ἔαρος..ὥρη Il.6.148; ὥρη εἰαρινή 2.471, 16.643, Od.18.367, etc.; so in Trag. and Att., ἦρος ὥρα or ὧραι, Ar.*Nu.*1008 (anap.), E.*Cyc.*508 (lyr.); ὥρα νέα Ar.*Eq.*419; νεᾶνις E.*Ph.*786 (lyr.); v. infr. 2. b. *summer*, θέρεος ὥρη Hes.*Op.*584, 664; ὥρα θερινή X.*Cyn.*9.20, Pl.*Epin.*987a, etc. c. *winter*, χείματος ὥρη Hes.*Op.*450; ὥρῃ χειμερίῃ Od.5.485, Hes.*Op.*494; χειμῶνος ὥρᾳ in winter, And.1.137; χιονοβόλος Plu.2.182e.—A. also names three seasons, *Pr.*454 sq.; an Egyptian division of the year, acc. to D.S.1.26.—A fourth first appears in Alcm.76, θέρος καὶ χεῖμα κὠπώραν τρίταν καὶ τέτρατον τὸ ϝῆρ; and in Hp.*Vict.*3.68, χειμών, ἦρ, θέρος, φθινόπωρον; ὥρας φαίνομεν ἡμεῖς ἦρος χειμῶνος ὀπώρας Ar.*Av.*709 (anap.); τετράμορφοι ὧραι E(?).*Fr.*943 (hex.): later, seven seasons are named, ἔαρ, θέρος, ὀπώρα, φθινόπωρον, σπορητός, χειμών, φυταλιά Gal.17(1).17. 2. esp. *prime of the year, springtime*, ὅσα φύλλα καὶ ἄνθεα γίγνεται ὥρῃ Od.9.51, cf. Il.2.468; παρὰ τὴν καθεστηκυῖαν ὥραν Th.4.6. b. in historians, *the campaigning season*, τὸν τῆς ὥρας εἰς τὸν περίπλουν χρόνον X.*HG*6.2.13; esp. in the phrase ὥρα ἔτους, Th.2.52, 6.70, Pl.*Phdr.*229a, *Lg.*952e, D.50.23, Thphr.*CP*3.23.2; εἰς ἔτους ὥραν next *season*, Plu.*Per.*10. 3. *the year* generally, τῆς ὥρης μέσον θέρος Hdt.8.12; ἐν τῇ πέρυσιν ὥρᾳ last *year*, D.56.3; εἰς ὥρας next *year*, Philem.116, Pl.*Ep.*346c, Lxx *Ge.*18.10, *AP*11.17 (Nicarch.), cf. Plu.*Ages.*22; also εἰς ἄλλας ὥρας *hereafter*, E.*IA*122 (lyr.); ἐς τὰς ὥρας τὰς ἑτέρας Ar.*Nu.*562 (lyr.); ἐκ τῶν ὡρῶν εἰς τὰς ὥρας Id.*Th.*950 (anap.); κἠς ὥρας κἤπειτα *next year* and for ever, Theoc.15.74; also ὥραις ἐξ ὡρᾶν Isyll.25; cf. ὥρασιν. 4. in pl., of *the climate* of a country, *as determined by its seasons*, Hdt.1.142, cf. 149, 4.199 (here perh. three *harvest seasons*); τὰς ὥ. κάλλιστα κεκρημένας Id.3.106; cf. Pl.*Criti.*111e, *Phd.* 111b; *climatic conditions*, Hdt.2.26. II. *time of day*, νυκτὸς ἐν ὥρῃ *h.Merc.*67,155,400; αἱ ὥ. τῆς ἡμέρας the *times* of day, i.e. morning, noon, evening, and night, X.*Mem.*4.3.4; δι' ὥραν ἡμέρας by *the time* of day (fixed for meetings), D.*Prooem.*49, etc.; πᾶσαν ὥ. τῆς ἡμέρας Arist.*Mete.*371$^b$31; μεσονυκτίοις ποθ' ὥραις *Anacreont.*31.1: without ἡμέρας or νυκτός, ἑκάστης ἡμέρας μέχρι τρίτου μέρους ὥρας Pl. *Lg.*784a; τῆς ὥρας μικρὸν πρὸ δύντος ἡλίου X.*HG*7.2.22; ψευσθεὶς τῆς ὥ. having mistaken the *hour*, And.1.38; ἐποίησαν ἔξω μέσων νυκτῶν τὴν ὥραν, i.e. they prolonged the day beyond midnight, D.54.26; τῆς ὥρας ἐγίγνετ' ὀψέ Id.21.84; ὀψίτερον τῆς ὥ. *PTeb.*793 xi 12 (ii B.C.); πολλῆς ὥρας *it being late*, Plb.5.8.3; ἤδη ὥρα πολλή *Ev. Marc.*6.35; ἄχρι πολλῆς ὥρας till *late in the day*, D.H.2.54. b. *duration, interval* or *lapse of time*, μετὰ ἱκανὴν ὥραν τοῦ κατενεχθῆναι τὸν πέλεκυν ἐξακούεται ἡ τῆς πληγῆς φωνή S.E.*M.*5.69; *length of time, term*, Ἄρτεμις ἐννέ' ἐτῶν δεκάδας βίον Ἀρτεμιδώρῳ ἔκχρησεν, τρεῖς δ' ὥραι (dat.) ἔτι προσέθηκε Προνοίη *IG*12(3).1350.3 (Thera, iii B.C.); ἐπὶ πολλὴν ὥ. for a long *time*, J.*AJ*8.4.4. 2. the νυχθήμερον was prob. first divided into twenty-four *hours* by Hipparch., ἐν πόσαις ὥραις ἰσημεριναῖς (equinoctial *hours*) ἕκαστον τῶν ἄστρων ἢ δύνει ἢ ἀνατέλλει 2.4.5, cf. Ptol.*Alm.*3.9, 4.9, al. b. in ordinary life the day from sunrise to sunset was divided into twelve equal parts called ὧραι (ὧραι καιρικαί when it was necessary to distinguish them from the ὧραι ἰσημεριναί, v. καιρικός 2c), ἡμέρα ἡ..δωδεκάωρος, τουτέστιν ἡ ἀπὸ ἀνατολῆς μέχρι δύσεως S.E.*M.*10.182; οὐχὶ δώδεκά εἰσιν ὧραι τῆς ἡμέρας; *Ev.Jo.*11.9; ὡράων ἀμφὶ δυωδεκάδι *AP*9.782 (Paul.Sil.); the time of day was commonly given without the Art., ὥρᾳ α *PHamb.*1. 96.3 (ii A.D.), τρίτης ὥρας Plu.*Rom.*12; ὀγδόης, ἐνάτης, δεκάτης ὥ., Id. *Alex.*60, *Aem.*22, *Ant.*68, etc.; but we have περὶ τὴν τρίτην ὥραν, περὶ τὴν ἑνδεκάτην, *Ev.Matt.*20.3,6, beside περὶ ἕκτην καὶ ἐννάτην ὥ. ib.5;

χθὲς ὥραν ἑβδόμην Ev.Jo.4.52, cf. IG5(1).1390.109 (Andania, i B.C.), etc.; ἐρωτᾷ σε Χαιρήμων δειπνῆσαι.. αὔριον, ἥτις ἐστὶν ιε, ἀπὸ ὥρας θ to-morrow the 15th at 9 o'clock, POxy.110 (ii A.D.): prov., δωδεκάτης ὥ., as we say 'at the eleventh hour', Plu.Crass.17. c. τὰ δυώδεκα μέρεα τῆς ἡμέρης παρὰ Βαβυλωνίων ἔμαθον οἱ Ἕλληνες Hdt. 2.109; here ἡμέρη means the νυχθήμερον, and the μέρεα were each = 2 ὧραι ἰσημεριναί; these double hours (Assyr. kaš-bu) are called ὧραι by Eudox., ἥμισυ ζῳδίου.., ὅ ἐστιν ὥρας ἥμισυ Ars 14.11, cf. 16.2; cf. δωδεκάωρος II. III. Astrol., degree of the zodiac rising at the nativity (cf. ὡρονόμος II, ὡροσκόπος II), ὥ. μεροποσπόρος, τεκνοσπόρος, Man.4.577,597; ἐξ ὥρης ἐσορῶν Ζεὺς Ἑρμείην Jupiter in the ascendant in aspect with Mercury, Id.3.186, cf. 32, al.

B. the fitting time or season for a thing (mostly without Art., even in Att.), freq. in Hom. (v. infr.); ὥρα συνάπτει Pi.P.4.247; ὧραι ἐπειγόμεναι Id.N.4.34; ὅταν ὥ. ἥκῃ X.Mem.2.1.2; but with Art., τῆς ὥ. ἐνθυμεῖσθαι Id.Cyn.8.6: freq. in later writers, τῆς ὥρας ἐπιγενομένης Plb.2.34.3, etc. 2. c. gen. rei, ὥρη κοίτοιο, μύθων, ὕπνου, the time for bed, tale-telling, or sleep, Od.3.334, 11.379, cf. Hdt.1.10; ὥρη δόρποιο Od.14.407; περὶ ἀρίστου ὥραν Th.7.81, X.HG1.1.13; πολυηράτου ἐς γάμου ὥρην Od.15.126; ἐς γάμου ὥρην ἀπικέσθαι Hdt. 6.61; γάμων ἔχειν ὥραν D.H.5.32; so εἰς ἀνδρὸς ὥραν ἥκουσα time for a husband, Pl.Criti.113d; ὥρη ἀρότου, ἀμήτου, Hes.Op.460,575; μέχρι ἀρότου ὥρης IG7.235.3 (Oropus, iv B.C.); καρπῶν ὧραι Ar.Ra. 1034 (anap.); ἡ ὥρα τῆς ὀχείας Arist.HA509$^b$20; τοῦ φωλεύειν ib. 579$^a$26, etc.; also ὥραν εἶχον παιδεύεσθαι I was of age to.. Is.9. 28. 3. ὥρα [ἐστίν] c. inf., it is time to do a thing, ἀλλὰ καὶ ὥρη εὕδειν Od.11.330, cf. 373; so also in Trag. and Att., E.Ph. 1584, Heracl.288 (anap.), Ar.Ec.30, Pl.Prt.361e, 362a; so δοκεῖ οὐχ ὥρα εἶναι καθεύδειν X.An.1.3.11, cf. HG7.2.13 (dub. l.): c. acc. et inf., ὥρα δ' ἐμπόρους καθιέναι ἄγκυραν A.Ch.661, cf. S.OT466 (lyr.): c. dat. et inf., X.Cyr.4.5.1, Pl.Tht.145b: in these phrases the inf. pres. is almost universal; the aor., however, occurs in Od.21.428, S.Aj.245 (lyr.), Ar.Ach.393 (where also ἐστί is added to ὥρα, as in Philyll.3, ἀφαιρεῖν ὥρα 'στὶν ἤδη τὰς τραπέζας); and the pf. in ὥρα πεπαῦσθαι Plu.2.728d: sts. the inf. must be supplied, οὐδέ τί σε χρή, πρὶν ὥρη, καταλέχθαι Od.15.394, cf. E.El.112 (lyr.), Ar.Ec.877; ὥρα κὴς οἶκον (i.e. ἰέναι εἰς οἶκον) Theoc.15. 147. 4. in various adverb. usages, τὴν ὥρην at the right time, Hdt.2.2, 8.19, X.Oec.20.16: but τὴν ὥ. at that hour, Hes.Sc.401; ταύτην τὴν ὥραν at this season, X.Cyn.9.1; [ἡ ἶρις] πᾶσαν ὥραν γίγνεται τῆς ἡμέρας Arist.Mete.371$^b$31; δείελον ὥρην παύομαι ἀμήτοιο A.R. 3.417; ὥραν οὐδενὸς κοινὴν θεῶν at an hour.., A.Eu.109, cf. E.Ba. 724, Aeschin.1.9; αὐτῆς ὥρας immediately, PMich. in Class.Phil.22. 255 (iii A.D.); ἐν ὥρῃ in due season, in good time, Od.17.176, Hdt. 1.31, cf. Pi.O.6.28, Ar.V.242, etc.; also αἰεὶ εἰς ὥρας in successive seasons, Od.9.135; ἐς τὰς ὥρας for all time, Ar.Ra.382 (lyr. cf. supr. A.I.3) (hence in an acclamation [ε]ἰς ὥρας πᾶσι τοῖς τὴν πόλιν φιλοῦσιν hurrah for.., POxy.41.29 (iii/iv A.D.)); οἱ ὧδε χέζοντες εἰς ὥ. μὴ ἔλθοιεν Milet.2(3) No.406, cf. ὥρασι; καθ' ὥραν Theoc.18.12, Plb.1. 45.4, cf. 3.93.6, etc.; opp. παρ' ὥρην AP7.534 (Alex.Aet. or Autom.), cf. Plu.2.784b, etc.:—πρὸ τῆς ὥρας X.Oec.20.16; πρὸ ὥρας Luc.Luct.13; πρὸ ὥρας τελευτῆσαι IG4$^2$(1).84.26 (Epid., i A.D.); πρὶν ὥρας Pi.P.4.43 (cf. πρίν A.II.4). II. metaph., the spring-time of life, the bloom of youth, Mimn.3.1; ὥραν ἐχούσας A.Supp.997, cf. Th.13,535; παῖδας πρὸς τέρμασιν ὥρας Ar.Av.705 (anap.); πάντες οἱ ἐν ὥρᾳ Pl.R.474d; οὐκ ἐν ὥ., = πρεσβύτερος, Id.Phdr. 240d; ἐὰν ἐπὶ ὥρᾳ ᾖ Id.R.474e; ἕως ἂν ἐν ὥρᾳ ὦσι Id.Men.76b; παυσαμένου τῆς ὥ. prob. in Id.Phdr.234a; ἀνθεῖν ἐν ὥ. Id.R.475a; τὴν ὥ. διαφυλάξαι ἄβατον τοῖς πονηροῖς Isoc.10.58; λήγειν ὥρας, opp. ἀνθεῖν, Pl.Alc.1.131e; ὡς ἐπιγιγνόμενόν τι τέλος, οἷον τοῖς ἀκμαίοις ἡ ὥρα Arist.EN1174$^b$33, cf. 1157$^a$8. 2. freq. involving an idea of beauty, φεῦ φεῦ τῆς ὥρας τοῦ κάλλους Ar.Av.1724 (lyr.); ὥρᾳ.. ἡλικίας λαμπρός Th.6.54; κάλλει καὶ ὥρᾳ διενεγκόντες Aeschin.1.134, cf. ib.158; καλὸς ὥρᾳ τε κεκραμένος Pi.O.10(11).104, cf. X.Mem. 2.1.22, Pl.Lg.837b; ἀφ' ὥρας ἐργάζεσθαι quaestum corpore facere, Plu.Tim.14, cf. X.Mem.1.6.13, Smp.8.21; τὴν ὥ. πεπωληκότες Phld.Rh.1.344 S.:—then, b. generally, beauty, grace, elegance of style, D.H.Pomp.2, Plu.2.874b, etc.; γλυκύτης καὶ ὥ. Hermog.Id.2.3, cf. Men.Rh.p.335 S., Him.Or.1.2; of beauty in general, χάρις καὶ ὥρα Plu.2.128d. 3. Ὥρα personified, like Ἥβη, Pi.N.8.1. III. = τὰ ὡραῖα, the produce of the season, fruits of the year, ἀπὸ τῆς ὥρας ἐτρέφοντο X.HG2.1.1.

C. personified, αἱ Ὧραι, the Hours, keepers of heaven's cloudgate, Il.5.749, 8.393; and ministers of the gods, ib.433; Ζεῦ, τεαὶ .. Ὧραι Pi.O.4.2; esp. of Aphrodite, h.Hom.6.5,12; also Ὧ. Διονυσιάδες, Καρνειάδες, Simon.148, Call.Ap.87; three in number, Eunomia, Dike, Eirene, daughters of Zeus and Themis, Hes.Th. 901; Ὧραι πολυάνθεμοι Pi.O.13.17, cf. Alex.261.6, Theoc.1.150, etc.: freq. joined with the Χάριτες, h.Ap.194, Hes.Op.75; worshipped at Athens, Paus.9.35.1; at Argos, Id.2.20.5; at Attaleia, BMus.Inscr.1044 (i B.C.).

ὡραία, ἡ, v. ὡραῖος I.3. II. v. ὥρα (B).

❋ ὡραΐζω, Att. contr. ὡρᾴζω, (ὡραῖος) beautify, adorn, Aristid. Quint.2.6:—but II. mostly Pass., bloom with youthful beauty, Cratin.272; αἱ παρειαὶ ὡ. Callistr.Stat.6; ἐν τρισὶν ὡραΐσθην LXX Si. 25.1; ἐν κάλλει Aristaenet.2.10; ὡραϊσμένη ἐπικτήτοις σοφίσμασι tricked out, Luc.Am.38:—so intr. in Act., ὡρᾴζων ἡλικίᾳ IG12(7). 53.7 (Amorgos, iii A.D.). 2. give oneself airs, behave affectedly, ὡρᾳζομένη καὶ θρυπτομένη Eup.358; ὡς ὡραΐζεθ' (leg. ὡρᾴζεθ') ἡ τύχη πρὸς τοὺς βίους Men.855; Meineke restores ὡρᾴζεται (cod. Rav. δρείζεται) for ὀρίζεται in Ar.Ec.202. 3. Med., make display (of one's oratory), Chor.Zach.1.8.

ὡραιό-καρπος, ον, with ripe or timely fruit, Tz.H.4.691. -κόμος, ον, studying dress or decoration, Suid. -ομαι, Pass., to be beautiful, LXX Ca.1.10, 7.1,6; ὡραιώθης μοι σφόδρα 2Ki.1.26. -πολέω, live with the young, Suid.:—but cf. ὡραπολεῖν. -πώλης, ου, ὁ, selling fresh fruits, also = ταριχοπώλης, Hsch.; also = ὁ τὴν ἀκμὴν πωλήσας, Id.

❋ ὡραῖος, α, ον, produced at the right season (ὥρα), seasonable, timely: esp. of the fruits of the earth, βίος or βίοτος ὡ. store of fruits gathered in due season, Hes.Op.32,307; ὡ. καρποί the fruits of the season, καρποὺς.. κατατίθεσθαι ὡραίους to store them up in season, Hdt.1.202: freq. in neut., ὡραῖα, τά, Th.1.120, 3.58, X.An.5.3.9, Pl.Lg.845e; ὡραίως τὰ ὡραῖα ἀποδιδόναι Hp.Aph.3.8; ὡραῖα.. ἀποτελεῖν ἱερά to render fruits of the season as sacred offerings, Pl.Criti. 116c, cf. Orac.ap.D.21.52; τρωκτὰ ὡ. X.An.5.3.12; ἄνθεα AP9.564 (Nicias); σῦκα Aret.CD1.3; also of animals, ὡ. ἄρνες yearling, AP6. 157 (Theodorid.); of tunnies at a year old (from six months to one year they were called πηλαμύδες), πηλαμὺς.. ὡραία θέρους τῷ Βοσπορίτῃ S.Fr.503; ὡ. θύννοι Ps.-Hes.ap.Ath.3.116b, cf. Hices.ib.116e, Archestr.Fr.38.9, Plaut.Capt.851; τάριχος ὡ. fish salted or pickled in the season, Alex.186.5; ἰχθύες ἐς τάγηνον ὡ. Babr.6.4; σαργάναι ὡ. pickling-tubs, Poll.7.27: hence generally, agricultural produce, εἶναι ἐνεχυρασίαν Αἰξωνεῦσιν ἐκ τῶν ὡ. τῶν ἐκ τοῦ χωρίου IG2$^2$.2492.8 (iv B.C.). 2. τὰ ὡραῖα, = τὰ καταμήνια, esp. at their first appearance, Hp.Superf.34. 3. Subst. ἡ ὡραία (in full, ὥρη ἡ ὡραίη Aret. SD1.4, Phryn.PSp.128 B., etc.), harvest-time, esp. the twenty days before and twenty days after the rising of the dog-star, μίμνει ἐς ὡραίην till harvest-time, A.R.3.1390. b. the campaigning-season, during which the troops kept the field, D.9.48, 56.30, Plb.3.16. 7. c. τὴν μὲν ὡραίην οὐκ ὕει it does not rain in the season (sc. of rain), Hdt.4.28. II. happening or done in due season, seasonable, ἄροτος, ἔργον, Hes.Op.617,642; πλόος ib.630; χειμῶνες Thphr.HP4.14.1; ὕδατα Id.CP2.2.1; σκαπάνη ib.3.16.1; τομὴ [καλάμου] Id.HP4.11.4; ὅτε ὡραῖον εἴη when the weather permitted, App.Pun.120. 2. metaph., (ὥρα (c) B) seasonable, due, proper, ὡραίων τυχεῖν, = νομίμων τυχεῖν (cf. ὅριος (A). III. 2), E.Supp.175: ἐν ὡραί[ᾳ ἐκκλησίᾳ] dub. in SIG668.4 (Delphi, ii B.C.); ἐνιαύτια ὡ. ib. 1025.37 (Cos, iv/iii B.C.), cf. Hsch. III. of persons, seasonable or ripe for a thing, c. gen., ἀνδρὸς ὡραίη Hdt.1.107, cf. Lys.Fr.4; γάμων or γάμου ὡραῖαι, Hdt.1.196, 6.122, cf. X.Cyr.4.6.9; ἐς ἥβην ὡραίαν γάμων E.Hel.12 (ὡραίων codd.); ὅστις οὐκέθ' ὡραῖος γαμεῖ Id.Fr.804; ὡ. γάμος seasonable marriage, A.Fr.55; also of old persons, ripe or ready for death, πατήρ γε μὴν ὡ. E.Alc.516; αὐτὸς δ', ἐν ὡ. γὰρ ἕσταμεν βίῳ, θνῄσκειν ἕτοιμος Id.Ph.968; θάνατος ὡ. X.Ages.10.3; σορὸς Ar.V.1365; ὡραῖος ἀποτέθνηκεν Plu.2.178e; so ὕλη ὡ. τέμνεσθαι Thphr.HP5.1.1. 2. in reference to age, in the prime of life, youthful, Hes.Op.695: hence in the bloom of youth, opp. ἄωρος, X.Smp.8.21, Pl.R.574c; ὡ. ἐὼν καὶ καλός Pi.O.9.94; παιδίσκη ὡραιοτάτη Ar.Ach.1148 (anap.), cf. Ra.291,514; παῖς ὡραῖος Id.Av.138: but not necessarily implying beauty, τοῖς τῶν ὡραίων προσώποις, καλῶν δὲ μή Pl.R.601b; ἄνευ κάλλους ὡραῖοι Arist.Rh. 1406$^b$37; cf. ὥρα (c) B II. 3. generally, of things, beautiful, graceful, LXX Ge.3.6, 2Ch.36.19, Ev.Matt.23.27; ἡ ὡ. πύλη τοῦ ἱεροῦ Act. Ap.3.10, cf. 3.2. IV. irreg. Sup. ὡραιέστατος Epich.186d. V. Adv. ὡραίως Hp.Aph.3.8.

ὡραιότης, ητος, ἡ, the ripeness of the fruits of the year, f.l. in Thphr.HP9.1.6. II. the bloom of youth, beauty, LXX Is.44.13, al.; σώματος X.Eph.1.1, Hld.2.1, al.: pl., X.Oec.7.43.

ὡραιόφθαλμος, ον, gloss on εὐῶπις, Sch.Pi.O.10(11).90.

ὡραϊσμός, ὁ, adornment, τοῦ σώματος, Plu.Agis 4; refinement, Id. 2.972d; with notion of effeminacy and affectation, LXX Je.4.30: metaph. of style, elegance, D.H.Comp.1, Plu.Fab.1.

ὡραϊστής, οῦ, ὁ, fop, AB225, Hsch. s.v. βαυκιζόμενος, EM192. 20.

❋ ὡρακιάω, faint, swoon away, Ar.Ra.481, Pax702, and in later Prose, as Phld.Acad.Ind.p.50 M., Lib.Decl.26.33, 31.34, Them.Or. 26.314b.—Moer.p.425 P. writes it with the aspir., as Att. for λιποψυχέω. Others wrote it ὠρακιάω as if for ὠχριάω, and this sense is given to the word by Aristaenet.1.10, Procop.Arc.10, Sch.Ar.Pax l.c.

ὡρακίζω, = foreg., EM823.33.

ὡρανιστήρ· ἱμάς, Hsch.

ὠρᾶνος, Aeol. for οὐρανός, Sapph.1.11, Alc.17 (but ὄρανος Sapph. 37,64, Alc.34):—also Dor. and Boeot. ὠρανός Alcm.23.16, Corinn. Supp.2.79, and ὠρανίαφι, Adv. in heaven, Alcm.59; cf. Boeot. Ὠρανία IG7.1804.1 (Thespiae).

ὡραπολεῖ· κατὰ τὴν εἰθισμένην ὥραν ἑκάστου ἔτους ἀναπολεῖν, Hsch.

ὡράριθμος [ᾰ], ον, reckoning the hours, Sch.Pi.P.4.336.

ὥρασι, ὥρασιν (also ὥρας, Men., v. infr.), Adv.: (old loc. pl. of ὥρα (c)):—in season, in good time, μὴ ὥρασιν ἵκοιτο, as an imprecation, may he not come in season, i.e. bad luck to him! Alex.266. 1, Luc.DMeretr.10.3; μὴ ὥρας σύ γε.. ἵκοιο Men.Pk.131; μὴ ὥρασ' ἵκοισθε (Dind. for ὥρας) Ar.Lys.1037 (troch.); ὁ μὴ ὥρασι that fellow—bad luck to him! ib.391; μὴ ὥρασιν ἱκοίμην, εἰ.. Luc.Salt.5.5; also μὴ σύ γ' εἰς ὥρας ἵκοιο Babr.53.7 (cf. ὥρα (c) B.I.4).—For the form, cf. θύρασι, Ὀλυμπίασι.

**ὠρεῖον**, τό, Cret. for οὐρεῖον (q. v.), *guard-house, fort*, *GDI*5075.79 (Latos, i B.C.): ὤρεια· φυλακτήρια, Hsch.

**ὠρεῖον**, τό, = Lat. *horreum*, *EM*697.32, *Gp.*2.28 tit.

**ὠρείτης**, v. ὠρίτης.

**ὠρείτροφος**, ον, poet. for ὀρείτροφος, of Dionysus, cj. in *AP*9.524.25.

**ὠρεσίδουπος** [ῐ], ον, poet. for ὀρεσίδουπος, *making a din on the mountains*, *AP*9.524.25 (Scaliger for ὠρεσίλοιπος; he also suggested -κοιτος).

**ὠρεσῐδώτης**, ου, ὁ, *one who brings on the seasons*, or *who gives the ripe fruits in their season*, epith. of Apollo, like ὠρηφόρος, ib.525.25.

**ὤρεσσιν**, v. ὤρ, ὄαρ. **ὤρετο**, v. ὄρνυμι.

**ὠρεύω**, *take care of, attend to*, c. acc., Hes.*Th.*903, cf. Hsch., Corn.*ND*1:—Pass., ib.29. (Hes. and Corn. ll. cc. use the word to expl. the Ὧραι; Hsch. glosses it by τὸ τῶν ἀγρίων νομῶν καὶ ἐθνῶν ἐπιμελεῖσθαι: cf. ὀρεύειν and οὐρεύω, of which ὠρεύω might be a Dor. form.)

**ὠρέω**, in pres. part. ὠρεόντων· φροντιζόντων, Hp.ap.Gal.19.157: but ὠρέοντα· χρονίζοντα, ὦρος γὰρ ὁ χρόνος καὶ ὡρογράφοι οἱ περὶ χρόνου γράψαντες, Hp.ap.Erot.: but the latter word may be imaginary, the reference being perh. to ὡραῖα ἐόντα in Id.*Loc.Hom.*38; neither has been found in our codd. of Hp.:—we have also ὠρήσαντα· φυλάσσοντα, and ὠρήσονται· φυλάσσονται, Hsch.; ὠρεῖν· φυλάττειν, ὅθεν καὶ ὁ θυρωρὸς λέγεται, Id., which together with *EM* 686.54, al., Corn.*ND*1, suggests that ὠρέω is coined by Grammarians to expl. words in -ωρός.

**ὥρη, ὤρη**, ἡ, Ion. for ὥρα, ὤρα.

**ὠρημάτων**· φυλαγμάτων, Hsch.

**ὠρητύς**, ύος, ἡ, = πήρωσις, Hsch. (Cf. πωρητύς.)

**ὡρηφόρος**, ον, *leading on the seasons*, or *bringing on the fruits in their season*, epith. of Demeter, *h.Cer.*54,192,492, Orph.*Fr.*49.102.

**ὡριαίνω**, = ὡραΐζω, -ομαι, Hsch.:—Med., Clearch.39.

**ὡριαῖος**, α, ον, (ὥρα (c) A.II) *an hour long*, διάστημα Hipparch.3.5.4, al., cf. S.E.*M.*5.63, Ptol.*Geog.*1.11.1, al.; μέγεθος Vett.Val.22.4.

**ὡριάς**, άδος, poet. fem. of ὥριος, Orph.*H.*10.19.

**ὠρίγγη**· ἑώρα, Hsch. (ὤριγγας v.l. for ὠλίγγας in Poll.2.67 seems to be different).

**ὠρίζεσκον**, v. sub ὀαρίζω.

**ὠρίζω**, 3 sg. ὠρίζει· ὑπνοῖ, ὁμιλεῖ, φροντίζει, μεριμνᾷ, ἀδολεσχεῖ, Hsch. (i. e. partly ὠρίζει fr. ὦρος I, partly ὠρ- = ὀαρ-, and partly ὡρίζει fr. ὥρα).

**ὡρῐκός**, ή, όν, (ὥρα) *in one's prime, blooming*, of the young people, Ar.*Ach.*272, *Fr.*235; ὡ. νέος Ael.*NA*14.5, cf. 4.8 (Comp.), Alciphr. 1.13; πάνυ γάρ ἐστιν ὡρικώτατα τὰ τιτθί', ὥσπερ μῆλον Crates Com. 40. II. Adv. -κῶς, πυνθάνει *you ask so maidenly, so prettily*, Ar.*Pl.*963; cf. ὥρα (c) B.II.

**ὡρῐμ-άζω**, (ὥριμος) gloss on ὑποπερκάζω, Sch.Od.7.126. **-αία**, ἡ (sc. ἄφεσις or μέθοδος), Astrol., *reckoning from the* ὥρα (c) A.II, Ptol. *Tetr.*131, Vett.Val.146.33, Id. in *Cat.Cod.Astr.*8(1).240, *Cod.Marc. Ven.*335 fol.384. **-ος**, ον (also α, ον *Leg.Gort.*, v. infr.), = ὡραῖος, *ripe*, καρπός Arist.*Fr.*571; ὡρίμη κριθή Sch.Ar.*Eq.*1233, Eust.1446.29; βότρυες, opp. ὄμφακες, *AP*9.316 (Leon.); ὀπώρα D.S.17.67: *timely, in season*, of fish, Nicom.Com.1.21: c. inf., τοῦ ὑπάρχοντός μοι κλήρου..ὡρίμου σπαρῆναι *PTeb.*54.7 (i B.C.); καιρὸς ὡριμώτατος εἴς τι *Gp.*9.9.7. 2. *marriageable*, fem. ὡρίμα *Leg.Gort.*8.39. 3. τὸ ὥριμον *bloom*, σευ τὸ ὡ. τέφρη κάψει Herod.1.38. **-ότης**, ητος, ἡ, *ripeness, seasonableness*, Sch.D Il.19.119.

**ὡρινθιᾶν**· ἐπείγεσθαι εἰς ἀπόπατον, Hsch.

**ὡριόκαρπος**, ον, *with ripe* or *timely fruit*, Orph.*H.*56.11.

**ὥριον**, Adv., Ion. for αὔριον, Gramm.post Greg.Cor.p.698 S.

⊕ **ὥριος** (A), α, ον, Pi.*P.*9.98; also ος, ον *AP*7.188 (Thall.), 9.311 (Phil.), Opp.*H.*1.689:—poet. form of ὡραῖος, *produced in season*, ὥρια πάντα *all the fruits of the season*, Od.9.131, Theoc.7.62, cf. Hes. *Op.*394, Theoc.15.112, *AP*9.329 (Leon.). II. generally, *in due season, seasonable*, ἔργα Hes.*Op.*392,422; γάμος ib.697; ᾠδίς Opp. l.c., cf. *AP*9.311 (Phil.); χρόνος ὡ. ἡμῖν ib.10.100 (Antiphan.); πλόος κώπαις ὡ. Arat.154: ὥριον (sc. ἐστί) c. inf., *it is time*.., Sol.27.9 (s.v.l.). 2. *youthful*, ἄνθος *Epigr.Gr.*319 (Philadelphia); *fresh*, ὥριον οἷά τε μῆλον κτλ. Archyt.Amphiss.2 (= Euph.11). III. ὥρια, τά, *the season*, νόσον ὥρια τίκτει Bion *Fr.*15.13.—This poet. form is also used in late Prose, τὸ ὡ. τῆς ἀκμῆς Hld.10.9; τὰ ὡ. D.L.2.139, cf. Him.*Or.*3.5. Adv. -ως Anon.ap.Suid.; but neut. sg. used as Adv., Arat.1076. 2. θαψάτωσαν καὶ τὰ ὡ. αὐτοῦ, καθὼς ἔθος ἐστίν, αὐτοὶ ποιησάτωσαν *his funeral rites*, *IG*9(1).39, cf. 42 (Phocis, ii B.C.).

**ὥριος** (B), ον, (ὦρος, *sleep*) *nightly*, χορός cj. Brunck in Mesom. *Sol.*22, where χρόνον ὥριον codd., fort. recte.

**ὥριος** (C), Dor., = οὔριος, v.l. (ap.Sch.) in Theoc.7.62, cj. in Hippod.ap.Stob.4.39.26.

**ὥρισμα**, ατος, τό, f.l. for ὅρισμα in Opp.*C.*4.23.

**ὡρισμένως**, Adv., (ὁρίζω) *definitely*, Arist.*Cat.*8ᵃ36,ᵇ17, *Top.*159ᵇ1, *Metaph.*1020ᵇ33, Plb.10.46.10, S.E.*M.*7.336; *with the definite article*, Chrysipp.*Stoic.*2.102; *regularly*, Sor.1.95.

**ὥριστος** or **ὤριστος**, Ion. crasis for ὁ ἄριστος, Il.11.288, al.

⊕ **ὡρίτης** [ῑ], ου, ὁ, *Ruler of the Seasons*, of Apollo, Lyc.352; Ἀπόλλωνος Ὠρείτου (sic) *Anecd.Stud.*267.

**Ὠρίων**, ωνος, ὁ, *Orion*, Od.5.121, 11.310,572, Telesarch.ap.S.E. *M.*1.262, Str.9.2.12, etc. II. the *constellation* named after him, Il.18.486,488, 22.29, Od.5.274, Hes.*Op.*598,609, Arist. *Mete.*361ᵇ23, *Pr.*941ᵇ24. III. a fabulous Indian bird, Str.15.1.69, Ael.*NA*17.22, Nonn.*D.*26.202. [ῑ in Hom.; ῐ Att., E.*Ion* 1153, *Cyc.*213, v. Choerob. *in Theod.*1.272 H.: we also find Ὠᾰρίων in Corinn.2, *Supp.*2.77, Call.*Dian.*265, and in Pi.*N.*2.12 (v.l. ὀαρίωνα); Adj. Ὠαριώνειος, α, ον, φύσις Id.*I.*4(3).49(67); the Homeric Ὠρῑων arose by contraction of Ὠα- and metrical lengthening of ι.]

**ὡρμέᾰται, ὡρμέᾰτο**, v. ὁρμάω. **ὤρνυεν, ὤρνῠτο**, v. ὄρνυμι.

**ὡρο-γενής**, ές, in pl., οἱ ὡ. θεοί *gods* (planets) *who preside over the several hours of the day*, *PMag.Leid.W.*1.30, cf. 9.37. **-γνωμονέω**, *tell the hour*, Dam.*Isid.*100. **-γρᾰφίαι**, αἱ, *annals*, D.S.1.26; cf. ὦρος (c) II. **-γράφος** [ᾰ], ὁ, *writing history by seasons* or *years, annalist*, Plu.2.869a; also *précis-writer* (or perh. *postmaster*), *POxy.* 710 (ii B.C.). **-δεσμος**, ὁ, *straw rope for binding sheaves*, Eust. 1162.32. **-δρομέω**, = ὡροσκοπέω, of a sign, Tz.*H.*1.476. **-δρόμημα**, ατος, τό, *space traversed in an hour*, *Cat.Cod.Astr.*1.23. **-θετέω**, *take note* of a thing *in casting a nativity*, τὸν Ἄρη καὶ τὸν Κρόνον *AP* 11.160 (Lucill.). II. *to be in the ascendant at the natal hour*, of one's ruling planet, ὡροθετεῖ σε Κρόνος ib.161 (Id.). **-κράτωρ**, ορος, ὁ, *the lord of the hour*, Ps.-Ptol.*Centil.*90.

**ὡρολογ-έω**, *tell of the* Ὧραι, Eust.1349.9; cf. sq. **-ητής**, οῦ, ὁ, *one that tells of the* Ὧραι (or possibly *reaps profit from*..), λαβάργυρος ὡ., of Prodicus, who composed a speech entitled Ὧραι, Timo 18, cf. Eust.1349.10. **-ιά[ρχης]**, ου, ὁ, *inspector of clocks*, prob. in *IGRom.* 3.1397 (Bithynia, iii A.D.). **-ικός**, ή, όν, *telling the hour*, Eust. ad D.P.223.⊕ **-ιον**, τό, *an instrument for telling the time, a dial* or *clock*, ὡ. σκιοθηρικόν the sun-*dial* of Anaximenes, Plin.*HN*2.187; a sun-dial (ὡρολόγιον) at Zea (Piraeus) mentioned in *PHaw.*81 (Att. periegesis of iii B.C., pap. of ii A.D.); ἀπὸ τοῦ σκιακοῦ ὡρολογίου *IGRom.*4. 293*a* i 35 (Pergam., prob. 127/6 B.C.), cf. Cleom.1.10sq., Gem.8.23, Plu.2.1006f, *CIG*1947 (loc. inc.), *Inscr.Cos*57, Suid. (who writes it ὡρολογεῖον); ὡ. ὑδραυλικόν a water-*clock*, = κλεψύδρα, cf. Aristocl. ap.Ath.4.174c, Plin.*HN*7.213, Bato 2.14; μηχανικὰ ὡ. Ach.Tat. *Intr.Arat.*25.6: the dimensions of a water(?)-clock are given in *POxy.*470.31 (iii A.D.). **-ος** (parox.), ὁ, *an Egyptian astrologer*, Chaerem.ap.Porph.*Abst.*4.8.

**ὡρό-μαντις**, εως, ὁ, *the hour-prophet*, of the cock, prob. in Babr. 124.15 (ὡρομάτην cod. Vat., ὡρονόμον Suid. s. v. πέταυρα). **-μέδων**, οντος, ὁ, *ruling the seasons*, of Phoebus, *IG*12(5).893 (Tenos, ii/iii A.D.), *Epigr.Gr.*1036.2 (Bithynia).

**ὡρονομ-εῖον** or **-νόμιον**, τό, = ὡρολόγιον, Alex.Aphr.*Pr.*1.95, Hld. 9.22. **-εύς**, ῆος, ὁ, = ὡρονόμος II, Antioch.Astr. in *Cat.Cod.Astr.* 1.108. **-εύω**, poet. for sq., Man.4.593, Doroth.ap.Heph.Astr. 3.30. **-έω**, *to be in the ascendant*, Man.1.58,339: c. acc., Κρόνος ὡρονομεῖ τετραπόδων γένεσιν *AP*11.383 (Pall.). **-ικός**, ή, όν, *of* or *for dividing and marking the hours*, κατασκεύασμα Sch.Ar.*Av.* 1693. **-ιον**, τό, v. ὡρονομεῖον. **-ος** (parox.), ὁ, *hour-divider*, i.e. *a dial* or *clock*, *AP*14.6; cf. ὡρόμαντις. II. in Astrology, = ὡροσκόπος II. 1, *ascendant*, Man.1.30,262, 3.120, Doroth.ap.Heph. Astr.2.24. 2. name of certain deities, οἱ δεκαδάρχαι καὶ ζῳδιοκράτορες καὶ ὡρονόμοι καὶ κραταιοί Dam.*Pr.*351.

**ὦρορε**, v. ὄρνυμι.

⊕ **ὦρος** (A), ὁ, = ἄωρος (c), *sleep*, Call.*Fr.*150 (cf. *PSI*11.1218*a*28); = ἡ νύξ, Hsch.; cf. ὥριος (B).

⊕ **ὦρος** (B), ὁ, Dor. for ὅρος (q. v.).

⊕ **ὦρος** (C), ὁ, (ὥρα) *a year*, Euph.58, Plu.2.677e, D.S.1.26, Ath.10. 423e. II. in pl., *annals*, esp. of Ion. writers, Luc.*Macr.* 14 (ubi vulg. ὅροι), Ath.13.572f (Alexis), Neanth.5 J., Duris 22 J., etc.; Σαμιακοὶ ὦ. Antig.*Mir.*120.

⊕ **ὦρος** (D), Aeol. crasis for ὁ ἔρος (better ὦρος), Theoc.30.9.

⊕ **ὡροσκοπ-εῖον**, τό, = ὡρολόγιον, Str.2.5.14, Gem.2.35, Boeth.ap. Eus.*PE*11.28; ὕδριον ὡροσκοπεῖον Hero *Spir.*1*Praef.*; also **-σκόπιον**, D.L.2.1, 6.104; τὰ ὕδρεια τῶν ὡροσκοπίων water-*clocks*, Simp. *in Ph.* 1335.14. II. ὡροσκόπιον, = ὡροσκόπος II, S.E.*M.*5.68. 2. *instrument for observing the* ὡροσκόπος, τῆς δι' ἀστρολάβων ὡροσκοπίων κατ' αὐτὴν τὴν ἔκτεξιν διοπτεύσεως Ptol.*Tetr.*108. **-έω**, Astrol., of a zodiacal sign or part of one, *mark by its rising the time of* birth, *to be in the ascendant*, τὸν χρόνον τοῦ ἀνίσχοντος ζῳδίου καὶ κατ' ἀκρίβειαν -οῦντος λαμβάνειν S.E.*M.*5.70, cf. Ptol.*Tetr.*33; τῆς ὡροσκοπούσης μοίρας Porph.ap.Stob.2.8.42. **-ησις**, εως, ἡ, Astrol., *observation of the* ὡροσκόπος II, S.E.*M.*5.99, Paul.Al.*S.*1, *Cat.Cod. Astr.*5(3).85. **-ία**, ἡ, = foreg., Ptol.*Tetr.*75, Porph.ap.Stob.2.8. 42. II. *observation of hours*, Sch.T Il.21.111. **-ικός**, ή, όν, *pertaining to a* ὡροσκόπος II, Ptol.*Tetr.*191, Vett.Val.156.2. **-ιον**, v. ὡροσκοπεῖον. **-ος** (parox.), ὁ, Astrol., *caster of nativities, astrologer*, τὰς τῶν ὡροσκόπων βοτάνας Gal.11.798. 2. Adj., *of the ascendant* (v. infr. II), φέγγεα Man.4.59, cf. 496. II. as Subst., ὡροσκόπος, ὁ, the sign or degree rising at the time of birth, *ascendant*, Ptol.*Tetr.*33, 130, S.E.*M.*5.12,50,61, Porph.ap.Stob.2.8.42. 2. pl., of certain stellar deities whose names agree in part with those of the δεκανοί II, from which, however, they are distd., τῶν λϛ' λαμπρῶν ὡροσκόπων *PLond.*1.98ʳ15, al., cf. Iamb.*Myst.*8.4.

**ὡροτρόφος**, ον, *fostering the seasons, bringing them on*, κοῦρος, of the sun, Orph.*H.*8.10, cf. 38.25.

**ὥρρα**· τηνικαῦτα, Hsch. **ὦρσε, ὦρτο**, v. ὄρνυμι. **ὠρτός**· βωμός, Id.

**ὤρυγγες**, οἱ, *striped* or *piebald horses* (including *zebras*), Opp.*C.* 1.317.

**ὠρῡγή**, ἡ, = ὠρυθμός, Hermesian.7.72 (dub. l.), Erinn. in *PSI*9. 1090.36, Plu.*Mar.*20, *Crass.*23, 2.590f; prop. of wolves, Poll.5.86, *Anecd.Stud.*104:—**ὠρυγμός**, ὁ, opp. ὑλαγμός, Ael.*NA*5.51, Poll. l.c.,

Longus 2.26 and 30; of a lion, v.l. in Theoc.25.217: and ⊛**ὤρυγμα**, ατος, τό, of the waves, *AP*6.233 (Maec., pl.).

**ὠρῦδόν**, Adv. *howling*, Nic.*Al.*222.

**ὠρυθμός**, ὁ, *a howling*, of dogs, ὠρυθμοῖς ὑλάει Opp.*C.*4.219 (but distd. fr. ὑλακή 'barking' by Q.S.14.287); of a lion, *roaring*, Theoc. 25.217 (v.l. ὠρυγμοῖο).

**ὠρυκτής**, οῦ, Dor. **-τάς**, ὁ, *howling*, λύκος ὠ. *Hymn.Is.*47.

**ὤρῦμα**, ατος, τό, = ὠρυγή, Lxx *Ez.*19.7.

⊛ **ὠρύομαι** [ῡ], fut. -ύσομαι Lxx *Ho.*11.10: aor. ὠρῡσάμην Pi.*O.*9. 109:—Ion. and poet. Verb, very rarely used in Att. (v. infr.), *howl*, prop. of wolves and dogs, Call.*Fr.*423, Theoc.2.35, Coluth. 116, D.S.1.87; of lions, *roar*, A.R.4.1339; of animals generally, Plu.2.973a, Lxx *Wi.*17.19; ὄρθιον ὤρυσαι Pi. l.c., cf. Lxx *Ps.*37(38). 9; of primitive folk, either in mourning, Hdt.3.117, or in joy, Id.4.75; ὥσπερ ἀπόπληκτοι..ὠρύονται Pl.Com.130; of the sea, D.P.83. II. trans., *howl over*, τῆνον μὰν θῶες, τῆνον λύκοι ὠ. Theoc.1.71; ὠ. ἐπί τινι Luc.*DMort.*10.13.—The Act. only in *AP*11.31 (Antip., dub. l.), Suid. (Skt. *rauti* (pl. *ruvanti*), *ruváti* 'bellow', Lat. *ru-mor*, Slav. *rev-ą*, *raju-ti.*)

**ὠρυτός**, ὁ, *a howling*, Theognost.*Can.*76.

**ὠρώρει**, v. ὄρνυμι. **ὠρωρύγμην**, v. ὀρύσσω.

⊛ **ὡς**:—Summary: **A.** as Adverb of Manner. **Aa.** ὧς and ὥς (with accent), *so, thus.* **Ab.** ὡς (without accent) of the Relat. Pron. ὅς, *as.* **Ac.** ὡς Relat. and Interrog., *how.* **Ad.** ὡς temporal, *when.* **Ae.** ὡς Local, *where.* **B.** ὡς, as Conjunction. **C, D.** various usages.

**A.** Adverb of Manner:

**Aa.** **ὥς**, Demonstr., = οὕτως, *so, thus*, freq. in Hom., Il.1.33, al.; ὣς εἶπ' Sapph.*Supp.*20*a*.11 (Epic style); in Ion. Prose, Hdt.3.13, al.; rare in Att., and almost confined to certain phrases, v. infr.2, 3; ὥς simply = οὕτως, A.*Ag.*930, Th.3.37, Pl.*Prt.*338a; ἀλλ' ὣς γενέσθω E.*Hec.*888, al. **2.** καὶ ὣς even *so, nevertheless*, Il.1.116, al.; οὐδ' ὣς not even *so*, 7.263, Od.1.6, al., Hdt.6.76; οὐδέ κεν ὣς Il.9.386: the phrases καὶ ὣς, οὐδ' ὣς, μηδ' ὣς, are used in Trag. and Att., S.*Ant.*1042, Th.1.74, 7.74; also later, *PCair.Zen.*19.10 (iii B.C., unaccented), *UPZ*146.40 (ii B.C.), *GDI* 1832.11 (Delph., ii B.C.), *IG*2$^2$.850.17 (iii B.C.); κἂν ὣς, εἴπερ μέλει σοι, ἀπόστειλόν μοί τινα *POxy.*120.11 (iv A.D.); δουλεύων καθὼς καὶ ὣς *GDI*2160 (Delph., ii B.C.); Thess. καὶ οὖς *IG*9(2).234.1 (iii B.C.); for this phrase the accentuation ὣς is prescribed by Hdn.Gr.2.932, al., cf. A.D.*Synt.*307.16, and is found in good Mss. of Homer; for the remaining uses under this head (Aa. 1, 3, 4) the accentuation ὥς is prescribed by the same grammarians. **3.** in Comparisons, ὥς.., ὡς.., *so.. as..*, etc.; and reversely ὡς.., ὣς.., *as.. so*, Il.1. 512, 14.265, etc.; in Att., Pl.*R.*530d; also ὥς τε..ὣς.., *as..thus..*, *h.Cer.*174–6, E.*Ba.*1066–8; οἷα..ὥς Id.*El.*151–5; ὥσπερ.., ὣς δὲ.. (in apodosi) Pl.*Prt.*326d. **4.** *thus, for instance*, Od.5.129, *h.Ven.* 218; ὥς shd. be accented in Od.5.121,125.

**Ab.** **ὡς**, Relat., *as*, Hom., etc.; prop. relat. to a demonstr. Adv., which is freq. omitted, κινήθη δ' ἀγορὴ ὡς κύματα μακρὰ θαλάσσης, i.e. οὕτως, ὡς.., Il.2.144 (φὴ Zenod.): it is relat. not only to the regular demonstr. Advs. ὥς (ὣς), τώς, ὧδε, οὕτως, αὕτως, but also to ταύτῃ, Pl.*R.*365d, etc. We find a collat. Dor. form ὧ (q.v.); cf. ὥτε. Usage: **I.** in similes, freq. in Hom., Il.5.161, al.; longer similes are commonly introduced by ὡς ὅτε, ὡς δ' ὅτε, ἤριπε δ', ὡς ὅτε πύργος [ἤριπε] 4.462: ἤριπε δ', ὡς ὅτε τις δρῦς ἤριπε 13.389, cf. 2.394; so later, Emp.84.1, etc.; ὡς ὅτε θαητὸν μέγαρον, πάξομεν Pi.*O.*6.2: ὡς ὅτε is rare in short similes, Od.11.368: ὡς is folld. by indic. pres., Il.9.4, 16.364: also by aor., 3.33 sq., 4.275, 16.823, al.; also by subj. pres. or aor., 5.161, 10.183,485, 13.334 (sts. ὡς δ' ὅτ' ἄν, 11.269, 17.520); cf. ὥστε A:—the Verb is sts. omitted with ὡς, but may be supplied from the context, ἐνδούπησε πεσοῦσ', ὡς εἰναλίη κήξ (sc. πίπτει) Od.15.479, cf. 6.20; θεὸς δ' ὣς τίετο δήμῳ Il.5.78; οἱ δὲ φέβοντο.., βόες ὣς ἀγελαῖαι Od.22.299: where ὡς follows the noun to which it refers, it takes the accent; so in Com., Ἀριστόδημος ὥς Cratin.151, cf. Eub.75.6; v. infr. H. **2.** *like as, just as*, ὡς οὗτος κατὰ τέκν' ἔφαγε.., ὣς ἡμεῖς κτλ. Il.2.326, v. supr. Aa. 3. **3.** sts. in the sense *as much as* or *according as*, ἑλὼν κρέας ὥς (i.e. ὅσον) οἱ χεῖρες ἐχάνδανον Od.17.344; ὦκα δὲ μητρὶ ἔννεπον ὡς (i.e. ὅσα) εἶδόν τε καὶ ἔκλυον *h.Cer.*172; τῶν πάντων οὐ τόσσον ὀδύρομαι..ὡς ἑνός Od.4.105; τόσον..ὡς Il.4.130; so in Trag., σοὶ θεοὶ πόροιεν ὡς ἐγὼ θέλω S.*OC*1124; ὡς ἐγὼ οὐκ ἔστιν ὑμῶν ὅστις ἐξ ἴσου νοσεῖ Id.*OT*60; in Prose, ὡς δύναται *as much as* he can, Democr.278; τὸ ῥῆμα μέμνημαι ὡς εἶπε Aeschin.3.72; ὡς μή = ὅσον μή, νέμεν ὅτι ἂν (= ἂν) βόλητοι ὡς μὴ ἰν τοῖ περιχώροι *IG*5(2).3.9 (Tegea, iv B.C.); cf. Ab. II. 2 infr. **4.** sts. after Comp., *compared with*, hence *than*, μᾶλλον πρέπει οὕτως ὡς..Pl.*Ap.*36d; ἅ γε μείζω πόνον παρέχει..οὐκ ἂν ῥᾳδίως οὐδὲ πολλὰ ἂν εὕροις ὡς τοῦτο Id.*R.*526c; οὐδενὸς μᾶλλον φροντίζειν ὡς..Plb.3.12.5, cf. 7.4.5, 11.2.9, Plu.*Cor.*36: μᾶσσον ὡς is dub. in A.*Pr.*629, and ⟨ἤ⟩ shd. perh. be inserted in Lys.7.12,31; cf. ὥσπερ IV. **II.** with Adverbial clauses: **1.** parenthetically, in qualifying clauses, ὡς ἔοικε, etc., Pl. *Smp.*176c, etc.: in these cases γε or γοῦν is freq. added, ὡς γοῦν ὁ λόγος σημαίνει *as* at any rate the argument shows, Id.*R.*334a; in some phrases c. inf., v. infr. B. II. 3. An anacoluthon sts. occurs by the Verb of the principal clause being made dependent on the parenthetic Verb, ὡς δὲ Σκύθαι λέγουσι, νεώτατον ἁπάντων ἐθνέων εἶναι (for ἦν) τὸ σφέτερον Hdt.4.5, cf. 1.65; ὡς ἐγὼ ἤκουσα, εἶναι αὐτόν Id.4.76; ὡς γὰρ..ἤκουσά τινος, ὅτι..X.*An.*6.4.18 codd.; ἀνὴρ ὅδ' ὡς ἔοικεν οὐ νεμεῖν (for οὐ νεμεῖ, ὡς ἔοικε), S.*Tr.*1238. **2.** in elliptical phrases, *so far as..* (cf. supr. Ab. I. 3) ὡς ἐμοί Id.*Aj.* 395 (lyr.); so ὥς γε ἐμοὶ κριτῇ Ael.*VH*2.41 and ὥς γ' ἐμοὶ χρῆσθαι κριτῇ E.*Alc.*801; ὡς ἐμῇ δόξῃ X.*Vect.*5.2; ὡς ἀπ' ὀμμάτων (sc. εἰκάσαι) to judge by eyesight, S.*OC*15: esp. in such phrases as οὐκέτι πολλὸν χωρίον, ὡς εἶναι Αἰγύπτου Hdt.2.8; οὐδὲ ἀδύνατος, ὡς Λακεδαιμόνιος *for* a Lacedaemonian, Th.4.84, cf. D.H.10.31; ὡς ἀνθρώποις Alcmaeon 1; φρονεῖ.. ὡς γυνὴ μέγα *for* a woman, S.*OT*1078; πιστός, ὡς νομεύς, ἀνήρ ib.1118; μακρὰν ὡς γέροντι..ὁδόν Id.*OC*20, cf. 385, *Ant.*62, etc.; ὡπλισμένοι ὡς ἐν τοῖς ὄρεσιν ἱκανῶς X.*An.*4.3.31; also with ἄν, μεγάλα ἐκτήσατο χρήματα, ὡς ἂν εἶναι Ῥοδῶπιν Hdt.2.135 codd. (ἂν secl. Krüger, Ῥοδώπιος cj. Valck.):—for ὡς εἰπεῖν and the like, v. infr. B. II. 3. **3.** ὡς attached to the object of the Verb, *as*, ἑωυτὸν ὡς ἐχθρὸν λυπέει Democr.88; ἔλαβεν ἀμφοτέρους ὡς φίλους ἤδη X.*Cyr.*3.2.25; ἐν οἰκήματι ᾧ ὡς ταμιείῳ ἐχρῆτο Pl.*Prt.*315d.—For the similar usage of ὡς with Participles and Prepositions, v. infr. C. **III.** with Adverbs: **a.** with the Posit., ὡς ἀληθῶς *truly*, Pl.*Phdr.*234e (cf. ἀληθής III. 1b: as if Adv. of τὸ ἀληθές); ὡς ἑτέρως *in the other way*, ib.276c, D.18.212 (Adv. of ὁ ἕτερος; v. ἕτερος V. 2) (v. infr. D. I. 1); ὡς ἠπίως, ὡς ἐτητύμως, S.*El.*1438 (lyr.), 1452; ὡς ὁμοίως *SIG*708.34 (Istropolis, ii B.C.), Lxx 4 *Ma.*5.21, 1 *Enoch* 5.3, *IG*7.2725.16 (Acraeph., ii A.D.); ὡς ἐναλλάξ Vett.Val. 215.9, 340.2; ὡς παντελῶς Id.184.26; ὡς ἄλλως Is.7.27, D.6.32; ὡς ἐνδεχομένως *PPetr.*2p.53 (iii B.C.); in ὣς αὔτως (v. ὡσαύτως) we have the Adv. of ὁ αὐτός, but the ὥς retains its demonstr. force, as does ὁ in Homer; ὡς ἀληθῶς, ὡς ὁμοίως, and ὡς παντελῶς may be modelled on ὣς αὔτως, with which they are nearly synonymous; so also ὡς ἑτέρως and ὡς ἐναλλάξ, which are contrasted with it. **b.** with Advbs. expressing anything extraordinary, θαυμαστῶς or θαυμασίως ὡς, ὑπερφυῶς ὡς, v. sub vocc.; ὡς is sts. separated by several words from its Adv., as θαυμαστῶς μοι εἶπες ὡς παρὰ δόξαν Pl.*Phd.*95a; ὑπερφυῶς δὴ τὸ χρῆμα ὡς δύσγνωστον φαίνεται Id.*Alc.*2.147c, cf. *Phd.* 99d. **c.** with the Sup., *as much as can be*, ὡς μάλιστα Th.1.141, etc.: ὡς ῥᾷστα *as* easily *as possible*, A.*Pr.*104; ὡς πλεῖστα Democr. 189; ὡς τάχιστα *as* quickly *as possible*, Alc.*Supp.*4.15, etc.; more fully expressed, ὡς δυνατὸν ἄριστα Isoc.12.153; ὡς ἐδύναντο ἀδηλότατα Th.7.50; μαχομένους ὡς ἂν δυνώμεθα κράτιστα X.*An.*3.2.6; ὡς οἷόν τε βέλτιστον Pl.*R.*403d; ὡς ἀνυστὸν κάλλιστα Diog.Apollon.3: ὡς and ὅτι are sts. found together, where one is superfluous, ὡς ὅτι μάλιστα Pl.*Lg.*908a; βοῦν ὡς ὅτι κάλλιστον *IG*2$^2$.1028.17 (ii/i B.C.); v. infr. G. **d.** with Comp., ὡς θᾶσσον Plb.1.66.1, 3. 82.1. **e.** in the phrases ὡς τὸ πολύ, ὡς ἐπὶ τὸ πολύ, Pl.*R.*330c, 377b; ὡς ἐπὶ τὸ πλεῖον for the more part, commonly, ὡς ἐπὶ πλεῖστον Th.2.34; ὡς ἐπὶ τὸ πλῆθος, ὡς πλήθει, Pl.*R.*364a, 389d; ὡς τὸ ἐπίπαν Hdt.7.50, etc.; ὡς τὰ πολλά Ael.*NA*12.17. **2.** with Adjs., **a.** Posit., ὑπερφυεῖ τινι..ὡς μεγάλῃ βλάβῃ Pl.*Grg.*477d. **b.** with Sup., ὡς ἄριστοι τὰς φύσεις Id.*Ti.*18d; ὅπως ὡς βέλτισται ἔσονται Id.*Grg.*503a; ὡς ὅτι βέλτιστον Id.*Smp.*218d. **c.** separated from the Adj. by a Prep., ὡς ἐς ἐλάχιστον Th.1.63, cf. D.18.246; ὡς ἐν βραχυτάτοις Antipho 1.18; ὡς ἐν ἐχυρωτάτῳ ποιεῖσθαι X.*Cyr.* 1.6.26, etc.

**Ac.** Relat. and Interrog., *how*, μερμήριζε..ὡς Ἀχιλῆα τιμήσειε Il. 2.3, cf. Pl.*R.*365a; ἐβουλεύοντο ὡς..στήσονται Hdt.3.84, etc.; οἷα δεῖ λέγειν καὶ ὥς Arist.*EN*1128$^a$1; ὡς πέπραται *how*, i.e. *at what price* the goods have been sold, *PCair.Zen.*149 (iii B.C.); so οὐκ ἔσθ' ὡς.. (for the more usu. ὅπως) nowise can it be *that..*, S.*Ant.*750; οὐκ ἔσθ' ὡς οὐ.., Id.*Ph.*196 (anap., Porson for οὐκ ἔστιν ὅπως οὐ); οἶσθ' ὡς πόησον; by a mixture of constructions for ὡς χρὴ ποιῆσαι or ὡς ποιήσεις, Id.*OT*543, cf. Hermipp.43, Men.916; οἶσθ' ὡς μετεύξει is f.l. in E.*Med.*600 (μέτευξαι Elmsley); similarly, οἶσθα.. ὡς νῦν μὴ σφαλῇς S.*OC*75. **2.** ὡς ἂν ποήσῃς *however* (*in whatever way*) thou mayest act, Id.*Aj.*1369, cf. Pl.*Smp.*181a; αὐτῷ ὥς κεν ἅδῃ, τὼς ἔσσεται A.R.3.350.

**Ad.** Temporal, *when*, with past tenses of the indic., ἐνῶρτο γέλως.., ὡς ἴδον Il.1.600: with opt., to express a repeated action, *whenever*, ὡς..ἐς τὴν Μιλησίην ἀπίκοιτο Hdt.1.17: rarely c. subj., to denote what happens under certain conditions, τῶν δὲ ὡς ἕκαστός οἱ μειχθῇ, διδοῖ δῶρον Id.4.172, cf. 1.132; later, ὡς ἄν c. subj., *when*, *PCair.Zen.*251 (iii B.C.), 1*Ep.Cor.*11.34, etc.; ὥς κα *Berl.Sitzb.*1927.170 (Cyrene); ὡς ἂν τάχιστα λάβῃς τὴν ἐπιστολήν *as* soon *as..* *PCair.Zen.*241.1 (iii B.C.), cf. Lxx 1*Ki.*9.13, *Jo.*3.8: in orat. obliq. c. inf., Hdt.1.86,94, al.: expressed more forcibly by ὡς..τάχιστα, some word or words being interposed, ὡς γὰρ ἐπετρόπευσε τάχιστα *as soon as ever..*, Id.1.65; ὡς δὲ ἀφίκετο τάχιστα X.*Cyr.*1.3.2: less freq. ὡς τάχιστα stand together, Aeschin.2.22: but this usage must be distd. from signf. Ab. III. 1c: folld. by demonstr., ὡς εἶδ', ὣς ἀνεπᾶλτο Il.20.424; ὡς ἴδεν, ὥς μιν ἔρως πυκινὰς φρένας ἀμφεκάλυψεν 14.294; also ὡς.., ἔπειτα 3.396; Κρονίδ. ὥς μιν φράσαθ' ὣς ἐόλητο θυμὸν ἀνωΐστοισιν ὑποδμηθεὶς βελέεσσι Κύπριδος Mosch.2.74; the second ὣς is repeated, ἁ δ' Ἀταλάντα ὡς ἴδεν, ὣς ἐμάνη, ὣς ἐς βαθὺν ἅλατ' ἔρωτα Theoc.3.41 (ὣς = εὐθέως, Sch.vet.), cf. 2.82; in Bion 1.40 the clauses with ὡς all belong to the protasis. **2.** ὡς appears to be f.l. for ἕως in ὡς ἂν αὐτὸς ἥλιος.. αἴρῃ S.*Ph.*1330, ὡς ἂν ᾖς οἷόσπερ εἶ Id.*Aj.*1117; cf. ὥσπερ III.1: but in later Gr. = ἕως, *while*, ὡς τὸ φῶς ἔχετε *Ev.Jo.*12.35,36; ὡς καιρὸν ἔχομεν *Ep.Gal.*6.10, cf. *Epigr.Gr.*646*a*5 (p.529); also *until*, τίθεται ἐπὶ ἀνθράκων ὡς ἀναξηρανθῇ *PLeid.X.*89 B.; ἔα ἀφρίζειν τὴν πίσσαν ὡς οὗ ἐκλείπῃ ib.37 B.; cf. *EM*824.43 (conversely ἕως for ὡς final, v. ἕως (B) A. I. 4).

**A.** e. Local, *where*, in dialects, Theoc.1.13, 5.101,103, *IG*9(2). 205.4 (Melitea, iii B.C.), *SIG*685.63, al. (Cretan, ii B.C.), *IG*12(1). 736.5 (Camirus), *GDI*5597.8 (Ephesus, iii B.C.).

**B. ὡς** as CONJUNCTION: I. with Substantive clauses, to express a fact, = ὅτι, *that*. II. with Final clauses, to express an end or purpose, = ἵνα, ὅπως, *so that, in order that*. III. Consecutive, = ὥστε, *so that*. IV. Causal, *since, because*.

I. with Substantive Clauses, with verbs of learning, saying, etc., *that*, expressing a fact, γνωτὸν.., ὡς ἤδη Τρώεσσιν ὀλέθρου πείρατ' ἐφῆπται Il.7.402, cf. Od.3.194, etc.: in commands, προεῖπεν ὡς μηδεὶς κινήσοιτο X.*HG*2.1.22: with Verbs of fear or anxiety, c. fut. indic., μηκέτ' ἐκφοβοῦ, μητρῷον ὥς σε λῆμ' ἀτιμάσει ποτέ S.*El.*1427, cf. X.*Cyr.*6.2.30; μὴ φοβοῦ ὡς ἀπορήσεις ib.5.2.12, cf. D.10.36; a sentence beginning with ὡς is sts., when interrupted, resumed by ὅτι, and vice versa, X.*Cyr.*5.3.30, Pl.*R.*470d, *Hp.Ma.*281c; so ὡς with a finite Verb passes into the acc. and inf., Hdt.1.70, 8.118: both constructions mixed in the same clause, ἐλογίζετο ὡς..ἧττον ἂν αὐτοὺς ἐθέλειν.. X.*Cyr.*8.1.25, cf. *HG*3.4.27: after primary tenses (incl. historic pres.) ὡς is folld. by indic., after historic tenses by opt. (sts. by indic., both constructions in ὑπίσχοντο..ἀμυνέειν, φράζοντες ὡς οὔ σφι περιοπτέη ἐστὶ ἡ Ἑλλὰς ἀπολλυμένη..ἀλλὰ τιμωρητέον εἴη Hdt.7.168): sts. c. opt. after a primary tense, κατάπτονται..λέγοντες ὡς Ἀρίστων..οὐ φήσειε Id.6.69, cf. 1.70, Th.1.38, Pl.*Chrm.*156b. **2.** with Verbs of feeling, χαίρει δέ μοι ἦτορ, ὥς μευ ἀεὶ μέμνησαι Il.23.648; ἄχος ἔλλαβ' Ἀχαιοὺς ὡς ἔπεσ' 16.600. II. with Final Clauses, *that, in order that*; in this sense ὡς and ὡς ἄν, Ep. ὥς κεν, are used with the subj. after primary tenses of the indic., and with the opt. after the past tenses, βουλὴν ὑποθησόμεθ'.., ὡς μὴ πάντες ὄλωνται Il.8.37; τύμβον χεύαμεν.., ὥς κεν τηλεφανὴς..εἴη Od. 24.83; ἡμεῖς δ' ἴωμεν ὡς, ὁπηνίκ' ἂν θεὸς πλοῦν ἡμὶν εἴκῃ, τηνικαῦθ' ὁρμώμεθα S.*Ph.*464; [νέας] διηκοσίας περιέπεμπον..ὡς ἂν μὴ ὀφθείησαν Hdt.8.7. b. rarely c. fut. indic., ὡς μὴ ὦν αὐτοί τε ἀπολέεσθε (cj. Cobet for ἀπόλεσθε) κἀμὲ τρώσετε, ἐς ἄλλον τινὰ δῆμον ἀποίχεσθε Hecat. 30J. **2.** ὡς is also used with past tenses of the indic. to express a purpose which has not been or cannot be fulfilled, τί μ' οὐκ ἔκτεινας, ὡς ἔδειξα μήποτε..; *so that I* never *should*.., S.*OT*1392; ἔδει τὰ ἐνέχυρα λαβεῖν, ὡς μηδ' εἰ ἐβούλετο ἐδύνατο ἐξαπατᾶν X.*An.* 7.6.23; cf. ἵνα B. I. 3, ὅπως B. I. ?. **3.** ὡς c. inf., to limit an assertion, ὡς μὲν ἐμοὶ δοκέειν Hdt.6.95, cf. 2.124; ὡς εἰπεῖν λόγῳ ib.53; or ὡς ἔπος εἰπεῖν, cf. ἔπος II. 4; ὡς συντόμως, or ὡς συνελόντι εἰπεῖν *to* speak shortly, *to* be brief, X.*Oec.*12.19, *Mem.*3.8.10; ὡς εἰκάσαι *to* make a guess, i.e. probably, Hdt.1.34, etc.; ὡς μικρὸν μεγάλῳ εἰκάσαι Th.4.36 (so without ὡς, οὐ πολλῷ λόγῳ εἰπεῖν Hdt. 1.61), v. supr. Ab. II. 1, 2. III. to express Consequence, like ὥστε, *so that*, freq. in Hdt., εὖρος ὡς δύο τριήρεας πλέειν ὁμοῦ in breadth *such that* two triremes could sail abreast, Hdt.7.24; ὑψηλὸν οὕτω.., ὡς τὰς κορυφὰς αὐτοῦ οὐκ οἷά τε εἶναι ἰδέσθαι 4.184; so in Trag. and Prose, A.*Pers.*437, al., S.*OT*84, X.*An.*3.5.7, etc.; ἀπέχοντας ἀπ' ἀλλάλων ὡς ἦμεν ϝικατίπεδον ἄντομον *Tab.Heracl.*1.75; οὕτως ..ὡς ὁμολογεῖν Jul.*Or.*5.164d; ὡς καὶ τοὺς τεχνίτας λανθάνειν *PHolm.* 9.13; also, like ὥστε, with Indic., οὕτω κλεινὴ ἐγένετο, ὡς..ἐξέμαθον Hdt.2.135, cf. S.*Tr.*590, X.*HG*4.1.33. **2.** ὡς after a Comp., μάσσον' ἢ ὡς ἰδέμεν Pi.*O.*13.113; μαλακώτεροι.. ἢ ὡς κάλλιον αὐτοῖς Pl.*R.* 410d; cf. ὥστε B. I. 2: with words implying comparison, ὀλίγοι ἐσμὲν ὡς ἐγκρατεῖς εἶναι αὐτῶν too few *to*.., X.*Cyr.*4.5.15, γραῦς εἶ, ὦ Ἐλπινίκη, ὡς τηλικαῦτα διαπράττεσθαι πράγματα too old *to*.. Stesimbr. 5J. **3.** ὡς is sts. omitted where the antecedent demonstrative is expressed, οὕτω ἰσχυραί, μόγις ἂν διαρρήξειας so strong, you could hardly break them, Hdt.3.12; ῥώμῃ σώματος τοιῇδε, ἀεθλοφόροι τε ἀμφότεροι ἦσαν Id.1.31. IV. Causal, *inasmuch as, since*, τί ποτε λέγεις, ὦ τέκνον; ὡς οὐ μανθάνω S.*Ph.*914, cf. E.*Ph.*843,1077, Ar.*Ra.*278: c. opt., μὴ καὶ λάθῃ με προσπεσών· ὡς μᾶλλον ἂν ἕλοιτο μ' ἢ τοὺς πάντας Ἀργείους λαβεῖν S.*Ph.*46. **2.** *on the ground that*.., c. fut. indic., Lys.30.27.

**C. ὡς** before I. Participles; II. Prepositions; and III. ὡς itself as a Preposition.

I. with Participles in the case of the Subject, to mark the reason or motive of the action, *as if, as*, ὡς οὐκ ἀΐοντι ἐοικώς Il.23.430 (v. infr. G); ἀγανακτοῦσιν ὡς μεγάλων τινῶν ἀπεστερημένοι (i.e. ἡγούμενοι μεγάλων τινῶν ἀπεστερῆσθαι), Pl.*R.*329a: most freq. c. part. fut., διαβαίνει.., ὡς ἀμήσων τὸν σῖτον Hdt.6.28, cf. 91; παρεσκευάζοντο ὡς πολεμήσοντες Th.2.7, etc.; δηλοῖς ὥς τι σημανῶν νέον S.*Ant.* 242; ὡς τεθνήξων ἴσθι νυνί Ar.*Ach.*325 (troch.): in questions, παρὰ Πρωταγόραν νῦν ἐπιχειρεῖς ἰέναι, ὡς παρὰ τίνα ἀφιξόμενος; Pl.*Prt.*311b; ὡς τί δὴ θέλων; E.*IT*557; with vbs. of knowing, ἐπιστάσθω Κροῖσος ὡς ὕστερον..ἁλοὺς τῆς πεπρωμένης Hdt.1.91; ὡς μὴ 'μπολήσων ἴσθι.. S.*Ant.*1063. **2.** with Participles in oblique cases, λέγουσιν ἡμᾶς ὡς ὀλωλότας they speak of us *as* dead, A.*Ag.*672; ὡς μηδὲν εἰδότ' ἴσθι μ' ὧν ἀνιστορεῖς S.*Ph.*253; τὸν ἐκβαίνοντα κολάζουσιν ὡς παρανομοῦντα Pl.*R.*338e; ἵνα μὴ ἀγανακτῇ ὑπὲρ ἐμοῦ ὡς δεινὰ πάσχοντος Id.*Phd.*115e, cf. Hdt.5.85, 9.54; νῦν δέ σου τὰ ἔργα φανερὰ γεγένηται οὐχ ὡς ἀνιωμένου ἀλλ' ὡς ἡδομένου τοῖς γιγνομένοις Lys.12.32; κτύπος φωτὸς ὡς τειρομένου ⟨του⟩ S.*Ph.*202 (lyr.); ἐν ὀλιγωρίᾳ ἐποιοῦντο, ὡς, ὅταν ἐξέλθωσιν, ἢ οὐχ ὑπομενοῦντας σφᾶς ἢ ῥᾳδίως ληψόμενοι βίᾳ made light of the matter, *in the belief that*.., Th.4.5.— Both constructions in one sentence, τοὺς κόσμους εἴασε χαίρειν ὡς ἀλλοτρίους τε ὄντας καὶ πλέον θάτερον ἡγησάμενος ἀπεργάζεσθαι Pl.*Phd.*114e, cf. X.*Cyr.*1.5.9. **3.** with Parts. put abs. in gen., νῦν δέ, ὡς οὕτω ἐχόντων, στρατιὴν ἐκπέμπετε Hdt.8.144; ἐρώτα ὅτι βούλει, ὡς τἀληθῆ ἐροῦντος X.*Cyr.*3.1.9; ὡς ὧδ' ἐχόντων τῶνδ' ἐπίστασθαί σε χρή S.*Aj.*281, cf. 904, A.*Pr.*760, E.*Med.*1311, Th.7. 15, X.*An.*1.3.6: so also in acc., μισθὸν αἰτοῦσιν, ὡς οὐχὶ αὐτοῖσιν ὠφελίαν ἐσομένην ἐκ τοῦ ἄρχειν Pl.*R.*345e, cf. E.*Ph.*1461: with both cases in one sentence, ὡς καὶ τῶν Ἀθηναίων προσδοκίμων ὄντων ἄλλῃ στρατιᾷ, καὶ..διαπεπολεμησόμενον Th.7.25, cf. Pl.*R.*604b. II. ὡς before Preps., ἀνήγοντο ὡς ἐπὶ ναυμαχίαν (v.l. -ίᾳ) Th.1.48, cf. X. *HG*2.1.22; φρύγανα συλλέγοντες ὡς ἐπὶ πῦρ Id.*An.*4.3.11; κατέλαβε τὴν ἀκρόπολιν ὡς ἐπὶ τυραννίδι, expressing the purpose, Th.1.126; ἀπέπλεον..ὡς ἐς τὰς Ἀθήνας Id.6.61; πλεῖς ὡς πρὸς οἶκον S.*Ph.*58; τὸ βούλευμ' ὡς ἐπ' Ἀργείους τόδ' ἦν Id.*Aj.*44: in these passages ὡς marks an intention; not so in the following: ἀπαγγέλλετε τῇ μητρὶ [χαίρειν] ὡς παρ' ἐμοῦ X.*Cyr.*8.7.28; also ὡς ἀπὸ τῆς πομπῆς Pl.*R.* 327c; ὡς ἐκ κακῶν ἐχάρη Hdt.8.101. b. later, in geographical expressions, of direction, προϊών, ὡς ἐπὶ τὸν Πηνειόν Str.9.5.8, cf. 13.1.22; ὡς πρὸς ἕω βλέπων Id.8.6.1, cf. 7.6.2; ὡς εἰς Φηραίαν (leg. Ἡραίαν) ἰόντων Id.8.3.32. III. ὡς as a Prep., prop. in cases where the object is a person, not a place: once in Hom., ὡς αἰεὶ τὸν ὁμοῖον ἄγει θεὸς ὡς τὸν ὁμοῖον Od.17.218 (v.l. ἐς τὸν ὁμοῖον, cf. αἶνος Ὁμηρικός, αἰὲν ὁμοῖον ὡς θεὸς..ἐς τὸν ὁμοῖον ἄγει Call.*Aet.*1.1.10; ἔρχεται..ἕκαστον τὸ ὅμοιον ὡς τὸ ὅ., τὸ πυκνὸν ὡς τὸ πυκνόν κτλ. (with v.l. ἐς) Hp.*Nat.Puer.*17), but possibly ὡς..ὡς *as*..*so*, in Od. l.c.; also in Hdt., ἐσελθεῖν ὡς τὴν θυγατέρα 2.121.ε΄; freq. in Att., ὡς Ἆγιν ἐπρεσβεύσαντο Th.8.5, etc.; ἀφίκετο ὡς Περδίκκαν καὶ ἐς τὴν Χαλκιδικήν Id 4.79; ἀπέπλευσαν ἐς Φώκαιαν..ὡς Ἀστύοχον Id.8.31; ναῦς ἐς τὸν Ἑλλήσποντον ὡς Φαρνάβαζον ἀποπέμπειν ib.39; ὡς ἐκεῖνον πλέομεν ὥσπερ πρὸς δεσπότην Isoc. 4.121; the examples of ὡς with names of places are corrupt, e.g. ὡς τὴν Μίλητον Th.8.36 (ἐς cod. Vat.); ὡς Ἄβυδον one Ms. in Id.8.103; ὡς τὸ πρόσθεν Ar.*Ach.*242: in S.*OT*1481 ὡς τὰς ἀδελφὰς..τὰς ἐμὰς χέρας is equiv. to ὡς ἐμὲ τὸν ἀδελφόν; in Id.*Tr.*366 δόμους ὡς τούσδε house = household.

**D. ὡς** in independent sentences: I. as an exclamation, *how*, mostly with Advbs. and Adjs., ὡς ἄνοον κραδίην ἔχες *how* silly a heart hadst thou! Il.21.441; ὡς ἀγαθὸν καὶ παῖδα λιπέσθαι *how* good is it.., Od.3.196, cf. 24.194; φρονεῖν ὡς δεινόν S.*OT*316; ὡς ἀστεῖος ὁ ἄνθρωπος *how* charming he is! Pl.*Phd.*116d; ὡς ἐμεγαλύνθη τὰ ἔργα σου, Κύριε LXX *Ps.*91(92).6, 103(104).24; in indirect clauses, ἐθαύμασα τοῦτο, ὡς ἡδέως..ἀπεδέξατο marvelled *at seeing how*.., Pl. *Phd.*89a. **2.** with Verbs, ὥς μοι δέχεται κακὸν ἐκ κακοῦ αἰεί *how* constantly.., Il.19.290, cf. 21.273; ὡς οὐκ ἔστι χάρις μετόπισθ' εὐεργέων *how* little thanks remain! Od.22.319; ὡς ὄχλος νιν..ἀμφέπει *see how*.., E.*Ph.*148; ὡς ὑπερδέδοικά σου *how greatly*.., S.*Ant.*82; so perh. ὡς οἰμώξεται Ar.*Ra.*279; ὡς ἅπανθ' ὑμῖν τυραννίς ἐστι Id.*V.*488 (troch.). II. to mark a wish, *oh that!* c. opt. alone, ὡς ἔρις..ἀπόλοιτο Il.18.107; ὡς ἀπόλοιτο καὶ ἄλλος Od.1.47, cf. S.*El.*126 (lyr.); also ὡς ἄν or κε with opt., ὡς ἂν ἔπειτ' ἀπὸ σεῖο οὐκ ἐθέλοιμι λείπεσθαι Il.9.444; ὥς κέ οἱ αὖθι γαῖα χάνοι 6.281. **2.** joined with other words of wishing, ὡς ὤφελες αὐτόθ' ὀλέσθαι 3.428; ὡς δὴ μὴ ὄφελον νικᾶν Od.11.548.

**E. ὡς** with numerals marks that they are to be taken only as a round number, *as it were, about, nearly*, σὺν ἀνθρώποις ὡς εἴκοσι X.*An.*3.3.5; also ὡς πέντε μάλιστά κῃ *about* five (v. μάλα III. 5), Hdt.7.30:—also with words compounded with numerals, δέπας.. ὡς τριλάγυνον Stesich.7; παῖς ὡς ἑπτέτης of *some* seven years, Pl. *Grg.*471c; δρέπανα ὡς διπήχη X.*Cyr.*6.1.30, cf. *An.*5.4.12; cf. ὡσεί III.

**F. ὡς** in some elliptical (or apparently elliptical) phrases: **1.** ὡς τί δὴ τόδε (sc. γένηται); *to what end?* E.*Or.*796 (troch.); cf. ἵνα B. II. 3c. **2.** *know that* (sc. ἴσθι), ὡς ἔστιν ἀνδρὸς τοῦδε τἄργα ταῦτά σοι S.*Aj.*39; ὡς τοῦτό γ' ἔρξας δύο φέρει δωρήματα Id.*Ph.*117; ὡς τῆσδ' ἑκοῦσα παιδὸς οὐ μεθήσομαι E.*Hec.*400, cf. *Med.*609, *Ph.*720; ὡς τάχ' οὐκέθ' αἱματηρὸν..ἀργήσει ξίφος ib.625 (troch.); so in Com., ὡς ἔστ' ἐν ἡμῖν τῆς πόλεως τὰ πράγματα Ar.*Lys.*32, cf. 499 (anap.), *Ach.* 333 (troch.), *Nu.*209; ὡς ἀλλ' ὥς, ἀπὸ τοῦ τείχους πάρεστιν ἄγγελος οὐδείς Id.*Av.*1119. **3.** ὡς ἕκαστος, ἕκαστοι, each *severally* (whether in respect of time, place, or other difference), ξυνελέγοντο..Κορίνθιοι δισχίλιοι ὁπλῖται, οἱ δ' ἄλλοι ὡς ἕκαστοι, Φλειάσιοι δὲ πανστρατιᾷ Th.5.57, cf. 1.107,113; πρώτη τε αὕτη πόλις ξυμμαχὶς παρὰ τὸ καθεστηκὸς ἐδουλώθη, ἔπειτα δὲ καὶ τῶν ἄλλων ὡς ἑκάστη [ξυνέβη] (ξ. secl. Krüger: ἀπὸ κοινοῦ ἐδουλώθη Sch. l. c.) Id.1.98; ἄλλοι τε παριόντες ἐγκλήματα ἐποιοῦντο ὡς ἕκαστοι ib.67, cf. 7.65; χρησμολόγοι τε ᾖδον χρησμοὺς παντοίους, ὧν ἀκροᾶσθαι ὡς ἕκαστος ὥρμητο, i.e. different persons ran to listen to different prophecies, Id.2.21; τὰς ἄλλας ὡς ἑκάστην που ἐκπεπτωκυῖαν ἀναδησάμενοι ἐκόμιζον ἐς τὴν πόλιν they made fast to the rest *wherever each* (ship) had been run ashore, Id.7.74; οἱ δ' οὖν ὡς ἕκαστοι Ἕλληνες κατὰ πόλεις τε ὅσοι ἀλλήλων ξυνίεσαν καὶ ξύμπαντες ὕστερον κληθέντες οὐδὲν πρὸ τῶν Τρωικῶν..ἁθρόοι ἔπραξαν the *various peoples* that were later called by the common name of Greeks, Id.1.3; ὡς ἑκάστῳ ἔργον προστάσσων Hdt.1.114; ὡς ἑκάστην (*one by one*) αἱρέοντες (sc. τὰς νήσους) οἱ βάρβαροι ἐσαγήνευον τοὺς ἀνθρώπους Id.6.31, cf. 79; ὡς ἑκασταχόσε D.C.41.9, al.; rarely with a Verb, ὡς ἕκαστος ἀπικνέοιτο Hdt.1.29, cf. Th.6.2: later ὡς follows ἕκαστος, ἑκάστῳ ὡς ὁ Θεὸς ἐμέρισεν μέτρον πίστεως *Ep.Rom.*12.3:—for the etymology v. infr. H; also ὡς ἑκάτεροι Th.3. 74 (v. infr. H).

**G. ὡς** pleonast. in ὡς ὅτι D.H.9.14, 2*Ep.Cor.*11.21, Sch.A Il.1. 264,129,396, 3.280, *AP*9.530, dub.l. in Str.15.1.57.

H. Etymology: this word is in origin five distinct words:

(1) ὡς '*as*' is the Adv. fr. the Relat. ὅς (I.-E. stem *yo-*); with ὡς βέλτιστος cf. Skt. *yácchrēṣṭáḥ* 'the best possible': (2) ὥς '*thus*' is the Adv. of a Demonstr. stem *so-* found in Skt. *sa*, Gr. ὁ, Lat. *sō-c* (*Gloss.*=*ita*, cf. Umbr. *esoc*); (3) ὡς postpositive (ὄρνιθες ὥς, etc.) constantly makes a preceding short closed syll. long in Hom., and must therefore have been ϝως; it may perh. be related to Skt. *vā*, a form of *va*, *iva* (=(1) *or* (2) *like*), Lat. *ve*, Gr. ἤ[ϝ]ε; (4) ὡς prep. '*to*' is of doubtful origin (perh. fr. *ὠς, cogn. with Lat. *ōs* 'face', Skt. *ās*: *ὠς τινα ἐλθεῖν like τί δέ σε φρένας ἵκετο πένθος;); (5) ὡς F.3 is prob. *ϝως, Adv. of ϝός the reflexive Adj., and means lit. *in his* (*their*) *own way* (or *place*); it is idiomatically placed before ἕκαστος (ἑκάτερος), cf. ϝὸν ϝεκάτερος *Leg.Gort.*1.18.

**ὦς**, τό, gen. ὠτός, Dor. for οὖς, Theoc.11.32; also a Hellenistic nom. analogically formed fr. ὠτός, ὠτί, etc. (v. οὖς), *Inscr.Délos* 1403 *Bb* 1.77, 1409 *Aa* 1.106 (both ii B.C.).

**ὦσα**, Ep. and Ion. for ἔωσα, aor. 1 Act. of ὠθέω, q.v.

* **ὡσάν**, or better **ὡς ἄν**, Ep. ὥς κε or ὥς κεν, v. ὡς B.II.1. 2. *as if*, *as it were*, κρότον τοιοῦτον, ὡς ἂν ἐπαινοῦντες.., ἐποιήσατε D. 21.14; ὡς ἂν συναγωγόν τι ἐχούσης τῆς ὁμοιότητος Democr.164; τὸν Κῦρον ἐπερέσθαι ὡς ἂν παῖς X.*Cyr.*1.3.8; ταῦτα προσδέχοιτ' ἂν ὡς ἂν οἰκεῖα Thphr.*CP*1.16.12; πολίτευμα ἔσται ὡς ἂν ἐν τοῖς νόμοις τοῖσδε *Abh.Berl.Akad.*1925(5).6 (Cyrene); ὡς ἂν ἐπὶ πίνακος καταγεγραμμένη Luc.*Alex.*17; παῖδα ὡραῖον ὡς ἂν Αἰγύπτιον Ael.*NA*4.54. 3. like ἅτε, ὡς ἂν τοῖς πλείστοις φίλος ὤν Luc.*Alex.*31. II. ὡς ἄν prob. f.l. for ἕως ἄν (v. ὡς AD.2).

**ὡσανεί** or **ὡς ἂν εἰ** (ὡς κἂν εἰ Arist.*Mu.*396$^b$1), *as if*, *as it were*, with Verbs, τὸ.. πνεῦμα ὡσανεὶ προδιαλύεται Id.*Pr.*934$^b$6; πόλις ἥτις ὡ. πρόσχημα..ἦν Plb.3.15.3; μήτε βλέπειν μήτ' ἀκούειν, ἀλλ' ὡ. βλέπειν καὶ ὡ. ἀκούειν Plu.2.961f; with a part., ὡ. προκαλούμενος Plb. 1.46.11; with Nouns, ὡ. σάρκες Arist.*Metaph.*1036$^b$10; ὡ. ἀμμῶδες Id.*Mir.*831$^b$30; μέγεθος ὡ. βοῦς ib.832$^b$15, etc.

**ὡσαννά**, Hebr. exclam. (*hôšî ʽāh-nâ*), *save now!* ὡ. τῷ υἱῷ Δαβίδ *Ev.Matt.*21.9.

**ὤσασκε**, v. ὠθέω.

**ὡσαύτως**, Adv. of ὁ αὐτός, *in like manner, just so*, used by Hom. only at the beginning of clauses with δέ inserted, ὡς δ' αὔτως.. Il.3.339, Od.9.31, al.; also in Hdt.1.215, al., Pl.*Phd.*102e, Arist.*Rh.* 1386$^b$30, al.; after Hom., in one word, ὡσαύτως καὶ..*in like manner as*..Hdt.7.86, etc.; c. dat., ὡς δ' αὔτως τῇσι κυσὶ οἱ ἰχνευταὶ θάπτονται Id.2.67; πολλοὶ συνεξῄκουν ὡ. ἐμοί S.*Tr.*372; ὥσπερ γάρ.., ὡ. δὲ σύ Id.*El.*27; opp. ὡς ἑτέρως, Arist.*SE*169$^a$31. 2. further strengthd., ὡ. οὕτως so *in like manner*, Pl.*Grg.*460d; ὡ. κατὰ ταὐτά Id.*Phd.* 78d.

**ὦσδε**, Dor. for ὦζε, 3 sg. impf. of ὄζω.

**ὡσεί** or **ὡς εἰ**, Adv. *as if, as though*; with various moods: I. c. opt., ἴσαν, ὡς εἴ τε πυρὶ χθὼν πᾶσα νέμοιτο Il.2.780, cf. 11.389, Od.9. 314, etc. 2. ὡσεί τε c. subj., ἐρίλησ' ὡς εἴ τε πατὴρ ὃν παῖδα φιλήσῃ Il.9.481. 3. ὡς εἰ or ὡς εἴ τε, c. indic., ἕποντ' ὡς εἴ τε μετὰ κτίλον ἕσπετο μῆλα Il.13.492; φιάλαν ὡς εἴ τις.. δωρήσεται Pi.*O.*7.1. II. in comparisons, *like, just as*, Il.16.59, Od.7.36, Hes.*Sc.*290, B.11.1, S.*Ant.*653, *El.*234 (lyr.), etc.: c. part., Il.5.374, Hes.*Sc.*194; ὡς εἴ τε Il.11.474; with verb supplied, Od.14.254, Pi.*P.*4.112; ὡσεί περ c. part., Hes.*Sc.*189, cf. Theoc.25.163 (nisi leg. εἰ περὶ σεῦ): ὡς εἴ πέρ τε with a noun, *h.Cer.*215. 2. ὡς εἴτε *as it were*, Pi.*P.*1. 44. III. with Numerals, or measures of time and space, *about*, ὡσεὶ τριήκοντα σταδίων μάλιστά κῃ Hdt.7.109, cf. X.*HG*1.2.9, Lxx *Ge.*24.55, al., *Ev.Matt.*14.21, al.

**ὡσία**, Dor. for οὐσία, Ocell.ap.Stob.1.20.3, Archyt.ib.1.41.2, cf. Pl.*Cra.*401c.

**ὦσις**, εως, ἡ, = ὤθησις, *thrusting, pushing*, Hp.*Aph.*3.26 (pl.); opp. ἕλξις, Arist.*Ph.*243$^a$17, *de An.*433$^b$25; of an injury to the skull, *depression*, Gal.ap.Orib.46.21.1: pl., *thrusts*, Plu.2.916d, Procl.*in Ti.* 1.297 D., al.

**ὡσιωμένως**, Adv. part. pf. Pass. of ὁσιόω, = ὁσίως, Poll.1.32.

**ὦσ-μή**, ἡ, *thrust, attack*, *P.Bremen* 1.4 (ii A.D.). -**μός**, ὁ, 'Hellenic' for the Att. forms ὠστισμός and ὠθισμός, D.S.2.19, Moer. p.424 P.

**ὥσπερ**, or **ὥς περ**, Adv. of Manner, *like as, even as*, ζῆν ὥ. ἤδη ζῇς S.*Ph.*1396; ἐσῴζετ' ἄν.., ὥ. οὐχὶ σῴζεται Id.*El.*994; but the Verb is more often left to be supplied, οὔ τι κατακρύπτουσιν.., ὥ. Κύκλωπες Od.7.206, cf. 2.333, Il.4.263, 14.50; ἔξεστί θ', ὥ. Ἡγέλοχος, ἡμῖν λέγειν..Ar.*Ra.*303; τεταγμένοι ὥ. ἔμελλον Th.4.93; τοῖς ἠτυχηκόσιν ὥ. ἐγώ D.45.1; Hom. freq. puts a word between ὡς and περ, e.g. ὡς σύ περ αὐτή, ὡς τὸ πάρος περ, ὡς ἔσεταί περ Od.19. 385, Il.5.806, 1.211; *as for instance*, ὅταν χορὸς..γίγνηται, ὥ. ⟨ὁ⟩ εἰς Δῆλον πεμπόμενος X.*Mem.*3.3.12; ὥσπερ differs from ὡς in Hom., in that it seldom has an antecedent expressed, as in Il.24.487, τηλίκου ὥ. ἐγών; also in Hes.*Th.*402, ὣς δ' αὔτως.., ὥ. ὑπέστη; but in Trag. and Att. ὥ. is very freq. after demonstr. words; before οὕτως, Meliss.3, Ar.*Av.*188; after it, S.*Tr.*475, etc.; ὥ. καὶ.., οὕτω καὶ..X.*Cyr.*7.5.75, cf. Pl.*R.*354b; ὥ..., ὧδε..S.*OT*276; τοιοῦτος ὥ. Pl.*Prt.*327d; αὐτοῦ ὥ. εἶχον *just as* they were, *then and there*, Hdt. 2.121.δ', cf. S.*Ant.*1235; εὐθὺς ὥ. εἶχεν X.*An.*4.1.19; εὐθὺς ὥ. ἔτυχε Id.*HG*3.1.19; τὰν τράπεζαν κάτθετε ὥ. ἔχει Sophr. in *PSI*11. 1214*a*2; καὶ τὸν δαελὸν σβῆτε ὥ. ἔχει *on the spot*, ib.14: c. gen., ὥ. ἔχει δόξης Pl.*R.*612d: strengthd., ὥ. γε *just exactly as*, Ar.*Nu.*673; ὥ. καί *even as*, ὡς καὶ ἐγώ περ Il.6.477; ὥ. καὶ ἄλλο τι Th.1.142, etc.: ὥ. also follows ἴσος, in Od.20.282, μοῖραν..ἴσην, ὡς αὐτοί περ ἐλάγχανον, cf. S.*El.*533; so after ὁ αὐτός, Pl.*Phd.*86a, D.9.33; after ὅμοιος, ὅμοιος ἀτμὸς ὥ. ἐκ τάφου πρέπει A.*Ag.*1311, cf. Th.4.34. 2. ὥσπερ ἄν c. subj., v. infr. III; c. opt., ὥσπερ ἄν τις..λέγοι Pl.*Phd.* 87b, cf. X.*HG*3.1.14; cf. ὡσπερεί II. II. to limit or modify an assertion or apologize for a metaphor, *as it were, so to speak*, ὥ. ἀκονιτί Th.4.73; τὸν ἐγκέφαλον ὥ. σεσεῖσθαί μοι δοκεῖς Ar.*Nu.* 1276, cf. *Pax* 234; ἅμα μὲν..ὥ. ὑπεφθόνει X.*Cyr.*4.1.13, cf. Pl.*Phdr.* 270d, *Cra.*384c; in later Gk. sts. after the word to which it refers, ἐσφιγμένον ὥ. Porph.*Chr.*26; βάθρον ὥ. Sch.Pi.*O.*8.33; στέφανος ὥ. τῶν πόλεων τὰ τείχη ib.42: freq. with parts., ὥ. ἐγγελῶσα S.*El.* 277; ὥ. ἐντεταμένον τοῦ σώματος Pl.*Phd.*86b; ὥ. τι τῶν ἄλλων εὐλόγως πεποιηκότες *as if* they had done, Lys.12.7; ὥ. ἐξόν *as if* it were in our power, X.*An.*3.1.14; σιωπῇ ἐδείπνουν, ὥ. τοῦτο ἐπιτεταγμένον αὐτοῖς Id.*Smp.*1.11, cf. *Mem.*2.3.3; with a change of construction, ὥ. τὸν ἀριθμὸν τοῦτον ἔχοντα ἀνάγκην.., καὶ οὔτε..οἷόν τε εἴη γενέσθαι Id.*HG*2.3.19; τὴν ὥ. ἐπὶ τοῦ δίφρου ἕδραν a seat *like* that used in the chariot, Id.*Eq.*7.5. III. rarely of Time, 1. ὥσπερ ἄν = ἕως ἄν, *so long as*, or *however long* (cf. ὡς AD. 2), ὥσπερ ἂν ζῶ S.*OC*1361 (sed leg. ἔωσπερ). 2. *as soon as*, Ar.*Pax*24. IV. after a Comp. (cf. ὡς AB. I. 4); οὐ μείους ὥ. χίλιοι Xenoph.3.4; ἧττον.. ὥ. X.*HG*2.3.16.—Cf. ὡσπερεί, ὥσπερ οὖν.

**ὥσπερ**, for ὥσπερ, barbarism in Ar.*Th.*1185,1192.

**ὡσπεράν**, *about*, ὡ. πεντήκοντα ποδῶν D.H.1.15.

**ὥσπερ εἰ** or **ὡσπερεί**, Adv. *just as if*, with indic., ὥσπερ εἰ παρεστάτεις A.*Ag.*1201; with opt., ὥσπερ τις εἴ σοι..μηδὲν διδοίη S.*OC* 776; τὸ "ὡσπερεὶ" φάναι to say '*as it were*', Longin.32.3; ὅμοια ὥ. εἰ..X.*Smp.*4.37: with Nouns or parts., *as it were*, ὡ. ψῆτταν Ar. *Lys.*115; ὡ. προκείμενον Id.*Ec.*537; ἃ ὡ. στοιχεῖα τῶν ἄλλων ἐστί Pl.*Cra.*422a. II. ὥσπερ ἂν εἰ or ὡσπερανεί (prop. elliptical for ὥσπερ ἂν ἦν, εἰ.., or the like), Id.*Grg.*479a, *Prt.*311b, Isoc.4.148, X.*Cyr.*1.3.2; Dor. ὥσπερ αἰκ ἐξ ἑνὸς κελεύματος κεχάναντι they gape *as it were* 'by numbers' Sophr.25; ὥσπερ οὖν ἂν εἰ with impf., Pl.*R.*420c: cf. ὥσπερ I. 2.

**ὥσπερ οὖν** or **ὡσπεροῦν**, Adv. *even as*. ὥ. οὖν ἀπώλετο A.*Ch.*96, cf. 888, *Ag.*1171. II. *as indeed, as in fact*, εἰ δ' ἔστιν (ὥσπερ οὖν ἔστι) θεός Pl.*Phdr.*242e, cf. *Ap.*21d.

* **ὥστε**, A. as Adv., bearing the same relation to ὡς as ὅστε to ὅς, and used by Hom. more freq. than ὡς in similes, when it is commonly written divisim, and is relat. to a demonstr. ὥς: sts. c. pres. Indic., Il.2.459 sq., 12.421, 13.703: sts. c. aor., ὥς τε λέων ἐχάρη 3.23: sts. c. subj. pres. or aor., 2.474 sq., 11.67, 16.428, Od.22.302: all three usages combined in one simile, with varied construction, Il.5.136–9:—the verb is sts. omitted, λάμφ' ὥς τε στεροπή 10.154: this usage of ὥστε is chiefly Ep. (Pi. uses ὥτε, q.v.), but it occurs in Alc.(?)27 (prob.), B.12.124 and sts. in Trag., κατώρυχες δ' ἔναιον ὥστ' ἀήσυροι μύρμηκες A.*Pr.*452, cf. *Th.*62, *Pers.* 424, *Ch.*421 (lyr.), S.*OC*343, *Ant.*1033, *Tr.*112 (lyr.). II. to mark the power or virtue by which one does a thing, *as being, inasmuch as*, like ἅτε, τὸν δ' ἐξήρπαξ' Ἀφροδίτη ῥεῖα μάλ', ὥ. θεός Il.3.381, cf. 18.518; ὥ. περὶ ψυχῆς *since it was* for life, Od.9.423; ὥ. ταῦτα νομίζων Hdt.1.8, cf. 5.83,101, 6.94.

B. as Conj. to express *the actual* or *intended result* of the action in the principal clause: I. mostly c. inf., *so as* or *for to* do a thing, twice in Hom., εἰ δέ σοι θυμὸς ἐπέσσυται, ὥ. νέεσθαι if thy heart is eager *to* return, Il.9.42; οὐ τηλίκος.., ὥ. σημάντορι πάντα πιθέσθαι not of such age *as to* obey a master in all things, Od.17.21; ῥηϊδίως κεν ἐργάσσαιο, ὥ. σε κεἰς ἐνιαυτὸν ἔχειν Hes.*Op.*44; ὥ. ἀποπλησθῆναι (ἀποπλῆσαι codd.) τὸν χρησμόν Hdt.8.96: freq. in Pi., *O.*9.74, *N.*5.1,35, al.; also in Trag. and Att. after demonstratives, οὔπω τοσοῦτον ἠπατημένος κυρῶ ὥστ' ἄλλα χρῄζειν S.*OT*595, etc.; this constr. is found in cases where (as in Il.9.42 supr. cit.) ὥστε seems superfluous; so after ἐθέλειν, Κύπρις..ἤθελ' ὥ. γίγνεσθαι τόδε E.*Hipp.*1327; after ἔστι, for ἔξεστι, S.*Ph.*656; after ψηφίζεσθαι, Th.5.17; after ἐπαίρειν, E.*Supp.*581; ἐπαγγελλόμενοι ὥ. βοηθεῖν Th.8.86; after words implying request, δεηθέντες..ὥ. ψηφίσασθαι Id.1.119; πεῖσαι ὥ. συγχωρῆσαι Id.8.45. 2. after Comparatives with ἤ, when the possibility of the consequence is denied (cf. ὡς B. III. 2), μέζω κακὰ ἢ ὥστε ἀνακλαίειν woes too great for tears, Hdt. 3.14; μεῖζον ἢ ὥστε φέρειν δύνασθαι κακόν X.*Mem.*3.5.17: but in Poetry ὥστε is sts. left out, νόσημα μεῖζον ἢ φέρειν S.*OT*1293; κρεῖσσον' ἢ φέρειν κακά E.*Hec.*1107 (rarely in Prose, Pl.*Tht.*149c); similarly with the Posit., ψυχρὸν ὥ. λούσασθαι *too* cold *to* bathe in, X.*Mem.*3.13.3; ἡμεῖς ἔτι νέοι ὥ. διελέσθαι *too* young *to*.., Pl.*Prt.* 314b; γέρων ἐκεῖνος ὥ. σ' ὠφελεῖν παρών E.*Andr.*80: this ὥστε is sts. omitted after words implying comparison, ὀλίγους εἶναι στρατιῇ τῇ Μήδων συμβαλέειν too few..Hdt.6.109; ταπεινὴ ἡ διάνοια ἐγκαρτερεῖν Th.2.61, etc. 3. ὥστε..ἄν is used with inf., of contingencies more or less improbable, οὕτως ἐκαέτο ὥστε μήτε..ἄλλο τι ἢ γυμνοὶ ἀνέχεσθαι, ἥδιστά τε ἂν ἐς ὕδωρ ψυχρὸν σφᾶς αὐτοὺς ῥίπτειν Th.2.49, cf. S.*OT*374, *El.*1316, D.8.35. 4. sts. implying *on condition that*.., like ἐφ' ᾧτε, παραδοῦναι σφᾶς αὐτοὺς Ἀθηναίοις, ὥστε βουλεῦσαι ὅ τι ἂν ἐκείνοις δοκῇ Th.4.37, cf. X.*An.*5.6.26. II. c. Indic., to express the actual or possible result with emphasis, οὐκ οὕτω φρενοβλαβὴς ὁ Πρίαμος οὐδὲ οἱ ἄλλοι.., ὥ. κινδυνεύειν ἐβούλοντο Hdt.2.120 (fort. delendum ἐβούλοντο); ἀσθενέες οὕτω, ὥ...διατετρανέεις Id.3.12; οὕτως ἀγνωμόνως ἔχετε, ὥ. ἐλπίζετε..; are you so foolish *that* you expect..? D.2.26, βέβηκεν, ὥ. πὰν ἐν ἡσύχῳ ἔξεστι φωνεῖν S.*OC*82, cf. *OT*533: freq. in X., *Mem.*2.2.3, al.; with ἄν and the impf. or aor. implying a supposed case, ὥστ', εἰ φρονῶν ἔπρασσον, οὐδ' ἂν ὧδ' ἐγιγνόμην κακός S.*OC*271; ὥστε οὐκ ἂν ἔλαθεν αὐτόθεν ὁρμώμενος Th.5.6: ὥστε τὴν πόλιν ἂν ἡγήσω πολέμου ἐργαστήριον εἶναι X.*Ages.*1.26. 2. at the beginning of a sentence, to mark a strong conclusion, *and so, therefore*, ὥστ'..ὄλωλα καί σε προσδιαφθερῶ S.*Ph.*75; ὥστ' οὐχ ὕπνῳ γ' εὕδοντά μ' ἐξεγείρετε Id.*OT* 65; ὥ. καὶ ταῦτα λεχθήσεται Arist.*Metaph.*1004$^a$22: c. imper., θνητὸς δ' Ὀρέστης, ὥ. μὴ λίαν στένε S.*El.*1172; ὥ. θάρρει X.*Cyr.*1.3.18, cf. Pl.*Prt.*311a; ὥ. ἂν βούλησθε χειροτονήσατε D.9.70 cod.A (–ήσετε cett.); before a question, ὥ. τίς ἂν ἀπετόλμησε..; Lys.7.28. 3. c. opt., with ἄν, Hdt.2.16: βρέφος γὰρ ἦν τότ'.., ὥστ' οὐκ ἂν αὐτὸν γνωρίσαιμ' E.*Or.*379, cf. S.*OT*857, Ar.*Ach.*943 (lyr.). b. c. opt. in orat. obliq., X.*HG*3.5.23; after opt. in principal clause, Id.*Oec.*1.13. 4. with subj., *in order that*, in Thessalian dialect, τὸς ταμίας φροντίσαι οὔστε..γενειθεῖ τᾶ πόλι ἃ δόσις *BCH*59.38 (Crannon); ἀντιλλαβέσθαι τᾶς πόλλιος (sic) οὔστε..ἐς πάντουν ἐγλυθεῖ τοῦν δανείουν ib.p.37. III. with part., instead of inf., after a part. in the principal clause, τοσοῦτον ἁπάντων διενεγκόντες, ὥσθ' ὑπὲρ Ἀργείων δυστυχησάντων Θηβαίοις..ἐπιτάττοντες κτλ. Isoc.4.64 (s. v.l.); οὕτω σφόδρα μισοῦντα τοῦτον, ὥστε πολὺ δὴ (ἂν Dobree) θᾶττον διαθέμενον κτλ. Is.9.16; ὥστε..δέον D.3.1. IV. πόλεμος σκληρὸς ὥστε λίαν *extremely*, Lxx 2*Ki.*2.17. V. in later Greek, folld. by Preps., Παρμένοντι κλειδὸς ὥ. ἐπὶ τὸ Διοσκούριον *Inscr.Délos* 316.83 (iii B.C.); ξύλον ὥ. ἐπὶ τὴν ἅμαξαν *IG*11(2)287*A*52 (iii B.C.); μόλυβδος ὥ. εἰς τὸ Κύνθιον ib.203*A*52 (iii B.C.); κριθῶν ὥ. εἰς τὰ κτήνη barley *for* the animals, *PCair.Zen.*251.5 (iii B.C.); ὥ. εἰς ξένια φοίνικας *PHal.*1.7.4 (iii B.C.). b. c. dat., *for*, χρεία αὐτοῦ ἐστὶν ὥ. Πισικλεῖ it is needed *for* P., *PCair.Zen.*241 (iii B.C.); ὥ. τοῖς χησίν *IG*11(2).287*A*45 (iii B.C.).

**ὠσ-τέον**, (ὠθέω) *one must thrust out*, D.Chr.70.8. **–της**, ου, ὁ, *one who thrusts* or *pushes*; σεισμὸς ὠ. an earthquake *with one violent shock*, Arist.*Mu.*396$^a$8 (pl.). **–τίζομαι**, fut. Att. ὠστιοῦμαι Ar.*Ach.*24:—Pass., Frequentat. of ὠθέομαι, *to push and be pushed about*, mostly c. dat. pers., *to jostle with* another, *jostle* him *and be jostled* by him, ὠστιεῖ Κλεονύμῳ Ar.*Ach.*844; δούλαισιν ὠστιζομένη Id.*Lys.*330 (lyr.); ὠστιοῦνται..ἀλλήλοισι περὶ πρώτου ξύλου Id.*Ach.* 24: abs., ἐς τὴν προεδρίαν πᾶς ἀνὴρ ὠστίζεται *jostles* for the first seat, ib.42, cf. *Pl.*330; so, Comically, τῶν..πλακούντων ὠστιζομένων περὶ τὴν γνάθον Teleclid.1.13. **–τικός**, ή, όν, *inclined to thrust, pushing*, ὠστικὴ..ἡ τοῦ πνεύματος φύσις Arist.*MA*703$^a$23; τὸ ὠ. *impetuosity*, Arr.*Epict.*4.1.84. Adv. **–κῶς** ib.2.9.5, M.Ant.9.3. **–τισμός**, ὁ, = ὠθισμός, Moer.p.424P. **–τός**, ή, όν, (ὠθέω) ὠστόν· τὸ ἀποδιωκτόν, Hdn.*Epim.*103.

**ὦσχη**, ἡ, = κληματίς, *EM*825.2, cf. Procl.ap.Phot.p.322B., Suid.

✱ **ὠσχός**, ὁ, in pl. ὠσχοί· τὰ νέα κλήματα σὺν αὐτοῖς τοῖς βότρυσιν, Hsch., cf. *AB*318: sg., Aristodem.ap.Ath.11.495f, cf. **οἰσχός·** κλῆμα βότρυας φέρον ὀργῶντας καὶ γενναίους, καὶ ὀσχοφόρια (v. sq.), τὰ τῆς ἀμπέλου κλήματα περιέχοντα βότρυας, παρὰ Ἀριστοφάνει, *EM*619.32 (v. infr.), whence Brunck conjectured ὀσχόν for the Aldine reading ὄρχον in Ar.*Ach.*997, where codd. and Sch. have the unmetrical κλάδον (one Ms. κάδον); perh. ὠσχόν shd. be read, as the ὠ- is corroborated by *EM*824.55, and by ὠσχοφόρια, etc.:—ὄσχοι, the reading adopted by Littré from three codd. in Hp.*Mul.*2.204, gives a poorer sense than ὄχοι (v. ὄχος II. 2), the reading of many good Mss. (incl. Vind. θ): ὄσχος in Sch.Od.5.38 is apparently f.l. for ὀσχεός, cf. Sch.A Il.24.94. [The ὠ- of this and the foll. words, for which ὀ- is an occasional v.l., is found in the best codd. and is corroborated by the position of the word in the ancient lexica.]

**ὠσχο-φορέω**, *celebrate the* ὠσχοφόρια, Phot. **–φόρια**, τά, one day of the Athen. festival Σκίρα, on which two chosen young men, sons of citizens, in women's dress, *carrying vine-shoots loaded with grapes* (v. ὠσχός), went in procession from the temple of Dionysus to that of Ἀθηνᾶ Σκιράς, Philoch.44, Plu.*Thes.*22, Alciphr.1.4,3.1. II. sg. **–φόριον**, τό, the sanctuary of Athena Σκιράς in Phalerum, Hsch., *AB*318, etc. **–φορικός**, ή, όν, *of* or *for the* ὠσχοφόρια, Ath.14.631b; μέλη ὠ. Poll.4.53, Procl.ap.Phot.p.322B. ✱ **–φόροι**, οἱ, *the young men who carried the vine-branches*, Hyp.*Fr.*87, Philoch.44, and Ister 13, all ap.Harp. (ὀσχο-).

**ὠτάκις**, ίδος, ἡ, a sea-plant, Dionys.*Av.*2.7.

**ὠτᾰκουστ-έω**, *listen, eavesdrop*, Hdt.8.130, X.*Cyr.*5.3.56, 8.2.10, D.19.288; ὠ. καὶ κατοπτεύειν τὰ συμβαίνοντα Plb.31.13.1: c. gen., Suid. **–ής**, οῦ, ὁ, *listener, eavesdropper*, of a person employed as *a spy* by tyrants, Arist.*Pol.*1313$^b$14, *Mu.*398$^a$21, Plb.16.37.1, Plu.2.522f.

**ὠταλγ-έω**, *have the ear-ache*, Dsc.4.64. **–ία**, ἡ, *ear-ache*, Id.2.179, 3.27, Poll.4.185, *Gp.*12.12.6. **–ιάω**, = ὠταλγέω, Dsc.2.169. **–ικός**, ή, όν, *suffering from ear-ache*, v.l. in Id.4.64.

**ὦ τᾶν**, v. τᾶν.

**ὠτᾰρᾶς**, = *auriculosus*, *Gloss.*

**ὠτάριον** [ᾰ], τό, Dim. of οὖς, *a little ear*, Anaxandr.43; ὠτάρι' ὕεια Alex.110.16; later simply = οὖς, *AP*11.75 (Lucill.); *Ev.Jo.*18.10. II. metaph., *handle* of a vessel, Parth.ap.Ath.11.783c; ὠτάρια κάδου *IG*7.3498.18 (Oropus, iii B.C.), cf. *BGU*781 i 15, *Inscr. Délos* 421.54 (ii B.C.). III. the *ormer* or *Haliotis*, Ath.3.87f.

✱ **ὦτε**, Dor. for ὥστε A. I, Pi.*N.*6.28, 7.62, *I.*4(3).18(36), *O.*10(11).86, *P.*10.54, Alcm.23.41, B.16.105, Corinn.*Supp.*2.65, *Lyr.Adesp.*ap. A.D.*Pron.*48.28. (For the accent, cf. Wackernagel *Beitr.z.Lehre vom Gr.Akzent* p.20; ὦτε· σὺν τῷ ῑ, ἀντὶ τοῦ ὥσειτε, Choerob. in *An.Ox.*2.281; this spelling (ᾧτε, ὧιτε) is found in Alcm. and cod. A of A.D. l.c., Corinn. l.c.)

**ὠτεγχύτης** [ῠ], ου, ὁ, *ear-syringe*, Dsc.*Eup.*1.56, Gal.6.439, *Hermes* 38.284.

✱ **ὠτειλ-ή**, ἡ, *wound*, esp. *a fresh, open wound*, Il. (acc. to Ammon. *Diff.*pp.104,144, opp. οὐλή); δεῖξεν..αἷμα καταρρέον ἐξ ὠτειλῆς Il.5.870; αἷμ' ἔτι θερμὸν ἀνήνοθεν ἐξ ὠ. 11.266, cf. 17.297; δόρυ χάλκεον ἐξ ὠ. εἴρυσε 16.862; ὠτειλὴν..δῆσαν ἐπισταμένως Od.19.456;—Aristarch. considered ὠτειλή as restricted in Hom. to a *wound inflicted hand to hand*, not by a missile, χαλκοτύπους ὠ. Il.19.25, and therefore he rejected as spurious 4.140,149, cf. Sch.Il.4.140, 11.266, 18.351. II. after Hom. (esp. in Hp.) generally, *wound*, whether recent or not, κίνδυνος ἂν εἴη συρραγῆναι τὰς ὠ. Hp.*Art.*11; also, *the mark of a wound, scar*, ὅταν τὰ ἕλκεα ἐς ὠτειλὰς ἴῃ ibid., cf. Ruf.*Ren.Ves. Praef.*: *ulcer*, Gal.19.157:—once in X., τὰ μὲν ἔπαθεν, ὧν τὰς ὠτειλὰς [φανερὰς add. codd. plerique] εἶχεν *An.*1.9.6, cf. Plu.*Cor.*14, 2.276d, Jul.*Caes.*309c. (Prob. fr. οὐτάω (so Sch.A Il.14.518); cf. οὐταμένη ὠτειλή Il.14.518, 17.86; Aeol. **ὀτέλλα** (sic) Jo.Gramm. *Comp.* (in Hoffmann *Die griechischen Dialekte* ii.488); cf. γατειλαί (for ϝατ-) and βωτ[ε]άζειν).) **–ῆθεν**, Adv. *from* or *out of the wound*, Orph.*L.*653. **–όομαι**, Pass., *cicatrize*, Hp.*Fract.*27.

**ὠτικός**, ή, όν, (οὖς) *of* or *for the ear*, ἰατρός Gal.*Thras.*24; φλεγμοναί Dsc.1.26.

**ὠτίον**, τό, prop. Dim. of οὖς, *auricle*, Dsc.*Eup.*1.63, cf. 62; but usu. = οὖς, *AP*11.81 (Lucill.), Lxx 1*Ki.*9.15, al., *Ev.Matt.*26.51, Arr. *Epict.*1.18.18, *PMag.Osl.*1.332. II. metaph., *a little handle*, προχύτου Hero *Spir.*1.9; χωρὶς ὠτίων ποτήριον Theopomp.Com.31, cf. Aët.1.138. 2. = ὠτάριον III, Xenocr.ap.Orib.2.58.130; gloss on τήθη, = λεπὰς ἀγρία, Sch.Nic.*Al.*396.

**ὠτιοφόρος**, ὁ, = ὠτοκάταξις, *AB*287 (where the word is distd. fr. ὀτιαφόρος, q.v.): also **ὠτιαφόρος**, *EM*826.27.

**ὠτίς**, ίδος, ἡ, (οὖς) *bustard*, *Otis tarda*, X.*An.*1.5.2 sq., Arist.*HA* 509$^a$4, al., Ael.*NA*5.24, Opp.*C.*2.407; cf. οὐτίς, ὀτίς. II. μυὸς ὠτίς, v. μυοσωτίς.

**ὠτο-γλῠφίς**, ίδος, ἡ, *ear-pick*, Pl.Com.148, *Hermes* 38.248, *Gp.*4.7.1; also **–γλῠφον**, τό, *Gloss.*:—Dim. **–γλύφιον**, τό, ib. **–ειδής**, ές, *like an ear, ear-shaped*, Ruf.*Anat.*32. Adv. **–δῶς** ibid.

**ὠτο-θλᾰδίας**, ου, ὁ, = ὠτοκάταξις, D.L.5.67. **–κάταξις**, ιδος, ὁ, *a boxer with thick* or '*cauliflower' ears*, Ar.*Fr.*98, cf. Poll.2.83, *EM*826.28, Suid. (ὠτοκαταξίας is f.l. in Poll.4.144). **–κλᾰδίας**, ὁ, = *auriflaccus*, *Gloss.* **–κοπέω**, *stun the ears by talking*, Hsch. **–κωφέω**, *to be hard of hearing*, Zonar. **–λᾰβίς**, ίδος, ἡ, *an instrument for laying hold of the ears*, τοὺς ὄρχεις..ἀποδεσμεῖν τῇ ὠ. *Hippiatr.* 99. **–λικνος**, ον, *with ears as large as a winnowing-fan*; οἱ Ὠτόλικνοι, name of a fabulous Indian tribe, Tz.*H.*7.635. **–πάροχος**, ον, (παρέχω) *supplying* or *having ears*, *Gloss.* **–πέτης**, ες, = *auritus*, ib. **–ρρῠτος**, ον, *having a running from the ears*, Hp.*Epid.*6.1.2.

**ὦτος**, ου, ὁ (on the accent v. Hdn.Gr.1.214), *a horned* or *eared owl*, ὁ δ' ὦτος.., περὶ τὰ ὦτα πτερύγια ἔχων Arist.*HA*597$^b$21, cf. Plu.2.961e, v.l. ib.52b: Ath.9.390d appears to identify it with the ὠτίς, but this is due to interpolation. II. *an easily deceived person, booby*, *Com.Adesp.*47, Ael.Dion.*Fr.*336. III. ὦτα· τὰ μὴ στρογγύλα, Hsch.; but ὦτοι λίθοι in *IG*4.823.66 (Troezen) is wrongly read, v. ὦ II.

**ὠτότμητος**, ον, *with ears slit* or *cropped*, Lxx *Le.*21.18, 22.23.

**ὠτώεις**, εσσα, εν, poet. Adj. *with ears* or *handles*, τρίπους Il.23.264,513, Hes.*Op.*657. (The older form οὐατόεις [q. v.] may originally have stood here, but has left no trace in codd.)

**ᾠύφιον**, τό, Dim. of ᾠόν, Theognost.*Can.*127; ωοιφια εικοσι *PLond.* 2.335.19 (ii A.D.).

✱ **ὠφέλ-εια**, ἡ, required by the metre (in iambics), S.*El.*944, Ar. *Th.*183; whereas **ὠφελία** is required in E.*Andr.*539 (anap.), *Fr.*78 (lyr.), Ar.*Ec.*576 (lyr.): the best codd. of Pl. have ὠφελία more freq. than ὠφέλεια (although B always has ὠφέλεια in *Phdr.*), and ὠφελία is found in *IG*1$^2$.69.24 (v B.C., Prose), Hyp.*Eux.*9, and freq. in Phld., as *Mus.*p.54 K., al.: Ion. **ὠφελίη** Hdt.5.98, al., *AP*6.187 (Alph.):—*help, aid, succour*, esp. in war, ἔπεμπον ἐς τὴν Ἐπίδαμνον..τὴν ὠ. Th.1.26, cf. 39; τὴν ὠ. παρέχειν τινί Id.3.13, cf. And.3.31; ὠ. ἀνδρὶ φέρειν E.*Fr.*78 (lyr.); ὠ. προσλήψεσθαι Th.2.7; ἀπό τινων εὑρίσκεσθαι Id.1.31; τῆς ὠ. μεταλαμβάνειν Id.1.39; τυγχάνειν Id.6.17; ἐπάγεσθαί τινας ἐπ' ὠφελίᾳ for *aid*, Id.1.3, cf. 5.38; ἀποχρήσασθαι τῇ ἑκατέρου ἡμῶν ὠ. to make full use of the *assistance* or *services* we both can give, Id.6.17; μετὰ τῶν κειμένων νόμων ὠφελίας Id.3.82, cf. D.H. *Th.*31; οὐδὲν ἰατρικῆς δεῖται οὐδ' ὠφελίας or *any other aid*, Pl.*Ly.* 217a, cf. *R.*559b; καὶ τοῖσιν ἑλκωθεῖσιν ὠφελίαν (ὠφέλειαν codd., unmetrically) ἔχει *Com.Adesp.*106.8. II. *profit, advantage*, βούλευμα ἀπ' οὗ..οὐδεμία ἔμελλε ὠφελίη ἔσεσθαι Hdt. l. c.; εἴ τις ὠφέλειά γε S.*El.*944; τὴν κοινὴν ὠ. φυλάξαι the common *interest* of all, Th.6.80; τίς ἂν εἴη ἡμῖν ὠ. εἰδόσιν αὐτό; Pl.*Chrm.*167b; opp. βλάβη, X.*Cyr.*6.2.13, Pl. (v. infr.2), etc.; opp. ζημία, X.*Mem.*2.3.6; ἐπ' ὠφελείᾳ ἐστί τι ib.1.4.4: c. gen. subjecti, τὴν ὠ. τὴν τῶν τειχέων their *utility*, Hdt.7.139: c. gen. objecti, ἐπ' ὠφελίᾳ τῶν φίλων for their *benefit*, Pl.*R.*334b; ὠφελίας ἕνεκα ib.398b; ἐναντία τῇ ἑαυτῶν ὠ. And.2.2; ἐν ὠ. ἐστί 'tis *of use*, X.*Vect.*4.35; after ὠφελεῖν, cf. ὠφελέω I.5. 2. *source of gain* or *profit, service*, freq. in pl., τὰς ὠ. τὰς ἐκ τῆς στρατείας..ἐσομένας Isoc.4.15; αἱ κοιναὶ ὠ. Lys.19.62; αἱ ἀπό τινος γιγνόμεναι ὠ. Isoc.4.29; ὠφελίας τε καὶ βλάβας ἀποδιδοῦσα Id.*R.*332d; αἱ παρὰ τῶν μισθοδοτούντων αὐτοὺς ὠ. D.15.32. 3. esp. *gain made in war, spoil, booty*, Plb.2.3.8, 3.82.8, *Rev. Arch.*6(1935).31 (pl., Amphipolis), Lxx 2*Ma.*8.20; ὠ. μεγάλαι καὶ λάφυρα Plu.2.255b; ὠφελείας ἀθροῖσαι Id.*Cleom.*12; πολλῆς ὠ. κυριεῦσαι D.S.15.36; τὴν χώραν γέμειν ὠφελείας Plb.3.80.3; τίθεσθαι τὰ χρήματα δι' ὠφελείας to regard as *booty*, D.H.7.37; so in the chase, *game*, X.*Cyn.*6.4; so of a thief, ὠ. ἑτοίμην καὶ κατειργασμένην ἀφῆκεν Antipho 2.1.4. (Prob. abstracted fr. οἰκ-ωφελία, which comes fr. οἶκον ὀφέλλειν 'to *increase* the οἶκος'; cf. ὄφελος.) **-έω**, fut. -ήσω Ar.*Av.*358, etc.: aor. ὠφέλησα Hdt.3.127, etc.: pf. -ηκα Hp.*Acut.*44, Pl.*Grg.*511e, etc.: plpf. ὠφελήκη Id.*Ap.*31d:—Pass., fut. ὠφεληθήσομαι And.2.22, Is.10.16, Hp.*Int.*35, X.*Cyr.*3.2.20; more freq. fut. Med. in pass. sense, ὠφελήσομαι Th.6.18, 7.67, Pl.*R.*343c, X.*Mem.*1.6.14, v.l. in Lys.19.61: aor. ὠφελήθην Th.2.39, 5.90, etc.: pf. ὠφέλημαι A.*Pr.*222, Pl.*Grg.*512a, etc.: plpf. ὠφέλητο Th.6.60: (ὄφελος):—*help, aid, succour*, first in Hdt. (v. infr.); opp. βλάπτω, Th.6.14, Pl.*Phd.*107d; opp. ζημιόω, Isoc.6.5.—Construction: **I.** abs., *to be of use* or *service*, τὰ μηδὲν ὠφελοῦντα A.*Pr.*44, cf. S.*Fr.*196, E.*IA*348(troch.), X.*Oec.*1.9; οὐδὲν ὠφελεῖ Th.2.87; τὸ πολλάκις ὠφελοῦν Isoc.8.35. **2.** c. acc. pers., *to be of service to, benefit*, Hdt.2.95, A.*Pr.*507; τὰς ψυχὰς ὠ. διδάσκοντες X.*Cyr.*2.3.23; ὠ. τινα ἔς τι *to be of use to* one towards a thing, Th.4.75; τί δέ μ' ὠφελήσουσ' οἱ ῥυθμοὶ πρὸς τἄλφιτα; how will rhythms *help* me to earn my bread? Ar.*Nu.*648: abs., ἐπὶ τοῖς δεινοῖσιν E.*Fr.*84; διὰ τῶν ὤτων Plu.2.38c, cf. 145b: c. part., αὐτοὺς ὠφελεῖ προσκείμενον E.*Hipp.*970. **b.** esp. of a general, *enrich* his soldiers by booty, Plu.*Aem.*29; τοὺς στρατιώτας ὠφεληκὼς ἀπὸ τῶν στρατειῶν Id.*Caes.*12; cf. ὠφέλεια II.3. **3.** in Poets also (v. Thom.Mag.p.408 R.) c. dat. pers., A.*Pr.*342, *Pers.*842, S.*Ant.*560, E.*Or.*666, 681, *Heracl.*681, Ar.*Av.*421 (lyr.); also in Antipho 6.38, and v.l. in Th.5.23; the compds. προσωφελέω, ἐπωφελέω, συνωφελέω also take both constructions. **4.** c. gen., dub. in οὐδεὶς ἔρωτος τοῦδ' ἐφαίνετ' ὠφελῶν S.*OC*436 (fort. leg. ἔρωτ' ἐς τόνδ'). **5.** c. acc. cogn., ὠφελίαν ὠ. τινα to *render* him a *service*, Pl.*R.*519e, cf. *Euthd.*275e; ὠφελίαν κοινῇ -οῦνται πάντες οἱ δημιουργοί Id.*R.*346c: with a neut. Adj., οὐδέν τινα ὠ. *to do* one no *service*, Hdt.3.126, E.*Alc.*875 (lyr.); πολλά, πλέον, πλεῖστον, ὡς πλεῖστα ὠ. τινα, Isoc.3.30, E.*Andr.*679, 681, Th.6.14. **II.** Pass., *receive help* or *succour, derive profit* or *advantage*, πρός τινος from a person or thing, Hdt.2.68; ἔκ τινος A.*Pr.*222, Antipho 3.2.3; ἀπό τινος Th.3.64, X.*Oec.*1.15, cf. Gorg.*Pal.*10; ὑπό or παρά τινος, Pl.*Grg.*512a, *Amat.*132d; ὠ. τοῦ νόμου *to derive benefit from..*, Antipho 5.17 (dub. l.); τινι *by* a thing, Th.3.67; διά τι ib.13; παρ' ἐμοῦ ὠφελεῖσθαι *to make something* out of me, Antipho 2.2.13; ἐκ τῶν ὑμετέρων *help themselves*, Lys.27.7: esp. of troops, *acquire booty*, πολλὰ παρὰ τὴν στρατείαν ὠ. Plu.*Cat.Ma.*10; ὠ. δι' ἁρπαγῆς Id.*Marc.*19; ὠφελεῖσθαι πρός τι *acquire advantage* towards a thing, X.*Cyn.*5.27: c. part., ὠφελεῖσθαι ἰδών *to be profited by* the sight of a thing, Th.2.39: c. adj. neut., οὐδὲν ὠφελουμένη S.*Ant.*550: πολλὰ ὠφελεῖσθαι οὐδὲν πονοῦντες X.*Cyr.*3.2.20. ⊛ **-ημα**, ατος, τό, *a useful* or *serviceable thing, service, benefit*, A.*Pr.*251; ἀνθρώποισιν ὠφελήματα ib.501; of a person, ὦ κοινὸν ὠφέλημα θνητοῖσιν φανείς ib.613, cf. E.*Tr.*703. **2.** ὠφελήματα *things good in themselves*, e.g. harmony, goodwill, opp. εὐχρηστήματα, *Stoic.*3.23, cf.136. **II.** generally, *use, advantage, profit*, τί δῆτα δόξης..ὠ. γίγνεται; S.*OC*259, cf. X.*Hier.*10.3; ὠφελήματα πατρίδος Id.*Ages.*7.2. **-ήσῐμος**, ον, *useful, serviceable, profitable*, πολλοὶ μὲν ἐχθροί, παῦρα δ' ὠ. S.*Aj.*1022; ὠ. [λόγος] Ar.*Av.*317 (troch.). ⊛**-ησις**, εως, ἡ, *helping, aiding*, hence, like ὠφέλεια, *use, service, advantage*, S.*OC*401; σοὶ γὰρ ὠ. οὐκ ἔνι Id.*El.*1031. **-ητέος**, α, ον, *proper to be served*, ὠφελητέα σοι ἡ πόλις X.*Mem.*3.6.3. **II.** **ὠφελητέον**, *one must serve*, τὴν πόλιν ib.2.1.28. **-ητικός**, ή, όν, *helpful, useful*, Ph.1.14, *Fr.*55 H., Arr.*Epict.*2.10.23, Aristid.Quint.2.9, Dam.*Isid.*296. **-ία**, v. ὠφέλεια. ⊛ **-ῐμος**, ον, rarely η, ον, Pl.*Chrm.*174d (dub. l.), *R.*607d:—*helping, aiding, useful, serviceable, beneficial*, sts. of persons, as Id.*Men.*98c, *R.*461b (Comp.), X.*Mem.*2.7.9: but more freq. of things, Th.2.46, etc.; τινι to one, E.*Ion* 138 (lyr.), Th.4.44, 7.64, etc.; ἔς τι for a purpose, Id.3.68; πρὸς τὰς πολιτείας Pl.*R.* 607d; ὑπέρ τινος X.*Cyr.*6.2.34; κρίνειν τι ὠ. Th.1.22; τὸ ὠ. as Subst., Pl.*R.*457d; τὸ ὑμῖν ὠ. Th.1.76, cf. E. l. c.: Comp. and Sup., -ώτερος, -ώτατος, Th.1.93, Pl.*R.*461b, *Tht.*179a. Adv. -μως X.*Mem.*4.4.1, Pl.*Grg.*470a, *Chrm.*163c: Sup. -ώτατα X.*Eq.*6.1.

**ὤφελλον**, Ep. for **ὤφελον**, aor. 2 of ὀφείλω.

**ὤχ, ὤχ**, a magical incantation against fleas, *Gp.*13.15.9.

**ὠχεί**, Egyptian name of ἀτράφαξυς, Ps.-Dsc.2.119.

**ὤχνων** (gen. pl.), dub. sens. in *POxy.*2146.11 (iii A.D.).

**ὤχρα**, ἡ, *yellow ochre*, Arist.*Mete.*$378^{a}23$, Thphr.*Lap.*40, *PCair.Zen.*764.13 (iii B.C.), Dsc.5.93, etc. **II.** in corn, = ἐρυσίβη, *mildew*, Lxx *De.*28.22.

**ὠχρ-αίνω**, *make pale* or *wan*, Orph.*A.*1308:—Pass., *to become so*, Sor.2.45; opp. ἐρυθραίνομαι, S.E.*M.*7.193, cf. Max.Tyr.34.2. **II.** intrans., *to be* or *become so*, Nic.*Th.*254. **-αντικός**, ή, όν, *making pale* or *wan*, only in Adv. -κῶς κινεῖσθαι, πάσχειν, of jaundiced patients, who see everything with a yellow tinge, S.E.*M.*7.192, 198. **-άω**, *turn pale* or *wan*, ὠχρήσαντα χρόα Od.11.529; of the sun, Arat.851. **-ία**, ἡ, = ὤχρα II, *EM*378.48. **-ίας**, ου, ὁ, *one of a pale complexion*, Arist.*Cat.*$9^{b}32$. **-ίᾱσις**, εως, ἡ, *a turning pale, paleness*, Sor.1.45, Plot.3.6.3; ἡ πολίωσις οἷον ὠ. Plu.2.364b: pl., ib.652d. **2.** = ὤχρα II, Thd.*Am.*4.9. **-ιάω**, = ὠχράω, *to be pallid*, Ar.*Nu.*103, *Ra.*307, *Com.Adesp.*342; ὠχριηκώς Hp.*Ep.*17; ὠχριήσας Babr.92.8; opp. ἐρυθριάω, ἐρυθραίνομαι, Arist.*Cat.*$9^{b}31$, *EN*$1128^{b}14$; of wine, Plu.2.692e.

**ὠχρο-ειδής**, ές, *pallid*, πόνος Suid. v. ἴκτερος, prob. in Dsc.5.104. **-λευκος**, ον, *of a whitish yellow* or *yellowish white*, ἄνθος Id.4.42; of wine, Gal.6.336. **-μέλᾱς**, αινα, ᾰν, *dark and sallow*, of sufferers from jaundice, Id.17(2).66; of a type of jaundice, Hp.ap.Herod.Med. in *Rh.Mus.*49.554.

**ὠχρ-όμμᾰτος**, ον, *pale-eyed*, Arist.*Phgn.*$812^{b}8$.

**ὠχρό-ξανθος**, ον, *of a pale yellow colour*, Gal.14.81. **-πελιός**, = *luridus, Gloss.* **-ποιός**, όν, *making pale*, gloss on Il.7.479 in cod.Mosqu.1.

**ὠχρός**, ά, όν, *pale, wan*, of complexion, E.*Ba.*438, Ar.*Nu.*1016 (anap.), *Pl.*422, etc.: esp. *pale-yellow, sallow*, τὸ δὲ ὠ. [γίγνεται] λευκοῦ ξανθῷ μειγνυμένου Pl.*Ti.*68c; of a frog, Batr.81; χρῶμα δ' ἀσίτων..γίνεται ὠχρόν Alex.162.9 (anap.); ὠχρὸς κἀνυπόδητος, of a Pythagorean, Theoc.14.6: freq. in Luc. of philosophers, *JTr.*1, al.; ὠ. καὶ αὐχμηρός, of a miser, Id.*Cat.*17; of bile, etc., Hp.*Int.*37, Gal.15.554; τὸ ὠ. τοῦ ᾠοῦ the *yolk* of the egg, Arist.*HA*$560^{a}21$; τὸ ὠ. the *colour yellow* (v. supr.), Id.*Cat.*$12^{a}18$; cf. ὤχρα.

**ὦχρος**, ου, ὁ (cf. Hdn.Gr.2.39), *paleness, wanness*, esp. *the pale hue* of fear, once in Hom., ὦχρός τέ μιν εἷλε παρειάς Il.3.35; also in Luc.*JTr.*1 (adapting Hom.) and late Poets, as Androm.ap.Gal.14.35, *AP*5.258 (Paul.Sil.). **II.** *birds' pease, Lathyrus Ochrus*, Antiph.301, Arist.*HA*$627^{b}17$ (pl.), Thphr.*HP*8.3.1, al., *CP*4.2.2, D.L.2.139.

**ὠχροσύνη**, ἡ, *pallor*, Antioch.Astr. in *Cat.Cod.Astr.*1.112.

**ὠχρότης**, ητος, ἡ, *pallor*, Pl.*R.*474e; χρόας Luc.*Icar.*5; opp. μελανία, Arist.*Cat.*$9^{b}22$: pl., Plu.2.84e; opp. ἐρυθήματα, Arist.*MA*$701^{b}31$.

**ὤχρωμα**, ατος, τό, *pallor*, interpol. in Suid.

**ὤψ**, ἡ, *EM*344.55, but ὁ, Ar.Byz. (v. infr.), Eust.1426.55 (v. infr.), gen. ὠπός, acc. ὦπα:—*eye, face, countenance*, Hom. and Hes., only in acc. sing.; εἰς ὦπα ἰδέσθαι τινί to look one in *the face*, Il.9.373; ἐπὴν ἔλθητε Διός τ' εἰς ὦπα ἴδησθε 15.147: abs., δεινὸς εἰς ὦπα ἰδέσθαι Od.22.405, cf. 23.107; θεῇς εἰς ὦπα ἔοικεν in *face* she is like the goddesses, Il.3.158; οὐ μὲν γάρ τι κακῷ εἰς ὦπα ἐῴκει Od.1.411; θεῇς εἰς ὦπα ἐΐσκειν Hes.*Op.*62.—masc. acc. pl., μεγάλους ὦπας Ar.Byz.ap.Ath.7.287b, cf. Ath.9.367a, Gal.12.804, Eust. l. c.; διγλήνους ὦπας Theoc.*Ep.*6.2, cf. *EM*233.32: but τὰ ὦπα Pl.*Cra.*409c: dat. ὤπεσσι Max.157. (Cf. ὄψ B.)

**ὠψά**, τά, = τὰ ὀπτητήρια, Hsch.

**ὠώ**, v. ὦ (ὤ).

**ᾠώδης**, ες, *egg-like*, ὑγρότης Arist.*HA*$565^{a}23$; σκώληξ Id.*GA*$733^{b}13$: *oval*, φιάλιον ὠιῶ[δες] *IG*$2^{2}$.1534.46 (iv B.C.).

# Greek-English Lexicon

## REVISED SUPPLEMENT

H. G. LIDDELL ROBERT SCOTT

H. STUART JONES RODERICK McKENZIE

# Greek-English Lexicon

## REVISED SUPPLEMENT

*Edited by*

P. G. W. GLARE

*With the assistance of*

A. A. THOMPSON

CLARENDON PRESS · OXFORD

1996

# PREFACE

The Greek–English Lexicon of Liddell and Scott was first published in 1843. In the 150 years which have passed since then it has gone through nine editions, the last being augmented by a Supplement published in 1968. This Supplement incorporated a considerable amount of new material, mainly taken from inscriptions and papyri, and also 'a good deal of information pertaining to literary sources, where the systematic reading of new editions, or ordinary consultation by scholars, has revealed the lexicon to be in need of revision'.

It had fallen to Dr M. L. West to see that Supplement through the press, and after its publication he kept custody of the slips from which it was printed and a collection of material that had been excluded from it. He did not undertake any further lexicographical work, but served as a receiving-point for any new material that happened to be sent to the Press. When he left Oxford in 1974 to take up a chair in London, he passed the archive to Mr (now Prof.) M. D. Reeve, then a Fellow of Exeter College.

In January 1979 Dr West presented to the British Academy a proposal for the preparation of a new Supplement. After some discussion a committee was set up to plan and cost the project in detail. It consisted of the following members: Prof. M. L. West (chairman), Prof. R. Browning, Dr J. Chadwick, Prof. A. M. Davies, the late Prof. D. M. Lewis, and Mr (now Prof.) P. J. Parsons. Early in 1981 the Council of the Academy, having come to an agreement with Oxford University Press, accepted the proposal and adopted the Supplement as one of the Academy's Major Research Projects. It was agreed that the project would run for ten years, and that a full-time editor would be needed. The post was advertised, and Mr P. G. W. Glare, who had amply proved his lexicographical competence and stamina by his labours on the *Oxford Latin Dictionary*, was appointed with effect from 1 August 1981. The Project Committee continued to monitor progress throughout with its original membership unchanged, except for the addition of Mr N. G. Wilson in 1989, and with the regular attendance at its meetings of representatives of the Press and of the British Academy.

In 1988, when it became clear that the undertaking was considerably greater than had at first been supposed, Dr Anne Thompson was appointed to the project as part-time Editorial Associate. Later in the same year Dr Carolinne White also joined the staff with the special function of checking the references, and proof-reading the print-out at all stages; she also became mainly responsible for the compilation of the lists at the beginning of the Supplement. Mrs Lorna Lyons acted as Secretary/Assistant throughout and, among multifarious duties, was entirely responsible for the keying-in of the text.

Much new material has become available since the publication of the first Supplement, and the incorporation of this is again the main aim of the new Supplement. The question of revision is altogether more complicated and re-examination of the entries in the first Supplement revealed the need to redraft many of them. How far revision of the main Lexicon should proceed is a more difficult question. It was evident from an examination of them that many articles require a more drastic rewriting than can be achieved by the addition, exclusion, or alteration of individual items. Minor changes may in fact only highlight shortcomings in the original articles.

For this reason and in view of the restricted staff and time available it has proved impossible to revise many articles which can now be seen to require changes. In a few cases new articles have been substituted for those appearing in the Lexicon, but these are mostly short ones. In longer articles it has been necessary to restrict changes to those which could be made within the existing framework of the article. It must also be explained that, although electronic retrieval facilities became available soon after the commencement of work on the Supplement, a systematic use of these was not made, since it would have involved a complete change in the scale and nature of the project.

At the time of the publication of the first Supplement it was felt that the Ventris decipherment of the Linear B tablets was still too uncertain to warrant the inclusion of these texts in a standard dictionary. Ventris's interpretation is now generally accepted and the tablets can no longer be ignored in a comprehensive Greek dictionary; however, for reasons explained in a note appended to this preface, Mycenaean forms are not included in the body of the articles, but attached at the end. Words written in the Cyprian syllabary are quoted in transcription as well as in a reconstructed alphabetical form, since the latter may be misleading. References to these have also been brought up to date.

The new inscriptions include many early ones in dialect, and advances in the classification and understanding of dialects since the last edition of Liddell and Scott mean that the information given in LSJ is not always reliable. While every effort has been made to explain new dialect forms and words, on many points recourse must be made to specialist works.

Words not already in LSJ but included in *A Patristic Greek Lexicon* (ed. Lampe, Oxford 1961) have not normally been added unless they help to explain related words which *are* in LSJ/Supplement. At the same time some words noted only from patristic sources, but used in a general, i.e. non-patristic/ecclesiastical sense, have been included if they have been overlooked by Lampe.

The occasional etymological notes in LSJ are frequently out of date. No attempt has been made to bring them up to date and readers are referred to the standard etymological dictionaries of Chantraine (*Dictionnaire Étymologique de la Langue Grecque*, Paris 1968) and Frisk (*Griechisches Etymologisches Wörterbuch*, Heidelberg 1960–70).

At the time of completion of this Supplement three fascicles of a new Spanish dictionary (*Diccionario griego-español* Madrid, 1980– ) have been published and these have been consulted with profit for those parts of the alphabet which they cover. New abbreviations in the Supplement have, where possible, been chosen to match those of the Spanish dictionary.

New words in the first Supplement were distinguished by the prefix of a cross(*); this practice has been continued, and in addition an upright cross (+) has been used to indicate those entries from the main dictionary which have been totally rewritten. A prefixed ° indicates a cross-reference to an article elsewhere in the Supplement, and ‡ means that readers should refer to the word so marked in both the Supplement and the main dictionary.

Vowel quantities are indicated on the same principles as in the main dictionary. To avoid misunderstanding all words in the new Supplement are so marked, not, as in the old Supplement, only the new entries. An exception is made in the case of late borrowings from Latin. At the time the borrowings were made the distinction of length was breaking down in both Latin and Greek, and to mark them according to classical principles would be meaningless. A number of other small changes have been made in printing conventions in line with modern practice and in the interests of greater clarity. Some of these will be found in the list of abbreviations; the rest are self-explanatory and will cause no problems.

New editions of texts are noted in the lists of Authors and Works, etc. References to them in the articles are normally indicated by the initial of the editor. No attempt has been made to update the references in the main work, except where a substantial change of text is involved, or in order to make cross-references consistent, or very occasionally where the original source of quotation is particularly difficult of access.

Thanks must go to the many scholars who have supplied material for the new Supplement. In particular, the bulk of the epigraphical material was collected by Dr Thompson. Substantial contributions in the field of papyrology were received from Dr Helen Cockle, Dr Revel Coles, and Vincent McCarren. Ivars Avotins contributed legal material, and generously made available the typescript of his book *On the Greek of the Novels of Justinian* in advance of publication. Prof. J. O. Urmson sent the typescript of his book *The Greek Philosophical Vocabulary*. Dr Elizabeth Tucker undertook the task of searching periodicals published since the last Supplement for extra material. The text has been read all or in part by Dr L. Holford-Strevens, Prof. Robert Renehan, and Dr Rudolf Wachter. Technical help with computing was given in the early stages by Dr Timothy Ashplant and since 1986 by Dr Jonathan Moffett. To all of these much gratitude is due.

The British Academy, by making annual grants from 1981 to 1992, has borne by far the largest share of the research costs of the project. Various other bodies have given single or multiple subventions, namely: Oxford University Press; the Jowett Copyright Trust; the Cambridge Classics Faculty; the Craven Committee; the Gaisford Memorial Fund; All Souls and Christ Church Colleges, Oxford; Trinity, Gonville & Caius, and St John's Colleges, Cambridge. The generosity of all these is gratefully acknowledged.

## NOTE ON MYCENAEAN AND CYPRIAN ENTRIES

The inclusion in an alphabetically arranged Lexicon of words spelled in a syllabic script raises obvious problems; this note is designed to explain the principles applied. The later editions of Liddell and Scott were able to record some of the new words and forms discovered by the decipherment of the Cyprian script by the simple expedient of devising a reconstruction which could be spelt in the Greek alphabet. This method is not satisfactory owing to the difficulty in some cases of selecting from a number of possible transcriptions. It was therefore decided to revise all such entries, and to insert as well as the alphabetic reconstruction the actual syllabic spelling, transliterated by the accepted system.

The decipherment of the Linear B script presented the same problem in a more acute form, so it was decided to include only a note of the corresponding Mycenaean form, usually at the end of an article, to warn the user that the word occurred in the Linear B texts. Here too the standard transliteration of the syllabic spelling is given, together with the probable reconstruction; but here the difficulty of choice is far greater, and such forms must be treated with suitable caution.

The two scripts are, despite considerable differences in both form and usage, clearly related, so it is convenient to describe them together. Both have signs for the five simple vowels, with no means of distinguishing vowel length, and for a range of consonants followed by each of the vowels. In both scripts the three orders of stops, unvoiced unaspirated, unvoiced aspirated, and voiced, are written with one series of signs, so that the choice is left to the reader. Thus a sign transcribed *ka* may be found in a reconstructed word as κα, χα or γα, *pa* as πα, φα or βα. However, although in Cyprian *ta*, *te*, etc. stand for τα, θα, δα, τε, θε, δε and so forth, Mycenaean has two series of signs, one restricted to the unvoiced, the other to the voiced dental stop. They are therefore transcribed *ta*, *te*, etc. in one case, but *da*, *de* in the other.

The other consonant series correspond to the appropriate Greek letter, with some exceptions. Mycenaean has only one series for liquids, transcribed *ra*, *re*, etc., but equivalent to λα, λε as well as ρα, ρε. In Cyprian these two sounds are allotted separate series of signs. The semi-vowel corresponding to the Greek digamma is regularly used in both dialects, and the signs are transcribed *wa*, *we*, etc. (in older publications also *va*, *ve* in Cyprian). This can be used, like Ϝ, to indicate a glide sound between υ and another vowel. Another semi-vowel, *ja*, *je*, etc. (also transcribed *ya*, *ye*) is used in both scripts to indicate the glide between ι and another vowel. But Mycenaean also uses this device to represent diphthongal ι before another vowel.

Another peculiarity of Mycenaean is the existence of a fourth series of signs for stops, which represents the inherited labio-velar sounds, which survived into Latin in the spellings *qu* and *gu*. These are conventionally transcribed *qa*, *qe*, etc. and must be understood to represent sounds such as $k^wa$, $k^we$, $kh^wa$, $kh^we$, $g^wa$, $g^we$, etc. Since there are no letters in the Greek alphabet for such sounds, reconstructed forms have been given in the spelling which such words show in classical times. Thus Mycenaean *-qe* will be found under τε, *qa-si-re-u* under βασιλεύς.

Both scripts have some additional signs with special values, some of which are disputed. Cyprian has a sign previously transcribed *za*, but now known to have the value *ga*; see γῆ, ἀγαθός. The value of *zo* is still unclear, but *xa*, *xe* correspond to Greek ξα, ξε. Mycenaean has many more abnormal signs: a number of doublets, probably all with special values, such as $a_2$ = ἁ, $a_3$ = αι, $ra_3$ = ραι, λαι. There is also a sign with the value *au*. The exact value of the signs transcribed $ra_2$, $ro_2$ is still uncertain, but it seems historically to continue *rya*, *lya*, *ryo*, *lyo*. The sign $pu_2$ usually has the value of φυ, and there is a special sign with the value *pte* (πτε).

Clusters of consonants in both scripts are written by adding extra vowels: Cypr. *ka-si-ke-ne-to-se* = κασιγνέτος, Myc. *a-re-ku-tu-ru-wo* = Ἀλεκτρύων. Double consonants are not written. In Cyprian a nasal is regularly omitted in writing before another consonant; in Mycenaean this principle is extended to include liquids (λ, ρ), sibilants (σ) and diphthongal ι. Thus Myc. *e-ka-ra* = ἐσχάρα, *e-ko-si* = probably ἔχονσι as in Arcadian.

The peculiarities of grammar and the scripts may be seen in specialist handbooks, such as C. D. Buck, *The Greek Dialects*, Chicago, 1955 for Cyprian, and M. Ventris and J. Chadwick, *Documents in Mycenaean Greek*, 2nd edn. Cambridge, 1973 or E. Vilborg, *A Tentative Grammar of Mycenaean Greek*, Göteborg, 1960. In the vocabulary there are a number of new words, mostly compounds which have no direct representative in classical Greek. These have been listed under a reconstructed form in the Greek alphabet, prefixed by an asterisk. Thus *to-ko-do-mo* is entered under *τοιχοδόμος, which although hitherto unattested must have existed as the noun on which the verb *τοιχοδομέω* is built. A new verb related to *κτίζω* is recorded under that form, since its 1st person singular is unknown; it does, however, explain the formation of Homeric *ἐυκτίμενος*. Likewise a verb meaning 'to row' is related to *ἐρέσσω*, but lacks the suffix -*σσ*-. The more speculative additions to the vocabulary have not been entered.

A fuller account of the evidence for particular Greek words in Mycenaean will be found in J. Chadwick and L. Baumbach 'The Mycenaean Greek Vocabulary', *Glotta*, 41 (1963) 157–271, also L. Baumbach, *Glotta*, 49 (1971) 151–190. For words in Mycenaean spelling there is now the *Diccionario micénico* (*Diccionario griego-español, anejo*) by F. Aura Jorro, Madrid 1985–93.

# I. AUTHORS AND WORKS

| | | | |
|---|---|---|---|
| T(L) | Teubner (Leipzig) | T(S) | Teubner (Stuttgart) |
| T(B) | Teubner (Berlin) | OCT | Oxford Classical Texts |
| B | Budé, Paris | | |

**Achaeus** tragicus, add 'Snell °*TrGF* 1 p. 115 [Achae. .. S.]'

**Achilles Tatius** scriptor eroticus, for 'iv AD' read 'ii AD'; add '*Leucippe and Clitophon*, E. Vilborg, Stockholm 1955 [Ach.Tat. .. V.]'

***Acta Alexandrinorum** [Act.Alexandr.] ii/iii AD, H. Musurillo, T(L) 1961.

***Acta Apostolorum Apocrypha**, R. A. Lipsius, M. Bonnet, Leipzig 1891–1903 [Hildesheim 1959] (3 vols.).

***Acta Petri et Pauli** v. °Acta Apostolorum Apocrypha.

***Acta Philippi** v. °Acta Apostolorum Apocrypha.

**Acusilaus**, add 'for Suppl. entries: Jacoby ‡*FGrH* no. 2: i (A) p. 47 [Acus. .. J.]'

**Adamantius**, add '*Vent.* = περὶ ἀνέμων, V. Rose, *Anecdota Graeca et Graeco-Latina* I, Berlin 1864 [Amsterdam 1963], p. 29 (cited by p.)'

**Aelianus**, end of line 2, insert '[Graz 1971]'; *NA*, add 'A. F. Scholfield, Loeb 1958–9 (3 vols.)'; *VH*, add 'M. R. Dilts, T(L) 1974'

**Aelius Dionysius**, add 'H. Erbse, *Untersuchungen zu den attizistischen Lexika*, Berlin 1950, p. 95'

**Aeneas Tacticus**, add 'A. Dain, A.–M. Bon, B 1967'

**Aeschines** orator, add 'V. Martin, G. de Budé, B 1927–8 [1962] (2 vols.); Sch. = Scholia, M. R. Dilts, T(L) 1992, [Sch.Aeschin. .. D.]'

**Aeschylus**, line 2, for 'A. Sidgwick' read 'D. L. Page' and for 'Oxford (OCT)' read 'OCT 1972'; Scholia, add 'O. L. Smith, T(L) i: 1976, ii (2): 1982'; line 6, for '*A.*' read '*Ag.*'; *Fr.*, add 'Radt °*TrGF* 3 [A.*fr.* .. R.]'

**Aeschylus Alexandrinus**, add 'Snell °*TrGF* 1 p. 312'

**Aesopus**, line 2, add 'A. Hausrath, H. Haas, H. Hunger, 1 (1) and (2), T(L) 1974[4]; B. E. Perry, *Aesopica* 1, Univ. Illinois 1952 [Aesop. .. P.]'

**Aëtius**, add 'Lib. i–viii, A. Olivieri, *CMG* viii 1, 2, Leipzig and Berlin 1935–50 [Aët. .. O.]'

**Africanus**, *Cest.*, add 'Les *"Cestes"* de Julius Africanus, J. R. Viellefond, Florence 1970 [Afric.*Cest.* .. V.]'

**Agathias**, line 2, add 'R. Keydell, Berlin 1967 [Agath. .. K.]'

***Agathodaemon** alchemista [Agath.Alch.] Berthelot °*CAlG*, pp. 115, 268.

***Agias Dercylus** historicus, Jacoby ‡FGrH no. 305: iii (B) p. 7 [Agias Dercyl. .. J.].

**Aglaias**, add '°*Suppl.Hell.* p. 7'

**Albinus**, add 'also known as ‡Alcinous'

**Alcaeus** lyricus, after 'iii p. 147' add 'E. Lobel, D. L. Page, *Poetarum Lesbiorum Fragmenta*, Oxford 1955 [1968 corr.], p. 112 [Alc. .. L.–P.]'

**Alcidamas**, *Soph.*, add '*Artium scriptores*, L. Radermacher, Vienna 1951 (= *SAWW* 227.3), p. 135 [Alcid.*Soph.* .. R.]'

**Alcinous** philosophus, add '(also known as Albinus q. v.)'; after '1892' insert '[1927]'; at end add '[Alcin.*Intr.* .. H.]'

**Alcmaeon**, after 'Diels' insert 'W. Kranz' and for 'i p. 131' read '[7] i p. 210'

***Alcmaeonis** poema epicum, vi BC, Bernabé °*PEG* p. 32 [*Alcmaeonis fr.* .. p. .. B.].

**Alcman**, add 'Page °*PMG* p. 2 [Alcm. .. P.]'

**Alexander Aetolus**, for 'Elegiacus' read 'tragicus et lyricus'; for 'iii BC' read 'iv/iii BC'

**Alexander Aphrodisiensis**, *Pr.*, add 'Bks. iii, iv, H. Usener, Berlin 1859'

**Alexander Ephesius** epicus, add 'in *Suppl.Hell.* p. 9'

***Alexander Myndius** historicus [Alex.Mynd.] i AD Apud Athenaeum. Jacoby ‡*FGrH* no. 25: i (A) 189.

**Alexander Trallianus**, add 'repr. Puschmann [Amsterdam 1963], cited in Suppl. by vol., p. and line'

**Amipsias**, add 'Kassel, Austin °*PCG* 2 p. 197 [Amips. .. K.-A.]'

**Ammonius** grammaticus, add 'K. Nickau, T(L) 1966'

***Amphilochius Iconiensis** scriptor ecclesiasticus [Amph.] iv AD *hom.* = *homiliae*, Migne °*PG* 39.36, Corpus Christianorum, series graeca, vol. 3, Leiden 1978.

**Anacreon**, add 'West °*IEG* (2) p. 30 [Anacr. .. W.]; Page °*PMG* p. 172 [Anacr. .. P.]'

**Anacreontea**, line 1, add '?i/vi AD'; at end add 'M. L. West, T(L) 1984 [*Anacreont.* .. W.]'

**Anaxagoras**, after 'Diels' insert 'W. Kranz' and for 'i p. 375' read '[7] ii p. 5'

**Anaxandrides** comicus, add 'Kassel, Austin °*PCG* 2 p. 236 [Anaxandr. .. K.-A.]'

**Anaxarchus**, after 'Diels' insert 'W. Kranz' and for 'ii p. 144' read '[7] ii p. 235'

**Anaximander** philosophus, after 'Diels' insert 'W. Kranz' and for 'i p. 14' read '[7] i p. 81'

**Anaximenes**, after 'Diels' insert 'W. Kranz' and for 'i p. 22' read '[7] i p. 90'

***Anaximenes Lampsacenus** rhetor [Anaximen. Lampsac.] iv BC *Rh.* = *Ars rhetorica*, M. Fuhrmann, T(L) 1966 (= Arist.*Rh.Al.* in *LSJ*).

**Anaxippus**, add 'Kassel, Austin °*PCG* 2 p. 299'

**Andocides**, add 'G. Dalmeyda, B 1930 [1966]'

**Andromachus**, add 'Heitsch °*GDRK* 2 p. 8'

***Andromachus** minor medicus i AD Apud Galenum [Androm.min.ap.Gal.].

**Anecdota Graeca** e codd. MSS. Bibl.Oxon., add '[Amsterdam 1963]'

***Anecdota Graeca e codicibus regiis** [*An.Boiss.*] J. Fr. Boissonade, Paris 1829–33 [Hildesheim 1962] (5 vols.).

***Anonyma de musica scripta Bellermanniana** [Anon.Bellerm.] D. Najock, T(L) 1975.

***Anonymi Alchemistae** [Anon.Alch.] Berthelot °*CAlG*.

**Anonymus**, add '*Vit.Arist.* etc., v. Diogenes Laertius'

*__Anonymus Argentinensis__ [Anon.Argent.] B. Keil, Strasburg 1902.

**Anonymus Londnensis**, read '**Londinensis**'; add 'W. H. S. Jones, Cambridge 1947'

**Anthologia Graeca**, line 6, after '1894–1906' add 'H. Beckby, Munich [1965–8][2] (4 vols.; I–XV = *Anthologia Palatina*, XVI = *Appendix Planudea*)'; at end add 'A. S. F. Gow, D. L. Page, *The Greek Anthology* 1: *Hellenistic Epigrams*, Cambridge 1965 (2 vols.) [*HE* .. G.–P.]; 2: *The Garland of Philip and Some Contemporary Epigrams*, Cambridge 1968 [*Garl.* .. G.–P.]; *Epigrammata Graeca*, D. L. Page, OCT 1975 [*EG* .. P.]; *Further Greek Epigrams. Epigrams before* AD *50 from the Greek Anthology and Other Sources*, D. L. Page (revised by R. D. Dawe, J. Diggle), Cambridge 1981 [*FGE* .. P.]; *Sch.AP* = *Scholia ad epigrammata arithmetica in Anthologia Graeca* (*scholia recentiora*), in *Diophanti Alexandri opera omnia*, P. Tannery, vol. 2 T(L) 1895 [(S) 1974]'

**Antidotus** comicus, add 'Kassel, Austin °*PCG* 2 p. 308'

**Antimachus Colophonius**, add 'West °*IEG* (2) p. 38 [Antim. .. W.]; B. Wyss, Berlin (Weidmann) 1936 [1974] [Antim. .. Wy.]; °*Suppl.Hell.* p. 20'

**Antiphanes Macedo** and **Megalopolitanus**, for these entries read '**Antiphanes Macedo** seu **Megalopolitanus** [Antiph.] i AD v. Anthologia Graeca'

**Antipho** orator, add 'L. Gernet, B 1954'

**Antipho Sophista**, after 'Diels' insert 'W. Kranz' and for 'ii p. 289' read '[7] ii p. 334'

**Antisthenes**, after 'Rhetor' add 'et philosophus' and at end add '*fr.* = *Antisthenis Fragmenta*, F. D. Caizzi, Milan 1966'

**Antoninus Liberalis**, add 'M. Papathomopoulos, B 1968 [Ant.Lib. .. P.]'

**Aphthonius**, after 'p. 19' insert 'H. Rabe, T(L) 1926'

*__Apollinaris Laodicenus__ scriptor ecclesiasticus [Apoll.] iv AD *Met.Ps.* = *Metaphrases in Psalmos* cited by volume and page of Migne °*PG*.

**Apollodorus** lyricus, line 1, add 'vi BC'; add 'Page °*PMG* p. 364 [Apollod.Lyr. .. P.]'

**Apollonius Rhodius**, add 'H. Fränkel, OCT 1961 [1986]; F. Vian, B 1974–81 (3 vols.); Sch. = *Scholia in A.R. vetera*, C. Wendel, Berlin (Weidmann) 1958[2]'

*__Appendix Proverbiorum__ [*App.Prov.*] E. von Leutsch, F. G. Schneidewin *Paroemiographi* i p. 379.

**Appianus**, after line 3, insert 'P. Viereck, A. G. Roos, E. Gabba, T(L) 1939 [1968[4]]'

*__Apuleius__ scriptor Latinus [Apul.] ii AD *Met.* = *Metamorphoses*, *Plat.* = *de Platone*, R. Helm, T. Thomas, T(L) 1931 [1963–70] (3 vols.).

**Apuleius** scriptor botanicus, after 'Basel 1560' insert '*Pseudo-Apulei Platonici Herbarius*, E. Howald, H. E. Sigerist, *CML* iv, Leipzig, Berlin 1927, p. 15'

**Aquila**, add 'L.–R.: v. °Vetus Testamentum'

**Aratus**, line 2, insert 'J. Martin, Florence 1956 [Arat. .. M.]'

*__Archelaus__ philosophus [Archel.Phil.] v BC, H. Diels, W. Kranz, *Vorsokr.* [7] ii p. 44.

**Archilochus**, line 2, after 'ii p. 383' insert 'West °*IEG* (1) p. 1. [Archil. .. W.]'

**Archippus** comicus, add 'Kassel, Austin °*PCG* 2 p. 538 [Archippus .. K.–A.]'

**Archytas Tarentinus**, after 'Diels' insert 'W. Kranz' and for 'i p. 322' read '[7] i p. 421'

**Aretaeus**, line 2, add '1958[2]'

**Ariphron**, add 'Page °*PMG* p. 422 [Ariphron .. P.], cited by line number'

**Aristaenetus**, line 1, add 'v AD'; add 'O. Mazal, T(L) 1971'

**Aristaeus Judaeus**, add 'A. Pelletier, Paris 1962'

**Aristarchus** tragicus, add 'Snell °*TrGF* 1 p. 89 [Aristarch.Trag. .. S.]'

**Aristides** rhetor, *Or.*, add 'F. W. Lenz, C. A. Behr, Leiden 1976 [Aristid. .. L.–B.]'; line 7, (*Rh.*): after 'ii p. 457' insert '[Munich 1966], W. Schmid, T(L) 1926 [Aristid.*Rh.* .. S., referring to Spengel's numeration in margin]; Sch. .. D. = W. Dindorf, Leipzig 1829 [Hildesheim 1964]'

**Aristides Milesius**, add 'Jacoby ‡*FGrH* no. 286: iii (A) p. 163 [Aristid.Mil. .. J.]'

**Aristides Quintilianus**, after 'iii AD' delete '(?)'; add 'R. P. Winnington-Ingram T(L) 1963, cited by p. and line'

*__Aristobulus Alexandrinus__ Judaeus ii AD A. M. Denis *Fr.Ps.Gr.* p. 217 [Aristobul.Alex. p. .. D.].

**Aristodemus**, for 'i BC' read 'iv AD'; add 'Jacoby ‡*FGrH* no. 104: ii (A) p. 493 [Aristodem. .. J.]'

*__Aristodemus__ mythographus historicus i BC Jacoby ‡*FGrH* no. 22: i (A) p. 186 [Aristodem.Myth. .. J.].

**Aristophanes** comicus, line 3, add 'V. Coulon, M. van Daele, B 1923–30 [revised 1963–73]'; *Fr.*, add 'Kassel, Austin °*PCG* 3(2) [Ar.*fr.* .. K.–A.]'; Scholia, add 'Fr. Dübner, Paris 1877 [Hildesheim 1969] [Sch.]; *Scholia in Aristophanis Equites*, Groningen/Amsterdam 1969: *Scholia vetera* .., D. Mervyn Jones [Sch. .. J.], *Scholia Tricliniana* .., N. G. Wilson [Sch. .. W.]; *Scholia vetera in Nubes*, D. Holwerda, Groningen 1977 [Sch. .. H.]'

**Aristophanes Byzantinus**, for 'Philosophus' read 'grammaticus' and add '*fr.* = *Fragmenta*, W. J. Slater (post A. Nauck), Berlin 1986'

**Aristopho** comicus, add 'Kassel, Austin °*PCG* 4 p. 1 [Aristopho .. K.–A.]'

**Aristoteles**, *Ath.*, add 'M. Chambers, T(L) 1986'; *Cael.*, add 'P. Moraux, B 1965'; *de An.*, add 'W. D. Ross, OCT 1956 [1963]'; *EE*, add 'R. R. Walzer, J. Mingay, OCT 1990'; *EN*, add 'I. Bywater, OCT 1894 [1962]'; *Fr.*, add '[Stuttgart 1967]; *Fr.lyr.*, = *fragmentum lyricum*, Page °*PMG* p. 444'; *GC*, add 'C. Mugler, B 1966'; *HA*, add 'P. Louis, B 1964–9 (3 vols.)'; *Metaph.*, add 'W. Jaeger, OCT 1957 [1973]'; *Mete.*, add 'F. H. Fobes, Cambridge, Mass. 1919 [Hildesheim 1967]'; *Oec.*, add 'B. A. van Groningen, A. Wartelle, B 1968'; *PA*, add 'P. Louis, B 1956'; *Ph.*, add 'W. D. Ross, OCT 1950 [revised 1973]'; *Po.*, add 'R. Kassel, OCT 1965 [revised 1968]'; *Pr.*, add 'C. E. Ruelle, T(L) 1922'; *Rh.*, add 'W. D. Ross, OCT 1959 [1969]'; *Rh.Al.*, add 'v. °Anaximenes Lampsacenus'; *Top.*, add 'W. D. Ross, OCT 1958 [revised 1970]'

**Aristoxenus**, *Rhyth.*, add 'L. Pearson, Oxford 1990'; add '*fr.* = *Fragmenta*, *Die Schule des Aristoteles* 2[2], F. Wehrli, Basel 1967 p. 10 [Aristox.*fr.* .. W.]'

**Arrianus**, for '*Epict.* .. 1894' read '*Epict.* .. ed. 2, 1916 [T(S) 1965]'; *Fr.*, add 'Jacoby ‡*FGrH* no. 156: ii (B) p. 837 [Arr.*fr.* .. J.]; *Fr. Phys.* = *Fragmenta de rebus physicis*, A. G. Roos, G. Wirth, T(L) 1968 vol. 2, p. 186ff.'; other works, add 'A. G. Roos, G. Wirth, T(L) 1967–8 (2 vols.); also v.s.v. °Periplus Maris Euxini'

**Artemidorus Daldianus**, add 'R. A. Pack, T(L) 1963 [Artem. .. P.]'

**Asclepiades Junior** medicus, add 'sts. known as Asclepiades Pharmacion'

**Asius**, for 'Lyricus' read 'elegiacus et epicus' and at end for 'p. 406' read 'p. 23; West °*IEG* (2) p. 46; *Fr.Ep.* = *Fragmenta Epica*, Bernabé °*PEG* p. 127'

*__Asterius__ sophista [Ast.Soph.] iv AD *Hom.* = *Homiliae in psalmos*, cited by volume and page of Migne °*PG*.

**Astydamas**, line 2, add 'Snell °*TrGF* 1 p. 198 [Astyd. .. S.]'

***Athanasius Alexandrinus** scriptor ecclesiasticus [Ath.] iv AD *Imag. Beryt.* = *Sermo in imaginem Berytensem*, two recensions, °*PG* 28.797, 805; *Sem.* = *Homilia de semente* °*PG* 28.144.

**Athenaeus** grammaticus, line 1, add '= Ath. epigrammaticus (q.v.)'; line 2, at end insert '[Stuttgart 1965–6] (3 vols.)'

**Athenaeus** mechanicus, line 1, at end, insert 'ii/i BC'; add '*Griechische Poliorketiker*, R. Schneider, *Abhandlungen der Gesellschaft der Wissenschaften zu Göttingen* (Phil.-hist. Klasse), N.F. 12 no. 5, Berlin 1912: cited by Wescher's p., given in Schneider's margin'

***Athenagoras Atheniensis** scriptor ecclesiasticus [Athenag.] ii AD *Res.* = *De resurrectione mortuorum* (ascribed to Athenag. but may be iii AD), W. R. Schoedel, Oxford 1972.

**Axionicus**, add 'Kassel, Austin °*PCG* 4 p. 20 [Axionic. .. K.–A.]'

**Babrius**, add 'B. E. Perry, Cambridge, Mass., Loeb 1965; [Ps.-Babr. .. C.] refers to Crusius' T ed. of 1897 by no. and p.'

**Bacchylides**, after '1905' add 'B. Snell, H. Maehler, T(L) 1970$^{10}$. [B. or B.*fr.* .. S.–M.]'

***Bardesanes** historicus Edessenus ii/iii AD Jacoby ‡*FGrH* no. 719: iii (C) p. 643 [Bardes. .. J.].

***Basilius Caesariensis** scriptor ecclesiasticus [Bas.Caes.] Migne °*PG* 29–32, 36.

***Basilius Seleucensis** scriptor ecclesiasticus [Bas.Sel.] v AD *HP* = *Homélies pascales*, M. Aubineau, Paris 1972.

**Bianor**, delete 'Idem .. q.v.'

**Bion**, for 'U. von Wilamowitz-Möllendorff$^{2}$, *Bucolici Graeci*, Oxford (OCT)' read 'A. S. F. Gow, *Bucolici graeci*, OCT 1952 [1969] p. 153'

**Bito**, add '*Greek and Roman Artillery*: *Technical Treatises*, E. W. Marsden, Oxford 1971 p. 65 [Bito .. M.]'

***Boeotica adespota** Page °*PMG* p. 345 [*Boeot.adesp.* .. P.].

***Bolus** philosophus et paradoxographus iii BC Giannini °*PGR* p. 377. See also °Pseudo-Democritus.

**Callimachus**, for 'Epicus' read 'poeta'; line 3, after '1921' insert 'R. Pfeiffer, Oxford 1949–53 (2 vols.)' to list of works add '*Dieg.* = *Διηγήσεις* (w. their own numeration and ref. to Call.'s text in parentheses), A. Vogliano in *PMil.Vogl.* i.18 (1937); Sch. = Scholia' at end for 'initial "P."' read 'letters "Pf." and those from his *Fragmenta nuper reperta* by "P."'; add '*VB* = *Victoria Berenices* °*Suppl.Hell.* p. 100'

**Callinus**, for 'Epicus' read 'Elegiacus' and add 'West °*IEG* (2) p. 47'

***Callisthenes Olynthius** historicus [Callisth.Olynth.] Jacoby ‡*FGrH* no. 124: ii(B) p. 631.

**Callistratus** Historicus, add 'Jacoby ‡*FGrH* no. 433: iii (B) p. 334 [Callistr.Hist. .. J.]'

**Callixinus**, read '**Callixenus**'; for 'iii BC (?)' read 'ii BC'; add 'Jacoby ‡*FGrH* no. 627: iii (C) p. 161'

**Carcinus** Tragicus, add 'Snell °*TrGF* 1 p. 210 [Carc. .. S.]'

**Carmen Aureum**, add 'D. Young, *Theognis* T(L) 1971$^{2}$ p. 86'

***Carmen Naupactium** Bernabé °*PEG* p. 123 [*Carm. Naup.* .. B.].

***Carmina Convivalia**, Page °*PMG* p. 472 [*Carm.Conv.* .. P.].

**Carmina Popularia**, add 'Page °*PMG* p. 450 [*Carm.Pop.* .. P.]'

**Catalogus Codicum Astrologorum**, for '1898' read '1898–1953 (12 vols.)'

***Cato** scriptor rei rusticae Latinus iii/ii BC *Agr.* = *De agricultura*, A. Mazzarino, T(L) 1962.

***Catullus, C. Valerius** poeta Latinus [Cat.] i BC R. A. B. Mynors, OCT 1958 [1972].

**Cephisodorus**, add 'Kassel, Austin °*PCG* 4 p. 63 [Cephisod. .. K.–A.]'

**Cercidas**, add 'Diehl °*Anth.Lyr.* 3$^{3}$ p. 141 [Cerc. .. D.$^{3}$]'

**Chaeremon** historicus, add 'P. W. van der Horst, Leiden 1987 [Chaerem.Hist. .. vdH.]'

**Chaeremon** tragicus, add 'Snell °*TrGF* 1 p. 215 [Chaerem. .. S.]'

**Chares** iambographus, add 'D. Young, *Theognis* T(L) 1906$^{2}$ p. 113; (app. the same as Chares Trag. q. v.)'

**Charisius**, add 'C. Barwick, T(L) 1925 [Charis. .. B.]'

**Charito**, add '*Charitonis Aphrodisiensis de Chaerea et Callirhoe amatoriarum narrationum libri octo*, G. Molinié, B 1979'

**Choerilus** Epicus, add 'Bernabé °*PEG* p. 187 [Choeril. .. B.]'

**Choeroboscus** *in Heph.*, add 'C. refers to Consbruch's edition, [T(L) 1906]'; *in Theod.*, add 'H. refers to Hilgard's edition, [Hildesheim 1967] (2 vols.)'

**Choricius**, add 'R. Förster, E. Richtsteig, T(L) 1929 [1972]'

**Cicero**, *Att.*, add 'W. S. Watt (part i), OCT 1965, D. R. Shackleton Bailey (part ii), OCT 1961'; before '*Fam.*' insert '*Div.* = *de Divinatione*, W. Ax, T(L) 1938 [1969]'; *Fam.*, add 'W. S. Watt, OCT 1982$^{2}$'

**Clearchus** comicus, add 'Kassel, Austin °*PCG* 4 p. 79 [Clearch.Com. .. K.–A.]'

**Clearchus** historicus, line 1, add 'et philosophus'; at end add '*Die Schule des Aristoteles* 3$^{2}$, F. Wehrli, Basel 1969 [Clearch. .. W.]'

**Clemens Alexandrinus**, line 2, add 'O. Stählin, L. Früchtel, U. Treu, Berlin 1985, 1970 (2 vols., = °*GCS* 52, 17)'; add 'Sch. = Scholia: 1 = °*GCS* 12; *Ecl.* = *Eclogae propheticae* (°*GCS* 17)'

***Columella, L. Junius** scriptor rei rusticae Latinus [Colum.] i AD H. B. Ash, M. B. H. Förster, F. S. A. Heffner, Loeb 1941–55.

**Coluthus**, line 1, add '**Colluthus** in Suppl. [Colluth.]'; at end add 'P. Orsini, B 1972'

***Comarius** alchemista, Berthelot °*CAlG* p. 289.

**Comica adespota**, add 'Austin °*CGFP* p. 223 [*Com. adesp.* .. A.]; D. refers to Demiańczuk's *Supp.Com.*'

***Consentius** grammaticus v AD Keil *Gramm.Lat.* vol. v p. 338.

**Corinna**, for 'vi BC' read '?v/iii BC'; add 'Page °*PMG* p. 326. [Corinn. .. P.]'

**Corpus Hermeticum**, add 'A. D. Nock, A. J. Festugière, B 1945–54 (4 vols.)'

**Cratinus** comicus, add 'Kassel, Austin °*PCG* 4 p. 112. [Cratin. .. K.–A.]'

**Critias**, after 'Diels' insert 'W. Kranz' and for 'ii p. 308' read '$^{7}$ ii p. 371. [Critias .. D.–K.]'; add 'Snell °*TrGF* 1 p. 172 [Critias .. S.]; West °*IEG* (2) p. 52 [Critias .. W.]'

***Critodemus astrologus**, v. *Cat.Cod.Astr.*

**Ctesias**, add 'Jacoby ‡*FGrH* no. 688: iii (C) p. 416 [Ctes. .. J.]'

***Cyranides** [Cyran.] i/ii AD de Mély °*Lapid.Gr.* (cited by p.); *Die Kyraniden*, D. Kaimakis, Meisenheim 1976 (cited by book, chapter and line).

**Cyrilli glossarium**, line 1, add 'v AD'

*__Cyrillus Alexandrinus__ scriptor ecclesiasticus [Cyr.Al.] v AD cited by volume and page of °*PG*.

*__Cyrillus Scythopolitanus__ scriptor ecclesiasticus [Cyr.S.] *Vit.Sab.* = *Vita Sabae*, E. Schwartz, *Texte und Untersuchungen zur Geschichte der altchristlichen Literatur*, Leipzig 1939.

**Damascius**, *Pr.*, add '[Brussels 1964]'; add '*in Phlb.* = *in Platonis Philebum scholia. Lectures on the Philebus Wrongly Attributed to Olympiodorus*, L. G. Westerink, Amsterdam 1959 (= Olymp. *in Phlb.* in *LSJ*)'

**Damoxenus** comicus, add 'Kassel, Austin °PCG 5 p. 1 [Damox. .. K.–A.]'

**Demades**, *Fr.*, add 'V. de Falco, Naples 1955²'

*__Demetrius Laco__ philosophus ii BC V. De Falco, Naples 1923 [Demetr.Lac. p. .. DF.].

**Demetrius Phalereus** rhetor, for 'iv BC' read 'i BC'; *Eloc.*, add '[Hildesheim 1965]'

*__Demetrius Scepsius__ grammaticus iii/ii BC R. Gaede, Diss.Greifswald 1880. Cited fr. Strabo or Athenaeus.

*__Demioprata__ [*Demioprat.*] cited from sources.

**Democritus** philosophus, after 'Diels' insert 'W. Kranz' and for 'ii p. 10' read '⁷ ii p. 81'; add '*fr.Orth* = *fragmentum Orth*, E. Orth, *Emerita* 26 (1958) p. 202'

**Demophilus**, *Sim.*, for '1900' read '1905'

**Demosthenes** orator, line 3, for 'Oxford (OCT)' read 'OCT 1903–31 [1967–74] (vols. 1, 2(1), 2(2), 3)'; add '*fr.* = *Fragmenta*, Baiter, Sauppe *Orat.Att.* ii p. 250'

**Demosthenes Ophthalmicus**, add 'cited also fr. Simon Ianuensis, *Clavis Sanationis*, Venice 1510'

**Dialexeis**, after 'Diels' insert 'W. Kranz' and for 'ii p. 334' read '⁷ ii p. 405'

**Dicaearchus** geographus, add '*Fragmenta*, *Die Schule des Aristoteles* 1², F. Wehrli, Basel 1967'

**Didymus**, *in D.*, add 'L. Pearson, S. Stephens, T(S) 1983 [Did.*in D.* .. P.–S.]'

**Dinarchus**, add 'N. C. Conomis, T(L) 1975'

**Dio Cassius**, add '*frr.* cited fr. Boissevain w. two figures, bks. w. three (i.e. book, chapter and paragraph).'

**Dio Chrysostomus**, add '*Orr.* 37 and 64 are now attrib. to ‡Favorinus philosophus'

**Diocles** medicus, add 'iv/iii BC'

*__Diodorus Cronus__ philosophus [Diod.Cron.] iv/iii BC *Die Megariker*, K. Döring, Amsterdam 1972 p. 28 (cited by no.) [Diod.Cron. .. D.].

**Diogenes Apolloniates**, after 'Diels' insert 'W. Kranz' and for 'i p. 416' read '⁷ ii p. 51'

**Diogenes Atheniensis**, add 'Snell °*TrGF* 1 p. 184 [Diog.Ath. .. S.]'

**Diogenes Cynicus**, after 'philosophus' add 'et tragicus [Diog.Sinop.]' and at end add 'Snell °*TrGF* 1 p. 253'

**Diogenes Laertius**, add 'H. S. Long, OCT 1964 [1966] (2 vols.)'

**Diogenes Oenoandensis**, add 'C.W. Chilton, T(L) 1967 [Diog.Oen.*fr.* .. C.]; *new frr.* ed. by M. F. Smith: nos. 1–4 in *AJA* 74 (1970) 56–62, nos. 5–16 in *AJA* 75 (1971) 358–89, nos. 39–51 in *Cahiers de philologie* (Lille) 1 (1976) p. 279 [Diog.Oen.*new fr.* .. S.]'

**Diogenes Sinopensis**, delete this entry (v. Diogenes Cynicus).

**Diomedes** grammaticus, line 1, add 'iv AD'

**Dionysius Bassaricon** auctor, v. Dionysius Periegeta.

**Dionysius Chalcus**, add 'West °*IEG* (2) p. 58'

**Dionysius Comicus**, add 'Kassel, Austin °*PCG* 5 p. 32 [Dionys.Com. .. K.–A.]'

**Dionysius Halicarnassensis**, *Opuscula*, add '[Stuttgart 1965] (2 vols.)'; *Vett.Cens.*, add '(= περὶ μιμήσεως B, repr. Usener–Radermacher [Stuttgart 1965] vol. ii pp. 197, 200, 202–16), also known as *Imit.*'

**Dionysius Periegeta**, add 'i/ii AD Heitsch °*GDRK* p. 61; *Dionysii Bassaricon et Gigantiadis Fragmenta*, E. Livrea, Rome 1973 (attrib. dub.) [Dionys.Bassar.*fr.* .. L.]'

**Dionysius Thrax**, Scholia, add '[Hildesheim 1965] [Sch.]'

*__Dionysius Tragicus__ iv BC Snell °*TrGF 1 p. 240* [*Dionys.Trag.* .. S.].

*__Dioscorus__ Thebanus (Aegypti) epicus et lyricus vi AD Heitsch °*GDRK* 1² p. 127 [Diosc.epic.].

**Diphilus** comicus, add 'Kassel, Austin °*PCG* 5 p. 47ff. [Diph. .. K.–A.]'

**Donatus**, add '*Ter.* = *Commentum Terenti*, P. Wessner, T(L) 1902–8 [1966] (3 vols.)'

*__Dorieus__ poeta, before ii AD, in °*Suppl.Hell.* p. 182 (*fr.* 396).

**Dorotheus**, add '*Die Fragmente des Dorotheos von Sidon*, V. Stegemann, Heidelberg 1939 [Doroth.*fr.* .. S.]'

**Dosiadas**, *Ara*, add '*Bucolici Graeci* A. S. F. Gow, OCT 1952 [1969] p. 182'

**Dromo** comicus, add 'Kassel, Austin °*PCG* 5 pp. 124 [Dromo .. K.–A.]'

**Duris** historicus, add 'Jacoby ‡*FGrH* no. 76: ii (A) p. 136 [Duris .. J.]'

**Empedocles**, line 2, for '*PPF* p. 74' read 'W. Kranz, *Vorsokr.* i⁷ p. 276, cited by letter and no. [Emp. .. D.–K.]'; line 4, for 'pp. 154, 199' read 'Berlin 1898 [1958] p. 154'

*__Ennius__ poeta Latinus [Enn.] iii/ii BC *Sat.* = *Saturae* I. Vahlen, T(L) 1928 [Amsterdam 1976].

**Ephorus**, add 'Jacoby ‡*FGrH* no. 70: ii (A) p. 37. [Ephor. .. J.]'

**Epicharmus**, line 2, add 'Austin °*CGFP* p. 52'

**Epictetus**, line 2, for '1894' read '1916² [Stuttgart 1965]'; add '*Sent.* = *Gnom.D* (*Sententiae Codicis Vaticani* 1144) H. Schenkl 1916² [1965] p. 478'

**Epicurus**, line 4, add 'G. Arrighetti, Turin 1973²'; *Sent.Vat.*, add '= Arrighetti p. 139'; at end add '*Epicuri et Epicureorum Scripta in Herculanensibus papyris servata*, A. Vogliano, Berlin, 1969'

*__Epiphanius Constantiensis__ scriptor ecclesiasticus [Epiph.Const.] iv/v AD *Opera omnia*, W. Dindorf, Leipzig 1859; *De XII gemmis*: cited without title fr. de Mély °*Lapid.Gr.* p. 193 (= Migne °*PG* 43.293); *Vita Epiph.* = *Vita Epiphanii* (Migne °*PG* 41.23).

**Erinna**, line 1, for 'Lyrica' read 'poetria' and add 'iv or iii BC'; line 2, add 'Diehl °*Anth.Lyr.* 1²(4) p. 207; °*Suppl.Hell.* p. 186'

**Etymologicum Genuinum**, add 'also in *Mélanges de littérature grecque, contenant un grand nombre de textes inédits*, M. E. Miller, Paris 1868 [Amsterdam 1965] and modern editions of portions by Lasserre, Berger, Alpers'

*__Euanthius__ grammaticus Latinus iv AD (*De comoedia. Commentum Terenti* prefixed to that of °Donatus) p. 62 in Kaibel *CGF* [Euanthius .. K.].

**Eubulus**, add 'Kassel, Austin °*PCG* 5 p. 188 [Eub. .. K.–A.]'

**Euclides**, add '*Catoptr.* = *Catoptrica* (vii p. 286 Heiberg)'

**Eunapius**, *VS*, add 'G. Giangrande, Rome 1956 (cited w. Boissonade's numeration) [Eun. .. p. .. B.]'; *Hist.*, add 'R. C. Blockley, *The Fragmentary Classicising Historians of the Late Roman Empire*, Liverpool 1983, vol. 2 p. 2 [Eun.*Hist.fr.* .. B.]'

**Euphorio**, line 2, add '°*Suppl.Hell.* p. 196'; line 3, add 'B. A. van Groningen, Amsterdam 1977 [Euph. .. vGr.]'

**Eupolis**, add 'Kassel, Austin °*PCG* 5 p. 294 [Eup. .. K.–A.]'

**Euripides**, line 2, for 'Oxford (OCT)' read 'OCT 1902–13 [1969–74] (3 vols.); J. Diggle, OCT 1981–94 (3 vols.); for *Hyps.*: G. W. Bond, Oxford 1963 [Eur.*Hyps.fr.* .. B.]; for *Ph.*: D. J. Mastronarde, T(L) 1988; for *Phaëth.*: J. Diggle, Cambridge 1970 [Eur.*Phaëth.fr.* .. D.]'; *fr.*, add 'B. Snell, suppl. to Nauck *TGF* p. 1027 [E.*fr.* .. N.–S.]'

**Eusebius** historicus, add 'Jacoby ‡*FGrH* no. 101: ii (A) p. 480 [Eus.Hist. .. J.]'

**Eustathius** episcopus, after 'Leipzig 1825–30' insert '[Hildesheim 1960] (3 vols.); *Commentarii ad Homeri Iliadem pertinentes*, M. van der Valk, Leiden 1971–87 (4 vols.) cited by page and line no. of ed. Rom. in margin'; add '*Eustathii Metropolitae Thessalonicensis Opuscula*, T. L. F. Tafel, Frankfurt am Main, 1832 [Amsterdam 1964]'

**Eutychianus**, for 'p. 365' read 'p. 369' and add 'Jacoby ‡*FGrH* no. 226: ii (B) p. 954 [Eutych. .. J.]'

***Evagrius** scholasticus [Evagr.Schol.] vi AD *HE* = *Historia Ecclesiastica*, cited by volume and page of Migne °*PG*.

***Excerpta Barocciana** [Exc.Barocc.] A. Nauck, *Lexicon Vindobonense*, Petersburg 1867 [Hildesheim 1967] p. 325.

**Ezekiel**, add 'Snell °*TrGF* 1 p. 288 [Ezek.*Exag.* .. S.]'

**Favorinus** philosophus, line 1, add 'ii AD'; add '*Exil.* = περὶ φυγῆς (= *PVat.* 11 p. 17, v. index III) (cited by column and line), A. Barigazzi, Florence 1966 [Favorin. .. B.]'

**Firmicus Maternus**, for line 2, read '*Math.* = *Mathesis*, W. Kroll, F. Skutsch, K. Ziegler, T(L) 1897–1913 [1968] (2 vols.)' and add '*De err.prof.relig.* = *De errore profanarum religionum*, K. Ziegler, T(L) 1907'

***Fragment eines griechischen Lexicons** [*Fr.Lex.*] *Philologus* suppl. 15 (1922) p. 115: *Fr.Lex.* I = *ex Codic. Monac.graec.* 263; p. 142: *Fr.Lex.* II = *ex Codic. Berol.graec.quart.* 13(C); p. 145: *Fr.Lex.* III = *ex Eudemi Codic.Parisin.* n. 2634.

**Fronto, M. Cornelius**, add 'M. P. J. van den Hout, T(L) 1988 [Fronto *Ep.* p. .. vdH.]'

**Galenus**, line 2, after 'Leipzig 1821–33' insert '[Hildesheim 1964–5; 20 vols.]'; for '*CMG* .. (in progress)' substitute '*CMG* 5.4(1).1 = Kühn 5.1–148; 5. 4.(1).2 = Kühn 5.181–805; 5. 4.(2) = Kühn 6.1–831; 5. 9.(1) = Kühn 15.1–223, 418–919, 19.182–221; 5. 9.(2) = Kühn 16.489–840, 7.643–65, 18(2).1–317; 5.10.(1) = Kühn 17.(1).4–302; 5.10.(2).1 = Kühn 17.(1).480–792; 5.10.(2).2 = Kühn 17.(2).1–344; 5.10.(3) = Kühn 18(1).196–299; (Kühn's numeration in margin in *CMG*) R. Charterius (w. Hippocrates), 13 vols., Paris 1639 [1679]'; *Subf.Emp.*, add '*Die griechische Empirikerschule, Sammlung der Fragmente und Darstellung der Lehre*, K. Deichgräber, Berlin 1930, p. 42 (cited by Bonnet's p., given in Deichgräber's margin)'; after '*Vict.Att.*' add '*in Pl.Ti.* = *in Platonis Timaeum commentarii fragmenta*, H. O. Schroeder, *CMG* Suppl. i, (1934) p. 9 (cited by p. and line)'

***Gargilius Martialis** scriptor de hortis [Garg.Mart.] iii AD, V. Rose, *Plinius* T(L) 1875 p. 133.

***Gelasius Cyzicenus** scriptor ecclesiasticus [Gel.Cyz.] v AD *HE* = *Historia Ecclesiastica*, G. Loeschke, M. Heinemann, Berlin 1918, (= °*GCS* 28).

**Gellius**, Aulus, add 'P. K. Marshall, OCT 1968 (2 vols.)'

**Geoponica**, line 1, add 'x AD'

***Gnomologium Vaticanum** [*Gnomol.Vat.*] L. Sternbach, *De Gnomologio Vaticano inedito* in *Wiener Studien* (*WS*), 9–11 (1887–9) [de Gruyter 1963].

**Gorgias**, after 'Diels' insert 'W. Kranz' and for 'ii p. 235' read '[7] ii p. 271'

**Gregorius Corinthius**, for 'xii AD' read '(?)x/xi AD'; *Trop.*, add '(an ancient work wrongly ascribed to Greg.), M. L. West in *CQ* N.S. 15.236; (cited by Spengel's p., given in West's margin)'

***Gregorius Magnus** scriptor ecclesiasticus Latinus [Greg.Mag.] vi AD cited by volume and page of °*PL*.

***Gregorius Nazianzenus** theologus [Gr.Naz.] iv AD *Carm.* = *Carmina* Migne °*PG* 37.397; *De vita sua* (= *Carmen* 11), C. Jungck, Heidelberg 1974.

***Gregorius Nyssenus** theologus [Gr.Nyss.] iv AD *Ep.* = *Epistulae*, G. Pasquali, Berlin 1925 [1959].

***Hegemon** epigrammaticus iii BC v. Anthologia Graeca.

**Hegesippus** epigrammaticus, line 1, add 'iii BC'

**Heliodorus** scriptor eroticus, add 'R. M. Rattenbury, T. W. Lumb, J. Maillon, B 1960[2] (3 vols.)'

**Hellanicus**, for line 2 read 'Jacoby ‡*FGrH* no. 4: i (A) p. 104 [Hellanic. .. J.]'

**Hellenica Oxyrhynchia**, add 'V. Bartoletti, T(L) 1959 [*Hell.Oxy.* .. B.], *Hellenica Oxyrhynchia*, P. R. McKechnie, S. J. Kern, Warminster 1988 [*Hell.Oxy.* .. M.–K.]'

**Hemerologium Florentinum**, add '*Die Kalenderbücher von Florenz, Rom und Leiden*, W. Kubitschek, in *Wiener Denkschriften* (*DAW*) 57 (1915) Abh. 3 [*Hemerolog.Flor.* .. p. .. K.]'

**Hephaestio** astrologus, add 'D. Pingree, T(L) 1973–4, cited by bk., chapter and numeration in the outside margin'

**Heraclides Lembus** historicus, add '*Pol.* = περὶ πολιτειῶν. *Excerpta politiarum*, M. R. Dilts, Durham 1971 (previously attributed to Heraclides historicus)'

**Heraclitus**, *All.*, add 'F. Buffière, B 1962'

**Heraclitus** philosophus, after 'Diels' insert 'W. Kranz' and for 'i p. 67' read '[7] i p. 139 [Heraclit. .. D.–K.]'; *Ep.*, for 'p. 409' read 'p. 280 (v. *Epistolographi* in °v)'

***Heras Cappadox** medicus i BC/i AD Apud Galenum. [Heras ap.Gal.]

***Hermerius Claudius** [Claud.Herm.] iv AD *Mul.* = *Mulomedicina Chironis*, E. Oder, T(L) 1901.

**Hermes Trismegistus**, v. °*Corpus Hermeticum*.

**Hero**, for '?ii/i BC' read '?i AD'; after '1914' add '[1976] (5 vols.)'; *Bel.*, add '*Greek and Roman Artillery: Technical Treatises*, E. W. Marsden, Oxford 1971, p. 17'; add '*Mech.* = *Mechanica* in vol. 2'

**Herodas**, add 'I. C. Cunningham, T(L) 1987'

***Herodes Atticus** sophista ii AD *Pol.* = περὶ πολιτείας, U. Albini, Florence 1968 [Herodes .. A.].

**Herodianus** grammaticus, line 3, add '[Hildesheim 1965]'; Hdn.*Epim.*, add '[Amsterdam 1963]'; add '*fr.* = *Fragmenta* H. Hunger, °*JÖByz* 16.1–33 [Hdn.*fr.* .. H.]'; *Philet.*, add 'A. Dain, Paris 1954'

***Herodicus** epigrammaticus iii/ii BC °*Suppl. Hell.* p. 247.

**Hesiodus**, add 'F. Solmsen, OCT 1970 [1990[3]]; *Fragmenta Hesiodea*, R. Merkelbach, M. L. West, Oxford 1967 [1990[3] w. Solmsen] [Hes.*fr.* .. M.–W.]; Sch. = *Scholia vetera in Hesiodi Opera et Dies*, A. Pertusi, Milan 1955 [Hes.Sch. .. P.]; *Scholia vetera in Hesiodi Theogoniam*, L. Di Gregorio, Milan 1975 [Hes.Sch. .. DiG.]'

**Hesychius** lexicographicus, add 'K. Latte, Copenhagen 1953–66 (*A–O*, 2 vols.). [Hsch. .. La.]'

**Hierocles Platonicus**, *in CA*, add 'F. G. Köhler, Stuttgart (T) 1974'

***Hieronymus Eusebius Stridonensis** scriptor ecclesiasticus [Jerome] iv/v AD *Ep.* = *Epistulae*, J. Labourt, B 1949–63 (8 vols.); *in Ep.Eph* = *Commentaria in Ep.Eph.*,

Migne °*PL* 26.439; *in Ezek.*, Migne °*PL* 25.15; *adv. Rufin.* = *Apologia adversus libros Rufini*, Migne °*PL* 23.398.

**Himerius**, *Or.*, add '*Declamationes et Orationes*, A. Colonna, Rome 1951 [Him.*Or.* .. C.]'

**Hippias Erythraeus**, line 1, add '[?Hellen.]'; at end add 'Jacoby ‡*FGrH* no. 421: iii (B) p. 317 [Hippias Erythr. .. J.]'

**Hippiatrica**, add '[1971] [*Hippiatr.* .. O.–H.]; *Hippiatr.Paris.* = *Hippiatrica Parisina* in vol. 2 p. 1 O.–H.'

**Hippocrates**, *Jusj.*, *Lex*, *de Arte*, *Medic.*, *Decent.*, *Praec.*, *VM*, *Alim.*, *Liqu.*, *Flat.*, add '*CMG* 1.1, I. L. Heiberg, T(L & B) 1927'; *Oct.*, *Septim.*, add '*CMG* 1.2.(1), H. Grensemann, Berlin 1968'; *Aër*, add '*CMG* 1.1.(2), H. Diller, Berlin 1970'; *Superf.*, add '*CMG* 1.2.(2), C. Lienau, Berlin 1973'; *Nat.Hom.*, add '*CMG* 1.1.(3), J. Jouanna, Berlin 1975'; *Morb.*, (iii), add '*CMG* 1.2.(3), P. Potter, Berlin 1980'

**Hippolytus**, at end add '(= °*GCS* 26); M. Marcovich, *Patristische Texte und Studien* 25, Berlin/New York 1986'

**Hippon**, after 'Diels' insert 'W. Kranz' and for 'i p. 288' read '$^{7}$ i p. 385'

**Hipponax**, add 'West °*IEG* (1) p. 110 [Hippon. .. W.]; H. Degani T(L) 1983 [Hippon. .. D.]'

**Homerus**, for line 2, read 'D. B. Munro, T. W. Allen, OCT 1912 [1969–74] (5 vols.)'; *Od.*, add 'P. Von der Mühll, T(S) 1984'; add '*fr.* = *Fragmenta*, OCT op. cit. v, p. 147; Davies °*EGF* p. 104 [Hom.*fr.* .. D.]'; Scholia in Homeri Iliadem: add 'H. Erbse, Berlin 1969–88 (7 vols.) [Sch.Il.]; J. Barnes in editione Homeri, Cambridge 1711 [Sch.D]; *Les Scolies genevoises de l'Iliade*, J. Nicole, Paris 1891 [Sch.Gen.Il.]; *Scholia minora in Homeri Iliadem*, V. de Marco, Rome 1946 [Sch.min.Il.]'; Scholia in Homeri Odysseam: add '[Amsterdam 1962] [Sch.Od.]'

**Horapollo**, add 'F. Sbordone, Naples 1940 [Horap. .. S.]'

***Horatius Flaccus, Q.** poeta Latinus [Hor.] i BC E. C. Wickham, H. W. Garrod, OCT 1912 [1975] *C.* = *Carmina*; *Sat.* = *Saturae*.

**Hymni Homerici**, line 2, add 'T. W. Allen, W. R. Halliday, E. E. Sikes, Oxford 1936$^{2}$ [1963]'

**Hymni Magici**, add '*PMag.* 1, 2, 3, 4 (v. °iii)'

**Hymnus ad Isim**, add 'W. Peek *Der Isishymnus von Andros*, Berlin 1930 [*Hymn.Is.* .. P.]; Y. Grandjean *Une nouvelle arétalogie d'Isis*, Leiden 1975 [*Hymn.Is.* .. (Maroneia)], cf. *SEG* 8.548–51, ib. 26.821, °*IKyme* 41'

**Hymnus Curetum**, add 'M.L. West, *JHS* 85(1965) p. 149 [*Hymn.Curet.* .. W.]'

**Hyperides**, line 2, add 'Ch. Jensen, T(L) 1917 [Stuttgart 1963]'

***Iambica adespota** West °*IEG* (2) p. 16 [*Iamb.adesp.* .. W.].

***Iamblichus** alchemista [Iambl.Alch.] Berthelot °*CAlG* p. 285.

**Iamblichus** philosophus, *Comm.Math.*, add '[U. Klein, Stuttgart 1975]'; *in Nic.*, add '[U. Klein, Stuttgart 1975]'; *Protr.*, add '[Stuttgart 1967] (both works cited by page and line of Pistelli)'; *VP*, add 'L. Deubner, T(L) 1937 [U. Klein, Stuttgart 1975]'

**Iamblichus** scriptor eroticus, add 'E. Habrich, T(L) 1960 [Iamb.*Bab.* .. Ha.]'

**Ibycus**, line 2, add 'Page °*PMG* p. 144 [Ibyc. .. P.]'

**Ilias Parva**, add 'Bernabé °*PEG* p. 71 [Il.Parv. .. B.]'

**Iliu Persis**, add 'Bernabé °*PEG* p. 86 [Il.Pers. .. B.]'

**Ion Chius**, line 1, add 'v BC'; line 2, add 'West °*IEG* (2) p. 78 [Ion Eleg. .. W.]'; line 3, add 'Jacoby ‡*FGrH* no. 392: iii (B) p. 276 [Ion Hist. .. J.]'; line 4, add 'Page °*PMG* p. 383 [Ion Lyr. .. P.]'; line 5, add 'Snell °*TrGF* 1 p. 96 [Ion Trag. .. S.]'

**Isaeus**, add '[1963]; fragments cited by the numbering of Baiter, Sauppe *Orat.Att.* ii p. 228'

**Isocrates**, line 2, add 'G. Mathieu, É. Brémond, B 1928[1963]–1962'

**Ister**, for '409' read '418' and add 'Jacoby ‡*FGrH* no. 334: iii (B) p. 168. [Ister .. J.]'

***Jerome**, v. °Hieronymus Eusebius Stridonensis.

***Joannes** alchemista [Jo.Alch.] Berthelot °*CAlG* p. 263.

***Joannes Gazaeus** exegeta vi AD [Jo.Gaz.] P. Friedländer, *Johannes von Gaza und Paulus Silentiarius: Kunstbeschreibungen justinianischer Zeit*, Leipzig/Berlin 1912 [Hildesheim 1969].

***Joannes Malalas** chronographus [Jo.Mal.] vi AD *Chron.* = *Chronographia*, 9–12 A. Schenk, *Die römische Kaisergeschichte bei Malalas*, Stuttgart 1931; 1–8, 13–18 Migne °*PG* 97.65.

**Juba, Rex Mauretaniae**, add 'Jacoby ‡*FGrH* no. 275: iii (A) p. 127. [Juba .. J.]'

**Julianus**, add 'J. Bidez, G. Rochefort, Ch. Lacombrade, B 1932–64 (4 vols., 1 (1), (2$^{2}$); 2 (1), (2))'

**Juvenalis, D. Junius**, for 'i AD' read 'i/ii AD'; for 'S. G. Owen' read 'W. V. Clausen' and add '1959'; add '*Sch.* = *Scholia*, P. Wessner, T(L) 1931 [1967]'

**Lasus**, add 'Page °*PMG* p. 364 [Lasus .. P.]'

**Leonidas** epigrammaticus, after '**Leonidas**' insert '**Tarentinus**' and add '[Leon.Tarent.] in Suppl.'

**Leonidas Alexandrinus**, add '[Leon.Alexandr.] in Suppl.'

***Leontius Byzantinus** scriptor ecclesiasticus [Leont. Byz.] vi AD *HP* = *Homélies pascales*, M. Aubineau, Paris 1972.

***Lesbiorum fragmenta adespota**, E. Lobel, D. L. Page, *Poetarum Lesbiorum fragmenta*, Oxford 1955 [1968], p. 292 [*Lesb.fr.adesp.* .. L.–P.].

**Leucippus**, after 'Diels' insert 'W. Kranz' and for 'ii p. 1' read '$^{7}$ ii p. 70'

***Lexicon Patmense** [Lex.Patm.] I. Sakkelion in *BCH* I (1877).

***Lollianus** scriptor eroticus ii AD A. Henrichs, Bonn 1972 [Lollian. p. .. H.].

**Longinus**, line 2, before 'cited without title' insert 'D. A. Russell, OCT 1968 [1974]'

**Longus**, add 'G. Dalmeyda, B 1960$^{2}$; M. D. Reeve, T(L) 1982 [1971]'

**Lucianus**, after 'Sophista' insert '[Luc.]'; line 4, after '(T) 1906–' add 'M. D. Macleod, OCT 1972–87 (4 vols.)'; line 5, after 'Scholia .. 1906' add '[1971]; other scholia in the Bipontine Edition, Zweibrücken 1789–93'; after '*Electr.* = *Electrum*' insert '*Epigr.* = *Epigrammata*'

***Lucianus** interpres Veteris Testamenti [Lcn.] iii/iv AD *Origenis Hexapla*, F. Field, Oxford 1875.

***Lucilius Gaius** poeta satiricus Latinus ii BC F. Marx, T(L) 1904–5 [Amsterdam 1963].

***Lucretius** = T. Lucretius Carus, poeta Latinus [Lucr.] i BC C. Bailey, OCT 1947 [1978].

**Lycophron**, line 2, after '1908' add '[1958]; L. Mascialino, T(L) 1964 (cited by line no.)'; *fr.*, add 'Snell °*TrGF* 1 p. 275'

**Lycurgus**, add 'N. C. Conomis, Leipzig (T) 1970'

**Lydus**, before '[*Mag.*]' and '[*Mens.*]' insert '[Stuttgart 1967]; [Lyd. .. p. .. W.] refers to p. of this edition'

**Lynceus**, for 'Cetera .. Athenaeum' read 'Prose writings cited fr. Athenaeus'

**Lyrica adespota**, add 'Page °*PMG* p. 484 [*Lyr.adesp.* .. P.], Page °*SLG* p. 106 [*Lyr.adesp.S.* ..]'

**Lysias**, for 'v BC' read 'v/iv BC'; line 2, for 'Oxford (OCT)' read 'OCT 1912 [1978]'

**Lysippus**, add 'Kassel, Austin °*PCG* 5 p. 618 [Lysipp. .. K.–A.]'

***Macarius Aegyptius** scriptor ecclesiasticus [Mac.Aeg.] iv AD *Hom.* = *Homiliae* cited by volume and page of Migne °*PG*.

**Macedonius Thessalonicensis**, add '[Maced.Thess. II] in Suppl.'

**Macho**, add 'A. S. F. Gow, Cambridge 1965 [Macho .. G.]'

**Maecius**, for 'i AD (?)' read 'i BC'

***Marcellus Empiricus** medicus Latinus [Marcell.Emp.] iv AD M. Niedermann in *CML* v, Leipzig, Berlin 1916.

***Marcellus Sidetes** poeta medicus [Marc.Sid.] ii AD E. Heitsch °*GDRK* 2 p. 17.

**Marcus Antoninus**, add 'J. Dalfen, T(L) 1987'

**Marcus Argentarius**, for 'vi AD ' read 'i AD '

**Marinus** biographus [Marin.] v/vi AD J. F. Boissonade, Leipzig 1814 [1966].

**Martianus Capella**, add 'A. Dick, T(L) 1925 [1969]'

**Matro**, add 'in °*Suppl.Hell.* p. 259, p. 266'

***Mela, Pomponius** geographus Latinus i AD C. Frick, T(L) 1880 [1968] (cited by bk. and short section).

**Meleager**, for 'i BC' read 'ii/i BC'

**Melissus**, after 'Diels' insert 'W. Kranz' and for 'i p. 176' read '$^{7}$ i p. 258'

***Melito Sardianus** scriptor ecclesiasticus [Melit.] ii AD *fr.* = *Fragmenta*, in *The Apostolic Fathers*, E. J. Goodspeed, New York 1950.

**Memnon**, for 'i AD ' read '?i BC/i AD '; add 'Jacoby ‡*FGrH* no. 434: iii (B) p. 336. [Memn. .. J.]'

**Menaechmus**, for 'iii BC' read 'iv/iii BC'; add 'Jacoby ‡*FGrH* no. 131: ii (B) p. 673 [Menaechm. .. J.]'

**Menander** comicus, lines 2/3, add 'F. H. Sandbach, OCT 1972, 1976 (revised w. appendix) [1990] [Men. .. S.]'; *Inc.*, add 'Sandbach [1990] p. 297'; *Mis.*, for '*Μισούμεναι*' read '*Μισούμενος*'; *Mon.*, add 'S. Jäkel, T(L) 1964 [Men. *Mon.* .. J.]'; to the list of plays add '*Asp.* = *Ἀσπίς*; *DE* = *Δὶς Ἐξαπατῶν*; *Dysc.* = *Δύσκολος*; *Sic.* = *Σικυώνιος*; *Th.* = *Θεοφορουμένη*'; at end add 'A. Körte, A. Thierfelder, T(L) 1938$^{3}$ [1955, w. addenda 1957], 1959$^{2}$ (2 vols.); *Arg.* = *Argumenta* in vol. i p. 146; *fr.* = *Fragmenta* in vol. ii [Men.*fr.* .. K.–Th.] or quoted from Sandbach'

**Menander** rhetor, add 'D. A. Russell, N. G. Wilson, Oxford 1981 [Men.Rh. .. R.–W.]'

**Menander Protector**, see also Anthologia Graeca.

**Mesomedes**, line 3, add 'Heitsch °*GDRK* 1$^{2}$ p. 24 no. 2 [Mesom. .. H.]'

**Metrodorus Chius**, for 'v BC' read 'iv BC'; after 'Diels' insert 'W. Kranz' and for 'ii p. 140' read '$^{7}$ ii p. 231'

***Mimi adespoti** [*Mim.adesp.*] in *Herodae mimiambi*, I. C. Cunningham, T(L) 1987 p. 36.

***Modestinus, Herennius** iurisconsultus Latinus [Modest.] iii AD *Dig.* = *Digesta* (q.v.).

**Moero**, for 'Epica iii BC' read 'poetria iv/iii BC'

**Molpis**, line 1, add 'ii/i BC'; add 'Jacoby ‡*FGrH* no. 590: iii (B) p. 704 [Molpis .. J.]'

**Moschio** paradoxographus, add '?iii BC Jacoby ‡*FGrH* no. 575: iii (B) p. 675 [Moschio .. J.]'

**Moschio** tragicus, for 'iv BC' read 'iv/iii BC'; add 'Snell °*TrGF* 1 p. 264 [Mosch.Trag. .. S.]'

**Moschus**, add 'A. S. F. Gow, *Bucolici Graeci* OCT 1952 [1969] p. 132 [Mosch. .. G.]'

**Moses** Alchemista, before 'ii AD ' insert '[Moses Alch.]'; line 3, for 'p. 139' read 'p. 39'

**Musaeus** philosophus, after 'Diels' insert 'W. Kranz' and for 'ii p. 179' read '$^{7}$ i p. 20'

**Musonius** philosophus, add '*fr.* K. = *Fragmentum*, in G. D. Kilpatrick, *CR* 63.94'

***Naevius** poeta Latinus [Naev.] iii BC *Trag.* = *Tragoediarum fragmenta*, E. V. Marmorale, Florence 1953.

**Nausiphanes**, after 'Diels' insert 'W. Kranz' and for 'ii p. 155' read '$^{7}$ ii p. 246'

***Nautarum Cantiunculae** ii/iii AD Heitsch °*GDRK* 1$^{2}$ p. 32 nos. 3–4.

**Neanthes**, add 'Jacoby ‡*FGrH* no. 84: ii (A) p. 191 [Neanth. .. J.]'

**Neophron**, add 'Snell °*TrGF* 1 p. 92 [Neophr. .. S.]'

***Nepos, Cornelius** scriptor Latinus i BC *Eum.* = *Eumenes*; *Dat.* = *Datames*, E. O. Winstedt, OCT 1904.

**Nessas**, after 'Diels' insert 'W. Kranz' and for 'ii p. 140' read '$^{7}$ ii p. 230'

**Nicaenetus**, add 'see also *Anthologia Graeca*'

**Nicander**, line 2, add 'A. S. F. Gow, A. F. Scholfield, Cambridge 1953'; for '*Alex.*' read '*Al.*' and for '*Ther.*' read '*Th.*'; after line 4 insert '*fr.* = *Fragmenta* [Nic. .. G.–S.]'; at end add '*Scholia in Nicandri Alexipharmaca*, M. Geymonat, Milan 1974 [Sch.Nic.*Al.* .. Ge.]; *Scholia in Nicandri Theriaka*, A. Cragnola, Milan 1971 [Sch. Nic.*Th.*]'

***Nicarchus I** epigrammaticus [Nicarch. I]. iv/iii BC v. Anthologia Graeca.

**Nicarchus** epigrammaticus, after 'Nicarchus' insert 'II'; add '[Nicarch. II in Suppl.]'

**Nicolaus Damascenus**, line 2, add 'Jacoby ‡*FGrH* no. 90: ii (A) p. 324. [Nic.Dam. .. J.]'

**Nicolaus** rhetor, line 1, add 'v AD '; *Prog.*, add 'sts. cited fr. *Rhetores Graeci* iii, L. Spengel, p. 447; sts. fr. *Rhetores Graeci* ii, Ch.Walz, p. 565, al.'

**Nicomachus** tragicus, line 1, add 'iii BC'; at end add 'Snell °*TrGF* 1 p. 285 (= Nicom. Alexandrinus, to be distinguished fr. Nicom.Atheniensis, v/iv BC, Snell *op.cit.* p. 154) [Nicom.Trag. .. S.]'

**Nicostratus** comicus, add 'Kassel, Austin °*PCG* 7 p. 74 [Nicostr.Com. .. K.–A.]'

**Nonius Marcellus**, add 'cited fr. Lindsay w. nos. fr. Mercerus' ed. [Non.Marc. .. M.]'

**Nonnus**, add 'R. Keydell, Berlin (Weidmann) 1959 (2 vols.); *Par.Ev.Jo.* = *Paraphrasis Evangelii Johannis*, A. Scheindler, T(L) 1881'

**Nossis**, for 'iii BC(?)' read 'iv/iii BC'

**Novum Testamentum**, line 2, add 'K. Aland et al., Stuttgart, 1968$^{2}$'

**Numenius Apamensis**, add '*fr.* = *Fragmenta*, É. des Places, B 1973 [Numen.*fr.* .. P.]'

**Olympiodorus** philosophus, *in Phlb.*, now attributed to °Damascius; *in Grg.*, add 'L. G. Westerink, T(L) 1970 (cited by page number)'

**Onosander**, read '**Onasander**'; after '1923' add '1962 [Onas. in Suppl.]'

**Oppianus Anazarbensis**, for '**Anazarbensis**' read '**Cilix**'; add 'A. W. Mair, Loeb 1928 [1963] p. 200'

**Oppianus Apamensis**, *C.*, add 'A. W. Mair, Loeb 1928 [1963] p. 1'

**Oracula Chaldaica**, line 1, add 'ii AD'; at end add 'É. des Places, B 1971 [*Orac.Chald.* .. P.]'

***Oracula Sibyllina** [*Orac.Sib.*] ii/iv AD J. Geffcken, Leipzig 1902 [1967] (= °*GCS* 8).

***Oracula Tiburtina** [*Orac.Tib.*] P. J. Alexander, Dumbarton Oaks 1967.

**Oribasius**, line 1, add 'J. Raeder, *CMG* 6, Leipzig, Berlin 1926–33 [Amsterdam 1964]; *Collectionum medicarum reliquiae* 6.1(1–2), 2(1–2), cited without title'

**Origenes**, add '*Adnot. in Gen.* = *Adnotationes in Genesim* °*PG* 17.11'

**Orphica**, *A.*, add '*Argonautiques orphiques*, F. Vian, B 1987'; *H.*, add 'W. Quandt, Berlin (Weidmann) 1962[3] [1973]; *Εὐχή* = *Εὐχὴ πρὸς Μουσαῖον* (v. *H.*)'; *L.*, add '[Hildesheim 1971], *Lithica Kerygmata*, G. Giannakis, Yannina 1987 [Orph.*Lith.Kerygm.* .. G.]'; *fr.*, add '[1963]'

***Ovidius Naso, P.**, poeta Latinus [Ov.] i BC/i AD *Am.* = *Amores*, E. J. Kenney, OCT 1961.

***Pachomius Tabennensis** scriptor ecclesiasticus [Pach.] *Poen.* = *Poenae monachorum*; *Reg.* = *Excerpta e regula*, L. Th. Lefort; in *Muséon* 37(1924) p. 9, 40(1927) p. 60.

**Palladas**, for 'vi AD' read 'iv/v AD'

**Palladius**, add '*Febr.* = *de febribus*, Ideler °*Physici* i p. 107'

***Palladius** auctor Latinus [Pallad.] ?iv AD *Agric.* = *Opus Agriculturae*, R. H. Rodgers, T(L) 1975.

***Palladius** episcopus Helenopolitanus [Pall.] iv/v AD *V.Chrys.* = *Dialogus de vita Iohannis Chrysostomi* P. R. Coleman-Norton, Cambridge 1928 [1958]; *Gent.Ind.* = *De gentibus Indiae et Bragmanibus περὶ τῶν τῆς Ἰνδίας ἐθνῶν καὶ Βραχμάνων* apud Pseudo-Callisthenem, W. Berghoff, Meisenheim 1967.

**Pancrates** epicus, add 'Heitsch °*GDRK* 1 p. 52'

**Pancrates** epigrammaticus, line 1, add 'iii/ii BC'; at end add 'in °*Suppl.Hell.* p. 286'

**Panyasis**, add 'Bernabé °*PEG* p. 171 [Panyas. .. B.]'

**Pappus**, add '*in Alm.* = *Commentarium in Ptolemaei Magnam Constructionem sive Almagesto* in *Commentaires de Pappus et de Théon d'Alexandrie sur l'Almageste*, I.: *Pappus*, A. Rome, Rome 1931 [1967]'

**Paulus Aegineta**, line 2, after '1921–1924' insert 'H. refers to p. and line of Heiber's ed.'

**Paulus Alexandrinus**, for 'page' read 'leaf'; add 'E. Boer, T(L) 1958 (cited by p. and line number)'

**Paulus Silentiarius**, add '*Ambo* = *Descriptio Ambonis*, P. Friedländer, *Johannes von Gaza und Paulus Silentiarius*, Leipzig/Berlin 1912'

***Pausanius Grammaticus** [Paus.Gr.] ii AD H. Erbse, *Untersuchungen zu den attizistischen Lexika*, Berlin 1950, p. 152.

**Pausanias** periegeta, add 'M. H. Rocha-Pereira, T(L) 1973–81 [1989[2]] (3 vols.)'

**Perictione**, for 'Philosophus' read 'philosopha Pythagorica'; add 'ii BC'

***Periplus Maris Euxini** [*Peripl.M.Eux.*] (in LSJ s.v. Arr.) °Diller *Trad.min.Gr.geogr.* p. 102.

**Periplus Maris Rubri**, add '*The Periplus Maris Erythraei*, L. Casson, Princeton 1989 [*Peripl.M.Rubr.* .. C.]'

**Perses**, line 1, add '?iv BC'

**Persius**, for 'S. G. Owen[2]' read 'W. V. Clausen' and add '1959'

**Phalaris**, for 'p. 439' read 'p. 409'

**Phanias** epigrammaticus, add 'iii BC'

**Pherecrates** comicus, add 'Kassel, Austin °*PCG* 7 p. 102 [Pherecr. .. K.–A.]'

***Pherecydes Atheniensis** historicus [Pherecyd.Ath.] v BC Jacoby ‡*FGrH* no. 3: i (A) p. 58.

**Pherecydes Lerius**, for 'vi BC' read 'Hellen.'; for 'F. Jacoby .. 58' read 'Jacoby ‡*FGrH* no. 475: iii (B) p. 434'

**Pherecydes Syrius**, after 'Diels' insert 'W. Kranz' and for 'ii p. 198' read '[7] i p. 43'

**Philemo** comicus, add 'Kassel, Austin °*PCG* 7 p. 221 [Philem. .. K.–A.]'

***Philetas Samius** epigrammaticus [Philet.Sam.] v. *Anthologia Graeca.*

***Philicus** lyricus [Philic.] iii BC °*Suppl.Hell.* p. 321.

**Philippides**, add 'Kassel, Austin °*PCG* 7 p. 333 [Philippid. .. K.–A.]'

***Philippus Pergamenus** historicus ii AD Jacoby ‡*FGrH* no. 95: ii (A) p. 446. [Philipp.Perg. .. J.].

**Philistus**, add 'Jacoby ‡*FGrH* no. 556: iii (B) p. 551 [Philist. .. J.]'

**Philo** mechanicus, before '1919, No. 12' insert '1918, no. 16' and for 'Wescher' read 'Thévenot'

**Philo Judaeus**, line 1, add 'i BC/i AD'; line 2, after '1915' add 'cited by vol. and p. of Mangey, given in margin of C.–W. ([de Gruyter 1962]) (Ph. 2.264–9 M. = v. 67–8 + i. 209–16 C.–W.; Ph. 2.437–44 M. = v. 324–35 C.–W.; Ph. 2.492.10–497.8 M. = vi. 89.11–97.3 C.–W.). References containing higher numbers than 2.600 will be found in T. Mangey's ed., London 1742, not in C.–W.'; line 3, after '1886' add 'cited by p.'

**Philodemus** philosophus, for '*D.* 1, 3 .. 1916, 1917' read '*D.* 1, 3 ..1915 no. 7, 1916 no. 4 [1916, 1917, Leipzig 1970]'; *Rh.*, add '[Phld.*Rh.* .. S.] refers to Sudhaus's edition, [1964] (2 vols. + Suppl.)'; at end add 'sts. cited by p. of A. Vogliano, *Epicuri et Epicureorum scripta in Herculanensibus papyris servata*, Berlin 1928. [p. .. V.]'

**Philolaus**, after 'Diels' insert 'W. Kranz' and for 'i p. 301' read '[7] i p. 398'

**Philoponus, Joannes**, after line 2, add '*Aet.M.* = *de Aeternitate Mundi*, H. Rabe, T(L) 1899 [1963]; *Dif.Ton.* = *Collectio vocum quae pro diversa significatione accentum diversum accipiunt* P. Egenolff, Breslau 1880 [p. 361 in *Lexica graeca minora*, K. Latte, H. Erbse, Hildesheim 1965]'

***Philoxenus Leucadius** lyricus [Philox.Leuc.] v/iv BC Page °*PMG* p. 433.

**Phlegon Trallianus**, *Mir.*, add '*De Mirabilibus*, A. Giannini, *Paradoxographorum Graecorum reliquiae* Milan 1965, p. 170'; *Fragmenta Historica*, add 'Jacoby ‡*FGrH* no. 257: ii (B) p. 1159 [Phleg.*fr.* .. J.]'

**Phoenix**, add '*Phoinix von Kolophon*, G. A. Gerhard, Leipzig/Berlin 1909 [Phoen. .. G.]'

***Phoronis** carmen epicum vii/vi BC Bernabé °*PEG* p. 118.

**Photius**, *Lexicon*, add 'repr. Naber [Amsterdam 1965]; Chr.Theodorides, Berlin 1982; vol. 1 (*Α–Δ*) [Phot. .. Th.]'; *Bibl.*, add 'R. Henry, B 1959–77 (8 vols., vol. 9: indices, J. Schamp 1991) [Phot.*Bibl.* p. (= paragraph) .. H.]'

**Phrynichus** Atticista, line 2, add '*Die Ekloge des Phrynichos* E. Fischer, Berlin 1974 (*Sammlung griechischer und lateinischer Grammatiker* I) [Phryn. .. F.]'

**Phrynichus** tragicus, add 'Snell °*TrGF* 1 p. 69 [Phryn. Trag. .. S.]'

***Physiognomici scriptores** [*Physiogn.*] R. Förster, T(L) 1893 (2 vols.).

***Physiologus** Graecus [*Phys.* A et B] ii AD F. Sbordone, Rome 1936.

**Pindarus**, line 2, add 'B. Snell, H. Maehler, T(L) 1971[5]'; *fr.*, add 'B. Snell, H. Maehler, T(L) 1975[4] [Pi.*fr.* .. S.–M.]'

**Pisander** epicus, add 'Heitsch °*GDRK* 2 p. 44'

***Pisander Camiraius** epicus vii/vi BC Bernabé °*PEG* p. 164.

**Plato** comicus, add 'Kassel, Austin °*PCG* 7 p. 431 [Pl.Com. .. K.-A.]'

**Plato** philosophus, line 2, for 'Oxford (OCT)' read 'OCT 1900–7 [1967]'; *Epigr.*, add '°*Anth.Lyr.* $1^3$ p. 102 [Pl.*Epigr.* .. $D.^3$]'; Scholia, add 'W. C. Greene, Haverford 1938 [Sch.Pl. .. G.]'

**Plotinus**, add 'P. Henry, H. R. Schwyzer, OCT 1964–82 (3 vols.); see also ‡Porph.*Plot.*'

**Plutarchus**, *Moralia*, line 2, after '1888–96' insert 'W. R. Paton et al., T(L) 1925 [1974]–1967 (7 vols.)'; line 3, for 'Wyttenbach' read 'Stephanus' edition 1599'; (*Vitae parallelae*) for '1881–65' read '1865–81' and add 'K. Ziegler, $T^4$ 1964–73 (3 vols.)'; *Fr.*, for 'pp. 150–2' read 'pp. 150–82'; add 'F. H. Sandbach, T(L) 1967 (= *Moralia* 7); *Galb.* = *Galba*; *in Arat.* = *quaestiones de Arati signis* (vol. vii, p. 102 B.)'; *in Hes.*, for 'p. 5' read 'p. 51'; *Nob.*, now regarded as humanist forgery; Ps.-Plu. *Vit.Hom.*, for '*Vita* .. p. 192' read '*de Vita et Poesi Homeri* (vol. vii, p. 329 B.)'; add 'B. refers to Bernardakis' edition'

**Poeta** de herbis, add 'Heitsch °*GDRK* 2 p. 23'

***Poliorcetici** scriptores [*Poliorc.*] *Poliorcétique des grecs*, C. Wescher, Paris 1867, cited by p. and line.

**Pollux**, add 'E. Bethe, T(L) 1900–31 [Stuttgart 1967] (2 vols.)'

**Polyclitus**, after 'Diels' insert 'W. Kranz' and for 'i p. 294' read '$^7$ i p. 391'

**Polystratus** Epicureus, add 'sts. cited by p. of Vogliano [p. .. V.], cf. °Philodemus'

**Porphyrius**, after '*in Harm.* .. Ptolemaeum)' add '*Porphyrios' Kommentar zur Harmonielehre des Ptolemaios*, I. Düring, Göteborg 1932'; *Plot.*, add '*Plotini opera 1*, P. Henry, H. R. Schwyzer, OCT 1964 pp. 1–38'; add '*Ep.Aneb.* = *Epistula ad Anebonem*, A. R. Sodano, Naples 1958; *Hist.Phil.* = *Historiae Philosophicae Fragmenta* in *Porphyrii Opuscula*, A. Nauck, T(L) $1886^2$ [1963]; *in Prm.* = *in Platonis Parmenidem commentaria*, p. 64 in *Porphyre et Victorinus*, vol. 2, P. Hadot, Paris 1968'

***Posidonius** Apamensis et Rhodius philosophus ii/i BC [Posidon.] vol. $I^2$ L. Edelstein, I. G. Kidd, Cambridge 1989; vols. II(i), II(ii) I. G. Kidd, Cambridge 1988.

**Posidonius** historicus, add 'Jacoby ‡*FGrH* no. 169: ii (B) p. 222 [in Suppl., Posidon.Hist. .. J.]'

***Possis** historicus iii/ii BC Jacoby ‡*FGrH* no. 480: iii (B) p. 444.

**Pratinas**, line 2, add 'Page °*PMG* p. 367 [Pratin. .. P.]'; line 3, add 'Snell °*TrGF* 1 p. 79. [Pratin. .. S.]'

***Probus Grammaticus**, Keil *Gramm.Lat.* vol. iv p. 3.

**Proclus**, *H.*, add 'E. Vogt, Wiesbaden 1957'; *in Alc.*, add 'L. G. Westerink, Amsterdam 1954 [Procl.*in Alc.* .. W.]'; *in R.*, add '[Amsterdam 1965], cited by vol. and p. [Procl.*in R.* .. K.]'; *in Ti.*, add '[Amsterdam 1965], cited by vol. and p. [Procl.*in Ti.* .. D.]'; *Inst.*, add '*Proclus. The elements of theology*, E. R. Dodds, Oxford $1963^2$ [1977] [Procl.*Inst.* .. D.]'; for '*Par.Ptol.* .. Basel 1554' read '*Par.Ptol.* .. Leiden 1635'; add '*Phil.Chald.* = *Eclogae de Philosophia Chaldaica*, in *Oracles chaldaïques*, É. des Places, B 1971 p. 206; *Sacr.* = περὶ τῆς καθ' Ἕλληνας ἱερατικῆς τέχνης, J. Bidez in *Catalogue des manuscrits alchimiques grecs* vi (1928) p. 148'; *Theol.Plat.*, add 'H. D. Saffrey, L. G. Westerink, B 1968–87 (5 vols.)'

***Proclus Constantinopolitanus** scriptor ecclesiasticus [Procl.CP] v AD *Hom.* 1–2 = *Homiliae*, Migne °*PG* 65.833, *Hom.* 26–34 in *L'Homilétique de Proclos de Constantinople*, F. J. Leroy, Vatican 1967.

**Procopius Caesariensis**, line 2, add 'G. Wirth (post J. Haury), T(L) 1962–4 (4 vols.)'

**Prodicus**, for 'v BC' read 'v/iv BC'; after 'Diels' insert 'W. Kranz' and for 'ii p. 267' read '$^7$ ii p. 308'

***Propertius, Sextus** poeta Latinus [Prop.] i BC E. A. Barber, OCT $1960^2$.

**Protagoras**, after 'Diels' insert 'W. Kranz' and for 'ii p. 219' read '$^7$ ii p. 253'

***Protagoras Nicaensis** astrologus [Protag.Nicae.] iii BC apud Hephaestionem astrologum.

***Pseudo-Acro** scholiasta [Ps.-Acro] vi/vii AD *Scholia in Horatium vetustiora*, O. Keller, T(S) 1902–4 [1967] (2 vols.) *C.* = *Carmina*.

***Pseudo-Archytas** philosophus [Ps.-Archyt.] cited fr. H. Thesleff, *The Pythagorean Texts of the Hellenistic Period*, Åbo 1965.

***Pseudo-Asconius** scholiasta [Ps.-Ascon.] i AD *in Verr.* = *Ciceronis Orationum Scholiastae*, T. Stangl, vol. ii (*commentarios continens*), Vienna/Leipzig 1912 [Hildesheim 1964].

**Pseudo-Callisthenes**, add 'W. Kroll, *Historia Alexandri Magni*, vol. i, Berlin 1926 [Weidmann 1959], cited by p. and line no. [Ps.-Callisth. .. K.]; *Recensio* λ, H. van Thiel, Bonn 1959 [ .. λ.]'

***Pseudo-Chrysostomus** scriptor ecclesiasticus [Ps.-Chrys.] v AD *HP* = *Homélies Pascales*, M. Aubineau, Paris 1972.

**Pseudo-Democritus**, add 'Diels, Kranz °*Vorsokr.* $^7$ ii p. 207 *frr.* B 298 ff. (sts. attributed to °Bolus). *Symp.Ant.* = περὶ συμπαθειῶν καὶ ἀντιπαθειῶν W. Gemoll, Striegau 1884 (sts. attributed to Nephalius, or °Bolus)'

***Pseudo-Dioscorides** medicus [Ps.-Dsc.], Wellmann op. cit. [Weidmann 1958] (3 vols.), under text of Dsc.

**Pseudo-Phocylidea**, add 'D. Young, *Theognis* T(L) $1971^2$ p. 95'

**Ptolemaeus** mathematicus, *Alm.*, cited by vol. and p. of Heiberg's ed. [Ptol.*Alm.* .. H.]; *Geog.*, for 'i–iii' read 'i–v'; add 'repr. Nobbe [Hildesheim 1966]'; *Harm.*, add 'I. Düring, Gothenburg 1930'; *Tetr.*, add '(= Ἀποτελεσματικά) F. Boll, E. Boer, T(L) 1940 [1957]'

**Ptolemaeus Chennos**, add 'sts. cited by p. of A. Westermann, Μυθογράφοι, Brunswick 1843'

**Pythagoras**, after 'Diels' insert 'W. Kranz' and for 'i p. 27, cf. p. 344' read '$^7$ i p. 96, cf. p. 446'; add '*Pyth.Sim.* = *Pythagoreorum Similitudines*, Mullach *FPG* i p. 488'

**Quintilianus**, *Inst.*, add 'M. Winterbottom, OCT 1970 (2 vols.)'

**Quintus Smyrnaeus**, line 1, for 'iv AD?' read 'iii AD'; add 'F. Vian, B 1963–9 (3 vols.)'

***Res Gestae divi Saporis** [*Res Gestae Saporis*] iii AD *Recherches sur les Res Gestae divi Saporis*, E. Honigmann, A. Maricq, Brussels 1953, p. 11.

***Romanus Sophista** [Roman.] vi AD περὶ ἀνειμένου, W. Camphausen, T(L) 1922.

***Rufinianus, Julius** rhetor Latinus [Rufin.] *Fig.* = *de Figuris*, in *Rhetores Latini Minores*, C. Halm, Leipzig 1863, p. 38 (cited by p. ).

**Rufus** Medicus, before '*Onom.*' insert '*fr.* = *Fragmenta*; *Interrog.* = *Interrogationes*, H. Gärtner, T(L) 1970' and before '*Ren.Ves.*' insert '*Oss.* = *de ossibus*; *Podagr.* = *de podagra*'

**Sallustius**, add 'G. Rochefort, B 1960'

**Sappho**, line 2, add '*Poetarum Lesbiorum Fragmenta*, E.

Lobel, D. L. Page, Oxford 1955 [1968], p. 2 [Sapph. .. L.–P.]'

***Satyrius** epigrammaticus i BC *AP* 6.11 (author now dist. fr. Satyrus).

**Satyrus** historicus, *Vit.Eur.*, add 'G. Arrighetti, Pisa 1964'

***Scaevola, Q. Cervidius** iurisconsultus Latinus [Scaev.] ii AD *Dig.* = *Digesta* (q.v.).

**Scolia**, add 'Page °*PMG* p. 472 [*Scol.* .. P.]'

***Scribonius Largus** medicus, [Scrib.Larg.] i AD G. Helmreich, T(L) 1887.

**Semonides** iambographus, add 'West °*IEG* (2) p. 97 [Semon. .. W.]'

**Semus**, line 1, add '?iii/ii BC'; add 'Jacoby ‡*FGrH* no. 396: iii (B) p. 285 [Semus .. J.]'

**Seneca, L. Annaeus**, add '*Ep.* = *Epistulae*, L. D. Reynolds, OCT 1965 (2 vols.)'

***Seneca, L. Annaeus** rhetor Latinus i BC/i AD *Contr.* = *Controversiae*, H. Bornecque, Paris 1932[2].

**Servius**, add '*A.* = *Aeneid*, Keil *Gramm.Lat.* vol. iv p. 403 (cited by vol., p. and line) [Serv. in *Gramm.Lat.* .. K.]'

**Sextus Empiricus**, for 'H. Mutschmann .. 1912' read 'H. Mutschmann, J. Mau, (indices by K. Janáček), T(L) 1912–62 (4 vols.)'

***Simeon Metaphrastes** scriptor ecclesiasticus x AD *Vit. Luc.* = *Vita Luciani*, Migne °*PG* 114.397.

**Simmias**, add '*Securis*, A. S. F. Gow *Bucolici Graeci*, OCT 1952 p. 174; see also Anthologia Graeca'

**Simon Atheniensis**, before '*Eq.*' insert '[Simon.Ath.] J. Soukup, Innsbruck 1911 (*Commentationes Aenipontanae*, E. Kalinka, no. VI)'; *Eq.*, add 'K. Widdra, T 1964'

**Simonides**, add 'West °*IEG* (2) p. 113 [Simon. .. W.]; Page °*PMG* p. 238 [Simon. .. P.] see also Anthologia Graeca'

***Socrates et Dionysius** de lapidibus scriptores *Lith.* = *Περὶ Λίθων*, *Les lapidaires grecs*, R. Halleux, J. Schamp, B 1985 p. 166 [Socr.Dion. .. H.–S.]; G. Giannakis, Yannina 1987 [Socr.Dion. .. G.].

***Solinus, C. Julius** geographus Latinus [Solin.] ?iii AD T. Mommsen, Berlin 1895[2] [1958].

**Solon**, add 'West °*IEG* (2) p. 120 [Sol. .. W.] *Lg.* = *Leges*, E. Ruschenbusch, *Historia* Einzelschr. 9, Wiesbaden 1966'

**Sopater**, add '*Sopatros the Rhetor*, D. Innes, M. Winterbottom, *BICS* 48, London 1988 [Sopat.Rh. .. I.–W.]'

**Sophocles**, for 'A. C. Pearson ..' read 'H. Lloyd-Jones, N. G. Wilson, OCT 1990 [L.-J.–W.]'; add '*fr.* = *Fragmenta*, Radt °*TrGF* 4 [S.*fr.* .. R.]; *Ichn.* = *Ἰχνευταί* (= *fr.* 314 in °*TrGF* 4); *Pae.* = Scholia, W. Dindorf, Oxford 1852; Scholia Vetera, P. N. Papageorgius, T(L) 1888 [Sch. .. P.]; Sch.*Aj.*, G. A. Christodoulou, Athens 1977'

**Sophron**, add 'A. Olivieri, *Frammenti della commedia greca e del mimo nella Sicilia e nella Magna Graecia*, Naples 1930, p. 169 [Sophron .. O.]'

**Soranus**, after '1882' insert '*Gynaeciorum libri iv, de signis fracturarum, de fasciis, vita Hippocratis secundum Soranum*, J. Ilberg, *CMG* 4, Leipzig/Berlin 1927 [*Gynaecia* cited by Rose's numeration]'

**Sosibius**, line 1, for 'iii BC' read 'iii/ii BC'; add 'Jacoby ‡*FGrH* no. 595: iii (B) p. 713'

**Sosiphanes**, add 'Snell *TrGF* 1 p. 261 [Sosiph. .. S.]'

**Sosylus**, add 'Jacoby ‡*FGrH* no. 176: ii (B) p. 903 [Sosyl. .. J.]'

**Statyllius Flaccus**, for 'Idem .. q.v.' read 'v. Anthologia Graeca'

***Pseudo-Stephanus** Alexandrinus [Ps.-Steph.] vi/vii AD °*Physici* 2 p. 199.

**Stesichorus**, before 'vii/vi BC' insert '(?)'; after 'iii p. 205' add 'Page °*PMG* p. 97 [Stesich. .. P.]; Page °*SLG* p. 5 [Stesich.*S.* 123 etc.]; Davies °*PMGF* p. 134 [Stesich. .. p. .. D.]'

**Strabo**, line 2, add 'G. Aujac et al., B 1966–89 (9 vols.), except for Bk. ix'

**Strato** Comicus, delete '(?)'; add 'Kassel, Austin °*PCG* 7 p. 618 [Strato Com. .. K.–A.]'

**Suetonius**, add '*Gramm.* = *de Grammaticis et Rhetoribus deperditorum librorum reliquiae*, I. Della Corte, Turin 1968; *περὶ βλασφημιῶν (καὶ πόθεν ἑκάστη)* and *περὶ τῶν (παρ' Ἕλλησι) παιδιῶν*, J. Taillardat, Paris 1967 [Suet.*Blasph.* .. T.; Suet.*Lud.* .. T.]'

**Suidas**, add 'A. Adler, T(L) 1928–38 [1967–71] (5 vols.) [properly *Suda*]'

***Synesius Cyrenensis** scriptor ecclesiasticus [Synes.] iv/v AD Migne °*PG* 66. *Calv.* = *Calvitii Encomium* °*PG* 66.1167; *Hymn.* = *Hymni*, Chr. Lacombrade, B 1978; *Insomn.* = *De Insomniis* °*PG* 66.1281; *Ep.* = *Epistolae*, A. Garzya, Rome 1979.

**Telestes**, for 'iv BC' read 'v/iv BC'; add 'Page °*PMG* p. 419 [Telest. .. P.]'

**Teucer Babylonius**, before 'i AD' insert '[Teuc.Bab.]' and delete '(?)'; for '6' read '16'; add '[Hildesheim 1967]'

**Thales**, after 'Diels' insert 'W. Kranz' and for 'i p. 1' read '7 i p. 67'

**Themistius**, *Or.*, add 'H. Schenkel, G. Downey, A. F. Norman, T(L) 1965–74 (3 vols., cited by no. of speech and p. of Hardouin, exc. no. 34, cited by p. of Dindorf)'

**Theocritus**, line 3, add 'A. S. F. Gow, Cambridge 1952[2] [1965] (2 vols.)'; before '*Beren.*' insert '*Adon.* = *εἰς νεκρὸν Ἄδωνιν* A. S. F. Gow *Bucolici Graeci*, OCT 1952 [1969] p. 166'; for '*Coma Berenices*' read '*Berenice*'; Sch., add '[1967]'

**Theodectes** Tragicus, add 'Snell °*TrGF* 1 p. 227'

**Theognis**, add 'West °*IEG* (1) p. 172'

**Theognostus**, add '1–84 K. Alpers, Hamburg 1964 [Theognost. .. A.]'

***Theon Alexandrinus** Mathematicus [Theon Al.] iv AD *in Ptol.* = *in Ptolemaeum*, in *Commentaires de Pappus et de Théon d'Alexandrie sur l'Almageste. II. Théon d'Alexandrie* A. Rome, Vatican 1936 (= Studi e Testi 72, 106); *Œuvres de Ptolémée*, M. Halma, vol. v, Paris 1821.

**Theon Smyrnaeus**, delete '*in Ptol.* .. Paris 1821.' N.B. in references, for 'Theo Sm. *in Ptol.*' read 'Theon Al. *in Ptol.*'

***Theophilus Antecessor** iurisconsultus [Theophil.Antec.] vi AD *Institutionum graeca paraphrasis Theophilo antecessori vulgo tributa*, E. C. Ferrini, 1884–97 [Aalen 1967] (2 vols.).

***Theophilus Antiochenus** scriptor ecclesiasticus [Thphl.Ant.] ii AD *Autol.* = *ad Autolycum*, R. M. Grant, Oxford 1970.

**Theophrastus**, *Char.*, add 'P. Steinmetz, Munich 1960–2 (2 vols.)'; *fr.*, add 'F. Wimmer, Paris 1855 [1931] (vol. 3)'; *Metaph.*, add 'W. D. Ross, F. H. Fobes, Oxford 1929 [Hildesheim 1967] [*Metaph.* p. .. R.–F.]'

**Theopompus** comicus, for 'v BC' read 'v/iv BC'; add 'Kassel, Austin °*PCG* 7 p. 708 [Theopomp.Com. .. K.–A.]'

**Theopompus** historicus, add 'Jacoby ‡*FGrH* no. 115: ii (B) p. 526, iii (B) p. 742 [Theopomp.Hist. .. J.]'

**Thespis**, add 'Snell °*TrGF* 1 p. 61 [Thespis .. S.]'

**Thucydides**, line 2, read 'H. S. Jones, J. E. Powell, OCT 1942[1] (rev.) [1974, 1976] (2 vols.)'; add 'Scholia, C. Hude, T(L) 1927'

**Timaeus Locrus**, add 'W. Marg, Leiden 1972 [Ti.Locr. .. M.]'

**Timotheus** Lyricus, line 2, add 'Page °*PMG* p. 399 [Tim. .. P.]'

**Tragica adespota**, add 'Kannicht, Snell °*TrGF* 2 [*Trag. adesp.* .. K.–S.]'

**Tryphiodorus**, line 1, at end add '[properly Triphiodorus; Triph. in Suppl.]'; add '*Oppian, Colluthus, Tryphiodorus*, A. W. Mair, Loeb 1928 [1963] p. 580'

**Tyrtaeus**, add 'West °*IEG* (2) p. 150 [Tyrt. .. W.]'

**Tzetzes, Joannes**, before '*Diff.Poet.*' insert '*Alleg.Il.* = *Allegoriae Iliadis* (*Prol.* = *Prolegomena*), J. F. Boissonade, Paris 1851 [Hildesheim 1967]'; *H.*, add 'A. M. Leone, Naples 1968 [Tz.*H.* .. L.]'

***Ulpianus, Domitius** iurisconsultus [Ulp.] ii/iii AD *Dig.* = *Digesta* q.v.

**Varro**, *LL*, add '[Amsterdam 1964]'; add '*fr.* = *Saturarum Menippearum fragmenta* R. Astbury, T(L) 1985 [Varro *fr.* .. A.]'

***Vegetius** veterinarius [Veg.] *Mul.* = *Mulomedicina*, E. Lommatzsch, T(L) 1903.

**Vettius Valens**, add 'D. Pingree, T(L) 1986'

**Vetus Testamentum Graece redditum A**, line 2, add 'A. Rahlfs, Stuttgart 1935 [1971] (2 vols.), L. Lütkemann, A. Rahlfs, *Hexaplarische Randnoten zu Isaias 1-16, aus einer Sinai-Handschrift* (*NGG* 1915 Beiheft); [.. (L.–R.)]'; after 'Heb. = 'Eβραῖος' insert 'Lcn. = Lucianus'; after 'Sm. = Symmachus (q.v.)' insert 'Syr. = ὁ Σύρος' **B**, after '*Ps.*' insert '*Ps.Sal.* = *Psalmi Salomonis*'

***Vita Aesopi** [*Vit.Aesop.*] *Aesopica*, B. E. Perry, Univ. Illinois 1952; (G) = *Vita Aesopi ex codice G Novaeboracensi Bibliothecae Pierponti Morgan* (Perry p. 35); (W) = *Vita Aesopi Westermanniana* (Perry p. 81).

**Xenocrates**, add '*Lap.* = *Λιθογνώμων*, M. Wellmann in *Quellen und Studien zur Geschichte der Naturwissenschaften und der Medizin*, P. Diepgen, J. Ruska, Band 4, Heft 4, p. 86 [426], Berlin 1935'

**Xenophanes**, for 'vi BC' read 'vi/v BC'; add 'West °*IEG* (2) p. 164; Diels, Kranz °*Vorsokr.*[7] i p. 113'

**Xenophon**, line 2, for 'Oxford (OCT)' read 'OCT 1900–20 [1968–71]'

**Xenophon Ephesius**, for 'ii AD?' read 'ii/iii AD'; add 'A. D. Papanikolaou, T(L) 1973'

**Zeno Eleaticus**, after 'Diels' insert 'W. Kranz' and for 'i p. 165' read '[7] i p. 247'

***Zenodotus Stoicus** epigrammaticus [Zenodotus] v. Anthologia Graeca.

**Zonaras**, line 1, add 'xii AD'; line 2, add '[Hildesheim 1967]'

# II. EPIGRAPHICAL PUBLICATIONS

*ABV = Attic Black-Figure Vase Painters*, J. D. Beazley, Oxford 1956.
*Amyzon = Fouilles d'Amyzon en Carie.* I: *Exploration, histoire, monnaies et inscriptions*, J. and L. Robert, Paris 1983.
*Antioch-on-the-Orontes = Antioch-on-the-Orontes* I–III, G. W. Elderkin et al., Princeton 1934–41.
*Ath.Agora = The Athenian Agora* Princeton 1953–. vol. 10: *Weights, Measures and Tokens*, M. Lang, M. Crosby, 1964; vol. 15: *The Athenian Councillors*, B. D. Meritt, J. Traill, 1974; vol. 17: *The Funerary Monuments*, D. W. Bradeen, 1974; vol. 19: *Inscriptions: Horoi, Poletai Records, Leases of Public Lands*, G. Lalande, M. Langdon, M. Walbank, 1991; vol. 21: v. °Lang *Ath.Agora.*
*Ath.Asklepieion = The Athenian Asklepieion: The People, their Dedications and their Inventories*, S. Aleshire, Amsterdam 1989.
*Baillet *Inscr. des tombeaux des rois* = J. Baillet, *Inscriptions grecques et latines des tombeaux des rois ou syringes*, 3 vols., Cairo 1920–6.
**BCH* suppl. 8, 9, v. index °IV.
*Bernand *Akôris* = É. Bernand, *Inscriptions grecques et latines d'Akôris*, Cairo 1988.
*Bernand *IMEG* = É. Bernand, *Inscriptions métriques de l'Égypte gréco-romaine: recherches sur la poésie épigrammatique des grecs en Égypte*, Paris 1969.
*Bernand *Inscr.Colosse Memnon* = A. and É. Bernand, *Les Inscriptions grecques et latines du Colosse de Memnon*, Paris 1960.
*Bernand *Les portes* = A. Bernand, *Les Portes du désert: Recueil des inscriptions grecques d'Antinooupolis, Tentyris, Koptos, Apollonopolis Parva et Apollonopolis Magna*, Paris 1984.
*Bernand *Pan* = A. Bernand, *Pan du désert*, Leiden 1977.
*Bile *Dial.crét.* = M. Bile, *Le Dialecte crétois ancien*, Paris 1988.
*Bithynische St. = Bithynische Studien. Bithynia Incelemeleri*, S. Sahin, Bonn 1978 (°*IGSK* 7).
*BMC = Catalogue of the Greek Coins in the British Museum*, F. G. Hill, London 1873–1927: the individual volumes are referred to as *BMC Ionia, BMC Caria*, etc.
*Bonner *Magical Amulets* = Campbell Bonner, *Studies in Magical Amulets* (Univ. Michigan Studies, Humanistic Series, 49), Ann Arbor 1950.
*Brixhe, Hodot *AMNS* = C. Brixhe, R. Hodot, *L'Asie Mineure du nord au sud. Inscriptions inédites*, Nancy 1988.
*Buck *Gr.Dial.* = C. D. Buck, *The Greek Dialects: Grammar, Selected Inscriptions, Glossary*, Chicago 1955.
*CCCA = Corpus cultus Cybelae Attidisque*, M. J. Vermaseren, 7 vols., Leiden 1977–89.
*CEG* = 1: *Carmina epigraphica graeca saeculorum viii–v a. Chr. n.*, P. A. Hansen, Berlin 1983; 2: *Carmina epigraphica graeca saeculi iv a. Chr. n. Accedunt addenda et corrigenda ad CEG 1*, Berlin 1989.
*CGIH = Corpus der griechisch-christlichen Inschriften von Hellas:* I. *Die griechisch-christlichen Inschriften des Peloponnes*, N. A. Bees, vol. i, Athens 1941.
*CID = Corpus des inscriptions de Delphes.* I: *Lois sacrées et règlements religieux*, G. Rougemont, Paris 1977; II: *Les comptes du quatrième et du troisième siècle*, J. Bousquet, D. Mulliez, Paris 1989.
*CIJud.*, add 'repr. [New York 1975]; vol. ii: *Asie–Afrique*, Rome 1952'
*CIRB = Corpus inscriptionum Regni Bosporani*, V. V. Struve, Leningrad 1965.
*CISem. = Corpus Inscriptionum Semiticarum*, E. Renan et al., Paris 1881–1951.
*Comptes et inventaires = Comptes et inventaires dans la cité grecque: Actes du colloque international d'épigraphie tenu à Neuchâtel du 23 au 26 septembre 1986 en l'honneur de Jacques Tréheux*, D. Knoepfler, N. Quellet, Neuchâtel/Geneva 1988.
*Corinth*, add 'vol. viii (3) *The Inscriptions 1926–1950*, J. H. Kent, Princeton, NJ 1966; vol. xv (3): Appendix I: *Inscriptions*, A. L. Boegehold, pp. 358 ff., Princeton, NJ 1984.'
*de Franciscis *Locr.Epiz.* = A. de Franciscis, *Stato e società in Locri Epizefiri* (*L'archivio dell'Olympieion locrese*), Naples 1972.
*Delph.*, for '3(1), (2)' read '3(1)–(6)'; for '1909' read '1909–76'; add '(also known as *FD*)'
*Demitsas *Maced.* = M. Demitsas, *Sylloge Inscriptionum Graecarum et Latinarum Macedoniae*, 2 vols., [Athens 1896] (Demitsas *Μακεδ.* in *LSJ*).
*di Cesnola *Salaminia* = Alessandro Palma di Cesnola, *Salaminia, Cyprus: The History, Treasures and Antiquities of Salamis*, London 1882.
*Didyma = Didyma*, Th. Wiegand. Bd. II: *Die Inschriften*, A. Rehm, Berlin 1958.
*Dubois *Dial.arcad.* = L. Dubois, *Recherches sur le dialecte arcadien*, 3 vols., Louvain-la-Neuve 1986.
*Dubois *IGDS* = L. Dubois, *Inscriptions grecques dialectales de Sicile*, Paris 1989.
*Dumont–Homolle *Mél.Arch.* = A. Dumont, Th. Homolle, *Mélanges d'archéologie et d'épigraphie*, Paris 1892.
*Dura*[1], *Dura*[2], add '*Dura*[3], Third season, H. T. Rowell, A. R. Bellinger, 1932; *Dura*[4], Fourth season, S. Gould et al., 1933; *Dura*[9], Ninth season, I: *The Agora and Bazaar*, F. E. Brown, C. B. Welles, 1944; III: *The Palace of the Dux Ripae and the Dolichenum*, M. Rostovtzeff et al., 1952.'
*EAM = Επιγραφές άνω Μακεδονιάς. τόμος Α': Κατάλογος Επιγραφών*, Th. Rizakis, G. Touratsoglou, Athens 1985.
*Edict.Diocl.*, add '*Diokletians Preisedikt. Texte und Kommentare*, S. Lauffer, Berlin 1971'
*Ephes.*, add '4 (3), 5 (1), Vienna 1951, 1944'
*Expl.arch. de Délos = Exploration archéologique de Délos.* xi: *Les sanctuaires et les cultes du Mont Cynthe*, A. Plassart, Paris 1928; xxx: *Les Monuments funéraires de Rhénée*, M.-Th. Couilloud, Paris 1974.
*Fouilles de Byblos = Fouilles de Byblos 1926–38*, M. Dunand, (Atlas 1, 2; Texte I–V), Paris 1937–73.
*Friedländer *Epigrammata* = P. Friedländer, H. B. Hoffleit, *Epigrammata: Greek Inscriptions in Verse, from the Beginnings to the Persian Wars*, Berkeley 1948.

*GDI*, add '[Hildesheim 1971]'

**Gonnoi* = *Gonnoi II: Les Inscriptions*, B. Helly, Amsterdam 1973.

*Guarducci *EG* = M. Guarducci, *L'epigrafia greca dalle origine al tardo impero*, Rome 1987.

**GVAK* = *Griechische Versinschriften aus Kleinasien*, W. Peek, Vienna 1980.

**GVAThess.* = *Griechische Versinschriften aus Thessalien*, W. Peek, Heidelberg 1974.

**GVI* = *Griechische Versinschriften*, W. Peek, Bd. I., Berlin 1955 [Chicago 1988].

*Hallock *Persepolis* = R. T. Hallock, *Persepolis Fortification Tablets*, Chicago 1969.

*Hatzopoulos *Actes de vente* = M. B. Hatzopoulos, *Actes de vente de la Chalcidique centrale*, Athens 1988.

**Hierapolis* = *Inschriften* in *Altertümer von Hierapolis*, W. Judeich, Berlin 1898.

**IApam.* = *Die Inschriften von Apameia (Bithynien) und Pylai*, T. Corsten, Bonn 1987 (°*IGSK* 32).

**IAskl.Epid.* = *Inschriften aus dem Asklepieion von Epidauros*, W. Peek, *Abhandl. der Sächsischen Akad. der Wiss. zu Leipzig*, 60(2) (1969).

**IAssos* = *Die Inschriften von Assos*, R. Merkelbach, Bonn 1976 (°*IGSK* 4).

**IBith.* = *Inschriften und Denkmäler aus Bithynien*, F. K. Dörner, Berlin 1941.

**ICilicie* = *Inscriptions de Cilicie*, G. Dagron, D. Feissel, Paris 1987.

**IClaudiopolis* = *Die Inschriften von Klaudiu Polis*, F. Becker-Bertau, Bonn 1986 (°*IGSK* 31).

**ICS* = *Les Inscriptions chypriotes syllabiques*, O. Masson, Paris 1964 [1985 with Addenda nova].

**IEphes.* = *Die Inschriften von Ephesos*, H. Wankel, R. Merkelbach et al., Bonn 1979–81 (°*IGSK* 11–17).

**IEryth.* = *Die Inschriften von Erythrai und Klazomenai*, H. Engelmann, R. Merkelbach, Bonn 1972–3 (°*IGSK* 1–2).

*IG*, $^{\times}$*IG* $1^3$ = *Inscriptiones Atticae Euclidis anno anteriores* (1) *Decreta et tabulae magistratuum*, D. M. Lewis, 1981–94. *IG* $2^2$, add 'fasc. ii (5220–13247) 1940'; *IG* $9^2$, add 'fasc. ii = *Inscriptiones Acarnaniae*, fasc. iii = *Inscriptiones Locridis Occidentalis*, G. Klaffenbach, 1957, 1968'; $^{\times}$*IG* 10.2(1) = *Inscriptiones graecae Epiri, Macedoniae, Thraciae, Scythiae*, pars 2: *Inscriptiones Macedoniae*, fasc. 1: *Inscriptiones Thessalonicae et viciniae*, C. Edson, 1972; $^{\times}$*IG* 12 suppl. = *Supplementum*, F. Hiller von Gaertringen 1939.

**IGBulg.* = *Inscriptiones Graecae in Bulgaria repertae*, G. Mihailov, vols. 1–4, Bucharest 1956–66; vol. $1^2$, Sofia 1970.

**IGC* = *Inscriptions de Grèce centrale*, F. Salviat, C. Vatin, Paris 1971.

**IGChr.* = *Recueil des inscriptions grecques-chrétiennes de l'Asie Mineure*, vol. I, H. Grégoire, Paris 1922 [Amsterdam 1968].

**IGLBulg.* = *Spätgriechische und spätlateinische Inschriften aus Bulgarien*, V. Beševliev, Berlin 1964.

**IGLS* = *Inscriptions grecques et latines de la Syrie*. Tomes 1–8(3), 13(1), 21(2), L. Jalabert, R. Mouterde, Cl. Mondésert, J.-P. Rey-Coquais, Paris 1929–86. (*Inscr.gr. et lat. de la Syrie* in *LSJ*).

**IGSK* = *Inschriften griechischer Städte aus Kleinasien*, Bonn (vols. listed separately acc. to provenance).

**IHadr.* = *Die Inschriften von Hadrianoi und Hadrianeia*, E. Schwertheim, Bonn 1987 (°*IGSK* 33).

**IHistriae* = *Inscriptiones Daciae et Scythiae minoris antiquae. Series altera: Inscriptiones Scythiae minoris Graecae et Latinae*. vol. I: *Inscriptiones Histriae et viciniae*, D. M. Pippidi, Bucharest 1983.

**IIasos* = *Die Inschriften von Iasos* I, II, W. Blümel, Bonn 1985 (°*IGSK* 28.1, 2).

**IIlion* = *Die Inschriften von Ilion*, P. Frisch, Bonn 1975 (°*IGSK* 3).

**IKeramos* = *Die Inschriften von Keramos*, E. Varinlioğlu, Bonn 1986 (°*IGSK* 30).

**IKios* = *Die Inschriften von Kios*, T. Corsten, Bonn 1985 (°*IGSK* 29).

**IKnidos* = *Die Inschriften von Knidos* I, W. Blümel, Bonn 1992 (°*IGSK* 41).

**IKyme* = *Die Inschriften von Kyme*, H. Engelmann, Bonn 1976 (°*IGSK* 5).

**IKyzikos* = *Die Inschriften von Kyzikos und Umgebung*. Teil I: *Grabtexte*, E. Schwertheim, Bonn 1980 (°*IGSK* 18).

**ILabraunda* = *Labraunda. Swedish Excavations and Researches*. vol. III(1) and (2): *The Greek Inscriptions*, J. Crampa, Lund 1969, Stockholm 1972.

**ILampsakos* = *Die Inschriften von Lampsakos*, P. Frisch, Bonn 1978 (°*IGSK* 6).

**IMagnes.Sipylos* = *Die Inscriften von Magnesia am Sipylos*, T. Ihnken, Bonn 1978 (°*IGSK* 8).

**IMiletupolis* = *Die Inschriften von Kyzikos und Umgebung*. Teil II: *Miletupolis. Inschriften und Denkmäler*, E. Schwertheim, Bonn 1983 (°*IGSK* 26).

**IMylasa* = *Die Inschriften von Mylasa*, W. Blümel, Bonn 1987–8 (°*IGSK* 34–5).

**INikaia* = *Katalog der antiken Inschriften des Museums von Iznik (Nikaia)*. Teil I, II 1–2, S. Sahin, Bonn 1979–82 (°*IGSK* 9, 10 (1), (2)).

**Inschr.Hierap.* = *Inschriften aus Hierapolis-Kastabala*, M. Sayar, P. Siewert, H. Täuber, Vienna 1989.

*Inscr.Cret.*, add 'II *Tituli Cretae occidentalis;* III *Tituli Cretae orientalis;* IV *Tituli Gortynii*, M. Guarducci, Rome 1939–50.'

*Inscr.Délos*, at beginning insert 'nos. 1–88, ed. A. Plassart, Paris 1950; nos. 89–104.33, J. Coupry, Paris 1972'; add '(6 vols.)'

**Inscr.Dura* = *Inscriptions from Dura-Europos*, R. N. Frye et al. in *YClS* 14.127–213.

*Inscr.Gr. et Lat. de la Syrie*, v. °*IGLS*.

*Inscr.Perg.* add '8(3) = *Altertümer von Pergamon viii (3). Die Inschriften des Asklepieions*, Ch. Habicht, Berlin 1969'

**Inv.Inscr.Palm.* = *Inventaire des Inscriptions de Palmyre*, J. Cantineau, Beirut 1930.

**IPamph.* = *Le Dialecte grec de Pamphylie*, C. Brixhe, Paris 1976.

**IParion* = *Die Inschriften von Parion*, P. Frisch, Bonn 1983 (°*IGSK* 25).

**IPhilae* = *Les Inscriptions grecques de Philae*, A. and É. Bernand. I: *Époque ptolémaïque*, II: *Haut et Bas Empire*, Paris 1969.

**IPhrygie* = *Nouvelles Inscriptions de Phrygie*, T. Drew-Bear, Zutphen 1978.

**IPrusa ad Olympum* = *Die Inschriften von Prusa ad Olympum*, T. Carsten, Bonn 1991 (°*IGSK* 39).

**IPrusias* = *Die Inschriften von Prusias ad Hypium*, W. Ameling, Bonn 1985 (°*IGSK* 27).

**IRhod.Peraea* = *The Rhodian Peraea and Islands*, P. M. Fraser and G. E. Bean, Oxford 1954.

**ISalamis* = *The Greek and Latin Inscriptions from Salamis*, T. B. Mitford, I. K. Nicolaou, Nicosia 1974.

**ISelge* = *Die Inschriften von Selge*, J. Nollé, F. Schindler, Bonn 1991 (°*IGSK* 37).

**ISestos* = *Die Inschriften von Sestos und der thrakischen Chersones*, J. Krauss, Bonn 1980 (°*IGSK* 19).

**ISmyrna* = *Die Inschriften von Smyrna*, I, II (1), G. Petzl, Bonn 1982–90 (°*IGSK* 23, 24 (1)).

**IStraton.* = *Die Inschriften von Stratonikeia*, M. Sahin, Bonn 1981–90 (°*IGSK* 21, 22).

**ITomis* = *Inscriptiones Daciae et Scythiae minoris antiquae. Series altera: Inscriptiones Scythiae minoris Graecae et Latinae.* Vol. II: *Tomis et territorium*, I. Stoian, A. Suceveanu, Bucharest 1987.

**ITrall.* = *Die Inschriften von Tralleis und Nysa.* I: *Die Inschriften von Tralleis*, F. B. Poljakov, Bonn 1989 (°*IGSK* 36(1)).

**ITyr* = *Inscriptions grecques et latines découvertes dans les fouilles de Tyr* (1963–74), I: *Inscriptions de la nécropole*, J.-P. Rey-Coquais, Paris 1977.

**IUrb.Rom.* = *Inscriptiones Graecae urbis Romanae*, L. Moretti, Rome 1968–79 (3 vols., the second in two parts).

*Jeffery *LSAG* = L. H. Jeffery, *The Local Scripts of Archaic Greece*, Oxford 1961. Revised edition with a supplement, A. W. Johnston 1990.

**JRCil.* = *Journeys in Rough Cilicia*, G. E. Bean, T. B. Mitford, 1: *1962–1963*, Vienna 1965; 2: *1964–1968*, Vienna 1970.

**Kafizin* = *The Nymphaeum of Kafizin: The Inscribed Pottery*, T. B. Mitford, New York 1980.

*Kalinka *ADB* = E. Kalinka, *Antike Denkmäler in Bulgarien*, Vienna 1906.

**Kerameikos* = *Kerameikos: Ergebnisse der Ausgrabungen* Bd. 1–13 (Archäologisches Institut des Deutschen Reiches/ Deutsches Archäologisches Institut), W. Kraiker, K. Kübler et al., Berlin 1939–88.

*Kontorini *AER* 1, 2 = V. Kontorini, 1: *Inscriptions inédites relatives à l'histoire et aux cultes de Rhodes au 2ᵉ et au 1ᵉ s. av. J.-C.*, Louvain-la-Neuve/Providence 1983. 2: *Ανέκδοτες Επιγραφές Ρόδου*, Athens 1989.

**Kouklia-Paphos* = *Les Inscriptions syllabiques de Kouklia-Paphos*, O. Masson, T. B. Mitford, Constance 1986.

**Kourion* = *The Inscriptions of Kourion*, T. B. Mitford, Philadelphia 1971.

*Kretschmer *GV* = P. Kretschmer, *Griechische Vaseninschriften*, Gütersloh 1894 [Hildesheim 1969, Chicago 1980].

**La Carie* = *La Carie: Histoire et géographie historique avec le recueil des inscriptions antiques*, L. and J. Robert, II, Paris 1954.

*Lane *CMRDM* = E. R. Lane, *Corpus Monumentorum Religionis Dei Menis*, Leiden 1971–8 (4 vols.).

*Lang *Ath.Agora* xxi = *The Athenian Agora.* vol. xxi: *Graffiti and dipinti*, M. L. Lang, Princeton 1976.

**Laodicée* = *Laodicée de Lycos; Le nymphée: Campagnes 1961–1963*, J. Des Gagniers, etc., Paris 1969.

*Lefebvre *RIGC* = G. Lefebvre, *Recueil des inscriptions grecques chrétiennes de l'Égypte*, Cairo 1967.

**Leg.Sacr.* = *Leges Graecorum Sacrae* I–II, J. Prott, L. Ziehen, Leipzig 1896–1906.

**Lindos* = *Lindos: Fouilles et recherches 1902–1914*, Chr. Blinkenberg, K. F. Kinch, II: *Inscriptions*, Chr. Blinkenberg, Copenhagen 1941 (2 vols.).

*MAMA*, add 'vol. vii, W. M. Calder, Manchester 1956; vol. viii, W. M. Calder, J. M. R. Cormack, Manchester 1962; vol. ix, B. Levick et al., London 1988'

**Meiggs–Lewis* = R. Meiggs, D. M. Lewis, *A Selection of Greek Historical Inscriptions to the End of the 5th Century* B.C., Oxford 1969 [1988].

*Mitchell *N. Galatia* = S. Mitchell et al., *Regional Epigraphic Catalogues of Asia Minor.* II: *The Ankara District: The Inscriptions of North Galatia*, Oxford 1982.

*Mon.Anc.Gr.*, add '*Res gestae divi Augusti: Das Monumentum Ancyranum*, H. Volkmann³, Berlin 1969'

*Moretti *IAG* = L. Moretti, *Iscrizioni agonistiche greche*, Rome 1953.

*Moretti *ISE* = L. Moretti, *Iscrizioni storiche ellenistiche.* I: *Attica, Peloponneso, Beozia* (nos. 1–70). II: *Grecia centrale et settentrionale* (nos. 71–132), Florence 1967 and 1975.

*OGI*, add '[Hildesheim 1970]'

**Orac.Tiburt.* = *The Oracle of Baalbek: The Tiburtine Sibyl in Greek Dress*, P. J. Alexander, Dumbarton Oaks 1967.

*Peek *AV* = W. Peek, *Attische Versinschriften. Abhandlungen der Sächsischen Akademie der Wissenschaften zu Leipzig, Phil.-hist. Klasse*, 69 (1980).

*Pouilloux *Rhamnonte* = *La Forteresse de Rhamnonte: Étude de topographie et d'histoire*, J. Pouilloux, Paris 1954.

*Ramsay *The Social Basis* = W. M. Ramsay, *The Social Basis of Roman Power in Asia Minor*, Aberdeen 1941.

*Rémondon *Phoebammon* = R. Rémondon et al., *Le Monastère de Phoebammon dans la Thébaïde* (ed. Ch. Bachatly), II: *Graffiti, inscriptions et ostraca*, Cairo 1965.

*Reynolds *Aphrodisias* = J. M. Reynolds, R. Tannenbaum, *Jews and Godfearers at Aphrodisias: Greek Inscriptions with Commentary*, Cambridge 1987.

**RIB* = *The Roman Inscriptions of Britain*, I: *Inscriptions on Stone*, R. G. Collingwood, R. P. Wright, Oxford 1965; *Epigraphic Indexes to RIB* I, R. Goodburn, H. Waugh, Gloucester 1983; II: *Instrumentum domesticum.* 1: *Military Diplomata, Metal Ingots, Tesserae, Dies, Labels and Lead Sealings*, S. S. Frere et al., Gloucester 1990.

*Robert *ATAM* = L. Robert, *À travers l'Asie Mineure*, Paris 1980.

*Robert *Castabala* = L. Robert, *La Déesse de Hiérapolis Castabala (Cilicie)*, Paris 1964, (= *Bibl.Arch.Inst.Fr. Istanbul* 16).

*Robert *DAMM* = L. Robert, *Documents de l'Asie Mineure méridionale: Inscriptions, monnaies et géographie*, Paris 1966.

*Robert *Ét.épigr.* = L. Robert, *Études épigraphiques*, 1ère série, 2ᵉ série (Repr. of *BCH* 52, 60), Paris 1928–36.

*Robert *Hell.* = L. Robert, *Hellenica*, 1–13, Limoges 1940–65.

*Robert *Les Gladiateurs* = L. Robert, *Les Gladiateurs dans l'Orient grec*, Paris 1940 [1971].

*Robert *OMS* = L. Robert, *Opera minora selecta: Épigraphie et antiquités grecques*, vols. 1–7, Amsterdam 1969–90.

*Robert *Villes* = L. Robert, *Les Villes de l'Asie Mineure*, Paris 1962.

*Roueché *Aphrodisias* = C. Roueché and J. M. Reynolds, *Aphrodisias in Late Antiquity: The Late Roman and Byzantine Inscriptions, Including Texts from the Excavations at Aphrodisias, Conducted by K. T. Erim*, London 1989.

**Salamine* = *Salamine de Chypre* XIII. *Testimonia Salaminia* 2: *Corpus épigraphique*, J. Pouilloux et al., Paris 1987.

**Samothrace* = *Samothrace, Excavations Conducted by the Institute of Fine Arts, New York University*, K. Lehmann, vol. 2 (1): *The Inscriptions on Stone*, P. M. Fraser, New York 1960.

*Schwyzer*, add '[Hildesheim 1960]'

**SEG* = *Supp.Epigr.* in *LSJ*, q. v. (vols. 1–25, 1923–71); new series, H. W. Pleket, R. S. Stroud et al., vols. 26–36, Leiden, Amsterdam 1976–7 [1979]–1986 [1989].

**Side* = *Side Kitabeleri: The Inscriptions of Side*, G. E. Bean, Ankara 1965.

*SIG*, add '[Hildesheim 1960]'

**Sokolowski* 1, 2, 3, = F. Sokolowski, 1: *Lois sacrées de l'Asie Mineure*, Paris 1955; 2: *Lois sacrées des cités grecques. Supplément*, Paris 1962; 3: *Lois sacrées des cités grecques*, Paris 1969.

*Stoian *Tomitana* = I. Stoian, *Tomitana*, Bucharest 1962.

**Suppl.epigr.ciren.* = *Supplemento epigrafico cirenaico*, G. Pugliese Carratelli, D. Morelli, in *ASAA* N.S. 23–4 (1961/2), 218–375.

*Świderek *La Propriété foncière* = A. Świderek, *La Propriété foncière privée dans l'Égypte de Vespasien et sa technique agricole d'après PLond. 131'*, Wrocław 1960.

*TAM*, add 'vol. iii: *Tituli Pisidiae*, R. Heberdey, Vienna 1941; vol. iv (i): *Tituli Bithyniae. Paeninsula Bithynica*, F. K. Dörner, M. B. von Stritzky, Vienna 1978; vol. v (i): *Tituli Lydiae: Regio septentrionalis ad orientem vergens*, vol. v (ii): *Regio septentrionalis ad occidentem vergens*, P. Herrmann, Vienna 1981, 1989'

**Thasos* I, II = *Recherches sur l'histoire et les cultes de Thasos* (École française d'Athènes, Études thasiennes III, V): I, J. Pouilloux, Paris 1954; II, C. Dunant, J. Pouilloux, Paris 1958.

**Tit.Calymn.* = *Tituli Calymnii*, M. Segre, *ASAA* N.S. 6–7 (1944/5) [Bergamo 1952].

**Tit.Cam.* = *Tituli Camirenses*, M. Segre, I. Pugliese Carratelli, *ASAA* N.S. 27–9 (1949/51), 141–318, 30–2 (1952/4), 211–46.

*Ugolini *L'Acropoli di Butrinto* = L. M. Ugolini, *Albania antica;* vol. iii: *L'Acropoli di Butrinto*, Rome 1942.

*Vidman *SIS* = L. Vidman, *Sylloge inscriptionum religionis Isiacae et Sarapiacae*, Berlin 1969.

*Wiegand *Palmyra* = T. Wiegand, *Palmyra: Ergebnisse der Expeditionen von 1902 und 1917*, Berlin 1932.

*Wolters *Kabirenheiligtum* = P. Wolters, G. Bruns, *Das Kabirenheiligtum bei Theben* I, Berlin 1940 (Kap. IV: *Inschriften*).

**Xanthos* = *Fouilles de Xanthos*, VII: *Inscriptions d'époque impériale du Létôon*, A. Balland, Paris 1981.

# III. PUBLICATIONS OF PAPYRI & OSTRACA

*BGU*, for '1895–' read '1895–1983 (15 vols.), [1–9 Milan 1972])'

*BKT*, for '1904' read '1904–39 (8 vols.)'

**CPap.Jud.* = *Corpus Papyrorum Judaicarum*, V. A. Tcherikover, A. Fuks, M. Stern, Cambridge, Mass., 1957–64 (3 vols.).

*CPR*, for 'vol. i .. etc.' read '1895–1986 (10 vols.), [Milan 1974]'

*Διηγήσεις*, add 'v. index °I s.v. Call.*Dieg.*'

*Gallo *Fram.biogr.* = I. Gallo, *Frammenti biografici da papiri* I, II, Rome 1975, 1980.

**GLP* = *Greek Literary Papyri*, D. L. Page, vol. i, Loeb 1942[2]; vol. iii, Loeb 1950.

**Gr.Roman-Papyri* = *Griechische Roman-Papyri und verwandte Texte*, F. Zimmermann, Heidelberg 1936.

*Milne *GSM* = H. J. M. Milne, *Greek Shorthand Manuals, Syllabary and Commentary; ed. from Papyri and Waxed Tablets in the British Museum, and from the Antinoë Papyri in the Possession of the Egypt Exploration Society*, London 1934.

**MPER* = *Mitteilungen aus der Papyrussammlung der Nationalbibliothek in Wien* (*Papyrus Erzherzog Rainer*) N.S. Vienna 1932–.

**OAbu Mena* = *Griechische Ostraka aus Abu Mena*, D. Wortmann (= *ZPE* 8.41).

**OAmst.* = *Ostraka in Amsterdam Collections*, R. S. Bagnall, P. J. Sijpesteijn, K. A. Worp, Zutphen 1976.

**OAshm.Shelton* = *Greek Ostraca in the Ashmolean Museum from Oxyrhynchus and Other Sites*, J. C. Shelton, Florence 1988.

**OBodl.* = *Ostr.Bodl.* in *LSJ*, add 'II: *Ostraca of the Roman and Byzantine Periods*, J. G. Tait, C. Préaux, London 1955; III: *Indexes*, J. Bingen, M. Wittek, London 1964 (sts. referred to as *OTait*).'

*OCambridge*, see *OBodl.* I pp. 153–73.

**ODouch* = *Les Ostraca grecs de Douch*, H. Cuvigny, G. Wagner, Cairo 1986 (2 vols.).

**OFlorida* = *The Florida Ostraka. Documents from the Roman Army in Upper Egypt*, R. S. Bagnall, Durham N.C. 1976.

**OHeid.* = *Griechische Papyrusurkunden und Ostraka der Heidelberger Papyrussammlung*, P. Sattler, Heidelberg 1963 (nos. 225–48 papyri, 249–88 ostraca).

**OLeid.* = *Greek Ostraka: A Catalogue of the Collection of Greek Ostraka in the National Museum of Antiquities at Leiden*, R. S. Bagnall, P. J. Sijpesteijn, K. A. Worp, Zutphen 1980.

**OLund* = *Ostraka aus der Sammlung des Instituts für Altertumskunde an der Universität zu Lund*, Lund 1979.

**OMich.* = *Ostr.Mich.* in *LSJ*.

*OPetrie*, see *OBodl.* I pp. 82–152.

**OROM* = *Ostraka in the Royal Ontario Museum.* I: *Death and Taxes*, A. E. Samuel et al., Toronto 1971.

*Ostr.*, add 'now known as °*OWilck.*'

*OStrassb.* = *Ostr.Strassb.* in *LSJ*.

*Ostr.Bodl.*, add '= °*OBodl.* I'

**OTait* = °*OBodl.*

**OWilck.* = *Ostr.* in *LSJ*; repr. w. addenda by P. J. Sijpesteijn [Amsterdam 1970].

**PAbinn.* = *The Abinnaeus Archive: Papers of a Roman Officer in the Reign of Constantius II*, H. I. Bell et al., Oxford 1962.

*PAlex.*, add 'sts. referred to as *PAlex.Botti*'

**PAlex.* (1964) = *Papyrus grecs du Musée Gréco-Romain d'Alexandrie*, A. Świderek, M. Vandoni, Warsaw 1964 (nos. 1–40, pp. 47–79).

**PAmst.* = *Die Amsterdamer Papyri* I, R. P. Salomons et al., Zutphen 1980.

**PAnt.* = *The Antinoopolis Papyri*, C. H. Roberts et al., London 1950–67 (3 vols.).

**PApoll.* = *Papyrus grecs d'Apollônos Anô*, R. Rémondon, Cairo 1953.

**Pap.Brux.* (series) = *Papyrologica Bruxellensia*, Brussels 1962–. XVII: Pt. II, Textes inédits, 1979 (= *PCongr.* XV).

**Pap.Bub.* = *Die verkohlten Papyri aus Bubastos*, J. Frösén, D. Hagedorn, (*Pap.Colon* XV) 1990.

**Pap.Colon.* (series) = *Papyrologica Coloniensia*, Cologne/Opladen 1964–.

**Pap.Flor.* XIX = *Miscellanea Papyrologica*, M. Capasso et al., Florence 1990 (= *Papyrologica Florentina* XIX).

*PBaden*, add 'Heft 5, 1934, Heft 6, 1938'

**PBatav.* = *Textes grecques, démotiques et bilingues*, E. Boswinkel, P. W. Pestman, Leiden 1978. (= *Pap.Lugd.Bat* XIX).

**PBeatty Panop.* = *Papyri from Panopolis in the Chester Beatty Library, Dublin*, T. C. Skeat, Dublin 1964, also known as *PPanop.Beatty*.

**PBerl.Möller* = *Griechische Papyri aus dem Berliner Museum*, S. Möller, Gothenburg 1929 (= *SB* 7338–50).

**PBerl.Zill.* = *Vierzehn Berliner griechische Papyri*, H. Zilliacus, Helsinki 1941.

**PBodm.* = *Papyrus Bodmer* Cologny-Geneva 1954– : 29 *Vision de Dorothéos*, A. Hurst, O. Reverdin, J. Rudhardt, 1984 (see also *ZPE* 75.82 ff.).

**PBon.* = *Papyri Bononienses*, O. Montevecchi, Milan 1953.

**PBouriant* = *Les Papyrus Bouriant*, P. Collart, Paris 1926.

*PBremen*, add 'repr. in *Berliner Akademieschriften zur Alten Geschichte und Papyruskunde* II p. 193 ff. U. Wilcken, Leipzig 1970'

**PBrooklyn* = *Greek and Latin Papyri, Ostraca and Wooden Tablets in the Collection of the Brooklyn Museum*, John C. Shelton, (= *Papyrologica Florentina* XXII) 1992.

**PCair.Isidor.* = *The Archive of Aurelius Isidorus in the Egyptian Museum, Cairo, and the University of Michigan*, A. E. R. Boak, H. C. Youtie, Ann Arbor 1960.

*PCair.Zen.*, add 'vol V: O. Guéraud, P. Jouguet, Cairo 1940 nos. (59)801–(59)853 [Hildesheim 1971, all 5 vols.]'

**PCarlsberg* cited by inv. no. and publication.

**PCharite* = *Das Aurelia Charite Archiv*, K. A. Worp, Zutphen 1980.

**PCol.* = *Columbia papyri.* I: *Upon Slavery in Ptolemaic Egypt* (*PCol.* inv. 480), W. L. Westermann, New York 1929; VII: *Fourth-Century Documents from Karanis*, R. S. Bagnall, N. Lewis, Missoula 1979 (nos. 124–91).

*PColl.Youtie = *Collectanea Papyrologica: Texts Published in Honor of H. C. Youtie*, A. E. Hanson, Bonn 1975–6 (2 vols.).

*PCongr.* xv = *Pap.Brux.* XVII.

*PCornell*, add '[1972]; sts. cited by inv. no. and publication'

*PDura = *The Excavations at Dura-Europos Conducted by Yale University and the French Academy of Inscriptions and Letters. Final report V.* I: *The Parchments and Papyri*, C. B. Welles, R. O. Fink, J. F. Gilliam, New Haven 1959.

*PEdfou = *Tell Edfou 1937, 1938, 1939. Fouilles franco-polonaises. Les Papyrus et les ostraca grecs*, J. Manteuffel et al. (*Univ.Joseph Pilsudski de Varsovie. Institut français d'archéologie orientale du Caire. Fouilles franco-polonaises* I–III), Cairo 1937–50.

*PErasm. = *Papyri in the Collection of the Erasmus University* (Rotterdam), I P. J. Sijpesteijn, Ph. A. Verdult, Brussels 1986; II : Ph. A. Verdult, Amsterdam 1991.

*PErlangen = *Die Papyri der Universitätsbibliothek Erlangen*, W. Schubart, Leipzig 1942 (sts. referred to as *PErl.*).

*PFam.Teb. = *A Family Archive from Tebtunis*, B. A. van Groningen, Leiden 1950 (= *PLugd.Bat.* vi).

*PFouad = *Les Papyrus Fouad I* (*Publ. de la Soc. Fouad I de Papyrologie: Textes et documents* III), P. Jouguet, O. Guéraud et al., Cairo 1939 [Milan 1976].

*PFouad I Univ. = *Fuad I University Papyri*, D. S. Crawford (*Publ. de la Soc. Fouad I de Papyrologie: Textes et documents* VIII), Alexandria 1949 [Milan 1976].

*PFreib.*, add '1927, Abh. 7; repr. of the 3 vols. [Milan 1974]; vol. iv: *Griechische und demotische Papyri der Universitätsbibliothek Freiburg*, (nos. 45–75), R. W. Daniel, M. Gronewald, H. J. Thissen, Bonn 1986'

*PGen.*, add 'II *Textes littéraires et documentaires* nos. 82–117, C. Wehrli, Geneva 1986.'

*PGiss.*, for '1910–12' read '1910–22 [Milan 1973]'

*PGiss.Univ. v. ‡*PUniv.Giss.*

*PGoodsp.Cair.*, for 'Chicago 1904' read 'Chicago 1902 [Milan 1970] (sts. known as *PCair.Goodsp.*)'

*PHamb.*, add '[Milan 1973]; II: B. Snell et al., Hamburg 1954; III: B. Kramer, D. Hagedorn, Bonn 1984'

*PHaun. = *Papyri graecae Haunienses*. I: *Literarische Texte und ptolemäische Urkunden*, T. Larsen, Copenhagen 1942; II: *Letters and Mummy Labels from Roman Egypt*, A. Bülow-Jacobsen, Bonn 1981; III: *Subliterary Texts and Byzantine Documents from Egypt*, T. Larsen, A. Bülow-Jacobsen, Bonn 1985.

*PHeid.*, add 'N.F. III, P. Sattler, Heidelberg 1963'

*PHels. = *Papyri Helsingienses* I *Ptolemäische Urkunden*, J. Frösén et al., Helsinki 1986.

*PHerm. = *Papyri from Hermopolis and Other Documents of the Byzantine Period*, B. R. Rees, London 1964.

*PHib.*, add 'Part II, E. G. Turner, M.-Th. Lenger 1955 (nos. 172–284)'

*PIand.*, for '1912' read '1912–38 (8 vols.)'

*PIndiana Univ. = *Indiana University Papyri*, V. B. Schuman in *CPh.* 43 (1948) p. 110.

*PKöln = *Kölner Papyri*, B. Kramer et al., Cologne/Opladen 1976–87 (6 vols.).

*PKöln Ketouba = *La Ketouba de Cologne: Un contrat de mariage juif à Antinoopolis*, C. Sirat et al., Cologne/Opladen 1986 (= *Pap.Colon.* 12).

*PLaur. = *Papyri from the Biblioteca Medicea Laurenziana*, R. Pintaudi, Florence 1976–83 (4 vols.).

*PLeit. = *Leitourgia Papyri*, N. Lewis, Philadelphia 1963 (= *TAPhA* 53 pt. 9; repr. as *SB* 10192 ff.).

*PLille*, add 'sts. cited by inv. no. and publication'

*PLond.*, add 'VI: *Jews and Christians in Egypt*, H. I. Bell, 1924 [Milan 1973] (= *PLond.* 1912–29 in *LSJ*); VII: *The Zenon Archive*, T. C. Skeat, 1974'

*PLond.*, 1912–29, v. for eg.

*PLouvre cited by inv. no. and publication.

*PLugd.Bat. (series) = *Papyrologica Lugduno-Batava*, Leiden 1941–: I = *PWarren*; II = °*PVindob.Bosw.*; XI = °*PVindob.Sijp.*; XIII = *Papyri selectae*, E. Boswinkel, P. W. Pestman, P. J. Sijpesteijn, Leiden 1965; XVII = *Antidoron Martino David oblatum. Miscellanea papyrologica*, E. Boswinkel, B. A. van Groningen, P. W. Pestman, Leiden 1968; XIX = °*PBatav.*; XX = *Greek and Demotic Texts from the Zenon Archive*, P. W. Pestman, Leiden 1980; XXV = *Papyri, Ostraca, Parchments and Waxed Tablets in the Leiden Papyrological Institute*, F. A. J. Hoogendijk, P. Van Minnen et al., Leiden 1991.

*PLund = *Aus der Papyrussammlung der Universitätsbibliothek in Lund*, (6 vols.), Lund 1935–52.

*PMacquarie cited by inv. no. and publication.

*PMag.*, add 'K. Preisendanz, A. Henrichs T(S) 1973–4[2]'

*PMag.Lond.*, add '(= *PMag.* 5, 6, 7, etc.)'

*PMasp.*, add '(also known as *PCair.Masp.*)'

*PMed. = ‡*PMilan.*

*PMed.Rez. = *MPER* vol. xiii; H. Harrauer and P. J. Sijpesteijn, *Medizinische Rezepte und Verwandtes*, Vienna 1981.

*PMerton*, i, for '1939' read '1948'; add 'vol. ii, B. R. Rees, H. I. Bell, J. W. B. Barns, Dublin 1959; vol. iii, J. D. Thomas, London 1967 (= *BICS Suppl.* 18)'

*PMich.*, add '*PMich.* I: = *PMich.Zen.* q. v. (nos. 1–120); II: *Papyri from Tebtunis* I, (= *PMich.Teb.*) A. E. R. Boak, Ann Arbor 1933 (nos. 121–8); *A Papyrus Codex of the Shepherd of Hermas*, C. Bonner, Ann Arbor 1934 (nos. 129–30); III: *Miscellaneous Papyri*, J. G. Winter, Ann Arbor 1933 (nos. 131–221); V: *Papyri from Tebtunis* II, (= *PMich.Teb.*) E. M. Husselman et al., Ann Arbor 1944 (nos. 226–356); VIII: = *Papyri and Ostraka from Karanis* ii, H. C. Youtie, J. G. Winter, Ann Arbor 1951 (nos. 464–521); IX: = *Papyri from Karanis* III, E. M. Husselman, Cleveland 1971 (nos. 522–76); XI: J. C. Shelton, Toronto 1971 (nos. 603–25); XII: G. M. Browne, Toronto 1975 (nos. 626–58); XIII: *The Aphrodite Papyri in the Univ. of Michigan Papyrus Collection*, P. J. Sijpesteijn, Zutphen 1977; XIV: V. P. McCarren, Chico, Calif. 1980; XV: P. J. Sijpesteijn, Zutphen 1982. Also sts. cited by inv. no. and publication'

*PMichael. = *Papyri Michaelidae*, D. S. Crawford, Aberdeen 1955.

*PMich.Teb.*, v. °*PMich.* II and V.

*PMich.Zen.*, add 'now often known as *PMich.* I'

*PMilan.*, I, add '2nd. ed. S. Daris, Milan 1967; II: S. Daris, Milan 1966 (nos. 13–87); also known as *PMil.* or *PMed.*; sts. cited by inv. no. and publication'

*PMil.Vogl. = I: *Papiri della R. Università di Milano* I, A. Vogliano, Milan 1937 [Milan 1966]. (*PUniv.Milan* in *LSJ*). II–VI: *Papiri della Università degli Studi di Milano*, various editors, Milan 1961–77. VII: *La contabilità di un'azienda agricola nel ii sec. d. C.*, D. Foraboschi, Milan 1981.

*PMoen. cited by inv. no. and publication.

*PMon. = *Veröffentlichungen aus der kaiserlichen Hof- und Staatsbibliothek zu München* I: *Byzantinische Papyri*, A. Heisenberg, L. Wenger, Leipzig/Berlin 1914 [Stuttgart (T) 1986]; II: *Papiri letterari greci della Bayerische Staatsbibliothek di Monaco di Baviera*, A. Carlini et al., Stuttgart (T) 1986; III: *Griechische Urkundenpapyri der Bayerischen Staatsbibliothek München*, D. Hagedorn et al., Stuttgart (T) 1986.

*PNag.Ham. = *Nag Hammadi Codices. Greek and Coptic Papyri*

*from the Cartonnage of the Covers*, J. W. B. Barns, G. M. Browne, J. C. Shelton, Leiden 1981 (= *Nag Hammadi Studies* vol. xvi).

*PNess. = *Excavations at Nessana*, I: *Introductory Volume*, H. D. Colt 1962; II: *Literary Papyri*, L. Casson, E. L. Hettich, Princeton 1950; III: *Non-Literary Papyri*, C. J. Kraemer jr., Princeton 1958.

*PNew York = *Greek Papyri in the Collection of New York University*. I: *Fourth Century Documents from Karanis*, N. Lewis, Leiden 1967.

*POsl.*, for '1925' read '1925–1936 (3 vols.)' and add 'I: *Magical Papyri*, S. Eitrem, Oslo 1925 (1–6), II: S. Eitrem, L. Amundsen, Oslo 1931 (7–64), III: S. Eitrem, L. Amundsen, Oslo 1936 (65–200).'

*POxford = *Some Oxford Papyri*, E. P. Wegener, Leiden 1942–8 (2 vols.).

*POxy.Hels. = *Fifty Oxyrhynchus Papyri*, H. Zilliacus et al., Helsinki 1979.

*PPalau Rib. cited by inv. no. and publication.

*PPanop. = *Urkunden aus Panopolis*, L. C. Youtie et al., Bonn 1980 (republ. fr. three articles in *ZPE* 7, 8 and 10; sts. referred to as *PPanop.Köln*).

*PPetaus = *Das Archiv des Petaus*, U. and D. Hagedorn, H. C. and L. C. Youtie, Cologne/Opladen 1969.

*PPhilad. = *Papyrus de Philadelphie*, J. Scherer (*Publ. de la Soc. Fouad I de Papyrologie: Textes et documents*, vii), Cairo 1947.

*PPrag. = *Papyri Wessely Pragenses*, L. Varcl, published in *Listy filologické* and *SB*.

*PPrag. I = *Papyri Graecae Wessely Pragenses*, R. Pintaudi et al., Florence 1988.

*PRainer Cent. = *Festschrift zum 100jährigen Bestehen der Papyrussammlung der Österreichischen Nationalbibliothek: Papyrus Erzherzog Rainer*, Vienna 1983.

*PRein.*, add 'repr. vol. I [Milan 1972]; II: *Les Papyrus Théodore Reinach*, P. Collart, Cairo 1940'

*PRev.Laws*, add 're-edited by J. Bingen in *SB* Beiheft 1, Göttingen 1952'

*PRyl.* add 'vol. iv: *Documents of the Ptolemaic, Roman and Byzantine Periods*, C. H. Roberts, E. G. Turner, Manchester 1952 [1965]'

*PSAA = *Papyri Societatis Archaeologicae Atheniensis*, vol. i, G. A. Petropoulos, Athens 1939 [Milan 1972].

*PSakaon = *The Archive of Aurelius Sakaon: Papers of an Egyptian Farmer in the Last Century of Theadelphia*, G. M. Parássoglou, Bonn 1978. (v. ‡*PThead.*)

*PSarap. = *Les Archives de Sarapion et de ses fils*, J. Schwartz, Cairo 1961.

*PSelect. = *Papyri selectae*, E. Boswinkel et al., Leiden 1965 (= *PLugd.Bat.* XIII).

*PSI*, for '1912–' read '1912–79 (15 vols.)'

*PSorb. I = *Papyrus de la Sorbonne*, I, H. Cadell, Paris 1966.

*PSoterichos = *Das Archiv vov Soterichos*, Sayed Omar, Cologne/Opladen 1979 (= *Pap.Colon.* viii).

*PStrassb.*, add '[Leipzig 1969]. II–VIII: *Papyrus grecs de la Bibliothèque Nationale et Universitaire de Strasbourg*, P. Collomp, J. Schwartz et al., Paris 1948 (vol. ii), Strasburg 1963–83'

*PTeb.*, add 'iv: J. G. Keenan, J. C. Shelton, London 1976'

*PThead.*, add '[Milan 1974]. II: *Aus den Archiven von Theadelphia*, L. Varcl *LFil.* (1961) p. 37 (nos. 1–61 re-edited as °*PSakaon*)'

*PThmouis = *Le Papyrus Thmouis* I, *colonnes 68–160*, S. Kambitsis, Paris 1985.

*PUG = *Papiri dell' Università di Genova*. I: M. Amelotti, L. Zingale Migliardi, Milan 1974; II: L. Zingale Migliardi, Florence 1980 also sts. cited by inv. no. and publication.

*PUniv.Giss.*, for '1924' read '1924–39 (6 vols.); *Indices*, K. A. Worp 1975'

*PUniv.Milan.*, add 'see °*PMil.Vogl.*'

*PUps.Frid = *Ten Uppsala Papyri*, B. Frid, Bonn 1981.

*PVarsov.*, add '[Milan 1974];also known as *PVars.*'

*PVatic.Aphrod. = *I papiri Vaticani greci di Aphrodito*, R. Pintaudi, Vatican 1980.

*PVat.*, add 'also known as *PMarm.*'

*PVindob.Barbara cited by inv. no. and publication.

*PVindob.Bosw. = *Einige Wiener Papyri*, E. Boswinkel, Leiden 1942 (= *PLugd.Bat.* II).

*PVindob.Salomons = *Einige Wiener Papyri*, R. P. Salomons, Amsterdam 1976.

*PVindob.Sijp. = *Einige Wiener Papyri*, P. J. Sijpesteijn (= *PLugd.Bat.* XI), Leiden 1963.

*PVindob.Tandem = *Fünfunddreißig Wiener Papyri*, P. J. Sijpesteijn, K. A. Worp, Zutphen 1976.

*PVindob.Worp = *Einige Wiener Papyri*, K. A. Worp, Amsterdam 1972.

*PWarren*, add '*The Warren Papyri*, M. David et al., Leiden 1941 (= *PLugd.Bat.* I)'

*PWash.Univ. = *Washington University Papyri* I, V. B. Schuman, Missoula 1980 (= *ASP* 17).

*PWisc. = *The Wisconsin Papyri*, P. J. Sijpesteijn, vols. I and II; Leiden 1967 (= *PLugd.Bat.* XVI), Zutphen 1977 (= *Stud.Amst.* XI).

*PWürzb.*, add 'repr. in *Berliner Akademieschriften zur Alten Geschichte und Papyruskunde* II, U. Wilcken, pp. 43–164, Leipzig 1970'

*P. XV Congr. = *Actes du XV^e Congrès International de Papyrologie* II: *Papyrus inédits* (*Papyrologica Bruxellensia* 17), Brussels 1979.

*PYale = *Yale Papyri in the Beinecke Library*, I, J. F. Oates, A. E. Samuel, C. B. Welles, New Haven/Toronto 1967 (= *ASP* 2).

*PYale Inv. = Yale papyri, cited by inv. no.

*PZen.Col.*, add 'vol. ii, W. L. Westermann et al., 1940 [Milan 1973] (= *PCol.* iv)'

*PZen.Pestm. = *Greek and Demotic Texts from the Zenon Archive*, P. W. Pestman, Leiden 1980 (= *PLugd.Bat.* xx).

*SB = *Sammelb.*, q. v., add 'VI–XVIII, E. Kiessling et al., Wiesbaden 1958–93'

*Schubart *Gr.Lit.Pap.* = W. Schubart, *Griechische literarische Papyri*, Berlin 1950.

*Stud.Pal.*, for '1901' read '1901–24 (23 vols.) [Amsterdam 1965–83]'

*Suppl.Mag. = *Supplementum magicum*. I: R. W. Daniel, F. Maltomini, Cologne/Opladen 1990 (= *Pap.Colon.* xvi.1).

*UPZ* II, for '1935' read 'Berlin 1935–57'

*Youtie *Scriptiunculae* = H. C. Youtie, *Scriptiunculae posteriores*, Bonn 1981 (2 vols.).

# IV. PERIODICALS

*AA = *Archäologischer Anzeiger* in *Jahrbuch des Deutschen Archäologischen Instituts* (*JDAI*) until 1982, then published separately, Berlin 1886– (*Arch.Anz.* in *LSJ*).

*AArch.Syr. = *Annales archéologiques de Syrie*, Damascus 1951–.

*AAWW = *Anzeiger der Österr.Akad. der Wissenschaften in Wien, Phil.-Hist.Klasse*, Vienna 1864–.

*ABSA = *Annual of the British School at Athens*, London 1895– (*BSA* in *LSJ*).

*AC = *L'Antiquité Classique*, Brussels 1932–.

*AD = *Ἀρχαιολογικὸν Δελτίον*, Athens 1915– (*Ἀρχ.Δελτ.* in *LSJ*).

*AE = *Ἀρχαιολογικὴ Ἐφημερίς*, Athens 1910– (*Ἀρχ.Ἐφ.* in *LSJ*).

*AEM = *Archäologisch-epigraphische Mitteilungen aus Österreich(-Ungarn)*, Vienna 1877–.

*AGWG = *Abhandlungen der Gesellschaft der Wissenschaften zu Göttingen*, Berlin 1843–.

*AHDO = *Archives d'histoire du droit oriental*, Brussels 1937–.

*AION(A) = *Annali dell'Istituto Universitario orientale di Napoli. Sezione di archeologia e storia antica*, Rome.

*AIPhO = *Annuaire de l'Institut de Philologie et d'Histoire Orientales et Slaves de l'Univ. Libre de Bruxelles*. Brussels 1932–.

*AJPh = *American Journal of Philology*, Baltimore 1880–.

*Anagennesis = *Ἀναγέννησις*, Athens 1981–.

*Anatolia = *Anatolia*, Inst. of Archaeol., Ankara Univ. 1956–.

*AncSoc = *Ancient Society*, Leuven 1970–.

*Ann.Mus.Gr.-R. d'Alex. = *Annuaire du Musée gréco-romain d'Alexandrie*, 1932–.

*APAW = *Abhandlungen der Preußischen Akademie der Wissenschaften*, Berlin (v. *Abh.Berl.Akad.* in *LSJ*).

*APF = *Archiv für Papyrusforschung und verwandte Gebiete*, T 1900– (*Arch.Pap.* in *LSJ*).

*AR = *Archaeological Reports*. Council of the Society for Hellenic Studies. The Management Committee of the British School of Archaeology at Athens, London 1959/1960–.

*Arch.Class. = *Archeologia classica*, Rome 1949–.

*ARW = *Archiv für Religionswissenschaft*, Leipzig 1943–.

*AS = *Anatolian Studies*, Journal of the British Institute of Archaeology at Ankara, London 1951– (*Anat.St.* in *LSJ*).

*ASAA = *Annuario della Scuola Archeologica di Atene e delle Missioni Italiane in Oriente*, Rome N.S. 1939–.

*ASAE = *Annales du Service des Antiquités de l'Égypte*, Cairo 1900– (*Annales du Service* in *LSJ*).

*ASMG = *Atti e Memorie della Società Magna Grecia*, Rome 1925–32, N.S. 1954–.

*ASNP = *Annali della Scuola Normale Superiore di Pisa, Classe di lettere e filosofia*, Pisa Serie III 1971–.

*Athenaeum = *Athenaeum. Studi periodici di letteratura e storia dell'antichità*, Pavia N.S. 1923–.

*BASO = *Bulletin of the American Schools of Oriental Research in Jerusalem and Baghdad*, Cambridge, Mass. 1919–.

*BASP = *Bulletin of the American Society of Papyrologists* New York, Columbia Univ. 1963/4–.

*BCAR = *Bullettino della Commissione Archeologica Comunale di Roma*, Rome 1872–. (*Bull.Comm.Arch.Com.* in *LSJ*).

*BCH*, add 'suppl. 8 = *Supplément* VIII*: Recueil des inscriptions chrétiennes de Macédoine du IIIe au VIe siècle*, D. Feissel, Paris 1983; suppl. 9 = *Supplément* IX*: L'antre corycien* II, Paris 1984 (ch. viii *Inscriptions*, J.-Y. Empereur)'

*BCO = *Bibliotheca Classica Orientalis*, Berlin 1956–.

*BCTH = *Bulletin archéologique du Comité des Travaux historiques et scientifiques*, Paris 1883–.

*BE = *Bulletin épigraphique* in *Revue des études grecques*, (*REG*; also sts. bound separately) 1938–.

*Belleten = *Türk tarih Kurumu, Belleten*, Ankara 1937–.

*Berytus = *Berytus*, Archaeological Studies published by the Museum of Archaeology of the American University of Beirut, Copenhagen 1934–.

*BICS = *Bulletin of the Institute of Classical Studies of the University of London*, London 1954–.

*BIFAO = *Bulletin de l'Institut Français d'Archéologie Orientale*, Cairo 1901– (*Bull.Inst.Franç.* in *LSJ*).

*BMB = *Bulletin du Musée de Beyrouth*, Paris 1937–.

*BSAA = *Bulletin de la Société Archéologique d'Alexandrie*, Alexandria 1898– (*Bull.Soc.Alex.* in *LSJ*).

*Byzantion = *Byzantion: Revue internationale des études byzantines*, Brussels 1924–.

*CE = *Chronique d'Égypte*, Brussels 1925–.

*Chiron = *Chiron: Mitteilungen der Kommission für alte Geschichte und Epigraphik des Deutschen Archäologischen Instituts*, Munich 1971–.

*CPh = *Classical Philology*, Chicago 1906– (*Class.Phil.* in *LSJ*).

*CPhil. = *Cahiers de philologie*, Lille 1976–.

*CRAI = *Comptes rendus de l'Académie des Inscriptions et Belles-Lettres* (cited by year; *CRAcad.Inscr.* in *LSJ*), Paris 1857–.

*CRIPEL = *Cahiers de recherches de l'Institut de Papyrologie et d'Égyptologie de Lille III*, Lille 1976–.

*CronArch = *Cronache di archeologia e di storia dell'arte*, Catania 1962–.

*Dacia*, add '48; N.S. Académie de la République populaire roumaine, Institut d'Archéologie, 1957–'

*DAW = *Denkschriften der Akademie der Wissenschaften in Wien*, Vienna 1850– (*Wiener Denkschr.* in *LSJ*).

*DOP = *Dumbarton Oaks Papers*, Cambridge, Mass. 1941–.

*EA = *Epigraphica Anatolica; Zeitschrift für Epigraphik und historische Geographie Anatoliens*, Bonn 1983–.

*EAC = *Études d'archéologie classique*, Paris 1955–.

*EHBS = *Ἐπετηρὶς Ἑταιρείας Βυζαντινῶν Σπουδῶν*. Athens.

*Emerita = *Emerita: Revista de lingüística y filología clásica*, Madrid 1933–.

*EPap = *Études de papyrologie*, Cairo 1932– (*Ét. de Pap.* in *LSJ*).

*Epigraphica = *Epigraphica*, Milan 1939–.

*GGA = *Göttingische gelehrte Anzeigen* (cited by year; *Gött. gel.Anz.* in *LSJ*).

*Gnomon = *Gnomon*, Berlin/Munich, 1925–.

*GRBS = *Greek, Roman and Byzantine Studies*, Durham, N.C. 1958–.
*Hellenica = *Ἑλληνικά: φιλολ., ἱστορ. καὶ λαογρ. περιοδικὸν σύγγραμμα τῆς Ἑταιρείας Μακεδονικῶν Σπουδῶν*, Thessalonica 1953–.
*HThR = *Harvard Theological Review*, Cambridge Mass. 1908– (*Harv.Theol.Rev.* in *LSJ*).
*IEJ = *Israel Exploration Journal*, Jerusalem 1950–.
*JA = *Journal asiatique*, Paris 1822–.
*JDAI = *Jahrbuch des Deutschen Archäologischen Instituts*, 1886– (*Jahrb.* in *LSJ*).
*JJP = *Journal of Juristic Papyrology*, Warsaw 1946–.
*JÖAI = *Jahreshefte des Österreichischen Archäologischen Instituts in Wien*, Vienna 1898– (*Jahresh.* in *LSJ*).
*JÖByz = *Jahrbuch der Österreichischen Byzantinischen Gesellschaft*, Verlag der Österr. Akad. der Wissenschaften, Vienna 1951–.
*JS = *Journal des savants*, Paris 1679–.
*JThS = *Journal of Theological Studies*, London 1900–57, Oxford 1958–.
*JWI = *Journal of the Warburg and Courtauld Institutes*, London 1937–.
*Kadmos = *Kadmos. Zeitschrift für vor- und frühgriechische Epigraphik*, Berlin 1962–.
*LFil. = *Listy filologické*, Prague 1874–1951, 1953–.
*Macedonica = *Μακεδονικά: σύγγραμμα περιοδικὸν τῆς Ἑταιρείας Μακεδονικῶν Σπουδῶν*, Thessalonica 1940–.
*MDAI(A) = *Mitteilungen des Deutschen Archäologischen Instituts (Athenische Abteilung)*, Berlin 1876–. (*Ath.Mitt.* in *LSJ*).
*MDAI(I) = *Mitteilungen des Deutschen Archäologischen Instituts (Istanbul Abteilung)*.
*MDAI(R) = *Mitteilungen des Deutschen Archäologischen Instituts (Römische Abteilung)*, 1886– (*Röm.Mitt.* in *LSJ*).
*MEFR = *Mélanges d'archéologie et d'histoire de l'école française de Rome*, Rome/Paris 1881– (= *Mél. de l'éc.fr. de Rome* in *LSJ*).
*MH = *Museum Helveticum*, Basel 1944–.
*Mnemosyne: *Bibliotheca Classica Batava*, Leiden 4th Ser. 1948– (older series: *Mnemos.* in *LSJ*).
*MUB = *Mélanges de l'Université Saint-Joseph*, Beirut 1906–. (= *Mélanges Beyrouth* in *LSJ*).
*Muséon = *Muséon: Revue d'études orientales*, Louvain(-la-Neuve) 1882–.
*NC = *Numismatic Chronicle*, London 1838–.
*NGG = *Nachrichten von der Gesellschaft der Wissenschaften zu Göttingen.* (cited by year; *Gött.Nachr.* in *LSJ*).
*OA = *Opuscula Archaeologica, Acta Instituti Romani Regni Sueciae*, Lund 1935–.
*OMRL = *Oudheidkundige Mededelingen uit het Rijksmuseum van Oudheden te Leiden*, Leiden 1909–.
*Orientalia = *Orientalia: commentarii trimestres editi a Facultate Studiorum Orientis Antiqui Pontificii Instituti Biblici*, Rome 1920–.
*PAAH = *Πρακτικὰ τῆς ἐν Ἀθήναις Ἀρχαιολογικῆς Ἑταιρείας*, Athens 1872–.
*PalEQ = *Palestine Exploration Quarterly*, London 1869–.
*PASA = *Papers of the American School of Classical Studies at Athens*, Boston 1882–97. (= *Papers of Amer. School at Athens* in *LSJ*).
*PBA = *Proceedings of the British Academy*, London 1903–.
*PP = *La parola del passato*, Naples 1946–.
*Philol.*, add 'suppl. = *Supplementband*'
*Phoenix = *Phoenix: The Journal of the Classical Association of Canada*, Toronto 1946–.
*QAL = *Quaderni di archeologia della Libia*, Rome 1950–.
*QIFG = *Quaderni dell' Istituto di Filologia Greca (Università di Cagliari)*.
*RA = *Revue archéologique*, Paris N.S. 1966– (= *Rev.Arch.* in *LSJ*).
*RAL = *Rendiconti della Classe di Scienze morali, storiche e filologiche dell'Accademia Nazionale dei Lincei*, Rome 1892–.
*REA = *Revue des études anciennes*, Paris 1899–.
*Rec.Pap. = *Recherches de papyrologie*, Paris 1961–.
*REG = *Revue des études grecques*, Paris 1888– (*Rev.Ét.Gr.* in *LSJ*).
*RFIC = *Rivista di filologia e d'istruzione classica*, Turin 1873– (*Riv.Fil.* in *LSJ*).
*RIDA = *Revue internationale des droits de l'antiquité*, Brussels 1952–.
*RN = *Revue numismatique*, Paris 1838–.
*RPh. = *Revue de philologie.* 3rd series 1927– (= *Rev.Phil.* in *LSJ*).
*SAWW = *Sitzungsberichte der Österreichischen Akademie der Wissenschaften in Wien*, Vienna 1849– (*Wien.Sitzb.* in *LSJ*).
*SCO = *Studi classici et orientali*, Pisa 1951–.
*SDAW = *Sitzungsberichte der Deutschen Akademie der Wissenschaften zu Berlin. Klasse für Philosophie, Geschichte, Staats-, Rechts- und Wirtschaftswissenschaften*, Berlin 1948–68.
*SHAW = *Sitzungsberichte der Heidelberger Akademie der Wissenschaften*, Heidelberg 1910–.
*SIFC = *Studi italiani di filologia classica*, Florence N.S. 1920– (*Stud.Ital.* in *LSJ*).
*SO = *Symbolae Osloenses*, Oslo 1922–.
*SPAW = *Sitzungsberichte der (Königlich) Preußischen Akademie der Wissenschaften*, Berlin 1882–1938 (*Berl.Sitzb.* in *LSJ*).
*TAPhA = *Transactions of the American Philological Association*, Cleveland, Ohio 1869– (*Trans.Am.Phil.Ass.* in *LSJ*).
*T&MByz = *Travaux et mémoires: Centre de recherches d'histoire et de civilisation byzantines*, Paris 1965–.
*Tyche = *Tyche: Beiträge zur alten Geschichte, Papyrologie und Epigraphik*, Vienna 1986–.
*VDI = *Vestnik drevnej istorii*, Moscow 1938–.
*WJA = *Würzburger Jahrbücher für die Altertumswissenschaft*, Würzburg 1946–, N.F. 1975–.
*WS = *Wiener Studien. Zeitschrift für klassische Philologie und Patristik*, Vienna 1879– (*Wien.Stud.* in *LSJ*).
*YClS = *Yale Classical Studies*, New Haven 1928– (*Yale Class. Studies* in *LSJ*).
*ZNTW = *Zeitschrift für die Neutestamentliche Wissenschaft und die Kunde der älteren Kirche*, Berlin 1902–.
*ZPE = *Zeitschrift für Papyrologie und Epigraphik*, Bonn 1967–.
*ZVS = *Zeitschrift für vergleichende Sprachforschung*, Berlin 1851–.

# V. GENERAL LIST OF ABBREVIATIONS

*abbrev. = abbreviation, abbreviated.
*abst. = abstract.
*_ACO_ = _Acta Conciliorum Oecumenicorum_, E. Schwartz, Berlin/Leipzig 1924–.
*add. = addenda.
*advl. = adverbial.
*Akkad. = Akkadian.
*_An.Boiss._, v. Anecdota Graeca in index °I.
*Anon.astr. = Anonymus astrologus.
*_Anon.in Herc._ = Scriptor Epicureus incertus, v. index °I s.v. Epicurus.
*Anon._Intr.Arat._ = Anonymi _Introductio in Aratum_ in _Commentariorum in A. reliquiae_, v. index °I s.v. Aratus.
*_Anth.Lyr._ = _Anthologia Lyrica Graeca_, E. Diehl, T(L) 1925; ed. 3, vol. i: fasc. 1–3, 1949–52; ed. 2, vol. ii: 1952.
_Apoc._, add 'v. Novum Testamentum'
*app. = apparently.
*Arg.Men., v. index °I s.v. Menander.
*arith. = in arithmetic.
*_ASP_ = _American Studies in Papyrology._
*assim. = by assimilation.
*astron. = in astronomy, astronomical.
*attrib. = attributed, attribution.
_BCH_, for '_BCH Suppl._' v. index °IV.
*_BE_ = _Bulletin epigraphique_ in _REG_ (v. index °IV); cited by volume of _REG_ and no. of Bulletin.
*Bile _Dial.crét._ v. index °II.
*Boll _Sphaera_, v. Teucer Babylonius in index I.
*_c._ = circa.
*_CAlG_ = _Collection des anciens alchimistes grecs_, P. E. M. Berthelot, Paris 1888 [Holland Press 1963, Osnabrück 1967].
*_CGFP_ = _Comicorum Graecorum Fragmenta in Papyris reperta_, C. Austin, Berlin 1973.
*_CGL_ = _Corpus Glossariorum Latinorum._
*chem. = in chemistry.
*Chr. = Christian.
*_CID_ v. index °II.
*_CIRB_ v. index °II.
*cl. = clause.
*_CML_ = _Corpus Medicorum Latinorum_, Leipzig/Berlin 1915–.
_Coll.Alex._, add '[1970]'
*colloq. = colloquial.
*comm. = commentary, commentator.
*concr. = concrete.
*Copt. = Coptic.
*corr. = correction.
*_CPap.Jud._ v. index °III.
*cpd. = compound.
*def. = definition.
*_Demioprata_ v. index °I.
*dial. = dialectal, in dialects.
*_Dieg._, v. Callimachus in index °I.
*Diller _Trad.min.Gr.geogr._ = A. Diller, _The Tradition of the Minor Greek Geographers_, American Philological Association 1952.
*dissim. = by dissimilation.
*dist. = distinguished.
*_EAM_ v. °index II.
*_EG_ = _Epigrammata graeca_, D. L. Page (OCT) 1975 [_EG_ .. P.].
*_EGF_ = _Epicorum Graecorum Fragmenta_, M. Davies, Göttingen 1988 [_EGF_ p. .. D.]'
*eleg. = elegist, elegiac.
*Epiph.Const. v. Epiphanius Constantiensis in index °I.
*epist. = epistola (epistle, letter).
_Epistolographi_, add '[Amsterdam 1965]'
*expr. = expressing.
*_FGE_ = _Further Greek Epigrams_, D. L. Page, Cambridge 1981.
_FGrH_, for 'Berlin 1923–' read 'Berlin 1923–9, Leiden 1926–58 [1954–60] (3 parts in 17 vols.); J. (= Jacoby) in Suppl. refers to this work'
*fig. = figurative(ly).
*foll. = following.
*_Fr.Lex._, v. Fragment in index °I.
*_Fr.Ps.Gr._ = _Fragmenta Pseudepigraphorum quae supersunt Graeca_, A. M. Denis, Leiden 1970.
*_Fs.Theocharis_ = _Διεθνές συνέδριο για την Αρχαία Θεσσαλία στη μνήμη του Δημήτρη Ρ.Θεοχάρη_, Athens 1992.
*funer. = funerary.
*_GDRK_ = _Die griechischen Dichterfragmente der römischen Kaiserzeit_, E. Heitsch, Göttingen 1963–4$^{2}$ (2 vols.).
*_GLP_, v. index °III.
*_GCS_ = _Die griechischen christlichen Schriftsteller der ersten drei Jahrhunderte_, Leipzig 1897–.
*_GVAK_, v. index ‡II.
*_HE_ v. Anthologia Graeca in index °I.
*Hellen. = Hellenistic.
*_IEG_ = _Iambi et elegi graeci ante Alexandrum cantati_, M. L. West, Oxford 1971–2 (2 vols.), 1989 (vol. 1$^{2}$), 1992 (vol. 2$^{2}$).
*_IGC_, v. index °II.
*_IGSK_, v. index °II.
*incl. = including.
*_Ind.Lect.Rost._ = _Index Lectionum in Academia Rostochiensi._
*inv. = inventory.
*iron. = ironically.
*_JRCil._ v. index °II.
*_Kafizin_, v. index °II.
*_Lapid.Gr._ = _Les Lapidaires de l'antiquité et du moyen âge._ Tome II: _Les Lapidaires grecs_, F. de Mély, C. É. Ruelle, Paris 1898.
*Lcn. = Lucianus interpres, v. index °I.
*lit.crit. = in literary criticism.
*Locr. = Locrian.
*_LW_ v. _LF_ in index II.
*Maced. = Macedonia(n).
*meton. = metonymical(ly).
*mil. = military.
*Miller _Mélanges_ v. Etymologicum Genuinum in index °I.
*_MPER_ v. index III.
*Myc. = Mycenaean.

*NWGk. = North-West Greek.
*obj. = object.
*onomat. = onomatopoeic.
*O.Pers. = Old Persian.
*Orat.Att.*, for '1839' read '1845'; add '[Hildesheim 1967]'
*ostr. = ostracon. (For *Ostr.* v. index III).
*parenth. = parentheses.
*Paroemiographi*, add '[Hildesheim 1958; w. Suppl., L. Cohn et al., Hildesheim 1961]'
**PCG* 2, 3(2), 4, 5, 7 = *Poetae comici Graeci*, R. Kassel, C. Austin, Berlin/New York: II: Agathenor–Aristonymus, 1991; III 2: Aristophanes, 1984; IV: Aristophon–Crobylus, 1983; V: Damoxenus–Magnes, 1986; VII: Menecrates–Xenophon, 1989.
**PEG* = *Poetarum epicorum Graecorum testimonia et fragmenta* 1, A. Bernabé, T(L) 1987.
*pers.n. = personal name.
**PG*, **PL* = *Patrologiae cursus completus, series Graeca*, J.-P. Migne, Paris 1857–68 (162 vols.); *Patrologiae cursus completus, series Latina*, J.-P. Migne, Paris 1844–55 (221 vols).
**PGR* = *Paradoxographorum Graecorum reliquiae*, A. Giannini, Milan 1965.
*phr. = phrase.
**Physici* = *Physici et medici Graeci minores*, J. L. Ideler, Berlin 1841–2 [Amsterdam 1963] (2 vols.).
**PMG* = *Poetae Melici Graeci*, D. L. Page, Oxford 1962 [1967].
**PMGF* = *Poetarum Melicorum Graecorum Fragmenta*, M. Davies, Oxford 1991.
**Poliorc.* v. Poliorcetici in index °I.
*pr. = preface.
*pred. = predicate, predicative.
*presum. = presumably.
*prolog. = prologus, prologue.
**PSI*, v. ‡index III.
*Pyth. or Pythag. = Pythagoras, Pythagorean.
**Pyth.Hell.* = *The Pythagorean Texts of the Hellenistic Period*, H. Thesleff, Åbo 1965.
*quot(s). = quotation(s).
*redupl. = reduplicated.
*ref. = reference.
*repr. = reprint(ed).
*republ. = republished.
rest., add 'restored'
*rev. = revised.
*Rhod. = Rhodian.
**RIB* v. index °II.
*Rom.imp. = (of) Roman imperial (date).
**Salamine*, v. index °II.
Sch., add 'Sch.Gen.Il., Sch.min.Il., etc, v. Homerus in index °I.'
Sext., v. Vetus Testamentum A in index I.
*sim. = similar.
**SLG* = *Supplementum Lyricis Graecis. Poetarum Lyricorum Graecorum fragmenta quae recens innotuerunt*, D. L. Page, Oxford 1974.
Sm., v. Vetus Testamentum A in index I.
**Socr.Rel.* = *Socraticorum reliquiae*, G. Giannantoni, Rome 1983–5 (4 vols.).
*Sophocles *Greek Lexicon* = E. A. Sophocles, *Greek Lexicon of the Roman and Byzantine Period (146 BC–1100 AD)*, New York 1887 [1951].
*sp. = spelling, spelt.
*spec. = specific(ally).
*subscr. = in subscriptione.
**Suppl.Hell.* = *Supplementum Hellenisticum*, H. Lloyd-Jones, P. J. Parsons, Berlin 1983.
*Syr. = Syrus interpres, v. Vetus Testamentum in index °I.
*tab.defix. = tabella(-ae) defixionis. (For *Tab.Defix.* v. index II).
*Taillardat *Images* = J. Taillardat, *Les Images d'Aristophane: Études de langue et de style*, Paris 1965.
*transf. = (in) transferred (sense).
*transl. = translating, translation of.
**TrGF* 1, 2, 3, 4 = *Tragicorum Graecorum fragmenta.* 1: *Didascaliae tragicae, catalogi tragicorum et tragoediarum, testimonia et fragmenta tragicorum minorum*, B. Snell, Göttingen 1971; *Ed. correctior et addendis aucta*, R. Kannicht, Göttingen 1986. 2: *Fragmenta adespota. Testimonia volumini 1 addenda. Indices ad volumina 1 et 2*, R. Kannicht, B. Snell, Göttingen 1981. [*Trag.adesp.* .. K.–S.] 3: *Aeschylus*, S. Radt, Göttingen 1985. 4: *Sophocles*, S. Radt (frr. 730a–g edidit R. Kannicht), Göttingen 1977.
*unexpld. = unexplained.
*unkn. = unknown.
*unpubl. = unpublished.
*van Brock *Vocab.medic.* = N. van Brock, *Recherches sur le vocabulaire médical du grec ancien*, Paris 1961.
*var. = variant (of).
*vbs. = verbs.
**Vit.*, for 'Anon. *Vit.Arist.*' and some other refs. containing '*Vit.*' see Diogenes Laertius.
*Vorsokr.*, substitute '*Vorsokr.*$^7$ = *Die Fragmente der Vorsokratiker*$^7$, H. Diels, W. Kranz, Berlin (Weidmann) 1954$^7$ (3 vols.)'
*w. = with.
*wd. = word.
*WGk. = West Greek.
*WIon. = West Ionic.
*Youtie *Scriptiunculae*, v. index °III.

# A

**ἀ- III**, delete ‘v. *ἀδάκρυτος*’

+**ἀάατος**, *ον*, (*ἀαάω*), in Il. ∪−−∪, in Od., A.R. ∪−∪∪, *admitting no error, infallible, νῦν μοι ὄμοσσον ἀ. Στυγὸς ὕδωρ* Il. 14.271; *τόξα .. μνηστήρεσσιν ἄεθλον ἀάατον* Od. 21.91, 22.5. **II** *invincible, κάρτος ἀάατος* A.R. 2.77.

**ἀᾱγής**, for ‘*hard*’ read ‘*unbreakable*’

**ἀάζω**, after ‘Arist.’ insert ‘*Mete.* $367^{b}2$’

**ἄαπτος**, omit ‘cf. *ἀπτοεπής*’

**ἆᾱς**, for ‘*ἀές*’ read ‘*ἄες*’

**ἀασιφρονία**, after ‘*folly*’ insert ‘Apollon.*Lex.*’

*__ἀάτη__, *ἡ*, v. °*ἄτη*.

*__ἄϝατι__, v. °*ἄβατι*.

**ἀβάθματα**, place after *ἀβαθής*.

+**ἀβᾰκέω**, (‡*ἀβακής*), *take no heed, οἱ δ’ ἀβάκησαν πάντες· ἐγὼ δέ μιν οἴη ἀνέγνων τοῖον ἐόντα* Od. 4.249.

**ἀβᾰκής**, delete ‘(*βάζω*) *speechless .. gentle*’ and substitute ‘*undisturbed*’; for ‘Sapph. 72’ read ‘Sapph. 120 L.-P.’

**ἀβάκητον**, after ‘Hsch.’ insert ‘(*ἀβάκτητον* La.)’

**ἀβᾰκιον 1 a**, add ‘Ammon.*Diff.* 1’ **b**, for ‘Plu.*Cat.Mi.* 90’ read ‘Plu.*Cat.Mi.* 70’ add ‘**c** *kneading-board, μάκτρα· ἀ. ἔνθα μάσσουσι τὸ ἄλευρον* Hsch.; cf. °*ἀβακίτης*.’ add ‘**4** *dish*, *PCair.Zen.* 71.1 (-*ειον*, iii BC).’

**ἀβᾰκίσκος**, for ‘*stone for inlaying*’ read ‘*panel*’ and add ‘(v. *REG* 80.325ff.)’

*__ἀβᾰκίτης__, *ὁ*, *dough-kneader*, *SEG* 33.1165 (Side, iii AD); cf. °*ἀβάκιον* 1 c.

*__ἄβᾰκος__, *ὁ*, *counting-board, abacus*, *OBodl.* i.262 (ii BC); cf. Lat. *abacus.*

*__ἀβάκτης__, *ὁ*, indecl., fr. Lat. *ab actis, records clerk*, *PFlor.* 71.509 (iv AD), *ἀβάκτις* *SB* 9106.3 (v AD).

**ἄβακτον**, delete the entry.

*__ἄβακτος__, *ον*, *ἄβακτον καὶ ἄβυκτον· τὸν μὴ μακαριστόν· Δωριεῖς δὲ τὸν ἀνεπίπληκτον καὶ ἀμεμφῆ* *AB* 323, Phot. α 24 Th.

**ἀβάκχευτος**, delete ‘generally .. Prose’; for ‘*Lap.*’ read ‘*Symp.*’ add ‘**2** *without Bacchic celebration, οὐδὲ ἀ. ἡ πηγὴ* Philostr.*Im.* 1.23.2; in oxymoron, *ἀ. θίασος* E.*Or.* 319. **II** *not drinking wine*, Nonn. *D.*17.96, 40.295.’

**ἄβᾰλε**, read ‘**ἆβᾰλε**’; after ‘*O that* .. !’ insert ‘Alcm. 111 P.’; for ‘Call.*fr.* 455’ read ‘Call.*fr.* 619 Pf.’

**ἄβαξ 1 a**, for this section read ‘*counting-board, abacus*, Arist.*Ath.* 69.1, *PTeb.* 793.6.4 (183 BC), *PFlor.* 1.50 (*RFIC* 1939.255)’ delete ‘*sideboard* .. **4**’ and after ‘(Delos, iii BC)’ add ‘Ammon.*Diff.* 1.’ **II**, delete the section (v. °*ἄβακος*).

**ἀβᾰρής II**, add ‘**2** *free from burden* (of taxation), Just.*Nov.* 59.7.’

+**ἀβαρκνᾷ**· *κομᾷ †τὲ Μακεδόνες* Hsch. (La.). **II** *ἄβαρκνα· λιμός* id.

*__ἀβᾶς__, v. °*ἀββᾶς*.

**ἀβᾰσάνιστος 1**, for this section read ‘*not tortured, ἀ. θνῄσκειν* J.*BJ.* 1.32.3; (transf.) *κημοῖς ὑπερῴαν ἀ.* Ael.*NA* 13.9; (fig., of style) D.H.*Vett.Cens.* 3 (207.19) (prob. interpol.); adv. -*τως* *without torment, ταῖς ἀκτῖσι τοῦ ἡλίου ῥᾳδίως καὶ ἀ. ἀντιβλέποντες* Ael.*NA* 10.1 ; Aesop. 177.1 P.; *without vexation*, Ael.*VH* 9.1 (*ἀβασκάνως* cj. Dilts)’

*__ἀβᾰσῐλευσία__, *state of being without a king, anarchy*, *UPZ* 196.83 (ii BC).

**ἀβάσκαντος**, for ‘*secure .. harm*’ read ‘*safe from the evil eye*’; line 4, after ‘Dsc. 3.91’ insert ‘voc. *ἀβάσκαντε* *Vit.Aesop.*(W) 30 P., of a being w. magical powers’

+**ἀβάστακτος**, *ον*, (*βαστάζω*), *that cannot be carried*, fig., *φορτίον ἀ. .. τὴν Καίσαρος διαδοχήν* Plu.*Ant.* 16; transf., *insufferable, χειρισμοῦ ἀ.* *PTeb.* 758.15 (ii BC). **II** *not removed*, *Inscr.Perg.* 8(3).37, (cf. *σημεῖον* I 3 fin.); adv. -*τως* Hsch.

*__ἄβατι__, perh. for *ἄϝατι*, dat. of **ἄϝας*, and related to *ἄτη*, *IPamph.* 3.6 (iv BC).

+**ἄβᾰτος**, *ον*, also *α*, *ον*, Pi.*N.* 3.21, *affording no passage, impassable, ὄρεα γὰρ ὑψηλὰ ἀποτάμνει ἄβατα* Hdt. 4.25, 7.176, S.*OT* 719, *ὕλη* Str. 5.4.5; of water, *ἅλς* Pi.*N.* 3.21; *ὡς δ’ αὔτως καὶ ὁ Παρθένιος ἄβατος* X.*An.* 5.6.9; fig., *τὸ πόρσω σοφοῖς ἄ. κἀσόφοις* Pi.*O.* 3.44; [*τὸ ἀγαθὸν*] *ἐν ἀβάτοις ὑπεριδρυμένον* Procl.*in Alc.* 319c W. **2** of holy places, *not to be trodden*, S.*OC* 167, 675, *ἕρπειν πλοῦτος .. ἐς τἄβατα καὶ πρὸς †τὰ βατά†* id.*fr.* 88.6 R.; *ἄ. ἱερόν* Pl.*La.* 183b, Porph.*Abst.* 4.11; *ἀβατώτατος ὁ τόπος* (i.e. cemetery) Arist.*Pr.* $924^{a}5$; transf., *undefiled, ψυχή* Pl.*Phdr.* 245a. **b** as subst., *ἄβατον, τὸ* Theopomp.Hist. 343 J., *IG* $4^{2}$.122.23 (Epid., iv BC); *Διὸς καταιβάτου ἄ.* *IG* $2^{2}$.4965 (Athens, iv BC). **3** of other places, *not affording access*, (*οἰκίαι*) *ἄ. τοῖς ἔχουσι μηδὲ ἕν*, Aristopho 4 K.-A.; *ἀ. ποιεῖν .. τὰς τραπέζας* Anaxipp. 3. **4** fig., *inaccessible* to a quality, etc., *φύσις .. ἄ. .. οἴκτῳ* Ph. 2.53; *κερδοσύνῃ ἄ.* *ZPE* 6.187.2b (Nicopolis). **II** *unavailable for sexual intercourse*, of fillies, *ἀδμῆτες ἔτι καὶ ἄβατοι* Luc.*Zeux.* 6; of a woman, id.*Lex.* 19. **III** of land, cities, etc., *untrodden, desolate, waste*, Lxx *Je.* 31.9, 39.43, 51.6. **IV** *marked by inability to walk*, w. ref. to gout, *ἄ. ἄστατος πόνος* Luc.*Ocyp.* 36. **V** *ἄβατον, τό*, an unidentified plant, Gal. 6.623.

*__ἀββᾶ__ or **ἀββᾶς**, *ὁ*, fr. Hebr. or Aramaic, *father*, of God, *Ev.Marc.* 14.36. **2** title of respect given to monks, esp. abbots, *ITyr* 200 (AD 609), *SEG* 30.1689, written *ἀβᾶ* 31.1430 (both Palestine, vi/vii AD), *PKöln* 111.19 (v/vi AD), *POxy.* 2480.31 (vi AD); see also *ἄππα, ἄππας*.

**ἀβέβαιος**, delete ‘of remedies, Hp.*Aph.* 2.27’

*__ἀβεβαίωσις__, *εως*, *ἡ*, = *ἀβεβαιότης*, *ἀ. τῶν πραγμάτων* Anon. *in Rh.* 117.34.

**ἀβέβηλος**, for ‘of persons, *pure*’ read ‘transf., *ἀβέβηλον καὶ τῆς τοιαύτης ἐπιθυμίας τόν ‹τε› καιρόν* [*ἐποίησεν*] i.e. made devoted to’

*__ἀβέλτης__, v. °*ἀβερτή*.

*__ἀβερτή__, *ἡ*, = *ἀορτή* II, *knapsack*, Suid., *ἀβέρτα* *Edict.Diocl.* 10.1a. Also **ἀβέλτης**, *ὁ*, *PMich.*IX 576.4 (v AD).

**ἀβήρ**, for ‘cf. *αὐήρ*’ read ‘cf. *αὔηρ*’

*__ἀβῐαστικός__, *όν*, *irresistible, ἀ. λόγος* *Suppl.Mag.* 95.12→ (v AD).

**ἀβίαστος 3**, for ‘*τὸ ἀπαθεί*’ read ‘*τὸ ἀπαθές*’ and for ‘Eus.*PE* 5.10’ read ‘Eus.*PE* 5,10.10’

*__ἀβίᾱτος__, *ον*, = *ἀβίαστος*, *not violent, ἀνήρ* *Trag.adesp.* in *NGG* 1922.25.

**ἄβιδα**, after lemma insert ‘(**ἀβίλλιον** La.)’

*__ἀβιτώριον__, *ου*, *τό*, fr. Lat. **abitorium*, cf. *abitus, latrine*, *IHistriae* 363.7.

**ἀβλαβής**, after ‘*ές*’ insert ‘*ἀβλάβη*[*ν*] (Aeol. acc.), Sapph. 5.1 L.-P.’; add ‘cf. °*ἀβλοπές*’

**ἀβλέφᾰρος**, for ‘*eyebrows*’ read ‘*eyelashes*’

*__ἀβλήχμων__· *ἀμβλύς* Hsch.

*__ἀβληχροποιός__, *όν*, *taking away strength*, a suggested interpr. of *ἀβληχρός* in *θάνατος ἀ.* Eust. 1676.57.

*__ἀβλίμαστον__· *ἄψαυστον* Hsch.

+**ἀβλοπές**· *ἀβλαβές. Κρῆτες* Hsch.

**ἀβλοπία**, for ‘cf. Hsch.’ read ‘v. °*ἀβλοπές*’

**ἀβοηθησία**, for ‘*helplessness*’ read ‘*state of being without help*’

**ἀβοήθητος**, line 3, delete ‘*fatal*’ **II**, for ‘*helpless*’ read ‘*lacking* or *cut off from help*’

**ἀβολαία**, delete the entry.

**ἄβολλα**, delete the entry (v. °*ἀβόλλης*).

*__ἀβόλλης__, *ου*, *ὁ*, Lat. *abolla, thick woollen cloak*, *POxy.* 1153.18 (i AD), *Stud.Pal.* 20.15.9 (ii AD), *Peripl.M.Rubr.* 6, *PMich.*inv. 3163 (*TAPhA* 92.258.5, iv AD); v. *κάροινον* II.

**ἄβολος**, for ‘(*βολή*)’ read ‘(*βολός*)’ **1**, for ‘also of an old horse .. *AB* 322’ read ‘cf. *οὐδέπω ἔχων τι ἐπὶ τῶν ὀδόντων γνώρισμα*, in Greek-Coptic glossary app. understood as *“packhorse”*, *Aegyptus* 6.186.72 (v. *Glotta* 60.80)’

*__ἄβολος__ (B), gender unkn., *woollen cloak*, Alciphr. 3.40.(1.23.)2 (cj.).

*__ἀβόρᾱτος__, *ὁ*, (perh. = *ἀϝόρατος* = *ἀόρατος*), kind of fish, *IGC* p. 98 A19 (Acraephia, iii/ii BC).

**ἀβουλέω I**, after ‘Id.*Ep.* 347a’ insert ‘D.*Ep.* 2.17’

**ἀβούλητος I**, transfer ‘Pl.*Lg.* 733d’ to section II after ‘or *will*’

**ἄβουλος**, line 4, for ‘Th. 1.120.7’ read ‘Th. 1.120.5’

**ἄβρα**, for ‘*favourite slave*’ read ‘*personal slave, maid*’; after ‘Luc.*Tox.* 14’ insert ‘Ezek.*Exag.* 19 S. (pl.)’

**ἀβραμύας**, add ‘(-*ίας* La.)’

**ἄβραχος**, delete the entry.

**ἄβρεκτος**, after ‘Hp.*Aff.* 52’ insert ‘Call.*fr.* 384.34 Pf.’

**ἁβροκόμης II**, delete ‘(with play on both meanings)’

*__ἁβρόπαις__, *παιδος*, *ὁ*, *ἡ*, *of pretty children, πάτρα* *RFIC* 1937.54 (Ptolemais).

+**ἁβροπενθής**, *ές*, *mourning effeminately*, A.*Pers.* 135.

*__ἁβρόπεπλος__, *ον*, *wearing delicate robes, Naΐδες ἁβρόπεπλοι* epigr. in *ZPE* 14.21 (Atrax).

*__ἁβρόπους__, *ποδος*, *ὁ*, *ἡ*, *delicate-footed*, gloss on *σαυκρόπους*, Hsch.

**ἁβρός**, line 5, for ‘*splendid*’ read ‘*delicate, luxurious*’; line 11, for ‘Stesich. 37 .. Sapph. 5’ read ‘Stesich. 37 P.; *σύ .. ἄβρως* ὀμ‹με›μείχμενον θαλίαισι νέκταρ οἰνοχόαισον Sapph. 2.14 L.-P.'; line 13, for '*Anacreont.* 41.3' read '*Anacreont.* 43.3 W.'

**ἁβρότης**, line 1, delete '*splendour*'; line 5, for 'in *the freshness of youth*' read 'μεγάλας, in circumstances of great *luxury*'

**ἀβρότονον**, add 'also as fem. pers. n., Plut.*Them.* 1, Men.*Epit. fr.* 1'

**ἀβροχικός**, after '= ἄβροχος' insert '*PVarsov.* 26.30 (iv/v AD)'

**ἀβροχίτων**, after '*Inscr.Cos* 5.11' insert '*Lindos* 197f5 (written -κιτ-, cf. κιτών)'

**ἁβρύνω**, line 4, delete '*wax wanton*'

**ἄβρωμος**, for 'Xenocr. 9' read 'Xenocr. 6'

**ἀβρωσία**, add 'prob. in E.*Hipp.* 136 (lyr.; codd. ἀμβροσίου)'

**ἄβρωτος I 1**, for 'ὀστᾶ Men. 129' read 'Men.*Dysc.* 452'

***ἀβστινατεύω**, *disinherit*, ἀ. τῆς τῶν πατέρων κληρονομίας Just.*Nov.* 89.3.

***ἀβστινατίων**, ονος, ἡ, *the fact of disinheriting*, *PMasp.* 97ᵛ.D82 (vi AD).

***ἄβυκτος**, ον, v. °ἄβακτος.

***ἄβυρσος**, ον, *lacking hide*, ἄ. .. ἡ τοῦ Ἀχιλλέως (sc. ἀσπίς) Eust. 911.62.

***ἀβύσσαιος**, ον, *lying at* or *coming from a great depth*, ὕδωρ Anon.Alch. 403.1, (v.l. ἐναβύσσ-).

***Ἀγαγύλιος**, ὁ, (sc. μήν), name of a month in Thessaly, *IG* 9(2).554 (Larissa), al.

**ἀγάζηλοι**, add 'cf. pers. n. Ἀγάζαλος *SEG* 24.383 (Delphi, iii BC)'

**ἀγάζω**, for '*exalt overmuch*' read '*act without moderation*' **II**, omit 'cf.'; add 'aor. part. ἀγασσαμένη Nic.*fr.* 74.15 G.-S.'

***ἀγᾰθημερία**, ἡ, *lucky day*, *PMich.* in *PBA* 15.131 (cf. -μερος *SEG* 31.1223 (Pisidia, Rom.imp.) and -μερίς ib. 1037 (Lydia, AD 210/11) as pers. n.).

**ἀγᾰθίδιον**, delete 'Paul.Aeg. 2.57'

***ἀγάθιον**, ου, τό, *poultice*, Paul.Aeg. 2.57 (124.20 H.).

***Ἀγάθιος**, ὁ, cult epith. of Zeus, *INikaia* 1061-7 (ii/iii AD).

***ἀγᾰθογνώμων**, ον, *of good opinions*, of a person, Heph.Astr. 3.45.4.

***ἀγᾰθοδαιμόνημα**, τό, astrol., *position in propitious region*, (v. ἀγαθοδαίμων III), Heph.Astr. 2.11.4, 11.

**ἀγᾰθοδαίμων**, delete 'less correct .. A.D.*Adv.* 60.15'

**ἀγᾰθοειδής**, at end add 'adv. -δῶς Procl.*Inst.* 25 D.'

**ἀγαθοεργασία**, delete the entry.

**ἀγᾰθός**, line 1, for 'ἀζαθός *GDI* 57' read '*a-za-ta-i* prob. = ἀγαθᾷ, *ICS* 220.4, *Kafizin* 135d, 136, al.' **I 6**, at the beginning insert 'as epith. of Hermes, *SEG* 26.137 (Attica, iv BC), ib. 35.1118 (Ephesus)' and after 'δαίμων' insert 'ἥρωες ἀ. of deceased souls, *SEG* 36.854 (Selinous, iii BC), *IUrb.Rom.* 301, 373; at Thasos, of heroized fallen soldiers, οἱ Ἀγαθοί, *Thasos* 141.3, 8, 11' **II 4**, ἐπ' ἀγαθῷ, add 'in epitaphs, *SEG* 31.797, 1533, etc. (Rom.imp.)' **III**, sup., add 'ἀγαθέστατε (voc.) Hyp.*fr.* 219b J. (ascribed to Euripides in codd.Phot.)' **IV**, line 2, for 'Hp.*Off.* 9' read 'Hp.*Off.* 4'

**ἀγᾰθύνω IV**, for '*do well*' read '*prosper*'

**ἀγαῖος** (A), before 'Hsch.' insert 'ἀγαῖον· ἐπίφθονον' and at end add 'τὰ τῶι Λυκείωι δάρματα καὶ τὰν ἀγαίαν μόσχον *CID* I 9 (iv BC)'

**ἀγαῖος** (B), delete the entry.

**ἀγακλεής**, line 3, after 'Pi.*I.* 1.34' insert '*AP* 9.26.5 (Antip.Thess.)'

***ἀγακλήεις**, εσσα, εν, *famous*, ἀγακλήεντι *MAMA* 1.267 (Laodicea Combusta).

**ἀγακλῠτός I**, for 'Il. 6.426' read 'Il. 6.436'

**ἀγαλλίᾱμα**, for '*transport of joy*' read '*cause of joy*' and add 'Lxx *Ps.* 118 (119).111; *Is.* 22.13, *Si.* 1.11'

**ἀγάλλω**, lines 7/9, for '*adorn* .. Pass., *glory*, *exult*' read 'med., εὔιον ἀγαλλόμεναι θεόν E.*Ba.* 157. **b** *honour* an occasion, γαμηλίους εὐνάς E.*Med.* 1027; med., τὰ γενέσια ἀγάλλεσθαι D.C. 47.18.6. **2** med., *glory*, *exult*'; line 15, for 'Pl.*Tht.* 176b' read 'Pl.*Tht.* 176d'

**ἄγαλμα** after lemma insert 'Cypr. *a-za-la-ma Kafizin* 292' **3**, before 'Hdt. 1.131' insert 'Jeffery *LSAG* p. 358 no. 49 (Egypt, Ion. letters, vi BC, written ἄκαλμα)' **5**, for 'expressed by painting or words' read 'metaph.'

***ἀγαλματικός**· ἀκουστής Hsch.

***ἀγαλματογλύπτης**, ὁ, *sculptor*, *IPhilae* 182 (iii AD).

***ἀγαλματογλύφης**, ὁ, *sculptor*, Aesop. 90.2 P.

**ἀγαλματογλύφος**, for '*Rev.Ét.* .. Aphrodisias)' read '*MAMA* 8.574 (Aphrodisias), *SEG* 32.1311 (Lycaonia)'

***ἀγαλματοθήκη**, ἡ, *place for a statue*, *SEG* 28.953.57 (Cyzicus, i AD).

***ἀγαλματομική**, ἡ, (sc. τέχνη), the art of *carving images*, Call.*Dieg.* iv.29 (*fr.* 100 Pf.) (perh. shortened for *ἀγαλματοτομ-).

***ἀγαλματοπώλης**, ου, ὁ, *seller of images*, Aesop. 99 tit. P.

**ἀγαλματοφορέω**, add 'of mankind, *bear the image* of God, τοῖς δὲ αὐτὸν ἐν ἑαυτοῖς ἀγαλματοφοροῦσι τὸν ποιητήν Athenag.*Res.* 12.6'

⁺**ἀγαλματοφώρας**, ὁ, *thief of temple adornments*, *Schwyzer* 424.13 (Elis, iv BC) (acc. sg. -φώρᾱν, unless -φῶρᾰν, nom. -φώρ).

**ἀγαλμοειδής**, delete the entry.

**ἄγᾰμαι I**, add '**6** w. imper., like Lat. *amabo*, in parenthesis, *please*, Cephisod. 3 K.-A.' **II 2**, after '(Od.) 23.64' insert 'w. dat. and gen., ἧιε, μή οἱ δῆμος ἐϋκλείης ἀγάσαιτο A.R. 1.141; w. gen. only, Pi.*Pae.* 8.75 S.-M.'

**Ἀγᾰμεμνόνεος**, after 'ειον' insert 'also two termin., Ἀ. δαὶς ἢ τράπεζα, a fatal feast, Eust. 1507.60' and after 'ιον' for 'Pi.; A.' read 'Pi.*P.* 11.20, A.*Ag.* 1499, *Ch.* 861'

**Ἀγᾰμέμνων**, delete 'Ἀγαμέμνονος .. 1507.60'

**ἄγᾰμος I**, after 'E.*Or.* 205' add 'in religious context, *celibate*, νικᾷ ἡ τύχη τῶν ἀγάμōν Robert *Hell.* 11/12.494 (Didyma, early Byz.)' **II**, delete '*fatal marriage*'

**ἄγαν**, add '**b** οὐκ ἄ. not *too*, not *particularly*, oft. iron., εἰμὶ δ' οὐκ ἄ. σοφή E.*Med.* 305, 583, *El.* 1105; οὐκ ἄ. σφ' ἐπῄνεσα id.*Ph.* 764, Ar.*Eq.* 598.'

**ἀγᾰνακτέω I**, for this section read '*shudder*, *quiver*, Hp.*Liqu.* 2, Heliod.ap.Orib. 46.7.8; of fermentation, Plu. 2.734e' **II 2**, after 'c. gen. rei' insert 'Lys. 14.39'

**ἀγάννῐφος**, after 'Il. 1.420' insert 'Hes.*fr.* 229.6, 15 M.-W.; *h.Merc.* 325' and at end add '*PMed.*inv. 71.82.18 (*Aegyptus* 52.90, i BC)'

***ἄγᾰνον**, v. ἤγανον.

**ἀγᾰνός 1**, add '**b** of things, of a crocus, *h.Cer.* 426; of water, *IEryth.* 224.12.'

**ἄγᾰνος**, delete the entry.

**ἀγᾰνῶπις**, for '*mild-eyed*' read '*of gentle appearance*'

**ἀγάομαι**, for 'only' read 'impf., ἀγᾶτο *was angry*, Hes.*fr.* 30.12 M.-W.' and delete 'and opt. .. Alc. 14'

**ἀγᾰπάω II**, add '**2** w. inf., *desire*, *MAMA* 1.176 (Laodicea Combusta).' **III 2**, after 'Pl.*R.* 475b' delete 'cf.'; after 'Antiph. 169' insert 'Is. 8.43'

**ἀγάπη I 1**, after '*love*' insert 'orig. in non-sexual sense but later w. some erotic connotation' and delete 'Lxx *Ca.* 2.7'; add '*IG* 14.2317 (Padua). **b** *loved one*, Lxx *Ca.* 2.7; cf. as pers. n., *SEG* 19.422 (vi BC).' **II**, for '*love-feast*' read 'the Christian *agape*' **IV**, delete the section (disputed text, v. *JThS* 18.142f., 19.209ff., 20.228ff.).

**ἀγᾰπητός**, lines 5/6, after 'αὐτῇ .. *To.* 3.10' insert 'τὸν υἱόν σου τὸν ἀ. Lxx *Ge.* 22.2, cf. *Am.* 8.10' **II 2**, after '*beloved*' insert 'Ἄδων ἀγαπατέ Theoc. 15.149' **III**, adv., add '*with acquiescence*, Luc.*Am.* 33'

**ἀγάστονος**, for '*much-groaning*' read '*loud-roaring*'; for '*loud-wailing*, *lamentable* .. 123' read '*loud-wailing* or *-howling* A.*Th.* 99, *AP* 14.123.3 (Metrod.), Nonn. *D.* 46.207; poet., of the pains of childbirth'

**ἀγαστός**, line 3, after '*An.* 1.9.24' insert 'Pl.*Lg.* 808c'; at end, for '(Pure Att. θαυμαστός)' read '(rare in Att. prose; ἀ. θεοῖς Pl.*Smp.* 197d is in parody of Gorgianic style)'

**ἀγατός**, delete the entry.

**ἀγαυρίᾱμα**, for '*insolence*' read '*pride*, *boastfulness*'

**ἀγαυριάομαι**, for '*insolent*' read '*proud*, *boastful*'

**ἀγγᾰρεία**, after 'Arr.*Epict.* 4.1.79' insert 'οἴνου ἐνγαρία (cf. mod. Gk. ἐγγαρεία) *BGU* 21.3.16 (iv AD); of a soldier's duty, *Cod.Just.* 12.37.19 pr.; ἀγγαρεία· δουλεία Hsch. (ἀγγαρρία La.)'

***ἀγγαριεύω**, = ἀγγαρεύω, *PCair.Isidor.* 72.32 (iv AD).

***ἀγγᾰρικός**, ή, όν, *concerning* ἀγγαρεία, cj. for αιγα- in *PCair.Preis.* 33.6 (iv AD).

***ἀγγάριος**, α, ον, *impressed for public service*, *PCair.Isidor.* 73.12 (iv AD); ἀπὸ τῆς ἀγγαρίου ib. 23, app. = ἀγγαρεία; masc. as subst. *workman*, gloss on Δᾶος Hsch.

**ἄγγᾰρος I 1**, delete 'Hdt. 3.126, X.*Cyr.* 8.6.17' at end for '(Assyr. *agarru*, "hired labourer")' read 'perh. cognate w. Aram. '*iggᵉrâ* "letter"; v. *Glotta* 49.97-100; earliest attestation in Gr. in pers. n. Ἀνγάριος, *Corinth* 15(3).1 (viii or vii BC)'

**ἀγγεῖον I 1**, line 10, after '1*Ki.* 9.7' insert 'κρέως ἀγγία *PRyl.* 627.72'; at end add 'ἐπὶ τῶν ἀνγήων (= ἀγγείων), of a particular office, *PPetaus* 86.11 (ii AD)' **2**, for this section read '*tank*, *reservoir*, Pl.*Lg.* 845e; transf., of the hollow of the sea-bed, Pl.*Criti.* 111a' **II**, line 4, after 'id.*PA* 692ᵃ12' insert 'of the eyes S.E.*P.* 1.49'

***ἀγγειουργός**, ὁ, *maker of vessels*, *IG* $2^2$.1576.69 (iv BC).

**ἀγγελία I 1**, line 3, delete 'ἀ. λέγουσα .. 114'; line 4, delete 'Il. 18.17'; for 'πέμπειν' read 'πέμπει .. ἀγγελίην λέγουσαν τάδε Hdt. 2.114'; penultimate line, after 'Hes.*Th.* 781' insert '(dub., cod. ἀγγελίῃ)'; at end add 'applied to official delegations, πολλὰς δ' ἀνγελίας πρὸ πόλεως κατὰ φῦλα διῆλθεν ἀνθρώπων *CEG* 416 (Thasos, vi BC); epigr. in *BCH* 116.599 (Ambracia, vi/v BC)' **I 2**, delete the section adding exx. to section I 1 **II**, delete the section (see end of section I 1).

***ἀγγελίαρχος**, *archangel*, *AP* 1.34, 35 (Agath.).

***ἀγγελίας**, Ion. **ἀγγελίης**, ὁ, v. ‡ἀγγελία I 1 (at end).

**ἀγγελιᾱφόρος**, add '= Lat. *frumentarius*, in sense of *imperial agent*, D.C. 78.15.1'

**ἀγγελικός 1**, add '**c** a name for the dactylic hexameter catalectic, Diom. 1.512.23, Sacerd. 6.507.20; also, the trochaic dimeter, Mar. Vict. 6.85.27.'

***ἀγγελιτείη**, app. 3rd sg. aor. opt. of vb., perh. = ἀγγέλλω, *Inscr.Cret.* 4.146.4 (iv BC).

**ἀγγέλλω**, line 4, for 'ἠγγείλαμην' read 'ἠγγειλάμην'

***ἀγγελοδείκτης**, ου, ὁ, revealer of ἄγγελοι (v. ἄγγελος I 4), *PMag.* 4.1374.

***ἀγγελόεις**, εσσα, εν, = ἀγγελικός, τιμή *SIFC* 2.397 (Crete).

**ἄγγελος I 2**, line 5, for 'ἐμῶν' read 'ἐπῶν' **4**, add 'Ἀγαθὸς Ἄγγελος *IStraton.* 1118, Θεῖος Ἄγγελος Οὐράνιος ib. 1307 (prob. pagan, v. *SEG* 31.1689)' **II**, add 'and of a goddess at Didyma, perh. also Artemis, *Didyma* 406.9-10 (ii AD); title of Zeus in Arabia, *SEG* 32.1539 (ii/iii AD)' at end add 'Myc. *a-ke-ro*'

***ἀγγλάριον**, τό, unexpld. wd., τὸ ἐπὶ τὴν πομπὴν ἀνγλάριον *Inscr.Cret.* 3.iii 7.13 (ii AD).

**ἄγγος**, after '*vessel*' read '*receptacle*'; after '*IT* 953, 960' add 'for dry substances, Aen.Tact. 29.6, 8; *cinerary urn*, S.*El.* 1118, 1205; *sarcophagus*, *IAssos* 72 (sp. ἄνγος)' **II**, for this section read '*box, chest*, or sim., Hdt 1.113; S.*Tr.* 622; adv. ἄγγοσδε, *to the receptacle*, Emp. B 100.12 D.-K.'

***ἄγγουρα·** ῥάξ, σταφυλή Hsch. (s.v. ἄγγορ-).

***ἄγγρεσις**, ιος, ἁ, Thess. = αἵρεσις B I 3, *choice*, *IG* 9(2).504.4 (Larissa, ii BC), dat. ἄγγρεσι, *BCH* 59.56.40 (cf. ἐφάνγρενθειν s.v. ἐφαιρέομαι; presupposes *ἄγγρειμι = ἀγρέω).

***ἀγγροφά**, v. °ἀναγραφή.

***ἀγγροφεύς**, v. °ἀναγραφεύς.

***ἀγδᾰβάτης**, ου, ὁ, perh., *member of some section* or *class of Persians*, A.*Pers.* 924 (codd.).

***Ἄγδιστις**, ἡ, Phrygian title of the mother goddess Cybele, voc. Ἀγγδιστι Men.*Th.fr.dub.* 20 S., acc. Ἄγδιστιν Str. 10.3.12, dat. Ἀνγδίσσῃ *SEG* 36.1201 (c.AD 200), dat. Ἀγδίσσιδι *IG* 12(2).524 (Methymna), Ἀνγδείσει Robert *ATAM* 239 (Pisidia, w. discussion of variants).

***ἀγέθλον**, τό, in pl., wd. of uncertain interpr., *IPamph.* 3.24 (Sillyon, iii BC).

**ἀγείρω**, line 4, after '*BC* 2.134' insert 'Aeol. (συν)αγάγρεται Alc. 119.10 L.-P.'; at end add 'Myc. 3 sg. *a-ke-re*'

***Ἀγελάα**, ἡ, = ἀγελείη, epith. of Athena, *Sokolowski* 2.19.89 (Athens, iv BC).

**ἀγελάζομαι**, after 'Act.' insert '*keep a flock*, Apoll.*Met.Ps.* 77.71 (*PG* 33.1429b)'

**ἀγελαιοκομικός**, add 'see also °ἀγελοκομική'

***ἀγελαιοκόμος**, ὁ, *keeper of a flock*, Pall.*V.Chrys.* 4 (v.l. ἀγελοκ-).

***ἀγέλαιος**, ὁ· ὁ ἀμαθής Phlp.*Dif.Ton.* p. 361.2.

**ἀγελαῖος II**, add '**3** math., *cubic*, *POxy.* 3455.8 (iii/iv AD).'

**ἀγελαρχέω**, add '*hold the office of* ἀγελάρχης, *Xanthos* 21.5 (iii AD)'

**ἀγελάρχης**, after '*Am.* 22' insert 'τῶν τράγων τὸν ἀγελάρχην Longus 2.31.2' at end add '**II** gloss on βουαγόρ, Hsch.'

**ἀγελαρχικός**, add 'cf. Procl. *in Ti.* 1.467.29'

***ἀγελάς**, άδος, ἡ, = φορβάς, Sch.A.R. 2.88b.

***ἀγελαστής·** ἔγχελυς Hsch.

***ἀγελαστοῦ·** ἀκακίας Hsch. (†ἀγελαστοῦ La.).

**ἀγελείη I**, after '= ἄγουσα .. *forager*' read 'or perh. *leader of the war-host* fr. *ἀγελήη' and add 'cf. °Ἀγελάα'

**ἀγέλη I**, at end omit 'but rare in early prose'

***ἀγελοκομική**, ἡ, (= ἀγελαιοκομική), *the art of keeping cattle*, Clem. Al.*Strom.* 1.7 (*GCS* 52.24.28).

***ἀγελοκόμος**, v. °ἀγελαιοκόμος.

**ἀγένειος**, for '*boyish* .. id.*Eun.* 9' read 'Alcm. 10(*b*).17 P.; Longus 1.16.2; τὸ ἀ. Luc.*Eun.* 9; (transf.) *puerile*, ἀγένειόν τι εἰρηκέναι id.*J.Tr.* 29'

***ἀγένειος** (B), ον, *not having children*, εἰ δὲ ἀγένειος εἴη Σαραπιὰς Ἀστοξένωι *GDI* 1891.29 (Delphi, ii BC); cf. ἀγενής III.

**ἀγενής II**, after 'S.*fr.* 84' insert '(anap.)'

**ἀγερμός**, after '(cf. ἀγείρω II 2)' insert '*Sokolowski* 3.175.12 (Cos, iv BC); ib. 48.A8 (Piraeus, ii BC)'

***Ἀγερράνιος**, v. °Ἀγριάνιος.

**ἄγερσις II**, for '= πανήγυρις' read '= ‡ἀγερμός'; add 'cf. ἄγαρρις'

**ἀγερωχία**, after '*arrogance*' insert '*pride*, Sapph. 7.4 L.-P.'; delete 'in good sense .. *revelry*'; after 'Lxx *Wi.* 2.9' for 'pl., *feats of mastery*' read '**II** pl., *bold feats*'

**ἀγέρωχος I**, line 5, for 'Hes.*Fr.* 14 ' read 'Hes.*fr.* 30(*a*).12 M.-W., ἀ. ὄψις D.H.*Comp.* 16'; for 'of *noble* actions' read 'of *lofty* actions'

**ἀγεσίφρων**, for '(fort. -οφρύων)' read '(ἀγεσόφρυν La.)'

***ἄγεστα**, ἡ, *bank of earth* (in siege warfare), cf. Lat. *aggestus, aggestum*, τὴν ἄγεσταν ἐργαζομένων Procop.*Pers.* 2.26.29. Also **ἀγέστον**, τό, Evagr.Schol.*HE* 4.27 (*PG* 86.2748c).

***ἀγέχορος** (or **ἀγε-**), όν, *leading the chorus*, Ar.*Lys.* 1281 (v.l. ἄγε χορόν).

**ἀγεωργησία**, for '*bad husbandry*' read '*lack of cultivation*'

**ἄγη II**, delete 'of the gods, *jealousy*'

**ἀγή** (A), after '*breakage*' insert '*PCair.Zen.* 15ʳ.27 (iii BC), etc., of pottery' and for '**1**' read '**b**' **2**, for '*place where* the wave *breaks, beach*' read '*breaking of the wave, surf*'

**ἀγηθής**, at end add 'S.*fr.* 583.10 R. (cj.)'

**ἀγηλᾰτέω**, add 'Nicom.Trag. 14 S.'

**ἀγηνόρειος**, delete the entry.

**ἀγηνορέω**, for '*to be valiant*' read '*to be proud* or *boastful*' add '**II** trans., *treat arrogantly*, ἀ. τοκῆας Euph. in *Suppl.Hell.* 415 ii 9.'

**ἀγήνωρ 1**, line 5, delete 'the Titans, Hes.*Th.* 641'

**ἀγήραος**, line 4, after 'Hes.*Th.* 277' insert 'ἀγείρω Corinn. 1 iii 25 P.' **1**, at end add 'θεῶν κῆρυξ ἀ. καὶ ἀθάνατος Hellanic.*fr.* 19(b) J.'

***ἀγηράσιος**, ον, = ἀγήρατος (A), βωμός *IUrb.Rom.* 128 (iv AD).

**ἀγήρᾱτος** (A), line 3, after '-ᾱτος' insert '*CEG* 548.4 (Attica), 721.2 (Aegeae, iv BC)'

***ἄγηρος**, ον, = ἀγήραος, *ageless*, Hes.*fr.* 25.28 M.-W.

***Ἀγησιτίμειοι**, ων, οἱ, name of a Rhodian guild, *Clara Rhodos* 2.203.

**ἀγητός**, line 5, after 'Sol. 5.3' insert 'abs., w. dat. of person affected, of a tomb, τὸ καὶ μακάρεσσιν ἀγητόν Theoc. 1.126; Opp.*C.* 1.364'

***ἁγιαστήρ**, ῆρος, ὁ, *consecrator*, *Tab.Defix.Aud.* 16 x 7 (Syria, iii AD).

***ἁγιαστί**, adv., *devoutly*, *Suppl.Mag.* 87.6 (iii/iv AD).

**ἅγιος**, after 'α, ον' insert '(θῴγιον = τὸ ἅγιον, Call.*fr.* 196.29 Pf.)' **I 2**, add 'as a title of Artemis at Ephesus, sup., *SEG* 31.960 (ii/iii AD), al.; of a god named Θεὸς Ἅ., *SEG* 32.1388 (Commagene), ib. 1551 (Arabia, iii AD); of (pagan or Jewish) ἄγγελοι, *SEG* 31.1080 (Galatia, ii/iii AD); of Christ, *SEG* 32.1617 (iv/v AD); of Mary, *Salamine* 234 (v/vi AD), *SEG* 30.1701 (Sinae, v AD); as a Chr. title, esp. of bishops, sup., *SEG* 30.1675 (vi AD), al.'

**ἁγιστύς**, for 'Call.*Aet.* 1.1.3' read 'Call.*fr.* 178.3 Pf.'

**ἁγιωσύνη II**, add '*Cod.Just.* 1.1.7 pr., al.'

**ἀγκ-**, for 'Poet.' read 'dial. or poet.'

**ἀγκάζομαι**, for 'λίθον .. 21.1' read '**II** *embrace* (cf. ἀγκαλίζομαι), καὶ δέ σ' .. ἀ[γκ]άσσαιτο Euph. in *Suppl.Hell.* 415 i 9.'

**ἄγκᾰθεν**, delete 'also .. 337'

***ἀγκᾰλῐδοπώλης**, ου, ὁ, *seller of* produce *in armfuls* or *bundles*, in quot., of firewood, Phot. α 179 Th.

**ἀγκᾰλίζομαι**, after 'Semon. 7.77' insert 'Mosch.Trag. 9.3 S.'

**ἀγκᾰλίς I 2**, after '*armful*' insert '*bundle*' **II**, for 'word' read 'use'; transfer 'J.*AJ* 5.1.2.' to section I 2.

**ἀγκᾰλισμα II**, for 'metaph.' read 'Ach.Tat. 2.37.6; transf.'

**ἄγκᾰλος**, add '*POxy.* 3354.9 (AD 257)'

**ἀγκής**, add '(ἀγκήεις La.)'

**ἀγκιστρεία**, add 'Ael.*NA* 12.43; (fig.) οὐδὲ ἀπαγορεύσω τὴν ἐμὴν -αν, εἰ καὶ δυσθήρατος ἡ γυνή Aristaenet. 1.17'

**ἄγκιστρον**, add 'of an anchor, *Trag.adesp.* 379 K.-S.; of a grapnel, *Poliorc.* 214.1'

**ἀγκιστρόομαι**, delete the entry (v. °ἀγκιστρόω).

***ἀγκιστρόω**, *fasten with hooks*, ῥαφαῖς ὑπὸ τὰς ἐπιπτυχὰς τὴν συμπλοκὴν ἀγκιστρώσαντες Hld. 9.15.2. **2** fig., *grip*, ἠγκιστρωμένος πόθῳ Lyc. 67. **II** *fit with hooks* or *barbs*, Plu.*Crass.* 25.

**ἀγκλάριον**, delete the entry.

***ἄγκλιμα**, ατος, τό, v. °ἀνάκλιμα.

**ἄγκοινα**, for 'Hes.*fr.* 245' read 'Hes.*fr.* 43(a).81 M.-W., Matro in *Suppl.Hell.* 534.59' **II**, for 'Alc. 18.9' read 'Alc. 326.9 L.-P.' and add 'later ἀγκοίνη *PCair.Zen.* 756.1 (iii BC)'

***ἀγκοπάζω**, v. °ἀνακ-.

**ἄγκος**, after 'E.*Ba.* 1051' insert '*Trag.adesp.* 445a K.-S.' add '**2** ἄ. φρείατος *well-shaft*, Alex.Aet. 3.29.'

**ἀγκτήρ 1**, for '*instrument for*' read '= Lat. *fibula, pin used in*' **4**, add 'ἀγκτῆρος δίκην shd. be restd. for ἀγκύρας δίκην in Lyd.*Ost.* 16 (cf. ἀκτῆρος (sic) δίκην id. in *Cat.Cod.Astr.* 11(1).146.10)'

**ἀγκτηριάζω**, add 'Archig.ap.Gal. 13.577, 661'

**ἀγκύλη I**, line 3, for 'B.*Fr.* 13.2' read 'B.*fr.* 17.2 S.-M., Anacr. 70 P.'; line 4, for 'Ath. 11.782d' read 'Ath. 15.667c'; line 6, for 'cf.' read 'Asclep.Jun.ap.Gal. 13.968.7, 969.1' **II 1**, add 'on a fighting ship, *loop* to contain a pole used for fire-throwing, Plb. 21.7.1'

***ἀγκῠλίδιον**, τό, dim. of ἀγκύλη, *loop, noose*, φιάλιον ἐπ' ἀγκ[υλ?]ιδίου *Inscr.Délos* 1442*B*59 (ii BC).

**ἀγκῠλιδωτός**, delete '*for a handle*'

**ἀγκῠλοβλέφᾰρον**, delete the entry.

***ἀγκῠλοβλέφᾰρος**, ον, *suffering from contraction of the eyelids*, Cels. 7.7.6.

**ἀγκῠλόγλωσσον**, after '*contraction of the tongue*' insert '*ankyloglossia*'

**ἀγκῠλοειδής**, add 'adv. -δῶς Erot. 76.3 (cj. for ἀγκυρο-)'

**ἀγκυλοκοπέω**, delete the entry.

***ἀγκῠλοκοπία**, ἡ, *hamstringing*, *PAbinn.* 15.15.

***ἀγκῠλόπεζος**, ον, = στραβοπόδης, *having twisted feet*, *Philol.*suppl. 15.1.143 (= *Fr.Lex.* II).

***ἀγκῠλόπρυμνος**, ον, *having a curved stern*, *Suppl.Hell.* 991.116 (poet. word-list, iii BC).

**ἀγκῠλος II 1**, for '*intricate*' read '*circuitous*'; delete '*catchy*' and 'in good sense *terse*'; transfer Alciphr. quot. to section II 2.

***ἀγκῠλοτόμον**, τό, *hooked instrument* used in tonsillectomy, Paul.Aeg. 6.30 (67.18 H.).

**ἄγκῡρα I**, add 'used as a grappling-iron, Plb. 21.27.5' **II**, add 'also unexpld. item in domestic inventory, *PMichael.* 18 iii 3 (iii AD)'

***ἀγκῡρειος**, α, ον, *for an anchor*, σχοινία *IG* 2².1609.101, *Inscr.Délos* 104-29.14 (both iv BC),; Ph.*Bel.* 100.34.

***ἀγκῡρίς**, ίδος, ἡ, perh. *small anchor*, *IG* 2².1550 (pl., iii BC). **II** gloss on κράδη III, some kind of theatrical machinery, Plu.*Prov.* 2.16.

**ἀγκῡροβολέω**, for 'Hp.*Dent.* 18' read 'Hp.*Oss.* 18'

**ἀγκῡροβόλιον**, add '*Peripl.M.Rubr.* 7.24'

***ἀγκῡροβόλος**, -ῳ δείπνῳ· -α Φοίνικες τὰ δεῖπνα, ἃ παρεσκεύαζον τοῖς τελώναις ἐκ τῶν λιμένων Hsch. (La.).

**ἀγκῡροειδής**, adv., add 'but v. °ἀγκυλοειδής'

***ἀγκῡρωμα**, τό, *anchor*, Sch.Ar.*Eq.* 762 J.

**ἀγκών I 1**, line 4, for '*Riv.*' read '*Amat.*' **2**, for '*arm*' read '*the bent arm, forearm and elbow*' **3**, for pres. def. read 'the corresponding part in animals' **II 1**, line 4, for '*ribs which support the horns*' read '*shoulders*'; line 5, for 'Semus 1, Hsch.' read 'Hsch., cf. Nic.*Al.* 562, Semus 1' **III**, line 3, delete 'Ath. 12.516a'

***ἀγκωνάριον**, τό, an item of clothing, perh. w. elbow-length sleeves, or an *armband*, *PVindob.*G 16846.2 (*Tyche* 2.6; written ἀγκονάριον, *c.*AD 640).

**ἀγκωνίζω**, add '**III** perh. *conduct canal water into side channels*, *PZen. Pestm.* 20 Suppl. C (p. 268).'

**ἀγκωνίσκιον**, for 'dim. of ἀγκών' read '*piece projecting at right angles to a structure, key* (in an organ)'

**ἀγκωνίσκος**, after '*Spir.* 1.42' insert 'for fastening a structure'

**ἀγκωνοφόρος**, for '*IG* 3.1280' read '*REA* 32.5 (Athens, i BC), *IG* 2².2361.8 (iii AD)'

**ἀγλαΐα**, line 3, after '*Or.* 4.148d' insert 'transf., of the Good, Numen.*fr.* 2.15 P.; of the intelligible world, Plot. 3.8.11'

***ἀγλάϊος**, α, ος, = ἀγλαός, Σιμωνίδου ἀγλαΐη παῖς *MAMA* 3.793 (Cilicia); epith. of Zeus, Διὸς Ἀγλαΐῳ *AA* 1966.342.

***ἀγλᾰοδίνης**, ου, ὁ, *having bright eddies*, *Suppl.Hell.* 991.106 (poet. word-list, iii BC).

***ἀγλᾰοειδής**, ές, *glorious in form*, epic. in *PLit.Lond.* 38.26.

**ἀγλαόθρονος**, after '*bright-throned*' insert '(or perh. to be derived fr. θρόνον *flowers*)'

**ἀγλᾰόκαρπος II**, delete the section.

***ἀγλᾰόκολπος**, ον, *fair-bosomed*, Pi.*N.* 3.56.

**ἀγλᾰομειδής**, after '*PLG* 3.639' insert 'ἀγαλμοειδ- codd.' and at end add '[ἀγ]λαομειδέσι Νύμφαις epigr. in *IGBulg.* 1579.5 (Augusta Traiana)'

***ἀγλᾰομήτης**, ου, ὁ, *with splendid wisdom*, epigr. in *SEG* 36.1198.8 (Hierapolis, iv AD).

***ἀγλᾰόμολπος**, ον, *of beautiful song*, *PHarris* 7 (ii/iii AD).

**ἀγλᾰόπεπλος**, add '*TAM* 3(1).590.1 (Termessos, iii AD)'

***ἀγλᾰοφορέω**, *to be the bearer of brightness*, Vett.Val. 344.8.

**ἀγλᾰόφορτος**, for '*proud of one's burden*' read '*carrying a splendid burden*'

†**ἀγλᾰόφωνος**, ον, *producing a splendid sound*, ἀ. ἀοιδός *Orac.Sib.* 12.173 (iii AD), of the Muses, Procl.*H.* 3.2.

***ἀγλᾰοχαίτας**, α, *bright-haired*, Pi.*fr.* 52g(e) S.-M.

***Ἀγλᾱπιός**, v. ‡Ἀσκληπιός.

**Ἄγλαυρος**, last line, read '(Hdt.) 8.53; μὰ τὴν Ἄγλαυρον Ar.*Th.* 533; Paus. 1.18.2, *IG* 2².3459, *SEG* 33.115'

**ἀγλᾰφύρως**, add 'Ath. 15.677f'

**ἀγλευκής**, add 'adv. -κῶς Philostr. *VA* 4.39'

**ἀγλευκιτάς**, add '(ἀγλευττας La.)'

***ἄγλευκος**, ον, = ἀγλευκής (q.v.), Sch.Nic.*Al.* 171a, b.

**ἄγλῑς**, at end for 'Call.*fr.* 140' read 'Call.*fr.* 495, 657 Pf.'

**ἄγλῠφος**, add '*uncarved*, κεφαλίς (column capital) *PHib.* 217.21, 29 (ii AD)'

**ἄγμα**, before 'Plu.*Phil.* 6' insert '*Inscr.Délos* 104-10.6 (iv BC), al.' and after it insert '(pl.)'

***ἀγμίεις**· παραθραύσεις Hsch. (La.).

***ἀγναβόν**, ?τό, kind of plant or tree, *Edict.Diocl.* 36.111, 112; cf. ἀρναβόν.

***ἄγναθος**, kind of fish, *IGC* p. 98 A10 (Acraephia, iii/ii BC).

***Ἀγναῖος**, ὁ (sc. μήν), name of a month at Halos, *IG* 9(2).109*a*28, 71 (ii BC); cf. °Ἁγνεών.

**ἄγναμπτος**, for 'B.8.73' read 'B.9.73 S.-M.; ἄ. νόον *A.Pr.* 163 (lyr.)'; before 'Orph.*L.*' insert 'σθένος'

**ἄγναπτος I**, line 1, delete 'hence *new*'; line 2, delete 'cf.'; at end add 'as subst., ἀλλ' Ἰουδαῖοι σαββάτων ὄντων ἐν ἀγνάπτοις καθεζόμενοι Plu. 2.169c' **II**, delete the section.

***ἀγνᾰφάριος**, *maker of* ἄγναφα, *unfulled cloth* or *garments*, *MAMA* 3.252b; Ἀλέξανδρος -ος ἐπίκλην Σακκᾶς *Bithynische St.* 7.II.2 (vi AD); (sp. ἀκν-) *MAMA* 3.622c, 767a.

**ἄγνᾰφος**, for 'foreg.' read '= ἄγναπτος *not fulled*, *PCair.Zen.* 92.16 (iii BC), *Peripl.M.Rubr.* 6'

***ἁγνεάρχης**, ου, ὁ, religious official at Ephesus, *IEphes.* 1044.15, 1045.5.

**ἁγνεία I**, add '*honourable public conduct*, *IEphes.* 213.7, 790, *SEG* 7.825.15 (Gerasa, ii AD), *IGLS* 21.117; at Ephesus in formula in agoranomic inscrs., κόρος· ἁγνεία *abundance and honesty*, *IEphes.* 938.7, al. **b** the quality associated by musical theorists w. the number seven, Aristid.Quint. 3.6.' **II**, add 'sg., *ritual purity*, of a period of *abstinence* or *fasting*, Chaerem.Hist. 10.6 vdH. (= Porph.*Abst.* 4.6), Plu. 2.353b, *IEphes.* 3263 (ii/iii AD)'

***ἁγνεῖον**· πηγαῖον Hsch. (perh. ἅγνειος "pure", sc. ὕδωρ).

**ἅγνευμα**, add 'E.*El.* 256'

**ἁγνεύω I 1**, line 6, after 'Luc.*Am.* 5' insert 'transf., ἄχρι] σὸν γένειον ἁγνεύῃ τριχός Call.*fr.* 202.69 Pf.'

**ἁγνεών**, add '**II** Ἁγνεών, ῶνος, ὁ (sc. μήν), name of a month at Magnesia, *Inscr.Magn.* 100*a*2, *b*20; cf. °Ἀγναῖος.'

†**ἁγνίζω**, fut. ιῶ (ἀφ-) Lxx *Nu.* 8.6; pf. ἥγνικα 1*Ep.Pet.* 1.22: (ἁγνός):- *make ritually clean, purify*, πόντου σε πηγαῖς E.*IT* 1039; ἁ. πυρσῷ μέλαθρον ib. 1216; Diph. 125.1 K.-A.; Hp.*Morb.Sacr.* 1.45; Lxx *Ex.* 19.10; *Act.Ap.* 21.24; w. gen., χέρας σὰς ἁγνίσας μιάσματος E.*HF* 1324; med., Lxx *Jo.* 3.5; Plu. 2.1105b. **2** *cleanse away* impurities, λύμαθ' ἁγνίσας ἐμά S.*Aj.* 655; E.*Or.* 429. **3** *purify* by funeral rites, S.*Ant.* 545; σῶμαθ' ἡγνίσθη πυρί E.*Supp.* 1211. **II** *consecrate*, Aristonous 1.17; sacrificial offerings, E.*IT* 705; A.R. 2.926; cf. E.*Alc.* 76.

**ἅγνισμα**, delete '*expiation*'

**ἁγνισμός**, delete '*expiation*'

**ἀγνοέω I**, add '**2** *not to know* a man (i.e. be a virgin), [ἡ ἀ]γνοήσασα ἄνδρα ἰς φθοράν Mitchell *N.Galatia* 468 (Byz.).'

**ἀγνοητικός**, for '*EE* 1246ᵃ48' read '*EE* 1246ᵃ38'

**ἄγνοια**, add '**III** *loss of consciousness*, Hipp.*Epid.* 7.85; *Prorrh.* 1.64.'

**ἁγνός I 2**, of Artemis, add '*unnamed*, ἁγνῆς θεοῦ *SEG* 32.218.43, 84'; add 'of Aphrodite, *SEG* 31.731 (all Delos, ii BC); in Chr. usage, *holy*, 1*Ep.Jo.* 3.4, *SEG* 30.1479 (Hierapolis, iii AD)' **II 3**, add '*SEG* 31.908 (Aphrodisias, iii AD); adv. -ῶς *with integrity*, *IEphes.* 712b (ii AD), al., *MAMA* 8.508 (Aphrodisias, *c.*AD 250)'

***ἁγνοτρᾰφής**, ές, *of pure nurture, pure*, δέμας *GVI* 643.10 (Egypt, i BC/i AD).

***ἁγνόφῠτος**, ον, *of pure stock*, *GVI* 1245.1 (Memphis, ii/iii AD).

**ἄγνῡμι**, line 19, after 'Hdt. 1.185' insert 'cf. ἐαγώς Arat. 46'

**ἀγνώμων I 1**, after 'Pi.*O.* 8.60' insert 'Aristarch.Trag. 3 S.' **3**, for 'of judges' read 'of judging *harshly*'

**ἄγνωστος II**, delete 'Pi. .. cf.'

**ἄγνωτος**, add 'Call.*fr.* 620 Pf. (v.l. ἄγνωστον). **II** w. gen., *ignorant* of, φωνὰν .. ψευδέων ἀ. Pi.*O.* 6.67.'

**ἀγορά I**, line 11, after '*AB* 327' insert 'in Crete, *SEG* 32.908 (Phaestos, vi BC)' and after 'in late prose' insert '(as Lat. *forum*) ἀ. δικῶν, *court of law* of provincial governor, τὰς πόλεις τὰς ἐχούσας ἀγορὰς δικῶν Modest.*Dig.* 27.1.6.2' at end add 'Myc. *a-ko-ra* (sense dub.)'

**ἀγοράζω 1**, delete '*occupy the market-place*' **2**, add 'κοιμητήριον .. ἀγορασθὲν .. παρὰ Φλαβίας Μαρίας *SEG* 29.641 (AD 507)' add '**4** *meet in assembly*, *SEG* 3.115.19 (Athens, iv BC).'

**ἀγοραῖος I**, line 3, after 'E.*Heracl.* 70' insert '*IG* 1³.42.5, in Crete, *SEG* 23.566 (Oaxus, iv BC)'; line 5, before 'generally' insert 'of Heracles, *SEG* 32.672 (Thrace, ii AD)' **III 1**, line 3, after 'Str. 13.4.12' insert 'Πέργη ἡ πρώτη τῶν ἀγορέων (cf. *conventus iuridici*), *SEG* 34.1306 (iii AD)'; line 4, before '*IGRom.* 4.790' insert 'also ἡ ἀγοραία, *IG* 12 suppl. 261 (Andros, i BC), *JRS* 30.148 (letter of Hadrian to Beroea); of a place used for market-day, τῷ τόπῳ τὴν καλουμένην ἀγορεῖον (sic) *SEG* 32.1149 (Magnesia ad Maeandrum, AD 209)' **2 b**, for this section read 'a weight, ἀγοραῖος λεῖτρα *EA* 16.141 (Nicomedeia, iii AD)' at end add 'Myc. *a-ko-ra-jo*'

***ἀγορᾱνομεῖον**, τό, = ἀγορανόμιον, *POxy.* 75.14 (ii AD), etc.

***ἀγορᾱνομεύω**, *to be* ἀγορανόμος, *SEG* 30.662 (Abdera, iii BC), unless error for -νομέω.

**ἀγορᾱνομέω**, add '**II** *preside in the assembly*, *IG* 9(2).517.10 (Larissa, iii BC).'

***ἀγορᾰσιαστικός**, ή, όν, = ἀγοραστικός, ἀπὸ ἀ. δικαίου *PLond.* 1727.32 (vi AD), *PMonac.* 4.16 (vi AD).

**ἀγόρᾰσις**, for '*PRyl.* 2.45.5' read '*PRyl.* 245.5'

**ἀγοραστής**, add '**II** *manager of a business*, *JEA* 39.84, *SEG* 24.1179 (Egypt, iii BC), al.'

**ἀγοραστός**, add 'perh. also *CIJud.* 98*'

**ἄγος** (A) **1**, add 'Cypr. *to-te-a-ko-se*, prob. τόδε ἄγος, on a lead tablet to provide a curse against tomb robbers, *ICS* 311 (= *Salamine* 7)' **2**, add 'ἁγι(α) (neut. pl.) *IPamph.* 3.13, *SEG* 34.989 (Sicily, i/ii AD)'

**ἄγρα III**, for 'Artemis' read 'Demeter' and for 'ib. 273' read '*IG* 1³.369.91, cf. Pl.*Phdr.* l.c.'

***ἀγρακόμας**, kind of bird (Pamphyl.), Hsch.

***ἀγραμματεύω**, *to be illiterate*, *SB* 5174.17, 5175.21 (vi AD), al.

**ἄγραμμος**, add '**II** = ἀγράμματος, *illiterate*, *PMeyer* 13.24 (ii AD).'

***ἀγραρεύω**, *lie in garrison*, *PGrenf.* 2.95.2 (vi AD), *SB* 7656.8, etc.; cf. °ἀγραρία.

***ἀγραρία**, ἡ, Lat. *agraria, garrison*, *PHerm.* 75.2 (v AD), etc. **2** as cult-title, Μητρὶ Θεῶν ἀγραρίᾳ *IGRom.* 1.92.

***Ἀγραστυών**, ῶνος, ὁ (sc. μήν), name of a month in Locris, *IG* 9²(1).721*C*2 (ii BC); also **Ἀγρεστυών**, **Ἀγροστυών**, *GDI* 1757, 1880.

***Ἀγρατέρα**, v. °Ἀγροτέρα.

***ἀγράφιος**, ον, perh. *not fit for writing on*, *PMich.*II 123ᵛ vii 25, 128.1(*a*)25 (both i AD). **II** subst. *note, blank roll*, used in business transactions, *PHarris* 104.12; *PMerton* 24.17. **2** v. ἀγραφίου γραφή.

**ἀγρεῖος 1**, add 'Θεοί *TAM* 2(1).148.7 (Lydia)' **2**, after '*boorish*' insert 'Alcm. 16.1 P.' and at end add 'neut. as adv. ἀγρεῖον .. ἐξεγέλασσε Call.*fr.* 24.13.Pf.'

**ἀγρειοσύνη**, delete '*clownishness* or'

***ἀγρελάτης**, ου, ὁ, (ἄγρα, ἐλαύνω) perh. *game-beater*, *POxy.* 1917.41 (vi AD).

**ἀγρέμιον**, (*prey*), add '*SB* 5301.2 (ἀκρ-), 8, 12 (pl., Byz.)'

***ἄγρενον**, v. ‡ἄγρηνον.

***ἀγρεσιθήρα**, app. epith. of Artemis, *POxy.* 3876 *fr.* 2.7 + *fr.* 6(*b*).2.

***Ἀγρεστυών**, v. °Ἀγραστυών.

***Ἀγρετέρα**, v. °Ἀγροτέρα.

**ἀγρέτης**, after 'Hsch.' insert '**b** title of magistrate or military leader in Crete, *BCH* 70.590 (Dreros, vii BC); cf. ἀγρεταί, ἀγρετεύω, °ἀγρήιον.' **II**, for 'from .. *fields*' read '*hunter* (ἄγρα) or *assembler* (ἀγείρω)'

**ἄγρευμα II 2**, for '*net* thrown over Agamemnon' read '*net* of fate'; at end add 'τύχης ἀγρεύμασιν Gorg. B 11.19 D.-K.'

**ἀγρεύς I**, of Apollo, add '*SEG* 35.491 (Atrax, *c.*200 BC)'

**ἀγρευτικός**, after 'Sch.E.*Ba.* 611' insert 'w. gen., Herm. *in Phdr.* p. 74'

**ἀγρεύω**, line 4, before '; of war' insert ', cf. ἀγρεύων αἷμα ταυροκτόνον ibid. 138' and after 'S.*fr.* 554' insert '*catch* by stealth, οὕτως .. ἂν .. ἥκιστα ὑπό τινων ἀγρευθεῖεν λάθρᾳ προσελθόντων Aen.Tact. 22.11; *capture* booty, id. 24.4' **2**, delete 'thirst for .. 138'

**ἀγρέω**, at end after 'cf. ἄργειτε' add 'ἐξαγρέω, ἐφάνγρενθειν (s.v. ἐφαιρέομαι 2), °ἀνhάγλημαι, ζωγρέω. Myc. 3 sg. aor. *a-ke-re-se*'

***ἀγρήγορος**, ον, *from which there is no waking*, τὸν ἀ. ὕπνον *CIG* 9449 (vi AD).

***ἀγρήιον**, τό, *meeting-place*, perh. in *Inscr.Cret.* 4.9 (Gortyn, vii/vi BC), cf. °ἀγρέτης I.

***Ἀγρήιος**, ὁ (sc. μήν), name of a month at Locri Epizephyrii, de Franciscis *Locr.Epiz.* 13, 22, 31, 34.

**ἀγρηνόν**, add 'also perh. ἄγρενον, rest. in D.P. 9.20'

**ἀγρία**, add '**II** = ἄγρωστις, Sch.Theoc. 13.42b.'

***ἀγριαγγούριον**, τό, *squirting cucumber*, expl. of ἀγριοσίκυον *AB* 1097 (ἀγρανγούρην cod.); cf. ἄγγουρον, ἀγγούριον *cucumber* in Sophocles *Greek Lexicon*.

***ἀγριάμπελος**· ἡ βρυωνία βοτάνη Hsch.

***Ἀγριάνια**· νεκύσια παρὰ Ἀργείοις. καὶ ἀγῶνες ἐν Θήβαις Hsch.; cf. ‡Ἀγριώνια.

***Ἀγριάνιος**, ὁ (sc. μήν), Aeol. Ἀγερράνιος, *IG* 12(2).527.45 (Eresus), name of a month at Sparta, *IG* 5(1).18*B*8, at Rhodes, ib. 12(1).906, at Epidaurus, ib. 4².109.2.13, at Illyria, *SEG* 36.565.5, at Cyprus, ib. 23.685(g), at Caria, ib. 14.715, at Lesbos (Eresus) l.c.; cf. ‡Ἀγριώνιος.

***ἀγριβρόξ**· ὀρίγανον Hsch.

***ἄγρινος**, ὁ, = ἀγρονόμος, *MAMA* 3.663 (Corycus); cf. ἄγρινοι· ἀγρονόμοι. καὶ οἱ παιδερασταὶ οὕτως Hsch. (La.).

***ἀγριόαιξ**, αιγος, ἡ, *wild goat*, Rhetor.in *Cat.Cod.Astr.* 7.225.9.

**ἀγριόεις I**, after 'Nic.*Al.*' insert '30' **2**, delete the section.

**ἀγριολειχήν**, add 'Aët. 8.16 (426.220 O.)'

**ἀγριόμορφος**, add 'ἀγριόμορφον ὄφιν *PLille* inv. 71 (*CRIPEL* 6.247, Hellen.)'

**ἄγριος I 2**, add '**b** subst. ἄγρια, τά, *weeds*, fig., ἄ. ψυχῆς Plu. 2.38c.'

**ἀγριοσίκυον**, add 'cf. ἀγριοσύκιον ἀγρανγούρην (read ἀγριοσίκυον ἀγριαγγούριον) καλεῖται *AB* 1097'

***ἀγριόσκορδον**, τό, *wild garlic*, Paul.Aeg. 7.3 (260.25 H.).

***ἀγριοσύκιον**, v. °ἀγριοσίκυον.

***ἀγριοχηνοπρυμνίς**, ίδος, ἡ (sc. ναῦς), *ship with wild goose as* ἀκροστόλιον, *PMonac.* 4.9 (vi AD; -πρήμνης pap.).

**ἀγριόω II 1**, add 'of way of life, τὸν ἀγριωμένον εἰς ἥμερον δίαιταν ἤγαγον βίον Mosch.Trag. 6.28 S.'

***Ἀγρίππαιος**, ὁ (sc. μήν), name of a month in Cyprus beginning Nov. 2, *Cat.Cod.Astr.* 2.144.17, al.

***Ἀγρίππηα**, τά, name of an athletic festival, *SIG* 1065.3.

***Ἀγριππήσιοι**, οἱ, name of a Jewish community at Rome, *CIJud.* 1.365, al.

***Ἀγριππίνειος**, ὁ (sc. μήν), an Egyptian month in Caligula's calendar, *APF* 9.225 (i AD; -νήου), *POxy.* 3780.8 (written Ἀγριππῖνος, i AD), etc.

**Ἀγριώνια**, for 'etc.' read 'at Thebes, *IG* 7.2447 (prob. i BC)'

**Ἀγριώνιος**, add '**II** (sc. μήν) name of a month in Boeotia, *IG* 7.3348, *SEG* 24.343, al., see also °Ἀγριάνιος.'

***ἀγροβάτας**, α, *ranging over the fields*, v.l. for -βότας in S.*Ph.* 214, E.*Cyc.* 54.

⁺**ἀγροβότης**, v. °ἀγροβάτας.

***ἀγρογειτνία**, ἡ, *adjacent plot*, *PMasp.* 151.112, al. (vi AD).

**ἀγροικικός**, after '*rustic*' insert '*SB* 7337.20 (inscr., 41 BC)'

***ἀγροϊώτικος**, ή, όν, *rustic*, μοῖραν ἔχων ἀγροϊωτίκαν Alc. 130.17 L.-P.

***ἀγρόκηπον**, τό, (or -πος, ὁ, masc.) *garden-plot*, *IG* 2².2776.145 (ii AD).

***ἀγροκωμήτης**, ὁ, *perh. member of rural assembly*, *TAM* 4(1).45.14 (Bithynia, Rom.imp.).

***ἀγρομυρίκινος**, ον, *of wild tamarisk*, *PHamb.* 12.19.

**ἀγρονόμος I 2**, add '**b** *farmer*, Opp.*H.* 4.602.'

**ἀγρός I**, after 'Od. 24.205' insert 'Call.*fr.* 489 Pf.' **2**, line 4, after '(Od.) 1.185' insert 'φροῦδοι πάλαι εἰσὶν εἰς ἀγρόν into the *countryside*, Men.*Dysc.* 776'; line 6, for 'τὰ ἐξ ἀγρῶν' read 'τὰ ἐκ τῶν ἀγρῶν' at end add 'Myc. *a-ko-ro*'

***Ἀγροστυών**, v. °Ἀγραστυών.

***ἀγρότας**, α, ὁ, perh. = ἀγρέτης I, *leader*, Alcm. 1.8 P., A.*Pers.* 1002 (codd., ἀγρέτ- cj.).

***Ἀγροτέρα**, ἡ, Ion. **-τέρη**, cult-title of Artemis, Il. 21.471, X.*Cyn.* 6.13, *EAM* 101, al.; worshipped at Agra in Attica, Arist.*Ath.* 58, *IG* 2².1028 (Athens, i BC), Paus. 1.19.6; *h*αγρατέρα (app. for *h*α ἀγρατέρα) *PP* 42.47 (Tarentum, vi BC), Ἀγρετέρα *IG* 2².4573 (iv BC), ἡ Ἀγροτέρα alone, X.*HG* 4.2.20, Ar.*Eq.* 660.

⁺**ἀγρότερος**, α, ον, (ἀγρός; cf. ὀρέστερος) *living in the wild*, ἡμίονοι, σύες, αἶγες Il. 2.852, 12.146, Od. 17.295; ἀγροτέρης ἐλάφοιο Hes.*Sc.* 407; φὴρ ἀ. Pi.*P.* 3.4; abs., ἀγρότεροι Theoc. 8.58; ἀ. καὶ νέποδες *AP* 6.11 (Satrius); of the nymph Cyrene, Pi.*P.* 9.6. **2** of rural inhabitants, *AP* 9.244 (Apollonid.), *APl.* 4.235 (id.). **3** of plants, *wild*, *AP* 9.384.8, cf. Nic.*Th.* 711, Coluth. 112, ὁδοῦ *MDAI(A)* 18.269. **4** v. °Ἀγροτέρα.

**ἀγρότης II**, delete the section amalgamating quots. w. section I (omitting 'Alcm. 23.8') **III**, delete the section.

**ἀγρυπνέω 2**, after 'Lxx *Da.* 9.14' insert '*SEG* 34.1243 (Abydos, v AD)'

***ἀγρυπνίστως**, adv. = ἀγρύπνως, *PLond.* 1660.12 (vi AD, -πτίστως pap.).

**ἄγρυπνος**, adv., add 'Aët. 2.93 (183.8 O.), Paul.Aeg. 1.87 (62.25 H.)'

**ἀγρυπνώδης**, at end add '(ed. ἀγρύπνῳ)'

***ἀγρῷος**, α, ον, *rustic*, *of the country*, Sch.Theoc. 3.1a.

**ἀγρώσσω**, line 3, after '*hunting*' insert 'Euph. 58.3 vGr.'

**ἀγρώστης I**, for 'Theoc. 25.48' read 'Theoc. 25.51' **II**, add 'adjectivally ἀγρώ[σ]ταισιν ἐπιύζων σκυ[λάκεσσι] *Suppl.Hell.* 939.21 (i/ii AD, hex.)'

***ἄγρωστος**, kind of grass, *PMil.Vogl.* 214.1.3, 7 (ii AD).

***Ἀγυαία**, ἡ, unkn. deity, *Sokolowski* 2.131 (Chios, v BC).

***Ἀγυεῖος**, v. °Ἀγυίηος.

**ἄγυια 1**, at end add 'Elean for Att. στενωπός acc. to Paus. 5.15.2'

**ἀγυιάτης 2**, for '(Phars.)' read '*SEG* 23.408 (both Pharsalus, iv BC; for doubts about the interpr. v. *BE* 1965.212)'

**Ἀγυιεύς 1**, add 'Ἀπόλλωνι Ἀγυεῖ *ITomis* 116(1).i 1, ii 2 (Rom. imp.)' **2**, add 'Cratin. 403 K.-A., Men.*fr.* 811 K.-Th. (both from Harp.)'

⁺**Ἀγυίηος**, ὁ, (sc. μήν), name of a month, *Schwyzer* 91.2 (iii BC), Ἀγυήιος ib. 92.2 (Argos, iii BC), *Inscr.Cret.* 4.197.11 (ii BC), Ἀγυεῖος *IG* 9²(1).638.6.2 (Naupactus, ii BC), *GDI* 1975.2 (Delphi, ii BC), *SPAW* 1936.371(*b*).4 (Potidania, ii BC).

**ἀγυμνάσία**, add 'Gal. 5.72.5'

**ἀγυμναστία**, add 'Gal. 5.91.3'

**ἀγύμναστος 2**, at beginning insert 'ἀ. φρενὶ E.*fr.* 598, πόνοις δέ γ' οὐκ ἀ. φρένας id.*fr.* 344'

***ἀγυοτόμητος**, *not divided into fields*, *POxy.* 3047.5, al. (iii AD).

**ἄγυρις 2**, for '*gathering* of herbs' read '*mixture, collection*, ἐν μὲν δὴ βοτάναις ἄγυριν λυγρῶν τε καὶ ἐσθλῶν'

⁺**ἀγύρτης**, ου, ὁ, (ἀγείρω) *wandering beggar, mendicant*, δόλιος ἀ., of Tiresias, S.*OT* 388, E.*Rh.* 503, 715, Lysipp. 6 K.-A., Hp. *Morb.Sacr.* 1.10, Clearch. 5 (= 49 W.), ἀ. καὶ μάντεις Pl.*R.* 364b; of priests of Cybele, Μητρὸς ἀ. *AP* 6.218 (Alc.Mess.); Γάλλοις ἀ. Babr. 141.1. **II** a throw of the dice, Eub. 57.5 K.-A. (On the accent cf. Hdn.Gr. 1.77)

**ἀγυρτικός**, for '*vagabond*' read '*mendicant*'; for '*juggling*' read '*of or belonging to mendicants*'; for '*jugglery*' read '*mendicancy*'

**ἄγχαυρος**, add '**II** subst., ὁ, *the time near dawn, morning twilight*, Call. *fr.* 260.64 Pf., Suid.; cf. Hsch. s.v. ἀγχοῦρος.'

⁺**ἀγχεμωλία**, ἡ, ἀνκεμō[λιαν] acc., prob. *law-suit* undertaken for a close relative, *Inscr.Cret.* 4.21.3 (Gortyn, vi BC); cf. °ἀντιμωλία, ἀμφιμωλέω.

***ἀγχιάλίτης**, ου, ὁ, *one who lives near the sea*, Steph.*in Rh.* 269.15 (pl.).

**ἀγχιβαθής 2**, add 'cj. for °ἀγχιβαφ- ib. 15.3'

***ἀγχιβαφής**, ές, *half-submerged*, Nonn.*D.* 15.3 (cod., cf. °ἀγχιβαθής).

***ἀγχίδικος**, Pythag. name for *six*, *Theol.Ar.* 38.

**ἀγχιθάλασσος**, add '-ος, ἡ, *coastland*, *EA* 14.22 l. 34 (Ephesus, i AD)'

**ἀγχίθεος**, after '*Od.* 5.35' insert '*h.Ven.* 200; of priests, *approaching god*, Luc.*Syr.D.* 31' deleting this ref. at end.

**ἀγχίθῠρος 1**, add 'fig., w. gen., γήραος ἀ. *AP* 7.726.4 (Leon.Tarent.)'

**ἀγχιμολέω**, delete the entry.

**ἀγχίμολος**, add 'ἀ]γχίμολοι rest. in A.*fr.* 168.28 R.'

**ἀγχινοία**, line 3, for 'etc.' read '*PVindob.Tandem* 2.5 (iii AD)'

*__ἀγχιπῦρα__, ἁ, (ἄγχω, πῦρ) *instrument for extinguishing altar-fire*, *SEG* 17.146.10 (Argos iv BC; but see *BE* 1988 p. 385 no. 586).

*__Ἀγχίσαιος__, ὁ (sc. μήν), name of a month in Cyprus beginning June 2, *Cat.Cod.Astr.* 2.146.12, 148.1.

*__ἀγχιστήδᾱν__, ἀνχιστἐδαν ἐπινεμέσθō, *amongst near kin*, *IG* $9^2$(1).609.5 (Naupactus, v BC); cf. ἀγχιστίνδην.

**ἀγχιστικός**, add 'ἀ. νόμος *Thasos* 192.4 (i AD)'

**ἀγχιστίνδην**, after 'Hsch.' add '(ἀγχιστάδην La.)'

**ἄγχιστος III**, at beginning insert 'neut. pl. as adv.'

*__ἀγχίτεξ__, εκος, ἡ, *near the birth*, *soon to bring forth*, Theognost.*Can.* 40 A.; cf. ἀγχιτόκος, ἐπίτεξ.

*__ἄγχνοος__, v. °ἔγχνοος.

**ἀγχόνη I**, for this section read '*rope for hanging*, *noose*, οἱ δ' ἀγχόνην ἅψαντο δυστήνῳ μόρῳ Semon. 1.18 W., A.*fr.* 47a.14 R., Neophr. 3.2 S., Apollod. 3.13.3, Plu.*Brut.* 31; in pl., ἐν ἀγχόναις θάνατον λαβεῖν E.*Hel.* 200; *HF* 154; αἱ ἀ. μάλιστα τοῖς νέοις Arist.*Pr.* $954^b35$. **2** transf., *hanging*, ἀγχόνης .. τέρματα A.*Eu.* 746; ἔργα κρείσσον' ἀγχόνης deeds too bad for *hanging*, S.*OT* 1374; τάδ' ἀγχόνης πέλας E.*Heracl.* 246; ταῦτ' οὐχὶ .. ἀγχόνης ἔστ' ἄξια id.*Ba.* 246; ταῦτα .. οὐκ ἀ.; Ar.*Ach.* 125.'

*__ἀγχονιμαῖα__ ξύλα, *gallows-trees*, Phot. s.v. ὀξυθύμια- (ἀγχονομ- cod.).

+**ἀγχοῦρος**· ὄρθρος· Κύπριοι. ἢ φωσφόρος καὶ οἱ σὺν αὐτῷ .. Hsch. (La.); see also °ἄγχαυρος.

**ἄγχουσα**, add 'Nic.*Th.* 638, 838; given as another name for ὀνοχειλές, Dsc. 4.24; for λυκαψός, id. 4.26'

**ἄγω**, line 4, for 'Sapph. 159' read 'Sapph. 169 L.-P.'; after 'Tim.*Pers.* 165' insert '(a barbarian speaks)'; after 'ἄξας' insert '(read ᾆξας)'; line 5, after 'ἄξαι' insert '(f.l.)'; after 'Antipho 5.46' insert 'συνᾶξα *GDI* 1772.17, 1791.8 (both Delphi, ii BC), ἄξατε Nonn.*D.* 1.11, 34, etc.'; delete '*SIG* 1 (Abu Simbel, vii/vi BC)'; line 6, after 'X.*Mem.* 4.2.8' insert 'ἄγωγα $Dura^4$ 122'; line 13, delete 'also .. 8.20' **I 3**, line 11, after '(Locr., v BC)' insert 'Plb. 18.5.1' **6**, after 'A.*Ag.* 406 (lyr.)' insert 'ἀπήμαντον ἄγων βίοτον Pi.*O.* 8.87' deleting this ref. in section IV 4. **II**, add '**7** *handle* or *carry* on the books, *POxy.* 290.7 (AD 83/4), *BGU* 820.2 (AD 187/8), 84.4 (AD 242/3), *PFay.* 40.8.' **V**, line 4, delete 'θεοὺς .. 924' at end add 'Myc. 3 sg. *a-ke*'

**ἀγωγαῖος**, add '**II** subst., ἀγωγαῖα, τά, perh. *entrance rites*, *APF* 16.175 (Chios, iv BC).'

**ἀγωγεύς I**, add '**4** generally, *director*, *organizer* of a festival, *Milet* 1(7) no.263 (iii AD).'

**ἀγωγή I 2**, for 'ὑμῶν' read 'ἡμῶν' **II 3**, line 6, after 'youth' insert 'Sosib. 4 J.'; line 7, for 'Δακεδαίμονι' read 'Λακεδαίμονι'

**ἀγωγός I**, after '*aqueduct*' insert '*SEG* 29.1157 (Lydia, Rom.imp.), *IEphes.* 3217(b).24' and after 'without ὕδατος' insert '*SEG* 31.953B (AD 113/20)'; at end add '*able to guide* or *influence*, ἀνθρώπων D.H.*Dem.* 22, cf. *Th.* 2'

**ἀγών II**, add 'καθεμένō τὠγῶνος *SIG* 38.32 (Teos, v BC), *IG* 5(2).113 (Tegea, v BC)' **III 6 b**, for '*power*' read '*urgency*, Cic.*Att.* 1.16.8'

*__ἀγωνάριον__, τό, dim. of ἀγών, *competition*, *Inscr.Cos* 43 (ii BC); εἰς ἀγωνάρια γυμνικά, *SEG* 38.1462.23 (Oenoanda, AD 124/6).

+**ἀγωνάρχης**, ου, ὁ, *organizer of contest* or *games*, S.*Aj.* 572, *IHadr.* 132.

*__ἀγώναρχος__, ὁ, an official in Boeotia, either in charge of games, or an equiv. of ἀγορανόμος in other cities (Sch.T Il. 24.1), *IG* 7.1817, *SEG* 23.271.3, cf. ib. 275, *IGC* p. 98 A1 (Acraephia, iii/ii BC, v. *SEG* 32.450).

**ἀγωνία 1**, add '**b** *trial*, οὐ .. τὴν ἀγωνίαν ὑπεισελθεῖν βουλομένοις Just.*Nov.* 49.1 pr.' **3**, for '*agony*' read '*anxiety*'

**ἀγωνικός**, add 'Ps.-Acro in Hor.*C.* 3.12.8; perh. also ἀγōνιϘὸν πόρο[ν] Lang *Ath.Agora* XXI K3 (vi BC)'

**ἀγώνισμα I**, add 'τὸ τελεώτατον τῶν ἀ. *SEG* 31.903.29 (Aphrodisias, iii AD, see also *BE* 1984.41)' **IV**, for '*plea*' read '*point at issue*'

*__ἀγωνιστήρ__, ῆρος, ὁ, *organizer of games*, perh. at *IG* 11(4).1053.30-1 (Delos; rest., v. *ZPE* 6.270).

**ἀγωνιστήριον**, for '*assembly*' read '(*judicial*) *contest*'

**ἀγωνιστήριος**, for '= ἀγωνιστικός' read '*of* or *associated with contests*' and add 'σάλπιγξ Poll. l.c.'

**ἀγωνιστικός I 1**, at end delete 'τὸ ἀ. ib. 219c, e'

**ἀγωνοδίκης**, add 'perh. at *SB* 10493.2 (AD 228)'

**ἀγωνοθεσία**, add 'also ἀγωνοθετία, *SEG* 7.825.14 (Gerasa, ii AD)'

**ἀγωνοθετέω I 2**, for 'Plb. 9.343' read 'Plb. 9.34.3'

**ἀγωνοθέτης 1**, add '*POxy.* 2611.14, al. (AD 192/3), Dor. ἀγωνοθέτας, *SEG* 30.1218 (Tarentum, iv BC); ib. 23.271 (Thespiae, iii BC)' **2**, after '*judge*' insert 'in any contest'

*__ἀγωνοθετία__, v. ‡ἀγωνοθεσία.

**ἀγωνοθετικός**, after '(Sparta)' insert 'τιμαί *SEG* 13.244 (Argos, i BC/i AD), *SEG* 23.317 (Delphi, i AD)'

*__ἀγωνοφῠλᾰκία__, ἡ, perh. *office of warden of the games*, *PRyl.* 90.2, al. (iii AD, unless to be read as ἀλωνο-).

*__ἀγώρις__, v. ‡ἀώριος.

*__ἄγωρος__, v. ‡ἄωρος (A).

*__αδα__· ἡδονή Hsch.; cf. *EM* 16.45, Arc. 105.

*__ϝᾰδᾱ́__, ἁ, Cret., *decree*, *decision*, *SEG* 37.352.A6 (Lyttos, *c.*500 BC); cf. ‡ἅδος (A), ‡ἅδημα, °ἅδισμα, ἅδιξις.

*__Ἄδαδος__, ὁ, the Syrian divinity Hadad, *Inscr.Délos* 2261, also Ἄδατος ib. 2258, (both ii/i BC); *Adadus*, Plin.*HN* 37.186; identified w. Zeus, *SEG* 31.731 (Delos, ii/i BC), ib. 28.1336 (Syria, ii/iii AD) (in some texts editors print Ἁ-).

**ἀδαίδαλτος**, for '*not carved*' read '*not ornamented*'

**ἀδαίετος**, add '*ZPE* 1.185.11 (oracle of Apollo Clarios, ii AD)'

*__ἀδαιτηί__, adv., perh. *without distinction*, *Inscr.Cret.* 4.51.13 (v BC).

**ἀδαίτρευτος**, for pres. def. substitute '*with no meat carved*'

**ἀδάκρῡτος I**, line 4, after 'ib. 106 (lyr.)' insert 'cf. Isoc. 19.27, Herodes *Pol.* 16 A.' **II 1**, add '*AP* 7.545 (Hegesipp.)'

*__ἀδᾰμαντίς__, ίδος, ἡ, a fabulous plant said to be found in Armenia and Cappadocia, Ps.-Democr.ap.Plin.*HN* 24.162.

**ἀδᾰμαντόδετος**, delete '(A.*Pr.*) 426' (v. °ἀκαμαντ-)

**ἀδᾰ́μαστος**, add 'adv. -τως Procl. *in Ti.* 2.314 D.'

**ἀδᾰ́μᾰτος**, last line, for 'restored by Elmsl.' read 'in all cases restored by edd.'

*__ἀδᾰμής__, ές, *invincible*, θεοί .. ἀδαμεῖς dub. in Swoboda *Denkmäler* 16 (Misthia in Pisidia).

*__ἀδᾱ́μιος__, v. ἀζήμιος.

*__ἀδαμμα__, *priest in cult of Agdistis*, Pouilloux *Rhamnonte* 140 no. 24.4 (prob. Phrygian, i BC).

*__ἀδαξησμός__, v. °ὀδαξησμός.

**ἄδαστος**, add '*SEG* 39.1001.4 (Camarina, ii/i BC)'

**ἄδδαυον**, for 'i.e. ἄζανον' read 'ἀδδανόν La.'; at end insert '(cf. ἀζαίνω)'

*__ἇδε__, adv., *in this manner*, *as follows*, *Schwyzer* 322 (Delphi, late v BC); ἆδ' ἔϝαδε Bile *Dial.crét.* no. 2 (Dreros, vii/vi BC); cf. ἆ δέ κα· ὅταν Κρῆτες Hsch. (La. p. 39).

+**ἀδεαλτόω**, app. *deface*, *erase*, αἰ δέ τιρ ἀδεαλτώhαιε τὰ(ν) στάλαν *Schwyzer* 424 (Olympia, iv BC); cf. ἀδηλόω, δεϝαλῶσαι s.v. °δηλόω.

**ἀδεής** (A), after 'Ep. ἀδειής, -ές' insert 'ἀδιής *IG* 12(3).552 (Thera); adv., ἀδιέως *SEG* 9.3.36 (Cyrene, iv BC)'

**ἀδέητος II**, after 'Ptol. *Tetr.* 159' insert '(cj.)'

**Ἀδειγάνες**, add 'v.l. πελιγᾶνες'

+**ἄδεικτος**, ον, *not indicated*, Ph. 1.197. **2** *invisible*, id. 1.618, al.

*__ἀδελιφήρ__· ἀδελφός, Λάκωνες Hsch.

*__ἀδελπιός__, v. °ἀδελφός.

*__ἀδελφεός__, v. °ἀδελφός.

**ἀδελφή**, line 3, after 'Ep. -ειή' insert 'Call.*fr.* 43.57 Pf.'; line 4, after '*OC* 535' insert 'ἀδευπιαί (nom. pl.) *Inscr.Cret.* 4.72 v 18; ἀδελφιά *GVI* 1275.9 (Thessalonica, ii AD)' add '**4** as cult epith., Νύμφηι Ἀδελφῆι *Kafizin* 35, al.'

*__ἀδελφιδεύς__, έως, ὁ, *nephew*, *Inscr.Délos* 1993 (i BC), *PGrenf.* 1.47.6 (ii AD).

**ἀδελφιδός**, delete '*beloved one*'

**ἀδέλφιον**, add '*SEG* 36.1182 (Galatia, v/vi AD), *SEG* 34.658 (Maced., iii AD, written -ιν)'

*__ἀδελφιός__, v. °ἀδελφός.

**ἀδελφίς**, add '**II** = ἀδελφή, *MAMA* 3.598 (Corycus).'

*__ἀδελφοθετία__, ἁ, app. *festival of brotherhood* or *rite of fraternal adoption*, οἱ πολῖται ἑορταζόντω παρ' ἀλλάλοις κατὰ τὰ‹ς› ἀ›δελφοθετίας *SEG* 30.1119 (Entella, Sicily, iii BC).

**ἀδελφόπαις**, add 'J.*AJ* 4.6.12'

**ἀδελφός I**, line 2, after '-εόο' insert '-ε‹ι›οῖο Call. in *Suppl.Hell.* 260A.5'; for 'Cret. ἀδελφιός .. 18.319' read 'nom. pl., -ειοί A.R. 3.731, Locr. ἀδελφεός *SEG* 23.358 (vi/v BC), Boeot. ἀδελφιός *SEG* 22.416 (Thebes, iv/iii BC); ἀδελπιός *Inscr.Cret.* 4.72.2.21 (Gortyn, v BC); ἀδευφιός ib. 4.208.A2 (ii BC)' **II 2**, at end for 'cf. Pl.*Smp.* 210b' read 'Lys. 2.64, Pl.*Smp.* 210b, Aen.Tact. 24.14.'

*__ἀδελφοσύνη__, ἡ, *fraternal* or *friendly sentiment*, *MAMA* 5.91 (Dorylaeum); as term of address, *fraternal kindness*, *CPR* 5.23.5, 10 (?v AD), *PMilan.* 87.5 (vi AD).

**ἀδελφότης III**, add 'ἀσπάζομαι τὴν ὑμετέραν γνησίαν ἀδελφ(ότητα) καὶ τὰ παιδία αὐτῆς *PVindob.Worp* 14.1 (vi/vii AD)'

*__ἀδεξίαστος__, ον, (δεξιάζω) *not to be trusted in an engagement*, Ptol.*Tetr.* 166.

*__ἀδεξιοβολία__, ἡ, *unskilful casting*, Ps.-Callisth. 24.30.

**ἀδέσποτος I**, add 'prob. in Alc. 207.3 L.-P.'

*__ἀδευπιά__, v. °ἀδελφή.

*__ἀδευφιός__, v. °ἀδελφός.

*__ἀδεφένδευτος__, ον, = Lat. *indefensus*, *undefended*, Just.*Nov.* 155.1.

**ἀδέψητος**, for '(δεψέω)' read '(δέψω)'

*ἀδή, v. °ϝαδά.
*ἀδηΐζω, app. *harbour, protect* (from the law), *SEG* 9.3.39 (Cyrene, iv BC); cf. ἀδεής (A).
*ἀδηληγάτευτος, ον, of taxes (app.) *not forming part of the delegatio* or *fixed rate, POxy.* 3424.5; cf. δηληγατεύω.
ἄδηλος, line 3, for 'hyaloid membrane' read 'capsule of the lens'
ἀδηλόω, add 'cf. perh. °ἀδεαλτόω'
ἄδημα, before 'Hsch.' insert '*decree, SEG* 28.1540 (Cyrene, i BC)'; at end add 'cf. °ϝαδά'
ἀδημονέω, line 2, after 'D. 19.197' insert '*Ev.Matt.* 26.37, *Ev.Marc.* 14.33'; line 6, delete 'which is found only .. derivation'
†ἀδήμων, ον, gen. ονος, *distressed,* Gal. 17(1).177, Eust. 833.15; v.l. Hp.*Epid.* 1.18.
*ἀδής, v. ἀηδής.
Ἀιδης or ᾄδης, line 1, after 'Dor. Ἀΐδας, α' insert 'Ἁΐδα (gen.) *SEG* 34.994 (Apulia, late iv BC); Thess. Ἁίδ[α]ο (gen.) *CEG* 120 (Demetrias), ἈϜίδαν (acc.) ib. 121 (Larissa, both *c.*450 BC)'; line 2, after 'anap.' insert 'voc. Ἄιδη, *h.Cer.* 347, Ἀΐδα epigr. in *Inscr.Cret.* 3.iv 39*B*11 (ii BC)'; line 3, after 'infr.' insert 'acc. Ἄϊδα (–⏑⏑) Arat. 299 M., Nic.*Th.* 181'; at end after 'Semon. 7.117' insert '*E.fr.* 936', after 'prob. in' read '*E.HF* 116 (lyr.)' and after '*S.OC* 1689' insert '(lyr.); ἀΐδεω *AP* 6.219.24 (Antip.Sid.), 7.711.8 (id.)'
ἀδηφαγέω, for 'of horses' read 'in part., of horses, = °ἀδηφάγος 1b'
ἀδηφάγος, lines 3/5, for 'ἀ. λύχνος' to end of article read '**b** t.t. for a category of horses at the games, Pherecr. 212 K.-A., Ar.*fr.* 758 K.-A. (both fr. Phot.), Theopomp.Hist. 250 J., *IG* 2².2311.55 (Athens, iv BC); cf. °ἀδηφαγέω; superl., Ach.Tat. 4.3.2. **2** fig., *eating up* fuel, money, etc., ἀ. λύχνος Alc.Com. 21; τριήρεις Lys.*fr.* 39, cf. Philist. 68 J.'
*Ἀδιαβηνικός, ὁ, Lat. *Adiabenicus, of Adiabene* in Syria, an imperial title, *TAM* 4(1).27; *ICilicie* 78 (both iii AD), al.
*ἀδιάβροχος, ον, *waterproof,* D.P. 2.1.
*ἀδιάβρωτος, ον, *not eaten through,* Paul.Aeg. 6.85.1 (127.7 H.).
ἀδιάγνωστος, add '*hard to read,* Ptol.*Tetr.* 47'
*ἀδιάγραφος, ον, perh. *without deduction,* δηνάρια *PDura* 29.8 (iii AD).
ἀδιάδοχος, add 'of Christ, *SEG* 32.1588 (Egypt, vi/vii AD)'
ἀδιάθετος, after 'Sch.Il. 22.487' insert '**b** perh. *not having one's schedule arranged,* Plu.*Cat.Ma.* 9.' **2**, delete 'Plu.*Cat.Ma.* 9' and after '(ii AD), al.' insert 'ἐξ ἀδιαθέτου (= Lat. *ab intestato*) Just.*Const.* Δέδωκεν 7, *Nov.* 1.1.1, *Cod.Just.* 1.5.15'
ἀδιαίρετος **I 1**, add 'ἐξ ἀδιαιρέτου equiv. of Lat. *pro indiviso, ISmyrna* 897 (ii/iii AD)'
*ἀδιάκλαστος, ον, *unbroken, Poliorc.* 257.9.
ἀδιᾱκόνητος, for 'ἐπιστολήν' read 'ἐντολήν'
ἀδιάλειπτος, after 'adv.' insert '-τον Sch.S.*OT* 198 P.'; at end add 'λε[ι]τουργήσαντι ἀδιαλείπτως Mitchell *N.Galatia* 178 (Rom.imp.)'
ἀδιάλῠτος **I**, after 'Hierocl. p. 17.23 A.' insert 'Procl.*Inst.* 48 D., al.; adv. -τως id. *in Ti.* 1.397.1'
*ἀδιαμέλητος, gloss on ἀφραδής, Hsch.
ἀδιαπᾰτητος, delete the entry (v. °ἀδιπάτητος).
ἀδιάπλαστος, add 'Gal. 4.662.16, 10.987.5, Athenag.*Res.* 17.2'
ἀδιάπνευστος **I**, add 'οἶνος νέος ἀ. Sm.*Jb.* 32.19'
ἀδιάπταιστος, add 'adv. -τως Procl. *in Ti.* 1.193.19'
ἀδιάπτωτος, line 2, after '*PRyl.* 77.46 (ii AD)' insert 'Iamb.*Protr.* 21 κ' (118.24 P.); *unfailing, without deficiency,* χρήματα *SEG* 36.788 (Samothrace, iii BC)'
ἀδιαρίπιστον, delete the entry.
*ἀδιαρρίπιστον, gloss on ἄκροτον, Hsch.
*ἀδιασάφητος, ον, *not made at all clear, unexplained,* Sch.Pi. (*Eustathii prooemium*) ed. Drachmann vol. 3 p. 286.3.
*ἀδιάσηπτος, ον, *not penetrated by putrefaction,* Paul.Aeg. 6.85.1 (127.7 H).
ἀδιάστολος, add '**II** *undistributed, UPZ* 180a 15.9 (ii BC), al.'
ἀδιάστροφος **III**, adv., line 2, before 'ἀφίεσθαι' insert '*without evasiveness*' and add '(*Cod.Just.*) 10.27.2.13'
ἀδιάσωστος, after 'Ptol.*Tetr.* 47' insert '(v.l.)'
ἀδιάτμητος, for '*not cut in pieces*' read '*not to be cut*'
ἀδίαυλος, add 'of the journey there, τὴν ἀ. ὁδόν *IG* 9(2).648.1'
ἀδιάφορος, add '**VII** *free of interest,* ἀρτάβαι *POxy.* 2351.24 (ii AD).'
ἀδιαχώριστος, after '*undistinguished*' insert 'Arist.*EE* 1219ᵇ34' and after 'Suid.' insert 'w. gen., *inseparable from, SEG* 8.574 (Fayûm, prob. iii AD)'
*ἀδιαψήφητος, ον, *without a vote,* i.e. by acclamation, ἀ. νε[ικήσας] *Delph.* 3(1).550.5.
*ἀδιγόρ· τρωξαλλίς, ὑπὸ Σκυθῶν Hsch. (La.).
*ἀδιεγγύ[ητος], *not making security, IMylasa* 830.2 (or ?ἀδιέγγυ[ος]).
ἀδιεξίτητος, after 'Ph. 1.554' insert 'τὸ -ον Procl.*Inst.* 94 D.'
ἀδιήγητος, after 'Cic.*Att.* 13.9.1' insert 'ἀδιήγηθ' ὅσα *indescribably many,* Men.*Dysc.* 405'
*ἀδιής, v. ‡ἀδεής (A).

ἀδικέω **II 2**, after 'X.*Eq.* 6.3' insert '*Apoc.* 7.2, 9.4, etc.; ἀδικεῖν τὸ ὕδωρ *damage* the water supply, *IEphes.* 3217A.11 (ii AD); ὃς δὲ ταύτην [σ]τήλην ἀδικήσῃ[· Mitchell *N.Galatia* 294'; at end add 'transf., τὸ μέτρον ἠδίκητο *violence was done to* the metre, D.H.*Comp.* 9'
*ἀδίκησις, εως, ἡ, *wrongdoing, PMasp.* 6.2 (vi AD).
ἀδικητικός, after 'Plu. 2.562d' insert 'Ar.Byz.*Epit.* 2.144'
ἀδῐκία, add '**III** cessation of judicial and all other public business in the event of war, etc., Arist.*Oec.* 1348ᵇ10.'
*ἀδιοβάντης, ου, ὁ, perh. fr. Lat. *adiuvans,* an official, *PAnt.* 96.12.
*ἀδίοπτος, ον, *opaque,* Alex.Aphr.*de An.* 148.4.
*ἀδιούτωρ, ορος, ὁ, Lat. *adiutor, assistant, PLond.* 1711.89 (vi AD), al.
*ἀδιπᾰτητος, ον, perh. *not thoroughly trodden* or *crushed,* πυρός *POxy.* 1259.15, 2125.20 (both iii AD), *PSI* 1053.8 (ii/iii AD).
*ἄδισμα καὶ ἄδμα· ψήφισμα, καὶ δόγμα Hsch.
ἀδιάστακτος, reverse the order of the first two refs.; before '*PTeb.*' insert 'ἀ. πάσης αἰτίας *not disputed* on any ground'
*ἀδιψάθεος, ὁ, (or -ον, τό), a shrub, app. = ἀσπάλαθος 1, Plin.*HN* 24.112 (v.l.).
*ἀδιψία, ἡ, *absence of thirst, Poliorc.* 203.4.
*ἄδμα, v. °ἄδισμα.
ἄδμητος, line 1, for 'poet. for ἀδάματος' read 'Dor. ἄδμᾱτος, B. 11.84 S.-M.' add '**3** *unconquered, AP* 7.723.'
*ἀδμινιστρατίων, ονος, ἡ, Lat. *administratio, official rank* or *function,* ἀπὸ κέρτας ἀ. *Cod.Just.* 6.48.1.10.
*ἀδμισσάριος, ὁ, Lat. *admissarius,* ταῦρος ἀ. bull *for breeding, Edict.Diocl.* 32.4.
ἀδμολίη, for 'Call.*Fr.* 338 .. Suid.' read 'Call.*fr.* 717 Pf. (v.l. -μωλίη, -μωλή)'
ἀδμωλή, after 'ἄγνοια' insert '*PAnt.* 60 (ii/iii AD), *CGFP* 204'
*ἀδμωλίη, v.l. for ‡ἀδμολίη, ‡ἀδμωλή.
*ἀδνοτατίων, ονος, ἡ, Lat. *adnotatio, imperial decision on a petition, SB* 9763.34 (v AD), *PMonac.* 14.85 (sp. ἀδνου-, vi AD).
ἀδοκίμαστος, add '**2** *unexamined, uninvestigated,* Just.*Nov.* 6.1.10.'
ἀδόκιμος **I**, after 'Pl.*Lg.* 742a' insert 'ἀ. ἀργύριον silver *that has failed the assayer's test,* Lxx *Pr.* 25.4, τὸ ἀργύριον ὑμῶν ἀ. your money is *not genuine, Is.* 1.22'
ἀδολεσχέω **II**, for 'Lxx *Ps.*68(69).12' read 'Lxx *Ps.*68(69).13'
ἀδολεσχία, for '*prating, garrulity*' read '*talk, chatter*' **II** and **III**, delete the sections transferring quots. to section I.
ἀδόνητος, add 'ἀστεμφεῖς καὶ ἀδόνητοι Agath. 1.21.8 K.'
ἄδοξος, line 2, after 'X.*Smp.* 4.56' insert '*Trag.adesp.* 423 K.-S.'
*ἀδόρωτος, ον, *not plastered,* prob. in *PMich.*v 253.5 (i AD, ἀδωρ- pap.).
ἅδος (B), after lemma insert '(or ἄδος)' and after '*decree*' insert '*sentence*'; for 'ἅδεῖν' read 'ἀδεῖν' and add 'perh. ϝαδόν acc. *SEG* 37.743.12-13 (Axos, iv BC); cf. °ϝαδά'
ἄδος, for 'ἦδος' read 'ἧδος'
ἀδούλωτος, after 'D.S. 1.53' insert '*Inscr.Perg.* 413 (i BC)'
*ἀδουσιάζομαι, *accept membership of,* φυλῆς καὶ δήμου καὶ φρατρίας ἀδουσιάσασθαι *IG* 2².553.15 (iv BC). **b** ἀδουσιασάμενοι· διελόμενοι, ὁμολογησάμενοι Hsch. (ἀδ- La.).
ἀδουσιασάμενοι, delete the entry.
*ἀδούσιον, *that is in agreement, BCH* 59.96 (Delphi, ii BC; unless read as pers. n. Ἀδούσιο[ς], v. *BE* 1953.93, ἀ.· ἐραστόν, σύμφωνον Hsch.
ἀδρᾰνεια, before 'Hdn. 2.10.8' insert 'Demetr.*Eloc.* 285 (-ία)'
ἀδρᾰνής, line 5, after '(Simp. *in Ph.*) 815.24' insert 'Procl.*Inst.* 7 D., τὸ μὲν ἀδρανὲς ὂν καθ' αὑτό, τὸ δὲ ἀπαθές ib. 80 D.'
Ἀδράστεια **1**, at end add 'or a goddess linked with but distinguished from Nemesis, Men.*fr.* 266 K.-Th., Nicostr.Com. 35 K.-A., *SEG* 33.645 (Rhodes, i BC); identified w. Fate, ἀνάγκη, etc., Chrysipp.*Stoic.* iii 292.15, cf. Orph.*fr.* 54'
*ἀδρασταδάραν, title of Persian official, Procop.*Pers.* 1.6.18.
*ἀδρεσπόνσουμ, Lat. *ad responsum,* title of official on the staff of a praetor, Just.*Edict.* 13.2; also -σον, Athanasius Scholasticus *coll.* 4.4 (Heimbach p. 54).
*Ἀδρεύς· δαίμων τις τῶν περὶ τὴν Δήμητραν, *EM* 18.36, cf. perh. cult-epith. in fragmentary dedication, *SEG* 31.745 (Naxos, Hellen.).
*Ἀδριάνειος, ον, *of Hadrian,* of a contest in his games, *SEG* 12.512 (Cilicia, ii/iii AD); Ἀδριάνεια, τά, festival at Athens named after Hadrian, *IG* 2².2050.18, 2067.17 (both ii AD), *TAM* 4(1).34; at Ephesus, *IEphes.* 618, 724, etc.
*Ἀδριανιών, ῶνος, ὁ, name of a month at Athens, *IG* 2².2050.14, 2067.197 (both ii AD).
*Ἀδριανονίκης, ου, ὁ, victor in the Hadrianic Games, *POxy.Hels.* 25.31 (AD 264).
*Ἀδριανός, ή, όν, *of* or *connected with Hadrian,* τῆς ἱερᾶς Ἀ. .. συνόδου *IG* 2².1350; of cities, Nicomedeia *TAM* 4(1).25, Tarsos *ICilicie* 30; Ἀ. γερουσία *IHadr.* 40; as a title of Zeus, *SEG* 33.1090 (Bithynia, i AD). **2** Ἀ. ὁ, sc. μήν, an Egyptian month = Choiak, *SEG* 31.1532 (Philae), *SB* 282, *BGU* 1616 (all ii AD); at Aphrodisias = Λῷος *ABSA* 59.29 no. 46.6. **3** neut. pl. subst. Ἀ., τά, *Hadrianic games,*

in Cilicia, Moretti *IAG* no. 87.23, at Smyrna, *IG* $2^2$.3169.26 (both iii AD).

***ἁδρομελής**, *ές*, *strong-limbed*, cj. in Emp. B 67.2 D.-K. (comp.).

**ἁδρός I**, line 4, after 'id. 20.85' insert 'of a sieve, *coarse*, *large-meshed* (comp.), *Gp.* 3.7.1; of measure, *full*, *μέτρον τετραχοινικὸν ἁ.* *SB* 10532.27 (AD 87/8)' **II 1**, add '**b** *grand*, Ael.*NA* 10.50 (comp.), Hsch.' and transfer to this '*οἱ ἁ.* *chiefs* .. *Ki.* 10.6' adding '*Je.* 5.5, *Jb.* 29.9, etc.' **2**, for '*fine, fat*' read '*well-grown, sturdy*' **3 c**, for '*ready to be laid*' read '*fully developed*'

**ἁδρόσφαιρος**, add 'Plin.*HN* 12.44'

***ἁδρότης**, v. ‡*ἀνδρότης*.

**ἁδροτής**, after lemma insert '(or ?-**ότης**)'

**ἁδρόχωρον**, delete '*full*, *χῶρον*'

**ἁδρυάς**, add 'Nonn.*D.* 2.92, 22.14, al.'

**ἁδρύνω**, line 2, after 'Thphr.*HP* 3.1.3' insert 'of a young girl, *εἰς γάμον* *AP* 6.281 (cj. Leon.Tarent.)' and at end add 'of children, Lxx *Jd.* 11.2, 4*Ki.* 18, al.; *solidify*, of ice, Ael.*NA* 14.26'

***ἀδρῠφής**, *ές*, *unscratched*, *undamaged*, *Iamb.adesp.* 38.14 W.

**ἀδῠνᾰμία**, line 2, after 'Hp.*VM* 10' insert 'Lys. 31.19, Pl.*Lg.* 646b'

**ἀδῠ́νᾰμος**, after '*weak*' insert '*without strength*, of a woman, *SEG* 35.227.28, 30 (tab.defix., Athens, *c.*AD 250)'

**ἀδῠνᾰσία**, for '= *ἀδυναμία*' read '*physical weakness*'; after 'Hdt. 3.79' insert '*military weakness*'; after 'gen.' insert '*incapacity* for'

***ἁδῠ́ποτος**, v. ‡*ἡδύποτος*.

***Ἀδυτηνή**, *ἡ*, name of a goddess, *θεὰ Βρυζη ἁγνὴ Ἀδυτηνή* *TAM* 5(1).533 (Maeonia, iii AD), al.

**ἄδῠτος**, add '[*ῡ* *SEG* 8.551.3 (i BC)]'

**Ἀδωνάρια**, for 'kind of .. *gifts*' read 'lines of verse in a particular kind of metre, *ἀ. πέμψας ἄρρυθμα*; cf. *Ἀδώνιος* II 2'

**Ἀδώνια**, after 'Pherecr. 170' insert 'Diph. 42.39 K.-A., *IG* $2^2$.1261.9 (Peiraeus, 302/1 BC), etc.'

**Ἀδωνιάζω**, add '*Ἀδωνιάζοντες* *SIG* 1113.2 (Rhodes, ii/i BC)'

***Ἀδωνιασταί**, *οἱ*, *guild of worshippers of Adonis*, *SEG* 4.168 (Caria, prob. i AD).

**Ἀδώνιος II**, add '**4** name of a month *SEG* 30.1119 (Sicily, iii BC).'

**Ἄδωνις I**, line 2, for '*ῶ*' read '*ῶ̄*' **2**, for 'cuttings planted' read 'corn, etc., grown'

***ἀδωσιδῐκέω**, *fail to pay one's due*, *PMich.*v 243.2, al. (i AD), *POxy.* 2351.58 (ii AD).

**ἀδωσιδῐκία**, add '*BGU* 1212.16 (i BC)'

**ἀδώτης**, line 2, for '*a*' read '*ἀ-*'

⁺**ἀέθλευμα**, v. °*ἄθλευμα*.

⁺**ἀεθλοθέτης**, v. ‡*ἀθλοθέτης*.

⁺**ἀεθλοσύνη**, v. °*ἀθλοσύνη*.

**ἀεί I 5**, after '*ἀείδασμος*' insert '(*αἰδασμος*)' and add 'Arc. *αἰ̂* *Schwyzer* 687.28 (Tegean decr. at Delphi, 324 BC)' **8**, after 'Boeot. *ἠί*' insert 'v.s.v., also °*ἠίν*' add '**10** *ἀή* *APAW* 1952(1).11 (Cos, in Lacon. dial., iii BC). **11** *ἀείσε* Steph. *in Hp.* 1.129.' at end for note in parenthesis read '(*αἰϝεί*, *CEG* 1, 344 (Phocis, vi BC); Cypr. *a-i-we-i* *ICS* 217.31; cf. *καταιϝεί* (°*καταεί*); see also °*ὐϝαίς*)'

**ἀειβλύων**, delete the entry.

***ἀείβουλος**, *ον*, *that is a perpetual counsellor*, *θεόκτιστον πρ(εσβύτερον) ὄντα, πάντων μύστην καὶ ἀείβουλον* *Inscr.Cret.* 2.xxiv 7.5.

**ἀειγενής 2**, for '*everlasting*' read '*born again and again*'

**ἀειγένητος II**, for '= *ἀειγενής*' read '*eternal*'

**ἀείγνητος**, for '*ον*, = *ἀειγενέτης*' read '*η*, *ον*, = *ἀειγένητος*'

**ἀείδελος I**, for '*dark* .. etc.' read '*obscure*, Hes.*fr.* 67b M.-W., Opp.*H.* 1.86, *C.* 3.489, *ἀ. ὠπήσασθαι* ib. 3.160'

⁺**ἀείδιος**, v. °*ἀΐδιος*.'

**ἀείδω**, line 8, delete 'Ar.*Lys.* 1243 (Lacon.)' and after 'Poets, as' insert 'Theoc. 22.135, Call.*Ap.* 30, *Dian.* 186'; line 24, after 'Pl.*Tht.* 164c' insert 'Ar.*fr.* 101 K.-A., *Av.* 41; = *μάτην λέγειν*, Phot. *α* 551 Th.'; at end add 'opp. *φράζειν* Str. 1.2.6' **II 1**, add '*τὸ ᾀδόμενον τοῦτο* *as the saying is*, Ael.*NA* 5.11' **2**, after 'B. 6.6' for 'etc.' read 'Arr.*An.* 1.11.2, 4.9.5, Philostr. *VA* 5.8'

**ἀείζωος**, line 3, after 'ib. 741' insert 'Pl.*Ep.* 8.356a'

**ἀεικέλιος**, after 'Il. 14.84' insert 'A.R. 2.1126, Nic.*Th.* 271'

**ἀεικής 1**, line 5, for '*meagre*' read '*unfitting*'; line 6, after '(Il.) 24.594' insert 'of persons, Od. 9.515 (v.l.), *h.Cer.* 83, 363, Call.*fr.* 344 Pf., A.R. 4.91' **2**, add 'Critias 7.11 S.'

**ἀεικί̄νητος**, after 'adv. *-τως*' insert '(prob. f.l. for *ἀκινήτως*)'

***ἀείκλαυστος**, *ον*, *to be for ever wept for*, *mourned*, *IG* 12(2).489.19 (Mytilene, i/ii AD). **2** *filled with perpetual lamentation*, *μέλαθρα* hymn ap.Hippol.*Haer.* 4.32 (= *GDRK* 53.4).

**ἀείκλαυτος**, delete '*μέλαθρα* .. 4.36' and substitute '*ἀεικλαύτῳ παρὰ τύμβῳ* *IKyme* p. 251 (*SEG* 29.1218, ii/i BC)'

***ἀεικοίματος**, *ον*, *sleeping everlastingly*, *Lyr.adesp.* 119.8 P.

***ἀείμνημα**, *τό*, gloss on *σκέλισμα*, Hsch.

**ἀείμνηστος**, add '*TAM* 4(1).138 (Bithynia, Rom.imp.), *SEG* 33.1106 (Paphlagonia, iii AD)'

**ἀειναῦται**, for 'at Chalcis' read 'or perh. association of sailors at Eretria, *SEG* 34.898 (Eretria, *c.*510/500 BC)'

**ἀειπάρθενος I**, for 'Sapph. .. *ἀϊπ-*)' read '?Alc. 304.5 L.-P. (*ἄϊ*[∪∪]*παρθενος* pap.)'; add 'of the Virgin Mary, *IEphes.* 4135.19; in epitaphs, of unmarried women, *BCH* suppl. 8 no. 23 (Edessa, v/vi AD), al.'

***ἀείπολος**, *ον*, *ever-moving*, *Orac.Chald.* 61(f).2 P.

***ἀειπρέπεια**, *ἡ*, *everlasting dignity*, *Corp.Herm.* 18.4.

**ἀείρω**, line 14, after 'E.*Hel.* 1597' insert '*Rh.* 54 (*αἰρ-* codd. in both places), Pl.*Lg.* 969a'; delete 'imper.' and after 'A.R. 4.746' insert '(v.l.)' **I 1**, penultimate line, after 'Hp.*Aër.* 6' insert 'but also of the *rising* of heavenly bodies, E.*Alc.* 450 (lyr.), Arat. 326, 405, 558 and so perh. in Alcm. 1.63 P.; intr., of heavenly bodies, *rise*, *ἕως ἂν αὐτὸς ἥλιος ταύτῃ μὲν αἴρῃ* S.*Ph.* 1331' **2**, add '*pick up* lots, *SEG* 30.1119.22 (found at Entella, iii BC)' **7**, add '*SEG* 30.1231 (med., Lugdunum, iii AD)' **III**, add '**3** *αἴ. ἀνά τι* *divide* by, *PRyl.* 27 i 1, al.; *αἴ. ἀπό τινος* *subtract* from, ib. 8.' **IV 1**, after 'B. 2.5' insert 'Pl.*Lg.* 969a' **3**, delete '*βοῦς* .. 27.5' and add '**b** *τοὺς βοῦς αἴ.* *perform* the bull-*hoisting*, *IG* $1^3$.82.29 (v BC), *IG* $2^2$.1028.10, 13, 28 (i BC), cf. *ἄρσις* I 1a; *ταῦρον ἀράμενοι* Paus. 8.19.2; cf. Thphr.*Char.* 27.5.' **4**, add '*μὲ ἔναι πόλεμον ἄρασθαι* *IG* $1^3$.105.35' **V 2**, add '**b** of rivers, X.*HG* 5.2.5, *AP* 9.568 (Diosc.).'

***ἀεισέβαστος**, *ὁ*, = Lat. *semper Augustus*, *Ephes.* 4(1) no. 33, *SEG* 9.356 (Cyrenaica), *BCH* suppl. 8 no. 81 (Thessalonica), (all vi AD).

***ἀείσειστος**, *ον*, *being always in a confused state of movement*, (opp. *ἀεικίνητος*) (cj. for *ἄσειστος* q.v.) D.L. 8.26 (cf. Thesleff *Pythagorean Texts* p. 235.1).

**ἀεισῑτία**, add 'pl., *ἀισειτιῶν* *SEG* 30.82 (Athens, *c.*AD 230)'

**ἀείσῑτος**, for '(in form *ἀϊσ-*)' read '(in form *ἀεισ-* or *ἀϊσ-*)' and add '*SEG* 28.94'

**ἀεκαζόμενος**, after '*πολλ' ἀ.*' insert 'Il. 6.458'

**ἀέκητῐ**, add 'Dor. **-ατι** B. 18.9 S.-M.'

**ἀεκούσιος**, line 3, after 'Democr. 240' insert '*ℎακόσι[α]* *IG* $1^3$.6B.5 (v BC)'

***ἀελιδρόμος**, *ὁ*, perh. *portico*, *BCH* 84.852 (Lissos, Crete).

**ἄελλα**, line 1, for 'Aeol. .. Hsch.)' read 'perh. Aeol. *ἄυελλα* *Lesb. fr. adesp.* 7 L.-P. (w. *υ* for *ϝ*; fr. Hsch., where cod. *αυεουλλαι* pl.), cf. °*Ἀελλώ*'; line 3, after '(Od. 5.) 304' insert 'Hes.*Th.* 874'; line 4, omit 'cf.' and transfer '13.334' to follow 'Il. 13.795' (line 3).

**ἀελλοπόδης**, add 'of a wild ass, Opp.*C.* 3.184, *θυγατέρες Λυκάβαντος ἀελλοπόδοιο τοκῆος* Nonn.*D.* 11.486'

**ἀελλόπος**, add '*ἀελλοπόδεσσ' ἐλάφοισι* Opp.*C.* 1.191'

**Ἀελλώ**, add 'perh. *Aϝε[λλώ]* on a vase, *SEG* 37.330 (Laconia, vi BC)'

**ἀελπής**, add 'neut. pl. as adv., Nic.*Al.* 125'

**ἄελπτος**, for '*unhoped*' read '*unlooked*'; line 4, delete '987 (prob. l.)' **II**, delete this section transferring '*h.Ap.* 91' to section I (see also °*ἄεπτος*) **III**, for '*hope*' read '*expectation*'; after 'S.*El.* 1263' insert 'in bad sense, A.*Supp.* 987'

⁺**ἄεμμα**, *τό*, *bow*, Call.*Dian.* 10, *Ap.* 33, Philet. in *Suppl.Hell.* 673.4; cf. *ἅμμα*.

**ἀένᾰος**, for '*ἀείνως*' read '*ἀείνως*'

***ἀένιος**, *α*, *ον*, *everlasting*, hymn in *Suppl.Hell.* 990.8 (perh. for *ἀέναος*).

***ἀεξίκᾰκος**, *ον*, *nourishing evil*, Nonn. *D.* 20.84.

**ἀέξω**, line 1, for 'twice in Trag.(lyr.)' read 'rare in trag.'; line 3, aor., add 'med., [*ἠ*]*έξαντο* Call.in *Suppl.Hell.* 287.9'; pass., add '*ἀεξήθησαν* Nonn.*D.* 45.150' **I 1**, before '*increase*' insert '*cause to grow* or *flourish*, *υἱὸν ἀ.* Od. 13.360; of plants, Od. 9.111'; after 'Od. 17.489' delete '*υἱὸν* .. 360'; after '(Od.) 15.372' insert '*δόμων ἀ. κάλλος* A.*fr.* 451n.5 R.'

***ἄεπος**, *ον*, *not uttering a word*, (dub. l.) Baillet *Inscr.des tombeaux des rois* 1402.

⁺**ἄεπτος**, *ον*, (*ἕπω*) *not to be dealt with*, *irresistible*, *fierce*, A.*Supp.* 908 (cj. *ἄελπτ'*), *Ag.* 141 (v.l. *ἀέλπτοις*), *fr.* 213 R. (or *ἄαπτ-*).

**ἀερικόν**, for '*tax on lights*' read 'name of a tax'

**ἀέρῐνος 3**, for this section read 'a precious stone, Ps.-Callisth. 1.4.13 (prob. f.l. for *ἀερίτης*)'

**ἀέριος II**, delete '*πῦρ* Hp.*Vict.* 1.10' (v. *ἠέριος*); at end add '**b** epith. of Zeus, *TAM* 5(1).616 (Lydia, AD 223/4 or 277/8); perh. also *θεός* *Expl.arch. de Délos* xi p. 276.'

**ἀέριπον**, delete the entry.

**ἀερί̄της**, add 'Anon.Alch. 360.13'

**ἄερκτος**, add 'Hsch. (cod. *ἀεριπ-*)'

***ἀεροκέλαδοι**· *πιτυοκάμπται* Hsch.

***ἀερόλευκος**, *ον*, app. *dull white*, Anon.Alch. 387.14 (perh. f.l. for *ἀκρό-*).

***ἀερολόγος**, *ον*, adj. without context in *PBrux.*inv. E7162.15 (*PP* 38.13; see also *Emerita* 56.236).

***ἀερομαντεῖον**, *τό*, *air-oracle*, *PMag.* 3.278.

***ἀερόμικτος**, *ον*, *mingled with the air*, *φώναισί τε ἀερομίκτοις* Orph.*fr.* 297; cf. *ἀερομιγής*.

***ἀερόμορφος**, ον, *air-formed*, Orph.*H.* 14.11, 16.1, 91.6 codd.; cf. ἠερόμορφος.

***ἀεροπετέω**, *cause to fly through the air*, ἀεροπέτησον τὴν ψυχὴν καὶ τὴν καρδίαν Λεοντίας *Suppl.Mag.* 43; pass., *PMag.* 36.111 (iv AD).

***ἀεροποτέομαι**, *fly through the air*, *Suppl.Mag.* 38 (ii AD); cf. °ἀεροπετέω and ποτάομαι, ποτέομαι.

**ἀεροριφής**, delete the entry (read -φερής).

***ἀεροφερής**, ές, *borne in the air*, *PMag.* 4.2508.

***ἄερσα**, v. ἔρση.

**ἀερσίλοφος**, add '**2** *lifting the crest of a mountain*, of a giant, Nonn.*D.* 48.44.'

**ἀερτάζω**, line 1, for '(Call.)*fr.* 19' read '*fr.* 261, 597 Pf.'

***ἀέρωμα**, ατος, τό, *patch* of ether *converted into air*, πρόσγεια ἀ. τοῦ αἰθέρος *Placit.* 2.30.6 (pl.).

***ἀέτιον**, τό, perh. dim. of °ἀετίς, *Inscr.Délos* 408.2 (ii BC); cf. ἀετός IV.

***ἀετίς**, ίδος, ἡ, *gabled stele*, *Sardis* 7(1).167 (iv AD).

**ἀετίτης**, add 'also **ἀετῖτις**, ιδος, ἡ, Plin.*HN* 37.187. **2** kind of convolvulus, Plin.*HN* 24.139.'

***ἀετόμορφος**, ον, *having the form of an eagle*, Procl.*in R.* 2.319 K.

**ἀετός I 1**, for 'S.*fr.* 885' read 'S.*fr.* 884 R.' add '**b** applied to vultures, *Ev.Matt.* 24.28, *Ev.Luc.* 17.37, *Apoc.* 12.14.' **3**, after 'Arat. 591' insert '(see also ‡ἄητος (A))' **II**, delete the section.

**ἀετοφόρος**, add '**2** *bearing an eagle*, of a coin, *Inscr.Délos* 1442*B*51 (ii BC).'

**ἀεχῆνες**, add 'cf. ‡ἀχήν'

**⁺ἀϝλανεως**, v. °ἀλανής.

***ἀζαβαρίτης**, v. °ἀζαραπατεῖς.

**ἀζαθός**, delete the entry.

**ἀζαίνω**, add 'cf. °ἄδδαυον'

**ἀζάλη**, add '(-ής La.)'

***ἄζαλμα**, v. °ἄγαλμα.

***ἀζάμιος**, v. °ἀζήμιος.

***ἀζαραπατεῖς**· οἱ εἰσαγγελεῖς παρὰ Πέρσαις Hsch., corr. to ἀζαβαρίτης, Ctes. 15 J.

**ἄζετον**, add '(πιστόν La.)'

**ἄζευκτος**, add 'ἀ. πόθοι *not joined in a (natural) pair*, Opp.*C.* 2.425'

**ἀζηλοπραγμόνως**, add '(s.v.l.)'

**ἀζήμιος**, after lemma insert 'dial. ἀζάμιος, *SEG* 34.849.18 (Mytilene, v BC), 25.447.12 (Alipheia, iii BC), 36.502.13 (Delphi, ii BC), also ἀσά[μιος] *Delph.* 3(1).342; ἀδάμιος *Schwyzer* 503a note (Coronea, *c.*200 BC), *Inscr.Cret.* 4.146.2 (iv BC), ἀττάμιος *Schwyzer* 424.7 (Elis, iv BC), *Inscr.Cret.* 4.183.15 (ii BC)' **2**, line 5, before 'Adv.' insert 'τὸ ἀζήμιον = Lat. *indemnitas*, *Cod.Just.* 1.3.55.4, 2.2.4.2'

***ἀζονίη**, ἡ, an unidentified plant, Claud.Herm.*Mul.* 988.

**⁺Ἀζόσιος**, ὁ, a month name at Epidaurus, *IG* $4^2$.103.127, al.; written Ἀζέσιος ib. 89; as epith. of divinities, θεῶν Ἀζοσίων ib. 434; Ἀζοσία, ἡ, ib. 410.13; cf. Αὐζησία s.v. °Αὐξησία.

***ἀζυγία**, ἡ, app. *bereavement*, *GVI* 2093.15.

**ἄζυγος**, add '*unyoked*, βοῦν ἄζυγον Dorieus in *Suppl.Hell.* 396.7'

***ἀζυμίτης**, ου, *unleavened*, ἐπὶ κολλυρῶν ἄρτων ἀζυμιτῶν Al.*Le.* 7.13.

**ἄζυξ**, for '*unyoked*' read '*that has not been yoked*'; after 'D.H. 1.40' insert 'B. 11.105, 16.20 S.-M.'

***Ἄζυρος**, ὁ, cult epith. of Apollo, *EA* 10.102.10.

**ἄζω** (B), after 'S.*fr.* 980' insert 'cf. Gal.*UP* 7.13' deleting 'so perh. .. *Th.* 99'

**ἄζωστος**, after '(Dreros, iii BC)' insert 'cf. πανάζωστος'

**ἀηδής**, after 'ές' insert 'contr. ἀδής cj. in Thgn. 296 W. (Aeol. acc. ἀυάδην Sapph. 22.5 L.-P., nom. pl. ἀυάδεες Alc. 259.11 L.-P.)'

**ἀηδία I 2**, after 'opp. ἡδονή' insert 'Men.*Dysc.* 435'

**ἀηδίζω**, pass., add '*SB* 4323.2 (Byz.)'

**ἀηδόνιος**, for '*Ra.* 684 .. *light*' read '*Ra.* 684; *like that of a nightingale*, Nicom.Trag. 13 S.; poet., of brief or fitful sleep'

**ἀηδών**, after 'ὁ, v. infr.' insert 'contr. ἀδών q.v.'

**ἄημι**, line 4, after '(Od.) 14.458' insert 'ἄεν A.R. 1.605, 2.1228'

**ἀήρ I**, line 3, after 'Thphr.*Sens.* 30' insert 'Triph. 669' **II**, add '**3** *space open to the air on a building, flat roof, terrace on a grave-monument*, etc., *Hierapolis* 158, Keil-Premerstein *Erster Bericht* no. 120, *PMonac.* 8.12, *PLond.* 1733.19 (both vi AD).'

**ἀήσσητος 2**, add 'as an imperial title (= Lat. *inuictus*), *SB* 4284.6 (AD 207), ἀηττήτων βασιλέων *POxy.* 3122 (AD 322)' at end add 'see also ‡ἀνήσσητος'

**⁺ἀήτη**, ἡ, Dor. **ἀήτα** Simon. 90 P., B. 17.91 S.-M., later **ἀήτης**, εω, ὁ, A.R. 4.1537, ου, X.Eph. 3.2.13, Hld. 1.22: masc. forms regular in Alex. and later poetry, also in some edd. of Il. 15.626, Od. 4.567, *blast* of wind, ἀνέμοιο .. δεινὸς ἀήτη (v.l. ἀήτης) Il. 15.626; pl. ἀνέμων .. ἀήτας ib. 14.254, Hes.*Op.* 621, cf. 645; Ζεφύροιο Od. 4.567, Νότοιο Hes.*Op.* 675 (fem.). **2** *wind, breeze*, ἀῆται Od. 9.139, Sapph. 2.10 L.-P., μεγάλαις ἀήταις id. 20.9 L.-P., Tim.*Pers.* 107, Call.*Del.* 318, *fr.* 110.53 Pf., Theoc. 22.9, ἀήτης μείλιχος A.R. 1.423, Q.S. 1.537, Nonn.*D.* 32.158, etc.; poet. wd., v. Pl.*Cra.* 410b.

**ἄητος** (A), add '[ἄη for ἄε w. play on ἄηται in 323]'

**⁺ἄητος** (B), ον, dub. sens., θάρσος ἄητον Il. 21.395 (= θάρσος ἄατον Q.S. 1.217); cf. αἴητος.

**⁺ἄητος** (C), ον, = ἄατος, ποηφάγος αἰὲν ἄ. Nic.*Th.* 783; ὁ ἀκατάπαυστος Hdn.Gr. 1.220; also ἄητοι· ἀκόρεστοι, ἄπληστοι παρὰ τὴν τροφήν, and ἀήτους· μεγάλας (A.*fr.* 3 R., ap. Hsch.).

***ἀηττησία**, ἡ, *invincibility*, Afric.*Cest.* p. 19 V.

**ἀθαλασσία**, delete the entry.

***ἀθαλάσσιος**, ον, of wine, *not mixed with sea-water*, *SEG* 39.959 (Eleutherna, ii/i AD); cf. ἀθάλασσος II.

**ἀθαλής**, after 'Ath. 12.254b' insert '(ἀειθαλές cod.)'

***ἀθανάτισις**, εως, ἡ, *deification*, D.C. 60.35.3 (cj.).

**ἀθάνατος I**, after 'Od. 24.47' insert 'in later cult Θεοὶ ἀθάνατοι *SEG* 33.1141 (Phrygia), 1187 (Lycaonia), of human beings in a continued existence after death, *IGBulg.* 796.4; οὐδεὶς ἀθάνατος formula in epitaphs, *SB* 3514, *SEG* 33.1276 (Jerusalem, i BC)' **II**, add 'of a boundary-stone, *SEG* 37.1036.5 (Calchedon, ii/iii AD)' **III**, add '**3** of imperishable, i.e. inanimate, property, in the formula θνατὰ (τνατὰ) καὶ ἀθάνατα *Inscr.Cret.* 1.xvi 17.12 (ii BC), 4.76*B* 8 (v BC), cf. *SEG* 9.1.§1.11 (Cyrene, iv BC); v. °θνητός.'

**ἀθάρη**, after '*porridge*' insert '*made of wheat*'

**⁺ἀθαρής**· ἄφθορος ἐπὶ γυναικός, ἐπὶ δὲ σιδήρου στερεός Hsch.

***ἀθαροφόρον**, τό, kind of vessel, presum. for holding ἀθάρη, *Kafizin* 133(a) (225/4 BC).

***ἀθεάφθειος**, ον, *unsulphurated*, of wine-jars, *BGU* 2205.16 (AD 590); cf. θεάφιον.

**ἀθεησίη**, place after 'ἀθεεί'

**ἀθελγής II**, after '*having no power to soothe*' insert 'or *charm*' and before 'al.' insert '42.248'

**ἀθέλητος**, after 'Hsch.' insert 's.v. ἀβούλητον'

**ἄθελκτος**, add '*Trag.adesp.* 665.29 K.-S.'

**ἀθεμελίωτος**, after 'Hsch.' insert 's.v. ἀτερμάτιστος'

***ἀθεμίζω**, Cypr. aor. inf. *a-te-mi-sa-i* ἀθέμισαι perh. *treat improperly*, *ICS* 311.2.

**ἀθέμιστος I**, delete '(the former .. Prose)'

**⁺ἄθεος** (A), *that is without God*, ἄθεος ἄφιλος, S.*OT* 661, *Ep.Eph.* 2.12; of things, *lacking divine nature*, παράδειγμα ἄ. Pl.*Tht.* 176e, *R.* 589e, Procl. *in Ti.* 1.368.6 D.; *having no connection with the gods*, ἀ. ὀνόματα Clearch. 86 W. **2** *godless, impious*, of persons, A.*Eu.* 151, S.*Tr.* 1036, E.*Or.* 925, *Ba.* 995; of actions, things, Pi.*P.* 4.162, B. 11.109 S.-M., A.*Pers.* 808, *Eu.* 540, E.*Andr.* 491, Ar.*Th.* 671, Gorg. 11a(36) D.-K. **3** *not believing in the existence of gods, atheist*, Pl.*Ap.* 26c; as a sobriquet, Cic.*ND* 1.23.63, S.E.*M.* 9.51; adv. -ως *in an unholy manner, dreadfully*, ἀ. ἐφθαρμένη S.*OT* 254, *El.* 1181, sup. -ώτατα, *El.* 124. **II** *impiously, godlessly*, Antipho 1.21, 23, Pl.*Grg.* 481a, 523b.

**ἀθερίνη**, add 'rest. in Hippon. 78.11 W.'

**ἀθέρμαντος**, at end add 'σώματα ἀ. Gal. 7.40.4'

**ἀθέσμιος**, after '*unlawful*' insert 'λέκτρον ἀ. Nonn.*D.* 25.16'

**ἄθεσμος**, add '*Trag.adesp.* 146a.5 K.-S.'

**ἄθεστος**, add '(= *Suppl.Hell.* 1066, cj. ἀπόθεστος)'

**ἀθέσφατος**, line 4, after '(Od.) 20.211' insert 'ἀ. φῦλ' ἀνθρώπων *h.Ap.* 298'

***ἀθετεία**, ἡ, *cancellation*, *PFam.Teb.* 9.15 (ii AD).

**ἀθετέω I 1**, add 'perh. *let fall into disuse*, ἐπὶ ἠθετημένου χώματος *SB* 11654 (AD 146/7)'

***ἀθετησία**, ἡ, *breach of faith*, Vett.Val. in *Cat.Cod.Astr.* 8(1).170 (acc. pl.).

***ἀθετητικός**, ή, όν, *treacherous*, *PMasp.* $353^v$.A12 (vi AD).

**ἄθετος II**, adv., for '= ἀθέσμως' read '*so as to set at naught*'

***Ἀθηνάδιον**, τό, *small image of Athena*, *POxy.* 1802 *fr.* 3.55 (ii/iii AD).

**Ἀθῆναι I**, delete '*IG* $1.373^{107}$' and at end add 'Th. 4.5; Σούνιον .. ἄκρον Ἀθηνέων Od. 3.278'

**Ἀθήναια**, τά, for '*IG* 3.1147' read '*IG* $2^2$.2119.22 (ii AD)' and add '*SEG* 35.218 (Athens, iii AD), Dor. Ἀθάναια *Schwyzer* 12.10 (Sparta, v BC)'

***Ἀθηναϊσταί**, οἱ, *guild of worshippers of Athena*, at Rhodes, *IG* 12(1).162.

**Ἀθήνη**, Ἀθηναίη, add '*ISmyrna* 739 (Ἀθηναέηι dat., *c.*600 BC), *SEG* 37.936 (Erythrae, vi BC)'; Ἀθηναία, add '*SEG* 32.1086 (Spain, vi BC)'; Ἀθάνα, add '*SEG* 35.419, 437 (Siphnian treasury at Delphi, vi BC)'; Ἀθαναία, for '*IG* $1.373^{108}$' read '*IG* $1^2$.499, *SEG* 30.380 nos. 1-4 (κἀθαναίαν, Tiryns, vii BC), *CEG* 375 (Laconia, vi BC)'; Ἀθανάα, for '*IG* 1.351' read 'ib. 711' add '**6** a type of aulos, Poll. 4.77.' at end add 'Myc. *a-ta-na*'

**Ἀθήνησιν**, (s.v. Ἀθῆναι), for this section read 'Ἀθήνησι(ν), Boeot. Ἀθάνασι Ar.*Ach.* 900, adv., *at Athens*, Th. 5.47, D. 17.28, 18.66'

**ἀθήρ**, for '*Lyr.adesp.* 2 B.' read 'Call. in *Suppl.Hell.* 253.1' **II**, after '*Cat.Mi.* 70' add '**b** of a tongue of fire, Eur.*fr.* 665a N.-S.' **III**, for this section read 'supposed *belly-fin* of the female tunny, Ath. 7.303d (quoting Arist.*HA* $543^a$14 where cod. has ἀφαρέα)'

***ἀθήριον**, τό, *wheat porridge*, *PPetaus* 36.3 (ii AD), *Stud.Pal.* 22.56.29 (ii/iii AD).

***ἀθηρώδης** (B), *gruel-like*, Paul.Aeg. 6.88.6 (133.16 H.).

***ἄθλευμα**, *ματος, τό*, in form *ἀέθλευμα*, = *ἄθλημα*, Eust. 1843.22 (pl.).

**ἀθλέω I**, at end add '2*Ep.Ti.* 2.5'

***ἀθλῐψία**, *ἡ*, *freedom from tribulation*, Critodem. in *Cat.Cod.Astr.* 8(1).259.

**ἀθλοθεσία**, after '*ἀθλοθέτης*' insert '*judging, awarding the prizes, Sokolowski* 1.49.B16 (Milet., ii BC)'

**ἀθλοθέτης**, add '*ἀεθλοθέτης IG* $2^2$.2193.2 (ii AD), *ἀεθλοθέτας SEG* 23.271.8 (Thespiae, iii BC)'

**ἆθλον**, *ἄεθλον*, add '*ἄϝεθλον IG* 5(2).75 (Tegea), *SEG* 30.52 (Athens, 430/20 BC), [*ἄ*]*ϝεθλα SEG* 26.472 (Tegea, vi BC), *hάϝεθλον SEG* 30.366 (Argos, 460/50 BC)'; line 5, for '*CIG* 776' read '*CIG* 7761'

**ἆθλος**, line 2, insert '*ἄϝεθλος SEG* 29.652 (Maced., 460/50 BC), *SEG* 30.1456 (Pontus, 470/50 BC)'; at end after '*IG* 5(2).75' insert '*SEG* 11.330 (Argos, v BC)'

**ἀθλοσύνη**, add '*BIFAO* 60.133; also **ἀεθλοσύνη** *AP* 5.293 18(Agath.)'

***ἀθλοφορεύς**, *ῆος, ὁ*, *victor*, *μάρτυρος ἀθλοφορῆος* Mitchell *N.Galatia* 211 (verse).

***ἀθμονάζειν**· *τὸ εἰς δῆμον* (i.e. Athmonon) *ἀφικνεῖσθαι τῆς Ἀττικῆς* Hsch.

**ἀθραγένη**, add 'Theophr.*Ign.* 64'

**ἄθρακτος**, add '*AB* 352'

**ἄθραυστος 2**, add '*invulnerable*, of a fortified place, *Pae.Delph.* 9; Plu.*Tim.* 18 (sup.)'

**ἄθρεπτος**, for 'Ar.Byz.*Epit.* 2.9.8' read 'Ar.Byz.*Epit.* 29.8'; for 'f.l. .. (Mel.)' read '*ἄ. καὶ ἀνάγωγοι γεγονότες ἄνδρες Act.Alexandr.* 1.2.6'

**ἀθρήματα**, add 'cj. Snell (*Glotta* 37.283) in Sapph. 44.9 L.-P.'

**ἀθροίζω**, line 8, after 'E.*Ph.* 495' insert '*put together, compile*, (in quots. in pass.), *τὴν νομοθεσίαν ἀθροισθῆναι ταύτην ἐγκελευόμενοι* Just.*Const. Δέδωκεν* 17, 20, 21' **2**, add 'so act. w. reflex. pron., *ἑαυτοὺς ἀθροίσαντες having pulled themselves together*, Ael.*NA* 9.43, cf. 10.48'

**ἄθροισις**, after 'E.*Hec.* 314' insert '*τὰς ἀθροίσεις καὶ τὰς πέμψεις .. ποιεῖσθαι* Aen.Tact. 4.12'

**ἀθρόος II 2**, for '*continuous*' read '*instantaneous*' and at end add 'v. *AJPh* 65.244/5' **V**, after 'Sup.' insert '*ἀθροώτατος* Isoc. 15.107'

**ἀθῡμέω**, lines 4/5, after 'id.*An.* 5.4.19' insert 'w. inf., *ἀ. ἐπιχειρῆσαι* Th. 7.21.3'

***ἀθῡμητής**, *οῦ, ὁ*, *one who is disheartened*, Phot. s.v. *ἄθυμος* (a 488 Th.).

**ἄθυρμα**, line 2, for 'Sapph.*Supp.* 20a.9' read 'Sapph. 44.9, 63.8 L.-P., *Inscr.Délos* 1441*A*i82 (ii BC)'; line 6, after 'Trag. and Com.' insert 'A.*fr.* 78c.50 R., Crates Com. 23 K.-A., Eup. 46 K.-A., E.*Hyps.fr.* 1 i 2 B.' and delete '*Com.adesp.* 839'

**ἄθῠρος II**, after '*unchecked*' insert '*ἀ. στόμα* Simon. 36.2 P.'

**ἀθῠροστομία**, after '= *ἀθυρογλωττία*' insert '*AP* 5.56 (Diosc.)' and for '*AP* 5.251' read '*AP* 5.252'

**ἀθύρω**, line 4, after 'A.R. 4.950' insert 'Pomp.Mac. 1.4 S.' **II 1**, add '**b** *λαῖφος ἀ. play with* the bedding, *h.Merc.* 152.'

⁺**ἀθύρωτος**, *ον*, *not fitted with a door* or *doors*, *οἰκία POxy.* 1699.6 (iii AD); of a pinax, perh. *without apertures* or *not shut up*, *Inscr.Délos* 1417A.12 (ii BC). **2** metaph., *ἀπύλωτον στόμα* Ar.*Ra.* 838 is read as *ἀθύρωτον σ.*, *unchecked* by Phot. α 495 Th., Suid.

***ἀθυσίαστον**, gloss on *ἀφαρκίδευτον*, Hsch. (*ἀρυτίδωτον* La.).

**ἄθῠτος I 1**, after '*omitted*' insert '*πελανός* E.*Hipp.* 147'

**ἀθῷος**, line 1, after '*ον*' insert 'Ion. **ἀθώϊος** *IG* 12(8).265.6 (Thasos, iv BC), al., Call. *VB* in *Suppl.Hell.* 260.7'

**ἀθῳόω**, for 'Iamb.*Bab.* 223' read 'Iamb.*Bab.* 5 Ha.'

**αἰ I**, add '*αἰ δὲ μὲ hυπερπαρσχ*[*ο*]*ῖιεν SEG* 30.380 no. 7 (Tiryns, vii BC)'

**ἀΐ**, read **ἀι(ν)** or **αἰι(ν)**.

**αἶα** (A), line 2, for 'cf.' read 'Stesich. 222(b).205 (p. 214 D.), Anacr. 3.1 P., Simon. 7.1 P.'

**αἶα** (B), omit '· *καὶ φυτόν .. ὁμώνυμος*'

**αἶα** (C), add '*αἶα .. καὶ φυτόν τι· ἔτι δὲ ὁ καρπὸς αὐτῷ ὁμώνυμος*, *EM* 27.24-26'

***αἰακώς**, *ἐμβαρύθων· ἐμπίπτων αἰακώς* Sch.Nic.*Al.* 541c.

**αἰᾱνής**, at end delete 'is dub.' and add 'perh. *Trag.adesp.* 700.24 K.-S.'

**Αἰάντειος**, delete '[penult. short Pi.*O.* 9.112]'; for '*festivals held in his honour*' read '*a festival held at Salamis in his honour, IG* $2^2$.1006.72, 1011.53, 1028.24'; after 'Zen. 1.43' insert 'Men. i p. 133 K.-Th. (cf. S.*Aj.* 303)'; add 'fem. *Αἰαντεία* name of a trireme, *SEG* 24.159 b.386-7 (Attica, iv BC); *Αἰάντειοι, οἱ*, *descendants of* (*Locrian*) *Ajax*, *Schwyzer* 366'

**Αἴᾱς**, at end, within the parentheses, add '*ΑἴϜας Schwyzer* 122(3), Corinthian vase'

***αἰβάλη**, Theognost.*Can.* 6 A., Hsch. (La. *αἰβάνη* cod.), Suid.; *αἰβαλέη*, Cyr.

⁺**αἰβάνη**, v. °*αἰβάλη*.

***αἰγάγριον**, *τό*, *meat of the αἴγαγρος* (*wild goat*), *Edict.Diocl.* 4.45.

**Αἰγαῖος**, after '*Aegaean*' insert '*πόντος* Ibyc. 1(*a*).28 P'; for '*mount Ida*' read 'a mountain near Lyctus'; after 'Hes.*Th.* 484' insert '*Αἰ. πεδίον*, a plain adjoining Crisa, id.*fr.* 220 M.-W.' **II**, for this section read '*Αἰγαῖον* (sc. *πέλαγος*), *τό*, *the Aegean*, Hdt. 7.55.1, Str. 2.5.21; also *-ος* (sc. *πόντος*), *ὁ*, Arist.*Mete.* 354$^a$14 (v.l.), Plu.*Cim.* 8.5'

**Αἰγαίων II**, add '**2** = Poseidon, Call.*fr.* 59.6 Pf., Philostr.*VA* 4.6, Lyc. 135, Hsch.'

**αἰγᾰνέη**, after 'Od. 4.626' insert '9.156, A.R. 2.829, Nic.*Th.* 170, Parth.in *Suppl.Hell.* 619, Opp.*H.* 1.712'

***αἰγάς**, *άδος, ἡ*, *goat*, Epich. 173 a Add. (p. vii K.), Hsch. (*Δωριεῖς*).

***αἰγειοπρᾱ́της**, *ου, ὁ*, *seller of goatskins*, Olymp.*in Grg.* p. 220.12 W.

**αἴγειος**, add 'cf. Myc. $a_3$-*za* (fem., <**aigyos*); see also ‡*αἴγεος*'

**αἴγειρος**, at end for 'of a seat .. 339' read '*a view from a poplar*, ref. to spectators watching from a vantage-point outside a theatre, Cratin. 372 K.-A.'

***αἰγεοθύτης**, *ὁ*, app. *sacrificer of goats*, written *ἐγεοθύτης SB* 11003.2 (iv/v AD), written *αἰγεωθήτης POxy.* 1136.3 (v AD); cf. °*αἰγοθύτης*.

**αἴγεος I**, add '*κρέα PCair.Zen.* 12.55 (iii BC); (sp. *αἴγιος Edict.Diocl.* 8.11); see also ‡*αἴγεος*'

**αἰγιάλειος**, add 'cf. Myc. $a_3$-*ki*-$a_2$-*ri-jo*'

**αἰγιᾰλίτης**, before '*ψῆφοι*' insert '*of* or *belonging to the shore*'

**αἰγιᾰλός**, add 'also *lake-shore* or *river-bank*, *PTeb.* 826.21 (172 BC), 998.5 (ii BC), *PRyl.* 171.13 (AD 56/7), *PPrag.* I 22.7, etc.'

***αἰγιᾰλοφόρητος**, (sc. *γῆ*), *ἡ*, *shore-land washed away* (by flooding), *PTeb.* 701(*a*).12 (ii BC).

***αἰγιᾰλοφῠλᾰκέω**, *hold office of αἰγιαλοφύλαξ*, prob. in *BGU* 12.24 (ii AD).

***αἰγιᾰλοφῠλᾰκία**, *ἡ*, *office of αἰγιαλοφύλαξ*, *PPetaus* 49.4 (AD 185).

**αἰγιᾰλοφύλαξ**, add '*PMich.*III 174.6, XI 617.4 (ii AD), *PFay.* 222 (iii AD), *PSI* 460.5 (iii/iv AD), etc.'

***αἰγιάριος**, *ὁ*, *goatherd* or ?*seller of goat's meat*, *Corinth* 8(3).556, 587 (*ἐγι-*, vi/vii AD).

**αἰγίκνημος**, after '*ον*' insert '(in quots., *-κνᾱμος*)'; at end add '*SLG* 387.4'

**Αἰγικορεῖς**, add '*Αἰκορεῖς* (for ?*Αἰκορεῖς*) *ITomis* 164(49), al.'

***Αἰγίκορος**, *ὁ*, a son of Pan, named because he glutted himself on goat's milk, Nonn. 14.75.

***αἰγίλουρος**· *κάραβος* Hsch.; cf. °*αἰγίπυρος*.

**Αἴγῑνα**, section *-ήτης*, add 'non-Att.-Ion. *-άτας SEG* 32.412 (Elis, v BC)'

***Αἰγῑναιοπώλης**, *ου, ὁ*, *seller of Aeginetan wares*, i.e. shoddy goods, *EM* 28.11; cf. °*Αἰγιναῖος*.

**Αἰγῑναῖος**, line 2, after 'Th. 5.47, etc.' insert '*Αἰγιναῖα· τὰ ῥωπικὰ φορτία EM* 28.10; cf. °*Αἰγιναιοπώλης*'

**αἰγινομεύς**, add 'Nic.*Al.* 39'

***αἰγιοπλᾰ́κινος**, *ον*, perh., *of goathair felt*, *χλανίδιν αἰγιοπλάκ*(*ινον*) *Stud. Pal.* 20.245.4 (vi AD).

**αἰγίοχος**, for 'Alc. 85, .. etc.' read 'Alc. 343 L.-P., etc., *IG* 5(1).238 (vi BC); subst., *AP* 9.224 (Crin.)'

**αἰγίπῡρος**, for '*rest-harrow, Ononis antiquorum*' read 'a thistle-like plant, perh. = *σκόλυμος*' and after 'Thphr. 2.8.3' insert '(codd.)' add '**II** glossed by *κάραβος*, Hsch., (dub., cf. °*αἰγίλουρος*).'

**αἰγίς IV**, add 'Gal. 19.127.14'

**αἰγίσκος**, add '*αἰγίσκον· αἶγα ἐκτομίαν* Hsch.'

***Αἰγλαπιός**, v. °*Ἀσκληπιός*.

***Αἰγλάτας**, v. ‡*αἰγλήτης*.

**αἴγλη**, add '**III** *καὶ ἡ θυσία δ' ὑπὲρ τοῦ κατακλυσμοῦ* {*ἡ*} *εἰς Δελφοὺς ἀπαγομένη αἰ. ἐκαλεῖτο· καὶ ποπάνου τι εἶδος, ἐν ᾧ διεπλάσσετο εἴδωλα. καὶ βόλος φαῦλος κυβευτικός αἰ. ἐκαλεῖτο. ἀλλὰ καὶ ἡ σελήνη. καὶ τοῦ ζυγοῦ τὸ περίμεσον καὶ παιδιά τις ἐκαλεῖτο αἰ. .. ἔνιοι δέ φασι σημαίνειν καὶ περιπόδιον κόσμον* Phot. α 527 Th., Suid.'

**αἰγλήεις**, line 4, after **αἰγλᾶς**' insert '*αἰγλάεντος ὠρανῶ* Alcm. 3 *fr.* 3 ii 66 P.'

**αἰγλήτης**, add 'cf. pers. n. *Αἰγλάτας IG* 5(1).222 (Sparta, *c.*500 BC), *SEG* 31.348 (Mantinea, v/iv BC)'

***αἰγοδόρας**, *ου, ὁ*, *goat-flayer*, name of the month *Ληναιών*, Sch.Hes.*Op.* 504.

***αἰγοθύτης**, *ου, ὁ*, *goat-sacrificer*, prob. in *Stud.Pal.* 10.252.19 (vi AD).

**αἰγόκερως**, add 'sp. *ἐυοκ- POxy.* 3353.10 (iii AD)'

***αἰγοκερωτή**, *ἡ*, perh. = *αἰγόκερας*, *fenugreek*, *Hippiatr.Paris.* 958 O.-H.

***αἰγοκρᾱ́νιον**, *τό*, *goat's head*, *Com.adesp.* 227 A.

**αἰγόλεθρος**, read '*αἰγόλεθρον, τό*'

**αἰγονομεύς**, for 'Nic.*Al.* 39' read 'Opp.*H.* 4.313' and add 'cf. ‡*αἰγινομεύς*'

***αἰγοτόμιον**, *τό*, *goat-sacrifice*, Ramsay *Cities and Bishoprics* 1.150.

***αἰγυλίς**· *λύγος* Hsch.

**Αἰγύπτιος**, add 'Myc. $a_3$-*ku-pi-ti-jo*, pers. n.'

**αἰγών I**, after '*ὁ*' insert '*goat-pen*, *PCair.Zen.* 771.14 (iii AD)'

***αἰγώνυχον**· *πόας εἶδος* Hsch.

**⁺αἰγωπός**, όν, *goat-eyed*, i.e. *yellow-eyed*, of men and animals, Arist.*GA* 779ᵇ1, 779ᵃ33, *HA* 492ᵃ3, Ptol.*Tetr.* 144 (αἰγοπ-).

**˟ἀΐδασμος**, v. ἀείδασμος.

**αἰδέομαι I 1**, add '**b** αἰ. μή .. *shrink with shame* from the possibility that, αἰ. γάρ, μή τις ἐμὲ κτείνειεν ἀνάρσιος ἀπτόλεμος χείρ Nonn.*D.* 23.65.' **2**, add 'perh. w. inf., Γλαῦκος, ἐσπλῖν αἴδεο *SEG* 30.869 (Leuce, v BC)'

**αἰδέσιμος**, line 3, after 'title' insert '*POxy.* 1969 (v AD), *PLond.* 1839.2'

**˟αἰδέστατος**, ον, prob. sync. form of sup. of αἰδεστός, *Act.Alexandr.* 9A vi 22.

**ἀΐδηλος I**, add 'neut. pl. as adv., μωμεύειν ἀΐδηλα make *malevolent* criticisms, Hes.*Op.* 756' **II**, line 2, delete 'Hes.*Op.* 756'

**˟αἰδίλης**, ὁ, Lat. *aedilis, aedile*, *Ann.Épigr.* 1927.173, *IGRom.* 3.238, *SEG* 6.555.

**ἀΐδιος**, line 1, add 'written ἀείδιος *TAM* 2.186a.13 (iv AD), Hsch.'; line 7, after 'Th. 4.63' insert '*APl.* 292'; line 8, after 'Plot. 2.1.3' insert 'κατ' ἀΐδιον *SEG* 1.327.13, ib. 24.1026.(b).15 (both Callatis, i AD); neut. as adv. ἐπὶ φιλότατι πιστᾶι κἀδόλοι ἀείδιον *Olympia Bericht* 7.207 (Sybaris at Olympia, v BC)'

**ἀϊδνής** (s.v. ἀϊδνός), delete the entry (see *Suppl.Hell.* 1097)

**˟αἰδοιόπληκτος**, ον, gloss on σαννιόπληκτος, Hsch., cf. *POxy.* 3329 i 6 (iii/iv AD).

**αἰδοῖος II 3**, add 'A.*Supp.* 194'

**˟Ἀϊδοκυνέα**, 'ας, ἁ, *Hades-cap* (v. κυνέη 2), S.*fr.* 269c.19 R.

**˟Ἀιδοναῖος**, v. ‡Ἀϊδωναῖος.

**ἀϊδρείη**, add 'dat. ἀϊδρείηφι Nic.*Th.* 409'

**ἀϊδρήεις**, delete 'εσσα' and add 'hypothetical adv. -έντως Sch.Nic.*Al.* 415a'

**Ἀϊδωνεύς**, line 4, after 'later poets' insert 'Euph. 98.4'

**˟Ἀϊδωνίς**, ίδος, fem. adj., *of Hades*, Λήθη *GVI* 1874.11 (Cnidos, ii/i BC).

**αἰδώς**, add '**IV** Chaldean name for the moon, Hsch.'

**αἰδῶσσα**, for 'αἴθουσα' read 'τῆς αὐλῆς τὰ τειχία'

**αἰεναοιδός**, delete the entry (read as two words).

**˟αἰέναος**, v. ἀέναος.

**αἰένυπνος**, delete the entry (read as two wds.: αἰὲν ὕπνον, L.-J.-W.).

**αἰζηός**, for 'of a *stout* ..' to the end read 'more often as subst., *able-bodied man* (as engaged in fighting, hunting, ploughing, etc., usu. in pl.), Il. 2.660, Od. 12.440, Hes.*Th.* 863, *Op.* 441, Call.*Jov.* 70, A.R. 4.268, Nic.*Al.* 176, *Th.* 343, etc.; (in parody) κραμένοις ἐπ' αἰζηοῖσι καυχᾶσθαι μέγα Cratin. 102 K.-A.'

**αἰθάλη I**, transfer 'Dsc. 5.75' to section II.

**αἴθαλος**, after '*smoke*' insert '*soot*'; at end add 'Myc. *a₃-ta-ro*, pers. n.'

**αἰθαλόω**, line 1, after '*El.* 1140' insert '*singe*, Arr.*Fr.Phys.* 3 (189.15 R.-W.)'

**αἰθέριος 1**, add '*IG* 12(2).484.9 (Mytilene), Robert *Hell.* 10.20 n. 6' **2**, add 'ψυχή(ν) αἰθερείαις α(ἰ)ῶσι (?) θέτο, σῶμα δὲ γα(ί)η *BCH* suppl. 8 no. 5 (Edessa, v AD)'

**αἰθερίτης**, after 'precious stone' insert 'perh. *turquoise*'

**˟αἰθεροδινής**, ές, *whirling in the ether*, orac. in *App.Anth.* 6.140.8.

**αἰθερολαμπής**, add '(cj.)'

**˟αἰθερολογία**, ἡ, *study of the ether*, Pythag. in D.L. 8.50.

**˟αἰθερύσσω**· τὸ ταχύνω Theognost.*Can.* 9 A.

**αἰθήρ**, line 1, after 'Hes.' insert '*Th.* 124'; line 2, after 'ἡ' insert 'Stesich. 32 i 4 P.' **1**, add '**b** personified, Ar.*Nu.* 578, Orph.*H.* 5.4, orac. in *ZPE* 1.185, II b line 11 (Phrygia, ii AD), Ἐθέρι ἀλεξιχαλάζῳ Robert *Hell.* 9.63 (Amasia).' **3 b**, delete 'cf. Arist.*Mu.* 392ᵃ5'

**⁺Αἰθιοπία**, s.v. Αἰθίοψ, Ion. -ίη, ἡ, *Ethiopia* (term loosely applied to the country southwards from Egypt), Hdt. 2.30.3, Th. 2.48.1.

**αἰθιοπίς** (s.v. Αἰθίοψ), **II**, *sage*, add 'Plin.*HN* 27.11; also app. another plant, ib. 24.163; αἰ.· φλομώδης πόα Hsch.'

**Αἰθίοψ**, line 2, for 'nom. Αἰθιοπεύς' read 'gen. sg. -οπῆος' and after '*Del.* 208' insert 'gen. pl. -οπήων Theoc. 17.87, A.R. 3.1192'; at end add 'Myc. *a₃-ti-jo-qo*, pers. n.'

**˟αἶθμα**· delete Hsch.

**˟Αἰθοπία**, ἡ, epith. of Artemis, Call.*fr.* 702 Pf., *IG* 12(2).92 (Lesbos), *AP* 6.269.3, 7.705.3 (Antip.Thess.).

**αἰθός I**, add 'perh. *black-* or *dark-complexioned*, S.*fr.* 269a.54 R.; cf. Αἰθίοψ' **II**, for '*shining*' read '*bronze-coloured*'

**αἴθουσα**, delete '(sc. στοά)'; for '*portico* .. *sun*' read 'some form of sheltered area on the outside of the μέγαρον'

**αἴθοψ**, delete '*flashing*'; for '*sparkling* (or *fiery*)' read '*fiery red*'

**αἴθρη**, add '**III** = °αἴθριον, *open court* in a house, τῆς πάσης οἰκίας ἀπό τε αἴθρας καὶ αὐλῆς .. *POxy.* 3355.6 (AD 535).'

**αἰθρηγενής**, add 'ἄνεμοι A.R. 4.765'

**αἰθρία**, after 'Ion. -ίη' insert 'poet. also **-ιάα** *Suppl.Hell.* 958.17 (prob.)'

**αἰθριοκοιτέω**, for 'Orib. 9.3.8' read 'Stob. 5.37.30'

**αἴθριος I**, after 'f.l. in S.*Ant.* 357' insert '(cj. ὑπαίθρεια)' **2**, epith. of Zeus, add '*SEG* 33.1052 (Cyzicus, ii BC), Robert *Hell.* 10.20/1 (Byzantium, i BC)' **III**, αἴθριον, for 'adaptation .. sense' read '*open court* in a house giving light to the surrounding rooms' and add 'cf. °αἴθρη III'

**αἴθυγμα**, line 1, delete '*glamour*'; line 2, delete 'cf.' and transfer 'Plu. 2.966b' to end of article adding 'Iamb.*Protr.* 5 p. 36.10 P.'

**αἰθύσσω**, line 4, after '(Nonn.*D.*) 48.689' insert 'φρένας B.*fr.* 20B.8 S.-M. (cod. Ath., cj. διαιθύσσω q.v.)'; after 'pass.' insert 'of winds, Euph.in *Suppl.Hell.* 415 i 23'

**αἴθω**, line 3, delete 'metaph.'; αἴθομαι, lines 6/7, after 'X.*Cyr.* 5.1.16, cf.' insert 'Theoc. 7.102' and after 'A.R. 3.296' insert 'ἐπί τινι Call.*fr.* 67.2 Pf.'

**αἴθων I**, for '*fiery, burning*' read 'of fire, etc., *dark red*' **II**, for 'of burnished .. Od. 1.184' read 'of bronze, bronze objects, *dark red* or *brown*'; at end add 'by poetic transf., of iron, Il. 4.485, Od. 1.184' **III**, after 'birds' insert '*reddish brown, tawny*' and for 'prob. of colour .. 559d)' read 'αἴ. θῆρες, i.e. *drones*, Pl.*R.* 559d; of bulls, Opp.*C.* 2.102; of a lion, ib. 3.54' **IV**, for 'metaph. .. *fiery*' read 'of complexion, *dark*, app. with the implication of manliness' and delete 'Hermipp. 46'

**αἰκίζω I**, add '**2** *inflict outrageously*, ἐμῆτίσαντ' α[ἰ]κισθέντα φόνον epigr. in *BCH* 116.599 (Ambracia, vi/v BC).'

**˟Αἰκορεῖς**, v. °Αἰγικορεῖς.

**˟αιλαι**, wd. of unkn. meaning perh. for ἐλαί(ου), αιλαι οἴνου ξ(έσται) *PRyl.* 627.74 (iv AD).

**˟αἰλέω**, v. ‡αἱρέω.

**αἴλινος 1**, after '*dirge*' insert 'ἁ μὲν εὐχαίταν Λίνον αἴλινον ὑμνεῖ Pi.*fr.* 128c.6 S.-M.'; after '(Diod.)' insert '*weaving-song*, Epich. 14'; add 'on an altar of Linos [Λ]ίνο̣υ Αἰλίνου *SEG* 33.303 (Epid., iv BC)'

**˟αὔλιψ**, unexpld. wd. perh. for αἰγίλιψ, Theognost.*Can.* 11 A.

**˟αἰλότριος**, v. °ἀλλότριος.

**˟αἰλουρόμορφος**, ον, *having the form of a cat*, (cf. ἱερακόμορφος), ξόανον Horap. 1.10 S.; εἰσὶ δὲ καὶ κανθάρων ἰδέαι τρεῖς. πρώτη μὲν αἰλουρόμορφος καὶ ἀκτινωτή ib.

**˟αἰλουροταφεῖον**, τό, *burial-place of sacred cats*, *OWilck.* 1486 (ii AD).

**αἷμα III 1**, add 'of the Hyperboreans, πολυχρονιώτατον αἷ. Call.*fr.* 67.7 Pf., *Del.* 282' **2**, add 'Theoc. 24.73, αἷμα θεῶν Call.*VB* in *Suppl.Hell.* 254.2'

**˟αἱμάζομαι**, *bleed*, *PWarren* 21.124 (iii AD).

**˟αἱμαλωπώδης**, ες, *bloodshot*, Paul.Aeg. 2.57 (124.12 H.).

**αἱμασιά**, for 'to lay' read 'gather stones for' add '**II** *walled enclosure*, *IG* 12(3).248, (5).872, *IMylasa* 255, etc.'

**˟αἱματεύω**, *furnish with blood*, ἓν τὸ ἄλλο αἱματευέι· καὶ ἓν τὸ ἄλλο γεννᾷ Anon.Alch. 22.4.

**αἱμάτη**, for 'Theognost.*Can.* 5.32' read 'Theognost.*Can.* 12 A.'

**αἱματία**, add 'cf. mod. Gk. αἱματιά, αἱμαθιά *blood-pudding*'

**αἱματοειδής**, add '*Orac.Tiburt.* 24, 25'

**αἱματόεις**, line 2, for '= αἱματηρός, Il. 5.82' read '*bloody*, Il. 5.82, Archil. 13.8 W., Tyrt. 10.25 W.' **4**, after 'etc.' insert 'Mimn. 14.7 W., φόνον Tyrt. 12.11 W.'

**αἱματοσταγής**, for 'cf. *Pers.* 816' read '*Pers.* 816 (v.l.)'

**˟αἱματοσφαγής**, ές, *proceeding from bloody slaughter*, πελανὸς αἱ. A.*Pers.* 816; cf. °αἱματοσταγής.

**˟αἱματοχάρμης**, ου, ὁ, *one who delights in blood*, *AP* 15.28.8.

**αἱματωπός**, add '*Trag.adesp.* 732 K.-S., *OBodl.* ii.2171; *blood-red*, χρῶμα Plu. 2.565c'

**˟αἱμαχάτης**, ου, ὁ, *red agate*, Plin.*HN* 37.139.

**˟αἱμογενής**, ές, *related by blood*, *SEG* 8.374 (Egypt, ii AD). **2** *producing blood*, *Suppl.Mag.* 90.A30, E↓6 (v/vi AD; sp. ημωγενη).

**˟αἱμοδρυφής**, ές, (δρύπτω), *drawing blood by scratching*, ἄλγη .. αἱ., w. ref. to rending cheeks in mourning, *IEphes.* 2101A (epigr.); cf. ἀμφιδρυφής.

**⁺αἱμοειδής**, ές, *having the appearance of blood*, Ph. 2.244 (cj. ἠθμο-, v.s.v. II).

**˟αἱμοποιός**, gloss on σκάραιβον, Hsch.

**˟αἱμοποτεῖν**, *drink blood*, gloss on δερκύλλειν (or δερμύλλειν), Hsch.

**⁺αἱμοπότις**, ἡ, *drinking blood*, epith. of Hecate, *PMag.* 4.2864.

**αἱμοπτυϊκός**, after '*blood*' insert 'Dsc. 2.85.3'

**⁺αἱμόρρυτος**, ον, (ῥέω) *flowing with blood*, αἱ. φλέβες *blood-vessels*, A.*fr.* 230 R.; *marked by efflux of blood*, νόσος *IG* 12(5).310.8 (Paros, ii AD, αἱμορυτ-).

**˟αἱμορυχία**, ἡ, *nosebleed*, Phryn.*PS fr.* 11.

**˟αἶμος**, ὁ, αἵμους· ὀβελίσκους, Hsch.

**˟αἱμοστατικός**, ή, όν, *styptic*, Alex.Trall. 2.199.18.

**˟αἱμοφθόρος**, Thespis 5 S., gloss on βροτολοιγός, Hsch.

**˟αἱμοφυής**, ές, *born of blood*, *Suppl.Mag.* 96.A25, E↓1, F*fr.* A4 (v/vi AD; sp. ημωφυη).

**αἱμόφυρτος**, after 'Posidon. 8' add 'transf., of fighting, Lyc. 1411, Nicom.Trag. 15 S.'

**˟αἱμόχρωμος**, ον, *blood-coloured, reddish*, of a cow, *PKöln* 55.5 (iii AD).

**˟αἱμοχύης**, ές, *shedding blood*, *Suppl.Mag.* 96.A26, E↓2 (v/vi AD; sp. ημοχυη).

**αἱμυλία**, add '*plausibility* (in argument, etc.), Ael.*NA* 5.49'

**αἱμύλος**, add '**2** *winning, seductive*, Democr. B 104 D.-K., *AP* 7.643 (Crin.), *GVI* 840.2, 698.2.'

***αἱμωβόλιον**, τό, *sacrifice of blood*, *CIG* 8558, cf. *CIL* 9.3015.

***ἀΐν**, v. ἀεί I 5.

***Αἰνεάδαιος**, ὁ, a month in a Cyprian calendar, *Cat.Cod.Astr.* 2.143 (see also *YClS* 2.213).

***Αἴνειος**, v. °*Αἰνικός*.

**αἰνελένη**, add 'Nic.*Th.* 310'

***αἰνεσίθῡμος**, ον, prob. f.l. for ἀλγεσί- (q.v.), orac. in *TAM* 3(1).34*D*65 (Termessus).

**αἰνετός**, after '*praiseworthy*' insert 'Cratin. 171.15 K.-A.'

**αἰνέω I**, line 9ff., delete 'ἐπαινέω .. usu.'; at end for '(both lyr.)' read '(anap., lyr.)' **III**, delete the section transferring quots. to section II 2.

***Αἰνιάρχαι**, οἱ, *magistrates among the Aenianes*, *IG* 9(2).5*b*15 (Hypata, ii BC).

***Αἰνιαρχέω**, *to be a magistrate among the Aenianes*, *IG* 9(2).7 (Hypata, ii BC).

***αἰνιγμᾰτοειδής**, ές, = αἰνιγματώδης, *enigmatic*, Zos.Alch. 241.26; adv. -ῶς, ἔμφατον· αἰ. εἰρημένον Hsch.

**αἰνιγμᾰτώδης**, at end for 'Arist.*Rh.* 1441$^{b}$22' read 'Anaximen. Lampsac.*Rh.* 1441$^{b}$22'

***Αἰνικός**, ὁ, a month in a Cyprian calendar, Madrid *Cod.Gr.* 95 (v. *YClS* 2.213; *Αἴνειος* cj.); *Hemerolog.Flor.* p. 24 K. has Ἄννιος.

**αἰνόγᾰμος**, for '*fatally*' read '*fatefully*'; after 'E.*Hel.* 1120 (lyr.)' insert 'λέχος αἰνογάμου .. Ἑλένης *Trag.adesp.* 644.40 K.-S.'

+**αἰνόγονος**, ον, *of terrible race* (supposed etym. explanation of Chaldaean), Ph.Epic. in *Suppl.Hell.* 681.7.

**αἰνόδακρυς**, for '= foreg.' read '*terribly wept for*'

**αἰνοδρῠφής**, for 'Antim.[107]' read '*Suppl.Hell.* 1002 (Antim. 156 Wy.)'

**αἰνολέων**, before 'Theoc. 25.168' insert 'Call. *VB* in *Suppl.Hell.* 257.21'

**αἰνόμορος I**, at end add 'Orph.*H.* 57.6' **II**, after '*h.Merc.* 257' insert 'of a mother who buries her sons, *CEG* 94.4 (?Athens, v BC)' and at end for '(Marcell.Sid.) 14' read 'Marc.Sid. 13'

***αἶνον**· τὸ ὕψος, ἢ ὁ ὄχθος τοῦ ὄρους Theognost.*Can.* 13 A.

**αἰνοπᾰθής**, add '*SEG* 26.405 (Corinth, Chr.). **2** *causing terrible suffering*, *Orac.Sib.* 5.185.'

**αἰνός**, line 3, after 'Od. 15.342' insert 'αἰνῷ φόβῳ Pi.*P.* 5.61, αἰ. ἄχος S.*Aj.* 706'; line 5, after '(Il.) 8.423' insert 'ματρὸς ὑπ' αἰνᾶς Phryn.Trag. 6.3 S.'

**αἰνοτάλᾱς**, delete 'Antim. [106] =' and for '(Call.)*fr.* 506' read '*fr.* 481 Pf.'

**αἰνόφυτα**, delete the entry.

***αἰνόφῠτος**, ον, *of terrible nature* (cf. °αἰνογόνος), Ph.Epic. in *Suppl.Hell.* 681.5.

**αἴξ**, line 2, after '*IG* 7.3171' insert 'acc. αἶγον dub. l. in *AJPh* 48.241 (Isauria, ii/iii AD)' **IV**, add 'Longus 2.15; αἶγες· τὰ κύματα. Δωρεῖς Hsch.'

***Αἰόληος**, α, ον, *Aeolian*, Alc. 129.6 L.-P.

**αἰολοβρόντης**, at end add '(cj. -βρέντ- Snell)'

+**αἰολόνωτος**, ον, *having a variegated back* or *upper surface*, Βρετανῶν αἰ. i.e. from staining or tattooing, Opp.*C.* 1.470, of fish (σάλπαι), id.*H.* 1.125; πόρδαλις αἰ. Nonn.*D.* 5.361; of patterning on a κρητήρ, ib. 37.660.

**αἰολόπρυμνος**, for '*gleaming*' read '*decorated*' and for 'B. 1.4' read 'B. 1.114 S.-M.'

**αἰολόπωλος**, add '**2** perh. *having the nature of a lively filly*, app. of a *hetaera*, Κυλιφάκ[η αἰ]ολοπ[ώλ]ῳ rest. in *SEG* 27.672 (Etruria, v BC).'

**αἰόλος**, at end add 'Myc. *$a_3$-wo-ro*, name of an ox'

***αἰολωπός**, όν, in dub. context, perh *of changeable appearance*, S.*fr.* 269a.56 R.

**ἀΐος**, delete the entry (v. αἰώς).

***ἄϊπαις**, παιδος, ἡ, *ever a girl*, *GVI* 1941.3 (Thisbe, ii/iii AD).

***ἧαιπερ**, v. °ὥσπερ II 4.

+**αἰπήεις**, εσσα, εν, *steep, precipitous*, Il. 21.87, A.R. 2.721, Euph. in *Suppl.Hell.* 418.15, Q.S. 1.304; *descending headlong*, αἰ. καταιγίς *AP* 7.273 (Leon.Tarent.).

***αἴποθεν**, *from the heights*, Thdt. in *Suppl.Hell.* 757.9.

**αἰπόλιον I**, add '*Schwyzer* 721.14 (Thebes-on-Mycale, v/iv BC)'

**αἰπόλος II**, add '(ἀίπολος La., cf. ἐμπολή *merchandise*)' add '**III** ὁ Ἑρμαφρόδιτος ὑπὸ Σινωπέων οὕτω καλεῖται Phot. α 634 Th.'

***αἰπολοφύλαξ**, ακος, ὁ, *overseer of goatherds*, *SB* 9415.7.2 (iii AD).

**αἶπος**, after 'A.*Ag.* 285, 309, etc.' insert 'E.*Ph.* 851, Theoc. 7.148'; delete 'hence αἰ.' to end.

**αἰπός**, delete 'αἰπόν, τό .. (Athens)'

**αἰπύκερως**, after '= ὑψίκερως' insert '*high-horned*' and add 'Theognost.*Can.* 14 A.'

**αἰπύς 1**, line 4, delete '*on high* .. 682' **2**, add 'of sounds, *high-pitched*, αἰ. ἰωή Hes.*Th.* 682; θεὸς αἰ. of Diomede, dub. sens. in Lyc. 630'

**αἶρα I**, after '*hammer*' insert 'Euph. 51.9' and for 'Call.*fr.* 129 .. Hsch.' read 'Call.*fr.* 115.12 Pf.'

***αἰράριον**, τό, Lat. *aerarium*, *public treasury*, esp. of the Roman fiscus, *IG* $2^2$.1119(a).10 (see also *SEG* 24.143), *Mon.Anc.Gr.* 9.12; of other provincial treasuries, Mitchell *N.Galatia* 414, στρατιωτικὸν αἰ. *MAMA* 4.139 (Phrygia, i AD); also **ἐράριον**, τό, *BMus.Inscr.* 4(2).1026 (Smyrna, *c.*ii AD); **ἀράριον** *La Carie* 177 (Sebastopolis).

***αἰράριος**, ὁ, Lat. *aerarius*, citizen of the lowest class, D.C. 57.71.

**αἵρεσις** (B) **II 1**, add '*good conduct* in public life, *SEG* 33.1039 (Cyme, ii BC), 639 (Rhodes, *c.*100 BC)' **2**, penultimate line, after '(*Act.Ap.*) 28.22' insert '*heretical sect*, *Cod.Just.* 1.1.5.3, al.' **III 1**, add '*condition* attached to a bequest, *Cod.Just.* 1.3.52.13, al.'

**αἱρετικός 2**, add '**b** *heretical*, of persons, *Cod.Just.* 1.5.18.8, al.' **4**, add '-ῶς ἔχοντος πρὸς τὴν πόλιν being *well-disposed* to .., *SEG* 7.62 (Seleucia in Pieria, ii BC)'

***αἱρετισμός**, ὁ, *adherence to unorthodox practices, heresy*, ἀργύριον αἱρετισμοῦ Lcn. 4*Ki.* 12.17.

**αἱρετιστής 2**, place 'τῶν λογῶν .. p. 12 C.' after 'Plb. 1.79.9, etc.'

**αἱρέω**, line 15, after 'εἱλάμην' insert 'Call.*fr.* 384.41 Pf.' and after '(Smyrna)' insert 'ἴλαντο, *Ath.Agora* xv 293.5 (i BC)'; line 18, Cret. forms, add 'inf. αἰλὲν *SEG* 27.631.B7 (Lyttos, *c.*500 BC)' **A II 4 b**, after 'Isoc. 18.15' insert 'w. two accs., δίκας εἶλεν Εὔπολιν δύο Is. 7.10' and transfer 'Is. 7.13' to follow **5 b**, at beginning insert 'of an amount or balance, *to be due*, αἱροῦντος (?sc. φόρου) γεομετρίας *BGU* 2484.5 (ii AD)' **B 1**, line 4, after 'Il. 22.119' insert '*receive, suffer*, κῆδος ἑλέσθαι A.R. 2.858, 3.692' **C I 1**, after '9.102' insert 'S.*Ant.* 406; ᾑρέθην .. ἐν μάχῃ E.*Supp.* 635' **II**, at end for 'always' read 'mostly'

**αἱρώδης**, add 'ὄλυρα *PTeb.* 857.18, 35 (162 BC)'

**αἶσα II 3**, line 3, for '*Inscr.Cypr.* 148' read '(*a-i-sa*) *ICS* 285.2; τὰν ψάφὸν τὰν τρίταν αἶσαν *Schwyzer* 84.17 (Argos, *c.*450 BC)'

**αἰσθάνομαι**, line 4, after 'Lxx *Jb.* 40.18' insert '(app. act. αἰσθάνω: οὐκ ἐσθάνετε ἀνθρώποις *POxy.* 3417.10, (iv AD), but could be misspelling of the middle)'; line 9, after 'E.*Hipp.* 603, etc.' insert 'w. cogn. acc., πᾶσαν αἴσθησιν αἰσθανομένῳ Pl.*Phdr.* 240d'

***αἰσθέσιον**· τὸ νοσερόν (read νοερόν) Theognost.*Can.* 16 A.

**ἀΐσθω**, add 'w. internal acc., αἰνὸν ἀΐσθων Opp.*H.* 5.311'

**αἰσῐμία**, after '*Eu.* 996' insert '*fairness*, ἐν αἰσιμίῃ .. ἄνυσσεν ἀρχήν *Inscr.Olymp.* 481 (iii/iv AD). **2** *oracle*, Call.*fr.* 18.9 Pf., cf. Theognost.*Can.* 16 A., *EM* 39.3, Suid.'

**αἰσιμῶ**, for 'Suid.' read 'Theognost.*Can.* 16 A., Zonar.'

**αἴσιος I**, add '**2** epith. of Poseidon at Delos, *Inscr.Délos* 1562, 1581, 1582, 1902.' **II**, for 'αἰ.' read 'αἰσία'

***ἄϊσιτος**, v. ‡ἀείσιτος.

**ἀΐσσω**, line 13 (p. 43 line 1), for 'of one .. enemy' read 'of men'; line 14, after '(Il.) 18.506' insert 'D. 25.52, 47.53; fig., Plot. 5.5.4'; at end after 'ἄ Lyr.' insert '(exc. μετ-ᾱΐξαις Pi.*N.* 5.43)'

**αἰσυμνάω 1**, for 'Call.*Iamb.* 1.162' read 'Call.*fr.* 192.6 Pf.' **2**, add 'ᾐσύμνας Ἐφέσου Call.*fr.* 102 Pf.'

**αἰσυμνήτης II 2**, add '*SEG* 31.984 (Teos, 470 BC)'

**αἰσυμνῆτις**, before 'Suid.' insert 'Call.*fr.* 238.10 Pf.; of a goddess, *Syria* 12.319 (Jerusalem)'

***αἰσύφιος**· δεινός (δειλός Kuster), ψευδής, ἀπατέων Hsch.; cf. ἀσύφηλος.

***Αἰσχλαβιός**, v. Ἀσκληπιός.

***αἰσχρία**, ἡ, *dirt*, Eust. 1853.28. **2** *dusk*, id. 1402.29.

***αἰσχρίασμα**, ατος, τό, *dusk*, Eust. 1401.29.

**αἰσχροκερδής**, add 'ἐσχροκερδοῦς ἕνεκεν .. *PVindob.Tandem* 4.18 (AD 312/314)'

**αἰσχροπρᾱγέω**, for '= αἰσχροποιέω' read '*behave basely*'

**αἰσχρός I** and **II**, transpose these sections. **II**, delete 'opp. καλός'

**αἰσχροσεμνία**, for '*avoidance of obscenity*' read '*euphemistic treatment of something indelicate*'

**αἰσχρουργέω**, for '*act .. masturbari*' read '*perform sexual perversions*'

**αἰσχρουργία**, combine examples under def. '*sexual perversion, obscenity*'

**αἰσχρουργός**, for '*obscene*' read '*sexually perverted*'

**αἰσχυντηρός**, after 'αἰσχυντηλός' insert 'Lxx *Si.* 26.15'

**αἰσχυντικός**, at end add '(dub., v.l. ἀναίσχυντα)'

***Αἰσωπίτανος**, α, ον, *made in the manner of Aesop*, i.e. having a sententious inscription, Αἰσωπίτανα κεραμίς *SEG* 39.1062 (Rhegium, i BC/i AD).

***ἀϊτάριον**, prob., a small bird of prey, *"little eagle"*, *PAmst.* 13 (v AD).

+**ἀΐτᾱς**, v. °ἀΐτης.

**αἰτέω I**, add '**6** *ask in marriage*, *Leg.Gort.* 7.51.' **II**, for '*ask for* .. = the Act.' read 'in sense not clearly dist. fr. act.'; lines 7/8, delete 'αἰτησάμενος .. Men. 476' add '**2** *borrow*, Th. 6.46.3, And. 4.29, Lys. 19.27; οὐ πῦρ γὰρ αἰτῶν, οὐδὲ λοπάδ' αἰτούμενος Men.*fr.* 410 K.-Th.; *ask for the services of*, Λύσανδρον ἄρχοντα Lys. 12.59.'

***ἀΐτης**, ου, ὁ, Dor. **ἀΐτᾱς**, *beloved youth*, ὁ μὲν εἴσπνηλος .. τὸν δ' ἕτερον πάλιν, ὥς κεν ὁ Θεσσαλὸς εἴποι, ἀΐτην Theoc. 12.14; of the favourite of a goddess Χρύσας (sc. Ἀθανᾶς) δ' ἀΐτας Dosiad.*Ara* 5; perh. also Lyc. 461 (ᾱ-, unless to be referred to ἀετός). **2** of a fish, (?*immature*), τὸν κεστρέα .. τὸν ἀΐτην καὶ ἄρσενα ἴσον *PTeb.* 701.44, 65 (iii BC).

**αἰτητής**, after '*petitioner*' insert '*PTeb.* 894 *fr.* 6.13 (ii BC)'

**αἰτία**, add '**VI** *illness, disease*, ποίᾳ αἰτίᾳ οὗτος ἐτελεύτησεν *Acta Philippi* 1, Hsch. s.v. ἀναγωγή.'

**αἰτιᾱτικός I 1**, add 'adv. -κῶς, ib. (Sch.Il.) 22.329'

**αἰτιᾱτός**, after 'Plot. 6.2.33' insert 'D.L. 9.97, Procl.*Inst.* 11 D.'

***αἰτιολογισμός**, ὁ, *explanation, justification*, Eus.*PE* 1.5.11 (cj., codd. αἴτιον λογισμόν, ἀπολογισμόν).

**αἴτιος II 2**, add 'prob. in Sapph. 67.6 L.-P.'

***ἀΐτις**, ιος, ἁ, *a beloved girl*, Alcm. 34 P.; cf. °ἀΐτης.

**αἰφνίδιος**, line 1, after 'A.*Pr.* 680' insert '(s.v.l.)'; after 'Th. 8.14' insert 'of fate, *IG* 12(7).52.3 (Amorgos)' adv. -ίως, for 'ib.' read 'Th.' and add '*IG* 12(7).397.4, 401.5 (Amorgos)' adv. -ιον, add '*Peripl.M.Rubr.* 45, 46 C.'

***αἴφνως**, = αἴφνης adv., *suddenly*, *GDRK* 49.5 (hymn to Sarapis), *SEG* 30.1480.3 (Phrygia, late Rom.imp.).

***αἰχμαῖος**, α, ον, *of a spear-point*, Eratosth. in *Suppl.Hell.* 398.

***αἰχμᾰλόω**, *take prisoner*, aor. pass. ᾐχμαλώθη *SEG* 8.595 (Egypt) (back-formation fr. αἰχμάλωτος).

**αἰχμή I 2**, after '*C.* 2.451' add 'of the teeth of monsters, Opp.*H.* 5.141, Philostr.*VA* 3.7' **II 1 b**, add 'of a sickle, Hes.*Sc.* 289' at end before 'cf. Lith. *iešmas*' insert 'form *αἰκσμά, Myc. *a₃-ka-sa-ma* (acc. pl.)'

**αἰχμητής I**, add 'αἰ. ἀλέκτωρ *a fighting* cock, *AP* 6.155 (Theodorid.)'

**αἰχμοφόρος**, at end add 'applied to praetorian guards, Hdn. 1.10.6'

***αἴχνιον**, τό, prob. name of a cult-object, *Inscr.Cret.* 1.v 23.4 (Arcades, ii AD).

**αἰψηροκέλευθος**, for 'Poet.ap.Apollod. 3.4.4' read 'hence of a dog named Βορῆς Epic. in *Coll.Alex.* p. 72 (= Apollod. 3.4.4)'

**ἀίω** (A), line 3, after 'Hdt. 9.93)' insert 'Cypr. ἀϝίω, fut. med. *a-wi-je-so-ma-i* ἀϝιῄσομαι, *Kouklia-Paphos* 237.5 (iv BC)' at end for 'ἄϊε .. 1.352' read 'ἄϊεις *MDAI(A)* 57.47 (i AD); ᾰϊ- is v.l. for ἀκου- in Il. 2.486, Od. 1.352, 353, Hes.*Op.* 213'

**αἰών**, line 2, delete 'apocop. .. 350' **II 1**, lines 3/4, for 'οἱ ἀπὸ .. 63.20' read '*in all time*, πρῶτος πάντων τῶν ἀπὸ τοῦ αἰ. Ῥωμαίων D.C. 63.20; ἕνα ἀπ' αἰῶνος ἀπαγόμενον γυμνασίαρχον *Act.Alexandr.* 11.67 (ii AD)'; after '*life long*' insert 'Simon. 36.12 P.' **3**, for 'cf.' read 'Heraclit. 52 D.-K., Sotad. 15.1, Nonn.*D.* 7.10' **B**, delete the section.

***αἰωνακτῖνοκράτωρ**, ορος, ὁ, *eternal lord of the sun's rays*, *PMag.* 1.201.

***αἰωνεργέτης**, ου, ὁ, *eternal worker*, Αἰωνεργέτα, κύριε Σάραπι *SEG* 35.1051 (Rome, i/ii AD).

**αἰώνιος 1**, add 'app. w. dittography, εἰς τειμὴν αἰωνιαιαν *Inv.Inscr.Palm.* vii 6 (i AD)' **2**, add 'of an office, *held for life*, αἰώνιον στεφανηφορίαν *SEG* 30.1390 (Lydia, c.AD 150)'

***αἰωνογυμνασίαρχος**, ὁ, *life gymnasiarch*, Κλαυδίου Συρίωνος ἑωνογυμνασιάρχου *POxy.* 2854.27 (iii AD).

***αἰωνοπῦρεῖον**, τό, *place of everlasting fire*, *Epigr.Gr.* 1140 b 8.

**αἰωνόφθαλμος**, for '*seeing with eternal eyes*' read '*eye of* Αἰών (personified)'; at end add '(v. *CRAI* 1985.438)'

**αἰώρα**, add '**IV** as a measure of capacity, τειμ(ῆς) μεικρᾶς αἰώρ(ας) οἴνο(υ) (δραχμαὶ) δ' *PMil.Vogl.* 307.112 (ii AD).'

**αἰωρέω**, after '*raise*' insert 'ὁ δὲ (sc. eagle) κνώσσων'; delete 'of the eagle .. feathers'; for '*swing* as in a hammock' read '*hold aloft*' delete '**2** *hang*' **II 3**, before 'Epicur.' for 'ψυχῆς' read 'φύσεως' and for '*Nat.* 22 G.' read '[34, 17] 5 A.'

**αἰώρημα**, add '**3** *that which is poised ready to fall*, E.*Supp.* 1047.'

***αἰώριον**, τό, dim. of αἰώρα, perh. *hoist*, *PUniv.Giss.* 10 ii 13 (ii/i BC).

***αἰώς**· ὁ αἰών. παρὰ Στησιχόρῳ, prob. in *Cod.Bodl.Auct.*T. II(11) f. 90, cf. Stesich. 69 P.

**ἀκᾶ**, delete the entry.

***ϝακάβα**, v. °Ἑκάβη.

***ἀκᾰδήμαρχος**, ὁ, ephebic official at Cyrene, *SEG* 20.742.11 (AD 161).

**Ἀκᾰδήμεια**, add 'cf. ‡Ἑκαδήμεια'

**ἀκαθαρσία 1 b**, after '(13 BC)' insert '*PSI* 787.22 (ii AD), *POxy.* 2109.45 (iii AD)' **3**, after '*impurity*' insert '*SEG* 19.427 (-ρτιαν Dodona, iv/iii BC)'

**ἀκάθαρτος I**, add '**4** *uncleared*, χώρα .. δύσορμος καὶ ἀκάθαρτος ῥαχίαις *Peripl.M.Rubr.* 20.'

**ἀκάθεκτος**, after 'Plu.*Nic.* 8' insert 'δρόμος ἀ. i.e. *stampede*, Hld. 4.21'

**ἀκαθοσίωτος**, add '*unholy*, *POxy.* 1865.8 (vi/vii AD); *dishonourable*, *PBerl.Zill.* 13.8 (vi AD)'

**ἀκᾰθυπερτέρητος**, after 'Ptol.*Tetr.* 157' add '190'

**ἄκαινα II**, add 'ἄκαιννα δεκάπος *SEG* 37.491 (Thessaly, v/iv BC)'

***ἀκαινιαῖος**, ον, *measuring one* ἄκαινα, *IEphes.* 3217a.9 (ii AD).

**ἄκαινον**, for 'Olymp. *in Metaph.* 43.1' read 'Olymp. *in Mete.* 113.1'

**ἀκαιρία I 1**, for 'Pl.*Phd.* 272a' read 'Pl.*Phdr.* 272a'

**ἀκαίριμος**, for 'ὅ τι .. *Lyr.adesp.* 86 A.' read 'ὅττι κεν ἐπ' ἀκαιρίμαν γλῶσσαν ἴῃ *Lyr.adesp.* 102 P.'

***ἀκαιροδᾰπᾰνία**, ας, ἡ, *untimely expenditure*, ἐξ ἐρωτικῆς τινος ἀφορμῆς ἢ ἀκαιροδαπανίας κακοπραγμονοῦσιν Heph.Astr. 2.36.22.

**ἄκαιρος I**, after 'A.*Pr.* 1036' insert 'ἄκαιρα μωμένους id.*fr.* 451c.21 R.' **II 1**, for '*importunate, troublesome*' read '*acting in an inopportune* or *untimely manner*'; add 'ἄ. ἐν ταῖς μετωνυμίαις *using* them *inappositely*, D.H.*Dem.* 5, cf. *Lys.* 5'

**ἀκακία** (A) **I**, add 'ἀκακίῃ Hp.*Mul.* 2.189'

***ἀκᾰκοποίητος**, ον, *undamaged*, *SB* 8754.18; cf. ἀκακούργητος.

**ἄκᾰκος I 1**, add 'ἀ. κόρην Men.*Dysc.* 222' **2**, add 'Pl.*Alc.* 2 140c'

**ἀκαλλιέρητος**, add 'Luc.*Bis.Acc.* 2, Philostr.*VA* 8.7.10'

***ἀκαλλίς**, ἡ, fruit of an Egyptian herb, Paul.Aeg. 7.3 (189.21 H.).

***Ἀκαμάντια**, τά, *feast of the Akamantes*, *SEG* 34.1644 (Cyrene, iv BC).

***Ἀκαμαντιάδες**, αἱ, (sc. ἡμέραι), *days of the festival of Akamantia*, *SEG* 34.1645 (Cyrene).

***ἀκᾰμαντόδετος**, ον, *indissolubly bound*, A.*Pr.* 426 (v.l. ἀδαμ-).

***ἀκᾰμαντοπόδᾱς**, 'α, ὁ, = ἀκαμαντόπους, χρόνος Synes.*Hymn.* 8.63.

***Ἀκάμας**, eponymous hero of the Acamantid tribe in Attica, Aeschin. 2.31, *SEG* 23.78(*b*)8 (iv BC); pl., guardian deities of the tribe, *IG* $2^2$.1358 ii 32-3.

**ἀκᾰ́μᾱτος**, at end delete 'ἄκᾰμᾰτος .. but'

***ἀκαμπτέω**, *behave uprightly*, ἐν τοῖς τόποις *PTeb.* 703.272 (iii BC).

**ἀκανθέα**, before '*PLond.*' insert '*PGoodsp.Cair.* 30.10.23 (ii AD)'

**ἀκανθεών**, after '*thorny brake*' insert '*POxy.* 1985.17 (vi AD)'

**ἀκανθίας 2**, for '*grasshopper*' read '*cicada*'

**ἀκάνθιον**, add 'see also °ἀχάντιον'

**ἀκανθίς I**, add 'Plin.*HN* 10.175, 205'

**ἀκανθοβάτης**, for '*walking* .. nickname of grammarians' read '*treading on thorns*, i.e. revelling in thorny passages, of pedantic grammarians'; after '**-βάτις**' insert 'ἀκρίδα .. ἀκανθοβάτιν'; for '(Leon.)' read '(Leon. Tarent.)'

**ἀκανθοπλήξ**, add 'also a play by Apollodorus, acc. to Suid.'

**ἄκανθος**, line 1, after 'ὁ' insert '(ἡ Dsc. 3.17)' add '**III** = ἀκανθίς I, Ael.*NA* 10.32.'

**ἀκανθών**, add '**2** *acacia*, *BGU* 2182.8 (AD 510).'

***ἀκάνθωτος**, ή, όν, *decorated with* ἄκανθαι, ἧλοι *Inscr.Délos* 1439*Abc*i45, 1450.47 (ii BC).

**ἀκάπνιστος**, add 'ἔλαιον ἀ. Aët. 15.13, κυρύον (= κηρίον) ἀκάπνυστον pap. in *SCO* 27.98'

***ἀκαρδάμῡτος**, ον, *unblinking*, v.l. in Opp.*C.* 1.208, 4.134; cf. ἀσκαρδάμυκτος.

**ἀκάρδιος I**, delete 'heartless .. *Je.* 5.21' add '**b** *senseless, witless*, Lxx *Je.* 5.21, *Pr.* 10.13, 17.16, *Si.* 6.20(21).'

**ἀκᾰρής II**, for 'Men. 835' read 'Men.*Dysc.* 695'

**ἀκᾰριαῖος**, add 'of a drop of flavouring, ἀ. χυμός Arist.*Sens.* 446ᵃ10'

**ἄκαρον**· τυφλόν Hsch.

**ἀκαρφής**, add '(dub., v. κατακαρφής)'

**ἄκασκᾶ**, after 'Cratin. 126' insert 'commentary on Pi. in *POxy.* 2451. *fr.* 14 i 10' and delete 'but .. *fr.* 28'

***ἀκαστόφρων**· συνετός Hsch.

**ἀκατάγνωστος**, add '*TAM* 4(1).130 (Rom.imp.)'; for 'Keil-Premerstein .. (iii AD)' read '*TAM* 5(1).224 (AD 189/90)'

**⁺ἀκαταιτίᾱτος**, ον, *not charged* or *accused*, J.*BJ* 1.24.8, 2.14.8, 4.3.10, al.

***ἀκατακλῑνής**, ές, *unbending*, Procl.*in Ti.* 3.258.22 D.

***ἀκαταληκτικῶς**, *indefinitely*, cj. in Arr.*Epict.* 2.23.46.

***ἀκαταλήρητος**, ον, *not gossiped about*, *POxy.* 3057.17 (i/ii AD).

**ἀκαταληψία**, for '*inability* .. term' read '*impossibility of direct apprehension*, term for Sceptic denial of Stoic doctrine of φαντασίαι καταληπτικαί, *impressions which carry a certainty of their truth*'; at end read 'S.E.*P.* 1.1, 236, 2.21'

**Ἀκάταλλος**, add '(iv BC)'

**ἀκατάμακτος**, add '*Hippiatr.* 34; cf. κατάμακτος'

***ἀκατάμεμπτος**, ον, *unexceptionable*, *SEG* 32.928 (Sicily, iv AD); adv. -ως, *IG* 12(7).231 (Amorgos).

**ἀκαταμέμπτως**, delete the entry.

**ἀκαταπᾰ́τητος**, delete the entry.

**ἀκατάπαυστος**, after 'D.S. 11.67, etc.' insert '*PMag.* 4.2364, *SEG* 27.1243.12'; after '-τως' insert 'Corn.*ND* 15' **II**, delete the section.

**⁺ἀκατάποτος**, ον, *not swallowed*, mistranslation of Hebr. *lōʾ yaʿălōs* in Lxx *Jb.* 20.18 (cf. Arabic *ʿalasa* "drank").

***ἀκαταργητί**, adv., perh. *without being excused work*, διὰ τὸ ἀκαταργηθεὶ αὐ[τὸ]ν λαμβάνειν τὸν προκείμενον μισθὸν *POxy.* 2875.26 (iii AD).

**ἀκαταστᾰσία I**, line 3, after 'etc.' insert '*fickleness*, *Lyr.Alex.adesp.* 1.7, *SEG* 35.221.15 (tab.defix., Attica, c.AD 250)'

**ἀκατάστᾰτος I**, add 'gramm., *irregular*, A.D.*Adv.* 134.19, *Synt.* 116.23' **II**, add 'Gal. 16.574.5, 17(1).557.10'

**ἀκαταχρημάτιστος**, for '*not encumbered with debt*' read '*not to be sold* or *used as security for a loan*' and for '*Sammelb.* 364 (Alexandria)' read '*SEG* 24.1189 (Alexandria, i AD)'

**ἀκάτειος II**, for this section read 'ἀκάτειον, τό, *small sail* (= ‡ἀκάτιον), Aen.Tact. 23.4 (cj.); prob. in fig. phr., w. pun on sense of "cup" (cf. ἄκατος II), Epicr. 9.1 K.-A., Ar.*Lys.* 64'

***ἀκατεργᾰσία**, ἡ, *lack of cultivation*, *SB* 5230.15 (i AD).

**ἀκατηγόρητος**, add 'ἀκαταγ- *SEG* 8.531.41 (Egypt, 57/6 BC)'

**ἀκάτιον**, for 'used by pirates' read '*CRAI* 1988.532-3.1, 7 (Ion. inscr., S. France, v BC)'; after 'Plb. 1.73.2, etc.' insert '**2** (unless ἀκάτειον should be read in these passages) kind of small sail, X.*HG* 6.2.27, Luc.*Lex.* 15, *JTr.* 46, *Hist.Conscr.* 45; in fig. phrs., Epicur.*fr.* 89 A.'

***ἀκαυμάτιστος**, gloss on ἀπρόσειλος, Hsch.

**ἄκαυστος 2**, after 'Thphr.*Lap.* 4' insert 'subst., οἱ ἄ., name given to "carbuncles" (in practice, prob. rubies), Plin.*HN* 37.92'

***ἀκέζομαι**, v. °ἀκέομαι.

**ἀκενόσπουδος**, for '*shunning vain pursuits*' read '*not courting useless trouble*'

**ἀκέομαι**, after '[ᾰ]' insert 'ἀκέζομαι Hld. 5.18.4 (v.l.)'; line 3, after 'Men. 863' insert 'ἀκεῦνται prob. in Hdt. 7.236'

**ἀκέραιος**, line 2, after 'Sch.Ar.*Pl.* 593' insert '*Dig.* 31.88.15' **II 2**, after '*perfect*' insert 'Pl.*Plt.* 268b' **II 3**, add '*naive*, *SEG* 35.214.16 (tab.defix., Attica, *c.*AD 250)'

***ἄκερμος**, ον, *without money*, prob. in Aesop.*Prov.* 39 P. (ἀκερρς cod.).

**ἄκερος**, add 'Gal. 2.430.18, 10.21.9'

**ἀκερσεκόμης**, line 1, after 'Dor.' insert 'nom. -κόμας *SEG* 37.1175.11 (Pisidia, ii AD)'

***ἄκερσος**, ον, *not shorn*, rest. in *PMasp.* 141 iii 11 (vi AD).

**ἀκεσίας**, delete the entry.

***Ἀκεσίας**, ου, comic name for a bad doctor, Ar.*fr.* 934 K.-A., Plu.*Prov.* 98, Phot. α 735 Th.'

***ἀκεστάλιος**, α, ον, unexpld. adj., ἀ. ὄρνιθες Stesich. 70 P.

***ἀκέστριον**, τό, *needle*, Eust. 1647.58.

***Ἀκεσώ**, ἡ, a goddess of healing, *IG* $4^2$.135 i 3 (Epid.).

**ἀκεύει**, delete the entry (v. °ἀκεύω).

***ἀκεύθω**, ἡ, = °ἀκεύω, Mitchell *N.Galatia* 234 (i AD).

***ἀκεύω**, prob. *look after*, *Inscr.Cret.* 4.72.2.17; cf. ἀκεύει· τηρεῖ. Κύπριοι Hsch.

***ἀκεφᾰλαίως**, adv. *without arrangement under headings*, *SEG* 8.694.9 (Luxor, iii/ii BC).

**ἀκέφᾰλος 1**, after 'J.*BJ.* 4.8.4' insert 'ζῷα Gal. 3.614, 631.7; of plants, τὸ δὲ γήτειον καλούμενον ἀκέφαλόν τι, i.e. *bulbless*, Thphr.*HP* 7.4.10' **2**, for '*without beginning*' read 'fig., of badly constructed arguments or narrative'

**ἀκέων**, after 'Od. 11.142' insert '*h.Cer.* 194, A.R. 3.85'

**ἀκή** (B), for 'ἀκὴν ἔχεν Mosch. 2.18' read 'ἀ. ἔχειν Call.*fr.* 238.9 Pf., A.R. 3.521, etc.' and add 'cf. ἀκήν'

**ἀκή** (C), delete the entry.

***ἀκηδεί**, adv., *carelessly* Theodos.Gr. p. 74.

**ἀκηδέω 1**, add 'w. acc., ἀ. τοὺς θεούς *FGrH* 153 F 7'

***ἀκηδιώδης**, ες, *exhausted*, *Vit.Aesop.*(G) 76 (ἀκιδ- cod.).

**ἀκήμων**, add 'perh. *silent*, *still*, οὐρανὸς ἀ. cj. in Plot. 5.1.2 H.-S. (addenda)'

**ἀκήριος** (A) **I**, delete 'ψυχαὶ .. *Fates*' and for 'Ps.-Phoc. 99' read 'Ps.-Phoc. 105 V.'

**ἀκήρωτος**, after '*unwaxed*' insert '*Inscr.Délos* 507.13 (iii BC)'

**ἀκιδνός**, at end delete '(*insipid* .. Brandt)' and for 'ἰατρός' read 'λογισμός' adding 'Hp.*Mul.* 12, 52'

**ἀκίδωτός I**, after '= foreg.' insert '*Inscr.Délos* 1421*Acd*18, 1450*A*21'

**ἀκίναγμα**, for pres. ref. read '*Suppl.Hell.* 1030'

**+ἀκῑνάκης**, ου, ὁ, acc. -άκεα Hdt. 3.118; gen -άκεος 4.62; acc. pl. -άκεας (v.l.) 3.128: *short straight sword* of Persian origin, ἀ. σιδήρεος, Pl.*R.* 553c, X.*An.* 1.2.27, D. 24.129, ἀ. ἐπίχρυσος; a Persian sword kept in the Parthenon, *IG* $1^3$.354.81, $2^2$.1394.11. **b** as an object of worship, Σκύθαι .. ἀκινάκῃ θύοντες Luc.*JTr.* 42; in an oath, οὐ μὰ τὸν ἀ. id.*Tox.* 38 [ăcīnăcēs in Hor.*Carm.* 1.27.5] cf. κινάκης.

**ἀκίνητος II 4**, add 'gramm. *unmodified*, of a wd. in its basic form, i.e. nom. sg. or 1 sg., Choerob. *in Theod.* 363.27 H.'

***ϝακίνθια**, v. Ὑακίνθια.

***ἄκιον**, unidentified domestic object, *POxy.* 1290.6 (v AD).

**ἀκιρός II**, add '(perh. Lat. *aquilo*)'

**ἀκίς I 2**, add '*IG* $4^2$(1).122.58, 60 (Epid., iv BC)' **4**, add 'of hostility, ἀκίσιν ὀφθαλμῶν ἐνήλατο Lxx *Jb.* 16.10'

**ἀκίσκλη**, after 'ἡ' insert '(or -ον, τό)'; add 'gen. pl. ἀκίσκλων or -ῶν, cf. Lat. *acisculus*'

***ἀκίτᾱλος**, unexpld. wd., Hdn.*fr.* p. 21 H.

***ἀκκήσσος**, ὁ, Lat. *accensus*, *supernumerary*, *IGRom.* 3.578, *Ann.Épigr.* 1929.89, *IEphes.* 1544.10 (ἀκκῆνσ-).

**ἀκκίζομαι 1**, before 'Ael.*Ep.* 9' insert 'as v.l. in'

***ἀκκοθήκιον**, τό, (?for ἀγγο-) *receptacle for vessels*, *PAnt.* 204.4 (vi/vii AD).

***ἀκκουβίκυλον**, τό, Lat. *accubiculum*, *dining-room*, *POxy* 2058.25 (vi AD).

***ἀκκουβιτάλια**, τά, Lat. *accubitale*, app. *couch-coverings*, *PBerl.Zill.* 13 (vi AD).

***ἀκκουβιτᾶρις**, Lat. *accubitalis*, τάπης ἀ. *of* or *for a couch* (°ἀκκούβιτος), *Edict.Diocl.* 19.34; neut. as subst., prob. *cover for a* (*dining*) *couch*, ἓν ἀκκουβιτάριν *POxy.* 3860.18 (iv AD).

***ἀκκουβίτιον**, τό, *dining-room*, *MAMA* 6.84 (ἀκουβ-).

***ἀκκούβιτον**, τό, *couch*, (sts. sp. ἀκουβ-), Ps.-Callisth. 1.21.9. **2** *bedroom*, *PLond.* 1724.30, 1733.19 (vi AD). **3** *dining-room*, Ath. *Imag.Beryt.* 2 (*PG* 28.805).

***ἀκκούβιτος**, ὁ, Lat. *accubitus*, *accubitum*, *couch*, *Edict.Diocl.* 19.34. **2** *bedroom*, *BGU* 2202.19 (AD 565).

***ἀκκουμβίζω**, = Lat. *accumbo*, *recline at table*, *Vit.Aesop.*(G) 40 (ἀκουμβήσωμεν cod.), Suid. s.v. πρόσκλιτον.

**ἄκλαστος**, for 'Thphr.*CP* 1.15.17' read 'Thphr.*CP* 1.15.1'

**ἄκλαυ(σ)τος I**, after 'A.*Eu.* 565' insert 'Luc.*Cat.* 5'

**ἀκλεής 1**, adv., after 'Antipho 1.21' insert 'Isoc. 4.84'

**ἀκλήρημα**, delete '*loss*' and 'Dicaearch. 1.25 (pl.)' and for 'etc.' read '(in pl.) *drawbacks* (including moral faults), Dicaearch. 1.25; *misfortunes*, *REG* 101.16.44, 61 (Xanthos, iii BC)'

**ἀκληρονόμητος**, after 'Eust. 533.32' insert '*not to be transmitted by will*, *SB* 9801.6 (ii/iii AD)'

**ἀκλόνητος**, after '*unmoved*' insert 'Palaeph. 52'

**ἄκλονος**, delete 'of a rider .. Palaeph. 52'

**ἀκλοπεία**, for '*administration*' read '*conduct*'

**ἀκμάδιον**, for 'Ps.-Mos.Alch.' read 'Moses Alch.'

**ἀκμαῖος I**, after '(A.)*Pers.* 441' insert 'Hippothoon 5 K.-A.' add '**III** *pointed*, sup., Hld. 9.19.4; cf. ἀκμή I.'

***ἀκμαιότης**, ητος, ἡ, *the prime of life*, Ptol.*Tetr.* 29.

***ἀκμάς**, άδος, ἡ, fem. adj. *seasonable*, ἀ. βουλῇ *Orac.Chald.* 37.1 P.

**ἀκμή III**, add 'personified, *SEG* 34.1446 (Syria, Rom.imp.)'

**ἀκμήν**, lines 1/2, for 'A.*fr.* 451 G, Men. in *Cod.Vat.Gr.* 122' read 'A.*fr.* 339a R., Men.*fr.* 715a K.-Th.'; line 4, after 'Theoc. 4.60' insert 'Call.*fr.* 781 Pf.'; line 7, for '*Cod.Vat.Gr.* 122' read '*Cod.Vat.Gr.* 12 (Reitzenstein *Ind.Lect.Rost.* 1892/3 p. 4)'

**ἄκμηνος**, for 'Call.*Fr.anon.* 4' read 'Call.*fr.* 312 Pf.' and add 'A.R. 4.1295, cf. ἄκμα'

**ἀκμής**, after '(Alph.)' insert 'perh. *that is in new condition*, προτομὰν ἀκμῆτα Antip.Sid.in *GLP* 1.107(4).2 (= *HE* 48 G.-P.)'

**ἄκμητος**, delete '**II** *not causing pain*'

***ἀκμινάλιον**, τό, cf. Lat. *agminalis*, *baggage-animal*, *POxy.* 3741.45 (AD 313).

***ἀκμονευτής**, οῦ, ὁ, *one who hammers* in a forge, Sm.*Is.* 41.7.

***ἀκμονίσκος**, ὁ, dim. of ἄκμων, *small anvil* on which coins were struck, *IG* $2^2$.1408.12 (iv BC).

**ἄκμων**, lines 1/2, delete 'orig. .. **II**' transferring Hes. quots. to following sense; last line, delete 'sling-'

***ἀκναμπτεί**, adv. *inflexibly*, Pi.*fr.* 70c.12 S.-M.

***ἀκναφάριος**, v. °ἀγναφάριος.

***ἄκνη**, ἡ, = ἴονθος II, *acne* or sim. skin condition, Aët. 8.14 (420.1 O.) (pl.).

**ἄκνημος**, for '*without calf*, of the leg' read 'of freaks of nature, *having no lower leg*'

**ἀκοιλάντως**, add 'ἀκυ- *Stud.Pal.* 142.21'

**ἀκοινώνητος II**, delete '*inhuman*, Cic.*Att.* 6.3.7' and 'cj. ib. 6.1.7 (v. ἀκοινονόητος)'

**ἀκολάστασμα**, delete 'Alciphr. 1.38'

***ἀκολαστότης**, ητος, ἡ, *indiscipline*, Asp. *in EN* 3.15.

**ἄκολος**, after 'Od. 17.222' insert 'Call.*Cer.* 115'

**ἀκολουθέω**, line 8, for 'Men.*Adul.fr.* 1' read 'Men.*Kol.fr.* 1.1 K.-Th.' **II 3**, add 'gramm., A.D.*Adv.* 163.16, *Pron.* 3.15' **4**, line 2, for 'Hippon. 55' read 'Hippon.*fr.* 79.9 W.' and delete '(s.v.l.)'

***ἀκολουθικός**, ή, όν, = ἀκόλουθος, *PCair.Zen.* 676.3 (iii BC).

**ἀκόλουθος 3**, adv., abs., add '*consequently*, *Cod.Just.* 1.4.32.3'

***ἀκομεντανήσιος**, = °ἀκομενταρήσιος, *PHarris* 94.7 (v AD), *SB* 2253.12.

***ἀκομενταρήσιος**, ὁ, fr. Lat. *a commentariis*, *official in charge of public records*, *IGRom.* 3.1264.

**ἀκόμιστος**, after '*S.Ichn* 143' insert '*GLP* 1.122.17 (anon., ii AD); *PAnt.* 58.11 (iv/v AD)'

**ἀκονάω**, line 3, after 'Arist.*Pr.* $886^b10$' insert 'Sosith. 2.18 S.'

**+ἄκονδος**· ἄχαρις. Κονδὰς γὰρ χάρις ἐστίν Hsch. (cf. perh. °κόννος).

**ἀκόνη**, add '**4** *small mortar* used by doctors, *Lapid.Gr.* 194.19.'

**ἀκονητής**, after '*sharpens*' insert 'or *polishes*, = Lat. *samiator*'; after 'σπάθης' insert 'περικεφαλαίας, etc.'; after '*Edict.Diocl.* 7.33' insert '*MAMA* 3.414 ([ἀ]κωνιτοῦ gen.), perh. to be restored in *Corinth* 8(1).245 (ἀκον[-, v. Robert *Hell.* 11/12.37-38)'

**ἀκονῑτί**, after 'D. 19.77' insert 'perh. Lacon. form **ασσκονικτει** *CEG* 372 (Laconian script at Olympia, vi BC), cf. perh. mod. Gk. σκόνη = *dust*'; add 'see also ἀκονητί'

**ἀκόνῑτον I**, delete 'dub. l. in Nic.*Al.* 42, cf.' and after '*AP* 11.123' insert 'perh. w. play on ἀκόνιτος (adj.)'

**ἀκοντίζω**, after 'Att. fut. -ιῶ' insert 'Boeot. inf. ἀκοντιδδέμεν *SEG* 32.496' **I 3**, for '*jettison* cargo' read 'πάντα .. ἠκοντίζομεν ἔξω τῆς νηός, i.e. jettisoned' **4**, for '*shoot forth rays*, of moon' read 'abs., of the moon, *dart its rays*'; after 'med.' insert 'of flames' add '**6** *direct* a stream of liquid, Ach.Tat. 4.18.6 V.; pass., *spout up* or *out*, τὸ αἷμα Alex.Trall. 1.13 p. 515.17 P.'

**ἀκόντιον**, add '**3** *goad*, ἀ. ἤτοι μάστιξ *Edict.Diocl.* 15.17. **II** = ἀκοντίας 1, kind of snake, Fronto *Ep.* p. 22.7 vdH.'

**ἀκοντιστήρ I**, add '**2** ἀκοντιστῆρες μόλυβοι perh. (*lead*) *jets* of a fountain, *IEphes.* 3214.16 (i AD).' **II**, lines 3/5, delete 'ἀκοντιστῆρες .. p. 89'

**ἀκοντοδόκος**, add 'Sch.Il. 16.361b, *Didyma* 496B9 (ii AD)'

**ἀκοός**, add '*Trag.adesp.* 279g.10 K.-S. **2** ἀκόοι, οἱ, *witnesses* to a transaction, *BCH* suppl. 22 p. 236 (Argos, v BC).'

**ἀκοπητί**, delete the entry.

**ἄκοπος II 2**, for '*removing .. refreshing*' read '*relieving pain*' add '**4** ἄ. (sc. λίθος), ἡ, kind of stone, Plin.*HN* 37.143.' **III 2**, after '*whole*' insert 'κέγχρου ἀκόπου *Edict.Diocl.* 1.5'

**ἄκοπρος I**, add 'Gal. 15.699.18'

***ἀκοράστως**, v. °ἀκόρεστος.

***ἀκορεσταίνω**· ἀκόρεστα πράττω Phot. α 800 Th.

**ἀκόρεστος I 1**, adv., add 'Cypr. *a-ka-ra-sa-to-se* perh. ἀκοράστως, *ICS* 264.2'

**+ἀκόρετος**, = ἀκόρεστος, edd. in A. *Ag.* 1117, 1143 (codd. -εστος).

**ἀκορία I**, add 'prob. *want*, *Tab.Defix.Aud.* 15.23 (Syria, iii AD)'

**ἀκόρσωτον**, add '(cod. ἀκόρωδον)'

***ἀκόρωδον**, v. °ἀκόρσωτον.

**ἀκοσκίνευτος**, add '*PTeb.* 1029.5 (ii BC)'

**ἀκοσμέω**, add '*not to observe religious ritual* or *discipline*, *IG* 5(1).1390.39 (Andania, i BC), ἄν τίς τι ἀκοσμέ[ι] *IG* $1^3$.82.25'

**ἀκόσμητος 3**, for '*unfurnished*' read '*undecorated*' and add '*SEG* 39.1055.9 (Neapolis, AD 194)'

**ἀκοσμία I 2**, add 'Plu. 2.926e' add '**III** *lack of adornment*, Gorg.*Hel.* B 11.1 D.-K.'

**ἄκοσμος I**, add '**b** *of loose morals*, χήρη *AP* 5.302.9 (Agath.); γυναῖκες Agath. 5.14.4 K.' **II**, after '(Jul.)' insert 'cf. καί νύ κε κόσμος ἄ. ἐγίνετο Nonn.*D.* 6.371'

**ἀκοστή**, add 'cf. κοσταί'

***ἄκοστος**, v. Αὔγουστος.

***ἀκούβιτον**, etc., v. °ἀκκουβ-.

***ἀκούρης**, ?ου, ὁ, *one having long hair*, perh. in *IG* 12(5).225 (cj. in *Philol.* 65.633, Paros, v B.C.).

**+ἀκούσιος**, *hakṓsios*, v. ‡ἀεκούσιος.

**ἄκουσμα 3**, after '*instruction*' insert 'Pl.*Ep.* 314a'

***ἀκοῦχος**, ὁ, some item of furnishing for a bedroom, *PMich.*inv. 4001 (*ZPE* 24.83, i/ii AD), *PBremen* 21.8 (i AD).

**ἀκούω II 2**, add '**b** *receive an order*, w. inf., μετὰ δεῖπνον ἄγειν τὸν νεανίαν ἀκούσασα οὕτως ἔπραττε Hld. 7.26.1.' **III**, add '**6** pass., *to be given a judicial hearing*, *Cod.Just.* 10.11.8.1.'

**ἄκρα 5**, add '*Inscr.Prien.* 4.51 (iv BC), Pouilloux *Rhamonte* no. 15.18, ἐν ταῖς τῶν ἄκρων πολιορ[κίαις] *MDAI(A)* 72.234 no. 64.28 (Samos)'

**ἀκρᾱ́αντος**, add 'A.R. 1.469, 4.387; n. pl. subst., Hom.*Epigr.* 4.14'

**ἀκρᾰ́δαντος**, after 'etc.' insert '*unaffected*, σῶμα οἴνῳ Clem.Al.*Paed.* 2.2.22'

**ἀκρᾱής**, delete '*si* ἀκραὲς .. 10.17.9'

**ἀκραινές**, after 'ἐγκρ-' insert 'ἀκρανές La.'

**ἀκραῖος**, for '= ἄκρος' read '*extreme*, *topmost*, etc.' **II**, before 'Aphrodite' insert 'Zeus, *Sokolowski* 1.56.13 (ii BC)'; after 'Paus. 1.1.3, 2.32.6' insert '*SEG* 32.1380 (Cyprus, AD 14)' add '**b** Ἀκρῆα, τά, a festival at Coronea, *Schwyzer* 503a.18 (*c.*200 BC).'

**+ἀκραιφνής**, ές, *pure*, *unadulterated*, ὕδωρ Ar.*fr.* 34 K.-A.; ἀήρ Hp.*Morb.Sacr.* 16, *Mul.* 1.11, etc., Anticl. 22 J., Lyc. 151. **b** of abstract things, ἀρετή *J.AJ Proem.* 4, ἀλήθεια Ph. 2.219, φύσις id. 2.374, πενία *AP* 6.191 (Corn.Long.); sup. Ph. 2.319; adv. -ῶς Ph. 1.100. **2** *unimpaired*, *intact*, ξυμμαχία Th. 1.19; of a fleet, id. 1.52.2, Pl.*Ax.* 2.366a, D.H. 6.14, Procop.*Aed.* 1.10; w. gen., *untouched* by, ἀ. τῶν κατηπειλημένων S.*OC* 1147, Lysipp. 9; adv. -ῶς Poll. 1.157. **3** *pure*, *innocent*, κόρης ἀκραιφνὲς αἷμα E.*Hec.* 537, *Alc.* 1052, Ph. 1.515.

**+ἀκρᾰ́σίων**, ωνος, ὁ, *intemperate person*, Cerc. 4.3.

***ἀκρᾰτευτής**, οῦ, ὁ, = ἀκρατής II 2, *lacking self-restraint*, ἀ. εἰς μοιχείαν Anon. *in Rh.* 120.30 (pl.).

**ἀκρᾱτίζομαι**, lines 5/6, after 'fut. -ιῶ' insert 'pf. part. ἠκρατικώς *Didyma* 286.8' and after '*breakfast*' insert 'τὴν πόλιν *Didyma* l.c.'

**ἄκρᾱτος I 2**, add 'of myrrh, σμύρνης ἀκράτου *Suppl.Hell.* 1164, Emp. B 128.6 D.-K.' **6**, for 'ἄ. καῦμα *AP* 9.71 (Antiphil.)' read 'ἄ. μανίην *AP* 12.115'

***ἀκρᾱτοχολής**, ές, *consisting of pure bile*, τὰ -ῆ διαχωρήματα Gal. 19.108; cf. ἀκρητόχολος.

***ἀκρεγιαιον**, an unknown bird, *PAmst.* 13.14 (v AD).

**ἀκρελεφάντινος**, add '*Inscr.Délos* 1409*Ba*ii47 (ii BC)'

**ἀκρεμών**, add '**2** *tentacle* of a polyp, Opp.*C.* 3.181.'

***ἀκρεοπαώνι(ν)**, a bird, app. a kind of peacock, *PAmst.* 13.3 (v AD); cf. πάων.

***Ἀκρῆα**, v. °ἀκραῖος II b.

**ἄκρηβος**, add '*Trag.adesp.* 656.18 K.-S.'

***ἄκρηστος**, v. °ἄχρηστος.

**ἀκρηχολία**, read '**ἀκρηχολίη**'

**ἀκρία**, before 'of Athena' insert 'perh. of Hera, *IG* 9(1).698 (Corcyra, iv BC)'

**ἀκρῑβάζω**, for '*proud*' read '*proved*'

**ἀκρῑβασμός**, after '3*Ki.* 11.34' insert '(cod. A)'; delete 'pl., ἀ. καρδίας *searchings* of heart'; for '*portion, gift*' read '*fixed allowance*'

**ἀκρῑβαστής**, delete '*inquirer*'

**ἀκρῑ́βεια I**, line 2, after 'Lys. 17.6' insert 'τὸν δὲ διαυγῆ χαλκόν, ἀκριβείης οὐκ ἀπολειπόμενον *AP* 6.210.4 (Philit.Sam.)'; line 6, after 'Arist.*Resp.* $478^b1$' insert 'ἐπ' ἀκριβείας Demetr.*Eloc.* 222'

**ἀκρῑβής I**, add 'adv. -βῶς, οὔτε ἀ. ὡπλισμένους of archers, Arr.*An.* 1.28.5'

**ἀκρῑβολογέομαι**, after '(Pl.)*Cra.* 415a' insert '*quibble*, Modest.*Dig.* 27.1.6.7'

**ἀκρῑβόω 1**, delete 'ἀ. τάδε .. X.*Cyr.*' and transfer '2.3.13' to follow 'X.*Cyr.* 2.2.9' in section 2; after 'Arist.*Pol.* $1279^b1$' insert 'of a work of art, εὖ σμίλησιν ἠκριβωμένην Call.*fr.* 202.66 (Add. II p. 119) Pf.' **2**, for '*investigate thoroughly*' read '*make sure of*'; delete '*inquire carefully of*' and after '*Ev.Matt.* 2.7' insert 'Longus 3.12.4'

**+ἀκρῑ́διον**, τό, *a little tip*, *spike*, καρπὸν .. ἔχει (βρόμος) ἐπ' ἄκρῳ ὥσπερ ἀκρίδια δίκωλα etc., Dsc. 2.94.

***ἀκρῑδοθήκη**, ἡ, *cage for locusts*, Longus 1.10.2 (v.l. -θήρα).

***ἀκριμακραγετα**, unexpld. wd. on an amulet, ἀ. κύριε βοήθι *SEG* 14.883 (Egypt, Rom.imp.), a magical wd., or perh. for ἀκριδο›μακρᾱγέτα *one who drives locusts far away*, *AJPh* 76.308-9.

**ἀκρις**, line 1, after 'ιος' insert '-εως *IG* 5(1).1370.6 (i BC); -ιδος in place-name Ἄκρις *SEG* 28.103.4; τῶι Ἡρακλεῖ τῶι ἐν Ἄκριδι ib. 19 (Eleusis, iv BC)'

**ἀκρίς**, after 'sg., in collective sense' insert '*PTeb.* 772.2 (iii BC)'

**ἀκριταγών**, add '(ἀκριτάγωνον La., ἀκριτόγωνον Fix)'

**ἀκρῑτοβάται**, add '(ἀκροβάται La.) cf. °ἀκροβάτης'

***ἀκρῑτόφῡλος**, ον, = ἄκριτος III 2, κλωστήρων γένη *SEG* 8.768.18 (Egypt); cf. φυλοκρινέω.

**ἀκροάομαι I**, after 'Pl.*Grg.* 499b' insert 'λέγοντος ἐμοῦ ἀκροάσονται id.*Ap.* 37d'; add 'perh. also act. form ἐλέλευσεν Πτολεμαίῳ .. ἀκροᾶσε (app. aor. inf.) τὸ πρᾶγμα *POxy.* 3398.12 (iv AD)' **2**, add '**b** *give a hearing*, *judge*, *Cod.Just.* 8.10.12.8.' **II**, for 'Th. 3.27' read 'Th. 2.37.3'

**ἀκροαπίς** should follow **ἀκροάομαι**

**ἀκρόασις**, for '**II** = ἀκροατήριον' read '**2** *lecture* (as a performance)'

**ἀκροᾱτήριον II**, add 'prob. in D.H.*Dem.* 15'

**+ἀκροβάτης**, *acrobat*, *PRyl.* 641.22 (iv AD); as a functionary in the cult of Artemis at Ephesus, *IEphes.* 27.459, 537, 941.4, etc.

**ἀκρόβατος**, delete the entry.

**ἀκροβελίς I**, for '*dart*' read '*spit*'

**ἀκροβηματίζω**, before 'Hsch.' insert '*Iamb.adesp.* 35.2 W.'

**ἀκροβολισμός**, after 'Aen.Tact. 39.6, etc.' insert 'fig., Ach.Tat. 1.10.4; as a military exercise, Pl.*Lg.* 804c'

***ἀκρόγωνον**, τό, *sharp corner*, *acute angle*, *PMasp.* 109.26 (vi AD).

**ἀκροδίκαιος**, for 'ἀκριβοδίκαιος' read '*eminently just*, Heph.Astr.*Epit.* 4.116.45; ἀ.· τὸ ἔσχατον τῆς δίκης Hsch,; comp., ὃς πάσης ἀρετῆς ὢν ἀκροδικαιότερος *MAMA* 8.569'

***ἀκρόδικος**, ον, = ‡ἀκροδίκαιος, *SEG* 35.1233.18 (Saittai, ii AD).

***ἀκρόθηκτος**, ον, *sharpened at the point*, ἀ. ἐγχέων E.*fr.* in Snell *Alexandros* p. 80.24.

**+ἀκροθῑ́νιον**, τό, *first-fruits of war*, *best of the spoils*, esp. as offered to the gods, E.*Ph.* 282, Th. 1.132.2, Pl.*Lg.* 946b; pl., Eumel. 12.1 B., Simon. 97 D., Pi.*N.* 7.41, Ἀθηναῖοι τ[ô]ι Ἀπόλλον[ι ἀπὸ Μέδ]ον ἀκ[ροθ]ίνια τêς Μαραθ[ô]νι μάχες *Delph.* 3(2).1 (489 BC), Hdt. 1.86.2, 90.4; transf., *choicest offerings*, *firstfruits*, A.*Eu.* 834; fig., τὰ .. Ἑλλήνων ἀκροθίνια i.e. Orestes and Pylades; Philostr.*Ep.* 61, *VS* 512.

**+ἄκροθις**, ἡ, acc. -θῖνα (this has been taken by some editors to be a var. form of the neut. pl. ἀκροθίνια), = °ἀκροθίνιον, Pi.*O.* 2.4, 10.57, *GDI* 2561.D47.

**ἀκροθώραξ**, delete '= ἡμιμέθυσος, Hsch., cf.'; for 'πεπωκότ'' read 'πεπωκότα'; for 'Diph. 46' read 'Diph. 45 K.-A., Hsch.'

***Ἀκροκαλλίστιος**, ὁ, epith. of Zeus at Delphi, *Delph.* 3(1).362 iii 14.

**ἀκροκέραια**, for 'κέρας VIII' read 'κέρας V 5'

**ἀκρόκομος I**, at end delete 'of goat's chin'

***ἀκροκωλοίφιον**, τό, *tip of the hoof* (written *acrocolefio*, abl. sg.), Veg.*Mul.* 3.1.2.

***ἀκρόλευκος**, ον, *white-tipped* or *-edged*, *Vit.Aesop.*(G) 92.

ἀκρόλῐθος, for '*IG* 4.558' read '*IG* 4.558.14' and after '(Argos)' add 'cf. Vitr. 2.8.11'

*ἀκρόλλιν, v. °ἀκρούλιον.

ἀκρολογέω, for '*gather at top*' read '*glean*'

ἀκρολοφίτης, for '*mountaineer*' read '*dweller on mountain tops*'; for '(Leon.)' read '(Leon.Tarent.)' and add '*APl.* 256'

*ἀκρόμεστος, ον, *brim-full*, cj. in *POxy.* 3722 *fr.* 1.8 (lemma in Anacr. commentary, ii AD; ].κρομεσ̣τ̣ου pap.).

ἀκρόνῠχος (A), line 4, after 'Nic.*Th.* 761' insert 'Posidipp. in *Suppl. Hell.* 698' and after '*Pr.* 942*23' insert '**2** = ἀκρόνυκτος, *PMich.*III 149 xi 9/11, cf. *Cat.Cod.Astr.* 8(2).84.5.'

*ἀκροξῐφίδιον, τό, *sword-point*, *PSI* 756.14 (Oxyrhynchus, iv/v AD), *Gloss.*

ἀκροπενθής, delete the entry.

ἀκρόπολις, after lemma insert '(poet. acc. ἀκροπόληα, Procl.*H.* 7.21)' **II**, line 2, after 'Simon. 137' insert 'Ἑλλάδος ἀ., of Sparta, *CEG* 819.12 (*c.*340 BC), Amyntas in *Suppl.Hell.* 44.8'

ἀκροπόλος I, delete 'cf.' and add '*h.Ven.* 54'

ἀκρόπρῳρον, add 'Cyran. 1.21.56 K.'

ἄκρος, line 1, after 'ἀκή A' insert 'w. secondary aspiration in Corcyran καθ' ἄκρον *IG* 9(1).690 (ii BC); cf. °ἀκροσκιρίαι' **I 2 a**, line 11, after 'E.*Ion* 1166' insert 'ἐπ' ἄκρα βέβηκας *APl.* 275.3 (Posidipp.)' **3**, delete the section adding example to section I 2 a, reading '*extreme* i.e. inmost' for '*inmost*' **III 2**, for 'Diph. 54' read 'Diph. 53 K.-A., μισθός Theoc.*Ep.* 8.5' **V 1**, add '*supremely*, ἄκρα σοφαὶ χέρες *APl.* 262'

ἀκροσκιρία, delete the entry, v. °ἀκροσκιρίαι.

*ἀκροσκιρίαι, αἱ, *heights covered with brushwood*, *Tab.Heracl.* 1.65,71 (written hακροσκιρίαις dat., -ιᾶν gen.; cf. σκῖρος).

*ἀκροσκόλιος, ον, *curved at the end*, Anon.Alch. 347.4.

ἀκροστῐχίς, after 'D.H. 4.62' insert '*GVI* 261.12 (Lycia, i/ii AD)' and after 'Cic.*Div.* 2.54.111' insert 'ἐπιθαλάμιον μετὰ ἀκροστοιχίδος τοῦ νυμφίου Dioscorus 23 tit.'

ἀκροστόλιον, add '*Inscr.Délos* 1403*Bai*40 (re-edited *SEG* 37.692, ii BC)'

ἀκροσφᾰλής I, before 'Plu. 2.713b' insert 'ἀ. ἴχνος Nic.*Al.* 242; διάνοιαν ὑγρὰν ὑπὸ τῆς μέθης καὶ ἀ. γεγενημένην' **II**, add 'subst. τὸ -ές, *hazardousness*, Longin. 22.4'

ἀκρότης II, place 'D.H.*Dem.* 2' after 'Diog.Oen.*fr.* 38' and delete 'cf.' and 'etc.'

*ἀκρούλιον, τό, perh. *woollen fringe* or some kind of garment, *Stud.Pal.* 20.245.19 (vi AD, ἀκρόλλιν); *PLugd.Bat.* xxv 13.22 (vii/viii AD), *PApoll.* 104.10-12 (viii AD).

ἀκρουροβόρη, add 'also masc., -βόρος, *PSI* 28.30 (iii/iv AD)'

*ἀκροφῠλάκιον, τό, *guard-post on a citadel*, *OGI* 254 (Babylon, ii BC) (pl.).

*ἀκρόχειρ, ὁ, *murderer*, *Hymn.Id.Dact.* 13, *EM* 53.37; cf. °ἀκρόχειρος.

ἀκρόχειρας, delete, and refer to °ἀκρόχειρ.

ἀκροχειρισμός, after '*wrestling with hands*' insert '*at arms' length*, opp. συμπλοκή'; add '(v. Robert *Hell.* 11/12.442 n. 4)'

ἀκρόχειρον, line 3, delete 'cf. *Hymn.Id.Dact.* 13'

*ἀκρόχειρος· ἀνδροφόνος Hsch.; cf. °ἀκρόχειρ.

*ἀκροχόρδονον, τό, kind of wart or *top of a wart*, Cyran. 35.5; cf. ἀκροχορδών.

*ἀκρόχρῡσον, τό, *gilding of the end(s)*, Anon.Alch. 378.17.

*ἄκρυτας, name of a bird, *PAmst.* 13.15 (v AD).

ἀκρωβέλια, after 'cod. -σβ-' insert 'edd. ἀκροβ-'

*ἀκρώμιος, ον, *of the acromion* (point of the shoulder), αὐτὴν τὴν σύνταξιν αὐτῶν ὀνομάζουσιν ἀκρώμιον ἁρμονίαν Gal. 2.766.

ἀκρωνῠχία, for '= ἀκρώρεια' read '*rock*, etc.'; add 'Philostr.*VA* 3.1'

ἀκρώνῠχος, after 'Plu. 2.317e' insert 'in uncertain sense, ἔν τε τοῖς ἀκρωνύχοις καὶ τῇ ταυροδιδαξίᾳ *Milet* 1(7).205*a* (p. 302)'

ἀκρώρεια, for '*mountain ridge*' read '*mountain heights*' and for 'Theoc. 25.31' substitute 'Call.*Dian.* 224'

*ἀκρώρειος, ον, *of mountain heights*, Orph.*H.* 32.4.

ἀκρωρεῖται, for '*ridges*' read '*tops*'; add 'sg. Ἀκρωρείτης, cult-title of Dionysus at Sicyon, Apollod.ap.St.Byz. s.v. Ἀκρώρεια; epith. of Pan, *HE* 2277 G.-P. (Leon.Tarent.), ib. 491 (Antip.Sid.) (-ριται pap.)'

ἀκρωτερῆσαι, after 'Hsch.' insert '(ἀκρωτηριάσαι La.)'

ἀκρωτηριάζω I 2, add 'Philostr.*VA* 7.4'

*ἄκτα, τά, Lat. *acta*, *official records*, *IGRom.* 1.421.20, *CIG* 29.27, *TAM* 4(1).39, *POxy.* 2725.21 (AD 71), *Inscr.Perg.* 8(3).24; also sg., οὔτε δι' ἄκτου βουλῆς *MAMA* 8.584.

ἀκταινόω, for 'Pl.Com.' to end of article substitute 'Pl.*Phd.* acc. to gloss. in *POxy.* 2087.22 (where read ἐξᾶραι, ‹ὑψ›ῶσαι) and Phryn.*PS* p.39 B.'

ἀκταῖος, add 'Myc. *a-ka-ta-jo* (pers. n.)'

ἀκτάριος, v. °ἀκτουάριος.

ἀκτέᾰνος, add 'of Δίκη, i.e. *incorruptible*, *BCH* suppl. 8 no. 87 (= *AP* 9.686)'

*ἀκτεινοβολή, v. °ἀκτινοβολή.

ἀκτέον I 1, add 'Plot. 1.3.1'

ἀκτεροί, add '(ἀκτέϊνοι La.)'

ἀκτή (A), line 5, for 'usu. of sea, coast .. rivers' read 'of river-banks' and transfer 'χλωρὰ ἀ. (S.*Ant.*) 1132, ἀκταὶ ἔναλοι Tim. *Pers.* 98 P.' to follow 'Il. 12.284 (line 2)' **2**, after '*into the sea*' insert '*cape, peninsula*' **II**, for 'generally, *edge*' read '*mound*'

*ἀκτήνδε, adv., *to the shore*, A.R. 1.318 (v.l. ἀκτὴν δ').

*ἀκτήρ, v. °ἀγκτήρ.

*Ἄκτια, τά, *Actian games*, *TAM* 4(1).34 (Delphi, Rom.imp.), *SEG* 34.1314 (Lycia, i AD), Ἄ. ἐν Νεικοπόλει *IG* 2².3169.17 (Athens, AD 253/7), Ἄ. ἐν Τύρῳ ib. 29, *SEG* 37.512 (Dodona, iii AD).

*Ἀκτιάς, άδος, ἡ, *festival of Actian Apollo*, *IG* 9²(1).583.9, 45, 69 (Olympia, iii BC). **2** the four-year period between the celebrations of the games held in honour of Augustus' victory at Actium, J.*BJ* 1.20.4, *SEG* 37.512 (Dodona, iii AD).

*ἀκτῑνηβολία, ας, ἡ, *emission of rays*, Man. 1.322. **2** *aspecting from the left*, id. 4.166.

*ἀκτῑνοβολή, ἡ, perh. = °ἀκτῖνοβολία 2, Anon.astrol. in *PMich.*III 149 xiv 28 (ἀκτεινο-, ii AD).

ἀκτῑνοβόλος, add 'of the sun, Melit.*fr.* 8b.24; as name of a horse, *SEG* 8.213.26 (Berytus, ii/iii AD)'

ἀκτῑνοκρᾰ́τωρ, add 'dub., v. °αἰωνακτινοκράτωρ'

*ἀκτῑνολαμπής, ές, *shining forth with its rays*, ἥλιος *Orac.Tiburt.* 22, 24, 29.

ἀκτινώδης, for '*like rays*' read '*appearing to give out rays*'; add '*Cat. Cod.Astr.* 11(2).163.5'

*Ἀκτιονίκης, ου, ὁ, *victor in the Actian games*, *BCH* 9.68.8 (-νείκης, Aphrodisias).

ἄκτιος, before 'ον' insert 'α'; add 'of Apollo, *IG* 5(1).29 (Sparta), of Arsinoe, *PEnteux.* 26.6 (iii BC)'

ἀκτίς I 1, add '**b** *day*, ἐν δὲ μονήρει .. ἀκτῖνι in *a single day*, Nic.*Al.* 401.' **3**, for '*Intr.*' read '*in Ptol.*' **II**, for '*spoke*' read '*cog*'

ἀκτίτης, for '*dweller on* .. **II**' substitute '*of* or *on a headland*, ἀ. καλαμευτής *AP* 6.304 (Phan.)'

ἄκτῐτος, add 'Myc. *a-ki-ti-to* (cf. °κτίζω)'

**ἄκτοινος, ον, Myc. *a-ko-to-no*, *not possessing an estate*.

*ἀκτουάριος, ὁ, Lat. *actuarius*, *keeper of records*, *PLond.* 237.20 (iv AD), *PMasp.* 229 (vi AD), *IGChr.* 211 (vi AD), *PAnt.* 190b31 (vi/vii AD), *Cod.Just.* 1.42.2, Just.*Nov.* 117.11; also ἀκτουάρις, *Dura*⁶ 292, ἀκτουριν *PBeatty Panop.* 1.21 (AD 298); also ἀκτάριος, *SEG* 26.1778 (Egypt), *PHarris* 96.14, 24 (i/ii AD), *BGU* 848.1 (iii AD), *IGBulg.* 1774, ἀ. σπείρης ib. 1835 (iii AD).

ἄκῡθος, delete 'c. gen. .. s.v.l.'

ἀκυθῶν, add '(ἄκυθον· ἄγρυπνον La.)'

ἄκῠλος, for 'ὁ' read 'ἡ' **II**, add '*IG* 1³.386.62, 387.69'

ἀκῠλωτός, add 'φιάλη *IG* 2².1421.48, 1425.93'

ἀκύμαντος I, line 2, for 'those of the stadium' read 'above the water-line'

ἀκύματος, add 'fig., *calm*, ἀ. βίους Lxx *Es.* 3.13b'

ἀκύμων (B), for 'of women' read 'of the womb'

ἀκῡρολογέω, for '*Lex.Vind.* 3.19' read 'Ps.-Hdn.Gr. in *An.Boiss.* 3.265, al.'

ἄκῡρος II, after '*power*' insert '*not sovereign*'; after 'Pl.*Tht.* 169e' insert 'τούτων μὲν οὖν ἄκυρός ἐστιν ἡ βουλή Arist.*Ath.* 45.4'

*ἀκῡρώσιμος, η, ον, *subject to cancellation*, μίσθωσις *PMich.*II 123ʳ viii 14 (i AD); πρᾶσις *PSI* 913ᵛ (add.) (i AD).

ἀκύρωσις, for '*BGU* 1282.35' read '*POxy.* 1282.35'

*ἀκώδωνος, ον, *without sound of* κώδων, μέλος ἀσάλπιγκτον καὶ ἀ. Steph.*in Rh.* 317.4.

ἀκώνητος, add '*PCair.Zen.* 743.3 (iii BC); Dor. ἀκώνατος, *Inscr.Cret.* 1.xvii 2*a*8 (Lebena, ii BC); cf. °ἀχώνευτος, κωνάω'

*ἀκώριαι· ἄκανθαι Hsch.; cf. ἀκορραί.

*ἀλαβαντικός, ὁ, wd. occurring in inventory of personal military equipment (app. from Alabanda in Caria), *PCol.* 188.16 (AD 320).

⁺ἀλᾰβαστοθήκη, ἡ, *case to contain alabastron* vase, Ar.*fr.* 561 K.-A., *IG* 2².1425.265 (iv BC), D. 19.237, also ἀλαβαστρουθήκα *BCH* 7.219 (Myrina); ἀλαβαστρουθήκη *PLond.* 402.28.

ἀλᾰ́βαστος, after 'ἡ' insert 'Poll. 7.177, 10.121'; for '*globular vase without handles*' read '*vase*'; line 4, for '*SIG* 102' read '*IG* 1³.421.207 (Athens, v BC)'

⁺ἀλᾰβάστρινος, η, ον, *of alabaster*, τράπεζα ἀ. *POxy.* 2058.25 (vi AD); neut. pl. as subst., *alabaster quarry*, *PRyl.* 92 i 1, ii 18 (ii/iii AD).

*ἀλᾰβαστροθήκη, ἡ, v. °ἀλαβαστοθήκη.

*ἀλᾰβαστροπώλης, ου, ὁ, *seller of alabaster-ware* or perh. *perfumes*, *PAnt.* 109.18 (vi AD).

*ἀλᾰβαστρωνίτης, ου, ὁ, *worker in an alabaster quarry*, *PSI* 822.5 (ii AD); ἀλαβαστ(ρωνιτῶν) *SB* 9904 (AD 154).

ἀλάβης, after 'a Nile fish' insert '*PTeb.* 701.41 (iii BC)'

⁺ἀλᾰβώδης, ες, *sooty*, *cindery*, Antim. 151.5 Wy., cf. Hsch.

ἀλαζονεύομαι, line 3, for 'Isoc. 12.74' read 'Isoc. 13.10'

*ἀλάζω, v. °ἀλλάσσω.

**ἀλαζών II 2**, for 'by Men.' read 'used by Plautus (*Mil.Glor.* 86)'
***ἀλαία**, v. ἀλαός II.
***ἀλαιθερές**· χλιαρόν. ἡλιοθερές Hsch.
**ἀλαιός**, delete the entry.
**ἀλᾰλαγμός I**, add '*bleating*, τῶν προβάτων καὶ τῶν κριῶν Lxx *Je.* 32.36'
**ἀλᾰλή**, for 'μύρου' read 'μύρον'
**ἄλᾰλος**, after '*IG* 14.1627' insert 'in curse, *SEG* 35.214.16, 216.25 (Athens, iii AD)'
***Ἄλανδρος**, ὁ, name of a god, θεὸς Ἄ. *SEG* 33.1172 (Lycia).
**ἀλανές, ἀλανέως**, delete the entries.
***ἀλανής**, -ές, app. *pressed together, acting together*: ἀ.· ἀληθές Hsch.; adv. -έως· ὁλοσχερῶς. Ταραντῖνοι id., ἀϝλανέōς, *Schwyzer* 412 (Elis, vi BC); cf. Aeol. ἀολλής.
***ἀλᾰοσκόπος**, ον, perh. *watching like a blind man*, cf. ἀλαοσκοπιά (-σκονος pap.) *PLond.* 1821.264 (*Aegyptus* 6.219).
**ἀλᾰπάζω**, line 2, for 'anap.' read 'dact., cf. λαπάσσω II'
**ἄλαρα**, add 'prob. the same as αὐαρά'
**ἅλας**, add 'prov., ὅτι οὐκ ἀνάνκη τῶν ἁλάτων ὧν ἐφάγαμεν ὁμοῦ κάδιον ἱστορῆσαι *PUniv.Giss.* 25.20 (iii AD), ἅλασιν ὕει, i.e. of great abundance, Suid.'
***Ἀλασιώτᾱς**, ὁ, dat. *a-la-si-o-ta-i*, cult-title of Apollo, perh. *of Alasia*, an ancient name of Cyprus, *ICS* 216(b).4 (*c*.375 BC).
***ἀλαστοτόκος** (dub.), ον, *giving birth in wretchedness*, ἐγὼν [μελέ]α καὶ ἀλασ[τοτόκος .. ] Stesich. *S*13.2 (p. 158 D.).
***ἁλᾰτάριον**, τό, *salt-cellar*, *BGU* 2360.10 (iii/iv AD).
**ἁλάτιον**, after 'ἅλας' insert '*IG* 4$^2$(1).123.60 (iii BC)'
***ἄλβολον**, Gallic name for βλήχων (q.v.), Ps.-Dsc. 3.31.
***ἀλβόμαυρον**, τό, prob. *grey dye* or *grey medicine*, *PVindob.*G 39847.929 (*CPR* 5.110; iv AD).
***ἀλγενήσιος**, ον, *dyed with seaweed*, *Edict.Diocl.* 24.9; cf. Lat. *algensis*.
**ἀλγεσίθῡμος**, add 'orac. in *TAM* 3(1).34.D65 (Termessus) (v.l., v. °αἰνεσίθῡμος, the reading in *TAM*)'
**ἀλγηδών I**, transfer 'Hdt. 5.18' to section III.
**ἀλγίων**, comp., add 'E.*Med.* 234, Isoc. 10.34'; sup., add 'Ar.*V.* 1117, Lys. 6.1, Th. 7.68.2, Opp.*H.* 2.624; neut. pl. as adv., S.*OC* 1174'
**ἀλδαίνω**, add 'to an aor. 2 of this verb app. belong the foll. participial forms: act., ἀλδών A.*fr.* 47a ii 17 R. (lyr.); med. ἐνάλδόμενον Nic.*Al.* 532 (v. ἐναλδαίνω), ἀλδομένη Q.S. 9.475 (s.v.l., v. ἀλθαίνω)'
**ἄλδομαι**, delete the entry.
***ἄλδω**, τὸ αὔξω, Hdn.Gr. 1.440, perh. a coined form for °ἀλδαίνω.
**ἀλέα** (B), last line, after '*fomentations*' insert 'Gal. 11.60.6'
***Ἀλέα**, ἡ, *h*αλέαι (dat.) *IG* 5(2).75 (Tegea, vi/v BC), Ion. Ἀλέη, title of Athena in Arcadia, Hdt. 1.66.4, X.*HG* 6.5.27, Men.*Her.* 84, Paus. 8.45.4.
**ἀλεαίνω**, for 'Archil.ap.Plu. 2.954f' read 'Archel.Phil. B 1a D.-K.'
***ἀλεαντρίς**, ίδος, ἡ, name of a fish, *Gp.* 20.7.1.
***ἄλεαρ** (B), ατος, τό, *coarse wheat meal*, Hdn.Gr. 2.472.12; pl., ἀλέατα *Milet* 3 p. 163 no. 31; w. metric lengthening, ἀλείατα Od. 20.108; late sp. ἀλήατος (gen. sg.) *SB* 5224.19, 40.
***ἀλέγη**, ἡ, unexpld. term used in hydraulic operations, *PPetr.* 3 p. 42 Fb2 (iii BC).
**ἀλεγύνω**, for '*heed, care for*' read '*occupy oneself with, take care of*'; add 'ἀγλαὰ ἔργ' ἀλεγύνειν, *h.Ven.* 11, A.R. 4.1203'
**ἀλέγω II 1**, delete 'cf. Simon. 37.10' **2**, line 2, after 'Hes.*Op.* 251' insert 'ἄχναν .. κύματος οὐκ ἀλέγεις, οὐδ' ἀνέμου φθόγγον Simon. 38.15 P.'
***Ἄλεια**, v. °Ἀλιεία.
⁺**ἀλείατα**, v. °ἄλεαρ (B).
***ἀλειμέντα**, τά, v. °ἀλιμέντα.
**ἄλειμμα**, after lemma insert 'Aeol. ἄλιππα *EM* 64.40, perh. ἄλει[ππα] Alc. 45.7 P.' add '**II** *application of unguents, anointing*, Hp.*Morb.* 2.66, *IG* 5(1).1390.106 (Messenia, i BC), 12(3).330.128 (Thera, iii/ii BC); meton., *gymnastic training*, *SEG* 9.4.10, 19 (Cyrene, i BC).'
**ἀλειμμάτιον**, add '*BGU* 2357 ii 12 (sp. ἀλιμμ-, iii AD)'
**ἀλέïος**, (ἀλεῖος La.), for 'Ἀλήϊος' read 'ἀλήϊος'
***ϝαλεῖος**, v. °Ἠλεῖος.
***ἀλειποτάκτως**, v. °ἀλιποτάκτως.
***ἄλειππα**, v. °ἄλειμμα.
***ἀλειπτηρία**, ἡ, perh. = ‡ἀλειπτήριον I, *SEG* 36.1097 (Sardes, iv/v AD).
**ἀλειπτήριον I**, line 2, for 'or in Roman .. *sudatory*' read 'or baths (perh. also general term for baths, v. *GRBS* 16.217ff.)' **II**, for this section read 'ἀλειπτήριον· γραφεῖον. Κύριοι; cf. perh. διφθεραλοιφός'
**ἀλείπτης 1**, add 'ἀ. Καίσαρος *Didyma* 108, ἀ. παίδων Σεβαστοῦ *IG* 2$^2$.7155'
**ἀλειπτικός**, for '*trained under him*' read '*devoted to athletics*'; after 'Ti.Locr. 104a' add 'cf. Alex.Aphr.*in Top.* 152.25'
**ἄλειπτος**, before 'adv.' insert 'name of a horse, *ICilicie* 49.B3 (Ἄλιπτος, vi AD)'
**ἄλειπτρον**, delete the entry.
***Ἀλεισία**, ἡ, epith. of Aphrodite, *Anecd.Stud.* p. 269.
**ἄλεισον**, for 'Call.*Aet.* 1.1.13' read 'Call.*fr.* 178.13 Pf.'
***ἀλειτηρός**, ὁ, adj., *sinning, offending against*, ἀνὴρ .. ἀ. Alcm. 79 P. (ἀλιτηρός codd.), κἀξ ἀλειτηροῦ φρενὸς S.*OC* 371; masc. subst., *sinner*, *CEG* 439 (ostr., Athens, v BC); adv. ἀλιτε̄ρôς *Schwyzer* 412 (Olympia, vi BC).
**ἀλειτουργησία**, for 'late word for Att. ἀτέλεια' read '= Lat. *immunitas*'
**ἀλειτούργητος**, after 'D. 18.91' insert 'Is.*fr.* 143'
***ἀλείτουργος**, ον, *exempt from* λειτουργίαι, *TAM* 2.224 (Sidyma; written ἀλιτούργου (gen.)).
**ἄλειφα**, for 'cf.' read 'Hippon. 58 W.' and for 'Call.*fr.* 12' read 'Call.*fr.* 7.12 Pf.'
****ἀλειφαζόος**, Myc. *a-re-pa-zo-o*, *a-re-po-zo-o*, *unguent-boiler*.
**ἄλειφαρ**, add 'Myc. *a-re-pa*'
**ἀλείφω 2**, after '(Ancyra)' insert '*train* an athlete, *PCair.Zen.* 60.2 (iii BC)' **3**, for '*polish*' read '*anoint* objects'
***ἀλειψανία**, ἡ, *lack, state of not having any left*, *SB* 6319.56 (ii/i BC).
***ἀλείψανος**, ον, *without relic*, κλῆσις Gr.Naz.*Carm.* 1.2.10.749 (*PG* 37.734).
⁺**ἀλεκτόρειος**, ον, (ἀλέκτωρ), *of a fowl*, ᾠὰ ἀ. Synes.*Ep.* 4.165; in the name of a laxative medicine, ἀ. καταπότιον Garg.Mart. 30; ἀλεκτορεία (sc. λίθος), ἡ, stone found in the gizzards of cocks, Plin.*HN* 37.144; neut. as adv., κοκκύζετ' ἀλεκτόρειον Gr.Naz.*Carm.* 2.1.11.1926 (*PG* 37.1164).
**ἀλεκτόριον**, add 'v. *BE* 1971.638'
**ἀλεκτορίς**, after '-ίδος' insert '(-ῖδος Herod. 6.100)' **I**, for 'used by Trag.' to end of section read 'Arist.*HA* 614$^b$10, Diocl.*fr.* 141, Herod. 6.100; used generically, .. τὸ τῶν ἀλεκτορίδων γένος· ὀχεύουσι γὰρ οἱ ἄρρενες καὶ ὀχεύονται αἱ θήλειαι τῶν ἀλεκτορίδων καὶ τίκτουσιν ἀεί Arist.*HA* 544$^a$31, 32'
**ἀλεκτρῠονώδης**, for 'πρὸς ἡδονάς .. end' read 'Eun.*Hist.* p.2.18 B.'
***ἀλεκτρῠώδης**, ες, *like a cock*, πρὸς ἡδονάς Eun.*Hist.* *fr.*71.2 B.
**ἀλεκτρύων**, add 'Myc. *a-re-ku-tu-ru-wo* (pers. n.)'
***Ἀλεκτρώνα**, ἁ, divinity or heroine at Ialysus, Rhodes, *IG* 12(1).677.4 (iii BC).
**ἀλέματος**, for 'Dor.' read 'Aeol. and Dor.'
***Ἀλεξάνδρεια**, τά, *festival in honour of Alexander the Great*, *OGI* 222.25/6 (Clazomenae, iii BC), Str. 14.1.31, *IG* 2$^2$.2226, (Athens, iii AD).
***Ἀλεξάνδρειος**, ον, *of Alexander*, μναῖ, i.e. of his standard, *SEG* 9.1.8, 9 (Cyrene, iv BC); δραχμὰς Ἀ. *SEG* 30.1073 (Chios, ?189/188 BC), *Didyma* 38.7 (i BC), 446.9 (iii BC).
***Ἀλεξανδρῑνός**, όν, *of Alexandrian workmanship*, *SEG* 33.946 (Ephesus, i AD).
**ἀλέξανδρος I**, delete the section **II**, add 'cf. Myc. *a-re-ka-sa-da-ra* (fem. pers. n.)'
***Ἀλεξεᾶτις**, ιδος, ἁ, epith. of the goddess Enodia, *IG* 9(2).576 (Larissa).
**ἀλέξημα**, for '*defence* .. 479' read '*remedy, medicine*'; add 'transf. A.*Pr.* 479'
**ἀλεξητικός**, for 'Alex.Aphr.*de An.* 162.16' read 'Alex.Aphr.*de An.* 162.26'
⁺**ἀλεξιάρη**, fem. adj., (ἀρή) *protecting against ruin*, νειός Hes.*Op.* 464; ῥάμνος Nic.*Th.* 861; masc. **ἀλεξιάρης** Hsch., which shd. perh. be restd. in Hes. l.c.
**ἀλεξίγᾰμος**, for 'Βάκχαι' read 'Νύμφαι'
**ἀλεξίκᾰκος**, after 'Hes.*Op.* 123 (as v.l.)' insert 'οἶνος .. πυρὶ ἶσον ἐπιχθονίοισιν ὄνειαρ .. ἀλεξίκακον Panyas. 16.13 B.'; line 4, after 'epith. of Heracles' insert '*Hesperia* 5.400.108-9 (Athens, iv BC), *SEG* 17.451 (Rome, ii/iii AD)'; add 'pl., divinities at Byzantium, Robert *Hell.* 9.56; of a bath, *ICilicie* 22 (v/vi AD); see also *SEG* 36.1325'
**ἀλεξίλογος**, delete 'dub. in'
**ἀλέξιον**, for 'cf. Phot.' read 'cf. ἀλεξήματα· τὰ βοηθήματα, Phot.'
**ἀλεξίπονος**, for 'S.(?)*Eleg.* 7' read 'of Asclepius, S.*Pae.* 1(*b*).(i).1 P.'; add 'of a stone, *Lapid.Gr.* 195.21; λουτρὸν *SEG* 33.773 (Ostia, iv AD)'
**ἀλεξιφάρμᾰκος I**, add '**2** fig., παιώνειόν τινα καὶ ἀ. .. λόγον Longin. 16.2, 32.4.' **II 1**, add 'ὥσπερ ἀ. ἐστι τοῖς ἀδικεῖν βουλομένοις D. 24.85'
***ἀλεξιχᾰλαζος**, ον, *warding off hail*, epith. of Αἰθήρ, Robert *Hell.* 9.63 (Amasia).
**ἀλεόμαι**, line 2, after '(v.l.)' insert 'A.R. 4.474' **2**, add '*Trag.adesp.* 705.10 K.-S.'
⁺**ἀλεός**· διάπυρος Hsch. **II** v. ἠλεός.
***Ἀλεπακίδαια**, τά, name of a farm at Messene, *IG* 5(1).1434 (i BC/i AD), cf. mod. Gk. ἀλεπού *fox*.
***ἀλέπῐδος**, ον, *not having scales*, ἰχθῦς Cyran. 1.1.8 K.
**ἀλέπιστος**, for '*not scaled*' read '*not having the scales removed*'
***ἀλέπῠρος**, ον, *free from husks*, κριθαί Hsch. s.v. ἀτυπῆδες (-ίδες La.).
***ἀλεστός**, *ground*, ἀλεστοῦ σίτου *POsl.* 155.16 (ii AD).
**ἄλεστρον**, after '*POxy.*' insert '736.8' and 'both' before 'i AD'; add 'also ἄλετρον *PPetr.* 3 p. 313 (iii BC), *SB* 7642.3 (iii BC)'

**ἀλέτης**, add 'of a man, *POxy.* 3169.91 (ii/iii AD), *PHib.* 268 int. (*c.*260 BC)'

***ἀλέτισσα**, ἡ, = ἀλετρίς 1, *POxy.* 2421.31 (iv AD).

**ἀλετός**, after 'Plu.*Ant.* 45' insert '2.289f, Ath. 14.618d'

**ἀλετρίς**, add 'cf. Myc. *me-re-ti-ri-ja* (for *me-* v. °ἄλευρον)'

***ἄλετρον**, τό, v. °ἄλεστρον.

**ἀλετών**, after '*millstone*' insert '*IG* $1^3$.422.24, al. (Athens, v BC)'

***ἀλευραττίς**· ἀγγεῖον εἰς ἄλφιτα Phot. α 932 Th. (ἀλεύραττις v.l.).

***ἀλευρητικός**, ή, όν, perh. *made of flour*, dub. in *PTeb.* 894 *fr.* 10.9 (ii BC, perh. read ἀλευριτ-).

**+ἀλευροδοῦντες**, οἱ, (cj. ἀλευροῦντες), kind of wheatcakes, Anticl. 23 J.

***ἀλευροκαθάρτης**, ου, ὁ, *one who sieves the flour*, *SEG* 33.1165 (Pamphylia, iii AD).

**ἄλευρον** (A), add 'see also ‡μάλευρον (Myc. *me-re-u-ro*)'

***ἀλευρόπωλις**, ιδος, app. fem. adj., *used for the sale of flour*, ἀλε[υρό]πωλις στωϊά *IG* 12(2).14.12 (Mytilene).

***Ἀλεύς**, title of Apollo, *SEG* 30.1218 (Tarentum, iv BC).

**ἀλέω**, line 3, after 'Hdt. 7.23' insert '*BGU* 1858, also part. ἠλεσμένος *Edict.Diocl.* 1.13-14'

**+ἀλεωρή**, Att. -ρά, ἡ, *means* or *place of escape*, *refuge*, *protection*, Il. 24.216, ὡς καὶ αὐτοί τινα ἀλεωρὴν εὑρήσονται Hdt. 9.6, A.R. 1.694, J.*BJ* 3.163, Opp.*H.* 1.790; w. obj. gen. δηΐων ἀνδρῶν ἀ. Il. 12.57, 15.533, βελέων ἀ. Ar.*V.* 615; of escape from conditions, situations, etc., λιμοῦ ἀ. Hes.*Op.* 404, Hp.*Praec.* 7, D.S. 3.34, J.*AJ* 18.147; of bodily protection, τὴν περὶ τὸ σῶμα ἀ. Arist.*PA* 679$^b$28, 687$^a$29, *HA* 488$^b$10.

***ἀλεωρία**, gloss (with πολυωρία) on ἄλεαρ, Hsch. (prob. corruption of °ἀλεωρά).

**ἄλη I 1**, line 2, after '(pl.)' insert 'E.*Med.* 1285' **2**, delete the section.

***ἄλη** (B), ἡ, Lat. *ala*, *IPrusias* 104.2 (ii AD), etc.

**ἁλή**, line 1, for 'only' read 'normally'; add 'rarely sg., τῶι ἥρωι τῶι ἐπὶ τῆι ἁλῆι *SEG* 21.527.38, al., τὴν ἁλ[λ]ὴν καὶ τὴν ἀγορὰν τὴν ἐν Κοίληι ib. 17 (Attica, 363/2 BC); cf. St.Byz. s.v. Ἁλαί· ἔστι καὶ λίμνη ἐκ θαλάσσης'

***ἀλήατος**, v. ‡ἀλείατα.

**ἀληγός**, add '2.912f, *BGU* 2353.14 (AD 115)'

**ἀληθάργητος**, for '*free from lethargy, energetic*' read '*unforgettable* (cf. ληθαργέω)'; for '*CIG* 2804 (Aphrod.)' read '*MAMA* 8.504.16, *IGChr.* 9'

***ἀληθέγγυος**, ον, *that guarantees truth*, Phot. α 938 Th.

**ἀλήθεια**, end of line 1, for 'ἀλάθεα' read 'Aeol. **ἀλάθεα**' and before 'neut.' insert 'also interpr. as' **I 2**, line 4, before 'Th. 4.120' insert '*in reality*'

**ἀληθής II**, add '**3** perh. *legitimate*, *IEryth.* 2(c).9 (v BC).' **III 2**, after 'Ar.*Ra.* 840' insert '(E.*fr.* 885)' and after '*Av.* 174' insert '*Pl.* 123, 429'

***ἀληθινοβάφος**, ὁ, (sp. ἀληθεινο-), *dyer* or *maker of best quality purple*, *ITyr* 137 (Chr.).

**ἀληθινόπινος**, read **ἀληθινόπῖνος**; for '*patina*' read '*pearls* (cf. πίνη II)'

***ἀληθινοπράσινος**, ον, *of real green*, *SB* 13597 (v AD).

**ἀληθῖνός I 2**, line 3, after 'ἰχθύς Amph. 26' insert '(cf. κάραβος ἀ. Macho 29 G.; the significance of the adj. is here uncertain)'

**ἀληθοεπής**, before 'Hsch.' insert '*Suppl.Hell.* 991.70 (poet. word-list, iii BC), ἀ. καὶ ἐτήτυμος *IStraton.* 1201.5'

**ἀλήμων**, for '(Leon.)' read '(Leon.Tarent.)' and after it insert 'D.P. 490, Opp.*H.* 3.455, Nonn.*D.* 1.528'; delete '- Ep. word'

**ἀληνής**, for 'prob. l. in Semon. 7.44' read 'Semon. 7.53 W. (codd., cj. ἀδηνής)'

***ἄληξ**, v. ‡ἄλιξ.

**ἀλήπεδον**, for '= Ἀλήιον πεδίον' read '*plain*, ἥξει δ' ἐρεμνὸν εἰς ἀλήπεδον φθιτῶν Lyc. 681'

**ἀλησία**, add 'perh. in *MAMA* 9.13 (i BC)'

**ἀλήτης**, for '*wanderer* .. exiles' read '*homeless wanderer*, *vagrant*, Od. 17.576, 18.18' **2**, after '**ἀλῆτις**, ιδος' insert '*GLP* 1.122.17' add '**II** ἀλῆται *the planets*, incl. sun and moon, Nonn.*D.* 5.68, al., *AP* 9.822.3.'

***ἀλητικός** (B), ή, όν, *of* or *for milling*, *PMil.Vogl.* 53.11, *PRyl.* 321.5 (sp. αλαι-).

**+ἀλητύς**, ύος, ἡ, *wandering* (cf. ἄλη), Call.*fr.* 10 Pf., Man. 3.379.

***ἀλητῶ**· τὸ πλανῶ *EM* 822, *Et.Gen.* 459.

**ἀλήτωρ**, add 'as Cret. pers. n., Perdrizet *Memnonion* 60 (iii BC), *Inscr.Cret.* 1.xxii 47 (ii BC); cf. ‡λείτωρ (λήτωρ)'

***ἀλήφατος**, ον, *crushed*, ἀλήφατον ἄνθος ἐ‹λ›αίης *SEG* 8.474.7 (Hermoupolis); ἀλήφατα (codd. ἀλί-)· ἄλφιτα ἢ ἄλευρα Hsch.

***ἀλθέσσω**, *heal*, *cure*, Aret.*SD* 1.13.4, 2.9.9.

**ἀλθήεις**, delete '645' (v. °ἀνθήεις).

***ἄλθησις**, εως, ἡ, *healing*, ἐναλθῆ· τὸν χρήζοντα ἀλθήσεως Sch.Nic.*Al.* 586i.

**ἄλθος**, add 'cj. in S.*fr.* 172 R.; pl. Nic.*Al.* 423 (v.l.)'

**ἁλία** (A), read **ἁλία** **I**, in Sicily, add '*SEG* 30.1117.4 (Entella, iii BC)'; add '*assembly* of a phratry, *CID* I 9.A21, al. (iv BC)'

**+ἁλία** (B), ἡ, *salt-box*, Archipp. 13, Stratt. 15 K.-A., Poll. 10.169; ἁλίην τρυπᾶν ἐν Θέμιδος οἴκῳ dig into *the salt-box* in the house of Themis, a mark of honest poverty, Ap.Ty.*Ep.* 7, cf. Call.*Epigr.* 47.1 Pf.

***ἁλιάδιον**, τό, kind of boat, *CPR* 10.2.4, 10.5 (early vii AD).

**ἁλιαία**, read **ἁλιαία** and after '= ἁλία (A) (ἀ-)' insert 'ἀλιαιίαν *SEG* 30.380 (Tiryns, vii BC)'; add 'in Arcadia, *Schwyzer* 666.6, *SEG* 25.443.10 (both Orchomenus, iii BC)'

***ἁλιάπους**, ποδος, ὁ, a bird, perh. *stormy petrel*, Achae. 54 S.

**ἁλιάς**, add '(employed in postal service) *PBeatty Panop.* 1.252 (AD 298), *POxy.* 2675.9 (iv AD)'

**ἁλίασμα**, read **ἁλίασμα** and add '*SEG* 35.999.19, 30.1119.33 (both Entella, iv and iii BC), *IG* 14.952.8 (Agrigentum, iii/ii BC), ib. 612.5 (Rhegium, ii BC)'

**+ἁλίασσις**, ιος, ἁ, *act of the assembly* or ἁλιαία, *IG* 4.554.5 (Argos, vi/v BC).

***Ἁλιασταί**, οἱ, religious association at Rhodes, *IG* 12(1).155 (ii BC); cf. Ἁλιάδαι.

**ἁλιαστάς**, read **ἁλιαστᾶς**

**ἀλίαστος**, for '*not to be turned aside*' read '*interminable*'; after 'Hes.*Th.* 611' insert 'A.R. 2.649; Musae. 318'; after 'Il. 24.549' insert 'Q.S. 4.17' **2**, for this section read 'of things, perh. *restless*, κῦμ' ἀλίαστον A.R. 1.1326 (cj. κῦμα λιασθέν)' **II**, substitute 'of persons, animals, *not to be stopped*, E.*Or.* 1479, Opp.*C.* 4.160, *H.* 2.590'; delete '-Ep. .. lyr.'

**ἁλίβαπτος**, for 'Nic.*Al.* 618' read 'Nic.*Al.* 605' and add '(v.l., ed. °ἁλίβλαπτος)'

**ἀλιβδύω**, delete 'expl. .. 269' (v. °ἁλιδ-).

***ἁλίβλαπτος**, ον, *hurt by the sea*, Nic.*Al.* 605 (v.l. ἁλίβαπτος).

**ἁλίβρομος**, for '*murmuring like the sea*' read '*sounding in the sea*'

**ἁλιβρώς**, add 'Diog.Oen.*fr.* 7 col. 2.6 (*AJA* 75.367)'

**ἁλίβρωτος**, for '*swallowed by the sea*' read '*gnawed by the sea*'

***ἁλιγενέτωρ**, ορος, ὁ, compd. of ἅλς (B) and γενέτωρ, *Suppl.Hell.* 991.64 (poet. word-list, iii BC, ἀλιγυνέτ- pap.); cf. °ἁλογενέτωρ.

**ἁλίγκιος**, line 1, after 'ον' insert '(also α, ον, B. 5.168 S.-M.)'

***ἁλίγνητος**, η, ον, = ἁλιγενής, *Suppl.Hell.* 991.58 (poet. word-list, iii BC).

***ἁλίγονος**, ον, = ἁλιγενής, *Suppl.Hell.* 991.66 (poet. word-list, iii BC).

***ἁλιδερκής**, ές, compd. from ἅλς (B) and δέρκομαι, *Suppl.Hell.* 991.57 (poet. word-list, iii BC).

**+ἁλιδίως**, *sufficiently*, ἁ. πονηρός Epich. 84.35 A., cf. Hsch. (ἀλ-).

***ἁλιδόνητος**, ον, *buffeted by the sea*, Gramm.ap.Ludwich *Aristarch* 2.665 (*Cod.Vindob.* 294), *Trag.adesp.* 720f K.-S. (= *Suppl.Hell.* 991.63, poet. word-list, iii BC).

**+ἁλίδονος**, ον, *driven by the sea*, codd. in A.*Pers.* 275.

**ἁλίδροσος**, after 'ον' insert 'app. *sprayed by the sea*' and for '*Lyr. Adesp.Oxy.* 219.11' read '*Lyr.Alex.adesp.* 4.11'

**ἁλιεία**, after 'Str. 11.2.4 (pl.)' insert 'Plu.*Tim.* 20, Ael.*NA* 14.20'

**Ἁλιεῖα**, delete the entry (v. °Ἁλίεια).

***Ἁλίεια**, τά, *festival of the Sun* in Rhodes, *Com.adesp.* 336, *IG* 12(1).72a (ii BC), Ἁλιέα ib. 730.17 (i BC), contr. Ἁλεῖα ib. 12.4, 58.19, Ath. 13.561e.

**ἁλιεινή**, for '*Edict.Diocl.* 21.2' read '*Edict.Diocl.* 21.2A, (Ἁλτείνη Laufer, cf. Lat. text *Altinata*)'

***Ἁλιεῖον**, τό, app. *temple of the Sun*, ἐπὶ [τ]ὰν κορυφὰν τοῦ Ἁ. *IG* 4.926.12 (Megara, iii BC).

**ἁλιευτής**, read '**ἁλιευτᾶς**, ᾶ' and for 'Cerc. 4.8' read 'Cerc. 7.9'

**ἁλιευτικός**, line 2, after '*An.* 7.1.20' insert '(ἁλιευτικόν, τό, *POxy.* 1846.1 (vi/vii AD))'

**ἁλιεύω**, after 'Luc.*Pisc.* 47' insert '*SEG* 24.1108'

**ἁλίζω** (A), line 3, for 'but ἡλ-' read 'ἡλ-'

**ἁλίζωνος**, after '*sea-girt*' insert '*Suppl.Hell.* 991.54, 67 (poet. word-list, iii BC)'; for '*Sos.* 24' read '*fr.* 384.9 Pf.'; after 'Sid.)' insert 'Nonn.*D.* 37.152, al.'

**ἁλικάκαβον**, read **ἁλικάκκαβον** (v.l. -κακα-)

**Ἁλικαρνασσίς**, add 'also of a tribe, *SEG* 33.1103 (Paphlagonia, ii/iii AD)'

***ἀλίκιον**, τό, perh. dim. of ἄλιξ 1, *groats*, *PHamb.* 192.24 (iii AD), *PRyl.* 629.293, 298 (iv AD, -κιν pap.).

***ἀλίκλα**, ἡ, Lat. *alicula*, light upper garment, *SB* 9834b.10 (iv AD).

**ἁλικνήμις**, for 'ἀπήνη .. car' read 'perh. *having spokes* (i.e. *wheels*) *that go through the sea*, applied to Poseidon's chariot, ἀπήνη ἁ.'

**+ἁλικός**, ή, όν, *of salt*, τὴν ἁλικὴν ὠνὴν *JHS* 74.97 no. 38.B8 (Caunus); ἁλική, ἡ, *salt-tax*, *PSI* 388.1 (iii BC), *PTeb.* 482 (iii, BC), *PHib.* 112.3, etc. **2** pl. = Lat. *salinae*, *salt-pans*, Charis. p. 33 K.

**ἁλικρήπῖς**, for '*at the sea's edge*' read '*bordered by the sea*'

**ἁλίκτῠπος**, for 'cf.' read 'ἁ. κῦμα E.*Hipp.* 754, *Anacreont.* 50.8 W.' and delete 'also .. (lyr.)'

**ἀλίμενος 2**, for '*shelterless, inhospitable*' read '*offering no refuge* or *protection*' and add 'γάμον A.*fr.* 154a.3 R.'

**ἀλῐμενότης**, for '*Peripl.M.Eux.* 37' read '*Peripl.M.Eux.* 25.2 (= 16ʳ.10 D.)'

***ἀλιμέντα**, τά, Lat. *alimenta*, *provisions*, *IEphes.* 805.6 (Rom.imp.); also ἀλειμέντα, *TAM* 2.278.22 (Xanthus, ?iii BC).

**ἀλιμενώτης**, for 'cf. Hsch.' read 'v. sq.'

***ἀλιμένωτον**· λιμένα μὴ ἔχοντα Hsch. (La.).

***ἀλιμμάτιον**, v. ‡ἀλειμμ-.

***ἀλιμονικός**, ή, όν, *of* or *concerned with provisioning*, fr. Lat. *alimonium*, ἀπὸ τοῦ ἀ. (λόγου) *PMich.*XI 613.3 (written ἐλιμ-, AD 415).

***ἁλίμοχθος**, ον, *toiling at sea*, *SLG* 364.8.

**ἁλιμῡρήεις**, after 'εσσα' insert '(fem. only at *Suppl.Hell.* 991.50, poet. word-list, iii BC)'; for '*into the sea*' read '*with salt water*'

**⁺ἁλιμῡρής**, ές, *flowing with salt water*, ἁ. βένθη, πόντος *GVI* 1833.5 (Salamis, Cyprus, ii BC), Orph.*A.* 68, ἀφρός *APl.* 180 (Democr.); of sea-washed rocks, etc., A.R. 1.913, Phanocl. 1.17, Opp.*H.* 2.258; of rivers at their mouths, Orph.*A.* 344, 462.

**⁺ἁλιναιέτας**, α, masc. adj., *dwelling in the sea*, δελφῖνες B. 17.97 S.-M. (ἐναλι- pap.).

**ἁλινδέω II 1**, delete '*to be twirled* .. 113' and substitute 'in erotic context, w. dat., Call.*fr.* 191.42 Pf.; μετά τινος, Herod. 5.30' **2**, lines 2/3, delete '*having grovelled*' and transfer '*frequent*' before 'ἠλινδημένος' in line 2. **3**, delete the section.

**ἁλινήκτειρα**, for '*the sea*' read '*brine*'

**⁺ἄλινσις**, ιος, ἁ, *application of stucco* or *whitewash*, τοῦ ἐργαστηρίου *IG* 4².102.39, *SEG* 24.277.A12 (both Epid., iv BC); cf. ἄλειψις (3).

**ἀλίνω**, for '*pound*' read '*grind*' and add 'cf. ἐναλίνω'

**ἅλιξ I**, add 'Dsc. 4.148, *Edict.Diocl.* 1.25; also written ἄληξ Hierocl.*Facet.* 222' **II**, delete the section.

***ἅλιξ (B)**, ικος, ὁ, Lat. *hallec*, *fish sauce*, Gp. 20.46.2.

**⁺Ἁλιονείκης**, ὁ, = Ἁλειονίκης, *victor in the Ἁλεῖα* (°Ἁλίεια) *at Rhodes*, *PLond.* 1178.67 (ii AD), *IGBulg.* 1574.3 (Rom.imp.).

**ἅλιος (B)**, line 3, after '(Od. 2.)318' insert '*h.Merc.* 549'; add 'perh. also in Ion., *fallow*, εἰ νέον ἀροῖ το[ὺς] ἁλίους ἀρότους *IG* 12(7).62.8 (Amorgos, iv BC)'

**ἅλιος (C)**, add '(Aeol. ἄλιος)'

**Ἁλιοτρόπιος**, add '(*c.*200 BC), perh. to be rest. at *GDI* 1338 (Dodona, (v. *BCH* 109.536))'

**ἀλίπαστος**, add '**2** neut. subst., dub. in Erinn. in *Suppl.Hell.*401.24.'

**ἁλίπλαγκτος**, for '*IG* 2.1660' read '*IG* 2².4968'

**ἁλιπλᾰνής**, after 'Lucill.)' add '6.223 (Antip.)'

**ἁλίπλοος II 1**, line 2, delete '*fisher*'

**⁺ἁλιπόρος**, ον, *travelling over the sea*, ἀνά τε νηῦς ἁλιπόρους *Lyr. Alex.adesp.* 36.2; *forming a sea-passage*, ἁλιπόρου διασφάγος Luc. *Trag.* 24.

***ἀλιποτάκτως**, adv., *without leaving one's post*, *SB* 9011.6 (ἀλειπο-, v/vi AD); cf. λιποτάκτης.

**⁺ἄλιππα**, v. °ἄλειμμα.

**⁺ἁλίρραντος**, ον, *sprayed by the sea*, ἀκτῇ ἐν ἁλιρράντῳ ἐπὶ πέτρῃ *Epic.Alex.adesp.* 8.1, *Suppl.Hell.* 991.55 (poet. word-list, iii BC), ἁλιρράντου .. πόντου *AP* 9.333 (Mnas.), 14.72.

***Ἆλις**, v. °Ἦλις.

**ἁλίσκομαι I 1**, after 'Pl.*R.* 468a' insert 'Is. 6.1' **II 2**, add 'of decrees, *to be invalidated*, τῶν ψηφισμάτων .. ἢ μενόντων κατὰ χώραν ἢ ἁλόντων D. 58.5'

**ἁλισμός**, add '*salt-incrustation*, *PZen.Col.* 95.6 (iii BC)'

**ἁλιστός**, add 'also -όν, τό, *bacon*, *Edict.Diocl.* 4.7'

**ἀλῐταίνω**, lines 4/5, for 'ἀλιταίνεται Hes.*Op.* 330: aor.' read '1 aor. subj. ἀλιτήνεται Hes.*Op.* 330 (pap.); 2 aor.'; line 9, for 'ἀλιταινητ' read 'ἀλιτήνεται'

**ἀλιτάνευτος**, for '*PMag.Par.* 1.1176' read '*PMag.* 4.1776'

***ἁλιτεγγής**, ές, perh. *moistened by the sea*, *Suppl.Hell.* 991.56 (cj. for ἁλιτεσχής, poet. word-list, iii BC).

***ἁλιτειχής**, ές, *walled by the sea*, Euph. in *Suppl.Hell.* 442.4.

**ἁλιτενής**, for '*projecting into the sea*' read '*extending along* or *into the sea*, νῆσοι *PHamb.* 119 iii 15 (iii BC)'

**ἀλῐτημα**, for '(Agath.) .. pl.)' read '9.154, 643 (all Agath.)'

**ἀλιτήμερος**, add 'Archil. 196a.39 W.²'

***ἀλιτήρ**, ῆρος, ὁ, = ἀλείτης, *EM* 65.24; cf. ἀλίτης.

**ἀλιτήριος 1**, add 'Lyc.*fr.* 2.8 S.' **II**, add 'of Zeus, *EM* 65.41; of Demeter (fem. ἀλιτηρία), ib. 65.40'

**⁺ἀλιτηρός**, v. °ἀλειτηρός.

***ἀλιτουργησία, ἀλίτουργος**, v. ‡ἀλειτ-.

***ἀλιτόφρων**, ον, *foolish*, Hsch. s.v. ὠλιτόφρονας (for ὁ ἀ- or ὦ ἀ-).

**ἀλιτραίνω**, for 'Hes.*Op.* 243' read 'Hes.*Op.* 241'

***ἀλιτρεύω**, *sin*, *MAMA* 1.235 (Laodicea Combusta).

**ἀλιτρόβιος**, for 'ἀλῐτρό-' read 'ἀλιτρό-'

***ἀλίτροπος**, ὁ, wd. of uncertain etym., app. meaning *sinner* or sim., Ps.-Phoc. 141 Y.

**ἀλιτρός**, for 'ἀλῐτρός, όν' read 'ἀλῐτρός, ά, όν' and at end delete 'fem. .. Semon. 7.7'

**ἀλῐτροσύνη**, read **ἀλῑτροσύνη**, and add 'Orph.*A.* 1231, *L.* 62'

**⁺ἀλίφατα**, v. °ἀλήφατος.

***ἀλῐφή**, ἡ, *painting*, τὴν ἀ. τῶν ξύλων *IG* 2².1682.29 (iii BC); cf. ἀλοιφή.

***ἀλῐφησις**, εως, ἡ, *painting*, *Delph.* 3(5).64.10 (sic ed., but perh. rest. ἀλιφῆ[ς] gen., v. °ἀλιφή.

**ἀλκαία I**, for 'Call.*fr.* 317' read 'Call.*fr.* 177.23 Pf., Nic.*Th.* 123, 225'

**ἄλκαρ**, line 4, after '*h.Ap.* 193' insert 'ἀναιδέος ὄθματος ἄ. Call.*fr.* 186.29 Pf.'; for 'Call.*fr.* 124' read 'id.*fr.* 304.2 P.'; after 'Aret.*CA* 1.1' insert 'Hp.ap.Gal. 19.75'

**ἀλκή I 1**, add '**b** περὶ ἀλκῆς, athletic contest at Athens, *IG* 2².2113.57, 2130.90 (both ii AD).' add '**2** fig., *strong point*, ἔν τινι τὴν ἀ. ἔχειν, of an author, D.H.*Th.* 23.'

**ἀλκήεις**, delete 'of patients' and for 'al.' read '(Aret.) *SD* 4.5 (p. 71.29 H.)'

**ἀλκηστής**, add '*Trag.adesp.* 585a K.-S.'

***ἀλκήτωρ**, ορος, ὁ, *protector*, Ramsay *Studies in Eastern Rom. Prov.* p. 128.

**ἄλκῐμος**, line 4, after '(Hdt. 1.)103' insert 'X.*Oec.* 4.15, 6.10, *HG* 7.3.1'

**ἀλκτήριον**, after '*against* a thing' insert 'Call.*fr.* 346 Pf. (pl.)'

**ἀλκυόνειον**, after 'Dsc. 5.118' insert '*PColl.Youtie* 87.10 (vi AD), ἀλκυόνυον *PTeb.* 273.34 (ii/iii AD)'

***ἀλκυονῖτις**, ιδος, fem. adj., *halcyon*, αἱ. ἁ (sc. ἡμέραι) *halcyon days*, Sch.Ar.*Ra.* 1309.

***ἀλκυονύτης**, unexpld. wd. in Theognost.*Can.* 44.

**ἀλλά**, before '**I**' insert 'usu. in first position, but occasionally post-poned, e.g. Call.*Jov.* 18, *AP* 5.9 (Rufin.), 5.17 (Gaet.), etc.' **I 2 a**, line 8, after 'Pl.*Phdr.* 262a)' insert 'ἀλλ' οὖν (without γε) E.*Ph.* 498, *Dig.* 50.6.6.2' **b**, line 4, after 'id.*Med.* 912' insert 'And. 2.26' **II 1**, line 11, after 'Od. 4.472' insert 'Hyp.*Dem.* 1, *Eux.* 1' **5**, after '*it is not* [*so*], *but* ..' insert 'D. 2.22, Pl.*Grg.* 453b, Arist.*Pol.* 1262ᵃ14'; after '(Pl.)*Smp.* 173b' insert '*Cra.* 436d'; after '(Ar.)*Ra.* 58, 498' insert 'E.*Ba.* 785, Pl.*Euthd.* 286b, Call.*fr.* 191.1 Pf.' **III 3**, ἀλλὰ γάρ, add 'after οὐ μόνον, *Cod.Just.* 1.40.13'

***ἄλλα**, v. °ἄλλη.

**ἄλλαγμα 3**, delete the section transferring example to section 2.

**ἀλλαγμός**, for '= foreg.' read '*change*, *transition*' and add '*Astrol.adesp.* in *PMich.*III 149 v 33'

***ἀλλάζω**, = ἀλλάσσω, ἀλαζέσθō δὲ ἀντὶ τō ἀρχō *IG* 9²(1).609.21 (Naupactus, vi/v BC).

**ἀλλακτικός**, line 2, for 'ἡ -κή .. *exchange*' read 'τὸ .. ἀλλακτικὸν (μέρος τῆς κτητικῆς τέχνης)' and after 'Pl.*Sph.* 223c' insert 'τῆς .. ἀλλακτικῆς (τέχνης) ib.'

***ἀλλαλο-**, v. ‡ἀλληλο-.

**ἀλλαμπᾶν**, add 'ἀλλάμπαν Musurus' and for '-χωρ' read '-χωριον'

**ἀλλάντιον**, add '*POsl.* 152.9 (i/ii AD), *PMich.*inv. 3731 ii 30 (*Tyche* 1.185, ii/iii AD)'

***ἀλλαξιμάριον**, τό, *change of clothes*, *Stud.Pal.* 20.245.25 (vi AD, written ἀλαξ-); sp. ἀλλαξαμάρνιον in *PMasp.* 6ᵛ.66 (vi AD); cf. ἀλλάξιμα.

**ἀλλάσσω III 1**, line 9, after 'Pl.*R.* 371c' insert 'w. dat. pers.'; line 10, for '*Lg.* 915d, e' read '*Lg.* 915d; abs., ib. 915 d,e' and before 'τοῦ παντὸς ἀ.' insert 'fig.' **2**, add 'med., *change residence*, *move*, εἰς .. *PMich.*III 203.9 (ii AD)' add '**VI** w. gen., *differ* from, ἀλλήλων D.H. *Dem.* 53; see also °ἀλλάζω.'

**⁺ἀλλᾰχόθι**, adv., *elsewhere*, *AP* 9.378 (Pall.), Jul.*Or.* 1.5c; *in another passage*, Demetr.*Eloc.* 156, A.D.*Synt.* 333.26, Plu. 2.20d.

**ἀλλᾰχόσε**, add '*elsewhere*, Just.*Nov.* 53.6.1'

***ἄλλη**, = ἀλλῃ, *Schwyzer* 148 (Megara, v BC), ἄλλη πη *SEG* 9.72.114 (Cyrene, iv BC); also Lesb. ἄλλα *IG* 12(2).645.49 (Nesos, iv BC).

***ἀλληλαναδοχή**, ἡ, *giving of mutual security*, *PMasp.* 170.15 (vi AD); dub. in *PLond.* 1661.19 (vi AD).

**ἀλληλεγγύη**, after '*security*' insert 'by which each debtor guarantees repayment of the whole debt, *PMasp.* 170.15'

***ἀλληλίσματα**, τά, *migration*, Favorin.*Exil.* 10.15 B.

***ἀλληλοκᾰκος**, ον, Aeol. **ἀλλᾱλο-**, *wronging each other*, τὼν ἀ. πολίταν Alc. 130.22 L.-P.

**ἀλληλομῑσέω**, add '*POxy.* 2343.21 (iii AD)'

***ἀλληλομολογία**, ἡ, *mutual agreement*, *PLond.* 1727.49 (vii AD).

***ἀλληλοφῐλία**, ἡ, Boeot. **ἀλλᾱλο-**, *mutual love*, *SEG* 37.389 (tab.defix., Hellen.).

**ἀλληλοφόνοι**, add 'adv. -ως Sch.A.*Th.* 734e S.'

**ἄλλιστος**, after '*inexorable*' insert 'Ἀϊδωνεύς Euph. 98 vGr.'

***ἀλλόγρᾰφον**, τὸ, perh. *copy of a document*, *SEG* 24.530 (Maced.).

**ἀλλοδᾰπός**, line 4, ἐν ἀλλοδᾰπῇ, add '*SEG* 30.1486 (Phrygia)'

**ἄλλοθι II**, add 'so perh. Od. 4.684' (ἄλλοθ' usu. referred to ἄλλοτε)

***ἄλλοι**, *to another place*, οὐδέ τι μυνάμενος ἄλλοι τὸ νόημμα Alc. 392 L.-P.

**ἀλλοῖος**, after 'ἄλλοτε ἀλλοῖος' insert 'Hes.*Op.* 483, Semon. 7.11 W.'; line 4, for 'every .. billet' read 'i.e. if you throw often, the throw will sometimes be good' and after '*Com.adesp.* 448' insert 'cf. Arist.*Div.Somn.* 463ᵇ21'

**ἀλλοιόω I 1**, after 'Pl.*R.* 381a, etc.' insert 'Mosch.Trag. 6.19 S.'

*__ἀλλοιωτέον__, *a change must be made*, Gal. 6.242.6.

*__ἀλλόκοιτος__, ον, *sleeping elsewhere*, Theognost.*Can.* 95.

**ἄλλομαι**, line 7, after 'ἁλέσθαι' insert 'Call.*fr.* 177.33 Pf.'

**ἀλλόμορφος**, for 'Hp.*Morb.* 4.93' read 'Hp.*Vict.* 4.93'

*__ἀλλοπάτριος__, ὁ, prob. *member of an alien community*, in context, non-Christian, Ramsay *Studies in Eastern Rom.Prov.* p. 224 (written ἀλλω-, Philadelphia, iii/iv AD).

**ἀλλοπίας**, add '*IGC* p. 98 A12 (Acraephia, iii BC)'

**ἀλλοπολία**, for '= ἀλλοδημία' read '*residence in a foreign city*'

**ἀλλοπολιᾶται**, add '*SEG* 37.752, (Lyttos, v BC)'

**ἄλλος** line 1, for 'Cypr. .. (Idalion)' read 'Cypr. αἶλος, ἄϝιλος (*a-i-la*, *Kafizin* 114a, *a-i-lo-ne ICS* 217.14, *a-wi-la Kafizin* 148, al.)' **II 3**, after '(X.)*Cyr.* 4.1.15' insert 'μὴ ἄλλα καὶ ἄλλα θορυβείτω Pl.*Ap.* 27b' **6**, line 2, after '*besides*' insert '*the rest of*, ἡ ἄλλη Ἑλλάς Th. 1.77.6, ἡ ἄλλη ψυχή Pl.*Men.* 88d, Procl. ad Hes.*Op.* 494' **III 2**, after 'c. gen.' insert 'ἄλλο τôν γεγραμένōν *IG* 9²(1).609 B 23 (Naupactus, vi/v BC)' **4**, after '*bad*' insert 'Hes.*Op.* 344'

**ἀλλος**, delete the entry.

*__ἄλλος__ (B), v. °ἠλέος.

**ἄλλοσε**, at end for '- by .. ἀλλαχοῦ' read 'for locative, by attraction to following relative' and add '*for another purpose*, Arist.*Ath.* 29.5'

**ἀλλοτριάζω**, add '**2** w. acc., app. *alienate*, *POxy.* 2267.8 (iv AD).'

**ἀλλοτριοπραγέω**, add 'Phlp. *in de An.* p. 528.23'

**ἀλλότριος**, after lemma insert 'αἰλότριος *Schwyzer* 411 (Elis); Cret. ἀλλόττριος, *Inscr.Cret.* 4.72 iii 12 (Gortyn, v BC)' **II 1 a**, add 'w. gen., φθόνου ἀ. *removed from it*, i.e. not the object of it, Luc.*Somn.* 7'

**ἀλλοτρίωσις**, add '**II** *alienation* of property, *BGU* 464.1 (ii AD).'

**ἀλλοφανής**, for 'Nonn.*D.* 14.156' read 'Nonn.*D.* 14.157'

+__ἀλλοφυής__, ές, *of a different kind* or *nature*, Nonn.*D.* 2.148, 4.419, *PMasp.* 19.7 (vi AD).

**ἀλλόχρως**, for '*looking strange* or *foreign*' read '*of a different colour* or *complexion*'; add 'in refs. to a theory (of Democritus and Anaxagoras) of perception by contrasts, Thphr.*Sens.* 27, 50, 54'

*__ἀλλύταρχος__, = ἀλυτάρχης, *SEG* 17.199.3 (Olympia, i AD).

*__ἀλλύτης__, v. ‡ἀλύτης.

*__ἀλλύω__, v. ‡ἀναλύω (B).

**ἄλλως II 1**, after 'E.*Hec.* 302' insert '*Or.* 709' **II 3**, line 8, after 'Philem. 51, etc.' insert 'ὡς ἄλλως, D. 6.32, Is. 7.27'

**ἅλμα**, for 'Epic. .. 32' read 'Euph. in *Suppl.Hell.* 453'

*__ἀλμενιχιακά__, τά, *almanac*, *astronomical list*, v.l. at Porph.*Ep.Aneb.* 2.12b (36), Eus.*PE* 3.4.1.

*__ἁλμυροδινής__, ές, *salt-eddying*, πόντος hymn in *Suppl.Hell.* 990.5 (iii BC).

**ἁλμυρός 3 a**, for 'Cerc. 19.37' read 'Cerc. 17.37'

*__ἁλμύρραξ__, ᾶγος, ὁ, prob., *efflorescence of potassium nitrate*, Plin.*HN* 31.106.

+__ἁλμυρώδης__, ες, *salty*, ῥεῦμα Hp.*Epid.* 1.26 ϵ'; χωρία Thphr.*CP* 3.17.2, J.*BJ* 4.8.2.

*__ἁλμώδης__, ες, *salty*, δάκρυον Hp.*Epid.* 4.35; πτύαλον id.*Coac.* 238; ἁλμωδεστέρα (οὖσα ἡ γῆ) πρὸς φυτείαν X.*Oec.* 20.12, Thphr.*HP* 8.7.6; of the bloom (χνοῦς) on certain fruit, id.*CP* 6.10.7.

**ἀλοάω I 3**, for '*destroy*' read '*batter down*'

*__ἀλογενέτωρ__, ορος, ὁ, = °ἁλιγενέτωρ, *Suppl.Hell.* 991.53 (poet. word-list, iii BC).

**ἀλογέω I 1**, line 4, for '*feel*' read '*be*'; add 'D.L. 1.32' **II 1**, delete '*to be .. indiscretion*' **2**, for '*out of one's senses*' read '*perplexed*'

**ἀλόγητος**, add '*UPZ* 110.205 (ii BC)'

*__ἀλογί__, adv. *irrationally*, Lib.*Decl.* 16.31 (s.v.l.).

**ἀλόγιστος I 1**, delete 'of persons, Phld.*Ir.* p.97 W.' (v. section 2) **II 2**, delete 'Men. 75'

*__ἀλογόμορφος__, ον, *having the form of an unreasoning animal* (cf. ἄλογος II), *Cat.Cod.Astr.* 8(1).173.

**ἀλογόομαι**, for '(prob. l.)' read '(dub. cj.)'

**ἄλογος I 2**, delete '*inexpressive* Pl.*Tht.* 203a' add '**3** *of which an account cannot be given*, *lacking explanation*, Pl.*Tht.* 203a.' **II**, after '*horse*' insert '*PKlein.Form.* 324.4 (vi AD)' **IV 1**, for '*incommensurable*' read '*irrational*' and for '(Euc.)*Def.* 10' read '*Def.* 3' add '**V** ἄλογος (sc. γραμμή), ἡ, critical sign marking corrupt or doubtful passage, Sch.A Il.16.613, Sch.Ar.*V.* 1282, *POxy.* 1788 p. 142, Isid.*Etym.* 1.21.27, Serv. ad Verg.*A.* 10.444.'

*__ἀλογότης__, ητος, ἡ, *lack of reason* (of animals), David *in Porph.* 209.24.

**ἀλόητρα**, after '*threshing*' insert '*SB* 7373.15 (AD 29); perh. ἀλώτρα (or ἀλώ⟨η⟩τρα) *PMich.*VIII 520.5 (iv AD)'

**ἀλοίδορος**, add '**II** = ἀλοιδόρητος I 2, *IUrb.Rom.* 836.6 (prob. i AD).'

**ἀλοιητήρ**, after '*thresher*' delete '*grinder*'; for '*grinders*' read '*threshers*'; for 'λιμός' read 'λιμὸν ἀλοιήτηρα βρότειον'

**ἀλοιμός**, add 'also **ἀλοιμμός**, *IG* 2².1663 (iv BC)'

**ἀλοιτηρός**, delete the entry.

**ἀλοίτης**, delete '= ἀλείτης' and after 'Emp. 10' insert 'Call.*fr.* 271 Pf.'

**ἀλοιφή 2**, after '(Od.) 18.179' add 'used by athletes, Hld. 10.31.5' at end add 'Myc. *a-ro-pa*'

*__ἀλοιφίς__, ἡ, *erasure*, *BGU* 2349.14 (ii AD) (α̣λυφις pap.).

**ἀλοκίζω**, after 'Ar.*V.* 850' insert 'of a wild boar attacking a hound, στήθη .. ἠλόκισ' *ploughed a furrow* in, epigr. in *Suppl.Hell.* 977.8 (iii BC)'; for '*scratched*, *torn*' read '*furrowed*'

*__ἁλοπέπερι__, ρεως, τό, mixture of *salt and pepper*, *Vit.Aesop.*(G) 52 P.

*__ἁλόποιος__, ον, *manufacturing salt*, Sch.Nic.*Al.* 519a.

*__ἁλοπόλιος__, ὁ, = ἁλοπώλης, *Stud.Pal.* 3.141 (vi/vii AD) (unless for ὁλοπόλιος *grey-headed*, cf. Achmes *Oneirocriticon* (T) p. 14.22, 16.15).

*__ἁλόπωλις__, ιδος, ἡ, *(female) salt-seller*, *IG* 2².12073 (iv BC), 2².11244 (-πōλις, i/ii AD).

*__ἄλορδος__, ον, *free from inward curvature*, v.l. in Hp.*Fract.* 8 (sup.).

*__ἅλος__, ἡ, = ἅλως, *IG* 14.352 ii 28ff. (Halaesa).

*__ἁλοτειχής__, ές, perh. *walled in by the sea*, *Suppl.Hell.* 991.52 (poet. word-list, iii BC).

**ἁλουργός**, add 'as masc. subst., *dyer* (of purple cloth), *PPrag.* I 25.9 (vi/vii AD)'

*__ἁλοφύλαξ__, ακος, ὁ, *guard* or *watchman employed in saltworks*, *PHib.* 275.14 (i/ii AD).

*__ἀλοχίς__, ίδος, = ἄλοχος, *wife*, *Cat.Cod.Astr.* 3.45.

**ἄλοχος I 1**, add 'also masc., *husband*, *Epigr.Gr.* 720.5'

*__ἀλπαιωνία__, v. °ἀλφ-.

*__ἄλπαρ__, τό, perh. *pleasing thing*, *comfort* (cf. ἄλπνιστος), *Inscr.Cret.* 1.xvi 6 ivA5 (Lato, iii/ii BC).

**ἄλπνιστος**, read **ἄλπιστος** and for 'Sup. .. Pi.*I.* 5(4).12' read '*sweetest*, *loveliest*, rest. in Pi.*I.* 5(4.12), A.*Pers.* 981 (understood as pers. n. by some edd.)'

**ἅλς** (A), line 1, delete 'dat. pl. ἅλασιν (v. infr.)'; lines 14/15, delete 'ἅλασιν .. Suid.' **IV**, delete 'possible .. certain in'; transfer 'ἅλες .. 685a' to section I 1.

**Ἄλσειος**, before 'ὁ' insert 'or **Ἀλσεῖος**'; add 'at Calymna, *Tit.Calymn.* 156, 172, al.'

**ἀλσηίς**, after 'A.R. 1.1066' add '4.1151'

**ἄλσος II**, at end, after '(A.)*Pers.* 111' insert 'δι' ἀλίρρυτον ἄλσος id.*Supp.* 868'

**ἀλτρός**, add '(ἀλτρόν La.)'

**ἀλύζω**, delete the entry (ghost-word).

*__ἁλυκή__, ἡ, kind of salted food, *BGU* 1069.2.9 (iii AD).

**ἁλυκός**, after 'Ar.*Lys.* 403' insert 'Pl.*Ti.* 65e'

+__ἀλυκρός__, ά, όν, *luke-warm*, Call.*fr.* 270 Pf., Nic.*Al.* 386 (comp.); cf. ἀλυκτρόν.

**ἀλυκτέω**, s.v. ἀλυκτάζω, after lemma insert '(A)'; after 'Hp.*Mul.* 1.5' insert 'Gal. 19.75'

**ἀλυκτέω**, (= ὑλακτέω), after lemma insert '(B)'

**ἀλυκτοπέδαι**, line 1, for '*bonds*' read '*shackles*, *fetters*'; after 'sg., *AP*' insert '12.160'

+__ἄλυκτος__, όν, *that cannot be escaped from*, φόνον .. ἄλυκτ[ον] *MAMA* 4.140.5 (*SEG* 30.1473) (Apollonia, Phrygia, AD 162/3), Suid., Zonar.

**ἄλυπος I**, add 'voc. freq. in epitaphs, *SEG* 23.262 (Zacynthus, ii BC), 31.1559 (Egypt, Augustan)'

**ἀλυσθαίνω**, after 'Nic.*Th.* 427' insert '*Al.* 141'

*__ἀλυσθενέω__, perh. *to be prostrated*, Call.*Del.* 212 (ἀλυσθενέουσα pap., ἀλυσθμαίνουσα codd.), cf. Hsch. ἀλυσθενεῖ· ἀσθενεῖ (ἀλυσθαίνει La.), cf. ἀλυσθένεια.

*__ἀλυσθμαίνω__, v. °ἀλυσθενέω.

*__ἀλυσία__, ἡ, *indissolubility*, ἀ. τοῦ κόσμου Procl.*in Ti.* 3.50.19 D.

**ἁλυσίδιον**, add '*Inscr.Délos* 1417*B*ii46 (ii BC), *BGU* 2328 (ἁλισείδιον, v AD)'

**ἁλυσιδωτός**, for 'ἁ. θώραξ' read 'θώραξ Lxx 1*Ki.* 17.5' and delete '(pl.)' after '6.23.15'

**ἁλύσιον**, add '*IG* 2².1533.20 (iv BC), *Schwyzer* 462.B51 (Tanagra, ii BC)'

**ἅλυσις 1**, add 'fig., μιᾷ .. ἁλύσει σκότους πάντες ἐδέθησαν Lxx *Wi.* 17.16'

*__ἁλυσιωτός__, ή, όν, *chained*, Pi.*fr.* 169a.28 S.-M.

*__ἀλυσκάνω__, = ἀλύσκω, Od. 22.330.

**ἀλύσκω**, delete '– *Ep. verb* .. *Her.* 7):'; after 'Pi.*P.* 8.16' insert 'Phryn. Trag. 6 S.'; line 6, for 'etc.' read 'A.R. 4.1505'

**ἀλυταρχέω**, for '*BCH* .. (Tralles)' read '*ITrall.* 136' and add '*IEphes.* 502.6, 1114.6, al., *SEG* 31.1288.7 (Side, AD 249/52)'

**ἀλυτάρχης**, add 'written ἀλλυτάρχης, *AE* 1905.255.2 (Olympia, iii AD); cf. ἀλλύτης s.v. °ἀλύτης'

**ἀλύταται**, add '(ἀλυτάρχαι· παρὰ Ἠλείοις La.)'

**ἀλύτης**, add 'ἀλλύτης *AE* 1905.255.4 (Olympia, iii AD)'

**ἄλυτος 1**, *not to be loosed*, add 'ἀ. .. δεσμοῖς Aristid.Quint. 1.3, *Cod.Just.* 8.10.12.7'

**ἀλυχή**, for 'Gal. 19.76' read 'Gal. 19.75'

**ἀλύω I 5**, delete the section. **III**, after 'trans.' insert '*to be distraught at*, τῶν σκελῶν .. τὴν ἧτταν ἀλυόντων Hld. 10.30.4'

*ἀλυώδης, ες, *marked by anxiety*, Hp.*Praec.* 14.
**ἄλφα 1**, add '*IG* 2².1425.95, al., *Schwyzer* 253.81 (Cos, iii/ii BC)'
**ἀλφάβητος**, add '*Orac.Tiburt.* 158'
***ἀλφαιωνία**, ἡ, *peony*, Cyran. 1.21.42 K. (ed. ἀλπ-); written ἀλφαωνία *Cat.Cod.Astr.* 8(1).187.
***ἄλφημα**, ατος, τό, *produce*, *Inscr.Délos* 502A13 (iii BC).
**ἀλφηστής I**, for 'lit. .. men' read 'prob. *eaters of bread*' **II**, add '*IGC* p. 98 A 8 (gen. ἀλφειστᾶο, Acraephia, iii/ii BC)'
**ἄλφι**, for 'cf. Str. 8.5.3' read 'Antim. 109 Wy.'
**ἀλφιτισμός**, for the pres. ref. read '*Inscr.Délos* 442A220' and add 'Hsch. s.v. παλαία'
**ἄλφιτον I**, for '*barley-groats*' read '*groats*, later sts. spec. *barley-groats*'; line 5, after 'Od. 14.429' insert '*Schwyzer* 725.4 (Miletus, vi BC)' **II**, for 'generally *meal*, *groats*' read 'w. grain specified' and add 'Pl.*Lg.* 849c, Paus. 1.18.7; see also αὔφιτα'
**ἀλφιτοφάγος**, delete '*-bread*'
**ἀλωή III**, for '(Arat.) 875' read '877'
**ἀλωνία II**, add 'written ἀλωνιεία *PTeb.* 727.21, 25 (ii BC)'
***Ἀλωνίτης**, ὁ, cult-title of Zeus, *SEG* 33.1167 (Side), *TAM* 5(1).166a (Saittae, i AD).
***ἀλωνοθεσία**, ἡ, *laying of a threshing-floor*, *PKlein.Form.* 810 (vi AD).
***ἀλωνοθέσιον**, τό, *threshing-floor*, εἰς τὸ ἀλονοθέσιον *PStrassb.* 680.5 (early vii AD).
***ἀλωνοφυλακέω**, *guard a threshing-floor*, *PCair.Zen.* 745.86 (iii BC).
**ἀλωνοφύλαξ**, add '*POxy.* 2714.19, *SB* 4525 (both iii AD)'
**ἀλωόφυτος**, after 'Nonn.*D.* 13.267' insert '(dub.; v.l., edd. °ἀλώφητος)'
**ἀλωπός**, after 'Hsch.' insert 'cf. ἀλώπα[ (sic), Alc. 69.6 L.-P.'
**ἀλωρῆται**, for '*salt*' read '*threshing-floor*'
***ἀλωροί**, οἱ, *guardians of the salt-pans*, *SEG* 32.869 (Hierapytna, Crete, ii AD).
**ἄλως**, after lemma insert '(perh. Cypr. *a-la-wo* (acc. and gen.), *ICS* 217.9, 18; see also ἄλων, °ἄλος)'; line 1, after 'ἄλωος' insert 'Nic.*Th.* 546, *fr.* 70.1 G.-S.'
**ἀλώσιμος I 1**, for '*easily beguiled*' read 'εὐεργεσία .. καὶ ἡδονὴ τὸ θηρίον τοῦτο (i.e. prospective friend) ἀλώσιμον .. ἐστιν' **II**, after '*conquest*' insert 'Τροίας .. ἀλώσι[μο]ν [ἆμ]αρ Stesich. *S*89.11 (p. 186 D.), cf. Ibyc. 1(*a*).14 P.'
***ἀλωτήριον**, τό, app. some component of a θυρίς, ἄλων (i.e. ἧλων) .. καὶ ἀλωτηρίων *IG* 4²(1).110.37.
**ἀλώφητος**, after 'Plu.*Fab.* 23' insert '2.1005e'; add 'Nonn.*D.* 13.267'
***ἆμα**, v. ‡ἄμη.
**ἅμα A 2**, delete definition 'partly .. partly .. ' (the examples belong to the preceding sense) **II**, at end, for 'Arist.*Metaph.* 1028ᵇ 27' read 'Arist.*Metaph.* 1068ᵇ 27' **C**, after 'D. 46.20' insert 'ἅμαν οἱ σταλογράφοι μόλωνσι *SEG* 37.340.17-18 (Mantinea, early iv BC)' and at end for 'A α II' read 'ἀ- II'
**ἀμᾶ**, for '*IG* 5(1)' read '*IG* 5(1).213.14, 86, ib. 1120.3, 10 (both v BC)'
***Ἀμαδρύες**, αἱ, = Ἁμαδρυάδες, Nonn.*D.* 15.416, cj. in 5.440.
**Ἀμαζών**, delete '**II** epith. .. Paus. 4.31.8'; after '-όνιος' insert '-η' and for 'Nonn.*D.* 37.17' read 'Nonn.*D.* 37.117'; add 'epith. of Smyrna, *SEG* 37.712.12 (epigr., Chios, ii AD)'
**ἀμαθής**, line 1, for '*stupid*' read '*lacking* or *incapable of understanding*'; line 5, for 'of .. *unmanageable*' read 'of class of animals (typified by wild boars)'; line 9, after 'E.*Ph.* 874' insert 'iron. ἐνδέχεται .. τὰς ξυμφορὰς τῶν πραγμάτων οὐχ ἧσσον -θῶς χωρῆσαι ἢ καὶ τὰς διανοίας τοῦ ἀνθρώπου Th. 1.140.1' **1 b**, delete the section transferring quot. to section 1 a. **2**, after 'of things' insert '*ignorant*, *uninformed*' and delete subsequent explanations in this section. **II**, delete the section.
**ἄμαθος**, for '*links* .. sea' read 'stretch of *sand*, *sands*'; after '*h.Ap.* 439' insert 'Euph. 44.2 vGr.'; add '(cf. Ἡαμαθόι, name of Nereid, *Schwyzer* 122.7, Corinthian vase at Caere)'
***ἀμαθούσιος**, ὁ, kind of jasper, Epiph.Const. in *Lapid.Gr.* 195.27.
***ἀμαιωτικός**, όν, neut. pl. τὰ ἀ. *spirits that prevent successful childbirth*, *BCTH* N.S. 19B.111 (Tunisia, ii/iii AD); cf. ἀμαίευτος, μαιωτικός.
**ἀμάλακτος I 1**, add '*not softened*, Gal. 7.40.5'
**Ἀμαλθεῖον**, for 'country-house .. 18' read '*shrine of Amaltheia*, Cic.*Att.* 1.16.15, 18'
**ἄμαλλα**, after 'S.*fr.* 607' insert 'Call.*fr.* 186.27 Pf.'; add '[ἀμ- pap. in Call. l.c.; cf. °ἀμαλλεῖον]'
**ἀμαλλεῖον**, add 'written *haμ-* in *IG* 1³.425.10 (Athens, v BC)'
**ἄμαλλος** (B), add '*cucumber*, *PColl.Youtie* 87.9 (vi AD)'
**ἀμαλογεῖ**, for '(prob. for ὁμο-)' read '(perh. for *ἀμαλολογεῖ)'
**ἀμαλός**, for 'παῖς Call.*fr.* 49 P.' read 'παῖς ἀμαλή Call.*fr.* 502 Pf.' and continue 'epith. of Zeus, *Lindos* 26.2 (*c.*400 BC); cf. Ἀμάλιος'
**ἀμάμαξύς**, read '**ἀμάμαξύς**' and before 'Matro *Conv.* 114' insert 'also ἀμαμ-'
**ἀμαμιθάδες**, read '**ἀμαμιθάδες**'; for 'Phot. p. 86 R.' read 'Phot. α 1112 Th.' and add 'cf. Hsch. (ἀμμαμηθάδης cod.)'
***ἅμαν**, v. °ἅμα.

**ἀμανῖται**, add '*PVindob.* G40851 B 7 (*JÖByz.* 33.5-6); sg., *PL* I/3 in *Tyche* 1.163.22 (vi/vii AD)'
**ἅμαξα I 1**, for 'Hes.*Op.* 453' read 'Hes.*Op.* 426, 453, 456' **II**, delete the section. **III**, add 'pl., of the Great Bear and Little Bear, Arat. 27' add '**2** *wagon-load* as unit of capacity, *Suppl. epigr.Ciren.* no. 104 (iii BC), *ZPE* 25.155 (vi AD).'
***Ἁμαξᾶς**, α, ὁ, *wagoner*, as a sobriquet, *IEphes.* 20 a 63.
***ἁμαξελάτης**, v. °ἁμαξηλάτης.
**ἁμαξεύς**, add '*Salamine* 22 (i AD)'
**ἁμαξηλάτης**, after '*wagoner*' insert '*PCair.Zen.* 176.281, 352 (iii BC); sp. ἁμαξελ- Agath. 2.6.4 K.'
**ἁμαξήποδες**, add 'see also ἁμαξόπ-'
**ἁμαξιαῖος**, for '*Com.adesp.* 836' read 'Polyzel. 7 K.-A.'
**ἁμαξικός**, add 'ὑποζύγια ἁμαξικά *PTeb.* 748.6 (iii BC)'
**ἁμαξίς**, after 'Hdt. 3.133' insert '*IG* 2².1673.11, 40 (iv BC)'
**ἁμαξίτης**, add '**II** epith. of Hermes, *BCH* 85.846 (Paros, Rom.imp.).'
***ἁμαξολάτης**, v. °ἁμαξηλάτης.
***ἀμάρα** (B), v. °ἡμέρα.
**ἀμαράκινος**, for '*Edict.* .. 16' read '*Edict.Diocl.* 36.99'; add 'ἀ., τό, sc. μύρον, *PCair.Zen.* 536.18 (iii BC)'
**ἀμαράντινος I**, add 'of colour, *PMasp.* 6ᵛ.82 (vi AD)'
**ἀμάραντος I**, at end delete 'neut. pl. .. *Im.* 1.9' **II**, after 'Poll. 1.229' insert 'Philostr.*Im.* 1.9'
**ἀμαράσαι**, for 'μαράσαι' read 'μαράσσαι, μαρίν'
***ἀμαρηγός**, ὁ, *digger of trenches*, Teuc.Bab. p. 46 B.
**ἀμάρηιος**, for '*in a conduit*' read '*channelled* (for irrigation)'
**Ἀμάριος**, of Zeus, add '*SEG* 35.304.15 (Epid., i AD)'; **Ἀμάριον**, close parentheses after 'Plb. 5.93.10' and delete rest of entry.
**ἁμαρτάνω II 1**, at end for '*EN* 1126ᵇ1' read '*EN* 1126ᵃ1' **2**, line 5, after 'ἁμαρτηθέντα' insert 'τα ἁμαρτανόμενα' and after 'X.*An.* 5.8.20' insert 'Isoc. 2.23, 8.39, D. 10.54, 17.21'
**ἁμάρτημα**, add '*delict*, Just.*Const.* Δέδωκεν 8'
**ἁμαρτία**, line 2, add 'of tragic heroes, Arist.*Po.* 1453ᵃ10, 16' **2**, delete 'Arist.*EN* 1148ᵃ3, al.'
***ἁμαρτωλικός**, ά, όν, app. = ἁμαρτωλός, Epich. 85.13 A.
**ἁμαρτωλός I 2**, add 'w. dat., ἔστω ἁ. θεοῖς χθονίοις *SEG* 33.1169 (Lycia, ii AD)'
**ἀμάστικτος**, for 'Sch.Pi.*O.* 1.32' read 'Sch.Pi.*O.* 1.33'
**ἀμάτα**, after '(Aetolia, iii BC)' insert 'adj. perh. in phr. ἀμάται τέχναι *Schwyzer* 309 (Dodona), nisi leg. ἅμα τᾶι τέχναι'
**ἀματροχιά 2**, delete 'by error for ἁρματροχιά'; for 'Call.*Fr.* 135' read 'Call.*fr.* 383.10 Pf.' and add 'cf. Porph. ad Il. 23.422'
**⁺ἀμαυρός**, ά, όν, (ός, όν Pl.Com. 20 K.-A.) *hardly seen*, *faint*, *dim*, εἴδωλον ἀ. Od. 4.824, 835, Sapph. 55.4 L.-P., ὄνειρος ἀ. Plu. 2.382f; of heavenly bodies, etc., Arist.*Mete.* 343ᵇ12, 344ᵇ29, 367ᵃ21, 375ᵃ30, Theoc. 22.21, Vett.Val. 6.15, Man. 2.117; of a lamp, Luc.*Tim.* 14, φλόξ Ph. 2.143; transf., of night, Luc.*Am.* 32. **b** of sight, X.*Cyn.* 5.26, Ph. 1.33, Gal. 14.776.4, 16.609.6; -ά or -ῶς βλέπειν, *dimly*, Hp.*Acut.*(Sp.) 55, *AP* 12.254 (Strat.), *IG* 14.2111; fem. subst. = ἀμαύρωσις 3, *PMag.* 13.235. **2** *inconspicuous*, *imperceptible*, ὅπου δ' ἂν ᾖ αὐταῖς ἀμαυρὸν τὸ ἴχνος X.*Cyn.* 6.21, Arist.*HA* 608ᵃ11, ἐντομὰς -οτέρας Thphr.*HP* 6.2.5, Lxx *Le.* 13.6; comp. adv. -οτέρως Gal. 9.249.8 (s.v.l.). **3** of sound, *faint*, Arist.*Aud.* 802ᵃ19, Ph. 2.204; -ῶς Plu. 2.590c. **II** *physically weak*, *feeble*, ἀμαυρῷ κώλῳ S.*OC* 182, φωτί 1018, χερσίν 1639, E.*HF* 124, ἀ. σθένος 231, Pl.Com. 20 K.-A., Arr.*Cyn.* 26.4; transf., of disease, *AP* 7.78 (Dionys.). **b** of faculties, ἀμαυρᾶς ἐκ φρενός A.*Ag.* 546, *Ch.* 157, ἀντίληψις Ph. 2.367. **2** of wine, *weak*, Ath. 1.34c. **3** of abst. things, *insubstantial*, *faint*, *vague*, κληδών A.*Ch.* 853, δόξα Plu.*Lyc.* 4, ἡδοναί id. 2.125c. **III** *obscure*, *unknown*, -οτέρη γενεή Hes.*Op.* 284, A.*Ag.* 466, E.*Andr.* 204.
**ἀμαυρόω, II**, line 7, for '*IG* 12(9).1129.22' read '*IG* 12(9).1179.22'
**ἀμαύρωσις 1**, after 'Hp.*Coac.* 221' insert '*dulling*, of sight in old age, Arist.*de An.* 408ᵇ20, Diog.Oen.*fr.* 57 I 5-6 C.' **2**, delete the section.
***ἀμαυρωτικός**, ή, όν, *dulling*, τὰ -ὰ τῆς ὀρέξεως Philum.ap.Aët. 9.20. **II** *invisible*, *POxy.* 3931.1 (iii/iv AD).
**ἀμαχεί**, delete '*without stroke of sword*'; line 2, after 'X.*An.* 1.7.9, etc.' insert '*Delph.* 3(1).506 (see also *SEG* 23.325, iv BC)'
**ἀμαχητηρία**, place after ἀμάχετος.
**ἀμάχητος I**, after '*unconquerable*' insert 'κέρδος Simon. 36.9 P.'
**ἄμαχος I**, line 3, after '(Ar.*Lys.*) 1014 (lyr.)' insert '*unsurpassable*, ἄ. γεωργός Men.*Dysc.* 775'; line 8, after 'ἄ. κάλλος' insert 'Men.*Dysc.* 193'; line 9, after 'Ael.*NA* 16.23' insert '*intractable*, ἄ. τρόπος Men.*Dysc.* 869' **II 2**, add '*ISmyrna* 550.8, adv. τὴν γλυκυτάτην γυναῖκα συνβιώσασαν .. ἀ., ἡδέως, εὐσεβῶς ἐτίμησεν *TAM* 5(1).717.5 (ii AD)'
***ἀμβαθμός**, v. °ἀναβαθμός.
**ἄμβαρ**, add 'also **ἄμπαρ**, Aët. 1.131 (66.17 O.)'
***ἀμβάριον** , τό, = ἄμβαρ, *PVindob.* G10.734 (*Analect.Pap.* 3.121, vi AD).

**ἄμβᾱσε**, for 'ἄμβᾰτος' read 'ἀμβᾰτός'
***ἀμβασμός**, v. °ἀναβασμός.
***ἀμβῐκισμός**, ὁ, *operation of an alembic*, Anon.Alch. 273.3.
**ἄμβιξ 1**, for '*spouted cup*' read '*vessel* narrowing towards the brim, cf. Hsch.'; for 'Posidon. 25' read 'Posidon. 67.25 E.-K.'; for 'Hsch., etc.' read '*EM* 80.18'; add 'see also ἄμβυξ'
***ἀμβιτεύω**, ?fr. Lat. *ambitus*, perh. *to seek after public service*, *POxy.* 2110.15 (iv AD), *to solicit*, *intrigue for*, Pall.*V.Chrys.* 61.9.
***ἀμβλατώριον**, τό, Lat. *ambulatorium*, *place for walking*, *walk* or *passage*, *IEphes.* 437 (pl.), *BE* 1961.783 (ἀμβλατούριον, Phoenicia).
**ἀμβλίσκω**, line 5, after '*Tht.* 150e' insert 'aor. 2 inf. ἀμβλῶναι Just.*Nov.* 22.16.1 (AD 536); cf. ‡ἐξαμβλόω'
***ἀμβλύχροος**, ον, *dull-* or *faint-coloured*, Petos. p. 342.8.2.
**ἀμβλυώσσω**, after '*weak sight*' insert 'A.*fr.* 25e.6 R.'
**ἀμβόλιμος II**, add 'v. *Schwyzer* 90.3, 91.2, 92.2 (perh. neut. subst., v. *BCH* 114.406); cf. ἀναβόλιμος, βόλιμοι'
***Ἀμβρακίδια**, τά, dim. of Ἀμβρακίδες, Herod. 7.57.
***ἀμβρᾰκόομαι**, quoted in conjunction w. ἀπαμβρακόομαι (q.v. for sense) Phot. α 1168 Th.
***ἀμβρότερος**, α, ον, *immortal*, of Artemis, Orph.*H.* 36.9 (cj. ἀγροτέρα).
**ἀμβρότιγνον**, add '(ἀμβροτῖνον· ἄμοιρον La.)'
**ἀμβροτόπωλος**, add '(codd. ἀμβρότα πώλου)'
**ἄμβροτος**, line 1, after 'Tim.*fr.* 7' insert '(= 4 P.) Cret. **ἄμορτος**, *Hymn.Curet.* 17 (dub.); neut. pl. as subst., *divine* or *undying things* (?*heavenly bodies*), Emp. B 21.4 D.-K.'
**ἄμβρυττοι**, delete the entry.
***ἄμβρυττος**, **ἀμβρύττιος**, = βρύσσος, kind of sea-urchin, Hdn.ap. Phot. α 1172 Th., Hsch.
**ἄμβων**, line 2, after 'Apollon.Cit. 1.7' insert 'acc. ἄββωνα *IG* 4.784 (Troezen)' **1**, for 'Call.*Aet.* 3.1.34' read 'Call.*fr.* 75.34 Pf.' **5**, for 'cf. *JHS* .. (Aspendus)' read '*platform in a synagogue*, *CIJud.* 781.4 (Side)'
**ἀμεθίστατος**, read '**ἀμεθέστατος**' and add '*PSarap.* 22.9, 27.26, al. (ii AD)'
**ἀμεθόδευτος 2**, add '*without sound method*, ἀμεθόδευτον .. ἐκκαλέσασθαι τὸν Περικλέα it is *bad procedure* to .., Sopat.Rh. 8.361.27 W.'
***ἀμεθυστίζω**, *resemble amethyst in colour*, Plin.*HN* 37.93.
**ἀμείβω A I 3**, for 'in Att. .. hence' read '*pass over from one side to the other*, Κρισαῖον λόφον ἄμειψεν Pi.*P.* 5.38, πορθμὸν ἀμείψας A.*Pers.* 70, E.*IA* 144' **5 b**, for '*dislodge*' read '*get rid of in exchange*' and insert 'ἀμεῖψαι κερασφόρον ἄταν E.*Hyps.fr.* 1 iii 29 B.' **II**, before '*rafters*' insert '*pitched*'; for 'Nonn.*D.* 37.588' read 'Nonn.*D.*37.592' **B II 1**, after 'S.*Tr.* 737' add '*put on as a change* (of clothing), E.*Ph.* 326'; add 'w. μετά, ἡ ψηφὶς μετὰ γῆρας ἀμιψαμένη νεότητα *Salamine* 202 (iv AD)'
**ἀμειδής**, for 'Orph.*A.* 1079' read 'Orph.*A.* 1075'
**ἀμείλικτος I**, add 'λοιμὸς ἀ. *SEG* 26.405 (Corinth, Chr.)' add '**III** = ἄμικτος, Hsch. (3548 La.); combined w. ἄχραντος, ἀκήρατος, etc., Procl. in *Ti.* 3.258.22 D., al.; cf. μειλικτός.'
**ἀμείλῐχος I**, after 'Sol. 32' insert 'πόντος *h.Hom.* 33.8, Anacr. 2*fr.* 1.16 P.'
**ἀμείνασις**, for 'ἡ δύοσμον' read 'ἡδύοσμον' and for '*EM* 83.50' read '*EM* 82.50'
**ἀμείνων I**, add 'used to denote curule (opp. plebeian) aediles, D.C. 53.33.3'
***ἀμειξία**, ἡ, *absence of communications*, *PLond.* 401.20, *PTeb.* 72.45 (ii BC), *Schwyzer* 195.7 (Cret. inscr. fr. Delos, ii BC); cf. ἀμιξία.
***ἀμειπτός**, ή, όν, *(capable of being) switched about*, app. of a siege-engine, Archil. 98.18 W.
**ἄμειψις I**, add '**2** *object received in an exchange*, Just.*Nov.* 7.5.2 (AD 535).' **II**, add '**3** *commutation*, i.e. money payment instead of payment in kind or payment in a different kind, *PMich.*XII 645.23, 28 (sp. ἀμιψ- and ἀμιμψ-, AD 304), *POxy.* 3795 (iv AD).'
***ἀμελγή**, ἡ, app. *milk-pail*, πελλίσι· ἐν ταις ἀμελγαῖς Sch.Nic.*Al.* 77b Ge.
**ἀμελητής**, for 'Gal. 3.827' read 'Gal. 3.327.13'
**ἀμελητί**, add '*without delay*, Just.*Edict.* 9 pr. (for ἀμελλητί)'
***ἀμελῖτῖτις**, acc. ιν, fem. adj., *lacking honey*, ἑορτή cj. in Herod. 5.85.
***ἀμέμαρον**, gloss on βούθουτον, Hsch. (s.v.l., ἀνέκφορον La.).
**ἄμεμπτος I 2**, adv., add '*SEG* 30.272 (Athens), *TAM* 4(1).208, 263 (Bithynia), *PPetaus* 24.29'
**ἀμεμφής I**, after '(A.)*Supp.* 581' insert 'Emp. B 35.13 D.-K.'; add 'adv. -φῶς Orph.*H.* 43.11, *MAMA* 8.413*a*17 (Aphrodisias); Ion. -φέως, Emp. B 35.9 D.-K.' **II**, delete 'adv. .. 11'
**ἀμεμψιμοίρητος**, adv. -τως, add '*SEG* 39.606.13 (Maced., ii BC)'
***ἀμέν**, v. °ἐγώ.
**ἀμενηνός**, line 1, after 'ή, όν' insert 'Luc.*Gall.* 5'
***ἀμένης**, -ητος, ὁ, *one lacking bodily strength*, *child*, Hdn.Gr. 2.684.
**ἀμένητος**, delete the entry (v. °ἀμενής).
***ἀμέρα**, v. ἡμέρα.
**ἀμέργω**, for '*Com.adesp.* 437' read 'Ar.*fr.* 406 K.-A.'

**ἀμέρδω II**, for this section read 'perh. = ἀμέργω, *pluck*, λειμώνιον ἄνθος ἀμέρσας (-ξας cj.) *AP* 7.657 (Leon.Tarent.), ἄμερσεν (-ξεν cj.) Nic.*Th.* 686' at end for 'cf. μέρδει' read 'cf. ‡μέρδει'
***ἀμεριμναῖος**, ον, = ἀμέριμνος, dub. in Ibyc.ap.Hdn.*fr.* 6 H.
**ἀμεριμνέω**, add '*Bithynische St.* III 2.10'
**ἀμέριμνος I**, line 2, after '*Eranos* 13.87' insert 'εἰς Ἀΐδαν ἀ. *SEG* 26.1808 (Egypt, Hellen.)' **III**, line 2, for 'either .. *celebrated*' read '*bringing more freedom from care*'
**ἀμέριστος I**, add '**2** rhet. ἀμέριστον (sc. σχῆμα), τό, repeated use of μέν without following δέ, Olymp. *in Grg.* 14.16 W. (p. 77 N.).'
***ἀμές**, v. ἐγώ (IV, line 3).
***ἄμεστος**, perh. *not occupied*, *PRyl.* 99.4 (iii AD).
**ἀμετάβᾰτος II**, for '*unextended*' read '*having no extent*'; at end for 'Epicur.*Ep.* .. U.' read 'τὰ ἀ. Epicur.*Ep.* [2].8 A. (cj., codd. -βολα)'
**ἀμετάβλητος**, after 'Ti.Locr. 98c' insert 'Sallust. I. 2, XVII.10'
**ἀμετάβολος**, for '= foreg.' read '*unchangeable*' **2**, add 'of pure vowels, *unchanging*, opp. diphthongs, S.E.*M.* 1.117, 118' add '**3** -βολον, τό, gramm., *liquid* (λ μ ν ρ), D.T. 632.7, Hdn.Gr. 2.393, Choerob.*in Theod.* 1.298.35 H.'
**ἀμετάκλητος**, delete 'ὀργή Hld. 2.10 (v.l. -βλητος)'
**ἀμετάληπτος**, add 'of words, *having no equivalent*, Eust. 490.38, al.'
**ἀμεταμίσθωτος**, add '*PSoterichos* 3.38, 42 (AD 89/90), *PTeb.* 378.29 (iii AD)'
***ἀμετανάτρεπτος**, ον, *unalterable*, *PLond.* 1660.37 (vi AD).
***ἀμετάπρᾱτος**, ον, *not to be sold again*, ἄσυλα καὶ ἀ. *IGBulg.* 995.3 (Philippopolis, iii AD).
***ἀμετάσχετον**, gloss on ἀσχαδές, Hsch. (dub., ἀκατά- cj.).
**ἀμετάτροπος**, add '*IG* 12(5).302.7 (Paros, i/ii AD)'
***ἀμετεπίγρᾰφος**, ον, *without change in its inscription*, *IG* 9(2).32.6 (Aenis).
**ἀμέτοχος**, add 'adv. -χως *without sharing* (in an action), Eust. 1946.32'
***ἀμετρησίη**, ἡ, = ἀμετρία, *excessiveness*, κερδέων ἀ., Philipp.Perg. 1 J.
**ἀμετρία**, add '**3** *absence of measure* or *rhythm*, διὰ τὴν ἐν τῷ ποδὶ πρὸς τὴν λύραν ἀμετρίαν Pl.*Clit.* 407c.'
**ἀμετροπαθής**, add '(codd. ἀμετριο-)'
**ἀμεύομαι II**, for this section read '*acquire by exchange*, aor. inf. ἀμεϝύσασθαι *Inscr.Cret.* 4.4.1 (Gortyn, vi BC), aor. subj. ἀμεύσονται *Inscr.Cret.* 1.xviii 1.3 (Lyttos, vi BC)'
**ἄμη**, after 'ἡ' insert 'also ἅμη Phryn.*PS* p. 107.10 (s.v. σκαφεῖον), ḥαμα *SEG* 24.361.15 (Thespiae, iv BC)' **1**, *shovel*, add '*PFreib.* 53.31 (i BC)' **2**, after '*pail*' insert 'or *scoop*, *SEG* l.c.'
**ἀμήνῑτος**, after '(A.)*Ag.* 649' insert 'Plu. 2.90d, 413d, 464c'; after '-τως' read 'A.*Ag.* 1036, Achae. 15 S.'; add 'also -τεί Archil. 89.10 W.'
***ἀμητορίδαι**, οἱ, = ἀμήτορες, (v. °ἀμήτωρ), Hsch. (cod.).
**ἄμητος II**, at end after 'Ammon.' insert '*Diff.* 38 N.'
**ἀμήτωρ I**, add '**2** ἀμήτορες, οἱ, designation of wandering minstrels in Crete, *EM* 83.15 (cf. Ath. 14.638b and °ἀμητορίδαι).'
**ἀμηχᾰνέω**, line 5, delete 'relative'; line 7, after 'Epicur.*fr.* 203' insert 'χῶτι τὸ φάρμακόν ἐστιν ἀμηχανέοντος ἔρωτος Theoc. 14.52'
**ἀμηχᾰνία II**, delete 'of things'; add 'Pi.*N.* 7.97'
**ἀμία** (A), add '*IGC* p. 98 A9 (Acraephia, iii/ii BC)'
**ἀμῐγής I**, after 'adv. -γῶς' insert 'Alcin.*Intr.* 10 (p. 164 H.)' **III**, for '*Proll.Ar.*' read 'in Anon.Cram.*Proll.Com.* XI c. II 9 K.'
**ἄμιθα**, for 'kind of *cake*, perh. = ἄμης' read 'perh. *provisions*' and add '*PHaun.* 22.11 (ii/iii AD)'
**ἄμικτος, III 1 a**, line 3, for 'Anaxil. 223' read 'Anaxil. 22.3 K.-A.'
***ἀμικτώριον**, τό, Lat. *amictorium*, *wrap*, *shawl*, *PFouad Inv.* 45.17 (*CE* 27.196, ii/iii AD); perh. *shroud*, *POxy.* 1535ᵛ.8 (iii AD).
**ἅμιλλα 2**, line 5, for 'Isoc. 10.15' read 'Isoc. 10.35'
**ἁμιλλάομαι I 1**, line 4, after '*contend*' insert '*Schwyzer* 726.15 (Miletus, v BC)'
**ἁμιλλητήρ**, add 'w. gen., *competitor in*, ἁμιλλητῆρας ἐρώτων Nonn.*D.* 6.12, 80'
**ἁμιλλητήριος**, add '*contest*, *Schwyzer* 726.14 (Miletus, neut. pl., v BC)'
**ἅμιλλος**, for the pres. ref. read 'Doroth.ap.Phot. α 1203 Th.' and add '*SEG* 21.527.61 (Athens, iv BC)'
**ἀμῑμητος**, after '*inimitable*' insert 'τὸν Ἀννίβαν ἀμίμητον παρεισάγοντες στρατηγόν Plb. 3.47.7; of Antony as a god, *OGI* 195.2 (i BC)'
**ἀμιναῖος**, add 'also Ἀμιννέος, Ἀμίννιος, *Edict.Diocl.* 2.4, 4A., Ἀμινναῖος, Dsc. 5.19'
***ἄμιον**, τό, perh. dim. of ἄμη, *small shovel*, περὶ τοῦ ἀμίου *Aegyptus* 15.273 (?iii AD).
**ἄμιππος**, after 'Xen.*HG* 7.5.23 (cj.)' insert '*Eq.Mag.* 5.13'
**ἀμίς**, for 'be .. (in contempt)' read 'put something (vile or common) to its intended purpose'
**ἀμίσαλλος**, after 'ap.*Et.Gen.*' insert 'v. Call.*fr.* 738 Pf.'
***ἀμίσαντος**, ον, unexpld. wd. in magical formula in *Inscr.Cret.* 2.xix 7.18 (iv BC).

**ἀμιχθᾰλόεις**, for '= ἄμικτος III, *inhospitable*' read 'obscure wd. expl. by ancient commentators as *"inhospitable"*, *"misty"*, etc.' and after '*h.Ap.* 36' insert 'ἀμιχθαλόεσσαν .. ἠέρα Call.*fr.* 18.8 Pf., Colluth. 208'

**ἀμμά**, add 'also perh. ἀμμή *IGLS* 99 (v. *SEG* 7.50)'

**ἅμμα I 5**, add 'Opp.*H.* 3.317' **6**, read 'as measure of length *POxy.* 669 (iii AD); = 40 πήχεις, Hero *Geom.* 23.14; = one-eighth of a σχοινίον, *VBP* IV 92 (*ZPE* 42.95), also as square measure, *SB* 6951; 11, al. (ii AD)' add '**7** *junction* of blood vessels, Pl.*Ti.* 70b.'

**ἀμμαμηθάδης**, for '= ἀμαμινθάδες (q.v.)' read 'corrupted fr. °ἀμαμιθάδες'

**ἀμμάς**, after 'ἡ' insert '*ISmyrna* 553.7 (i/ii AD), *PMich.*III 208.9 (ii AD)'; add 'cj. in Simm. 11'

**ἀμματίζω**, after '*bind*' insert 'Poet.*de herb.* 63, Hsch.'

**ἀμμεδαπάν**, add '(Aeol. for ἡμεδαπήν)'

**°ἀμμή**, v. °ἀμμά.

**°ἀμμηγία**, ἡ, *conveyance of sebakh*, i.e. powdery earth used as manure, *PSoterichos* 1.24 (AD 69), κοπρηγία καὶ ἀ. *PFlor.* 143.6 (iii AD), *PBerl.Leihg.* 23.10 (-εία; iii AD).

**ἀμμία**, add 'cf. fem. pers. n. Ἀμμία'

**°ἄμμῐγα**, v. ‡ἀνάμιγα.

**ἄμμινος**, add '*SB* 7644.10 (iii BC). **2** app. *sandy-coloured*, κύτη (= κοίτη) ἀ. *POxy.* 3201.6 (iii AD); ἐρίων ἀ. *SB* 12314.16.'

**°ἀμμίτης**, ου, ὁ, name of precious stone, Isid.*Etym.* 16.4.29 ([*h*]*ammites*).

**°ἀμμῖτις**, ιδος, ἡ, name of precious stone, prob. = °ἀμμίτης, Plin.*HN* 37.167 (*hammitis*).

**ἀμμόγειος**, add 'as part of a village name, ἀ. Σέντρυφις *PVindob.Bosw.* 3.8 (iii AD)'

**ἀμμοδύτης**, delete 'διψάς'

**°ἀμμόνιον**, τό, (ἀναμένω), perh. *fine levied on defaulters*, *CID* I 9.A48 (Delphi, iv BC); for formation cf. καμμονίη.

**ἀμμορία** (A), lines 1/2, for 'Ζεὺς .. ἀνθρώπων' read 'εὖ οἶδεν (Ζεύς) .. μοῖράν τ' ἀμμορίην τε καταθνητῶν ἀνθρώπων'; add 'perh. *what is not the portion* (of any party), epigr.ap.D. 7.40'

**ἀμμορία** (B), delete the entry.

**°ἀμμοσκᾰφεῖον**, τό, (ἄμμος, σκαφεῖον) prob. kind of scoop used by sand-diggers, *BGU* 1521 (iii BC).

**°ἀμμόχρωμος**, ον, *sand-coloured*, of a donkey, *CPR* 7.36.6 (iv AD).

**ἀμμόχωστος**, add 'Wilcken *Chr.* 1.227.1 (-χοστος; Fayûm, iii AD), *PCol.* 172.17 (iv AD)'

**Ἀμμωνιακή**, add '*PTeb.* 273.35 (iii AD)'

**°Ἀμμωνῖται**, οἱ, *association of worshippers of Ammon*, *SEG* 33.1056 (Ἀμμωνειτ-, Cyzicus, ii AD).

**ἀμνᾱμος**, after 'etc.' insert 'Hsch., also **ἄμναμμος**, *grandson*, *SEG* 18.744.9 (Cyrene, ii AD), cf. Κυρηναῖοι τὰ ἔκγονα τῶν ἐκγόνων ἀμνάμους καλοῦσι Ar.Byz.*fr.* 235 S.; αμ *CPap.Jud.* 428.4 (Egypt, ii AD) may be abbrev. for this wd.; also ἡ ἄμναμμος *granddaughter*, *Inscr.Cret.* 1.98 (p. 212).B 1-2 (Lyttos, Rom.imp.)'

**ἀμνᾱ́μων** (A), after 'ὁ' insert '*grandson*, Call.*fr.* 338, rest. in 110.44 Pf.'

**ἀμνάς**, after '*lamb*' insert '*PCair.Zen.* 576.3, al. (iii BC), Theoc. 8.35 (pl.)'

**ἀμνή**, after '*ewe-lamb*' insert '*IG* 1³.250.A16 (Attica, v BC)'

**ἀμνημοσύνη**, add '*loss of memory*, *Cat.Cod.Astr.* 8(1).189.24, 192.23'

**ἀμνήμων I 1**, add '**b** *suffering from loss of memory*, *Cat.Cod.Astr.* 8(1).192.23.'

**ἀμνησικάκέω**, for '*bestow* .. τινός' read 'w. gen. of offence, *overlook* an offence, ἀμνησικακεῖν ὧν εἴργασται Ἀντώνιος'

**ἀμνήστευτος**, for 'E.*fr.* 815' read 'E.*fr.* 818'

**ἄμνηστος**, after lemma insert 'dial. ἄμνᾱστος'

**ἀμνίς**, after 'Theoc. 5.3' insert '5.139'

**ἀμνοκόπος**, add '(ἀμνοκόμος cj. La.)'

**°ἀμνός**, ὁ, (or ἡ, Theoc. 5.144, 149, *AP* 5.205), *lamb*, esp. *sacrificial lamb*, an older animal than ἀρήν; ἐτῆρας ἀμνοὺς θεοῖς ἔρεξ' ἐπακτίοις S.*fr.* 551, Ar.*Av.* 1559, ἀμνὸν κριτόν *SEG* 26.136.19-20 (sacrificial calendar, Attica, iv BC), Arat. 1106, ἰσομάτορα ἀμνόν Theoc. 8.14, *AP* 6.282 (Theod.); ἐσόμεθ' ἀλλήλοισιν ἀμνοὶ τοὺς τρόπους, i.e. *meek*, Ar.*Pax* 935; metaph., ὁ ἀ. τοῦ Θεοῦ *Ev.Jo.* 1.36; fem. also ἀμνή (-ά), ἀμνίς, ἀμνάς qqv.

**°ἀμόγως**, adv. *without tiring*, *POxy.* 2331 iii 20 (pap. ἀλόγ-; verse, iii AD).

**°ἄμοθος**, *lacking a battle*, cj. in Nonn.*D.* 25.308; cf. μόθος.

**°ἀμοιβᾰδίζω**, gloss on Lat. *alternor*, w. ἀμφιβάλλω, Dosith. p. 430 K.

**ἀμοιβάζω**, add '**II** *reward*, ἀμοιβάσασθαι αὐτὸ ταῖς πρεπούσαις τειμαῖς *IEphes.* 4337.12-13 (i AD).'

**ἀμοιβή**, after lemma insert 'dial. ἀμοιβά (Pi., ἀμοίβᾱ Sapph. 133.1 L.-P.); also ἀμοιϝά (v. infra)'; line 5, for 'χαρίεσσα .. (Corinth)' read 'χαρίϝετταν ἀμοιβ[άν] (or ἀμοιϝ-) *CEG* 326 (Thebes, viii/vii BC), [χα]ρίεσ(σ)αν ἀμοιϝάν *CEG* 360 (Corinth, vi BC)' add '**IV** ἐπ' ἀμοιβῆς *on the other hand*, κείνων δ' οὔτε τι θῆλυ πέλει γένος, οὔτ' ἐπ' ἀ. ἄρσενες Opp.*H.* 1.765 (v.l. ἀπ' ἀ., ὑπ' ἀ.).'

**ἀμοιβός I**, add '*successor in office*, Just.*Nov.* 58'

**°ἀμοίρᾰτος**, ον, *exempt from fate*, ἀμοίρατον ἐς χρόνον ἔλθοις Dioscorus 4.10 H.

**°ἀμοιρόγᾰμος**, ον, *excluded from* or *having no part in marriage*, κοῦρος *IG* 12(5).1104 (Syros, ii AD).

**ἀμόλγιον**, after 'Theoc. 25.106' insert 'gloss on γαυλός, Sch.Od. 9.223'

**ἀμολγός**, add '**II** *milking-pail* (cf. mod. Gk.), also wooden *container* for wine, *EM* 86.11-12. **III** *milker, exploiter*, Paus.Gr. α 90, *EM* 86.13.'

**°ἀμολυβδοχόητος**, ον, *not fixed with lead*, λίθοι *IG* 7.3074.4 (Lebadea, ii BC).

**ἀμόλυντος II**, for '*not* .. *stain*' read '*solid enough not to make a mess*'; delete 'cf.' and insert 'Heras ap.Gal. 13.432.18'

**ἀμόρα**, add 'cf. Hsch.'

**ἀμορβεύω**, after '*attend*' insert 'ἀμορβεύεσκεν Call.*fr.* 271 Pf. (ἀμορμ- codd.)'; for '*let follow, make follow*' read '*give as burden, load on to*'

**ἀμορβός I**, for 'Call.*Hec.* 6' read 'Call.*fr.* 301 Pf.'

**ἀμόργης**, add 'acc. -ητα *PCair.Zen.* 839.3 (iii BC)'

**ἀμορτης**, add 'see also ἀμορβίτης, ἀμοργίτας, °ἀμυρίτης'

**°ἀμορφέω**, *to be shapeless*, Plot. 6.7.32.

**ἀμορφία II**, add 'of literary style, *inelegance*, D.H.*Comp.* 18, 19'

**ἁμός** (B), delete 'ἀμόθι'

**°ἀμούμαντις**, εως, ὁ, dub. sens. in Ps.-Callisth. 1.4.3 (cod. A; perh. ἀμμόμαντις, *diviner by sand*).

**ἀμουσία I**, for 'E.*fr.* 1020' read 'E.*fr.* 1033'

**ἀμόχθητος**, after '= sq.' insert 'ἀμόχθητον .. δίαιταν Alc. 61.12 L.-P.'

**°ἄμπαιδες**· οἱ τῶν παίδων ἐπιμελούμενοι παρὰ Λάκωσιν, Hsch. (perh. fr. °ἀμφίπαιδες or cf. ἀναπαιδεύω).

**ἀμπαίνεθαι**, add '(s.v. ‡ἀναφαίνω I 3)'

**ἀμπαιστήρ**, for '*IG* 4.1484' read '*IG* 4²(1).102' and add '(lapis ἀνπ-)'

**ἀμπαλίνορρος**, delete the entry.

**°ἀμπᾰλίνωρος**, ον, *returning*, Cratin. 78 K.-A., Philetaer. 11 K.-A.

**ἄμπᾰλος**, for '*auction*, *SIG* .. (Aetol., iii BC)' read '*contract*, *IG* 9²(1).188.15 (Melitea, iii BC)'

**°ἄμπανσις**, ἁ, acc. ἄνπανσιν, *act of adoption*, *Leg.Gort.* 4.10.33; cf. ‡ἀναφαίνω I 3.

**°ἀμπαντός**, ὁ, *adopted one*, *Leg.Gort.* 4.10.7 (ἀνπ-).

**°ἀμπαντύς**, ἁ, dat. -υῖ (or ύι), *state of adoption*, *Leg.Gort.* 4.10.48-9.

**°ἄμπαρ**, v. ‡ἄμβαρ.

**°ἀμπείθω**, v. ‡ἀναπείθω.

**ἀμπελεών**, for 'poet.' read 'non-Att.'; add '*AP* 6.226 (Leon.Tarent.)'

**ἀμπελικός**, line 2, add 'καρποί *PLond.* 163.16 (i AD), κτῆμα *BGU* 2127 (ii AD); also -κόν, τό, *OAbu Mena* 11'

**ἀμπέλινος I**, after 'Id. 2.37, 60' insert 'Antim. 85 Wy.'; add 'of colour, *PHamb.* 10.27 (ii AD)'

**ἀμπέλιον**, add '**2** *vineyard*, *PStrassb.* 29.39 (iii AD).'

**°Ἀμπελίτης**, ὁ. cult-title of Zeus in Phrygia, *SEG* 33.1144, etc.

**ἀμπελίων**, after '*bird*' insert '*Edict.Diocl.* 4.34'

**ἀμπελόεις**, after 'Il. 2.561' insert 'and acc. fem. pl. ἀμπελόεις Nic.*Al.* 266'

**°ἀμπελοῖνος**, ὁ, app. *grape-wine*, *SB* 4486.6 (vi/vii AD, pl.).

**ἄμπελος II**, before '*vineyard*' insert '*land planted with vines*' and after it 'Hatzopoulos *Donation du roi* 17, line 19 (Cassandreia, iii BC), *PRev.Laws* 36.5 (iii BC), *PAvrom.* 1A10, al., *Apoc.* 14.18, 19, *POxy.* 1631.21, 29 (iii AD)'

**°ἀμπελοσκάφος**, ὁ, *vine-digger*, A.*fr.* 46a.18 R.

**°ἀμπελοτόμος**, ον, *for pruning vines*, δρέπανον *TAM* 5(1).318.19-20 (ii AD), Hsch. s.v. βίσβης.

**ἀμπελουργός**, add 'ἀ. οἱ, association of worshippers of Dionysus, *SEG* 32.488 (Tanagra, *c.*100 BC). **2** ἀμπελουργός, όν, adj., δρέπανον ἀμπελοργόν *IG* 1³.422.143 (Athens, v BC), cf. *IG* 2².1526.8.'

**°ἀμπελοφόριμος**, ον, *vine-bearing*, γῆ *PMasp.* 151.105 (AD 570).

**ἀμπελόφυτος**, add '*PMasp.* 151.125 (vi AD)'

**°ἀμπελοχελώνη**, ἡ, *pent-house* or *mantlet*, Poliorc. 214.5.

**ἀμπελωνίδιον**, add '*PCair.Zen.* 309.6 (iii BC)'

**ἀμπεχόνη I**, for '*fine shawl* .. men' read '*covering for the body, wrap*' and for 'Pherecr. 108.28' read 'Pherecr. 113.28 K.-A., Theoc. 27.59, 60, *APl.* 306 (Leon.Tarent.)' **2**, for 'etc.' read 'Pl.*Chrm.* 173b, *Lg.* 679a'

**°ἀμπλᾰκιῶτις**, ιδος, fem. adj. applied to ἱερὰ νόσος, Poet.*de herb.* 175.

**ἄμπνυτο**, line 2, after 'al.' insert 'but see ἔμπνυτο'; add '[ἄμπνῦτο, Nonn.*D.*34.342]'

**°ἀμπούλλιον**, τό, *small flask*, dim. fr. Lat. *ampulla*, *PLond.* 191.16 (ii AD), *SB* 9238.19 (ii/iii AD).

**°ἄμποχος**, ὁ, (ἀμπέχομαι), *guarantor*, Sicilian wd., *SEG* 34.940.5, 39.996.6 (both Camarina, iv/iii BC and ii/i BC), ib. 4.62.4 (Morgantina, ii/i BC), Hsch.

**ἀμπτᾶσα, ἀμπταίην**, delete 'ἀμπτᾶσα'

**ἀμπῠκάζω**, for '*bind front hair*' read '*place a diadem* or *headband on, crown*'
***ἀμπῠκόω**, *tie a headband on*, Phot. α 1256 Th. (ἀμπυκοῖς).
**ἀμπύκωμα**, add 'prob. in A.*Supp.* 235 (pl.)'
***ἄμπυλλα** (or -η), ἡ, Lat. *ampulla*, *BGU* 40 (ἀνπ-, ii/iii AD); sp. ἄμβουλλα *POxy.* 3993.8 (ii/iii AD).
***ἀμπυλλάριον**, τό, app. *holder* or *container for flasks*, *CPR* 5 Skar 455 (iv AD).
**ἄμπυξ 2**, for '*headband*' read '*headstall*' at end add 'Myc. *a-pu-ke* (pl.), sense II; cf. *a-pu-ko-wo-ko* = *ἀμπυκϝοργός, fem. occupational term'
**ἄμπωτις**, line 1, after 'ιος' insert 'dat. ιδι D.C. 39.40, pl. -ιδες Longin. 9.13' **I 1**, line 2, for 'πλημμυρίς' read 'πλημυρίς or πλήμη'; line 4, delete '*ebb and flow, tides*' **3**, add 'Longin. l.c.'
***ἀμτύριον**, τό, (for ἀμιτύριον), *cheese flavoured with caraway*, *PCair.Preis.* 38.11 (iv AD).
**ἀμυγδάλη I**, after 'Theophr.*HP* 1.113' insert 'Men.*fr.* 133 K.-Th.' add 'forms ἀμυσγέλα, ἀμυσγύλα at Cyrene, *SEG* 9.32, 43 (iii/ii BC)'
**ἄμῠδις II**, at end after 'late Ep.' insert 'Call.*fr.* 295 Pf.'
**ἀμυδρός I**, at end delete 'ἀ. ἔχειν .. $668^a3$' **2**, for this section read 'of movement, *indistinct, imperceptible*, Aret.*CA* 2.3 (127.28 H.), *SD* 1.12 (53.18 H.); τυπαί Nic.*Th.* 358 (comp.); of creatures, etc., *imperceptible in movement*, ib. 195, 373; 158 (sup.)'
***Ἀμυκλάδια**, τά, dim. of Ἀμύκλαι, kind of shoe, *IG* $1^3$.422.244 (Athens, v BC).
**Ἀμυκλαῖος**, add 'cult-title of Apollo at Idalion, *SEG* 25.1071 (iii BC). **2** ὁ (sc. μήν), name of month at Argos, *SEG* 34.282 (iv BC), *BCH* 98.776 no. 2 (iii BC), at Gortyn, *Inscr.Cret.* 4.182.23 (ii BC).'
***ἀμυκτηρίστως**, adv. *without disparagement*, ἀκούων ἀ. *Vit.Aesop.*(G) 87.
**ἄμῠλος II**, delete 'cf.' and insert 'Pherecr. 113.17 K.-A., Metag. 6.11 K.-A.'
**ἀμύμων**, line 2, after 'Hsch.' insert 'hence traditional interpr. *blameless*'
**ἀμυντήριον**, line 3, for 'Plu. 2.714f' read 'Plu. 2.714e'
**ἀμύντης**, for pres. refs. read '*Trag.adesp.* 585b K.-S. (oxyt. acc. to Hdn. 1.78.5; paroxyt. in Phot. 1270 Th.); cf. pers. n. Ἀμύντας, -ης'
**ἀμύντωρ I**, for 'Il. 13.384 .. etc.' read 'Il. 15.610, 13.384 (v.l.), Od. 2.326 (pl.), Call.*fr.* 635 Pf.'
**ἀμύνω** (A) **I 1 b**, line 5, after 'Th. 3.67' insert 'w. ἐπί added, Ἀπόλλωνα .. αὗταί φασιν αἱ ποιήσεις ἀμῦναι Κούρησιν ἐπὶ τοὺς Αἰτωλούς Paus. 10.31.3' **2**, add '**c** w. acc., *aid, succour*, Nic.*Th.* 868.'
**ἄμυξις**, for '*tearing, rending, mangling*' read '*scratching, laceration*' and delete '*irritation*'
***ἀμυρίτης**, ου, ὁ, prob. = ‡ἀμορίτης, Aq., Sm. 2*Ki.* 6.19.
***ἄμυρος**, ον, interpr. by gramm. as *watery* but prob. *malodorous*, ἀμύρους τόπους S.*fr.* 512 R. **2** *devoid of perfume*, *Orac.Sib.* 5.128.
***ἀμυσγέλα, ἀμυσγύλα**, v. ‡ἀμυγδάλη.
**ἀμύσσω I**, line 7, delete '*tear in pieces, mangle*'
**ἄμυστις**, after 'ιδος' insert 'written ἄμυσσιν (acc.) *SEG* 30.938 (graffito, Olbia, vi/v BC)' **I 1**, for 'Call.*Aet.* 1.1.11' read 'Call.*fr.* 178.11 Pf.'
**ἀμυχή I 1**, add 'γενύων τ' ἀμυχάς E.*fr.* 925a N.-S.; μετὰ ἀμοιχῆς *POxy.* 3195.46 (AD 331)' add '**3** *scratched surface*, Plu. 2.473e.'
***ἀμφαγνοέω**, v. ἀμφιγνοέω.
***ἀμφᾰδά**, adv. v. ‡ἀμφαδόν.
**ἀμφάδιος I**, add 'λέκτρα *AP* 5.219 (Paul.Sil.); φιλίη ib. 267.5 (Agath.)'
**ἀμφᾰδόν**, after 'A.R. 3.615' insert 'also neut. pl. ἀμφαδά, *APl.* 4.296 (Antip.Sid.), cj. in Posidipp. in *Suppl.Hell.* 705.17'
**ἀμφαεικής**, add '(**ἀμφάϊκος** La.)'
**ἀμφακλής**, add '(ἄμφακες La., v. ‡ἀμφήκης)'
**ἀμφαλλάσσω**, for '*change entirely*' read '*transform*' add '**II** *exchange*, *PMich.*III 149.18.15 (ii AD).'
**ἄμφανσις, ἀμφαντός, ἀμφαντύς**, delete the entries (v. °ἄμπανσις, etc.)
**ἀμφάνω**, delete the entry (v. ‡ἀναφαίνω I 3)
***ἄμφαρμος**, ον, archit., *having joints on both sides*, ἀ. λίθος *MDAI(I)* 19/20.238.12, 242 (Didyma).
**ἀμφαϋτέω**, add '*shout on all sides*, στρατός Archil. 196a.51 $W^2$.'
**ἀμφᾰφάω I**, add 'part. ἀμφαφόωμενος Archil.*fr.* 196A W.'
**ἀμφεικάς**, after '(Cos)' insert '*IStraton.* 9.2 (ἀμφικ-, ii BC)'; at end delete 's.v. ἀμφ' εἰκάς'
***ἀμφειλύω**, *wrap, enfold*, Philet. 17.1. (tm.).
***ἀμφέλιξ**, ικος, *coiled, twisted*, Erinn. in *Suppl.Hell.* 401.41 (rest.).
**ἀμφελύτρωσις**, delete the entry.
**ἀμφήκης**, after lemma insert 'Dor. ἀμφάκης (B., S. ll.cc.)' **I**, add '**b** subst., τὤμφακες *axe*, Sophr. in *GLP* 1.73.7.' **II**, after 'Luc.*JTr.* 43' add '(v.l. ἀμφήρης, °ἀμφήχης)'
**ἀμφημερῖνός**, after 'Hp.*Epid.* 1.6' insert '*Nat.Hom.* 15, *Morb.Sacr.* 1.6'
***ἀμφήχης**, v. °ἀμφήκης.
**ἀμφί C II 2**, add 'App.*Syr.* 20' **E**, after 'Od. 6.292' insert 'ἀμφὶ δ' ἐκτύπουν πέτραι S.*Tr.* 787, E.*Hipp.* 770, *Ion* 224, *Ph.* 325' at end add 'Myc. *a-pi*'

**ἀμφιάζω**, line 9, for 'Them.*Or.* 13.235a' read 'Them.*Or.* 20.235a' and for 'Lxx *Jb.* 40.5' read 'Lxx *Jb.* 40.5(10)'; add '°ἐμφιέζω'
**ἀμφίᾰλος**, for 'S.*Ph.* 146' read 'S.*Ph.* 1464'
**Ἀμφιαράϊα**, τά, s.v. Ἀμφιάραος, add 'Ἀμφιάραα *IG* $2^2$.2196.12 (c.AD 200), Ἀμφιαίρεια *IG* $2^2$.2237.58 (iii AD); see also Ἀμφιεραία'
**Ἀμφιάραος**, line 1, -ηος, add 'Hes.*fr.* 25.34 M.-W.'; add 'also Ἀμφιέρ- *SEG* 31.438 (Boeotia, iv BC), *IG* $2^2$.4452 (Rhamnous, iii BC)'
***Ἀμφιάρειον**, τό, *temple of Amphiaraus*, Str. 9.2.10.
**ἀμφίασμα**, delete 'Luc.*Cyn.* 17' (read ἀμφίεσμα)
**ἀμφιασμός**, add '*SB* 10228.2.16 (AD 125)'
***Ἀμφιασταί**, οἱ, name of healing cult association, *SEG* 31.807 (Eretria, ii BC).
***ἀμφιάστωρ**, ορος, ὁ, *cloak, wrap*, Sch.Gen.Il. 3.134.
***ἀμφιάτωρ**, gloss on κόλωψ, Hsch.
**Ἀμφίβαιος**, for 'ἀμφίγαιος' read 'ἀμφίγειος'
**ἀμφιβάλλω I 1 b**, for 'built chamber *over* him' read 'built the chamber round it' **c**, line 6, for '*like a net*' read '*like a mantle*' **IV 2**, after 'Alciphr. 1.37' insert 'εἴ τις πρὸς μίαν τῶν εἰρημένων ἁγίων συνόδων ἀμφιβάλλει .. *Cod.Just.* 1.1.7.20, ἀμφιβάλλετε πρὸς ἐμέ *PMasp.* 295.19 (vi AD)'
***ἀμφιβαρής**, ές, v. ‡ἀμφικέλεμνον.
**ἀμφίβληστρον 1 b**, add 'E.*fr.* 697'
**ἀμφίβλητος**, delete the entry (v. °ἀμφίβληστρον).
**ἀμφιβόητος 2**, for this section read '*celebrated all around*, *AP* 9.241 (Antip.Thess.), *APl.* 278 (Paul.Sil.), Nonn.*D.* 26.141'
**ἀμφιβολεύς**, for '*fisherman*' read '*one who fishes with a net*' and add '*PCornell* 46.6 (ii AD)'
***ἀμφιβολεύω**, *fish with a casting-net*, *PSI* 901.13, 22 (i AD).
**ἀμφίβολος I**, after '*encompassing*' insert 'A.*Th.* 298' deleting this ref. in section II 1.
***ἀμφιβῶτις**, ἡ, fem. adj., *celebrated all around*, Ion Trag.*fr.* 35 K.-S.; cf. ἀμφιβόητος.
**ἀμφίβωτος**, delete the entry (v. °ἀμφιβῶτις).
**Ἀμφιγυήεις**, for pres. def. read '*with bent legs, bandy*' and add 'epith. of the bird αἴγιθος, Call.*fr.* 469 Pf.'
***ἀμφίγῠος**, ον, *curved on both sides* (of the blade), *leaf-shaped*, ἔγχεσιν ἀμφιγύοισιν Il. 13.147, Od. 24.527, ἀ. δούρασιν, A.R. 3.1356. **2** fig., of antagonists, perh. *keen on either side*, S.*Tr.* 504.
***ἀμφιδαής**, ές, *two-edged*, ἀ. ἡ ἀμφοτέρωθεν κόπτουσα μάχαιρα, Suid.
***ἀμφιδάνης**, v. °ἀφιδάνης.
**ἀμφιδεῖδιον**, delete pres. ref. and read '*IG* $2^2$.1424a.183, $2^2$.1428.75'
**ἀμφιδέξιος**, add '**6** as epith. of Apollo, Cypr. *ta-pi-te-ki-si-o-i* τά(μ)φιδεξίοι *ICS* 335.'
***ἀμφιδέσφάγανον** (sic), delete the entry.
**ἀμφίδετος**, for '*bound* or *set all round*' read '*with a string attached to either end* (of a bow-drill)'
***ἀμφιδήμᾱ**, ἁ, either *personal adornment* or *footwear* (cf. ἀμφιδήσασθαι· ὑποδήσασθαι Hsch.) ἀντιδήμας (gen.) *Inscr.Cret.* 4.43*Ab*11; ἀντιδέμας ib. 72 v 40, 75*B*3 (all Gortyn, v BC).
**ἀμφιδῖνεύω**, after 'πυρήια' insert 'codd. in'
**ἀμφίδοξος II**, line 3, delete '*causing doubt*'
**ἀμφιδρόμια**, line 4, after 'Lys.l.c.' insert 'seventh, acc. to Hsch. s.v. δρομιάμφιον ἦμαρ (δρομιάφιον ἦ. S.) = *Suppl.Hell.* 1075'
**ἀμφίδῠμος**, after 'λιμένες ἀ.' insert 'i.e. on both coasts' and after 'ἀκταί' insert 'i.e. accessible to ships from both sides'
**ἀμφιέννυμι**, line 1, after '-ύω' insert '*IG* $1^3$.7.11 (v BC)'; line 6, for 'poet. part.' read 'part. ἠμφιεσμένη Hippon. 2 W., poet.'; line 7, delete 'ἀμφὶ .. Il. 19.393' (v. °ἵζω).
**ἀμφιέπω I 1**, add 'Hes.*Th.* 696' **II 1**, line 3, for '*dressed*' read '*prepare*'; for '*do honour .. to*' read '*devote oneself to*'; delete 'prob. in E.*Med.* 480, etc.'
**ἀμφίεσμα**, after '(Pl.)*R.* 381a' insert 'Luc.*Cyn.* 17 (also pl.)'
**ἀμφιεσμός**, add '*SEG* 33.1039.74-5 (Cyme, Aeolis), *Didyma* 38 (both ii BC), *PDura* 20.12 (ii AD), cf. 14.9'
**ἀμφιετηρίς**, after '*festival*' insert '*OGI* 51.27 (Egypt, iii BC)' and for '*SIG* .. 69' read '*IG* $2^2$.1368.69'
**ἀμφιετής**, after 'Orph.' insert '*H.* 53.1'
***ἀμφιθᾰλάσσιος**, ον, *surrounded by sea*, Phot. s.v. ἀμφιπλήκτοις α 1363 Th.
**ἀμφιθάλασσος**, add 'as the name of a horse, *ICilicie* 49 (Rom.imp.)'
**ἀμφιθᾰλής 1**, for '*blooming*' read '*flourishing*'; for 'Call.*Iamb.* 3.1.3' to the end read 'esp. of young persons taking part in religious or agonistic rites, for auspicious reasons, Call.*fr.* 75.3 Pf., *SEG* 32.1243.4 (Cyme, Aeolis, i BC/i AD), *Inscr.Magn.* 98.19, *MAMA* 9.30 (ii AD)'
***ἀμφιθᾰλιτεύω**, of a Laconian officer, app. *perform the function of an* ‡*ἀμφιθαλής* or *be in charge of the ἀμφιθαλεῖς*, *SEG* 11.677c (p. 250 Add., ἀπιϛαλιτ-, ii/i BC), 677 (ἀνφιθαλειτ-, time of Augustus).
**ἀμφιθάλλω**, delete '*full*'; for '(Antip.)' read '(Antip.Sid.)' and after it insert '*flourish about*, ib. 9.221 (Marc.Arg.), 12.93 (Rhian.)'

**ἀμφίθετος**, for '*that will stand on both ends*' read '*that can be used either way up*'; add 'Antim. 24.1 Wy.'

**⁺ἀμφιθηγής**, *ές*, *two-edged*, *ξίφος*, S.*Ant*. 1309 (lyr.).

**⁺ἀμφίθηκτος**, *ον*, *two-edged σάγαρις*, *AP* 6.94 (Phil.).

***ἀμφικαπνίζω**, *make smoke round*, Archil. 89.1 W.

**ἀμφικάρηνος**, for '*two-headed*' read '*having a head at either end*'

***ἀμφικατέργω**, *shut in all round*, *Orac.Sib.* 2.295; cf. *κατείργω*.

**⁺ἀμφικέλεμνον**· *ἀμφιβαρές, οἱ δὲ τὸν βασταζόμενον ὑπὸ δύο ἀνθρώπων δίφρον, οἱ δὲ ἀμφίκοιλον* Hsch. (-‹κοιλον› *ξύλον* La.); cf. *ἀμφικελέμνους· ἀμφιβαρεῖς* Phot. α 1333 Th.

**ἀμφικέφἄλος**, after '*ον*' insert 'also *η*, *ον* (*SEG* 29.146.5, iv BC, in sense II)' **II**, for '*IG* 1.227*d*' read '*IG* 1³.421.206'

**ἀμφίκλαστος**, after '*AP* 6.223' add '(Antip.Sid.)'

**ἀμφικλάω**, after '*break all in pieces*' insert '(in quots., fig.)'

**ἀμφίκομος**, add '**3** subst., *ὁ*, precious stone, Plin.*HN* 37.160, also known as *ἐρωτύλος* (v.s.v. sense IV.)'

***ἀμφικουρία**, Ion., -*ρίη*, *ἡ*, dub. sens., Archil. 146.9 W.

**ἀμφίκρᾶνος**, for '= *ἀμφικάρηνος*' read '*having heads on either side* or *all round*'; add '*Trag.adesp.* 586a K.-S.'

**ἀμφίκροτος**, for '*IG* 3.82' read '*IG* 2².3118'

**Ἀμφικτύονες**, line 3, after 'esp. at Delphi' insert 'Hdt. 7.200.2'; line 4, for '*IG* 2.545.16' read '*CID* I 10.16'

**Ἀμφικτυονικός**, add 'written *Ἀμφικτιονικός*, *CID* I 10.6, 42'

***ἀμφίκῡφος**, *ον*, *doubly convex*, *κεραμίδες* *Inscr.Délos* 456*A*6 (ii BC).

**ἀμφίλἄλος**, for 'Ar.*Ra.* 979' read '*χείλεσιν ἀ.* Ar.*Ra.* 680'

**ἀμφιλάφης 3**, add '*ἔρις* Nonn.*Par.Ev.Jo.* 7.167' **4**, add '*ὄχλος* ib. 12.81' **5**, for '*great*' read '*wide-ranging*'

**ἀμφιλειπής**, after 'Mar.Vict. 2559' insert '(p. 110.31 K., *amphilipes*)'

**ἀμφίλογος**, after '*ον*' insert 'dial. **ἀμφίλλ-** treaty in Th. 5.79.4, *IG* 5(2).343.A11 (Orchomenus, Arcadia, iv BC), *SEG* 25.447.5 (Aliphera, Arcadia, iii BC), 23.305 (Delphi, ii BC)'

**⁺ἀμφιμήτορες**, *οἱ*, *αἱ*, Dor. *ἀμφιμᾶτ-*, *children with two rival mothers*, i.e. a natural mother and a stepmother, (v. *CQ* 37.498ff.), A.*fr.* 73b.4 R., E.*Andr.* 466 (lyr.); sg. in Hsch.; cf. ‡*ἀμφιπάτορες*.

**ἀμφιμῡκάομαι**, after 'Od. 10.227' add '*δῶμα ἀμφιμέμυκεν* epigr. in *SEG* 30.172 (late Hellen.)'

**ἀμφίον**, before 'D.H. 4.76' insert 'Call.*fr.* 177.31 Pf. (pl.)'

**ἀμφιπαίω**, for '*spike, transfix*' read '*impale*' and for '*IG* 4.951' read '*IG* 4²(1).121.92' add '**2** = *ἀμφισβητέω*, *Inscr.Cret.* 4.80.12 (Gortyn, v BC).'

**ἀμφιπάτορες**, for 'cf. *ἀμφιμήτορες*' read 'Poll. 3.24 (but perh. wd. invented on the model of ‡*ἀμφιμήτορες*, v. *CQ* 37.498ff.)'

**ἀμφιπῐάζω**, for '*squeeze all round, hug closely*' read '*enfold in one's grasp*'

**ἀμφιπίπτω**, line 4, for 'Parth. 8.4' read 'Parth. 7.3'

**ἀμφιπλέκω**, after 'Opp.*H.* 4.158' insert '*Anacreont.* 42.6 W.'

**ἀμφιπλήξ**, after 'Id.*Tr.* 930' insert '*σφῦραι AP* 6.205 (Leon.Tarent.)'

**ἀμφιπολεύω 2**, transfer '[*τὰς κούρας*] .. Od. 20.78' to section 3 and 'Hes.*Op.* 803' to section 1, line 2, after '*h.Merc.* 568' **3**, line 2, delete 'Q.S. 13.270'; add '*to be slave to*, *χείροσιν ἀ.* Q.S. 13.270'

**ἀμφιπολέω II**, for '*roam with*' read '*attend on*' add '**III** abs. *roam up and down*, A.R. 4.1547.'

**⁺ἀμφίπολος**, *ον*, as subst., *servant, attendant*: fem., Od. 1.331, 6.199, etc.; *λάβετ' ἀμφίπολοι γραίας ἀμενοῦς* E.*Supp.* 1115; w. other substs., *ἀ. ταμίη*, *γραῦς* Il. 24.302, Od. 1.191; masc., Pi.*O.* 6.32. **2** *servant of god* or *cult*: fem., *θεᾶς ἀμφίπολον κόραν* E.*IT* 1114, *Διός* *IG* 14.2111, D.H. 1.50; masc., *SEG* 11.314.12 (Argos, vi BC), Pi.*Pae.* 6.117, E.*fr.* 992, *τῶν θεῶν* Phld.*D.* 1.13, Plu.*Comp.Demetr.Ant.* 3, *IG* 9(1).683 (Corcyra). **3** *ἀ. Διὸς Ὀλυμπίου* title of magistrate at Syracuse, D.S. 16.70. **II** *frequented*, *τύμβος* Pi.*O.* 1.93. Myc. *a-pi-qo-ro*.

**ἀμφιπονέομαι II**, for this section read '*to be troubled about*, *χὠς ὄρος ἀμφεπονεῖτο .. αὐτόν* Theoc. 7.74; pass. *τὰ ἀμφιπονεόμενα* *neighbouring parts affected by the disorder*, Hp.*Mul.* 2.135'

***ἀμφιπῠκάζω**, *wreathe, deck round*, *ἀμφιπυκάσσας* *Eleg.adesp.* in *POxy.* 3723.3 (ii AD, unless to be read as two wds.).

**ἀμφίπῠλος**, add '(or perh. -*ον*, *τό*, *doorway*)'

***ἀμφίροος**, *ον*, *that has streams flowing around* or *on both sides*, attested in place-name *Ἀμφίροος*, *SEG* 36.336.16 (Argos, iv BC).

**⁺ἀμφισᾰλεύομαι**, *rock up and down astride*, *AP* 5.55 (Diosc.).

**ἀμφισκέπαρνος**, for '*λίθοι*' to the end read 'archit., of a right-angle block in door-frame, *λίθος* *Didyma* 25.A19, B26, 26.A29, 55, al.'

***ἀμφισταδόν**, adv., *on both sides*, *SEG* 37.1537.9 (Arabia, c.AD 400).

**ἀμφιτίθημι**, line 2, for 'Thgn. 847' read 'Thgn. 848'

**ἀμφιφἄής**, after 'Arist.*Mu.* 395ᵇ14' insert '(cj. -*φανής*)' add '**II** of the new moon, *shining at either horn*, Nonn.*D.* 4.281 (v.l. *ἀρτιφαής*), 22.349; cf. *ἀμφιφανής* 2.'

**ἀμφιφἄνής 1**, add 'Arist.*Mu.* 395ᵇ14 (v.l.)'

***ἀμφιφάων**, *οντος*, *ὁ*, (cf. *ἀμφιφῶν*), *visible on all sides*, *τόπον* *Orac.Chald.fr.* 158.2 P.

**ἀμφιφορεύς**, add 'Myc. *a-pi-po-re-we* (pl.)'

**ἀμφιχάσκω**, for '*gape .. for*' read '*open the mouth wide* so as to swallow'; add 'w. cogn. acc., *ἀμφιχανὼν ὀλίγον στόμα* Opp.*H.* 1.223'

**ἀμφίχωλος**, add '**II** in metre, *halting at both ends*, of an iambic line that has a long for the normal short in both the first and the last metron, Sacerd. 523.10, 531.6.'

**ἀμφόδιον**, after 'of sq.' insert '*BGU* 1579.10, 1580.11 (both c.AD 119)'

***ἀμφοδογραμματεύς**, *έως*, *ὁ*, *secretary of an ἄμφοδον* II, *POxy.* 2131.11 (iii AD), *PLond.* 935.1, 936.1 (both iii AD).

**ἄμφοδον II**, delete 'hence .. *town*' and after 'Lxx *Je.* 17.27' insert 'as administrative unit'

***ἀμφόδους**, v. ‡*ἀμφώδων*.

**⁺ἀμφόδων**, v. ‡*ἀμφώδων*.

***ἀμφοκέραιος**, *ον*, *two-handled*, *POxy.* 1343 (vi AD; -*κέρυια* pap.; for **ἀμφικ-*).

***ἀμφοράριον**, *τό*, dim. of *ἀμφορεύς*, *PGot.* 17ʳ.17 (vi/vii AD, sp. -*φολ-*); see also °*ὀμφαλάριον*.

**ἀμφορεύς I 1**, line 5, after 'wine in' insert '*Schwyzer* 725.9 (Miletus, vi BC)' and for '[Ar.]*fr.* 299' read 'Ar.*fr.* 310 K.-A.; for oil, given as prizes at the Panathenaea, *IG* 1³.422.41-60 (Athens, v BC), cf. *Hesperia* 27.178ff.' at end add 'Myc. *a-po-re-we* (pl.)'

**⁺ἀμφορίσκος**, *ὁ*, dim. of *ἀμφορεύς*, Magn. 7 K.-A., *IG* 2².1640.19 (354 BC), D. 22.76.

**ἀμφορίτης I**, for this section read 'a *δίαυλος* race at Aegina *run by bearers of amphorae* and called '*Ὑδροφόρια*, Call.*Dieg.* viii.23 (*fr.* 198 Pf.), *EM* 95.3 (*ἀμφιφορίτης*)'

***ἀμφοροθῡνω**, *provoke to strife*, *πεζὸν .. Ἄρη* *Polemon* 2.57 (epigr., Thess., iii BC).

**ἀμφότερος I 2**, line 5, before 'Pi.*P.* 4.79' insert 'Il. 7.418'

**ἀμφοτέρωθεν**, add 'Myc. *a-po-te-ro-te*'

***ἀμφουριασμός**, *ὁ*, *deed of transfer of landed property*, *SEG* 3.674.3, 46, al. (Rhodes, ii BC).

**⁺ἀμφούριον**, *τό*, (*οὖρος* = *ὅρος*) prob. *copy of a declaration of transfer*, *PHal.* 1.253 (iii BC), *SEG* 3.674.40 (Rhodes, ii BC).

***ἀμφύνω**, v. °*ἀναφύω*.

**ἄμφω**, add '**2** adv., like *ἀμφότερον* (s.v. *ἀμφότερος* I 2), Nonn.*D.* 11.187, *AP* 9.25.3 (Leon.Tarent.).'

**ἀμφώδων**, for '*οντος*, *ὁ*, *ἡ*, (*ὀδούς*)' read '*ον*, Arist.*PA* 663ᵇ36 (-*ουν* id.*HA* 507ᵇ34), gen. -*οντος*'; after 'ruminants' insert 'Hp.*Art.* 8'; after 'al.' add 'neut. pl. subst., *ἀμφώδοντα δὲ ἄνθρωπος ἵππος ὄνος* Ael.*NA* 11.37' **II**, for '*ass*' read 'applied to an ass'; for '*ἀμφόδων*; cf. *ἀμφόδους*' read '*ἀμφοδ-* as from *ἀμφόδων* or **ἀμφόδους*'

**ἀμφώτιξ**, after lemma insert '(*ἄμφωτις* La.)'

**ἄμφωτις II**, after 'A.*fr.* 102' insert 'Pl.Com. 256 K.-A.'

***ἀμωλώπιστος**, *ον*, *not bruised*, Plu. 2.1091e (cj.).

**ἀμώμητος**, after '-*ον*' insert '[also -*η*, -*ον* Hes.*fr.* 185.13 M.-W., *SEG* 37.908 (Ephesus)]'; line 3, after 'Ph.*fr.* 69 H.' insert '*ἐκ λειμῶνος ἀ.* *AP* 4.1.31 (Mel.)'

**ἄμωμον**, add '*Apoc.* 18.13'

**ἄμωμος**, add 'adv. -*ως*, *IHadr.* 120 (Chr.)'

***ἄμωροι** (v.l. in Od. 12.89), = *ἰχθυοφόροι*, *EM* 117.26.

***ἄμωρος** (B), dub. sens., Call.*fr.* 686 Pf.

**ἄν** (B), add 'also in Arc. inscr., *ἂν δέ τις .. μὴ φᾶτοι* *SEG* 37.340.21 (Mantinea, early iv BC)'

**ἄν** or **ἀν**, after 'Ep.' insert 'and dial.'

**ἀνά**, line 1, after '*ὄν*' insert 'also Arc., Cypr. *ὐν*' **C III**, after '*Ev.Luc.* 9.14' insert '*PMich.*III 145.3 iv 1, 11 (ii AD)' and after '*Ev.Matt.* 20.10' insert 'Dioph. 5.12'

**ἄνᾰ** (A), delete 'and always as address to gods' and add 'E.*Rh.* 828, Call.*fr.* 24.3 Pf., *Epigr.* 34.1 Pf.'

**⁺ἄνᾱ** (B), Dor. for °*ἄνη*.

**ἀνάατος**, after '*IG* 5(2).357.177' insert '(v. *SEG* 31.351)'

**ἀναβαθμός**, add '**2** Ep. *ἀμβαθμός*, *ἀ. πετρώδεας* rocky *ascents*, Nic.*Th.* 283 (cj.).'

**ἀνάβαθρον**, after 'Tralles' insert 'cj., but now read as *τὸ πᾶμ βάθρο[ν]*, *ITrall.* 240.4'; add '*ἀνά[β]α̣θρον* *PTeb.* 793 viii 1 (ii BC), cf. *anabathra* (pl.), Juv. 7.46'

**ἀναβαίνω A II 6**, lines 4/5, delete '*ἀ. ἐπὶ τὸν ὀκρίβαντα .. Eq.* 149' and transfer '*ἀνάβηθι* [Ar.] *V.* 963' to follow 'of witnesses in court' add '**b** of the "entrance" of an actor, Ar.*Ach.* 732, *Eq.* 149, *V.* 1341; for *ἀ. ἐπὶ τὸν ὀκρίβαντα* Pl.*Smp.* 194b, v. *ὀκρίβας*.' add '**11** *rise, be promoted* (cf. Lat. *ascendo*), *θεσπίζομεν μηδένα .. εἰς τὰς ῥηθείσας ἱερατείας ἀναβαίνειν* *Cod.Just.* 1.3.52, *οὐκ ἔτι πρὸς τὰ μείζω τῆς ἱερωσύνης ἀναβήσεται γέρα* Just.*Nov.* 6.1.2. **12** astron., = *ἀναβιβάζω* II 10, Palch. in *Cat.Cod.Astr.* 6.63.8, al.' **III 1**, add '**c** of anger, *rise* or *surge up*, Lxx 2*Ki.* 11.20, al.' **IV**, after 'of discourse' insert '*τοῦτο μέν νυν τοιοῦτόν ἐστι, ἀναβήσομαι δὲ ἐς τὸν κατ' ἀρχὰς ἤϊα λέξων λόγον* Hdt. 4.82' and after 'Democr. 144ᵃ' insert 'Hp.*Gland.* 7, *Morb.* 4.45, X.*Eq.* 1.4'

**ἀναβακχεύω**, for '(E.) *Or.* 337' read '(E.) *Or.* 338'

**ἀναβαλλαγόρας**, add '(*ἀναβαλλογήρας* La.)'

**ἀναβάλλω A I 3**, for 'Ctes.*fr.* 30' read 'Ctes. 1(p).γ J.' **4**, after '*cause to spring up*' insert 'ὕδωρ Call.*fr.* 546 Pf.' **7**, delete the section transferring quot. to section 1 **B 1**, line 3, after 'c. acc.' insert 'μέλος Theoc. 10.22' **II 1**, add 'ἀ. προσελθεῖν Men.*Dysc.* 126' **V**, delete the section.

***ἀνάβαπτος**, ον, *tinged, dyed*, κάμβαπτον cj. in Philic. in *Suppl.Hell.* 680.60.

**ἀνάβᾰσις**, add '**V** astron., *rising*, Heph.*Astr.* 1.23.18; ἀ. ἡλίου *noon altitude* of sun, *Cod.Vat.Gr.* 1058.431$^v$.'

***ἀνάβασμα**, ατος, τό, *stair*, Hsch. s.v. σκάλα.

**ἀναβασμός**, line 2, after 'Paus. 10.5.2' insert '*ITrall.* 240.6'; at end for '*SIG*$^2$587.308' read '*IG* 2$^2$.1672.308 (iv BC); also form ἀμβασμός *Didyma* 35.17 (ii BC); cf. ἀμβαθμός s.v. °ἀναβ-'

***Ἀναβατηνός**, ὁ, cult-title of Zeus, *IHadr.* 9.

***ἀναβέβροχε**, v. ‡ἀναβέβρυχε.

**ἀναβέβρῡχε**, for '*gushed* or *bubbled up*' read '*gushes* or *bubbles up*'; after 'Zenod.' insert 'and edd.' and add 'cf. *βρόχω'

***ἀνάβηξις**, εως, ἡ, *expectoration*, αἵματος ἀναβήξεως Gal. 8.287.6.

**ἀναβήσσω**, add '*Morb.* 2.49'

**ἀναβῐβάζω II 6**, for 'cf. *POxy.* 513.27' read 'pass., ἕνεκα τοῦ .. τὴν προκειμένην οἰκίαν .. ἀναβεβι‹βά›σθαι εἰς δραχμὰς χειλίας because it *has had its price raised* (by overbidding), *POxy.* 513.27 (ii AD)' add '**11** *reckon* time *back*, ἀπό γε τῆς ἐκβολῆς τῶν βασιλέων ἐπὶ τὸν πρῶτον ἄρξαντα .. ἀναβιβασθεὶς ὁ χρόνος D.H. 1.75.1.'

**ἀναβῐβασμός**, add '**4** *overbidding*, *PTeb.* 295.10 (ii AD).'

**ἀναβῐβαστέον**, add '**2** *one must move* a word *farther back* (in construing), Sch.Pi.*N.* 4.14a.'

**ἀναβῐώσκομαι II**, after 'aor.' insert 'ἀνεβιωσάμην Crates Com. 52 K.-A.'

**ἀναβλαστάνω**, line 3, for 'Pl.*Lg.* 835d' read 'Pl.*Lg.* 845d' and after 'Plu. 2.366b' insert 'ἄρδω σ' ὅπως ἀμβλαστάνῃς Ar.*Lys.* 384'

**ἀναβλέπω I 3**, add 'ἀναβλέψατε εἰς ὕψος τοὺς ὀφθαλμοὺς ὑμῶν Lxx *Is.* 40.26'

**ἀνάβλησις**, for 'Call.*Ap.* 45' read 'Call.*Ap.* 46'

***ἀναβλητέον**, *one must postpone*, ἀλλὰ ταῦτα μὲν ἐν τῷ παρόντι ἀναβλητέον, πρότερον δὲ .. Plot. 6.8.1.

**ἀναβλύες**, after 'Hsch.' add '(ἀνάβλυδες La.; cf. σύγκλυδες)'

**ἀναβλύζω**, delete 'fut. .. *Exag.* 137' (read ἀναβρυήσει)

**ἀναβλυσθαίνω**, (after ἀναβλυστάνω), add 'Procl. *in Ti.* 1.119, 120 D.'

**ἀναβολεύς II**, for pres. def. read '*lever used in surgical operations*'

***ἀναβολέω**, *put on*, ἀνεβολήσατο ὡς ἔνδυμα ζῆλον Aq.*Is.* 59.17.

**ἀναβολή I 1**, add '**b** *laying* of bricks, rest. in *IG* 2$^2$.1661.7; cf. ἀναβάλλω I 5.' **2**, line 2, for '*that which* .. *mantle*' read 'that part of a garment which hangs loose at the back'; line 3, before 'of the *toga*' insert 'of the ἱμάτιον, ἐξ ἀ. τοῦ ἱματίου εἵλκυσεν (αὐτόν) *Vit.Aesop.*(G) 15, 28'; line 4, after 'Nic.*Dam.* p. 119 D.' insert 'ἀφεῖλε τῶν μανδυῶν αὐτῶν τὸ ἥμισυ ἕως τῆς ἀναβολῆς i.e. up to just below the waist, Lxx 1*Chr.* 19.4'

**ἀναβολικός**, ἀναβολικόν, τό, for this section read 'Egyptian tax, used to cover costs of military clothing, *PAmh.* 2.131.15 (ii AD), *POxy.* 1135.2 (iii AD), *PThead.* 34.26, *Pap.Lugd.Bat.* xxv 62.8 (both iv AD)'

**ἀναβόλιμος**, add 'see also ‡ἀμβόλιμος'

***ἀνάβολον**, τό, *wrap*, *POxy.* 936.24 (iii AD), *PTeb.* 413.10 (ii/iii AD).

***ἀναβομβέω**, *blare*, λιγυρὴ δ' ἀνεβόμβεε σάλ[πιγξ] *GDRK* 32.80.

**ἀναβράζω**, add '**2** τήνδ' ἕωλον ἀναβεβρασμένην Ar.*fr.* 51 K.-A., interpr. in Phot. s.v. (α 1404 Th.) by ἀνακεκινημένη; prob. there is allusion to a *réchauffé*; cf. ἀναβρασμός. **3** *toss up*, ῥάβδον Lxx *Ez.* 21.26.'

***ἀναβροχέω**, *flood*, τὸ πεδίον *PSI* 168.22 (ii BC).

***ἀναβρύχω**, delete 'Eust. 1095.6'

**ἀναβρύω**, after lemma insert 'fut. ἀναβρυήσει (ἕλκη πικρά) Ezech.*Exag.* 137 S.'; add '*SEG* 31.1474 (Arabia, AD 575/6)'

**ἀναβώνες**, read 'ἀνάβωνες'

***ἀναγαργάλικτα**, τά, *gargles* Hp.*Aff.* 4.

**ἀναγγελία**, for '*SIG* 598.11' read '*Inscr.Magn.* 91.11 (decr. at Delphi, ii BC)' and add '*PP* 42.121 (Cos, iii/ii BC), *IKyme* 13 i 9, *SEG* 37.1006 (Troas, both ii BC)'

**ἀνάγειον**, after 'ἀνάγαιον' insert 'Ph. 2.476'; for '*Reise*' read '*Reisen*'

**ἀναγεννάω**, after 'Pass.' insert 'Sallust. 4.10'

**ἀναγεύω**, add '*PMich.*VIII 473.28 (ii AD)'

***ἀναγίγνομαι**, in tm., perh. *rise up*, ἀνὰ μὲν θυμὸς [ἔ]γεντο θε[ῆ]ς Call.*fr.* 63.6 Pf.

**ἀναγιγνώσκω I 2**, after 'Pi.*I.* 2.23' insert 'Philostr.*VA* 1.31' **II**, line 2, delete 'dub. in *GDI* 5075' add '**b** in textual criticism, *adopt as a reading*, Sch.Ar.*Pax* 594 H.'

**ἀναγκάζω**, after lemma insert 'ἀνακκάζω *IG* 9$^2$(1).706A 16' **I 1**, after 'Hdt. 5.101' insert 'in weakened sense *exert pressure on*, Th. 8.41.3, 76.1'

**ἀναγκαῖος I 1**, add 'ἐν καιροῖς ἀναγκαίοις *SEG* 37.957 (Claros, ii BC)' **II 4**, for '*indispensable* .. *minimum*' read '*forced* on one *by necessity, indispensable*, D. 50.38, 54.17; w. ref. to a minimum standard, *absolutely necessary, essential*, οὐδὲ τἀναγκαῖα ἐξικέσθαι Th. 1.70.2, παρασκευή 6.37.2, Lys. 31.18, Is. 4.20'; delete 'less freq. .. 6.37' **5**, add '**b** prob. an honorary title, *kinsman* (cf. συγγενής III), in *OGI* 315.49, 763.31 (letters of Attalus II and Eumenes II).' **7**, add 'Epiph.Const. in *Lapid.Gr.* 196.22 (comp.)' add '**8** lit. crit., *sparing* of words, opp. περιττός, of Sophocles, D.H. *Vett.Cens.* 2.11; opp. ἀστεῖος and ἡδύς, of Lycurgus, ib. 5.3.'

***ἀναγκεπάκτης**, ου, ὁ, *bringer of compulsion*, *PMag.* 4.1361.

***ἀναγκεπόπτης**, ου, ὁ, *overseer of necessity*, *PMag.* 7.355.

**ἀνάγκη**, after lemma insert 'Dor. ἀνάγκᾱ' **I 1**, at end after 'c. inf.' insert 'D.Chr. 31.105, 114' **2 a**, add 'of the rules of rhetoric, ῥητόρων ἀνάγκας *Anacreont.* 52.2 W.' **II**, delete the section.

***ἀναγκίτης**, ου, ὁ, name for ἀδάμας, *ob id quidam eum ananciten vocavere*, Plin.*HN* 37.61, τόν ῥα παλαιγένεες μὲν ἀναγκίτην (cj., codd. ἀνακτ.) ἀδάμαντα κλεῖον Orph.*L.* 192.

***ἀναγκῖτις**, ιδος, ἡ, app. = °ἀναγκίτης, Plin.*HN* 37.192.

**ἀναγκοφᾰγέω**, after 'ἀναγκοτροφέω' insert '(?)Ephor. in *PLit.Lond.* 114.12'

***ἀνhαγλημαι**, Pamph. pres. imper. 3 sg. ἀνhαγλέσθō *let him take upon himself, undertake*, *IPamph.* 3.15 (iv BC); cf. ‡ἀγρέω.

**ἀναγλύφω**, after '(Lydia, i AD)' insert '*SEG* 26.1835 (epigr., Cyrene, i AD)'

***ἀναγνέω**, = ἀνάγω, ὕμνον Lasus 1 P.; cf. ἀγνέω, διεξαγνέω.

**ἀνάγνιστος**, delete '*unpurified*'

**ἄναγνος**, add 'J.*Ap.* 1.306'

**ἀνάγνωμα**, delete the entry.

**ἀναγνώστης I**, add '**2** *one who reads and expounds*, Lxx 1*Es.* 9.42. **3** *reader*, office in the Christian church, *POxy.* 3787, *Cod.Just.* 1.3.44, *BCH* suppl. 8 no. 142 (?vi AD).'

**ἀνᾰγόρευσις**, after '(Cnidus)' insert '*SEG* 28.60 (Athens, iii BC), *IHistriae* 58.22, 59.23 (ii BC)'

***ἀνᾰγορία**, ἡ, *public announcement*, *PFay.* 66.4 (ii AD), *SB* 6951 (ii AD). **2** *roll-call, muster*, *POxy.* 2902.24, 2903, etc. (all iii AD).

**ἀναγρᾰφεύς**, after 'έως' insert 'Dor. **ἀγγροφεύς** *IAskl.Epid.* 42.65 (c.370 BC)'; line 2, for '*IG* 1.61' read '*IG* 1$^3$.104.5 (409/8 BC)' **II**, for '*IG* 2.192c, cf. 191' read '*IG* 2$^2$.1700.215 (335/4 BC), al.' **III**, for '*plan* .. 33' read '*template*, *IG* 2$^2$.1666 (iv BC), 2$^2$.244' add '**IV** *secretary*, Phld.*Acad.Ind.* iii 37.'

**ἀναγρᾰφεύω**, before '*IG* 14.757' insert 'rest. in'

**ἀναγραφή**, after lemma insert 'Dor. **ἀγγροφά** *IG* 4$^2$(1).103.140 (Epid., iv BC)'

**ἀναγράφω**, after lemma insert 'Thess. ὀνγράφω *IG* 9(2).461, 517.21, 45'; ἀγγράφω, add '*SEG* 32.1586 (Naucratis, v BC)' **I 1**, line 7, for 'ἀναγρψάσαθαι' read 'ἀναγράψασθαι' **II 2**, add '**b** *enter in a list*, pass., of eclipses, εἰ [ἔκλειψις] ἐν ταῖς ἀναγραφείσαις εὑρίσκεται Hero *Dioptr.* 35.' add '**V** *repaint* (ornamentally), *Inscr.Cret.* 3.ii 1.11 (ii BC).'

**ἀναγρετόν**, add 'cf. νήγρετος· ἀνάγρετος, id.'

***ἀναγχίστευτος**, ον, *having no kindred*, *GVI* 819.11 (Phrygia, iii AD).

**ἀνάγχω**, delete '*hang up*' and add 'transf., *deprive of life*, τῷ λιμῷ *PMasp.* 20.12 (vi AD)'

**ἀνάγω I 5**, for '*conduct* the choir' read '*lead* the dance' **9**, line 3, after 'Id.*Aph.* 3.25' insert 'πνεῦμα .. ἀνηγάγετο Call.*Ep.* 43.2 Pf.'; after '*draw* a line' insert 'up to' **12**, add 'τῆς ἀναχθεί[ση]ς ἀμπέλου *PPetaus* 127.8 (ii AD)' add '**13** *transfer* land *to a higher category, upgrade*, *BGU* 2060.13 (AD 180).' **II 5**, for 'Pl.*Lg.* 915c' read 'Pl.*Lg.* 915d' **10**, add '*Carm.Pop.* 5.1 P.' at end add 'Myc. inf. *a-na-ke-e*, dub. sens.'

**ἀναγωγή I 1**, after 'X.*HG* 1.6.28' insert 'D. 33.25, 49.6' add '**c** *bringing up* from the shore, quayside, or sim., *Didyma* 41.45.' **II 7**, for 'Ath. 9.395a' read 'Ath. 9.394f'

**ἀναγωνίατος**, add '*PBaden* 48.12 (ii BC)'

***ἀναγώνιος**, ον, *free from care*, ὥστε περὶ γε τούτου ἀναγώνιος ἴσθι *PAmst.* 89.1 (AD 3).

**ἀναγώνιστος**, add '*uncontested*, τῶν .. ἀ. δευτερείων τῆς αὐλῳδίας, *SEG* 19.335.50 (Tanagra, i BC)'

**ἀναδαίομαι**, for 'v. ἀναδατέομαι' read 'pass., *to be distributed*, γᾶς ἀναδαιομένας orac. in Hdt. 4.159.3'

**ἀναδᾰτέομαι**, after '*redistribute*' insert 'ἀνδάζαθαι = ἀναδάσασθαι, *Inscr.Cret.* 4.5.2 (vii/vi BC)'; delete 'pass. .. 4.159'

**ἀνάδειγμα**, add 'see also ‡ἄνδεργμα'

**ἀναδείκνῡμι I**, after '*exhibit, display*' insert 'τὸν μάργον ὄνδειξαι θέλω, perh. *show up*, prob. in (?)Sapph. 99 i 24 L.-P.' **II 2**, for '*dedicate*' read '*consecrate*'

**ἀναδενδραδικός**, add '*PSoterichos* 1.8 (AD 69), 2.8 (AD 71)'

**ἀναδενδράς**, add '(ἀναδενδρᾶς (pl. -ᾶδες), acc. to Seleuc.ap.Phot. α 1454 Th.)'

**ἀναδέχομαι**, at beginning insert 'poet. **ἀνδ-** Pi.*P.* 2.41, Orph. *A.* 1133' **II 6**, add '**b** *recover* (the use of limbs), *MAMA* 4.266 (Dionysopolis).'

**ἀναδέω III**, for 'Plu. 2.222e' and '(Plu.) 343a' read 'Plu. 2.322e' and '(Plu.) 243a'

***ἀναδημιουργέω**, *reverse, annul, in one's capacity as* δημιουργός, *IG* 12(8).264.5 (Thasos, iv BC).

**ἀναδίδωμι**, line 1, add 'Cypr. aor. perh. ὑνέδωσε *Kafizin* 217 (221/200 BC)' **I 2**, add 'ἀναδοθεισᾶν ψάφων *SEG* 23.208 (Messene, i AD)' **II 5**, for '*present* by name' read '*nominate*' and add '*appoint*, *PMich.*xi 604.4 (iii AD, v. *BASP* 12.111-2)' **III**, add '**3** *assign* a liturgy, *BGU* 2475.5 (AD 138).' **V**, add '**2** *give back, return*, *BGU* 1149.23, *Cod.Just.* 1.2.17.3.'

**ἀναδῑνεύω**, for '*whirl*' read '*revolve, rotate*'

**ἀναδῑφάω**, for '*grope after*' read '*bring to light by probing, unearth*'

***ἀναδιχάζω**, v. ‡ἀνδιχάζω.

***ἀναδοσία**, ἡ, *repayment*, *Stud.Pal.* 20.114.15 (v AD).

**ἀνάδοσις II 1**, add 'ἀ. σπερμάτων *POxy.* 1031, *SB* 9358 (both iii AD)' add '**IV** *giving back, return*, Just.*Nov.* 7 pr., 46.6.'

***ἀναδούλωσις**, εως, ἡ, *re-enslavement*, Just.*Nov.* 78.2 pr.

**ἀνάδρομος**, add '**II** as masc. subst., *path which turns back on itself*, of a labyrinth, σφαιρικοὺς ἀναδρόμους Anon.Alch. 39.19.'

***ἀναδυτήριον**, τό, *niche*, app. for statuette, *SEG* 6.718 (Pisidia, Rom. imp.).

**ἀνείρω**, lines 3/4, for '*lift up in one's arms, carry off*' read '*raise from a position on the ground* or *other surface*, E.*Phaëth.* 81 D. (tm.)'

***Ἀναείτεια**, τά, festival of Artemis Anaïtis, *IGRom.* 4.1634.7 (Philadelphia, Asia).

***Ἀναεῖτις**, ιδος, ἡ, a Persian goddess, (cf. OPers. *Anāhitā-, the unblemished one*), *TAM* 5(1).172 (AD 93/4), *SEG* 29.1152 (ii/iii AD); identified w. Artemis, ib. 33.1007 (dat. Ἀναεῖτι, Lydia, ii AD), *IGRom.* 4.1611.9, 17.

**ἀναέξω**, after 'Coluth. 247' insert '*raise in status, advance*, Nonn.*D.* 8.183, 9.100'

**ἀναερτάζω**, for '= sq.' read '*raise up, lift up*'

***Ἀναζαρβαῖος**, ον, *from Anazarba* in Cilicia, a description of clothing, *PKöln Ketouba* l. 14.

**ἀναζεμα**, read 'ἀνάζεμα'

**ἀναζῠγή**, add '*PHamb.* 91.8 (ii BC)'

**ἀναζωγρέω 2**, for 'Nonn.*D.* 19.102' read 'Nonn.*D.* 19.104'

**ἀναζώννῡμι**, for 'Nonn.*D.* 19.73' read 'Nonn.*D.* 19.75'

**ἀναζωπῠρέω II**, after 'act.' insert '*recover one's spirits*'

***ἀναθάλλωσις**, εως, ἡ, *flourishing condition*, *PMasp.* 2 iii 22 (vi AD).

**ἀνάθεμα I 2**, add 'ἔσται ἡ ψυχὴ ἀν[αθε]μας (sic) *TAM* 5(1).21 (Chr.)' **II**, add '*SEG* 37.195 (Attica, Chr.)'

***ἀναθέσιμος**, ον, *votive*, πινάκια *Inscr.Délos* 1442*B*35 (ii BC).

**ἀναθεωρέω**, after 'Thphr.*HP* 8.6.2' read '(pass.) D.S. 12.15, Longin. 7.3'

***ἀναθεώρησις**, εως, ἡ, *close examination*, Plu. 2.19c; *further reflection*, D.S. 13.35, Cic.*Att.* 9.19.1; κατὰ τὴν ἀ. Longin. 23.2; ἐδόκει .. μεγάλην ἔχειν ἀ., i.e. *food for thought*, D.S. 13.34, cf. 35, Cic.*Att.* 14.15.1, 14.16.2.

**ἀναθήκη**, add '*loading* (on to wagons), ἐπ' ἀναθήκει *IG* 2².1666A.35 (iv BC)'

**ἀναθηλέω**, add 'fig., *AP* 5.264 (Paul.Sil.)'

***ἀναθηρεύω**, *hunt out*, ἀ[να]θηρ[ε]ύσαντες Did.*in D.* 12.15.

**ἀναθρεπτικός**, add 'adv. -κῶς Gal. 10.487.13'

**ἀνάθρεψις**, add 'Gal. 13.74.4, id.*Thras.* 7'

**ἀναθρώσκω**, add 'ἄνθρωσκε S.*fr.* 422 R.; E.*Or.* 1416 (tm.)'

***ἀναθῡμιάζω**, gloss on ἀτμίζω, Hsch.

***ἀναιβᾰσίη**, ἡ, Ion. ίη, = ἀνάβασις, *ascent*, prob. in epigr. in *IG* 2².4831 (rest. [ἀν]αιβασίη, iv AD).

**ἀναίδεια**, for '*shamelessness*' read '*lack of proper restraint* or *consideration, intemperateness*' **II**, delete 'cf. ὕβρις'

**ἀναίδην**, delete the entry (read ἀνέδην).

***ἀναιδής**, ές, (αἰδώς) *lacking in restraint, intemperate*, of Agamemnon, (ὦ μέγ' ἀναιδές Il. 1.158, of Penelope's suitors, Od. 1.254, al., (ὦ θρέμμ' ἀναιδές S.*El.*622, D. 8.68. **2** of conduct, character, etc., κυδοιμὸς ἀ. Il. 5.593, ἐλπὶς ἀ. Pi.*N.* 11.45, λόγοι τῶν ἀναιδῶν ἀναιδέστεροι Ar.*Eq.* 385, ἀ. γνώμη D. 21.91; neut. subst., ἐπὶ τὸ ἀναιδέστερον τραπέσθαι Hdt. 7.39, εἰς ἀναιδὲς .. δός μοι σεαυτὸν S.*Ph.* 83, βλέφαρα πρὸς τἀναιδὲς ἀγαγών E.*IA* 379, ἔνθα τἀναιδὲς κρατεῖ *Trag.adesp.* 528 K.-S. **3** -δῶς adv. S.*OT* 354, E.*Alc.* 694, Ar.*Th.* 525, Pl.*R.* 556b; sup. -έστατα Heraclit. 15 D.-K. **II** of things, *unable to be stopped*, ὀστέα λᾶας ἀναιδὴς ἄχρις ἀπηλοίησεν Il. 4.521, ἀναιδέος .. πέτρης 13.139; of Sisyphus' stone, Od. 11.598; of abst. things, θάνατος Thgn. 207, Pi.*O.* 10.105.

***ἀναιδομᾰχέω**, *quarrel insolently*, *POxy.* 2997.41 (ii/iii AD).

***ἀναιδόφθαλμος**, ον, gloss on κυνάμυια, Sch.Gen.Il. 21.394.

**ἀναίμακτος**, for 'Pyth.' read 'Pythag.' and add '*AP* 6.324 (Leon. Alexandr.), etc.'

**ἄναιμος I**, add 'sup., Plu. 2.913f.'

**ἀναιμωτί**, after 'Ph. 1.323, al.' insert 'J.*BJ* 4.1.6' and after 'Gal. 2.604' insert 'Opp.*C.* 4.453'

**ἀναίνομαι**, line 2, after 'Alciphr. 3.37' insert 'ἀνήνατο Call.*fr.* 178.11 Pf. (v.l.)'

***ἀναιρετός** (B), όν, *taken up*, of foundlings, *BGU* 1058.11 (i BC), *POxy.* 73.26 (i AD), etc.

**ἀναιρέω**, line 1, after '*Com.adesp.* 18.6 D.)' insert 'Pamph.aor. ἀνhε̄λε *IPamph.* 3.1 (iv BC), see also °ἀνhάγλημαι, Aeol. aor. inf. ὀννέλην Alc. 130.27 L.-P.' **II 1**, add '**b** *worst, bring down* enemies, D. 6.15, 18.18.' **2**, add '**b** *get rid of*, στάσιν Alc. l.c., Pi.*fr.* 109; νεῖκος Theoc. 22.180.'

**ἀναισθησία 2**, after '*obtuseness*' read 'Isoc. 7.9, D. 18.128, 22.64, al.'

**ἀναίσθητος I 1**, after '*feeling*' insert 'Hp.*VM* 15'; for 'Thrasymach. 1' read 'Thrasym. 1 D.-K.' and transfer to sense 2, adding there 'Isoc. 15.218, D. 5.15, 17.22, 18.120'

**ἀναισῑμόω**, line 4, for '*he used up*' read '*she used up*'

**ἀναισίμωμα**, add 'Call.*fr.* 196.45 Pf.'

**ἀνᾱΐσσω**, line 7, after 'Hp.' insert '*Morb.Sacr.* 1'

**ἀναιωρέω**, after 'Nonn.*D.*' insert '2.457'

**ἀνακᾰθαίρω**, after lemma insert 'Dor. ἀγκοθ-, v. infra' **II 3**, add 'εἴ τι πρότερον ἀτελὲς ἢ συγκεχυμένον ἐδόκει, τοῦτο καὶ ἀνακαθᾶραι καὶ τέλειον ἐξ ἀτελοῦς ἀποφῆναι Just.*Nov.* 7 pr. **b** *expound* or *declare*, [δόγματα] Porph.*Plot.* 3.'

**ἀνακάθαρσις**, after 'εως' insert 'Dor. ἀνκαθάρσιος (gen.) *IG* 4²(1).106.25; ἀγκ-, *IAskl.Epid.* 52.A25, rest. in 32 (both Epid., iv BC)'

**ἀνακαινίζω**, line 2, after 'Hsch.Mil. 4.33' insert 'ἀνεκενίσθη εἰ (= ἡ) γέφυρα *BE* 1972.293, *MAMA* 7.190 (both Hadrianoupolis), *SEG* 37.1442 (Dura, ii AD)'

**ἀνακᾰλέω**, line 1, after 'ἀγκ-' insert 'ὀγκ-' **II 1**, after '*appeal to*' insert 'Πάον' ὀνκαλέοντες ἐκάβολον Sapph. 44.33 L.-P.' **2**, after 'Lys. 15.2' insert '*proscribe*, App.*BC* 4.25; *be invited*, ἀνακαλεῖσθαι δὲ αὐ[τὸ]ν εἰς προεδριὰν ὑπὸ τοῦ ἱεροκήρυκος *Amyzon* 3.13 (iii BC)' **III 1**, add '**b** *revoke* legal transaction, *Cod.Just.* 1.3.55.2.'

**ἀνακᾰλυπτήρια II**, add 'Pherecyd.Syr. 2 D.-K., Sch.E.*Ph.* 682'

***ἀνακᾰλυψις**, εως, ἡ, *disclosure*, Plu. 2.70f, 518d.

***ἀνακάρδιον**, τό, *upturned twig* of the mulberry tree, Cyran. 1.12.27 K.

**ἀνακάς**, delete the entry.

***ἀνακάταξις**, εως, ἡ, *refracture*, Paul.Aeg. 6.109 (162.27 H.).

**Ἀνάκεια**, τά, add 'Ἀνάκια *IG* 1³.258.6 (v BC)'

**ἀνάκειμαι I 1 b**, transfer 'χρύσεοί κ' .. 10.33' to follow '(Pl.)*R.* 592b' in previous sense **II**, line 7, for 'εἰς θάνατον .. 18.1.1' read '**b** w. εἰς, *to be assigned* or *given over* to, εἰς θάνατον ἦν ἀνακείμενα τοῖς ἀλογήσασι J.*AJ* 17.6.5, λιμὸς εἰς ὑστάτην ἀνακείμενος ἀναισχυντίαν 18.1.1, εἰς τὸ σωφρονεῖν ἀνέκειτο ἡ ἐπιτήδευσις τοῦ βίου 18.3.4; so w. ἐπί, τὴν ἐπὶ τῷ θανεῖν ἀνακειμένην ἐπιστολήν 18.8.9, D.C. 37.18; also w. dat., *to be assigned* to, Plu.*Arist.* 15, Lyc. 1.' **III**, add '**b** *to be laid up* by sickness, *PMich.*xi 624.27 (vi AD).'

**Ἀνακεῖον**, τό, add 'Ἀνάκιον *IG* 2².1400.44'

***ἀνάκεστος**, ον, = ἀνήκεστος, perh. erron., on analogy of εὐάκεστος, Hp.ap.Erot. (ἀνήκ- in *Acut.* 39); for 'ἀνᾱκ-' see °ἀνήκεστος.

**ἀνακεφαλαιόομαι**, add '**2** *recapitulate*, *Ep.Eph.* 1.10.'

**ἀνακήρυξις**, after '*proclamation*' insert '*SEG* 33.639 (Rhodes, ii/i BC)'

**ἀνακηρύσσω**, after 'Att. -ττω' insert 'dial. ἀνακᾱρ-, *IG* 5(2).16.6 (Tegea, iii BC), *SEG* 23.208.24 (Messene, i AD); ὀγκᾱρ-, *IG* 12 suppl. (2).2.6 (Mytilene, iii BC)'

***Ἀνάκια**, v. ‡Ἀνάκεια.

***Ἀνάκιον**, v. ‡Ἀνάκειον.

**ἀνακίρνᾰμαι I**, for 'φιλίας .. friendship' read 'χρῆν .. μετρίας εἰς ἀλλήλους φιλίας θνητοὺς ἀνακίρνασθαι'

**ἀνακλάζω**, add '**b** of a cry, *arouse*, τίς ἠχ[ο]ς ἡμᾶς ἐκ δόμων ἀνέκλαγε; *Trag.adesp.* 649.11 K.-S.'

**ἀνακλέπτω**, after lemma insert 'perh. 3 sg. imper. in ἐμὲ μεδὲς ἀνκλετέτο *SEG* 34.1019 (Kylix, Salernum, vi BC)'

***ἀνακληρόω**, *reallot*, Sch.Pi.*O.* 110a.

**ἀνάκλητος**, after lemma insert '**I** *recalled*, S.*fr.* 1008 R.; ἐν ἀνακλήτῳ (λόγῳ) formula in financial documents, app. of the amount carried forward at the end of each month, *CASA* 3.43ff. (Tauromenium, v. Dubois *IGDS* no. 186). **II**'

**ἀνάκλῖμα**, add '**II** part of a ship where the κυβερνήτης reclines (κατακλίνεται), Poll. 1.90 (written ἄγκλιμα).'

**ἀνακλιντήριον**, delete the entry; v. °ἀνακλιτήριον.

**ἀνάκλιντρον**, delete 'also' and after 'τό' insert 'cf. °ἐπίκλιντρον'

**ἀνάκλῐσις II**, at end for '*bench* .. 277*d*' read 'perh. *chair with back*, *IG* 1³.423.209, *JHS* 12.232 (Cilicia)'

***ἀνακλῐτήριον**, τό, *back* or *armrest of a chair* or *couch*, Erot. s.v. ἀνακλισμοῦ, *Hist.Aug.* 2.5.7; *chair with back* or *armrests*, *SEG* 17.545.5 (Pisidia, Rom.imp.).

**ἀνακλύζω 2**, before 'Plu. 2.590f' insert 'Cleobul.ap.D.L. 1.90, ἀνακλύζῃ δὲ θάλασσα (vv.ll. ἀναβλύζῃ, περικλύζῃ)'

***ἀνακολᾰφή**, ἡ, = Lat. *subsumen*, *Gloss.*

***ἀνακολᾰφίς**, ίδος, ἡ, = Lat. *replica*, *Gloss.*

**ἀνακολλητικός**, after '*glueing*' insert 'or *sticking*'

**⁺ἀνακολυμβάω**, *dive and fetch up*, Thphr.*HP* 4.6.4, *Inscr.Délos* 440*A*52 (ii BC).

**ἀνακομβόομαι**, delete the entry.

***ἀνακομβόω**, *tuck up*, χιτῶνας *Vit.Aesop.*(W) 77a: med., *Gp.* 10.83.1.

**ἀνακομῐδή 4**, after '*bringing up*' insert '*conveyance*, ἀ. τοῦ .. σίτου *SEG* 24.344 (Oropus, ii BC)'

***ἀνακόμῐσις**, εως, ἡ, *restoration*, *Stud.Pal.* 20.114.11 (v AD).

***ἀνακομιστής**, ου, ὁ, *conveyer* (of goods), *POxy.* 3124.9 (AD 322).

***ἀνακομιστικός**, ή, όν, *bringing back*, Hsch. s.v. νόστιμον ἦμαρ.

***ἀνακοπάζω**, *check*, *restrain*, *Inscr.Cret.* 3.iv 37.14 (Itanos, i BC; ἀγκ-).

**ἀνακόπτω I 3**, after 'Thphr.*Char.* 25.2' add '*propel* a ship *back to land*, Arat. 346'

**ἀνακοσμέω**, add '**2** *decorate*, στεφάνναιν .. ἀ. Corinn. 1(*a*) i 27 P. (dub.).'

**ἀνακουφίζω**, for 'of the ship of state' read 'fig., of a drowning man' add '**II** *subtract*, *Cat.Cod.Astr.* 8(1).146.15.'

**ἀνακούφισμα**, for '*a relief*' read '*raising the body* from a prone position by using the arms'

***ἀνακούω**, *listen further*, Sch.S.*El.* 81 P. (S. codd. κἀνακούσωμεν, edd. κἀπ-).

***ἀνακραδαίνω**, aor. part. -δάνας gloss on ἀμπεπαλών, *PBerol.* in E. Ziebarth *Aus der antiken Schule*² (Bonn 1913) p. 32.

**ἀνακραδεύω**, add '(ἀνακραδάω La.)'

**ἀνακράζω 1**, line 5, after 'etc.' insert 'τηλικοῦτ' ἀνεκράζετε .. ὥστε D. 21.215'; line 7, for 'a relat.' read 'ὡς'; line 8, delete 'τηλικαῦτ' .. 215' **2**, after 'animals' insert 'Stesich. *S*88 ii 21 (p. 185 D.)'

**ἀνακρεμαστήρ**, for 'Orib. 54.31.20' read 'Orib. 24.31.20'

***Ἀνακρεοντικός**, όν, *Anacreontic*, of a metre, Isid.*Etym.* 1.39.7.

***ἀνακρίμνημι**, = ἀνακρεμάννυμι, Pi.*Pae.* 8.79; cf. °κρίμνημι.

**ἀνακρΐνω I 2**, after 'Antipho 2.3.2' insert 'γενήν Call.*fr.* 203.54 Pf.'

**ἀνακροτέω**, at end for 'in Hexam.ap.Diogenian. 3.67' read 'in hex.in Diogenian. 3.97'

**ἀνακρούω I 1**, after 'Aen.Tact. 18.6' insert 'Arat. 193'; line 3, after 'Plu.*Alc.* 2' insert 'cf. δοχμὸς ἀνακρούων θηρὸς πάτον Nic.*Th.* 479; *put* a ship *astern*, νῆα A.R. 4.1650; fig., ἀ. τοὺς μνηστῆρας τῆς ἐς τὴν Πηνελόπην ὕβρεως Aristid.Quint. 2.10 (p. 74.19 W.-I.)' **2**, delete 'ἀπὸ .. 4.1650' **II 1**, add '**b** *pull back*, κάλωας A.R. 1.1277; ἡνίας Sch.Ar.*Av.* 648b.'

**ἀνακρύπτω**, add '(cj. ἐνέκρυφε)'

***ἀνακρωτόφονος**, gloss on γυρτεύς, Hsch.

***ἀνακτένιον**, τό, kind of comb, *PRyl.* 627.168 (iv AD).

***ἀνάκτερος**, α, ον, Myc. *wa-na-ka-te-ro*, *royal.*

**ἀνάκτησις**, add 'written ἄγχτησις *PRein.* 7.14 (ii BC)'

**ἀνακτητικός**, for '*recuperative*' read '*restorative*', w. gen., *from*, σίκυς .. ἀ. λειποθυμιῶν ὀσφραινόμενος Dsc. 2.135'

**⁺ἀνακτΐτης**, v. °ἀναγκίτης.

**ἀνακτορία**, after lemma insert 'Ion. -ίη'; after 'A.R. 1.839' insert 'Parth. in *Suppl.Hell.* 640.1, *Orac.Sib.* 4.66, epigr.ap.Paus. 10.12.6'

***ἀνακτορίζω**, *to be ruler*, of an emerald, ὁ δὲ .. ὑποχλωρίζων λέγεται σμάραγδος ἀνακτορίζων Socr.Dion.*Lith.* 1.13 G. (†ὑακτορίζων† codd., v. H.-S.).

**⁺ἄνακτωρ**, ορος, ὁ, *ruler*, *lord*, usu. of gods, A.*Ch.* 357, E.*IT* 1414, ἀ. πόλεως (of Astyanax), *Tr.* 1217, ἀνάκτορι θήκατο τέχνας (i.e. Poseidon) *AP* 6.4 (Leon.Tarent.); pl., Cerc. 4.38, Ptol.*Tetr.* 122.

**ἀνακυλίνδω**, read '**ἀνακῠλινδέω**'

**ἀνακύπτω**, line 3, after 'Thphr.*Char.* 11.3' insert 'Men.*Dysc.* 537'

***ἀνακώσιος**, ον, adj. fr. ἄναξ in dialect of Rhegium, Sch. D.T. p. 542 H., cf. Ibyc. 60(*a*) P., and χαριτώσιος.

**ἀνᾰλᾰλάζω**, after 'E.*Ph.* 1395' insert 'Astyd. 2a.16 S.'

**ἀναλαμβάνω I 8**, add '*Cod.Just.* 1.3.45.14' **II 1**, add '**b** w. ref. to confiscation by the Ptolemaic kings, *SB* 8008.31 (260 BC), τὰ ἴδια αὐτῶν ἀναληφθήσεται εἰς τὸ βασιλικὸν *UPZ* 112 viii 18 (203/2 BC), *PTeb.* 1001.15 (ii BC).' **3**, add '**b** med., *recover*, *be convalescent*, Gal. 10.679.7.'

***ἀναλδαίνω**, *make to spring up*, Nonn.*D.* 40.390.

**ἀναλδής**, after 'Hp.*Aër.* 15' insert 'of stars, Arat. 394'; for 'ἄρουραι .. *fruiting*' read 'neut. pl. as adv., *feebly*, φυταλιαί .. ἀναλδέα φυλλιόωσαι'

**ἀναλεαίνω**, add '**II** ἀναλεαίνει· σχολάζει. Ταραντῖνοι Hsch. (La.; cf. ἀναλεῖ).'

**ἀναλέγω II**, after 'Plu.*Lyc.* 1' insert 'μῆκος δὲ ἀμήχανον χρόνου ἐν βραχεῖ ἀναλεγόμενον Max.Tyr. 28(22).5e' **III 1**, after '*read through*' insert '*AP* 9.63 (Asclep.)' add '**b** act., *read out*, *recite*, *SEG* 31.985.D14 (Teos, v BC), D.C. 37.43.2, 53.11.1.'

***ἀναλείωσις**, εως, ἡ, *covering with powder*, ὅταν μετὰ τοῦ κουφολίθου ἀναλείωσιν ξηραίνεται Pelag.Alch. 254.

***ἀναλεκτήριον**, *bag* or *other container*, Aq. 1*Ki.* 17.40.

**ἀναλέκτης**, add 'Sen.*Ep.* 27.7'

**ἀνάλεκτος**, add 'παιδία ἀ. *SB* 4425.3.21 (ii AD)'

**ἀνάλημμα III**, for '*sun-dial* .. 9.7.7' read '*projection* on a plane of circles and points on the celestial sphere, Hero *Dioptr.* 35, Ptol.*Anal.* p. 202.26 H., al., Papp. 4.246 H.; used for the construction of a sun-dial, Vitr. 9.6.1, 7.6'; for '*CIG* 2681' read '*Ilasos* 249' and transfer to section II.

***ἀναλημπτός**, ή, όν, *confiscated*, *PSI* 104.14 (ii AD), *PMich.*inv. 148ᵛ 1.10 (ii AD, *ZPE* 27.127).

***ἀναλημπτρίς**, v. ‡ἀναληπτρίς.

***ἀναλημψιακός**, ή, όν, *of* or *belonging to a reception* (ἀνάληψις I 6), *corona analempsiaca CIL* 14.2215.11 (Nemi).

**ἀναληπτρίς**, before 'Gal.' insert 'Sor.*Fasc.* 41, 42 (-λημπ-)' and after '323' add '*Hippiatr.* 50 O.-H.'

***ἀναλήψιμος** (written -λήμψ-), ον, of goods, *liable to be reclaimed*, *resumable*, *SB* 9016.1.20 (ii AD).

**ἀνάληψις I 1**, after '(Hp.)*Off.* 9' insert 'Gal. 18(2).414.1, 416.7, 417.1 al.' **3**, before '*acquirement*' insert '*taking up* or *on*, φορτίων *Peripl.M.Rubr.* 55' **6**, add 'δόντα καὶ ἀ. καὶ ταυροκαθάψια *SEG* 32.660 (Thrace, ii/iii AD)' **II 1**, add '*recovery* of things previously paid out, Just.*Nov.* 1.3'

**ἀνᾱλίσκω**, line 10, pf. pass., add 'ἀνέλōται *SEG* 35.13 (Attica, early v BC)' **I 1**, line 17, after '(D.) 18.66' insert 'περὶ αὐτοὺς *Cod.Just.* 1.3.41.14'

***ἀνᾰλῐφος**, ον, τὸ -ον *lack of the means of anointing oneself*, *Ilasos* 248.44 (ii AD).

**ἄναλκις**, add 'w. gen., ὅπλων *lacking strength of weapons*, Opp.*H.*1.578'

**ἀναλλοίωτος**, at end for 'Thphr.*CP* 6.10.1' read 'Thphr.*CP* 6.10.3'

**ἄναλλος**, after '*topsy-turvy*' insert 'v.l. for ἔναλλος in Theoc. 1.134, *AP* 5.299.9 (Agath.)'

**⁺ἀνάλμῠρος**, ον, ἀνάλμυροι· ἄναλοι ἢ οὐχ ἁλμυροί Dios.Gloss.ap.Gal. 19.79.

**ἀναλογία I**, add '**3** *proportionate share*, *PMichael.* 42 A, *POxy.* 1892, *SB* 9153 (all vi AD).'

**ἀναλογιστικός**, after '*analogical*' insert 'Epicur.*fr.* [26]28.6, [31]16.23 A.'

***ἀνᾰλόητος**, ον, *unthreshed*, *PMich.*inv. 3207.2 (*ZPE* 100.74, ii BC).

**ἀναλύζω**, delete 'lit. .. hence'; for 'vulg. ἀνωλύζεσκε' read 'ἀνωλύζεσκε codd.'

**ἀνάλῠσις I 1**, add 'perh., from mortality, *POxy.* 3010.29 (ii AD)'

***ἀναλῠτέος**, *that must be dissolved*, Plot. 4.7.2.

**ἀναλῠτικός**, add '**3** in magic, *releasing* from a spell, *PMich.*III 154 (iii/iv AD).'

***ἀναλυτρόομαι**, *redeem* a pledge, *PMasp.* 23.21 (vi AD).

***ἀναλύτρωσις**, εως, ἡ, *redemption*, *PMasp.* 167.13 (vi AD), *Stud.Pal.* 3.339.4 (vi AD).

**ἀναλύω** (A), delete the entry.

**ἀναλύω** (B) **I 2**, add 'med., ἐπὶ τôι ἀλλυσαμένōι ἔμēν *Leg.Gort.* 6.49, al., cf. Hsch. s.v. ἀναλυσάμενος' **II 1**, transfer 'in med.' to follow '*unloose*' and after '*Del.* 237' insert 'μίτρας for sexual intercourse, Hes.*fr.* 1.4 M.-W.; μίτρην in child-bearing, Call.*Del.* 222' **5**, before '*reduce*' insert 'math.' and after '*Geom.* 5.8' insert '*PMich.*III 145.3 iii 2, 3 vi 6' **7**, add '[ἀλλ' ὅτε δὴ τριτάτας] τεκέων ἀνέλυον ἀνάγκας *SEG* 25.752 (epigr., Callatis, ii BC)' **II**, delete the section (v.II 2), and substitute '*unsettle*, Philostr.*VA* 5.35.' **III 2**, add 'ἐξ εὐωχίας, Call.*Dieg.* iv.38 (*fr.* 102 Pf.)'

**ἀναλφάβητος**, add 'Ath. 176e, *App.Anth.* 5.12'

**ἀνάλωμα**, add 'see also ἄλωμα'

**ἀνᾰλωσις I**, add '*Bull.Soc.Alex.* 10.28.28 (ἀνήλ-, i BC)'

**ἀνᾰλωτος**, line 2, after '(Hdt.) 8.51' insert 'of the Nile, ἀ. .. καὶ δύσμαχος τοῖς ἐπιβουλεύουσιν Isoc. 11.13'

**ἀναμαρμαίρω**, for '*move quickly*' read '*cause to blaze*, ὅτε .. ἀναμαρμαίρουσιν πῦρ ὀλοὸν πιμπρᾶσαι' and after 'A.R. 3.1300' add '(pap. ἀναμορμύρουσιν)'

***ἀνᾰμαρτέω**, *to be sinless*, Herm.*fr.* 7.2 N.-F.

**ἀναμαστεύω**, after '(for fugitives)' insert '*IRhod.Peraia* 357.9 (ii BC)'

**ἀναμασχᾰλιστήρ**, for pres. def. read 'article of female dress, perh. the same as, or similar to, ἀναληπτρίς' and add '*IG* 2².1408.5 (prob.), Hsch.'

**⁺ἀναμᾰχομαι**, *renew the fight*, *fight over again*, Hdt. 5.121, 8.109.2, Th. 7.61.3. **2** *fight* an argument *over again*, ἀ. τὸν λόγον Pl.*Hp.Ma.* 286d, *Phd.* 89c. **II** *fight back and retrieve* a defeat, περιπέτειαν Plb. 1.55.5, νίκην Memn. 58 (38.7 J.), Jul.*Or.* 1.24c; transf., *make good* loss, damage, etc., ἡ φύσις τὴν φθορὰν ἀ. Arist.*GA* 755ᵃ31, ἀ. τὰ ἁμαρτανόμενα Thphr.*CP* 3.2.5, Aret.*CD* 2.6 (165.9 H.).

**ἀναμείγνῡμι**, line 1, for 'B.*fr.* 16' read 'B.*fr.* 20B.9' and add 'ὀμμ(όν-) Sapph. 2.15, 44.24, 30' **II 1**, at beginning insert 'μύρρα καὶ κασία λίβανός τ' ὀνεμείχνυτο Sapph. 44.30 L.-P.'

**ἀναμερισμός**, add '**II** *distribution* of burdens, *PSI* 684.12 (iv/v AD).'

**ἀναμετρητής**, add '*SB* 4295.3, Ptol.*Judic.* 4.5'

**ἀνάμῐγα**, for '*promiscuously*, *confusedly*' read '*so as to be mingled together*'; after '*IG* 5(1).726' insert 'Theoc.*Ep.* 5.3, Κυκλάδες ἄμμιγα νῆσοι Heph.Astr. 1.1.102' and delete 'also τινός ib. 22'

**ἀναμίγδην**, add 'w. dat., Nic.*Al.* 557'

**ἀναμιμνήσκω**, line 2, for 'Sapph.*Supp.* 23.10' read 'Sapph. 94.10

L.-P.' **II 1**, add '*recollect*, τετάρτῃ .. ἡμέρᾳ ἀναμιμνήσκομαι ἐμαυτοῦ καὶ αἰσθάνομαι οὐ γῆς εἰμι Pl.*Mx.* 235c'
**ἀναμίξ**, after 'Th. 3.107' insert 'Arat. 104, *AP* 4.1.8 (Mel.)'
**ἀναμίσγω**, lines 3/4, for 'γέλως .. 7.3 P.' read '[πλοῦτος] ἀναμίσγεται ἄτῃ Sol. 13.13 W., Call.*fr.* 24.3 Pf., *Del.* 217'
**ἀναμισθόομαι**, delete the entry.
***ἀναμισθόω**, Dor. ἀμμ-, *let anew*, *IG* 11(2).142.5 (Delos, iv BC); pass. *Tab.Heracl.* 1.111.
**ἀνάμνησις 2**, for this section read '*commemoration* of a dead person, *TAM* 4(1).272 (Bithynia, Rom.imp.); cf. τοῦτο ποιεῖτε εἰς τὴν ἐμὴν ἀνάμνησιν *Ev.Luc.* 22.20, 1*Ep.Cor.* 11.24' transferring 'Lxx *Nu.* 10.10' to section 1.
**ἀναμνηστικός I**, add 'adv. -κῶς, *by way of recollection*, Alcin.*Intr.* p. 178.7 H.' **II**, for this section read '*suggestive*, *reminiscent*, Demetr.*Eloc.* 287. **2** *indicative of the past*, σημεῖα Gal. 1.313.'
**+ἀναμοχλεύω**, *unbar* gates, E.*Med.* 1317. **II** *raise by leverage*, ἀρθρεμβόλοις ὀργάνοις .. τὰς πόδας .. ἐξ ἁρμῶν ἀναμοχλεύοντες ἐξεμέλιζον Lxx 4*Ma.* 10.5, τὴν Ὄσσαν Luc.*Cont.* 4; in reducing dislocations, Gal. 18(1).403.7.
**ἀνάμπυξ**, add 'Myc. *a-na-pu-ke* (pl.)'
***ἀναμφιβόητος**, ον, perh. *not renowned*, οὐδ' ἀναφιβό[η]τον *GDRK* 27ʳ.22.
**ἀναμφίβολος**, adv. -ως, add '*without question*, *Stud.Pal.* 3.124.4 (*ZPE* 75.256), ἀ. καὶ ἀναντιρρήτως *PMasp.* 116.6 (vi AD)'
**ἀναμφίλογος**, adv., after 'X.*Cyr.* 8.1.44' insert '*Oec.* 6.3' and after 'id.*Ages.* 2.12' insert '*Oec.* 4.7'
**ἀναμφισβήτητος**, adv., add '*PGen.* 103 I 19 (ii AD)'
**ἀναμφόδαρχος**, for 'ἀμφόδαρχος' read 'ἀμφοδάρχης'
**ἀνανδριεῖς**, for 'cf. ἀναριεῖς' read 'v. Ἐνάρεες'
**ἀνανεάζω**, for 'Phyrn.' read 'Phryn.' and for 'Lxx 4*Ma.* 7.14' read 'Lxx 4*Ma.* 7.13'
**ἀνανέμω 2**, after '*over*' insert '*GVI* 1210.2 (Eretria, v BC), perh. in graffito on vase, *ho* δὲ γράψας τὸν ἀννέμο(ν)τα πυγιξεῖ *SEG* 35.1009 (Sicily, early v BC)'
**ἀνανεόομαι I**, add '*restore* (buildings, etc.), *SEG* 24.880 (Thrace, iii AD), *TAM* 4(1).355, *Salamine* 212 (vi AD), *Cod.Just.* 8.10.12.2. **2** *reaffirm*, an obligation, *Zeitschr.d.Savigny-Stiftung* 56.101 (Dura, i AD).'
**ἀνάνευσις**, delete '(νέομαι .. Hsch.'
**ἀνανεύω II**, after '*throw the head up*' insert 'to God, in prayer, *PKöln* 111.6 (v/vi AD)'
**ἀνανέωσις I**, add '**2** *reaffirmation*, of an obligation, *POxy.* 1105.21 (i AD); so perh. ib. 274.20 (v. supr.). **3** *restoration* of building, *CPHerm.* 95.15 (iii AD), *POxy.* 1752.2 (iv AD), *SEG* 30.1787 A, *Salamine* 212 (both vi AD), *Cod.Just.* 1.12.17.1.'
**ἀνανεωτής**, add 'as imperial title, ἐπὶ τοῦ θεοφιλεστάτου καὶ ἀνανεωτοῦ τῶν ἱερῶν δεσπότου *SEG* 31.641 (iv AD)'
**ἀνανήφω**, transfer 'D.Chr. 4.77' to follow '2*Ep.Ti.* 2.16' and add to it 'M.Ant. 6.31'
***ἀνάνοικτος**, gloss on ἀχανής (ἀχανανεῖ cod.), Hsch.
***ἀναντώδης**, ες, *uphill*, *steep*, Hsch. s.v. κνῆμαι.
**ἄναξ** line 2, after 'etc.' insert 'Cypr. *wa-na-xe* *ICS* 211, Myc. *wa-na-ka*' **I**, at end for 'The irreg. .. gods' read 'For the irreg. voc. ἄνα, v.h.v.' **II**, line 5, for '(' substitute ',' and lines 6/7, for 'cf. Isoc. .. 911)' read 'esp. in Cyprus, Clearch. 25, cf. Isoc. 9.72, *ICS* 211, 220(b)2; of Creon, S.*OT* 85, cf. 911' **III**, add 'Mitchell *N.Galatia* 25'
***ἀνάξιππος**, ὁ, ἡ, *master* or *mistress of horses*, Λάρισα B. 14B.10 S.-M.
***ἀναξίχορος**, ον, *ruling the dance*, κοῦραι prob. in B.*fr.* 65(a).11 S.-M.
***ἀναξοή**, Dor. -ξοά, ἡ, *polishing*, *smoothing*, rest. in *IG* $4^2$(1).102.66 (Epid., iv BC).
**ἀναξυρίδες**, line 1, for 'eastern nations' read 'Persians'; line 2, after 'X.*An.* 1.5.8' insert 'ἀ. Περσικαί Max.Tyr. 20(14).8c' and delete 'Hdt. 1.71, cf.'; line 3, for 'Hdt. 3.87, etc.' read 'Hdt. 7.64.2'
***ἀναπαιστήρ**, ῆρος, ὁ, *door-knocker*, *IG* $4^2$(1).102.79 (Epid., iv BC) (ἀνπ-).
**ἀνάπαλιν**, add '**V** *upside down*, ἀ. πέτεσθαι Ael.*NA* 10.14.'
**ἀναπαλλοτριώτος**, delete the entry (read ἀ[νεξαλλο]τριώτους, see *AJPh* 62.197).
**ἀναπάλλω**, line 3, after '*Ra.* 1358' insert 'so intr., ἀμπάλλοντι id.*Lys.* 1310'
**ἀνάπαλος**, delete 'κατ' ἄμπαλον .. (Thess.)' **II**, for 'Ath. 14.631d' read 'Ath. 14.631b'
**ἀναπαριάζω**, for 'Ephor. 107' read 'Ephor. 63 J., prob. in Lib.*Ep.* 555.3 (ἀνεπυρρίσσε codd.)'
**ἀνάπαυλις**, add 'perh. also ἄμπ-, rest. in *SEG* 30.1444 (?ii AD)'
**ἀνάπαυμα I 2**, add 'ἄμπαυμα μόχθων καὶ φύλαγμα σωμ[άτων] ἔθεντο *TAM* 4(1).303' **II 2**, add 'ἀπὸ ἀναπαύματος φακοῦ *PWürzb.* 14.18 (ii AD), ἀπὸ ἀ. λαχανοσπέρμου *PBouriant* 17.15 (iii AD), *PCair.Isidor.* 99.24, 100.18 (iii AD)'
**ἀνάπαυσις 1**, add 'of the repose of death, Mitchell *N.Galatia* 467, *SEG* 26.1672 (Jerusalem, v AD), *ICilicie* 21 (vi AD)'
**ἀναπαυστήριος II 2**, add 'τὸ τῶν νοσούντων ἀ. Procop.*Aed.* 5.3.20; of the tomb, *TAM* 4(2).269'
***ἀναπαύστρια**, ἡ, *giver of rest*, of Easter Day, Leont.Byz.*HP* 1.2.6.
**ἀναπαύω II 2 c**, ἀ. alone, add '*SEG* 29.640, 643, 644; ἀνεπάη ὁ μακάριος Τιμόθεος ib. 34.1466; ἀ. τῇ ψυχῇ ib. 31.1419 (both Palestine, iii/iv and vi AD)' add '**e** μετά τινος *sleep* with (sexually), E.*Cyc.* 582, Macho 286 G., Plu.*Alex.* 2.'
**ἀναπείθω**, line 1, for 'Arc. ἀμπ-' read 'Arc. 3 sg. aor. subj. ἀμπείσῃ (sense 3 infra)' **2**, add 'app. *exact*, *demand*, *Cod.Just.* 10.19.9'
**ἀναπελάσας**, for 'ὀλιγ-ηπελίη' read 'εὐηπελής'
**ἀναπέμπω II 3**, add 'τὸ δὲ μὴ νῦν κατὰ Ἀττικοὺς ἀναπέμπεται (i.e. μή νυν) Sch. E. *Med.* 584'
***ἀναπεσσεύομαι**, med. or pass. part., perh. of counter or sim., *move along*, *PMichael.* 4.4 (ii AD).
**ἀναπετάννυμι**, last line, after '*Stoic.* 1.58' insert 'ἀναπεπταμένη .. βλασφημία Plu.*Them.* 21'
**ἀναπηδάω**, line 5, after 'ib. 1.3.9' insert 'in mounting a horse, ἐπὶ τοὺς ἵππους ἀναπηδᾶν id.*Eq.Mag.* 1.5, 17'
***ἀναπηδύω**, v. ‡ἀναπιδύω.
**ἀναπηρτισμένως**, add '(cj.); v.l. ἀναπηρτημένως (*fr.* 298a Marrone)'
**ἀναπιδύω 1**, add 'Lxx *Pr.* 18.4 (sp. -πηδ-)'
**ἀναπιεσμός 1**, for '= foreg.' read '*forcing up*'
**ἀναπίμπλημι II 2**, after 'Pl.*Ap.* 32c' insert 'τὴν πόλιν ἡμῶν πονηρᾶς δόξης ἀναπλήσει D. 20.50, 24.205, Aeschin. 2.88, Din. 1.25' and transfer here 'D. 20.28' fr. section II 1; after 'so in pass.' insert 'Aeschin. 2.72, Procl.*Inst.* 13 D.'
**ἀναπίπτω 5 b**, after 'sickness' insert 'Arr.*Epict.* 2.18.3'
**ἀνάπλασις**, add 'Gal. 13.824.5'
**ἀναπλέκω 1**, add 'ἀ. βοστρύχους D.H.*Th.* 19'; for 'ἀμπλ-' read 'ἀνπεπλεγμένας' **2**, after 'metaph.' insert 'διαλόγους D.H.*Comp.* 25'
**ἀνάπλευσις I**, add 'Crito ap.Gal. 13.794.10'
**ἀναπληρόω I 6**, add '*complete*, *finish*, τὰ αὐτὰ ἔργα ἀναπληροῦν *Cod.Just.* 8.10.12.9a'
***ἀναπληρωματικός**, *expletive*, of particles, Charis. p. 226 K.
***ἀναπλωτικός**, ή, όν, *forming into a simple whole*, Procl.*in R.* 1.90.5 K.
**ἀναπνέω IV**, for '*breathe* the horse' read '*allow* the horse *to breathe*' add '**2** *rouse to consciousness*, Nic.*Th.* 547 (s.v.l.).'
**ἀναπνοή IV**, after '*breathing organ*' insert 'αὗται (sc. αἱ φλέβες) .. ἡμῖν εἰσιν ἀναπνοαὶ τοῦ σώματος τὸν ἠέρα ἐς σφᾶς ἕλκουσαι Hp.*Morb.Sacr.* 4'
**ἀναποικός**, delete the entry.
***ἀναπόγραπτος**, ον, *unregistered*, *IG* $2^2$.1100.33 (Athens, ii AD).
***ἀναποδέω**, = ἀναποδίζω II, ἀναποδοῦσιν ἐπὶ τὴν μονάδα Plu. 2.876f; ἀπὸ τῆς μονάδος ἀναποδῶν ibid., cf. Pythag.ap.Stob. 1.10.12.
**ἀναποδίζω II**, delete 'ἐπὶ τὴν μονάδα .. (corr. Heeren)'
**ἀναποδιστικός**, before '*in retardation*' insert '*retrograde*, of planets, Ptol.*Tetr.* 113'
***ἀναποδόομαι**, *grow new feet*, in quot., of scorpions, Lyd.*Mag.* 1.42.
**ἀναποδόω**, delete the entry.
***ἀναπομπαζόμενον**· ἐν ἀναπολήσει γινόμενον Hsch.
**ἀναπομπή**, add '**III** *divorce* of wife by husband, *CPR* 24.30 (ii AD).'
**ἀναπόμπιμος 1**, add '*IG* $1^3$.21 (Athens, 450/449 BC)'
**ἀναπομπός II**, for '*distributor* of bread to soldiers' read '*one who delivers* supplies, etc.'
**ἀναπορεύομαι**, add '**b** πολλὴ ἀκαθαρσία ἀναπορεύεται καὶ λεύκη comm. in Alc. 306(14) ii 10 L.-P., where ἀ. glosses ὀνστείχει.'
**ἀναπόρριφος**, after '(ἀπορρίπτω)' insert '(sp. ἀναπόριφος *BGU* 446.5, 2049.12, al.)'; after '*free from blemish*' insert 'ὄνος'; add 'δοῦλος *SB* 7533.50 (ii AD). **2** *irrefundable*, δραχμαί *PSarap.* 10.8 (ii AD), ἀρραβῶνα *BGU* 446.5.'
***ἀναπότρεπτος**, ον, *not to be departed from*, *PMasp.* 98.4 (vi AD).
**ἀναπράσσω**, after '*OGI* 669.20' insert '(Egypt, i AD)'
***ἀναπροζύμιον**, τό, *product of fermentation*, Iambl.Alch. 286.10.
***ἀναπρηνίζω**, *knock down*, *lay flat*, cj. in Nonn.*D.* 18.271.
**ἀναπτύσσω**, line 4, before 'δέλτων' insert 'ἀ. πίνακα A.*fr.* 281a.22 R.' and for 'E.*fr.* 370' read 'E.*fr.* 369'; line 5, after '*Ion* 39' insert 'φαρέτρας πῶμα B. 5.75 S.-M.'; line 7, after '*Im.* 2.17' insert 'fig., εἰ καὶ αὐτὸ τὸ εἶδος ἕκαστον πρὸς αὐτὸ ἀναπτύττοις Plot. 6.7.2'; line 12, after '*Tr.* 622' insert 'Antim. 22 Wy.'
**ἀνάπτω I 3**, at end after 'med.' insert 'like act., χάριν ἀ. τινί A.R. 2.214'
***ἀναπτωτήριον**, τό, item of equipment app. associated with a *candelabrum*, *CIL* 14.100.
***ἀναπυγίζω**, intensive of πυγίζω, perh. to be understood fr. ἀπυγίζει (= ?ἀπ-), *SEG* 37.817 (vase, Salerno, 480/470 BC), unless ‹ἐ›πύγιζε[ι] is to be read.
***ἀναπυριάω**, *re-subject to a vapour-bath*, Hp.*Mul.* 2.133.
***ἀναπυρριάζω**, v. °ἀναπαριάζω.

**ἀναπωλέω**, for '*CIG* 2266.11 (Delos)' read '*Inscr.Délos* 502*A*11 (ii BC)'

**ἀναπωμάζω**, add '*DAW* 1896(6).64.125 (Cilicia) (v. *ZPE* 15.46)'

**ἀνάρβηλα**, after 'δέρματα' insert '‹ξέουσι›'

**ἀναργῠρία**, before '*non numeratae pecuniae*' insert '*exceptio*'; for '*Cod.Just.* 4.21.16' read '*Cod.Just.* 4.21.16.1; ἀναργυρία alone, *Cod. Just.* 4.21.16.4'

**ἀνάργῠρος**, add 'of physician, *who practises without asking money*, ἔγραψεν .. θαύματα τῶν ἁγίων ἀναργύρων Κοσμᾶ καὶ Δαμιανοῦ Suid., s.v. Χριστόδωρος Θηβαῖος'

***ἀναρδής**, *ές*, *moistureless*, γούνατα Euph. in *Suppl.Hell.* 443.6; λοιμός hex. orac. in *ZPE* 1.185.20 (Hierapolis, iii AD).

**ἄναρθρος II**, add 'τῇ ἀνάρθρῳ φωνῇ Cels. in *Dig.* 33.10.7.2'

**ἀνᾱριστέω**, for 'v.l. in Hp.*Acut.* 28' read 'Hp.*Acut.* 30, Gal.*Consuet.* p. 13'

**ἀνᾱρίτης**, after lemma insert '(Hsch.), Dor. -τᾶς'; at end for '(ἀνηρ-)' read '(ἀνηρίτης)'

**ἀνᾰροτρίαστος**, add 'gloss on ἄσκαλα, Sch.Theoc. 10.14'

**ἀναρπάζω I**, add 'pass., of garment, δίπλακες .. ἀναρπαζόμεναι τοῖς ὤμοις *caught up* at the shoulders, Lyd.*Mag.* 2.4' **II 2**, add '**b** ἀ. εἰς ἐλευθερίαν calque of Lat. *eripere in libertatem*, *take from the owner and set free*, Just.*Nov.* 5.2.1; sim., ἀ. εἰς εὐγένειαν *give status of being ingenuus to*, ib. 22.11.'

**ἀναρραψῳδέω**, for '*begin singing*' read '*recite again*'

***ἀνάρρηγμα**, *τό*, *breach*, *EM* (s.v. ἀνὰ ῥῶγας μεγάροιο); app. *bursting out*, ὠκυάλοις ποδῶν ἀναρρήγμασιν *Trag.adesp.* 450a K.-S.

**ἀναρρίπτω II**, after 'Ar.*fr.* 673' insert 'Critias Trag. 7.27 S.'

**ἀναρρῑχάομαι**, line 3, for 'ἀρριχάομαι' read '°ἀρριχάομαι'

**ἀναρροιβδέω**, line 3, after 'cf. (Od.) 236' insert '*A.fr.* 217 R.'; line 4, after 'Paul.Aeg. 3.10' insert '*snort*, *AP* 9.769.4 (Agath.)'

**ἀναρροιζέω**, for 'Plu. 2.979e' read 'Plu. 2.979d'

**ἀνάρσιος I**, add 'perh. in pass. sense, *abhorred*, *hated*, A.R. 2.343'

***Ἀναρσιτική**, *ἡ*, cult-title of Demeter, *SEG* 33.1166 (-ειτηκή, Side, Pamphylia).

***ἀνάρτᾱς**, app. Dor. form of ἀναρίτης, Ath. 3.86b.

**ἀναρτάω I 1**, for 'χέρρας ὐμ' read 'χέρρ' ἀπύ μ'' and for 'Alc.*Supp.* 4.21' read 'Alc. 58.21 L.-P.' **2**, add 'w. gen., τῆς ἐκείνου πίστεως τὸ πᾶν ἀνηρτήσατο Just.*Nov.* 73.4'

***ἀναρτικός**, *ή*, *όν*, *used for suspension*, gloss on ἀρτάνη, Sch.S.*OT* 1266 (perh. ἀναρτ‹ητ›ικήν).

**ἀναρχᾰΐζω**, for 'πόλιν' read 'πατρίδ''

**ἀναρχία III**, add '*IG* $2^2$.1713.12, also at Thasos, *Thasos* 28.37 (-ίη, iv BC)'

**ἀνασαβρῶσαι**, add '(ἀνασαρῶσαι La.)'

**ἀνασάξιμον**, for pres. ref. read '*IG* $2^2$.1587.13, al. (iv BC)'

**ἀνασειράζω**, for '*hawser*' read '*rope, trace*, etc.' and after 'metaph.' insert 'E.*Hipp.* 237' **2**, delete '*draw* .. 237'

**ἀνασείω I**, add '**4** *shake up*' and transfer here 'ὑδρίαν *IG* $2^2$.204.36' fr. section 3 add '**III** abs., *make trouble*, Men.*Epit.* 241; = ἐπηρεάζω, Phot. s.v. ἀνασείειν.'

***ἀνασελγαίνομαι**, *behave wantonly*, codd. in Ar.*V.* 61 (ἐνασ- Herm.).

**ἀνασεύομαι**, for 'pass.' read 'med.'

***ἀνασήπω**, *leave to decompose*, Anon.Alch. 21.13.

**ἀνάσιλλος**, add 'v. °ἀνάσιμος'

**ἀνάσῑμος 1**, add 'Herod. 4.67 (v.l. ἀνάσιλλος)'

**ἀνασῑμόω**, add '**II** pass., *to be curved at the end*, Hero *fr.* 2.1.294.'

**ἀνασκάπτω 1**, add 'ἀναμέτρησις χωμάτων· ἕκαστος τῶν ἐπιχωρίων ἀνασκάπτι πέντε ναύβια *POxy.* 2847.22 (iii AD)'

**ἀνασκᾰφή**, after '*digging up*' insert '*PLille* 1$^r$.8 (iii BC)'

***ἀνάσκᾰφος**, *ον*, *accursed*, *POxy.* 1854 (vi/vii AD).

**ἀνασκευάζω**, line 3, for 'Philostr.*VS* 1.17.3' read 'Philostr.*VS* 1.17.2' **I 2**, add '*destroy* a funerary monument, *TAM* 4(1).376 (aor. inf. ἀνασκεβάσ[ε]), v. *Hellenica* 11/12.389-9' **6**, add '*reverse* a judgement, *PColl.Youtie* 66.37 (AD 253/60)'

**ἀνασκιρτάω**, before 'Philostr.' insert 'perh. *alert*'

***ἀνασκολοπισμός**, *ὁ*, *impalement*, Nigidius Figulus in Lyd.*Ost.* p. 74 W. (pl.).

***ἀνασκῠβᾰλίζω**, *defile*, *IG* $2^2$.13221 (iii AD).

**ἀνασοβέω**, after 'Pl.*Ly.* 206a' insert '*Ep.* 7.348a'; add 'transf., γυνὴ ἀνασεσοβημένη τοὺς τρόπους *SB* 9421.18 (iii AD)'

**ἀνάσπᾰσις**, add '**2** *raising*, *lifting up*, κίονος, μελάθρων *SB* 10299.140, 144 (iii AD).'

**ἀνασπαστός 1**, for 'but mostly .. Asia' read 'uprooted from one's home, country, etc.' add '**3** *that can be tightened* (of noose), *AP* 6.109 (Antip.Sid.).'

**ἀνασπάω I 6**, for '*pucker*' read '*raise*' and for 'οἱ τὰς ὀφρῦς .. Arist.' read 'οἱ τὰς ὀφρῦς ἀνεσπασμένοι πρὸς τὸν κρόταφον those *whose* eyebrows *rise* towards the temples, Arist.'

**ἀνασπογγίζω**, after '*Ulc.* 4' insert 'Antipho 5.45 (v.l. ἀπο-)'

**ἄνασσα**, line 1, for parenthesis read '(Cypr. *wa-na-sa-se* Ϝανάσσας *ICS* 6; 7.4; [Ϝ]άναΨα *IPamph.* 3.29, v/iv BC)'

**ἀνάσσω**, line 4, after 'Ϝανάσσω' insert '*SEG* 11.336 (the Larissa at Argos, vii BC); ἐϜαναssαντο Jeffery *LSAG* p. 168 no. 7 (*c.*575/550 BC)'

***ἀνάστᾱμα**, v. ‡ἀνάστημα.

***ἀναστᾰσία**, *ἡ*, *erection, construction*, *BGU* 2375.20 (i BC). **II** *removal, displacement*, Anon.astr. in *APF* 1.495.16.

**ἀνάστασις II d**, add 'ἕως ἀναστάσεως *BCH* suppl. 8 no. 119 (Thessalonica, *c.*AD 300)'

**ἀνάστᾰτος I 1**, add '*Trag.adesp.* 394 K.-S.' **2**, line 2, for 'δόμους τιθέναι' read 'οἴκους τιθέναι' **4**, delete the section transferring quot. to section I 1.

**ἀναστείχω**, add 'Aeol. **ὀνστείχει**, Alc. 306(14) ii 3 L.-P.'

**ἀνάστημα**, add 'also ἀνάσταμα *SB* 10771 (223/2 BC)' add '**6** *garrison*, Lxx *1Ki.* 10.5. **7** *hub* of wheel, Sm.*Ez.* 1.18.'

**ἀναστομόω**, line 4, for 'med., φάρυγος ἀναστόμου' read 'φάρυγος ἀναστόμου (med. ἀναστομοῦ, cj.)'

**ἀναστοφᾰ́γος**, after 'Paus. 8.42.6' add '(v.l. °ναστο-)'

**ἀναστρέφω A I 1**, line 7, for 'τῆς' read 'τὰς'; add 'τοῦτο ἔμπαλιν ἀνέστραπται *is reversed* or *inverted*, (X.) *Hier.* 4.5, cf. *Cyr.* 8.8.13, Arist.*Mech.* 854$^a$10' **II 2**, add '*PCair.Zen.* 815.4 (257 BC), *PMich. Zen.* 55.7 (240 BC), Lxx *Ge.* 8.11, 18.14' **B II**, for '*dwell in* a place' read 'med., *roam over* a place, *go up and down* in it, *sojourn*' deleting '*go to* a place *and dwell there*'; line 5, after 'Th. 8.94' insert 'στέρνοις *AP* 5.237.6 (Agath.)' **III 2**, delete the section.

**ἄναστρος**, add 'also ἄ. σφαῖρα, of the sphere beyond the fixed stars, Aristid.Quint. 3.12'

**ἀναστροφή II 3**, add 'Thess. **ὀστροφά** *BCH* 59.55 (Larissa)' **7**, for 'Plu. 2.112c' read 'Plu. 2.112d'

***ἀνασυρτόλις**, *εως*, *ἡ*, *one who lifts her clothes* (applied to a *hetaera*), Hippon. 135a W.

**ἀνασῠ́ρω I 1**, line 1, after '*up*' insert 'ὕδωρ Aq.*Is.* 30.14'; line 5, for '*obscene*' read '*exceeding the bounds of decency*' and after 'Anacr.ap.Phot. p. 123 R.' delete '*lacking in decency*' **2**, delete the section, placing quot. after 'Clearch. 14' (line 2).

**ἀνασῴζω**, lines 3/4, for '*rescue* .. 1165$^b$22' read 'ἐάν τι ἀπολωλὸς πυνθάνωνται, ἀνασῴζειν *IG* $1^3$.32.22 (Eleusis, v BC); ἀ. φίλον ἀλλοιωθέντα Arist.*EN* 1165$^b$22; *preserve from*, ἀπὸ φόνου ἔρρυτο κἀνέσωσέ μ' S.*OT* 1351'

**ἀνασωσμός**, for 'Aq.*Ge.* 45.1' read 'Aq.*Ge.* 45.7'

***ἀνασωστέον**, *one must restore*, ταῦθ' ἡμῖν φυλακτέον ἐστὶ καὶ ἀ. διαφθειρόμενα Gal. 10.838.3.

**ἀνασωφρονίζω**, after '*sobriety*' insert 'Sch.Gen.Il. 14.436'

***ἀνάταλος**, unexpld. wd. in Hdn.*fr.* 8$^v$ p. 21 H.

**ἀνατᾰράσσω I**, for '*stir up* the mud' read 'poet. ἀνταρ- Sol. 37.8 W.; *stir up*, a settled liquid (in quots., abs.), Sol. l.c.'; for '*thick*' read '*turbid, cloudy*'

**ἀνάτᾰσις 2**, after '*threats* of violence' insert 'Clearch. 2'

**ἀνατείνω I 4**, add 'generally *offer*, πᾶσαν .. τὴν ἑαυτῶν ζωὴν εἰς τὸν φιλάνθρωπον ἀ. θεόν *Cod.Just.* 1.3.41.1; εὐχὴν καὶ πρεσβείαν ἀ. ὑπὲρ διαμονῆς ὑμῶν καὶ σωτηρίας *PMasp.* 2 iii 24 (vi AD)' **6**, delete '*pucker*' and add 'cf. ‡ἀνασπάω I 6' **III**, after 'food' insert '(medic.), Arr.*Epict.* 3.22.73: trans., *impose abstinence*, *starve*' and after 'Arr.*Epict.* 2.17.9' add 'generally, *starve*, ὄνους Sch.Call.*fr.* 1.43 Pf.'

**ἀνατέμνω I 2**, for 'Arist.*Spir.* 478$^a$2' read 'Arist.*Spir.* 478$^a$27' **II**, for 'Aeschin. 3.166' read 'D.ap.Aeschin. 3.166 (dub.)'

**ἀνατεταμένον**, for 'ἐλξίνη' read 'ἑλξίνη'

**ἀνατίθημι**, line 1, for 'pf. .. etc.' read 'poet. and dial. ἀντ-, Pi.*O.* 3.30, *IG* 7.3055 (Lebadea, iv BC), *Inscr.Cret.* 4.72 xi 14; Cypr., Thess. ὀντίθημι: 3 sg. aor. *o-ne-te-ke* *ICS* 265, al.; ὀνέθεκε *IG* 9(2).1027 (Larissa, v BC), ὀνέθεικε *SEG* 34.483 (Atrax, *c.*200 BC); Cypr., Arc. ὐντίθημι: 3 sg. aor. *u-ne-te-ke* ὐνέθεκε *ICS* 181, 3 pl. imper. aor. ὐνθεάντω *SEG* 25.447 (Aliphera, iii BC)'; for other inflexional forms see also s.v. τίθημι **I 2**, delete 'in Prose' and after 'person' insert 'πάντα θεοῖς ἀνέθηκαν Ὅμηρός θ' Ἡσίοδός τε Xenoph. 11.1 D.-K.' **II 1**, line 7, after '(Jaffa)' insert 'med., *dedicate*, *Rev.Bibl.* 34.579 (Jerusalem)' add '**b** *install* in a priesthood, *SIG* 1011.12 (Chalcedon, iii/ii BC).' **B I 1**, line 3, freq. like act., at end add 'also *dedicate*, ναὸν .. ἄνθετ' *SEG* 37.1175.9 (eleg., Pisidia, ii AD)' **3**, add '*defer, put off*, τὴν ζήτησιν Ath. 2.47a' **II 2**, after 'metaph.' insert 'ἀναθέσθαι ὥσπερ πεττὸν τὸν βίον οὐκ ἔστιν Antipho Soph. 52 D.-K., cf. Socr.ap.Stob. 4.56.39'; after '(Pl.)*Men.* 89d' insert 'Men.*fr.* 80 K.-Th.'

***ἀνατῐθηνητέον**, *one must nurse, foster*, θυμόν, πικρίαν, Muson.*fr.* K.

***ἀνατμητέος**, *α*, *ον*, *that is to be dissected*, Gal. 2.481.5.

**ἀνατοκισμός**, add '*SEG* 38.1462.21 (Oenoanda, ii AD)'

**ἀνατολή I 4**, add 'ἀντολαί .. Καΰστρου, Nic.*Th.* 635' **II**, add '**2** in pl., *growth*, of grass, *PTeb.* 703.51 (iii BC), *Aegyptus* 5.130.25 (ii BC).'

**ἀνατομή I**, add '**2** *breaking up* of coins (prior to re-minting), τὰ πρὸς ἀνατομὴν *Inscr.Délos* 461*Bb*49 (ii BC).'

***ἀνατομία**, transl. Lat. *apertio, dissection*, Cael.Aur.*CP* 1.8.57.

***ἀνατρᾰπελος**, ον, *overturned*, πάντα δ' ἀνατράπελα Call.*fr.* 7.30 Pf.

***ἀνατρεκιδδέτω**, unexpld. wd. in *Inscr.Cret.* 4.95 (v BC).

**ἀνατρέπω II 4**, add '*Cod.Just.* 6.4.4.13; act., *make null and void*, *Cod.Just.* 7.62.35'

**ἀνατρίζω**, for '*chirp* aloud' read '*screech, squawk*' and for 'al.' read 'codd.'

**ἀνατύπωμα**, for '*Stoic.* 1.214' read 'Zeno *Stoic.* 1.19 (D.L. 7.61)'

**ἄναυδος I 1**, lines 4/5, after '*without speaking*' insert 'τέλεος καιρὸς ἄναυδος τάδ' ἐπαινεῖ A.*fr.* 47a ii 25 R.'

⁺**ἀναυλεί** or **ἀναυλί**, *free of freight charge*, *POxy.* 3250.8 (*c.*AD 63); cf. ἀναυλεί χωρὶς ναύλου Suid.

**ἄναυλος** (A) for '*flute(s)*' in this article read '*aulos (auloi)*' **I 1**, after 'E.*Ph.* 791' insert 'ἀ. βρέγμα (dub., cj. ἄναυδον) A.*fr.* 451h.8 R.'

**ἄναυλος** (B), for 'αὐλίον' read 'αὔλιον'

**ἀναυμαχίου**, add 'Poll. 8.42-43'

**ἀναφαίνω I 3**, line 5, for 'ἀμφ-' read 'ἀμπ-'; for '*Leg.Gort.* 10.34,al.' read '*Inscr.Cret.* 4.72.10.34, 11.18'; add 'ἀντ- ib. 10.43, 48' **II 2**, for '*to be declared* king' read '*to be seen manifestly to be* king'; line 4, for 'romancer' read 'speech-writer'

**ἀναφαίρετος**, line 2, after '(i AD)' insert 'Iamb.*Protr.* 5 (p. 36.14 P.)'; line 4, after '(iii AD)' insert 'Procl.*Inst.* 105 D.'

**ἀναφᾰλακρος**, for '*forehead-bald*' read '*having a receding hairline*'

**ἀναφᾰλαντιαῖος**, after 'foreg.' insert 'Ptol.*Tetr.* 143'; add 'Heph.Astr. 2.2.31, 32, 34'

**ἀναφᾰλαντος**, for '*forehead-bald*' read '*having a receding hairline*'

**ἀνάφανσις**, delete the entry.

***ἀνάφαυσις**, εως, ἡ, *flash*, Anon. *in Ptol.Tetr.* 5 (v. *MH* 41.70).

**ἀναφέρω I 1 b**, add 'of archives, περὶ τῶν γραμμάτων τῶν μνημονικῶν τῶν τε ἀνενειγμένων εἰς τὸ ἱερόν .. *SEG* 33.679.4 (Paros, ii BC)' add '**c** astron., in pass., *rise* above the horizon, Hypsicl. 9.8, al.' **2**, line 3, after '(Plu.)*Alex.* 52' insert 'abs., *sob in breathing*, Hp.ap.Gal. 19.80' add '**7** pass., *to be seconded, detached* of troops, *Salamine* 75.3 (ii BC), *BGU* 2024.8 (AD 204).' **II 7**, line 3, for '(v. supr. I 2) Hdt. 1.116' read 'Hdt. 1.116.2 (cf. supr. I 2)'; line 4, after 'Theopomp.Com. 66' insert 'Men.*Sic.* 368, *fr.* 369 K.-Th.' **10**, add '**b** *recall, remember*, Isoc. 5.32, Plu. 2.607e, App.*BC* 1.121, al.'

**ἀναφθείρομαι I**, for 'cf. φθείρω' read 'cf. ‡φθείρω II 1'

**ἀναφλάω**, after '-φλάω' insert 'τὸ αἰδοῖον'

**ἀναφορά I 1**, add '**b** *lifting* or *carrying up*, λίθου Demetr.*Eloc.* 72.' **2 d**, for 'of a sign' read 'above the horizon, Hypsicl. 9.8, al.' add '**3** perh. *duct carrying must from the wine-press to the fermentation vat*, δεῖ .. τὸν ληνεῶνα ὅλον κατηλεῖφθαι πάντοθεν λειοτάτοις κονιάμασι, καὶ οὐχ ἧττον τὰς ἀναφοράς *Gp.* 6.1.3.' **II 4**, add '*SEG* 32.1611 (ii/iii AD)' **9**, delete the section. **III**, delete the section.

**ἀναφορεύς**, for '*bearer, bearing-pole*' read '*carrying-pole*'

**ἀναφορέω**, add 'Cypr. *u-na-po-re-i* perh. ὐναφορεῖ *Kafizin* 266b'

**ἀναφορικός II**, add 'νόσος ἀ. Ptol.*Tetr.* 87'

**ἀναφρίζω**, add 'app. describing a medical symptom, Men.*Asp.* 453'

***ἀναφυή**, ἡ, *bud, shoot*, Aq.*Za.* 6.12.

***ἀναφυλάσσω**, *keep, guard*, *Epic.Alex.adesp.* 9 ii 19, *PDura* 29.8 (iii AD).

**ἀνάφυξις**, add '(perh. read ἀνάψυξις, cf. Jul.*ad Them.* 258c)'

**ἀναφῡσάω III**, for '*blow the flute*' read '*tune up* on the pipe' and before 'κύκνοι' insert 'cf., of swans'

**ἀναφύσησις I**, delete 'Plb. 34.11.17' **II**, for '*prelude* in flute-playing' read '*blowing* in playing the aulos'

**ἀναφῡσητός**, after '*blown up*' insert 'Moses Alch. 312.7'

***ἀναφυτέω**, *foster the growth of*, ἀναφυτοῦντος ὅλον τὸ προκείμενον πωμάριον *SB* 9907.24 (AD 388).

**ἀναφύω I 2**, add 'Sm.*Jb.* 14.9' **II**, for this section read 'ἀναφύομαι *come into being, grow up*, Pherecyd. 22(a) J., Hdt. 4.58, ἀναφυομένης ἐκ γῆς πόας Pl.*Plt.* 272a; also act. (intr.), ἢν γὰρ ἀποθάνῃ εἷς τις πονηρός, δύ' ἀνέφυσαν ῥήτορες Pl.Com. 186 K.-A. **b** transf., διαβολαί Plu.*Thes.* 17, δίκαι id.*Per.* 37; act., πάλιν ἀπορία τις ἀναφύει Phlp. *in de An.* 195.12. **2** *grow again*, act. (intr.), ἀναφῦναι τὰς τρίχας Hdt. 5.35.3, τὸ ἀνδρεῖον ἀνέφυ Luc.*DMort.* 28.2. **b** transf., ἀναφύντος τοῦ δήμου Aeschin. 2.177; in form ἀμφύνει, οὐχ ἥκιστα γὰρ τῷ στομάχῳ ἐς ἔκλυσιν ἡ νοῦσος ἀμφύνει (s.v.l., cj. ἐμφ-) Aret.*CA* 2 (bk. 6).3.8.'

**ἀναφωνέω I 3**, for this section read '*proclaim*, intr., of slaves making declaration of liberty, πλὴν ὅτι τοὺς δούλους οὐ χάριτι τῶν δεσποτῶν ἀλλὰ ἀναφωνήσαντας ἐλευθερωθῆναι λέγει Artem. 1.56 p. 63.7 P.; cf. Plu.*Cic.* 27.6, *Cod.Just.* 6.4.4.6'

***ἀναφωνητικός**, ή, όν, *exclamatory*, Eust. 1964.47; adv. -ῶς, *as an exclamation*, Eust. 1044.53, Sopat.Rh. 8.335.10 W. (cj. I.-W.; -φωνικῶς W.).

**Ἀναφωνητικῶς**, delete the entry.

**ἀναχάζω II**, for 'pass.' read 'med.' twice.

**ἀναχαιτίζω I 2**, after 'D. 2.9' insert 'Men.*Sam.* 209'

**ἀναχάσκω**, add 'of the cervix, Alcmaeon 3 D.-K.; Hp.*Superf.* 32, *Vict.* 1.30'

**ἀναχέω**, line 4, after 'Arr.*An.* 6.18.5' insert 'of water reaching inland, εἰς τοὺς ἐσωτάτους τόπους ὁ Περσικὸς κόλπος ἀναχεῖται *Peripl. M.Rubr.* 35'

**ἀναχωρέω**, line 1, for 'Locr., Cret. ἀνχ-' read 'Locr. inf. ἀνχōρεῖν *IG* $9^{2}$(1).718.7, 27 (v BC), Cret. ἀνκōρε̄ν *Inscr.Cret.* 4.72 xi 10 (Gortyn, v BC)' **I 2**, line 7, for '*IG* 9 .. 334' read '*IG* $9^{2}$(1).718.7, 27'; add '*withdraw* to place of refuge, *go into hiding*, of strikers, *PTeb.* 26.18, 41.14 (both ii BC); of slaves, *PHib.* 71.6 (iii BC); of offenders, *PTeb.* 5.6 (ii BC)' **IV 1**, delete '= συγχωρέω .. *Arc.* 10' (read ἐνεχώρησαν) **2**, delete the section.

**ἀναχώρησις I**, add '**b** *turning back*, Ph. 2.539.' add '**V** ἀ. τῶν ὄντων, calque of *"cessio bonorum"* Just.*Const.Δέδωκεν* 7d.'

**ἀναχωρητής**, add '*SEG* 33.1366 (-ιτής, Nubia, vi AD), *PAnt.* 202b9'

**ἀνάχωσις** (s.v. ἀναχώννυμι), place the article after 'ἀναχωρίζω'; add 'rest. in *JÖAI* 3.56'

**ἀναψησμός**, add '*SB* 9699.622 (AD 78/9), *PWürzb.* 22.13 (ii AD), *BGU* 2264 I 5, II 7 (AD 198)'

**ἀναψηφίζω**, before 'Th. 6.14' insert '*IG* $1^{3}$.250*A*12 (Attica, v AD)'

**ἀνάψυξις 1**, after 'Posidon. 72' insert '*refreshment*, *SEG* 36.1277 (Mesopotamia, iii AD)'

**ἀναψύχω I 3**, line 1, after 'metaph.' insert 'ὂν δ' ἔψυξας ἔμαν φρένα καιομέναν πόθῳ Sapph. 48 L.-P., cf. Thgn. 1273 W.'; line 2, for 'Call.*Hec.* 1.1.7' read 'Call.*fr.* 260.7 Pf.'

***ἀνγλάριον**, v. °ἀγγλάριον.

***ἄνγρεσις**, v. °ἄγγρεσις.

**ἀνδαβάτης**, for '*gladiator*' read '*a type of gladiator who fought blindfold*' and add 'cf. Cic.*Fam.* 7.10.2'

***ἀνδαιθμός**, ὁ, *redivision, redistribution* of land, *IG* $9^{2}$(1).609.2 (Naupactus, vi/v BC); cf. δαιθμός, ἀναδασμός, ἄνδαιτος.

**ἁνδάνω**, lines 4/5, aor., add '3 sg. ἔϝαδε *SEG* 23.530 (Dreros, vii BC), ἔβαδε *Inscr.Cret.* 1.xvi 1.2 (Lato, iii BC), ἇδε *SEG* 18.772 (Berenice, Cyrenaica, iv BC; cf. °ἅδημα)' **I**, line 9, after 'Od. 2.114' insert 'Alcm. 1.88, 45, 56.2 P.' add '**b** *rejoice in*, w. dat., *AP* 6.299 (Phan.).' **II**, line 4, for 'so' read 'cf.' and delete 'cf. Od. 2.114'

**ἄνδεμα** κτλ., delete '**ἀνδεσμός**'

**ἄνδεργμα**, after lemma insert '(ἄνδειγμα La.; cf. ἀνάδειγμα)'

***ἀνδηρεύων**, ὁ, app. = ἀνδηρευτής, *PUniv.Milan.*inv. 100 (*Acme* 9(2).59.17).

***ἀνδηρικός**, όν, *determinative*, ὁ Δημόκριτος ἔλεγε ταῦτα δὴ τὰ ἀνδηρικὰ ὀνόματα, ἕν, μηδέν, ῥυσμόν, τροπήν, διαθιγήν Democr.*fr.Orth.*

**ἀνδίκα**, for 'ἀναδίκη' read '***ἀναδίκη**'

**ἀνδίκτης**, for 'Call.*Fr.* 233' read 'Call.*fr.* 177.33 Pf.' and add 'cf. perh. **ἀνδικτήρ**, ῆρος, δούνακας ἀνδικτῆρας *AP* 6.296 (Leon.Tarent.) (cj. Lobeck, ἀντυκτῆρας cod.)'

⁺**ἀνδῐχάζω** (s.v. ἄνδιχα), *cut in two, cleave*, in a riddle about an oyster, *Epigr.adesp.* in *Suppl.Hell.* 983.7 (unless [ἄ]ν διχάσῃ is to be read). **2** app. *to be of divided opinion*, αἴ κ' ἀνδιχάζοντι τοὶ ξενοδίκαι *IG* $9^{2}$(1).717.10 (Khaleion, W. Locris, *c.*450 BC).

**ἀνδρᾰγᾰθία**, line 3, after '*the character of an upright man*' insert '*integrity*' and after 'Phryn.Com. 1' insert 'Isoc. 3.44, 6.105, D. 22.72, 24.180'; add '*IG* $1^{3}$.97.13 (412/11 BC)'

**ἀνδρᾰδέλφη**, after '*husband's sister*' insert '*MAMA* 1.324 (Phrygia)'

**ἀνδρᾰδελφος**, after '*brother-in-law*' insert '*MAMA* 1.363, 369, 8.167' and after 'Suid.' insert 's.v. γαλόῳ, also fem. *sister-in-law*, ib.'

**ἀνδρᾰκάς** (B), delete '*man's*'

***ἀνδρᾰποδική**, ἡ, *tax on slaves*, MacDowell *Stamped Objects from Seleucia* pp. 41, 42, 64, *YClS* 3.30-3, 37, 38 (Uruk, Babylonia).

**ἀνδρᾰποδιστί**, adv., *like a slave*, prob. in *PTeb.* 765.13 (ii BC).

**ἀνδρᾰποδον I**, add 'not dist. fr. δοῦλος Th. 1.139.2, 7.27.5'

***ἀνδρασώτειρα**, ἡ, *saviour of men*, epith. of Isis, *POxy.* 1380.55 (ii AD).

***Ἀνδρέας**, ὁ, cult-title of Zeus in Phrygia, *SEG* 26.1367, 33.1153, al.

**ἀνδρεία I**, add '**2** as honorific title, *PVarsov.* 17.9, 12 (ii AD), τὴν σὴν ἀνδρείαν *PAmh.* 2.82.5 (iii/iv AD). **3** personified, the deity *Virtus*, *SEG* 33.945 (Ephesus), 35.1377 (Hierapolis, iii AD), *BGU* 2150.13 (v AD).'

***ἀνδρεῖζομαι**, *be bold*, *POxy.* 3302 (AD 300/1).

**ἀνδρεῖος II**, for '*stubborn*' read '*bold*'; after 'Luc.*Ind.* 3' insert 'sup. as honorific title, *SEG* 23.296 (Lebadeia, iii AD), *PLips.* 119 ii 3 (iii AD), *Aegyptus* 9.123 (v AD)' **IV**, delete the section.

***ἀνδρεϊστέον**, *one must play the man*, Men.*Kith.* 76.

**ἀνδρειφόντης**, for 'ἀνδρότης' read 'ἀνδροτής'

***ἀνδρεοκαταμάκτης**, ου, ὁ, temple-official, perh. one who rubs down men after bathing, or perh. who polishes statues, *SB* 7336.25 (iii AD); cf. καταμάκτης, καταμάσσω.

***ἀνδρεοπλάστης**, ὁ, app. = ἀνδριαντοπλάστης, *modeller of statues*, *CPR* 14.47.1 (vi/vii AD).

***ἀνδρεοφονικός**, όν, *of homicide*, κὰτ τὸν ἀ. τεθμόν *IG* $9^{2}$(1).609.A13 (Naupactus, vi/v BC).

**ἀνδρεών**, for '*IG* 14 .. (Segesta)' read '*IPamph.* 3.8 (ἀδριιῦνα acc. sg., iv BC); Dor., *IG* 14.291 (Segesta), perh. here public meeting place; cf. °ἀνδρήιον'

***ἀνδρήιον**, τό, building where public feasts (for men) were held, *Inscr.Cret.* 4.4.4 (Gortyn, vii/vi BC), 5.1.8 (Axos, vi/v BC), al.

***Ἀνδριάντεια**, τά, name of festival involving the dedication of statues, also called the *Nea Adrasteia*, *MAMA* 6.76 (Phrygia).

**ἀνδριαντίδιον**, for pres. ref. read '*Inscr.Délos* 442*B*167 (ii BC)' and add '*SEG* 34.1087.4 (Ephesus, i AD)'

**ἀνδριαντίσκος**, delete '*puppet*'

**ἀνδριαντουργός**, delete '(ἔργον)' and add '*SEG* 33.1139 (Hierapolis, Phrygia, ii/iii AD)'

**ἀνδριάς**, add 'Myc. *a-di-ri-ja-te* (dat. sg.)'

**+ἀνδρίζω**, med., *come to manhood*, Ar.*fr.* 772 K.-A., Hyp.*fr.* 228, τῷ σώματι ἀνδρίζεσθαι, Luc.*Anach.* 15. **II** *make physically strong* or *manly*, τοὺς γεωργοῦντας X.*Oec.* 5.4. **2** *endow with moral strength*, Pl.*Tht.* 151d; med., *take courage, be resolute*, X.*An.* 4.3.34, Arist.*EN* 1115$^b$4, Lxx *Jo.* 1.6, 1*Ep.Cor.* 16.13, D.C. 50.24.7. **III** med., *perform the man's part in sexual intercourse*, D.C. 79.5, ἐπὶ τὸ παιδάριον Lcn. 4*Ki.* 4.35, Philostr.*Ep.* 54, Ach.Tat. 4.1.2 V.; cf. of a eunuch, ἐπὶ γυναῖκα Philostr.*VA* 1.37. **2** of a woman, *behave* (*dress*) *like a man*, Philostr.*Im.* 1.2.

**ἀνδρικός I 2**, for this sense read 'of things, *suitable for a man*, i.e. *large*, Eub. 56.1 K.-A.; also, *having great force*, σεισμοί Ael.*VH* 6.9'

**ἀνδρισμός**, add 'cf. *SB* 5948. **II** = Lat. *capitatio*, *poll-tax*, *PRyl.* 658.8 (iv AD).'

**ἀνδροβάμων**, for pres. ref. read '*Inscr.Cret.* 3.3.25.2, 26.5, etc. (Hierapytna, i AD)'

***ἀνδροβλής**, ῆτος, ὁ, *struck by* (or *striking*) *a man*, *Trag.adesp.* 645.12 K.-S.

***ἀνδρόβουλος**, ον, *having the will* or *purpose of a man*, A.*Ag.* 11, Phryn.*PS* p. 31 B.; cf. γυναικόβουλος.

***ἀνδρογύναιος**, ον, of a man, *having a womanish nature, effeminate*, Lxx *Pr.* 19.12(15).

***ἀνδρόγυνον**, τό, *married couple*, Cyran. 1.2.26 K. (pl.), 3.22.3 K. (sg.).

**ἀνδροδάμας II**, add 'Anon.Alch. 5.12; variety of haematite acc. to Plin.*HN* 36.146, 37.144'

***ἀνδροκίδαλος**, ὁ, or -ον, τό, ἐπώνυμον ἀνδροκιδάλου, gloss on κρίθων, Hsch., but La. reads ἀνδρὸς μοιχαλίου.

***Ἀνδρόκλειος**, ον, *of Androklos*, the founder of Ephesus, Ἀνδρόκλειος πόλις *IEphes.* 1064.

***Ἀνδροκλωνεῖον**, τό, app. *club building* or *tomb of Androklos*, rest. οἰνοδ[οτή]σαντα ἐν τῷ Ἀνδροκλω. [..] *SEG* 34.1107 (Ephesus), v. °Ἀνδρόκλειος.

***ἀνδροκόμος**, ον, *caring for one's husband*, Sch.Pl. p. 407 G.

**ἀνδροκτόνος**, for 'Hdt. .. *Cyc.* 22' read 'σὺν ἀ. B. 18.23 S.-M.; of Amazons, Hdt. 4.110.1; of Cyclops, E.*Cyc.* 22. **2** *slayer of her husband*, S.*fr.* 187 R.'

**ἀνδρολέτειρα**, as adj., add '*Suppl.Hell.* 1168.3 (epic.)'

***ἀνδρολέτης**, ου, ὁ, *slayer of men*, of Ares, *GVI* 1552.6 (Panderma, ii/i BC).

**+ἀνδροληπτέω**, *capture men*, *IG* 4$^2$.68.64 (Epid., iv BC).

***ἀνδρομανία**, ἡ, (*male*) *homosexual lust*, *Orac.Tiburt.* 123.

***ἀνδρόμαξ**, ὁ, perh. kind of bird, *OFlorida* 15.4 (ii AD).

**ἀνδρόμεος**, after 'Il. 11.538' insert 'αἵματος ἀ. Hes.*Sc.* 256' and after '[A.R.] 4.581' insert 'μήδεά τ' ἀνδρομέοισι πανείκελα Opp.*H.* 1.581'

**ἀνδρομητόν**, for 'ἀνέδραμον' read 'ἀναδραμεῖν'

**ἀνδροτής**, after 'Il. 16.857, 24.6' read '(vv.ll. ἀδρ-, ἁδρ-)'

**ἀνδροφόνος**, lines 3/4, for 'rarely exc.' read 'in Hom. usu.' **I 1**, after '*murderous*' insert 'ἀνδροφόνους .. Ἰλιάδας E.*Hec.* 1061'

***ἀνδροφυλάκιον**, τό, *guardhouse*, *Sardis* 7(1).17.10.

***ἀνδροφύλαξ**, *guard*, *PCol.* 2.4 ii 2 (sp. ἀνδρω-).

**ἀνδρόω II**, after 'E.*HF* 42' insert 'Pl.*Smp.* 192a, Arist.*EN* 1180$^a$2' **III**, after '*sum*' insert 'Cratin. 318 K.-A.'

**ἀνδρών**, after 'X.*Smp.* 1.4, etc.' insert 'in inscrs. freq. of the dining-hall of religious associations, *SEG* 33.639 (Rhodes, *c.*100 BC), *Syria* 26.55 (Palmyra)' and at end for 'Ion. -εών (q.v.)' read 'dial. -εών (‡q.v.)'

**ἀνδρωνύμιον**, delete the entry (v. *JHS* 106.184).

***ἄνδρωσις**, εως, ἡ, *arrival at manhood*, *PMich.*III 149.5.27 (ii AD).

**ἀνέβραχε**, for '*βράχω' read 'βραχεῖν'

**ἀνεγείρω III**, after 'of buildings' insert 'and other structures' and add '*SEG* 32.1389 (Commagene, i/ii AD), *ITomis* 384.15 (iii/iv AD), *SEG* 32.1540 (Arabia)'

**+ἀνέγερσις**, εως, ἡ, *waking up, rousing*, Iamb.*Protr.* 20 (p. 103.16 P.); pl. ἀνεγέρσεις βακχεύοντες (i.e. performing rituals to rouse), Plu. 2.378f. **II** *erection* of buildings or structures, *SEG* 26.1672 (Jerusalem, v AD), *PMich.*XI 624.12 (vi AD).

**ἀνεγκέφαλος**, add '**b** transf., *brainless*, *PLond.* 1075.19 (vii AD).'

***ἀνέγλιπος**, ον, *unfailing*, καρπός *SEG* 8.548.13 (Fayûm, i BC).

**ἀνέθιστος**, add '**2** of persons, *unused*, μαλακίαις (?)Ephor. in *PLit.Lond.* 114.16.'

**ἀνείδεος**, after 'Ael.*NA* 2.56' insert 'Sallust. 17.6'

***ἀνείκητος**, v. ‡ἀνίκητος.

**ἀνείλησις 3**, for '*twisting of the body*' read '*folding* or *doubling up of the body*'

**ἀνειλλω**, after 'ἀνειλέω' read 'med., *roll oneself up* Pl.*Smp.* 206d. **II** *unroll, unfold* Pl.*Criti.* 109a.'

**ἄνειμι I 1**, lines 2/3, after 'Hdt. 3.85' insert 'πρὸς ἡλίō ἀνιόντ[ος] towards the East, *SEG* 32.161 (Athens, 402/1 BC)' **3**, for 'v. supr. 1' read 'cf. ἀναβαίνω II 3'

**ἀνείμων**, add 'Call.*fr.* 7.9 Pf., Ph. 2.225, Nonn.*D.* 35.107, 47.281'

**ἀνεῖπον**, line 3, after '*proclaim*' insert 'ὃν Ὡπόλλων ἀνεῖπεν ἀνδρῶν σωφρονέστατον πάντων Hippon. 63.2 W.'

***ἀνειρήνευτος**, ον, *irreconcilable*, Hsch. s.v. ἀσύμβατον.

**ἀνείσακτος**, add 'Iamb.*Protr.* 21 (p. 106.17 P.); of those not properly taught medicine, Gal. 13.563.3'

***ἀνεισφόρητος**, ον, *exempt from taxation*, *SIG* 612B5 (Delphi, ii BC).

**ἀνέκαθεν I**, add 'Plu.*Thes.* 33.3' **II 1**, add 'Plu.*Num.* 1.2'

***ἀνεκδυσώπητος**, ον, quoted as equiv. of Lat. *inexorabilis*, Dosith. p. 392 K.

**ἀνεκθέρμαντος**, adv. -ως, add 'Paul.Aeg. 7.19.3 (375.24 H.)'

**ἀνέκλυτος**, after '*indissoluble*' insert '*IG* 12(7).393 (Amorgos, i/ii AD)'

***ἀνεκπολέμητος**, ον, app. *invincible in war*, Dosith. p. 392 K.

***ἀνέκτακτον**, τό, in accounts, *total not itemized*, *PMasp.* 57 i 4, iii 8 (vi AD).

**ἀνεκτέος**, after 'Ar.*Lys.* 477' insert '*Trag.adesp.* 382 K.-S.'

**ἀνεκτός II**, after 'without neg.' insert 'Isoc. 5.11, 8.126, 10.1, 12.110'

**ἀνεκφοίτητος**, add 'τῶν ἐκεῖ Syrian. *in Metaph.* 109.25'

**ἀνέκφραστος 2**, delete the section.

***ἀνέλεγχος**, ον, *irrefutable*, *SEG* 26.788 (funerary epigr., Byzantium).

***ἀνέλκυσις**, εως, ἡ, *hauling up*, Sch.Th. 7.25.

***ἀνελληνόστολος**, ον, *wearing non-Greek dress*, cj. in A.*Supp.* 234 (v. ἀνέλλην).

**ἀνεμομαχία**, add '*Cat.Cod.Astr.* 11(2).168.16, 17'

**ἄνεμος**, add 'Myc. *a-ne-mo*'

***ἀνεμόσουριν** (acc.), name of *whirlwind* said to be derived from a fan similarly called used by ladies in Alexandria, Olymp. in *Mete.* 200.19 (Alexandrian wd.; perh. corrupt for *ἀνεμόσυριν (σύρω) or °ἀνεμούριον).

**ἀνεμόσυρις**, delete the entry.

**ἀνεμοτρεφής**, last line, for 'cf.' insert 'ἀ. πυλάων Simon. 107 P.'

**ἀνεμούριον**, add '**2** *fan*, ἀνεμούρ(ιον?) βιβραδ(ικόν?) dub. in *PRyl.* 627.165 (iv AD).'

**ἀνεμόφοιτος**, for 'v. sub ἠνεμ-' read 'v. ‡ἠνεμ-'

**ἀνεμοφόρητος**, after '*carried by the wind*' insert 'prob. in comm. in Sapph. 90 iii 23 L.-P. (ἀν[εμ]οφορητο[ pap.)'; for 'dub. sens.' to end read 'of spirits who have no rest, *PMag.* 15.8, 14 (iii AD)'

**ἀνέμφατος**, lines 4/5, for 'p. 434' read 'p. 530' and for 'pp.434, 450' read 'p. 543'

***ἀνενάριθμος**, ον, *not reckoned in*, *PMasp.* 97$^v$.D61 (v AD).

**ἀνενδεής 1**, after '*AP* 10.115' insert 'αὐτὸ .. τὸ θεῖον ἀνενδεές Sallust. 15.1'; adv. -εῶς, for '*faultlessly, unexceptionably*' read '*in a way that lacks nothing, generously*' and add '*IEphes.* 728.25'

**ἀνενδοίαστος**, adv., add 'Iamb.*Protr.* 20 (p. 96.8 P.)'

**ἀνενεχύραστος**, after '*distraint*' insert '*PTeb.* 817.22 (ii BC)'

***ἀνενῆλιξ**, ικος, ὁ, ἡ, of children, *not of age*, *MAMA* 6.225 (Apamea).

***ἀνενοχλησία**, ἡ, *freedom from disturbance*, *SEG* 36.1051.9 (Miletus, ii AD).

**ἀνέντατος**, for 'Theopomp.Com. 71' read 'Theopomp.Com. 72 K.-A., κλίνη *Inscr.Délos* 1416*A*i38 (ii BC)'

**ἀνέντροπος**, after 'Hsch.' insert '*irreverent*, Sm.*Ez.* 7.24'

**ἀνεξαλλοτρίωτος**, for '*unalienated*' read '*not assigned to anyone else, inalienable*, of property'; for 'cf. *Ath.Mitt.* 3.58 (Lydia)' read '*IEphes.* 3245.19; esp. of tombs, *SEG* 24.1206 (Egypt, i BC), *AJA* 36.453 (S.Galatia, iii AD)'

***ἀνεξάρπαστος**, ον, perh. *not to be robbed*, *POxy.* 2712.14 (AD 292/3).

**ἀνεξέλεγκτος**, after lemma insert 'Cret. neut. pl. ἀνεξέλεντα *SEG* 35.989.19 (Cnossus, ii/i BC)'

**ἀνεξέταστος**, after '*examined*' insert 'Isoc. 9.42' and after 'Aeschin. 3.22' insert 'Scaev.*Dig.* 33.8.22.2'

**ἀνεξία**, for '*endurance* .. word' read 'dub. wd., app. requiring sense *abstinence, forbearance*, or sim.'

***ἀνεξιδιαστός**, όν, *not to be appropriated*, dub. reading in Ramsay *Cities and Bishoprics* 2.475.

**ἀνεξίλαστος**, after '*implacable*' insert '*SEG* 29.1179 (AD 108/9)'

**ἀνεξοδίαστος**, for pres. refs. read '*ISmyrna* 228.6, *INikaia* 283.4, 1231.8, *IStraton.* 258, 316, *IGBulg.* 1007 (Philippopolis, iii AD)'

**ἀνέξοδος I 2**, place after section II **II**, for this section read '*not going out of doors* or *in public*, Plu. 2.242e, 426b; because of *illness, weather*, *Vit.Aesop.*(G) 59, *BGU* 2350.11 (?ii AD); fig., of attitudes, etc., διάνοια Plu. 2.610a, λόγοι 1034b, βίος 1098d'

***ἀνέξοχα**, gloss on ἔμπηρα, Hsch.

**ἀνεπάγγελτος 1**, add '*IGBulg.* 388 bis 3 (Istria, ii BC)' *ἀνεπάνοδος, ον, *not returning*, Heph.Astr. 3.47.

ἀνέπᾰφος, after 'ον' insert '(fem. -η *IGRom.* 1.892.10 (Panticapaeum, c.ii AD)'; line 2, after '*seizure*' insert 'D. 56.38, 40'; line 4, after '*unencumbered*' insert '*PMich.*x 583.15 (i AD)'

*ἀνεπεύθυνος, ον, app. = ἀνυπ-, *BGU* 1262.19 (iii BC), *PFrankf.* 1.87 (iii BC).

ἀνεπηρέαστος, after 'ον' insert '(fem. -η *CIJud.* 1.65 (Panticapaeum, iii AD))'

ἀνεπίβλητος, for '*inattentive, heedless*' read '*unheeded*' add '**II** *not required to make payment*, *PFlor.* 323.12 (vi AD).'

*ἀνεπιγιγνώσκω, *not to recognize as correct*, *BGU* 874.7.

*ἀνεπιγραφέω, *set down, record*, Zos.Alch. 219.

ἀνεπίγρᾰφος **1**, line 3, for '*IG* 2 .. al.' read '*IG* 2².1514.28 (iv BC), [τρί]πους ἀ. *SEG* 34.95 i 86 (Attica, ii BC)' and add 'w. gen., ἀ. ὁλκῆς καὶ νομίσματος *Didyma* 468.13 (ii BC), cf. 469.7. **b** of books, *without title*, λόγοι D.H.*Dem.* 13.'

ἀνεπιδάνειστος, after '*not mortgaged*' insert '*PTeb.* 817.22 (ii BC)'

ἀνεπίδετος, after 'Hp.*Fract.* 20' insert 'Gal. 16(2).543.6'

*ἀνεπικωλῡτί, adv. *without let or hindrance*, *MAMA* 6.83 (Attouda).

ἀνεπικώλῡτος, after '*unhindered*' insert 'ἀ. τὰν κράναν *SEG* 23.398b.10 (Thestia, Aetolia, ii BC)'; adv., *without let or hindrance*, add '*PKöln* 232.11 (iv AD)'

ἀνεπίληστος, add 'Sch.Call.*Lav.Pall.* 87'

ἀνεπίλῠτος, for '*unbandaged*' read '*not having one's dressing changed*'

*ἀνεπιμέμπτως, adv., *blamelessly*, ζῶν ἀλύπως καὶ ἀ. *IPrusa ad Olympum* 108.

*ἀνεπιμηνίευτος, ον, *free from the obligation of serving as* ‡ἐπιμήνιος, *SEG* 8.529.40 (Egypt, ii BC).

ἀνεπίξεστος, for 'Them.*Or.* 26.388b' read 'Them.*Or.* 26.322b'

ἀνεπισήμαντος **II**, for '*without an attack of* ἐπισημασία (q.v.)' read '*not showing the symptoms* (v. ἐπισημασία)'

*ἀνεπίσπαστος, ον, *not subject to seizure*, *PMasp.* 151.143 (vi AD).

ἀνεπιστάθμευτος, after 'Plb. 15.24.2' insert '*IGBulg.* 315.17 (Mesambria)'

ἀνεπιστρεψία, for '*want of regard*' read '*inattention*' and add 'ostr. in *CGFP* 318 (Philadelphia, iii BC), *PSI* 152 ii 13 (ii AD)'

ἀνεπίστροφος, add '**3** *whence there is no return*, οἰκία (neut. pl.) .. νεκύων ἀ. Bernand *IMEG* 33.23 (ii BC).'

ἀνεπίτακτος, for '*control*' read '*dictation*'

ἀνεπίτᾰτος, for '*not to be* .. **2**' read '*that does not admit of heightening*' and after 'μᾶλλον' add 'S.E.*M.* 10.272'

*ἀνεπιτυχία, ἡ, *failure*, Cyran. 1.22.15 K.

ἀνεπίφαντος, before '*insignificant*' insert '*inconspicuous*, Ptol.*Tetr.* 170'

*ἀνεπίφορος, ον, *not admissible in evidence*, *POxy.* 1716.17 (iv AD).

ἀνεπιχείρητος **1**, after 'Plu.*Caes.* 25' insert '*intact*, *IGRom.* 4.661.17 (Acmonia, i AD)'

*ἀνεπίψογος, ον, *blameless*, Aristid.Quint. 3.9 (p. 108.5 W.-I.).

*ἀνεραυνάω, v. ‡ἀνερευνάω.

ἀνέργαστος, add '*raw, untreated*, of hides, *Edict.Diocl.* 8.6a, 9, al.'

ἀνέρεικτος, add 'Gal. 19.81'

⁺ἀνερεύγω, *throw up, disgorge*, Men.*Asp.* 451, ἀνήρῠγεν ἀτμόν (aor. 2) Nonn.*D.* 1.239, ἰωήν ib. 485; of rivers, εἰς θάλασσαν Arist.*Mu.* 392ᵇ16, A.R. 2.744.

ἀνερευνάω, before '*POxy.* 1468.18' read 'ἀνεραυνῶσα .. τὰ ἔγγραφα'

ἀνερεύνητος **1**, add '*unexplored*, *Peripl.M.Rubr.* 18, 66'

ἀνερίθευτος, add 'adv. -τως *OGI* 7.4'

*ἄνερμος, ον, unexpld. wd., neut. pl. subst., ἄνερμα τοῦ ἱ[ερ]οῦ ἀργύρου *IG* 2².1544.24 (Eleusis, iv BC).

ἀνέρπω, for 'Call.*Ap.* 110' read 'Call.*Ap.* 111'; add 'w. acc., *climb*, τείχε' ἀ. Arat. 958'

*ἄνερσις, εως, ἡ, (ἀνείρω) *stringing up*, cj. in Plu. 2.156b.

ἀνέρχομαι **I 2**, add '**b** = ἀνέχω B 2, *jut out*, D.P. 400.' add '**4** *rise in rank* or *status*, τί γὰρ ὅτι πρὸς ἱερωσύνην ἄτερος αὐτῶν ἀνῆλθεν; Just.*Nov.* 89.9 pr.' **II 1**, add '*come up* from a village to a capital, *CPR* 8.29.4 (iv AD)' **3**, for '*brought home to* you' read '*brought before* your *bar*' and for 'ἀνερχομένῳ is corrupt' read 'ἀναερχ- is v.l. for ἐπανερχ- and unmetrical ἀνερχ-'

ἄνεσις **2**, line 3, after 'Plu. 2.102b, etc.' insert '*rest*, of the dead, *BCH* suppl. 8 no. 180, *ICilicie* 35'; line 5, after '(Thisbe)' insert '*exemption from liturgy*, *BGU* 2474.10 (ii/iii AD)'

ἀνέσσυτο, for 'pass.' read 'med.'

ἀνέστιος, for 'metaph.' to end read 'of crayfish, Opp.*H.* 2.417; transf., of the soul, Max.Tyr. 14.8 (8.8 H.). **2** *unoccupied, tenantless*, ὄστρακον, οἰκητῆρος ἀνέστιον οἰχομένοιο Opp.*H.* 1.325.'

ἄνετος, add 'Myc. *a-ne-ta* (neut. pl.), of dues, *remitted*'

ἄνευ, last line but two, for 'as always in Arist.' read 'e.g. Arist.'

ἀνευρετής, add within parenthesis 'iv BC'

*ἀνευρησιλογήτως, adv., *without subterfuge*, *SB* 7663.17 (i AD).

*ἀνευσυνθετέω, *fail to observe a contract*, prob. in *BGU* 1738.32 (i BC).

⁺ἀνεφάλλομαι, *leap up* at, ἀνεπᾶλτο Il. 20.424, ἀνεπάλμενος A.R. 2.825 (see also ἀναπάλλω).

*ἀνεφάμιλλος, ον, *unrivalled*, καλοκἀγαθία prob. in *PAmh.* 2.145.6 (iv/v AD).

⁺ἀνέφαπτος, ον, *that cannot be reclaimed*, of manumitted slaves, *SEG* 26.720.13 (Epirus, iii BC), 32.623 (Bouthrotos, Illyria, ii BC), *IG* 9²(1).705.10, *GDI* 1684.6 (both Delphi, ii BC).

ἀνέφικτος, after '*unattainable*' insert 'Aristeas 223'

*ἀνεφόρητος, ον, app. *not watched over* (by evil), *unenvied*, ἀνεφόρ[η]τος εὐδαίμων *SEG* 19.372(b).7 (Thespiae, Rom.imp.); cf. ἐφοράω 2.

ἀνεχέγγυος, for '*unwarranted*' read '*not relied upon, not regarded as reliable*' and delete 'because .. themselves'

ἀνέχραζεν, add '(ἀνέχραυεν· ἀνέχριμπτεν, ἀνήρειδεν, ἐκούφιζεν La.; cf. ἐγχραύω)'

ἀνέχω, line 12, after '(v. infr. C II)' insert '3 pl. pf. ἠνέσχονται *PKöln* 240.11 (vi AD)' **A I 5 b**, at end for 'his anger' read 'a show of anger' **II**, after 'Th. 6.86' insert 'Ar.*fr.* 632 K.-A., D.*Prooem.* 41.3' **C II 3**, after 'Od. 22.423' insert 'E.*Andr.* 340, *Tr.* 101' and after 'D. 19.16' insert 'M.Ant. 5.33.6'

ἀνεψιᾰδοῦς, after 'ὁ' insert '(-ιδοῦς Sch. A.R. 3.359)'; for '*first cousin's son*' read '*first cousin once removed* (not always dist. fr. second cousin, cf. Poll. 3.28)'; delete all after 'Is. 11.12' inserting '45.54' after 'D. 44.26'

ἀνεψιός, add '*first cousin once removed*, D. 43.41, 49; ἀνεψιῶν παῖδες *second cousins*, Is. 7.22, 11.2, D. 43.51; also sg. ἀνεψιοῦ παῖς Is. 11.10, al. (v. *Glotta* 48.76)'

ἀνεψιότης, after '*cousins*' insert '*IG* 1³.104.15, 21 (409/8 BC)'

ἄνεω, add 'but found w. sg. verb, Od. 23.93'

*ἄνεως· ἄφωνος καὶ τὸν νοῦν ἐκπεπληγμένος Gal. 19.81.

⁺ ἄνη, Dor. ἄνᾱ Alcm. 1.83 P. (ἄν-, unless ἄνα = ἁ ἄνα is read), ἡ, *fulfilment*, Alcm.l.c., A.*Th.* 713, Call.*Jov.* 90.

ἄνηβος, line 2, after 'cf.' insert 'Sol. 27.1 W.'

ἀνηθοποίητος **1**, add 'n. sg. subst. Marcellin.*Vit.Thuc.* 57' **2**, for '*unprincipled*' read '*morally unformed*' and for 'Cic.*Att.* 10.10.5' read 'Cic.*Att.* 10.10.6'

ἀνήκεστος, before '*incurable*' insert 'Dor. ἀνᾱκ- B.*fr.* 20 D.9 S.-M.'

ἀνηλᾰκάτος, for '*unable to spin*' read '*lacking a distaff*'

ἀνηλεγής, after 'Q.S. 2.414' add 'and read by Hdn. in A.R. 1.785'

ἀνηλέητος **II**, add 'Nicom.Trag. 16 S.'

ἀνήλειπτος, ἀνήλιφος, at end after 'Hp.*Ep.* 17' add '(ἀνήλιπος cod.)'

⁺ἀνηλιοδείκτης, ου, *one that points the direction without the aid of the sun*, *PMag.* 4.1374.

ἀνήλιος, add 'Plu. 2.330d, Luc.*Nec.* 9, *Luct.* 2, ἀ. οἶκος Gal. 13.778.2'

ἀνηλιποκαιβλεπέλαιος, for '*unanointed* (?)' read '*having a lamp-oil look* (i.e. bleary-eyed from reading late)' and add '(v. *FGE* p. 476 P.)'

ἀνήλῐπος, add '*EM* 107.14, Hp.*Ep.* 17.6 (cod., cj. ἀνήλιφος)'

*ἀνηλίπους, ποδος, ὁ, ἡ, *barefooted*, *IKios* 19.3 (ἀνιλίποδες, i AD).

*ἀνηλόω, = ἀναλόω, v. ‡ἀναλίσκω.

*ἀνήλωσις, v. ‡ἀνάλωσις.

ἀνήλωτος, after '*not nailed*' insert 'καλίκων στρατιωτικῶν ἀ. (Lat. *caligae militares sine clabo*) *Edict.Diocl.* 9.6'

ἀνημέρωτος, for '*untilled*' read '*uncleared*'

*ἀνηνεχυῖαν· ἀναφέρουσαν Hsch.

ἀνήνῠτος **1**, after 'E.*Hel.* 1285' insert 'Critias Trag. 1.14 S.' **2**, neut. pl. as adv., add 'πονοῦσιν Pl.*R.* 531a, Theoc. 15.87'

ἀνηπελίη, for 'εὐηπελίη' read 'εὐηπελής'

ἀνήρ, line 1, after 'ἀνδρί' insert '(Pamph. ἀδρί Hsch.)'; line 11, before '*beast*' insert '*god* or' **III**, add 'ἀνήρ, of statue personifying this athletic category, *RA* 1987.99 (Hierapolis, Phrygia, iii AD)' **VI 1**, add 'transl. of Lat. *vir* in honorary titles and designations, ἀνδρὸς διασημοτάτου *IEphes.* 3217 (ii AD); τοὺς τρεῖς ἄνδρας (*triumviros*) Plb. 3.67.6'

*ἀνηροσίη, ἡ, *lack of cultivation*, *Orac.Sib.* 3.542.

ἀνήσσητος, add '*ASAA* 30/32(1952/4).290 no. 66.4 (Rhodes)'

ἀνθαιρέομαι **I**, add 'D.C. 43.46.2, 48.32.3'

ἀνθαιρετιστής, add '*PMich.*III 149 xviii 16 (pl., ii AD)'

*ἀνθαιρετιστικόν, τό, astrol., *exchange of qualities between the "conditions"*, *PMich.*III 149 viii 28; cf. αἵρεσις B II 4.

*ἀνθαιρετός, όν, *favourite*, as name of a horse, *SEG* 7.213.28 (tab. defix.; Palmyra, ii/iii AD).

ἀνθάπτομαι, line 4, after 'Th. 8.97' insert 'cf. περὶ τῆς μισθοφορᾶς .. μαλακωτέρως ἀνθήπτετο (sc. τοῦ πράγματος) 8.50.3 (or delete περί leaving μισθοφορᾶς as gen. constr. w. vb.)' **II 2**, delete all after 'E.*Med.* 55, 1360'

*ἀνθαρπάζω, *seize by way of reprisal*, *Hell.Oxy.* 8.3 M.-K.

ἀνθέμιον **2**, for '*IG* 1.322' read '*IG* 1³.474.47' **3**, for 'of gold .. *quality*' read 'dub., Hebr. in this passage app. means *bowl of a lamp*'

ἀνθεμίς, add '**3** in temple, perh. either *flower-shaped support* for dedication or *floral ornament* (cf. ἀνθέμιον 2), *Ath.Asklepieion* IV 66.'

ἄνθεμον, add '**5** dub. item in temple account, cf. ἀνθεμίς, *IG* 1³.472.142, 146, 149.'

ἀνθεμωτός, add '*Inscr.Délos* 1439*Abc*i47 (ii BC)'

***ἀνθερίκη**, ἡ, = ἀνθέρικος (*asphodel-stalk*), cj. in *AP* 12.121 (Rhian.) (codd. ἀθερ-).

**ἀνθέρῐκος I 1**, after 'Thphr.*HP* 7.13.2' insert 'Theoc. 1.52' **II**, for this section read 'applied to sim. flowering stalks, ἀνθέρικον νῦν εἴρηκε τὸ ἄνθος τῆς σκίλλης· κυρίως γὰρ τὸ ἄνθος τῶν ἀσταχύων Sch.Arat. 1060'

**+ἀνθέριξ**, ῐκος, ὁ, *flowering stem of asphodel*, Il. 20.227, Hes.*fr.* 62 M.-W.

**Ἀνθεστήρια**, line 3, for '(Teos)' read '(Teos, v BC), *SEG* 31.985.D6 (Abdera, v BC)'

**ἀνθεστηριάδας**, add '(ἀνθεστρίδες La.)'

***ἀνθεστρίδες**, αἱ, perh. *marriageable girls*, *Tit.Cam.* 148; cf. ‡ἀνθεστηριάδας.

**ἀνθέω I**, add '**3** *have an efflorescence* or *secretion*, Hp.*Morb.Sacr.* 5.2.'

**ἄνθη**, add '**3** *efflorescence*, χαλκοῖο πάλαι μεμογηότος ἄνθην (i.e. verdigris or perh. cuprous or cupric oxide) Nic.*Al.* 529.'

**ἀνθήεις**, after 'εσσα, εν,' insert '*abounding in flowers*, ἄκανθος Nic.*Th.* 645'; for '*bright-coloured*' read '*coloured as though with flowers*'

**+ἀνθηλᾶς**, ᾶ, ὁ, perh. *flower- or papyrus-merchant*, *PLond.* 387.21, *PPrag.* I 25.8 (both vi/vii AD) (v. °ἀνθήλη).

**ἀνθήλη**, after 'Dsc. 1.85' insert 'Str. 5.26, *PUniv.Giss.* 13.4 (refers in both of these to commodity, perh. head of the papyrus or similar plant, v. *ZPE* 75.155-6)'

***ἀνθηρεύομαι**, *to be in bloom*, Hsch. s.v. χλοάζει.

**ἀνθηρός II 1**, line 3, after '(Plu.*Pomp.*) 2.50b' insert '*blooming*, τά τε εἴδεα τῶν ἀνθρώπων εὔχροά τε καὶ ἀνθηρά ἐστι Hp.*Aër.* 5'

***ἀνθιεράομαι**, *to be* ἀνθιερεύς, *IG* $2^2$.1368.5 (Athens, ii AD).

***ἀνθιερεύς**, έως, ὁ, *deputy-priest*, *IG* $2^2$.1368.9, 27, al. (Athens, ii AD).

***Ἀνθινός**, ὁ, cult-title of Apollo, *IGBulg.* 1723.

***ἀνθίνης**, ου, of wine, *flavoured with flowers*, Gal. 19.81 (s.v.l.), Hsch.

**ἀνθίστημι II 1**, line 7, after 'X.*Smp.* 5.1' insert 'ἐὰν δέ τις περὶ τούτου πράγματος ἀνθίστηται *IEphes.* 4101.4 (i/ii AD)'

***Ἀνθιστήρ**, ῆρος, ὁ, a divinity, perh. Dionysus, *IG* 12(3).329 (gen. Ἀνθισ[τῆ]ρος, Thera, iii/ii BC); cf. Ἀνθεστήρια.

***ἀνθοβᾰτέω**, *walk on flowers*, μαλακὴν ἀνθοβατεῦσα πόη[ν Honestus in *SEG* 13.344(*i*) (epigr., Thespiae, i BC/i AD).

**ἀνθοβαφής**, delete 'γῇ *IG* 7.1802'

**ἀνθοκομέω**, add 'Cyr.Al. in *PG* 73.620A.'

**ἀνθοκόμος 1**, add 'βελέμνῳ (of Eros), Nonn.*D.* 7.194, μάστιγι (of Dionysus) ib. 17.20'

***ἀνθοράω**, = ἀντιβλέπω, ἀντοψόμεθα τὰ θεῖα ἐναργῶς Alb.*Intr.* 5 (p. 150.12 H.), dub. in *PFreib.* 2.5 in *NGG* 1922.33.

***ἀνθοριστικός**, ή, όν, *belonging to a counter-definition*, Fortunat.*Rh.* 1.13, *An.Ox.* 4.15.25.

**ἄνθος** (A) **I 2**, after '*surface*' insert 'κύματος ἄ. Alcm. 26.3 P.' **II 1**, line 3, after 'Thgn. 994' insert 'χροιῆς ἄνθος ἀμειβομένης Sol. 27.6 W.'; line 5, after 'id.*R.*601b' insert 'in epitaphs, metaph., of children, ἔνθα κατάκιτε νέον ἄνθος *SEG* 36.1183 (Galatia, v/vi AD), Ποπλικία .. ῥόδον ἐρχόμενον ἄνθος *TAM* 5(1).481.6' add '**3** *finest quality*, *flower*, καὶ σὺ λαβὲ ἡδύσματα, τὸ ἄνθος Lxx *Ex.* 30.23.'

**ἀνθοσμίας**, for 'Pherecr. 108.30' read 'Pherecr. 113 K.-A., Longus 4.10.3'

***ἀνθοτόκος**, ον, *bringing forth flowers*, Bernand *IMEG* 20.6 (ii BC).

**ἀνθρᾰκεύς**, after '*charcoal-maker*' insert 'Men.*Epit.* 81'

***ἀνθρᾰκηγός**, ον, *charcoal-carrying*, *BGU* 2353.12 (ii AD).

**ἀνθρᾰκηρός**, for these refs. read '*Inscr.Délos* 509.40 (iii BC), Alex. 211 K.-A. (m. pl. subst.)'

**ἀνθρᾰκίδες**, add 'cf. ἐπανθρακίδες'

**ἀνθρᾰκινος 2**, add 'cf. *anthracina*, *charcoal-coloured garments*, Varro in Non.Marc. 550 M.'

***ἄνθρᾰκις**, εως, ἡ, *carbuncle*, *PLond.* 77.28 (vi AD).

**ἀνθρακίτης**, for '*gem*' read '*mineral*'

**ἀνθρακῖτις**, for '*coal*' read '*gem-stone*'

***ἀνθρᾰκοβᾰτης**, ου, ὁ, *one who walks on coals*, Ps.-Steph. in *Physici* 2.201.15.

**ἄνθραξ I**, add 'ἄνθρακες ὁ θησαυρὸς πέφηνεν, of illusions destroyed, Zen. 2.1, cf. Luc.*Philops.* 32, *Tim.* 41, al.'

**ἄνθρυσκον**, for '*chervil*, *Scandix australis*' read 'plant, perh. one or more species of *Anthriscus*'

**ἀνθρωπεύομαι**, for 'Herm.ap.Stob. 1.41.68' read '*Corp.Herm.* 25.8 N.-F.'

***ἀνθρωπιμαῖος**, α, ον, *humane*, Sch.Gen.Il. 23.98.

**ἀνθρώπινος I**, after 'Lys. 6.20' insert 'κατὰ τὸ ἀνθρώπινον Th. 1.22.4, οὐκ ἀνθρωπίνης δυνάμεως βούλησιν ἐλπίζει 6.78.2' **II**, adv., line 4, for 'And. 2.6' read 'And. 1.57, 2.6'; delete 'Of the three' to end.

**ἀνθρωπόδηκτος**, add 'n. pl. subst., *wounds caused by the bite of a man*, Gal. 13.432.3, 558.3, al.'

**ἀνθρωπόθεν**, before '*humanitus*' insert '(parox.)'

**ἀνθρωπόλεθρος**, after 'Suid.' insert 'Sch.Gen.Il. 21.421'

***ἀνθρωπομορφίτης**, ου, ὁ, *anthropomorphic god*, Isid.*Etym.* 8.5.32.

***ἀνθρωποπρεπής**, ές, *befitting a man*, *PMonac.* 8.5 (vi AD).

**ἄνθρωπος 3 a**, after 'Paus. 4.26.5' insert 'Sopat.Rh. 8.160.15 W.' **6**, at end for 'simply, *brother*' read 'without derogatory sense, ἄνθρōπε hὸ(ς) στείχε[ι]ς καθ' ὁδὸν *CEG* 28 (Attica, vi BC)' **7**, line 2, after '1*Ep.Tim.* 6.11' insert 'so prob. τῆς θεοῦ τὸν ἄ. Call.*fr.* 193.37 Pf.' **II**, last line, delete 'Aeschin. 3.137' at end add 'Myc. *a-to-ro-qo*'

**ἀνθῠλακτέω**, for 'Ael.*HA* 4.19' read 'Ael.*NA* 4.19'

***ἀνθυλλοπρᾱ́της**, ου, ὁ, *florist*, *PMasp.* 156.8 (ἀνθυλο-, vi AD).

***ἀνθυλλοπρᾱτική**, ἡ, *trade of florist*, *PMasp.* 156.12 (ἀνθυλο-, vi AD).

***ἀνθυλλοπρᾱ́τισσα**, ἡ, fem. of -πράτης, *PMasp.* 156.5 (ἀνθυλο-, vi AD).

**ἀνθυπαλλάσσω**, add '**II** *pledge as security for a debt*, *PIand.* 142 i 13 (pass., ii AD).'

**ἀνθυπηρετέω**, add '**II** *act as deputy* ὑπηρέτης, *IG* $2^2$.1945.5.'

***ἀνθυπήχησις**, εως, ἡ, *answering echo*, [τῆς λύρα]ς *PBerol.*inv. 13426.18$^v$ in Gercke-Norden *Einl. in die Altertumswiss.* 1(9) p. 42 (T(L) 1924).

**ἀνθυποφαίνω**, delete the entry.

**ἀνιάζω**, at end delete 'metri gr.'

**ἀνιᾰρίζω**, delete 'Dor. for ἀνιερίζω' and add 'cf. ἱερίζω'

***ἀνιᾱροποιός**, ον, *causing painful things*, ἀνιαρὲ ἀντὶ τοῦ ἀνιαροποιέ Sch.Theoc. 2.55.

***ἀνίᾱσις**, εως, ἡ, *sadness*, Sm.*Ez.* 23.33.

**ἀνῑᾱτος I 1**, add '**b** *uncured*, ἐξάρθρημα Gal. 10.220.15.'

**ἀνίᾰχω**, after '*cry aloud*' insert 'E.*Or.* 1465 (lyr.)'; add '[ῐ except where augmented]'

**ἀνιγρός**, delete 'Call.*Iamb.* 1.164 (prob.)' and for 'Call.*Aet.* 3.1.14' read 'Call.*fr.* 75.14 Pf.'

***ἀνιεράω**, *dedicate*, perh. in Myres *Cesnola Coll.* p. 548 no. 1903 (Cyprus, i AD).

**ἀνιερόω**, after lemma insert '(Arc. 3 sg. aor. opt. ὑνιερõσει, *SEG* 11.1112, vi/v BC)'

***ἀνίημα**, ατος, τό, *grief*, Baillet *Inscr. des tombeaux des rois* 1087.

**ἀνίημι II 7 a**, line 1, after '*relax*' insert 'τὰς ὀφρῦς ἄνες ποτ' Men.*Dysc.* 423' **8**, after 'Hdt. 2.113, 4.152' insert 'of snow, E.*Ba.* 662, χειμῶνος ἀνέντος Theoc. 18.27' **b**, after '(Hdt.) 2.121.β'' insert 'Th. 1.129.3'

***ἀνῐκᾰνέω**, *not to meet the requirements*, *SB* 9066.23 (ii AD).

**ἀνίκητος I**, add 'as epith. of var. divinities, *SEG* 24.903 (Thrace, ii/iii AD), 36.616 (Edessa, iii AD), of Roman emperors (Lat. *invictus*), *SEG* 33.18 (Athens), 23.199 (Taenarum, both iii AD)'

***ἀνίκλιον**, τό, unidentified garment, *SEG* 7.417 (Dura, iii AD).

***ἀνικμαίνω**, = ἀνικμάζω, cj. in Nic.*Al.* 524.

**ἀνίκμαντος**, after 'Lyc. 988' insert '(cj.)'

**ἀνῑ́λαστος**, add '*PMag.* 4.1776'

***ἀνῑ́λατος** (sp. **ἀνείλατος**), ον, *implacable*, *IGLS* 1.119, 212, 47 iii 7 (unless to be taken as ἀνήλατος) (i BC).

**ἀνῑμάω**, read '**ἀνῑμάω** (cf. καθῑμάω)'; for '*draw up*, *raise* water .. (ἱμάντες )' read '*draw up* from well'; after 'Sor. 1.93' insert 'Iamb.*Protr.* 21 (p. 105.24 P.)'

**ἀνῑ́μησις**, add 'for the public baths, *POxy.* 2569.5-6 (iii AD)'

***ἀνῑμητής**, οῦ, ὁ, *one who draws water*, for the public baths, *SB* 10555.5, 8, al. (ἀνειμητ-, iii AD).

***ἀνίουλος**, ον, *not having the first growth of hair on the cheeks*, Nonn.*D.* 11.373, 38.167.

**ἄνιππος 1**, for '*without a horse to ride on*' read '*not having a horse*' and add 'Pi.*Pae.* 4.27'

**ἄνις**, add 'rest. in Call.*fr.* 3.1 Pf.'

***ἀνῐσόκυκλα**, τά, app. system of gears, as used in a hoisting machine, Vitr. 10.1.3.

***ἀνῐσομεγέθης**, ες, *of unequal size*, Hipparch. 2.1.12.

**ἄνῐσος**, add '**2** *unequalled*, ἄνισος ἀρεταῖς παναρχόντων γόνος Diosc. in *GDRK* 17.6.'

**ἀνῐσοσθενής**, for 'Gal. 5.415' read 'Gal. 4.415.11'

**ἀνῐσότονος**, for '*not in unison*, Ptol.*Harm.* 2.2' read 'music., *of unequal pitch*, φθόγγοι Ptol.*Harm.* 2.2, 3.2; *varying in pitch*, ψόφοι ib. 1.4'

**ἀνίστημι A**, line 2, aor. 1, add 'ἀνέστᾱσε (3 sg., dial.) *SEG* 27.1116 (Egypt, v BC), ἠνέστησα *SEG* 6.377 (Lycaonia, Chr.)' **3**, *raise from the dead*, add 'Mitchell *N.Galatia* 87, cf. sense B 3' **5**, line 5, after '*Brut.* 1' insert 'in funerary inscrs. sts. w. dat. of pers., acc. of monument, etc., not expressed, Mitchell *N.Galatia* 22' **B**, line 3, imper., add 'ἄστα *SEG* 34.994 (vase, Apulia, late iv BC), ἄνστα Theoc. 24.36' **I 5**, delete 'Τυφῶνα .. codd.'

**ἀνιστόρητος II**, add '*unheard of*, i.e. nothing like it before, [τῆς] σκληρᾶς σιτοδείας ἐκ τῆς γενομένης ἀ. ἀπορίας *SEG* 24.1217.10 (Thebes, Egypt, i BC = *OGI* 194)'

**ἀνίσχυς**, add 'as subst., ἐπὶ ἀφ[ανίσει] καὶ ψύξει καὶ ἀνίσχυϊ tab.defix. in *SEG* 35.216.18 (Attica, iii AD)'

**+ἀνίσωμα** (A), ατος, τό, *equalizing portion* or *part*, of wine, Ath. 10.447a; of masonry, *Inscr.Délos* 507.4, 5 (iii BC).

***ἀνίσωμα** (B), ατος, τό, *unevenness* in the tooth of young horses, *Hippiatr.* 95.15 O.-H.

***ἀνκεμōλία**, v. °ἀγχεμωλία.

*__ἀννάλιος__, ον, Lat. *annalis*, *annual*, *Cod.Just.* 1.3.45.9, neut. pl. as subst., ib. 1.3.55.1.

__ἄννησον__, after 'Dsc. 3.56)' insert '__ἄννησσον__ *Inscr.Délos* 440*A*64 (ii BC)'

*__Ἄννιος__, v. °*Αἰνικός*.

__ἀννίς__, add '*IG* 7.3380 (Boeotia; parox. acc. to ed.)'

*__ἀννω__, ἡ, v. °*ναννω*.

*__ἀννῶνα__, (or *ἀννώνα*), ἡ, Lat. *annona*, *corn-supply*, *PTeb.* 404.12 (iii AD), *IGRom.* 3.409; also *ἀννώνη* *IGLS* 262.12, *OGI* 200.16, *POxy.* 1192.4 (iii AD); gen. pl. *ἀννόνων* *Cod.Just.* 1.4.18, 1.44.1; *ἄννονα* or *ἀννόνα* Suid.

*__ἀννωνάριος__, ὁ, *official administering the annona*, *ZPE* 22.101.26 (iv AD).

__ἀννωναρχέω__, add '(= *TAM* 4(1).189.8)'

*__ἀννωναταμίας__, ου, ὁ, = *praefectus annonae*, rest. in *IEphes.* 4330.10 (iii AD).

__ἀννωνέπαρχος__, add '*Cod.Just.* 1.44.2 (*ἀννον-*)'

+__ἀννώνη__, v. °*ἀννῶνα*.

__ἀννωνιακός__, add '-*ιακή*, ἡ, *corn-supply*, *PWisc.* 32.13 (i AD), *PMichael.* 40.20 (vi AD)'

__ἀννωνικός__, add '-*ικόν*, τό, *bread*, *BGU* 2358.7 (iv AD), *CPR* 7.42 i 2, al. (v AD), *Stud.Pal.* 8.978.2 (vii AD)'

*__ἄννως__, -ως, ἡ, kinship term, perh. *grandmother*, *IG* 9(2).877 (Larissa); cf. *ἄννις*, Lat. *anus*.

__ἄνοδος__ (B), add '__V__ *advancement*, *promotion*, Just.*Nov.* 6.5.'

__ἀνόδυρτος__, add '__2__ *unmourned*, *Salamine* 199 (?i AD).'

__ἀνόζεστα__, after 'fort. *ἀπόζεστα*' insert '*ἀνόζωτα* La.'

__ἀνοηταίνω__, after 'Pl.*Phlb.* 12d' insert '*Ep.* 359c'

*__ἀνοητίζω__, *to be stupid*, Aq.*Je.* 10.8.

__ἀνόητος__ __I 2__, after '*province of thought*' insert 'Parm. 8.17 D.-K.'

*__ἄνοθεν__, adv. = *ἄνωθεν*, *PHib.* 110.66, al. (iii BC); cf. *ἔξοθεν*, *κάτοθεν*.

__ἄνοια__, after 'Thgn. 453' insert 'Ion. and poet. __ἀνοιΐη__, Hippon. 75.3 W.; Aeol. __ἀνοΐα__, Alc. 112.1, 119 L.-P.'

__ἄνοιγμα__ __I__, add '*opening* from water-pipe, *tap*, *SEG* 31.953.A12, B5, 10 (Ephesus, ii AD), perh. *sluice-gate*, *Syria* 62.83.17'

*__Ἀνοιγμοί__, οἱ, festival at Miletus, *Didyma* 382.8, 385.1.3, al.

__ἀνοίγνῡμι__, line 10, before 'v. infr.' insert 'also intr.' __I 2__, for '*ἔργ' ἀναιδῆ*' read '*μὴ .. ἀνοίξῃς .. ἃ πέπονθ' ἀναιδῶς*'

__ἀνοικοδομέω__ __II__, line 2, after 'etc.' insert '*SEG* 31.1548 (Egypt, ii AD)'

__ἄνοιξις__, add '__2__ *opening* of a business, *πρὸς ἄνοιξιν καπηλείου* *POxy.* 2109.10 (AD 261). __II__ *aperture* of a garment, *ἀνύξεως καὶ ὑποραφῆς ὁλοσειρικοῦ ἱματίου* *Edict.Diocl.* 7.49 (*ἀνυξ-*).'

__ἀνολβέω__, after lemma insert 'Ep. -*είω*'

__ἀνόλβιος__, after '= sq.' insert '*BCH* 85.848 (funerary epigr., Paros)'

__ἄνολβος__ __1__, line 4, before 'Thgn.' insert 'Archil. 88 W.'

__ἀνολισθάνω__, for 'Call.*fr.* 96' read 'Call.*fr.* 191.75 Pf.'

__ἀνομία__ __1__, add '*ἐξάλιψο(ν) τὰς ἀ. μου καὶ τὰ παραπτώματά μου* *SEG* 31.1562.5 (?Egypt, Chr., iv/v AD); cf. °*ἀνόμιον*'

__ἀνόμιμος__, add '*PMag.* 36.140 (iv AD)'

*__ἀνόμιον__, τό, *transgression*, *wrong-doing*, *ἐξάλιψον τὸ ἀνόμιον αὐτῆς* Guarducci *EG* 4 p. 459 no. 2.12 (Nubia, Chr., v AD); cf. °*ἀνομία*.

__ἀνόμοιος__, after 'Arist.*Pol.* 1277ᵃ5' insert '*τῆς ἀνομοίου μίξεως σύμβολον* Hld. 3.14.2' add '__3__ *not equal to*, *not suited for*, *ἄπορος .. καὶ ἀνόμοιος πρὸς τὴν λ[ι]τουργείαν καὶ τὴν ὑπηρεσίαν* *PPetaus* 12.9 (ii AD).'

__ἀνομοιόω__ __I__, after 'Pl.*Tht.* 166b, al.' insert 'Procl.*Inst.* 36, 110 D.; act. in this sense, Hsch. s.v. *ἀπεοίκασιν*'

__ἀνομολογέομαι__ __I 1__, line 3, after '[Pl.]*Tht.* 164c' insert '*ἀνομολογησάμενος παρ' αὐτοῦ* *getting his agreement*, Pl.*Smp.* 199b' __2__, add '[Pl.] *Amat.* 136e'

*__ἀνομολογέω__, *disagree*, Porph.*Gaur.* 13.7.

__ἀνομολόγητος__ __II__, after 'Ptol.*Tetr.* 47' insert '(v.l.)'

__ἀνομόλογος__, after 'S.E.*M.* 8.331' insert 'Ptol.*Tetr.* 47'

__ἀνομολογούμενος__, delete 'for a verb *ἀνομολογέομαι* .. does not occur'

__ἄνομος__ __I 1__, line 2, after 'E.*Ba.* 995' insert '*IHadr.* 100 (epigr.)'

*__ἀνόνειρος__, ον, *dreamless*, *ὕπνος* Porph.*Gaur.* 12.7.

__ἀνόνητος__ __I__, for 'Cerc. 4.4' read 'Cerc. 4.6'

__ἄνοος__, line 1, after '*ουν*' insert 'also nom. pl. *ἄνοες* in *SEG* 35.220.17 (Attica, iii AD; cf. nom. pl. *εὔνους*)'

__ἄνοπλος__, line 2, after 'Pl.*Euthd.* 299b' insert 'Ion Trag. 53e S., Ezek.*Exag.* 210 S., *AP* 9.320 (Leon.Tarent.)'; at end for 'on the form v.' read 'cf.'

*__ἀνοράσσω__, var. of *ἀνορύσσω*, *Inscr.Cret.* 1.xviii 64.4 (Lyttos, iii AD).

__ἀνοργίαστος__ __1__ and __2__, for '*orgies*' read '*mystery rites*' __II__, add 'Iamb.*Protr.* 21 *κη'* (p. 122.18 P.)'

+__ἀνορίνω__, Aeol. impf. *ὀννώρινε*, *disturb*, *παίσαις .. ὀ. νύκτας* Alc. 72.9 L.-P.

*__ἀνορύγή__, ἡ, *digging up*, *excavation*, *PRyl.* 95.8 (*ἀναρ-*, i AD); *θεμελίου* *SAWW* 149(5).14 (iv AD).

*__ἀνόρυξις__, εως, ἡ, *digging up*, *SB* 4774.9.

__ἀνορύσσω__ __1__, add '*σάρκας ἀ.* *EA* 13.21 no. 6 (Phrygia or Lydia)' at end add 'see also °*ἀνοράσσω*'

*__ἀνορῠχή__, ἡ, *digging*, prob. in *PMasp.* 283.1.16 (vi AD).

__ἀνοσία__, after lemma insert '(A), Ion. -*ίη*' __I__, add 'Hp.*Praec.* 6' __II__, delete the section.

*__ἀνοσία__ (B), (*ἀνόσιος*), ἁ, Cypr. *a-no-si-ja*, *impiety*, *ἀνοσίja* Ϝοι *γένοιτυ* *ICS* 217.29 (Idalium, v BC).

__ἀνοσιότης__, add '*Cod.Just.* 1.11.10'

__ἀνοσιουργία__, add 'Iamb.*Protr.* 13 (p. 71.4 P.)'

__ἄνοσμος__, add 'of wine, *PZen.Col.* 108.5 (iii BC)'; for 'but *ἄοσμος* (q.v.) was preferred' read 'cf. *ἄοσμος*'

__ἀνόστεος__, add '__2__ *shell-less*, of eggs, Nic.*Al.* 296 (codd., *ἀνόστρακα* G.-S.).'

__ἀνόστητος__ __II__, add '*ὅροι* *Trag.adesp.* 658.17 K.-S.'

__ἄνοστος__ __II__, before 'Thphr.' insert '*γένοιτο αὐτῷ τὰ νόστιμα ἄ.* *SEG* 6.802.23 (Salamis, Cyprus)'

__ἀνούᾰτος__, for '*ear*' read '*ears*' and delete '*without handle*'

*__Ἄνουβις__, ιδος, (-*ιος* *Inscr.Délos* 2098, acc. -*ιν* D.S. 1.18, voc. *Ἄνουβι* *IKios* 21) ὁ, the Egyptian dog-headed deity *Anubis*, Call.*fr.* 715 Pf., *Inscr.Délos* 2039 (ii BC), *POxy.* 1256.12 (iii AD).

__ἀνούλεγοι__, after lemma insert '(__ἀνούλιοι__ La.)'

__ἀνοχ[ικ]ός__ __I__, after lemma insert '(__ἀνοχαῖος__ La.)'

__ἀνόχῡρος__, delete the entry.

*__ἀνπανάμενος__, v. ‡*ἀναφαίνω* I 3.

*__ἀνπανσις__, __ἀνπαντός__, v. ‡*ἀμφαν-*.

+ __ἄνπερ__, v. °*ἐάνπερ*.

*__ἀνπιδήμα__, v. °*ἀμφιδήμα*.

*__ἄνπυλλα__, v. °*ἄμπυλλα*.

__ἄνσατον__, after lemma insert '(__ἀνσάττεν__ La.)'

__ἀντᾰγωνία__, delete the entry.

*__ἀντᾰγώνισμα__, ατος, τό, gloss on *ἅμιλλα*, Phot. α 1201 Th.

__ἀντᾰγωνιστής__, add '*τῶν εὐτυχούντων ἀνταγωνιστὴς φθόνος* *Trag. adesp.* 167 K.-S.'

*__ἀντᾰγωνοθετέω__, *act as deputy to ἀγωνοθέτης*, *IG* 10(2).133.5 (ii AD).

__ἀνταίρω__ __I__, add '__2__ *ἀνταίρουσιν· ἀντιλέγουσι· Σοφοκλῆς Θυέστῃ* (*fr.* 265 R.) Hsch.'

__ἀντᾰκαῖος__ __2__, for '*ἀν καῖον*' read '*ἀντακαῖον*'

__ἄνταλλος__, add 'also as pers. n. *Ἄνταλλος* *IG* 2².6514, etc. (v. Robert *Hell.* 11.208 n. 2)'

__ἀντᾰμείβομαι__ __III__, delete '*again*'

__ἀντᾰμειψις__, after '*requital*' insert 'Aristeas 259, *BGU* 1816.18 (i BC)'

+__ἀντᾰμοιβός__, *ίν*, (epic form *ἀντημ-*) *substitute*, *given in exchange*, Call.*Del.* 52. __2__ *requiting*; *τὰ ἀ.*, *reprisals*, *PMasp.* 151.257 (vi AD).

+__ἀνταναιρετέος__, ον, *to be set off against* (a sum), *PTeb.* 61b.220 (ii BC).

__ἀνταναιρέω__, add '__5__ *counteract with equal strength*, *ἰσχυρὸν στόμα ἔχει, ὡς καὶ σιδηρᾶ ἀνταναιρεῖν*, of parrot's beak, Cyran. 3.52.4 K.'

*__ἀντανάπαιστος__, ὁ, metrical foot (◡‒‒◡◡), Diom. 1.481.29 K.

*__ἀντανατέλλω__, astrol., *rise in opposition*, *PMich.*III 149 xi 5 (ii AD).

*__ἀνταναφορά__, ἡ, *official counter-report*, *BGU* 1859.B.11 (i BC).

__ἀντάξιος__ __2__, add 'Ach.Tat. 3.23.1 V., Hld. 10.18.3'

+__ἀνταπᾰμείβομαι__, *answer in turn*, Tyrt. 4.6 W., Call. in *Suppl.Hell.* 238.8.

__ἀνταποδίδωμι__ __I__, delete '__2__ *take vengeance*' and include exx. in section I 1.

__ἀνταπόδοσις__ __II 1__, add '*ἀ. τῶν ἐκλείψεων* *return* of eclipses, *Cat. Cod.Astr.* 8(2).126.6'

+__ἀντάποινα__, v. *ἀντίποινα*.

*__ἀνταπόμνυμι__, 3 pl. imper. -*υόντων*, *make a counter-declaration on oath*, *SEG* 9.1.11 (Cyrene, iv BC).

*__ἀνταποπάλλω__, of earthquakes, *thrust back in the opposite direction* (opp. single shock), Arist.*Mu.* 396ᵃ8.

__ἀνταποστέλλω__, line 3, for 'an echo' read 'a reflection'

__ἀνταποφαίνω__, add 'med., *ἀ. γνώμην* *put forward a counter*-proposal, J.*AJ* 19.2.2'

__ἀνταρκέω__ __II__, after 'c. part.' insert '*ἀκμάζων τῇ ὠκύτητι ἀντήρκεσε* Paus. 6.13.4'

__ἀνταρσία__, add '*ἀνταρσίας γενομένης ἐν τοῖς Ἀθηναίοις* Arist.*fr.* 667 R. (*Vita Arist.* vulg.)'

__ἄνταρσις__, add 'Sm.*Is.* 8.12'

*__ἀνταρχιδικαστής__, οῦ, ὁ, *deputy ἀρχιδικαστής*, *PSI* 1105.5 (ii AD), 1255.3 (iii AD).

*__ἀνταρχιερεύς__, έως, ὁ, *deputy high-priest*, *SB* 9016.1.1, 2.1 (ii AD), *POxy.* 3026.19 (ii AD).

__ἀνταυλέω__, for '*flute*' read '*pipe(s)* or *aulos*'

*__ἀντᾰχάτης__ *λίθος*, = *ἀντιαχάτης*, Socr.Dion.*Lith.* 40 H.-S., Plin.*HN* 37.139.

__ἀντέγκλημα__, after 'or -*charge*' insert 'Quint.*Inst.* 7.4.8'

*__ἀντειρήναρχος__, ὁ, *deputy εἰρήναρχος*, *SEG* 6.700, 711 (Pamphylia).

*__ἀντειρωνεύομαι__, *use εἰρωνεία in reply*, Sch.Gen.Il. 1.132.

__ἀντεισάγω__ __I__, add '__2__ *bring in as replacement* for shortfall, Just.*Nov.* 43.1 pr.'

**ἀντεισᾰγωγή**, add '**2** *replacement* of shortfall in funds, Just.*Nov.* 43.1 pr.'

**ἀντεισοδιάζω**, add '*SEG* 14.639.E20 (sp. ἀντισ-, Caunus, i AD; in uncertain sense, app. w. ref. to entering port)'

***ἀντεισπράττω**, *exact in return*, *SEG* 29.127.E82 (ii AD).

**ἀντέκτιστος**, delete the entry.

***ἀντέκτιτα**, τά, gloss on ἀντίτιμα, Hsch. (ἀνέκτιστα cod.).

***ἀντελία**, ἁ, = ἀντολίη, *Boeot.adesp.* 41 *fr.* 2.3 P. (pl.).

**ἀντεμβάλλω**, after 'Dsc. 2.49' insert 'ἀντεμβαλλόμενα καλοῦμεν τὰ ἀντὶ τῶν ἄλλων ἐμβαλλόμενα φάρμακα Gal. 19.721.4'

**ἀντεμβριάζειν**, add '(ἀντεμβιάζειν La.)'

***ἀντεμόνιον**, τό, *antimony*, Anon.Alch. 334.2.

**ἀντεμφᾰνίζω**, add '*make out a case before*, τῷ τε δήμ[ῳ] ἀντεμφανιοῦμεν *PZen.Col.* 11.10 (iii BC)'

***ἀντενᾰγωγή**, ἡ, *countersuit*, *Cod.Just.* 7.51.5.1.

***ἀντένδειξις**, after '*counter-indication*' insert 'Gal. 10.630.14'

***ἀντέντευξις**, εως, ἡ, *counter-petition*, *summons*, *PHib.* 203.7, 16 (iii BC).

**ἀντεξανίστᾰμαι**, add 'transf., of the principle of cold in relation to heat, Plu. 2.946d (v.l. ἀντεξίσταμαι, q.v.)'

**ἀντεξῐσάζω**, for 'Sch.Od. 11.308' read 'Sch.Od. 11.309'

**ἀντεπιστᾰ́της**, for the ref. read 'Bernand *Les Portes* 32 (*SB* 7027.4)' and within parenth. add 'ii AD'

***ἀντεπιτροπεύω**, astrol., *to be associate-ruler*, *PMich.*III 149 xvii 7, 11 (ii AD).

**ἀντεραστής**, after 'Ar.*Eq.* 733' insert 'X.*Cyn.* 1.7, Pl.*Amat.* 132c'

**ἀντερείδω I**, for '*clasping* hand in hand' read '*thrusting out* hand *towards* hand'

***ἀντερῐδαίνω**, = ἀντερίζω, Nonn.*D.* 36.28.

**ἀντερῶ**, after 'S.*Tr.* 1184' insert 'πρὸς τὰ ἀντειρημένα *Stoic.* 2.8'; add 'see also ἀντιλέγω'

**ἀντέρως II**, add 'pl., *IG* 12(5).917.6 (Tenos, i BC)' **III**, for 'name of a *gem*' read 'kind of amethyst'

***ἀντευγνωμονέω**, *perform a service duly in place of another*, prob. in *PSI* 1037.42 (iv AD).

**ἀντευεργέτημα**, add '*PLit.Lond.* 138 viii 40 (i AD, -γέμητα pap.)'

**ἀντευποιέω**, after '(Arist.)*Rh.* 1374ᵃ24' insert 'Arr.*Epict.* 2.14.18'

***ἀντεφάπτομαι**, *seize by way of reprisal*, *PMeyer* 8.8 (ii AD).

***ἀντεφηβαρχέω**, *to be deputy overseer of ephebes*, *IGBulg.* 14.7 (Dionysopolis, iii AD).

**ἀντεφόρμησις**, after '*attack*' insert 'Th. 2.91.4 (v.l. ἀντεξ-)'; for 'Hld. l.c.' read 'Hld. 8.16'

**ἀντήδην**, delete the entry.

***ἀντηδίς**· ἱκετευτικῶς Hsch. (La. cod. -δης), cf. Theognost.*Can.* 163.

⁺**ἀντημοιβός**, v. °ἀνταμ-.

**ἀντηρίς I**, add 'in building, ἀντειρίδας .. τοῦ βαλανείου *Pap.Lugd.Bat.* xxv 46.8 (late ii AD), unless in sense II'

**ἀντί I**, line 7, after 'witnesses' insert 'ἀντὶ τô ἀρχô *BCH* 87.3 (vi/v BC)' **III 2**, add 'Just.*Const.* Δέδωκεν 22; ἀνθ'οὗ, w. pers. n., *alias*, *BGU* 406.2.16, *PBasel* 10.5 (both ii AD)' **B**, add 'Hes.*Th.* 893' **C 7**, for '*counter*, as ἀντίφορτος' read 'as ἀντίγραφος' add 'Myc. *a-ti- in compds.*'

**ἀντιάζω I 1**, after '(Hdt.) 4.80, etc.' insert 'φλέγει με περιβόητος ἀντιάζων (Ares) S.*OT* 192', for 'abs.' read 'transf.' and after '(Pi.)*O.* 10(11).84' insert 'πρὸς μέλος ἠντίασεν *accompanied* the song, sc. by dance and gesture, *APl.* 287 (Leont.)' **2**, delete 'Ἄρεα ἀντιάζω S.*OT* 192'

***ἀντίαος**, ὁ, epith. of Zeus, god *of suppliants*, Alc. 129.5 L.-P., rest. in Sapph. 17.9 L.-P.; cf. ἀνταῖος II.

**ἀντιᾰχᾰ́της**, for 'dub.' read 'prob.'

**ἀντιβάλλω I**, lines 1/2, delete '(the acc. pers. being understood)' **II**, of Mss., add '[ἐ]κγεγραμμένον καὶ ἀντιβεβλημένον ἐκ τεύχους χαρτίνου διαταγμάτων ἐκ τοῦ ἐν Μαγνησίᾳ ἀρχείου *SEG* 32.1149 (Magnesia ad Maeandrum, AD 209), cf. *ISmyrna* 598.1 (ii AD)'

**ἀντιβίην**, after '(Il.) 5.220' insert 'A.R. 1.1002, 2.758'

**ἀντίβιος 1 b**, after '*enemy*' insert 'ἀντιβίοισι τύραννε *h.Hom.* 8.5'

***ἀντιβλεπόντως**, adv. from pres. part. of ἀντιβλέπω, *facing*, καθεσθέντα ἀ. τῷ κάμνοντι Paul.Aeg. 6.114 (168.5 H.).

**ἀντιβλέπω**, add 'Pherecr. 224 K.-A.'

***ἀντίβλησις**, εως, ἡ, expl. of ἀντιβολία, Hsch. s.v. κατ' ἀντιβολίαν.

***ἀντιβολάδιον**, τό, a surgical instrument, gloss in *Hermes* 38.281.

***ἀντιβουκολέω**, *practise trickery upon in return*, Aesop. 28 P.

***ἀντίβους**, ὁ, ἡ, sacrificed *instead of an ox*, οἶς ἀν[τ]ίβους *Sokolowski* 3.18 i 64 (Erchiae, Attica, iv BC); cf. ἀντίβοιος, ἐπίβοιον.

**Ἀντιγόνειος** (s.v. Ἀντίγονος), add 'of a tetrachm, *Ath.Asklepieion* v 106 (244/3 BC)'

**Ἀντίγονος**, add '**b** position in board game app. resembling backgammon, *AP* 9.482.17 (Agath.).'

***ἀντιγραμματεύς**, έως, ὁ, *deputy* γραμματεύς, *IG* 2².2067.225 (ii BC).

**ἀντιγρᾰφεῖον**, for pres. refs. read '*IEphes.* 14 (i BC), 1024.12 (ii AD, both sp. -ῖον)' and add '*SEG* 33.1039.79 (Aeolian Cyme, ii BC, sp. -ῖον)'

**ἀντιγρᾰφεύς**, add 'legal and administrative official of the emperor, Just.*Const.* Δέδωκεν 9; senate official, Lyd.*Mag.* 3.27'

**ἀντιγρᾰφή II**, add 'legal term at Paros, *SEG* 33.679.27 (ii BC), significance uncertain' **IV**, add 'Modest.*Dig.* 27.1.12.1'

***ἀντιγρᾰ́φιον**, τό, *medical prescription*, *PMerton* 12.13 (i AD); cf. °ἀντίγραφος II.

**ἀντίγρᾰφος I**, add 'ποιήσασθαι ἀ. ἐκ τῶν στηλῶν τὰ ἀναγεγραμμένα *IG* 2².120.22' **II**, after 'as subst.' insert 'Dor. ἀντίγροφον, *IG* 4².68.81 (Epid., iv BC), *Inscr.Cret.* 1.viii 10.5 (Cnossus, iii/ii BC), *IG* 12(3).248.22 (Anaphe, ii BC), *SEG* 25.640 (W.Locris, ii BC)' and add '*written reply*, *PSI* 584.29, *PCair.Zen.* 375.14 (both iii BC), *PKöln* 166.14 (vi/vii AD); *prescription*, Orib.*fr.* 97'

**ἀντιγρᾰ́φω II 2**, for '*keep a counter-reckoning* .. (cf. ἀντιγραφεύς)' read 'of clerk, *check*' and delete 'simply *check*'

**ἀντιγυμνᾰσιαρχέω**, add '*PLund* 4.9'

***ἀντιγυμνᾰσίαρχος**, ὁ, *deputy gymnasiarch*, Str. 14.5.14 (v.l., al. ἀντὶ γυμνασιάρχου).

***ἀντιδείκνῡμι**, *counter-indicate*, τὸ ἀντιδεικνύμενον Gal. 1.166.15, 18, 14.666.5.

**ἀντιδέχομαι**, add 'w. gen., *accept*, *exchange* one thing for another, Call.*fr.* 75.45 Pf. (tm.)'

***ἀντιδηλόω**, *inform in turn*, *reply*, pap. in *Tyche* 1.163.19 (vi/vii AD).

**ἀντιδιαγρᾰφή**, after 'ἡ' insert '*PSI* 571.4 (iii BC)'

**ἀντιδιαίρεσις II**, add 'Gal. 1.386.9, 11.128.11, 14'

***ἀντιδιαιρετικός**, ή, όν, *opposite*, *contrasted in a dichotomy*, David *in Porph.* 214.13/14.

***ἀντιδιάλεξις**, εως, ἡ, unexpld. wd., *ASAA* 3/5(1941/3).94 i 8 (Lemnos, ?ii BC).

***ἀντιδικαιολογέομαι**, *make a counter-claim*, *counter-plead*, *PMonac.* 14.25, *PMich.*XIII 659.21 (both vi AD).

**ἀντιδίσκωσις**, add '*An.Ox.* 3.405.8'

**ἀντιδομή**, delete '*opposed* or'

**ἀντίδοτος I**, add '**b** *given in return*, ἕλκος Nonn.*D.* 29.166.'

**ἀντιδωρεά**, add 'Just.*Nov.* 2 pr. 1'

***ἀντιενείριος**, ον, dub. sens., (cf. perh. ἀντιάνειρα) μητέρες ἀντιενίριοι, *IKourion* 127.2, 136.2, etc.

***ἀντιεξάγω**, *expel in turn*, *BGU* 1273.34 (iii BC).

**ἀντίζῠγος**, after '*correspondent*' insert 'Diog.Ath. 1.9'

***ἀντιζῶ**, *live instead*, βίον κοινόν *CIJud.* 1.144 (Rome).

**ἀντίθεμα**, add '*Didyma* 39.5, cf. 32.14, 15, 41.12, 17'

**ἀντίθεος I**, add '*in place of a god*, i.e. falsely similar to a god, Hld. 4.7.13, Iamb.*Myst.* 3.31, *PMag.* 7.635' **II 2**, delete the section.

**ἀντίθεσις**, line 6, for '*by negation*' read 'involving *use of the contradictory*'

**ἀντιθέω II**, add 'Nonn.*D.* 1.498'

**ἀντίθροος**, before 'Coluth. 118' insert 'Nonn.*D.* 13.44'

**ἀντίθῠρος**, add '*SEG* 33.880 (Ephesus, perh. masc. subst.)'

***ἀντικαθιστάνω**, *substitute*, *IG* 2².1099.24 (ii AD); also **ἀντικαθιστάω** Just.*Nov.* 16.1.

**ἀντικαθίστημι II 1**, add 'D.C. 48.53.1'

***ἀντικαταίνετοι**, οἱ, financial officials at Epidaurus, *IG* 4².109 ii 150 (iii BC).

**ἀντικατάλλαξις**, for '*BGU* 1210.177' read '*PGnom.* 177'

**ἀντικατάστᾰσις**, add '**2** *preliminary hearing before a strategus*, *BGU* 2241.3.'

***ἀντικατατῐ́θημι**, *put back*, *replace*, ἀντικαταθεῖναι ὁπόσον ἂν λάβοι Agath. 4.21.7 K.

***ἀντικατεργᾰσία**, ἡ, *tillage* of plot *in lieu of* another, *PMeyer* 1.6 (ii BC).

**ἀντικατηγορέω II**, for this section read '*predicate by interchange*, τινὰ ἀλλήλων D.H.*Th.* 24'; renumber old section II as III adding 'Sch. Iamb.*Protr.* 6'

***ἀντικάτοχος**, ον, *holding fast on the other side*, Anon.Alch. 419.9.

**ἀντίκειμαι III**, add '**b** ὁ ἀντικείμενος *the Devil*, *Cod.Just.* 1.4.34.9.'

***ἀντικήνσωρ**, ὁ, Lat. *antecessor*, class of law-teacher under Justinian, Just.*Const.* Δέδωκεν 9, 11.

***ἀντικνήμη**, ἡ, *shin*, *PLond.* 1821.179 (*Aegyptus* 6.179; vi AD).

***ἀντικνημία**, ἡ, *shin*, *SB* 5274.9 (iii AD).

***ἀντικονταίνω**, v. ἀντικοντόω.

**ἀντικοσμητεύω** (s.v. -ήτης in *LSJ*), for pres. ref. read '*IG* 2².2079 (ii AD)' and add '*SEG* 33.158.11 (Athens, iii AD)'

**ἀντικρίνω**, add 'Ael.*NA* 6.61'

**ἀντίκριος**, read '**ἀντίκρῑος**' and for 'Aen.Tact. 22.7' read 'Aen.Tact. 32.7'

***ἀντίκροκος**, ὁ, kind of aquatic plant, *Hippiatr.Paris.* 712.

**ἄντῐκρῠς**, line 3, for 'εἰς τὸ' read 'εἴσω (pap.)'

***ἀντικῠ́ριος**, ὁ, app. *one serving as his master's deputy*, *POxy.* 3239.45 (gloss., iii AD).

⁺**ἀντιλᾰ́βεύς**, έως, ὁ, *handle*, included in inventory of a sailing-ship's furnishings, *PCair.Zen.* 756.4 (iii BC).

**ἀντιλαμβάνω II 2**, for this section begin '*give a helping hand to*, οὐκ ἀντιλήψεσθ' E.*Tr.* 464; transf., *come to the assistance of, help*, w. gen., ἀντιλλαβέσθαι τᾶς πόλλιος, *BCH* 59.37.17 (Crannon, ii BC), ἀ. Ἑλλήνων, D.S. 11.13, etc.'

**ἀντιλέγω**, line 4, delete 'pf. ἀντείρηκα; fut. pass. ἀντειρήσομαι'; line 12, after 'Id. 1.28' insert '*urge in opposition*' **2**, delete 'πρὸς τὰ ἀντειρημένα .. *Stoic.* 2.8' (v. ἀντερῶ).

**ἀντιληπτικός 1**, line 4, after '*Stoic.* 2.230' insert 'ἡ δὲ γευστικὴ αἴσθησίς τε καὶ δύναμίς ἐστι .. ἀντιληπτική τε καὶ κριτικὴ τῶν γευστῶν Alex.Aphr.*de An.* 54.1'

**ἀντιλογία 3**, delete the section.

**ἀντιλογίζομαι**, add 'X.*Ath.* 1.16'

***ἀντιλύω**, *set free in turn*, *IG* 2².1225.18 (iii BC).

***ἀντιμᾰχεία**, ἡ, = ἀντιμάχησις, *An.Ox.* 3.171.24.

***ἀντιμειδιάω**, *smile in return*, *Vit.Aesop.*(G) 32.

**ἀντιμερίζομαι 2**, after 'Hsch.' insert 's.v. ἀντιδιαιρεῖται'

**ἀντιμεσουρᾰνέω**, after 'Ptol.*Tetr.* 33' insert '(v.l., al. μεσουρ-)'

**ἀντιμετάβᾰσις**, delete the entry.

**ἀντιμισθία**, add '*ICilicie* 35.8 (sp. ἀνταμισθεία, vi AD)'

***ἀντιμίσθωσις**, εως, ἡ, prob. *contract of lease executed by the lessor* as opposed to one executed by the lessee, *PMichael.* 43.23, 24 (vi AD), *PMasp.* 66.3, 107.18 (vi AD); cf. ἀντίπρασις.

**ἀντιμνηστεύω**, add 'Charito 8.7'

**ἀντίμοιρος**, after 'ον' insert '*having opposite fortunes*'

**ἀντίμολπος**, for '*song*, sleep's *substitute*' read 'i.e. song acting as a substitute for sleep'

**⁺ἀντίμορφος**, ον, *corresponding in shape*, τῶν ἀντιμόρφων χαρακτήρων ἀγράφους εἰκόνας Luc.*Am.* 44; adv. -φως, *in a contrary form*, Plu.*Crass.* 32.

***ἀντίμουσος**, ον, *sounding in answer*, μέλος Rh. 1.493.22.

***ἀντιμωλία**, ἡ, expld. as δίκη εἰς ἣν οἱ ἀντίδικοι παραγίνονται Hsch. s.v. μωλεῖ (ἀντιμολία cod.); ἀντ]ιμōλίαι rest. in *Inscr.Cret.* 4.13*b* (Gortyn, vi BC); cf. ‡ἀντίμωλος, °ἀγχεμωλία, ἀμφιμωλέω, ἀμφιμῶλος.

**ἀντίμωλος**, for '= ἀντίδικος' read 'ἀντίμōλος *adversary* in law-suit' and add '*Inscr.Cret.* 4.13*a*.1 (Gortyn, vii/vi BC), 2.v 10.4 (Axos, vi BC)'

***ἀντιναύτης**, ου, ὁ, *substitute sailor*, *SEG*.39.1180.64 (Ephesus, i AD).

**ἀντινέμομαι**, for '*bestow*' read '*receive*' and add 'act. prob. in *SEG* 11.343 (ἀ]ντινενέμων, Argos, iii BC)'

***ἀντινοέω** or **-νοέομαι**, *hold opposing views*, fut. part. ἀντινοησόμενος *PMasp.* 97.49 (vi AD).

***ἀντίνῡ**, τό, the letter *N* written in reverse, and representing a note in the musical scale, Alyp.*Diat.* 5, 13, *Chrom.* 5, 8.

**ἀντίξοος**, line 5, after 'A.R. 2.79' insert 'ἀ. .. διχο[φροσύνην] Call.*fr.* 43.73 Pf.'

**⁺ἀντίον**, τό, *the upper cross-beam* of a loom, Ar.*Th.* 822, *POxy.* 264.4 (i AD), Poll. 7.36, 10.125; as standard of comparison for a spear-shaft Lxx *2Ki.* 21.19, *1Ch.* 11.23.

**ἀντίος II**, as adv., add '**5** *in opposite ways*, ἀντία δεσμεύων Hes.*Op.* 481.'

***ἀντίουρος**, ὁ, = ἄνθορος, *opposite boundary* or *boundary stone*, *IEphes.* 3516.

**Ἀντιόχειος**, add '**II** *of the city of Antioch*, of weights, *IGLS* 1071 (d), (f), etc.; neut. pl. subst., Ἀντιόχεια, τά, *Inscr.Prien.* 59.21 (decr. of Laodicea, *c.*200 BC).'

***Ἀντιοχεών**, ῶνος, ὁ, name of month at Smyrna, rest. [Ἀντι]οχεών, *REA* 38.26; (previously read as Ὀχεών); also rest. [Ἀντιοχ]εῶνι, in *MAMA* 6.5.16 (Laodicea, iii BC).

***Ἀντιοχήσιος**, α, ον, *from Antioch*, Lat. *Antiochensis*, στιχάριον Ἀ. *PFouad* 74.6 (v AD), *POxy.* 1978.4, al. (sp. -χύσιος, vi AD).

***Ἀντιοχισταί**, οἱ, *partisans of Antiochus*, Plb. 21.6.2.

***ἀντίπανον**, τό, Lat. *antepannus*, *embroidered cloth*, Hsch. s.v. παρατούριον.

***ἀντιπανουργέω**, *practise trickery against* someone, Sch.Gen.Il. 3.325.

**ἀντιπαραβαίνω**, for '*PLips.* 298' read '*PLips.* 29.8'

**ἀντιπαράδοσις**, add '**II** *return of hired property*, *SB* 9305.5 (iv AD), Just.*Nov.* 64.1.'

**ἀντιπαράθεσις**, after '*contrast*' insert 'D.H.*Comp.* 18'

**ἀντιπαράκειμαι 1**, add 'Str. 11.8.2, *Peripl.M.Rubr.* 61' **2**, after 'τινί' insert 'D.H.*Dem.* 26'

***ἀντιπαραμένω**, *remain in service as compensation*, *Stud.Pal.* 22.36.14 (ii AD), *PMich.*inv. 5191a (*BASP* 22.255, iii AD).

**ἀντιπαρίστημι**, for 'Ptol.*Geog.* 8.1.14' read 'Ptol.*Geog.* 8.1.4'

***ἀντιπατρίδιον**, τό, dim. of ἀντιπατρίς, *PCair.Zen.* 38.11 (iii BC).

***Ἀντιπατρισταί**, οἱ, *followers of the philosopher Antipater*, Antip.*Stoic.* 3.246.

***ἀντίπατρος**, ὁ, perh. title of Mithraic initiate in one of the grades of initiation, *Dura*⁷·⁸ 119; cf. πατήρ v.

**ἀντιπελαργέω**, after '*cherish in turn*' insert 'as a stork cherishes its parent, Cels.ap.Orig.*Cels.* 4.98'; delete '*cherish in place .. parent*'

**ἀντιπελάργωσις**, before '*Com.adesp.* 939' insert '*return of benefits*'

**ἀντιπέρᾱν**, after 'A.R. 2.177, al.' insert 'w. gen., ἀντιπέρην γὰρ ἀείρεται Ἀρκτούροιο Arat. 405'; add 'see also ἀντιπέρα'

***ἀντιπεράω**, *cross to other side of* a river, *PFouad* 87.25 (vi AD).

**ἀντιπεριάγω**, add 'transf., *divert*, ἀντιπεριάγοντα τὴν ψυχὴν τῆς ἐς τὸ πονεῖν σχολῆς Ach.Tat. 1.6.3'

***ἀντιπεριέχω**, *enfold* or *encompass in turn*, ἀντιπεριέχει γὰρ ἄλληλα τὰ ἴσα κατά τι ἀντίστροφον Dam.*Pr.* 377.

**ἀντιπεριποιέομαι**, add '**2** part. as gloss on ἀρνύμενος, Hsch.'

**ἀντιπεριωθέω**, add 'Alcin.*Intr.* p. 175.24 H.'

**ἀντίπηξ**, for '*wheeled* .. infants' read 'prob. *a basket with a hinged lid*'; after 'Eust. 1056.46' insert 'cf. Hsch. s.vv. ἀντίπηξ, ἀντίπηγα'

**ἀντιπλάδη**, add 'τειχῶν ἐπιστάται τῆς ἀντιπλάδης *IEryth.* 23.4 (iv BC)'

**ἀντιποιέω I**, after '*in return*' insert 'τί A.*fr.* 78c.57 R.' **II**, lines 2/3, for 'τῶν σπουδαίων' read 'παιδείας'

**⁺ἀντίπους**, πουν, of position on the earth, *situated diametrically opposite*, Pl.*Ti.* 63a, Arist.*Cael.* 308ᵃ20, Cic.*Acad.Pr.* 2.39.123; εἰ γάρ εἰσιν ἀντίποδες ἡμῶν .. τῆς γῆς τὰ κάτω περιοικοῦντες Plu. 2.869c, Eratosth. 16.19; in the opposite hemisphere and under the opposite meridian, Cleom. 1.2; on the opposite side of the same hemisphere, Str. 1.1.13.

**ἀντίπρᾱσις**, for '*PLond.ined.* 2227' read '*SB* 6612.18'

**ἀντιπροβολή**, add 'τοῖς ἐξ ἀντιπροβολ[ῆ]ς κ̣αταστα̣θεῖσι [ταμίαις] *ISmyrna* 711.10 (late Rom.imp.)'

***ἀντίπροικον**, τό, = Lat. *donatio propter nuptias*, *PLond.* 1708.50 (vi AD).

**ἀντιπροπίνω II**, for 'προπίνω I 2' read 'προπίνω II 3'

**ἀντιπρόσωπος**, after 'X.*Cyr.* 7.1.25' insert 'τοῦ ἀ. θεάτρου id.*Eq.Mag.* 3.7'

**ἀντίπτωμα**, for '*stumble against* .. 29' read '*cause of stumbling*, Lxx *Si.* 35(32).20(25); *conflict*, ib. 34(31).29(39)'

***ἀντιπωλέω**, *sell in opposition to* (a state monopoly), *PTeb.* 709.14 (ii BC).

**ἀντιρρητορεύω**, add 'Lxx *4Ma.* 6.1'

***ἀντίρριζον**, v. ἀντίρρινον.

***ἀντισέβεια**, ἡ, *mutual reverence*, *PBremen* 37.11 (ii AD).

***ἀντισέληνος**, ον, *like the moon*, A.*fr.* 204c.6 R.

**ἀντισήκωμα**, add 'ἀ. ψελλίων *SB* 1962 (ostr., iv/v AD)'

**ἀντίσκηνος**, for pres. ref. read '*IEphes.* 2041' and add 'σινδ(όνιον) ἀντίσκ(ηνον) perh. cloth *screen*, *PVindob.* G25737.12 (*ZPE* 64.75, vi/vii AD)'

***ἀντίσκιον**, τό, *azimuth*, Ptol.*Anal.* pp. 193, 195 H.

***ἀντισκρίβας**, α, ὁ, *deputy scribe* (v. °σκρείβας), *PSI* 768.17 (v AD).

**ἀντισπάω II**, for '= ἀντέχομαι' read '(cf. ἀντέχομαι)'; after '*seize*' insert '*and hold back*'

***ἀντιστεφᾰνόω**, *crown in return*, *IG* 2².2969 (pass., iv BC).

**ἀντιστήκω**, add '*stand opposite* or *in front*, Serv. in Verg.*Georg.* 2.417'

**ἀντίστοιχος**, add 'Anon.Lond. 20.5'

**ἀντιστρᾰ́τηγος**, at beginning insert 'Aeol. ἀντιστρόταγος *SEG* 29.741'

***ἀντιστρᾰτιώτης**, add '*substitute soldier*, *SEG* 39.1180.64 (Ephesus, i AD).'

**ἀντιστρέφω IV, 3**, for '*opposites*' read '*contradictories*'

**ἀντιστροφή III 3**, for '*opposite*' read '*contradictory*'

**ἀντίστροφος VII, 1**, for 'ἀπόστροφος' read 'ἀπόστροφος II 1'

***ἀντισύγγρᾰφος**, ον, *executed by both parties*, *PMonac.* 7.6 (vi AD). **II ἀντισύγγραφον**, τό, *copy*, *counterpart* of legal instrument, *PDura* 19.18 (i AD), 32.19 (iii AD).

**ἀντισύγκλητος**, for 'Marius' read 'P. Sulpicius Rufus'

***ἀντισχολαστής**, οῦ, ὁ, *rival lecturer*, Suid. s.v. Ἀδριανός.

***ἀντισυνίστημι**, *set up in opposition*, εἰ τὰ κατὰ σχέσιν ὑφεστῶτα ἀντισυνίστησιν ἄλληλα Dam.*Pr.* 82.

***ἀντιτᾰγής**, ές, *belonging to the opposite order*, Dam.*Pr.* 56.

***ἀντιτᾰμιεύω**, *serve as deputy treasurer*, inscr. in *Studi off.a E.Ciaceri* p. 257 (Rhodes, iii AD).

**ἀντιτάσσω II 3**, read '*set oneself against, match*' and delete '(Pass.)'

**ἀντίτεχνος**, delete 'cf. *Lg.* 817b'; after 'w. gen.' insert 'τοῦ καλλίστου δράματος Pl.*Lg.* 817b'

**ἀντιτῑμάω II**, add '*IG* 12(2).526a.18-19, b.21-2'

**ἀντιτῑμωρέομαι**, add 'pf. pass. κινδύνους ἐκφυγόντα ἀντιτετιμωρῆσθαι τοὺς πολεμίους *SEG* 13.206.12 (Messenia, ii/iii AD)'

***ἀντιτοξότης**, ου, ὁ, *counter-archer*, Afric.*Cest.* 50.69 V.

**ἀντιτορέω**, for 'τετορεῖν' read 'τορέω'

**ἄντῑτος**, line 1, for 'which occurs in Hsch.' read 'cf. Sch.Il. 24.213 τὸ τέλειον ἀντίτιτα, ἵν' ᾖ ἀντιτιμώρητα'; line 2, for '*requited, revenged*' read '*done in requital* or *revenge*'; at end delete 'cf. Call.*Iamb.* 1.160'; add 'A.*Ag.* 1429 (cj.)'

**ἀντιτρέφω**, add 'Phld.*Epicur.* p. 72 V.'

***ἀντιτῡπητικός**, ή, όν, *resistant, solid*, Taurus ap.Phlp.*Aet.M.* 520.10 R.

**ἀντιτῡπία**, add '**II** of sounds, *clash, dissonance*, D.H.*Comp.* 20, al.'

ἀντίτῠπος I 1, line 4, for '(S.*Ph.*) 1460 (lyr.)' read '(S.*Ph.*) 1460 (anap.)' 2 c, line 2, after '(Berytus)' insert '[Εἰκ]όνος ἀντίτυπον καθορ[ᾶτε *TAM* 5(1).33'; line 3, after '(iv AD)' insert '*LW* 1639.13 (Caria)'

*ἀντίφαντος, ον, perh. *shining in one's face*, A.*fr.* 451i.10 R.

+ἀντιφᾰρα, ἡ, dub. (φάρω, N.W. Greek for φέρω, perh. contraction fr. ἀντιφάρεα for *ἀντιφέρεια), ἀ.· ἀντιλογία. μάχη. ζάλη. οἱ δὲ μητρυιά Hsch., *EM* 114.19.

*ἀντιφαρής, ές, dub., perh. N.W. Greek for *ἀντιφερής, *opposed* to, *the rival* of, ἀντιφαρές· ἐναντίον Hsch.; perh. also ἀντιφαριν (for ἀντιφαρῆν = -φερῆ) Λάκωνι .. Ἀλκμᾶ[νι Alcm. 13(a).8 P.

ἀντίφᾰσις, for 'ἐξ ἀντιφάσεως συλλογισμός .. not day' read 'ἐξ ἀ. διαιρετικὸς συλλογισμός disjunctive syllogism w. *contradictory alternatives*'

ἀντιφᾰτικός, after '*contradictory*' insert 'Alex.Aphr. *in Top.* 580.16'; delete 'only in'

ἀντιφέρω, line 5, for 'cogn.' read 'of respect'

ἀντιφῐλοφρονέομαι. for pres. def. read '*treat with kindness* or *affection in return*' and delete 'also, *rival*'

*ἀντιφρακτικός, ή, όν, *obstructive*, Phlp. *in de An.* 365.34.

ἀντιφωνέω II, add 'Just.*Nov.* 4.1'

ἀντιφώνησις, add 'II = Lat. *constitutum*, *promise to pay* an existing debt, *PFlor.* 343.3 (v AD), Just.*Nov.* 136.1.'

+ἀντιφωνητής, οῦ, ὁ, *one who promises repayment* of a debt, *POxy.* 136.39 (vi AD), Just.*Nov.* 4.1.

ἀντιχᾰλεπαίνω, for '*to be embittered against*' read '*to show rancour in return*'

*ἀντιχέλυσμα, v. ἀντιχάλημα.

ἀντίχρησις, add '*Dig.* 13.7.33'

*ἀντίχωμα, ατος, τό, *embankment*, *AE* 1923.39.34 (Oropus, iv BC).

ἀντίψαλμος, add 'prob. rest. in A.*fr.* 451e.13 R.'

ἀντίψῡχος 1, for '*given for life*' read '*given in exchange for life*'; add 'ἀντίψυχον, τό, *ransom given in exchange for a life*, ἀντίψυχον αὐτῶν λαβὲ τὴν ἐμὴν ψυχήν Lxx 4*Ma.* 6.29, 17.21; cf. ἀντίλυτρα, ἀντίψυχα Hsch. s.v. περίψημα'

ἀντλέω I, add 'for irrigation, ἀντλοῦντ(ες) εἰ[ς] τὸ νεόφυτ[ον] *PMil.Vogl.* 308.30, al. (ii AD)'

ἀντλησμός, add 'sp. ἀντλισμός in *PBerl.Leihg.* 23.15 (iii AD)'

+ἀντλητός, ὁ, *irrigation*, *PMich*.II 123ʳ ii 30 (i AD). *PFlor.* 369.6 (ii AD).

ἀντλήτρια, for '*DDeor.* 2.1' read '*DMeretr.* 2.1'

ἀντλιαντλητήρ, after '*bucket*' insert 'Ar.*fr.* 486 K.-A.' and for 'Men. 30' read 'Men.*fr.* 269 K.-Th.'

ἄντλος I, neut. form τὸ ἄντλον, add 'Sch.A.*Th.* 796h' 2, after '*bilge-water*' insert 'πὲρ μὲν γὰρ ἄντλος ἰστοπέδαν ἔχει Alc. 326.6 L.-P.'

ἀντοικοδομή, for '*IG* 12(1)' read '*IG* 12(3)'

ἄντοικος, for pres. def. read 'pl., *those who live between the same meridian lines, but on the opposite side of the equator*'

*ἀντολεύς, έως, ὁ, *riser*, of Apollo, *PMag.* 2.108.

ἀντολίη 1, after 'personified' for pres. ref. read '*PMag.* 2.93, Orph.*H.* 12.12, 78.5'

ἀντόμνῡμι II, for 'Antipho 1.18' read 'Antipho 1.8'

ἄντομος, for '*stake* or *pale*' read '*divider*, hence *unploughed land between plots*, *baulk*, *Tab.Heracl.* 1.15, 2.13, al.; cf. ἀντόμους· σκόλοπας Hsch. (perh. erron.)'

ἀντορύσσω, delete 'metaph.' and after 'ὀφθαλμούς' insert '*gouge out each other's* eyes'

ἄντρον I, add 'referring to a model of a cave, Ath. 5.200c' II, for '*inner chamber, closet*' read 'transl. Hebr. *'armôn* (fortified tower of palace)'

ἀντροφυής, for '*born in caves*, ἀυθίαι' read '*hollow by nature*, πέτραι'

*ἀντροφύλαξ, ἄκος, ὁ, *guardian of the cave*, in Bacchic worship, *IUrb. Rom.* 160.3B.28 (Latium, ii AD).

*ἀντυγάς, άδος, ἡ, = ἄντυξ I 1, rest. in Call.*fr.* 115.16 Pf.

*Ἀντώνεια, τά, shortened form of °Ἀντωνεινεῖα, *IG* 2².3015, al. (iii AD), perh. in *SEG* 30.1524.2 (Lycia), *TAM* 5(2).1024 (sp. -ῆα, Thyatira), Ἀντώνηα Γετεῖα Ὀλύμπια Robert *Laodicée* p. 285 (sp. -ῆα).

*Ἀντωνεινεῖα, τά, name of various festivals instituted in honour of Antonine emperors, Robert *Hell.* 11-12.350 (Ancyra), *AS* 39.50 (Balboura), *CRAI* 1970.20 (from Delphi, naming five different states); also Ἀντωνῖνα Robert *Laodicée* p. 293.

ἀντωνῠμικός, after 'D.H.*Amm.* 2.12' insert '(v.l. ἀντωνυματικόν)'

*ἀντώνυμον, τό, = ἀντωνυμία, A.D.*Pron.* 4.5.

ἀνυβριστί, delete the entry.

ἀνύβριστος I, after '*not insulted*' insert 'esp. of property, *free from outrage, inviolate*'; add 'adv. -α, τὴν ἐξουσίαν ἐχούσης τῆς θεοῦ ἀνύβριστα *SEG* 24.498a (Leucopetra, Maced., ii AD)' II, adv., add 'cj. in Anacr. (11(*a*).5 P.)'

*ἀνῠγιαίνω, *return to health*, Bataille *Hatshepsout* no. 36.1 (v. Van Brock *Vocab.med.* 157 no. 1).

*ἀνυγραντέον, *one must moisten*, Aët. 7.20 (269.19 O.).

*ἀνυγραντικός, ή, όν, *moistening*, δύναμις Plu. 2.659c.

ἀνυμφής, delete the entry.

*ἀνύμφιος, ον, *unmarried*, τὴν ἀνύμφ[ι]ον κόρην rest. in *Didyma* 567.1.

ἄνυμφος I, add 'of Helen, τὴν ἄνυμφον πόρτιν Lyc. 102; of Europa, Mosch. 2.41 G.' II, add 'of a man who died unmarried, *Salamine* no. 192 (ii/i BC)'

+ἀνῠόδρομος, ον, perh. *finishing the race*, *Lesb. fr.adesp.* 11 L.-P.

*ἀνυπάλλακτος, ον, *not pledged*, *PMasp.* 309.35 (vi AD).

*ἀνυπᾰναγκαῖος, ον, *voluntary*, *BGU* 741.37 (ii BC).

ἀνύπεικτος, before 'Suid.' insert 'Paul.Aeg. 2.43 (125.8 H.)'

ἀνυπεξαιρέτως, for '*exception*' read '*reservation*'

ἀνυπέρβλητος 1, adv. -τως, add '*IHistriae* 57.11'

*ἀνυπέρβολος, ον, *not increased*, of rent, *PMil.Vogl.* 267.32 (ii AD).

ἀνυπερθεσία, for '*immediateness, haste*' read '*immediate rejection*'

ἀνυπερθετέω, for pres. def. read '*reject immediately*' and after 'ib.' insert '57.21, 59'

ἀνυπεύθῡνος I, add '3 *not liable to reproach*, Just.*Nov.* 25.3.'

+ἀνῠπηνος, ον, Dor. -ᾱνος, app. *having no moustache*, Alcm. 10 (*b*).18 P., Eust. 1353.47; cf. ἀνύπηνον· ἀγένειον Hsch.

ἀνυπόδῐκος, line 1, delete 'Plu.*Cat.Mi.* 11' and before '*action*' insert '*legal*'; add '*SEG* 33.1039.84 (Aeolian Cyme, ii BC); *freedom from liability*, ἀλλὰ καὶ τῷ γραφείῳ τὸ ἀνυπεύθυνον καὶ τὸ ἀ. ἐπίστευσεν Plu.*Cat.Mi.* 11, *BGU* 1273.35 (iii BC)'

ἀνυπόθετος I, adv., for '*not hypothetically*' read '*not giving the conditions* or *situation*' add 'III *not mortgaged*, *TAM* 2.261*b*16.'

*ἀνυπόθηκος, ον, perh. *without external suggestion* or *pressure*, τοῦ βίου προαίρεσιν πεποιημένος -ον καὶ ἀναντι[.. Maiuri *Nuova Silloge* 443 (Cos).

ἀνυπόκρῐτος III, for 'in a .. sentence' read 'preceding clause which is not the apodosis' and for 'p. 24' read 'pp. 24, 27'

+ἀνυπόληπτος, ον, *disreputable, discreditable*, Anon. *in Rh.* 82.38, *PLand.* 132.8 (vi/vii AD).

+ἀνυπόμνηστος, ον, perh. *not the subject of any petition* or *challenge*, *PFlor.* 323.13, *PMasp.* 151.143 (both vi AD); dub. sens. in Phld.*Piet.* 98.

ἀνύποπτος 3, delete '*unhesitatingly*' and transfer quot. to section 1.

ἀνυπόστατος I, line 4, after 'D. 54.38' insert 'πολέμιοι Isoc. 3.71' II, add '5 in legal terminology, *without a basis, invalid*, of the institution of an heir, *Cod.Just.* 6.48.1.27, of a will, Theophil.Antec. 2.13 pr.'

ἀνυπόστολος, add 'τὰν τᾶς πόλιος ἀνυπό[σ]τολον εὐχαριστίαν *SEG* 26.1817.58 (Arsinoe, Cyrenaica, ii/i BC)'

ἀνυπόστροφος 1, for 'Orph.*H.* 56' read 'Orph.*H.* 57'

*ἀνυποσφρᾱγίς, ίδος, (sic) *not under seal*, *PMasp.* 151.11 (vi AD).

*ἀνυποτελής, ές, *not subject to charges*, *PMasp.* 98.14 (vi AD).

ἀνυποτίμητος, -τως, add '*without calculating the cost*, *Didyma* 287.20'

ἀνυτικός 1, line 3, for 'of persons .. (Sup.)' read 'J.*BJ* 5.9.2 (comp.), of persons, 1.17.8 (sup.)'

*ἄνυτος, ή, όν, *feasible*, S.E.*M.* 1.81.

*ἀνυφόρατος, ον, *unexceptionable*, *BGU* 1730 (i BC).

ἀνυψόω, for '*PGen.* 51.27 (iii AD)' read '*PGen.* 51.27 (iv AD)'

ἀνύω I 2, add '*AP* 7.474; *defeat*, ἀθλητὰς ἤνυσε *GVI* 263.4 (Phrygia, ii AD)' 9, add 'b *collect*, χρήματα δημόσια *Cod.Just.* 10.30.4.6, 10.19.9.4.'

*ἀνφάδιος, acc. to Hsch. variant of ἀφάδιος (s.v.).

ἄνω (B) A II d, add 'τᾶι ἄνω πόλι καὶ τᾶι κάτω (referring to Gortyn) *SEG* 23.563.2 (Axos, iii BC); also *out to sea*, Il. 24.544'

*ἀνωβλεπής, ές, *turned upwards*, καρδίον ἀ. μορέας Cyran. 1.12.39 K.

ἄνωγα, line 3, after 'E.*Or.* 119' insert 'Call.*fr.* 628 Pf.'; line 14, for 'ἄνωγον *Inscr.Cypr.* 135 H.' read 'Cypr. *a-no-ko-ne* ἄνωγον *ICS* 217.2 (Idalium, v BC)'

ἀνωγή, add 'ἀχράντοισιν ἀνωγαῖς *Salamine* no. 202 (iv AD)'

ἄνωθεν I 2 b, for 'τῆς .. 12' read 'ὅς ἂν βάλλῃ τὰ ἐκ(κ)[α]θάρματα ἄνōθεν τῆς ὁδō *IG* 12(5).107 (Paros, v BC), Ar.*Ach.* 433, *Av.* 1526' II 1, after '*from farther back*' insert 'Hp.*VM* 3' and add 'σύμμαχος ἄνωθε (sc. Νεικομήδεια) *long-time* ally, *TAM* 4(1).25.9'

ἀνωθέω 2, after 'Hp.*Art.* 80' insert 'Sch.Arat. 346'

ἀνώϊστος (A), after 'Il. 21.39' insert 'μῦθον ἀ. A.R. 3.670, πότμῳ ἀ. id. 3.800, *AP* 7.564' and after 'A.R. 1.680' insert 'al.'

ἀνωμᾰλία III, add 'περιόδων D.H.*Comp.* 22'

ἀνωμᾰλοκράς, add '(ἀνωμαλόκουρος· ἀνωμάλως κεκαρμένη, οἱ δὲ λελυμένως La.)'

ἀνωμολόγητος, delete the entry.

ἄνωνις, after 'v.l. .. 485a' add '(= *Suppl.Hell.* 1138)'

ἀνωνῠμία, add 'Alex.Aphr. *in Metaph.* 493.31'

*ἀνωνύμιος, ον, *nameless* or *unspeakable*, ὄρνις *Carm.Pop.* 13 P. (dub.).

ἀνώνυμος I 3, after '*unspeakable*' insert '[Τρο]ίας .. ἀλώσι[μο]ν [ἆμ]αρ ἀ. Ibyc. 1(*a*).14 P.' II, at end for 'Herod. 6.14' read 'Herod. 5.45'

+ἄνωξις· βούλευσις Hsch.; cf. ἄνωγα.

+ἄνωρος, ον, *not of age, minor*, *Leg.Gort.* 7.29; *untimely*, ἄ. ἀποθανών

Hdt. 2.79 (v.l. ἄωρος), ἐνθάδ' ἄνωρος ἐὼν ἔθανον *CEG* 171.1 (Egypt, v BC); *unripe, sharp,* ἄνωρον· ὀξύν Hsch.; cf. ἄωρος (A) 2; adv. -ως, [πολλὰ γο]δσα, ὅτ' ἀνδρῶς ὄλετο ὃν ἀγαθός *CEG* 117.2 (Pharsalus, v BC).

***ἀνώρροπος**, ον, *tending upwards,* of heat, Olymp. *in Phd.* p. 244 N.; κατὰ τὸ ἀ. Phlp. *in GC* 229.20.

***ἀνωτέρειος**, α, ον, *belonging to the upper portion, APF* 1.64 (ii BC).

**ἀνώτερος**, after 'Nic.Dam. p. 25 D.' insert 'ποιήσει .. ναυαγίων ἀνώτερον will make him *superior* to shipwrecks, Dionysius in *WS* 20.319'

**ἀνωφάλακρος**, delete the entry.

**ἀνωφελής**, add 'form *νωφελής, Myc. *no-pe-re-a₂* (neut. pl.), of wheels, *unserviceable*'

**ἀνωφέλητος I**, add 'ἀ. καὶ θεοῖς ἐχθρός Stratt. 68 K.-A.' **II**, delete 'ἀ. .. 9 D.'

**ἀνώχυρος I**, delete '= ἀνόχυρος' and add 'so prob. *PZilliac.* 1.24 (ii BC); cf. ἀνοχυρόομαι'

**ἀξία I 2**, add 'like Lat. *dignitas*: *rank, office,* κόμητος ἀξίαν *Cod.Just.* 12.33.8.2, *class,* τῇ τῶν μεγαλοπρεπεστάτων ἰλλουστρίων ἀξίᾳ Just.*Nov.* 15.1 pr.; in the church, *office, Cod.Just.* 1.3.41.19; *class,* τῆς ἱερατικῆς ἀξίας ib. 1.2.24.15'

**ἀξιάγαστος**, add '*PHerm.* 2 (iv AD)'

***ἀξιάζω**, = ἀξιόω, *think it right, expect that, SEG* 38.1476.99 (Xanthos), *ILampsakos* 34.33, *IEryth.* 121.5 (all iii BC).

**ἀξιάω**, delete the entry (v. °ἀξιάζω).

**ἀξίνη 2**, add '*Alcmaeonis* 1.3 p. 33 B.' **3**, add 'Call.*Cer.* 6.35, S.*Ant.* 1109 (perh. here used for digging; cf. *AB* 62.9, as expl. of σκαφεῖον, mod. Gk. ἀξίνα *pickaxe*)'

**ἀξινίδιον**, after 'foreg.' insert '*PTeb.* 794.13 (iii BC), *PCair.Zen.* 783.12 (pl., iii BC)'

***ἀξῑνογλυφία**, *cutting into with an axe, Phys.* B. 164.2.

***ἀξῑνογλύφω**, *cut into with an axe, Phys.* B. 164.1, 169.1.

***ἀξῑνομαντεία**, ἡ, *divination by axes,* Plin.*HN.* 36.142.

***ἄξῑνος** ὁ, = ἀξίνη, (distd. fr. πέλεκυς) *SEG* 24.361.14 (Thespiae, iv BC).

***ἀξιοδότας**, α, ὁ, *having the entitlement to give, IG* 9²(1).609.17 (Locris, v BC).

**ἀξιόζηλος**, add 'Ael.*NA* 6.15, 43'

**ἀξιοζήλωτος 1**, for '= foreg.' read '*enviable, admirable*' and add '*TAM* 2.767.23 (Lycia), *IG* 12(7).231.4 (Amorgos, ii/i BC); adv. -ως, *BMus.Inscr.* 925.21 (Branchidae, i BC)'

**ἀξιόλογος**, for 'ἀλίθοι' read 'ἀ. λίθοι' **2**, add 'as honorific title, of Apollo, *POxy.* 1578.iii.2, 2153.1.27; of prominent citizens, sup., *MAMA* 8.508, 509 (Aphrodisias), *Didyma* 156, 168; of women, *IHadr.* 68, *ITrall.* 240 (all iii AD)'

**ἀξιόνῑκος**, after '*victory*' insert 'Cratin. 171.2 K.-A.'; after 'X.*Cyr.* 1.5.10' insert 'τὸν ἀ. δεκάπρωτον *SEG* 31.372 (Olympia, ii AD)'; add 'adv. -κως, *Didyma* 194.12'

***ἀξιοπᾰθεῖ**, gloss on βρενθύεται, Hsch. (ἀναξιο- La.).

***ἀξιοπᾱ́μων**, ον, gen. ονος, perh. *worthily endowed,* Lyr.ap. Favorinus *Exil.* 11.6 B.

**ἀξιοπρεπής**, add 'adv. -πῶς, *SEG* 37.501 (Phthiotic Thebes, vi AD)'

**ἄξιος I 3 b**, line 4, for 'Lys. 22.18' read 'Lys. 22.8' and after it insert 'ἵν' ὡς ἀξιώτατον ὑμῖν πωλοῖεν id. 22.11, ἀξιώτερον τὸν σῖτον ὠνήσεσθε, εἰ δὲ μή, τιμιώτερον 22.22'

***Ἀξιοττηνός**, ὁ, epith. of the divinity Μήν, *TAM* 5(1).251, *SEG* 37.1000, 1001 (Lydia, ii/iii AD).

**ἀξιοχρεία**, for '*CPH* 97.13' read '*CPHerm.* 97.13'

***ἀξιοχρέων**, ονος, = ἀξιόχρεως, *SPAW* 1937.156 (Miletus, iii BC), *Delph.* 3(3).239.17 (ii BC).

**ἀξιόχρεως II**, adv., add 'Modest.*Dig.* 50.12.10'

***ἀξιοχρήματος**, ον, *worth money,* οἱ ἀγαθοὶ οὐκ ἀ. λέγονται ἀλλ' ἀξιόλογοι Steph.*in Rh.* 304.17.

**ἀξιόω II 2**, line 6, after '*PEleph.* 19.18' insert '*request* (someone), ἠξίωσα τοὺς δεσπότας *INikaia* 767 (iv AD)' **III 2**, line 6, after 'D. 21.101' insert '*consent, allow,* ὁ θεὸς ἀξιώσι ἡμᾶς προσκ(υνεῖν) ἐν οἰγίᾳ (= ὑγιείᾳ) *POxy.* 1837.16 (vi AD), 1857.4 (vi/vii AD)'; line 10, after 'X.*Oec.* 21.4' insert 'οὐκ ἠξιώθην καταφιλῆσαι τὰ παιδία μου *I was not allowed* .., Lxx *Ge.* 31.28' add '**4** ἀ. ὥστε w. inf., Macho 328 G.' **IV 2**, penultimate line, after 'II 2)' insert 'Pl.*Phd.* 86d' add '**V** ἀξιομένων (τῶν δεῖνα), official designation in *BCH* 50.401 (Thespiae).'

**ἀξίωμα I 2**, add 'Moschio Trag. 9.9' **3**, add '*office, post, Cod.Just.* 12.33.8.3, *rank, class,* Just.*Nov.* 38 pr. 3 (pl.)' **II 1**, add '*decree* displayed in public (as Lat. *libellus*), Αὔγουστος Σαμίοις ὑπὸ τὸ ἀξίωμα ὑπέγραψεν *SEG* 32.833 (Aphrodisias, i BC)' **3**, after '*request, petition*' insert '*SIG* 656.6 (Abdera, ii BC)'

**ἀξιωμᾰτικός I 1**, add '**b** neut. pl. subst., *meretricious payments, subsidies, Cod.Just.* 1.5.20.7.' **3**, delete the section transferring exx. to section I 2.

**ἀξίωσις I 2**, add 'ἀ. τῶν ὀνομάτων Th. 3.82.4' **II b**, add 'public *petition* (for the holding of market-days), *SEG* 32.1149 (Magnesia ad Maeandrum, iii AD)' **IV**, delete the section.

**ἀξουγγία**, at end for 'ὀξούγγιον' read 'ὀξύγγιον'

**ἀξῠλία**, after 'Hes.*fr.* 314 M.-W.' insert 'Call.*fr.* 176.4 Pf.'

**ἄξῠλος I**, for '*with no timber* .. wood' read '*having no timber,* i.e. devoid of large trees, ἄξυλος ὕλη'

**ἄξων I 1**, add 'sp. αὔξων *POxy.* 1986 (vi AD)' **II**, after '*axis*' read 'Plu.*Sol.* 23, 25, Plu. 2.779b, Ammon.*Diff.* 57, Sch.Ar.*Av.* 1354; sg., πρῶτος ἄχσōν *IG* 1³.104.10, D. 23.31, Luc.*Eun.* 10' at end add 'Myc. *a-ko-so-ne* (pl., in sense I 1)'

**ἀοζία**, add '(of husband and wife)'

**ἄοζος**, for 'Call.*Del.* 249' read 'Call.*fr.* 563 Pf., *Del.* 249 (cj.)'; add 'fem., τὰν .. ἄ., *SEG* 15.385.2 (Dodona, v BC; unless erron, for τὸν); v. also ἄζος'

**ἀοιδή 3**, add '**b** of a book of poems, *AP* 4.1.1 (Mel.).'

**ἀοίδιμος**, at beginning insert 'Boeot. ἀϜύδιμος Corinn. 40 *fr.* 5(*a*).8 P.' **I**, line 2, before 'προφάταν (Pi.*Pae.* 6.6)' insert '*full of song, skilled in song*'; at end for '*notorious, infamous*' read '(cf. Od. 24.200 s.v. ἀοιδή 4)'

***ἀοιδολαβράκτας**, α, ὁ, *boaster in song,* cj. in Pratin.Trag. 6.6 S.

**ἀοιδοπόλος 2**, for 'Aus.*Ep.* 14' read 'Aus.*Ep.* 10'

**ἀοιδός I 1**, line 4, for 'Arist.*Metaph.* 983ᵃ4' read 'Sol. 29 W.' **II 1**, after '*musical*' insert 'τὴν ἀοιδὸν ἀκρίδα *AP* 7.198 (Leon.Tarent.); comp., ἀοιδοτέρα Alcm. 1.97 P.; sup.'; after 'cf.' insert 'Phanocl. 1.22'; add 'comp. adv. φθέγξετ' ἀοιδότερον *AP* 11.195 (Diosc.)' **2**, add '*AP* 9.424 (Duris), sup. *SEG* 11.773 (epigr., Sparta, iv AD)' **III**, delete 'cf. δοῖδος'

**ἀοίκητος I**, add 'Isoc. 4.148, 15.22'

***ἀοῖος**, v. ἠοῖος.

**ἀολλίζω I**, add 'Τρώων ἀόλλιζον φάλαγγας B. 15(14).42 S.-M.'

***ἀόξοος**· ἀδιάγλυφος Hsch. (La.).

**ἀόρᾱτος**, add 'see also °ἀβόρατος'

⁺**ἀοργησία**, ἡ, *deficiency in the passion of anger,* Arist.*EN* 1108ᵃ3, 1126ᵃ3. **2** *restraint in respect of anger, self-control,* Plu. 2.452 (title), Nic.Dam. 103w J., Andronic.Rhod. p. 575 M., Gal. 5.30.18.

**ἀοριστιαίνω**, for '= sq.' read '*to be in an indeterminable state,* Alcin.*Intr.* 26 (179.28 H.), *to be indeterminate*'

**ἀοριστία 2**, add 'Procl.*Inst.* 117 D.'

**ἀορτήρ 1**, add 'Pherecr. 41 K.-A.'

**ἀόρτης I**, before '(Maced.)' insert '*PSI* 858.37 (iii BC)'

**ἀοσμία**, for 'Thphr.*CP* 6.16.3' read 'Thphr.*HP* 6.6.5'

**ἀοσσητήρ**, after 'Od. 4.165' insert 'Call.*Ap.* 104, *fr.* 18.4 Pf.'

***ἀουνδίκιος**, unexpld. wd., referring to land belonging to the ταμιεῖον rather than κτήτορες, *POxy.* 3205.14, 23, 35, etc. (iii/iv AD).

***ἄπ**, v. °ἀπό.

***ἀπᾶ**, v. °ἀββᾶς.

**ἀπαγγελία I 1**, delete 'in Psychology .. Plot. 4.6.3' and add '**3** *recitation* or *repetition from memory,* Plot. 4.6.3.'

**ἀπαγγέλλω**, add '**III** *recite* or *repeat from memory,* Synes.*Ep.* 111, Sch.*Ar.V.* 1109 (in dramatic rehearsals), Suid. s.v. Καλλιφάνης.'

**ἀπάγγελσις**, add 'rest. in *Hesperia* 26.52 no. 9 line 1 (iv BC)'

**ἀπαγγελτικός I**, after '*reporting*' insert 'Alcin.*Intr.* 4 p. 154.30 H.'

***ἀπαγγισμός**, ὁ, (ἄγγος), *decanting, PCol.* 239 (iv AD).

***ἀπαγκάζομαι**, *lift away,* ἀπὸ μὲν .. λίθον ἀγκάσσασθαι Call.*fr.* 236.1 Pf.

***ἀπαγκίστρωσις**, εως, ἡ, *barbed form,* Sch.Gen.Il. 21.474 (pl.).

**ἀπαγκωνίζομαι I**, for '*bare the elbows*' read '*thrust the elbows away from the body*'

**ἀπαγλαΐζω I**, after '*Pers.* 20' insert 'Agath. 2.15, 5.14 K.'

**ἀπάγνῡμαι**, add 'pf. part. act. ἀπεαγώς *broken, IG* 2².1447.15 (iv BC); [στέφανος] *Inscr.Délos* 385*a*23 (ii BC)'

**ἀπᾰγορεύω I**, line 11, after 'Arist.*Pol.* 1298ᵃ38' insert 'w. acc., ὁ νόμος .. αὐτῇ ἀπαγορεύει τὴν τοῦ παιδὸς διαδοχὴν Just.*Nov.* 22.40'; at end add 'abs., *make a prohibition, SEG* 33.1468 (Ptolemais, Cyrenaica, ii/i AD)' **III**, for this section read '*speak from,* ἀπὸ τō λάō (ὃ ἀπαγορεύοντι, lit. *from the stone from which they speak, Leg.Gort.* 10.36, rest. in 11.13' add '**IV** (perh. transl. Lat. *renuntio*) *announce, proclaim,* Just.*Nov.* 117 epilogos.'

***ἀπάγριος**, ον, perh. *domesticated, tame,* πρόβατο(ν) ἀπάγριν on mosaic depicting a sheep and a bird, *SEG* 34.1439 (Apamea, Syria, vi AD).

***Ἀπαγχομένη** (ἀπάγχω), title of Artemis in Arcadia, Call.*fr.* 187 Pf., Paus. 8.23.7.

**ἀπάγω II**, add 'med., perh. *get oneself back, return, OFlorida* 1.4' **IV 3**, for 'And. 4.181' read 'And. 4.18' add '**4** *carry off to execution,* D.S. 13.102.3, J.*BJ* 6.2.7, *Ev.Luc.* 23.26, *POxy.* 33 iii 15.' **V b**, for 'Arist.*APr.* 29ᵇ9' read 'Arist.*APr.* 29ᵇ8' add '**VII** *weigh short, weigh less than the supposed weight, Inscr.Délos* 1417*A*ii68 (ii BC), al.; cf. ἄγω VI.'

***ἀπᾰγώγιμος**, ον, *which is to be delivered,* σῖτον .. ἀ[πα]γώγιμον *SIG* 360.47 (Cherson.Taur., iii BC, v. *BE* 1950.151).

***ἀπᾱέτωμα**, ατος, τό, = ἀέτωμα, *IG* 2².1685*B*4.4.

***ἀπαθῷος**, ον, unexpld. wd., Hdn.*fr.* p. 19 H.

**ἀπαίδευτος I**, add '**3** *uncontrolled, unrestrained*, *Trag.adesp.* 523 K.-S., J.*AJ* 19.2.9; τὸ ἀ., *lack of control*, ib. 17.9.3.'

***ἄπαιδος**, ον, *childless*, ἄπαιδος καὶ ἀδιάθετος *PSI* xx *Congr.* 16.8 (iv AD).

**⁺ἀπαίνῡμαι**, v. °ἀποαίνυμαι.

**ἀπαίρω I**, line 4, delete 'in (E.)*IT* 967 .. πειρατήρια' and transfer quot. to section II 2 (*depart*).

**ἀπαιτέω I 1 a**, line 10, after 'Arist.*EN* 1164ᵃ17' insert 'ποινὰς ἀ. Jul.*Or.* 2.59a'; at end, w. inf., add 'ἀ. αὐτοὺς πάντα πληροῦν *Cod.Just.* 1.3.45 pr.; w. ἵνα, ib. 6.4.4.16a' **b**, delete the section. **II 2**, line 3, after 'Lxx *Wi.* 15.8' insert 'ποινὰς ἀ. Jul.*Or.* 2.58a'

***ἀπαιτήσιμος**, ον, *subject to dues*, *PMichael.* 34.4 (vi AD); cf. ἀπαιτήσιμον, τό.

**ἀπαίτησις**, add 'Lxx *Ne.* 5.10, *Sir.* 34(31).31, *2Ma.* 4.27, πληρῶσαι τὴν τῆς εἰκόνος ἀ. satisfy the *requirements* of the picture, Ael.*VH* 2.44'

**ἀπαιτητής**, add '*Cod.Just.* 10.19.9.4'

**ἀπαιωρέομαι I 1**, delete '*hover about*' and add 'Arr.*Tact.* 34.4' **I 2**, delete the section. **II**, for '*lift up* a garment' read '*hold up, lift* from the ground' and add 'pass. Luc.*Astr.* 19'

**ἀπακρῑβόομαι I**, line 4, after 'of persons' insert 'ἐκ τοίης ὤνθρωποι ἀπηκριβωμένοι ὀστῶν ἁρμονίης *AP* 7.472.7 (Leon.Tarent.)'

**ἀπᾰλαιστρος I 1**, after '*unskilled in wrestling*' insert 'or perh. *incapable of physical exercises*'; add '*SEG* 27.261.B28 (Beroea, ii BC), *IMagnes.Sipylos* 34'

***ἀπαλάκιστος**, ον, *unsweetened*, Anon.Alch. 11.2.

**ἀπαλγέω**, for '*put away sorrow for*' read '*work out* one's *grief for*'

***ἀπᾰλεξιάρη**, prob. fem. subst. or adj., *she who wards off ruin*, *POxy.* 2819.11 (hex. fragment); cf. ἀλεξιάρη, ἀπαλεξίκακος.

**ἀπᾰλεξίκᾰκος**, delete 'f.l. in'

**ἀπᾰλέξω I 1**, add 'poet.ap.Pl.*Alc.* 2.143a'

**⁺ἀπᾰλίας**, ου, ὁ, *immature animal*, D.L. 8.20 (text dub.).

***ἀπᾰλιος**, ον, of animals, *young, immature* (opp. τέλεος, *full-grown*), *Sokolowski* 2.22.8 (Epid., iv BC), Hsch.

**ἀπάλλαξις**, add '**2** *relief* from a disease, Hp.*Nat.Hom.* 8.'

**ἀπαλλάσσω A I 1**, line 3, after 'And. 1.59' insert 'τοῦ ζῆν Pl.*Ax.* 367c' **II**, line 3, for 'E.*Med.* 786' read 'Ar.*Pax* 568'; line 8, delete 'τοῦ ζῆν .. 367c' **B II 2**, delete 'Pl.*Phd.* 81c'

**ἀπαλλοτριόω 3 b**, for 'Pl.*Ti.* 65d' read 'Pl.*Ti.* 65a'

***ἀπᾰλόθροος**, ον, *softly-sounding*, ἦχος Nonn.*D.* 48.606.

**ἀπᾰλοιφή I**, before '*Gloss.*' insert '*SEG* 33.1177.10 (Lycia, i AD)'

**ἀπᾰλοκροκῶδες**, add '*CIL* 13.10021.188'

**ἀπᾰλός I**, line 5, for 'Sapph.*Supp.* 23.16' read 'Sapph. 94.16 L.-P.'; line 6, for 'Alc.*Supp.* 14.5' read 'prob. in Alc. 39(a).5 L.-P.' and for 'Sapph. 76' read 'Sapph. 82(a) L.-P.'; line 7, for 'Ead.*Supp.* 25.13' read 'id. 96.13 L.-P.'; line 11, for 'of *raw* fruit .. X.*Oec.* 19.18' read 'of fresh fruit, κολοκύνταις .. ἀπαλωτέραις Alc. 117(b).9 L.-P., Hdt. 2.92.4, X.*Oec.* 19.18'

**ἀπᾰλοχρώς**, add 'Heras ap.Gal. 13.511.15'

***ἀπᾰλόψῡχος**, gloss on γλυκύθυμος, Hsch.

**ἀπᾰλύνω 1**, delete '*make plump*, opp. ἰσχναίνω'; add 'Gal. 18(2).840.5, 841.7' add '**3** *make gentle, calm* κῦμα θαλάσσης ἀπαλύνεται γαλήνῃ *Anacreont.* 46.4 W.'

***ἀπᾰμαύρωσις**, εως, ἡ, *removing of dimness*, Zos.Alch. 211.1.

**ἀπᾰμάω** (A), add 'λαιμὸν σιδήρῳ Il. 18.34'

**ἀπαμβρᾰκόομαι**, for parenth. to the end read '(cf. °ἀμβρακόομαι) Pl.Com. 66 K.-A.'

**ἀπᾰμέρδω**, after '= ἀπαμείρω' insert '*deprive of*' and add 'w. acc. of pers. and gen. of thing, *GVI* 1547.7 (Rome, ii AD)'

***ἀπᾱμία**, v. °ἀφαμία.

**ἀπᾰναίνομαι**, for 'Pi.*N.* 5.60' read 'Pi.*N.* 5.33' and add 'A.R. 1.611, Lxx *Jb.* 5.17'

***ἀπαναφέρω**, *bring back*, aor. inf. ἀπονιγ[κ]ῆν *SEG* 37.340 (Mantinea, iv BC).

***ἄπανδρος**, ον, *having no husband*, *BGU* 2462.14 (ii AD).

***ἀπανηγύριστος**, ον, *unfit for a festival speech*, Eust. 1569.56.

**ἀπανθίζω**, after 'A.*Ag.* 1662' insert '(dub.)'

***ἀπανθρᾰκισμός**, ὁ, gloss on ἀποκραιπαλισμός, Hsch. (dub.).

**ἀπάνθρωπος II 1**, after 'S.*fr.* 1020' insert 'ἀ. ἄνθρωπος Men.*Dysc.* 6'

***ἀπάνονα**, gloss on φόρβον, Hsch.

**ἀπάνουργευτος**, read **ἀπανούργευτος**

***ἀπανούργητος**, = ἀπανούργευτος, Sch.E.*Ph.* 469.

***ἀπανταίνω**, *meet*, ἀνερχομένου ἔρχομε ἀπαντάνω σου *PAmst.* 56.6 (vi AD).

***ἀπαντᾰχόσε**, *in every direction*, Gal.*UP* 12.5, 15.4.

**ἀπαντάω I 1**, add '**d** *approach with a request*, *POxy.* 1242 (iii AD).' **2 a**, add 'αἰ[δέ] ἀπαντᾶι *if someone attacks*, *SEG* 23.563 (Axos, iii BC); *counter* an argument, ἴσως ἂν .. τοῖς εἰρημένοις ἀπαντήσειας; of a jury, *face, deal with* a line of argument, D. 21.24, 31.36' **II 1**, add 'abs., Μενουθ[εσ]ιὰς ἀπαντᾷ νῆσος *comes upon one, comes next*, *Peripl.M.Rubr.* 15'

**ἀπαντή**, add '*SEG* 37.1186.41 (Pisidia, iii AD)'

**ἀπάντησις I**, for '= foreg.' read '*the action of going out to meet* an arrival, esp. as a mark of honour'; delete '*escort*' and add 'Cic.*Att.* 8.16.2, 9.7.2, 16.11.6'

**ἀπαντητήριον**, before '*PIand.* 17' insert '*IGLS* 1.1316 (Apamea), *SEG* 32.1496 (Palestine), 36.1222 (Isauria, all v or vi AD)'

***ἀπαντοτρόφος**, ον, *nurturing everything*, γαῖα Cyran. 1.7.40 K.

**ἅπαξ I 1**, line 1, for '*once only, once for all*' read '*on one single occasion*'; line 8, after 'Lxx *2Ki.* 17.7' insert '**b** math., of a term taken *once*, Papp. 100.24, *PMich.*III.145.3 iv 6 (ii AD)'; after 'Pl.*Men.* 82c' insert 'ἀ. μετρεῖ Papp. 12.7'; add 'πρὸς ἅπαξ, of payment made *once*, a lump sum, *Cod.Just.* 6.48.1.14' add '**III** *sometimes*, A.D.*Adv.* 170.18, *Conj.* 252.22, Thom.Mag. p. 200 R., al.'

**ἀπαξαπλῶς**, for '*in general*' read '*at one go, at one and the same time*'

**ἀπαξία**, add 'Iamb.*Protr.* 20 (94.24 P.)'

**ἄπαξις**, after '*arrest*' insert '*and taking before the magistrates*'

**ἀπαράβατος** line 7, for '3 act.' read '4 act.' and after 'adv. -τως' add 'Herod.Med.ap.Aët. 9.2'

***ἀπαραβίαστος**, ον, *inviolable, indefeasible*, Polystr. p. 88 W.

**ἀπαράβλητος**, add '*IStraton.* 303.8; perh. *not to be set aside*, *CPR* 5.11.6 (?iv AD)'

***ἀπαράβροχος**, ον, '*without excess dampness*, of a grain cargo, *PRoss.-Georg.* 2.18.129, al. (ii AD), *PMich.*inv. 3781.6 in *ZPE* 62.140 (v AD); cf. ἄβροχος, mod. Gk. παραβρέχω'

**ἀπαραδειγμάτιστος**, for '*not liable to censure*' read '*inconspicuous* (cf. °εὐπαραδ-)'

***ἀπαράδοτος**, ον, *not transferred*, *PFam.Teb.* 15.62 (ii AD).

**ἀπαραίτητος I**, add '*Trag.adesp.* 495 K.-S.'

**ἀπαρακάλυπτος**, adv. -τως, add 'Hld. 8.5.6'

**ἀπαράκλητος I**, add 'adv. -τως, *SEG* 7.62 (Seleucia in Pieria, ii BC)'

**ἀπαραλήκτως**, delete the entry.

***ἀπαράπ‹ε›ιστος**, gloss on ἄπιστος (app. in sense *disobedient*), Hsch.

***ἀπαράπτωτος**, ον, *firm*, *Poliorc.* 200.4.

**ἀπαράσημος II**, for this section read '*without a title*, of a speech, Antipho 2.1 tit., Lys. 21 tit.'

**ἀπαρατήρητος**, before 'adv.' insert '*not requiring special precautions*, i.e. *favourable*, ἔστι δὲ εἰς τὸ πλεῦσαι ἀπαρατήρητος (ὥρα τοῦ Ἡλίου) *Cat.Cod.Astr.* 11(2).131.18'; add '*without supervision* or *hindrance*, *Didyma* 314.10 (ii AD, v. Robert *Hell.* 11/12.465)'

**ἄπαργμα I**, after '= ἀπαρχή (q.v.)' insert 'perh. in *IHistriae* 101 (vi BC, v. *SEG* 33.582), *IG* 9(2).1135.6 (epigr., Demetrias, i AD; see also *SEG* 23.451)'

**ἀπαρενθύμητος**, delete the comma after '*considering*'

**ἀπαρήγορος**, for '*Epigr.Gr.* 344.2 (Mysia)' read 'epigr. in *IHadr.* 80 (ii AD)'

**ἀπάρθενος**, delete 'virgin wife and widowed maid'

**ἀπᾰριθμέω I**, add '**2** of an instrumentalist, *measure out* a rhythm, ἐπὶ τῶν ὀργάνων D.H.*Comp.* 25.'

**ἀπαρκέω II**, for this section read 'pass., *to be contented*, Cerc. 18 ii 13, Lyc. 1302'

**ἀπαρκτίας**, after '*Gloss.*' insert '*IEryth.* 304.4 (i BC), πρὸς ἀπαρκίαν *Peripl.M.Rubr.* 30'

**ἀπαρνέομαι**, lines 1/2, after 'Pl.*Grg.* 461c' insert 'also -ηθήσομαι S.*Ph.* 527' and after 'Att.' insert '(also Herod. 4.74)' for '*deny utterly*' to end of article read '*say no* to an assertion, *deny* a fact, Hdt. 6.69.2, Antipho 2.3.4, S.*Tr.* 480, καὶ νῦν γέ φημι κοὐκ ἀναρνοῦμαι E.*El.* 1057, Pl.*Tht.* 165a; w. inf., ἀπαρνήσονται δ' εἰκότως .. Ἀλέξανδρον αὐτοὺς ἠρεθικέναι Phld.*Rh.* 1.359.12; w. μή, τὸν τἄμ' ἀπαρνηθέντα μὴ χρᾶναι λέχη E.*Hipp.* 1266; w. double neg., τίνα οἴει ἀπαρνήσεσθαι μὴ οὐχὶ .. ἐπίστασθαι Pl.*Grg.* 461c; ellipt., φημὶ δρᾶσαι κοὐκ ἀπαρνοῦμαι τὸ μή S.*Ant.* 443. **2** in logic, *deny* a proposition, opp. κατηγορεῖν, Arist.*APr.* 41ᵃ9; in pass. sense, ib. 63ᵇ37. **II** *refuse to accept, reject*, ὅτ' Ἀχαιιάδες μιν ἀπηρνήσαντο πόληες ἐρχομένην Call.*Del.* 100; θεούς Luc.*Peregr.* 13; w. things as obj., Arist.*EN* 1127ᵇ25, Lxx *Is.* 31.7, Nonn.*D.* 47.478. **b** *refuse to recognise, deny*, ὅτι .. πρὶν ἀλέκτορα φωνῆσαι, τρὶς ἀπαρνήσῃ με *Ev.Matt.* 26.34, *Ev.Marc.* 14.30, etc.; refl., *Ev.Matt.* 16.24, etc. **2** *refuse* or *reject* a course of action, Hp.*Praec.* 12, τὸν .. Ἁρμόδιον ἀπαρνηθέντα τὴν πείρασιν Th. 6.56.1, Pl.*Sph.* 217c, Herod. 4.74, D.C. 51.7.1; w. inf., Hp.*Ep.* 9.328.12; abs., S.*Ph.* 527.'

**ἄπαρσις**, after '*departure*' insert 'Dicaearch.*fr.* 34 W.'

**ἀπάρτησις I 2**, delete 'metaph. .. 5.1.2' **II**, add 'Plot. 5.1.2'

**⁺ἀπαρτί**, adv. *exactly, just*, ἡμέραι ἀ. ἐνενήκοντα, Hdt. 5.53, ἀ. ἐναρμόζειν πρός τι Hp.*Art.* 73, ἀ. ἐν καιροῖσι id.*Acut.* 41. **II** (w. intensifying force) *altogether, absolutely*, φρόνιμος ἵν ἀ. ταύτης τῆς τέχνης Telecl. 39 K.-A., Pherecr. 77 K.-A., τί .. ἀποτίνειν τῷδ' ἀξιοῖς; – ἀ. δή που προσλαβεῖν παρὰ τοῦδ' ἐγὼ μᾶλλον, id. 93, Ar.*Pl.* 388. **III** often written as two words ἀπ' ἄρτι *from now on*, οὐ μή με ἴδητε ἀπ' ἄρτι, ἕως ἂν εἴπητε .. *Ev.Matt.* 23.59, 26.64, *Ev.Jo.* 14.7, *Apoc.* 14.13; w.

pres. tense, ἀπ' ἄρτι λέγω ὑμῖν πρὸ τοῦ γενέσθαι, ἵνα πιστεύητε .. *EvJo.* 13.19.

**ἀπαρτίζω II 1**, line 1, after 'Plb. 31.12.10' insert '*ἡ σύμβιος .. ἀπήρτισαν ἑαυτοῖς* .. of a funerary monument, *SEG* 30.1548 (Cilicia, iv/vi AD); *Νέστωρ ἀπή[ρτι]σεν* app. an artist's signature, Robert *Villes* p.169 (Lycia, Rom.imp.)'; line 6, after 'J.*AJ* 3.6.7' insert '*χαλεινοῦ ἱππικοῦ μετὰ τοῦ μασήματος ἀπηρτισμ(ένου) horse's bridle ending in a bit*, i.e. with bit attached, *Edict.Diocl.* in *SEG* 37.335 iii 5; (cf. mod. Gk. *ἀπαρτίζω form, constitute*)'

**ἀπᾰρύω I 2**, for 'Epic.ap.Arist.*Po.* 1457$^b$14' read 'Emp. 138'

**ἀπαρχή 2**, line 7, after 'Hdt. 4.88' insert '*τὰ ἐξ ἀπαρχᾶς δοθέντ[α* *SEG* 23.566 (Axos, iv BC)' **6**, for this section read 'app. *a board of officials* sent by a city to order the affairs of a colony, *IG* 12(8).273, 280, 283, 285 (Thasos, vi BC, v. esp. *BCH* 107.185); cf. *ἀπάρχης*'

**⁺ἄπαρχος**, ὁ, *commander*, A.*Pers.* 327 (v.l. *ἐπ-*), *Ag.* 1227.

***ἀπάσχαρος**, v. °*ἀπέσχαρος*.

**ἀπᾰτάω**, lines 1/2, impf., after 'Ion.' insert '*ἀπάτασκον* Cercop. 3'; at end after 'Pl.*Prt.* 323a' insert 'w. inf., *συνέσεσθαι ἀπατώμενον* Hld. 1.30.6'

***ἀπατενίζω**, gloss on *degenero*, Dosith. p. 436 K. (nisi leg. *ἀπαγενίζω*).

**ἀπᾰτερθε I**, adv., add '*h.Merc.* 403' **II**, add '*far short of, unlike*, *οὐκ ἀ.* Opp.*H.* 1.725'

**ἀπάτη II**, at the beginning insert '*the act of deceiving*, *ἐν ἐκείνοις .. ἡγεῖται τὸ πιθανόν, κἂν ᾖ ψεῦδος, διὰ τὴν ἀ. τῶν θεωμένων* Plb. 2.56.12, hence ..'

**ἀπᾰτήμων**, for 'Zos. 1.52' read 'Zos. 1.57'

**ἀπᾰτήνωρ I**, after 'Tryph. 137' insert 'Nonn.*D.* 26.118' **II**, for pres. ref. read 'Euph. in *Suppl.Hell.* 418.25'

**ἄπᾱτος**, before the pres. ref. insert '*Inscr.Cret.* 2.xii 3.5, 11.15 (Eleutherna, vi BC); impers. w. dat. *τοι .. δικασσταῖ .. ἄπατον ἤμην* *Inscr.Cret.* 4.42 B.11-14' and after it add 'impers. w. acc., *τὸνς πρειγ[ίσ]τονς .. πράδδοντας ἄπατον ἔμεν* *Inscr.Cret.* 4.80.11-12; cf. *ἄνᾱτος* II 2'

**Ἀπατουρεών**, written **Ἀπατουριών**, add '*SEG* 30.977 (Olbia, v BC), *Thasos* 18.5 (v BC), *Inscr.Prien.* 51 (ii BC), *SEG* 30.1353 (Miletus, ii/iii AD)'; written **Ἀπατοριών**, add '*Thasos* 171.29 (i BC), *SEG* 33.679 (Paros, ii BC)'

**Ἀπᾰτουρία**, for 'Aphrodite' read 'Athena'; after '*Ἀπατούρη*' insert 'title of Aphrodite' and after '(Panticapaeum)' add '(iii AD), *Ἀπατόρης* on vase, prob. of Aphrodite, *SEG* 30.879 (Berezan, v BC)'

**ἀπατρία**, delete the entry.

**ἀπαυαίνω**, delete '*make to wither* .. 3.10.7'

***ἀπαυγή**, ἡ, *radiance*, Call.*fr.* 273 Pf. (*ἀγαυ-* codd.).

**ἀπαυδάω II**, add 'app. in *ICS* 318 A II 3 (vi BC)' **III**, at end for '*πόνοις*' read '*πόθοις*'

**ἀπαυθᾱδιάζοντες**, med., add '*refuse to admit one is in the wrong*, Arr.*An.* 4.9.6'

**ἀπαυλία** (*ἀπαυλία*), for '*EM* 119.14 is confused' read '*EM* 119.14 and Hsch. are confused'

**⁺ἀπαυλόσῠνος**, ον, *away from one's shelter*, *AP* 6.221 (Leon.Tarent., s.v.l.).

**ἀπαύξησις**, delete 'hence, *disesteem*'

**ἀπαυστί**, for 'sq.' read '*ἄπαυστος*'

**ἀπαφρίζω**, to act. exx. add 'Gal. 14.13.7'

***ἀπεγγόνη, ἀπέγγονος**, v. °*ἀπέκγονος*.

***ἀπεγγυάω**, *pledge, give security*, *ἀπενγυάτω ὁ [κατειπὼν τὴν ἀπενγύην]* *Thasos* 7.7 (v BC, see also *SEG* 36.790).

***ἀπεγγύη**, ἡ, *security*, rest. in *Thasos* 7.8 (v BC), v. °*ἀπεγγυάω*.

**ἀπέδῑλος**, after 'Nonn.*D.* 5.407, al.' insert 'fig., *[ἀπ]εδῖλος ἀλκά* i.e. perh. coming without delay, Alcm. 1.15 P.'

**⁺ ἀπειδοποιέω**, *give final form to*, *κατεξέσθη τὸ ὑπέρθυρον καὶ ἀπειδοπο[ι]ήθη* *Didyma* 32.19.

**ἀπειθής I 2**, line 3, for '*impracticable*' read '*inexorable*'

***ἀπειθόω**, *to be disobedient*, *Inscr.Délos* 1417*B*ii150 (ii BC).

**ἀπειλέω** (B) **I**, line 3, after 'Il. 23.863, cf. 872' insert 'Call.*fr.* 18.6 Pf.' **II 3**, at end delete 'Theocr. 24.16' and add '**b** *order with threats*, w. inf., Theoc. 24.16, A.R. 3.607.'

***Ἀπείλων**, ωνος, ὁ, Cypr. *a-pe-i-lo-ni* (dat.), = *Ἀπόλλων*, *ICS* 215.4 (Tamassos, elsewh. *Ἀπόλλων*); cf. ‡*Ἀπέλλων*.

**ἄπειμι** (A), add 'Myc. 3 pl. pres. *a-pe-e-si*, part. *a-pe-o*'

**ἄπειμι** (B) **I**, at end, *μηνὸς ἀπιόντος*, add '*IG* $4^2$.83 (Epid., i AD), 7.506, *Ilion* 51.30, 63.2, 4; *μη(νὸς) Λῴου θ' ἀπιούσῃ* *TAM* 5(1).129, *μη(νὸς) Δύστρου ς'.. ἀ(πιούσῃ)* ib. 93 (Saittae, iii AD)'

**ἀπεῖπον**, line 4, after 'med.' insert 'fut. *ἀπεροῦμαι* *AP* 12.120 (Posidipp.)' **IV 1**, add 'Thgn. 89'

**ἀπειράκις**, add '*ἐξ ἀ. ἀπείρων*, Procl.*Inst.* 1 (p.2.10, 11) D.'

***ἀπείραντος**, ον, = *ἀπέραντος*, *boundless*, Pi.*P.* 9.35.

**ἀπείρᾰτος I**, add '(v.l., edd. *ἀπειρίτῳ*)'

**ἀπειρέσιος**, line 2, after 'Od. 11.621' insert 'Thgn. 8'; line 5, delete '(Q.S.) 3.386'

**ἀπείρῐτος**, after 'al.' insert 'cj. in Pi.*O.* 6.54 (v. *ἀπείρᾰτος*)'; add 'also sg., A.R. 3.971, Q.S. 3.386; Lacon. **ἀπήριτος** Alcm. 7.14 P.'

***ἀπειρόμογος**, ον, *unused to toil*, *ἀ]πε[ιρ]ομόγῳ Διονύσῳ* *PMich.*inv. 4926a (*ZPE* 93.157, iii AD).

**ἄπειρος** (B), line 3, delete '*πλῆθος* Hdt. 1.204' and add '*πεδίον .. πλῆθος ἄπειρον ἐς ἄποψιν* Hdt. 1.204' to previous group.

***ἄπειρος, Ἄπειρος** (C), v. *ἤπειρος* III.

***ἀπειρότεχνος**, η, ον, *having unlimited skills*, *Φοίβη ἀ.* orac. ap.Lyd.*Mens.* 3.10.

**ἀπειρότοκος**, for 'Antip.Sid.' read 'Antip.Thess.'

**ἀπείρων** (B), add '*δι' ἀπείρονα γαῖαν* E.*Phaëth.* 243 D., Chaerem.Hist. 10 vdH.'

***Ἀπειρώτας** [ᾱπ-], v. ‡*ἠπειρώτης* III 2.

**ἀπέκ**, add 'Q.S. 4.540, 14.230, *ἀπὲκ ἀέρος* *PMich.*XIII 665.21, 30, 60 (vi AD)'

**ἀπέκγονος**, for pres. ref. read '*AP* 13.26 (?Simon., = Page *FGE* no. 36)'; add 'also *ἀπέγγονος* *Cod.Just.* 6.4.4.10, Just.*Nov.* 91.1; also fem., *ἀπεκγόνη* Theophil.Antec. 3.6.4'

**ἀπεκδέχομαι I**, add '*μαστῷ πόρτιν ἀπεκδέχεται* *AP* 9.722 (Antip. Sid., = Page *EG* 3595, v.l. *ὑπεκ-*)'

***ἀπεκλείπω**, *go away and leave*, *τὸν βίον* *BCH* 10.302.34 (Alabanda, ii BC).

***ἀπεκτίθημι**, *remove and reject*, *[μύρμηκες] τῶν καρπῶν τὰς ἐκφύσεις ἀπεκτιθέασιν* Cels.ap.Orig.*Cels.* 4.83.

***ἀπελαστικός**, ή, όν, *capable of driving away*, *μιασμάτων* Sch.Theoc. 2.35, Eus.*PE* 4.1.9.

**ἀπελαύνω**, line 5, after 'pf.' insert '*ἀπελήλαμαι* Alc. 130.23 L.-P.' **II**, after '*driven away*' insert '*ἀπὺ τούτων* Alc.l.c.'

***ἀπελέκιστος**, ον, = *ἀπελέκητος*, *IG* $2^2$.1678*b*A7 (iv BC).

**ἀπελευθεριάζω**, add '**II** prob. *emancipate, manumit*, *τὰν .. ἀπηλευθεριασ(σ)μέναν ὑπὸ Σωτηρίχου* *Delph.* 3(3).388.4 (i BC).'

***ἀπελευθερίζω**, *emancipate, manumit*, *Delph.* 3(3).311.10 (i BC).

**⁺ἀπελλάζω**, *hold an assembly*, Plu.*Lyc.* 6, *ἀπελλάζειν· ἐκκλησιάζειν. Λάκωνες* Hsch.

**ἀπέλλαι**, after '*ἐκκλησίαι*' insert '*τὰ δὲ ἀπελλαῖα ἄγεν Ἀπέλλαις καὶ μὴ ἄλλαι ἁμέραι* *CID* I 9.A31, cf. D3 (Delphi, v BC)'

**ἀπελλαῖα**, after 'Delph.' insert 'v BC'

**Ἀπελλαῖος**, for 'etc.' read 'in Lydia *SEG* 29.1184 (AD 152/3); also at Ephesus (beginning Oct. 24) and elsewhere, *Hemerolog.Flor.* p. 79 (p. 22 K.), *Cat.Cod.Astr.* 2.149.1'

***ἀπελλογαρίζω**, *render an account*, *PLond.* 1708.104 (vi AD).

**Ἀπέλλων**, for 'cf. *Ἀπείλων* *Inscr.Cypr.* 140 H.' read 'cf. °*Ἀπείλων*'

***ἀπεμβλέπω**, *look away and within*, i.e. *concentrate on looking within*, v.l. in Pl.*Chrm.* 160d.

**ἀπεμπολάω**, after 'pass.' read '*ἀπεμπολώμενοι*, *disposed of by sale*, Ar.*Ach.* 374, *Ἰθακησίαν τινὰ ὑπὸ Φοινίκων ἀπεμποληθεῖσαν* *Certamen* 26'

**⁺ἀπεμπολή**, ἡ, app. *sale*, Call.*fr.* 203.27 Pf.; *ἀπεμπολήν· ἀπαλλαγήν. πρᾶσιν. ἐμπορίαν* Hsch., *ἀ.· ἀπόστασις, ἡ μετὰ ἀπάτης πρᾶσις, καὶ ἐμπορία* Suid.

***ἀπέμφᾰσις**, εως, ἡ, *false sense-impression*, opp. *ἔμφασις*, Carneades ap.S.E.*M.* 7.169.

**ἀπενᾰρίζω**, add '*ἀπηναρίσθη* Hippon. 68.7 W.'

***ἀπενεκτική**, (sc. *πτῶσις*), ἡ, *ablative* case, Dosith. p. 392 K.

***ἀπένθεια**, ἡ, *absence of mourning*, dub. cj. in A.*Ag.* 430 (codd. *πένθεια*).

**ἀπενθής**, after '*grief*' insert 'or *lamentation*'

***ἀπενθησία**, ἡ, app. *relief of misfortune* or *grief*, *SEG* 36.970.A6 (Aphrodisias, iii AD).

***ἀπέννοια**, ἡ, prob. calque on Heb. *m^ezimmāh* (evil devices) *craft, cunning*, Aq.*Ps.* 138(139).20.

**ἀπεξαιρέω**, add '*ἀπὸ δ' ἐξείλετο θεσμὸν μέγαν* Anacr. 61 P.'

***ἀπεξαρθρέω**, *dislocate*, *PRyl.* 529.37 (iii AD).

**ἀπεξηγέομαι**, for 'cj. in X.Eph. 5.9' read 'X.Eph. 5.9. (cod.)'

**ἄπεπλος**, delete 'i.e. *in her tunic only*, of a girl' and after 'Pi.*N.* 1.50' insert '*Pae.* 20.14'

***ἀπερανός**, ὁ, or *-όν*, τό, name of a plant, Paul.Aeg. 4.22.2 (344.17 H.).

**ἀπέραντος II**, line 2, for 'A.*Pr.* 1087' read 'A.*Pr.* 1078'

**ἀπεράω I**, after '*disgorge*' insert '*ἀπὸ σφαγὴν ἐρῶν* A.*Ag.* 1599'

**ἀπεργάζομαι III 2**, for 'Pl.*Riv.* 135e' read 'Pl.*Amat.* 135e'

**ἄπεργος**, add '**III** *ἄπεργον*, τό, *unworked part* of ashlar, *spall* or *offcut*, *λίθοι ἀ. ἔχοντες* *IG* $2^2$.1666.A98, B48, 70 (Eleusis, iv BC), cf. *ἀργός* (B) II 1.'

**ἀπερείδω I 1**, add 'of a scorpion *planting* its sting, Ael.*NA* 16.27'

**ἀπέρεισμα**, after 'Hsch.' insert 's.v. *ἀπόσκημμα*'

**ἀπερίγραπτος**, add '*not marked for exclusion* or *"bracketed"* *ἀπερ[ί]γρα(πτος) ἄν (αὕτη, sc. ?ᾠδή)* Sch.Alcm. 3 *fr.* 1 P.'

**ἀπερικάλυπτος**, delete the entry (v. °*ἄπαρα-*).

***ἀπερίμετρος**, ον, *boundless, infinite*, Apul.*Plat.* 190.

**ἀπερίσπαστος**, line 4, for 'Plu. 2.521c' read 'Plu. 2.521d'

***ἀπερίστροφος**, ον, *unable to turn, immovable*, Afric.*Cest.* p. 8 V.

**ἀπερίτμητος I**, add '(non-Jewish instance) *PCair.Zen.* 76 (iii BC)'
**ἀπερίτρεπτος**, after 'adv. -τως' insert '*irrefutably*'
**ἀπερίττωτος**, for 'φύσις' read 'φυτόν'
**ἀπερύκω 1**, med., last line, read 'later in act. sense στυγερὰς δ' ἀπερύκεο νούσους Maced.*Pae.* 31; w. gen., *rescue* from, ἀπερύκεο νούσου Nic.*Al.* 608'
**ἀπέρχομαι I 3**, delete 'κἆτ' .. 689' **4**, read 'w. part. indicating outcome of action κἆτ' ὀφλὼν ἀπέρχεται Ar.*Ach.* 689, πλέον ἔχοντες ἀπέρχεσθε Isoc. 17.57, Men.*Dysc.* 52, Plu.*Ages.* 7, Aristid.Mil. 2.2 J.'
*__ἀπεστενωμένως__, adv., *in a restricted manner*, Simp. *in de An.* 44.37.
*__ἀπέσχᾰρος__, ον, *scab-removing*, ζίριον (i.e. ξηρίον) ἀπάσχαρον (sic) *PMed.Rez.* 12.17.
*__ἀπέταιρος__, ὁ, one who is not a member of a ἑταιρεία, *Leg.Gort.* II 5, 25; cf. ἀφέταιρος.
**ἀπέτηλος**, add 'comp., *AP* 9.231 (Antip.Thess.)'
*__ἀπευδοκέω__, *satisfy*, τινὰ τῆς τιμῆς in respect of the price, *PLeid.*P. 3 (ii BC).
**ἀπευλῠτέω**, add 'so prob. *PMich.*v. 243.9 (i AD)'
**ἀπευτακτέω**, to act. exx. add '*PSI* 360.19 (iii BC), *PTeb.* 40.22 (ii BC), *PRyl.* 578.9 (i BC)'
**ἀπευχᾰριστέω**, after '*show gratitude*' insert 'τοὺς ἀσπασαμένους τε αὐτὸν .. καὶ ἀπευχαριστήσοντας ἐπὶ τοῖς γεγον[ό]τοις εὐεργετημάτοις *Delph.* 3(3).239.9 (ii BC)' and after 'τινί' insert '*BGU* 2418.9 (ii BC), *GVI* 1232.7 (ii/i BC)'
*__ἀπέφατο__ (A)· ἀπέθανεν Hsch. (v. θείνω).
*__ἀπέφατο__ (B)· ἀπείπατο. ἀπεφήνατο Hsch.
⁺__ἀπέφθῐθον__, v. ἀποφθίνω.
**ἄπεφθος**, line 2, after '*refined* gold' insert 'Ibyc. 1(*a*).43 P.'
**ἀπέχω III 1 c**, for this section read '*to be distant from* in time, ἀπόσχων τεσσαράκοντα μάλιστα σταδίους μὴ φθάσαι ἐλθὼν Th. 5.3.3; προειπὼν ὅτι οὐδὲ ἐκεῖνος ἀπέχει μακρὰν τῆς τοῦ βίου τελευτῆς Aeschin. 1.14.6, ἀπεχούσης δὲ χρόνον ἱκανὸν τῆς .. ἡμέρας D.S. 20.110.1' **IV**, *have* or *receive in full*, add 'D.*fr.* 23 S.'
**ἀπεψία**, add 'ἀπεψίαις χρώμενος *IG* 4².126.3 (Epid., ii AD)'
**ἀπηθέω**, add 'also ἀφηθέω (q.v.); cf. ἠθμός'
**ἀπηλεγέως**, for 'A.R. 4.687' read 'A.R. 4.689'
⁺__ἀπηλλαγμένως__, adv., *in a way which is free from*, ὀργῆς ἀ. ἐπιψηφίζειν J.*AJ* 17.124, Alcin.*Intr.* p. 164.15 H.
**ἀπήμαντος I**, read '*free from harm* Od. 19.282; *free from sorrow* or *misery*, Hes.*Th.* 955, Simon. 526.3 P., ἀ. βίοτος Pi.*O.* 8.87, A.*Ag.* 378 (lyr.); in later prose, *IStraton.* 10.18 (Panamara, i BC), Sopat.Rh. 8.264.27 W.'
⁺__ἀπηναῖος__, α, ον, *belonging to a wagon*, ὀρῆες Call.*fr.* 85.5 Pf.
**ἀπήνη 2**, after 'Str. 4.5.2' add '*state chariot*, poet. symbol of the *sella curulis*, καθαρῆς μετὰ μόχθον ἀ[π]ήνης *IEphes.* 1310'
**ἄπηρος**, for 'Hsch.' read 'Suid. s.v. ἄπηρα'
**ἀπηρτημένως**, after 'Plu. 2.105e' insert '(v.l.)' **II**, at beginning, insert '*discontinuously*, of hymns, μὴ ἀπηρτημένως ἀλλὰ συνεχῶς πλάττειν Men.Rh. 341.20 R.-W.'; after 'M.Ant. 4.45' add '(codd.)'
**ἀπηχέω I 2**, for this section read '*cause to ring out* or *resound*, φωνάς Arr.*Epict.* 2.17.8, Ph. 1.693, 2.44' **II**, delete 'to be discordant .. 2.44'
**ἀπήχημα 1** and **2**, for these sections read '*echo* (in quots., fig.) Pl.*Ax.* 366c, ὕψος μεγαλοφροσύνης ἀπήχημα Longin. 9.2, ἔτι γὰρ ἀπήχημα φέρουσι τῆς ἐκεῖ ζωῆς Procl.*in Alc.* p. 99 C., p. 135 C.' **3**, add 'Paul.Aeg. 6.90.2 (137.10 H.)'
**ἀπηχής**, for 'Aristid.*Or.* 40(5).8' read 'Aristid.*Or.* 29(40).8'
*⁺__Ἀπῐδᾱνῆες__, οἱ, *Peloponnesians*, Call.*Jov.* 14, A.R. 4.263, Rhian. 13.
**ἀπίθανος III**, line 5, after 'Id.*Pseudol.* 16' insert 'ἀπίθανος ἐν τῷ λαλεῖν Men.*Dysc.* 145'
*__ἄπικες__, οἱ, Lat. *apices*, *conical hats*, τὰς καλουμένας ἄπικας ἐπικειμένοι ταῖς κεφαλαῖς D.H. 2.70.
**ἄπικρος**, after 'Ptol.*Tetr.* 158' add '(v.l.); app. *without sting*, *ineffectual*, γένηται καὶ ἀσθενὴς καὶ ἄπικρος *SEG* 35.223.7 (tab.defix., Athens, iii AD)'
*__ἀπιομήδης__, ες, (= ἠπιο-), *having kindly purposes*, rest. in Pi.*Pae.* 7.7 (pap. ἀπιομ[ήδ]ει).
**ἄπιον 2**, delete the section. add '**II** Lat. *apium*, Paul.Aeg. 7.4; written ἄποιον in Orib.*fr.* 52.'
**ἄπιος** (A) **I 1**, for '*CP* 1.15.2' read '*CP* 1.15.1'
**Ἆπις I 1**, after 'Hdt. 2.153, etc.' add '(dat. Ἄπι); in Syria, *SEG* 31.1383 (dat. -ιδι, ii AD)'
**ἀπίσσωτος**, for 'Str. 11.10.2' read 'Str. 11.10.1'
**ἀπιστέω II 1**, after '*disobey*' insert 'Antipho *fr.* 21'
**ἀπιστία 2**, add '(σημεῖον) τεράστιόν τε καὶ βροτοῖς ἀπιστία *source of disbelief*, Ezek.*Exag.* 91 S.'
**ἄπιστος II**, line 3, transfer 'ὦτα .. Hdt. 1.8' to the end of section I 1 and for '*credulous*' read '*trustworthy*'
**ἀπίσωσις**, add 'εἰς τὴν ἀφίσωσιν τῶν μερῶν *PDura* 19.14 (i AD)'
*__ἀπίτῡρος__, ον, *free from husks*, κριθαί Hsch. s.v. ἀτυπῆδες (ἀτυπίδες La.).
**ἄπλαστος**, after '**II**' read 'app. = ἄπλατος, (w. which it frequently coexists as a variant), Hes.*Th.* 151, *Op.* 148'
**ἀπλᾰτής**, line 2, after 'id.*Top.* 143ᵇ14' insert 'Euc. in *PMich.*III 143.3'
**ἄπλᾰτος**, line 3, for '(whence it must be restored .. A.*Pr.* 373' read 'cj. for ἄπληστος in A.*Pr.* 371'; line 7, delete 'E.*Med.* 151 (lyr.)' **2**, after '= ἄπλετος' insert 'χρόνου μῆκος Archestr. 59.9; σταδίων *EG* 1613 P. (Posidipp.)'
**ἀπλετομεγέθης**, for '*unapproachably great*' read '*immensely great*'
**ἄπλετος**, line 2, after 'S.*Tr.* 982' insert 'ἰχθύες A.R. 1.574'
**ἄπληγος**, after '(πληγή)' insert '*not bearing marks of blows*, *PRein.* 92.11 (iv AD)'
*__ἀπληκεύω__, *bivouac*, Suid. (perh. ἀπληκ‹τ›εύω).
*__ἄπληκτον__, τό, *bivouac*, *PLond.* 1416.23, Suid.
**ἄπλητος**, for 'Ep. .. *great*' read '= ἄπλετος, *immense*, *monstrous*, ἰσχύς Hes.*Th.* 153 (s.v.l.); ὄτοβος ib. 709; χόλος *h.Cer.* 83'; add 'neut. sg. as adv., ἄπλητον κοτέουσα Hes.*Th.* 315, cf. *Sc.* 268, Semon. 7.34'
*__ἄπλιος__, ον, adj., applied to a textile, often coupled w. μονόβαφος, *Edict.Diocl.* 24.5, 29.20, al.; neut. subst., in inventory of items taken on a journey, *PRyl.* 627.161 (iv AD); v. °ἁπλόος III e.
*__ἁπλόγραμμος__, ον, app. *drawn in a single line*, *Poliorc.* 237.8.
**ἄπλοια**, after '(E.)*IT* 15' insert '*Trag.adesp.* 637.13 K.-S.'
**ἁπλοϊκός**, add '**b** *simple-minded*, Hld. 1.11.'
**ἁπλόος**, line 1, after 'ον' insert '(Cret. as two-termin. adj. acc. fem. pl. ἁπλόονς, *Inscr.Cret.* 4.72 I 48 (Gortyn); voc. ἁπλόε *Inscr.Délos* 1533.3 (Antisthenes of Paphos, hex.))' **I a**, add 'τὰς στοὰς τάς τε ἁ. καὶ τὰς διπλᾶς τοῦ ἱεροῦ perh. *single-aisled*, *SEG* 30.1535 3 (ii AD); neut. subst., perh. *original* of a document, τῆς ἐπιγραφῆς ἁπλοῦν ἀπετέθη εἰς τὸ ἀρχεῖον *SEG* 30.1352 (Miletus, iii AD), cf. τὸ δὲ συναίρεμα τοῦτο δισσὸ(ν) γρα(φὲν) ἐπὶ τῷ ἁπλο(ῦν) συνηγηθῆναι *PTeb.* 340.16 (iii AD)' add '**c** *flat*, *plane*, ἁπλοῖ πήχεις *POxy.* 2145.6 (ii AD); opp. καμαρωτικοί, ib. 921ʳ (iii AD).' **II c**, *simple-minded*, add '*Cod.Just.* 1.3.29.1' add '**d** *in good condition*, *sound*, ἐὰν οὖν ᾖ ὁ ὀφθαλμός σου ἁπλοῦς .. ἐὰν δὲ ὁ ὀφθαλμός σου πονηρὸς κτλ. *Ev.Matt.* 6.22, *Ev.Luc.* 11.34.' **III 1 a**, add 'neut. as subst., τὸ ἁπλόον *simple penalty*, *Inscr.Cret.* 4.41 I 4 (Gortyn)' **c**, for this section read 'of coinage, *unmixed*, i.e. of pure alloy, δραχμαί *SEG* 12.226.9 (Delphi, iv AD), *ABSA* 23.95 no. 20 (Thessalonica), χρυσοῦ νομισμάτια *PMasp.* 41' add '**e** of a quality of ἱματισμός, perh. of *single* size, *plain* or *fine* (unadulterated), *Peripl.M.Rubr.* 24, 28; cf. °ἁπλοπάλλιον, °ἄπλιος, °ἁπλουργός.'
*__ἁπλοπάλλιον__, τό, *cloak* or *cloth* of a certain quality, perh. *single* or *plain*, *PVindob.* G41673 (*Tyche* 1.88; vi/vii AD); cf. °πάλλιον, °ἁπλόος III e.
*__ἁπλοπότιον__, τό, wd. in list of foodstuffs, *PRyl.* 627.88 (iv AD), precise meaning uncertain.
**ἁπλότης II 1**, after 'D.H.' insert '*Is.* 4' add '**4** *ignorance*, *backwardness*, Just.*Nov.* 73.9.'
**Ἅπλουν**, for '*IG* .. Larissa)' read '*IG* 9(2).1027, 9(2).512.19 (both Larissa, v and ii BC)'
*__ἁπλουργός__, ὁ, kind of textile worker, *JHS* 56.79 (Laodicea ad Lycum), v. °ἁπλόος III e.
*__ἄπλυντος__, = ἄπλυτος, Sch.Nic.*Al.* 469a Ge.
**ἄπλυτος**, line 2, after 'Semon. 7.5' insert 'σήσαμον *IG* 1³.422.151 (Athens, v BC)'
**ἅπλωμα**, add 'perh. *open space*, in front of rooms of a monastery, *SB* 5174.5, 9, 16 (vi AD)'
**ἁπλῶς II 1 b**, after 'D. 18.308, etc.' insert 'ἁπλόως καὶ ἀδόλως *Inscr.Cret.* 4.174.8 (ii AD)'
*__ἁπλωστί__, adv. = ἁπλῶς II, cj. in A.*Ch.* 121.
**ἄπλωτος**, add '**2** *not transportable by water*, σῖτος *PTeb.* 703.73 (iii BC, s.v.l.).'
*__ἁπλωτός__, όν, *spread out*, δίκτυον .. ἁ. *AP* 6.185.3 (Zos., cj.); *prostrate*, Sisyphus *fr.* 1.6 (cj. for πλωτός, v. *Byzantion* 6.468).
**ἄπνοος II 2**, after '*lifeless*' insert 'Call.*Epigr.* 5.9 Pf.' add '**4** *without scent*, Call.*fr.* 43.14 Pf.'
**ἀπό**, line 3, after 'etc.' insert 'w. apocope, ἀπ πατέρω[ν] Alc. 6.17 L.-P., ἀτ τᾶς πρεισβείας *IG* 9(2).517.12 (Larissa, iii BC)' **A I 2**, add 'indicating distance already travelled, εἰσπλεόντων ἀπὸ χιλίων ὀκτακοσίων σταδίων *Peripl.M.Rubr.* 1, al.' **9**, add 'ἀσπό(ρου) ἀπὸ κρι(θῆς) of unsown land *formerly* under barley, *BGU* 2441.118 (i BC)' **II**, line 10, ἀφ' ἧς, add 'Lxx 1*Ma.* 1.11, *Ev.Luc.* 7.45, *Act.Ap.* 24.11, 2*Ep.Pet.* 3.4'; line 18, after '(iv AD)' insert 'ἀ. προέδρων *PFlor.* 71.521, al.'; line 19, after 'Hdn. 7.1.9, etc.' insert 'ἀπὸ πριμιπιλαρίων = *e primipilaribus* (indicating soldier's rank on discharge), Roueché *Aphrodisias* 10.2 (iv AD)'; add 'ἐνδημῶν ἐν τῇ πόλει ἡμῶν ἀπὸ χρόνων years *since*, i.e. for years, *SEG* 31.576.12 (Larissa, ii BC)' **III 6**, lines 17/18, for '*by* word .. *Ag.* 813)' read '*by* words (sc. by swearing falsely), Hes.*Op.* 322; *from* tongues (which may lie), A.*Ag.* 813; *orally*, Hdt. 1.123'; add 'ἀπὸ τριῶν *three times*, *BGU*

2157.15 (v AD)' **B**, line 2, for 'ἀπὺ τᾷ ζᾷ *Inscr.Cypr.* 135.8 H.' read 'Cypr. *a-pu-ta-i za-i ta-i-pa-si-le-wo-se* ἀπὺ τᾶι γᾶι τᾶι βασιλῆος *ICS* 217.8' **D 3**, for 'ἀπαλγέω .. ἀπανθίζω' read 'ἀπανθέω, ἀποζέω'

**⁺ἀποαίνῠμαι**, also **ἀπαίνῠμαι**, *strip off, remove*, τί τινος Il. 13.262; ἀπαιν- Il. 11.582, Mosch. 2.66 G. **2** *take away, deprive one of*, θεὸς δ' ἀποαίνυτο νόστον, Od. 12.419, 17.322.

**ἀποβάθρα**, add 'S.*fr.* 415 (unless ἀπόβαθρα, q.v., is read)'

**ἀποβαίνω**, after 'fut. -βήσομαι' insert 'Cret. fut. part. ἀποβᾱσιόμενον *Inscr.Cret.* 1.xvii 10 A 7' **I 1**, for 'Lys. 2.24' read 'Lys. 2.21' **2**, for 'E.*Hec.* 142' read 'E.*Hec.* 140' **II 2**, for 'Plb. 26.6.15' read 'Plb. 25.2.15'; for 'Th. 5.4' read 'Th. 5.14'; add 'ἵν' εἰς βέλτιον ἀποβῇ τὸ φοβερόν Men.*Dysc.* 418' **3**, delete 'cf. 5.14'

***ἀποβάλσᾰμον**, τό, = ὀποβ-, *BGU* 34.5.13.

**ἀπόβᾰσις I 1**, add '**b** *fall* in river level, opp. ἀνάβασις I 3, *Peripl.M.Rubr.* 63.'

**ἀποβᾰτήριος I**, add 'of Asclepius, *Iasos* 227'

**ἀποβιβρώσκω**, after '*eat off*' insert 'Zen. 6.44'

**ἀποβιόω**, add '*SEG* 24.911 (Thrace, iv AD)'

**ἀποβλέπω I 3**, add 'ἀκρωτήριον .. ἀπόβλεπον εἰς ἀνατολήν *Peripl. M.Rubr.* 30, καθ' ὃ μέρος ἀποβλέπει τὴν ἤπειρον ib.'

**ἀποβλώσκω**, add 'pf. ἀπὸ .. μέμβλωκεν Call.*fr.* 384.5 Pf.'

**ἀπόβρασμα**, *chaff*, add 'Gal. 19.116'

**ἀποβρασμός**, for '*throwing off of scum*' read '*boiling over, ebullition*; in quot. applied to *ejaculation* of semen'

***ἀποβρόχω**, *swallow up*, ἀπέβροξεν δ' ἄχρις ἐπ' ὀμφαλίου *AP* 7.506 (Leon.Tarent.).

***ἀποβυρσόω**, = Lat. *decorio, skin*, Dosith. p. 436 K.

**ἀποβώμιος II 2**, delete the section.

**ἀπογᾰλακτισμός**, add 'Aët. 4.29 (370.27 O.)'

**ἀπογάλακτος**, add '(but perh. to be read as ἀπὸ γάλακτος)'

**ἀπόγειος I 1**, add 'of persons, ἀπόγειος ὄψομαι Luc.*Lex.* 15' **II 2**, delete the section.

**ἀπογεισόω**, after '*crown with a cornice*' insert 'or *replace the cornice*'

***ἀπογείσωσις**, εως, ἡ, *provision* or *replacement of a cornice*, *Inscr.Délos* 366A7 (iii BC).

***ἀπόγευμα**, ατος, τό, *tasting*, Cyran. 1.7.88 K., etc.

**ἀπογιγνώσκω**, for '*IG* $2^2$.457.30' read '*IG* $2^2$.457.18'

***ἀπογόμωσις**, εως, ἡ, *unloading*, *PAnt.* 108.4/5 (iv AD), *PVindob.Worp* 8.28 (iv AD).

***ἀπογομωτής**, οῦ, ὁ, *stevedore*, *POxy.* 3867.17, 18 (vi AD).

**Ἀπογονικός**, for '*Hemerolog.Flor.*' read 'beginning Oct. 24, *OGI* 583.15 (Cyprus, i AD)'

**ἀπόγονος**, line 5, after 'ἀπογόνη' insert '*great-grand-daughter, female descendant*, *SEG* 1.399.5, *IEphes.* 3072.17'

**ἀπογράφω**, after lemma insert '(Arc. ἀπυ-, *SEG* 37.340.18 (Mantinea, iv BC))' **I**, add '**2** *alter* or *cancel in copying*, *CID* I 10.10 (iv BC).'

**ἀπογυμνόω 2**, add 'Ezek.*Exag.* 47 S.'

***ἀπογῠναικόομαι**, pass., *to be made effeminate*, Agatharch. 101, Cyran. 1.10.52 K.

**ἀποδακρύω I 1**, add 'abs., Aristox.*fr.hist.* 90, cf. *AB* 427' **II**, delete the section.

**ἀποδεής**, for '*empty*' read '*not completely full*'; after 'Plu. 2.967a' insert '*SEG* 30.1663 (Ai Khanoum, ii BC)' add '**II** *of poor quality, inferior*, ἀποδεῆ χαρτία *Pap.Lugd.Bat.* XIII 6.6 (i AD).'

**ἀποδείκνῡμι**, after lemma insert '(ἀπυ- *SEG* 34.1238, Aeolis, *c.*200 BC)' **A I 1**, line 5, for '*SIG* 134.2' read '*SIG* 134b.22' **I 5 a**, pass., add 'of places *assigned* for anchorage, ὁρμίζεσθαι .. ἐν τοῖς ἀ. τ[ό]ποις *PHib.* 198.112 (iii BC), τῶν ἀ. ὅρμων τῆς Ἐρυθρᾶς θαλάσσης *Peripl.M.Rubr.* 1' **II 1**, at end, *consul designatus*, add 'of other magistrates, *Laodicée* no. 5 p. 281, *IPrusias* 6.2'

**ἀποδειλιάω 2**, add 'πράσσειν μὴ ἀ. J.*AJ* 19.1.19'

**ἀπόδειξις I 1**, add '**b** *display, demonstration*, ἐν τοῖς] ὅπλοις ἀπόδειξιν ἐποιήσαντο .. *SEG* 26.98.' **3**, add 'w. subordinate cl., ἀ. ὡς τὰ τούτων ἀδικήματα .. γέγον' αἴτια D. 18.42; *document providing proof*, *BGU* 1141.12, *POxy.* 257.19 (both i AD), *Cod.Just.* 4.21.16.3, 4'

**ἀποδεκατεύω**, add '*dedicate a tithe*, τῷ θεῷ *SEG* 9.72.56 (Cyrene)'

**ἀποδέκτης**, line 3, after '*IG* 12(8).608' insert '*SEG* 33.679 (sg., Paros, ii BC)'

***ἀποδεκτικός**, ή, όν, *receptive*, Hierocl.*Prov.*ap.Phot.*Bibl.* 465 b 15.

**ἀπόδεξις I**, add 'ἀγάπησις ἀπόδεξις παντελής Pl.*Def.* 413b'

**ἀποδέρω**, line 2, after '(Hdt.) 4.60' insert 'Theoc. 25.278' **2** and **3**, for these sections read '**2** *strip back the foreskin of*, by causing an erection, Ar.*Lys.* 739, 953. **3** *strip the fibres from* stalks of mallow, etc., ibid. 739 (w. pun on section 2).'

**ἀποδέχομαι I 1**, add 'φόρτους *Peripl.M.Rubr.* 26'

**ἀποδημέω 2**, at end for 'ἄλλοσε ἀ. Pl.*Lg.* 579b' read 'οὐδαμόσε ἀ. Pl.*R.* 579b'

**ἀποδημία**, add '**b** applied to the absence of a prefect from Alexandria on visits to the Egyptian χώρα (q.v. II 3), *PGiss.* 44, Act.Alexandr. vii A 134, 137, ix A 11.7.'

**ἀπόδημος**, for 'Plu. 2.799f' read 'Plu. 2.799e'

**ἀποδιαστέλλω**, for '*divide* .. (ii BC)' read '*assign, apportion*, *PTeb.* 740.30 (ii BC), *PTaur.* 8.22, 48 (ii BC)'

***ἀποδιατίθημι**, *alienate*, Sopat.Rh. 8.169.5 W.

**ἀποδιδάσκω**, add 'Herodes Atticus *Pol.* 18'

**ἀποδιδράσκω 1**, line 9, transfer 'of runaway slaves' before 'σώματα ἀποδράντα' in line 11, and in its place read 'οὔτε ἀποδεδράκασιν .. οὔτε ἀποπεφεύγασιν'

**ἀποδίδωμι**, line 2, after 'Hsch.' insert 'form ἀπυ-, Myc. 3 sg. aor. *a-pu-do-ke*; (for other forms v.s.v. ‡δίδωμι)'

**ἀποδῐκάζω**, add '*SEG* 31.358 (Olympia, v BC), rest. in *Inscr.Cret.* 4.22*B* (vii/vi BC)'

**ἀποδικέω**, for 'X.*HG* 1.7.21' read 'X.*HG* 1.7.20'

**ἀποδιοπόμπησις**, add 'Epict.*Diss.* 2.18.20'

**ἀποδοκιμάζω**, for 'τὸ ποιεῖν τι' read 'w. articular inf.' and add 'Isoc. 5.75'

**ἀποδόσιμος 2**, for this section read '-μον, τό, *an order to hand over* money or goods, *PSI* 237.6 (v/vi AD), *PMich.*XV 742.2, *CPR* 5.18.12, al. (both vi AD)'

**ἀπόδοσις I 3**, delete the section. **II 2**, add '**b** in metre, *responding section* in antistrophic compositions, Sch. metr. Pi.*O.* 2 p. 58 D., al.' at end add 'form ἀπυ- Myc. *a-pu-do-si*'

**ἀποδοχή I**, add '**4** *acknowledgement of receipt*, ἀποσταλείσης ἀποδοχῆς *POxy.* 3121.15 (iv AD).'

***ἀποδοχικός**, όν, μέτρον ἀ., a measure of capacity (= 42.25 choenices), *PLond.* 1940.11, 15; cf. δοχικός, παραδοχικός.

***ἀποδρακωνάριος**, ὁ, *ex-standard-bearer*, *PAmst.* 45.7 (AD 501).

**⁺ἀποδρομή**, ἡ, *run-in* or *lay-by* for boats, ὁ δὲ τόπος ἀλίμενος καὶ σκάφαις μόνον τὴν ἀ. ἔχων *Peripl.M.Rubr.* 3.

**ἀποδῠρομαι 1**, after '*lament bitterly*' insert 'w. acc., *CEG* 13 (funerary, Attica, vi BC)'; line 3, for 'τινί .. (dub.)' read '*complain bitterly*, w. inf., πολλῶν ἀποδυρομένων πολειτῶν ὑπὸ τῶν ἐπαρχικῶν ἐξελαύνεσθαι *SEG* 30.568 (= *EAM* 186, ii AD)'

**ἀποδῠτήριον**, in the palaestra, add '*SEG* 32.147 (Attica, iv BC)'

**ἀποδύω II 2**, lines 4/6, delete 'οἱ ἀποδυόμενοι .. Lys.*fr.* 45.1'; after '*IG* 14.256 (Phintias)' insert 'ἀπεδύσατο εἰς τὴν αὐτὴν παλαίστραν Lys.*fr.* 75.1'

***ἀποδώτης**, ου, ὁ, = ἀποδοτήρ, *PMasp.* 126.7 (vi AD).

***ἀποέπαρχος**, ὁ, *ex-eparch (prefect)*, *PLips.* 42 (AD 391).

**ἀποζάω 1**, after '*to live off*' insert '*h.Ap.* 539 (tm.)' **2**, for this section read '*make a living*, πονηρῶς Luc.*Tox.* 59, μόλις Ael.*NA* 16.12, μόνον Lib.*Orat.* 11.253'

**ἀποζεύγνῡμι**, after '*part*' insert 'τὰς ἀντονομασίας ἀπὸ τῶν ὀνομάτων D.H.*Comp.* 2, id. 7.67 (pass.)'

**ἀπόζευξις**, add '**b** *separation*, εἰ δὲ οὕτως ἐχούσης τῆς Ἀφροδίτης ἀπόζευξις γένοιτο Heph.*Astr.* 3.9.34.'

**ἀποζέω 2**, add '**b** *to be cleaned by boiling, be boiled out*, ἡ ληνὸς πεμπταία ἀπέζεσεν καὶ κατηλείφθη *BGU* 1549 (iii BC), cf. 1550.'

**⁺ἀποζημιόω**, gloss on corrupt form ἀπίθετο in Hsch.

***ἀπόθεμα**, ατος, τό, *thing stored away*, Sm.*Ez.* 27.27 (pl.).

**ἀποθεόω I**, after 'μετὰ τὸ ἀποθεωθῆναι' insert 'i.e. after the burial' add '**b** *consecrate as a burial-place*, ἀπεθέωσα τὴν λάρνακα *IGRom.* 3.1480 (Iconium).'

**ἀποθερᾰπεύω 2**, *cure*, add 'ἀ. ὀφθαλμού[ς] *Suppl.Mag.* 32 (v/vi AD)' add '**3** *restore, make good* a loss, εἰ δὲ βλάψει τὸ πρᾶγμα .. τὴν ζημίαν ἀποθεραπεύει *Cod.Just.* 1.2.24.6.'

***ἀποθερμαίνω**, *warm up*, οὐ πολὺ μὲν ἔπιον, ἀλλ' ὅσον ἀποθ[ερ]μανθῆναι Lollian. B 1 23 (p. 122 H.), perh. in *PMed.*inv. 70.16.2 in *CE* 52.97.

**ἀπόθετος I 1**, add 'of a person, *hidden away*, Philostr.*Her.* 19.3'

**ἀποθέωσις**, after '*deification*' insert 'also *burial* (*CIG*, v. infr.)'

***ἀποθηκάριος**, ὁ, *storekeeper*, Teuc.Bab. p. 51 B., *IGChr.* 10.4, *MAMA* 3.534, etc. (Corycus, var. sp., including ἠπο- 431, ὠπο-), *SEG* 37.620 (Thrace, Chr.).

**ἀποθήκη I 1**, after '*storehouse*' insert 'or *storeroom*' and add 'τὴν ἐξέδραν σὺν τῇ ἐν αὐτῇ ἀποθήκῃ διστέγῳ *Sardis* 7(1).12 (ii AD), *POxy.* 2729.31, 33'

**ἀποθησαυρισμός**, add 'Antioch.Astr. in *Cat.Cod.Astr.* 11(2).109.3'

***ἄποθι**, Arc. adv., *far away, apart*, *SEG* 36.376 (Lykosoura, ii BC); cf. °ἄπυθεν, ἄποθεν.

**ἀποθλίβω I 1**, after 'D.S. 3.62' read 'Nic.*fr.* 86, ἄρδην με τῆς οἰκείας ἀποθλίψει χώρας Luc.*Jud.Voc.* 2' **3** and **4**, for these sections read '**3** *squeeze dry, wring*, τὰ κράσπεδα Diph. 43.30; cf. ἐνουρέω. **4** *press forcibly against, crush*, Nic.*Th.* 314, Lxx *Nu.* 22.25, *Ev.Luc.* 8.45.'

***ἀπόθραυμα**, ατος, τό, = ἀπόθραυσμα, *Inscr.Délos* 1442*B*9 (ii BC).

**ἀποθριγκόω**, after '*furnish with coping*' insert 'or *replace the coping*'

***ἀποθρίγκωσις**, εως, ἡ, *furnishing with coping* or *replacing the coping*, *IG* 4.823.39 (Troezen, iv BC).

***ἀποθρυόομαι**, pass., (θρύον) pf. part. ἀποτεθρυωμένοι *bent like rushes*, v.l. for ἀποτεθρυμμένοι in Pl.*R.* 495e ap.Tim.*Lex.*, cf. Sch. ad loc., Suid.

**ἀποθύμιος**, after 'Hdt. 7.168' insert 'οὐδ' ἔστιν ὅπως ἀποθύμια ῥέξω

Call.*Del.* 245'; add 'used app. mistakenly in opposite sense, νεκρῶν δ' ἀποθύμια ῥέζει(ν) epigr. in *SEG* 39.449.11 (Tanagra, v AD)'

***ἀποθῠσία**, ἁ, pl., some kind of ritual, perh. *distribution after a sacrifice*, ἐποίησεν δὲ καὶ τοῖς κατοιχομένοις .. καὶ ταῖς ἀποθυσίαις καὶ χονδρογάλα *SEG* 32.1243.35 (Aeolian Cyme, i BC/i AD).

***ἀποῐέρωσις**, εως, ἡ, = ἀφιέρωσις, *Albania* 5.43 (Apollonia in Illyria).

**ἀποίητος III**, add 'of persons, *unsuitable* for office, *PPetaus* 93.126, [ε]ἰς χρίας ib. 26.9; w. dat. ἀποίητον τῇ πολιτικῇ ἐργασίᾳ *Vit.Aesop.*(G) 2'

**ἀποικέω II**, line 3, delete 'c. acc., .. (s.v.l.)'; for 'Corinth *was inhabited by me at a distance*' read 'Corinth *was dwelt far from* by me'

**ἀποικία I 1**, at end for 'Aeschin. 2.176' read 'Aeschin. 2.175' and add 'of Roman colony, Plb. 2.19.12, etc., Ἀ. Πατρέων as translation of *Colonia Patrensis*, *SEG* 18.64 (Athens, i AD)'

**ἀποικιστής**, delete ref. to Men.Rh.

**ἄποικος II**, for this section read '**1** of cities, *settled as a colony*, πόλεις ὁπόσαι τῆς γῆς τῆσδ' εἰσὶν ἄποικοι Ar.*Lys.* 582; πόλιν Σινωπέων ἄποικον ἐν τῇ Κολχίδι χώρᾳ X.*An.* 5.3.2, 6.2.1. **2** subst. ἄποικος, ὁ, *colonist*, Hdt. 5.97, Th. 1.25, 38, 7.57, *IG* 1$^3$.46-7; poet., of iron, Χάλυβος Σκυθῶν ἄ. A.*Th.* 728.'

***ἀποίνιμος**, ον, *carrying no penalty*, cj. in Hes.*fr.* 124.1 M.-W.

**ἀποιωνίζομαι**, add 'Dosith. p. 430 K.'

**ἀποκᾰθᾰρίζω**, after '*purify*' insert 'wine, *CPR* 8.82.6 (vii AD), transf., ἑαυτόν'

**ἀποκάθαρμα**, add '*that which is sifted out* of grain, *PMasp.* 2.iii.11 (pl., vi AD)'

**ἀποκαθαρτικός**, after '*cleansing*' insert 'Thphr.*Sens.* 84'

**ἀποκαθεύδω I**, for 'of a woman .. 399' read 'used for ἀποκοιτέω by Eup.*fr.* 431 K.-A.; τουτέστι γυναῖκα χωρίζεσθαι ἀνδρὸς καὶ ἀφίστασθαι Suid. α 3332'

**ἀποκαθιστάω**, before 'v.l.' insert 'Duris 7 J., D.S. 1.78.2'

**ἀποκαθίστημι I 1**, add '*rebuild, restore* buildings, etc., *SEG* 34.1122 (Ephesus, i AD), *IHadr.* 44, *TAM* 5(1).517, *SEG* 31.1295 (Oenoanda, all ii/iii AD)' **2**, add '*deliver* goods which have been ordered, οἱ δὲ ἐργολαβήσαντες ὑϊκὸν ἢ οἰνικὸν μ[ὴ] ἀποκαταστήσαντες *SEG* 31.122 (Attica, ii AD)' **3**, add 'τὴν προγαμιαίαν δωρεὰν ἀποκατέστησε καὶ δέδωκε τῷ παιδί Just.*Nov.* 2 pr. 1' add '**5** app. in calque on Lat. *rationes reddere*, ἄχρι ἂν τὰς ψήφους ἀποκαταστήσωσιν Scaev.*Dig.* 40.5.41.4.'

**ἀποκαίω 1**, add '**b** *consume by fire, burn up*, Arist.*Pr.* 928$^a$20, Luc.*Tox.* 61, *IG* 10(2).260.B9 (iii AD); cf. ‡ἀπόκαυσις III.' at end add 'form ἀπυ- Myc. pf. part. pass. *a-pu ke-ka-u-me-no*.'

***ἀποκαλά**, ἡ, tentatively given as a gloss on φορμός in *Lex.Rhet.* in *AB* 315.

**ἀποκᾰλυμμα**, for '*a revelation*' read '*uncovering* (of the head)'

**ἀποκᾰλύπτω 1**, add 'ἀ. τὸ ὠτίον τινος *uncover* a person's ears, i.e. make a thing known to him, Lxx 1*Ki.* 9.15, 2*Ki.* 7.27, etc.'

**ἀποκάμπτω 1**, after 'X.*Eq.* 7.14' insert 'ἵνα ἀπ[ο]κάμψῃ καὶ ἀσχη[μονήσῃ] *SEG* 35.218.15 (tab.defix., Attica, iii AD)'

**ἀποκαρπίζω II**, in med., *harvest* (in quot., dates), *BGU* 2127.12 (AD 156).

***ἀποκάρπωσις**, ἡ, ἀ. νεκρῶν perh. *exploitation of* or *profiting from* corpses, *BGU* 2462.8 (ii AD).

**ἀποκαρτέρησις**, add 'Charito 6.2'

**ἀποκατάγνῡμι**, add 'pf. part. intr. -εαγώς *broken off*, *Inscr.Délos* 1439*Abc*i47 (ii BC)'

***ἀποκαταράομαι**, = *deprecor*, Dosith. p. 431 K.

**ἀποκατάστᾰσις**, add '= Lat. *restitutio*, *restoration* of property, *Cod.Just.* 1.3.52.13; ἡ εἰς ἀκέραιον ἀ. = Lat. *in integrum restitutio*, Just.*Nov.* 119.6'

***ἀποκατῶρυξ**, ῠγος, ἡ, reading of codd. in Thphr.*CP* 5.9.11, perh. due to confusion of ἀπῶρυξ and κατῶρυξ.

**ἀπόκαυσις**, add '**II** *loss involved in melting down* gold votive offerings, prob. rest. in *IG* 2$^2$.1495.4, 13 (iv BC), cf. *NC* 1951.109-110, and °ἀφέψησις. **III** *burnt offering*, name of a type of sacrifice, prob. where the whole offering is consumed, *SEG* 32.1423.9, 11 (Syria), Mitchell *N.Galatia* 257 (both ii AD); cf. °ἀποκαίω 1, °ἀποκαυσμός.'

**ἀποκαυσμός**, for 'Judeich .. p. 142' read '*BCH* 38.52; cf. °ἀπόκαυσις III'

**ἀποκείρω**, line 3, for 'ἀπεικείρατο' read 'ἀπεκείρατο'

**ἀπόκενος**, after 'Hero *Spir.* 2.24' add '*PCair.Zen.* 680.3 (iii BC)'

***ἀποκενωτέον**, *one must evacuate*, Archig.ap.Aët. 9.35.

⁺**ἀποκηδεύω**, *complete the funeral rites of*, Hdt. 9.31, *SEG* 6.220 (Phrygia).

**ἀποκηρύξιμος**, for the pres. ref. read '*IG* 2$^2$.1013.5 (ii BC)'

**ἀποκηρύσσω**, after 'Att. -ττω' insert 'dial. ἀποκᾱρ-' **II 1**, add 'also act., ἀποκηρύξας τὰ τέκνα *POxy.* 2342 (ii AD)' **IV**, before pres. ref. insert '*SEG* 32.623 (ἀπεκάρυξε, Buthrotum, ii BC)' add '**V** *proclaim, declare*, πατρογέροντας *IEphes.* 26.24 (ii AD).'

**ἀποκλαίω**, after '-έκλαυσα' read '*mourn for, lament*, θανόντα Thgn. 931, τύχας A.*Pr.* 637, ἐμαυτόν Pl.*Phd.* 117c; abs. Hdt. 2.121. γ'; w. internal acc., στόνον S.*Ph.* 695 (lyr.); med. ἀποκλαύσασθαι κακά S.*OT* 1467, τὴν πενίαν Ar.*V.* 564, E.*fr.* 563; abs. Luc.*Syr.D.* 6'

**ἀποκλείω I 2**, add 'as Lat. *excludere*, *exclude from inheritance*, w. acc., (τῆς κληρονομίας understood) *Cod.Just.* 6.4.4.14b-14c, 19a'

***ἀπόκλεμμα**, τό, (*amount of*) *theft*, ἀποτεισάτω τὸ ἀπόκλεμμα πενταπλοῦν, τὸ δὲ νοσφισμὸν ἡμιόλιον *PMich.*x 587.29.

**ἀποκλέπτω**, add 'τὰ ἀποκλαπέντα Heph.Astr. 3.37 in *Cat.Cod.Astr.* 8(1).154'

***ἀποκλήζω**, *discard*, τοῦτ' (sc. ὄνομα) ἀποκληζομένη *IG* 2$^2$.3575 (Eleusis, ii AD).

**ἀποκληΐω**, delete 'later -κλήζω *IG* 3.900'

**ἀπόκληρος II**, add '*PCornell* 12.14 (iii AD), *Cod.Just.* 6.4.4.14'

**ἀποκληρόω I 2**, after '*assign by lot*' insert 'δικαστήρια Luc.*Bis.Acc.* 4, 12'

***ἀποκλησία**, ἁ, *committee*, *IG* 9$^2$(1).609.A11 (Naupactus, vi/v BC).

**ἀποκλῑμάκωσις**, for '*ladder*' read '*flight of steps*' and add '*SEG* 26.1449 (also Cilicia)'

**ἀποκλίνω I**, line 3, after '*h.Ven.* 168' insert 'τυτθὸν ἀποκλίνασα καρήατα Call.*Del.* 236'; line 4, after '*slope away*' insert 'ἀπὸ δ' ἐκλίθη ἔμπαλιν ὤμοις φοίνικος ποτὶ πρέμνον Call.*Del.* 209' **III 1**, add '**b** of ships, *tilt over*, *Peripl.M.Rubr.* 46.' **2**, add 'of ships, *JHS* 74.98 *E*19 (Caunus, i AD)'

**ἀποκλύζω I**, add 'Anacr.*epigr.* 3.4 P. (tm.)'

***ἀποκλώθω**, perh. *bring about* (death) *by spinning*, μοῖραν .. οὐκ ἀπέκλωσε θεὸς *Inscr.Cret.* 1.v 42 (i/ii AD).

***ἀποκοιλαίνω**, *hollow out*, *AE* 1923.45 (Oropus).

***ἀποκοιτία**, ἡ, *absence for a night*, *PSI* 1120 (i BC/i AD).

**ἀποκολυμβάω**, add 'Clearch. 73 (ἀποκυμβ- codd. plerique)'

**ἀποκομιστικός**, add 'ἀποκομιστική (sc. πτῶσις), ἡ, Dosith. p. 401 K.'

***ἀποκομματικός**, ή, όν, *abbreviated*, ἀ. λεξείδιον, Phot. s.v. ψό.

⁺**ἀποκοντόω**, perh. *bring near*: pass. ὥστε τέμνεσθαι τὰς παρακειμένας ἀγκύρας ἀντέχειν ἀποκοντουμένας ?*shortened*, *Peripl.M.Rubr.* 40 (acc. to others: *thrust out*); cf. in description of Theodora's lewd behaviour, τὰ ὀπίσω ἀποκοντῶσα τοῖς τε διάπειραν αὐτῆς ἔχουσι καὶ τοῖς οὔπω πεπλησιακόσι Procop.*Arc.* 9.23 (v.l., codd., edd. ἀποκεντ-); cf. mod. Gk. αποκοντά *near*, απόκοντος *very short*.

**ἀποκοπή IV**, delete the section.

**ἀπόκοπος II**, for '*precipitous*, ὄρη' read '*abruptly ending, sheer*, ἀκρωτήριον *Peripl.M.Rubr.* 12, ὄρη ib. 32, βυθός ib. 40'

**ἀποκόπτω III**, for 'E.*Tr.* 628' read 'E.*Tr.* 627' add '**IV** pass., ἀποκοπῆναι *lose the scent*, *AB* 428, cf. Hsch.'

***ἀποκορᾰκόω**, *unfasten*, *BE* 1971.647 (Hierapolis); cf. ‡κορακόω, κατακορακόω.

***ἀποκοσκῐ́νημα**, ατος, τό, *that which is sifted out of grain*, *PMasp.* 2.iii.11 (pl., vi AD).

***ἀπόκοσμος**, ὁ, Cret. *one who has served in the office of* κόσμος (v.s.v. III), or *one who is not a* κ. (v. *SEG* 37.752), *SEG* 35.991.A5 (Lyttos, c.500 BC), 23.566.14 (Axos, iv BC).

**ἀποκραιπᾰλάω I**, after '*sleep off a debauch*' insert 'Men.*Dysc.* 457'

**ἀποκρέμᾰμαι**, delete the entry.

**ἀποκρημνίζω**, add '**2** pass., of pulse, *to be precipitate*, Gal. 8.662.12, 942.18.'

**ἀπόκρῐμα 2 b**, for this section read '*judgement* pronounced by Emperor after hearing oral presentations, *PTeb.* 286.1 (ii AD), *PMich* IX 529 (III AD)'

**ἀποκρίνω I**, add '**4** pass., w. εἰς, *to be classed as*, Luc.*Syr.D.* 10.'

⁺**ἀποκρῐσιάριος**, ὁ, *agent* or *envoy*, *POxy.* 144.14, *IEphes.* 1296, *Cat.Cod.Astr.* 5(3).93.22, 7.155.22 (all Byz.); οἱ ἐν τοῖς μοναστηρίοις διατρίβοντες μὴ ἐχέτωσαν ἐξουσίαν ἐξιέναι .. ὑπεξαιρουμένων τῶν καλουμένων ἀποκρισιαρίων *Cod.Just.* 1.3.29 pr., Just.*Nov.* 133.5.

**ἀπόκρῐσις II 4**, for the pres. ref. read 'Chor. 3.59' and add '*Cod.Just.* 1.3.29.1, Just.*Nov.* 123.25'

**ἀπόκρῐτος**, add 'neut. subst., φυλάττεσθαι .. τὸ ἀ. τοῖς ἀπολιμπανομένοις app. *opportunity for defence*, Lat. *servata .. absentibus defensione*, *Cod.Just.* 10.11.8.7a'

**ἀποκρούω II**, for '*knock off* .. 12' read '*break up* or *off, damage*, μηδὲ λωβήσασθαι μηδὲν ἢ ἀποκροῦσαι *IG* 2$^2$.13200.12 (ii BC), *SEG* 35.209.13 (Attica, ii AD)'

**ἀποκρύπτω II**, lines 4/5, delete 'cf. Th. .. αὐτούς)'; line 6, delete 'ἀποκρύπτουσι .. 179' add '**b** abs., *disappear*, Hes.*fr.* 290 M.-W., Th. 5.65, *Schwyzer* 708.3, 6, 9.'

***ἀπόκτανσις**, εως, ἡ, *killing*, Anon. *in Rh.* 146.1.

***ἀποκτένισμα**, ατος, τό, *combings*, τὰ ἀ. τοῦ στιππύου prob. in *PCair.Zen.* 176.42 (iii BC).

**ἀποκυβιστάω**, delete the entry.

**ἀποκῡδαίνω**, for '*IG* 3.1367' read '*IG* 2$^2$.11636'

**ἀποκῠλίω**, after '*roll away*' insert 'λίθους *AE* 1923.39 (iv BC)'

**ἀποκωλύω I**, before 'X.*Hier.* 8.1' for 'ποιεῖν' read 'φιλεῖσθαι'

***ἀπόλᾱος**, ον, *formally excluded* from an association, *banned*, ἀ. ἔστου [ἀ]τ τᾶς συγγενεί[ας] *SEG* 36.548 (Metropolis, Thessaly, iii BC).

**ἀπόλαυσις II 1**, add 'ἐπίτροπος ἀπὸ τῶν ἀπολαύσεων transl. of Lat. *a uoluptatibus, procurator, overseer of imperial entertainments*, *SEG*

36.556 (Epirus, ii AD); also ἐπὶ τῶν ἀ. *IEphes.* 852.18 (i/ii AD); Ἀπόλαυσις personified: *SEG* 26.438.4 (mosaic, Argos, v AD)'

**ἀπολέγω I 2**, add '*challenge* a juror, *SEG* 9.8.28 (edict of Augustus)' **II**, add '**2** *fail to appear*, of goods to be delivered, *BGU* 1564.12 (ii AD).'

**ἀπολείβω**, after 'Hes.*Th.* 793' insert 'A.*Ag.* 69 (anap., cj., codd. ὑπο-)' and delete 'metaph. .. *Com.adesp.* 39'

**ἀπολείπω**, line 1, aor. ἀπέλειψα, add '*Carm.Aur.* 70' **I 2**, after 'S.*Ph.*' insert '1158' **C II** 2, after 'Id. 27.2' insert 'ἐμοῦ πολὺ ἀπολελειμμένου τῶν ἐμαυτοῦ κακῶν Lys. 1.15'

**ἀπολειτουργέω**, after '*service*' insert '*PCair.Zen.* 35.3 (iii BC)'; add 'ἀ. τὸν βίον *fulfil one's obligations to* this life, *PLond.* 1708.29 (vi AD)'

**⁺ἀπολείχω**, *lick*, ἕλκη *Ev.Luc.* 16.21 (v.l.); *lick off*, αἷμα Dionys.Bassar. 20ᵛ.6 L., Ath. 6.250a; w. partit. gen., φόνου A.R. 4.478.

**ἀπόλειψις**, add '**IV** *legacy, bequest*, *SEG* 32.1537.5 (Gerasa, ii AD), ἐξ ἀπολείψεως *MAMA* 8.451.12, (Aphrodisias).'

**ἀπόλεμος I 1**, delete 'cf.' and insert 'Hp.*Aër.* 16 (comp.)'

**ἀπολεπίζω**, add 'Hsch. s.v. ἀποσκόλυπτε'

***ἀπόλεσις**, εως, ἡ, *loss*, Hippod.ap.Stob. 4.34.71.

**ἀπολήγω I 2**, for 'opp. γίνεται' read 'opp. ἐπιγίνεται' **3 b**, after '(ii BC)' insert '*Peripl.M.Rubr.* 33'

***ἀποληκῡθίζω**, app. *make a loud* or *hollow sound*, πλαταγωνίσας· ἀποληκυθίσας, ψοφήσας Hsch.

**ἀπολιμπάνω**, for 'ἀέκων .. 23.5' read 'ἀέκοισ' ἀ. Sapph. 94.5 L.-P.' and add 'in pass., *to be absent*, Just.*Nov.* 6.2'

**ἄπολις I**, add '**3** w. ref. to lack of Roman citizenship, Ulp.*Dig.* 32.1.3, Marcian.*Dig.* 48.19.17.1.'

**ἀπολισθάνω 2**, after 'Ar.*Lys.* 678' insert 'βίοιο *AP* 7.273 (Leon.Tarent.)'

**ἀπολίτευτος II 3**, delete the section.

**ἀπόλλῡμι**, line 5, 'freq. in tmesis in Ep.', add 'also occasionally in prose, e.g. Meliss. 7.5'

**Ἀπόλλων I**, line 5, delete 'Ἀπόλλων A.*Ch.* 559'; add 'pl., of Apollo as honoured in various cults, *IG* 2².1945.1; first syllable sts. lengthened in epic in oblique cases, e.g. Od. 9.198, *h.Ap.* 15' add '**III** in month name, μηνὸς Ἀπόλλωνος (app. gen. of god's name) at Chaleum (Locris), *Delph.* 3(3).38 (i BC); *GDI* 1931.1 (Delphi, end ii BC); cf. Ἀπολλώνιος II.'

**Ἀπολλώνεια**, after 'τά' insert 'festival at Myndos, *Inscr.Cos* 104.14' add '**2** Ἀ. Πύθια *games in honour of Apollo* at Hierapolis, *JÖAI* 30 *Beibl.* 203 (Ephesus, iii AD).'

**Ἀπολλωνιασταί**, add '*Inscr.Délos* 1757 (i BC), etc.'

**Ἀπολλώνιος III**, -ώνιον, add 'also **Ἀπολλωνιεῖον**, *SEG* 9.73.4 (Cyrene, ii/iii BC)'

**ἀπολογέομαι I 2**, for 'Aeschin. 1.92' read 'codd. in Aeschin. 1.70'

***ἀπολογικόν**, τό, v.l. for ἀπολογητικόν, Arist.*Rh.Al.* 1421ᵇ10 (*PHib.* 26.300), Syrian. *in Hermog.* 2 p. 11 R., Fortunat.*Rh.* 2.15.

**ἀπολούω 2**, med., add '*perform* ritual *ablutions*, *Peripl.M.Rubr.* 58'

**ἀπολοφύρομαι**, for '*bewail loudly*' read '*bewail to the full*' and for 'abs. *indulge one's sorrows to the full*' read 'of lamentation for the dead'

**ἀπολύσιμος**, after '**II**' insert 'ἀ. ἀρχαί *discharged, no longer subject to* εὔθυνα, D. in *Lex.Min.* 160' add '**b** of priests, temples, *tax-exempt*, *PTeb.* 292.6, 293.6.'

**ἀπόλυσις I**, add '**5** κατ' ἀπόλυσιν, *in an absolute construction* or *form*, A.D.*Pron.* 46.17, 81.25; id.*Adv.* 172.12.' **II 1**, line 2, delete '*separation*, .. Arist.*GA* 718ᵃ14' add '**2** *separation* on the completion of sexual intercourse, Arist.*GA* 718ᵃ14, 718ᵃ32, 756ᵇ3.'

**ἀπολῠτικός**, add '**II** *absolute, simple*, prob. in Dosith. p. 406 K.'

**ἀπόλῠτος 3**, add '**b** *absolute, independent*, A.D.*Pron.* 81.28.'

**ἀπολύω A III 4**, add '*defray the cost of*, τὴν .. διάβασιν (*bridge*) ἀ. *AS* 12.199' **II**, add '**b** of laying down an office, ἐκ τῆς ἀγωνοθεσίας *SEG* 3.367.31 (Lebadea, ii BC).' **B IV**, add '**2** *pass clear of*, Arist.*Cael.* 272ᵃ24, 26, 272ᵇ3, 10, 26.' **C I**, after 'X.*Cyr.* 6.2.37' insert 'ἀπολελυμένος λεγιῶνος *IPrusias* 31 (i AD)'; add '*to be exempted*, *have remission* from liturgy, *PFlor.* 312.4-5 (i AD), *BGU* 2474.9 (ii/iii AD)' **II**, add '**3** *to be separated after* sexual intercourse, Arist.*GA* 718ᵃ1, 731ᵃ21.'

**ἀπολωτίζω**, for '= ἀπανθίζω .. κόμας' read '*pluck off* a person or thing regarded as a flower, τίς ἄρα μ' .. ἀπολωτιεῖ;'

**ἀπόμαγμα I 2**, add '(pl.); transf., of a person, *Vit.Aesop.*(G) 14'

**ἀπομαίνομαι**, for '*go mad*' read '*recover from madness*' and add 'Men. *Sam.* 491, Aret.*SD* 1.6'

***ἀπομακκόω**, *strike dumb*, [Ζεὺς Τρωσου] ἀπεμάκκωσεν αὐτὸν ἐπὶ μῆνας τρεῖς *SAWW* 265(1).58.4 (Lydia, ?i/ii AD); see also *BE* 1971.511; cf. μακκοάω.

***ἀπομάλᾰκος**, ον, *soft, effeminate*, ἐναντίως δὲ λάγνους, θηλυψύχους, φιλοκόσμους, ἀπομαλάκους Heph.Astr. 2.15.15.

**ἀπομάσσω**, penultimate line, delete 'c. gen.'

**ἀπομαστίδιον**, for '*suckling*' read '*weaned child*'

**ἀπομειουρισμός**, for '*curtailment*' read '*tapering off*'

**⁺ἀπομειόω**, *make less*, οὐδὲν παντελῶς τῶν ἄλλων παραγραφῶν ἀπομειοῦντες Just.*Nov.* 111.1, cf. 108.1; pass., [τὰ τέλη ..] ἀπομειωθῆναι *IEphes.* 38.7 (?v AD), ἡνίκα ἡ τῆς προσόδου μηδαμῶς ἀπομειοῖτο ποσότης *Cod.Just.* 1.2.17.1.

**ἀπομείρομαι 1**, for '*distribute*' read '*take as one's portion*'

***ἀπομελᾰνισμός**, ὁ, = °ἀπομέλανσις, Comarius Alch. 291.17.

**ἀπομέλανσις**, for '= λεύκωσις' read '*blackening*'

***ἀπομελάνωσις**, εως, ἡ, = °ἀπομέλανσις, Zos.Alch. 210.15.

**ἀπομέμφομαι**, after 'E.*Rh.* 900 (lyr.' insert 'dub.'

**ἀπομένω**, after 'Polyaen. 4.6.13' add 'Just.*Nov.* 123.36'

**ἀπομεριμνάω**, add '**2** *to be free from anxiety*, pap. in *JEA* 21.53 (vi AD).'

***ἀπομεριστός**, όν, *set aside*, *PVindob.Boswinkel* 6.4 (iii AD).

**ἀπομέτρησις**, after '*measuring out*' insert 'of land, *SEG* 34.477.5 (Atrax, ii BC)' and after '*distribution*' insert 'κλιμάτων καὶ ἐθνῶν'

***ἀπόμῑμος**, ον, *imitator*, *IMylasa* 468.2.

***ἀπομίσθωσις**, εως, ἡ, *letting out for hire*, ἀπομίσθωσιν ποιήσασθαί τινος *Arch.f. Religionswiss.* 10.211 (Cos, ii BC).

***ἀπόμμᾰτος**, ον, *blind*, *PLond.* 1821.268 (*Aegyptus* 6.193).

**ἀπόμοιρα**, add '**3** tax on produce, *OBodl.* 43, 60, etc., *OCambridge* 8, *OPetrie* 52, *BGU* 1336-1346 (iii/i BC).'

***ἀπόμοσις**, εως, ἡ, *denial on oath*, Hsch. s.v. μά.

**ἀπομύζουρις**, for 'obscene name of a courtesan' read '*fellatrix* (cf. μύζουρις)'

**ἀπομύσσω II 1**, add '**b** *reject with contempt*, Hsch. s.v. ἀπέπτυσεν λόγους.' **III**, add '[κ]αὶ χαλκοῦν ἀπομυσσέτω [λυχνίσκον] *SEG* 31.851 (Italy, i AD)'

**ἀπομύω**, delete the entry (v. ἐπιμύω).

***ἀπομώρωσις**, εως, ἡ, *the act* or *process of enfeebling*, τῆς διανοίας Archig.ap.Aët. 6.27 (170.16 O).

**ἀποναίω II**, add 'Call.*fr.* 43.51 Pf.'

**ἀπονέμω I**, pass., *to be assigned*, add 'ἀπονενεμῆσθαί τε αὐτῷ προεδρίαν ἐν τοῖς αὐτοῖς ἀγῶσιν *IG* 2².1064 (Athens, c.AD 230)'

**ἀπόνοια 2**, add '**b** *lack of constraint, impropriety*, Thphr.*Char.* 6.1.'

***απονομάζω**, *name for, dedicate*, w. dat. [Διὶ] ἀμπέλων δύω ὄρχους ἐκ τῶν πεκουλαρίων *EAM* 22.4 (ii/iii AD).

**ἄπονος I 2**, add 'Nicoch. 5 K.-A.' **b**, after 'Aret.*SA* 2.1' insert 'w. gen., τῆς πλε(υ)ρᾶς ἀ. *SEG* 6.213.10 (Eumenea)'

**ἀπονοστέω**, add 'Pi.*N.* 6.50'

**ἀπονοσφίζω**, add 'med., χὴ πικρὴ Μοῖρ' ἀπενοσφίσατο *IG* 10(2).368.6 (epigr., ii AD)'

***ἀπονουμεράριος**, ὁ, = Lat. *exnumerarius*, *POxy.* 2004.2 (v AD) (-νομιρ- pap.).

**ἀπονῠχιστικός**, for '*polishing to the nail*' read '*trimming the nails*' and after 'τέχνη), ἡ' insert '*An.Ox.* 4.248.11'

**ἀπονωτίζω**, add '**II** med., *put down* a load *from one's back*, Hsch. s.v. νωτίσασθαι.'

**ἀποξενόω I 1**, line 3, add 'fig., τὸ γὰρ ὀρεγόμενόν του ἐνδεές ἐστιν οὗ ὀρέγεται καὶ τοῦ ὀρεκτοῦ .. ἀποξενώμενον Procl.*Inst.* 8 D.' **4**, for '*disguise oneself*' read '*act as a stranger*'

**ἀποξυλόομαι**, after '*become hard like wood*' insert 'Men.*Dysc.* 534'

**ἀποξύω 1**, after 'φάρμακον' insert '(sc. ἔλαιον)' **2**, at end delete 'Med., .. D.Chr. 32.44'

**ἀποπαιδαριόω**, for 'dub. sens.' read 'prob. *treat as a small boy* or *slave boy*'

***ἀπόπᾱν**, adv., *totally*, Procl.*in Ti.* 2.111.29.

**ἀπόπαξ**, add '*IG* 1³.435.50, 77 (v BC, cf. *Hesperia* 8.76)'

***ἀποπαραφέρω**, *deliver, hand over*, ἀποπαρε[νε]χθῦναι (sic), *SB* 9906.16 (iii AD).

**ἀποπειράομαι II**, add '*make a sexual attempt* on, Sch.Ar.*Nub.* 1063a'

**⁺ἀποπέκω**, *comb out*, med. ὡς ἀπὸ χαίταν πέξηται Call.*Lav.Pall.* 32. **II** *shear off*, ἀποπέπεκται· ἀποκέκαρται Hsch.; *cut off AP* 6.155 (Theorid.).

***ἀποπεμπτήρια**, τά, *means of getting rid of*, Hsch. s.v. καταστατήρια.

**ἀποπεμπτικός**, for pres. ref. read 'Men.Rh. p. 333.4, 10, p. 336.5, 6, 12 R.-W.'

**ἀπόπεμπτος**, delete 'cf. Hsch.'

***ἀποπετρόομαι**, *turn into stone, petrify*, of coral, ἐγχρονίζουσαν δὲ πλέον ἀποπετροῦσθαι Orph.*Lith.Kerygm.* 20.8 H.-S.

***ἀπόπηγμα**, ατος, τό, unexpld. wd. in broken context, *PMich.* III 149.13.32.

**ἀποπίεσμα**, for '*pressure* .. bent' read '*outward pressure*' and add '**II** = ἐκπίεσμα I, ἐλαιῶν Hsch. s.v. ψεαδερτῶν (written -πίασμα).'

**ἀποπίμπλημι I**, add 'perh. *fill up* a cup, [ἀ]ποπίπλη on shard, *SEG* 30.940 (Olbia, v BC)'

***ἀποπιτῠρισμα**, ατος, τό, = πιτύρισμα (which is v.l.), Arc. 20.

**⁺ἀπόπλᾰνος**, ον, *wandering away*, ὄρπηξ Paul.Sil.*Ambo* 197. **II** as subst., ἀ., ὁ, = ἀποπλάνησις, κυκᾶν τοῖς ἀντιθέτοις, τοῖς πέρασι .. τοῖς ἀποπλάνοις .. νουβυστικῶς Cratin.Jun. 7 K.-A. **b** perh. *conjuror* or sim., ἀ. κακοί· γόητες Hsch.

**ἀποπληρόω III 2**, add '*POxy.* 1255.16 (iii AD) **b** pass., *receive in full*, *PHamb.*inv. 410.11 (*JEA* 34.100; ?vi AD).'

**ἀποπλήρωσις**, add '**3** *bleeding, blood-letting*, (cf. Lat. *depletura*), *Edict. Diocl.* 7.21.'

**ἀποπλοκή**, add '*separation* of married couple, prob. in *PRyl.* 154.31 (i AD); cf. *ἀποπλέκω*'

**ἀπόπλοος** (A), delete '**2** *voyage home* or *back*' (include quots. under '*sailing away*')

**ἀπόπλυσις**, add 'Pelag.Alch. 254.18'

*__ἀποπλύτης__, *ου, ὁ, washerman*, Teuc.Bab. p. 46 B.

**ἀποπνέω I 2**, for '*exhale, evaporate*' read '*evaporate from*, w. gen.' **3**, delete 'in Com.'

**ἀποπνίγω 1 a**, at end after 'D. 32.6' insert 'X.*Eq.Mag.* 8.4, Men.*Dysc.* 668'

*__ἀποποιμαίνω__, *cherish, guide through, βίον POxy.* 3722 *fr.* 1.5, cf. *fr.* 28.3 (lemmata in Anacr. commentary, ii AD).

*__ἀπόπομπον__, gloss on *ἀποτάξιον*, Hsch.

*__ἀποπραιπόσιτος__, *ὁ, formerly praepositus, PMasp.* 127.23, *PLond.* 1687.23; *ἀ. κάστρου PMasp.* 296.3, *IPhilae* 224 (all vi AD).

*__ἀπόπρᾱσις__, *εως, ἡ, sale, Inscr.Délos* 353*A*38 (iii BC).

**ἀποπρηνίζω**, add '(cj. °*ἀνα-*)'

**ἀπόπρῑσις**, add 'Gal. 10.442.5'

**ἀπόπρισμα**, add '[*θυ*]*ίνων ἀποπρισμάτων Inscr.Délos* 1409*Ba* ii35 (ii BC)'

**ἀποπροάγω**, for '*in the second rank*, of things neither good nor bad' read 'of things neither good nor bad, but *negatively advanced*, i.e. *degraded* below the zero point of absolute indifference'

**ἀπόπροθι**, add '**b** prep. w. gen., A.R. 3.313, 372, 1065.'

**ἀποπροθορεῖν**, for '*spring far from*' read '*leap forward from*'

**ἀποπροΐημι 1**, for '[*κύνα*]' read '*τὸν δὲ τέταρτον*'

**ἀποπτερνίζω**, for pres. def. read '*trip up* (an opponent) *by twisting his heel*'

**ἀποπτίσσω**, add '*ἄρτοι ἀπεπτισμένοι* loaves *made from husked grain*, Philostr.*Gym.* 44'

**ἀποπτοέω**, for 'Call.*Fr.anon.* 93' read '*Suppl.Hell.* 1046'

**ἀπόπτυγμα**, for '*IG* 2.652.*A*20' read '*IG* $1^3$.469.23 (v BC), $2^2$.1388.20, etc.'

*__ἀποπωλέω__, = *ἀπομισθόω*, *Πολέμων* 1.32 (Demetrias, iii BC).

*__ἀποπωνίω__, v. *ἀποφωνέω*.

**ἀπορέω** (B) **I 1**, w. inf., add 'Pl.*Ti.* 44e'

**ἀπόρθωμα**, add '*Delph.* 3(5).74.15'

**ἀπορία III**, add '**4** *low yield, infertility*, of land, *Cod.Just.* 1.2.17.1.'

**ἀπόρνῡμαι**, add '*h.Ap.* 29, Mimn. 9.5 W.'

**ἄπορος III**, add '**4** *low-yielding, infertile*, of land, *PGen.* 67.7 (iv AD), *Cod.Just.* 1.2.17.1; neut. as subst., *unproductive land*, *PUniv.Giss.* 13.7 (i AD).'

**ἀπορρέω**, line 3, after 'Ath. 9.381b' insert '*ἀπέρευσα* Opp.*C.* 2.193; 3 sg. pf. *ἀπερρύηκε* Archil. 196a.27 W.' **I**, add 'w. internal acc., *γεννητικὴ .. δύναμις τὰς ἀεννάους τῶν θείων προόδους .. ἀπορρέουσα* Procl.*Inst.* 152 D.'

**ἀπορρήγνῡμι I 2**, after 'App.*BC* 2.81' insert 'of *breaking* bad news, Demetr.*Eloc.* 216' **II 2**, add 'pf. part. fem., *ἄλλην* (sc. *φιάλην*) .. *ἀπερρωγεῖαν* (sic) *μέρος τι Inscr.Délos* 1432*Bb* ii19 (ii BC)'

**ἀπορρήσσω**, add '**ἀπορρήττω** Ph. 2.304'

**ἀπόρρητος II 1**, penultimate line, after 'D.S. 15.20' insert '*φίλοι ἀ.* *secret* friends, Aen.Tact. 11.7' **III**, adv., add '*surreptitiously*, Ael.*NA* 7.42'

**ἀπόρροια I 3**, after '*συναφή*' insert 'Ptol.*Tetr.* 52' and after 'Gem. 2.14' insert 'Ptol.*Tetr.* 3'

*__ἀπόρρῠμα__, *ατος, τό, drainings* from grapes, *PAvrom.* 1*B*34 (i BC). **II** liquid measure = $\frac{1}{2}$ *σαΐτης* of 22 *ξέσται*, used for consignment of coins, *PColl.Youtie* 84 (iv AD).

*__ἀπορρωγή__, *ἡ*, = *ἀπόρρηξις*, Hsch. s.v. *ῥωγαί*.

**ἀπορρώξ II**, lines 8/9, delete '*ἀπορρὼξ τῆς πόλεως* .. 99d'

*__ἀπορυτιάζων__, *οντος, ὁ*, unexpld. title of ephebic official at Cyrene, *SEG* 9.51 (iii BC), 19.741.10 (i AD).

**ἀποσᾰφηνίζω**, delete this entry (transfer quot. to *ἀποσαφέω*).

*__ἀποσείρωμα__, *τό, something filtered off*, anon.medic. in *PColl.Youtie* 4.10 (iii AD).

*__ἀποσειρωτόν__ (v.ll. *-σιρ-*, *-σηρ-*), *τό*, (*σειρά*) *linear measure* (opp. *μέτρον*, *liquid measure*), Lcn. 1*Ch.* 23.29.

**ἀποσείω 1**, med., add '*unleash* a storm, *Βορέου χεῖμ' ἀποσεισαμένου SEG* 33.634 (epigr., Rheneia, ii BC)'

**ἀποσεμνύνω**, for '*extol, glorify*' read '*reverence*' and add 'Hld. 1.22, Charito 2.4' **II**, for '*give oneself solemn airs*' read '*adopt an aloof stance, move to a more exalted plane*'

**ἀποσεύω**, for '*chase away*' read '*rid oneself of*' and before '*AP* 9.642' insert 'w. ref. to excretion'

**ἀποσημείωσις**, add '*record* of inscription, *ἀ. ἐτέθη ἐπὶ τὸ βασίληον MDAI(I)* 15.124.6 (Miletus, ii AD; v. *SEG* 30.1353)'

**ἀποσῐώπησις 3**, delete the section.

*__ἀποσκάζω__, *limp away*, Hsch. s.v. ‡*κανάζοντα*.

*__ἀποσκᾰφή__, *ἡ, side-trench, PRyl.* 583.62, al. (ii BC), Choerob. *in Theod.* 2.103.12.

*__ἀποσκᾰφία__, *ἡ, excavation, IG* 9(2).522.18 (Larissa, iii/ii BC).

**ἀποσκευή I**, add 'Anon. *in Rh.* 146.1' **II**, delete 'Lxx *Ge.* 34.29' add '**2** soldier's *encumbrances*, i.e. *family*, *PBaden* 48.9 (ii BC), *UPZ* 110.199 (ii BC); *dependants*, Lxx *Ge.* 46.5, al.'

**ἀποσκλῆναι**, after 'pf.' insert '*ἀπεσκληκός* Hld. 8.8' and after 'fut.' read 'med. *ἀποσκλήσῃ you will perish with cold*, *AP* 11.37 (Antip.)'

**ἀποσκληρύνω**, after '*CP* 3.16.2' insert '*AP* 6.298 (Leon.Tarent.)'

⁺**ἀποσκολύπτω**, *strip the skin off*, S.*fr.* 423; (spec.) *circumcise*, Ael.Dion. α 162 E., Hsch., glossed by *κεκακουχημένος POxy.* 2328 ii 5/6 (i/ii AD); *pull back the foreskin*, Archil. 39 W.

**ἀποσκορᾰκισμός**, for '*casting off utterly*' read '*execration*'

**ἀποσμῡ́χομαι**, delete the entry.

**ἀποσοβέω I**, after '(Ar.) *V.* 460' insert '*μάρτυρας PEnteux.* 86.6 (iii BC); *send away*, *ἀ. με εἰς τὴν διόρυγα καὶ εἰς τὸ χῶμα PKöln* 104.14 (vi AD)'

**ἀποσόβησις**, after '*scaring away*' insert '*PLond.* 1724.49 (vi AD)'

*__ἀποσπάθιον__, *τό*, perh. *knife*, *PHamb.* 223.11.

⁺**ἀποσπᾰλᾰκόω**, *reduce to the condition of a σπάλαξ* (blind-rat), *ὁ τᾶς Δίκας ὀφθαλμὸς ἀπεσπαλάκωται* Cerc. 4.19.

**ἀποσπάς II**, for this section read 'as subst., *something torn off*, *σταφυλῆς ἀποσπάδα πεντάρρωγον*, i.e. five grapes pulled off from a bunch, *AP* 6.300 (Leon.Tarent.); spec., *slip* for propagation, *Gp.* 10.23, 11.9, 16; transf., *branch* of a river, Eust. 1712.6'

**ἀπόσπαστος**, after '*separated*' insert '*PBerol.* in Gercke-Norden *Einl. in die Altertumsw.* 1(9) p. 42'

**ἀπόσπληνος**, for 'Apul.*Herb.* 79' read 'Apul.*Herb.* 80'

**ἀποσπογγίζω**, after 'Antipho 5.45' insert '(v.l. *ἀνα-*)'

*__ἀποσπορά__, *ἡ, sowing*, *PCair.Isidor.* 34.5, 38.8 (both iii AD), *PCol.* 136.40, 51.

*__ἀπόσταθμον__, *τό, weight remaining* after deduction, esp. of the part of a victim reserved for the god, *Thasos* I p. 451.

**ἀπόσταξις**, add '**2** *distillation*, Moses Alch. 303.10.'

*__ἀποστάριος__, *ὁ*, = °*ἀποστασάριος*, *PKlein.Form.* 1161 (v/vi AD).

*__ἀποστασάριος__, *ὁ*, perh. *butler*, *SB* 4640-2, 10990.16-26 (v/vi AD).

**ἀποστασίου I**, add 'D.H.*Din.* 12'

**ἀποστᾰτέω**, line 1, after '*aloof from*' insert '*ἀπό τινος Thasos* 174c5'

**ἀποστέλλω**, add '**V** *give off, convey* a mental or sense impression, *ἡ καρὶς .. κινουμένη .. δόξαν τινὰ ἀποστέλλει μελλούσης .. παριέναι* Ael.*NA* 1.15; *τοὺς .. ὀφθαλμοὺς ἀποστέλλειν κυανοῦ χρόαν* id. 4.52; *ὁ ταὼς .. πρὸς τοὺς ἔξωθεν φόβον ἀποστέλλει* id. 5.21.'

**ἀποστεφᾰνόω**, delete '*discrown*' and insert '*Inscr.Olymp.* 225.21 (AD 49)'

*__ἀποστέφω__, *honour with libations*, *ψυχῇ θ' ἡρώων πένθος ἀποστέφετε* (= *-ται*) prob. to be read in *IGBulg.* 200, v. *ZPE* 9.186-7; cf. perh. *ἀποστεφήσῃ*, gloss on *ἀποέρσει* Hsch. (v. *εἴρω* (A)).

**ἀποστηθίζω**, after '*by heart*' insert 'Dam.ap.Suid. s.v. *Σαλούστιος*'

**ἀπόστημα 3**, add '*PMich.*XIII 660.8 (vi AD)'

**ἀποστημᾰτώδης**, add 'Paul.Aeg. 4.23 (345.9 H.)'

**ἀποστήριξις**, add '**2** *taking of a firm stance*, Gal.*Parv.Pil.* 2 (pl.).'

**ἀποστολεύς I 2**, for '*IG* 2.$809^b$20' read '*IG* $2^2$.$1629^b$252' add '**3** *harbour official in charge of freight consignments*, *PLond.* 1940.3 (iii BC), Aen.Tact. 29.12.'

**ἀποστολή I 1**, for 'cf. *IG* 2.238.15' read '*sending of ambassadors*, *IG* $2^2$.477.15, D.H. 8.64, of *συνθέωροι*, *SEG* 33.671.11 (= *OGI* 42, Cos, iii BC, in Dor. form *-ά*)' add '**b** *consignment* of goods, *ὁ πρὸς ταῖς ἀ. PLond.* 1963.6 (iii BC), *PCair.Zen.* 299 (pl., iii BC).' add '**5** prob. calque on Hebr. *shelaḥ*, *shoot* (where context requires prob. "cheek"), Lxx *Ca.* 4.13.' **II**, after '**2**' insert '*exile*, Lxx *Je.* 39(32).36, *Ba.* 2.25' (renumbering pres. section 2 as 3)

**ἀποστολικός**, add '**2** of an apostle, Clem.Al.*Prot.* 1.44, with the quality of an apostle, id.*Strom.* 2.20.116; of the Christian church, *apostolic*, *BCH* suppl. 8.235 (iv AD), *PRyl.* 471.5 (v AD), *Cod.Just.* 1.1.5.1; neut. subst., *gospel quotation*, Clem.Al.*Ecl.* 25 (p. 143.23), esp. of St. Paul's letters, *Pap.Lugd.Bat.* XXV 13.52, 53 (vii AD).'

**ἀπόστολος II 1**, for '*IG* 2.$809^b$190' read '*IG* $2^2$.1629.243' add '**8** = Lat. *litterae dimissoriae*, *PCol.*inv. 1696 in *ZPE* 10.135, cf. *Dig.* 50.16.106.'

**ἀποστόμωσις**, after '*πόρων*' insert 'perh. f.l. for *ἀναστομ-* in'; after 'Arist.*Pr.* $888^a$28' add 'but cf. *IG* 4.823.44 (Troezen, iv BC)'

**ἀποστρᾰτεύομαι**, add '*Dig.* 27.1.8 pr., 27.1.8.1'

*__ἀποστράτωρ__, *ορος, ὁ, ex-στράτωρ* (q.v.), *Syria* 6.232 (Der'a, iii AD); but prob. *ἀπὸ στρατόρων* shd. be read; cf. *ἀπό* II.

**ἀποστρέφω A II**, add 'Din. 2.23' **B II 1**, w. acc., add 'Even. 2.5' add '**4** w. acc. and inf., *shrink from saying*, Plu. 2.387c.'

*__ἀποστρεψῐκάκος__, *ον, averting evil*, epith. of Zeus, Bonner *Studies in Magical Amulets* p. 172.

**ἀποστροφή III**, rhet., add 'of an adjuration' and transfer 'Longin. 16.2' to follow.

**ἀποστῠγέω**, line 1, after '*-έστυξα*' insert '*AP* 6.48'

*ἀποστῡλόω, dub. sens., Delph. 3(5).85.8 (iv BC).

+ἀποσῡκάζω, gather the fruit from fig-trees, Amips. 33 K.-A. (pass.); fig., of cheats or the like, Ar.Eq. 259. 2 ἀποσυκάζειν· σῦκα ἐσθίειν Hsch.

ἀποσυμβιβάζω, add 'PUps.Frid 10.17 (iii AD), PMilan. 86.5 (v AD)'

*ἀποσυμμᾰλάσσω, make into a paste, ἐν κηρῷ ἀποσυμμαλαχθεὶς καὶ ἐπιπλασθεὶς μετώπῳ Cyran. 62 (v.l. συμμαλ-, v. ib. 2.16.5 K.).

ἀποσυνίστημι, add '3 reserve money for a purpose, Didyma 488.22. 4 ἀποσυνιστῶ gloss on Lat. amando, Dosith. p. 435 K.'

+ἀποσυντάσσω, revoke an order, prohibit, w. μή and inf., PSI 418, PLond. 1979.17 (both iii BC).

*ἀποσῠοκεφᾰλόω, change so as to have a pig's head, Cels.ap.Orig.Cels. 5.64.

ἀποσῡρίζω, for 'pass. .. VH 2.5' read 'give out whistling sound, in pass., ἀπὸ τῶν κλάδων κινουμένων τερπνὰ .. μέλη ἀπεσυρίζετο Luc.VH 2.5' add '(ἀποσυριεῖς Lxx Is. 30.14 is prob. f.l. for ἀποσυρεῖς)'

ἀπόσυρμα I 1, add 'Erot. 93.8'

ἀποσύρω, add 'also perh. Lxx Is. 30.14, v. °ἀποσυρίζω'

ἀποσφάζω, pass., add 'Hp.Nat.Hom. 6'

ἀποσφήλωσις, delete the entry.

ἀποσφίγγω, add 'AP 10.210 (Lucill.)'

ἀπόσχᾰσις I, add 'ἀ. τῶν σκελῶν scarification, Orib.Syn. 8.3.22'

ἀπόσχημα, delete the entry.

*ἀποσχῆναι· ἀπενεχθῆναι Suid.

+ἀποσχολάζω, take one's recreation, ἐν τούτοις (sc. amusements) ἀποσχολάζειν Arist.EN 1176ᵇ17, ἐν ταῖς ἀγοραῖς Ael.VH 9.25, τῷ οἴνῳ ib. 12.1, παρά τινι Ps.-Hdt.Vit.Hom. 5, 34.

*ἀποσχολέομαι, to be busy or preoccupied, PKöln 317.39 (vi AD).

ἀποσῴζω II, get off safe, add 'νὴ Δί' ἀπεσώθητέ γε Men.Dysc. 434'

*ἀποτακτάριος, ὁ, assessor, SB 9608.4.

ἀποτᾰμιεύομαι, add 'act., An.Ox. 3.195.11'

ἀπότᾰσις 2, for 'Plu. 2.670d' read 'Plu. 2.670c'

ἀποτάσσω I, add 'b register, ὁ γυμνασίαρχος .. ἀπέταξεν τοὺς ὑφ' ἑαυτῶι γενομένους ἐφήβους CRAI 1939.222.A13, 224.B11, 230 (Dalmatia, i AD).'

+ἀποταυρόομαι, pass., to be changed into a bull (or cow), w. internal acc. in mixed metaphor, τοκάδος δέργμα λεαίνης ἀποταυροῦται δμωσίν E.Med. 188; cf. ταυρόομαι; of Io, Erot. s.v. κερχνώδεα.

+ἀποτεκμαίρομαι, find by following signs, trace, πόρους A.R. 4.1538.

ἀποτέλεσμα 3, after 'finished product' insert 'Trypho Trop. p. 196 S.'

*ἀποτελεσμός, ὁ, completion, result, SEG 8.464.38 (Egypt).

ἀποτελέω II, delete the section.

ἀποτελωνέομαι, for 'PLond.ined. 2092' read 'PLond. 1979.10' and add 'PStrassb. 238.13, 14'

ἀποτέμνω I 1, line 8, for 'PMag.Par. 1.38' read 'PMag. 4.38; abs. execute (by decapitation), Cod.Just. 10.11.8.2 (cf. ib. 9.1.20)'

+ἀποτηγᾰνίζω, also ἀποτᾰγηνιζω (Sotad.Com. l.c., Alex. 178.11 K.-A.), eat off the frying-pan, eat broiled, Pherecr. 128 K.-A., Phryn. Com. 60 K.-A. 2 broil, Macho 421 G., Sotad.Com. 1.1 K.-A.

*ἀποτηγάνισμα, ατος, τό, rendered-down fat, lard, τοῦ κροκοδείλου Cyran. 2.22.6, 22.9 K.

ἀποτήκω, line 3, for 'τρία τάλαντα' read 'τέταρτον ἡμιτάλαντον'

ἀποτῐ́θημι I 1, line 3, delete '"pigeon-hole"' 2, after 'a child' insert 'Leg.Gort. 3.49, al.' II 3 b, after 'bury' insert 'Call.Epigr. 19.1 Pf., D.C. 73.5, 76.15 (Pass.)' add 'c lay charges, ὅταν παρ' αὐτοῖς ἀποτεθείη τις αἰτίασις κατά τινος Cod.Just. 1.4.29.8, τὸν κατ' αὐτοῦ τὴν αἰτίασιν ἀποθέμενον Just.Nov. 96.2.1.' 6, after 'Str. 10.5.2' insert 'ἀ. τὸ βάρος PBremen 63.4 (ii AD), Artem. 5.30' add '10 put down, record, τά τε γὰρ καλούμενα παρὰ πᾶσι πρῶτα ἐν τέσσαρσιν ἀπεθέμεθα βιβλίοις Just.Const. Δέδωκεν 3, 7c, 7e.'

ἀποτῑμάω II, add '3 reckon, assess numbers, Phleg. 12.6 J.'

ἀποτῑ́μησις II 2, after 'valuation' insert 'of a ἡρῷον, SEG 30.1354 (Miletus, iii AD)'

ἀποτίνῡμι, add '= ἀποτίνω'

ἀποτίνω I 3, add 'ἀ. πέντε δραχμάς SEG 23.76 (Attica, iv BC), ἀ. προστείμου .. δραχμὰς δέκα .. ib. 31.122 (Attica, ii AD)'

*ἄποτις, ιδος, app. fem. adj., abstaining from drink, Suid.

*ἀπότιστος, ον, unwatered, PTeb. 1126.1 (ii BC).

ἀποτμήγω 2, after 'c. gen.' insert 'Parm.fr. 4.2 D.-K.'

ἀποτομάς 3, delete the section transferring quot. to the beginning of section 2.

*ἀπότομον, τό, dub. sens., BGU 1546 (iii BC), perh. offcut.

ἀπότομος I 2 b, add 'Lxx Wi. 18.15' c, add '(v. Robert Les gladiateurs 258ff.)' add '6 neut. subst. pl., of land cut off and enclosed for private use, τὸν ἀποτόμōν καὶ τὸν δαμοσίōν IG 9²(1).609.2 (Naupactus, v BC); cf. ἀποτέμνω II 2.'

*ἀποτόσῑτος, ον, without food or drink, dub. in Sophr. in PSI 1214d7.

ἀποτρεπτικός 2, add 'τῶν δεινῶν Ps.-Luc.Philopatr. 8' deleting this ref. in section 1

ἀποτρέπω II 2, add 'τὸ ξύμπαν περὶ Πλαταιῶν οἱ Λακεδαιμόνιοι οὕτως ἀποτετραμμένοι ἐγένοντο Th. 3.68' 3, after 'E.IA 336' delete '(lyr.), cf. Th. 3.68'

ἀποτρέχω, after lemma insert 'Dor. ἀποτραχ- SEG 26.700.7 (Dodona, iii BC), Inscr.Cret. 1.xxii 4 c 5 (Olous, iii/ii BC), see also τράχω s.v. τρέχω' I, add 'w. inf., avoid, χρωτίζεσθαι ἀ. Lyr.Alex.adesp. 36' II, delete the section.

ἀποτρῑ́βω II, for this section read 'rub down a horse, X.Eq. 6.2. b ἀ. τὸ αἰδοῖον, masturbate, Macho 181 G., med., Plu. 2.1044b.'

ἀπότριπτος, add 'σφυρίς perh. used, worn out, PSoterichos 4.17 (i AD); κτήνη (beasts of burden) SB 7621.22, al. (iv AD)'

ἀποτρόπαιος, before 'ον' insert 'α' I, line 3, for 'CIG 464' read 'SEG 21.541 i 33 (Attica, iv BC), IG 2².4852, Sokolowski 2.116.A3-4 (Cyrene, ii BC); also of Zeus and Athena, Sokolowski 1.25.59, 82, 146 (Erythrae, iii BC), Sokolowski 2.88β3 (Lindos, ii BC), cf. ib. a1 (iv BC); of Athena alone, IG 14.957 (Rome); of Zeus, Inscr.Perg. 8(3).161 p. 169 line 19 (both ii AD)'; add 'neut. subst., the sanctuary of Apollo Apotropos, SEG 9.72.6 (Cyrene, iv BC)'

ἀποτροπάομαι, add 'act., = ἀποτρέπω, v.l. ἀποτροποῶμεν in Il. 20.119'

ἀποτροπία, -ίη, add 'perh. distance, inaccessibility of a divinity, IStraton. 543.16 (iii/ii BC)'

ἀπότροπος I, add 'εἴ τις .. ἀπότροπος οἴκαδ' ἀπέλθοι Panyas. 13.5 (nisi leg. ὑπο-)' II, add 'of Apollo, SEG 9.72.6 (Cyrene, iv BC)'

ἀποτροφή, line 1, after 'PSI .. pl.)' insert 'food for the poor, Cod.Just. 1.2.25 pr., maintenance for soldiers, ib. 10.27.2.12'

ἀποτρόφιμος, add 'ἀ., τά, subsistence, rest. in PMasp. 151.268 (vi AD)'

*ἀποτρῡπάω, bore through or gouge out, ὀφθαλμὸν ἀπετρύπησα τὸν τοῦ βασκάνου i.e. to avert evil, prob. w. sens. obsc., on phallic representation, SB 6295. 2 ἀποτρυπῶν· λάθρα ἐξιών Hsch.

ἀποτρῡπῶν, delete the entry.

ἀποτρώγω 2, w. gen. nibble at, for 'metaph. .. swathe' read 'transf., of a reaper, ὃς νῦν ἀρχόμενος τᾶς αὔλακος οὐκ ἀποτρώγεις'

*ἀπότττημα, ατος, τό, siftings, riddlings, IG 2².1672.218 (pl.); cf. διαττάω.

ἀποτύμβιος, delete the entry.

+ἀποτυμπᾰνίζω, (later -τυπ- PEnteux. 86.6, 8 (iii BC), UPZ 119 (ii BC), POxy. 1798.1.7), put to death, execute (whether by judicial sentence or less formally; perh. originally cudgel to death, but this is not specified in the quots.), Lys. 13.56, D. 8.61, 9.61, 19.137, Arist.Rh. 1383ᵃ5, 1385ᵃ10, PEnteux. l.c., UPZ 119.37, Plu.Dio 28, Sull. 6, id. 2.523a, 778e, 1049d, Euph.Fr.Hist. 173 vGr., Lxx 3Ma. 3.27.

ἀποτυμπᾰνισμός, for 'crucifixion' read 'prob. destruction'

ἀπότῡπος 1, add 'b decorated with repoussé figures, φιάλη Inscr.Délos 442B183, σκύφοι ib. 30 (ii BC).'

ἀποτύπτω 2, for 'cease to .. mourning' read 'finish beating the breast'

*ἀπότυψις, εως, ἡ, perh. repoussé work, Inscr.Délos 1441Aii62, 1450A161 (both ii BC); perh. error for ὑπότυψις (q.v.).

*ἀπούατος, ον, ill-sounding, ill-omened, ἄγγελος Call.fr. 315 Pf. (fr. misinterpretation of ἀπ' οὔατος Il. 18.272).

ἀπουλόω, add 'also ἀφουλ- Paul.Aeg. 6.47 (87.17 H.); pass., id. 6.40.3 (79.13 H.)'

ἀπούλωσις, add 'also ἀφούλ-, Paul.Aeg. 6.9 (54.5 H.), 6.58 (97.24 H.)'

ἀπουλωτικός, add 'also ἀφουλ- Paul.Aeg. 6.5 (48 H.)'

ἀπούλωτος, delete the entry (see ἀμωλώπιστος).

ἀπούρας I, after '4' insert 'w. acc. and gen., νόστου τόνδε στόλον .. ἀπούρας A.R. 3.175. 5'

ἀπουσία II, add 'deficit incurred in reminting old coins, NC 1950.1-22'

ἀπουσιάζω, after 'Sor. 1.87' add 'cf. ἀπουσία III'

ἀποφαίνω A I., for 'ἀ. παῖδας .. by her' read 'ὡς ἐκ ταύτης παῖδας ἀποφανῶν i.e. claim that children by her are his legitimate offspring'; after 'Is.' insert '3.30, 73, 79' II 4, transfer 'πρίν .. Ra. 845' to section 3, and after 'Lys. 31.2' insert 'b pronounce, of the Areopagus' B I 1, add 'b appear as, be shown to be, τῆς θαλάσσης .. κατὰ μικρὸν εἰς πέλαγος ἀποφαινομένης Peripl.M.Rubr. 26.'

ἀπόφᾰσις (A), line 1, delete 'opp. κατάφασις'

ἀπόφᾰσις (B), for 'διαίτης' read 'δίκης' and after 'cf. 33.21' insert 'of a report made by the Areopagus, Din. 1.1'

ἀποφέρω III, after 'returns, etc.' insert 'ἀ. γραφὴν κατά τινος κακώσεως D. 58.32; ἀπηνέχθη ἡ κατὰ τοῦδε τοῦ ψηφίσματος γραφή (sc. παρανόμων) Aeschin. 3.219'

ἀποφεύγω, add '4 fail to meet an obligation, default, Just.Nov. 120.8.'

ἀπόφημι, line 1, add 'pf. ἀποπέφηκεν Arist.Met. 1012ᵃ16 (s.v.l.)' II, add '3 w. acc. of predicate, κλεινὴν οὐκ ἀ. I do not deny that you are famous, AP 9.550 (Antip.).'

ἀποφθῐνύθω I, add 'νούσοι .. ἀποφθινύθουσι βροτοῖσι Orph.H. 68.3, καρποὶ .. ἀποφθινύθουσι orac. in Paus. 9.17.5' II, delete '2 diminish'

ἀποφθίνω II 2, for 'most freq. .. plpf. form ἀπέφθιτο[ῐ]' read 'most freq. in med. or pass., perish, die, esp. in aor. 2 form ἀπέφθῐτο'

*ἀποφλισκάνω, pay off, ἔχεις τὸ χρέος .. ἀποφληθέν Tz.H. 13.607.

**ἀπόφλω**, delete the entry.
**ἀποφοιβάζω**, add 'Certamen 35'
**ἀποφορά II**, for '*effluvia*' read '*effluvium, bad smell*' and add 'also *scent* ῥόδων Dsc. 4.45, οἴνου *Gp.* 7.7.5'
**ἀποφόρησις**, add '**2** perh. *removal*, *GDI* 3362.45.'
**ἀποφόρητος**, after '*carried away*' insert 'τὰ παρατιθέμενα ἔστω ἀ. *IG* 12(7).515.65 (Amorgos, ii BC)'; add 'δεῖπνον ἀ. *IStraton.* 270.13'
**ἀπόφορος 1**, for '*not .. suffered*' read '*that is given off* (cf. ἀποφορά II 1)'
**ἀποφράς**, after 'Luc.*Pseudol.* 12' insert 'w. ellipsis of ἡμέρα Sallust. 18, p. 34.5'
**ἀποφράσσω**, add 'fig., ἁπλῶς εἰπεῖν ἀποφράττειν αὐτοῖς τὴν δεῦρο ἄνοδον Paul.*Dig.* 49.1.25'
***ἀποφροντίστης**, ου, ὁ, *ex-φροντιστής* (local government official), *PMich.*xv 736.7 (vi AD).
**ἀποφώλιος**, line 4, after '(Od.) 11.249' insert '*uneducated, wild*, ἐξ ὀρέων ἀ. ἀγροιώτης Philet. 10.1'
**ἀποφωνέω**, add 'cf. ‡φωνέω I 3'
**ἀποχᾰραξις I**, add 'of a footprint, Sch.S.*Aj.* 2' **II**, for this section read '?*gap*, *Didyma* 32.4, 34.17 (pl.)'
**ἀποχειροτονέω II 3**, for 'Ar.*Pax* 668' read 'Ar.*Pax* 667'
**ἀποχή I**, add '**2** astron., *elongation*, Ptol.*Alm.* 6.2.462.6, al.' **III**, for '*PTeb.* 11.14' read '*PHib.* 162 (iii BC), *PTeb.* 11.18'
***ἀποχλωριαίνω**, *become pale*, *Vit.Aesop.*(G) 43: also **ἀποχλωριάω**, ib. 54.
***ἀποχονδρόομαι**, *become cartilaginous*, Paul.Aeg. 6.96.1 (149.21 H.).
**ἀποχράω A I 2 a**, add 'ἀποχρεῖ *suffices*, *SEG* 9.72.40 (Cyrene)' **3 a**, at end for 'D. 17.31' read 'D. 17.13' add '**C** (cf. χράω B) *lend*, 3 pl. fut. -χρήσουσι *PCair.Zen.* 107.5 (iii BC); med., *borrow*, *PMerton* 4.6 (iii BC).'
***ἀποχρηστεύομαι**, *to be unaccommodating*, *PTeb.* 777.8 (iii BC).
**ἀπόχῦμα 1**, add '*drainage water*, *PMich.*xi 617.9 (ii AD)'
**ἀπόχῦσις**, add '*drainage ditch*, *BGU* 2354.2 (ii AD)'
**ἀποχωρέω I 1**, add 'of slaves, *run away*, ἡμῶν *PCair.Zen.* 15$^v$.41 (iii BC)'
**ἀποχώρησις II**, for '= ἀπόπατος 2' read '*latrine*, *PMich.*i 38.31 (iii BC)'
**ἀποψέ**, add '*PLond.* 1081.1 (pap. -α, vii AD); cf. mod. Gk. απόψε'
**ἀπόψημα**, after '*refuse*' insert '*PCair.Zen.* 9 (iii BC)'
***ἀπόψηστος**, ον, *scraped off, made level*, ἡμιχοινίκια *IG* 2$^2$.1013.21.
**ἀποψηφίζομαι**, add '**V** act., *count off*, i.e. (?)*reject*, (?)ἄχρ(ε)ι(α) *Dura*$^4$ 127.'
***ἀποψηφοποιέω**, gloss on *praefragor* (?*disfranchise*), Dosith. p. 432 K.
**ἄποψις**, add '**III** *surface*, *Syria* 18.372 (Palmyra).'
**ἀποψοφέω**, delete '**II** *sound loudly*' and for 'φωνή' read 'φώκη'
**ἀπόψυγμα**, add 'cf. ‡ἀποψύχω III'
**ἀπόψυξις**, delete '*evaporation*'
**ἀπόψῡχος**, for '*frigid*' read 'prob. *lifeless*'
**ἀποψύχω I 1**, add '**b** *evaporate, lose flavour*, Sm.*Ez.* 17.9.' **II 1**, delete 'they *got* the sweat *dried off* their tunics' **III**, add 'cf. ἐναποψύχω'
**ἀποψωλέω**, delete '*a lewd fellow*' and add 'id.*Pax* 904, *Lys.* 1136, *Th.* 1187b, *Pl.* 295'
***ἄππαμα**, τό, Boeot. for ἀναπ- (cf. ἀνακτάομαι, ἀππασάμενος), pl., τἀππάματα *the debts to be recovered*, *IG* 7.3172.163, al. (Orchomenus, iii BC; but some interpret as τὰ ππάματα = τὰ κτήματα).
**ἄππας II**, add 'διὰ τοῦ ἄππα καὶ ἐπιτρόπου μου *Inscr.Cos* 352.6'
***ἀππεισάτου**, v.s.v. ἀποτίνω.
**ἀπρᾱγία**, add '*futility*, Sm.*Pr.* 12.11, 28.19'
***ἀπραγμᾰτικός**, όν, perh. *inalienable* or *not to be mortgaged*, *SEG* 34.1339 (Iconium, iii AD).
**ἀπραγμοσύνη I 1**, for '*freedom from politics, love of a quiet life*' read '*freedom from involvement in affairs, tranquillity*' and add 'Just.*Nov.* 100.1, 147.1'
**ἄπρᾱγος**, for '= ἀπράγμων' read '*futile, ineffective*'
***ἀπραίδευτος**, ον, (cf. Lat. *praedor*) *not sacked*, Phot. α 344 Th.
**ἄπρακτος I 2**, line 4, after 'Th. 6.48' insert 'codd., edd. -τους'
**ἄπρᾱτος**, after 'Aeschin. 2.23' insert '*not for sale*, ἄπρατον εἰς αἰεί *SEG* 34.1136, *ISmyrna* 228.6 (ii AD), v.l. in Plu.*Galb.* 17; neut. pl. subst., *things left unsold*, *PPetaus* 13.19 (AD 184/5)'
**ἀπρεπής**, add '**III** *improper, illegal* (use of water), *IEphes.* 3217.A12 (ii AD).'
***Ἀπρίλιος**, α, ον, Lat. *Aprilis*, *PLond.* 130.44 (ii AD, -λει-), *POxy.* 899 i 7 (iii AD, -λλι-), al., *SEG* 34.1469 (Palestine, vi AD).
***ἀπροαισθήτως**, adv. *unforeseeably*, Eurysus ap.Stob. 1.6.19.
**+ ἀπρόβουλος**, ον, *unforeseeing*, ἀπροβούλῳ (cj., cod. -ως) .. ὕπνῳ A.*Ch.* 620 (lyr.).
***ἀπρόγραπτος**, ον, *which has not yet been published*, *PPetr.*ined. in *APF* 33.24.8 (iii BC).
**ἀπροϊδής**, add 'δαίμων ἀπροιδής *IG* 14.1892'
**ἄπροικος**, after 'Lys. 19.15' insert 'Men.*Dysc.* 308'
***ἀπροϊσία**, ἡ, *seclusion*, Sch.E.*Hipp.* 132.
**ἀπροκοπία**, add 'Heph.Astr. 2.32.10, 3.6.6'
***ἀπρόκρῐτος**, ον, *not pre-judged, free from praeiudicium*, *Cod.Just.* 7.62.36.
**ἀπροόρᾱτος II**, for 'Ph. 2.268' read 'Ph. 2.269'
**ἀπρόσβᾰτος**, for 'νοῦσος' read 'νόσος'
**ἀπρόσδεκτος II**, transfer '*unacceptable* .. Porph.*Marc.* 24' to section I, after 'S.E.*P.* 2.229'
**ἀπροσδιόνῡσος I**, add '**2** of a person, *not suited to Bacchic rites*, Hld. 3.10.2.' **II**, transfer 'Plu. 2.612e, Luc.*Bacch.* 6' to section I 1.
***ἀπροσήκων**, ον, app. *no one's property*, εἶναι τὸ .. σῶμα ἐλεύθερον, ἀπρόσηκον, μηδενὶ μηδὲν προσῆκον *Delph.* 3(6).116.8 (i AD).
**ἀπρόσθετος**, after '*added to*' insert 'δηνάρια *PDura* 29.8 (iii AD)'
***ἀπροσκοπία**, ἡ, (προσκόπτω) *safety, freedom from accident*, *SB* 7352 (ii/iii AD).
**ἀπρόσκοπος** (B) **I**, after '*unseeing*' insert 'or perh. *not seen beforehand*'
**ἀπρόσλογος**, after '*not to the point*' insert 'Artem. 1.11'
***ἀπροσμᾰχητος**, ον, *irresistible*, Sch.Hes.*Th.* 295 (p. 58.16 G.), ib. 319b (p. 62.5 G.).
***ἀπροσοδίαστος**, ον, *not yielding income*, *IGRom.* 3.422.19 (Ariassus); cf. ἀπρόσοδος II.
**ἀπρόσοδος II**, add '**b** *unsalaried*, *BCH* 83.363.25 (Thasos, i BC).'
**ἀπροσποίητος**, before 'in adv.' read '*SEG* 3.226.14 (Athens, ii AD)'
***ἀπροσπολίη**, ης, ἡ, *loss of* one's *attendant*, rest. in *IG* 12(8).92.9 (Imbros, ii/i BC).
***ἀπροσπόριστος**, ον, of property, *not acquired from the property of the paterfamilias*, Just.*Nov.* 84.1.2.
**ἀπρόσφορος**, add '*not applicable*, δικαστής i.e. not competent, *Cod.Just.* 3.1.12.2; w. gen., κἂν τοῦ ἐνάγοντος ἀπρόσφορος ib. 7.51.5.1'
**ἀπροσωπόληπτος**, add 'prob. voc. -λημπτε, to a divinity, *IGLS* 343.6 (lapis -λημιε)'
**ἀπροτίελπτος**, add 'χάρμα orac. in *ZPE* 1.184.22 (Guarducci *EG* 4 p. 103)'
**ἀπροφάσιστος I 1**, line 3, after 'Timocl. 8' insert '(cf. perh. ἀ. in καλός inscr., *SEG* 35.252, vi BC)'; adv., add 'neut. as adv., pl., *AP* 7.721 (Chaeremo), sg., ib. 5.250 (Paul.Sil.)'
***ἀπροφήτευτος**, ον, *not having a* προφήτης, ἐνιαυτός *Didyma* 237 II 10 (?i AD).
**ἄπταιστος**, line 3, after '*Am.* 46' insert '*unerring*, D.H.*Dem.* 52'
**ἀπτήν I**, delete 'metaph. of men' and after '*Com.adesp.* 1291' insert '= A.*fr.* 337 R.'
***ἀπτής**, = ἀπτώς, *Inscr.Olymp.* 164 (iv BC).
**+ἄπτιστος**, ον, *not winnowed* or *husked*, Hp. *VM* 14; of loaves, *made from unhusked grain*, Philostr.*Gym.* 43.
**ἄπτρα**, for 'ἄπτριον' read 'ἀπτρίον' and add 'cf. ἀπτρήν (= -ίον) Gregorius Magnus in PL 77.178C, (mod. Gk. dial. ἀφτρί)'
**ἅπτω A I 1**, after '(to hang herself) 11.278' insert 'οἱ δ' ἀγχόνην ἅψαντο Semon. 1.18' **B**, *set on fire*, after 'A.*Ag.* 295' insert 'w. gen., Th. 4.100.4' **III**, delete the section.
**ἀπτώς**, delete 'ἀ. δόλος .. 9.92'; add 'fig., of wrestlers and their art, σὸν κατ' ἀγῶνα ἀπτῶτ' ἀγγέλλω παῖδα κρατεῖν *Lindos* 699.*b*2 (epigr., ii BC), νεικήσας ἀγῶνα ἀπτώς *SEG* 31.1287 (Side, Rom.imp.)'
***ἀπτωτί**, adv. *without falling*, in wrestling, φῶτας δ' ὀξυρεπεῖ δόλῳ ἀ. δαμάσσαις Pi.*O.* 9.92.
**ἀπύ**, add 'also Myc., Cypr. *a-pu*'
***ἀπῡγίζω**, v. °ἀναπυγίζω.
**ἄπῡγος**, add 'Comp., *AP* 11.327'
***ἀπῦγων**, gloss on διχόνδις, Hsch.
**ἀπῦθεν**, after 'Aeol.' insert 'or Arc., Cypr.'
**ἀπύρετος**, add at end '(interpol.)'
**ἀπύρηνος**, after '*without*' insert 'or *with only a residual*'; delete 'φοῖνιξ' and add 'Arist.*Met.* 1023$^a$1'
**ἄπῡρος I 1 a**, add 'Alcm. 17.3 P.' **3**, for '*unfermented*' read '*not heated*' and for 'Alcm. 117' read 'Alcm. 92(*a*) P.' **6**, insert def. '*made without the use of fire*' and add 'Pl.*Plt.* 287e'
**ἄπυστος I 1**, for 'Sapph.*Supp.* 25.19' read 'Parm. 8.21, Call.*Del.* 215, *Cer.* 9' **II**, add 'Call.*fr.* 611, 680 Pf.'
**ἀπφά**, add 'Suid., *AB* 441'
**ἄπωθεν**, line 1, before 'Q.S. 6.647' insert 'Call.*fr.* 194.97, 197.25 Pf.'
**ἀπωθέω**, line 1, after 'ἀπῶσα' insert '*AP* 9.326.5 (Leon.Tarent.)'
**ἀπώμοτος II**, add '*one who denies on oath* that he has done a thing, *Inscr.Cret.* 4.72 xi 28'
**ἀπωνέομαι**, for '*buy, purchase*' read '*sell*' and after 'ἀπωνηθήσεται' insert '*will be sold*'
**ἀπώρωτος**, add 'Paul.Aeg. 6.110 (163.9 H.)'
**+ἄπωτος**, ον, perh. *deaf*, on votive offering in the shape of an ear, Cypr. *to-po-to-e-mi*, perh. τō 'πότō ἠμί *ICS* 289.
**ἄρα B 4**, for 'v. sub τοι II 2' read 'v. sub τοι III'
**ἆρα A**, at end for 'Id.*fr.* 931' read 'S.*fr.* 931' **B**, for 'almost always' read 'generally'

**ἀρά I 2**, for this section read '*ex-voto dedication*, *ISmyrna* 739 (Ion. acc. ἀρήν, *c*.600 BC), Cypr. *a-ra*, *Rantidi* 44 (vi BC), perh. in *ICS* 107, *Inscr.Cret.* 1.xxv 3, xxi 7 (both near Gortyn), *SEG* 23.593 (Gortyn, i BC)'

***Ἀραβάρχης**, ου, ὁ, *ruler of Arabs*, applied by Cicero to Pompey, *Att.* 2.17.2. **II** title of official, *controller of customs*, esp. in Egypt, orig. E. of Nile, *OGI* 202.9, Juv. 1.130; dissim. **Ἀλαβάρχης**, J.*AJ* 18.6.3, al.; also in Lycia and Euboea, *OGI* 570, *IG* 12 suppl. 673 (Chr.).

**Ἀραβαρχία**, before '*office*' insert '*rule over Arabs*, J.*AJ* 15.6.2. **II**' and add '*OGI* 674 (i AD)'

**ἄραβδος**, delete the entry.

**Ἀρᾰβικός**, s.v. Ἀραβία, add 'as Lat. *Arabicus*, title conferred on Septimius Severus, *TAM* 4(1).27, *ICilicie* 78, etc. **2** name of a god in Arabia, Θεὸς Ἀ. *SEG* 32.1540 (Gerasa, Rom.imp.).

**Ἀρᾰβισσα**, s.v. Ἀραβία, before 'St.Byz.' insert '*Arabian woman*, *RDAC* 1975.142-3 (Cyprus, late Hellen.), *AD* 25.74 no. 22 (in Att. epitaph, i BC), *SB* 11169.13 (ii AD)'

***Ἄραβος** (B), ὁ, *Arab*, for phrase κατ' Ἀράβους v.s.v. °Ἄραψ.

**ἀραγμός**, add 'Plu. 2.594e'

**ἄρᾰδος**, for '*palpitation* of the heart' read '*agitation*'

**ἀραιόστῡλος**, for 'Vitr. 3.31' read 'Vitr. 3.3.1'

***ἀραιόφρῡς**, -υος, ὁ, *having scanty eyebrows*, in description of a slave, *POxy.* 3054.16 (sp. ἀρεο-, iii AD).

**ἀραίωμα**, after 'Plu. 2.980c' insert 'Longin. 10.7' and at end delete '*a little bit*, Longin. 10.17'

***ἀρᾰ́κινος**, η, ον, *of* or *from aracus*, χόρτος *PVindob.Worp* 3.19, perhaps = χορτάρακος; ἄχυρον *BGU* 2151.18.

***ἀρᾰκόομαι**, med., *sow with aracus*, *PSI* 1021.19 (ii BC).

***ἀρᾰκοφόρος**, ον, *producing aracus*, *PMich.*I 31.26 (iii BC).

**ἀράομαι I**, line 1, after 'Aeol.' insert 'pres. ind. ἄρᾱμαι Sapph. 22.17 L.-P.' and for '*Supp.* 5.22' read '16.22 L.-P.'; line 2, for 'Sapph. 51' read 'Sapph. 141.7-8 L.-P., Cypr. *a-ra-wa-sa-tu*, ἀρϜάσατυ *ICS* 343a (p. 404); later ἠρᾰσάμην *AP* 5.47 (Rufin.)' **2**, add '*h.Hom.* 6.16' **3**, line 1, for 'Sapph. 51' read 'Sapph. 141.7-8 L.-P.' **4**, add 'abs. Cypr. ἀρϜάσατυ, *ICS* 343a; cf. °ἀρά I 2'

***ἀράριον**, τό, v. °αἰράριον.

**ἀρᾰρίσκω B I**, line 5, after 'etc.' insert '2 sg. ἠρήρεισθα Archil. 172.3 W.' **2**, line 2, for 'Il. 10.553' read 'Od. 10.553' **V**, last line, for 'Pl.*Epigr.* 6' read '*AP* 7.35 (Leon.Tarent.)' at end add 'Myc. pf. part. *a-ra-ru-ja* (fem. pl. = ἀραρυῖαι), *a-ra-ru-wo-a* (neut. pl. = *ἀραρϜόhα), *fitted*'

***ἄρασιν**· ἀράχνην Hsch. (after ἀρᾶσαι).

**ἀράσσω I**, for '*smite*, *dash in pieces*' read '*strike violently*' and for 'of any violent .. Pi. l.c.' read 'often w. implication of noise, χαλκέαις δ' ὁπλαῖς ἀράσσεσκον χθόνα (βόες) Pi. l.c.'; line 5, after 'συναράσσω' insert 'exc. in Od. 5.248 (v.l. ἄρηρεν)'; line 7, for 'horses' read 'oxen' **2**, add 'Sch.Il. 2.801'

***Ἀράτειος**, ἡ, name of kind of fig-tree, Thphr.ap.Ath. 3.77a.

**ἀρᾱτός II**, add 'neut. ἀρητόν as adv., *gladly*, prob. for ἄρητον in Call.*Del.* 205' add '**III** Ἀρητος, title of Heracles in Macedonia, *MDAI(A)* 27.311 no. 18 (Edessa), Hsch.'

***ἀραχνέω** (or -όω), perh. *remove cobwebs*, *ZPE* 8.57.

**ἀράχνη V**, for '*sundial*' read '*hemispherical dial* devised by the astronomer Eudoxus of Cnidos'

***ἀραχνιάω**, *to be covered with cobwebs*, Nonn.*D.* 38.14.

**ἀραχνιόω I**, delete 'act. in same sense, Nonn.*D.* 38.14'

***ἀραχνοποιέω**, *make a (spider's) web*, Cyran. 2.16.12 K.

**ἀραχνοϋφής**, add '*Suppl.Hell.* 1071'

**ἄραχος**, add '*Schwyzer* 603 (Corope, vi/v BC)'

**Ἄραψ**, after '*Arab*' insert '*IG* $2^2$.8361-2 (iii and ii BC)'; after 'J.*BJ* 1.19.4' insert 'in dates, κατ' Ἄραβας referring to the Macedonian calendar adopted by the Arabs, *SEG* 30.1687, 34.1468 (both Palestine, vii and vi AD), also κατ' Ἀράβους ib. 34.1467 (Palestine, vi AD)'; after '*Pae.Delph.* 11' insert 'γένος Ἄραβα *IG* $9^2$(1).624(d).4'

***Ἀρβακτις**, εως, ὁ, name of an Egyptian divinity, *OGI* 52 (iii BC), Bernand *Les Portes* 23 (ii BC).

***ἀρβελλάριον**, τό, kind of knife, used for pig-slaughter, *POxy.* 3866.3, 7 (vi AD); cf. ‡ἄρβηλος.

**ἄρβηλος**, for '*semicircular knife* .. leather-workers' read '*leather-worker's knife*, having a semicircular blade with two semicircles cut away from the straight edge'

**ἀρβυλίς**, add '**II** ἀρβυλίδα· λήκυθον. Λάκωνες Hsch.; cf. ἀρυβαλλίς II.'

**ἀργαπέτης**, add 'see also °ἀρκαπάτης'

***ἄργεθμον**, τό, = ἄργεμον I, Cyran. 1.16.15 K. (v.l. ἄργεμος).

**Ἀργεῖος**, after 'α, ον' insert 'quadrisyll. (Ἀργεΐων) in E.*Hec.*'; add 'cult-epith. of Hera, Il. 4.8, Hes.*Th.* 12 (-είη) *SEG* 30.366, (Argos), 30.648 (Vergina), 30.1456 (Sinope, all v BC)'

***Ἀργειώνη**, ἡ, *the Argive* (i.e. *Greek*) *woman*, sc. *Helen*, Hes.*fr.* 23(a).20, 217.6, 136.10 M.-W. (rest.), Theognost.*Can.* 700.

**ἀργεννός**, add 'prob. of chalky soil, Rhian. 54, Nic.*Th.* 67; form ἀεργενν- by false association w. ἀργός (B), *POxy.* 3536.3 (hex., ε erased but required metrically, iii AD)'

***ἀργεντάριος**, ὁ, Lat. *argentarius*, *BGU* 781 vi 8 (i AD), *SEG* 2.421 (Maced.), etc.

***ἀργενταρίτης**, ου, ὁ, *cashier*, *CPR* 14.41.7 (vi/vii AD).

**ἀργέντινος**, after '*silvery*' insert '*Stud.Pal.* 20.46.32 (ii/iii AD)'

**ἀργέω**, after lemma insert 'form ἀεργέω, *SEG* 30.1175.5 (tab.defix., Metapontum, iii BC; but ἀργ- in line 9)' **I**, add 'as legal term, abs., *to be inoperative*, *Cod.Just.* 6.4.4.11a, *to be nullified*, *cancelled*, ib. 1.3.55.2-3, Just.*Nov.* 110.1'

**ἀργήεις**, after 'εσσα, εν' insert 'nom. fem. pl. ἀργήεις Nic.*fr.* 74.26'; line 3, for '(v.l. ἀργινόεντι)' read '(cj.; ἀργινόεντι codd.)'

**ἀργής**, line 5, delete 'φύσις Orph.*H.* 10.10'

**ἀργηστής 1**, for '*glancing*, *flashing*' read '*shining*, *bright*'; add 'of the wind, cf. ἀργεστής B. 5.67 S.-M.' **2**, for 'κύκνοι' read 'ταῦροι'

***ἀργητός**, ή, όν, *lying idle*, *unused*, κέλλαι λ ὧν ἀργηταὶ οὖσαι δ *PMich.*XI 620.114 (iii AD).

**ἀργιβρέντας**, for pres. ref. read 'Pi.*fr.* 52m.9 S.-M.'

***ἀργίζω**, *to be unemployed*, *idle*, *SB* 9699.197, 201, etc., rest. fr. abbrev. ἀργι, but could be ἀργῖ = ἀργεῖ.

***ἀργιζώστη**, ἡ, (or -της, του, ὁ), *white bryony*, Cyran. 9 (1.1.108 K.); cf. ἀρχεζῶστις.

**ἀργιλλοφόρητος**, delete the entry.

**ἄργμα**, add '*CEG* 246 (v BC)'

**Ἀργολικός**, after '*Rom.* 21' insert 'Call.*fr.* 114.19, 384.22 (Add. II) Pf.'

***ἀργολογία**, ἡ, *empty talk*, Hsch. s.v. βατ‹τ›ολογία.

**ἀργομέτωπος**, add '*IG* $2^2$.463.40 (rest.)'

**Ἄργος**, accentuate thus.

**ἀργός (B) I 2 a**, line 5, before 'adv.' insert '*Iamb.adesp.* 39 W.; ἀργοί (sc. ἡμέραι), *holidays*, Porph.*Plot.* 5' **II 1**, add 'ἀργύρου ἀργ(οῦ) *POxy.* 3628.10 (v AD)'

***ἀργῠρᾰμοιβήϊον**, τό, *bureau de change*, Duchêne *La stèle du port*, *Fouilles du port* I p.20 l.42 (Thasos, v BC).

**ἀργῠρᾰμοιβικός**, add 'ἀργυραμο]ιβικὴ τράπεζα *PRev.Laws* col. 73, 3-4'

**ἀργῠρᾰμοιβός**, delete '*banker*' and before 'Theoc. 12.37' insert '*assayer*'

***ἀργῠρᾶς**, 'α, ὁ, *silversmith*, *BGU* 1034.15 (ii AD).

**ἀργῠράφιον**, add '*SB* 12084.6 (i AD)'

**ἀργύρεος**, line 1, after 'οὖν' insert '(fem. -εος, τὴν ἀργύρεον τράπεζαν Lanckoroński *Städte Pamphyliens und Pisidiens* 1.58.20, τὰς ἀργυρέους Μούσας *SEG* 32.1269 (Phrygia, Rom.imp.)); Lacon. ἀργύριος Alcm. 1.55 P.' **I**, line 4, for 'Pl.*Lg.* 801d' read 'Pl.*Lg.* 801b'; add 'fig., of a lover, *SEG* 31.847 (Thasos, rock inscr., iv BC)' **II**, add 'also neut. pl. ἀργυρᾶ *POxy.* 2729.6 (iv AD), *PStrassb.* 330 (iv AD)'

**ἀργῠρίζομαι**, add '*earn money* (in quot., of prostitutes), Ath. 13.569d'

***ἀργῠρικέλαιον**, τό, lit. *silver oil*, perh. extract of *mercurialis annua* (λινόζωστις), *ODouch* 34.7.

***ἀργῠριοθήκη**, ἡ, *money-box*, *AB* 443.6, Suid.

**ἀργύριον I 1**, delete '(v. Poll. 9.89)' and transfer to sense I 2, *money*; add 'ἀ. Ἀττικόν *Attic coinage*, *SEG* 26.72.3 (iv BC; see also ib. 28.49); ἀ. μεγάλον *large silver coinage*, *SB* 5174.8 (vi AD), opp. μικρόν *PVindob.Sijp.* 10.10-12 (vi AD)' **II**, add 'app. this sense in Lang *Ath.Agora* XXI He 15, p. 78 (amphora graffito, ii AD)'

**ἀργύριος II**, delete the section (v. °ἀργύρεος).

**ἀργῠρίς**, line 1, after 'ἴδος' insert '(acc. ἄργυριν Alcm. 3 *fr.* 3 ii 77 P.)'

***ἀργῠροζώμιον**, τό, *silver wash*, Zos.Alch. 214.4.

**ἀργῠροκοπεῖον**, -κόπιον, before pres. ref. insert 'rest. in *SEG* 26.6 (coinage decree, Athens, v BC)'

**ἀργυροκόπος**, add '*SEG* 26.72.54 (Athens, 375/4 BC)'

***ἀργῠροκόραλλος**, ἡ, *silver-coral*, name of a metal, Anon.Alch. 361.3.

***ἀργῠρόκρᾱνος**, ον, *with silver head*, ἀνήρ (referring to the emperor Hadrian), *Orac.Sib.* 5.47.

**ἀργῠρολογέω**, add '**2** *take money* (for consultations), Aesop. 161 P.'

**ἀργῠρολόγος**, add '**II** ἀ., οἱ, financial officials, *Samothrace* II (1)5.14 (ii BC).'

**ἀργῠρόπαστος**, for '*silver-broidered*' read '*silver-plated*' and add 'of a coin, prob. in *Inscr.Délos* 1442*B*50 (ii BC)'

***ἀργῠροπλάστης**, ου, ὁ, *silversmith*, *SB* 6259 (v/vi AD).

***ἀργῠροπρᾱ́της**, ου, ὁ, *silver-merchant*, *IGChr.* 98 (v AD), *PSI* 76 (vi AD).

**ἀργῠροπρᾱτικός**, for pres. ref. read '*Cod.Just.* 4.21.22.5, Just.*Nov.* 4.3 (p. 27.43), 136'

**ἀργῠρόρρυτος**, for '*beside a silver stream*' read '*silver-streaming*'

**ἀργῠρορῠχή**, for '*Mon.Ant.* 23.8' read '*Mon.Ant.* 23.78'

**ἄργῠρος**, add 'Myc. *a-ku-ro*'

***ἀργῠροστατήρ**, ῆρος, ὁ, *silver stater*, dub. in Hsch. s.v. γλαῦκες Λαυριωτικαί.

**ἀργῠροτᾱμίας**, add 'τῶν φυλάρχων *TAM* 4(1).42'

**ἀργῠρότοξος**, add '*CEG* 326 (?Thebes, Boeotia, vii BC), 337 (the Ptoion, *c*.500 BC)'

***ἀργῠροφύλαξ**, ακος, ὁ, *keeper of silver, IEphes.* 4233 (iii AD).

***ἀργῠροχοϊκός**, ή, όν, *of the* ἀργυροχόος, ἡ ἀ. (sc. τέχνη) Phlp. *in GC* 70.14.

**ἀργῠροχόος**, add '*IEphes.* 585, *SEG* 34.1094 (Ephesus), 31.1592 (Asia Minor)'

**ἀργυρόω I**, add '**2** *make in silver*, Cypr. *a-ra-ku-ro-se* ἀργύρω̄σε *ICS* 307.'

⁺**ἀργῠρωματικός**, ή, ον, γῆ kind of earth used for polishing silver, *IEphes.* 27.542, 549.

**ἀργῠρωμάτιον**, after 'dim. of ἀργύρωμα' insert '*PCair.Zen.* 44.9, al. (iii BC), *Inscr.Délos* 1441*A*ii104'

***ἀργῠρωματοφῠλάκιον**, τό, *storehouse for keeping silver plate, PCornell* 1.130 (iii BC).

***ἀργύρωσις**, εως, ἡ, *silvering*, Zos.Alch. 214.6.

***ἀργῠρωτός**, ή, όν, *silvered*, rest. in *IG* $2^2$.1473.11 (iv BC).

***ἀρδάλιον**, τό, ἀρδάλια· τοὺς πυθμένας τῶν κεραμίδων, οὓς ἔνιοι γοργύρας καλοῦσιν Hsch.

**ἄρδαλος**, add 'cf. Lat. *ardalio, busybody*'

**ἀρδάνιον**, after '= ἀρδάλιον' insert 'used esp. for ritual purification at funerals'

**ἄρδην II**, after '*wholly*' insert 'esp. w. ref. to destruction' and add 'D. 19.61, 27.26, Isoc. 14.19'

**ἄρδις I**, after 'Hdt. 4.81' insert 'Call.*fr.* 70 Pf.'

**Ἄρειος**, after lemma insert 'or ἄρειος'; line 7, after '(Hdt.) 4.23' insert 'Ἀραβίας τ' ἄρειον ἄνθος A.*Pr.* 420, στέφανος E.*Ph.* 832, ὅπλα D.C. 44.17.2'

**Ἄρειος πάγος**, line 2, delete '1.38a (prob.)'; line 3, before 'D. 18.133' insert '*SEG* 12.87'; line 4, for 'βουλὴ Ἀρεία' read 'βουλὴ Ἀρεία'; line 6, for 'Isoc. 7.37' read 'Isoc. 7.38'; line 7, after 'id.*Ath.* 59.6' insert 'w. ref. to the Council of the Areopagus as the type of political integrity'

**ἀρείων**, add 'cf. Myc. *a-ro₂-a* (neut. pl.) perh. *ἄρροhα or *ἄρyoha'

***ἀρέοφρυς**, v. °ἀραιόφρυς.

**ἀρεσκεύομαι**, add '**b** *please, oblige*, *BCH* 83.499.51, 53 (i AD).'

**ἀρέσκω I 3**, add 'ἀρεσκομένου Χαρίτεσσιν *AP* 7.440 (Leon.Tarent.)' **III**, line 4, after '*Tht.* 172d' insert 'Just.*Const.* Δέδωκεν 20a'

**ἀρεστήριον**, add '*AE* 1923.39 (Oropus, iv BC)'

**ἀρετᾱλόγος**, at end after '*SIG* 1133' insert '(Delos, i BC)' and after 'cf.' insert '*IG* 11(4).1263'

***Ἀρέταρχος**, ὁ, cult-title of Zeus, *INikaia* 1076 (Rom.imp.).

**ἀρετηφόρος**, add 'poet., **ἀρεταφόρος**, ἡ, of a temple-road (cf. λαοφόρος I 2), *Lindos* 487.23 (iii AD)'

**ἀρηβώ**, delete '*Peripl.M.Rubr.* 12'

**ἀρήγω I 1**, add 'Gal. 13.707.3'

**ἀρηγών**, after 'masc. in' insert '*Suppl.Hell.* 1163'

***Ἀρηϊσταί**, οἱ, members of an association of worshippers of Ares Enyalios, *SEG* 33.945 (Ephesus).

**ἀρήν**, line 1, delete 'only in Inscrr.' and insert 'Phryn.*PS* p. 9 B., Poll. 7.184, Aesop. 155 tit. P.'; line 4, after 'dat. ἀρνάσι' insert 'Arat. 1104' **I**, add 'ἀρὲν κριτός *IG* $1^3$.234.22 (v BC), ἄρνα παμμέλαιναν *SEG* 21.541 col. i 9 (Attica, iv BC)'

**Ἄρης**, line 2, delete '(never contr.)' and in line 3, after '*fr.* 16' insert 'contr. Ἄρευς *AP* 9.322.9 (Leon.Tarent)' add '**IV** the Arabian Ares, identified w. a local war god, *SEG* 33.1301, 36.1374 (Hauranitis, Rom.imp.).' at end add 'Myc. *a-re*'

**ἀρθμός**, add 'Myc. *a-to-mo*, referring to group of men, exact sense uncertain'

**ἄρθρον**, τὰ ἄρθρα, *genitals*, add 'Ael.*NA* 3.47, μοιχὸς ἑάλω ποτέ, ὡς ὁ ἄξων φησί, ἄρθρα ἐν ἄρθροις ἔχων Luc.*Eun.* 10'

**ἀρθροπέδη**, after 'Phan.' insert 'prob. corrupt'

**ἀρία**, add 'Eup. 491 K.-A.'

**ἀρίγνως**, read '**ἀριγνώς**'

**ἀριδάκρυος**, add 'Call.*fr.* 700 Pf.'

**ἀρίζηλος**, line 5, after 'ib. 519' insert 'Call.*Epigr.* 51.3 Pf.' **II**, delete the section.

**ἀριθμέω 1**, line 9, after '*AP* 11.349 (Pall.)' insert 'the years of one's life, i.e. live so long, γήραι ἀριθμ[ή]σασ' ἐννέα ἐτῶν δεκάδας *CEG* 592.4 (Athens, *c*.300 BC)'; line 10, for 'πλίνθους' read 'τὰς ἐπιβολάς'

**ἀρίθμησις I 1**, after '*IPE* $1^2$.32*B*35 (Olbia)' insert 'Just.*Nov.* 18.10' add '**3** *report of collection* made by tax collectors, *PMich.*x 577, 582 (i AD), *PLond.* 1157 (ii AD).'

**ἀριθμητής**, add '*PUG* inv, DR61.c.3 (Atti Napoli III 900, 165 BC), Just.*Nov.* 73.7.1'

**ἀριθμητικός III**, for '*Sammelb.* 4415.14' read '*SB* 4415.4'

**ἀρίθμιος II**, after 'D.P. 263' insert 'Call.*fr.* 110.61 Pf.'

**ἀριθμός I 2**, add '*expenditure in cash*, opp. γράμματα (estimate on paper), Pech-Maho lead in *ZPE* 82.161 (v BC), *SEG* 2.582 (Teos, iii/ii BC)' **II**, after 'Hdt. 8.7' insert 'ναῶν δ' εἰς ἀριθμὸν ἤλυθον E.*IA* 231' **VIII**, for '*Dem.* 52' read '*Dem.* 54' **IX**, before '*line*' insert '*number of lines* in a book, Plb. 39.8.8, Luc.*Hist.Conscr.* 16. **b**'

**ἀρικύμων**, add '*Steril.* 219'

⁺**ἆριν**, v. ἄρρις.

⁺**ἆρις**, v. ἄρρις.

**ἀρίς II**, for this section read '*bow-shaped sluice*, also called φράκτης, Procop.*Aed.* 2.3.18, 21'

**ἀριστεία**, at end before 'Cic.*Att.*' insert 'Hdt. 2.116'

**ἀριστεῖα 1**, line 4ff., delete 'ἀ. τῆς θεοῦ .. *IG* 2.652*A*30, al.' and for 'ἀριστεῖον' to end of section read 'in sg., Ion. -ήιον, *SEG* 37.994 (-ήϊιον, Priene, vi BC), *MDAI(A)* 87.153-4 no. 24 (Samos, v BC), Hdt. 8.11.2, -εῖον, *SEG* 31.1590 (ii BC, unkn. provenance, on bracelet); used esp. of golden crown, *IG* $2^2$.1388.30, 1635a*A*32, *SEG* 18.200-202 (Samian inscrr. at Delphi, iv BC), D. 22.79, *Amyzon* 24, *IStraton.* 1321, Luc.*DDeor.* 2(22).3'

**ἀριστεῖος**, add '*SEG* 17.584, *ILS* 8863 (both ii AD); of a person, *MAMA* 1.234 (Phrygia, -ῆον)'

**ἀριστερός 1**, add 'τούτου τοῦ ἡρώου ἡ ἐν ἀριστ‹ε›ροῖς ‹κ›λείνη *IEphes.* 3456; without a prep., neut. pl. adv., ἀριστερὰ εἰσιόντων *Inscr.Délos* 1416*A*i34 (ii BC). **b** ἐπ' ἀριστερὰ γράφειν write *from right to left*, Artem. 3.25; ἐπ' ἀριστερὰ περιβεβλῆσθαι, have dressed *leftwards*, id. 3.2.4.' **2**, add 'simply ἀριστερᾶς, *Inscr.Délos* 1441*A*ii95 (ii BC)' **4**, at end for 'τῷ ἀριστερῷ' read 'τῇ ἀριστερᾷ'

**ἀριστεύς**, at end delete '*CIG* 2881 (Milet.)' and for '(Cibyra)' read '(Cibyra, v. *SEG* 32.1306), *IGBulg.* 150.3 (Odessus), $2^2$.3733.15 (Athens, ii AD); an official at Miletus, *Didyma* 84.13'

***Ἀρίστη**, ἡ, epith. of Artemis, Paus. 1.29.2.

***ἀριστήριον**, τό, = ἀριστητήριον, *BCH* 28.262.13.

**ἀριστητήριον**, for pres. ref. read '*IStraton.* 270.6, 17.7 (both ii AD), *PZilliac.* 6.26 (vi AD)'

**ἀριστητικός**, delete 'Eup. 130'

***Ἀριστ[ι]ασταί**, οἱ, in Boeot. form -[ι]αστή, *devotees of Ariste*, *Schwyzer* 463.3 (*SEG* 26.614, Tanagra, iii/ii BC) or **Ἀριστ[η]ασταί**, *devotees of Aristaeus*, cf. *ZPE* 25.135.

**ἀριστίζω**, after '(Ar.)*Av.* 659' insert 'Sosith. 2.21' and after 'Acraephia' insert '*SEG* 26.1826.21 (Cyrene, ii AD)'

***ἀριστίνδα**, adv. = ἀριστίνδην, *IG* 7.188.9 (Pagae, iii BC).

**ἀριστίνδας**, add '-δης *SEG* 11.501.1 (Sparta, ii AD)'

**ἀριστίνδην**, line 2, for '(*IG*) 9(1) .. -δαν' read '(*IG*) $9^2$.717.12 (Locr., -αν, v BC)'

⁺**ἀριστογᾰλάτιας**, ὁ, app. *leading citizen of Galatia*, Mitchell *N.Galatia* 287 (Chr.).

**ἀριστόμαντις**, after 'εως' insert '(-ιδος *IG* 9(1).645)'

**ἄριστον**, read '**ἄρ-**'

**ἀριστοπολῑτεία**, after '(Sparta)' insert '*SEG* 31.372 (Olympia, ii AD)'

**ἀριστοπόνος II**, delete the section and add 'Nonn.*D.* 44.79' to section I.

**ἄριστος**, line 1, at end insert 'Thess. Ἀσ(σ)το-, for Ἀριστο- in pers. n., e.g. Ἀσ(σ)τόμαχος, *Schwyzer* 567.13, 569' **III**, adv., add '*SEG* 33.1105 (Paphlagonia, ii/iii AD)'

**ἀρίφρων**, after '*prudent*' insert 'ἡγητῆρες *IEphes.* 452.5 (iii AD)'

***ἄρκα**, ἡ, Lat. *arca, coffin*, *IG* 14.2327.

**Ἀρκαδία, Ἀρκαδικός**, transfer to before and after Ἀρκαδίζω.

***Ἀρκάδισσα**, ἡ, female *Arcadian*, *Ann.Mus.Gr.-R. d'Alex.* 1935-9.121 no. 7 (Alexandria), Iamb.*VP* 267.

***ἄρκανος**, ὁ, an unidentified fish, perh. = ἄκαρναν, *IGC* p. 98 A11 (Acraephia, iii/ii BC).

***ἀρκᾰπάτης**, ου, ὁ, = ἀργαπέτης, prob. as hereditary title, *Dura* 20.4 (ii AD).

**ἀρκαρικός**, add 'Just.*Edict.* 13.20'

**ἀρκάριος**, after 'Lat. *arcarius*' insert '*treasurer*' and add '*Inscr.Perg.* 8(3).99 (-ις), ib. 125, *SEG* 36.970.B56 (ἀρκά abbrev. Aphrodisias), τῆς ἐκκλησίας *Cod.Just.* 1.2.24.16'

***ἀρκεθεωρέω**, = ἀρχιθεωρέω, rest. in *IG* $2^2$.365*b*7.

**ἀρκεθέωρος**, for '*IG* 2.181 *a*' read '*IG* $2^2$.365*a*7, 10, etc. (Athens, 323/2 BC)' and add 'rest. in *Hesperia* 37.375 (iv BC)'

***ἀρκέτιον**, τό, name of a metal, Anon.Alch. 326.26.

**ἀρκευθίς I**, delete 'Thphr. .. -θος)'

**ἄρκευθος**, add '**V** prob. = ἀρκευθίς 1, Thphr.*Od.* 5, *Inscr.Cret.* 4.184.16 (ii BC).'

**ἀρκέω III 3**, add 'Just.*Const.* Δέδωκεν 17'

⁺**ἀρκήλα**, (in *LSJ* proparox.), ‹τὸ› ζῷον. Κρῆτες τὴν ὕστριχα Hsch. (La.).

**ἄρκηλος**, for '*young* .. panther, ibid.)' read 'an animal exhibited by Ptolemy II, Callix. 2; acc. to Ael.*NA* 7.47 *young leopard* (but some say a different species, ibid.)'

**ἄρκιος** (A) **II**, line 3, for 'he' read 'it'

**ἄρκος** (A), add '**IV** = ἄρκτος II, servant of Artemis, *SEG* 9.72.98 (iv BC).'

**ἄρκος** (B), add 'prob. in Nic.*Al.* 43'

*ἄρκος (C), ὁ, *sarcophagus, coffin*, *IG* 14.2326, al.; cf. °ἄρκα.

*ἀρκτεία, ἡ, *service as* ἄρκτος II, Hsch.

*ἀρκτόμῦς, υος, ὁ, *marmot*, Jerome *Ep.* 106.65.

ἄρκτος, add 'see also ‡ἄρκος (A)'

Ἀρκτοῦρος I, add 'ἁρκτοῦρος *IG* $1^3$.2.9' add 'III ἀρκτοῦρος = ἄρκτιον, Dsc. 4.105, cf. Hsch.'

ἄρκῦς, metaph., add 'ὅταν δ' ἔρωτος ἐνδεθῶμεν ἄρκυσιν Dicaeog. 1b.1 S.'

*ἀρκυστάσιον, τό, *line of hunting nets*, X.*Cyn.* 6.6.

ἅρμα I 1, add 'w. ref. to curule triumph, δὶς ἐ[πὶ κέλητος ἐθριάμβευσα καί], τρὶς [ἐ]φ' ἅρματος *Mon.Anc.Gr.* 2.9' add 'Myc. *a-mo-ta* (pl.), *wheels*'

ἁρμακιάς, add 'cf. perh. ἕρμαξ and mod. Gk. ἁρμακᾶς *dry stone wall*'

*ἁρμακίς, ίδος, ἡ, *section* or *parcel of land*, *PNess.* 31.15 (vi AD), al.

*ἁρμαμέντον, τό, *arsenal*, Just.*Nov.* 85.1, ζῷα διαφέροντα τοῦ θίου ἁρμαμέντου *BCH* 116.397 (?Constantinople, vi AD).

*ἄρμαρα, τά, kind of incense, *PMag.* 4.1.1294, 1990.

*ἁρμαραύσιον, τό, type of sleeveless military garment, cf. late Lat. (Goth.) *armilausa*, *PMich.*xiv 684.11 (-ιν), *PMonac.* 142.3 (ἐρμ[ε]λαῦσον, both vi AD).

*ἁρμάριον, τό, Lat. *armarium*, *EM* 146.56.

ἀρμαρίτης, read ἁρμαρίτης.

ἁρμᾰτάρακτα, before 'τά' insert 'or ἁρματοτάρακτα' and for '(for ἁρματο-ταρ-)' read '(ἁρματορ- pap.)'

ἁρμάτειος, line 2, after 'X.*Cyr.* 6.4.9' insert 'D.H. 5.47 (-τίου)'

*Ἁρμᾰτεύς, έως, ὁ, epith. of Hermes, *IEryth.* 201d.31 (iii BC).

ἁρμάτιον I, after 'ἅρμα' insert '*PLond.* 1973.3 (iii BC)'; before '*Gloss.*' insert '*SB* 7263.3 (iii BC), *Inscr.Délos* 1441*A*i43 (ii BC)' and add 'title of poem by Theopompus of Colophon, Ath. 4.183b'

ἁρματῑ́της, add 'II of horses, *drawing chariots*, *PCair.Zen.* 673.5 (iii BC), *PLond.* 1930 (259 BC).'

*ἁρμᾰτοκολλιστής, οῦ, ὁ, *chariot-maker*, *PHarris* 97.3 (iv AD).

ἁρμᾰτοπηγός, add '*OAshm.Shelton* 119, 130, al.'

+ἁρμᾰτοτροχιά, ἡ, = °ἁρματροχιά, Luc.*Dem.Enc.* 23, Ael.*VH* 2.27.

*ἁρμᾰτοφορέω, pass., *to be carried in a chariot*, *Hymn.Is.* 37 (Maroneia).

*ἁρματροχιά, Ep. -ιή, ἡ, *wheel-track of a chariot*, Il. 23.505, Ph. 1.312, Q.S. 4.516.

*ἁρμένια, τά, small tools, Hero *Aut.* 24.2, Sch.Opp.*H.* 1.222.

Ἀρμενία, after lemma insert 'poet. -ίη, *AP* 16.61 (Crin.), *SEG* 34.1409 (Cappadocia, Rom.imp.)'

+Ἀρμενιακός, ή, όν, *Armenian*, Str. 11.14.2; adopted as title by Roman emperors, *victor in Armenia*, *IG* $2^2$.2090a2, *ICilicie* 12, *ISelge* 13.10, *Salamine* 163 (all ii AD); μῆλα Ἀ. *apricots*, Dsc. 1.115; χρυσοκόλλα Ἀ., form of malachite, id. 5.89; also λίθος Ἀ., Alex.Trall. 1.427.16, Cyran. 6.6.1 K., *PHolm.* 88.

ἁρμενίζω, add 'Cyran. 31, 86, al.'

+Ἀρμενικός, ή, όν, Armenian; μηλέα Ἀ. *apricot*, Gal. 12.76.16, also τὸ Ἀ. *PRyl.* 629.227 (iv AD); λίθος Ἀ. Dsc. 5.105.

+Ἀρμένιος, ον, *Armenian*, ἐξ Ἀρμενίου ὄρεος Hdt. 1.72; -ον, τό, a mineral, Dsc. 5.90; cf. λίθος Ἀρμενικός.

*ἁρμενοπετής, ές, gloss on Lat. *ueliuolus*, *P.XV Congr.* 3.50.

*ἁρμενορᾰ́φος, ὁ, *sail-maker*, *MAMA* 3.293, al. (Corycus), *SEG* 37.715 (mosaic, Chios).

ἁρμενοφόρος, before 'gloss' insert '*carrying sails*'

*ἁρμίγεροι, οἱ, Lat. *armigeri*, *POxy.* 1888.2 (v AD, ἑρμ- pap.), Lyd.*Mag.* 1.46.20.

*ἁρμιλλίγεροι, οἱ, Lat. wd. indicating military rank, equiv. of βραχιάτοι, ψελιοφόροι Lyd.*Mag.* 1.46.19.

*ἁρμίως, *at once*, Gal. 19.86.2; cf. ἁρμοῖ.

ἁρμόδιος, after 'α, ον' insert 'also ος, ον, Longin. 12.5, Just.*Nov.* 123.21.1' II, after 'Pi.*N.* 1.21' insert 'παρεχόντων .. τἆλλα ἁρμόδια *CID* I 7.A18 (Andros, v BC)'

ἁρμόζω, line 10, after 'ἁρμόχθην' insert '*Olympia Bericht* 7.207 (3 pl. ἁρμόχθεν, Sybarite inscr. at Olympia, vi BC)' I 1 a, for 'πόδα ἐπὶ' read 'πόδας ἐπὶ' and for 'foot' read 'feet'; line 15, for 'Simon. 182' read '*AP* 7.431.4 ([Simon.])' 4 b, after 'c. acc.' insert 'Ael.*NA* 13.21' 5, lines 4/5, for 'Simon. 184' read '*AP* 7.25.4 ([Simon.])' II 1 a, line 1, after 'armour' insert 'or masonry'; add '*IG* $2^2$.244.88, 100, 463.72' add '6 as Lat. *competo*, *to be legally in force, to be due to someone*, *CodJust.* 1.5.13 pr., 6.4.4.23.' at end add 'Myc. pf. part. pass. *a-ra-ro-mo-te-me-na* (fem. pl.)'

*ἁρμοκούστωρ, ὁ, v. °ἁρμοροκούστορ.

ἁρμονία I 4, delete 'νεύρων καὶ' IV 4, add 'πανηγυρικὴ τῆς λέξεως ἁ. D.H.*Dem.* 45, cf. *Isoc.* 3, al.' add 'VIII ancient name for a *plane geometrical proportion*, Aristid.Quint. 3.6.'

*ἁρμοροκούστορ, Lat. *armorum custos*, *SB* 1592 (Nubia), ἁρμοκούστωρ *OBodl.* 2022 (ii AD), ἑρμοκούστωρ *PHamb.* 88, ἁρμικούστωρ *PWisc.* 14.5 (all i AD).

ἁρμός 3, for this section read '*joint in the body*, τὰς χεῖρας καὶ τοὺς πόδας ἐξήρθρουν καὶ ἐξ ἁρμῶν ἀναμοχλεύοντες ἐξεμέλιζον Lxx 4*Ma.* 10.5, *Hippiatr.* 34'

ἁρμοστής I, add 'b *harmonizer*, τῶν ὅλων (of Alexander), Plu. 2.329b.' 2, add '(dub., prob. reading δικασταί)' 3, delete '= *triumvir*, App.*BC* 4.7'; for '= *praefectus*' read '*governor* (in Roman contexts)' and add 'Luc.*Peregr.* 9, App.*Hisp.* 38'

ἁρμοστικός, add 'ἐνέργεια Procl.*in Ti.* 1.358.15, 2.216.22'

ἄρμυλα, add 'cf. ἀρβύλη'

ἀρναβόν, add 'cf. °ἀγναβόν'

*ἀρναβωράτιον, τό, product mentioned in price list, perh. dim. of ‡ἀρναβόν, *POxy.* 3766.104 (gen. pl. -βωρατιων), rest. in 3733.20 (both iv AD).

ἀρνακίς, for '*sheepskin coat*' read '*sheepskin*'

ἄρνειος I 2, add 'Call.*fr.* 26.1 Pf.'

ἀρνέομαι, line 4, aor. med., add '*CodJust.* 1.1.7.11, 7.62.36, al.' 3, add 'w. dat., εὐχωλῇσι Orph.*L.* 176; act. (in sense 2), Fronto *Ep.Gr.* 5.6 H.'

+ἀρνηΐς, ιδος, fem. adj., *connected with lambs*, ἀρνῇδας (mutilated papyrus) Call.*fr.* 26.2 Pf.; ἐν ταῖς ἡμέραις ἃς καλοῦσιν ἀρνηΐδας Clearch. 79; θυσίαν ἄγουσι καὶ ἑορτὴν ἀρνηΐδα (ἀρνίδα codd.) Conon 19, all referring to an Argive festival, prob. in the lambing season, in which stray dogs were killed.

+ἀρνίς, v. °ἀρνηΐς.

*ἀρνοκτᾰσία, ἡ, *killing of lambs*, Rh. 3.607.9.

ἄρνῠμαι, line 2, delete 'Pl.*Lg.* 969a' (v. °ἀείρω); lines 3/4, for statement in parentheses read 'augm. 3 sg. ἥερετο *SEG* 33.716 (Histiaea, v BC); ἤρετο occurs as v.l. for ἤρατο; cf. ἀείρω' I, four lines from end, delete 'δίκαν ἁρέσται .. (Locr.)' add '2 w. gen., φήμης ἄρνυνται ἀθανάτου *Clara Rhodos* 6/7.529 (Nisyrus).'

ἀροτήρ 1, add '*PTeb.* 886.69, 99 (ii BC), *POxy.* 2241.12, 41 (iii AD)' 2, add 'fig., *cultivator*, of poet, [Πιερίδων ἀ]ροτῆρι orac. in *SEG* 27.678.11 (Ostia, ii/iii AD)'

ἀροτήσιος, add 'b epith. of Zeus, *Syria* 36.77-8 (Hippos, iii AD).'

ἀροτρεύς, after '= sq.' insert 'Arat. 1075, al.'

ἀροτριάζω, delete the entry.

ἀροτρίᾱμα, add 'pl., = γεννήματα, app. *fruits of the earth*, Hsch. (after ἀρώματα)'

*ἀροτρίασμα, ατος, τό, gloss on ἄρομα, Suid.

ἀροτριάω, for '= ἀρόω' read '*plough*'; after 'Babr. 55.2' insert '*IEphes.* 3217A.8 (ii AD)'; add 'fig. ψεῦδος Lxx *Si.* 7.12, τὰ ἄτοπα *Jb.* 4.8'

ἄροτρον II, add 'μήτε φυτοῖς μήτε ἀρότροις ἀνοίγεσθαι referring to water conduit, *IEphes.* 3217B.28 (ii AD)'

ἀροτρόπους, for '*Ju.*' read '*Jd.*'

*ἀροτρόω, *plough*, prob. in Alc. 120.8 L.-P. (ἀροτρώμμε[, athematic); cf. ἀροτροῦντος Inv.OL 1988.25.4 in *ZPE* 78.145 (sp. ἀρω-, v AD).

*ἀρουᾶλος, Lat. *arualis*, ἀδελφὸς ἀ. *Mon.Anc.Gr.* 4.7.

*ἄρουλλα, Lat. *arula*, gloss on ἐσχάρα, Sch.Ar.*Ach.* 888.

ἄρουρα, lines 2/3, for '*Inscr.Cypr.* 135.20 H.' read '*ICS* 217.20' add 'IV as goddess = Γῆ, Nonn.*D.* 1.154, al.' at end add 'Myc. *a-ro-u-ra*'

*ἀρουρατίων, ωνος, ἡ, tax assessed in proportion to area of land, *PLips.* 62 ii 21, *POxy.* 3397.22 (both iv AD), 3634.1 (v AD), *PMasp.* 329.11.8 (vi AD).

*ἀρουρίδιον, τό, dim. of ἄρουρα, *PSI* 476.1 (iii AD).

ἀρούριον, after 'ἄρουρα' insert '*PSI* 974.6 (i/ii AD)'

ἀρόω II 2, line 2, after '(Tanagra)' insert 'med., [Νέστορα ..] Πυλία .. ἀρόσατο χθών *GVAK* 47.1 (Cilicia, i BC)'

ἁρπᾰγή, for '*rape*' read '*forcible abduction*'

ἁρπάγη 1, for 'Men. 829' read 'Men. 657'; before 'Poll.' insert '*flesh-hook*'; after 'Poll. 6.88' insert '10.98'

*ἁρπᾰγηδόν, = ἁρπάγδην, gloss on *raptim*, Dosith. p. 412 K.

ἁρπᾰ́γιον, add 'II name of an eye-salve, *CIL* 13.10021.93.'

ἁρπάζω I 1 (p. 246a, line 7), for 'χάρπάσαι' read 'χἀρπάσαι'; add 'fig., of death, λοιμὸς ἀμείλικτος κ(αὶ) ἀνάρσιος ‹ἥ›ρπασε‹ν› Πλουτεύς *SEG* 26.405' add 'III *take away*, ἁ. εἰς ἐλευθερίαν, of releasing a slave, cf. Lat. *eripere in* or *ad libertatem*, *CodJust.* 6.4.4.7, Just.*Nov.* 144.2.4; cf. °ἀφαρπάζω.'

+ἅρπακτός, ή, όν, *taken without being earned* (i.e. by work), χρήματα δ' οὐχ ἁρπακτά· θεόσδοτα πολλὸν ἀμείνω Hes.*Op.* 320. 2 *taken hurriedly, snatched* (i.e. by seizing an opportunity), πλόος Hes.*Op.* 684. 3 *taken illicitly, stolen*, ὑμέναιοι Nic.*fr.* 108.

ἁρπᾰλίζω 1, after 'med.' insert 'τόδ' ἁρπαλ[ί]ζομ[αι] Archil. 24.4 W.'

ἅρπαξ II 1, add '(but perh. humorous personification, "*Grabber*")'

ἅρπᾰσος, for 'a .. *prey*' read 'name of a bird, Call.*fr.* 43.61 Pf.'

ἁρπαστός 1, add 'by death, *SEG* 34.325.6 (Megalopolis, *c.*100 BC), cf. *Salamine* 193.10 (ii AD)' 2, add 'b an eyesalve, *CIL* 13.10021.153.'

ἀρπεδόεις, for 'ἐρπεδίζω' read 'ἐρπεδό‹ε›σσα'

*ἀρπεδόνιον, τό, name of a gemstone, Socr.Dion.*Lith.* 23.2 G.

ἄρπεζα, at beginning add '(perh. ἄρπεζα; cf. ὑπάρπεζος)'

ἄρπεζος, for '*BCH* 46.405 (Mylasa)' read '*IMylasa* 254.2 in *EA* 19.16 (i BC)' and add '*LW* 327.6 (Olympus)'

ἅρπη, add 'Sosith. 2.19'

***Ἀρποκράτης**, ους, acc. ην, ὁ, Egyptian divinity, *AP* 11.115 (Lucill.), Plu. 2.358e; sp. -χράτας, *IG* 9(2).591 (Larissa, i BC), -χράτης, *IPhilae* 3, 4, *SEG* 24.413 (Ambracia, all iii BC); also Καρποκράτης Vidman *SIS* 88 (Chalcis, iii/iv AD).

***Ἀρποκρᾰτιακός**, ὁ, kind of physically deformed person (fr. °Ἀρποκράτης, who was premature and weak in lower limbs, acc. to Plu. 2.358d), Ptol.*Tetr.* 124.

***Ἀρποκρᾰτικός**, ή, όν, *with the nature of* °Ἀρποκράτης, prob. *weak* or *deformed*, Heph.Astr. 1.1.99, 2.9.5.

**ἀρρᾰβών 1**, add '*pledge*, of an object, perh. in *SEG* 38.1036.7 (Gaul, Pech-Maho, v BC), Lxx *Ge.* 38.17, 18' **2**, for 'Men. 697' read 'Men.*fr.* 688 K.-Th., ὀλέθρου κοὐχ ἑταίρας ἀρραβών Python 1.18', deleting 'Lxx *Ge.* 38.17, 18'

***ἀρρᾰβωνιακός**, ή, όν, *marking betrothal*, περιθέματα (*necklaces*) ἀ. Hsch. s.v. κάθορμα.

***ἀρρᾰβωνίζομαι**, add '*PCair.Zen.* 250.3 (iii BC); med. *betroth to oneself*, fut. ἀρραβωνίσομαι (-ησ- cod.) αὐτόν *Vit.Aesop.*(W) 30; ἀρραβωνίζεται· ἀρραβῶνι δίδοται Hsch.'

**ἀρρενικός 1**, form ἀρσ-, add 'Lxx *Ex.* 13.15, Ezek.*Exag.* 13'

**ἀρρενογονία**, add 'Heph.Astr. 2.7.3, 2.8.3. **2** *descent* or *relationship reckoned through males*, τοὺς ἐξ ἀρρενογονίας αὐτοῦ *Cod.Just.* 6.4.4.23, term expld. at Theophil.Antec. 1.10.1 (p. 40.28ff.).'

**ἀρρενοκοίτης**, after '*AP* 9.686' insert '(Maced., iv/vi AD, v. *BCH* suppl. 8 no. 87)'

**ἀρρενόομαι**, add 'act., **ἀρρενόω**, *make male* or *masculine*, *represent as male*, Heraclit.*All.* 71'

**ἀρρενώδης**, after '*brave*' insert 'Sch.BT Il. 8.39'

**⁺ἀρρενώπας**, (s.v. ἀρρενωπός in *LSJ*), ὁ, comic term for an androgynous person, Cratin. 417 K.-A., cf. Eust. 827.29.

**ἀρρενωπός**, after 'Luc.*Fug.* 27' insert 'ἀρσενωπέ (addressed to Athena), *PKöln* 245.10 (iii AD, verse)'

**ἀρρεπής**, delete 'of a balance' and after '*inclining to neither side*' insert 'Gal. 2.266.12, 760.6, *UP* 6.16, 12.9, *CMG* 5.10(2).1.21.2'

**ἀρρευμάτιστος II**, add 'Gal. 11.301.8, 18(2).844.14'

**ἀρρεψία**, for 'etc.' read 'rest. in *SB* 7183.3 (iii BC, ἀρεψ- pap.)'

**ἄρρηκτος**, after 'ον' insert 'also η, ον, *PASA* 2.352 (Cappadocia), Aeol. αὔρηκτος acc. to Hdn.Gr. 2.271, Eust. 548.31'

**⁺ἀρρητοποιέω**, *do unmentionable things to*, i.e. *fellate*, Artem. 1.79 passim.

***ἀρρητοποιΐα**, ή, βρίμη· .. γυναικεία ἀ. Hsch.

**ἀρρητοποιός I**, for '*practising such vice*' read '*practising fellatio*' and add 'Sch.Ar.*Eq.* 1287' **II**, delete 'pedantically'

**ἄρρητος I**, line 2, delete 'ἄνδρες .. *Op.* 4'; at end after 'Id.*El.* 1012' add '*not spoken of*, ἄνδρες .. ῥητοί τ' ἄ. τε Hes.*Op.* 4; ἄρρητος τελετή *CEG* 317 (Athens, v BC); Arat. 2, 180'

***ἀρρητοῦργος**, ον, *indulging in fellatio*, γίνονται δὲ εὐνοῦχοι ἢ ἑρμαφρόδιτοι .. ἢ ἀρρητοῦργοι γυναῖκες Heph.Astr. 2.13.12.

**ἀρρίγητος**, delete '*daring*' and for '*AP* 6.219' read '*AP* 6.219.7 (Antip.Sid.)'

**⁺ἀρρῐχάομαι**, (ἀριχάομαι Arist.*HA* 624ᵃ34), *clamber, climb*, Hippon. 137 W., Arist. l.c.; cf. ἀναρριχάομαι.

**ἄρρῐχος**, line 2, after '(Diosc.)' insert 'cf. *EM* 149.30, *AB* 446.30, which give masc. in Ion., fem. in Att.'; line 3, for '162' read '62' and after 'Amorgos' insert 'iv BC'

***ἄρροπος**, ον, *not inclining the scale*, of a weight, *IGLS* 1272*a* (Laodicea ad mare, ii AD); *inflexible*, δικαστὴς ἄ. Gr.Naz. in *PG* 37.662A, cf. Att. pers. n. Ἄροπος, app. *unwavering, steady*, *SEG* 26.207 vi 2 (iii/ii BC), *IG* 2².2452.17 (ii BC), etc.; cf. ἀρρεπής, °ἔρροπος, °σύρροπος.

**ἄρρῡπος**, add 'cf. ἀρύπαρος'

**⁺ἀρρύσιος**, ον, (sp. ἀρυ-), *not liable to seizure*, *IG* 9²(1).706A.3 (Oianthea, iii BC); cf. ῥύσιον.

**ἀρρωστία 1**, after 'Hp.*VM* 6, etc.' insert 'τὴν τοῦ σώματος ἀ. D. 24.160, Isoc. 19.21'

**ἄρρωστος 1**, after 'Plu. 2.465c' insert 'comp. ἀρρωστότερος τῷ σώματι Isoc. 16.33'

***ἀρσατικός**, ή, όν, adj., otherwise unexplained, describing a quality of coinage, νομίσματα *Stud.Pal.* III 59.3, *CPR* 1.30 *fr.*ii 44, *BGU* 314.15 (all vi/vii AD).

***ἄρσεα**, v. °ἄρσια.

**ἀρσενίκιον**, add 'written ἀρσενίκην, i.e. ἀρσενίκιν, Anon.Alch. 318.7'

***ἀρσενοβάτης**, ου, ὁ, *sodomite*, Hsch. s.v. παιδοπίπας.

**ἀρσενόθηλυς**, add 'Serv.*Aen.* 10.89'

***ἄρσενος**, ον, = ἄρσην, *POxy.* 744.9 (i BC), *PMich.*III 203.6 (i/ii AD).

***ἀρσενόω**, trans., *turn to arsenic*, Anon.Alch. 269.3.

***ἀρσενωπός**, v. °ἀρρενωπός.

**ἄρσην 1**, at end after '*the male sex*' insert 'A.*Supp.* 951' add **'b** *directed towards males*, i.e. *homosexual*, ἔρως Cerc. 9.15; πῦρ *AP* 9.77 (Antip.Sid.); πυρσοί ib. 12.17. **c** Pythagoreans regarded odd numbers as male, Plu. 2.288c, cf. 264a.' **2**, delete 'Id.*Supp.* 951' **4**, delete 'but also .. 3.9.3'

***ἄρσια**, τά, designation of a place-name, ἀπὸ τᾶς λεγο[μέν]ας παρὰ τὰ ἄ. *Delph.* 3(4).42.13 (ii BC); cf. perh. ἄρσεα· λειμῶνες Hsch.

**Ἀρσινόεια**, add 'sg. τὸ Ἀρσινοεῖον, *temple of Arsinoe*, in Cyprus, *SEG* 25.1072 (Idalium, iii BC), at Philadelphia, *Aegyptus* 22.197, at Alexandria, Plin.*HN* 36.38, 37.108'

**ἄρσις I 1 a**, for 'as an athletic feat .. (pl.)' read 'bull-*hoisting*, ritual act performed by ephebi at Eleusis, *IG* 2².1006.78 (pl., ii BC); cf. °ἀείρω IV 3 b, °Βοάρσαι, °Βοάρσιον' and add 'σημείου ἄρσις v. σημεῖον I 3'

**ἄρσος**, delete the entry (v. °ἄρσια).

**ἀρτάβη II**, for 'varying from 24 to 42 χοίνικες' read 'normally containing 40 χ.'

**ἀρτᾰμέω**, add 'prob. in A.*fr.* 281a.35 R.'

**Ἄρταμις**, after '-μίτιον' insert '-μάτιος'

**ἄρτᾰμος 1**, add '*Trag.adesp.* 148'

**ἀρτάω II**, add **'3** δικαὶ ἠρτημέναι, calque on Latin *lites pendentes*, Just.*Const.* Δέδωκεν 23.'

**ἀρτεμής**, for 'Call.*Iamb.* 1.227. -Ep. word' read 'Call.*fr.* 194.28 Pf., whence rest. in Hippon. 105.6 W.'

**ἀρτεμία**, after '*health*' insert 'Pi.*N.* 11.12 (cj.), id.*fr.* 52m.3 S.-M. (prob.)'

**Ἄρτεμις**, gen. -ιτος, add 'Myc. *a-te-mi-to*'; Ἄρταμις, gen. -ιτος, add '*SEG* 31.356A (Elis, vi BC);' dat. Ἀρτάμι, add 'cf. Ἀρτέμι app. in *SEG* 31.356B (Elis, iv BC)' at end add 'see also Ἄρτιμις'

***Ἀρτεμῖσιακόν**, τό, name of silver mine at Laurium, *IG* 2².1582.38, 114, al. (iii BC).

***Ἀρτεμῖσιάς**, άδος, ή, *period of the Artemisian games*, *IGRom.* 4.1609, 1610 (Hypaepa).

**Ἀρτεμίσιος**, Dor. Ἀρταμίτιος, add '*IG* 4².108.110 (Epid., iv/iii BC), also Ἀρταμάτιος, de Franciscis *Locr.Epiz.* 31.6 (iv/iii BC)'; after 'Plu.*Alex.* 16' insert '*SEG* 34.1221 (Saettae, i AD), 24.614 (Maced.), 32.1394 (Commagene, both ii AD), 36.1288b (Syria, ii/iii AD), etc.; answering to May, *PLond.* 229.30 in *Hermes* 32.274 (Seleucia, ii AD), cf. *Hemerolog.Flor.* p. 73 (p. 10 K.)'

**Ἀρτεμῖσιών**, add '*SEG* 24.574 (Torone, end iv BC), 33.1056.A3 (Cyzicus, ii AD)'

**ἄρτημα II 1**, for '*IG* 2.834 *c* 13' read '*IG* 1³.387.40'; add '(in *IG* l.c., al., ἄ. may mean *counter-poise weights*, v. *Hesperia* 13.186 and °ῥυμός)'

**ἀρτί 1**, line 3, after 'Pl.*Cri.* 43a' insert 'Theoc. 23.26', deleting this ref. fr. line 5; line 7, after '(iii AD)' insert 'for ἀπ' ἄρτι read °ἀπαρτί' **2**, add 'ᾤχετο φεύγων ἄρτι μὲν εἰς Μυτιλήνην, ἔπειτα δ' εἰς Χίον Charon.Lamps.*fr.* 9 J.'

**ἀρτίγᾰμος**, after '*just married*' insert 'A.*fr.* 168.20 R. (lyr.)'

**ἀρτῐγένειος**, after '(Diod.)' insert '*GVI* 854 (Egypt), epigr. in *SEG* 26.456 (Laconia, both ii/iii AD)'; after 'Nonn.*D.* 18.135' insert 'Sch.Call.*fr.* 2 Pf.'

**ἀρτῐδαής**, add '*SEG* 3.543 (Thrace, ?iii BC)'

***ἀρτίδομος**, ον, *closely fitting*, ἀρτιδόμῳ δ' ἐκάθητο λιθοστρώτῳ παρὰ χώρῳ codd. Nonn.*Par.Ev.Jo.* 19.13.

**ἀρτῐλιθία**, after 'in masonry' insert '*IG* 2².1671.36 (Attica, iv BC)'

***ἀρτίουλος**, ον, *just having the first growth of beard*, *Limes de Chalcis* p. 214 no. 50 (i AD).

***ἀρτιόφρων**, ονος, adj., *in full possession of one's faculties*, perh. in A.*fr.* 451r.3 R. (ἀρ[τιόφ]ρων, nisi leg. ἀρτίφρων).

**ἀρτῐπᾰγής II**, add 'app. also in καὶ λοετροῦ πολὺς ὄλβος, ὃν ἀρτιπαγοῦς ἀπὸ γαίδης ὤπασεν *Milet* 1(9).343 (Chr. epigr.), but precise signif. uncertain'

**ἀρτίπους I 1**, add **'b** (ἀρτίπος) *in good health*, *AP* 5.287.4, 9.644.5 (both Agath.).' **2**, add 'S.*Tr.* 58' **II**, delete the section.

**ἄρτῐσις**, add **'2** *preparation*, *PCair.Zen.* 771.27 (iii BC).'

***ἀρτίτῠπος**, ον, *newly made*, cj. for ἀντι- in Nonn.*D.* 39.11.

**ἀρτιφᾰνής**, add 'E.*Phaeth.* 67 D.'

**ἀρτίφρων**, add 'see also °ἀρτιόφρων'

**ἀρτιφυής**, add **'III** app. = ἀρτίφρων, *GVI* 1917.9 (Cyme, ii BC).'

***ἀρτοδοτέω**, *give bread*, *Vit.Aesop.*(G) 19 (-δωτ- cod.).

***ἀρτοθέσιον**, τό, *bread-store*, *PBrooklyn 15.2* (vi AD).

***ἀρτοκόλλυτος**, ὁ, *baker*, *PHamb.* 56.v.4, vi.8 (vi/vii AD).

***ἀρτοκοπέω**, *keep a bakery*, Cumont *Fouilles de Doura-Europos* 385 no. 22; cf. ἀρτοποπέω.

**⁺ἀρτοκοπία**, ή, *bakery*, *PMich.*x 586.7 (i AD), *OMich.* 257.2 (sp. ἀρτε-, iv AD); also *PThead.* 31.35, 36.21 (s.v.ll., iv AD).

**ἀρτοκόπος**, add 'cf. Myc. *a-to-po-qo* (no doubt the original form)'

**ἀρτόκρεας**, for '(Lydia)' read '(Sardes, v. Robert *Hell.* 11/12.480-1)'

**⁺ἀρτολάγῡνος**, ον, *consisting of bread and bottle*, πτωχῶν πανοπλίη ἀρτολάγυνος *AP* 11.38 (Polem.).

**ἀρτοποιέω**, before 'Longus' insert 'Ctes.*fr.* 11 J.'

***ἀρτοπράτισσα**, ή, fem. of ἀρτοπράτης, *BCH* 4.205 no.27 (Isauria, v/vi AD).

**ἀρτόπτης 2**, after '*pan for baking bread*' insert 'Plaut.*Aul.* 400' and after 'Plin.*HN* 18.107' add '(perh. misunderstood by Pliny as meaning *baker*), Poll. 10.112'

***ἀρτοπτρίς**, ίδος, fem. adj., *used for baking bread*, ἐσχάρα ἀ. *PCair.Zen.* 692.12 (iii BC).

**ἀρτοπώλης**, for '*AJA* 18.33' read '*AJA* 18.68 (= *Sardis* 7(1).166)' and before it insert 'Arist.*Ath.* 51.3'

**ἀρτοπωλικόν**, for pres. ref. read '*IG* 2².1707.4 (iii BC)'

***ἀρτοφᾰγία**, ἡ, *eating of bread*, *Sokolowski* 3.177.37 (Cos, iv BC).

***ἀρτοψῡγεῖον**, τό, *place for cooling bread*, *POxy.* 3355.6 (ii AD), *PSI* xx *Congr.* 16.7 (iv AD; both written -ψυγιον; cf. ὑδροψυγεῖον).

**ἄρτῡμα**, line 3, after 'Anaxipp. 1.5' insert '*PPetaus* 28.19 (ii AD)' **II**, delete '(cf. ἄρτημα)'

***ἀρτῡματηρά**, ἡ, *tax on spices*, *PHels.* 37.4, 16 (ii BC).

***ἀρτῡματοθήκη**, ἡ, *box for spices*, *SB* 9509.3 (iii AD).

**ἀρτῡματοπώλης**, add '*BGU* 1898.209 (ii AD), *POxy.* 3739.7 (iv AD)'

**ἀρτύς**, add 'rest. in Call.*fr.* 80.19 (Add. II) Pf.'

**ἀρτύω I**, add 'ἐὰν δὲ τὸ ἅλας ἄναλον γένηται, ἐν τίνι αὐτὸ ἀρτύσετε; *Ev.Marc.* 9.50, *Ev.Luc.* 14.34'

**†ἄρυα**· τὰ Ἡρακλεωτικὰ κάρυα Hsch.

**ἀρυβάσσαλον**, after 'κοτύλη' insert 'ἢ φλάσκων'

***ἄρῠσις**, εως, ἡ, *drawing up* of liquids, ποτοῦ Afric.*Cest.* p. 39 V.

**ἀρυστήρ**, line 1, for '= ἀρυτήρ' read 'kind of cup used as ladle, esp. for wine' and for '*Supp.* 4.9' read '58.9 L.-P.'; line 3, for 'Call.*Aet.* 1.1.17' read 'Call.*fr.* 178.17 Pf.'; last line, after '*liquid measure*' insert '*SEG* 33.63 (amphora, Athens, *c.*500 BC)'

**†ἄρυστις**, εως, ἡ, perh. = °ἀρυστήρ, *cup*, τὰς ἀρύστεις ὧδ' ἔχουσ' ἐκώμασας S.*fr.* 764 R., (but ἀρύστεις· τὰς ἀπνευστὶ πόσεις Hsch., Phot. α 2918 Th. app. error for ἀμύστεις).

**ἀρύστῐχος**, for 'dim. of ἀρυτήρ' read 'kind of cup'; after 'Aegina' insert 'v BC'; add 'on an Ionian container, perh. for perfume, *SEG* 32.724 (Berezan, vi BC)'

**ἀρυστρίς**, for '= ἀρύταινα' read '= °ἄρυστις'

**ἀρῠ́ταινα**, for 'fem. of ἀρυτήρ' read 'kind of cup used as scoop in the baths' and add 'Ar.*fr.* 450 K.-A., *PHels.* 2.9 (ii BC)'

***ἀρῠταίνιον**, τό, dim. of ἀρύταινα, *Inscr.Cret.* 1.xvii 2*a*9 (Lebena, ii BC).

**ἀρῠτήρ 1**, before '*ladle*' insert '= °ἀρυστήρ'

**ἀρύω** (A), line 1, after '[ᾰ]' insert '[ῠ, in late poets also ῡ, as *AP* 9.37 (Stat.Flacc.), Nonn.*D.* 14.46]'

***Ἀρχᾰ́γᾰθος**, ὁ, epith. of Zeus, app. *source of all good things*, *INikaia* 1071.2, 10 (i/ii AD).

**ἀρχάγγελος**, after '*archangel*' insert '*ICilicie* 116, *POxy.* 1151.42 (both v/vi AD), esp. of Gabriel or Michael'

**ἀρχᾱϊκός**, before 'interpol.' insert '*Inscr.Délos* 1426*B*i42, 1428ii50 (ἀρχαιϊκ-, ii BC)'

***ἀρχαιόθεν**, adv. *from early times*, ἐξ ἀρχεόθεν *MAMA* 7.559.5.

**ἀρχαιολογέω I**, for '*discuss* .. Th. 7.69' read '*say the same old things*, Th. 7.69' and before 'ἀ. τὰ Ἰουδαίων' insert '**2** *discuss antiquities*'

**ἀρχαιολογία**, lines 3/4, title of works, add 'Dionysius of Halicarnassus'

***ἀρχαιολόγος**, ὁ, *dramatic performer, mime*, *IG* 2².2153.7 (prob., cf. Robert, *REG* 49.235ff.), *Gloss.* s.v. *Atellani.* **2** = Lat. *antiquarius*, perh. *expert copyist of old texts*, *Edict.Diocl.* 7.69.

**ἀρχαιο-μελῐ-σιδωνο-φρῡνίχ-ήρᾰτος**, for 'ἀρχαῖα μελι- codd.' read 'v.l. ἀρχαία μελι-'

**ἀρχαιόπλουτος**, add 'Cratin. 171.70 K.-A.'

**ἀρχαῖος II**, after 'of persons' insert '*ancient, venerable*'; add 'τῆς ἀρχέας (sic) ἁγίας Μαρίας *ITyr* 187'

**ἀρχαιρεσία I**, add 'in sg. = Lat. *comitia*, Plb. 1.52.5, but cf. section II'

**ἀρχαιρεσιακός**, add '*SEG* 27.938.14 (Tlos, v AD)'

***ἀρχαιρέσιοι**, οἱ, perh. = αἱρεσιάρχαι, *SEG* 16.696.8 (Caria, Rom. imp.).

***ἀρχάρχων**, οντος, ὁ, perh. *chief magistrate*, *SEG* 9.869 (Numidia).

**ἀρχέβακχος**, for '16' read '6'

**ἀρχεδέατρος**, for '*chief seneschal*' read '*chief* °ἐδέατρος'; add '*SEG* 18.730 (Cyrene, ii BC), *PTeb.* 728.4 (ii BC); also ἀρχελέατρος *UPZ* 202.1.5 (ii BC)'

***ἀρχεδέκᾱνος**, ὁ, v. °ἀρχιδέκανος.

**ἀρχεζῶστις**, add 'also -ζῶστρις Orib. 14.62.1; cf. °ἀργιζώστης'

***ἀρχεθεωρία**, v. °ἀρχιθ-.

**ἀρχεθέωρος**, after '(Delos, iii BC)' insert '*SEG* 28.60 (Athens, iii BC)'; add 'cf. ‡ἀρχιθέωρος'

***ἀρχεία**, v. °ἀρχήια.

**ἀρχεῖον I 2**, after '(Dyme, ii BC)' insert '*SEG* 23.305 iii 15 (treaty at Delphi, ii BC)'; add 'ὁ ἐπὶ τῶν ἀ. *SEG* 34.1107.7 (Ephesus), δι' ἀρχήου perh. = *per tabularium*, *IEphes.* 13 i 15, 16, etc. (i AD)' **II**, pl. exx., add 'generally, *public offices*, Isoc. 7.24'

**ἀρχεῖτις**, add '*SEG* 31.791 (Thasos, ii/iii AD), perh. late sp. for -ῖτις; cf. Lat. *architidis* (gen.), as Assyrian epith. of Venus, Macr.*Sat.* 1.21.1'

***ἀρχελέατρος**, v. °ἀρχεδέατρος.

**ἀρχέμπορος**, add '*IG* 10(2).564.7 (iii AD), *SB* 10529b.31 (iii/iv AD); voc., as title of respect, *Vit.Aesop.*(G) 12'

***ἀρχενδρομῑ́της**, ου, ὁ, perh. *chief runner* or *footman*, *BGU* 1834.6 (i BC, -δρωμ- pap.).

**ἀρχέπλουτος**, for '= ἀρχαιόπλουτος' read '*having control of wealth*'

***ἀρχέποδες**, v. °ἀρχέφοδος.

***ἀρχεπολία**, ἁ, perh. *board of city magistrates*, dub. rest. in *SEG* 9.72.132 (Cyrene, iv BC).

***ἀρχερᾰνεύς**, έως, ὁ, = ἀρχερανιστής, rest. in *ASAA* N.S. 1/2.195, n. 2 (Rhodes, iii AD).

**ἀρχερᾰνιστής**, for pres. ref. read 'in Attica, *IG* 2².1339.4, *SEG* 37.103.4 (both i BC), in Rhodes (gen. sg. ἀρχερανιστᾶ), *IG* 12(1).9.1 (i BC)'

***Ἀρχερᾰνίστρια**, τά, festival of the ἀρχερανισταί in Attica, *BCH* 84.658 (Acharnae, ?i BC).

***ἀρχέσκοπος**, ὁ, title of religious official, *IG* 9(2).1322.1 (Halmyros, iv BC) (pl.).

***ἀρχέταιρος**, ὁ, *president* of a religious association, *Inscr.Dura* 2.8 (i AD).

**ἀρχέτας**, add 'E.*Phaëth.* 100 D.'

**ἀρχέτῡπος II**, delete 'opp. ἀπόγραφον .. *Is.* 11, cf.'; add 'also masc. ἀρχέτυπος, ὁ, opp. ἀπόγραφος, D.H.*Is.* 11. **b** *ledger*, Cic.*Att.* 12.5c (pl.).'

**ἀρχεύω**, w. dat., add 'Antim. 27 Wy.'

**ἀρχέφηβος**, add 'also **ἀρχιέφηβος**, inscr. in *SB* 9997.5 (?Memphis, iii AD)'

**ἀρχέφοδος**, add 'app. athematic inflexion in ἀρχέφοδα (acc.), *PAberd.* 60.2 (i/ii AD); -δι (dat.), *PGen.* 107.11 (ii AD); cf. ἀρχέποδες app. same sense, as if fr. *ἀρχέπους, Ps.-Callisth. 1.31 β, γ, v.l. ἀρχέφοδοι'

**ἀρχή**, after lemma insert 'dial. ἀρχά Pi.*O.* 2.58, etc., Lesb. ἄρχα *IG* 12(2).1.8 (Mytilene, iv BC)' **I 1 a**, at end for '[ὁ ἄνθρωπος] .. 3.3.4' read 'ἡ ἀρχὴ ἐν τῷ πράττοντι Arist.*EN* 1110ᵇ4, cf. 1140ᵃ13, al., Plot. 3.3.4'; add 'μη(νὸς) Γωρπιέου (sic) ἀρχῇ *at the beginning* of the month, *SEG* 32.1442.4 (Syria, vi AD)' **b**, add 'ἐν ἀρχῇ *in the beginning, at the outset*, inscr. in *Phoenix* 43.319.9 (Arsinoe, Hellen.); of all time, Lxx *Ge.* 1.1, *Ev.Jo.* 1.1' **3**, for '*corner*' read '*extremity*'; add 'of road or street, Lxx *Ez.* 16.25, 21.20(25)' **5**, for '*branch*' read '*head*' **6**, add 'al., *Ps.* 138(139).17 (pl.)' **II 3**, line 8, after 'Antipho 6.42' insert 'ἐπὶ [τῆ]ς ἀρχῆς *during his term of office*, *ICilicie* 70' **5**, for '*command*, i.e. *body of troops*' read '*company, band*' add '**8** Dor. -ά, part of the νόμος κιθαρῳδικός, Poll. 4.66.'

***Ἀρχηγέσιον**, τό, *precinct of Apollo Archegetes*, *Inscr.Délos* 316.115 (iii BC), 461*Ab*49 (ii BC).

***ἀρχηγετεῖον**, τό, building for commemoration or worship of a founder or tutelary hero, *SEG* 12.373.15 (Cos, iii BC).

**ἀρχηγέτης 1**, lines 3/4, title of Apollo, at Cyrene, add '*SEG* 9.7.26 (ii BC)'; add 'at Apamea (Syria, in Dor. form), *BE* 1976.721'; line 7, for '*IG* 2.1191' read '*CEG* 314 (Rhamnous, v BC), *IG* 2².2849 (ii BC)'; line 11 (fem. ἀρχηγέτις), for 'cf. *BMus.* .. ii AD)' read 'of Artemis, *Inscr.Magn.* 16.21 (iii BC), *IEphes.* 27.20 (ii AD), of Leto, *SEG* 38.1476.17 (Xanthos, iii BC)'; add 'pl. -γέται, applied to female deities (the Erinyes), *Suppl.Mag.* 42A.8 (iii/iv BC)' **2**, for 'generally *leader, chief*' read '*chief ruler*'

***ἀρχήγισσα**, ἡ, Jewish title, fem. of °ἀρχηγός, μνῆμα Περιστερίας ἀρχηγίσις (i.e. -ίσσης) Robert *Hell.* 1.26 (see also *SEG* 33.1602, Thessaly, v/vi AD).

**ἀρχηγός II 2**, add 'ἀγγέλων ἀρχηγέ of archangel Michael, *SEG* 30.1266 (Caria, Byz.); as Jewish title, *CIJud.* 731g (see also *SEG* 33.1602, vi AD)'

***ἀρχήια**, ἁ, Cret., *magistracy, period of office*, *Inscr.Cret.* 4.233.3 (Gortyn, iii BC), al.; ἀρχεία *SEG* 33.729 (Amnisos, i BC); sense uncertain in *SEG* 23.366.18 (Axos, iv BC).

**ἀρχηΐς**, add 'Plu. 2.364e, *Delph.* 3(1).466.5 (ii AD)'

**ἀρχῐᾰριστάς**, add 'also ἀρχιεριστάς *Tit.Cam.* 9.11, 11.14, etc. (iii BC), ἀρχιαριστής *Tit.Cam.* 53.3 (ii BC)'

***ἀρχιατρίνη**, ἡ, app. fem. of ἀρχιατρός, *MAMA* 7.566 (-ιειατρηνα lapis); Robert *Epitaphes* p. 177.

**ἀρχιᾱτρός**, after 'of communities' insert 'τῆς [Ἐ]φεσίων πόλεως *IEphes.* 3055.16, *SEG* 27.1262 (Aphrodisias), ἀ. καὶ ἱεροφάντης *TAM* 5(1).268, τοῦ σύμπαντο[ς] ξυστοῦ Robert *Hell.* 9.25 (Thyatira, ii/iii AD)'

***ἀρχιβαλιστάριος**, ὁ, *chief ballistarius*, *SEG* 7.989 (Philippopolis, Syria, ii AD).

***ἀρχιβάπτης**, ου, ὁ, *chief* βάπτης *(dyer)*, *IEJ* 7.76-7 (= *Beth She'arim* 188, iii/iv AD) (-βαφθ-).

***ἀρχιβασιλιστής**, ὁ, *chief of the* °βασιλισταί, corr. to *SB* 1106.2 in *SEG* 34.1605 (?iii BC), previously read as ἀρχιβουλευτής.

**ἀρχιβασσάρα**, for the pres. ref. read '*IGBulg.* 401.16 (Apollonia ad Pontum), *IUrb.Rom.* 160 i B24 (ii AD)'

***ἀρχιβάσσᾰρος**, ὁ, *chief of the* βάκχοι, *IUrb.Rom.* 160 i B5 (ii AD).

**ἀρχιβούκολος II**, add '*IGBulg.* 1517.17 (iii AD), *SEG* 17.320 (Abdera, ?iii AD), *Epigr.Gr.* 1036a (Perinthus)'

**†ἀρχιβουλευτής**, v. °ἀρχιβασιλιστής.

***ἀρχιβωμιστής**, οῦ, ὁ, *chief priest*, *SEG* 7.893 (Gerasa, i AD).

***ἀρχιγάλλαρος**, ὁ, *chief °γάλλαρος*, prob. in *IGBulg.* 1517.19 (Philippopolis, iii AD).

***ἀρχιγερουσιάρχης**, ου, ὁ, *chief of Jewish board of elders*, *SEG* 26.1178 (Rome, iii/iv AD).

***ἀρχιγερουσιαστής**, οῦ, ὁ, *chief member of a board of elders*, *IPrusias* 25.3 (iii AD).

**ἀρχιγέρων**, after '*Sammelb.* 2100.5 (i BC)' insert '*IFayoum* 38.2 (i AD)'

**ἀρχιγεωργός**, add 'voc., as title of respect, *Vit.Aesop.*(G) 12'

**ἀρχιγραμμᾰτεύς**, add 'ἀ. ξυστοῦ *SEG* 23.395.4 (Corcyra, ?ii AD), *PLond.* 1178.82 (ii AD), *IUrb.Rom.* 246.B1, 2 (iv AD)'

***ἀρχιδέκᾱνος**, ὁ, *chief δεκανός*, *SEG* 16.813.5 (Arabia, iii AD), *IGChr.* 269 (Aphrodisias); also ἀρχε- *MAMA* 8.46 (Lystra).

**ἀρχιδιᾱ́κονος**, before pres. ref. insert '*ICilicie* 39, *BCH* suppl. 8 no. 281 (both v/vi AD), *SEG* 31.1446 (Palestine, vii AD), *JRS* 16.68 (Eumeneia)'

***ἀρχιδιᾱ́κων**, = ‡ἀρχιδιάκονος, *Inscr.Phryg.* 77.

***ἀρχιδικαστικός**, ή, όν, *of the* ἀρχιδικαστής, ἀρχή, *PVindob.Salomons* 5.15 (ii AD), ὑπηρέτης *PSI* 1328.56 (iii AD).

***ἀρχιδρᾰγᾱ́της**, ου, ὁ, *chief field-warden*, *JÖAI* 30 *Beibl.* 24 (Ancyra, iii AD); cf. δραγατεύω.

***ἀρχιεπισκοπή**, ἡ, *archbishopric*, Epiph.Const. in *PG* 42.185A.

**ἀρχιεπίσκοπος**, before pres. ref. insert '*IEphes.* 495 (iv AD), *PBaden* 65.20, *SEG* 30.1711 (Palestine, vi AD), *BCH* suppl. 8 no. 91, *Salamine* 206, 219 (vi/vii AD)'

**ἀρχιεράομαι**, after lemma insert 'ἀρχιαρ-, *SEG* 35.1416 (Pamphylia, Rom.imp.)'

**ἀρχιερᾱτεύω**, line 1, within parentheses add 'also ἀρχιερετεύω, *BCH* 51.89 (Panamara)'

**ἀρχιέρεια**, line 1, after '(Olympia)' insert '*SEG* 31.900 (Aphrodisias, i AD), *IGBulg.* 66.2, *IEphes.* 430.20 (ii AD)'

**ἀρχιερεύς**, line 1, before 'Ion.' insert 'Aeol. **ἀρχείρευς**, *IG* 12(2).239.6, **ἀρχίρευς**, ib. 249.5, al.'; line 5, after '(iii AD), etc.' insert 'ἀ. δι' ὅπλων of gladiatorial games, *IGBulg.* 1572.3, al.'; add 'in Chr. Gk., *MAMA* 1.208, *SEG* 37.501 (Thessaly, vi AD). **2** name of tenth month in a Cyprian calendar, *YCLS* 2.213f.'

***ἀρχιεριστάς**, v. °ἀρχιαριστάς.

***ἀρχιεριστέω**, *to be* ἀρχιεριστάς, *Tit.Cam.* 23.15, 27.15 (iii BC).

**ἀρχιεροθύτης**, after lemma insert 'Dor. -θύτᾱς'; add '*SEG* 33.643 (Rhodes, ii/i BC), *ISelge* 17.7 (Rom.imp.), ἀρχιιεροθύτας *Lindos* 70.5 (iii BC)'

**ἀρχιερωσύνη**, after '(Daphne, ii BC)' insert '*IHistriae* 57.20 (pl., referring to a woman, ii AD)'; add 'also **ἀρχιιερ-** *SB* 8267.12 (i BC)'

***ἀρχιέφηβος**, ὁ, v. °ἀρχέφηβος.

**ἀρχιζάκορος**, delete the entry (read ἀρχινᾱ-).

**ἀρχιζάπφης**, for the pres. ref. read '*Inscr.Délos* 2628a (ii BC)'

***ἀρχιζωγρᾰ́φος**, ὁ, *master-painter*, *master-decorator*, *BE* 1958.516 (Georgia, iv AD), Eust.*Op.* 307.23.

***ἀρχιζώστη**, ἡ, v. °ἀργιζώστη.

**ἀρχιθεωρία**, add 'also ἀρχε- Din. 1.81, *SEG* 28.60.60 (Athens, iii BC)'

**ἀρχιθέωρος**, after '(Delos, ii BC)' insert '*SEG* 37.709.A2 (Epirus, iii/ii BC)'; **ἀρχιθέαρος**, add '*SEG* 26.487.(1)6 (Megara, ii AD)'; add 'also **ἀρχεθέαρος** *CID* I 7.A5, 8, 23 (Andros, v BC)'

**ἀρχιθῐᾰσεύω**, delete the entry.

⁺**ἀρχιθῐᾰσῑτεύω**, *lead a thiasos*, *Inscr.Délos* 1778.5, 1779.6, 1782.7 (ii/i BC).

**ἀρχιθῐᾰσίτης**, for '*IG* 11(4).1228.4' read '*IG* 11(4).1228.2' and add '*SEG* 6.718.5 (sp. -ειτ-, Pisidia, Rom.imp.)'

**ἀρχιθῠρωρός**, add '*PTeb.* 790.1 (ii BC)'

***ἀρχιθύτης**, ου, ὁ, *he who leads the sacrifice*, perh. for *archbishop*, *IEphes.* 1356 (Chr.).

***ἀρχιιατρίνη**, v. °ἀρχιατρίνη.

***ἀρχιιερωσύνη**, ἡ, v. °ἀρχιερωσύνη.

**ἀρχικός I 2**, after 'Isoc. 4.67' insert '*emanating from* or *pertaining to a magistracy*, ἀ. πρόσταξις *Cod.Just.* 1.2.20, ἀ. ὄχλησις ib. 1.3.45.70' add '**4** in Roman contexts, *curule*, δίφρος ἀ. D.C. 43.14.5, 43.48.2, 53.30.6.'

**ἀρχικῠβερνήτης**, for '*pilot*' read '*navigator*' and add 'ἀ. ὢν τοῦ σύμπαντος στόλου D.S. 20.50.4'

**ἀρχικῡνηγός**, add '*SEG* 23.271.26 (ἀρχικ[ου]ναγύ nom. pl., Boeotia, iii BC); app. *chief*, of gladiatorial rank, *IIlion* 126.4 (Rom.imp.)'

***ἀρχίλαρχος**, ὁ, written ἀρχιίλ-, *chief of the* ἴλαρχοι, *ASAA* N.S. 61.342 (proto-Corinthian alabastron, *c.*700 BC; ?pers. n.).

***ἀρχιλᾱτόμος**, ὁ, *chief quarryman*, Bernand *Pan* 28.3, (iv AD).

***ἀρχιμᾰγᾰρεύς**, έως, ὁ, *chief of the rite of the μάγαρον*, *IG* 10(2).1.65.3 (Thessalonica, iii AD).

**ἀρχιμαγειρεύς**, delete the entry.

**ἀρχιμανδρίτης**, add '*IGLS* 2143c, *PKöln* 112.12 (v/vi AD), *CPR* 10.122.12, *PMasp.* 242.4 (both vi AD)'

***ἀρχιμᾰχαιροφόρος**, *chief of the armed police*, *PMich.*XI 656.6 (sp. -μ[α]χερ-, i AD).

***ἀρχιμεταλλάρχης**, ου, ὁ, *chief controller of mines*, Bernand *Pan* 51.6 (AD 11).

**ἀρχίμῑμος**, for '*chief comedian*' read '*chief actor in a mime*'

***ἀρχιμονάζων**, οντος, ὁ, *chief monk*, wax tablet in *ZPE* 56.90 (v/vi AD).

***ἀρχινᾱκόρος**, v. °ἀρχινεωκόρος.

***ἀρχιναυπηγός**, ὁ, *head shipbuilder*, *PRyl.* 640.19 (iv AD).

***ἀρχιναυφῠ́λαξ**, ακος, ὁ, *chief ναυφύλαξ* II, *ASAA* 2(1916).136 (Rhodes, i BC).

**ἀρχινεᾱνίσκος**, add '*IUrb.Rom.* 160 i B22 (ii AD)'

***ἀρχινεωκορέω**, *hold the office of* ἀρχινεωκόρος, *IG* 10(2).1.114.9, etc. (Thessalonica, i/ii AD); see also ἀρχινακορέω.

**ἀρχινεωκόρος**, add 'also ἀρχινᾱκόρος *IG* 10(2).1.244.7, prob. in *IGLS* 1263 (Laodicea ad mare, both ii AD)'

***ἀρχινεωποιΐα**, ἡ, office of ἀρχινεωποιός, *Wien.Anz.* 1893.103 no. 11 (sp. -νεοπ-, Aphrodisias).

***ἀρχιοικιστᾱ́ς**, ᾶ, ὁ, *commissioner for foundation of a colony*, *IG* 9²(1).2.10 (Thermon, iii BC, pl.).

***ἀρχιοικοδόμος**, ὁ, *master-builder*, *Fouilles de Byblos* II 76 no. 7186, *PKöln* 197.2 (v/vi AD), *SEG* 8.781.10 (Syene, vi AD).

***ἀρχιπαστοφορία**, ἡ, *the office of* ἀρχοπαστοφόρος, *PMich.*inv. 5598.22 in *ZPE* 63.297 (ii AD).

***ἀρχιπερίπολος**, ὁ, *chief of patrols*, *Rev.Bibl.* 1.246 (Caesarea, vi AD).

**ἀρχιποίμην**, add '*SEG* 19.782 (ἀρχ[ιπ]οίμην, Pisidia, Rom.imp.)'

***ἀρχιποσία**, ἡ, *position of president of a drinking-party*, Porphyrio ad Hor.*Carm.* 2.7.25, al.

***ἀρχιποτᾰμίτης**, ου, ὁ, *chief ποταμίτης*, *PHerm.* 69.6, 21 (v AD).

***ἀρχιπρεσβῠ́τερος**, ὁ, *chief presbyter*, *IGLS* 21.57 (vi AD).

**ἀρχιπροστᾰτέω**, for 'συναγωγῆς' to end read 'in a military *koinon*, *SB* 626 (= *IFayoum* 16.4, ii BC)'

⁺**ἀρχιπροστάτης**, ου, ὁ, *chief of a military koinon*, *SB* 5959 (iii/iv AD) in *CE* 27.290.

***ἀρχιπροφήτης**, ου, ὁ, *chief προφήτης*, *PGen.* 7.5 (i AD), *PHerm.Rees* 3.26 (iv AD).

***ἀρχιπρῠτᾰνεία**, -ία, ἡ, *office of chief president*, *Didyma* 570, 157 1 *a*.

**ἀρχιπρῠ́τᾰνις**, after 'εως' insert '(but -ιδος *Didyma* 252.7, etc., -ίδων ib. 272.5'

**ἀρχιραβδοῦχος**, before '*chief lictor*' insert '*chief of the* ῥαβδοῦχοι (q.v. sense 2), *PWisc.* 50.9 (ii AD)'

***ἀρχισῑτολόγος**, ὁ, *chief σιτολόγος*, *SB* 6800.3 (iii BC), *PTeb.* 792.10 (ii BC).

***ἀρχισῑτωνέω**, *to hold the office of* °ἀρχισιτώνης, *JRCil.* 2.19.6 (sp. -σειτ-, iii AD).

***ἀρχισῑτώνης**, ὁ, *chief officer in charge of grain supply*, *Side* 114.4 (sp. -σειτ-); cf. σιτώνης.

***ἀρχισταβλίτης**, ου, ὁ, *chief stableman*, perh. honorific title, *PPrincet.* 145.11 (vi AD), *POxy.* 1908.5 (vi/vii AD).

**ἀρχιστολιστής**, before '*keeper*' insert '*chief*' and add 'Bernand *Les portes* no. 1 (Antinooupolis, i BC)'

***ἀρχίστολος**, ὁ, = °ἀρχιστολιστής, rest. in *IEphes.* 1244 ([ἀρχ]ί-, ii AD).

***ἀρχιστράτωρ**, ορος, ὁ, title of an equestrian official, *TAM* 3.52.8 (Termessus, ii AD).

***ἀρχισύμμᾰχος**, ὁ, *chief messenger* or *courier*, *PFlor.* 5.93.4, *PMich.*inv. 3706.16 in *JÖByz* 36.25, *CPR* 14.6.7 (both v/vi AD), *POxy.* 1866.4 (vi/vii AD).

⁺**ἀρχισυνᾰγωγέω**, *to be leader of a religious association*, *IG* 10(2).1.288 (Thessalonica, ii AD).

***ἀρχισυνᾰγώγης**, ου, ὁ, = ἀρχισυνάγωγος, *CIJud.* 336 (Rome, iii/iv AD).

***ἀρχισυνᾰγώγισσα**, ἡ, fem. of °ἀρχισυνάγωγος 2, *CIJud.* 731c (v. *SEG* 38.913, Crete, iv/v AD).

**ἀρχισυνάγωγος I**, for this section read 'ὁ, ἡ, *leader of a religious association*, *SB* 623 (i BC), *IGRom.* 1.782 (Perinthus). **2** *leader* or *elder of a synagogue*, Jewish honorary title, *Ev.Marc.* 5.22, al., *IG* 14.2304, Ramsay *Cities and Bishoprics* 2 no. 559; of women, *ISmyrna* 295 (Rom.imp.), *CIJud.* 756 (Caria, iv/v AD).'

⁺**ἀρχιτεκτοσύνη**, ἡ, *art* or *skill of an architect*, *BCH* 10.500 (Pisidia), *IMylasa* 468.7.

**ἀρχιτέκτων I 1 a**, add 'τῆς θεοῦ *IEphes.* 536, 1061, 1600.6 (Rom.imp.)' add '**c** ἔπαρχος -τεκτόνων, = Lat. *praefectus fabrum*, *IG* 2².3546 (Eleusis, i AD), cf. *ABSA* 56.23 (Paphos, ii BC).'

***ἀρχίτοκος**, ον, perh. *ruling childbirth*, ὠδῖνες *MDAI(A)* 56.128 (Thespiae, Hellen.).

**ἀρχιυπηρέτης**, after 'ἀρχυπερέτης' insert '*RA* 6.31.8, 17 (Amphipolis, ii BC)' and transfer existing entries to sp. ἀρχιυπ-

***ἀρχιφρᾰ́τωρ**, ορος, ὁ, *president of a phratry*, *IGLS* 232.

**ἀρχιφρουρέω**, after '(Thess.)' insert 'al., *SEG* 36.635 (Maced., iii AD)'

**ἀρχίφρουρος**, add '*PSI* 938 (vi AD)'

**ἀρχιφῠλᾰκίτης**, add '*IFayoum* III 209 (= *SEG* 33.1359, ii BC)'

***ἀρχιφῡλέτης**, ου, ὁ, = ἀρχίφυλος, *TAM* 3(1).121 (Termessus).

**ἀρχογλυπτάδης**, for '*son of*' read 'humorous patronymic for'

***ἀρχόμαος**, ὁ, perh. a religious official, *SEG* 38.945 (Megara Hyblaea, vi BC).

***ἀρχοντεία**, ἡ, *archonship*, *TAM* 2.612 (Teos).

**ἀρχοντεύω**, add '*IHadr.* 40.7 (ii AD)'

**ἀρχοντικός 1**, add '*of the authorities*, τὴν ἀρχοντικὴν τιμουρίαν ὑποστῆν(αι) *SEG* 37.200 (Athens, Chr.), εἰς ἀρχοντικόν *to the authorities*, *PMich.*XIII 660.5 (vi AD); ἀρχοντικῶν καὶ δημοτῶν app. *people of rank and commoners*, *POxy.* 2346.23 (iii AD); applied to angels, Cels.ap.Orig.*Cels.* 6.27' **2**, for this section read 'in particular, referring to Roman offices: of *praefectus*, *SB* 9152.9; of *praeses*, *CPR* 5.17.8 (v AD); of *ex-consul*, *IG* 14.756a (Naples, i AD); of *duumviralis*, ib. 1789 (Rome)'

**ἀρχός I 2**, for this section read 'as ἄρχων, *chief magistrate*, ἀ. Τειχιό(σ)ης *Didyma* 6 (Miletus, vi BC), *IG* $9^2$.609.21 (Naupactus, c.500 BC), ἀ. καὶ Ϝοικιάται *SEG* 26.449.6 (Epid., v BC), *ICS* 2.1 (Paphos, iv BC), *IG* 7.3301 (Chaeronea, ii BC), *Inscr.Cret.* 4.250.3 (i BC)'

***ἀρχοωνία**, v. °ἀρχωνεία.

***ἀρχυλωρός**, ὁ, *chief* ὑλωρός, Thessalian office, rest. in *SEG* 34.565 ([ἀρχυ]λουρός, Pherae, ii BC).

**ἄρχω I 1**, line 4, after 'and 2' insert 'ὁ ἄρχων τᾶς δίκας *Leg.Gort.* 11.51 (v BC)' **4**, add 'so med., ἀρχόμεναι θυμέλας Posidipp. in *Suppl.Hell.* 705.4' **6**, line 2, after '*begin*' insert '*mark the beginning of*' and line 3, before 'Lex ap.' insert '*Thasos* 18.5, 13 (v BC)' **II 3**, add 'aor. part. designating past holders of the archonship, Εὐκλείδην τὸν ἄρξαντα Archipp. 27.3 K.-A., *SEG* 23.647 (Cyprus, i AD), *TAM* 4(1).238; cf. ἄρχων'

**ἄρχων II 2**, add 'πρῶτος ἄρχων *IPrusias* 7.7, 38.7 (Rom.imp.)' **3**, *ruler* of a synagogue, add '*CIJud.* 347 (pl.)' at end add 'see also ‡ἄρχω II 3'

***ἀρχωνεία**, ἡ, office of ἀρχώνης, form ἀρχοωνήαν (acc.), *IEphes.* 4101.17 (ii AD).

**ἀρχωνέω**, for '*BCH* 1.410 (Callipolis)' read '*IParion* 5.3, cf. Robert *Hell.* 9.81'

**ἀρωγός I**, add 'neut. pl. as subst. (sc. φάρμακα), Gal. 11.95.8'

**ἄρωμα** (A), line 2, delete 'prob. in *Suppl.Epigr.* 1.414 .. pl.)'

***ἀρωμᾰτίτης**, ου, ὁ, *aromatic*, ἀ. οἶνος Dsc. 5.54, κάλαμος Gal. 11.405.

***ἀρωμᾰτῖτις**, ἡ, fem. of ἀρωματίτης, σχοῖνος ἀ. Str. 16.2.16; as subst., *precious stone*, Plin.*HN* 37.145.

***ἀρωμᾰτοποιόν**, gloss on ζειρίς, Hsch. (La.; -ποιεῖν, ζειρεῖν cod.).

**ἀρωμᾰτοφόρος 2**, add 'rest. in *IEphes.* 1076, title of a religious official'

**ἀσᾰμινθος**, add 'S.*fr.* 204 R.; Myc. *a-sa-mi-to*'

***ἀσᾰμιος**, v. °ἀζήμιος.

***ἀσᾰρίτη**, = ὀροβάγχη, Sch.Cyr.

**ἀσαρκέω**, for 'causal, *make lean*' read 'intr. *to be lean*'

**ἆσᾰρος**, for 'Sapph. 77 (Comp.)' read 'Sapph. 103.11 L.-P., 91 L.-P. (comp.)'

**ἀσάω**, after 'Thgn. 593' insert 'Alc. 39.11 L.-P. *MAMA* 8.361.7'

***ἀσβέστιον**, τό, prob. *limestone*, *PNess.* 54.9 (vi/vii AD, pl.).

**ἄσβεστος**, after 'Il. l.c.' insert 'φάεος .. ἀσβέστου Call.*Dian.* 118'

**ἀσβολάω**, delete the entry.

**ἀσβολόω**, for 'Macho .. 3.16.3' read 'Macho 372 G., Arr.*Epict.* 3.16.3; as sobriquet of the descendants of Damon, Plu.*Cim.* 1'

**ἀσεβέω**, line 5, after '[Xen.]*Cyn.* 13.16' insert 'ἀσεβήτω πὸτ τᾶρ Ἀθανᾶρ *SEG* 35.389.7 (Elis, iv BC)'

**ἀσεβής**, after 'A.*Supp.* 9 (anap.)' insert 'μήτ' ἔρδειν μήτε λέγειν ἀσεβῆ Thgn. 1180'

**ἄσειρος**, add '= ὁ ἄδετος χιτών, Cyr.'

**ἀσείρωτος**, add '**2** *not having a border* (or *worn without a belt*), τὸν φαιλόνην (for φαινόλην) μου τὸν ἀσίρωτον *PYale* 82.8 (ii/iii AD).'

**ἄσειστος**, after 'D.L. 8.26' insert '(but see also °ἀείσειστος)'

**ἀσελγής**, line 1, for '*brutal*' read '*unconstrained*'; line 3, for 'generally, *outrageous*' read 'of natural forces' and add 'οἷον αὖ τὸ πνῖγος, ὡς ἀσελγές Pherecr. 191 K.-A.'

**ἄσεπτος**, add 'E.*Ba.* 890, *IA* 1092'

**ἄση I 2**, for 'Sapph. 1.3 .. 14.11' read 'Sapph. 1.3 L.-P., Alc. 39(*a*).11 L.-P., Anacr. 2 *fr.*1.8 P.' **3**, delete the section.

***ἀσηκρῆτις**, ὁ, Lat. *a secretis*, Procop.*Arc.* 14.4, cf. Lyd.*Mag.* 3.20.

**ἀσημείωτος I**, for 'Ph. 1.121' read 'Ph. 2.121'

***ἀσήμινος**, η, ον, *made of silver*, *PIand.* 103.15 (vi AD, ἀσίμ-), *PMich.*XIV 684.14 (vi AD, -ενος).

***ἀσήμιον**, τό, *silver plate*, *PHamb.* 227.15 (iii AD), *PSI* 825.13 (iv/v AD, both sp. ἀσήμιν), ἀργύρεον βάρος ἤγουν τοῦ ἀσημίου Sch.Nic.*Al.* 54a; cf. ἄσημος I 2 and mod. Gk. ἀσήμι.

**ἄσημος II**, add 'χρη]σμοὺς ἀσάμους Stesich. 222(b).247 (p. 215 D.)' **III**, add '**e** of days on which critical signs are absent, Gal. 9.751.9, 776.10.' **IV**, add 'Κόρινθος ἄστρον οὐκ ἄσημον Ἑλλάδος *Trag.adesp.* 128'

**ἀσήμων**, add 'adv. ἀσημόνως Phld.*Mort.* 37'

**ἄσηπτος**, for '*Acacia tortilis*' read '*Acacia* (*shittim*) *wood*'

***ἀσήτωρ**, ορος, ὁ, *sick at heart*, Antim. in *Suppl.Hell.* 65.1 (prob. nomen agentis fr. ἀσάω, but expld. by Sch. as τοῦ ἀνιωμένου τὸ ([ἦ]τ[ο]ρ).

**ἀσθενέω 2**, add 'εἰ μὲν οὖν μὴ συνεβεβήκει τὰ κοινὰ τῆς πόλεως ἀσθενεῖν *SEG* 38.1476.A50 (Xanthos, iii BC)' add '**II** trans., *weaken*, *cause to fall*, Lxx *Ma.* 2.8.'

***ἀσθέταιροι**, οἱ, unit of Macedonian infantry, Arr.*An.* 2.23.2, 4.23.1, 5.22.6, 6.21.3, 7.11.3 (codd., vv. ll. ἀσθέτεροι, cj. πεζέταιροι).

***ἄσθιπποι**, οἱ, *unit of Macedonian cavalry*, τοὺς ἀσθίππους ὀνομαζομένους D.S. 19.29.2 (v.l. ἀνθίππους); cf. °ἀσθέταιροι.

**ἆσθμα III**, line 3, after '(Agath.)' insert 'ἀ. πυρός ib. 7.210 (Antip.Sid.)'

**ἀσθμάζω**, add 'med. aor. part., *PMag.* 13.522'

**ἀσθμάομαι**, delete the entry.

**ἀσθμᾰτώδης**, add 'Gal. 7.949.8, 959.3, 16.662.14 (*CMG* 5.9.(2).85.17)'

**Ἀσία**, after '*Asia*' insert '(perh. orig. a name for Lydia and then extended to all the hinterland of Ionia and eventually over the continent) Hes.*fr.* 180.3 M.-W., Archil. 227 W., Mimn. 9.2, Sapph. 44.4 L.-P.'

**Ἀσιᾱγενής**, Ion. Ἀσιηγενής, add '*IEphes.* 600A'

**Ἀσιᾱνός**, before 'ή, όν' insert 'Ion. **-ηνός**, Hp.*Aër.* 16, al.'; add 'Ἀσιανῶν θίασος a fraternity for worship of Dionysus, *SEG* 31.633B (Maced., ii AD)'

**Ἀσιαρχία**, add '*Milet.* 1(9).339 a 5, b 4 (iii AD)'

**Ἀσιάς** (s.v. Ἀσία in *LSJ*), line 4, after 'Euph. 34' insert 'Ἀσίδι .. αἴῃ Hes.*fr.* 165.11 M.-W.'

**ἀσίδηρος I**, add '**b** δόρατα ἀσίδηρα = Lat. *hastae purae*, D.C.ap.Zonar. 7.21.' **II**, for '*sword*' read '*weapon*'; before 'βίος' insert 'w. ref. to the Golden Age'; after 'Max.Tyr. 36.1' insert '*without a tool*, χείρ *AP* 9.52 (Carph.)'

***ἀσῐδήρωτος**, ον, ῥυμοί, *not strengthened with iron*, *IG* $1^3$.386.22; v. °ῥυμός IV.

**ἄσιλος**, delete the entry.

**ἀσινής II**, after 'Hdt. 1.105' insert 'X.*Eq.* 5.1'

***Ἀσιονίκης**, ου, ὁ, *victor in the Asian games*, *IG* 4.206 (i BC), *MAMA* 8.418.31 (Aphrodisias), *Inscr.Perg.* 8(3).71.

**ἄσιος**, add 'form ἄσϝιος, cf. Myc. *a-si-wi-ja*, pers. n., *a-si-wi-ja*, epith. of Potnia'

**ἀσίρακος**, delete '= τρωξαλλίς'

***ἀσῐτητέον**, *one must fast*, Gal. 10.807.10.

***Ἀσκαηνός**, ὁ, cult-title of the deity Men, in Antioch, *SEG* 30.1503, 31.1138, etc., in Aphrodisias, Reynolds *Aphrodisias* 29.15, 32.7 (Ἀσκαιν-, both i BC).

**ἀσκάλαφος**, add 'cf. mythical name associated with an owl, Ἀσκάλαφον .. Δημήτηρ ἐποίησεν ὦτον Apollod. 2.5.12'

***Ἀσκαληπιακόν**, etc., v. °Ἀσκληπ-.

**ἀσκαλία**, add 'prob. in *POsl.* 48.6 (i AD, pl., -λει- pap.)'

**ἀσκᾰλος**, add 'orac. in *IEphes.* 1252.7 (ii AD)'

**ἀσκᾰλώνιον**, add '**II** ἀ., τό, vessel of unknown size used as measure of capacity, οἴνου ἀσκαλώνια δ' τραγημάτων ἀσκαλώνιον α'. *PHerm. Rees* 23 (iv AD), *POxy.* 1924.3 (v/vi AD), κοῦφον ἀσκαλόνιν ibid. 10, *PKlein.Form.* 1204.4 (vi AD).'

***Ἀσκαλωνῖτις**, ιδος, fem. adj., *of Ascalon*, γάστρα Zos.Alch. 210.15, Anon.Alch. 418.24.

**ἀσκάνδης**, add 'see also ‡ἀστάνδης'

**ἀσκάντης I**, after 'Ar.*Nu.* 633' insert 'Call.*fr.* 240 Pf.'

**ἀσκᾰρίζω**, for 'Att. form .. euph.' read '= σκαρίζω, *palpitate*' and before 'Hp.*Nat.Puer.* 30' insert 'Hippon. 33.2 W.'

**ἀσκαύλης**, add '*PSAAthen.* 43ᵛ i 3, al. (ii AD)'

**ἄσκᾰφος**, add 'rest. in Pratin. 3 P.'

**ἀσκέδαστος**, after '*not scattered*' insert 'Alc.*Intr.* 25 (p. 177.21, 27 H.)'

**ἄσκεπος**, *defenceless*, for the pres. ref. read 'ἤριπε .. ἄ. of the city of Sparta, Amyntas in *Suppl.Hell.* 44.5'

**ἄσκεπτος II 2**, add 'ἀσκέπτους νεκύων εἰς θαλάμους epigr. in *Salamine* 192 (ii/i BC)'

**ἀσκέρα**, for 'Herod. 2.32' read 'Herod. 2.23' and add 'dub. in *IG* $1^3$.422.163 (Athens, v BC; perh. ἀσκηρά)'

**ἀσκέω I 3**, delete the section. **II 2**, line 5, after 'metaph.' insert 'δαίμον' ἀσκήσω .. θεραπεύων Pi.*P.* 3.109; ἀσκεῖται Θέμις id.*O.* 8.22'

**ἄσκημα**, for 'in warfare .. chariots)' read '*form of warfare, military practice*'; add '*object of practice, art*, D.H.*Comp.* 3.5'

**ἀσκητέος II**, ἀσκητέον, add 'Muson.*fr.* K.'

**ἀσκητήρ**, add 'Myc. *a-ke-te-re* (pl.) *decorator, finisher*'

***ἀσκητήριον**, τό, *monastery*, *Cod.Just.* 1.3.53.3, al.; also *nunnery*, ib. 1.3.46.5.

***ἀσκητής**, οῦ, ὁ, *one who is in training for athletics*, Ar.*Pl.* 585, Pl.*R.* 403e, Isoc. 2.11, Διόνυσος ἀ., title of comedy by Aristomenes, cf. οὗτός ἐστιν ὁ τῆς ἀληθείας ἀσκητὴς ὁ πρὸς τὰς τοιαύτας φαντασίας γυμνάζων ἑαυτόν Arr.*Epict.* 2.18.27. **2** *one who exercises himself in any art* or *discipline*, ἀ. τῶν καλῶν κἀγαθῶν ἔργων X.*Cyr.* 1.5.11, λόγων D.H.*Is.* 2.1, σοφίης *IG* $2^2$.11140.2 (ii AD), φρονήσεως Ph. 1.59, 1.643, al.; of things, καρτερίας ἀσκητὴν λογισμόν id. 1.89, ὁ νοῦς ὁ ἀσκητής 1.91. **3** *monk, hermit*, Ath.*Apol.Const.* in *PG* 25.632a, al.

**⁺ἀσκητικός**, ή, όν, *concerned with* or *relating to physical training*, νόσημα Ar.*Lys.* 1085, βίος Pl.*Lg.* 806a, μελέται Ph. 1.646; of persons, id. 1.552; as subst., τοιαῦτα ὑφηγεῖται τῷ ἀ. ἡ ὑπομονή id. 1.551; neut., τὸ ἀσκητικόν *training* Epict. 3.12.6; adv. -κῶς Poll. 3.145.

**⁺ἀσκήτρια**, ἡ, *ascetic woman, nun*, *Cat.Cod.Astr.* 7.225.29, *MAMA* 1.174.1 (Laodicea Combusta), *SEG* 28.1576 (v/vi AD), *Cod.Just.* 1.3.45.9, Just.*Nov.* 59.3.25; Myc. *a-ke-ti-ri-ja*, *decorator, finisher.*

***ἀσκιᾱτρόφητος**, ον, *used to unsheltered life, hardy*, ?Com.ap.Phot. 264 Th.

**ἄσκιος I**, before 'αὐγή' insert 'Λακεδαίμων *AP* 7.723'

**ἀσκίπων**, line 2, after '(Theodorid.)' insert 'Posidipp. in *Suppl.Hell.* 705.24'

***Ἀσκλᾱπ-**, v. ‡Ἀσκληπ-.

***ἀσκλατάριος**, ὁ, dub. sens., *SB* 6951ᵛ.34 (ii AD) (cf. perh. medieval Lat. *sclata, exclate* = *scindula, stick* or *rafter*).

**Ἀσκληπιακός** (s.v. Ἀσκληπιός), add 'σκάφιον *Inscr.Délos* 320*B*56 (iii BC); -κά, τά, *fund for the expenses* of Asclepios' festival, *IG* 12(5).544.B 2.9 (Ceos, iv/iii AD); neut. subst. sg., in form Ἀσκαληπιακόν, name of mine in Attica, *SEG* 32.233 (iv BC)'

**ἀσκληπιάς**, add '**4** pl., *haemorrhoids*, Cyran. 41 (1.21.64 K.).'

**Ἀσκληπιασταί** (s.v. Ἀσκληπιός), add 'Ἀσσκηπιαστῶν (sic, gen. pl.) *ZPE* 70.152 (Chios, iii BC)'

**Ἀσκληπίεια** (s.v. Ἀσκληπιός), add 'also Ἀσκληπεῖα *SEG* 31.594 (Ephesus, ii AD), 32.1089 (Africa, *c.*300 AD), Ἀσκλᾱπίεια *SEG* 23.212 (Messene, i BC/i AD), Ἀσκλᾱπεῖα *IGRom.* 4.1064 (Cos)'

**Ἀσκληπιεῖον** (s.v. Ἀσκληπιός), add 'Ἀσκλᾱπιεῖον *IG* 7.1780 (Thespiae), Ἀσκλᾱπιῆον *IGBulg.* 1².315.20 (Mesambria, i BC)'

**Ἀσκληπιός**, line 1, after '-ᾱπιός' insert 'Αἰσκλαπιός *IG* 4².136 (Epid., vi/v BC); Αἰσχλαβιός *IG* 4.356 (Corinth); Ἀσσκλαπιός *IG* 4.1172.3 (Epid.); Ἀσκαλ[α]πιός *IG* 9(2).397 (Scotoussa); Ἀσκαλπιός *Inscr.Cret.* 4.182.6 (Gortyn); Lacon. Ἀγλαπιός *IG* 5(1).1313 (v BC), *SEG* 12.371.5 (Cos, iii BC), Αἰγλαπιός ib. line 3, (cf. Ἀγλαόπης (Lacon.) and Αἰγλάηρ Hsch.); Cypr. Ἀσκαπιός *SEG* 30.1678 (but *a-sa-ka-la-pi-o-i* in syllabic version, Syria, iv/iii BC); cf. pers. n. Ἀσ(σ)κηπιάδης, etc., v. *ZPE* 70.152-6); dat. sg. hαισκλαπιεῖ (? from hαισκλαπιεύς) *IG* 4².151 (Epid., vi/v BC)' and after 'etc.' add 'pl., *statues of A.*, *Inscr.Délos* 1417*B*i147 (ii BC)'

***ἀσκόμισθοι**, οἱ, *those who let wineskins for hire*, συνεργασία ἀσκομίσθων *IEphes.* 444.9.

***ἀσκοναυτοποιός**, ὁ, *maker of rafts supported on inflated skins*, *BE* 1964.495 (Palmyra, iii AD).

***ἀσκοποιός**, ὁ, *maker of wineskins*, *BE* 1964.495 (Syria), *IGLS* 9158, 9159, 9160 (Bostra); = Lat. *utrarius*, *Gloss.* 3.307.

**ἀσκός**, add '**6** dub. sens. app. denoting some metal object, *IG* 2².1544 (iv BC), v. °ἐξάγιστος, ἀκκόρ.'

***ἀσκότεινος**, ον, *free from darkness*, gloss on ἀνέσπερον Hsch.

***ἀσκότιστος**, ον, gloss on ἀνέσπερον, Cyr.; cf. °ἀσκότεινος.

***ἀσκοφύσιον**, τό, *bellows made from skin*, Anon.Alch. 349.3.

***ἀσκόω**, *fit with leather pads*, *IG* 2².1604.13.29, 38 (iv BC); cf. ἄσκωμα 1.

**ἀσκύλευτος**, after '*stripped*' insert '*GVI* 1603.11 (Acraephia, iii BC)' and add 'Sopat.Rh. 8.51.11 W.'

**ἄσκωμα 1**, add '*IG* 2².1604.32, al. (iv BC)' **2**, for pres. def. read '*the fully-developed female breast*'

**ἆσμα**, for 'ἄττω' read 'ἄττομαι'

***ᾀσμᾰτογρᾰ́φος**, ὁ, *song-writer*, Tz. ad Lyc. p. 1 S.

***ἀσμένεια**, ἡ, *pleasure, satisfaction*, *PFlor.* 294.13 (vi AD).

**ἀσμενιστός**, after '*welcome*' insert 'Cic.*Att.* 9.2a.2, 9.10.9'

**ἀσοφία**, for '*folly, stupidity*' read '*lack of skill* or *judgement*'

**ἄσοφος**, for '*unwise, foolish*' read 'lacking *skill* or *understanding*'; after 'Pi.*O.* 3.45' insert 'Φοίβου τ' ἄσοφοι γλώσσης ἐνοπαί E.*El.* 1302, ἄσοφοι καὶ ἀκρατεῖς X.*Mem.* 3.9.4'

**ἀσπαίρω**, line 6, after 'of an infant' insert '*h.Cer.* 289'

**ἀσπᾰ́λᾰθος 1**, at end for 'Thphr. 9.7.3' read 'Thphr.*HP* 9.7.3'

***ἀσπαλακίτης**, ὁ, name of a stone, Socr.Dion.*Lith.* 50 H.-S., al.

***ἀσπᾰρᾰγῡλιοκογχῡλεύς**, έως, ὁ, *purple-fisher who uses a weel* (γυλιός) *made of* ἀσφάραγος, w. haplology, *MAMA* 3.681 (ἀσπαραγυλιωκονχ-, Corycus).

***ἀσπαράκιον**, v. °ἀσφ-.

***ἀσπερμολόγητος**, ὁ, epith. of Jesus Christ, app. *not humanly conceived*, *PMasp.* 188.1 (vi AD).

**ἀσπιδεῖον III**, for '= ἀσπίδιον (?)' read 'perh. *votive panel* (portrait)'

***ἀσπῑδῆος**, α, ον, Boeot. for *ἀσπίδεος *of shields*, ἆθλα ἀ. *IG* 7.2712.23 (Acraephia).

**ἀσπῑδίσκη** (s.v. ἀσπιδίσκος), line 2, for '*SIG* .. ii BC)' read '*Inscr.Délos* 442B.32 (ii BC); as part of a brooch, πορπίον ἀ. ἔχον ib. 1417A.3'

**ἀσπῑδίσκος**, after 'ἀσπίς' insert '*small shield*, votive in character, *IG* 2².47.7 (iv BC)'; after 'Sch.Il. 5.743' insert 'ornamental *boss* or *button*, ἀσπιδίσκοι λίθων ἑτέρων Aristeas 75; on high priest's ephod, Epiph.Const. in *Lapid.Gr.* 198.17; *disc* on each end of the crossbar of a cithara, Hsch.'

**ἀσπίς 1**, line 1, after 'al.' insert 'κοίλη Tyrt. 19.7 W. (cf. Mimn. 13a.2 W.), Alc. 357.6 L.-P.' add '**b** ἡ ἐξ Ἄργους ἀσπίς, name of games at the festival of Hera at Argos in Roman times, *IG* 2².3145 (i AD), v. *SEG* 33.296), etc., *IG* 14.746.18 (i/ii AD), *SEG* 34.1316 (Xanthos, i AD).'

**ἄσπονδος**, penultimate line, delete '(lyr.)'

**ἄσπορος I**, add 'γαῖα Moschio Trag. 6.25.5; as fem. subst., *SEG* 23.305 ii b8 (Delphi, ii BC)' **IV**, after 'Nonn.*D.* 2.221, al.' insert 'of Attis, ib. 25.311'

***ἀσπροειδής**, ές, *tending to whiteness*, Socr.Dion.*Lith.* 26.10 H.-S.

***ἀσπροπώλισσα**, ἡ, *seller of incense*, cf. ‡ἀσπρός III, *ITyr* 17B (Chr.).

**ἄσπρος II**, for 'ἄ. γράμματα .. very late)' read '*colourless, white*, ἄ. γράμματα "*invisible*" writing, *Cat.Cod.Astr.* 1.108.1; *white*, *Stud.Pal.* 20.245.4 (v. *ZPE* 76.113, vi AD), dist. fr. λευκός, καρακάλλιον λευκὸν λινεγαῖον ἄ. *PSI* 14.1427.19 (vi AD)' **III**, add 'cf. perh. mod. Gk. ἀσπρούχι'

***ἀσπρόχρους**, -ουν, *white-coloured*, *Cat.Cod.Astr.* 5(4).170.

**ἄσσα**, line 5, after 'Cratin. 6' insert 'ποιεῖν ἄττα Pl.*R.* 339d'

***ἀσσκονικτεί**, v. °ἀκονιτί.

**ἄσσον** I, line 7, for 'A. *fr.*6' read 'A. *fr.*66 R.'

**Ἀσσύριος**, after 'adj.' insert 'Ἀ. γράμματα, name given to various oriental scripts, id. 4.87 (prob. cuneiform), Th. 4.50 (prob. Aramaic); cf. °Σύρος; ξεῖνος' and delete 'al.'

**ἀστᾰγής II**, at end after '*in a stream*' insert 'Call.*fr.* 317 Pf.'

**ἀστᾰκός I**, after '*lobster*' insert 'Epich. 30'

**ἀστάνδης**, after 'Plu.*Alex.* 18, 2.326f' add '340c, Ath. 3.122a (cj.) Hsch.'; add 'see also ἀσκάνδης'

***Ἀστάρτη**, ἡ, Dor. -ᾱ, Phoenician goddess, *SEG* 36.316 (Corinth, v BC), J.*AJ* 1.118, Plu. 2.357b.

**ἀστᾰσία**, add '**II** *unsettled conditions*, in political sense, Sch.Th. in *DAW* 67 no. 2 p. 11.'

***ἀσταταρία**, ἡ, *candlestick*, *Stud.Pal.* 8.941, *PVindob.*G 25737.6 in *ZPE* 64.75; cf. στατάριον, medieval Lat. *cereostata statarii.*

***ἀστᾰτί**, adv. of ἄστατος, perh. in Sophr. in *Stud.Ital.* 10.249.

**ἄστᾱτοι** (or **ἀστᾶτοι**), read this for **ἄστᾰτοι** and add 'Lyd.*Mag.* 1.46 (p. 48.8 W.), sg., *SEG* 33.1195 (Cappadocia, i/ii AD), ib. 7.86 (Syria, ii AD), *IGRom.* 3.1206 (Palestine)'

**ἄστᾰτος**, after 'of persons .. Onos. 3.3' insert 'τύχῃ δ' ὡς ἀστάτῳ πιστευτέον ἑταίρᾳ Iamb.*Protr.* 2'

**ἀστᾰφίς I**, line 2, for 'Tegea' read 'Laconia'; line 5, delete '**σταφίς** .. Theoc. 27.9' and substitute 'see also ‡σταφίς'

**ἀστᾰ́φῡλος**, for 'Aus.*Ep.* 12.24' read 'Aus.*Ep.* 8.24 (p. 243.24 P.)'

**ἀστέγαστος**, delete 'Gal. 17(2).153' (v. °ἀστέγνωτος)

***ἀστέγνωτος**, ον, *uncovered*, Gal.*CMG* 5.10.(2).2.208.10.

**ἀστεῖος**, adv. -ως, add '*nicely, well*, Erasistr.ap.Gal. 9.206.17'

**ἀστειότης**, add '**2** in Rhetor Anon. in *PLit.Lond.* 138 ii 12 app. *citizenship.*'

**ἀστεϊσμός**, for '*wit*' read '*witticism*'; after 'D.H.*Dem.* 54' insert '(pl.)'

**⁺ἀστεμφής**, ές, *motionless, immobile*, σκῆπτρον .. ἀστεμφὲς ἔχεσκεν Il. 3.219, ἀ. οἷη νέκυς Opp. *H.* 2.70; neut. adv. ἀστεμφὲς ἔκειτο Mosch. 4.113. **II** *firm, immovable*, οὐδός Hes.*Th.* 812, θεμέλιος Amph.*Hom.* 1.1; of men, animals, Anacr. 22 P., ἀ. κύων i.e. Cerberus *Trag.adesp.* 658.2 K.-S., ἀστεμφής .. τίγριν ἐλαύνων Nonn.*D.* 11.70, 28.14, *not giving way, unflinching*, Theoc. 13.37, Opp.*H.* 2.446, *C.* 4.174, Agath. 1.21, pr. n. of a Titan, Emp.B 123 D.-K.; adv. -έως Od. 4.419, 459. **2** of bonds, etc., *firm, fast*, ποδάγρη *AP* 6.296 (Leon.Tarent.), ζυγόν Opp.*H.* 1.417, δεσμός 2.84, Nonn.*D.* 40.324. **III** of abst. things, *unmoved*, βουλή Il. 2.344, βίη A.R. 4.1375, δύναμις Plot. 6.8.21; adv. ἀστεμφῶς τὸν βίον διενήξατο Marin.*Procl.* 15. **2** of atmospheric conditions, *unchanging*, νύξ *AP* 9.424 (Duris); neut. adv. ἀλωαὶ .. ἀστεμφὲς μελανεῦσαι Arat. 878.

***ἀστεοπρόσωπος**, ον, *with refined face*, epith. of a boy in paederastic rock inscr., *SEG* 32.847.A16 (Thasos, iv BC).

***ἀστέραρχος**, ὁ, *ruler of the stars*, Ἥλιος *Cat.Cod.Astr.* 9(2).162, 163.

**ἀστεργᾰ́νωρ**, for '*without love of man*' read '*refusing marriage*'

**ἀστερίζω**, add '*turn into stars*, *Placit.* 2.13.3'

**ἀστέριος**, add '**VI** ἀστερία, sc. λίθος, ἡ, a precious stone, Plin.*HN* 37.131.'

***ἀστερομαρμᾰροφεγγής**, ές, *gleaming with stars white as marble*, *Lyr.adesp.* 9 P. (iii BC).

**ἀστεροπός**, add 'as the name of a Cyclops, = Στερόπης, Euph. 51.11'

**ἀστερόφοιτος II**, add 'κόσμου φύσις *PMag.* 4.2552 (= *Hymn.Mag.* 20.26)'

**ἀστή**, add '*PMerton* 5.2'

***ἄστη**, ἡ, Lat. *hasta*, *spear*, δώροις δεδωρημένῳ .. [στε]φάνῳ τειχικῷ ἄστῃ καθαρᾷ οὐηξίλλῳ *IEphes.* 680.16 (i/ii AD). **2** *auction*, *PBeatty Panop.* 2.138, 139 (iv AD).

**ἄστηνος**, after '*miserable*' insert 'Call.*fr.* 275 Pf.' and add 'cf. δύστηνος'

**ἀστήρ I 1**, lines 3/4, for 'ἀ. Ἀρκτοῦρος .. etc.' read 'ἀ. Ἀρκτοῦρος

[Hes.*Op.*] 566, etc.; πλόον ἠελίῳ τε καὶ ἀστέρι τεκμήρασθαι A.R. 1.108' **II**, add 'τὸν ἀγαπητὸν ἀστέρα τῆς οἰκουμένης Them.*Or.* 16.213a' **V**, for this section read 'one or more plants of the *Aster* genus, Nic.*fr.* 74.66, ἀ. Ἀττικός Dsc. 4.119' add '**X** app. part of a bath-house, *SB* 9921.16 (iii AD).'

*__ἀστιάριος__, ὁ, Lat. *hastiarius* (*hastili-*), *grade of cavalry officer*, *SB* 11591.17, 11592.17 (iv AD), *BGU* 1024.5, 8 (iv/v AD, cf. *Berichtigungsl.* 7.17).

*__Ἀστιάς__, άδος, fem. adj., epith. of Artemis at Iasos, Plb. 16.12, *IIasos* 88.3, 92.8, 248.6 (all Rom.imp.).

**ἀστῐβής 1**, add 'X.*Mem.* 3.8.10 (sup.)' **3**, for this section read 'of holy places, *not to be trodden*, ἄλσος S.*OC* 126, Ps.-Hdt. *Vit.Hom.* 21'

*__ἄστῐγος__, ον, *unmarked*, of a corpse, dub. in *PRein.* 92.12 (iv AD).

**ἀστικός I 1**, line 2, for 'epith. of Hecate' read 'epith. of Enodia Ϝαστικά' **II 2**, delete 'ἀστικά .. ἀγροίκως'

*__ἀστίλιον__, τό, cf. Lat. *hastile*, *shaft*, *spear*, *Edict.Diocl.* 14.4 (ἀ- ed.), *SB* 9017.9 (i/ii AD).

*__ἀστιοπόλων__, gen. pl., dub. sens., *IEphes.* 454 (ii/iii AD).

**ἄστολος**, at end read '(sch. ad loc., cod. ἄστονος)'

**ἄστοργος 1**, after '*without natural affection*' insert 'Achae.*fr.* 2.4 S.'

**ἀστός**, lines 1 ff., for 'dist. from πολίτης, ἀστός' read 'dist., prob. wrongly, fr. πολίτης as' add '**II** w. gen., *dweller in*, ἐρημάδος ἀ. ἐρίπνης Nonn.*D.* 25.272; cf. 17.40.'

**ἀστοχέω**, after 'rare in poetry .. *Lyr.Alex.adesp.* 4.21' insert '*Trag.adesp.* 658.2 K.-S.' add '**II** *disregard*, w. gen., τοῦ καλῶς ἔχοντος *PTeb.* 798.14 (ii BC); τοῦ προσώπου Callisth.Olynth. 44.'

⁺__ἀστραβιστήρ__· ὄργανόν τι, ὡς δίοπτρον Hsch.; cf. ἀστραφιστήρ.

**ἀστρᾰγάλη**, after 'for ἀστράγαλος' insert 'Il. 23.88 (v.l.)' and after 'Herod. 3.7' insert '*AP* 6.309 (Leon.Tarent.)'

**ἀστρᾰγᾰλίζω**, add '**II** ἀστραγαλίσαι ἐπὶ τῶν ὑποποδίων perh. describes some method of fastening statues, *Inscr.Cret.* 3.ii 1 8 (ii BC).'

*__ἀστρᾰγᾰ́λιον__, τό, dim. of ἀστράγαλος, *IG* 2$^2$.1533.32, 4$^2$.103.91 (Epid., both iv BC).

**ἀστρᾰ́γᾰλος III**, for '*wrist*' read '*knuckle*' and for 'Lxx *Da.* 5.5, 24' read 'Thd.*Da.* 5.5, 24' **VI**, add 'κατεγλύψαμεν ἀστράγαλον *Didyma* 39.20'

**ἀστρᾰγᾰλωτός**, line 2, for 'Posidon. 9' read 'Posidon. 8'

*__ἀστραγεύτως__, adv., (στραγγεύομαι) *without delay*, prob. in *BGU* 1760.7 (i BC, cf. *Berichtigungsl.* 3.23).

*__ἀστραπαία__, ἡ, a precious stone, Plin.*HN* 37.189, Eust. 827.26.

**ἀστρᾰπαῖος**, before 'α, ον' insert '[-πᾱος (< -παιος), Orph.*H.* 15.9, 20.5]'; for '*IGRom.* .. (Bithyn.)' read '*INikaia* 701, 702 (Rom.imp.); cf. °ἀστραποποιός'

**ἀστρᾰπή**, lines 4/5, personified, add '*Pap.Lugd.Bat.* xxv 8 i 8 (iii AD)'

**ἀστρᾰπηφορέω**, for 'Ar.*Pax* 722' read 'E.*fr.* 312 N. (Ar.*Pax* 722)'

**ἀστρᾰ́πιος**, delete the entry.

*__ἀστρᾰποποιός__, ὁ, *maker of lightning* (title of Zeus), *INikaia* 1505 (Rom.imp.); cf. °ἀστραπαῖος.

**ἀστράπτω II**, after '*flash* or *glance like lightning*' insert 'ὄμματα ἀστράπτοντα Il.Pers. 5.8 B.'

⁺__ἀστρᾰ́τευτος__, ον, *not having done military service* (usu. w. implication of avoidance), Ar.*V.* 1117, Lys. 9.15, D. 24.102, 107, 119, Aeschin. 3.176, ἀ. καὶ λιποτάκτης Ph. 1.144; adv. -τως Poll. 1.159.

**ἀστρᾰτήγητος II**, add 'Sopat.Rh. 8.193.18 W. (v.l. ἀστράτηγος)'

*__ἀστρᾰτηγικῶς__, *not in the manner of a good general*, Sch.Gen.Il. 2.74 (v.l. ἀστρατηγητικῶς).

**ἀστρᾰφιστήρ**, for 'dub. sens. .. ἀστραβιστήρ' read '= °ἀστραβιστήρ (cf. κισσύβιον, κισσύφιον), *IG* 2$^2$.1628.522, 1629.998 (both pl., iv BC)'

**ἄστρεπτος**, for '*without turning the back*' read '*without turning round*'

**ἀστροθέτης**, add '*PHarris* 55.18 (ii AD)'

**ἀστροΐτης**, after '*astriotes*' insert '(nisi leg. *astrites*, cf. Mart.Cap. 1.75 D.)'

*__ἀστρολογογεωμέτρης__, ου, ὁ, *astrological geometrician*, Phld.*Epicur.* 2.6.3 p. 60 V.

**ἄστρον**, line 7, for 'Arist.*Cael.* 290$^a$20' read 'Arist.*Cael.* 290$^a$23'; line 13, after 'S.*OT* 795' insert 'ὑπ' ἄστρα *beneath the stars* i.e. in the open air, *Salamine* 199 (i AD)'

**ἀστρονόμημα**, after '*observation of the stars*' insert 'humorous personification applied to Thales' and add '(= *Suppl.Hell.* 797)'

*__ἀστρόπληκτος__, ον, *star-struck*, Gal. 14.402, Jo.Alch. 266.14.

**ἀστροχί̄των**, add '*Suppl.Hell.* 1051'

**ἄστυ**, line 5, before 'pl.' insert 'dat. ἄστυι *SEG* 30.622 (Maced., i AD)' at end add 'Myc. *wa-tu*; also in compd. pers. n.'

**ἀστῠ́αρχος**, delete the entry.

**ἀστῠνομικός**, add 'as subst., Roman municipal official, Paul.*Dig.* 43.10.1 (cj. ἀστυνόμος)'

**ἀστῠόχος**, at end for '(Ϝαστ-; cf. ἄστυ fin.)' read 'Ϝαστυόχος *IG* 5(2).77 (Tegea, cf. ἄστυ fin.)'

**ἄστῠρον**, for 'Call.*fr.* 19 .. *Hec.* 1.1.6' read '*fr.* 11.5, 75.74, 260.6, 261.2 Pf.'

**ἀσύγγνωστος II**, for 'Gal. 1.13' read 'Gal.*Protr.* 7 (comp.)'

⁺__ἀσυγκόλλητος__, ον, *not soldered on* or *together*, *PVindob.Salomons* 2.2 (ii/iii AD), Sch.Il. 14.200.

**ἀσύγκρῐτος I 2**, add 'of a person, τῷ ἀσυγκρίτῳ ἀδελφῷ *SEG* 33.1196 (Cappadocia, i/ii AD), *IHadr.* 158'

**ἀσῡλεί** or **-ί**, for '*inviolably*' read '*with immunity from* σῦλαι (*seizure on account of reprisals*)'

**ἀσῡλία**, line 3, for 'in inscrr.' read '**b** *immunity from* σῦλαι'

**ἀσυλλόγιστος I 2**, add 'see also °ἀσυλλόχιστος'

*__ἀσυλλόχιστος__, ον, perh. f.l. for °ἀσυλλογιστ-, *not calculated*, of a debt, *PRyl.* 585.10 (ii BC).

**ἄσῡλος I 1**, add 'epith. of Artemis at Perga, *IGRom.* 3.797, *ABSA* 17.231'

**ἀσύλωτος**, delete the entry.

**ἀσυμφᾰνής**, adv. -νῶς, add 'Phlp.*in GC* 55.1'

*__ἀσυνᾰφής__, ές, *disconnected*, Corn.*Rh.* 141 (p. 377 H.).

**ἀσυνδεξίαστος**, add '(v.l.)'

*__ἀσυνειδησία__, ἡ, *lack of conscience*, *POxy.* 3770.12 J. (iv AD).

*__ἀσυνείσφορος__, ον, *not contributing*, Rh. 3.573.5.

**ἀσυνέξωστος**, after 'of an athlete' insert 'perh. *not thrown out of the arena of competition* i.e. unbeaten'

**ἀσύνετος**, line 1, after 'Hp.*Fract.* 31' insert 'prob. in Alc. 67.2 L.-P. (ἀσύνν-)'

**ἀσυνήμων**, add '*Trag.adesp.* 664 ii 23 (both ἀξυν-)'

**ἀσύνθετος II**, line 3, after '*Ep.Rom.* 1.31' insert 'Ptol.*Tetr.* 166'

*__ἀσυνόδευτος__, ον, expl. of *incomitatus* in Virgil glossaries, *PSI* 756.29, *PNess.* 1.965.

**ἀσύντροφον**, for 'βάκτος' read 'βάτος (A) 1'

**ἀσῠ́ρής**, for '*lewd*, *filthy*' read '*dirty*, *filthy*, βρέγμα Herod. 4.51; τἀσυρέ̂ *dirt*, *refuse*, *IG* 1$^3$.2.11 (Marathon, v BC)' and before 'ἄνθρωπος Plb. 4.4.5' insert '**2** *morally debased*, *foul*'

**ἀσύστᾰτος**, add '**9** ἀ. ὀνόματα names of persons *not appointed*, *PLond.* 1249.5 (iv AD).'

*__ἀσυσχημᾰ́τιστος__, ον, *not in* (*astrological*) *relation*, Heph.Astr. 3.7.

**ἀσύφηλος**, add 'ἡ νεότης ἀσύφηλος ἀεὶ θνητοῖσι τέτυκται *Eleg.adesp.* 25.1 W.'

*__ἀσφαλάνθιον__, τό, app. = ἀσπάλαθος, *camel's thorn*, *POxy.* 3733.20, 3766.103 (iv AD).

**ἀσφάλαξ**, add '*SEG* 38.1237.11 (Lydia, iii AD)'

**ἀσφάλεια**, line 1, after 'ἡ' insert 'sp. ἀσπ- *SEG* 23.437 (Thessaly, iii BC)' **I 1**, add '**b** *safeguarding*, *security* of structures, property, etc., ἐποίησαν τὴν τῶν θυρίδων ἀσφάλειαν *CIJud.* 766 (Phrygia, i AD), *IEphes.* 3217.26 (ii AD).' **3**, after 'Lit. Crit.' for '*circumspection*' read '*caution* in use of words, D.H.*Dem.* 2'

⁺__ἀσφάλειος__, ον, also **-ιος** and **-εος**, *that gives a guarantee*, κατὰ τήνδε τὴν ἀσφάλειον *PCair.Isidor.* 105.9 (iii AD), *BGU* 96.6 (iii AD), *PPanop.* 21.18 (iv AD); neut. subst., ὑπὲρ ὑμετέρου ἀσφαλίου *PRainer Cent.* 84.6 (iv AD). **II** epith. of Poseidon, Ar.*Ach.* 682, Paus. 3.11.9, 7.21.7, Plu.*Thess.* 36; form -εος, *Didyma* 132.2, 14 (ii BC); form -ιος, Opp.*H.* 5.680, *IG* 5(1).559.14 (Amydae), Aristid.*Or.* 46(3).1.

*__Ἀσφάλεος__, v. °ἀσφάλειος.

**ἀσφᾰλής I 5**, after 'rhythm' insert 'D.H.*Dem.* 24, al.'; adv., add 'D.H.*Dem.* 26' add '**IV** epith. of Poseidon, = ‡Ἀσφάλειος, *IG* 4$^2$.555 (Epid.).'

**ἀσφᾰλίζω I**, for '**b** *secure* .. in Med.' read '**2** *ensure the safety* or *security of*, *BGU* 829.9 (i AD); esp. in med.' **II 1**, add '*make provision for* in will, *POxy.* 2348.41 (iii AD)' add '**3** *give security*, Modest.*Dig.* 27.1.15.17, 50.12.10.'

⁺__Ἀσφάλιος__, v. °ἀσφάλειος.

**ἀσφάλισμα**, add '**II** in pl., gloss on λέπαδνα, Sch.Gen.Il. 5.730.'

**ἄσφαλτος**, after '*bitumen*' insert 'Alc. 124.7 L.-P. (rest.)'

*__ἀσφᾰράγιον__, τό, written ἀσπαράκιον, dim. of ἀσφᾰ́ρᾰγος (B), *PMich.*inv. 3731 ii 36 (*Tyche* 1.185; ii/iii AD).

**ἀσφᾰ́ραγος** (B), at end (form ἀσπ-) add 'Lang *Ath.Agora* XXI Hd 11 (ii/iii AD)'

**ἀσχημᾰ́τιστος II**, after 'D.H.*Pomp.* 5' insert '*Rh.* 9.13'

**ἄσχημος**, after 'late form for ἀσχήμων' insert '(but Ἄσχειμος as pers. n., *SEG* 25.662, Thessaly, iv BC)'

**ἀσώδης II**, delete '*slimy*'; for '(lyr.)' read '(anap.)' and add 'cf. ἀσώδης· ἀμμώδης Hsch.'

**ἀσώμᾰτος I**, add '**2** *lacking a body*, νέκυς ἀ., i.e. a skull, *AP* 9.52 (Carph.).'

**ἀσωτεῖον**, for 'Longus 4.17' substitute 'Poll. 9.48'

*__ἀτ__, v. °ἀπό.

*__Ἀτᾱβῡριασταί__, οἱ, Διὸς Ἀ. *worshippers of* Zeus *Atabyrios*, *Lindos* 391.31, 392a.12, *IG* 12(1).937.4 (near Lindos, i/ii AD).

*__Ἀτᾱβῠ́ριον__, τό, or **-ιος**, ὁ (ὁ Ἀτάβυρις Str. 14.2.12), mountain in Rhodes, Ζεῦ πάτερ, νώτοισιν Ἀταβυρίου μεδέων Pi.*O.* 7.87, Str. l.c.

*__Ἀτᾱβύριος__, epith. of Zeus in Rhodes and Agrigentum, *ISelge* T 52 (Rhodes, Mt. Ataviro, iv BC), *Lindos* 339 (i AD), *IG* 12(1).891.7 (Lindos, ii AD), Plb. 9.27.7, App.*Mith.* 26.

**ἀτακτέω**, line 5, for '*POxy.* 275.24' read '*POxy.* 275.25'

**ἄτακτος II**, line 5, after '(Pl.*Lg.*) 840e' insert 'of persons, *immoral*, ἀ. τὸν τρόπον *Vit.Sapph.* in *POxy.* 1800 *fr.*1 i 17' add '**4** *unassessed*, πόλις *IG* $1^3$.277.31.' **B** adv., add 'ἄτακτα παίζει *Anacreont.* 59.26 W.'

**ἀτάλαντος**, for '*equal in weight, equivalent to, like*' read '*equal* in some respect *to*' and add 'ἀ. ἀπάντῃ, Emp.B 17.19 D.-K.'

**ἀτᾰλός**, delete 'ἀ. χερσί .. A.*Pers.* 537 (anap.)'; at end for 'Sup. .. *IG* 1.402*a*' read 'sup. ἀταλότατα παίζει *CEG* 432 (viii BC)'

***ἀτᾰνύω**, = τανύω, aor. imper. ἀτάνυσσον, Diosc.epic. 4.16, aor. subj. ἀτανύσσῃς ib. 6.28, w. χεῖραν and dat., *help*, ib. ll.c., 3.25, 13.14, etc.

**ἀτάομαι II**, line 4, after 'Gythium' insert 'cf. ἀγατᾶσθαι (i.e. ἀϝατ-)· βλάπτεσθαι Hsch.'

**ἀτᾰρ 1**, line 11, delete 'sts. after ἐπειδή .. Il. 12.144' **2**, for 'Pl. and Trag.' read 'Attic, except in the orators'; after 'S.*OT* 1052' insert 'Cratin. 200 K.-A., Ar.*Pax* 177, *Av.* 144, al.' **3**, after '(Il.) 270' insert '12.144' and delete 'also in Com., Cratin. 188'

**ἀταρπῑτός**, for 'Ion.' read 'poet.'

**ἄτε II**, line 5, delete 'ἄ. .. A.*Th.* 140 (lyr.)'

***ἀτεγγής**, ές, = ἄτεγκτος II, [οὐ]θε[ί]ς οὕτως ἐστὶν ἐν ἀν[θ]ρώποισιν ἀτενγής *IG* $2^2$.12236.7 (iii BC).

**ἄτεγκτος II**, delete 'Ar.*Th.* 1047'

***ἀτειρήεις**, εσσα, εν, = ἀτειρής II, Nonn.*D.* 35.226.

**ἀτειρής II**, add '**2** *patient in suffering*, *Anacreont.* 56.1 W.'

***ἄτεις**, ὁ, acc. sg. ἄτειν, perh. name of degree of kinship, *MAMA* 3.53 (Cilicia); cf. ἄττα (B).

**ἀτείχιστος**, after 'Lys. 33.7' insert 'τᾶς πόλιος ὑπαρχοίσας ἀτιχίστω *SEG* 28.1540.13 (Cyrenaica, i BC)'

⁺**ἀτέκμαρτος**, ον, *lacking any demarcation*, ἐρημία Plu.*Luc.* 14, θάλασσα Nonn.*D.* 13.537; neut. pl. as adv., fig., ἐπὶ μὰν βαίνει τι καὶ λάθας ἀτέκμαρτα νέφος Pi.*O.* 7.45. **2** *having no sign* or *indication* for the purpose of interpretation, prediction, etc., χρηστήριον Hdt. 5.92γ, μοῖρα (sup.) A.*Pers.* 910, δέος Th. 4.63.1, Pl.*Lg.* 638a, Orph.*A.* 1150; of persons, Ar.*Av.* 170; w. inf., ἀτέκμαρτον προνοῆσαι Pi.*P.* 10.63; adv. -τως *without any indication*, X.*Mem.* 1.4.4. **II** (dub.) *boundless, unlimited*, γαστήρ (i.e. appetite) Opp.*H.* 2.206 (s.v.l.).

**ἀτεκνόω**, after '*make childless*' insert 'πάτρα γάρ μ' ἀτέκνωσε my country *has robbed* me *of children* (by depriving me of life in her service), Bernand *IMEG* 13.11 (Egypt)'

***ἀτεκτόνευτος**, ον, expl. of *infabricatus* in Virgil gloss., *PNess.* 1.854 (vi AD).

**ἀτέλεια**, line 1, before 'Cret.' insert 'Ion. -είη *SEG* 36.982.C8 (Iasos, v BC)' **I**, add '**2** *ineffectualness*, *Schwyzer* 167*a*.*A4*, *B2* (Selinus, v BC).'

**ἀτέλειος**, add '*BMC Caria* no. 20 (Alabanda, Rom.imp.)'

**ἀτέλεστος I**, add '**2** of children cut off before reaching maturity, *MUB* 13.26.1, *IHadr.* 151 (Rom.imp.).' **IV**, add 'neut. pl. as adv., Arat. 678' add '**V** *unfinished*, of buildings, *POxy.* 3691.6 (AD 138).'

**ἀτελής I 2**, line 3, after 'ib. 40' insert 'of a discussion, Pl.*Prt.* 314c' **II 1**, line 2, after '*ineffectual*' insert 'καπνός Simon. 36.3 P.'; line 3, after 'Pl.*Smp.* 179d' insert 'of things, ἔρημον καὶ ἀ. φιλοσοφίαν λείποντες id.*R.* 495c' **III 1 a**, add 'τοῦ σώματος *Inscr.Prien.* 174.6 (ii BC)' **b**, add 'Cypr. *a-te-li-ja* (n. pl.), *ICS* 217.23'

**ἀτενής I**, add '**5** *of close texture, compact*, γῆ ἀ. καὶ σκληρά Plu. 2.640e.' **III**, for 'Hp.*Prorrh.* 1.24' read 'Hp.*Prorrh.* 1.124'

**ἄτερ II**, line 4, for 'also in late prose' read 'in prose, ἀ. ἐμέο *SEG* 37.665 (N. shore Black Sea, *c.*400 BC), ἀ. τῆς Πτολεμαίου γνώμης ib. 9.1.42 (Cyrene, iii BC)'

**ἀτεράμων**, after 'Ar.*Ach.* 181' insert '*V.* 730' and for 'Eub. 1 D.' read 'Eub. 22 K.-A.'

**ἄτερθε II**, add 'Nic.*Th.* 242'

**ἄτερος**, add '*IG* $4^2$.40.11, 15, 41.12, al.; Myc. $a_2$*-te-ro* (= ἅτερον)'

**ἀτερπής**, line 4, for 'Simon. 37.6' read 'Simon. 38.10 P.'

***ἀτέρυι**, Aeol. adv., *in a different place*, Theognost.*Can.* 160; cf. ἀτέριγε.

***ἀτέρωτα**, Aeol. for °ἑτέρωτε, *at another time*, κἀτέρωτα Sapph. 1.5 L.-P., cf. A.D.*Adv.* 1.194.5.

**ἀτεχνής**, add 'adv. ἀτεχνέως in sense of Att. ἀτεχνῶς *TAPhA* 65.105 (Olynthus, iv BC)'

**ἀτεχνία**, after 'Hp.' insert '*VM* 9'

⁺**ἀτέω**, only part. ἀτέων *reckless, heedless*, Il. 20.332, Hdt. 7.223.3; but indic., w. gen., Μουσέων Call.*fr.* 633 Pf.

**ἄτη**, line 1, for 'αὐάτα' read '**ἀυάτα**' and after '(ἀϝ-)' insert 'Alc. 70.12 L.-P., Pi.*P.* 2.28, 3.24, *Lyr.adesp.* 55 P., poet. ἀάτη Call.*fr.* 557 Pf.' and delete 'v. infr.'

**ἄτηκτος I**, add 'Pl.*Sph.* 265c, *Ti.* 60e, al.'

***ἀτηρεύεσθαι**, *act mischievously*, Hsch. s.v. σικελίζειν.

**ἀτηρής**, delete the entry.

**Ἀτθίς 1**, line 2, after 'be read)' insert '*AP* 12.55 (?Artemo)' add '**b** Ἀτθίδες, αἱ, *maidens of Attica*, Call.*fr.* 178.4 Pf.'

**ἀτίζω**, last line, after 'A.R. l.c.' insert 'app. w. inf., ἐρέσθαι .. ἄτισσε id. 2.9'

**ἀτῑμάζω**, line 6, after 'ἄκοιτιν' insert '(also ἠτίμασεν v.l. in Il. 1.11)'

***ἀτῑμᾰσία**, ἡ, = ἀτιμία, Favorin.*Exil.* 17.6, 22.45 B.

**ἀτῑμάω**, line 4, for 'ἠτίμασεν' read 'ἠτίμησ' (v.l. ἠτίμασεν)'

**ἀτῑμία I 2**, add 'as transl. of Lat. *infamia*, Just.*Nov.* 22.22 pr.'

***ἄτῑμιος**, ον, *worthless*, *PMasp.* 1.25 (vi AD).

**ἀτῑτάλτας**, for the pres. ref. read '*Inscr.Cret.* 4.15 (Gortyn, vii/vi BC)'

⁺**ἄτλᾱς**, αντος, ὁ, ἄτλας· ἄτολμος, ἀπαθής Hsch. **2** perh. *insensible, unresponsive*, ἀλλ' οὐκ ἀ. γὰρ βάσανος ἢ Λυδὴ λίθος S.*fr.* 91a R.'

**ἄτλητος 1**, add 'ἄτλητα πεπονθώς Thgn. 1029'

**ἀτμένιος**, for '*toilsome, prepared with trouble*' read '*used by slaves*, i.e. *common*'

**ἀτμή**, after 'Hes.*Th.* 862' add '(v.l.), Dieuch. 15.5 (Orib. 4.7.1)'

**ἀτμήν**, for 'Call.*Aet.* 1.1.19' read 'Call.*fr.* 178.19 Pf.'

**ἀτοκία**, add 'Gp. 12.38.1'

**ἀτόκιος**, after '*medicine for causing it*, Hp.*Mul.* 1.76' read '*a contraceptive* or *abortifacient*, Dsc. 1.77.2, 3.130, 3.134.2, Sor. 1.60 (*CMG* IV p. 45.1, 2, 4, 17)'

**ἀτονέω**, add '**b** *suffer loss of strength*, tab.defix. in *SEG* 35.227.29 (Athens, iii AD). **II** transl. of Lat. *deficio*, *fail to make a claim*, *Cod.Just.* 6.4.4.14d. **2** of a condition, *fail to occur*, Theophil.Antec. 3.1.7.'

**ἄτονος I**, line 1, for 'of the limbs' read 'of the physique' and after 'Hp.*Aër.* 3 (comp.), 19' insert 'Arr.*Epict.* 3.16.7; *deprived of strength*, tab.defix. in *SEG* 35.215.3 (Athens, iii AD)' add '**3** gramm., *unaccented*, Eust. 907.15.'

***ἀτοπέω**, *misconduct oneself*, *PTeb.* 711.5 (ii BC).

**ἀτόπημα 3**, for '*offence*' read '*outrage*' and add '*PFlor.* 5.60.11'

**ἀτράκτιον**, after 'pl.' delete '(written ἀτράκτεια)' and insert '*Inscr.Délos* 1442 B 56 (ii BC)'

**ἄτρακτος II**, after '(S.)*Tr.* 714' insert 'E.*Rh.* 312, *AP* 5.188 (Leon. Tarent.)' and for 'specially Lacon.' read 'in Lacon. apophthegm'

**ἀτρακτῠλίς**, for 'used for making spindles' read 'resembling a spindle covered w. wool' and add 'δοκίδας ἀτρακτυλίδος X.*Cyn.* 9.15'

***ἀτράκτῠλον**, τό, = ἀτρακτυλίς, prob. in Epich. 161.

**ἀτρᾰπός**, line 2, after 'Il. 17.743' insert 'also Alcm. 102 P., *ISmyrna* 521.8 (ii/i BC), Nonn.*D.* 41.39'

⁺**ἀτραυμᾰ́τιστος**, ον, *unwounded, free from wounds*, διάθεσις Aët. 7.9 (261.20 O.); title given to successful boxers, *Entretiens Hardt* 14.236; poet. πόνοι, i.e. not arising fr. wounds, Luc.*Ocyp.* 36.

**ἀτρᾰ́χηλος I**, add 'χιτῶνα .. ἀτράχηλον, i.e. without opening for the neck, Apollod.*Epit.* 6.23'

**ἀτρεκής II 1**, line 3, after 'ad loc.)' insert 'cf. *AP* 5.267 (Agath.)'

**ἀτρέμᾱ 3**, add 'Lyc.*fr.* 2.8 S.'

***ἀτρῑᾱκοστολόγητος**, ον, *not subject to a tax of one-thirtieth*, *IIlion* 52.20 (ii BC); see *Sokolowski* 2.9.20.

⁺**ἄτριον** (A), v. ‡ἤτριον.

***ἄτριον** (B), τό, Lat. *atrium*, Ἴσιδος ἐν ἀτρίῳ *APF* 2.439.42 (ii AD), *IGRom.* 1.1048, 1175 (both Egypt, ii AD) the *Atrium Magnum* at Alexandria, *PFouad* 21.4, *SB* 8247; written ἄτρειον *IStraton.* 15.7, 664.4 (both Caria, i AD); in a private house, *POxy.* 2406 (ii AD).

***ἀτρῐχία**, ἡ, *hairlessness*, Cyran. 35 (1.16.12 K.).

**ἄτρομος**, add 'of personified Φύσις, Orph.*H.* 10.26'

**ἀτροπάμπαις**, for 'dub. sens. in' read '= °παῖς II'; add 'cf. πρᾱτοπάμπαις'; for parenth. note at end read '(ἀτρο- perh. w. syncope fr. ἄτερο(ς))'

**ἄτροπος 3**, delete the section transferring quot. to section 2.

**ἀτρῠ́γετος**, line 1, for 'later η, .. 900' read 'also η, ον Stesich. 32 i 4 P., *IG* $2^2$.3575.9 (ii AD)'; for '*unharvested, barren*' read 'sens. dub., acc. to sch. *unharvested, barren*; ἀτρυγέτοιο· ἀκάρπου ἀβύσσου καὶ ἀπείρου Hsch.'; line 4, after '*h.Cer.* 67, 457' insert 'αἰθέρος ἀτρυγέτας Stesich. l.c.; ἀ. χθών Nonn.*D.* 6.101'

***ἀτρυγόνιστος**, ον, dub. sens., πρόβατα *SB* 8003.20 (iv AD).

**ἀτρῠ́πητος**, add 'ἀ. ψῆφος Poll. 8.123, Phot. s.v. τετρυπημένη ψῆφος (v. τρυπάω 1); rest. in *Lindos* 410 iii 6 (i AD)'

**ἄτρῡτος 1**, add 'ἄτρυτος ἐν πόνοις *Trag.adesp.* 163 K.-S.'

***ἄτρωγλος**, ον, *lacking an aperture, not perforated*, ἀ. καὶ ἄτρητοι Ptol.*Tetr.* 150.

**ἄτρωτος II**, add 'ὅπλον *AP* 12.115, cf. ὅπλα .. ἄρρηκτα καὶ ἄτρωτα δι' ἅπερ σέ φασιν ἄτρωτον εἶναι Antisth.*Od.* 7'; to metaph. exx. add 'μοῖρ' ὦ λιταῖς ἄτρωτε δυστήνων βροτῶν Moschio Trag. 2.2' **III**, add 'of institutions, *Cod.Just.* 1.2.17 pr., Just.*Nov.* 120.11.epilogos'

**ἀττᾰγεινός**, for 'Dorio ap.Ath. 7.322c' read 'Dorio ap.Ath. 7.322e'

***ἀτταγήνη**, ἡ, fem. of ἀτταγήν (cf. Lat. *attagena*), *Edict.Diocl.* 4.30.

***ἀττακίτης** (sp. -ήτης), ου, ὁ, kind of cake, *PGoodsp.Cair.* 30.7.21, al. (ii AD); cf. perh. ἀττανίτης.

***Ἀτταλικός**, ή, όν, *on the Attalic standard*, δραχμή *Inscr.Perg.* 260.13. **2** name of medicinal compound, ἄλλη ἐκ τῶν Μαντίου δυνάμεων Ἀτταλική Asclep.ap.Gal. 13.162.16.

**ἀττάμιος**, v. ‡ἀζήμιος.

**ἀττᾰνίτης**, add '*PStrasb.* 339.7, 12 (*c.* AD 200)'
**ἀττᾰρᾰγος**, after 'Ath. 14.646c' insert 'Sch.Hippon.118 D12 W.'
**Ἀττικίζω I**, add '[D.] 58.37, Isoc. 8.108'
**Ἀττῐκός I**, add '**2** of weight-standard, ταλάντων Ἀ. *SEG* 33.861 (Caria, ii BC); fem. subst., *Attic drachma*, Ἀττικὰς φ' *IMylasa* 455, Ἀτ(τ)ικὰς ιβ' *TAM* 4(1).250, etc.'
**ἀτῠλωτος I**, delete the section.
**ἀτύμβευτος**, add '*EA* 19.58 (Sinope, Rom.imp.)'
**ἄτῠπος I**, add '*balbus et blaesus et atypus isque qui tardius loquitur*, Ulp.*Dig.* 21.1.10; humorous transl. for pr. n. *Balbus*, Cic.*Att.* 12.3.2 (cj.)'
**ἀτῡφία**, add 'M.Ant. 11.6'
**ἄτῡφος**, after 'Timo 9.1' insert '(*Suppl.Hell.* 783), Cic.*Att.* 6.9.2, Ael.*VH* 2.20, 4.9'
**ἀτῠχέω 1**, add 'w. internal acc., τῶν ἀτυχησάντων τὴν τῶν Μανιχαίων ἀσεβῆ πλάνην *Cod.Just.* 1.5.15' **3**, line 3, after 'Eup. 114' insert 'οὐθενὸς ἀ. τοῦ δήμου τῶν δικαίων *IG* 2².275.5, 360.41'
***ἄτω**, ἰάπτεται· ἄτει, βλάπτει Sch.Nic.*Al.* 251c Ge.
**ἀτῶμαι**, for 'v. ἀτάω' read 'v. ἀτάομαι'
**αὖ IV**, delete the section.
***ἀυάδεες, ἀυάδην**, v. °ἀηδής.
***αὐαντήρ**, ῆρος, ὁ, *he that parches*, epith. of Zeus, *IG* 2².2606 (iv BC) (prob.).
**αὐαρά**, add 'cf. ἄλαρα'
**αὐγάζω I**, line 3, before '*AP* 9.221' insert 'Call.*fr.* 85.15 Pf.' **II 1**, for 'sun' read 'heavenly bodies' and add '(ἀστέρες) αὐγάζοντες ἀεὶ νυκτὸς ζοφειδέα πέπλον Orph.*H.* 7.10, *AP* 5.123 (Phld.)'
**αὐγή 1**, add 'also *light* (*rays*) of the moon, *h.Hom.* 32.12, Plu. 2.658b, f.' **2**, add '**b** ἐννέα αὐγὰς ἠελίου nine *days*, Nic.*Th.* 275.' **5**, after 'eyes' insert '*h.Merc.* 361'
***Αὐγουστάλης**, ὁ, Lat. *Augustalis* (subst.), *SEG* 29.614 (pl., Maced., Rom.imp.).
***αὐγουσταλιανός**, ή, όν, fr. Lat. *augustalis*, τάξις *POxy.* 1882.4, 8 (vi AD), *PWash.Univ.* 6.4 (vi/vii AD), Just.*Edict.* 13.2.
**⁺Αὐγουστάλιος** (s.v. Αὔγουστος), ὁ, *priest in the cult of Augustus*, *MAMA* 1.169, 216, 283 (Laodicea Combusta), Just.*Edict.* 13.1 pr. **2** title given to the prefect of Egypt, Lyd.*Mag.* 2.3 (p. 57.24 W.), *PStrassb.* 255.9; of Thebais, *SB* 7439.6 (vi AD).
**Αὔγουστος I**, add 'ἀεισέβαστος Ἄγουστος (sic) *SEG* 9.356.2 (Cyrenaica, AD 501); fem., as title of Empress, Εὐδοκίας Αὐγούστης *SEG* 32.1502 (Palestine, *c.*AD 455); as title of a legion, *SEG* 31.626 (Αὐγοστ-, Maced., *c.*AD 200)' **II**, for this section read 'the month *August*, Plu.*Num.* 19; καλανδῶν Αὐ. *Cat.Cod.Astr.* 2.145, al., μη(νὶ) Ἀγούστου *TAM* 4(1).356, written Ἄκοστος *SB* 9529.12 (vi/vii AD)'
**αὐδάζομαι 2**, after '*name*' insert 'w. double acc., Nic.*Th.* 464'; after 'Lyc. 892' and after 'Id. 360' insert '(v.l.)'
**αὐδάω II 2**, line 3, for 'A.*Th.* 1048' read 'A.*Th.* 1042, 1043'
**αὐδή 1**, after 'Il. 1.249' insert 'θεῷ ἐναλίγκιος αὐδήν 19.250, Od. 1.371, 9.4, Sapph. 1.6 L.-P. (αὔδα)'
**αὐδήεις**, add '(contr. **αὐδῆς** Hdn.Gr. 2.618)'
***αὐδιτώριον**, τό, Lat. *auditorium*, *hall of justice*, *IEphes.* 3009 (sp. αὐδειτ-), Just.*Nov.* 50 pr.
**Αὐδυναῖος**, after '*IG* 12(3).254' insert '(Anaphe, iii BC)' and add 'Αὐδον- *SB* 7341.2 (iii AD) and note on p. 53; Αὐδν- *SEG* 29.1161, Αὐδνίος *SEG* 31.989 (Lydia, ii AD), Αὐδαναῖος *SEG* 7.1.15 (Susa, i AD), Αἰδοναῖος *SEG* 25.712 (Thessalonica, ii AD)'
**⁺αὐεοῦλλαι** or **ἄυελλα**, v. °ἄελλα.
**αὐερύω II**, for this section read '*suck up, absorb*, αὐ. τὸ φίλημα *AP* 5.285.5 (Agath.); of leeches, Opp.*H.* 2.603'
***Αὐζησία**, v. °Αὐξησία.
**αὐθᾰδεια**, for '*wilfulness, stubbornness*' read '*concern for one's own interests, self-interest, self-centredness*' and add '*PCair.Isidor.* 74.11 (IV AD)'
**αὐθᾰδης 1**, for '*self-willed, stubborn*' read '*acting to please oneself, self-regarding*' and add 'E.*El.* 1117' **2**, add '*not concerned to please others*, αὐ. κάλλος, of the style of Thucydides, D.H. *Comp.* 22' **3**, after '-έστερον' insert 'Th. 8.84.2'
**αὐθᾰδιάζομαι**, delete 'J.*BJ* 5.3.4'
**αὐθαίμων**, add '*AP* 6.14 (Antip.Sid.)'
**αὐθαίρετος**, at end delete '*independently*, Luc.*Anach.* 34'
**αὖθε**, for 'αὖθέ περ' read 'ἀλ(λ)' αὖθε πὲρ γᾶς τᾶσδε ..'; after 'Cierium' insert 'v BC'
**αὐθέκαστος 1**, line 4, for 'Ph. 2.51' read 'Ph. 2.519' **3**, at end before 'Phld.*Vit.* p. 30 J.' insert 'Aristo ap.'
***αὐθεντεύω**, = αὐθεντέω, *Cat.Cod.Astr.* 8(3).196.12.
**αὐθέντης 1** and **2**, invert order of these sections; for '*murderer*' read '*perpetrator of a murder* or *death*' and delete '*suicide*'
**αὐθεντία 1**, add '**b** as honorary appellation (of praetorian prefect), Just.*Nov.* 111 epilogus.'
**αὐθεντικός 2**, line 4, after 'Ptol.*Tetr.* 182' insert 'σπουδὴ *IMylasa* 134.2, 6 (ii BC)' add '**3** subst., αὐ. τό, *original copy*, *PFam.Teb.* 31.13 (ii AD), v. °ἔκβασος.'
***αὐθεντόπωλος**, ὁ, *son* (*slave*) *of the master*, Sch.Aristid. p. 54.10 D.
***αὐθῆμαρ**, v. αὐτῆμαρ.
**αὐθημερῐνός**, add '**5** τὸ αὐ. τοῦ ἡλίου solar *longitude for given date*, Cod.Vat.Gr. 1058.265ʳ.10.'
**αὐθήμερος II**, add 'also **αὐταμερόν** Herzog *Heilige Gesetze von Kos* 8*B*21, *Tit.Cam.* 218, *Schwyzer* 633.9 (Aeol., Eresos ii/i BC)'
**αὖθι 3**, after 'Call.*Dian.* 241' insert '*fr.* 197.49 Pf.'; add 'see also αὖθε'
**αὖθις**, lines 2/3, after '(id.*OC*) 1438' insert 'E.*fr.* 35, codd. in *Supp.* 679, al.; Ar.*Av.* 1326'; before 'Adv.' insert 'Cret. αὖτιν *Leg.Gort.* 4.3' **III**, after 'Pl.*Ap.* 24b' insert 'sim. ἐπ' αὖθις ἀγωνοθετοῦντος καὶ προκαθεζομένου τοῦ ἀνδρός μου, ἐπ' αὖθις δὲ τῶν ἐξ ἐμοῦ γεννηθησομένων τέκνων Modest.*Dig.* 50.12.10'
***αὐθοπτικός**, ή, όν, v. αὐτοπτικός II.
***αὐθόριστος**, ον, *self-defining*, David *Proll.* 14.23.
**αὐθυπόστᾰτος**, adv., add 'Procl.*Inst.* 41, 86 D.'
**αὖλαξ**, line 2, for '(q.v.)' read 'A.*Th.* 593, S.*OT* 1211, E.*Ph.* 18, Emp.B 100.3 D.-K.'
***Αὐλαρίοκος**, ὁ, epith. of Apollo, *IGBulg.* 1859, 1860 (both ii AD).
***Αὐλαρκηνός**, ὁ, epith. of Apollo, *IGBulg.* 802, 841, *SEG* 37.652 (Bosphorus, *c.*AD 100), also Αὐλαρχ- *IGBulg.* 801.
**αὐλέω I 1**, for '*flute*' read '*aulos*'; line 4, after 'Plu.*Alc.* 32' insert 'w. ellipsis of μέλος (or sim.), αὔλει, Παρθενί, Πανός Men.*Dysc.* 432' **II**, for 'generally, *play*' read '*play* any wind instrument'
**αὐλή I - III**, for these sections read '*enclosed courtyard* (in a farm, palace, private house, etc.), Il. 4.433, 6.247, 11.774, Od. 14.5, Hdt. 3.77.2, Ar.*V.* 131, Pl.*Prt.* 311a, *SIG* 1044.17 (Halic., iv/iii BC), Theoc. 25.99, 27.36; in a temple, ἱεροῦ *IG* 2².1299.28 (Eleusis, iii BC), Lxx *Ps.* 83(84).3. **2** w. ref. to the whole complex of buildings enclosing the courtyard, *court, hall* or sim., Ζηνὸς αὐ. Od. 4.74; τὴν Διὸς αὐλήν A.*Pr.* 122 (lyr.); ἀγρονόμοις αὐλαῖς S.*Ant.* 786 (lyr.); χαλκοδέτοις αὐλαῖς ib. 946; id.*Ph.* 153; used as equiv. of Lat. *villa*, D.H. 6.50.'
***αὐλήεις**, εσσα, εν, *living in an* αὐλή, Arist.*fr.* 171, cj. for αὐδήεσσα in Od. 5.334.
**αὔλημα**, for '*piece of music for the flute*' read '*performance on the aulos*'
**αὔλησις**, for '*flute-playing*' read '*aulos-playing*'
**⁺αὐλητήριον**· τόπος παρὰ Ταρεντίνοις Hsch.; transf., of a noisy place, σύμμικτον ὥστε γλεῦκος αὐλητήριον *Trag.adesp.* 420 K.-S. (s.v.l.).
**αὐλητής**, for '*flute-player*' read '*piper*'
**αὐλητικός**, passim, for '*flute*' read '*aulos*'
**αὐλήτρια**, after 'αὐλητρίς' insert '*Hesperia* 37.368 (Athens, iv BC)' and add 'Arc. 95.15'
**αὐλητρίς**, for '*flute-girl*' read '(*female*) *piper*' and for 'Simon. 178' read '*AP* 5.159.1 ([Simon.])'
**αὐλιάδες**, for 'nymphs *protecting cattle-folds*' read 'prob. *cave-dwelling* nymphs'
***Αὐλιδεία**, ἡ, title of Artemis, *SEG* 25.542 (Aulis, Rom.imp.).
**αὐλίζομαι**, line 8, for 'Eup. 322 (= 347 K.-A.)' read 'Eup. 347 K.-A., *spend the night in the open*, *SEG* 23.305 (Delphi, ii BC, act. form αὐλιζόντω)'
**αὔλιον**, after 'τό' insert '(parox. in pap. at Call.*fr.* 181.6 Pf.)'; delete '*country house, cottage*' and transfer '*h.Merc.*' to follow '*stable*, etc.'; for 'prov. .. Cratin. 32' read 'βοῦς ἐν αὐλίῳ, prov., of what is discarded as useless, Cratin. 32 K.-A., Longus 4.18.3' add '**III** any *dwelling*, *AP* 9.424 (Duris).'
**αὔλιος**, line 2, for 'Call.*fr.* 539' read 'Call.*fr.* 177.6 Pf.'
**⁺αὖλις**, ιος, ἡ, *place for passing the night in, bivouac*, ἐγγὺς .. νηῶν .. αὖλιν ἔθεντο Τρῶες Il. 9.232; meton., εἰ .. ἄγχι .. νὺξ αὖλιν ἄγει Nic.*Th.* 58. **2** *accommodation* for cattle, etc., *h.Merc.* 71, *h.Ven.* 168, E.*Cyc.* 363, Call.*Dian.* 87, Theoc. 25.18, *AP* 6.221 (Leon.Tarent.). **b** *resting-place* for birds, wild animals, Od. 22.470, Theoc. 25.169, Arat. 1027.
**αὐλο-**, in compds. of αὐλός for '*flute*' read '*aulos*'
**αὐλοβόας**, '*IG* 3.82' read '*IG* 2².3118.6 (Attica, ii AD)'
**αὐλοποιός**, add '*SEG* 18.36.A433 (Attica, iv BC)'
**αὐλός 1**, for '*pipe, flute, clarionet*' read '*oboe-type musical instrument, reed-pipe, aulos*'; lines 8/9, for 'pl., αὐλοί .. (Aegina)' read '**b** pipe of a compound instrument: of organ, Simp.*in Ph.* 681.7; of syrinx, *IG* 4.53 (Aegina, Rom.imp.). **c** Τυρρηνὸς αὐλός, = ὕδραυλις, Poll. 4.70.' **3**, add 'pl., = Lat. *tibiae*, *cannon-bones* of a horse, *shanks*, Opp.*C.* 1.189' at end add 'prob. Myc. *au-ro*, part of chariot (cf. section I 2)'
**ἀὐλότης**, add '(cj. ταὐτότης)'
***αὐλοφύλαξ**, ακος, ὁ, app. *house-watchman*, *PCair.Zen* 292.58 (iii BC).
***αὐλύδριον**, τό, dim. of αὐλή, *small house with courtyard*, *PSI* 915.4 (i AD, -ίδρ- pap.), *PMich.*II 123ʳ.19.33, 21.36, al. (i AD), *PSoterichos* 25.20 (ii AD), *PAbinn.* 63.5 (iv AD).
**αὐλών 3**, add '*Peripl.M.Rubr.* 25'
**⁺αὐλωνίζω, -ίζουσα**· ἐν αὐλῶσιν (ἐναύλως cod.) διάγουσα Hsch.
**αὐξάνω**, line 13, after 'Pl.*R.* 497a' insert 'later **αὐξέω**, ηὔξουν D.C.*fr.* 89.3 (ηὔξουν cod.), αὐξοῦνται Plu. 2.724f, αὐξούμενον dub. in

*GVI* 1903.3 (Megara, iii AD), αὐξῶν Ps.-Aristid.*Rh.* 1.505 S., cf. Procop.Gaz.*Ep.* 86' **I 1**, for '*increase* .. Pi.*fr.* 153, etc.' read '*cause to grow*, δενδρέων δὲ νομὸν Διώνυσος .. αὐξάνοι Pi.*fr.* 153 S.-M.; *increase*' **5**, after 'name of a *fallacy*' insert '(= σωρίτης)' **II 2**, line 2, delete '*grow* up'

**Αὐξησία**, add 'also **Αὐζησία**, *IG* 4.1588.28 (Aegina, v BC)'

**αὔξησις 1**, add 'in logic, ὁ περὶ αὐξήσεως λόγος (= σωρίτης) Plu. 2.1083a'

***αὐξήτειρα**, ἡ, *she who gives growth* or *increase*, of Artemis, oracle in *ZPE* 92.269 (Ephesus, ii AD).

**αὐξητέον**, before 'Men.' insert 'Arist.*Rh.* $1376^{b}7$'

**αὔξι**, add '*BCH* suppl. 8.291 (iv/v AD); also **αὔξε** *SEG* 34.1306 (Pamphylia, iii AD); **αὔξησι** *SEG* 34.1418 (Cyprus, ii/iii AD)'

**αὔξις**, add '*PMich.*XI 617.15 (AD 145/6)'

**αὐξίς**, before 'Nic.*Al.* 469' insert 'but dub. sens. in'

***αὐξιφάής**, ές, of the moon, *increasing its light*, *waxing*, Heph.Astr. 2.36.1, Man. 5.174, al., *Cat.Cod.Astr.* 8(4).217.19.

**αὐξίφωνος**, delete the entry.

***αὐξίφως**, φωτος, of the moon, *increasing in light*, *waxing*, Heph.Astr. 2.33.9, 2.36.6, al.

**αὐξίφωτος**, add 'Σελήνη Heph.Astr. 2.35.4, 2.36.15'

**αὐξομείωσις**, add '**III** *gradation*, ἀ. τῶν ἀξιωμάτων Ptol.*Tetr.* 176.'

***αὐξομειωτικός**, ή, όν, *varying in period*, *Cat.Cod.Astr.* 7.194.18.

***αὔξων**, v. °ἄξων.

**αὖος**, line 2, for 'Philostr.*VS* 1.21.1' read 'Philostr.*VS* 1.20.2'

**ἀϋπνία**, after 'Pl.*Lg.* 807e' insert '*Trag.adesp.* 664.26 K.-S.'

**ἄϋπνος**, line 3, after 'S.*Aj.* 880' insert '[φρου]ρεῖν ἀΰπνοις φυλακαῖσιν orac. in *SEG* 30.175.14 (Athens, iv BC)'

**αὔρα 1**, delete 'esp. a cool breeze .. morning' **2**, for 'metaph. .. Ar.*Av.* 1717' read '*exhalation*, *effluvium*, θυμιαμάτων αὖραι Ar.*Av.* 1717'; after 'Dionys.Com. 2.40' read 'transf. *influence*, αὔρη φιλοτησίῃ Opp.*H.* 4.114, δαίμονος αὐ. *AP* 6.220.9 (Diosc.)' **3**, add 'μικρά τις ἀπελείπετο αὔρα βοηθείας Ph. 2.559' **5**, for 'Gal. 8.94' read 'Gal. 8.194.17'

***αὐράριος**, ὁ, Lat. *aurarius*, *goldsmith*, *MAMA* 1.214, 281, al. (Laodicea Combusta), 3.254, 348b (Corycus); pl., guild in Miletus w. reserved area in the theatre, τόπος αὐραρίων Βενέτω(ν) *BE* 1977.82 (see also *SEG* 36.1053 note); but some connect w. *aurarii sunt laudatores vel fauctores*, i.e. *supporters*, *Gloss.* 5.616.1, Serv.ad *Aen.* 6.816, 204; *qui favoribus splendidos, hoc est claros, faciunt*, Priscian.*Inst.* 3.509.33.

**αὔρηκτος**, for 'Hdn.Gr. 2.171' read 'Hdn.Gr. 2.271'

**αὔριον III**, line 3, after 'S.*OC* 567' insert 'also ἡ ἐς αὔριον Ps.-Hdt.*Vit.Hom.* 433'

***αὐροχάλκειος**, ον, = ὀρειχάλκινος, θύραι *CISem.* 2.3914 (Palmyra, ii AD), also -κεος, λάμναι *Hippiatr.Paris.* 346 (II 56 O.-H.).

***αὐρόχαλκος**, ον, *of gilded bronze*, Ἔρωτες *IEphes.* 3015.3 (iii AD), *Edict.Diocl.* 15.63a.

**αὑσαυτοῦ**, add '[Βακ]χυλὶς Δαματρίου αὑσαυτὰν καὶ τὸ[ν υἱόν (?)] Εὔφορβον Νίκωνος θεοῖς *SEG* 23.224 (Messene, Rom.imp.); also cf. αὐτοσαυτόν'

**αὐσόν**, add 'prob. for αὖον; but cf. αὐσὸς δέ ἐστιν ἡ κάμινος παρὰ τὸ ἀτμόν τινα ἀφιέναι David *Proll.* 41.15'

**Αὐσονία**, line 3, after 'ib. 363, al.' insert '**Αὐσώνιοι**, Hsch.' and after 'also' insert 'Αὔσων, ὁ, *AP* 11.24'; line 4, after 'aborigines):' insert '**Αὐσονιῆες**, D.P. 333, al.'

***Αὐσονίδης**, ου, ὁ, *Italian*, Αὐσονίδην .. ἀγακλυτὸν Ἀντωνῖνον *IG* $2^2$.3411.7 (ii AD).

***Αὐσονικός**, ή, όν, *Italian*, Mosch. 3.94.

***Αὐσονίτης**, ου, ὁ, masc. ethnic, *Italian*, Lyc. 593; fem. adj. -ῖτις, -ιδος, id. 44, 702, 1355.

**αὔτανδρος**, line 3, after 'Sosyl. p. 31 B.' insert 'Call.*fr.* 7.33 Pf.'

**αὐτάρ**, after '*IG* $1^2$.1012' insert 'vi BC'; for '*Inscr.Cypr.* 57 H.' read '*a-u-ta-ra*, *ICS* 235, 242, al.'

***αὐταρχία**, ἡ, *absolute rule*, D.C. 45.1.3, 53.4.3, 54.12.2.

**αὑταυτοῦ**, penultimate line, after 'Sophr. 19 (-τᾶς Pors.)' insert 'cf. ‡αὐσαυτοῦ, αὐτοσαυτόν'; delete 'also αὐτοῦτα' to end.

**αὖτε II 2**, after '(A.)*Ag.* 553' insert 'Democr.*fr.* 172 D.-K.'; antepenultimate line, delete 'not in prose'

**αὐτεῖ**, line 1, after 'αὐτοῦ' insert 'Alcm. 1.79 P.'; line 2, after 'αὐτί' insert 'Corinn. 39 *fr.* 7.5 P.'

***αὐτενεργητικός** or **αὐτοεν-**, ή, όν, = αὐτενέργητος, Choerob. *in Theod.* 2.19.25.

**αὐτενίαυτος**, add 'w. advl. sense, *in the same year*, ἐπ[ὶ δ' ἐσ]πετο αὐτενίαυτο[ς] καὶ πόσις *SEG* 30.578 (Maced.)'

**αὐτεξουσιότης**, add '**2** *freedom from patria potestas*, Just.*Nov.* 81.1 pr.'

***αὐτεφόδιος**, ον, *paying one's own travelling expenses*, *SEG* 33.861.20 (Euromos, ii BC), *IKeramos* 14.20 (i AD).

**ἀϋτή**, at end after 'Corc.' insert 'early vi BC'

**αὐτῆμαρ**, add 'Call.*Del.* 46, Coluth. 199, also αὐθῆμαρ *CEG* 815.2 (Epid., iv BC), 894.13 (Delphi, iv BC)'

+**αὐτημερόν**, v. αὐθημερόν.

**αὐτίκα**, line 1, after 'Adv.' insert 'Lesb. αὔτικα, Sapph. 31.10, 44.13, 30.2 L.-P.'; line 4, for 'Sapph.*Supp.* 20a.13' read 'Sapph. 44.13 L.-P.' **I 2**, add 'in phr. w. prep., ἐπωλήθη πρὸς αὐτίκα *SEG* 37.917.B3 (Erythrae, v/iv BC)' **3**, add '**b** perh., *at length*, A.R. 2.946, 3.23, 521, 4.1547.' **II**, line 3, for 'Pl.*Prt.* 395e' read 'Pl.*Prt.* 359e'

+**αὖτις, αὖτιν**, v. ‡αὖθις.

**αὐτίτης II**, after '*home-made*' insert '(or perh. for αὐτοέτης, cf. αὐτοετίτης)'

**ἀϋτμή**, add '[disyllabic in Hes.*Th.* 862, s.v.l.]'

***αὐτοανεξοδίαστος**, ον, *absolutely unsaleable*, *INikaia* 127 (Rom.imp.).

**αὐτογένεθλος**, for 'sq.' read 'αὐτογενής' and for '*Orac.Chald.* 32' read 'πατρικὸς νόος *Orac.Chald.* 39 P.'

***αὐτογεννήτωρ**, ορος, ὁ, *self-originator*, δεῦρό μοι, ὁ αὐτογεννήτωρ θεέ *Suppl.Mag.* 65.31 (iii AD).

**αὐτόγρᾰφος**, for 'τὸ αὐ. *one's own writing*' read 'ἔλεγχος'; add 'τὰ .. τῶν παλαιῶν αὐτόγραφα ψηφίσματα *original drafts*, Posidon. 253.152 E.-K.'

**αὐτοδάκής**, after 'Hsch.' insert '(= *Suppl.Hell.* 1072)'

***αὐτοδιαφορά**, ἡ, *absolute differentia*, Simp. *in Cat.* 276.25, 30.

**αὐτοδίδακτος**, line 2, after '(lyr.)' insert 'ὃν Πιερὶς αὐτοδίδακτον θῆκ' *SEG* 37.1175.10 (Cremna, Pisidia, ii AD)'

**αὐτοδόξαστον**, after '*abstract*' insert 'Alex.Aphr. *in Top.* 572.17'

**αὐτοέν**, after 'τό' insert 'gen. αὐτοενός Procl.*Inst.* 4 D.'

***αὐτοενεργητικός**, v. °αὐτοενεργητικός.

***αὐτοένωσις**, εως, ἡ, *absolute union*, Plot. 6.1.26.

**αὐτοεξούσιος**, add 'see also αὐτεξούσιος'

***αὐτοεξουσιότης**, v. ‡αὐτεξουσιότης.

**αὐτοετής**, after 'J.*AJ* 3.9.3' insert 'i.e. *holding an office in the same year* (as another office), προφήτης *Didyma* 270, 278.3, 283, etc.; cf. αὐτοετεις ἱεροὺς .. στεφάνους ib. 229 II 8 (metr., all Rom.imp.)'

***αὐτοζώη**, ἡ, *absolute life*, Plot. 3.8.8.

**αὐτόζωος**, add '*GVAK* 25.6'

**αὐτοκάβδᾱλος II**, for '*buffoons, improvisers*' read '*reciters of improvised verses*' and transfer 'Eup. 200 (for which read 192.195 K.-A.)' to section I

**αὐτοκᾰσιγνήτη**, add 'λελίητο νέεσθαι αὐτοκασιγνήτηνδε A.R. 3.647, *Suppl.Hell.* 1168.4'

**αὐτοκᾰσίγνητος**, add '*IHadr.* 168.3 (ii/iii AD)'

**αὐτοκέλευθος**, at end for '[Nonn.*D.*] 21.167' read '[Nonn.*D.*] 21.169'

***αὐτοκῑβώτιον**, *the ideal box*, Alex.Aphr. *in Metaph.* 553.23.

**αὐτοκῑνησία**, after '= sq.' insert 'Alex.Aphr. *in Top.* 297.23'

**αὐτοκίνητος**, after '*PMasp.* 122.3 (vi AD)' insert '*Cod.Just.* 1.3.43.4, al.'

**αὐτοκρᾰτωρ I 3**, add '**b** the seventh month in Cyprus (in honour of Augustus), *Hemerolog.Flor.* p. 72 (p. 8 K.).'

***αὐτόκῠβος**, ὁ, *the ideal cube*, Alex.Aphr. *in Metaph.* 816.30.

**αὐτόκυκλος**, after '*form of circle*' insert 'Alex.Aphr. *in Metaph.* 816.29'

***αὐτολείπω**, *leave behind*, τέσσαρας αὐτολιπὼν υἱούς *BCH* 25.21 (Bithynia, Rom.imp.).

***αὐτόλευκος**, ον, τὸ αὐ, *ideal whiteness*, Alex.Aphr. *in Metaph.* 771.1.

+**αὐτολήκῠθος**, ὁ, *one who carries his own oil-flask*, *a parasite* or sim., Antiph. 17 K.-A., Men.*fr.* 91, 182 K.-Th., Luc.*Lex.* 10, Plu. 2.50c; adopted as a sobriquet by a group of young men about town, D. 54.14.

***αὐτολόγος**, ὁ, *the very word*, Cels.ap.Orig.*Cels.* 2.31.

**αὐτολόχευτος**, add 'Nonn.*D.* 37.68, *PMag.* 4.458'

***αὐτόλῠρος**, ον, ποιητὴς αὐ. poet *who accompanies himself upon the lyre*, *PBremen* 59.14 (ii AD).

**αὐτομᾰθεια**, delete 'also **-μᾰθία**'

***αὐτόμαργος**, ον, dub. sens., prob. in A.*fr.* 451i.5 R.

***αὐτοματάρειον**, τό, *vessel for spontaneous digestion* of minerals, dub. in Olymp.Alch. 91 (v.l. αὐτῷ τῷ βοταρίῳ, i.e. βωταρίῳ).

***αὐτοματάριος**, ὁ, *maker of automata*, *POxy.* 2873.21 (-ις, iii AD).

***Αὐτομάτειος**, ον, of °Αὐτομάτη, -είου sc. ὕδατος *PMilan.* 17.18.

***Αὐτομάτη**, ἡ, name of a spring at Argos, Call.*fr.* 65.1, 66.8 Pf., *PMilan.* 17.14.

**αὐτομᾰτίζω**, add '**5** *prophesy spontaneously*, ὁ Ἀπόλλων αὐτομάτιξεν Βάττῳ *SEG* 9.3.24 (Cyrene, iv BC), Aristid. *Or.* 28(49).103, Ath. 1.31b; pass., Sch.E.*Andr.* 445.'

**αὐτομᾰτισμός**, for 'Phleg.*Mir.* 1' read 'Phleg. 36.1.4 J., D.H.*Comp.* 25'

**αὐτόμᾰτος II**, line 7, after 'X.*An.* 1.3.13' insert 'παρὰ τοῦ αὐ. Aen.Tact. 6.2' **III**, adv. -τως, add 'αὐ. ἤνθησα καὶ ἤκμασα *SEG* 33.1406.11 (Termessus, ii/iii AD)'

***αὐτόμεγα**, τό, *absolute size*, πρὸς αὐ. (gen. indecl.) Plot. 3.6.17.

***αυτομενις**, unexpld. item in temple inventory, αυτομενις ξυλ(ιν-) περικεχ(ρυσωμεν-) α' *POxy.* 3473.13 (ii AD), *BGU* 387 ii 4 (ii AD).

**αὐτομόλησις**, add 'Arr.*fr.* 10 J.'

**αὐτομολία**, add '**II** pl., *suckers* or *shoots* of trees, Poll. 7.146; cf. μολεύω.'

**αὐτόμολος 1**, add '*volunteer*, in unpublished inscr. listing αὐτόμολοι, app. a Maced. garrison, *SEG* 37.280 (Argos, iv BC)'
**αὐτονοέω**, shd. precede **αὐτονομέομαι**.
***αὐτονομαστί**, adv., *by its very name*, Gal. 17(2).26.
**αὐτόξῠλος**, for '*of one piece of wood*' read '*of wood in its natural state*, i.e. rough, unpolished, etc.'
***αὐτοοικία**, ἡ, *ideal house*, Alex.Aphr. *in Metaph.* 553.23.
***αὐτοουρᾰνός**, ὁ, *the very heaven*, Alex.Aphr. *in Metaph.* 198.15.
***αὐτοπᾰτήρ**, ὁ, *the very father*, Alex.Aphr. *in Metaph.* 126.13.
***αὐτόπερᾰς**, ᾰτος, τό, *abstract limit*, Procl. *in Prm.* p. 875, Anon. *in Cat.* 67.32, Simp. *in Cat.* 337.31.
***αὐτόπλᾰτος**, τό, *ideal plane*, Alex.Aphr. *in Metaph.* 127.10.
***αὐτοποιέω**, *create by oneself*, Numen.*fr.* 16.11 P.
**αὐτοποιός**, after 'S.*OC* 698 (lyr.)' insert '(αὐτόποιος codd., perh. fr. ποία = πόα)'; delete '*made by one's own hand*' to end. add '**II** αὐτοποιόν, τό, *abstract quality*, Alex.Aphr. *in Metaph.* 563.1.'
***αὐτοποσότης**, ητος, ἡ, *quantity in itself*, Simp. *in Cat.* 130.12.
**αὐτοπρᾱγία**, add 'Iamb.*Protr.* 21 ιδ' (115.3 P.)'
***αὐτοπραξία**, ἡ, *privilege of collecting one's own taxes*, *IG* 9²(1).137.20 (Calydon, ii BC).
**αὐτόπρεμνος**, add 'Eup. 260.25 K.-A. (s.v.l., pap. αὐτόπρυμνος)'
**αὐτοπροαίρετος**, add '*SEG* 36.1051.6 (Miletus, ii AD)'
***αὐτοπῡρᾰμίς**, ίδος, ἡ, *the ideal pyramid* (v. πυραμίς I 2), Alex.Aphr. *in Metaph.* 816.29.
**αὐτοπῡρίτης**, for 'Luc.*Pisc.* 44' read 'Luc.*Pisc.* 45'
***αὐτόρρευστος**, ον, = αὐτόρρυτος, Ps.-Democr.ap.Moses Alch. 313.9; Anon.Alch. 20.2.
**αὐτόρῠτος**, add 'μέλι *Lyr.Alex.adesp.* 37.10'
**αὐτός**, line 2, after '*Leg.Gort.* 3.4, al.' insert 'ἀτός *PHal.* 1.130 (iii BC), *PTeb.* 812.9 (ii BC), *SEG* 29.771 (Thasos, ii BC)' **I 1**, for '*one's true self* .. Il. 1.4' read '*one's real* (*bodily*) *self*, opp. an εἴδωλον or sim., Il. 1.4, Od. 11.602' **3**, add 'οὐκ αὐτὸς ὁ Πλοῦτος not *only* .., Theoc. 10.19' **4**, add 'absol., αὐτὸ .. ὅ ἐστι καλόν Pl.*Smp.* 211c, *Cra.* 432d, Arist.*Met.* 991ᵃ5, al., Iambl.*Protr.* 8' **8**, add '*inclusive*, of a date, ἕως Μεχεὶρ καὶ αὐτοῦ Wilcken *Chr.* 157.16 (Hermopolis, iii AD), cf. *POxy.* 270.42 (i AD), etc.' **10**, add '**f** combined w. ἐκεῖνος for greater precision or emphasis (v. R. Janko *CQ* 35.20ff.), Od. 24.321, Hdt. 2.115.6, Ar.*Ec.* 328, Pl.*Smp.* 192b, etc.' **11**, add 'A.R. 1.199' **IV 1**, add 'Ath. 6.270b' **2**, delete the section. **3**, add 'X.*An.* 1.9.21, Pl.*Smp.* 204a, Aen.Tact. 11.10; also pl. αὐτὰ ταῦτα Pl.*Prt.* 310e' **V 2**, after 'Αὐτοθαΐς' insert 'cf. Herod. 6.59' at end add 'Myc. *au-to-jo* (gen.); cf. *au-to-te-qa-jo* pers. n. = *Αὐτοθηβαῖος'
**αὐτοσαυτόν**, add 'cf. αὑσαυτοῦ, αὑταυτοῦ'
**αὐτόσε**, add '**2** without spatial sense, αὐ. προστίθημι Pl.*Men.* 73d, Metag.*fr.* 6.4.'
⁺**αὐτόσοφος**, ον, *endowed with innate wisdom*, Rh. 3.530, Tz.*H.* 8.437; neut. subst., *innate cleverness*, ἣν αὐτόσοφον ὁ τέκτων *PTurner* 8 (ii AD).
***αὐτοστερεόν**, τό, *ideal solidity*, Alex.Aphr. *in Metaph.* 127.10, 128.3.
***αὐτοσυμφυής**, ές, *naturally united by itself*, Porph.*Antr.* 5 (cod. αὐτοφυής).
**αὐτοσύστᾰτος**, add 'opp. ἑτεροσύστατος, Choerob. *in Theod.* 2.411.22 H.'
***αὐτοσφαῖρα**, ἡ, *ideal globe*, Alex.Aphr. *in Metaph.* 636.16.
**αὐτοσχεδιαστής**, add 'αὐ. (pl.) πολέμων perh. *engaging at will* in wars, cj. in Vett.Val. 78.4 (75.1 P.)'
**αὐτοσχέδιος II**, add 'neut. subst. τὰ αὐ., *extemporaneous speeches*, Plu. 2.842c'
**αὐτοσχεδόν 1**, add 'Hes.*Sc.* 190'
***αὐτοσχῆμα**, ατος, τό, *ideal shape*, Alex.Aphr. *in Metaph.* 742.25, Procl. *in Ti.* 2.136.14.
**αὐτοτελής I 1**, add '**c** of a body of citizens, *sovereign, independent*, J.*AJ* 14.7.2.' **5**, delete '*sufficing for oneself*: also'
***αὐτοτετρᾰγωνον**, τό, *ideal square*, Alex.Aphr. *in Metaph.* 823.20.
***αὐτότευκτος**, ον, *self-made, natural*, rest. in A.*fr.* 73b.2 R.
**αὐτότης**, delete the entry (v. *Mnemosyne* (4th ser.) 37.89-93, read ταὐτότης).
**αὐτουργός I 1**, for '*self-working* .. 18.2; αὐ.' read '*self-reliant, unassisted*, αὐτὸς αὐτουργῷ χερί S.*Ant.* 52' **2**, for '**b** metaph.' read 'αὐ. γίγνομαι *do* a thing *oneself* (not delegating it), Aen.Tact. 18.2'
***αὐτοῦτα**, Sicilian reflexive in -τα, gen. sg. αὐτοῦτα *IG* 14.287, 288b (both Segesta, iii/ii BC); pl. αὐτῶντα *SEG* 30.1119.19, 26 (Nakone, c.300 BC), Dubois *IGDS* no. 189.13 (Centuripa, ii BC), *IG* 14.316 (Thermae Himeraeae, ii/i BC); acc. pl. αὐτούστα Dubois l.c. lines 3, 5; dat. pl. αὐτοῖστα *SEG* l.c. line 27.
***αὐτοφαείνομαι**, *shine with one's own light*, δαίμων ἀπηνὴς αὐτοφαεινομένην ἔσβεσα δᾶδα γάμων *GVI* 228.4 (Bithynia, ii/iii AD).
***αὐτοφάνεια**, ἡ, *appearance in person*, Procl.*Sacr.* p. 152.6.
***αὐτοφθόνος**, ον, *radically* or *essentially malicious*, κακία ἀ. *An.Bachm.* 2.352.14.
***αὐτοφῐλοτίμημα**, ατος, τό, *act of voluntary generosity*, καὶ περ[ὶ π]ολλῶν αὐτοφιλοτειμημάτων εἰς ἡμᾶ[ς] *IEphes.* 22.15 (ii AD).
***αὐτόφλεψ**, φλεβος, ἡ, *an actual vein*, opp. ἐοικός τι φλεβί, Ruf.*Onom.* 206.
**αὐτοφόνος 1**, add 'perh. in this sense, unexpld. wd. in list of sacred laws, *SEG* 9.72.132 (Cyrene, iv BC)' and transfer 'παλάμη .. Leont.)' to section 2
⁺**αὐτόφορτος**, ον, *transporting one's own baggage* or *cargo*, A.*Ch.* 675, S.*fr.* 251, Cratin. 266 K.-A. **2** of ships, *together with their cargo*, αὐτοφόρτους ὁλκάδας Plu.*Aem.* 9, 2.467d.
**αὐτοφυής I 3**, line 10, before 'Comp.' insert 'κόρη κάλλος αὐτοφυὲς καὶ ὅμοιον αὐτομάτῳ φυτῷ φέρουσα Aristaenet. 1.7.4' **II**, adv., add 'Procl.*Inst.* 205 D.'
**αὐτόφῠτος 1**, after '*self-engendered*' insert '*grown spontaneously*, of Prometheus' liver, which was renewed automatically, Nonn.*D.* 2.300'
**αὐτόφωρος II**, for 'mostly in the phrase .. *in the act*' read '(being) *in the very act of crime, red-handed*, κολάζων .. αὐτοφώρους Th. 6.38.4; esp. in phr. ἐπ' αὐτοφώρῳ λαμβάνειν or sim.'
**αὐτοχειλής**, for 'S.*fr.* 138' read 'S.*fr.* 130 R.'
**αὐτοχειρία II**, line 2, after '= αὐτοχειρί' insert 'τὸν νεὼν ἐξεποίησεν αὐτοχερίῃ Robert *Hell.* 9.78 (Mysia, vi BC)'
**αὐτόχθων I**, add 'title of Μήτηρ θεῶν *SEG* 24.498, 26.729 (both Maced., ii AD; see also *SEG* 33.532)' **II**, line 2, after '(ii AD)' insert '(πόλις) *IStraton.* 15.2 (Panamara, i/ii AD)'; line 4, for '*urbanitas, racy of the soil*' read 'ἀ. *urbanitas, authentic national*, i.e. *Roman, manners*'
**αὐτόχροος, -χρους 1**, after '*colour*' insert '*PCair.Zen.* 92.6 (iii BC)'
**αὐτόχῠτος**, line 1, for '*poured out of itself, self-flowing*' read '*flowing spontaneously*' and for 'θάλαμος .. 96.102' read 'Hes.*fr.* 204.140 M.-W.'
**αὐχένιος I**, add '**3** *neck-like*, ὅλοσχοι Nic.*Th.* 871; αὐχένιαι κεφαλαί (of columns), *MDAI(I)* 19/20.238.14, 24 (Didyma, ii BC).'
***αὐχενοπλήξ**, ῆγος, ὁ, ἡ, *struck in the neck*, Hippon. 102.6 W.
**αὐχέω II 2**, line 3, for 'A.*Pr.* 340' read 'A.*Pr.* 338'
**αὔχη**, after lemma insert 'dial.' and add 'Ibyc. 220.13, 221.5 S.'
**αὐχήεις**, add '[θυμοῦ ἐξ] αὐχήεντος *SEG* 24.1243 (Egypt, Chr.)'
**αὔχημα I**, for this section read '*cause for pride* or *boasting*, S.*OC* 710, 713, Th. 7.75.6, Aq.*Is.* 3.18 (L.-R.)'
**αὐχήν II 6**, add 'ἀετο[ῦ α]ὐχένα *SEG* 31.1349.8 (Cyprus, i AD)' add '**7** part of spindle, prob. end to which thread is attached, ἀντία γ', ὦ Μοῖραι, γαμψοὺς ἐπεθήκατε ἀτράκτοις αὐχένας *GVI* 1681.8 (Rhenea, ii/i BC).'
**αὔχησις**, for 'Th. 6.16' read 'Th. 6.16.5, Aq.*Pr.* 4.9, al.'
**αὐχμηρός 2**, after '*squalid*' insert 'χεῖρες Anacr. 2 *fr.* 1.4 P.' add '**4** of literary style, *arid*, D.H.*Dem.* 45, al.; ῥήτορες id.*Din.* 8.'
**αὐχμός**, add '**5** *disregard of niceties of toilet, unkempt state*, Arr.*Epict.* 3.22.89.'
**αὖχος**, add '*SEG* 30.1486 (Phrygia)'
**αὔω** (B) **2**, line 2, for '(Il.) 13.475' read '(Il.) 13.477'; after 'Od. 9.65' insert 'Tim. 11 P.'; last line, after 'diphthong' insert 'except in *Hymn.Is.* 59 [ῠ]'
***αὐωρο-**, v. °ἀωρο-.
***ἀφάγγρειμι**, *take away, subtract*, τὸ χοῦρον ἐμε[τρεί]θει ἀφανγρειμενᾶν τᾶν ὀδοῦν καὶ τᾶν ἐνόδουν *IGC* p. 11.14 (Larissa, iii BC); cf. ἀφαιρέω, ἐφανγρενθεῖν s.v. ἐφαιρέω.
***ἀφᾰγιστεύω**, app. *perform apotropaic rites*, κἀφαγιστεύσας ἶ χρή S.*Ant.* 247 (but see °ἐφαγ-).
***ἄφᾰγος**, ον, *fasting*, Sch.A.R. 4.1295.
⁺**ἀφᾱδία**, ἡ, *enmity*, Eup. 376 K.-A.
***ἀφάεσται, ἀφάετοι**, (?ἐ), med. inf. and 3 sg. subj. of Arc. vb. meaning *pay*, [ἀφάε]σται δαρχμὰς τριάκοντα· εἰ δὲ μὲ ἀφάετοι Jeffery *LSAG* p. 214 no. 2 (see also Dubois *Dial. arcadien* pp. 195ff., Pheneos, c.500 BC); cf. °ἐξάετοι, perh. also ‡ἀφαιάσαι.
**Ἀφαία**, for '*IG* 4.1580' read '*SEG* 32.356, 37.260 (vi and v BC), Paus. 2.30.3, Ant.Lib. 40.4'
**ἀφαιᾶσαι**, add '(ἀφαιμάσαι· δαπανῆσαι, ἀπολειτουργῆσαι, etc., La.)'
**ἀφαίρεσις I**, add '**4** *wrongful deprival*, *POxy.* 3611.8 (iii AD).' **II 2**, after 'Gramm., *removal*' insert 'of letters, words, etc., μετασκευῆς .. ἀφαιρέσεως λέγω καὶ προσθήκης καὶ ἀλλοιώσεως D.H.*Comp.* 6, 9'
**ἀφαιρετικός I**, add '**2** ἀ. πτῶσις *ablative* case, Dosith. p. 392 K.'
**ἀφαιρετός 1**, after 'Pl.*Plt.* 303e' insert 'Arist.*EE* 1241ᵇ23, al.'
**ἀφαιρέω**, line 1, after 'Ion. ἀπαιρέω' insert 'cf. Thess. °ἀφάγγρειμι' **II 4**, for 'cf. Lys. 23.10' read 'Lys. 23.9'; after 'Aeschin. 1.62' insert 'cf. ὥστε ἀφηρεῖτ' αὐτὸν ὡς ἐλεύθερον ὄντα Isoc. 17.14, 49'
***ἀφᾰκέομαι**, aor. imper. ἀφ[α]κεσάσθω, *repair damage*, *Sokolowski* 2.27.11 (Argos, vi BC).
**ἀφάλλομαι**, line 1, for 'ἀφάλασθια' read 'ἀφάλασθαι'
**ἀφᾰμαρτάνω**, line 1, delete 'Orph.*A.* 643'
***ἀφᾰμαρτέω**, *wander off*, Orph.*A.* 643 (v.l. ἀφομ-).

*__ἀφαμία__, ἁ, Cret. term, perh. type of land-holding, ἐν ἀπαμίαις *Inscr.Cret.* 2.12.16 Ab 2 (Eleutherna, vi BC), app. same wd. as in τὰν Ἐξάκωντ[ος] ἀφαμίαν, landscape feature used as boundary mark, *SEG* 26.1049.72 (Lato, ii BC); cf. Ἀφαμιῶται.

**ἀφάνεια II**, ἀφανία, add 'καὶ ἐν ἀργίαι καὶ ἐν ἀφανί‹αι› *SEG* 37.215 (Attica, tab.defix., ?iv BC)'

**ἀφανής 1**, add 'w. gen., ‹φ›θι‹ό›μενοι κείμεθα γῆς ἀφανεῖς *CEG* 520.9 (Athens, *c.*360 BC)' **4**, add '**b** = Lat. *incertus* or *incerta persona*, one who is not precisely designated or whose existence is uncertain, ἐπίτροπος ἀφανέσιν οὐ δύναται δοθῆναι *Cod.Just.* 6.48.1.28, 6.48.1.2.'

**ἀφανίζω I 6 b**, add 'μῆλα .. ἠφάνισται *BGU* 38.11'

**ἄφαντος**, transfer 'θεοῖς .. Epimenid. 11' fr. section 3 to section 1; at end of that section, for '*invisible*' read '*blotting out, obscuring*' and add 'θύελλαι Alc. 298.12. L.-P.'

**ἀφᾱρής**, before 'Euph.' insert 'cj. in' and add 'cf. *Tav.Lign.Cer.* 66.1.20 (vi AD)'

**ἀφαρκίδευτον**, add '(ἄγρυπτον, ἀρυτίδωτον La.)'

**ἀφαρπᾰγή**, add 'Sol. 4.13 W. (s.v.l.)'

**ἀφαρπάζω**, aor. 1 pass., add 'ἀφαρπαχθεῖσα epigr. in *SEG* 37.489 (Larissa, iv/v AD)', cf. aor. pass. forms given s.v. ἁρπάζω' add '**2** *transfer* to a changed status (cf. Lat. *eripere*, εἰς εὐγένειαν ἀφαρπάζονται *Cod.Just.* 6.4.4.3 (v.l. ἀφ' οὗ ἁρπάζονται).'

*__ἀφάρπαξ__, αγος, ὁ, unclean bird, one of the *raptores*, Al.*Le.* 11.19.

**ἀφαυαίνω 1**, after 'Thphr.*HP* 3.18.9' insert '*CP* 3.10.8'

*__ἄφαυστος__, ον, *inexplicable*, Plot. 6.6.7 (s.v.l.).

**ἀφαύω**, add 'prob. in Ar.*Pax* 1144 (codd. ἄφευε)'

**ἀφεδριατεύοντες**, add 'also sg., *SEG* 23.271 (Thespiae, iii BC)'

**ἀφειδέω I**, for 'abs. .. E.*IT* 1354' read 'abs., ἀφειδήσαντες *putting aside restraint* or *inhibition*, Hp.*Art.* 37, E.*IT* 1354, τὸν ἄριστον ἀφειδήσαντες ἕλεσθε ὄρχαμον ἡμείων A.R. 1.338'

**ἀφειδής I 1**, line 3, for 'ἀ. πρὸς τὸν ἔρωτα Call.*Epigr.* 47.7' read 'ἀφειδέα ποττὸν Ἔρωτα Call.*Epigr.* 46.7 Pf.' add '**b** abs., *uncontrollable*, ἀφειδῆ ταῦρον, ὃν οὐχ αἱροῦσ' ἀνέρες οὐδὲ δέκα Aristocl. in *Suppl.Hell.* 206.'

**ἀφέλεια**, line 2, after 'style' insert 'D.H.*Is.* 16'

**ἀφελής**, delete '(φελλεύς)' and section I. **II 1**, add '*AP* 5.42 (Rufin.)'; at end, adv., add 'comp. Ael. *VH* 7.1' **b**, for this section read 'w. pejorative force, Μένων ἀφελές ostr. in *MDAI(A)* 80.118 nos. 30-2 (Athens, v BC)' **2**, add 'cf., in apparent allusion to Cratinus' style, Κρατίνου .. ὃς πολλῷ ῥεύσας ποτ' ἐπαίνῳ διὰ τῶν ἀφελῶν πεδίων ἔρρει Ar.*Eq.* 527'; adv., add 'ὅτι φυσικῶς πως εἴρηται καὶ ἀ. D.H.*Is.* 7'

**ἀφέλκω I**, add '*take off* a lid, πῶμαт' ἄφελκε κάδων Archil. 4.7 W.' **II**, delete 'κάδων .. Archil. 4'

**ἀφελληνίζω**, line 2, for '-ηλλήνισθη' read '-ηλληνίσθη'

**ἄφεσις 2 a**, add 'ἔντιμος ἄφεσις = Lat. *honesta missio*, *honourable discharge*, *CPR* 7.21.12 (iv AD)'

**ἀφεσοφῠλάκία**, read 'ἀφεσιοφυλακία' and add 'v. *PBremen* p. 44'

**ἀφέταιρος**, for 'cf. ἀπέταιρος' read '**II** subst., *one who is not a member of a* ἑταιρεία or *society of free citizens*, *Leg.Gort.* 2.5, al. (v BC); *one who is not a member of the association of Epilykoi*, *SEG* 35.989.11 (Knossos, ii/i BC).'

**ἀφετήριος 5**, for '*gate* of a sluice' read 'ἀφετήριαι, αἱ, *sluice-gates*' and add '*outlet* of conduit, *POxy.* 2146.6 (iii AD), v. °ἐξομβριστήρ'

**ἀφέτης I 1 c**, add '*OAshm.Shelton* 174, 176'

**ἀφεύω**, line 1, for 'Semon. (v. infr.)' read 'Semon. 24.1 W.' **2**, delete the section.

**ἀφέψᾰλος**, add 'θ[οίν]η δ' [εἰ]μὶ βροτοῖσιν ἀφέψαλος i.e. *uncooked*, *Suppl.Hell.* 983.6 (iii BC)'

**ἀφέψησις**, for 'Sch.Lyc. 156' read '**2** *boiling*, sc. of Pelops by Tantalus, Sch.Lyc. 157. **3** *refining*, of gold, *IG* 2².1496.201.'

**ἀφέψω**, add '**3** simply *boil*, ἀφεψήθη, of Pelops, Sch.Lyc. 157.'

**ἀφή I**, add 'Men.*fr.* 197 K.-Th.' **II 1**, delete the section. **2**, add '**b** pl., *the senses, perceptions*, Pl.*Ax.* 365a.'

**ἀφήλικος**, for '= sq.' read '= ἀφῆλιξ II, *POxy.* 2134.8, al. (ii AD)'

**ἀφῆλιξ II**, add '*BGU* 907.2, *POxy.* 2474.21, Modest.*Dig.* 26.5.21, Just.*Nov.* 100.2 pr.'

*__ἀφημερεία__, ἡ, *absence for a day*, *PSI* 1120.3 (i BC/i AD).

*__ἀφηρωϊσμός__, ὁ, *canonization as a hero*, *IG* 12(7).515.6 (Amorgos, ii BC).

**ἄφθα** (A), delete '*infantile*' and add 'Marc.Sid. 101'

**ἄφθαρτος I**, add '**2** *unaltered*, Ἑλληνικά 7.179 (Chalcis, iii BC).'

*__ἄφθαστος__, ον, perh. *not* (*to be*) *overtaken*, τῇ κακίᾳ ἄφθαστοι *Cat.Cod.Astr.* 11(2).136.16; cf. adv. ἀφθάστως.

**ἄφθῐτος**, line 1, add 'fem. ἀφθίτα Mesom. 3.16' **2**, line 3, for 'Simon. 184' read '*AP* 7.25.1 ([Simon.])'; add 'adv. -ως, ἀφθίτως βιοτεύειν *Orac.Sib.* 5.303' **3**, add 'neut. as adv., *CEG* 862.6 (Olympia, iv BC)'

**ἀφθώδης**, add 'Crito ap.Gal. 12.933.15'

*__ἀφιδάνης__, ου, ὁ, name of gem, Xenocr.*Lap.* 108, cf. Plin.*HN* 37.147 (*amphidanes*).

**ἀφίδρῡμα I**, for '*thing set up*, esp. *image* of the gods' read '*image set up in honour of a god*'; delete 'Str. 12.5.3' and add 'D.S. 15.49' **2**, delete the section. **II**, for this section read '*temple* or *shrine* copied fr. an original, Cic.*Att.* 13.29.1, Str. 6.2.5, ἱερὸν Ἀσκληπιοῦ ἀ. τοῦ ἐν Τρίκκῃ 8.4.4'

**ἀφιδρύω**, add 'med., ὃν .. ἀνέστησέν τε καὶ ἀφειδρύσατο *GVAK* 14'

**ἀφίημι** (A), line 9, after 'Il. 23.841, etc.' insert 'ἀφέωκαμεν (1 pl.) *SEG* 20.325.3 (Hyrcania, iii BC), ἀφέωκε (3 sg.) *PCair.Zen.* 502.4/5 (iii BC), *IG* 9(2).1042.11 (Gonnoi, i AD)'; line 15, transfer 'Arc.inf. .. (Tegea, iv BC)' to line 18 to follow '*IG* 5(2).6.14'; line 17, before 'plpf.' insert 'part. ἠφειμένους *ASAA* N.S. 3/4(1941-2).97.6 (Lemnos, i BC)' **II 1 b**, add 'of manumission, ἀφέω τοῦτον τὸν ἐπτάδουλον Herod. 5.75, cf. Hippon.*dub.fr.* 190 De., *SEG* 32.622, 623 (Illyria, ii BC)'

*__ἀφῐκετεία__, ἡ, *intercession*, *IKnidos* 220.6 (iii/ii BC).

*__ἀφῐκετεύω__, *intercede for a suppliant*, *SEG* 9.72.132, 138 (Cyrene, iv BC), *SEG* 39.729 (Lindos, iii BC); cf. ἀφίκτωρ.

*__ἀφῐλανθρώπητος__, ον, = ἀφιλάνθρωπος, *BGU* 1785.10 (i BC).

*__ἀφῐλόκερδος__, ον, *not devoted to gain*, *SAWW* 265 i 55 no. 12.4.

*__ἀφῐλοπόνητος__, ον, *not given devoted attention*, *Vit.Aesop.*(G) 51.

*__ἄφῑμος__, *unbridled*, ἵππος *Trag.adesp.* 328g K.-S.

**ἀφιππεύω**, after 'Hld. 4.18' insert '(v.l.), Charito 3.7.2'

**ἀφιπποτοξότης**, for 'v. ἀμφιππoτ-' read '*bowman on horse-back*, D.S. 19.29 (nisi leg. ἀμφ-), cf. Plu. 2.197c (v.l. ἀμφ-)'

*__ἄφισμα__, ατος, τό, app. *image* set up in a temple, τοῦ ἀπολωλότος ἀφίσματος τοῦ Ἀφαίστου *BCH* 116.335 (Argos).

**ἀφίστημι B**, line 2, for 'Men. 375' read 'Men.*fr.* 158, 317 K.-Th.'; line 24, after 'Th. 7.28' insert 'w. gen., μὴ ἀποστήσεσθαι Ὀξυρύγχων πόλεως *depart from*, *PKöln* 148.6 (ii AD)'

*__ἀφίστησις__, εως, ἡ, *relinquishing*, τῶν ἑτέρων of his other claims, *Dura*[7,8] 428 (parchment 40; i AD).

*__ἀφίσωσις__, v. °ἀπίσωσις.

**ἄφλαστον**, delete 'Asclep.Tragil. 31 J., Sch.'

**ἀφλέγμαντος 1**, adv., add 'Heras ap.Gal. 13.557.12'

**ἀφνειός**, line 4, after 'c. dat.' insert 'Hes.*fr.* 240.2 M.-W.'

**ἀφνύει**, delete the entry.

*__ἀφνῠνω__, v. °ἄφνυω.

*__ἀφνύω__, *enrich*, ῥυδὸν ἀφνύονται Call. in *Suppl.Hell.* 287.3 (ἀφνύνται Suid.); ἀφνύει· ἀφνύνει. ὀλβίζει Hsch.

**ἄφοβος 1**, at end after 'Pl.*Lg.* 682c' insert 'Arist.*EE* 1228ᵇ26'

*__ἀφοδευτήριος__, α, ον, ἀ. δίφρους *latrine-stools*, Hsch., s.v. λάσανα; neut. subst. *privy*, ἀπόπατος λέγεται τὸ ἀ. Sch.Ar.*Pl.* 1184.

**ἀφολίδωτος**, add 'rest. in *Inscr.Délos* 104-5.31'

*__ἀφομαρτέω__, v. °ἀφαμαρτέω.

**ἀφομοίωσις**, add '**2** perh. *levelling*, ἀ. τοῦ χωρίου *IG* 4.823.66 (Troezen, iv BC).'

**ἀφοπλισμός**, add '*Cod.Just.* 1.4.26.16'

**ἀφοράω**, line 1, after 'aor. ἀπεῖδον' insert 'ἀφίδω *Ep.Phil.* 2.23 (codd.)' **I 1 b**, add '*Peripl.M.Rubr.* 35'

*__ἀφορί__, adv. *without paying rent*, ἀφορὶ ἕξουσιν (sc. τὴν γῆν) *PTeb.* 737.27 (ii BC); ἀφορεί *PFlor.* 384.54 (*Berichtigungsl.* 2.60, v AD).

**ἀφορίζω II 2 b**, add 'Just.*Nov.* 123.11 pr.'

**ἀφόρισμα**, add 'τὰ ὄρη καὶ τὰ ἀφορίσματα perh. *boundaries marked off* or *borders*, *IG* 2².30.18 (pl.; Attica, iv BC)'

**ἀφορισμός II 1**, add '**b** *excommunication*, *Cod.Just.* 1.3.38.2.'

*__ἀφορμάριος__, ὁ, *one who makes excuses*, *SB* 7168.4 (v/vi AD, pl., written ἀφορμαροι).

*__ἀφορμία__, ἡ, *deterrent*, *Vit.Aesop.*(G) 16.

**ἀφορμίζομαι**, add 'ἀφορμισάμενοι cj. for ὑφ-, Th. 2.83.3; act., perh. *push off* a boat from the shore, (τὸ πορθμεῖον) pap. in *SHAW* 1923(2).23 (pap. ἐφ-)'

*__ἀφορολόγιστος__, ον, = ἀφορολόγητος, Ps.-Callisth. 72.10 K.

**ἀφοσιόω II 1**, add 'D. 47.70' **2 c**, add 'Isoc. 12.269'

**ἀφοσίωσις 2**, after 'Plu.*Eum.* 12' insert 'ἀφοσιώσεως χάριν Modest.*Dig.* 27.1.13.6'

*__ἀφουλόω__, v. ‡ἀπουλ-.

†__ἀφουλωτικός__, v. ‡ἀπουλ-.

**ἀφρατίας**, add '(ἀφραττίας La., i.e. ‹ ἀφρακτ-, perh. cf. Ἄφραττος)'

**Ἄφριος**, for 'Ἀρχ.Ἐφ. 1913.219' read '*AE* 1913.219, Ἄφροι (gen. sg.) *BCH* 59.56 (Larissa, ii AD)'

**ἀφρογενής**, add 'Hes.*Th.* 196 (prob. interp.; -γενειαν codd.)'

*__Ἀφροδῑσιακόν__, τό, name of a mine in Sunium, *IG* 2².1587.5 (iv BC).

*__Ἀφροδῑσιακός__ (B), *of Aphrodisias* (in Caria), of a type of marble workmanship, ζῴδια Ἀ. *SEG* 33.946 (Ephesus, i AD), *IEphes.* 3803b.8 (iv AD).

*__ἀφροδισιαρχέω__, *preside over the festival of Aphrodite*, Ἀφροδεισία ἀ[φ]ροδεισιαρχήσασα Ἀφροδίτᾳ χαριστήριον *SEG* 25.595, 596, both of women (Phocis, i AD; ii BC acc. to *BE* 1970.305).

**ἀφροδισιάς II**, for 'ἄκορος' read 'ἄκορον' and add 'cf. Ps.-Dsc. 1.2'

**Ἀφροδῑσιαστής 3**, add '*SEG* 26.614 (Tanagra, iii/ii BC)'

*__Ἀφροδῑσιδεῖον__, τό, *sanctuary of Aphrodite and Isis*, *IG* 4².742.5 (Epid., ii/iii AD), but Ἀφροδισι[δ]είωι *Sokolowski* 2.25.A5 (= Ἀφροδίσιον).

**Ἀφροδίσιος I**, line 3, after 'Semon. 7.48' insert 'λόγοι ib. 91 W., cf. Ael.*NA* 6.1' **II 1**, line 3, after 'X.*Mem.* 2.6.22' insert 'cf. 1.3.8' and delete 'also as concrete .. 1.3.8' **III 1**, after '*PPetr.* 3 p. 113' insert '*Inscr.Délos* 1442*B*31, 33 (ii BC)' add '**V** epith. of Zeus, *IG* 12(5).220 (Paros, iii BC).'

**Ἀφροδισιών**, add '*SEG* 30.533 (Phthiotic Thebes, ii BC), *IIasos* 47.1 (iv BC)'

**Ἀφροδίτη**, after lemma insert 'Dor. -ῖτᾱ Alcm. 1.17 P., etc., Aeol. voc. -ῖτᾰ (proparox.) Sapph. 1.1. L.-P., etc; Ἀφορδῖτᾱ *Inscr.Cret.* 1.9.1.27 (Dreros, iii/ii BC); cf. pers. n. Ἀφορδίσιυς *IPamph.* 21, etc.' **I**, add 'pl., Call.*fr.* 200a Pf., cf. Ἀφροδείταις Καστνιήτισιν (*sic*) *SEG* 17.641 (Aspendos, early Rom.); as statue of A., *SB* 9834a.7 (iv AD)'

***ἀφροδιτολειτορεύω**, *serve as priestess of Aphrodite*, *SEG* 27.206 (sp. -λιτ-, Larissa, i BC/i AD).

***ἀφροειδής**, ές, *foam-like*, Sch.Hes.*Th.* 191a.

**ἀφρόνιτρον**, add 'Plin.*HN* 20.66, al.; also **ἀφόνιτρον** *PRyl.* 629.101, al. (iv AD)'

**ἀφρός I 1**, add 'personified as a Nereid, *SEG* 31.1387 (Syria, iv AD)'

***Ἄφρος**, α, ον, *African*, i.e. from the Roman province, τάπης *Edict.Diocl.* 19.35, al.; Ἄφροι, of the Carthaginians, Suid. s.v.

**ἀφροσέληνος**, add '**II** = λιβανωτίς, Ps.-Apul.*Herb.* 80.'

**ἀφροτόκος**, add '*Eleg.adesp.* in *POxy.* 3723.2 (ii AD)'

**ἀφρούρητος**, after lemma insert 'Dor. ἀφρούρᾱτος *IAskl.Epid.* 25.4 (iii BC)'; after '*ungarrisoned*' insert 'as a privilege, i.e. *free from military occupation*, *IAskl.Epid.* l.c., *SEG* 37.1003.19 (Sardis, iii/ii BC), *IIlion* 45.14 (ii BC)'

***ἀφρωραῖος**, α, ον, *beautiful in the foam*, Ἀφροδίτη *PMag.* 4.3232.

**ἀφύη**, after 'Ar.*Ach.* 640' insert 'id.*fr.* 520 K.-A., Hermipp. 14 K.-A., Call.Com. 10 K.-A., Aristonym. 2 K.-A.'; at end delete 'not used in sg. .. τιμή'

*** ἀφῡλισμός**, ὁ, *removal of solid matter*, of clearing of ditches, *PMich.*VI 380.6 (ii AD), *OMich.* 802.7 (AD 296), *PNew York* 2.5 (iv AD); cf. °ἐφυλισμός, παρυλισμός; of straining of wine, *OMich.* 12 (iii AD).

**ἀφυπνόω II**, after '*Ev.Luc.* 8.23' insert '*Vit.Aesop.*(G) 127, Aesop. 252 P.' and for 'v.l. ὑφυπν-' read 'cj. for ὑφυπν-'

**ἀφύσσω I 2**, for '*sound, probe*' read 'medic., *draw off fluid from* a wound, *drain*' **II**, penultimate line, after 'σπειρήματ' insert '(codd. πειρήματ)' and at end read 'Trag. only in E.ll.cc., Ion Trag. 10 S., Ezek.*Exag.* 250 S.'

**ἀφυστερέω II**, add 'v.l. in *Ep.Jac.* 5.4 (pass.)'

**ἀφωνία I**, add 'στήλη δὲ φωνῶ ἀντ' ἀ‹φ›ωνίας βίου *IUrb.Rom.* 1322.6 (= *IG* 14.1977)'

***ἀφῶτε**, *from the time that*, *SEG* 37.340.12 (Mantinea, iv BC).

**Ἀχαία I**, add 'of Athena, Arist.*Mir.* 840ᵇ2' **II**, transfer '(acc. to Hsch. .. id.)' to the end of section I. add '**III** οἱ δὲ ἔρια μαλακά, Hsch. s.v. Ἀχαία; cf. perh. ἀπὸ ἀχάης *POxy.* 1978.4, al. (vi AD).'

**Ἀχαΐα** (s.v. Ἀχαιός), for this entry read '**Ἀχαιΐα** later **Ἀχαΐα**, ἡ, *Achaea*, a region of the northern Peloponnese, τὴν νῦν καλεομένην Ἀχαιΐην Hdt. 7.94, Th. 1.115.1, Paus. 7.1.1, etc. **2** region of Thessaly (Achaea Phthiotis), Hdt. 7.173.1, Str. 9.5.6, etc. **3** the Roman province of Achaea, J.*BJ* 1.26.4, D.C. 58.25.5, etc.'

***Ἀχαιϊάς**, άδος, fem. adj., *Achaean*, Ἀχαιϊάδες .. πόληες Call.*Del.* 100, γυναῖκες Nonn.*D.* 47.636. **II** fem. subst., *Achaean* (*Greek*) *woman*, Il. 5.422, Od. 2.101. **2** *Achaea*, *SEG* 13.226.6 (Corinth, ii AD), *BCH* 50.444.85 (Thespiae, iv AD).

**Ἀχαιικός**, add 'comp. -ωτέρα ὑπόθεσις Plb. 24.9.2'

***Ἀχαιΐς**, later **Ἀχαΐς**, ίδος, ἡ, *Achaean*, Ἀχαιΐδα γαῖαν Il. 1.254, προσβολὴν Ἀχαιΐδα A.*Th.* 28, νεὼς .. Ἀχαιΐδος E.*Hel.* 1544, Ἀχαΐδας πόλεις X.*HG* 7.1.43, Ἀχαιΐδα .. κούρην A.R. 3.639. **II** fem. subst., *Achaean woman*, Il. 2.235. **2** *Achaea*, Il. 3.75, A.R. 3.1081.

***ἀχαιοπόρφῠρος**, ον, *of Achaean purple*, δελματικοφόριον ὀνύχινον ἀχαοπόρφυρον (sic) *SB* 11075.7 (v AD).

**Ἀχαιός 1**, add '**b** Θεὸς Ἀ. name of a god in Asia Minor, *SEG* 33.1542, 1543 (Rom.imp.).'

***ἀχαιόσημος**, ον, of clothing, *with an Achaean stripe*, *POxford* 15.10 (iii AD); also **ἀχαο-** *SB* 11075.10 (v AD).

**ἀχάντιον**, add 'Eust. 468.33'

**ἄχᾰρις I 1**, add 'of speech, D.H.*Lys.* 12, *Is.* 20' **2**, line 3, after '(Hdt.) 7.52' insert 'ἄ. τιμή id. 7.36.1' delete '**II** *ungracious* .. Hdt. 7.36.1' for 'χάρις ἄχαρις' to end read '**3** in phr. χάρις ἄχαρις *lacking the essential quality of* χάρις, A.*Ag.* 1545, κακῆς γυναικὸς χάριν ἄχαριν ἀπώλετο E.*IT* 566, *AP* 9.322.'

***ἀχᾰρῖτος**, ον, *lacking charm, unpleasant*, τὰ δέ μοι παθήματα ἐόντα ἀ. μαθήματα γέγονε Hdt. 1.207.1; δῆμον εἶναι συνοίκημα ἀχαριτώτατον id. 7.156.3; ἀχαριτωτάτου προσώπου (sc. of the Cyclops) Demetr.*Eloc.* 130; Plu.*Sol.* 20; of style, Demetr.*Eloc.* 139 (comp.); adv. οὐκ -τως ἔφη Ath. 7.281c; Hermog.*Id.* 2.11; D.C. 66.9.5. **2** in phr., χάρις ἀχάριτος *lacking the essential quality of* χάρις, A.*Ch.* 44, E.*Ph.* 1757.

***ἀχασμώδητος**, ον, *not having hiatus*, Rh. 3.544.11.

**ἄχειρ**, add '**b** *having no holes for the arms*, χιτῶνα ἄχειρα καὶ ἀτράχηλον Apollod.*Epit.* 6.23.'

***ἀχειρής**, ές, *lacking hands*, καρκίνοι Batr. 298.

***Ἀχελωΐδες** (sc. πόλεις), dub. sens., app. of towns situated on or near rivers or lakes, A.*Pers.* 869.

**Ἀχελῷος II**, add 'Ar.*Lys.* 381, E.*Andr.* 167; Ἀχελῷον πᾶν ὕδωρ Εὐριπίδης φησὶν ἐν Ὑψιπύλῃ Macr.*Sat.* 5.18.12; as a divinity, object of cult worship, *Sokolowski* 3.18.B24 (Attica, iv BC), 96.35, 38 (Myconus, *c.*200 BC); at a fountain, *BCH* 113.610 (Messene)'

***ἀχέρνιπτος**, ον, *not to be used for ritual washing*, ὕδωρ A.*fr.* 273a.12 R.

***Ἀχεροντίς**, ίδος, fem. adj., *of Acheron*, Ἀ. λίμνην *GVI* 731.9 (ii/iii AD).

***Ἀχερουσίς**, ίδος, fem. adj., *of Acheron*, A.R. 2.728, *AP* 5.204 (Mel.), Λήθης Ἀχερουσίδος *IG* 10(2).1.368.1 (epigr., Thessalonica, ii AD).

**ἀχεύω**, line 3, for 'cf. Sapph.*Supp.* 1.11' read 'ἀχεύων Sapph. 5.11 L.-P.'

**ἀχήν**, line 1, delete '= ἠχήν (q.v.)'; for 'dat. pl.' to end read 'ἀχήν· ἄπορος Hsch., dat. pl. ἀχή‹ν›εσσιν *IStraton.* 543.7 (epigr., Lagina, iii/ii BC), see also ἠχῆνες, ἀεχῆνες'

***ἀχθαίνω**, *carry a burden of sorrow, ache*, πολλὸν δὲ περὶ φρεσὶν ἀχθήνασα Call.*fr.* 63.7 Pf.

**ἀχθέω**, add '(ἀχθίσας La., v. ἀχθίζω)'

**ἀχθηρός**, add 'v.l. in Phalar.*Ep.* 122'

**ἄχθος I**, add '**b** as a measure, φρ[υγά]νων ἄχθος, καὶ ξυλέων ἄχθος *Inscr.Cos* 39.14 (iv/ii BC).'

***ἀχθοφορικός**, ή, όν, *of* or *from bearing burdens*, Eust. 1577.44.

***ἀχι**, v. °ἠχι.

**Ἀχίλλειος**, line 1, before 'Ἀχιλλέϊος' for 'poet.' read 'Aeol.'; add 'τὸ Ἀχίλλειον temple with tomb of Achilles at Sigeum, Str. 13.1.39, 46, Ion. -ήιον Hdt. 5.94.2'

**Ἀχιλλεύς**, add '**III** *image of the sun thrown on a ceiling by a moving mirror*, Hero *Deff.* 135.12.' at end add 'Myc. *a-ki-re-u* pers. n.'

**ἀχλῠόεις**, line 1, delete 'δεσμός .. Hdt. 5.77' (v. °ἀχνυόεις)

**ἀχλύς**, line 1, after '*mist*, Od. 20.357' insert 'Arist.*Mete.* 367ᵇ17, 373ᵇ12, Plb. 34.11.15, Str. 6.2.8' **2**, add 'Iamb.*Protr.* 21 ιδ' (115.18 P.)' at end delete 'Mostly poet. .. supra 2.'

***ἄχμα**, ματος, τό, app. *cargo*, τὰ δ' ἄχματ' ἐκπεπ[.].άχμενα Alc. 208 ii 7 L.-P., cf. perh. 167.7.

***ἀχνάζω**, ἀχνάζει· ἄχθεται, μισεῖ, ψέγει Hsch.; cf. °ἀχνάσδημι.

***ἀχνάσδημι**, Aeol., *to be miserable*, Alc. 349A L.-P.

**ἄχνη**, line 2, for '*foam, froth*' read '*spray*'

***ἀχνῠόεις**, εσσα, εν, *grief-laden*, δεσμῷ ἐν ἀχνυόεντι σιδήρεῳ cj. in *CEG* 179 (*c.*506 BC), *GVI* 238.1 (Rom.imp.).

***ἀχνύς**, ύος, ἡ, *grief*, *Suppl.Hell.* 1031; personified, cj. in Hes.*Sc.* 264, cj. in Hld. 2.14.5.

***ἀχόνωδες**, dub. sens., φιδάκναι ἀχόν‹ω›δες *IG* 1³.422.302 (v BC); cf. °χονδήν.

**ἀχορτασία**, for '*ravenous hunger*' read '*the state of being unsatisfied* (by food)'

**ἀχόρταστος**, for '*unfed, starving*' read '*unfilled, unsatisfied*' and add 'Cyran. 1.6.14 K.'

**ἀχραής**, after 'ψυχρὸν ἀ.' insert '(cj., cod. ἀκραές)'

**ἄχραντος**, add 'Iamb.*Protr.* 21 α' (108.24 P.), Procl.*Inst.* 154, 156 D.'

**ἀχρεῖος I 1**, add 'of objects, *unserviceable*, φιάλη *IG* 7.303.10 (Oropus, iii BC); of garments, *SEG* 38.1210.8, al. (Miletus, ii BC), τὴν ἐσθῆτά μου διέρρηξεν καὶ ἀχρίαν ἀπέδιξεν *SB* 7449.12 (v AD)' **II**, after 'as adv.' insert '*in a manner out of keeping with one's character* or *situation*'

**ἀχρεοκόπητος**, after lemma insert 'of debts, dues, *that cannot be remitted*, ἐπ[ικε]φάλια .. ἀχρε[ω]κόπητα *SB* 11379.8 (ii AD)

**ἀχρημάτιστος III**, for this section read 'perh. *having no business*, Bernand *Akôris* 28'

***ἀχρής**, ές, = ἄχρους, *pallid with fear*, acc. to *EM* 182.47, v. (?)Call.*fr.* 742 Pf.

**ἀχρήσιμος**, add '*PColl.Youtie* 77.6 (iv AD)'

**ἄχρηστος**, add '**V** perh. *deprived of civil rights*, *Meiggs-Lewis* 2 (Dreros, vi BC).'

**ἄχρι II 1**, after 'Lxx *Ge.* 44.28' insert '**b** *for the duration of, until the completion of*' and add 'ἄχρι τῆς ζωῆς Just.*Nov.* 7 pr.; also *by the end of*, ἤλθομεν πρὸς αὐτοὺς .. ἄχρις ἡμερῶν πέντε *Act.Ap.* 20.6' **III 1**, delete '*so long as*' and add '**b** *so long as, whilst*, Call.*fr.* 195.23 Pf., *AP* 7.472.15 (Leon.Tarent.).'

***ἀχρύσωτος**, ον, *not gilded*, *Inscr.Délos* 1417*A*i150 (ii BC).

***ἀχρωμία**, ἡ, *effrontery, insolence*, *PPetaus* 26.14 (ii AD), *Gloss.* 2.254.

**ἀχῠρηγέω**, before '*BGU* 698.22' insert '*PCair.Zen.* 176.145, al. (iii BC)'

**ἀχῠρικὸν** τέλος, delete this entry (v. °ἄχυρον).

**ἀχύριος**, for '= ἀχυρός' read '*building to hold chaff* or *straw* (cf. °ἀχυρός)'; add 'prob. *chaff*, *PLand.* 146.6.8 (ii BC)'

**ἄχῠρον I**, add '*OBodl.* i 237; app. used for grain and chaff together as separated from the straw, Theoc. 10.49, see Gow ad loc. and

*CQ* 49.227. **2** pl., *straw*, Hp.*Prog.* 4 (transferred from section I 1), *SEG* 9.11, 13, 41, 18.743, etc. (all Cyrene, iv/ii BC).'

***ἀχῠροπόρος**, ον, ὁ, *chaff-seller*, cj. in *MAMA* 3.487 (Corycus, perh. erron. for -πώλης).

**ἀχῠρός**, for 'Ar.*fr.* 10 D.' read 'Ar.*fr.* 234 K.-A. (anap.)' and for 'should be read' read 'seems required by the metre in Ar.l.c.; elsewh. ‡ἀχύριος is possible; *storehouse for chaff* or *straw*, ἀ.· ὁ ἀχυρών. ἀχυροδόκη. ἀποθήκη τῶν ἀ. Hsch.'

**ἀχῠρόω**, after 'Polioch. 2' insert 'in building walls'

**ἄχῠτος**, add 'dub. sens., app. *not liquid*, *dry*, πλακοῦντες ἀ. *PCair.Zen.* 707.18 (iii BC)'

**ἀχώνευτος**, add '*not coated with pitch* (v. χωνεύω and cf. ἀκώνητος), *PCair.Zen.* 741.31; also -ητος, ib. 742.9 (both iii BC)'

**ἀχώριστος I**, add '**3** *irremovable*, πᾶσαν πόλιν .. ἔχειν ἐκ παντὸς τρόπου ἀχώριστον .. ἐπίσκοπον *Cod.Just.* 1.3.35 pr.'

**ἀψευδέω I**, add 'as a legal requirement, *not to commit fraud*, ὁ μὲν τοίνυν εἷς νόμος κελεύει ἀψευδεῖν ἐν τῇ ἀ[γορᾷ] Hyp.*Ath.* 14; D. 20.9' **II**, after '*observe faithfully*' insert 'ἀψευδήων (1 sg. subj.) ἂν τὰν συϝ(Ϝ)οικίαν'

**ἀψεφέω**, delete the entry.

**ἀψεφής**, add 'cf. pers. n. Ἀψεφίων And. 1.43, etc.'

**ἀψίκορος**, line 4, for 'Posidon. 41' read 'Posidon. 36 J.'

***ἀψίμοθος**, ον, *kindling conflict*, *provocative*, Nonn.*D.* 28.92 (ὀψι- cod.).

**ἀψινθᾶτον**, add '*wine flavoured with wormwood*, *Edict.Diocl.* 2.18'

***ἀψινθοκραής**, ές, *mixed with wormwood*, οἶνος *An.Boiss.* 3.410.

**ἄψινθος**, add '*BGU* 2358.3 (iv AD)'

**⁺ἀψίς**, Ep. and Ion. **ἀψίς, ῖδος**, ἡ, acc. ἄψιν Hes. l.c., *outer part of a wheel*, *felloe*, Hes.*Op.* 426, Hdt. 4.72.3, E.*Hipp.* 1233; fig., Ar.*Th.* 53; of water-wheel, *PLond.* 1177.200 (ii AD), *PFlor.* 218.4 (iii AD), *PThead.* 20.10 (iv AD); of potter's wheel, Nicaenet. 5. **b** *rim*, *band*, A.R. 3.138; perh. ξύλον εἰς τὰς ἀψίδας τοῖς σφονδύλοις τοῦ κίονος *IG* 11(2).161.*A*70 (Delos, ii BC). **2** *segment* of circle, Arist.*Mete.* 371ᵇ28, 29; spec. *semicircle*, Hero *Geom.* 18.1. **3** *semicircle* of seats, D.C. 61.17.2, *GVI* 656.9. **II** *concavity*, *hollow* of a net, ἀψῖσι λίνοιο Il. 5.487, D.P.*Au.* 3.9, Opp.*H.* 4.146. **III** *arch*, Hld. 10.6.2, Lib.*Or.* 11.202; *triumphal arch*, D.C. 53.22.2, 55.2.3, 68.1.1, *CPHerm.* 127ᵛ.2.22; *arch* of bridge, *IGRom.* 3.887.7 (Cilicia). **2** *the vault of heaven*, Pl.*Phdr.* 247b, Archestr. in *Suppl.Hell.* 164.2, Luc.*Bis Acc.* 33. **3** the *curved* (visible) *course* of the sun or moon, τὴν ἡμερίαν ἁψῖδα E.*Ion* 88, σελάνας ἐς δεκάταν ἀψῖδα i.e. the tenth month, *Hymn.Is.* 38; also, the *course* of a planet in relation to the earth, Plin.*HN* 2.63, 64.

**ἄψογος**, after 'Poll. 3.139' insert '*ISmyrna* 550.9'

**ἄψος**, for '*juncture*, *joint*' read 'in pl., *limbs*' (deleting those wds. fr. line 3); add 'Od. 18.189, A.R. 3.676, Nic.*Th.* 332, τὰ δ' ἡμίβρωτα κέχυνται ἄψεα Opp.*H.* 2.294, Q.S. 1.252'

**ἀψοφητί**, before 'Pl.*Tht.* 144b' insert 'οἷον ἐλαίου ῥεῦμα ἀ. ῥέοντος'; add 'Plot. 3.8.5'

**⁺ἄψυκτος**, ον, *uncooled*, codd. in Pl.*Phd.* 106a. **2** fem., name of a precious stone, Plin.*HN* 37.148.

**ἀψῡχέω**, add '**2** *to be faint-hearted*, *lack courage*, *SEG* 35.989.20 (Cnossus, ii/i BC), Phot. α 3491 Th.'

**ἄψῡχος II**, add 'of dogs, X.*Cyn.* 3.2.3'

**ἄω** (A) **II**, delete the section (v. ἀέσκω).

**ἄω** (C) **I**, line 4, after '*satiate*' insert 'w. acc. and gen.' and at end after '(Il.) 5.289' insert 'cf. 9.489, 18.281, al.; w. acc. and dat., Il. 11.818; w. acc. only, ib. 24.211' add '**2** *administer liberally*, Nic.*Th.* 676, *Al.* 305, 331.' **II**, delete 'mostly'

***ἀωϊλιασταί**, οἱ, *excavators*, *PCair.Zen.* 745.58 (iii BC); cf. °ἀωΐλιον 2.

**ἀωΐλιον**, for '2 *cubic* πήχεις' read '*the cube of a royal double* πῆχυς' and after 'p. 118' insert '**2** the ἀ. being used to measure earth or sand removed, οἱ τὰ ἀ. ἐργαζόμενοι are *excavators of earth*, *PCair.Zen.* 745.61 (iii BC), cf. *PHib.* 1.100ʳ.3 (iii BC).'

**ἀωρί**, add 'ἔστιν ἀ. *AP* 12.116'

**⁺ἀώριος**, α, ον, *out of season*, *untimely*, of unripe fruits, Thphr.*CP* 2.2.2, Nonn.*D.* 2.78; *born at the wrong time*, of Dionysus, i.e. as a man, not as other immortals, Nonn.*D.* 20.206; of persons who die prematurely, *CEG* 75 (ἀhόριος, Athens, v BC), fem. pl. -ιαι ib. 696 (Peraea, iv BC); τὸν ἴδιον ἀγώριν (= ἀώριον) *Side* 114.9 (Rom.imp.); cf. mod. Gk. ἀγόρι *young boy*, ἄγωρος s.v. °ἄωρος; transf., ἀ. τύμβος *AP* 7.600 (Jul.Aegypt.).

***ἀωρόβιος**, ον, cj. for δορόβιος, *SEG* 23.659 (Cyprus, iii AD).

**⁺ἀωροθάνής**, ές, *of untimely death*, rest. in *ISmyrna* 533.6 (ii BC), *SEG* 28.1101, 1206.13, αὐωρο- *AA* 48.124 (all Phrygia, iii AD).

**ἄωρος** (A), after 'ον' insert '[α, ον *MAMA* 7.345, *SEG* 26.1717 (Egypt, iii/iv AD)], ἄhορος *CEG* 45 (Athens, vi BC), αὔωρος *MAMA* 7.313.3, ἄγωρος *SEG* 2.202 (Thespiae, iii/iv AD), cf. ἄγουρος, alleged by Eust. 1788.56 to be Thracian and Att. for *youth* (cf. ἄγωριν, s.v. °ἀώριος)'; line 2, after 'θάνατος' insert '*Carm.Conv.* 1.4 P.'; line 4, before 'ἄ. θανεῖν' insert 'of persons, οὐκ ἂν ἄωρος ἐὼν μοῖραν ἔχοι θανάτου Sol. 27.18 W.'; line 10, after 'Plu.*Sull.* 2' add 'neut. pl. as adv., *untimely*, *Anacreont.* 59.20 W.'; at end add 'see also ἄνωρος'

**ἄωρος** (C), delete this entry (v. °ὦρος C).

**ἀωροσύνη**, for 'dub. in *Epigr.Gr.* 414' read 'Bernand *IMEG* 73.4 (Abydus, ii AD)'

***ἀωρότης**, ητος, ἡ, *immaturity*, τὴν σή[ν] ἀωρότηταν κὲ ἀθαλάμευ[τον] ἡλικίαν *SEG* 6.140.10 (Phrygia, iv AD), but perh. f.l. for ἀωροτάτην.

**⁺ἄως**, v. ‡ἕως.

**ἄωτον**, for '*the choicest* .. wool' read '*nap* or *pile* of wool'; for 'once of the *finest linen*' read 'of linen'; line 7, for '(Call.)*Hec.* 1.4.3' read '(Call.)*fr.* 260.57 Pf.'

**ἄωτος**, ον, for 'dub. in .. 1.138' read 'prob. in Call.*fr.* 399 Pf.'

# B

***β-**, for transcriptions of Lat. wds. beginning with 'v' see also **οὐ-**.

**βαβάκινος**, add '(βαβάκινον ‹καὶ βάκινον› La.)'

***βαβαλιστήριον**, τό, *cradle*, *Gloss.* 2.361.

***βαβαλίστρια**, ἡ, *cradle*, Leont.Byz.*HP* 1.2.4.

***βάβᾱλος**, v. ‡βέβηλος.

***βαβούλιον**, gloss on κύμβαλον, Hsch.; cf. °βακύλιον.

***βαβουτζικάριος**, ὁ, name for person suffering from λυκανθρωπία, Cyran. 66 (2.23.18 K.), Suid. s.v. Ἐφιάλτης.

**⁺βάβρηκες·** τὰ οὖλα τῶν ὀδόντων. οἱ δὲ σιαγόνας. οἱ δὲ τὰ ἐν τοῖς ὀδοῦσιν ἀπὸ τῆς τροφῆς κατεχόμενα Hsch.; cf. βάρηκες.

***βαβύη·** χείμαρρος. οἱ δὲ πόλις (?πηλός) Hsch.

***Βᾰβῠλωνάριος**, ὁ, *maker of Babylonian shoes* or *garments*, *SEG* 8.138*a* (Palestine); cf. °καλιγάριος.

***Βᾰβῠλωνικός**, ή, όν, *Babylonian*, *Edict.Diocl.* 8.1, al.

**Βᾰβῠλώνιος**, add 'λίθος σάρδιος ὁ Β. οὕτω καλούμενος Epiph.Const. in *Lapid.Gr.* 194.5, Cyran. 6.8.1 K.'

**βαβύρτᾱς**, after 'Hsch.' insert 'as pers. n., *IG* 1³.1157.18 (Athens, v BC), Plb. 4.4.5 (a Messenian), Maiuri *Nuova Silloge* p. 250 no. 3 (Hellen., ?Rhodes), *Delph.* 3(6).87.16 (ii BC), etc.'

***βαγεύει·** πλανητεύει Cyr. (cf. Lat. *vagor*).

***βαγινάριος**, ὁ, Lat. *vaginarius*, *scabbard-maker*, epitaph in *ZPE* 82.225 (Stobi, v/vi AD), Lyd.*Mag.* 1.46.

**βάγος**, add '= ἄγος (B)'

**⁺βαγός**, app. error by Hsch. for ἀγός.

**βᾰδιστηλάτης**, add '*carriage-driver*, *PWash.Univ.* 49.11 (i BC)'

**βᾰδιστικός II**, add '-ὰ πορεῖα *carriage-animals*, *PLond.* 1973.3 (iii BC)'

**βάδιστοι**, add '(but βά‹ρ›διστοι· β‹ρ›αδύταται La.)'

***βάζιον**, τό, a mineral (cf. πάζιον), *SEG* 20.670.7 (= Bernand *Pan* 51.6, i AD); sp. βασιον in *OGI* 660.3 (= Bernand *Koptos* 41, i AD); cf. Copt. *basion*.

**βαθάρα**, add '(dub., placed after βαταίνει β 320; cf. perh. °βαιθάρα)'

**βαθμίς I**, add 'ἔστρωσεν σὺν βαθμεῖσι *IGLS* 4034 (ii AD)'

**βαθμός I 1**, for 'Lxx .. 1127' read 'βαθμοῖς νυμφικοῖς ἐπεστάθη ὁ μοιχός *Trag.adesp.* 519 K.-S., ἐπὶ βαθμὸν οἴκου Lxx 1*Ki.* 5.5, πύργον [κα]ὶ βασμόν *GDI* 5524.10 (Cyzicus); *rung* of ladder, Luc.*Trag.* 221 (βασμ-), *Edict.Diocl.* 14.6' **2** and **3**, delete the sections. **II**, of a genealogy, add 'Modest.*Dig.* 27.1.14.1, Just.*Nov.* 118.4'

**βᾰθόημι**, add 'β]αθόην[ rest. in Alc. 288.2 L.-P.'

**βάθος 1**, line 4, after 'Pl.*R.* 528b' insert 'μετρητικὴ δὲ μήκους καὶ ἐπιπέδου καὶ βάθους *Lg.* 817e' **2**, after 'Plu.*Pomp.* 53' insert 'β. σεμνότητος Callistr.*Stat.* 10' **3**, for '*bathos*' read '*profundity*'

**βαθρικόν**, for '*base*' read '*pedestal with steps*' and delete '*stairway*'

***βαθρικός**, ή, όν, *of a* βάθρον, τὸν δὲ ἀνδ[ριάν]τα ἀνέστησεν .. ἐπισκευάσας τὸ ὑπὸ πατρὸς γε[γον]ὸς β. ἔργον *BCH* 10.501 (Pisidia).

***[β]αθρόθυμα**, ατος, τό, dub. sens., *IG* 1³.425.36 (v BC).

**βάθρον 1**, add 'cf. ἀλλὰ μὴν καὶ ἡ γῆ τούτου (sc. τοῦ ἠέρος) βάθρον Hp.*Flat.* 3' **3**, add '**b** *horizontal timber* (?*sill*) at the bottom of a door, ξύλα εἰς βάθρα ταῖ(ς) θύραις τῶν πυλίδων *IG* 2².1672.149.' **4**, add '*SEG* 37.713 (Chios, Rom.imp.)' **6**, add 'also β. Ἱπποκράτειον Gal. 18(1).303.12, 351.6, 747.34'

***βάθρος**, ὁ, = βάθρον, *Hierapolis* 269.

**⁺βᾰθύγλωσσος**, ον, glossed by ἐλλόγιμος, Hsch., Suid. (also v.l. in Lxx *Ez.* 3.5; cf. °βαρυγλ-).

**βᾰθῠδῑνήεις**, add 'Il. 21.603'

**βᾰθῠδίνης**, ου, add 'Orph.*H.* 38.17'

***βᾰθύκερως**, ωτος, *having deeply-curving horns*, epith. of Isis, *Lyr. Alex.adesp.* 36.5 (= Mesom. 5.5 H.).

**βᾰθῠκνήμῑς**, after '*greaves*' insert 'Ἄρεος θύγατρα' add '**2** = βαθύκνημος, ἐρίπνη Nonn.*D.* 9.273.'

**βᾰθῠκύμων**, for '*deep in waves*' read '*having deep waves*' and after 'Nonn.*D.* 23.320' insert 'βαθυκύμονος Ὠκεανοῖο D.P. 56'

***βᾰθῠλιμενίτης**, ου, ὁ, *presiding over a deep harbour*, epith., prob. local, of Apollo, *SEG* 15.766 (Artake nr. Cyzicus, ii/i BC), 33.1054 (Cyzicus, i BC).

**βᾰθύνω II**, intr., for '*sink deep* .. 2.402' read '*go down* or *penetrate deeply*, ὅταν αἱ .. ῥίζαι βαθύνωσι Ph. 2.402; of the mind's eye, id. 1.248; w. intent to hide, βαθύνατε εἰς κάθισιν Lxx *Je.* 30.2, 25'

**βᾰθύπλουτος**, add 'A.*fr.* 451g.3 R. (anap.); metaph., β. κραδίη *APl.* 40 (Crin.)'

**⁺βᾰθύπορος**, ον, wd. in broken context, perh. *having deep paths*, *Lyr. adesp.* 7(*c*).9 P.

**βᾰθύρροος**, add 'Ezek.*Exag.* 13'

**βᾰθύς**, line 2, add 'acc. fem. βαθέην Il. 17.466' **I 2 b**, comp., add '*Edict.Diocl.* 25.2' **3 b**, line 5, for '*AP* 7.170' read '*AP* 7.197 (Phaënn.)'; line 6, after 'Luc.*DMar.* 2.3' insert 'of death, v.l. in *AP* 7.170 (Posidipp. or Call.)' **4**, add '**b** *not easily offended*, of persons, Chrysipp.*Stoic.* 2.243.'

**βᾰθύτης**, for 'of mental *profundity*' read '*slowness to take offence*'

**⁺βᾰθύφωνος**, ον, calque on Hebr. *ʿimkê-sāphâ*, i.e. *of unintelligible speech*, Lxx *Is.* 33.19.

***βᾰθύχειλος**, ον, = °βαθύφωνος, Lxx *Ez.* 3.5.

**βαΐα**, add '*IG* 14.839 (ed.: pers. n.), epitaph in *Glotta* 16.277 (Constantinople, vi AD), Suid. s.v. τεθή'

***βαίθ**, or **βέθ**, representing Hebr. *bath*, Graecized as βάτος (C) q.v., β. ἐλαίου Lxx 3*Ki.* 5.25.

***βαιθάρα**, ἡ, (perh. βαίθαρα, τά), dub. sens., ἐλαιῶν β. *PAberd.* 192.5 (ii/iii AD), prob. a measure; cf. °βαίθ, βάτος (C), ‡βαθάρα.

**βαίνω**, line 4, delete '*Eu.* 76'; line 16, after 'Il. 1.428' insert '2 sg. aor. ἐβήσαο *h.Ap.* 141 (intr.), 3 sg. ἐπ-εβάσατο Call.*LavPall.* 65 (trans.)'; line 19, after 'Th. 1.123, 8.98' insert 'περ-βέβαται Alc. 119.9 L.-P.' **A II 1**, delete 'in act. .. Them.*Or.* 21.248b)' and then read 'of the male, *mount*, *cover*, Pl.*Phdr.* 250e, Arist.*HA* 575ᵃ13; (fut.) med., Thgn. 185, Achae. 28'

***βαιοιελυπίου**, Egyptian word for a kind of boat, *PTeb.* 701.260, *PPetr.* 3.129a.11, al., *PLille* 25.43 (all iii BC).

**βαιός**, line 14, after '*a little*' insert 'Hes.*Op.* 418'; line 15, after '(S.)*Tr.* 335' insert 'also πρὸς βαιόν *APl.* 212.4 (Alph.)'

***βαίουλος**, ὁ, dub. sens., *GVI* 1112.11 (Bithynia, ii AD); cj. in Hsch. s.v. οἴσυλος (= Lat. *baiulus*).

**⁺βαίτη**, ἡ, *cloak made of skins*, ἐκ τῶν ἀποδαρμάτων καὶ χλαίνας ἐπιέννυσθαι ποιεῦσι συρράπτοντες κατά περ βαίτας Hdt. 4.64.3, Sophr. 38, Theoc. 3.25, Herod. 7.128. **II** *tent of skins*, S.*fr.* 1031 R. **2** *covered building* in a market-place, *IG* 5(2).268.48 (Mantinea *c.*10 BC/*c.*AD 10), *Inscr.Magn.* 179.12, 15 (i AD), *SEG* 26.1652.5 (Syria, ii AD).

**βαιτοφόρος**, delete 'prob. for βαττ- in'

***βαιτύλιον**, τό, dim. of βαίτυλος, in pl., Ph.Bybl.ap.Eus.*PE* 1.10, Dam.*Isid.* 94, 203.

**βαίτῠλος**, add 'prov. βαίτυλον ἂν κατέπιες, of greedy persons, Apostol. 9.24; a precious stone, Plin.*HN* 37.135; as title of Zeus, cf. Semitic *bethel*, Διὶ βετύλῳ *SEG* 7.341 (Dura, iii AD)'

**βαιών I**, for this section read 'kind of fish (= βλέννος acc. to *EM* 192.52), Epich. 64 (Ath. 7.288a)' **II**, add 'cf. βάϊς, βάϊον II'

***βακάνιον**, τό, dim. of βάκανον, *POsl.* 48.10 (i AD).

**βάκανον**, for '*cabbage*' read 'perh. *Althaea cannabina*' and delete 'also *cabbage-seed*'

***βᾰκέλας**, α, ὁ, = βάκηλος, cj. in Alex.Aet. 9.2 (*Coll.Alex.* p. 127; codd. ‡μακ-).

**βάκηλος I**, add 'Suet.*Blasph.* 52 T.' at end add 'cf. κάβηλος, app. same wd. w. metath.'

**βάκκᾰρις**, dat., for 'Hippon. 41' read 'Hippon. 104.21 W., βακκάρει Achae. 10'

***βάκκερα**, ἡ, plant sacred to Dionysus, Cyran. 22 (1.8.8 K.).

***βάκρον**, v. °βάκτρον.

**βακτηρία**, see also βατηρία.

**βακτήριον**, for 'dim. of βακτηρία' read 'var. of βακτηρία'

***βακτηριοφόρος**, gloss on καλαυρόψις, Hsch.

***βακτρᾶς**, 'α, ὁ, *dealer in* βάκτρα, *SEG* 34.221 (?Athens, iv AD).

**βάκτρον**, add 'app. Cypr. var. *pa-ka-ra* (pl.) βάκρα, *shafts* of bronze lances, *ICS* 218, cf. 368a (Add. p. 415, v BC)'

***βακύλιον**, gloss on κύμβαλον, Hsch.; cf. °βαβούλιον.

***Βακχάζω**, in expl. of Διαγόρας, .. διὰ τὸ τοὺς μύστας βακχάζειν, τουτέστιν ᾄδειν τὸν Ἴακχον δι' ἀγορᾶς βαδίζοντας Hsch. s.v. Διαγόρας.

***Βακχεασταί**, οἱ, *worshippers of Bacchus*, *IGBulg.* 20.3 (Dionysopolis, iii BC); cf. Βακχιαστής.

**Βακχεία**, line 3, after 'E.*Ph.* 21' insert '*Bacchic rite*, Ael.*VH* 13.2'

**Βακχεῖον 2 b**, for this section read '*sanctuary* or *shrine of Bacchus*, *SEG* 37.601 (Thrace, iii AD); cf. β.· τελεστήριον, νάρθηξ Hsch.'

***Βακχειώτης**, ου, ὁ, epith. of Dionysus, *Lyr.adesp.* 318 in *SLG*; cf. ‡*Βακχιώτης*.

**Βακχιαστής**, add 'cf. °*Βακχεασταί*'

**Βακχικός**, after 'D.S. 1.11' insert '*βαχχικὸς ὀρχηστής* epigr. in *IClaudiopolis* 83'

**Βάκχιος** (s.v. *Βάκχειος*) **II**, as subst., add 'Ar.*Ach.* 263, E.*Ba.* 67, 225, etc., *Ion* 550; *ὦ Βάχχιε* Philod.Scarph. 10'

**Βακχιών**, add 'at Ceos (Poessa), *IG* 12(5).1100.4 (v BC)'

**βακχιώτης**, after 'lyr.' insert 'Dor. *-τᾶς*' and add 'cf. °*Βακχειώτης*'

**Βάκχος**, after lemma insert '(sp. *Βάχχ-* *SEG* 26.683, Thessaly, iii BC), etc.'

***βᾰλάβαθρον**, v. °*μαλάβαθρον*.

**βᾰλᾰνάγρα**, line 1, for '*key* .. *βάλανος* II 4' read '*key* or *hook for pulling out the bolt-pin of a door*'; line 2, for 'in pl. = *βάλανος* II 4' read 'also, *bolt-pin*' and add '*App.Anth.* 5.17 (Hedyl.)'

**βᾰλᾰνάριον**, add '*SEG* 7.417.12 (Dura, iii AD)'

**βᾰλᾰνεῖον I**, add '*ἐπὶ βαλανείων* = Lat. *a balneis*, *IG* 5(1).669, *IG* 14.1052, *Ann.Epigr.* 1938.84, *PLond.* 1178.59 (ii AD)'

***βᾰλᾰνειοφύλαξ**, ἄκος, ὁ, *caretaker of the baths*, dub. l. in *OMich.* 102 (iv AD).

**βᾰλᾰνευτικός**, add '*τὸ -όν* *bath tax*, *Pap.Lugd.Bat.* xxv 24.3 (AD 94)'

**βᾰλᾰνικός**, add '*-οῦ* sc. *ἐλαίου* *PSI* 481.6'

**βᾰλᾰνισσα**, add '*Suppl.Mag.* 42 (Hermoupolis, iii/iv AD)'

**βάλᾰνος II 7**, for '*ballot-ball*' read '*lot*'

***Βαλβίλλεια** (-ηα), τά, *games in honour of Balbillus*, held in Ephesus, *IG* 14.746 (sp. *Βαρβ-*, Naples, i AD), etc., *SEG* 34.1314 (Lycia, c.AD 90), *IEphes.* 642, 686, al.; also held at Smyrna, ib. 1123.

**βάλερος**, add 'also *βάλλερ[ος]* *IGC* p. 99 B29 (Acraephia, iii/ii BC)'

**βαλιδικός**, delete the entry (v. *ZPE* 7.54).

***βαλλαντᾶς**, 'α, ὁ, *maker of βαλλάντια*, *ITyr* 95 (ed.: pers. n.).

**βαλλάντιον I**, for '[Simon.] 178' read '*AP* 5.159.3 (Simon.)'; add 'perh. *bag containing fixed sum of money*, *PBeatty Panop.* 2.93, 94, 97'

***βάλλερος**, v. °*βάλερος*.

**βαλλίζω**, delete 'in Sicily and Magna Graecia' and add '*GVI* 1112.11 (Bithynia, ii AD), *IHadr.* 101 (ii AD)'

***βαλλιστάριος**, ὁ, Lat. *ballistarius*, Lyd.*Mag.* 1.46, *SEG* 7.154 (E. of Palmyra); also *βαλλιστράριος* *IGChr.Russie* 7, Just.*Nov.* 85.2.

**βάλλω A I**, line 4, for '*ἐλβὼν*' read '*ἐλθὼν*' **II 1**, line 5, delete 'in prose abs.'; line 7, after 'Th. 4.33' insert 'cf. Call.*fr.* 191.79 Pf.' **2 b**, line 3, after '(S.)*Ph.* 1028' insert 'esp. of *throwing* into prison, *εἰς φυλακήν β.* *Ev.Matt.* 18.30, *Apoc.* 2.10, Arr.*Epict.* 1.1.24, al., *PTeb.* 567 (i AD)' **6**, line 6, before '*pour*' insert '*lay the foundations* of, *ἄστυ βαλεῖν* A.R. 2.849; cf. infr. B. I 4' **7**, line 3, after 'metaph.' insert 'abs. Call.*Epigr.* 8.4.Pf.'; for '*εὖ* or *καλῶς*' read '*καλῶς* or *εὖ*' **II**, add '**8** *bury illicitly* in a tomb, *SEG* 37.1086 (Pontus, ii/iii AD), *MAMA* 6.325 (iii AD), 1.167 (c.AD 400), *TAM* 2.1148, 4(1).283, Ramsay *Cities and Bishoprics* 1.233.80.' **B I 2**, add '**b** *cast* lots, *πάλους ἐβάλοντο* Call.*fr.* 119.2 Pf.'

***βαλνικάριος**, ὁ, *bath attendant*, *Corinth* 8(3).534 (v/vi AD).

***βάλτιον**, τό, *belt*, *PMich.*III 217.19 (-ιν, iii AD, cf. Lat. *balteus*).

***βάλτιος**, ὁ, *belt*, *Edict.Diocl.* in *SEG* 37.335 iii 17, al. (written -ις).

**βαμβαίνω**, for '*chatter with the teeth*' read '*make inarticulate sounds, babble, mumble*, etc.'

**βαμβᾰκύζω** (s.v. *βαμβαίνω*), for pres. ref. read 'codd. in Hippon. 32.3 (v. °*βαμβᾰλ-*)'

***βαμβᾰλιαστύς**, ύος, ἡ, *babbling*, v.l. for *κρεμβ-* in *h.Ap.* 162; cf. *βαμβαίνω, βαμβαλύζω*.

**βαμβᾰλύζω** (s.v. *βαμβαίνω*), before 'Phryn.' insert 'cj. in Hippon. 32.3 W., *Iamb.adesp.* 38.4 W.'

**βάμμα II**, for this section read 'something in which food is dipped, e.g. vinegar (glossed by *ὄξος*, Sch.Nic.*Al.* 49, al.), Nic.*Th.* 87, 622, *Al.* 369, al.; *β. σίμβλων* = *ὀξύμελι*, id.*Al.* 49'

***βάνατα**, ἡ, app. some kind of garment, *Edict.Diocl.* 19.55, 57, perh. cf. Lat. *pannus*.

**βάναυσος II 1**, add 'Iamb.*Protr.* 5' **3**, for 'later, *fastidious*' read '*rude, coarse-mannered*'

***βάνδον**, τό, also *βάνδα*, τό, Sch.Procl. *in Ti.* 1.462.11, *military standard* (Goth. *bandwa*), Procop.*Vand.* 2.2.1. **2** *company of infantry*, *IGLBulg.* 89.3 (vi AD), perh. also *IApam.* 136. **3** *military area*, Sch.Procl. l.c.

***βανδοφόρος**, ὁ, *standard-bearer*, Procop.*Vand.* 2.10.4.

***βανιάτωρ**, ορος, ὁ, Lat. *balneator*, *PKlein.Form.* 980.2 (vi AD).

**βανωτός**, for '*vase*' read '*jar*'

**βάπτης**, add '**II** name of gem, Plin.*HN* 37.149.'

**βαπτίζω 1**, line 7, after 'J.*BJ* 4.3.3' insert 'transf., *overwhelm, flood*, *ἐλευθέραν ἀφῆκε βαπτίσας ἐρρωμένως* Aristopho 13 K.-A.' **2**, delete 'Aristopho 14.5'

**βαπτιστήριον**, add '**II** *baptistery*, *SEG* 32.1065 (Rome, Chr.).'

***βαπτιστός**, ή, όν, dub. sens., *βαπτιστοῖο* .. *μελάθρου* *GVI* 134.3 (Tyana, iii AD).

***βάπτρον**, τό, *charge for dyeing*, *SB* 12314.16 (ii AD).

**βάπτω I 1 - 3**, for these sections read '*immerse* in a liquid, *dip*, *ὡς δ' ὅτ' ἀνὴρ χαλκεὺς πέλεκυν* .. *εἰν ὕδατι ψυχρῷ βάπτῃ* (so as to temper the red-hot steel) Od. 9.392; *ἔβαψεν ἰούς* S.*Tr.* 574; *χιτῶνα τόνδ' ἔβαψα* ib. 580; *β. εἰς ὕδωρ* Pl.*Ti.* 73e, cf. Emp. 100.11; *τάρια θερμῷ* Ar.*Ec.* 216; *εἰς μέλι, εἰς κηρόν* Arist.*HA* 605ᵃ29, *de An.* 435ᵃ2, *β. τὸν δάκτυλον ἀπὸ τοῦ αἵματος* Lxx *Le.* 4.17; pass., *βαπτόμενος σίδηρος* iron *in process of being tempered*, Plu. 2.136a. **b** of slaughter in trag., *ἐν σφαγαῖσι βάψασα ξίφος* A.*Pr.* 863; *ἔβαψας ἔγχος εὖ πρὸς Ἀργείων στρατῷ*; S.*Aj.* 95; *φάσγανον εἴσω σαρκὸς ἔβαψεν* E.*Ph.* 1578 (lyr.); in later prose, *εἰς τὰ πλευρὰ β. τὴν αἰχμήν* D.H. 5.15. **2** *colour by immersion, dye*, *β. τὰ κάλλη* *dye* the beautiful cloths, Eup. 333; *β. ἔρια ὥστ' εἶναι ἁλουργά* Pl.*R.* 429d; *εἵματα βεβαμμένα* Hdt. 7.67.1; *τρίχας βάπτειν* *AP* 11.68 (Lucill.); poet., *φᾶρος τόδ' ὡς ἔβαψεν Αἰγίσθου ξίφος* A.*Ch.* 1011; humorously, *βάπτειν τινὰ βάμμα Σαρδιανικόν* *dye* one in the [red] dye of Sardes, i.e. give him a bloody head, Ar.*Ach.* 112; fig., *βέβαπται β. κυζικηνικόν* *he has been dyed in* the dye of Cyzicus, i.e. is a thorough coward, id.*Pax* 1176 (v. Sch.); transf., of gilding and silvering, Ps.-Democr. p. 46 B. **3** *dip* a vessel in order to draw water, *ἀρύταιναν* .. *ἐκ μέσου βάψασα τοῦ λέβητος ζέοντος ὕδατος* *draw* water *by dipping* the bucket, Antiph. 25, cf. Thphr.*Char.* 9.8; *βάψασα ποντίας ἁλός* (sc. *τὸ τεῦχος*) *having dipped* it *so as to draw* water from the sea, E.*Hec.* 610; cf. *ἀνθ' ὕδατος τᾷ κάλπιδι κηρία βάψαι* Theoc. 5.127.'

**βάραγχος**, delete the entry.

**βάραθρον**, add '**IV** pl., gloss on *λάσανα*, Hsch. (*τὰ βάθρα* La.).'

**βάρακος**, after 'Hsch.' insert 'a freshwater fish in *IGC* p. 99 B 21 (Acraephia, iii/ii BC)'

**βάρβαξ**, add 'comic gloss in *CGFP* 343.7; cf. pers. n. *Βάρβακς* *IG* 12(3).543 (Thera, vii BC); *Βάρβακος* *Inscr.Cret.* 2.xi 3.6, 19 (Dictynna, i BC)'

***βαρβᾰρικάριος**, ὁ, *brocade-maker*, *Edict.Diocl.* 20.5, 7, *ITyr* 122.

**βαρβᾰρικός I**, add '*πρεσβείας* .. *βαρβαρικάς* i.e. *embassies to non-Greeks*, *IHistriae* 12.9 (iii BC)'

**βαρβᾰρισμός**, add '**II** *siding with non-Greeks*, in quot. spec. Persians, *SEG* 22.506.9 (Chios, letter of Alexander).'

***βαρβᾰρόλεξις**, εως, ἡ, *use of foreign speech*, Consentius p. 386 K.

***βαρβᾰρόμῡθος**, *uttered in a foreign tongue*, cj. in Ar.*Pax* 753 (v. *βορβορόθυμος*).

***βαρβᾰρόστομος**, ον, *speaking in a barbarous manner*, *Trag.adesp.* 696 K.-S.

***Βαρβίλληα**, τά, v. °*Βαλβίλλεια*.

**βάρβῐτον** (s.v. *βάρβιτος*), after 'as' insert 'sts.'; delete 'Neanth. 5' and for 'etc.' read '*AP* 7.23b, ib. 588 (Paul.Sil.), Nonn.*D.* 42.253'

**βάρβῐτος**, for '*musical instrument of many strings* .. Theoc. 16.45)' read 'type of bowl lyre with long arms'; delete 'freq. used for *the lyre*'; line 3, for 'etc.' read 'Theoc. 16.45; in 4th century distd. fr. *κιθάρα* and *λύρα* Arist.*Pol.* 1341ᵃ40, Anaxil. 15 K.-A.'; line 4, for '(*Anacreont.*) 14.34' read '15.34 W. and *AP* 7.25 (Simon.)'; at end add '*βάρμιτος* Aeol. acc. to *EM* 188.21; cf. *βάρμος*'

**βάρδοι II**, delete the section.

***βάρδος**, ὁ, dub. sens., (refers to commodity which is purchased), *BGU* 276.11 (iii AD); cf. perh. °*βαρδόσημος*.

***βαρδόσημος**, ον, dub. sens., adj. applied to garment, *POxy.* 3860.20 (iv AD); cf. °*βάρδος*, or perh. = *παρδο-*, *with marks like a leopard*.

**βᾰρέω**, line 1, after 'Aeol. *βορ-*, v. infr.' insert 'line 7, but see also °*βορέομαι*' **I 1**, line 3, after 'Id.*Sol.* 7' insert 'Hdn.*Philet.* 212'; line 7, transfer '*κῆρ* .. 25.17' to section II line 8, after 'pass., pres.' add '**3** *charge with a legal obligation*, *Cod.Just.* 6.4.4.18, Just.*Nov.* 43 pr.'

***Βαρζοχαρα**, ἡ, epith. of the Iranian goddess Anaitis, *BE* 1968.538 (i BC) (see also *ZVS* 84.207 for etym.).

***βαριοτομέω**, *cut* (in quot., papyrus) *from a boat*, *BGU* 1121.20.

**βᾶρις 2**, at beginning for 'later' read 'wd. of uncertain origin, distinct. fr. *βᾶρις* 1'; for 'Kalinka .. 142' read '*IGBulg.* 400.5' and before it insert '*Didyma* 492.18, etc. (iii BC), *Inscr.Magn.* 122 d 4-8 (Rom.imp.)'; last line, transfer '(Egyptian word)' to the end of section 1.

***βαρκαῖος**, ὁ, kind of fish, Theognost.*Can.* 52.

***βάρμῐτος**, v. °*βάρβιτος*.

***βάρμος**, ὁ, = *βάρβιτος*, Alc. 70.4 L.-P., Phillis ap.Ath. 636c; also *βάρωμος* Sapph. 176 L.-P. (acc. to Euph. 180 vGr.) but perh. read *βάρμος*.

**βάρνᾰμαι**, for '*IG* .. (Corc.)' read '*CEG* 145.2 (Corc., c.600 BC), 155.2 (Paros, 476/5 BC), 6.2 (Athens, ?447 BC), al.'

**βάρος II**, add 'the *burden* of the womb, *ἐκύησε ἐγ γαστρὶ Κλεὼ βάρος* *IG* $4^2$.121.9 (Epid., iv BC), *ἀποθέσθαι τὸ β.* *PBremen* 63.4 (ii AD), Artem. 5.30, *θηκαμένη τὸ β.* *SB* 5718' **VII**, add 'of language, D.H.*Dem.* 34, *Th.* 23 (in both places coupled w. *τόνος*)' add '**X** *legal obligation*, Just.*Nov.* 1.1.2.'

***βᾰρουλκός**, ὁ, "*weight-lifter*", an arrangement of interacting cogs described by Hero, and the title of a work by him, Papp. p. 1060.6 H.; also **βαρυολκός**, Olymp. in *Alc.* 191.15.

***βᾰροφίτης**, ου, ὁ, app. *crusher of snakes*, magical inscr., *SEG* 33.1551 (Egypt, iii AD), perh. also in *IGLS* 1098.

**βᾰρυᾱής I**, for '*breathing hard*' read '*marked by deep breathing*'

**βᾰρύβρεμέτης**, add 'epigr. in *SEG* 34.1308 (Side, i BC/i AD)'

***βᾰρυγαύτης**, ου, ὁ, garment, perh. the same as παραγαύδης, *PMich.*xv 752.42 (ii AD).

+**βᾰρύγλωσσος**, ον, *heavy of tongue*, i.e. *hesitant in speech*, λαός Lxx *Ez.* 3.5; *vitriolic*, of Hipponax, Suet.*Blasph.* 39 T.

**βᾰρύδουπος**, for last ref. read '*IHadr.* 80.13 (ii AD) and add 'Coluth. 55'

**βᾰρυηκοΐα**, add 'Gal. 12.533.6, Sever.*Clyst.* p. 18 D.'

**βᾰρυκάρδιος**, for '*heavy, slow of heart*' read '*having base inclinations*'

***βᾰρυκηδής**, ές, *causing great sorrow*, πότμος Bernand *IMEG* 67.7, ἄχθος *GVI* 1397.3 (Pisidia, ii AD).

**βαρύλλιον**, add '*levelling instrument*, Elias *in Porph.* 21.31, *in Cat.* 117.100'

**βάρυμηνις**, add 'of Pan, Orph.*H.* 11.12, of Zeus, ib. 20.4, of Dionysus, id. 45.5'

**βᾰρύμοχθος I**, add '**2** *greatly distressed*, *AP* 12.132 (Mel.).'

**βαρύνω I 2**, line 4, for 'Simon. 184.5' read '*AP* 7.25.5 ([Simon.])'; add 'ὄμματά τ' ἀστράπτοντα βαρυνόμενόν τε νόημα Il.Pers. 4.8 B.' add '**3** *charge with a legal obligation*, Just.*Nov.* 39.1 pr.'

+**βᾰρυολκός**, ὁ, v. °βαρουλκός.

**βᾰρυπένθητος**, for '*mourning heavily*' read '*deeply mourned*'

***βᾰρυπεψία**, ἡ, *indigestion*, *Corp.Herm.ad Amm.* in *Physici* 1.395.22.

**βᾰρύς I 1**, line 3, after 'Arist.*Cael.* 310ᵇ25' insert 'Ath. 3.115e' **2**, lines 10/11, delete '*indigestible*, Ath. 3.115e' **4**, add 'of oaths, ὅρκος γὰρ οὐδεὶς ἀνδρὶ φηλήτῃ βαρύς S.*fr.* 933 R.; Call.*fr.* 75.22 Pf.' **II 4**, delete the section. **III 1**, penultimate line, delete '(οὐ opp. οὔ)'

***βᾰρυσμός**, ὁ, = βαρύτης I, β. τοῦ σώματος ὅλου Gal. 7.466.1 (s.v.l.).

***βᾰρυσταθμία**, ἡ, *full weight*, of coinage, *PLond.* 1405.3 (see also *ZPE* 85.298, AD 709).

**βᾰρύσταθμος**, after 'Ar.*Ra.* 1397' insert 'τὰ πράγματα .. βαρύσταθμα *fr.* 415 K.-A.'

**βᾰρύστομος 3**, for '*cutting deeply*' read '*heavy-bladed*'

**βᾰρυτῑμέω**, for 'τιμουλκέω' read 'τιμιουλκέω'

**βᾰρύφθονος**, add '*EA* 13.19 no. 4, *GVI* 1375 (both Phrygia, Rom.imp.)'

***βᾰρύχειρ**, χειρος, ὁ, ἡ, *heavy for the hands*, παλά epigr. in *Lindos* 699b.1 (ii BC).

***βάρωμος**, v. °βάρμος.

***βαρών**, ῶντος, ὁ, Lat. *baro*, *blockhead*, *BGU* 836.1 (vi AD).

**βᾰσᾰνίζω I**, line 5, after '*prove*' insert 'τὸ πρᾶγμα Pl.*Euthd.* 307b' **II**, for 'αἰωνίοις' to end of section read 'fig., of the earth as being tortured to yield its produce, Philostr.*VA* 6.10. **b** *to be subjected to cruel treatment, be racked*, *Ev.Matt.* 8.6, θηρίοις βεβασανισμένοις Philostr.*VA* 1.38; of things, πλοῖον .. βασανιζόμενον ὑπὸ τῶν κυμάτων *Ev.Matt.* 14.24; *to be racked by emotions*, *SEG* 31.895 (Africa).'

**βᾰσᾰνιστήριον I**, delete 'of the stocks' and transfer 'Sm.*Je.* 20.2' to section II **II**, add 'Lxx 4*Ma.* 8.12, al.'

***βᾰσᾰνιστός**, ή, όν, *tested*, σφραγίδιον β. *IG* 2².1542.13 (iv BC).

**βᾰσᾰνος II**, lines 4/5, for 'βάσανον .. *Lg.* 648b' read 'w. λαμβάνειν, *make a test*, τῶν πολιτῶν .. β. .. λαμβάνειν ἀνδρείας τε πέρι καὶ δειλίας Pl.*Lg.* 648b; δυνάμεις β. λαβοῦσαι *being tested*, D.H.*Dem.* 16'

***βασᾰρα**, v. °βασσάρα.

+**βᾰσείδιον**, v. °βασίδιον, °βασίδιος.

***βᾰσίδιον**, τό, dim. of βάσις, *base*, σὺν τοῖς ὑπὸ τοὺς πόδας βασιδίοις χαλκοῖς *Inscr.Délos* 1417*B*i36 (ii BC), *SB* 9238.20, 9321.11 (both ii/iii AD).

***βασίδιος**, ον, *fitted with a base*, *BGU* 781 iii 6 (i AD), *CPR* viii 62.23 (vi AD).

**βᾰσῐλεια**, line 1, for 'βασιλέα' read 'βασίλεα'

**βᾰσῐλεία I 2**, add '**b** *position of queen*, Lxx *Es.* 1.19.' **4**, delete the section. at end add 'Myc. *qa-si-re-wi-ja*, precise sense obscure'

**βᾰσῐλεΐδης**, for '*prince*' read '*descendant of kings*' and add 'S.*Ant.* 941 (cj.)'

**βᾰσῐλειον I 1**, add '**c** *dominion, reign*, τὴν Τύχην .. τοῦ ἀνεικήτου βασιλείου *BCH* suppl. 8 no. 59 (Maced., iv AD).' **IV**, for 'at Olbia, *IPE* 1.105' read 'later of festivals founded by Hellenistic kings, *IG* 2².3779.19 (iii BC)'

**βᾰσῐλειος**, lines 4/5, delete 'used by Trag. in lyr.' **3**, after 'Crates Com. 2' insert 'of a type of fig, β. σῦκα Philem.Lex.ap.Ath. 3.76f, Poll. 6.81'

**βᾰσῐλεύς**, line 1, for 'Cypr. .. 135 H.' read 'Cypr. *pa-si-le-wo-se* βασιλῆϜος *ICS* 15, 217.6, al.'; lines 2ff., nom. pl., add 'Elean -ᾶες (v. infra, II 2)' **I 1 b**, add 'Θεῷ Βασιλῖ *TAM* 5(1).167 (Saittae, iii AD)' **IV 2**, delete 'β. σῦκα .. Poll. 6.81' (v. °βασίλειος) and substitute 'of rivers, [ποταμῶν ἡμε]τέρων β. Call.*fr.* 7.34 Pf.: sup., π. βασιλεύτατος ἄλλων D.P. 353' at end delete words in brackets and add 'Myc. *qa-si-re-u*, *chief* (not *king*)'

**βᾰσῐλεύω I 1 a**, line 9, after 'Lxx 1*Ma.* 1.16' insert 'τῶν πρὸ ἡμῶν βεβασιλευκότων Just.*Const.Δέδωκεν* pr.'; at end transfer 'hence .. *Sull.* 12' to line 10 to follow 'Arist.*Pol.* 1284ᵇ39, etc.' and add '(s.v.l.)' **c**, after 'cf.' insert '*IG* 2².4067 (βασιλει- lapis)'

**βᾰσῐληΐς 1**, add 'of Rome, Ῥώμης βασιληΐδος *IHadr.* 61 (ii AD), *IEphes.* 802'

***βᾰσῐλίδιον**, τό, name of an eye-salve, Asclep.Pharm.ap.Gal. 12.788.16.

**βᾰσῐλικός I 2**, line 4, after 'γεωργοί' insert 'i.e. cultivators of royal land leased to them'; add 'of coinage of Diocletian, νομίσματα β. *TAM* 4(1).352' add '**5** *of the master of a feast* (συμποσίαρχος), β. νόμους description of works by Xenocr., Speus. and Arist., Ath. 1.3f.' **II 2**, add '**b** *nave* of a church, *AD* 12.69 (Lesbos)' **3 d**, add 'perh. fig., of an Epicurean doctrine, Diog.Oen.*fr.* 51'

+**βᾰσίλιννα**, ἡ, (person having some of the characteristics or functions of a) *queen*, D. 59.74, Men.*fr.* 652a K.-Th.

***Βᾰσίλιος**, ὁ, name of a Cretan month beginning 23 Aug., *Hemerolog.Flor.* p.77 (p. 18 K.).

**βᾰσιλίς I 1 a**, for 'Imperial *princess*' read '*empress*' add '**c** = Lat. *regina sacrorum*, *IGRom* 4.1687.' add '**III** ὑπόδημα γυναικεῖον καὶ αὐλητικόν Eratosth.ap.Hsch. s.v. βασιλίδες; cf. βασιλίσκος v 1.'

**βασίλισσα 2**, at end delete 'also βασίλιννα .. 907' add '**5** as title of goddesses, of Demeter, Mitchell *N.Galatia* 129, of Isis, *SEG* 24.1244 (both Rom.imp.).'

***βάσιον**, v. °βάζιον.

**βασκαίνω**, after 'evil eye, etc.' insert '*CEG* 455 (Amorgos, vi BC), Euph.*fr.* 175'

**βασκᾰνία 1**, add 'personified, Call.*fr.* 1.17 Pf., *PMag.* 4.1451'

**βάσκᾰνος II 1**, add '**b** *mean, niggardly*, Lxx *Prov.* 23.6, 28.22, *Si.* 14.3, 18.18, 37.11.'

***βασκαντήρ**, ῆρος, ὁ, = βάσκανος, Euph. in *Suppl.Hell.* 429.23.

**βασκαύλης**, for 'perh. = Lat. *vasculum*' read 'vessel, perh. = Lat. *bascauda*; cf. also μασκαύλης'

***βασκέλειον**, τό, prob. for βασκαύλειον, dim. of βασκαύλης, ἐλέου β. *PColl.Youtie* 84.10 (iv AD).

**βάσκον**, delete the entry (v. ‡βάσκω).

***βάσκυλα**, τά, Lat. *vascula*, *PRyl.* 27.82 (iv AD).

**βάσκω**, for 'only imper.' read 'usu. imper.', and at end for '(βάσκου .. Hsch.)' read 'ἔβασκε Alc. in *SLG* 262(a) ii 10, βάσκε· πορεύου Hsch., βάσκον· ἐχώρουν id.; see also ‡ἐπιβάσκω'

**βασσάρα II 1**, add 'Λυδῶν δὲ χιτών τις βασάρα (sic) Διονυσιακός, ποδήρης Poll. 7.60'

***βάσσος** (B), (**βᾶσσος** La.) οὐδετέρως· ἡ βῆσσα Hsch.

***βαστᾰγεύς**, έως, ὁ, perh. *carrier of sacred objects*, *Inscr.Délos* 2628.

**βαστᾰγή**, add '*Cod.Just.* 12.57.3'

**βαστάζω I 2**, add 'Sm.*Pr.* 4.8' **IV**, delete the section transferring exx. to section II 2 (act.) at end for 'Plb.' read 'Arist.'

**βαστέρνιον**, line 1, delete '*Cod.Just.* 8.10.12' add '**2** perh. some kind of covered passage in a building, *Cod.Just.* 8.10.12.'

***βαστέρνος**, ὁ, prob. = βαστέρνιον, Hdn.*fr.* p. 26 H.

**βαστραχαλίσαι**, add 'also βαστραχηλίζει Hsch. (La.)'

***βασυμνιάτης**, ου, ὁ, perh. *maker of* βασυννίαι, *MAMA* 3.645 (Corycus).

***βάταλον**, τό, *clapper for marking time*, cf. °κρούπεζα 2, Sch.Aeschin. 1.126, Phot. s.v. κρούπεζαι.

**βᾰτάνη**, add '*PAlex.* (1964)31.4 (iii/iv AD)'

**βατάνιον**, add 'see also πατάνιον'

**βᾰτεία**, delete the entry (v. °βατία).

***βᾰτελλίκιον**, v. °πατελλίκιον.

***βατέρνος**, dub. sens., Hdn.*fr.* p. 26 H.

**βᾰτεύω**, for 'perh. *trample, damage*' read '*cover* (of animals)'

**βᾰτήριον**, delete the entry (v. °βατήριος).

***βᾰτήριος**, α, ον, *of* or *connected with* (*animal*) *copulation*, μηδ' ἀλόγοις ζῴοισι βατήριον ἐς λέχος ἐλθεῖν Ps.-Phoc. 188.

**βάτης**, delete '*treads* or' and for 'expld. .. ἀναβάτης' read 'β. πίθηκος· ἀναβάτης Hsch.'

***βᾰτιά**, ἡ, *thicket*, Pi.*O.* 6.54 (-εία, -ία codd.).

**βᾰτῐᾰκιον**, add '*PCair.Zen.* 120.2 (iii BC)'

**βάτιον**, add '*AB* 224'

**βᾰτον**, add '*SB* 11064 (i AD)'

**βάτος** (C), after 'ὁ' insert '(v. °βαίθ)'; delete '= Egypt. ἀρτάβη or Att. μετρητής'

**βᾰτός**, for '*permissible*' read '*possible*' and add 'Marcellin.*Vit.Thuc.* 35, Just.*Const.Δέδωκεν* 12'

**βᾰτρᾰχειος**, after 'Ar.*Eq.* 523' insert '(edd. nonnulli βατραχειοῖς, v. βατραχειοῦς s.v. βατραχιοῦν)'

**βατραχίτης**, add 'Cyran. 39.27 (1.21.3 K.)'

***βατραχῖτις**, ιδος, ἡ, (sc. λίθος), = βατραχίτης, *PSI* 1180.52 (ii AD).

***Βᾰτρόμιος**, v. °Βοηδρόμιος II.

***Βᾱτρομιών**, v. ‡Βοηδρομιών.

**+βαττολογέω**, *talk aimlessly, waffle*, *Ev.Matt.* 6.7, Simp. in *Epict.* p. 91 D.

***βάττος**· τραυλόφωνος, ἰσχνόφωνος Hsch. (false inference from Hdt. 4.155).

***βαυβύζω**, *bark*, of a dog, *PMag.* 36.157.

**βαυβώ**, add '(acc. to Hsch., s.h.v.)'

**βαυκᾰλιον**, add '**II** as a capacity measure, containing 3,000 bricks, *POxy.* 2197.3, al. (vi AD).'

***βαυκίδια**, τά, dim. of βαυκίδες, Poll. 7.94.

**+βαυκός**, ή, όν, app. *soft, effeminate* or sim., Arar. 9 K.-A.; cf. βαυκά· ήδέα Hsch.

***βαυκύων**, ό, app. *barking dog*, *PMag.* 4.1912 (ref. to Cerberus).

**βαῦνος**, add 'the properisp. accent is Attic acc. to Trypho and Philemon ap. Hdn.*fr.* 53 H.'

**βᾰφή I**, line 5, delete 'prob. poet. for σιδήρου β. in' and 'v. Sch. ad loc.' **II**, line 3, for 'the saffron-*dyed robe*' read '*sprinklings* of saffron'

***βαφωρι-**, article of women's dress (perh. cf. μαφόριον), *PNess.* 18.37 (vi AD).

***βαχχ-**, v. ‡βακχ-.

**βάψιμος**, add '*PMich.*inv. 3731 i 13 (*Tyche* 1.185, ii/iii AD)'

**βδελύσσομαι I 1**, delete '*to be sick*' **2**, after 'id.*Ach.* 586' insert 'Pl.*R.* 605e' add '**3** w. part., *to be sick of* doing, καρυκκοποιοὺς προσβλέπων βδελύσσομαι Achae.*fr.* 12 S.' **II**, delete '*cause to stink*'

**βέβαιος I 1 b**, add 'in Locr. as κύριος, *valid, in force*, τεθμὸς ὅδε περὶ τᾶς γᾶς βέβαιος ἔστō *IG* 9².609.1 (Naupactus, *c.*500 BC)' **II** adv., add 'βεβᾶως Alc. 344 L.-P.'

**βεβαιόω I 1**, add '**b** w. inf., *affirm*, β. ἀναπλεῖν ἐθέλειν D. 32.19.'

**βεβαιωτήρ**, add '*IG* 9².612.9, etc. (Naupactus, iii BC), 394.9, etc. (Stratus, ii BC)'

**βεβαιωτής 1**, add 'ὧν ἁπάντων ἐναργέστατος ἦν βεβαιωτάς *IAskl.Epid.* 36.9 (iv BC)'

**βέβηλος**, line 1, after 'ον' insert 'also η, ον, *Thasos* 18.4 (v BC)'; after 'Dor.' insert 'βάβᾱλος *SEG* 9.72.9, 21 (Cyrene, iv BC)'; after 'βέβαλος' insert 'Theoc. 3.51, 26.14'

**βέβρῡχε**, for 'v. βρύχω' read 'v. βρυχάομαι'

***βέδοξ**, ό, app. some kind of garment or covering, β. Νωρικὸς κάλλιστος ἤτοι βῆλον *Edict.Diocl.* 19.56, 58.

**βέδυ**, after 'Phryg.' insert 'Clem.Al.*Strom.* 5.8.46, 5.48.5'

***βεῖκουλον**, τό, Lat. *vehiculum*, ἔπαρχος βεϊκούλων *IGRom* 4.1057.

***βεκάς**, v. °ἑκάς.

**βέκος**, add 'β.· ἀνόητος Hsch.'

***βεκτοῦρα**, ή, Lat. *vectura, conveyance, transport*, *Edict.Diocl.* 17.3-5.

***βελέαγρον**, τό, or -ος, ό, *instrument for extracting weapons from wounds*, Aët. in J.G.Schneider ad Nic. *Al.* 511 p. 243 (Halle 1792).

***βελεβέκη**· βελόνη Hsch.

**βέλεμνον**, add 'E.*Andr.* 1136'

***βέλλερα**, ἄλλως. βέλλερα τὰ κακὰ λέγει Sch.Hes.*Th.* 325 (expl. of name Βελλεροφόντης).

**βελλούνης**, after 'τριόρχης' insert 'Λάκωνες'

**βελοθήκη**, for 'Lib.*Decl.* 30.9' read 'Lib.*Descr.* 30.9'

***βελομαντεία**, ή, *casting lots by shaking marked arrows from a quiver*, Jerome *in Ez.* 21.24 (*PL* 25.206).

***βελονίστρια**, ή, *needlewoman*, title of play by C.Decius Laberius, Nonius Marcellus p. 104.25.

**βελοστᾰσία**, for '*range* or *battery of warlike engines*' read '*artillery emplacement*'; add 'Lxx 1*Ma.* 6.20'

**βελόστᾰσις**, after 'foreg.' insert 'Lxx *Je.* 28(51).27 (pl.)'

***βελότρωτος**, ον, *wounded by a missile*, Cyran. 112 (4.28.7 K.).

**βελουλκέω**, add 'Paul.Aeg. 6.88.3 (131.22 H.)'

**βελτίων**, at end for '[ῐ Att., but βέλτῑον Mimn. 2.10]' read '[Att. usu. ῐ, but ῑ A.*fr.* 309.3 R., Eup. 336 K.-A.; also in Mimn. 2.10 W.]'

**βελτίωσις**, add 'ἀπὸ βελτιώσεως χέρσου *SB* 10891 i 18, al.'

***Βελφαῖον**, τό, the Thetonian treasury at Delphi (or the sanctuary of Delphian Apollo at Thetonium), *IG* 9(2).257.10 (Thetonium, v BC); cf. Βελφοί, etc.

***Βελχάνια**, v. Ϝελχάνια.

**βέμβιξ I**, add '**2** *spinning movement* of dancers, Ar.*V.* 1531.'

***βενεφικιάλιος** (A), ό, = °βενεφικιάριος, (in quot., one who provides medical aid for veterans), Lyd.*Mag.* 1.46.

***βενεφικιάλιος** (B), ό, wd. incl. in list of criminal types, Just.*Nov.* 13.4 pr.

***βενεφικιάριος**, ό, Lat. *beneficiarius*, *IGRom.* 3.110, etc; abbreviated βφ, *SEG* 32.1551 (Arabia, ii AD).

***βενεφίκιον**, τό, Lat. *beneficium*, βενεφίκιν, *PFlor.* 296.49 (vi AD), Just. *Edict.* 4.1.

***Βενεφρανός**, ον, *of Venafrum*, name of kind of olive oil, ἐλαίου Βενεφράνου Heras ap.Gal. 3.1042.12.

***βενέω**, v. °βινέω.

***Βεννάρχης**, ου, ό, *official in the cult of Zeus Bennios*, *INikaia* 1206 (-αιρχης).

***Βεννεύω**, dub. sens., *MAMA* 1.390 (Phrygia), perh. *worship Zeus Bennios.*

***Βέννιος**, epith. of Zeus, *IGRom.* 4.535 (Phrygia), *SEG* 28.980 (Bithynia, AD 210).

***βένος**, τό, dub. sens., *SEG* 6.550 (Pisidia).

***βεραιδαρικός**, *of* or *typical of a veredarius*, Lyd.*Mens.* 1.32.

**βερβέριον**, for '*shabby garment*' read 'kind of headdress'

***Βερενίκειος**, α, ον, *of Berenice*, Theoc. 15.110, Call.*fr.* 110.62 Pf.

***βεριδάριος**, = βερεδάριος, Hsch. s.v. οὐεριδάριος.

**βερίκοκκον**, add 'see also °πραικόκκιον'

***βέρνα(ς)**, v. °οὐέρνας.

***βεστιάριον**, τό, Lat. *vestiarium*, Modest.*Dig.* 34.1.4 pr., Suid., etc.; also **βιστ-**, Hsch.

***βεστιάριος**, ό, Lat. *vestiarius, clothes-dealer*, *POxy.* 3867.22, *Stud.Pal.* 3.50.1 (both vi AD).

***βεστιαρίτης**, ου, ό, dub. sens., (perh. = °βεστιάριος, or person connected w. *bestiae*), *CPR* 8.56.15 (v/vi AD); sp. βηστ- *Stud.Pal.* 20.157.2 (vi AD).

**βεστίον**, add '*CPR* 14.41.1 (vi/vii AD), cf. Lat. *vestis*'

***βετ(ε)ρανός**, v. ‡οὐετ-.

***βεττάριον**, τό, dub. sens., perh. dim. of βέττον, *PHib.* 211.5 (iii BC).

**βεττονίκη 3**, for 'κέστρος' read 'κέστρον I 1'

**βεῦδος I**, for 'Sapph. 155 .. 11.4 (pl.)' read 'Sapph. 177 L.-P., Call.*fr.* 7.11 Pf. (pl.), Parth. in *Suppl.Hell.* 646.6 (pl.)'

**βήκη**, add 'Theognost.*Can.* 109'

**βηλόθυρον**, add 'also **οὐηλόθυρον** *PGrenf.* 2.111.14 (v/vi AD)'

***βῆλον**, τό, Lat. *velum, covering* or *cloth*, *CIG* 2758 ii B8, 4283.16; also **οὐῆλον** *POxy.* 2128.8 (ii AD), *Edict.Diocl.* 19.56, cf. *Gloss.* 3.92.58 β. *pallium*, 270.39 καταπέτασμα, κρήδεμνον *velum.*

**βῆμα**, line 3, for '*footfall*' read '*walk, gait*' and for 'Sapph.*Supp.* 5.17' read 'Sapph. 16.17 L.-P' **I 2**, add '**b** β. ποδός *a step*, as a very short distance, Lxx *De.* 2.5.' add '**4** *imprint of a foot* offered as a dedication, *IG* 11(4).1263, *Inscr.Délos* 2080.' **II 2 b**, add 'D.C. 57.7.2, Modest.*Dig.* 27.1.13.10' add '**5** *grade, rank*, *Cod.Just.* 12.33.8.2.'

**βημᾰτιστής I**, for 'Ath. 10.442c' read 'Ath. 10.442b'

***βηρυλλίτης**, ου, ό, a precious stone, *Cat.Cod.Astr.* 8(2).169.8.

**βήσαλον**, after '*brick*' insert 'Moses Alch. 300.13'

***βησαρτης**, ό, app. official in Bacchic cult, *IG* 10(2).1.244 i 16 (Thessalonica, ii AD), perh. also ib. 259.3 (i AD).

***βηστιαρίτης**, v. °βεστιαρίτης.

***βήχω**, *to cough*, χελύσσεται· ταράσσεται, ‹βήχει› Sch.Nic.*Al.* 81d Ge.

**βηχώδης 2**, add 'Gal. 13.56.12'

**βῐα II 2**, line 7, after 'etc.' insert 'πρὸς βίαν ἐπίνομεν Ar.*Ach.* 73'; line 8, after 'D.S. 20.51' insert 'εἰς βίαν Men.*Dysc.* 396'; add 'πὲρ βίαν πώνην Alc. 332 L.-P. (πρὸς βίαν cod.)'

***βιᾱθᾰνᾰτος**, ον, = βιαιοθάνατος, *SEG* 6.803 (Cyprus, iii AD).

**βῐαιοθᾰνᾰτέω**, add 'cf. °βιοθανατέω'

***βῐαιολεχής**, ές, *wedded by force*, Dain *Inscr.du Louvre* 60.11 (Heraclea ad Latmum).

***βῐαι]όπρᾱτος**, or **βι]όπρατος**, ον, *subjected to compulsory sale of one's property*, prob. in *PRyl.* 617.10 (iv AD).

***βῐάρπᾰγος**, ον, *life-robbing*, βιαρπάγου Λήθης *Suppl.Mag.* 42.21.

***βῐάρχης**, ου, ό, = βίαρχος, *PMich.*xi 612.5 (vi AD).

***βῐαρχία**, ή, *office of* βίαρχος, *Cod.Just.* 1.31.1.

**βῐαρχος**, add '*SEG* 34.1292 (Phrygia), *Cod.Just.* 12.20.3; written βίορχος in *LW* 2037 (Arabia, iv AD)'

***βῐασάνδρα**, ή, *coercing men*, epith. of Ἄρκτος, *PMag.* 7.696, *RPh* 1930.249 (Egypt, tab.defix.).

**βῐᾱτᾱς**, after '*mighty*' insert 'Alcm. 1.4 P.'

***βιατικόν**, τό, Lat. *viaticum*, *BGU* 423.9, *PGoodsp.Cair.* 30 xli 18 (both ii AD).

***βῐᾰφορέω**, *violate*, τὸ παρὰ τὴν συγγραφὴν βεβιαφορημένον μέρος *BGU* 1844.25 (i BC).

**βιβλιαφόρος**, after 'D.S. 2.26' insert '**βυβλιαφόρος** *PRyl.* 555.2 (iii BC), *POxy.* 710.2 (ii BC), *SEG* 24.1221, 1222 (Egypt, iv AD)'

**+βίβλινος** (A), v. βύβλινος.

***Βίβλινος** (B), η, ον, *Bibline*, kind of vine and wine, Β. οἶνος Hes.*Op.* 589, E.*Ion* 1195, Theoc. 14.15; ὁ τῆς Βιβλίνης ἀμπέλου Ach.Tat. 2.2.2; from Thracian place-name acc. to Epich.*fr.* 174, but Βίμβλινος from a Naxian river acc. to Semus *fr.* 13 J.; cf. Βίμβλινος Lang *Ath.Agora* xxi L45 (iv AD), Hsch. (Βίβλ- La.).

**βιβλιογράφος**, add 'see also °βιβλογράφος'

***βιβλιοκατᾰγωγεύς**, έως, ό, **βυβλ-**, perh. *forwarder of documents*, *PSI* 1410.15 (ii AD).

**βιβλιοπώλης**, add '**βυβλιο-**, *POxy.* 2192.37 (ii AD), see also βιβλοπ-'

**βιβλιοφῠλᾰκέω**, for '*to be a librarian*' read '*to be a keeper of archives*'

***βιβλιοφῠλᾰκικός**, ή, όν, **βυβλ-**, *of or for a keeper of archives*, MacDowell *Stamped Objects from Seleucia* 39, *YCLS* 3.47 (Uruk).
**βιβλιοφῠλᾰκιον**, add '**βυβλ-** *ABSA* 42.202 (Cyprus, Rom.imp.)'
**βιβλιοφύλαξ**, add '*PGiss.* 58 (ii AD), *POxy.* 1256 (ii AD)'
*****βιβλίς**, ίδος, ή, βιβλίδες· τὰ βιβλία ἢ σχοινία τὰ ἐκ βίβλου πεπλεγμένα *EM* 197.30; Aeol. βίμβλις (in broken context), ἐν βιμβλίδεσσι Alc. 208(a).ii 6 L.-P.
***βιβλογρᾰ́φος**, ὁ, Att. for βιβλιογράφος, acc. to Gramm. in Reitzenstein *Ind.Lect.Rost.* 1892/3 p. 4, Phryn.*PS* p. 52 B. cod.
***βιβραδ[ικός]**, ή, όν, fr. Lat. *vibrare, vibratory*, ἀνεμούρ[ιον] β., dub. in *PRyl.* 627.165.
***βίδυν**, = βίδην, ψαλεῖ βίδυν *Trag.adesp.* 656.27 K.-S.
***βίετος**, v. °βίοτος.
***βιζάκιον**, τό, *small stone, pebble*, Suid., Zonar.
*****βιζάριον**, τό, prob. *camel suckling her young*, βιζάριν *Aegyptus* 6.188 (*PLond.* 1821); cf. °βυζαστρία.
***βίζια**· *mamillae* Gloss. (perh. for βυζία, cf. mod. Gk. βυζί).
**Βῑθῡνιάρχης**, after '*Bithynia*' insert '*and of its festivals*' and for '*OGI* 528.10 (Prusias), al.' read '*IPrusias* 3.1, 5.3, al. (Βει-, ii/iii AD), *Inscr.Perg.* 8(3).551, *INikaia* 726'
***βικαριανός**, ή, όν, *of a* °βικάριος, Just.*Nov.* 26.2.2.
***βικαρία**, ή, Lat. *vicaria, office of vicar* in an imperial diocese, [τοῦ ἁ]γνοῦ κόμητος καὶ ἀπὸ βικαρίας *Salamine* 207 (v/vi AD).
***βικάριος**, ὁ, Lat. *vicarius, governor of a diocese*, *Epigr.Gr.* 929.2 (iv AD), *Cod.Just.* 12.37.19 pr., *SEG* 36.663 (Thrace, v/vi AD); see also °οὐικάριος.
***βικεννάλιον**, v. °οὐικεννάλια.
**βῖκία**, for '*Edict.Diocl.* 17.6' read '*Edict.Diocl.* 1.30, 17.6a'
**βῖκίον**, after 'βῖκος' insert '*PCair.Zen.* 7 (iii BC)'
**βῐκίον**, add '*Edict.Diocl.* 1.30A'
***βίκλα**, ή, prob. *watch-post* (for *βίγλα, cf. Lat. *vigilia*), *POxy.* 1862.29; cf. °οὐίγιλ.
**βῖκος 1**, after '*cask*' insert 'Hippon. 142 W.' **3**, after '*measure*' insert 'of land' and add 'ψιλοὺς τόπους ἀδ[ε]σπότους βίκων τεσσάρων *POxy.* 3334.8 (i AD)'
**βιλλαρικός**, for 'perh. = Lat. *villaticus*' read 'perh. for *βηλαρικός *used for screening* or *veiling*'
**βιλλᾶς**, add 'perh. pers. n.'
*****Βίμβλινος**, v. °Βίβλινος.
***βίμβλις**, v. °βιβλίς.
***βίνδιξ**, ικος, ὁ, Lat. *vindex*, in quots., app. *official concerned with tax collection*, Just.*Nov.* 128.5, 134.2.
*****βῑνέω**, (**βενέω** v. infra) coarse wd. for *to have sexual intercourse*, Hippon. 84.16 W., Ar.*Ra.* 740; w. acc. pers., γυναῖ]κα βινέων Archil. 152 W., Ar.*Av.* 560, etc.; pass., Ion. impf. iterative, βινεσκόμην of male prostitute, id.*Eq.* 1242; of the woman, Eup. 385.2 K.-A., Philetaer. 9.4 K.-A.; app. understood as illicit, opp. marital, intercourse, Sol.*Lg.* 52b R. [βενέω Lang *Ath.Agora* XXI C2 (vi BC), C 14 (v BC), perh. in *Inscr.Olymp.* 7 (v BC; Elean), prob. represents βειν-; many codd. and papp. have βειν-].
***βιξιλατίων**, ωνος, ή, Lat. *vexillatio, military detachment*, *IGRom.* 3.418.5 (pl.); see also °οὐιξ-.
**βῐοθάλμιος**, for '*strong, hale*' read '*productive of life*'
***βῐοθᾰνᾰτέω**, = βιαιο-, Sch.A.Il. 13.393.
**βῐόκουρος**, add 'also **οὐιόκουρος** Keil-Premerstein *Dritter Bericht* 129.2 (iii AD)'
***βῐοκωλῡσία**, ή, *suppression of violence*, *POxy.* 2046.56 (vi AD).
*****βῐολόγος**, ὁ, kind of mimic actor or mime, *IG* 14.2342, *POxy.* 1025.7 (iii AD), *IGRom.* 1.552 (Salona), *IGLS* 9407 (Bostra, Chr.), *GVI* 515n (Citium, ii BC).
***βῐοποριστέω**, *make a living*, οὐ μικρὰ β. Aesop. 56 P.
**βῐόπρᾱγος**, add '*POxy.* 1477.14 (iii/iv AD)'
*****βῐόπρᾱτος**, v. °βιαιόπρατος (cf. ‡βιόπραγος).
**βίος II**, line 8, after 'Iamb.*VP* 30.170' insert 'στοὰν ἐπισκευάσειν ἐκ τοῦ ἰδίου βίου i.e. at (his) own *expense*, *SEG* 23.207.19 (Messene, i BC/i AD)' **III**, line 4, after 'Luc.*DDeor.* 13.1' insert 'οὐδέπω (τὰ γεγραμμένα) τῷ β. παραδέδωκας id.*Hes.* 2; χάριν τούτου ἐκαλούμην μέγας ἐν τῷ βίῳ *Lyr.Alex.adesp.* 4.19' **V**, add 'βίους συνταξάμενοι D.H.*Amm.* 1.3; βίον ἀναγράψαντες ib. 6'
***βῐοστερέτις**, ιδος, ή, *depriving of life*, Μοῖρα *GVI* 845.2 (Panticapaeum, ii/i BC).
**βῐοτεία**, add '**2** *livelihood, maintenance*, εἰς τὴν κοινὴν βιοτείαν *POxy.* 3491.12 (ii AD).'
***βῐοτερπής**, ές, *delighting in life*, orac. in *IEphes.* 1252.6 (ii AD), epigr. in Geel *Catal.MSS.Lugd.Bat.* p. 18 no. 54.
**βίοτος**, line 1, after 'Ep.' insert 'βίετος *Inscr.Cret.* 1.xvi 7.10 (Lato, ii/i BC)'
**βῐοφθόρος**, add 'epigr. in *BCH* 85.848 (Paros)'
***βιόχρηστος**, ον, *useful for life*, *Menandro qui* βιόχρηστα *scripsit*, Plin.*HN* 1.19, 20. al.
**βῐόω**, line 8, delete 'v.l. for βιοίη in'; line 14, delete '(opp. ζάω *live, exist*)' add '**3** aor. part., of one who has lived and is now dead, *SEG* 29.663 (Thrace, v/iv BC), δίδωσιν δὲ καὶ κηδευτικὸν τοῖς βιώσασιν *Xanthos* 67.30 (ii AD).
**βιπίννιον**, after 'Lat. *bipennis*' insert '*small axe*'; for pres. ref. read '*Edict.Diocl.* 7.36'
***βίρριον**, τό, dim. of βίρρος, *cloak*, *PUniv.Giss.* 32.17 (iii/iv AD; βεί[ρι]ον).
**βίρρος**, for '*Edict.Diocl.* 19.26, al.' read '*Edict.Diocl.* 7.43, al., βίρος ib. 7.42'; for 'Suid. .. βύρρος.)' read 'also **βίρρον**, Suid.; **βύρρος**, *BGU* 814.8 (iii AD), *SEG* 7.431'
***βιστιάριον**, v. °βεστιάριον.
**βίττακος**, for 'ψίττακος' read 'ψιττακός *parrot*'
**βῐωφελής**, line 1, after '*useful for life*' insert 'Varro *Sat.Men.* 340'
***βῐωφέλιμος**, ον, *helping life*, Heph.Astr. 2.21.15.
**βλᾰ́βη 2**, line 2, for 'cattle' read 'animals'
***βλᾰβοποιέω**, *damage, harm*, ἐβλαβοποίησαν .. φοίνικας δύο *PGen.* 107.7 (Arsinoite, i AD).
***Βλαγανῖτις**, ιδος, ή, epith. of Artemis in Macedonia, *SEG* 37.539 (Metochi); also Ἀ. ἐν Βλαγάνοις ib. 590, 592 (Vergina, both ii AD), fr. place-name, perh. meaning "place of frogs"; cf. βλαχάν, and θεὰ τῶν βατράχων ib. 540 (Aegeae, iii AD).
*****βλᾰδᾰρός**, ά, όν, = πλαδαρός, *flaccid*, cj. in Gal. 19.88; β.· ἐκλελυμένον. χαῦνον Hsch.
***βλᾰδεῖς**· ἀδύνατοι, ἐξ ἀδυνάτων Hsch.
***βλᾰδόν**· ἀδύνατον Hsch.
***βλαισοπόδης**· βάτραχος Suid.; cf. **βλαισόπους** (s.v. βλαιτόνους).
**βλαστέω**, (s.v. βλαστάνω), lines 1/2, for 'interpol.' and 'corrupt' read 'dub.' twice.
***βλασφημολόγος**, ὁ, *blasphemer*, Leont.Byz. *HP* 1.8.30.
***βλάττιος**, α, ον, Lat. *blatteus, purple*, καμίσια β. *Stud.Pal.* 20.245.10 (*ZPE* 76.113, vi AD); -ον, τό, *purple garment*, Lyd.*Mens.* 1.21.
***βλαττόσημος**, ον, *having purple stripes*, *Edict.Diocl.* 29.11, al.
***βλᾰχά**, v. βληχή.
**βλαχάν**, after 'Hsch.' add 'cf. βλίκανος'
**βλαψῐτᾰ́φος**, line 1, for '*IG* 14.934.4' read '*IG* 14.943.4'
*****βλέθρα**, v. πλέθρον.
**βλεμεαίνω**, for '*exult*' read 'prob. *glower*'
**βλέμμα**, for 'Antiph. 235' read 'Antiph. 232 K.-A., Men.*Dysc.* 258'
**βλέννα**, add 'cf. πλένναι, πλεννεραί'
**βλέπω**, line 1, after 'etc.' insert 'Dor. **γλέπω** in ποτιγλέπω (v. °προσβλέπω), cf. γλέφαρον' **II 2**, *have regard* to, after 'Arist.*Pol.* $1293^b$14' insert 'εἰς τὴν ταμειακὴν ἐξουσίαν βλέπον Just.*Nov.* 30.5 pr.' **III 2**, after '(S.)*Aj.* 962' insert 'ζώντων φρονούντων βλεπόντων Aeschin. 3.94; X.*Cyr.* 8.1.22'
**βλεφᾰρίζω**, after '*wink*' insert 'Clem.Al.*Paed.* 3.70'
**βλέφᾰρον**, line 1, after 'τό' insert 'dat. pl. -εσσι Nonn.*D.* 5.480, 15.408'
**βλεφᾰροσπάξ**, for '*arching the eyebrows*' read 'prob. *pulling out the eyebrows* or *eyelashes*'
***βλησκούνιον**, gloss on γληχών, Sch.Nic.*Al.* 128b Ge.; cf. βληχώνιον.
***βλήσκω**, iterative form of the pres. stem of βάλλω, τὴν .. βλησκομένην βοτρυῖτιν (βλισκ-, -την codd.) Zos.Alch. 207.6.
***βλήχησις**, εως, ή, *bleating*, Alex.Aphr.*Pr.* 3.168.
**βλήχων**, line 4, after 'gen.' insert '[γ]ληχῶνος (-ῶ- pap.) Hippon. 84.4 W.'; line 6, after 'Ar.*Ach.* 874' insert 'γληχώ Nic.*Al.* 128' add '**II** *pubic hair*, Ar.*Lys.* 89.'
**βλῐτομάμμας**, add 'Sch.Pl.*Alc.* 1.118e'
**βλίτον**, add 'Antiph. 275 K.-A.'
***βλιτυρίστριαι**, αἱ, female singers of a cult lament, Cyr., v. *Univ. di Cagliari: Quaderni dell'Ist. di Filol. gr.* 2.104.
**βλῐχᾰνώδης**, read βλῐχ- and delete 'of fish'
**βλοσῠρότης**, after '*grimness*' insert 'Antioch.Astr. in *Cat.Cod.Astr.* 11(2).109.7'
**βλοσῠρωπός**, add '*AP* 5.299.7 (Agath.)'
***βλόψ**, onomat. wd. expr. sound of drops falling into water, cf. Eng. "plop", καὶ τῆς δικαστικῆς ψήφου ἦχος ὡς ὁ τῆς κλεψύδρας παρὰ Ἀττικοῖς βλόψ Hsch. s.v. κόγξ; Eust. 768.12.
***βλυάζω**, *produce, give birth to*, Ar.*fr.* 609 K.-A.; cf. βρυάζω.
**βλύζω**, delete 'Orph.*A.* 599' and insert '*AP* 11.24 (Antip.Sid.)'
**βλυστάνω**, for 'sq.' read 'βλύω'
**βλύω**, line 1, after '= βλύζω' insert 'ἔτι βλύοντι φόνῳ Nic.*Th.* 497'; after 'φόνῳ' insert '(v.l. φόνου)'
**βλωθρός**, after 'ά, όν' insert 'Ep. also **γλωθρός** Hes.*fr.* 204.124 M.-W.'
**βλώσκω**, line 2, aor. 2, after 'etc.' insert '(ἔμολα epigr. in *INikaia* 223.3)'; add 'used in prose in Arc., *arrive*, ἔβλωσκον ἰμ Μαντινέαν .. ἆμαν οἱ σταλογράφοι μόλωνσι *SEG* 37.340.16, 18 (Mantinea, iv BC)'
***βοᾱγεία**, (for -γία), ή, *conveyance of oxen*, Αὐρηλ(ίου) Ἀνεικήτου .. ἄρξαντος βοαγείαν *POxy.* 3565.4 (AD 245).
**βοᾱθόος**, add 'Βοαθοῖος *Delph.* 3(6).19.1, al.; Βαθοῖος ib. 134.3'

***Βοάρσαι**, οἱ, guild of *bull-hoisters*, *IG* 12(1).102.8, Maiuri *Nuova Silloge* 18.27 (both Rhodes); cf. °ἀείρω IV 3 b.

***Βοάρσιον**, τό, *contest connected with bull-hoisting*, ἀγωνοθέται Βοαρσίου *IG* 12 suppl. 646.21 (Chalcis, iii AD).

**βοαύλιον**, after 'dim. of sq.' insert '*AP* 7.717'

***βόγγλωττος**, v. ‡βούγλωσσος.

**βόειος II 1**, add 'Cret. βοῖα *Inscr.Cret.* 4.65.6 (Gortyn, v BC)'

**βοεύς**, add '*h.Ap.* 407'

**βοηγία**, ἡ, add '**II** *public service connected with such contests*, *GDI* 5633.3 (Teos).'

**βοηγοί**, delete the entry.

***βοηγός**, ὁ, *ox-driver*, title of certain religious officials at Miletus, *Didyma* 199.5, 16 (pl.), 19, 262.7, 263.8.

**Βοηδρόμια**, add 'also Βοᾱδρόμια *SEG* 25.445.32 (Arcadia, ii BC)'

**Βοηδρόμιος II**, add 'also **Βατρόμιος** at Calymna, *Tit.Calymn.* 79A.49, 88.38, 41, 94A.9; at Cos, *APAW* 1928(6).10.50'

**Βοηδρομιών**, add 'also Βατρομιών *SEG* 33.681 (Paros, ii BC)'

**βοήθεια I**, line 2, after '(Thermon)' insert '**βοάθεια** *SEG* 23.547 (Crete, c.200 BC)' **III**, add '**2** *staff* or *aides* of an official, *Cod.Just.* 10.30.4.12, Just.*Nov.* 7 epilogos.'

**βοηθέω**, lines 2/4, for 'Ion. **βωθέω** .. iv BC)' read '**βωθέω** Hdt. acc. to Eust. 812.59, *AP* 12.84 (Mel.), βωθέοντες· βοηθοῦντες Hsch.'; after '**βοᾱθοέω**' insert 'Pi.*N.* 7.33, *SEG* 30.1117, 1118, 1121 (Entella)'; line 4, after '(Thermon)' insert 'βοᾱθέω *SEG* 25.847 (Telos, c.300 BC), 23.547 (Crete, c.200 BC)' **1**, add 'w. gen., βοήθησον τῆς μεικρᾶς *Suppl.Mag.* 13 (iv AD)'

**βοηθητικός**, line 4, after '(Arist.)*HA* 515^b^9' insert 'of medic. treatment, *promoting a cure*, D.L. 3.85' add '**2** *of a* βοηθός, τὰ -ά, *fees for assistance*, *PMich.*XI 624.5 (vi AD).'

**βοηθός**, line 3, after 'Pl.*R.* 566b, al.' insert '= Lat. *adiutor*'; add 'as honorific title, β. καθόλου τῆς Ἀρσινοϊτῶν πόλεως *CPR* 10.25.5 (AD 526/7); written βοιθός, *SEG* 8.483.4 (Egypt, i BC), cf. *OWilck.* 1084.11 (ii BC)'

**βοηλᾰτέω**, after 'Opp.*C.* 4.64' insert '(v.l. °βροχηλατέω)'

**βόησις**, after '*shout for assistance*' insert 'Plu. 2.171d'

***βόθρευμα**, ατος, τό, *pit*, *Poliorc.* 212.4.

**βόθῡνος I**, add 'Lxx 2*Ki.* 18.17, 4*Ki.* 3.16, *Is.* 24.17, etc.; *Ev.Matt.* 12.11, etc.'

**βοίδιον**, add 'also βουείδιον *SB* 9920 ii 19.9 (vi AD)'

***βοιθός**, v. °βοηθός.

***βοῖπις**· γῆ βουνώδης Theognost.*Can.* 19.

**βοϊστί**, after '*ox-language*' insert 'Iamb.*VP* 61'

***Βοιώταος**, η, ον, (?for *Βοιωταῖος), = Βοιώτιος, Δήμητρος Βοιωτάης *SEG* 17.396 (Chios, iv BC).

**Βοιωταρχέω**, add '*SEG* 25.553 (Onchestus, iv BC): also **Βοιωταρχίω**, *IG* 7.2407.12, 2408.12 (iv BC)'

**Βοιώτιος** (s.v. Βοιωτός), for 'Hes.*fr.* 132, etc.' read 'Hes.*fr.* 181 M.-W., etc.; also as subst., ἀγῶνες Βοιωτίων Pi.*O.* 7.85'

***βοκάλιοι**, οἱ, Lat. *vocales*, *singing rope-dancers*, *POxy.* 2707.7 (βοκ[άλιοι], vi AD).

**βολαῖος**, for '(βολή) *violent*' read '(βόλος) *caught in the net*'

***βόλβαξ**, ακος, ἡ, app. edible bulbous plant, *PMich.*VIII 496.16 (ii AD).

^+^**βόλβῐτον**, τό or **βόλβῐτος**, ὁ (βόλβιθος *PMag.* 4.1440) = βόλιτον, *dung, excrement* (less acceptable form acc. to Phryn. 335), Hippon. 92.9; 144 W., Thphr.*HP* 5.5.3, Dsc. 2.167, Archig.ap.Gal. 12.173.

***βολένη**· τὸ κρέας τὸ περὶ τὸ στόμα τῆς γαστρός Theognost.*Can.* 48 A.

***βολεός**, όν, *heaped*; βολεοὶ λίθοι, series of cairns acting as boundary marks at a place in Epidaurus, *SEG* 11.377.16 (Hermione, ii BC), βολεοὶ λίθων κύκλοι *IG* 4^2^.75.33 (ii BC); **Βολεοί** alone, treated as place-name, Paus. 2.26.3.

***βολευταί**, gloss on δανδαρίκαι, Hsch.

**βολή 4**, line 4, for '*radiance*' read 'snow-*falls*'

**βολίζη**, delete 'Cretan word in'

^+^**βόλῐμον**, τό, (s.v. βόλῐμοι) *sacrificial victim* (slaughtered with an axe), *SEG* 22.508 (Chios).

**βόλῐμος**, add '*lead tablet*, τοὺς ἐν τῷ βολίμωι γεγραμμένους πάντας *SEG* 30.1175 (Italy, iii BC); cf. περιβολιβόω'

**βολίς 3**, delete 'ἀστραπὴ βολίς (sic)' and transfer '(Lxx) *Za.* 9.14' to section 1. **4 b**, delete the section transferring ref. to section 4a.

**βολῑ́τινος**, delete 'σκέλος Cratin.*inc.* 17 Mein.'

***βολλευτήριον**, v. ‡βουλευτήριον.

**βόλομαι**, line 4, delete 'cf. A.R. 1.262'

***βόλτιον**, gloss on °βότις, Hsch.

^+^**βομβαύλιος**, ὁ, comic conflation of βομβύλιος and αὐλός, *"drone-piper"*, Ar.*Ach.* 866.

**βόμβος**, add 'of the sonorous utterance of tragedy, Μελπομένης βόμβον ἀπεπλάσατο (sc. an actress) *AP* 5.222.4 (Agath.)'

**βομβῠκίας**, for '*flutes*' read '*pipes*'

***Βομβῠλεία**· ἡ Ἀθηνᾶ ἐν Βοιωτίᾳ Hsch.

^+^**βομβῠλία**· κρήνη ἐν Βοιωτίᾳ Hsch.

**βομβῠλιάζω**, for 'βορβορύζω' read '°βορβορύζω'

**βομβῠλιός II**, add 'Antisth.*Protr.fr.*ap.Poll. 6.98, 10.68, Ion Trag. 64 S.'

**βόμβυξ II 1**, for '*flute*' read '*pipe*' and add 'cf. Dor. **Βομβύκα** Theoc. 10.27, name of a piper' **2**, for '*cap of a flute*' read 'included among parts of an αὐλός'

***βοο-**, for βοῦς compds. see also βου-.

***βοοκλοπίη**, ἡ, *theft of oxen*, Firm.*Err.prof.relig.* 5.2; cf. βουκλόπος.

***βοόκρημνος**, ον, *having banks occupied by cows*, βοοκρήμνοιο .. ἴχνος Ἀράτθου Call.*fr.* 646 Pf. (s.v.l., see also °βούκρανος).

**βοοκτᾰσία**, after '*of oxen*' insert '*AP* 6.115 (Antip.), 263 (Leon.Tarent.)'

***βοόκτιστος**, ον, = βούκτιτος, of Thebes, *founded through the action of a cow* (i.e. where a cow lay down), Ps.-Callisth. 55.10.

**βοοσσόος**, line 2, for 'βουσσόον' read 'βουσόον (v.l. -σσ-)'

***βοοτροφέω**, *to rear oxen*, Heph.Astr. 3.5.24; cf. °βουτρόφος.

^+^**βόρασσος**, ὁ, name for the fruit enclosed in the spathe of the date-palm, Dsc. 1.109.5 (perh. Semitic).

***βορατ**[.., kind of fish, cf. perh. °ἀβόρατος, *IGC* p. 98 A20.

***βορατίνη**, ἡ, kind of juniper, cf. βόρατον, Aq.*Ca.* 1.17.

^+^**βόρατον**, τό, one or other species of *juniper*, D.S. 2.49, Dsc. 1.76, Sm.*Ps.* 103(104).17, *Ca.* 1.17, *Is.* 60.13 (cf. Hebr. *b^e^rôt*).

**βορβορόθῡμος**, add '(cj. °βαρβαρόμυθος)'

**βορβορυγμός**, add 'Gal. 14.122.5'

***βορβορύζω**, *rumble*, seethe, esp. internally, ἐβορβόρυζε δ' ὥστε κύθρος ἔτνεος Hippon. 29a W.; Hp.*Int.* 6.

***βορδόνιον**, τό, *mule*, Cyr.S.*Vit.Sab.* 44.

***βορεαῖος**, ὁ, (sc. ἄνεμος) *north wind*, *IG* 12(3).357; cf. βορειαῖος.

**Βορέας**, after '**Βορρᾶς**, ᾶ' insert '(also Βορροῦ Aristonym. 7 K.-A.; cf. °Βορρόθεν)'; add 'see also βορεύς'

**Βορεάς II**, add 'βορεὰς .. ἀήτα B. 17.91 S.-M.'

***Βορεασταί**· Ἀθήνησιν οἱ ἄγοντες τῷ Βορέᾳ ἑορτὰς καὶ θοίνας, ἵνα ‹οὔριοι› ἄνεμοι πνέωσιν. ἐκαλοῦντο δὲ Βορεασμοί Hsch.

**βόρειος I**, add '**3** name of variety of *iaspis*, Plin.*HN* 37.116.'

***βορέομαι**, *feed oneself*, v.l. (*POxy.* 2221) in Nic.*Th.* 394 (v. βοτέω); perh. to be understood in Sapph. 96.17 L.-P. (v. βαρέω).

***βόρεος**, α, ον, = βόρειος, *Didyma* 27A24, 67 (iii BC).

***βορίζω**· ἐβόρισεν· ἐσίτισεν Hsch.; cf. perh. πορίζω.

***βορολίβας**, α, ὁ, *the north-west*, ἐν τῷ βορολίβᾳ τοῦ οὐρανοῦ *PMag.* 4.1647 (s.v.l.).

***βορρόθεν**, adv. *from the north*, Teuc.Bab. p. 67 B.

**βορρόλιψ**, delete '*PMag.Par.* 1.1646'

^+^**βόρυες**, οἱ, kind of animal found in desert or semi-desert country, Hdt. 4.192.2.

^+^**βοσκάδιος**, α, ον, *free-grazing*, χήν Nic.*Al.* 228.

**βοσκάς I**, for this section read '*greedy*, νηδύς Nic.*Al.* 782. **2** of birds which feed themselves, *not artificially fed*, ὀρταλίς Nic.*Al.* 293; Aët. 9.30; cf. βοσκός II.'

**βόσκημα**, sg., add 'coll. στερέσθω τοῦ βοσκήματος *IG* 12(9).90.12 (Tamynae, iv BC)'

**βοσκός II**, after '(*Edict.Diocl.* 4.) 22' insert 'φασιανὴ βοσκή (sic), βοσκὴ τρυγών ib. 20, 26'

**Βοσπορᾱνός** (s.v. Βόσπορος), add '*TAM* 4(1).239'

**Βοσπόριος**, after '(S.)*Aj.* l.c.' insert 'name of month at Rhegion near Byzantium, *Belleten* 23.552, al. (i AD)'

**Βοσπορίτης**, add '*SEG* 25.272 (Attica, iv BC)'

**βοστρῠχίτης**, add '**II** by-product of firing of copper ore, formed like bunches of grapes, Anon.Alch. 6.8.'

***βοστρῠχῖτις**, ιδος, ἡ, precious stone, perh. *moss-agate*, Plin.*HN* 37.150, 191.

**βόστρῠχος**, line 1, pl. -α, add 'Nonn.*D.* 1.133, *AP* 5.218.4 (Agath.)'

***βοτανιάτης**, ου, ὁ, *herbalist*, *MAMA* 4.93 (Robert *Noms indigènes* p. 141).

***βοτᾰνοφᾰγία**, gloss on ποηφαγία, Hsch.

**βότειος**, add 'δέρματα βότια *POxy.* 3505.4 (ii AD)'

***βότεος**, α, ον, = βότειος, *of a sheep*, βόεα μηδὲ βότεα (sc. ἱερεῖα) μὴ ποτάγειν Maiuri *Nuova Silloge* 17 (Rhodes).

**βοτέω**, delete 'Ep. .. cf.'; for 'pass. .. 394' read 'med., *feed on*, Nic.*fr.* 74.46 G.-S., *Th.* 394; see also °βορέομαι)'

**βοτήρ**, add 'Theoc. 25.139, A.R. 3.592, 4.1248'

***βοτήραρχος** (or ?-άρχης), ὁ, *chief herdsman*, *Trag.adesp.* 721.4 K.-S.

***βοτηρίδιον**, v. ‡ποτηρίδιον.

^+^**βότις**, ιος, ἁ, Sophr. 64 (acc. to Ath. 286d kind of fish, or possibly plant); βότις· βόλτιον Hsch.

**βοτόν**, for '*beast*' read '*farm animal*'; add 'ἐν βοτοῖς Alcm. 1.47 P., βοτὸν τέλευν *SEG* 9.72.31, al. (Cyrene)'; last line, delete 'but also of birds'

**βοτρῡηφόρος**, add 'Orph.*H.* 30.5 (-οφόρον codd.)'

**βοτρυίτης**, delete the entry.

***βοτρυῗτις**, ιδος, ἡ, form of *calamine* (sc. καδμεία), Dsc. 5.74, Plin.*HN* 34.101, Gal. 12.220.9. **2** = ἀρτεμισία I 2, Poet.*de herb.* 26.

***βοτρυοκαρποτόκος**, ον, *bearing bunches of grapes*, *Lyr.adesp.* 9 P.

**βοτρυοστέφανος**, for 'dub. in *IG* 3.3688' read '*IG* 2².11387 (*CEG* 550.3, iv BC)'

***βοτρυοφόρος**, ον, *bearing bunches of grapes*, epith. of the vine, Cyran. 11 (1.1.162 K.); of a coin, *bearing the representation of a bunch of grapes*, δραχμή *Inscr.Délos* 1450*A*108 (ii BC).

**βότρυς**, line 1, after 'ὁ' insert '(ἡ, Nic.*Al.* 185)' and for 'heterocl. pl. βότρυα, τά Euph. 149' read 'βότρυα (Euph. 149) cited as exceptional acc. sg. by Theodos.*Can.* p. 234 H.'

**βοτρυώδης**, for '= βοτρυοειδής, E.*Ba.* 12' read '*full of grapes*, ἀμπέλου .. βοτρυώδει χλόῃ E.*Ba.* 12; βοτρυώδη .. χάριν οἴνας ib. 534'

***βοτρυωτός**, ή, όν, *ornamented with bunches of grapes*, *Inscr.Délos* 1408*A*ii4, 1444*Aa*16 (ii BC).

**βούβαλις**, after '*A.Fr.* 330' insert '*S.fr.* 792 R.' add '**II** v. βούταλις.'

**βουβάρας**, after '*EM* 206.18' insert '(= Eup. 436 K.-A.)'

**Βουβαστεῖον**, add '*PColl.Youtie* 19.15 (AD 44)'

**βουβίλιξ**, transfer the article before **βουβόσιον**.

**βουβότης**, add 'cf. Myc. *qo-u-qo-ta*, pers. n.'

**βούβρωστις**, after '*Epigr.Gr.* 793' insert '(= *SEG* 30.1473, ii AD)'

**βουβωνίσκος**, add 'Gal. 18(1).776.17, 827.1'

**βούγλωσσος**, add 'Boeot. βογγλώτ[τω] (gen.) *IGC* p. 98 A17 (Acraephia, iii/ii BC)'

***Βουδιών**, ῶνος, ὁ, month name, *SEG* 36.1116.A7 (Cyzicus, iv BC).

**βουδόρος II 1**, add 'prob. in *IG* 1³.405.9 (v BC)'

***βουεργέτης**, coined as expl. of βουγάϊε, Sch.Gen.Il. 13.824.

**βουθοίνης**, after 'ὁ' insert 'only in Dor. form **βουθοίνας**'

**βούθουτον**, after 'ἀμέμαρον' insert '(ἀνέκφορον La.)' and add 'cf. βούθυτος'

**βουθυτέω**, line 2, after 'E.*El.* 785' insert 'Aeschin. 3.77' and delete 'also in later prose'

**+ βουκαῖος**, ὁ, *man in charge of oxen*, Nic.*Th.* 5; βουκαῖοι ζεύγεσσιν ἀμορβεύοντες ὀρήων id.*fr.* 90; prob. pers. n. in Theoc. 10.1, 57, but expld. as βουκόλος by Sch.; = ἄγροικος, acc. to Eust. 962.12; cf. ‡βοῦκος.

***βουκελλάριον**, τό, ingredient in the preparation of nard, Aët. 1.131 (66.26 O.).

***βουκελλάριος**, ὁ, Lat. *bucellarius*, *member of armed escort of military* or *civil functionaries in Egypt*, *POxy.* 150.1, 156.2, *BGU* 836.8, 12 (all vi AD).

***βουκελλάτης** (?-τᾶς), ὁ, prob. *baker of* βούκελλαι, *PErlangen* 81.49, cf. *CPR* 5.118.

***βουκέλλιον**, τό, *small loaf*, Paul.Aeg. 3.14.3 (158.21 H.), sp. βουκέλιον *PVindob.*G 39847.457 (*CPR* 5.97).

**βούκερας**, for '-αος' read 'gen. -αος Nic.*Al.* 424, -ατος *Edict.Diocl.* 1.18'; for '= τῆλις .. *Al.* 424' read '*fenugreek*, ll.cc.'

**βουκέφαλος 1**, add 'as pr. n. = Βουκεφάλας, *Gp.* 16.2 1, Hsch.'

***βουκία**, ἡ, or **βούκιον**, τό, kind of cake or biscuit, *POxy.* 397 (i AD), 155.4 (vi AD); (perh. = mod. Gk. βούκα "mouthful" fr. Lat. *bucca*).

***βούκινον**, τό, Lat. *bucinum*, *trumpet*, Anon.Alch. 330.4.

***βουκκᾶς**, ᾶ, ὁ, *biscuit-maker*, *Stud.Pal.* 20.148 (vi AD), *PBaden* 31.21 (βουκᾶς), v. *ZPE* 54.93 (previously read as pers. n.); cf. βούκελλα, °βουκέλλιον.

***βοῦκλεψ**, v. βόκλεψ.

***βοῦκλος**, ὁ, kind of jar, Zos.Alch. 140.15, Anon.Alch. 267.14.

***βουκόλα**, ἡ, *female member of an association of* βουκόλοι, cf. -κόλος II, *IG* 4.207.3 (Cenchriae, Rom.imp.).

**βουκολέω I 1**, add '**c** fig., *feed* in one's mind, φροντίσιν πάθος A.*Ag.* 669; med., τόνδε πόνον id.*Eu.* 78.' **2**, delete ':– med. .. *Eu.* 78' **II**, delete 'πάθος .. 669'

**βουκολιασμός**, add 'see also °-ισμός'

**βουκολικός II 1**, add '**b** β. τό, prob. garment or ceremonial cloth used by a βουκόλος II 2, *BGU* 2427.6, 11 (?iii BC).'

**βουκόλιον**, after '*cattle*' insert '*h.Merc.* 288'

***βουκολισμός**, ὁ, = βουκολιασμός, Trypho ap.Ath. 14.618c; v.l. for -ιασμός, ib. 619a.

***βουκόλισσα**, ἡ, *cowherd*, *SB* 10447ʳ.ii.53 (iii BC).

***βουκολιστής**, ου, ὁ, *herdsman*, *PMil.Vogl.* 212ʳ.viii.9, xi.21.

**βουκόλος**, add 'Myc. *qo-u-ko-ro*'

**βουκονιστήριον**, for '*bullring*' read 'app. some kind of arena (the meaning of the prefix is disputed)'

**+βουκόπος**, ὁ, *butcher*, *IEphes.* 2.31, 32 (iv BC); gloss on βουπλήξ Hsch.

**βοῦκος**, add 'glossed by ἄγροικος, Eust. 962.12; by βουκόλος, Nic.ap.Sch.Theoc. 10.38'

**βουκράνιον**, for '*ox-head*' read '*ox-skull* (with the horns)'

**βούκρανος**, for 'Call.*fr.* 203' read 'dub. cj. (βοοκράνοιο) in Call.*fr.* 646 Pf.; cf. °βοόκρημνος'

***βούκρας**, Myc. *qo-u-ka-ra*, *adorned with an ox-head*.

***βουκτέανος**, ον, *possessing oxen*, Call.*VB* in *Suppl.Hell.* 260A.8.

***βουκτόνος**, ὁ, *ox-killer* (as a religious office), *IG* 2².4629.

**βουλαῖος I**, add 'as title of emperor Hadrian, *IG* 5(1).1352'

***βοῦλβα**, ἡ, Lat. *volva*, *vulva*, sow's *womb*, in list of meats, *Edict.Diocl.* 4.4, *bulba* μήτρα *Gloss.* 2.534.46.

**βουλεῖον**, add '*SEG* 23.207.19 (Messene, Augustus); Arc. βωλήιον *SEG* 37.340.21 (Mantinea, iv BC)'

**βουλεύς**, add '*SEG* 26.402 (Corinth), 723 (Illyria, both Hellen.)'

**βούλευσις II 2**, add '*IG* 2².1631.394 (Athens, iv BC)'

**βουλευτήριον**, after 'τό' insert 'Aeol. βολλ- *IKyme* 13.71 (ii BC)' **II**, line 1, of local βουλαί, add '*Cod.Just.* 1.4.34.10, Just.*Nov.* 38 pr. 1, etc.'; line 3, after 'E.*Andr.* 446' insert '(so perh. in A.*Th.* 575, v. βουλευτήριος)'

**βουλευτήριος**, add '(but this may be °βουλευτήριον II)'

**βουλευτής 1**, add 'in a local council or *curia*, *Cod.Just.* 1.4.34.10, Just.*Nov.* 101.2, etc.'

**βουλευτικός I 1**, add 'in Roman provincial government, τάγμα Mitchell *N.Galatia* 195 (AD 126), *SEG* 33.1123 (Phrygia, iii AD)'

**βουλευτός I**, add 'Call.*Lav.Pall.*38'

**βουλεύω B**, for '**5** rarely folld. by relat.' read '**b** *deliberate*, *consider*, folld. by clause' and transfer all to section 1.

**βουλή**, line 1, for 'Dor. **βωλά** .. 18.90' read 'Dor. **βωλά** (q.v.)' and add 'Cret. ϝωλᾶς (gen., dub.) *SEG* 37.752.6 (Lyttos, v BC)' and after 'Aeol. **βόλλα**' insert 'Alc. 130.20 L.-P. (rest.)' **I 2** and **3**, for these sections read '**2** *counsel*, *advice*, Il. 1.258, 2.202; κακὴ β. Hes.*Op.* 266; πρᾶτος .. καὶ βουλᾷ καὶ χερσὶν ἐς Ἄρεα *IG* 9(1).658 (Ithaca); νυκτὶ δὲ βουλὴν διδοὺς Hdt. 7.12.1; νυκτὶ βουλήν .. δίδου Plu.*Them.* 26; τούτοις οὐκ ἔστι κοινὴ β. Pl.*Cri.* 49d, X.*Cyr.* 7.2.6, βουλῆς ὀρθότης ἡ εὐβουλία Arist.*EN* 1142ᵇ16; ἐν νυκτὶ β. .. διδοὺς ἐμαυτῷ Men.*Epit.* 252; μαχέσασθαι οὐκ ἐποιεῦντο βουλήν Hdt. 6.101.2; in pl., οἵ τέ μοι αἰεὶ βουλὰς βουλεύουσι Il. 24.652, A.*Pr.* 221, *Th.* 842; ἐν βουλαῖς μὲν ἄριστον *Epigr.Gr.* 854, ἐν βουλαῖσι κράτιστος *IG* 2².3669.8 (iii AD). **3** *deliberation*, *consideration*, τὰ .. γενόμενα ἐν β. ἔχοντες Hdt. 3.78.1, 8.40.1, Arist.*EN* 1112ᵃ19, D. 9.46; οὐδεὶς περὶ τούτου προτίθησιν οὐδαμοῦ βουλήν id. 18.192; ὅπως δ' ἂν βουλὴν ἀγάγοιεν Polyaen. 7.39, ἐν β. ἐγίνοντο πότερον .. D.H. 2.44.' **II**, line 7, after 'X.*HG* 5.29' insert 'in Lesbos, Alc. 130.20 L.-P.' add '**2** *rank of membership of the* βουλή, Δελφοὶ .. Δελφὸν ἐποίησαν καὶ βουλῇ ἐτείμησαν *Delph.* 3(1).219, *IEphes.* 1615.19.'

**βούλησις III**, add 'ἐν τελευταίᾳ βουλήσει *Cod.Just.* 6.4.4.1, 27'

**+βουλογραφέω**, *carry out the enrolment of senators*, *OGI* 549.2 (Ancyra, iii AD).

**+βουλογραφία**, ἡ, *function of enrolling senators*, *IGRom.* 3.206 (Ancyra).

***βουλογράφος**, ὁ, *clerk to the council*, *GDI* 1172.37 (Elis, Hellen.; form βωλογράφορ).

**βούλομαι I 1**, line 26, w. inf. fut., add 'βουλόμενοι ἐξ αὐτέων παῖδας ἐκγενήσεσθαι Hdt. 4.111.2, Th. 6.57.3, Iamb.*Protr.* 16 (p. 83.27 P.)'; add 'w. legal instruments, etc., as subject, *Cod.Just.* 1.3.45.13, 1.3.52.5' **2**, line 3, delete 'later' and after 'c. acc.' insert 'ἄνδρες τὰ Συρακοσίων βουλόμενοι Th. 6.50.3, cf. ib. 82.4' **II**, for 'Att. usages' read 'in var. spec. usages' **4**, add 'Democr. 173 D.-K.'

**βουλυτός**, line 1, delete '(sc. καιρός)'

**βούμαστος**, after 'so in' insert '*PCair.Zen.* 33.15 (iii BC)'

***βουναῖος**, α, ον, *of* or *belonging to the hills*, app. of a kind of wine, Lang *Ath.Agora* XXI I45 (vi AD); cf. βουναία.

***βούνευρον**, (dub.), gloss on κίσσηρις, Hsch.

**βουνιάς**, add 'cf. μουνιαδικόν'

**βούνιον I 1**, add '*PMag.* 3.333' **II**, delete the section (v. °βουνίον).

***βουνίον**, τό, dim. of βουνός, *hill*, *Inscr.Prien.* 42.41 (ii BC), as place-name, *Inscr.Magn.* 122; cf. mod. Gk. βουνί.

**βουνός I 2**, before 'σίτου' insert '**3** as measure of quantity' and add '*JJP* 18.190 (ii/iii AD)'

**βουπόρος**, add '**2** subst., perh. = *ox-spit*, βουπόρος Ἀρσινόης μητρὸς σέο (app. ref. to Mt. Athos) Call.*fr.* 110.45 Pf.'

**βούπρῳρος I**, add 'σημαίνει δὲ καὶ τὴν βουπρόσωπον Hsch. (*Trag. adesp.* 587b K.-S.)'

***βοῦργος**, ὁ, Lat. *burgus*, *tower*, *fort*, *BE* 1962.315 (Palestine, Byz.).

**βουρδών**, after '*Edict.Diocl.* 14.10' insert '(βουδρών ib. 11.4a)'

**βουρδωνάριος**, add '*BE* 1958.301 (Egypt, Chr.); also βουρδουνάριος, Teuc.Bab. p. 43.4 B.'

**βουριχάλλιον**, for pres. def. read 'some kind of carriage, prob. *pony-cart*' and add 'perh. -χάλιον, i.e. dim. of late Lat. **buricale*, cf. *buricus*'

***βουριχᾶς**, 'α, ὁ, *pony-dealer* or *drover*, *IEphes.* 551 (late Rom.imp.; cf. *manni equi dicuntur pusilli, quos vulgo burichos vocant* Porphyrio ad Hor.*C.* 3.27.7).

**βοῦς I a**, add 'ἐν δὲ Συρίᾳ .. οἱ βόες, ὥσπερ αἱ κάμηλοι, κάλας ἔχουσιν ἐπὶ τῶν ἀκρωμίων Arist.*HA* 606ᵃ15' **b**, for this section read 'w. ἄγριος, applied to var. non-domesticated species, Arist.*HA* 499ᵃ4, *Mir.* 842ᵇ33' **c**, delete the section. **d**, for 'βούφθαλμος' read 'βούφθαλμον' **IV**, add '**b** kind of cake, *Sokolowski* 1.42*B*6, 43.3 (Miletus, v BC).' at end add 'Myc. *qo-o* (prob. acc. pl.)'

**βουστᾰσία**, add '*Cat.Cod.Astr.* 11(2).181.14'

**βοῦτις**, add '*Edict.Diocl.* 13.17 ([βο]ῦττις)'

***βούτμημα**, ατος, τό, *furrow*, gloss on τμήγας, Hsch.

***βουτοί**· τόποι παρ' Αἰγυπτίοις, εἰς οὓς οἱ τελευτῶντες τίθενται Hsch.

**+βουτρόφος**, ὁ, *rearer of oxen*, *JHS* 54.143.69 (decr., pl., Delos, ii BC), Poll. 1.249, *EM* 209.54; cf. βοοτρόφος.

***βουτῠ́πιον**, gloss on δάροσος (°δάρος), Hsch.

**βούτῡρον**, add '*Peripl.M.Rubr.* 14, 41'

***βουφονία**, Ep. -ίη, ἡ, *sacrifice of oxen*, Call.*fr.* 67.6 Pf.

***βουφόντης**, ου, ὁ, *ox-slaying*, λίς Euph. in *Suppl.Hell.* 418.17.

***βοῦφος**, ὁ, nocturnal bird, Cyran. 86 (3.8.1 K.); cf. mod. Gk. μποῦφος.

**βοών**, add '*IG* 1³.425.42 (Athens, v BC; βο‹ῶ›νι lapis)'

**βοώνης**, add 'at Delos, *Inscr.Délos* 399*A*17 (ii BC)'

**βοωτέω**, add 'βωτέω Theognost.*Can.* 48 A., Suid. (Lacon.)'

***βοωφόρος**, ὁ, official in Bacchic cult, *IG* 10(2).1.244 i 4 (Thessalonica, ii AD).

**+βρά**· ἀδελφοί (Illyrian) Hsch.

**βρᾰ́βευμα**, add 'Leont.Byz.*HP* 1.5.6'

**βρᾰβεύς I 2**, delete the section transferring quots. to section 1, *judge, arbitrator*

**βρᾰβευτής II**, add '*TAM* 5(1).234, 515 (Rom.imp.)'

**βραγχώδης 1**, add 'Gal. 13.4.14'

**βρᾰ́δῑνος**, insert '(= Ϝράδ-)' and for 'Sapph. 90, 104' read 'Sapph. 102, 115 L.-P., Alc. 304 ii 9 L.-P.'

***βρᾰδῠγᾰμέω**, *be late in marrying*, Heph.Astr. 1.1.190.

**βρᾰδῠδῑνής**, add '(cj.)'

***βρᾰδῠ́θω**, *move slowly*, Nic.*Th.* 372 (v.l. μινύθ-).

**βρᾰδῠλόγος**, read βραδύλογος.

**βρᾰδῠπειθής**, for '*AP* 5.286 (Agath.)' read '*AP* 5.287.7, 299.7 (both Agath.)'

***βρᾰδυπλοΐα**, ἡ, *slow voyage*, *POxy.* 2191.8 (ii AD).

**βρᾰδύς**, line 3, βάρδιστος, add 'Theoc. 15.104'; line 9, comp. adv. βράδιον, add 'Plu. 2.459f, 460a'

***βρᾰδυστομέω**, *be slow of speech*, *Trag.adesp.* 668.13 K.-S.

**+βράθυ**, τό, name of various trees or shrubs of the genus *Juniperus*, Dsc. 1.76, Cyran. 12.1 (1.2.1 K., v.l. βράθυος).

**βρακάριος** (s.v. βράκαι), for '*breeches-maker*, ib. 18' read '*maker of trousers, tailor*, *Edict.Diocl.* 7.42'; add '*IGChr.* 262 (Aphrodisias), βρικάριος (sic) *MAMA* 3.597 (Corycus) is perh. the same wd., see also βρεκάριος'

**βράκια** (s.v. βράκαι), dim. βράκια, for '*IG* 5 .. Asine' read '*Edict.Diocl.* 7.46'

**+βράπτω**, βράπτειν· ἐσθίειν, κρύπτειν, ἀφανίζειν. τῷ στόματι ἕλκειν. ἢ στενάζειν Hsch.; see also s.vv. ἔβραπτεν, ἔβραψεν in Hsch.; cf. μάρπτω.

**βρᾰ́σις**, add 'fig. of anger, cj. in Plot. 4.4.28'

**βράστης**, add '**2** *winnower*, *PMich.*I 53.6 (pl. (s.v.l.), iii BC).'

***Βραυρωνία**, ἡ, title of Artemis, *IG* 1³.369.89, 2².1401 (iv BC), *SEG* 25.445 (Arcadia, ii BC).

***βραχιᾶτοι**, οἱ, *bracelet-wearers* (legionary rank in the late empire), Lyd.*Mag.* 1.46.

**βρᾰχίων**, at end for 'as a .. 478' read 'of strength of arm, νέοι βραχίοσιν E.*Supp.* 738'

**βρᾰχύνω**, for 'Pl.*Per.*' read 'Plu.*Per.*'

**βρᾰχῠ́ποτος**, delete the entry (refer quot. to -πότης).

**βρᾰχύς**, line 1, after 'ῠ' insert 'Aeol. **βρόχυς** (q.v.); cf. βρόσσων'; line 8, for 'Men. 726' read 'Men.*fr.* 544 K.-Th., βραχὺ *soon*, *Anacreont.* 52A.4 W.' **5**, after 'D.T. 631' insert 'S.E.*M.* 1.100ff.' and delete 'etc. .. S.E.*M.* 1.113'

**βρᾰχῠ́της 3**, after 'of a syllable' insert 'or vowel' **6**, after 'Rhet.' insert '*conciseness of expression*, ἡ τοιαύτη β. κόμμα ὀνομάζεται Demetr.*Eloc.* 9'

**βρέβιον**, for 'Lat. *brevis*' read 'Lat. *brevium*'; βρέουιον, add '*POxy.* 3628.1 (v AD)'

**βρέγμα I 1**, after '*front part of the head*' insert '(anat.) *sinciput*' and add 'A.*fr.* 451h.8 R. (lyr.), Call.*fr.* 37.3, 177.28 Pf.'; delete '(prob. from βρέχω .. 24)'

**βρεκτός**, after '*soaked*' insert 'βρεκτῶν τε κομάων Euph. in *Suppl.Hell.* 442 *fr.* 2.7'

***βρεμέθω**, = βρέμω, Jo.Gaz. 2.145.

**Βρετᾰνικός I**, add 'as imperial title, D.C. 60.12, *SEG* 34.1268 (Bithynia, AD 189), *ICilicie* 78 (AD 209/211); βρυτανικῆς (sic) τέχνης prob. *tin-working*, *PKöln* 101.9 (iii AD)'

***Βρεταννίς**, ίδος, fem. adj., *British*, νήσοιο Β[ρ]εταννίδος *GDRK* 1².79 no 22.4.

**βρέτας 1**, add 'of a statue of Artemis, epigr. in *SEG* 23.220(b) (Messene, i AD)'

**βρέφος II**, for '*new-born babe*' read '*baby, child*'; after '[not in S.]' insert 'Theoc. 15.14, Call.*Cer.* 100, *fr.* 487 Pf.'; after 'in later prose' insert 'β. διετές *Delph.* 3(6).39.11, 57.10'

***βρεφοτροφεῖον**, τό, *institution for the maintenance of infants*, *Cod.Just.* 1.2.22 (pl.).

***βρεφοτρόφος**, ὁ, official in charge of βρεφοτροφεῖον, *Cod.Just.* 1.3 tit.

**βρεφώδης**, for 'Diog.Oen. 9' read 'Diog.Oen.*fr.* 9.12 C. (rest.)'

**βρέχω**, line 5, (aor. 2), after 'but' insert 'βρεχεῖσα Men.*Dysc.* 950'; line 6, after 'Wilcken *Chr.* 341.6 (ii AD)' insert 'and aor. pass. subj., βρεχῶσιν *PHib.* 90.8 (iii BC)'; lines 19/20, delete 'but also intr.' **II**, line 2, after '(ii AD)' insert 'ἔβρεξεν ὁ Ζε[υ]ὸς θεῶ οὐραγός orac. in *SEG* 31.1575 (Cyrene, ii AD)'

***βρεχώδης**, ες, = βροχμώδης, *damp*, rest. in Diog.Oen.*fr.* 9.8 C. (rest.).

**+βρία**, η, expld. as πόλις (in Thracian), Str. 7.6.1, βρίαν· τὴν ἐπ' ἀγροῖς κώμην Hsch.; in false etym. expl. of Μεσημβρία, ἀπὸ [Μέ]λσα καὶ βρία epigr. in *IGBulg.* 345.4; so in Str. l.c. and St.Byz. s.v. Μεσημβρία.

***βριάριον**, τό, app. dim. of °βρία, *little settlement*, *Peripl.M.Rubr.* 58 (cj. φρούριον).

**βρίζα I**, after 'Gal. 6.514' insert '*Edict.Diocl.* 1.3'

***βριζόμαντις**· ἐνυπνιόμαντις Hsch.

**βρίζω II**, delete the section.

***βρίζω** (B), perh. *pick, gather*, καρποὺς ξύλων D.Chr. 35.18; cf. βρίζει· ἐσθίει, πιέζει, κύει Hsch.

***βρῑθυεργός**, ὁ, *powerful worker*, of an architect, epigr. in *IHadr.* 132 (ii AD).

**βρῑθύς**, delete 'once in Trag.' and for 'id.*Eleg.* 5' read '(A.)*fr.* 353a R.'

**βρίθω I 3**, add '(= *SEG* 30.1473)' **III 2**, line 6, transpose 'συμποσίων .. 3.12' to section I 2 (after 'Od. 15.334')

***βρικάριος**, v. °βρακάριος.

***βριλών**, 'ωνος, ὁ, β.· ὁ βαλανεύς Theognost.*Can.* 35.

**βρῑμός**, before 'μέγας' insert '*mighty*, *Carm.Pop.* 16 P.'

***Βρῑσαῖος**, ὁ, title of Dionysus, *EM* 214.5, St.Byz. s.v. Βρῖσα.

**βρῑσόμᾰχος**, add 'perh. in *POxy.* 3876 *fr.* 3.4 (Stesich.)'

***βρίσχος**, v. ὑριχός.

***Βρῑτομάρπεια**, τά, *festival of Britomarpis*, *Inscr.Cret.* 1.xvi 5.43 (Latos, ii BC); cf. Βριτομάρτια (s.v. Βριτόμαρτις).

***Βρῑτόμαρπις**, ά, = Βριτόμαρτις, acc. -ιν, *Inscr.Cret.* 1.xviii 9 c 7 (Lyttos, ii BC), 1.vii 4 2 (Cret., Chersonesus, ii BC), al.

**Βριτόμαρτις**, etc., add 'cf. °Βριτομαρπ-'

***βριττανδρα**, perh. fem. adj. *prevailing over men*, *Suppl.Mag.* 42.30 (iii/iv AD).

**βρογχωτήρ**, delete the entry (v. °βροχωτήρ).

**βρόμος** (A), line 4, after 'A.*Th.* 476' insert 'Aq.*Ez.* 23.20'

**βρόμος** (B) **1**, add '*Edict.Diocl.* 1.17'

**βρονταῖος**, add '**2** βρονταία (sc. λίθος), ἡ, name of a precious stone, Plin.*HN* 37.150.'

**βροντάω**, after '*JHS* 5.258, etc.' insert 'Mitchell, *N.Galatia* 13, 77, *SEG* 32.1275 (Dorylaeum), in Bithynia, *INikaia* 1504, al.; *SEG* 35.1419 (Pamphylia)'

**βρότειος** (A), add 'Emp. 6.3 D.-K.'; form βρότεος, before 'Pi.*O.* 9.34' insert 'Simon. 76.6 P. (cj.)'

***βρότειος** (B), α, ον, *gory*, λαιμοί E.*Heracl.* 822 (cj. βοείων), id.*IA* 1083; cf. βροτόρις.

**βροτήσιος**, after 'Hes.*Op.* 773' insert 'φῦλα Alcm. 106 P.'

**βροτοβάμων**, add '(cj. βοτοβάμων *mounting flocks*)'

***βροτοείκελος**, ον, *like a human being*, εἶδος *Inscr.Cret.* 2.xxiv 13.12 (epigr., Rhethymna, iv AD).

**βροτόεις I**, add 'Hom.*fr.* 7, Stesich. *S*15 ii 13 (p. 160 D.)'

**βροτολοιγός**, last line, 'ἔρως .. end' read 'Ἀίδης *AP* 1.56, Ἄρης ib. 6.91 (Thallus), 9.323 (Antip.Sid.), ἔρως ib. 5.180 (Mel.), 9.221 (Marc.Arg.)'

**βροῦκος**, after 'Ion. acc. to Hsch.' insert 'but as pers. n. elsewh., *SEG* 9.46.8, 35 (Cyrene, iv BC), 32.281 (Athens, iii BC)'; βρεῦκος, after 'Cret. acc. to Hsch.' insert 'cf. pers. n. *SIG* 737.3, 11 (Cret. at Delphi, i BC)'; add 'cf. βραύκη, βρόκος, βρύκος'

**βροῦνος**, add 'Hdn.*fr.* p. 27 H.'

***βροῦχος**, v. βροῦκος.

***βροχεύς**, έως, ὁ, *net-maker*, *PAmst.*inv. 21 (*ZPE* 9.49, iv/v AD).

***βροχηλᾰτέω**, *drive into snares*, v.l. in Opp.*C.* 4.64 (v. βοηλατέω).

**βροχίς I**, after 'Opp.*H.* 3.595' insert '(pl., *meshes* of a fishing net), *snare for birds*, *AP* 9.76 (pl., Antip.Sid.)'

**βρόχυς**, for 'Sapph. 2.7' read 'Sapph. 31.7 L.-P. (βρόχεα, neut. pl. as adv., *a little while*)'

***βροχωτήρ**, ῆρος, ὁ, *neck-hole* in a garment, J.*AJ* 3.7.2.

**βροχωτός 2**, for '*twisted, corded*, of chain work' read 'as transl. of Hebr. wd. app. meaning *finely-woven*'

**βρῠάζω**, line 1, delete 'aor. ἀν-εβρύαξα Ar.*Eq.* 602'

**βρύαθμον**, delete 'cf. *Hymn.Is.* 89 (dub. sens.)'

***βρυάθων**, dub. wd. in *Hymn.Is.* 89 (perh. part. of βρυάθω = βρυάζω).

**βρυάκτης**, for '*jolly*' read '*wanton*'
**βρῦγμα**, delete '*gnawing*'
***βρυδακίζειν**· ἐκτείνειν Hsch. (La.); cf. ‡βρυλλιχίζειν.
***βρυδαλίχα**· πρόσωπον γυναικεῖον Hsch. (remainder of gloss corrupt).
***βρύζα**, ἡ (= °ὄβρυζα), χρυσοῦ β. *refined gold*, *Edict.Diocl.* 30.1a.
**βρύζω**, delete 'dub. sens. in Archil. 32.2' (v. °μύζω (B))
**βρυκεδανός**, after 'μακρός' insert '(cj. μάργος)'
**βρύκω II**, for '*grind*' read '*snap*'
**βρυλλιχίζειν**, after 'Hsch.' insert '(cj., cod. °βρυδακίζειν)'
***βρύλλω**, dub. sens., βρύλλων Ar.*Eq.* 1126: expld. by Sch. as ἐξαπατώμενος, also ὑποπίνων, μεθύων, etc.
***βρῠόεις**, εσσα, εν, *growing luxuriantly*, νέον βρυόεντα θύμου στάχυν Nic.*Al.* 371, 478. **2** *full of luxuriant growth*, βρυόεντος .. ποταμοῖο id.*Th.* 208, ἐνὶ βρυόεντι .. κόλπῳ Nonn.*D.* 1.206, 21.180, al.
**βρύον I**, transfer 'Arist.*HA* 591$^{b}$12' to follow 'β. alone' and after it insert 'Thphr.*HP* 4.6.6' and 'Theoc. 21.7' (from section II)
**βρύσσος**, add 'E.*fr.* 955b (cf. ἄμβρυττος). **2** *pudenda muliebria* (cf. βύττος), ὅς κατευδούσης τῆς μητρὸς ἐσκύλευε τὸν βρύσσον Hippon. 70.8 W.'
***βρυτανικός**, v. °Βρετανικός.
***βρῡχή**, ἡ, *roaring, bellowing*, Opp.*H.* 2.530, Q.S. 5.392. **2** *crashing*, A.R. 2.83.
**βρῡχηδόν**, for '*gnashing*' read '*snapping*'
**βρύω 2**, after 'c. gen., *to be full of*' insert 'βρύουσι φιλοξενίας ἀγυιαί B. 3.16'
**βρῶμα II 2**, for '*Ep.Je.* 12' read '*Ep.Je.* 11'
**βρωμάομαι I**, add 'βρωμωμένου· ὀγκωμένου Hsch.' for '**III** etc.' read '**II** ἐβρώμησε (ἐβρωμήσατο La.)· βρώσεως ἐδεήθη Hsch.'
**βρωμᾰτίζω**, add '*Vit.Aesop.*(G) 45'
**βρωμάτιον**, add '*Pap.Lugd.Bat.* xxv 73.3 (vi AD)'
**βρωμήεις**, add 'also **βρωμέεις**, Hdn.Gr. 2.921.1, al.'
**βρωτός II**, add 'Aen.Tact. 8.4'
***Βύβλιος**, η, ον, *from Phoenician Byblos*, of a kind of wine, Archestr. ap.Ath. 1.29b.
***βυβλι-**, see also βιβλι-.
**βύβλος I 2 a**, delete the section transferring 'Thphr.*HP* 4.8.4' and 'Hdt. 2.96.2, Plot. 2.7.2' to section 1. **b**, delete 'sg., *strip of* β. .. Ph. 2.522' and transfer 'Ph. 2.522' and 'Pl.*Plt.* 288e' (from 2 a) to section 3
***βυζάστρια**, ἡ, gloss on τίτθη, Hdn.*Philet.* p. 81 Dain; cf. mod. Gk. βυζάστρα, *wet-nurse.*
**βύθιος I**, for '*Hymn.Is.* 71' read '*Hymn.Is.* 161'
***βῠθοκλόνος**, ον, *convulsing the deep*, *PMag.* 4.1363.
**βῠθός a**, add 'Βυθός, personified, in mosaic, *SEG* 31.1387 (Apamea, Syria, iv AD)' **b**, add '*deep track*, Nic.*Th.* 570'
**βῡκάνητής**, after 'Plb. 2.29.6' insert '30.22.11'
**βῡκάνιστής**, delete 'Plb. 30.22.11'
**βύκτης I**, add 'A.R. 3.1328, Orph.*A.* 125'
**βυλλόω**, add 'also ἐβύλλων· ἔβρυον, ἐπλήθυον Hsch.'
**Βύνη**, after '*Leucothea*' insert 'Call.*fr.* 91 Pf.'
***βῦνις**, εως, prob. = βύνη, *malt*, *PMag.* 12.426, 433, *PMil.Vogl.* 278.18, al.
***βυρίτιον**, app. *kind of garment*, cf. perh. ‡βίρρος, στιχαρομαφόρην β. *PWash.Univ.* 58.3 (V AD).
**βυρρός II**, delete the section (v. °βύρρος).
***βύρρος**, v. °βίρρος.
**βυρσεῖον**, after '*tan-pit*' insert '*tannery*, *PTeb.* 801.2 (ii BC)'
**βυρσοδεψέω**, add '*IG* 1$^{3}$.257.9 (Athens, v BC)'
***βυρσοφώνης**, ου, ὁ, *sounding with hides*, of Salmoneus, imitating thunder with drums, S.*fr.* 10c.6 R.
***βύσαλον**, τό, *brick*, Anon.Alch. 334.10.
***βυσσικός**, ή, όν, made of βύσσος, Marcian *Dig.* 39.4.16.7.
**βύσσινος 1**, add 'fig., τὸν βασιλεῖ μέλλοντα μετὰ παρρησίας διαλέγεσθαι βυσσίνοις χρῆσθαι ῥήμασι i.e. with soft words, Plu. 2.174a'
**βυσσοδομέω** (s.v. -δομεύω), add '*SEG* 29.1444 (Oenoanda, *c.*AD 200)'
**βυσσόθεν**, after 'Call.*Del.* 127' insert '*from the depths* of the earth, id.*fr.* 202.59 Pf. (Add. II)'
**βύσσος**, add '**II** a dye, Suid. s.vv. βυσσόν and βύσσινον.'
***βυσσοφαντεῖον** (for *βυσσυφ-), τό, *workshop for weaving linen*, *PMagdola* 36 (*BASP* 22.131).
* **βωθέω**, v. °βοηθέω.
**βωθύζειν**, add 'βωθύσσειν Theognost.*Can.* 48 A., Zonar.'
**βωλάκιον**, add '*lump of earth*, Afric.*Cest.* p. 82 V.'
**βῶλαξ**, add 'Lxx *Jb.* 7.5'
***βωλοκοπέω**, *break up* soil, *harrow*, Ar.*fr.* 800 K.-A., Hp.*Ep.* 17, Ael.*Ep.* 19, *PLond.* 131$^{r}$ iii 50 (i AD), *PMil.Vogl.* 305.96, al. (ii AD); w. acc., τὸν χοῦν *IG* 2$^{2}$.1672.45 (Eleusis iv BC), τὴν γῆν ib. 60; transf., app. *beat up*, of violent sexual assault, epigr. in *IG* 9$^{2}$(2).253 (Thyrreum, iii BC); cf. ἀρόω II 2.
***βωλοκόπημα**, ατος, τό, *harrow*, *occa* βωλοκόπημα *Gloss.Philox.*
**βωλοκόπος**, add '*occiliator* (= *occillator*, *harrower*), *Gloss.*'
**βωλόκρῖθον**, add '*PCair.Zen.* 292.437 (iii BC)'
**βῶλος 3**, add '**b** a precious stone, Plin.*HN* 37.150.' at end after 'masc. in Arist. l.c.' insert '(elsewhere in Arist., fem.)'
**βωλοστροφέω**, for '*turn up clods in ploughing*' read '*break up clods after ploughing*' and add '*BGU* 2126 ii 10 (iii AD)'
**βωλοστροφία**, after '*clods*' insert '*PHib.* 282.22 (i/ii AD), *Gloss.*'
***βωλοστροφικός**, ὁ (or -όν, τό) perh. *harrow*, *POxy.* 3805.111 (vi AD).
***βωλοτρόφος**, ον, *feeding the tilth*, or **βωλότροφος**, *fed by silt*, *Hymn.Is.* 176 (s.v.l.).
**βωμικός**, for '= βώμιος' read '*having a base* or *pedestal*'
**βωμίς**, add '**2** prob. *base* (of sarcophagus), *SEG* 17.632, *BE* 1950.204 (both Perge, Rom.imp.).'
***βωμίσκος**, ὁ, dim. of βωμός, *altar* (in quot., a model in a mechanical contrivance by Hero), Hero *Spir.* 1.38, al. **b** name for the constellation Ara, Ptol.*Alm.* 8.1. **2** app. kind of bandage shaped to the form of an altar, Gal. 18(1).823.11. **3** *base* of molar teeth, Poll. 2.93. **II** geom., *solid figure* consisting of a truncated pyramid, Hero *Deff.* 114, Theo Sm. p. 41 H., Nicom.*Ar.* 2.16, Syrian. *in Metaph.* 143.7, al. **b** *plane figure* formed by the elevation of such a figure, *quadrilateral*, Papp. 878.
**βωμολοχεύομαι**, for '*play the buffoon, indulge in ribaldry*' and '*play low tricks*, in Music' read '*play antics, clown*' and add 'Isoc. 15.284'
**βωμός 1**, delete 'but' and add '*platform* or *floor* of a tomb, on which sarcophagi were placed, *TAM* 4(1).231, *MAMA* 6.191a (Apamea), 8.545 (Aphrodisias), etc.' **2**, delete 'mostly' **3**, for this section read '*funerary altar*, *MAMA* 6.19 (Laodicea), etc.'
***βωμοφόρος**, ὁ, *altar-carrier*, *SEG* 16.741 (Pergamum, Rom.imp.).
***βώνυσοι**· ἄποικοι, βουκόλοι Suid., cf. Theognost.*Can.* 48 A.
***Βωρεῖς**, οἱ, one of the Ionic tribes, *SIG* 57.3 (Miletus, v BC), etc.; sg. Βωρεύς, έος, ὁ, member of this tribe, *IEphes.* 945a, 1431, al.; also **Βορεύς**, ib. 1578a.7 (ii AD, also at Tomi).
**βωρίδιον** (s.v. βωρεύς), add '*POxy.* 2728.33 (iii/iv AD), *PRyl.* 629.88 (βορ-, iv AD)'
***βώσεσθε**, v. °βόσκω.
**βωσίον**, after 'dub. sens.' insert 'perh. = βωτίον'
***βωτέω**, v. °βοωτέω.
**βωτῐάνειρα**, for 'Hes.*Cat.* .. 1.16' read 'rest. in Hes.*fr.* 165.16 M.-W., Alcm. 77 P.'
**βώτωρ**, transfer 'βώτορες ἄνδρες' to precede 'Il. 12.302'

# Γ

**γᾰ**, after 'Ar.*Ach.* 775' insert '(in the mouth of a Boeotian); *SEG* 11.244 (Sicyon, v BC)'

**γαβαθόν**, for 'cf. ζάβατος' read 'cf. ζαβατός 2, καβαθα'

**γάβενα**, add 'cf. mod. Gk. γαβάνη'

**γαβεργόρ**, add '(γαβεργός La.)'

**γαγγᾰλίζω**, for 'but the contrary is stated' read 'γαργ- said to be correct form'

***γαγγᾰλισμός**, ὁ, γαργαλισμός· γαγγαλισμός, ἡδυπάθειά τις Hsch.

+**γάγγᾰλος**· ὁ εὐμετάθετος καὶ εὐρίπιστος τῇ γνώμῃ καὶ εὐμετάβολος Hsch.

+**γαγγᾰμεύς**· ἁλιεύς, ὁ τῇ γαγγάμῃ ἐργαζόμενος Hsch.

**γαγγάμη**, add 'σαγήνη ἢ δίκτυον ἁλιευτικόν. καὶ σκεῦος γεωργικὸν ὅμοιον τῇ κρεάγρᾳ Hsch.'

**Γαγγητικός**, delete 'a fragrant .. *Iwarancusa*'; after '*Peripl.M.Rubr.* 63' insert '(Γαγγιτικός Casson); cf. Γαγγῖτις νάρδος'; for a description of the plant see also Plin.*HN* 12.42.

**γάγγραινα**, add '**2** = μέροψ (bird), Cyran. 92 (3.30.3 K.).'

**γαγγραινικός**, add '**2** *used in cases of gangrene*, Gal. 13.739.13.'

***γᾱδαισία**, v. °γεωδαισία.

**Γάδειρα**, etc., delete marks of quantity and add '[Γᾱ- Pi. l.c., cf. Lat. *Gādes*; Γᾰ- Theodorid. in *Suppl.Hell.* 744, *AP* l.c., D.P. 11, al., *Anacreont.* 14.25 W.]'

***γᾱϝεργέω**, v. °γεωργέω.

***γᾱϝεργός**, v. °γεωργός.

***Γαζαῖοι**, οἱ, *inhabitants of Gaza*; in a dating formula, κατὰ .. Γαζαίους τοῦ εχʹ ἔτους ἰνδικτιῶνος ηʹ *SEG* 34.1467 (Palestine, vi AD).

***γαζαρηνοί**, οἱ, (Aramaic *gāzerīn*) *astrologers*, Lxx *Da.* 2.27, 4.7, 5.7.

**γαῖα I 2**, delete 'the forms .. etc.'

+**γαιᾶται**· κερτομεῖ. καταμωκᾶται Hsch.; cf. γαιῶ· τὸ κερτομῶ καὶ διαβάλλω Theognost.*Can.* 22 A.

***γαιάτης**, ου, ὁ, *dweller on earth*, St.Byz. s.v. γῆ.

***γαιεῖος**, v. °γαιήϊος.

***γαιηϊάς**, fem. adj. = γαιήϊος, St.Byz. s.v. γῆ.

**γαιήϊος II**, add 'also γαιεῖος, βρότεον γένος ἠδὲ γαιεῖον *Didyma* 496*B*4 (ii AD)'

***Γαιῆος**, ὁ, name of a month in Caligula's calendar in Egypt, *PTeb.* 492, *OStrassb.* 68 (AD 41); also Γάϊος, in full Γ. Σεβαστός *OBodl.* ii 469, 470, al.

***γάϊνος**, v. °γήϊνος.

+**γαιώδης**, v. ‡γεώδης.

**γάλᾰ I 3**, transfer 'οὐδ' εἰ γ. λαγοῦ .. Alex. 123 (= 128 K.-A.)' to section I 1, after 'Theoc. 24.3'

**γᾰλᾰθηνός**, add 'Simon. 38.8 P.'

***γάλαιθος**, unexpld. wd., anon.ap.*An.Ox.* 2.318.

**γᾰλακτίτης I**, add 'Plin.*HN* 37.162'

***γᾰλακτῖτις**, ιδος, ἡ, = γαλαξίας II, Plin.*HN* 37.162.

***γᾰλακτοδότρια**, ἡ, *giving of milk*, ἡ τῶν ἀναγεννηθέντων γ. Ps.-Chrys.*HP* 5.2, Leont.Byz.*HP* 1.6.2.

***γᾰλακτοποιός**, όν, = γαλακτοποιητικός, βοτάνη Hdn.Gr. 1.395.

**γᾰλακτοποτέω**, for '(Written .. p. 111 V.)' read '(shd. be written **-πωτέω** acc. to Ammon. 399 N., s.v.l.)'

***γᾰλακτοπότος**, ον, *sucking*, χοίρου γαλακτοπότο[υ] *Edict.Diocl.* 4.46 (v.l.).

***γᾰλακτορρύω**, *flow with milk*, Procl.CP *Hom.* 29.18.

**γᾰλακτοφόρος**, add '**2** γαλακτοφόροι, οἱ, *milk-carriers*, *OBodl.* i 304 (ii BC).'

**γᾰλαξίας II**, add '= γαλακτίτης I, Plin.*HN* 37.162'

+**γαλαρίας**· ἰχθύς, ὁ ὀνίσκος Hsch. (see also γαλλερίας, καλλαρίας, °γελαβρίας).

**Γαλάται**, add 'sg. -τας *IG* 9²(1).624c5 (Naupactus, ii BC)'

**γᾰλεάγρα**, after '*weasel-cage*' insert '*IG* 1³.422.139 (Athens, v BC)' add '**II** *winepress*, Hero *Mech.fr.* (Arabic text) 3.17 (2.238 N.-S.).'

***γᾰλεάριος**, Lat. *galearius*, *soldier's servant*, *SEG* 19.787 (Pisidia).

**γᾰλεός I**, after 'small *shark*' insert 'Philox.Leuc.*fr.* (*b*).11 P.'; add 'γαλιῶ μέδδονος *IGC* p. 99 A40 (Acraephia, iii/ii BC)'

***γᾰλεοψοποιέω**, *prepare a dish of dogfish*, Archestr. in *Suppl.Hell.* 188.9 (γαλεοψοποιούντων cj., γαλῇ ὀψοποιούντων cod.).

**γάλερος**, after '*AB* 229' insert 'neut. as adv., *GLP* 123.1'

**γᾰλεώνυμος**, add 'Orib.*Syn.* 4.17.7'

**γᾰληναίη**, add 'Call.*Epigr.* 5.5 Pf., *AP* 7.640 (Antip.Thess.), Opp.*H.* 1.460'

***γᾰληνοποιός**, ὁ, *one who makes calm*, gloss on στορεύς, Hsch.

**γᾰληνότης**, add '**II** as title, *Serenity*, *MAMA* 3.197 (Corycus), *ICilicie* 118.8, *PFlor.* 75.5 (all vi AD), Just.*Nov.* 124.4.'

***γαλίβδολον**, τό, = °γάλιψις, Paul.Aeg. 7.3 (203.3 H.).

***γάλιψις**, ἡ, plant said to resemble ἀκαλήφη (prob. in sense I), Paul.Aeg. 7.3 (203.3 H.).

***γάλλαρος**, ὁ, member of a Dionysiac cult-society, prob. in *IGBulg.* 401.15-16 (Apollonia in Thrace; pl.); γ.· Φρυγιακὸν ὄνομα Hsch.; cf. °ἀρχιγ-.

**γαλλερίας**, add 'cf. γαλαρίας, καλλαρίας'

***γαλλεωρ**, ὁ, accent unkn.; app. designation of man's trade or occupation, *BGU* 1614.Ci5 (i AD).

***Γαλλικός**, ή, όν, *Gallic*, θάλασσα Ptol.*Geog.* 2.10.2, of garments, βάνατα γ. *Edict.Diocl.* 19.57, etc.; σαβάνων Γ. ib. 28.57; designating military units, εἴλης (sic) βʹ Γαλλικῆς *ala* II *Gallorum*, *SEG* 38.683 (Maced., ii AD), λεγεώνων Γαλλικῆς καὶ αʹ Ἰλλυρικῆς ib. 34.1598.5 (Egypt, iv AD).

**γάλοως**, **γάλως**, add 'prob. in *SEG* 31.1004.8 (Saittai, ii AD)'

**γαμβρά**, after '*sister-in-law*' insert '*PMich.*II 123ᵛ viii.10 (i AD), γαμβ-pap.)'

**γαμβρός**, line 1, after 'ὁ' insert 'also γαρβρός (sic) *SEG* 31.1031.5 (Saittai, ii AD); cf. γαβρός ib. 1004.7' and after '*A.Ag.* 708 (pl.)' insert 'Plu. 2.620a'

**γᾰμελα**, for '*Michel* 995*B*36' read '*CID* 1.9A 24-25, B 36, equiv. of Att. γαμήλια'

**γᾰμετή**, add 'as name of a chariot horse, *SEG* 26.1837 (Leptis Magna, iv AD), sp. γαμητ- *BCH* 4.199, 7.237 (both Isauria), 503 (Philadelphia), *IG* 3.3479'

**γᾰμέτης**, before 'Euph. 107.3' insert 'Call.*fr.* 228.12 Pf.' and after 'Dor.' insert 'nom. γαμέτᾱς Call. l.c.'

**γᾰμέω I 2**, for this section read '*take as a lover* or *concubine*, Od. 1.36; οὐχὶ χατέρας πλείστας ἀνὴρ εἷς Ἡρακλῆς ἔγημε δή S.*Tr.* 460; βιαίως E.*Tr.* 44. **b** *have sexual intercourse with*, Luc.*Asin.* 32, *AP* 5.94 (Rufin.).' **3**, of the woman, add 'εἶθ' ὕστερον ἔγημε τὸν φθείραντα Arg.Men.*Her.* 3; abs., 1*Ep.Cor.* 7.34, Charito 3.2.17, Just.*Nov.* 97.6 pr.'

***γᾰμητή**, v. ‡γαμετή.

***γᾰμητιάω**, *be eager for sexual intercourse*, *Vit.Aesop.*(W) 103.

+**γᾰμίζω**, *give in marriage*, *Ev.Matt.* 24.38, A.D.*Synt.* 280.11; pass. *Ev.Matt.* 22.30, *Ev.Marc.* 12.25, *Ev.Luc.* 17.27. **2** *make* a woman *one's wife*, 1*Ep.Cor.* 7.38.

**Γᾰμίλιος**, after 'Epirus' insert 'and elsewhere' and add '*SEG* 30.990 (Corinth, iv/iii BC)'

***γαμμάτιον**, τό, of an ornament, *a little* (representation of) *gamma*, *EM* 766.7.

+**γαμματίσκιον**, τό, = °γαμμάτιον, Lyd.*Mag.* 2.4.

**γᾰμοκλόπος**, add 'of Κύπρις, *Inscr.Cret.* 3.iv 37.5 (Hellen. epigr.)'

**γᾰμος VI**, Γάμος, add 'also at Argos, *SEG* 30.356 (300 BC)'

***γᾰμοστολίη**, ἡ, perh. *wedding-dress*, *MAMA* 7.229.

***γᾰμότης**, ητος, ἡ, *state of marriage*, σώφρων ἐν γαμότητι, περίφρων ἐν βιότητι *GVI* 1737.5 (Syria, iii AD).

**γαμφηλαί**, for 'once in sg.' read 'also in sg.' and insert 'v.l. in Moero 1.6'

+ **γᾰνάεις**, εσσα, εν, *glorious*, prob. in Pi.*Dith.* 4(h).7 S.-M.

***γανᾱλός**, unexpld. wd. in Hdn.*fr.* p.21 H.

**γᾰνάω II 2**, for this section read 'γανάοντες *glorifying*, A.*Supp.* 1019 (cj., cod. γανάεντες)'

***γανίς**, ίδος, ἡ, Egyptian liquid measure (in quots., of oil), *OMich.* 253, 254 (iii/iv AD).

**γάννος**, for '= γλάνος' read '*hyena*'; add '(Phrygian and Bithynian acc. to Hsch. (γάνος cod.))'

***γᾰνοπετεῖν**, v. γανυτελεῖν.

**γάνος** (A) **2**, add 'στάζει ἐνὶ κραδίῃ γλυκερὸν γ. Opp.*H.* 1.275' **3**, add 'γάνος .. οἴνας *IG* 2².3783.5' **4**, delete the section (read γᾶν ὅς).

**γᾰνος** (B), for 'dub. in .. (Mytilene)' read 'τῶν γανων dub. interpr. in *IG* 12(2).58.(a)17 (Mytilene, Rom.imp.), cf. perh. *ka-no-se*, *ICS* 309.12, but this may be second element of a longer wd.'

**γᾰνόω I**, line 4, for 'ἑοῖς .. (Philae)' read 'νέοις ἐγάνωσεν ἰάκχοις

*IPhilae* 159.3 (i AD)'; line 6, for 'Ph. l.c., al.' read 'Ph. l.c. [1.121], al.' and after it insert '*enjoy*, τί δεῖ (δη pap.) γανοῦσθαι τοῦτο; A.*fr.* 78c i 19 R.' delete '**II** *tin, lacquer*' incorporating quots. in section I.

**γάνῠμαι**, add 'γάνυται δέ τ' ἀκούων Hom.*fr.* 4'

**γάνωσις 1**, add 'fig., of style, *lustre*, cj. in Longin. 30.1'

**γᾰνωτός**, add 'Anon.Alch. 316.11'

**γᾱοδίκαι**, add '*BCH* 116.200 (Phocis, iii BC)'

***Γάος**, ὁ, name of a divinity associated with Persephone, *SEG* 34.940.4 (Camarina, iv/iii BC).

**+γᾰπεδον**, v. °γήπεδον.

**γᾰράριον**, add 'prob. l. in Sch.Nic.*Th.* 526b C.'

**γαργαλισμός**, add 'see also °γαγγαλισμός'

**γάργᾰρα**, add 'χρημάτων .. γ. *Trag.adesp.* 442 K.-S.'

**γαργᾰρίζω**, add 'freq. in Lat. borrowing, Varro *LL* 6.96, Cels. 4.2.8, Plin.*HN* 28.129, etc.'

***γαργᾰρισμάτιον**, τό, *gargle*, Marcell.Emp. 15.19; written *gargal-* ib. 14.28.

**γᾰροπώλης**, add '*POxy.* 3749.6 (iv AD)'

**γᾰρος**, neut., add '*PRyl.* 629.88 (iv AD)'

**γαστήρ I 2**, line 9, for 'com. of one who has nothing to eat' read 'i.e. eat sparingly' **II**, add 'by synecdoche, for the mother, Just.*Nov.* 54 pr., 156.1' **III**, for this section read 'archit., precise significance uncertain but app. some form of bulge, τὸ κα[τάζευγ]μα τὸ hυπὸ γαστέρα ἐπὶ τὸ ἐπ[ιστύλιον ..] *IG* 1³.474.253, τὰ τρήματα τῶν γαστρῶν *Inscr.Délos* 504 A 7 (iii BC), [τὴν κα]ταγλυφὴν τῶν ἐν αὐτοῖς γαστρῶν *Didyma* 39.4 (ii BC), but for these last two some assume nom. γάστραι'

**γάστρα IV**, add '**2** *womb*, Sor. 1.3.9.'

**γαστρᾰφέτης**, add 'Bito 64.4 M., al.'

**γαστρίαν**, after 'διάνοιαν' insert '(read διάρροιαν La.)' and after 'Hsch.' insert 'so γαστρίῃ Hippon. 118.9 W., expld. by Sch. ad loc. as γαστρὸς ἀλγηδών'

**γαστρίμαργος**, add '**II** -γα, ἁ, a kind of fish, *IGC* p. 100 B33 (Acraephia, iii/ii BC).'

**γαστροκνήμιον**, add '*BGU* 975.11 (i AD, written καστρο-)'

**γαστρόπτης**, for '*vessel for cooking sausages*' read 'perh. *belly-shaped cooking vessel*'; add '*IG* 2².1638.67 (Delos, iv BC), etc.'

***γασυνδάνη**, ἡ, name of gem, Xenocr.*Lap.* 109.

***γᾱτομέω**, Dor. form of γεωτομέω, *cleave the ground*, A.R. 2.1005, Lyc. 268, 1396.

**γᾱτόμος**, add 'see also γεωτόμος'

**γαυλός I 1**, for '*water-bucket* .. (Delos)' read '*water-bucket*, A.R. 3.758, used for raising water from a well, Hdt. 6.119.3, γ. μοι χρύσεος φρείατος ἐκ μυχάτου Alex.Aet. 3.20, *IG* 11.146.A29, etc. (Delos, iii BC, v. *BE* 1960.168)'; add '*wine-cask*, οἰνηρὸν ἀγγεῖον Suid.'

**γαυριάω**, line 3, for 'φυσῶντα καὶ γαυριώμενον' read 'γαυριώμενος'; line 5, after 'of persons' insert 'Semon. 10a W.'; at end for 'Anon.*Oxy.* 220iii3' read 'anon. metrical treatise in *POxy.* 220 v 3'

***γαυροειδής**· ὁ ὑπερήφανος Suid.

**γαῦρος**, line 4, epith. of ἔφηβοι, add 'Robert *Hell.* 1.127-31 (Eretria)'

**γαυρόω**, pass., add 'ταῦρος ὥς γαυρούμενος Ezek.*Exag.* 268 S.'

***γαυρῡ́νομαι**, *pride oneself*, δῶρα ἀμισῶς ἀποδίδων γαυρύνομαι *IHadr.* 24.7 (ii/iii AD), app. w. word-play on pers. n. Γαῦρος.

***γᾱωρύχιον**, v. °γεωρύχιον.

**+γέγειος**, α, ον, *ancient*, Hecat. 362 J.; βόες Call.*fr.* 277 Pf.; λόγος ib. 510; comp. -ότερος, γ. .. νίκης σύμβολον ib. 59.5.

**γέγωνα**, line 3, for 'ἐγεγώνειν' read 'ἐγεγώνει'; line 10, before '-είτω' for 'impf.' read 'imper.' **1 b**, for '*speak* .. sound' read '*make an effectual sound*' and after 'γεγωνεῖ' insert 'ἂν μὴ λεῖον ᾖ τὸ πληγέν'

**+γέη**, v. °γῆ.

**γείνομαι I**, for this section read '(for the forms γεινόμενος, γεινόμεθα v. °γίγνομαι)' **III**, line 2, delete 'in pass. sense' and after 'Call.*Cer.* 58' insert '*Del.* 260, etc.'

***γεΐνος**, v. °γήϊνος.

**γειόθεν**, for 'Call.*fr.* 35c' read 'Call.*fr.* 110.49 Pf. (v.l. γηόθεν)'

***γεισεπίστῠλον**, τό, *cornice-architrave*, *MAMA* 6.370 (Synnada, iii AD).

***γεισηποδίζω**, *furnish a corbel for the cornice*, ὅσ[αι δὲ] τῶν παρ[ό]δω[ν στ]ενότεραί εἰσι[ν] καὶ γεγεισηποδι[σ]μέ[ναι λιθ]ίνωι γεισηποδίσματι *Hesperia* 9.68.113 (= new *fr.* of *IG* 2².463.113, Athens, iv BC); cf. γεισηποδίζειν· τὸ προσβάλλειν τὰ γεῖσα ἐν τοῖς τοίχοις Hsch.; also γεισιποδίζω Is.*fr.* 113.

**+γεισηπόδισμα**, τό, *corbel supporting a cornice*, *IG* 2².463.114 (Athens, iv BC); γεισιπόδισμα Is.*fr.* 113.

**+γεισήπους**, ποδος, ὁ, *cornice-support*, *IG* 2².463.51 (Athens, iv BC), app. referring to *dentils* beneath a cornice, *Inscr.Délos* 104.24.17.

**+γεισιποδίζω**, -πόδισμα, v. °γεισηπ-.

***γειτνεύω**, *be a neighbour, border* on, *PMich.*x 581.13 (ii AD), *PCornell* 11.8, see also °γειτνιεύω, γειτονεύω.

**γειτνία**, add '*BGU* 94, *PKöln* inv. 1695 (*ZPE* 10.104, iv AD; sp. γιτν-); Γιτνεία Ἁμαξικὴ *quarter near the chariot-gate*, Robert *Hell.* 11/12.410 n. 1 (Apamea, Syria)'

**γειτνίᾱσις I 2**, add '**b** *guild of neighbours*, τῇ ἱερᾷ Λητοῦς γειτνιάσει *TAM* 3(1).765.11 (Termessus); cf. °γειτονίασις.'

***γειτνιεύω**, *be a neighbour, border* on, *PFlor.* 60.7 (iii AD); w. dat., *POxy.* 2190.57 (ii AD), *BGU* 2061.7, 30 (iii AD) (see also °γειτνεύω).

**γείτνιος**, delete the entry (v. °γειτνία).

**γειτονία 2**, add 'Lang *Ath.Agora* xxi L8 181 (iv BC; sp. γιτ- ib. 31.1035 (Lydia, ii AD)), *MAMA* 7.301'

***γειτονιάρχαι**, οἱ, *magistrates of a* γειτονία or *ward*, Robert *Hell.* 11/12.410 n. 1 (Constantinople).

***γειτονίᾱσις**, εως, ἡ, *group* or *guild of neighbours*, *IGRom.* 4.548 (Orcistus, prob. iii AD); in connection w. a shrine, γ. Ἀχιλλέως Ἰητῆ‹ρ›ος *TAM* 3(1).348 (Termessus); cf. °γειτνίασις I 2b.

***γειτόνισσα**, ἡ, *(female) neighbour*, *PSI* 876.5 (v/vi AD).

**γειτοσύνη**, add '*INikaia* 1202 (ii AD), *REG* 2.24 (Acmonia, iii AD)'

**γειτόσυνος**, for 'ον' read 'η, ον'; add 'τὰ γειτόσυνα *IG* 9(2).301.13 (Tricca, ii BC)'

**γείτων I**, lines 7/8, for 'ἐν γειτόνων .. Men.*Pk.* 27' read 'ellipt., ἐν γειτόνων δ' οἰκοῦσα living *in the neighbourhood*, Men.*Pk.* 27, cf. *Dysc.* 25' **II**, at end after 'Jul.*Or.* 2.72c' insert 'fig., γείτονα πότμου ἥβητήν Nonn.*D.* 11.97; νέος .. Ἀΐδι γείτων ib. 11.214' and after 'neut. γεῖτον' insert '*IG* 1³.426.67 (Athens, v BC)'

***γέλα**, ἁ, *hoar-frost*, cited by St.Byz. (γέλαν· πάχνην) as Sicilian or Oscan wd. in explanation of place-name Γέλα (s.v.); cf. Lat. *gelu*.

***γελαβρίας**, ὁ, name of a fish, *IGC* p. 99 A39 (Acraephia, iii/ii BC); cf. γαλλερίας, γαλαρίας.

**γελάω**, line 1, delete 'Ep.' **I 1**, after '*laugh*' insert '*smile*'

**+γελγοπωλέω**, app. *sell fancy goods*, etc., Hermipp. 11 K.-A., Hsch.

**γελγοπώλης**, for '*garlic*' read '*fancy goods*'

**Γελέοντες**, add 'also Γλέοντες *Sokolowski* 2.10.A35, 47 (Athens, v BC)'

**γέλλαι**, add '(cf. ἐλλίζων)'

**γελοιάζω**, delete 'only pres.' and insert 'aor. inf. γελοιάσαι Hsch. s.v. γελυνμάξαι'

***γελοίασμα**, ατος, τό, gloss on ψιά, Hsch.

**γελοῖος**, line 3, after 'Thgn. 311' insert 'παρέξαι τὰ γελοῖα A.*fr.* 47a ii 15 R.'

***Γελώιος**, ὁ, month name, Γελωίου ἕκται ἐπὶ δέκα *SEG* 39.996 (Camarina, ii/i BC).

**γέλως II**, line 2, after '*food for laughter*' insert 'πολὺς ἀστοῖσι φαίνεαι γ. Archil. 172.4 W., Semon. 7.74 W.'

**γέμω 1 a**, add 'of a tomb, *SEG* 34.1469 (Palestine, AD 588)'

**+γενάρχης**, ου, ὁ, *founder* or *head of family* or *race*, Call.*fr.* 229.1 Pf., Lyc. 1307; of Cronos, Orph.*H.* 13.8; epith. of Heracles, *IG* 5(1).497 (Sparta), al.; of Abraham, Ph. 1.513, of Abraham, Isaac and Jacob, id. 1.646. **b** transf., of the 70 elders, Ph. 2.111; of the ἐθνάρχης at Alexandria, id. 2.527.

**γενεά I 1**, lines 10/11, for 'πατριὰ καὶ γ. .. (Elis)' read 'πατριὰν .. καὶ γενεάν *gens* and (immediate) *family*, *Schwyzer* 409 (Elis, vi BC), pl. *children*, *Schwyzer* 424 (Elis, iv BC)' **3**, add '*SEG* 33.765 (form γενιά, Italy, iii/ii BC)' **II 3**, add '*birth*, γ. ἑτέρη, of Dionysus, *APl.* 257'

**γενεᾱλογία**, add 'γενεολογία dub. l. in Max.Tyr. 23.1'

**γενεαρχικός**, add 'Just.*Nov.* 21.1'

**γενέθλη I 3**, after '*birth*' insert '*parturition*, *AP* 6.272 (Pers.); metonym. *that which gives birth* to, [κ]υδαλίμαν θέον πάντων γενέθλαν Alc. 129.7 L.-P.'

***γενεθλιάς**, άδος, ἡ, (sc. ἡμέρα) *birthday*, *GVI* 2039.2 (Mytilene, ?i/ii AD).

**γενέθλιος**, after 'also α, ον Lyc. 1194' insert 'η, ον Call.*fr.* 202.21 Pf.'

**+γενειόλης**, ου, voc. γενειόλα, *bearded*, epith. of Hermes, Call.*fr.* 199.1 Pf.

**γένειον 1**, for '*part covered by the beard, chin*' read '*beard*' and combine w. section 2. **5**, for 'dub. sens.' read 'perh. some form of clamp or fastening' add '**6** *barbel* of a fish, Ael.*NA* 15.11.'

***γενεολογία**, v. °γενεαλογία.

***γενέρωσος**, η, ον, Lat. *generosus*, *of noble birth*, *IEphes.* 1540, *JÖAI* 23 *Beibl.* 171.118.

**γενεσιακός**, add 'κατὰ τὸ γ. *BGU* 1843.12 (i BC)'

**γενέσιος III**, add '**2** ὁ Γενέσιος name of month, *Hesperia* 27.75 (*c.*200 BC).' **III**, line 2, delete '*the birthday of*'

**γενεσιουργέω**, add 'Herm.*in Phdr.* p. 169 A.'

**γένεσις II 2**, add '*SEG* 7.904 (Gerasa)'

**γενέτειρα I**, add 'of Aphrodite, as mother of the imperial family, *Venus Genetrix*, *SEG* 30.1253 (Caria, i AD)'

**γενέτης**, add 'see also °γονέτης'

**γένημα**, add '**b** perh. *year*, in respect of its produce, *BGU* 2269.15 (ii AD).'

***γενημᾰτογράφος**, ὁ, *sequestrator*, *PLond.* 454.b4 (iv AD).

**γενημᾰτοφύλαξ**, add '*PGen.* 86 (?ii BC)'

***Γενιακός**, ὁ, epith. of Apollo, *IGRom.* 1.740.

**γενικός I 1**, line 3, after 'Phld.*Sign.* 18, 19, etc.' insert 'opp. to ἰδικός (*particular*), *Cod.Just.* 3.2.2.1, 6.48.1.8'; line 4, after '-κῶς' insert 'Cic.*Att.* 1.14.2'; add 'comp., Cic.*Att.* 9.10.6 (cj.)'

**γέννᾰ I 1**, add 'pl. πάντες δὲ βροτοὶ χ[άρεν σαῖς, ὦ Β]άκχιε, γένναις Philod.Scarph. 10'

**γεννάδας**, add 'w. non-Dor. inflexion, συμβίῳ γεννάδῃ καὶ ἑαυτῇ Mitchell *N.Galatia* 109'

**γενναῖος I**, add '**4** sup., as honorific epith., *PLond.* 1645.25, *SB* 4299.28, *PRyl.* 177.16 (all iii AD), ὁ γενναιότατος καὶ ἐπιφανέστατος Καῖσαρ *PAmh.* 148.4 (v AD), *BCH* suppl. 8.63 (Maced., v/vi AD).' **II**, line 3, after 'Pl.*Lg.* 844e' insert 'μᾶζαι id.*R.* 372b; καρποί D. 18.309' **III 1**, at end after 'Ps.-Callisth. 1.38' insert '-ότερον D.H.*Dem.* 26'

**γέννημα I 2**, delete the section transferring ref. to section 1.

**γεννῆται** (s.v. γεννητής II), add 'D. 59.55, al.; transf. in sg., πῶς οὖν οὐ σοὶ πρώτῳ μέτεστι τῆς τιμῆς, ὄντι γεννήτῃ τῶν θεῶν Pl.*Ax.* 371d'

***γεννήτριος**, ον, *of childbirth*, ὠδῖνες γ. Ps.-Callisth. 13.6 (cj., cod. γεννητηρ-).

**γεννήτωρ**, add 'transf., ὧν δή εἰσι καὶ οἱ ποιηταὶ πάντες γεννήτορες Pl.*Smp.* 209a'

**γένος V 3 c**, *produce*, add '*Peripl.M.Rubr.* 10, 14' add '**5** ἐν γένει *as concerning all, generally*, Just.*Nov.* 7.9.1.'

**γέντα**, for 'Call.*fr.* 309' read 'Call.*fr.* 322, 530 Pf.'

***γέντη**, ἡ, app. *flesh, meat*, θεὸς γέντης μὴ γεύεσθ[αι] *IGBulg.* 2083.7 (Rom.imp.); cf. ‡γέντα.

**γεοθαλπής**, for '*CIG* 3769' read 'orac. in *TAM* 4(1).92.1'

***γεουχία**, ἡ, *landowning*, *SEG* 8.448*a*, 24.1191(*a*) (Egypt); *estate*, *PMich.*VIII 503.3 (ii AD), *PPrincet.* 69.1.

***Γεραιστιασταί**, οἱ, participants in the festival of τὰ Γεράστια (s.v. °Γεράστιος), *IG* 4.757*B*12 (Troezen, ii BC).

**γέρᾰνος III**, for the pres. def. read 'name of a dance instituted by Theseus on Delos' add '**b** cult-offering at Delos of unkn. nature, ἡ καλουμένη γέρανος *IG* 11(2).161.B61-2, γέρανος ἀργυρᾶ *Inscr.Délos* 296*B*48-49, etc.'

**γερᾰρός 1**, line 2, for 'a table *of honour*' read '*grand, splendid* table' **3**, line 4, after '*IG* 2.2116' insert '12(3).420 (Thera)'

**γέρᾰς**, line 2, after 'γέρᾱ' insert 'S.*El.* 443' at end add 'Myc. *ke-ra*'

**γεράσμιος**, after 'ον' insert 'or α, ον' **II**, after '*honoured*' insert 'μαῖαν ὡς γερασμίαν A.*fr.* 47a.6 R.'

**Γεράστιος**, add '**II** τὰ Γ. festival in Euboea, Sch.Pi.*O.* 13.159; masc. οἱ Γ. participants in it, ibid. (see also °Γεραιστιασταί).'

**γερδίαινα** (s.v. γερδιός), add 'Ταπάϊς γερδία(ινα) *PColl.Youtie* 36.5 (*PVindob.Gr.*inv. 39867; AD 184)'

**γερδιακός**, after '*PGrenf.* 2.59.10' insert 'γερδιακή, ἡ, *weaving*, *BGU* 2041.9 (AD 201)'

***γερδικός**, ή, όν, *of weaving*, *POsl.* 140.2, 13 (ii BC).

**γερεᾱφόρος**, add 'see also ‡γερηφόρος'

***γερητηρία**· ἀπώλεια Hsch. (γ 429 La.; cf. γέρρω).

**γερηφόρος**, add '(= *Tit.Calymn.* 250.3)'

***γερῖνος**, ὁ, kind of fish, Marc.Sid. 37; cf. γέρυνος.

***Γερμανίκεια**, τά, festival in honour of a Germanicus, *IG* 2².2067.115, 2068.207, etc. (ii AD).

***Γερμανίκειος**, ὁ, Egyptian month (= Pachon) in Caligula's calendar, *SB* 6705, *PLond.* 1171ᵛ.*c*13, *POxy.* 3780.9 (-νίκιος) (all AD 42).

***Γερμανικός**, ὁ, title of Roman emperors, D.C. 55.2.3, al., *Amyzon* 68 (Caligula), *SEG* 34.1122 (Nero), etc. **II** Egyptian month (= Thoth) under Domitian, *BGU* 1.260, *PLond.* 259.138, *PFay.* 110, *POxy.* 266.

***γεροῖα**, τά, v. °Ϝεροῖα.

**γερόντειος**, add '**II** γεροντεῖον, τό, *body of elders*, *senate*, cf. γερόντιον II, [τῶν ἐν τῷ γερ]οντείῳ φερομένων rest. in *Berytus* 12.127/8 (Cyrene, ii/i BC).'

**γεροντία**, add 'Nic.Dam.*fr.* 103(3) J.'

**γεροντικός**, line 2, after 'Pl.*Lg.* 761c' insert 'ὅπλον Call.*Epigr.* 1.7 Pf.'

**γεροντοδῐδάσκᾰλος**, add 'Varro *Sat.Men.*tit. p. 32 A.'

***γερός**, ά, όν, adj. used in description of buildings, γερὰ καὶ στεγνὰ καὶ τεθυρωμένα *Inscr.Délos* 1417*C*89, 58 (ii BC); cf. mod. Gk. γερός *strong, sturdy.*

**γερουσία I 1**, line 3, after 'BC)' add 'local γ. in Erythrae, *SEG* 37.938, in Phrygia, Ramsay *Cities and Bishoprics* no. 549 (Acmonia), sim. in other places'; add 'γ. of Jews in Alexandria, Ph. 2.527' at end add 'Myc. *ke-ro-si-ja*'

***γερουσιάζω**, *to be a member of a* γερουσία, *IG* 12(8).389 (Thasos).

**γερουσιακός**, add '*Sardis* 7(1).17.2'

***γερουσιαρχέω**, *to be president of elders*, *IGBulg.* 1906, *IEJ* 4.252.

**γερουσιάρχης**, add '*SEG* 36.946 (Italy, iv AD), *CIJud.* 803 (Syria, iv AD)' add '**2** Dor. -ᾱς, *president of* γερουσία, *SEG* 1.327.16 (Callatis, i AD).'

***γερουσιάρχισσα**, ἡ, fem. of γερουσιάρχης, *IG* 10(2).1.177.10 (Thessalonica, iii AD).

**γερουσιαστής**, line 2, for 'iii BC' read 'iii AD'; add '*INikaia* 1242 (i/ii AD), *IHistriae* 57.26, 193.B1, 13 (ii AD), *SEG* 31.635 (Maced., ii/iii AD)'

***γερροφῠλάκια**, ἡ, form of guard, *SEG* 28.1484 (Egypt, 116 BC).

**γέρων I 2**, add 'in religious cult, οἱ τᾶς Οὐπησίας ἱεροὶ γέροντες *SEG* 23.215, 216 (Messene, ii/iii AD)' **II**, line 4, for 'πόνος' read 'πίνος', delete following parenth. and for '(S.)*OC* 1258' read '(S.)*OC* 1259'; line 7, after 'Plu.*Pel.* 2' insert 'transf., γέροντος ἤδη χρόνου πολιὰ Luc.*Am.* 12'; line 8, for '(for ἀρχαῖα)' read '*things characteristic* or *worthy of an old man*' and add '*EM* 227.9 (s.v.l.)' **III**, add 'Herod. 12.3' add 'Myc. *ke-ro-te* (pl., sense I), *ke-ro-ta* (neut. pl., sense II, of cloth)'

***Γετικός**, ή, όν, *of the Γέται*, a tribe in the region of the Istros, ἵπποι Ael.*NA* 15.24, ἀλαλαγμοί Arr.*Tact.* 44.1, Γετικὴ χθ[ών] epigr. in *SEG* 25.823 (Dacia, ii AD).

**γεῦμα I**, add 'οἴνου παλαιοῦ πρώτου γεύματος app. *of first quality* or *first of the season*, *Edict.Diocl.* 2.8, 9, ἐλαίου ὀμφακίνου δευτέρου γ. ib. 3.2' **II**, add 'w. ref. to function not precisely explained, οἱ ἐπὶ τὸ γ. πραγματευόμενοι *IEphes.* 728.34 (iii AD)'

**γεύω I**, at end after 'Herod. 6.11' insert 'ναὸν ἱερουργημάτων J.*AJ* 8.4.5' **II 3**, add 'ὁ θανάτο(υ) γευσόμενος *ITyr* 126'

**γέφῡρα**, line 1, after 'Stratt. 47.5' insert '(= 49.5 K.-A.) codd. βλ-' and after 'Hsch.' insert 'cf. also βουφάρας'; line 7, for '*limits* of the battlefield' read '*earthworks*'

***Γεφῡραία**, epith. of Demeter at Athens, *EM* 229.4, St.Byz. s.v. Γέφυρα.

***Γεφῡραῖος**, epith. of Apollo, *IG* 2².4813.

***γεφῡρίς**· πόρνη τις ἐπὶ γεφύρας, ὡς Ἡρακλέων. ἄλλοι δὲ οὐ γυναῖκα, ἀλλὰ ἄνδρα ἐκεῖ καθεζόμενον ‹ἐπὶ› τῶν ἐν Ἐλευσῖνι μυστηρίων συγκαλυπτόμενον ἐξ ὀνόματος σκώμματα λέγειν εἰς τοὺς ἐνδόξους πολίτας Hsch.

***γεωβᾰφής**, ές, adj. describing some method of dyeing, perh. with a kind of earth used as colouring agent or mordant, χλαμύς γ. *PCair.Zen.* 92.3 (iii BC) ποδείων γ. ib. 23; cf. γῆ IV.

**γεωγράφος**, for 'ον, *earth-describing*: Subst.' read 'ὁ' and add 'cf. γαιογράφος'

**γεωδαισία**, add 'also γᾱδαισία *distribution of land*, *IG* 9²(1).609.11 (Naupactus, *c.*500 BC)'

**γεωδαίτης**, for 'Call.*Oxy.ined.*' read 'pl., Call.*fr.* 43.64 Pf. (codd. γαιοδόται, cf. °γεωδότης)'

**γεώδης I**, line 1, after 'Pl.*Phd.* 81c' insert 'Plb. 2.15.8 (codd. γαι-)' and at end add 'fig., of faculties, *dull, torpid*, Plu. 2.625c'

***γεωδότης**, ου, ὁ, perh. *assigner of land*, Ἡγησίου γεωδότο[υ εὐεργ]εσίας ἕνεκεν *EA* 16.65.5 (Saittai, ii BC).

**γεωμέτρης**, for 'ib. 28' read '*BGU* 12.28' and after it insert '*SEG* 34.477 (Thessaly, ii BC); sp. γεομ- *SEG* 32.1287 (Phrygia, iii AD), *ISmyrna* 893 (i AD), *TAM* 4(1).173 (Bithynia); cf. γαιομέτρης'

**γεωμορία II**, add '*Lyr.adesp.* in *SLG* 414(d).10'

***γεωμόριον**· τὸ τῆς γῆς μόριον Hsch., see also °γημόριον.

**γεώπεδον**, for pres. def. read '*holding of land, estate*'; add 'cf. γάπεδον'

**γεωργέω**, after lemma insert '(Thess. °γαοργέω, Boeot. 3 sg. fut. γαϜεργείσι *BCH* 60.182.11 (Thespiae, iii BC))'

**γεωργία I**, add '**3** *cultivation period*, *PRainer Cent.* 123.16 (AD 478).'

**γεώργιον I**, add 'Lxx *Ge* 26.14, *Pr.* 6.7, *Je.* 28(51).23' **III**, delete the section.

**γεώργισσα**, add '*PSI* 1021.31 (ii BC)'

**γεωργός**, after lemma insert 'Lacon. γαβεργός (i.e. γαϜεργός)· ‹ὁ› ἀγροῦ μισθωτής Hsch. (La.), Boeot. γαεργός *BCH* 60.178.6 (Thespiae, iii BC)'

***γεωρῠχικός**, ή, όν, *of* or *concerning mining*, γεωρυχικὸν νόμον *SEG* 39.1180.78 (Ephesus, i AD).

***γεωρῠ́χιον**, τό, *tunnel, mine*, *SEG* 39.1180.81 (Ephesus, i AD); in Dor. form γᾱωρύχιον, *Inscr.Cret.* 1.v 19 B 24 (Arcades, ii/i BC).

**γεωτόμος**, add 'see also γᾱτόμος'

***γεωφάγος**, ὁ, *earth-eater*, περὶ γεωφάγων, Plu. title in Lamprias' catalogue (vii p. 477.191 B.); cf. γαιη-, γηφάγος.

**γῆ**, line 3, after 'γαῖα' insert 'gen. γέης Roueché *Aphrodisias* 37.13 (v AD); acc. γέην Hatzopoulos *Actes de vente* II p. 23.5 (Chalcidice); γέαν *ICilicie* 49'; line 6, for 'Cypr. ζᾶς *Inscr.Cypr.* 135.50 H.' read 'Cypr. *za-i* γᾶι *ICS* 217.8, 17, al.' **I 1**, line 11, after '(A.)*Pers.* 629, etc.' insert 'ποιησάτω τὰ ποτὶ Γᾶν (καὶ) τὰς ἀλλαθεάδας *Delph.* 3(3).22.12, 3(6).40.3; as a goddess, Hdt. 4.59.1 (Scythia), Th. 2.15.4, *SEG* 31.748 (Tenos, iv BC), Πλούτων καὶ Γᾶ καὶ Ἑρμᾶ ib. 35.1011 (Sicily, i BC), 31.917b (Aphrodisias, i AD)'; line 13, after 'S.*OT* 416' insert 'ἐν γᾶι *SEG* 32.914 (Entella, iv/iii BC)' **2**, add 'as that to which dead bodies are reduced, Thgn. 878, *Anacreont.* 32.12 W.'

**γηγενής I 3**, for 'ib.' read 'Lxx'

**γῆθεν**, add '*Com.adesp.* 133.3, see also °γειόθεν'

**γηθέω**, 3 lines fr. end, after 'Sotad. 15.4' insert 'γηθομένη τειμαῖς

*MAMA* 9.48.7 (Aezani, iii AD), abs., λωφᾷ τε τῆς ὀδύνης καὶ γέγηθεν Pl.*Phdr.* 251c, Plu. 2.372f'; add 'Pl.*Phd.* 85a'

**γήϊνος**, after 'η, ον' insert '(also γέϊνος Hsch. s.v. γηγενῶν, Dor. γάϊνος, ον, *SEG* 9.72.118 (Cyrene, iv BC))'

**γήτης**, add '**II** = αὐτόχθων, St.Byz. s.v. γῆ.'

**γημόριον**, add 'perh. mistake for μημόριον, v. *BE* 1987.400, but cf. °γεωμόριον, °γημόρος'

**γημόρος**, line 4, Att. γεωμόρος, add 'app. iron., καὶ νέκυς γεωμόρος εἴης epigr. in *SEG* 34.1247.3 (Miletoupolis, ii AD); cf. ‡γημόριον' and after 'μείρομαι)' insert 'see also γειομόρος'; line 5, οἱ γāμόροι in Sicily, add '*Marm.Par.* 52, Dubois *IGDS* no. 219.3 (v BC)'

**γήπεδον**, for '*plot of ground*' read '*estate, land*' **II**, for 'γάπεδον' read '°γάπεδον'

**γῆρας II**, line 3, for 'Arist.*HA* 600b20' read 'Arist.*HA* 601a17'

**γηράσκω**, line 11, γηρεῖς, add '*Iamb.adesp.* 4 W.'

**γηροβοσκός**, add '*POxy.* 3555.8 (i/ii AD)'

**γηροκομεῖον**, add '*SB* 4845 (-ῖον Byz.)'

**γηροκόμος**, add '**II** (in pass. sense, proparox.) *nursed in old age*, γενέτις *GVI* 1823.6 (Naucratis, ii BC).'

**γηροτρόφος**, add 'εἰ .. παῖδες ἔσονται [γη]ροτρόφοι Ἰσοδήμωι *JHS* 87.133 (lead tablet, Dodona)'

**γήρῡμα**, after 'pl.' insert 'γāρύματα μαλσακά Alcm. 4 *fr.* 1.5 P.'

**⁺γητομέω, -τόμος**, delete the entry (v. °γεωτ-).

**˟γῐγαντοπαντορήκτης**, ου, ὁ, (in Gnostic mythology) *he who shatters all giants*, amulet in *MB* 18.32.

**˟γῐγαντοπνικτορήκτης**, ου, ὁ, *he who throttles and shatters giants*, amulet in *MB* 18.32.

**˟γῐγαντοπτορήκτης**, ου, ὁ, (perh. for γιγαντοπαντ-) *he who shatters all giants*, amulet in *MB* 18.32.

**˟γῐγαντορήκτης**, ου, ὁ, voc. -ρηκτα, *he who shatters giants*, amulets in *MB* 18.32, *MUB* 15.76, *ARW* 28.269, *Hesperia* 20.326, *SEG* 33.1551 (Egypt, iii AD).

**˟γῐγαντοφόντης**, ου, ὁ, voc. -φόντα, *giant-slayer*, amulet in *Hesperia* 20.326.

**γίγγλᾰρος**, for 'kind of *flute* or *fife*' read 'kind of small aulos'

**˟γιγγλίζειν** τὸ ἀπειλεῖν οἱ ἰδιῶται λέγουσι *AB* 1.88.

**⁺γιγγρί**· ἐπιφώνημά τι ἐπὶ καταμωκήσει λεγόμενον. καὶ εἶδος αὐλοῦ Hsch., Hdn.Gr. 1.506.

**γίγνομαι**, line 3, after 'ib. 7.3303' insert 'Cret. **γίννομαι** *Inscr.Cret.* 4.184.9, 232.2 (both Gortyn, ii BC)'; line 4, after 'ἐγενάμην' insert '*SEG* 34.1107 (Ephesus), *IEphes.* 3239 (ii/iii AD)'; line 8, after '(γη-το)' insert 'Ep. also has γειν- for γεν- in the forms γεινόμεθ' Il. 22.477, Hes.*Sc.* 88, γεινόμενος Il. 20.128, 24.210, Od. 4.208, Hes.*Th.* 82, cf. Alc. 39(*a*).8 L.-P.' **I 1**, add 'εὖ γεγονότας *free-born*, Just. *Const.* Δέδωκεν 7' **II** and **II 1, 3**, for 'folld. by' read 'with' **3 c**, line 3, γ. εἴς τι, add 'εἰς ἄλλο τι γιγνόμενον Pl.*Ti.* 57a, ὅταν δὲ εἰς πύον γίνεται Gal. 16.71.4'; lines 6/7, delete 'ἐς Λακεδαίμονα .. 4.634)'; lines 15/16, after 'ἐπὶ ποταμῷ' insert 'ἐν τῷ προθύρῳ' and for 'Hdt. 1.189, etc.' read 'Hdt. 1.189.1, Pl.*Prt.* 313c'; three lines from end for 'Hdt. 7.22' read 'Hdt. 8.22.2'

**γιγνώσκω**, line 7, after 'Pi.*P.* 4.120' insert 'perh. 1 sg. *PAnt.* 58.27'; line 14, delete 'and in past tenses'

**⁺γίννος**, ὁ, alleged offspring of mare by mule, Arist.*HA* 557b25, *GA* 748b34; of other mixed or defective parentage, Hsch. s.v. (also s.v. ἴννος); prob. refers to horse or mule of less than normal size, Str. 4.6.2, *BCH* 66/67.181 (Abdera), γῖνος *IG* 12(1).677.23 (Ialysus, both iv BC); also ἴννος (ἰννός cod.) Hsch.; cf. ὕννος, Lat. *ginnus, hinnus.*

**˟γίνυμαι**, v. γίγνομαι.

**˟γισγίνη**, γισγῖνόσημος, v. °ὕσγιν-.

**γλᾰγερός**, delete '**2** *soft, plump*' transferring exx. to section 1.

**⁺γλάζω**, perh. *distil*, μέλι Pi.*fr.* 97 S.-M. (s.v.l.); cf. γλάγος.

**γλᾶθις**, for 'dub. sens. .. pl.)' read 'acc. pl. -ιας, epigr. in *Inscr.Cret.* 3.iv 38.5 (pl., i BC)'

**⁺γλακτοπᾱγής**, ές, *rigid with milk*, γλακτοπαγεῖ μαστῷ epigr. in *ISmyrna* 541.7 (i AD).

**γλᾰρίς II**, delete the section.

**˟γλαυκάνεα**, τά, perh. some product of mining operations, *IG* 12(8).51.22 (Imbros, ii BC).

**γλαυκινίδιον**, read '-ῐνίδιον'

**γλαύκῐνος**, read '**γλαύκῖνος**' **II**, for this section read 'ἐλαίου γλαυκίνου oil *of* or *flavoured with* γλαύκιον I, *Edict.Diocl.* 36.100; neut. subst., a perfumed unguent, Mart. 9.26.2, Pompon.*Dig.* 34.2.21.1 (Lat. *glaucina* pl.)'

**γλαυκόμματος**, add '*FGE* 160 P., Pisander Lav. 18 H.'

**γλαυκός II**, after 'Hegesianax 1' insert 'αἱ δύο (sc. ζῶναι) μὲν γλαυκοῖο κελαινότεροι κυάνοιο Erastosth. 16.4' at end add 'cf. Myc. *ka-ra-u-ko* pers. n.'

**˟γλαυκοφθαλμία**, ἡ, *cataract*, Cyran. 106 (4.9.5 K.).

**˟γλαυκοφόρος**, ον, *bearing* (i.e. stamped with) *an owl*, τετρᾶχμα Ἀττικά *Inscr.Délos* 1429*B*ii22, rest. in 1428ii76 (ii BC).

**γλαυκοχαίτης**, for 'Choerob. in *Cod.* .. f. 200' read '*An.Ox.* 2.317.24'

**γλαυκῶπις**, epith. of Athena, add '*CEG* 392 (Himera, vi BC), S.*OC* 706'

**γλαύξ**, line 3, before 'Epich. 166' insert 'γλαύχς *IG* 5(1).832 (Laconia, vi BC)'

**γλᾰφῠρός II 2**, of dishes, add 'Astyd. 4 S.' **III 4**, of music, add 'μέλη D.H.*Dem.* 26'

**˟Γλέοντες**, v. °Γελέοντες.

**˟γλεύδιον**, τό, perh. *mallet*, παῦγλα ἤτοι γλεύδια (v.l. λεύδια) *Edict.Diocl.* 15.43.

**γλευκᾰγωγός**, for '*new wine*' read '*must*'

**⁺γλευκάω**, in gloss γλευκήσας· ‹ὑπὸ› γλεύκους γενόμενος ἔκλυτος καὶ παρειμένος, ἀπὸ τῶν οἴνῳ νέῳ μεθυσθέντων› Hsch. (La.).

**˟γλευκῑνίτης**, ου, ὁ, = γλευκίτης, Paul.Aeg. 7.3 (246.20 H.).

**γλεύκινος 1**, delete 'Androm.ap.Gal. 13.1039' and add 'γλεύκινον, τό, a preparation of γλεῦκος, Androm.ap.Gal. 13.1039'

**γλευκοπότης**, for '*new wine*' read 'γλεῦκος'

**γλεῦκος I 1**, for '*sweet new wine*' read '*unfermented grape-juice, must*' and add '*IG* 1³.237.4, 12 suppl. 347 (both v BC)' **2**, delete the section adding 'Gal. 6.575.17' to section 1. at end add 'form *δλεῦκος, Myc. *de-re-u-ko* (cf. etym. note on γλυκύς)'

**γλέφαρον**, for 'Aeol.' read 'dial.'

**γλίσχρασμα**, for 'Aret.*CA* 1.9' read 'Aret.*CA* 5.1.7, 5.10.5-6'

**γλίσχρος II 1**, adv., sup. -ότατα, read 'ἕλκουσιν .. γλισχρότατα σαρκάζοντες ὥσπερ κυνίδια Ar.*Pax* 482' **2**, adv., add 'οὐ γλίσχρως ἀλλ' ἀληθινῶς Isoc. 5.142'

**γλίσχρων**, for '*niggard*' read '*glutton*'

**γλῖχομαι**, after lemma insert '(γλῐ- Ar.*fr.* 104 K.-A., *AP* 9.334 (Pers.))' and at end delete '(γλῐ- .. Hdn.Gr. 1.37)'

**˟γλοιάφιον**, τό, perh. *glue*, *SB* 9408(2).53, 9409(1).83, (6).38 (sp. γλυ-); cf. γλία.

**γλοιός I**, line 4, delete 'generally, *oily sediment* in baths'; add 'as a term of abuse, Ar.*Nu.* 449' **II 1**, delete the section. add '**4** *sordid, mean*, Suid., adv. -ῶς prob. in Timocr. 1.10.'

**˟γλουθίον**, τό, dim. of γλουτός, prob. reading (unless γλουθρός as dial. form of γλουτός is accepted) in *ABSA* 21.172 (Lydia).

**˟γλουθροῦς**, ὁ, = γλουτός, *buttock*, inscr. in *Talanta* 10/11.88 (Lydia, Rom.imp.).

**γλουρός**, after '*AP* 15.25.7' for '(Besant.)' read 'cj., cod. ταγχούρου, see τάγχαρας'

**γλούτια II**, delete the section (v. °γλουτός).

**γλουτός II**, for this section read '*the great trochanter*, Gal. 2.773.17; pl., γλουτοί· τὰ τῆς κοτύλης σφαιρώματα *the trochanters*, Hsch.'

**˟γλυάφιον**, v. °γλοι-.

**γλῠκάδιον**, after 'Hsch.' add 'in form γλυκάδιν *Dura*⁴ 151 (iii AD)'

**γλῠκαίνω**, pass., after 'Hp.*Aër.* 8' insert 'X.*Oec.* 19.19'

**˟γλῠκᾰσία**, ἡ, *kind feeling, affection*, *SB* 6263.29.

**˟γλῠκελαία**, ἡ, *sweet olive*, prob. in *SB* 5747 (κεράμιον) γλυκυελεῶν; acc. pl. written κλοκελέας H.I. Bell, *Jews and Christians in Egypt* no. 1918.15.

**γλῠκέλαιον**, delete '*Sammelb.* 5747.8 (γλυκυέλ-)'

**γλῠκερός**, add 'sup. -ώτατος *SEG* 31.846 (Italy, iii AD)'

**γλῠκίζω I**, add '*SEG* 25.790 (Histria, ii BC), 32.1243 (Cyme, i BC/i AD)'

**⁺γλῠκῠμείλῐχος**, ον, *sweetly gentle*, *h.Hom.* 6.19.

**γλῠκύμηλον**, for '= μελίμηλον, *sweet-apple*' read '*apple grafted on to a quince*' and add '*PMich.*XIV 680.13 (iii/iv AD)'

**γλῠκύνους**, add 'epigr. in *SEG* 33.1110 (Paphlagonia, iii AD)'

**γλῠκύπικρος**, before '*AP*' insert 'rest. in Pi.*fr.* 128b.7, Sophr. in *PSI* 1214*d*3'; line 3, delete '"a gilded pill"'

**γλῠκύς I 1 a**, add 'sup. adv. γλυκύτατα *most delightfully*, D.L. 4.59' **2**, add 'w. ellipsis of ὀφθαλμός, οὐ τὸν ἐμὸν τὸν ἕνα γλυκύν, ᾧ ποθορῷμι ἐς τέλος Theoc. 6.22' **II 1 b**, delete the section.

**˟γλῠκῠφεγγής**, ές, *giving sweet light*, ἥλιος *SEG* 8.548.10 (Hymn to Isis, i BC).

**γλύπτης**, add '*EA* 19.51 (Sinope, Rom.imp.), *Stud.Pal.* 20.260.9 (vi/vii AD)'

**γλυπτός 2**, after 'Lxx *De.* 4.25' insert 'εἰς θεὸν γλυπτόν *Is.* 44.17'; γλυπτόν, τό, for '*Is.* 44.10' to end read 'τὰ γλυπτὰ τῶν θεῶν *Ex.* 34.13, ἐπικατάρατος ἄνθρωπος, ὅστις ποιήσει γλυπτὸν *De.* 27.15, *Jd.* 2.2, 4*Ki.* 17.41, al.'

**γλῠφικός**, add 'Philostr.Jun.*Im.proem.* 15'

**˟γλῠφοποιός**, ὁ, *sculptor*, Porphyrio ad Hor.*C.* 4.8.6.

**γλύφω II**, for '*note down* .. τόκους' read 'τόκους γ. *mark down interest*, cf. τοκογλύφος'

**˟γλωθρός**, dial. for ‡βλωθρός, Hes.*fr.* 204.124 M.-W.; cf. γλήχων = βλήχων.

**γλώξ**, for '*beard of corn*' read '*ear of corn* (in quot., millet)'

**γλῶσσα I 2**, after 'E.*Hipp.* 612' insert 'τά τ' ἐκ ποδῶν σιγηλὰ καὶ γλώσσης ἄπο σῴζοντες, i.e. not speaking, id.*Ba.* 1049'; lines 6ff., for 'ἀπὸ γλώσσης .. A.*Ag.* 813' read 'ἀπὸ γλώσσης *by word of mouth*, *orally*, αἶνος .. ὃν ἐν δίκᾳ ἀπὸ γλώσσας Ἄδραστος .. φθέγξατ' Pi.*O.* 6.13; Hdt. 1.123.4, Th. 7.10, Arr.*An.* 2.14.1; in contexts contrasting wds. w. thoughts, actions, etc., Hes.*Op.* 322, Thgn. 63, τοῦ νοῦ θ' ὁμοίως κἀπὸ τῆς γλώσσης λέγω S.*OC* 936; contrasted with writing, Cratin. 122; οὐκ ἀπὸ γλώσσης not from *mere word of mouth*, but after full argument, A.*Ag.* 813' **3**, for this section read 'meton., *speaker*, μεγίστη γ. τῶν Ἑλληνίδων i.e. Pericles, Cratin. 324 K.-A., S.*Ichn.* 151 R., Herod. 6.16, *AP* 7.345' **III 1**, add 'Eup. 442 K.-A.; of trumpet, Poll. 4.85; cf. γλῶσσαί τινες σαλπίγγων ἢ αὐλῶν ταῖς ὀπαῖς (sc. of organ-pipes) προστιθέμεναι Simp.*in Ph.* 681.7'

**γλώσσαλγος**, delete '*itching* .. 510a'; add 'γ. ἦθος *Trag.adesp.* 562 K.-S.'

+**γλωσσάομαι**, pf. part. γεγλωσσαμένος, *tongued*, γεγλωσσαμέναν κακκαβίδων ὄπα prob. in Alcm. 39 P.

**γλώσσημα II**, for '*dart*' read '*spear*'

**γλωσσίδιον**, add '**III** *tenon*, Sch.Hes.*Op.* 426.'

(**γλωσσ**)**ίδος** (post γλωσσίδιον), delete the entry.

***γλωσσίς**, v. ‡γλωττίς.

***γλωσσόζωμος**, ὁ, *broth made from tongue*, *Vit.Aesop.*(G) 52.

**γλωσσοκομεῖον**, line 8, for '*cage*' read '*chest*' and delete 'rejected by Phryn. 79'; at end after 'also masc. -κομος .. (Pamphylia)' insert 'dub. gender, Aq.*Ge.* 50.26'

**γλωσσόκομον**, add '*box of lock into which key is inserted*, Gal. 14.638.12'

***γλωσσοπέτρα**, ἡ, a (perh. imaginary) precious stone, Plin.*HN* 37.164.

**γλωσσοποιός**, add 'also γλωττοποιός· ὁ τὰς αὐλητικὰς γλωσσίδας ποιῶν Hsch.'

+**γλωσσοστροφεῖν**, v. °γλωττοστροφέω.

**γλωττίς I**, add 'form γλωσσίς, *Hippiatr.* 130.138'

***γλωττοποιός**, v. °γλωσσοποιός.

**γλωττοστροφέω**, after 'Ar.*Nu.* 792' insert '(prob. nonce-word), γλωσσοστροφεῖν· περιλαλεῖν καὶ στωμύλλεσθαι Hsch.'

***γλωττοτόμιον**, τό, dim. of °γλωττοτόμον, *Inscr.Délos* 1450.180 (ii BC).

***γλωττοτόμον**, τό, or **-τόμος**, ὁ, app. = γλωσσόκομον, *chest*, *Inscr.Délos* 1432*Ab*ii73, 1439*Abc*72, 1441*A*ii104 (ii BC); γλοττοτόμῳ ib. *A*i75, 86.

**γλωχίν 2**, add '*corner* of a chair-frame, Call.*Del.* 235' **4**, for this section read 'topogr. *corner*, πυμάτην .. ἐπὶ γλωχῖνα νέμονται D.P. 184, θαλάττης γ. Agath. 5.22'

***γλωχῑνόομαι**, *to be made barbed*, Eust.*Opusc.* 292.33.

***γνᾰθιος**, ον, γ. λίθος, app. = °γνάθος III, Cyran. 14 (1.3.2 K.).

**γνᾰθος**, add '**III** hard variety of stone, Cyran. 13 (1.3.9 K.).'

**γνάμπτω**, at end delete 'Nic.*Th.* 423' (read γναπτ-)

***γνάπτρα**, τά, *cost of fulling*, *BGU* 1558.7 (iii BC), *PCair.Zen.* 398.7 (iii BC).

**γνάπτω**, for 'γνάμπτω, id.' read 'κνάπτω, q.v.'

**γνᾰφαλλον**, add 'see also s.v. κνέφαλλον'

**γνᾰφαλλολόγος**, after '*flock-picker*' insert 'prob. incl. other stages in wool preparation' and add '*PFreib.* 60.5 (AD 181)'

***γνᾰφαλλος**· πτίλον Hsch.

*[**γ**]**νᾰφαλλοϋφάντης** or [**κ**]**ναφ-**, ου, ὁ, *flock-weaver*, *IG* $2^2$.7967 (v BC).

***γνᾰφήσιος**, ἰχθῦς, kind of fish, Cyran. 106 (4.12.1 K.).

***γνάψιμος**, ον, *cleaned by fulling*, *POxy.* 4004.13 (v AD).

**γνάψις**, add '*SB* 9834b.3 (iv AD)'

**γνήσιος I 2**, line 7, before 'Gal. 15.748' insert 'D.H.*Lys.* 12' add '**3** *dear*, τῇ γλυκυτάτῃ τεκούσῃ Μελ[τ]ίνῃ καὶ γνησίᾳ γυναικὶ Ἀμμίᾳ *MAMA* 4.305, 8.595; sup. *IG* 10(2).1.403 (Thessalonica, vi AD).'

**γνησιότης I**, add '*legitimate status* in marriage, Just.*Nov.* 89.9 pr.'

***γνόφαλλον**, τό, v. κνέφαλλον.

***γνοφεντινάκτης**, ου, ὁ, (ἐντινάσσω) *shaker* or *hurler in darkness*, of a thunder- or lightning-deity, *PMag.* 4.181.

**γνόφεον**, for 'Id.' read 'Hsch.'

***γνοφερός**, v. °δνοφερός.

***γνοφοειδής**, = γνοφώδης, *Gr.Roman-Papyri* 8.43.

***γνόφος**, after '*darkness*' insert 'Lxx *Ex.* 10.22, al.'

**γνοφώδης**, add 'see also °γνοφοειδής, δνοφώδης'

**γνύξ**, for 'Arat. 921' read 'Arat. 591; αἰεὶ γνύξ id. 615'

**γνύποντι**, delete the entry.

***γνυπόομαι**, (γνυπτ- La.) *to be depressed*, in pf. part. ἐγνυπωμένον· ταλαίπωρον. κατηφές, Hsch.; also ἐγνυπώθη· τρυφᾷ. καὶ τὸ ἐναντίον, id.

+**γνυπτέω**, *to be weak* or *feeble*, Hsch. s.v. γνυπτεῖν, γνυπτοῦντι (cod. γνυποντι).

**γνῶμα**, delete '*test*'; for 'of an ass's teeth, Arist.*HA* 577$^b$3' read 'applied to certain teeth as indication of age, τούτους (ὀδόντας) δὲ γνῶμα καλοῦσι, τοὺς τετάρτους Arist.*HA* 577$^a$22, 577$^b$3, καὶ γνῶμ' ἔχει. τὸ γνῶμα γοῦν βέβληκεν ὡς οὖσ' ἑπτέτις *Com.adesp.* 572, 573'

**γνωμεισηγητής**, delete the entry (v. *JEA* 21.238).

**γνώμη II 1**, line 13, for 'ἕτερον' read 'ἑτέρῳ' **III 1**, add '**c** *consent, approval*, *PSI* 967.18 (i/ii AD), *PFam.Teb.* 38.10 (AD 168).'

***γνωμῐδιώκτης**, ου, ὁ, (for γνωμιδιοδι-) *one who hunts after sententious maxims*, Cratin. 342 K.-A.

***γνωμοδίκᾱ**, ἁ, *verdict, judicial decision*, *BCH* 93.76 (Phocis, ii BC).

**γνωμολογία 2**, for this section read 'usu. in pl., *aphoristic saying, maxim*, Plb. 12.28.10, D.H.*Dem.* 46, Plu.*Cat.Ma.* 2, *Fab.* 1; sg., title of collection of aphorisms, Suid. s.v. Θέογνις'

**γνωμονικός II**, after 'Procl.*Hyp.* 5.54' insert '*SEG* 36.1153 (sp. -ηκός, Bithynia)'

**γνώμων I 1**, add 'title of magistrate, *Inscr.Cret.* 4.14 (Gortyn, vii/vi BC, pl.)' **II 1**, after '*square*' insert 'Thgn. 805' add '**b** κατὰ γ. *perpendicularly*, Oenopides ap.Procl. *in Euc.* p. 283 F.' for '**V**' read '**III**' and after '*AB* 233' add 'κατὰ γνώμονα *PMich.*III 145 iii 5.5 (ii AD)'

**γνωρίζω I 3**, add '*give legal recognition to* children, Just.*Nov.* 6.1.4'

**γνώρῐμος**, line 3, for '(Pl.)*Lg.* 798e' read '(Pl.)*Lg.* 798a' **I 3 b**, for '*pupil*' read '*adherent*' **c**, delete the section transferring 'Lxx *Ru.* 3.2' to section 3 a.

**γνωριστής II**, for '*diviner*' read '*wizard*, prob. as calque of Hebr.; cf. °γνώστης'

***γνωσία**, ἁ, Arc. = γνῶσις I 1, to be read in *IG* 5(2).262.15 (Mantinea, v BC; v. *SEG* 39.393).

**γνωσίδῐκα**, delete the entry (v. °γνωσία).

**γνῶσις 1**, add 'recorded in writing, Arist.*Ath.* 53.2' add '**VI** pl., *accounts*, ἐπίτροπον γνώσεων τῶν ἐξοχωτάτων καθολικῶν, = Lat. *procurator rationum summarum*, *APAW* 1932(5).46.'

**γνωστεία**, add '*Stud.Pal.* 22.50.3 (iii AD, -τια pap.)'

**γνωστεύω**, before '*to be witness*' insert '*to be personally acquainted with*, τινα *PTeb.* 816 i 8 (ii BC)'

**γνώστης**, for 'esp. *one who knows the future, diviner*' read '*wizard*'

**γνωτοφόνος**, for '*murderer of another's brother*' read '*murderer of a brother*'

***γοᾱτήριον**, v. °γοη-.

**γοάω**, see also °γόημι.

**γόγγρος I**, add '*IGC* p. 99 A36 (Acraephia, iii/ii BC)'

+**γογγυλίδιον**, τό, dim. of γογγυλίς, *turnip*, *CPR* 9.28 (written κογκυλίδ-, v/vi AD). **II** = καταπότιον, Hp.ap.Erot. (γογγυλίδα codd.), Gal. 19.91.

**γογγῠλίς**, add 'Crates Com. 30 K.-A.'

**γογγύλλω**, for '*round*' read '*turn round*' and add 'cf. συγγογγύλλω'

**γογγῠλος**, line 2, after '*IG* $1^2$.372.22' insert 'cf. Call.*fr.* 606 Pf.' **II**, for '(proparox. .. *Th.* 855' read 'unexpld. use in Hdn.Gr. 1.164'

***Γόγγῠλος**, ὁ, name of a deity, Διονύσου Γονγύλου *IG* 10(2).1.259 (Thessalonica, i AD).

***γόημι**, = γοάω, Erinn. in *Suppl.Hell.* 401.18.

***γοητήριον**, τό, **γοᾱ-**, perh. *magic practice*, (ε)ἰσάγομεν εὖ γοατήρια terracotta in H. Kenner *Das Phänomen der verkehrten Welt* (Bonn 1970) p. 30.

**γοῖ II**, delete the section.

***γοί** (B), v. °οὔ.

**γοῖτα**, delete '(leg. ὗς)' and add 'cf. γοτάν'

**γοιταί**, add 'cf. γοσταί s.v. °κοσταί'

***γομόρ**, Hebr. measure, *homer*, Lxx *Ex.* 16.16, 1*Ki.* 16.20, *Ez.* 45.11, *Ho.* 3.2.

**γόμος I 2**, add '*PCol.Zen.* 2.8 (iii BC)'

**γομφιάζω**, for '*have pain in the back teeth*, or *gnash* them' read '*grind* the back teeth'

**γομφιασμός**, after lemma insert 'prob. the same as γομφίασις'

**γόμφος I 1**, at end for 'χαλκοί' read 'χαλκοί' **2**, add '**b** *eschar caused by cautery*, *Hippiatr.* 96. **c** *projection* on the shoulder of a horse, ib. 26.'

**γομφόω 1**, add '*cause* teeth *to be embedded in the manner of nails*, Gal. 2.754.9'

***γονάγρα**, ἡ, *gout in the knee*, Cyran. 95 (3.36.46), 109 (4.18.14 K.).

***γονέτης**, ου, ὁ, = γενέτης, *father*, *IHadr.* 120.3 (Chr.epigr.).

**γονή I 1**, after '(S.)*Ant.* 641' insert 'Just.*Nov.* 22.20.1'

***γονίζω**, *stock with offspring*, pass. pf. part. περιστερῶνα γεγονισμένον *PRyl.* 581 ii 8 (ii BC); so prob. *SB* 7814.32 (iii AD).

**γόνιμος 3 b**, for 'Antiph.' read 'Antiphil.'

**γόνυ**, line 8, delete 'but Γόννα .. Eust. 335.39' and for 'Alc.*Supp.* 10' read 'Alc. 44.7 L.-P., hyper-Aeol. acc. pl. γόννα acc. to St.Byz. s.v. γόννοι, Eust. 335.39; dat. pl. γόννοις Theoc. 30.18'; before 'E. has γουνάτων' insert 'S. has γούνατα *OC* 1607' **I 2**, line 5, after 'v. sub κάμπτω' insert 'ἐς γόνυ ἕζεσθαι *kneel*, Luc.*Syr.D.* 55'

**γονῠαλγής**, add 'Gal. 17(2).605.4, 7'

***γόνυγρον**· τὰ ἄκαρπα καὶ ξηρὰ πεδία Hsch. (cj. τὴν ἄνυγρον La.).

***γονῠπεσος**, ὁ, *Kneeler*, as a nickname, Δημήτριος ὁ γ., a grammarian, Hdn.Gr. 2.61, Sch.Gen.Il. 13.137, Sch.T Il. 15.683.

**γοργεύω 2**, add 'μέχρι τῆς ἀριθμήσαιως γόργευο (= γόργευου) ὅσον δύνῃ ποεῖν καὶ ἀπετῆσαι *PMich.*x 577.9 (i AD), *BGU* 1097'

**γοργίειος**, add 'γοργίεια, τά, festival at Delos, *Inscr.Délos* 366*A*133 (iii BC)'

***γόργιλον**, τό, = σέσελι, Paul.Aeg. 7.3 (205.25 H.).

***γοργοκτόνος**, ον, *Gorgon-killing*, of Athena, poet. in *PKöln* 245.8 (iii AD).

***γοργόμματος**, ον, *fierce-eyed*, Heph.Astr. 3.45.3.

***γοργόπλοος**, ον, *swift-sailing*, *An.Par.* 4.200.22.

**γοργός 1**, after '*A.Th.* 537' insert 'νῦν δ' ἐς γυναῖκα γοργὸς ὁπλίτης φανεὶς κτείνεις μ' E.*Andr.* 458, 1123, τὸ .. ἀντιμετώπους προσελαύνειν ἀλλήλοις γοργόν X.*Eq.Mag.* 3.11'; after '*IG* 3.1079' add '*Milet* I 7.308 no. 222, 9.176 no. 356' **2**, after 'of persons' insert 'Ar.*Pax* 565'

**Γοργοτομία**, for 'Str. 8.6.2' read 'Str. 8.6.21'

**γόργῡρα**, add 'pl., ἀρδάλια· τοὺς πυθμένας τῶν κεραμίδων, οὓς ἔνιοι γοργύρας καλοῦσιν Hsch. **II** (in Ion. form γοργύρη) prob. as pr. n. = Γοργώ, τῆι Ἥρηι ἀνέθεσαν .. γοργύρην χρυσῆν *SEG* 12.391 (Samos, vi BC).'

***γοργῠ́ριον**, τό, dim. of γόργυρα, *subterranean channel*, prob. in *ABSA* 26.220 (Sparta).

***γοργωπιάσκω**, ἐγοργωπίασκεν· ἀτενὲς ἔβλεπεν Hsch.

**γοργῶπις** (s.v. γοργώψ), add 'also as designation of a lake, γ. λίμνη A.*Ag.* 302'

**γοργωπός**, after '*grim-eyed*' insert 'in some case w. allusion to the Gorgon'

***Γορδιάνεια**, τά, festival in honour of Gordian, *IG* 2².2239.189, 2242.29 (iii AD).

***γόρνα** or **γόρνη**, ἡ, = Syriac *gūrnā*, *amphora*, *burial urn*, γόρνης ἕνα ἥμυσυ *IGLS* 269.

***γοσταί**· αἱ κριθαί Theognost.*Can.* 44 A.; cf. κοσταί, °κόσταια.

***γουνάριος**, ὁ, Lat. *gunnarius*, *furrier*, *Corinth* 8(1).148, *IGLBulg* 99.4, 100.4, 102.8, al. (sts. γουνν-, all vi AD).

**⁺γούντη**, ἡ, (wd. of unkn. origin) *tomb*, *CIJud.* 767 (Phrygia).

**⁺γουτάριον**, τό, perh. *tomb*, *MAMA* 6.277 (Phrygia); cf. °γούντη.

***γουπνάριος**, ὁ, = Lat. *gubernator*, *CPR* 10.57.

***γουργᾰθός**, v. °γυργ-.

**⁺γράα**, ἡ, αἱ λεγόμεναι γράαι, in context after mention of water-snakes, some kind of dangerous aquatic creature, fr. Skt. *grāhá-* *Peripl.M.Rubr.* 38.

***γράβακτον**, v. °κράββατος.

**γράβατος**, delete the entry.

***γράδος**, ὁ, Lat. *gradus*, *stepped pedestal*, *IGBulg.* 992, 993, *MAMA* 4.343.

**γραῖα**, after '**γραίη**' insert 'Babr. 104.5' and after '**γραία**' insert 'Theoc. 7.126 (also sp. γρέα *POxy.* 2860.11, *OAmst.* 85.11)'

**Γραικίτης** (s.v. Γραικός), after 'ὁ' insert '*Greek style*, ἐν δὲ Γραικίταις πέπλοις'

***Γραικολατῖνος**, ον, *Graeco-Latin*, of the name Zeno which is used in both languages, *Orac.Tiburt.* 159.

**Γραικός**, add 'adv. -ῶς, *in the Greek manner*, *Orac.Tiburt.* 158'

***Γραικόστᾰσις**, εως, ἡ, Lat. *Graecostasis*, platform or tribunal in the Roman forum, reserved for foreign envoys, Varro *LL* 5.155, Cic.*QF* 2.1.3, Plin.*HN* 7.212, etc.

***γραιούδια**· οἱ παρ' ἡμῖν ἐφθοὶ ὄμφακες Suid.; cf. γραῖα II, ‡γραῦς II.

***γραίοψις**, εως, ἡ, *having the face of an old woman*, *Dura*⁹ 1.213.19 (iii AD, γρε-).

**γράμμα**, after 'Doric γράθμα' insert '*SEG* 30.380 (Tiryns, vii BC)' **II 5**, add 'as unit of currency, *TAM* 4(1).269.7 (Rom.imp.), *BCH* suppl. 8.159 (Thessalonica, v AD)'

**γραμμάριον**, add 'abbrev. ΓΡ on bronze weight (for pl.), *SEG* 32.1626 (v/vi AD)'

**γραμμᾰτεῖον I 2**, add 'also perh. of a receipt, *CPR* 5.12.5 (iv AD)' add '**V** app. some premises occupied by an association of artists, τὸ κοινὸν τῶν ἐν τῶι κατὰ Κύπρον γραμματείωι περὶ τὸν Διόνυσον τεχνιτῶν *Salamine* 83.5 (ii BC).'

**γραμμᾰτεύς 1**, line 3, after 'Th. 7.10' insert 'τὸν γραμματέα τὸν κατὰ πρυτανείαν καὶ τοὺς ἄλλους γραμματέας τοὺς ἐπὶ τοῖς δημοσίοις γράμμασιν *IG* 2².120.15 (Athens, 353/2 BC), γραμματὶ πολιτικῶν *POxy.* 3185.1 (iii AD)'; line 5, after '*UPZ* 110.145 (ii BC)' insert 'τοῦ γραμματέως τῶν δυνάμεων *Salamine* 89 (ii BC)' add '**b** as transl. of Hebr. *šōṭēr*, Lxx *Ex.* 5.6, *Nu.* 11.16, *Jo.* 1.10, al.; *sop̄rim* or "scribes", 2*Ki.* 8.17, *Ne.* 8.1, *Ev.Matt.* 2.4, *Ev.Marc.* 1.22, al.'

**γραμμᾰτικός II 2**, line 3, for 'Cyrene' read 'Cumae'

**γραμμᾰτιστής**, after lemma insert 'dial. -ᾱ́ς'; after '(Thespiae)' insert '*SEG* 30.990 (?Corinth, iv/iii BC), 32.497 (Thespiae, iii BC)'

**γραμμᾰτοεισᾰγωγεύς**, for '*schoolmaster: governor*' read 'minor official (military or civil): transl. Hebr. *šōṭēr*'

***γραμμᾰτοτρώξ**, ῶγος, ὁ, *"nibbler of letters"*, wd. in Hdn.Gr. 2.643.

**γραμμᾰτοφῠλᾰκεῖον**, add '*SEG* 19.854.6 (Pisidia, ii AD)'

***γραμμᾰτοφῠλᾰκέω**, app. *serve as* γραμματοφύλαξ, rest. in *Xanthos* no. 16 (Lycia).

**γραμμή II**, for '= βαλβίς .. *winning-point*' read '*finishing-line*'

**γραμμοειδής**, add '**2** perh. *having the form of a letter*, Afric.*Cest.* 1.2 p. 117 V.'

***γρανᾶτα**, τά, Lat. *granata*, *pomegranates*, Anon. *in Rh.* 74.10, 176.5.

**γραπτός II**, add 'also sg., συνθέμενοι γραπτὸν πρὸς αὐτούς *IG* 7.4130.4 (Acraephia, ii BC), ἐν τοῖ γραπτοῖ *SEG* 35.665.B19, 27, al. (Ambracia, ii BC)'

**γράπτρα**, after '*copying*' insert '*PMich.*II 123ᵛ vi 9, ix 31 (i AD)'

**γραστίζω**, for pres. refs. read '*Hippiatr.* 98; pass., *Gp.* 16.1.11, *CPh* 19.234, *PCair.Zen.* 158 (both iii BC)'

***γραστολόγος**, ὁ, *fodder-collector*, *Stud.Pal.* 20.213 (*Berichtigungsl.* II 2.165, vi AD) or *γραστολογία, (*Berichtigungsl.* VIII 471).

**γραῦς I**, line 6, after 'D. 19.283' insert 'γ. κορώνη Call.*fr.* 260.50 Pf.' **II**, for '*scum* of boiled milk' read '*scum* forming on the top of heated liquids' add '**b** perh. *froth* on fresh milk, Nic.*Al.* 91. **c** ἡ ἐν τοῖς χείλεσι τῶν ποταμῶν (ποτηρίων La.) γραμμή i.e. the line of scum along river-banks, Hsch.' add '**V** a throw at dice, Hsch.' at end add 'Myc. *ka-ra-we* (pl.); see also γρεῦς'

***γραφέας**, ὁ, app. equiv. of γραφεύς, Πύρρō(γ) γρ[α]φέας· καὶ Φαρίξενος καὶ τοὶ μαστροὶ *SEG* 31.358 (v. *Olympia Bericht* 10.234 no. 30, v BC); cf. γραφής.

***γρᾰφεία**, ἡ, (?)*painting*, *CID* II 101 i 11 (iv BC; unless termination of longer wd.).

***γρᾰφιάριον**, τό, app. some item connected with writing (?desk), *PAmh.* 2.181 (iii AD).

**γρᾰφικός I 2**, add '**b** *forming the perfect pattern of*, Plaut.*Ps.* 519, *Trin.* 936, 1024.'

***γρᾰ́φιον**, τό, *prescription*, τῆς διαλυτικῆς *PMerton* 12.23 (i AD); cf. °ἀντιγράφιον. **2** a kind of poll-tax, *IEphes.* 13 i 3, al. (i AD); see also γραφεῖον.

**γρᾰφίς II**, for 'in pl. = *paintings*' read '*painting*, *APl.* 36 (Agath.), 80.4 (id.)' and after 'Nonn.*D.* 25.433' insert '(pl.)'

***γρᾰφύνα**, ἡ, dub. sens., *IAskl.Epid.* 52 A 47 (iv BC).

**γρᾰ́φω**, line 2, γεγράφηκα, add '*IG* 11(4).1026 (Delos, ii BC)'; line 10, after '*Leg.Gort.* 1.45, al.' insert 'ἠιγραμμένο *SEG* 38.13.B5 (Rhamnous, early v BC)'; line 11, after 'Dor.' insert 'γεγράβαται (pl.) Dubois *IGDS* 121 (Camarina, v BC, tab.defix.)'; line 18, before 'Pl.*R.* 420c' insert '*paint* a statue' **II 3**, κληρονόμον γράφειν, add '*Cod.Just.* 1.2.25 pr., 1.3.45.4' **6**, line 3, for 'etc.: abs. (sc. νόμον) D. 18.179' read 'D. 18.179, etc.' **8**, add 'ὁ δὲ γράφων ἡμεῖν ἀναγορευσάτω *IG* 12(5).655.12 (Syros, ii/iii AD)' **B 1**, lines 3/4, for 'ἐγραψάμην .. D. 56.6, etc.' read '*cause to be written*, *dictate*, Hdt. 3.128.2, ἐγραψάμην τότ' εὐθὺς ὑπομνήματα, ὕστερον δὲ κατὰ σχολὴν ἀναμιμνησκόμενος ἔγραφον Pl.*Tht.* 143a; συγγραφήν D. 56.6, etc.'; add '*cause to be painted*, Hdt. 4.88.1, *AP* 6.355 (Leon.Tarent.)' **2**, for '*IG* 1².374.16, ib. 2.115ᵇ21' read '*IG* 2².19.b8, al.'; add '*IG* 2².856.6, al.'

**γράω**, line 1, for 'Call.*fr.* 200' read 'Call.*fr.* 551 Pf. (v.l. κράω)'; line 2, for 'γράσθι .. (Golgoi)' read 'Cypr. *ka-ra-si-ti* perh. γράσθι (imper.) *ICS* 264.1'

**γρᾱώδης**, for '= γραϊκός' read '*typical of* or *proper to an old woman*'

***γρεάγρα**, γρέγρα, v. °κρεάγρα.

***γρηγοροόφθαλμος**, ον, *with watchful eyes*, Tz.*Alleg.Il.Prol.* 671, 675.

***γρήϊος**, ον, Ion. for *γρᾴϊος, *of an old woman*, εἶδος Call.*fr.* 490 Pf.; μορφή Nic.*fr.* 62 G.-S.; ἴχνος prob. in Euph. in *Suppl.Hell.* 415 ii 6.

**γρῖπος I**, for '= γρῖφος' read '*net*'

***γρῑφάνη**, ἡ, *rake*, *Poliorc.* 212.3.

***γρῑφεύς**, έως, ὁ, = γριπεύς 1, Opp.*C.* 4.259.

**γρῖφος 1**, for '*basket*, *creel*' read '*net*'

***γρῖφος**, ον, *obscure*, comp. and sup., γριφότερος, -τατος, *An.Boiss.* 4.61; cf. γρίφον· τὶ ἀσαφές Hdn.*Epim.* 16.

**γρονθονεύεται**, after lemma insert '(γρονθων- La.)' and delete 'βρενθύεται'

***γρόνθων**· ἀναφύσησις, ἣν πρώτην μανθάνουσιν αὐληταὶ καὶ κιθαρισταί Hsch.

**⁺γρουνός**, ὁ, v. ‡γρυνός.

**γρύζω**, line 3, after '*mutter*' insert 'Hippon. 70.6 W.'; line 5, after '(Ar.)*Ra.* 913' insert 'Pl.*Euthd.* 301a'

**⁺γρυήλιον**· ῥωχμὴν (cod. ῥωσμ-) δρυός Hsch.

**γρύλλος 1**, add '*PSorb.*inv. 2381 (*ZPE* 78.153, ii AD)' **2**, read 'painting by Antiphilus of such a person, subsequently used generically, Plin.*HN* 35.114, *POxy.* 2331 ii 9 (iii AD)'

**γρῡνός**, add '(γρουνός is v.l. in all three places)'

***γρυπάλιον**, v. γρυπάνιος.

**γρῡπάνιος**, for 'also -άνιον .. Hsch.' read 'see also °γρυπάλιον'

***γρῠτάρης**, ου, ὁ, prob. = γρυτοπώλης, Sch.Ar.*Pl.* 17.

**γρύτη 2**, after '*frippery*' insert '*Peripl.M.Rubr.* 30'

**γρῡτοδόκη**, add '(γρυτ- codd.)'

**γρῡτοπώλης**, after '*small wares*' insert 'Maiuri *Nuova Silloge* 466 (Cos, i BC/i AD), *ISmyrna* 719.6 (i AD)'

**γρύψ I**, after '*griffin*' insert 'Hes.*fr.* 152 M.-W.'

**γρῶνος II**, γρώνη, after '*hole*' insert '*cavity*'; delete '**2** *hollow vessel*, *kneading-trough*' and for '(Leon.)' read '(Leon.Tarent.)'

**γῠάλας**, after 'ὁ' insert 'or **γυάλα**, ἡ' and for '*a* Megarian *cup*' read 'a kind of cup, attributed in quots. to Megarian and Macedonian sources'; add 'cf. γυλλάς' *__γύαρχος__ or **γυάρχης**, ου, ὁ, official of unkn. function, *PHib.* 260.3 (iii BC).

**γύης**, after lemma insert 'dial. γύας' **II 1**, after '*field*' insert '*SEG* 39.996.2 (Camarina, ii BC)' add '**5** type of *dike* or *embankment*, *SB* 9699.82, 90 (i AD); cf. Swiderek *La propriété foncière* p. 60.'

**γυήτης**, after 'Hsch.' insert 'Theognost.*Can.* 19'

**γυιοπέδη**, add 'transf., in sg., of the paralysis inflicted by the electric ray, Opp.*H.* 2.85'

*__γυιοφθόρος__, ον, *destroying the limbs*, (v.l. θυμοφθ-) Nic.*Th.* 140.

**γυιόω**, line 2, for '*wound*' read '*disable*' and add 'Hp.*VM* 9'

**γυλιός, γύλιος**, add '**III** γύλιον· χοῖρον ἢ λέοντα. σημαίνει δὲ καὶ τὸν Ἡρακλέα *EM* 244.24, Theognost.*Can.* 19.'

**γύλλινα**, add 'cf. Theognost.*Can.* 19'

**γυλλός**, after '*block of stone*' insert 'sacred to Apollo'; after '(Milet., v BC)' insert 'γ.· κύβος ἢ τετράγωνος λίθος Hsch.; v. Pfeiffer ad Call.*fr.* 114.2 sq.'

**γυμνάζω I 2**, delete the section. **II 2**, for '*investigate*' read '*discuss*' and add '*PFlor.* 338.4 (iii AD), *PTrinity College* inv. D 28.53 (*CE* 44.313, iii AD), *Cod.Just.* 7.62.36'

**γυμνᾰσιαρχέω**, line 4, after '(Lys.) 6.60' insert 'of a female, *IEphes.* 3239A.10 (i/ii AD)'

**γυμνᾰσιαρχία**, after '*office of gymnasiarch*' insert 'as a λειτουργία' and after 'Pl.*Ax.* 367a' insert 'Isoc. 16.35'

**γυμνᾰσιαρχικός**, add 'γυμνασιαρχικόν, τό, *fund administered by the gymnasiarch*, *BCH* 37.91.19 (Beroea)'

**γυμνᾰσιαρχίς**, add '*PMilan* inv. 69.01 ii.6 (*Aegyptus* 60.126)'

**γυμνᾰσίαρχος**, fem., add '*TAM* 3.58 (ii/iii AD), al.'

**γυμναστικός I**, add 'νεανίσκοι γ. *members of an organization of young men participating in athletic exercises*, *SEG* 29.1201 (Lydia)'

**γυμνητής II**, add 'Str. 16.4.17; transf., *lacking the necessities of life, destitute*, γ. βίοτος, of Diogenes the Cynic, *AP* 7.65 (Antip.Sid.)'

*__γυμνιεύω__, *to be destitute*, *PRoss.-Georg.* 3.28 (iv AD).

**γυμνικός**, add '**2** -κός, ὁ, *acrobat*, of a child, *SEG* 30.1231 (Lugdunum, iii AD; sp. -κως).'

*__γυμνόλοπον__, τό, variety of chestnut, τῶν δὲ καστάνων τὸ μὲν Σαρδιανόν, τὸ δὲ λόπιμον .. τὸ δὲ γυμνόλοπον Sch.Nic.*Al.* 271b Ge.

*__γυμνομάχος__, ὁ, = γυμνής II 1, Tyrt.23a.14 W.[2].

*__γυμνοπᾰγής__, ές, *freezing because of (their) nakedness*, Tim.*Pers.* 99 P.

**γυμνοπερίβολος**, add 'app. *without covering garment*, καὶ μαστειγοφόρους κʹ .. ἐν ἐσθῆσι λευκαῖς γυμνοπεριβόλους καὶ σὺ[ν ἀσπ]ίσι καὶ μάστιξι *SEG* 38.1462.64 (Oenoanda, ii AD)'

**γυμνός 5**, for '*lightly-clad*, i.e. *in the undergarment only*' read '*stripped*, i.e. with one's main garment removed'

**γυμνόω 1**, add 'ἀτιμωθεὶς τῶν ὄντων γυμνούσθω *Cod.Just.* 1.3.35.1, 1.3.44.1' **3**, for '*lay aside*' read '*strip off* a garment' and add 'so perh. in Call.*fr.* 191.30 Pf.'

*__γῠναικᾰδέλφη__, ἡ, *wife's sister*, *SEG* 33.1103 (Paphlagonia, ii/iii AD).

**γῠναικάδελφος**, after '*wife's brother*' insert 'Mitchell *N.Galatia* 385 (?iv AD)'

*__γῠναικ(ε)ιάριος__, ὁ, *manager of* γυναικεῖον (°γυναικεῖος II 4), *Cod.Just.* 11.8.13.

**γῠναικεῖος I 1**, delete 'Thphr.*Char.* 2.9'; add '**b** ἀγορὰ γ. *woman's market*, i.e. where female clothing, ornaments, etc., are sold, τὰ ἐκ γυναικείας ἀγορᾶς Thphr.*Char.* 2.9, Men.*fr.* 390 K.-Th.' **II**, add '**4** γυναικεῖον, τό, (textile) *factory employing women*, *Cod.Just.* 11.8.2, al., *JÖAI* 23 *Beibl.* 205 (Heraclea-Perinthus).'

*__γῠναικεράστρια__, ἡ, (*female*) *lover of women*, of Sappho, *POxy.* 1800 *fr.* 1 i 18.

*__γῠναικογένεια__, ἡ, *relationship through females*, πρὸς -γένειαν on the *female side*, *PSI* 1016.26 (ii BC), κατὰ γ. *PGen.* 104.15 (ii AD).

**γῠναικοκρᾰτέομαι**, add '*AP* 10.55 (Pall.)'

**γῠναικονόμος**, add '*PHib.* 196.11, 18 (iii BC)'

**γῠναικοπίπης**, for '(ὀπιπτεύω)' read '(ὀπιπεύω)'; add 'prob. in Sch.Hippon. 118.D9 W.'

*__γῠναικοτρᾰφής__, ές, *brought up by a woman*, Hsch. s.v. τηθαλλαδοῦς.

*__γῠναικοϋφής__, ές, *woven by women*, γυναικυφῆ interpr. as acc. sg. in *PSI* 341 (*ZPE* 66.59).

**γῠναικοφίλης**, for 'Theoc. 8.[60]' read 'Theoc. 8.60'

*__γῠναικόω__, *make a woman of* by sexual experience, παρθένος οὐδέποτε γυναικουμένη Ph. 1.683. **2** *make* one with abnormal male characteristics *into a complete woman*, Hp.*Epid.* 6.8.32. **II** *make womanish* or *effeminate*, τὰ σώματα μαλακότητι καὶ θρύψει γυναικοῦντες Ph. 2.21.

**γύναιος I**, add 'Myc. *ku-na-ja* (fem.), *decorated with the figure of a woman*'

**γύνανδρος**, for '*of doubtful sex, womanish*' read 'of a man, *womanish, effeminate*'

**γύος**, for '= γύης II' read '*field* (esp. as enclosed by dikes, opp. γῆ χέρσος)'; before 'etc.' insert '*BGU* 1132.10, *CPap.Jud.* 142'

*__γυπαιετούς__, bird name, perh. error for γρυπ- or °ὑπαιετούς, Suid.

*__γύπη__, ἡ, *hollow cavity*, Call.*fr.* 43.71 Pf., γύπη· κοίλωμα γῆς. θαλάμη. γωνία Hsch. and cf. id. s.v. γύπας; in Hsch. also, perh. by folk-etymology, *vulture's nest.*

**γῡπιάς**, add '(or ?*hollow*, cf. °γύπη)'

**γύπινος**, add 'πτερά *Edict.Diocl.* 18.10'

*__γῡπίς__, ίδος, ἡ, = γυπιάς, in place-name, ἐκ τᾶν γυπίδων πετρᾶν *SEG* 34.384 (Delphi, ii BC).

*__γῡπόμορφος__, ον, *having the form* (head) *of a vulture*, epith. of Isis, hymn in *POxy.* 1380.66 (ii AD).

**γύπωνες**, after 'Sparta' insert 'οἱ δὲ γ. ξυλίνων κώλων ἐπιβαίνοντες ὠρχοῦντο, διαφανῆ ταραντινίδια ἀμπεχόμενοι' and add 'cf. ὑπογύπωνες'

**γυργάθιον**, add 'Anon.Alch. 360.15'

**γυργᾰθός**, after '*creel*' insert '(or perh. *net*)' and after 'Luc.*DMeretr.* 14.2' insert 'esp. a *bread-basket*, cf. Hsch. s.v. γυργαθόν'; at end after 'Aristaen. 2.20' add 'also γουργαθός *Vit.Aesop.*(G) 18, al.'

*__γυργαθώδης__, ες, *resembling a* γυργαθός, Hsch. s.vv. σαργάναι and σεγάνιον.

**γῡρητόμος**, for '*tracing a circle*' read 'perh. *trenched* (cf. γῦρος 2)'

**γυρῖνος**, after '*tadpole*' insert 'or *frog*'

**γῡροειδής**, after '*round*' insert '*PMag.* 3.139'

**γῡρός**, line 4, for 'γ. πάλη .. *Gym.* 11' read 'of wrestling, *contorted*, Philostr.*Gym.* 11, 35'

**γῡρόω III**, for '*coil oneself up*' read '*curve* or *arch oneself*'

**γυρτόν**, after 'σκύφον' insert '(κυφόν Vossius)'

**γύρωσις**, for 'γῦρος' read '(γῦρος 2)' add '**II** *giddiness, reeling*, Aq.*Is.* 19.17.'

**γύψ**, after 'Eus.*PE* 3.12)' insert 'gen. pl. γυπάων Opp.*C.* 4.392'

**γυψίζω**, add 'in sealing a jar, *PMich.*XII 657.17 (ii/iii AD)'

**γύψινος I**, after '*gypsum*' insert 'στεφάνιον *Inscr.Délos* 1452*B*11 (ii BC)' **II**, add 'Ἰσιδώρου τὸ γύψινον (on a plaster-cast of a horse's nose-piece), *BE* 1960.95 (iii/ii BC)'

*__γυψοκόπος__, *one who powders gypsum*, *ITyr* 31.

**γύψος**, for '**III** *cement*' read '(II) **2** plaster made from gypsum'

*__γωνά__, ἡ, perh. = γωνία, *SEG* 7.1047 (Syria).

**γωνία I**, add '**5** *spike of corn*, Sch.Hes.*Sc.* 398. **6** *edge, point* of a sword, Eust. 563.18.'

**γωνιαῖος I**, add 'and γωνιεῖος *PRyl.* 567.3 (iii BC)' add '**III** γωνιαία (sc. λίθος), ἡ, a precious stone, Plin.*HN* 37.164.'

**γωνιόομαι**, after 'Dsc. 3.7' insert 'Eust.*Op.* 292.33'

**γωνίωσις**, add '**II** *sharp point*, Sch.Gen.Il. 8.297.'

**γῶνος**, add 'acc. to Theognost.*Can.* 50 A., oxyt. in the sense of ἕδος (cf. γουνός), properisp. as παιδιὰ παλαιστρική'

**γωρῡτός**, for '*quiver*' read '*bow-case*'; line 2, for 'Od. 21.54, cf. Lyc. 458' read 'ὅς οἱ περίκειτο φαεινός Od. 21.54; so prob. in Lyc. 458. **2** *quiver*' at end delete 'wrongly .. 1898.21'

# Δ

**δαγνόν**, delete '(leg. ἀδινόν)'

**δᾶγύς**, delete 'used in magic rites'; add 'gen. pl. δαγ[ύ]δων Erinn. in *Suppl.Hell.* 401.21'

**Δαδᾶφόρια**, for pres. ref. read '*CID* I 9.D4 (Δαιδᾶφ[ό]ρια, iv BC)'

**δάδινος**, add 'σπάθη δ. Heras ap.Gal. 13.781.13'

**δᾴδιον 1**, after '*little torch*' insert 'δ. χρυσοῦν ἐπὶ βάσεως *Inscr.Délos* 1417*A*i80 (ii BC), al.'

***δᾳδοσχίστης**, ου, ὁ, *one who splits pine-brands*, *IG* $2^{2}$.1557.29.

**δᾳδουχία**, after '*torch-bearing*' insert '*SEG* 30.93 (Eleusis, i BC)'

***δᾳδουχικός**, ή, όν, of a δᾳδοῦχος I 1, ἱεροφαντικῶν καὶ δ. οἴκων *IG* $4^{2}$.84.30 (Epid., i AD).

**δᾳδούχιον**, delete the entry.

**δᾳδοῦχος I 1**, add 'also fem., *AJA* 37.239 (Latium, ii AD); of Persephone, *IG* 12(5).229.23 (Paros)'

**δᾳδοφόρος**, for 'B.*fr.* 23.1' read 'δαϊδοφόρε B.*fr.* 31.1 S.-M., *IG* $2^{2}$.5146; δᾳδοφόροι μελανείμονες of the Furies, *Suppl.Hell.* 1154'

**Δάειρα**, Δαῖρα, add 'also, of Hecate, Δαῖραν μουνογένειαν A.R. 3.847'

***δαελόν**· διάδηλον Hsch.; cf. δίαλον ib.

**⁺δαελός**, Syracusan form of δᾶλός, τὸν δαελὸν σβῆτε ?Sophr. in *PSI* 1214.13; cf. δαλός .. καὶ δαελὸς παρὰ Σώφρονι *EM* 246.35.

**δαημοσύνη**, add 'Max. 454'

**δαήμων**, line 1, after 'gen. ονος' insert 'contr. pl. **δῦμονες** (codd. δαήμονες) perh. in Archil. 3.4 W. (for v.l. v. °δαίμων B)' **4**, after 'Democr. 197' insert 'w. κατὰ πόλεμον Arr.*Tact.* 12.1'

**δᾱήρ**, line 1, before 'dat.' delete 'Men. 135' and insert 'gen. written δῆρος *IKios* 53.3, cf. gen. pl. infra'

***δάθιος**, v. °ζάθεος.

***Δαιδάλειος**, α, ον, *of* or *named after Daedalus*, ἀγάλματα ἃ ἐκαλεῖτο Δαιδάλεια *Lindos* 2C.61, cf. Ar.*fr.* 202 K.-A., D.S. 4.30.1; neut. subst. *sanctuary of Daedalus*, *Ath.Agora* XIX P5, 11, 12, 22 (written -ειον and -εον, Athens, iv BC); cf. Myc. place-name *da-da-re-jo(-de)* (neut. acc.).

***δαιδᾰλικός**, ή, όν, *skilfully wrought*, δαιδαλικοὺς λιβάνους Σμύρνης *Suppl.Hell.* 1062.

**δαίδᾰλος II**, last line, for 'Argos' read 'Plataea'

**δαιθμός I**, add '*IG* $9^{2}$(1).609.10 (Naupactus, v BC), cf. °ἀνδαιθμός, δασμός'

***δαϊθρᾰσής**, ές, (δάϊς) gen. δαϊθρασέος *bold in battle*, Euph. in *Suppl.Hell.* 415 i 7.

**δαϊκτήρ 1**, for 'Alc. 28' read 'cj. for διακτήρ *Lesb.fr.adesp.* 6 L.-P.'

***δαιμονᾱ́**, ᾱ, *distribution*, prob. in Alcm. 65 P., cj. in A.*Eu.* 727.

**δαιμονιόπληκτος**, for '= δαιμονιόληπτος' read '*afflicted by evil spirits*' and after 'Ptol.*Tetr.* 169' insert 'Rhetor. in *Cat.Cod.Astr.* 8(4).165'

***δαιμονιόπλοκος**, ον, *exposed to assaults of evil spirits*, *in their grip*, v.l. for δαιμονιόπληκτος, Rhetor. in *Cat.Cod.Astr.* 8(4).165; cf. θεόπλοκος.

***δαιμονοκλησία**, ἡ, *invocation of spirits*, Anon.Alch. 397.15 (sp. δημ-).

***δαιμονώδης**, = δαιμονιώδης, φαντασία *IGLS* 220 (iv/v AD).

**δαίμων I**, lines 4/5, for '*Divine .. Deity*' read 'unspecified agency affecting human fortunes' **2**, for '*the power.. lot* or *fortune*' read 'merging into the sense *fortune*, *lot*, but still often conceived as an active agency'; transfer 'στυγερὸς .. (Od.) 11.61' to section 1, line 6, after '11.792'; after 'Antipho 3.3.4' insert 'ἔδωκε τῇ τύχῃ τὸν δ. surrendered his *fortunes* to events, E.*Ph.* 1653' **B**, for this section read '= °δαήμων, *knowing*, δαίμονες μάχης Archil. 3.4 W., but δᾶμονες shd. prob. be written'

**δαΐξανδρος**, after '*man-destroying*' insert 'δ. πολέμō *CEG* 798.1 (Delphi, iv BC)'; add '(= *GVI* 1153)'

**δάϊος I 1**, line 6, before 'φόβημα δαΐων' insert 'ἐγχέων'; add 'of armour, *warlike*, A.R. 1.635, *AP* 6.128 (Mnasalc.)'

***Δαῖρα**, v. Δάειρα.

**δαΐς**, after 'ἡ' insert 'nom. sg. written **δαές** in *Inscr.Délos* 1442*B*23 (ii BC)' **1**, add 'of wedding torches, [οὐ]δὲ γὰρ οὐ δαΐδων καὶ παστάδος ἔλλαχεν ἡμ[αρ] epigr. in *IEphes.* 2101A.3'

**δάϊς**, before '(δαίω A)' insert 'ἡ'; add 'cf. Myc. *da-i-qo-ta*, compd. pers. n. (app. = Δηιφόντης)'

***δαίστωρ**, ὁ, perh. *consumer* or *?slaughterer*, δαίστορας ἀλλοτρίων epigr. in *SEG* 26.1215.

**δαίτης**, after 'E.*fr.* 472.12' insert '(dub.), δαίτας· μεριστάς Hsch.; pers. n. Δαίτης a Trojan hero of feasting, Mimn.*fr.* 18 W.'

***δαιτῐκλῠτός**, 'α, ον, *famed for feasts*, Κορίνθου δειράδ' ἐποψόμενος δαιτικλυτάν (codd. δαῖτα κλυτάν) Pi.*O.* 8.52.

**δαῖτις**, delete the entry.

***Δαιτίς**, ἡ, epith. of Aphrodite, *IEphes.* 1202.5 (iii AD).

***δαιτόποινος**, ον, unexpld. wd. in poet. word-list, *Suppl.Hell.* 991.27.

***Δαίττης**, ου, ὁ, epith. of Apollo and Artemis, Ἀπόλλωνι καὶ Ἀρτέμιδι Δαίτταις *SEG* 7.17 (Susa, ii BC); τοῦ Ἀπόλλωνος καὶ τῆς Ἀρτέμιδος τῶν Δαιττῶν *OGI* 244.22 (Daphne, ii BC).

**δαιτῠμών**, after 'Od. 7.102, 148, al.' insert 'Alcm. 98 P.'

**δαίω** (A) **I**, lines 14ff., mostly metaph. sense, after '(Il.) 2.93' insert 'οἰμωγὴ .. δέδηε Od. 20.353, Ὅμαδός τε Φόνος τ' Ἀνδροκτασίη τε δεδήει Hes.*Sc.* 155'

***Δάκεια**, τά, games celebrating Trajan's conquest of Dacia, *Corinth* 8(1).77.

***Δᾱκικός**, ή, όν, *Dacian*, τὸ ἀγώνισμα τοῦ Δακικοῦ ἅρματος *PColl.Youtie* 69.9 (AD 272); as title of Roman emperors, *SEG* 31.1124 (AD 104), 24.486 (AD 114).

***δακνᾶς**, ᾶ, ὁ, *biter*, Phryn.*PS* p. 64 B., gramm. in Gaisford *Choerob.* 1 p. 43.

**δάκος I**, at end for 'β. δάκος' read 'βλοσυρὸν δ.'

**δακρῠόεις**, add 'see also ‡ζακρυόεις'

**δακρῠρροέω 1**, line 3, for 'δακρυροοῦν' read 'δακρυρροοῦν'; add 'ἀπ' ὀμμάτων κλάον πρόσωπον καὶ δακρυρροοῦν *Trag.adesp.* 447 K.-S.'

***δακρῠστᾰγής**, ές, *marked by flowing tears*, δακρυσταγεῖ [γ]όῳ Tim.*Pers.* 100 P.

**δακρῡτός**, add 'δακρύτ' ἄγαν E.*El.* 1182, πᾶσιν δακρυτὸς *Amyzon* 65 (ii BC)'

***δακρῠχοέω**, *shed tears*, *GVI* 969.8 (Lydia, i AD).

**δακρύω I 3**, add 'τὸ κόμμι *Peripl.M.Rubr.* 29' **II**, before 'A.*Ag.* 1490' insert 'Simon. 48 P.'

***δακτῠλιδάριος**, ὁ, *maker* or *seller of rings*, rest. in *ITyr* 166 (δακτυλιδ-, Rom.imp.).

**δακτῠλίδιον**, delete '[λῐ]'

**δακτῠλικός**, for 'αὐλὸς .. Ath. 4.176f' read 'name of kind of aulos, Ath. 4.176f; also of a cithara (also called °Πυθικός), Poll. 4.66'

**δακτύλιος II 2**, add 'Plu. 2.518d'

**δακτῠλόδεικτος**, delete 'cf. *PLond.ined.* 1821' and add '**b** in a Greek-Coptic gloss. given as name for the first finger, *PLond.* 1821.306 (vi AD).'

***δακτῠλοκλείδιον**, τό, *finger-ring-key*, *PFouad I Univ.* 8.12 (ii AD, δακτυλοκλίδιν pap.), cf. ib. 8.

**δάκτῠλος I 1**, add '**b** δ. θεοῦ, the *finger* of God, as symbol of divine agency, Lxx *Ex.* 8.19, *Ev.Luc.* 11.20.' **2**, add '**c** pl., *joints* of a beetle's tarsi, Horap. 1.10.' **VI**, for this section read 'kind of shell-fish, *dactyli*, *ab humanorum unguium similitudine appellati*, Plin.*HN* 9.184'

***Δακύτιος**, ὁ, epith. of Hermes, *Inscr.Cret.* 4.174.60 (Gortyn, ii BC).

**Δαλμᾰτεῖς**, lines 3/4, Δαλματική, Δελμ-, add 'also Δελματικόν, τό, *PSI* 900.7 (iii/iv AD), *POxy.* 1741.15 (iv AD), var. Δελμάτιον *POxy.* 1026.16 (v AD)'; line 6, δερματίκιν, add '*PMich.*III 218.14 (-ιον, iii AD)'

***δαλμᾰτικομαφόριον**, τό, attested only in form δελματικο-, *Dalmatian cloak*, *SB* 10988 (iv AD), 11075 (v AD), cf. °δαλματικομαφόρτης.

**⁺δαλμᾰτικομᾰφόρτης**, ου, ὁ, *Dalmatian cloak with hood*, *Edict.Diocl.* 22.5, al., δελμ- *POxy.* 1273.12 (iii BC); δελματικομαφόλτου *Edict.Diocl.* 22.13, δελματικομαφέρτ[η]ς ib. 19.43.

***δαλμᾰτικομᾰφόρτιον**, τό, dim. of δαλματικομαφόρτης, δελματικομαφέρτιον *Edict.Diocl.* 19.8,, δερματικομαφόρτιν *POxy.* 114.5 (ii/iii AD), *PMichael.* 18.2, 4 (iii AD), cf. ‡μαφόρτης.

***Δαλμάτιον** (**Δελμ-**), τό, app. = Δελματίκιον (for which it may be an error), *POxy.* 1026.16 (v AD).

**δᾶλός II**, for this section read '*smouldering ember*, fig., of a youth who no longer inflames a man with homosexual love, *AP* 12.41 (Mel.)'

***Δαλφοί**, v. Δελφοί.

**δᾰμάζω**, line 4, after 'Od. 14.367' insert 'inf. δμῆσαι Hsch.'

**δᾰμᾰλίζω**, for 'codd.' read '*Lyr.adesp.* 415.7 S.'

**δᾰ́μᾰρ**, after 'A.*Pr.* 834' insert 'S.*OT* 930, al, E.*Alc.* 930, *Andr.* 4, al., Eup. 171 K.-A., Lex ap.Lys. 1.30, D. 23.55'

***δᾰμᾰσίβιος**, ον, app. *subduing life*, δα]μαισιβίου (sic) epigr. in *Inscr.Cret.* 1.xvi 52 (i AD).

**Δαμασκηνόν**, add 'see also °*Δαμασκηνός*'

***Δαμασκηνός**, *ή, όν*, *of* or *from Damascus*, *οἱ Δ.* Str. 16.2.20, *ἡ Δ.* (*χώρα*) 16.2.16; of cloth, *damask*, *ἐνδρομίς .. Δαμασκηνή* *Edict.Diocl.* 19.6, *καμάσιον Δαμασκινόν* *SB* 7033.41 (v AD). **II** *Δαμασκηνοί, οἱ*, *damsons*, *οἱ Δ.* *PRyl.* 630.80, al. (iv AD), *PFreib.* 4.67 (ii/iii AD, gen. pl. of masc. or neut.); cf. *Δαμασκηνόν*.

**δᾰμαστικός**, add '*δμήτειρα· δαμαστική* Hsch.'

***δᾰμάστρια**, gloss on *δμήτειρα*, Hsch., Sch.Gen.Il. 14.259.

**δαμασώνιον I**, for '= *ἄλιμος*' read '= *ἄλιμον*, s.v. *ἄλιμος* II'

**δᾰμᾰ́τειρα**, after '*δαμαντήρ*' insert 'Call.*fr.* 267 Pf.'

**Δᾱμᾱ́τριος**, add 'see also *Δημήτριος* I'

+**δᾱμεύω**, v. °*δημεύω*.

**δᾱμία**, delete the entry.

**Δᾱμία**, add '*Λοκαία* (for *Λοχ-*) *Δαμία* *IG* 12(3).361 (Thera)'

***δᾱμιεργέω**, v. °*δημιουργέω*.

***δᾱμιοργία**, *ἁ*, *meeting of the* *δαμιοργοί*, *IG* 4.493 (Mycenae), cf. *δημιούργιον* II.

***δᾱμιοργίζω**, perh. *serve as* *δαμιοργός*, app. aor. part. *δαμιοργίσōσα περτέδοκε* *IPamph.* 17 (iii BC; unless to be read as *δαμιοργὶς ὅσα*).

***δᾱμιοργίς**, *ιδος, ἁ*, perh. fem. of *δαμιεργός*, v. °*δαμιοργίζω*, *δημιουργίς*.

**δάμνια**, add '(*δάμνιον* v.l. for *δ' ἀμνίον* in Od. 3.444)'

***δᾱμονομέω**, *hold the office of* **δαμονόμος* (app. a local magistrate), *IG* $9^2$(1).138.14 (Calydon, iv/iii BC).

***δᾱμοσιεργός**, *ὁ*, = *δημιουργός*, *SEG* 23.305 ii 20 (Delphi, 190 BC), cf. °*δαμοσιοργία*.

+**δᾱμοσιοργία**, *ἁ*, *eligibility for public office*, *GDI* 3052.10 (Chalcedon).

***δᾱμοσιόω**, v. °*δημοσιόω*.

***δᾱμοτεύομαι**, v. °*δημοτεύομαι*.

**δᾱμώματα**, add 'also *δημώματα· παίγνια* id.'

***δᾱ́μων**, v. °*δαήμων*.

**Δᾰναΐδαι**, after '*descendants of Danaus*' insert 'used for the Greeks generally' and add 'E.*Hec.* 503, *Tr.* 447, al.'

**δᾰνᾰ́κη**, after '*ἡ*' insert 'and **δανάκης**, *ου, ὁ*'; add '(see also note to Call.*fr.* 278 Pf.)'

***δάνας** (B), Semitic word for *wine-jar*, *Dura*$^4$ p. 122; cf. Akkadian *dannu*(*m*).

***δάνδηξ**, *ηκος, ὁ*, kind of large dog, Ps.-Callisth. 2.33 cod. B.

**δᾰνείζω I**, before 'fut.' insert '(cf. *δανίζω*)'; line 6, after '*lend*' insert 'Sol.*Lg.fr.* 68 R.' **2**, line 2, for '*ἀπό τινος*' read '*παρά τινος*'

**δᾰ́νειον**, for 'Men.*Mon.* 97' read 'Men.*Mon.* 759 J.' and add '*SEG* 38.1476.A52 (Xanthos, iii BC)'

**δᾰ́νεισμα**, line 2, after 'Th. 1.121' insert '*δ. πράττειν* Just.*Nov.* 4.1'

**δᾰνειστής I**, after '*creditor*' insert 'D. 34.7, Plu.*Sol.* 13' deleting the latter ref. in section II; add 'also *δανιστής* *TAM* 5(1).231.11'

**δᾰνειστικός**, after 'etc.' insert '*ἐργασία* *money-lending* business, Thphr.*Char.* 23.2'; *ὁ δ.*, for '= *δανειστής*' read '*moneylender*'

**δᾰνίζω**, for 'Lxx *Pr.* 19.14' read 'Lxx *Pr.* 19.17'

***δᾰνιοκαρπία**, *ἡ*, *usufruct*, *BGU* 2338.9 (ii AD).

***δανιστής**, v. °*δανειστής*.

***Δάνκλε̄, Δανκλαῖοι**, v. °*ζάγκλη* II (*Ζάγκλη*).

**δᾱνός**, add 'Call.*fr.* 243 Pf.'

**δᾰ́νος** (A) **II**, add 'Ammon.*Diff.* p. 82 N.'

**δαόν**, add 'prob. error for *δοάν*, cf. *δήν*'

**δᾰπᾰνάω I 1**, add 'w. *περί*, *τῶν .. περὶ τοὺς κληρικοὺς .. δαπανωμένων* *Cod.Just.* 1.3.42 pr., Just.*Nov.* 59.2'

**δᾰπᾰ́νη I**, for '*cost*' read '*outlay*' **II** delete '*money spent*' and transfer exx. to section I

**δᾰπᾰ́νημα**, after lemma insert 'dial. *δαπάνᾱμα* *SEG* 31.572.A8 (Thessaly, *c.*200 BC)' and for '*cost*' read '*outlay*'

**δᾰπᾰ́νησις**, add '*κράτησον τὴν ἐπιστολὴν εἰς δαπάνησίν σου* *Stud.Pal.* 20.125.3 (v. *ZPE* 76.112)'

***δᾰπᾰνητέον**, *one must use up*, *consume*, Aët. 9.108(98).

+**δᾰπᾰνητής**, *ου, ὁ*, *defrayer of expenses*, *PMich.*XII 658.7 (iii AD), *EM* 40.44.

**δᾰ́πᾰνος**, after 'Th. 5.103' insert '*κόλλοψ* *AP* 12.42 (Diosc.)'

**δᾰ́πεδον**, line 4, *ground*, add 'Aen.Tact. 37.6'

**δάπτης**, for '*eater*, *bloodsucker*' read '*devourer*'

***δαράτα**, *ἁ*, app. kind of bread, offered in religious ceremonies, *μή δέκεσθαι μήτε δαρατᾶν γάμελα μήτε παιδήια* *CID* I 9.A24 (iv BC), cf. °*δάρατος*.

+**δάρατος**, *ὁ*, or **-ον**, *τό*, kind of bread, *τὸν ἄζυμον ἄρτον .. δάρατον* Nic.*fr.* 134 G.-S.; said to be Thess., equiv. Maced. *δράμις*, Seleuc.ap.Ath. 3.114b; *τὸ δά[ρατον]* rest. in *Schwyzer* 603 (Coropa, Magnesia, vi/v BC), cf. °*δαράτα*, also *δαρόν* s.v. *δαρός*.

***Δαρδᾰνικός**, *ή, όν*, poet. *Trojan*, *Δ. .. σκήπτροις* *AP* 9.155 (Agath.); *ἡ Δ.* *Dardania*, a river in the Troad, Str. 13.1.43, in Illyria, ib. 7.5.1; *χλαμὺς Δαρδανικὴ* *Edict.Diocl.* 19.69, 70.

**Δᾱρεικός**, for 'a Persian gold coin' read 'gold coin, originally Persian, later Maced.' and add '*IG* 7.3055.13, al. (Lebadeia), *Delph.* 3(5).61 ii A1, al. (both iv BC; v. *SEG* 29.445, 458)'; after '**Δαρικός**' insert '[ῐ Herod. 7.102]'

***Δαρζάλεια**, *τά*, games at Odessus in honour of the *μέγας θεός* Derzelas or Darzalas, *BCH* 52.395 (on coins); (for the god v. *IGBulg.* 47, 768, al.).

+**δαρκνά**, v. ‡*δραχμή*.

***δαρμός**, *a flogging*, *flaying*, Hsch. s.v. *μάστιγας*.

***Δάρρων**· *Μακεδονικὸς δαίμων, ᾧ ὑπὲρ τῶν νοσούντων εὔχονται* Hsch.

**δάροσος**, add '(*δάρος* La.)'

**δαρτός**, before 'Paul.Aeg. 6.61' insert 'Ruf.*Anat.* 61'

**δασμός**, add 'see also °*δαθμός*'

**δασμοφορέω**, add '**II** *exact tribute from*, w. acc., Call.*Dieg.* iv.7 (*fr.* 98 Pf.).'

+**δασπλής**, *ῆτος*, masc., fem. adj., *horrid*, *frightful*, *δασπλῆτα Χάρυβδιν* Simon. 37 P., Call.*fr.* 30 Pf., *δασπλῆτες Εὐμενίδες* Euph. 98 vGr., *δασπλῆτε δράκοντε* Nic.*Th.* 609, *μάχαιρα* Nonn.*D.* 22.219, *γυναῖκες* 46.210, al., Hsch.; also app. *δασπλήτης* *An.Ox.* 1.149.

+**δασπλῆτις**, fem. adj. = *δασπλής*, *θεὰ δ. Ἐρινύς* Od. 15.234, *Ἑκάτα δασπλῆτι* Theoc. 2.14.

**δάσσω**, for the pres. ref. read '*Suppl.Hell.* 1068'

***δαστήρ**, *ῆρος, ὁ*, *land-commissioner*, *IG* $9^2$(1).116 (pl., Aetolia).

**δᾰσῠγρᾰφέω**, for 'Hdn.*Epim.* 25' read 'Hdn.*Epim.*ap.Bast *Epistula Critica*, *Appendix* p. 25'

**δᾰσῠ́θριξ**, for '*hairy*' read '*having thick hair*' and after it insert '*δασύτριχος .. τράγοιο* Theoc. 7.15'

**δασυκνήμις**, before 'Nonn.*D.* 14.81' insert '*δασυκνήμιδι Φιλάμνῳ*'

***Δᾰσυλλιεῖον**, *τό*, *sanctuary of* *Διόνυσος Δασύλλιος*, *Sokolowski* 3.90.10 (Moesia, ii BC).

**δᾰσῠ́νω IV**, for this section read 'in prohibition, *μηδένα .. δασύνειν τὴν οἰνοποσίαν, μηδὲ ἀκοσ̣[μ]ίαν παρέχειν* perh. *gulp*, *BGU* 2371.4 (i BC)' and renumber pres. section IV to V. **2**, *of breathing*, for '*rapid*' read '*thick*'

**δᾰσῠπόδειος**, delete '*τὸ δ.* *the species hare*'

**δᾰσῠ́ς I 1**, add 'of snakes, *rough*, *scaly*, Arist.*HA* 607$^a$32' **II 2**, after 'D.H.*Comp.* 14' insert 'comp., *τὸ β̄ τοῦ μὲν* (sc. *φ̄*) *ψιλότερόν ἐστι, τοῦ δὲ* (sc. *π̄*) *-ύτερον* *nearer to an aspirate*, ib.' and after 'adv. *-έως*' insert '*λέγεται* ib.'

**δᾰτέομαι I**, line 4, for 'Diog. .. infr. II)' read 'in pass. sense Il. 1.125, etc., in act. sense Q.S. 2.57' **II**, line 6, for 'Diog.Apoll. l.c.' read 'Diog.Apoll. 3' add '**2** *break up into lots for sale*, *sell off*, *κὰ(Ϝ) Ϝοικίας δάσασσθαι τὰς ἄνοδ' ἐάσ(σ)ας* *IG* 5(2).262.17 (Mantinea, v BC = Dubois *Dial.arcad.* p. 95); prob. also in *ἀλλὰ τὰ μὲν πολίων ἐξεπράθομεν, τὰ δέδασται* Il. 1.125.' at end add 'Myc. aor. (*o-*)*da-sa-to*, pf. (*e-pi-*)*de-da-to* (*-δέδαστοι*), cf. adj. *e-pi-da-to* (= **ἐπίδαστος*)'

**δᾰτήριος**, for '*α, ον*' read '*ον*'

**Δᾱτισμός**, for 'the Median commander at Marathon' read 'the ref. is obscure'

***Δατυιος**, *ὁ*, name of a month at Dodona, *SEG* 15.384.19 (iv BC).

**δαῦκος** (A), at end delete 'also **δαυχμός** .. *Al.* 199' (v. °*δαυχμός*)

**δαῦκος**, read **δαῦκος** (B)

***δαυνός**, perh. *fiery*, A.*fr.* 41a R. (**δαϜ-νός*, v. *δαίω* (A)).

**δαυχμός I**, for 'v. *δαῦκος*' read '= *δάφνη πικρά*, Nic.*Th.* 94, *Al.* 199 (acc. to Sch.Nic.*Th.* 94)'

**δαύχνα**, after '*ἀρχιδαυχναφορέω*' insert '‡*συνδαυχναφόρος*'

+**Δαυχνᾱφόριος**, v. °*Δαφνηφόριος*.

**δαφνήεις**, add 'contr. **δαφνῆς, ῆντος**, Choerob. *in Theod.* 1.360, al.'

***δαφνηρεφής**, *ές*, *δαφνηρεφέων μυχάτων* *covered with laurel*, Porph. ap.Eus.*PE* 6.3.239a.

**δαφνηφᾰ́γος**, delete 'hence *inspired*'

**δαφνηφορέω**, line 2, delete 'Paus. 9.10.4'; line 3, after '(Hdn.) 7.6.2' insert 'serve as °*δαφνηφόρος* I 2, Paus. 9.10.4 (twice)'

**Δαφνηφόριος**, add 'Cypr. *Δαυχνᾱφόριος*, *ta-u-ka-na-po-ri-o* (gen.) *ICS* 309.3'

**δαφνηφόρος I 2**, add '*δαφνᾱφόρος*, *wearing* (crown of) *bay*, title of boy-priest of Apollo Ismenius, Paus. 9.10.4' **II**, delete 'at Thebes, Paus. 9.10.4'

**δαφνίς 2**, delete the section transferring ref. to section 1; add 'Alex. Trall. 5.4'

**δαφνόκοκκον**, add 'Aët. 7.114 (385.2 O.)'

**δαφνών**, add 'as pr. n., *POxy.* 3917.10 (ii AD)'

***δάχμα**, *τό*, = *δῆγμα*, Nic.*Th.* 119 (codd. also *δηχ-*, *δαγ-*), 128, al.

**δαψῐλής I 1**, *-εστέρως*, after 'Ptol.*Tetr.* 58' insert '(v.l.)'

***δᾰ́ω II**, *δάε, ἔδαε*, add 'A.R. 3.529; perh. also *δαείης* *h.Merc.* 565'

**δέ II 3**, implying causal connection, add 'A.*Supp.* 190, S.*Ph.* 741, E.*Ph.* 689, Ar.*Av.* 935; also in prose Th. 1.86.2, Pl.*Cra.* 426a, Lys. 12.68' line 34 of article, for '**II**' read '**III**' **B**, add 'but cf. *οὐ δὲ βίηφιν* Od. 9.408, *οὐ δ' εἰδώς* Pl.*Smp.* 199a' at end add 'Myc. *-de*, e.g. *da-mo-de-mi pa-si*, *δᾶμος δέ μίν φασι*'

**-δε**, at beginning for 'an enclitic post-position' read 'a post-position';

add '(It is uncertain whether -δε is enclitic, cf. A.D.*Adv.* 179.5, 181.13, Hdn.Gr. 1.498.) Myc. -*de*'

***δεϝαλῶσαι**, v. °δηλόω.

**δεγμόν**, add '(ὅρμον La.)'

**δέδηε, δεδήει**, after 'v. δαίω (A)' insert 'and °δέω (A)'

**δεδίσκομαι II**, delete the section.

***δεδίσσω**, v. °δειδίσσομαι.

**δέησις I 2**, written *petition*, delete 'written'

***δεητός**, όν, *needed, necessary*, Plu. 2.687e.

**δεῖ I 1**, line 9, for '(X.) *Oec.* 7.20' read '(X.) *Oec.* 8.9, Pl.*Phlb.* 33b' add '**b** (in the protasis of a condition in which one apologizes for pressing a point) *if I had to go so far as to* .., or sim., πόσους εἴποιμ' ἂν ἄλλους, εἴ με μηκύνειν δέοι Ar.*Lys.* 1132, εἰ δεῖ τι καὶ σκῶψαι Pl.*Men.* 80a.'

**Δεῖα**, add 'Δ. Σεβαστὰ οἰκουμενικὰ ἐν Λαοδικείᾳ *IEphes.* 1605.5, 11 (ii AD); Δ. Κομόδεια τὰ πρώτως ἀχθέντα ἐν Λαοδικείᾳ *ITrall.* 135.15 (ii AD, v. *Laodicée* p. 283)'

***Δειγαία**, ἡ, Maced. cult-epith. of Artemis, *SEG* 37.590 (Vergina, ii AD), 591 (-έα, iii AD); see also ib. 539 (unpublished inscrs. from Metochi; also sp. Διγαία).

**δεῖγμα 1**, line 1, for '*sample, pattern*' read '*material example, sample*'; line 2, after '*POxy.* 113.5 (ii AD)' insert 'of a sealed sample of goods sent for approval, *PPetaus* 57.4 (ii AD)' and before 'τοῦ βίου' insert '*immaterial example, model*, etc.'

***δειγματοκαταγωγεύς**, έως, ὁ, *official charged with the delivery of sealed samples*, *PBerol.*inv. 7441 (*Eos* 58.63ff., iii AD).

***δειδία**· ἡ σκοτία νύξ Suid.

**δειδίσκομαι**, at beginning insert 'also δεδίσκομαι'; line 6, after 'Od. 7.72' insert 'Call.*fr.* 87, 186.12 Pf.' and after '*welcoming*' insert 'Od.' add '**III** = δειδίσσομαι I, Ar.*Lys.* 564.'

**δειδίσσομαι**, at beginning delete 'impf. .. *Lys.* 564'; line 9, delete 'D. 19.291, *Prooem.* 43'; line 10, for 'cf. δεδίσκομαι II' read 'act. in this sense, Sch.B Il. 24.569, Suid.'

**δείδω**, line 16, before '3 sg.' insert '2 sg. δείδιας *AP* 12.138 (Mnasalc.)'; line 23, after 'etc.' insert 'pf. part. fem. δειδυῖα A.R. 3.753'; line 27, after '(Nonn.*D.*) 35.30' insert 'late Ep. pres. part. fem. δειδιόωσα Jo.Gaz. 2.248'

**δεικανάω II**, at end after 'Od. 18.111' insert 'χερσὶ δὲ καὶ μύθοισιν ἐδεικανόωντο A.R. 1.884'

**δείκελον 2**, add 'Parth. in *Suppl.Hell.* 653, *AP* 5.260 (Paul.Sil.), 9.505'

**+δεικηλίκτας**, α, ὁ, *actor in burlesque* or sim., Plu.*Ages.* 21 (codd. δικ-), 2.212f, Hsch. s.v. δίκηλον.

***δεικηλιστής**, οῦ, ὁ, Atticized form of δεικηλίκτας, Ath. 14.621e, f.

***Δείκνιος**, ὁ, name of a month, *SEG* 17.829.11 (provenance uncertain, *c.*200 BC).

**δείκνυμι 2**, add '**b** pf. part. pass. δεδειγμένος = *designatus*, ὕπατος [τὸ] γ', δεδειγμέ[νος] τὸ δ' *SEG* 9.165, cf. 167 (Cyrene, i AD).' **6**, line 2, for 'προθυμίαν' read 'δύναμιν'

**δεικτήριον I**, for '*place for showing*' read '*stage* or *room for a spectacle* or *exhibition*, *PPetr.* 3.142 (app. for the mysteries of Adonis), τὸ λογεῖον τοῦ δ. *SEG* 23.207 (Messenia, Augustus); applied to Theophrastus' σχολή D.L. 2.37; defined as ἄμβων or ἀκροατήριον by Bas.Sel. in *PG* 85.612D' **II**, delete the section.

**δεικτικός**, add '**III** subst. δεικτικός (sc. δάκτυλος), ὁ, *index finger*, Cael.Aur.*TP* 5.21.'

**δεικτός**, add '**3** *capable of being shown* (opp. described), *demonstrable*, Gal. 8.678.13.'

**δειλαίνω**, after 'aor. pass.' insert 'ἐὰν δὲ δειλανθῇ *if he shows himself a coward*, Lxx *1Ma.* 5.41'

**δείλαιος**, line 1, within parentheses add 'Ion. fem. -η, epigr. in *SEG* 33.849.5 (Mauretania, i AD)'; line 3, after 'S.*OT* 1347' delete '(lyr.)'

***δειλανδρία**, ἡ, *cowardice*, Suid.

**δεῖλαρ**, for 'Call.*fr.* 458' read 'Call.*fr.* 177.17 Pf.'

**δειλιάω**, add 'Ezek.*Exag.* 267 S.'

**δειμαίνω**, line 1, for 'only .. 2.439)' read 'Ep. impf. δειμαίνεσκε Q.S. 2.439: aor. part. δειμή[ναντες Euph. in *Suppl.Hell.* 428.4'; line 2, for 'Pl.*R.* 330c' read 'Pl.*R.* 330e'

**δειμός I**, add 'Chrysipp.*Stoic.* 3.123 (pl.)'

***δείμυλος**, unexpld. wd. in Theognost.*Can.* 61.

**δεῖνα I**, line 2, gen. τοῦ δεῖνατος, add '*PMich.*II 122 *passim* (i AD)'; at end after '(D.) 20.106' add 'quasi-adj. κατὰ τὴν δεῖνα πόλιν *Cod.Just.* 1.12.3.5' **II**, at end after '(Ar.) *Pax* 268' insert 'Men.*Dysc.* 897'

***δεινόθυμος**, ον, gloss, w. σχέτλιος, on οὐλόθυμος, Hsch.

***δεινολέων**, οντος, ὁ, gloss on αἰνολέων, Call. in *Suppl.Hell.* 258.21, (see also 257.21).

**δεινοπροσωπέω**, for 'περί' read 'ὑπὲρ (codd. ὑπὸ)'

***δεινόφρων**, gloss on λυκόφρων, Hsch.

**δεῖξις II**, for '*display*' read '*public performance*'

***Δεῖος**, v. ‡Δῖος; also Δεῖα, Δῖα.

**δειπνοκλήτωρ II**, add 'Παβακ τοῦ δειπνοκλήτορος *Res Gestae Saporis* p. 17 l. 58 (Persepolis, iii AD)'

**δειπνολόχος**, for '*laying .. parasite*' read '*lying in wait for a dinner*, i.e. greedy' and add 'cf. βωμολόχος'

**δεῖπνον 1**, add '**b** *sacrificial meal*, *IG* 12(7).515.53 (Amorgos, ii BC).'

**δειπνοποιέω**, med., add 'Aen.Tact. 7.3'

**δειπνοποιός**, add '*IG* 12(1).579 (Rhodes)'

**δειπνοσοφιστής**, for '*one .. kitchen*' read '*learned man at a dinner party*'

**+δειπνοφορία**, ἡ, *solemn procession with food-offerings*, in honour of Herse, Pandrosos, and Aglauros, Is.*fr.* 151; in honour of Artemis, Men.*Kith.* 95.

***δειπνοφοριακός**, ή, όν, πομπή *marked by the carrying of food-offerings*, *IEphes.* 1577.(a)9.

***δειραγχής**, ές, cj. for °δειραχθής, cf. δεραγχής.

**+δειραχθής**, ές, of a hunter's noose, *oppressing the neck*, ἅμμα *AP* 6.179 (Arch., s.v.l., v. °δειραγχής).

**δειρή**, line 2, after '(v. infr.)' insert 'ep. gen. δειρῆφι Opp.*C.* 1.176' **I 2**, add '**b** *mane* of a lion, Ael.*NA* 17.26.' **II**, for this section read '*col* of a mountain, Nic.*Th.* 502, Hermesian. 7.54 (prob.); pl., Pi.*O.* 3.27, 9.59' at end, line 2 of parenthesis, for 'Arc. δερϝά .. (Orchomenus)' read 'Arc. δερϝά *Schwyzer* 664 (Orchomenus, iv BC)'

**δειρόπαις**, for pres. def. read '*giving birth to young via the throat*'

**+δείς, δενός**, in quots. only in neut. δέν and in juxtaposition w. οὐδέν or μηδέν, *something, anything*, καὶ κ' οὐδὲν ἐκ δενὸς γένοιτο Alc. 320 L.-P., μὴ μᾶλλον τὸ δὲν ἢ τὸ μηδὲν εἶναι Democr. 156 D.-K. (back-formation fr. οὐδείς).

***δεισάης**, ές, *smelling of filth* (abusive term for a homosexual), Suet. *Blasph.* 64 T. (formed fr. δεῖσα on model of δυσαής; cf. δείσοζος).

***δεισακεία**, v. °δισάκκιον.

***δεισαλέος**, α, ον, *polluted*, Clem.Al.*Protr.* 4.55; δεισαλέον, gloss on μόλυχνον, Hsch.

**δεισιδαιμονία 1**, add '*PBonn.*inv. 2 (*JJP* 18.43, ii AD)'

***Δειφίλεια**, v. °Διφίλεια.

**δέκα**, line 1, after 'indecl.' insert 'but gen. δέκων *Schwyzer* 688.D13 (Chios, v BC); Arc. δέκο Dubois *Dial.arcad.* p. 196.6 (Pheneus, vi/v BC), cf. δυόδεκο'

***Δεκάβριος**, v. °Δεκέμβριος.

**δεκαδαρχέω**, add '*SEG* 19.742.9 (Cyrene, prob. ii AD); *SEG* 33.684 (Paros); pass. δεκαδαρχούμενοι *being ruled by a board of ten*, Sopat.Rh. 8.27.14 W.'

**δεκαδάρχης I**, = Lat. *decurio*, add 'Arr.*Tact.* 42.1'

**δεκάδαρχος I**, delete 'Plb. .. 42.1'; add '= Lat. *decurio*, Plb. 6.25.2 (gen. pl.; nom. sg. could be -άρχης), *EA* 17.26 (Cilicia), *SEG* 32.1473 (Syria, both iii AD)'

**δεκαδιστής**, add 'see also δεκατισταί'

**δεκαδύο** (s.v. δέκα), add 'also -δύω *Milet* 1(7).204*b*12 (i AD); neut. δεκαδύα *SEG* 26.672 (Larissa, *c.*200 BC)'

**δεκαέξ** (s.v. δέκα), add 'also δεκαέξε *SEG* 26.672 (Larissa, *c.*200 BC)'

**δεκαεπτά** (s.v. δέκα), add 'see also ‡δεχεπτά'

**δεκαετηρία** (s.v. -έτηρος), after 'ἡ' insert '*CIG* 8610 (Egypt, iv AD)'

**δεκαέτηρος**, add 'see also δεκέτηρος'

**δεκάζω I**, pass., add 'Ael.*VH* 2.8'

***δεκακορίνθιος**, ὁ, coin with value of 10 (Corinthian) staters, de Franciscis *Locr.Epiz.* 8 (iv/iii BC), cf. °πεντακορίνθιος.

**+δεκαμηνιαῖος**, α, ον, *amounting to ten months*, χρόνος Plu.*Num.* 12; of children born in the tenth month of pregnancy, βρέφη Alex.Aphr.*Pr.* 1.40, *IKyme* 41.19 (i BC).

**δεκάμηνος 3**, delete 'subst. δεκάμηνον, τό' and leave quots. to follow '*Placit.* 5.18.1'

**δεκάμνους**, add '(prob. as adj.) δεκάμνων (νόμισμα) X.*Lac.* 7.5'

**δεκαναῖα**, add 'Plb. 24.6.1'

***δεκανεύω**, *hold the office of* δεκανός, *decurio*, *IGBulg.* 917, 1401 *bis* (both Philippopolis, iii AD).

***δεκάξυλος**, ον, *ten* ξύλα (v. ξύλον V) *in length*, δέσμαι *OTheb.* 144 (i AD).

***δεκαπάλαστος**, ον, *ten palms long*, *Inscr.Délos* 1442*B*67 (ii BC).

**δεκάπεδον**, delete the entry.

***δεκάπεδος**, ον, *measuring ten feet*, *IG* 4².106.25, 116.12, 13, 21 (Epid., iv and iv/iii BC), etc.; τὸ δ. *per ten foot length*, ib. 109 i 127, etc.

***δεκαπενταέτης**, ές, *fifteen years old*, *GVI* 988.5 (Larissa, ii/iii BC).

***δεκαπεντάρουρος**, ὁ, *holder of fifteen* ἄρουραι, *PMich.*inv. 6167 (*ZPE* 33.200; AD 201), *Stud.Pal.* 17.23.369 (iii AD), *PVindob.Tandem* 18.16 (v/vi AD).

**δεκαπέντε** (s.v. δέκα), add 'δεκαπένδε *SEG* 6.728.66 (Perge, i BC)'

**δεκάπλεθρος**, add '*measuring ten* πλέθρα, *Inscr.Cret.* 1.v 21 (Arcades)'

***δεκαποδία**, ἡ, *space of ten feet*, *Delph.* 3(5).74 (iv BC).

**δεκάπους**, add 'also δεκάπος, ἄκαινα δ. *SEG* 37.491 (Magnesia, Thessaly, v/iv BC)'

***δεκάπρωσις** (sic), εως, ἡ, app. = δεκαπρωτεία, δ. τῆς κολω[νίας] *IGRom.* 4.222.

**δεκαπρωτεία**, for 'δεκάπρωτοι' read 'δεκάπρωτος' and for '(Syllaeum)' read '(Syllium, written -πρωτία)'

**δεκᾰπρωτεύω**, add '*Salamine* 128 (ii AD), *SEG* 34.1093 (Ephesus, ii/iii AD)'

***δεκᾰπρωτικός**, ή, όν, *having held the* δεκαπρωτεία, γένος *IGRom.* 3.406 (Pisidia).

**δεκάπρωτοι I**, add '(unless dat. of *δεκαπρώτης)'

***δεκάργῠρος**, ὁ, or -ον, τό, name of coin, *POxy.* 3874.46 (iv AD).

***δεκᾰρουρία**, ἡ, *estate of ten* ἄρουραι, *PMich.*v 238.79 (i AD).

**δεκάρτᾰβος**, after 'ἀρτάβαι' insert '*BGU* 1773.15 (i BC)'

**δεκάς I 1**, for this section read '*group* or *company of ten*, Il. 2.126, Hdt. 3.25.6; ἡ Ἀττικὴ δ. the ten Attic orators, Luc.*Scyth.* 10; of ships, A.*Pers.* 340; of slaves, *BCH* 59.453 (Chios, v/iv BC). **b** ἐτέων δ. *decade*, Call.*fr.* 1.6 Pf., *CEG* 477 (Athens, 400/390 BC), al., epigr. in *IKyzikos* 521 (i BC), etc.' add '**3** *select group*, ἧς καὶ σὺ φαίνῃ δεκάδος E.*Supp.* 219.'

**⁺δεκάσημος**, ον, *consisting of ten units*, in prosody, of short syllables, Mar.Vict. p. 49 K.; in music, of time-units, Aristid.Quint. 1.14.

**δεκαστάδιον**, for '*race-course* .. *IG* 4.951.79' read '*sign marking the distance of ten stadia*, *IG* $4^2$(1).121.79'

***δεκαστάσιος**, ον, *worth ten times its weight*, of gold as compared with silver, v.l. in Poll. 9.76, prob. in *IG* $1^3$.376.110, 122 (*NC* 10(1930).24).

***δεκάστομος**, ον, *ten-mouthed*, *Trag.adesp.* 653 K.-S. (or [δω]δεκάστομος *twelve-mouthed*).

**δεκᾰταῖος I**, for '*for ten days*' read '*of* or *appropriate to the tenth day*, i.e. having been in that condition for nine days' and add 'Gal. 9.935.14' add '**III** *of* or *belonging to a tithe* (δεκάτη), rest. in Call.*fr.* 186.3 Pf.'

**δεκᾰτάλαντος**, line 2, after 'Ar.*fr.* 276' insert 'neut. as subst., Poll. 9.54'

***δεκᾰταρχέω**, *be a* δεκάταρχος, *SEG* 33.683 (Paros, ii/i BC, new reading of *IG* 12 suppl. 210).

***δεκᾰταρχίς**, ίδος, fem. adj., *of a decurio*, δεκαταρχίδι τειμῇ *GVI* 730 (Palestine, iii AD).

**δεκάταρχος**, add '*SEG* 4.594.18 (Colophon, Rom.imp.)'

**δεκᾰτέσσᾰρες**, s.v. δέκα, add 'δεκατέταρες Lang *Ath.Agora* XXI He 2'

**δεκάτευμα**, for 'Call.*Ep.* 40' read 'Call.*Epigr.* 39 Pf.' and add '*AP* 6.290 (Diosc.)'

**δεκάτευσις**, for '*decimation*' read '*offering of every tenth man to a god*'

**⁺δεκᾰτευτής**, οῦ, ὁ, *tithe-farmer*, Antipho *fr.* 10, *IG* $2^2$.1609.97 (Athens), 7.2227.4 (Boeotia).

**δεκᾰτεύω I 1**, add 'med., *give as tithe*, ἄσσ' ἀπὸ λικμητοῦ δεκατεύεται *AP* 6.225 (Nicaenet.)' **II 2**, after '*divide into ten sections*' insert 'or (as Lat. *decuriare*) *organize into units* (v. *Athenaeum* 46.273ff.)' **III**, for 'D.ap.Harp.' read 'Did.ap.Harp. s.v. δεκατεύειν'

**δεκᾰτηφόρος**, Dor. δεκαταφόρος, add 'Cypr. *te-ka-ta-po-ro-se Kafizin* 117b, al.'

**δεκᾰτισμός**, add 'Cypr. *te-ka-[ti]-si-mo-i* δεκατισμôι prob. *collection of tithe*, *Kafizin* 266b.1'

**δέκᾰτος I**, add 'τόκος δ. *10% interest*, *SEG* 33.1041.27 (Aeolian Cyme, ii BC)' **II 1**, (δεκάτη) after '*tithe*' insert 'Eumel.*fr.* 12.1 B., τῆι Ἥρηι ἀνέθεσαν δεκάτην ἔρδοντες *SEG* 12.391 (Samos, vi BC)' **5**, add '*SEG* 24.486 (Maced., AD 114)'

***δεκᾰτός**, ή, όν, *tithed*, i.e. *subject to payment of one-tenth of one's substance*, *SEG* 9.72.34 (Cyrene, iv BC).

**⁺δεκᾰτόω**, *take tithes of* a person, Lxx *2Es.* 20.37(38), *Ep.Hebr.* 7.6; pass., ibid. 7.9.

***δεκᾰτωνέω**, *act as tithe-farmer*, *TAM* 5(1).195 (i/ii AD).

**δεκᾰτώνης**, add '*TAM* 2(1).1.19 (ii BC), Poll. 6.128'

***δεκᾰχους**, ουν, *holding ten* χόες, Arist.*Ath.* 67.2.

***Δεκέμβριος**, ὁ, *December*, ἐν τῷ Δεκεμβρίῳ Plu. 2.272d; as adj., Δεκεμβρίαις εἰδοῖς id. 2.287a, Δ. καλανδῶν Jul.*Ep.* 376a, μεὶς Δ. *SEG* 25.346 (Corinth), 33.1270 (Palestine, vi AD); Δεκάβριος *PIand.* 654.3 (*APF* 1958.14).

**δεκέτης**, line 1, for 'ου, ὁ' read 'ες'; add 'δεχέτης *GVI* 678.8 (Crete, iii/ii BC)'

**δεκήρης**, for '*with ten banks of oars*' read 'prob. *having ten oarsmen to each "room"*'

***δέκο**, v. °δέκα.

***δεκόβολον**, v. °δεκώβολον.

***δεκουρία**, ἡ, Lat. *decuria*, ἐπίλεκτον κριτὴν ἐκ τῶν ἐν Ῥώμῃ δεκουριῶν *IGRom.* 3.778.9 (Attalea).

***δεκουρίων**, ωνος, ὁ, *member of municipal council*, *IGRom.* 1.499 (Lilybaeum). **2** *cavalry officer*, *IGRom.* 3.1231 (Arabia), 1.1336 (Egypt), 4.1156 (Lydia), al. **3** *foreman of a slave household*, *IGRom.* 4.102.

***δέκρετον**, τό, Lat. *decretum*, *decree*, Just.*Nov.* 67.4, al.

**δεκτήρ**, after '*receiver*' insert 'of offerings, etc.'; add 'θυμάτων δεκτῆρα βωμόν inscr. in *SHAW* 1971.2, no. 3 (Sparta, Rom.imp.)'

**δέκτης**, add 'epigr. in *SEG* 39.443.36 (Tanagra, v AD). **II** *heir*, *IG* 9(2).522.27 (Larissa, iii/ii BC).'

**δεκτικός 1**, add '**b** *welcoming, hospitable*, πηγὴ ζ[ω]τική, δεκτική *BCH* suppl. 8 no. 103 (v AD).'

**δέκτρια**, after 'fem. of δεκτήρ' insert '*receiver, welcomer*'; for 'Archil. 19' read '*FGE* p. 149 P. (ps.-Archil., iii BC or later)'

**δεκώβολον**, for pres. ref. read '*IG* $2^2$.1537.23 (δεκώβολ[ον], iii BC)' and add '*PCair.Zen.* 111.12 (δεκόβολον, iii BC)'

**δέλεαρ**, add 'see also βλήρ'

**δέλλει**, after 'leg. βάλλει' insert 'La.'; add 'cf. ἐσδέλλω s.v. ἐκβάλλω, ζέλλω ἔζελεν'

**δέλλις** (B), for '*Annuario* 3.144 (Pisidia)' read '*SEG* 2.710.13 (Pednelissus, i BC)'

***δελμᾰτικομᾰφόριον**, etc., v. °δαλμ-.

**δέλτα I**, after 'δέλτα' insert 'Achae. 33'

***δελτικός**, ή, όν, app. *recorded on a tablet*, [δημοσί]ᾳ δελ[τ]ικῇ διαθ[ήκῃ *IEphes.* 2061 ii 22 (Rom.imp.).

**δελτογράφημα**, for '*official receipt*' read '*official document provisionally recorded on a wooden* or *wax tablet*' and add '*Chiron* 19.133.30 (Sardes, i BC), *ABSA* 59.22 no. 16 (Aphrodisias, Rom.imp.)'

**δέλτος** (B), line 1, for entry in parentheses read '(δάλτος Cypr. = δέλτος, *ta-la-to-ne* δάλτον *ICS* 217.26)' **I**, add 'δ. Διός, of *tablet* on which men's offences are conceived of as recorded, A.*fr.* 281a.21 R., E.*fr.* 506, Luc.*Merc.Cond.* 12 (pl.)'

***Δελφαῖος**, ὁ, epith. of Apollo, *IGC* p. 11.13 (Larissa, ii BC); see also °Βελφαῖον.

***δελφάκτιν**, unexpld. wd. in Choerob. *in Theod.* 1.267 H.

**⁺δέλφαξ**, ακος, ὁ, ἡ, (cf. Ath. 9.375a) *pig*, acc. to Ar.Byz.ap.Ath. l.c. full grown, opp. χοῖρος; masc., S.*fr.* 671, Cratin. 155 K.-A., Epich. 100.4, Pl.Com. 118 K.-A., Sopat. 5, Anaxil. 12 K.-A.; fem., Hippon. 145 W., Hdt. 2.70, Ar.*fr.* 520.6 K.-A., Eup. 301 K.-A., Theopomp.Com. 49 K.-A., Arist.*HA* $573^b$13, *IG* $2^2$.1367.7.

***Δελφικός**, v.s.v. Δελφοί.

***δελφίνειος**, α, ον, *of the dolphin*, στέαρ Cyran. 108 (sp. -νιος 4.17.6 K.).

***δελφῑνέλαιον**, τό, *oil of dolphin*, Cyran. 4.15.3 K.

***δελφῑνηρός**, όν, *abounding in dolphins*, A.*fr.* 150 R. (s.v.l.).

**δελφῑνοφόρος I**, delete the section (v. °δελφινηρός). **II**, add 'Poll. 1.85'

**δελφίς II 2**, for 'Opp.*H.* 3.290' read '*sinker* placed in mouth of dead fish used as bait, Opp.*H.* 3.290, 4.81'

**Δελφοί**, at end delete entry for Δέλφιος.

***δέλφον**, word alleged to be old Greek term for 'one', in etym. of ἀδελφός, Numen.*fr.*54 P.

***Δέλφῡνα**, ἡ, name for the serpent killed by Apollo, Call.*fr.* 88 Pf., also (?)Δελφύνης, ὁ, ibid.; Δελφύνη, ἡ, A.R. 2.706, Nonn.*D.* 13.28.

**δέμα I**, add '**b** *bundle*, *BGU* 2208.15 (AD 614).'

**δέμας I 3**, for '= πόσθη, Pl.Com. 173.10' read '*flesh*, as euphem. for penis, Pl.Com. 189.10 K.-A.'

**δεμάτιον**, after 'δέμα' insert '*bundle*, *Edict.Diocl.* 6.37'

**δεμελέας**, after 'δεμβλεῖς' insert '(δεμελεῖς La.)'

**δέμνιον**, add 'Myc. *de-mi-ni-ja* (pl.)'

***δεμνιοπετής**, ές, *taking to one's bed*, Nic.Dam.*fr.* 44 J.

**δέμω**, after 'pres.' insert '(*IEphes.* 3.8 (iii BC))'; at end add 'Myc. fut. part. *de-me-o-te* δεμέοντες; cf. compds. *na-u-do-mo*, *to-ko-do-mo* (v. °ναυδόμος, °τοιχοδόμος)'

***δενδρᾰχάτης**, ου, ὁ, *dendritic agate*, Plin.*HN* 37.139, Orph.*Lith.Kerygm.* 3.1 G., Socr.Dion.*Lith.* 41; paraphrased as ἀχάτης δενδρήεις Orph.*L.* 236.

**δενδρήεις I 2**, after 'ἀχάτης' insert '*dendritic* agate'

**δενδρίτης**, after 'Mart.Cap. 1.75' insert '(sc. λίθος) an Indian stone resembling coral, Cyran. 1.4.2 K., al.' **II**, delete the section

**δενδρῖτις**, add 'fem. subst., name of precious stone, Plin.*HN* 37.192'

***δενδροβάτης**, ου, ὁ, acrobat who had to *climb trees* in the amphitheatre to escape wild beasts, *Gloss.* (Lat. *arborarius*).

***δενδρόκλων**, ωνος, ὁ, *twig*, Socr.Dion.*Lith.* 19 G.

**δενδρολίβᾰνον**, for '*Gp.* 11.15 tit.' read '*Gp.* 16.1'

**δενδροτομέω**, delete 'but usu.' to end of article and substitute 'as a hostile action, Th. 1.108.2; humorously, of a flogging, δ. τὸ νῶτον Ar.*Pax* 747'

**δενδροτόμος**, add '*ZPE* 96.53 (Egypt, v/vi AD)'

**δενδροφόρος**, for 'Theodor.ap.Ath. 14.621b' read 'Sotad. 2'

**δενδρόω II 2**, for 'Plot. 3.4.1' read 'Plot. 3.4.2'

**⁺δενδρυάζω**, *dive and remain under water* (associated by popular etymology w. δρῦς), Eust. 396.29, Hsch., *EM* 256.4; fig., app. of constricted type of voice production, Ael.Dion. δ 7 E.

**δενδρύφιον**, after 'Dsc. 1.108' insert 'in statuary, *Inscr.Délos* 1416*A*i91 (ii BC)'; for '*toy tree*' read 'part of a working model made by Hero'; at end for 'Thphr.*HP* 4.7.2' read 'Thphr.*HP* 4.7.3'

**⁺δενδρύω**, *dive under water*, *IG* $4^2$(1).122.20 (Epid.); cf. °δενδρυάζω, δρυάσαι s.v. δρυάζειν, δρύεται.

***δενδρώτης**, app. masc. adj. *wooded*, Theognost.*Can.* 44.

***Δενδυρίτης·** *κροκόδειλος* Hsch. (La.); (app. = Egyptian ethnic *Τεντυρίτης*).

***δεξάριον,** *τό*, perh. some kind of female ornament, *δεξάρια ζυγὴν* [*μίαν*] *PSI* 183.6 (v AD).

***δεξίαμα,** *ατος*, *τό*, v.l. for *δεξίωμα*, E.*fr.* 324.1 (*PRoss.-Georg.* 1.9), S.*OC* 619.

***δεξιοκοιτέω,** *sleep on the right side, Physici* ii p. 195.

**δεξιόομαι I,** at end after 'E.*Rh.* 419' insert 'Men.*Dysc.* 948'

**δεξιός I,** at end after '*δεξιά* as adv.' for 'Plb. 3.82.9 (s.v.l.)' read 'E.*Hipp.* 1360' **IV,** after 'Pl.*Hipparch.* 225c' insert '*τὴν καλλίπαιδα, τὴν τρόπον* [*τε*] *δεξιάν* epigr. in *SEG* 36.293 (Athens, iii AD)' at end add 'Myc. *de-ki-si-wo*, pers. n.'

***δεξιόχωλος,** *ον*, *lame in the right leg*, (*dexiocholus* in Lat.), Mart. 12.59.9 (s.v.l.).

**δέξις I,** add 'Pl.*Lg.* 761d'

**δεξίωμα II,** after 'S.*OC* 619' insert '(v.l. °*δεξίαμα*)'

***Δεξίων,** *ὁ*, title said to have been given to Sophocles after his death, *ἀπὸ τῆς τοῦ Ἀσκληπιοῦ δεξιώσεως EM* 256.7.

**δέον,** add '*τὰ δέοντα necessaries, maintenance, PMich.*x 587.8 (AD 24/5), *UPZ* 42.45 (AD 162)'

**δέος,** line 12, after 'Th. 3.33' insert 'folld. by *τοῦ μή* w. inf. Hld. 1.33.4'

**δέπας,** line 3, after 'Stes. 7' insert 'A.*fr.* 74 R.'; add 'form **δίπας*, Myc. *di-pa* (*di-pa-e*, dual), *vessel with up to four handles*'

***δέπυρα,** v. °*γέφυρα*.

**δεράγχη,** for '*collar*' read '*noose*'; for 'Antip.' read 'Antip.Sid.'

**δεραγχής,** add 'see also °*δειραγχής*'

**δέραιον,** *collar*, add 'Arr.*Cyn.* 5.8'

**δεραιοπέδη,** for '*collar*' read 'kind of snare for birds'

***δεραιοῦχος,** *ον*, of a noose, *neck-holding*, *AP* 7.473 ( Aristodic., cj.).

**δερβιστήρ,** add 'cf. *δεριστήρ*'

***δέριον·** *torquis*, Charis. p. 40 K. (var. of *δέραιον*).

**δεριστήρ,** add 'cf. *δερβιστήρ*'

***δέρκηθρον,** *τό*, unexpld. wd., Ph.Epic. in *Suppl.Hell.* 683.2.

**δέρκομαι,** line 1, after 'Hsch.' insert 'epigr. in *Didyma* 567.1 (ii/i BC) and perh. in Pi.*fr.* 52w(i) S.-M.' **I 2,** add '**c** of mental perception, *τὴν σὺ νόῳ δέρκευ* Emp. 17.21 D.-K.'

**δέρμα,** after lemma insert 'Delph. *δάρμα* q.v.'

**δερμᾰτηρά,** add '*ὠνὴν δερματηρᾶς PColl.Youtie* 32.7 (AD 199)'

⁺**δερμᾰτίκιον,** v. ‡*δαλμ-*.

**δερμᾰτιον,** add '*PCair.Zen.* 353.15 (iii BC)'

***δερμᾰτόκολλα,** *ἡ*, *glue extracted from skins*, Anon.Alch. 380.10.

***δερμορράφιον,** *τό*, large kind of needle, Sch.Ar.*Pl.* 301 (*Mnemos.* (ser. 4) 10.58).

⁺**δέρρις,** *εως*, *ἡ*, also *δέρσις* Th. 2.75.5, *curtain, screen* of skin or hide, later of any material, Eup. 357 K.-A., Pl.Com. 267 K.-A., Myrtil. 1 K.-A., Lxx *Ex.* 26.7, al., *IG* 5(1).1390.35 (Andania, i BC). **2** hung before fortifications to check missiles, Th. l.c., Ph.*Bel.* 95.34, *AP* 12.33 (Mel.), D.S. 20.9, Apollod.*Poliorc.* 142.2, Polyaen. 3.11.13. **b** on shipboard as a protection against waves, Cic.*Att.* 4.19.1. **II** *cloak* or sim., perh. fr. similarity to Hebr. *aderet*, Lxx *Za.* 13.4.

**δέρω,** line 7, after 'Il. 23.167' insert 'of Marsyas, *δεδαρμένον* Timocl. 19.1 K.-A.'

**δέσις I,** add 'also perh. *soldering*, *MAMA* 8.430' **III,** delete the section.

⁺**δέσκαλος,** v. °*διδάσκαλος*.

***δέσμευσις,** *εως*, *ἡ*, *binding*, *τοῦ χόρτου PCair.Zen.* 180 (iii BC).

**δεσμεύω II,** delete the section.

**δέσμη 2,** add '*PCair.Zen.* 782 b.5, *PZen.Col.* 113.12 (both iii BC), *PYale* 38.8'

**δεσμίδιον,** for '(= *δέσμη* 2b)' read '*small bundle*' and add 'Erasistr.ap.Gal. 11.215.5'

**δεσμός I 2,** sg. collect., add 'A.*Pr.* 97, *fr.* 190 R., E.*Hipp.* 1237, (the state of) *being bound*, Pl.*R.* 378d, 390c' **4,** add 'perh. also Call.*fr.* 191.41 Pf. (v. addenda)' at end add 'Myc. *de-so-mo*, prob. *belt* for sword'

***δεσμοφῠλᾰκέω,** *to be a gaoler*, *PCair.Zen.* 354.11 (iii BC).

**δεσμοφύλαξ,** after '*gaoler*' insert '*PTeb.* 777.5, 791.17 (pl.) (both ii BC), *Dura* [7,8] p. 171 no. 875 (ii AD)'

**δέσποινα 3,** add 'pl. *Δέσποιναι*, of Demeter and Kore, Paus. 5.15.4, 10; *IG* 5(1).230 (Sparta)'

**δεσπόσυνος II 1,** add '*AP* 12.169 (Diosc.), *Laodicée* p. 362 no. 19 (i AD); of a praetor, Bernand *IMEG* 24.8 (Egypt, ii AD)'

**δεσποτεύω,** add '**b** *rule as bishop*, *Ann.Épigr.* 1971.454 (Lesbos, v AD).'

**δεσπότης I 1,** line 2, after '*lord*' insert 'Tyrt. 7.1 W., Sapph. 95.8 L.-P., etc.'; line 4, after '(A.)*Pers.* 169' insert '*δέσποτα πάτερ POxy.* 3356.13 (i AD)' **3,** add '*θεῷ δεσπότῃ Πλούτωνι EAM* 15 (ii AD)'

**δεσποτικός I 2,** *imperial*, add '*ἐπίτροπος χωρίων δεσποτικῶν IG* 10(2).1.351.3 (Thessalonica, iv AD). **b** neut. subst., some form of tax or payment, *JÖAI* 1 *Beibl.* 115; pl., *CPR* 7.26.20 (vi AD).'

**δεσπότις,** add 'epith. of the nymph at Kafizin, *Kafizin* 9 (iii BC), al.'

**δεῦμα,** delete the entry.

**δεῦρο,** after 'Aeol. *δεῦρυ*' insert 'prob. in Sapph. 2.1 L.-P., cf.' line 3, delete 'late *δευρεί* .. iv/v BC)' (v. *Tyche* 7.225) **I 2 d,** delete the section transferring quot. to section 2 c. at end add 'in Myc. compd. *de-we-ro* (*-a$_3$-ko-ra-i-ja*), name of district'

**δευσοποιός,** after '*δ. φάρμακα*' insert '*Trag.adesp.* 441 K.-S.'

**δεύτᾰτος,** delete 'prob. f.l. in' and after 'Pi.*O.* 1.50' insert '*AP* 5.108 (Crin.)'

**δεῦτε,** line 4, delete 'rarely'; for 'Sapph. 60, 65' read 'Sapph. 53, 128 L.-P., *Lyr.adesp.* 286 ii 8 S.'; line 5, after 'E.*Med.* 894' insert 'and Com., *δ. δή* Men.*Dysc.* 866'

**δευτερᾰγωνιστέω,** for '*play second-class parts*' read '*act in the second role* in a play'

⁺**δευτερᾰγωνιστής,** *ὁ*, *actor who takes the second role*; transf., *one who speaks second in support of a case*, D. 19.10, Luc.*Peregr.* 36, Hsch.

***δευτεραρχέω,** *to be the second magistrate*, prob. in *JÖAI* 23 *Beibl.* 121 ([*δευ*]*τερ-*, Thrace, Rom.imp.).

**δευτερεύω,** add '**b** *hold the position of second-in-command* or *deputy*, *UPZ* 2.159.13 (iii BC).'

**δευτεροβόλος,** for '*shedding the teeth a second time*' read '*having shed the second group of teeth, i.e. the medial incisors*'

***δευτερογᾰμέω,** *marry for the second time*, Just.*Nov.* 2.2.1, al.

***δευτερόγᾰμος,** *ον*, *married for the second time*, Just.*Nov.* 137.1.

**δεύτερος I 2,** line 6, for 'X.*Cyr.* 2.2.1' read 'X.*Cyr.* 2.2.2' **II 1,** line 3, for 'very much *behind*' read 'easily *second to*'; line 5, delete '*δ. παιδὸς σῆς* E.*Tr.* 618' **2,** neut. as adv., *twice*, add 'Just.*Nov.* 137.4'

⁺**δευτερόω,** *do a second time, repeat*, *περὶ δὲ τοῦ δευτερῶσαι τὸ ἐνύπνιον* Lxx *Ge.* 41.32, *λόγον Si.* 7.14, *ὁδόν*, i.e. go back, *Je.* 2.36; ellipt., 1*Ki.* 26.8, *ἐὰν δευτερώσητε, ἐκτενῶ τὴν χεῖρά μου ἐν ὑμῖν* 2*Es.* 23.21. **II** *to be second*, dub. in Lxx *Je.* 52.24 (v.l. *δευτερευ-*).

**δευτήρ,** for '*kettle, cauldron*, Demiopr.' read '*vessel for mixing a dry mass with liquid*, Demiopr.' and for 'cf. *δεῦμα*' read 'cf. *δεύω* (A) I 2'

**δεύω** (A) **I 2,** add '*Inscr.Perg.* 8(3).161 (ii AD)'

**δεύω** (B) **I,** at end after '(Eresus)' insert 'Alc. 117(*b*).30 L.-P.' and for 'Alc. *Oxy.* 1788.15 ii 3' read 'id. 119.5 L.-P.' **II,** line 2, after 'Od. 6.192' insert 'part. (athematic inflexion) *δεύμενος* Sophr. 36, *BCH* 59.38 (Crannon)'; add '*οὐδέ τι θυμὸς ἐδεύετο δαιτὸς ἐΐσης* Il. 1.468, al., Od. 16.479, al.'

**δεχεπτά,** add '*SEG* 33.1475 (Cyrenaica, i/ii AD); cf. *δεκαεπτά* s.v. *δέκα*'

***δεχέτης,** v. °*δεκέτης*.

**δέχομαι,** line 1, *δέκομαι*, add 'also Dor. *SEG* 30.1123 (Sicily, iii BC); Arc., *SEG* 37.340.10 (Mantinea, iv BC)'; line 2, for 'impf.' read 'aor.'; line 10, imper. *δέξο*, add '*h.Merc.* 312, Orph.*H.* 18.3'; line 11, inf. *δέχθαι*, add 'Il. 1.23' **I,** line 6, *accept* as legal tender, add '*SEG* 26.72 (Athens, 375/4 BC)' **II 1,** add '*receive* sexually, *πρὸς ἔργον ἀφροδίσιον ἐλθόντ' ἑταῖρον ὀντινῶν ἐδέξατο* Semon. 7.49 W.' at end add 'Myc. aor. med. (*o-*)*de-ka-sa-to*, also *de-ko-to*, cf. *δέκτο*'

**δέω** (A), line 3, after 'And. 4.17 (prob.)' insert 'intr. pf. *δέδηα*, *to be bound*, Nic.*Al.* 436'; line 10, after 'Din.*fr.* 89.15' insert 'v. °*καταδέω*' at end add 'Myc. pf. part. pass. *de-de-me-no*'

**δέω** (B), line 6, after '*√δεϝ*' insert 'cf. *δεύω* (B) I' **I 2,** add 'w. fut. inf. Pl.*Ap.* 37b' **II,** delete 'part. *δεύμενος* id. 36' (v. °*δεύω* (B)) **1 b,** add 'w. acc. and inf., *εἰ μὲν γὰρ μηδὲν δέονται χρηστοὺς αὐτοὺς εἶναι* Isoc. 11.43'

**δή,** line 6, after 'A.*Th.* 214 (lyr.)' insert 'also *δὴ τότε δή*, Opp.*C.* 2.271, Q.S. 10.224, Orph.*A.* 1270, Nonn.*D.* 22.299'

**δῆγμα I,** add '**2** *tooth* of a fish-hook, Opp.*H.* 4.444 (pl.).'

**δηγμός 2,** after 'Thphr.*HP* 4.4.5' insert 'Nic.*Al.* 119 (sp. *δηχμός*)'

**δηθά,** after '(Il.) 5.587' insert 'Od. 1.49, 120, 2.255, al.'

**δῆθεν II,** add 'Luc.*Alex.* 39, Ach.Tat. 2.1.1, Aen.Tact. 11.4, *Cod.Just.* 1.3.44.5, etc.'

**δηϊόω,** line 12, delete 'said by Sch. .. Eumel.(*fr.* 9)' and insert '*δῄιον AP* 6.122.4 (Nic.)'

***δηκόκτα,** *ἡ*, Lat. *decocta, decoction*, Gal. 10.467.17.

***δηλάβρα,** *ἡ*, fr. Lat., *winnowing-fan*, *δ. ἤτοι πτύον Edict.Diocl.* 15.44; cf. *πτύον· ventilabrum, delabrum, Gloss.* 2.425.47, *delabra: ption* ib. 522.25.

**δηλᾰδή,** add 'D.Chr. 9.13, *Cod.Just.* 1.3.52.15, etc.'

***δηλάτωρ,** *ὁ*, Lat. *delator, informer*, *BCH* 59.152 (Philippi).

**δηληγᾰτεύω,** add '*SEG* 32.1554.A49, 56 (Arabia, vi AD), Just.*Nov.* 130.5 (cf. Lat. *delegatio, delego*)'

**δηλητήριος,** *δ. τό*, *poison*, add 'M.Ant. 6.36.2'

**δηλητηριώδης,** after '*noxious*' insert 'Zos.Alch. 201.15'

**Δήλιος,** add '**V** *Δάλιος* (sc. *μήν*) *ὁ*, name of a month, *Inscr.Cos* 30.1, 367.55, *Lindos* 465 i (ii AD), *Tit.Calymn.* 88.46, etc., *SEG* 25.1110 (Cyprus, Hell.).'

°**Δηλίτης**, *καὶ Δηλίτης ὁ εἰς Δῆλον ἐρχόμενος χορός, Καλλίμαχος* St.Byz. (s.v. *Δῆλος*).

**δῆλος III**, for '*Urim*' read '*symbols of revelation* of the Urim' and after 'Lxx' insert '*Nu.* 27.21'

**δηλόω**, after lemma insert 'Arc. aor. inf. *δεϝαλῶσαι SEG* 37.340.21 (Mantinea, iv BC)' **II 2**, line 2, for '*δηλώσει* .. *R.* 497c' read 'so perh. *δηλώσει* Pl.*R.* 497c'

**δήλωσις 3**, for '*Urim*' read '*symbol of revelation* of the Urim' and add '(Lxx) *Ex.* 28.30, 1*Es.* 5.40'

°**Δημαρχεξούσιος**, *ὁ*, name of month (Apr./May) in an Augustan calendar from Cyprus, Madrid MS. in *JÖAI* 8.112 (-*εξάσιος*), *IGRom.* 3.930 (Soloi, prob. i AD); named *Δήμαρχος* acc. to *Hemerolog.Flor.*, v. *YCLS* 2.213.

**δημαρχία**, add '**III** [*θ*]*εοί· δημαρχία ἡ μέζων*, heading of an Attic sacrificial calendar, precise significance disputed, *Sokolowski* 3.18 (Erchiae, iv BC).'

**δήμαρχος 1 b**, add 'in Egypt, Hdt. 3.6' **2**, after '*plebis*' insert '*SIG* 601 (Teos, 193 BC), *SEG* 31.1300 (Lycia, ii AD)' add '**II** v. °*Δημαρχεξούσιος*.'

**δηματρεύεσθαι**, add '(*δημαστ-* La.; app. corruption of *δηθὰ στρεύγεσθαι* Il. 15.512)'

°**δημεκδικέω**, *to be a* °*δημέκδικος*, *ACO* 3.102.19 (vi AD).

°**δημέκδικος**, *ὁ*, = Lat. *defensor civitatis, public advocate*, *PMasp.* 353$^{v}$.A26 (vi AD).

**δημεύω I**, pass., later of persons, delete 'later' and insert '*αἴ τις* .. *ἒ δικάσ*[*ζοι*] *ἒ δικάσζοιτο* .. *τρέτō καὶ δαμευέσθō ἐνς Ἀθāναίαν* .. *have his property confiscated for the benefit of Athena*, *IG* 4.554.5 (Argos, vi/v BC)' **III**, add '*τὰ κοινὰ καὶ δεδημευμένα* Plu. 2.243d'

**δημεχθής**, for 'Call.*fr.* 472' read 'Call.*fr.* 486 Pf.' and add '*Trag.adesp.* 337a K.-S.'

**δημηγορικός**, for '*suited to public speaking* .. X.*Mem.* 1.2.48' read '*of, concerned with* or *typical of public* (*political*) *speaking*, *οὐχ ἵνα δημηγορικοὶ ἢ δικανικοὶ γένοιντο* X.*Mem.* 1.2.48'; line 3, delete '*popular*'

**Δημήτηρ**, line 1, after 'Arc.' insert 'Cypr.' **1**, add 'used in pl. for Demeter and Kore, *Δαματέρων καὶ Διὸς Δαματρίου Lindos* 183 (ii BC), *Δαμάτερσιν οἶν κνεῦσαν* ib. 671 (Camirus, i BC)'

°**Δημητρίειος** *δραχμή*, coin minted by Demetrius Poliorcetes, *Inscr.Magn.* 33.20.

**Δημητριών**, after '*SIG* 380' insert 'at Chalcidice, *SEG* 37.576.5 (?Polichne, iv BC)'

°**δημήτρουλος**, *ὁ*, *hymn in honour of Demeter*, Semus 23 J.; cf. *οὖλος* (D), *καλλίουλος*.

**δημιόπρāτα**, before 'Ar.*V.* 659' insert '*δēμιόπρατα IG* $1^3$.85.3'; add 'Ion. *-πρητ- Inscr.Délos* 72 (v BC)'

°**δημιοπρᾱ́της**, v. ‡*δημοπράτης*.

**δήμιος**, line 1, delete '*δημίην* .. (Cypr.)' **I**, add 'advs. *-ίως*, *-ιωστί*, Theognost.*Can.* 160, Eust. 1899.57. **2** *οἱ δάμιοι*, magistrates at Dreros, *Meiggs-Lewis* 2 (Dreros, vii/vi BC).' **II 1**, add '*OAshm. Shelton* 51' add '**3** *δημίην Κύπριν· πόρνην* Hsch.La. (cod. *δημίην· πόρνην. Κύπριοι*); cf. *Δημίασι πύλαις· κοιναῖς, ἐπεὶ προεστήκεσαν ἐν ταῖς πύλαις αἱ πόρναι* Hsch. (for other expls. v. Hsch. s.v.).' **III**, for this section read '*vulgar, coarse*, *δήμια λαβράζουσι* Nic.*Al.* 160' at end add 'form *δᾱ́μιος*, Myc. *da-mi-jo*'

**δημιουργέω**, after lemma insert 'dial. *δᾱμιοϝοργέω*, *δᾱμιοργέω*, Cyren. *δᾱμιεργέω*' **II a**, *hold office of δημιουργός*, add '*ἐπὶ τōνδεōνὲν δᾱμιοργόντōν SEG* 11.314 (Argos, vi BC); *κὰ ὄζις τότε δᾱμιοϝοργε̄ͅ* Dubois *Dial.arcad.* p. 196 (Pheneus, *c.*500 BC); *ἰν τῶι ὕστερον ϝέτ*[*ε*]*ι ἠ Νικῆς ἐδαμιόργη SEG* 37.340.23 (Mantinea, iv BC); athematic part. *δᾱμιεργέντων SEG* 9.11.2, 12.2 (Cyrene, iv BC)'

**δημιούργημα**, line 3, for 'Jul.*Or.* 2.54b' read 'Jul.*Or.* 2.54a'; line 5, for 'Ph. 1.208' read 'Ph. 1.207'

**δημιουργία II**, add '*SEG* 30.1518 (Side, iii AD)'

°**δημιουργίς**, *ίδος*, *ἡ*, (sc. *ἀρχή*) *office of δημιουργός*, *ὑπὲρ τῆ*[*ς*] *δ*[*η*]*μιου*[*ρ*]*γίδος MAMA* 3.103; see also °*δαμιοργίς*.

**δημιουργός I 1**, line 6, after 'Pl.*R.* 529e' insert 'Call.*Dieg.* vii.30 (*fr.* 196 Pf.)'; line 7, delete 'Men. 518.12 (fem.)' and after 'Alexandr.Com. 3' insert 'esp. fem. of the bridal attendant who made wedding cakes, Men.*fr.* 451.12 K.-Th., Poll. 3.41, Sch.Ar.*Eq.* 647' **II**, *δᾱμιοργός*, add 'Locr., *IG* $9^2$(1).609.22 (Naupactus, *c.*500 BC), 717.15 (Chalium, v BC), Arc., *SEG* 37.340.20 (Mantinea, iv BC); also of women, *IGRom* 3.794, 802 (Pamphylia)' **III**, delete the section.

°**δημιωστί**, v. °*δήμιος*.

°**δημογραμμᾰτεύς**, *έως*, *ὁ*, title of local government official, *Cod.Just.* 10.71.4.

**δημοεγερτής**, delete 'Suid.' and substitute 'Suet.*Blasph.* 83 T.'

**δημόθεν I 2**, after '*people*' insert 'Call.*fr.* 93.15 Pf.' and add '**III** *from the town*, *AP* 9.316.2 (Leon.Tarent.).'

**δημοθοινέω**, add '*SEG* 30.340 (Aegina, ii AD)'

**δημοθοινία**, add 'sp. *δημοθυνία IStraton.* 202.19, 266.23, al.'

°**δημοκατάρᾱτος**, *ον*, *cursed by the people*, Thd.*Pr.* 11.26.

°**δημοκῆρυξ**, '*υκος*, *ὁ*, *public herald*, *MAMA* 4.351 (Eumeneia).

**δημόκοινος 1**, add 'transf., *ἀνδροφόνων καὶ δημοκοίνων θίασος* Ph. 2.559'

°**δημόκομπος**· *στωμύλος* Suid. (perh. *-κόπος*).

°**δημοκόπιον**, *τό*, = *δημοκοπία*, *POxy.* 2400.5 (iii AD).

°**δημοκοπίς**, *ίδος*, *ἡ*, *ἣν δὲ καί τι ὑπόδημα*, *δημοκοπίδες* Poll. 7.89 (s.v.l.).

**δημοκόπος**, for 'Ph. 2.47' read 'Ph. 2.520'

**δημοκρᾰτία II**, for 'Paus. 1.3.2' read 'Paus. 1.3.3'

⁺**Δημοκρίτειος**, *ον*, *of Democritus of Abdera*, *ἡ Δημοκρίτειος φιλοσοφία* S.E.*P.* 1.213; masc. subst., *follower of Democritus*, Ael.*VH* 12.25; pl., Plu. 2.1108e.

**δημοποιήτος**, add 'Aeschin.*Ep.* 12.13'

**δημοπρᾱ́της**, add 'vv.ll. *δημιοπράτης*, *δημοπράτα*'

°**δημόπρᾱτος**, *ον*, *sold as state property*, Ph. 2.539; cf. *δημιόπρατα*.

**δῆμος III 1**, personified, add '*IHistriae* 19.14 (ii BC), '*Ηλίωι καὶ τῶι Δήμωι ICilicie* 83 (ii/i BC), *εἰς τὸ ἐράριν δήμου Ῥωμαίων Laodicée* p. 325, *Δήμῳ Ῥωμαίων SEG* 30.1253 (Aphrodisias, i AD), *IEryth.* 32, 33, al., etc.' **IV**, add 'transl. Lat. *vicus*, *IEphes.* 4101 (ii AD)' at end add 'form *δᾶμος*, Myc. *da-mo*, prob. *a body of people, community*'

°**δημοσάριος**, *ον*, app. fr. °*δημοσιάριος*, *belonging to the state*, *τὸ δημοσάρδριον POxy.* 3423.12.

**δημοσιεύω I**, add '**6** *make publicly known, expose*, *Cod.Just.* 1.1.3.3, Just.*Edict.* 7.2 pr.' **II**, before 'Ar.*Ach.* 1030' insert '*IG* $1^3$.164.13 (440/25 BC)' add '**2** *appear before the people*, Just.*Nov.* 161.1.1.'

**δημόσιος I 1 a**, line 5, after '(Halic.)' insert '*οἱ δ. θεοὶ Sokolowski* 1.79.3 (?Pednelissus, i BC)'; add 'stamped on vessels, weights, etc,. to denote public ownership, *SEG* 31.374 (v/iv BC), *Ἀργείων δᾱμόσιον* 36.332 (Nemea, Hellen.), etc.' **2**, add '= *δημοτικός* I 1, *γράμματα IG* 12(5).14.6 (Ios, ii/iii AD)' **III 1**, neut., add '**e** pl., *public lands*, *IG* $9^2$(1).609.3 (Naupactus, *c.*500 BC).' **2 a**, add 'sg., *SEG* 33.679 (Paros, ii BC)' **b**, add 'Just.*Nov.* 128.10, al.' add '**c** *public sacrifices* or *victims*, *IG* $1^3$.35.12 (Athens, v BC), *SEG* 31.416.29 (w. rhotacism, *δημορίōν*, Oropus, iv BC), etc. **d** ?*public affairs* or *business*, *SEG* 30.380 (Tiryns, vii BC). **e** *public baths*, sg., R. Stillwell *Antioch-on-the-Orontes* (1933-6) no. 112; (-*ιν*), pl., *CRAI* 1945.379.9 (Berytus, Byz.).'

⁺**δημοσιουργία**, v. ‡*δᾱμοσιοργία*.

**δημοσιόω**, after lemma insert 'Elean 3 sg. opt. *δᾱμοσιοίᾱ*, pres. inf. *δᾱμοσιῶμεν Schwyzer* 424 (Olympia, iv BC)'

°**δημοσιωνικός**, *ή*, *όν*, *νόμος* law *relating to revenue-leases*, *SEG* 14.639.A11, al. (Caunus, i AD), 35.1439.16 (Myra, Lycia, ii AD).

**δημοσιώνιον**, after '*office*' insert '(building)' and add '*SEG* 35.1439.5 (Lycia, ii AD)'

**δημοσίωσις**, add '**2** *engagement in public affairs*, Vett.Val. 1.7.'

°**δημόσῠνος**, *η*, *ον*, = *δημόσιος*; *-η* prob. *at public expense*, *IG* $2^2$.4658 (Athens, iv/iii BC).

**δημοσώστης**, add '*SEG* 16.428.7 (Callatis, i AD), *ITomis* 19(b).5 (ii/iii AD)'

**δημοτελής I 2**, add '*SEG* 33.679 (Paros, ii BC)'

**δημότερος**, after lemma insert 'perh. Cypr. *ta-mo-te-ro-ne δᾱμοτέρōν* (gen. pl.) *Kourion* 218 (v BC)' **I**, for 'poet. for .. 3.606' read '*of the land*, *γυναῖκες* A.R. 1.783; abs., id. 3.606 (v.l. *δημογέρουσιν*); Dor. *δᾱμο-* Call.*fr.* 228.71 Pf.'

°**δημότευκτος**, *ον*, *furnished by the people*, *λίθοι Sardis* 7(1).181 (i AD).

**δημοτεύομαι**, for 'pass.' read 'med.' and add 'Dor. *δᾱμ-* rest. in *BCH* 50.17 vii 4 (Law of Cadys, Delphi, iv BC)'

**δημότης II**, add 'opp. *ξένος*, *SEG* 31.416.9 (= *IG* 7.235, Boeotia, iv BC)'

**δημοτικός II 1**, add '**b** *τὸ -όν*, *the populace*, Just.*Nov.* 102.2.'

°**δημοφίλητος**, *ον*, as honorific title, *beloved of the people*, *ἀρχίατρος καὶ δ. IGBulg.* 150 (Odessus).

**δημοχᾰ́ρης**, add 'epigr. in *ICilicie* 49 (iii/iv AD)'

⁺**δήμωμα**, v. ‡*δαμώματα*.

**δημωφελής**, adv. *-λῶς*, for '(Iotapata)' read '(Iotape)'

⁺**Δήν, Δῆνα**, v. *Ζεύς*, lines 15/6.

**δήν**, line 1, within the parentheses add 'see also *δαόν*' **1**, (p. 388), delete 'cf. 16.736, δ. *δὴ* .. *φίλοι ὦμεν* Thgn. 1243' add '**3** perh. in local sense *far away*, Thgn. 494, 597; w. gen., *far away* from, Il. 16.736.'

**δηναιός I 1**, neut. as adv., add 'A.R. 1.334, 3.590' **II**, for this section read '*occurring, coming*, etc., *after a long time, late*, *δηναιοὶ* .. *εἰσαφίκοντο* A.R. 4.645, (*τὰ ἱρὰ*) *δηναιὰ πατὴρ ἐκόμισσεν* Maiist. 8, *δηναιὸν ἀδελφεὸν* .. *νοστήσαντα* Opp.*H.* 4.154'

**δηνάριον**, add '*IG* 9(2).1092 (Thessaly); also **δινάριον** *Inscr.Délos* 1439*Abc*83, 1441*Ai*89, 1449*Aab*ii23, 36 (ii BC); *δειν-* *IG* 9(2).1104.14 (Thessaly, i BC), etc. **2** collect., *Roman money*, δ. *χρυσοῦν καὶ ἀργυροῦν Peripl.M.Rubr.* 8, 49.'

°**δηπόσιτον**, *τό*, Lat. *depositum*, *PSI* 1063.5 (ii AD).

°**δηποτᾶτος**, masc. adj. Lat. *deputatus*, *sent from the provinces to the*

*Emperor*, ἑκατόνταρχον δε[σ]ποτᾶτον *centurio d.*, *IApam.* 8.5 (iii AD).

**δήποτε 1**, delete αἰεὶ δ. Th. 8.73; *at length*' add '**b** *sometimes*, Nic.*Th.* 683, *Al.* 133, 383.' **2**, add '**b** αἰεὶ δ., *always, whenever it might be*, Th. 8.73.5.'

**δηριάομαι**, penultimate line, for 'οὐκ ἄν τοί' read 'οὐκ ἄν οἱ θηρῶν'

**δῆρις**, after 'A.*Supp.* 412' delete '(lyr.)'; after '(only in acc.)' insert 'Hes.*Sc.* 241, 251, Ibyc. 30(*b*) P., B. 5.111 S.-M.; of athletic contests, Hes.*Sc.* 306 (all acc.)'

***δησέρτωρ**, ορος, ὁ, Lat. *desertor*, *PFlor.* 362.3 (iv AD).

***δησιστάχυς**, υος, ὁ, *binder of corn*, orac. in Paus. 8.42.6 (cj.).

**δῆτα**, line 4, after 'answers' insert 'or in corroboration of what has been said'; line 8, after '(lyr.)' insert 'E.*El.* 673, 676'; lines 11/12, delete 'also .. cf. 676'

***δητύω**, ἐδήτυεν· διεῖλεν, διῄρει Hsch.

***δηφήνσωρ**, ορος, ὁ, Lat. *defensor*, *PLips.* 35.12 (iv AD), *PHerm.* 19.4 (iv AD), 69.3 (v AD).

***δηχμός**, v. ‡δηγμός.

***Δηωΐς**, ίδος, ἡ, *daughter of Deo* or *Demeter*, i.e. *Persephone*, *Didyma* 496*B*11 (ii AD); cf. Δηωΐνη.

**διά**, line 2, after 'anastroph.' insert '(but after its case in Hes.*Op.* 3, Tyrt. 4.2)'; lines 3/4, delete 'also .. which' **A I 1**, add '**b** *for a distance of*, φόρετρον δ. σχοίνων γ' *PMich.*III 145 III col.v.9 (ii AD); cf. 3, 5.' **III 2**, line 2, after 'thing is made' insert '*AP* 6.282 (Theod.), Plb. 14.1.15'; add 'in Marcell.Emp. 8.199, 210, al., collyria are named διὰ μίσυος, δ. χολῆς (diamisyos, diacholes), etc.' **IV a**, line 5, after 'δι' ἀπεχθείας γίγνεσθαι' insert '(i.e. *become an object of hatred*)'; add 'δι' εὐχῆς εἶναι *to be the object of one's prayer*, *PBremen* 20.6 (ii AD), *Aegyptus* 15.267 (ii/iii AD); διὰ σπουδῆς εἶναι Ael.*NA* 7.45, al.' **C**, for 'δ. πρό (v. supr. A I 1)' read 'δ. πρό (v. °διαπρό)'

**διαβάλλω II**, for 'αὐτῷ' read 'αὐτῇ' and for 'him' read 'it (the πόλις)' **III**, line 7, delete 'Hdt. 8.22'; line 9, after 'Isoc. 15.175' insert 'πρὸς τὴν ὠμότητα τοῦ υἱοῦ διαβληθείς Luc.*Macr.* 14, Arr. *Epict.* 2.26.3'; transfer '*to be brought into discredit* .. Lys. 7.27, 8.7' to section v 1 line 8 (after 'Pass.') **V 1**, lines 7/8, delete 'or πρός' and '*Macr.* 14' **VII**, delete the section.

**διάβασις 2**, delete '*bridge*'

**διαβήτης 2**, for 'cf. ib. 2.1054.10' substitute 'ὀρθοὺς πρὸς τὸν διαβήτην πανταχῆι *Inscr.Délos* 104-4.7 (iv BC)'

***διαβητικός**, ή, όν, *made straight by rule*, *Stud.Pal.* 20.211.9 (v/vi AD, v. *ZPE* 71.117).

**διαβήτινος**, delete the entry.

***διαβήτρια**, ἡ, a kind of priestess, Μητερείνῃ διαβητρίᾳ Περασίας *EA* 19.20 (Mopsuestia, ii AD).

**⁺διαβιάζομαι**, *force a way through*, τῶν φλεβῶν διαβιαζόμενον καὶ ξυνεπίστρεφον sc. πνεῦμα Pl.*Ti.* 84d; of plants penetrating the soil in germination, Thphr.*CP* 2.17.7; abs., *advance with force*, Lxx *Nu.* 14.44. **2** w. inf., *compel* to go, etc., E.*IT* 1365. **II** *overcome, master*, δ. τὴν ἀσθένειαν τῇ συνηθείᾳ τῇ πρὸ τοῦ Plb. 23.12.2.

**διαβιβρώσκω**, line 1, after 'Gal. 13.553' insert 'aor. 3 pl. διέβρον (?read -ων) Call.*fr.* 177.31 Pf.'

**διαβοάω**, line 5, for '(Plu.)*Per.* 9' read '*Per.* 19'

**διαβουλία**, delete the entry transferring refs. (both gen. pl.) to διαβούλιον I.

**διαβρεχής**, add '(cod., v.l. -βραχής, cj. -βραχείς, aor. part. of διαβρέχω)'

***διαβρύκω** or **-βρύχω**, *gnaw through* or *utterly devour*, πρῶτον γάρ μιν ἐλοῦσα γαλῆ μέσσον διέβρυξεν *PMich.*inv. 6946 (*ZPE* 53.13.6, Hellen. mock epic).

**διάγγελμα**, for '*message, notice*' read '*command*'

**διάγγελος 2**, delete the section transferring refs. to section 1.

**διαγειτονία**, delete the entry (v. °διαγονία).

**διαγελάω 1**, abs., add 'S.*fr.* 171'

**διαγίγνομαι**, line 9/10, delete 'he *was never anything* but a theorist' and preface quot. with '*spend one's life* doing'

***διαγκυλίζομαι**, v. ‡διαγκυλόομαι.

**διαγκυλόομαι**, after '(v.l. -ισμένος' insert 'cf. διηγκυλίσθαι Hsch.'

**διαγλύφω 1**, lines 3/4, for 'διαγλυφέντες .. athletes' read 'οἱονεὶ διαγλυφέντες καὶ διατορευθέντες, of men in good physical condition'

**διαγνώμων**, add 'subst. *arbiter*, *PMich.*XIII 659.56, al. (vi AD), κατὰ κρίσιν καὶ μεσιτίαν τοῦ κοινοῦ διαγνώμονος ib. 81, 99, *Cod.Just.* 8.10.12.7a, Just.*Nov.* 125.1'

**διάγνωσις II**, add 'διαγνώσεως = Lat. *in cognitione*, *Edict.Diocl.* 7.73'

**διαγογγύζω**, for pres. refs. read 'ἐπί τινα Lxx *Ex.* 15.24, *Nu.* 14.2; ἐπί τινι *Jo.* 9.18, *Si.* 31.24; κατά τινος *Ex.* 16.7, *Nu.* 16.11; πρός τινι Hld. 7.27; absol. Lxx *De.* 1.27, *Ev.Luc.* 15.2, 19.7'

***διαγονία**, ά, some kind of family group, *ASAA* 2(1916).140 (iii BC), Maiuri *Nuova Silloge* 18, to be read in *IG* 12(1).922, *Clara Rhodos* 2.175 (ii BC), 203, *Lindos* 219.7 (ii BC), 454.9 (i AD).

**διαγορεύω**, line 5, after 'App.*BC* 1.54' insert 'w. ὥστε, Just.*Nov.* 58'

**διάγραμμα I**, add '**c** *enclosure*, ξένον μηδένα ἐντὸς τοῦ δ. παρ[απ]ορεύεσθαι *BCH* 33.23 (Pontus, ii BC).' **III**, add '*BGU* 1053, 1054, etc.'

**διαγραφάριος**, add '*PKlein.Form.* 31 (vi AD)'

**διαγραφή II**, line 3, after '*description*' insert 'Longin. 32.5'

**διαγράφω I 1 a**, for 'Philostr.*VS* 2.2.7, *Her.* 2.1' read 'Philostr.*VS* 2.1.7, *Her.* 2.2' **IV**, after 'Ar.*Nu.* 774 (pass.)' insert 'διαγράφω τοὺς ἱππέας Ar.*Lys.* 676, ἡ .. λῆξις τοῦ κλήρου διεγράφη Is. 5.17' **V**, add 'pass., *be paid, receive money*, *SEG* 33.1039.54 (Aeolian Cyme, ii BC)'

**διάγω I 1 a**, add 'perh. also *take to court*, *Cod.Just.* 1.33.4, Just.*Nov.* 123.8, al.'

**διαγωγή**, line 2, after '*carrying across*' insert '*SIG* 135 (Olynthus, 393 BC)'

**διαγωνίζομαι**, line 4, after 'περί τινος' insert 'Aeschin. 1.132' and delete this ref., w. def. in line 6.

**διάδεσμος**, add 'Gal. 8.90.14, 11.181.4, 11.230.7'

**διάδηλος**, after 'Arist.*HA* 613$^b$1' insert '*clearly visible, conspicuous*, *SEG* 23.207.39 (Messene, Augustus)' add '**2** *distinguishable as such, recognizable*, of the foetus in a miscarriage, *SEG* 9.72.107 (Cyrene, iv BC).'

**διάδημα I**, add 'φέρε τὸ διάδημα τὸ χάλκινον *OBodl.* i 262 (ii BC)'

***διαδιδασκαλία**, ἡ, *teaching, education*, *PMasp.* 295 i 29 (v AD).

**διαδιδράσκω 3**, delete the section transferring ref. to section 1.

**διαδικέω** (A) **1**, after 'Plu. 2.196c' insert 'D.C. 40.55' **2**, delete the section.

**⁺διάδικος**, ὁ, *opponent in a lawsuit*, Just.*Edict.* 7.1; cf. διάδικος (διὰ δίκης La.)· τὸ εἰς δίκην καλεῖν. Ἀττικοί Hsch.

**διάδομα**, for '*distribution of money*' read '*distribution of goods* or *money*' and add '*SEG* 32.1306.7 (Lycia, i AD), *Didyma* 360 (ii AD), *Kourion* 111.11 (AD 114)'

**διαδοξάζω**, after 'Pl.*Phlb.* 38b' insert 'Antisth.*Aj.* 9'

**διαδοχή I 2**, add 'dist. fr. κληρονομία, *Cod.Just.* 1.5.18.3, Just.*Nov.* 118.4. **b** *the assets of the deceased*, Just.*Nov.* 22.48 pr.'

**διάδοχος 3**, add '**b** dist. fr. κληρονόμος, *Cod.Just.* 1.3.55.4, 1.4.26.1.' **4**, w. dat., add 'neut. pl. as adv., διάδοχά σοι γόνυ τίθημι γαίᾳ *in turn*, E.*Tr.* 1307, *Andr.* 1200' **5**, for this section read 'abs. *taking over as a replacement*, πεντήκοντα τριήρεις διάδοχοι πλέουσαι Th. 1.110.4; also, *in succession to each other*, i.e. in relays, Hdt. 7.22.1; neut. pl. as adv., *in turn*, E.*Andr.* 200' **6**, add 'διάδοχος τῆς στρατηγίας *POxy.* 3975.3 (ii AD)'

***διαδρανής**, ές, *very ineffective*, of planets, δ. εἰσὶν τοῖς ἀποτελέσμασιν *PMich.*III 149 xi.17 (ii AD); cf. ἀδρανής.

**διαδρομή I 1**, after 'Arist.*Mete.* 341$^a$33' insert 'Ptol.*Tetr.* 102' **6**, add '*Cod.Just.* 1.3.45.1b'

***διαζευγίζω**, *separate*, w. gen., ἣν .. μεσηλικίης διεζεύγισε .. Ἅδης *MAMA* 7.263.

**διάζευγμα**, for 'dub. sens. .. canal' read 'some sort of a connecting structure (cf. διάζωμα 4), *bridge, mole* or sim.' and add 'perh. spec. the *Mole* at the Piraeus, Thphr.*Char.* 23.2'

**διαζεύγνυμι 1**, line 8, after 'Pl.*Lg.* 784b' insert 'ἐὰν δὲ διαζυγῶσιν ἀλλήλ(ων) οἱ γαμοῦντ(ες) *POxy.* 3491.18 (ii AD)'

**διάζευξις 1**, after 'Pl.*Phd.* 88b' read '*separation, divorce*' and after '(Pl.)*Lg.* 930b' insert '*Cod.Just.* 1.3.52.15, Just.*Nov.* 22.14; *segregation*, ἡ δ. τῶν γυναικῶν in Crete, Arist.*Pol.* 1272$^a$23'

**⁺διάζομαι**, *set* the warp *in the loom*, ἐδιάσατο τοὺς ἑπτὰ βοστρύχους τῆς κεφαλῆς αὐτοῦ (sc. of Samson) Lxx *Jd.* 16.14, *Is.* 19.10, Sch.Ar.*Av.* 4; fig., Aq.*Ps.* 138.13; app. in pass. sense, ὁ δ' ἐξυφαίνεθ' ἱστός, ὁ δὲ διάζεται Nicopho 13 K.-A. (s.v.l.).

**διάζωμα**, line 2, for '*girdle, drawers*' read '*loincloth*'

***διαζωματικός**, ή, όν, *of* or *for a* διάζωμα 3, πίνακες *Inscr.Délos* 1442*B*42 (ii BC).

**διαζώννυμι II**, after '*encompass*' insert 'of the rainbow, (in tm.) ἔζωσε διά .. οὐρανὸν ἶρις Arat. 940'

**διάημι**, add 'pass., *to be blown through*, Nic.*fr.* 74.41, see also ζάημι'

***διαθαλάμευσις**, εως, ἡ, *seclusion in a chamber*, Eust. 782.48.

**διάθεσις II 1 b**, delete '*propensity*'; for 'πρός τινα Sch.E.*Hec.* 8' read '*partiality*, Favorin.*Exil.* 16.43 B., Sch.E.*Hec.* 886; in complimentary address, perh. *graciousness, condescension*, τὰ γράμματα τῆς σῆς ἱερᾶς διαθέσεως *CPR* 8.28.4, *PAmh.* 2.145.23, 26 (iv/v AD)'

**διαθετικός**, add '**b** unexpld. wd., perh. *relating to sale*, *PTeb.* 847 intr. (ii BC).'

**διαθρυλέω I**, add 'τοὺς πάλαι παρ' ὑμῖν διατεθρυλημένους (λόγους) Isoc. 15.55'

**διαθρύπτω II 2**, for this section read 'med., perh. *behave in an affectedly coy manner*, ἃ δὲ καὶ αὐτόθε τοι διαθρύπτεται Theoc. 6.15; of doctor's manner towards his patient, Gal. 17(2).148.12'

**διαιθύσσω II**, for 'B.*fr.* 16.4' read 'B.*fr.* 20B.8 (see also ‡αἰθύσσω)'

**διαινέω**, add 'δ. περί w. gen. perh. to be read in *IG* 5(1).1379.5 (Messenia, ii/i BC)'

**διαίνω**, add 'διᾶναι· σμῆξαι, πλῦναι Hsch.'

***διαιπετής**, ές, *falling through*, ἀστὴρ ὠρανῶ δ. Alcm. 3 *fr.* 3 ii 67 P.

***διαϊπνίτης**, ου, ὁ, app. *thoroughly oven-baked* (cf. ‡ἰπνίτης), διαϊπ[νίτης] τυρός *Sokolowski* 3.90.5 (Callatis, ii BC).

***διαίρᾰσις**, v. °*διέρασις*.

***διαίρεμα**, v. °*διέραμα*.

**διαίρεσις II**, *dividing, distribution*, add 'of land, Plb. 3.40.9' **VI**, add '*division by punctuation*, Arist.*Po.* 1461ᵃ23'

**διαιρετός I 1 b**, for '*having divisions*' read '*set apart from each other*'

**διαιρέω II 1**, lines 6/7, for 'τοῖς δικάζουσι .. Lib.*Or.* 52.4' read 'οἱ παρακαθήμενοι .. τοῖς δικάζουσι διελόμενοι τὰ ὦτα, σφῶν δὲ μᾶλλον ἢ τῶν συνδίκων αὐτοὺς ἀναγκάζοντες ἀκροᾶσθαι, i.e. *dividing* their attention, Lib.*Or.* 52.4'; (pass.), add '(ποταμοὶ) διῃρημένοι κατὰ σταθμοὺς *Peripl.M.Rubr.* 15'

**διαίρω III**, delete 'intr. .. *over*' and add '*Peripl.M.Rubr.* 25, al.'

**διᾰΐσσω**, of sound, add 'Pl.*Ax.* 364a'; line 8, delete 'Anaxag.ap.'

**δῐαιτα I**, line 1, after '*mode of life*' insert 'ἀμόχθητον .. δίαιταν Alc. 61.12 L.-P.; ἀνδρῶν δ. Pi.*P.* 1.93' **III 2**, delete the section.

**δῐαιτάω I 2**, last lines before 'δίαιταν' insert 'in respect of diet, regimen, etc.'; add 'J.*AJ* 14.246' **II**, for this section read '*act as arbitrator in, settle, arbitrate on* a dispute, etc., Pi.*P.* 9.68, Theoc. 12.34; νείκη D.H. 7.52, Hld. 10.10.2, w. cogn. acc., δ. δίαιταν Arist.*Ath.* 53.5, κρίσεις J.*AJ* 14.117; abs., Is. 2.29, Phld.*D.* 1.22, 24; w. dat., οὗτος διαιτῶν ἡμῖν D. 21.84; *act as mediator*, Ὀκταουία οὖν ἐχώρει πρὸς Καίσαρα διαιτήσουσα αὐτοῖς App.*BC* 5.93. **2** *exercise office over* as arbitrator, οἱ .. τὴν Οἰνῇδα καὶ τὴν Ἐρεχθῇδα διαιτῶντες D. 47.12; *govern*, πόλιν Pi.*O.* 9.66. **3** *administer, organize*, τὰ ἐκ τῶν διαθηκῶν δ. Luc.*Tox.* 23, τἆλλα οἷς τὸ πολυτελὲς τῶν ἐδεσμάτων ὁ Θεαγένης διήτησεν Hld. 3.10.3. **b** *deal with, settle*, δ. τῆς ψυχῆς τὸ αἰδούμενον Hld. 4.6.1, 7.28.1. **4** *pass judgement on* persons or problems, Str. 1.2.1, 2.2.1, 2.3.8.'

**δῐαίτησις**, after '*way of life*' insert 'Plu. 2.500b' add '**2** perh. *arbitration*, *SEG* 23.180.9 (Cleonaea, 145 BC).'

**διαιτητέον I**, add 'Gal. 11.35.12'

**δῐαιτητικός I**, for '*of* or *for diet* .. *dietetics*' read '*of* or *concerned with regimen*: ἡ δ. (sc. τέχνη) that part of medicine so concerned'; after 'Hp.*Acut.*(*Sp.*) 54' insert 'D.L. 3.85'

***δῐαιτία**, ἡ, *way of life*, *SEG* 30.86.B36 (Athens, letter of Hadrian).

**+δῐαιτός**, ὁ, *arbitrator*, *BCH* 59.96 (Delphi), *APF* 15.75 (Dodona), Hsch.

**διακᾰής**, πυρετοί, add 'Gal. 10.759.11, 11.65.2'; metaph., add 'ὅλως ἐξηρέθιστο ἤδη καὶ δ. ἦν ὁ σατράπης Hld. 8.2.3'

**διακάθαρσις II**, add '*PSoterichos* 4.26 (AD 87)'

**διακαθίζω II**, for '= foreg.' read '*maintain a siege*'

**+διακᾰλίνδω**, *roll along*, μισθωτοῖς το[ῖς δ]ιακαλίσασιν τὰ ξύλα *IG* 2².1672.158; cf. κυλίνδω.

***διᾱκᾰ́σιοι**, v. °*διακόσιοι*.

**διᾱκᾰ́τιοι**, add '*SEG* 32.908 (Phaestus, Crete, vi BC), *IG* 9²(1).609.8 (Naupactus, c.500 BC)'

**διακατοχή**, = *bonorum possessio*, add 'Just.*Const.* Δέδωκεν 7, *Nov.* 18.5'

**διακεάζω**, for 'cf. A.R. 4.392' read '(understood by A.R. 4.392 as *burn*)'

**διάκειμαι II 2**, at end delete 'of a gift .. 7.3.17' **3**, add '*Cod.Just.* 10.11.8.5, Just.*Nov.* 159 pr., al.'

***διακέλευσις**, εως, ἡ, *exhortation*, λόγος δ. ἔχων τῶν εἰς τοὺς πολέμους Did.*in D.* 13.60.

**+διακέντησις**, εως, ἡ, *the action* or *process of piercing*, τί ἐστιν δ.; [ἔστι]ν ἡ διὰ βελόνης τῶν σωμάτων τομή *APF* 2.2; of the teeth in dentition, Hp.*Dent.* 11.

***διακέντητον**, τό, sc. κολλύριον, name of an eyesalve, Aët. 7.79 (326.11 O., v.l. δικέντ-), 7.114 (389.16 O.).

***διακῐθᾰρισμός**, ὁ, *competition in* κιθαρισμός, *Inscr.Cos* 59.

**διακῑνέω I 1**, for this section read '*move about, agitate*, Ar.*V.* 688, Hp.*Art.* 9, 30, *Vict.* 4.9; med., Hdt. 3.108.4' add '**III** intr., *walk round*, διακινῶ μηθὲν ποιῶν *PMich.*VIII 465.16 (ii AD), *Vit.Aesop.*(G) 76.'

***διακλᾱρόω**, v. ‡διακληρόω.

***διάκλειμα**, ατος, τό, wd. of unkn. meaning (app. deriv. of διακλείω), τόμια ἀργυρᾶ καὶ διακλείματα *Inscr.Délos* 104.17 (iv BC).

**διακλέπτω**, before 'med., *steal away*' insert '*remove* a person *by stealth*, μία τοίνυν σωτηρίας ἐλπὶς διακλέψαι τὴν γυναῖκα Charito 5.2.9'

**διακληρόω**, after '(Dyme, iii BC)' insert 'w. εἰς, τὰν δὲ βουλὰν διακλαρῶσαι εἰς ἡμιόγδοον καὶ τριακάδα καὶ φυλὰν καὶ φάτραν *SEG* 30.990.21 (decr. at Delos, iv/iii BC)'; pass., add 'καθὼς ἁ χώρα διεκλαρώθη *BCH* suppl. 22 p. 237 (Argos, Hellen.)'

**διακλήρωσις 1**, after '*apportionment*' insert '*PDura* 19.6 (i AD)'

**+διακλονέω**, *shake violently*, ὅλος διακλονούμενος *Vit.Aesop.*(G) 18; διακλονῶν· διασείων. δονῶν Hsch.

***διακλυσμάτιον**, τό, *little clyster*, Gal. 17a.610.4.

**+διακναίω**, pf. διακέκναικα Pherecr. 155.20 K.-A., *grate to bits*, ὄψιν E.*Cyc.* 487; humorously, w. ref. to making of a salad, πόλις διακναισθήσεται Ar.*Pax* 251. **2** *ruin utterly, destroy*, διακναιομένης κάμακος A.*Ag.* 65, E.*Med.* 164, *Alc.* 109; δ. Ὀρέστην (i.e. the play, of a bad actor) Stratt. 1. **3** *make sore, ulcerate*, ἢν δὲ ῥερυπωμένα ᾖ καὶ νέμηται, καὶ τὸν πελαστάτω χῶρον διακναίῃ Hp.*Mul.* 1.66, 2.120. **4** *wear* or *waste away*, ἡ ἀσιτίη δ. Hp.*Morb.* 1.13, οἵαις αἰκείαισιν διακναιόμενος A.*Pr.* 94, μόχθοις δ. ib. 541, πόθος μ' ἔχει διακναίσας Ar.*Ec.* 957; cf. τὸ χρῶμα διακεκναισμένος id.*Nu.* 120.

**+διακνημόομαι**, διεκνημώσατο· διέφθειρε Hsch.

**διακοιρᾰνέοντα**, add '(prob. fr. Il. 4.230 πολέας διὰ κοιρανέοντα)'

**διακολάπτω**, for '*dress stone with a chisel*' read '*cut through with a chisel*'

**+διακολλάω**, *stick throughout*, Luc.*Ind.* 16. **2** *cover with a layer of decorative materials*, id.*Hipp.* 6, *POxy.* 3473 (AD 161/9).

***διακολπῑτεύω**, *smuggle*, *PTeb.* 709.9, 14 (ii BC); cf. °κολπιτεύω.

**διακομῐδή I**, after '*carrying over*' insert '*transport*' **II**, delete the section transferring quot. to section I, adding '*SEG* 34.558.39 (Larissa, ii BC)'

**διακομπέω**, for 'Posidon. 41' read 'Posidon. 36 J.'

**διᾱκονέω I 1**, antepenultimate line, after 'Luc.*Asin.* 53' insert 'τὰ μειράκια διακονούμενα *Merc.Cond.* 16' add '**III** διακονῆσαι· κατεργάσασθαι. ἀπολέσαι. βλάψαι. Hsch. (s.v.l.).'

***διᾱκονητής**, οῦ, ὁ, official of unkn. function, *PMasp.* 2 iii 19, 60.1, 126.73, *PAnt.* 95.2 (all vi AD).

**διᾱκόνισσα**, add '*MAMA* 7.69 (iv AD), *Cod.Just.* 1.2.13, al.'

**διᾱ́κονος I 1**, line 3, for '(S.)*fr.* 133' read '(S.)*fr.* 137 R.' and add 'epith. of Hermes, Ἑρμεῖ διακόνῳ *SEG* 30.326.8 (Athens, i AD)' **2**, line 5, fem., add '*TAM* 4(1).355, *SEG* 37.367 (Patrae, vi AD)'

***διᾱκοντισία**, ἡ, = διακοντισμός, Robert *Ét.Anat.* 401 n.2 (Cos).

**διακοπή I**, line 2, after '(Gal.) 18(1).27' insert 'also *the act of cutting, incision*'; after 'Plu.*Mar.* 19' insert 'Archig.ap.Gal. 8.90.15'

***διακοπτικός**, gloss on δήϊος, δάϊος, Sch.Gen.Il. 14.422, Sch.E.*Andr.* 826.

**διακόπτω 1**, line 3, after '*gash*' insert 'διακέκομμαι τὸ στόμα Men.*Sam.* 679' deleting this passage (*Sam.* 334) fr. section 3; at end delete 'so διακέκοπται .. Suid.' and insert '**b** *cut through* a base coin, so as to invalidate it, *SEG* 26.72 (Athens, 375/4 BC), Suid.'

**διακόρευσις**, add '*Lindos* 487.12 (iii AD)'

**διακορεύω**, delete 'Ar.*Th.* 480'

**διακορέω**, add 'Ar.*Th.* 480'

***Διακός**, ή, όν, prob. *of Zeus*, νόμος *IG* 12(2).58.8 (Mytilene, i BC).

***διᾱκοσιόδραχμος**, ον, *of 200 drachmae;* neut. pl. subst., *loans of 200 drachmae* (sc. prob. δάνεια), *IG* 1³.248.36.

**διᾱκόσιοι**, after 'Ion. διηκ-' insert 'Cypr. διακάσιοι *ti-wi-ja-ka-si-a-se*, perh. δϝιjακασίας (acc. fem. pl.) = διακοσίας, *ICS* 318 A III 1'

**διᾱκοσιοκαιτεσσᾰρᾰκοντάχους**, for '*two-hundred-and-forty-fold*' read '*having a yield of two-hundred-and-forty-fold*'

**διᾱκοσιοντάκις**, for 'Suid.' read 'Alex.Aphr. *in Top.* 586.8 W.'

**διᾱκοσιοντάχους**, for '*two-hundred-fold*' read '*having a yield of two-hundred-fold*'

**διᾱκοσιοστός**, after 'Written' insert 'διακοσαστή *PCair.Zen.* 15ʳ.39 (iii BC)'

**διακοσμέω II**, pass., add 'of a building, *SEG* 37.1541.5 (Gerasa, vi AD)'

***διακόσμιος**, ον, *pervasive throughout the universe*, Simp. *in de An.* 28.3.

**διακρᾱτέω I 2**, add '*Cod.Just.* 10.11.8.5'

**διακρέκω**, add 'prob. in Sapph. 99 i 4 L.-P.'

***διακρηνάω**, Dor. -κρᾱνάω, perh. *mingle with spring water*, οἷον δὴ τόκα πῶμα διεκρανάσατε (v.l. διεκρανώσατε: see foll.), Νύμφαι Theoc. 7.154.

**διακρηνόω**, delete '*make to flow*' and after 'πῶμα' insert 'διεκρανώσατε (glossed by *EM* w. ἀνεψύξατε, but see °διακρηνάω)'

***διακρῑβεύω**, *work out* or *determine exactly*, ἐπιλέγει .. δεήσει διακριβεύειν τὰς οὕτω τῶν ἐνιαυτῶν εὑρισκομένας διαθέσεις Heph.Astr. 2.11.120.

**διακρῐδόν**, for '*eminently*' read '*by a clear margin, decidedly*'

**διάκρῐσις I**, add '**3** *dividing up* (of land), αἱροῦνται δὲ τρεῖς ἄνδρες ἐπὶ τὴν διάκρισιν καὶ διανομὴν Plu.*TG* 13.' **IV**, add '**2** *parting of hair*, Poll. 4.140.' **VI**, for '*a bandage*' read 'a method of bandaging (ἐπίδεσις)'

**διακρούω III**, for '*hinder, entangle*' read '*interrupt*' and add 'τὸ συνεχὲς τῆς ἁρμονίας D.H.*Comp.* 22'

**διακρύπτω**, med., add 'D. 41.17 (s.v.l.)'

***διακτήρ**, v. °δαϊκτήρ.

**διάκτορος**, line 2, for 'δ. alone' read ''Ἑρμείαο διακτόρου'

**διάκτος**, delete the entry (v. ‡δρακτόν).

**διακῠβεύω**, after '(Plu.*Rom.*) 2.128a' insert '*Vit.Aesop.*(G) 81' and delete 'περί .. 70d'

***διακῡσοσᾰλεύω**, in broken context, app. *waggle the bottom*, Stratt. in *CGFP* 220.8(b) ii 96.

**διάκων**, add '*SB* 5124.207, al. (ii AD); as Jewish office, *CIJud.* 805 (Apamea, vi AD); fem., *IEphes.* 3415 (ii/iii AD)'

**διαλαμβάνω III 4**, add '*Peripl.M.Rubr.* 20'

**+διάλαυρος**, ον, *bordered on all sides by streets*; fem. subst., διάλαυρος· οἰκία μεγάλη πανταχόθεν λαύραις διειλημμένη, ἡ λεγομένη περιάμφοδος Hsch., Eust. 1921.58; neut. subst., sc. χωρίον, *SEG* 23.398 (Aetolia, ii BC).

**διαλεαίνω I**, for this section read '*smooth, rub, massage*, διαλεαινομένων τῶν ἄκρων Arch.ap.Gal. 13.169.13'

**διαλέγω A II**, after 'Ar.*Lys.* 720' insert 'διαλέξαντι τὸ θύρετρον *BCH* 32.69 (Delos)' **B 1**, three lines from end after 'Plu.*Per.* 7' delete '*reason* .. *Marc.* 18'

***διαλειπτικός**, ή, όν, *intermittent*, Gal. 9.284.17, 328.9.

**διάλευκος**, for '*quite white*' read '*white, marked with white*' and insert 'Pi. *fr.* 169.24 S.-M.'

**διάληξις**, for 'of an inheritance' read '*by lot*'

**διάληψις III 2**, for '*Annales* .. 42' read '*SB* 6152.26, 6153.28 (i BC)'

**διάλῐθος**, add 'as subst., app. a piece of jewellery set with stones, διόπας, διάλιθον, πλάστρα Ar.*fr.* 332.10 K.-A.'

**διαλλάσσω IV 1**, for this section read 'intr., w. dat., *differ* in some respect, δ. ταῖς ἡλικίαις Arist.*EN* 1161ᵃ5, κλήσει οὐ φύσει D.H. 1.29, τῇ ἐγκλίσει διηλλαχός A.D.*Synt.* 70.11; abs., τὸ διαλλάσσον τῆς γνώμης Th. 3.10.1, οὐ ταὐτὸ δ' ἐστὶ τοῦτο, πολὺ διήλλαχεν Dionys.Com. 2.10. **b** *differ* from, w. dat. and internal acc., διαλλάσσοντες εἶδος .. οὐδὲν τοῖσι ἑτέροισι Hdt. 7.70.1; w. gen., Plb. 2.37.11; w. πρός, Aristid.*Or.* 35(48).16; w. ἀπό, Modest.*Dig.* 27.1.13 pr.'

**διαλογή 4**, add '*Salamine* 90 (ii BC)'

**διαλογίζομαι III**, delete the section.

***διαλόγῐσις**, εως, ἡ, = διαλογισμός (in quot., II), Polystr. p. 81 W.

***διαλογογρᾰ́φος**, ὁ, *writer of dialogues*, Syrian.*in Hermog.* 1.95 R.

**δίᾱλον, διᾱ́λας**, add 'cf. δεϝαλῶσαι s.v. °δηλόω'

**διαλῡμαίνομαι II**, pass., add 'D.*Ep.* 1.12'

**διάλῠσις 6**, add 'Charis. p. 283 K.'

**διαλῡσίφῐλος**, add 'epigr. in *SEG* 24.1238 (Egypt, Hellen./Rom.imp.)'

**διαλῠ́της**, add '**2** *mediator*, *Ath.Agora* XIX 4b.6 (iii BC, pl.).'

**διαλῠτικός II**, add 'διαλυτική, ἡ (sc. ἔμπλαστρος), *resolvent plaster*, *PMerton* 12.22 (i AD)'

***διάλῠτον**, τό, *asyndeton* (= διάλυσις 6), Charis. p. 283 K.

**διαλῠτός II**, add '**2** *capable of being taken to pieces*, κλίμακες Plu.*Arat.* 6.'

**διαλύω I 7**, add '**b** transf., *pay for*, τὴν παρρησίαν Macho 162 G.'

**διαμανθᾰ́νω**, for '*learn by inquiry*' read '*learn in detail*' and add 'E.*Hyps.fr.* 60.6 B.'

**διαμαρτᾰ́νω 3**, adv. διημαρτημένως, add 'Call.*Dieg.* ix.12 (*fr.* 201 Pf.)'

**διαμαρτία II**, after 'Luc.*Sacr.* 1' insert '(v.l.)'

**διαμαρτῠρία 1**, for pres. def. read '*sworn testimony to a fact that affects admissibility of an action at law*'

**διαμᾰσάομαι I**, after '*chew up*' insert 'Ar.*Th.* 494 (cj.)'

**διαμαστῑγόω**, for 'Pl.*Grg.* 524c' read 'Pl.*Grg.* 524e'

**⁺διαμαστῑ́γωσις**, εως, ἡ, *prolonged beating*, name given to Spartan custom used to test the endurance of boys, Plu. 2.239d.

**διαμᾰ́χησις**, for 'Gal. 9.921 (ap.Aët. 5.24)' read 'Aët. 5.24 (16.14 O.)'

***διαμᾰχίζομαι**, *strive earnestly*, διαμεμάχισται ἡ ψυχή μου ἐν αὐτῇ (sc. σοφίᾳ) LXX *Si.* 51.19(25).

**διᾰμείβω 2**, add '**c** transf., *complete* a period of time, δεκάδας δέκ' ἐτῶν διαμείψας *CEG* 477 (Attica, *c.*400/390 BC).'

***διαμελεϊστί**, v. μελεϊστί.

***διαμελίστρια**, ἡ, *one that dismembers*, (ἡμέρα), ἡ τοῦ λογικοῦ ἀμνοῦ δ. (i.e. the Passover) Leont.Byz.*HP* 1.2.5; cf. °διαμερίστρια.

**διαμένω**, add 'impers. διαμένει, -μεμένηκε, etc., *the practice continues, has continued*, etc., w. acc. and inf., Paus. 9.36.6, al.; w. dat. and inf., Arist.*Ath.* 8.1, Paus. 7.17.14, 27.8, al.'

***διαμερές**, v. °διαμπερές.

***διαμερίστρια**, ἡ, *one that divides up*, (ἡμέρα) ἡ .. τοῦ λογικοῦ ἀμνοῦ δ. Ps.-Chrys. *HP* 2.6; cf. °διαμελίστρια.

**διάμετρον**, add 'perh. also *payment* in lieu, *PHib.* 110.14 (pl., iii BC), *PCornell* 3.25 (iii BC)'

**διαμηρίζω**, for '*femora diducere, inire*' read '*part the thighs of*'

***διαμήριον**, τό, perh. *payment for sexual intercourse*, ἀπόδος τὸ δ. Kretschmer *GV* 89.

**⁺διαμηρισμός**, ὁ, *sexual intercourse*, Zeno *Stoic.* 1 (pl.).

**διαμίγνῡμι**, for 'Plu. 2.1131e' read 'Plu. 2.1132e'

***διαμίμνω**, *continue unchanged, persist*, Democr.ap.Thphr.*Sens.* 55.

***διαμισθωτής**, οῦ, ὁ, *tenant of state land*, *BGU* 2490.14 (ii/iii AD, s.v.l.).

**διαμισθωτικόν**, add '*PGiss.* 64.7 (ii AD)'

**διαμνημονεύω 2**, for 'X.*Cyr.* 1.1.2' read 'X.*Cyr.* 1.2.2'

**διαμονή**, for pres. def. read '*continuance in good* or *unchanged condition*'; add 'in prayers for the well-being of the imperial family, *SEG* 31.1124 (Phrygia, AD 104), 32.672 (Thrace, AD 144)'

**διάμονος**, after '*permanent*' insert 'δ. καὶ βέβαια *SEG* 4.598.50 (i BC)'

**διαμπερές**, after lemma insert 'διαμερές *CEG* 108.9 (Eretria, vi BC)' **II**, for '*Supp.Epigr.* 1.409 (Eretria)' read '*CEG* l.c.'

**διαμπερέως**, add 'Stesich. 222(b).281 (p. 216 D.), Theoc. 25.120'

***διάμφοδος**, gloss on διέλθυρις, Hsch.

**διαμώκησις**, for 'Ath. 5.200b' read 'Ath. 5.220b'

***διαμωμάομαι**, strengthd. for μωμάομαι, Sch.Pi.*O.* 6.124.

**διαναβάλλω**, after 'med.' read '*Cod.Just.* 1.3.45.7, Hsch. s.vv. διακρούεσθαι and διαπονδαρίζει'

***διαναίω**, aor. διένασσα, *establish in different places*, Hes.*fr.* 33(a).3 M.-W.

***διαναρρίπτομαι**, *postpone, put off*, Hsch. s.v. διαπονδαρίζει; cf. πυδαρίζω.

**διαναυμᾰχέω**, for '*maintain a sea-fight*' read '*fight a sea-battle through to a decision*'

**διαναῦσαι** (s.v. διανάω), after lemma insert '(διαναυσθλοῦσθαι cj. La.)'

**⁺διανάω**, *flow through, percolate*, Thphr.*fr.* 171.11; transf., of a container, Plu.*Aem.* 14.

**διανέμησις**, add '**2** *transfer of ownership*, Just.*Nov.* 17.18.1.'

***διάνευμα**, ατος, τό, app. *gesture of the body*, Φρυγίων διανεύματα Χαρίτων Ar.*Th.* 122 (dub., cj. δινεύματα).

**διανεύω I**, add '**2** *gesture with the body*, Luc.*Salt.* 64.'

***Διᾱ́νη**, ἡ, the goddess *Diana*, *SEG* 34.1306 (Pamphylia, iii AD).

***διανήφω**, perh. *lose potency*, διένηφε δ' οὖν καὶ κατὰ μεικρὸν εἰς ὕδωρ Diog.Oen.*fr.* 7 col. 2.8 (*AJA* 75.367).

**διανθής I**, add 'ἀσφόδελος Nic.*Th.* 534' **II**, delete the section.

**διανίστημι I**, add 'fig., κἂν γὰρ εἰ .. πρὸς τὴν ὑπὲρ αὐτῶν διαναστῶμεν ἐκδίκησιν Just.*Nov.* 129 pr.'

**διανοέω II**, add 'w. ὡς, εἰ γάρ καὶ διανοεῖταί τις ὡς δεῖ Pl.*Alc.* 1.109c'

**διανόημα**, line 4, delete 'esp. *whim, sick fancy*' and add 'Hp.*Vict.* 1.2'

**διανόησις**, add '**III** ἀπελευθερωθεὶς κατὰ διανόησιν prob. *by* (*declared*) *intention*, *IG* 9(2).109*b*19 (Thessaly, ii BC), cf. ib. 1301.9, where [κατὰ διανό]ησιν δ[έ is distd. fr. κατὰ διαθήκην.'

***διάντομαι**, διήντετο· διάζετο ἱστόν Hsch.

**διᾰνύω**, line 9, before 'pass.' insert 'med., πέντε διαινυσάμην ἐνιαυτούς *IGRom.* 4.608 (Phrygia, iv AD)'

**διαξέω**, add 'διεξεσμένα, fig., of style, Poll. 6.141'

***διάξυστος**, ον, perh. *fluted*, ἐπὶ στυλίδος διαξύστω *ILesb.* 6 B 10.

**διαξύω**, add '**2** *ruffle in passing*, Γαλάτεια .. διαξύουσα γαλήνην Nonn.*D.* 39.258. **3** app. *scratch through*, διαγράφειν· διαξύειν, ἀπαλείφειν, ἀκυροῦν Hsch., *AB* 1.238.'

***διαπᾰλαιόω**, strengthd. for παλαιόω, προπυλῶνος διαπαλαιωθέντος *POxy.* 2272.6 (ii AD).

**διαπᾱσῶν**, after 'divisim' insert 'Pherecr.*fr.* 31 K.-A.'

**διᾰπειλέω**, add '*threaten* a penalty, θάνατος τῷ παραβαίνοντι διηπειλεῖτο Hld. 5.25.2'

**διάπειρα**, add 'D. 44.58, 56.18, τὸ πρᾶγμα εἰς διάπειραν καὶ λόγον κατέστησαν Aeschin. 1.184, Just.*Nov.* 5.2 pr.'

**διαπειραίνω**, add 'perh. in reversed tm. in *h.Merc.* 48 (πειρήνας διὰ νῶτα); but cf. περαίνω IV'

**διαπειράομαι**, after '*proof of*' insert 'ἔπεσιν δ. (sc. τοῦ πατρός) Od. 24.240 (v.l. in *PRyl.* 53, iii/iv AD)'

**διαπέρᾱμα**, for '*strait of the sea*' read '*crossing*'

**διαπεράω III**, delete 'ὕδωρ .. Eub. 151' and before 'Luc.*DMort.* 20.1' insert 'τὸν πορθμέα τοῦτον, ὅς σε διεπέρασε'

**διαπέρθω**, add 'διεπέρσατε Δύμιον ἄστυ Antim. 28.2 Wy.'

**διαπεττεύω**, for '*gamble*' read '*subject to a throw of the dice*' and delete '*try* one's luck *at play*'

**διάπηγα**, for '*panels*' read '*cross-pieces*' and for '3*Ki.* 7.31, 32' read 'v.l. in 3*Ki.* 7.17 (31, 32)'

**διάπηγμα**, delete '*partition*' and add 'Aq. 4*Ki.* 16.17'

**διαπηδάω 2**, delete 'medic.' and for '*ooze through*' read '*let moisture through*' add '**II** *contend in jumping*, D.Chr. 8.12.'

**διαπίνω**, for '*drink one against another*' read '*carry on drinking*'

**διαπίπτω III**, *perish*, add 'Just.*Nov.* 15.5.1'

***διαπιστόομαι**, *confirm, prove*, Aristodem. 16.2 J.

**⁺διάπλασμα**, ατος, τό, *moulding, shaping*, Sch.Ar.*V.* 614, τὸ δ. τοῦ τύπου *Vit.Aesop.*(G) 88.

**διαπλαστικός**, for 'Alex.Aphr.*Pr.* 1.47' read 'Alex.Aphr.*Pr.* 2.47'; add '*capable of being formed*, ταῖς τῶν ἐμβρύων διαπλαστικῶν φύσεσι Alcin.*Intr.* p. 178.28 H.'

**διαπλᾰτύνω**, for 'X.*Lac.* 2.5' read 'X.*Lac.* 2.6'

**διαπληκτίζομαι**, for '*spar*' read '*fight* with the hands' and delete '*τινί*' before 'Luc.*Anach.* 11'

**διαπλοκή**, add '**III** *intertwining*, ἐπὶ ταῖς διαπλοκαῖς τῶν παλαισμάτων Philostr.*Gym.* 11.'

**διάπλοκος**, after '*plaited*' insert 'Aristeas Judaeus 75'

**διάπλοος II**, add '**4** *strait*, *AP* 7.666 (Antip.Thess.).'

**διαπνέω I 2**, delete the section transferring quot. to section 1, prefixed by 'abs.' add '**2** *break wind*, Suid. s.v. ἀποψοφεῖν.'

**διαποιέω**, for '*PTheb.Bank*' read '*Theb.Ostr.*'

**διαπολῑτεία**, for '*party-strife*' read '*political conflict*'

***διαπολλύω**, gloss on διολλύω, Hsch.

**διαπονέω I 3**, add '*Vit.Aesop.*(G) 3'

**διᾰπορέω**, line 2, after 'aor. pass.' insert 'διαπορηθείς Pl.*Sph.* 217a' **II**, lines 5/6, delete 'Med. .. 217a'

**διαπορθμεύω I 2**, line 3, after 'Iamb.*Myst.* 1.5' insert 'also Max.Tyr. 14.8 (of interpreters)'

**διάπρᾱσις I**, add '*SEG* 38.1462.9 (Oenoanda, ii AD)'

**διαπράσσω II 2**, add 'Plu. 2.404a'

**διαπρᾱΰνω**, for 'Philostr.*VA* 6.14' read 'Philostr.*VA* 6.13'

**διαπρέπω I 2**, for 'ἐπί τινι .. D.C. 68.6' read 'πάνυ .. διαπρέψαντα ἐν τῇ ὀρχηστικῇ Luc.*Salt.* 9; w. ἐπί, πλεῖστον .. ἐπ' ἀνδρείᾳ .. διέπρεπε D.C. 68.6'

**διάπριστος**, for 'Demioprat.' read '*Demioprat.*'; add '*IG* $1^3$.422.13-14 (Athens, v BC), $2^2$.2500.56'

**διαπρίω III**, after 'διαγοράζει' insert '(dub.)'

**⁺διαπρό**, prep., w. gen. *straight through*, Il. 4.138, δόρυ δ' ὀφθαλμοῖο διαπρὸ καὶ διὰ ἰνίου ἦλθεν 14.494. **II** as adv., Il. 5.66, 7.260, etc., Od. 22.295, 24.524, *h.Ven.* 114.

***διαπροαιρέομαι**, strengthd. for προαιρ-, Sch.Pi.*O.* 6.140.

**⁺διαπτερόω**, *brush* or *clean out*, Hp.*Acut.* 58, Aret.*CD* 1.8; διαπτερῶσαι· ἀνευρῦναι, διαστῆσαι Hsch.

***διαπτῠχής**, ές, *split apart*, Philox.Leuc. (b).29 P.

**διάπῡρος 2**, add 'Gal. 12.1003.8, 9, 12' **3**, after '(Pl.)*Lg.* 783a (sup.)' insert 'Men.*Dysc.* 183'

**διαπῡ́ρωσις II**, add '*scorching* by the sun, Ptol.*Tetr.* 56'

***διαπωτάομαι**, *direct one's flight*, πᾷ μοι φθογγὰ διαπωτᾶται φοράδην; S.*OT* 1310 (pap., codd. διαπέταται).

***διᾰ́ρᾱμα**, v. °διέραμα.

***διᾰρᾱμᾰτία**, ἡ, *lading* or *conveying of corn*, as a public service, *PSI* 1103.9 (ii AD); cf. °διέραμα.

***διαρᾰπίζω**, *beat up*, *PTeb.* 798.15 (ii BC).

***διᾰ́ρᾰσις**, εως, ἡ, v. °διέρασις.

***διαργῠρόω**, *decorate with silver*, ᾠὸν στρούθειον διηργυρωμένον *PMich.*II 9$^r$.3 (iii BC).

**⁺διᾰ́ρημα**, v. °διέραμα.

**διάρθρωσις 3**, line 3, for '*distinctness*' read '*analysis*'

**διᾰρίθμησις**, add 'ψήφων *SEG* 9.8.32 (Cyrene, Aug.)'

**διάριον**, add '*Cod.Just.* 12.17 pr.'

**διαρκέω I 1**, line 4, for 'δ. πρός τινα .. etc.' read '*have resources* to meet, ἵνα καὶ διαρκέσῃς πρὸς τοῦ πένθους τὸ μέγεθος Luc.*Luct.* 24'

**διαρκής 2**, for 'sup. .. Them.*Or.* 11.146a' read '*having staying power*, ἵπποι Them.*Or.* 11.146a; transf., of a race, Paus. 6.13.3'

**δίαρμα II**, add 'Cleonid.*Harm.* p. 206 J.'

**διαρμόζω 2**, pass., add 'of musical instrument, *to be regulated* in pitch, διηρμοσμένον ἦν συρίγγιον, ᾧ τὴν φωνὴν οἱ ἁρμονικοὶ σχέδην ἐπ' ἀμφότερα διὰ τῶν τόνων ἄγουσι Plu. 2.456a'

***διᾰ́ροσις**, εως, ἡ, gloss on σφύρωσις, Hsch.

**διαρπᾰγή**, add '*SEG* 32.1128.13 (Ephesus, 39/8 BC)'

**διαρπάζω II 3**, for 'Nonn.*D.* 48.290' read 'Nonn.*D.* 48.920'

**διαρραίνω**, line 4, for 'Philostr.*Im.* 7.27' read 'Philostr.*Im.* 1.27'

**διαρραίω**, fut. med., add 'διᾰραίσομαι Tim. 791.133 P.' **II**, for this section read '**2** *divide* or *break up*, ῥωχμαὶ (wrinkles) σάρκα διαρραίουσι, i.e. break up the surface of, Marc.Sid. 80.'

***διάρ(ρ)αντος**, ον, *speckled* or *brindled*, Lxx *Ge.* 30.32.

**διαρρᾰφή**, add '*APF* 2.2.13'

**διαρρέπω**, for '*oscillate: halt in one's gait*' read '*tilt sideways as one walks*, of a person with one leg shorter than the other'

**διαρρέω II**, after '*waste away*' insert 'διέρρυε[ν] Sapph. 98(*b*).9 L.-P.'

**διαρρήγνῡμι**, add '**2** *rescind* will or other document, cf. Lat. *testamentum rumpere* and sim., Just.*Nov.* 107.2.'

**διαρρήδην**, line 3, for 'Lys. 1.20' read 'Lys. 1.30'

**διάρρησις**, after 'Pl.*Lg.* 932e' insert 'Poll. 2.128'

**διαρρίπτω I 3**, add '**b** *cause to go off in a wrong direction*, Arr.*Cyn.* 16.3, ὁ μὲν (sc. λαγωὸς) ἐξελίξας τὸν δρόμον καὶ διαρρίψας τὴν κύνα ib. 17.3.'

**διαρρῐφή**, for 'Dor.' read 'dial.' and add 'a (variously explained) rite at a feast, *SEG* 32.1243.38 (Aeolian Cyme, 2 BC/AD 2)'

**διάρρους**, before 'D.S. 13.47' insert '*IG* 7.4255.21 (Oropus, iv BC)'

**διάρτᾰβος**, add '**b** *of two* ἀρτάβαι, σφυρίδες *SB* 6801$^r$.20, 24 (iii BC).'

***διάρτης**, ου, ὁ, ποταμῶν δ. *one who raises* water from rivers, Teuc.Bab. p. 46.9 B.

***διαρτία**, ἡ, *mould*, *form*, σωματικὴν διαρτίαν Sch.Nic.*Al.* 227c Ge.

***διασᾰλᾰκωνεύω**, = διασαλακωνίζω, Hsch. s.v. διασα‹λα›κώνισον.

**διασᾰλᾰκωνίζω**, after 'Ar.*V.* 1169' insert 'Hsch.'

**διασᾰλεύω**, line 5, for '(Luc.)*Merc.Cond.* 35' read '(Luc.)*Merc.Cond.* 33'

**διασᾰφέω**, add '**b** *state plainly* something previously expressed figuratively, *Ev.Matt.* 13.36, J.*AJ* 5.293. **c** *make known officially*, *declare*, τὸ διασεσαφημένον ἐκφόριον *PTeb.* 105.39 (103 BC).'

***διασᾰφής**, ές, *very clear*, *Kafizin* 146(a) (iii BC).

**⁺διασᾰφητικός**, ή, όν, *declaratory*, διαφορὰ τοῦ ἤ συνδέσμου A.D.*Conj.* 221.16, 23; cf. *EM* 415.27, Sch.B Il. 1.117; adv. -κῶς, Sch.T ibid. **II** *explanatory*, Sch.Ar.*An.* 825, *An.Ox.* 1.118.

**διάσεισις II**, add '*UPZ* 1.9'

**διάσημος II**, sup., add 'adv., μεταπαρέλαβεν διασήμοτατα τὴν δαιδουχίαν *SEG* 30.93.5 (Eleusis, 20/19 BC)'

**Δῑάσια**, add 'also festival at Thasos, *SEG* 21.541.A38 (iv BC)'

***διασιαίνω**, for *διασικχαίνω, *loathe utterly*, Sch.Luc.*Tim.* 7; cf. δικχαίνω.

**διασκάπτω**, line 2, for 'ἰσθμόν' read 'Μίμαντα'

**⁺διασκᾰρῑφάομαι**, *scratch up*, in fig. phr., τὰς εὐτυχίας .. διεσκαριφησάμεθα καὶ διελύσαμεν Isoc. 7.12; act., διασκαριφῆσαι· ἐπὶ ὀρνέων τῶν τοῖς ὄνυξι σκαλευόντων τὴν γῆν κυρίως λέγεται Hsch.

**διασκευάζω II**, line 2, after 'Plu.*Ant.* 24' insert 'τὴν θεὸν διεσκευασμένην καταπληκτικῶς D.S. 4.51'

**διασκευαστής**, add '**II** dub. sens., w. ref. to some activity of a person under the influence of Aphrodite, Ptol.*Tetr.* 164.'

***διασκεῦος**, τό, pl. διασκεύη *equipment*, Roueché *Performers and partisans* no.1 (Aphrodisias, v/vi AD).

**διασκηνέω II**, delete the section transferring 'X.*Cyr.* 3.1.38' to section I.

**διασκοπέω I**, add 'w. inf., διεσκεψάμεθα μέσην τινὰ τῷ πράγματι τάξιν ἐπινοῆσαι Just.*Nov.* 22.26 pr.'

**διασκορπίζω**, line 1, after '*scatter abroad*' insert '*disperse*' and after 'al.' insert 'Ael.*VH* 13.46'

***διασκορπιστής**, οῦ, ὁ, *winnower*, λικμηταί· διασκορπισταί Hsch.

**διασπᾰθάω I**, add '*SB* 10567.9 (iii AD)'

**διασπᾰράσσω I 1**, after 'A.*Pers.* 195' insert '*Suppl.Hell.* 996.7'; pass., add 'Memn. 8.8 J.'

**διάσπᾰσις II**, delete the section (v. °διάστασις).

**διάσπαστος**, delete the entry.

***διασπᾰτᾰλάω**, *squander*, *PHarris* 67 ii 7 (ii AD).

**διασπάω**, add '**4** *squander*, *dissipate*, Just.*Nov.* 38 pr. 1.'

**διασπείρω**, line 4, delete '*squander*'

***διάσταθμον**, τό, perh. *ration*, *allowance*, *PCair.Zen.* 320.8 (iii BC).

**διασταλμός**, add '*PWash.Univ.* 8.2 (vi AD)'

**διασταλτικός II**, for this section read 'v. °διαστατικός' add '**III** medic., *diastolic*, Gal. 9.298.3.'

**διάστᾰσις I 1**, add 'Plu. 2.721a' **III**, line 2, for 'Arist.*Top.* 142$^b$5' read 'Arist.*Top.* 142$^b$25'

**διαστᾰτικός**, after '**3**' insert 'of music, *exciting*, *exalting*, Ptol.*Harm.* 1.12, 3.11, Cleonid.*Harm.* 13, Aristid.Quint. 1.12, 19 (διασταλτικός occurs as ms. reading or variant in some of these passages)' **3**, renumber this section as **4** inserting before 'adv.' '*separating*, *distinguishing*, ἐν τῇ λαλιᾷ διαστατικός τῶν ὀνομάτων D.L. 4.33'

**διαστέλλω I 4**, for '*pronounce*' read '*state explicitly*'

**διάστεμα**, before '*PRyl.*' insert '*interval*'; add '*distance*, δύο ἡμερῶν ἐστι τὸ δ. *PBremen* 15.30'

**διάστημα I 1**, add 'ἐν τῷ τοῦ πλοὸς δ. in the *course* of the voyage, X.Eph. 1.14.7; see also ‡διάστεμα'

***Δῑαστής**, οῦ, ὁ, *worshipper of Zeus*, *BCH* 46.342 (pl., Teos).

**διάστησις**, delete the entry.

**διαστίζω 3**, for '*brand*' read '*distinguish*, *differentiate*'

***διαστικός**, ή, όν, (διάζομαι) *of weaving*, ἡ δ. (sc. τέχνη) τῶν ἀραχνῶν Theodos.Gr. p. 53 G.

**διάστιξις**, for '*branding*' read '*distinction*, *differentiation*' and add 'Just. *Nov.* 112.1'

**διαστολεύς II**, for '*cashier*, title of official ' read 'some local financial official '

**διαστολή I 4**, for this section read '*itemized list*, *schedule* of payment, *BGU* 2493.13 (i/ii AD), *PTeb.* 363.1 (ii AD), *BGU* 652, al. (iii AD)' **II 2**, add 'Anon.Bellerm. 11'

**διαστρέφω I 1**, line 4, after '*to be warped*' insert 'of wood, Pl.*Prt.* 325d'

**διαστροφή 2**, add 'ἐκ διαστροφῆς, opp. κατὰ φύσιν, Jul.*Or.* 6.202c' **4**, add 'δίχα ζημίας καὶ διαστροφῆς *Cod.Just.* 11.1.1.1'

**διάστῡλος II**, for this section read '*intercolumniation*, *SEG* 35.1109, 1110 (Ephesus, iii AD), 37.851 (Aphrodisias, iv AD), *MAMA* 8.498'

***διασυλλαμβάνω**, perh. *keep*, *preserve* in specified condition, *PGiss.*inv. 245.6 (*Pap.Brux.* 7.78, ii AD).

**διασῡρίζω**, line 1, delete 'f.l. in' and substitute 'διασυριζόντων (ἰκτίνων)'

**διασύρω**, lines 2/3, delete '*tear in pieces* .. *pull to pieces*, i.e.' **II**, for '*break up*, *disperse*' read '*keep apart*' add '**IV** abs. *prolong one's stay*, *linger*, *POxy.* 3867.4 (vi AD).'

**διασφαλίζομαι**, after 'Orib. 8.7.3' insert '*SEG* 38.1462.B16 (Oenoanda)'

**διασφάλλω**, after 'Luc.*Abd.* 17' insert '*pervert*, νόον Neophr.(?) in *PLit.Lond.* 77 *fr.* 2.12'

**⁺διασφετερίζομαι**, *appropriate*, *usurp*, v.l. in Ph. 2.130, *PLond.*inv. 2222 (*Mnemos.*(ser. 4) 40.413, AD 319).

**διασωστής**, for '*policeman*' read '*guide*'

**διασωστικός**, add 'Alcin.*Intr.* p. 182.32, 183.4 H.'

**διατᾰγή**, add '**b** perh. *order*, *requisition*, *BGU* 2347.5 (iii AD).'

***διαταγματάριος**, ὁ, an official in the service of a *dux* (δούξ), *PAnt.* 96.11 (vi AD).

**διατάκτης**, after '*assigner of posts*' insert 'Ptol.*Tetr.* 82' add '**2** gloss on κοσμήτωρ 1, Sch.Hom. in *POsl.* 12 iii 16. **3** title of Roman official in Egypt, *SB* 6026 (iii AD).'

**διατακτικός**, delete 'Ptol.*Tetr.* 82'

**διαταξίαρχος**, add '*MDAI(A)* 37.302 (Pergamum, ii AD)'

**διάταξις II 2**, add 'of other decrees and regulations, κατὰ τὴν Γεντιανοῦ διάτα‹ξ›ιν *SEG* 30.568.17 (Maced., ii AD)'

**διατάσσω I 2**, line 2, for 'Th. 4.103' read 'Th. 4.130.3'

**διατείνω**, line 1, for '*keep stretched out*' read 'of a surgeon, in setting a bone'; line 3, for 'τινὰ ὑπὲρ λεχέων' read 'Δωρίδα τὴν ῥοδόπυγον ὑπὲρ λεχέων διατείνας' **B I 1**, line 5, after 'X.*Mem.* 3.7.9' insert '*strain*, of a woman in childbirth, Al.*Mi.* 4.10'; line 6, for '*prevented*' read '*exerted themselves to prevent*'

**διατειχισμός**, for '*fortifying*' read '*walling off*'

***διατεκταίνομαι**, διετεκτήνατο· ἐμηχανήσατο Hsch.

**διατελέω I**, for '*bring quite to an end*' read '*carry through to the end*' **II 1**, line 3, for 'And. 1.38' read 'And. 1.138' **2**, add '**c** *remain* in a place, κατ' οἶκον Aen.Tact. 10.13, cf. 3.6, 7.1.'

**διατέμνω 1**, line 3, after 'Hdt.' insert '2.41.3'; lines 5ff., delete 'τι ἀπό τινος' to end of article and substitute 'fig., διατετμηκότα τὴν πολιτείαν *split apart*, Aeschin. 3.207. **2** *divide into two*, τὸ μέτρον D.H.*Comp.* 26; w. gen., *separate* from, τὴν μὲν διετέμομεν ἀπ' αὐτῆς Pl.*Plt.* 280b.'

**διατενής**, add 'of the pulse, *strained*, Gal. 8.943.2 (unless διάτονος is read)'

***διατετυπωμένως**, v. διεσκευασμένως.

**διατήρησις**, add '*SEG* 25.687 (Thessaly, Hellen.)'

**διατίθημι A I**, add '*h.Ap.* 254' **II 1**, add '**b** w. double acc., οὐδὲν δ. αὐτὸν δεινόν *gave* him no ill-*treatment*, Aristodem. 5.3 J., cf. 8.1. J.' add '**3** *subject to sexual practices*, Ptol.*Tetr.* 164, 166, 187, al.' add '**IV** *compose, settle* (cf. B 4), Just.*Nov.* 159.3, ib. epilogos.'

**⁺διατίλλω**, *pull out the hair from*, κουραῖς .. διατετιλμένης φόβην S.*fr.* 659.7 R., λαβών με τῆς κόμης διέτιλεν Lxx *Jb.* 16.12.

**διατίμησις**, after '*valuation*' insert '*SEG* 34.558.52 (Larissa, ii BC)' and after '*assessed value*' insert 'διατιμήσεις ἀποτινέτων *RA* 6.31.16 (decr., Amphipolis, ii BC), *Cod.Just.* 6.4.4.4, al.'

***διάτῑμος**, ον, *honoured*, *OGI* 615.4 (iii AD) (sup.).

**διατῑνάσσω II**, after '(E.)*IT* 282' insert 'Aristo 13 iii W.'

**διατμήγω**, line 6, pass. διέτμαγεν, add 'διέτμαγον (act. intr.) v.l. in Il. ll. cc., also in A.R. 2.298, 3.1147 (cj. διέτμαγεν in both passages)'

***διατοίχιον**, τό, dim. of διάτοιχος II, *Milet* 7 p. 56.

***διατόμιον**, τό, dim. of διατομή in uncertain sense, *Inscr.Délos* 1442*B*41 (ii BC).

**⁺διάτομος**, ον, v.l. for διχότομος (in same sense) in Mart.Cap. 7.738, 8.864.

**διατόναιον**, after '(iii BC)' insert '*Inscr.Délos* 1417*A*i73'; for '*curtain-rod*' read '*cross-support*'; after 'so -τόνιον' delete '*curtain-hook* or *ring*'

**διάτονος I 2**, add '**b** διάτονα, τά, *cross-supports*, *Inscr.Délos* 290.216 (iii BC).'

***διατόξευσις**, εως, ἡ, = διατοξεία, Robert *Ét.Anat.* 401 n.2.

**διατοξεύω**, line 2, for 'Hld. 5.32' read 'Hld. 5.33 (32.5; v.l. τοξ-)'

**διάτορος I**, add 'adv. -ως *by piercing*, S.*fr.* 314.316 R.'

**διατρᾰχηλίζομαι**, delete the entry.

***διατραχηλίζω**, *keep holding in a neck-lock*, in quot. pass., Teles p. 10 H.; transf., *hold in one's grasp*, ἐν ταραχῇ καὶ πλάνῃ δρόμοις ὀλεθρίοις καὶ παραφόροις διατραχηλιζόμενος Plu. 2.501d.

***διατρᾰχηλισμός**, ὁ, *state of being forced down in a neck-lock*, in quot. fig., Plu. 2.317b (v.l., v. διαταραχή).

**διατρέπω I**, line 5, for 'Epicur. p. xxviii U.' read 'Epicur. [1] 119.4 A., *turn to new business* (of one's own accord), Onas. 42.2' **II 1**, delete the section.

**διατρέφω**, pass., add 'X.*Vect.* 1.1, D. 19.249, Isoc. 4.153, 6.78'

**διατρέχω II 2**, add '*Cod.Just.* 10.19.9.1, Just.*Nov.* 93 pr.' add '**III** abs. *contend in running*, D.Chr. 8.12.'

**διάτρησις**, add '**3** *tunnel*, Ael.*NA* 16.15.'

**διατρῐβή I 2 d**, after '*school*' insert 'of rhetoric, Aeschin. 1.175' **III**, add 'Men.Rh. p. 335, 336, al.'

**διατρῖβω III**, *put off by delay*, add 'Men.*fr.* 265 K.-Th.'

**διατροπή 1**, for '*fiasco, débâcle*' read '*upset*'

**διατροφή**, line 3, for '*means of subsistence*' read '*food, nourishment*'

***διάτροχος**, ον, *running* or *extending through*, *Inscr.Délos* 500*A*19 (iii BC).

***διατρῠφής**, ές, *pulverized*, Nic.*Th.* 709 (s.v.l.).

**διατυγχάνω**, delete the entry.

**διατῠπόω 3**, add '[δι]ετυπώθησαν ἐπιμελεῖσθαι i.e. were appointed as ἐπιμεληταί *SEG* 11.464 no. 24 (Sparta, AD 359), *SIG* 3.908 (Megara, AD 401/2)'

**διατύπωσις I 3**, for 'Alex.*Fig.* 3.25' read 'Alex.*Fig.* 1.24' **II**, add '**2** term for tax assessed in money or kind in accordance with the schedule, = Lat. *delegatio*, *PCol.* 137.3 (AD 301/2), *PCair.Isidor.* 42 (AD 303).'

**διαυγάζω II**, after '*J.AJ* 5.10.4' insert '(v.l. διυπνισθείς)'

**διαυγής**, line 4, after 'of stars' insert '*shining through* clouds'; line 5, transfer 'of gems .. 204' to follow '*AP* 9.227 (Bianor)';add 'of style, *transparent*, D.H.*Dem.* 5'

***διαύλη**, ἡ, = δίαυλος I 1, *SEG* 29.147.8 (pl., Athens, ii/iii AD).

**⁺δῐαυλία**· ὅταν δύο ᾄδωσι Hsch., cf. *EM* 269.30.

**δῐαύλιον**, for '*flute*' read '*aulos*'

**δίαυλος I 1**, for '*double pipe* .. *course*' read '*track running up one side of a stadium and back down the other* or the *race* along it'; add 'Hp.*Vict.* 2.63' **b**, delete the section. **2**, add 'of an outward and return voyage through a strait, E.*Tr.* 435' **II 1**, delete the section.

**διαφᾰνής I 2**, for '*red-hot*' read '*glowing with heat, incandescent*' and for 'Hdt. 2.9' read 'Hdt. 2.92.5'

***διάφαργμα**, v. ‡διάφραγμα.

**διάφᾰσις**, line 2, for 'ἐκφάσεις' read 'ἐμφάσεις' and for 'Plu. 2.354b' read 'Plu. 2.354c'; transfer 'Cic.*Att.* 2.3.2' to precede 'metaph.' add '**b** *gap* or *space in a construction through which light can pass*, *IIasos* 22.9.'

**διάφαυμα**, add '*PSI* 939.4 (vi AD)'

**διαφερόντως II 2**, add '*Cod.Just.* 1.2.24 pr.'

**διαφέρω II 3**, after '*distract*' insert 'τινὰς λόγοισι E.*HF* 76' **4**, for '*give each man* his vote' read '*vote on this or that side*'; add 'also ψᾶφον δ. *put* a question *to the vote*, *BCH* 87.3 (Locr., v BC); pass., περὶ τούτου ψήφου διενεχθείσης *BCH* 86.58.25 (Maced., ii AD)' **III 3**, line 6, after 'matters' insert 'E.*Hyps.fr.* 60.46 B.' **4**, line 3, after 'Th. 3.39' insert 'μηδὲν τῶν τυχόντων Isoc. 1.48, X.*Mem.* 4.2.2'; after 'Alex. 36.6' insert 'X.*Mem.* 4.2.1; ἐπί τινι ibid. (v.l.)'; line 9, after 'abs., *excel*' insert 'εἴς τι X.*Cyr.* 1.1.6' **8**, line 2, before 'of persons' insert 'τινος *MAMA* 3.421 (Corycus), al., *IG* 10(2).1.790 (Thessalonica, iv AD)' **IV**, line 8, after '(D.) 9.8' insert 'cf. Plu. 2.80d (w. nom. part.)'

**διαφεύγω 2**, delete 'δ. τὰ πολλὰ .. Jul.*Or.* 7.228a' add '**b** *to be beyond the competence of*, αἴτιον .. τοῦ διαφεύγειν τοὺς παρὰ τοῖς Ἕλλησιν ἰατροὺς τὰ πολλὰ νοσήματα Pl.*Chrm.* 156e, Jul.*Or.* 7.228a.'

**διαφημίζω**, after '*J.BJ* 1.33.3' insert 'impers., *JÖAI* 23 *Beibl.* 16 (ii AD)'

**διαφθείρω I 4**, *lose by miscarriage*, after '*Is.* 8.36' insert 'of dogs, X.*Cyn.* 7.2'

***διάφθερμα**, ατος, τό, *abortion*, *SEG* 28.421 (Arcadia, before ii AD).

**διαφθορά II**, concr., add '**2** *means of ruin* or *destruction*, οὗτοί (sc. οἱ σοφισταί) γε φανερά ἐστι λώβη τε καὶ διαφθορὰ τῶν συγγιγνομένων Pl.*Men.* 91c, *Grg.* 464c.'

***διαφίστημι**, *provoke*, βασιλέα εἰς ὀργήν *Sardis* 7(1).20.16 (vi AD).

**διαφοιτάω I**, for '*wander, roam*' read '*wander throughout* a place'; delete '*go backwards and forwards*'; after 'of a report' insert 'δ. τῆς πόλεως D.Chr. 34.20'

**διαφορά VII**, for this section read 'perh. *deficit*, *PEnteux.* 27.10 (iii BC)'

**διαφορέω I 4**, for '*tear in pieces*' read '*scatter in pieces*' and add 'fig., ὕψος τὰ πράγματα πάντα δ. Longin. 1.4'

***διαφορητέον**, *one must disperse*, Archig.ap.Gal. 12.676.13.

**διάφορος I 2**, w. gen., add 'Is. 12.10' **II 4 b**, at end transfer 'D.L. 6.9' to section 4 a.

**διαφορότης**, after 'Pl.*R.* 587e' insert '*Phlb.* 13a, *Prm.* 141c, etc.'

***διαφορτόομαι**, *transport*, *Vit.Aesop.*(G) 18.

**διάφραγμα I**, after lemma insert 'διάφαργμα *IAskl.Epid.* 52 A 10 (iv BC)' and after '*Inscr.Prien.* 99.19' insert '*SEG* 32.643.13 (Koroneia, ii AD)'

**διαφράζω**, for 'only in pf. διαπέφρᾰδε' read 'usu. in redupl. aor. 2 διεπέφρᾰδε; also unredupl. διέφρᾰδον *Inscr.Cret.* 1.xvi 7 (Lato, ii/i BC)'

**διαφυή III**, add '*BGU* 2333.15 (AD 143/4)'

***διαφύλλω**, διέφυλλε· διέτιλλε. διέτεμεν Hsch. (perh. corruption of *διεφύλλιζε).

**διαφύομαι II**, delete the section transferring 'Emp. 17.10' to section I.

**διάφῠσις II**, add '= κτηδών, Sch.A Il. 21.169'; for '*division*' read '*divergent form* or *growth*, *bifurcation*'

**διάφυσον**, add '(διάφυσος La.)'

**διαφωνέω 2**, delete 'Plb. 21.43.23' **3**, for '*desert*' read '*to be missing*' **b**, of persons, add 'τῶν ἐπιλέκτων τοῦ Ἰσραὴλ οὐ διεφώνησεν οὐδὲ εἷς Lxx *Ex.* 24.11, *Nu.* 31.49, 1*Ki.* 30.9, *Ju.* 10.13'; of things, add 'Plb. 21.43.23' add '**4** of wine, *be of poor quality*, *BGU* 1994.5 (240 BC).'

***διάφωσις**, εως, ἡ, *the centre of a house open to the light* (cf. αἴθριον), *UPZ* 180a.1.10, al. (ii BC).

***διαχᾰλιγμός**, ὁ, (χάλιξ) *intermediate layer of rubble*, *Inscr.Délos* 507 *bis* 6 (iii BC).

**⁺διαχειριστικόν**, τό, *charge for measuring grain*, *PLond.* 1940 (iii BC).

**διαχέω I 4**, after 'Philostr.*VS* 2.10.1' insert 'διαχεῖ .. τὸν Ἀπόλλω καὶ ποιεῖ χαίροντα id.*Im.* 1.26' add '**b** of the effect of smooth sounds upon the ear, D.H.*Comp.* 15, cf. II 4.' **II 2**, add 'fig., of facts, *leak out*, J.*AJ* 19.1.7'

**διάχλωρος**, add '*BGU* 2328.5 (v AD)'

**διαχρέμπτομαι**, add 'Theoc. 15.99 (pap., codd. διαθρύπτεται)'

**διάχρῡσος**, add '**2** *gilded*, φιάλη ἔκτυπος δ. *IG* 11(2).161*B*69 (Delos, 279 BC).'

***διαχωννύω**, = διαχόω, Hsch. s.v. διαχοῦ.

**διαχωρισμός**, add 'δίεσιν· διαχωρισμόν Hsch. (perh. in sense "divorce")'

***διαχωριστικός**, ή, όν, *separating*, καιρώματα γὰρ τὰ δ. τῶν στημόνων πλέγματα Hsch. (s.v. καιροσέων).

***διάχωρον**, τό, *section, division* of a building, *AD* 12.39 (Eresus).

***διαψαλμός**, ὁ, *competition in* τὸ ψάλλειν, inscr. in Ziebarth *Gr.Schulwesen*² p. 145 (Cos, ii BC).

**διαψάω I**, add 'med., διεψήσατο· διεκάθαρε Hsch.'

***διαψηλάφημα**, ατος, τό, *unrhythmical passage of instrumental melody*, Anon.Bellerm. 3, 85.

**διαψήφισις**, add 'used to render Lat. *rogatio*, ἔφη διαψήφισιν προθήσειν περὶ τοῦ νόμου App.*BC* 1.12(51)'

**διαψῐθῠρίζω II**, for '*whisper among themselves*' read '*spread gossip by whispering*'

**διάψῑλος**, before '*uncultivated*' insert '*bare, bald*, ψηνός· ψεδνός, διάψιλος Hsch.'

***διαψωμίζω**, aor. διεψώμισε (-ησε cod.), compd. of ψωμίζω in corrupt entry in Hsch. s.v. διεψήσατο (perh. separate lemma).

***δῐβολίς**, ίδος, ἡ, = διβολία II, Ps.-Callisth. 24.15.

**δίβος**, for '*square on the draught-board*' read 'position in board-game app. resembling backgammon'

***Διγαία**, v. °Δειγαία.

**δίγαμμα**, add 'the symbol used with uncertain significance, Cic.*Att.* 9.9.4 (s.v.l.)'

***Διγένης**, epith. of Apollo, in uncertain significance (perh. variant of Διογενής II), *Tit.Cam.* 47.20 (ii BC).

**δίγλωσσος II**, for this section read '*double-tongued*, στόμα *AP* 9.273 (Bianor); fig., Lxx *Si.* 5.9, 14, 6.1. **2** app. *loose-tongued*, Lxx *Pr.* 11.13.'

***δῐγλώχῑς**, ῑνος, *having two barbs*, neut. pl. -ινα, βέλη Paul.Aeg. 6.88.2 (130.1 H.).

**διγονία**, for '*double parturition*' read '*birth in two stages* (i.e. production internally of an egg and hatching)'

***δίγυον**, τό, *measure of two* γύαι, Hsch. s.v. γύης.

**δῐδακτικός**, add '**II** [δάκτυλος] δ. *fore*-finger, *PLond.* 1821 in *Aegyptus* 6.194.304.'

**δῐδασκᾰλία I 2**, add 'ἕνεκεν διδασκαλίας λογικῆς Sch.Hes.*Th.* 720 p. 97.17'

**δῐδασκᾰλικός 2**, after 'sc. ὁμολογία' insert 'or συγγραφή' at end add '*PMich.*III 121ʳii 12, xi 13, xii 6 (AD 42); sp. διδεσκ- ib. 123ʳii 34 (AD 45/7)'

**δῐδασκᾰλιον II**, for 'Plu.*Lyc.* 14' read 'Plu.*Lyc.* 13'

**δῐδάσκᾰλος**, lines 1/2, within parentheses, fem., add 'also ἡ δέσκαλος (sic) *BGU* 332.9 (ii/iii AD); cf. Mod.Gk. δάσκαλος' **I**, add 'as ephebic office, Arist.*Ath.* 42.3' at end add 'Myc. *di-da-ka-re* (?loc.)'

**δῐδάσκω**, add '**IV** med., *instruct an advocate*, ἐδιδαξάμην .. Χρυσάμμωνα ῥήτορα *POxy.* 2343.8 (iii AD).'

***δῐδεσκαλική**, v. °διδασκαλικός.

***διδιπλοῦν**, τό, a measure of capacity, = 2 διπλᾶ, *BGU* 2175.8 (v/vi AD), *SB* 9295.11 (vi AD), *CPR* 14.4.9 (vi AD): v. *Aegyptus* 55.54ff.

**δῐδράσκω**, line 2, for '*Tab.Defix.Aud.* 26' read 'tab.defix. in *RhM* 56.85'

**δῐδραχμία**, for '*BGU* 741 iii 3' read '*BGU* 748 iii 5' and before this quot. insert '*PTeb.* 281 (ii BC)'

**δῐδραχμιαῖος**, add '**2** δ. τόκος *interest at 2 drachmas per mina per month*, *PHamb.* 28.5 (ii BC).'

**δῐδραχμος IV**, δίδραχμον, after 'τό' insert 'τὸ τέταρτον τῆς οὐγκίας Hsch.' and for '*half-shekel*' read '*shekel*'

**Δῐδῠμαῖος**, line 3, after 'of Apollo' insert 'Call.*fr.* 191.57 Pf.'

**Δῐδῠμεύς** (s.v. Διδυμαῖος), add '*SEG* 30.1352 (Miletus, iii AD)'

**δῐδῠμητόκος**, add 'θεὰ διδυματόκε i.e. Leto, Orph.*H.* 35.1'

**δῐδῠμόζῠγος**, for '*with a pair of horses*' read '*twin-yoked*, i.e. consisting of two moving, acting, etc., together'

**δίδῠμος I**, add '**b** Διδύμη as title of legion (transl. Lat. *Gemina*), ληγίωνος τρεῖς καὶ δεκάτης Διδύμης Mitchell *N.Galatia* 289.' **II**, add 'cf. Myc. *di-du-mo*, pers. n.'

***δῐδῠμωτός**, ή, όν, *forked*, γλῶσσα Cyran. 14 (1.4.16 K.).

***δίδυφον**, v. ‡δίζυφον.

**δίδωμι**, line 1, after '**δίδω**' insert '*POsl.*inv. 1460.7 (*Aegyptus* 31.179, i AD), δείδει (for δίδει) *PMich.*inv. 337 (*ZPE* 22.67, iv AD)'; line 8, inf., add 'δίδειν epigr. in Keil-Premerstein *Erster Bericht* No. 140 (i AD)'; line 16, for 'Lacon. ἔδον' read 'ἔδον Hes.*Th.* 30' and after '*B*1' insert '(Lacon.); Cypr. *e-tu-wa-n(o)* ἔδυϝαν *ICS* 217.6'; line 23, delete 'Cypr. .. ib. 6' and insert 'Cypr. inf. *to-we-na-i* δοϝέναι, *ICS* 217.5, also *to-e-na-i* δοέναι, *ICS* 306.6; Myc. 3 pl. *di-do-si*; pass. 3 sg. *di-do-to* δίδοτοι; fut. 3 sg. *do-se*, pl. *do-so-si*; aor. 3 sg. *do-ke*; pf. pass. part. *de-do-me-na*' **I 4**, add '**b** *consign, deliver*, ἔδωκεν εἰς κναφεῖον Macho 413 G.' **5**, line 4, after 'D. 21.87, 24.13' insert 'δ. ψήφισμα *propose*, Aeschin. 2.13' **II 1**, lines 2/3, after 'Il. 5.397' insert 'cf. Hippon. 39.1 W., Pl.*Phdr.* 254e' and after 'Od. 24.65' insert 'cf. Lib.*Or.* 1.245' **5**, add '*cause to be, make*, δώσω πάντας τοὺς ὑπεναντίους σου φυγάδας Lxx *Ex.* 23.27, δώσω τὴν Ἱερουσαλὴμ εἰς μετοικίαν *Je.* 9.10'

**διέ** (s.v. δῖε III), add '*SEG* 31.572.B15 (Crannon, c.200 BC), 33.460.12 (Larissa, ii BC)'

**διεγγυάω**, after lemma insert '(aor. διενεγυήσαμεν· ἐνεχυρισάμεθα Hsch.)'

**διεγείρω I**, add 'ὄρωρεν· διήγειρε Sch.Nic.*Al.* 339d Ge.'

**δίεδρος II 1**, add 'also δίεδρος, ὁ or ἡ, *Didyma* 467.12' **2**, for '*chaise-longue*' read '*double seat*, στρωμάτιον ὥστε τῷ μήκει ἐπὶ δίεδρον ᾖ μικρῷ μεῖζον, διπρόσωπον *PCair.Zen.* 241 (iii BC)' and for 'Antyll.' read 'Herod.Med.'

***διεικάτιοι**, v. °διακόσιοι.

**διειλύομαι**, for '*slip out of*' read '*wriggle through*'; add '*wind across*, χαίτη διειλυθεῖσα καρήνου Nonn.*D.* 4.364'

**διεῖπον II**, med., for '*fix upon, agree*' read '*state fully*' and add 'Clearch. 2'

**διείργω**, line 1, after '**διέργω**' insert 'aor. 2 opt. διεργᾰθοι Hsch.; cf. ἐργαθεῖν'

**διέκ**, after 'etc.' insert 'also w. acc., διὲξ τὸ μύρτον Archil. 32 W., διὲκ πέτρας ἐλάσειαν A.R. 2.558, 3.73'

**διεκβολή II**, for '*estuary*' read '*outlet* of river' and add 'Lxx *Ez.* 47.11'

**διεκδρομή**, after 'Ptol.*Tetr.* 102' insert '(v.l., v. °διαδρομή)'

**διεκπεραιόομαι**, add 'Sopat.Rh. 8.362.16 W.'

**διεκπίπτω**, line 2, after 'Ph.*Bel.* 57.3' insert 'J.*AJ* 14.15.3'

***διεκφυγγάνω**, *come safely through* an illness, etc., ἡ δὲ νοῦσος σπερχνή τε καὶ θανατώδης, καὶ ὀλίγαι διεκφυγγάνουσιν αὐτὴν καὶ μελεδαινόμεναι Hp.*Nat.Mul.* 38.

**διελίσσω**, add '**2** *cause to revolve*, οὐρανόν *SEG* 7.14.8 (Susa, Hymn to Apollo, i AD).'

**δίεμαι I**, add 'A.R. 2.330, Nic.*Th.* 755' **II**, for 'A.*Pers.* 701 (lyr., cod. Med. δείομαι)' read 'cj. in A.*Pers.* 701 (v. ‡δίω)'

***διενεγυήσαμεν**, v. °διεγγυάω.

***διένεξις**, εως, ἡ, app. = διαφορά, Sch.Th. 2.37 (cj., cod. διενίξας).

**διενοχλέω**, after 'Luc.*Symp.* 14' insert 'πρὶν ἂν .. διενοχλήσειε τὸν ἄνδρα στέλλουσα γράμματα Just.*Nov.* 22.14 pr.'

***διεξάπτω**, app. = ἐξάπτω B II, *set fire to, burn*, Gal. 8.415.8.

**διεξαρκέω**, after '*suffice*' insert 'ἐς τὸ ὀφθῆναι Hp.*de Arte* 11 (v.l.)'

**διέξειμι II**, line 2, after '(Hdt.) 7.77, etc.' insert 'ἐπαινῶν καὶ διεξιών τινας ὡς φιλανθρώπως ἔχουσι D. 23.13'

**διεξελαύνω**, add 'A.R. 3.879'

***διεξευκρῑνοῦμαι**, *make a thorough investigation* of, *PHeid.Gr.*inv. 1281 (*Scritti in onore di O.Montevecchi* ed. E. Bresciani, Bologna 1981, p. 406).

**διέξοδος I**, add '**6** *outcome, result*, D.S. 4.35.'

***διεξοχετεύω**, *channel through and out*, τάφρον .. διεξοχετεύουσαν ἐκ τῶν .. ἀμπέλων τὸ καταφερόμενον ἐξ αὐτῶν ὕδωρ ἐπὶ τὸ χείμαρρον ὑποκείμενον ῥεῖθρον *SAWW* 265(1).8.9 (Lydia, i BC/i AD).

***διεπιβουλεύω**, *compete in forming designs* on, τῷ γάμῳ Max.Tyr. 20.4 (v.l. δὴ ἐ.).

***διεπιτροπή**, ῆς, ἡ, app. = ἐπιτροπή, the region administered by an ἐπίτροπος, *PNag.Hamm.* 22(h).1.

**διέπω**, line 2, after '(Il.) 24.247' insert 'χορούς *h.Pan.* 23'

**⁺διέρᾱμα**, ατος, τό, (ἐράω (B), but sense I perh. influenced by διαίρω), kind of small boat, *POxy.* 3250.24 (AD 63), *BGU* 2027 (AD 296); also διάραμα *PBremen* 48.28 (ii AD), *PMil.Vogl.* 189.6 (AD 208); διάρημα Procop.*Aed.* 6.1; διαίρεμα *PThead.* 26.13, διέρεμα ib. 27.19 (both late iii AD). **II** kind of vessel used in straining or decanting, Plu. 2.1088e.

**⁺διερᾱμᾰτίτης**, ου, ὁ, *owner* or *operator of* διεράματα, *POxy.* 1197.14 (iii AD); see also °διαραματία.

**διέρᾱσις**, after lemma insert '(ἐράω (B), but perh. confused w. διαίρεσις)'; for '*lading*' read '*transport*' and add 'also διάρασις *PMil.Vogl.* 189.8, 11 (AD 208), διαίρεσις *POxy.* 2568.16 (iii AD)'

**διερείδω II**, after 'E.*Hec.* 66' insert 'D.H. 3.20'

**διερέσσω 2**, for 'E.*Tr.* 1258 (lyr.)' read 'E.*Tr.* 1258 (anap.)'

**διερευνάω**, after 'Plb. 14.2.1' insert 'ποία φροντίς, ποῖος δὲ λόγος διερευνᾶται παρὰ τοῖσιν; Epicr. 10.5 K.-A.'

**διερμηνευτής**, add 'Hsch. s.v. ὑποφῆται'

**διερός I**, add 'θνατὸς δ' οὔ κ[ε]ν ἀνὴρ διερὸ[ς] τὰ ἕκαστα εἴποι Ibyc. 1(*a*).26 P.' **II**, line 1, delete 'after Homer' and after '*liquid*' insert 'αὐην καὶ διερήν (sc. ἄροσιν) Hes.*Op.* 460; coupled w. τραφερός, Dionys.Bassar.*fr.* 34(b)+(c).3 L.'; line 3, for 'of birds .. *Nu.*

337' read 'of clouds, Ar.*Nu.* 337 (s.v.l.)'; line 11, after '(*soaked through*)' insert 'so Arist.*de An.* 423ᵃ24'

**δίερσις**, line 2, after 'Aen.Tact. 31.18' insert '(διαιρέσει cod.)'

**διέρχομαι I 1**, after 'Ar.*Av.* 181' insert 'διὰ παντὸς τοῦ μήπω μεμαχημένου τῶν ἐναντίων .. διελθεῖν Th. 7.43.7' **2**, for '*pass through, complete*' read '*complete the course of*' and add 'Sol. 36.17 W.'

**δίεσις I 1**, add '**b** *sifting, careful investigation*, Lxx *Wi.* 12.20 cod *H.*'

**διεστραμμένως**, after 'Hld. 2.19' add 'δ. τε καὶ ἀτάκτως Gal. 15.583.17'

**διευημερέω**, transfer the entry to follow διευεργετέω.

***διευθυντής**, οῦ, ὁ, = διευθυντήρ II, Vett.Val. 42.24.

**διευθύνω I**, after '*keep straight*' insert 'εὐθεῖαν ὁδὸν εὐθύνων ἢ διευθύνειν γε ὀφείλων Modest.*Dig.* 27.1.10.3' and before 'Ph. 1.327' insert 'in fig. phr.' add '**IV** intr., euphem. = *relieve oneself*, Aq. 1*Ki.* 24.4.'

**διευκρῑνέω II**, for '*examine thoroughly, elucidate*' read '*subject to a critical judgement, appraise*' and add 'Cic.*Att.* 7.8.3, *hoc* διευκρινήσεις πρόβλημα *sane* πολιτικόν ib. 7.9.2'

**διευλᾰβέομαι**, for '*take good heed to*' read '*treat with caution*'; for 'δ. μὴ .. ib. 789e' read 'δ. μὴ .. στρέφηται ib. 789e' and delete following 'but'

**διευλῠ́τησις**, add '*POsl.* 130.13 (i AD)'

**διευλύτωσις**, add '*Cod.Just.* 1.2.17.1'

**διευτελίζω**, for 'Ael.*VH* 14.49' read 'Ael.*VH* 14.48'

**διέχεια**, after 'Sch.Ar.*Pax* 938' insert 'κατὰ διέχειαν after an *interval*, Heph.*Poëm.* 10'

**διεχθραίνω**, add 'Aesop. 172 P.'

**δίζημαι II**, add 'Simon. 9, 37.22 P., Thgn. 83, al., Pi.*fr.* 51a.3 S.-M.'

**δίζῠφον**, add '*PGen.* 117.6 (iii BC), *AP* 9.503.2 (Pall.), διζῠ- ibid. 1 (s.v.l.); also **δίδυφον** *SB* 9907.19 (AD 388)'

**διηγημᾰτικός**, line 2, for 'ποίησις' read 'μιμητική'

**διήγησις**, add '*written* or *formal statement*, *POxy.* 3955.26 (AD 611); also to be read ib. 1892.42 (AD 581), 2420.21 (AD 610)'

**διηθέω I 1**, add '*isolate by filtering*, (ἔστιν) τόπος .. χρυσίῳ, ὅθεν διηθεῖται Lxx *Jb.* 28.1'

**διήκω II**, line 3, for '(but in an inverted constr.' read 'abs.' and delete closing bracket.

***διημίεκτον**, τό, app. *a double* ἡμίεκτον, *SEG* 16.495 (Chios, iii/ii BC).

***διήμῐσυς**, εια, υ, *dealing in half-measures*, τέλεον καὶ οὐ διήμισυν δεῖν τὸν νομοθέτην εἶναι Pl.*Lg.* 806c.

**διηνεκής**, line 5, at end insert 'τῷ διηνεκεῖ βίῳ *in the whole course of his life*, *SEG* 32.1243.6 (Aeolian Cyme, i BC/i AD)'; adv. διηνεκέως, add '*SEG* 32.1243.29 (Aeolian Cyme, i BC/i AD)'; lines 14/15, εἰς τὸ διηνεκές, for '*JHS* 33.338' read '*SEG* 30.568'

**διήνεμος**, add '**2** *swift as the wind*, διηνέμοις τε ταρσοῖς *Anacreont.* 58.3 W.'

**δῐ́ηρης II**, for '*with .. oars*' read '*having two files of rowers on either side*'

***δῐ́θηκος**, ον, *containing two coffins*, of a tomb (λατόμιον), *JÖAI* 23 *Beibl.* 204 (Thrace, Rom.imp.).

**δῐθύραμβος**, line 1, after 'ὁ' insert 'διθύραμφος Att. vase in *SEG* 16.40 (v BC)'

**δῐ́θῠρος**, line 2, after 'Porph.*Antr.* 3' insert 'κιβωτὸς δ. *IG* 1³.421.200 (Athens, v BC)'

***δῐθῠ́σᾰνος**, ον, *having two tassels* or *fringes*, Hsch. s.v. κέρκυ.

***διϊκᾰνοδοτέω**, *give surety*, *SEG* 39.1180.102, 124 (Ephesus, i AD).

**διϊκνέομαι**, for '*go through, penetrate*' read '*penetrate* or *carry as far as*' **2**, add '*h.Cer.* 416'

**διϊπετής**, add 'cf. °διαιπετής'

**διϊππεύω**, add 'Arg. ii in Ar.*Pax*; τοῦ πότου διϊππεύοντος the drinking-bout *proceeding*, *Vit.Aesop.*(G) 68'

**διΐπταμαι**, after 'Arist.*Mir.* 839ᵃ23' insert '*SEG* 37.529 (Epirus, iii BC)'; add 'act. part. ὡς ὀρνέου διιπτάντος ἀέρα Lxx *Wi.* 5.11'

**διϊστάω**, delete 'D.T. 642.31'

**διΐστημι I 4**, for 'Ath. 7.305d' read 'Ath. 7.303d' **III**, at end for '*spread*' read '*stretch from one point to another*'

**διϊσχῡρίζομαι II**, after '(Pl.)*Ep.* 317c' insert '*PMich.*XIII 659.14 (vi AD)'

***διϊσχῠ́ρισις**, εως, ἡ, *affirmation*, Epicur. 31[21].8 A.

**Διῖσωτήρια**, add 'cf. °Διοσωτήρια'

***διϊτητικός**, ή, όν, *penetrable*, Phlp. *in GC* 214.27.

**⁺δῑκᾰδία**, ἡ, *vessel with the capacity of two kadoi*, *IG* 2².1695.3, *Ath.Asklepieion* III 17 (both iii BC).

**δικάζω I 2 a**, lines 10/11, after 'X.*Cyr.* 1.2.7' insert 'transf., δ. ἀνδρεία τινὶ τὸ γύναιον *adjudges*, Procop.Gaz.*Ecphr.* p. 169 B.' **4**, add 'also w. dat. of thing, ὁ δικάζων τῇ ὑποθέσει *Cod.Just.* 4.21.22.6, Just.*Nov.* 15.3.2'

**δῐκαιοδοτέω**, line 2, after 'c. acc.' insert 'rei'; add 'of the person, *decide in favour of*, πρὸς τὴν κολωνείαν ἐδικαιοδότησα ὑμᾶς *Thasos* 186.3-4 (i AD)'

**δῐκαιοδότης**, after 'generally' insert '*OGI* 646'

**δῐκαιοκρίτης**, add '*Orac.Tiburt.* 101'

**δῐκαιολογικός**, after '*judicial*' insert '*PGrenf.* 2.7a.10 (iii BC)'

**δῐκαιοπρᾱγέω**, add '**2** pass., *receive satisfaction*, *POsl.* 40.18 (ii AD).'

**δίκαιος A 1**, lines 3/4, for '[Γαλακτοφάγοι] δικαιότατοι' read 'Ἀβίων .. δικαιοτάτων ἀνθρώπων' **3**, delete 'euphem.' add '**4** as title of god, Ὅσιος καὶ Δίκαιος Mitchell *N.Galatia* 45, 242, etc., Ὅσιος Δίκαιος *SEG* 34.1294 (Phrygia), etc.' **B I 1**, add '**c** of measures, *exact*, Lang *Ath.Agora* XXI Ha 25, 27 (iii AD).'

**δῐκαιοσύνη I 1**, before 'Pl.*R.* 433a' insert 'Lys. 2.14, 12.5' **2**, delete the section transferring exx. to section 1. **III**, after 'personified' insert 'E.*fr.* 486'

**δῐκαιότης**, after lemma insert 'Dor. δικαιότας *SEG* 30.119 (Entella, Sicily, iii BC)' and after 'Pl.*Prt.* 331b' insert '*Gorg.* 508a'

***δῐκαιοῦχος**, ον, *upholding justice*, *AA* 1934.168 (Olynthus, iv BC).

**δῐκαιοφᾰνής**, add 'Modest.*Dig.* 27.1.15.11'

***δῐκαιόφρην**, ενος, = *δικαιόφρων, *righteous-minded*, epigr. in *AEM* 19.109 (Callatis).

***δῐκαιοφροσύνη**, ἡ, *sense of justice*, *SEG* 38.1310 (δικεο- Phrygia, Rom. imp.).

**δῐκαιόω I**, delete the section. **III 1**, after '*punish*' insert 'νόμος .. δικαιῶν τὸ βιαιότατον Pi.*fr.* 169.2 S.-M.' and after 'pass.' insert 'δικαιωθείς *brought to justice*, A.*Ag.* 393 (lyr.)'

**δῐκαίωμα 1 c**, line 1, after '*documents* in a suit' insert '*SEG* 17.415.4 (Thasos, iv BC)'

**δῐκᾰνικός II 1**, add 'comp., D.H.*Vett.Cens.* 5.2'

**δῐκᾰ́σιμος**, add 'D.*fr.* 11'

***δῐκαστᾰγωγία**, ἡ, *function of* δικασταγωγός, *Delph.* 3(1).362 i 28.

**δῐκαστᾰγωγός**, for '*to their homes*' read '*to* and/or *from their homes*' and after '(ii BC)' insert '*SEG* 11.491 (Sparta, ii AD)'; add 'cf. Πολέμων 1.119ff. no. 422.6'

**δῐκαστήριον**, add '**3** pl., *hearings*, *POxy.* 3126.10 (AD 328).'

***δῐκαστορεύω**, *serve as a magistrate*, (prob. δικάστωρ, unattested equiv. of δικαστής) ϘόλουϘος δικαστορεύϝων ἔτευξε ὁ Παισιάδας τὸ τέγος *SEG* 29.548 (Thessaly, *c.*550 BC).

**δῐκεῖν**, line 2, for 'δίεπει' read 'διέπει' and add 'δικεῖν γὰρ τὸ βάλλειν Corn.*ND* 34 (cj., cod. δίκειν)' **1**, after '(E.)*HF* 498' insert 'w. advl. acc., μᾶκος δὲ Νικεὺς ἔδικε πέτρῳ ὑπὲρ ἁπάντων Pi.*O.* 10.72' deleting the ref. fr. section 2.

***δῐκέλᾰδος**, ον, perh. *with two sounds*, Hsch. s.v. κέρκυ (q.v., διστέλεχος La.).

**δῐ́κελλα**, for '*fork*' read '*hoe* or *mattock*' and add '*IG* 2².1673.51, Men.*Dysc.* 375, 390, al.'

***δῐκελλευτής**, οῦ, ὁ, = δικελλίτης, *PCair.Zen.* 788.20 (iii BC).

***δῐκέλλιον**, τό, dim. of δίκελλα, *two-pronged hoe* or *mattock*, *BGU* 2361a ii 13 (iv AD), *PVindob.* G14271 (*Aegyptus* 61.87, vi AD).

**δῐ́κελλον**, add '[perh. read **δίκελλον**· ‹δίκελλα›. **δικραδές**· τὸ ἐξ ἑνὸς ‹πυθμένος› δύο κλάδους ἔχον Hsch., cf. La. ad loc.]'

**⁺δῐκέντητον**, v. °διακέντητον.

**δῐκέραιος**, after 'Antip.' delete '(?)'

**δῐ́κερας**, for 'Callix. 2' read 'Callix. 2(34) J.' and add 'drinking-vessel, Theocl. 3'

***δῐκεράτιον**, τό, name of a tax, cf. °τετρακεράτιον *REG* 70.120 (Palestine, vi/vii AD).

**δίκη I 2**, after 'c. gen.' insert 'ἰκτίνου δίκην Semon. 12 W.' **II 1**, add 'referring to the constellation *Virgo*, Max. 208, Nonn.*D.* 6.249' **IV 2 b**, add 'δ. γράφειν write *a speech for the courts*, Demetr.*Eloc.* 229' **3**, line 11, for '(E.)*Heracl.* 852' read '*SIG* 167.37'

***δικηλιστής**, v. °δεικηλιστής.

***δῐκῑτωνία**, ἡ, v. °διχιτωνία.

***δῐ́κιων**, ον, *having two columns*, [πρόθυρον] *IG* 1³.426.67 (Athens, v BC).

***δῐκληρία**, ἡ, perh. *allotment in two sections*, *Ath.Agora* XIX L7.9 (iv BC).

**δῐκόλλῠβος**, read '**δικόλλυβον**, τό'

**δῐκολογέω**, add '*Cod.Just.* 2.7.19'

**δῐκολόγος**, after '*advocate*' insert 'Phld.*Rh.* 1.38.7'

***δῐκορία**, ἡ, *double pupil* (eye disorder), Cyran. 34 (1.16.20 K.).

**δῐκορίᾱσις**, add 'pl., Cyran. 75 (v.l. δικορία, 2.40.32 K.)'

**δῐκόρυμβος**, add 'Philostr. *VA* 2.3'

***δῐκόρωνον**, τό, *pair of crows*, *Vit.Aesop.*(G) 77.

**⁺δικρᾰ́δεστος**, prob. ghost-word: v. ‡δίκελλον.

***δῐκρᾰδής**, ές, *having two branches*, v. °δίκελλον.

***δῐκρᾱνισμός**, *digging in* of manure, *PSoterichos* 4.27 (AD 87).

**δίκροος**, add 'also πρὸς τοῖς [δ]ικροῖς on the *zygomatic bones* (which are forked), *APF* 4.271 (iii AD)'

**δίκροτος I 2**, subst., δ., τό, add '*SEG* 33.684 (Paros)'

**δίκρουνος**, delete '*with two springs*' and for 'a vase *from* .. *poured*' read 'vase *with two spouts*, Antisth.Paph. in *Philol.* 101.105.16'

**⁺Δικταῖος**, α, ον, *of* or *belonging to Dicte*, mountain in Crete, A.R. 1.509, Call.*Jov.* 47, *Dian.* 199, *Epigr.* 22.3 Pf., Str. 10.4.12; Myc. *di-ka-ta-jo*.

**δικτῠαρχέω**, delete '*in the cult* .. (less prob.)' and for '(Callipolis)' read '(Parium)'

⁺**δικτῠβόλος**, ὁ, *fisherman* (one who casts nets), *AP* 6.4 (Leon.Tarent.), 6.105 (Apollonid.), 9.370 (Tib.Ill.), Opp.*H.* 4.578.

***δικτῠΐσκος**, ὁ, *railing in lattice-work*, *An.Par.* 4.21.14.

**Δίκτυννα**, add '*Inscr.Cret.* 2.xvii 1.15 (Lisos, iii BC), *Amyzon* 14.3, 15.3 (iii BC)'

***Δικτυνναϊσταί**, οἱ, association of worshippers of Dictynna, *IMylasa* 179.4 (Rom.imp.).

**δίκτῠον 4**, add '*IAskl.Epid.* 52A.42 (iv BC)'

**δικτῠοπλόκος**, for 'Poll. 7.139' read 'Poll. 7.179' and add '*SPAW* 1934.1032 (tab.defix., Attica, iii BC)'

***δικτῠουλκέω**, *haul up with nets*, Call.*Dieg.* viii.14 (*fr.* 197 Pf.).

***δίκτυς** (B), = δίκτυον (in quot., sense 4), Alex.Polyh.ap.Eus.*PE* 9.34.11.

**δικτῠωτός**, after 'θυρὶς δ. *lattice-window*' insert '*PMich.*I 38.18 (iii BC)'; add 'also δικτυωτή, ἡ, Lxx *Jd.* 5.28, Hsch.'

***δῐκωμία**, ἡ, *group of two villages*, *INikaia* 1551 (iii AD), *IPhrygie* 26.

**δίλασσον**, add '*PVindob.Worp* 24.4 (iii/iv AD)'

**δῐλημμα**, after '*ambiguous proposition*' insert 'Serv.*Aen.* 2.675, 10.449, Jerome *adv.Rufin.* 3.3'

**δῐλιτρον**, add 'χρηστοῦ δίλειτρον *IG* 14.2417.2'

**δῐλωρος**, for 'dub.sens.' read '*having two* λῶροι (?epaulettes or sim.)' and add 'στιχαρίων δ' ἐρεῶν διλώρων *SB* 9305.7 (iv AD), δίλωρον ἕν ib. 11075.9'

⁺**δῐμαλλος**, ον, perh. *made with two fleeces*, *Gloss.*; app. neut. subst., διμάλλων ζυγ(οῦ) *PMerton* 41.10 (v AD).

***δῐμάτιον**, τό, *double* μάτιον, *PLond.* 1718 *passim* (vi AD).

**δῐμηνία**, delete the entry (v. *Anc.Soc.* 21.33).

***δῐμήνιος**, ον, *two months old*, *PMich.*XII 658.7.

***διμισσωρία**, ἡ, Lat. *dimissoria*, *BGU* 27.13 (ii/iii AD).

**δῐμῐτος**, delete 'καυσία'

⁺**δῐμιτρος**, ον, *having a double headband*, καυσίαις διμίτροις Plu.*Demetr.* 41.

**δίμνους**, δίμνουν, τό, add '*SEG* 39.1752 (ii/i BC)'

**δῐμοιραῖος I**, add '**2** σιτηρέσια τὰ καλούμενα διμοιραῖα *double annona*, *SEG* 8.355 (Egypt, vi AD).' **II**, delete '*PMasp.* .. (vi AD)'

**δῐμοιρία I 1**, add '*IEphes.* 4337.15 (i AD)'

**δῐμοιριαῖος**, add 'τόκος *PMasp.* 126.38, al. (vi AD)'

**δῐμοιρίτης I 1**, add 'διμοιρίτην ἢ τριμοιρίτην Luc.*JTr.* 48' **2**, for 'Id.' read 'Arr.' **II**, delete '*mate* .. 48'

**δίμορφος**, add '*Com.adesp.* 386'

**δῑνάζω**, add 'δίνασεν ὄμμα B. 17.18 S.-M.'

***δινάριον**, v. °δηνάριον.

**δίνευμα**, for 'prob. in Ar.*Th.* 122' read 'Ar.*Th.* 122 (cj.)' and after 'X.*Eq.* 3.11' insert 'cj., codd. and most edd. δὴ νεύματα)'

**δῑνεύω, δῑνέω**, line 8, for '*whirl*' read '*swing round in a circle*' **I 2**, add 'Λευκίππην ἔπι δίνεαι Anacr. 23 P. (ἐπιδίνεαι codd.)'

**δίνη 4**, add 'Opp.*H.* 4.420'

**δίνω**, line 2, for '(v.l. περὶ)' read '(v.l. πέρι)'

**Διο-**, delete the entry.

**διό**, after '*on which account*' insert 'Hdt. 7.6.4'; διὸ καί, add 'Arist.*Ath.* 3.6, al., *Peripl.M.Rubr.* 10, al.'

**Διοβλής**, for '*hurled*' read '*struck*'

**Διογένητος**, delete 'contr. for Διογένητος' and add 'Hes.*fr.* 60 M.-W.'

**διοδεύω**, line 3, for 'Arr.*Epict.* 2.23, 26' read 'Arr.*Epict.* 2.23.36'; add '*PCair.Zen.* 367.33 (240 BC); med., *BGU* 1273.56 (222/1 BC), *IEJ* 16.59.28 (*c.*200 BC)'

***διόδιος**, ἁ, app. = δίοδος, *BCH* 116.200.6, 7 (Phocis, iii BC).

**δίοδος I**, add '*right of way*, *SEG* 30.568 (Maced., ii AD); *"street"* in a military camp, δίοδον .. ἣν καλοῦσι πέμπτην Plb. 6.30.6'

**διόδους**, before '*Gloss.*' insert '*Edict.Diocl.* 15.47'

***δῐόζια**, τά, perh. *forked branches*, Hippon. 92.5 W.

**Δῐόθεν**, add 'Il. 24.561, Hes.*Sc.* 22, Thgn. 197, Pi.*N.* 4.61, 6.13, A.*Ag.* 470, *Ch.* 306, *Pr.* 1089, *Supp.* 437, E.*fr.* 916.6'

**διοικέω I 1**, line 18, before 'pass.' insert 'in ref. to the imperial secretary *ab epistulis*, ἐπιστολὰς διοικεῖν D.C. 72.7.4, 78.13.4'; lines 21/3, delete 'pf. pass .. cf. 40' add '**c** *manage*, *control* a person, Alciphr. 2.2.' **2**, for this section read '*contrive*, *bring about*, τὸ εὔπρεπὲς δ. D.H.*Rh.* 9.3; med., D. 18.178; δ. οὕτως ἀδίκους πλεονεξίας id. 44.38, cf. 40; ὁ ἕτερα λέγων καὶ ἕτερα διοικούμενος λόγος D.H.*Rh.* 9.4, cf. 8.10, 9.10. **b** *furnish*, *procure*, decr.ap.D. 24.27, τόκους *SIG* 672.73 (Delph., ii BC), *SPAW* 1936.380 (Thestia, ii BC), Wilcken *Chr.* 167.26 (ii BC). **c** *provide for* a person, τὴν ἀδελφήν D. 24.202, διοίκει κἀμὲ καὶ τὴν μητέρα Men.*Dysc.* 739, Str. 14.2.24.' **5**, delete the section.

**διοίκημα**, add '*administrative act*, *IG* 12 suppl. 365 (pl., Thasos, ii BC)'

**διοίκησις I 1**, line 6, before 'ἕοπως' insert '*provision*, *funds*' add '**b** *ordering*, *government*, τῶν ἐνθάδε (i.e. in the world) Aristid.Quint. 2.2; τῶν ὅλων id. 3.26.' **II**, add 'group of provinces as an administrative unit of the church, *Cod.Just.* 1.3.45.6'

**διοικοδόμησις**, for '*fortification*' read '*walling off*'

**διολκή**, add '**III** = παρολκή I, *delay*, *PMich.*VIII 486.8, *PFam.Teb.* 24.93 (both ii AD).'

⁺**δίολκος**, ὁ, passageway for the transport of cargo-boats (and occasionally warships), spec. across the isthmus of Corinth, Str. 8.2.1.

⁺**Διομανής**, διομανεῖς· ὑπὸ Διὸς μαινόμεναι· ἢ τῷ Διὶ βουλόμεναι μάχεσθαι διὰ μανίαν Hsch.

***Διόμβρια**, τά, name of festival, *SEG* 1.327.14 (Callatis, i AD).

**διομολογέω II**, add 'abs., Aen.Tact. 24.5'

**Δῐονῡσιάς I**, add '**5** a precious stone, Plin.*HN* 37.157.'

**Δῐονύσιος II**, add '*SEG* 25.744 (Callatis, ii BC), 39.1001.1 (Camarina, ii/i BC)'

***Δῐονῡσίς**, ίδος, ἁ, *female votary of Dionysus*, *SEG* 11.610.3 (Sparta, ii AD).

**Δῐόνῡσος**, line 3, for 'and **Δεύνυσος**' read 'Ion. **Δεύνυσος**', before 'also **Δίνυσος**' insert 'Aeol.' and after '(Amorgos)' insert '**Δινύσō** (gen., Berezan, v BC), Aeol. Δίννυσος *SEG* 32.1243.12 (Cyme, i BC/ i AD); Ζόννυσσος Alc. 129.9 L.-P., Ζόννυσος *IG* 12(2).69 (Mytilene, ii AD)'; at end add '[Δ]ιϝονύσου *SEG* 29.360 (Argos, iv BC) cf. pers. n., Διϝονύσεις *IPamph.* 77 (Aspendos, ii BC), etc. Myc. *di-wo-nu-so*'

***Δῐονῡσοτροφικός**, ή, όν, *concerned with the sustenance of Dionysus*, βωμός Robert *Ét.Anat.* 289 (Paphlagonia, Rom.imp.).

**Διοπετής**, line 1, after '*from Zeus*' insert 'i.e. from heaven' and after 'E.*IT* 977' insert 'ἀστήρ id.*fr.* 971'

**διοπεύω**, for '*captain*' read 'δίοπος' and add 'διοπεύειν· ἐπιμελεῖσθαι νεώς Hsch.'

**διόπη**, for '*IG* 2.652*B*26' read '*IG* $2^2$.1388.76 (Athens, iv BC)' and add '*Inscr.Délos* 104.51 (iv BC)'

***Διοπλήξ**, ῆγος, ὁ, ἡ, *struck by Zeus*, Hippon. 19.1 W.

***Διόπομπος**, ον, *sent by Zeus*, αἰετός Sch.Pi.*I.* 6.53.

**δίοπος** (A) **I**, add 'cf. as pers. n. *SEG* 34.939 (Camarina, vi BC)' **II**, for '*captain of a ship*' read 'a ship's officer'

**διοπτήρ**, add 'also διοτήρ· κατάσκοπος Hsch.'

***διοργᾰνισμός**, ὁ, *apparatus*, Zos.Alch. 252.17.

**διοργάνωσις**, add 'Iamb.*Protr.* p. 117.12 P.'

**διορθόω II**, line 7, for '(Plb.) 12.28.5' read '(Plb.) 11.28.5'

**διόρθωμα II**, add '*SEG* 23.305 (Delphi), 34.558 (Larissa, both ii BC)'

**διορθωτής 1**, as transl. of Latin *corrector*, add 'perh. δι]ορθωτὴν Γαλ[ατίας ἐπαρχείας] Mitchell *N.Galatia* 414'

⁺**διορία**, ἡ, *interval*, *Vit.Aesop.*(G) 82, cf. ib.(W).

**διορίζω**, line 1, fut., add '-ίσω E.*Melanipp.Capt.fr.* 6.26'

***διορκόω**, *swear solemnly*, *SEG* 9.3.15 (Cyrene, iv BC).

**διορμίζω**, after 'D.S. 20.88' insert '*Peripl.M.Rubr.* 39, 55'

***δίορον**, τό, *dividing-line* between day and night in an ἀνάλημμα, Hero *Dioptr.* p. 304 S.

***Διορύγίτης**, ου, ὁ, title of Asclepius, *IApam.* 5, 6 (-είτης).

**δῖος I 2**, add '*TAM* 4(1).48.8 (Rom.imp.); in word-play, cf. II, οἱ μὲν δὴ οὖν Διὸς δῖόν τινα εἶναι ζητοῦσι τὴν ψυχὴν τὸν ὑφ' αὑτῶν ἐρώμενον Pl.*Phdr.* 252e' at end add 'Myc. *di-wi-jo* (variant *di-u-jo*), neut. subst., *shrine of Zeus*; *di-wi-ja* (var. *di-u-ja*), app. name of a goddess'

**Δῖος**, before 'ὁ' insert '(in inscr. freq. **Δεῖος**, sts. **Δῆος**' at end add 'Myc. *di-wi-jo-jo* (gen.)'

**Δῐόσδοτος**, add 'διόσδοτον ἀρχάν Pi.*fr.* 137.3 S.-M.'

**διοσκέω**, for 'Anacr. 3' read 'Anacr. 14.3 P.' and delete 'διαπολέσαι, διαφθεῖραι'

**Δῐόσκοροι**, line 3, after '*h.Hom.* 33.1, etc.' insert '*IG* 12.3.359 (Thera, viii/vii BC)'; dual, add 'Διοσκόρō *BCH* 102.51 (Attic vase, vi BC), oblique -οιν app. in *SEG* 30.1456 (Pontus, v BC)' add '**IV** σημεῖον ἐν θυτικῇ, Hsch. s.v. Διόσκουροι.'

**Διοσκουριασταί**, add '*BCH* 10.425 (Cedreae, ii BC)'

***Διοσσωτηριασταί**, οἱ, an association (κοινόν) connected w. the Διοσωτήρια, *Lindos* 683 (i BC).

***Διοσ(σ)ωτήρια**, τά, *festival of Zeus Soter* at Rhodes, Maiuri *Nuova Silloge* 19 (iii/ii BC); cf. Διισωτήρια.

⁺**διοτήρ**, v. °διοπτήρ.

**διότι I 2**, before 'Henioch.' insert 'Pl.*Ion* 536d' at end add 'see also διεκί'

⁺**διού**, v. °δύο.

**δῐούγκιον**, add '**2** *sixth of an estate*, *Cod.Just.* 4.6.6.16c, Just.*Nov.* 18.5.'

**διουργέω**, delete the entry (cf. *Delph.* 3(1).457.9).

**διοχλίζω**, add 'Sch.Nic.*Al.* 452a Ge.'

**δίπαις**, for 'Cypr. .. 93 H.' read 'Cypr.*ti-pa-se*, δίπας *ICS* 84.3'

***δῐπᾰλαστος**, ον, = διπάλαιστος, *Inscr.Délos* 1442*A*47 (ii BC).

⁺**δίπαλτος**, ον, *"doubly brandished"*, δίπαλτα πολεμίων ξίφη, app. swords brandished by two men, E.*IT* 323; δίπαλτον .. κεραυνοφαὲς πῦρ (?forked), id.*Tr.* 1103. **2** perh. *brandishing with two hands*, πᾶς .. στρατὸς δίπαλτος ἄν με χειρὶ φονεύοι S.*Aj.* 408.

***Δῑπᾰνάμια**, τά, festival at Rhodes, *ASAA* 8/9(1925/6).317 (i BC), *Clara Rhodos* 6/7.437 (Camirus, i AD), *Lindos* 490.11 (ii AD); cf. Μάναμος.

***δίπεμπτον**, τό, *two-fifths*, *BGU* 2331.12 (AD 91).

**διπλάδιος I**, for 'Antip.' read 'Antip.Thess.'

**διπλάζω I**, add 'δίπλαζ' ἕκαστον κῶλον *Trag.adesp.* 166.3 K.-S.'

**δίπλαξ I**, line 1, after 'Il. 23.243' insert 'λώπη Theoc. 25.254'

**διπλάσιος 1**, add 'διπλάσιοι γίγνονται ταῖς προθυμίαις *they become twice as eager*, Onas. 23.2' **2**, add 'ἐκ διπλασίων *doubly*, *Cod.Just.* 10.11.8.4b' **4**, adv., add 'Gal. 13.872.10'

**διπλεθρία**, for '*IG* 9(1).693.20 (Corc.)' read '*Inscr.Cret.* 2.x 1.20, 22 (Cydonia)'

**δίπλειον**, for '*PPetr.* 2 p. 42' read 'διπλεῖōι θōιέστō *IG* 9²(1).717.8 (Chalium, v BC)'

**διπλῆ**, line 1, after '*Gort.* 2.7' insert '(v BC), διπλῆ *Inscr.Cret.* 4.13i (Lap. διπληι, Gortyn, vii/vi BC)'

***δίπλησον**, aor. imper. *multiply by two*, perh. erron. for δίπλωσον (διπλόω) *PCair.* 10758 (vi AD).

***διπλόγραμμος**, ον, *having double lines*, *Poliorc.* 233.5.

***διπλοείλητος**, ον, *double-turned* (the precise sense is unclear) ἀστερίσκος, Hero *Stereom.* 1.77.

**διπλόη I**, delete 'but usu.' and add '**2** *dual nature*, Plu. 2.441d, Aristid.Quint. 2.8.' **II 2**, delete 'cf. 441d' and insert 'ἦν μὲν γὰρ ἐξ ἀρχῆς διπλόη τις ὕπουλος ὥσπερ ἐν σιδήρῳ Plu.*Per.* 11.3'

***διπλοία**, ἡ, = διπλεία, *Inscr.Cret.* 2.xii 5.6, 13.3 (Eleutherna, vi BC).

**διπλοΐς I**, for 'Antip.' read 'Antip.Sid.'

**διπλοκάριος**, add 'cf. °δουπλικάριος'

**διπλόος I**, delete 'properly of cloaks and articles of dress' add '**7** *having a double* or *composite nature*, ταύρου μεμῖχθαι καὶ βροτοῦ διπλῇ φύσει E.*fr.* 997.' **II**, add 'ἐν διπλῷ *doubly*, *Cod.Just.* 1.1.7.22, Just.*Nov.* 123.2.1' **III**, delete 'in trag.' and add 'A.R. 1.588, *AP* 7.198 (Leon.Tarent.)' add '**VI** διπλοῦς, ὁ (sc. (?)πίναξ), *contract* or *copy of a contract*, *MAMA* 8.413.(c), al. (Aphrodisias, Rom.).'

**διπλός**, line 1, after '(cf. ἁπλός)' insert 'Emp. 17.1, 16 D.-K.'

**διπλόω**, line 2, after 'Vett.Val. 159.27' insert '*duplicate*, διπλόσσαι (sic) τὴν κλεῖδαν ostr. in *ZPE* 62.69 (Mons Claudianus, ii AD)'

**δίπλωμα II**, for this section read '*double document* (a certificate written out twice, on papyrus or on a diptych, and closed or rolled with one copy forming the interior which was sealed), *BGU* 1113.9 (i BC), *ISmyrna* 236b.18 (i AD), δ. γάμων *BGU* 388.31 (ii AD), *SB* 10530 (ii AD), δ. Ἑλληνικόν *PVindob.Bosw.* (iii AD); prob. of a licence, δ. ὄνων *BGU* 213 (ii AD), δ. ἵππων *PAmh.* 2.92.21 (ii AD); of a travel permit, "*passport*", Cic.*Att.* 10.17.4, *Fam.* 6.12.3; of an order enabling a traveller to use the public post, Plu.*Galb.* 8, *OGI* 665.25 (Egypt, i AD)'

***διπλωμάτιον**, τό, dim. of °δίπλωμα II, *POxy.* 2730.3 (iv AD).

**δῐποδιάζω**, for 'fut.' read 'Dor. (or Lacon.) aor. 1 subj.'

***Δῐπολιασταί**, οἱ, association connected w. the Διπολίεια, *Hesperia* 9.331 (Athens, iv BC).

**διπρόσωπος 1**, add 'στρωμάτιον .. δ. *PCair.Zen.* 241 (iii BC)'

**δίπτῠχος II**, add 'δίπτυχον ἄτην, of the death of a brother and sister, epigr. in *SEG* 34.1290 (Phrygia, Rom.imp.); δίπτυχα ὀρχεῖσθαι (sc. σχήματα) Aristid.*Or.* 28(49).129' **III**, add '*Cod.Just.* 1.1.7.22'

***δίρ**, v. °δίς.

**δίρκος**, for '= φθείρ III' read '*louse*'

***δί(ρ)ρυτος**, ον, perh. *flowing in two ways*, *Poliorc.* 214.9.

**δίς**, add 'δϝίς *SEG* 26.407 (Isthmia, vi BC); also Lacon. δίρ *IG* 5(1).302.5'

***δῐσακκία**, ἡ, = δισάκκιον, *POxy.* 2424.34 (ii/iii AD), δεισακεία μία *PColl.Youtie* 84.12 (iv AD), *POxy.* 1923.6 (v/vi AD), *Stud.Pal.* 20.67.38.

***δῐσάρχων**, οντος, ὁ, *twice* ἄρχων, *CIJud.* 1 p. 505 (v. *BE* 1959.259).

***δῐσεπίτρῐτος**, ον, διπλάσιος καὶ δ. [λόγος] two and *two-thirds* times as great, the ratio *8:3*, Theo Sm. p. 56 H.

***δῐσευποσιάρχης**, ου, ὁ, *one who holds the office of* εὐποσιάρχης *twice*, *Dacia* N.S. 1.182.7 (Callatis, i AD).

***δίσεφθος**, ον, *twice boiled*, Gal.*CMG* 5.4.(2).206.4, 312.19, 326.12.

**δίσημος I-III**, for these sections read '**I** in prosody or music, containing two time-units, χρόνος Aristox.*Rhyth.* 2.10, μέγεθος ib. 2.31, πούς Aristid.Quint. 1.14; cf. ἔστι γὰρ μακρὰ παρὰ τοῖς μουσικοῖς τεσσάρων χρόνων, ἣν καὶ δίσημον καλοῦσιν ὡς διπλασίαν τῆς παρὰ τοῖς μετρικοῖς μακρᾶς Elias *in Cat.* 189.9. **II** (of vowels), *having two quantities*, i.e. long or short, Sch.D.T. p. 38 H. **III** *having two meanings*, Sch.Od. 9.106.'

**δισθανής**, for '*twice dead*' read '*dying twice*'

**δισκεύω**, pass., add '*to be hit by a quoit*, *GVI* 815.4 (Pamphylia)'

**δισκέω**, add 'Anacr. 19 P.'

**δίσκος II 4**, after '*gong*' read 'Lxx 2*Ma.* 4.14, Plu.*Per.* 6, S.E.*M.* 5.28, 69'

***δισκούσσωρ**, ὁ, Lat. *discussor*, *auditor*, (= λογοθέτης), *SEG* 8.310.6 (Palestine, vi AD).

***δισκοφᾰνής**, ές, *disc-shaped*, ἄρτους δισκοφανεῖς δύο *SEG* 39.449.9 (Tanagra, v AD).

**δισκοφόρος**, for '*bringing .. discus*' read 'τὴν δ. (sc. χεῖρα) *holding the quoit*'

**+δισμῡριεπτᾰκισχῑλιοστός**, ή, όν, *twenty-seven thousandth*, Gal. in *QSGNM* Bd. 3 [Heft 4].336[128].

***δίσορος**, ον, on stele, perh. tomb *having two* σοροί, *SEG* 6.101 (see also 26.1835, Cotiaeum).

**δισπερίοδος**, delete the entry.

***δισποντάρχης**, ου, ὁ, *one who holds the office of* ποντάρχης *twice*, *ITomis* 116 ii 6 (ii AD).

**δισσός I 1**, add 'διττόν, neut. as adv., *twice*, *ITrall.* 89'

**διστάζω**, line 5, after 'Plu. 2.62a' insert 'ὡς οὐ .. Longin. 28.1'

***δίσταθμος**, ὁ, *double camp*, given in Hebr. letters as equiv. of Mahanaim, *Midrash* to *Ps.* 33 (Tarbiz ii.507).

***διστάξιμος**, ον, *doubtful*, Papp. *in Alm.* p. 93.

**δίστεγος 1**, add '*SEG* 6.672 (Pamphylia), *MAMA* 8.498 (Aphrodisias), *Sardis* 7(1).12; neut. subst. *two-storey building*, *BE* 1971.644 (Hierapolis)'

***διστέλεχος**, cj. for °δικέλαδος, Hsch.La. (s.v. κέρκυ).

**δίστοιχος**, add 'prob. of a χορός, A.*fr.* 78c.ii2 R.'

**δίστομος II**, add '-ος, ἡ, *double axe*, Nonn.*D.* 30.141'

***δίστῡλον**, τό, *colonnade with two rows of pillars*, *Princeton Exp.Inscr.* 419a.

***δισφῡλαρχία**, ἡ, *tenure of* φυλαρχία *twice*, *ITomis* 123.2 (ii AD).

***δισφύλαρχος**, ὁ, *holder of the office of* φύλαρχος *twice*, *ITomis* 123.1 (ii AD).

**δίσχοινος**, add 'τὸν γύαν .. δ. τὸ εὖρος *SEG* 39.996.3 (Camarina, ii BC)'

**δίσωμος**, add '**2** *designed to contain two bodies*, καμάρα *Sardis* 7(1).163, κοιμητήριον δίσωμον *T&MByz* 7.316 n. 10 (Thessalonica, AD 535).'

**δῐτάλαντος**, add 'Poll. 9.54'

**+δῐτοκέω**, *bear two at a birth*, Arist.*GA* 772ᵃ35. **2** *bear twice*, id.*HA* 558ᵇ23, Nic.*fr.* 73.1 G.-S.'

***δῐτομή**, ἡ, *splitting* of reeds, *POxy.* 3354 (iii AD).

**δῐτομία**, for '*second cutting*' read '*splitting*'

**+διττάμενον**· ἀρνούμενον. Κρῆτες Hsch.; perh. read ἀνύμενον (v. *PP* 23.365).

**διτταχῶς**, add '*PHamb.* 128.60 (iii BC)'

***διττότης**, ητος, ἡ, *ambiguity*, Anon. *in SE* 57.25.

**διῠδᾰτίζω**, for 'Sch.Il. 6.302' read 'Sch.Il. 2.307'

**διϋλισμα**, add 'Ps.-Democr. p. 41 B.'

***διυπερβάλλομαι**, *outdo*, *surpass*, *SEG* 38.1462.9 (Oenoanda, ii AD).

***διυπέχω**, *submit* oneself, διυπ[έχ]ω ἐμαυτόν *SB* 10724.18 (iii AD).

***διυπόκειμαι**, *to be detailed below*, *PSorb.* 20 (AD 253).

***διυποκολλάω**, *attach* a document *at the end*, *POxy.* 3365 (AD 241).

**διυφή**, add '*PCair.Zen.* 423 (iii BC)'

***δῐφάρετρος**, ον, epith. of τόξον, *equipped with two quivers*, epigr. in *Inscr.Cret.* 4.243 (ii BC, -αλε- lap.).

**διφάω**, line 1, for 'only pres., *search after*' read '*probe*, *poke into*, *seek for by delving*'

**διφθέρα I**, at end before 'used for' insert '*page* of a codex, Afric.*Cest.* p. 16 V. (pl.)' and for 'bindings' read 'casings' **II**, for '*anything made of leather*, *leather jerkin*' read '*upper-garment made from animal skins*, typically worn by country people, slaves, etc.' at end add 'Myc. *di-pte-ra*; also in compd. *di-pte-ra-po-ro*'

**+διφθεράλοιφος**, ὁ, Cypr. *ti-pe-te-ra-lo-i-po-ne*, διφθεραλοίφōν (gen. sg.) *ICS* 143, *schoolmaster*, γραμματοδιδάσκαλος παρὰ Κυπρίοις Hsch.; cf. perh. °ἀλειπτήριον II.

**+διφθερίας**, ου, ὁ, person wearing a °διφθέρα II, Luc.*Tim.* 8, Poll. 4.137; on the stage, Varro *RR* 2.11.11.

**διφθέριον**, add '*piece of leathery tissue*, *Hippiatr.* 58'

***διφθεροποιός**, ὁ, *leather-worker* or *parchment-maker*, *MAMA* 6.44 (Colossae; sp. -πύς for -πύος).

***Δῑφίλεια**, τά, Τραιάνεια, a festival at Pergamum, *IEphes.* 4114, 1605.9 (Δει-).

**δῐφορέω II**, (pass.), add '**2** *to be repeated*, Sch.Il. 9.26.'

**δίφορος I 1**, add 'humorously applied to one Ephorus who paid his fee to his teacher twice, Hsch.' **II**, delete the section.

**δίφραξ**, add 'in the original version of A.R. 1.789 acc. to Sch. ad loc.'

**διφρηλᾰτέω**, after 'E.*Rh.* 781' insert 'Theodect. 17'

**διφρίον**, before 'Tim.' insert '*chair* or *stool*, διφρία ξύλινα δύο *Inscr.Délos* 1417*B* ii77 (ii BC)'

**δίφρος I**, line 8, delete '*travelling-car*' and transfer '*litter* .. D.C. 60.2' to section II. **II**, line 4, after '*seat of office*' insert '*Inscr.Cret.* 4.160*B*3 (iv/iii BC, pl.)'; after '*throne*' insert 'Call.*Jov.* 67'; add 'δ. γυναικεῖος *obstetric stool*, *POxy.* 3491.8 (ii AD)'

**διφρῠγής**, subst., add 'Heras ap.Gal. 13.779.17'

**δίφῠής**, line 6, after 'δ. Ἔρως' for '*sexual intercourse*' read '*of double nature*, i.e. *androgynous*' add '**3** *bearing two crops* (in the year), [γῆς] χόρτῳ διφυοῦς *PWarren* 2.16 (vi AD), cf. *PLond.ined.* 1769aᵛ.2. **4** δ. (sc. λίθος), ἡ, a precious stone, Plin.*HN* 37.157.'

**δίφυιος III**, after 'ζιφ-' insert 'ib. 409.6' add '**IV** δίφυιον νυκτός· τὰ δύο μέρη, τὸ δίμοιρον Hsch.'

**δίφωνος**, add '*Peripl.M.Rubr.* 20'

*__δῐχαλκαῖος__, α, ον, *costing two chalci*, *PCair.Zen.* 19.5 (iii BC).

*__δῐχαλκηρός__, όν, app. adj. fr. unkn. flower name, στέφανοι διχαλκηροί *PAlex.* 22.2 (ii AD).

**δῐχαστός**, add '**2** *divided in two equal parts*, τὴν δὲ γῆν .. καὶ τὴν ἀγορὰν .. νείμασθαι διχαστὴν ἑκάτερος *Ath.Agora* XIX L4a.18 (iv BC).'

*__δίχθα__, ἡ, a perfume, *Edict.Diocl.* 36.85, 86.

**διχθάδιος**, line 1, after 'Il. 14.21' insert 'φονέας Call.*fr.* 177.32 Pf., A.R. 3.397'; line 2, delete 'simply, *two*'

*__δῐχῐτωνία__, ἡ, *double* (perh. *lined*) χιτών, *PTeb.* 514 (sp. δικιτ-, pl., ii AD).

*__δῐχοίνῐκον__, τό, *measure of two* χοίνικες, Ar.*Nu.* 640.

**διχοινικός**, delete the entry.

*__δῐχόνιον__, τό, *two-*χοῦς *jar*, *POxy.* 3942.20, al. (AD 606).

⁺__δῐχονοέω__, *to be in two minds*, *PMich.*inv. 203 (*ZPE* 29.290).

*__δῐχότης__, ητος, ἡ, *state of being cut in half*, of a phase of the moon, *PMich.*III 149 xi 34.

**δῐχοτομέω** **2**, add 'fig., τῷ υἱέῳ μου .. τῷ διχοτομήσαντί με τοῦ πολοέ(τι)ον ζῆν i.e. who has condemned me to live alone, etc., *MAMA* 8.252b'

*__δίχρῡσον__, τό, *coin of value of two* χρυσοῖ, *Inscr.Délos* 338*Ba*14.

*__δίχῠτος__, ον, *formed by fusion of two* (metals), πέταλον Maria Alch. ap.Zos.Alch. 146.16.

*__δίχωρος__, ον, app. *having two compartments*, [οὐ]εστάριον γυναίκιον δ. *PMasp.* 340$^v$.41.

*__διψάκιον__, τό, = δίψακος I, Anon.Alch. 20.3.

**διψάς** **II 1**, add 'cf. δ.· ἔχις. ὕδρα. καὶ σημεῖον ἐν θυτικῇ ἐπὶ τοῦ ἥπατος Hsch.'

**διψάω** **2**, line 5, w. inf., add '*AP* 6.335 (Antip.Thess.)'

*__διψέλλιον__, τό, *double armlet*, *PRainer Cent.* 161.29 (?v AD).

**δίψησις**, for 'cf. δίψα' read '(v.l. δίψης)'

**δίψιος**, add '**III** Δίψιος (sc. μήν), ὁ, name of month at Larissa, *BCH* 59.515 (iii BC).' at end add 'Myc. *di-pi-si-jo-i* (dat. pl.), prob. divinities'

**δίω**, last line, for 'f.l. for δίεμαι, id.*Pers.* 700' read 'w. inf., δίομαι μὲν χαρίσασθαι, δίομαι δ' ἀντία φάσθαι id.*Pers.* 700, 701'

*__διωβελιαῖος__, v. ‡διωβολιαῖος.

**διωβολιαῖος**, add 'also **διωβελιεῖος** (sic) *JHS* 74.87.30 (Caunus, ii BC)'

**διώβολον**, add '*IG* 1$^3$.236.10'

**διωγμείτης**, delete the entry.

*__διωγμίτης__, ου, ὁ, *policeman* in some Asian cities (v. *SEG* 33.1591), *BCH* 52.409 (Pisidia), *IGRom.* 4.580 (Aezani, sp. -είτης).

**διωθέω** **I 1**, at end for 'Pl.*Ti.* 67e' read 'Pl.*Ti.* 68a'

**διώκω**, line 3, after 'διώξομαι' insert 'A.*fr.* 204b.5 R. (lyr.)' **3**, line 3, after 'X.*Mem.* 2.1.34' insert '(v.l. διώκει)' **III 3**, for 'Simon. 29' read 'Pi.*fr.* 107ab.(a)3 S.-M.' and add 'Ἰάονι τόνδε λαῷ παιᾶνα διώξω Pi.*Pae.* 2.4 S.-M.'

**διωλένιος**, line 1, for 'Antip.' read 'Antip.Sid.'

**διωμοσία**, add 'also app. during the proceedings, *Cod.Just.* 12.37.19.4, Just.*Nov.* 22.44.2'

**Διώνη** **I**, add 'with a cult at Dodona, *SEG* 23.474 (Διώνᾱ, iv/iii BC); app. identified w. Hecate, ib. 34.1436 (Apamea, iii AD)'

**Δῐωνῡμία**, add 'Hsch. s.v. Βάκχου Διώνης'

⁺__διωρία__, ἡ, *interval*, J.*BJ* 5.9.1, cf. διωρίαν· διαζυγίαν, διαχωρισμόν Hsch.; δ. ἐσχάτως ἀδόκιμον· ἀντ' αὐτοῦ δὲ προθεσμίαν ἐρεῖς Phryn. 16 F.; see also °διορία.

**δῐώροφος**, for '*with two roofs* or *stories*' read '*having roofs at two levels*'

**δίωτος**, add 'cf. fem. subst. *diōta* Hor.*Carm.* 1.9.8'

**δμωΐς**, add 'Plu.*Cam.* 33.4'

**δμῶος**, after lemma insert 'or **δμωός**' and delete 'Call.*Hec.* 1.4.15 (pl.)'

**δνοφέος**, read 'δνόφεος'; for 'B. 15.32' read 'B. 16.32 S.-M.; v.l. for δνοφερός in Hes.*Th.* 736 (*POxy.* 2649); cf. γνόφεον, ζόφεος'

**δνοφερός**, at end for 'Hp.*Morb.Sacr.* 16' read 'Hp.*Morb.Sacr.* 13' and add 'see also °γνοφερός'

*__δνοφοείμων__, ον, gen. ονος, *clothed in dark robes*, rest. in *IG* 2$^2$.3606 (verse, Attica, ii AD).

*__δοάκιστα__· ἀσφαλέστατα Theognost.*Can.* 52 A., Cyr. (ineditus).

**δόγμα** **1**, for '*that which seems to one*' read '*that which seems right* or *reasonable*'; add 'as a course of action, Pl.*Ti.* 90b, *Lg.* 854b' **2**, add 'of other ordinances, etc., Ῥωμύλου .. τύμβος καὶ δόγματα ταῦτα *SEG* 32.1256 (Bithynia). **b** *decree* granting a privilege, μηδὲ δόγμα τινὶ διδόναι πολιτείας ἢ χρήσεως τόπων δημοσίων *SEG* 30.568 (i AD).'

⁺__δογμᾰτογρᾰφέω__, *draft a decree*, *IEphes.* 27.427, al. (AD 104), 4101a; *serve as* δογματογράφος, *MAMA* 9.15 (Rom.imp.).

**δογμᾰτοποιΐα**, add 'Alcin.*Intr.* 36'

*__δοιάκι(ς)__, = δυάκις, epigr. in *SEG* 33.891.11 (Lydia, ii BC).

**δοῖδυξ**, add 'Lys.*fr.* 62a'

**δοιοί**, add 'form *δϝοιός, cf. Myc. *du-wo-jo, dwo-jo*, pers. n.'

*__δοιώδεκα__, poet. for δυώδεκα, *twelve*, Q.S. 2.595 (v.l.).

**δοκεύω** **1**, add '*Lyr.adesp.* 7 P.' **2**, for 'Arat. 987, al.' read 'Arat. 1128' and after 'c. gen. .. id. 813' insert '1136'

**δοκέω** **1**, add 'part. τὰ δεδοχμένα *Delph.* 4(4).357.14 (iii BC)' **I**, line 1, after 'δέχομαι II 3)' insert 'w. acc., ἀνέμοιο, ὑετοῖο κελεύθους Arat. 803/4' **1 a**, lines 3/5, delete 'rarely .. X.*An.* 5.7.26' **b**, add 'A.*Ag.* 1649' **2**, before 'mostly' insert 'w. two accs., τούτους τί δοκεῖτε; what *do you think* about them? X.*An.* 5.7.26'; line 3, delete 'Ar.*Pax* 47'; line 4, before 'πῶς' insert 'δ. μέν S.*El.* 61, 547, *OC* 995, Ar.*Pax* 47'; for 'to .. remarked' read '*you cannot think* how much, how well, etc.; cf. οἴομαι VI 1' **3 b**, lines 3/5, delete 'rarely .. 650' **II 4**, line 4, after 'Pl.*R.* 487d' insert 'without dat., X.*An.* 4.5.1, etc.'; at end delete 'without μοι, X.*An.* 4.5.1' and insert 'not parenth., opp. τὸ ἀληθές, *in seeming*, J.*AJ* 19.2.1; w. subj. ἐπὶ κῶμον δοκεῖ ἴωμεν Antiph. 197 K.-A., ἢ δοκεῖ τοὺς θεοὺς ὑμνοῦντες σφόδρα τιμῶμεν; Pl.*Epin.* 980b' **5**, line 6, after 'E.*Hec.* 295' insert '*Ep.Gal.* 2.2; δοκέων, opp. ἀδόκητος, Pi.*N.* 7.31, *Trag.adesp.* 482 K.-S. (lyr.)'

⁺__δοκή__, glossed by ὑπόνοια, Hdn.Gr. 1.313; δόκαι· ἐνέδραι, παρατηρήσεις Hsch., δοκάν· θήκην id., δοκήν· δόκησιν, δοχήν id.

**δοκῐμάζω** **II 1**, at end delete 'ἐκπονεῖν .. *Mem.* 1.2.4' **3**, after '*think fit* to do' insert 'Macho 371 G.'

**δοκῐμαστής**, for '*money-changer*' read '*scrutineer of currency, assayer*' and add '*SEG* 26.72.5, al. (Athens, 375/4 BC)'

*__Δοκῐμᾰτογλύφος__, ὁ, *carver of Dokimeion marble*, Λιμναῖος καὶ Διομήδης ἀδελφοὶ ἀγαλματογλύφοι Δοκιματογλύφοι Δοκιμεῖς ἀνέθηκαν *SEG* 32.1311 (Iconium).

**δοκῐμεῖον**, add '**II** perh. *test-sample* of precious metal from which offerings have been made, *CID* II 102 iia 5ff., *IG* 2$^2$.1424a.313ff., 7.303 (Oropus, iii BC), *Inscr.Délos* 1449*Aab*ii32 (ii BC).'

**δοκῐμή**, add '**3** *characteristic feature*, Epiph.Const. in *Lapid.Gr.* 194.18.'

*__Δοκῐμηνός__, όν, *made of marble from Dokimeion*, *BE* 1971.642 (Hierapolis).

⁺__δόκῐμος__, ον, (α, ον, *Tab.Heracl.* 1.103) *reliable, dependable*, Alc. 6.12 L.-P., Heraclit. 28 D.-K. (sup.), Democr. 67 D.-K.; w. inf., δόκιμος δ' οὔτις .. εἴργειν A.*Pers.* 87. **2** *acceptable, approved*, ὕμνος Pi.*N.* 3.11, κριθὰ καθαρὰ δ. *Tab.Heracl.* 1.103. **b** *approved, examined*, of naval stores, δόκιμα καὶ ἐντελῆ *IG* 1$^3$.498-500 (v BC); of metal, coin *certified, approved*, ἀργύριον D. 35.24, *PLond.* 938.6 (iii AD), χρυσοῦ δοκίμου κεφαλαίου 991 (vi AD). **3** *esteemed, distinguished*, ἀνδρὸς δοκίμου ἐν Μήδοισι Hdt. 1.114.3, 124.3, 152.3, al., οἰκίης .. ἐὼν δοκίμου 5.66.1, ποιηταί Phld.*Po.* 1.11, 2.12, J.*BJ* 1.35, *AJ* 6.191, al. (all sup.); of rivers, Hdt. 7.129.2; w. dat. δοκιμώτατος Ἑλλάδι E.*Supp.* 277; w. παρά, Ἀρταχαίην, δόκιμον ἐόντα παρὰ Ξέρξῃ Hdt. 7.117.1. **4** adv. -μως, *surely, for certain*, Parm. 1.32 D.-K., A.*Pers.* 547, X.*Cyr.* 1.6.7.

⁺__δοκῐμόω__, = δοκιμάζω, Hsch.; ἢν δοκιμώσῃς (sc. τὴν γραφήν) *if you approve*, Ps.-Pherecyd.ap.D.L. 1.122.

**δοκίμωμι**, add 'cf. δοκίμοι Theoc. 30.25, 26 (3 sg., cj.)'

**δοκίς** **I 1**, add 'Opp.*H.* 4.536'

**δοκός**, line 5, for '*one who has swallowed a poker*' read 'of a stiff or inflexible speaker' and for 'Ar.' read 'Arist.'

**δόκος** **I**, add '**b** perh. *expectation*, *LW* 1170.14.' **II**, add '(perh. δοκός)' add '**III** ἐς δόκον· ἐς ἐνέδραν Hsch.'

*__δόλαντρον__, τό, *horn for carrying grease*, δ.· κέρας γλοιὸν ἔχον, ᾧ ἁμαξεῖς χρῶνται εἰς τὸν ἄξονα Hsch.; also **δόλατρον**, Theognost.*Can.* 52 A.

**δόλιος**, line 6, after 'Hermes' insert '*SEG* 37.1673 (Cyrenaica, vi BC)'

*__δολῐχαδρόμος__, v. δολιχοδρόμος, °δολιχοδρομεύς.

*__δολῐχαῖος__, ὁ, = δόλιχος, *SEG* 29.147.6 (Athens, c.AD 200).

**δολῐχαυλος**, add '*Certamen* 126'

*__δολῐχεύς__, έως, ὁ, *competitor in the* δόλιχος (race), *ABSA* 26.213 (Sparta, ii AD), Pi.*O.* 12 tit. (v.l.).

**δολῐχεύω**, add 'fig., of a runner in the race of life, *SEG* 35.1427 (Side, iii AD)'

*__δολῐχοδρομεύς__, έως, ὁ, = δολιχοδρόμος; δολιχ[ο]δρομέ[α] rest. in *PASA* 3.413 (Kara Baulo, Asia Minor), but δολιχαδρόμον is possible.

**δολῐχόπους**, delete the entry.

**δολῐχός** **I**, add 'A.*Pr.* 284' at end add 'cf. Myc. pers. n. *do-ri-ka-o*, compd. *do-ri-ka-no*'

**δόλιχος**, after 'opp. στάδιον' insert '*IG* 5(1).222 (Laconia, vi BC)' **II**, for pres. def. read '*a leguminous plant*'

**δολομήδης**, for 'f.l. in Simon. 43' read 'Simon. 70 P. (cj.)'

**δολοπλόκος**, line 2, after 'Sapph. 1.2' insert 'L.-P., Simon. 36.9 P.'

*__δολοποιέω__, *practise fraud*, *MAMA* 3.225 (Corycus).

**δόλος** (A) **2**, add 'Hdt. 9.90.3, Pl.*R.* 548a, X.*An.* 5.6.29, *HG* 7.1.46, Plb. 4.87.4, al.'

**δολοφροσύνη**, add 'A.R. 4.687'

**δόλοψ**, for '*lurker in ambush*' read '*scout, spy*, Theognost.*Can.* 52 A.' and add 'also glossed by μάστροπος Hsch.'

**δολόω**, line 1, after '*take by craft*' insert 'Hes.*fr.* 33(a).18 M.-W.' **II**, line 2, for 'Dsc. 1.81' read 'Dsc. 1.68'; for '*alloy*' read '*give a disguised harmful effect to*'

**δόλωσις 2**, for '*alloying*' read '*making noxious with a disguised admixture*'

**δόμα** (A) **1**, add 'δ. ἀναπόδοτον *PCair.Zen.* 825.3 (252 BC), *UPZ* 2.8 (ii BC), *SEG* 37.851 (Aphrodisias, iv AD)' **2**, delete the section.

***δομεστικός**, ὁ, Lat. *domesticus*, title of palace official, *SEG* 32.1554 (Arabia), *ICilicie* 89, Just.*Nov.* 30.70.2 (all vi AD), etc.

***Δομιτιανός**, ὁ, name of month in Egypt (= Phaophi), μὴν Δ. *POxy.* 237 viii 43, *PLond.* 259.99 (both under Domitian).

**δομοτέκτων**, add '*JÖAI* 23 *Beibl.* 183 (Thrace), *IGBulg.* 690'

***Δονάκεια**, τά, *festival founded by Δόναξ* at Delos, *Inscr.Délos* 366A54, al. (iii BC).

**δονακοφοίτης**, delete the entry.

**δόναξ**, line 2, delete '(δονέω "a reed *shaken with the wind*")' **II 3**, delete 'or *limed reed*' and after '(Apollonid.)' insert '6.27 (Theaet.), 28 (Jul.), 29 (id.), Opp.*H.* 3.74; *limed reed*, *AP* 6.109 (Antip.Sid.)' **4**, for this section read 'used in the construction of a lyre, ἕνεκα δόνακος, ὃν ὑπολύριον ἔνυδρον ἐν λίμναις τρέφω Ar.*Ra.* 232'

**δονέω I 1**, line 5, before 'pass.' insert 'A.*fr.* 311.3 R.; med., Βορέης .. δεδονημένος Nonn.*D.* 1.69, 2.80'

**δόξα III 1**, line 2, for 'first in Sol. .. 34' read 'πρὸς ἁπάντων ἀνθρώπων αἰεὶ δόξαν ἔχειν ἀγαθήν Sol. 13.4, 34' add '**5** *an honour conferred on one, distinction*, τὰς .. Ἑλληνικὰς δόξας καλλίστας ἡγούμενοι Lxx 2*Ma.* 4.15. **b** accorded to things, δόξαν .. ἀπομέρισον τῇ προτετιμημένῃ .. ἡμέρᾳ ib. 15.2.'

**δοξάζω II**, for '*magnify*' read '*hold in honour*' and add '*OFlorida* 17.10'

**δοξαστής I**, add 'Antisth.*Aj.* 8' **II**, add '*AB* 1.242'

***δόραντον**, prob. corruption for °δόλαντρον, Hsch.

***δορᾰτοδέξιος**, ον, *holding a spear in the right hand*, poet. in *PKöln* 245.9 (iii AD).

**δοριάλωτος**, after 'Plb. 23.10.6' insert '*SEG* 32.833 (Samos, 38 BC)'

***δορίδαπτος**, ον, *"consumed by the spear"*, *Suppl.Hell.* 991.98 (poet. word-list, iii BC).

**δορίκρᾶνος**, for '*spear-headed*' read '*forming a spearhead*' and add '(cj. δουρικρανοῦς, as fr. δουρικρανής)'

**δορίμᾰχος**, add 'cf. as pers. n., *SEG* 34.281e (Corinth, vi BC)'

***δορίπληκτος**, ον, Ion. **δουρί-** A.*Th.* 278, *struck by the spear*, λάφυρα δαΐων .. δουρίπληχθ' A.l.c., Sch.E.*Andr.* 653.

**δορίς**, for 'Call.*Aet.* 3.1.11' read 'Call.*fr.* 75.11 Pf.'

***δορίσκηπτρος**, Dor. **-σκαπτρος**, ον, *ruling by the spear*, Antip.Sid. in *EG* 3616 P.

***δορίστεπτος**, ον, = δοριστέφανος, Ῥωμαίων ἀρχάν prob. in Limen. 46.

**δορκάδιον**, after 'τό' insert '**ζορκάδιον**, *Cat.Cod.Astr.* 8(2).164.12'

***δορκᾰδοθήρας**, ου, ὁ, *gazelle-hunter*, *PCair.Zen.* 744.1 (iii BC).

**δορκάς**, after 'ἴορκος Opp.*C.* 2.296, 3.3' insert 'ἴορκες Hsch.' add '**II** *dice made of deerhorn*, Herod. 3.63; cf. δορκαλίδες.'

**δορκών** I (s.v. δορκάς), add '*PColl.Youtie* 55.20'

***δοροδόκιον**, τό, *beam*, *transom*, *PMerton* 39.5, 12 (iv/v AD, pl.); cf. δουροδόκος.

**δόρπον**, add 'S.*fr.* 734'

**δορποφόρος**, add 'Δορποφόρων ἱερόν *SEG* 28.708 (Paros, iv BC)'

**δόρυ**, lines 6 ff., for 'dat. δορί or δόρει .. Choerob.*in Theod.* 1.346' read 'dat. δορί; δόρει A.*Supp.* 846, S.*OC* 620, 1314, 1386, Achae.29 (all edd. for metrical requirements, codd. δορί)' **I 2**, *ship*, add 'δ. νήϊον A.R. 3.582; δόρυ alone, *AP* 7.665 (Leon.Tarent.), Opp.*H.* 3.213, *C.* 4.265' **II 1 a**, add 'as symbol of judicial court, [δέκ]α ἀνδρ[α ἐπὶ τῶν] ὑπὸ δόρυ κρι[τηρ]ίων, cf. Lat. *decemvir ad hastam*, *Xanthos* 48' add '**II** Boeot. pl. δόρα, as measure of length, *REG* 10.29 (Thespiae, iii BC).'

**δορυθαρσής**, for 'also -θρασής' read 'also δοριθρᾱσής' and add 'epigr. in *SEG* 37.751.9 (Lato, *c.*100 BC)'

**δορύκνιον**, after 'τό' insert '(also sp. δορυχν-)'

***δορύπαλος**, gloss on ἐγχέσπαλος, Hsch.

**δορυσσόος**, add 'Nonn.*D.* 13.49, 14.305, etc.'

***δόρωμα**, ατος τό, prob. = δόρωσις, *PMich.*I 37.9 (iii BC).

**δόρωσις**, add '*IG* 2².1682.30 (iii BC)'

**δόσιμος**, after 'η, ον' insert 'Boeot. δότιμος, *liable to be handed* or *paid over*, τὸ ἅλωμα ἅπαξ δότιμον *SEG* 25.556.25 (Haliartus, *c.*210/200 BC)'

**δόσις I 1 b**, add '*Peripl.M.Rubr.* 32' **II 1**, add 'ἐν δόσει *as a gift*, ἔδωκεν ἐν δόσει τοῖς τε νῦν αὐτοῦ καὶ ἐσομένοις μύσταις *IG* 10.2(1).259 (Thessalonica, i AD)'

****δοσμός**, ὁ, Myc. *do-so-mo*, *contribution*; deriv. adj. *do-si-mi-jo* (cf. ἀπυδοσμός, -δόσμιος, s.v. ἀπο-).

**δοσοληψία**, add '*PLond.* 1727.45 (vi AD, -λημψ- pap.)'

**δότειρα**, add 'Aeol. πολέμου δότε[ρ]ραν (or -τε[ι]-) Alc. 298.9 L.-P.'

***δότιμος**, v. °δόσιμος.

***δουακα**, unkn. aromatic, *Peripl.M.Rubr.* 8.

**δουκηνάριος I**, add '*BCH* suppl. 8.267 (Thasos, v/vi AD), δωκενάριος *SEG* 7.1097 (Arabia)'

***δουκιανός**, ή, όν, *of* or *belonging to the dux*, ἐξουσία *PMasp.* 283.1.3 (vi AD).

**δουκικός**, add '*Epigr.Gr.* 446.6 (Arabia, iv AD), δουκικῆς τάξεως *PMasp.* 23.5 (AD 569); *SEG* 32.1554a.20 (Arabia, vi AD)'

***δουκτάριον**, τό, cf. Lat. *ductarius*, *a rope used for hauling*, *Edict.Diocl.* in *SEG* 37.335 iii 4.

**δουλᾰγωγέω 2**, add '*Suppl.Mag.* 38.9'

**δουλᾰγωγός**, add '*Vit.Aesop.*(G) 91 (s.v.l., cj. δουλαγωγία)'

**δουλεία**, line 1, after 'also' insert '**δουλίη** Sol. 36.13 W.' add '**IV** legal *servitude*, *Cod.Just.* 8.10.12.3.'

**δούλειος**, line 1, delete 'Pi.*fr.* 223'

**δουλελεύθερος**, add '*POxy.* 2238.11 (vi AD)'

**δουλεύω 3**, for '*render a service*, τινά' read '*behave as a servant*, ἀλλήλοις' add '**4** pass., *to be served*, *Vit.Aesop.*(G) 31, al.'

***δούλη**, v. ‡δοῦλος II.

**δουλικός 1**, add 'app. written δουλιδός, *BGU* 2548.6 (ii AD)' **2**, add 'neut. as subst., *slave*, *Peripl.M.Rubr.* 13 (pl.); *slave* or *place of burial of a slave*, [Α]ὐρηλίου Ποπλίου .. ἡ μάκρα σὺν τῷ δουλικῷ *MAMA* 3.795 (Rough Cilicia)'

**δουλοκοίτης**, add 'μὴ πρόσιθί μοι, δουλοκοῖτα *Vit.Aesop.*(G) 49 (-κόπα cod.)'

***δουλοπαράσῑτος**, ὁ, *parasite of slave origin*, *Dura*[9] 1.217 (iii AD).

**δοῦλος** (A) **I**, line 4, after '(q.v.)' insert 'for the distinction between δοῦλος and οἰκέτης cf. Chrysipp.*Stoic.* III.86, Ammon.*Diff.* 45'; line 7, after 'A.*Pers.* 242' insert 'of the subject of Roman emperor, *IG* 4.204 (Corinth, vi AD)' **II**, line 6, after 'etc.' insert 'δοῦλα τοῦ θεοῦ τρία ἀδέλφια *SEG* 36.1182; fem. as subst., ἡ δούλη τοῦ θεοῦ ib. 1186 (both Galatia, v/vi AD)' at end add 'Myc. *do-e-ro*, *do-e-ra* (fem.)'

**δοῦλος** (B), delete the entry (v. °δοῦμος).

***δουλοχείρων**, ονος, ὁ, *one worse than a slave*, *PMasp.* 353.18 (vi AD).

***δουμοπύραιθοι**, οἱ, members of an association connected w. worship of Cybele, in Lat. transcription *dumopiretis* (dat. pl.), *JDAI* 44.132-6 (Moesia, ii AD); cf. πύραιθοι.

***δοῦμος**, ὁ, religious association, perh. a Maeonian wd., Hippon. 30 W., *AP* 7.222.3 (Phld.); *TAM* 5(1).179 (Lydia, ii AD); ἱερὸς δ. ib. 536 (iii AD), etc.; app. an association of women in *IGBulg.* 1925.20 (Hadrian); perh. δοῦμος (cj., δοῦλος cod.)· ἡ οἰκία ἢ τὴν ἐπὶ τὸ αὐτὸ συνέλευσιν τῶν γυναικῶν Hsch.

**δούξ**, after '= Lat. *dux*' insert '*commander of a military district*'; add 'ἀπὸ δουκῶν *of ducal rank*, *PMich.*XI 611.4 (AD 412)'

***δουπλικάριος**, ὁ, Lat. *duplicarius*, military title indicating the receipt of double pay, *PAmh.* 108.3 (ii AD), *SEG* 8.346 (sp. δοφλικάρις, Palestine, v AD); also **δουπλικιάριος** (var. as in Lat.) *PGrenf.* 2.51.5 (-ιάρις, ii AD), *SEG* 8.608.9 (Egypt, ii/iii AD), *PBerol.*inv. 7347 (*JJP* 19.93, iii AD).

**δοῦπος**, at end, rare in prose, add 'Hld. 1.30, 9.8'

**δούρειος**, at end, add 'form *δόρϝειος, Myc. *do-we-jo*'

**δούριος**, add 'Paus. 1.23.8, Q.S. 12.110, Hsch.'

**δουρίπηκτος**, delete the entry (v. °δουρίπληκτος).

***δουρίπληκτος**, v. °δορί-.

**δοχαῖος**, for 'κραδίην .. δοχεῖον)' read 'subst. δοχαίη, ἡ, *receptacle*, Nic.*Al.* 21 (s.v.l.)'

**δοχεῖον**, add '**b** *reservoir*, *Lindos* 289, 290 (i BC), *SEG* 37.282 (Argos, ii AD).'

**δοχεύς**, add '**II** = ὑποδοχεύς, *receiver*, *host*, *IG* 12 suppl. 365.11 (Thasos).'

***δοχμάς**, άδος, fem. adj. *slanting*, ὁδός *Delph.* 3(4).42.8.

**δόχμιος I**, for 'ἐμβάνειν' read 'ἐμβαίνων'

**δράγμα**, after '(δράσσομαι)' insert 'also δράχμα Nic.*Th.* 667; Cypr. *ta-ra-ka-ma-ta* δράγματα *Salamine* 2 (*c.*600 BC)'; for '*handful*; esp. .. *truss*' read '*the amount that can be grasped in the hand*, δράχμα χερὸς πλήσας Nic. l.c.; cf. δράγμα· τὸν τῆς σταφυλῆς βότρυν, καὶ τὰς φοινικίνας βαλάνους Hsch., esp. in reaping' for '**II** later, *uncut corn*' read 'applied to crops still standing'

**δραγμᾰτηγέω**, add '*BGU* 1511.8 (iii BC)'

**δραγμᾰτηγία**, add '*BGU* 1513 (iii BC)'

***?δραγμᾰτολογία**, ἡ, app. *gleaning*, rest. fr. ἀπὸ δραγματολ(..) *POxy.* 3473.32 (ii AD).

***δραγματολόγος**· ὁ τὰ δράγματα συνάγων Hsch.

***δραϝεός**, ά, *cauldron*, *CEG* 344 (pl., Phocis, vi BC); cf. δραιόν.

**δράκαινα**, for '*dragon*' read '*serpent*, applied esp. to mythical beings'

***δράκιον**, τό, word of dub. sense in inventory of clothing, *PRyl.* 627.14 (iv AD).

**δρακονθόμῑλος**, for '*of dragon brood*' read '*swarming with serpents*'

***δρᾰκονῖτις**, ιδος, ἡ, = δρακοντίας 4, Plin.*HN* 37.158.

**δρᾰκόντειος**, for 'Luc.*Philops.* 4' read 'Luc.*Philops.* 24'

***δρᾰκοντέλιξος**, ον, *covered with coiling snakes*, *Suppl.Mag.* 42.2, 63 (iii/iv AD).

***δρᾰκοντιοῦς**, perh. *snake-coloured*, -οῦντα Ps.-Callisth. *Γ* 1.7.1 (unless to be taken as part. of *δρακοντιόω *"turn into a snake"*).

***δρᾰκοντόστηθος**, ον, *having the breast adorned with snakes*, of Athena, φένγαστι, δρακοντόστηθε poet. in *PKöln* 245.9 (iii AD).

**δράκος II**, add 'Poll. 2.147'

**δρακτόν**, for '*small vase*' read 'measure of capacity, perh. a quarter of a ξέστης' and add '*MAMA* 8.492, *SEG* 6.185 (Sebaste), *Laodicée* p. 265.15'

***δρακτός**, ή, όν, adj. applied to unguents used by athletes, app. *grasped by the hand*, i.e. *solidified* (opp. *liquid*), δρακτοῖς ἐλαίοις *MAMA* 8.484, 485, δ. ἄλειμμα *BCH* 10.520 no. 19 (Nysa).

**δρᾰ́κων I**, line 2, delete '*dragon*' and 'interchangeable with ὄφις' **IV 4**, for '*dragon*' read '*snake*'

***δρᾰκωνάριος**, ὁ, *bearer of the serpent-standard*, *MAMA* 1.218 (Laodicea Combusta), *PLond.* 113.1.86 (vi AD), *SEG* 32.1554.A36 (Arabia, vi AD).

***δρᾱμᾰτοθέτης**, ου, ὁ, *one who arranges a dance*, rest. in *SB* 7336.

**δράξ I**, *handful*, add 'Lxx *Le.* 2.2, 5.12, 3*Ki.* 17.12, *Ez.* 13.19' **II**, *hand*, add 'Poll. 2.144, Lxx *Ez.* 10.2'

**⁺δρᾰ́πᾰνον**, v. ‡δρέπανον.

***δρᾱπετᾰγωγεῖον**, τό, *prison for runaway slaves*, *BGU* 1881.7 (sp. -ώγιον, i BC).

**δρᾱπετεύω**, add '*PStrassb.* 612.23 (Arsinoe, ii AD), *PKöln* 281.10 (vi AD)'

**δρᾱσείω**, add 'Ar. *V.* 168'

**⁺δρᾱ́σῐμος**, ον, *that can be done*, A. *Th.* 554.

**δράσσομαι I 1**, after 'Il.l.c.' insert 'Archil. 223 W.' **II**, line 2, after '*catch*' insert '*APl.* 275.10 (Posidipp.)'

**δραστέος II**, δραστέον, add 'Pl. *Phlb.* 20a, *Criti.* 108d, *Lg.* 626a, al.'

**δραχμή**, for 'δράσσομαι .. Plu. *Lys.* 17)' read '(δράσσομαι), **δαρκνά** *GDI* 4985, *Leg. Gort.* 1.32, al.; **δαρκμά** *GDI* 5071 (Knossos); **δαρχμά** ib. 1154 (Elis), *IG* 5(2).3 (Tegea), *SEG* 24.361 (Khorsiai, iv BC), Hsch.; **θραχμά** *SEG* 23.392 (Corcyra, vi BC): *handful*, ὀβελίσσκων δαρχμαὶ τριάκοντα πέντε *SEG* 24.361 (Khorsiai, 386/380 BC))' for '**I**' read '**II**' **2**, after 'Pl.Com. 174.17' insert 'Men. *Epitr.* 159'; at end delete '**δαρχμή** .. δαρκνά'

**δραχμιαῖος 2**, add 'Heras ap.Gal. 14.203.14'

**δραχμίον**, delete the entry.

***δράψ**, ᾶπός, ὁ, perh. = δραπέτης, Ar. *fr.* 809 K.-A.

**δράω** (A), line 10, after 'freq. in trag.' insert 'and in prose, e.g. Antipho 2 δ 5, al., Hp. *Epid.* 4.43, al., D.S. 5.55.6, al., Ph. 1.44, al., etc.' **2**, add '**b** abs., *work*, of poison, Plu. 2.258c.' **II**, delete '*IG* $1^2$.4'

**δρεπανηΐς**, for 'poet. for foreg.' read '*of the sickle* or *sickle-shaped*, Ζάγκλης .. δρεπανηΐδος ἄστυ'

**δρέπανον**, line 1, for '(q.v.)' read '*SB* 9834b.37 (iii AD)' **2**, after '*pruning-knife*' insert '*IG* $1^3$.422.143 (Athens, v BC), Ar. *Ra.* 576' **3** & **4**, for these sections read '**3** *weapon with a curved blade*, Hdt. 5.112.2, 7.93; cf. of blades attached to a war-chariot, X. *Cyr.* 6.1.30.'

**δρεπᾰνουργός**, for '*sword-maker, armourer*' read '*sickle-maker*'

**δρηστήρ I**, after 'Od. 16.248' insert '*server*, δ. κυπέλλων, of Ganymede, Nonn. *D.* 10.259, al.' and after '(Od.) 19.345' add 'A.R. 3.700'

***δρῑλοπότης**, ου, ὁ, *cup in the form of* δρῖλος, Sch.Juv. 2.95 (codd. *drillopotae*).

**⁺δρῖλος**, ὁ, perh. *worm*, in pers. n. Βροῦκος Δρίλου *SEG* 32.281 (Attica, iii BC); cf. κροκόδιλος, δρίλαξ. **2** *limp penis*, *Suppl.Hell.* 975.1 (ostr., iii BC), *AP* 11.197 (Lucill.), *IG* $9^2$(1).733 (δρειλ-, mosaic, Amphissa, iii AD); cf. δ., δρίλλος· *verpus*, *Gloss.*

**δρῑμύλος**, for 'ὄμμα .. eye' read 'ὄμματα δ. *piercing* eyes'

**δρῑμύς II**, line 5, after '*Cond.* 18' insert '*PCair.Zen.* 33.15 (iii BC; gen. masc. δριμίος)'

**δρίφος**, add 'Theoc. 15.2 (*PAntin.*, codd. δίφρ-); δ. Συρακούσιοι *EM* 287.50, Hsch.'

***δρίωτος**, v. °τρίωτος.

***δρόγγος**, ?*troop*, cf. late Lat. *drungus*, Theognost. *Can.* 46 A.

**δρομάς**, line 2, for 'ἄντυξ δ.' read 'ἄμπυξ δ.'

***δρομάω**, add 'pres. part. δρομέων, *CEG* 815.2 (Epid., iv BC)'

**δρομεύς**, line 3, for 'Call. *fr.* 555' read 'Call. *fr.* 441 Pf., cf. Simon. 1 P.' **3**, delete the section (v. *ZPE* 93.149).

**δρομιάφιον**, add '(δρομιάμφιον Salmasius, cf. *Suppl.Hell.* 1075)'

**δρομικός**, comp., add 'Φήμη ὕδατος ὑγροτέρα, πνεύματος δρομικωτέρα, Ach.Tat. 6.10'; sup., add 'Ach.Tat. 7.16'

**δρομικότης**, for '*fleetness* .. 18' read 'hypothetical derivative of δρομικός, Simp. *in Cat.* 214.18'

***δρομίσσω**, unexpld. wd. in Theognost. *Can.* 14.

**δρόμος I 1**, line 4, after 'Luc. *Dom.* 10' insert 'δρόμους ἀπελαύνω τὸν ἵππον ride off *at a gallop*, Aristid. *Or.* 49(28).5'; line 7, after 'D. 19.273' insert '*a day's run* (for ship), *Peripl.M.Rubr.* 9, 15, al.' **2**, add 'in fig. phrs. referring to the course, Pl. *R.* 613d, *Cod.Just.* 1.3.55.3, *SEG* 31.1440 (Palestine, AD 614)' add '**5** perh. *runner, courier*, *PBodm.* 28.19.' **II 3**, line 4, after '(Itanos, iii BC)' insert 'cf. Call. *fr.* 261.3 Pf.'; line 7, after 'Str. 17.1.28' insert 'cf. Call. *fr.* 715 Pf.'

**δρόμων I**, add 'prob. in *SB* 9855.4 (ii AD)'

**δροσερός 1**, add 'δ. Γαλατία *SEG* 32.1502.11 (Palestine, v AD)' **2**, add '*AP* 5.292.4 (Agath.)'

**δροσίζω I**, line 3, after 'D.L. 7.152' insert 'δροσιζέσθω .. πρόποσις *AP* 5.134 (Posidipp.)' **II**, after 'Arist. *Pr.* 939$^b$38' insert 'ἐὰν μὴ δροσίσῃ *PMil.Vogl.* 60.4 (ii AD)'

**δρόσος I 4**, for this section read '*surface moistness*, τὸ καθαρόν τε καὶ Ἀττικὸν ὥσπερ δρόσον καὶ χνοῦν ἀποδρεπομένους Plu. 2.79d; on the genitals, Ar. *Nu.* 978' **II**, delete 'in sg. .. Call. *Hec.* 1.2.3' and add 'cf. δρόσους· ἀχρείους. Κύπριοι Hsch.'

***Δρούσαιος**, ὁ, month in Cyprus beginning 2 Apr., prob. in *Cat. Cod.Astr.* 2.144.14.

***Δρουσιεύς**, έως, ὁ, Egyptian month (= Epeiph) in Caligula's calendar, *PLond.* in *PRyl.* ii p. 381 (AD 40), *CPR* 242.16, 36 (AD 40); also Δρουσεύς, *Atti* XVIII *congresso intern. di papirologia* (1984) pp. 1107-13, *PSI* 908.19 (AD 43; dat. Δρυσεῖ).

***Δρουσιλλῆος**, ὁ, Egyptian month (= Pauni) in Caligula's calendar, μὴν Δ. *BGU* 1660.12, *PMich.*inv. 622 (*JEA* 13.185, both AD 41).

**Δρυάς I**, before 'Plu.' insert 'Pl. *Epigr.* 26 D.$^3$'

**δρῠ́ινος**, line 3, for 'Antip.' read 'Antip.Thess.'

***δρῠ́μιος**, α, ον, Cypr. *tu-ru-mi-o-ne*, *of* or *belonging to a copse*, perh. proper name of stream, *ICS* 217.19 (Idalium).

**δρῡμός I**, add 'spec. of wet or irrigable land, *PWisc.* 31.5, 34.6, al. (ii AD)' **II**, add 'parox. δρύμα, acc. to gramm. in Reitzenstein *Ind.Lect.Rost.* 1890/91 p. 9'

***δρῡμόχορος**, ον, *having wooded dancing-places*, Κιθαιρὼν δ. eleg. in *POxy.* 3723.12.

**δρύος**, delete the entry.

***δρῠοσάνδραξ**, gloss on σαννίς, Hsch.

***δρῠοστέφᾰνος**, ον, *wearing crown of oak-leaves*, δρυοστεφάνοις .. Λυκαίοις *CEG* 814.8 (Argos, 350/325 BC).

***δρῠοφόρος**, ον, *bearing oak-branches*, of a thiasus in a Bacchic cult, *IG* 10(2).1.260c.11 (sp. δροιο-, Thessalonica).

**δρῠ́οχοι I**, add 'defined as *ribs* of a ship, = νομεῖς, Procop. *Goth.* 4.22'

**δρῦς**, line 2, after '(Thyrrheum)' insert 'masc. also in *POxy.* 2113.18 (iv AD)' and after '*Schwyzer* 664.23' insert '(Arcadian Orchomenus, iv BC)'; line 6, for 'gen. δρυός .. verse, Hes. *Op.* 436' read 'δρυός scanned as monosyllable in Hes. *Op.* 436'; line 7, for 'originally *tree* .. trees' read 'etym. *tree*, cf. δρῦν ἐκάλουν οἱ παλαιοὶ πᾶν δένδρον Sch.Il. 11.86, Hsch., but usu. denoting any of various kinds of oak' and add 'S. *Tr.* 766, Paus. 8.1.6'; line 16, before 'prov.' insert 'applied to unspecified kinds of tree, E. *Cyc.* 615' **II**, delete the section. **IV**, delete the section.

**δρύσσομαι**, delete the entry.

**δρῠτόμος**, add 'Myc. *du-ru-to-mo*'

**δρῠ́φακτος 1**, add '*IG* 12(3).326.25 (Thera, ii AD)'

**δρύφειν**, delete the entry (v. °δρύφω).

***δρύφω**, app. = δρύπτω, κἠπὶ τᾶι μύλαι δρυφήται κἠπὶ ταῖς συναικλίαις Alcm. 95(*a*) P.; δρύφειν· περαίνειν Hsch., δρυφόμενοι· φθειρόμενοι id.

**⁺δρύψελον**, τό, app. *flake, paring* of bark, peel, etc., ῥίζης δρύψελα Ποντιάδος Parth. in *Suppl.Hell.* 642, σελίνου δ. ib. 643; cf. δρύψελ[λ]ον· τὸ λέμμα, ὁ φλοιός *Et.Gen.*, δρύψελα (cod. -αλα)· πέταλα δρυώδη Hsch.

**⁺δρύψια**, τά, app. *scrapings*, δ. τυρῶν *AP* 6.299 (Phan.).

**δρωπᾰκιστής I**, add '*SEG* 37.1434 (Apamea, ii AD)' add '**II** applied to one who uses wax for peeling the gold from gilded statues, Sch.Juv. 13.151.'

***δρώπᾰκος**, ὁ, *depilator*, *SB* $10447^r$.ii.51.

**δρώψ**, add 'cf. Clem.Al. *Strom.* 5.48.5, δ. δὲ ὁ λόγος ὁ δραστικός ib. 9'

***δῠανδρία**, ή, = Lat. *duumviratus*, *SEG* 19.830, 37.1176, 1177, 1179, etc. (Pisidia, ii/iii AD).

***δύασμα**, ατος, τό, *duplication*, Schubart *Gr.Lit.Pap.* 36.31.

***δύβρις**, = θάλασσα, Asclep.Myrl.ap.Sch.Theoc. 1.118.

***δύγαστρον**, v. °ζύγαστρον.

**δυερός**, after '*miserable*' insert 'Call. *VB* in *Suppl.Hell.* 257.24, δυερὴν μοῖραν *EA* 13.3-4 no. 496 (Mylasa, Rom.imp.)'; for '*IG* 3.1337' read '*GVI* 1029 (Athens, Rom.imp.)'

***Δύμαινα**, fem. adj., *of the* Δυμᾶνες, Δ. φυλή Call. *fr.* 703 Pf.; pl. subst., Alcm. 4 *fr.* 5.4 (rest.), 10(*b*).8 P., Euph. 47.

***Δῠμᾶναται**, οἱ, the people of the tribe of Δυμᾶνες (at Sicyon), Hdt. 5.68.2.

***Δῠμᾶνες**, οἱ, name of tribe in Dorian cities, rest. in Tyrt. 19.8 W., *SEG* 25.394 (Epid., iv BC), St.Byz.

***Δῠμᾰνίς**, ίδος, = °Δύμαινα, Δυμανίδος ἠπείροιο *Suppl.Hell.* 1173.

**δύνᾰμαι I 2 b**, add '*Cod.Just.* 1.3.44.1, Just. *Nov.* 47 pr.' **II 3 a**, line 3, after 'Th. 7.58' insert '(prob. interp.)' and add 'λοιδορίαν οὐκ ἔχουσαν ἔλεγχον ὁ λόγος αὐτῷ δύναται Gorg.*Pal.* 29, σκοπεῖν ἕκαστον τί δύναται τῶν ῥημάτων Strato Com. 1.44 K.-A.'

**δύνᾰμις II 5**, add 'D.S. 4.51' and for '*PMag.Leid.* v 8.12' read '*PMag.* 12.257' **V 2**, for this section read 'math., *square root*, Pl.*Tht.* 147d, e; limited to surds, ibid. 148a'

**δυναστεία II**, line 4, for 'Roman Senate' read 'triumvirates'

**δυναστευτικός**, after '(Arist.*Pol.*) 1272$^b$3' insert '*holding a position of power*'

**δυναστεύω I**, p. 453, line 5, before 'Pass.' insert 'of χαρακτῆρες τῆς λέξεως, *stand out, be most important*, D.H.*Dem.* 8'

**δῠνᾰτέω 1**, add '*Ep.Rom.* 14.4, 2*Ep.Cor.* 9.8; w. impers. constr., δυνατῖ .. τῷ κυρίῳ θεῷ .. παρασχῖν *POxy.* 3819.9 (iv AD)'

**δῠνᾰτός**, after lemma insert '(Boeot. sp. διουνατόν *SEG* 28.449.13)' **I 3**, add 'of a goddess, *TAM* 5(1).250' **II**, line 6, after 'ἐς τὸ δ.' insert 'Simon. 36.14 P.'

***δῡνω**, v. δύω.

**δύο**, line 3, after 'Inscrr.' insert '(Boeot. sp. δουο *BCH* 60.179.31; διούο, διού *IG* 7.3193.1, 5; *SEG* 3.356.4)'; line 4, after 'Thess. fem. δύας ib. 9(2).517' insert 'neut. δύα *SEG* 26.672.10 (Larissa, 200/190 BC);'; line 6, dual δυεῖν, add 'Men.*Dysc.* 327'; line 13, dat. δυοῖσι, add 'Hippon. 92.6 W.'; line 14, δυοῖς, add 'Hsch.' at end add 'Myc. *dwo*, instr. *du-wo-u-pi*'

***δυόβολος**, ὁ, *double obol*, *PPetr.* ii.44.25, *SB* 5729.9 (both iii BC); also **δυόβολον**, τό, *OBodl.* 643, 984 (both AD 36); see also διώβολον.

**δυοκαίδεκα**, add 'gen. -δέκων Alc. 349(*c*) L.-P.'

**δυοκαιδεκάδελτος**, add '*Cod.Just.* 6.4.4 pr., etc.'

***δυοτριακοστόν**, τό, *thirty-second part*, *PGen.* 116.13 (iii AD), *PCornell* 20(a).54, 75 (iv AD); written δυτριακοστόν *PMich.*v 322.(*a*)23, al. (i AD).

***δυοτρίαντον**, τό, *thirty-second part*, *PCornell* 20.13, al. (iv AD).

**⁺δύπτης**, ὁ, *diver*, Lyc. 73, Opp.*H.* 2.436; of birds, καύηκες Call.*fr.* 522 Pf., κηρύλος Lyc. 387.

**δυσάγγελος**, before 'Nonn.*D.* 20.184' insert 'Call.*fr.* 125.3 Pf.' and after it add 'al.'

**δυσάθλιος**, add 'epigr. in *SEG* 38.605.4 (Maced.)'

**δυσάλυκτος**, add '*GVAK* 16 (Hadrianopolis)'

**δυσανακόμιστος**, add '**2** *involving a difficult return*, ἐπάνοδοι Ptol.*Tetr.* 196. **3** *having difficulty in convalescing*, Gal. 18(1).718.13.'

**δυσανάληπτος II 1**, add '*finding difficulty in convalescing*, Gal. 13.213.7, 1048.6'

***δυσανάφορος**, ον, *slow-rising*, of constellations, Serv. ad Virg.*G.*1.32 (Daniel).

**⁺δυσάνεμος**, v. °δυσήνεμος.

***δυσανεύρετος**, ον, *hard to find* or *get at*, ἐπειδὴ δυσανεύρετός ἐστιν ἡ ἐσχάτη ῥίζα τοῦ ἠρυγγίου Cyran. 21 (1.7.90 K.).

**δυσανιῶν**, delete the entry.

***δυσανίως**, = δυσάνιος, Critias 42 D.-K.: neut. δυσανίων, τό, Plu. 2.106d (-ιῶν codd.).

***δυσάνυστος**, ον, *difficult in execution*, πρᾶξις *Cat.Cod.Astr.* 8(1).250.

**δυσαπάλλακτος**, add 'Hp.*Nat.Hom.* 15, etc., Pl.*Ti.* 85a'

***δυσαπόπλυτος**, ον, *hard to wash out*, Sch.Pl.*R.* 429e.

***δυσαπόρρυτος**, ον, *flowing away with difficulty*, Gal. 11.529.9.

**δυσαπότροπος**, for '*IG* 2.1660' read 'orac. in *IG* $2^2$.4968 (Athens, iv BC)'

**δυσαπούλωτος**, add 'also **δυσαφούλωτος** Paul.Aeg. 6.40.3 (79.8 H.)'

**δυσᾰρεστέω**, line 3, for 'δ. ὅτι' read 'δ. ὅτε τις ..'

**δυσαυλία**, add 'prob. rest. in *A.fr.* 78c i 7 R. (pl.)'

**δυσαυχής**, for '*idly boasting, vain-glorious*' read '*haughty, unapproachable*'

***δυσαφούλωτος**, v. ‡δυσαπούλωτος.

***δυσβάϋκτος**, ον, *marked by doleful howling*, τεῖνε δὲ δυσβάυκτον βοᾶτιν τάλαιναν αὐδάν A.*Pers.* 575.

***δύσβροχος**, ον, *poorly-watered*, *BGU* 1185.20 (i BC).

**δυσγενής**, add '**III** *cowardly*, adv., δυσγενῶς ἔχειν πρὸς ψυχρολουσίαν Agathin.ap.Orib. 10.7.5.'

**δυσγρίπιστος**, add '(the sophist Stagirius in Gr.Nyss.*Ep.* 26)'

**δυσδιαφορησία**, add 'Gal. 1.220.2'

**δυσδιαχώρητος II**, add 'Gal. 15.760.18'

**δυσεγκαρτέρητος**, add 'prob. in Plu. 2.36b, sp. δυσεκκ- in Phld.*D.* 1.12; cf. ἀνεκκαρτέρητος'

**δυσειδής II**, delete the section.

**δύσεικτος**, add 'adv. -τως, Paul.Aeg. 6.112.3 (166.5 H.)'

**⁺δυσεκκαρτέρητος**, v. °δυσεγκ-.

**δυσέκλειπτος**, add 'Ach.Tat. 6.11.1'

**δυσεκλήπτως**, delete '(leg. δυσεξάλειπτον)'

**δυσέκφευκτος**, line 1, delete 'Tim.*Pers.* 130'; line 2, for 'Tim.*Pers.* 140' read 'Tim. 15.129 P., *hard to reach in escaping*, ib. 119 P.'

**Δυσελένα**, add 'E.*IA* 1316'

**δυσέμβολος II**, add 'γῆν .. πυρὸς γέμουσαν ῥεύμασιν δυσεμβόλοις Carc. 5.7 S.'

***δυσεμπέλαστος**, ον, *making approach difficult*, θάλασσα *An.Par.* 1.179.

**δυσεντερία**, line 1, after 'ἡ' insert 'Ion. -ίη' and add 'in horses, *BCH* 66-7.181 (Abdera, iv BC)'

**δυσεξάλυκτος**, after '*avoid*' insert 'λοιμός Keil-Premerstein *Erster Bericht* p. 9 (Troketta), cf.'

***δυσεξέταστος**, ον, *hard to search out*, Ptol.*Harm.* 1.8.

**δυσεξῶθωτός**, for '*not easily displaced outwards*' read '*not easily rid of its bumps*'

**δυσεύρετος 2**, add 'τὸ στόμα τοῦ .. ποταμοῦ δυσεύρετόν ἐστιν *Peripl.M.Rubr.* 43'

***δύσεφθος**, ον, *hard to boil*, Aët. 3.8 (267.14 O.).

**δύσζηλος I 1**, for '*exceeding jealous*' read '*harmfully jealous*' **2**, for '*eager*' read '*eager to no purpose*' **II**, for '*rivalling in hardship*' read '*unenviable*' and delete 'αἰθυίησι'

***δυσηβόλιος**, ον, unexpld. wd. in Call.*VB* in *Suppl.Hell.* 257.29.

**δυσηκοΐα**, after 'Vett.Val. 109.31' insert 'Heras ap.Gal. 12.610.10'

**δυσηλεγής**, for 'Thgn. 795' read 'Mimn. 7.1 W.'

**δυσήλιος**, add 'δυσηλίους φάραγγας Mosch.Trag. 6.5 S.'

**δυσημερία**, add 'Plu. 2.168c, 467e, 741a'

**δυσήνεμον**, delete the entry.

***δυσήνεμος**, ον, Dor. δυσάνεμος, *afflicted by adverse winds*, δυσάνεμοι στόνῳ βρέμουσιν ἀντιπλῆγες ἀκταί S.*Ant.* 591, Plu. *in Hes.* 82 S., δυσήνεμον· δυστάραχον, τὸ κακοὺς ἀνέμους ἔχον Hsch.

**δυσήνῠτος**, delete 'also δυσήνυκτος'

***δυσθερᾰπεία**, ἡ, *difficulty of treatment*, Hp.*Aff.* 20, 22, Aët. 7.45 (297.17 O.).

**δυσθετέω I**, add '*to be in difficulty*, Call.*Dieg.* iv.40 (*fr.* 102 Pf.)'

***Δύσιος**, ὁ, month-name, *SEG* 34.1209 (Maeonia).

**δυσκάθαρτος I**, *hard to purge*, add 'of patients, Gal. 11.353.13'

***δυσκατάσχετος**, ον, *difficult to stop*, of haemorrhage, Afric.*Cest.* p. 61 v$^1$.

**δυσκέλᾰδος**, add 'perh. w. ref. to arrows, *Suppl.Hell.* 939.4'

***δύσκερκος**, ον, *having a harmful tail*, ἔστι δὲ αὕτη (sc. σαύρα) δ. Sch.Theoc. 2.58.

***δυσκληρία**, ἡ, *misfortune*, Just.*Nov.* 22.22.1.

***δύσκλωστος**, ον, *spun with adverse effect*, μίτος Μοιρῶν *MAMA* 5.30.

**δυσκρᾱσία**, line 2, for 'Plu.*Stoic.* 3.216' read 'Plu.*Stoic.* 2.216'

***δυσκρᾰταιος**, ον, *harmfully mighty*, δυσκράτεε Τυφῶν *SEG* 35.221.11 (tab.defix., Athens, iii AD).

**δυσκρᾰτητος**, add '*Hymn.Is.* 21 (Maroneia)'

***δύσμα**, ατος, τό, *sunset, west*, *Inscr.Délos* 1417 *C*73 (ii BC).

**δύσμᾰχος**, add '**II** *fighting in vain*, Nonn.*D.* 48.452.'

**δύσμεικτος II**, after '*unsocial*' insert 'subst. δύσμικτον, τό, *unsociability*, Gal. 8.689.11'

**δυσμεναίνω**, add '*Trag.adesp.* 535 K.-S.'

**δυσμενής**, add 'δῦμενές *SEG* 11.1112 (Arcadia, vi/v BC)'

***δυσμετᾰγωγος**, ον, *hard to tame* or *break in*, θρέμμα Afric.*Cest.* p. 22 v$^1$.

**δυσμή II**, add 'πρὸς δυσμήν *Amyzon* 28.11 (ii BC)' at end, δυθμή, add 'Pi.*I.* 4.65 S.-M.'

***δυσμηνῑτης**, ου, ὁ, *wrathful man* (cf. μηνιτής), Ptol.*Tetr.* 159.

**δυσμήνῑτος**, delete 'ψυχαί Ptol.*Tetr.* 159 (-ίτας)'

***δυσμῐαῖος**, ον, *western*, τὸ δυσμιαῖον μέρος *PNess.* 16.12.

***δυσμῑγής**, ές, *harmfully mixed*, Sch.Call.*VB* in *Suppl.Hell.* 251.25.

***δυσμογέω**, app. *suffer distress*, *Lyr.adesp.* in *SLG* 458 i 3.

***δυσμοιρία**, v. ‡δυσμορία.

**δύσμοιρος**, add '*SEG* 34.1247 (Miletoupolis, ii AD)'

**δυσμορία**, add 'also δυσμοιρία *Salamine* 193 (ii AD)'

***δυσμορφής**, ές, = δύσμορφος, rest. in *Hymn.Is.* 115 P. (Andros).

**δύσορμος I**, add '*Peripl.M.Rubr.* 10, 20, 43'

***δυσουριᾰκός**, ή, όν, *suffering from suppression of urine*, Firm. 4.15.2.

**δυσπαίπαλος**, after '*rough*' insert 'of animals, their skins, etc.' and add 'of snakes, Opp.*C.* 2.270'

**δυσπαρηγόρητος**, add '*IG* 12(7).239 (i/ii AD)'

**δυσπέμφελος**, line 4, after '(Hes.)*Op.* 618' insert 'Herodicus in *Suppl.Hell.* 494.5' and after 'Nonn.*D.* 2.550' insert '13.75, 22.171, 24.64'

**δυσπιστία**, after '*disbelief*' insert 'Zos.Alch. 209.8'

**δύσποτμος**, add 'Anacr. 1 *fr.* 7 P. (s.v.l.)'

**δυσπρᾱγία**, add '*SEG* 38.340 (tab.defix., Camarina, v BC)'

**δύσρῑγος**, add 'prov. δυσριγότερος χελώνης· ἐπὶ τῶν εἰς ὁτιοῦν γλισχρευομένων Macar. 3.41'

**δύσσοος**, for '*Riv.* .. 266' read '*hoι δὲ πάντες δύσσοοι SEG* 38.340 (tab.defix., Camarina, v BC)'

***δύσσταλτος**, ον, (στέλλω) *hard to check*, *Hippiatr.* 9.1.

***δυσστρᾰτοπέδευτος**, ον, *ill-suited for encamping*, Aen.Tact. 8.1.

***δύσσφαλτον**· δύσμαχον Hsch.

**δύσταλτος**, delete the entry (v. °δυσσ-).

**δυστερπής**, add 'κεῖμαι .. δυστερπεῖ τῇδ' ἐνὶ πέτρῃ *GVI* 959.3 (Thespiae, ii/iii AD)'

**δύστηνος I 2**, before 'μόχθος δ. Pi.*P.* 4.268' insert 'δ. .. νοῦσοι Semon. 1.12 W., δ. μόρῳ ibid. 18'
**δυστλήμων**, add '*S.fr.* 555.8 R.'
**δυστοκία II**, for '= δυστεκνία' read '*unsuccessful* or *unlucky childbirth*' and add 'epigr. in *SEG* 25.752 (Moesia, ii BC)'
***δύστοπος**, ον, *difficult*, Sch.Clem.Al. 1.296.31; adv. sup., Suid.
**δυστρᾰτοπέδευτος**, delete the entry (v. δυσσ-).
**Δύστρος**, add 'cj. in Anaxipp. 1.41 K.-A., *SEG* 32.1395 (Commagene, ii AD), 31.990 (Lydia, iii AD), *Kafizin* 267a (iii AD)'
**δυστῠχία**, after '*ill fortune*' insert 'Thgn. 1188'
**δυσυπνήτως**, delete the entry (v. ‡δυσύποιστος).
**δυσύποιστος**, add 'adv. -ως, ἔχειν πρός τι Agathin.ap.Orib. 10.7.27 (-υπνοιστ-)'
**δύσφαλτος**, delete the entry (v. °δύσσφαλτον).
**δυσφημέω**, add 'Hippon. 78.8 W. (broken context)'
**δύσφθαρτος**, for '*not easily spoilt*' read '**2** of (ingested) food, *not easily broken down*' and add 'Gal. 8.42.5'
**δύσφορος**, line 5, for 'δύσφορόν [ἐστι]' read 'πειρῶμαι μηδέποτε ὑπερπίμπλασθαι· δύσφορον γάρ' **I 3**, delete the section.
***δυσφρόνα**, ἁ, = δυσφροσύνη, cj. in Pi.*O.* 2.52.
**δυσφροσύνη**, delete 'E.*Tr.* 597' add '**II** *ill-will, malice*, E.*Tr.* 597.'
***δυσχερασμός**, ὁ, *irritation, anger*, Phld.*Lib.* p. 80 O.
**δυσχερής**, line 1, delete '(χείρ)'
**δύσχρηστος**, after 'adv. -τως' insert 'ἔχειν to be *intractable*, Men.*Dysc.* 249'
**δῠσώνης**, for pres. def. read '*one who is unskilled at shopping*'
**δῠσωπέω**, line 3, after 'X.Eph. 4.5' insert 'so perh. δυσωπήσας λίνα Μοιρῶν, of Apollo, *Didyma* 217.13 (hex. poem or oracle)' **III**, add '*through being dazzled*, Ael.*NA* 8.10, 10.14'
**δῠ́τη**, for '*shrine*(?)' read '*well* or *reservoir*'; after 'Cabireum' insert 'Thebes, ii BC'; add '*AE* 1948/9.136, A17, 18, 20 (Epid., iv BC)'
***δῠτορύκτᾱς**, α, ὁ, ?*excavator*, *IAskl.Epid.* 52A.24, 28-32, al. (iv BC).
***δυτριᾱκοστόν**, v. °δυοτριακοστόν.
**δυώδεκᾰ**, add 'gen. pl. δυωδέκων *SEG* 12.391 (Samos, vi BC); δοώδεκα *SEG* 24.361 (Thespiae, iv BC)'
**δῠωδεκάβοιος**, add '*Suppl.Hell.* 991.80 (poet. word-list); see also δωδεκάβοιος'
**δῠωδεκᾱῖς**, delete 'Att.' and insert 'also **δωδεκᾱῖς**'; for '*SIG*[2] .. ii BC)' read '*CID* I 9.D34 (v BC)'; after 'etc.' insert 'δωδεκαΐδα βούπρῳρον *SIG*[3] 604.9 (Delphi, ii BC)'
***δῠωδεκᾰ́πεδος**, ον, *twelve foot long*, *CID* II 113.26 (iv BC).
***δυωδεκάσημος**, v. °δωδ-.
**δῶ**, add 'Myc. *do-(de)*, acc. w. -δε, *to the house (of)*'
**δωδεκάβοιος**, add 'see also δυωδεκάβοιος'
***δωδεκᾰδραχμία**, ἡ, *twelve-drachma tax* on boats, *PMich.Zen.* 60.2 (iii BC).
**δωδεκάθεος II 1**, add 'perh. τὸν Ἀξιοττην[ὸν ἐν] τῷ ἐκεῖ δωδεκάθην καθήμ[ενον *SEG* 29.1179 (Lydia, AD 108/9)'
***δωδεκαῖος**, ὁ, or -αῖον, τό, *coin worth twelve* (?obols), *RA* 3.40 (Amphipolis, iii/ii BC), 6.32 (ib., ii BC).
***δωδεκαΐς**, ίδος, ἡ, v. °δυωδεκαΐς.
***δωδεκᾰκέφᾰλος**, ον, *twelve-headed*, δ. δράκοντα *IGChr.* 210 *ter* 6 (Arcesine).
***δωδεκάκιστος**, η, ον, perh. *one of a group of twelve*, *Suppl.Mag.* 47 (ii/iii AD), 42.30, 49 (iii/iv AD), *BMus.Inscr.* 949.
**δωδεκάμηνος**, for '-μηνον, τό' read '-μηνος, ἡ'
***δωδεκάπλησον**, aor. imper. *multiply by twelve*, perh. erron. for δωδεκάπλωσον (°δωδεκαπλόω) *PCair.* 10758 (vi AD).
***δωδεκαπλόω**, *multiply by twelve*; v. °δωδεκάπλησον.
***δωδεκᾰποδία**, ἡ, *length of twelve feet*, *SEG* 25.394.C15.
**δωδεκᾰ́πους**, after '*long*' insert '(sc. σκιᾶς or στοιχείου)' and for 'Men. 364' read 'Men. 304.3 K.-Th.'
**δωδεκάσημος**, add 'in prosody, *of the length of twelve short syllables*, Mar.Vict. p. 49 (*duod-*)'
***δωδεκάστολος**, ον, *forming a squadron of twelve*, Αἰνιάνων δὲ δωδεκάστολοι νᾶες ἦσαν E.*IA* 277 (s.v.l.).
***δωδεκάστομος**, v. °δεκάστομος.
**δωδέκατος I**, add '-ον, neut. as adv., *for the twelfth time*, *SEG* 36.1207.3 (Milyas, Pisidia, 5/4 BC)' **II**, after 'ἡ' insert '*the twelfth day of the month*, *SEG* 32.117 (Athens, iii BC), 33.1039 (Aeolian Cyme, ii BC), etc.; δυωδεκάτη Hes.*Op.* 774, δυωδεκάτᾱ *SEG* 25.744 (Callatis, ii BC)'
***δωδεκαχαλκία**, ἡ, *tax of twelve* χαλκοί, *PHib.* 112.8 (iii BC, abbrev.).
***δωδεκέτηρος**, ον, *twelve years old*, *GVI* 665.5 (Maced., i AD).
***δωδεκέτης**, ες or -ετής, ές, *twelve years old*, Call.*Ep.* 21, Plu.*Aem.* 35, παῖδα δυωδεχέτη epigr. in *IG* 10(2).1.368 (Thessalonica, ii AD); δωδεχετῆ *CEG* 709.5 (Halic., iv BC); fem. -έτις, ιδος, *CEG* 591.2 (*c.*350/325 BC), *AP* 11.70 (Leon.Tarent.); see also δωδεκαέτης.
**Δωδωναῖος**, after 'α, ον' insert '*of Dodona*, esp. as epith. of Zeus'; after 'Cratin. 5' insert '*SEG* 34.592 (Epirus, i BC); of Zeus identified w. Hadrian, *SEG* 37.521 (Epirus, ii AD)'; prov., add 'τὸ Δωδωναῖον ἄν τις χαλκίον ὃ λέγουσιν ἠχεῖν .. Men.*fr.* 60.3 K.-Th.'
***Δωδωνεύς**, έως, ὁ, *of Dodona*, epith. of Zeus, Hsch.
**Δωδώνη**, line 3, heterocl. forms, add 'dat. -ῶνι *S.fr.* 455 R., Call.*fr.*483 Pf.; acc. -ῶνα Euph. 4 vGr.'
***δωκενάριος**, v. ‡δουκηνάριος.
**δωλέννετος**, delete 'cf. sq.'
**δωλοδομεῖς**, delete '(cf. δοῦλος .. to be born)'
**δωμᾰ́τιον**, delete '*IG* 12(8).442.8' (v. *Glotta* 50.68)
***δωμᾰτουργία**, ἡ, *structure*, ἐνηλλάγη ἡ δ. πᾶσα τῆς βασιλικῆς *IEJ* 11.184 (Sepphoris, vi AD).
**δώμημα**, add '*IKnidos* 303.1 (i BC)'
***δώμησις**, εως, ἡ, *building*, *AA* 19.8 (Milet., pl.), δώμησις· οἰκοδομή Hsch.
***δωμητύς**· κατασκευή Hsch.
**δωμήτωρ**, add 'epigr. in *Fs. Theocharis* p. 399 l. 7 (Nemea, ii AD)'
***δωνατίουον**, τό, Lat. *donativum, donative, gratuity*, *POxy.* 1047.4 (iv AD); also δωνάτιον *PBeatty Panop.* 2.162, 164, al. (AD 300).
**δωράκινον**, add '*PMich.*XIV 680.9 (-εινον, iii/iv AD); cf. ῥοδάκινον'
***δωράκιον**, τό, = δωράκινον, *PRyl.* 630.419, al. (iv AD).
**δωρεά**, line 1, for '*IG* 1[2].77' read '*IG* 1[3].131.20' **I 1**, add 'κατὰ *mortis causa* δωρεάν *Cod.Just.* 1.3.45 pr., τὴν πρὸ γάμου δωρεάν ib. 1.3.52.15' **II**, line 4, after '(iv BC)' insert 'also δωρεᾶς *ISmyrna* 600.17 (ii AD), Robert *Ét.Anat.* 388 (Limyra in Lycia)'
***δωρεακός**, ὁ, *official* or *employee of a* δωρεά I 2, *BGU* 1540.3 (iii BC); cf. χρειακός.
**δωρεαστικός**, add '*CPR* 10.122.8 (vi AD)'
**δωρέω I**, line 3, after 'pass.' insert 'ἐκ θεῶν .. μηχαναὶ δωροῦνται Sch.Pi.*P.* 1.74'
**Δωριάζω I**, add 'Sch.E.*Hec.* 933, Hsch.'
**Δωριεύς II**, add 'as the name of phratry at Argos, *SEG* 30.355 (iv BC)'
**Δωρικός**, add 'w. ref. to architecture, γεῖσα Δ. *IG* 2[2].1666.A55 (iv BC)'
***Δώριος**, ον, (fem. α, Pi.*O.* 1.17, 3.5, *N.* 5.37, *I.* 2.5) *Dorian*, Δ. μέλος Pi.*fr.* 67 S.-M., Δώριον χορείαν Pratin.Lyr. 1.17, *AP* 7.436 (Hegemon), Δώριος (ἁρμονία) Arist.*Pol.* 1276[b]9, 1290[a]22, *D.* γλυφάς Ph. 1.666, Δ. τόνου Plu. 2.1135a, D.Chr. 33.42, Iamb.*VP* 24.1, Nonn.*D.* 25.21. **b** of the Isthmus of Corinth, Ἰσθμὸς Δ. Pi.*N.* 5.37; w. ref. to the Isthmian games, id.*I.* 2.15, 8.64.
***δωρίσκος**, ὁ, compound foot scanned –◡◡–◡, Diom. 482.2.
**δωρίτης**, add 'Sch.Pi.*O.* 8.101'
**δωρογραφία**, delete the entry.
**δῶρον I 1**, w. gen., add 'σχολῆς τὸ δῶρον E.*Tr.* 911' add '**b** δῶρα στρατιωτικά (= Lat. *dona militaria*), *TAM* 2.1201A (ii AD).' at end add 'Myc. *do-ra* (pl.)'
**δωροτελέω**, add 'w. acc., *make a benefaction of*, δωροτελεῖ μναμεῖο[ν] *SEG* 33.735 (= Bile *Dial.Cret.* no. 35, Cydonia, *c.*400/350 BC)'
**δωροφόρος**, add 'Callix. 2.32 J.'
***δωρύφιον**, τό, *wedding-gift*, *PHamb.* 87.11 (ii AD), Mitteis *Chr.* 290ii7 (vi AD).
**δώς**, add '(perh. to be read as a pr. n.)'
**δωσίβιος**, for '*Mus.Belg.* 16.70' read 'eleg. in *BCH* 50.529 (Marathon, ii AD)'
***δωσίπῡγος** (or **δοσί-**), ον, adj. applied to sexually compliant woman, Suid., s.v. ἀφελές.
**δωτήρ**, line 1, for 'ἐάων' read 'ἑάων' add '**2** *donor*, of the dedicator of a building, *IGLS* 9027; see also δοτήρ.'
**δωτῑνάζω**, for pres. def. read '*collect donations*'
***δωτίνᾱσις**, ιος, ἁ, *letting* of land, *BCH* suppl. 22.237 (Argos, Hellen.).
***δωτῑνᾱτήρ**, ῆρος, ὁ, *officer in charge of* °δωτίνασις, *BCH* suppl. 22.237 (Argos, Hellen.).
***δωτῑνάω**, *let* land, in pass., ἁ. χώρα .. κατεμερίσθη κατὰ γύας δωτιναμένας *BCH* suppl. 22.237 (Argos, Hellen.).
**δωτίνη**, after '*gift, present*' insert 'w. notion of obligation or reciprocity, as to a ruler or host'; line 2, delete '*give as a free gift*' **II**, for this section read 'Dor. δωτίνα *rent* for land, *Sokolowski* 3.59.8, 11 (Calauria, iii BC), *BCH* suppl. 22.237 (Argos, Hellen.)'
**δώτωρ**, line 1, for 'ἐάων' read 'ἑάων'
***δώω**, v. ζῶ.

# E

**ἐᾱ́ν**, line 2, after '(iv BC))' insert 'ἰάν *Hesperia* 33.385 (Eretria, vi BC), Dubois *IGDS* 15.5 (Sicily, vi BC), ἐάμ (before labial), ἐά (before μ), *IG* $1^3$.1 (*c.*500 BC)'

**ἑᾱνός I**, at end for 'Sapph. (?)122' read 'Sapph. 156 L.-P.' **II 1**, add 'cf. ἰανόν· ‹λεπτὸν› ἱμάτιον Hsch. La.'; at end add 'Myc. *we-a$_2$-no-i* (dat. pl.)'

**⁺ἐάνπερ, ἤνπερ, ἄνπερ**, strengthd. for ἐάν, ἤν, ἄν (cf. εἴπερ), *that is to say if*, ἐάνπ. A.*Pers.* 529, E.*Med.* 727, Pl.*Tht.* 166b, etc.; ἐάνπερ γε id.*Phd.* 89b; ἤνπ. Ar.*Lys.* 551, X.*Cyr.* 4.6.8; ἤ. γε id.*Eq.* 10.11; ἄνπ. Pl.*Ti.* 90c, *Lg.* 631c, D. 20.22.

**ἔαρ** (A), add 'see also ‡ἦρι'

**ἐᾰρῑνός**, after 'εἰαρινός' insert 'Ϝειαρινός *IG* 7.1919 (Thespiae, pers. n.)'; after 'Plb. 3,34.6' insert 'ἠρινοῦ X.*HG* 3.2.10'; after 'E.*Supp.* 448' insert 'φθέγμασιν ἠρινοῖς Ar.*Av.* 683'; after '*PCair.Zen.* 33.13 (iii BC)' insert 'ἠρινῶν· τῶν θυννίδων τῶν τῷ ἔαρι τεταριχευμένων *AB* 1.263.10'; after 'neut. as adv., *in springtime*' insert 'Alc. 115(a).10 L.-P.' at end, adv., read 'ἦρις ὡς (ἠρινῶς La.)· ἐαρινῶς Hsch.' add '**2** metaph., of beauty, ἀμεθύσου .. ἐ. τις ὥρα Hld. 5.13.'

***ἐαρῑ́της**, ου, ὁ, name given to a precious stone, ἀγλαΐας δ' ἐαρίτην τὸν αἱματίτην λίθον φησί Sch.Nic.*Al.* 314e Ge.

**ἑαυτοῦ**, line 5, after '*SIG* 774.2 (Delph., i BC)' insert 'ἀτοῖς, ἀτῶν *SEG* 29.771.18, 23 (Thasos, ii BC)'; lines 8/9, for '**ϝιαυτοῦ** .. p. 34' read '**ϝιαυτô** *Inscr.Cret.* 4.47.5 (Gortyn, v BC)'; lines 9/10, after '*IG* 9(2).517.16' insert 'acc. pl. fem. εὑτάς, *BCH* 59.55.18 (Larissa, ii BC)'; line 11, for 'Alc. 78' read 'Hes.*Th.* 126'

**ἐάω**, add '**III** *leave behind one*, τέκνα *MAMA* 6.215 (Apamea, iii AD), cf. ib. 124 (Heraclea Salbace; aor. med.), θυγατέρας *SEG* 24.911.18 (Thrace, iv AD); *bequeath*, ἀνδριάντα πλατ(ε)ίᾳ *MAMA* 6.176 (Apamea).'

**ἑάων**, read '**ἐάων**'

**ἑβδέματος** (s.v. ἑβδεμήκοντα), for 'ον' read 'α, ον'

**ἑβδεμήκοντα**, add 'ἑτ̣δ̣εμεικοντα *SEG* 26.672.34 (Larissa, 200/190 BC)'

***ἕβδεμος**, v. °ἕβδομος.

**⁺ἑβδομᾱγέτης**, ου, ὁ, *ruler of the seventh*, τὰς δ' ἑβδόμας (sc. πύλας) ὁ σεμνὸς ἑβδομαγέτας ἄναξ Ἀπόλλων εἵλετ' A.*Th.* 800; Procl. *in Ti.* 3.200d.

**ἑβδομαῖος I**, add '**3** *belonging to the seventh generation*, Sm.*Ge.* 4.24. **4** epith. of Apollo, Ἑτδομαῖος *BCH* 113.638 (Atrax).'

***ἑβδομαϊστής**, οῦ, ὁ, *one who celebrates the* ἑβδομαῖον, *SEG* 32.244 (Attica, iv BC).

***Ἑβδομαιών**, ῶνος, epith. of Apollo, *IEryth.* 207.87 (ii BC).

***ἑβδομάριος**, ὁ, app. title of functionary in the imperial palace, *ITyr* 88.

**ἑβδόματος**, for 'ον' read 'η, ον' and add 'Hes.*Op.* 805, *fr.* 362 M.-W., etc.'

**ἑβδομήκοντα**, add 'see also ‡ἑβδεμήκοντα'

***ἑβδομηκοντάδραχμος**, ον, *having a salary of seventy drachmas*, *PMich. Zen.* 66.11 (iii BC).

***ἑβδομηκοντᾰετής**, v. °ἑβδομηκοντούτης.

***ἑβδομηκοντᾰρουρικός**, η, ον, *consisting of seventy* ἄρουραι, *PVindob.* G39919 (*ZPE* 50.135, 24 BC).

***ἑβδομηκοντοστός**, ή, όν, *seventieth*, Mitchell *N.Galatia* 325 (AD 247); cf. ἑβδομηκοστός.

**ἑβδομηκοντούτης**, add 'also **ἑβδομηκοντᾰέτης** *SEG* 6.138.3 (Phrygia, -μαικ-)'

***ἑβδομοκούρης**, ὁ, temple official, *IEphes.* 10.24, 1042.11 (iii AD).

**ἕβδομος**, after lemma insert 'ἕβδεμος, α, ον *SEG* 9.72.101 (Cyrene, late iv BC)' **3**, for this section read 'ἕβδομα, τά, *festival celebrated on the seventh day after birth*, Call.*Dieg.* ix.26, cf. ib.*fr.* 202.22 Pf.; *seven-day marriage feast*, Lxx *Ge.* 29.27'

***ἑβδομοστᾰ́της**, ου, ὁ, *religious functionary of the seventh rank*, *SEG* 32.1484 (Sidon, i/ii AD).

***ἐβένωσις**, εως, ἡ, *the process of turning ebony-black*, Anon.Alch. 419.22.

***ἐβί**, v. °ἐπί.

***ἐγγαΐδιον**, τό, *small plot of land*, cj. rest. in *PAmh.* 2.36, *SB* 4638 (v. *ZPE* 41.256, both ii BC).

***ἐγγαιέω**, = ἐγγαέω, *SEG* 17.197 (Olympia, i BC), 37.370 (Augustus; = *Inscr.Olymp.* 335).

***ἐγγᾰμιστός**, ή, όν, *betrothed*, ἑδνωτήν· ἐγγαμιστὴν νυμφίῳ Hsch. (ἢ νύμφιον Cyr.).

**ἐγγαρέω**, delete the entry (v. ἐγγαιέω).

**ἐγγαστρῐ́μῡθος**, for '*ventriloquist* .. means' read 'one who speaks from the belly'

**ἐγγάστριος**, add 'ἐγγάστριον, τό, *foetus*, *Cat.Cod.Astr.* 8(1).175, al.'

***ἔγγαστρος**, ον, *situated in the womb*, Hsch. s.v. συλλήψεται.

**ἐγγέαβλος**, after lemma insert '(-**κλος** La.)'

***ἐγγένημα**, v. °ἐκγένημα.

**ἐγγεύομαι**, for 'pass.' read 'med.'

**ἐγγήρᾱμα**, delete 'Cic.*Att.* 12.25.2' and add '**b** *place to grow old in*, Cic.*Att.* 12.25.2, 29.2, 44.2.'

**ἐγγίζω II 1**, after 'Plb. 18.4.1' insert 'τοῖς τελείοις D.H.*Comp.* 14'

**ἐγγλοψούμενα**, after lemma insert '(ἐγχλοιούμενα La.)'

**ἐγγομφόω**, delete 'pass. .. 25.6.4)'

***ἐγγονία**, ἡ, *grandchildren*, *SEG* 33.765 (Heraclea, Lucania, iii/ii BC) (for ἐκγ-, cf. ἔγγονος).

***ἐγγόνιον**, τό, *grandchild*, *IGLS* 1335 (ἐγον-, iv AD), *CIJud.* 590 (sp. ινγόνιν, v/vi AD) (for ἐγκ-, cf. ἔγγονος).

**ἔγγονος 1**, add 'ἔγγονοι *grandchildren*, *Cod.Just.* 1.3.41.2, παῖδες .. καὶ ἔγγονοι καὶ ἀπέγγονοι ib. 6.4.4.15'; 3 lines fr. end, after 'ca.300 BC' insert 'and are synonymous in *IG* $1^3$.426.62 (Athens, v BC)'; last line, after '(Samos, iv BC)' insert '*IG* 12(3).1296.22 (Thera, ii BC)'

**⁺ἔγγραυλις**, εως, ἡ, *anchovy*, ἐγγραύλεις, οἱ δὲ ἐγκρασιχόλους καλοῦσιν αὐτάς Ael.*NA* 8.18, Opp.*H.* 4.470.

**ἔγγρᾰφος I**, line 2, subst., add '*SEG* 33.1039.90 (Aeolian, Cyme, ii BC); also sg., *SEG* 30.1349 (Miletus, ii AD)'

**ἐγγρᾰ́φω**, at end for '(perh. written ἐκγρ- *SIG* 742.29)' read '(app. written ἐκγρ- *SIG* 742.29, *GDI* 5496.10, 15)'

**ἐγγυάω 2**, med., add '*PHarris* 65.7 (AD 342)' **II 1**, add 'spec., *act as fideiussor*, Just.*Nov.* 4.1'

**ἐγγυεύω**, add 'Arc. pf. ἰνγεγύευκε *SEG* 25.447.18 (Aliphera, iii BC)'

**ἐγγῠ́η**, line 1, for 'Delph.' read 'Delos'

***ἐγγῠητήριον**, τό, *security*, *guarantee*, *SEG* 38.1036 (lead tablet, Gaul, v BC).

**ἐγγῠητής**, add '*POxy.* 3576.16 (AD 341); spec., = Lat. *fideiussor*, Just.*Nov.* 4.1, 99 pr.'

**ἐγγῠητικός**, add '*PLond.* 1494.11 (Byz.)'

**ἐγγῠητός**, add 'ἀστὸν ἐξ ἀστῆς ἐγγυητῆς αὐτῷ γεγενημένον D. 57.54; fem. subst. ἐξ ἐγγυητῆς ἢ ἐξ ἑταίρας Is. 3.6, 24'

**ἐγγυήτρια**, add '*POxy.* 3938.15 (AD 601)'

**ἐγγῠ́θεν 4**, add '**b** οἱ ἐ. those within a given legal relationship, Just.*Nov.* 91.2.'

**ἐγγῠθήκη**, after 'Hegesand. 45' insert '*Inscr.Délos* 372*B*30 (iii/ii BC)'

**ἐγγυμνάζω**, lines 2/3, delete 'ἐν σοὶ .. *Phdr.* 228e' add '**II** 'ἐκκλήτους ἐγγυμνάζειν calque on Lat. *appellationes exercere*, *launch appeals*, Just.*Nov.* 41 pr., 112.3 pr.

***ἐγγῠοβεβαιωτής**, οῦ, ὁ, *guarantor*, *PKöln* 232.2, 3, al. (iv AD).

**ἔγγῠος II**, lines 4/5, for '*IG* 9(2).4' read '*IG* 9(2).5*b*14'

**ἐγγῠ́ς I**, line 5, after '(A.)*Eu.* 65' insert 'τὸν ἔνγιστά σοι μένοντα *POxy.* 3314.23 (iv AD)'

***ἔγγων**, ονος, ὁ, ἡ, *grandchild*, *CIJud.* 1.140 (Rome); (prob. for ἐκγ-, cf. ἔγγονος, etc.).

**ἐγγώνιος I**, adv., add 'Gal. 18(1).815.1'

**ἐγδάκτῠλος**, for '*IG* 2.$809^b$195' read '*IG* $2^2$.1629.428, 429, *SEG* 3.137 iii 12 (Athens, iv BC)'

**ἐγείλασαν**, add '(ἐγείλησαν· συνήλασαν La.)'

**ἐγείρω**, lines 5/6, aor. pass., add 'redup. γεγέρθη κρῖνε (sic) ζôντας καὶ νεκρούς, of Christ, *Suppl.Mag.* 23 (v AD)' **I 1**, delete 'ἐ. τινά .. (lyr.)' and add 'med. τόν γ' ἔγρεο Nic.*Al.* 456' **2**, line 3, after 'ib. 510' insert 'cf. λόγος .. ἐ. ὀργάς Lxx *Pr.* 15.1'; add 'w. gen., *cause to rise from*, μὴ .. εὐνᾶς ἐγείρετε E.*HF* 1050 (lyr.); τὸν μὲν λέχους ἤγ̣ε̣ι̣ρ[α *Trag.adesp.* 664.29 K.-S.' **4**, after 'Luc.*Alex.* 10' insert 'τίτλον πε[ρὶ] τύμβῳ ἔγειρεν Mitchell *N.Galatia* 338' **III**, after '*oneself*' insert 'Ar.*Ra.* 340, E.*IA* 624 (both imper. ἔγειρε)' and add 'ἔγειρε ἐς τὸ μέσον *Ev.Marc.* 3.3'

**ἐγεργεῖ**, add '(ἐγερτί· γρηγόρως La.)'

**ἐγέρσῐμος**, add '*PAnt.* 57 *fr.*$(a)^v$.35'

***ἐγέρτης**, ου, ὁ, *one who rouses up*, τὸν τῶν νεκρῶν ἐγέρτην Leont.Byz. *HP* 1.4.5.

**⁺ἐγϝηληθίωντι**, v. ἐξείλλω 2.

**ἐγκαθαρμόζω**, for 'Ar.*Lys.* 682' read 'Ar.*Lys.* 681'

**ἐγκαθίζω I 2**, line 2, for 'pass.' read 'med.'

°**ἐγκαθιστάω**, *appoint*, *Cod.Just.* 1.3.45.3, Just.*Nov.* 57.2.

**ἐγκαθίστημι I**, add '**2** *put* a cargo *on board*, *PWarren* 5.6 (*Aegyptus* 13.242, ii AD).'

**ἐγκαίριος**, for '*PGrenf.* 1.64' read 'in *PGrenf.* 1.64 εὐκαιρείαν (= εὐκαιρίαν) is prob.'

**ἐγκαίω IV**, add 'w. acc., Διὶ .. ἀμνὸν καὶ ὄρνιν *Mél.Glotz* 872 (Maced., ii AD)'

**ἐγκᾰλέω II 1**, c. gen. rei, add 'Demad. 61 B.' **2**, line 3, for 'ἐ. τινὶ περί' read 'ἐ. περί'

°**ἐγκᾰλυμμα**, ατος, τό, *wrapping, cover*, *SEG* 38.1210.4 (Didyma, ii BC).

**ἐγκᾰλύπτω I**, pass., transfer fr. section II 'And. 1.17' and add 'Thgn. 1045'

°**ἐγκαμψικήδαλος**, ον, *onion-eating*, Luc.*Lex.* 10.

**ἐγκᾰνάσσω**, after 'E.*Cyc.* 152' insert '(cj.)'

**ἐγκᾰνᾰχάομαι**, read '**ἐγκαναχέομαι**'

**ἐγκάπτω**, for '*gulp down greedily*' read '*take a mouthful of*' **II**, delete the section (v. °ἐγκαπύει).

°**ἐγκαπύει**· ἐμπνεῖ Hsch. (cj. Toll for ἐγκάπτει· ἐκπνεῖ).

**ἐγκάρδιος**, after 'ον' insert '(ος, α, ον Horap. 1.7)' and after '*in the heart*' insert 'ψυχή Horap. l.c.' **II 2**, for 'Roussel .. 236' read 'χαλκοῦν *Inscr.Délos* 1442*B*58; ξύλινον ib. 59' add '**III** ἐγκαρδία (sc. λίθος), ἡ, gem with the shape *of a heart* on it, Plin.*HN* 37.159.'

°**ἐγκαρπίζω**, w. acc. and gen., *make fruitful* with; fig. τοὺς δὲ καὶ ὑπνώοντας ἑῆς ἐνεκάρπισεν ἀλκῆς *Orac.Chald.* 118.2 P.

**ἔγκαρπος**, add 'ἔγκαρπον· ἔγκυον Suid.'

°**ἐγκαταβλέπω**, ἐγκατάβλεψον, gloss on ἰνκαπάταόν, Hsch.

**ἐγκαταγρᾰ́φω**, add '*write a curse against* *SEG* 16.573.14 (Selinous, v BC)'

**ἐγκαταδαρθάνω II**, for '(Plu. 2.)688f' read '(Plu. 2.)688e'

**ἐγκαταλαμβάνω I**, add 'transf., ἔθανον λοιμοῦ ν[ε]φει ἐνκαταληφθείς *MAMA* 9.79 (ii AD). **2** *come and see* a person, ἐὰν ῥᾷον ἔχῃς ἐνκατάλαβε ἡμᾶς *PMich.*XI 624.7 (vi AD).'

**ἐγκαταλέγω I 1**, add 'Call.*fr.* 64.7 Pf.'

**ἐγκατάλειμμα 2**, add 'Alex.Aphr. 63.3' **3**, delete the section transferring exx. to section 1.

**ἐγκατάλειψις**, add '**b** *excess, residue*, *SB* 9066 ii 13 (ii AD).'

°**ἐγκατάλοιπον**, τό, *deficit*, suggested reading in *IGBulg.* 2265.18 (?i AD).

°**ἐγκαταλοχίζω**, *enter in a register*, v.l. in Lxx 2*Ch.* 31.18 (v. °καταλοχία).

**ἐγκαταναίω**, add 'perh. in hymn in *SEG* 32.1020.3 (Italy, ii/iii AD)'

**ἐγκαταπήγνῡμι 1**, line 3, after 'Il. 9.350' insert 'ἐγκαταπήγνυσι (τῷ Χρυσίππῳ) τὸ ξίφος Plu. 2.313e' **2**, delete the section.

**ἐγκαταπλέκω**, add 'fig., w. acc. and dat., D.H.*Comp.* 12'

°**ἐγκαταρδεύω**, *water* or *irrigate in*, τινι, fig., Polystr. p. 87 V.

°**ἐγκαταρρήγνῡμι**, *come violently down upon*, of a wind, *Gr.Roman-Papyri* 8.24.

**ἐγκατασκήπτω I**, add 'ὅταν τι ναοῖς ἐγκατασκήψῃ μύσος *Trag.adesp.* 466.2 K.-S.'

**ἐγκατασπείρω**, after 'Ph. 2.673' insert '(cj. for κατέσπειρεν 2.420)'

**ἐγκατατᾰράσσω**, add '(dub., edd. ἕλικα τεταραγμένην)'

**ἐγκατατίθημι II**, add 'of burial, ζῶντες ἐγκατεθόμεθα τὴν θήκην *TAM* 4(1).374'

°**ἐγκαταφῠτεύω**, *plant in, implant*, Hsch. s.v. ἰνκαφότευε.

°**ἐγκατέρχομαι**, *come down into a place*, εὐθέως οὖν μνησθήσῃ αὐτῷ ἵνα ἐνκατέλθῃ *PMil.Vogl.* 279.10 (i AD).

**ἐγκατέχω II**, pass., add '**2** *to be caught up* in, τέσσαρσι χρείαις ἐγκατασχεθήσεται παρὰ τοὺς νόμους Modest.*Dig.* 27.1.4 pr.'

**ἐγκατοικοδομέω I**, for this section read '*to build on* or *into*, στρωτῆρας *IG* $2^2$.463.59, 60 (iv BC); impers. pass., φρούρια δ' ἔστιν ᾗ ἐπὶ τῶν καρτερῶν ἐγκατῳκοδόμηται Th. 3.18.4'

°**ἐγκαυλέω**, v. °ἐκκαυλέω.

**ἔγκαυμα**, add '**IV** *fuel*, *PHels.* 12.12, 20 (AD 163), *POxy.* 2206.9 (vi AD), (in this sense app. the same as ἔκκαυμα).'

°**ἐγκαύσιμος**, ον, *painted in encaustic*, *IG* $4^2$.109 iii 63 (Epid., iii BC).

**ἔγκαυσις**, add '**III** *heating*, τῇ τῶν δημοσίων βαλανείων ἐγκαύσει Just.*Edict.* 13.16 (in this sense app. the same as ἔκκαυσις).'

**ἐγκαυστήρια**, add 'sg., *Ath.Asklepieion* IV 84'

**ἔγκαυστος**, add 'fem. -ᾱ, *Lindos* 420*a*24, *b*34 (i AD)'

**ἐγκαυχάομαι**, for '*pride oneself on*' read '*glory, exult in*' and add 'Lxx *Ps.* 51(52).1, 96(97).7, 105(106).47 (perh. the same as ἐκκαυχάομαι)'

**ἐγκαψικίδαλος**, delete the entry (v. °ἐγκαμψι-).

°**ἔγκειμαι**, *to lie on* or *in*, ἐπεὶ οὐκ ἐγκείσεαι αὐτοῖς (sc. εἵμασι) Il. 22.513; Hdt. 2.73. **b** *to be situated on* or *in*, Pl.*Cra.* 402e, *R.* 616d, Thphr.*HP* 5.3.6, Arat. 138, δοιὰ μετώπῳ ἔγκειται .. φάη Nic.*Th.* 292, *IG* 14.1389 i 27, J.*AJ* 8.83(3.6), βελῶν .. πολλῶν ἐπὶ τοῖς τραύμασιν ἐγκειμένων Plu.*Fab.* 16, Hld. 1.14. **c** *to be* in a plight, situation, etc., πόθῳ Archil. 193.1 W., βλάβαις S.*Ph.* 1318, E.*And.* 91, *Hel.* 269, μόχθοις id.*Ion* 181, Plb. 14.9.5. **2** *to exist* or *be present in*, ἐγκείμενον ἔχοντας ἔρωτα Plot. 4.4.40, 5.7.2, 6.1.13, al. **b** *to be included* or *involved in*, ἐπειδὴ ἐν σώματος λόγῳ ἔγκειται μέγεθος Plot. 3.6.16, 6.7.3. **II** of hostile forces, *to press hard on*, Th. 1.49.7, 144.3, X.*HG* 3.5.20, 5.2.1; τοὺς κατὰ πλευρὸν ἐγκειμένους J.*BJ* 2.543(19.7), *AJ* 14.417(15.4), Hld. 8.16.5; in argument, policy, etc., Ar.*Ach.* 309, ἐνέκειντο τῷ Περικλεῖ Th. 2.59.2, 5.43.1; of afflictions, περὶ τῆς ἐγκειμένης σοι ἀλγηδόνος Sch.S.*OC* 513, ὑπέκκαυμα γίνεσθαι τοῦ ἐγκειμένου πόθου Hld. 1.24.2. **2** *to press one's point, be insistent* or *urgent*, X.*Eph.* 2.13, ἰδὼν αὐτὴν σφόδρα ἐγκειμένην Ach.Tat. 5.16.7, Hld. 10.30.8; w. adj., πολλὸς ἐνέκειτο λέγων Hdt. 7.158.1, Th. 4.22.2, D. 18.199. **3** *to apply oneself* to task, policy, etc., ἰσχυρῶς ἐγκείσονται Th. 1.69.3, ἐ. ἐπὶ τὰ πονηρά Lxx *Ge.* 8.21, ἐγκεῖσθαι πρὸς τὴν ζήτησιν Ach.Tat. 6.10.2. **b** *to be devoted* to a person, οὕνεκ' ἐγὼ μὲν τὶν ὅλος ἔγκειμαι Theoc. 3.33, Herod. 5.3.

**ἐγκεκαροῦται**, add '(ἐγκεκλάρωται· ἐγκαταλέγει La.)'

**ἐγκέλευμα**, add '*word of command*, ἀφ' ἑνὸς ἐ. J.*AJ* 19.1.14'

°**ἐγκενίδες**, αἱ, *side-planks*, *EM* 310.38; cf. ἐπηγκενίδες.

**ἐγκεντέω II**, delete the section transferring quot. to section I and add 'cf. ἐκκεντέω'

**ἐγκεντρίζω I**, for '*goad, spur on*' read '*sting, bite*'; add 'cf. ἐκκεντρίζω'

**ἐγκεραυλέω**, for 'Phrygian flute' read 'Phrygian aulos'

°**ἐγκεύθω**, poet. **ἐνικεύθω**, *conceal, contain*, σορὸς ἥδ' ἐνικεύθει Ἑρμαῖον *SEG* 6.635 (Termessus, ii AD).

**ἐγκεφᾰ́λιον**, for 'ἐγκέφαλος I' read 'ἐγκέφαλος II' and add '*PCornell* 50.11 (i AD)'

**ἐγκηδεύω**, add '*SEG* 31.1304 (Lycia)'

°**ἐγκήρυκτος**, ον, verb. adj. fr. ἐγκηρύσσω (q.v.), Theognost.*Can.* 83.

**ἐγκῐλῐκίζω**, add 'cj. in Ar.*fr.* 107 K.-A.'

**ἐγκινδῡνεύω**, add 'Just.*Nov.* 134.2'

°**ἐγκισσάω**, *to come into heat*, Lxx *Ge.* 30.38, 39, 41, 31.10.

**ἐγκλαστρίδια**, add 'cf. ἐκκλαστρίδιον'

**ἐγκλάω**, form ἐνικλάω, add 'Call.*fr.* 75.22 Pf.'; line 2, for 'σωομένους' read 'σωομένοις'

°**ἔγκλειστος**, ὁ, *hermit*, *SEG* 8.39 (Scythopolis, vi AD), *PHaun.* 26.3 (vi/vii AD).

**ἐγκλέφωνος**, add '(ἐγκλησίφωνος La.)'

**ἔγκλημα I**, lines 6/7, for 'γίγνεται .. Lys. 10.23' read 'τίνος ὄντος ἐμοὶ πρὸς ὑμᾶς ἐγκλήματος; *with what complaint against me* of an offence *respecting you?* Lys. 10.23, 16.10; γίγνεται .. παισὶ πρὸς ἀλλήλους .. ἐγκλήματα X.*Cyr.* 1.2.6'

°**ἐγκληρονομέω**, *inherit*, dub. in *PDura* 24.31 (ii AD).

**ἐγκλῐδόν**, line 1, for 'ἐ. ὄσσε βαλοῦσα *aslant* or *askance*, A.R. 3.1008' read 'ἐ. ὄσσε βαλοῦσα *casting her eyes down*, A.R. 1.790, 3.1008'

**ἔγκλιζε**, add '(ἐγέλλιζε La.; cf. γελλίζειν)'

**ἐγκλίνω I**, add '**8** pass., *lie down, pass the night*, perh. of incubation in a temple, *PLit.Lond.* $53^v$.10 (Ionic iambics).'

**ἔγκλῐσις I 4**, after 'a singer's' insert 'or speaker's' and add 'D.H.*Dem.* 54'

**ἐγκλυστέον**, add 'Aët. 16.64, 89 Z.'

°**ἐγκοιλόομαι**, *to be hollowed out*, Paul.Aeg. 6.118.2 (176.10 H.).

**ἐγκοιμάομαι 1**, *sleep in* a temple, add '*Inscr.Perg.* 8(3).161.14 (ii AD)'

**ἐγκοίμησις**, add '**2** gloss on ἔναυλος, Sch.Hes.*Th.* 129 (29.8 Di G.).'

**ἐγκοιμητήριος**, after '-τήριον, τό' for '*grave*' read '*dormitory* for performing incubation'; add '*Inscr.Perg.* 8(3).161, 11, al. (ii AD), *IG* $4^2$.127.7 (iii AD)'

**ἐγκοιμήτριον**, add 'also adj. -ιος, -ιον, ἐγκοιμήτριν ὀθόνιον *PPar.* 53.8'

**ἐγκοίμητρον**, line 2, after 'Ammon. p. 140 V.' insert 'written ἐκκ- *PBaden* 48.4 (ii BC)'

**ἐγκόλαψις**, delete '4.1484.265 (Epid.)'

**ἐγκοληβάζω**, for 'κόλοις' read 'κόλαις (sic)'

**ἐγκολλάω**, add '**2** *cement on*, τῶν λίθων τὰ κροιά *AE* 1923.39.68 (Oropus, iv BC).'

°**ἐγκόλοβος**, ον, *rather short* in stature, *POxy.* 3477.9 (AD 270).

**ἐγκολπίας**, add 'Seneca *QN* 5.8.1'

**ἐγκολπόω**, med., add '*appropriate*, ἅπαντα τὰ κατέλιψεν ἐνκολφωσάμενος (sic) *PCair.Isidor.* 64.6 (*c.*AD 298)'

**ἐγκόμβωμα**, for 'a sort of *frock* .. clean' read 'kind of over-garment' and for 'Thd.*Is.* 3.20' read 'Sm.*Is.* 3.20'

**ἐγκονέω**, line 5, after 'Ar.*Av.* 1324' insert 'ep. impf. ἐγκονέεσκον Euph. in *Suppl.Hell.* 415 i 16'

**ἐγκόνῑμα**, delete the entry.

**ἐγκότημα**, for '= sq.' read '*object of anger*' and before 'Hsch.' insert 'ἐ.· ὀργή'

°**ἐγκότιος**, ον, = ἔγκοτος I, ὑμεῖς δαίμονες ἐνκότιοι αὐτῷ γένοισθε *SEG* 6.802 (Cyprian Salamis, ii/iii AD).

°**ἔγκοψις**, εως, ἡ, app. some form of enamelling process, Anon.Alch. 323.7, 22.

**ἐγκρᾰτεύομαι**, delete '*force oneself* to do a thing'

**ἐγκρᾰτής III**, add '**3** *member of the Encratite sect*, *SEG* 6.348, 349

(Lycaonia, iv AD).' **IV** adv. **2**, line 2, after 'φέρειν τι' insert 'Men.*Dysc.* 770'

***ἐγκρᾱτία**, poet. -ίη, ἡ, *sect of Encratites, SEG* 6.488.6 (Isauria, iv AD).

**ἐγκρίνω 2**, line 3, after '*HG* 4.1.40' insert 'w. dat., ἐνικρινθῆναι ὁμίλῳ A.R. 1.227'

**ἐγκρίς**, for '*a cake made with oil and honey*' read 'kind of cake' and before 'Ph. 1.214' insert 'δύο ἐγκρίδες, ἡ μὲν ἐκ μέλιτος, ἡ δ' ἐξ ἐλαίου'; for 'also expld. .. Hsch.' read 'ἐγκρίδες· πέμμα ἐλαίῳ ἑψόμενον καὶ μελιτούμενον. ἔνιοι δὲ ἀμανίτας (ταγηνίας La.) Hsch., ἐγκρίς· γλύκασμα (?-υσμα) ἐξ ἐλαίου ὑδαρές id.'

***ἐγκρῑτής**, οῦ, ὁ, *judge who admits* entrants to athletic contests, *DAW* 44.30 (Hieropolis Kastabala, pl.).

**ἐγκροστόω**, for '*Suppl.Epigr.* 2.698' read '*SEG* 17.596.7 (Pamphylia, ?iii AD), perh. in *Corinth* 8(1).318 (v. Robert *Hell.* 11/12.52)'

**ἐγκρύπτω 2**, add 'Arist.*Juv.* 470ᵃ16 (pass.)' **3**, add 'pass., ἑρπετὰ δ' ἰλυοῖσιν ἐνέκρυφεν (-φθεν v.l.) Call.*fr.* 336 Pf.'

⁺**ἔγκρυψις**, εως, ἡ, *covering over*, of fire with ashes, Arist.*Juv.* 470ᵃ12; of planets, *PMich.*III 149 x 40 (ii AD).

**ἐγκτάομαι**, add '*IG* 2².43.37 (Athens, 378/7 BC)'

**ἔγκτησις**, lines 1/2, for 'Dor. .. εως, ἡ' read 'εως, ἡ, **ἔκτησις** *IG* 9²(1).19.12 (Thermus, iii BC), Dor. **ἔγκτᾱσις**, Thess. **ἔντᾱσις** (q.v.), see also ἔμπᾱσις'; line 5, after '(Sparta)' insert '*IG* 1³.227.21 (Athens, v BC)'

**ἔγκῡδον**, add '(ἐγκυδές La.)'

**ἐγκῡέομαι**, delete the entry.

***ἐγκῡέω**, w. acc., *to become pregnant with*, χόλον *AP* 7.385 (Phil.); pass., *to be carried in the womb*, Theon *Prog.* 2.

***ἔγκυθρον**, τό, in pl. app. contents of χύτραι, perh. grape-juice, *SEG* 34.1213 (ἐνκ-, Lydia, ii AD); cf. ἐγχύτριαι, κύθρος, etc.

**ἐγκυκλέομαι III**, add 'Philod.Scarph. x 124'

***ἐγκυκλιακός**, ή, όν, *of* or *for the* ἐγκύκλιον (ἐγκύκλιος IV), λόγος *BGU* 914.5 (ii AD), cf. *PMich.*II 123ʳ xxii 31, 123ᵛ vii 16, 19 (i AD); ὁ ἐ. the official collecting the ἐγκύκλιον, *POxy.* 2281.3 (ii AD).

**ἐγκύκλιος I**, add '**2** ἐγκύκλιον, τό, *semicircular exedra*, Petersen-Luschan *Reisen in Lykien* 257.' **III 3**, add 'ἐπιστολὴ ἐ. Lxx *Da.* 4.34b'

**ἔγκυκλος II**, before 'ἔγκυκλον' insert '*having a border all round*, ταινία *PCair.Zen.* 696.5 (iii BC); ἱμάτιον Phot. s.v. παράπηχυ'

**ἐγκῡμονέω**, for '*conceive*' read '*carry in the womb*'; add 'pass., *Cod.Just.* 6.48.1.3'

**ἐγκύπτω**, add 'ἐγκύψας κάτω Ar.*Ra.* 804, ἐγκύψας καὶ ἐκτείνας τὴν κέρκον Pl.*Phdr.* 254d'

***ἐγκῡριεύω**, *to be in control*, Callistr.Hist. 5 J.

**ἐγκῡσίκωλος**, read '**ἐγκῡσίχωλος**'

***ἔγκωλον**, τό, v. δαῖμα.

**ἐγκωμιαστής**, add '*SEG* 32.502 (Thespiae, ii AD)'

**ἐγκωμικός**, delete the entry.

**ἐγκώμιος I**, delete the section.

***ἐγό**, v. ἐγώ.

**ἐγρηγορέω**, delete the entry.

**ἔγρηνται**, add 'cf. ‡ἀγρέω'

**ἐγρήσσω**, after 'A.R. 2.308' insert '*Trag.adesp.* 664.21 K.-S.'

***ἐγροάς**· στόμα ἢ πόρου .. Hsch.; cf. ἐκροή, ἔκροια.

**ἔγρω**, delete the entry.

**ἐγχαδές**, after 'ἐγχαλές' insert 'or ἔγχαλις (La.)'

**ἐγχᾰλῑνόω 3**, for 'metaph. of reins' read 'of veins'

**ἔγχαλκος I**, delete '*in* or *with brass*' and add 'Men.*Mon.* 492 J.'

**ἐγχάραξις I**, add 'Gal. 11.322.6'

**ἐγχᾰράσσω I**, line 5, after 'Jul.*Or.* 7.217a' insert 'fig., ἐνεχάραξε .. τὸ θεῖον αὐτῷ τὸ τῶ παντὸς λόγω σύσταμα Archyt.in Iamb.*Protr.* 4 (p. 18.26 P.)' **II**, *scarify*, add 'Gal. 11.321.18'

**ἐγχᾰρίζομαι**, add 'ἐνκεχαρισμένος dub. sens., in tomb curses, Mitchell *N.Galatia* 129, 362'

**ἐγχάσκω II**, add 'Ar.*Nu.* 1436, *Lys.* 271'

**ἐγχείη**, add 'Myc. *e-ke-i-ja*, cf. *e-ke-i-ja-ta*, pers. n.'

**ἐγχειρέω 2**, add 'of tomb robbers, *SEG* 30.1546 (Cilicia, iv/vi AD)'

***ἐγχειρής**, ές, *that is to hand*, cj. in B. 10.11 S.-M.

**ἐγχειρίδιον 1**, for this section read '*hand-weapon, sword*, Hdt. 1.12, 214, Th. 3.70.6, Lys. 4.6, Lxx *Ez.* 21.3, 4, 5. **b** rendering Hebr. *hereb̲* as used in stone-cutting, Lxx *Ex.* 20.25. **c** rendering Hebr. *kid̲ôn* (spear), Lxx *Je.* 27(50).42.' **4**, delete the section.

**ἐγχειρογάστωρ**, for 'Cleanth. .. 16' read 'Anon.ap.Ath. 1.4d'

***ἔγχειρον**, τό, pl. ἔγχῑρα *wages*, *IG* 2².1126.4; cf. °ὔχηρος.

****ἐγχειρόποινος**, Myc. *e-ke-ro-qo-no*, *wage-earner.*

**ἔγχελυς**, line 3, for 'ἐγγέλεων' read 'ἐγχέλεων'; line 5, after 'Arist.*HA*' insert 'gen. sg. ἐγχελιουος *IGC* p. 100 B31 (Acraephia, iii/ii BC)' add '**b** τυφλὰς ἐ. *penises*, Archil. l.c.'

⁺**ἔγχῑρα**, v. °ἔγχειρον.

**ἐγχηρωτύλει**, after lemma insert '(**ἐγχήροντι δύη** La.)'

**ἐγχλίω**, for '[ῐ]' read '[ῑ]'

**ἔγχνοος**, add 'Nonn.*D.* 22.25 (cj., ἄγχ- cod.)'

**ἔγχος**, add 'Myc. *e-ke-si* (dat. pl.)'

**ἐγχοῦν**, add '(ἔγχουτον Meineke)'

**ἔγχουσα**, add 'Amips. 3 K.-A.'

**ἐγχρίμπτω I**, add 'ἐ. αὐτοῖς τὰ κέντρα of bees *planting* their stings, Ael.*NA* 17.35'

**ἔγχρῑσις I**, add 'Asclep.Jun.ap.Gal. 12.746.9, 753.2'

**ἐγχρονίζω I**, line 4, for 'ἐν τόπῳ' read 'ἐν αὐτῇ, sc. τῇ Ἀλεξανδρείᾳ'

***ἐγχρωτάζω**, *to be smeared on*, ἡ βούπρηστις ἐγχρωτάζουσα εἰς τὰ χαλινὰ λίτρῳ ὁμοίαν ἔχει τὴν γεῦσιν Sch.Nic.*Al.* 337a Ge.

****ἐγχυσεύς**, ὁ, Myc. *e-ku-se-we* (pl.), *funnel.*

**ἐγχυτρίστρια I**, for '*EM* 313.41' read 'Suid. s.v.; καὶ ὅσαι τοὺς ἐναγεῖς καθαίρουσιν αἷμα ἐπιχέουσαι ἱερείου, καὶ θρηνητρίας, .. ib.'

***ἐγχωνεύω**, *fill up*, of a method of sealing tombs, ἐγχωνεύσει τοὺς πελεκείνους *SEG* 17.633.9 (Perge).

**ἐγχωρέω I 1**, add '**c** pres. part., *fitting*, τὸν ἐγχωροῦντα τρόπον Just.*Nov.* 4.1, *Cod.Just.* 12.60.7.2.'

**ἐγχώριος II**, for '*of .. rustic*' read '*of* or *belonging to one's estate, domestic*'

**ἐγώ I**, line 3, after '(lyr.)' insert 'Cypr. *e-ko-ne* ἐγών before consonant, *ICS* 213a' and after 'A.D.*Pron.* 51.4' insert 'ἐγό, verse in *POxy.* 2331.17, 19 (iii AD; for text see *CR* 7.191)'; line 6, after 'ἐμίνγα' insert 'Sophr. 86, A.D.*Pron.* 81.20, ἐμίγγα' and transfer to section II. **II**, line 3, for 'Sapph. .. 23.7' read 'Sapph. 94.7 L.-P.' and after 'ἐμεῖο' insert 'Il. 1.174, al., read by Zenodotus at Il. 14.118, al., A.R. 1.829, al.'; line 5, after 'dat. ἐμοί' insert '(strengthened w. γε, ἔμοιγε)' and after 'enclit. μοι' insert 'Cypr. *o-mo-i-po-si-se* ὅ μοι πόσις *ICS* 84.2'; line 7, for 'ἐμίν' read 'ἐμῑν'; line 9, at end for 'Cypr. .. H.' read 'Cypr. *mi* = με *ICS* 234, 235' **III**, line 4, after 'νῷν' insert 'A.*Ch.* 234' **IV**, line 3, Dor. ἁμές, add 'also ἁμέν ib. viii 10.7 (Cnossus, iii/ii BC)'; line 5, delete 'Herod. 1.46'; line 9, after '*Pron.* 95.3' insert 'cf. A.R. 2.616'

**ἐδαλάχθη**, for 'Id.' read 'Hsch.'

***Ἐδαλιεύς**, ῆϝος, ὁ, *inhabitant of Idalion*, Cypr. *e-ta-li-e-we-se* Ἐδαλιῆϝες, *ICS* 217.2.

⁺**ἐδᾰνός**, όν, unexpld. epith. (cf. ἑδανή), ἐλαίῳ ἀμβροσίῳ ἑδανῷ Il. 14.172, *h.Ven.* 63 (cj.), ἑδανοῖο .. οἴνης Nic.*Al.* 162, 181.

**ἐδάφιον**, add '**2** *small plot of ground*, rest. in *IG* 7.2808a.29.'

**ἔδᾰφος 1**, add 'fig., *foundation*, Longin. 8.1' **2**, add 'fig., [πάθη ψυχῆς] καταλύειν εἰς ἔ. Plu. 2.515c'

**ἐδέατρος**, for 'among the Persians .. *seneschal*' read '= ἐλέατρος, *steward* or sim. domestic officer'; add 'cf. ‡ἀρχεδέατρος'

**ἔδεος**, add '(ἔδος La.)'

***ϝhεδιέστᾱς**, ᾶ, ὁ, *private citizen*, = ἰδιώτης, Buck.*Gr.Dial.* 83 (Argos, vi BC).

***ἔδικτον**, v. °ἤδικτον.

***ϝέδιμνος**, v. ‡μέδιμνος.

***ἑδνῆστις**, ἡ, acc. sg. -ιν, *paid for by a bride-price*, Call.*fr.* 67.10 Pf.

**ἕδνον IV**, add 'χαρίσιον ἕ. Call.*fr.* 383.1 Pf.'

**ἑδνόω II**, med., for pres. defs. read '*seek in marriage*'; for 'Hes.*fr.* 94.47' read 'Hes.*fr.* 200.7 M.-W.'

**ἕδος I 3**, delete '*seated*' and after 'Paus. 8.46.2' insert 'D.C. 51.1, 59.28'; for 'ἕ. ὑπαίθριον D.C. 51.1' read 'D.C. 48.14'

**ἕδρα I 3**, line 7, after 'D.C. 57.21' insert 'archit., *Inscr.Délos* 104-4.5 (iv BC)'

**ἑδραῖος II**, line 6, after 'Ath. 11.496a' insert ''Εδραία epith. of γῆ, *SEG* 12.513 (Cilicia, i AD)'

**ἕδρασμα**, add 'meton., of Cerberus, στυγοῦ σκότους ἕδρασμα *Suppl.Mag.* 42 (iii/iv AD)'

***ἕδρευμα**, ατος, τό, some unidentified fitting in a building, *Pap. Lugd.Bat.* XIII 21.6, 12 (i AD).

**ἑδρικός**, add '**2** masc. subst., perh. *stone for foundations*, *BE* 1966.512 (Tauromenium, Sicily).'

***ἑδρύσκη**, v. °ὑδρίσκη.

**ἐδωδός**, after 'Hp.*Aër.*' insert '4'

***ἑδωλή**, ἡ, *seat*, *Naukratis* ii.68.

***ἐέ**, exclam., v. ἔ.

**ἐέλμεθα, ἐελμένος**, add 'but ἐελμένοι is for ἐελδόμενοι in Keil-Premerstein *Erster Bericht* 9 (Lydia, ii AD)'

⁺**ἐητύς**, v. °ἐυτής.

**ἔθειρα II**, a bird's *feathers*, add 'B. 5.29 S.-M.'; add 'of pubic hair, ἐπὶ κτενὸς ἔσκον ἔθειραι Call.*fr.* 343 Pf.'

⁺**ἐθειράς**, άδος, ἡ, = ἔθειρα (in quot., sense II), Sch.Theoc. 1.34.

**ἐθέλω**, line 10, after '46.47)' insert 'med. (or pass.) θέλοιτο *Cod.Just.* 1.4.19.11'; line 12, delete 'nor in Aeolic'; line 14, after '(Milet., iv BC)' insert '*IG* 2².851.15 (224/3 BC)'; line 15, after 'both forms in' insert 'Sapph. 1.17, 24 L.-P.'; line 16, delete 'trag. never use ἐθέλω exc. in augmented forms ἤθελον, -ησα' **I 6**, add 'S.*El.* 585, Macho 383 G., Herod. 8.6' **7**, folld. by subj., add 'E.*Ba.* 719, *Anacreont.* 10.1 W., *Ev.Matt.* 13.28, *Ev.Luc.* 9.54'

***ἐθετῶ**· τὸ σκοπῶ Theognost.*Can.* 9 A.

**ἐθημολογέω**, delete the entry.

**ἐθήμων**, delete 'c. dat., ἐλπίδι'

**ἐθίζω I**, pass., add 'Diog.Sinop.*fr.dub.* 9 S.'

**ἔθιμος**, line 4, after 'etc.' insert '*ἔθιμοι ἡμέραι days fixed by custom* for slave's service to a divinity, *SEG* 26.729, 37.590 (both Maced., ii AD)'

**ἐθμοί**, after '*δεσμοί*' insert '(*ἑσμοί* Solmsen)'

***ἐθνιάρχης**, ου, ὁ, = *ἐθνάρχης* I 2, *CIJud.* 1.719 (Argos).

**ἔθνος I 3**, after '*PPetr.* 3 p. 67 (iii BC)' insert '*PKöln* 260.3 (iii BC)'

***ἐθνῦμών**, *όνος, ὁ*, app. = *ἔθνος*, Hdn.Gr. 1.33, 2.735.

**ἔθος**, line 7, *ἐξ ἔθους*, after '(Arist.*EN*) 1103ᵃ17' insert '*SEG* 31.122 (Attica, ii AD), *according to custom*, *τὸν ἐξ ἔθους τριῶν μυριάδων τόκον* Modest.*Dig.* 50.12.10'

**ἔθω**, line 12, for '*εἰώθοσιν*' read '*εἰωθόσιν*'

**εἶ**, before 'indecl.' insert '*τό*'

**εἰ**, line 2, for '*ἤ Inscr.Cypr.* 135.10 H.' read '*e-ke* ἐ̄ *κε* (= *ἐάν*) *ICS* 217.10, 23' **A 2 b**, *εἴθε*, w. inf., add 'Ps.-Phoc. 45' add '**e** *εἴθε γάρ*, = *εἰ γάρ*, Diog.ap.D.L. 6.52, Hsch., Suid. s.v. *εἰ γάρ*, Phot. α 504 Th., Sch.Vet.A.*Th.* 550; condemned by Moer. p. 161 P.' **B II**, line 5, after '*εἰκ* alone ib. 3.21' insert 'also perh. orac. in Hdt. 1.174, B. 13.228 S.-M.'; line 7, after '(Pi.)*P.* 4.266, al.' insert '*εἴ τι ἐάν* (= *ἐάν τι*) *BGU* 2494.16 (iii AD)' **VII 3 a**, line 5, *εἰ μή τι, ἀλλά*, add 'Pl.*R.* 502a, 509c' **e**, delete '*siquis alius*'

**εἶα**, at end after 'S.*Ichn.* 87' insert '*fr.* 221.4 R. (v. *POxy.* ix Pl.iv)'

***εἰαριήτης**, ου, ὁ, (*ἔαρ* B) = *αἱματίτης, λίθος* Aglaïas in *Suppl.Hell.* 18.19; cf. *Ἀγλαΐας δ' ἐαρίτην τὸν αἱματίτην λίθον φησί* Sch.Nic.*Al.* 314e.

**εἰβάτας**, read '**εἰβᾱτάς**'

**εἴβω**, add 'cf. *εἰφθῇ· εἴβηται* Hsch.'

***εἰδάλιμος** (B), η, ον, v. °*ἰδάλιμος*.

***εἶδε**, v. °*ἤδη*.

***εἴδεος**, ον, (*εἶδος*) *having form*, Zos.Alch. 205.8. (Formed after *ἀνείδεος, πανείδεος*.)

**εἰδήμων**, after '*AP* 9.505.4' insert '9.496 (Ath.)'; before 'Hermog.' insert 'Rhet.Anon. in *POxy.* 410.27'

**εἰδογράφος**, for '*classifier of literary forms*' read '*classifier of forms* (in quots., *musical categories*)'

**εἰδομᾱλίδας**, add 'also -ίδης Suet.*Blasph.* 63 T.'

**εἰδοποιία 2**, for 'Rhet. *descriptive quality* .. 18.1' read 'transf. *ταῖς τῶν σχημάτων εἰ.* by means of the *specific characters* of the figures, Longin. 18.1'

**εἶδος I 2 b**, after 'Apollon.Perg.*Con.* 1.14, 21, al.' insert 'perh. also applied to a section of a city laid out on a rectangular grid, *POxy.* 2975.5 (AD 198)' **III**, add '**4** *special proposition*, i.e. one belonging to particular subject, opp. *τόπος*, Arist.*Rh.* 1358ᵃ31.' add '**V** unexpld. use, *χιλίαρχοι λογχοφόροι εἴδους Βιθυνῶν δευτέρων BSAA* 7.64.'

***εἰδοσύνη**, ἡ, *knowledge*, *IEphes.* 452 (iii AD).

**εἰ δ' οὖν**, for 'v. *εἰ* VII 4c' read 'v. *εἰ* VII 3c'

⁺**εἰδοφόρος**, ὁ, *frieze*, *Inscr.Délos* 442*B*232 (ii BC), *MAMA* 8.560.

***εἴδω A**, line 3, after '(Balbilla)' insert 'Cypr. *e-wi-te ἔϝιδε ICS* 379 (addenda p. 423)'; line 4, after '*ἰδεῖν*' insert '*Ϝιδε͂ν CEG* 375 (Laconia, vi BC)' **II**, add '**4** *think* that something is so, w. acc. and inf., A.R. 1.718, 1024.' **B**, line 1, delete '*I see with the mind's eye*'; line 11, for '*ἴσᾱμι*' read '‡*ἴσᾱμι*'; line 19, transfer 'also *ἰδέμεν* Pi.*N.* 7.25' to section A, line 5, after 'Ep. *ἰδέειν*'; line 21, for 'Pl.*Smp.* 119a' read 'Pl.*Smp.* 199a' **1**, w. gen. (12 lines fr. end), add 'perh. also Men.*fr.* 434 K.-Th., *Dysc.* 385' **3**, at end after 'with part. omitted' insert 'D. 4.18' **5**, add '**b** w. *ὅτε*, Il. 14.71, Od. 16.424, E.*Hec.* 110, *Tr.* 70.' at end add 'Myc. 3 sg. aor. (*o*-)*wi-de*'

**εἰδωλολατρία**, add '*Cod.Just.* 1.11.10.4'

**εἴδωλον I 3**, add '**b** *image* imprinted in sand, Ar.*Nub.* 976.' add '**VI** *Εἴδωλον* the constellation *Hercules*, Arat. 64, Nonn.*D.* 1.256.'

**εἰδωλόπλαστος**, for '*ideal*' read '*imagined*'

**εἶθάρ**, for 'Antim. 16.5' read 'Antim. 20.5 Wy., Call.*fr.* 31b Pf. (Add. II)'

**εἰθισμένως**, add '*POxy.Hels.* 37.6 (s.v.l., AD 176)'

***εἴθυνα**, v. °*ἴθυννα*.

**εἰκάζω II**, line 4, after 'cf. (Hdt.) 4.31' insert 'Pl.*R.* 488a'

**εἰκᾰθεῖν**, line 2, after '(S.)*Ph.* 1352' insert 'opt. *εἰκάθοι* A.R. 3.849'

**εἰκαῖος 1**, add '*casual*, *offhand*, *σφίγξις* Heliod.ap.Orib. 50.9.10' **3**, for this section read '*ordinary*, *taken at random*, Call.*fr.* 334 Pf., Nic.*Th.* 394, *ξύλα* Iamb.*Comm.Math.* 4'

**εἰκάς I**, line 1, for 'B.*Scol.Oxy.* 1361 *fr.* 1.5' read 'B.*fr.* 20B.5 S.-M.'; line 2, delete '(Hes.*Op.*) 820' (v. °*μετεικάς*); lines 3/7, for 'Epicur. .. *Lg.* 849b' read 'Ar.*Nu.* 17, And. 1.121, Epicur. [1]18, 8 A.; *μετ' εἰκάδα, μετ' εἰκάδας* are used in referring to days in the month later than the 20th, Men.*fr.* 265.3 K.-Th.: in Att. inscrr. (cf. Arat. 1149-52) they are usu. counted backwards fr. the end of the month, thus *δευτέρα μετ' εἰ.* = the 29th (or in a 29-day month the 28th), *τρίτη μετ' εἰ.* = the 28th (or 27th).' at end add 'see also *ἰκάς*'

**εἴκασμα I**, after 'A.*Th.* 523 (lyr.)' insert '*Γύ[γην γὰρ ὡ]ς ἐσεῖδον, [ο]ὐκ εἴκασμά τι Trag.adesp.* 664.18 K.-S.'

**εἰκασμός**, add '**b** *estimate* of yield on land, *PCair.Zen.* 147.3 (iii BC); of price, Aq.*Ge.* 26.12.'

***εἰκαστήριον**, *τό*, perh. *place for an image*, Nonn.*D.* 13.517 (cod. *ἰκ*-).

**εἰκῇ I 1**, delete 'D. 28.5' add '**2** *without good cause*, D. 28.5, 30.20, *UPZ* 108.24 (i BC).' **II**, add '*ITyr* 17' add '**IV** perh. = *εἰκότως, probably*, Antiph. 216.7 K.-A.'

**εἰκοβολέω**, for '*talk at random*' read '*guess*'

**εἰκοβολία**, for '*talking at random*' read '*guessing*'

***εἰκόνη**, ἡ, *image*, *PMil.Vogl.* 150.11 (ii AD).

**εἰκονίζω 1**, for 'from a pattern' read 'a document' **2**, for '*draw up an official description*' read '*verify the identity of*' and add '*BGU* 2475.6 (ii AD)'

**εἰκόνιον**, add '*εἰς ἰκόνια τῶν Σεβαστῶν POxy.* 3792.19 (iv AD)'

**εἰκόνισμα**, line 1, for 'S.*fr.* 573' read '*Trag.adesp.* 700a.3 K.-S.'

**εἰκονισμός II**, after '*PLond.ined.* 2196' insert '(*JEA* 52.135)'; at end for 'Sen.*Ep.* 95' read 'Sen.*Ep.* 95.66'

**εἰκονιστής**, for '*registrar*' read '*scribe, copyist*'

***εἰκονοφόρος**, ὁ, = Lat. *imaginifer, carrier of the emperor's effigy*, Lyd.*Mag.* 48.4, *MAMA* 9.131.

**εἰκός II**, add '*ἐὰ[ν μὴ ἐπι]θῶσιν κατὰ τὸ εἰκός SEG* 30.61.A39 (Athens, iv BC)'

**εἰκοσᾰβοιος**, add '*εἰκοσόβοιον Suppl.Hell.* 991.79 (poet. word-list, iii BC)'

**εἰκοσᾰγωνος**, after '*τὸ εἰ.*' insert 'i.e. the dodecahedron'

***εἰκοσαδράχμιος**, ον, Cret. **ἰκᾰτιδάρκμιος** *SEG* 27.631.A13 (-*ίος* acc. pl., Lyttos, vi BC).

***εἰκοσᾰδραχμος**, ον, *of twenty drachmae*, *τιμή PLond.* 1157ᵛ.8 (iii AD); also **εἰκοσίδραχμος** *PTeb.* 373.12 (ii AD).

**εἰκοσᾰέτης**, add 'see also *εἰκοσέτης*'

**εἰκοσᾰετία**, add '*PCol.* 175.44 (AD 339), *IKeramos* 31'

***εἰκοσᾰκότυλον**, *τό*, *measure of twenty κοτύλαι*, *SEG* 16.496 (Chios).

**εἰκοσᾰμηνος**, for '(Leon.)' read '(= Theoc.*Ep.* 16)'

**εἰκοσάπρωτοι**, for '*OGI* 629.10 (Palmyra)' read 'Petersen-Luschan *Reisen in Lykien* 38' and add '*SEG* 38.1462.15, al. (Oenoanda, ii AD); also in sg., ib. 28'

***εἰκοσέτηρος**, ον, = *εἰκοσέτης*, *Corinth* 8(3).305 (iii AD).

**εἰκοσέτης**, for '(Cypr.)' read '(Cyprus)' and add '*GVI* 1081 (Ephesus, i AD); fem., *SEG* 3.543 (Thrace, iii BC)'

***εἰκοσήμερος**, ἡ, *period of twenty days*, *SEG* 17.829, *Pap.Lugd.Bat.* xx 3.14 (iii BC).

**εἴκοσῐ**, line 4, *Ϝίκατι*, add '*ἴκατι BCH* 61.334 (Drerus, vi BC), *SEG* 37.422 (Phocis, v BC), *ἴκατιν* (before consonant) Call.*fr.* 196.32 Pf., *φίκατι IPamph.* 17, 18 (iii/iv BC)'

***εἰκοσίδραχμος**, v. °*εἰκοσάδραχμος*.

***εἰκοσιεννεαέτης**, ες, *twenty-nine years old*, *GVI* 816.4 (Egypt, iii AD).

***εἰκοσιεπτάς**, άδος, ἡ, *the number twenty-seven*, Procl. *in Ti.* 2.213.32, 215.22 D.

***εἰκοσῐπενταέτηρίς**, ίδος, ἡ, *period of twenty-five years*, *Cat.Cod.Astr.* 11(2).112.1, 113.12 (both pl.).

**εἰκοσῐπεντᾰρουρος**, add '*OMich.* 90.2 (ii BC)'

***εἰκοσῐποδία**, ἡ, *space of twenty feet*, prob. in *IG* 2².1654.38, see J.M. Paton *The Erechtheum* (Harvard 1927) 420.

***εἰκοσόβοιος**, v. °*εἰκοσάβοιος*.

⁺**εἰκόσορος**, ep. *ἐεικ-*, ον (*εἴκοσι, ἐρ-/ὀρ-* as in *ἐρέτης*), *having twenty rowers*, Od. 9.322, Teles p. 27 H.; applied derogatorily to courtesan, *ὁλκάδος AP* 5.161 (Asclep.), ib. 204 (Mel.); as subst., *εἰ.* (sc. *ναῦς*), ἡ, D. 35.18, *AP* 6.222 (Theodorid.).

**εἰκοστός I**, add 'neut. subst., *twentieth year* (sc. *ἔτος*), *SEG* 26.482 (Dyme, ii/iii AD)' **II**, add '*SEG* 30.979 (Olbia, *c.*500 BC)'

***εἰκοτολογικός**, ή, όν, *based on εἰκοτολογία*, *λόγοι* Procl. *in R.* 1.284.5.

⁺**εἰκότως**, adv. fr. *εἰκώς* (v. *ἔοικα*), Ion. *οἰκότως* Hdt. 2.25.2, 7.50.1. **I** *suitably, in keeping with*, *ἀπουσίᾳ .. εἶπας εἰ. ἐμῇ* A.*Ag.* 915. **II** *reasonably, fairly*, A.*Supp.* 403, S.*OC* 432, 977, *αὐτοὶ οὐκ εἰ. πολεμοῦνται* Th. 1.37.1, 2.93.1, Isoc. 12.101, And. 1.142, Pl.*Epin.* 979d, X.*Cyr.* 8.8.20, Plu. 2.409f; at the end of sentences, Th. 1.77.5, D. 1.10, Pl.*La.* 183b; in constr. w. acc. and inf., *σθένειν τὸ θεῖον μᾶλλον εἰ. ἔχει* E.*IT* 911, cf. *Or.* 737, *τοὖτ' εἰ. δὴ δοκεῖ ἀνδρῶν ἀγαθῶν .. ἔργον εἶναι* And. 1.140.

**εἴκω I 1**, line 6, for 'Gal. 18(1).97' read 'Gal. 18(2).97' **2**, add 'Alcm. 83 P., Ps.-Phoc. 220' **III**, delete the section (v. D.Page *Sappho and Alcaeus* (Oxford 1955) 23).

**εἰκών**, line 4, after 'Maiist. 15' insert '(these forms may come fr. ***εἰκώς**, declined like *αἰδώς*)' and after 'acc. pl. *εἰκούς*' insert 'A.*fr.* 78a.1 R. (rest.)'; line 5, for '*Ϝεικ- Inscr.Cypr.* 151 H.' read 'Cypr. *we-i-ko-na Ϝεικόνα ICS* 276'

***Εἰλαῖος**, v. *Ἰλαῖος*.

**Εἰλείθυια I**, pl., add '*SEG* 24.226 (Attica)' add **b** transf., *ὃ δὲ καλοῦσιν οἱ μάντεις Εἰλειθυίας ἄφεδρον* Theoph.*HP* 5.9.8; cf. *τὰ ἐκ τῶν ξύλων ἐκφυόμενα καὶ μάλιστα ἐκ τῶν ἐλατίνων ἃ καλοῦσιν οἱ* μάντεις -ας id.*CP* 5.4.4.' at end add 'also Ἐλίθιουια *IG* 7.3385, Εἰλειθούα 7.3391 (both Boeotia, ii BC); Εἰλειόθυια *SEG* 24.1163 (Gortyn, ii/iii AD), ℎιλέθυια *SEG* 35.37 (Attic vase, vi BC), Ἰλυθει[ Lang *Ath.Agora* XXI G8 (iv BC), Ἐλυθία *SEG* 31.1586, Lacon. Ἐλευσία *ABSA* 12.348 (ii/i BC), Myc. *e-re-u-ti-ja*'

*__Εἰλειθυιαῖα__, τά, festival at Delos, *Inscr.Délos* 401.22, 440*A*69, 461*Bb*53 (all ii BC).

**Εἰλείθυιον**, add 'Ἰλειθυεῖον rest. in *Ath.Agora* XIX L6.98, **Ἰλύθειον** *Inscr.Délos* 1403*Bb*i97, ii37; also **Ἰλύθυιον** ib. 1421*Bb*ii2 (both ii BC)'

**εἰληδόν**, after '= ἰληδόν' insert 'εἰληδὸν ἐσμεύουσιν rest. in Call.*fr.* 191.28 Pf.'

**εἰληθερής**, for 'cf. ἐλαθερής' read 'also **ἐλαιθερής**, ἐλαιθερὲς ὕδωρ *Suppl.Hell.* 1019; ἐλāθερής Hsch.'

**εἴλημα I**, add 'ἐν ἰλήματι καινῷ λεντίῳ *POxy.* 3060.6 (ii AD)' **II 1**, delete the section (read ἀνείλημα). **2**, add 'perh. also *book-roll*, Aq.*Je.* 43(36).2' **III**, add '*JRCil.* 1.24 (late Rom.imp.)' add '**V** Lacon. Ϝήλημα, v. βήλημα.'

**εἰλῆς εἶ**, after '**εἰλῆς**' insert '(**εἴληος** La.)'

*__εἴληφα__, **εἰληφώς**, v. λαμβάνω.

**εἰλίονες**, add 'cf. °ἰλίων'

*__εἶλον__, v. αἱρέω.

+__εἰλόπεδον__, τό, θ' εἰλόπεδον read by some edd. for ‡θειλόπεδον in Od. 7.123; cf. *EM* 449.29, Eust. 43.38.

**εἴλῡμα**, add 'form Ϝέλῡμα, Myc. *we-ru-ma-ta* (pl.)'

**εἰλυτά**, delete the entry.

*__εἰλύτας__, v. °ἐλλύτης.

**εἴλω**, line 6, after 'Il. 13.408' insert '3 pl. ἄλεν 22.12'; line 8, after '(Il.) 13.524' insert 'κατα-Ϝελμένος *Leg.Gort.* 10.35 (v BC); also Ϝευμέναν *Schwyzer* 177.14 (Gortyn, v BC)'; lines 13/14, for 'J.*AJ* 12.1.9' read 'J.*AJ* 12.2.9' **B**, line 7, after 'ib. 8' insert 'cf. ἀμφὶ κῆρες εἰλεῦνται Call. in *Suppl.Hell.* 253.1' **C**, line 4, for 'Call. *Iamb.* 1.144' read 'Call.*fr.* 191.83 Pf.' and add 'perh. *unroll*, μὴ .. ἐπ' ὀμφαλὸν εἴλεε (imper.) βίβλον *AP* 9.540.1'

*__εἵλως__, v. °ἵλαος.

**εἶμα**, line 2, for '(but gen. fem. Ϝήμας 5.40)' read 'see also °Ϝῆμᾱ'; after '(Od.) 10.542' insert 'ἀπὸ κρόκεον ῥίψαις Ἰάσων εἶμα Pi.*P.* 4.232'

*__εἱματιστής__, οῦ, ὁ, *servant in charge of clothes*, *La Carie* 18 (ii AD).

**εἰμί** (*sum*), lines 1/2, for 'Cret. .. 4959a' read 'Dor. ἠμί *Schwyzer* 273 (Rhodes, vi BC), *Inscr.Cret.* 2.x 7.2 (ἐμί, Cydonia, v BC), ib. xii 31a.3 (ἠμί, Eleutherna, ii BC), etc.'; line 10, after 'Sapph. 1.28' insert 'L.-P., *AP* 9.318 (Leon.Tarent.)'; line 12, for '*CIG* 2664' read '*BMus.Inscr.* 918 (Halicarnassus, ii/iii AD)' and after 'al.' insert 'pl. ἤτωσαν Mitchell *N.Galatia* 129; cf. ἐξήτω *AS* 12.209, 211 (Cilicia)'; line 13, after 'ἔστωσαν' insert '(rare, and often altered to ἔστων; but cf. E.*Ion* 1131, Pl.*Sph.* 231a, *Lg.* 737e, 762d)'; line 15, for 'ii BC, ib. $2^2$.1328' read 'iv BC, *SEG* 9.1.13, cf. *IG* $2^2$.1328; so codd. in Pl.*R.* 352a, codd. BT in id.*Sph.* 231a' and after 'ib. 1126' insert 'Boeot. ἔνθω *IG* 7.3172.88'; line 17, delete '*IG* 7.3172.165'; line 18, after 'εἰῃ 9.245, etc.' insert 'ἦν *POxy.* 1061.13 (i BC), etc.'; line 25, inf., εἶναι, add 'Stesich.*fr.suppl.* 15 i 7 P.'; line 27, ἔμεν, add 'Theoc. 25.116, Call.*fr.* 67.20 Pf.', ἦμεν, add '*SEG* 30.356 (Argos, *c.*300 BC)', εἶμεν (in *IG* 12(1).155.100 written ειμμ-), add 'Stesich.*fr.suppl.* 102.5 P.'; lines 25/27, inf. ἔμμεναι, Aeol., add '*IKyme* 13 i 18 (iii BC)', ἔμμεν, add 'also Thess., *Schwyzer* 590.20 (Larissa, iii BC)', εἶμεν, add 'also Boeot., *SEG* 32.496 (Thespiae, iii BC)'; line 30, εἴμειν, add 'Stesich.*SLG* 102.5 P.', εἶν, add 'Stesich.*SLG* 15 i 7 P.'; lines 31/4, for '*SIG* 135.4' read '*SIG* 135.3'; part., after 'Ep. ἐών, ἐοῦσα, ἐόν' insert 'gen. ἐόντος *SEG* 32.356 (Aegina, vi BC)', for 'ἰών .. 23 H.' read '*i-o-ta* ἰόντα *ICS* 217.23', for '*IG* 7.3172.15' read '*IG* 7.3172.116'; after 'Theoc. 28.16' insert 'ἦσσα *SEG* 9.11.17 (Cyrene, iv BC)' and after 'ἔασσα' insert '*PAE* 1931.89 (Dodona, vi/v BC), ἔασα *SEG* 11.112, 37.340.6 (vi/v and iv BC, both Arcadia); gen. ἐόνσας *SEG* 29.529 (Larissa, ii/i BC); acc. sg. ἔντα *Lyr.adesp.* 62 P.'; line 36, delete 'ἐᾶσα .. (Messene)'; line 38, after 'dat. pl. ἔντασσι ib. 104' insert 'Thess. εἴντεσσι *SEG* 36.548.2 (Matropolis, iii BC)'; line 47, delete '(wh. is v.l. in Pi.*I.* 1.26)'; line 48, delete 'Erinn. 4.4'; line 50, after 'Sophr. 59' insert 'Pi.*I.* 1.26 (v.l.), Erinn. 4.4'; line 51, after '(Delph.)' insert 'also Arc. *IG* 5(2).6.37 (iii BC), Cypr. *e-se* *ICS* 398'; line 56, after 'Epidamnus, iii BC)' insert 'cf. ἐξῆν· ἐξεγένοντο Hsch., v. °ἔξειμι (B)'; p. 488a line 1, after '*GDI* 1696' insert '*SEG* 16.255.17 (Argos, ii BC)'; line 2, after '(lyr.)' insert 'ἦσκε Alcm. 74 P.' at end of para. add 'Myc. pres. 3 pl. *e-e-si* (form ἔℎενσι); part. *e-o* ἐℎών (masc. sg.), *e-o-te* ἐℎόντες (pl.); *a-pe-a-sa* ἀπ-έℎασσαι (fem. pl.); fut. 3 pl. *e-so-to*' **A IV**, line 7, for 'X.*Cyr.* 2.3.16' read 'X.*Cyr.* 2.3.18'; lines 10/11, w. relat. particles, add 'w. ὅποι, E.*Alc.* 113, w. ᾗ, Pl.*Lg.* 721b'; line 13, delete 'in questions expecting a neg. answer' **VI**, lines 6/7, delete 'imper.' and 'ἔστω .. 10.7' **C I**, add 'καλῶς ἔσται Men.*Dysc.* 571' **E I**, for 'phrases .. do a thing' read 'limiting phrases' and after 'Pl.*Plt.* 300c' insert 'ἀριθμὸν εἶναι id.*Ep.* 337c'

**εἶμι** (*ibo*), line 2, after '3 sg. εἶσι' insert 'εἶτι *SEG* 9.72.57, 88 (Cyrene, iv BC)'; line 3, after 'compd.' insert 'πρόσει Epict.*Ench.* 32.2'; line 5, after 'Sophr. 48' insert 'εἴῃ (lapid. *EIEI*) *Inscr.Cret.* 4.81.7 (Gortyn, v BC), (ἐπ-) *SEG* 9.72.3 (Cyrene, iv/iii BC)'; line 9, for 'Il. 24 .. (Crete)' read 'dub. in Il. 24.139, Od. 14.496, Hes.*Op.* 617'; line 11, after 'Str. 9.2.23' insert '*SB* 6152.22, 6153.25 (Egypt, i BC)'; line 12, delete '(προσ-εῖναι .. 353)' **I**, add 'Myc. fut. part. *i-jo-te* ἰόντες (masc. pl.)' **II 1**, add '*SEG* 9.72.88 (Cyrene, iv BC)' **VI 2**, add 'E.*Ba.* 365, *Heracl.* 455, etc.'

*__εἰμιμναΐῆος__, v. °ἡμιμναϊαῖος.

**ἕϊν**, v. οὗ.

**εἰνᾰετής**, add 'also εἰνέτης Call.*Dian.* 14; cf. ἐνναέτης, °ἐννεέτης'

**εἰνᾰ́τερες**, line 4, (acc. sg.), add 'cf. τὴν ἰανάτερα *TAM* 5(1).682, 754 (prob. loan-word)'

*__Εἰνᾰτίη__, *from the city* Εἴνατος in Crete, epith. of Ilithyia, Call.*fr.* 524 Pf., St.Byz. s.v. Εἴνατος; Ἐλεύ]θυιαν Βινατίαν *Inscr.Cret.* 4.174.76 (Gortyn, ii BC), cf. ib. 61.

*__εἰνέτης__, v. °εἰναετής.

**εἴπερ II**, line 2, after 'etc.' insert 'εἰ μή πέρ γ' ἅμα αὐτὴ γένοιτ' ἂν γραῦς τε καὶ νέα γυνή Ar.*Nu.* 1183' **III**, for this section read 'w. an ellipse, *if* what precedes is inevitable, is a valid assumption, etc. Ar.*Nu.* 227, Pl.*Lg.* 667a, 900e; ἀλλ' εἴπερ, Pl.*Prm.* 150b, *R.* 497e, Arist.*EN* $1101^a12$, $1155^b30$, $1174^a28$'

**εἶπον**, line 3, after 'Pi.*O.* 4.25' insert '3 sg. ἦπε *Clara Rhodos* 9.221 (Lindian decree, v BC)'; line 5, for 'Dor.' read 'Aeol.'; line 6, ἔειπα, add 'Pi.*N.* 9.33'; lines 8/9, for 'persons' read 'person' and delete 'and imper.'; line 11, εἰπάτω, add 'X.*Ath.* 3.6'; line 13, before 'part.' insert 'opt. εἴπαιμεν Pl.*Sph.* 240d; εἴπειεν Arist.*Ath.* $75^a24$, *Top.* $159^b35$' and after 'εἴπας' insert 'Hdt. 8.102.1, 9.42.4, al., Longin. 1.2'; line 17, Ϝεῖπαι, add '*SEG* 32.908 (Phaestus, vi BC)' **I 1 b**, add 'μέλος Call.*Del.* 257, Nonn.*D.* 43.392; ὑμηναίους Call.*fr.* 75.43 Pf. (ειδον pap., εἶπον Pf.)' **III**, at end after 'Herod. 6.26' insert 'folld. by ὅπως and fut. ind., Men.*Dysc.* 237'

**εἶπος**, delete the entry (v. °ἶπος).

**Εἰρᾰφιώτης**, line 2, for 'Call.*fr.anon.* 89' read '*Suppl.Hell.* 1045'

**εἰρεσία I 1**, line 5, for 'close to her *throbbing* breast' read 'beside the *rhythmic beating* of her breast (cf. ἐρέσσω II 1)' **II 1**, line 2, for 'Antip. (?)' read 'Antip.Thess.'; insert 'Opp.*H.* 5.301'; transfer 'Th. 7.14' to section I 1. **2**, delete the section transferring exx. to section I 1.

**εἴρην**, for '*who .. year*' read '*aged between thirteen and nineteen, teenager*'; add 'Call.*fr.* 487 Pf.; ἰρήν in Hdt. 9.85.2; ἴρανες· οἱ εἴρενες. οἱ ἄρχοντες ἡλικιώταις. Λάκωνες Hsch.; cf. μελλείρην, ‡τριτίρενες'

*__εἰρηναρχία__, ἡ, *office of* εἰρηνάρχης, εἰρηναρχίαι ε', i.e. five tenures of office, *Didyma* 157 II (b).

**εἰρήνη I**, line 3, after 'E.*Med.* 1004' insert 'καὶ πολέμō καὶ εἰρήνης *in peace and war* *SIG* 110 (Rhodes, 410/8 BC), *SEG* 31.969 (Erythrae, iv BC), 30.990.17 (decree from Delos, iii BC), etc.. **2** *assurance, making safe*, ἐξ ἀλληλενγύης τῇ εἰρήνῃ τοῦ αὐτοῦ Ἀμουλοῦ pap. in *Mnemosyne* (series 3) 3.236 (iv AD). **3** as the condition of the dead, cf. section IV, *TAM* 4(1).357, *SEG* 33.764 (Italy, iv AD).' fourth line from end, ἰράνα, add '*SEG* 30.360 (Argos)'; after '(*IG*) 7.2407' insert 'Rhod. ἰρήνα *Schwyzer* 278 (v BC)'; for 'but Cret. .. 508.5' read 'w. aspirate χιρήνας (= καὶ ἱ-) *Inscr.Cret.* 186.B5, 184.a7, Thess. ℎιρένα *SEG* 23.415 (Pherae, v BC), ℎιράνα *SEG* 26.461 (Sparta, v BC)'

**εἰρηνικός 3**, add 'οἱ δὲ κατοικοῦντες εἰρηνικώτεροι *Peripl.M.Rubr.* 8'

*__εἰρηνόφρων__, ονος, ὁ, ἡ, *peaceably-minded*, *MAMA* 8.321.

*__εἰριπόνος__, ον, = εἰροπόνος, Simon. 113 P.

*__εἰρκτήριον__, τό, = Lat. *carcer*, Charis. p. 32 K.

*__εἰροπλόκος__, ὁ, *wool-weaver*, *IG* $2^2$.13178 (iv BC).

*__εἵρους__, **εἰρούισσα**, v. ‡ἥρως, ‡ἡρώϊσσα.

*__εἰροφόρος__, ον, *wearing wool*, Νίοβος εἰ., title of play attributed to Ar., Hdn.*fr.* 29 H. (cf. ἐριοφόρος).

**εἴρω** (A), line 2, after '(v. infr.)' insert 'εἰρμένος Call.*fr.* 657 Pf. (v.l. εἰργμ-), prob. in Poll. 6.75 (codd. εἰργμ-)'; line 6, delete 'τὸ .. Plot. 2.3.7'

**εἴρω** (B), line 3, after '(Od.) 11.137' insert '3 pers. εἴρει Arat. 739; impf. εἶρεν B.17.20, 74 S.-M.'

**εἰρωνευτικός**, add 'οἱ λόγοι τοῦ Γοργίου εἰ. εἰσιν ἅπαντες Anon. *in Rh.* 190.5'

*__εἰρωνων__, gen. pl., word occurring in price-lists of spices, *POxy.* 3733.25, 3766.107 (both iv AD).

**εἰς**, line 8, after 'vowels' insert '(exc. Sapph. 44.23, 26 L.-P.)'; line 11, after '(Crete)' insert 'also **ἰσς** (for *ἰνς) *Inscr.Cret.* 2.v 1.12 (Oaxos, vi/v BC), but **ἰς** ib. 9.13, *IPamph.* 3.4' **I 1 b**, delete 'and Ion.' and for 'Hdt. 4 .. Ar.*Av.* 619' read 'in Pindar e.g. ἐς ἄνδρας *O.* 2.38, ἐς θεόν ib. 7.31, but not freq.; in Hdt. and Att. where persons stand for country or region, ἐς τοὺς συγγενέας Hdt. 4.147.3; ἐς ἀνθρώπους ἀπόρους Th. 1.9.2; ἐς Πισίδας X.*An.* 1.1.11; also of coming before an assemblage, εἰς ὑμᾶς *before* your court, Pl.*Ap.* 17c, D. 18.103, etc. (cf. ἐς τὸν δῆμον Th. 5.45.1, etc.); also χωρεῖν ἐς and the like, of attacking, Th. 4.95.3, X.*An.* 3.2.16, etc. ἕξει ἐς τὸν ἄνδρα Ar.*Eq.* 760. (in εἰς Ἄμμωνα id.*Av.* 619, Ἄ. is the place, cf. Str. 17.1.42.)' **2**, line 12, after 'D.S. 14.117' insert 'τὰ παιδία εἰς τὴν κοίτην εἰσίν *Ev.Luc.* 11.7; εὑρέθη εἰς Ἄζωτον *Act.Ap.* 8.40' **II**, of time, add 'w. ellipsis of acc., ἐς ἔτους φανέντος ἄλλου *Anacreont.* 56.14 W.' **2**, at end for 'Th. 4.63 (v. εἰσαῦθις)' read 'v. °εἰσαῦθις'; after 'Ar.*Pax* 367' insert 'cf. Arat. 770, 1103 (prob.)'; add 'ἐς ἄχρι, v. ἐσάχρι' **IV 3**, line 4, after 'Ar.*Ach.* 686' insert 'εἰς βίαν Men.*Dysc.* 396' **V 2**, add '**b** *as, by way of,* εἰς μεγάλην .. χάριν *AP* 5.287.10 (Agath.), cf. 7.614.14 (id.); εἰς μισθόν Ps.-Hdt. *Vit.Hom.* 4.'

**εἷς**, line 1, after 'μιᾶς, ἑνός' insert '(acc. εἶνα only Hdn.Gr. 1.546), Myc. *e-me* (masc. dat. = ἑνί)' **1 g**, line 6, after 'Luc.*Salt.* 12' insert 'so ἕνα παρ' ἕνα *SEG* 31.825 (Sicily, ii BC), μίαν παρὰ μίαν *on alternate days, Suppl.Mag.* 10 (iii/iv AD); so παρὰ μίαν Plb. 3.110.4'; line 9, after 'Ael.*NA* 5.9' insert 'ἐν ἑνί *taken together, total* (of prices), *BCH* 60.119.6 (Delph.)'; add 'διὰ μιᾶς *after a day's break, Suppl.Mag.* 34 (vi AD)' **h**, line 2, after 'Th. 8.109' insert '(s.v.l.)' **i**, for this section read 'μίαν, as adv., *once, POxy.* 1593, *BGU* 984 (both iv AD); rptd. μίαν μίαν, app. *from time to time, S.fr.* 201' add '**j** εἷς εἷς τῷ Ἐλεαζάρ καὶ εἷς εἷς τῷ Ἰθαμάρ *one each* .. (app. in imitation of Hebr. constr.), Lxx 1*Ch.* 24.6.'

**εἰσαγγελία I 1**, add '(s.v.l.; cj. προσαγγελία)'

**εἰσαγγέλλω I 1 b**, add 'for honorific purposes, τῇ βουλῇ *Amyzon* 35, *IMylasa* 126.2 (iii/ii BC)'

**εἰσάγω I 3**, add '**b** *bring in* water supply, *SEG* 31.1363 (Cyprus, i AD), 26.784.9 (Thrace, ii AD), *IEphes.* 3217.(b)21 (ii AD), etc.' **II 3 a**, transfer 'A.*Eu.* 580, 582' to follow 'of the εἰσαγωγεύς'; for 'D. 24.10' read 'οὐδ' αἰσχύνει φθόνου δίκην εἰσάγων D. 18.121; cf. εἰ γραψάμενοι τὸν νόμον καὶ εἰσαγαγόντες εἰς ὑμᾶς λῦσαι δυναίμεθα id. 24.10'

***εἰσᾰγωγεῖον**, v. ‡εἰσαγώγιον.

**εἰσᾰγωγεύς I**, add 'official under the ἀγωνοθέτης who admitted the contestants, *SEG* 16.258 (Argos, ii AD)'

**εἰσᾰγωγή I 3**, add 'ἐσαγωγὰν καὶ ἐξαγωγάν *SEG* 32.1586 (Egypt, v BC)'

**εἰσᾰγώγιμος**, line 2, for 'Arist.*Oec.* 1345$^{a}$21' read 'Arist.*Oec.* 1345$^{b}$21'

**εἰσᾰγώγιον**, add '*SEG* 14.639.(E)9 (Caunus, i AD): also -εῖον *SEG* 33.115.26 (Athens, iii BC), *Hesperia* 11.295.16 (Athens, ii BC). **b** *import duty, SEG* 37.859.B16 (Caria, ii BC), *PHels.* 36.5 (ii BC), *IEphes.* 13 i 24 (i AD). **2** *office of the* εἰσαγωγεῖς at Samos, *BCH* 59.478 (Samos, ii BC).'

**εἰσᾰεί**, add 'also ἐσαεί *IG* 2$^{2}$.1064 (c.AD 230), *Hesperia* suppl. 6, no. 31.14 (Athens, iii AD)'

**εἰσᾰΐω II**, add 'ἐσαΐειν Hp.*Mul.* 1.4; ἐσαΐει ib. 1.9'

**εἰσᾰκοντίζω**, line 1, delete '*at,* τινά'

**εἰσᾰκούω I 1**, at end after '*Ev.Matt.* 6.7' add '*SEG* 34.1220 (Lydia)'

**εἰσάκτης**, add 'gloss on εἰσηγητής Hsch. **2** *tax-collector, PMich.* VIII 989.4 (ostr., iii AD).'

**εἰσᾰλείφω**, delete '*anoint,* Aristid. 2.292 J.'

**εἰσᾰμείβω**, for '*go* .. τεῖχος' read '*allow to enter*'

***εἰσάμην**, v. ἵζω I 2.

**εἰσάμην III**, delete the section.

**εἰσαναβαίνω**, add 'of the dead, ψυχὴ δ' αἰθέρα εἰσανέβη epigr. in *SEG* 37.198 (Attica, i BC/ii AD), *Corinth* 8(3).658 (v/vi AD)'

***εἰσανδρόω**, Ep. ἐσ-, *fill with men,* A.R. 1.874 (v.l. ἐπ-).

***εἰσανέχω**, *jut out,* A.R. 1.1360, 4.291; w. acc., *jut out into,* id. 4.1578.

***εἰσᾰνύω**, prob. f.l. for ἀνύω in *Cat.Cod.Astr.* 8(1).168 (Vett.Val.), cj. in *Suppl.Hell.* 962.17.

***εἰσαπαντάω**, *meet, encounter, PMerton* 65.8 (ii AD).

***εἰσαπόλλῡμι**, *lose into* (in quot., a well), Men.*Dysc.* 681 (pap.; perh. read ἐξαπ-).

***εἰσᾰράσσω**, Att. -ττω, *drive in disorder into,* Hdt. 4.128.3, ἐσαράξαντές σφεας ἐς τὰς νέας 5.116, D.C. 43.40.3, τὴν .. ἵππον .. ἐς τοὺς πεζοὺς ἐσήραξε id. 51.26.1.

***εἰσαῦθις**, **ἐσαῦθις** (or **εἰς, ἐς αὖθις**), *for another* (*later*) *occasion,* ἐ. ἀναβάλλεσθαι Ar.*Ec.* 983, Th. 4.63.1, Pl.*Euthphr.* 15e, *Smp.* 174e; *on another occasion, later,* εὐτυχοῦσι δέ οἱ μὲν τάχ', οἱ δ' ἐσαῦθις, οἱ δ' ἤδη βροτῶν E.*Supp.* 551.

**εἰσβαίνω I 2**, add '**b** *embark on, begin* an action χορεῖον εἰσέβαινε ῥυθμόν *began,* Men.*Dysc.* 951.' **II**, line 2, after 'E.*Alc.* 1055' delete '(lyr.)'

**εἰσβάλλω II 1**, line 6, for 'country' read 'region, place' **4**, after '*begin*' insert 'D.H.*Lys.* 17'

**εἰσβᾰτικόν**, after 'τό' insert '*entrance fee, POxy.* 2239.21 (vi AD)'; for 'tax in Egypt' read 'unexpld. sense'

***εἰσβῐάζομαι**, *force one's way in,* ὁ μὲν γὰρ ὢν οὐκ ἀστὸς εἰσβιάζεται Ar.*Av.* 32, *OGI* 736.6 (Fayûm), *PPetr.* 3 p. 39 (iii BC); w. πρός, D.S. 14.9; w. εἰς, ἐς τὸν Βόσπορον D.C. 42.47; transf., D. 39.33 εἰς τὰ πρῶτα γένη Plu. *Num.* 1.

***εἰσβοηθέω**, *bring help* to, *SEG* 38.1476.96 (Xanthos, 206/5 BC).

**εἰσβολή 2 b**, add '*entrance* to a bay, *Peripl.M.Rubr.* 5' **3**, *proem, preface,* add 'Arg.E.*Med.*'

**εἰσγρᾰφή**, add '**II** *inscription,* τιμῶν (on statues), *IGRom.* 3.739 ix 60 (Rhodiapolis, ii AD, pl.).'

***εἰσδημέω**, *pay a visit* to another country, Ἀθήναζε Eun. *VS* p. 491 B.

**εἴσειμι**, add 'see also ‡ἔνσειμι'

***εἰσείρω**, app. *fasten on,* Hsch., s.v. ἵρεται.

**εἰσελαστικός**, for '*celebrated by a triumphal entry*' read '*carrying the privilege of a triumphal return to one's native land* or *city*'

**εἰσελαύνω**, line 1, after '-ελάω' insert 'Eretrian εἰρελάω q.v.'

***εἰσένεκτον**, τό, perh. *entrance-passage,* τὸ περίβολον καὶ τὸ ἐν αὐτῷ εἰσένεκτον *MAMA* 4.85 (Phrygia), 7.323 (Lycaonia), Ramsay *Cities and Bishoprics* I 163 (Pisidia).

***εἰσεργάζομαι**, *perform rites* to, Κρονίω(νι) παιδίο(ις) εἰσεργα(ζομένοις) *PMil.Vogl.* 212$^{r}$ i 12.

**εἰσέρχομαι**, line 11, after '*visit*' insert 'Men.*Asp.* 428'

***εἰσέτῐ**, adv., *still, yet,* Call.*Del.* 189, Mosch. 2.19.45, *AP* 6.271 (Phaedim.), Theoc. 27.19; εἰσέτι νῦν Phanocl. 1.28, A.R. 1.1354; εἰ. νῦν γε id. 2.717; εἰ. καὶ νῦν Call.*Dian.* 77.

**εἰσευπορέω**, after lemma insert 'Thess. ἐνευπορέω *IG* 9(2).66a.5, 13 (Lamia, ii BC)'

**εἰσέχω I**, add 'Arr.*Ind.* 32.11, 43.2'

**εἰσηγέομαι 2**, add 'pass., διάταξιν, σωφρόνως μὲν εἰσηγηθεῖσαν κοσμίως δὲ τεθειμένην Just.*Nov.* 87.7'

***εἰσθεάομαι**, *gaze upon,* τὸ .. εἰσθεᾶσθαι γῆν ὅλην τ' οἰκουμένην Ezek. *Exag.* 87 S.

**εἰσθλίβω**, for 'Them.*Or.* 14.197a' read 'Them.*Or.* 15.197a'

**εἰσῐτήριος**, εἰσιτήρια (sc. ἱερά), add 'or before a battle'; at end, sg., add '*entrance charge, Didyma* 314.10 (ἰσ-, ii AD); cf. mod. Gk. εἰσιτήριο *ticket*; see also °ἐνετήρια'

***Εἰσιτῠχή**, v. °Ἰσιτύχη.

***εἰσκήρυξις**, εως, ἡ, *proclamation* by sending a herald, *SEG* 33.1039.37 (Aeolian Cyme, ii BC).

***εἰσκλεῖστρον**, τό, perh. *rod, BGU* 2361a ii 11 (iv AD; written εἰσκλῖστρον).

**εἴσκλησις**, for '*summons*' read '*invitation*' and add 'εἴσκλησις εἰς τοὺς Διονυσιακοὺς ἀγῶνας *SEG* 21.506.20 (Athens, iii AD), 30.82.11 (Athens, c.AD 230)'

***εἰσκόλαψις**, ιος, ἁ, *carving, SEG* 25.383 (Epid., iv BC, ἰσκ-).

**εἰσκομίζω I**, add 'οὐδέ[να δὲ ἄλλον τινὰ] ἐξέσται εἰσκομισθῆναι σορ[ῷ] *SEG* 34.1401 (Lycaonia)'

**εἴσκρῐσις II**, for '*enrolment, admission*' read '*examination* for admission to priesthood, guild, etc.' and add '*PLond.* 329.7, *PTeb.* 598 (both ii AD)'

**εἰσκρῐτικόν**, add 'by priests on admission, *Stud.Pal.* 22.184.25 (ii AD), *PTeb.* 294.20 (AD 146), *SB* 9320.33 (AD 171)'

***εἰσκρύπτω**, app. intr. *hide, go into concealment, SEG* 24.1224 (form εἰσκρύβω; Egypt, v AD).

**εἰσκυκλέω I**, for '*wheel in* .. *spectators*' read '*wheel in* (metaphor prob. derived fr. the use of stage machinery)'

**εἰσνέομαι**, delete '[Thess.]'

**εἰσόδιος I**, after '*PPetr.* 2 p. 54 (iii BC)' insert '*entrance fee* of society, *Inscr.Délos* 1521.17 (ii BC)'

**εἴσοδος II 2**, add '*entrance* on a magistracy, *OGI* 458.15 (i BC)' **II 4**, after 'Lys. 1.20' insert '*SEG* 35.219.4 (ἰσ-, tab. defix., Athens, iii AD)' and after 'of a doctor' insert 'Hp.*Decent.* 12, 13, Men.*Mon.* 659 J.'

**εἰσοιχνέω**, add 'epigr. in *IG* 10(2).1.368.7 (Thessalonica, ii AD)'

**εἰσόκε I**, w. subj., add 'epigr. in *BCH* suppl. 8.5 (Edessa, iii AD)' add '**III** *when,* w. aor. ind., A.R. 2.857 (v.l. εἰσότε).'

**εἴσομαι**, after lemma insert '(A)' and for 'II' read 'εἴσομαι (B)' adding 'Ἀμφίνομος δ' Ὀδυσῆος ἐείσατο κυδαλίμοιο Od. 22.89'

***εἰσόμνῡμι**, aor. ἐσσώμο[σ]σαν, app. *swear* to a thing, *SEG* 23.271.61 (Thespiae, 220/208 BC).

***εἰσονομάζω**, *name, designate, SEG* 32.1423 (Syria, ii AD).

**εἰσοπτρίζω**, line 2, for '(Plu. 2.)141c' read '(Plu. 2.)141d'

***εἰσοπτρομαντεία**, ἡ, *divination by mirrors,* rest. in *PMag.* 13.752 (iv AD).

**εἰσορμάω**, line 1, read '*impel into,* E.*IA* 151 (cj.); transf., πάλιν εἰσώρμησα τὸν ἄρσενα Δωρίδι Μούσῃ ῥυθμόν *AP* 7.707 (Diosc.)'

**εἰσορμίζω**, line 1, after '*bring into port*' insert 'epigr. in *SEG* 23.395.A10 (Corcyra, ii AD)'

**εἴσοψις**, for '*spectacle*' read '*observation, attention*'

**εἰσπλέω 2**, after 'Pl.Com. 183' insert '*sail in* (with merchandise), *import,* Lys. 22.17, 21'

**εἴσπλοος 2**, add 'ἔσπλῶν καὶ ἔκπλῶν *SEG* 36.982.C9 (Iasos, v BC)'

**εἰσποιέω I 2**, add 'pass., Arr.*An.* 4.11.5'

**εἰσπορεύω**, for 'pass.' read 'med.' and add 'Aen.Tact. 18.1, 15, al.'

**εἴσπραξις I**, add 'τῆς ἰσπράξεως τοῦ πυροῦ *PPetaus* 53.12 (ii AD)'

***εἰσπρῖάμαι**, *buy up*, aor. εἰσεπρίατο *IG* $2^2$.1629.698, ἐσπριάσθω *SEG* 26.72.40 (iv BC).

***εἰστελής**, ές, dub. sens., ἡμέραι εἰστελεῖς, followed in context by ἡμέραι ἀργυρικαί, *SB* 7551.24, 34 (ἰστ-, ii AD).

***εἰστήλην**, for εἰς στήλην (v. °στήλη).

**εἰστίθημι 3**, delete the section.

***εἰσφέννω**, perh. for εἰσφαίνω or εἰσφέγγω, *shine in*, *PAnt.* 64.18 (vi AD).'

**εἰσφέρω**, line 2, aor., add 'εἰσήνικα *SEG* 7.381, 382 (Dura, ii AD)' **I 1**, add 'καὶ μηδένα ἰσφέριν ἀλλότριν νεκρόν into the tomb, *SEG* 24.1189 (Egypt, i AD)'

**εἰσφορά**, line 1, after '(εἰσφέρω)' insert 'dialect form ἐμφορά *SEG* 23.398 (Aetolia, ii BC)' **III**, after '*proposal*' insert 'Arist.*Pol.* $1322^b$14'

**εἰσχέω**, line 1, after '(s.v.l.)' insert 'ἐσχέαι *Thasos* 10.8 (iv BC)'

***εἰσχύνω**, = εἰσχέω, πετρῶν ἀφ' ἧς οὐκέτ' αὐτὸν εἰσχύσεν Diog.Oen. *new fr.* 7 ii 1 S. (*AJA* 75.367).

**εἰσωπός 2**, add 'Simon. 13.12 W.$^2$'

**εἰσώστη**, for '*tomb*' read '*niche*'; delete '(Caria)' and add 'oft. written ἰσ-, e.g. *MAMA* 8.537.3, 582.1'

***εἰσωφόριος**, ον, *inner*, of garment, στιχάριον *POxy.* 1684.4, 8 (iv AD; εἰσο-, ἰσο- pap.).

**εἶτᾰ I 1**, line 8, after '*SIG* 1171' insert 'εἶτ' αὖθις D.H.*Comp.* 18' **II**, add 'κᾆτα after part., Ar.*Eq.* 392, cj. in Pl.*Lg.* 861c'

**εἰτακεῖν**, add 'v. °ἰτάω'

**ἐκ**, line 1, for 'also .. 135.5 H.' read 'also in Cypr. before consonant, if *xe* is accurate transcription, *e-xe-to-i wo-i-ko-i* ἐξ τôι ϝοίκōι *ICS* 217.5, al.; Cypr. also *e-se* ἐς *Kafizin* 218b, 266b, al.'; line 2, form ἐξ, add 'also before δ *IPamph.* 3.19'; line 3, ἐς, add '[*h*]ε̄ρακλέος ἐς Θεσπίας *SEG* 30.541 (vase, Epirus, v BC); ἐς Λαρίσας *SEG* 24.571 (Maced., iv BC); ἐος Corinn. 1 col. 3.34 P.'; line 8, w. dat., add 'ἐξ ἐ[πι]τε̄ρίιᾳ *IPamph.* 3.4' **I 4**, line 5, after 'cf. (Il. 18.) 432' insert 'ἐξ ἀλλᾶν Pi.*O.* 6.25' **5**, line 4, for 'sate .. Hdt. 3.83' read 'remained *in* the middle, i.e. neutral, Hdt. 3.83.3' and transfer to the end of section I 6 (cf. μέσος III 1 c). **III 2**, add 'w. pers. n. to express metronymic, τῶ ἐκ Πεισῶς *SEG* 33.724 (Amnisos, Crete, i BC)' **9 d**, after 'Space' insert 'ἐκ δέκα ποδῶν *by* ten feet, Eup. 102.3 K.-A.' add '**10** indicating proportionate share of inheritance, εἰ μέντοι τοὺς μὲν παῖδας ἔκ τινος μοίρας γράψαιεν κληρονόμους, ἐξωτικοὺς δὲ ἐξ ἑτέρας Just.*Nov.* 22.20.2, al. (cf. Lat. *ex*).'

***ἑκάβη**, ἡ, v. °'Εκάβη.

**'Εκάβη**, ἡ, Dor. ϝεκάβα *Schwyzer* 122(4), *Hecabe*, the wife of Priam, Il. 6.293, al.; app. meton. for a pig because of her fertility, ἐν τοῖς Ὀρφικοῖς οἱ χοῖροι ἑκάβαι προσαγορεύονται Orph.*fr.* 46 K.

**'Εκαδήμεια**, add '[*h*]όρος τε̂ς *he*καδημείας *SEG* 24.54 (vi BC) cf. pers. n. ϝhεκάδαμος *Schwyzer* 452.5 (Tanagra, v BC)'

**'Εκαέργη** (s.v. 'Εκάεργος I), add 'epith. of Artemis, *SEG* 31.934 (Caria)'

**ἑκάλλιθμος**, add '(ἑκάλιμος La.)'

**ἑκάς**, add '**III** *severally* or *apart*, Nic.*Th.* 345 (perh. by misinterpr. of Hes.*fr.* 233.2 M.-W.).' at end add 'βεκάς· μακράν Hsch.'

**ἕκαστος II 1**, add 'τὰ ἕκαστα Il. 11.706, Od. 12.16, τὰ ἕκαστα διαρρήδην ἐρέεινον *h.Merc.* 313, Ibyc. 1(*a*).26 P., A.R. 1.339' **III 2**, add '**b** w. ellipsis of ἡμέρα, ἐφ' ἑκάστης *each day*, Just.*Nov.* 40 epilogus; sim. καθ' ἑκάστην ib. 43.1.1.'

**ἑκάστοτε**, add 'ἐπιμέλειαν ποιήσασθαι .. τοὺς πρυτάνεις τοὺς ἑκάστοτε γινομένους *IPriene* 59.24 (v. *Laodicée* p. 250)'

**ἑκᾰτᾱβόλος**, add 'of Apollo, Simon. 6 *fr.* 1(*a*).6 P., Pi.*P.* 8.61, *fr.* 2.2 S.-M.; ἑκαταβόλων Μοισᾶν ἀπὸ τόξων id.*O.* 9.5'

**'Εκᾰταῖος II**, for 'or 'Εκάτειον .. 804' read '(-ειον in Ar.*V.* 804, *Lys.* 64 is v.l. in Sch.' and for 'Ar. l.c.' read 'Ar.*V.* 804'

**+ἑκᾰτερέω**, ἑκατερεῖν· τὸ πρὸς τὰ ἰσχία πηδᾶν ἑκατέραις ταῖς πτέρναις Hsch. (but cf. ἑκατερίς).

**'Εκάτη**, line 1, delete 'lit. *she who works her will*'

***'Εκατηφόρια**, τά, festival at Eretria, *IG* 12 suppl. 646.12 (Chalcis, iii AD).

**ἑκᾰτόγγυιος**, line 1, delete 'or *bodies*'; line 2, for '100 maidens' read '50 maidens'

**ἑκᾰτόμβαιος II**, delete the section (v. *BCH* 98.562 no. 24).

**'Εκᾰτόμβιος I**, add '*SEG* 36.548.20 (Thessaly, iii BC), *SEG* 38.665 (W.Maced., *c.*100 BC)'

**'Εκᾰτόμβοια**, add ''Εκατόμβοια δόλιχον ἐν Ἄργει *SEG* 30.489 (at Delphi, v BC)'

***ἑκᾰτονέξε** (= ἑκατονέξ), *one hundred and six*, *SEG* 26.672.18 (Larissa, ii BC).

***ἑκᾰτονεττά** (= ἑκατονεπτά), *one hundred and seven*, *SEG* 26.672.44 (Larissa, ii BC).

***ἑκᾰτοντᾰδικός**, ή, όν, of the ἑκατοντάς, Sch.Procl. *in Ti.* 2.332.20, 26.

**ἑκᾰτοντᾰμᾰχος**, add 'also **ἑκατοντομάχος**, Bonner *Studies in Magical Amulets* 163'

***ἑκᾰτοντᾰρουρικός**, όν, consisting of 100 ἄρουραι, -ὸς κλῆρος *PMoen.* inv. 17.9.

**ἑκᾰτοντάρχης**, add '*SEG* 33.1306 (Arabia, i AD), *TAM* 4(1).285 (Rom.imp.); written ἑκατονθάρχης *IGRom.* 3.1367 (Gerasa)'

**ἑκᾰτόνταρχος**, add '*INikaia* 1551.14, *SEG* 31.905 (Aphrodisias), *POxy.* 3029.4 (iii AD)'

**ἕκᾰτος**, line 2, after '(Il.) 20.295' insert 'Alcm. 46 P., ἱερῆος Ἀπόλλωνος ἑκάτοιο epigr. in Mitchell *N. Galatia* 74a (i AD)' and after 'ὁ' insert 'Il.'; line 3, for 'Simon. 26 A' read 'Simon. 68 P.'

***ἑκᾰτοστάριος**, ὁ, *collector of the* ἑκατοστή, *BMB* 7.78 (v. ἑκατοστός II) (Berytus, v AD).

**ἑκᾰτοστηρία**, delete '*PCair.Zen.* 12.76, al.'

**ἑκᾰτοστός I**, add '*IG* $1^3$.182.8 (*c.*420/405 BC)' **II**, after 'Plu.*Luc.* 20' add 'cf. τὸν ἀπὸ τρίτου μέρους τῆς ἑκατοστῆς τόκον Just.*Nov.* 2.4'

**ἑκᾰτοστύς II**, add 'as military unit, Arr.*An.* 6.27.6'

***ἐκβᾰδιστέον**, *one must go out*, Sch.Hes.*Th.* 732a (98.11 Di G.).

**ἐκβακχεύω**, line 7, intr. in act., add 'E.*Tr.* 169'

**ἐκβάλλω I 1**, after '*carry out* to sea' insert 'of a river, ὕδωρ ἐς θάλασσαν ἐκβάλλων *Peripl.M.Rubr.* 38' **2**, add '*cause to be thrown* from chariot, *SEG* 34.1437 (Dyria, v/vi AD). **b** *send out* to a task, *PMich.*XI 618.15 (ii AD), *OMich.* 655.4.5, *PRyl.* 80.1.' **III**, line 8, after 'Thphr.*HP* 4.8.4' insert '*vomit*, τὰ σπλάγχνα Plu. 2.831c' **IX 2**, delete the section.

**ἐκβαρβᾰρόω**, pass., add 'Isoc. 9.47'

**ἐκβᾰσᾰνίζω**, line 2, for 'Philostr.*VA* 2.31' read 'Philostr.*VA* 2.30'

**ἔκβᾰσις**, add '**VI** *withdrawal*, in legal sense, αὐθεντικὸν ἐκβάσεως τόπων *PFam.Teb.* 31.13 (ii AD).'

**+ἐκβασμίδωσις**, εως, ἡ, *stepped pedestal*, *IEphes.* 1627.5.

**+ἐκβάσμωσις**, εως, ἡ, = °ἐκβασμίδωσις, *IGRom.* 4.514, *BCH* 4.381 (both Pergamum).

**ἐκβᾰτήριος I**, add '**2** Ἐκβατηρία, epith. of Artemis in Siphnos, *IG* 12(5). p. xxvii no. 1454, Hsch. s.v.' **II**, add 'Them.*Or.* 4.61a (βακτηρίας cod.)'

***ἐκβᾰτικός**, ή, όν, *concerning the laying down of office*, τὰ ἐ. βιβλία *POxy.* 3601.10 (AD 202).

***ἐκβδάλλω**, *drain off*, ἠὲ καὶ ἐκβδήλαιο καταχθέος ἕρματα γαστρός Nic.*Al.* 322.

**ἐκβῐάομαι**, delete 'Act., .. *Jd.* 14.15'

**ἐκβῐαστικός**, for '(s.v.l.); cf. ἐκβιβ-' read '(v.l., ed. ἐκβιβ-)'

**ἐκβῐβάζω II**, add 'ἐζήτει ἐκβιβασθῆναι τὴν συνθήκην *Vit.Aesop.*(W) 72, cf. τὴν συνθήκην ἐκβίβασον (ἐμ- cod.) ibid.(G)'

**ἐκβῐβασμός**, delete 'Aq. .. 23' add '**II** *expulsion*, μορφωμάτων Aq. 1*Ki.* 15.23.'

**ἐκβῐβαστικός**, after '*oppressive*' insert 'Ptol.*Tetr.* 155'

**ἔκβῐος**, add 'Sch.Od. 11.134'

**ἐκβλύω**, after '**ἐκβλύζω**' insert 'I'

**+ἐκβλώσκω**, v. ἐκμολεῖν.

**ἐκβόησις**, add 'πολλάκις ἐκβοήσεσι κεχρῆσθαι κατὰ τὴν ἁγίαν ἐκκλησίαν κατὰ Ἰωάννου *PMich.*XIII 659.42 (vi AD)'

***ἐκβοητικός**, ή, όν, of musical συστήματα, *suited to shrill cries*, Aristid. Quint. 2.14.

**ἐκβολεύς**, for '*inspector of dikes*' read 'ἐ. χωμάτων *one who assigns work on the dikes*' and add '*PPetaus* 86.6 (ii AD), *PMich.*XI 618.14 (i AD), *POxy.* 1301 (iii/iv AD)'

**ἐκβολή VII 1**, add '(perh.) Sch.E.*Med.* 1 (v.l. ὑπερβ-)'

***ἐκβουτῦπόομαι**, *to be changed into a cow*, S.*fr.* 269a.37 R.

**ἐκβράζω IV**, for '*boil over*, of water' read '*surge out*, dub. in'

**ἔκβρᾰσις 1**, after 'Suid.' add 's.v. Καλλισθένης'

***ἐκγαιζεσθαι**, wd. of uncertain sense, *MDAI(A)* 68.4 (Samos, i AD).

**ἐκγέννημα**, add 'also ἐγγέννημα *DAW* 85.31 (Cilicia, pl.)'

***ἐκγόνιον**, τό, dim. of ἔκγονος, τέκνοις καὶ -ίοις *TAM* 3(1).378 (Termessus).

**ἔκγονος**, **ἔσγονος**, add '*SEG* 29.502 (Thessaly, iii BC)' **2**, at end after 'id.*Phdr.* 275d' insert 'of animals, *IG* $1^3$.426.62 (but ἔγγονα ib. 63) (Athens, v BC)'

**ἐκγράφω II**, delete '*IG* $1^2$.84.28, Decr.ap.And. 1.77 (Pass.)'

**+ἐκγρῡτεύω**, *rummage out*, ἐκγρυτεύσῃ· ἐξερευνήσῃ Hsch.

***ἐκδαίνῡμαι**, *eat out of* the pot, imper. -δαίνυσο Nic.*fr.* 68.8 G.-S. (cod. -δαίνεο, v.l. ἐξαίρεο).

***ἐκδᾰμάζω**, *make tender*, Aesop.fab.Syntip. 5 p. 530 P.

**ἐκδᾰνείζω**, add 'ἐγδανείζεσθαι *IG* 12(7).515.10 (Amorgos, ii BC)'

**ἐκδᾰνεισμός**, *IG* 12(7).515, add 'sp. ἐγδ-' and after '*BGU* 362 xiv 21 (iii AD)' insert 'οἱ ἐπὶ τοῦ ἐκδανεισμοῦ *POxy.* 2848.5 (iii AD)'

***ἐκδᾰνειστεία**, ἡ, = ἐκδάνεισις, ἐκδανεισμός, rest. in *ASAA* 30/32(1952/4).295, no. 67.26, 31 (Rhodes).

***ἐκδάπτω**, *devour out of*, in tm., ἐκ μέλαν εἶαρ ἔδαπτεν Call.*fr.* 523 Pf. (cj. ἔλαπτεν).

*ἐκδάω, learn, pres. not in use, aor. pass. ἐξεδάην A.R. 4.1565, Man. 6.469.

ἐκδέκτωρ, for 'one who .. toil A.fr. 194' read 'neut. pl. -ορα, ἐκδέκτορα πόνων (animals) relieving men from toils, A.fr. 189a R.'

ἐκδέχομαι 7, add 'ὁ στέφανος τῷ βασιλεῖ, ὃν ἐξεδέξατο, Ἀπολλώνιος Ἐπικύδει PCair.Zen. 36.26, 636.4 (iii BC), PPetr. 3.64.(b)6 (iii BC). b stand surety on behalf of, PSI 349.1 (254/3 BC), PZen.Col. 121.3 (181 BC).'

*ἐκδημητής, οῦ, ὁ, one who goes abroad, Rhetor. in Cat.Cod.Astr. 7.205.11.

ἐκδῐδύσκω, add 'AP 5.309 (Diophan.)'

ἐκδίδωμι I 5, add 'ἐκδότω στεφάνους τις ἡμῖν, δᾷδα Men.Dysc. 963'

*ἐκδῐκαιωτήρ, ῆρος, ὁ, Cret. ἐσζικαιωτήρ, official responsible for exacting penalties, SEG 37.752.8 (Lyttos, c.500 BC).

ἐκδῐκέω I 1, for '2Ki. 4.8' read '4Ki. 9.7, Ho. 1.4'

ἐκδίκησις, add 'Lxx Ex. 7.4, Jd. 11.36, Sir. 5.7, Je. 11.20, al.'

ἐκδικία 1, add 'SEG 30.1384.6 (Lydia, AD 301)' 2, delete the section.

*ἐκδῐκιον, τό, penalty, δώσει .. ἐγδεικίου δηνάρεια πεντεκειχείλεια (sic) INikaia 1331.14.

ἔκδῐκος II 1, before 'cf.' insert 'ἔ. ἀνάγκη prob. in B.fr. 20a.13 S.-M.' 3, add '= defensor civitatis, CPR 5.9.4 (iv AD), Cod.Just. 1.4.22.1'

ἐκδιοικέω, for 'collect dues, etc.' read 'alienate (property)' and before 'al.' insert '700.38 (ii BC), IIasos 4.20 (ἐγδ-, ii BC)'

ἐκδιοίκησις, for 'collection of dues' read 'alienation (of property)'

*ἐκδῐομαι, = ἐκδιώκω, subj. ἐδδίεται Inscr.Cret. 4.88 (Gortyn, v BC), cf. ἐπιδίομαι.

ἐκδῐφάω, after 'aor. 1' insert 'Hippon. 85.8 W.'

ἐκδῐώκω, add 'fig., πάντα τὰ αἰσχρὰ ἐξεδίωκεν X.Ages. 3.1. II prosecute, perform, τὸ ἔργον UPZ 81 iv 18 (ii BC).'

ἔκδοσις I 3, add 'τὴν δὲ ἔγδοσιν τῶν στηλῶν i.e. perh. of the contract for, SEG 29.1089.19 (Caria, i BC)' 4, add 'Hyp.Dem. 5' 5 a, after 'Ael.Tact.Praef. 4' insert 'of decree, τῆς ἐγδόσεως τῶν προειρημένων SEG 23.447.31 (Thessaly, ii AD)'

*ἐκδοχεία, ἡ, office of ‡ἐκδοχεύς, PMich.I 26.3 (ἐγδ-).

ἐκδοχεῖον, before 'Peripl.M.Rubr. 27' insert 'entrepôt'

ἐκδοχεύς, after 'agent' insert 'or receiver'

*ἐκδοχικός, ή, όν, explicative: adv. -κῶς, Demetr.Lac. pp. 3-4 DF.

*ἔκδοχος, ὁ, = ἀνάδοχος II, surety, PSI 584.14 (iii BC).

*ἔκδραχμον, τό, = ἑξάδραχμον, the sum of six drachmas, Hsch.

ἔκδραχμος, delete the entry.

ἐκδρομάς, for 'one who has outrun the age of youth' read 'one who has gone to excess'

*ἐκδῠγήρας, adj., shedding its slough (cf. γῆρας II), of a serpent, cj. in Dosiad.Ara 14.

+ἔκδῡμα, ατος, τό, that which is taken off the body, spoils, expl. of exuviae in Virgil gloss., PNess. 1.1020, PSI 756.47 (both v AD), AP 5.199 (Hedyl., v.l. ἐνδ-).

ἐκδύσια, add '(cf. the ephebic ceremony cited s.v. ἐκδύω I 3)'

ἐκεῖ, line 1, for 'Sapph. 51' read 'Sapph. 141.1 L.-P.' and after it insert 'Ion. κεῖ, q.v.' and delete 'Dor. τηνεῖ' add 'IV perh. in that matter, SEG 30.568.6 (Maced., i AD).'

ἐκεῖθεν, for 'Dor. τηνῶθεν, τηνῶθε' read '(for τηνῶθεν, τηνῶθε v.hh.vv.)'

ἐκεῖθι, for 'Dor. τηνόθι Theoc. 8.44' read '(for τηνόθι v.h.v.)' II, delete the section.

ἐκεῖνος, line 5, Aeol. κῆνος, for 'Sapph. 2.1' read 'Sapph. 31.1 L.-P., Thess. κένὁ (gen.) SEG 23.415 (Pherae, v BC) (also Dor., Inscr.Cret. 4.41.4 (Gortyn, v BC), SIG 1025.25 (Cos, c.300 BC))'; for 'Dor. τῆνος' read '(for τῆνος v.h.v.)'

ἐκεῖσε II, after 'Hp.Vict. 2.38' insert 'A.R. 4.1217, al.'

*ἐκεχείριος, α, ον, of games, etc., marked by a cessation of public business, SEG 31.1288.5 (Side, iii AD), Inscr.Magn. 100.25.

ἐκζητέω, add 'III search out, weigh, observe, Lxx Ps. 60(61).8, 118(119).94.'

ἐκζήτησις, for 'research' read 'speculation'

ἐκζωόομαι, for 'worms' read 'living creatures'

ἐκζωπῠρέω, for 'rekindle' read 'cause to blaze up'

ἐκζωπύρησις, for 'rekindling' read 'causing to blaze up'

ἐκηβόλος, line 1, for 'Dor.' read 'dial.' and add 'Ϝεκᾱβόλοι ἀργυροτόξσοι CEG 326 (Boeotia, early vii BC), Ϝεκᾱβόλοι Ἀπέλ(λ)ονι CEG 370 (at Delphi, vi BC, perh. Lacon.), Πάον' .. ἐκάβολον Sapph. 44.33 L.-P.'; line 3, after 'of Artemis' insert 'CEG 425 (ℎεκηβώ[λωι], Chios, vi BC)'; line 7, after 'Agath. 3.17' insert 'neut. pl. as subst., prob. slings, J.BJ 2.17.5'

ἔκθαμβος, for 'Tab.Defix. 5.20' read 'Tab.Defix.Aud. 271.20 (Hadrumetum, iii AD)'

*ἐκθέβεν, v. ‡ἐκθέω.

*ἐκθεῖος, ὁ, uncle's son, cousin, Rev.Bibl. 41.577 (Syria).

ἔκθεμα, add 'II (as transl. of Hebr. rāmāh, perh.) platform for displaying goods, Lxx Ez. 16.24.'

ἐκθέμεναι, delete the entry.

ἐκθεόω I, add 'ὑπὸ τῆς εὐτυχίας τῆς περιλαβούσης αὐτὸν τότε ἐκθεούμενος assuming the attributes of divinity, Ael.VH 2.19'

*ἐκθεραπευτέον, one must cure completely, Gal. 6.440.9.

ἐκθερίζω, for 'PEdgar 27' read 'PCair.Zen. 155'

ἔκθεσις I, add '3 giving out, allocation, ὁ αἱρεθεὶς ἐπὶ τὰν φυλα(κὰν) καὶ ἔχθεσιν τοῦ ἐλαίου SEG 39.774.7 (Rhodes, i BC).' X, for this section read 'arrears of payment, PMich.XII 656.11 (i AD), POxy. 583.136 (vi AD), Hsch.'

ἐκθέτης, add '2 app. a kind of basket, PMich.XIV 680.22 (iii/iv AD).'

*ἐκθέτωσις, εως, ἡ, perh. projection on a building, La Carie 185.3 (Kidrama); cf. ἐκθέτης 1, ἔκθεσις VII 1.

ἐκθέω, add 'ἐκθέβεν· ἐκτρέχειν Hsch.'

ἐκθηλύνω, for 'soften, weaken' read 'make soft or weak like (that of) a woman' and add 'Gal. 13.392.15, 949.18'

*ἐκθῐνόω, silt up completely, SEG 14.615.11 (ἐχθεινο[ί]η[τ]ε. tab.defix., Rome, ii/iii AD); cf. ἀποθινόομαι.

ἐκθλίβω 1, add 'γένος ἀνθρώπων ἐκτεθλιμμένων τὴν ῥῖνα (i.e. with flattened noses) Peripl.M.Rubr. 62'

ἐκθνήσκω II, for 'Luc.Hist.Conscr. 27' read 'Luc.Hist.Conscr. 20'

+ἐκθοράξει (ἐκθοράψει La.)· ἐκδιώξει. ἀπὸ τοῦ ἐκθορεῖν Hsch.

ἐκθρῴσκω, for 'start up .. DMar. 2.3' read 'start up, Luc.DMar. 2.3; ἀπὸ τοῦ ὕπνου id.Herm. 71'

ἐκκᾰθᾰρίζω, add 'cf. Lat. excatarisso, colloq. clean out of money, Petron. 67.10'

*ἐκκάθαρμα, ατος, τό, offscouring, τὰ ἐκ[α]θάρματ[α] (sic) IG 12(5).107.2 (Paros, early v BC).

*ἐκκαθοράω, look down from, w. gen., Q.S. 8.430.

ἐκκαίδεκᾰ, add 'Ϝεκαίδεκα PP 42.42.8 (Tarentum, vi BC)'

ἐκκαιδεκαέτης, add 'cf. ἐκκαιδεκέτις, °ἐκκαιδεχέτης'

*ἐκκαιδεκάπεδος, ον, sixteen feet long, IG $4^2$.109 ii 139 (Epid., iii BC).

ἐκκαιδεκᾰταῖος, add 'Afric.Cest. p. 22 V.'

ἐκκαιδέκᾰτος, add 'fem. subst. (sc. ἡμέρα), the sixteenth day, SEG 34.396.2 (-δεκέτᾱ, Delphi, i AD); neut. subst., name of weight, BMB 8.62 no. 28, p. 63 no. 35, al.'

*ἐκκαιδεχέτης, ου, ὁ, = ἐκκαιδεκαέτης I, GVI 1352.1 (Britain, iii AD).

*ἐκκακκᾰβίζω, perh. pour from a κακκάβη, Anon.Alch. 441.10.

ἐκκᾰλέω IV, after 'Med.' insert 'appeal to, ἐκκαλέσθω ἐς βολὴν SEG 16.485.13 (Chios, vi BC)' and after '(Plu. 2.)178f' insert 'SEG 29.127 ii 15, 20 (Athens, c.AD 100); w. ἀπό, SB 11222.12 (AD 332); ἐκκαλούμενος = Lat. provocator, Hdn. 1.15.6'

ἐκκᾰλύπτω, line 5, after 'E.IA 872' insert 'med., οὐδεὶς ὄκνος πάντ' ἐκκαλύψασθαι λόγον Critias 1.5 S.'

ἐκκαυλέω, after lemma insert '(ἐγκ- codd. in Arist.Pr. 926ᵃ26, Thphr.HP 1.2.2)'

ἐκκηρύσσω II 2, add 'Lys. 3.45'

ἐκκλαστρίδιον, add 'cf. ἐγκλαστρίδια'

ἐκκλείω, add '5 shut off, enclose a place, SEG 36.935 (Rome).'

ἔκκλημα, for 'Jahresh. 14.168' read 'Schwyzer 366A21' and for 'Foed. .. B 20' read '328ᵃiiB20'

ἐκκλησία, after lemma insert 'Thess. ἐκκλεισσία BCH 59.38 (Crannon)' II 2, add 'SEG 33.1272 (Palestine, vi AD)'

ἐκκλησιάζω I 1, add 'abs., ἐξοπλασίαν .. ποιησάμενος ἐκκλησιάζειν ἐπεχείρει sc. the president of an assembly, Arist.Ath. 15.4'

ἔκκλησις 1, after 'appeal' insert 'BGU 1756 (i BC)'

ἔκκλητος 3, after 'appeal' insert 'δίκας ὀκόσαι ἂν ἔκκλητοι γένωνται Schwyzer 687B12 (Chios, c.600 BC)'; after 'IG $2^2$.111.74' insert '(Athens, iv BC)'

ἐκκλυστέον, for 'Aët. 16.89' read 'Paul.Aeg. 6.73.2 (114.31 H.)'

*ἐκκοίτιον, τό, = ἐκκοιτία, RA 3(1934).40 (Amphipolis, iii/ii BC).

ἐκκολυμβάω, at end for 'App.Syr. 6' read 'App.Syr. 56'

ἐκκομίζω I, add '5 export, SEG 35.1439.11 (Lycia, ii AD).'

ἔκκοπος, add 'ταῖς πράξεσιν Cat.Cod.Astr. 8(1).184 (s.v.l., cj. ἐγκοπτικός)'

ἐκκόπτω I 2, after 'X.HG 6.5.37' insert 'ἐκκοπτομένης ἀμπέλου POxy. 2847.5 (iii AD)' b, add 'Lys. 28.6' 7, add 'c abs., make meaning clear, make sense, οὐκ ἐκκόπτει ἡ γραφή Sch.Pi.P. 4.195a.' II, delete the section (v. ἐγκόπτω IV).

ἐκκορέω, for 'prov. .. Horap. 1.8' read 'ἐκκόρει, κόρει, κορώνας, marriage cry of dub. form and significance, Carm.Pop. 35 P., given as ἐκκορὶ κορὶ κορώνη Horap. 1.8; see also °κορικορώνη'

ἐκκρέμαμαι II, add '2 pay attention to, hang on the words of, ὁ λαὸς .. ἐξεκρέματο αὐτοῦ ἀκούων Ev.Luc. 19.48.'

ἔκκρουσις I, for 'beating out, driving away' read 'the act or process of forcing a thing from its position'

ἐκκρούω I 1 b, add 'pass., ἐὰν δὲ δυοῖν φερομένοιν ἀπὸ τῆς αὐτῆς ἰσχύος τὸ μὲν ἐκκρούοιτο πλεῖον τὸ δὲ ἔλαττον Arist.Mech. 849ᵃ7'

ἐκκυέω, add '(cj. °ἐγκυέω); τοὺς δ' ἑτέρους τρεῖς πέδας (= παῖδας) ὅτ' ἐξεκύησα epigr. in SEG 33.1082.12 (Nikaia)'

*ἐκκῠκάω, stir up, (tm.), ἐκ δ' ἀφάντοις .. ἐκύκα θυέλλαις Alc. 298.12 L.-P.

*ἐκκῠλίω, = ἐκκυλίνδω, *roll out*, τὰς ἐμπροσθίους ὁπλὰς μετεωρίζοντες ἐξεκύλιον τοὺς ἐλατῆρας Agath. 3.27.4, 4.18.5; (see also ἐκκυλίομαι).

**ἐκκῡμαίνω II**, for 'Pass., *to be cast up by the waves*' read 'of the sea, *to cast ashore*, Heraclit.*All.* 79.7; pass.'

**ἐκκῡνηγέσσω**, add 'fut. -έσω, cj. in A.*Eu.* 231'

**ἐκκῡνηγετέω**, for 'prob. in A.*Eu.* 231' read 'cj. in A.*Eu.* 231' and add 'Lyc. 1025'

**ἐκκύπτω II**, delete the section transferring ref. to section I.

*ἐκκῡρόω, *confirm completely*, *SB* 9121.8 (pap. -κοιρ-, i AD).

*ἐκλακέντα, gloss on ἐκκολλαβήσαντα, Hsch.

**ἐκλαμβάνω IV**, for 'ἔργα ἐ. = ἐργολαβέω, *contract to do work*' read 'ἔργα, etc., ἐ., *contract to perform*' and add 'τοῖς ἐξειληφόσι τὴν ἑξεδραχμίαν τῶν ὄνων *POxy.* 1457 (4/3 BC), *PRyl.* 95.5 (AD 71/2), *PTeb.* 40.4 (ii AD); ἐξέλαβον τὴν ζυτηράν *PHib.* 133 (iii AD)' **V 2**, after '*PGen.* 74.8 (iii AD)' add 'Just.*Nov.* 90.4 pr.'

**ἔκλαμψις I**, add '**2** *inflammation*, Sm.*Le.* 13.26.'

**ἐκλανθάνω II**, line 2, after '**ἐκληθάνω**' insert '(Aeol. **ἐκλᾱθάνω** rest. in Sapph. 25.5 L.-P.)' **1**, for '*make* one .. c. gen. rei' read '*make* one *forgetful* of, w. gen.' and after 'Od. 7.220' insert 'Ἥρης ἐκλελαθοῦσα κασιγνήτης ἀλόχου τε *h.Ven.* 40'

*ἐκλαχμός, ὁ, *apportionment by lot*, *PNess.* 21.19 (vi AD).

**ἔκλειγμα**, for pres. def. read '*medicine to be licked from a spoon, electuary*'

**ἐκλειγμᾰτώδης**, for '*lozenge*' read '*linctus*'; add 'v.ll. ἐλιγμ-'

**ἐκλεικτικός**, for '*made into a lozenge*' read '*made into a linctus*'

**ἐκλειόω**, before 'Alex.Trall.' insert 'Asclep.Jun.ap.Gal. 13.744.14'

**ἔκλειψις II 2**, add 'ἔκλειψις ὑγροῦ Arist.*Pr.* 937ᵃ13'

*ἐκλείωσις, εως, ἡ, *complete pulverisation*, Anon.Alch. 7.7.

**ἐκλεκτικός I 1**, delete '*moral*' and add 'w. gen. D.H.*Lys.* 15' **II**, delete 'Gal. 14.684 (v. *ZPE* 72.241)'

*ἐκλέπτυνσις, εως, ἡ, *reduction to a fine state*, Zos.Alch. 251.16.

**ἐκλέπω**, add 'ὃς (sc. eagle) τρία μὲν τίκτει, δύο δ' ἐκλέπει, ἓν δ' ἀλεγίζει Musae.*fr.* 3 D.-K., *Trag.adesp.* 328.1 K.-S.'

**ἐκληψις** 2, after '*PTeb.* 38.11 (ii BC)' add '*Cod.Just.* 1.2.24.2'

*ἐκλικμόω, = ἐκλικμάω, dub. in *PTeb.* 727.27 (ii BC).

**ἐκλιστράω**, for '*slap*' read '*lightly touch, graze*, given as colloq. equiv. of λίζω'

**ἐκλογεύς**, add 'Antipho *fr.* 52; ἐ. φόρων applied to Roman *procurator*, Ph. 2.575'

**ἐκλογή I 5**, delete the section. add '**III** ὑπὲρ ἐκλογῆς in *PRyl.* 157.6 (ii AD) of payment for the *superior value* (perh. orig. for the *right of choosing*), made by the recipient of the better portion in division of property, cf. *PFlor.* 47.14 (iii AD; exchange of property). **2** perh. *balance* in accounts, σὺν καὶ τῇ ἐγλ(ογῇ) *BGU* 362 vi 10 (iii AD; also read as τῇ ἐκλόγῳ and as τῇ ἐκ λόγου w. fem. noun understood); cf. ib. 64.10 (iii AD).'

*ἐκλόγισμα, ατος, τό, *salary*, *SEG* 20.180.8 (Paphos, ii BC, εγλ- lapis), *BGU* 1749.12 (i BC).

**ἐκλογιστής 1**, add '*SEG* 31.122.30 (Attica, ii AD)' **2**, add 'φόρου διοικήσεως ἐξ ἀναπομπῆς ἐκλογιστοῦ *POxy.* 3170.257 (iii AD)'

**ἐκλογιστία**, add '*PLond.* 1708.159 (vi AD). **2** *office of* ἐκλογιστής, *POxy.* 1436.23 (ii AD), *PGiss.* 48.1 (iii AD).'

**ἔκλογος** (A) **II**, delete the section.

*ἔκλογος (C), ὁ or **ἔκλογον**, τό, perh. *payment in arrears, balance*, Ostr. 47 in *PFay.*, but the compd. is doubtful. Cf. °λόγος I 1 c.

*ἐκλοιδορέω, *abuse verbally*, καὶ ἐξελυδόρησεν καὶ ἀνέσ{ο}υρεν αὐτή⟨ν⟩ *POxy.* 2758.11 (AD 110/2).

**ἐκλοχεύω**, line 3, after 'E.*Hel.* [258]' insert 'Lyc. 88'

**ἐκλοχίζω**, add '**II** μαιούμενος· ἐκλοχίζων Hsch.'

**ἔκλῠτος III**, *weak*, add 'of an athlete, *SEG* 35.213.16 (ἐγλ-, tab.defix., Athens, iii AD)'

**ἐκλύω I**, at end delete 'abs. .. 531' **II 3**, at end for '*cease*' read '*lose force*'

**ἐκμᾰγεῖον I**, for this section read '*cloth for wiping*, Meyer *Ostr.* 62.5 (ii BC), Archig.ap.Gal. 12.621.7, Paul.Aeg. 1.57 (38.9 H.); used in simile w. ref. to the spleen, οἷον κατόπτρῳ παρεσκευασμένον καὶ ἕτοιμον ἀεὶ παρακείμενον ἐκμαγεῖον Pl.*Ti.* 72c, cf. ὅτιπερ ἐκμαγεῖόν ἐστι αἵματος μέλανος (sc. ὁ σπλήν) Aret.*SD* 1.15'

**ἐκμάθησις**, add '**2** *learning by heart*, εἴ τις .. ἀμελοίη .. τῆς ἐκμαθήσεως τῶν ψαλμῶν Bas.Caes. in *PG* 31.1305c; cf. Ἑλληνικά 8.66 (Lydia).'

**ἐκμαίνω**, line 8, after 'passion' insert 'Τροΐω ὐπ' ἄνδρος (or -ω ἐπ' ἄνδρι) ἐκμάνεισα, of Helen, Alc. 283.5 L.-P.'

**ἔκμακτος**, for '*express*' read '*moulded, modelled*' and add 'τύπος *IG* 2².1534.64 (iii BC)'

**ἐκμᾰλάσσω**, add 'pass., ἡ αἴσθησις of the effect of pleasing sounds, D.H.*Comp.* 12 (v.l. μαλ-)'

**ἐκμαρτῠρέω I**, line 2, after '(A.)*Ag.* 1196' insert 'ἐπὶ τοῖς δικάζōσιν before those judging the case, *IEphes.* 1678B (vi BC)'; line 3, after 'Aeschin. 1.107' insert 'ἐγμαρτυρῶν ὑπὲρ τῆς εὐνοίας τῶν πολιτῶν *Amyzon* 15.12 (215 BC)' add '**2** *acknowledge publicly*, med., ἐκμαρτυρεῖσθαι τὴν αὐτὴν ὁμολογοῦσαν τὸν γεγονότα αὐτῇ ἐκ τοῦ Χαιρήμονος υἱόν *POxy.Hels.* 35.25 (AD 151).'

**ἐκμάσσω I**, add '**3** *polish, scour*, ἀπεικονίσματα γῇ ἀργυρωματικῇ (q.v. in Suppl.), *IEphes.* 27.542, 545 (AD 104).'

*ἐκμήδομαι, *devise*, Αἰγύπτῳ κακὰ σημεῖα καὶ τεράστι' ἐξεμήσατο Ezek.*Exag.* 226 S.

**ἔκμηνος 1**, subst., add 'fem., ἁ ὑστέρα ἔγμεινος *BCH* 60.183.31 (Boeotia, iii BC)'; add 'cf. ἐξαμηνός'

*ἐκμηρίζω, *remove thigh-bones*, *IEphes.* 10.8, 1201a.7.

*ἔκμισθος (B), ὁ, perh. *leasing*, Θεοφίλῳ βοηθ(ῷ) ὑπὲρ ἐκμίσθου καὶ μετρήσεως *PVindob.Tandem* 17.29 (vi/vii AD).

*ἐκμογέω, *labour at*, ἱμερτὰν ἐξεμόγησα τέχναν epigr. in *SEG* 34.325 (Arcadia, *c.*100 BC); cf. ἐκμοχθέω.

**ἐκμοχθέω 3**, add 'φιλοσοφοῦντες ἐκμοχθοῦσί τι Diog.Sinop.*fr.dub.* 6.1 S.'

*ἐκμῡθέομαι, *speak out*, Theoc. 25.3 (tm.).

*ἐκνεόω, *renew*, τὸν σῖτον καὶ τὰ ξύλα, Ἑλληνικά 7.179 (Chalcis, iii BC).

*ἔκνευμα, ατος, τό, gloss on κλειτύς: κλιτύν· τὸ ἀπόκλιμα, ἔκνευμα, ἐξοχήν Sch.Nic.*Al.* 34c Ge.; cf. ἀπόνευμα.

⁺ἐκνεύω, *turn aside by a movement of the head*, πάντα γὰρ ὁπόσα ἂν δύσκολ' ᾖ περὶ τὸ πρόσωπον ὁ ἵππος ἐκνεύειν πέφυκεν ἄνω X.*Eq.* 5.4, μὴ ἐκκρούσῃ (τὸ προβόλιον) ἐκ τῶν χειρῶν τῇ κεφαλῇ ἐκνεύσας, sc. the boar, id.*Cyn.* 10.12. **2** *cause to move aside by a movement of the head, nod aside*, ἡμᾶς .. ἐξένευσ' ἀποστῆναι πρόσω E.*IT* 1330. **II** *turn the head, look round*, Lxx 4*Ki.* 23.16. **2** transf., *turn aside, bend one's course to*, E.*IT* 1186, εἰς θάνατον id.*Ph.* 1268; πρός τι τῶν ἡδονῆς φίλτρων ἐκνενευκότα Ph. 1.297; w. gen., τῶν παρόντων Plot. 6.7.34. **III** w. acc., *avoid by turning, dodge*, Phld.*Sign.* 27, Ph. 1.146, Orph.*A.* 458, ξίφος Hegesias ap.D.H.*Comp.* 18, πληγήν D.S. 17.100. **2** *shun, avoid*, Themist.*Or.* 34.6.

**ἐκνῑκάω I 1**, add '*prevail over so as to compel*, w. inf., αὐτοὺς ἀναστῆναι ἐξενίκησαν Ael.*NA* 17.41; so pass., τὰ θηρία ἐκνικᾶται ἐμπεσεῖν ib. 8.10' add '**III** perh. *recover possession of at law* (= Lat. *evincere*), *IGRom.* 4.914.6 (v. *ZPE* 48.269); cf. °ἐκνίκησις.'

⁺ἐκνίκησις, εως, ἡ, *recovery of possession at law, eviction* (= Lat. *evictio*), *Cod.Just.* 1.3.38(39), Just.*Const.* Δέδωκεν 5.

**ἐκοντήν**, for '= foreg.' read '= ἑκοντί, *SEG* 18.343.45 (Thasos, i BC/i AD)'

*ἐκουβίτωρ, v. °ἐξκ-.

**ἐκπαγλέομαι II**, after 'A.*Ch.* 217' insert 'κάλλος ἐκπαγλούμενον *fr.* 451n.5 R.'

**ἐκπᾰθής I**, adv., add 'Ath. 10.443d'

**ἐκπᾰλής**, add '**2** (*carried*) *out of orbit*, Plu.*Lys.* 12 (cj., Coraes for ἐκ παλμῶν).'

**ἐκπᾰλιγκοτεῖν**, for '(prob.)' read '(cod. ἔκπαλιν κοτεῖν)'

*ἐκπάρθενος, ον, *deprived of virginity*, Sch.Theoc. 2.40.

*ἔκπεισμα, ατος, τό, (written ἔκπισμ-), *consideration, inducement*, *PCair.Isidor.* 80.6, 13 (AD 296), 81.13 (AD 297).

**ἐκπέμπω I 1**, at end for 'etc.' read '*Trag.adesp.* 664.29 K.-S.'

**ἐκπεράω I 1**, add '*reach*, A.R. 4.329 (tm., s.v.l.)'

**ἐκπέσσω**, after '**-ττω**' insert 'later -πτω Plu. 2.683d, Ath. 3.83f'

**ἐκπέτομαι**, line 3, after '(Chios)' insert 'ἐξεπταμένη (sic) *IEryth.* 302.2 (iii BC); καὶ ἐπεὶ ἐκ τᾶς ἰδίας ἐξεπέτομες καὶ ἐπλανώμεθα *SEG* 30.1123.10 (Entella, Sicily, iii BC)'

*ἐκπέφαται, pf. pass. of *ἐκθείνω cf. θείνω II, *remove by killing*, ἐκ δ' αἰὼν πέφαται Il. 19.27.

**ἐκπηδάω 1**, add 'in a frenzy, *Suppl.Mag.* 42.17 (iii/iv AD)'

**ἐκπίνω 2**, line 3, after 'Antiph. 3, etc.' insert 'ἐκπῖθι τὸ φρέαρ εἰσπεσών Men.*Dysc.* 641'; add 'w. dat., ἔχων σκύπφον Ἐρξίωνι τῷ λευκολόφῳ ἐξέπινον Anacr. 88 P.'

**ἐκπιπράσκω**, delete 'cf. Poll. 7.9'

**ἐκπίπτω**, line 6, delete 'After Hom. .. ἐκβάλλω' **2**, add 'δίκης ἐκπίπτειν *lose one's case* (cf. Lat. *causa cadere*), *Cod.Just.* 2.2.4.2; abs., *lose one's position*, εἰ .. ὑπὲρ τὸν εἰρημένον ἀριθμὸν γένηται χαρτουλάριος, ἐκπίπτει ib. 1.2.24.13' **3**, add '**b** of a wrestler, *be thrown*, *SEG* 35.213.8 (tab.defix., Athens, iii AD); fig., of an unsuccessful lover, ib. 219.10.' **8**, add 'ὡς ἤδη ἥ τε ποίησις ἐξεπεπτώκεε καὶ ἐθαυμάζετο ὑπὸ πάντων Ps.-Hdt.*Vit.Hom.* 36' add '**18** of time, *run out*, Just.*Nov.* 158.1.'

**ἐκπλᾱγής**, add '*possessed, maddened*, *AP* 9.603 (Antip.Sid.)'

⁺ἐκπλεθρίζω, to carry out form of exercise in which one runs up and down within a πλέθρον, reducing the distance each time until a single step is reached, Gal. 6.133.18.

**ἔκπλεθρος**, for 'in ἔ. ἀγών .. *narrowing*' read 'ἀγών E.*El.* 883; κῶλον ἐκπλέθρου δρόμου prob. in id.*Med.* 1181 (v.l. ἔκπλεθρον)'

⁺ἐκπλέκω, *unfold* a document, ἐκπέπλεκται *PDura* 31.59 (AD 204); fig. διάνοιαν Alex.*Fig.* 2.1. **2** *PTeb.* 768.17 (ii BC, dub.), *arrange, settle*, ἔχω ἕως οὗ ἐκπλέξω ὃ ἐν Ἀλεξανδρείαι μετέωρον *PBremen* 17.10, cf. ib. 11.35 (pass.; both ii AD). **b** without object, *to be ready*, *PStrassb.* 73.18 (iii AD).

***ἐκπλεονεξία**, ἡ, *wrong* done to someone, *Pap.Lugd.Bat.* XIII 18.7 (iv AD).

**ἔκπλεος 1**, add 'εἰκόνων Fronto *Ep.* 1.4'

**ἐκπλέω I**, line 3, delete 'ἔξω τοῦ Ἑλλησπόντου id. 5.103' and add 'ἐκπλώσαντες .. ἔξω τὸν Ἑλλήσποντον Hdt. 5.103.2' to section II 1.

**ἐκπλήγδην**, for '*terribly*' read 'glossed by ἐκπληκτικῶς' and after 'Suid.' insert '*in terror* or *amazement*, Theoc. 24.56 (*PAntin.*, συμπλήγδην codd.)'

**ἐκπληρόω I**, add '**6** *complete* task or project, *Cod.Just.* 8.10.12.9a, 9b.'

**ἐκπλήσσω I**, add '*throw off course*, in quot. fig., S.*Aj.* 33'

**ἔκπλοος I**, add 'καὶ ἔσπλον καὶ ἔκπλον ἀσυλ[εί] *SEG* 36.982.C9 (Iasos, 500/450 BC)'

**ἐκποιέω II**, add '**2** dub. sens., Hippon. 7 W.' **IV**, for '*cause* .. **2** *permit*' read '*permit*, Thphr.*CP* 1.14.1, 2'

**ἐκποίησις IV**, add '*PMich.*XIII 659.102 (vi AD)'

***ἐκπολῡωρέω**, *take care of*, κατὰ πάντας τρόπους -ηθεὶς Anon. in Herc. 176 p. 48 V.

**ἐκπομπή I**, add '*Cod.Just.* 12.37.18'

**ἐκπονέω 6**, for this section read '*exert oneself to obtain*, E.*Ion* 1355, *Hel.* 1514' **7**, after '*to digest*' insert '*by taking exercise*'; after '(X.)*Cyr.* 1.2.16' insert 'Arist.*Pr.* 877ᵃ18' add '**11** *exert oneself over* or *in the matter of*, E.*Andr.* 1052.'

**ἐκπορεύω**, line 3, after 'etc.' insert 'w. acc., ἐξόδους *SIG* 1219.15 (Gambrea, iii BC); τὰ λόχια *Milet* 1(7).204*b*9 (v. °λόχιος III)'

***ἐκποριστικός**, ή, όν, *providing*, w. gen., τῶν ἀναγκαίων Procl.*in R.* 1.216.14.

⁺**ἐκπορνεύω**, *commit fornication*, Lxx *Ge.* 38.24, *Ez.* 16.16, *Ep.Jud.* 7; med., Poll. 6.126; w. εἰς, *resort to for fornication*, Lxx *Num.* 25.1. **b** *resort immorally* to false gods, ἐκπορνεύσωσιν ὀπίσω τῶν θεῶν αὐτῶν ib.*Ex.* 34.15, *Jd.* 2.17, *Ez.* 20.30. **II** *prostitute* or *cause to fornicate*, τὴν θυγατέρα ib.*Le.* 19.29, *Ez.* 16.33. **b** *seduce into immoral practices*, ib. 2*Ch.* 21.11, 13.

**ἐκπράκτης**, add 'Cret. **ἐσπράττας**, *Inscr.Cret.* 4.87.1 (v BC), al.'

**ἐκπρεμνίζω**, add 'see also ἐσπρεμμίττεν'

**ἐκπροφέρω**, after 'Man. 6.733' insert 'cj. in Orph.*H.* 71.7'

**ἐκπτύω I**, line 2, before '*AP* l.c.' insert 'Ar.*V.* 792' **II 1**, delete the section.

**ἔκπτωσις**, line 2, for '*projection* of rays from the sun' read '*projection* of vision from the eyes'

**ἐκπῡέω**, add 'Heras ap.Gal. 13.775.3'

**ἐκπῡητικός**, add 'Gal. 12.328.1, 771.8'

***ἐκπωλή**, ἡ, Dor. **-πωλά**, *selling, sale*, χαλκωμάτων *Lindos* 419.143 (i AD).

**ἐκπωμᾰτοποιός**, after '*cup-maker*' insert '*LW* 2741 (Citium)'

***ἐκπώνω**, Aeol. for -πίνω, ποτήριον prob. in Alc. 376 L.-P. (tm.).

**ἔκρηγμα II 1**, add '*breach* in a dike or sim., Wilcken *Chr.* 386.6 (iii BC), Lxx *Ez.* 30.16 (v.l. ἔκρημα), *SB* 7174.18 (i AD) (ἐκχρηγμα)' **3**, add 'cf. perh. φλεγματόεν ἔ. *Suppl.Hell.* 1116'

**ἐκρήσσω**, before 'Theano' insert 'Gal. 11.786.4'

**ἐκρίπτω**, after 'A.*Pr.* 932' insert '*cast off* a garment, App.*BC* 2.126'

**ἐκρομβέω**, add 'ἐξέσται τῷ [βου]λομένῳ τὸ εἰσενεχθὲν ἀλλότριον πτ[ῶμα] ἢ ὀστᾶ ἐκρομβῆσαι *TAM* 5(2).1143.16'

**ἔκροος II**, add '**2** *outlet channel*, τὸν ἔγρουν *SEG* 39.442.2 (Oropus, iv BC).'

**ἐκσᾰόω**, add 'epigr. in *Salamine* 204 (v AD)'

***ἐκσειασμός**, ὁ, app. *purgation*, *OLeid.* 1.12 (ii BC).

***ἐκσπάστης**, ου, ὁ, *one who draws out*, cj. for σκεπαστής in Lxx *Ps.* 70(71).6; cf. ὁ ἐκσπάσας με in *Ps.* 21(22).10.

**ἐκσπεύδω**, after 'Ar.*Th.* 277' insert '(s.v.l.)'

⁺**ἐκστᾰδιος**, ον, prob. *going outside the bounds of the stadium*, Luc.*Nav.* 39 (v.l. ἑκστάδιος, *six stades long*).

***ἐκστᾰσιον**, τό, *surrender* of property to a creditor (cf. Lat. *cessio bonorum*), Just.*Nov.* 135.1.

***ἐκστρανήιος**, ὁ, *stranger*, opp. συγγενής, *TAM* 3(1).481 (Termessus); also **ἐκστράνιος** ib. 608 (ἐξτρ- 541); **ἐκτράνιος** *SEG* 3.208 (Athens, iii AD); cf. Lat. *extraneus*.

**ἐκστρᾰτεύω II 2 a**, delete the section.

**ἐκστρέφω**, after lemma insert 'perh. also ἐκστράφω *SEG* 30.380 no. 6 (ἐξστ- Tiryns, vii BC)'

**ἐκστροφή**, add '**V** *diversion from the proper purpose*: ἐπ' ἐκστροφῇ to the *prejudice* of the rightful owner, *Studi in onore di P.Bonfante* (Milan 1930) 3.64 (ii AD), prob. in *PGnom.* 10 (ii AD), teste Schubart; *PBerl.Möller* 2.17 (i AD).'

***ἔκστρωσις**, εως, ἡ, perh. *preparation of bedding* (or *laying of roads*), *PBeatty Panop.* 1.260 (AD 298).

***ἐκστρώστης**, ου, ὁ, perh. *organizer of bedding* for imperial visitations (or *of road-laying*), *PBeatty Panop.* 1.256, 259, 262, 263 (AD 298).

**ἐκσῡρω**, add 'pf. pass., *PVat.* 11ʳ viii 22, al. (ii AD)'

***ἐκσφηκόω**, τοὺς θύρσους ἐξεσφηκωμένους φοροῦντα, perh. *wasp-waisted*, Hsch. s.v. κάθαπτος (expl. of E.*fr.* 752).

***ἐκσφούνγευσις**, εως, ἡ, *discharge* of soldiers, *POxy.* 1204.6 (iii AD).

***ἐκσφουνγεύω**, = Lat. *expungo*, *discharge* soldiers, *POxy.* 1204.19 (iii AD).

**ἐκσῴζω**, line 6, after 'Pass.' insert 'Eup. 260.24 K.-A. (parody of S.*Ant.* 1128)'

**ἐκτᾰδόν**, add 'epigr. in *SEG* 37.1537.8 (Arabia, *c*.AD 400)'

**ἔκτακτος II**, add 'ἐν ἐκτάκτῳ *PBeatty Panop.* 1.361 (AD 296); adv. -τως, *separately, individually*, ib. 231, 233, 264, 266'

**ἐκταμιεύομαι I**, add '*entrust* to the keeping of a subordinate, ἐρίφους *PCair.Zen.* 429 (iii BC)'

**ἐκτανθαρύζω**, add '(**ἐκτονθορύζω** La.)'

**ἐκτᾰνύω 3**, add 'Εὐψύχι Ταήσι μητρῷον μόρον ἐκτανύσασα σωφροσύνῃ καὶ φιλανδρίᾳ *SB* 5037'

**ἐκταρσόομαι**, for '= ταρσόομαι' read 'pass., *to be stretched*'

***ἐκτασμός**, ὁ, unexpld. agricultural operation (cf. °ἐκτασσω II), *PMil. Vogl.* 52.50, 87 (ii AD).

**ἐκτάσσω I**, add '**2** *muster*, λαόν Lxx 4*Ki.* 25.19.' **II**, for this section read '*carry out* (an unexpld.) agricultural operation, ἐργάτης ἐκτάσσων *PMil.Vogl.* 69.A94, B55, 62 (ii AD), *SB* 9379.2.12 (ii AD), 9410(5).3 (iii AD); cf. ἐκτάσσοντα· χαράσσοντα, γράφοντα Hsch.' add '**III** ἐξετάγη .. εἰς, *was appointed* or *assigned to* a liturgy, *BGU* 2251.2-3 (ii AD).'

**ἐκτείνω I 2**, after 'X.*HG* 6.5.19' insert 'abs. ἐξέτειναν ἐπὶ τὴν Γαβαα Lxx *Jd.* 20.37' add '**3** *extend to*, ἡ προσηγορία .. καὶ ἐπὶ τοὺς ἐγγόνους ἐκτείνεται Modest.*Dig.* 27.1.2.8.' **IV**, for this section read '*pronounce* a vowel or syllable *long*, A.D.*Adv.* 159.21, interpol. in D.H. 2.58; pass., id.*Comp.* 14, A.D.*Pron.* 27.2, al.' **V**, delete the section.

**ἐκτεκνόω**, med., add 'Cret. ἐστετέκνωται *Inscr.Cret.* 4.72 viii 24'

**ἐκτένεια**, line 2, delete '*gush, empressement*'

**ἐκτέος II**, ἐκτέον, *one must have*, add 'Pl.*R.* 535b, *Amat.* 138e, D. 58.60' **2**, add 'Pl.*R.* 468a'

**ἕκτη**, after lemma insert 'Ϝέκτᾱ *SEG* 23.392 (Corcyra), 31.397 (Haliartus, both vi BC)' **III**, add '*SEG* 36.790.5 (Thasos, *c*.480 BC)' add '**IV** *sixth day* (in a month, etc.), ἡ πρώτη ἕκτη Hes.*Op.* 785, opp. ἕκτη ἡ μέσση 782; ἕκτη ἐπὶ δέκα *SEG* 21.541 i 45 (Attica, iv BC), ἕκται ἐφ' ἰκάδα *SEG* 30.1117.3 (Entella, iii BC).'

**ἐκτήκω I 2**, add 'Mosch.Trag. 9.9 S.' **II 2**, add 'Cratin. 196 K.-A.'

**ἐκτημόριοι**, delete all after 'Plu.*Sol.* 13' (v. °ἐκτήμορος)

***ἐκτημόριον**, τό, *a sixth part*, S.E.*M.* 10.140, Protag.Nicae. ap.Heph.Astr. 3.30.37.

***ἐκτήμορος**, ον, οἱ ἐκτήμοροι = ἐκτημόριοι, Arist.*Ath.* 2.2. **II** ὁ ἐκτήμορος (sc. κύαθος), a liquid measure, Herod. 1.80, cf. μέτρῳ ἐ. *PSI* 30.5, 10.

**ἐκτίθημι II 1**, add '**c** *grant* a benefit, *Cod.Just.* 10.30.4.8.'

**ἐκτίλλω II 1**, after 'Hippon. 84' insert '(dub.; = 114A W.)'

**ἐκτῑμάω II**, add 'χρήματα *SEG* 9.72.43 (Cyrene, iv BC)'

⁺**ἐκτίμητρα**, τά, Dor. -ατρα, some form of honorific offerings, *IKnidos* 138.3 (iii BC).

**ἐκτῑναγμός**, for 'perh. *winnowing* or *threshing*' read '*harvesting* of olives *by shaking from the tree*' and add '*PPrag.* I 110.7 (iii AD)' add '**2** *disposal, sale* of stock, *PFlor.* 209.13 (iii AD).'

**ἐκτῑνακτρον**, for '*winnowing-shovel*' read 'pl., *payment for* the work of *harvesting olives* (cf. ἐκτιναγμός 1)'

**ἐκτῑνάσσω I 1**, add '**b** *scatter, shower* missiles, ἐξετίναξαν τὰς σχίζας εἰς τὸν λαόν Lxx 1*Ma.* 10.80.' **II**, for '*make a disturbance*' read 'of the bowels, *be in violent motion*'; delete '*make a thorough* .. (ii BC)'

**ἐκτῑνω 1**, add '**b** *render accounts for*, ἐκτῖσαι τὰ τῆς κληρονομίας Modest.*Dig.* 19.2.49 pr.' **II 1**, add 'abs., *Inscr.Cret.* 4.14, al. (vii/vi BC)'

***ἐκτίον**, τό, perh. dim. of ἕκτη *a sixth*, *PUniv.Giss.* 25.6 (iii AD).

⁺**ἐκτιστής**, οῦ, ὁ, *payer in full*, *PSI* 1435.6 (i AD), Hsch.

**ἐκτοκίζω**, for '*exact interest*' read 'w. cogn. acc., οὐκ ἐκτοκιεῖς τῷ ἀδελφῷ σου τόκον ἀργυρίου'

***ἐκτοκισμός**, ὁ, *interest*, *SEG* 33.1039.72 (Aeolian Cyme, ii BC).

⁺**ἐκτομάς**, άδος, ἡ, πυλὶς ἐ. *wicket-gate*, Aen.Tact. 24.5, 28.2; also ἐ. alone *Stud.Pal.* 20.211.9 (v/vi AD).

**ἐκτομή II**, add '**4** *piece* of weaving, *PTeb.* 703.95 (pl.), 113 (iii BC).'

***ἐκτονέω**, perh. *unstring*: fig., ἐκτετόνημαι *POxy.* 3724 *fr.* 1 iv 30 (list of epigrams, i AD).

**ἐκτοπισμός I**, add 'perh. ἐκτοπισμοὺς στρατοπέδων Scymn. 26 (*GGM* 1.196, s.v.l.)'

**ἔκτοπος II 2**, line 3, after 'Thphr.*CP* 6.18.12' insert 'οἰκία Men.*Dysc.* 624; θέα ib. 690'; line 5, after '(Arist.)*Mir.* 833ᵃ14' insert 'Men.*Dysc.* 824'

'**Εκτόρειος** (s.v. ἕκτωρ), add 'irreg. fem.'Εκτόρεια χείρ E.*Rh.* 762 (cj.)'

**ἕκτος**, after 'Il. 2.407, etc.' insert 'λεγιῶνος ἕκτης *IGRom.* 4.266 (iv

AD), μηνὸς ἕκτου *SEG* 34.389 (Delphi, ii BC)'; after 'Plu. 2.268a' insert 'ἕκτον, τό, *sixth part*, *SEG* 24.486 (Maced., AD 114)'

**ἐκτός II**, for 'abs. .. Plb. 2.4.8' read 'w. definite art., τὰ ἐκτός *external things*, Plb. 2.4.8, etc.; ἐκ (or ἐγ) τῆς ἐκτός = ἔκτοσθε, *Didyma* 25*A*9, *B*21, al. (ii BC)'

**ἔκτοσθεν**, line 5, for '*delirious*' read '*wandering in mind*'

**ἔκτοτε**, after 'Luc.*Sol.* 7' add 'ἐ. κατὰ μηδένα τρόπον εἴπῃς, ἀλλ' ἐξ ἐκείνου Phryn. 31'

***ἐκτράνιος**, v. °ἐκστρανήιος.

***ἐκτραορδινάριοι**, οἱ, Lat. *extraordinarii*, name of specially selected troops, Plb. 6.26.6.

**ἐκτρᾰπελόγαστρος**, after 'ον' insert '(or -**γάστωρ**, ορος)'

**ἐκτρᾰπελος II**, delete the section, incorporating quots. in section I.

**ἐκτρέπω I 1**, line 6, after '*turn off* or *aside*' insert 'w. acc. of route taken' and after 'Hdt. 1.104' insert '*turn aside from*, τῶν ἐκτρεπομένων τὰς βασιλικὰς .. ὁδοὺς στρατιωτῶν *SEG* 13.492 (Caria, iii AD)'

**ἐκτρέχω 1**, add '**b** *leave the* ἀγέλη on completion of ephebic training (become a δρομεύς 2), ἐπεί κ' ἐγδρ‹ά›μωντι *Inscr.Cret.* 1.xvi 5.21.'

**ἐκτρίβω III**, add '**2** *ease by rubbing*, *massage*, συνέκαμψέ τε τὸ σκέλος καὶ ἐξέτριψε τῇ χειρί Pl.*Phd.* 60b.' **V 1**, for '*Class.Phil.* 19.234' read '*PCornell* 1.194' **2**, for '*wipe out*' read '*wipe clean*'

**ἐκτρῡχόω**, add 'Arr.*An.* 4.28.7'

**ἔκτῠπος I 1**, add 'sg., *Inscr.Délos* 104.96 (iv BC)'

**ἐκτύπωσις I**, add 'Lxx 3*Ki.* 6.35, Alcin.*Intr.* p. 162.35 H.'

⁺**ἔκτῡφος**, ον, *free from delusion*, *veracious*, Μοῦσα Oenom.ap.Eus.*PE* 5.21.

**ἐκτῡφω**, line 1, for '(sic, post ἐξήια)' read '(ἐξέθυψεν La.)'; line 4, for '*swelled up* with weeping' read '*was inflamed* with weeping' and add 'Men.*fr.* 439 K.-Th.'

***ἐκτῠχίζω**, *dress with the* τύχος (*mason's hammer*), in Att. fut. ἐκτυχιεῖ, ὁμαλῶς *IG* 2².1670.20.

**ἔκτωρ II**, add 'cf. Myc. *e-ko-to*, *e-ko-to-ri-jo*, pers. nn.'

**ἑκῠρά**, after '*mother-in-law*' insert '(at first only *husband's mother*, acc. to Ar.Byz.ap.Eust. 648.55)'; add '*MAMA* 7.321, 576'

***ἑκῠρεύς**, έως, ὁ, = ἑκυρός, *GVI* 1422 (Antioch, i AD).

**ἑκῠρός**, after '*father-in-law*' insert '(at first only *husband's father*, acc. to Ar.Byz.ap.Eust. 648.53)'; after 'Jul.*Or.* 3.127c' insert 'ὑκερός (w. metathesis of vowels or misspelling), *SEG* 31.1007 (Lydia, ii AD)'

**ἐκφαίνω**, line 2, after 'Il. 13.278' insert 'aor. 2 -εφάνη Il. 19.46, etc.; 3 pl. -έφανεν Pi.*O.* 13.18' add '**III** intr., *appear*, Nic.*Th.* 855.'

**ἔκφανσις**, add 'Aristobul.Alex. p. 216 D. (cf. °ἔκφαυσις)'

***ἐκφαντεύω**, *reveal*, *make known*, *SEG* 37.1001.18 (Katakekaumene, Lydia, ii/iii AD).

**ἐκφαντικός**, add 'perh. adv. -ικῶς *clearly*, Aristobul.Alex. p. 217 D. (v.l. ἐμφ-)'

***ἐκφαύλισμα**, ατος, τό, expl. of σκυβαλισμός Hsch.

***ἔκφαυσις**, εως, ἡ, *radiation*, v.l. in Aristobul.Alex. p. 216 D. (v. °ἔκφανσις).

**ἐκφέρω II 3**, at end for 'Isoc. 5.36' read 'Hdt. 5.36.2' **11**, add 'perh. μόνης τῆς ὑπεροχῆς, ἐάν τις ᾖ, ἐκφερομένης *POxy.* 2411 (AD 173)' add '**VI** math., *divide*, παρὰ τῶν ϛʹ (by six) *Cat.Cod.Astr.* 8(1).173.'

**ἐκφεύγω 3 a**, add 'δίκην *be acquitted*, A.*Eu.* 752'

***ἐκφευκτέον**, *one must avoid*, Archig.ap.Gal. 13.168.4.

**ἐκφλαυρίζω**, for 'f.l.' read 'cj.'

***ἐκφλῠᾱρίζω**, *treat contemptuously*, *slight*, Eust. 3.3, 1416.37, 1675.56; also in codd. of Plu. 2.680c, *Pomp.* 57 (v. ἐκφλαυρ-).

**ἐκφοιτάω**, add '**II** *divulge*, Ael.*fr.* 45 (quoted by Suid. l.c.).'

**ἐκφορά I 1**, add '**b** *bier*, *SEG* 9.4.16 (Cyrene, i BC).'

***ἐκφόρησις**, εως, ἡ, *carrying out*, Arg.E.*Cyc.*, prob. in *BGU* 1774.6.

**ἐκφόριον II**, add '*SEG* 38.1462.29 (Oenoanda, ii AD)' add '**III** *export*, Just.*Edict.* 13.5 (unless neut. of *ἐκφόριος, *exportable*).'

⁺**ἐκφορτίζομαι**, *unload a cargo*, *POxy.* 36 (ii/iii AD); fig., ἐξημπόλημαι κἀκπεφόρτισμαι πάλαι S.*Ant.* 1036.

***ἐκφορτισμός**, ὁ, *unloading*, *POxy.* 36 (ii/iii AD).

**ἐκφύης**, after '*abnormally developed*' insert 'v.l. in *AP* 5.56(55).6 (Diosc.)'

**ἐκφυλάσαι**, add '(perh. for ἐκφυλλάσαι, cf. °ἐκφυλλάζω)'

***ἐκφυλλάζω**, *strip of leaves*, fig., ἐξεφύλλασεν γένος A.*fr.* 154a.13 R.; cf. perh. ἐκφυλάσαι.

**ἐκφυλλοφορέω**, add 'Δείναρχος ἐν τῇ κατὰ Πολυεύκτου ἐκφυλλοφορηθέντος ἐνδείξει Harp. s.v. παλιναίρετος'

**ἔκφῠσις II 2**, add 'of horse, *spring of the neck*, Simon. Ath.*Eq.* 6, *Hippiatr.* 115'

***ἐκφωτίζομαι**, *to be illuminated*, Plu. 2.922e.

**ἐκχέζω**, for '= Lat. *ecacare*' read '*excrete*'; add '*Inscr.Cret.* 1.xvii 9.12 (Lebena, ii BC, sp. ἐσχ-)'

**ἐκχέω**, line 2, for 'fut. .. χέω)' read '(-χέω in E.*Supp.* 773 is pres. subj.)' **I 1 b**, line 2, after 'Men. l.c.' add '*empty*, κελέβην Call.*fr.* 246 Pf.' **3**, add '[εὐπραξίαν] *see it slip away*, A.*fr.* 154a.20 R.'

**ἐκχλοιόομαι**, add 'Gal. in *CMG* 5.9.(2).151.11, 13 (vv.ll. ἐκλύεσθαι, ἐνοχλεῖσθαι)'

**ἐκχοΐζω I**, after '*dig out*' insert '*POxy.* 2272.66 (ii AD)'

**ἐκχράω I**, add 'φωνήν Posidipp. in *Suppl.Hell.* 705.12'

***ἐκχῠμενίτας**, v. παλινεκχυμενίτας.

**ἐκχύμωμα**, add 'Gal. 12.804.5, 13.385.12, 17'

***ἐκχῠσία**, ἡ, app. = ἔκχυσις 1, *PKöln* 234.9 (AD 431).

**ἐκχωρέω II**, after '*cede*' insert 'cf. °ἐκχώρησις II 2' and add '*PMich.*II 123 (AD 45/7), *SB* 10880, 10881 (AD 302)'

**ἐκχώρησις II 2**, for '*deed of surrender*' read '*withdrawal from a property*, *cession*' and add '*PSI* 1144 (AD 100), *PMich.*VI 238 (AD 145/6), *SB* 10880,10881 (AD 302)' add '**3** *transfer of right to sue* (Lat. *cessio actionum*), *Cod.Just.* 4.35.24, Just.*Nov.* 72 pr.'

**ἐκχωρίζω I**, add '**2** *confiscate*, *take away*, Lxx 1*Es.* 4.44, 57.'

**ἑκών**, after 'ἑκόν' insert 'Dor. fem. ἕκασσα *SEG* 9.72.87 (Cyrene, iv BC), ἑκοῖσα ib. 89'

**ἕλα I**, after 'γέλαν' insert 'εἵλη' and add 'also **ἔλα**: dat. ἔλᾳ cj. in Pi.*fr.* 123.10 S.-M.'

***Ἐλαγάβαλος**, epith. of the god Helios, Θεῷ Ἡλίῳ Ἐλαγαβάλῳ *SEG* 33.1254 (Emesa, iii AD); also **Ἐλεγάβαλος** D.C. 78.31, etc.; cf. Ἐλαιβάριος.

***ἐλαγμάτιον**, v. ‡ἐλασμ-.

**ἐλάδιον II**, for '*a little oil*' read '*olive oil*'

⁺**ἐλᾱθερής**, v. ‡εἰληθερής.

**ἐλαία**, line 1, after 'Att. **ἐλάα**' insert 'also Aeol., Alc. 296(*b*).2 L.-P. [-ᾱ-]' **II**, for 'but ἐλάα is simply .. etc.' read 'while ἐλάα is generally the Attic form, cf. *IG* 1³.84.33, 2².1013.21, 2492.36, etc., both forms appear in *IG* 1³.422.84, 89, 118 (Athens, v BC)' at end add 'form *ἐλαίϝα, Myc. *e-ra-wa*'

**ἐλαιήεις I**, insert 'θαλλὸν ἐλαιήεντα Nonn.*D.* 11.510' and transf. 'φλοιός Nic.*Th.* 676' to section II.

**ἐλαιηρός 3**, delete the section.

***ἐλαιθερής**, v. ‡εἰληθερής.

**ἐλαϊκός**, fem. subst., add '*olive-oil tax*, *PHamb.* 182.10, 16 (iii BC)'

**ἐλάϊνος 3**, add 'ἐλαίου ἐλαΐνο[υ] *SEG* 30.1663 (Bactria, ii BC)'

***ἐλαιοβαστάκτης**, ου, ὁ, *olive-carrier*, *ITyr* 35 (sp. ἐλεο-).

**ἐλαιόγᾱρον**, add '*PWash.Univ.* 59.14 (v AD)'

***ἐλαιόκαρον**, τό (written ἐλεό-), perh. *caraway oil*, *PVindob.*G 39847.456 (*CPR* 5.97, iv AD).

**ἐλαιοκονία**, after '*oil*' insert 'Zos.Alch. 141.11'

**ἔλαιον**, after 'τό' insert 'Cypr. *e-la-i-wo* ἐλαίϝō (gen.) *Salamine* 1 (*c.*600 BC)' **I**, add 'pl., αἱ δὲ κόμαι θυόεντα πέδῳ λείβουσιν ἔλαια (i.e. drops) Call.*Ap.* 38' at end add 'form ἔλαιϝον, Myc. *e-ra₃-wo*, *e-ra-wo*'

***ἐλαιονοπαράδεισος**, v. ‡ἐλαιωνο-.

***ἐλαιοποιέω**, *manufacture oil*, *PSI* 1030.12 (ii AD).

***ἐλαιοπρᾱ́τισσα**, ἡ, *female oil-dealer*, *PPanop.* 24.2 (*ZPE* 10.117; AD 323/6).

***ἐλαιοπωλέω**, *carry on trade of oil-merchant*, Θατρῆν ἐλαιοπωλοῦσαν *PSI* 1239.10, ἐλεοπωλοῦ(ντας) *PLaur.* 187.14 (ii AD).

**ἐλαιοπώλης**, add '*IEphes.* 2.44 (iv BC), *EA* 16.47 (Sinope, iv BC)'

***ἐλαιόπωλις**, ιδος, ἡ, *female oil-seller*, rest. in *PMasp.* 287 iv 23, *OBodl.* 2355, (?iii AD; sp. ἐλε-).

***ἐλαιοπώλισσα**, ἡ, *female oil-seller*, *SB* 10978 (AD 320).

**ἐλαιοτρίβιον**, after '*oil-press*' insert '*IGLS* 1509 (ἐλεο-)'

***ἐλαιουργικός**, ή, όν, *belonging to oil-manufacture*, μέτρον *POxy.* 2350 i 9 (iii AD), etc.

***ἐλαιούργισσα**, ἡ, *female oil-worker*, *PGot.* 22 (vi AD).

***ἐλαιοφοινῑκών**, ῶνος, ὁ, *grove of olive-trees and palms*, *CPR* 7.46.9 (Hermopolis Magna, early ii BC).

***ἐλαιοχρηΐστᾱς**, α, ὁ, = ἐλαιοχρίστης, as a member of a ship's crew, *Clara Rhodos* 8.228.9 (Rhodes, i BC).

**ἐλαιοχρίστης**, for '*municipal official responsible for supply of oil*' read '*one who rubs a person down with oil* after exercise'

**ἐλαιοχρίστιον**, add '*SEG* 37.859.10 (Heracleia on the Latmos)'

**ἐλαιρός**, add '*Edict.Diocl.* in *SEG* 37.335 iii 15'

**ἐλαιών** for '*PCair.Zen.*57.2' read '*PCair.Zen.*157.2'

**ἐλαιωνοπᾰράδεισος**, add 'also ἐλαιονο- *Pap.Lugd.Bat.* xxv 21.13 (78 BC)'

***ἐλαιωνοφοινῑκοπᾰράδεισος**, ὁ, *olive and date orchard*, *PVindob.Bosw.* 8+9.9 (*BASP* 14.96, AD 331).

⁺**ἐλᾰ́σιος**, ὁ, *one that drives away*, τοὺς δὲ τὰς ἐπιληψίας ἀποτρέπειν δοκοῦντας ἐλασίους μὲν ὀνομάζουσι (sc. at Argos) Plu. 2.296f.

**ἔλᾰσις**, add '**5** *rowing*, Ael.*NA* 13.2.'

**ἐλασμάτιον**, before 'Dsc.' insert '*Inscr.Délos* 1443*A*i148, ii61, 1449*Aab*ii21 (ii BC)'; add 'also ἐλαγμ- *Inscr.Délos* 1441*A*ii85 (ii BC)'

***ἐλασσοδαφία**, ἡ, prob. sim. to λειψεδαφία, *loss of soil*, *PRyl.* 677.9 (i AD).

**ἐλασσονέω**, delete the article.

**ἐλασσόω I 1**, add '*Cod.Just.* 10.27.2.10'

**ἐλάσσων I 3**, add 'ἐπὶ τὰ ἐλάσσονα *in the least detail*, *SEG* 33.1034.B13 (Aeolis, iii BC)' **III**, add '**2** ἐλάσσων τὴν ἡλικίαν *under age*, *minor*, Just.*Nov.* 1.4.1, 22.19.'

***Ἐλάστερος**, ὁ, epith. of Zeus, *AE* 1948-49.1 (Paros, v BC).

**ἐλάτη III**, delete '(but .. 5)' and add '**2** the fruit enclosed by the spathe, Dsc. 1.109.5.'

**ἐλᾰτήρ II**, transfer 'Call.*Jov.* 3' to section I.

**ἐλαττονέω 2**, for this section read '*grow less*, Lxx 3*Ki.* 17.14; *be missing*, *PMagd.* 26.9, 12 (iii BC), *BGU* 1195.19 (i BC)' **3**, for '(*PMagd.*) 11.22' read 'Lxx 3*Ki.* 11.22'

**ἐλαύνω**, line 3, after '(Hp.)*Nat.Mul.* 32' insert 'inf. ἐλάσσειν *AP* 7.427 (Antip. Sid.)' and for '(ἐλάσσω (παρ-)' read '(παρελάσσεις'; line 21, pres. ἐλάω, add 'Tim.*Pers.* 210 P.'; line 25, after 'A.R. 3.872' insert '*GVI* 1844.3 (Rome, ?ii AD)' **I 1 b**, add 'ἐλαύνων ἐργ(άτης) *drover*, *SB* 9379 ii 11, al.' **III 2**, at end for 'generally .. 3.74' substitute '**b** metaph., *drive as a team*, Pi.*N.* 3.74; *set in motion*, A.*Ag.* 701 (lyr.).'

**ἐλάφειος**, after 'ον' insert '(perh. also 3 termin., πήραν ἐλαφείαν v.l. Longus 3.15.3)' and after '(iii AD)' insert '*of deerskin*, Longus l.c. Myc. *e-ra-pe-ja* (fem.)'

**ἐλάφιος**, add '**II** = ἐλάφειος, κέρας *Inscr.Délos* 104.21 (iv BC), *Edict. Diocl.* in *SEG* 37.335 ii 17. Myc. *e-ra-pi-ja* (fem.) *of a deer*'

***ἐλᾰφοκερᾰτίτης**, ου, ὁ, a precious stone, Orph.*Lith.Kerygm.* 4.

**ἔλᾰφος**, add 'cf. Myc. *e-ra-po ri-me-ne* = ἐλάφων λιμένει (dat.), place-name = *Deer-harbour*'

**ἐλαφρία II**, add '*ICilicie* 36 (vi AD)'

**ἐλαφρός III 1 b**, for '*gentle, mild*' read '*adaptable*' and delete 'cf.'

**ἐλαφρόω**, after '= sq.' insert 'Plu. *in Hes.* 41'

***ἐλᾰφώδης**, ες, *deer-like*, comp. -έστερον Eun. in Phot.*Bibl.Cod.* 77.

**ἐλᾰ́χιστος I 1**, add 'adv. -τως, *to the least degree*, Damocr.ap.Gal. 13.1057.15' add '**5** *least in rank* or *estimation*, *Ev.Matt.* 25.40, etc., *BCH* suppl. 8.225 (Philippi, v/vi AD), *SEG* 33.1316, al.'

**ἐλᾰχύς**, line 4, for 'Archyt.Amphiss. 2, Euph. 11' read 'Archyt.Amph. 2 = Euph. 188.2 vGr.'; line 5, after 'Nonn.*D.* 37.314' insert 'masc. ἐλαχὺν δόμον Call.*fr.* 525 Pf.; ἐγὼ δ' εἴην οὐλαχύς id.*fr.* 1.32'

**ἐλᾱών**, after '= ἐλαιών' insert '*PCair.Zen.* 788.18, 27 (iii BC)'

***ἐλβούνιον** or **ἐλβύνιον**, τό, some kind of comestible, *PSI* 862.9 (iii BC), *PHerm.* 23.8 (iv AD); cf. perh. ἔλπος, ἔλφος.

**ἔλδομαι** and **ἐέλδομαι**, w. gen., add 'σοὶ δ' εἰ πλούτου θυμὸς ἐέλδεται Hes.*Op.* 381'

**ἐλέατρος**, for '= ἐδέατρος' read '= ‡ἐδέατρος'

**ἐλεάω**, add '*IKyme* 41.37 (*Hymn.Is.*)'

**⁺ἐλεγαίνω**, glossed variously by τὸ παραφρονεῖν, τὸ ὁπωσδήποτε ἀκολασταίνειν, ἀσελγαίνειν *EM* 152.50, 327.6 (perh. invented, as etym. of ἀσελγαίνειν).

**⁺ἐλεγεία**, ἡ, *literary poem in elegiacs*, Arist.*Ath.* 5.2, 3, Thphr.*HP* 9.15, etc. **2** *elegy* as genre, Μίμνερμος .. ποιητὴς ἐλεγείας Str. 14.1.28, cf. 13.1.48, 4.8; δι' ἐλεγείας (gen. sg.) *in elegiacs*, Plu.*Cim.* 4.9, Suid. s.v. Θέογνις, al. **3** in pl., = ἐλεγεῖα, *elegiacs*, Parth.*praef.*, Plu.*Cim.* 4.10.

**ἐλεγεινή**, add 'cf. ἀλεγεινός'

**ἐλεγείνω**, delete the entry.

**⁺ἐλεγεῖον**, τό, *distich consisting of hexameter and pentameter, elegiac couplet*, Critias 4.3 W., Th. 1.132.2, Arist.*Po.* 1447$^b$12, D.S. 19.1; in pl., *elegiacs*, whether forming complete poem or not, Pherecr. 162.10 K.-A., Pl.*R.* 368a, D. 19.252, Arist.*Rh.* 1375$^b$32; of poet's whole output, ib. 1405$^a$33, etc.; of inscriptions, Lycurg. 142; of single couplet, D. 59.98. **2** *poem in elegiacs*, *CEG* 819.13 (Lacon. epigr. at Delphi, iv BC), D.S. 10.24, 11.14, Plu.*Flam.* 9, *Them.* 8, Sch.Pi.*O.* 13.32 (all of four-line dedications); of literary poems, Str. 14.6.3, D.H. 1.49, Paus. 7.18.1. **II** *pentameter*, Heph. 1.5, 15.14, 15, Sch.D.T. 20.13, al.; cf. Pl.*Hipparch.* 228d. **III** without metrical connotation, *epitaph*, Ps.-Hdt.*Vit.Hom.* 36, D.Chr. 4.135. **2** in pl., *lament, song* of *woe*, Luc.*Tim.* 46.'

**ἐλεγειοποιός**, before 'ὁ' insert '(Dor. -γηο- *AP* 13.21 (Theodorid.))'

**⁺ἔλεγος**, ὁ, *sung lament*, inscr.ap.Paus. 10.7.6 (pl.), Ar.*Av.* 217 (lyr., pl.), E.*IT* 146 (lyr., pl.), *Hel.* 185 (lyr.), A.R. 2.782 (pl.). **2** ἔλεγοι name of an aulodic nome, Ps.-Plu. 2.1132d. **II** in pl., = ἐλεγεῖα, *elegiacs*, Call.*fr.* 7.13 Pf., *AP* 4.1.36 (Mel.), 11.130.3 (Poll.); ἱλαροὶ ἔ. id. 10.19.5 (Apollonid.).

**ἐλεγχής I**, add 'comp. ἐλεγχότερος *Eleg.adesp.* in *Suppl.Hell.* 964.20 (s.v.l.)'

**ἔλεγχος** (B) **III**, add '**2** app. = ὁ ἐλέγξας, *informer*, *TAM* 2(3).991.6 (Lycia).'

**ἐλέγχω II 5**, add 'Call.*fr.* 84 Pf., Nonn.*D.* 1.42'

***ἐλεεινολόγημα**, ατος, τό, *appeal to pity*, Sch.T Il. 21.70.

**ἐλεθαινομένη**, add 'cf. °ἐλεγαίνω'

***Ἐλειθῡαιών**, ῶνος, ὁ, last month of the year at Tenos, *IG* 12(5).872.75 (iii BC).

**ἐλειοδίακτος**, delete the entry.

***Ἐλείτας**, ὁ, Cypr. *e-le-i-ta-i* (dat.), title of Apollo, *ICS* 215(b).

**ἐλείτης I**, add '*PMil.Vogl.* 69.50, 122, ib. B107 (ii AD)' **II**, delete the section.

**ἐλελίζω** (A) **III**, line 4, for 'Simon. 29' read 'Pi.*fr.* 107a.3 S.-M.'

**⁺ἐλελίζω** (B), *utter a wavering* or *warbling sound* (ἐλελεῦ): of the noise made by troops going into battle, ἐφθέγξαντο. πάντες οἷον τῷ Ἐνυαλίῳ ἐλελίζουσι X.*An.* 1.8.18, τῷ Ἐνυαλίῳ ἠλέλιξαν ib. 5.2.14; of bird's trill, E.*Ph.* 1514; med., Ar.*Av.* 213, E.*Hel.* 1112; of inanim. things, ἡ (sc. ἀσπίς) δ' ἐλέλιξεν ἐνόπλιον Call.*Del.* 137.

**ἐλελίσφᾰκος**, before '*salvia*' insert 'plant, uncertainly identified w.' and add 'Nic.*Th.* 84. **II** app. = ἐλελίσφακον II, πόα τις ὁμοία δικτάμῳ Hsch.'

**⁺ἐλελύζω**, = ὀλολ-, γύναικες δ' ἐλέλυσδον ὅσαι προγενέστεραι Sapph. 44.31 L.-P. (v.l. ὀλόλ-).

**ἔλεμος**, add '(ἐλεμόσπερμα La.); cf. °ἐλίμαρ'

***ἐλενίδιον**, τό, dim. of ἐλένιον 2, *elecampane*, *POxy.* 2570 iii b 11, 3733.26, 3766.108 (all iv AD); cf. *helenidi* (gen.) *Edict.Diocl.* 34.88 in *ZPE* 34.183.

***ἐλεόπολις**, v. °ἐλέπολις.

***ἐλεορέω**, *to be overseer of marshland pasture*, *IEryth.* 17 (iv BC).

**ἐλέπολις**, add 'also ἐλεόπολις Lxx 1*Ma.* 13.43, 44' **II**, delete 'invented by Demetrius Poliorcetes' and add 'Lxx 1*Ma.* l.c.'

***Ἐλευθέρα**, ἡ, *Liberty* (as goddess), *SEG* 17.680, *EA* 16.116, also perh. *IGRom.* 3.700 (all Lycia).

**Ἐλευθεραί**, add 'Ἐλευθερᾶθεν *IG* $1^2$.943.96'

**ἐλευθερία 1 a**, add 'implying freedom from taxation, *SEG* 32.833 (Samos, 38 BC)' **b**, add '*IG* $9^2$(1).624.a8, al. (Naupactus, ii BC), Just.*Const.* Δέδωκεν 7b, Theophil.Antec. 1.12.6; *manumission-document*, *MAMA* 4.279 (Dionysopolis)' add '**5** personified as goddess, *Epigr.Gr.* 903 (Sardis, iv AD).'

**ἐλευθερικός**, add 'ἔδωκε τὸ ἐλευθερικὸν τέλες (sic) Πολυξένῳ *SEG* 37.450 (Thessaly, ii/iii AD), *ITyr* 45'

**ἐλευθέριος I 2**, line 6, after '(Arist.)*Pol.* 1340$^b$10' insert 'τύμβος *AP* 7.178 (Diosc.), 185 (Antip.Thess.)' **III**, add '*IMylasa* 207.5, etc., *SEG* 34.558.15 (Larissa, ii BC)'

**ἐλευθερόπαις**, add 'eleg. in *AD* 10(1926) παράρτημα 49 (Phalanna, iii BC)'

**ἐλεύθερος I 1 b**, delete '*married woman*, Ath. 13.571d'; after '*POxy.* 1872.8 (v/vi AD)' insert '*PVindop.Worp* 14.2 (vi/vii AD), *PGron.* 10.17'; delete 'but, *freedwoman* .. (Vienne)' **2**, after 'D.S. 4.46' insert 'also ἐλευθέρα τήρησις *POxy.* 3346.5 (early iii AD)' **II**, add '**2** in cultural or moral sense, opp. δημιουργός Pl.*Prt.* 312b, *Lg.* 848a, *R.* 405a, 431c.' at end add 'Myc. *e-re-u-te-ro*, *free*, of contributions, *not payable*'

**ἐλευθερόω**, add '**3** *manumit*, *Cod.Just.* 6.4.4.10, also perh. *emancipate*, ib. 6.4.4.25.' at end add 'Myc. aor. *e-re-u-te-ro-se*, *allowed free*'

**ἐλευθερωτής**, add '**2** *manumissor*, *Cod.Just.* 6.4.4.24, Just.*Nov.* 78.4.1, etc.'

**Ἐλευθία**, delete 'Ἐλευθώ'

***Ἐλευθώ**, = Εἰλείθυια, Call.*Del.* 276 (cj.), *AP* 7.604 (Paul.Sil.), 9.268 (Antip.Thess.), cf. Hsch.

**ἐλεύθω**, line 2, for 'Ibyc.*Oxy.* 1790.18' read 'Ibyc. 1(*a*).18 P.; 3 sg. ἔλευσεν Pi.*fr.* 70d.39 S.-M.'

***Ἐλευσία**, v. °Εἰλείθυια.

**Ἐλευσίνιος II**, for '*Eleusis*' read '*Athens*'

**Ἐλευσίς I**, add 'Ἐλευσεῖν *GVI* 1058 (Eleusis, iii/iv AD)'

**⁺ἐλεφαντάρχης**, ου, ὁ, *master of elephants*, Phylarch. 31 J., Plu.*Demetr.* 25, Lxx 2*Ma.* 14.12; spec., *commander of squadron of sixteen elephants*, Ascl.*Tact.* 9, Ael.*Tact.* 23.

**ἐλεφάντειος**, add 'Myc. *e-re-pa-te-jo*, *made of ivory*'

***ἐλεφαντιᾰκός**, ή, όν, *suffering from elephantiasis*, Firm. 3.5.30; also -τικός, id. 8.26.13.

**ἐλεφάντινος 1**, after 'Alc. 33.1' insert '(= 350.1 L.-P.), λύραι ἐλεφάντιναι *IG* $1^3$.345.47' **2**, add 'perh. so used by Alcm. 10(*b*).6 P.'

***ἐλεφαντιώδης**, ες, *suffering from elephantiasis*, Antyll.ap.Aët. 3.9 (p. 269.10 O.).

**ἐλεφαντουργός**, subst., add '*SB* 10258 ii 14 (iv AD)'

**ἐλέφᾱς II**, add '*IG* $1^3$.457.22 (442/1 BC), *CID* II 62 ii A 5, Lxx *Ez.* 27.6; *ivory statue*, χὀ βωμὸς χἐλέφας *SEG* 32.356 (Aegina, vi BC)' **III**, add 'Al.*Jb.* 2.7' at end add 'Myc. *e-re-pa*'

***Ἐλήγηρις**, εως, ἡ, epith. of Demeter (διὰ τὸ ὑπὸ τῆς τοῦ ἡλίου ἕλης γηρᾶν), Eust. 1197.53.

**ἕλιγμα I**, add 'perh. *hairband*, πορφυρεῦν .. κόμης ἕλιγμα *AP* 6.211 (Leon.Tarent.)' **III**, delete the section.

**ἑλίκη III**, add 'Myc. *e-ri-ka*, *willow*'

**ἑλῐκοβλέφᾰρος**, for '*with ever-moving eyes, quick-glancing*' read '*having curling eyelashes*'

**ἑλῐκός**, for '*eddying* .. *fr.* 290' read 'perh. *meandering* (but *black* acc. to Sch.), of river, Call.*fr.* 299 Pf.' and before 'χορεία' insert '**II** *circling*'

**ἑλικτός I**, lines 4/5, for 'a *wheeled* ark' read 'prob. *plaited* basket'; line 6, before 'Theoc. 1.129' insert 'i.e. wrapped round with bands'; line 7, before 'comp.' insert 'ἐλ{ε}ικτὸν κεφαλίδα Jos.*Jer.* 43(36).2' add '**b** ἑλικτά, τά, app. kind of vessel, *Inscr.Délos* 442*B*210 (ii BC).'

**Ἑλῐκών**, add '**III** experimental instrument used by musical theorists, Ptol.*Harm.* 2.2.'

**Ἑλῐκωνίδες**, add 'Ibyc. 1(*a*).24 P.'

**Ἑλῐκώνιος II**, add '*SEG* 15.784 (Sinope, iii BC)'

**ἑλίκωψ**, for '*with rolling eyes* .. spirits' read 'epith. of uncertain sense, perh. *with rolling eyes*'; line 4, for 'Sapph.*Supp.* 20a.5' read 'Sapph. 44.5 L.-P.' and after it insert 'Alc. 283.16 L.-P.'; after '*P.* 6.1' insert 'ἑ. .. λαγωοί Nonn.*D.* 48.900'; add 'expld. as *black-eyed* by Sch.Il. 1.98, *Et.Gud.*, Eust. 57.1, etc., cf. °ἑλικός'

***ἐλίμαρ**· κέγχρῳ ὅμοιον ἢ μελίνη ὑπὸ Λακώνων Hsch. (La.); cf. ‡ἔλεμος, ἔλυμος III.

***ἐλιμονικός**, v. °ἁλιμονικός.

**ἔλῐνος**, for 'later ἔλινος' read 'later ἔλῑνος' and after 'Nonn.*D.* 12.299' insert '(cod. σελίνοις)'; cf. ‡ἐλίνοφόρος'

**ἐλῑνοφόρος**, delete 'Ep. εἰλ-' and after 'ib. 17.333' insert '(v.l.)'

**ἐλίνύες**, add 'cf. ἡ παρὰ τὸ ἐλινύειν τὸ ἡσυχάζειν γέγονεν ἐλινὺς καὶ Ἐρινύς Sch.Hes.*Th.* 472 (p. 75 Di G.)'

**ἐλῑνύω**, line 5, delete 'μὴ ἐλινύειν Hdt. 1.67' **3**, line 2, after 'cf.' insert '1.67' add '**II** trans., *bring to rest, halt*, πότμον ἐλινύσειεν Call.*fr.* 330 Pf.'

**ἕλιξ** (A), for 'epith. of oxen .. *rolling*' read 'epith. of oxen: the original significance is unknown; it was interpreted by Alexandrian scholars as *"black"* and perh. used by Theoc., etc. in this sense'

**ἕλιξ** (B) **III 1**, line 2, before 'Thphr.' insert 'Hes.*Sc.* 295' **2**, add '**b** of palm, *AP* 4.1.50 (Mel.).' **4**, at end for '*feelers*' read '*tentacles*', for '(Antiphil. Byz.)' read '(Antiphil.)' and after it insert '*feelers* of the prawn, Ael.*NA* 16.13'

**ἑλίσσω I 3**, add 'ἑ. τὸ μέλος *trill* its song, of the nightingale, Ael.*NA* 5.38' **4**, add '**b** = ἀνελίσσω I 1, i.e. *read*, γράμματα (= συγγράμματα) Call.*fr.* 468 Pf.; βίβλον Posidipp. in *Suppl.Hell.* 705.16, cf. *AP* 9.161.1 (Marc.Arg.).'

**ἑλίχρῡσος**, after 'ὁ' insert '(-ον, τό Dsc. 4.57)'

**ἑλκητήρ**, for 'harrow' read 'rake'

**ἑλκόω I 2**, add '**b** *produce ulceration by cautery*, πέλματα *PMerton* 12.20 (i AD).'

**ἑλκυστός II**, for '*refined, fine-drawn* oil .. Stratonicea' read 'oil *which may be drawn* by the users *IStraton.* 15.10, 197.12, al.' and add '*SEG* 11.492.11 (Sparta, ii AD); ἀλείμματα ἑ. *IGRom.* 3.804 (Aspendus); γυμνασιαρχία ἑ. *IStraton.* 210.8, 219.3'; transfer 'cf. ἑλκυστῷ· λείῳ Hsch.' to section I 1.

**ἕλκυστρον 2**, for 'φορβεύα' read 'φορβεια'

**ἕλκω**, line 5, delete '*IG* 11(2).287.B61 (Delos, ii BC)' **I 2**, add 'med., *APl.* 306, 307 (Leon.Tarent.)' **II 1**, for 'barge-pole' read 'paddle' **4**, add '**b** καθ' ὃν τόπον .. καὶ ὁ ῥοῦς ἕλκει *towards which place the current sets*, *Peripl.M.Rubr.* 13.' **6**, at end for 'εἰκλυσμένων' read 'εἱλκυσμένων'

**ἑλκώδης I**, add 'adv. -δῶς, *so as to produce ulceration*, Gal. 17(2).620.16, 621.3'

**ἑλκωτικός**, add '**II** ἑλκωτική, ἡ, (sc. ἔμπλαστος), kind of plaster producing ulceration by its caustic properties, *PMerton* 12.15 (i AD).'

**ἐλλᾶθι**, after 'ἴληθι' insert '(v. *ἴλημι)'; after 'B. 10.8' insert 'Simon. 54 P. (s.v.l.)'; for 'Call.*fr.* 121' read 'Call.*fr.* 7.13 Pf.'

**ἐλλαμβάνω I**, for '*Supp.Epigr.* .. ii BC)' read 'ψάφος ἐλλάβοιεν *BCH* 66/7.144 (Thess. inscr. at Delphi, iii BC)'

***ἐλλαμπρύνομαι**, *distinguish oneself, shine*, μηδὲ τούτῳ ἐμπαράσχητε τῷ τῆς πόλεως κινδύνῳ ἰδίᾳ ἐλλαμπρύνεσθαι Th. 6.12.2, App.*BC* 3.66; without dat., Luc.*Dom.* 1. **2** *glory in*, τῷ ἔργῳ D.C. 73.10, πρὸς τὰς φίλας ἑ. λόγοις J.*AJ* 18.3.4.

**Ἑλλᾱνοδίκαι I**, after 'Paus. 5.9.5 sq.' insert 'at the Olympic games of Alexandria, *SEG* 8.658 (sg., Coptos, iii AD)'

***ἔλλατε**, v. ‡ἔλλαθι.

**ἔλλειμμα**, line 3, after '(D.) 22.44' insert 'ostr. cited *OBodl.* 49 note'

**ἐλλειπόντως**, after 'Plot. 1.3.6' insert '*deficiently, with insufficient force*, Simp. *in Epict.* p. 38 D.'

**ἐλλείπω I 1**, after 'E.*El.* 609' insert 'Th. 5.103.1'

**ἐλλείχω**, add '*take in by licking*, Hp. *Mul.* 1.8'

**ἔλλετε**, for 'Call.*fr.* 292' read 'Call.*fr.* 1.17 Pf.' and delete 'cf. ἔλλατε (v. ἔλλαθι)'

**Ἕλλην III**, lines 4/5, delete 'Πυλῶν Ἑλλήνων D. 18.304'

**Ἑλληνάρχης**, add '*IPrusias* 5.1, 46.2'

**Ἑλλήνιος II**, after 'Hdt. 2.178' insert 'ἐν τῶι Ἑλλᾱνίωι *SEG* 32.1586.17 (Naucratis, v BC)'

**Ἑλληνίς II 1**, add 'pl., Hyp.*Epit.* 36' **2**, add '*Ev.Marc.* 7.26'

**Ἑλληνιστί**, for '*PTaur.* 1$^v$4' read 'Mitteis *Chr.* ii.31 v 4'

**Ἑλλήσποντος**, line 5, after 'Aegean' insert '*AP* 7.705 (Antip.Thess.)'

**ἐλλῐμενίζω**, for 'Ar.*fr.* 455' read 'ἐλλιμενίζεις ἢ δεκατεύεις Ar.*fr.* 472 K.-A.' and add 'also ἐνλ- Hsch.'

**ἐλλῐμένιος I**, add 'as epith. of Hera, *IG* $2^2$.5148, cf. λιμένιος'

**ἐλλῐμενιστής**, for '*farmer*' read '*collector*'

***ἐλλίμην**, ενος, ὁ, perh. an area of the agora, τὰ ποτ' ἐνλίμενα (cf. ‡λιμήν III) *SEG* 37.494.11 (Matropolis, Thessaly, iii BC).

**ἐλλῑπής II 1**, add 'ἐ. ἐπὶ τῆς τραπέζης αὐτοῦ Lxx *Si.* 14.10' **2**, add '-εστέρως J.*AJ* 19.1.17'

***ἐλλῑτές** or **ἐλλιστές**, wd. of unkn. meaning in Epich. 183.

**ἐλλόγιμος I**, add 'sup., as honorific title, ὁ ἐλλογιμώτατος συνήγορος τοῦ Θηβαίων φόρου *SB* 7033.21 (v AD), *POxy.* 1886.1 (v/vi AD)'

**ἐλλογιμότης**, add '**II** as complimentary address, παρακαλῶ τὴν σὴν ἐ. *your notability*, *POxy.* 1885.11 (vi AD).'

**ἐλλοπίης**, delete the entry.

**ἐλλῠ́της**, add 'also εἰλῠ́τᾱς (acc. pl.), *Sokolowski* 3.74.4, 6 (Lebadea, iv BC)'

***ἐλλυχνιδᾶς**, ᾶ, ὁ, *lamp-wick maker*, Παύλου ἐνλυχνιδᾶ *SEG* 32.375 (Argos, Chr.).

**ἐλλύχνιον**, add '**3** τὸ τοῦ ποδὸς ἐ. = θέναρ, Cyr.'

**ἔλμινς**, add 'λίμινθες· ἔλμινθες Hsch.'

**ἕλος**, line 3, for '*Inscr.Cypr.* 135.9 H.' read 'Cypr. *e-le-i*, *ICS* 217.91' **2**, add 'glossed by σύμφυτος τόπος, ἢ χεῖλος ποταμοῦ, Hsch.; cf. ἔλη· σύνδενδροι τόποι id.' at end add 'cf. Myc. *e-re-e* (dat.), place-name'

***ἐλοτρεφής**, ές, gloss on ἐλεόθρεπτος, Hsch.

***Ἐλουσία**, title of Demeter, Ἐλουσία· Δημήτηρ παρὰ † Ἀλφουσίοις Hsch.; also Ἐλουία, Δαματ[ρὸ]ς ἱεροὶ Ἐλουίας *SEG* 30.1174 (Corinthian jug, iii/ii BC).

***ἐλπῐδηφόρος**, ον, *bringing hope*, Theognost.*Can.* 95; also as pers. n., *IG* 12(2).76.e7 (Mytilene), etc.

**ἐλπιδοκοπέω**, add '*PKöln* 166.13, *SB* 10525.3 (both vi/vii AD)'

**ἐλπίς**, line 1, before 'v. ἔλπω' insert 'ϝελπίδα *CEG* 10.9 (Athens, v BC)' and for '*hope, expectation*' read '*expectation* (whether of good or bad)' **I 1**, at end before 'S.*Ant.* 330' for 'beyond *hope*' read 'i.e. otherwise than I expected' **2**, for '*object of hope*' read '*basis of one's hopes* or *expectations*' **II**, delete the section, transferring quots. to section I 1.

**ἐλπωρή**, before 'ἡ' insert '(-α Alc. 119.11 L.-P.)'

***Ἐλυγεύς**, ὁ, epith. of Dionysus in Samos, Hsch. (post ἐλίγαινον; cj. Ἐλεγ-, Ἐλελ-, al.).

**ἔλῠμα**, read '**ἔλῡμα**, in obl. cases by metr. lengthening ἐλῡματ-'; for '*stock*' read '*share-beam*' and after 'Hsch.' insert '(cf. εἴλυμα)'

**ἐλύμνιαι**, add 'Myc. *e-ru-mi-ni-ja*'

**ἔλῠμος**, for 'ὁ' read 'ον' **I** and **II**, for these sections read '*curved*: αὐλοὶ ἔλυμοι pipes, also acc. to Ath. 4.176f called Phrygian, of which the left-hand one of the pair was crooked at the end, S.*fr.* 450, 644 R., Call.Com. 23 K.-A., Cratin.Jun. 3 K.-A., Poll. 4.74; cf. ἔλυμοι· τὰ πρῶτα τῶν αὐλῶν, ἀφ' ὧν ἡ γλωσσίς Hsch. **2** perh. a stringed instrument, Ath. 14.636f. **II** ἔλυμοι· .. καὶ ἡ τῆς κιθάρας καὶ τοῦ τόξου θήκη Hsch.'

**ἐλυτροειδής**, for 'Antyll.ap.Orib. 44.23.75' read 'Antyll.ap.Orib. 44.20.75'

**ἔλυτρον 2**, *shell* of crab, add 'ἀρτιφύτοισιν .. ἐλύτροις Opp.*H.* 1.303'

**(ϝ)ελχάνιος** (s.v. Ϝέλχανος), add 'cf. Cypr. pers. n. *wa-la-ka-ni-o*, perh. gen. Ϝαλχανίō *ICS* 299.4'

**ϝέλχανος**, after 'Crete' insert '*Inscr.Cret.* 1.xxiii 5 (Ϝευχ-, Phaestus)'

***ἔλψ**, ἐλπός, ἡ, = ἐλπίς, φίλōν ὄλεσεν ἔλπ' ἀγαθέν *CEG* 51 (Athens, *c.*510 BC).

**ἐλώριον**, pl., add 'Opp.*H.* 4.429'

**ἐμαυτοῦ**, line 7, for 'in pl. .. etc.' read 'pl. υἱῷ καὶ ἐμαυτοῖς *PASA* 2.278 (Armenia); (ἡμῶν αὐτῶν, etc. are normally used)'

***ἐμβαθμός**, ὁ, perh. *entrance*, ἐ. τοῦ .. κάστρου *PNess.* 24.3 (vi AD, pl.).

**ἔμβαθρα**, delete the entry.

***ἔμβαθρον**, τό, *right of entry*, *PAvrom.* 2B9 (i BC). **II** pl., ἔμβαθρα, τά, kind of shoes, Poll. 7.93.

**ἐμβαίνω I 5**, add '**c** *enter into possession*, εἰς κτήματα *IEphes.* 4.75, al. (iii BC); of the lessee of sacred land, w. acc., τὰν γᾶν *IG* 7.1739.5 (Thespiae): abs., ib. 9, al. **d** *enter* or *join* a society, *SEG* 31.122.39 (Attica, ii AD). **e** perh. *reach the age of*, ἐμβαίνοντες εἰς τὰ ιζ' ἔτη *IGLS* 607, cf. °ἐπαναβαίνω.' **II**, add 'in fut., of the ἀρχά that assigns sacred land to a lessee, *IG* 7.1739.10, *Mél.Navarre* p. 353 (both Thespiae)'

**ἐμβάλλω I 1**, add '**b** *put into* an already occupied tomb, Ramsay *Cities and Bishoprics* 1.233.80, *SEG* 6.219 (Phrygia), *TAM* 4(1).231.' **3**, line 5, after 'Pl.*R.* 344d' insert 'Men.*Dysc.* 352' **III 1**, after '*one's own*' insert 'ἐν δὲ κλήρους ἐβάλοντο Il. 23.352' **3**, for '*fall upon*' read '*throw in*, i.e. stuff oneself with' **4**, add '*SEG* 34.558.37 (Larissa, ii BC), *Peripl.M.Rubr.* 32'

***ἔμβᾱμα**, ατος, τό, *statue*, *IRhod.Peraia* 13.3 (iv/iii BC).

**ἔμβαμμα**, add '*Inscr.Dura* 198'

**ἐμβάπτω**, med., add 'X.*Cyr.* 2.2.5'

***ἐμβᾰρέω**, *to be reluctant, hesitate*, *BGU* 1816.9 (i BC).

**ἔμβᾰρος I**, delete the section.

***Ἔμβᾰρος**, ὁ, a proverbially cunning hero, οὐκ Ἔμβαρος εἶ, Men.*fr.* 368 K.-Th., cf. id.*Phasm.* 80 S., Paus.Gr.*fr.* 163, Suid. (Hsch. ἔμβαρος·

ἠλίθιος, μῶρος is due to abridgement of οὐκ Ἔ. εἶ· ἠλίθιος εἶ, cf. id. s.v. οὐκ ἔ. εἶ).

+**ἐμβᾰρύθω**, *to be heavy*, Nic.*Th.* 324; *to be oppressive*, ib. 468, 512, id.*Al.* 541 (v.l.).

***ἐμβᾰσίλευμα**, ατος, τό, *realm*, Μίλατος .. Φοίβου κλυτὸν ἐ. epigr. in *Didyma* 229 ii 9 (66 BC).

**ἔμβᾰσις I 5**, add '*lease of sacred land*, *IG* 7.1739.18; *rent* under such a lease, ib. 12, 13, *Mél.Navarre* p. 353' **II**, for this section read '*means of walking*, ὑπαί τις ἀρβύλας λύοι τάχος, πρόδουλον ἔμβασιν ποδός A.*Ag.* 945; in periph. for cows' legs, δίχηλον ἔμβασιν E.*Ba.* 740' **III**, add '**2** *tomb*, *BE* 1964.631 (cf. °ἐμβατός II b).' add '**IV** *pedestal*, Javolenus *Dig.* 32.100.3.'

**ἐμβᾰτεία**, add '*BCH* 22.402'

***ἐμβᾰτευτικός**, ον, *ius* ἐμβατευτικόν "the right *of setting foot on*", perh. the right of a *superficiarius* to use what is on the surface of another's land, Ulp.*Dig.* 27.9.3.4.

**ἐμβᾰτεύω I**, line 3, for 'E.*El.* 595' read 'E.*fr.* 696.3'; line 6, after 'S.*OT* 825' insert '*enter*, πόλιν E.*El.* 595' add '**V** glossed by ζητέω, Hsch. s.vv. ἐμβατεῦσαι, ἐμβατεύσας.'

+**ἐμβᾰτέω**, = ἐμβατεύω I, Nic.*Th.* 147 (v.l. -βροτ-), 804 (v.l. -βοτ-); med., w. acc., Lyc. 642. **II** prob. f.l. for °ἐμβοτέω.

***ἐμβατή**, v. ‡ἐμβατός.

+**ἐμβᾰτήρ**, ῆρος, ὁ, perh. *footway*, *terrace*, prob. in *IG* 4.481.2 (Nemea), *Ath.Agora* XIX L4b.15 (iii BC), cf. Hsch.'

**ἐμβᾰτήριος I**, add 'ἐ. αὐλούς Poll. 4.82'

**ἐμβάτης**, add '**III** perh. *ditch* or *fosse*, (cf. ἐμβατή) τοῦ τύχου (= τοίχου) τούτου σὺν ὅλου τοῦ πέλματος καὶ τοῦ ἐμβάτου ἐπὶ .. *SEG* 37.727 (Samos, Byz.).'

**ἐμβᾰτός I**, after '*accessible*' insert '*APl.* 95 (Damag.)' **II**, fem. subst., add '**b** *tomb*, *AD* 21(1966).335.'

***ἐμβᾰφεία**, ἡ, *dipping in*, Moses Alch. 313.24.

***ἐμβᾰφής**, ές, *dipped in*, Moses Alch. 309.9.

**ἐμβάφιον**, after 'Hdt. 2.62' insert '*SB* 9158.6 (v AD), *CPR* 8.66.9 (vi AD)'

+**ἐμβῐβαστέον**, *one must cause to enter*, Herod.Med.ap.Orib. 10.38.3, *Gp.* 14.7.18.

**ἐμβῐόω**, line 2, after 'Philostr.*Her.* 2.3' insert 'ἐνδεδιωκότα (= ἐμβεβιωκότα) *Schwyzer* 62.120 (in sense II, Heraclea, iv BC)'

**ἐμβλέπω**, line 3, after 'cf. D. 19.69' insert 'ἐ. ἀγάλματι Men.*Dysc.* 677, παρθένῳ ib. 682'

**ἔμβλημα 2**, add 'written **ἔμβληθμα** (s.v.l.) in *IG* 11(2).287*B*134 (Delos, iii BC). **b** fig., ἔμβλημα σωφροσύνης epigr. in *SEG* 36.399 (Dyme, *c*.100 BC).'

***ἔμβλητος**, ον, *used as inlay*, *inlaid*, πίνακας ἐμβλήτους γραφὰς ἔχοντας *Inscr.Délos* 1403*Bb*ii18, 1417*A*ii36 (ii BC).

+**ἐμβολάδιον**, τό, *little portico*, *JHS* 18.308 (Mopsuestia, v. *ICilicie* p. 129).

***ἐμβολάρχης**, ου, ὁ, *official in charge of loading of ships*, (ἐμβολή I 3), *POxy.* 3612.4 (iii AD), *CPR* 7.26.11 (vi AD).

***ἐμβολαρχία**, ἡ, *control of the loading of ships* (ἐμβολή I 3), *PMerton* 90.11, 22 (iii/iv AD).

***ἐμβολάτωρ**, ορος, ὁ, *collector of dues*, *POxy.* 126.15, *PMasp.* 54 i 7 (both vi AD), etc.

***ἐμβολευτικόν**, τό, wd. of uncertain reading and sense, *PTeb.* 847.17 (ii BC).

**ἐμβολεύω**, add '**2** perh. colloq., *appropriate*, τῆς πράσεως τὴν τιμὴν ἐνεβόλευσε *POxy.* 2342.9 (ii AD).'

**ἐμβολή I 3**, after '*POxy.* 62.11 (iii AD)' insert '*Peripl.M.Rubr.* 32' **II 2**, after 'E.*HF* 869' insert 'ταῦρος λέοντος ὡς βλέπων πρὸς ἐμβολήν id.*fr.* 689.4' **4**, line 3, after 'ἐσβάλλει' insert 'ἡ τῶν ὑδάτων εἰς τὰ πεδία ἐμβολή *PHels.* 6.4 (ii BC)'

**ἐμβόλιμος 1**, add 'Ξανδικοῦ ἐμβολίμου ιγʹ *SEG* 31.1046 (Sardis, before 9 BC)'

**ἐμβόλιον IV**, add '*Inscr.Délos* 372*B*30 (200 BC)'

***Ἐμβολῖται**, οἱ, a guild at Ephesus centred on the Ἔμβολος (v. °ἔμβολος 8), *IEphes.* 3059.11.

**ἔμβολος 3 a**, before 'Pi.*P.* 4.191' insert 'Hippon. 28.3 W.' **4**, for '*wedge-shaped order of battle*' read 'military or naval formation in the form of ram' **8**, line 1, after '*portico*' insert 'or *colonnaded street*'; line 2, delete '*Ephes.* 3 No. 8'; add 'spec., a street in Ephesus, *IEphes.* 3008.12, al.'

**ἐμβόσκομαι**, add 'also act., *MDAI(A)* 68.5 (Samos, i AD), *IStraton.* 513.55 (iii AD)'

***ἐμβοτέω**, *pasture* animals in a place, *AP* 7.657 (Leon.Tarent., cj.).

**ἔμβρεφος**, for '*boy-like*' read '*having a child in the womb*, in quots., of women who died in pregnancy' and add 'epigr. in *LW* 116 (Teos)'

***ἐμβρῑμέω**, *to be indignant*, w. dat., Stilpon in *Lex.Patm.* in *BCH* 1.151 (*Rh.Mus.* 32.477).

**ἐμβρῡκω**, add 'ὅτʼ ἐμβρύξῃσιν (v.l. ὅταν βρύξῃσιν) Nic.*Th.* 271'

***ἐμβρύμιον**, τό, *papyrus mat* or *cushion*, *PFouad I Univ.* 26.5 (pl., i AD), *PPetaus* 33.7 (AD 184/7), *PCol.* 240 (iv/v AD).

+**ἐμβύθιος**, ον (fem. -η *AP* 9.227 (Bianor), cj. in 423 (id.)), *existing* or *situated at the bottom of the sea*, ἐ. θαλάμας Isid.Char. 20, πέτρα *AP* 7.504 (Leon.Tarent.). **2** of water, *deep*, κρηνῖδες D.H. 1.32, 6.13.

***ἔμβυσμα**, ατος, τό, perh. *stopper*, *plug*, *PIand.* 144ᵃ2 (pl., ἐνβ-; iii AD); cj. in *CGFP* 289.4.

***ἐμέτερος**, α, ον, = ἡμέτερος, *POxy.Hels.* 49.12 (iii AD).

**ἐμετήριος**, add 'Gal. 11.173.1'

**ἐμετοποιέομαι**, add 'act., dub. in *IG* 14.2577.13 (Xanten)'

**ἐμμᾰνής**, line 5, for '-έστερος' read '-έστερον' and transfer 'Comp. .. Luc.*Am.* 14' to last line after 'Eun.*VS* p. 455 B.'

***ἐμμέλεια** (B), ἡ, *authority* of a local official, *CPR* 5.12.5 (AD 351).

**ἐμμελής II 3 b**, after '*suitable*' insert 'A.*fr.* 78c ii 22 R. (sup.)' **III 3**, add 'σὲ γάρ φη Ταργήλιος ἐμμελέως δισκεῖν Anacr. 19 P.'

**ἐμμενής**, adv. -νέως, add 'epigr. in *IStraton.* 543.8'

**ἐμμενύτρωτος**, add '(ἐμμεσότροπος La.)'

**ἐμμένω**, line 1, fut., insert '-μενίω *SEG* 33.638 (Crete, late ii BC)' and after 'Th. 1.5' insert '3 sg. aor. opt. ἐμ[μ]έναι *SEG* 36.548.8 (Matropolis, iii BC)'

***ἐμμεσότροπος**, v. °ἐμμενύτρωτος.

***ἐμμετροποιός**, όν, *composing in regular metres*, Phld.*Po.* in *Eos* 29.19 (ἐνμ-).

**ἔμμηνος II**, add '**4** of an official, *serving for a month*, *SEG* 33.1039.77 (Aeolian Cyme, ii BC).'

***ἔμμομφος**, Arc. (?)ἴνμομφος, v. ‡μόμφος.

**ἔμμονος I**, add 'of dyes, *fast*, Hsch. s.v. δευσοποιόν'

***ἐμόρμησεν**· ἐπενόησεν Hsch.; cf. μερμαίρω.

***ἐμμόχλιον**, τό, *socket for a bar*, K. Kourouniotes Ἐλευσινιακά i.190 (Eleusis), Poll. 10.23.

**ἐμός II 2**, add 'of lovers, Μυΐσκος ἐμὸς ἡδύς graffito in *BCH* 106.12 no. 57 (Thasos, iv BC)' **II 3**, delete '*PEdgar* 4.6 (iii BC)' and insert '*BGU* 37.3 (i AD)'; add 'ἐξ ἐμοῦ *from my funds*, Mitchell *N.Galatia* 240'

**ἐμπᾰγή**, for '*suretyship*' read '*trap*'

**ἐμπάθεια II**, after 'Ptol.*Tetr.* 92' insert '(v.l.)'

**ἔμπαιγμα**, for '*jest, mocking, delusion*' read '*raillery, mocking*'

**ἐμπαίζω I 1**, add 'w. εἰς, ἐμπαῖξαι εἰς οἱανδήποτε ἐκκλησιαστικὴν κατάστασιν Just.*Nov.* 123.44'

+**ἔμπαις**, παιδος, ἡ, *with child*, ἡ παῖς γὰρ ἔμπαις ἐστίν Cratin. 318 K.-A., ἔμπαις· ἐγκύμων Hsch. **2** *having children*, Muson.*fr.* 15A (p. 78 H.).

**ἔμπαισμα**, before 'Eust.' insert '*Inscr.Délos* 1412*a*7 (ii BC)'

**ἐμπαίω II**, add 'εἴ τε ῥᾴθυμός τις ἐμπέπαικεν Plu. 2.52c' add '**2** *fall into*, εἰς ἄρκυν Lyc. 105 (v.l.).'

**ἔμπᾰλιν I a**, add 'ἡ ἐ. θύρα door *leading out again*, Luc.*Merc.Cond.* 42'

**ἔμπᾰμα**, delete the entry (v. °ἄπαμα).

**ἐμπαρέχω**, line 4, for '*give* oneself *up* as his tool ' read '*hand* oneself *over* into his power'

**ἐμπαρίσταμαι**, delete the entry (v. °ἐμπαρίστημι).

***ἐμπαρίστημι**, pf. part. act. intr., *stand by*, Hld. 7.19.1 (v.l.).

**ἔμπᾱς** (A), line 4, for 'Call.*Ep.* 14' read 'Call.*Epigr.* 12, *fr.* 726 Pf.'

**ἔμπᾱσις**, Boeot., add 'also ἔνπασις *SEG* 32.476 (Onchestus, iv BC)'

***ἐμπασμός**, ὁ, *strewing*, *SEG* 33.1056 (Cyzicus, ii AD).

**ἐμπαστήρας**, after lemma insert '(**ἐμπιστ-** La.)'

**ἔμπατον**, add '(ἔμπαστον· κατανθιζόμενον La.)'

**ἐμπέδιος**, add '**2** = ἔμπεδος 2, *constant, unfailing*, *LW* 1522 *bis* (Cyme) (s.v.l., cf. *IKyme* 4).'

***ἐμπεδόμητις**, ιδος, ὁ, ἡ, *of steadfast counsel*, *IG* $2^2$.12318.7 (verse, iii BC).

+**ἐμπελάδην**, ἔμπλην· ἐμπελάδην, συνεγγύς Apollon.*Lex.*; app. in temporal sense, *just*, Nic.*Al.* 215.

**ἐμπελᾶνα**, add 'cf. perh. εὐχὰν ἐμπελάνω̄ν, rest. in Dubois *IGDS* 54 (Selinus, vi/v BC)'

**ἐμπελάω**, delete '*IG* 14.271 (Selinus)'

***ἐμπεπείρακται**· ἐμπεπόδισται Hsch. (cj. ἐμπεπέδηται La.).

**ἐμπέρᾰμος**, add 'Spartan pers. n. (vii BC), Paus. 4.20.5'

***ἐμπεριπλέκω**, *enfold*, Alcm. 13(b).10 P. (dub.).

**ἐμπερονάω I**, med., add 'οἶμαί σε τὸν ἐπʼ ἀριστέρʼ ἐμπερονώμενον Men.*fr.* 691 K.-Th.'

**ἐμπήγνῡμι I**, line 5, after '(Ar.) *V.* 437' insert 'στήλαις .. ἐνπηγνυμέναις ἐκεῖ *SEG* 34.1243 (Mysia, v AD)'

**ἐμπήκτης**, for pres. def. read '*one who inserts the* πινάκια *of potential jurors*, etc., *into the slots of the* κληρωτήριον'

**ἐμπηνός**, add '(ἐμπηγός La.)'

**ἐμπήσσομαι**, add 'Aët. 7.21 (269.22 O.)'

**ἐμπῖλια**, for '*bandage* .. νακτά' read 'νακτά· τοὺς πίλους. καὶ τὰ ἐμπίλια Hsch.'

+**ἐμπῑπίσκω**, aor. ἐνέπῑσα, Pi.*fr.* 111.1 S.-M.: *give to drink*, Nic.*Al.* 519; transf., Pi.l.c.; med., *soak in* ὕδατι, ὄξει, Nic.*Th.* 573, *Al.* 320; pass., *to be administered in*, νύμφαις (sc. water) ἐμπισθέν id.*Th.* 624.

**ἐμπιπράσκω**, delete 'Hsch. (Pass.)'

**ἐμπίπτω 1 b**, add 'of adjoining houses, *ICilicie* 124 (i/ii AD)' **3**, add '**c** of things, *come one's way*, ἀντιφορτίζονται τὰ ἐμπεσόντα *Peripl.M.Rubr.* 14.' **10**, for '*desert*' read '*go over to*'

**ἐμπίσιον**, add '(ἐμπίσειον La.)'

***ἐμπίστευτος**, ὁ, *trustee*, Vett.Val. 379.17 P.

**ἐμπιστεύω**, add '**III** pass., w. inf., *to be assured*, ἐνπιστευθεὶς ὑπὸ τούτου ἔχειν *POxy.* 2347.4/5 (iv AD).'

***ἐμπιστῆρας**, v. ‡ἐμπαστῆρας.

**ἐμπλἄνάομαι**, line 2, after '-πλανωμένη' insert 'ἑαυτῇ'

**ἐμπλάσσω I 5 a**, after '(Gal.) 15.204' insert 'Nic.*Al.* 79'

**ἔμπλαστρον**, add 'in Latin transcription *emplastrum*, Cato *Agr.* 39.2, etc.'

***ἐμπλείω**, *fill up*, Nic.*Al.* 613.

***ἔμπληγος**, ον, = ἐμπληγής, *An.Bachm.* 1.43.30.

**⁺ἐμπλήδην**, adv., *together with*, w. dat., Nic.*Al.* 129.

**ἐμπλήθομαι**, add 'act. intr., Q.S. 13.22 (cj.)'

**ἐμπλόκιον 1**, delete the section. **2**, add 'Macho 257 G.'

**ἔμπλουμος**, add '*PVindob.* G25737 (*ZPE* 64.77, vi/vii AD)'

***ἐμπνευμἄτώδης**, ες, *flatulent*, Androm.Min.ap.Gal. 13.982.8.

**ἐμπνευμάτωσις 2**, add 'Heras ap.Gal. 14.203.4'

**ἔμπνευσις**, for '*on-breathing*' read '*the action of breathing on*'

**ἐμπνέω II 2**, add 'ἐπιθυμίαν Jos.*Jer.* 28(51).11c'

**ἔμπνοος I**, add '**2** of blood, *aerated*, opp. θολερός, Philostr.*Gym.* 30.'

**ἐμποδίζω**, line 2, after '*Gp.* 2.49.1' insert 'pf. inf. ἐνπεποδικέναι *IEphes.* 4101.19 (ii AD)'

**ἐμπόδισμα**, for 'D. 3.4' read 'D. 3.7'

**ἐμποδοστἄτέω**, delete 'also **ἐμποδιοστατέω**'

**ἐμποιέω III**, at end after 'etc.' insert '(in pass. aor. *PAvrom.* 2*B*13)'

**ἐμποίησις II**, for this section read '*installation*, κλαι[κός] *SEG* 25.383.193 (Epid., iv BC)' and renumber present section II as III; after '*claim to*' insert '*PMich.*III 121ʳ ii 9.5 (i AD)'

**ἐμπολάω I 2**, line 2, after '(S.)*Ant.* 1037' insert 'νυνὶ δὲ πεντήκοντα δραχμῶν ἐμπολῶ i.e. *sell* for .. , Ar.*Pax* 1201' deleting this ref. in section II 1.

**ἐμπολέμιος 1**, add 'τὰ ἐ. *war-material*, prob. for τὰ ἐν πολεμίᾳ in Afric.*Cest.* 32 V.'

**ἐμπόλημα I**, add 'ἡ Μιλησία σμάραγδος, ἐ. τιμηέστατον *Trag.adesp.* 109 K.-S.'

**ἐμπόλιον**, after lemma insert '= ἐμβόλιον'; for '*casing for dowel*' read '*dowel*' and add '*Inscr.Délos* 104-4.6 (iv BC)'

**ἐμπομπεύω**, after '*walk in procession*' insert 'Sopat.Rh. 8.178.19 W.'

**ἐμπονέω I**, for this section read '*work on*, ἀργὸς δὲ ἡ γῆ χηρεύουσα τῶν ἐμπονούντων Alciphr. 3.25.1; w. acc., ἢ ἐνπονεῖν ἢ ἀγοράζειν ἢ κατέχειν δημοσίαν γῆν *SEG* 30.568 (Maced., ii AD)'

**ἔμπονος I**, delete 'Ezek.*Exag.* 208'

***ἐμπορητικός**, ή, όν, = ἐμπορικός, Isid.*Etym.* 6.10.5.

**ἐμπορία I 1**, at end delete 'cf. D. 56.8' **II**, line 2, after 'X.*Vect.* 3.2' insert 'D. 56.8 (pl.)'

***ἐμποριακός**, ή, όν, prob. f.l. for -ίαρχος (= ‡-ιάρχης), in *SIG* 880.28 (Maced., ii/iii AD).

***ἐμποριαρχέω**, *act as* ἐμποριάρχης, *SEG* 34.1107 (Ephesus).

**ἐμποριάρχης**, for '*supervisor of trade*' read '*headman of an* ἐμπόριον I 1 b' and add '*INikaia* 1071.11 (ii AD)'

***ἐμποριδονήτας** (ἐμποριοδ- La.)· ἐνοικίου πρακτῆρας Hsch.

**ἐμπόριον I 1 a**, add '*ISmyrna* 713'

**ἔμπρακτος**, line 6, after '(D.S. 13.)70' insert 'w. gen., ἐ. παιδείας *educated*, *Vit.Aesop.*(G) 81'

***ἐμπράσσω**, perh. *bring about*, *effect*, ἀπὸ .. αὐτε̄̃ς (sc. Ἄτροπος) ἐνπραχθέσεται [ἐν τῶι βίωι κα]λά *Kafizin* 219 (iii BC).

**ἐμπρέπω**, line 2 for 'cod. Med.' read 'codd.'

***ἐμπροθεσμί**, adv., perh. *punctually*, *PCol.* 176.8 (-εί, AD 325).

***ἐμπρολείπω**, *leave behind*, *predecease*, *Bithynische St.* III 16.7 (iii AD).

**ἔμπροσθεν**, line 4, after 'E.*Hipp.* 1228' insert 'Arcad. ἴνπροσθε *SEG* 25.447.17 (Aliphera, iii BC)' **II**, as prep., **1**, add 'Lxx *Ge.* 24.7, 16, etc.'

**ἐμπύλαι**, delete 'cf. τιτύπαι' and add '(ἐμπύλαιαι (sc. κρῆναι)· νυμφαῖα La.)'

**ἐμπῦρίζω**, after 'ἐμπυρεύω' insert '*PCair.Zen.* 387.3 (iii BC)'

**ἐμπῦρισμός**, add 'used to render Hebr. wd. meaning some sort of blight of cereal crops, Lxx 3*Ki.* 8.37'

**ἐμπῦριστής**, add 'ἐ. ἄγγελον Lxx 4*Ma.* 7.11'

**ἐμπῦρίφοιτος**, for '*dwelling*' read '*going about*' and for 'Orph.*H.* 1.33' read 'Orph.*Εὐχή* 33'

**ἔμπῦρος I**, add '*made with the aid of fire*, Pl.*Plt.* 287e' **III 2**, line 4, delete 'hence .. S.*El.* 405'; last line, delete 'dub. sens. in *PCair.Zen.* 14.17' add '**b** vessel for burning incense, or sim., S.*El.* 405, *PCair.Zen.* 14.17, *IG* 2².1534.94, *SEG* 29.1205 (Sardis, iv AD).'

**ἐμπῦρόω**, add '*SEG* 37.1003.8 (Sardis, iii/ii BC)'

***ἐμπῦρωδής**, ές, *marked by inflammation*, τῶν ἐμπυρωδῶν ἑλκώσεων ἢ νομῶν Heph.Astr. 2.13.19.

**⁺ἐμύς** or **ἐμύς**, ὕδος, ἡ, (also ὁ Arist.*HA* 600ᵇ22, s.v.l.), *marine* or *fresh water chelonian*, *turtle*, Arist.*HA* 558ᵃ8, al., Thphr.*fr.* 171.1 (codd. μῦς).

**ἐμφαίνω I 2**, after '*display*' insert 'λόγον Emp. 3.4 D.-K., ἐρατὸν δέμας id. 62.7' **4**, add '*IG* 5(2).6.24 (ἰνφ-, Tegea); (pass.), *SEG* 37.340.22 (Mantinea, iv BC)'

***ἐμφάλσωμα**, v. °ἐμφάρσωμα.

**ἐμφᾰνής II 3**, add 'sup. θεῶν ἐνφανέστατον, of Antoninus Pius, *AS* 7.147 (Derbe, AD 157), *IGRom.* 3.704 III B.16' **b**, line 3, after 'cf.' insert 'ἐμπανία (masc. acc. sg.) δειξάτω *Inscr.Cret.* 4.47.32 (v BC)' add '**d** of documents, (*made*) *public* or *official*, τῶν .. δημοσίων ἀποδείξεων ἐμφανῶν ἐν ὑπομνήμασι γινομένων Just.*Nov.* 46.1.'

**ἐμφᾰνίζω**, line 2, after '*PSI* 4.400.2 (iii BC)' insert 'Thess. ἐνεφανίσσοεν (= ἐνεφάνιζον, 3 pl.) *Schwyzer* 590.12 (Larissa, iii BC)'

**ἐμφᾰνισις 3**, for this section read '*entering* of documents *into official records*, Just.*Nov.* 15.3 pr.'

**ἐμφᾰνισμός**, add 'dub. sens., *AAWW* 1962.5.33 (Lycia, i AD)'

***ἐμφανόω**, = ἐμφανίζω, *enter* private documents in public records, ἐν ὑπομνήμασιν ἐμφανωθῆναι *Cod.Just.* 4.21.22.7, Just.*Nov.* 134.3.

**ἐμφαντάζομαι I 1**, before 'M.Ant.' insert 'Alcin.*Intr.* p. 164.13 H.'

***ἐμφάρσωμα**, ατος, τό, perh. *inset woodwork*, *Didyma* 254.4 (ii AD; pl., ἐνφ-); also ἐμφάλσωμα *ABSA* 51.154.

**ἔμφᾰσις I 1**, line 3, (κατ' ἔμφασιν), after 'id.*Mu.* 395ᵃ29' insert '*obliquely*, Sopat.Rh. 8.229.13 W., al.' **2**, after 'Arist.*Div.Somn.* 464ᵇ12' insert 'Men.*fr.* 722.2 K.-Th.' and add '*true sense-impression*, opp. ἀπέμφασις, Carn.ap.S.E.*M.* 7.169'

**ἐμφέρω III 1**, for 'τὰ ἐμφερόμενα .. *matters*' read 'τῶν ἐμφερομένων τοῖς πράγμασι μορίων καὶ τόπων'

***ἐμφθείρω**, *cause to perish in*, ἐμφθορέων· ἐμφθειρομένων Sch.Nic.*Al.* 176d Ge.

***ἐμφιέζω**, or **-άζω**, *clothe*, perh. coined (like ἀμφιάζω) as back-formation from ἠμφίεσμαι, etc. (ἀμφιέννυμι); pf. part. ἀγάλματα .. ἐμπεφιεσμένα *ISmyrna* 753.22 (i AD); κλεῖν .. ἐμπεφιασμένην ib. 25.

**ἐμφιλόσοφος**, add 'ἡ ἐμφιλόσοφος ἐπιστήμη Sch.Iamb.*Protr.* 5; adv. **-φως** Sch.Luc.*Pisc.* 26, Sch.Aristid. p. 482 D.'

**ἐμφιλοχώρως**, for 'Ptol.*Harm.* 3.11' read 'Ptol.*Harm.* 2.11'

**ἐμφοβέω**, add 'οὐκ ἐμφοβήσῃ *you will* not *be terrified*, Favorin.*Exil.* 25.29'

**ἔμφοβος II**, adv. **-βως**, add '*SEG* 26.1717 (Antinoupolis, iii/iv AD)'

***ἐμφορά**, ἡ, Cypr. *i-po-ra-se*, ἰ(μ)φορᾶς *ICS* 318 (Salamis, *c.*600 BC), *special contribution*, *SEG* 32.456.26 (Boeotia, iii BC), ib. 23.398 (Thestia, ii BC).

**ἐμφόρβιος II**, for this section read 'ἐμφόρβιον, τό, *pasture-tax*, *AJP* 56.375 (pl., Colophon, iv BC), Hsch.'

**⁺ἐμφορβισμός**, ὁ, Arc. **ἰνφ-**, *imposition of pasture-tax*, *IG* 5(2).3.2 (Tegea, iv BC).

**⁺ἐμφορβίω**, Arc. **ἰνφ-**, *impose pasture-tax*, *IG* 5(2).3.3, al. (Tegea, iv BC).

**ἔμφορος I**, add '**2** *paying rent*, *PCair.Zen.* 310.3, 328.133 (iii BC).' add '**III** *full of*, *EM* 677.30.'

***ἐμφράγνῦμι**, = ἐμφράσσω, Ael.*NA* 4.15 (pass.).

***ἐμφρόνιμος**, ον, = ἔμφρων, prob. in *OGI* 383.106 (Commagene, i BC).

**ἔμφρων II 2**, delete 'Thgn. 1126'; line 4, after '*Hipparch.* 226c' insert 'θεὸς ἔμφρων (app. = Σωφροσύνη) epigr. in *INikaia* 752' add '**3** *mindful*, w. gen., v.l. in Thgn. 1126.'

**ἔμφῦλος I 1**, line 4, after '*kinsman*' insert 'Hes.*fr.* 190.2 M.-W. (prob.)'; line 7, after '(Hierapytna)' insert 'transf., πέτρῃσι βαθείαις ἐ. *at home in*, Opp.*H.* 1.249'

***ἐμφύνω**, *arise*, or *grow in*, Aret. p. 22.7, 28.17, 29 H., al; cf. ἐμφύω II 1 (intr.).

**ἐμφῡσιόω**, after lemma insert 'ἐνιφ- *GLP* 123.42'

**ἐμφῠτεία**, for 'Thphr.*HP* 1.6.1, 2.1.4, al.' read 'Thphr.*HP* 2.1.4, *CP* 1.6.1: sg., ib. 1.6.5, 5.6.10'

**ἐμφῠτευσις**, for '*tenure of such a holding*' read '*tenure with right to plant*' add '**2** *planting in* a place, *SEG* 24.614.11 (Maced., ii AD).'

**ἐμφῠτευτής**, add 'ἀναγνώστης καὶ ἐμφυτευτὴς τῆς κτήσεος *Inscr. Olymp.* 656 (v/vi AD)'

**ἐμφῠτευτικός**, add '*si ius* ἐμφυτευτικὸν *vel* ἐμβατευτικὸν *habeat pupillus*, Ulp.*Dig.* 27.9.3.4 (perh. because of early date not connected w. ἐμφύτευσις 1, q.v., but some provincial institution)'

**ἐμφῠτεύω**, line 1, for '*implant*' read '*plant* in a place, ἀμπέλους D.Chr. 7.27; *SEG* 24.614.17 (Maced., ii AD)' **II**, for this section read '*grant* ἐμφύτευσις *on* land, *PMasp.* 298.39 (vi AD), Just.*Nov.* 7.3.3, *Cod.Just.* 1.2.24.5, Theophil.Antec. 3.24; med., *hold* land *on such tenure*, *Cod.Just.*, Theophil.Antec. ll.cc.'

**ἐμψάω**, for 'Call.*Fr.* 121' read 'Call.*fr.* 7.13 Pf.'

***ἔμψογος**, ον, prob. = ἐπίψογος I, *PTeb.* 276.1 (ii/iii AD).

***ἐμψυκτέον**, *one must cool*, Gal. 2.127.14.

***ἐμψῡχοποιέω**, *endow with life*, Heph.Astr. 3.7.13.

**ἔμψῡχος 2**, add 'Alcid.*Soph.fr.* 15(28) R.'

**ἐμψῡχόω**, after '*AP* 9.774 (Glauc.)' insert '*enliven*, Sopat.Rh. 8.58.28 W.'

**ἔμψυχρος**, before 'Thphr.' insert 'cj. in'

**ἐν**, line 3, for '*Inscr.Cypr.* 135.9 H., al.' read '*ICS* 217.9, 27' and add 'also sts. in Crete, *Inscr.Cret.* 2.xii 16 Ab 2, 3 (Eleutherna, vi BC), 2.v 1.5 (Axos, vi/v BC)' **A I 1 a**, delete 'ἐν αὐτῷ εἶναι' to end of section and add 'w. place-name indicating place of residence, Νικοβούλη ἐν Ἐφέσῶι καλή *SEG* 31.763(a) (Thasos, iii BC), al.; also w. gen., ἐν κώμης Φεβίχεως μεγάλης *CPR* 5.15.3, *PVindob.Sijp.* 7.2, *Stud.Pal.* 20.127.6 (all v AD)' **2**, line 9, for 'ἐν αὐτοῦ .. Ar.*V.* 642' read 'in fig. phr., ἐν αὐτοῦ εἶναι *to be in control of oneself*, ἐν σαυτοῦ (v.l. σαυτῷ, cf. sense I 6) γενοῦ S.*Ph.* 950' **5 a**, at end for 'v. ὁ' read 'v. ὁ A VIII 6' **6**, line 8, after 'E.*Alc.* 278' insert 'ἐν τῷδε κἀχόμεσθα σωθῆναι λόγῳ; id.*Heracl.* 498 (v. °ἔχω C v)'; add 'ἐν ἑαυτῷ *in control of oneself*, Hp.*Morb.* 1.30, X.*An.* 1.5.17' **11**, line 2, after 'Th. 1.9' insert 'ἐν Διομήδεος ἀριστείῃ Hdt. 2.116' **II 3**, w. subst., (ll. 6 ff.) add 'ἰ(ν) τύχαι *i-tu-ka-i Kafizin* 169(a).1' **IV 1 b**, add '*IG* $9^2$(1).748 iii 49 (Myanian treaty at Delphi, *c.*190 BC)' **B**, w. acc., add 'Pi.*P.* 2.11, 5.38, *N.* 7.31, etc., Corinna *fr.* 1 col. i.21 P.; in Boeot., Thess., NWGk. inscr., *IG* $9^2$(1).748 iii (Delphi), 31.572 (Krannon, ii BC), *IG* 9(2).1226.21 (Larissa), etc.; Cypr. *i-ta-ti-o-ne* ἰ(ν) τὰ(ν) θιόν *ICS* 217.27' **C 3**, before 'S.*Aj.*' insert 'Pi.*fr.* 70b.10, 11, 15 S.-M.' at end add 'Myc. only in compds., e.g. *e-ne-e-si* (v. ‡ἔνειμι)'

*__ἐνᾱβύσσαιος__, v.l. for °ἀβύσσαιος.

**ἐνᾰγής II**, add '*involving such a curse*, θεοῖς δ' ἐναγέα τέλεα πελομένων καλῶς ἐπίδρομ' A.*Supp.* 123'

**ἐνᾰγισμός II**, add 'also sg., *SEG* 23.207.13 (Messene, Augustus)'

+**ἐναγκῠλίζω**, med. = ἐναγκυλάω, Poll. 1.136; pass., *to be fitted into a loop*, Plb. 27.11.5.

**ἐναγλαΐζομαι**, add 'act., *set gloriously in*, τὸν νέον εὐσεβέων χώρῳ ἐναγλάϊσον *GVI* 1154 (Samos, ii/i BC)'

**ἔναγχος**, add 'Pl.*Chrm.* 155b, *Tht.* 147c, D. 11.5, 13.32, etc.'

**ἐνᾰγώνιος**, add '**IV** *alarmed, distressed*, Arg.Ar.*Pax* 1.7.'

**ἐνᾰείρομαι**, add '(v.l. ἀν-)'

**ἐνᾱέριος**, before '*in the air*' insert '*inhabiting* or *situated*' and add 'M.Ant. 12.24'

**ἐναιθέριος**, after '*in upper air*' insert 'Arat. 532'

**ἐναίθομαι**, add '*BSAA* 8.60 (Gizeh)'

*__ἐναιμής__, ές, *covered with blood*, Ἄρηος .. ἐναιμέος orac. in Robert *DAMM* 92 (Sydra, i BC, hex.).

*__ἐναίμιος__, ον, = ἔναιμος, *Trag.adesp.* 627 K.-S.

**ἔναιμος I 1**, line 2, after 'Hdt. 3.29' insert 'A.*fr.* 451m.33 R.'

**ἐναίρω**, line 1, after 'ἤνᾰρον' insert 'Ibyc. 1(*a*).2 P.'

**ἐναίσιος I**, before 'D.C. 38.13' insert 'Pl.*Lg.* 747d' **II**, for '= foreg. II 1' read '*favourable*'

**ἐνᾰ́κις**, for '**ἐννεάκις** is' read '**ἐννεάκις** *Lindos* 421*a*5 (i AD)'

*__ἐνᾰκισμῡ́ριοι__, αι, α, *ninety thousand*, App.*Hann.* 4.

*__ἐνᾰκόλουθος__, ον, *accordant, in conformity with*, Simp. *in de An.* 250.16.

**ἐνᾰκόσιοι**, add '**ἠνακάτιοι** *SEG* 9.2.59 (Cyrene, iv BC)'

**ἐνᾰκοσιοστός**, delete the entry.

**ἐνᾰ́λειπτος**, for '*anointed with*' read '*applied as ointment*'; add 'form *ἐνάλιπτος, Myc. *e-na-ri-po-to*, of a chariot frame, prob. *painted*'

*__ἐναλθής__, ές, *undergoing medical treatment*, Nic.*Al.* 586 (v.l. ἀν-).

*__ἐνᾰλῑναιέτης__, v. °ἁλιναιέτας.

+**ἐνᾰλίνω**, Cypr. pf. part. pass. *i-na-la-li-si-me-na* ἰναλαλισμένα *write on, inscribe*, *ICS* 217.26.

**ἐνᾰ́λιος**, line 7, after '(lyr.)' insert 'Ζεῦ ἐ. prob. in A.*fr.* 46a.10 R.'; at end, prose exx., add 'Gal. 10.128.18, 131.3, 15.754.3'

**ἐναλλαγή II**, after 'Lyd.*Mag.* 2.16' add '*Cod.Just.* 6.4.4.23'

**ἐναλλοίωσις**, after '*alteration*' insert '*PSI* 483.3 (iii BC)'

**ἐνάλλομαι 2**, add 'fig., ὑμῖν ῥήμασιν Lxx *Jb.* 16.5'

*__ἔναλλος__, ον, *contrary, other*, v.l. in Theoc. 1.134 (v. ἄναλλος), *AP* 5.299 (Agath.); adv. -λως Plu. 2.1045e.

**ἐνᾰ́μαρτος**, after '*faulty*' insert 'Cyran. 5 (prolog. 81 K.), *Gloss.*'

**ἐνᾰμείβω**, add '**2** intr., *alternate*, prob. in Pi.*N.* 11.42.'

**ἐνᾰμοιβᾰδίς**, add '(codd., edd. ἐπ-)'

**ἐναναστρέφομαι**, for 'Stob. 3.1.49' read 'Stob. 4.1.49'

*__ἐνανατέλλω__, *rise in*, ἐναντέλλουσα Nonn.*D.* 28.231 (s.v.l.).

**ἐνανθρωπέω**, add '*Aegyptus* 55.60 (version of Creed, cf. *homo factus est*), cf. *Cod.Just.* 1.1.5.1'

*__ἐνανθρώπησις__, εως, ἡ, *incarnation*, *TAM* 4(1).372, *Cod.Just.* 1.1.5.3.

**ἐναντῐ́βιος**, adv., add 'Od. 14.270, 17.439'

**ἐναντῐοβουλία**, for '*contrary purpose*' read '*the fact of intending the opposite of what one says*'

**ἐναντῐόβουλος**, for '*of contrary purpose*' read '*intending the opposite of what one says*'

**ἐναντῐολογέω**, before 'abs.' insert 'Epicur. [31.9]7 A.'

*__ἐναντῐολόγος__, ὁ, *person who maintains the contrary*, Simp. *in Ph.* 131.31.

**ἐναπερείδω II 2**, delete 'Pass., *to be so fixed* .. ib. 23'

**ἐναπόγρᾰφος**, add 'γεωργὸς ἐ. *POxy.* 2479.7 (vi AD)'

*__ἐναποθέρομαι__· ἐνδέχομαι Hsch.

*__ἐναπόκλειστος__, ον, *recluse*, *Cat.Cod.Astr.* 8(1).264.

**ἐναπολαμβάνω I**, after 'Pass.' insert 'Hp.*Prog.* 11'

**ἐναπολαύω**, after '*enjoy*' insert 'Sopat.Rh. 8.237.24 W.' and after '(vi AD)' insert 'Favorin.*Exil.* 20.26 B.'

**ἐναπομάσσω**, line 2, after 'Plu. 2.99b' insert '*rub off* an image *upon*, κατόπτρῳ Ach.Tat. 5.13'; line 4, delete 'to be .. 5.13'

**ἐναπονίζω I**, med., add 'ἐκπώματα Poll. 6.100'

**ἐναποσπάω**, add 'transf., ἐναποσπωμένων τῶν ἀγροίκων *Syria* 34.281.28 (Hama, i AD)'

**ἐναποτελέω**, after '*produced*' insert 'in a place'

**ἐναποτίθεμαι**, line 4, *include* (in a written work), add 'Just.*Const.* Δέδωκεν 5'

**ἐνάπτω II**, add 'fig., perh. λυγρὸν θρῆνον ἐναψαμένη epigr. in *IG* $10^2$(1).368 (Thessalonica, ii AD)'

**ἐνάργεια II**, add '**b** of the manifestation of a god, ἐποιήσαντο (sc. Zeus and Hecate) προφανεῖς ἐναργείας *IStraton.* 1104.4 (ii AD).'

**ἐναργής I 1**, line 7, ἐ. τινὰ στῆσαι, for 'to set him *bodily before one*' read 'to set him *in clear view*' **3**, add '**b** of style, *vivid*, D.H.*Isoc.* 2, *Is.* 3.'

**ἐνᾰ́ρετος**, after lemma insert 'also ἰνάρετος Hsch.' **I**, add '**b** in honorific addresses, τῷ δεσπότῃ μου τῷ τὰ πάντα ἐναρέτῳ Ἀπφοῦτι νο[τ(αρίῳ)] *POxy.* 1834, 1872, 1873 (all v/vi AD).'

**ἐνᾰρηφόρος**, add '*Epigr.Gr.* 856*a*7 (Hypate)'

*__ἐνᾰρίστερος__, α, ον, *situated on the left*, *Inscr.Délos* 1441*A*i71 (ii BC); adv. -τερα, *PCol.Zen.* 81.15, al. (iii BC), *Inscr.Délos* 1439*Abc*ii55 (ii BC), Roussel *Cultes Égyptiens* p. 213 (Delos, ii BC).

**ἔνᾰρος**, for '*Rev.Ét.Gr.* 24.415' read '*Inscr.Cret.* 3.4.6.6, 7 (Itanos, iii BC)'; before 'Hsch.' insert '*Clara Rhodos* 2.171.12'

*__ἔναρσις__, εως, ἡ, *uprooting*, συκαμίνου *Inscr.Délos* 356*bis**A*27 (iii BC).

+**ἐναρσφόρος**, ον, = ἐναρηφόρος, Hes.*Sc.* 192, Alcm. 1.3 L.-P.

*__ἐνάρτησις__, εως, ἡ, *fitting up, installation*, μηχανῆς *Didyma* 39.44 (ii/i BC).

*__ἐναρχή__, ἡ, *period* or *term of office*, *SEG* 34.1304 (Pamphylia, Rom. imp.).

**ἐνάρχομαι I 2**, add 'pass., περίβολον ἐναρχθέντα *SEG* 6.424 (Iconium)' **II**, (act.), add '*POxy.* 3350.11 (AD 330)'

*__ἐνᾰ́τειρα__, ἡ, *sister-in-law*, cf. ‡εἰνάτερες, *JRS* 18.176 no. 51 (Gerasa).

**ἐνᾰτεύω**, add '*Thasos* 10a.1 (iv BC)'

+**ἐνᾰ́τηρ**, v. ‡εἰνάτερες.

**ἔνᾰτος**, line 2, after 'εἴνατος' add 'Ion., *Thasos* 18.5'; line 3, after 'iii BC)' insert 'Cret. **ἤνατος**, *SEG* 9.72.102 (Cyrene, iv BC), *Inscr.Cret.* 4.181.5 (ii BC); εἴνατον ἡμιτάλαντον $8\frac{1}{2}$ *talents*, Hdt. 1.51.2; fem. subst. (sc. ἡμέρα), Hes.*Op.* 772, *SEG* 21.541 ii 27 (Attica, iv BC); as market-day (cf. Lat. *nundinae*), ib. 1149 (Magnesia on the Maeander, AD 209)'

**ἐναυγής**, delete the entry.

**ἐναύλιος**, add '**II** epith. of Zeus, perh. as god of the farm, Robert *Hell.* 10.34 (Thrace).'

**ἐναυλιστήριος**, for '*habitable*' read '*providing lodging* or *shelter*' and for 'Antip.' read 'Antip.Sid.'

**ἔναυλος (A) II**, line 3, after '*HF* 371' insert 'of mountain caves, A.R. 1.1226 (pl.)' **III**, delete the section.

**ἔναυλος (B) I 1**, for '*flute*' read '*aulos*' **2**, line 6, after 'Plu. 2.17d' insert 'cf. Call.*fr.* 384.6 Pf.'

+**ἔναυσις**, εως, ἡ, *kindling*, ὑδάτων τε πηγαίων ‹ὀχετείαν› καὶ πυρὸς ἔναυσιν Plu.*Cim.* 10. **2** *incitement, stimulus*, Did.ap.Porph. *in Harm.* p. 26 D.

*__ἐναυτόθῐ__, adv. *at the said place*, *PTeb.* 798.5 (ii BC).

**ἐναύω (A)**, line 9, delete 'of poets, *draw* inspiration' and for following quotation read '῎Εφεσον ὅθεν περ οἱ τὰ μέτρα μέλλοντες τὰ χωλὰ τίκτειν .. ἐναύονται Call.*fr.* 203.14 Pf.'; penultimate line, delete 'ἐπαύω'

*__ἐναφῆλιξ__, ικος, ὁ, ἡ, = ἀφῆλιξ II, *minor*, *PFam.Teb.* 7.22 (ii AD).

**ἐναφίημι II**, add 'ἀπελθοῦσα τὴν μορφὴν ἐναφῆκέ μου τοῖς ὀφθαλμοῖς *left the imprint of her beauty in my eyes*, Ach.Tat. 1.19 (v.l. ἐπ-)'

*__ἐναφωρισμένος__, η, ον, *separated*, Plot. 6.4.12; cf. ὁρίζω, ἀφωρισμένως.

**ἔνβενος**, add '(ἔνβεννος La.)'

**ἐνδαγεῖ**, add '(ἐνδαμεῖ· ἐμμένει La., but perh. dat. of *ἐνδα(Ϝ)ής, cf. δάος)'

+**ἐνδαίνῡμαι**, *feast on*, ἐνδαινυ[.. *Thasos* 128 (iv BC); Ath. 7.277a (s.v.l.).

**ἐνδαίω (B)**, delete the entry.

**ἔνδακρυς**, add 'Ezek.*Exag.* 211 S.'

*__ἐνδαναία__· ἐρημία Hsch. (La.).

**ἐνδᾰ́πιος**, line 1, before 'Mosch. 2.11' insert 'Nicaenet. 6.4'

+**ἐνδᾰτέομαι**, *assign, apportion*, βέλεα θέλοιμ' ἂν .. ἐ. S.*OT* 205, ἐ. λόγους ὀνειδιστῆρας E.*HF* 218, λόγου ὑπόστασίν τινι Aristid.Quint. 2.2; pass. ἐνδεδασμέναι ἡλικίαι Iamb.*VP* 31.201. **2** *mention specially*, τὸ δυσπάρευνον λέκτρον ἐ. S.*Tr.* 791; in dub. context, δίς τ' ἐν τελευτῇ τοὔνομ' (sc. of Polynices) ἐνδατούμενος A.*Th.* 578; pass. Nic.*Th.* 509. **II** *divide into pieces*, Lyc. 155.

**ἐνδαψῐλεύομαι I**, add 'Suid. s.v. Φιλίσκος Κερκυραῖος'

**ἐνδεής 6**, line 3, after '*E.fr.* 898.8' insert 'ἐ. πράττειν Men.*Dysc.* 280'

**ἔνδεκα II 2**, add 'also at Thespiae, *SEG* 32.504 (iv BC)'

***ἐνδεκάβριος**, app. = *November*, *SB* 9529.4 (vi/vii AD).

***ἐνδέκαρχος**, ὁ, *member of a board of eleven magistrates*, *SEG* 23.271.54 (Thespiae, iii BC).

**ἐνδέκᾰτος**, add 'in legionary title, ἐν λεγιῶνι ἐνδεκάτῃ Κλαυδίᾳ *SEG* 24.911 (Thrace, iv AD)'

**ἔνδενδρος**, for 'prob.' read 'rest., nisi leg. Ἐ[λαστέ]ρο, *c.*500 BC'; add 'γῆς ἐνδένδρου *wooded*, *SEG* 38.619.7, 13, 18 (Cassandrea, iii BC)'

**ἐνδέξιος I 2**, line 4, for 'ἐνδεξία' read 'ἐνδέξια' and after '*Inscr.Prien.* 19.46 (iii BC)' insert 'τῆς ἐνδέξια φλιᾶς *Inscr.Délos* 1413*b*27, 1439*Abc*i54 (ii BC)'

***ἐνδέσμιος**, ον, *tied in a bundle*, Sor.ap.Gal. 13.42.15.

**ἔνδεσμος I**, for this section read '*anything tied up*, *bundle*, *package*, Lang *Ath.Agora* XXI B9 (v BC), ἐ. ἀργυρίου Lxx *Pr.* 7.20, Dsc. 3.83' and transfer 'Lxx 3*Ki.* 6.10, al.' to section II.

***ἔνδεσμος** (B), ον, *tied* or *bundled up*, Luc.*Lex.* 10.

**ἐνδεύω** (B), add '*soak* with, πατρὸς κόλπους ἐνιδεύσας αἵματος .. νοτίοιν *GVI* 874.7 (Smyrna, ?ii AD)'

**ἐνδέχομαι III 3**, acc. abs., add 'Arist.*de An.* 407$^b$21, etc.'

**ἐνδέω** (A), after lemma insert 'pf. part. pass. ἐνδεμένον *SEG* 37.1001.9 (Katakekaumene, Lydia, iii AD)' **I**, line 8, for 'also οὐρανὸς [ἀστράσιν]' read 'κύκλοις οὐρανὸν' **III**, for this section read 'med., *bind* by spells, ἐνδούμενοι τὰ δαιμόνια J.*AJ* 8.2.5'

**ἐνδέω** (B), line 4, for 'indentical' read 'identical'; line 5, after '(Pl.)*Phd.* 74d' insert 'abs., Aeschin.Socr. 8 D.'

**ἐνδημία**, form ἐνδαμία, add 'also other non-Att.-Ion. dialects, *SEG* 31.574.7 (Larissa, ii BC), etc.'; add 'of life on earth, opp. death, *ICilicie* 59 (v/vi AD)'

**ἐνδιαβάλλω 2**, for '*stand in the way as an adversary*' read '*cause to turn aside*'

**ἐνδῐαίτημα**, add '*deck-house* on a boat, Arr.*fr.* 19 (pl.)'

***ἐνδῐαιτητήριον**, τό, *dwelling-place*, Sch.Hes.*Th.* 129 (p. 29.8 G.).

**ἐνδιαλλάσσω**, after 'pass. -αγμένος, ὁ' read '*male prostitute*, Aq. 3*Ki.*22.47; also by analogy -αγμένη, ἡ, (*female*) *prostitute*, Aq.*Ge.* 38.21, *De.* 23.18'

**ἐνδίδωμι V 2**, add 'Aeschin.*Ep.* 9.1' **3**, add 'Al.*Le.* 14.56'

***ἐνδικτίων**, v. °ἰνδ-.

**ἐνδῑνεύω**, for '= sq.' read '*go round and round* in a place'

**ἔνδιος II 2**, delete the section.

**ἐνδίφριος**, after 'αὐτῷ' insert 'ἱκέτης'

**ἔνδοθεν 2**, add 'Simon. 74.6 P.'

**ἔνδοθι 1**, add 'κεῖται .. τῷδ' ἔνδοθι τύμβῳ *SEG* 34.1271 (Paphlagonia, iii AD)' **2**, add '**b** w. acc., *to within*, A.R. 4.1235.'

**⁺ἐνδοθίδιος**, v. °ἐνδοσθ-.

***ἐνδομῠχία**, ἡ, (?) *secretiveness*, Antioch.Astr. in *Cat.Cod.Astr.* 11(2).109.6; pl., expl. of *latebrae* in Virgil gloss., *PNess.* 1.278, 360 (vi AD).

**ἐνδόμῠχος I**, add '**3** *domestic*, Cic.*Att.* 5.14.3, 5.21.14.'

**ἔνδον I**, line 2, before 'D. 27.10' insert 'Pl.*Smp.* 213c' deleting this ref. in line 6 add '**6** like ἐντός I 3, *on this side of*, Plu.*Cim.* 13.4.'

**ἐνδοξάζομαι**, add '(first two exx. perh. med., *display one's glory*)'

**ἔνδοξος I 1**, add 'as honorific form of address, app. = Lat. *illustris*, *Cod.Just.* 1.4.22 pr.; sim. sup. ἐνδοξότατος ib., Just.*Nov.* 22.14, *POxy.* 1974.1, 1982.3 (v AD), *PLond.* 1780.80 (vi AD); = μεγαλοπρεπέστατος (Lat. *magnificentissimus*), *Cod.Just.* 4.59.1.1; also = Lat. *gloriosissimus*, Just.*Nov.* 7 epilogus'

**⁺ἐνδόρωμα**, ατος, τό, app. *plastering of lime* on the inside of a sarcophagus, σὺν τῷ ἐνδορώματι (unless in error for ἔνδο⟨ν⟩ δορώματι) *ISmyrna* 243 (see also ib. II(2) p. 369).

**ἔνδος**, after '(Delph.)' insert '*SEG* 9.11ff. (Cyrene, iv BC)'

**ἐνδοσθίδια**, delete the entry.

***ἐνδοσθίδιος**, α, ον, *belonging inside* the building, *Leg.Gort.* 2.11 (sp. ἐνδοθ- for ἐνδοσθ-); neut. pl. subst. = ἐνδόσθια, *entrails*, *IG* 4².40.17 (Epid.); see also ἐντοσθίδια.

**ἐνδόσιμος I**, add '**2** neut. subst., *period of grace*, *respite* (= Lat. *laxamentum*), Just.*Nov.* 72.6.' **II**, add '**2** ἔστω δὲ ἐνδοσιμώτερα τὰ γυμνάσια *less strenuous*, Philostr.*Gym.* 52.'

**ἐνδοτέρω I 1**, add '*Peripl.M.Rubr.* 40'

**ἐνδρομίς II 2**, after '(Herod.Med.ap.Orib.) 38.1' insert 'κρεβατταρία *Edict.Diocl.* 19.5'

**ἔνδῠμα**, add '[ἔνδῠμα *AP* 6.280; cf. ὑπένδυμα q.v.]'

***ἐνδῠνᾰμάω**, = ἐνδυναμόω, Heph.Astr. 3.4.4.

**ἐνδῠναστεύω I**, add 'Procl.*Inst.* 159 D.'

***ἐνδῠτή**, ἡ, *dress*, *PHarris* 88.22 (v AD).

**ἐνδῠτός 2**, line 2, for 'Simon. 179.10' read '*AP* 6.217.10 ([Simon.])'

**ἐνδύω I 1**, line 10, after '*Ep.Eph.* 4.24' insert 'ἐνέδυ θεόν *APl.* 290 (Antip.Thess.)' **2**, line 7, after 'Pl.*Phd.* 89d' insert '*make an indentation* in coastline, κόλπος .. ἐπὶ βάθος ἐνδύνων εἰς τὴν ἤπειρον *Peripl.M.Rubr.* 32, 42'

***ἐνδωρότερον**· ὠμότερον. ἀκρατέστερον Hsch.; cf. ζωρός.

**ἐνέδρα**, add '**IV** *anus*, Hsch. s.v. ῥινοβόλους ἀνέμους; cf. ἔνεδρος II.'

**ἐνεδρεία I**, add '*Vit.Aesop.*(G) 55 P.'

**ἔνεδρος I**, add '**2** *holding office*, *SEG* 33.1177.44 (Myra, i AD).'

**ἐνείλλω**, for '*wrap up*' read '*roll up tight*'

**ἔνειμι**, line 1, after 'ἔνι' insert '(written ἔνει *Inscr.Délos* 4442*A*8, 68 (ii BC))'; line 2, delete '3 sg. ἔνι freq. for'; line 4, after 'Od. 21.288' insert 'repeated, S.*fr.* 314.191, Ar.*Lys.* 545' **II 2 a**, at end for 'Plb. 21.4.14' read 'Plb. 21.2.14' at end add 'Myc. 3 pl. pres. *e-ne-e-si*, part. *e-ne-o*'

**ἕνεκᾰ**, line 5, after 'Sch.Pi.*O.* 7.10)' insert 'also **ἔνεχεν** *MAMA* 1.197 (Laodicea Combusta)'; line 14, after 'Hdt. 3.122, etc.' insert 'Mitchell *N.Galatia* 322' before '**1**' insert 'also app. w. acc. εὐχὴν ἕνεκεν Mitchell *N.Galatia* 198, μνήμην ἕνεκεν ib. 277' **II 1**, for 'Call. .. 287' read 'Call.*fr.* 75.6 Pf. (ἕνεκ'), ib. 1.3 (εἵνεκεν), cf. Hes.*fr.* 180.10 M.-W.' **2**, add 'Call.*fr.* 6 Pf. (ἕνεκ')' at end add 'Myc. *e-ne-ka*, prep. w. gen., preceding case'

**ἐνελίσσω 1**, line 3, delete 'ὀλίγῳ .. Nic.*Al.* 287' add '**3** med., *whirl round* in, ὀλίγῳ ὄγμῳ Nic.*Al.* 287.'

**ἐνεματίζω**, add '*use as an enema*, Herod.Med.ap.Aët. 9.2'

***ἐνενηκονθεκταῖος**, ον, (occurring) *on the ninety-sixth* (*day*), Gal. 7.501.10.

***ἐνενηκονθήμερος**, *of* or *lasting ninety days*, *PMich.*III 149 xi 19 (ii AD); **ἐνενηκοντᾱ́μερος** Petos. 359.2.

***ἐνενηκοντᾰεξάπηχυς**, υ, *ninety-six cubits long*, *PSI* 905.6 (i AD), represented by symbols in *PTeb.* 382.9 (i BC) and *PMich.*II 121$^r$.3 xi 1 (i AD).

***ἐνενηκοντᾱ́μερος**, v. °ἐνενηκονθή-.

***ἐνενηκοστόεκτος**, η, ον, *ninety-sixth*, *PWisc.* 9.15, 22 (ἐνενηκόσεκτος pap., AD 183), *PKöln* 94.27, 40 (prob. ἐνενηκόσθεκτος pap., AD 213).

**ἐνεξουσιάζω II**, for '*usurp authority*' read '*stand on one's rights*'

**ἐνεός 1**, add '*PMich.*XV 723.8 (iv AD)'

**ἐνεοστᾰσία**, for '*standing dumb*' read '*inability to utter*, Κύπριν δ' ἐνεοστασίη λάβε μύθων'

**⁺ἐνεπίσκημμα**, ατος, τό, *claiming as owed to oneself some part of property confiscated from another by the state*, Harp., Poll. 8.61; *such a claim on behalf of a tribe*, *IG* 1³.429.8 (v BC), *Ath.Agora* XIX P26.512, 528 (iv BC).

**ἐνεπισκήπτομαι 1**, for '*claim .. state*' read '*claim as owed to oneself some part of property confiscated from another by the state*'; after 'Poll. 8.61' insert '*make such a claim for a tribe* or *religious group*, κοινὸν ὀργεώνων *Ath.Agora* XIX P5.31; ib. P26.515 (both iv BC)'

**ἐνέπω**, line 3, delete '(anap.)'

**ἐνεστιάομαι**, for '*give an entertainment*' read '*feast*'

***ἐνευπορέω**, v. ‡εἰσευπορέω.

**ἐνεύχομαι**, add 'w. ὥστε and inf., *SEG* 30.1382.C20, *IG* 12(3).330.14 (Thera); w. inf. alone, *IG* 5(1).1208.50'

**ἐνεχῠρασμός**, after '= ἐνεχυρασία' insert '*PEnteux.* 87$^v$.3 (iii BC)'

***ἐνεχῠρέω**, = ἐνεχυράζω, prob. in *SB* 9834 b 48 (iv AD).

**ἐνεχῠριάζω**, add 'aor. inf. -ιάξαι'

***ἐνεχῠ́ρίαξις**, ιος, ἁ, *taking of a pledge*, *BCH* 50.16 (Delphi, iv BC).

***ἐνεχῠρίζομαι**, = ἐνεχυράζομαι (v. -άζω), Hsch. s.v. διενεγ(γ)υήσαμεν.

***ἐνεχῠρῐμαῖος**, α, ον, *pawned*, *held in pawn*, βοῦς ἐνεχυριμαῖος τὰ πολλὰ ἔξω βλέπει· ἐπὶ τῶν ἀμελουμένων καὶ πρὸς τοὺς ἐπιμελουμένους ἀφορώντων *Paroemiographi* suppl. p. 75 no. 30.

**ἐνέχῠρον**, after 'τό' insert 'Boeot. **ἐννέχυρον** *Mél.Navarre* 353 (Thespiae), Cret. **ἰνέκυρον** inscr. in *JHS* 69.34 (Oaxos, vi/v BC)'; add 'in Rom. law = Lat. *pignus*, *Cod.Just.* 4.24.1, Just.*Nov.* 8.5 pr., al.'

***ἐνήκοος**, ον, *obedient*, w. dat. and gen., *JA* 1958.3.10 (Kandahar, Inscr. of Aśoka).

**ἐνήλᾰτον I**, for 'S.*Fr.* 315' read 'S.*fr.* 314.316 R.'

***ἐνήλᾰτος**, gloss on γλίσχρος, Hsch.

**ἐνῆλιξ**, for '*in the prime of manhood*' read '*adult*, *grown-up*' and add 'μήπω ἐ. οὖσα *SEG* 37.1000 (Katakekaumene, Lydia, ii AD)'

**ἐνῆμαι**, read **ἔνημαι**.

***ἐνήμῐσυ**, v. °ἰνιμίνα.

**⁺ἐνήνοθε**, v. ἀνήνοθε; also in compds. ἐπ-, κατ-, παρ-ενήνοθε.

***ἐνηφι**, v. ἔνος (B).

**ἔνθᾰ I 1**, add 'in epitaphs, τίθησί με .. ἔνθα *ITrall.* 219 (Tralles, i AD), *SEG* 30.1479 (Phrygia, before AD 216), ἔνθα κῖτη Θεώδωρος *ITyr* 9 (Chr.)'

**ἐνθάδε**, after lemma insert 'Cypr. *i-ta-de* ἰνθάδε *ICS* 11, 213a'

***ἐνθᾰλᾰμεύω**, *embed*, (λίθος) ᾧ ἡ βήρυλλος ἐνθαλαμεύεται Eust.ad D.P. 1010.

**ἐνθεαστικός I**, line 3, after 'Syrian. *in Metaph.* 42.14' insert 'ἔχειν ἐ. Men.*Dysc.* 44'

**ἐνθεμέλιοι**, add '*IEphes.* 1073, *SEG* 34.1127 (Ephesus)'

***ἐνθεμολογέω**, *collect* (*financial*) *deposits*, or perh. *produce*, *SEG* 14.547 (Poeessa, Ceos, v BC, see also *ABSA* 84.295 n. 39); cf. θημολογέω.

**ἐνθένδε**, add 'late **ἐνθένδεν** Chor. 28.2 cod. (p. 312 F.-R.)'
**ἐνθερμαίνω**, add 'ἐξ ὧν ἂν διψῷεν οἱ ἐνθερμανθέντες Gal. 17(2).103.8'
+**ἐνθηκάριος**, ὁ, perh. *storeman*, *SEG* 19.553 (-ις, Cos, Chr.).
**ἐνθήκη I**, add '*SEG* 16.754 (Phrygia)' **II**, after '*capital*' insert '(financial)' and add 'Hsch. s.v. ἀφορμή. **2** perh. *security* or *deposit*, δοὺς ἐνθήκην ὅσα ἔχω ἐν χερσίν *PHaun.* 21.9.'
**ἔνθηρος I**, add 'ἐσθημάτων τιθέντες ἔνθηρον (i.e. verminous) τρίχα A.*Ag.* 562, ἐνθήρου (i.e. maggoty) ποδός S.*Ph.* 698, πᾶν ὅσον ἔνθηρον ἦν τοῦ τόπου Ael.*NA* 6.63' **II**, delete the section.
**ἐνθρήνιον*, τό, *wild bee's nest*, Sch.Nic.*Al.* 547b.
**ἐνθρίζειν**, for 'ἐνέθριξε' read 'ἐνέθριξεν (ἐνέθρεξεν La.)'
**ἔνθρυπτος**, τὰ ἔ., delete '*sops* or' and add 'Aristid.*Or.* 46'
**ἐνθρώσκω**, line 4, delete '*kicked* him on the hip'; after 'D.C. 74.14' insert 'comm.in Alc. 306.9.4 L.-P.'
**ἐνθύμημα II**, for '(X.*HG*) 5.4.52' read '(X.*HG*) 5.4.51'
**ἐνθῡμία**, add 'v.l. in Longus 4.17.1'
**ἐνθῡμιστός**, delete '(nisi leg. -ητόν)' and add 'ἐ. αὐτῷ ἔστω *Thasos* 141.5 (iv BC); ἐ. εἶναι *BCH* 64-5.176 (Thasos, i BC)'
***ἐνθῴϊος**, ον, = ἐπιθώϊος, *Thasos* 150.14 (iv BC).
**ἐνῐαύσιος II**, after '*annual*' insert 'ὀλολύγα Alc. 130.35 L.-P.' at end add 'cf. Myc. *e-ni-ja-u-si-jo*, pers. n.'
**ἐνῐαυτοκράτωρ**, add 'Heph.Astr. 2.27.6'
**ἐνῐαυτός I 2**, line 10, for 'five' read 'four' **II**, delete the section.
**ἐνίημι I 8**, delete the section.
***ἐνικεύθω**, v. °ἐγκεύθω.
***ἐνικλάω**, v. ‡ἐγκλάω.
**ἐνικνέομαι**, add 'cod. in Thphr.*CP* 5.13.1'
***ἐνικρίνω**, v. °ἐγκρίνω.
***ἐνίλλω** (B), v. ἐνείλλω.
+**ἐνιλλώπτω**, *eye lasciviously*, Ael.Dion.ι 8 E., Clem.Al.*Paed.* 3.70 (who equates with βλεφαρίζω).
**ἐνίστημι A 2**, add '*Cod.Just.* 1.2.25 pr., med., Just.*Nov.* 101 pr.' **3**, line 7, after 'Plu.*Arat.* 16' insert 'ἐνστήσας βασκανίην *AP* 5.218.10 (Agath.)'; add 'also pres. οὐκ ἀγνοῶ .. ὅσον ἔργον ἐνίσταμαι Isoc. 12.36'
***ενίψογος**, v. ἔμψογος.
+**ἐνλιμενίζω**, v. °ἐλλιμ-.
**ἐνναέτης** (A), add 'also ἐννηέτης *IHadr.* 69 (Rom.imp.); ἐννεέτης *GVI* 1118.3 (Piraeus, iv BC); see also ἐννεαέτης'
**ἐνναέτης** (B), after '= ἐνναετήρ' insert 'Epigr.ap.D. 7.40, Call. in *PAnt.* 113.1(a)13'
***ἐνναία**, ἡ, perh. *spring, fountain*, *SEG* 19.181.1, 182.1, also perh. in *IG* $2^2$.2491.7 (Attica, iv BC), Phot.; see also °ἐννοαί.
***ἐνναούγκιον**, τό, = Lat. *dodrans*, *three-quarters* of an inheritance, Just.*Nov.* 18.2, al.
***ἐννάπηχυς**, v. ἐννεάπηχυς.
***ἐνναύων**· πρὸς τῷ ναῷ διάγων, ἱκετεύων Hsch. ε 2715 (La.); cf. ἐναύω C, ναεύω, ναύω II.
**ἐννέα**, line 1, for 'Dor... (q.v.)' read '**hεννέα** *Tab.Heracl.* 2.17, al., *IG* 4.1588.16 (Aegina, v BC); WGk. **ἐννή** *CID* II 5 ii 43, 52 (iv BC), *SEG* 9.1.32, **ἐννῆα** ib. 9.3.16 (both Cyrene, iv BC); cf. ἐννή· θ' Κυρηναῖοι Hsch.' at end add 'Myc. cpd. form *e-ne-wo-*'
***ἐννεάδραχμος**, ον, *costing nine drachmae*, *IG* $2^2$.408.13 (iv BC).
**ἐννεακαιδέκατος**, add 'fem. subst. (sc. ἡμέρα) *the nineteenth day*, *SEG* 32.1149 (Magnesia on the Maeander, AD 209); neut. as adv. *for the nineteenth time*, *AS* 36.137ff., no. 1 (Pisidia, 5/4 BC)'
**ἐννεακαιδεκέτης**, add 'form -δεχέτης *GVI* 1214.3 (Pholegandros, ? iii/ii BC)'
***ἐννεάκεντρος**, ον, *having nine* (i.e. *many*) *stings*, Sch.Nic.*Th.* 781 = Nic.*fr.* 37; cf. ἐννεάδεσμος.
**ἐννεάκις**, after '= ἐνάκις' insert '*Lindos* 421a5 (i AD)'
**ἐννεάπηχυς**, add 'also ἐννάπηχυς *PFlor.* 167.14, 215.3 (iii AD)'
***ἐννεάπῠλον**, τό, *precinct with nine gates*, of the Pelasgikon at Athens, *AB* 419.
***ἐννεάχῑλιοι**, αι, α, *nine thousand*, (see also ἐννεάχιλοι), epigr. in *SEG* 30.483 (Thespiae).
***ἐννεέτης**, v. °ἐνναέτης (A).
**ἐννεόβολον**, delete the entry.
***ἐννεόβολος**, ον, *accruing at the rate of nine obols*, τόκοι *BGU* 1161.10 (i BC).
***ἐννεόμφαλος**, ον, *"having nine knobs"*, name of kind of sacrificial cake, πόπανον ῥαβδωτὸν ἐννεόμφαλον *Inscr.Perg.* 8(3).161.
***ἐννεός**, v. ἐνεός.
+**ἐννή**, v. ‡ἐννέα.
***ἐννηετής**, v. °ἐνναέτης (A).
***ἔννιος**, wd. of unkn. meaning, Hdn.*fr.* p. 27 H.
***ἐννοαί**· πηγαί Hsch. (La.) (cod. ἔννοιαί, cf. °ἐνναία, νόα).
***ἔννοσος**, ον, *morbid*, σαπρία Aët. 7.11.
**ἔννῡμι**, line 7, after 'Od. 14.529' insert 'Arc. 3 sg. aor. subj. Ϝέσἕτοι (unless = Ϝέσἕτοι, subj. of pres. *Ϝέστοι, cf. ἐπίεσται s.v. ἐπιέννυμι) *SEG* 11.1112 (Pheneos, *c.*500 BC)'
**ἐνό, ἔνο**, add 'graffito in *ZPE* 12.268 (Sicily, *c.*420 BC)'
***ἐνοδιάζω**, app. = ἐφοδιάζω, τὸ ὀφίλον τούτοις ἐνοδιάζζεσθαι ἀργύριον παραδόντω (sic) *Lindos* 419.70 (i AD).
**ἐνόδιος I 1**, add 'οἳ πρῶτοι κακοεργὸν ἐχαλκεύσαντο μάχαιραν εἰνοδίην i.e. the highwayman's knife, Arat. 132' **II**, Ἐνοδία alone, add 'Ἐπάγαθος δῶρον Ἐννοδίᾳ *SEG* 31.1584; w. epiths., Ἐννοδίας Μυκαικᾶς *IGC* p. 11.28 (Larissa), Ἐ. Ἀστικά *IG* 9(2).575, etc.'
**ἔνοδμος**, for '*sweet-smelling, fresh*' read '*strong-smelling, pungent*'
+**ἔνοδος**, ἡ, prob. Thess. for εἴσοδος, *way in, entrance*, *IGC* p. 11.14 (Larissa).
**ἐνόζῠγος**, delete the entry.
***ἐνοικήτειρα**, ἡ, *inhabitant* (fem.), [πό]ντου .. ἐνοικήτιραι .. [Ν]ηρῆδες epigr. in *Inscr.Cret.* 3.iv 37.1.
***ἐνοικιάζω**, *let*, *PLond.* 1735.11 (vi AD), v. *Kapsomenakis* 97.
**ἐνοίκισμα**, add '*PMich.*III 188.16 (ii AD)'
***ἐνοικοδόμημα**, ατος, τό, *building in a place*, cj. in Pl.*Lg.* 760e (pl., codd. ἐν οἰκοδ-).
**ἔνοικος 1**, add '**b** *worker in an establishment*, Just.*Nov.* 43.1.2.'
***ἐνόλμιον**, τό, part of the ὅλμος (in a reed-pipe, v. ὅλμος II 5), Hsch. s.v. καταστομίς (ἐνόλβιον cod.).
***ἐνομμᾰτίζω**, = ἐνομματόω, *Hymn.Is.* 18 (Maroneia).
**ἐνοπή 2**, add 'Emp. 62.8 D.-K.'
**ἐνόπλιος I**, after 'Anon.Vat. 64' insert 'δρόμος *Didyma* 201.14'
**ἔνοπλος III**, for 'portrait-statue *in armour*' read '*representation on a shield*'
**ἐνοπτρικοί I**, after '*geometers*' insert 'Alex.Aphr. *in Mete.* 141.17'
**ἐνοργείας**, add '(ἐνορταλίας La.)'
**ἐνόρκιος I 1**, for this section read '*bound by an oath*, Pi.*O.* 2.101, *Inscr.Olymp.* 22(f).6 (decree of Megara Hyblaea and Selinous, vi BC); *faithful to an oath*, *SEG* 30.1117.8, 1118.10 (both Entella, iii BC)'
**ἔνορκος II a**, add 'used to express Latin *foederatus*, (πόλεις) ὅσαι ἑαυτὰς ἐγκεχειρίκεσαν ἐπὶ συνθήκαις ἔνορκοι App.*BC* 1.102'
**ἐνορμάω**, add '*rush upon*, w. dat., ἐνθορεῖν καὶ ἐνορμ[ῆσαι τ]οῖς τοῦ Φιττακοῦ νώτ[οις comm.in Alc. 306.9.5 L.-P.'
**ἐνόρμιον**, after '*harbour-dues*' insert '*BGU* 1834.11 (i BC), *PFay.* 104.8 (iii AD)'
***ἐνορταλίας**, v. °ἐνοργείας.
**ἔνορχις**, add '**II** an unidentified precious stone, *enorchis* (sc. λίθος) *candida est divisisque fragmentis testium effigiem repraesentat*, Plin.*HN* 37.159.'
**ἔνος** (C) **2**, line 3, after 'acc. to' insert 'Plu.*Sol.* 25.4'; lines 4/5, for 'Hes.*Op.* 770' read '*IG* $2^2$.1241.26, 28, Sch.Ar.*Nu.* 1131; but in Hes.*Op.* 770 *the first of the month*'
**ἐνουλίζομαι**, add 'perh. also of a woollen textile, [ζώμ]ατα δύο ἐνουλισ[μένων] Τηνίων *SEG* 37.692.43 (Delos, ii BC)'
**ἐνούσιος 3**, delete the section.
**ἐνοχή**, add 'Just.*Const.* Δέδωκεν 7e; also in uncertain sense, Διονύσις τὴν ἐ. ἀνέθηκα Robert *Hell.* 10.14 (Phrygia)'
**ἐνοχία**, add '*PMich.*XV 740.25 (vi AD)'
**ἐνοχλέω I 1**, line 9, *be unwell*, add '*PPetr.* 2.25(a).12 (iii BC), *PCair.Zen.* 812.5 (257 BC)' add '**b** *subject to pressure*, ἐνοχληθέντες παρὰ τῶν .. ἐπισκόπων *Cod.Just.* 1.3.45.7; w. dat., *put pressure* on, Just.*Nov.* 80.3.'
***ἐνοχλής**, ές, *troublesome*, *PLond.*inv. 2226.17 (*Pap.Flor.* XIX 517, AD 308).
**ἔνοχος**, after lemma insert 'Arc. ἴνοχος *SEG* 25.447 (Alipheira, iii BC)' **I 1**, add '*abs.*, *held fast*, of anchor, *AP* 7.506 (Leon.Tarent.)'
**ἐνόω**, add '*cause* a wound *to close*, Hld. 1.8.5'
**ἐνραβῶς**, after lemma insert '(**ἐνραβδώσας** La.)'
***ἐνρευμᾰτίζομαι**, *to be full of* or *affected by rheum*, *APF* 4.270 (iii AD).
**ἔνρυθμος**, *possessing rhythm*, add 'τραγῳδίας epigr. in *SEG* 31.1072 (Herakleia, Pontus, Rom.imp.)'
**ἔνσειμι**, after 'Cret.' insert 'and Arg.'; after '*Leg.Gort.* 5.36' insert '*Schwyzer* 84.21 (cj., ἐνσ[ lapis, v BC)'
**ἐνσεισμός**, delete 'of engines of war'; add 'cf. ἐνσείω II'
**ἐνσείω**, line 2, after 'ἐνσέσεικα' insert 'Men.*Dysc.* 581' **4**, add 'Gal. 18(2).922.9, 924.3'
**ἔνσημος I**, delete 'f.l.' add '**III** of garments, *striped* or perh. *embroidered*, *POxy.* 1273.13, 14 (iii AD).'
***Ἐνσῑτάρχιος**, epith. of Zeus, perh. *ruler of the guests*, ΔιϜὸς Ἐνσιταρ[χ]ίου *SEG* 30.351 (Kleonaia, iv BC).
***ἔνσκαμβος**, ον, *crooked*, gloss on ἔγγαυσος, Hsch.
+**ἐνσκηνόω**, v.l. for σκηνόω, Lxx *Ge.* 13.12.
***ἐνσκολῐεύομαι**, perh. *twist oneself, twist and turn*, Lxx *Jb.* 40.19(24) (passage corrupt in Hebr.).
**ἐνσκοπέομαι**, substitute 'in Hld. 8.10.1 is f.l. for ἀνασκ-'
+**ἐνσόριον**, τό, *niche* in a sepulchre, *ISmyrna* 190, 192, al., ib. 211 (sp. ἐσσόριν), *AJA* 18.68 (Sardes, iii AD).

***ἐνσπόνδια**, τά, = σπονδαί, ἐ. ποῖμεν *Schwyzer* 491.14 (Thespiae, ?ii BC).

**ἔνστᾰσις I 3**, *inheritance*, add '*Cod.Just.* 1.2.25 pr.' **II 2**, at end delete 'ὀνύχων'

***ἐνστρᾰτεύομαι**, *serve in a (military) unit*, οὐδὲ χρήματα εἰσῆγον ἐφ' ᾧ ἐνστρατεύσασθαι Agath. 5.15.3 K.

**ἐνστρέφω 2**, delete the section.

**ἐνστρηνές**, after lemma insert '(ἐνστηνές La.)'

**ἐνσχίζω**, add '*PMich.*IX 576.3 (iii AD)'

**ἐνσωμᾰτόω**, pass., add 'Alcin.*Intr.* p. 178.10, 36 H.'

***ἐνταλματικός**, ὁ, unexpld. wd., app. expr. some rank or occupation, *BCH* 33.86 (Cappadocia, Byz.); cf. perh. ἐντολικάριος.

**ἔντᾰσις II**, after 'Hp.*Epid.* 3.1.β'' insert 'Gal. 11.207.11'

**ἐντᾰτός**, after '*stretched*' insert '*IG* $2^2$.1541.23-25 (Athens, iv BC)'

**ἐντᾰφή**, add '**2** *tomb*, τεθῆναι αὐτὸν ἐν τῇ ἐ. *IEphes.* 614c.26 (i AD).'

**ἐνταφιαστής**, for '*undertaker, embalmer*' read '*one who prepares for burial*' and for 'of the Bactrian dogs' read 'of Bactrian dogs, reputed to be kept for the disposal of corpses'

**ἔντεα**, sg., read 'Archil. 5.2, 139.5 W., Hes.*fr.dub.* 343.18 M.-W.'

**ἐντείνω III 2**, after 'pass.' insert 'ἐντέταμαι *APl.* 236 (Leon.Tarent.)'

**ἐντέλεια II**, for '*GDI* 1339.11 (Dodona)' read '*SEG* 23.471 (iv BC), 26.701 (*c.*205 BC), 37.511 (ii BC, all Dodona)'

+**ἐντελέω**, *complete* term, πεντεάδας δισσὰς ἐντελέσας ἐτέων epigr. in *SEG* 33.848 (Mauretania, i AD); in uncertain context, Phld.*Ir.* 12 W.

**ἐντέλλω II**, delete the section transferring exx. to section I.

**ἐντέμνω II 2**, for this section read '*tap* (the root of) plant to extract the sap, Thphr.*CP* 6.11.14, 15, al.: so fig., ὕπνου τόδ' ἀντίμολπον ἐντέμνων ἄκος (also expld. as "shredding") A.*Ag.* 17'

**ἐντενής**, delete 'only' and add 'adv. ἐντενίως *Inscr.Cret.* 4.168.10 (iii BC)'

+**ἐντέριον**, τό, dim. of ἔντερον, in quot. used in a slighting description of sexual intercourse, ἐντερίου παράτριψις M.Ant. 6.13.

***ἐντερίς**, ίδος, ἡ, = αἱμορροΐς I, Cyran. 29.27 (pl.).

**ἐντερειδής**, add '(s.v.l.)'

**ἔντερον II**, delete 'but *worm-casts*'

**ἐντερόνεια**, delete '= ἐντεριώνη'

**ἐντεσϊεργός**, add 'also **-ουργός** Hsch.'

***ἐντετραίνω**, *pierce*, aor. 1 part. ἐντετράνας *IG* $2^2$.1665.18, 1672.176 (both Athens, iv BC).

**ἐντεῦθεν**, after '**ἐνθεῦτεν**' insert '**ἐντεῦθε** dub. in Chor. 29.50 (p. 327 F.-R.)' **I**, at end delete 'ἐντεῦθεν .. Men.*Pk.* 184'

**ἐντευκτικός**, after '*affable*' insert 'Phld.*Rh.* 1.222.10, 13'

**ἔντευξις 2 b**, for '*manners, behaviour*' read '*manner of encounter* or *converse*'

**ἐντευτλᾰνόομαι**, delete 'Aret.*CA* 1.2'

**ἐντεύχω**, after 'ἐρυθήματα' insert 'Aret.*CA* 1.2 (p. 101.18 H.)'

**ἐντηρέω**, delete 'Procop.*Arc.* 4'

**ἐντί̆θημι**, line 1, for 'aor. 1 inf.' read 'aor. 2 inf.' **2**, add '**c** *place* in the tomb, *TAM* 4(1).264 (Rom.imp.), *SEG* 30.1557 (Cilicia, iv/vi AD).'

***ἐντί̆μιος**, ον, = ἔντιμος, sup. -ώτατος *IG* 12(7).410.8 (Aegiale).

**ἔντῑμος I 1**, add 'ἔνθα κῖτε ὁ Ῥεββὶ Ἀββᾶ Μάρις ὁ ἔντιμος *SEG* 29.968 (Naples, iv/v AD)' **III**, add '*highly-priced*, ἔντιμον κατέλιπον τὸν σῖτον D. 56.9'

***ἐντί̆ναγμα**, ατος, τό, *a hurling, shower*, χαλάζης Aq.*Is.* 28.2, cf. 32.2; v. ἐντιναγμός.

**ἐντολή**, add '*instruction* in will, *TAM* 5(1).18; also representing Lat. *mandatum*, Just.*Nov.* 4.1'

**ἐντολικάριος**, add '*PCol.* 175.50, 63, 70 (AD 339)'

***ἐντόλιον**, τό, dim. (in form) of ἐντολή, *PBremen* 20.8 (ii AD).

+**ἐντόλιος**, ον, prob. = φιλέντολος, *SB* 2654 (Jewish).

**ἐντομίς I**, add 'Lxx *Je.* 16.6; perh. also in this sense, ὁ πρῶτος ῥυμὸς σὺλ λίνοις καὶ πίττει καὶ κηρῶι ὥστε μέσον εἶναι τῶν ἐντομίδων τῶν ἐν τει θεραπείαι *Inscr.Délos* 1444*Aa*19 (ii BC)' **II**, for this section read '*niche* or *cavity* in a tomb, *IG* $10^2$(1).308, 478, al. (Thessalonica)'

**ἔντομος**, lines 4/5, for 'Call. .. x 38' read 'Call.*fr.* 43.80, 694 Pf.'

**ἔντονος I 2**, line 5, after 'Pl.*Tht.* 173a' add 'ἔ. τι φθεγξαμένη Nic.Dam. 68 J.'

***ἐντορνεία**, ἡ, app. *defensive breastwork* of warship, *SB* 9215.11 (250 BC), v. ἐντορνία.

**ἐντός 2**, add 'Isoc. 4.144, 15.110' **II**, lines 3/4, after 'id. 2.76' insert 'cf. ἐκ (or ἐγ) τῆς ἐντός *Didyma* 25*A*22, *B*20, al. (ii BC)' and for 'ib. 49' read 'Th. 2.49.2'

+**ἐντοῦθα**, = ἐνταῦθα, *Schwyzer* 792 (Cumae, v BC), 811.17 (Oropus, iv BC, ἐντôθα); perh. ἐντοῦθε 792a (Cumae, iv BC, v. *SEG* 4.93).

**ἐντρᾰπελος**, for '*shameful*' read '*false, deceitful*'

**ἐντρέφω**, lines 2/3, delete 'Med. .. :-'; line 4, after '*in*' insert 'Hp.*Aër.* 12' add '**2** med., φυτὰ ἐνθρέψασθαι *bed* them *in*, Hes.*Op.* 781.'

**ἐντρέχεια**, line 2, after 'Gal. 14.213, cf. 306' insert 'as honorific title, *POxy.* 3350.6 (AD 330), διὰ τοῦτο ἐπιδίδωμι τῇ ὑμῶν ἐντρεχείᾳ *PMasp.* 91, 92, al. (vi AD)'

**ἐντρῐβής 2**, add 'Max.Tyr. 12(6).2'

**ἐντροχάζω II**, delete the section.

+**ἐντρῠγάω**, *gather in* grapes or other fruit, Moeris s.v. ἄρριχος, *PPrincet.* 39.7 (iii AD, ἐντρυκ-).

**ἐντρύχομαι**, delete the entry.

***ἐντρῡχόω**, *harass, wear down*, [πόλις] πολεμίοις -ωθεῖσα Memn. 20.3 J., D.C. 38.46 (codd.).

**ἐντύ̆λη**, delete the entry (read 'ἐν τύλῃ').

***ἐντῠλιγμός**, ὁ, *swaddling cloth*, gloss on σπείρημα, Sch.Nic.*Al.* 417b.

**ἐντύ̆νω**, line 4, after 'A.R. 1.235' insert '4.1191' **I**, at end transfer 'A.R. 4.1191' to follow 'A.R. 1.235'

**ἐντῠπάζω**, for '*enwrap* .. (Pisidia)' read '*carve* or *mould on*, *TAM* 3(1).922.2 (Termessus, ii/iii AD)'

**ἐνυαίνειν**, after lemma insert '(ἐννᾱνεῖν La.; cf. ὑηνέω)'

**Ἐνῡάλιος**, line 2, for 'written' read 'τὀνυϝαλίō (gen.) ἰαρά *SEG* 11.327 (Argos, vii BC), Ἐνυϝαλίο ib. 23.187 (Mycenae, vi BC)'; line 4, after 'cf.' insert '*SEG* l.c.' **II**, line 3, for '*Lyr.*..*desp.* 108' read '*Lyr.adesp.* 109(*b*) P.'; at end for 'ῠ .. metri gr.' read 'ῡ, exc. *Lyr.adesp.* l.c.; cf. Ἐνῡώ' at end add 'Myc. *e-nu-wa-ri-jo*'

***ἐνυβριστής**, οῦ, ὁ, gloss on λωβητῶν, Hsch.

**ἔνυγρος**, add '**V** ἔ. (sc. λίθος), ἡ, a precious stone, perh. *chalcedony*, Plin.*HN* 37.190 (v.l. *enydros*).'

**ἔνυδρις I**, read 'cj. in Ar.*Ach.* 880'

**ἔνυδρος**, add '**5** v. °ἔνυγρος.'

**ἐνυπνιόμαντις**, add 'cj. in Semus 20 J. (ἡ ἐν ὕπνῳ μάντις in Ath. 335a)'

**Ἐνῡώ**, after 'Il. 5.333' insert 'Ἐνhυọ[ῖ] *SEG* 35.1014 (Naxos, Sicily, *c.*600 BC)' and for 'ib. 592' read 'Il. 5.592'

***ἐνφ-**, v. ἐμφ-.

**ἐνωδάς**, after lemma insert '(ἐνώλας La.; cf. οὖλος B)'

**ἐνώδιον**, read '**ἐνῴδιον** (cf. *IG* $2^2$.1544.20 (iv BC))' and add 'written ἐνόδιον *SB* 7260.2*b*8, 3*a*2 (pl.) (i AD)'

**ἐνωμοτάρχης**, lines 2/3, transfer 'Arr.*Tact.* 6.2' to follow 'Ascl.*Tact.* 2.2'

**ἐνωνά**, after 'Chaeronea' insert 'ii BC' and add '*SEG* 34.355.8 (Leuctra, iv BC), *SEG* 39.400 (Orchomenos, 225/200 BC)'

**ἐνώπιος I**, add '*SB* 7817.56 (AD 201)' **II**, as prep. w. gen., add 'Lxx *Ge.* 11.28, etc.; w. ref. to personal service, ib.*Jd.* 20.28, 1*Ki.* 16.21; *in the eyes* or *opinion of*, translating Hebr. *bᵊ 'ênê*, ὁδοὶ ἀφρόνων ὀρθαὶ ἐνώπιον αὐτῶν ib.*Pr.* 12.15, εἰ εὗρον χάριν ἐνώπιον τοῦ βασιλέως *Es.* 5.8'

**ἕξ**, add 'Thess. ἕξε, *SEG* 13.394 (iii BC); Myc. in cpd. *we-pe-za*, prob. *six-foot*'

**ἐξάγγελος II**, add 'Hsch.'

**ἐξάγιον**, after 'τό' insert '(Lat. *exagium*)' add '**II** *part payment*, *POxy.* 3955 (AD 611).'

+**ἐξάγιον**, τό, = Lat. *sextula*, Orib. in *CMG* vi 2.2 p. 231 R., Suid. s.v. στατήρ.

***ἐξᾰγῐσις**, εως, ἡ, perh. *purification*, *IG* $1^3$.8.23 (Sunium, v BC).

**ἐξάγιστος II**, for this section read '*taboo*, ἃ δ' ἐξάγιστα μηδὲ κινεῖται λόγῳ S.*OC* 1526, cf. Hsch.' add '**III** perh. *deconsecrated*, *SEG* 34.116.26 (Eleusis, 394/3 BC), σίγλοι καὶ ἀσκοὶ ἐξάγιστοι *IG* $2^2$.1544.22 (329/8 BC), cf. ib. 1453.10; v. *Hesperia* 25.100/1.'

***ἐξάγκᾰλος**, ον, (ἀγκάλη III) *containing six sheaves*, *PBerol.* $13062^v$ in *PMilan.* pp. 27-29.

**ἐξᾰγορεία**, for '*excantation* .. *confession*' read '*confession of sin* as means of obtaining cure of disease, coupled with θεοφορία and with ἐνθουσιασμός' and add 'Lxx *Ps.Sal.* 9.6'

**ἐξᾰγόρευσις II**, after 'Ptol.*Tetr.* 154' add '(v.l., ed. ἀγορία)'

**ἐξᾰγορευτής**, for '*one* .. sins' read '*one who practises* ‡ἐξαγορεία, δεισιδαίμονας ἱεροφοιτοῦντας ἐ.'

**ἐξᾰγορευτικός**, add '**2** perh. *of confession-cures*, δρόμου ἐξαγορευτικοῦ Ἀφροδείτης *POxy.Hels.* 23.30 (AD 212).'

**ἐξᾰ́γω I 2**, line 5, after 'Chrysipp.*Stoic.* 3.188' insert 'Plu. 2.242d' **II**, add '*IG* $1^3$.61.37, al. (v BC)' **III**, add '**2** *utter* a judgement, *Cod.Just.* 7.45.15.'

**ἐξᾰγωγεύς II**, add 'perh. in *Inscr.Délos* 399*A*98 (ii BC)'

**ἐξᾰγωγή I 3**, *exportation*, add 'ἐσαγωγὰν καὶ ἐξαγωγάν *SEG* 32.1586 (Lindian decree, Naucratis, v BC)' **II**, add '*IG* $1^3$.236.9 (v BC)'

**ἐξᾰγωγίς**, after '*drain*' insert '*IG* $4^2$.116.2 (Epid., iv/iii BC)'

**ἑξᾰ́γωνος I**, add '**2** ἑξάγωνον, τό, *hexagon*, *PKöln* 52.15, 17, 19, etc. (AD 263).'

**ἑξᾰδάκτυλος**, add 'see also ‡ἑγδάκτυλος'

***ἐξᾰδελφῐδῆ**, ἡ, *great-niece*, rest. in Dain *Inscr.du Louvre* 56.4 (Miletus).

***ἐξᾰδελφιδοῦς**, ὁ, *great-nephew*, *BCH* 87.203 (Delphi, iii AD).

**ἐξᾰ́δελφος I**, fem., add 'Ἡραῒς ἡ ἐξάδερφος τοῦ ἱερέος *IEphes.* 3415 (ii/iii AD); cf. mod. Gk. ξάδερφος'

***ἑξαδραχμιαία**, ἡ, = ἑξαδραχμία, *OBodl.* 1078 (ii AD).

**ἑξάδραχμον**, add 'see also °ἔκδραχμον'

***ἐξάδραχμος**, ον, *costing six drachmae*, συρίας ἐ. rest. in *PHib.* 51.6 (iii BC).

**ἐξᾰδῠνᾰτέω**, line 2, after 'Plu.*Alc.* 23' insert 'w. gen., ἐ. τοῦ προτιθέμεν *IG* 9²(1).583.9 (Acarnanian decree at Olympia, iii BC); περί τινος ib. 69'

**ἐξᾴδω I 2**, for '*sing the* ἔξοδος .. chorus' read '*sing aloud*' and add '(s.v.l.)' **II 1**, add 'περίπτωμα σχοῦσα καὶ ἐξᾳσθεῖσα *TAM* 5(1).331'

***ἐξαέτοι**, 3 sg. subj., perh. *pay a fine*, *IG* 5(2).261.10 (Mantinea, v BC); cf. °ἀφάεσται, ἀφαέτοι.

**ἐξαιθρᾰπεύω**, add '*Amyzon* 2 (321/320 BC)'

**ἐξαιθριάζω**, after 'pass.' insert 'ὕδωρ' and for '*Com.adesp.* in *PLond.ined.* 2294' read '*Com.adesp.* 274.20 A.'

**ἐξαιμᾰτωσις**, add '*PMich.*III 149 iv 21 (ii AD)'

**ἐξαίρεσις II**, before '*place where cargoes are landed*' insert '*unloading*, *Didyma* 39.37 (ii BC)'

**ἐξαιρετός I**, line 2, for 'ἐξαίρετα' read 'ἐξαιρετά' **II 2**, after 'And. 3.7' insert 'ἐ. [νῆες] *reserve* squadron, *IG* 2².1612.39, al. (Athens, iv BC)' **3**, add 'ἐξαιρετόν, perh. as adv. in *PWarren* 19.1 (ii AD)'

**ἐξαιρέω II**, add '**3** *make an exception of, exempt*, *Cod.Just.* 1.3.41.8, 11.1.1 pr., al.' **IV 1**, add 'Isoc. 17.14'

**ἐξαίρω II 1**, line 2, delete 'ἐκ'

**ἐξαΐω**, delete the entry.

**ἐξᾰκανθίζω**, for '*pick out* .. *holes in*' read '*deck with thorns*; fig., *denigrate*'

**ἐξᾰκανθόομαι**, add 'Gr.Nyss.*Ep.* 28 (p. 83.10 P.)'

***ἐξᾰκεράτιον**, τό, measurement of weight = 6 κεράτια, *PFlor.* v 112.6, 113.8, 116.10, 122.9.

***ἐξᾰκεστήρ**, ῆρος, ὁ, *the one who remedies evil*, τρεῖς θεοὺς ὀμνύναι κελεύει Σόλων, ἱκέσιον καθάρσιον ἐ. Sol.*Lg.* 44b R.

**ἐξᾰκεστήριος**, after '*remedying evil*' read 'as a divine epith., v.l. in Sol.*Lg.* 44b R. (v. °ἐξακεστήρ), θεοί D.H. 10.2.6, Ἐξακεστήριος· ὁ Ζεύς. καὶ ἡ Ἥρα Hsch.'

***ἐξᾰκισχῑλιοστός**, ή, όν, *six-thousandth*, Hsch. s.v. κοδράντης.

**ἐξᾰκολουθέω 1**, add '**b** *take up* an action, e.g. a fight, instituted by another, *SEG* 31.122 (Attica, ii AD).'

**ἐξᾰκόσιοι**, form ϝεξακάτιοι, add '*SEG* 23.393 (Corcyra, late vi BC)'

**ἐξᾰκουστος**, add '**3** *heard out, listened to*, πᾶσιν ἀνθρώποις Cyran. 25.'

***ἐξακτορεύω**, *hold office of* ἐξάκτωρ, *POxy.* 2110.18 (iv AD).

***ἐξακτορικός**, ή, όν, *of an* ἐξάκτωρ, τάξις, rest. in *POxy.* 126.4 (vi AD).

**ἐξᾰλᾰπάζω**, at end after 'Theoc. 2.85' insert '(v.l.)'

**ἐξᾰλειπτρον**, for '*unguent-box*' read '*unguent-flask* or *-basin*' add '**2** perh. *trinket-box*, ἐξάλειπτ[ρον τ]ορευτὸ[ν] χρυσοῦ[ν] ἐν ὧι βασ[ίλει]ον *PLond.* 1960.12.'

**ἐξαλλᾰγή 2**, add '**b** *departure from common idiom*, D.H.*Dem.* 13.'

**ἐξαλλάκτης**, add 'Hsch. s.v. κλοτοπευτής'

***ἐξάλοβος**, ον, *six-lobed*, Ar.Byz.*Epit.* 2.168.

**ἔξᾰλος**, add '**II** *away from the sea*, Eust. for ἐξ ἁλός in Od. 11.134, 23.281.'

**ἐξᾰμαρτᾰνω II**, for 'ἐξημαρτήθη' read 'ἐξαμαρτηθῇ' and add to the ref. '(s.v.l.)'

**ἐξᾰμάω** (B), for '= ἐξαφύσσω' read '*scrape out*'

**ἐξαμβλόω**, line 2, delete 'prob. f.l. for -ῶσαι in'

**ἐξαμβλῠνω**, for 'Dsc. 1.88' read 'Dsc. 1.69.4; τοὺς δικαστάς *PLit.Lond.* 138 viii 7'

***ἐξᾰμεινόω**, *amend, improve* an expression, Cratin. 171.72 K.-A.

**ἐξᾰμετρος**, add 'ἐξάμετρον, τό, *measure of six metra*, *CPR* 6.74.7 (AD 301)'

***ἐξᾰμηνιεῖος**, α, ον, = ἐξάμηνος II, *PCair.Zen.* 340.5, 27 (iii BC).

**ἐξᾰμηνος 2**, for 'ἑ. (sc. χρόνος), ὁ' read 'ἑ. (sc. περίοδος), ἡ' and after '*half-year*' insert 'Hdt. 4.25'; delete this ref. at end of section and substitute '*SEG* 33.464 (Larissa, 27 BC)'

⁺**ἐξαμναῖος**, α, ον, = ἐξάμνους: πολῖται ἐ., citizens who have acquired their status for six minae, or perh. who have a potential annual income of six minae, *IEphes.* 2001.9 (iii BC; v. *SEG* 37.882).

***ἐξᾰμυξος**, ον, *having six wicks*, λύχνοι *IUrb.Rom.* 106.9; cf. μύξα II 2.

**ἐξαναβαίνω**, add 'Il. 24.97 (v.l. εἴσανα-)'

***ἐξᾰναγκος**, ον, *necessary*, ἐξάνανκα πραττέσθω *SEG* 31.122 (Attica, ii AD).

***ἐξαναπάλλω**, med. sync. aor. κορυφᾶς .. ἐξανέπαλτο *sprang up out of*, Ibyc. 17.4 P.

**ἐξανᾰριθμέω**, for '*IGRom.* 4.661.34' read '*IGRom.* 4.661.3'

***ἐξαναστησείω**, *want to get up again*, ἰλυσπώμενον δὲ αὐτὸν ἔτι καὶ ἐξαναστησείοντα Agath. 3.4.6 K.

***ἐξαναστροφή**, ἡ, *turning upside-down, total change*, Sch.Hes.*Th.* 253b (p. 52.7 G.).

**ἐξανατέλλω 1**, add '**b** *cause to arise, bring into view*, νῦν δὲ Τιμόθεος μέτροις ῥυθμοῖς τ(ε) ἑνδεκακρουμάτοις κίθαριν ἐξανατέλλει Tim. *Pers.*231 P.'

***ἐξανατρέφω**, *bring up, rear*, πέδα τὸν κοινὸν ἐξαναθρέψας epigr. in *SEG* 26.645 (Thessaly, *c.*AD 400).

**ἐξαναφαίνω**, add '**2** *give birth again to*, of a mother, *CEG* 605.1 (Piraeus, iv BC).'

***ἔξανδρος**, *bereaved of a husband*, Hsch. s.v. χήρωσε.

**ἐξανέχω II**, add 'Ar.*Nu.* 1373'

**ἐξανθέω II 1**, after 'of wine' insert 'perh. *lose its bouquet*'

**ἐξάνθημα**, add '**II** ἀκάνθης ἐξανθήματα *thistledown*, Hsch. s.v. γήρεια.'

**ἐξανίημι I 1 a**, after 'Call.*Del.* 207' insert 'ἐξανέηκεν ἄναξ .. πηγήν epigr. in *Didyma* 159 iii 7 (iii AD)'

**ἐξάντλησις**, add '*SB* 10283.10 (ii BC)'

***ἐξαξεστιαῖος**, ον, = ἐξάξεστος, οἴνου ἐξαξεστιαῖα ἐβδομηκονταεννέα *PMich.*XIII 674.5 (vi AD).

**ἐξάξεστος**, add '*PMich.*XIII 667.17 (vi AD)'

***ἐξαούγκιον**, τό, *six-twelfths*, i.e. *one-half* (of an inheritance), Just.*Nov.* 18.1; also -ούγγιον ib. 2 pr. 1.

**ἐξᾰπᾰτη**, add 'D. 20.98, 45.46'

***ἐξαπελεύθερος**, ὁ, *freedman*, *Syria* 27.238 (iii AD); cf. ἐξαπελευθερόω.

***ἐξαπηθέω**, *strain off* from something, Nic.*Th.* 707-8 (tm.).

***ἐξάπλησον**, aor. imper. *multiply by six*, perh. irreg. for ἐξάπλωσον (ἐξαπλόω) *PCair.* 10758 (vi AD).

**Ἑξᾰπολις**, add 'of Greek cities on the Euxine, *IGRom.* 1.634.3, al.; in Cyrenaica, *SEG* 20.727.3 (ii AD)'

**ἐξαπόλλῡμι II**, add 'Emp. 12.2'

**ἐξάπρυμνος**, for '*stems*' read '*sterns*'

***ἐξάπτερος**, *six-winged*, Theognost.*Can.* 89.

**ἐξαπτέρῠγος**, add '*Orac.Tiburt.* 44'

**ἐξᾰράομαι II**, delete the section (v. °ἐξαρέσκομαι).

***ἐξάρεον**, τό, *central area in a temple enclosure*, Jo.Mal. 9.287 (v. *ZPE* 43.140).

**ἐξᾰρέσκομαι 2**, add 'Aeschin. 3.116'

***ἐξαριθμοζῠγοκαμπανοτρῡτᾰνίζω**, *count and weigh out with a steelyard*, (?)Jul.*Ep.* 205 (s.v.l., ed. ἐξ ἀριθμοῦ ζυγῷ Καμπανῷ τρυτανίσας).

**ἔξαρνος**, line 4, before 'ἐ. ἦν τοῦ φόνου' insert 'τοῦ δὲ τρίτου (sc. ταλάντου) ἔξαρνος γίγνεται Isoc. 21.3'

**ἐξαρπάζω**, line 7, after 'S.*OC* 1016 (s.v.l.)' insert 'D. 18.133'

**ἐξαρτίζω I**, after '(Mytilene)' insert 'a statue, *SEG* 24.1038 (Callatis, iii AD)' **II**, for '*equip and dispatch*' read '*furnish for a voyage*'

***ἐξαρτιστήρ**, ῆρος, ὁ, *fitter*, Ὀλυμπίῳ ἐξαρτιστ(ῆρι) *PRyl.* 641.11 (iv AD).

**ἐξαρτιστήριον**, after '*equipment*' insert '*PRyl.* 641.8 (iv AD)'

**ἔξαρχος 2**, line 2, after '*chorus*' insert 'E.*Ba.* 140'

**ἐξάρχω 4**, *rule*, add 'Just.*Nov.* 6 pr.'

**ἑξάς**, add '*SEG* 32.1601.24 (Nubia, iv/v AD)'

**ἐξασελλάνωμεν**, add '(ἐξασελγαίνωμεν La.)'

***ἔξασθμα**, ατος, τό, *exhalation*, *PMag.* 13.10.

***ἐξατίλιον**, τό or -ιος, ὁ, perh. a fish (?cf. Lat. *saxatilis*), *PRyl.* 630*. 332, al. (iv AD).

***ἐξάτμῐσις**, εως, ἡ, = ἐξατμισμός, Zos.Alch. 138.5 (lemma).

***ἐξάτροχος**, ον, *having six wheels*, *Poliorc.* 239.9.

⁺**ἐξαυλέω**, *wear out by playing the pipe*, ἐξηυλημέναι γλῶτται αἱ παλαιαί Poll. 4.73.

**ἐξαυστήρ**, for '[ἐξ]αυστήρ .. ib. 689' read '*IG* 2².1640.27, 1641.39'

***ἐξαύστης**, ου, ὁ, = ἐξαυστήρ, *Inscr.Délos* 372*B*26, 379.15 (ii BC).

**ἐξαυτῆς**, delete 'Thgn. 231, Aen.Tact. 22.29'

**ἐξαῦτις III**, add 'A.R. 4.455'

**ἐξάχαλκος**, delete the entry.

**ἐξᾰχειρ**, after '(Luc.)*Tox.* 62' insert 'epith. of Hecate, *PMag.* 4.2119'

**ἐξᾰχοίνῑκος**, add '*PTeb.* 210, *PTurku* 1.34 (*Tyche* 6.101; both ii BC); -ον, τό, measure of six choenices, *IEphes.* 3437'

**ἐξαχῠρόω**, read '**ἐξᾰχῠριόω**'

**ἐξᾰχῶς**, add 'ἅρματα ἑ. ἁμιλλώμενα *six at a time*, D.C. 75.4'

***ἐξδέκατος**, η, ον, *sixteenth*, *GVI* 440.4 (Cappadocia, ?ii/iii AD).

***ἔξε**, v. °ἐξ.

***ἐξέβενος**, ἡ, precious stone, *exhebenum* .. *candidam, qua aurifices aurum poliant*, Plin.*HN* 37.159.

***ἐξεγγόνη**, ἡ, *great-granddaughter*, *BCH* 87.202 (Delphi, iii AD).

⁺**ἐξεγγύη**, ἡ, *surety, security*, Is. 5.3.

**ἐξεγείρω**, add '**II** *erect* a building, *Salamine* 204 (v AD).'

**ἐξέδρα**, ἡ, delete separate definitions and substitute '*an open recess* or *alcove with seating* (whether accommodating small group or large gathering)'

**ἔξεδρος I 1**, for 'id.*Rh.* 1406ᵃ31' read 'Alcid.ap.eund.*Rh.* 1406ᵃ31' **2**, metaph., add 'Ath. 5.187f'

**ἐξεικάζω**, line 2, after 'X.*Hier.* 1.38' insert 'med., *model*, τὰ πόπανα πρῶτος ἐξηκάσατο *IG* 2².4962.17 (iv BC)'

**ἐξεικάττιοι**, for '*Supp.Epigr.* .. ii BC)' read '*BCH* 66/7.144 (iii BC)' and add 'also ἐξεικατι (sic) *SEG* 26.672.27'

**ἐξείλησις**, for '*release, escape* from' read '*twisting free* of'

**ἐξείλλω**, add 'cf. ἐγείλασαν'

*__ἐξειλώτισεν·__ ὡς ἐπὶ †τοῦ λωτοῦ† ἐξεπόρθησεν Hsch. (but prob. fr. ἐξειλωτίζω, *make into a helot*).
__ἔξειμι__ (B), add 'ἐξῆν· ἐξεγένετο· ἢ δύνατον ἦν Hsch. (La.)'
__ἐξείρω II__, delete the section transferring quots. to section I.
*__ἐξελαίωσις__, εως, *anointing with oil*, Anon.Alch. 345.4.
__ἐξελεύθερος__, line 1, after '*freedman*' insert '*SEG* 22.509 (Chios, vi BC), *IEryth.* 2.B21 (v BC)'
__ἐξέλικτρον__, add '*PCornell* 29 (iii/iv AD)'
__ἐξελίσσω I 1__, line 5, after '(Plot.) 2.4.9' insert 'Procl.*Inst.* 93 D.'
*__ἐξενεχυρασία__, ἡ, = ἐνεχυρασία, *APF* 15.93.5 (ii AD); cf. ἐξενεχυριάζω.
*__ἐξενιαυτέω__, *serve to the end of one's year of office*, -ῆσαι τὴν πρυτανείαν Sch.Pi.*N.* 11.10.
*__ἐξέο__, = ἐκ σέο, *IG* 12(5).472.13 (Oliarus), 14.2012*Cb*2 (Rome), *SEG* 19.456.7 (Thrace, ii AD).
__ἐξεπομβρέω__, for '*rain on*' read '*send rain*'
__ἐξέρᾱμα__, add 'Philum.*Ven.* 4.13'
*__ἐξέρᾰνος__, ὁ, *expelled from the ἔρανος*, *SEG* 31.122.44 (Attica, ii AD).
__ἐξεράω II 2__, add 'med., *pour out for oneself*, ἔλαιον ἐξηρασάμην *Com.adesp.* 289.17 A.'
__ἐξεργάζομαι I 5__, add '*POxy.* 2812.19'
__ἐξεργᾰτης__, delete the entry.
__ἐξέρεισμα__, add 'in pl., *buttresses*, *SEG* 4.270 (Panamara)'
__ἐξερεύγομαι I__, add 'λόγους *APl.* 328 (Barb.)'
__ἐξερέω__ (B) __II 2__, add 'A.R. 2.695, 4.1546'
*__ἐξέρκετον__, τό, = Lat. *exercitus*, *army*, *POxy.* 3872 (vi/vii AD).
__ἐξέρπω__, line 1, aor., add 'ἐξῆρψα Lxx *Ps.* 104(105).30' __III__, for this section read 'w. internal acc., *crawl*, *swarm* with, ἐξῆρψεν ἡ γῆ αὐτῶν βατράχους Lxx *Ps.* 104(105).30'
__ἐξέρχομαι I 1 c__, add 'in chariot-racing, *leave the starting traps*, *Hesperia* 54.221 no. 6, *Tab.Defix.Aud.* 234-238 (all ii/iii AD)' __III 1__, add 'of conditions, *be fulfilled*, *Cod.Just.* 6.4.4.17a'
__ἐξεσία__, add 'nom. pl. prob. in Call.*fr.* 80+82.22 Pf. (Add. II)'
__ἔξεστι__, line 1, imper., add '(ἐξήτω *SEG* 20.94.13 Cilicia, ?ii AD)'; inf., add '(WIon. ἐξεῖν *TAPhA* 65.105.10 Olynthus, iv BC)'; add 'ἐξόν in periphrastic constr. w. εἶναι (expr. or understood), ἡ .. δούλη .. ἐτόλμησεν .. ἰδεῖν ἃ οὐκ ἐξὸν (sc. ἦν) αὐτῇ Is. 6.50, καὶ οὐκ ἦν ἐξὸν καταπεσεῖν Luc.*As.* 16, Modest.*Dig.* 27.1.13.5'
__ἐξετάζω__, after 'ἐξετάσω' insert 'Ar.*Ec.* 729, etc.'
*__ἐξεταιρέω__, *prostitute*, ἐπὶ τῶν ἐκδεδιητημένων καὶ ἐξηταιρημένων ἀρρένων Suet.*Blasph.* III (tit.) T.
*__ἐξετᾰσιμος__, ον, *subject to scrutiny*; n. pl. subst., of documents, *SB* 7173.29 (ii AD).
__ἐξέτᾰσις__, line 4, after 'D. 18.246' insert 'Call.*Epigr.* 59.3 Pf.'
__ἐξέτεροι__, delete the entry (v. °ἐξέτερος).
*__ἐξέτερος__, η, ον, *some other*, ἐξετέρην θανάτου φύξιν Nic.*Th.* 588; pl., νοῦσοι ἐξέτεραι ib. 744; masc. pl. subst., ib. 412.
__ἐξέτι__, add '**2** app. in local sense, *from*, A.R. 1.976 (s.v.l.).'
__ἐξευλᾰβέομαι__, add 'Plu. 2.31b, 85e, al.'
*__ἐξευχᾰριστέω__, *give token of gratitude*, prob. in *MAMA* 4.288 (Dionysopolis).
__ἐξέφηβος__, add '*Milet* 1(7).203*b*26 (ii BC)'
__ἐξέχω I 2 b__, for '(Ar.)*fr.* 389' read '(Ar.)*fr.* 404 K.-A., Stratt. 48 K.-A.'
__ἐξηγητεία__, add '*POxy.* 2127.6 (iii AD)'
__ἐξηγητής II__, add '**4** local official in Egypt, Ἑρμοπολίτου (sc. νομοῦ) *PAmh.* 85.2, cf. 86.1 (both i AD); of Alexandria, Str. 17.1.12, *BGU* 1073.3 (iii AD).'
__ἐξηγητικός__, add '**III** *of* or *belonging to an* ἐξηγητής, ὑπηρέτης *PTeb.* 397.28 (ii AD); ἐξηγητικόν, τό, the *board* or *body of* ἐξηγηταί, *POxy.* 1413.9 (iii AD).'
__ἐξηκονθημερίσια__, delete the entry (v. °ἐξηκονθημερήσια).
*__ἐξηκονθημερήσια__, τά, *provision of sixty days' quarters and forage*, *PCair.Zen.* 341(*b*).5 (iii BC; sp. -ίσια).
__ἐξήκοντα__, line 1, for 'Ϝεξ-' read 'Ϝεξέκοντα' and add 'Ϝεξέϙοντα *SEG* 23.393 (Corcyra, 525/500 BC)'
*__ἐξηκοντάδραχμος__, ον, *of sixty drachmae*, *Stud.Pal.* 5.101.7.
*__ἐξηκονταείς__, μία, έν, *sixty-one*, *SEG* 26.672.35 (Larissa, early ii BC).
__ἐξηκοντάς II__, before 'Str.' insert 'Eratosth.ap.'
__ἐξήμαρε__, add '(ἐξημάρευσε La.; cf. ἀμαρεύων ib.)'
__ἑξῆς__, line 1, after '**ἐξείης**' insert '(ἐξέης perh. in *SEG* 37.575.6 (Chalcidice, iv BC), **ἐξείας** Isyll. 79 = *IG* $4^2$.128.74)' and after 'Dor.' insert '**ἐξᾶς** *ASAA* 14-16(1952/4)290.663 (Rhodes)'; line 5, for 'πάντας ἑ. .. 657.2' read 'κατὰ τὸ ἑξῆς *Peripl.M.Rubr.* 7, 15, al.' **3**, delete 'καὶ τὰ ἑ. .. etc.' **4**, add '**c** καὶ τὰ ἑ. *and so on in sequence*, *PTeb.* 319.34 (iii AD), Longin. 23.4, etc.'
__ἐξηχευη__, delete the entry (v. °ἐξηχεύομαι).
*__ἐξηχεύομαι I__ = βακχεύομαι, Hsch. s.v. βακχευθεῖσα. __II__ = *stupeo*, *Gloss.*
__ἐξῐδιάζομαι 1__, add 'Phryn. 172 F. (cited as non-Att.)'
__ἐξῐδιόομαι__, add 'J.*AJ* 1.6.2, al. **2** = ἐξιδιάζομαι 2, ib. 14.1.3.'
*__ἐξῐεριστέω__, Dor. ἐξιαρ-, = ἐξιεριστεύω, *Tit.Cam.* 40.15 (iii BC).'
__ἐξίημι I 2__, delete 'ἐς θάλασσαν'
__ἐξικνέομαι II 3__, for 'abs.' read 'w. adv. or advl. phr.' and transfer 'E.*Ba.* 1060' to exx. w. gen. in section II 2.
*__ἐξιόντως__, adv., perh. *in course of time*, *MAMA* 6.83 (Attouda).
__ἐξῐσόω I 1__, line 7, after '*rival*' insert 'Sapph. 96.22 L.-P.'
__ἐξίστημι B II 1__, add 'abs., = Lat. *bonis cedere*, *Cod.Just.* 9.4.6.8' **6**, for 'of language .. *usage*' read 'of a subject, etc., *to be removed from everyday concerns*'
__ἐξισχῠω II__, delete the section.
+__ἐξῖτᾱλα__, v. ‡ἐξίτηλος.
__ἐξῖτηλος__, add '**II** neut. pl. subst., ἐξίταλα· ἀναλώματα Hsch.'
__ἐξίτης__, add 'also **ξείτης**, **ξεῖτος**, **ξεῖθος**, *BCH* 8.501ff.'
__ἐξιτητήρια__, add '*SEG* 26.98.25 (Athens, iii BC)'
*__ἐξκέπτωρ__, ὁ, Lat. *exceptor*, *a minute-clerk* or sim. attached to a magistrate, *PKöln* inv. 1699.4 (*ZPE* 10.143, AD 332), *PMich.*XI 624.31 (vi AD), *POxy.* 943.6 (vi/vii AD); also ἐξκήπτωρ *PMich.*XIV 683.1 (v AD).
*__ἐξκουβίτωρ__, ορος, ὁ, Lat. *excubitor*, *soldier of the imperial guard*, *Corinth* 8(3).541, 558a (Chr.), *SEG* 34.927 ([ἐ]κουβίτωρ, Crete, all v/vi AD).
*__ἐξκουσατεύω__, *excuse* (from a duty), τοῦ πρώτου .. καλουμένου ἐξκουσατεύοντος ἑαυτὸν ὁ μετὰ ταῦτα ἐκαλεῖτο *Cod.Just.* 6.4.4.20a.
*__ἐξκουσατίων__, ονος, ἡ, Lat. *excusatio*, *grounds for being excused*, Modest.*Dig.* 27.1.13 pr.
*__ἐξκουσᾶτος__, ὁ, Lat. *excusatus*, *excused*, *exempt*, Just.*Nov.* 59.2; also **ἐξσκ-** *PAnt.* 33.37 (iv AD).
*__ἐξκουσεύω__, = °ἐξκουσατεύω, Just.*Nov.* 43.
__ἐξοδεία__, add '**III** *passing away*, Lxx (A) *Ez.* 26.18; cf. ἐξοδεύω II.'
__ἐξοδεύω__, add '**III** *expend* (money), *SEG* 30.1383.A10 (AD 301).'
__ἐξοδιασμός I__, delete the section (v. ἐξιδιασμός). __II__, before '*payment*' insert '*expenditure*, Lycurg.*fr.* 22 B.'
*__ἐξοδιαστικός__, ή, όν, *used for payment*, μέτρον prob. in *POxy.* 494.17 (ii AD).
__ἐξόδιος II 3__, for '*a feast* .. *Exodus*' read '*outgoing*, *terminating day of a feast*'
__ἔξοδος__ (A) __III 1__, after '*death*' insert 'Lxx *Wi.* 3.2'
__ἐξόθεν__, delete the entry (read ἐξ ὅθεν).
__ἔξοθεν__, add '**2** *apart from*, *besides*, *SEG* 26.437 (Argos, Chr.).'
__ἐξοιδίσκομαι__, delete the entry.
*__ἐξοιδίσκω__, = ἐξοιδέω, Gal. 9.521.7,; med., Hp.*Morb.* 2.57, Gal. 6.790.1.
__ἐξοκέλλω I 2__, for 'metaph. *drift into*' read 'fig., *run aground* (on the reef of)' __II__, metaph., add 'A.*fr.* 154a.3 R.'
__ἐξολεθρεύω__, add '*SEG* 32.1601.32 (Nubia, iv/v AD)'
__ἐξολισθάνω__, line 4, for 'of leaves' read 'of stags' horns'
*__ἐξομβριστήρ__, ῆρος, ὁ, *conduit for carrying off rain-water*, *PMich.*V 252.4 (i AD), *POxy.* 2146.6 (pl., iii AD).
__ἐξόμνῡμι II 1__, add '**b** (Boeot. 3 pl. aor. **ἐσσώμοσσαν**) of magistrates swearing themselves in, *SEG* 23.271.61 (Thespiae, iii BC).'
__ἐξομόργνῡμι__, line 6, delete 'parodied by'
__ἐξονομάζω II__, for '*call by name*' read '*give a name* to persons or things' and add '*Carm.Naup.* 1.1 B.'
*__ἐξονῠχιστής__, οῦ, ὁ, *scrutinizer*, λέξεων ἐ. *Poliorc.* 200.14; cf. ὀνυχίζω III.
*__ἐξονῠχιστικός__, ή, όν, *connected with paring the nails*, ἡ ἐ. (sc. τέχνη) Sch.D.T. 298.22.
*__ἐξοξέω__, *give accurate edges to*, ἐ. ἁρμούς *Inscr.Délos* 500*A*44, 46 (iii BC).
__ἔξοπτος__, after '-ος, ον' insert '(ος, η, ον freq. in pap.)'; after 'Hp.*VM* 14' insert '*PAmh.* 99a.9, *PRyl.* 164.7'
*__ἐξορέγομαι__, app. *stretch out*, orac. in *IEphes.* 1252.12 (ii AD).
+__ἐξορθρίζω__, dub., ἀπὸ μήτρας ἐξωρθρισμένης Aq.*Ps.* 109(110).3; cf. ἐκ γαστρὸς πρὸ ἑωσφόρου Lxx, ἐκ μήτρας ἀπὸ πρωῒ Th., etc.
__ἐξορία__ (s.v. ἐξόριος II), add '*Cod.Just.* 9.47.26 pr., etc.'
__ἐξορίζω__ (A), line 1, after 'aor. subj.' read 'Cypr. *e-xe o-ru-xe*, perh. ἐξορύξε̄ (fr. -ορϜιξ-) *ICS* 217.12, al.'; line 2, after '*banish*' insert '*expel*'
__ἐξορκίζω 1__, add 'Aeschin. 2.85, 87' **2**, add 'sp. ἐζορκ- *SB* 11247'
__ἐξορμέω__, for pres. def. read '*lie offshore*'
__ἔξορμος II__, delete the section.
__ἐξόρνῡμι__, add 'ἐξώρετο θεῖος ἀοιδός *Suppl.Hell.* 1185'
*__ἐξόροφος__, ον, *that belongs outside the house*, *outdoor*, [τὸν δ' ἐ]ξόροφον οὐ μιανεῖ *SEG* 9.72.17 (Cyrene, iv BC).
*__ἔξορρος__, ον, (ὀρός) *sapless*, *dry*, cj. in Thphr.*HP* 1.11.3 (codd. ἔξορθος).
*__ἐξόρυξις__, εως, ἡ, *excavation*, τοῦ ὄρους *BCH* 44.252 (Ptoion, i BC).
__ἐξορύσσω II 2__, add 'so perh. in Hippon. 104.35 W.'
+__ἔξος__, Dor. for ἔξω, *CID* II 34 ii 58 (iv BC), *SEG* 9.11ff. (Cyrene, iv BC), cf. *An.Ox.* 2.164.
__ἐξοστεΐζω__, line 1, for 'prob. l.' read 'cj.'

**ἐξότε**, add 'orac. in *Didyma* 496*A*3'

***ἐξουδένημα**, ατος, τό, *object of contempt*, ἐ. ἀνθρώπων Lxx *Ps.* 21(22).7, *Da.*(Thd.) 4.14(17).

**ἐξουθένημα**, delete the entry (v. °ἐξουδένημα).

**ἐξουσία I 1**, add '*licence* conferred on teachers of Jewish law, *Ev.Marc.* 1.22'; add 'πατρικὴ ἐ. *patria potestas*, Modest.*Dig.* 26.3.1.1, *CPR* 6.12.3 (AD 300/1). **b** = Lat. *imperium*, μηθενὸς ἐν ἐκείναις (ὑπαρχείαις) ἐξουσίαν μείζω εἶναι τῆς σῆς *PKöln* 10.10 (Augustus).'

**ἐξουσιάζω 1**, transfer 'D.H. 9.44' after 'Lxx *Ec.* 8.4'

***ἐξοφθαλμέω**, perh. = ἐξοφθαλμιάζω, *PAlex.* p. 36, no. 318.

**ἔξοχος II 1 a**, add 'Hes.*Op.* 773' add '**d** ἐπίτροπος .. τῶν ἐξοχ[ωτά]των καθολικῶν (= Lat. *procurator summarum rationum*), *Inscr.Perg.* 8(3).44.'

***ἐξπεδῖτος**, ον, *ready for action*, ἐξπεδῖτοι, εὔζωνοι, γυμνοί, ἑτοῖμοι πρὸς μάχην Lyd.*Mag.* 1.46; ἐν ἐξπεδίτῳ *in a state of readiness*, Just.*Nov.* 117.11.

**ἐξπελευστής**, delete the entry (v. °ἐξπελλευτής).

***ἐξπελλευτής** (**ἐξπελευστής** *Cod.Just.* 10.19.9.1), οῦ, ὁ, *collector* of taxes, κώμης Ἀφροδίτης *PFlor.* 291.6, cf. *PLond.* 1038 (both vi AD); of arrears, *Cod.Just.* l.c., Just.*Nov.* 128.6; (Lat. *expello*; cf. *compulsor*).

***ἐξσκούσατος**, v. °ἐξκουσ-.

**ἐξυβρίζω II**, add 'of water in flood, Lxx *Ez.* 47.5'

***ἐξῠδᾰτάω**, = ἐξυδατόω, Heph.Astr. 3.6.10.

***ἐξῠδᾰτισμός**, ὁ, *changing into water*, Zos.Alch. 197.10.

**ἐξυδρίας**, before 'Ach.Tat.' insert 'cj. in'

***ἐξυπτιόω**, = ἐξυπτιάζω, pass., *live luxuriously*, Phot. s.v. πεταχνοῦνται; cf. Hsch. s.v. πεταλοῦνται.

**ἐξῠφαίνω I 1**, line 3, delete 'Nicopho 5' and after 'pass.' insert 'ὁ δ' ἐξυφαίνεθ' ἱστός, ὁ δὲ διάζεται Nicopho 13 K.-A.'

**ἐξυψόω**, for '*elevate*' read '*transform into an elevated style*'

**ἔξω I 1 a**, add 'w. ref. to the movement of dislocated bones away from the body, Hp.*Mochl.* 16, *Art.* 64' **2 a**, add 'ἔξω ἐγένετο *became distracted*, Hp.*Epid.* 5.80' **b**, line 8, ἔ. τοῦ πράγματος, add 'Is.*fr.* 22'

***ἐξώβολος**, ον, *consisting of six obols*, Hsch. s.v. λεπτὰς καὶ παχείας; neut., *sum of six obols*, *OStrassb.* 67 (i AD, ἐξόβ-).

**ἔξωθεν II a** after '1*Ep.Ti.* 3.7' insert '*those outside a (particular) relationship*, Just.*Nov.* 1.1.3' **b**, for 'X.*An.* 5.7.24' read 'X.*An.* 5.7.21' **c**, add '*Cod.Just.* 1.2.17.15; abs., *besides*, *MDAI(A)* 51.13 (lapis ἐσ-, Cos), *JHS* 15.112 (Lycia), *TAM* 2.247.11, etc.'

**ἐξωθέω I 1**, penultimate line, after 'S.*OC* 428' insert '**b** *debar, exclude*, αὐτὸν .. ἐξωθείτω καταλόγων *Cod.Just.* 1.4.34.9.'

**ἐξώλεια I**, add 'ἐξξόλειαν *IG* $9^2$(1).609.15 (Naupactus, vi/v BC)' add '**II** *abandoned* or *abominable conduct*, Horap. 2.65.'

***ἐξώλεος**, ον, = ἐξώλης, *IMylasa* 476 (Rom.imp.).

**ἐξώλης II**, add 'ἐ.· κίναιδος Hsch.'

**ἐξωμίς**, line 4, after 'X.*Mem.* 2.7.5' insert '*SEG* 34.122.47 (= *IG* $2^2$.1673, Eleusis, iv BC)'

**ἐξωμοσία I**, add '**2** = Lat. *cautio iuratoria*, *Cod.Just.* 10.11.8.7, Just.*Nov.* 134.9.1.'

**ἐξωπῠλῖται**, after 'organized body' read 'app. connected w. burial work, *TAPhA* 71.650 (ostr., iii AD), *PGrenf.* 2.72.4 (iii/iv AD), *BGU* 34 ii 21 (iv AD)'

**ἔξωρος 2**, w. gen., add 'ἔξωρον .. τῶν ἐρωτικῶν Philostr.*Her.* 11'

***ἐξώρροπος**, ον, *inclining outwards*, Phlp. *in APo.* 439.7.

**ἐξώστης 4**, add 'Theophil.Antec. 4.6.2'

**ἐξώτατος**, (s.v. ἐξωτάτω), add '*Peripl.M.Rubr.* 4 C. (cod. ἐσω-, v. *CQ* N.S. 30.495)'

**ἐξωτικός 1**, before 'ή, όν' insert '(ἐσω- *RPh* 10.121)'; after '*foreign*' insert '*unguenta exotica* Plaut.*Most.* 42'; line 4, after '(Iasos)' insert '*RPh* l.c. (Perinthus)' add '**b** *Graecia exotica, overseas* i.e. *colonial Greece*, Plaut.*Men.* 236. **c** *being outside a (particular) legal relationship*, Just.*Nov.* 48.1 pr.'

***ἐξωφάκαι** (or -**άκες**), αἱ, kind of haemorrhoids, Cyran. 29 (v.l. ἐξωχάδας, v. °ἐξωχάδες), 103 (v.l. ἄνθρακας).

***ἐξωχάδες**, αἱ, *external haemorrhoids*, Cyran. 1.12.31, 2.30.13 K., al.

**ἐοικότως**, delete the entry (v. °εἰκότως).

***ἐόργη**, ἡ, τορύνην, ἣν καὶ εὐέργην ὠνόμαζον καὶ ἐόργην Poll. 6.88, 10.97.

**ἑορταστικός**, add '*PSI* 791 (vi AD)'

**ἑός**, Boeot., add 'ϝϝοῖ (dat.) *CEG* 444(i) (at Delphi, ?*c.*550 BC)'

**ἐπαγγελία**, after lemma insert 'Thess. ἐπαγγελλία *BCH* 59.38 (Crannon, in quot., sense 3)' **3**, ἐξ ἐπαγγελίας, add '*SEG* 30.1274 (Caria, *c.*AD 200)'

**ἐπαγγέλλω 6**, for this section read 'med., *propose, ask* as a concession or favour, D. 19.41, 193'

**ἐπάγγελμα 4**, add '*Cod.Just.* 1.3.41.26'

**ἐπαγλαΐζω I**, add 'Ps.-Hdt. *Vit.Hom.* 192'

**ἔπαγρος**, line 2, for 'Call.*Hec.* 1.4.10' read 'Call.*fr.* 260.64 Pf.'

**ἐπάγρυπνος**, delete 'Aristaenet. 1.27' and add 'Ἄμμων ἐπάγρυπνος ὀπτ‹ή›ρ *IUrb.Rom.* 141; adv. -ως *SEG* 29.250 (Attica, Chr.)'

**ἐπάγω I 8 a**, line 4, after 'D. 47.28' insert 'abs., ἐφόρων καὶ γερόντων ἐπαγόντων *BSAA* 39.133 (Euesperides, iv BC)'

**ἐπᾰγωγή 1**, add '*bringing in, introduction* of a water-supply, *PAvrom.* 1*A*27' **3**, add '**b** *visitation*, Ἑκάτης φάσκων ἐπαγωγὴν γεγονέναι Thphr.*Char.* 16.7.' **4 b**, delete "Ἑκάτης .. 16.7' **7**, for this section read '*trouble, distress* Lxx *Si.* 2.2, 3.28, al., 23.11 (pl.), *Is.* 14.17'

**ἐπᾰγωγός**, add '**III** οἱ ἐ., officials in tax-farming company, *Michel* 1225.16 (Cyzicus, i BC). **IV** *supply-pipe*, *IG* $4^2$.116.19 (Epid., iv/iii BC, pl.).'

**⁺ἐπάγων**, οντος, ὁ, kind of pulley, = ἀρτέμων II, the guiding pulley of a system, Vitr. 10.2.9.

**ἐπαείδω 2**, add 'πείθειν ἐπᾴδουσ' ὥσθ' ὁμαρτεῖν μοι πέτρας E.*IA* 1212' add '**3** *relate* a story *about*, w. dat., μῦθον τῷδε τῷ ζῴῳ ἐπᾷσαι Ael.*NA* 6.51, 16.5, λόγον ib. 12.30.'

***ἐπᾱέτιον**, τό, *top of gable*, ἐ. ξύλινον μεμολυβδωμένον *Inscr.Délos* 421.17, 442*B*168 (ii BC).

**ἔπαθλον**, line 1, for 'etc.' read '1262 (cj.)' and at end add 'cf. παρ' οὐδενὶ κεῖται τὸ "ἔπαθλα" ἢ μόνῳ τῷ Εὐριπίδῃ Sch.E.*Ph.* 52'

**ἐπάϊκλα**, delete the entry.

***ἐπαῖκλον** or **ἐπάακλον**, τό, (αἶκλον) *additional meal, dessert*, Dor. for ἐπιδειπνίς, ἐπιδόρπασμα, Ath. 14.664f; pl., Pers.*Stoic.* 1.101.454, Sphaer.*Stoic.* 1.142.630, Molpis 2b J.; also **ἐπαίκλεια** or **ἐπαῖκλεια**, Apion ap.Ath. 14.642e.

**ἐπαινέτης II**, delete the section.

**ἐπαινέω**, line 8, after '(*Schwyzer*) 623.34)' insert 'also Dor., *REA* 33.210.16 (Theangela, decree of Troezen, iii/ii BC)'; line 13, delete '= αἰνέω .. Att.)' **I 4**, delete the section transferring quots. to section I 2. **II**, for '= παραινέω .. *advise*' read '*express one's approval of* a course of action, *recommend*' **IV**, delete the section.

**ἐπαινός**, add '**2** *praiseworthy*, Triph. 52, Mitchell *N.Galatia* 103.'

**ἐπαινουμένως**, add 'Just.*Nov.* 82.1.1'

**ἐπαιονάω**, line 1, delete '(intr.)'

**ἐπαίρω I 2**, add 'in fig. phr., ἐπάραι κύριος τὸ πρόσωπον αὐτοῦ ἐπὶ σέ (transl. Hebr. idiom, i.e. show favour) Lxx *Nu.* 6.26' **4**, add '*raise oneself* in bed, prob. in Call.*fr.* 191.43 Pf.' **5**, line 1, for 'Gal. 6.264' read 'Gal. 6.265.1'

**ἐπαισθάνομαι 1**, add 'Hes.*fr.* 204.120 M.-W.'

**ἐπαιτιάομαι**, penultimate line, delete 'to it'

**ἔπαιτον**, delete 'τό' and for 'dub. sens. in' read 'perh. adv., *approximately*' and add '*PGen.* 113.8 (sp. ἐπαίετον), 114.8 (sp. ἐπάαιτον) (both iii AD)'

***ἐπαιχμάζω**, *attack with a spear*: transf., of mating wild boars, Opp.*C.* 1.389.

**⁺ἐπαιωρέω**, *hold suspended* over, ξίφος .. τοῖς αὐχέσιν ἐπαιωρούμενον Hdn. 5.2.1, πέτρον ἐπῃώρησε καρήνων Nonn.*D.* 4.456. **b** med., *poise threateningly* above or over, Plu.*Fab.* 5; Σκύθαι τοῖς μέσοις ἐπαιωροῦντο Them.*Or.* 8.119c; of conditions, τοῖόν σφιν ἐπὶ δέος ᾐωρεῖτο A.R. 1.639, τὰ ἐκτὸς ἐπῃωρημένα Ph. 1.650, κίνδυνον οὐκ ἐπαιωρούμενον ἀλλ' ἤδη παρόντα Hdn. 1.9.10. **2** *hold poised for action*, ἄκουε .. τὰ ὦτα ἐπαιώρησας Ph. 2.125; med., w. dat., *hold oneself poised* for, ἐπαιωρεῖσθαι πολέμῳ Plu.*Pel.* 29, τοῖς πράγμασι id.*Tim.* 2. **3** *cause to rest on the top* or *surface* of, τρίχας .. καὶ τὰ ὅμοια ἐπαιωρηθήσεσθαι διὰ τὴν κουφότητα Dsc. 5.75.11, 5.92, ἐ. πτερὸν ἠέρι πολλῷ *GVI* 1765.5, fig., αἶσιν (εὐτυχίαις) ἐπῃώρησας ἀεὶ βίον *AP* 7.645 (Crin.), ἐλπίσιν ἐπαιωρούμενοι Luc.*Alex.* 16, Hdn. 2.9.1. **II** med., *rise, swell*, ὄγκος ἐπαιωρεύμενος ἔξω Aret.*CA* 1.7, *SD* 1.14.

**ἐπακμάζω**, line 2, after '*come to its height*' insert 'Longin. 13.4'

***ἐπᾰκολουθητής**, οῦ, ὁ, *concurring party*, *PColl.Youtie* 67.8 (AD 260–1).

***ἐπᾰκολουθία**, ἡ, = ἐπακολούθησις, Sch.Hes.*Th.* 245b.

**ἐπάκριος I**, add '*SEG* 21.541 v 60 (Attica, iv BC)' **II**, add '**2** ἐπάκριοι, οἱ, a party at Athens in the time of Solon, Plu. 2.763d; cf. πεδιεῖς, πάραλος.'

**ἐπακροάομαι**, line 2, for 'Hld. 2.17' read 'Hld. 2.16'

**ἐπακτήρ**, after 'Il. 17.135' insert 'Call.*Jov.* 77, Opp.*C.* 1.481' and for 'later' read 'also'

**ἐπακτός I 2**, line 2, after 'Pi.*O.* 10(11).89' insert 'E.*Ion* 290, 592'; lines 6/7, delete 'ἐ. πατήρ .. *Ion* 592'

**ἐπᾰλειπτέον**, add 'Gal. 10.498.11'

**ἐπᾰλείφω**, after lemma insert '(app. ἐπᾱλ- Alcm. 80 P.)'

**ἐπᾱλής**, for '*open to the sun, sunny*' read '*exposed to the fire*'; for '(nisi .. ἀλής)' read '(or perh. *crowded*, cf. ἀλής)'

**ἐπάλλαξις 3**, delete 'διαιτημάτων .. 385 (pl.)'

**ἐπαλληλία**, line 4, for 'Gal. 19.679' read 'Gal. 19.680.1'

**ἐπάλληλος II 1**, for 'by *one another's* hands' read 'by *hands used against each other*'

**⁺ἐπᾰμερος**, v. ἐφήμερος.

**ἐπᾰμύντωρ**, after 'Od. 16.263' insert 'as title of Apollo, *SEG* 31.559 (Delphi, iv BC)'

***ἐπαμφιάζοντες·** ἐπενδύοντες Hsch.

**ἐπαμφόδιος**, delete the entry.

**ἐπάμων**, for 'cf. Hsch. (pl.)' read 'ἐ. (cod. ἐπάλλων)· δοῦλος λάτρις Hsch. (La.), ἐπάμονες· ἀκόλουθοι id. (ἐπ- Schmidt)'

**ἐπαναβαίνω I 3**, add '**c** perh. *reach the age of*, w. εἰς, *IGLS* 607; cf. °ἐμβαίνω.'

**ἐπαναβάλλω III**, add 'pass., of *deferred* payment, *IG* 11(2).142.1, 3, 4 (Delos, iv BC)'

**ἐπαναγκάζω**, omit '*by force*' and add '*IG* 12(7).515.85 (Amorgos, ii BC)'

**ἐπᾰνάγκης**, line 2, for 'And. 1.12' read 'And. 3.12' **2**, add 'ἡ δὲ δημοθοινία [γε]νέσθω ἐν τῷ γυμνασίῳ ἐπάναγκες *as is required*, *IG* 12(7).515.106 (Amorgos, ii BC)'

**ἐπᾰ́ναγκος I**, add 'neut. as adv., *PMich.*inv. 1410.11 (*JJP* 18.158)'

**ἐπανάγω III 2**, for this section read 'εὖ ἐ. *enjoy health* or *prosperity*, *get on well*, τῷ σώματι Apollon.Perg.*Con.* 1 pr.; sim., w. other advs. μετρίως, ἱκανῶς ἐ., *PTeb.* 755.6 (ii BC), *UPZ* 110.6 (ii BC); στενῶς ἐ. ib. 60.15 (ii BC)'

***ἐπαναδύω**, dub. sens., cf. ἀναδύομαι, Dor. aor. 2 part. ἐπανδύς, prob. = *ἐπαναδύς, Sophr. in *PSI* 121*d*11.

**ἐπανακᾰλέω I**, delete the section.

**ἐπανάληψις**, add '**III** *recapture*, Just.*Const.* Δέδωκεν pr.'

***ἐπαναμισθόω**, *let afresh*, *BCH* 60.182 (ἐπαμμ-, Thespiae, iii BC).

**ἐπανανεόομαι**, add '*restore*, ἐπανανεωσάμην τὴν (sic) ἐκτησάμην ποίαλον (= πύαλον) *TAM* 4(1).352'

**ἐπαναποδίζω**, add 'ἐπαναποδιστέον Arist.*GC* $317^{b}19$'

***ἐπανάπωλος**, ον, *resold to a further party* (in quot., of contracts), *IG* 7.3074.3 (Lebadea, ii BC).

**ἐπανάστασις I 3**, after '(Th.) 8.21' insert '*SEG* 31.985A (Teos, v BC), ib. 28.60.12 (Attica, iii BC)'

**ἐπαναστρέφω II**, for 'Pass., *return to the surface*' read 'med., *turn oneself over*'

**ἐπανατέλλω II**, lines 6/7, delete '*show oneself* .. A.*Ch.* 282' and add 'w. dat., *rise close behind*, Arat. 341; *grow up in consequence of*, A.*Ch.* 282'

**ἐπανατίθημι**, for '*lay upon*' read '*shift* a load, weight *on to*' and after 'metaph.' insert '*PPetr.* II 4.1+4.9 (256 BC; v. *ZPE* 59.62)'

**ἐπαναφέρω I 3**, add '*report*, ἐπαναφέρω σοι περὶ τῆς αὐτῆς γεωργίας *POxy.Hels.* 13.4, 10 (i AD)'

**ἐπαναχέω**, add 'also ἐπαγχ-, v.l. in A.*Ag.* 1137 (cf. ἐπεγχέω)'

**ἔπανδρος**, add 'sup. *La Carie* p. 98 no. 5'

**ἐπανδρόω**, add '**2** *fill with men*, Λῆμνον A.R. 1.874 (v.l. ἐσ-).'

**ἐπανερωτάω**, after '*question again*' insert 'or *further*' and after 'Pl.*Clit.* 409d' insert 'Demetr.*Eloc.* 288'

**ἐπάνεσις I**, add '**2** *relaxation*, *remission* of dues, καθόλου ἐπάνεσις ἔστω τοῦ τελωνοῦ *SEG* 39.1180.47 (Ephesus, i AD)'

**ἐπανήκω**, add 'of an estranged lover returning, Heph.Astr. 3.9.34'

**ἐπανθέω II**, add 'w. internal acc., [ὃς] μὲν γὰρ παριαῖσιν ἐπήνθει παῦρον ἴουλον epigr. in Mitchell *N. Galatia* 392.17' **III**, delete the section.

**ἐπάνθισμα**, add '**II** dub. sens., ἐ. [ἱα]ρεῖ Διονυσίωι *IAskl.Epid.* 51.7 (p. 44) (iii BC).'

**ἐπανοίγω**, for '*open*' read '*open up again*' and add 'εἰ δέ τις τολμήσει ἐπανῦξε τὴν σορόν *TAM* 4(1).267, *IEphes.* 3327 (both ii/iii AD)'

**ἐπανορθόω**, line 2, for 'Lys. 1.70' read 'Lys. 2.70' add '**4** *repair*, *restore* artefacts, τὰ δημόσια ὅπλα .. ἐπανορθοῦν τε καὶ ἀνανεοῦν Just.*Nov.* 85.2.'

**ἐπανόρθωσις**, add '**b** *restoration*, *reconstruction* of buildings, etc., *IG* $9^{2}$(1).583.59 (Acarnanian decr. at Olympia, iii BC), *IG* 12(5).1030 (Paros, ?i BC).'

**ἐπανορθωτής**, add 'ἐπανορθωτὴν Ἀσίας *SEG* 31.910 (Aphrodisias, iii AD)'

**ἐπαντλησμός**, for '= foreg.' read '*artificial irrigation*, *PBremen* 30.4 (ii AD)'

***ἐπάντλιον**, τό, kind of machine for irrigation, *SB* 12524.21 (i BC).

**ἐπάνω I 1**, add 'οἱ ἐπάνω *those above the earth*, *the living*, *INikaia* 1282, 1450, al.' **2**, line 3, after '(Tenos, iii BC)' insert 'οἱ ἐπάνω γῆς = οἱ ἐπάνω (v. supra) *INikaia* 1395'; at end after 'Val. 48.5' insert 'ἐ. εἴλης, = Lat. *praepositus alae*, *SEG* 6.167 (Temenothyrae, Phrygia)' add '**4** *up-country*, *inland*: ἐπάνω τοῦ λιβός *inland in a westerly direction*, *Peripl.M.Rubr.* 15; τούτων ἐπάνω ib. 47.'

**ἐπαποθνήσκω**, for '*die after* another' read '*add oneself* to *in death*, *die in addition* to, οὐ μόνον ὑπεραποθανεῖν ἀλλὰ καὶ ἐπαποθανεῖν τετελευτηκότι'

***ἐπαπολισθάνω**, of perspiration, *stream off* a person, *POxy.* 1381.130 (ii AD).

**ἐπαπορέω**, line 3, ἐπαπορεῖταί τι, omit 'τι' and substitute 'impers.'

**ἐπαποστέλλω I**, add '**2** *send in addition* on a mission, expedition, or sim., pass. ἐ. ὑπὸ Ἀγησιδάμου *Inscr.Cret.* 1.xvi 35 (Lato, ii BC).'

**ἐπᾰράομαι**, add '**7** w. acc. and inf. with μή, *conjure* (deities) to prevent an occurrence, *SEG* 6.784 (Cilicia, ii/iii AD).'

**ἐπᾰρᾰρίσκω I**, add '[λίθον] γυίοις ἐπήραρε Euph. 9.14' **II**, lines 5/6, for '*well-fitted* .. Nonn.*D.*' read '*made fast*, Hes.*Op.* 601, 627: ἐφάρμενος, *suited*, w. dat., Nonn.*D.* 7.78'

***ἐπάρδεια**, ἡ, *irrigation*, *POxy.* 3354.27 (AD 257).

**ἐπάρδια**, delete the entry (v. *ZPE* 41.256).

***ἐπᾰρετέω**, *requisition* or *take for use*, κτήνη, πλοῖα *PTeb.* 5.182, 252 (ii BC); cf. ἡ ἐν ἀρετῇ κειμένη γῆ (v. ἀρετή I 2 b).

**ἐπάρκεια**, add '*SEG* 25.653 (Thessaly, ii BC)'

**ἐπαρκής I**, delete the section transferring quots. to section II.

**ἔπαρμα I**, add '**2** *raised bank* or *platform*, ἔθηκεν ἔπαρμα ὕψος πήχεις ἑξήκοντα, πλάτος αὐτοῦ πήχεων ἑξήκοντα Lxx 2*Es* 6.3; ὄχθοι δὲ γῆς ἐπάρματα Ammon.*Diff.* p. 108 V. (369 N.). **3** app. *a weight lifted* by a strong man, ἔ. Φαβατίωνος *SEG* 23.666 (Cyprus, iii AD).' **II 2**, delete the section. add '**III** wd. occurring in inventory of utensils, *SEG* 24.361.10 (Thespiae, 386/380 BC).'

**+ἐπαρτής**, ές, *ready* for action, use, etc., ἐπαρτέες εἰσὶν ἑταῖροι Od. 8.151, 14.332, ἐπεὶ δμώεσσιν ἐπαρτέα πάντ' ἐτέτυκτο A.R. 1.234, 3.299. **II** app. *hanging*, Opp.*H.* 5.359, πολλαὶ δ' οὐρανόθεν καὶ ἐπαρτέες ἐκ νεφελάων .. ἐπόρνυνται φηγοῖς .. πηγυλίδες Orph.*fr.* 270.

**ἐπαρχεία I**, add 'also app. of a bishop's reign, *SEG* 31.1474 (Arabia, vi AD)'

**ἐπαρχεῖον**, delete the entry.

***ἐπάρχειος**, ον, *of* or *pertaining to an* ἔπαρχος: -ειος, ἡ, *province*, *IPE* $1^{2}$.54 (Olbia), *IGBulg.* 1690.e30 (Pizus); sp. -ιος, *IG* 14.1078*a*.7, *IGRom.* 1.580 (Nicopolis ad Istrum), *POxy.* 2106.4 (iv AD). **2** cult-title of Zeus, *of the province*, *ICilicie* 109 (AD 99).

**ἐπαρχή**, after 'Oropus' insert 'v. *SEG* 31.416 (iv BC)'

**ἐπαρχία**, line 14, for 'of Carthage, *empire*' read 'in general, *subject territory*' and add 'Plb. 1.15.10, 1.75.5, al.'

***ἐπαρχιακός**, ή, όν, *provincial*, Modest.*Dig.* 26.5.21.4; neut. pl. subst., *dowry*, Cod.Sinait. in *BCH* 4.452.

**ἐπαρχικός I**, add '**2** ἐπαρχικός, ὁ, *ex-prefect* (cf. ἔπαρχος I 2), *OGI* 578.14 (Tarsus, iii AD), *SEG* 8.647 (Egypt, iv AD). **b** employee in the office of an ἔπαρχος, *ITyr* 12, *MAMA* 3.374, 416, 691.'

***ἐπάρχιος**, v. °ἐπάρχειος.

***ἐπαρχῑτικός**, ή, όν, *of a province* (Lat. *provincialis*), ἐπαρχειτικῶν ἀγρῶν *Mon.Anc.Gr.* 8.23.

**ἔπαρχος I 1**, delete '*commander* .. ἄπαρχος' (v. °ἄπαρχος). **2**, line 3, after '(Plu.)*Brut.* 51' insert 'ἔ. ἀρχιτεκτόνων *IG* $2^{2}$.3546 (Eleusis, i AD)'; line 7, after '(Sidyma)' insert 'ἐπάρχῳ λεγ(ιῶνος) ια' Κλαυδίας *SEG* 33.1194 (Cappadocia, i/ii AD), ἔπαρχος ἱππέων *ITomis* 127 (ii/iii AD)' **II**, add 'ἔ. ἐξουσία *BCH* 11.351 (Laodicea), cf. ἐπαρχικός I'

**ἐπασσῠ́τερος I**, add 'Stesich. S139.7'

***ἐπασχᾰλάω**, *to be indignant at*, w. dat., ἐπασχαλόων .. κυδοιμῷ Nonn.*D.* 36.413; Aeol. pres. part. ἐπα[σχάλαντες] συμφόραισι rest. in Alc. 69.1 L.-P., cf. 306 i 18/19 L.-P.

***ἐπᾰ́τερθεν**· ἐπέκεινα Hsch.

**ἐπαυλέω, ἐπαύλημα**, for '*flute*' read '*aulos*'

**ἐπαύλιον III**, delete the section.

***ἐπαύλιος**· ἡ τῆς αὐλῆς ὁδός Suid., Zonar.

**ἔπαυλος**, after 'Od. 23.358' insert '(v.l. ἐν-)'; delete 'A.R. 1.800' and add 'Hes.*fr.* 66.1 M.-W.' **2**, after '*home*' insert 'Hes. l.c.'

***ἐπαυξητικός**, ή, όν, *increasing*, *intensifying*, Sch.E.*Hipp.* 518.

**ἐπαυρέω II 1 a**, lines 2/3, delete 'μόχθων .. Pi.*N.* 5.49'; line 9, transfer 'Hdt. 7.180' to section b; add 'w. acc., μόχθων ἀμοιβάν Pi.*N.* 5.49; κτῆσιν *AP* 9.332 (Noss.)'

**ἐπαυχμέω**, for '*send drought* .. ἐπαυχμήσας' read '*cause a drought*'

**ἐπᾰφάω**, line 3, after 'c. gen.' insert 'Ἄρκτου Arat. 93'

**ἐπᾰφή I 1**, add '**b** ἐπαφῇ τῆς σελήνης as cause of the birth of Apis, Plu. 2.718b.' **III**, for 'prob. *external claim*' read 'perh. *skin-disease*' and add '*BGU* 2111.14 (ii AD)'

***ἐπάφησις**, εως, ἡ, *touching*, cj. in Nicostr.ap.Stob. 4.22.102 (pl.).

**ἐπαφίημι 1**, line 5, after 'Alciphr. 1.22' insert 'transf., τὴν ὀργὴν εἴς τινας J.*AJ* 19.2.2' **2**, after 'Thphr.*CP* 2.5.5' insert '(Schneider)'

**Ἐπᾰ́φιος**, delete the entry (v. °Ἐπάφριος).

***ἐπαφορμίζομαι**, *look for a pretext*, *Vit.Aesop.*(W) 58.

***ἔπᾰφος**, ον, app. *attached*, i.e. *staked* or *trained*, ἐὰν .. ὀλιγωρήσῃ τὴν ἄμπελον καὶ μὴ ποιήσῃ αὐτὴν ἔπαφον *PAvrom.* 1*A*26, 1*B*27 (i BC; v. *JHS* 35.55).

***Ἐπάφριος**, epith. of Dionysus, Orph.*H.* 50.7 (ἐπάφιε codd.), 52.9; cf. Ἀφριος.

**ἐπάχθεια**, add '*PKöln* 110.4 (v/vi AD)'

***ἐπβάσκω**, v. °ἐπιβάσκω.

***ἐπεγγράφω**, *register in addition*, Plu. 2.278d.

**ἐπεγκλίνω**, add 'ἐ. νοῦν *incline* the mind, *direct* it to something, *Orac.Chald.* 1.2 P.'

***ἐπεγρήγορος**, ον, *alert*, *watchful*, Plu.*Brut.* 36.2, Horap. 1.60 S.

***ἐπεγρία**, ἡ, *wakefulness*, Iamb.*VP* 3.13.

***ἐπέγχωσις**, εως, ἡ, *the action of heaping on top* (in quot., in building up a dike), *PBremen* 14.7 (ii AD).

**ἐπεί**, line 1, after '**ἐπειδή**' insert '(Thess. **ὀπειδεί** *SEG* 27.202 (Larissa, iii BC), and so perh. **ὀπεί κε** = ἐπειδάν, *BCH* 59.55, *SEG* 31.575.31 (Larissa, both ii BC))' **A II**, line 5, add 'w. κα in Doric ἐπεί κα πέντε ϝέτεα hēβōντι *IG* 5(2).159.4 (at Tegea)' **B 1**, *for otherwise*, add 'so also ἐπειδή Mitchell *N.Galatia* 257 (AD 140)'

**ἐπείγω IV 3**, add 'Gal. 9.309.3, *SEG* 30.1390B (Lydia, ii AD)' add '**V** *impose* a penalty, θέματα, ἐφ' ὧν ἐξ ἀρνήσεως διπλάσια τὰ τῆς καταδίκης ἠπείγετο *Cod.Just.* 1.3.45.7a.'

**ἐπεῖδον**, after 'ἐπιδεῖν' insert 'late aor. inf. ἐφιδῆσαι *PTeb.* 751.10 (ii BC)'

**ἐπεὶ ἤ**, add 'and ἤ adv. I 2'

**ἐπείκτης**, add '**II** *collector*, χρυσοῦ στεφάνου *POxy.* 1413.25 (iv AD); written **ἐπίκτης** *POxy.* 1428.3 (iv AD).'

***ἐπείλῠμα**, ατος, τό, *wrapping*, *POxy.* 1765.16 (iii AD; pl., sp. -ειλύμματτα).

**ἔπειμι** (A) **II**, add 'Call.*Epigr.* 50.3 Pf.'

**ἔπειμι** (B) **III 1**, delete 'χώρους Hdt. 5.74'

**ἐπείσακτος**, for '*SIG* 1231' read '*TAM* 4(1).276' and add 'Procl.*Inst.* 201 D.'

**⁺ἐπεισβαίνω**, *to go into so as to make an approach* or *attack*, ἐπεσβαίνοντες ξὺν τοῖς ὅπλοις ἐς τὴν θάλασσαν Th. 2.90.6, 4.14.2, ἵππῳ εἰς θάλασσαν X.*HG* 1.1.4; fig., ἐχόμενοι .. ὥς τινος ἀσφαλοῦς πείσματος ἐπεισβαίνωμεν εἰς τὸν νῦν λόγον Pl.*Lg.* 893b.

**ἐπεισκρίνομαι**, delete the entry.

***ἐπεισκρίνω**, *bring in on top of* or *in succession*, pass., Hp.*Alim.* 5; med., οὐσία ἀεὶ ῥεῖ τε καὶ ἑτέρα ἀνθ' ἑτέρας ἐπεισκρίνεται S.E.*P.* 3.82.

**⁺ἐπεισκυκλέω**, *roll* or *trundle in one after another*, θεὸν ἀπὸ μηχανῆς ἐπεισκυκληθῆναί μοι τοῦτον ᾤμην Luc.*Philops.* 29; fig. ὁ δ' Ἄττης .. καὶ ὁ Κορύβας .. πόθεν ἡμῖν ἐπεισεκυκλήθησαν; id.*Deor.Conc.* 9, *Hist.Conscr.* 13, ἀσάφειαν ἡμῖν τοσαύτην S.E.*P.* 2.210, Gal. 8.575.5, ἕτερα ἑτέροις ἐπεισκυκλούμενα Longin. 11.1, 22.4.

**ἐπεισπαίω**, after '*Com.adesp.* 439' insert 'ἀγῶσι *thrust oneself into*, prob. in *PLond.* 1912.92 (i AD)'

**ἐπεισφέρω**, line 5, add 'εἰ δέ τις ἕτερον νέκυν ἐπισενέγκ[η] *TAM* 4(1).249 (ii/iii AD)'

***ἐπείτοιγε**, introducing a final alternative or resort, *or else*, *otherwise*, *Cod.Just.* 1.3.45.10, al., Just.*Nov.* 1.1.2, 17.3, al.

**ἐπεκδῐκέω**, add 'cf. *TAM* 3(1).418 (ii AD), al.'

***ἐπεκκεντέω**, *stab*, *pierce*, Sm.*Za.* 12.10.

***ἐπεκονίθη**· κατωρύχθη Hsch.

**ἐπεκτείνω I 1**, after 'Arist.*EN* 1097ᵇ12' insert 'τὴν αὐτὴν .. νομοθεσίαν καὶ ἐπὶ γυναιξὶ παρθενευούσαις ἐπεκτείνομεν *Cod.Just.* 1.3.52.14' add '**6** *expand* in value, τὰς προσόδους Str. 17.1.15.' **II 2**, add 'Macho 208 G.' **III**, delete the section.

**ἐπελαύνω I 1 b**, add 'ἐπελ[ά]σтō *SEG* 30.380 (Tiryns, vii BC)'

**ἐπελέγχω**, add '*disgrace*, *put to shame*, Thgn. 1011 (tm.)'

**⁺ἐπελεύθω**, aor. 1 ἐπήλευσα, *bring to*, *Inscr.Cret.* 4.41 i 9, al. (Gortyn, v BC), *Leg.Gort.* 3.45, al., *GVAK* 32.15.5.

**ἐπέλευσις**, add '**4** *assault*, *PMich.* VI 423-424.4 (ii AD), *POxy.* 69.15 (ii AD).'

**ἐπεμβάλλω 3**, line 5, for 'thou .. *intrudest* thyself' read 'you *impose* yourself'

**ἐπεμπηδάω II**, for this section read '*leap upon*, Gal. 8.556.15'

***ἐπεμπόδων**, adv., = ἐμποδών, *MAMA* 4.279 (Dionysopolis).

**ἐπεμφέρω**, add '*bring in*, *serve*, *IG* 12(7).515.49 (Amorgos, ii BC)'

***ἐπεναντίον**, *contrary to*, ἐπεναντίον τούτῳ *PFlor.* 294.43 (vi AD).

**ἐπενδύτης**, line 3, after 'Lxx 1*Ki.* 18.4' insert '*PMich.*inv. 1648.12 (*AJP* 65.257; ii AD)'

***ἐπενδύτιον**, τό, dim. of ἐπενδύτης, *SEG* 39.1278 (Katakekaumene, Lydia, ii AD).

***ἐπενεκτέον**, *one must give a name to*, Gal. 9.813.5; cf. ἐπιφέρω I 6.

**ἐπενήνοθε 2**, for '*had passed*' read '*has passed*'

**ἐπενθάπτω**, add '*TAM* 4(1).264 (Rom.imp.), *INikaia* 766'

**ἐπενίημι**, for '*compress* the pulse' read '*exert on*, πόσον ἀρκεῖ τῆς θλίψεως ἐπενεῖναι τοῖς οὕτως ἔχουσιν'

**ἐπεντίθημι**, after 'pass., *to be put in besides*' insert 'of additional (unauthorized) burial in a tomb' and add '*TAM* 4(1).239 (Rom.imp.)'

**ἐπέξειμι**, add 'παλαιὰς ἀπεχθείας Arr.*An.* 1.9.6'

***ἐπεξελέγχω**, *denounce*, *TAM* 3(1).823 (Termessus).

**ἐπεξεργάζομαι 4**, add 'ὑπέρ τινος Ptol.*Tetr.* 117'

**ἐπεξεργᾰσία**, after 'Ptol.*Tetr.* 117' insert '(v.l.)'

**ἐπεξορκίζω**, add '**b** *conjure*, w. acc. of deity invoked, Swoboda *Denkmäler* 18 (Pisidia).'

**ἐπέραστος**, line 2, after '(Luc.)*Im.* 10' insert '*AP* 5.299.1 (Agath.)'

**ἐπεργάζομαι 3**, delete the section. add '**III** *contrive in addition*, εὔνους γὰρ γεγονὼς τοὐμῷ πατρὶ .. κατὰ πόδας θανατοῦ μοῖραν ἐπειργασάμην epigr. in *SEG* 32.611 (Thessaly, i BC).'

**⁺ἔπεργος**, ον, *aiding the business*, *useful*, *PSI* 619.8 (iii BC). **2** -ος, ὁ, *assistant*. *SB* 5680.3 (iii BC). **II** -ον, τό, *work*, *effort*, ὃν (νηόν) ἀκαμάτοισιν ἐπέργοις .. ἐξετέλεσσεν epigr. in *SEG* 37.1537 (Arabia, c.AD 400). **2** *work done in addition* to payment of rent, τοῦ μισθώματος καὶ τῶν ἐπέργων ἁπάντων ἀπότεισμα *IG* 12(7).62.15 (Amorgos).

**ἐπέρεισις**, line 2, for 'Gal. 2.386' read 'Gal. 2.387.17'

***ἔπερθα**, adv., = ὕπερθεν, Alc. 208(*a*).ii.8 L.-P.; cf. °κατέπερθεν.

**ἐπέρχομαι**, line 2, after 'ἐπῆλθον' insert '(Cret. part. ἐπευθών, *Inscr.Cret.* 4.168.17 (iii BC))' **I 3**, add 'neut. part. used abs. w. ἄλλως, *haphazardly*, *as it came to mind*, ἄλλως ἐπελθόν, οὐκ ἐξεπίτηδες ἤρετο Luc.*DDeor.* 20.4, cf. Apollod. 1.9.16'

**ἐπερωτάω 5**, add '*Cod.Just.* 2.12.27.2, Just.*Nov.* 162.1 pr.'

**ἐπερώτησις 1**, add 'τὰν μαντείαν καὶ ‹ἐ›περώτασ[ιν *SEG* 30.85.18, 25 (Delphian letter, i BC)'

**ἐπές**, add 'w. gen., app. w. assim., ἐπὲ ϝέργō Dubois *Dial.Arcad.* p. 196 (Pheneus, c.500 BC)'

**ἐπεσθίω I 2**, for 'Thphr.*CP* 6.4.7' read 'Thphr.*CP* 6.4.6'

**ἐπέτης**, masc., add '*PRyl.* 627.146, al. (iv AD); Myc. *e-qe-ta*, title of high official; deriv. adj. *e-qe-si-jo*'

**ἐπετήσιος**, for 'ἐγχρονίσας .. *Epigr.Gr.* 815' read '᾽νχρονίσας ἐφετήσιον (*annual sacrifice*) οὐκ ἀπέδωκε epigr. in *SEG* 33.736 (Crete, ii AD)'

**ἐπευάζω**, add 'cf. ἐφευάζω'

***ἐπευθών**, v. °ἐπέρχομαι.

**ἐπευνάζω**, read '**ἐπευνάζομαι**'

**ἐπευωνίζω**, after 'D. 23.201' insert 'τὴν ἀγορὰν ἐπευωνίζων *SEG* 38.1462.9 (Oenoanda, ii AD)' add '**2** intr. of prices, *get lower*, *PCair.Zen.* 363.14 (iii BC; ἐπεων-).'

***ἐπηβολέω**, dial. ἐπᾱβ-, *achieve mastery*, *knowledge*, etc., of, w. acc., *Iamb.adesp.* 38.11 W.; w. gen., Pi.*Pae.* 6.182.

**ἐπηβολή**, line 1, after '*Leg.Gort.* 5.50' insert 'also Boeot. *SEG* 3.342.16 (Thebes, iii BC)'

**ἐπήβολος I 1**, line 3, after 'Hdt. 9.94' insert 'ἀμφοτέρων ἐ. Call.*fr.* 384.44 Pf.'; last line, after 'Hld. 10.20' insert '*hitting the mark*, *effective*, ὁρμή A.R. 2.1280; μῆτις id. 4.1380' **2**, last line, delete 'πάντεσσιν .. 4.1380' **II**, for this section read '*having been attained*, ἐπήβολός ἐστ' ἀλεωρή A.R. 1.694, ἐπήβολος ἅρματι νύσσα id. 3.1272'

**ἐπήκοος II**, lines 5ff., abs., add '*SEG* 30.519-526 (Corcyra, c.500 BC); of Apollo, Mitchell *N.Galatia* 154,; of Hermes, *Salamine* 44 (ii/i BC)'

**ἔπηλυς II**, after 'neut. sg.' insert 'ἔπηλυ πλῆθος Heraclit.*Ep.* 9.6'

**ἐπήλυσις**, for '*assault*' read '*onset*' and after it insert 'Archil. 196A.50 W., Call.*fr.* 331 Pf.'; add 'ποταμοῦ (sc. the Nile) *GDRK* 60 ii 1'

**ἐπηλύτος**, add 'Lxx *Jb.* 20.26'

***ἐπήμενοι**, v. ἔφημαι III.

**ἐπηρεάζω I** and **II**, combine these sections under definition '*treat vexatiously*, *obstruct*' **III**, add 'Gal. 9.283.9, 14'

**ἐπηρεασμός**, line 1, for '*despiteful treatment*' read '*vexatious* or *obstructive conduct*'; line 3, after 'cf. (Arist.*Rh.*) 1382ᵃ2' insert 'Men.*Dysc.* 178'

**ἐπηρεαστής**, for '*insolent person*' read '*ill-disposed* or *hostile person*'

**ἐπήρεια**, line 1, delete '(ἐπί, ἄρος)' and for '*insulting treatment*, *abuse*' read '*hostile* or *obstructive attitude* or *conduct* (so in subsequent glosses)'; add 'μείζονα ἐπήριαν προσάγουσιν οἱ πρακτῆραις *PCol.* 174.7 (iv AD)'

**⁺ἐπήρης**, ες, of ships, *equipped with oars*, νῆες A.R. 1.235 (pap.), πλοῖα Agatharch. 83, κελήτιον Arr.*An.* 5.7.3; transf., ἐ. πτερύγεσσιν Max. 415.

**ἐπητύς**, for '(This .. ἐδ-η-τύς)' read '(etym. obscure)'

**ἐπί**, line 1, after '(iii BC)' insert 'sp. ἐβί *GVI* 1990.9 (Egypt, ii/i BC), 817.5 (Arcesine, Amorgos, ii/iii AD)' **B I 1 c**, line 2, after '(lyr.), etc.' insert 'δῶρα δεχόμενον ἐπὶ τοῖς τῆς πατρίδος συμφέρουσιν Din. 2.26' **II 1**, add 'ἐπὶ τοῖς ἄστροις .. καὶ μάλιστα ἐπὶ κυνί Arist.*HA* 600ᵃ3-4' **III 3**, line 4, for '*on condition that* .. ' read '*on condition that*, w. fut. indic.' and delete 'in orat. obliq.'; line 5, after '(Hdt.) 7.154' insert 'Pl.*Ap.* 29c'; line 6, after 'Th. 1.126' insert 'ὁρκίσας ἐφ' ᾧ .. ἔσται *SIG* 684.26 (Dyme, ii BC)' **6**, at end delete 'ἐ. θυγατρί .. 4.154' add '**8** *in the presence of*, ἐπὶ τοῖς δικάζōσιν *IEphes.* 1678 (vi BC).' **C I 1**, add '**c** arith., *multiplied by*, *PMich.* III 145.3.5.6, al.; τέσσαρες μονάδες ἐπὶ η' γίνονται λβ' Papp. 26.10; ἐπόησα τὰς ε' ἐπὶ τὰς ᾱ *I multiplied five by a thousand*, *PMich.* III 145.3 vi 4.' **5**, line 8, for 'Th. 1.50, cf. 62' read 'Th. 1.62.6, cf. 50.2' **II 1**, add '**b** ἐφ' ἔτος, v. ‡ἐφέτος II.' **2**, add '*up to now*, τῶν γ' ἐπὶ τάδε γεγενημένων Isoc. 9.37' **III 2**, at end delete 'κρείσσων ἐπ' ἀρετήν Democr. 181' **E I**, add 'also *item*, introducing an entry in accounts, ἐπί· ἔδωκα κτλ. *SEG* 7.387, cf. 381, al. (Dura, iii AD)' at end add 'Myc. *e-pi* (w. dat.)'

***ἐπιάλης**· ὁ ἐφιάλτης Hsch.

**⁺ἐπιάλτης**, v. ‡ἐφιάλτης.

**ἐπιάομαι**, delete the entry (cf. *Schwyzer* 369.22).

***Ἐπίασσα**· Δήμητρος ἐπώνυμον Hsch.

**ἐπιβάθρα 2**, for this section read '*landing-place*, Plb. 3.24.14 (pl.), Ael.*NA* 12.15. **b** transf., *place offering means of approach*, *"stepping-stone"*, *"gangway"* or sim., ἵνα, ἐὰν πρόθηται διαβαίνειν αὖθις εἰς τὴν Ἀσίαν, ἐπιβάθραν ἔχοι τὴν Ἄβυδον Plb. 16.29.2; Plu.*Demetr.* 8; fig., γάμον ἐ. τισὶ γενέσθαι J.*AJ* 11.8.2, τῷ ἑξῆς λόγῳ Arr.*Epict.* 1.7.22, Plot. 1.6.1, Gal. 9.149.18.'

***ἐπίβαθρον**, τό, *embarkation fee, passage-money*, καὶ δέ κεν ἄλλ' ἐπίβαθρον .. δοίην Od. 15.449, Call.*Del.* 22 (pl.), *PCair.Zen.* 753.34, 36 (pl., iii BC), D.S. 1.96, *Et.Gen.*, Suid.; transf., of a sacrifice before embarkation, A.R. 1.421 (pl.), ὅ γε πελαργὸς ἐπίβαθρόν τι τῆς ‹διαίτης› δίδωσιν Plu. 2.727f. **II** something on which to sit or rest, of a stool, *AP* 9.140 (Claudian.), of a perch, ib. 9.661 (Jul.Aegypt.). **III** *ladder* or *steps*, *PSI* 171.27 (pl., dub., ii BC); perh. τὠπίβαθρον τῶ θρόν[ω] τ̣ὸ̣ χρύ[σι]ο̣ν̣ (part of Zeus' statue at Olympia) Call.*fr.* 196.23 Pf.

**ἐπιβαίνω II 1**, add '**c** *take possession*, w. gen., ἐπιβαίνειν τῶν προσηκόντων αὐτοῖς πραγμάτων *Cod.Just.* 1.3.52.7; w. dat., ib. 10.11.8.7a.'

**ἐπιβάλλω I 1**, add 'med., *cast* lots *for*, καὶ ἐπὶ κλήρους ἐβάλοντο Od. 14.209' **4**, delete 'in Med. .. 23.27' **6**, delete 'βλαστούς ib. 3.5.1' **II 5**, add '**b** ὁ ἐπιβάλλων in law, *the next in succession*, *Leg.Gort.* 7.36, 11.42, al.' **6 b**, delete the section. **III 2 a**, line 4, delete '*take possession* .. 14.209' **IV 1**, for 'Pass. .. *put upon*' read 'med., *place* upon (sc. ὀϊστούς)' **2**, before '*to be set over*' insert 'pass.'

**ἐπιβαρύνω**, add 'Hsch. s.v. ἐπεζάρηκεν'

**ἐπιβάσκω**, add '**2** perh. *encroach on*, Thess. 3 sg. pres. ἐπβάσκει *IGC* p. 10.8, al. (Larissa, ii BC).'

**ἐπιβατήριος III 2**, after '*disembarkation*' insert '*IGRom.* 4.1542 (Smyrna, ii AD)'

**ἐπιβάτης 4**, for '*male quadruped*' read '*stallion*, w. ref. to its function in breeding'

**ἐπιβατός II**, for 'παίων' read 'παιών (but cf. Παιάν ad fin.)'

***ἐπιβηματίς**, ίδος, ἡ, *step* (at the foot of a structure), *ISmyrna* II(2). p. 355 ix (ii/iii AD).

***ἐπιβήτωρ**, ορος, ὁ, *one who sets foot on* or *dwells in*, ὕλης οὐρανίας Orph.*fr.* 353. **b** *one that moves upon*, θοῶν ἐπιβήτορα κύκλων ἵππον (i.e. the Trojan horse) Triph. 307. **2** *one who goes on board*, νεὼς ἐ. λαόν (i.e. crew) *AP* 7.498 (Antip.Sid.); νηῶν ἐ. ἄνδρας (= ἐπιβάτας) Opp.*H.* 5.298. **II** *one who mounts* a horse, etc., ἐ. ἵππων Od. 18.263, Simm. 1.3; of tamer of wild animals, θηροδιδασκαλίης ἐ. Man. 4.245. **b** transf., adj. ἐ. παλμῷ Nonn.*D.* 20.113. **2** of a male animal used for breeding, συῶν ἐπιβήτορα κάπρον Od. 11.131; Theoc. 25.128.

**ἐπιβιάζομαι**, for '*constrain besides*' read '*use force against* (in tomb robbery)' and add '*SEG* 17.632.10 (Perge, Rom.imp.)'

***ἐπιβιβάζω**, (fut. -βιβῶ Lxx *Ho.* 10.11), *cause to go on board*, ἐπ' ὀλίγας ναῦς τοὺς ὁπλίτας .. ἐπιβιβάσαντες Th. 4.31.1. **2** *cause to mount* on, ἐπιβιβάσατε τὸν υἱόν μου .. ἐπὶ τὴν ἡμίονον Lxx 3*Ki.* 1.33, ἐπιβιβάσας .. αὐτὸν ἐπὶ τὸ ἴδιον κτῆνος *Ev.Luc.* 10.34, pass., Apollod. 3.1.1; fig., Aristid.*Or.* 30(10).23. **b** app. *put to the plough* (calque Heb.), Lxx *Ho.* 10.11. **c** *set* or *place* on, ἐπιβίβασον τὴν χεῖρά σου ἐπὶ τὸ τόξον Lxx 4 *Ki.* 13.16. **d** *cause to ride* or *tread* over, ἐπιβίβασας ἀνθρώπους ἐπὶ τὰς κεφαλὰς ἡμῶν Lxx *Ps.* 65(66).12, ἐπεβίβασας εἰς θάλασσαν τοὺς ἵππους σου Lxx *Hb.* 3.15, 19.

**ἐπιβιόω**, for 'only in' read 'impf. ἐπεβίουν Just.*Nov.* 66.1.4, aor. 1 part. ἐπηβιώσασα *SEG* 31.342 (Sparta, Rom.imp.)'

**ἐπιβλέπω**, after 'Lxx *Le.* 26.9' insert '(ἐπιγλέποι· ἐπόψεται Hsch. La., cod. ἐπιπλέγοι; cf. ποτιγλέπω)' **I 1**, add 'abs. *SEG* 36.552.14 (Thessaly, ii BC)' **2**, add '**b** w. acc., of the gods, *watch over*, Call.*fr.* 602.2 Pf.; cf. ἐφοράω 1.' **3**, for this section read '*face* in a particular direction, ἐπιβλεπέτω δὲ τὸ μὲν κοῖλον αὐτῶν ἄνω, κάτω δὲ ἡ ἀποτομή Dsc. 5.120'

***ἐπίβλημα**, ατος, τό, *cloth thrown over as a covering*, Nicostr.Com. 13.3 K.-A., Gal.*UP* 11.12; as coverlet, bedspread, *IG* 12(5).593.4 (Iulis, v BC), Plu.*Cat.Ma.* 4, Arr.*An.* 6.29.5, Gal. 14.638.18, Sor. 1.85. **b** included among items of clothing, *IG* 1³.403.61, 2².1514.31, Lxx *Is.* 3.22. **c** used to patch clothing, *Ev.Matt.* 9.16, *Ev.Marc.* 2.21, etc. **d** as an outer bandage, Paul.Aeg. 6.92 (146.4 H.).

***ἐπίβλησις**, εως, ἡ, chemical operation expld. as συλλείωσις κατασπωμένη, Anon.Alch. 7.5.

**ἐπιβοάω I 4**, add 'med., *TAM* 2(3).838*e*19 (Lycia, ii AD)'

**ἐπιβοήθεια**, add '*SEG* 32.1128.11 (Ephesus, i BC)'

**ἐπιβόητος I**, for 'Aeschrio 8' read '*AP* 7.345'

***ἐπιβολᾰδοποιός**, ὁ, *maker of* *ἐπιβολάδες (perh. mantles or wrappers) or *of* *ἐπιβολάδια (dim. of ἐπιβόλαιον), *IG* 2².11175 (iv BC).

**ἐπιβόλαιον**, add 'Hsch. s.v. καυνάκαι'

**ἐπιβολεύς**, add '**2** gen. pl., dub. sens., *IG* 4².110*A*40 (Epid., building accounts, iv/iii BC).'

**ἐπιβολή I**, add '**6** *landfall*, *Peripl.M.Rubr.* 55.' **II 3 b**, add '*extra payment*, *APAW* 1952(1).12' add '**4** *compulsory allocation* of land to proprietors on which they were obliged to pay taxes, *BGU* 2023.11-12 (AD 198/201).'

***ἐπίβολον**, τό, *linch-pin*, Gorg.ap.Poll. 1.145.

**ἐπιβουλεύω I 4**, add 'μὴ ἐπιβουλεύσῃ‹ς› τῷ τάφῳ *SEG* 33.311 (Laconia, Chr.)'

***ἐπιβρίζω**, = ἐπιβρίθω, Nonn.*D.* 20.347, al.

**ἐπιβρῑ́θω**, after 'Porph.*Abst.* 1.43' insert 'Plot. 5.3.15'

**ἐπιβρύκω**, at end after 'Herod. 6.13' insert 'cf. ἐπιβρύκων (pap. -βρυχον ante corr.) Hippon. 104.15 W.'

**ἐπιβωμίς**, add '*TAM* 4(1).45.9'

**ἐπίγαιος**, add 'of evil spirits, *PMasp.* 188ᵛ (vi AD)'

**ἐπιγαμβρεία**, add 'also **ἐπιγαμβρία**, *PHarris* 202.8'

**ἐπιγάμβρευσις**, add 'gloss on κηδεία Exc.Barocc. 324'

**ἐπιγᾰμέω**, add '**II** med., of the woman, *marry as a second husband*, w. dat., Sch.Pl.*Mx.* 235e.'

**ἐπιγᾰμία II b**, add 'οἱ κατ' ἐπιγαμίαν οἰκεῖοι Modest.*Dig.* 26.6.2'

**ἐπιγδουπέω**, add 'w. dat., κύμβαχος .. ἐπεγδούπησε κονίῃ *fell with a thud* on, Nonn.*D.* 36.218'

**ἐπίγειος**, line 2, before 'opp.' insert 'ὕδατα ἐ. *on the surface of the ground*, Thphr.*CP* 2.5.1'

**ἐπιγεννάω**, add 'σὺν τοῖς ἐπιγεννωμένοις *with* (*her*) *descendants*, *SEG* 24.498(*a*) (Maced., ii AD)'

**ἐπιγεννητός**, add '**b** gramm., *agnomen ex aliqua virtute forinsecus quaesitum, quod ἐπιγεννητόν Graeci dicunt*, Diom. p. 321 K.'

**ἐπιγίγνομαι II 3**, add '*Cod.Just.* 1.2.17.2a' add '**7** *come additionally into being*, Emp. 17.30 D.-K.'

**ἐπιγιγνώσκω IV 2**, add '*Cod.Just.* 3.10.1.1'

***ἐπιγλέποι**, v. °ἐπιβλέπω.

**ἐπιγλισχραίνω**, add 'Gal.*CMG* 5.9(1).245.17'

***ἐπιγλωσσάομαι**, Att. -ττάομαι, *utter forebodings*, μηδ' ἐπιγλωσσῶ κακά A.*Ch.* 1045, cf. Hsch. s.v. ἐπιγλωσσῶ; περὶ τῶν Ἀθηνῶν δ' οὐκ ἐπιγλωττήσομαι τοιοῦτον οὐδέν Ar.*Lys.* 37; w. gen., *against*, ταῦτ' ἐπιγλωσσᾷ Διός A.*Pr.* 928.

**ἐπιγνώμων**, after '*judge*' insert '*SEG* 30.380.6, 7 (Tiryns, vii BC)'

**ἐπίγνωσις I 1**, add '**b** *recognition* (as mark of honour), *approval*, *SEG* 34.553.8 , 23.447.13 (both Demetrias, ii BC).'

**ἐπιγογγύζω**, add 'gloss on ἐπιμύζω Sch.Gen.Il. 8.457'

***ἐπίγομος**, ὁ, *additional cargo*, *PUG* inv. DR 48 (*ZPE* 65.173). **II** measure of capacity, Ἰωάνω ἐλαίο(υ) ἐπιγό(μους) γ' μετρητὰς ϛ' *SB* 7365 (AD 104).

**ἐπιγόνειον**, for 'Egyptian .. μάγαδις' read 'musical instrument with forty strings, prob. a board zither' and add 'perh. also ἐ. (codd. ἐπιτόνιον) ψαλτήριον Ath. 10.456d'

**ἐπιγονή I 1**, line 4, after 'θρεμμάτων' insert 'Androt. 55 J.' **I 2**, add '**b** πυρὸς συντέχνου μυρίας ἐπιγονάς *benefits resulting from* fire, Anon.ap.Suid. s.v. Ἀρίσταρχος Τεγεάτης.' **II**, for 'later apptly. .. Πέρσης τῆς ἐ.' read 'Πέρσης τῆς ἐπιγονῆς member of the lowest class of Greek settlers in Egypt; later, applied to Hellenizing Egyptians'

**ἐπίγονος II 2 c**, at end delete 'τῷ Ἐπιγόνου .. (Cnidus)'

**ἐπιγράβδην II**, for '*like lines*' read '*in the form of letters*'

**ἐπιγραμμᾰτογράφος**, add '*SEG* 28.1493 (Egypt, ii BC)'

**ἐπιγραμμᾰτοποιός**, add 'of Posidippus, *IG* 9²(1).17*A*24 (Thermus, iii BC); Ps.-Plu.*Vit.Hom.* 84 (of Antipater of Sidon)'

**ἐπιγρᾰφή**, after lemma insert 'ἐπιγροφά *IAskl.Epid.* 52 A 16 (iv BC), cf. γροφά' **1 a**, add 'εἰκόνα χαλκέαν ἐπὶ τῶ αὐτῶ βάματος ἐπιγραφὰν ἔχοισαν *IKyme* 13' **3**, add 'ἐν τῶι δ[ι]κρότωι ὧι ἐπιγραφὴ Δη[μή]τηρ *SEG* 33.684 (Paros)'

**ἐπιγυμνάζω**, for 'Pass., .. abs.' read 'med., *take exercise*, Hp.*Insomn.* 88'

***ἐπίγῡος**, ον, *imminent*, *PEnteux.* 15.5 (iii BC), cf. ὑπόγυιος I.

**ἐπιγώνιος I**, for '*at the angle*' read '*situated at a corner*' and after 'Nicom.*Ar.* 1.19' add 'of buildings, etc., οἰκία *SB* 9902A ii 30 (iii AD), ψιλός ib. K 10, πύργος ib. Q ii 6'

***ἐπιδαίομαι** (A) (δαίω A), *to burn with passion* for, w. dat. and acc. of respect, κίχλης δ' ἐπιδαίεται ἦτορ (κόσσυφος) Opp.*H.* 4.173.

**ἐπιδαίομαι** (B), for 'dub. sens.' read 'prob. corrupt'; delete 'Pass. .. Hes.*Th.* 789' (v. °ἐπιδατέομαι)

**ἐπιδάκνω**, delete 'med.' and transfer 'Nic.*Al.* 19, 121' to follow 'pass.'

**ἐπιδᾱμιοργός**, after 'al.' insert '(-ουργός *BCH* 52.174 (Delphi, i BC))'

***ἐπιδᾰτέομαι**, *allot*, Ὠκεανοῖο κέρας, δεκάτη δ' ἐπὶ μοῖρα δέδασται Hes.*Th.* 789.

**ἐπιδέρκομαι**, add 'w. dat., *AP* 12.87.5 (Mel., tm.)'

**ἐπιδερμίς I**, add '**2** *conjunctiva*, Ruf.*Onom.* 28.'

**ἐπίδεσμος**, add 'cf. Myc. *o-pi-de-so-mo* (pl.), *bindings*'

**ἐπιδετόν**, add 'Hp.*Hum.* 5'

**ἐπιδευής I**, *in need of*, w. gen., add 'Theoc. 25.50'

**ἐπιδεύομαι II**, for 'later c. acc. rei' to end read 'perh. w. acc., ἀλκήν (codd., ἀλκῆς cj., ed.) A.R. 2.1220; act. τεθνάκην δ' ὀλίγω 'πιδεύσην φαίνομαι cod. in Sapph. 31.15 L.-P. (v. ἐπιδευής II); ἀρχόμενος φείδου πάντων, μὴ τέρμ' ἐπιδεύῃς Ps.-Phoc. 138'

**ἐπιδέω** (B) **II 2**, add 'Ἐννοδίᾳ Θεᾷ Νίκανδρος Παρμενίωνος εοὐχὴν ἐπιδεώμενος *EAM* 98 (ii AD)'

**ἐπιδημέω III**, line 8, after 'Philostr.*VS* 1.22.4' insert '*BCH* 52.172

(Delphi, Hellen.), τὸς ἐγ Κῶι ἐπιδαμεῦντας *SEG* 33.675.7 (Cos, ii BC)'

**ἐπιδημητικός II**, add 'Just.*Nov.* 134.1'

**ἐπιδημία 1**, add 'as the title of a work by Ion Chius, Ath. 13.603e; *visit of inspection*, *PLond.* 1259 (iv AD); transf., βραχυτάτου δὲ τοῦ τῆς ἐπιδημίας ὄντος ἐν τῷ βίῳ χρόνου Plu. 2.117f' **4**, add '*SEG* 39.733 (Rhodes, i BC)'

**ἐπιδήμιος**, add '**5** epith. of Zeus, *MDAI(A)* 19.372 no. 4 (Bithynia, ii AD).' at end add 'cf. Myc. *o-pi-da-mi-jo* (pl.)'

**ἐπίδημος 2**, line 2, before 'οἱ ἐπίδᾱμοι' insert 'τôν ἐπιδέμōμ (sic) *IG* 1³.3.5'

***ἐπιδίδημι**, *bind*, Hsch. s.v. λαμπάδιον.

**ἐπιδίδωμι I**, add '**8** *nominate* to an office, *BGU* 1022.16 (AD 196).'

***ἐπιδιετὲς** ἡβῆσαι, written by some editors for ἐπὶ διετὲς ἡβ., e.g. Hyp.*fr.* 192; cf. διετής 1.

***ἐπιδῐκεύομαι**, = ἐπιδικάζομαι, *SEG* 37.340.23 (Mantinea, iv BC).

**ἐπίδῐκος II 1**, add 'w. παρθένος Men.*Asp.* 349'

**ἐπιδῐμερής**, for '*containing* 1⅔' read '*standing in the proportion of 5:3*'

**ἐπιδίομαι**, add 'A.*Eu.* 357 (tm., s.v.l.)'

**ἐπιδίφριος II 1**, add 'cf. τοὺς ἄγαν ἀχρείους καὶ μόνον τοῦ λαιμοῦ ὄντας ἀνθρώπους ἐπιδιφρίους καλοῦσι Arethas ad D.Chr. 7.110, p. 105 Sonny (Kiev, 1896)'

***ἐπιδοκεύω**, *watch*, tm. ἀλλ' ἐπὶ καὶ τὰ δόκευε περισκοπέων ὑετοῖο Arat. 987. **2** *look out for, expect*, ἀλλ' ἐπὶ χεῖμα δόκευε id. 1018.

**ἐπίδομα**, add '*SEG* 1.276.14 (Maced., ii AD) (pl.)'

**⁺ἐπιδόρπιος**, ον (α, ον Ath. 4.130c), *used for the purposes of dinner* or *as an accompaniment* to it, ὕδωρ Theoc. 13.36, ἐ. τρύφος μάζης Lyc. 607, 661, θήρη Opp.*C.* 2.7; cf. of the stomach, τεύχεος ἐπιδορπίου Nic.*Al.* 21; app., *postprandial* τράπεζαι Ath. l.c.

***ἐπιδοτέον**, *one must administer*, Gal. 12.516.16.

**ἐπιδρομή II**, ἐξ ἐ. *cursorily*, add 'Ptol.*Tetr.* 55'

**ἐπιδυσ‹ω›χεῖν**, add '(ἐπιδυοχεῖν· ἐπιτωμάζειν La.; cf. δυοχοί Hsch.)'

**ἐπιείκεια**, after lemma insert 'ἐπείκεια *ISelge* 17 (Rom.imp.)'

**ἐπιεικής III 1**, line 2, after 'Hdt. 2.92' insert 'ἐ. πάλαι Pl. *Tht.* 142a'; line 4, after '*Hell.Oxy.* 13.5' insert 'ἐ. ἔντιμον D. 56.9'

***ἐπιενεχῠρέω**, med. pf. ἐπιενεχύρειμαι *receive as additional pledge*, *SB* 9834.b56 (iii AD); cf. ἐπενέχυρον.

**ἐπιέννῡμι**, line 9, after 'Il. 14.350' insert 'γᾶν ἐπιέμμενοι Alc. 129.17 L.-P.'

***ἐπιζᾱής**, ές, *blowing strongly against*, prob. in *Gr.Roman-Papyri* 8.28.

***ἐπιζᾰμενής**, ές, *violently angry*; perh. neut. as adv., ἐπιζαμενὲς κοτέουσα Nic.*Th.* 181 (read by edd. as ἐπὶ ζαμενὲς κοτέουσα); cf. ἐπιζάφελος.

**ἐπιζᾰρέω**, after '= ἐπιβαρέω' insert '*fall heavily upon*'; add 'Sch.Od. 22.9: pf. ἐπεζάρηκεν Hsch.'

**ἐπιζάω**, add '*PMil.Vogl.* 207.33 (iii/ii BC)'

**ἐπιζέω**, line 2, for 'Stob.*App.* p. 9 G.' read 'Stob. 1.31.8'

**ἐπιζητέω 1**, add '**c** *miss, regret* the dead, *IUrb.Rom.* 452.9.' add '**5** *examine medically*, τινά Ptol.*Tetr.* 9.'

**ἐπιζήτησις 3**, for '*rendering .. examination*' read '*claim, demand*'; add 'for taxes, μετὰ μετοχ[ων τὴν] ἐπιζήτησιν *PHels.* 38.2, ἐ. παντοπωλίου *OBodl.* 81.2 (ii BC)'

***ἐπιζήτητος**, ον, *missed, regretted*, *IUrb.Rom.* 1012.

**ἐπίηρα I**, line 4, delete 'Antim. 87'; at end of article after 'ἦρα' insert '(B)'

**ἐπιθαλάμιος II**, add 'also neut., Sch.Sapph. 103.17 L.-P. (s.v.l.), D.H.*Comp.* 25, Serv.*A.* 1.31'

**⁺ἐπιθάλλω**, *bloom upon*, Plot. 5.3.11 (v.l. ἐπιβάλλειν).

**ἐπιθᾰ́νᾰτος I**, for '*sick to death*' (twice) read '*terminally ill*'; -τως ἔχειν, add 'Alex.Aphr.*Pr.* 3.175'

**ἐπιθέατρον**, after '*theatre*' insert 'or perh. *seats above the* διάζωμα'

**ἐπιθέτης II**, for '*IG* 3.1280*a*' read '*Sokolowski* 2.26.10 (Tiryns, vi BC), *IG* 2².2361*A*17'

**ἐπίθετος I**, add '**4** rhet., *adventitious, artificial*, κόσμοι D.H.*Dem.* 1; φράσις ib. 4.'

**ἐπίθημα 2**, add '*SEG* 35.209.17 (Marathon, ii AD)'

**ἐπιθλίβω**, for '*press upon the surface*' read '*press down on*'; after '*tread*' insert 'Σκορπίον Arat. 84'; after 'Nonn.*D.* 7.91' insert 'of a gravestone pressing on the dead, *AP* 7.655 (Leon.Tarent.)'

**ἐπιθολόω**, before 'Max.Tyr.' insert '*cover with muddy water*'

**ἐπιθραύω**, add '*cripple*, Sopat.Rh. 8.332.3 W.'

**ἐπίθῡμα**, after '*victim*' insert '*SEG* 19.335.55 (Tanagra, i BC)'

**ἐπιθῡμέω**, line 3, delete '[Men.] ap.Clem.Al.*Strom.* 5.119' and after 'Lys. 20.3' insert 'w. acc. of thing, μηδὲ βελόνης ἔναμμ' ἐπιθυμήσῃς Men.*fr.* 683.11 K.-Th., Teles p. 42.12 H.'

**ἐπιθύμιος**, add '**2** νῦ]ν δέ μοι οὔτε .. [ἐστ'] ἐπιθύμιον οὔτε .. w. inf., it is not *in* my *desires* or *on* my *mind*, Ibyc. 1(*a*).11 P.; cf. καταθύμιος II.'

**ἐπιθύριον, ἐπίθῠρον**, for '*lintel*' read '*ornamental fitting on a door*'

***ἐπιθῠσία**, ἡ, = ἐπίθυσις, rest. in *IG* 12(1).762*A*23.

**ἐπιθύω II**, add '*PMag.* 4.1497'

**ἐπιθῳ̈ος**, for '*under penalty of a fine*' read '*involving the penalty of a fine*'

***ἐπικαθάπτω**, aor. pass. ἐπικατήφθη, gloss on ἐπὶ ἑάφθη, Sch.Gen.Il. 13.543; v. ἑάφθη.

**ἐπικαθίστημι 3**, after 'Plb. 2.2.11' insert 'ὁ μετὰ τὴν Φλαμινίου τελευτὴν ἐπικατασταθείς (sc. ὕπατος) id. 3.106.2'

***ἐπικαίνισμα**, ατος, τό, *novel* or *strange event*, *Cat.Cod.Astr.* 8(3).195.6.

**ἐπικαίριος I 2**, after 'X.*Oec.* 15.11' insert '*AP* 7.477 (Tymn.) (s.v.l.)'

**ἐπικαίω I**, add '**2** metaph. in pass., *be inflamed with passion for*, τινί Ath. 1.23d; ἐπί τινι Sch.Ar.*Lys.* 221.' **II 1**, line 2, after 'Pl.*Ep.* 340d' insert 'Men.*Dysc.* 754' **3**, add '*make* a mark *by branding* on, ἐπικεκαῦσθαι βουσὶ καὶ ἡμιόνοις ῥόπαλον Str. 15.688'

***ἐπικάλυψις**, εως, ἡ, *covering over*, Plu. 2.266e.

**ἐπικαμπής**, add 'of a promontory, *Peripl.M.Rubr.* 40'

**ἐπικαρπία 1**, add '**b** perh. amount of output imposed as a condition on a cultivator, *Inscr.Cret.* 4.43*Ba*9 (v BC).' **2**, *usufruct*, transfer 'D.H. 3.58' to section 1, and substitute 'Modest.*Dig.* 31.34.7, Just.*Nov.* 18.3'

**ἐπικάρσιος I 1**, after '*at an angle*' insert 'ἀπέκλινε δ' ἄρ' αὐχένα .. ἐπικάρσιον Stesich. *S*15 ii 15' and add 'fig. σάφ' οἶδ' ὅτι πάντα βροτοῖς Ζεὺς ἐπικάρσια τέμνει *Trag.adesp.* 482 K.-S.' **2**, delete the section transferring ref. to section III. **III**, for '*striped garment*' read '*transversely woven garment*'

**ἐπικαταβολή**, add '*PEnteux.* 14, 15 (iii BC), *PTeb.* 817 (182 BC)'

**ἐπικαταλαμβάνω I a**, line 3, after '(Epid.)' insert 'fig., of misfortunes, Sch.E.*Hipp.* 732' add '**c** *reach* a place, ἐπικαταλαμβάνομεν τὴν Ὀξυρυγχιτῶν *POxy.* 3932.4, ἐπικαταλήμψομαι τὴν πόλιν *PMasp.* 82.3 (both vi AD).'

**ἐπικαταλείπω**, for pres. ref. read '*SEG* 6.550 (Pisidia)'

**ἐπικατᾰράομαι 1**, add '*SEG* 34.1212 (Lydia)'

***ἐπικατασκευή**, ἡ, *building extension*, τοῦ θεάτρου *TAM* 2.420 (Patara).

***ἐπικατατομή**, ἡ, *carrying of mine-workings beyond one's boundaries*, *Ath.Agora* XIX P26.304, P27.97, 106 (iv BC).

**ἐπικαταχέω**, add 'Heras ap.Gal. 12.594.11'

**ἐπικατέχω**, add 'pass., of land, *to be subject to a further claim*, *PMich.*II 121ʳ2 ii 1.9 (i AD)'

***ἐπικατήφθη**, v. °ἐπικαθάπτω.

**ἐπικατορύσσομαι**, delete the entry.

***ἐπικατορύσσω**, *bury*, *SPAW* 1934.1030 (tab.defix.).

***ἐπικαυχάομαι**, *vaunt oneself*, Hsch. s.v. ἐναροκτάντας.

**ἐπίκειμαι II 2**, add '*insist* or *harp on*, τοῖσδε Emp. 113 D.-K.' **4**, for '*to be imposed*' read '*to be applied to*'

**ἐπικείρω I**, add 'ἀνδρῶν οὓς νῦν δαίμων ἐπέκειρεν A.*Pers.* 921 (v.l. ἀπ-)'

**ἐπικερδαίνω**, add 'Plu.*Ant.* 93'

***ἐπικερδία**, ἡ, *interest on money*, *BGU* 2140.9 (AD 432).

***ἐπικεφᾰλίς**, ίδος, ἡ, perh. *bearing* or *axle-box*, Poliorc. 220.22.

***ἐπικέφᾰλος**, ον, *allocated per head*, ἐ. ὀβολός *CID* II 10A i 14.

**ἐπίκηρος I a**, line 4, delete 'βίος Call.*Ep.* 59' **2**, after '*hazardous*' insert 'βίος Call.*Epigr.* 58.3 Pf.'

**ἐπικηρῡκεύομαι I 2**, add 'πρὸς Λακεδαιμονίους ἐπικηρυκεύεσθαι D. 20.52'

**ἐπικηρύσσω I**, add '**4** *propose*, ψήφισμα rest. in *SEG* 19.124.21 (Athens, ii BC).'

**ἐπικίχρημι**, delete the entry (v. ‡ἐπιχράω (C)).

***ἐπικίων**, ονος, ὁ, *architrave* (or a section of it), *SEG* 20.142 (Cyprus, ii BC).

**ἐπικλάζω**, for '*sound to*' read '*add one's sound to*'; add '*shout to*, Arr.*Cyn.* 16.8'

**⁺ἐπικλαίω**, Att. -κλάω, *add tears* to an action just completed, Ar.*Th.* 1063, App.*Pun.* 53; w. dat., *weep in response* to, Nonn.*D.* 30.114.

**ἐπικλασμός**, for 'dub. .. (ii AD)' read '**2** *additional taxes* or *dues, extra levy*, ὁ ἐσόμενος ἐ. τοῦ ἐνεστῶτος γ' (ἔτους) *PTeb.* 391.27 (i AD), *POxy.* 899.9 (ii/iii AD), *BGU* 920.22 (ii AD), etc.'

**ἐπικλάω II 2**, add '(μουσικὴν) ἐπικεκλασμένην τοῖς μέλεσιν Plu. 2.397b' add '**III** perh. *transfer* a charge to someone, *PPhilad.* 1.47 (ii AD), *POxy.* 3792.31 (iv AD), τὸ .. λάχανον ἀποτιμῶνται καὶ τὴν τούτου διατίμησιν ἐπικλῶσι τῷ λαμβάνοντι κηπουρῷ Just.*Nov.* 64.1.'

**ἐπικλεής**, line 1, after '*famous*' insert 'Simon. in *POxy.* 3965 *fr.* 2.14'

**ἐπικλείω (B) 2**, after 'A.R. 1.18' insert '(cj.)'

**ἐπικλεσαιδόνα**, after lemma insert '(**ἐπικλεηδόνα** La.)'

**ἐπίκλην 1**, add 'w. τό, Ἀνδρέας οὗ τὸ ἐπίκλην Κομιτᾶ *BCH* suppl. 8.247 (Philippi, ?v AD)' **2**, at end after '*IG* 14.1018.6' insert 'Poll. 9.104'

**ἐπίκληρος**, lines 1/2, read '**ἐπίκληρος**, ον, Dor. -κλᾱρος: ἡ -ος, *heiress*' etc. **3**, for this section read '**II** astrol., *occupying a* κλῆρος II 4, χρηματίζοντες ἀστέρες λέγονται οἱ ἐπὶ δυνάμεως ἐπίκεντροι ἢ ἐπίκληροι *Cat.Cod.Astr.* 8(4).225.'

**ἐπικληρόω 1**, line 5, after '(Samos, iv BC)' insert '*BCH* 57.493 (Temnos, iii BC), cf. 496)'

**ἐπίκλητος II 1**, for this section read 'subst., *invited guest*, Ar.*Pax* 1266,

Men.*Dysc.* 608. **b** *supernumerary guest* (i.e. one brought by an invited guest), Plu. 2.707a.'

**⁺ἐπίκλιντρον**, τό, part of couch, perh. *elbow- or head-rest*, Ar.*Ec.* 907 (lyr.), *fr.* 41 K.-A., *IG* 1$^3$.422.286 (v BC), 2$^2$.1541.26, 11(2).144.66 (both iv BC), Gal. 18(1).344, *Gp.* 13.14.9, Poll. 6.9, 10.34; cf. ‡ἀνάκλιντρον.

***ἐπικλοπάδαν**, *slily, craftily*, σιγᾷ δ' ὅ γ' ἐπικλοπάδαν ἐνέρεισε μετώπῳ Stesich. *S*15 ii 6.

**ἐπίκλοπος**, add 'transf. epith., ὠκεῖαν ἑλὼν καὶ ἐπίκλοπον ἄγρην Opp.*H.* 3.270'

**ἐπικλύζω I 2**, line 2, for 'E.*Tr.* 1327' read 'E.*Tr.* 1326'

***ἐπίκλωσμα**, ατος, τό, variant for °μετάκλωσμα (q.v.), Cyran.prol. l. 82 K.

***Ἐπικνίσιος**, ὁ, (κνῖσα) epith. of Apollo, *Tit.Cam.* 120.

**ἐπικοινάομαι**, before '*consult*' insert 'w. dat.' and add '*SEG* 23.474 (Dodona, iv/iii BC)'

**ἐπικοινόω II**, after 'Pl.*Lg.* 631d' insert '(but perh. med. governing γάμους)'

***ἐπικονδύλιον**, τό, *knuckle-ring*, *POsl.* 46.17 (iii AD).

**ἐπικόπτω 5**, delete the section.

***ἐπικορύσιος**, ον, (*located*) *on the helmet*, Myc. *e-pi-ko-ru-si-jo* (dual); cf. *o-pi-ko-ru-si-ja* (neut. pl.).

**ἐπικοτέω**, add 'unless to be read as ἐπιζαμενὲς κοτέουσα, v. °ἐπιζαμενής)'

**ἐπικουρία**, add '**IV** form of land-tax paid in barley, *PCair.Isidor.* 11 ii 27 (iv AD).'

***ἐπίκουρος** (B), ον, prob. *ready for shearing*, *PCair.Zen.* 771.6 (iii BC); cf. κουρά.

**ἐπικουφίζω II 2 a**, add 'χρήμασι Arr.*An.* 2.18.4'

**ἐπικουφισμός**, add '*PAlex.* p. 40 no. 271 (v AD)'

**ἐπικραδαίνω**, for '*wave on high*' read '*brandish* at'

**ἐπικραίνω**, add '**2** *confirm, guarantee*, w. inf., A.*Supp.* 13 (anap.); w. acc., id.*Eu.* 949 (anap.); med., w. acc., ib. 969 (anap.); pass., ib. 347 (lyr.).'

***ἐπικρᾱνιον**, τό, = ἐπίκρανον I, *headdress*, *Lindos* 487.7 (iii AD, pl.).

***ἐπικρᾱνιος**, ον, *placed on the head*, στεφάνωμα Hsch. s.v. κράδεμνον.

***ἐπικραστίζω**, *pasture* horses, *PTeb.* 724.2 (ii BC).

**ἐπικρᾰτής**, for '*master* of a thing: only Comp.' read '*having the mastery*, Sch.E.*Ph.* 1058; esp. comp.'; after 'Hes.*Sc.* 321' insert 'Stesich. *S*40.24'

**ἐπικρᾰτητικός**, delete the entry.

**⁺ἐπικρᾰτύνω**, *increase the force, potency*, etc., *of, strengthen*, νοῦσον Hp.*Morb.* 4.49, ἐπικρατύνειν· ἐπισχύειν, ὀχυροῦν Hsch.

**ἐπικρῖμα**, add '*IMylasa* 132.2'

**ἐπικρίνω I 1**, line 8, after '2*Ma.* 4.47' insert 'ib. 3*Ma.* 4.2' **II 2**, after '*POxy.* 39 (i AD)' insert 'ἐπικριθείς one included in a category of recipients of grain, ib. 2892 i 7 (AD 269), 2894 ii 8 (AD 270), etc.'

***ἐπίκριος**, ον, *roosting*, prob. in Nic.*Th.* 198.

**ἐπίκρισις II**, add '*PMich.*XIV 676.5, 19 (AD 272)'

**⁺ἐπίκροκον**· ἐπανθητόν (σπαθητόν La.) Hsch.; the name of a woman's garment, Paul.ex Fest. p. 82 M., etc.

**ἐπικρούω I**, for '*jeer at* .. Ath. 13.579b' read '*impugn*, Macho 240 G.; cf. Ἀριστοφάνης δ' ἐν Πλούτῳ καὶ τῷ ἐπικρούσασθαι ἐπὶ τοῦ νουθετῆσαι κέχρηται Arist.*fr.* 432 K.-A.'

**ἐπικτηνίτης**, for '*drover*' read '*head ostler*' and add '*IGBulg.* 1519 (sp. -είτης)'

**ἐπικῡδής**, add 'sup. οἱ ἐπικυδέστατοι Ἀθηναίων Philostr.*VA* 8.15'

***ἐπικύρημα**, ατος, τό, gloss on κύρμα, Sch.Gen.Il. 17.151.

***ἐπικώκῡτος**, ον, *lamented over*, *GVI* 1279 6.6 (Callatis, ii/iii AD).

**ἐπικωκύω**, add 'w. tm., ἐπ' οὐλοὰ κωκύσαντες *GVI* 1990.3 (Egypt, ii BC)'

***Ἐπικωμαῖος**, ὁ, epith. of Apollo at Thurii, Thphr.*fr.* 97.3.

**ἐπίκωμος**, add '*BGU* 2430.43 (i BC)'

***ἐπίκωμος** (B), *staying* or *residing in a* κώμη, Call.*fr.* 384.49 Pf.

**ἐπιλᾰλέω**, for '*interrupt in speaking*' read '*speak against*'; for '*charm*' read '*utter spells against*'

**ἐπιλαμβάνω II 1 a**, after 'Th. 2.51' insert 'of sleep, Hp.*Ep.* 5.28' **b**, line 3, after 'Pl.*Epin.* 974a' insert 'abs., ὡς νὺξ ἐπέλαβεν Memn. 40.2' **III 1**, line 3, before 'c. gen.' insert 'usu.'; add 'w. acc., *Ev.Luc.* 9.47, 23.26' add '**b** of taking hold of a person to help him, Lxx *Si.* 4.11, *Ep.Heb.* 2.16, Sch.A.*Pers.* 742 codd.; cf. ἀντιλαμβάνω II 2.'

***ἐπιλάσκω**, pf. -λέληκα, *fill with squawking*, Opp.*H.* 3.247 (tm.).

**ἐπιλέγω I 3**, pass., add 'ἀπὸ χωρίου ἐπιλεγωμένου Πίβρου (i.e. *known as*), *SEG* 26.790 (Byzantium, vi AD)' **III 1**, line 2, after 'ταῦτα' insert 'B.5.136 S.-M.'; delete 'rare in trag. .. A.*Ag.* 1498 (anap.)' (passage corrupt)

**ἐπιλεκτάρχης**, for '*commander* .. *band*' read 'title of certain Aetolian officers'

**ἐπίλεκτος 2**, add '**d** ἐ. κριτής = *selectus iudex*, *IGRom.* 3.778.9 (Attalea).'

**ἐπιλήθω II 2**, add 'w. acc., ἵνα τοὺς μεταξὺ κινδύνους ἑκὼν ἐπιλάθωμαι Demad. 11'

**ἐπιλήκητος**, after lemma insert '(**ἐπιλήμητος** La.)'

**ἐπιληκῠθίστρια**, for '*comic nickname* .. *bombastical*' read '*one who utters with a booming voice*, applied derogatorily to the muse of Mnasalcas'

**ἐπιλήνιος I**, delete 'ἐπιλήνια .. *C.* 1.127' **II**, add '**3** ἐπιλήνιον, τό, perh. *wine-vat*, Opp.*C.* 1.127; cf. ὑπολήνιον and Suid. s.v. τριπτῆρα.'

**ἐπιληψία II**, add '*SEG* 30.1794 (iii AD)'

***Ἐπιλιμένιος**, α, ον, *dwelling by the harbour*, title of Hera, *IG* 12 suppl. 409 (Thasos); of Aphrodite, *SEG* 28.1596 (Aegina, v BC).

**Ἐπιλίμνιος**, add 'cf. Myc. *o-pi-ri-mi-ni-jo*, pers. n.'

***ἐπιλῑνεύω**, = ἐπιλινάω, Hsch. s.v. λινοπτάζει.

***ἐπιλίτραις** (**ἐπιλιτρίς** La.)· τὸ μέσον τοῦ ζυγοῦ Hsch.

**ἐπιλλίζω 2**, for '*blink*' read 'perh. *fix the gaze*'

***ἐπιλλύζω**, v. ἐπιλύζω.

**ἐπιλογιστέον**, for '*reckon*' read '*consider*'

**ἐπίλογος I**, add 'prob. also Aeol., cf. κα]τ' ἐπίλλογ[ον Alc. 204.2 L.-P. (κατ' ἐπιλογισμόν Sch.)' **II**, add '**4** last part of the νόμος κιθαρῳδικός Poll. 4.66.'

**ἐπίλογχος** (B), add '*POxy.* 2894.13, 2896.2 (both iii AD)'

***ἐπιλοιπογρᾰφέω**, perh. *carry over additionally*, (cf. λοιπογραφέω), *PTeb.* 718.9 (ii BC) (dub.).

**ἐπίλοιπος**, add 'cf. Myc. *o-pi-ro-qo*'

***Ἐπίλῠκοι**, οἱ, members of a religious group, *SEG* 35.989 (Knossos, ii/i BC).

**ἐπίλῠσις**, add '**6** perh. *loss of skin* by peeling, or sim., ἄλφος καλεῖται ἡ ἐ. ἡ καλουμένη μελανία ἡ περὶ τὰς παρειὰς γινομένη ἐκ τοῦ ἡλιακοῦ καύσωνος Lxx Sch.*Le.* 13.39 (perh. read ἐπίχυσις).'

***ἐπιλῠτέον**, *one must solve the question*, ἐ. οὕτως Sch.Pi.*O.* 6.23.

***ἐπιλώγεον**, v. ἐπιλόγεον.

**ἐπιμάζιος**, add 'Nonn.*D.* 3.380, Triph. 345, Poll. 2.8'

**ἐπιμαίομαι I**, at end after 'Timo 5.7' insert 'w. acc., *search for*, Arat. 89' **II 1**, add 'transf., of darkness, abs. Orph.*A.* 121' **III**, delete the section.

**ἐπιμαρτῠρία II**, add 'Heph.Astr. 2.32.11'

**ἐπίμαρτυς**, line 2, for 'Call.*Aet.* 3.1.48' read 'Call.*fr.* 75.48 Pf., *AP* 12.129 (Arat.)'

**ἐπιμείγνῡμι II**, line 3, for '(Hld.) 5.33' read '5.34'

**ἐπίμεικτος 2**, add 'εἰσὶν δὲ ἐπίξενοι καὶ ἐπίμικτοι Ἀράβων τε καὶ Ἰνδῶν *Peripl.M.Rubr.* 30'

**ἐπιμελαίνομαι**, delete the entry.

***ἐπιμελαίνω**, *blacken on the surface*, Arist.ap.Stob. 1.29.1; med., as symptom of mortification, Hp.*Fract.* 35; of the tongue, id.*Morb.* 3.6; of ripening fruit, Thphr.*HP* 3.15.6.

**⁺ἐπιμέλᾱς**, αινα, αν, *having a black surface*, Thphr.*HP* 3.8.7, 6.5.3; subst., kind of gem, *epimelas est, cum candida gemma superne nigricat* Plin.*HN* 37.161.

**ἐπιμέλεια**, line 13, for 'Isoc. 6.154' read 'Isoc. 5.154'; line 15, after 'Is. 7.14' insert 'ἵνα ἐν ἐπιμελείᾳ τῆς κόρης γενώμεθα Men.*Dysc.* 228'

**ἐπιμελέομαι**, form -μέλομαι, add 'ἐπιμέλεσθον *IG* 12(2).6.23 (Mytilene, iv BC)'

***ἐπιμελετής**, οῦ, ὁ, = ἐπιμελητής, εἴλης *IGRom.* 3.642 (Temenothyrae); pl., *Schwyzer* 491.15 (-τᾶς, Thespiae, ?ii BC).

**ἐπιμελής I**, line 1, for '*careful* or *anxious about*' read '*careful about* or *attentive to*' add '**3** adv. -λῶς χλωροί *remarkably* sallow, Str. 14.2.3 codd.' **II**, line 5, for 'made him *anxious*' read '*became a matter of interest* or *concern*'

**ἐπιμελητεύω**, add 'τῆς πόλεως *IG* 2$^2$.1103.14 (ii AD), 3546.17 (Eleusis, i/ii AD), etc.'

**ἐπιμελήτρια**, for 'fem. of ἐπιμελητής' read '*woman in charge of domestic arrangements, welfare*, or sim.' and add '*PMasp.* 97.(D)35 (vi AD)'

**⁺ἐπιμερής**, ές, *superpartient*, of ratios which are not multiple (n:1), superparticular (n+1:n), multiple superparticular (nm+1:n), nor reciprocal to these, Theo Sm. p. 76 H., Nicom.*Ar.* 1.17, al.; cf. ‡ἐπιμόριος.

**ἐπιμερισμός**, line 4, delete '*parsing*'

**⁺ἐπίμερος**, ον, = ἐφίμερος, Alcm. 1.101 P., Semon. 7.51.

**ἐπιμετρέω I**, delete the section. **II**, for pres. def. read '*measure out in addition*' and add 'Hes.*Op.* 397, Hdt. 3.91.3'

**⁺ἐπιμηθής**, ές, *thinking after one acts*, i.e. *hasty*, Theoc. 25.79; adv. -θέως *on second thoughts*, Herod. 3.94.

***ἐπιμηκάζω**, *bleat at*, Eust. 1761.26.

***Ἐπιμηλίδιος**, ἡ, *protectress of sheep*, epith. of Apollo at Camirus, *Tit.Cam.* 135 (iii BC).

**⁺ἐπιμηνίη**, ἡ, Ion., *magisterial college of the* ἐπιμήνιοι, (cf. *JHS* 82.4), *SIG* 58.11 (Miletus, v BC).

**ἐπιμήνιος II 2 b**, for 'Plb. 31.12.13' read 'Plb. 31.20.13'

**ἐπιμηχᾰνάομαι II**, add '*devise to meet the need*, Opp.*H.* 1.322'

**ἐπιμιμνήσκομαι** (not -μνῄσκ-) **1**, add 'σταφυλαὶ δρεπάνης ἐπιμιμνήσκονται *AP* 11.37 (Antip.Thess.)'

***ἐπίμισθος**, ον, *in receipt of payment, paid*, ἡ πρώτη σύνοδος οὐκ ἐ[πί]μισθος συνήχθη *IEphes.* 17.58 (i AD).

***ἐπίμιτρον**, τό, part of a loom, perh. *rod-heddle*, *POxy.Hels.* 34.5 (AD 101), *POxy.* 264.4, 2773.14 (i AD; v. *Berichtigungsl.* VIII).

***ἐπιμνήμων**, ονος, ὁ, official at Alabanda, *BCH* 10.312, 313.

**ἐπιμοιράομαι**, for '*receive* .. grave' read '*grant as one's due share*, ἐ. κόνιν sc. for burial'

***ἐπιμοιρᾰσία**, ἡ, *allocation of one's due share*, Sch.Hes.*Th.* 565 (p. 86.12 DiG.).

⁺**ἐπιμορῐασμός**, ὁ, *formation of a ratio of the form n+1:n*, Iamb.*in Nic.* p. 108 P.

**ἐπιμόριος**, for pres. def. read '*having a ratio of the form n+1:n, superparticular*'

**ἐπιμορμῠ́ρω**, for '*murmur*' read '*froth, bubble*' and add 'med., ἐπιμορμύρεται *An.Ox.* 3.220'

**ἐπιμῠ́ρομαι**, delete '*An.Ox.* 3.220' (v. ἐπιμορμύρω).

**ἐπιμύω II**, add 'also of ranks in battle, *PBerol.* 6926.B iii. 22'

**ἐπιμωκεύω**, delete the entry.

**ἐπίμωμος**, after '*blameworthy*' insert 'Ptol.*Tetr.* 163'

***ἐπίναιον** (A), τό, = ἐπίνειον, *Inscr.Cret.* 4.146.

***ἐπίναιον** (B), τό, *addition to a temple*, *ICS* 1(b), sp. Cypr. *e-pi-na-e*[-*a*] *ICS* 1(a).

***ἐπίνακτον** (-**νάκτιον** La.)· τὸν ἐπιδιδόμενον ἔξω‹θε› ναύτην Hsch. (cod. ἐπίνακτιν).

**ἐπινάστιος**, delete '*taken as a stranger into a country*'

***ἐπινεβεύω**, aor. part. fem. ἐπινε[β]εύσασσα, *perform some (particular) service to Artemis*; cf. °νεβεύω, *SEG* 34.493 (Atrax, c.200 BC).

***ἐπινειόθι** or ἐπὶ νειόθι, *towards the bottom*, A.R. 4.1615.

**ἐπίνειος** (s.v. ἐπίνειον), add 'τὰς ἐπινείους κώμας *PBeatty Panop.* 2.47, 102 (iv AD); -οις .. τόποις ib. 110'

**ἐπινέμω I 1**, add '**c** *give extra* or *further grazing to* a flock, Longus 1.8.'

**ἐπινίκιος I**, add '**2** epith. of Zeus, *ICilicie* 16; of Hermes, ib. 17.' **II 2 a**, add 'perh. particular festival at Athens, *SEG* 26.184 (iii AD); games celebrating a victory, *IEphes.* 671, 721, al.'

**ἐπίνῑκος**, line 2, after '(dub. l.)' insert 'τὸν ἐπινίκον ἀέθ[λ[ον] *SEG* 30.499 (Delphi, vii BC); as epith. of Heracles, Ἡρακλεῖ ἐπινίκ[ῳ] *SEG* 29.569 (Thessaly; unless -[ίῳ] is read)'; add 'rest. in Call.*Dieg.* viii.21 (*fr.* 198 Pf.)'

***ἐπινοστέω**, *return*, τῇ πατρίδι Sch.Pi.*O.* 7.36 (v.l.).

**ἐπινυκτίδιος**, add 'cj. in (?)Call.*fr.* 775 Pf.'

**ἐπινυμφεύομαι**, after '*contract a second marriage*' insert 'or perh. *become betrothed* (v. *SEG* 33.669)'

**ἐπινωμάω I**, for '*bring* .. τινί' read '*visit*, w. dat.' and before 'σώματα' insert 'w. acc.'

⁺**ἐπινῶς**· τὸ λίαν Suid.; also v.l. (for ἐπιμανῶς) and Sch. in Luc.*VH* 2.25.

⁺**ἐπινωτίζω**, *put on one's back*, E.*HF* 362; med., Paus.Gr.*fr.* ε 6 E. **II** acc. to Hsch. = ἐφορμάω, Archipp. 5 K.-A.

***ἐπιξενεύω**, *lodge with* or *at*, στρατιωτῶν ἐπιξενευσάντων τῷ οἴκῳ μου *POxy.* 3581.13 (iv/v AD).

**ἐπίξενος 2**, for '*stranger*' read '*person residing away from his normal* or *registered domicile*' and add '*SB* 4251.3 (i AD), *PFay.* 24 (AD 158), *Peripl.M.Rubr.* 30'

**ἐπίξηνον**, delete '*executioner's block*'

**ἐπιξοά**, for '*IG* 4.1484.84 (Epid.)' read '*IG* $4^2$.103.17 (Epid., iv BC)'

**ἐπιξῠ́ω 1**, add 'Crito ap.Gal. 13.863.6'

***ἐπιϝοικίζω**, v. ἐποικίζω.

***ἐπιϝοικοδομέω**, v. ἐποικοδομέω.

***ἐπίολπος**, ον, *expected*, Q.S. 14.291, 295 (codd., cj. ἐπίελπτος).

***ἐπιονειδίζω**, v. °ἐπονειδίζω.

⁺**ἐπιοπτεύω**, v. ‡ἐποπτεύω.

**ἐπιορκέω**, line 2, forms ἐφι-, after '(Smyrna, iii BC)' for 'etc.' read '*PTeb.* 78/7 (ii BC), *IG* 5(1).1390.6 (Andania, i BC); sp. -ίω *SEG* 33.638 (Crete, ii BC)'

**ἐπιορκία**, add 'ἐφιορκίας γυναικίας *SEG* 33.1119 (Phrygia, iii AD)'

**ἐπιόσσομαι**, add '**2** abs., *keep watch*, *GVI* 1178 (Rhod.Peraea, ?ii BC).'

**ἐπιόψομαι**, line 2, after 'aor. 1' insert 'inf. ἐπιόφσασθ[αι *IG* $1^3$.3.4 (Marathon, v BC)' add '**II** *supervise*, *IG* $1^3$ l.c.'

***ἐπιπαιδειάζειν**· τὸ μὴ ‹ἐν καιρῷ› θύειν φρατρίαν. Λάκωνες Hsch. (La.; cod. ἐπιπαίζειν).

**ἐπίπαιμα**, after lemma insert '(ἐπίπταιμα La.)'

***ἐπιπαλλᾰκεύομαι**, *take concubines*, Sch.E.*Andr.* 216.

***ἐπιπαρωθέω**, *thrust aside, deflect*, *PMich.*III 149 xii 26, 37 (pass., ii AD).

**ἐπίπᾱς**, after '*AP*' insert '7.490 (Anyt., v.l.)'; delete '(Strat.)'; add 'οὐ μείους ὥσπερ χείλιοι ὡς ἐπίπαν *a thousand in all*, Xenoph. 3.4 W.'

***ἐπιπασσᾰλεύω**, *peg upon, nail upon*, A.*fr.* 78a.19 R.

**ἐπιπαστέον**, add 'Aspasia ap.Aët. 16.94'

***ἐπιπατρίδιον**, τό, *patronymic*, τὰ ὀνύματα κὴ τὰ ἐ. *AD* 1931-2(14) Pl. iii 4 (Thespiae, iii BC).

**ἐπίπεδος I**, add '**2** τὰ ἐ. (sc. γῆς) the *surface* of the earth, opp. τᾶς γᾶς ὑπένερθε (= Pi.*fr.* 292), Pl.*Tht.* 173e.' **III 1**, add '**b** τὸ ἐπίπεδον *face* of a solid figure, Simp.*in de An.* 68.7.'

**ἐπιπέλομαι**, for 'so of a storm' read 'of blindness'

**ἐπίπεμπτος II**, for this section read 'ἐπίπεμπτον, τό, *one-fifth* (whether or not considered as an additional sum): of the votes in a trial, Ar.*fr.* 212 K.-A., Eup. 75 K.-A.; as a fine, penalty, or sim., Lxx *Le.* 5.16, *IG* 7.3073.1 (Lebadea, ii BC)'

**ἐπιπέμπω II 1**, add 'as an °ἐπίπλοος (A) III a; pass., ἐ. ὑπὸ το[ῦ] τριηράρχου *GDI* 4335 (Rhodes, ii BC)'

**ἐπιπεντεκαιδέκατος**, add '**b** ἐ. τό, *one-fifteenth in addition*, *PLille* 29.1.8 (iii BC).'

**ἐπιπήγνῡμι II**, insert at beginning '*plant* or *fix on top*, σῆμα τύμβ[ῳ] *MAMA* 1.370 (Phrygia)'

**ἐπιπλέκω II**, add '**2** prob. *swindle*, τινά *PEnteux.* 48.7, 10 (iii BC).'

***ἐπιπλευστής**, οῦ, ὁ, perh. = °ἐπίπλοος (A) III b, *PIand.* 150 ii 16.

**ἐπιπλέω III**, add '**b** *to be an* °ἐπίπλοος (A) III a, Plb. 16.5.1 (Rhodian ship).'

**ἐπίπληξις 2**, transfer 'Lxx 2*Ma.* 7.33' to section 1.

**ἐπίπλοος** (A) **I 3**, delete the section. add '**III** ἐπίπλοος, ὁ, gloss on δίοπος Harp. **a** *officer in charge* of a ship, appointed by a trierarch to command in his stead, *Clara Rhodos* 8.228 (i BC), Arr.ap.Suid. s.v.; ἐπίπλοι τριήραρχοι *SEG* 29.799 (Rhodes, Hellen.). **b** *agent* of the state *in charge* of a cargo of corn, in Egypt, *POxy.* 276.3 (i AD), *PLond.* 301.10 (ii AD), *PGrenf.* 2.46.7 (ii AD); cf. °ἐπιπλέω III.'

***ἐπιπλωία**, ἡ, the office of an °ἐπίπλοος III b, *POxy.Hels.* 20 i 9 (AD 138).

**ἐπιπνέω I 1**, line 4, after 'Od. 4.357' insert 'w. acc., Call.*Del.* 318' **II 3**, delete 'c. acc., .. 3.121' **III**, before 'Pass.' insert 'w. acc. *inspire*, Call.*fr.* 260.50 Pf., A.R. 3.937, Nonn.*D.* 3.121'

***ἐπιπολέω**, *go up to* or *upon*, Sch.Hes.*Th.* 2 (p. 2.14 DiG.).

**ἐπιπολή I 1**, add '**b** sg., some defined area in Nemea, ὧρος ἐπιπολᾶς *SEG* 34.285 (Nemea, iv BC).'

***ἐπιπολιορκέω**, *besiege in addition*, Arr.*fr.* 10 J.

***ἐπιπολυπραγμονέω**, *inquire further into*, w. acc., Ptol.*Tetr.* 120.

**ἐπιπομπή 2**, for '*enchantment*' read '*charm*' and add 'tab.defix. in *SEG* 35.214.15, etc. (Athens, iii AD)'

***ἐπίπομπος**, ον, perh. *outlawed* or *banished*, ἀποτεισάτω .. τριάκοντα μνᾶς .. καὶ ἐ. ἔστω *IG* $9^2$(1).138.11 (Calydon, iv/iii BC).

**ἐπιπορπίς**, delete 'νυμφᾶν' and after '*AP* 6.274' insert '(cj.)'

**ἐπιπρεπής**, after '*becoming*' insert 'τὰν ἐπιπρεπέα χάριν *SEG* 23.220 (Messene, i AD)'; add 'adv. -έως, epigr. in *Lindos* 177 (ii BC)'

⁺**ἐπιπρίω**, *gnaw at*, τὸ γένειον *AP* 7.531 (Antip. Thess.). **2** *grind* the teeth, ἐπιπρίσῃσιν (-βρι- codd.) ὀδόντας Call.*fr.* 332 Pf., Hsch.

**ἐπιπρό**, for '*right through, onwards*' read '*further, beyond that*' and add 'Call.*fr.* 238.22 Pf.'

***ἐπιπροσδέομαι**, *ask in addition*, *PColl.Youtie* 26.2 (AD 156).

**ἐπιπροσθετέω 2**, delete the section.

**ἐπιπροσθέω**, line 6, for '*stands* .. *view of*' read '*the centre is in line with the extremes*'; line 10, for 'Longin. 32.1' read 'Longin. 32.2'

**ἐπιπροστῐ́θημι**, add 'pass. aor., Hp.*Alim.* 4'

⁺**ἐπίπταισμα**, ατος, τό, *stubbing* of the toes, τὰ δὲ ὑπὲρ τοὺς δακτύλους κρούματα πταίσματα. Ἀριστοφάνης δὲ καὶ ἐπιπταίσματα αὐτὰ καλεῖ Poll. 2.199 (Ar.*fr.* 818 K.-A.; see also ἐπίπαιμα).

***ἐπιπτερύσσομαι**, aor. ἐπεπτερύχθην, *fly in pursuit of*, Cyran. 86 (3.6.3 K.).

**ἐπίπτησις**, add 'ὕπνου Afric.*Cest.* p. 38 V.'

**ἐπιπτύσσω**, line 3, for 'abs. .. *folds*' read '*corrugate*'

**Ἐπιπυργῑδία**, add 'epith. of Artemis at Eleusis *SEG* 30.93 (20/19 BC)' and 'also masc., ἥρωι Ἐπιπυργιδῖοι *Sokolowski* 2.19.86 (Athens, iv BC)'

**ἐπιπώλησις**, add 'also applied (in one ms.) to the middle section (85-152) of Theoc. 25'

**ἐπίρραμμα**, after '*Gloss.*' insert '**ἐπίραμμα** *Inscr.Délos* 1409*Ba*ii118 (ii BC)'

**ἐπιρράπτω 2**, add 'Hsch. s.v. κάθαπτος'

***ἐπιρρᾰχῖτις**, ιδος, fem. adj. *spinal*, ἀρτηρίαι *Hippiatr.* 33.5.

***ἐπίρρεγμα**, ἐπίρεγμα· ἐπίθυμα Hsch.

**ἐπιρρέζω 1**, add 'ἐπιρέξαι· ἐπιθῦσαι. ἐπαγαγεῖν Hsch.'

**ἐπιρρέπω I 2**, add '**b** *be impending*, δί[κ]ην ἐπιρρέ[π]ουσαν ἐδε[δοίκ]ειν Antipho *fr.* 1a col. 1.'

**ἐπιρρέω 2**, line 7, for '(Pl.)*Tht.* 177e' read '(Pl.)*Tht.* 177c'

**ἐπιρρήγνῡμι**, after 'A.*Pers.* 1030 (lyr.)' insert 'ἵνα καὶ σοὶ ἐπιρρήξαιμι χ[ιτῶνα Call. in *Suppl.Hell.* 287.13'; add 'pass., of a storm, *burst*, ἐπιρραγέντος ὑετοῦ Ael.*NA* 7.8'

**ἐπίρρημα II**, add '**2** ἐ. σχετλιαστικόν *interjection* expressing distress,

D.T. 642.2, A.D.*Pron.* 34.30, *Adv.* 127.19, Sch.Ar.*Nu.* 1; [ἐ.] θαυμαστικά D.T. 642.7; ἐ. θρηνητικόν Tz. ad Lyc. 31.' **III**, delete the section.

**ἐπίρρητος I**, add 'Philostr.*VA* 1.12, 5.7, *Ep.* 38; sup., Origenes *Cels.* 3.50'

***ἐπίρρῑν**, ῑνος, *long-nosed*, *POxy.* 3617.9 (ἐπίριν, iii AD); cf. ἐπίρρινος.

**ἐπιρριπίζω**, for 'dub. sens. in' read 'w. dat., *fan into flame*, in quot. fig.'

**ἐπιρρίπτω I**, add '**6** *put* oneself *forward*, τοὺς βουλομένους ἐπιρρίπτειν ἑαυτούς (sc. to become tutors) Modest.*Dig.* 26.5.21.6.' **II**, delete the section.

**ἐπίρριψις**, add '**2** *imposition*, τελῶν *IMylasa* 601.7 (sp. ἐπιρειψιν).'

**ἐπίρροια**, after 'D.S. 5.25' insert '*POxy.* 2341.5, *PLond.* 934 (*Tyche* 1.8; both iii AD); ὑδάτων .. ἐπιρροίαις *conduits*, Luc.*Phal.* 1.3'

**ἐπιρροιβδέω 1**, for '*croak so as to forebode rain*' read '*make a whirring or rushing sound*'

**ἐπιρροφέω**, line 4, delete 'Archig.ap.'

**ἐπιρρυθμίζω**, delete '*dress* oneself simply' and insert 'Chaerem. 1.3 S.'

**ἐπίρρῠσις I**, add '**2** in irrigation, *water-intake*, *PTeb.* 703.31, 37 (iii BC).'

**ἐπιρρύσμιος**, for '*adventitious*' read '*remoulding*'

***ἐπισᾰλᾰγέω**, *move violently towards* one, tm. σαλαγεῦντος ἔπι δροσεροῖο Νότοιο Opp. *C.* 4.74 (v.l. σελαγ-).

***ἐπισεβάζω**, *consecrate*, εὐχαριστήριον ἐπισεβάσας τὰ τῶν προγόνων *TAM* 4(1).76 (Bithynia; cf. κατασεβάζω).

**ἐπίσειστος I**, add '**b** σειστὰ ἐξ ἀμφοτέρων τῶμ μερῶν ἐπίσειστα earrings *to be worn pendant* on both sides, *Inscr.Délos* 461*Ba*5 (ii BC).'

**ἐπισείω 1**, add 'φόβον ἐ. Lib.*Or.* 56.11'

**ἐπίσημα** (form ἐπίσᾱμα), for '*Schwyzer* 607' read '*grave-marker*, *SEG* 24.405'

**ἐπισημαίνω II**, add '**2** *give a signal for action*, Men.*Pk.* 476, Phot. p. 153.17.'

**ἐπισημᾰσία I**, line 4, after 'cf. (Cic.*Att.*)14.3.2 (sg.)' insert '*TAM* 5(1).48 (ii/i BC)'

**ἐπισημειόομαι**, add '**II** *indicate*, w. acc. and inf., Memn. 60.3.'

**ἐπίσημον I**, line 4, after 'Plu.*Thes.* 6' insert '*Peripl.M.Rubr.* 47'

**ἐπίσημος I**, add '**2** ἐπίσημα, τά, *badges* or *tokens of office* (app. calque of Lat. *insignia*), Just.*Ed.* 8.3.4.' **II 3**, add 'ἐπίσημοι ἡμέραι *feast-days*, *IGRom.* 4.860 (Laodicea ad Lycum)' add '**5** *conspicuous*, ἐν ἐπισήμοις τόποις *SEG* 24.1217 (Egypt, 39 BC).'

***ἐπισιλλαίνω**, *ridicule*, Sch.Pi.*N.* 4.60.

**ἐπισκαλμίς**, add 'Agath. 5.22.2 K.'

**ἐπισκάπτω II**, for this section read '*cover by digging* or *hoeing*, *PSoterichos* 1.25 (AD 69), 2.21 (AD 221), τὰ σπαρέντα τὸ μὲν κάλλιστον δι' ἀνθρώπων ἐπισκάπτεσθαι *Gp.* 2.24.1, Hsch. (s.v. ἐπισκαφεύς)'

**+ἐπισκᾰφεύς**, έως, ὁ, *one who hoes in seed*, Hsch.

**ἐπισκέπτης**, add 'of official dealing with the determining of land under cultivation within a nome, *PMich.*inv. 341 (*ZPE* 36.80; ii/iii AD)'

***ἐπισκεπτίτης**, ου, ὁ, app. = ἐπισκέπτης, *inspector*, *MAMA* 7.190, *IApam.* 130.

**ἐπισκέπτομαι**, after lemma insert '(also act., Hsch.)'

**ἐπισκέπω**, for 'med.' read 'pass.'

**ἐπισκευάζω I**, add '**4** *prepare*, *construct*, Mitchell *N.Galatia* 117, ἐπισκευάσαντες τὸ μνῆμα τῷ Δομετιανῷ ib. 179.'

**ἐπισκευή I**, add 'πὲρ τᾶς ἐπισκευᾶς τοὶ γυμνάσσοι *SEG* 33.460 (Larissa, ii BC)' **II**, add '**2** sg., *furniture*, Memn. 4.5 J.'

**ἐπισκευόω**, delete 'Ἐφ.Ἀρχ. .. (Crete)'

**ἐπίσκεψις 1**, add 'w. implication of calling to account or punishing, Lxx *Nu.* 16.29, *Je.* 9.23, 23.12, etc.' add '**4** *oversight*, *charge*, Lxx *Nu.* 3.36, 1 *Ch.* 24.3.'

**ἐπισκηνόω**, after '*to be quartered in*' insert '*SEG* 33.870 (Caria, *c.*203 BC)'

**ἐπισκήπτω II 3**, add '**b** *rely*, *base oneself* on, τοῖς τῆς διαθήκης ἐπισκήψαντες ῥήμασιν Just.*Nov.* 159.1.' **III**, add 'also of accusations for homicide, Lys. 3.39, Is.*fr.* 137'

**ἐπισκῐάζω**, add '**5** *follow closely in pursuit*, Arr.*Cyn.* 16.3.'

**ἐπισκιρρόομαι**, add '(dub., ed. σκιρ-)'

***ἐπισκοπάζω**, *inspect*, dub. rest. in *POxy.* 3410.9 (iv AD).

**ἐπισκοπεία**, add '**2** (sp. -σκοπία) office of ἐπίσκοπος (in quot., inspector of weights), *BE* 1971.61 (Palestine).'

**ἐπισκοπεύω**, for '= sq.' read '*keep watch over*' add '**b** *serve as* ἐπίσκοπος in the supervision of building operations, *Syria* 29.317 (Arabia, iii AD). **c** *to be a bishop*, *BCH* suppl. 8 no. 2 (Edessa), *SEG* 37.479 (Thessaly, both v/vi AD).'

**ἐπισκοπέω 5**, add '*to be a bishop*, *SEG* 37.479 (Thessaly, v/vi AD), *Cod.Just.* 1.3.41.6'

**ἐπισκοπή I**, add '**2** *visitation*, *punishment*, Lxx *Is.* 24.22, 29.6.'

**+ἐπισκοπία**, v. °ἐπισκοπεία.

***ἐπισκόπιον**, τό, *office of the* ἐπίσκοπος, *PSI* 1310.26 (ii BC).

**ἐπίσκοπος** (A) **3**, line 2, delete '*municipal*'; add '*inspector of weights and measures*, *BE* 1971.61 (Palestine)' **4**, add 'in the more fully developed ministry, *bishop*, Ἐπιφάνης ἐπι[σ]κόπου Εὐγενίου Mitchell *N.Galatia* 135, *SEG* 31.1396 (Syria, v AD), etc.'

**ἐπισκοτέω**, add 'ὑπὸ .. τῆς αἰσθήσεως ἐπισκοτεῖσθαι Iamb.*Protr.* 3 (p. 13.6 P.)'

**+ἐπίσκῡρος**, ὁ, ball game played between two teams, Hsch., Poll. 9.103, Sch.Pl.*Tht.* 146a; also ἡ ἐπίσκυρος (sc. παιδιά) Poll. 9.104; see also °σκῦρος.

***ἐπισκῦρος**, ὁ, sens. dub., Κεκροπίης τευμήσατ' ἐπίσκυρος Εὐρύκλεια *Suppl.Hell.* 1044.

**+ἐπισμᾰρᾰγέω**, *crash upon*, Opp.*H.* 2.159; *resound*, id.*C.* 2.78; w. cogn. acc., ἐ. ὕμνον τινί Nonn.*D.* 48.965.

**+ἐπισμήχω**, *smear* on, κωκύει ῥοδαλῇσιν ἐπισμήχουσα (sc. dust) παρειαῖς Opp.*C.* 1.501.

***ἐπισμικρῡ́νω**, *belittle*, Corn.*Rh.* p. 378 H.

**ἐπίσπαστρον I 2**, add '*Inscr.Délos* 1417*A*ii10'

**ἐπισπάω**, line 2, after '(E.)*Andr.* 710' insert 'Tim.*Pers.* 15.144 P.' **3**, add '*draw in* a net, Sol. 23.3'

**ἐπισπέρχω II 1**, intr., for '*rage furiously*' read '*hasten on*'

**+ἐπισπορά**, ἡ, *sowing of one* (*parasitic*) *plant on another*, Thphr.*CP* 2.17.10. **II** *second sowing*, *sowing of an after-crop*, *PTeb.* 27.37, al., 375.14 (both ii AD).

**ἐπισπορία**, for '= foreg.' read '*oversowing*'

**ἐπισπουδάζω I**, delete '*further*' and before '*Pr.*' insert '*bring about in haste*, ὕπαρξις ἐπισπουδαζομένη'

**ἐπισπουδαστής II 2**, add '*PColl.Youtie* 16.25 (109 BC)'

**ἔπισσαι, ἔπισσον**, delete the entries.

***ἔπισσος**, α, ον, *later*, *subsequent*, Hecat. 363 J., Μνημοσύνης ἧδ' ὧδε γόνου χαρίεντος ἔπισσα (?)Call.*fr.* 735 Pf., ἔπισσον· τὸ ὕστερον γενόμενον Hsch.; cf. μέτασσαι.

***ἐπίσσοχον**· ἀκόλουθον Hsch.

**ἐπίσταθμος I**, line 3, delete 'neut. pl. .. 4.173' and insert 'perh. humorously, of an image, Call.*Epigr.* 24 Pf.' **II**, for '*quartermaster* .. *AB* 253' read '*governor* appointed over a city or state, Isoc. 4.120; ἐ. Καρίας ib. 162, cf. *AB* 253, *EM* 364.36; in uncertain application, Plu. 2.612c: fig., ψυχὴν ἐ. σωμάτων Aristid.Quint. 2.2' **1 b** and **2**, delete these sections.

**ἐπίσταλμα II**, after '*Cod.Just.* 7.37.3.1c' insert '*requisitioning order*, *CPR* 8.37.12 (iv AD), *PMerton* 100.2, 6 (vii AD)'

**ἐπίστᾰμαι IV 1**, after 'Od. 21.406' insert 'cf., by back-formation, οὔπω .. νείκεος ἠπίσταντο Arat. 108'

**ἐπιστᾰ́σιον**, add '*EAM* 87.8 (ii BC)'

**ἐπιστᾰ́σιος**, after 'Plu.*Rom.* 18' insert 'fem. ἐπιστασίη, epith. of Aphrodite, perh. as patron of the ἐπιστάται, *Thasos* 1 p. 234 no. 24 (iv BC)'; delete etym. note and substitute '(ἐφίστημι, cf. perh. °ἐπίστασις VI)'

**ἐπίστασις II 1**, add '**c** *remission* of fever, Erasistr.ap.Gal. 11.208.13, 16.' **3**, delete 'κατὰ τὴν ἐ. .. (Samos. vi BC)' **V**, after 'Cypr.' insert '*e-pi-si-ta-i-se*' and for '*Inscr.Cypr.* 144 H.' read '*ICS* 264.3' add '**VI** *apparition*, *presence* (divine or heroic), *SEG* 30.1080 (Samos, *c.*500 BC), ib. 1517 (Perge, v/iv BC), Robert *Hell.* 11/12.544 (Miletus, ii AD).'

**ἐπιστατεία**, add '**IV** app., *fee for the superintendence of cargo*, *BGU* 2274 i 4 (AD 155).'

**ἐπιστεγάζω**, add '*PMerton* 76.32 (ii AD)'

***ἐπίστεγος**, ον, *roofed*, οἰκήματα *IRhod.Peraea* 352 A27, 353 A13, B10 (all iii/ii BC).

**ἐπιστείχω**, add 'χείματι δ' οὔποτε φασὶν ἐπιστείχειν ἁλὸς ὕδωρ πουλύποδας Opp.*H.* 2.241'

**ἐπιστένω 1**, add 'ἐπέστενε δ' αἶα νέκυσσι Q.S. 8.88'

***ἐπιστέργω**, *give one's love to*, *GVI* 728.8 (Cappadocia, ii/iii AD).

***ἐπιστήκω**, *superintend*, ἐπίστηκε (imp.) *PMich.*inv. 1610 (*ZPE* 35.104); ὁ -ων, *superintendent*, *PMich.*VIII 515.2 (iii AD).

**ἐπιστήμη I**, add '**3** perh. *discipline*, *sense of order*, Zos. 1.7.2, 2.32.2, 33.5, cf. δημοσία ἐ. ?*public order*, *POxy.* 3123.8 (AD 322).' **II**, line 3, for 'πλέως' read 'πλέων'

**ἐπίστιος II**, delete the section (v. ‡ἐφέστιος).

***ἐπιστολᾱφορία**, ἡ, *office of letter-carrier*, *PPetaus* 84.3 (AD 185), *POxy.* 3095.10 (AD 217/8).

**ἐπιστολεύς**, after '*secretary*' insert '(= Lat. *ab epistolis*)' and add '*OGI* 679, Phryn. 203, 356'

**ἐπιστολή 2**, add '**b** *letter of appointment*, *Cod.Just.* 12.33.8.2.'

**ἐπιστοληφόρος**, add 'also **ἐπιστολοφόρος**, ἐ. πρὸς Κλυταιμήστραν Weitzmann *Illustrations in Roll and Codex* (Princeton, 1947) p. 20 (Megarian bowl, iii BC), *PMich.*III 217.21 (iii AD), *PSI* 887.4 (vi AD)'

**ἐπιστολῑμαῖος**, line 2, after 'Ph. 2.533' insert '*POxy.* 3296.14 (iii AD)'

**ἐπιστολογρᾰφεῖον**, form ἐπιστολᾱ-, add '*BCH* 58.291 (ἐπιστωλαγραφῖον, Caria, iii BC)'

***ἐπιστολογρᾰφέω**, *to be a secretary*, *SB* 7638.15 (iii BC).

**°ἐπιστολοφόρος**, ὁ, v. ‡ἐπιστοληφόρος.

**ἐπιστομίζω I**, at end after 'ἐπεστομίσθη' insert '(sc. Πῶλος, with a play on his name)'

**ἐπιστρᾰτεία**, add 'D. 13.24, Paus. 8.25.4'

**ἐπιστρεπτικός**, add '**II** *capable of turning* one from mental aberration, Horap. 2.117.'

**°ἐπιστρέφειον**, τό, app. = ἐπιστρέφεια, *POxy.* 3304.19 (AD 301).

**ἐπιστρέφω I 1 b**, after 'Plb. 1.47.8, 50.5' insert 'in a διέκπλους manoeuvre, Sosyl. 1 J.' **II 4**, for 'E.*Andr.* 101' read 'E.*Andr.* 1031' **5**, at beginning for 'pf. part. pass.' read 'pf. pass. ἐπέστραμμαι *to be vehement*, Longin. 12.3'

**ἐπιστρωφάω**, add '**II** *spin, rotate*, ἀχθινὸν ἐπιστρωφήσατ' ἄτρακτον epigr. in *SEG* 37.990 (Miletus, ii BC).'

**ἐπισῡκοφαντέω**, add '*PHels.* 1.23 (ii BC)'

**°ἐπισύμβᾰμα**, ατος, τό, *supervenient accident*, Anon. *in Cat.* 48.3.

**°ἐπισυμβῐόω**, *live in second marriage with*, *SB* 7333 (s.v.l.; AD 186/7).

**ἐπισυνᾰγω I**, pass., add 'of contributions of money, *SEG* 31.122 (Attica, ii AD)'

**ἐπισυνάπτω I 1**, add '**b** intr., *follow on without a break*, ἐπισυναπτούσης τῆς ἡμέρας Onas. 42.10.'

**°ἐπισυναρμόζομαι**, med., of a woman, *join* (*herself*) *in a second marriage*, ἀνδρί *PFam.Teb.* 13.56 (ii AD).

**°ἐπισυνέρχομαι**, *come together towards*, ἐκ τῶ ἀδήλω ἐς τὸ ὁρατὸν ἐπισυνερχόμενα Hippod.ap.Stob. 4.34.71.

**°ἐπισυντῑμάομαι**, *make an additional valuation of*, τοὺς τόπους *PBremen* 24.11 (ii AD).

**⁺ἐπισῡρίζω**, *make a whistling sound* at, Arr.*Tact.* 35.4, Nonn.*D.* 1.71, 170.

**ἐπισύρω I 1**, add '**b** w. dat., *cause to go along* with, *attach* to, ὁρίζω τὸ ταύτης τέλος ἀεί ποτε βασιλικὸν ἐνέλκεσθαι καὶ ἐπισύρεσθαι καὶ ἐπαναστρέφεσθαι τῇ ἐμῇ περιουσίᾳ *PMasp.* 151.135, *PFlor.* 294.41 (both vi AD).'

**°ἐπισφᾰλερός**, ά, όν, *stumbling*, Nic.*Al.* 33.

**ἐπισφίγγω**, line 3, for 'ἐ. τοὺς ἀναγωγέας .. *tight*' read 'χρυσοῖς .. ἀνασπαστοῖς ἐπέσφιγγε τῶν βλαυτῶν τοὺς ἀναγωγέας'

**ἐπισφρᾱγίζω I 2**, after 'Vett.Val. 354.19' insert 'ἐ. τῇ ἰδίᾳ δυνάμει *Vit.Aesop.*(G) 91' **II 2**, line 3, before '(Pl.)*Phd.* 75d' delete 'prob. cj. in'

**°ἐπισφρᾱ́γισμα**, ατος, τό, *appendix, postscript*, Afric.*Cest.* p. 48 V. (title of section).

**ἐπισφρᾱγιστής**, add '*sealing inspector* who placed official seal on state granaries, *POxy.* 2841.12 (AD 85), *Stud.Pal.* 20.32.10, *PKöln* 94.9, 29, *SB* 10270(42).7 (all iii AD)'

**°ἐπισχολάζω**, *study* with, Πυθαγόρας .. τοῖς Μάγοις ἐπισχολάσας *SEG* 33.802B ii 27 (i AD).

**°ἐπισχῡρίζω**, *enforce*, *Suppl.Mag.* 45.53 (v AD).

**ἐπίσχω I**, line 2, for '[σελάννα] .. Sapph.*Supp.* 25.9' read 'intr., *reach* or *extend* over, φάος ἐπίσχει θάλασσαν ἐπ' ἀλμύραν Sapph. 96.9 L.-P.' **III 1**, add 'μικρὸν δ' ἐπίσχες Men.*Dysc.* 255 (dub.)'

**°ἐπισῴζω**, *continue to save*, Εἰλειθυίῃ σωζούσῃ ἐπισωζούσῃ εὐχήν *IG* 2².4793 (ii AD).

**ἐπίσωτρον**, line 3, ὀπίσσωτρον, add '*PMasp.* 279.20 (vi AD)'

**ἐπιτᾰγή 2**, add 'κατ' ὀνίρου ἐπιταγήν *TAM* 4(1).60'

**ἐπιτάδε**, for 'in Mss.' read 'written'

**ἐπιτάκτης**, add 'as the name or title of a god, *Pap.Lugd.Bat.* xxv 8 iii 1 (after AD 231)'

**ἐπιτακτικός**, at end after '-κῶς' insert 'Arist.*EE* 1249ᵇ14'

**ἐπίταλον**, after lemma insert '(ἐπιταδόν La.)'

**ἐπιτάξ III**, for 'Call.*Aet.* 1.1.9' read 'Call.*fr.* 178.9 Pf.' and delete 'dub. in *Iamb.* 1.239'

**ἐπιταξίδια**, add 'cf. perh. ‡ἐπιτοξίς'

**°ἐπιτᾰρᾰχώδης**, ες, *troubled, disordered*, Ἄρης Κρόνῳ ἐπιμερίζων μῆνας καὶ ἡμέρας ἐπιταραχώδεις τοὺς χρόνους σημαίνει Heph.Astr. 2.32.10.

**ἐπίτᾰσις**, add '**7** *development of the plot* of a play, between πρότασις and καταστροφή, Donat. in *CGF* p. 69.'

**ἐπιτᾰ́φιος I**, line 4, after 'Luc.*Eun.* 4' insert 'Certamen 63' add '**2** *neniae* ἐπιτάφια Charis. p. 33 K.' **II**, for 'ἐπιτάφια .. ἀγών' read 'Ἐπιτάφια, τά, festival in honour of the dead'

**ἐπίτεγξις I**, add 'Gal. 18(2).570.4'

**ἐπιτείνω I 1**, line 3, for 'Id. 4.201' read '(Hdt.) 4.201.1; βαρὺν ζυγὸν αὐχένι Call.*fr.* 4 Pf.' **2 c**, line 2, after 'Arist.*Pol.* 1308ᵇ4' insert 'ἐπετάθη πάντων .. τιμὴ J.*AJ* 9.14.2'

**ἐπιτέλεια II**, add '*SEG* 23.448 (Thessaly, ii/iii AD); personified, καὶ Δίκαι καὶ Ἐπιτελείαι τῶν ἀγάθων *SEG* 36.750 (Lesbos, iv BC)'

**ἐπιτέλειος**, add '**2** *brought to fulfilment*, ἐπιτελειᾶν δὲ τᾶν εὐχᾶν γενομενᾶν *SEG* 23.547.17 (Crete, 201/200 BC).'

**°ἐπιτελευτάω**, *die in addition*, *SB* 8979 (AD 180).

**ἐπιτέλλω** (B), for 'Pass.' read 'med.'; line 3, after 'intr. in Act.' insert 'Il.Parv. 9 B.'

**°ἐπιτελωνέω**, app. *pay* (tax), *IMylasa* 601.8 (i BC); cf. τελωνέω II.

**ἐπιτέμνω I**, add '**3** = τέμνω II 2, ὅρκια ἐπιταμνέτω *SEG* 16.485.30 (see also ib. 35.921) (Chios, vi BC).'

**ἐπίτερα**, after lemma insert '(ἐπιτερῇ La.)'

**⁺ἐπιτέρμιος**, ον, *marking the end, final*, ..] δ' ὁρᾶτε τοὐπι[τ]έρμιον γάμου A.*fr.* 154a.5 R.; ἐπιτέρμιον· ἐπὶ τοῦ τέρματος, οἷον ἐπὶ τοῦ τέλους Hsch.; Ἐπιτέρμιος title of Hermes, id.

**ἐπιτέταρτος**, for 'ratio of 4:3' read 'ratio of 5:4'

**ἐπιτετρᾰέβδομος**, for '*one plus four-sevenths*' read '*standing in the proportion of 11:7*'

**°ἐπιτετραίνω**, *perforate, bore*, τὰς παραετίδας (sc. δοκοὺς) ἆραι καὶ τὰς δοκοθήκας ἐπιτρῆσαι *IG* 11.161*A*55 (Delos, 279 BC).

**ἐπιτετρᾰμερής**, for '*one plus four-fifths*' read '*standing in the proportion of 9:5*'

**ἐπιτετράπεμπτος**, for '= foreg.' read '*standing in the proportion of 9:5*'

**ἐπίτευγμα**, line 2, delete '*coup*'

**°ἐπιτευτάζειν**· πραγματεύεσθαι ἢ σκαιωρεῖν Did.*Plat.* p. 245.

**ἐπιτήδειος**, after 'α, ον' insert '(ος, ον Th. 5.112.3)' **I**, add 'εἰ μὴ .. ἡλικίας καὶ τέχνης ἐστὶν ἐπιτήδειος *Cod.Just.* 11.8.16 pr.'

**ἐπιτηδειότης I 1**, add '*potentiality, capacity*, Alex.Aphr. *in APr.* 184.7, *in Top.* 400.3'

**⁺ἐπιτηλίς**, ίδος, fem. adj. μήκων .. ἐ., perh. the same as μήκων κερατῖτις (Dsc. 4.65), Nic.*Th.* 852.

**°ἐπίτηνα**, adv., Dor. = ἐπέκεινα, δωρεὰν τὰν ἐπίτηνα τῶ *hάλη*κος de Franciscis *Locr.Epiz.* 23.11, 30.14, 31.9.

**ἐπιτηρέω I**, line 2, after 'καιρόν' insert 'Men.*Dysc.* 291' **II 1**, after 'App.*BC* 4.39' insert 'of guardian deities, *Peripl.M.Rubr.* 32' **2**, add '*attend* to business, ὅταν τις τῶν τριῶν ἀνδρῶν ἐπὶ τῆς καταστάσεως τῶν δημοσίων πραγμάτων ἐπιτηρῷ *SEG* 31.952.10 (Ephesus, Trajan)'

**ἐπιτηρητής 2**, add 'ἐπιτηρητοῦ οὐσιακῶν *PPetaus* 75.7 (AD 184)'

**⁺ἐπιτηρία**, ἡ, = ἐπιτήρησις (in quot. sense 2), ἐξ ἐ[πι]τηρίᾱ *IPamph.* 3.4 (iv BC).

**ἐπιτίθημι A III 1**, add '**b** *add* statements, etc., D.H.*Isoc.* 14, *Is.* 7 (pass.); ἐ. ὅτι ib. 4.' **IV**, line 6, after '(D.) 49.42' insert 'Men.*Dysc.* 308'

**ἐπιτῑμάω II 1**, add 'abs., *inflict punishment*, Decr.ap.D. 18.74' **2 b**, add 'D. 18.294'

**ἐπιτῑ́μησις II 2**, for '*heightening* .. *term*' read '*rejection* of one term in favour of another (usually a stronger term)' add '**III** *estimated value*, *PWisc.* 15 (AD 236).'

**ἐπιτῑ́μιος**, delete the entry (v. *BCH* 58.497).

**ἐπίτῑμος I**, add 'adv. -ως, w. ref. to completion of, or discharge from, duty, *with honour*, *La Carie* 172, *IGRom.* 1.648, Mitchell *N.Galatia* 178, Modest.*Dig.* 27.1.8 pr., 6' **II 1**, add '*PCol.Zen.* 100 (iii BC)' **2**, add '*PTeb.* 38 (113 BC)'

**°ἐπιτιμωρέω**, *avenge*, πατρί Sch.E.*Or.* 775; med., *avenge oneself*, Sch.E.*Med.* 465.

**°ἐπιτίτλωσις**, εως, ἡ, *title* of a criminal charge, Steph.*in Rh.* 286.1, v. ἐπίγραμμα 4.

**°ἐπιτοιχογρᾰ́φος**, ὁ, *writer of graffiti*, *SEG* 29.974 (s.v.l., Ostia, Rom.imp.).

**ἐπιτόνιον**, line 2, delete 'prob. in' and after 'Ath. 10.456d' insert '(cj. °ἐπιγόνειον)'

**ἐπιτοξίς 1**, for 'dub. sens. in' read 'name of some ritual object, cf. prob. ἐπιτοξίδες· ἀγκυρίδες σιδηραὶ δίβολοι Phot. ε 1768'

**°ἐπίτοπος**, ον, *positioned* in a place, Plb. 3.40.4.

**°ἐπιτρᾰπεζίδιον**, τό, perh. *small tray* or *table-ornament*, ἐ. ἀργυροῦν ἔχον στεφάνην *Inscr.Délos* 1439*Cb*20 (ii BC).

**ἐπιτρᾰπέζιος I**, add 'neut. pl. subst., *tableware*, ἐπιτραπέδι[α (sic) Lang *Ath.Agora* XXI B13 (iv BC)'

**°ἐπιτρᾰπεζόω**, med., perh. *provide extra food*, *SEG* 18.21.9 (Athens, ii BC); cf. °ἐπιτραπέζωμα.

**⁺ἐπιτρᾰπέζωμα**, ατος, τό, *dish served as an extra*, prob. *dessert*, Pl.Com. 76 K.-A.

**ἐπιτρέπω**, lines 2/3, for 'Cret. fut. inf. .. 5024.12' read 'Cret. 1 sg. -τραψίω *Inscr.Cret.* 1.xviii 9 c 13 (Lyttos, ii BC), inf. -τραψῆν ib. 4.174 A12, 14 (Gortyn, ii BC)'

**ἐπιτρέφω II**, pass., add 'Hp.*Nat.Hom.* 12'

**ἐπιτρέχω II 2**, add '**b** *pervade*, of literary qualities, D.H.*Dem.* 13, 41.'

**ἐπιτρῐμερής**, for '$1+\frac{3}{4}$' read '*standing in the proportion of 7:4*'

**ἐπιτροπεύσιμος**, for '*subject to wardship*' read '*capable of acting as guardian* in Roman law'

**⁺ἐπιτροπέω**, *govern*, w. acc., βυθίην Κύπρον ἐπιτροπέων *IG* 2².3662.10 (Eleusis, ii/iii AD); w. gen., ἐπιτροπ[έω]ν Θηβηΐδος *SEG* 8.724 (Egyptian Thebes, ii AD), Bernand *Inscr.Colosse Memnon* 36.

**ἐπιτροπή II 1**, add 'used to render Lat. *tutela*, *Cod.Just.* 6.4.4.20a'

**ἐπιτροπία**, add 'τοῦδ' ἔλαχ' ἀθανάτων ὅστις ἐπιτροπίην epigr. in *IMylasa* 496.11 (*EA* 13.4). **2** *guardianship*, *POxy.* 2133.13 (iii AD); cf. ἐπιτροπή II.'

**ἐπιτροπικός II**, add '*IGBulg.* 514' add '**III** -ική, ἡ, *power of attorney*, *PPhilad.* 16.7, 14 (ii AD) (s.v.l.).'

**ἐπίτροπος I 1**, add '*PMich.*xv 733.1, *POxy.* 1973.5, 2033.1 (all vi AD)' **II**, add 'Modest.*Dig.* 19.2.49 pr., 27.1.13 pr.'

**ἐπιτρώγω II**, for 'generally, *eat*' read '*eat as an accompaniment*, ἅλας'

**ἐπιτυγχάνω**, line 1, aor., add 'ἐπέτυχα *SEG* 34.1212 (Lydia)' **III 1**, line 2, for 'εὐχωλᾶς *Inscr.Cypr.* 134 H.' read '*ta-se e-u-ko-la-se* [*e*]*-pe-tu-ke* τᾶς εὐχὀλᾶς ἐπέτυχε *ICS* 220.4'; at end after 'abs.' insert '*Com.adesp.* 357' **4**, add 'ποιήματα D.S. 16.92.3'

***ἐπιτῡρόομαι**, *turn cheesy, curdle*, Nic.*Al.* 364 (v.l. ἐπιθρομβ-).

**ἐπιτῠχία 2**, add 'Alcid. 15.4 R.'

***ἐπιΐζω**, *yell at*, w. dat., *Suppl.Hell.* 939.21.

**ἐπιφαιδρύνω**, after 'A.R. 4.663' add '(v.l. περι-)'

**ἐπιφαίνω II**, delete '*dawn*' and insert 'μήτε δὲ ἡλίου μήτε ἄστρων ἐπιφαινόντων *Act.Ap.* 27.20; transf., θεὸς κύριος καὶ ἐπέφανεν ἡμῖν Lxx *Ps.* 117(118).27'

**ἐπιφανής II 1**, add 'ἡμέραι *Mél.Glotz* 290.28 (sup.; Delphi, ii BC)' **3**, add 'title of Aphrodite, *SEG* 13.458.28 (Thasos, ii/i BC); of Artemis Iakinthotrophos, *SEG* 38.812 (Cos, iii/ii BC); sup., of Roman Emperors, *SEG* 31.932, 940 (Caria, AD 293/305)' **III 1**, add 'comp. adv. ἐπιφανεστέρως Gal. 9.249.7, 9'

**ἐπιφαύσκω**, line 2, after '(Lxx *Jb.*) 31.26' insert 'Orph.*H.* 50.9 (s.v.l.)'

***ἐπιφερία**, ἡ, dub. sens. in context relating to land allocation, perh. *attached* or *marginal land*, *PAlex.* 14.4, 13 (ii/iii AD).

**ἐπιφημίζω I 1**, add 'Arr.*An.* 5.3.1' **III 1**, add 'med. aor. ἐπεφημίξαντο Arat. 442'

**ἐπιφθίνω**, add '**2** *die in addition*, ἁ δὲ πολυθρήνητος ἐπέφθιτο μήτερι κούρα epigr. in *ICilicie* 41 (i BC).'

**ἐπιφῐλοτῑμία**, delete the entry (v. *SEG* 29.139).

***ἐπιφλυκτίς**, ίδος, ἡ, *pimple* or *blister*, Hsch. s.v. ὀλοφυκτίς (perh. f.l. for ἐπινυκτίς, cf. Phot.).

**ἐπιφορά I 1**, add 'of land granted to soldiers, *PHamb.* 168.7, 9 (iii BC)' add '**b** as pay category (indicating rank), *BGU* 2367.8 (iii BC).'

**ἐπιφόρημα**, add '**II** *additional fee*, prov. Ἀβυδηνὸν ἐ., of a petty nuisance, Ath. 14.641a.'

***ἐπιφόριμα**· ἐπὶ δέρμα (ἐπίδρομα La.) Hsch.

**ἐπιφροσύνη**, line 2, after 'Od. 5.437' insert 'Thgn. 1100'

***ἐπιφυτευτικός**, ή, όν, i.e. *held by the tenure of* ‡ἐμφύτευσις, *Dura*[6] 429 (parchment).

**ἐπιφύω II**, penultimate line, after '(Plu.)*Pomp.* 51' insert '*PMonac.* 1.46 (vi AD)'

**ἐπιφώνησις**, add '**V** *interjection*, A.D.*Adv.* 121.15.'

**ἐπίχᾰρις**, adv., add 'Isoc. 15.132, id.*Ep.* 6.6'; delete 'Boeotian ἐπιχαρίτως dub. l. in Ar.*Ach.* 867'

**ἐπίχαρμα**, add '**III** *cause for joy*, E.*Phaëth.* 93 D., cf. Hsch.'

**ἐπίχειρον I**, add 'Lxx 2*Ma.* 15.33' **II 1**, line 2, after 'Theoc.*Ep.* 18.8' insert 'εὐδοξίας ἐ. Pi.*Pae.* 14.31 S.-M.'; line 3, after 'ironically in' insert '*Trag.adesp.* 664.20 K.-S., Call.*fr.* 260.59 Pf.'

**ἐπιχειροτονέω 2**, delete 'τοὺς προέδρους .. hence' add '**3** *put to the vote*, lex ap.D. 24.39.'

***ἐπιχιτώνιος**, ον, Myc. *e-pi-ki-to-ni-ja* (?neut. pl.), prob. *ornaments on a tunic*.

**ἐπίχνοος**, add 'Gal. 16.553.2'

**ἐπιχράω** (B), line 1, after 'ἐπέχρᾱον' insert '(3 sg. ἐπέχρα Nic.*Th.* 14)'

**ἐπιχράω** (C) **I**, for this section read '*lend*, τάγματα ὧν ἐπέχρησε δύο Καίσαρι Plu.*Pomp.* 52; ἐπιχρήσας ἑαυτὸν εἰς ἀπαλλοτρίωσιν *ISmyrna* 212.11' **II 2**, add '**b** w. dat., *occupy oneself with*, Iamb.*Protr.* 20 (96.4 P.).'

***ἐπιχρεμετίζω**, *neigh at*, Q.S. 8.57.

**ἐπίχρῑσις**, add '**2** *coating with paint*, *IG* 4².109 i 130 (Epid., iii BC).'

**ἐπίχῠμα II**, add '*BGU* 2333.13 (ii AD)'

**ἐπιχύνω**, for '*JHS* 19.73 (Galatia)' read 'Mitchell *N.Galatia* 78'

***ἐπιχῠσίδιον**, τό, dim. of ἐπίχυσις III, *Inscr.Délos* 1408*A*i32, 1443*A*ii45 (ii BC).

**ἐπίχῠσις III**, for '*beaker* or *wine-jug*' read '*pouring-vessel*'

**ἐπιχῠτήρ**, for '= ἐπίχυσις III' read '*vessel for pouring* oil into a lamp'

***ἐπιχώρημα**, ατος, τό, perh. *leave, permission*, *PRyl.* 222 *fr.* (ii AD), *PWash.Univ.* 1.22 (rest.), 23.

***ἐπιψέλλως**, adv. *incoherently*, γράφειν *PTeb.* 763.14 (ii BC).

**ἐπιψηφίζω I 1**, line 2, before 'D. 22.9' insert 'Th. 6.14.1' **2**, delete 'Th. 6.14, etc.' **III**, add 'ἐπιδεὶ ἐπεψαφίτταto ὁ δᾶμος ἀποδόμεν Νικαρέτη‹ι› *IG* 7.3172 viii 112'

***ἐπιψήχω**, dub. sens., βῶλον ἐπιψήχων πυροφόροις βοτάναις *GVI* 1165.2 (near Sardes, ii AD), v. *RPh.* 31.19.

***ἐπιώβολος** τόκος, interest at $16\frac{2}{3}$%, *Inscr.Délos* 442*C*61 (ii BC).

***ἐπιωπής**, ές, *watchful, vigilant*, κλυτὴν ἐπιωπέα κούρην orac. in *ZPE* 92.269 (Ephesus, ii AD).

**ἐποδύρομαι**, add 'cj. in Apollod. 1.9.8 (codd. ἀποδ-)'

**ἐποίζω**, delete the entry.

**ἐποικία I**, add 'v.l. for ἀπ- in Pi.*O.* 1.24'

**ἐποικίζω III**, for '*bring into cultivation*' read '*settle on*'; add 'ἐπιϝοικίξ[ε]ιτη *BCH* 60.182.25 (Thespiae, iii BC)'

**ἐποίκιον II**, add 'w. place-names, ἀπὸ ἐποικίου Γεννέσυ ὅρων Ἀπαμέων *IG* 14.2327, 2329, etc.'

***ἐποικιοφύλαξ**, ακος, ὁ, *settlement-guard*, *POxy.* 3518 (iii AD).

***ἐποικιώτης**, ου, ὁ, *inhabitant of an* ἐποίκιον, *PFlor.* 180.7 (iii AD).

**ἐποικοδομέω**, after lemma insert 'ἐπιϝοικοδομέω *BCH* 60.182.25 (Thespiae, iii BC)'; line 2, after 'D. 55.25' insert 'Men.*Dysc.* 376 (cj.)'

**ἔποικος I 3**, last line, for 'Call.*Aet.Oxy.* 2080.69' read 'Call.*fr.* 43.67 Pf.'

**ἐποικτίζω**, med., add 'ὃν [ὁ] πᾶς δῆμος ἐπῳκτίσατο epigr. in *SEG* 39.972.9 (Lato, ii BC)'

**ἐποιμώζω**, add 'τέκνοις τοῖς τεθνηκόσιν A.*fr.* 154a.7 R. (s.v.l.)'

**ἐποίχομαι I 2**, add 'A.*Ch.* 956'

**ἐποκέλλω 2**, add 'fig. ἐποκέλλοντες δὲ εἰς τὸ ῥωπικὸν καὶ κακόζηλον Longin. 3.4'

***ἐπονειδίζω**, *insult*, στίγματα μὴ γράψῃς ἐπονειδίζων θεράποντα Ps.-Phoc. 225; also ἐπιον- *PIand.* 97.4 (iii AD).

**+ἐπονήμενοι, ἐπονᾱ́μενοι**, dub. lect. and sens., Alc. 5.9, 33(*b*).4, 119.17 (L.-P.).

**ἐπονομάζω 3**, line 2, after 'so and so' insert 'κάπωνύμασσαν ἀντίαον Δία they *entitled* Zeus god of suppliants, Alc. 129.5 L.-P.'

**ἐποξίζω**, add '*Vit.Aesop.*(G) 63'

**ἐποπτεύω I 2**, add '*IEryth.* 2C.1 (v BC), ἐπιοπτευέτω καὶ ὑποζυγὴν ἔναι ib. 4'

***ἐπορθοβοάω**, *lift up* a cry, ἵνα πατρὶ γόους νυχίους ἐπορθοβοάσω E.*El.* 142 (s.v.l.).

**ἔπος**, line 1, after '(v. infr.)' insert 'Cypr. *we-po*, perh. ϝέπο(ς), *ICS* 264.1'

***ἐπούλων**, ωνος, ὁ, ἑπτὰ ἀνδρῶν ἐπουλώνων (transl. Lat. *septemvirum epulonum*, *board of seven in charge of public feasts*), *IEphes.* 3033, 3034.

**ἐπούλωσις**, add 'Heras ap.Gal. 13.765.15'

**ἐπουλωτικός**, add 'Heras ap.Gal. 13.765.13'

**ἐπουράνιος 1**, add 'τῷ μεγάλῳ Θεῷ Ὑψίστῳ καὶ Ἐπουρανίῳ *SEG* 31.1080 (Galatia, ii/ii AD), cult-title of Zeus, *INikaia* 1114, 1115 (ii/iv AD)'

**ἐπουρίζω I**, add 'S.*fr.* 442.7 R.'

**ἔπουρος I**, after 'S.*Tr.* 954 (lyr.)' add '*carried by a favourable breeze*, id.*OT* 194'

**ἐποφλισκάνω**, add '**2** simply *owe*, Just.*Nov.* 121.1, *Edict.* 9 pr.'

**ἐποχέομαι**, line 1, after 'med.' insert 'athematic pres. part. ἐποχήμενος Nonn.*D.* 8.229, al.' **3 a**, line 2, after '*transcend* the lower' insert 'τὸ ἀγαθὸν ἐποχούμενον ἐπὶ τῇ οὐσίᾳ Numen. *fr.* 2 P.'

**ἐποχή III 2 a**, add '*position* or *orbit* of planets, Nicom.*Harm.* 3 (pl.)' **3**, delete the section.

***ἐπόχησις**, εως, ἡ, = ἐποχή III 2, Iamb.*VP* 15.65 (s.v.l.).

***ἐπόχθων**, ονος, ὁ, app. error for ἐπίχθων, = ἐπιχθόνιος 1, opp. ὑπόχθων, of a δαίμων, *SEG* 7.213.6 (tab.defix.; Beirut, ii/iii AD).

***ἐπόχιμος**, ον, *suspended*, of payments, *PTeb.* 337.3 (ii/iii AD); cf. ἐποχή II 2.

**ἐπόψιος**, line 1, for 'Arat. 258' read 'Arat. 81, 258' **II**, add 'Ἐ. Ζεύς. καὶ Ἀπόλλων Hsch.'

**ἔποψις I**, add '**2** perh. *façade*, οἰκοδόμησαν τὴν ἔποψιν Θεῷ Κρόνῳ M.Dunand *Le Musée de Soueïda* (Paris 1934) no. 198 (ii AD).'

**ἔπρεσε**, for 'πρήθω' read 'πίμπρημι'

**ἑπτά**, after 'indecl.' insert 'Cret. ἑττά *Inscr.Cret.* 1.viii 5A.9 (iii BC)'

**ἑπταγράμμᾰτος**, add '*PMag.* 12.8.6'

***ἑπταέτηρος**, ον, *seven years long*, φύλοπιν ἑ. Nonn.*D.* 25.3.

**ἑπτᾰετής I**, after '*seven years old*' insert '*IG* 9²(1).431.1 (Acarnania, ii/i BC)'

**ἑπτᾰέτις** (s.v. ἑπταετής), add '*GVI* 1508 (Gaza, Ptolemaic)'

**ἑπτακαιδέκατος**, add 'Thess. ἑττακαιδεκότα *SEG* 29.529 (*BCH* 104.643)'

**ἑπτᾰκᾰ́τιοι**, add '*SEG* 25.387.A22 (Epid., iv BC)'

***ἑπτᾰκελλάριον**, τό, perh. *chest*, or sim., *with seven compartments*, *PAnt.* 93.31 (iv AD, -ρον pap.).

***ἑπτᾰκλᾰ́δος**, ον, *having seven branches* or *shoots*, Ps.-Callisth. 131.2.

***ἑπτᾰ́μετρον**, τό, of capacity, *seven* (*standard*) *measures*, *PFlor.* 356.11 (i/ii AD).

**ἑπτᾰμήκης**, delete the entry.

**ἑπτᾰ́μηνος II**, add '*PTeb.* 342.30 (ii AD; v. *AncSoc* 21.33)'

***ἑπτάξῠλος**, ον, *containing seven sticks*, or *seven* ξύλα (v. ξύλον V) *in length*, δέσμαι *OTheb.* 144 (i AD).

**+ἑπτᾰπᾰ́λαιστος**, ον, *seven palms long*, S.E.*M.* 9.321; also **-πάλαστος** *IG* 1².373.237, *PPetr.* 3.41ᵛ.5 (iii BC), *Inscr.Délos* 1442*B* 66 (ii BC).

***ἑπτάπλησον**, aor. imper. *multiply by seven*, perh. erron. for ἑπτάπλωσον (°ἑπταπλόω) *PCair.* 10758 (vi AD).

***ἑπταπλόω**, perh. *multiply by seven*, v. °ἑπτάπλησον.

**ἑπτᾰ́ρουρος**, add '*PColl.Youtie* 16.3 (109 BC)'

***ἑπτάστεγος**, ον, *having seven stories*, *POxy.* 2719.9 (iii AD).

***ἑπτάστολος**, ον, *wearing seven* στολαί, of a devotee of Isis, ἱεροφόρος ἑ., *AE* 1931.174 (Samos).

***ἑπτάστροφος**, ον, *consisting of seven strophes*, Heph.*Sign.* 4.

***ἑπτασφόνδῠλος**, ον, *having seven segments*, of the scorpion's tail, Cyran. 46 (1.24.7 K.); transf., ἑ. μοι ῥήματα εἶπας *Vit.Aesop.*(G) 31.

**ἑπτάτονος**, for '*B.Scol.Oxy.* 1361 *fr.* 1.2' read '*B.fr.* 20*B*.2 S.-M. (of a βάρβιτος)'

***ἑπταύχενος**, ον, app. *seven-necked* (in broken context), Dain *Inscr.du Louvre* 60.28 (Heraclea ad Latmum).

**ἕπω** (A), line 2, after 'Il. 6.321' insert 'ἀμφὶς ἕπουσιν = ἀμφέπουσιν *honour*, Nic.*Th.* 627 (v.l.)'

**ἕπω** (B), **I 10**, add 'part., w. month name, Ἀμυκλαίου ἑπομένου *SEG* 34.282 (Nemea, iv BC)'

**ἐπωβελία 1**, add 'Aeschin. 1.163'

**ἐπῳδή**, line 5, after 'A.*Pr.* 174' insert 'id.*fr.* 281a.20 R., Hp.*Morb.Sacr.* 1' **II**, add 'Zen. 5.68 (Archil. 201 Q.)'

***ἐπωδύνιος**, ον, = ἐπώδυνος, *GVI* 1675.2 (Tomi, ii/iii AD).

***ἐπώζω**, *wail* over, τέκν]οις ἐπώζει ζῶσα τοῖς τεθνηκόσιν perh. to be read in A.*fr.* 154a.7 R. (pap. ἐποιμώζουσα, Αἰσχύλος Νιόβῃ μεταφορικῶς· ἐφημένη τάφον τέκνοις ἔπωζε .. τοῖς τεθνηκόσιν Hsch. s.v. ἐπῳζειν); cf. also Ar.*Av.* 266.

**ἐπῴζω**, for 'Cratin. 108' read 'Cratin. 115 K.-A. (ἐπωάζ- cod. Ath.)' and delete '*cluck* .. Ar.*Av.* 266'

**ἐπωλένιος**, after '(*h.Merc.*) 510' insert '(ὑπ- codd.)'

**ἐπωμάδιος I**, for '*on the shoulders*' read '*situated on the shoulders*' and add 'Arat. 249'

**ἐπώμιος**, add 'Myc. *e-po-mi-jo* (dual), *shoulder-pieces* of armour'

**ἐπώμοτος I**, after '*Tr.* 427' insert 'in broken context -- δε]κα λεβήτōν ἐπόμοτον ἦμ[εν --, *Inscr.Cret.* 4.8 (vii/vi BC)'

**ἐπώνια I**, sg., for pres. ref. read '*SEG* 37.917.A5, al. (Erythrae, v/iv BC), *IEryth.* 201 (iii BC)'

**ἐπωνυμία**, add '**II** *office of* °ἐπώνυμος II 2 c, τὴν ἐ. τῶν Σαραπιαστῶν *BCH* 51.220.3 (Thasos, prob. ii BC).'

**ἐπωνύμιον**, after 'τό' insert '*title*, ?Alc. 304 i 10 L.-P.'

**ἐπώνυμος II 2 a**, add 'later, of a patron or benefactor, *Hesperia* suppl. 6, no. 24.1 (Athens, ii AD)' add '**c** official of Sarapiastae whose name appeared in their decrees, *BCH* 51.220, 221 (Thasos, prob. ii BC).'

**Ἐπωπετής**, before 'Hsch.' insert '*SEG* 21.541 iii 20 (Erchiae, Attica, iv BC)'

***ἐπώπια**, τά, perh. *eyebrows*, Call.in *Suppl.Hell.* 238.7.

***ἐπωστός**, όν, *capable of being pushed forward*, Eratosth.ap.Eutoc.*in Archim.* p. 94 H.

**ἐπωτίδες**, add 'also applied to similar fittings on a trolley used for transporting marble drums, ἐπωτίδες εἰς τὴν λιθαγωγίαν *IG* 2$^{2}$.1673.34. **II** sg. ἐπωτίς, ίδος, ἡ, *bandage for the ear*, Gal. 12.488 Charterius (σπωτίς cod.).'

**ἔρᾰμαι**, lines 5/6, delete 'poet. .. 19'

**ἔρᾰνος I 2**, add 'Epich. 87.1'

**ἐραπίδα**, add '(ἐράπεδα· ἃ ἡμεῖς δαπέδα La.)'

***ἐράριον**, v. αἰράριον.

**ἐρᾰσιχρήματος**, add 'Philostr.*VA* 1.35'

***ἐράσκομαι**, = ἐράω, *GVI* 280.2 (Thrace, iii AD).

***ἐρασμίβωμος**, ον, *having lovely altars*, ἐρασμιβώμοις θύμασιν δωρουμένη *PKöln* 125 i 3 (s.v.l.).

**ἐράσμιος**, after 'X.*Mem.* 3.10.3' insert 'Pl.*R.* 402d, al.'

**ἐραστής**, add '**3** name given to white spots on the finger nail (cf. ψεῦδος II 2), Alex.Aphr.*Pr.Anecd.* 2.58.'

**ἐραστός**, line 3, for '[Simon.] 178.1' read '*AP* 5.159.1 ([Simon.])'

**ἐρᾰτεινός**, after '(Pi.)*fr.* 122.7' insert 'σωφροσύνην ἐρατεινήν epigr. in *SEG* 25.299 (Attica, iv BC)'

**ἐρᾰτός**, line 6, delete 'παίδων' **2**, delete 'ἀνδράσι .. Tyrt. 10.29' and substitute 'epigr. in *ZPE* 44.102 no. 12 (Pisidia)'

***ἐρᾰτόφρων**, ονος, ὁ, *friendly*, rest. in epigr. in *SEG* 15.620.6 (Ostia, iii AD).

**ἐραυνητικόν**, add '*PCornell* 3.5 (iii BC), *PMerton* 15.28, 33 (AD 114), also **ἐρευνητικόν** *PCair.Zen.* 753.35, 40, *PTeb.* 867 (iii BC)'

**ἐράω** (A), line 2, form ἐρέω, add 'Anacr. 14.1, 83.1 P.'; line 4, after 'ἐρᾶσθαι' insert 'Men.*Epit.* 432'; lines 5/6, for 'also .. ἔραμαι)' read 'med. ἐρᾶται Plu. 2.753b is suspect' and add 'pf. pass. Cypr. *e-re-ra-me-na*, ἐρεραμένα, *ICS* 264.2' **I 2**, delete 'without sexual reference'

***ἔρβουλον**, τό, ?*vetch*, *Edict.Diocl.* 1.8a; cf. Lat. *ervum.* **2** an Italian wine, Ath. 1.27c.

**ἐργάζομαι**, lines 4/5, aor., add 'Thess. 3 sg. ἐργάξατο *IG* 9(2).1027b (?Atrax, v BC); ἐϝεργάσ(σ)ατο *SEG* 11.379 (Hermion, v BC)'; line 6, after 'iv BC' insert 'also ἠργάσετο Robert *Hell.* IX.40, εἰργάσετο Ramsay *Cities and Bishoprics* 1.338 no. 186, both in sculptors' signatures' **I**, add '**2** w. dat., *work for, serve*, Lxx *Je.* 34(27).6, 35(28).14, *Ba.* 1.22.' **III 1**, add 'of skins, *treated, tanned*, *Edict.Diocl.* 8.10, *BCH* suppl. 8 no. 85 (Thessalonica, v/vi AD)'

**ἐργᾰ́νη**, line 3, for '*APr.*' read 'A.*Pr.*'

***ἐργᾰνοφύλαξ**, ακος, ὁ, name of an occupation, app. some kind of watchman, *BGU* 1988 b 3 (s.v.l. ?ὀργανο-, iii BC).

**ἐργᾰσία II 3**, at end transfer 'of sexual *intercourse*, Arist.*Pr.* 876$^{a}$39' to section I 1 **b**, add 'Demad. 8, *Act.Ap.* 16.16, 19' **II 5**, line 2, delete '(non legit Sch.)'

**ἐργᾰ́σιμος II 2**, add '*energetic*, of a person, Nic.Dam.*fr.* 61 J.'

**ἐργαστηριακός**, for '*practising a handicraft*' read '*working in an* ἐργαστήριον'

**ἐργαστήριον 1**, add 'of a local θησαυρός with its branches, *PTeb.* 722.7 (ii BC), al.; app. of a medical clinic, *SEG* 30.1175 (Italy, iii BC)'

**ἐργαστής**, after '-τής' insert '(Cret. ϝεργαστάς Bile *Dial.crét.* no. 27, Axos (vi/v BC)'; after '(Thyatira)' insert '*PIand.* 8.150 ii 16 (iii AD)'

**ἔργαστρα II**, after '*IG* 2$^{2}$.839.85' insert '(but this may belong under section I)'

***ἐργάστρια**, ἡ, fem. of ἐργαστής, prob. in Sch.E.*Med.* 408.

***ἐργᾰτηγός**, ὁ, app. *foreman, overseer*, Μουσ.Σμυρν. 1884/5 p. 79.

***ἐργᾰ́της**, form ϝεργάτᾱς, Myc. *we-ka-ta*, (pl., *-ta-e* dual), of oxen.

**ἐργᾰτικός**, add '**2** -κόν, τό, *payment for labour*, *PCornell* 3.15 (iii BC), *Inscr.Délos* 440*A*72, 79 (ii BC).'

**ἐργεπιστάτης**, add '*SEG* 30.1254.10 (Aphrodisias, AD 102/116)'

***ἐργεπόπτης**, ου, ὁ, *overseer*, *JHS* 12.263 (Cilicia).

**ἔργμα**, add 'Hes.*Op.* 801, *Th.* 823'

***ἐργμός**, = εἱργμός 2, δεσμῶν ἐ. *SPAW* 1937.156 (Aetolian decree, Miletus, iii BC).

**ἐργοδιωκτέω**, for '*to be a taskmaster*' read '*to be an overseer*'

**ἐργοδιώκτης**, for '*taskmaster*' read '*overseer*' and add '*PHarris* 100.11, *POxy.* 2195.128, 2197.176, al. (all v/vi AD); perh. also τῷ ἐργοδιώτῳ (sic) Mitchell *N. Galatia* 161.8'

**ἐργοδότης**, add '*IMylasa* 895 in *EA* 13.7.17 (ii BC)'

**ἐργολᾰβέω**, add '**III** *victimize*, ἠργολάβησέν με *PMich.*VI 425.13 (ii AD).'

***ἐργολᾰβικόν**, τό, *contractor's fee*, *PMich.Zen.* 62.13 (iii BC).

**ἐργολᾰ́βος**, line 3, after 'Them.*Or.* 21.260b' insert '*PRyl.* 577.11, 16 (ii BC)'

**ἔργον**, line 1, ϝέργον, add '*SEG* 28.37.3(b) (amphora from S. Italy, vi BC); ib. 32.496.19 (Thespiae, iii BC)'; line 2, after 'τό' insert 'see also °ἔργος' **III 1**, add 'of a monument, *SEG* 30.1383.A11 (Lydia, AD 301), Mitchell *N.Galatia* 142, al.' **III 2**, add 'D. 28.13'

⁺**ἐργοπόνος**, ὁ, *one who toils* or *labours*, *AP* 11.9 (Leon.Tarent.), Nic.*Th.* 831; w. gen. indicating occupation, ἐργοπόνοι κρατεροὶ θήρης ἐρικυδέος Opp.*C.* 1.148; ἐ. ἐλέφαντος Man. 1.298; epigr. in *SEG* 31.1284 (Pisidia); fem., of Athena, as patroness of crafts, Coluth. 195. **2** one destined for toil, *drudge*, *Cat.Cod.Astr.* 7.198.

***ἔργος**, τό, = ἔργον, gen. sg. [ἔ]ργεος *Epigr.Gr.* 321.3 (Lydia, ii/iii AD), dat. pl. ἔργεσι ib. 343 (Germae).

***ἐργοστᾰσιάρχης**, ου, ὁ, *workshop foreman*, *BpW* 1910.310 (Rhodes).

***ἐργοτόχιος**, ὁ, perh. = ἐργοδόχος, ?*contractor*, *MAMA* 3.487 (Corycus).

**ἔργω I**, add '**2** *hold together, keep shut*, ἄλλικα .. ἐεργομένην ἐνετῇσιν Call.*fr.* 253.11 Pf.' **II 3**, add '**c** *shun*, *Inscr.Cret.* 4.176.25 (ii BC).'

***ἐργωνικός**, ὁ, prob. = ἐργώνης, *MDAI(A)* 24.204 (near Pergamum).

**ἔρδω**, line 9, for 'aor. 1 ἔϝερξα *Inscr.Cypr.* 146 H.' read 'aor. 1 Cypr. *e-we-re-xa*, perh. ἔϝερξα, *ICS* 261' **2**, line 4, after 'Hdt. 1.131' insert 'δεκάτην *SEG* 12.391 (Samos, vi BC)'

**ἐρέα**, add '**b** applied to other materials resembling wool, ἐρέας λαγείας νωτιαίας *Edict.Diocl.* in *SEG* 31.911.10.'

**ἐρεβίνθιον**, add 'sg. in collective sense, *PVindob.* G40805 (*ZPE* 50.129 (iv AD)'

**ἐρέβινθος II**, delete '*Ach.* 801'

**ἐρεβῶπις**, for '*gloomy-looking*' read '*having the face of a creature from Erebus*, of a gorgon'

**ἔρεγμα**, for '*bruised corn*' read '*crushed corn, pulse*, etc.' and add 'ἐμψίουσα· ἐρέγματα διδοῦσα Hsch.; also **ἔριγμα**, φακῶν ἢ ἐρεβίνθων ἐρίγμασι Hp.*Coac.* 621, ξὺν κριθέων ἐρίγματι id.*Mul.* 2.195, Sch. Gen.Il. 17.295, Al.*Le.* 2.16'

**ἐρέγμῐνος**, for '*made of bruised beans*' read 'made into ἔρεγμα'

**ἐρεγμός I**, add '**ἐριγμός**· ὁ λεγόμενος διεσχισμένος κύαμος Apollon.*Lex.* s.v. ἐρικόμενος'

**ἐρεείνω I 3**, delete the section transferring '*h.Merc.* 533' to line 3 after 'Il. 6.145'

*°**Ἐρεθειβιάζω**, = Ἐρεθειμιάζω, *Tit.Cam.* 87.7.

***ἐρεθρύδανον**, v. °ἐρυθρέδανον.

**ἐρείδω I 1**, line 20, for 'τι' read 'τινά' **III 2**, add 'transf. of words in a sentence, D.H.*Comp.* 22'

**ἐρεικτός**, add 'also ἐρεικτή, ἡ, Phot. s.v. πολφοί'

**ἐρείπω**, line 6, aor. 1 pass., add 'ἠρείφθην, epigr. in *IEryth.* 308 (i AD)'; line 14, after 'metaph.' insert 'ἄνεμός τέ μιν .. δείματι ἔρειπεν Simon. 38.5 P.' **II**, lines 5/6, delete 'metaph., .. 37.3'

**ἐρέκτης**, add '*PPrag.* I 25.12 (vi/vii AD)'

***ἐρεοπλῠτικος**, v. °ἐριο-.

*ἐρεουργός, ὁ, = ἐριουργός, *MAMA* 3.275, al. (Corycus): written -ωργός, ib. 435.

ἐρεοῦς, add 'app. fem. subst. *woollen garment*, παραθήκην ἔδωκί τινι ἐρεᾶν π[ρά]σινον Mitchell *N.Galatia* 242.10; form *ϝερϝέεος, Myc. *we-we-e-a* (neut. pl.)'

ἐρέπτομαι, line 3, after '(*AP*) 7.20' insert '([Simon.])'

ἐρέπτω **II**, delete the section.

ἐρεσιμήτρην, after lemma insert '(**ἐρεσιμετρίην** La.)'

*ἐρεσκῷος, ον, unexpld. wd., Hdn.*fr.* p. 19 H.

ἐρέσσω, line 2, delete '(earlier ἐλαύνω)' **I**, add 'ἔρεσσε *go on your way* (by land), Leon.ap.Stob. 4.52.28' **II 1**, add 'pass., in fig. phrase, of a woman in sexual intercourse, *AP* 5.54 (Diosc.)' add 'cf. Myc. inf. *e-re-e* fr. stem ἐρε-, *row*'

ἐρέτης, add 'Myc. *e-re-ta*'

ἐρετμόν **II**, add 'Pl.Com. 3.4 K.-A.'

ἐρετμός, add '**II** *oar*, Orph.*A.* 278.'

ἔρετο, add 'v. ὄρνυμι, line 23'

Ἐρέτρια, line 2, after 'etc.' insert 'Ἐρετριᾶθεν, adv., *from Eretria*, *IG* 12(9).272 (Eretria, v BC)'

Ἐρετριάς, after 'ἡ' insert '*the land of Eretria*, *SEG* 31.804 (Eretria, iv BC)'; penultimate line, before '*a kind of clay*' insert 'γῆ Ἐρετριάς'

Ἐρετρικός, add 'τὸ Ἐ., an unguent, *PPetr.* 2.34.8 (iii AD)'

ἐρευθέδανον, add 'see also °ἐρυτρέδανον'

ἔρευθος, add 'pl., Arat. 837'

*ἐρεύνησις, εως, ἡ, *investigation*, *EM* s.v. Ἐριούνιος.

*ἐρευνητικόν, v. °ἐραυν-.

ἐρεφύλλινον, delete the entry.

*ἐρεφύλλινος, ον, adj. referring to an unidentified plant, στέφανοι ἐ. *PAlex.* 22.5 (ii AD), ἄνθος ἐ. *PMag.* 13.25.

ἐρέχθω, add '(ἐριχθ-, as read by Apion in the Homeric passages)'

ἐρημαῖος, line 2, for '*silent*' read '*empty*'; add 'neut, sg. as adv., ἐρημαῖον βοόωντες Arat. 1003 (cj.), Q.S. 12.513'

*ἐρημεῖος, α, ον, = ἔρημος, χώρη *EAD* 469.3 (Myconus).

ἐρῆμος **II**, add '**4** of a vessel, *empty*, Lang *Ath.Agora* XXI Hb6 (ii AD).' add 'Myc. *e-re-mo* (subst. describing land)'

ἐρημοτελωνία, for pres. def. read '*farming of taxes for passage through the desert*'

ἐρημοφῠλᾰκία, for '*maintenance of this force*' read '*tax paid for protection of desert travellers*'

ἐρημόω **II**, add '**3** *clear out*, *get rid of*, ὕρακας Nic.*Al.* 37.'

*Ἑρησίειον, τό, *temple of the Egyptian god* Ἑρῆσις, Bernand *Les Portes* 1 (i BC).

ἐρητύω **3**, add 'also w. part. ὅς μιν θαρσύνεσκεν, ἐρητύων ἀχέουσαν A.R. 4.1054'

*ἐρθυρίς, v. ἐρῑθῡρίς.

*ἐρίβρυχμος, ον, = ἐρίβρυχος, Q.S. 3.171 (codd.); cf. βρυχμή, βρυχμός.

ἐρίβρῡχος, after 'Q.S. 3.171' insert '(cj.)'

\+ἔριγμα, v. ‡ἔρεγμα.

\+ἐρίγμη, ἡ, = ‡ἔρεγμα, Sch.Ar.*Ra.* 508.

*ἐριγμός, v. ‡ἐρεγμός.

ἐρίδιον, add 'prob. in Cerc. in *POxy.* 1082 *fr.* 32 (ἐρίδια τριβ[)'

*ἐρῐδισμός, ὁ, *strife*, *contention*, *Cat.Cod.Astr.* 8(3).196.3.

*ἐρίδρομος, ον, *fast-running*, Nonn.*D.* 23.28 (cod.).

ἐρίζω, line 8, delete 'Pass.' and '(in act. sense)'; line 16, after 'c. inf.' insert '*urge*, Plu.*Comp.Per.Fab.* 3; w. acc. & inf.' **I 2**, line 8, after 'Hdt. 5.49' insert 'w. gen. pers., οὐδὶς γὰρ ἐδύνατο τούτου ἐρίζειν epigr. in *WS* 53.152 (near Iconium, prob. iii AD)' **II 1**, line 3, for 'also in pf. pass.' read 'abs., Pi.*O.* 1.95' **2**, delete the section.

ἐρῑθᾰκος, after 'ἐρίθυλος' insert '°ἐρύθακος'

ἐρῑθεύομαι **II 1**, after 'Arist.*Pol.* 1303ᵃ16' insert 'μηδὲ ἠρειθεῦσθαι ἐπὶ κακοσχολίᾳ μηθέν *Delph.* 3(1).362 i 31'

ἐρῑθευτός, add 'εἵνεκεν τοῦ λαβεῖν ἐριθευτοὺς (τοὺς) δικαστάς *Delph.* 3(1).362 i 33'

ἐρίθεχνα, delete the entry.

ἔρῑθος, add '**III** epith. of Artemis, *IG* 2².5005 (Ἐρει-; Athens, ii AD).'

ἐρίκτῠπος, add 'of Zeus, Archil. 91.42 W.'

ἐρῑνεός, line 1, after 'ὁ' insert '(ἡ, Apollod.*Epit.* 6.3)'

*ἔρῑνος (B), η, ον, *woollen*, *Dura*⁴ 93 (iii AD); cf. ἐρεινοῦς.

Ἐρῑνύς, line 5, before 'E.*Med.*' insert 'A.*Th.* 700 (lyr.)'; after '(anap.)' insert 'Choerob. *in Theod.* 1.331' **II**, add 'Thebais *fr.* 2.8' add 'Myc. *e-ri-nu*'

\+ἐριοκάρτης, ου, ὁ, (κείρω) *shearer* or worker who shaved roughness from woollen cloth to provide a smooth finish, *PMich.*II 123ʳ iii 9, xvii 35 (i AD), *PFreib.* 60 (ii AD), *PFlor.* 71.438, al. (iv AD).

*ἐριοκαρτία, ας, ἡ, *wool shearings*, *BGU* 2295.5 (AD 157/8).

ἔριον, add 'pl., meton., of the part of the market where wools are sold, Teles p. 13 H.; ἔ. Σηρικόν perh. *raw silk*, *Peripl.M.Rubr.* 64'

ἐριόξῠλον, before 'cf. ἐρεόξ-' insert 'τὰ ἐ., *SB* 9026.11, 13 (ii AD)'

*ἐριόξῠλος, ον, *made of cotton*, τὸν χιτῶνα .. τὸν ἐ. *POxy.* 3991.14 (ii/iii AD).

*ἐριοπλῠτικός, όν, *of* or *for fulling*, κόπανον· ξύλον. ὄργανον ἐρεοπλυτικόν Hsch.

ἐριοπώλης, add '*IEphes.* 454 (ii/iii AD), *SEG* 30.1382 (Lydia, AD 301), *TAM* 4(1).174 (Rom.imp.)'

*ἐριοπωλικός, όν, *of wool-selling*, *POxy.* 3455 *fr.* (iii/iv AD).

*ἐριοραβδιστικός, όν, ἐργαστήριον ἐριοραβδιστικόν *fulling workshop*, *PBon.* 24a 8-9, b 16-17, c 11 (AD 135).

ἐριούνιος, line 2, after 'of uncertain meaning' insert 'perh. *speedy* (cf. οὔνει, οὔνιος, οὖνον) or *thieving* (cf. οὔνης, οὔνιος)'; add '*Trag.adesp.* 588 K.-S.'

ἐριουργός, add 'ἡ συνεργασία τῶν ἐριοργῶν *SEG* 29.1198 (Saittai, AD 223/4); see also °ἐρεουργός.'

ἐρίπνη, add 'ἐκ .. τῶν λόφων τῶν ὑπεράκρων, οὓς ἐρίπνας οἵ τε νομευτικοὶ φιλοῦσιν ὀνομάζειν καὶ ποιητῶν παῖδες Ael.*NA* 14.16'

\+ἐριπτοίητος, ον, *wildly excited*, Nonn.*D.* 17.198, 28.13.

*ἐρισκός or ἐρισκός, ὁ, perh. = ὑριχός (or possibly ῥίσκος), *PMich.*II 121ʳII.ii 8 (i AD), Suid. s.v. κώθωνες; v. °πλυτάριος.

*ἐρισφᾰλής, ές, *very unsteady*, ἴχνος Nonn.*D.* 47.63.

ἐρίτῑμος, line 3, after 'Ar.*Eq.* 1016' insert '(in mock oracle)'

ἐρίφειος, add 'δέρμα ἐρίφειον ἀνέργαστον *Edict.Diocl.* 8.17 (δέρμα ἐρίφιον ἄνεργον *SEG* 37.335 ii 11)'

*ἐρίφλοισβος, ον, *loud-roaring*, Nonn.*D.* 39.295.

ἔρῐφος **I**, line 1, for '(ἡ .. Crete))' read '(ἡ, *Inscr.Cret.* 4.260 (ii BC), *POxy.* 2887 i 3 (?i/ii AD))'; line 2, for 'Alc. l.c.' read 'Alc. 71.1 L.-P.' add '**2** *cinaedus pilosus*, *AP* 11.216.6 (Lucill.).'

ἑρκίτης, after 'Ath. 6.267c' insert '*An.Ox.* 2.45.7' and for 'written ἑρκῆται in Hsch.' read 'Hsch. cod. ἑρκῆται'

ἕρμα **II**, for 'Ael.*NA* 17.35' read 'Ael.*NA* 17.25' at end add 'Myc. *e-ma-ta* (pl.), *shoe-laces*'

ἑρμᾰγέλη, for '*Hermae*' read '*Hermeses*' and add '(humorously, for the offspring of a promiscuous woman)'

Ἑρμάδιον, for 'Keil-Premerstein .. 117' read '*IEphes.* 3334.11 (i AD)'

ἑρμάζω **I**, add 'pass., id.*Fract.* 26 (v.l. ἡρμόσθαι)'

Ἑρμαϊκός **I**, add '-όν, τό, name of a mine at Laurium, *IG* 2².1588.4, 5 (iii BC)'

ἕρμαιον **I 1**, add 'Men.*Dysc.* 226' **3**, for this section read '*tomb*, *MAMA* 4.178 (Apollonia), 4.250 (Tymandos)' **II**, add '**3** app. = Ἑρμῆς I 2, *herm*, Str. 17.1.50 (pl., s.v.l.).'

Ἑρμαιών, for 'at Halicarnassus' read 'in Caria'; after '*SIG* 45.4 (v BC)' insert '*SEG* 29.1089 (i BC)'

*Ἑρμᾶνιος, ὁ, name of a month at Scarpheia, *Delph.* 3(4).159.2.

ἑρμᾰτίζω **II 1**, after 'Plu. 2.967b' insert '*load up with ballast*, τοῖς τὴν ἅμαξαν ἑρματίσασιν καὶ ἀπαγαγοῦσιν *Inscr.Délos* 372*A*101 (200 BC)'

*ἑρμελαῦσον, v. °ἁρμαραύσιον.

ἑρμή, after 'Hsch.' insert '*Didyma* 486.26'

ἑρμηνεία, add '**II** *office of* ἑρμηνεύς in an Egyptian sanctuary, *SB* 9355.1, 2 (ii AD, -νια pap.).'

ἑρμηνεύς **I**, add 'transf., οὗτος (sc. ὁ ἐγκέφαλος) γὰρ ἡμῖν ἐστι τῶν ἀπὸ τοῦ ἠέρος γιγνομένων ἑ. Hp.*Morb.Sacr.* 16'

ἑρμηνεύω **I**, add 'transf., διό φημι τὸν ἐγκέφαλον εἶναι τὸν ἑρμηνεύοντα τὴν σύνεσιν Hp.*Morb.Sacr.* 17'

Ἑρμῆς, line 6, for 'later' read 'also' and before 'Call.' insert 'Hes.*Op.* 68, *h.Pan.* 28' **I 1**, add 'identified with the Emperor Tiberius, Τιβερίωι Καίσαρι Ἑρμεῖ *IEphes.* 3420' **3**, at end delete 'hence, .. 37.19' **II 1**, add '"Ἑ. ἡ τελευταία πόσις Poll. 6.100; Phot.' at end add 'form Ἑρμάhᾱς, Myc. *e-ma-a₂*'

ἑρμίν, before 'Herod.' insert 'Hippon. 79.8 W. (perh. w. pun on Ἑρμῆς; cf. *EM* 376.40)'

*Ἑρμογένειοι, οἱ, a Rhodian guild, Ἀφροδισιαστᾶν Ἑρμογενείων κοινόν *SEG* 3.674.34, al. (ii BC).

Ἑρμοκοπίδης, add 'Epicur. 104.8 A.'

*ἑρμόλυχνον, τό, *lighting of lamps before herms* in honour of the dead, cj. in *IG* 2².1368.151 (τό θ' ἑρμ. for τὸ θερμόλυχνον): see *JÖAI* 24.168.

ἔρνος **I 1**, add 'Alcm. 3.68 P.' **II 1**, line 3, delete '"Ηρακλέος .. 2.121'

*ἐρογλέφᾰρος, ον, *showing love in one's eyes*, Χάριτες Alcm. 1 i 21 P.

ἐρόεις, line 2, after '(lyr.)' insert 'μορφά Ibyc. 1(*a*).44 P.; πηκτίς Anacr. 28.2 P.'

*ϝεροῖα, τά, *tales*, καλὰ ϝεροῖ' ἀϊσομ[έναν Corinn. 2 *fr.* 1(b).2 P.; written Γεροῖα as title of her poems, prob. in Ant.Lib. 25 P.

ἔρος (A), line 4, after 'Thgn. 1064' insert 'εἰς ἔρον ἦλθε Sapph. 15(*b*).12 L.-P.'

*ἐρουθρός, v. °ἐρυθρός.

ἑρπετώδης, add '*Corp.Herm.* 10.7'

\+ἑρπηστήρ, v. °ἑρπυστήρ.

\+ἑρπηστής, v. °ἑρπυστής.

\+ἑρπυστήρ, ῆρος, ὁ, *creeping thing*, whether insect, small mammal, reptile or mollusc, Androm.ap.Gal. 14.37, Opp.*H.* 1.305, al., id.*C.*

3.110; as adj., ὄφεις ἑ. id.*C.* 3.411, Orph.*L.* 49. (Freq. ἑρπηστ- in codd., but wrongly.)

+**ἑρπυστής**, οῦ, ὁ, = °ἑρπυστήρ, Nic.*Th.* 9, Androm.ap.Gal. 14.38, Opp.*H.* 3.345; of a mouse, *AP* 9.86 (Antiphil.). **b** *guinea-worm*, *Hippiatr.* 58. **2** adj. *crawling*, of a baby, *AP* 9.302 (Antip.Thess.); *creeping*, of ivy, ib. 11.33 (Phil.). (Freq. ἑρπηστ- in codd., but wrongly.)

**ἕρπω 1**, for '*move slowly*' read '*move on the ground*'; of infants, add 'Arist.*HA* 501ᵃ3'; add 'of flocks, ib. 610ᵇ24, of snakes, ib. 696ᵃ9'; at end for 'an animal that *walks* on its teeth' read 'humorously, of the belly' **2**, line 4, after '(Cos)' insert 'ἕρπεν ἐπὶ τὰ[ν] προκειμέναν χρήιαν *SEG* 35.989.22 (Cnossus, ii/i BC)' and for 'cf. καθέρπω' read 'cf. καθέρπω II'

*__ἔρρηγμα__, ατος, τό, unexpld. wd. in *PCair.Zen.* 499.38 (iii BC).

*__ἔρροπος__, ον, quoted with °σύρροπος in unspecified sense by Sch.D.T. p. 465.5 H.

**ἔρρω** (A), line 17, after 'opt.' insert 'ἔρροι νὺξ αὕτα καὶ δαίμων E.*Tr.* 204'

**ἐρρωμένος**, lines 3/4, after 'Lys. 24.7' insert '*strong, muscular*, ἄνδρες Hp.*Fract.* 15'; after 'Pl.*Phdr.* 268a' insert 'exclamatory, ὦ βίας ἐρρωμένης Men.*Inc.* 23 S., ὦ πολυτίμητοι θεοί, ἐρρωμένου πράγματος ib. 57 S.'

**ἕρση**, line 5, after 'Hes.*Sc.* 395' insert 'ἕρσῃ δὲ θαλερὸς .. ἀμαρακός Chaerem. 14.16 S.'

**ἑρσήεις**, for 'metaph., of a corpse' read 'transf., *moist, wet*'; add 'ὄστρεά θ' ἑρσήεντα Opp.*H.* 1.317'

**ἔρσην**, comp., add 'ἐρσέντερος *BCH* 81.584 (Dodona)'

**ἐρῠθαίνω**, after '*blush scarlet*' insert '*AP* 9.322 (Leon.Tarent.)'

*__ἐρύθακος__, ὁ, prob. = ἐρίθακος, Hdn.*fr.* p. 20 H.

*__ἐρυθρέδᾰνον__, τό, = ἐρευθέδανον, *PCair.Zen.* 326 *bis* 24 (app. misspelt ἐρεθρύδ-, iii BC).

**ἐρυθρῖνος 2**, add '*SEG* 23.326.14 (Delphi, iii BC)'

*__ἐρυθρονεφής__, ές, *surrounded by red clouds*, ἥλιος *Cat.Cod.Astr.* 8(1).138.

**ἐρυθρός**, line 3, for 'but the metre .. Choerob. *in Theod.* 2.76' read '-ότερος Anaxandr. 23 K.-A., Dromo 1 K.-A., Choerob.*in Theod.* 2.76 H.' **I 1**, delete 'a ship painted with vermilion' and after 'Orac.ap.Hdt. 3.57' insert '(interpreted as a red-painted ship)' **2**, add 'ἐρυθρά, ἡ, *redness* (as a medical complaint), *Suppl.Mag.* 88' add '**4** ἐρυθρός, ὁ, kind of fish, *IGC* p. 99 B1 (ἐρουθρ-, Acraephia, iii/ii BC).' at end add 'Myc. *e-ru-ta-ra* (fem.)'

*__ἐρύθρω__, = ἐρυθαίνω, Sm.*Is.* 63.1 (pass.).

**ἐρῠθω**, after '= ἐρεύθω' insert 'part. -ουσα (-οισα) Call.*fr.* 80.10 Pf.'

**ἔρῠμα 2**, add 'E.*Ba.* 55'

*__ἔρυμος__· ὁ ῥυμός Theognost.*Can.* 64.

**ἐρῠσίπτολις**, add 'Call.*fr.* 626 Pf.'

+**ἐρῠσίχθων**, ονος, ὁ, ἡ, *grubbing up the earth*, v.l. in Strato Com. 1.19; cf. °ῥηξίχθων.

**ἐρύω** (A), line 5, delete '(in Hdt. .. εἵλκυσα)' **2**, add '**b** *draw up*, ἐρύσσαι ὀφρύας *AP* 5.216.3 (Agath.).' **B I 3 a**, add 'αὐτμάν *sniff, inhale*, *AP* 6.219.10 (Antip.Sid.)'

**ἐρύω** (B), line 12, after 'A.R. 2.1208' insert 'part. ῥυμένη hymn in *SEG* 8.548.27 (Egypt, i BC)'; line 13, after '(Il.) 20.195' insert 'Aeol. pres. or fut. inf. ῤύεσθαι Alc. 129.20 L.-P.' **5**, line 13, after 'c. gen.' insert 'ἀνθρώποι[ς] θα[ν]άτω ῤύεσθε Alc. 34.7 L.-P.' at end add 'Myc. athematic 3 pl. (*o*)-*u-ru-to*, *Ϝρυντοι'

**ἔρχομαι**, lines 7/8, after 'Lys. 22.11' insert '*fr.* 47'; lines 14/15, delete 'imper. ἐνθέ Aristonous 1.9'; line 16, after 'iv BC)' insert 'ἐυθών (ἐπ-) *Inscr.Cret.* 4.168*.17 (III BC), cf. ib. 1.xxiv 2.5, ἦνθον (πορτ-) *Schwyzer* 186.11 (Gortyn, ii BC)'; line 20, after '*AP* 14.44' insert 'ἐρτ(ε)ῖν = ἐρθεῖν, *POxy.* 1069.31, *PMich.*VIII 516.10 (both iii AD)'; line 24, after '(Cyrene)' insert '1 sg. plpf. ἠληλούθειν Call.*fr.* 265 Pf.' **IV**, add 'w. inf. ἤλυθεν .. μαθεῖν Neophr. 1.1 S.'

**ἐρῶ**, line 2, delete 'Nic.*Th.* 484' and for 'Ath. 9.400a' read 'Ath. 9.400b'

**ἐρωή**, before 'ἡ' insert '(Aeol. **ἐρωΐα** Theoc. 30.6)' **II**, before '*escape*' insert '*respite*, Theoc. 30.6'

*__ἐρωμενᾰγοράστης__, ου, ὁ, gloss on *amicarius, procurer*, Diom. p. 326 K.

**ἐρωμένιον**, add 'Lucr. 4.1166'

*__ἐρωμενοπάροχος__, as °ἐρωμεναγοράστης.

*__ἐρωμενοπώλης__, as °ἐρωμεναγοράστης.

**ἔρως**, add '**V** οἱ Ἔρωτες, members of a religious association, *JÖAI* 14 *Beibl.* 46 (Lydia, ii AD).'

**ἐρωτάω III**, after '*entreat*' insert '(use disapproved of in Hermog.*Meth.* 3)'

*__Ἐρωτίδιον__, τό, = Ἐρωτάριον, *IG* 11(2).287*B*7 (Delos, iii BC, pl.).

**ἐρωτικός II**, add '**b** -ός, ὁ, *lover*, *AP* 5.216.7 (Agath.).'

**ἐρωτίς II**, add 'Nonn.*D.* 32.28'

**ἐς II**, = ἐκ, add 'also Thess.*GDI* 1329.1a.15, Boeot. *BCH* suppl. 6(1980).211-212 (v BC), *SEG* 30.567 (iv BC); ἐσς *GDI* 713b.8, etc.'

*__ἔσαν__, v. °ἵζω.

*__ἐσζικαιωτήρ__, v. ἐκδικ-.

**ἐσθίω**, line 2, after 'Hes.*Op.* 147' insert 'εἴσθιον Antiph. 166 K.-A., Timocl. 35 K.-A.'

**ἐσθλός**, line 2, at end insert '[ἐσλ- scanned short Pi.*O.* 13.100, al.]'

**ἔσθος**, add '*h.Hom.* 31.13'

*__ἐσίταμον__· δηλοῖ δὲ τὴν πρόσοδον Theognost.*Can.* 16 A.; prob. = ‡ἐσσίταλα.

+**ἔσκε**, = εἰς ὅ κε (i.e. ἔστ' ἄν), *until*, ἔσκε μάχηται Archil. 15 W.

*__ἐσκλητόρ__· ὁ δοκιμαζόμενος Hsch. (La.).

*__ἐσμεύω__, (ἑσμός) *swarm*, rest. in Call.*fr.* 191.28 Pf. (pap. [..] μεύουσιν).

*__ἐσοχάδες__, αἱ, *internal piles*, Ps.-Gal. 14.495 (lemma, ἐσωχ-), Cyran. 2.30.13, 4.28.26 K.

*__ἐσπασμένως__, adv., *with convulsions*, Gal. 7.810.17.

**Ἑσπερία**, for '*Western* .. 1.49' read '*West*, *Epigr.Gr.* 823.3'

**Ἑσπερινός**, line 3, for ''Εσπέρινος' read ''Εσπερινός'

**ἑσπέριος**, line 2, after 'E.*HF* 395 (lyr.)' insert '*Peripl.M.Rubr.* 18' **I**, line 6, after 'Pi.*P.* 3.19' insert ''Ερίφοι *setting in the evening*, Theoc. 7.53' **II**, line 2, delete 'ἐρίφοι Theoc. 7.53'

**ἑσπερίτης**, for 'D.L.' read 'D.S.'

**ἔσπομαι**, for 'ἕπομαι q.v.' read 'ἕπομαι (v. ἕπω)'

**ἑσπόμην**, add '(v. ἕπω)'

*__ἐσπράττας__, ὁ, v. °ἐκπράκτης.

**ἐσσήν** (A), lines 3 and 5, for 'Call.*Aet.* 1.1.23' read 'Call.*fr.* 178.23 Pf.'

**ἐσσηνεύω**, for pres. ref. read '*IEphes.* 969.1, 1578b.7, al '

**ἐσσηνία**, for pres. ref. read '*IEphes.* 956.2, 957.13, al.'

*__ἔσσηρος__· ὁ μάντις Theognost.*Can.* 16 A.; cf. ἐσσήτιοι.

**ἐσσήτιοι**, add 'cf. °ἔσσηρος'

**ἐσσίτᾱλα**, for '(cf. ἐξίταλα' read '(cf. ἐξίτηλος)'

*__ἐσσόριον__, v. ‡ἐνσόριον.

**ἔσσων**, delete the entry.

**ἔστασαν**, for '(but the v.l. ἵστασαν is to be preferred)' read '(v.ll. for ἵστασαν)' and add 'E.*Heracl.* 937 (cod., edd. ἵστασαν)'

*__ἔστᾰσις__, ιος, ἡ, *placing*, θυρᾶν *IAskl.Epid.* 52A.14, 49.

**ἔστε**, lines 5/6, delete 'ἔσκε .. f.l.' (v. °ἔσκε). **III**, add '**2** w. gen., of time, ἔ. τᾶς τριακάδος *Clara Rhodos* 2.171.'

*__ἐστεκνοόμαι__, v. ‡ἐκτεκνόω.

**ἑστία I 2**, add 'Modest.*Dig.* 27.1.12.1, *PLips.* 41.10, *PGrenf.* 78.10' **II**, line 2, add ''**Ιστία** *SEG* 30.1117 (Entella, Sicily, iii BC)'

*'__Ἑστιαικός__, ή, όν, v. °'Ιστιαϊκός.

*__ἑστιασμός__, ὁ, = ἑστίασις, *TAM* 2.201 (Sidyma, pl.).

**ἑστιᾱτικός II**, for '*fund* .. Delos' read '*a fund* for temple-expenses *deposited in the sanctuary of Hestia*'; add '*Inscr.Délos* 365.5'

**ἑστιᾱτορία 2**, before 'ii AD' insert 'ἱστια-'; add 'also εἰστια- *PTeb.* 598, ἱστα- *PMich.*II 123ʳ xvii 25'

**ἑστιᾱτόριον**, before '*IG* 11(2)' insert '*SEG* 11.244 (Sicyon, vi/v BC)'

**ἑστιοῦχος I 3**, for 'ψόλος .. (prob.)' read 'σέλας A.*fr.* 204b.4 R. (lyr.), cf. *fr.* 492b.2' add '**II** functionary in the cult of Hestia, *IEphes.* 1060.12, 1070.3, al. (iii AD); cf. °ὑπεστιοῦχος.'

**ἔστωρ**, after lemma insert '(A)'; for '*peg* .. reins through' read '*peg* near the end of the chariot-pole, over which was passed a ring (κρίκος), prob. for holding the yoke in place'

*__ἔστωρ__ (B), ορος, ὁ, *founder*, *IUrb.Rom.* 1155.88.

*__ἐσχάδις__, adv., unexpld. wd. in Theognost.*Can.* 163.

**ἐσχάρα**, line 2 to end, read '**I** *place for a fire*, Τρώων πυρὸς ἐσχάραι Il. 10.418; esp. in domestic use, πῦρ μὲν ἐπ' ἐσχαρόφιν μέγα καίετο Od. 5.59, ἡ δ' ἧσται ἐπ' ἐσχάρῃ ἐν πυρὸς αὐγῇ 6.305, 7.153, 20.123, E.*Cyc.* 382, Plu.*Marc.* 17.11. **2** transf., *hollow scab formed over wound caused by cautery*, etc., Hp.*Morb.* 2, Arist.*Prob.* 863ᵃ12, Pl.Com. 200.4 K.-A., Diosc. 1.56, Gal. 10.315.3. **b** *hollowed out wood* in which fire-drill is rotated, Thphr.*HP* 5.9.7, *Ign.* 64. **c** *external female genitals*, Ar.*Eq.* 1286. **II** *container for fire, brazier, fire-basket*, etc., used for domestic heating, Plu. 2.180e; for cooking, Ar.*Ach.* 888, *V.* 938, *PCair.Zen.* 692 (iii BC); in religious ritual, πρὸς ἐσχάρην Φοίβου A.*Pers.* 205, νυκτίσεμνα δεῖπν' ἐπ' ἐσχάρῃ πυρὸς ἔθυον id.*Eum.* 108, S.*Ant.* 1016, E.*Andr.* 1240, *Ph.* 274; carried in procession, X.*Cyr.* 8.3.12, Callix. 2; not clearly distinguished from sense "*altar*", D. 59.116, *Inscr.Délos* 104.142, al. **2** transf., *grid* or *lattice-work* forming the base of var. structures: καὶ ποιήσεις αὐτῷ (sc. θυμιαστηρίῳ) ἐσχάραν ἔργῳ δικτυωτῷ χαλκῆν Lxx *Ex.* 27.4; as the base of a ballista or sim., Vitr. 10.11.9, Ph.*Bel.* 92.13.' add 'Myc. *e-ka-ra*, *brazier*'

**ἐσχᾰρίς**, after '*brazier*' insert 'Ar.*fr.* 946 K.-A.' add '**2** app. *platform* on a trolley used for transporting marble, ἐσχαρὶς ἐπὶ τὸν λίθον παγεῖσα *IG* 2².1673.63.'

**ἐσχᾰρίτης**, for '*over the fire*, Antidot. 3' read '*in the ashes*, Hp.*Vict.* 2.42, Antid. 3 K.-A.'

*__ἐσχάρωθεν__, unexpld. wd. in Theognost.*Can.* 156.

*__ἐσχάρως__, unexpld. wd. in Theognost.*Can.* 156.

**ἔσχᾰτος**, line 1, after 'Arat. 625' insert '628'

***ἐσχημένως**, *at once, immediately*, *PMag.* 4.1876.

**ἐσώτατος**, add 'ἐν .. τοῖς ἐσωτάτοις τόποις *Peripl.M.Rubr.* 42'

**+ἐσωτικός**, v. °ἐξωτικός.

**ἐτάζω 1**, line 5, after '(prob. l.)' insert 'ἔτασον ἐκεῖσε *Cat.Cod.Astr.* 8(1).190'; at end for '*reveal, unmask*' read '*prove by test*' and after 'τινα' insert 'cj. in'   **2**, after '*Ge.* 12.17' insert 'pass., ἐν ἀσθενείαις ἢ κινδύνοις *Cat.Cod.Astr.* 8(1).256'

**ἑταιρεύομαι**, add 'act. pres. part., Hsch. s.v. σκαφίον, pf. part. ἡται[ρ]ευκώς *SEG* 27.261 (Maced., ii BC)'

**ἑταιρέω I**, for '*keep company with*' read '*act as a courtesan* (or the male equivalent)' and add 'Ar.*Pax* 11'

**ἑταιρίζω**, after lemma insert 'ἑτᾰρ- Il. 13.456, Call.*Dian.* 206'

**ἑταιρικός I 3**, add 'cf. *equitum alae quae Hetaerice appellabatur* Nepos *Eum.* 1.6'

**ἑταιρίστρια**, for '= τριβάς' read '*lesbian*'

**ἑταιροποιέομαι**, add 'also act., as expl. of Lat. *sociare* (Verg.*A.* 1.600), pap. in *Aevum* 1(1927).65'

***ἑταρίζω**, v. ἑταιρίζω.

**ἐτασμός**, add '*PSorb.* I.9 (iii AD)'

**ἐτέα**, for 'Theognost.*Can.* 7' read 'Theognost.*Can.* 17 A.'

**Ἐτεόκρητες**, add 'Str. 10.4.6, D.S. 5.64.1'

***ἐτέολβος**, ον, perh. *having honourable wealth*, epigr. in *JRS* 57.43 no. 8 (Lycia).

**ἐτεός**, add 'form ἐτεϝός, cf. Myc. *e-te-wo-ke-re-we-i-jo*, patronymic of Ἐτεϝοκλέϝης (Ἐτεοκλῆς)'

***ἑτεροβᾱ́μων**, ον, gen. ονος, perh. *one-legged* or *limping*, κόρη orac. in *DAW* 42(2).3 (iv AD).

**ἑτερόγλαυκος**, add '*PPetr.* 2 p. 115 (iii BC); of the eyes, Ps.-Callisth. 1.13 codd. B,C'

***ἑτερογνωμονέω**, *to be of a different way of thinking*, τῇ ἐκείνου ἐννοίᾳ *PRyl.* 463.9 (iii AD; fragment of a Gnostic gospel).

**ἑτεροειδής**, line 2, after 'Arist.*HA* 508ᵇ11' insert 'v.l. for ἐντερο-)'

**ἑτεροκρᾱνικός**, add 'adv. -κῶς, Paul.Aeg. 7.4.4 (276.11 H.)'

**ἑτερομήκης 2**, add '**b** of ὁ ἄρτιος ἀριθμός, *made up of one species of length only*, being the sum of two even or of two odd numbers, Iamb. *in Nic.* p. 12 l. 17 P.; cf. ἀμφιμήκης.'

***ἑτερόμμᾰτος**, ον, app. = ἑτερόφθαλμος (in one or other sense), in quot., of horses, Afric.*Cest.* p. 24 V.

**ἑτεροπλᾰτής**, add '*Poliorc.* 263.6'

***ἑτερόριστος**, ον, *defining other things*, opp. °αὐθόριστος, David *Proll.* 14.23.

**ἕτερος**, lines 1/2, for 'Dor. .. v. infr.)' read 'non.-Att.-Ion. ἅτερα *IG* 4².40.11 (Epid., iv BC), etc.; Myc. *a₂-te-ro*'   **I 1**, add 'ἅτεροι πότεροι, v. ‡πότερος III'   **II a**, add '(acc. to Sch.Aeschin. 2.116 the use of ἕτερος for ἄλλος is Attic)'   **III**, line 6, after '*Ep.Gal.* 1.6' insert 'ἑτέραν καὶ ἑτέραν ὁδόν two *different* ways, D.Chr. 42.3'   **2**, add 'οὕτερος δαίμων Call.*fr.* 191.63 Pf., εὔχεται μὲν ὁ νοῦν ἔχων τὰ βελτίονα, προσδοκᾷ δὲ καὶ θάτερα Plu. 2.474c'   **IV 1 b, c**, for 'θατέρᾳ' read 'θητέρᾳ'   **V 1**, τοῦ σκέλους .. Philostr.*VA* 3.39, delete '= ἑτεροσκελὴς εἶναι' and transfer ex. to section 3.

***ἑτεροσεβέω**, *depart from established forms of worship*, Vett.Val. 4.15.1 (p. 174 P.).

**ἑτερόσκῐος**, read '*throwing shadows only one way* (only north or only south), of those who live between the polar circles and the tropics (cf. ἀμφίσκιος I, περίσκιος)'

***ἑτεροσύστᾰτος**, ον, *subsisting by means of something else, dependent*, of the subjunctive mood, opp. αὐτοσύστατος, Choerob. *in Theod.* 2.411.22 H.

**ἑτερότης**, opp. ταυτότης, add 'Plot. 5.3.10, 6.2.15'

***ἑτεροϋπόστᾰτος**, ον, *subsistent in something else* (cf. ὑπόστατος II), Elias *in Cat.* 162.2.

**ἑτερόφθαλμος I**, for 'metaph., of the proposed destruction of Athens' read 'fig., of Greece, envisaged as deprived of one of its chief cities'

**ἑτέρσετο**, for 'τερσαίνω' read 'τέρσομαι'

**ἑτέρωθι III**, add '(s.v.l., v. °ἑτέρωτε)'

**ἑτερώνιος**, for '*another's property*' read '*foreign, introduced from outside*, Theognost.*Can.* 17 A.'

***ἑτέρωτε**, *at another time*, A.D.*Adv.* 1.193.14, 194.4, cj. in Hdt. 3.35.5 (Aeol. ἑτέρωτα acc. to A.D. ib., cf. °ἀτέρωτα).

***ἐτησιακός**, ή, όν, *etesian*, kind of vine at Arretium, Plin.*HN* 14.36.

**ἐτησιάς**, for 'poet. fem. of sq.' read 'fem. adj., *etesian*'

**ἐτήσιος**, line 1, for 'and in Hp. η, ον' read 'also Ion. η, ον'   **2**, after 'Arr.*Ind.* 2.21' insert 'predicatively σὺ μέν, φίλη χελιδών, ἐτησίη μολοῦσα Anacr. 25.2 W.'; after 'adv. -ίως' insert '*PBerl.Leihg.* 23.9 (iii AD)'

***ἐτητῠμέω**, *to be true*, ἐ]τητυμέοντα[ς] .. ὀνε[ίρους *Suppl.Hell.* 922.1 (iii BC).

**ἐτητῠμία**, for 'Call.*Aet.* 3.1.76' read 'Call.*fr.* 75.76 Pf.'

**ἐτήτῠμος II**, line 2, for 'Archil. 62' read '*h.Ap.* 64, Archil. 110 W., A.R. 1.142, al.'

***Ἐτηφίλα**, ᾱ, title of Persephone in Mytilene, *IG* 12(2).222.3, 263.4, cf. Ἐταιφίλη· Περσεφόνη Hsch.; in pl. = Demeter and Persephone, *IG* 12(2).255.3.

***Ἐτηφίλιος**, epith. of Hadrian as devotee of Persephone, *Hesperia* 32.78/9 no. 164 (Mytilene, ii AD), v. °Ἐτηφίλα; dub. reading and accent, Ἐτηφιλια *IG* 12(2).239.9 (Mytilene), cf. ib. suppl. p. 10.9.

**ἔτι I 2**, after 'Pl.*Prt.* 310c' insert 'X.*HG* 2.4.11'

**ἑτοιμόδακρυς**, add 'Sch.E.*Med.* 903'

***ἑτοιμολογία**, ἡ, *talkativeness*, *Vit.Aesop.*(G) 88a, Hsch. s.v. προφορά.

**ἕτοιμος III**, adv. -οτέρως, add 'Gal. 2.312.13, 11.622.14'

**ἔτος 1**, add 'πολλὰ τὰ ἔτη (expression of wish for a long life), *IEphes.* 1192(3)'   at end, ϝέτος, for '*Inscr.Cypr.* 135.1 H.' read 'Cypr. *we-te-i* (dat.) *ICS* 217.1, al., Myc. *we-te-i-we-te-i* (redupl. dat.), *annually*' and add 'ϝετέων *SEG* 30.380 (Tiryns, vii BC), ϝετ[ι]ια *IPamph.* 3.5 (Pamphylia, iv BC); ἔτος is found in inscriptions, papyri and codd., e.g. *IG* 9²(1).2.11, 31, 32 (Thermus, iii BC, written *HΕΤΕΩΝ*), πένθ' ἑτέων *GVI* 1576.7 (Capri, i/ii AD), καθ' ἔτος *BGU* 538.31 (AD 100); cf. °δεχέτης, ἐφέτειος, etc.)'

**ἐτός** (B), for 'ἐτά .. anon. 283' read 'ὡς ἐτά *how truly*, (?)Call.*fr.* 780 Pf.; adv. ἐτῶς id.*fr.* 75.39 Pf. and perh. *fr.* 203.16 Pf.'

**ἔττακαν**, after lemma insert '(**ἔττασαν** cj.)'

***ἐττία**· ἑστία Hsch.

***ἐτῠμόγλωσσος**, ον, *true of tongue*, *Suppl.Hell.* 991.71 (poet. word-list, iii BC).

***ἐτῠμόμαντις**, εως, ὁ, *prophet of truth*, *Suppl.Hell.* 991.69 (poet. word-list, iii BC).

***ἐτῠμόφανος**, ον, unexpld. wd., *Suppl.Hell.* 991.72 (poet. word-list, iii BC) (perh. -φαμος = -φημος; cf. ψευδόφημος).

***ἐτῠμοφάς**, dub. reading and accent, *Suppl.Hell.* 991.73 (poet. word-list, iii BC).

**εὖ I 1**, at end after 'D. 5.2, etc.' add 'εὖ .. ὁ ἀποφηνάμενος .. εἴπας .. Longin. 1.2, cf. Cerc. 5.12.   **b** εὖ δίδωμι, of gods, etc., bestow *good*, S.*OT* 1081, E.*Alc.* 1004; w. dat., S.*OC* 642.'   **III**, add 'in pl., πολλῶν γὰρ τῶν εὖ δύναται τυχεῖν Arist.*Cael.* 292ᵇ3'   at end add '*e(h)u-* in Myc. compd. pers. names, as *e-u-me-de* (= Εὐμήδης)'

**εὐαγγελίζομαι**, line 8, after 'J.*AJ* 18.6.10' and after 'Alciphr. 3.12' insert '(codd.)'; after 'Hld. 2.10' insert '(v.l. σοι)'

**εὐαγγέλιον I**, line 6, after 'Aeschin. 3.160' insert '*Laodicée* p. 265.12 (see also p. 273)'   **II 1**, add '**b** esp. *announcement of an emperor's accession*, J.*BJ* 4.10.6 (pl.), cf. *PBerol.* in *POxy.* 7 p. 150 (sg.).'

**Εὐαγγέλιος I**, add 'fem., epith. of goddess Μήτηρ, *IMiletoupolis* 17 (sp. -εία, ii/i BC)'   **II**, after 'month' insert 'beginning in late Apr.' and add 'p. 72 (p. 8 K.)'

***Εὐαγγελίς**, ίδος, ἡ, (prob.) title of priestess of Hera, *MDAI(A)* 68.47.22 (= *GDI* 5702, Samos, iv BC).

***εὐάγγελμα**, ατος, τό, = εὐαγγέλιον, ἐπὶ τοῖς τῶν ἡμετέρων ἀγαθῶν [εὐ]αγγέλμασι *MDAI(A)* 48.100 (Nicopolis ad Istrum, late ii AD).

**εὐάγγελος**, at end, title of Hermes, add '*IG* 12(5).235 (Paros, i AD).   **II** -ος, ὁ, *gospeller*, *POxy.* 3958.13, 36, 42 (AD 612).'

**εὐᾱγής** (A) **3**, line 3, delete 'ὕμνοι *AP* 7.34 (Antip.Sid.)'

***εὐᾰγία**, ἡ, *holy offering*, εὐαγίας δ' ἐπὶ τοῦδε (sc. τοῦ βωμοῦ) τελείετε μηνὸς ἑκάστου orac. in Ramsay *Studies in Eastern Rom.Prov.* p. 128.

**εὐαγκής**, for '*with sweet glades*' read '*having lovely glens*'

***εὐάγκρῐτος**, ον, = εὐανάκριτος *easy to judge*, of an indisputable victor, *IG* 7.2470 (Thebes, iv/iii BC).

**εὐαγρέω**, for 'Ath. 7.297f' read 'Ath. 7.297e' and add '*AP* 9.337 (Leon.Tarent.)'

**εὐάγωγος II**, add 'of parts of the body, *easily controlled*, Philostr.*Gym.* 35'   **III**, add '(cj. for εὐαγῶς; εὐλαβῶς Lambinus e cod.Tornes.)'

**εὐᾰ́ερος**, add 'εὐϝάϝερος app. in Lacon. pers. nn. Εὐβάβερος *IG* 5(1).154, cf. Εὐβαβερίσκος *SEG* 11.552.6, 528 (all ii AD)'

**εὐᾱής I**, add 'Ezek.*Exag.* 244 S.'

**εὔαθλος I**, add 'εὔϝαθλος, on a terracotta ball, *SEG* 39.940 (Eretria, vii BC)'

**εὐαί**, after 'εὐοῖ' insert '*SEG* 32.779 (Berezan, graffito, vi BC)'

***εὐακία**, ἡ, *easy healing*, *PAnt.* 66.iʳ.7.

**εὐάμπελος**, after 'Str. 3.3.1, al.' insert 'ὕλη Nonn.*D.* 12.300, Φρυγίη ib. 34.214'; add 'Οἰνεύς Nonn.*D.* 43.54'

**εὐανακόμιστος**, for 'of health' read 'to health'

***εὐανδρησία**, ἡ, *manliness*, *Trag.adesp.* 193 K.-S. (s.v.l.).

**εὐανθής**, after 'ές' insert '(fem. εία, Orph.*H.* 10.11)'   **II 1**, add 'εὐ. ῥόδα Chaerem. 13 S.'

***εὔανθος**, ὁ, name of a stone, Cyran. 16 (1.5.2 K.) (but τὸν εὐάνθη λίθον ib. 17 (1.5.27 K.)).

**εὐάνιος**, add 'as pers. n., *IG* 12(3).783, *SEG* 26.476 (vi BC), ib. 11.244 (c.500 BC)'

**εὐάντητος I**, add 'Orph.*H.* 2.5, 3.13, etc., Nonn.*D.* 27.178, 35.316, 39.207'

**εὐαρχία**, after '*government*' insert '*IEphes.* 44.8 (c.AD 440)'

**εὔαρχος I 1**, delete the section.   **II**, after '*beginning well*' insert 'μύλος Lyc. 233'

***εὐάσκητος**, ον, *well-crafted*, [εὐ]άσκητον μνῆ[μα] rest. in *MAMA* 1.171 (Laodicea Combusta).

**εὐαστήρ**, for '*Arch.Pap.* 7.4' read 'Dionys.Bassar.*fr.* 19.17 L.' and add '*AP* 6.154 (Leon.Tarent. or Gaet.)'

**εὐβαφής I**, add 'of mosaic, εὐβαφεέσσι λίθοισιν *Gerasa* p. 484, no. 327 (vi AD)'

***εὐβίαστος**, ον, *easily constrained*, Simp. *in Cael.* 267.23.

***εὐβοή**, ἡ, name for the nightingale, Cyran. 16 (1.5.1, 4 K.).

**εὐβολέω**, add '**2** *to be lucky* (in hunting), Call.*Dieg.* ix.4 (*fr.* 200b Pf.).'

***εὐβότανος**, ον, *having plentiful grass*, Hsch. s.v. ποιήεντι.

**εὐβουλεύς**, add '*GVI* 2030 (Syros, ii/iii AD)'

**εὐβριθής**, for '*laden with fine* yarn' read '*well-weighted*'

**εὔβωλος**, delete the entry.

***εὔβους**, ὁ, ἡ, acc. εὔβων (v.l. εὔβουν), *rich in cattle*, *h.Ap.* 54.

***εὔγαμος**, ον, *having a happy* or *successful marriage*, *AP* 9.59 (Antip. Thess.), Heph.Astr. 1.1, Nonn.*D.* 1.27; transf., εὐνή ib. 13.352, ὕδωρ (sc. of the river Adonis) 20.144.

**εὐγένεια**, add '**6** *free-born status*, *Cod.Just.* 6.4.4.3, Just.*Nov.* 89.9 pr.; also *legitimate birth*, ib. 74.2 pr.'

**εὐγένειος**, add '**b** *having a sturdy jaw*, δελφὶς δ' ἠυγένειος Opp.*H.* 2.565.'

**εὐγενής I 1**, add 'ἄνδρα εὐ. prob. = Lat. *patricium*, *Inscr.Perg.* 8(3).21.21 (ii AD). **b** *freeborn*, Modest.*Dig.* 27.1.1.4, Just.*Nov.* 22.11; also, *of legitimate birth*, ib. 89.15.1. **c** sup. in honorific address, masc. *POxy.* 1664.15 (iii AD), *PLond.* 1023.1 (v/vi AD), 1319.4 (AD 544/5); fem., *ITyr* 37.'

**εὐγενία**, after '*AP* 7.337.6' insert '*Didyma* 496*B*10 (oracle, ii AD); εὐγενίῃ epigr. in *SEG* 32.1608 (Cyrene, iii AD)'

***εὐγηρασία**, ἡ, = εὐγηρία, *PMag.* 13.783.

+**εὐγλαγής**, ές, also **εὔγλαγος**, ον, Lyc. 307, metaplast. dat. εὔγλαγι *AP* 9.744 (Leon.Tarent.); *abounding in milk*, Q.S. 13.260, v.l. for περιγλ- in Il. 16.642 ap.Ath. 11.495c; epith. of Hermes, *AP* l.c.; *milky*, *fresh*, θάλος Lyc. l.c.; *with milky juice*, Nic.*Th.* 627.

***εὔγλυφος**, ον, *easily engraved*, of a gem, Xenocr.*Lap.* 90.

**εὐγνωμονέω II**, for '*reward*' read '*pay what is owing to*' and add '*PSI* 303.14, *PMasp.* 243 (Byz.), *POxy.* 3584.7 (v AD)'

**εὐγνωμοσύνη**, add '**3** *repayment*, *SB* 9770.6 (vi AD).'

***εὔγνωτος**, ον, = εὔγνωστος (in quot., sense 1), epigr. in *SEG* 31.335 (Laconia, ii/iii AD, s.v.l.).

***εὔγραφος**, ον, = εὐγραφής I, στήλη *AEM* 19.99 (Moesia Inferior).

**εὔγυρος**, for '*tortuous* (= γυρός, q.v.)' read '*well-curved*, (in quot., w. ref. to wrestler's stance)'

**εὐδαιμονισμός**, add '**b** perh. *funeral celebration*, *PHib.* 202.2 (iii BC).'

**εὐδαιμοσύνη**, add '**b** app. personified (cf. εὐδαιμονία 2 b), ἡμέρα Εὐδαιμοσύνης *IGRom.* 4.661.5 (Acmonia, i AD).'

**Εὐδαίμων 3** add 'in epitaphs, *SEG* 25.1143 (Cyprus, ii/iii AD), v. *BE* 1967.659'

**εὐδάμνας**, add '(**εὐδάμας** La.)'

**εὐδείελος I**, add 'in prose, ἐπὶ τὰν κολουάδα τὰν εὐδείελον decr. in *BCH* 116.200.9 (Phocis, iii BC), cf. Str. 9.2.41'

***εὔδειλος**, ον, = εὐδείελος, τέμενος Alc. 129.2 L.-P.

**εὔδενδρος**, add 'in lyr. also ἠΰδενδρος, B.17.80 S.-M. (εὐδ. pap.)'

**εὐδερκής**, add '**2** app. *easily seen*, A.*fr.* 281a.30 R.'

***Εὐδήμεια**, τά, festival at Delos, *Inscr.Délos* 371*B* 51 (iii BC).

***εὐδιάδοχος**, ον, gloss on εὔκηλος, Sch.Gen.Il. 17.371.

**εὐδιάκριτος**, add '**3** perh. *having its parts well separated*, i.e. open, ὄμμα Simp.*in Cael.* 75.1.'

***εὐδιάλεκτος**, ον, *easy to talk to*, *PMag.* 8.28.

**εὐδιάφθορος I**, add '**2** of food, *easily broken down*, Xenocr.ap.Orib. 2.58.145, opp. δυσφθαρτότερα, Dsc. 1.105.' **II**, delete '*easily going bad* .. 105'

**εὐδιάω**, for 'of persons' read 'of living creatures' and add 'εὐδιόωντι .. ὄρνιθι Arat. 278, δελφῖνες .. εὐδιόωντες A.R. 4.933'

**εὐδίδακτος**, for '*docile*' read '*receptive to teaching*' and add '*CIJud.* 1.190 (Rome)'

**εὔδιος I**, delete 'εὐδίja *O Berl.Sitzb.* 1911.639, cf.'; after 'neut. .. as adv.' insert 'τὸν εὔδι' ἰαύονθ' *E. HF* 1049 (cj.)' at end for '(For εὐδιϝος' to end of article read '[ῐ in verse, except Orph. l.c., Arat. l.c.; cf. ἔνδῖος]'

***εὐδιφής**, ές, *carefully exploring*, χείρ prob. in Androm. in *GDRK* 62.102.

+**εὐδοκιμάζω**, *consider good*, Origenes.*Adnot.in Gen.* 7.4 (*PG* 17.13a).

**εὐδοκίμησις**, add '*SEG* 31.903.8 (Aphrodisias); in an honorific address, καταξειώσῃ ἡ σὴ εὐδοκίμ(ησις) *PNess.* 24.4, *PBerol.*inv. 25022 (*Aegyptus* 70.43, both vi AD)'

**εὐδόκιμος**, add 'sup. as honorific epith., Mitchell *N.Galatia* 186, *POxy.* 1898.38, *PLond.* 1708.167, *PMasp.* 94.5, etc. (all *c.*vi AD)'

***Εὐδοσία**, ἡ, *Benefaction*, name of a ἡρωΐνη, Πολέμων 1.246 (iv BC).

**εὐδράνεια**, for '*bodily strength and health*' read '*vigour*' and add '*GGA* 1897.407 (Phrygia, ii/iii AD; εὐδρανίην)'

**εὔδρομος**, add '**III** (δρόμος II 3) of a city, *having fine public walks*, *App.Anth.* 3.281.4 (εὐ̆-)).'

**εὐδυκήμερος**, delete the entry.

***εὐδώμητος**, ον, *well-built*, ἄγυια epigr. in *IParion* 52.9 (ii AD).

***εὐδωσιδικέω**, *pay one's dues satisfactorily*, *POxy.* 2351.33 (ii AD), opposite of °ἀδωσιδικέω.

***εὐέγερτος**, *easily aroused*, Hierocl.*in CA* 8 p. 32 K.

**εὐέγρετος**, delete the entry.

**εὐέθειρα**, for 'Anacr. 76' read 'Anacr. 73 P.' and add 'Simon. 14 *fr.* 84.6 P.'

**εὔεικτος**, after '*soft*, *yielding*' insert 'Alcin.*Intr.* p. 175.2 H.'

**εὐέκβατος**, add 'Gal. 15.709.7'

***εὐεντέλιος**, α, ον, *fully developed*, ἄμπελος *PNess.* 34.2 (vi AD).

**εὐέντευκτος**, adv. -τως, add '*IMylasa* 603.7'

**εὐεπίβατος II**, after 'Ph.*Bel.* 94.40' insert 'of a single person, J.*AJ* 19.1.14' and for 'id.' read 'Ph.'

**εὐεπίθετος**, add '**2** *easy to apply oneself to*, Alcid.*Soph.* 3.'

***εὐέπιος**, = εὐεπής, *Et.Gud.*

**εὐεπιχείρητος II**, for '*readily attempting*' read '*easily persuaded* or *tempted*'

**εὐεργεσία**, after '-εσίη' insert 'Cypr. *e-u-we-re-ke-si-a-se*, εὐϝεργεσίας *ICS* 261'

***Εὐεργεσιασταί**, οἱ, an association celebrating the Εὐεργέσια, *CRAI* 1951.256 (Syria, i AD).

**εὐεργέτεια**, for 'iv BC' read 'ii BC'

**εὐεργέτης**, add 'Dor. -**ας** *SEG* 31.306 (Argos, Hellen.)'

**εὐεργέτις**, after 'E.*Alc.* 1058' insert '*IG* $9^2$(1).582.19, 23 (Magnesia, 207 BC), *Salamine* 81.5 (ii BC)' add '**2** = τορύνη (*ladle*), Miller *Mélanges* p. 405, *EM* 762.34.'

**εὐεργέω**, for '*BGU* 1118.27, al. (i BC)' read '*PKöln* 144.31 (ii BC); perh. also in *BGU* 1119.30 (i BC)'

***εὐέργη**, ἡ, app. = °εὐεργέτις 2, Poll. 10.97; cf. °ἐόργη.

**εὐέργημα**, for '*JHS* 22.366' read '*MAMA* 8.317'

***Εὐέρνειος**, name of a month in Sicily, *SEG* 30.1120.17 (Entella, iii BC or later).

**εὐετηρία I**, after 'X.*HG* 5.2.4, etc.' insert 'D. 10.49'; add '*SEG* 32.1243.33 (Aeolian Cyme, 2 BC/AD 2)'

**εὔζηλος II**, for '*enviable*' read '*glorious*'

**εὔζυξ**, read 'ἐΰζυξ' and for '*AP* 5.55' read '*AP* 5.56 (Diosc.)'

**εὐζωΐα**, add 'Iamb.*Protr.* 5 p. 36.24 P.'

**εὐηγορία**, after lemma insert '(**εὐᾱγ-**)' and add '-αγορία Pi.*Pae.* 2.67 S.-M.'

**εὐήθης I 1 b**, delete the section.

**εὐήκοος 3**, add 'epith. of Aphrodite, Ἀφροδίτῃ Εὐακόοι *SEG* 31.515 (Boeotia, iv BC)'

**εὐηλάκατος**, add 'Pi.*Pae.* 7(a).4 S.-M.'

***εὐήλικος**, ον, = εὐῆλιξ, *Vit.Aesop.*(G) 32.

+**εὐῆλιξ**, ικος, ὁ, ἡ, *of* or *characteristic of the prime of life*, i.e. early adulthood, εὐ. προσώπου Men.*Dysc.* 950. **2** *of good stature*, Polem.*Phgn.* 5, Lyd.*Mag.* 1.23.

**εὐημερία 3**, add 'Certamen 94'

**εὐήμερος 1**, add 'ἄγεν .. εὐάμερον keep *holiday*, *Inscr.Cret.* 1.xix 3.39 (Malla, ii BC), cf. ib. 3.iii 3.2 (Hierapytna, iii BC)' **2**, after '*happy*' insert 'ξὺν τύχαις εὐ. A.*fr.* 451k(a).3 R.'

**εὐήνωρ I**, add '**2** *involving a man of honourable status*, γάμων εὐ. θεσμός Orph.*A.* 885.'

**εὐθάλεια**, add 'ὑπὲρ εὐετηρίας καὶ εὐθαλείας πόλεως *SEG* 36.1095 (Lydia, iii AD)'

***εὐθελγής**, ές, *bewitching*, dub. in *Hymn.Is.* 104 P., v. πολυθελγής.

***εὐθέμεθλος**, ον, *set on good foundations*, Γαῖαν *h.Hom.* 30.1 (ἠϋ-).

**εὐθενέω I**, line 4, after 'D. 18.286' insert 'Men.*Dysc.* 275'

**εὐθενιακός**, add '*POsl.* 83.5, 6 (iii/iv AD)'

***εὐθέρα**· μέρος τι τῆς νεώς Hsch.; cf. ἐνθύριον.

**εὔθετος 2**, at end before 'adv.' insert 'w. gen., εὐ. τῆς ἀρχιερωσύνης inscr. in *SB* 8267.12 (i BC)'

**εὐθημονέομαι**, delete the entry.

***εὐθημονέω**, *keep in good order*, θὤπλα λάζευ καὶ γνάθους εὐθημόνει *Trag.adesp.* 381 K.-S.; med., Pl.*Lg.* 758b. **2** intr., *be in good order* Simp.*in Ph.* 1067.24.

**εὐθηνία I 1**, add '*POxy.* 2479.26 (vi AD)'

***εὐθηνίαρχος**, ὁ, = εὐθηνιάρχης, *POxy.* 1417.28 (iv AD).

**εὔθρονος**, after '*with beautiful seat* or *throne*' insert '(or *adorned with beautiful flowers*, cf. θρόνον)'

**εὐθυμάχος**, for 'Simon. 137' read '*AP* 7.442.1 ([Simon.])'

**εὐθυμέω II**, pass., add 'εἰρήνης .. γενομένης εὐθυμέονται *make merry*, Arr.*Ind.* 12.4'

**εὐθυμία I**, add 'Hp.*Lex* 4, *Hymn.Is.* in *SEG* 8.549.33'

***εὐθυνέω**, act as εὔθυνος II, *INikaia* 1083, 1153 (see also *SEG* 31.1069).

**εὐθύνω I**, add '**4** w. internal obj., *drive a straight* path (in quots. fig.), Modest.*Dig.* 27.1.10.3, εὐθύνει τὴν ἀτραπὸν τοῦ παντὸς βίου Ph. 1.271, 297.' **III 3**, *censure*, add 'A.D.*Pron.* 81.6, *Adv.* 171.1'

**εὐθυόνειρος**, after 'Arist.*Div.Somn.* 463$^b$16' insert '*EE* 1248$^a$40' *εὐθῠϝορία, εὐθυορία, v. °εὐθυωρία.

**εὐθύπορος** I, after 'metaph.' insert '*with a straight course*, εὐ. λά[χος] A.*fr.* 168.11 R. (lyr.)'

*εὐθῠ́(ρ)ρῑνος, ον, *straight-nosed*, *PLips.* 2.6 (i AD), 5.2.7 (iii AD).

**εὐθύς** A 2, line 10, ἐξ εὐθείας, add '*CodJust.* 1.3.42.1' **B II 1**, line 14, after 'Pl.*Tht.* 186b' insert 'Modest.*Dig.* 27.1.6.8'

**εὐθύτης** II, add '*rightness*, τὴν ἄκραν εὐ. τοῦ θείου νόμου D.Chr. 36.23'

*εὐθῠ́τοκος, ον, *new-laid*, of an egg, Cyran. 101 (3.55.3 K.).

*εὐθῠφορικός, ή, όν, *directed in a straight line*, κίνησις Phlp. *in GC* 134.18.

**εὐθῠωρία**, before 'ἡ' insert '(**εὐθυορία** in *SEG* 11.405.36 (Epid., iii/ii BC) and *SEG* 11.377.18 (Hermione, ii BC), copies of the same text)'

**εὐθύωρος**, neut. as adv., add 'Antipho *fr.* 39 T.; Ion. neut. pl. as adv., ‹ἰ›θύωρα *SEG* 26.845.13 (Berezan, *c.*500 BC)'

**εὐθώρηξ**, *well-mailed*, read '*equipped with a good corslet*' and for 'μύες Marcell.' read 'of mussels, Marc.'

**εὐιάς** (s.v. εὐιακός), add 'τὰς ἱερὰς προφυγὼν εὐιάδας εἰς Ἀΐδην *SEG* 31.633B (AD 171/2; εὐιάδας scanned as trisyll., v. *ZPE* 52.288)'

**εὐίερος**, line 1, for '*Pae.Oxy.* 675.14' read '*POxy.* 675.14'; line 3, after '*holy*' insert 'σάκος Theoc.*Ep.* 4.5'; add 'Orph.*H.* 7.2, 12, al.'

*εὐῑλᾰσία, ἡ, app. *propitiation*, *SEG* 32.1269 (sp. εὐειλ-; Phrygia, Rom.imp.); cf. εὐιλασία· εὐπειστία Hsch.'

**εὐΐλᾰτος**, add '*SEG* 30.1180 (Pompeii, i BC)'

**Εὔιος** I, add '**2** transf., *wine*, Εὔ. γέροντα πολιὸν ἤδη Men.*Dysc.* 946.' **II**, add '**2** masc. or neut. as subst., *Bacchic cry*, Εὔιον ἀείσειε .. Διονύσῳ Nonn.*D.* 15.131, Βάκχον .. Εὔια παππάζοντα ib. 48.954, ταῖς βάκχαις ἐκδιδόντα τὸν Εὔιον Him.*Or.* 46.4.7 C.' add '**III** fem. Εὐία (sp. -εία), name or title of a priestess, *IG* 10(2).1.260*B*2 (Thessalonica, iii AD).'

**εὐϊώτης**, after '*Lyr.Alex.Adesp.* 22' insert 'cf. *An.Ox.* 1.86.29'

*εὐκᾱλέω, v. °εὐκηλέω.

*εὐκᾱμία· ἡσυχία, ἤτοι εὐφημία (Dor.), *EM* 392.5; εὐκαμίαν νυν παρέχεσθε Sophr. in *GLP* iii 73.14; cf. κημός.

**εὐκαμπής**, line 5, after 'τὸ εὐ. τῶν μελῶν' insert 'i.e. the fine modulations of the melodic line (v. καμπή III 1)'

**εὔκαρπος**, line 1, delete 'of women, *h.Hom.* 30.5'; line 4, after 'S.*Aj.* 671' insert 'of men, *blessed with good crops*, *h.Hom.* 30.5'

*εὐκατάακτος, ον, = εὐκάτακτος, *easily shattered*, δόξα Sch.Pi.*N.* 8.58.

*εὐκατάγνωστος, ον, *easily recognizable*, εὐκατάγνωστον εἶναι ἑαυτῷ συνιστοροῦντα .. *it is easily perceived* that he is conscious .. (cf. καταγιγνώσκω I) Mitteis *Chr.* II.31 viii 11 (ii BC), cf. *EM* 400.6.

**εὐκατασκεύαστος** 2, add '**b** adv. -τως, *in a well-contrived way*, Sch.E.*Hec.* 1288.'

*εὐκατάσπαστος, ορ, *easily pulled down*, *SEG* 7.265 (Sidon, ii BC).

**εὐκέραστος**, add 'γλῶτταν prob. in Cratin. 171.63 K.-A.'

*εὐκηλέω, Dor. -κᾱλέω, εὐκαλεῖ· ἀτρεμίζει Hsch.

**εὐκηλήτειρα**, add '(s.v.l.)'

**εὐκλεής**, line 3, before 'dat.' insert 'gen. shortened to εὐκλέος *Inscr.Délos* 1658.6 (i BC)'; line 4, for 'Id.' read 'Pi.'; line 14, before 'adv.' insert 'sup. in honorific address, *POxy.* 1983.3 (vi AD)'

**εὔκλειᾰ** I, line 5, delete 'ἄγαλμα'

*Εὔκλειος, ὁ, name of a month, *SEG* 24.1021 (Callatis, iii BC).

**ἐϋκνήμῑς**, add '**III** = εὔκνημος I, Nonn.*D.* 18.60 (s.v.l.).'

*εὐκολοδιάβλητος, ον, *easy to slander*, Anon. *in Rh.* 72.28.

**εὔκολπος**, add '**3** *having a fair bosom* i.e. *a welcoming embrace*, *GVI* 2020.6 (Corinth, ii/i BC).'

**εὐκόμιστος** 2, add 'Simp. *in Cael.* 267.23'

**εὐκοσμία**, add '*adornment*, *decoration*, *SEG* 31.1472 (Arabia, AD 603)'

*εὐκόσμιος, ον, *decent in appearance* Hsch. s.v. κίδαρις (adv. -ίως, q.v.).

**εὔκουρος**, add 'in uncertain sense, *Rev.Bibl.* 42.250 (Syria)'

**εὐκταῖος** 2, add 'Ἀρτέμιδι εὐκτέᾳ *SEG* 32.1260 (Paphlagonia, ii AD)' **3**, adv., add '*GVI* 788.9 (Pontus, ii/iii AD)'

**εὐκτέανος** (A), after '(A)' insert 'Ep. ἐϋκτ-' add '**2** *costly*, Q.S. 14.271.'

*εὐκτερής, ές, *who has been given rich funeral honours*, epigr. in *Lindos* 698.7 (*c.*200 BC).

**εὐκτήριος** I, add '*SEG* 34.1292 (Phrygia, late Rom.imp.)' **II**, add '*SEG* 37.1541 (Gerasa, vi AD)'

**ἐϋκτίμενος**, for '= εὖ .. *dwell in*' read 'epith. of land, or sim., of unknown meaning' and at end after 'Od. 24.226' insert 'in Homeric imitation, Ῥώμης .. ἐϋκτιμένης *SEG* 11.773 (Sparta, iv AD), cf. Myc. *ki-ti-me-na*'

**ἐΰκτῐτος**, before '= ἐϋκτίμενος' insert '(εὐκτ- in Anacr. 13.5 P.)'; after 'B. 3.46' insert 'δόμος εὔκτιτος *Lyr.adesp.S* 414.13'

**εὐλᾰβέομαι** II 3, delete '*quietly*' **III**, add 'imper. εὐλάβει *Com. adesp.* 239.7 A.'

*εὐλᾰλία, ἡ, *eloquence*, Hsch. s.v. προφορά.

**εὐλή**, for pres. def. read '*larva* of the fly or other insect, *maggot*, *grub*, *worm*, etc.'; line 4, delete 'of common worms' and insert 'οἷον εἰ εὐλαὶ ἐν σαπέντι μέρει τοῦ φυτοῦ γίγνοιντο Plot. 4.3.4'

**εὐλίβᾰνος**, after 'Aristonous 1.23' insert '*SB* 6699.2 (inscr., iii BC)'

**εὐλῐπής** 1, add 'ὄρνεον *PLond.* 2741 iv 71 in *SHAW* 14(1923).16 (iii AD)'

*ἐΰλλιστος, ον, *favourably received*, θυηλαί orac. in *Didyma* 496*B*3 (oracle, ii AD).

*εὐλόβρωτος, ον, *worm-eaten*, *An.Par.* 4.182.21 (εὐλοβρώτειος cod.).

**εὐλογέω** II 1, add 'pres. part. as a form of address in a letter, τῷ εὐλογο[υ]μένῳ .. υἱ[ῷ]'

**εὐλογία** II, add 'Lycurg. 46, Isoc. 7.76' **III 1**, add '*TAM* 4(1).374, 375'

*εὐλοιδόρητος, ον, *open to abuse*, Men.*Sic.fr.* 2 S., Plu. 2.757a.

*Εὐλοχία, = εὔλοχος, epith. of Artemis, *Gonnoi* 173.3 (iii BC).

**εὔλοχος**, add '**II** of women, *fertile*, *fruitful*, Nonn.*D.* 31.111, 38.134, 44.309; transf., of the earth, ib. 1.294.'

**εὐλῠτέω**, add '*SEG* 39.1180.48, 87 (Ephesus, i AD).'

**εὔλῠτος** I, add '**6** fig., mentally *supple*, ἀγχίνοια Alcid.*Soph.* 16, cf. ib. 20, 34.'

**εὐλῠτόω**, delete the entry.

*εὐλῠ́τωσον (εὐλύτρωσον La.)· ἀπάλλαξον Hsch.

**εὐμᾰ́θεια**, line 3, after 'Ion. -ίη' insert 'Call.*Epigr.* 48.1 Pf.'

**εὐμᾰρέω**, add 'δυνάμεις τὰς εὐμαρεούσας, of the plant θύρσιον, Cyran. 23 (1.8.10 K.)'

**εὐμᾰρής** I 1 b, delete the section transferring quot. to follow '*Trag.adesp.* 383' in section II.

**Εὐμένειος** II, add '-ειον, τό, *sanctuary of Eumenes*, *Inscr.Perg.* 8(1).240 (ii BC)'

**εὐμενέτειρα**, add '*SIFC* 2.389 (Crete, Chr.)'

*εὐμενηστικός (εὐμενιστικός La.): gloss on μειλικτήριος Hsch.

*Εὐμενίδειος, ὁ, name of a month in Sicily, *SEG* 30.1117 (Entella, iii BC), ib. 1118, 1120.

**εὐμετάβολος**, add 'adv. -λως, Hsch. s.v. ἐμπλήγδην'

**εὐμήκης**, add '**4** εὐ. (sc. λίθος), ἡ, a precious stone, Plin.*HN* 37.160.'

*εὐμήνῡτος, ον, perh. *easily detected*, Theognost.*Can.* 83.

*εὐμίτρης, ου, ἡ, a precious stone, Plin.*HN* 37.160.

**εὐμνηστος**, line 2, before 'χρηστήριον' insert '**II** *of which it is good to make remembrance*, or *celebrated*'

**εὐμοιρία**, add 'personified, *SB* 642, 1625 (ii/iii AD)'

**εὐμοιρίτης**, add 'perh. also fem. **εὐμοιρῖτις**, ιδος, rest. in *SEG* 36.573 (Illyria, vi AD)'

**εὔμοιρος**, add 'euphem., of the dead, *PHaun.* 17.9 (ii AD), *PUniv.Giss.* 20.10'

**εὔμολπος**, for '*sweetly singing*' read '*melodious*' and after it insert 'εὐμόλποις ὑμ[εναίοις] A.*fr.* 168.19 R. (lyr.), εὐμόλπῳ .. ἄνακτι λύρης'

**εὔμορφος**, add 'of style, *elegant*, D.H.*Dem.* 18: adv. -φως, Luc.*Salt.* 71 (comp.), Sch.Luc.*JTr.* 12'

**εὔμωλος**, after '-ότατον' insert '(-ύτατον La. app. fr. *εὔμωλυς, cf. μῶλυς)'

**εὐνάζω**, line 2, for 'Simon. 184.10' read '*AP* 7.25.10 ([Simon.])' **2**, line 5, for 'Simon. l.c.' read '*AP* l.c.'; last line, for 'Call.*Aet.* 3.1.1' read 'Call.*fr.* 75.1 Pf.'

**εὐνάης**, delete the entry.

*εὐνάης, ές, (νάω) *fair-flowing*, B. 1.75, 9.42 S.-M., Call.*fr.* 65.1 Pf.

**εὐναῖος** II 2, add '*Trag.adesp.* 589 K.-S., Call.*fr.* 727 Pf.'

*εὐναστήριον, τό, *grave*, E.*Or.* 590 (codd.), Lyc. 583; cf. εὐνατήριον.

**εὐνατήριον**, delete '(εὐαστήριον .. E. ll.cc.)'

**εὐνέτης**, for '= εὐναστήρ' read '*bedfellow*, *husband*' and after '(lyr.)' insert 'E.*El.* 803'; fem. -ις, add '*GVI* 1262.2 (Telus, ii/i BC)'

*Εὐνίκειον, τό, app. *sanctuary of* a hero *Eunicus*, *IG* 9²(1).757b (Amphissa, ii BC).

**εὖνις** (B), after '(E.*IA*) 807' insert 'Call.*fr.* 55.1 Pf.'

**εὐνομία** I 1, at end for 'οἱ ἐπὶ τῆς εὐνομίας .. (Lato)' read '**b** name of a Cretan magistracy, *Inscr.Cret.* 1.xiv 2.2, al. **c** w. gen., *peace from*, τόξων εὐ. *APl.* 212.4 (Alph.).' **4**, add 'pl., epigr. in *SEG* 29.1139 (Miletus, iv/v AD)'

**εὔνομος** I 1, add '**b** *law-abiding*, *SEG* 6.796 (Cappadocia, iii AD).' transferring 'ἄνδρες Pl.*Lg.* 815b' to this section.

**εὔνοος** 1, line 4, after '*friendly*' insert 'θῦμος Alc. 129.9 L.-P.'; line 9, comp. Ion. εὐνοέστερος, add '*Amyzon* 186.8 (ii BC)'; at end before '*EM* 394.5' insert '*IG* 12 suppl. 693.10 (Eresus, iii AD)' **2**, adv. εὐνόως, after 'διακείμενος' insert '*SEG* 30.533.A3 (Thessaly, ii BC)'

*εὐνουχικός, ή, όν, *of* or *relating to eunuchs*, μοῖραι Vett.Val. 14.26.

**εὐνοῦχος** I 1, before 'Hdt. 3.130' insert 'Hippon. 26 W.' **II**, add 'app. in complimentary sense, of a faithful wife, *SEG* 28.1536 (Egypt, Rom.imp.)'

**εὔξενος** I, add 'app. a title of the descendants of Antenor, founder of Padua, Εὐξείνοι[ς] Ἀντηνορίδα[ις] *SEG* 30.1132 (Aquileia, ii AD)'

**εὐοδία**, after '*journey*' insert 'E.*fr.* 308 cod. Sch.Ar.*Vesp.* 757'; after 'A.*fr.* 36' insert '*PVindob.* G39995 (*CE* 56.305, iii AD)'

*εὐόκερως, v. ‡αἰγόκερως.

**εὐόνυξ**, for '*claws*' read '*operculum*'

**εὐοπλία**, add '**II** pl., *feats of arms*, Aristid.Quint. 2.10.'
**εὔοπλος**, add 'of Athena, εὔοπλε καὶ ἀρσενωπέ, poet. in *PKöln* 245.10 (iii AD)'
**εὐοργία**, for 'sic' read 'εὐπειστία La.'
†**εὔοργος**, ον, *good-tempered*, S.*fr.* 33a R.; adv. -ως E. in *POxy.* 3317.14 (= E.*fr.* 165 where εὐλόγως or cj. εὐλόφως is read).
***εὐοχθεία**, ἡ, *abundance, plenty*, ὅρσει δὲ πολύλλιτον εὐοχθείαν Robert *DAMM* p. 92 (Syedra, i BC; hex.).
**εὐπἄγής**, for '*well-woven*' read '*close-woven*' and after '*BGU* 1564.10 (ii AD)' insert '*PBeatty Panop.* 2.22 (AD 300); of words, *well-assembled*, i.e. with a euphonious arrangement of letters, Demetr.*Eloc.* 176'
**εὐπαιδευσία**, add '*SEG* 24.491 (Maced., AD 202)'
**εὔπαις**, add '(so perh. in Ar. l.c., *noble son* of Apollo, cf. καλλίπαις II)'
**εὐπἄλής I**, after 'A.R. 2.618' insert 'οὐ]τι γὰρ εὐπαλές ἐστι *Lyr.adesp.* 14.9 P.' **II**, add '*BCH* 107.875 (unless pers. n.)'
***εὐπαραδειγμάτιστος**, ον, *well-exhibited*, i.e. *clearly showing*, Ptol.*Tetr.* 170.
†**εὐπάρθενος**, ον, *having a beautiful maiden* or *maidens*, εὐ. ἄστυ Triph. 51, Nonn.*D.* 39.188, 42.462, 43.430; εὐ. εὐνήν ib. 16.311. **II** (*that is a*) *beautiful, blessed*, or sim., *maiden*, εὐ. Δίρκα E.*Ba.* 520, *AP* 6.287 (Antip.Sid.).
**εὐπαρόξυντος**, add 'Paul.Aeg. 7.4.9 (278.16 H.)'
***εὐπᾰτάγος**, ον, *fine-sounding*, ἠχῆς εὐπατάγου perh. of drums and cymbals, *POxy.* 3723.14 (elegy, ?ii AD); cf. εὐκέλαδος.
**εὐπἄτειρα**, for 'Men. 616 (with v.l. εὐπατέρεια)' read 'Men.*Dysc.* 968'
***Εὐπᾰτορισταί**, οἱ, guild of worshippers of Mithridates Eupator at Delos, *Inscr.Délos* 1567 (i BC).
**εὐπατρίδης I**, add '*Kafizin* 50'
**εὐπἄτωρ**, add '**III** epith. of kings, e.g. Antiochus V, App.*Syr.* 46 §236.'
**εὐπειθής**, add '**2** *satisfied*, of a contracting party, *PMich.*XI 604.22, *POxy.* 2769.26 (both iii AD).'
**εὔπεπτος 1**, add 'adv. -τως, εὐ. ἔχειν πρός τι *have an appetite* for, *Vit.Aesop.*(G) 3'
**εὐπερίπᾰτος**, add '**II** of persons, *able to walk easily*, *Cat.Cod.Astr.* 11(2).191.31.'
**εὐπῖδαξ**, read '**εὐπῖδαξ**'
**εὐπῑθής**, act., add 'E.*Andr.* 819 (codd. εὐπειθ-)'
†**εὔπῑλητος**, ον, expl. of εὔστιπτος Sch.A.R. 2.30; dub. l. in Arist.*Sens.* $438^a15$ (comp.).
**εὔπλεκτος**, delete 'also η, ον .. (cj. for ἀπλ-)'
**Εὔπλοια** (εὔπλοια II), add 'of Isis, *Inscr.Délos* 2153 (ii BC)'
***εὔπλουμος**, ον, *well-embroidered*, *PAnt.* 44.13 (iv/v AD).
**εὐποδία**, add '*SEG* 23.109 (Attica, ii AD)'
**εὐποιΐα**, line 3, before 'εἰς πλῆθος' insert 'Thphr.*fr.* 584A.100 F.'
**εὐπόλεμος**, after '*h.Mart.* 4' insert '*CEG* 10.4 (Athens, v BC), Ἀρετή ib. 102.2 (Athens, *c.*400 BC)'
**εὐπορέω II**, after '*furnish*' insert 'Hp.*Cord.* 11'; line 5, after '(iii AD)' insert 'also abs., *make provision*, rest. in *JRS* 27.19 (Galatia)' and omit 'hence in'
**εὐπορία I**, add '**3** *power, might*, Aq.*Ps.* 109(110).3; concr., of an armed force, Lxx 4*Ki.* 25.10(cod. A), Aq.*Is.* 36.2.'
**εὔποτος II**, after '*good to drink from*' insert 'ποτέριον *CEG* 454 (Ischia, viii BC)'
**εὔπους I**, line 3, after '*fleet of foot*' insert 'εὐ. νύμφαν Sapph. 103.5 L.-P.'; for 'Call.*fr.* 48' read 'Call.*fr.* 302 Pf.' and add 'Ὧραι Nonn.*D.* 38.131, 331'
**εὔπραξις**, add '(cf. pers. n., Εὔπραχσις, Lang *Ath.Agora* XXI D7 (vi BC))'
***εὐπρᾱτικός**, ή, όν, *of a cheap kind*, ζῦτος *BGU* $1069^r9$ (iii AD).
***εὐπρόσεκτος**, ον, *cherished*, τέκνον *BCH* 58.343 (Caria).
***εὐπροσώνῠμος**, ον, *of good name, honoured*, τὴν εὐ. ἡμῶν πόλιν Act. Alexandr. IX col.vi.17.
**εὐπροσωπία**, add '*BGU* 1787.12'
**εὐπρόσωπος**, line 1, after 'Anaxandr. 9.5' insert 'of Pan, hymn in *IG* $4^2$.130.19' **3**, delete the section.
***εὐπτέρυξ**, ῠγος, ὁ, ἡ, = εὐπτέρυγος, ἐϋπτερύγεσσι πελείαις *GVI* 655.9 (Trachonitis, ii/iii AD).
**εὐρέκτης**, add 'also **ἐϋρρέκτης** epigr. in *Inscr.Olymp.* 481 (iii/iv AD); (cf. pers. n. *IG* $1^3$.319.14, Athens, 432/1 BC)'
†**εὕρεμα**, v. ‡εὕρημα.
**εὐρετός**, add 'w. θεός in uncertain significance, Mitchell *N.Galatia* 138'
**εὑρέτρια**, add '*Hymn.Is.* in *SEG* 8.548.3 (Fayum, i BC)'
**εὕρημα**, line 1, delete '(q.v.)' **I**, add '(form εὕρεμα) Hp.*Vict.* 1.2, Str. 16.2.24, *AP* 7.411 (Diosc.), Babr.*Prooem.* ii 2, *PMag.* 13.299' **III**, add '*sum* specified in a tender, *IG* 7.3074.3 (Lebadea, ii BC)'
**εὑρησῐλογία**, add '*casuistry, quibbling*, *PAlex.* 10.11 (i AD), *BGU* 2042.15 (AD 105), *PNess.* 26.21 (AD 570)'
**εὔρῑπος**, add 'Myc. *e-wi-ri-po*, place-name; cf. deriv. adj. *e-wi-ri-pi-ja*'
**εὑρίσκω I**, add '**7** pass., *to be found, be present*, *Cod.Just.* 1.2.17.2.'
**εὐροέω II**, add 'τοῖς εὐρ‹ο›οῦσι καὶ θέουσι prob. in Plu. 2.375d'
***εὔροιζος**, ον, *ringing true*, of gold, Ps.-Callisth. 2.41.1 cod.C.
**εὔροπος**, line 1, εὐ. ἅμμα, for 'an *easy-sliding* noose' read 'clasp *that easily overturns* (a bull)'
***ἐϋρρᾰθάμιγξ**, ιγγος, adj. *copiously dripping*, Nonn.*D.* 5.258, 33.101.
**εὐρύαναξ**, read '**εὐρῠάναξ**'
**εὐρύβατος II**, add 'often coupled w. Φρυνώνδειος (q.v.)'
***εὐρύβοτος**, ον, *having broad pastures*, πατρίδος εὐρυβότου epigr. in *SEG* 38.734 (Thrace, iii/ii BC).
**εὐρυθμοκάρηνος**, **-κερως**, delete the entries.
**εὔρυθμος 3**, add 'κείοσιν εὐρύθμοις epigr. in *SEG* 37.1537 (Arabia, *c.*AD 400)'
***εὐρῠκάρηνος**, ον, *having a broad head*, σιγύνης Opp.*C.* 1.152, Πίθος Nonn.*D.* 20.127.
***εὐρύκερως**, ωτος, *having spreading horns*, Opp.*C.* 2.293, v.l. in Mosch. 2.153.
**εὐρῠκόων**, ωντος, fem. κόωσα, unexpld. wd. (cf. Hsch. s.v. -κόωσα) used as epith. of οὐρανός, poet. in *PAnt.* $56B(a)^r.6$; of νύξ, Hsch.; of the sea-goddess Ceto, Euph. 116 vGr. (for suffix, cf. perh. Λαοκόων).
**εὐρυκόωσα**, delete the entry.
**εὐρύνωτος**, add '*Suppl.Hell.* 991.46 (poet. word-list, iii BC)'
**εὐρύπρωκτος**, for '*wide-breeched*' read '*having a wide anus*' and add '*SEG* 26.1708 (Egypt, early v BC)'
***εὐρύρροος**, ον, = εὐρυρέεθρος, cj. in A.R. 4.269.
**εὐρύς**, lines 3/4, for 'Asius 13' read 'Asius *Fr.Ep.* 13.3 B.' at end add 'in Myc. compd. names, as *e-u-ru-da-mo* (= Εὐρύδημος)'
***εὐρύσμωλος** (v.l. **εὐρύσωλος**), unexpld. wd., Arc. 57.14 B.
**εὐρῠ́σορος**, for '*with wide bier* or *tomb*' read 'of a tomb, perh. *holding a wide sarcophagus*, or sim.'
**εὐρῠχορος**, add '**2** *widespread, far-flung*, οὐκ ἔθανεν γάρ, ζώσης εὐρυχόροιο τέχνης ἀρεταῖσι μαθητῶν *GVI* 742.7 (Rome, ii/iii AD).'
†**εὐρώδης**, ες, prob. *mouldy* (= εὐρώεις) S.*Aj.* 1190 (lyr.).
**Εὐρωπαῖος**, after '*European*' insert 'Hp.*Aër.* 16, 23'
**Εὐρώπη**, after 'Pi.*N.* 4.70' insert '(Εὐρώπαν ποτὶ χέρσον perh. as adj.)'
***εὐρωτίας**, ου, ὁ, a precious stone, Plin.*HN* 37.161.
**ἐΰς**, add 'used for Lat. *pius*, Ἀντωνῖνος εὐς *SEG* 12.1502 (Palestine, v AD)'
**εὐσέβεια 1**, add 'εὐσεβίας χάριν *SEG* 31.1533 (Egypt, *c.*AD 200)' **3**, add '**b** as an honorific title, *SEG* 34.1243.6 (Abydus, v AD), etc., τὸ τῆς ἡμετέρας εὐσεβείας ἐπώνυμον συντεθείκαμεν βιβλίον Just.*Const.* Δέδωκεν 1.'
†**Εὐσέβεια**, τά, games founded at Puteoli by Antoninus Pius in honour of Hadrian, *IG* $2^2$.3169/70.16, 14.737.8, 7.49.23, Artem. 1.26.
**εὐσεβέω**, line 4, for 'εὐ. τὰ πρὸς θεούς' to end of article read 'θύουσα καὶ εὐσεβοῦσα τοῖς θεοῖς *PRyl.* 112(a).4 (iii AD); w. internal obj., εὐσεβεῖν τὰ πρὸς θεούς S.*Ph.* 1441; εὐ. τὰ περὶ τοὺς θεούς Isoc. 3.3; pass., ἵνα τοῦτο εὐσεβηθῇ Pl.*Ax.* 364c. **2** trans., *reverence*, εὐ. θεούς A.*Ag.* 338, E.*Tr.* 85, *Ph.* 1321; pass., Ph. 2.201.'
**εὐσεβής I 2**, add 'also of other monarchs, *SEG* 30.1697 (prob. sup.; Palestine, AD 585). **c** as the title of a legion (= Lat. *Pius*), λεγ(ιῶνος) ια´ Κλαυδίας εὐσεβοῦς πιστῆς *SEG* 33.1194 (Cappadocia, i/ii AD), *Xanthos* 50.7.' **II**, add '**2** *venerable*, *AP* 9.360 (Metrod.).' add '**IV** εὐ. (sc. λίθος), ὁ or ἡ, a precious stone, Plin.*HN* 37.161.'
***εὐσεβουργός**, όν, *doing pious service*, *SEG* 6.66 (Ancyra).
**εὔσειστος**, add '**2** w. ref. to the eyes, εὔσειστοι τὰ ὄμματα gloss on κλαδαρόμματοι, Hsch.'
**εὔσελμος**, add 'σωτῆρες εὐσέλμων νεῶν *Trag.adesp.* 463 K.-S.'
***εὔσεμνος**, ον, *august*, σπείρης *IG* 14.925 (Portus Trajani, ii/iii AD).
**εὔσημος II**, after 'Hp.*Mochl.* 16' insert 'Gal. 9.776.16'
**εὐσῑτέω**, add 'Gal. 17(2).526.11, 13'
***εὔσκηνος**, ον, *well-staged, beautiful on the stage*, χορεία *AE* 1931.117 (Miletus, ii BC).
**εὔσοια**, add 'dub. in Alc. 286(*a*).6 L.-P.'
***εὐσόλοικος**, ον, *irregular but permitted* (in regard to speech), Eust. 1287.37.
***εὔσοφος**, ον, prob. *very learned, well-skilled*, τὸν εὐ. καὶ πανάριστον *PASA* 3.175 (Isauria).
**εὐσπάρτεος**, add '(*Suppl.Hell.* 1078)'
**εὔσπειρος**, for '*well-wreathed*' read '*well-coiled*'; for 'Antip.' read 'Antip.Sid.'
**εὐστάθεια**, line 2, after '(Strat.)' insert '*Didyma* 496*B*13'
**εὐσταθμος**, line 3, after 'νομίσματα' insert '*POxy.* 1932.6 (v AD)'
***εὐστάσία**, ἡ, = εὐστάθεια 1 personified, poet. in *Inscr.Perg.* 8(2).324.15.
**ἐϋστείρη**, delete the entry.
***εὔστειρος**, α, ον, poet. **ἐΰστ-**, *having a good keel*, Call.*fr.* 18.4 Pf. (uncertain gender in broken passage), ἐϋστείρης .. νηός A.R. 1.401.
**εὔστεκτος**, delete the entry.

*εὐστέφιος, α, ον, = εὐστέφανος II, γαῖα *BCH* 59.148 (Philippi).
εὐστόν, transfer the entry before εὔστοργος.
εὔστοργος, add '**II** *loving*, μήτηρ *JRS* 18.30 (Upper Tembris valley).'
εὐστόρθυγξ, for '*consisting .. branch*' read 'perh. *well-spiked*'
εὔστοχος **II 3**, after 'ἄγρη' insert '*AP* 6.13 (Leon.Tarent.)'
εὔστρεπτος **I**, add '*close in texture*, expl. of εὔστιπτος, Sch.A.R. 2.30'
εὐστροφάλιγξ, for '*curly*' read '*whirling*'; for 'Antip.' read 'Antip.Sid.'
εὔστρωτος, after '*h.Cer.* 285' insert 'Alc. 283.8 L.-P.'
+εὐσύγκρῐτος, ον, *well-constituted* or *-compounded*, ὄμμα Simp.*in Cael.* 75.2; in Epicurean philosophy, Diog.Oen. 1 ii 14, 2 iii 4.'
*εὐσυμβούλευτος, ον, *easy to advise*, Ps.-Callisth. 30.7.
εὐσύνδετος, add 'Heph.Astr. 3.20.5'
εὐσυνείδητος **I**, add 'adv. -τως, εὐσεβῶς .. καὶ -τως ἔχων *MAMA* 8.413e'
εὐσύνθετος **I 2**, add '**b** *well put together*, κέκλεικε τοῦτο μαρμάροις εὐσυνθέτοις *CIJud.* 1.653 (Syracuse), *SEG* 34.327 (Tegea, Chr.).'
*εὐσυννόητος, ον, *easy to comprehend*, Simp.*in Cael.* 264.16.
εὐσύνοπτος **II**, for '*easily taken in by the mind*' read '*easily comprehended*' and add 'Is.*fr.* 161'
*εὐσῦριγξ, ιγγος, perh. *melodious with the sound of pipes*, μέλαθρον Nonn.*D.* 3.320.
*εὐσχεθής, ές, *good to handle*, εὐσχεθὲς .. τόξον Hes.*fr.* 33(a).32 M.-W.
εὐσχημονίζω, for '*train, educate*' read '*treat properly, maintain adequately*'
*εὐσχημονισμός, ὁ, *proper maintenance*, *GDI* 1708.16 (Delphi, ii BC).
εὔσχημος, after 'adv. -μως' insert 'Chor. 29.77 p. 335 F.-R.'
εὐσχήμων **II 2**, add 'sup. in honorific address, ἀγωνοθετοῦντος τοῦ εὐσχημονεστάτου Αὐρ. Διοτίμου *SEG* 30.1524 (Lycia, iii AD)'
*εὐ]τακτία, ἡ, app. *good order*, εὐ]τακτίῃ rest. in *SEG* 26.551 (Coronea, iii BC).
εὔτακτος **I 2**, add 'in epitaphs, esp. of slaves, *SEG* 34.1483 (Palestine, iii/ii BC)' **II**, after 'of payments' insert '*PStrassb.* 228 (iii BC)'
εὔταρσος **1**, for '*delicately winged*' read '*well-operculated*' and for 'grasshopper' read 'cicada'
*εὐτᾰφία, ἡ, *good burial*, ζῶον ἐλευθερίῃ [καὶ] νέκυν εὐταφίῃ *MAMA* 9.76.
εὖτε **I 1**, line 5, delete 'δὴ τότε γε 22.182'; line 7, after '(Od.) 20.56' insert '22.182'
εὐτεκνέω, add '*Trag.adesp.* 681.9 K.-S.'
εὐτεκνία **I**, add '**2** *easy birth*, Epiph.Const. in *Lapid.Gr.* 197.4.'
εὐτέλεια **I 2**, add '**b** as term of self-depreciation, ἡ εὐτέλειά μου *POxy.* 1165.1, 8 (vi AD).'
εὐτελής **I**, add '**3** of words, style, etc., *undistinguished, commonplace*, Arist.*Rh.* 1408ª13, Demetr.*Eloc.* 70 (comp.); of the speaker, ib. 100; adv. -λῶς, ib. 167 (sup.), D.H.*Dem.* 18 (comp.). **4** *belonging to the lower orders*, *Cod.Just.* 11.41.7, Just.*Nov.* 12.1.' **II**, add 'οἱ εὐτελεῖς κληρικοί *SEG* 37.195 (Attica, Chr.); freq. as pr. n. *IG* 12(9).126 (Styra, v BC), *SEG* 26.368, etc. (Attica, iv BC)'
*εὐτερπίη, ἡ, *delight*, *Hymn.Is.* in *SEG* 8.549.18 (Egypt, i BC).
*εὔτης· ἀγαθότης Hsch. (La.; v. ἐητύς).
εὐτλήμων, after 'δόξῃ' insert '(v.l. ἐν τλήμονι)'
εὐτονέω, add 'Iamb.*Protr.* 21 λβ' p. 124.9 P.'
εὐτονία **a**, add 'εὐ. τοῦ ἔργου w. ref. to a circus athlete, *Delph.* 3(1).216.5'
εὐτράπεζος **2**, add '*good to eat*, Xenocr. 9'
εὐτρᾰπελεύομαι, add 'Sch.Pl.*Euthphr.* 24c G.'
εὐτρεπίζω **II**, delete '*conciliate*' and 'pass. in med. sense'; add 'humorously, w. ref. to appropriation of another's possessions, *AP* 9.316 (Leon.Tarent.)'
εὐτρίαινα, add '(εὐρυτρ. codd.)'
εὔτρῐχος, add 'ἄνδρα εὔτριχον *Cat.Cod.Astr.* 11(2).190.10'
εὔτροπος **II**, after 'Sch.Od. 1.1' insert 'Sopat.Rh. 8.56.33 W.'; of diseases, add 'Gal.in *CMG* 5.9(2) 114.25, 129.17, 142.18'
εὐτρόχᾰλος **I**, after '*quick-moving*' insert 'ἅμαξαι A.R. 1.845' **II**, for 'ἐϋτροχάλῳ' to end of section read '**III** *well-rolled*, ἀλωή Hes.*Op.* 599, 806.'
εὔτροχος **I**, line 4, delete 'εὐ. κύκλος .. 19' **III**, after '*round*' insert 'E.*Ion* 19'
*εὐτρύγιον (or ?εὐτρύτιον), τό, item in list of comestibles, etc., otherwise unexpld., *BGU* 2358.15 (iv AD).
εὐτῠκάζομαι, add 'act., Call.*fr.* 177.32 Pf.'
εὐτῠχέω **II**, for this section read 'act., *have the good fortune to obtain, attain to*, παρὰ τῶν Σεβαστῶν στέφανον *IEphes.* 3070.13, Men.Rh. 439.10 R.-W., Sopat.Rh. 8.247.18, 328.19 W.'
εὐτύχημα, add '*SEG* 31.903.9 (pl., Aphrodisias, iii AD)'
εὐτυχής **I**, lines 2/3, comp., after 'S.*Aj.* 550' insert 'masc. ending for fem., *SEG* 30.1485 (Phrygia, iv AD)' add '**2** sup. as honorific title (= Lat. *felicissimus*), *SB* 4678.11, *POxy.* 1042, 1896, *PLond.* 1723 (all vi AD).' **II**, after 'at close of letter, D.H.*Amm.* 2 fin.' insert '*SEG* 30.812'; add 'at the end of an inscr., *SEG* 31.635 (Maced., ii/iii AD), etc.'

εὔυμνος **II**, for this section read '*making beautiful song*, ῥήματα *Suppl.Hell.* 980.3'
+εὐυπάντητος, ον, *easily approached*, *IGBulg.* 390.6; adv. -ως, *VDI* 1960(3).154 (Chersonese).
*εὐυπόστᾰτος, ον, *staunch, steadfast*, Afric.*Cest.* p. 18 V.
*εὐφᾰνής, ές, *illustrious*, *IGRom.* 3.739ᵛ.5 (Rhodiopolis, ii AD; sup.).
*εὐφᾰρέτρειος, α, ον, *having a beautiful quiver*, Ἄρ]τεμιν εὐφαρέτρειαν orac. in *ZPE* 92.267 (Ephesus, ii AD).
εὐφᾰρέτρης, add '*SEG* 23.126.3 (Attica, i BC)'
εὔφημος **I 1**, lines 4/5, for 'moving the lips of *reverent* thought' read 'uttering the words of *auspicious* thought'
εὔφθαρτος, **I 2**, **II**, for these sections read '**II** of food, *easily broken down*, Diph.Siph.ap.Ath. 2.68f, Gal. 8.34.5.'
εὔφθογγος, line 2, after 'λύρῃ' insert 'Margites 1.3 W.'
εὐφρᾰδής **1**, adv., for '*eloquently*' read '*prudently, wisely*' and add '*IG* 2².5201, *CRAI* 1968.423 no. 6'
εὐφραίνω, line 7, after 'Ar.*Ach.* 5' insert 'pf. part. εὐφραμμένος Hsch. s.v. κεκραιπαληκώς' **II**, add 'w. ref. to sexual fulfilment, Ar.*Lys.* 165, 591'
εὐφραντός **1**, for 'Sch.E.*Hec.* 100' read 'Sch.E.*Hec.* 98'
*Εὐφράνωρ, ορος, ὁ, epith. of Zeus, *ABSA* 49.12 (Dorylaeum).
*εὐφρονέω, *be in good heart*, *CIJud.* 303.
εὐφρονέων, delete final parenth.
εὐφρόνη **II**, add 'cj. in Orph.*H.* 9.8'
*Εὐφρονίσιοι, οἱ, name of group of Corybantes, *IEryth.* 201a.62 (iii BC).
εὐφροσύνη **II**, add '**2** title of Isis, Ἴσιδι Εὐφροσύνῃ *Inscr.Délos* 2107 (i BC).'
εὐφωνία **I 1**, after 'X.*Mem.* 3.3.13' insert 'D. 19.339'
*εὐφώτιστος, ον, *well-lighted*, Simp.*in Cael.* 457.12.
εὐχαίτης, add 'of Dionysus, *AP* 9.524'
εὐχᾰρακτος, add 'Procl.CP *Hom.* 28.29'
εὔχᾰρις **I**, add '**2** *graceful*, of diction, Demetr.*Eloc.* 173; of style, D.H.*Din.* 81.'
*εὐχᾰριστεύς, έως, ὁ, *bestower of favours, benefactor*, nom. pl. -ῆς *SEG* 38.1476.108 (Xanthos, iii BC).
εὐχαριστέω **2**, line 5, after '1*Ep.Cor.* 1.4, etc.' insert 'med., *show gratitude*, μεταξὺ ἀχαρίστων τε .. καὶ εὐχαριστουμένων παίδων Just.*Nov.* 22.48 pr.'
εὐχᾰριστητικός, for '= -ιστικός' read '= εὐχαριστικός' and after '(Ph.) 177, 371' insert '*IGRom.* 3.704iii*B* 6 (Cyanae)'
εὐχᾰριστία **1**, add 'Θεῷ Ἡλίῳ Ἐλαγαβάλῳ Μαιδουας Γολασου εὐχαριστίας ἀνέθηκεν *Philol.* 127.257 no. 2 (Emesa, iii AD)'
εὐχάριστος **I**, for 'εὐχάριστα .. (Cyprus)' read 'Cypr. *e-u-ka-ri-ta* εὐχάριστα, *acceptable gifts*, *Kafizin* 117b, 303' and add 'πλείονα εὐχάριστα πεποίηκεν τῇ συνόδωι *SEG* 32.453 (Boeotia, ii BC)' **III**, add 'cult-title of Zeus, *INikaia* 1085 (iii AD).'
εὐχάριτος, add 'fem. εὐχαρίτη, ἀρχήν epigr. in *Inscr.Délos* 36 (iv/iii BC); adv., εὐχαρίτως ἄρξας rest. in epigr.ib. 37'
εὐχέρεια **IV**, add 'εὐ. τῆς βολῆς poet.ap.Ath. 15.667e (εὐχειρία codd.)'
εὐχερής **I 1**, line 8, for '(Pl.)*Tht.* 184c' read '(Pl.)*Tht.* 184b' **III**, before 'Batr. 62' insert 'πρᾶγμα Damox. 2.10 K.-A.' and after it 'μελέτη Plu.*Dem.* 2'; after 'adv. -ρῶς' insert 'ἐργάζεσθαι Hp.*Fract.* 30' and add 'διὰ τὴν ἔνδειαν τῆς τροφῆς εὐχερῶς ἀπολλύμενοι *Peripl.M.Rubr.* 29'
εὐχή **1**, line 5, delete 'εὐχὴν ἀνέστησεν .. i/ii AD)' add '**b** *votive offering*, καλλίγραπτον εὐ. A.*fr.* 78a.12 R. (lyr.); εὐχὴν ἀνέθηκεν *IG* 12(3)458, etc., cf. *Samothrace* p. 49; without verb, in a dedication, Δάματρι εὐχάν *SEG* 33.765 (Heracleia, Italy, iii/ii BC), Γεννάδης Ἀπόλλωνι εὐχήν *SEG* 30.1474 (Phrygia), 1604 (Cyprus).'
+εὔχλοος, ον, Ep. ἐΰχλ-, *characterized by green vegetation*, πόλις Βερόη Nonn.*D.* 41.15 (cj.); epith. of deities assoc. w. vegetation, εὐχλόου Δήμητρος S.*OC* 1600.
εὔχομαι **II 1**, line 6, delete 'cf. .. codd.' add '**4** aor. part. in dedications, Κυρίῳ Ἀσκληπιῷ Ἀμφείων .. εὐξάμενος ἀνέθηκεν *SEG* 30.719 (Thrace, ii/iii AD).' **III 3**, after '*declare*' insert '(acc. to Sch.Pi.*O.* 6.88a so used in Laconian)' add 'Myc. 3 sg. pres. ind. *e-u-ke-to* (= *εὔχετοι)'
*εὐχόρευτος, ον, *excelling in the dance*, of Pan, poet. in *IG* 4².130 19 (Epid.).
εὔχορος, delete the entry (v. ‡εὔρυχ-).
*εὔχους· χώνη, Σαλαμίνιοι Hsch.
*εὐχρήσιμος, ον, *performing beneficial service*, *GDI* 3011.5 (Megara, iv BC).
εὐχρηστία **I 1**, after 'Chrysipp.*Stoic.* 3.168' insert '*PMil.Vogl.* 11.7 (ii AD)' **2**, add '*Inscr.Magn.* 58.12 (iii BC); εὐχρηστίας ποιεῖσθαί τινι *advance* him money or money's worth, *BGU* 1731.8, 1732.8 (both i BC)'
εὔχρηστος, add 'τὸ τρ[ύβ]λιον τό[δ]ε εὔχρεστον *Kafizin* 49 (221/0 BC)'
εὐχρωτέω, delete the entry.
εὐχῡμία **II 2**, delete the section.

**εὐχωλή I 1**, for '*Inscr.Cypr.* 94 H.' read 'Cypr. *e-u-ko-la* ευχōλά *ICS* 85, 220(b).3' **2**, after '*offering*' insert 'εὐχōλέν *IG* $1^3$.618 (Athens, vi BC), *Naukratis* ii p. 65.776, 777; εὐχōλὰν ἀνέθεκε *SEG* 30.1150 (Heracleia, Italy, *c*.iv BC), *AP* 6.137 (Anacr.)'

**εὔψοφος**, add 'adv. -ως Sch.Theoc. 11.57'

**εὔψῡχος**, adv. -χως, for this section read '*courageously*, X.*Eq.Mag.* 8.21, Plb. 5.23.9, al., Lxx 2*Ma.* 7.20; *magnanimously*, *IGRom.* 4.860.12'

**εὐώδης**, add '**2** εὐῶδες, τό, *sweet-smelling medicament*, Hp.*Epid.* 4.30, *Superf.* 24.'

**εὐωνίζω**, add '**2** *make cheaper*, τὴν ἀπο[ρίαν] *LW* 3.1661 (Lydia).'

**εὐώνῠμος** (A) **III**, line 2, after '*from the left*)' insert 'εὐ. πλευρωμάτων A.*Th.* 888' add '**IV** εὐώνυμοι, οἱ, a body of troops in Cyprus, *ABSA* 56.21 (ii BC).'

**εὐωρία I**, add 'Lib.*Ep.* 434.4'

***εὐωχήτρια**, fem. adj., *festal*, (ἡμέρα) ἡ τῶν ποτῶν εὐ. Leont.Byz.*HP* 1.2.5.

**εὐωχία**, add 'Astyd. 4.1 S.'

**+ἐφᾰγιστεύω**, *perform rites over* the dead, S.*Ant.* 247 (κάφα-, also interpreted as καὶ °ἀφα-).

***ἐφαγνίζω**, *perform rites over* the dead, τὰ πάντα S.*Ant.* 196 (v.l. ἀφ-).

**ἐφάλλομαι**, at end delete 'εἰς τοὐπίσω .. Gal. 6.145'

**ἔφαλος**, add 'form *ὀπίhαλος, Myc. *o-pi-*$a_2$*-ra* (neut. pl.) *coastal regions*'

***ἐφάνγρενθειν**, v. ἐφαιρέομαι.

**ἐφαπτίς**, for '*soldier's upper garment*' read 'kind of cloak, worn esp. by soldiers' and add 'Str. 11.14.12'

***ἔφαπτον**, τό, kind of cloak, cf. ἐφαπτίς, Callistr.ap.Sch.Ar.*Av.* 933.

**ἐφάπτω**, line 5, for 'she *had made fast* (i.e. perpetrated)' read 'he (sc. Hyllus) by his anger *had fastened on her* (i.e. doomed her to)' **II 5, III**, delete the sections.

**ἐφαρίξαντο**, at end of parenth. add 'ἐφατίξαντο· ἐψηφίσαντο La.'

**ἐφαρμογή**, add 'ἐφαρμογάν Ps.-Archyt. p. 30.19'

**ἐφαρμόζω II 1**, add '**c** σῆμα ἐ. *build* or *set in its place*, *AP* 7.295.7 (Leon.Tarent.).'

**ἐφέδρα II 1**, delete the section. **2**, add 'orac.ap.Phleg.*Mir.* 3'

**ἐφέδρᾰνον 3**, add 'Gal. 18(1).747.12'

***ἐφεδρευτής**, οῦ, ὁ, *one who lies in wait*, Sch.Pi.*N.* 4.155.

**ἐφεδρεύω II 2**, for '*draw a bye*' read '*wait one's turn* (having drawn a bye in the first round)' add '**5** *attend* at a meeting, [ταῖς ἐκκλησί]αις ἐφεδρεύοντες *SEG* 29.116 (Athens, iii BC).'

***ἐφεδρίς**, ίδος, ἡ, *throne*, Call.*fr.* 196.37 Pf.

**+ἐφεκτός**, όν, *on which judgement is to be suspended*, S.E.*P.* 3.55.

**ἔφεκτος**, line 2, after 'D. 34.23' insert '*BCH* 80.53 (Sigeum, ii BC)'

***ἐφελιώμενος**, app. epith. of oxen, of unkn. meaning, cf. perh. ἔφηλις II 1, *OGI* 456.22 (Mytilene, i BC).

**ἐφέλκω I 1**, add '**b** of circumstances, *bring* to a place, εἰς ἃς δήποτέ σε ὑπαρχείας τὰ κοινὰ τῶν Ῥωμαίων ἐφέλκοιτο *PKöln* 10.7-9 (i BC).' **3**, delete the section transferring 'E.*Cyc.* 151' to section I. add '**IV** w. inf., dub. in *JRS* 40.78.6 (Cyrene; letter of Hadrian), v. °ἐφολκέω.'

***ἐφενέπω**, *proclaim*, *SEG* 12.371.3 (Spartan decree engraved at Cos, iii BC) (ἐπι- + ἐνέπω, w. aspirate transferred fr. ἐνhέπω > ἐνέπω).

**ἐφεξῆς**, after lemma insert 'non-Att.-Ion. -ᾶς *BCH* suppl. 22 p. 237 (Argos, Hellen.)' **II 1**, for 'esp. with πᾶς' read 'combined w. πᾶς, all *without exception*' **3**, add '**b** *subsequently*, κρατήσει .. οὗτος ὁ νόμος .. ἐπὶ τοῖς ἐφεξῆς Just.*Nov.* 18.5, *Cod.Just.* 1.3.55.1.'

**ἐφέπω II 1**, line 2, for 'Simon. 142.2' read '*AP* 7.296.2 ([Simon.])' **B II 2**, add 'Thgn. 217, 1073'

**ἐφερμηνευτικός**, after '*explanatory*' insert 'Alex.Aphr.*in Metaph.* 745.10'

***'Ἐφεσηΐς**, ίδος, ἡ, *a celebration of the* (μεγάλα) Ἐφέσεια, used in dating, *BMus.Inscr.* 605.10 (Ephesus, ii AD).

**Ἐφέσια**, τά, add 'also Ἐφέσηα *IEphes.* 859a'

**Ἐφέσιος**, add 'epith. of Artemis esp. at Ephesus, *SEG* 33.939, etc.; at Alea, Paus. 8.23.1'

**ἔφεσις I 2**, after '*appeal*' insert 'or *referral* (v. *SEG* 28.4)' **II**, after 'Pl.*Lg.* 864b' insert '(s.v.l., cj. ἄφεσις)'

**ἐφέσπερος**, add 'ἐφέσπερον δαίουσα λαμπτῆρος σέλας *Trag.adesp.* 407 K.-S.'

**ἐφέστιος I**, add '**2** of sacrifices *offered at the* (*public*) *hearth*, οἷς *SEG* 12.371.17 (Spartan decree engraved at Cos., iii BC); cf. ἐνέστιος.' **IV**, for this section read 'fem. subst., a drink, perh. particular mark of hospitality, πίνουσα τὴν ἐπίστιον Anacr. 82.4 P. (expld. by Ath. as ἀνίσωμα)'

**ἐφέτειος**, after '(Apollonis)' insert '*TAM* 5.1206.9 (-τήϊος; Apollonis); *of the present year*, *PFam.Teb.* 3.23 (AD 92)'

**ἐφέτης III**, add 'as adj., παρὰ τῷ ἐφέτῃ δικαστῇ Just.*Nov.* 93.1'

**+ἐφετινός**, ή, όν, *of the present year*, χόρτος *POxy.* 1482.12 (ii AD), αἶγες, ἐρίφια *PMasp.* 141.6ᵛ.9, 12 (vi AD); as name of a category of ephebes, *IG* 12 suppl. 690.10.

**ἐφετός II**, delete the section.

***ἐφέτος** (unless to be taken as two words **ἐφ' ἔτος**), adv. *this year*, *IG* 5(2).433.7 (Megalopolis, ii BC), so **ἐφέτους** (or **ἐφ' ἔτους**) *Stud.Pal.* 22.23.9 (i AD; pap. εφετους), *PMich.*VIII 473.10 (ii AD); mod. Gk. φέτος.

***ἐφεύδω**, = ἐγκοιμάομαι 1, part. fut. ἐφευδησίονσαν *Inscr.Cret.* 1.xvii 3, 9 (Lebena).

**ἐφεύρεμα**, for '*IG* $2^2$.1119.6 (iii AD)' read '*SEG* 24.143 (Attica, Augustus)'

**ἐφευρίσκω I 1**, line 3, for 'Sapph.*Supp.* 4.9' read 'Sapph. 15(*b*).9 L.-P.'; line 9, after 'Sapph.l.c.' insert 'Πενία, τί σ' ἡμεῖς τηλικοῦτ' ἐφεύρομεν; Men.*Dysc.* 209'

***ἐφευροκλέψ**, unexpld. wd., Theognost.*Can.* 97 (cf. νακοκλέψ; perh. better parox.).

**ἐφηβεία 1**, add '*AP* 7.467 (Antip.Sid.)'

***ἐφήβειον**, τό, = ἐφήβαιον, *SPAW* 1934.1049 (tab.defix.).

**ἐφηβεύω**, after lemma insert 'aor. ηφήβευσαν *Inscr.Délos* 2594.4 (ii BC), pf. part. ηφηβευκότων *OGI* 178.5 (Egypt, i BC)'

**ἐφηβικός I**, add '**2** ἐφηβική (sc. παιδιά), ἡ, alternative name for the game °ἐπίσκυρος, Poll. 9.104.'

**ἔφηβος**, after lemma insert '**ἐπηβ-** *SEG* 9.72.40 (Cyrene, iv BC)' **I**, add '**3** as adj., ἐκ νηπίας ἡλικίας καὶ οὔπω τὴν ἔφηβον ἐκβάσης *Cod.Just.* 1.3.52.1, Just.*Nov.* 72 pr.'

**ἐφηβότης**, add 'cf. perh. Pamph. ἐφ[ι]ιειιόται[ *IPamph.* 3.9'

**ἐφηβοφύλαξ**, add '*AJA* 58.236 (Nicopolis)'

**ἐφηγέομαι**, add '**II** *be in charge of*, ἐφηγείσθω γε αὐταῖς (sc. ταῖς ἐπαρχείαις) ἀνὴρ εἷς Just.*Nov.* 28.2.'

**ἐφήγησις**, add '**II** *conducting* of arbitrators along disputed boundary, *Delph.* 3(1).362 i 14, 15, 25.'

**ἔφηλις II**, for '(Hp.)*Mul.* 2.215' read '(Hp.)*Mul.* 3.215'

**ἔφημαι**, line 5, for 'Id.*fr.* 157' read 'id.*fr.* 154a R.'; delete '(ἐφιμένη cod. Hsch.)'

***ἐφημερησία**, ἡ, perh. *day's work*, *PHeid.* 328.9 (iii AD).

**ἐφημερία**, add '**II** *division of guards* on duty, οἱ ἐκ τῆς μέσης ἐ. *SEG* 7.29 (Susa, i BC), cf. ib. 30.'

**ἐφημέριος**, add '**II** subst. -ιον, τό, *space of a day*, *MDAI(A)* 56.125 (nr. Sardis).'

**ἐφήμερος**, Dor. ἐπάμ-, add 'Theoc. 30.31, *CEG* 139 (Troezen, *c*.500 BC)' **III 2**, add 'neut. sg. adv., *within the same day*, *CEG* l.c.'

**ἐφθέος**, delete '*to be*'

***ἔφθιον**, τό, some kind of boiled food (?soup), *OAshm.Shelton* 74, 76, al. (sp. ἔπτιν).

***ἐφθιοπώλας**, ου, ὁ, *seller of cooked food*, *PUG* II 71.3 (vi AD).

**ἐφθός I 1**, add 'of perfumed oil, *BCH* 59.440 (Acraephia, i AD)'

**ἐφιάλτης**, line 2, add 'Dor. Ἐφιάλτᾱς (as pr. n.), *BCH* 109.94 no. N7'; line 3, after 'Alc. 129' insert '(= 406 L.-P.), Macr.*Somn.* 1.3.7'; line 4, after 'Od. 11.308' insert '*Salamine* 355 (amphora, vi BC)'

**ἐφιδύη**, for '(Theognost.*Can.*) 7.30' read '18 A.'

**ἐφίερον**, for '*IG* 3.74' read '*IG* $2^2$.1366.24'

**ἐφίημι B II 1**, after 'Isoc. 2.25' insert 'τυραννίδος Pl.*Ep.* 8.354c'

**ἐφικνέομαι I 1**, line 3, delete 'with a stick' and insert 'οὐκ ἐδύναντ' ἐπίκεσθαι (i.e. reach the apple) Sapph. 105(*a*).3 L.-P.' add '**5** ἐ. ἐς *approach* in similarity, *resemble*, Luc.*Syr.D.* 15.' **III**, delete the section.

**ἐφίμερος**, line 1, after 'ον' insert 'also °ἐπίμερος'

***ἐφινίους**· τὰς ἐπὶ τοῦ ἰνίου σάρκας Hsch. (La.; ἐφινους cod.).

**ἐφιορκέω**, after '= ἐπιορκέω' insert '*SEG* 23.320(*a*) (Delphi, iv BC)'

**ἐφιππάζομαι 3**, delete 'Palaeph. 52' add '**4** *drive*, Palaeph. 52.'

**ἐφιστάνω II 2**, line 3, for 'Ammon.*in APr.* 68.10' read 'Ammon.*in APr.* 60.18'

**ἐφίστημι A I**, add 'esp. *place* gravestone *over*, Ἀγαθόκλεια .. τῷ ἀνδρὶ .. ἐπέστησεν *BCH* 37.202 (Chios, ii BC), *SEG* 23.640 (Paphos, iv BC), cf. *GVI* 97'

**+ἐφιστορέω**, *inquire of* an oracle, ἐ. τὸν Δία .. περί .., Ἠπειρωτικὰ Χρονικά 1.254 (Dodona, iv BC, ἐπιστ-); cf. ἐφιστορεῖν· ἐπερωτᾶν Hsch.

**+ἐφοδευτής**, οῦ, ὁ, *one who goes the rounds*, of one who patrols roads as a guard, *POxy.* 1033.10, 15 (iv AD); as a spy, transl. Hebr. *rāgal*, Aq.*Ge.* 42.9.

**ἐφόδιος I**, add '**2** fem. Ἐφοδία, title of Artemis (or Hecate), *SEG* 36.329 (Nemea, archaic).'

**ἔφοδος** (C) **I 2**, add '**c** *approach* to a piece of land, *access-road*, *Mél.Navarre* p. 354.6, cf. *IG* 7.1740.6 (both Thespiae, iii BC).' **II**, line 1, for 'A.*Eu.* 375' read 'A.*Eu.* 370'

***ἐφολκέω**, *drag one's feet*, *delay*, *IG* 12 suppl. p. 213 (= *FGrH* 502) iv.19-20; w. inf., *delay to*, dub. in *JRS* 40.78.6 (Cyrene; letter of Hadrian).

**ἐφόλκιον 2**, for 'generally *appendage*' read '*baggage*' and transfer 'Plu.*Pomp.* 40' to section 1. **3**, for this section read 'ἐ.· διὰ τοῦ ι τὸ πηδάλιον Hsch.'

**ἐφολκίς**, add '**3** part of a ship, = ῥινωτηρία, Poll. 1.86.'

**ἐφομαρτέω**, add '(Arr.)*Cyn.* 16.8, *Fr.Phys.* 6 (p. 194.11 R.-W.)'

**ἐφορᾱτικός**, add '**II** prob. *obvious, apparent, BGU* 2380.8 (265 BC).'
**ἐφορμαίνω**, add '**II** *meditate, ponder*, Opp.*H.* 3.503.'
**ἔφορος II**, line 4, after '*Test.Epict.* 4.1' insert 'at Cyrene, Heraclid.Lemb.*Pol.* 10, 18 D.'
**ἐφυβριστής**, after 'Ptol.*Tetr.* 165' add '(v.l., v. sq.)'
**ἐφύβριστος I**, after 'Vett.Val. 71.18' insert 'Ptol.*Tetr.* 165'; add 'adv., -τως, *intemperately*, Posidon. 7 J. **2** *scornful, contemptuous*, ἔλεγχος ἐφύβριστος Lxx *Wi.* 17.7' **II**, delete the section.
**ἐφυδριάς**, add 'sg., Call.*fr.* 66.2 Pf.'
°**ἔφῡλος**, ον, *wooded*, τόπος *SEG* 37.100.76, 96, al. (Athens, iv BC), prob. also in *SEG* 3.117.15 (Oropus, iv BC).
**ἐφύμνιον**, for '(Call.)*Sos.* 8.4' read '(Call.)*fr.* 384.39 Pf.'
**ἐφύπερα**, add '*SEG* 23.678 (Cyprus, ii BC)'
**ἐφύπερθε**, line 3, for 'Simon. 183.7' read '*AP* 7.24.7 ([Simon.])'
°**ἐφυπερῷος**, α, ον, *upper*, οἶκος *Inscr.Délos* 1416*B* ii1 (ii BC).
**ἐχεμῡθέω**, add '*PCair.*inv. 3733(17A)(19).5 (*Atti Napoli* III 840, vi AD)'
**ἐχενηΐς II**, for 'a small .. 505ᵇ19' read 'name of various fish. **1** *blenny* or *goby*, Arist.*HA* 505ᵇ19. **2** *sucking-fish* and *lamprey* (authors confuse the two).'
**ἐχετογνώμονες**, add '(codd; cj. ὀχετο-)'
°**Ἔχετος**, epith. of Apollo, *SPAW* 1927.8 (Locris, v BC).
**ἐχεφροσύνη**, add '*SEG* 36.629 (Maced., Chr.)'
⁺**ἐχέφρων**, ον, gen. ονος, *sensible, prudent*, ἀνὴρ ἀγαθὸς καὶ ἐ. Il. 9.341, Od. 13.332; freq. as epith. of Penelope, 4.111, etc.; adv. -όνως D.S. 15.33. **II** of (normally) inanimate things, animals, etc., *endowed with a mind*, ἐχέφρονα νῆα Nonn.*D.* 1.91, νεβρὸς ἐχέφρων 5.538, 7.227, 16.226, πέτρον ἐχέφρονα Orph.*L.* 369; cf., of the gestures of a mime, ἐχέφρονι .. σιγῇ Nonn.*D.* 19.218.
°**ἔχθεμα, ἔχθεσις**, v. ‡ἐκθ-.
**ἐχθές**, line 5, for 'only form used' read 'best-attested form'
**ἔχθιστος 2**, line 3, after 'X.*An.* 3.2.5' insert 'cf. οἱ ἔχθιστοι οἱ ἐμοί Antipho 5.85'
**ἔχθρᾱ**, line 1, before 'Ion.' insert '(ἐχθρᾶν *AP* 11.340 (Pall.))'
°**ἐχθρᾰλέος**, α, ον, app. *hateful*, Nic.*Al.* 594 (v.l. ἐχθομένη).
**ἐχθρία**, add '*PMich.*VIII 516.10 (iii AD; ἐκθ-)'
°**ἔχθῡμα**, v. °ἔκθυμα.
**ἐχθύσῃ**, after lemma insert '(-σσῃ La.)'
**ἔχθω** (A), line 5, after '(Od.) 14.366' insert 'σφετέρῳ δ' ἤχθοντο τοκῆι Hes.*Th.* 155'
°**ἐχίδνηκτος**, ον, *bitten by a viper*, Theognost.*Can.* 96.
**ἔχιδνα**, line 2, delete 'prob. of a *constrictor snake*' and after '*Act.Ap.* 28.3' insert 'spec., of the female, Arist.*Mir.* 846ᵇ18'
**ἐχῑνέες**, for pres. def. read '*spiny mice, Acomys* sp.' and after '(v.l. ἐχῖνες)' insert 'Ael.*NA* 15.26'
**ἐχῑνόπους**, add 'Plin.*HN* 11.18'
**ἐχῖνος II 2**, for pres. def. read '*jar* in which were sealed various documents relating to impending court cases (v. *Hesperia* suppl. 19.3f.)'
**ἐχῐόδηκτος**, for '= ἐχιδνόδηκτος' read '*bitten by a viper*'
**ἔχῐς II**, delete '636'
**ἔχμα**, add 'Myc. *e-ka-ma-te, -ma-pi* (instr. sg. and pl.), prob. *strut* (of table)'
°**ἐχόμενα**, adv. pres. part. of ἔχομαι, *in succession* or *next*, *SB* 4325 vi 9, viii 5 (iii AD), *PPetr.* 2 p. 118 (iii BC), cf. *PLond.* 267.3 (ii AD). **2** w. gen., *near*, Lxx *Jd.* 19.14, *Ps.* 139(140).6, *Am.* 2.8; *next to, adjoining*, *PPetr.* 3 p. 2.22 (iii BC), *PStrassb.* 29.36 (iii AD). **b** w. gen. of person, *with, beside*, δόξον ἐμὲ εἶναι ἐ. σου *PCol.* in *CPR* 30.145.24 (i/ii AD), cf. *PGiss.* 77.11 (ii AD). **II** *immediately*, *PSI* 514.8 (iii BC).
**ἐχομένιον**, before '*coriander*' insert 'plant, sts. identified as'; add 'also ὀχομ- *POxy.* 2284*B*6 (iii AD)'
°**ἐχόνομα**, = °ἐχόμενα, as prep. w. gen., *OFlorida* 14.7 (ii AD), *PPetaus* 29 (ii AD), *PMich.*VIII 510.15 (ii/iii AD), etc.
⁺**ἐχόντως**, adv. fr. part. of ἔχω, *in the manner of one having*, εἰ μὲν οὖν ἀφρόνως ἢ καὶ νοῦν ἐ. ταῦτ' ἐδόξαζον Isoc. 5.7, Pl.*Lg.* 686e; cf. ἆρ' οὐκ .. ἐχόντως ἑαυτὸν τὸν νοῦν φήσομεν .. ἀποκρίνασθαι; δικαίως καὶ λόγον ἐ. Isoc. 7.60.
**ἐχῠρός I 1**, after '*secure*' insert 'ἐς δ' ἐ. λίμενα Alc. 6.8 L.-P.'
°**ἐχύρωσις**, εως, ἡ, *strengthening*, πρὸς ἐχύρ[ωσιν πυ]λῶν *PBeatty Panop.* 1.386, 390, 406 (AD 298); cf. ὀχύρωσις.
°**ἐχῠσία**, ας, ἡ, app. for *ἐκχυσία (= ἔκχυσις), perh. *scoop*, *PKöln* 234.9 (AD 431).
**ἔχω** (A), line 4, after 'inf.' insert 'ἐξέμεν Il. 5.473' and for 'Call.*Aet.* 3.1.27' read 'Call.*fr.* 75.27 Pf.'; seven lines before 'A', after '(Il.) 21.345' insert 'cf. B.26.15 S.-M.' and after 'Od. 11.279' insert 'Pi.*fr.* 52u.17'; after 'Isoc. 19.11' insert 'Pl.*Prt.* 321c (s.v.l.)' **A I 1**, add '**b** *have* an ἀγών, i.e. a victory in it, *to one's credit*, *Delph.* 3(1).554, *IG* 14.1102.14 (Rome); Ἀσκλήπεια ib. 737.9 (Neapolis; all ii AD).' **II 1**, add '**b** of hunters, fishermen, *to have caught*, Certamen 326, cf. Ar.*Nu.* 733.' **3**, line 5, after 'etc.' insert 'but ὀϊστούς, ἄρδιν ἔ. *have in one's flesh, in one's heart*, Call.*Epigr.* 37.5 Pf., *fr.* 70 Pf., cf. *AP* 6.9.3 (Mnasalc.)' **4 a**, after 'Arist.*Pol.* 1335ᵇ18' insert 'Sm.*Mi.* 6.14' **5**, delete the section transferring exx. to section 9 (*check, stop*) **8**, line 21, delete 'ἕξει .. (Laodicea)'; add '**b** *support, sustain* an action, πόλεμον Il. 14.100.' **B I 4**, add '*be concerned* with, [ἔ]ξι πρὸ[ς] τὸν Θεὸν [ὅσ]τις κρείνι δ[ικαίους καὶ ἀδίκους] Mitchell *N.Galatia* 246; *JRS* 14.88 (Laodicea)' **II 2**, add 'ὡς ἔχω w. vb. of movement, *immediately, quickly*, Hdt. 2.121. δ, Th. 3.30.1, Ar.*Eq.* 488, Lys. 376, Men.*Dysc.* 559; w. vb. of speaking, *in a straightforward manner, directly*, Isoc. 9.30, 15.311' **III 3**, add 'Paus. 9.38.10, 10.28.2' **IV 1**, add '**b** πιών .. τρίτην ταύτην ἡμέραν ἔχω, i.e. it is two days since I drank, Alciphr. 3.32.' **2**, add 'ληρεῖς ἔχων Cratin. 208 K.-A.' **C I 3**, line 6, of time, add 'τῇ ἐχομένῃ ἡμέρᾳ *SEG* 31.122 (Attica, c.AD 121/2); τῆι ἐχομένηι εἰς Κροκοδίλων πόλιν καταπλέωμεν *PKöln* 262.5 (iii BC)'; at end for 'τὰ ἐχόμενα .. Isoc. 6.29)' read 'τὰ ἐχόμενα, *what follows*, Pl.*Grg.* 494e (s.v.l.), Isoc. 6.29' **V**, for 'pass. .. B I' read '*stand, be*, cf. B I 1, II' and add 'see also °ἐν A I 6' at end add 'Myc. 3 sg. and pl. *e-ke, e-ko-si*; inf. *e-ke-e*; part. *e-ko, e-ko-te* (masc. sg. and pl.); cf. compd. pers. n. *e-ke-da-mo, e-ke-me-de*'
**ἔχω** (B), for '3 sg. aor. 1 .. *Inscr.Cypr.* 66 H.' read 'Cypr. *e-we-xe*, perh. ἔϜεξε, *brought as an offering*, *ICS* 245'
**ἑψητός II**, add 'Eup. 5, 16 K.-A., *IGC* p. 99 B2 (Acraephia, iii/ii BC)'
°**ἕωθε**, = ἕωθεν, *Didyma* 384.4.
**ἕωθεν 1**, add 'ἕωθεν ἑκάστης ἡμέρας *SEG* 37.1019 (Pergamon, ii AD)'
**ἑωθινός 1**, line 2, after 'Ar.*Ach.* 20' insert '*IG* 1³.68.30'; after 'Bato 5.3' insert 'Alciphr. 1.34, cf. perh. Macho 314 G. (s.v.l.)'; line 8, delete 'cf. .. (dub. l.)'
**ἕωλος 2**, at end delete 'of payments .. AD)' (v. *OBodl.* i 49).
**ἐώρα**, after 'αἰώρα' insert 'I 2'; for 'Ael.Dion.*fr.* 23' read 'Ael.Dion. α59 Erbse, cf. Phot., Suid. **II**' after 'Arist.*fr.* 515' insert 'codd. Ath.' and after 'αἰ- codd.' add 'Poll.'
**ἕως** (B) **A I 2**, at end delete 'ἕ. οὗ .. 8.32' **6**, line 3, after 'X.*Cyr.* 5.1.25' insert 'ἕως ὅτε περίεισι *for as long as they live*, *Cod.Just.* 6.48.1.15'; line 4, after 'later Gr.' insert 'Lxx *Jd.* 3.30, al.', for 'Gem.l.c.' read 'Gem. 8.32' and after 'etc.' insert 'ἕ. ἂν οὗ Macho 454 G.' **III b**, add 'exceptionally ἕως ἂν ὅσου ζῷ *as long as* she may live, *Sokolowski* 1.79.7 (?Pednelissos, i BC)'
**Ἑωσφόρος**, line 2, after 'Pi.*I.* 4(3).24' insert '*Trag.adesp.* 664.27 K.-S.' add '**II** transf., of illustrious persons (cf. ἀστήρ II), Ἀονίης Πολύδωρον Ἑ. ἀστέρα πάτρης Nonn.*D.* 5.208.'

# Z

**ζâ**, delete the entry (v. γῆ). for 'Cypr. *za-ne*' v. °ὐϝαις.

***ζαβέρνα**, ἡ, *bag*, *Edict.Diocl.* 11.2, 7, 7a.

***Ζαγκλαῖοι**, οἱ, *inhabitants of Zancle* (v. sq.), Hdt. 6.23.2, 3, al.; Δανκλαῖοι Dubois *IGDS* 2 (Elis, vi BC).

**ζάγκλη II**, for this section read 'old name of Messene in Sicily, Hdt. 6.23.2, Th. 6.4.5, etc.; also Δάνκλε̄ν Dubois *IGDS* 3 (Elis, vi BC), Δάγκλᾱ, perh. in *SEG* 26.1122 (Syracuse, vii BC)'

**ζάημι**, after 'Hsch.' insert 'fem. ζάεισαι dub. in (?)Alc. 261(*b*).7 L.-P.'

**ζᾱής**, add 'Q.S. 3.619'

**ζάθεος**, after '(E.*Tr.*) 1075 (lyr.)' insert 'Boeot. δάθιος Corinn. 1(*a*).i.13 P.'; line 6, delete 'ἄνεμοι Hes.*Th.* 253'; at end delete 'later' and after 'of persons' insert 'Corinn.l.c., Philod.Scarph. 139'

***ζάκαρπος**, ον, *fruitful*, Cyr., v. *QIFG* 2.104.

**ζακορεύω**, add 'w. gen., τοῦ .. Ἀσσκληπιοῦ *IG* $2^2$.4521*a* (ii AD)'

***ζακορία** (**ζακόρια** La.)· θυσία Ἀφροδίτης Hsch.

**ζακρυόεις**, after '*freezing*' insert 'or (= δακρυόεις) *full of lamentation*'

**+ζἄλάω**, *rage*, transf. of a skin eruption, ἀμφὶ δὲ γυίοις χειμερίη ζαλόωσα πέριξ βέβριθε χάλαζα Nic.*Th.* 252.

**+ζαλλεύω**, v. ζηλεύω.

***ζαμβῦκη**· μουσικὸν ὄργανον Hsch., Phot.

**ζἄμενής**, delete 'neut. as adv. .. Nic.*Th.* 181' (v. °ἐπιζαμενής).

**ζαμίλαμπις**, transfer to follow ζαμία and add 'Plin.*HN* 37.185'

**ζἄπεδον**, after 'Paros' insert '*c.*500 BC'; add 'also cj. in *h.Cer.* 283, Stesich.*S* 15 i 17 P.'

**ζάπλουτος**, add 'Lat. *saplutus*, Petron.*Sat.* 37.6'

***ζάρωμα**, ατος, τό, *wrinkle*, ῥυτίδας ἤτοι ζαρώματα Cyr.

***ζάτρἄφος**, ον, app. *well-fed*, Alcm. 134 P.

**ζαχρεῖος**, after '*needy*' insert 'ἔπη *of sore need*, prob. in A.*Supp.* 194.

**+ζέα**, v. ‡ζειά.

**ζειά**, lines 1/2, after 'ἡ' insert 'also **ζεά** D.H. 2.25, Dsc. 2.89, 3.74, *Hippiatr.* 1 p. 8; **ζεή** *PPetr.* 2 p. 69 (iii BC)' and for '*one-seeded .. monococcum*' read '*emmer, Triticum dicoccum*'; lines 7ff., for 'ζειὰ .. Gal. l.c.' to end of article read 'Thphr.*HP* 8.9.2, al. (where ὄλυρα is a cultural variety); including also *one-seeded wheat, Triticum monococcum*, ζέα δισσή· ἡ μὲν γὰρ ἁπλῆ ἡ δὲ δίκοκκος καλεῖται Dsc. 2.89 (v.l. ζειά) = Gal. 6.517.17. **2** = λιβανωτὶς κάρπιμος, Dsc. 3.74. **II** *the roof of a horse's mouth*, Hippiatr. l.c.'

***Ζειρήνη** (**-νίς** La.)· Ἀφροδίτη ἐν Μακεδονίᾳ Hsch.

**ζεστάκρατα**, add 'also sg., Paul.Aeg. 7.5.13 (283.14 H.)'

**ζετραία**, add '(v.l. ζεταία)'

**ζευγίον**, for '= ζύγον III 2' read '*yoke*'

**ζεύγλη I 2**, delete '–Not .. Prose.'

**ζεῦγμα I 2**, for this section read 'applied to a bridge of boats, Plb. 3.46.2, 4, τὰ ζ. τῶν ποταμῶν D.H. 9.31, Plu. 2.174e; also, to boats lashed together to form a floating platform, id.*Marc.* 14, 15. **b** applied to a normal bridge, *AP* 9.147 (Antag.).' add '**III** a constellation, Vett.Val. 10.2.'

**ζευγματικόν**, delete the entry (v. °ζευγματικός).

***ζευγμἄτικός**, ή, όν, πλοῖον ζ. some kind of cargo transport, *POxy.* 2415.44 (iii AD); w. ellipsis of πλοῖον, ib. 56. **2** -όν, τό, app. a type of customs-duty, *PLond.* 3.1157.6, al., *POxy.* 2129.4, 3180.5 (all iii AD).

**ζεῦγος II 2**, for this section read '*double-reed mouthpiece*, Arist.*Aud.* $804^a13$, Thphr.*HP* 4.11.4, 6' **IV**, at the beginning insert 'a land measure, *SEG* 37.859.C6 (Heracleia on the Latmos, late 2 BC); cf. ζυγόν X' at end add 'Myc. *ze-u-ke-si* (dat. pl.), *pair*'

***ζεύκτρα**, ἡ, app. some form of bond or fastening, ζεύ[κ]τρας σχοίνιναι perh. *plaited-reed ropes*, *BGU* 2361a i 2 (iv AD).

***Ζευξάνθιος**, epith. of Poseidon, *AE* 1933 Chron. p. 1 (Crannon).

**ζεῦξις I**, for 'oxen' read 'animals' add '**2** *yoked beasts*, Sch.E.*Ph.* 847.'

**Ζεύς**, dat., add 'Ζί *SEG* 31.364 (Olympia, *c.*500 BC)'; line 24, for 'Aeschrio 8.5' read '*AP* 7.345' **IV**, Διὸς ἡμέρα, add '*SEG* 30.1212 (Rome)' add 'Myc. *di-we* (dat.), *di-wo* (gen.); (see also δῖος)'

**ζεφύριος III**, add 'cape in Egypt, St.Byz.'

**ζεφῦρῖτις**, for '= foreg. III, .. ζεφυρῆτις 1' read 'epith. of Arsinoe-Aphrodite, from her temple at Zephyrion in Egypt, St.Byz. s.v. Ζεφύριον, Call.*fr.* 110.57 Pf., *Epigr.* 5.1 Pf., Posidipp. 12.7, 13.3 (*EG* 1624, 1630 P.) (prob. corr. of Ζεφυρηΐδος, v. ζεφυρῆτις 1)'

**Ζέφῠρος**, add 'cf. Myc. *ze-*$pu_2$*-ro*, pers. n.; *ze-*$pu_2$*-*$ra_3$, description of women, ?from place-name'

**ζέω I 3**, add 'ὅθεν καὶ Ὅμηρος .. "ἔζεσεν αἷμα" Arist.*EN* $1116^b29$, Theoc. 20.15' at end add 'Myc. fut. ?pass. part. *ze-so-me-no* (dat.)'

**ζηλεύω**, after '= ζηλόω' insert 'Aeol. imper. 3 pl. ζαλλευόντω̄ν Alc. 5.10 L.-P.'

**ζηλοδοτήρ**, for '*giver of bliss*' read 'as epith. of Dionysus, *giver of success, good fortune*'

**ζῆλος II**, add 'ζῆλον ἔχο̄σ' .. τὸμ μακαριστότατον *CEG* 538.2 (Attica, iv BC)' **III 2**, for 'esp. .. *style*' read 'of oratorical style, *showiness*'

**ζηλόω**, after '(ζῆλος)' insert 'Thess. pf. inf. ἐζᾱλουκέμεν *BCH* 59.55 (Larissa, ii BC)' **I**, line 5, after 'Lxx *Si.* 9.1' insert 'ἐπί τινι ib.*Ps.* 72(73).3' **II**, line 3, after '(D.) 20.141' insert 'ἔργον .. φαῦλον ζ. Men.*Dysc.* 289'

**ζημία**, line 1, after 'Dor. ζᾱμία' insert '[τὰ]ν ζᾱμίιαν *SEG* 30.380 no. 7 (Tiryns, vii BC)'

**ζημιόω**, after lemma insert 'Cret. pres. inf. ζᾱμιόμε̄ν *Inscr.Cret.* 2.v 1.4 (Axos, vi BC); δᾱμιόμε̄ν ib. 4.80.6 (Gortyn, v BC), Boeot. pres. part. δᾱμιώοντες *Schwyzer* 528.14 (Orchomenos, iii/ii BC)' **II**, line 3, after 'Pl.*Lg.* 936a' insert 'w. acc. δαρκνᾶν *Inscr.Cret.* l.c.'

***ζήνη**, ἡ, *goldfinch*, Cyran. 89 (3.14.1 K.).

***ζητάριος**, ὁ, Lat. *cetarius*, *fishmonger*, *SB* 9152.9 (AD 492).

**ζητητής II**, add 'also a sim. officer at Mylasa, *IMylasa* 132.1'

**ζιγγίβερις**, for 'perh. .. *singaber*)' read '(cf. Skt. *śṛṅgavera-*, prob. orig. Dravidian)'

***ζινίχια**, ἡ, unkn. substance in list of metals, Anon.Alch. 25.3.

**ζμάραγδος** and derivatives, v. ‡σμαρ-.

***ζμηνών**, v. °σμηνών.

***ζόμβρος**, ὁ, kind of bull or bison, *AP* 9.300 tit.

***Ζόννυσος**, v. °Διόνυσος.

***ζορκάδιον**, τό, = δορκάδιον, *Cat.Cod.Astr.* 8(2).164.12.

**ζοφερός 1**, add 'E.*fr.* 868'

**ζοφοειδής**, add 'μολίβου ζοφοειδέος Nic.*Th.* 256, νυκτὸς πέπλον Orph.*H.* 7.10, cf. 18.8, 71.9'

**ζόφος 1**, add 'E.*Hipp.* 1416'

***ζτε̄ραῖος**, α, ον, Arc. adj. of uncertain sense (cf. ζειρά), used in description of a garment, ζ. λο̂πος *SEG* 11.1112 (Pheneos, vi/v BC; v. Dubois *Dial.arcad.* pp. 197/8).

**ζύγαινα**, after '*shark*' insert 'A.*fr.* 46a.9 R.'

***ζυγάς**, άδος, ἡ, v.l. for ξυστάς, Poll. 7.147 (v. °ξυστάς).

**ζῠγάστριον**, after 'of sq.' insert '*IAskl.Epid.* 52.B63-66'; add '*IG* $4^2$.118.61, 63'

**ζύγαστρον**, after 'τό' insert 'Boeot. **δύγ-** *SEG* 24.361.23 (Thespiae, 386/0 BC)'

***ζῠγία** (B), ἡ, = ζεῦξις, νυμφίδιαι ζ., i.e. wedlock, *GVI* 653 (Syros, ii/iii AD).

**ζύγιος II**, before 'epith. of Hera' insert '*of marriage, nuptial*, ζ. .. θαλάμων *GVI* 1431 (Athens, ii AD)' **III**, for 'κώπη' to end of section read '**b** *of a* ζυγίτης or ζυγῖται, κώπη *IG* $2^2$.1604.71; κῶπαι ib. 1607.59, 1609.51 (all iv BC), Polyaen. 5.22.4.'

**ζῠγομἄχέω 1**, add 'Plu. 2.445c' **2**, after '*Com.adesp.* 207' insert 'Men.*Dysc.* 17'

**ζῠγόν**, line 1, after 'in various senses' insert 'in Lxx masc. where determinable, exc. neut. pl. *Le.* 19.36' **I 2**, add 'w. ref. to a bridge, A.*Pers.* 72' **II 1**, after 'φόρμιγξ' insert 'and sim. instruments' and add 'Thphr.*HP* 5.7.6' **III 2**, for '*panels* of a door' read '*cross-pieces* of a door'; delete 'cf. ζευγίον' **IV**, add '*PColl.Youtie* 92.28 (AD 569)' **VIII**, of the chorus, add 'Sch. Ar.*Pax* 733 D.' **X**, add 'cf. ‡ζεῦγος 4'

**ζῠγοποιός**, add '*AD* 24.300 (Thessalonica; see also *SEG* 33.495)'

**ζῠγοστἄσία**, add '**b** = ζυγοστάσιον, *weigh-house*, *PLond.* 301.11 (ii AD).'

**ζῠγοστάσιον 2**, for '*Cod.Just.* 11.28.1' read '*Cod.Theod.* 14.26.1'

**ζῠγοστἄτέω I a**, add '*weigh out, allot*, τοῖς θεοῖς τὰς τιμάς Max.Tyr. 39.5'

**ζῠγοστάτης**, add '*PAlex.* 40.2 (iv/v AD), *Corinth* 8(1).158; of Hermes (as patron of ἀγορανόμοι), *Illion* 4.9'

***ζύγωσις**, εως, ἡ, *weighing* of money, prob. in *CPR* 8.40.3 (iv AD).

**+ζῡθοπώλης**, v. °ζυτο-.

*__ζῦμάριον__, τό, _ferment_, Anon.Alch. 20.3 (mod. Gk. ζυμάρι _dough_).
__ζῦμουργός__, after '_leaven_' insert '_POxy._ 754 (i AD)'
__ζῡμόω 2__, delete 'γῆν Gal. 10.964'
*__ζῦτικός__, ή, όν, _of beer_, τιμή _PMich._II 121$^r$4.vi 2 (i AD); -κόν, τό, _beer-tax_, _PTeb._ 337 intr. (ii/iii AD), _PLond._ 254$^v$.70 (ii AD).
*__ζῦτοπώλης__, ου, ό, _beer-seller_, _PMil.Vogl._ 278.22 (ii AD), _BGU_ 2280b.1 (AD 276); ζυθο- _POxy._ 85 iv 4 (iv AD).
__ζῶ__, line 17, before 'Cret. __δώω__' insert 'Boeot. __δώω__ _Schwyzer_ 509.14 (Lebadea, iii BC), etc.'; line 20, after 'ἔζωσα' insert 'Call._fr._ 191.39 Pf.' __I 1__, add 'part., on a tablet set up to a person in his/her lifetime, ζώσῃ φρονο[ύ]σῃ Πρωτογένης ἀνέστησεν συμβίῳ Ἀργυρίδι Mitchell _N.Galatia_ 93, cf. φρονέω IV lines 13ff.; also of a survivor in a joint epitaph, ib. 108, _SEG_ 30.595 (Maced., ii/iii AD)'
*__ζώγιος__, v. °ζῶκος.
__ζωγράφημα__, add 'Plu._Tim._ 36, id. 2.64a, etc., _SEG_ 36.1287 (Syria, Chr.)'
*__ζωγράφησις__, εως, ή, _painting_, _ISmyrna_ 685.3 (iv AD).
__ζωγρᾰφητός__, add 'prob. in _Dura_$^4$ p. 93'
__ζωγρᾰφία II 1__, add '_Inscr.Magn._ 107.13 (ii BC), Phld._Rh._ 2.166 S.'
__ζωγρᾰφος__, delete '(ζωγρ- without iota' and 'so ζωγραφία' to end of article.
__ζωγρέω I__, pass., add 'Isoc. 12.194' __II__, line 2, after '(quoted by Aret._CA_ 2.3)' insert 'perh. _activate_, ἐπὶ φλογὶ ζωγρηθεῖσα χαλβάνη Nic._Th._ 51 (v.l. μοιρηθεῖσα)'
__ζῳδιᾰκός__, after 'Adv. -κῶς' insert '_according to_, or _by the zodiac_' and after 'Vett.Val. 22.12' insert '137.27, al.'
__ζῴδιον II__, add 'Vett.Val. 22.12'
__ζῳδιωτός__, after '= ζῳωτός' insert 'λάρναξ _Inscr.Délos_ 1409_Ba_ ii36 (ii BC)'
__ζωή I 2__, add 'ἐν ζωῇ _during_ (_his_) _lifetime_, _Cod.Just._ 1.3.45.8' __II__, add 'Myc. _zo-a_'
*__ζωητόκος__, ον, = ζωοτόκος, Theognost._Can._ 87.
__ζωθαλπής__, after 'Nonn._D._ 1.454' insert 'ζωθαλπέες Ὧραι ib. 16.397' and delete 'fem. ζώθαλπις' to end.
+__ζωϊτός__ or __-τόν__, app. some form of sculptured figure(s), _Inscr.Délos_ 104-24.26 (iv BC); cf. ζῳοφόρος I.
*__ζῶκος__, ό, ζ. ἐστι πτηνόν· οἱ δὲ ζώγιον (vv.ll. ζύγγιον, etc.) φασι, οἱ δὲ ἴρπην. ἔστι δὲ εἶδος λευκοῦ γυπὸς νεκροβόρου Cyran. 17 (1.6.9 K.).
*__ζωκρός__, = ζωρός, comp. ζωκρότερον _GVI_ 1815.7 (Naxos, i/ii AD).
__ζωκτήρ__, add '_PAbinn._ 4.8 (iv AD; but perh. for ζευκτ-, cf. °ζωκτήριον)'
*__ζωκτήριον__, τό, unexpld. item in an account, perh. = ζευκτήριον, _BGU_ 2357 ii 15 (iii AD).
__ζωμᾰρυστρον__, add '_PAlex._ 31.8 (iii/iv AD)'
__ζωμός__, after 'fish, etc.' insert 'Asius 14.3 W.'
__ζωνάριον__, add '_Inscr.Délos_ 1442_A_52 (146/5 BC), _PMich._XV 740.8 (vi AD)'
__ζώνη__, line 1, after '(ζώννυμι)' insert 'Cret. τώνā, Hsch.' __I 1 c__, transfer this section to follow section II 1 b __3__, prov., add 'Philostr._VA_ 2.31'
__ζώννῡμι I__, for pres. def. read '_surround with a belt_ or _girdle_, _gird_' and add 'σεαυτόν _Ev.Jo._ 21.18' __II__, for pres. def. read '_fasten_ or _secure one's dress with a belt_ or _girdle_ as a prelude to action' and add '_Act.Ap._ 12.8'
*__ζωνοβαλλάντι(ο)ν__, τό, _belt-purse_, pap. in _Eos_ 32.30 (v/vi AD).
*__ζωνομᾰχαιρα__, ή, _a knife carried in the belt_, _dagger_, Sch.B Il. 19.252.
*__ζωνοπώλης__, ου, ό, _belt-seller_, _SEG_ 39.1176B 10 (_BE_ 1993 p.489 no.196, Ephesus, i AD).
__ζωογόνος__, for '_animals_' read '_living things_'
*__ζῳολογικός__, ή, όν, _concerning animals_, τὰς πραγματείας Ἀριστοτέλους τὰς ζ. Sch.Luc. 131.9.
__ζῷον I__, add 'extended to include plants, Pl._Ti._ 77a; cf. also Arist._PA_ 681$^a$33' __II__, add 'sp. δῶια (pl.), _SEG_ 32.1612 (iii BC)' __III__, for 'till after the middle of the fifth cent. BC' read 'before Semonides'
__ζῳοπλαστέω__, delete '_mould to the life_' and 'analogous to ζωγραφέω'
__ζῳοπλάστης II__, add 'Heph.Astr. 2.19.15, Ptol._Tetr._ 180'
*__ζωοποιός__, όν, _bringing about_ (_supernatural_) _life_, of a holy person, _PLond._ 1303.2 (_Tyche_ 6.198, AD 498).
+__ζῳοπώλης__, ου, ό, ζωοπώλᾱς· ὁ τὰ ἱερὰ ζῶα πιπράσκων. καὶ ὁ τόπος ζωοπωλίς (-πώλιον L.Dindorf) Hsch.
+__ζωοπωλίς__, ᾰ́, (sc. ἀγορά), _animal-market_, v. ζῳοπώλης; gen. sg. ζωπωλίδος rest. in _GDI_ 5224 I 12 (Tauromenium; v. Dubois _IGDS_ 186).
__ζωός__, line 1, after '__δωός__' insert '(or δοός)'; line 2, for 'ΖωϜόθεμις _Schwyzer_ 684' read '_zo-wo-te-mi-se_, perh. ΖωϜόθεμις _ICS_ 354'; line 5, after 'A._Eleg._ 3' insert 'of a surviving relative, on an epitaph, Διοσκουρίδης Μουκασου .. ζωὸς ἑαυτῷ καὶ Σουρᾳ Μουκασου συνβίῳ _SEG_ 30.596 (Maced., AD 106); masc. pl. as subst., the _living_, Il. 23.47, etc.; ἐν ζωοῖσι καὶ ἐν Ἀΐδαο δόμοισι epigr. in _ISmyrna_ 550.2'
__ζωοτόκος__, before 'opp. ᾠοτόκος' insert '_viviparous_'
*__ζωοφθόρος__· καὶ σαλαμάνδρα. καὶ ἀγγεῖον νεκροῦ Hsch. (La.; cod. -φόρος).
__ζωπύρωσις__, for '_kindling_' read '_fanning into flame_'
*__ζώπωλις__, v. °ζωοπωλίς.
__ζωροποτέω__, for 'Call._fr._ 109' read 'Call._fr._ 178.12 Pf. (v.l. ap. Ath. 10.442f)'
__ζωρός__, line 5, after 'Arist._Po._ 1461$^a$14' insert 'Plu. 2.677c-678c'; line 6, after 'Ephipp. 10' insert 'Philum._Ven._ 2.3, 4.2'; at end for note in parenth. substitute '__2__ app. understood by Empedocles (from Homer) as _"mixed"_, Emp. 35.15 D.-K.'
__ζωστήρ__, line 4, after 'Pi._fr._ 172' insert 'E._HF_ 415, _Heracl._ 217' __III 1__, for '_stripe marking certain height in the ship_' read '_one of the horizontal rows of planking forming the external shell of a boat_' __IV 2__, after 'Zoster' insert '_IG_ $2^3$.369.67' and delete '(sed leg. ζωστήριος)'
__Ζωστήριος__, add '__3__ Ζωστήρια, τά, festival of Apollo Zoster, _AD_ 11.40 (Attica).'
__ζώστρα__, for '_head-band_, _fillet_' read '_encircling band_ or _ribbon_'
__ζώφυτος I__, add 'sp. σόφυτος _PMich._IX 540.8 (AD 53)'
__ζώωσις__, add 'Aq._Ge._ 45.5'

# H

**ἤ** (A), line 1, after 'Ep. also **ἠέ**' insert '(q.v. in Suppl.)' **A I 3**, add '(ἤ ..) ἢ ἔπειτα *either* .. *or* (failing that), Il. 13.742-3, 20.120, 24.356; but in Alc. 129.19 L.-P. ἤπειτα (= ἢ ἔπειτα) introduces the more desirable alternative' **3**, add 'S.*Ph.* 983, E.*Alc.* 628, And. 1.33, X.*Ath.* 2.12' add '**4** ἢ καὶ *and/or*, *PPetaus* 25.8 (ii AD), *CPR* 5.11.12 (?early iv AD).' **B 1**, line 7, after '*Tab.Heracl.* 1.121' insert 'ἰν τῶι ὕστερον Ϝέτ[ε]ι ἢ Νικῆς ἐδᾶμιόργη *in the year after* .. *SEG* 37.340.23 (Mantinea, iv BC)'

**ἤ** (C) **1**, for this section read 'Cypr. *e-ke*, v. εἰ' **2**, for 'Cret. for *when*' read 'Cret. **ἔ**, *starting from the time when*'

**ἦ**, adv., **I**, line 7, delete 'ἦ δῆτα S.*OT* 429'

**ᾗ I**, Dor. **ᾇ**, add 'ᾆι ὕδωρ ῥεῖ *Inscr.Cret.* 4.182.11 (Gortyn, ii BC); *hᾶι* μὲν .. *hᾶι* δὲ *on this side* .. *and on that*, *Tab.Heracl.* 1.81' add '**2** of time, ᾆι ὄκ(α) *from that time when*, *Inscr.Cret.* 4.72 v 4.' **II**, add '**4** = ἵνα, *in order that*, *Inscr.Cret.* 4.41 ii 11 (v BC), 168*.24 (iii BC).'

***ἡβαδόν**, v. °ἡβηδόν.

***ἡβάζω**, = ἡβάω, *cum vero* ἡβάζοντα *(significat)*, *pubes puberis (declinatur)*, Charis. p. 542 K.

**ἡβάω 1**, for '*attain* or *have attained puberty*' read '*to have passed puberty, be a young adult*' **2**, penultimate line, for 'Simon. 183.3' read '*AP* 7.24.3 ([Simon.])'

**ἥβη I 1 c**, for pres. def. read '*legal puberty*, at Athens attained at the age of sixteen' **II**, delete 'Dor. .. Theoc. 5.109'

**ἡβηδόν**, after lemma insert 'Dor. ἡβᾱδόν *Tit.Calymn.* xii 10'

***ἡβοκᾶτος**, ὁ, v. °ἡουοκᾶτος.

***ἡβότᾱ**, ᾱ, *young men* (collect.), perh. in *hε*Ϝόταισι (dat. pl.) *IPamph.* 3.7 (iv BC).

**ἠγάθεος**, Πυθώ, add 'Od. 8.80, *h.Hom.* 24.2, B. 3.62, 5.41 (ἀγ-); Ἑλλάς *Carm.Pop.* 21.1 P.'

**ἥγανον**, add 'also Boeot. τυροκνασστίδες τρῖς, Ϝαγάνω δύο *SEG* 24.361.19 (Thespiae, iv BC)'

**ἡγέμαχος**, add 'Dor. ἁγέμαχος, Simon.*fr.eleg.* 11.14 W[2].'

**ἡγεμόνεια**, add 'Dor. **ἁγ-**, ὅρος Ἀρτέμιδος Ἀγεμονείας Ὀρθωσίας *IG* 12(5).894 (Tenos, ii BC)'

**ἡγεμονέω**, add 'τὸ ἡγεμονοῦν *ruling principle*, Plot. 4.7.7'

**ἡγεμόνη**, add 'of Hecate, Orph.*H.* 1.8, of Physis, ib. 10.12'

**ἡγεμονικός II 2**, before '= *consularis*' insert '*of a* ‡ἡγεμών II 1 c, οὔτε διὰ ψηφίσματος οὔτε δι' ἐντεύξεως ἡγεμονικῆς *MAMA* 8.554'

**ἡγεμών II 1 a**, line 5, after 'Th. 8.89' insert 'στρατηγοῖς ἱππάρχαις, πεζῶν ἡγεμόσι *Amyzon* 10 (iii/ii BC)' **c**, add 'title of officials at Istria, *IHistriae* 6.1, al. (iii/ii BC); leader of ephebes at Athens, *SEG* 26.176.61 (AD 170/1–175/6); magistrate at Chalcis, *SEG* 29.806 (120/100 BC)' add '**d** as divine title, τ[ὸν Ἑρ]μῆν τὸν Ἡγεμ[όνα] *SEG* 23.547.53 (Crete, 201/200 BC)'.

**ἡγέομαι**, line 1, for 'irreg.' read 'Cret.'; line 4, after 'cf. περιηγ-' insert 'καθηγ-' **I 1 f**, before 'of logical priority' insert '*come earlier, precede*, *Cod.Just.* 1.2.24.9' **II 3 d**, add '*SEG* 30.1688 (Palestine, AD 576/8), 30.1704 (Arabia, vi AD)'

**ἠγερέθομαι**, line 2, after 'impf.' insert '(exc. ἠγερέθεσθε A.R. 2.632)'

⁺**ἡγεσία**, ἡ, *leading the way, guiding*, Amph.*hom.* 4.7.231 (117 D.), Gr.Naz.*Carm.* 1.1.8.91 (*PG* 37.453a), ἡγεσίης· ὁδηγίας Hsch.

**ἡγέτης**, fem. -έτις, add 'πολύσκιος ἡγέτις ὄρφνης Jo.Gaz. 2.289'

**ἡγηλάζω**, at end for 'ὑφηγηλάζω' read '°ὑφηγηλάζω'

*Ἡ**γησιαστής**, οῦ, ὁ, *imitator of Hegesias* of Magnesia, *Didyma* 181.6.

***ἡγητορεύω**, *hold office of* ἡγήτωρ II, *ABSA* 56.37 no. 99 (Cyprus, Ptolemaic).

**ἡγήτωρ I**, add 'E.*Med.* 426 (ἀγ-)' **II**, for 'ἀγήτωρ' read 'ἀγήτωρ (ἀγ- cod.)'

**ἡγός**, after '= ἡγεμών' insert '*Hesperia* 5.95 (Athens, iii AD)'

***ἡγουμενικός**, ή, όν, *of* or *for a leadership*, *PMich.*II 123[r] viii 5 (i AD).

**ἤγουν**, last line, after '*or*' insert 'Vett.Val. 138.12' and after '*POxy.*' insert '2085 *fr.*3.15, 16 (ii AD)'

**ἠδέ II**, lines 7/8, after '*AP* 9.788.9' insert 'also ἠδὲ .. τε Orph.*H.* 10.27'; line 9, delete '*Ch.* 1025'

***ἡδέοσμον**, τό, or **-οσμος**, ὁ, v. °ἡδύοσμον.

**ἤδη**, before 'adv.' insert 'Thess. **εἶδε̄** *BCH* 59.37 (Crannon, ii BC)'

***ἤδικτον**, τό, Lat. *edictum*, D.H. 5.73.1, *BCH* suppl. 8.85 (Thessalonica, v/vi AD), Just.*Const.* Δέδωκεν 5, 21; also **ἔδικτον** Plu.*Marc.* 24.

**ἥδομαι II**, add 'w. dat., Chrysipp.*Stoic.* 3.108.4, 115.39, 116.19'

**ἡδονή I 1**, fourth line from end, for 'take *pleasure* in them' read 'regard them with *favour*' **II**, *taste, flavour*, add 'Hp.*Vict.* 1.23; also, *scent*, Heraclit. 67 D.-K.'

***ἡδονίς**· οἱ δὲ ἀφύδιον Cyran. 18 (1.7.2, 15 K.).

**ἦδος I**, add 'Lib.*Or.* 1.274'

***ἡδύβολος**, ον, *thrown, shot, precipitated*, etc., *with agreeable effect*, ἡ. ὀϊστῷ Nonn.*D.* 48.472 (cj. for °ἡδυμόλος), ἡδυβόλου νιφετοῖο Jo.Gaz. 2.129.

**Ἡδύλειος**, add '(nisi leg. κύλιξ ἡδυ(πότις) λεία, v. *RPh.* 64.45)'

**ἡδῠλίζω**, add '**2** ἡδυλίσαι· συνουσιάσαι Hsch.'

**ἡδῠλισμός**, add '**2** ἡδυλισμός· συνουσία Hsch.'

**ἡδῠλογία**, delete 'in pl.'

**ἡδῠλύρης**, delete 'epith. of Apollo' and for '*Philol.* 71.6' read '*CEG* 816.2'

***ἡδῠμόλος**, ον, *coming with sweetness*, dub. in Nonn.*D.* 48.472 (v. °ἡδύβολος).

***ἡδύμοχθος**, ον, *to whom toil is sweet*, γεωργὲ ἡ. epigr. in *SEG* 18.456.7 (Caria, Rom.imp.).

***ἥδυνσις**, εως, ἡ, *causing of pleasure*, Olymp.*in Grg.* 242.11 W.

***ἡδῠοινέω**, *produce sweet wine*, *PCair.Zen.* 446.8 (iii BC).

**ἡδύοσμον** (s.v. ἡδύοσμος II), after 'Str. 8.3.14' insert '*Ev.Matt.* 23.23'; after 'Dsc. 3.34' insert 'also **-οσμος**, Hsch.; **ἡδέοσμος** or **-ον** *ISmyrna* 728.14 (ii/iii AD), *SB* 4483.12, 4485.3'; after 'as trisyll.' insert '*ISmyrna* l.c. (hex.)'

**ἡδύπνοος 1**, after 'Pi.*I.* 2.25' insert 'of a poet, *AP* 4.1.11 (Mel.)'

***ἡδῠποτέω**, *imbibe delicious drink*, epigr. in *SEG* 26.1835.3 (Cyrene, ii AD).

**ἡδῠπότις**, for '*something* .. cup' read '*cup for delicious drink*, a kind of κύλιξ' and after 'ib., ii BC)' insert 'called κύλιξ, *IG* 11(2).287*B*75'

**ἡδύποτος**, after 'of a cup' insert '*hᾱδύποτος* *SEG* 34.370 (Boeotia, *c.*500 BC), 34.462 (graffito, Phocis, Hellen.)'

**ἡδύς II**, add 'attached to the name of a loved one, Πυθίων ἡδύς *SEG* 32.847 no. 30, Μυΐσκος ἡδύς ib. no. 31, al. (Thasos, erotic graffiti, all iv BC)' **III**, adv., add 'Dor. ἁδέως, *SEG* 26.426.10 (Argos, *c.*AD 200)'

***ἡδῠφυεία** (or **-φυΐα**), ἡ, *sweetness of disposition*, rest. in *Vit.Philonid.fr.* 55b.1 (p. 949).

**ἡδύφωνος**, add 'adv. -ως, Poll. 2.113'

**ἡδῠχᾰρής**, add '**II** *(he) who delights in luxury*, title of comedy by Theopompus, Theopomp.Com. 14 ff. K.-A. (p. 715).'

**ἡδύχροος I**, add 'name of a bath-house monument (*pleasant to the skin*, w. ref. to water, or *of a pleasant colour* w. ref. to marble), *Laodicée* 19 (pp. 362-3)'

**ἠέ**, after '*whether*' insert 'but for **ἤ** (A) B 1 in μελεδαντὸς ἀνδράσιν ἠὲ πάρος (without μᾶλλον) epigr. in *BCH* 50.529.2 (Marathon, ii AD). [In some passages of Hellen. and later verse, where the second syll. is long by position, the first syll. is short: Numen.ap.Ath. 7.328a, Nic.*fr.* 50, 74.19 G.-S., Nonn.*D.* 34.47, v.l. in Max. 127.]'

**ἠέριος**, add 'see also ‡ἀέριος'

**ἠερόθεν**, for '*from air*' read '*from the air*' and add 'Nonn.*D.* 34.284'

⁺**ἠερόμικτος**, v. °ἀερο-.

⁺**ἠερόμορφος**, v. °ἀερο-.

**ἠερόποιταν**, add '(ἠεροποίναν La.)'

***ἠεροποῖτις**, ιδος, ἡ, wd. of uncertain meaning, *Suppl.Hell.* 991.31 (poet. word-list, iii BC); cf. perh. ἠερόποιταν, εἰαροπῶτις.

**ἠήν**, add 'Men.*Dysc.* 465 (ην pap.)'

**ἠθάς I 2**, after 'E.*Andr.* 818' insert 'τῶν ἠθάδων καὶ συνεστηκότων ῥητόρων D. 22.37'

***ἠθητής**, οῦ, ὁ, *one who strains* wine, rest. in *PHib.* 268.15, *CPR* 13.20.3 (both iii BC).

***ἠθητός**, ή, όν, *strained*, *PCair.Zen.* 436.2 (iii BC).

**ἠθικός II 1**, add '**b** ἠθικοί, οἱ, *types of moral character, typical characters*, τοῖς ἰδίως ὀνομασθεῖσιν ἠ., οἷον λίχνοις ἢ δειλοῖς Hermog.*Id.* 2.2.' **2**, at end after '(Plu.)*Alex.* 52' add '= ἐν ἤθει (v. ‡ἦθος), Sch.E.*Hipp.* 307, etc.'

**ἠθμός**, read '**ἠθμός**' and for '*SIG* 2 .. ἠθμός, ὁ' read 'written *hε̄*θμόν (acc.) *Schwyzer* 731 (Attic text, Sigeum, vi BC), ἰθμός *Stud.Pal.* 20.46.18 (ii/iii AD)'

***ἠθμωτός**, ή, όν, *equipped with a filter*, ὀξίδες ἠθμωταί graffito in *RAL* 1993 p.72 (Attic crater, iv BC).

**ἠθοποιέω II**, add 'D.L. 3.18'

**ἦθος II 2 b**, add 'ἡ δ' ὀφρὺς ἐπίκειται τῷ τοῦ ὀφθαλμοῦ ἤθει Philostr. *VA* 7.28' **4**, add '**b** ἐν ἤθει (λέγειν) *in an assumed character*, ἐν ἤ. εὐνοίας Call.*Dieg.* vii.23 (*fr.* 195 Pf.); also *so as to convey a meaning indirectly*, ἐν ἤ. καὶ εἰρωνείᾳ Sch.E.*Hec.* 26, cf. Sch.E.*Or.* 750; μετὰ ἤθους Sch.E.*Ph.* 388.'

**ἡΐ**, add 'also ἡΐν *Boeot.adesp.* 39 i 3 P.'

**ἤϊα** (A), after '**II**' insert '(prob. a different word'; line 4, after 'Pherecr. 161' insert 'ἄχυρα καὶ ἔϊα *IG* $1^3$.422.85 (Athens, v BC)'; add 'cf. εἰαί, εἶοι'

**ἠΐθεος I 1**, add 'D. 59.22'; as adj., add 'τὸν ἠ. (βίον) Antip.*Stoic.* 3.255'

**ἤϊος**, add 'Orph.*Εὐχή* 7'

**ἠκής**, add '(perh. only inferred fr. ἀμφήκης, εὐήκης)'

**ἥκω**, line 3, transfer 'Gal. 6.56' to line 13 (fut.); line 6, after 'ἥκατε' insert 'Call.*fr.* 177.13 Pf.'

**ἠλᾰκάτη**, add 'cf. Myc. *a-ra-ka-te-ja*, *spinning-woman*'

***ἠλᾰκάτιον**, τό, dim. of ἠλακάτη, *Inscr.Délos* 1442*B*56 (ii BC; pl.); cf. ἠλεκάτιον.

**ἡλάριον**, after '*nail*' insert 'Zos.Alch. 236.9'

**ἠλάσκω**, add 'Lyc. 575'

***Ἠλεῖος**, α, ον, *Elean*, Il. 11.671, etc.; Elean Ϝᾱλεῖος *Schwyzer* 409.1 (vi BC), *SEG* 31.364 (*c.*500 BC).

***ἠλέκτραι**· τὰ ἐν τοῖς κλινόποσι τῶν σφιγγῶν ὄμματα Phot.

**ἠλεκτρίς II**, add 'sg., of one such island, A.R. 4.505'

**ἠλεός**, for 'ἄλλος .. 110' read '**ἀλλος** dub. in *Lesb.fr.adesp.* 5.3 L.-P., Pi.*N.* 4.39 (cj.)'

**Ἡλιάδης**, add 'see also Ἀλιάδαι (s.v. ἀλιάδης)'

**ἡλιαία I 1**, add 'at Delos, *Inscr.Délos* 442*B*113 (ii BC)' at end add '(perh. ἡλ-, v. Dover on Ar.*Nub.* 863, etc.)'

**ἡλιακός**, add 'ἡλιακόν, τό, *place exposed to the sun, solarium*, *PKöln* 230.13 (ii AD)'

**ἡλιαστήριον**, for '*place for drying fruit*' read '*room open to the sky used for drying fruit*' and add '*PVindob.Salomons* 12.9 (AD 334/5)'

*****Ἡλίεια**, τά, *festival of the Sun*, *IG* $2^2$.3779.21 (iii BC); see also °Ἁλίεια.

**ἤλιθα II**, at end for 'cf. 140' read 'see also ἤλιθος'

**ἠλιθιάζω**, add '*to be foolish* or *senile*, Procop.*Arc.* 9.50'

**ἠλίθιος**, after lemma insert '*hēλίθιον* *CEG* 37 (Attica, vi BC)' **I**, add '-ον as adv., *in vain*, *CEG* l.c.' **II**, line 4, of persons, after 'X.*Smp.* 3.6' insert 'Simon. 37.37 P., Is. 9.11, D. 7.26, 31.11, 47.30'; for 'ἠλίθιόν [ἐστι] .. Antiph. 58' read 'as complement of inf., ὥστε ἐν ὁποιᾳοῦν τέχνῃ τὸ κατὰ γράμματ' ἄρχειν ἠλίθιον Arist.*Pol.* 1286ᵃ12, *Rh.* 1395ᵃ6, τῷ γὰρ καθορῶντι τῶν ἀϊδίων τι ἠλίθιον περὶ ταῦτα σπουδάζειν id.*fr.* 59'

***ἤλῐθος**, ον, *useless*, Nic.*Al.* 140.

**ἡλικία I 1**, line 7, for 'X.*HG* 6.1.4' read 'X.*HG* 6.1.5' **II 1**, add 'κατ' ἁλικίαν *according to age group*, *SEG* 37.340.17 (Mantinea, iv BC), καθ' ἁλικίαν *Inscr.Magn.* 20.23'

**ἧλιξ**, line 3, after 'A.R. 2.479' insert 'ἠ. χαίτην Call.*Del.* 297' add '**3** Cypr. *wa-li-ka* Ϝάλικα *of the same kind, similar*, *Kafizin* 117b, 159, al. (unless to be taken as Ϝᾱλίκα (ἡλίκος)'.

***ἡλιοβολή**, ἡ, ἁλιοβολή· σύνοδος ἡλίου ἅμα καὶ σελήνης Λάκωνες Hsch.

***ἡλιόγονος**, ον, *born of the sun*, *PMag.* 3.331.

**ἡλιοδρόμος**, add '**2** an Indian bird, Cyran. 89 (3.15.1, 2 K.).'

***ἡλιοδύσία**, ἡ, *sunset*, Hsch. s.v. γελοδυτία.

**ἡλιοθερής**, add 'Hsch. s.v. ἀλαιθερές'

**ἡλιοκάμῑνος**, add '*TAM* 5(1).517 (ii AD)'

***ἡλιοκογχύλιον**, τό, wd. of uncertain meaning, Anon.Alch. 32.6.

***ἡλιοκόσμιον**, τό, wd. of uncertain meaning, Anon.Alch. 32.6.

***ἡλιορόδιος**, ον, ἀγών the festival Helieia at Rhodes, dub. in Sch.Pi.*O.* 7.146a Dr.

**ἥλιος**, line 4, Dor. ἅλιος, add '*Schwyzer* 173.50 (Chersonesus Taurica, iv/iii BC), *Inscr.Cret.* 1.ix 1A28 (Dreros, iii/ii BC)'; lines 5/6, Aeol. ἀέλιος, add '*SEG* 34.492 (Atrax, *c.*200 BC)' **II**, add '**3** ἡμέρα ἡλίου a day of the week, *"Sunday"*, *SEG* 31.830 (Catane, iv/v AD), *IG* 14.142 (Syracuse).'

**ἡλιοσέληνος**, at end for 'Procl.*de sacrificio* .. p. 8)' read 'Procl.*Sacr.* p. 149 B.; Tz.*Alleg.Il.Prol.* 980'

**Ἡλιοσέρᾱπις**, add 'also **Ἡλιοσάραπις** (dat. -σαράπει) *IGRom.* 3.93 (Sinope)'

***ἡλιόφεγγος**, ον, = ἡλιοφεγγής, εἶδος *Lapid.Gr.* 175.14 (cf. Plin.*HN* 37.181).

***Ἦλις**, ιδος, ἡ, *Elis*, Il. 2.615, etc.; Elean Ϝᾶλις, dat. Ϝάλει *SEG* 12.371.38 (iii BC).

**ἡλίτης**, for 'Procl.*de sacrificio* .. p. 8)' read 'Procl.*Sacr.* p. 149 B.'

**ἡλοκόπος**, add '*EA* 19.27 (Pessinus, Chr.)'

***ἧλος**· τόπος οὕτω καλούμενος, ἐν ᾧ οὐδὲν φύεται Hsch.

**ἧλος I 2**, add '*IG* $2^2$.1673.33, 41'

**ἠλοσύνη**, for '= ἠλιθιότης' read '*irrational behaviour, witlessness* (cf. ἠλεός)' and after 'Nic.*Al.* 420' insert '*madness* (of the Proitides), Hes.*fr.* 37.15 M.-W. (ἠλ- pap.)'

***ἡλουργός**, ὁ, *nail-maker*, *Stud.Pal.* 8.955 (*ZPE* 76.110, v/vi AD).

**ἡλόω**, add '**III** *bristle*, app. by confusion of Heb. *sāmar* and *sᵉmōr* (cf. καθηλόω II), Aq.*Ps.* 118(119).120.'

***Ϝῆμᾱ**, ἡ, = εἶμα, τά .. τρίτρα τᾶς Ϝήμας *Inscr.Cret.* 4.43*Ab*10, 4.72 v 40.

**ἧμαι**, line 2, for 'ἧστε' read 'ἧσθε'; line 5, after 'κάθημαι)' insert 'irreg. 3 sg. εἵατο (παρ-) Call.*fr.* 497 Pf.'

**ἥμαιθον**, add '*IG* 12(1).891.1 (Rhodes, ii BC)'

**ἦμαρ**, line 1, ἆμαρ, add 'Cypr. *a-ma-ta* (pl.), *ICS* 318 B vi' **I 1**, add 'fig., of life, τριέτης λίπεν ἦμαρ *SEG* 23.632 (hex., Cyprus, ii BC)' **II**, add 'Cypr. *a-ma-ti-a-ma-ti*, ἄματι ἄματι *day by day*, *ICS* 318 B v2 (*c.*600 BC)'

***ἡμᾰ́τιον**, v. °ἱμάτιον.

**ἡμεδᾰπός**, line 3, after '(sc. γῆ)' insert 'Ath. 4.138f'; add 'see also °ἀμμεδαπάν'

**ἡμέρα**, line 2, after 'etc.' insert 'Arc. ἁμάρα *IG* 5(2).3.9, al. (*c.*400 BC)'; line 5, after '*IG* $1^2$.49.6, al.' insert 'cf. κατ' ἡμέραν *IG* $2^2$.1656.3 (394 BC)' **I 5**, add 'διὰ τὸ ἐνλιπέσθε ἡμέρας *days of observance*, *SEG* 34.1210.5 (Saittai, ii AD)' **II**, add '**4** ὅσαι ἡμέραι, v. ὁσημέραι.' **III**, line 10, after 'ἐν τρισὶν ἡ.' insert 'Hdt. 8.66.1' **III**, line 16, ἐπί w. acc., add 'ἐφ' ἡ(μέρας) ε' *for five days*, *PGen.* II 92 (i AD)' **IV**, for 'as pr. n., *the goddess of day*' read 'personified as a goddess' and add '*SEG* 31.922 (Aphrodisias, i/ii AD)'

***ἡμερείσιος**, v. ‡ἡμερήσιος.

**ἡμερήσιος II**, after lemma insert '(sp. -είσιος *IG* $4^2$.742.1 (Epid., ii/iii AD)' and add 'δρόμους ἡ. *Peripl.M.Rubr.* 15' **III 1**, after 'D.L. 7.181' insert 'ἡμερείσια sc. ἱερά, *daily sacred rites*, *IG* l.c.' add '**4** ἡ. κύκλος the circle of the sun's course *on a given day*, Hero *Dioptr.* p. 304 S.'

***ἡμερία** (B), Ep. -ίη, ἡ, = ἡμερότης, *culture* of plants, hex. in *POxy.* 1796.19 (= Heitsch *GDRK* 50, ii AD).

**ἡμερινός**, add 'φύλακες ἁμερινοί *SEG* 30.703A (Mesambria Pontica, ii/i BC)'

**ἡμέριος I**, line 4, after '*mortals*' insert 'E.*IA* 1331, Nic.*Th.* 346'

***ἡμεροκωμία**, ἡ, *daytime revelry*, Epicur. [104] 1 A.

**ἡμερολεγδόν**, line 1, after 'A.*Pers.* 63 (anap.)' insert '*IG* $2^2$.458.6 (iv BC)'

**ἥμερος I 2**, line 2, after 'δένδρεα (Hdt.) 4.21, 8.115' insert 'w. ellipsis of noun, τῶν ἡμέρων *SEG* 33.1034.A3 (Aegae, Aeolis, iii BC)'

**ἡμεροσκόπος**, for '*day-watcher*' read '*(daytime) look-out*'

**ἡμερούσιος**, add 'adv. -ιον, pap. in *Tyche* 1.163 (vi/vii AD)'

**ἡμέτερος**, ἡμέτερόνδε, add '*h.Cer.* 163, A.R. 1.704'

**ἡμιᾰρούριον**, add '*PAlex.* 26.16 (ii/iii AD)'

***ἡμιᾰρούριος**, ον, *measuring half an aroura*, prob. in *PLugd.Bat.* xxv 21.5 (i AD).

**ἡμιγύναιξ**, after lemma insert 'or -**γύνη**'; after '*half-woman*' insert 'i.e. eunuch' and for 'Simon. 179.9, Suid. s.v. ἄρρεν' read '*AP* 6.217.9 ([Simon.])'

***ἡμιγύνης**, acc. -ην, ἡ, = ἡμιγύναιξ, *OBodl.* 2171.6 (Elephantine, ii AD).

**ἡμιδεής**, for '*AP* 5.182 .. -δαής in' read '*PSI* 428.24, cj. for -δαής in *AP* 5.183 (Posidipp.) and'

***ἡμίδιον**, τό, *one half*, *PMerton* 39.3 (iv/v AD; v. *PFreib.* IV p. 34).

***ἡμιεκᾰτοστιαῖος**, α, ον, *half one-hundredth*; ἡ. τόκοι *interest of 0.5% monthly*, i.e. 6% p.a., *PNess.* 46.6 (AD 605).

***ἡμιεκτᾰ́νιον**, τό, half *ἐκτάνιον, a monetary value (cf. perh. ἕκται Φωκαΐδες), τρίτον ἡ., = $2\frac{1}{2}$ ἑκτάνια (cf. ἡμιτάλαντον), *SEG* 38.1036.4 (lead tablet, Gaul, v BC); also **ἡμιοκτάνιον** ib. 3, 12, either var. or = half *ὀκτάνιον (an eighth fraction).

**ἡμίεκτον**, after '*half-ἑκτεύς*' insert 'Hippon. 21 W. (scanned ‒‒◡)'

**ἡμιθᾰλής**, for '*half-green*' read '*half-fresh*, i.e. wilting'

**ἡμιθᾰνής**, add 'epigr. in *SEG* 30.1421.6 (Bithynia, i BC)'

**ἡμιθέα**, add 'a Carian goddess: see J.M. Cook and W.H. Plommer *The Sanctuary of Hemithea at Kastabos* (1966) p. 58 (*c.*300 BC)'

**ἡμιθωρᾰ́κιον**, for '*front plate of the* θώραξ' read '*half-θώραξ*'; add '*RA* 6(1935).31.7 (Amphipolis, ii BC)'

***ἡμικᾰ́βινος**, ον, app. *measuring half a* κάβος, οἴνου ἡμικαβίνου *PRyl.* 629.247 (iv AD).

***ἡμικᾰ́βιον**, τό, dim. of °ἡμίκαβος *PRyl.* 629.91 (iv AD).

***ἡμίκᾰβος**, ὁ, half a κάβος, *PRyl.* 629.186 (iv AD).

***ἡμικερᾰ́τιον**, τό, *half a* κεράτιον (v. κεράτιον II), *CRAI* 1945.379.4 (Berytus, v AD), *BGU* 2142.3 (v AD).

**ἡμικόλλιον**, add '**II** *half-strip of papyrus*, *PMich.* II 123ʳ vii 39 (i AD; ἱμι-).'

**ἡμικρᾱνία**, add 'cf. ἑτεροκρανία'

**ἡμικρᾱ́νιον**, add '*PMasp.* 141.11ʳ.20 (vi AD)'

**ἡμίκρᾱνον**, add 'also *pain on one side of the head* (?*migraine*), *Suppl.Mag.* 32 (v/vi AD)' *__ἡμικτεύς__, ὁ, *half a medimnus*, *hημικτέος* (gen.) de Franciscis *Locr.Epiz.* no. 23 (formed after ἑκτεύς).

__ἡμικύλινδρος__, add 'of an apse in elevation, Procop.*Aed.* 1.1.32'

__ἡμιλίτριον__, add '*SEG* 36.1342A (Palestine)'

__ἡμίλιτρον 2__, add '*IEphes.* 558 (iii AD), ib. 3437a (both -λειτρ-), *Edict.Diocl.* 19.15'

__ἡμίμετρον__, add 'rest. in *IG* 4.523 (Argive Heraeum)'

__ἡμιμναῖον__, add 'Ion. __ἡμιμνήϊον__ *IG* 12(5).123*b* (Paros), cf. *IEphes.* 1b.1 (vi BC), __ἡμιμνοῦν__ *IEphes.* 3437a'

*__ἡμιμνᾱϊαῖος__, ον, Boeot. εἱμιμνᾱΐῆος, *weighing half a mina*, *IGC* p. 99 B18 (Acraephia, iii/ii BC); also __ἱμιμνᾱΐῆος__ ib. B22.

*__ἡμιμύριος__, ον, *five thousand*, παρέχοντος ἐτησίως κάλαμον ἡμιμύριον *PBerl.Leihg.* 23.9 (iii AD).

__ἡμίνα I__, add '(ἰνιμίνα· ἐνήμισυ cod.; cj. ἰν ἱμίνᾳ (or ἡμίνᾳ)· ἐν ἡμίσει)' __II__, add '__b__ ἱμίνα· χοῖνιξ Hsch.'

*__ἡμίνομον__, τό, *half a* νόμος III, rest. in *SEG* 4.48 (Tauromenium, i BC).

__ἡμίξεστον__, delete '(Alexandrian .. 121b)'

__ἡμιοβόλιον__, transfer the article before ἡμιόγδοον and add 'cf. ἡμιωβόλιον'

__ἡμιόγδοον__, add '__II__ a division of the citizen body, τὰν δὲ βουλὰν διακλαρῶσαι εἰς ἡ. καὶ τριακάδα καὶ φυλὰν καὶ φάτραν *SEG* 30.990.22 (decree found at Delos, prob. of Phlius, iv/iii BC).'

__ἡμιόδελος__, delete the entry.

*__ἡμίοδος__, ἡ, *field-path*, *BGU* 2159.8 (AD 485).

*__ἡμιοκτάνιον__, v. °ἡμιεκτάνιον.

__ἡμιόλιος I__, after '*half as much* or *as large again*' insert 'ἡμιόλια .. τὰ χρήματα Isoc. 17.19'; line 7, after 'Arist.*HA* 629ᵃ13' insert 'as nickname of the general Theodotus, Plb. 5.42.5, 79.5'; to neut. exx. add '*IG* 12(7).515.32 (Aegiale, ii BC); fem. σὺν ἡμιολίᾳ *with*, i.e. *including*, *50% interest*, *PLugd.Bat.* XVII 4'

__ἡμιονικός__, delete 'ὁδὸς .. Str. 6.3.7'

__ἡμιονίτης__, add '*CPR* 13.11.41 (iii BC)'

__ἡμίοπος I__, for this section read '*half-holed*: ἡ. αὐλός type of small aulos (app. w. half the normal number of holes), Anacr. 30 P., *A.fr.* 91 R.; equated with αὐλὸς παιδικός in Ath. 4.182c; cf. ἡμίοπος· αὐλὸς ὁ ὑποτεταγμένος τῷ τελείῳ. μεταφορικῶς δὲ ἡμίοπος θράσος Hsch.' __II__, add 'ἡμίοπ(α) (neut. pl., in list of kitchen equipment) perh. *half-size*, Lang *Ath.Agora* XXI B14 (iv/iii BC)'

__ἡμίοπτος__, add '*Trag.adesp.* 327f.2 K.-S.'

*__ἡμιόρυκτος__, ον, *half-dug*, λάκκος *PVat.* 11ᵛ ii 39, v 9 (ii AD).

__ἡμιούγκιον__, after 'Gal. 13.558' add '__-όγκιον__ in *BGU* 781.5.17, 18'

*__ἡμιροδία__, ἡ, = ἡμιρόδιον, *Inscr.Délos* 1442*B*52 (ii BC).

__ἡμιρρήνιον__, delete 'fem. __-ρρηνιαία__, ἡ, ib. 35'

*__ἡμίρροπος__, ον, *half turning the scale*, in quot. transf., οἷον ἡμίρροπός τις ἐκ χαλκίτεως εἰς μίσυ μεταβολή Gal. 12.228.2.

__ἡμιρρόπως__, add 'Gal. 17(2).507.8'

__ἡμισάκιον__, add '*IG* 1³.422.152-4 (Athens, v BC)'

*__ἡμίσιος__ (B), = ἥμισυς, *MAMA* 1.301 (Phrygia); also __ἡμύσιος__ *AJA* 36.455 (S. Galatia).

*__ἡμῐσοαγκωνοειδής__, ές, *shaped like an elbow*, Bito 58.9.

*__ἥμισον__, v. ἥμισος.

*__ἡμιστάθμιον__, τό, *half a* στάθμιον, *PMich.* II 127 ii 4 (AD 45/6).

__ἥμισυς__, line 11 at end add 'also acc. sg. fem. ἡμίσῃ *PTeb.* 815 *fr.* 10 ii 8 (iii BC); Boeot. fem. *hέμιττα* *SEG* 24.361 (sp. *hμ-*, Thespiae, iv BC; cf. ἡμίτεια)' p. 774a, line 3, ἥμισσον, add '*SEG* 31.825 (Halaesae, Sicily, ii BC)'; line 5, after 'Aug.)' insert 'Aeol. __αἴμισυς__ *IG* 12(2).1.9, 11 (Mytilene, iv BC), Theoc. 29.5' __II 1 a__, line 14, after 'Pi.*N.* 10.87' insert 'Call.*Dian.* 90'; lines 15/16, transfer 'regul... 601c' to the end of section I 1, and for '*half-done*' read 'ῥηθέν *half said*'

__ἡμισφάγής__, after '*half-slain*' insert 'Ps.-Callisth. 21.13'

⁺__ἡμισφήκιον__, τό, archit., *half-*σφήξ, *half-chevron*, *Inscr.Délos* 403.17 (ii BC); cf. °σφήκιον, σφηκίσκος.

*__ἡμίσωμα__, ατος, τό, *half-solid* (i.e. *vaporous*) *substance*, Anon.Alch. 7.14.

*__ἡμισωράκιον__, τό, *a half-*σώρακος, τοξευμάτων *IG* 2².1424*a*.344 (Athens, iv BC).

__ἡμίτεια__, after 'ἡ' insert '(fem. of *ἥμιτυς)'; add 'also __ἡμίτεα__ *IG* 7.2712 (Acraephia; cf. *BCH* 62.156); __ἡμιτία__ *SEG* 16.848 (Caesarea, ημμlapis)'

*__ἡμιτέλειος__, ον, *half-complete*, ἀριθμητικόν *SB* 4415.12, *BGU* 330.6 (both ii AD).

*__ἡμιτετάρτεον__ or __-τετάρτεων__, τό, *half a* τεταρτεύς, *IG* 1³.250.A20, 25, B3 (Attica, v BC).

__ἡμιτέταρτον 1__, add '*SEG* 31.154(b) (*hε̄μι-*, Attica, v BC)'

*__ἡμιτία__, v. ‡ἡμίτεια.

*__ἡμίτονον__, τό, *semitone*, Alex.Eph. in *Suppl.Hell.* 21.15, 19.

*__ἡμιτρῐβᾰκός__, όν, *half-worn*, στρῶμα Pach.*Reg.* in *PG* 40.952a.

__ἡμιτριβής__, add 'written εἱμιτριβ-, *PMich.*inv. 3163.9, 13 (*TAPhA* 92.258, iii AD)'

__ἡμιτριταῖος__, for '*half*.. fever' read 'of a fever, *semitertian*'

__ἡμιτύβιον__, after 'Samos, iv BC)' insert '[ἡ]μιτυβίων ἐπ[πορικῶ]ν ἱστούς *PHels.* 7.6 (ii BC)'

__ἡμιφανής__, add 'Gr.Naz. in *PG* 37.764a'

__ἡμιχοαῖος__, add 'w. dissim. of aspirates, ἡμικοαῖα (n. pl.) *SEG* 35.134.31 (Athens, iv BC)'

__ἡμίχοον__, line 2, after 'ἡμίχα' insert '*Inscr.Délos* 104.132 (364 BC), Lang *Ath.Agora* XXI B15 (iv BC)'

__ἡμιχρῡσους__, for '-χρῦσος' read '-χρῦσον, τό'; add '*SEG* 34.95.36, al. (Athens, ii BC)'

__ἡμιωδέλιον__, add '*SEG* 30.1222.B1 (Tarentum, iv/iii BC)'

*__ἡμοιρικοί__ (-ρηκώς La.)· μὴ μετέχοντες (-χων La.), Hsch.; cf. ἄμοιρος.

*__ἡμουλίτρινος__, ον, = ἡμιλιτριαῖος, κόβαθρον ἡ. *PCol.* 188.9 (AD 320).

*__ἡμύσιος__, v. °ἡμίσιος (B).

__ἦν__, for 'φημί' read 'ἠμί'

*'__Ηναῖος__, ὁ, name of month, *Hesperia* 27.75.14 (*c.*200 BC, unknown provenance).

*__ἠνᾰκᾰτιοι__, v. ‡ἐνακόσιοι.

*__ἤνατος__, v. °ἔνατος.

__ἠνεμόεις 1__, add 'οὐρανὸν ἠνεμόεντα *h.Ven.* 291'

__ἠνεμόφοιτος__, add 'also __ἀνεμόφοιτος__ Sch.Lyc. 1119'

*__ἠνεμόφωνος__, ον, *having the sound of rushing wind*, βροντή Jo.Gaz. 2.164.

__ἡνία__ (B), line 3, after 'sg.' insert '*A.fr.* 132b.4 R.' at end add 'form ἀνία, Myc. *a-ni-ja* (fem. pl.)'

__ἠνίκα 2__, add 'without ἄν, *Cod.Just.* 1.3.52.1, 6.4.4.1, al.'

__ἡνιορράφος__, add '*MAMA* 3.741 (ιωραφ-, Isauria, Chr.)'

⁺__ἡνιοχαράτης__ (ἡνιοχάρτης La.)· διδάσκαλος ἱππικῆς τῶν νέων. Λάκωνες Hsch.

__ἡνιοχεύς__, add '__2__ transf., *ruler*, *governor*, *SEG* 33.940 (Ephesus, ?V AD); cf. ἡνίοχος I 4.'

__ἡνιοχεύω__, line 3, for 'ἀνιόχευεν' read 'ἔπι .. ἀνιοχεύων'

__ἡνιοχέω__, delete 'prose form of ἡνιοχεύω'; line 4, *drive*, add 'abs. ὁμολογῶ ἑκουσίως .. ἡνιοχῖν [σ]οι ἐ[π]ὶ τοῖς σοῖς ἵπποις *POxy.* 3135 (?AD 273/4)'

__ἠνορέη__, add 'Hes.*Th.* 516'

__ἤνπερ__, add 'etc.'; v. °ἐάνπερ'

**__ἦος__, v. ἕως.

*__ἠουοκᾶτος__, ὁ, Lat. *evocatus* (mil. rank), Βάλβιλλος ἠουοκᾶτος *IGRom.* 1.78, *MAMA* 6.376; also ἠβοκᾶτος *IGBulg.* 1570.4 (iii AD).

__ἠπᾰνία__, add '*AP* 9.368.4 (Jul.)'

*__ἠπᾰτημένως__, adv. (ἀπατάω), *mistakenly*, *erroneously*, Olymp. *in Grg.* 251.13 W.

__ἤπειρος I__, after 'Timocr. 8' insert 'pl., Theoc. 17.77, epigr. in *IPhilae* 142.1 (7 BC), Nic.*Th.* 827' __II__, add 'w. spec. ref. to its coastline, *Peripl.M.Rubr.* 38, 41, al.'

__ἠπειρώτης III 2__, add 'Isoc. 4.157, al., Φίλων Ἠπειρώτας καλός *SEG* 31.770(a) (Thasos, Hellen.); also Ἀπειρώτας *IG* 9²(1).17.63 (iii BC, etc.)'

__ἤπερ__, for 'v. ἤ (A)' read 'ἀρείοσιν ἠέ περ ὑμῖν Il. 1.260, al; πρότερον ἤπερ πρὸς Λακεδαιμονίους Hdt. 1.77.2, cf. ἤ (A) B 1; also Amphis 33.2 K.-A., but doubtful in Attic prose (codd. Th. 6.40)'

__ἠπεροπεύς__, after 'Od. 11.364' insert 'Hom.*Cercop.fr.* 1.1' and add 'as adj., δόλον ἠπεροπῆα Nonn.*D.* 2.7, ἠπεροπῆι .. μύθῳ ib. 11.116'

__ἠπεροπεύω__, delete 'used only in pres. and impf.'

*__ἠπητικόν__, τό, *repair shop*, *OBodl.* 1046 (ii AD).

__ἤπητρον__, after '*wages*' insert '*OMich.* 1.8 (iii BC)'

*__ἠπιόβουλος__, ον, *of gentle counsel*, *GVAK* 10 (Halicarnassus, Hellen.).

__ἠπιόδωρος__, add 'app. of a doctor, epigr. in *IEphes.* 3821'

__ἤπιος I 1__, add 'epigr. in *TAM* 5(1).19'

__ἠπιόχειρ__, delete 'prob... 84.8' and add 'epigr. in *Bithynische St.* III 3.5, Ἀσκληπιὸν ἠπιοχεῖρα *SEG* 37.840 (Chester, iii/iv AD)'

*__ἠπιόχειρος__, ον, = ἠπιόχειρ, Orph.*H.* 23.8, 84.8.

*__ἠποθηκάριος__, v. °ἀποθ-.

__ἠρα__ (B) __I__, add 'μηδοσύνας ἦ. τίνων Simm.*Securis* 1'

"__Ηρα 1__, delete 'an oath of Athen. women' and add '*hε̄ρᾶι* (dat.) *SEG* 36.341 (Argos, vi BC), *SEG* 30.1176.B2 (Metapontum, vi/v BC), 30.1456 (Pontus, 470/450 BC)' at end delete etym. note and add 'Myc. *e-ra*; Cypr. *e-ra-i* (*dat.*) *ICS* 90.5'

'__Ηραῖος I__, τὰ Ἡ., add '*CID* I 9 D4 (iv BC), *IStraton.* 316.2, etc.' __II__, 'Ηραῖος, add '*SEG* 34.940 (Camarina, iv/iii BC), *SIG* 279.17 (Mysia, iv BC)'; 'Ηραιών, add '*Amyzon* 28 (ii BC)'; add 'also 'Ηραών, *hε̄ραō-νος* (gen.) *IG* 12 suppl. 549 A6 (Eretria, v BC); 'Ηρεῶνος (gen.) *SEG* 26.691 (Phthiotic Thebes)' add '__III__ 'Ηραία, ἡ, = Ἥρα, *SEG* 13.236 (Mycenae, *c.*500 BC).'

'__Ηρακλέης__, line 3, after 'Prose' insert 'Cypr. [*e*]-*ra-ke-le-we-se*, 'Ηρακλέϝης *ICS* 415'; line 14, after ''Ηρακλῆν' insert '*Inscr.Délos* 1416*A*i17, al. (ii BC), *SEG* 31.122.31 (Attica, *c.*AD 121/2)'; line 16, for 'later 'Ηρακλες' read 'also 'Ηρακλε̄ς *CEG* 396 (Metapontum, 525/500 BC)' add '__3__ name of a plaster used to staunch blood, Gal. 13.858.5.'

*'__Ηρακλειασταί__, οἱ, guild of *worshippers of Heracles*, *SEG* 31.122.4

(Attica, *c*.AD 121/2), *IHistriae* 57.32 (ii/iii AD); also **Ἡρακλεϊσταί**, *IG* 12(1).162 (Rhodes), *SEG* 24.1037 (Moesia, ii/iii AD).

**Ἡρακλεῖδαι**, add '*SEG* 34.487 (Atrax, *c*.200 BC)'

***Ἡρακλείδιον**, τό, dim. of Ἡρακλέης, ὦ κάλλιστον Ἡρακλείδιον Achae. 26 S.

**Ἡράκλειος**, line 2, add '**-ηος** *INikaia* 1202' and add ref. to section VI **II 1**, for '*temple* .. Hdt. 2.44, al.' read '*temple* or *sanctuary of Heracles*, Hdt. 2.44.5, al., Paus. 9.11.6' **2**, add '*SEG* 31.985.D8 (Teos, v BC), *Inscr.Perg.* 8(3).3 (ii BC)'

***Ἡρακλεϊσταί**, v. °Ἡρακλειασταί.

**Ἡρακλείτειος**, for 'α, ον' read 'ον'; add 'Arist.*Ph.* 185ᵃ7, *Metaph.* 987ᵃ33'

**Ἡρακλεῶτις**, add '*SEG* 25.274 (Attica, Rom.imp.)'

***Ἡραών**, v. °Ἡραῖος.

**ἠρέμᾰ 2**, for 'dub. in Luc.*Merc.Cond.* 28 codd.' read 'Luc.*Merc.Cond.* 28, *Icar.* 9'

**ἠρεμέω**, line 1, for 'hyperdor.' read 'Dor. (cf. ἀράμεν, ἀραμέναι; Tsakonian αραμού *remain*)' **.1**, add 'app. euphem., of the dead, *SEG* 30.976 (graffito, Olbia, iv BC)'

**ἠρέμησις**, for 'hyperdor.' read 'Dor.'

**ἠρεσίδες**, before '*EM*' insert 'παρθένοι αἳ καλοῦνται ἠ. (or Ἡ.) Agias Dercyl. 4 J., cf. Call.*fr.* 65 Pf. adn.; Hsch.'

***ἠρεσιώνης**, ὁ, some kind of priestly official, (cf. perh. εἰρεσιώνη), *Hesperia* 40.316 line 5, ib. 32.48 no. 69.6; to be rest. in *IG* 2².1825.71, 3680.11 (all Attica, iii AD).

**-ήρης 2**, add 'when compounded w. numerals (e.g. τριήρης) it indicates the number of files of rowers along each side of the ship'

**ἦρι**, after '*in the morning*' insert 'Call.*Jov.* 87'; at end for '(Cumae)' read '(Cumae, vii/vi BC); (acc. to some edd. here ἦρι is dat. of ἔαρ (A))'

**ἠρῐγένειον**, for '= ἠρύγγιον, Hsch.' read 'ἠ. (-νιον La.)· τὴν ἠρύγγιον πόαν Hsch.'

**⁺ἠρῖνός**, v. ‡ἐαρινός.

***ἠρῖνοτόκος**, ἠρινοτόκου· ἀπὸ τῶν ποιμνίων τῶν κατ' ἔ‹τ›ο‹ς› φόρους τελούντων ἔαρι Hsch.

***ἠριπότην**· ἡμέραν ἐξ ἡμέρας .. Hsch.

***ἠρογάτωρ**, ὁ, Lat. *erogator*, official in charge of distribution of supplies, *SEG* 32.1554 (Arabia, vi AD).

***ἠρόδοτος**, ον, *given in spring*, *An.Ox.* 3.350.7.

***Ἡροξείνια**, τά, *feast in honour of the Heroes*, *Sokolowski* 2.69.3 (Thasos, iv BC); also **Ἡρωιξείνια**, *Thasos* 192.23 (i AD).

***Ἡροσούρια**, τά, an Attic festival, perh. connected with fair winds in spring, *Sokolowski* 3.18.B28 (Erchiae, iv BC); cf. Ἡροσάνθεια, Ἡροφάνεια.

***ἠρτυλημένος** (-λιμ- cod.)· ἠρτυμένος Hsch.

**ἦρυς**, add 'but perh. sp. of ἡρωίς'

***ἡρωάς**, άδος, ἡ, = ἡρωΐνη I, Corinn. 11(*b*).2 P.

***ἡρῴδιον**, τό, dim. of ἡρῷον, *TAM* 1.73 (Cyanae).

**ἡρωϊκός I 2**, add 'ἔδοξεν τῇ πόλει τειμάς τε αὐτῷ ἡρωικὰς ψηφίσασθαι *SEG* 23.319 (Delphi, ii AD)'

**ἡρωΐνη I**, add 'pl. Ἡρωῖναι, Attic deities, *Sokolowski* 3.18.A19 (Erchiae, iv BC)'

**ἡρωΐς I 2**, add 'Ἀφροδεισίᾳ ἡρωΐδι *SEG* 34.1028 (Italy, ii/iii AD)' **II 1**, after 'ἡρωικός' insert 'θεαρίας Pi.*Pae.* 14.36 S.-M.'

**ἡρωϊσμός** (s.v. ἡρωΐζω), for '*worship*' read '*cult*' and add '*SEG* 33.946.8 (Ephesus, i AD).

**⁺ἡρώϊσσα**, ἡ, contr. ἡρῷσσα, (Thess. εἰρούισσα *AE* 1931.178) *female hero, demigoddess*, A.R. 4.1309, 1358, *AP* 6.225 (Nicaenet.). **2** *deceased woman*, *IG* 5(1).610 (Sparta), al., 12(5).325 (Paros), *SEG* 24.398 (Thessaly, iii/ii BC).

***ἥρων**, ωνος, ὁ, Syracusan for ἥρως, ἡρώνεσσι Sophr. 154.

**ἡρώνα**, add '(also read as εἰρώνα = *ἱερωνή (i.e. ἱερωνία), v. *ZPE* 49.187ff.)'

**ἡρῷον 1**, before 'Hdt. 5.47' insert 'Ἑρϝο̃ον τὸν ἐν Θέβαις *SEG* 37.283 (Argos, *c*.550 BC)'

**ἡρῷος**, for 'πούς .. etc.' read 'ἡ. πούς *AP* 7.9 (Damag.)'

**ἥρως**, line 1, for 'signf. III' read 'signf. II', add '(Thess. εἴρους *AE* 1931.178)' and, gen. ἥρωος, add '*hḗrōos* *SEG* 37.286 (Argos, v BC)'; line 4, after 'Orac.ap.D. 43.66' insert 'ἥρωτι *IGBulg.* 362, 1727, 1750'; line 8, delete 'ἡρώνεσσι .. 154.1' **I 3**, add 'a Thracian horseman divinity, *IGBulg.* ll.cc., *SEG* 31.638 (Maced.), etc.' add '**4** of great writers of the past, Phld.*Rh.* 1.200, Longin. 4.4, 14.2, 36.2.'

**ἡρωστής**, delete the entry.

**Ἡσιόδειος**, add 'τῶν σ[υν]θυτάων τ[ᾶμ] Μωσά[ων τῶ]ν Εἰσιοδείων *IG* 7.1785 (Thespiae)'

**Ἡσίοδος**, for 'Aeol. Αἰσ-' read 'hyperaeolic Αἰσ-'

**ἡσσάομαι**, line 1, delete 'Th. 3.57'; line 6, after 'etc.' insert 'Hellen. ἑττηθήσεσθε *PSI* 340.21, ἑσσηθείς *PHib.* 197.53 (both iii BC)'

**ἠστός**, add 'Dam. in *Phlb.* 124.1, al.'

**ἡσῠχάζω I**, add '**c** of rights, *lapse, be suspended*, αἱ δὲ λοιπαὶ πατρωνικαὶ διακατοχαὶ ἡσυχαζέτωσαν *Cod.Just.* 6.4.4.21a.' **II a**, add 'Sol. 4c.1 W.'

**ἡσῠχῇ 1**, line 3, after '*gently*' insert 'Hippon. 26.1 W.'

**ἡσῠχία 4 a**, at end, pl., for these entries read 'τὰς ἡ. ἄγειν Ephor. 236 J., Ath. 3.114a; ἔχειν id. 11.493f'

**ἦτορ**, line 2, after 'codd. Ath.' insert 'Pi.*Pae.* 6.12 S.-M.'

**ἤτριον**, line 2, for '(Leon., pl.)' read '(Leon.Tarent., pl.), (*AP*) 15.27 (Simm.)'

**⁺ἦτω**, v. ‡εἰμί.

***Ἡφαίστειος**, α, ον, *of* or *belonging to Hephaestus*; neut. pl. subst., *works of Hephaestus*, Call.*fr.* 202.57 Pf. (Add. II). **2** the name of a month, cf. Ἡφαίστιος, *SEG* 37.453.19 (sp. -ειος, Thessaly, ii/iii AD).

***Ἡφαιστιασταί**, οἱ, *worshippers of Hephaestus*, *SEG* 30.1004 (Rhodes, ii/i BC).

**Ἡφαιστιεῖον** (s.v. Ἡφαιστεῖον), before '*temple of Ptah*' insert '*temple of Hephaestus* at Athens, *SEG* 26.98 (iii BC)'

***Ἡφαίστιον**, τό, = Ἡφαιστεῖον, *IG* 1³.472.2 (Athens, v BC).

***ἡφαιστίτης**, ου, ὁ, λίθος, a mineral, Cyran. 18, 19 (1.7.2, 17 K.).

***Ἡφαιστόπους**, *having a foot like Hephaestus*, i.e. *lame*, Olymp. *in Alc.* 160.9 sch. W.

**Ἥφαιστος**, line 1, at end insert 'Ηέφαστος Jeffery *LSAG* 77 no. 24 (vase, Athens, *c*.550 BC), Kretschmer *GV* p. 127' add 'cf. Myc. *a-pa-i-ti-jo*, pers. n. (cf. Ἀφάστιος *IPamph.* 149, ii BC)'

**Ἡφαιστότευκτος**, add 'Ἡ. πανοπλίαν Procl.*Chr.* p. 106.2'

**Ἡφαιστόχειρος**, for 'Choerob.*Orth.* in *AB* 1380' read '*An.Ox.* 2.317'

**ἠχέω**, line 5, for 'grasshopper' read 'cicada' **II**, at end after 'S.*OC* 1500' insert 'of long vowels, πολὺν ἠχεῖται χρόνον D.H.*Comp.* 14; (ἁ βάρβιτος ..) Ἔρωτα μοῦνον ἠχεῖ *Anacreont.* 23.4 W.'

**ἦχι**, add 'Dor. ἆχι *Suppl.Hell.* 1034-1035'

**ἠῷος**, add 'cf. Myc. *a-wo-i-jo*, pers. n.'

**ἠώς I 4**, at end for '*IG* 7.235' read '*SEG* 31.416'

# Θ

**θᾰάσσω**, add 'prob. in Sapph. 73(*a*).7 L.-P.'

**θᾶκος**, after 'θῶκος' insert '(also Men.*Dysc.* 176)' **I 3**, add '*IEphes.* 455 (ii AD)'

**θᾰλάμη I 1**, line 3, after 'polypus' insert '*h.Ap.* 77'; line 6, after '(E.)*Ion* 394 (pl.)' insert 'of the *underground shrine* of Rhea, Nic.*Al.* 8 (pl.) and Sch., cf. Phot. and Hsch. s.v. θαλάμαι' at end add 'cf. Myc. *ta-ra-ma-ta*, pers. n.'

**θᾰλᾰμίς**, add '**2** prob. *funerary monument*, *SEG* 31.1126 (Phrygia, AD 150/200).'

***θᾰλᾰμίσκος**· κοιτωνίσκος Cyr.

**θᾰλᾰμίτης**, for pres. def. read '*a member of the lowest file of rowers* in a trireme'

**θάλασσα**, line 1, after 'Att.' insert 'Boeot.' and after parentheses insert 'Lac. θάλαθ(θ)α *SEG* 26.461.7 (Sparta, v BC), Cret. θάλαθθα (ii BC)' **4**, for this section read 'applied to a trench (perh. fr. similarity to Hebr. *tᵉʿālāh*), Lxx 3*Ki.* 18.32, 35, 38' **5**, for '*laver*' read '(*artificial*) *pool made of bronze*' and add '3*Ki.* 7.23'

**θᾰλασσαῖος 1**, add 'Boeot. θαλαττῆον, τό, *produce of the sea*, *IGC* p. 98 A4, 5 (Acraephia, iii/ii BC)'

**θᾰλασσίγονος**, delete the entry (read °θαλασσό-).

***θᾰλάσσινος**, η, ον, *of the sea*, ἐπὶ θαλασσίνηι ὁδ[?ῶι] (i.e. *leading to the sea*) *Delph.* 3(1).362 iii 15. **2** *sea-like*, prob. *dyed purple*, *thalassina vestis*, Lucr. 4.1127; cf. θαλάσσιος III.

**θᾰλάσσιος**, line 2, after 'E.*IT* 236' insert 'Luc. *VH* 2.46'; line 7, before 'πεζοί' insert 'μόσχος θ. *seal*, *Edict.Diocl.* 8.37, θ. νεκρός of a shell used as a trumpet (cf. Ath. 10.457f), Thgn. 1229'; line 9, delete 'θ. .. 1229' **3**, for '= ἁλουργής' read '*dyed purple*'

**θᾰλασσίτης**, add '**2** kind of hyacinth stone, Epiph.Const. in *Lapid.Gr.* 196.24.'

**θᾰλασσοβᾰφής**, add '*sea-coloured*, of a stone, Epiph.Const. in *Lapid.Gr.* 197.21'

***θᾰλασσόγονος**, ον, *born from the sea*, θαλασσογόνου Παφίης Nonn.*D.* 13.458.

***θᾰλασσοδίαιτος**, ον, *dwelling in the sea*, *APAW* 1943(14).8 (Chalcis, iii AD).

**θᾰλασσοειδής**, add 'epith. of (Jewish) God, *sea-like*, prob. w. ref. to his immensity, *PMag.* 4.3068'

***θᾰλασσόζωνος**, ον, *sea-girt*, prob. in *Suppl.Hell.* 991.68 (poet. word-list, iii BC).

**θᾰλασσομᾰχέω**, for '*fight by sea*' read '*combat the sea*, in quot., of a κυβερνήτης'

**θᾰλασσομάχος**, for '*fighting by sea*' read '*combating the sea*'

**θᾰλασσοπόρος**, add 'Nonn.*D.* 20.376, 21.187, 40.531, 43.425'

***θᾰλασσοσέρις**, ἡ, name of a plant, Aët. 7.114 (388.7 O.).

**θᾰλασσουργός**, before 'ὁ' insert 'also **-οεργός** *GVI* 1859 (Teos, ii/i BC)'

**θάλαττα**, etc., after 'Att.' insert 'Boeot.'

**θᾰλεα**, line 3, for 'Alcm. 10' read 'Alcm. 15 P., cf. Pi.*Parth.* 2.36 S.-M.' and for 'θαλέεσσιν .. *Fr.anon.* 31' read 'τὼ μὲν ἐγὼ θαλέεσσιν ἀνέτρεφον Call.*fr.* 337 Pf.'

***θᾰλειοι**, οἱ, *devotees of* Θάλεια III 2, *IEryth.* 201 a 62 (iii BC).

**θᾰλερός II**, line 6, for 'the *thick and frequent* sob' read '*mighty* lamentation'; line 8, after 'A.*Th.* 707 (lyr.)' insert 'but v. °θελεμός'

**θᾰλία I**, pl., add 'X.*Hier.* 6.2 (cf. Lac. pers. n.)'

***θαλικτάριον**, τό, = θάλικτρον, *PMed.Rez.* 12.13 (sp. θαλκιτάριον, vi/vii AD).

**⁺θαλιοποιοί**· οἱ τὰ σκυτούμενα κιβώτια, καὶ τοὺς δερματίνους ῥίσκους ἐργαζόμενοι Hsch. (cf. σαλία, θολία; but **θαλλικοποιοί** La., cf. °θάλλικα).

***θαλκιτάριον**, v. °θαλικτάριον.

***θαλλέομαι**, *put out shoots*, *BGU* 2157.15 (AD 485).

***θάλλικα**· σάκκου εἶδος Hsch.

***θαλλικοποιοί**, v. °θαλιοποιοί.

**θάλλινος**, στέφανος, add '*SEG* 30.1892 (Maced., iii BC)'

***θαλλίς**· μάρσιππος μακρός Hsch., Afric.*Cest.* p. 47 V.

***θαλλισμός**, ὁ, *special monetary provision in will*, *PMil.Vogl.* 84.9 (ii AD); cf. θαλλός III.

***θαλλοδοτέω**, *distribute branches* at a shrine, *POxy.* 3094.40, 43 (AD 217/8; cf. θαλλός III).

***θαλλόομαι**, prob. *produce shoots*, of a date-palm, *BGU* 2158.3-4 (V AD).

**θαλλός I**, line 7, after 'etc.' insert 'also w. apposition, θαλλῷ στεφάνῳ *IG* 12(1).160, 161, *ASAA* 8/9(1925/6).322 (Rhodes)' **I**, add '**2** as cult-title of Zeus, Δεὶ Θαλλῷ εὐχήν *SEG* 32.1282; Διὶ Θαλῷ 37.1171 (both Phrygia, Rom.imp.), al.'

**θάλλω 3**, after '*to be fresh, active*' insert 'πατρίδ' ἀν' ἱμερτὰν πένθος ἔθαλλε τότε epigr. in *BCH* 116.599 (Ambracia, vi/v BC)'

**θάλος**, add '**II** *victor's wreath, crown*, Pi.*I.* 7.24, *fr.* 70a.14 S.-M.; fig. κλεινᾶν Συρακοσσᾶν θάλος Ὀρτυγία id.*N.* 1.2, *Lyr.adesp.* 1029.3 P. **III** *well-being*, cf. θάλεα, epigr. in *BCH* 85.849 (Paros, Rom.imp.).'

***θαλπίζω**, *cherish, look after*, *PNag.Ham.* 70.17.

***θάλπιον**· θερμότερον Cyr.

**θάλπω II 3**, for '*hatch*' read '*brood over*' **III**, add '**4** *prefer, favour*, Theophil.Antec. 2.20.3.' **IV**, line 2, after 'θάλψαι' insert '(s.v.l.)' and for '*to live*' read '*keep oneself warm*'; for 'Leon.' read 'Leon. Tarent.'

**θᾰλυκρός**, for first quot. read 'ἃ πάντῃ πάντα θαλυκρὸς ἐγώ Call.*fr.* 736 Pf.'

**θᾰλύσια 1**, for '*offerings* .. Artemis' read '*harvest-offerings to the gods*'; line 2, delete 'later'; add '*offerings of any first fruits*, Nonn.*D.* 47.493, 48.224'

***θᾰλυσμοσύνη**, ἡ, dub. sens., epigr. in *ITomis* 241(77).10 (Rom.imp.).

**θάλψις II**, add 'Just.*Const.Δέδωκεν* 1'

**θᾰμέες**, line 7, after '(Il.) 12.287' insert 'θαμειαὶ σφενδόναι Archil. 3.1 W., Panyas. 4.2'

***θαμνίον**, τό, dim. of θάμνος, Gal. 12.108.18.

**θαμνομήκης**, for '*a long .. bush*' read '*of the length equal to the height of the bush*'

**θάμνος**, add 'Emp. 9.2, 20.6, 117.2 D.-K.'

***θαμνοῦχος**, ον, *full of bushes*, ἐν ὑψηλοῖσι θα[μν]ούχοι[ς cj. in A.*fr.* 73b.3 R.

**⁺θᾰμῠρίζω**, prob. *celebrate the cult of Thamyris*, Θαμυριδδόντων Πισάνδρω, Δαμοκλεῖος *SEG* 32.503 (Thespiae, 400/350 BC); cf. θαμυρίζει· ἀθροίζει, συνάγει Hsch.

**θᾰνᾰτήσιος**, for 'Afric.*Cest.* 14, 16 .. Thévenot)' read 'Afric.*Cest.* p. 28 V. (v.l. -ήσιμος), p. 30 V.'

**⁺θᾰνᾰτιάω**, = θανατάω I, anon.ap.Suid. **II** = θανατάω II, Luc. *Peregr.* 32, S.E.*M.* 9.153.

***θᾰνᾰτοσυνάρτης**, ου, ὁ, *joiner-together of deaths*, *PMag.* 4.1372.

***Θάξιος**, ὁ, month-name (app. = Θάσιος II), *SEG* 33.1039.57 (Aeolian Cyme, ii BC).

***θάομαι**, line 6, after 'Theoc. 15.23' insert '(v.l.)' **II**, add '1 pl. aor. subj. θασῶμες Theoc. 15.23 (*PAntin.*)'

**θάπτω**, line 8, after 'Hes.*Sc.* 472' insert 'θάπτουσι κατακαύσαντες ἢ ἄλλως γῇ κρύψαντες Hdt. 5.8'; line 10, after 'cremation' insert 'E.*Antiop.* p. 21 A.'

**Θαργήλια**, add 'Θαργήλιος as title of Apollo, *SEG* 30.977(a) (Olbia, v BC)'; form Ταργ- as pers. n., add '*SEG* 33.659 (Rhodes)'

**Θαργηλιών**, after 'Athens' insert 'and elsewhere' and add '*SEG* 30.977(c) (Olbia, v BC), 33.679'

***Θαρησιεῖον**, τό, prob. = °Ἐρησιεῖον, *SB* 9628 (*SO* 57.77).

**θαρσέω I 4**, add 'ἐξ ἀνθρώπων as far as men are concerned, Epicur.*Sent.* 6; ἀπὸ τῶν ἔξωθεν ib. 39'

***θαρσικάριος**, v. ταρσικάριος.

***Θαρσικός**, v. Ταρσικός.

***θᾶς**, Lesb. = Ion. τέως (q.v. I 2), Alc. 70.8, 206.6 L.-P.; cf. ἆς.

**Θάσιος II 1**, add 'cf. °Θάξιος'

**θάσσω**, after '(E.)*Hec.* 36' insert 'τίς ἐπ' αὐλείοισι θύραις θάσσει; Ar.*V.* 1482'

**Θαύλιος**, add 'epith. of Zeus at Atrax, *SEG* 34.490 (*c.*200 BC), Θαύλιος (cod. Θαῦμος) ἢ θαῦλος· Ἄρης Μακεδόνιος Hsch.'

**θαῦμα I 2**, for '*mountebank-gambols*' read '*acrobatic feats*, *IG* 1³.757 (500/480 BC)' and after 'cf. (X.*Smp.*) 7.3 (sg.)' insert 'Max.Tyr. p. 344 H.'

**θαυμάζω 2**, add 'pass., w. deponent force, θαυμασθῆναι βασιλέα σάρκινον Lxx *Es.* 4.17p.'

**θαυμάσιος I 1**, add 'sup. as honorific epith., γραμματεύς *PLond.* 1842.4, ἰατρός *PMasp.* 6.ii.14, προνοητής *POxy.* 206.6 (all vi AD)'

**θαυμᾰσιότης II 2**, add '*PGrenf.* I 56.7 (vi AD)'

**θαυμαστός**, line 1, insert 'σαυμαστά (n. pl.) Alcm. 4 *fr.* 1.4 P. (v. *POxy.*

2388)'; line 7, after 'c. gen.' insert '*ῥαστώνης* Pl.*Lg.* 648c'; lines 8/9, delete '*πλέοσι* .. 9.122'

**θαυσήκρι**, add '(**θαυσίκριον** La.)'

**θεά I**, add '**2** as the title of empresses; of Julia Domna, *SEG* 24.953 (Moesia, AD 198).' at end, monosyll., add 'also Herod. 4.11'

**θέᾱ I 1 a**, line 5, for '*τινός* at the *sight of*' read '*τῇ αὐτοῦ* angry at his *gazing* (at the fallen enemy)'

***θεαγεία**, *ἡ*, the office of *θεαγός*, *POxy.* 3974.18 (AD 165/6).

**θεᾱγός**, for '*priest* .. *gods*' read '"*god-bearer*", a priest concerned with the transporting of sacred images'; delete '*PTeb.* .. (ii BC)' and for 'etc.' read '*θ. Θοήριος PTeb.* 61(*b*).59 (ii BC; pl.), *θ. Σούχου* ib. 121.76 (pl.), 133 (i BC), *θ. Θοηρείου ἐξαγορείων καὶ ἑτέρου Σιντάνω λεγομένου* pap. in *JEA* 20.21.9 (iii AD; pl.), cf. ib. 28'

***Θεᾰδέλφεια**, *τά*, a Ptolemaic festival, *SEG* 1218.9 (Xanthos, iii BC), *Inscr.Olymp.* 188 (-*εα*, ii BC; cf. *Hesperia* 4.90), *PSI* 431.

**θέαινα**, after '*θεά*' insert '**θεαίνη** Nonn.*D.* 6.123' and after 'Od. 8.341, al.' insert '*h.Ap.* 311'

**θέᾱμα**, add '**2** in act. sense, *gazing* at, *αἰθέρος θεάμασιν* Chaerem. 14.4.'

**θεάομαι**, line 7, after '(Od.) 5.74' insert 'perh. Cypr. *e-ta-we-sa-to ἐθαϝέσατο ICS* 319' **I**, add '**5** *see*, i.e. consult, *βουλόμενος ἰατρὸν ὀφθαλμῶν θεάσασθαί τινα* Luc.*Nigr.* 2.' **II**, line 3, after 'Hsch.' insert 'dub. in Men.*Epit.* 564'

***θέαπνον**, *τό*, unkn. product in a medicinal recipe, *PAmst.*inv. 148 (*Mnemos.* series 4, 30.146); cf. *θεάφιον*.

***θεᾱτράλιος**, *α*, *ον*, cf. Lat. *theatralis*, *of the theatre*, Just.*Nov.* 63.1.

**θεᾱ́τρια**, add '*SEG* 25.306 (Attica, i BC)'

**θεᾱτρίζω I**, for this section read '*perform in the theatre*, *οἵ τε ἀγων*[*ιζ*]*όμενοι πάντες καὶ οἱ κατὰ καιρὸν θεατρίζοντες Gerasa* 192.18 (ii AD), Suid.'

**θεᾱτρικός 2**, add '**b** of style, *showy*, D.H.*Isoc.* 12.15.'

**θέᾱτρον**, line 4, for '*Act.Ap.* 19.20' read '*Act.Ap.* 19.29'

**θεᾱτροτορῦνη**, for '*stage-pounder*' read '*one who rouses the theatre-audience*' and delete 'who was a clumsy dancer'

**θεάφιον**, add 'Charis. p. 32 K.; cf. *θειάφιον*'

**θέεινος**, add 'written **θόειν-** *PMich.*inv. 3163.7 (*TAPhA* 92.258; iii AD)'

**θεηγόρος**, add '*παντὸς ἔργου καὶ θεηγόρου λόγου Trag.adesp.* 118b K.-S. (perh. Chr.)'

†**θεηδόχος**, *ον*, *recipient of deity*, *οὖδας ἀρούρης* Nonn.*D.* 13.96.

†**θειασμός**, *ὁ*, *divine possession* or *frenzy*, *θειασμοῖς κάτοχοι γυναῖκες* D.H. 7.68; *θειασμοῦ* (*ἐπιρρήματα*) D.T. 642.17. **2** *inspired utterance*, *ἄγαν θειασμῷ προσκείμενος* Th. 7.50.

***θειάφιον**, see also ‡*θεάφιον*.

***θεικᾱ́**, *ά*, v. °*θήκη*.

**θειλόπεδον**, for pres. def. read '*area exposed to the sun* used for drying grapes' and add '*IMylasa* 843.6'

***θειογρᾰφικός**, *ή*, *όν*, *theological*, *ἱστορίαι* Rh. 3.541.22.

**θεῖον** (A), add '**II** = *ἐλελίσφακον*, Dsc. 5.107, Poet.*de herb.* 93.'

**θεῖος** (A), line 2, after 'Bion.*fr.* 15.9' insert 'Cret. *θιήιος SEG* 27.631.4, 6'; delete 'late' and after '**θήϊος**' insert 'Alc. 45.8 L.-P.' **II 1**, add 'in Lydian dedications, Keil-Premerstein *Dritter Bericht* no. 30 (ii AD), cf. *TAM* 5(1).186, *IStraton.* 519' at end add 'Myc. *te-i-ja* (fem.)'

**θεῖος** (B), after '*ὁ*' insert '**θῖος** *IG* 12(1).72b (Rhodes, i BC), perh. *δεῖος SEG* 31.1004 (Lydia, AD 101/102)'; after '(Balbilla)' insert 'Dor. *θῆος* (q.v.)'

**θειόστεπτος**, delete the entry.

**θειοτελής**, delete the entry.

**θειότης II**, add '**2** attribute of Roman emperors personified as deity, *SEG* 30.1253 (Aphrodisias, i AD).' at end add 'see also *θεότης*'

***θείς** (A), *θεῖσα*, *θέν*, gen. *θέντος*, aor. part. of *τίθημι* (q.v.).

***θείς** (B), *θέν*, gen. *θενός*, = °*δείς*, *ἡ δὲ γῆ ἦν θὲν καὶ οὐθέν* Thd.*Ge.* 1.2.

**θειώδης** (B), for '*divine*' read '*supernatural*, *marvellous*, *ἔτι δὲ τούτου θειωδέστερον συνεμαρτύρουν* Eun.*VS* 459' and for '*PMasp.* 451.42, 56' read '*PMasp.* 317.27'

***θείωσις**, *εως*, *ἡ*, *consecration*, by initiation, Plu. 2.351f; see also *θέωσις*.

†**θελεμός**, *ον*, app. *quiet*, *placid*, *ποταμοὺς δ' οἳ διὰ χώρας θελεμὸν πῶμα χέουσιν* A.*Supp.* 1027, *θελεμωτέρῳ πνεύματι* id.*Th.* 707 (cj.); *θελεμόν· ἥσυχον* Hsch.; glossed by *θεληµός* Hdn.Gr. 1.171; adv. -*μῶς· ἡσύχως* Hsch.

**θελήμων**, add 'of persons, *willing*, A.R. 4.1657'

***θελησμός**, *ὁ*, *volition*, Hdn.*fr.* p. 24 H.

***θέλκαρ·** *θέλγμα* Hsch.

**θέλκτρον**, delete the entry.

***θελκτώ·** *κολακευτική* Phot., Suid.

**θελξῐμελής**, for '*IG* 3.400' read 'hex. in *IG* 2².5200 (iii AD)'

***Θελξίνη**, *ἡ*, epith. of Hera, *SEG* 26.1211 (Velia, iv BC).

**θέλξις**, add 'prob. in D.H.*Th.* 33'

**θελοντής**, add '(in S.*Aj.* 24 prob. reading *κἀγὼ 'θελοντής*)'

**θέλυμνα**, delete the entry.

***θέλυμνος**, *η*, *ον*, *close-packed*, *dense*, *θ. τε καὶ στερεωπά* Emp. 21.6 (codd. *θέλημνα*, *θέλημα*; cf. *προθέλυμνος*, *τετραθέλυμνος*).

***Θελχίνια**, v. *Τελχίνιος*.

†**θέλω**, v. *ἐθέλω*.

**θέμα I 1**, after 'Plu. 2.116a, b' insert '*bank account*, *deposit*, *PCharite* 38.4 (iv AD)'; after '*PTeb.* 120.125 (i BC)' insert '*receipt* acknowledging deposit of grain, *PMich.*XI 604.16 (iii AD), *POxy.* 2769.14 (iii AD)' **6**, for this section read '*platform serving as base for monument*, *ἡ σορὸς καὶ τὸ βαθρικὸν καὶ τὸ ὑποκείμενον θέμα Hierapolis* 208, cf. 124, al., *TAM* 4(1).140, rest. in *MAMA* 6.19'

**θεματοποιέω**, add '**II** *place in position*, *θ*]*εματοποήσας τὰς γεφύρας καὶ κατασκευάξας τὰς ὁδούς IRhod.Peraia* 601.4 (Hellen.).'

**θέμεθλα**, at end delete 'Call.*Dian.* 248' (v. *θέμειλον*, s.v. °*θεμείλια*) and insert '*θέμεθλα· ἕδραι, βάθρα, θεμέλια* Hsch.'

**θεμείλια**, line 3, after 'Opp.*H.* 5.680' insert 'fig., *θ. πήγνυτο χάρμης the foundations of battle were being laid*, Nonn.*D.* 17.135, cf. 29.324, 43.3: sg. **θεμείλιον** Nic.*Th.* 608, *Inscr.Délos* 290.202 (iii BC)'; line 4, after '**θέμειλον**' insert 'Call.*Dian.* 248'

**θεμελιόθεν**, add 'also **θεμελιᾶθεν** *IGLS* 9121 (V AD); **θαιμηλιῶθε** *BE* 1959.459 (Syria, Chr.)'

**θεμέλιος I**, add '*οἰκοδομήθη ἐκ θεμελίων SEG* 31.1473 (Arabia, AD 562)'

**θεμελιοῦχος**, of Poseidon, add '*SEG* 30.93.17 (decr., Eleusis, 20/19 BC)'

**θεμελίωσις**, add '*IG* 11(2).199*A*88 (Delos, iii BC)'

**θεμερός**, (not **θέμ-**), after 'Hsch.' insert '*θ. ὀπί* Pi.*N.* 7.83 cod. D'

***θεμιονείκης** (i.e. -*νίκης*), *ου*, *ὁ*, *winner of a θέμις* II, *TAM* 2.688 (Cadyanda).

**θέμις**, line 4, after 'Pi.*O.* 13.8' insert 'Pl.*R.* 380a (cf. *Θέμιτι IG* 7.1816.2)' **II**, add 'gen. *θέμεως MAMA* 4.124, 132 (Metropolis), *Schwyzer* 686a (Pamphylia, ii BC)' **IV**, add '*SEG* 37.491 (dat. -*ιστι*, Magnesia, v/iv BC), 26.717.8 (dat. -*ιτι*, Epirus, iv BC)'

***θεμισσόος**, *ον*, *preserving justice*, *SEG* 36.1198.12 (Phrygia, iv AD).

**θεμιστεύω I**, after 'Od. 11.569' insert '*λαοῖς θεμιστεύσοντα Trag.adesp.* 664.30 K.-S.' **II**, add '**b** w. dat. and inf., *in* (oracular) *answer enjoin* on one to .., *PAAH* 1932.52.2 (Dodona, iv BC).'

**θεμιστοπόλος I**, add 'Hes.*fr.* 10(a).25 M.-W., *θεμιστοπόλῳ δέ τε βουλῇ* epigr. in *SEG* 13.277.11 (Patrae, iv/v AD)'

**θεμιστός I**, after '= *θεμιτός*' insert 'Archil. 177.3 W.'; add 'as pers. n., *SEG* 32.756 (Berezan, vi/v BC)'

**θεμῑτεύω**, for 'orgies' read 'rites' and delete 'metri gr.'

**θεμῑτός**, line 6, for '*τὰ μὴ θεμίτ' ἦν* .. dub. l. in' read '*εἶδε τὰ μὴ θεμιτά*'

**θεοβλᾰβής**, add '**2** *heaven-inflicted*, *ἄχη θεοβ*[*λαβῆ* rest. in S.*fr.* 269c.30 R.'

**θεογένειος**, add 'also -**γένιος** *POxy.* 3780.5 (AD 40/2)'

**θεογενής**, add 'as epith. of Caesar, *SEG* 30.1245 (Aphrodisias, i BC/i AD)'

***θεογηθής**, *ές*, *rejoicing in god*, *Didyma* 344.5, epigr. in *IGBulg.* 2086.2.

***θεόγνητος**, *ον*, *born of a god*, *Suppl.Hell.* 991.89 (poet. word-list, iii BC).

**θεόγνωστος**, add '**2** fem. subst., another name for *βράθυ*, Cyran. 12 (1.2.1 K.).'

***Θεοδαισία**, *ά*, = *Θεοδαίσια*, *τά*, *IG* 12(2).68.9 (Lesbos, ii AD).

**Θεοδαίσιος** (s.v.*Θεοδαίσια*), as the name of a month, add '*ἐπὶ Ἀλεξάνδρου*, *Θεοδαισίου SEG* 30.1637 (Rhodian amphora, Paphos, Hellen.)'; form *Θευδ-*, add '*SEG* 39.1008 (Morgantina, iv/iii BC)'

***θεοδέκτρια·** *θεὸν δεδεγμένη* Hsch. (La.; -*δέκτορα* cod.).

**θεοδέκτωρ**, delete the entry.

**θεόδμητος**, after '(Pi.)*fr.* 87.1' insert 'Lacon. *σιόδματος* Alcm. 2(iv).5 P.'

**θεοδόσιος**, add '(as pers. n., *Θōδοσιος IG* 1³.1151, Attica, v BC, etc.)'

**θεοειδής**, add 'see also *θεειδής*, *σιειδής*, °*σιοειδής*'

***θεοθελής**, *ές*, *willed by the gods*, Sch.B Il. 14.120.

***θεοκοίμητος**, *ον*, *resting in God*, *IG* 14.88 (Syracuse, Chr.).

**θεοκολέω**, add 'see also *θευκολέω*'

**θεοκόλος**, add '**θευκόλος** de Franciscis *Locr.Epiz.* 21.6; see also °*σιοκόλος*'

***θεοκόρος**, *ὁ*, gloss on *σιοκόρος*, Hsch.

***θεόκραντος**, *ον*, *ordained by the gods*, A.*Ag.* 1488.

**θεόκρῖτος**, add '**2** gloss on *Δάν* (Hebr. = *judge*), J.*AJ* 1.19.7.'

**θεολογία**, for '*science of things divine*, Pl.*R.* 379a' read '*talk about gods*, Pl.*R.* 379a; *science of things divine*'

**θεολόγος**, lines 6/7, for '*BMus.Inscr.* .. ii AD)' read 'as an official title, *θεολόγου ναῶν ἐν Περγάμῳ IEphes.* 22.4, 645.6, 1023.4, etc.'

**θεομᾰχέω**, add 'X.*Oec.* 16.3, D.S. 14.69, Philostr.*VA* 4.44'

***θεομήδεα**, *τά*, *counsels of God*, *Gerasa* 327 (vi AD).

***θεομῑμᾶτος**, *ον*, hyperdor. = *θεόμιμος*, Hippod.ap.Stob. 4.1.95 (p. 102.12 Thesleff).

**θεομῖσής I**, after '*θεοφιλής*' insert 'Ar.*Av.* 1548' **II**, delete 'Ar.*Av.* 1548 (ubi v. Sch.)' and '(*θεομίσης* v.l. in Ar. l.c.)'

***Θεοξενιακά**, τά, *fund for the expenses of the Theoxenia*, *IG* 12(5).544*B*2.9 (Ceos, iv/iii BC).

**θεοπάτωρ**, add 'of a Roman Emperor, *MDAI(A)* 75.121.21 (Samos, i AD)'

**θεοπειθής**, after '*to God*' insert '*IG* $4^2$.424.5 (iii AD), 551.2'

**θεόπλοκος**, before '*Cat.Cod.Astr.*' insert 'Rhetor. in'

**θεόπνοος**, add 'perh. of a priest of Apollo at Claros, *Laodicée* 12c p. 337'

**θεοποιός I**, add 'maker of statues of gods, Ἐπαφρᾶς θεοποιὸς ἐποί[ησε] *SEG* 32.1381 (Paphos, ii BC)'

**θεοπόλος**, delete the entry.

**θεοπροπέω**, for '*prophesy*' read '*explain the will of the gods*' **II**, add '*Ephes.* 4(3) p. 294 no. 62 (θαιο-)'

**θεοπροπία**, for '*prophecy*' read '*statement of the will of the gods*'

**θεοπρόπος I 1**, line 1, for '*prophetic*' read '*divining*'; delete 'ἔπος .. lyr.' add '**b** τοὔπος τὸ θ. *the oracle*, S.*Tr.* 822 (lyr.); πολλὰ .. θεοπρόπα .. χρησεῖ Call.*Lav.Pall.* 125.' **2 b**, delete the section.

***θεοπρόσπλοκος**, ον, *very religious*, Ptol.*Tetr.* 71 (where Proclus paraphrases προσπλεκόμενοι πρὸς θεούς), 155, 159.

***θεοπρόσπολος**, ον, *dedicated to the service of God*, v.l. for prec. in Ptol.*Tetr.* 71, 155.

**θεός**, line 1, Lacon. σιός, after 'v. infra' insert 'and s.v. ‡σιός' and θιός, add 'Arg. θιιôι (dat.) *SEG* 36.341 (*c.*550 BC)'; line 2, for '*Inscr.Cypr.* 135.27 H.' read '*ICS* 217.27, 219 (both fem.), 267.2, al.'; line 5, after 'Τιμόθεε' insert 'ep. gen. and dat. sg. and pl. θεόφιν Il. 17.101, 14.318, al.' **I 1 a**, add 'κατὰ πρόσταγμα σὺν θεοῖς πᾶσι *SEG* 35.989 (Cnossus), in dedications, etc., θεοῖς πᾶσιν ib. 25.867 (Telos, both ii/i BC), etc. (cf. Myc. *pa-si-te-o-i*)' add '**g** as a statue, τὸν θεὸν .. ἐκ τῶν ἰδίων ἀνέσ(σ)τησε *TAM* 4(1).70.' **III**, line 5, after 'not in Com.' insert 'exc. Men.*Pk.* 397' at end add 'Myc. *te-o*'

**θεόσδοτος**, add 'Θεόζοτος (as pers. n.) *SEG* 32.610 (Pharsalus, *c.*350 BC); cf. Θεοζοτίδης *SEG* 28.46 (Attica, 403/2 BC)'

***θεοστεφής**, ές, *crowned by god*, *Epigr.Gr.* 1064.10 (Constantinople, vi AD).

**θεοστῠγής**, for '*hated of the gods*' read '*hated by the gods* (*God*)' and add 'S.*fr.* 269a.22, E.*Cyc.* 396'

**θεοσύλης**, after '*sacrilegious*' insert 'Alc. 298(*a*).4 L.-P., *Iamb.adesp.* 35.10 W.'

***θεόσῡλις**, fem. adj. *sacrilegious*, ῥῖνα θεόσυλιν rest. in Hippon. 118.1 W.

***θεοταρβής**, ές, *god-fearing*, *Suppl.Hell.* 991.38 (poet. word-list, iii BC).

**θεότης**, add 'see also ‡θειότης'

**θεοτόκος**, add '*SEG* 30.1701 (Sinai, v AD). **2** *giving birth to gods*, γῆ rest. in orac. in *TAM* 2.174*B*11 (Sidyma, ii AD).'

***θεότροπος**, ον, *godlike in character*, of a queen, *BMC Bactria* p. 43.

**θεουδής**, at end after '(Q.S.) 3.775' insert 'where the adj., applied to ὄμβρος and νῆσος respectively, perh. = θεσπέσιος'

**θεοφάνια**, add '*SEG* 30.1073 (Chios, perh. *c.*189/8 BC)'

***Θεοφάνικά**, τά, prob. *fund for the expenses of the Theophania*, *IGRom.* 4.950 (Chios, i BC/i AD), cf. Robert *OMS* 1.523 n. 3.

**θεοφῐλής I**, line 4, as honorific epith., delete 'in Egypt' and add '*SEG* 31.641 (Thessalonica, AD 361/3), 37.367 (fem. sup., Patrae, vi AD)'; lines 7/8, delete 'θεοφιλές .. Plu. 2.30f'

**θεοφίλητος**, add 'Socr.*Ep.* 35'

**θεόφῐλος**, add 'of a person, *SEG* 32.1442 (Syria, AD 542)'

**θεοφορέω**, name of play of Menander, add '(*OCT* ed. Sandbach p. 143)'

**θεοφορία**, add 'Myc. *te-o-po-ri-ja*, perh. name of a festival'

**θεοφόρος I**, add '-φόρος, ὁ, as title of functionary in a Bacchic association, *AJA* 37.244 (pl.; Latium, ii AD)'

**θεοφροσύνη**, add 'Euph.in *Suppl.Hell.* 443.4 (s.v.l.)'

***θεοφύλακτος**, ον, *protected by God*, τῶν γαλινοτάτων καὶ θεοφυλάκτων ἡμῶν βασιλέων Μαυρικίου καὶ Θεοδοσίου *ICilicie* 118 (AD 596).

**θεόχρηστος**, add 'pers. epith., *APAW* 1925.5, p. 18 no. 2.5 (Cyrene, iii AD)'

⁺**θέπτανος**· ἁπτόμενος Hsch. (θεπτάνων La., cf. θεπταίνων· ἁπτόμενος Cyr.; perh. misreading of θειγγάνων = θιγγάνων).

**θεράπαινα**, add 'also **θεράπεινα** *SEG* 31.1387 (Apamea, iv AD)'

**θερᾰπεία II**, add '**2** *treating*, ἐγχώριος θ., according to native (Egyptian) custom i.e. embalming, *CPR* 6.1.14 (AD 125). **3** *remedying* of a situation, Just.*Nov.* 4.1, οὐδὲ τοῦτο ἀρκεῖ πρὸς τελειοτάτην τοῦ πράγματος θεραπείαν ib. 69.3.1. **b** *financial compensation*, *remuneration*, id.*Edict.* 9.2 pr.'

**θεράπευμα II 2**, add '**b** *thing to be treated*, *case for treatment*, δύσκολον θ. τὴν ἀδολεσχίαν Plu. 2.502b.'

***θερᾰπεύσιμος**, ον, *repaired*, *POxy.* 3595.36, 3596.33, 3597.33 (all iii AD).

**θερᾰπευτέον II**, add '**4** *one must remedy* a legal difficulty, Just.*Nov.* 4.1.'

***θερᾰπευτήριον**, τό, wd. of uncertain sense, app. relating to the preparation or supply of wine, περὶ δὲ τῶν οἰναρίων ὑπερεθέμεθα τὰ θ. εἰς τὸ μέλλον *POxy.Hels.* 50.17 (iii AD).

**θερᾰπευτής I**, add '*worshipper of Asclepius*, *Inscr.Perg.* 8(3).71' **II**, add '**3** perh. *caulker* (cf. °θεραπεύω), θ. ναυπηγός *OGIS* 674.'

**θερᾰπευτικός II 2**, add 'δύναμις θ. Epiph.Const. in *Lapid.Gr.* 194.8'

**θερᾰπεύω II 10**, add 'of embalming, ζῷον Horap. 1.39 S., cf. *UPZ* 162 ii 22 (ii BC), *APF* 13.76; also, of some process connected with shipbuilding, perh. *caulk*, *PBeatty Panop.* 2.271 (AD 300)'

***θεραπνεύω**, *to be a* θεράπων, Ἀθηνᾶ 20.216, 217 (Chios).

**θεράπνη II**, add 'Orph.*A.* 950, 1208 (pl.); cf. θεράπναι· αὐλῶνες, σταθμοί Hsch.'

**θεράπων I**, line 9, for 'Cypr.' read 'Cyprus' **II**, after '*servant*' insert '(whether slave or free)' and delete 'in Chios, *slave*' at end add 'perh. Myc. *te-ra-po-ti* (dat.) (?)pers. n., cf. *te-ra-po-si-jo*, pers. n.'

⁺**θερειγενής**, ές, *produced* or *coming into being in summer*, θερειγενέος .. κυμίνου Nic.*Th.* 601; of the Nile flood, ὕδάτων Nonn.*D.* 26.229, Νείλοιο θ. οἶδμα 26.238.

**θέρειος II**, after 'Plb. 5.13, al.' insert '*Delph.* 3(3).237.10 (ii BC)' **III**, for 'Nic.*Th.* 460' read 'Nic.*Th.* 469'

**θεριστής**, add 'Sosith. 2.21 S.'

***θέριστον**, τό, = θέριστρον, Phot.

**θερίστριον**, add 'Eub. 101 K.-A., *Vit.Aesop.*(G) 32'

**θερμαντήριος II**, after '= θερμαντήρ' insert '*IG* $1^3$.421.96 (Athens, v BC)'

**θερμαντικός**, add '**II** *hot*, *lustful*, of a bull, Horap. 1.46 S. (sup.).'

**θέρμαστις**, for 'perh. .. garment' read 'name of a garment, παρυφὴν ἔχει θέρμαστιν'

***θερμάστριον**, τό, app. some vessel or implement, θ. σιδηροῦν παλαιόν *Inscr.Délos* 1417*A*ii58, cf. Hsch. s.v. σχίνδαν.

**θερμαστρίς**, line 5, after 'Hsch.' insert 'used by a painter, prob. for encaustic work, *PCair.Zen.* 782(a).50, 61 (iii BC)'

***θέρμαυστις**, εως, ἡ, = θερμαστρίς III, *IG* $1^3$.421.97-8 (rest.; Athens, v BC), *IG* $2^2$.*Add. et Corr.* 1424a.287.

**θερμαύστρα**, for 'f.l. .. (q.v.)' read '= θερμάστρα, Call.*Del.* 144 (codd.), *IG* 11(2).144*B*19 (late iv BC)'

***θέρμαυστρον**, τό, or ος, ὁ, *portable brazier*, Heracleo and Ar. Byz.ap.Hdn.*fr.* p. 28 H.

***θερμέλᾰτος**, ον, *struck hot*, Moses Alch. 304.7.

***θερμέλη**· ἡ θέρμη Suid.; cf. ἕλη.

**θέρμη II 1**, add 'also sg., Orph.*H.* 59.3'

**θερμημερίαι**, add '**2** *warm days* in winter, Diocl.*fr.* 141 W. (ap.Orib.*inc.* 40.41).'

***θερμηνός**, ή, όν, *of hot springs*, Μητρὶ Θ. εὐχήν Robert *Hell.* 10.78 (S.E. of Dorylaeum).

**θέρμιον**, add '*OFlorida* 14.12'

***Θέρμιος**, ὁ, name of month, *Hesperia* 27.75 (*c.*200 BC, unkn. provenance). **2** as title of gods: of Apollo, *IG* 12(2).104 (Mytilene); also fem. **Θερμία** of Artemis, ib. 12(2).67.14 (Mytilene), 544 (Methymna).

**θερμοδοσία**, after 'ἡ' insert '*administering of hot drinks*'

**θερμοδότις**, for '*bath-attendant*' read '*one who serves hot food* or *drink*'

***Θερμόλοια**, τά, festival at Gortyn, *Inscr.Cret.* 4.143.3 (Gortyn, iv BC).

**θερμόλυχνον**, add 'also read as °ἑρμόλυχνον (i.e. τό θ' ἑρμ.)'

**θερμομῑγής**, for '*half-hot*' read '*mixed with heat*'

**θερμοπερίπᾰτος**, for pres. ref. read '*IGBulg.* 615 (AD 184/5)'

***θερμοπώλης**, ου, ὁ (written -πολ-), *keeper of a cook-shop*, *MAMA* 3.165 (Corasium), 719 (Corycus).

**θερμός I**, add '**2** *warm*, of living creatures, in quot. *"still alive"* LXX *Je* 38(31).2.' **II 1**, add '**b** of a situation, *dangerous*, τὰ γὰρ πράγματα θερμὰ γε[ίνεται *SB* 10556.28 (iii AD). **c** of speech, *vehement*, Philostr.*VS* 1.25.10.' **III 3**, delete the section. **4**, add '*hot baths*, *Thermae*, Ἀδριανῶν θ. *POxy.* 54.14 (iii AD); τῶν μειζόνων θ. ib. 473.5 (ii AD)'

**θέρμος**, add 'Lyc.*fr.* 2.10 S.'

**Θερμοῦθις** (to precede θερμουργία), add 'as title of Isis, Bernand *Les Portes* 24 (i BC), 3 (ii AD)'

***θερμοφῠλάκιον**, τό, app. a cooking utensil for keeping food hot, θερμοφυλάκιον ὁλκ(ῆς) λι(τρῶν) ζ' *PWash.Univ.* 59.12 (v AD).

***θερμοψῡχέω**, *to be hot* (in temper) or *agitated*, *POxy.* 3860.7 (iv AD).

***θεροκαυσώδης**, ες, *causing summer heat*, *PMag.* 4.1359.

***Θερσῑτοκτόνος**, ὁ, *killer of Thersites*, Ἀχιλλεὺς Θ. title of play by Chaeremon, Stob. 1.6.5 (1.85 W.) (cf. *SEG* 33.322).

***θεροόλη**, ἡ, unexpld. wd., Arc. 109 B., Theognost.*Can.* 111.

**θέρσος**, after 'θάρσος' insert 'Alc. 206.2 L.-P.'

***θερσύς**, v. °θρασύς.

***θεσίδιον**, τό, *position* (for coffin or sarcophagus), *burial-place*, *ITyr* 72, 130, al. (sp. -ιν).

**θέσις**, line 2, after 'Pi.*O.* 3.8' insert '= ἡ ποίησις παρὰ Ἀλκαίῳ, *EM* 319.31' **III**, line 4, after '(Amorgos)' insert 'οἱ εἰς θέσιν .. δεδομένοι (cf. Lat. *in adoptionem dare*) *Cod.Just.* 6.4.4.21' add '**IX**

*burial-place, grave*, *SEG* 30.1349 (Miletus, c.AD 180/200), ib. 1479 (Phrygia, before AD 216), etc.'

**θέσκελος**, delete 'perh. *set in motion by God* (κέλλω) and so'; line 3, after 'Call.*fr.anon.* 385' insert '*divine*, εἶδος, opp. βροτοειδέα μορφήν, Nonn.*D.* 47.718'

**θεσμοθέτις**, for '= θεσμοφόρος' read 'fem. of θεσμοθέτης'

**θεσμοπόλος**, add '*GVAK* 38 (Pisidia, v AD)'

**θεσμός**, line 2, for 'Locr. τετθμός .. v BC)' read 'W.Locr. τεθμός *IG* 9²(1).609.A1 (vi/v BC)' **I 2**, add '**b** *jurisdiction*, ἐν ἁπάσαις ταῖς πόλεσιν ὅσας ὁ ἡμέτερος κατέχει θεσμός Just.*Nov.* 2.5 epilogos, 7 epilogos.' **3**, add '**b** ἐρόεις καὶ ἄλκιμος εἰν ἑνὶ θεσμῷ *in combination, at once*, Nonn.*D.* 29.29 (s.v.l.).' **III**, add '**2** perh. = θήκη 2, *ARW* 10.403 (Cos, iii BC).'

***θεσμοτόαρος**, ὁ, *guardian of the law* (functionary in Arcadia), *BCH* 111.169.19 (Mantinea, iv BC).

***θεσμοφοριακός**, ή, όν, *belonging to the Thesmophoria*, St.Byz. s.v. Κάλατις.

***θεσμοφοριαστής**, οῦ, ὁ, *one who celebrates the Thesmophoria*, *IG* 12(1).157 (i AD).

**Θεσμοφόριος II**, month-name, add '*SEG* 30.1637 (Rhodes)'

**Θεσμοφοριών**, add '*Amyzon* 14 p. 146 (202/1 BC)'

**θεσμοφόρος**, after 'of Demeter' insert 'Dubois *Dial.arcad.* p. 196 (Pheneos, c.500 BC)'

***θεσμοφῠλᾰκέω**, *act as* θεσμοφύλαξ, Petersen-Luschan *Reisen in Lykien* no. 19 *o* 5.

**θεσμοφύλαξ**, at end, Boeot. τεθμοφούλαξ, add '*SEG* 32.456.21 (Haliartus, c.235/0 BC)'

**θεσπέσιος III**, after 'θεσπεσίηθεν .. Emp. 96.4' insert '(prob. f.l. for θεσπεσίῃσιν)'

**θεσπίζω I**, add '**2** *reveal*, δίκταμον .. ἀθάνατοι τὴν αὐτοὶ θέσπισαν ἡμῖν Poet.*de herb.* 75.' **II**, after 'Ph. 2.38' insert '(s.v.l.)' **III**, add 'of other rulers, in quot., of Lycurgus, w. inf., Sch.B Il. 1.534'

**θέσπισμα 2**, add 'generally, *ordinance*, τὰ τῶν ἀρχόντων θ. Sch.B Il. 8.12'

***θεσπιστήρ**, ῆρος, ὁ, *prophet*, epigr. in *SEG* 15.620.5 (Ostia, iii AD).

***Θεσσᾰλιώτας**· ἐναγι[α]σμός τις παρὰ Λάκωσι, Hsch. (Θεσσαλώπας· ἐναγισμός La.).

***θέστας**, α, ὁ, *suppliant*, prob. to be understood in vase inscr. θεστᾶν μνάμων *SEG* 34.966 (nr. Gela, c.350 BC).

**θέσφᾰτος I 2**, add 'Luc.*Philops.* 38, *Syr.D.* 36'

**θετικός III**, lines 5/6, for '*addressed* .. feeling' read '*more abstract*'

**θετός II**, add 'perh. also *TAM* 4(1).276'

***θευκόλος**, v. ‡θεοκόλος.

**θέω** (B), after '*IG* 14.1389 ii 24' insert 'cf. χλωραθέω'

***θεώδης**, ες, = θεοειδής, Heph.Astr. 3.7.13 (comp.).

**θεώρημα II 1 c**, add 'Plot. 3.8.4, τὸ θεωροῦν μου θεώρημα ποιεῖ ὥσπερ οἱ γεωμέτραι θεωροῦντες γράφουσιν Plot. 3.8.4, 3.8.6, Iamb.*Protr.* 2 p. 9.12'

**θεωρητικός II**, add '*Cod.Just.* 11.1.2'

**θεωρία**, line 2, after 'Dor. **θεᾱρία** (v. infr.)' insert 'also Arc. *BCH* 111.168.10 (Mantinea, iv BC)' **III 2**, add 'ὁκοίη .. τῶν ἐν γῇ φυομένων θεωρία Hp.*Lex* 3' **3**, add '*Didyma* 279*a*11, 152.10 (θυορ-), 329.12 (θεορ-) (all pl.)'

**θεωρικός II**, add '**b** *fee paid to* θεωροί, *SEG* 12.372*B*10 (Cos, iii BC).'

**θεωρίς I 1**, add 'S.*fr.* 765 R.' add '**3** by confusion = θυωρίς (sc. τράπεζα), Poll. 4.123.'

**θεωροδοκία**, (θεαρο-), add '*SEG* 31.535 (Delphi, c.320 BC)'

**θεωρός**, lines 11/12, form θεαρός, add 'Ion. inscr. from Andros in *Hesperia* 18.59.A33 (Delphi, 425 BC)'; penultimate line, after 'θιαρός' insert '*Inscr.Cret.* 2.xii 11 (Eleutherna, vi/v BC)'

**θεωροσύνη**, add 'also **θεωρωσ-** rest. in *SEG* 23.180 (Cleonaea, 145 BC)'

**Θῆβαι**, line 1, after 'Il. 9.381' insert 'Ἐρόōν τôν ἐν Θέβαις *SEG* 37.283 (Argos, vi BC)'; line 2, after '(Il.) 4.406' insert '*CEG* 787, Call.*Del.* 87, 88 (Egyptian), *GVI* 943 (Demetrias, iii BC), 870 (Tanagra, ii BC); Myc. *te-qa*'

**Θηβαϊκός**, after 'ή, όν' insert '*of* or *from the Thebais*' and after 'Hdt. 2.4, etc.' add '*SEG* 33.946.12 (Ephesus, i AD), of wine, *POxy.* 3740.17, 3762.16, 3765.4 (iv AD)'

**Θηβαῖος**, add 'epith. of Zeus (*of* Egyptian *Thebes*), Jeffery *LSAG* p. 415 no. 49 (Naucratis, vi BC); cf. Myc. *te-qa-ja*, fem. pers. n., *au-to-te-qa-jo* masc. pers. n.'

**θηητός**, after 'Tyrt. 10.29' insert 'cj.'

***θηήτωρ**, ορος, ὁ, = θηητήρ, Nonn.*D.* 22.57.

**θηκαῖος**, add 'of a bronze hydria used as an urn for ashes, θηκαία Αὐτονοεία *SEG* 33.472 (Thessaly, v BC)' **II**, add '*IMylasa* 470 (sp. θηκαῖν)'

**θήκη 1**, after '*chest*' insert 'for money or other things' and after 'X.*Oec.* 8.17, etc.' add 'θ. καλάμων *Edict.Diocl.* in *SEG* 37.335 iii 17 (θήκην καν[νῶν ib. 10.17 L.)' **2**, add '*GVI* 1613 (Attica, ii AD), *TAM* 4(1).354, 374, 376; perh. also masc. θῆκος *SEG* 32.1530' **3**, at beginning insert 'θ. σπάθης *Edict.Diocl.* 7.37'

**+θηκίον**, τό, *chest*, *PFay.* 104.5 (iii AD). **2** *tomb*, *IG* 12(3).1238 (Melos, iii/iv AD), *SEG* 32.317 (Athens, Chr.); cf. Hsch. (both senses).

**θηκοποιέω**, pass., add '*PHels.* 31.14 (160 BC)'

***θηλαστήριον**, τό, *establishment of wet-nurses*, *BGU* 1854.6 (?i AD).

**θηλή II**, add '**2** part of the θυμιατήριον, *Inscr.Délos* 443*Bb*143 (ii BC).'

**θηλητήρ**, add 'cf. θηρατήρ'

***Θηλούθιος**, ὁ, v. Θειλ-.

***θηλῠκάρδιος**, ἡ, sc. λίθος, a precious stone, Plin.*HN* 37.183.

***θηλῠκόσωμος**, ον, *having the body of a woman*, Ps.-Callisth. 1.5.

**θηλῠμᾰνέω**, add 'sim., of animals, Sch.B Il. 23.295' add '**II** *to be over-luxuriant*, of trees, as etym. of προθέλυμνος, Andromachus in Sch.B Il. 13.130; cf. μάχλος 2a and ‡καθυλομανέω.'

**θηλυπρεπής**, after 'Chor.*Lyd.* 7' insert 'θηλυπρεποῦς φωτός, perh. Heracles, *Didyma* 501.9'

***θηλύρριζος**, ἡ, sc. λίθος, a precious stone, Plin.*HN* 37.183.

**θῆλυς**, line 5, delete 'acc. fem. .. Nic.*Al.* 42' **I 1 c**, add 'n. pl., *females*, τοῖς θήλεσι (opp. τοῖς παιδικοῖσι) E.*Cyc.* 584' **2**, at end for 'murder *by women*' read 'murder *of women*' **II 3**, add 'of stones, Theophr.*Lap.*(*fr.* 5) 30' **III**, for 'Seleuc.ap.Ath. 650d' read 'Seleuc.ap.Ath. 658d'

***θῆμνες**, gloss on θιάλλαι, Hsch. (but perh. distortion of entry ib. s.v. θίλα).

**θημολογέω**, add '(prob. corrupt; ἐχημολόγει Meineke)'

**+θημωνιά** (**θιμ-** v.ll. and edd. in Lxx) *heap, pile*, Lxx *Ex.* 8.10, *Jb.* 5.26, *Ca.* 7.2, *Si.* 20.28, *Ze.* 2.9, etc., Aq., Th.*Jb.* 21.32, Eust. 1539.16; also **θειμωνειαί** and **θημονιά** Hsch. (-μων- Schmidt).

***θημωνιάζομαι**, *to be heaped up*, Al.*Ex.* 15.8.

**θην**, add 'Pi.*fr.* 203.1 S.-M., A.R. 2.915, Cerc. 4.35'

**θήνιον**, add 'prob. in *Inscr.Cret.* 1.xvii 18 (Lebena, i BC)'

**θήρ**, line 1, after 'also ἡ' insert 'Nic.*Th.* 814' **2**, line 3, after 'Ar.*Av.* 1064 (lyr.)' insert 'of a centipede, Nic. l.c.'

**θήρα**, add '**V** *snare* (transl. Hebr. *rešet* "net"), Lxx *Ps.* 34(35).8, *Ep.Rom.* 11.9.'

**θηραγρέτης**, delete 'E.*Ba.* 1020 (lyr., s.v.l.)'

***θηραγρευτής**, οῦ, ὁ, *hunter*, cj. in E.*Ba.* 1020 (cod. θηραγρότ-).

**Θηραϊκόν** or **Θήραιον**, add '*IG* 2².1415.25, 1421.126, al. (iv BC, Θήραιον or Θήραια)'

**θήρᾱμα**, add '**2** *snare*, E.*IA* 963.'

**θηρᾱτήρ**, add 'see also θηλητήρ'

**θήρατρον**, line 3, after 'Max.Tyr. 16.5' insert 'of the tentacles of an octopus, Ael.*VH* 1.1'

***θήραφος**, ὁ, *spider*, Cyran. 62 (2.16.1 K.).

**θηράω I 2**, line 4, after 'A.*Ag.* 1194' insert '(cj.)'

**θήρειος I**, add '**2** = θηριακός, φάρμακα Aristid.*Or.* 48(24).64.'

***θηρέστατος**, η, ον, perh. *most devoted to hunting*, ὁ γὰρ θηρέστατος ἦεν *Suppl.Hell.* 970 i 20.

**θηρευτικός 2**, add 'ἄλλαι πᾶσαι ἐπιστῆμαι θηρευτικαί τινές εἰσι .. τῶν ἀγαθῶν Iamb.*Protr.* 5 p. 27.3'

**θηρεύω II 2**, at end after 'Phld.*Rh.* 2.5 S., al.' insert 'θ. ἀκοήν, of birds, *Lyr.adesp.* 118.2 P.'

**θηρίδιον**, for '*animalculae*' read '*animalcules*'

***Θηρικλείδιον**, τό, (*small*) *vessel made by Thericles* or *in his style*, Θ. οὐκ ἔχον οὔτε ὦτα οὔτε πυθμένα *Inscr.Délos* 1450*A*137 (ii BC).

**Θηρίκλειος**, add 'also sp. Θυρεικλεῖος *Kafizin* 40, 41, 46'

**θηριοδεῖκται**, for '*exhibitors of wild beasts*' read 'perh. *snake-charmers*'

**θηριοδήκτης**, delete the entry.

***θηριοδιώκτης**, *Marsus*, *Gloss.*

***θηριομάχιον**, τό, *contest with wild beasts*, *TAM* 2.508.12 (Pinara, pl.).

**θηρίον I 2**, add 'of snakes, *Act.Ap.* 28.4, of vermin, etc., Dsc. 1.75' **3 b**, delete the section. **IV**, add 'also, any of constellations symbolized by animals, v.l. in Lxx *Je.* 10.2' at end add 'see also °σηρίον'

**θηριοτρόφος I**, after '*keeping wild beasts*' insert 'Ptol.*Tetr.* 179'

**θηριώδης II 2**, add 'Hp.*VM* 7, Critias 19.2 S., D.S. 1.8.1; adv. Isoc. 3.6, 4.28'

***θηριωνῠμία**, ἡ, *name derived from a wild beast*, *Orac.Tiburt.* 143.

**θηριώνῠμος**, add '*Orac.Tiburt.* 136'

**θηρόβοτος**, add 'θηροβότου .. κολώνης Nonn.*D.* 16.259; θηρόβοτος, ἡ, *beast-haunted wilderness*, Phalar.*Ep.* 147.4'

***θηροδίαιτος**, ον, *living like wild beasts*, *Didyma* 496*B*6 (ii AD).

**+θηροκόμος**, ὁ, *keeper of a wild animal*, Hld. 10.27.3.

**θηροκτόνος**, add 'see also σηροκτόνος'

**θηρομᾰχία**, delete '*IGRom.* 3.631 (Xanthus)'

***θηρομάχια**, τά, *wild beast fights*, *TAM* 2(2).287.14.

**θηρόπεπλος**, for 'Cerc. 10 .. Timae. 80' read 'Stratonic.ap.Timae. 16 J.'

**θής I**, add '**4** *temple servant*, prob. in Call.*fr.* 186.14 Pf.'

**θησαυρός II 1**, add 'of the imperial treasury, ὁ θησαυρὸς τοῦ κυρίου *SEG* 34.1306.12 (Perge, iii AD)'
**θησαυροφύλαξ**, transfer 'Vett.Val. 85.23' to section II.
**Θησεύς**, add 'Myc. *te-se-u*, pers. n.'
***θίας**, α, ὁ, Rhodian = θεῖος (B), *Lindos* 198.7 (ii BC), al., *Clara Rhodos* 2.193 (ii BC), al.
**θιᾰσῑτικός**, add '*PEnteux.* 20.5, 9 (iii BC)'
**θίᾰσος I**, add 'Alcm. 98 P.'
***θῑβοῦχος**, ὁ, *basket-carrier*, Swoboda *Denkmäler* 217 (Palaia Isaura, s.v.l.).
**θιβρός II**, after 'Euph. 81' insert 'cf. θίρρον· τὸ τρυφερόν, Theognost.*Can.* 15.20'
**θῑγάνα**, for '*Schwyzer* .. (Delph.)' read '*CID* I 9.639 (iv BC)'
**θιγγάνω I 1**, w. acc., add 'Alcm. 58.2 P., S.*Ant.* 546, Pherecr. 10.4 K.-A.' add '**4** w. dat., *be adjacent* to, τὰ θιγγάνοντα τῷ ἰαρῷ τεμένια *REA* 44.35.45 (Olus, ii BC).'
**θικέλιον**, after lemma insert '(**θίκελιν** La.)'
***θιμωνιά**, ἡ, v. °θημωνιά.
***θῖος**, v. ‡θεῖος (B).
**θίς I 2**, add '**c** *hill*, Lxx *Ge.* 49.26, *De.* 12.2, *Jb.* 15.7.'
**θλίβω II**, lines 5/6, delete 'θλιβομένα .. Theoc. 21.18'
**θλῖψις 3**, add 'from famine, τὰν τῶν ἰδίων συνπολιτᾶν θλῖψιν *SEG* 26.1817.38 (Cyrenaica, ii/i BC)'
**θνῆσις**, add 'προβάτων καὶ βοῶν θνῆσις γενήσεται *Orac.Tiburt.* 125'
**θνητογᾰμία**, add 'Sch.Il. 1.5'
***θνητόγονος**, ον, = θνητογενής, epigr. in *SPAW* 1932.862.
**θνητός 1**, after 'Hdt. 1.216, 2.68' insert 'παντοῖα .. εἴδεα θνητῶν Emp. 115.7' add '**b** τὰ τνᾱτά (= θνητά), property in cattle, animals, *Leg.Gort.* 5.39 (v BC), etc., v. °ἀθάνατος.'
**θοάζω** (C), delete the entry.
***θοάω**, v. °θωάζω.
***θοιναρμοστρέω** (?), *serve as* θοιναρμόστρια, aor. part. in Lacon. form σειναρμοστρήἀά perh. to be read in *IG* 5(1).229.2 (i BC/i AD), cf. *ABSA* 45.266, n. 13.
**θοιναρμόστρια**, after 'σειναρμόστρηα ib. 229' add '(dub., v. °θοιναρμοστρέω)'
***θοινᾱτᾱ́ς**, ᾶ, ὁ, = θοινάτωρ, τᾶς Δάματρος *Dacia* 3/4.451 (Callatis, i BC, pl.); also **θοινητής**, οῦ, *SEG* 24.975 (sp. θοινειτ-, Moesia, ii AD).
***θοινητής**, v. °θοινατάς.
***θολέρησις**, εως, ἡ, *turbidity*, cj. in Plu. 2.383d.
**θολερός II**, after 'adv. -ρῶς' insert 'Man. 6.178'
***θολίδιον**, τό, dim. of θόλος, *IG* $2^2$.1534.280 (Athens, iii BC).
***θόλιος**, α, ον, *of the Tholos* (at Athens), *Hesperia* suppl. 4.145 (ii BC).
***θολοποιέω**, *make muddy*, τὸ ὕδωρ Aesop. p. 542 P.
**θόλος**, add '(θόλος as wd. of two genders, S.E.*M.* 1.148; for masc. v. sense II)' **II 2**, add 'Gal. 18(1).777.5; also fem. in this sense *SEG* 12.1503 (Palestine, *c.*AD 455)'
**θοός** (A), line 2, after 'etc.' insert 'Βιττίδα .. θοήν Hermesian. 7.77'; line 12, after 'motion' insert 'Ἄϊδος' and for 'Antim. 71' read 'Antim. 187.2 W.'; add 'comp. θανάτοιο θοώτερος ἵξεται αἶσα Nic.*Th.* 120' add '**II** interpreted as *"sharp"* by Hellen. writers (cf. Str. 8.3.26 w. ref. to Od. 15.299, where it may be a proper name) θοοῖς .. γόμφοις A.R. 2.79, θοῶν .. ὀδόντων 3.1281, θοοῖς πελέκεσσιν 4.1683, *AP* 9.157, Q.S. 4.417, 14.305.' at end add 'in Myc. cpd. *pe-ri-to-wo*, pers. n. = Πειρίθοος'
**θοός** (B), delete the entry (v. °θοός (A)).
**⁺θοόω**, perh. *urge on*, Od. 9.327. **II** *excite*, ἐν πυρὶ .. φωνὴν τεθοωμένος, of Cerberus, Hermesian. 7.11, Nic.*Th.* 228, λύσσῃ τεθοωμένος Opp.*H.* 1.557, 2.525.
**θοράνας**, after lemma insert '(**θόρανδε** La.)'
**θορή**, add 'Aret.*SD* 2.5.1 (71.11 H.), al.'
***θορηνεύς**· ὁ ξιφίας ἰχθύς Hsch. (cod. θορηνεῦσαι).
***θόρνη**, ἡ, perh. *mating*, *PDerveni* xvii 1 (*ZPE* 47.*10; late iv BC).
**θόρνυμαι**, after 'Nic.*Th.* 130' insert 'thematic forms, θορνύεται Theognost.*Can.* 46 A.'; add 'act. part. θορνύς *mating*, Nic.*Th.* 99.'
**θορῠβέω II**, after '(Th.) 6.61' insert '*Cod.Just.* 1.3.52.9'
***θουννόκειτ**( ?ος), v. °θυννόκητος.
**θουράω**, for '*leap upon*, c. acc.' read '*leap impetuously* upon, ἐπ' ἀρσένων .. λέκτρα θουρῶσαι βροτῶν'
**θούριος**, add 'epith. of Ares, *SEG* 31.1285.7 (Pisidia, Rom.imp.)'
***θρᾰ́γᾰνα**, τά, perh. *mortar and pestle*, θ. διπλόα *SEG* 24.361.16 (Thespiae, 386/0 BC).
**θραγμός**, for '*crackling*' read 'perh. *ground flour*'; for 'cf. θραύω' read 'cf. °θρωγμός, perh. also °θραττεύομαι'
***Θρᾳκαρχέω**, *to hold the office of* °Θρᾳκάρχης, *IGBulg.* 1183.
***Θρᾳκάρχης**, ου, ὁ, *president of the provincial council of Thrace*, *IGBulg.* 1170, 1559, al., *SEG* 31.677.B6 (Thrace, ii/iii AD).
**Θρᾴκιος**, add 'Θρεΐκιος Hippon. 72.5, 127 W.'
**θρᾱνίδιον**, add '*IG* $1^3$.421.140 (Athens, v BC)'
**⁺θρᾶνις**, ὁ, *sword-fish*, = ξιφίας, τὸν θράνιν hελόντε *AE* 1937(3).833ff. (Eleusis, v BC); Xenocr. 8; cf. θρανίας.
**θρᾱνίτης I**, transfer 'Ar.*Ach.* 162' to section II inserting before it 'ὁ θρανίτης λεώς'
**θρᾱνογρᾰ́φος**, for '= τοιχογράφος' read 'app. *writer of graffiti*'
**θρᾶνος I 1**, add 'defined as *tanning-bench*, Sch.rec.Ar.*Eq.* 369' **II 1**, add 'S.*fr.* 269a.41; *roof-beam*, ἀπὸ θράνω λέλακα γλαύξ Alcm. 1.86 P.' **2**, before 'θ. ποικίλος' insert 'in the προστάς of a house'
**Θρᾷξ**, for 'Call.*Aet.Oxy.* 2079.13' read 'Call.*fr.* 1.13 Pf., al.' and for 'Ion. dat. pl. .. Archil.*Supp.* 4.48' read 'Θρέϊξ rest. in Archil. 42.1, 93a.6 W.'
***θρᾰσύαιγις**, ιδος, perh. *headlong, impetuous* or sim., *Lyr.adesp.* 7(*e*).12 P.
***θρᾰσύδης**, ες, *bold*, *PMich.*III 149 xi 23 (ii AD).
**θρᾰσυμήχᾰνος**, add 'Ἄρης cj. in Simon. 70.2 P.; cf. αἰγίς II, ἐπαιγίζω'
**θρᾰσυπτόλεμος**, add 'epigr. in *IUrb.Rom.* 69 (iii/iv AD)'
**θρασύς**, line 1, after 'Philem. 20 (s.v.l.)' insert 'Aeol. **θερσύς** (2 termin.), gen. ύος *IGC* p. 11 l. 24 (*c.*iii BC; cf. °Θροσία)' **1**, line 2, after 'Il. 8.89, etc.' insert 'as epith. of Athena, Pi.*N.* 3.50, *IGC* l.c.'
***θρᾰσυτολμία**, ἡ, *effrontery*, Act.Alexandr. 10.34 (ii/iii AD).
**θρᾰσύφωνος**, add '*Suppl.Hell.* 986.4'
**θρᾴττα**, add '*IGC* p. 99 B3 (Acraephia, iii/ii BC)'
***θραττεύομαι**· συντρίβομαι, συγκόπτομαι Hsch. (La., s.v.l.; cf. θράσσω).
***θραυμάτιον**, τό, dim. of θραῦμα (in quot., sense I): pl., ἀργυρᾶ *Inscr.Délos* 1450*A*115 (ii BC).
**θραῦσμα II**, for 'in leprosy, *scab*' read '*break in the skin, sore, ulcer*'
**θραύστης**, delete the article (read pers. n. [Τι]θραύστης).
***θραυστικός**, ή, όν, *that breaks up*, θραυστικὰ .. τῶν λίθων Aët. 3.152 (324.13 O.).
**θραύω**, line 4, after 'Pl.*Lg.* 757e (v.l. -τεθραυσμένον)' insert 'cf. ἀποτεθραυμένην *Inscr.Délos* 1450*A*33, but περιτεθραυσμένην ib. 35 (ii BC)'
***θρειστίον**, τό, = °θρισσίον, *PWisc.* 6 (AD 210/1).
**θρέμμα**, add '**II** *nourishment*, Pl.*Plt.* 289b.'
**θρέομαι**, line 1, for 'only in pres.' read 'usu. pres.' and add 'impf. θρεύετο poet. in *IG* $4^2$.616.4 (Epid., iv BC)'; after 'women' for 'θρέομαι' read 'θρεῦμαι'
**θρεπτάριον**, add '*INikaia* 1376.9 (Rom.imp.), *BCH* suppl. 8.62 (Beroea, iv/v AD)'
**θρεπτήριος III 2**, after 'Hes.*Op.* 188' insert 'A.R. 1.283'
**θρεπτός I**, for 'as Subst. .. Lxx *Es.* 2.7' read '*brought up in another household, fostered*, παῖς θρεπτή Lxx *Es.* 2.7. **2** masc., fem. as subst., *domestically raised slave* (= Lat. *verna*), Lys.*fr.* 215 S., Pherecr. 130 K.-A.'; after 'Plin.*Ep. ad Traj.* 65, etc.' add 'fem., *SEG* 37.453.11 (Thessaly, ii/iii AD); also neut., (?sc. παιδίον), *SEG* 31.1004.9 (Lydia, AD 101/2); fig., *fosterling* (of the Nile), describing Sosibius, a Greek born in Egypt, Call.*fr.* 384.28 Pf.' add '**3** cult-name of Triptolemus, *Sokolowski* 3.10*A*69 (Athens, *c.*400 BC).'
**θρεσκός**, add 'cf. φιλόθρεσκος'
***θρηναύλης**, ου, ὁ, *player of aulos for dirges*, *PSAA* $43^v$ i 13 (ii AD).
**θρηνήτρια**, add '*SEG* 8.621.18 (Egypt, ii AD)'
***θρηνία**, ἡ, ἐνταῦθα δὲ τὴν ἀληθῆ μέλισσαν λέγει, ἣν ἔνιοι θρηνίαν φασὶ καὶ πληθυντικῶς θρήνια Sch.Nic.*Al.* 547b G.; cf. perh. τενθρήνη.
***θρηνικόν**, (sc. μέτρον), τό, *anapaestic monometer*, Serv. in *Gramm.Lat.* 4.461.31 K.
***θρηνοτόκος**, ον, *engendering lament*, μολπή *GVI* 1244 (Athens, ii/iii AD; less prob. to be read as θρηνότοκος *born of lament*).
**θρῆνυς**, add 'form *θρᾶνυς, Myc. *ta-ra-nu*'
**θρησκεία 1**, add 'in honour of the dead, τὴν τοῦ ἥρωος θ. *SAWW* 265(1).12.51 (Nakrason, i BC/i AD), *TAM* 2.247 (AD 146), al.'
**θρησκώδης**, add 'sup. [θρη]σκωδέστατα rest. in *IG* $2^2$.1074.15 (ii AD), cf. *AJP* 70.300'
**θριαί II**, add 'Call.*fr.* 260.50 Pf.'
**θρίαμβος I 1**, after 'Cratin. 36' add '*AP* 13.6 (Phal.)'
**θριγκός**, at end after 'θριγγός v.l. in Plu. l.c.' insert 'Longus 4.2'; for '*SIG* 1231.6' read '**τριγχός** *TAM* 4(1).276.6'
**θρίγκωμα**, for 'cj. .. 15.11.3' read 'J.*AJ* 15.11.3, cj. for τριχώματα in E.*IT* 73'
**θρῐδᾰκηΐς**, for '*of the lettuce*' read '*lettuce-like*'
**θρίδαξ**, line 4, after 'θίδραξ' insert 'Arr.*Epict.* 2.10.9, 3.24.44' and after 's.v. θιδρακίνη' insert '**θύδραξ**, *PRyl.* 627.151, 629.233'
**⁺θρίζω**, aor. ἔθρισα, v. θερίζω.
**θρῖνάκη**, for 'Call.*fr.* 46 P.' read '(?)Call.*fr.* 799 Pf.' and for 'θρίνακ' ἦν' read 'θρίναχ' ἦν'
**Θρῖνάκιος**, add '*AP* 7.714'
**θρίξ**, add '**IV** (pl.) kind of seaweed, μνία καλεῖταί τινα .. καὶ τρίχες Ael.*NA* 13.3.'
***θρισσίον**, τό, dim. of θρίσσα, *POxy.* 1923.9 (v/vi AD).
***θρίσσος** (B), ὁ, Thessalian name for kind of snake, Afric.*Cest.* p. 16 V.

**θρίψ II**, add 'cf. perh. pers. n. *Θριφόνδας SEG* 2.192 (Tanagra, vi BC; v. *MH* 43.256)'

**θροέω**, line 7, after '(troch.)' insert 'of the wind, ἀδύ τοι ἐν χλωροῖς πνεῦμα θροεῖ πετάλοις *APl.* 228 (Anyt.)' **II**, for 'causal' read 'trans., *boo* a speaker, ἐν ἐκκλησίᾳ -ούμενος *Gnomol.Vat.* in *WS* 10.224' and before '*scare*' insert '2'

**θρόμβωσις 2**, add 'Gal. 18(2).446.14'

**θρονισμός**, after '*enthronement*' insert '(in mystery rites)'

***θρονιστήριον**, τό, app. *place for a throne*, Ps.-Callisth. 38.1 (v.l.).

***θρονοθήκη**, ἡ, *box of herbs* or *drugs*, Babylonian Talmud, Kelim ch. 13 p. 42 (in Hebr. letters).

***θρονόμαντις**, εως, ὁ, *diviner by θρόνα, magic herbs*, *APAW* 1943(14).8 (Chalcis, iii AD).

**θρόνος I 1**, add 'of an honorific seat in the theatre, *SEG* 30.82.7 (Athens, *c.*AD 230)' **2**, add 'θ. ἀνθυπάτων = Lat. *sella curulis*, *SEG* 33.940 (verse, Ephesus, ?v AD). **b** transf., for the occupant of a seat of authority, *Cod.Just.* 1.3.52.11, Just.*Nov.* 82.1.1.' at end add 'Myc. *to-no* (prob. in sense I 2 = *θόρνος; in compd. also θρονο-, *to-ro-no-wo-ko* = °θρονοϝοργοί)'

**θρόνωσις**, add 'cj. in *Orac.Sib.* 8.49'

***Θροσία**, ἡ, epith. of Artemis, perh. = θρασεῖα, *Πολέμων* 1.249 (Larissa), *SEG* 34.481 (Atrax, *c.*150 BC).

**θρυαρίς**, add '(**θρυγανίς**· ψίαθος La.)'

**θρῦϊνος**, add '*PLond.* 122.103 (iv AD)'

**θρύμμα**, add 'θρύμματα· κλάσματα ἄρτου Hsch.'

**θρυμμᾰτίς**, add 'cf. θρυματίς· κρηπίς Theognost.*Can.* 20'

***θρῠοκόπος**, ὁ (or -κοπεύς, έως, ὁ), *cutter of rushes*, *POxy.* 2243*a*84 (vi AD).

***θρῠοτιλτής**, οῦ, ὁ, *rush-gatherer*, *PHarris* 97.3 (iv AD).

***θρύπτειρα**, fem. adj., *that breaks up and disperses*, θ. κονίη, *lye*, Nic.*Al.* 370 (v.l. ῥύπτ-).

***θρυπτεύεται**· ὑπερηφανεύεται Hsch. (La.; cod. θρημνεύεται).

**θρύπτω II 2 b**, delete the section. **c**, delete '*bridle up*' and add 'ὄμματι θρυπτομένῳ with a look *of feigned reluctance*, *AP* 5.287.8 (Agath.)'

**θρύσκα**, add '(due to wrong division of ἄν/θρυσκα Sapph. 96.13 L.-P.)'

⁺**θρύψιχος**, prob. *effeminate*, θ.· τρυφερός Hsch.; θ.· φοβερός Theognost.*Can.* 20.

***θρωγμός**· τρίβος Theognost.*Can.* 20.

***θρωμός**· ᾠὰ δικτύου Theognost.*Can.* 20.

**θρώσσει**, add '= ἅλλεται, Theognost.*Can.* 20; cf. θρῴσκω'

**θυαλόν**, after lemma insert '(θυαλοῦν La.; cf. θυηλέομαι)'

**θυάω**, add 'θυᾶν· καπρᾶν. ἐπὶ ὑός Hsch.'

**θῠγάτηρ**, line 1, insert 'Lacon. συγάτηρ *SEG* 11.677a, c'; at end add 'Myc. *tu-ka-te*'

**θῠγατριδοῦς**, after '*OGI* 529.23 (Sebastopolis)' insert 'τοῦ -οῦς *ABSA* 45.277 (Laconia, i/ii AD)'

**θῠγατροποιία**, add '*SEG* 31.937 (Caria, iii/ii BC)'

***θύδραξ**, v. °θρίδαξ.

**θῠεῖον**, add 'perh. also θῖον *POxy.* 3354.15 (AD 257)'

***θῠή**, ἡ, *burnt sacrifice*, Philoch. 194 J.

***θῠηδόκος**, ον, = θυοδόκος, Antip.Sid. in *Inscr.Délos* 2549.3, v. *Hermes* 76.411.

**θυηκόος**, add '*IGRom.* 3.73 (Claudiopolis)'

**θῠηπολία**, after 'Ion. -ίη' insert 'dial. θυᾱ- *SEG* 23.639 (Paphos, iv/iii BC), *BCH* 10.424 (Cedreae)'

**θῠηπολικός**, add 'Θυηπολικόν, title of work attributed to Orpheus, Suid. s.v. Ὀρφεύς'

**θυιάς**, line 2, for 'θύω' read 'θύω (B)' **I**, add '**b** pl., *nymphs associated with Dionysus' revels*, Alcm. 63 P.'

**θυίω II**, after 'Hes.*Th.* 131 (pap.)' insert 'Anacr. 2.17 P.'

**θῠλάκιον I**, add 'of money-bag, Lxx *To.* 9.5'

**θῠλακίς**, delete 'Nic.*Th.* 852' add '**II** adj., = θυλακῖτις, μήκων θ. Nic.*Th.* 852.'

**θύλᾰκος**, line 1, before 'Hdt. 3.46' insert 'Epich. 113'

**θῦμα**, last line, before '*Supp.Epigr.*' insert 'Babr. 97.12'

**θῡμαίνω**, after 'Ar.*Nu.* 610' insert 'Call.*fr.* 24.2 Pf.'; add 'med., θυμαίνεται· (θυμαίνει La.) ὀργίζεται Hsch.'

**θύμαλλος**, for 'an unknown *fish*' read 'a fish, perh. *grayling*'

**θῠμάλωψ**, add '**2** οἱ δὲ καλούμενοι νῦν τῶν ἀμπέλων ἐπίτραγοι θυμάλωπες ἐλέγοντο Poll. 7.152.'

**θῡμᾱρής**, line 3, after '(Od.) 17.199' insert 'δαῖτας θ. Call.*Cer.* 55'; line 6, after 'A.R. 1.705' insert '(cj. θυμηδές)'

**θῠμέλη II d**, add 'εἰν θυμέλαισι κλυταῖς epigr. in *SEG* 35.1427.8 (Side, iii AD)'

**θῡμηδής**, add 'Q.S. 14.312, 340'

***θῡμιαντήριον**, v. °θυμιατήριον.

***θῡμίασμα**, ατος, τό, = θυμίαμα, *incense*, *PMag.* 4.2575, 2643.

***θῡμιᾱτηρίδιον**, τό, dim. of θυμιατήριον (in quot., sense I 1), *Inscr.Délos* 1416*A*i34 (ii BC).

**θῡμιᾱτήριον**, after 'θυμιητ-' insert 'also **θυμιαντήριον** *EAM* 104' and for '*censer*' read '*incense-burner*' and add '*Kafizin* 302(b) (iii BC), *EA* 13 p. 7 no. 895 (ii BC)'

**θῡμίατρον**, add '*IEphes.* 1004, al.'

**θῡμιάω I 2**, add 'βῶμοι δὲ τεθυμιάμενοι λιβανώτῳ cj. in Sapph. 2.3/4 L.-P. (δεμιθυμ- ostr.)'

**θῡμοειδής 2 a**, add 'Hp.*Aër.* 16'

**θῡμόεις**, add 'Call.*fr.* 238.23 Pf.'

***θῡμοιδής**, ές, *irascible*, A.*fr.* 281a.32 R. (cj.).

***θῡμοκόρυμβος**, ὁ, *spike of thyme*, *PVindob.* G10734 (*Analect.Pap.* 3.121, vi AD).

**θύμον**, line 3, after '**θύμος**, ὁ' insert 'Nic.*fr.* 92'; for '*Cretan thyme*, *Thymbra capitata*' read 'some kind of thyme or sim. plant' **2**, delete the section transferring exx. to section 1.

**θῡμός I 1**, add '**b** as exhaled upon something, Κυρίου Lxx *Is.* 30.33; as the vehicle of snakes' venom, ib. *De.* 32.33 (bis), *Am.* 6.12.' add '**4** *membrum virile*, Hippon. 10 W. (but cf. Hdn.Gr. 1.169 θύμος δὲ τὸ μόριον ἢ ἡ βοτάνη and θύμος (B)).'

**θῡμοφθόρος**, after 'Nic.*Th.* 140' for '(v.l. γυιοφθ-)' read '(v.l., v. °γυιοφθ-)'

**θύννα**, for 'f.l. in Hippon. 35.2' read 'Hippon. 26.2 W.'

**θυννάς**, add 'θυννάδες· τεμάχη ταρίχου Hsch. (cf. °θυννίς 2)'

**θυννίς**, line 2, after 'ἡ' insert 'θυνίδω[ν] (gen. pl.) *SEG* 23.326.15 (Delphi, iii BC), θουννίδων *IGC* p. 99 B7 (Acraephia, iii/ii BC)' and delete 'prob. .. Hippon. 35.2' add '**2** θυννίδες· θύννων τεμάχη, ὑποκοριστικῶς Hsch.'

***θυννόκητος**, ὁ, name of a sea-fish, *IGC* p. 98 B4 (sp. θουννόκειτ-, Acraephia, iii/ii BC).

**θύννος**, add 'cf. θύννον· τὸν ὄρκυνον λέγουσι· τὴν δὲ πηλαμίδα θυννίδα Hsch.'

⁺**θυννώδης**, ες, *like a tunny*, εἶδος θ. ἰχθύος Hsch. s.v. πρημάδες (v. ‡πρημνάς); *typical of a tunny*, ἄπαγε, θυννῶδες τὸ ἐνθύμημα (i.e. stupid) Luc.*JTr.* 25.

**θύος I**, for '*burnt sacrifice*' read '*a substance producing a fragrant smell when burnt*, *incense*, or sim.' and add 'Hp.ap.Gal. 19.104' **2**, for this section read '*fragrant oil*, Nic.*Al.* 203, 452' at end add 'Myc. *tu-wo*, *aromatic substance*'

***θύρ**, θυρός, ὁ, θύρ· πτηνόν Cyran. 22 (perh. misspelling of θήρ).

**θύρα I 1**, add 'applied to symbolic door on tomb, Mitchell *N.Galatia* 242, *MAMA* 7.323, *IPhrygie* 4.24, 32' **3**, line 7, after 'S.E.*M.* 1.43' insert 'cf. παρὰ θύρας ἀπαντᾶν answer beside the point, Olymp. *in Grg.* 23.2, 26.11, 25 W.' add '**10** *leaf* of a writing tablet, Poll. 4.18.'

**θῠραῖος I 4**, add 'ἀρετὴ .. οὐκ ἐκ -ων τἀπίχειρα λαμβάνει E.*fr.* 908a'

⁺**θύρεθρα**, τά, = θύρετρα, Maiist. 28, Hsch.

**θῠρεός I**, for '*stone* .. shut' read '*stone used to block an entrance*' **II**, line 2, after 'Callix. 2' insert '*AP* 6.129 (Leon.Tarent.)'

**θῠρίδιον**, add '**2** *niche*, *POxy.* 2058.24 (vi AD).'

**θῠριδωτός**, after 'κιβωτός' insert '*IG* 1³.425.19 (Athens, v BC)'

**θύριον**, add 'ἀνέστησε θύριν μν[ήμης χάριν] Mitchell *N.Galatia* 245'

**θῠρίς I**, add '**4** *wall niche*, *SB* 7574 (ii AD), *PRoss.-Georg.* III 1 (iii AD).'

**θυρξεύς**, for 'Achaea' read 'Lycia'

***θῠροκρουστέω**, app. *knock on a door*, *PMich.*III 149.18.9.

***θῦρος**, ὁ, kind of fish, Marc.Sid. 10 (s.v.l.).

***θῠρουρικός**, v. °θυρωρ-.

***θύρσις**, ιδος or εως, ἡ, = °βάκερα, Cyran. 22 (1.8.1 K.).

**θυρσίτης**, add '**2** θ. λίθος stone resembling coral, Cyran. 22 (1.8.1 K.).'

***θυρσοκλόνος**, ὁ, = θυρσοτινάκτης, of Dionysus, *GVAThess.* 29; applied to Egyptian god, prob. identified w. Dionysus, *APAW* 1943(14).8 (Chalcis, iii AD).

**θυρσοκόμος**, after '*keeper*' insert 'Διόνυσος θ. Ps.-Callisth. 7.9'

**θῠρών**, add '**2** pl., perh. *tablets made to resemble doors* for stage purposes, *PFouad I Univ.* 14; cf. θυρῶνας· τὰς σανίδας. καὶ τὰς εἰσόδους Hsch.'

***θῠρωρικός**, ή, όν, **θυρουρ-**, *of a door-keeper*, ἄρτος *POxy.* 1890.11 (vi AD). **II** subst., θυρουρικόν, τό, *porter's lodge*, *SB* 9898.9 (*c.*AD 220), *PMich.*XI 620.9 (AD 239/40).

**θῠρωρός**, for 'Cypr. .. 215 H.' read 'Cypr. *tu-ra-wo-? perh.* θυράϝο[ρος] *ICS* 417'; add 'as ephebic rank, *SEG* 29.152 (Athens, AD 175/6)'

**θῠσία I**, line 2, before 'v.l. in Batr.' insert '*h.Cer.* 312, 368'

**θῠσιαστήριον**, add '**2** *sanctuary*, *AD* 12.27, 69; *IHadr.* 121.'

**θῠσιαστής**, add '*BCH* 8.49 (Maced.); pl., members of a cult-society, *IGRom.* 1.832 (Abdera)'

***θύσιν**, τό, v. °θύσιον.

***θύσιον**, τό, perh. *censer*, *CPR* 8.66.5 (vi AD).

***θύσκον**, τό, object for religious use, *CPR* 8.66.8, 15 (vi AD); cf. perh. θυίσκος.

**θύσσομαι**, add '(perh. due to wrong division of ἐσκίαστ' αἰθυσσομένων Sapph. 2.7 L.-P., but cf. Sch.Pi.*P.* 4.411)'

**θύτης**, after 'or *diviner*' insert 'Call.*fr.* 194.25 Pf.'

***θῦτόν**, τό, *sacrificial meat*, Hsch. s.v. θυαλόν.

**θύω** (A), line 14, after 'Pi.*O.* 13.69' insert 'θύεται [ῠ] id.*Pae.* 6.62 S.'; line 15, delete '*Cyc.* 334'

***Θῠωνίδας**· ὁ Διόνυσος παρὰ Ῥοδίοις. τοὺς συκίνους φάλητας Hsch.; cf. Θυωναῖος.

***θῠωνοφόρος**, ὁ, religious official of uncertain function, ἐλθόντι ἐπὶ τὸ Καπετώλιον μόνῳ ἄνευ τοῦ θυωνοφόρου *SEG* 29.807 (Chalcis, Rom.imp.).

**θυωρός**, for '*BCH* 11.161' read 'epigr. in *SEG* 30.1272.7'

**θωάζω**, for '*pay the penalty*' read '*penalize, fine*', deleting this in line 2; after '*IG* 1².4.7, 12' insert 'also **θωϊάω** *Thasos* 141.6 (v/iv BC)'; line 3, after '*Michel* 995 *D* 19' add '(v BC)'; add '(fut. θοάσει *IG* 2².1362.14 may be copied fr. an earlier version w. ο = ω)'

**θωή**, line 3, for 'Ion. also' read 'Arg. **θωϊᾱ́** *IG* 4.555; Ion.'; after 'Archil. 109' insert '= Call.*fr.* 195.22 Pf. (θωΐῃ pap.; cf. ἀθῷος)'

***θωπάζω**, app. = θωπεύω, scholiast in *JThS* 47(1946).70.

***θωπεῖον**, τό, a nocturnal bird, Cyran. 89 (3.16.1 K.).

**θώπτω**, add 'θώπτει· σκώπτει. θεραπεύει Hsch.'

***θωρᾱκαῖος**, α, ον, equipped with a θώραξ (sense I 1), [λιβανωτίδα ἔχουσαν νίκη]ν ἐπὶ τοῦ πώματος θωρακαίαν *Inscr.Délos* 1417*B*ii53 (ii BC).

**θωρᾱκεῖον I 1**, add 'supporting a sarcophagus, *MAMA* 8.556b'

**θώραξ II**, add '**c** pl., *breast* of a chicken, Nic.*Al.* 388.' **III**, add 'Archimel. in *Suppl.Hell.* 202.10 (pl.)' at end add 'Myc. *to-ra-ke* (pl.)'

**θώρηξις**, add 'cf. θώρηξις· οἰνοποσία. καθόπλισις Hsch.'

**θῶσθαι**, line 1, for 'A.*fr.* 49' read 'A.*fr.* 47a.2.20 R.'

# I

**ῐ**, for '*Inscr.Cypr.* 135.24 H.' read '*ICS* 217.34'
**ἰά**, add 'E.*Hipp.* 585'
**ἰαίνω**, line 4, after 'later poets' insert 'Call.*fr.* 80.8 Pf.'
**ἰακχάζω**, add '**III** ἰακχάζει· φυλλολογεῖ Hsch.; cf. perh. ἰάκχα.'
**ἰακχαῖος**, add 'of person, *Salamine* 43 (ii/iii AD)'
**Ἴακχος I 1**, after 'Ar.*Ra.* 398' insert '*SEG* 30.914 (Olbia, iv BC)'
**ἰάλεμος I**, after '*dirge*' insert 'Pi.*fr.* 128e.(b)6 S.-M.'
**ἰάλλω**, line 2, after 'Dor. ἶᾱλα' insert 'aor. pass. ϝιάλε̄ Dubois *IGDS* 11 (Himera, *c*.475/50 BC), Lacon. decr. in *Inscr.Délos* 87.2 (v BC)' **I 1**, at end after 'so later' insert '*utter* a cry, ἰάλλων φρικαλέον βρύχημα Nonn.*D.* 6.182, μυκηθμὸν ἰ. ib. 198'
**Ἰᾱλυσός**, at end, adj. Ἰηλύσιος, before 'D.P. 505' insert 'Anacr. 4 P.'
***ἴαμαι**, v. °ἰάομαι.
***ἰᾱμᾰτικός**, ή, όν, *curative*, Cyran. 10 (1.1.118 K.), Epiph.Const. in *Lapid.Gr.* 197.20 (cf. mod. Gk. ἰαματικός).
**ἰαμβεῖος II 1**, delete 'in pl., *iambic poem*, Luc.*Salt.* 27' **2**, delete the section.
**ἰαμβίζω I**, delete '*assail in iambics*'; add 'ἰαμβίζειν· τὸ λοιδορεῖν, κακολογεῖν· ἀπὸ Ἰάμβης τῆς λοιδόρου Hsch.'
**ἰαμβικός**, line 3, after 'Ath. 15.629d' insert 'comp. -ώτερος *SEG* 15.517 (iii BC)'
**ἰαμβιστής**, for pres. def. read '*performer of* ἴαμβοι (v. °ἴαμβος II)'
**ἰαμβοποιέω**, for '*parody*' read '*satirize*'
**ἴαμβος I**, add '*AP* 14.15.3. **2** *iambic trimeter*, *AP* 14.15.1.' **II–III**, for these sections read '**II** *poem* written in iambic, trochaic or epodic metre, esp. of a scurrilous or satiric nature, καί μ' οὔτ' ἰάμβων οὔτε τερπωλέων μέλει Archil. 215 W., ἐν ἰάμβῳ τριμέτρῳ Hdt. 1.12.2, ἴαμβον Ἱππώνακτος Ar.*Ra.* 661, Pl.*Ion* 534c, *Lg.* 935e, Arist.*Rh.* 1418^b^29, *Po.* 1448^b^33, Clearch.ap.Ath. 14.620c, Str. 8.3.30, Ath. 14.645f. **b** applied app. to prose pieces by Asopodorus, ἐν τοῖς καταλογάδην ἰάμβοις Ath. 10.445b. **2** transf., a person as the subject of such a poem, Luc.*Pseudol.* 2. **3** (see quot.) ὕστερον δὲ ἴαμβοι ὠνομάσθησαν (οἱ αὐτοκάβδαλοι) αὐτοί τε καὶ τὰ ποήματα αὐτῶν Semus 24 J.'
**+ἰαμβύκη**, ἡ, musical instrument, prob. = °σαμβύκη I 1, Eup. 148.4 K.-A., prob. in Arist.*Pol.* 1341^a^41 (speculatively dist. fr. σαμβύκη by later antiquaries, Phillis ap.Ath. 14.636b, Hsch., Phot., Suid.).
***ἰάν**, = °ἐάν.
***ἰανάτηρ**, v. °εἰνάτερες.
**+ἰᾰνογλέφᾰρος**, ον, *dark-eyed*, Alcm. 1.69 P.
***ἰανόν**, v. ‡ἑανός.
***Ἰανουάριος**, α, ον, Lat. *Ianuarius*, εἰδ]οῖς Ἰανουαρία[ις the Ides *of January*, *SEG* 18.495.8 (Smyrna, ii AD), μη(νὸς) Ἰανουαρίου Mitchell *N.Galatia* 441.
**ἰάομαι**, line 1, before 'Hp.*Loc.Hom.* 24' insert 'Pi.*P.* 3.46'; line 2, for 'ἰjᾶσθαι *Inscr.Cypr.* 135.3 H.' read '*i-ja-sa-ta-i* perh. ἰjᾶσθαι but more likely fr. athematic ἴαμαι *ICS* 217.3, cf. pr. n. Ἰαμενός' **II**, for 'act. .. 1236' read 'act. only in ff.ll.'; for '*Ev.Luc.* 6.17' read '*Ev.Luc.* 6.18'
**Ἰάονες**, after 'Ἰάων rare' insert 'Hes.*fr.* 10a.23 M.-W. (as eponym, rest.), A.*Pers.* 950, 951 (s.vv.ll., app. ⏑⏑–), Pi.*Pae.* 2.3 S.-M.'; add 'Ἰήονες Call.*fr.* 7.29 Pf.; **Ἰηονίη** *AP* 16.295.2; cf. Myc. *i-ja-wo-ne* (dat.), pers. n.'
**ἰάπτω** (A), at end after 'Theoc. 2.82' insert 'ἰαφθῆναι· ἀποθανεῖν. πεσεῖν. φθαρῆναι Hsch.'
**ἰάπτω** (B) **I 1**, add '**b** w. acc. and dat., *inflict on*, βουβῶσι τυπὴν ἀλίαστον ἰάπτει Nic.*Th.* 784, *Al.* 187.'
**+ἰάραξ**, v. ‡ἱέραξ.
***ἰαρεῖον**, v. ‡ἱερήϊον.
**+ἰαριγμόν**, χαράν. καὶ θροῦν. Κρῆτες Hsch.
**Ἰάς**, at end for '[ῐ, .. 2.21.]' read '[ῐ, cf. *AP* 7.83, but ῑ in arsi Nic.l.c., *App.Anth.* 2.21]'
***Ἰᾱσίς**, ίδος, ἡ, *daughter of Iasus*, *Io*, Call.*fr.* 66.1 Pf.
***ἰασμός**, ὁ, *shouting, crying aloud*, v.l. in Aq.*Je.* 32.16.
**ἴασπις**, line 2, after 'ἡ' insert '(also ὁ, *AP* 9.750 (Arch.))'
***ἰασσεῖν**· θυμοῦσθαι. δάκνειν Hsch.
**ἰᾱτήρ**, for 'Cypr. .. 135.3 H.' read 'Cypr. *to-ni-ja-te-ra-ne* τὸν ἰjατῆραν *ICS* 217.3'; at end add 'Myc. *i-ja-te*'
**ἰᾱτής**, add 'perh. also νούσων εἰη[τήν] rest. in epigr. in *IG* 2^2^.5935 (ii AD, cf. *SEG* 26.284)'
**ἰᾱτικός**, after '*healing*' insert 'Pl.*Ti.* 87b'
**ἰᾱτρεῖον II 1**, add '*Inscr.Perg.* 8(3).161 (pl., ii AD)'
**ἰᾱτρίνη**, add 'as epith. of Μήτηρ θεῶν, *IG* 2^2^.4714 (i BC/i AD), al.'
***ἰᾱτρίσκος**, ὁ, *contemptible physician, quack*, Sch.D.T. 228.3.
**ἰᾱτρόμαια**, add '*MAMA* 3.292 (-μεα, v. *SEG* 37.1854)'
**ἰᾱτρός**, after lemma insert '(written ϝιατρ-, *SEG* 31.834, Megara Hyblaea, vi BC)'; after 'ὁ' insert '(ἡ)' **I**, of Apollo, add '*SEG* 30.880 (Berezan, vi BC), 30.977 (Olbia, v BC)' and add 'of Asclepius, Paus. 2.26.9, *SEG* 26.1818 (Cyrene, ii AD)'; at end for '*midwife* .. s.v. μαῖα' read 'μαῖα καὶ ἰατρὸς Φανοστράτη *CEG* 569 (Acharnae, iv BC), Hellad.ap.Phot.*Bibl.* 531a'
**ἰᾱτροσοφιστής**, add 'of one who practises magic arts and divination, Ps.-Callisth. 1.3'
**ἰαύω II**, after 'c. acc. and gen.' insert '*cause to rest* from'
**ἰάχω 3**, line 6, after 'E.*El.* 707' insert '(dub., cj. ἰαχεῖ)'
***Ἰᾱώ**, indecl., *Yahweh*, D.S. 1.94, orac.ap.Macr.*Sat.* 1.18.20, *PMag.* 3.149, 211, al., *SEG* 32.1082 (Spain, iii AD).
***Ἴβηρ**, ηρος, ὁ, *Iberian*, Hdt. 7.165, Th. 6.2.2, *GVI* 1001.12 (Rhodes, *c*.100 BC); cf. Hsch. ἴβηρ· χερσαῖόν τι θηρίον· ἀφ' οὗ καὶ Ἴβηρες.
**ἰβῐοτάφος**, add '*PFouad* 16 (ii BC)'
**ἶβις**, for pres. def. read 'one or other species of *ibis*'
***ἰβύκη**· εὐφημία Hsch.; cf. ἴβυς.
**+ἴγα**· σιώπα. Κύπριοι Hsch. (= σίγα).
***ἰγμαμένος**, v. ‡ἰκμάω (B).
***Ἰδαλιάνιος**, ὁ, a month at Termessus, *TAM* 3(1).4.15 (ii AD).
**ἰδάλιμος**, add '(prop. εἰδ- or εἰδάλιμος)'
***Ἰδάλιον**, τό, city in Cyprus, Theocr. 15.100 [initial ῑ perh. metri gratia, cf. Verg.*Aen.* 1.693], Cypr. *e-ta-li-o-ne* Ἐδάλιον, *ICS* 217.1, see also Ἐδαλιεύς.
**ἰδαλίς**, add '(ἰδάλιος La.)'
**ἰδᾰνός**, for 'χάριτες .. 535' read 'Χάριτες Call.*fr.* 114.9 Pf., Musae. 76 (prob.), Hsch.'
***Ἰδᾰ́της**, ὁ, title of Zeus in Crete, *SEG* 23.547.51 (Olous, *c*.200 BC).
**ἰδέ I**, add 'Cypr. *i-te*, introducing a new sentence, *ICS* 217.26' **II**, for this section read 'Cypr. introducing an apodosis, *in that case, then*, *ICS* 217.12, 24'
**ἰδέατος**, for 'ἰδήρατος' read 'καλὸς ἀνήρ'
**ἴδη I**, line 3, before 'in sg.' insert 'ἴδηφιν· ἴδαις (-ες cod.), Βοιωτοί Hsch.'
**ἰδήρατος**, add 'as pers. n., *IG* 2^2^.10366 (Skione, iv BC)'
***ἰδῐαστικός**, ή, όν, app. *having a peculiar nature*, ἰδιαστικῶν ἤγουν ἰδιοποιῶν Eustr. *in APo.* 82.34.
***ἰδιόκοιτον**· ἰδιόρρυθμον Hsch. (perh. read -κοπον).
**ἰδιόκτητος**, line 3, after '*Cod.Just.* 10.3.7' insert 'χω(ρίου) ἰ. *ICilicie* 33 (iii/iv AD)' and after '*PTeb.* 5.111 (ii BC)' insert '*land belonging to one's own people*, Onas. 6.13'
***ἰδιόλογος**, ὁ, = ὁ ἴδιος λόγος (v. ἴδιος II 1 b), cj. in Str. 17.1.12, cf. *CIL* 10.4862.
**ἰδιοξενοδόκος**, for pres. ref. read '*SEG* 26.670.16 (Doliche, late ii BC)'
**ἰδιοποιός**, add '**II** *acting on one's own initiative*, *POxy.* 2407.12 (iii AD).'
**ἰδιοπρᾱγέω**, add 'Phlp. *in de An.* p. 455.30, al.'
**ἴδιος I 3**, add '**b** τὰ ἴδια, *one's own funds, one's private resources*, ἐκ τῶν ἰδίων, *at one's own expense*, *AS* 35(1985).50 (Pisidia, AD 150), *SEG* 31.167.7 (Eleusis, AD 162/9), Mitchell *N.Galatia* 193; also sg., ἐκ τοῦ ἰδίου *SEG* 30.1617 (Cyprus, 44/31 BC), *IHadr.* 24 (ii/iii AD), ἀπὸ τῶν ἰδίων *ICilicie* 124 (i/ii AD).' **4**, add 'τὸν ἴδιον συμβιωτήν *fellow-townsman*, *SEG* 29.1185 (Lydia)'; *relatives*, add 'Mitchell *N.Galatia* 1, *TAM* 4(1).77' **5**, add '*SEG* 25.539 (Aulis, iii BC)' **6 b**, after 'no. 133' insert 'ἰδίῳ (sc. θανάτῳ) ἔθανον *BCH* 52.391 (Thasos)' and add 'cf. Phalar.*Ep.* 147.4' **II 3**, add '**b** of words, = κύριος A II 5, opp. τροπικός, Aristid.*Rh.* 1 p. 468 S.' **V**, add 'ἰδιαίτατος· ἴδιος, ὑπερθετικῶς Hsch.' **VI 1**, add '**b** = ἰδίᾳ, τῶν ἰ. (sc. ἐρδομένων) *Schwyzer* 728.13 (Miletus, *c*.400 BC).' at end add 'καθ' ἰτδίαν *BCH* 59.37 (Crannon)'
**ἰδιοσπορέομαι**, after '*labour*' insert '*PBaden* 90.39 (iii AD)'
***ἰδιοσυστάτως**· καθ' ὑπόστασιν ἰδίαν Hsch.
**ἰδιοφυής**, before 'Archelaus' insert 'a writer called '
**ἰδιόχειρος**, add 'adv. -χείρως *with his own hand*, Sch.*AP* 7.432'
**ἰδιώτης II 3**, after 'D.H.*Dem.* 2' insert '(without λόγος, id.*Lys.* 3,

4)' **III 1**, of prose writers, add 'Pl.*Lg.* 890a' **IV**, delete the section. at end add 'see also °*Fhεδιέσταs* (after °ἔδεος)'

**ἴδμων**, add 'w. inf., ἴδμων .. σημήνασθαι ἀϋτμήν Opp.*C.* 1.480'

**ἰδνόομαι**, act., add 'ἰδνῶν· κάμπτων Hsch. La. (cod. ἴδμων)'

**ἴδος**, for 'Call.*fr.* 124 (prob.)' read 'Call.*fr.* 304 Pf. (cod. εἴδεος)'

**ἰδού II 3**, for this section read 'in answer to a summons with following question, *"yes"*, *"here I am"*, (*what do you want?*, or sim.) ἰδού· τί ἔστιν; Ar.*Nu.* 825, *Eq.* 157.'

**ἴδρις**, line 9, after 'Vett.Val. 4.19' insert 'w. acc. of respect, οὐδὲν ἴδρις S.*OC* 525 (lyr.), ἴδριες οὐδέν id.*Tr.* 649 (lyr.); ταῦτ' οὐκέτ' ἴδρις id.*fr.* 269a.31 R.'; lines 9/10, delete 'οὐδὲν .. (lyr.)'

***ἰδροσύνη**, ἡ, *the state of being fixed*, *GVI* 1487.2 (pl., Phrygia, iii AD).

**ἵδρῡμα I 1**, for 'Call.*Aet.* 3.1.73' read 'Call.*fr.* 75.73 Pf.' **2**, add 'of a funeral monument, *ISmyrna* II(2) p. 357, no. xii'

**ἱδρύω I 2**, add 'of words in a sentence, *to be placed*, D.H.*Comp.* 6'

**ἱδρῷον**, for '*cloth* .. (ii BC)' read '*cloth for covering horses, donkeys*, etc., *when heated*, *PTeb.* 796.11 (ii BC), *PSI* 527, etc.; ὀνικά *PCair.Zen.* 720.4 (iii BC)'

**ἱδρώτιον**, add 'pl., Aët. 3.3 (261.19 O.)'

***ἰδύαι**· τρίχες Hsch.

**ἱερᾱγέω**, add '*PVat.Gr.* 65 in *Tyche* 5.102.2 (iii BC)'

**ἱεράζω**, add '**II** trans., = ἱερόω, *Princeton Exp.Inscr.* 653 (Syria).'

***ἱερᾱκάδιον**, v. °ἱερακίδιον.

**ἱερᾱκάριος**, add '*MAMA* 3.17, 79 (Cilicia)'

**ἱερᾱκίδιον**, for pres. ref. read '*Inscr.Délos* 1416*A*19 (ii BC); also written -άδιον ib. 1452*A*9 (ii BC)'

***ἱερᾱκῖτις**, ιδος, a plant, = ἱεράκιον I, Cyran. 75, *PMag.* 4.902.

**ἱερᾱκόμορφος**, add 'ἀνδριάντες Ἀπόλλωνος ἱερακομό(ρφου) χαλ(κοῖ) γ' *POxy.* 3473.10 (ii AD)'

***ἱεραμφοδίτης**, ου, ὁ, *inhabitant of the sacred quarter*, *SEG* 30.1449 (-είτης, Pontus, AD 257/8).

**ἱερανθεσία**, for 'only Dor.' read 'dial. ἱαρ-'; add '*SEG* 36.516, 517 (Delphi, i AD); (second element < -αναθεσία)', cf. °ὡνανθεσία'

**ἱερᾱνομέω**, delete the entry (v. *Glotta* 50.77).

**ἱέραξ II**, add 'cf., ἱάραξ· ἰχθὺς ποιός, Δωρικώτερον· διὰ τὸ ἐοικέναι τῷ πτηνῷ. καὶ λύχνος ὁ πρὸς τὰ ἱερά Hsch.'

***ἱερᾱπολία**, ἡ, office of ἱεραπόλος, epigr. in *SEG* 13.422 (Delos, iii BC).

**ἱερᾱπόλος**, add 'ἱαρᾱ- *SEG* 39.1008 (Morgantina, *c.*iii BC)'

**ἱερᾱτεύω**, line 2, after '(perh. i BC)' insert '*IG* 10(2).1.95 (ii/i BC), 114 (ii AD), etc.'; line 7, after 'Hdn. 5.6.3' insert 'ἱερατεύσαντα πρὸ πόλεως *MAMA* 7.406'; line 8, med., add '*SEG* 31.635 (Maced., ii/iii AD)'

**ἱερᾱτικός**, line 5, after 'Dam.*Pr.* 399' insert 'ἱ. γράμματα, βίβλος *PTeb.* 291 ii 41, 43 (ii AD)'

**ἱεραύλης**, for '*flute-player*' read '*aulos-player*'

***ἱερᾱφάντρια**, v. °ἱεροφάντρια.

**ἱερᾱφόρος**, after '*SIG*² 754 (Pergamum)' add 'also fem., *IG* 7.2681 (Thebes)'

**ἱέρεια**, line 1, after 'ἡ' insert 'ἵρεια epigr. in *IG* 2².3606.15 (ii AD)'; line 5, after 'al.' insert '(acc. pl. τὰς ἱερῆς *Inscr.Cos* 386.9)'; line 6, after '(Thebes)' insert 'ἱάρηια *SEG* 23.566.9, al. (Axos, Crete, iv BC), Aeol. ἴρεα *JÖAI* 5.141.19 (Eresus, ii/i BC)'; after '*BCH* 6.24 (Delos, ii BC)' insert 'in Jewish context, *CIJud.* 1007 (iv AD)' at end add 'Myc. *i-je-re-ja*'

**ἱερεία III**, for this section read 'Cypr. *ta-ni-e-re-wi-ja-ne* τὰν ἱερεϜίαν τᾶς Ἀθάνας prob. *sanctuary*, *ICS* 217.20'

**ἱερεῖον**, Ion. **ἱερήιον**, add '*SEG* 30.1283 (Didyma, vi BC)' **II**, of sucking pigs, add '*PMich.Zen.* 84.3, *PZen.Col.* 46.5 (both iii BC)' at end add 'Myc. *i-je-re-wi-jo*'

**ἱερειτεύω II**, add '*IG* 10(2).1.156'

**ἱερεύς**, line 1, for 'Cypr. .. 59 H.' read 'Myc. *i-je-re-u*; Cypr. *i-je-re-u-se* ἰjερεύς *ICS* 7.3, gen. *i-e-re-wo-se* ἱερῆϜος *ICS* 234'; line 3, before 'Ion. nom.' insert 'Lesb. nom. **ἴρευς**, acc. εἴρεα, ἴρεα, *IG* 12(2).102, 242.4, 239.8, al.'; line 5, after '*GDI* 4841 (Cyrene)' insert 'ἱαρεύς *SEG* 29.361 (Argos, *c.*400 BC)'; line 9, for '*Inscr.Cypr.* 100 H.' read 'Cypr. *i-je-re-se* ἰjερές *ICS* 4'

**ἱερεύω 1**, add '**b** *to be a priest*, w. dat. ἱερεύοντος δὲ τῷ Ἀσκλαπιῶι *SEG* 32.622 (Illyria, ii BC); w. gen. ἱερε[ύ]οντος δὲ τοῦ Ἀσκλαπιοῦ *SEG* 32.623 (Illyria, ii/i BC).'

***ἱερεωτική** (sc. τέχνη), ἡ, perh. *art of priesthood*, Poll. 7.210.

**ἱέρισσα**, add 'in Jewish use, Μάριν ἱέρισα χρηστή *CIJud.* 15.14 (Egypt, 28 BC)'

***ἱερόγαλλος**, ὁ, title of priest, *TAM* 3(1).740 (Termessus).

***ἱερογραμμᾰτεία**, ἡ, work-place of a ἱερογραμματεύς, *Pap. Lugd. Bat.* XIII 21.16.

***ἱεροδούλη**, ἡ, = (ἡ) ἱερόδουλος, *AS* 10.48 no. 96 (Pisidia), *TAM* 2(3).1023, 3(1).567.

***ἱεροεθνής**, οῦς, ὁ, *person of priestly stock*, *POxy.* 3470.16, 3471.14 (both AD 131), *CPR* XV 32.8 (ii/iii AD).

***ἱεροζωμουργοί**, οἱ, *makers of mash* for the Apis bull, *PRoss.-Georg.* 5.16.16 (ii/iii AD; -ζομ- pap.).

***ἱεροθᾱλής**, ές, *having sacred branches*, Orph.*H.* 40.17.

**ἱεροθαλλής**, delete the entry.

***ἱεροθῠσία**, ἡ, in Dor. form ἱᾰρο-, *sacrifice*, *SEG* 9.13.20 (Cyrene, iv BC).

**ἱεροθῠ́της**, after '(Euboea, iii BC)' insert '*SEG* 32.330 (Athens, Rom.imp.)'; add 'Arg. ἱᾰροθύται *BCH* suppl. 22 p. 235 (v BC)'

**ἱερόθῠτος**, subst., add 'sg., *SEG* 18.596.15·(Babylonia, iii AD)'

***ἱεροῑ̈ᾰτροι**, οἱ, *priestly doctors* who attended the Apis bull, *PRoss.-Georg.* 5.16.15 (ii/iii AD).

***ἱεροκαλλίνῑκος**, ον, *holy and victorious*, *Lyr.adesp.* 19 P.

***ἱεροκηρῡκεία** (-κᾱρυκ-), ἡ, office of a ἱεροκῆρυξ, *ASAA* 30/32(1952-4).295, no. 67.23 (Rhodes).

**ἱεροκηρῡκεύω**, add '*SEG* 37.973.7 (Claros, AD 172/3)'

**ἱεροκῆρυξ**, line 2, for 'prob. in *IG* 1².6.89' read '*IEphes.* 2.53, 10.22, al., *IStraton.* 503.6 (318 BC)'

***ἱεροκώμη**, ἡ, *sacred village*, *CIG* 5069 (Nubia, iii AD).

**ἱερόμαντις**, add 'fem., τὴν -ιν, *AE* 1945-7.106 (Thessaly)'

***ἱερομνημονεία**, ἡ, office of ἱερομνήμων II 2, *IEphes.* 4324.5 (i BC, -ηα lapis).

**ἱερομνημονέω**, add 'athematic part. ἱαρομναμονέντες L.Gasperini *Le laminette iscritte dal repostiglio dell'Agorà di Cirene* (*Giornata Lincea* 3 Nov. 1987, Cyrene, iv BC)'

**ἱερομνήμων**, after 'ονος, ὁ' insert 'ἱαρομμνάμονα *SEG* 30.380 (Tiryns, vii BC), ἱαρομνᾱμ- *SEG* 34.282 (Nemea, iv BC), 23.271 (Thespiae, iii BC)' **II 1**, add 'Ar.*fr.* 335 K.-A.' add '**4** a precious stone, Plin.*HN* 37.160.'

**ἱερομοσχοσφρᾱγιστής**, add '*PGrenf.* II 64.1 (ii/iii AD, ἱαιρο- pap.)'

***ἱεροναύτης**, ου, ὁ, *sailor on a sacred vessel*, *Inscr.Délos* 50 (iv BC), *ITomis* 98.4 (Rom.imp.).

**ἱερονίκης**, after 'Luc.*Hist.Conscr.* 30, etc.' insert 'w. ref. to exemption from taxes, τῶν ἱερονικῶν καὶ ἀτελῶν *BGU* 2122.1 (AD 108)'; at end add 'Aeol. **εἰρονεικ-** *IG* 12(2).68.11 (Mytilene, ii AD)'

***ἱερονῑκοτελοῦσα**, ἡ, *giving victory in sacred games*, epith. of Isis, *Hymn.Is.* in *POxy.* 1380.78 (ii AD, written ἱερω-).

***ἱερονόμᾱς**, ὁ, Aeol. **ἰρο-** = °ἱερονόμος, Θεοφάνης ὁ εἰρονόμας *SEG* 29.741 (Mytilene, after AD 138).

***ἱερονομία**, ἡ, *office of* °ἱερονόμος, Robert *Hell.* 6.70 (Thyatira).

**ἱερονόμοι**, delete the entry.

***ἱερονόμος**, ὁ, Aeol. **ἰρονόμος** *SEG* 34.1234 (Aeolis, *c.*200 BC), *official in charge of sacred rites*, *SIG* 982.23, *IGRom.* 4.461 (Pergamum), *IIlion* 31.24, 32.20, al.; of the *pontifices* at Rome, D.H. 2.73; as pers. n., *SEG* 31.348 (Mantineia, v/iv BC).

***ἱεροπλᾰτεῖται**, οἱ, *occupants of a* °ἱεροπλατίη, *IHistriae* 57.32 (early iii AD).

***ἱεροπλᾰτίη**, ἡ, = ἱερὰ πλατεῖα, *sacred street* or *square*, ἱ. τῶν φιλόπλων *Milet* 2(3).134 no. 403.

***ἱεροποϊκόν**, τό, *fund for the* ἱεροποιός, *Inscr.Délos* 1521.23.

**ἱεροπρεπής**, adv., add 'neut. pl. sup. -έστατα *IHistriae* 57.36 (early iii AD)'

***ἱεροπρόσπλοκος**, ον, *devoted to religious matters*, Ptol.*Tetr.* 159 (v.l.), 181.

**ἱεροπρόσπολος**, for 'Ptol.*Tetr.* 159' read 'Ptol.*Tetr.* 181 (v.l.)'

**ἱερόπτης**, add 'as pers. n., *IG* 2².12237 (*c.*400 BC), *SEG* 23.155 (Attica, mid iv BC)'

**ἱερός**, line 2, after 'Orac.ap.Hdt. 8.77' insert 'cf. ἱερὸς ἕδρη Arat. 692'; line 3, ἱαρός, add '*SEG* 30.1176.F5 (Metapontum, vi BC), 31.368 (Olympia, v BC)' and Aeol. ἶρος, add 'εἰρ- *SEG* 32.1243.45 (Cyme, i BC/i AD)' **I**, add 'Stesich. 8.3 P.' **II 3 b**, after 'Od. 24.81' insert 'ℎιαρὸς Χαροπ[ί]νος· ℎιαρ[ὸς] Ἀρισστόδαμος *Schwyzer* 66.6 (Messenia, early v BC)' **c**, add 'τοῦ εἱεροτάτου βαφίου *ITyr* 28 (Rom.imp.)' add '**d** sup. as honorific epith. of Caesars, *PLond.* 948, *POxy.* 1114.20, *Stud.Pal.* 20.51 (all iii AD).' **III 1**, add 'ὁ ἐπὶ τὰ ἱερά *SEG* 32.218.203 (Athens, 89/8 BC)' **2**, line 1, after 'Ion. ἱρόν' insert 'B. 3.15, E.*Hel.* 1002, *IT* 969, etc.' **5**, add '*IPamph.* 3.1 (Sillyon, iv BC)'; fem., add 'ℎιαρᾶν μίστωμα de Franciscis *Locr.Epiz.* 23' **IV 4**, add 'also ἀφ' ἱεροῦ Pl.*Lg.* 739a' **10**, add 'cf. ἱ. ῥάχις *AP* 9.644.7 (Agath.)' line 6 fr. end, after 'Theoc. 5.22' insert 'in iambics, Lyc. 950, 1350 (καθιερώσει)' at end add 'Myc. *i-je-ro* (in sense II 2, *owned by a deity*)'

**ἱεροσαλπικτής**, for '(*CIG*) 2983 (Ephesus)' read '*IEphes.* 1034, al.'

**ἱεροσκοπέομαι**, add 'act., Hsch. s.v. ἱερᾶται'

**ἱεροσκόπος II**, add '*IKeramos* 31, *IEphes.* 1004, al.'

**ἱεροσῡλία**, add 'Is. 8.39'

***ἱερόσῡλις**, fem. adj., expl. of °θεόσυλις, Sch.Hippon. 118.1 W.

**ἱερόσῡλος**, for '*sacrilegious person*' read '*pilferer*'

**ἱεροτᾰμιεύω**, add 'med. aor., *BCH* 1.291 (Ephesus, ii AD)'

***ἱεροτίθηνοι**, οἱ, *tenders* of the Apis bull, *PRoss.-Georg.* 5.15.12, 16.1 (ii/iii AD).

**ἱερουργέω I**, add 'Dor. ἱᾰρωργ- *Inscr.Cret.* 1.23.4 (Phaestus, ii BC)'

**ἱερουργός**, add '*PVindob.Worp* 21.1 (v/vi AD); form ἱεροϜοργός Myc. *i-je-ro-wo-ko*'

***ἱερουσιάρχης**, ου, ὁ, late sp. for γερουσιάρχης, *CIJud.* 1.405 (Rome): εἱεροσάρχης, ib. 408 (Rome).

***ἱεροφάντειος**, ον, = ἱεροφαντικός, rest. in epigr. in *TAM* 2(2).418.5 (Lycia).

**ἱεροφάντης**, add '*IEphes.* 10.11, 47.39, al., *POxy.* 2782.2 (ii/iii AD)'

**ἱεροφαντικός**, after '*Alex.* 60' insert 'οἶκοι *IG* $4^2$.84.30 (Epid., i AD)'

**ἱεροφάντρια**, add 'also ἱεραφάντρια *ISelge* 15.4 (Rom.imp.)'

**ἱεροφύλαξ 1**, after 'cj. Markl.' insert ', ἱεροῦ φύλακες Diggle'; add '*Sokolowski* 3.155.5 (Cos, iii BC), *IG* $9^2$(1).1.95, etc. (Phystium, ii BC)'

**ἱερόφωνος**, for '*with sacred voice*' read '*making a holy utterance*'; for 'f.l. for ἱμερό- in Alcm. 26.1' read 'Alcm. 26.1 P. (cj. ἱμερο-)'; after '*IG* 14.914' insert 'D.Knibbe *Der Staatsmarkt* (Vienna, 1981) p. 170/1 no. 10 (Ephesus, iii AD; v. *SEG* 31.950)'

**ἱερόω**, add '*hold to be sacred*, οἱ πρῶτοι τοῦτο τὸ νόσημα ἱρώσαντες v.l. ἀφιερω- Hp.*Morb.Sacr.* 1'

**ἱέρωμα**, for '*consecrated object, offering*' read '*sacred image*'; line 2, for 'ἱαρώματα .. ἀρώματα)' read 'ἱαρώματα *Inscr.Cret.* 4.145.7 (Gortyn, iv BC)'; line 3, delete 'ἱαρ[ώ]ματα *IG* 4.917 (Epid., iv BC; read ἱαρ[ε]ῖα τὰ)'

***ἱερώνας**, α, ὁ, *buyer of sacrificial victims*, *IG* 12 suppl. 120.13 Rhodes, (iii BC); rest. in *Inscr.Cret.* 3.3.3A91 (iii/ii BC); cf. βοώνης.

***ἱερωνέω**, *act as* °ἱερώνας, *Lindos* 449.12 (i/ii AD).

**ἱερωνία**, for 'dub. sens. in' read '*purchase of sacrificial victims*'

**ἱερωσύνη**, line 3, after 'etc.' insert '**ἱεροσύνη** *SEG* 34.1095 (Ephesus, iii AD), **ἱερειοσύνᾱ** *IG* 5(1).1114.21, 25 (Laconia)'; line 4, after 'D. 59.92' insert 'in Chr. use, Mitchell *N.Galatia* 493 (εἱερ-), *Cod.Just.* 1.3.43.10, etc.'; at end, pl., add '*SEG* 32.825 (Paros, ii BC)'

**ἵζω**, line 3, after 'etc.' insert '3 pl. ἕσαν Il. 19.393'; line 4 (and I 1, line 7), for 'ἕσσαντα' read 'ἵσσαντα' (changing ref. to *SEG* 9.71.134 (Cyrene, iv BC)) **I 1**, add '**b** *set* or *settle* in place, λέπαδνα Il. 19.393.' **2**, line 6, for '[ἥ]σσαντο .. iii BC)' read 'ἵσσαντο *BCH* 81.477 (Argos, iv BC)' and add 'w. deity as obj., *set up* in form of cult-statue, etc.' and transfer here 'Thgn. 12' fr. line 4, adding 'Call.*fr.* 200b Pf., *Del.* 309' **III 1**, line 3, for '*Berl.Sitzb.* 1927.169 (Cyrene)' read '*SEG* 9.72.122 (Cyrene, iv BC)'

**ἵημι**, at end of the note on quantity (lines 29ff.) delete 'with variation .. *Carm.Pop.* 1' **I 2**, add 'w. partit. gen., οἱ δὲ ὄνοι .. οὕτω δὴ μᾶλλον πολλῷ ἵεσαν τῆς φωνῆς Hdt. 4.135.3' **5**, line 2, after '(Il.) 5.513' insert 'E.*Rh.* 291' **II 2**, line 3, after '(Il.) 2.589' insert '(so in act., εἵεσαν ἐκτελέσαι poet. in *BCH* 50.406 (Thespiae))'; line 4, before '11.168' insert 'Il.'

**ἰήρια**, delete the entry.

***ἱήρια**, τά, unexpld. wd. in *Inscr.Cret.* 4.145.4 (Gortyn, iv BC).

***ἱῆτε**, 2 pl. imper. formed fr. ἰή, dub. l. in Pi.*Pae.* 6.122 S.-M.

***ἰθαινάθῡμος**, ον, cited as compd. of ἰθαίνω Theognost.*Can.* 81 (cf. sq.).

**⁺ἰθαίνω**, perh. *gladden*, ἴθαινε θυμόν anon.ap.*An.Ox.* 1.61, ἰθαίνειν· εὐφρονεῖν (? εὐφραίνειν) Hsch., med. ἰθαίνεσθαι· θερμαίνεσθαι id.; supposed etym. of ἰθαγενής A.D.*Adv.* 187.25 (prob. cogn. w. ἰθαρός).

**ἰθᾰρός I**, for 'Alc.*Supp.* 4.18' read 'Alc. 58.18 L.-P.; ἰθαραῖς .. λογάσιν *with glad eyes*, Call.*fr.* 85.15 Pf.; ἰθαρὸν (v.l. ἱκανὸν) γόνυ id.*Cer.* 132'

**ἰθῐ**, line 1, for 'Adv.' read 'exclam.'

***ἴθμη**, ἡ, *way, passage*, Theognost.*Can.* 112, Sch.Opp.*H.* 1.738; cf. εἰσίθμη, ἴθμα. (For the accent see C.A. Lobeck *Paralipomena grammaticae Graecae* (Leipzig, 1837) p. 395.)

***ἰθμός**, v. °ἠθμός.

***ἰθουλίς**, ίδος, ἡ, Boeot. name of a fish, perh. = ἰουλίς, *IGC* p.99 B10 (Acraephia, ii BC).

***ἰθῠβάτης**, ου, masc. adj. *running in a straight line*, κανών cj. in *AP* 6.62 (Phil.).

***ἰθῠβέλεια**, ἡ, *straight-shooter*, of Artemis, oracle in *ZPE* 92.269 (Ephesus, ii AD).

**ἰθῠδικος**, for '*righteous*' read '*giving right judgement*'

**⁺ἴθυμβος**, ὁ, the name of a type of performer or performance, ἴθυμβος· γελοιαστής. καὶ τὸ σκῶμμα. ἀπὸ τῶν ἰθύμβων ἅτινα ποιήματα ἦν ἐπὶ χλεύῃ καὶ γέλωτι συγκείμενα. καὶ ᾠδὴ μακρὰ καὶ ὑπόσκαιος Hsch.; καὶ ἴθυμβοι ἐπὶ Διονύσῳ καὶ καρυατίδες ἐπὶ Ἀρτέμιδι Poll. 4.104; cf. θρίαμβος, ἴαμβος, etc.

**ἴθῡνα**, add 'εἴθῡνα *SEG* 17.377.14 (Chios, v BC)'

***ἰθύνοος**, ον, perh. *fair-minded*, ἰθυνόων .. θεσμῶν Nonn.*D.* 41.353.

**ἰθυντήρ**, line 2, delete '*IG* 9(1).390 (Naupactus)'

**ἰθύνω 3**, add '*Cod.Just.* 1.4.33.2 (AD 534)'

**ἰθῠπόρος**, add '**2** *giving a straight voyage*, of winds, Opp.*H.* 5.677.'

**ἰθυπτίων**, line 1, after 'Il. 21.169' insert '(also read by Zenod. at 20.273 s.v.l.)'; line 3, after 'Zenod.' insert 'and Callistr.'

**ἰθύς** (A), after 'cases)' insert 'perh. also ειθεία, ἁ ὁδὸς ἁ ειθεία (nisi leg. ἀὲ ἰθεία) *SEG* 35.991.B5 (Lyttos, *c.*500 BC)' **II 2**, at end after 'Hp.*Off.* 3' insert 'ἐς ἰθὺ *in length*, Call.*fr.* 196.26 Pf.'

**ἰθύς** (B) **1**, for this section read '*straight line*, πρὸς ῥόον ἀΐσσοντος ἀν' ἰθύν Il. 21.303, ἐπεὶ δὴ σφαίρῃ ἀν' ἰθὺν πειρήσαντο Od. 8.377, μηκός τε καὶ ἰθὺν *in outstretched length*, Nic.*Th.* 398'

**ἰθῠτενής**, delete '*upright, perpendicular*' and 'metaph.'

**ἰθύφαλλος III**, for 'metaph., *lewd fellow*' read 'adopted as a group-name by an association of young men'

***ἰθύωρα**, v. ‡εὐθύωρος.

***Ἰθωμαῖα**, τά, games at Messene in honour of Zeus Ithometas, *SEG* 23.208 (Messene, i AD), Paus. 4.33.2.

**ἰθών**, add 'perh. in *POxy.* 3729.19 (AD 307)'

**ἱκᾰνοδοσία**, add '*POxy.* 3807.36 (AD 28)'

**ἱκᾰνοποιέω**, add '*SEG* 4.648.11, 37.1001 (Lydia, ii AD)'

**ἱκᾰνός I 1**, at end delete 'ὁ Ἰ. the Almighty Lxx *Ru.* 1.21' **2**, delete the section. **III 1 a**, lines 3/4, for 'later' read 'also' and after '*amply*' insert 'Hp.*Epid.* 5.49'

**ἰκάς**, after '*twentieth* of the month' insert '*SEG* 23.530 (Crete, vii BC)'

**ἰκαστός** (s.v. Ϝίκατι), add 'Ϝικαστή (sc. ἁμέρα) *IG* 7.3172.109 (late iii BC)'

***ἰκᾰτιδάρκμιος**, v. °εἰκοσαδράχμιος.

***ἰκᾰτιείς**, = εἰκοσιείς, *SEG* 26.672.47 (Larissa, *c.*200 BC).

***ἰκᾰτιεννέα**, = εἰκοσιεννέα, *SEG* 26.674.4 (Larissa, ii BC).

***ἰκᾰτιπέμπε**, = εἰκοσιπέντε, *SEG* 26.672.23 (Larissa, *c.*200 BC).

**ἴκελος**, add 'as pr. n. Ϝίκελος *BE* 1990.863 (Selinous, *c.*500 BC)'

**ἱκεσία**, line 4, for '*AP* 5.215' read '*AP* 1.34.8, 5.216.2' **2**, for '*AP* l.c.' read '*AP* ll.cc.'

**ἱκέσιος II 1**, of Zeus, add '*SEG* 33.244d, e (*h*ικ-, Attica, archaic)' at end after 'A.R. 2.215' add '*AP* 5.300.5 (Paul.Sil.)'

***ἱκετεύσιμος**, ον, *of a suppliant*, Hsch. s.v. προστροπαίων.

**ἱκετευτέος**, add 'X.*Mem.* 1.5.5 (s.v.l.)'

***ἱκετέω**, = ἱκετεύω (in quot., sense 4), *PTeb.* 2d^v^.9.

***ἱκετηριάς**, άδος, ἡ, = ἱκετηρίς, perh. eleg. in *POxy.* 3723.10 (ii AD).

**ἱκετήριος II 1**, line 3, after 'A.*Supp.* 192' insert '(ἱκετ- cod.)'

**ἱκέτης**, line 2, after 'ὁ' insert 'Arg. ἱκέτᾱς *Schwyzer* 97 (Argos, vi BC), cf. Lacon. Διο*h*ικέτα (= Διὸς ἱκεσίου) *Schwyzer* 1'; add 'cf. Myc. *i-ke-ta*, pers. n.'

**ἱκετικός**, before 'Adv.' insert '*BGU* 1053 ii 6 (i AD); ἱερὰ ἄσυλα καὶ ἱ. *IStraton.* 1101.3 (ii AD)'

**ἱκέτις**, add 'E.*Hel.* 1238'

**ἰκμαίνω**, add '**II** *express* (liquids), *cause to be exuded*, Nic.*Al.* 97.'

**ἰκμᾰλέος 1**, add 'of the noise emitted by the parrot-wrasse, φθέγγεται ἰ. λαλαγήν Opp.*H.* 1.135'

**ἴκμαρ**, add 'Antim.in *Suppl.Hell.* 57.4'

**ἰκμάω** (A), after 'Id.' insert 'cf. ἀνικμάω, ἀπικμάω'

**ἰκμάω** (B), for 'pf. part. .. *Inscr.Cypr.* 135.3H.' read 'part. *i-ki-ma-me-no-se*, ἰκμαμένος *wounded*, *ICS* 217.3'

**ἰκνέομαι II 3 b**, add 'A.*Supp.* 333'

**ἴκρια**, before 'τά' insert '[ῑ by nature, see Ar.*Th.* 395, Cratin. 360 K.-A.]'; for 'sg. v. infr. III' read 'sg. Hsch., see also infr. III' **II 1**, add 'perh. *balcony*, *PDura* 19.9 (i AD)' **3**, delete the section adding quots. to section II 2 **III**, after 'Nic.*Th.* 198' insert 'so perh. pl. in *PRein.* 2065.35 (*JJP* 11/12.66; ii AD)'

**ἰκριοποιέω**, for '*Rev.Phil.* 50.69' read '*SEG* 4.448.5, 449.21'

***ἴκταιον**· τὸ τρόφιμον, Theognost.*Can.* 15 (perh. read ἰκμαῖον).

**ἰκταῖος**, delete 'with penult. short'

**ἴκτερος I**, add '**2** *rust* on plants, Lxx 2*Ch.* 6.28, al.' **II**, add 'cf. χαραδριός'

**ἰκτῖς**, after '*marten*' insert 'A.*fr.* 47a.2.10 R. (lyr.)'

**ἵκω**, line 2, after 'Trag.' insert 'exc. in A.*fr.* 6 R.'; line 7, insert 'asigmatic aor. *h*ῖκαι *IPamph.* 3.9 (iv BC)'; at end delete '– ἷκοντ' .. 36'

***ἶλαξ**· ἡ πρῖνος, ὡς Ῥωμαῖοι καὶ Μακεδόνες Hsch. (cf. Lat. *ilex*).

**ἱλάομαι**, add 'act. ἱλάοντες· ἐξευμενιζόμενοι, ἐξιλεούμενοι Hsch.'

**ἵλαος**, line 2, after 'Ar.*Th.* 1148)' insert '*h*ίλαος *IG* $9^2$.609.A16 (Naupactus, *c.*500 BC)'; line 7, after 'Pl.*Phd.* 95a' insert 'εἵλως (= ἵλεως) *Sokolowski* 1.29.13 (Metropolis in Ionia, iv BC)' **III**, adv., add '*Kafizin* 291 (iii BC)' line 3 fr. end, after 'Theoc. 5.18' insert '*AP* 6.334 (Leon.Tarent.)' at end add 'see also ‡εἰλής'

***ἱλαότι**, v. ἵλημι.

**ἱλᾰρός I**, add 'sup. -ώτατα (adv.), epigr. in *SEG* 23.206.20 (Messenia, ii/iii AD)'

***ἱλαροφυΐα**, ἡ, *cheerful nature*, Dioscorus in *Byz.-neugr.Jahrb.* 10.342.

**ἰλάρχης**, line 3, for '*praefectus turmae*' read '*decurio*'

**ἴλαρχος**, add 'Ϝίλαρχος *SEG* 23.271.16 (Thespiae, 220/208 BC)'

**ἱλάσκομαι I 1**, line 10, delete 'c. part. .. *O.* 7.9' add '**b** *reverence* sacred things, ἱερόν A.R. 2.808, Posidipp.ap.Ath. 7.318d.' **2**, add 'νέκταρ χυτὸν .. ἀεθλόφοροις ἀνδράσιν πέμπων .. ἱλάσκομαι Pi.*O.* 7.9'

**ἱλαστήριος II**, add '**4** app. some item of water-raising equipment, *POxy.* 1985.11 (vi AD); perh. a separate wd. ἱλαστ- for ἐλαστήριος = ἐλατήριος.'

*Ἱλαστηριών, ῶνος, ὁ, name of a month at Caunus, Robert *Hell.* 7.174.60 (Smyrna, ii BC).

*Ἱλάων· ἥρως, Ποσειδῶνος υἱός, ἀφ' οὗ Ἀριστοφάνης ἐν Τριφάλητι (*fr.* 567 K.-A.) Ἱλάονας ἔφη τοὺς φάλητας μεταφέρων Hsch.

*ἵλημι, for 'Dor. **ἵλᾰθι**' read 'Dor. and Ep. **ἵλᾰθι**, Call.*Cer.* 138, *fr.* 638 Pf., A.R. 4.1014' and after 'Luc.*Epigr.* 22' insert 'etc.'

**ἴλια**, add 'cf. ἴλιον'

**Ἰλιακός I**, after '*Trojan*' insert 'Call.*fr.* 114.25 Pf.' add '**2** Ἰλιακά, τά, festival at Ilium, *Ilion* 52.17 (ii BC).'

*ἰλιγγιζόμενον· συστρεφόμενον Hsch.

**ἰλιγγιώδης**, transfer the article before **ἴλιγγος**.

**ἴλιγγος 3**, add '*Peripl.M.Rubr.* 40'

*Ἰλίεια, τά, festival of Athena at Ilium, *IG* $2^2$.3138 (Athens, iv BC), Hsch.

**ἴλιον**, add 'cf. ἴλια and Lat. *ilia*'

*ἰλίων, ονος, ὁ, = σύγγαμβρος, Choerob. in *An.Ox.* 2.221; cf. εἰλίονες.

*ἶλκα· γλοιός, ῥύπος Theognost.*Can.* 15, Hsch.

*ἰλλᾰτίζω, app. = ἰλλάζω, *PAlex.* 26.19 (ii/iii AD).

**ἰλλός**, add 'of the feet, ?*twisted*, ἰλλοί τε πόδες *Suppl.Hell.* 1026'

*ἰλλούστριος, ὁ, cf. Lat. *illustris*, as rank, *SEG* 36.1326 (Palestine, vi AD), *Cod.Just.* 40.20.16 pr., Just.*Nov.* 15.1 pr.; sp. ἴλλυστρος *MAMA* 3.504.

**ἴλμη**, add 'cf. εἴλεα, εἶλος'

*Ἰλύθειον, Ἰλύθυιον, v. °Εἰλείθυιον.

**ἰλυσπάομαι**, line 1, for '*crawl*, like a worm' read '*move like a snake* or *worm*'; line 3, before 'Ael.*NA* 8.14, 9.32' insert 'of other creatures, *move convulsively*, *wriggle from side to side*, *squirm*' and after it insert 'act. ἰλισπῶντες· συνειλοῦντες Hsch.'

**ἰλυώδης**, last line, for 'τὸ -ῶδες' read 'εἰ μηδὲν ἔχουσα διεφθορὸς ἐν ἑαυτῇ μηδ' ἰλυῶδες'

*ἰμαγινιφέρ, ὁ, Lat. *imaginifer*, *PBeatty Panop.* 2.297 (AD 300), *SB* 8430.3.

*ἱμαῖος, ον, *of hauling* or *drawing*, ἱμαῖον (sc. ᾆσμα) kind of work-song, ἀείδει καὶ πού τις ἀνὴρ ὑδατηγὸς ἱμαῖον Call.*fr.* 260.66 Pf.; so ἱμαῖος (sc. ᾠδή) ἡ ἐπιμύλιος καλουμένη, ἣν παρὰ τοὺς ἀλετοὺς ᾖδον Trypho ap.Ath. 14.618d, cf. Sch.Ar.*Ra.* 1297, Hsch.

**ἱμαντόδετος**, add 'κολλήματα Ps.-Callisth. 120.2 K.'

*ἱμαντοπαικτική (sc. τέχνη), ἡ, *sparring with boxing-thongs* (opp. serious boxing), Eustr.*in EN* 10.17, 16.9.

**ἱμαντόπους**, for '(ἱμάς .. **1**' read 'having a malformation or abnormality of foot or leg, the nature of which is uncertain, = Lat. *loripes*'

**ἱμαντοσκελής**, for 'Tz. l.c.' read 'Apollod. l.c.'

**ἱμᾱ́ς I 1 b**, after 'etc.' insert '(in 23.363 has also been taken as *lash* of a whip)' **d**, for this section read '(naut.) *lifts*, *PZen.Col.* 100, *PCair.Zen.* 754, 756 (all iii BC)' **2**, add '**k** title of book of problems by one Anaxagoras, Anaxag.A 40 D.-K.' at end for 'always ῑ' read 'regularly ῐ, but v. ἱμάω'

**ἱμάσθλη**, line 2, after '*Eranos* 13.88 (pl.)' insert 'fig., δαιμονίης κακότητος ἐβακχεύθησαν ἱμάσθλῃ Nonn.*D.* 9.39, al.'

*ἱμᾰσιοπώλης, v. °ἱματιο-.

**ἱμάτιον**, at end after 'εἱματισμός' add 'Dor. **ἡμάτιον** *SEG* 9.13.15 (Cyrene, iv BC)'

**ἱμᾰτιοπρᾱ́της**, add '*MAMA* 3.619 (Corycus), *BCH* suppl. 8.157 (vi AD), *PKlein.Form.* 969 (vi/vii AD)'

**ἱμᾰτιοπώλης**, add 'ἱμασιοπώλης *UPZ* 7.8'

**ἱμᾰτιοπωλικόν**, add 'also **-ική**, ἡ *PErasm.* 5'

**ἱμάω**, after 'from a well' insert 'Men.*Dysc.* 191'

**ϝιμβάναι**, add 'cf. °ἵμψας'

**Ἴμβρος**, line 1, for 'ὁ' read 'ἡ'; before 'epith. of Pelasgian Hermes' insert 'masc.'

**ἱμείρω II**, add 'Democr. 223 D.-K.'

*ἵμερα· τὰ πρὸς τοὺς καθαρμοὺς φερόμενα ἄνθη καὶ στεφανώματα Hsch.; cf. °ἴσμερα.

**ἱμερόεις**, at end after 'of persons' insert 'Hes.*Th.* 359'

**ἵμερος I 1**, line 2, for 'raised' read 'roused'; line 5, after '(Od.) 4.113' insert 'τῶν ἀντερώντων ἱμέρῳ πεπληγμένοι A.*Ag.* 544' deleting this ref. in lines 12/13 **II**, line 2, delete 'only in' before 'neut. as adv.' and add 'sup. *APl.* 16.182 (Leon.Tarent.)'

*ἱμερόφοιτος, ον, *wandering in a frenzy of desire*, Nonn.*D.* 15.227.

**ἱμερτός**, add 'fem. as pr.n. Ἱμερτή· τὸ πάλαι ἡ Λέσβος Hsch.'

*ἵμεστος (ἱμέσιτος La.)· δίκη (Sicel) Hsch.

*ἱμητήρ, ῆρος, ὁ, κάδον ἱμητῆρα bucket *for raising water*, dub. in *Inscr.Délos* 1417*A*i146 (ii BC).

*ἱμιμναῖῆος, v. °ἡμι-.

*ἱμίτραον· ὑπόζωσον, Πάφιοι Hsch. (perh. = ἐμμίτρασον, fr. *ἐμμιτράω; ἱμιτραιον· ὑπόζωστρον La.).

*ἰμπεράτωρ, ορος, ὁ, Lat. *imperator*, *IG* 5(1).1454.3 (i BC), *Thasos* 175 i 11.

*ἰμφειβλατώριον, τό, *cloak fastened with a fibula*, *Rev.Phil.* 1937.106 (Pessinus, ii AD); cf. °φιβλατώριον, Lat. *infibulo*.

*ἰμφορά, ἁ, perh. Cypr. for εἰσφορά, *contribution*, *i-po-ra-se* ἰ(μ)φοράς *ICS* 318 A III.

*ἵμψας· ζεύξας. Θετταλοί Hsch.; cf. ϝιμβάναι, °Ἴμψιος.

*Ἴμψιος, ὁ, epith. of Poseidon in Thessaly, *Fs.Theocharis* p. 381.

**ἵνα B II 3 c**, line 3, delete 'cf.' and for 'Pl.*Ap.* 26d' read 'Pl.*Ap.* 26c' add '**IV** w. τοῦ and inf., ἱ. τοῦ τὰ ὅλα συντελεσθῆναι *OGI* 5.15 (letter of Antigonus Monophthalmus, iv BC).'

*ἰνάρει· μαστεύει Hsch.; cf. νάρειν.

*ἰνᾰ́ρετος, v. °ἐνάρετος.

**ἰνάσσω**, for 'Call.*Fr.anon.* 126' read '*Suppl.Hell.* 1036'

*Ἰνᾰ́χεια, τά, festival of Leucothea in Crete, Hsch.

*Ἰνᾰχίδαι, οἱ, *descendants of Inachus*, *Argives*, E.*IA* 1117, *SEG* 35.267c (Argos, late iv BC), *Suppl.Hell.* 1088.

*Ἰνᾰχίη, ἡ, poet. for Argos, epigr. in *SEG* 11.325 (Argos, iv/v AD).

*Ἰνᾰ́χιος, = Ἰνάχειος, Call.*Epigr.* 57 Pf.

**ἰνδάλλομαι**, add '**3** trans., *deem like*, D.Chr. 11(12).53, S.E.*M.* 11.122.'

**ἴνδαλμα**, for '*IG* 3.1403' read 'epigr. in *IG* $2^2$.12142 (iii AD)'

*Ἰνδία, ἡ, *India* (the actual area is not defined), Luc.*Alex.* 44, *SEG* 31.1116 (Phrygia, Rom.imp.).

*ἰνδῐκοβᾰ́φος, ὁ, *indigo-dyer*, Anon.Alch. 418.22.

**ἰνδῐκοπλάστης**, delete the entry.

*ἰνδῐκοπλύντης or **-πλύτης** (-πλεύστης cod.), ου, ὁ, *dyer*, *Gloss.*, cf. *BCH* 77.658.

*ἰνδῐκοπλῠ́τιον, τό, *dyer's shop*, *PAmst.*inv. 62 (*Mnemosyne* ser. 4 30.146, ii AD).

**Ἰνδικός I**, after 'Hdt. 3.98' insert 'Ἰνδική alone, Hdt. 3.106.2, Lxx *Es.* 3.12, *SEG* 24.1225 (Philae, i BC); σίδηρος Ἰνδικὸς καὶ στόμωμα καὶ ὀθόνιον Ἰνδικόν *Peripl.M.Rubr.* 6'

*ἰνδικτίων, ωνος, ἡ, Lat. *indictio*, *SEG* 26.1697 (Palestine, *c.*AD 299/300), 31.1389(a) (vi AD), al., also ἐνδικτίων *ICilicie* 118 (AD 596).

*Ἰνδοκτόνος, ὁ, = Ἰνδοφόνος, applied to Egyptian god, *APAW* 1943(14).8 (Chalcis, iii AD).

*ἰνιμίνα· ἐνήμισυ Hsch.; v. ‡ἡμίνα I.

*ἰνιορᾰ́φος, v. ‡ἡνιορρ-.

**ἶνις**, masc., add 'A.*Supp.* 251, *AP* 15.26 (iii BC), *IG* 14.1374 (ii AD)'; fem., add '*Inscr.Délos* 1533.9'; line 3, delete 'Trag. only in lyr.'; at end for '*Inscr.Cypr.* 101, al.' read '*ICS* 15c (vi BC), 7.5 (iv BC), al. (masc.)'

*ἰνκαφότευε, v. °ἐγκαταφυτεύω.

*ἰνκόλας, ὁ, acc. -αν, Lat. *incola* in sense *resident alien*, Modest.*Dig.* 27.1.13.12, 50.1.35.

*ἴνσπεκτον, τό, *inspection*, *review*, *SEG* 27.1139.34 (Ptolemais in Cyrenaica, vi AD).

*ἰνστρουμεντάριος, ὁ, Lat. **instrumentarius*, *keeper of documents*, ἰ. ταβουλαρίων *MAMA* 1 p. xiv, Lyd.*Mag.* 3.19, 20.

*ἰντερκαλάριος, α, ον, Lat. *intercalarius*, *Inscr.Prien.* 71, 76 (late i BC).

*Ἰνύνια· ἑορτὴ ἐν Λήμνῳ Hsch.

**ἰνώδης**, line 3, delete '*sinewy*, X.*Cyn.* 4.1'

**ἰξαλῆ**, at end after 'Theognost.*Can.* 14' insert '**ἰττέλη** prob. in Poll. 7.211, 10.57'

**ἰξευτής**, after '*bird-catcher*' insert '*AP* 9.337 (Leon.Tarent.)'

**ἰξία III**, add 'Plu.*Mar.* 6'

*ἰξύας· ἰχθύς τις Hsch.

**ἰξώδης**, add 'adv. -δῶς Archig.ap.Aët. 6.8 (137.11 O.), Gal.ap.Aët. 9.10'

*ἰόβας (ἰόβλης La.)· κάλαμος παρὰ Κρησίν Hsch.

*ἰοβρυχέουσα· ἀνιωμένη. πικραινομένη Hsch.

*ἰόβρωτος, prob. *devoured by rust*, Hsch.

*ἰοδερκής, ές, *looking with dark eyes*, Κύπρις (?)B.*fr.* 61 S.-M.

*ἰόζωνος, ον, *having a purple girdle*, Call.*fr.* 110.54 Pf., Hsch.

*ἰόκολπος, ον, *wearing a purple robe*, Sapph. 21.13, 30.5, 103.6, 7 L.-P.

**Ἰόνιος**, for '*of*, or *called after*, *Io*' read '*Ionian*'; before 'across which Io swam' insert 'explained as that'

*ἴορκες, αἱ, v. ‡δορκάς.

**ἰός** (B), line 2, after 'Ruf.*fr.* 118' insert 'Gal. 16.621'

**ἰός** (C), line 3, after 'Gal. 12.218' insert 'applied loosely to gold and silver, *Ep.Jac.* 5.3'

*ἰός (D), ὁ, = υἱός, *BICS* suppl. 10.34, *SEG* 23.640 (both Cyprus, iv BC).

**ἰοστέφᾰνος**, line 2, after '*h.Hom.* 6.18' insert 'ϝιοστεφάνοι Ἀφροδίται *SEG* 32.395 (Laconia, archaic)'

**ἰού 2**, line 2, delete '*Grg.* 499b'

*ἰούγερα, τά, Lat. *iugera*, *IMylasa* 272, 273, al. (iii/iv AD).

*ἰοῦγον, τό, Lat. *iugum*, *unit of land* (for assessment purposes, the area depending on use and quality), Just.*Nov.* 17.8 pr., al.

**Ἰουλαῖος**, line 3, Ἰούλιος, add 'the month *of July*, Lang *Ath.Agora* XXI Hc9, Mitchell *N.Galatia* 424'

*Ἰουλιεύς, έως, ὁ, name of a month in Egypt, = Choiak, *Stud.Pal.* 22.173.16 (AD 40), *PMich.ined.* 1285 (v. *JEA* 13.185).

*ἰούλιος, ὁ (or -ον, τό), app. fiscal unit (in contexts in conjunction w. ζυγοκέφαλον and °ἰοῦγον), Just.*Nov.* 17.8 pr., al.

ἰουλίς, add 'cf. °ἰθουλίς'

ἴουλος IV, for 'Arat. 959' read 'Arat. 957'

ἰουλοφόρος, for pres. ref. read '*GVI* 385'

ἰουλώδης, for '*scolopendra-like*' read '*millipede-like*'

*Ἰούνιος, μὴν Ἰ., the month *June*, *Corinth* 8(1).145 (AD 446), *SEG* 30.1711.4 (Arabia, AD 596); perh. also Ἰόνιος *Inscr.Cret.* 4.181.3 (ii AD).

*Ἰουστινιανός, ή, όν, *of Justinian*; Νουμίδαι Ἰουστινιανοί, body of soldiers stationed in Egypt, *BGU* 2197.7 (vi AD).

*ἰοχάλκιον, τό, *verdigris*, rest. in Anon.Alch. 20.2.

*ἰόχαλκος, ὁ, *verdigris*, Anon.Alch. 281.1.

ἰπνασία, add '(ἰπναστά La.)'

*ἴπνασμα· κάπνη Hsch. (La.) (v. ἴπαμα).

ἰπνευτής, delete 'prob. for ἰπνίτης .. (Phan.)'

*ἰπνεύτης, ου, (-ᾱς, ᾱ) ὁ, = ἰπνίτης, ἰπνεύτα φθόϊος *AP* 6.299 (Phan.; ἰπνέστα cod.).

ἰπνίτης, at end delete 'ἰ. φθοῖς .. -ευτής)'

*ἰπνιών, ῶνος, ὁ, Cret., = ἰπνών, *Inscr.Cret.* 4.73A9 (Gortyn, v BC).

*ἰπνοκοδόμαν (cj. for ἰπνοδόμαν, q.v.)· τὴν φρύκτριαν. Κρῆτες Hsch. (La.).

*ἰπνός, ὁ, *domestic oven*, Semon. 7.61, Hdt. 5.92 η', Hp.*Mul.* 1.220.4, Antiph. 174.4 K.-A., Archestr. in *Suppl.Hell.* 177.4, Diph. Siph.ap.Ath. 2.54a; as a source of warmth, προσιόντες εἶδον αὐτὸν θερόμενον πρὸς τῷ ἰπνῷ Arist.*PA* 645ª20; used for heating water, Dsc. 5.88. **b** *kiln*, ἀπὸ τοῦ κεραμέου ἰπνοῦ Hp.*Epid.* 4.20, perh. also id.*Morb.* 2.47. **2** *room containing an oven* (a large *oven* could be understood in some cases), Ar.*V.* 837, *Av.* 437, App.*BC* 4.2.22. **3** a kind of *brazier* filled with glowing charcoal to provide light out of doors, Ar.*Pax* 841, *Pl.* 815, *SIG* 1027.13 (Cos, iv/iii BC), Ael.*NA* 2.8. **4** Ἀριστοφάνης (369 K.-A.) δὲ ἐν Κωκάλῳ καὶ τὸν κοπρῶνα οὕτως εἶπεν Hsch. s.v. ἰπνός, perh. based on a misunderstanding; Myc. *i-po-no*.

ἶπος 1, delete '(815 ?)' and after 'id. 7.41' insert 'ἶπον Call.*fr.* 177.33 Pf.'; delete 'cf. εἶπος'

ἵππα, delete 'as pr. n. .. *H.* 48.4'

*ἱππᾰπαῖ, comic adaptation of the rowers' cry (ῥυππαπαῖ) for horses imagined as rowing warships, Ar.*Eq.* 602.

ἱππάριον, add '**4** name of an eye-disease, Cyran. 35 (1.16.20 K.). **5** bird resembling the χηναλώπηξ, Hsch.'

ἱππάρχης, lines 1/2, for 'Samothrace' read 'Cyzicus'

ἱππᾰσία I 1, add '*SEG* 26.121.42 (Athens, i BC)'

ἱππαστήρ, for 'ὁ, .. μύωψ' read 'masc. adj., *used in riding*, μύωψ'

*ἱππᾰφεσία, ἡ, = ἱππάφεσις, prob. in Ps.-Callisth. 20.1.

ἵππειος 1, add '**b** ἱππεία, ἡ (sc. νευρά), *horsehair bowstring*, Hsch.' at end add 'Myc. *i-qe-ja* (fem.), epith. of goddess Potnia'

ἱππέλᾰφος, for '(Arist.*HA*) 499ᵇ2' read '(Arist.*HA*) 499ª2' and add 'Tim.Gaz.ap.Ar.Byz.*Epit.* 131.15'

ἱππεύς I 1, after '(Il.) 23.262' add 'Hes.*Sc.* 305'

ἱππεύω IV, add 'w. perlative acc., *drive over*, οὐρανὸν ἱ. Nonn.*D.* 23.239'

ἱππιᾰναξ, for '*king of horsemen*' read '*commander of horsemen*'

ἱππικός I 2, add 'of a cavalry unit (σπεῖρα), *SEG* 33.1266 (Palestine, i AD)' add '**4** -κός, ὁ, *groom*, *POxy.* 922.6 (vi/vii AD).'

ἵππιος II, line 3, after 'ἀγών' insert '*IG* 11(2).203A67 (Delos, iii BC)' add '**IV** fem. as subst. in Myc., = *chariot*, *i-qi-ja*.'

ἱππιοχαίτης, for '*shaggy with horsehair*' read 'of a helmet-plume, *horsehair*'; add 'also ἱπποχαίτης, Hsch.'

*ἱππιόχαρμος, ον, = ἱππιοχάρμης, *Suppl.Hell.* 991.20 (poet. word-list, iii BC).

*Ἱπποδαμάντειος· οἶνος ποιὸς ἐν Κυζίκῳ Hsch.

*ἱπποδᾰμεια, ἡ, *tamer of horses*, χεῖρα ἱπποδάμειαν (w. ref. to charioteer) Euph. 127 vGr.; as pers. n., Il. 2.742, etc.

ἱππόδᾰμος, delete 'fem. Ἱπποδάμεια' to end.

ἱπποδῑνητος, add '*Suppl.Hell.* 991.19 (poet. word-list, iii BC)'

*ἱπποδιώκτης, ου, ὁ, perh. = ἱππηλάτης, Theocr. 14.12, ἱπποδιώκτας· ἡνίοχος Hsch. **2** a kind of mounted gladiator, *ISmyrna* 404, *Sardis* 7(1).162. **3** functionary in the circus (sts. acting also as ἀφέτης "*starter*"), *OAshm.Shelton* 93, 97, al.

Ἱπποδρόμιος I, add 'in Thessaly, *BCH* 79.446.36, 447.19 (ii BC)'

ἱππόδρομος I, add 'in poet. ref. to the sun's chariot, E.*IT* 1138'

*ἱπποζύγιος, ὁ, gloss on ἐρυσάρματας (acc. pl.), Sch.Gen.Il. 15.354.

ἱππόθεν, add '*from horseback*, *IG* 7.1828.6 (Thespiae, c.AD 125, metr. dedication of Hadrian); of one falling *off his horse*, ἱ. ὠλίσθησε Nonn.*D.* 36.208'

*ἱπποθοίνην· τὴν μεγάλην εὐωχίαν Hsch. (La.).

ἱπποθόρος, after 'mules' insert 'Anacr. 32 P.'

*Ἱπποκαθέσια, τά, (καθίημι I 2) *Horse-Races*, name of a festival at Rhodes, *Tit.Cam.* 153.8 (iii BC), *ASAA* 30/32(1952/4).256, 258 (i BC).

*ἱπποκενταυροδελφίς, ῖνος, ἡ, imaginary creature (depicted on a seal), *PBatav.* 30.2 (ii AD).

ἱπποκοινάριον, for '*Raccolta* .. 374' read '*SB* 7182.45 (late Ptolemaic)'

*ἱπποκομικός, ή, όν, *of a groom*, *POxy.* 1858.4 (vi/vii AD).

ἱπποκύων, add 'title of Menippean satire, Varro *fr.* 220 A.'

ἱππόλοφος, add '*Suppl.Hell.* 991.15 (poet. word-list, iii BC)'

*Ἱππολύτειον, τό, *shrine of Hippolytus*, Ἀφροδίτης ἐν Ἱππολυ[τείῳ *SEG* 22.47.66 (Attica, v BC); app. incorporating a gymnasium, *IG* 4.754 (Troezen).

ἱππομᾰνής I, add '**2** *mad on horses*, Nonn.*D.* 37.275, Sch.BT Il. 5.25.'

*ἱππόμαυρος, ὁ, app. *Moorish horseman*, ἱππόμαυροι σκουτάριοι *Stud. Pal.* 20.98 (AD 348).

ἱπποπᾰρηος, read 'ἱπποπάρηος'

*ἱπποπείρης, ου, ὁ, *experienced in horses*, Anacr. 72.6 P.

*ἱππόπορνος, ὁ, ἡ, *vulgar prostitute* (cf. ἵππος VII), Men. i p. 101 K.-Th., Alciphr. 1.38, al.; facetiously interpr. as *mounted prostitute*, Diog.ap.Ath. 13.565c.

ἱπποπότᾰμος, for '-ποτάμις' to end read '-ποτάμιος, ὁ, *PMag.* 13.319, *POxy.* 1220.21 (-ις, iii AD)'

*ἱππόριζος, ὁ, *a medicament for horses*, *Hippiatr.* 1.88.10.

ἵππος I 1, line 11, after 'Lys. 19.63' insert 'of the west wind imagined as a horse, Call.*fr.* 110.54 Pf.; applied as sobriquet to sexually intemperate women, Ael.*NA* 4.11. **b** name given to small boats at Gades having a horse as figure-head, Posidon.Hist. 28 J.' **2**, add '**b** ἱ. ἀργυροῦς, Corinthian coin bearing a figure of Pegasus, E.*fr.* 675.' **IV a**, delete the section. at end add 'Myc. *i-qo*'

ἱπποσείρης, delete the entry (v. °ἱπποπείρης).

ἱπποστᾰσία, add 'Ps.-Callisth. 18.16 K.'

ἱπποστάσιον, after 'Lys.*fr.* 56 S.' insert 'Sm.*Da.* 11.45'

ἱππόστᾰσις, after '*stable*' insert '*IG* 4².109 iii 91 (Epid., iii BC)'

ἱπποσύνη, line 3, for '(= *IG* 1².946)' read '(= *IG* 1³.1181)' and insert 'E.*Or.* 1392'

ἱπποτέκτων, add 'Call.*fr.* 197.3 Pf.'

ἱππότης (A) I, line 3, after 'Il. 2.336, etc.' insert 'ἱππότᾰ as gen., Arat. 664'; after 'S.*OC* 59' insert 'X.*Eq.* 8.10'; line 5, after 'Ascl.*Tact.* 10.2' add 'dial. pers. n. Ἰκκότας *SEG* 36.626 (Maced., iv BC)'

ἱππότιγρις, for '*a large* kind of *tiger*' read '*zebra*' delete 'cf. ἵππος VII' and add 'Tim.Gaz. in Haupt *Opusc.* iii 283'

*ἱππότις, ιδος, ἡ, (*female*) *driver of horses*, Triph. 670, Nonn.*D* 1.172. **2** adj. *used by drivers*, ζώνη *APl.* 336.

ἱπποτροφέω, add '**2** *perform the liturgy of* ἱπποτροφία, *SEG* 33.1053 (Mysia, ii BC).'

ἱπποτροφικός, add '-κά, τά, prob. *literary works on horse-rearing*, Hsch. s.v. σφυροδέται'

ἱπποτρόφος II 2, add '*JRS* 18.174 (Gerasa, prob. iii AD)'

ἵππουρος 1, add '*IGC* p. 99 B11 (Acraephia, iii/ii BC)' add '**4** gloss on σκίουρος, *squirrel*, Hsch.'

*ἱπποφᾰτης, ου, ὁ, *slayer of horses*, *Suppl.Hell.* 991.16 (poet. word-list, iii BC).

*ἱπποφονία, ἡ, *sacrifice of horses*, Ps.-Callisth. 125.3.

ἱπποφόρβιον I, for 'Arist.*HA* 576ª20' read 'Arist.*HA* 576ᵇ20'

ἱπποφορβός 2, for 'flute' read 'aulos' at end add 'Myc. *i-po-po-qo-i* (in sense 1, dat. pl.)'

*ἱπποχαίτης, v. °ἱππιοχαίτης.

*Ἵπτα, ἡ, *Hipta*, nurse of Dionysus, Orph.*H.* 48.4, 49; μητρὶ Ἵπτᾳ *ABSA* 21.169 (Maeonia), al., cf. ἵπτα· ὁ δρυοκόλαψ ἐθνικῶς. καὶ Ἥρα Hsch.

ἵπταμαι, before 'Mosch. 3.43' insert '*APl.* 275.4 (Posidipp.)'; add 'Phryn. 297 F.'

*ἰρᾶν, v. °εἴρην.

ἱρέα, delete the form.

*ἴρην, v. °εἴρην.

*ἰρίτης, ου, ὁ, name of a stone, Socr.Dion.*Lith.* 51.1 G.; cf. *iritis*, Plin.*HN* 37.138.

ἱρμοφόρος, delete the entry (v. °φορμοφόρος).

ἱρών, delete the entry (v. °οἱρών).

ἰρωστί, add 'Semon. 24.2'

ἶς (B), line 2, after 'Od. 9.538' insert 'cj. in Pi.*P.* 4.253'

ἰσάζω I, add '*to make level*, Nonn.*D.* 43.132' **II 1**, add 'A.R. 3.1045'

*ἰσαίων, ωνος, ὁ, ἡ, *having an equal span of life*, Hes.*fr.* 1.8 M.-W.

ἴσᾱμι, add 'part. ἴσαις *AP* 7.718 (Noss.)'

*ἰσαντινόϊος, ον, *equivalent to the Antinoan games*, ἀγών *JEA* 37.87 (Memphis, iii AD), *PGiss.Univ.*inv. 252 (*ASP* 1.20).

ἰσᾰριθμέω, add 'Aristid.Quint. 3.19'

*ἰσατέον· γνωστέον. ἰστέον Hsch.

*Ἰσαυρικός, ή, όν, *made in Isauria*, στιχάριον Ἰ. *PVindob.* G16859 (*Tyche* 2.10, vi AD).

Ἰσεῖον (s.v. Ἰσιεῖον), add 'sp. Ἰσῖον *SEG* 26.1777 (Egypt, Ptolemaic)'

ἰσημερινός, add '-ή, sc. τροπή, on a sundial, *SEG* 31.931 (Aphrodisias, v AD)'

**ἰσήρης**, line 2, for 'ῥαιβοῖσιν ἰσήρεες' read 'ῥοικοῖσιν ἰσήρεες ἄντα παγούροις'

***ἰσθμή**· φρόνησις Theognost.*Can.* 14; cf. ἰσμή.

**ἰσθμιάζω I**, after '*Isthmian games*' insert 'A.*fr.* 78a.34, 75 R.'

**Ἰσθμιᾰκός**, add 'πίτυν -ήν epigr. in *SEG* 37.712 (Chios, ii AD)'

**Ἰσθμιάς**, line 1, before 'ἄδος' insert '(also **Ἰθμιάς**, *SIG* 36*A*26 (Delphi, v BC))'

***Ἰσθμιάτης**, ου, ὁ, = Ἰσθμιαστής, *Inscr.Délos* 1441*A*i53 (pl., ii BC).

**Ἰσθμικός**, add '**II** παῖδες Ἰ. *boy competitors of the age fixed for the Isthmian games*, *SIG* 1065.9, al. (Cos, i BC/i AD); without παῖδες, *SEG* 3.335.7, al. (Thespiae, ii AD).'

**ἴσθμιον II 2**, add 'ἴσ[θ]μιον ‹φ›ρεατ(ος) Lang *Ath.Agora* XXI K1 (vi BC)'

**Ἰσθμιονίκης**, after 'B. 9.26' insert add 'Lang *Ath.Agora* XXI L12'

**ἰσθμός I 2**, after '*fauces*' insert 'Nic.*Al.* 80, 508' **II 4**, transfer '*Inscr.Délos* ll. cc.' to section II 1.

***Ἰσιάστησις**, εως, ἡ, *the worshippers of Isis collectively*, *PColl.Youtie* 14.24 (132/1 BC).

**Ἰσιδεῖον**, add 'sp. Εἰσιδεῖα *IG* 12(5).606 (Ceos)'

**ἰσῑκιάριος**, add '*MAMA* 3.343 (Corycus), εἰσικι[άριος] *SEG* 35.1110 (Ephesus, iii AD), *PRyl.* 640.10, 641.30, al. (iv AD, εἰσ-, εἰσσ- papp.)'

**+ἰσῑκιομάγειρος**, ὁ, *sausage-maker* or *-seller*, *PMich.*inv. 3780 (*ZPE* 62.133, AD 458), *SB* 9456 (AD 594).

**ἰσῑκιον**, line 2, for 'Ath. 9.376b' read 'Ath. 9.376d'

***ἰσῑκιοπώλης**, ου, ὁ, *sausage-* or *mince-seller*, *PLond.* 1028.12 (vii AD).

**Ἶσις**, line 3, after 'etc.' insert 'Εἴσεως (gen.) *ASAA* 30/32(1952/4).264, no. 11 (Rhodes)'

***Ἰσιτῠ́χη**, ἡ, goddess combining the natures of Ἶσις and Τύχη (Fortuna), *SEG* 30.708, *CIL* 14.2867 (in Roman letters); sp. Εἰσιτύχη *CIL* 4.4138.

**ἴσκω** (B) **III**, add '**2** *call, name*, w. double acc., A.R. 4.1718.'

**ἴσμα**, delete the entry.

***ἰσμαίνει**, v. ἰσθμαίνω (s.v. ἴσθμα).

***ἴσμερα**· τὰ εἰς τοὺς καθαρμούς Hsch.; ἰσμέρα· τὸ εἰς τοὺς καθαρμούς, Theognost.*Can.* 14; cf. °ἵμερα.

**ἰσμή**, add 'cf. °ἰσθμή'

***Ἰσμήνιος**, epith. of Apollo, [Ἀπόλλον]ι hισμ[ενίοι ..] *SEG* 22.417 (Thebes, vi BC), Hdt. 1.52, Paus. 2.10.5, Hsch.

**ἰσόγραφος**, for 'Timo 30.2' read 'Timo in *Suppl.Hell.* 804.2' and add 'see also °ἰσόκραγος'

**ἰσόδρομος**, line 2, delete 'abs.' and insert 'νάεσσιν'

**ἰσοδῠνᾰμέω**, line 3, after 'A.D.*Pron.* 41.15, al.' insert 'Aristid.*Rh.* 1 p. 485 S., al., Hermog.*Id.* 1.11 p. 284 R.'

**ἰσοκέφᾰλος**, for 'Ibyc. 16' read 'Ibyc. 4.3 P.'

***ἰσόκλητος**, ον, prob. *similarly named*, epigr. in *Lindos* 698.17 (*c.*200 BC; v. *Hermes* 77.208).

***ἰσοκράγος**, ον, *equally noisy*, cj. for ‡ἰσόγραφος.

***ἰσολεξία**, ἡ, app. *use of a succession of words of equal length*, Rh. 6.328.1.

**ἰσόμοιρος**, line 1, after 'ον' insert 'or α, ον'; line 2, after '(Gort.' insert 'vii/vi BC'; line 6, after '(Melos)' insert 'λαμβάνωσιν διανομὴν .. ἀνὰ δραχμὰς ἰσομοίρας *in equal portions*, *IEphes.* 4123.11' **2**, delete 'κίβισιν'

**ἰσόνεκυς**, for '*dying* .. Sch.' read '*virtually dead*, E.*Or.* 200 (lyr.)'

**ἰσονέμειος**, add '*ISmyrna* 574.9 (iii BC)'

**ἰσοπᾰλής 2**, for '*equivalent, equal*' read '*equal in force, value, effect*, etc.' and add 'Pl.*Ti.* 62e'

***ἰσοπάρθενος**, ον, *resembling a maiden*, in an address to the moon, κύων *PMag.* 4.2251.

**ἰσοπᾰχής**, at end after 'codd.' add 'cf. °ἰσόπηχυς'

**ἰσόπηχυς**, add 'in Sch.Pi.*O.* 6.154, Sch.Ar.*Av.* 1283, ἰσοπήχεις is perh. confused w. ἰσοπαχεῖς'

**ἰσοπολῖτις**, add 'τῆς ἰ. καμίνου Lxx 4*Ma.* 13.9 (s.v.l., sense unclear)'

**ἰσοπῡ́θιος**, add '*SEG* 31.1287 (Pamphylia, Rom.imp.)'

**ἰσόρροπος I 2**, add 'ἐπιχείρημα Democr. 26 D.-K.; comp., Sch.B.Il. 12.421' **II**, line 2, for 'πορεύεσθαι' read 'εὐήνια ὄντα'

**ἰσόρυθμος**, delete the entry.

**ἴσος**, line 2, after 'Hsch.' insert 'Ϝίσος *SEG* 37.340.4 (Mantinea, early iv BC)'; line 10, after 'Pl.*R.* 441c' insert 'θυγατέρας ἓξ καὶ ἴσους ἄρρενας (i.e. *as many*) Plu. 2.312c, ἡμέρας .. ἑπτὰ καὶ ἴσας νύκτας Luc.*VH* 2.1' **IV 2**, line 2, after 'D. 14.6' insert 'ἄχρι τῆς ἴσης id. 5.17'; line 8, ἐξ ἴσης, add '*SEG* 30.1382 (Lydia, AD 301)'; line 18, after 'Plb. 1.18.10' insert 'ἐπ' ἴσῃ, etc.; ἐπὶ τᾶι ϜίσϜαι [καὶ τ]ᾶι ὁμοίαι *on fair and equal terms*, *Schwyzer* 175.2 (Gortyn, v BC or earlier); ἐπὶ τοῖς ϜίσϜοις καὶ τοῖς ὑμοίοις id. 665 A[1].4 (Orchomenus Arcadiae, iv BC); ἐφ' ἴσηι καὶ ὁμοίηι id. 708[a] (Ephesus, iv BC)'

**ἰσοστάσιος 1**, line 5, after 'Dam.*Pr.* 91' insert 'ἰ. μύρον Hsch.'

***ἰσόστῡλον**· τὸ στοιχηδόν Hsch. (La.) (after ἰστυάζει, v. ἰστυλόν).

**ἰσότης III**, add '**2** *equability* of weather, *Cat.Cod.Astr.* 8(3).196.4.'

**ἰσότῠπος II**, add 'Nonn.*D.* 2.553'

**ἰσουράνιος**, add 'γένεθλα *MDAI(A)* 56.122 (Smyrna), epigr. in *SEG* 28.541.6 (Maced., Hellen.)'

**ἰσοφόριος**, delete the entry; v. °εἰσωφόριος.

**ἰσοχρόνιος**, line 3, after 'Ptol.Tetr. 36' insert '(v.l.)'

***ἰσόχωρος**, ον, gloss on ἰσόπεδος, Hsch.

**ἰσόψῡχος**, add '**3** *precious as life*, Sch.E.*Andr.* 419.'

**Ἰσπανός**, for "Ἰσπανόν' (line 1) to end read "Ἰσπανόν, τό, kind of oil, Gal. 10.790.13, 822.8, 12.513.9; see also ‡Σπανός'

***ἰσπνιᾶται**, οἱ, *ropes*, Theognost.*Can.* 14.25.

***ἰστάκη**· δρέπανον. Βοιωτοί Hsch., Theognost.*Can.* 14.

**ἵστημι I**, line 2, after 'E.*Supp.* 1230' insert 'καθίστη Ar.*Ec.* 743' and after 'Il. 9.202' insert 'προσίστα Macho 20 G.' **II 1**, line 3, for 'Dor. σταθί' read 'Dor. and Aeol. στᾶθι' and for 'Sapph. 29' read 'Sapph. 138.1 L.-P'; line 9, after 'Hdt. 7.152' insert 'Aeol. pf. part. fem. παρεστάκοισαν Alc. 298.7 L.-P.'; line 11, after 'ἕσταθι' insert 'Od. 22.489, Ar.*Av.* 206'; line 17, before '*POxy.* 68.32' insert '*Inscr.Délos* 1443*C*6 (ii BC)'; line 3 fr. end, delete 'hence' and after 'Hom.*Epigr.* 15.14' insert 'Ar.*Lys.* 634, Pl.*Smp.* 220d, D. 20.37, cf. Th. 3.37.3, 102.6 (καθ-), Pl.*R.* 587b (ἀφ-)' **A III 5**, add 'ἐστάθησαν ἕως ἐνταῦθα οἱ λόγοι Ἱερεμίου *have been established*, Aq.*Je.* 51(28).64' **B II 1**, line 6, after 'Arist.*HA* 588[a]8' insert 'ἔστη τὸ αἷμα the blood was *staunched*, Lxx *Ex.* 4.25'

**Ἰστιαϊκός**, add 'also **Ἰστιαιικός**, *Inscr.Délos* 1429*B*ii35, al.; ib. **Ἑστιαικός**, ib. 1441*A*ii108 (ii BC)'

***ἱστιᾱτικός**, ή, όν, *of a fund* for temple-expenses *deposited in the sanctuary of Hestia*, ἀργύριον *Inscr.Délos* 449*A*33 (ii BC).

***ἱστιορρᾰφεῖον** (-φῖον), τό, *sail-mender's workshop*, *Inscr.Délos* 1416*B*i92 (ii BC).

**+ἱστιορρᾰ́φος**, ὁ, *sail-stitcher*, Poll. 7.160; as a term of opprobrium, Ar.*Th.* 935; also ἱστιαρράφος *PCair.Zen.* 754.1 (iii BC; -αράφος), gramm. in Reitzenstein *Ind.Lect.Rost.* 1892/3 p. 4.

***ἱστιοφόρος**· ἀρμενοφόρος. καὶ ἱστοφόρος Hsch.

**ἱστοβοεύς**, line 4, after 'Paus. 9.37.4' insert 'also, *pole* of a waggon, Opp.*C.* 1.532.' and delete 'Acc. ἱστοβόην' to end.

***ἱστοβόης**, ὁ, acc. -βόην, *plough-tree*, *AP* 6.104 (Phil.).

****ἱστόεις**, εσσα, εν, form ἱστόϜεις, Myc. *i-to-we-sa* (fem.), *fitted with an upright part*.

***ἱστοπένδιον**, v. °στιπένδιον.

***ἱστοποιός**, ὁ, *loom-maker*, *MAMA* 3.693 (Corycus).

**ἱστοπόνος**, after '*working at the loom*' insert 'ἱστοπόνοι μείρακες *Lyr. adesp.* 57(a) P.'

**ἱστός II 1**, add 'στίχης ἀπὸ ἱστοῦ *Edict.Diocl.* 7.56' **III**, for '*leg*' read '*shank*, κώλων .. ἱστοί'

***ἱστοτέλεια**, fem. adj. *mistress of the loom*, of Athena, Nonn.*D.* 6.154, 37.312, 45.49.

**ἱστοφόρος**, after 'Hsch.' add 's.v. ἱστιοφόρος'

**Ἰστριᾱνός**, line 3, for 'Ar.*fr.* 88' read 'Ar.*fr.* 90 K.-A.'; add 'm. pl. subst., *inhabitants of Istria*, D.C. 38.10.3, etc.'

***Ἰστριεύς**, έως, masc. adj., *of Istria*, Lyc. 74.

**ἱστών**, add 'epigr. in *SEG* 30.1429 (Nicaea, ?i AD)'

**ἵστωρ I**, add 'glossed by συνθηκοφύλαξ, Hsch. (s.v. ἴστορας)'

**ἰσφαίνειν**, add 'Theognost.*Can.* 14'

***ἴσφατον**· βίαιον πεπραγμένον Hsch. (βιαίως πεπληγμένον La.); cf. °ἰσφαίνειν.

**+ἰσχᾰ́διον**, τό, dim. of ἰσχάς, *fig*, Ar.*Pl.* 798, *IG* 4[2].742.45 (Epid.).

**ἰσχᾰδοκάρῠον**, add 'written **σχαδο-** *Mél.Glotz* 872.14 (Maced., ii AD)'

***ἰσχαίνω**, v. °ἰσχναίνω.

**ἰσχᾰλέος**, form ἰσχν-, add 'Hp.*Mul.* 1.17'

**ἰσχάς I 1**, after '*fig*' insert 'Hippon. 8 W.'; add 'in epigrams based on pun on the senses of *fig* and, transf., *anus*, *APl.* 240.1, 8 (Phil.), 241.2, 5 (Marc.Arg.); pl., meton., *stalls where dried figs are sold*, Teles p. 13 H.'

**ἰσχέπλινθα**, after '(perh. *door-jambs*)' insert 'or perh. *sockets to secure lintel and sill*'

***ἰσχῐαλγικός**, όν, *suffering from pains in the hips*, *Inscr.Cret.* 1.xvii 9 (Lebena).

**ἰσχναίνω 2**, line 2, for 'σφυδῶντα' read 'σφριγῶντα' and for 'A.*Pr.* 382' read 'A.*Pr.* 380' at end delete 'In the metaph. sense'

***ἰσχνοπρεπεῖς**, gloss on συναγέσκεο, Hsch.

**ἰσχνός 3**, adv. -νῶς, add '*slightly*, τὸν ἰ. ὀξύν Archig.ap.Gal. 8.87.7, 106.15, 107.5'

**ἰσχνόφωνος**, line 2, delete 'Gal. 17(1).186' (v. °ἰσχο-).

***ἰσχόφωνος**, ον, *having a constriction in one's voice*, Gal.in *CMG* 5.10(1).94.10; also v.l. for ἰσχνο- in Hdt. 4.155.1, cf. *AB* 100.

**ἰσχῡρίζομαι II 1**, line 4, for '*persist* .. Th. 7.49' read 'τοσαῦτα λέγων ἰσχυρίζετο kept *insisting* on these points in discussion, Th. 7.49.1; cf. abs. μή τι καὶ πλέον εἰδὼς ὁ Νικίας ἰσχυρίζηται i.e. *lest N.'s insistence might not be based on superior knowledge*, ib. 4' **2**, add 'Din. 1.8'

**ἰσχῡροπαίκτης**, for '*one who plays valiantly*' read 'app., *one who performs feats of strength for entertainment*'

**ἰσχῡρός**, line 3, after 'Hp.*Art.* 50' insert 'of drink, *potent*, ἰ. ποτόν Luc.*Nigr.* 5' *ἰσχῡρόστομος, ον, *having a strong mouth*, i.e. beak, Cyran. 87 (3.12.2 K.).

ἰσχύς I 2, add 'personified, *Pap.Lugd.Bat.* xxv 8 i 5 (after AD 231)' 3, line 2, after 'A.*Pr.* 214' insert 'κατ' ἰσχύος τρόπον id.*fr.* 281a.20 R.' 5, add 'also of works of art, D.H.*Is.* 4'

ἰσχύω 2, add 'c *to be able to, succeed in*, εἰ δὲ οὐκ ἰσχύσειε παρὰ τοῦ δανεισαμένου λαβεῖν ἢ εἰς μέρος ἢ εἰς ὁλόκληρον Just.*Nov.* 4.1, 22.15.1.'

ἴσχω III 3, add 'εὖ κτερέων ἴσχοντα A.R. 4.1536'

ἰσωνία, after 'Ar.*Pax* 1227' insert 'Lys.*fr.* 48 S., *PSI* 670 (iii BC)'

*ἴσωρος, ον, *equal in age*, θυγατέρες μόνωροι καὶ ἴσωροι *IEryth.* 525.6 (cj., Rom.imp.).

ἴσως IV, add 'Arist.*Ath.* 33.1'

*ἰσώστη, v. °εἰσώστη.

Ἰτᾰλίδης, delete 'Call.*fr.* 448' and substitute '*Orac.Sib.* 4.104'

*Ἰτᾰλίης, ητος, ὁ, Ion. for *Italian*, Antioch.Hist.ap.D.H. 1.12.

Ἰτᾰλίς, add '2 *period of the games called* Ἰταλικά, *IG* 14.748 (Naples, ii AD).'

Ἰτᾰλός, after 'as Adj.' insert 'Call.*fr.* 669 Pf. (prob.; ῐτ-)'

*ῑτᾰμότης, ητος, ἡ, *initiative, enterprise, boldness*, Pl.*Plt.* 311a, Plu. 2.715e, [Simon Ath.]*Eq.* 11; in pejorative sense, Jul.*Or.* 7.225, συγγραφέως Plb. 12.9.4.

*ἰτάω, *go*, inf. pf. ἰτάκειν Hsch. (εἰτακεῖν cod.); cf. ἐπανιτάω, ἰτητέον, εἰσιτητήριον.

ἰτέϊνος, add '*PAlex.* 27.4 (ii/iii AD; sp. ειτοειν-)'

ἰτεόφυλλος, for '*Annuario* 4/5.463' read '*SEG* 4.187.16, 19'

ἰτεών, for '*willow-ground*' read '*willow-plantation*' and add '*PKöln* 163.10 (iii AD)'

*ἴτη· συρισμός. ῥοῖζος Hsch.

*ἴτηλος, η, ον, app. *effective, operative*, εἴ καὶ παραμείν[ηι τέ]ως ἁ ὠνὰ ἴτηλος ἔστω *IG* 9²(1).621 (Naupactus, ii BC); cf. ἴτηλον· τὸ ἔμμονον καὶ οὐκ ἐξίτηλον Αἰσχύλος Γλαύκῳ Ποτνιεῖ (*fr.* 42 R.) Hsch.

*ἰτράριος, ὁ, *maker of* ἴτρια, *MAMA* 3.459, 598 (Corycus), *ITyr* 33B.

ἴτριον, transfer to follow ἰτρίνεος.

ἰτριοπώλης, add 'cj. in *CIG* 4434 (Pompeiopolis in Cilicia)'

*ἰτρόγᾰλα, ακτος, τό, app. kind of rich cake, Olymp. *in Grg.* p. 164.10 W., Suid.

ἴττα, delete the entry (v. °Ἴππα).

ἴττιον, after 'Hsch.' add '(dub., cod. ἴττεο)'

Ἴτῠλος, add 'app. also = Ἴτυς, *SEG* 30.1142 (Italy, Augustan)'

ἴτῦς, line 5, for '*arch* of the eyebrows' read '*rim* of the eyes' and add 'βλεφάρων .. πυρόεσσαν ἴτυν *APl.* 140'; last line, after '(Gal.) 10.448' insert '*vault* of heaven, or perh. *orbit* of stars, ἐς ὑψιπόρων ἴτυν ἄστρων Nonn.*D.* 2.575, al.; of the Milky Way, γαλαξαίην ἴτυν ib. 6.338; ἀν' οὐρανίαν ἴτυν rest. in Theoc. 24.172'

Ἰτωνία, add 'at Coronea, *SEG* 28.458 (vase, vi/v BC); at Larissa, ib. 34.558.64 (ii BC); at Haliartus, ib. 32.456.8 (iii BC)'

Ἰύγγιος, add 'Ὕγγιος *BCH* 79.449-51 (Skotoussa)'

*ἴυγμα, ατος, τό, *shout*, A.*fr.* 46a.17 R. (pl.).

ἴφθῑμος, line 1, for '*stout, strong*, of bodily strength' read 'wd. of uncertain origin, app. implying power, virility and sim. qualities'

ἶφι (A), line 1, after 'ἴς' insert '(A)'; add 'Myc. *wi-pi-no-o*, pers. n.'

*ἰφίμωλος· δυσχερής Hsch. (La.) (cod. ἴφικλος q.v.).

ἴφυον, add '(app. also an edible plant, Hsch.; cf. Ar. l.c.; v. *JS* 1988.165-6)'

ἰχαίνω, for 'Call.*Aet.* 1.1.22' read 'Call.*fr.* 178.22 Pf.'

*ἰχάλη· ἧπαρ ὑός, ἐσκευασμένος ἰχθύς. ἢ κίχλη τὸ ὄρνεον Hsch., cf. °ἴχλα.

ἰχθύα II, for pres. def. read 'vessel, prob. type of *lekanis*'

ἰχθῠακός I, for '*Cat.Cod.Astr.* 1.160' read '*Cat.Cod.Astr.* 1.166'

ἰχθῠβολέω, for '*strike, harpoon fish*' read '*fish*'

ἰχθῠβόλος II, for this section read '(pass., proparox.) *consisting of a catch of fish*, θήρα *AP* 6.24, δεῖπνα Opp.*H.* 3.18'

ἰχθύβοτος, for 'Epic.*Oxy.* 213ᵛ.15' read '*Epic.Alex.adesp.* 3.36'

ἰχθύδιον, for 'Archestr.*fr.* 45.18' read 'Archestr. in *Suppl.Hell.* 176.15' add 'II *the constellation Pisces*, *SEG* 7.364 (Dura-Europos, AD 218).'

*ἰχθύειος, α, ον, *made of fish*, γάρον τὸν ἰχθύειον S.*fr.* 799a R.

ἰχθυοβόλος, add 'in *PTeb.* 868.5 ἰχθυοβ[ may represent a noun ἰχθυοβόλον, τό, *harpoon, trident*'

*ἰχθυόγρῑπος, ὁ, prob. *basket-trap for fish*, *PTeb.* 868.4 (ii BC); the wd. may be ἰχθυογρῑπεύς = γριπεύς.

ἰχθῠοθήρας, after '*fisherman*' insert 'Plu. *in Hes.* 8'

ἰχθῠοφᾰγος, line 3, for 'Arabian Gulf' read 'Red Sea'

ἰχθῠοφόρος 2, for '-φόρος, ὁ, .. (Epid.)' read '-φόρος, ὁ, *fish-carrier*, i.e. *itinerant fishmonger*, *IG*.4².123.21 (Epid.)'

ἰχθῦς, line 4, before 'Alex. 261.9' insert 'Emp. 21.11 D.-K.'

ἰχθῠσιληϊστήρ, for '*a stealer of fish*' read '*fish-pirate*, humorous term for a fisherman'

*ἴχλα, ἡ, kind of fish = κίχλη II, *IGC* p. 99 B8 (Acraephia, ii BC), Hsch.; cf. °ἰχάλη.

ἴχματα, after 'Id.' insert 'read for ἴχνια by Zenod. and Ar.Byz. in Il. 13.71'

*Ἰχναῖος, α, ον, *of Ichnae* (in Macedonia), of Themis, *h.Ap.* 94, of Nemesis, *AP* 9.405 (Diod. Sard.), Lyc. 129; (in Thessaly) Ἴχναι, ὅπου ἡ Θέμις Ἰ. τιμᾶται Str. 9.5.14.

ἰχνάομαι, for '= ἰχνεύω' read 'glossed by ἰχνοσκοπέω'

ἰχνευτής I 1, add 'also of a work on plagiarism, Porph.ap.Eus.*PE* 10.3; adj., ἰ. κινωπέτου Nic.*Th.* 195' II, after 'Hdt. 2.67' insert 'S.*fr.* 314.305 R.' and delete 'Nic.*Th.* 195'

ἰχνηλατέω, add 'ἰχνηλατῆσαι· ἐκ τῶν ἰχνῶν ζητῆσαί τινα ψηλαφῆσαι, ἢ τὰ ἴχνη ἐλάσαι Hsch.'

ἰχνηλάτης, for '*APl.* 4.289' read '*APl.* 289'

ἴχνιον 2, after '*remnant*' insert 'νομογραφίης Call.*fr.* 43.91 Pf.; σπινθῆρος *AP* 12.31 (Phan.)'

ἴχνος 1, add 'b of sound, ἴχνος αὐτῆς μαιομένη Opp.*H.* 3.391, ἴχνος .. βληχῆς *C.* 4.96.' 2, delete 'Herod. 7.20' and insert '*AP* 6.219.11 (Antip.Sid.)' 3, *sole of a shoe*, add 'perh. also Herod. 7.20 (in damaged text)' 6, for this section read '*track, route*, Lxx *Ge.* 42.9, 12; in the name of a tax, ἴχνους ἐρημιοφυλακίας *PFay.* 75, 76, al., *PLond.* 1266, *PLips.* 82 (all ii/iii AD)' 7, add '*TAM* 5(1).524 (AD 184/5)'

ἰχώρ I, delete 'later .. A.*Ag.* 1480 (anap.)' transferring ref. to section II 2. II, line 2, delete 'of the blood'

ἴψον, after lemma insert '(ἰψών La.)'

ἰώ, add 'Sapph. 86.7 L.-P., X.*Cyn.* 6.17'

ἰωά (B), for 'Call.*fr.* 1.40 P.' read 'Call.*fr.* 228.40 Pf.'

ἰώδης I 2, delete the section transferring the refs. to section I 1.

ἰωή, line 6, after 'Hes.*Th.* 682' insert '(s.v.l.)'

ἰωκή, add 'ἰωκαί· διώξεις. ὁρμαί Hsch.'

Ἰωνικός 1, add 'b Ἰ. ῥῆσις *long-winded* (opp. Spartan terseness), Ath. 13.573b.' add '4 archit., γεῖσα *IG* 2².1666*B*9 (iv BC), κεφαλὴ Ἰ. *Ionic capital*, *Didyma* 39.53, cf. 39.24 (ii BC).'

*Ἰωνογενής, ές, *Ionian*, epith. of Ephesus, *Inscr.Olymp.* 225.11 (AD 49).

ἴωψ, after lemma insert 'Boeot. ϝίωψ *IGC* p. 99 B12 (Acraephia, ii BC)'

# K

***κᾰ**, form of κάτ (= κατά, v. κατά F), used before τ, mainly in inscrs. which do not write double letters, κὰ(τ) τὸν θεθμόν *Schwyzer* 57.A8 (Tegea, v BC), κὰ(τ) τῶνδε *IG* 9²(1).718*A*1 (Naupactus, v BC); also occasionally in later inscrs., κὰ(τ) τοὺς νόμους *SIG*² 860.9 (Delphi, ii BC), but usu. the result of haplography, κατὰ ‹τὰ› εἰω[θότα] *IG* 2².334.15 (Athens), κατὰ ‹τὰ› δόξαντα .. τῇ βουλῇ *Inscr.Magn.* 179.33 (ii AD); also in compds., v. καβαίνων.

***κᾰ** (B), Cypr. = °κάς *and*, usu. before vowel, *ICS* 217.5, 220.1, but also before consonant, *ka-to-pa-ti-ri* κὰ(ς) τô(ι) πατρί *ICS* 167, al.

**κᾰβαλλαρικός** (s.v. καβάλλης), after '(*Edict.Diocl.*) 19.22' add '*PNess.* 18.28 (vi AD)'

***κᾰβαλλάριος**, ὁ, *horse-driver*, Teuc.Bab. p. 42 B.

***κᾰβάλλειον**, or **κᾰβάλλιον**, τό, *working horse*, *RA* 86(1925).259 (Callatis), Hsch. **2** ἡ πρώτη τοῦ τρικλίνου κλίνη, διὰ τὸ ἀνάκλιτον id. **3** = κόλλοψ I 1, Sch.Ar.*Ra.* 510 (colloq.; written καβάλιον).

**κᾰβάλλης**, after '*caballus*' insert '*AP* 9.241 (Antip.Thess.); cf. pers. n. Καβαλλᾶς *IEphes.* 1437 (iv BC)'

***καβάτωρ**, ορος, ὁ, Lat. *cavator*, *gem-cutter*, *PKlein.Form.* 607, 813 (both vi AD).

***καβιαία**, ἡ, the area which can be sown with a *qab* (v. κάβος) of grain, *PNess.* 24.5, 12 (vi AD).

**καβιδάριος**, add '*MAMA* 3.118 (Corasium)'

***καβίδιον**, τό, app. *small jar* or sim. vessel, *BGU* 2359.9 (iii AD), *PRyl.* 627.346 (iv/v AD), *PStrassb.* 35.7 (iv/v AD), etc.; cf. χαβίτια, χαβότια.

***καβιθακάνθιον**, τό, an unknown musical instrument, Anon.Alch. 438.10.

***καβικλάριος**, ὁ, = Lat. *clavicularius*, *keeper of a prison*, *MAMA* 3.648 (Corycus), *IEphes.* 1347 (v. *SEG* 37.915); cf. Lyd.*Mag.* 3.8 cod.

***καβλή**· μάνδαλος τῶν θυρῶν. Πάφιοι Hsch. (= καταβλής).

***καβόνιον**, τό, a measure, ἄρτων καβόνιον *PMag.* 13.1013; (pap. ἄρτων χαβωνίων); cf. κάβος.

***καβουρᾶς**, ᾶ, ὁ, *crab-fisher*, *IEphes.* 4282 (cf. mod. Gk. κάβουρας *crab*).

***κάγ**, sp. of shortened form of κατά before γ, κὰγ γόνυ Il. 20.458 (v.l. κάκ); perh. also Hes.*Op.* 533, Sapph. 101.2, 5 L.-P. (cf. κατά F).

**καγκαίνω**, delete '(Cf. κέγκω)'

***κάγκαμον**, τό, kind of gum, Dsc. 1.24, Plin.*HN* 12.98, *Peripl.M.Rubr.* 8, Hsch.

**κάγκανον**, after 'κακκαλία' insert '(στρύχνον (q.v., sense 4) ὑπνωτικόν)'

***καγκελλάριος**, ὁ, financial official in the late imperial service, Lyd. *Mag.* 3.36, 37, *PMasp.* 5.19 (vi AD).

***καγκέλλιον**, τό, *lattice*, *railing*, fr. Lat. *cancelli*, *Stud.Pal.* 20.151.18 (vi AD, -κελλιν pap.)

***καγκελ(λ)οειδῶς**, adv. *in the form of a lattice*, *criss-cross*, Hippiatr. 117.

**κάγκελλον**, delete the entry (v. sq.).

***κάγκελλος**, ὁ, and -ον, τό, Lat. *cancellus*, *latticed barrier* or *balustrade*, masc. pl. *POxy.* 2146.12 (iii AD), *Side* 58, Hsch. (s.v. δρύφακτοι, sp. -ελοι); neut. sg., Sch.Theoc. 8.58, Sch.Ar.*Eq.* 641 (sp. -ελον); pl., ib. 675 (sp. -ελα); gender indeterminate, sg., *PRyl.* 233.4 (ii AD, sp. καγγ-); pl., *IG* 7.1681; cf. κάγκελλον αὐτὸ οἱ Ῥωμαῖοι καλοῦσιν ὑποκοριστικῶς ἀντὶ τοῦ δικτύδιον ὅτι πρωτοτύπως κάγκρους αὐτοὶ τὰ δίκτυα λέγουσιν, ὑποκοριστικῶς δὲ καγκέλλους Lyd.*Mag.* 3.37. **II** a system of measure of capacity (gender indeterminate), μέτρῳ τῷ κ. ἀρτάβας ἕνδεκα τέταρτον *POxy.* 1447 (i AD), σί(του) καν(κέλλῳ) 127.1 (vi AD), 3936.22, etc.

***καγκελλωτός**, ή, όν, *trellised* or *latticed*, καγκελωτὴ θύρα Sch.Ar.*V.* 124, Poll. 8.124, καγγελωτὴ διαβάθρα *PRyl.* 233.3 (ii AD), [θυ]ρίδα κανκελλωτήν *SEG* 17.545.8 (Pisidia, Rom.imp.), Hsch. s.vv. κιγκλίδες, δικτυωτή.

**κάγκελος**, delete the entry (v. °κάγκελλος).

**καγκελωτή**, delete the entry (v. °καγκελλωτός).

***κάγχαλος**· κρίκος ὁ ἐπὶ ταῖς θύραις. Σικελοί Hsch.

***κάγχασος**, ὁ, name of throw at dice, Poll. 7.204.

***καδᾶς**, ὁ, *maker of* κάδοι, ὁ υἱὸς τοῦ κατὰ Κολοτσε *Aegyptus* 10.73-5.

***καδδίζω**, *reject on a vote*, τὸν δὲ οὕτως ἀποδοκιμασθέντα κεκαδδίσθαι (codd. κεκαδδεῖσθαι, cj. (ἐκ)κεκαδδιχίσθαι) λέγουσι Plu.*Lyc.* 12.

**κάδδῐχος**, delete 'hence, *voting-urn* .. ibid.'; for 'also' read '2'; after '*Tab.Heracl.* 1.52' insert '(gen. κάδδιχος, fr. athematic κάδδιξ)' add '**3** οἱ τοῖς θεοῖς θυόμενοι ἄρτοι κάδδιχοι Hsch. (s.v. κάδδιχον)'

**κᾱδεστής**, read **κᾱδεστάς**.

**Καδμῖλος**, line 3, after '**Κασμ-**' insert '*Iamb.adesp.* 58 W.'; line 4, for 'Call.*Fr.* 409' read 'Call.*fr.* 723 Pf.'

**Καδμίς**, ίδος, ἡ, *descended from Cadmus*, Ibyc. 21 P.

**καδμῖτις**, ιδος, ἡ, precious stone, perh. *calamine*, Plin.*HN* 37.151.

**κᾰδος**, after 'ὁ' insert 'Cypr. *ka-to-se* *ICS* 318 Aiv, Bv, al.' **III**, delete the section (v. *CEG* 438).

***κάδουκος**, η, ον, Lat. *caducus*, of a bequest, *that becomes void* (because of the legal incapacity of the legatee), *caducary*, Just.*Const.* Δέδωκεν 6b.

***καϝοικία**, v. °κατοικία.

**καθά**, after 'καθ' ἅ' for '*according as*, *just as*' read 'in all its senses'; for 'Men.*Mon.* 551' read 'Men.*Mon.* 848 J., ἔδοξε τᾶι ἁλίαι καθὰ καὶ τᾶι βουλᾶι *SEG* 30.1117 (Sicily, iii BC)' add '**b** *where*, Paus. 8.42.13, Gal. 2.82.7.' **II**, line 3, after 'D. 37.16, etc.' insert 'Thess. **καττάπερ** *IG* 9(2).234 (Pharsalus, iii BC)'; line 5, after '(nisi leg. καίπερ)' insert 'καθάπερ ἐνμανεῖς ὄντες *IStraton.* 10.17'; at end add 'see also °καθάσσα'

**καθαίρεσις I 4**, for this section read '*drawing down*, τὰς ἐκλείψεις ἡλίου καὶ σελήνης καθαιρέσεις τῶν θεῶν Sch.A.R. 3.533'

**καθαιρετικός**, add 'adv. -κῶς *putting an end to*, Sopat.Rh. 8.383.14 W.'

**καθαιρέω II 1**, add '**b** *lay flat*, *fell* (in quots., in boxing), δὶς τοὺς ἴουλον ἀνθεῦντας, ἄνδρας δὲ Πίσῃ δὶς καθεῖλε πυκτεύσας Herod. 1.53, Theoc. 22.115.' **3**, for '*raze to the ground*' read '*knock down* buildings, etc.'; add 'of natural forces, οἰκίας καθειρημένης *PColl.Youtie* 13.6 (170 BC)'

**καθαίρω I 6**, for 'metaph. = μαστιγόω' read 'transf., *beat up*' and add 'Men.*Dysc.* 901'

**καθάπαξ**, after 'Adv.' insert 'also **κατάπαξ** *SEG* 24.151 (Attica, iv BC)' **I**, after '*once for all*' add '*irrevocably*'; line 6, before 'οὐδὲ κ.' insert '**II** *once*' at end delete '*singly*, Plb. 3.90.2'

**καθαπτής**, delete the entry (v. sq.).

**καθαπτός II**, for this section read '**2** *plucked*, of stringed instruments, ἐντατὸν .. καὶ καθαπτὸν sc. ὄργανον Aristocles ap.Ath. 4.174c. **II** *hanging*, *suspended*, fem. subst. of type of vessel, γάστρας καὶ καθαπτάς *PSI* 420.26 (iii BC).'

**κᾰθάρειος**, line 8, after 'Plb. 11.9.5' insert 'ἱματίου καθαρίου *Edict.Diocl.* 7.48 in *SEG* 37.335 i 9; of wood, *trimmed*, ῥαβδίων καθαρίων id. 12.19a'; line 9, for '*Sammelb.* .. 230 (pl.)' read '*PMag.* 5.230; without ἄρτος *SB* 5730 (iv/v AD)'

**καθαρειότης 1**, line 2, after 'X.*Mem.* 2.1.22' insert '*PHarris* 193.7 (ii AD)'

***κᾰθᾰρεοσύνη**, ἡ, = κάθαρσις, *SB* 10278.21 (i/ii AD).

**κᾰθᾰρεσις**, delete the entry (read καθαίρεσις).

***κᾰθᾰρεύς**, έως, ὁ, *purifier*, dub. in *IG* 1³.250.B37 (Athens, v BC).

**κᾰθᾰρίζω I**, line 6, after '(Andania, i BC)' insert '*clear* a building site, *Pap.Lugd.Bat.* xxv 46 (ii AD)'

**κᾰθᾰρισμός**, add 'w. ref. to polishing of marble, *PMil.Vogl.* 304.16 (AD 166)'

**κάθαρμα I 1**, line 3, after 'Str. 3.2.8' insert 'σιδήρου (καὶ) καθάρμ(ατος) μνᾶς κδ' *SB* 7365.92 (iii AD)'

**κᾰθᾰροποιέω II**, after 'encumbrances' insert '*PDura* 25.10, 32 (ii AD)'

**κᾰθᾰροποίησις**, add '*PLond.* 1724.50 (vi AD)'

***κᾰθᾰροπώλης**, ου, ὁ, *seller of pure bread*, *PTeb.* 872.19, 22 (?iii BC); cf. ‡καθαρός I 2.

***κᾰθᾰροπώλισσα**, ἡ, fem. of καθαροπώλης, τῇ καθαροπολίσσῃ *PPrag.* I 97.1 (iv AD).

**κᾰθᾰρός I 2**, line 6, before 'κ. ἄρτος' insert 'of flour, bread, *free from bran*, *bolted* (sts. combining sense of ritual purity)'; delete 'of *white* bread'; line 7, after '(Gal.) 19.137' insert 'also καθαροί alone, *PTeb.* 884.12, 16 (iii BC)' and after '*PTeb.* 93.36 (ii BC)' insert '*Tab.Heracl.* 1.103' **3**, line 14, before 'c. gen.' insert 'κ. οὔασιν, with *clear* (unblocked) ears (in quot., fig.), Posidipp. in *Suppl.Hell.* 705.2, cf. *auribus puris* Prop. 2.13.12' **b**, line 4, after '*POxy.* 633 (ii AD)' insert '*Cod.Just.* 6.4.4.16, Just.*Nov.* 1.2.2' **II 5**, after '*correctly*' insert 'κ. γράφειν ἢ λέγειν D.H.*Lys.* 2' add '**7** perh. of weight, contents, *net*, καθαροῦ λ(ίτραι) Lang *Ath.Agora* XXI Hd 10 (ii AD).'

**κᾰθᾰρότης 6**, after 'style' insert 'Hermog.*Id.* 1.2, al.'

**κᾰθᾰρουργεῖον**, add '*Stud.Pal.* 10.233.3.7 (v AD), *PAlex.* 32.10 (v AD)'

**κᾰθᾰρουργικός**, add '*PAlex.* 32.11 (v AD)'

**κᾰθᾰρουργός**, add '*PAlex.* 32.4 (v AD)'

**κᾰθάρσιος III**, add 'so prob. in Ael.*VH* 14.7'

**κάθαρσις III**, add '*pruned wood*, *prunings*, LXX *Ez.* 15.4' **V**, add 'τῇ τῶ[ν] ἐνόντων φυτῶν πάντων καὶ φοινίκων δικ[αίᾳ] καθάρσει *PVindob.Salomons* 8.15 (?AD 325)'

**˟κᾰθάσσα**, i.e. καθ' ἄσσα, = καθά, *Milet* 3.136 (iv BC).

**καθέδρα II 3**, delete the section transferring quot. to section II 1. add '**V** καθέδρα· θυσία Ἀδώνιδος, and καθέδραι· πένθους ἡμέραι ἐπὶ τετελευτηκόσι Hsch., cf. *AB* 1.268.'

**καθέζομαι II 1**, add '**b** *remain inactive*, ἐκαθέζετο ὁ Κῦρος ἀμφὶ τὴν περὶ τὸ φρούριον οἰκονομίαν X.*Cyr.* 5.3.25.'

**καθείργνῡμι 2**, after 'Ar.*Nu.* 751' insert 'transf.'; add 'καθεῖρξα βοήν *Trag.adesp.* 664.24 K.-S.'

**καθεῖς**, for 'εἷς καθεἷς *Ev.Marc.* 14.19, etc.' read 'cf. εἷς 1f' add '**2** *each individual*, ὁ δὲ καθεὶς ἄνθρωπος δεήσεις περὶ τοιούτων ἐννοιῶν μὴ ἐπιδότω *Cod.Just.* 10.16.13 pr.'

**καθεκτός**, add '**III** καθεκτόν· ἐφικτόν, καταληπτόν Hsch.'

**καθελίσσω**, line 1, after '(v. infr.)' insert 'Aeol. aor. (?med. part.) κατελιξαμε[ν- Sapph. 98(a).4 L.-P.'

**˟καθελκτικός**, ή, όν, *downward-drawing*, *virtus* κ. *peristalsis*, Macr.*Sat.* 7.4.14.

**καθέλκω I 2**, line 2, for 'δρῦν' read '[..]'; for 'Call.*Aet.Oxy.* 2079.9' read 'Call.*fr.* 1.9 Pf.' and add 'Zeno *Stoic.* 1.23.18'

**κάθεμα**, after '*collar*' insert '*PTeb.* 761.12 (iii BC)' and after 'Antiph. 319' add '*POsl.* 46.11 (iii AD)'

**κάθεσις**, add '**III** κάθεσιν· καταγωγήν, οἴκησιν Hsch.'

**κάθετος**, add '**4** κάθετον, τό, perh. a chamber beneath the surface or the floor of a grave monument, *MAMA* 6.335.3 (Acmonia).'

**καθεύδω I**, line 9, after 'Timocl. 16.2' insert 'prov. ἐπ' ἀμφότερα τὰ ὦτα κ. Aeschin.Socr. 54, cf. Men.*fr.* 333.2 K.-Th.'

**˟καθεψητέον**, *one must boil down*, Gal. 13.613.5.

**καθηγεμών**, add 'κ. ἐφήβων inscr. in *JEA* 37.87 (Memphis, iii AD)'

**καθηγέομαι 2**, add 'pass., καθηγηθείς (written -ηκηθ-) *having been told*, *PMich.*VIII 497.12 (ii AD)' add '**7** = ἡγέομαι, *think*, Is. 5.14 (s.v.l.).'

**˟καθηγέτις**, ιδος, ἡ, *leader*, *guide*, κ. θεά *MAMA* 8.419.

**κάθημαι 4**, add 'of a god, θεὸν τὸν καθήμενον ἐπάνω τοῦ ὄρους παλαμναίου, etc., *SEG* 31.1594'

**˟καθημερήσιος**, α, ον, *daily*, μισθός *Stud.Pal.* 22.36.10 (ii AD).

**˟κάθθηκε**, v. κατατίθημι.

**⁺καθθηρατόριον**, v. °κασσ-.

**καθιγνῦσαι**, for '(Apptly. .. καθαγνίσαι)' read '(perh. corrupt for καθαγνίσαι, but cf. ἴγνυς s.v. ἴκνυς)'

**καθῐερόω**, line 1, add 'Boeot. καθιᾰρόω *SEG* 23.271.33 (220/08 BC)'; line 6, after 'καθιερωμένος' delete '[ῑ]'; at end add 'also [with ῑ] by Lyc. 950, 1350; see also °καταϊερόω'

**˟καθῐέρωμα**, ατος, τό, *dedicated offering*, Phot.

**καθίζω I 1**, add 'prov. ἐπ' οὐδεϊ φῶτα καθίσσαι i.e. robbed him of all his possessions, *h.Merc.* 284' **5**, after 'X.*Cyr.* 2.2.15' insert '*Smp.* 3.11'

**καθίημι I 2**, of plays, add 'Plu. 2.839d'

**˟καθίκω**, *go down*, καθίκ[ειν] prob. rest. in Call.*fr.* 191.38 Pf.; cf. ἵκω, παρίκω.

**καθιππεύω 1**, after 'Opp.*H.* 2.515' insert 'w. gen., Nonn.*D.* 2.646, ποταμοῖο 23.156, 40.348, etc.' **2**, add 'w. gen., ἐλεφάντων Nonn.*D.* 1.25'

**κάθισις**, add '**III** app., *place of refuge*, βαθύνατε εἰς κάθισιν Lxx *Je.* 30.2, 25.'

**καθιστάνω**, add 'pass. inf. καταστάνεσθαι *SEG* 31.122 (Attica, *c.*AD 121/2)'

**καθίστημι A I 1**, at end, *set up*, *erect*, for '*Inscr.Cypr.* 94, 95 H.' read 'Cypr. *ka-te-se-ta-se* κατέστασε *ICS* 85, 86' and add 'πύργους *SEG* 24.154.9 (Attica, iii BC), βωμόν *TAM* 4(1).56' add '**4** *pay* fines, prices, etc., *Inscr.Cret.* 4.14 (vii/vi BC), al.' **B**, line 1, for 'aor. 2' read 'aor. 1 and 2' and after 'S.*OC* 23' add 'οὔτε καταστήσαντες (οἱ ἁλιεῖς) ἐπὶ θέαν X.*Oec.* 16.7, *Cod.Just.* 1.2.25 pr.' **1 b**, add 'E.*Hec.* 531' **4**, add 'of style, D.H.*Lys.* 9' **8**, after 'πρός τινα' insert 'κατέστην πρὸς αὐτοὺς καὶ ἐδίδουν ἀντίγραφα τῶν δικαιωμάτων *PPetr.* in *APF* 33.24.6 (iii BC)'

**καθό**, add '**III** *where*, Str. 2.5.31, J.*BJ* 3.7.7, Poll. 2.185.'

**κάθοδος**, line 1, for 'Demeter' read 'Persephone'

**καθολικός I**, line 10, after 'Dam.*Pr.* 310' add 'of the Chr. church, *SEG* 34.1341 (Lycaonia), *BCH* suppl. 8.62, 233, al. (Maced., iv/v AD), *Cod.Just.* 1.1.5 pr.'

**˟καθολικότης**, τητος, ὁ, *the office of the* καθολικός (in quot. w. ref. to the sum owing to him), *POxy.* 3408.27, 3423.20 (iv AD).

**˟κάθολον**, τό, *the total sum*, ὁ δὲ μὴ δοὺς τὸ κάθολον ἐξέρανος ἔστω *SEG* 31.122.44 (Attica, AD 121/2).

**καθοπλίζω I**, line 4, after 'Lxx 4*Ma.* 3.12' insert 'fig., τὸ μὴ καλὸν (cj. ἄκος καλὸν) καθοπλίσασα δύο φέρειν S.*El.* 1087' **II**, delete the section.

**καθορμίζω 1**, add 'fig. in med., *lay to rest*, σῶμα *GVI* 788.10 (Bithynia, ii/iii AD)'

**καθόρμιον**, at end delete 'κάθορμον Hsch.'

**˟καθόρμιον** (B), καθόρμια· τὰ ἐνόρμια Hsch.

**καθοσιόω 1**, add '**b** pf. pass. part. qualifying titles of imperial officials, δομεστικοί *POxy.* 1982.4 (v AD), ἀκτουάριος *PMasp.* 320.2 (vi AD), κεντηνάριος *Stud.Pal.* 20.139.5 (vi AD), Φλαβιάλις Mitchell *N.Galatia* 450.'

**⁺καθότι**, Ion. κατ-, for καθ' ὅ τι, *as*, κ. γέγραπται *SIG* 577.18 (Miletus, iii/ii BC), *PKöln* 219.15 (iii/ii BC), 193.8 (v/vi AD). **II** *for the reason that*, Plb. 4.25.3. **III** *where*, Paus. 6.20.10. See also ‡κατά B IV 1.

**καθῡλομᾰνέω**, add 's.v.l.; cf. °θηλυμανέω'

**˟καθυπεμφαίνω**, *give a faint indication of*, τέλος Eust. 1568.28.

**˟καθυπερδέξιος**, ον, *possessing superiority*, epith. of Zeus, Robert *Hell.* 10.63; cf. °ὑπερδέξιος.

**καθύπερθε**, line 2, after 'Ion. κατύπερθε' insert 'Aeol. °κατέπερθεν'

**˟καθυπερῷος**, α, ον, perh. *upper*, of a room, *Inscr.Délos* 1406*B*14 (ii BC; force of prefix unclear in broken context).

**˟καθύπο**, adv. *underneath*, Ps.-Democr.Alch. p. 51 B.

**καθύφεσις**, before 'Poll. 8.143' insert 'Sopat.Rh. 8.280.25 W.' add '**II** *decline*, *recession*, ἡ τιμὴ τοῦ οἴνου ἐνταῦθα πάνυ ἐν κατυφέσει ἐστίν *POxy.* 3507.18 (iii/iv AD).'

**καθυφίημι II 2**, add 'Men.*Epit.* 402'

**καθυφίσταμαι**, for 'Jul.*Or.* 4.163d' read 'Jul.*Or.* 5.163d'

**καθώσπερ**, add '*Ep.Hebr.* 5.4, v.l. in 2*Ep.Cor.* 3.18'

**καί A V**, after 'correlative' insert '*both* .. *and*, *as* .. *so*' add '**2** τε .. καί and καὶ .. τε, v. τε A II.' **B 7**, for 'assent' read 'consent' **8**, after '(Pl.)*Lg.* 663d' insert 'at the beginning of a law, καὶ ἐάμ μὴ 'κ [π]ρονοί[α]ς [κ]τ[ένει τίς τινα *IG* 1[3].104.11, D. 24.39' **C 1**, for 'ἔγνωκα .. etc.' read 'Pi.*P.* 10.58, Call.*fr.* 1.15 Pf., al., Euph. 51.7' **D**, add 'καὶ ὁ, written as χο *Schwyzer* 80[2], κο *SEG* 31.696 (N.shore, Black Sea, v BC)'

**καιετάεσσαν** (s.v. καιάδας), after 'Od. 4.1' insert '(so Eust., but καιτάεσσαν Sch. ad loc.)'; for 'Call.*Fr.* 224' read 'Call.*fr.* 639 Pf. (so Eust. ibid., but καιτα- Sch.Od. l.c. and *POxy.* 2377 Front 6)'

**˟καιλούριον**, τό, app. = κολλούριον, occurring in context with ψωμία (ψωμία), *SB* 1975 (pl., v AD).

**⁺καίμιον**, v. °κέμιον.

**καινέω**, delete the entry.

**˟καινοκέρᾱμος**, ὁ, *new wine-jar*, *PSI* 1249.27, 1250.3 (both pl., iii AD); cf. °παλαιοκέραμος.

**καινόκουφον**, add '*PKlein.Form.* 968 (iv AD; v. *Tyche* 7.230), *CPR* 14.2.15 (vi/vii AD)'

**καινολόγος**, add 'gloss on εὑρεσιεπής, Sch.Pi.*O.* 9.120'

**καινοπᾰθέω**, delete the entry (v. °κενο-).

**καινός II**, line 3, delete 'οὐκ .. Tim.*fr.* 21'

**˟καινούργημα**, ατος, τό, *innovation*, Just.*Nov.* 84 pr.

**καίνῡμι I**, line 10, after '(Od.) 2.158' insert 'τό[ξα ..] τάδε δώσω παλά[μα]ισιν ἐμαῖσι κεκασμένα .. [ἐ]πικρατέως βάλλειν Stesich. 40.23 P.' at end add 'w. acc. of thing, ὀδμή .. λειμῶνος ἐκαίνυτο λαρὸν ἀυτμήν Mosch. 2.92'

**καίνω**, line 2, after 'Theoc. 24.92' insert '(codd., κανεῖν cj.)'; add 'ἐκάνετ' ἐκάνετε E.*fr.* 588'

**καιρικός 1**, for this section read '*suitable for the occasion*, *IG* 2[2].3800.8'

**καίριος II 1**, add '**b** *of the moment*, *extempore*, *GVI* 1924 tit. (Rome, i AD).' **III**, add '*vital*, *essential*, Longin. 1.1; sup., id. 10.1'

**καιρός III 1 a**, add 'καιρὸν εὑροῦσα τοῦ γραμματοφόρου finding an *opportunity* to avail oneself of, *PMich.*inv. 430 (*Glotta* 58.177); personified, Ὀλυμπῖō *SEG* 26.1211 (Velia, v BC), Καλοὶ Καιροί *SEG* 34.279 (Corinth, iv AD), 34.1448 (Syria, Rom.imp.)' **b**, line 4, after 'Pl.*Cri.* 44a' insert 'ἐμ παντὶ καιρῶι *at every opportunity*, *SEG* 30.990 (Delos, *c.*325/275 BC)'; line 6, after '*BGU* 15.10 (ii AD)' insert '*Cod.Just.* 1.4.22.2; also κατὰ τὸν καιρόν *SEG* 31.575 (Thessaly, 171 BC)' **IV**, line 2, for 'to his *advantage*' read 'to your *advantage*'

**˟καιρωτός**, ή, όν, app. *well-woven*, Call.*fr.* 383.13 Pf.; cf. καῖρος.

**˟καίσαπος**, ὁ or ἡ, or -ον, τό, Greek name of kind of lettuce, acc. to Plin.*HN* 20.59 (*caesapon* acc.).

**Καισάρειος**, τὸ K., after '*temple*' insert 'or *shrine*' and add 'at Xanthos, Lycia, *SEG* 30.1535 (after AD 152), *POxy.* 1683.19 (sp. κησ-, iv AD)'

**˟Καισᾰρήσιος**, α, ον, *of* or *from Caesarea*, ὀθόνιον *PMasp.* 6[v].85 (vi AD).

**˟Καισᾰρογερμᾱνίκεια**, τά, *games in honour of Germanicus*, *SEG* 23.638.7 (Cyprus, AD 18 or 19).

**καιτάεις**, for 'f.l. .. Od. 4.1' read 'v. °καιετάεσσαν'

**καί τοι II**, line 6, after 'E.*fr.* 953.10' insert '(= Men. i p. 143 K.-Th.)'

**καίω II**, add '**6** part. as epith. of a fire-god, Καίοντος Μάνδρου *IKyme* 37.5.'

**κᾰκαγγελία**, add 'Hp.*de Arte* 1'

**κᾰκάγγελος**, add 'Call.*fr.* 260.48 Pf.'

**˟κᾰκάγωγία**, ἡ, *bad behaviour*, *BGU* 1816.13 (i BC).

**κᾰκανδρία**, after '*unmanliness*' insert 'A.*fr.* 132a.4 i 2 R.'

**˟κᾰκεπίτροπος**, ὁ, *felonious guardian*, διὰ τὴν τῶν κ. πλεονεξίαν *PMed.Bar.* 15[r] (*Aegyptus* 66.7.42, ii BC).

**κάκη**, add '**3** pl., app. *troubles*, κἀγὼ ἔχο μου τὰς κάκας *POxy.* 3417.13 (iv AD).'

***κᾰκήμερος**, ον, *experiencing a bad day* (opp. καλήμερος), *AP* 9.508 (Pall.).

**κακιθά**, add '**κακιθή** Theognost.*Can.* 109'

**κακιθής**, delete the entry.

***κᾰκινκάκως**, adv., (κακὴν κακῶς) *with much trouble*, *Vit.Aesop.*(G) 19.

**κακκάβιον**, add '*PAlex.* 31.3 (iii/iv AD)'

**κᾰκόβουλος I**, add 'adv. -ως, ἀφραδέως· κακοβούλως, ἀνοήτως Sch. Nic.*Al.* 502b Ge.'

**κᾰκοδοξία I**, after 'Pl.*R.* 361c' add 'Sopat.Rh. 8.15.9 W.'

**κᾰκόδουλος I**, add '*Vit.Aesop.*(G) 26, 28'

**κᾰκοδρομία**, for '*bad passage* (by sea)' read '*unlucky journey*, alluding to Icarus' flight'

**κᾰκόδωρος**, before 'Suid.' insert 'Sch.S.*Aj.* 665' and after it add '*Πανδώρη* κ. Euph. in *Suppl.Hell.* 415 ii 1 (prob.)'

**κᾰκόζηλος**, add '**2** *jealous, spiteful*, φθόνου κακοζήλου *IMEG* 114 iv 13 (Panopolis).'

**κᾰκόηχος** (s.v. κακοηχής), add '*Cat.Cod.Astr.* 11(2).189.9'

**κᾰκομῑλία**, for '*bad intercourse* or *society*' read '*evil association* or *company*'

***κᾰκομνήμων**, ονος, ὁ, prob. = μνησίκακος, title of mime by D.Laberius, Gell. 16.7.8.

**κᾰκομουσία**, for '*corruption of music*' read '*the quality of offending against the principles of art*'

**κᾰκονοέω**, add 'w. acc., *bear malice towards*, *PHaun.* 10.21'

**κᾰκοπᾰθέω**, line 3, after 'D. 18.146' insert 'Men.*Dysc.* 348, 371'

***κᾰκοπάθημα**, ατος, τό, gloss on ὄτλημα, Hsch.

**⁺κᾰκοπάρθενος**, ἡ, *evil maiden*, Μοῖρα *AP* 7.468 (Mel.).

***κᾰκοπίαστος**, ον, *hard to hold, unmanageable*, gloss on ἀμήχανος, Sch.Gen.Il. 10.167.

***κακοπόδινος**, ον, *whose coming brings bad luck*, *REA* 62.357 (cf. mod. Gk. κακοπόδαρος).

***κᾰκοποιεία**, ἡ, *evil-doing*, Jos.*Jer.* 9.3(2).

**κακός**, add 'Myc. comp. *ka-zo-e* (pl.) < **kakyos-es*'

**κᾰκόσῑτος 2**, for 'Ἀρχ.Δελτ. 2 App. 47' read '*IG* 9²(1).253 (iii BC)'

***κᾰκοστομᾰτίζω**, *speak ill of*, κακ]οστοματισθήσε[ται *PMerton* 11.56.9 (ii AD).

**κᾰκοσυνθεσία**, after 'Hsch.' add 'Sch.bT Il. 15.16'

***κᾰκοσύστᾰτος**, ον, in Lat. *cacosystatae* (sc. *controversiae* or *materiae*), *scarcely forming a coherent whole*, Fortunat.*Rh.* 1.3 (distd. fr. *asystatae*).

**κᾰκοτεχνέω I 1**, add 'Men.*Dysc.* 310' **II 2**, add '*IG* 1³.21.48 (Athens, ?450/49 BC)'

***κᾰκοτέχνησις**, εως, ἡ, *fraud*, *SB* 9109 (AD 31), rest. in *PColl.Youtie* 19.26 (AD 44).

***κᾰκοτήϊος**, α, ον, *evil*, oracle in *ZPE* 92.269 (Ephesus, ii AD).

**κᾰκότροπος I**, for '*malignant*' read '*having evil ways, evil-living*' and insert 'Sapph. 71.4 L.-P. (prob. rest.), Ar.*fr.* 717 K.-A., decr. in *SEG* 30.80.11 (Athens, i BC)'; before '*PMasp.*' insert '*POxy.* 2342.12 (AD 102)'

**κᾰκουργέω I 1**, line 4, after 'Pass.' insert 'τάδε κακουργεῖται Aen.Tact. 18.2' **II 4**, after 'Pl.*R.* 416a' add '(s.v.l.)'

**κᾰκουχία**, line 4, transfer 'Alex. 80' after 'Pl.*R.* 615b' in line 2 and before 'Vett.' insert 'Plu. 2.112c'

**κᾰκόψογος**, delete 'cf. Ptol.*Tetr.* 166'

**κᾰκόω**, line 5, for 'A.*fr.* 156' read 'A.*fr.* 154a.9 R.'; line 10, for 'ἐκάκωτο' read 'ἐκεκάκωτο'

***κᾰλᾰθᾶς**, ᾶ, ὁ, *basket-maker*, καλαθᾶτες *PAmst.*inv. 21 (*ZPE* 9.49, iv/v AD).

**κᾰλᾰθηφόρος**, add 'καλαθηφόρος, ἡ, (*female*) *basket-bearer*, καλατηφόρῳ Νεσμείμεως *POxy.* 2781.2 (ii/iii AD), *IEphes.* 1060, 1070a, al. (iii AD)'

**κᾰλᾰθίσκος II**, for 'Men. 1018' read 'Men.*fr.* 855 K.-Th.' and transfer to section I 1 before 'Theoc. 21.9'

**κᾰλᾰθος I 1**, after 'esp. for wool' insert 'καλάθου μείμημα τρόπαιον as a symbol of wifely virtue, *SEG* 36.1260 (Paphos, late ii AD)'

***κᾰλαθρον**, τό, *basket*, = κάλαθος, *SB* 13273 (Ptolemaic).

***κᾰλᾰθωνία**, ἡ, *provisions* (in a basket), *CRAI* 1945.378 (Beirut, Byz.).

***κᾰλᾰϊκός**, ὁ, name of a stone, Socr.Dion.*Lith.* 50.1 G.

**κᾰλᾰϊνος I**, line 4, after 'καλαεινου)' insert '*PCair.Isidor.* 58.14 (iv AD, καλλιείνων pap.)'

**κᾰλᾰϊς II**, for this section read 'app. some kind of sacrificial animal, *IG* 4².40.5, 41.6 (Epid., *c.*AD 400)'

***κᾰλᾰκᾰγᾰθιος**, = τῶν καλῶν κἀγαθῶν, epith. of Zeus, *SEG* 6.550 (Pisidia).

**κᾰλᾰμαῖος**, delete 'καλαμαία, ἡ, a kind of *grasshopper*'

**κᾰλᾰμαύλης**, add '*PSAAthen.* 43ᵛ i 9 (ii AD), *PSorb.*inv. 2381 (*ZPE* 78.153)'

**⁺κᾰλᾰμευτής**, οῦ, ὁ, *angler*, *AP* 6.167 (Agath.), 10.8 (Arch.). **2** perh. *catcher with a limed reed* (also understood as *gleaner*), Theoc. 5.111.

***καλαμεύω**, κεκαλαμευμένοι (cod. κεκαλαμινθευμένοι)· καλάμη γεγονότες Hsch.

**κᾰλᾰ́μη**, line 1, after '*straw of corn*' insert 'whether cut or left standing' **I 1**, add 'metaph., as a typically fragile material, μεμνημένος .. ἐξ οἵης ἡρμόνισαι καλάμης *AP* 7.472.16 (Leon.Tarent.)' **2**, delete the section, transferring material to section 1.

***κᾰλᾰμίδιον**, τό, *reed-crop*, *PFreib.* 56 (i/ii AD), *PVindob.Worp* 5.24 (AD 169).

**κᾰλᾰμίζω**, add '**II** *grow reeds*, *PMich.*XIII 666.21 (vi AD).'

**⁺κᾰλᾰμίνθη**, ἡ, name of var. kinds of mint, or sim. plant (three varieties mentioned by Dsc. 3.35), Ar.*Ec.* 648, Thphr.*CP* 2.16.4, Gal. 11.882.18, 19.731.5, ἡ ἔνδροσός τε καὶ νοτερὰ καλαμίνθη Ael.*NA* 9.26, Hsch.; also -μίνθα Philum.*Ven.* 7.9, 14.6, Phot.

**κᾰλᾰ́μῐνος II**, add 'μέλι τὸ καλάμινον τὸ λεγόμενον σάκχαρι *Peripl. M.Rubr.* 14'

**κᾰλᾰμῑ́της I**, add '**2** name of kind of green frog, Plin.*HN* 32.122.'

**κᾰλᾰμῖτις**, for 'ἡ, = καλαμαία' read '*of* or *associated with the cornstalks* (ἀκρίδα) τὴν καλαμῖτιν; cf. ‡καλαμαῖος'

**κᾰ́λᾰμος**, line 1, after '*reed*' insert 'Alc. 115.9 L.-P.'; line 2, after 'Th. 2.76' insert 'in building, *IG* 2².463.68, 1663.1 (Athens, iv BC), cf. καλαμίς 5' **II 1**, add '**b** = δόναξ ὑπολύριος (v. ὑπολύριος), S.*fr.* 36 R., cf. *h.Merc.* 47. **8**, add '**b** used in hairdressing, κ. τινα ἔχουσιν ἀεὶ ἐν αὐτῇ τῇ κόμῃ ᾧ ξαίνουσιν αὐτὴν ὅταν σχολὴν ἄγωσι D.Chr.*Enc.Comae* p. 386 B.'

**κᾰλᾰμοστεφής**, for '*covered*' read '*crowned*'

**κᾰλᾰμουργία**, add '*POxy.* 729.4 (ii AD), *PVindob.Salomons* 8.30 (AD 325)'

**κᾰλᾰμών**, add '*IMylasa* 803.10, 814.9'

***καλανδαρικά**, τά, = καλανδικά, *SEG* 9.356.69 (Ptolemais in Cyrenaica, vi AD).

**κᾰλᾰσῑρις**, add '*SEG* 38.1210.5 (-σειρις, Didyma, ii BC)'

***καλαυδάκη**, ἡ, *headband*, gloss on ἀναδέσμη, Sch.AT Il. 22.469-70 (Sch.T -δεύκη).

***καλαυδάκιον**, τό, *headband*, *SB* 9122.10 (i AD).

**κᾰλαῦροψ**, for '*shepherd's* .. herd' read '*herdsman's staff*, which was thrown to control cattle'; at end for '*BSA* .. Pamphylia' read '*SEG* 17.552 (Pisidia)'

***Καλαφωνία**, ἡ, perh. = Κολοφωνία (s.v. Κολοφώνιος), *BMB* 7.78 (Berytus, v AD).

***καλεα**, ?τά, perh. some kind of surgical appliances or instruments, καλεα μοτεα στερεα *SEG* 29.972 (Magna Graecia, iv BC).

***καλενδάριον**, τό, Lat. *calendarium*, *Ann.Épigr.* 1910.169 (Laodicea Combusta).

**⁺καλέχες**, v. καταλέχομαι.

**κᾰλέω I 2**, line 4, after 'E.*Ion* 1140' insert 'ἐπ' ἔριφον καὶ χοῖρον κ. prov. for an invitation to a choice meal, Alc. 71.1 L.-P.' add '**7** *designate as heir* to, Just.*Nov.* 22.48 pr., 53.6 pr.; w. πρός, *Cod.Just.* 1.5.18.3; w. εἰς, ib. 1.5.18.9.'

***καλεων**, ὁ, prob. non-Hellenic name of some cult-object, *Inscr.Cret.* 1.v 23.9 (Arcades, ii AD).

**κᾰλήμερος**, for '*bringing a fair day*' read '*enjoying a good day*'

**κᾰλιά**, line 3, transfer 'A.R. 1.170, 4.1095' to follow 'Hes.*Op.* 301, 307' in line 2; for '*Anacreont.* 25.7' read '*Anacreont.* 25.3, 7 W.'

***καλιγαρικός**, ή, όν, *of* or *pertaining to boots*, περὶ φορμῶν καλικαρικῶν (sic) *Edict.Diocl.* 9.1.

***καλιγάριον**, τό, = καλίγιον, Sch.Luc.*Cat.* 15.

***καλιγάριος**, ὁ, Lat. *caligarius*, *bootmaker*, *MAMA* 3.235 (Corycus), *SEG* 8.45 (Palestine, iv/v AD); κ. Βαβυλωνάριος *maker of Babylonian shoes*, *MAMA* 3.616; sp. καλικ- ib. 3.131 (Corasium), *SB* 10258 ii 17 (iv AD); καλκ- *MAMA* 3.30 (v/vi AD).

**καλίγιον**, add 'καλλίγιον *SEG* 7.423 (Dura, iii AD); καλίκιον *Edict.Diocl.* 9.5A; also prob. **καλλίκιν** *PRyl.* 627.34 (iv AD)'

**καλίζομαι**, add '(καλια- La.)'

**κάλικα**, delete the entry (v. °κάλιξ).

***κάλιξ**, ιγος, ἡ, = Lat. *caliga*, *Edict.Diocl.* 9.5, οἱ τὰς ἀπὸ κάλιγος στρατείας .. στρατευσάμενοι i.e. common soldiers, Modest.*Dig.* 27.1.10 pr.

**κᾰλῐός**, add '**4** perh. *shrine*, *PVindob.Salomons* 2.20 (ii/iii AD).'

***καλκουλάτωρ**, ὁ, Lat. *calculator*, *accountant*, Modest.*Dig.* 27.1.15.5. **2** *arithmetic teacher*, καυκουλάτορι (sic) ὑπὲρ ἑκάστου παιδός *Edict.Diocl.* 7.67.

**⁺καλλαϊνοποιοί**, οἱ, *makers of a green dye*, *OBodl.* 45 (ii BC); also καλλαϊνιο- *PBodl.ined.* c.88(P).

**καλλᾰρίας**, add 'cf. γαλαρίας, γαλλερίας'

***καλλεανός**, v. καλάϊνος.

***καλληλακανία**, ἡ, app. shrub, perh. same as °καλωλακάνθη, *PCornell* 25ᵛ.10 (28/3 BC).

**⁺καλλίᾱς**, ου, (Lacon. **καλλίαρ** Hsch.) ὁ, humorous or euphemistic term for an ape, Din.*fr.* 6.2, Gal. 18(2).236, 611; Ion. καλλίης Herod. 3.41. **II** name for ἀνθεμίς (v.s.v. 2), Dsc. 3.137.1.

**καλλίγονος**, masc., add 'of Zeus, epigr. in *SEG* 31.962 (Ephesus, Rom.imp.)'

***καλλίγραπτος**, *beautifully drawn* or *painted*, *A.fr.* 78a.12 R.

***καλλιγράφισσα**, ἡ, *female calligraphist*, *SEG* 7.196 (Beirut, v/vi AD).

***Καλλίδρομος**, ὁ, name of a month in Crete, *IG* 12(5).868.25 (decr. at Tenos).

**καλλιέλαιος**, add '[Arist.] *de Plantis* 820ᵇ40'

**καλλιεπέω**, before 'Them.' insert 'D.H.*Dem.* 5'

**⁺καλλιεργέω**, *work* or *construct beautifully*, Phlp.*in Ph.* 327.1; *beautify with mosaic, paved work or sim.*, καλλιεργῶν καὶ σκάπτων Quint.*Ps.* 140.7; τὴν στρῶσιν *make* the *beautiful* paved-work, *Inscr.Olymp.* 656.8 (v AD); τὴν πᾶσαν ἐκαλιέργησεν (sic) τρίστῳον *DOP* 6.87 (Nicopolis, vi AD); πόλεις καὶ ναούς *An.Par.* 1.168. **2** *improve* land *by cultivation*, *SB* 5168.27 (ii AD).

***καλλιεργικός**, ή, όν, *characterized by good cultivation*, πρὸς ἐργασίαν καλλιεργικήν *PCornell* inv. II.38.15 (*Rec.Pap.* 3.33; AD 388).

**καλλίεργος**, add 'epith. of Athena, *IG* 4².408 (Epid., iii AD), 485 (Epid.), Procl. *in Ti.* 1.169.4; cf. ἐργάνη'

***καλλιέτης**, ες, *having a prosperous year*, *SEG* 9.173, 186 (both Cyrene, ii AD), 18.750 (Cyrene, iii AD).

***καλλιθέμειλος**, ον, *having fine foundations*, epigr. in *SEG* 37.1537 (Arabia, vi AD).

***καλλίθρονος**, gloss on χρυσόθρονος, Hsch.

***καλλιθυγάτηρ**, *having a beautiful daughter*, Δηὼ καλλιθύγατρα *Didyma* 496 (*ZPE* 7.207).

***καλλιθύεσσα**, Ἰὼ καλλιθύεσσα· καλλιθύεσσα ἐκαλεῖτο ἡ πρώτη ἱέρεια τῆς Ἀθηνᾶς (Ἀνθείας ‹Ἥρας› La.) Hsch.

**καλλίκαρπος II**, for this section read 'epith. of Dionysus, *ICilicie* 78 (AD 209/11), Mitchell *N.Galatia* 155 (Rom.imp.); identified w. Domitian, *JÖAI* 18 *Beibl.* 55 (Anazarba)'

**καλλικέρας**, add 'Pi.*fr.* 169a.50 S.-M. (Sch. -κερως)'

***καλλικίθων**, v. °καλλιχίτων.

***καλλίκλωνος**, ον, *having beautiful twigs* or *sprays*, Ast.Soph.*Hom.* 1.4.

***Καλλικόραι**, αἱ, title of nymphs, *SEG* 34.639 (Maced., ii AD).

***Καλλικράτειοι**, οἱ, name of a Rhodian guild, *Clara Rhodos* 2.203.

**κάλλιμος**, add 'Certamen 222, *h.Hom.* 31.5'

**καλλίνικος I**, after '(Paros)' insert 'epith. of Heracles, *Salamine* 45 (ii BC)'

**καλλιπάρηος**, add 'Λατωΐδι καλλιπαράωι *SEG* 37.1175 (Pisidia, ii AD)'

**καλλιπρόσωπος**, after '*face*' insert 'Anacr. 1 *fr.* 1.3 P., graffito in *SEG* 31.847.28 (Thasos, iv BC)'

**καλλίρροος**, add 'of water-nymphs, καλλιρόοισι θεαῖς epigr. in *SEG* 37.1239 (Lycaonia)'

**καλλιστεῖον**, line 2, after 'Sch.Il. 9.129' insert 'τῷ κρίναντι τὰ κ. Πριάπῳ *AP* 6.292 (Hedyl.)'

**καλλιστέφανος**, line 1, after '*beautiful-crowned*' insert 'of Aphrodite, *CEG* 454 (Pithecusae, viii/vii BC; cf. Jeffery *LSAG*² p. 235)'

**καλλίσφυρος**, line 3, after 'Od. 5.333' insert 'Alcm. 1.78 P.'

**καλλιτέχνης**, delete 'pl. -τέχνεις *Epigr.Gr.* 796' (v. °καλλίτεχνος)

**καλλίτεχνος**, add 'of Athena, epigr. in *ZPE* 15.226 (Attica)'

***καλλιχίτων**, ωνος, *wearing a beautiful* χιτών, καλλικίθōνι [χο]ρίōι (prob. reading) *CEG* 785 (v BC).

**καλλίχοιρος**, before 'Arist.' insert 'interpol. in'

**καλλιώνυμος**, for 'sens. obsc., *Com.adesp.* 1023' read 'μεταφέροντες δέ τινες τὴν λέξιν καὶ ἐπὶ τοῦ αἰδοίου ἔτασσον ἀνδρός τε καὶ γυναικός Hsch.'

**κάλλος 3**, line 3, after 'Pl.*Phd.* 110a' insert 'Call.*fr.* 7.11 Pf.'

**κάλλυνθρον**, for '*sweeper, duster* made of palm-leaves' read '(palm-) *frond*'; add 'cf. °κάλυτρα'

***Κάλλων**, ωνος, ὁ, epith. of Dionysus, *SEG* 18.279, 280, al. (Rhegion nr. Byzantium, i AD).

**καλλωπίζω II 2**, line 2, for 'also κ. ὅτι ..' read 'ἐνδείξασθαι καὶ καλλωπίσασθαι ὅτι ..'

**καλλωπισμός II 2 b**, after '*embellishment*' insert 'D.H.*Th.* 29, al.'

**καλλωπίστρια**, add 'transf., ἡ ἡμέρα .. ἡ τῆς ἀναστάσεως ἔθιμος καὶ τῆς χάριτος καλλωπίστρια Ps.-Chrys.*HP* 2.5, Leont.Byz.*HP* 1.2.4'

***κᾰλόδουλος**, ον, *treating slaves well*, *Vit.Aesop.*(G) 26.

***κᾰλόζηλος**, ον, *eager for beauty, having good taste*, Ptol.*Tetr.* 165.

***κᾰλοίδιον**, v. °καλῴδιον.

**κᾰλοκᾰγᾰθία**, after '*goodness*' insert 'Ar.*fr.* 205.8 K.-A.'

**κᾰλόκαιρος**, after '= *bonum tempus*' insert '*fair season*' and add 'epigr. in Robert *Hell.* 9.51 (Attalea, i/ii AD); cf. mod. Gk. καλοκαίρι *summer*'

***κᾰλοκοίμητος**, ον, (in quots. sp. -κυμ-) *resting well*, of the dead, *IG* 14.2290, 2293, al. (Italy, v AD), *BCH* suppl. 8.166 (Thessalonica, v/vi AD), etc.

***κᾰλοούνυμος**, v. °καλώνυμος.

**⁺κᾱλοπέδῖλα**, τά, (κᾶλον), *wooden shoes, clogs* (also interpr. as *hobble* for cows during milking), Theoc. 25.103 (codd. κωλ-).

***κᾰλοπόδῖνος**, ον, *whose coming brings good luck*, *REA* 62.357 (Syria, v AD); cf. mod. Gk. καλοπόδαρος.

***κᾰλοποίητος**, ον, *well-made*, Moses Alch. 314.27.

***κᾱλοποιός**, v. °καλωποιός.

**κᾰλός A I 2**, add '*SEG* 32.847 (erotic graffiti, iv BC)' **b**, for this section read 'as epith. of Artemis, ἃ καλά A.*Ag.* 140 (cj.); καλλίστη, Paus. 1.29.2, 8.35.8, *IGLS* 182 (Beroea); also of Hera, *SEG* 33.704 (Thasos, iv BC)' **II 1**, line 11, after 'Th. 5.59, 60' insert 'ὅπου ἂν δοκεῖ ἐν καλλίστῳ εἶναι *SEG* 25.486.19 (Boeotia, iii BC); [ὑπὲρ] τοῦ γενέσθαι τῶν διασαφουμένων τὴν διεξαγωγὴν κατὰ τὸ κάλ(λ)ιστον *SEG* 26.677 (Larissa, ii BC)' **B**, add 'cf. mod. Gk. καλύτερος' **C II 1**, add 'ἱερατεύσαντες καλῶς *properly*, *SEG* 30.1420 (Bithynia, Rom.imp.). **b** τὸ καλῶς ἔχον *what is right and fair*, *PPetr.*2 p. 19(1) (iii BC), *UPZ* 12.46 (ii BC).' **2**, add '**b** in expression of welcome, χέρετε παροδῖτε καὶ καλὸς ἤλθατε *SEG* 26.791 (Byzantium, vi AD; cf. mod. Gk. καλώς ἤρθατε *welcome*); also written at the end of an epitaph, *SEG* 31.1041 (Lydia, iii AD).' **5**, after 'Aeschin. 3.232' insert 'καλά γ' ἐπόησε he *deserved* it, Men.*Dysc.* 629' **10**, comp., add 'perh. also καλιτέρōς *GDI* 1156 (Elis, vi BC)'

**κάλπᾰσος**, add 'sp. καλπασσ- *POxy.* 3931.27 (iv/v AD)'

***καλπίδιον**, τό, dim. of κάλπις, graffito on oenochoe, *SEG* 35.33 (Athens, viii BC).

**κάλπις**, line 6, after '*cinerary urn*' insert '*AP* 7.444.6 (Theaet.)'

***καλτάριος**, ὁ, *shoemaker*, *BCH* 7.243 (Chr.).

***κάλτις**, ὁ, an Indian gold coin, *Peripl.M.Rubr.* 63.

**κᾰλῠβός**, after '*chamber*' insert 'decr. in *SEG* 14.656.14 (Caunus, ii BC)' and for '*Epig.Gr.* 260 (Cyrene)' read '*GVI* 1254 (Cyrene, iii/ii BC)'

**κᾰλύδριον**, add '*Inscr.Délos* 1429*B*ii84 (ii BC)'

***κᾰλῠκοειδής**, ές, = °καλυκώδης, of the chrysanthemum, Cyran. 44 (1.22.8 K.).

**⁺κᾰλῠκώδης**, ες, *having the form of a bud*, τὰ τοῦ καρύου καλυκώδη περικάρπια Thphr.*HP* 3.5.6, ὅταν ᾖ καλυκῶδες (τὸ ἄνθος) ib. 3.10.4; transf., ἐνθάδε Κλειτόριος κεῖται δρῖλον καλυκῶδες .. (i.e. either "immature" or "not erect") epigr. in *Suppl.Hell.* 975.1 (iii BC).

***κᾰλῠκωπός**· εὐόφθαλμος Hsch. (La.; cod. καλυκοντος).

***κᾰλύκωσις**, εως, ἡ, perh. *budding flower*, Aq.*Is.* 35.1, *Ca.* 2.1.

**κάλυμμα 3**, for '*skull*' read '*dura mater*' **10**, delete the section (v. °καλυμμάτιον) and substitute 'perh. *lid* of a dish, Lang *Ath.Agora* XXI L19 (Hellen.)'

**⁺κᾰλυμμάτιον**, τό, dim. of κάλυμμα (in quots. app. sense 9), Ar.*fr.* 70 K.-A., *Didyma* 39.55 (καλυμμαν lapis; ii BC).

**κάλυξ I 2**, line 2, delete 'κισσοῖο .. Theoc. 3.23'; line 5, after '*h.Cer.* 427' insert '(στέφανον) ἀμπλέξας καλύκεσσι Theoc. 3.23' **II**, add 'Call.*fr.* 80.5 Pf.' add '**IV** καλύκων· τῶν ὀμματοφύλλων Hsch. **2** κάλυξ· .. ἔνιοι ἔμβρυα ἀποδιδόασι κάλυκας id.'

**⁺κάλυξις**, εως, ἡ, (s.v.l., κάλυξι (dat. pl.) La.) **I** = κάλυξ I 2, Hsch. **II** = κάλυξ II, Id.

***κάλυτρα**· σπάθαι φοινίκων. σκόλοπες, χάρακες, σταυροί Hsch.

**κάλυψ**, delete the entry.

**κάλυψις**, add 'perh. also *IAskl.Epid.* 52.A43 (iv BC)'

***κάλφομαι**, verb cited in explanation of ἀκαλήφη (*nettle*) and κνίδη, Sch.Nic.*Al.* 201a Ge.

**κάλχη I 1**, add 'Lyc. 864'

**κᾰλῴδιον**, after 'Th. 4.26' insert 'Men.*Dysc.* 580'; add 'καλοίδιον *PCol.Zen.* 43 (iii BC)'

***καλωλακάνθη**, ἡ, perh. shrub of the genus *Acacia*, *PColl.Youtie* 24.20 (AD 121/2); cf. °καλληλακανία.

***κᾱ́λων**, v. °κήλων.

**κᾰλώνυμος**, add 'Εὐφροσύνη καλοούνομε (sic) *GVI* 1856 (Aegiale, ii/iii AD)'

***κᾰλῶπις**, ιδος, fem. adj. *having a beautiful face* (or eyes), Περσεφόνην δὲ καλώπιδ[α] *SPAW* 1934.1046 (tab.defix.).

***κᾱλωποιός**, ὁ, app. *rope-maker*, Φιλιστίδας .. hο [κ]αλōποιό(ς) Dubois *IGDS* 130 (Gela, *c.*500 BC); (also interpr. as κᾰλο-, i.e. *shipwright*).

**κάλως**, line 5, after 'κάλωας' insert 'A.R. 1.566'; line 6, for '*reef*' read '*halyard*'

***κᾰμᾰκίς**· κοσμάριον, ὃ τοὺς πλοκάμους περιέχει. ἔνιοι σύριγγα Hsch.

**κάμαξ**, line 1, for 'infr. 3' read 'infr. 2, 3'

**κᾰμᾰ́ρα**, line 1, after 'Ion. -η' insert 'also **καμέρα** *IGRom.* 3.1057.6 (Syria, ii AD)' **I**, line 4, for '*vault* of a tomb .. (Teos)' read '*burial chamber*, ἡ θύρα τῆς καμάρας *IEphes.* 3704, *IHadr.* 75, *TAM* 4(1).188, etc.'; line 7, for '*tester-bed*, Arr.*An.* 7.25.4' read 'perh. *meeting-room*, *LW* 2220, 2240 (Syria)'

***καμαράριος**, ὁ, Lat. *camerarius*, *personal servant*, *POxy.* 1300.7 (v AD, καμαλ- pap.).

***καμάρια**· κοιτῶν καμάρας ἔχων Hsch.

***κᾰμᾰρος** (B), app. = καμάρα I, *LW* 2426*b* (Syria).

**κᾰμάρωσις I**, add '*SEG* 16.470.16 (Thera, i/ii AD)'

**καμάσιον**, add '*PLand.* 125.2 (iv AD), *PHeid.* 333.28 (v AD); cf. ‡καμίσιον'

**κᾰμᾰτηρός II**, delete 'Pass.' **2**, for '*toiling*' read '*patient of toil*, ψυχαί Max.Tyr. 39.3'; add 'gloss on φάλαγγες, Sch.Ar.*Ra.* 1349'
***καμβαών**, v. ‡καμπαγών.
***κάμβειν**, τό, perh. = °κομβίον, *TAM* 5(1).706.
***κάμβειος**, ὁ, a kinship term (cf. °κάμβειν), *SEG* 31.1031 (Lydia, ii AD).
***καμελαύκιον**, τό, *cap*, *SB* 9754.3 (AD 647).
***καμέρα**, v. ‡καμάρα.
***καμηλαῖος**, ὁ, *camel-driver*, *PBaden* 31.22 (v. *ZPE* 54.93).
**κᾰμηλάριος**, after '*camel-driver*' insert '*Edict.Diocl.* 7.17 (rest.), *POxy.* 1870.7 (v AD)'
***κᾰμηλία**, ἡ, perh. *camel-load*, *PVindob.* G39847.803 (*CPR* 5 p. 107, iv AD).
***κᾰμήλινος**, η, ον, *of a camel*, τριχῶν .. καμηλίνων *Edict.Diocl.* in *SEG* 37.335 iii 11.
***κάμηλις**, εως, ἡ, *female camel*, *BGU* 2106.3-4 (AD 142).
***καμηλιών**, ῶνος, ὁ, unkn. object, costing 3 obols, *SB* 10241$^v$.6 (i AD).
**κάμηλος**, add '**3** *camel's load*, *PGrenf.* 50 (ii/iii AD), *PWisc.* 47 (iv AD), etc.'
**κάμῑλος**, for 'Sch.Ar.*V.* 1030' read 'Sch.Ar.*V.* 1035'; line 2, after 'τρυπήματος' insert '(v.l. τρήματος)'; add 'perh. also *ICilicie* 108 (sp. καμηλ-, v/vi AD)'
***κᾰμῑνάριος**, ὁ, *furnace-man*, *ITyr* 111.
**καμίνιον**, add '*BGU* 2361a i 4 (iv AD)'
**κᾰμῑνοκαύστης II**, add '*POxy.* 2272.22 (ii AD)'
**κάμῑνος**, add '**2** part of a ship, Hsch. **II** κάμινοι· εὔπλευροι βόες, ἰσχυροὶ καὶ εὐίσχιοι id.'
***κᾰμῑσᾰγοραστής**, ὁ, *seller of shirts*, *Corinth* 8(3).522 (καμισογ-, iv AD).
**κᾰμίσιον**, at end for 'κάμασος .. different' read 'cf. ὑποκαμίσιον, late Lat. *camisia*; see also κάμασος, ‡καμάσιον'
***καμμορέων**· κακοπαθῶν Hsch.
**κάμνω I 1**, add 'οἴκους Philet. 8' (from section 3). **3**, for this section read 'aor. med., (w. pred.), *render by toil*, οἵ κέ σφιν καὶ νῆσον ἐϋκτιμένην ἐκάμοντο Od. 9.130'
***καμπάγια**, τά, gloss on ξυρίδες, Suid. (-άκια), Phot.; cf. Lat. *campagus*, καμπαγών, ξυρίς II.
**καμπαγών**, for pres. ref. read '*Edict.Diocl.* 9.11 (καμβαών ib. 11A0)'
**καμπεσίγυιος**, add '*Suppl.Hell.* 1082'
**κάμπη I 2**, after '*ornament* of this shape' insert '*IG* 2$^2$.1425.251 (Athens, iv BC)' **II**, delete '*Indian*'
***καμπιδούκτωρ**, ορος, ὁ, Lat. *campiductor*, *-doctor*, *drill-master*, *MAMA* 1.168 (iv AD).
***κάμπιστρον**, τό, Lat. *campestre*, *loin-cloth*, *Ann.Épigr.* 1907.29 (Aphrodisias), *PRyl.* 627.341, al. (iv AD).
**καμπτήρ**, add '**III** prob. = κάμπτρα, *Inscr.Délos* 104-28*bB*19.'
***καμπτίον**, τό, some kind of case or container, *SB* 9834b.23 (iv AD).
**κάμπτρα**, add 'cf. καρδοπεῖον· .. ἡ κάμπτρα ὅπου τὰ ἄλευρα μάσσουσιν Hsch.'
**κάμπτω I**, line 13, after '*bend* the knee in worship' read 'Lxx 1*Ch.* 29.20, 1*Es.* 8.73, etc., *Ep.Rom.* 11.4; intr., of the knee, ἐμοὶ κάμψει πᾶν γόνυ Lxx *Is.* 45.23; of a person, ὃς ἂν κάμψῃ ἐπὶ τὰ γόνατα Lxx *Jd.* 7.5, 4*Ki.* 1.13, ἔκαμψεν ὁ βασιλεύς 2*Ch.* 29.29'
**καμπῠλόπρυμνος**, after '*stern*' insert '*Suppl.Hell.* 991.115 (poet. word-list, iii BC)'
**⁺καμπύλοχος**, ον, compd. of καμπύλος and -οχος (ἔχω), in uncertain sense, κερκίδες Orph.*fr.* 33.
**κάμψα**, add '*PVindob.* G25737 (*ZPE* 64.77, vi/vii AD)' and after 'κάψα' insert '*PLaur.* 188.7 (iii AD), *PHeid.* 333.8 (v AD)'
**καμψάκιον**, after 'καψάκιον' read '*POxy.* 2273.6 (iii AD), κ.· γλωσσόκομον Hsch.'
**καμψάριος**, add 'see also καψάριος'
***καμψίγουνος**, ον, *bending the knee*, *Suppl.Hell.* 991.29 (poet. word-list, iii BC).
**καμψίον** (s.v. κάμψα), add 'καμψίν *PCornell* 29 (iii/iv AD)'
**καμψίουρος**, for 'v. σκίουρος' read 'as subst., = σκίουρος, Hsch.'
***καμψίχειρ**, χειρος, adj., *bending the hand*, *Suppl.Hell.* 991.28 (poet. word-list, iii BC).
**⁺κανᾰβιουργός**, v. °καννᾰβ-.
**κάνᾰβος**, at end for 'cf. κίναβος' read 'cf. κινάβευμα, κίνναβος'
***καναθρέω**, *beat with rods*, *PMich.*inv. 3690 (*ZPE* 1.97, ii/iii AD).
**κάναθρον**, for '*cane* or *wicker carriage*' read '*carriage furnished with wicker-work*' and after 'X.*Ages.* 8.7' insert 'Plu.*Ages.* 19'
***κανάλιον**, τό, *culvert*, dim. of Lat. *canalis*, pap. in *AHDO* 1.267 (Dura).
***κανανικλάριος**, ὁ, app. some minor official, perh. form of Lat. *canalicularius*, *PColl.Youtie* 66.28, 38 (AD 253/60), *POxy.* 2925 (*c.*AD 270) (also interpr. as corrupt form of ‡κανονικάριος).
**κᾰναστραῖα**, add 'sg., καναστ[ραῖ]ον δριωτόν *Inscr.Cret.* 4.145.6 (Gortyn, v/iv BC)'
**κάναστρον**, delete 'dub. .. Crete)' (v. °καναστραῖα)
**κᾰνᾰχέω**, add 'φωνήν Posidipp. in *Suppl.Hell.* 705.12'
***κᾰνᾰχισμός**, ὁ, = καναχή, *Orac.Chald.* 61c P. (pl.).
***κανδηλάπτης**, ου, ὁ, *candle-lighter*, Teuc.Bab. p. 42 B.
**κανδήλη**, add '*Corinth* 8(3).618'
***κανδιδάριος**, ὁ, Lat. *candidarius*, *baker of white bread*, *MAMA* 5.254 (-άρις, Nacolea), *SEG* 39.649 (-άρις, ii/iii AD).
***κανδιδᾶτος**, ὁ, Lat. *candidatus*, *candidate for office*, κανδιδᾶτον αὐτοκράτορος *IG* 4.588.9 (Argos, ii AD), etc.; κυαίστορα κ. *IEphes.* 677 (ii/iii BC), *IGRom.* 1.134, *SEG* 30.1556 (Cilicia, iv/vi AD).
**⁺κανδύλη**, v. °κανδυτάνης.
**⁺κανδῠτᾰλις**, delete the entry (v. °κανδυτάνης).
***κανδυτάνης**, ὁ, *clothes-press*, Diph. 39 K.-A., Men.*Sic.* 388; κανδυτάναι καὶ κανδύλαι· ἱματιοθῆκαι Hsch.; pl. -ᾶνες Poll. 7.79, κανδύτανες· ἱματιοφορίδες· οἱ δὲ εἶδος ἰχθύος· ἔστι δ' ὅτε τὸ αἰδοῖον Phot. **2** the name of a kind of rat found in Babylonia, Ael.*NA* 17.17.
***κάνειος**, α, ον, Myc. *ka-ne-ja* (neut. pl.), *made of basketry*.
**κάνεον**, line 2, pl. κανᾶ, add 'Hld. 3.2, X.*Eph.* 1.2.4'
**⁺κάνης**, ητος, ὁ, *reed-mat*, D.H. 2.23, Plu.*Sol.* 21, in gnomic remark, ὁ κάνης δὲ τῆς κοίτης ὑπερέχειν μοι δοκεῖ, app. of trivialities being given precedence over important things, Crates Com. 14 K.-A.; cf. Phot.s.v.; used for winnowing, Poll. 6.86.
***κανθᾰρίας**, ου, ὁ, *gem in scarab form*, prob. = κάνθαρος VI, Plin.*HN* 37.187.
**κανθᾰρίς I**, line 3, delete 'pl.' and insert 'Gal. 12.363.14'; line 5, delete 'so .. 363' add '**III** = καπνός II, Ps.-Dsc. 4.109.'
**κάνθαρος IV**, add '*IGC* p. 98 A6 (Acraephia, iii BC)'
**κανθήλια I**, at end add 'Myc. *ka-tu-ro*$_2$ (gen. pl.), cf. *ka-tu-re-wi-ja-i* (dat. pl. of deriv.), perh. *saddle-bags*, may reflect a form κανθυλ-, cf. κανθύλη'
**κανθός I 2**, for 'Call.*fr.* 150' read 'Call.*fr.* 177.28 Pf.' **II**, after '*wheel*' insert 'Polyaen. 7.21.3'
**κάνίσκος** (s.v. κᾰνίσκιον), after '*Gloss.*' insert '**κανίσκον**, τό, *Inscr.Délos* 372*B*25 (iii/ii BC)'
***κᾰνίτης**, ὁ, *basket-maker*, rest. in *IEphes.* 454.
**⁺καννᾰβάριος**, ὁ, *worker in hemp*, *IEphes.* 454; = *stupparius*, *Gloss.*
***καννᾰβᾶς**, ᾶ, ὁ, *tow-seller*, in quot., as pers. n., *TAM* 5(2).1298.18, cf. Καννᾰβίων, pers. n. *IMylasa* 463.
***καννᾰβιουργός**, ὁ, app. = καννάβαριος, *Tab.Defix.* 87$^a$7 (sp. καναβ-; iv BC).
**κᾰνονικάριος**, add 'see also °κανανικλάριος'
**κᾰνόνιον II**, for '*compass*' read '*ruler* or *measuring-rod*'
**κᾰνονίς I**, after '(Phil.)' insert 'cf. °ἰθυβάτης' **II**, read 'perh. *upright of a door-frame*, *IG* 2$^2$.1672.155' add '**IV** *column of slots* in a °κληρωτήριον (sense I), Arist.*Ath.* 64.2.'
**κᾰνονισμός**, add '**2** *ordering*, *regulation*, *PHamb.* 234.2 (vi AD).'
**κᾰνονωτός 1**, after '(iii BC)' insert 'cf. *PCair.Zen.* 847.5 (w. note)'
***κᾰνοῦν**, v. κάνεον.
***κάνψη**, gen., name of a relation, *MAMA* 3.745; gen. pl. κανψίων *LW* 1784 (Tarsus); perh. also gen. sg. [κ]ανψίου Rott.*Kleinas.Denkm.* 374 no. 89 (*SEG* 34.1411); cf. Tsaconian *kambzi* 'child'.
**Κάνωβος**, add 'in title of Zeus, identified with Helios and Sarapis, *SEG* 24.1192 (Egypt, ii AD)'
**κανών I 3**, lines 8/10, for 'μολίβδινος κ. .. κῦμα)' read 'μολίβδινος κ., flexible *rule* that can be adjusted to curved outlines, Arist.*EN* 1137$^b$31' **II 7**, add '**b** *rent*, *Cod.Just.* 1.4.32 pr.' add '**8** in athletics, τὸ μέτρον τοῦ πηδήματος Poll. 3.157; prob. also in *SEG* 15.501 (Rhodes).'
***καπανεύς**, v. °σκαπανεύς.
***καπβολαία**, v. °καταβολαία.
**Καπετώλια**, add 'Καπετώλ[εια ἐν Ῥώμῃ] *SEG* 37.712 (Chios)'
***Καπετωλιάς**, άδος, ἡ, *a celebration of the Ludi Capitolini*; meton., *victory in these games*, δύ' ἔχω καὶ Καπετωλιάδας epigr. in *SEG* 37.712.4 (Chios, ii AD).
**Καπετώλιον**, add '*citadel* in any town, *SEG* 29.807 (Chalcis, late Rom.imp.)'
**κᾰπηλεία**, add '**2** *shop*, ἐπρίατο οἴκησιν καὶ τὰ‹ν› καπη[λ]είαν τὰν Δίων[ος] *SEG* 34.940 (Camarina, *c.*400 BC).'
**κᾰπηλικός I**, line 2, for 'ἀργύρωμα .. 111' read 'τὸ -ικόν, ἡ -ική, kind of cup, *IG* 11(2).110.24, 124.39, al. (all Delos, iii BC)'
**⁺κᾰπητόν**, v. °καπιτόν.
***κᾰπιστρον**, τό, Lat. *capistrum*, *halter*, κ. ἱππικόν *Edict.Diocl.* in *SEG* 37.335 iii 10.4, rest. in *Edict.Diocl.* 10.4.
***καπιτατίων**, ωνος, ἡ, Lat. *capitatio*, *allowance of food* or *fodder*, Just.*Nov.* 8.2, al.
***κάπιτον**, τό, (perh. formed as sg. of Lat. *capita*) *daily ration of fodder*, *PHerm.* 39.2 (v AD), Lyd.*Mag.* 1.46; in general, *ration allowance*, *PHerm.* 78.3 (v/vi AD); cf. κ.· παράβλημα ἀλόγων Hsch.
**καπνία**, add 'Myc. *ka-pi-ni-ja*, *chimney*'
**καπνίζω**, add '**III** *heat over steam*, βαλανεῖον *PBremen* 56*b*.5 (ii AD).'
***καπνισμός**, ὁ, *smoking* (in quots., process employed to give pottery a dark grey colour), *POxy.* 3596.15, 3597.20 (iii AD).
**⁺καπνοβᾰτης**, ου, ὁ, in pl., *walkers through smoke*, name given to the

Mysians, app. in respect of some religious observance, Posidon.ap.Str. 7.3.3.

**καπνόομαι**, delete the article (v. °*καπνόω*).

***καπνόω**, *smoke* (a beehive), *AP* 9.226 (Zon.). **II** pass., *to be turned to smoke*, i.e. burnt up, Pi.*P.* 5.84, E.*Supp.* 497, *Tr.* 8.

**καπνώδης 1**, add '**b** *producing smoke* when burned, *φύλλον* D.Chr. 66.5.' **2**, delete '*φύλλον* .. 66.5'

**κάπος**, add '**II** *καὶ ὁ τοῦ φοίνικος φλοιός, ἐν ᾧ κέκρυπται ὁ καρπός. καὶ ἡ πρώτη ἔκφυσις* Hsch. s.v.'

**κάπουπλος**, add '(*καπουστάς· φάρυγξ* La.)'

***καπουστάς·** *φάρυγξ* Hsch. (La.) (v. *κάπουπλος*).

***Καππαδοκαρχία**, *ἡ*, *Presidency of Cappadocia* (of its council and festival) as part of Imperial cult, *Dig.* 27.1.6.14.

**καππᾰ́ριον**, before '*Gloss.*' insert '*BGU* 227.19 (ii AD)'

**κάπρος**, add '**III** disease of bees, Hsch.'

**κᾰπῦ́ρια**, add 'Ath. 3.113d'

**κᾰπῠρόομαι**, after '*become crackly*' insert 'Str. 11.13.2'

***καπύσσων·** *ἐκπνέων* Hsch.

**κᾰπύω**, after 'aor. 1' insert '*ψυχὴν οὔ τι*'; for '*κεκαφηώς*' read '*καπύσσων· ἐκπνέων* Hsch.; cf. *ἀποκαπύω* (from which it may be a back-formation), perh. also *κεκαφηώς*'

**κᾰρᾱ** (A), line 1, after '*τό*' insert '(v. infr.)'; line 19, after '*Anacreont.* 50.9' insert 'nom. *κάρη* is fem. in Q.S. 11.58, and so acc. *κάρη* (nisi leg. -*ην*) id. 13.241' at end add 'Myc. *ka-ra-a-pi* (instr. pl.)'

**κάρα** (B), for 'Id.' read '*Inscr.Cret.* 1.xvii 12*A*1 (Lebena), Hsch.'

***κᾱρᾰβιάριος**, *ὁ*, *fisher of crayfish* (?or *boatman*, cf. *κάραβος* III), rest. in *ITyr* 24A.

**Κᾰραιός**, add 'also *Κεραιός* *IG* $2^2$.2360 (ii BC), *Καραός* *IG* $9^2$(1).434.1 (Astacus, ii BC)'

**κᾰρᾰκάλλιον**, *τό*, add '*PL* ι/3 l. 26 (-*ιν*, *Tyche* 1.164, vi/vii AD)'

***καρακέριον**, *τό*, perh. corruption of foreg., *PVindob.* G39847.846 (*CPR* 5.108, iv AD).

**κᾰρᾱνιστήρ**, delete '*touching the head*'

**κάρβᾱνος**, after 'A.*Supp.* 914' insert 'S.*fr.* 269a.54'

***καρβᾶς**, *ὁ*, occupational term, perh. *charcoal-merchant*, *OGI* 697 (Egypt) v. *Amyzon* p. 136 no. 32.

**καρβᾰ́τινος**, add 'cf. *crepidas* .. *carpatinas* Cat. 98.4'

**κάρδακες**, add 'cf. Nepos *Dat.* 8.2'

***καρδᾰμέα**, *ἡ*, = *καρδάμη* or *κάρδαμον*, *OBodl.* 2183.4 (iv AD).

***καρδᾰμογλῦ́φος**, *ὁ*, *one who chops κάρδαμον* (humorous term for a miser), Hsch. s.v. *κυμινοπρῖσται*; cf. *κυμινοπριστοκαρδαμογλύφος*.

**κάρδᾰμον**, add 'cf. Myc. *ka-da-mi-ja*'

**καρδία I 1**, line 4, after '(E.)*Hipp.* 1274' insert '*κραδία* epigr. in *SEG* 37.1175.13 (Pisidia, ii AD)' and for 'Sapph. 2.6' read 'Sapph. 31.6 L.-P., Alc. 207.9 L.-P.' add '*καρδίαν μὴ ἐσθίειν* (and sim. phrs.) D.L. 8.17, 18, Iamb.*Protr.* p. 108.5, 123.3 P., Pythagorean saying meaning (acc. to D.L.) *"not to waste one's soul in pain and grief"*, (acc. to Iamb.) *"not to break up the unity of the universe"*' **III**, add '**2** of a golden crown, perh. *core* or *framework*, *Inscr.Délos* 1449*Aab*ii 13 (ii BC).' **V**, add 'cf. *Ἠελίου κραδίην* (= the planet Mercury) Nonn.*D.* 38.392'

**καρδῐᾰκός II**, after '*heart disease*' insert 'Cic.*Div.* 1.81'

***καρδίδιον**, *τό*, *twig* of the mulberry tree, Cyran. 29 (1.12.21 K.).

**καρδῐοειδής**, add 'adv. -*ῶς*, *PWarren* 21.82 (iii AD)'

***καρδῐοστᾰ́λακτος**, *ον*, *dropping from the heart*, *κ. δάκρυον* epigr. in *IGChr.* 295 (Megiste).

***καρδῐοτομέω**, *cut the heart from*, tab.defix. in *SEG* 30.326 (Athens, v/vi AD; v. *Glotta* 58.64).

**καρδῐουργέω**, after '*καρδιουλκέω*' insert '*draw out the heart*' and add '*IEphes.* 10.7 (iii AD)'

***καρδόπιον**, *τό*, dim. of *κάρδοπος*, *κ. λίθινον ἐπὶ βάσεως τετραγώνου* *Inscr.Délos* 1417*A*i70 (ii BC); Hsch. (sp. *καρδοπεῖον*).

**κάρδοπος**, line 1, after 'Ar.*Ra.* 1159' insert '*κ. λιθίνη* *IG* $1^3$.422.4, 11, *κεραμεία* ib. 9 (Athens, v BC)'

**Κάρειος**, after '*ὁ*' insert 'epith. of Apollo at Hierapolis, *ASAA* 41/42(1963/4).353 (?ii/i BC), 360 (?ii AD)'; before '(sc. *μήν*)' insert '**II**'

***Κᾱρία**, *ἡ*, *Caria*, a region of Asia Minor, later Roman province, Hdt. 1.142.3, al., Paus. 1.29.7, Str. 2.5.31, *SEG* 31.1116.

**Κᾱρικός**, add '**VI** name of a coital posture, *ὄντα γ' ἐν Ἀθήναις Καρικοῖς χρῆσθαι σταθμοῖς* Macho 310 G.; *δηλοῖ δὲ καὶ ἀφροδίσιον σχῆμα αἰσχρόν* Hsch.'

**κάρκαρον**, after 'Sophr. 147' insert 'cf. Lat. *carcer* (*carcar*)'

⁺**καρκῐνάς**, *άδος*, *ἡ*, *crab*, Artem. 2.14, Opp.*C.* 2.286. **b** spec. *hermit crab*, Gal. 6.717.12, Ael.*NA* 7.31, Opp.*H.* 1.320, 542.

⁺**καρκῐ́νηθρον**, v. ‡*καρκίνωθρον*.

**καρκῐ́νος IV 1**, add '**b** *crane*, = *μηχανὴ λιθαγωγός*, Poll. 10.148.' **5**, add 'instrument similar to the *διαβήτης*, Papp. *in Alm.* p. 70 R.'

**καρκῐνόω I**, for 'Pass. .. ib. 3.23.5' read '*cause* roots *to spread out crabwise*, i.e. *intertwined on the surface*, *ὁ χειμὼν πιλώσας καὶ καρκινώσας τὰς ῥίζας* Thphr.*CP* 3.23.5; *κεκαρκινωμένος*, of roots, so *spread out*, id.*HP* 1.6.3, *CP* 3.21.5, *PPetaus* 22.31 (AD 184/7)'

**καρκῐνώδης II**, add 'n. pl. as subst.' and transfer 'Dsc.*Eup.* 2.72' from beginning of section.

**καρκῐ́νωθρον**, add 'Plin.*HN* 27.113; cf. *καρκίνηθρον* = *polygonos*, *Gloss.*'

⁺**κάρμα·** *γλεῦκος. τὸ πρῶτον ἀποθλιβόμενον διὰ τῶν χειρῶν. καὶ κούρευμα* Hsch.

***καρνάριος**, *ὁ*, Lat. *carnarius*, *butcher*, *PFlor.* 207.5, 214.3, al. (iii AD), *POxy.* 2331 ii 12 (-*ις*, iii AD).

**Κάρνειος**, add '*IG* 5(1).222 (Laconia, *c.*530/500 BC), *Inscr.Cos* 38.11, al.'

**κάρνον II**, delete 'hence .. al.'

**κάρνυξ**, add '*τὴν σάλπιγγα Γαλάται* Hsch. (La.) (*κάρνον*, q.v., cod.)'

***καροῦσθαι·** *ὠνεῖσθαι* Hsch.; also *καρούμενος· ὠνησάμενος* ib.

**καρουχάριος**, add '*χαρουχα*[.. *ITyr* 205 (unless *χαρουχᾶ*, gen. of *χαρουχᾶς*, is read in same sense)'

**κᾰρόω**, line 2, of wine, add '*τὴν ψυχήν μου κάρωσον* *Anacreont.* 52A.3 W.'

**καρπεύω**, line 2, for 'Corc.' read 'Cret. decree at Corcyra, iii BC'

⁺**κάρπιον**, *τό*, tree found in India, Ctes.*fr.* 45.47 J.

**Κάρπιος**, add 'of Dionysus, *Πολέμων* 6.17/18, *Rev.Phil.* 35(1911).124 (both Larissa)'

**καρπιστής**, for '*emancipator*' read '= Lat. *adsertor*, *vindex* (cf. *RIDA*, ser. 3, 6, pp. 190-3)'; add '*SB* 9801.7 (ii/iii AD)'

**καρπογόνος**, add '*IG* 12(1).783.6 (Lindos) = *AP* 15.11.6'

**καρποδαιστάς**, after '*ᾱ*' insert 'or -**δαίστᾱς**, *ᾱ*'

***καρποδότης**, *ὁ*, *giver of fruit*, *Διὶ Βροντῶ‹ν›τι καὶ Δὶ Καρποδότῃ* *INikaia* 1085 (iii AD), 1084.

***καρποθᾰ́λεια**, fem. adj., *rich in fruit*, cj. in epigr. in *Didyma* 496*B*3 (ii AD; v. *ZPE* 7.207).

***καρποθηκείτας**, *ου*, *ὁ*, perh. *granary superintendent*, *IRhod.Peraia* 603.2(ii BC).

***Καρποκράτης**, v. °*Ἁρποκράτης*.

⁺**καρπολογέω**, *prune the fruiting boughs* of: pass., of trees, Thphr.*CP* 1.15.1. **II** *serve as καρπολόγος* II, *SIG* 1000.29 (Cos).

**καρπολόγος II**, add 'also at Colophon and elsewhere, decr. in *AJPh* 56.362.37; cf. °*καρπολογέω* II'

***καρπόμετρον** (?), *τό*, (rest. fr. abbrev. *καρ.*) an undefined measure, *SEG* 31.374 (Olympia, vi/v BC).

**καρπός** (A), line 7, after 'of grapes, Il. 18.568' insert 'of fruit from trees, Od. 11.588, 19.112' at end add 'Myc. *ka-po*'

**καρπός** (B), line 2, after '(E.*Ion*) 891' insert '*καρποὶ χειρῶν* Hp.*Aër.* 20'

***καρπότεξ**, *τεκος*, adj. *bearing fruit*, epith. for a month, Dionys.Trag. 121 S.

**καρποτρόφος**, after '*Milet.* 7.64' insert '*ICilicie* 78 (iii AD)'

**καρποφόρος**, of Demeter, add 'rest. in *SEG* 30.1341.5 (Miletus, ii/i BC)'

**καρπόω I 1**, line 2, after 'A.*Pers.* 821' insert 'med., *Inscr.Cret.* 4.43*Aa*3 (v BC)'

**κάρπωμα II**, for this section read '*an offering* (properly of fruits, but used by Septuagint translators to cover offerings of all kinds, mainly animal victims), Lxx *Ex.* 29.25, *Le.* 1.4, *Jo.* 22.26, etc.'

**καρπωνία**, for '*fruit-buying*' read '*purchase of a crop*'; add 'sp. -*εία*, *PMich.*v 238.34 (AD 46), *PLond.* 168.7 (AD 162), etc.; (meton.) *the crop so purchased*, *PSoterichos* 4.5 (AD 87), *SB* 9132 (iii/iv AD)'

**κάρπωσις I**, add '*SEG* 37.77.10 (Athens, iv BC)' **II**, after '*offering of fruits*' insert 'including animal offerings (cf. °*κάρπωμα*)'; after 'Lxx *Le.* 4.10' insert '22.22, *Jb.* 42.8, *Si.* 30.19'

***καρραρικός**, *ή*, *όν*, *of a wagon*, *τροχός* *Edict.Diocl.* 15.30.

***καρσανάριος**, *ὁ*, unkn. occupational term, *MAMA* 3.421, 422 (Corycus).

**καρτερέω I**, transfer '*ἀκούων* .. 241' fr. line 10 to follow 'Arist.*Pol.* 1287*b*27' in line 5 of section II, prefixing 'w. part.'

***καρτερόθροος**, *ον*, *loud-voiced*, *κ]αρ[τ]ερόθρουν βριαρό[ν τ]ε* *PRyl.* 15.10 (= Heitsch *GDRK* no. 11; ii AD).

**καρτερός I 2**, after 'Thgn. 480' insert '*ὅκου δὲ μὴ αὐτοὶ ἑωυτῶν εἰσι καρτεροὶ ‹οἱ› ἄνθρωποι* Hp.*Aër.* 16' **3**, sup., add 'Thrasym. 1 D.-K.' **6**, add '**b** w. part., *having discretion in*, *οἱ πολέμαρχοι θωϊῶντες κ. ἔστων* *Thasos* 141.6 (iv BC).'

***καρτέω**, v. ‡*κρατέω*.

***κᾰρῡδᾶς**, *ὁ*, *nut-seller*, *SEG* 32.1611 (ii/iii AD).

**κᾰρῠ́διον**, add 'written **καροιδ**- *PRyl.* 629.185, al. (iv AD)'

***κᾱρύζω**, v. *κηρύσσω*.

**κᾰρῠ́κινος**, for '*dark-red*' read '*brown*'

**κᾰρῡκοποιέω**, after '*καρύκη*' insert 'in quot. fig., i.e. *stir things up*'

***κᾰρῠοφῠ́λαξ**, *ακος*, *ὁ*, *guard set over a nut-plantation*, *PSI* 297.19 (v AD).

**κᾰρῠόφυλλον**, add '*PAlex.* 36.6 (iv/v AD), *PColl.Youtie* 87.4 (vi AD)'

***κᾱ́ρυσσα**, Aeol. fem. of *κῆρυξ*, *BCH* 59.473 (Mytilene), prob. in *IG* 12(2).255 (ib.).

**κᾰρῠωτός 1**, for '*date*-palm, *date*' read 'name of variety of date' and add 'D.S. 2.53, *PCornell* inv. II 38.18 (*Rec.Pap.* 1964 p. 32, n. 4)'

***κάρφη**, ἡ, *dry straw, hay*, or sim. material, X.*An.* 1.5.10, *SEG* 9.11, al. (Cyrene, iv BC), Arr.*An.* 1.3.6, κάρφην· φορυτόν Hsch.

**καρφίον**, add '**3** *fenugreek* (= κάρφος v), *ICilicie* 108 (v/vi AD).'

**κάρφος I**, line 5, after '*AP* 10.14 (Agath.)' insert 'κάρφη· ξύλα λεπτά, καὶ ξηρά Hsch.' add '**2** *hay* (cf. κάρφη), *SEG* 9.35 (Cyrene, iii BC).' **II**, add 'cf. καρπίζω (B)' **V**, add 'Plin.*HN* 24.184'

**καρχᾰρίας**, add '*IGC* p. 98 A5 (Acraephia, iii/ii BC)'

**καρχᾰρόδους**, line 1, after 'neut. -όδουν' insert 'Choerob.*in Theod.* 1.347' and after 'Plot. 6.7.9' insert '(v.l.)'

**καρχᾰρόδων**, add 'Nonn.*D.* 41.210'

***καρχᾰρόπεπλος**, ον, *having a saw-toothed peplos*, of Hecate, χαρχαρόπεπλε *PMag.* 7.701.

***καρχαρόστομος**, α, ον, *jagged-toothed*, χαρχαροστόμα σκύλαξ *Suppl.Mag.* 42.1, 63 (iii/iv AD).

**καρχήσιον II**, for '*mast-head of a ship*' read 'naut., *truck*'

**κάς II**, delete the section.

***κάς** (B), Arc. and Cypr. = καί, *IG* 5(2).261, 262 (Mantinea, v BC), Cypr. *ka-se*, *ICS* 92, 217.1, al., also *ka*, v. °κᾰ (B).

**κασάνδρα**, delete the entry.

***κασαπανα** (pl.), transcription of Middle Iranian *karshapana*, type of punch-marked coins, *SEG* 33.1223(c) (Bactria, ii BC).

**κᾰσία**, lines 1/2, for '*Cinnamomum iners*' read '*Cinnamomum cassia* or sim. species' and after '(Thphr.) *Od.* 30' insert '*Peripl.M.Rubr.* 8, al.'

**κᾰσιγνήτη**, line 2, for 'Hippon. 34, cf. 70$^a$' read 'Hippon. 48, 103.10, 144 W.'; line 3, for 'Cypr... (q.v.)' read 'Cypr. *ka-si-ke-ne-ta* κασιγνέτα *ICS* 164, var. *ka-si-ne-ta-i ICS* 153; cf. καινίτα'

**κᾰσίγνητος I**, line 5, after 'Ps.-Luc.*Philopatr.* 11' insert 'applied to a half-sister, E.*Ion* 467 (lyr.)' **II**, line 5, after '(Eresus)' to end of article read 'Cypr. *ka-si-ke-ne-to-ne* κασιγνέτōν *ICS* 217.14, al.; Thess. κατίγνειτος rest. in *IG* 9(2).894, *SEG* 31.575.16 (Larissa); Lesb. κασίγνᾶτος *IKyme* 13 i 16 (ii BC)'

***κᾰσιεύς**, ὁ, app. acc. κασιέα, *brother*, *SEG* 37.494.4 (Thessaly).

***κάσινος**, η, ον, perh. *of* κασῆς, ἱδρῴου κασίνου *APF* 5.392.31 (i AD).

**κάσιοι**, delete the entry.

***Κάσιος** (A), ὁ, cult-title of Zeus, Ach.Tat. 3.6, *SEG* 24.1196, etc. (Egypt); in Syria, *AP* 6.332, *SEG* 36.1301; in Sicily, *SEG* 34.980 (Syracuse, ii BC); also **Κάσσιος** epigr. in *SEG* 23.477 (Epirus, i BC).

***κάσιος** (B), ὁ, *brother*, app. in Mitchell *N.Galatia* 14 (Rom.imp.). **b** κάσιοι· οἱ ἐκ τῆς αὐτῆς ἀγέλης ἀδελφοί τε καὶ ἀνεψιοί Hsch.

**κάσις**, line 3, after '*sister*' insert 'Anacr. 25 P.' and for 'Call.*Aet.* 3.1.23' read 'Call.*fr.* 75.23 Pf.'; add 'also πάν[τες γὰρ πέλομε]ν κάσιες poet. in *Hesperia* 5.95.28 (iii AD)'

***Κασιωτικός**, ή, όν, *of* or *made in Casiotis*, κάτοπτρον δίπτυχον Κασιωτικόν *POxy.* 3491.7 (ii AD).

***Κασμῖλος**, ὁ, v. ‡Καδμῖλος.

***κάσος**, v. °κάσσος (A) and (B).

***Κασσανδρίζω**, *side with Cassander*, Polyaen. 4.7.6.

***Κασσεῖα**, τά, *games in honour of Cassius* (prob. Cassius Apronianus, father of Cassius Dio), *TAM* 2.428 (Patara).

***κασσηρατόριον**, Lacon. = *καθηρατόριον, *hunt*, an athletic contest at Sparta, *IG* 5(1).279 (i/ii AD), al.; also **καθθηρα-** ib. 274 (-τόριν), 288 (-τόριον).

**Κασσιέπεια**, add 'Luc.*Salt.* 44, *SEG* 31.1394 (Palmyra, iii AD), 31.1387 (Apamea, iv AD), Nonn.*D.* 33.296'

***Κάσσιος**, v. °Κάσιος.

**κασσῐτέρινος**, add 'of coins (prob. with core of tin, plated with silver), *Inscr.Délos* 1442*B*51 (ii BC)'

**κασσῐτεροποιός**, add 'κασιδεροποιός *PTeb.* 414.34 (ii AD), κασειδεροποιός *SB* 9375 (ii AD)'

**κασσῐτερουργός**, for '*tinker*' read '*tin worker, tinsmith*'; add 'Heph.Astr. 2.19.16'

**κάσσος**, add 'written κάσος, prob. in *BGU* 759.17 (ii AD)'

***κάσσος** (B), ὁ, also κᾶσος, Lat. *casus*, *occasion, occurrence*, Just.*Nov.* 53.5.1, 97.4. **II** *part, portion* of an estate, ib. 2.4, 123.40.

**κασσύω**, add '**III** καττύεσθαι· Ὑπερείδης· τὸ ὑποδεδέσθαι, ἀπὸ τῶν καττυμάτων Phot.'

***Κασταλίς**, ίδος, fem. adj. *of Castalia*, νύμφαι Theoc. 7.148.

***καστελλίτης**, ου, ὁ, perh. = Lat. *castellarius*, *man in charge of a reservoir*, *PLond.* 1652.6 (iv AD).

***κάστελλος**, ὁ, or **κάστελλον**, τό, Lat. *castellum*, *fort*, *Res Gestae Saporis* 12, Procop.*Aed.* 2.5.9. **2** *water-reservoir*, *PLond.* 1177.65, al. (ii AD), *Stud.Pal.* x 205 (vi AD), Hsch.; (masc. forms in *Res Gestae Saporis*, Procop. and Hsch., elsewhere indeterminate).

***καστελλοφύλαξ**, ακος, ὁ, *guardian of the fort*, app. a Persian court-official, *Res Gestae Saporis* 63.

***Καστνιῆτις**, ιδος, ἡ, title of Aphrodite, *of Mt. Kastnion* in Pamphylia, Call.*fr.* 200a Pf., Str. 9.5.17; in pl., *JHS* 78.65 (Aspendos).

**Καστόρειος II**, after 'Dsc. 2.24' insert 'δέρμα καστόριον *Edict.Diocl.* 8.31'

**καστορίδες II**, for '*sea-calves, seals*' read '*beavers*'

***κάστρα**, τά, and later **κάστρον**, τό, Lat. *castra, castrum*, *SEG* 34.309 (Sparta, *c.*AD 200), *IGRom.* 3.237, *PFay.* 50, etc.

***καστρένσιος**, v. °καστρήσιος.

***καστρησιανός**, ὁ, Lat. *castrensianus*, *soldier of the frontier guard* stationed in a fort or permanent camp, *SEG* 9.356.46, 80 (Ptolemais in Cyrenaica, vi AD), *PMasp.* 126.62 (vi AD).

***καστρήσιος**, α, ον, also **καστρένσιος** *IEphes.* 852 (Trajan), *of a military camp* or *station*, ἐπίτροπος κ. = Lat. *procurator castrensis*, *Inscr.Dessau* 8856; pl. subst. = Lat. *castrenses milites*, prob. in *SEG* 8.643 (Ptolemais, Egypt); cf. γαστρισι[ .. *POxy* 1001 (AD 572). **II** *of the (Byzantine) imperial court*: μόδιος (ἡμιμόδιος) κ. Hero *Mens.* 1.204.4, *Hippiatr.* I p. 425.27.

***καστροκνήμιον**, v. ‡γαστρο-.

***κάστυ**, τό, scribe's *equipment*, Aq., Thd.*Ez.* 9.2 (Hebr. *qeset* fr. Egyptian *gstj*); perh. to be read in *IG* 14.2413.17.9, 25 (Jewish amulet fr. Sicily), cf. *Aegyptus* 33.172.

**Κάστωρ**, add 'Myc. *ka-to*, *ka-to-ro* (gen.), pers. n.'

**κάτ**, add 'κατά (A) F'

**κᾰτά**, line 1, after 'A.D.*Synt.* 309.28' insert 'cf. κ. δονακώδεος ὕλης epigr. in *SEG* 16.702 (Caria, ii/iii AD), and' **A II 3**, after 'Hdn. 6.7.8' insert 'cf. Luc.*Pisc.* 7' add '**8** Locr., *in accordance with*, κα τῶνδε *IG* 9(1)$^2$.718.1; κα τᾶς συμβολᾶς ib. 717.15; καθ' ὧν ib. 267.9.' **B II 3**, add 'κατὰ μηδὲν *in nothing, in no respect*, *SEG* 33.1041 (Aeolian Cyme, ii BC)' **III 2**, add 'κ. πόδα ὑπέλαβες of *immediately* seizing what has been said, Pl.*Sph.* 243d' **IV 1**, add 'καθ' ὅ τι *in what way*, *IG* 1$^3$.35.7, Th. 1.82.6; κατ' ὅ τι *for what reason, for the reason that*, Hdt. 6.3, 7.2.3'

**καταβαίνω**, line 5, after '(Ar.)*Ra.* 35' insert 'Men.*Dysc.* 633 (-βαι pap.)' **II**, add '**6** *pass to a less lofty style*, D.H.*Dem.* 13, 25. **7** *descend* (genealogically), Just.*Nov.* 3.3 epilogus.'

**καταβάλλω I 7**, pass., after 'Isoc. 12.8' insert 'καταβεβλημένα ἔπη Philostr.*Her.* 2.19'

**καταβᾰτικός**, add '**2** κ. κύκλος a vertical great circle passing through the zenith and a star, Ptol.*Anal.* pp. 191, 205 H. (Lat. *descensivus*).'

**καταβᾰτός I**, after 'Porph.*Antr.* 23' insert 'subst., καταβατή, ἡ, perh. *path down, descent*, κατεσκεύασα τὴν καταβατὴν σὺν τῇ ἐπικειμένῃ σορῷ Dumont-Homolle *Mél.Arch.* 378 (Perinthus)' **II**, add 'esp. *column* of days in an ἐφημερίς, Cod.Vat.Gr. 1058.328$^r$.6, al.'

***καταβᾰφικός**, ή, όν, *effected by* καταβαφή, καῦσις Zos.Alch. 208.5.

**καταβιβρώσκω**, add 'σίδηρος καταβεβρωμένος ὑπὸ τοῦ ἰοῦ *IG* 2$^2$.1672.310 (iv BC)'

***καταβίων**, app. a kind of garment, βάνατα Νωρικὴ διπλῆ ἤτοι καταβίων *Edict.Diocl.* 19.55.

***καταβίωσις**, εως, ἡ, the *living out of one's life, spending one's days*, Cic.*Att.* 13.1.2, D.S. 18.52, App.*BC* 4.16.

**καταβλάπτω**, pass., add 'inf. καταβλάπεθαι (= -βλάπτεσθαι) *Inscr.Cret.* 4.42*B*11 (Gortyn, v BC)'

***καταβλάστημα**, ατος, τό, *shoot, plant*, Hsch. s.v. πρέμνα.

**κατάβλημα III**, for '*payment*, dub. in' read 'perh. *support* for a statue'

***καταβολαία**, ἁ, in Thess. form καπβολαία, a land measure, subdivision of a πελεθρ(ι)αία, *SEG* 26.672, 675, 676 (Larissa, iii BC).

**καταβολαῖον**, add '*PMich.*IX 540 (AD 53)'

**καταβολή I 1 a**, add 'δρεπάνη (or δρέπανον) εἰς καταβολήν *sickle for reaping* or *pruning hook*, *SB* 9834b37 (iv AD)' **2**, before 'D. 59.27' insert '*SEG* 26.72.7 (Athens, 375/4 BC)'

**κατάβολος**, add '**III** *payment of an instalment*, de Franciscis *Locr.Epiz.* p. 16 n. 2, p. 24 n. 10, etc. (iv/iii BC), *Mél.Navarre* 357 (Thespiae, iii BC).'

**καταβῠθίζω**, for 'πολεμίοις .. i BC)' read 'πολέμοις καταβυθισθεῖσαν τ[ὴν πόλιν] *IPE* 1$^2$.34.7 (*SEG* 37.670, Olbia, *c.*200/175 BC)'

**καταγγίζω**, add 'καταγγίζω ε[ἰς σ]άκκους *PMil.Vogl.* 214$^r$.i.16 (AD 154)'

***καταγγίσιμος**, η, ον, *packed in bottles* or *jars*: n. pl. as subst., *BGU* 2355.10 (ii/iii AD).

**καταγγισμός**, add '*PMil.Vogl.* 250.2 (AD 167)'

***καταγγιστής**, ὁ, *bottler, packer*, *SB* 10258 ii 11 (iv AD).

**κατάγειος I**, add 'of the gods of the underworld, Θεοῖς καταγαίοις *SEG* 33.844 (Africa Proconsularis)'

**καταγῑνέω II**, delete the section transferring quot. to section I.

***καταγκτηρία**, ἡ, app. some form of fastening, μοχλοὶ ταῖς καταγκτηρίαις παλαιοὶ κατεχρήσθησαν εἰς σφῆνας καὶ σφύρας καὶ πιεστῆ[ρας *IG* 2$^2$.1672.304 (Eleusis, 329/8 BC).

**καταγλαΐζω**, after '*glorify*' insert 'τινὰ μνημείοις *SEG* 4.633.10 (Sardis, iii/iv AD), cf.'

**καταγλισχραίνω**, pass., add 'Gal. 15.654.10, 11, 680.8'

**κατάγλῠφος**, add '*Iiasos* 8.2 (AD 135/6)'

***καταγμάτιον**, τό, dim. of κάταγμα (B) I, *Inscr.Délos* 1441*A*i67 (ii BC).

**κατάγνῡμι**, line 7, after '(Hes.*Op.*) 693' insert 'also part. κανάξαντες Call.*fr.* 260.53 Pf.'

**κατάγνωσις II**, add '*the record of a judgement*, law in D. 24.63'

**καταγοράζω**, pass., add 'ἐάν τι τῶν καταγορασθησομένων σωμάτων πάθῃ *SEG* 33.1039.75 (Cyme, ii BC)'

**καταγορασμός**, add 'τὸν .. καταγορασμὸν τῶν σωμάτων *SEG* 33.1039.69 (Cyme, ii BC)'

*__καταγρᾰ́φιον__, τό, perh. form of poll-tax, *IEphes.* 13 i 3, 23 (i AD, cf. *SEG* 37.884).

**κατάγρᾰφος II**, for '*drawn* .. 1.4.5' read '(seen as) *drawn from the side*, of stars, Hipparch. 1.4.5; of a portrait-bust, *GVI* 979 (Panticapaeum, i AD) add '**III** (as Lat. loan-word) *figured, catagraphosque Thynos* Cat. 25.7.'

**καταγρᾰ́φω II 5**, add '*SEG* 16.573, 39.1020A.2 (both Selinous, v BC), ib. 31.837 (Phintias, Sicily, ii/i BC)'

*__καταγρέω__, *overcome*, σιγὰ δ' ἐν νεκύεσσι, τὸ δὲ σκότος ὄσσε καταγρεῖ (cj., cod. Stob. κατέρρει) Erinn. in *Suppl.Hell.* 402.2 cf. κατάγρμμι.

**καταγρῡπόω**, for 'Schneid.' read 'Winckelmann'

**κατᾰγυιόω**, add 'Gal. 15.665.11, 12'

**κατάγχω I**, add 'Plu.*Dio* 57.2 (cj.)'

**κατᾰ́γω I 1**, line 8, after '*PGrenf.* l.c.' insert 'κατάξω δὲ ὑμεῖν καὶ ὕδωρ *SEG* 32.460.11 (Boeotia, AD 125)'

**κατᾰγωγεύς**, after '*BGU* 92 (ii AD)' add '(dub., cj. °χοιροκαταγωγεύς) *OLund.* 10.2 (iii AD). **2** *transporter* of goods, *PHels.* 7 (ii AD).'

**κατᾰγωγή I 2**, add '**b** *forwarding to the coast*, *SEG* 34.558 (Larissa, ii BC), πρὸς παράλημψιν καὶ κ. βιβλίων *PRyl.* 83.4 (ii AD).' **4**, *shelter* for cattle, add '*PVindob.Salomons* 12.5 (AD 334/5)'

**καταγώγιον III**, after '*festival of the return*' insert 'of Aphrodite' and after '*SIG* 1109.114 (ii AD)' add '*IEphes.* 661.20 (ii AD)'

**κατᾰγωγίς**, add '**III** epith. of Artemis, *SEG* 9.13.12 (Cyrene, iv BC); v. *SEG* 39.1714. **IV** σκεῦος πεντηρικόν. καὶ κράσπεδον. καὶ παράλωμα Hsch., i.e. = παράρρυμα 1.'

**κατᾰγωνίζομαι**, line 1, delete 'τινας' and substitute 'κ. τὸν ἐργώδη γέροντα Men.*Dysc.* 965'; line 3, after 'Dam.*Isid.* 122' insert 'abs., J.*AJ* 4.6.12'

†__καταδάκνω__, *seize with the teeth, bite*, ἡ μὲν (sc. μύραινα) τοῦ ἀντιπάλου τὰ κέντρα (i.e. spines or prickles) .. οὐκ ἐννοοῦσα καταδάκνει Ael.*NA* 1.32.

**καταδακτῠλίζω**, for '*feel with the finger*, sens. obsc.' read '*make an obscene gesture at with the middle finger*'

†__καταδακτῠλικός__, ή, όν, w. gen., *inclined to make an obscene gesture* at, Ar.*Eq.* 1381 (prob. nonce-wd.).

**καταδαρθάνω**, line 4, after 'A.R. 2.1227' insert '(v.l. -ον)'

**καταδεής** (A) **I 2**, (compar.), add 'used to describe plebeian (opp. curule) aediles, D.C. 53.33.3'

**καταδείκνῡμι 1** and **2**, combine these sections under def. '*make known* something that one has discovered, devised, invented, etc., *introduce*'

*__καταδέκτρια__, ἡ, app., *one who admits* to a place, epith. of sea-goddesses, Βύνης καταδέκτριαι cj. in ?Call.*fr.* 745 Pf.

**κατάδενδρος**, after '*thickly wooded*' insert 'Dicaearch. 1.1'

**καταδέρκομαι**, after 'aor. 2 κατέδρᾰκον' insert 'Pi.*N.* 4.23'

**κατάδεσις II**, for this section read '*binding by spells*, in pl., Pl.*Lg.* 933d'

**κατάδεσμος II**, for '-δέσμοις τοὺς θεοὺς πείθοντες' read 'βλάψει ἐπαγωγαῖς τισι καὶ καταδέσμοις'

**καταδέχομαι**, after lemma insert 'κ]αδδέκεται *Lesb.fr.adesp.* 27 L.-P.' **3**, for this section read '*accept* into a class or category, Str. 16.1.6'

**καταδέω** (A), before 'fut.' insert 'contr. -δῶ *Tab.Defix.* 101, 100a (both iv BC), al.'

†__καταδημᾰγωγέω__, *attain by the arts of a demagogue*, w. acc. and inf., Arr.*fr.* 150 J.; pass., *to be won* by such arts, Plu.*Cleom.* 13. **2** *disadvantage by demagogic means*, ἀδελφούς id. 2.482d; pass., id.*Per.* 9.

*__καταδημεύω__, *confiscate*, rest. in *Thasos* 150.17, 21, see *REA* 61.289.

*__καταδιαβαίνω__, *come down across*, *POxy.* 2331 ii 11 (= Heitsch *GDRK* no. 11, iii AD).

**καταδιαιρέω 3**, add 'med., *interpret*, σημεῖον *Vit.Aesop.*(G) 81'

**καταδίδημι**, after 'al.' insert '*SEG* 37.215 (Athens, ?iv BC)'

*__καταδιδράσκω__, *overrun*, μέλαθρα τῷ πυρὶ καταδέδρακεν Sch.V E.*Tr.* 1303.

**καταδίδωμι I**, add 'τοὶλ Λατōσίοις *Inscr.Cret.* 4.58 (v BC)' add '**2** *distribute among*, δέρμα τοῖς [ἀεὶ ἱερασο]μένοις *SIG* 624.37 (ii BC).'

**καταδῐκάζω I**, line 6, after 'Luc.*DMort.* 29.2' insert 'w. acc. of person convicted, *CodJust.* 4.20.13.2, Just.*Nov.* 69.2.1'; line 16, after '(Artem.) 5.21' insert 'w. πρός, *condemn* to, κατεδικάσθησαν .. πρὸς θηρ[ία *PPetaus* 9.10 (AD 185)'

**καταδίκη**, after lemma insert 'Arc. καδίκας acc. pl., *SEG* 25.447.8 (Aliphera, iii BC, in sense 2)' **1**, add 'καταδίκαν γράψαι *SEG* 31.351 (Arcadia, *c.*300 BC)'

**καταδίψιον**, add 'see also *Suppl. Hell.* 1083'

**καταδρέπω**, add 'Pl.*Ti.* 91d'

**καταδρομή I 2**, delete 'cf. D.H.*Th.* 3' and after 'Plb. 12.23.1' insert 'w. obj. gen., D.H.*Th.* 3, *Pomp.* 1'

*__καταεικοβολέω__, *conjecture from probabilities*, Sch.Pi.*I.* 2 inscr.

*__κατᾱ́ερος__, ον, *situated in the air*, *Hymn.Is.* 28.

†__καταέρρω__, v. ‡καταίρω.

*__καταέσας__ (cod. -έσσας)· κατακοιμηθείς Hsch., cf. ἀέσκω.

**κατάζευγμα**, add 'rest. in *IG* 1³.474.252'

*__καταζώγρᾰφος__, ον, *painted over with pictures*, ἰστήλη *GVI* 133.1 (Galatia, ii/iii AD).

*__κατάζωσις__, εως, ἡ, *girding*, name of Bacchic rite, *IUrb.Rom.* 160 ii A.1 (Latium, ii AD); cf. κατάζωσμα II.

**καταζωστικός**, for 'τὸ κ. .. *robes*' read '*K.*, τό, an Orphic poem app. concerning the girding of initiates'

*__καταζώστρη__, ἡ, *lace* for fastening the κόθορνος, Herod. 8.33 (s.v.l.).

†__κατάημι__, fut. καταήσεται· καταπνεύσει Hsch.; in undetermined sense, καταήσσατο Alc. 296.2 L.-P.

**κατάθεσις 1**, for 'κ. κλάδων .. *Gp.* 9.5.1' read '*Gp.* 4.3.4, 9.5.1, 6.1' **2**, add '*SEG* 33.169B i 3 (Athens, iv BC)' **4**, add 'θείων μηνιμάτων (v.l. καθέσεις) Aesop. 56 P.' **7**, add '*SEG* 34.1262 (Calchedon, AD 452)' add '**8** *laying down* on the ground, περικομιδῇ καὶ κ. χελώνης, as a charm, *Gp.* 1.14.9. **9** *arrangement*, διπλῇ τῇ καταθέσει τῶν κλάδων D.S. 2.53 (perh. read καθέσει). **10** *mortgage*, *Inscr.Cret.* 4.43*Ba*7 (v BC), cf. κατατίθημι I 4b.'

**καταθλέω**, add '**III** *spend on athletic contests*, *Inscr.Délos* 316.114 (iii BC), 372*A*117 (iii/ii BC), al.'

**καταθνητός**, add 'Thgn. 897'

**καταθῡ́μιος**, line 1, after 'Eumel. 1.13' insert 'Call.*Lav.Pall.* 33, 69, Muson.*fr.* 14 p. 74 H.' **II**, for '*according to one's mind*' read '*that is in accordance with one's wishes, close to one's heart*' and add 'ἐμοὶ καταθύμιον ἄνδρα *SEG* 30.1565 (Cappadocia), etc.'

*__καταθυτός__, ά, όν, *to be used in sacrifice*, ζέκα μναίς κα ἀποτίνοι .. κα(τ)θυταὶς τοὶ Ζὶ Ὀλυνπίōι *Schwyzer* 409.4, 410.5 (rest.), 418.6 (all Elis, vi/v BC).

**κᾰταί**, add 'cf. κ. δονακώδεος ὕλης epigr. in *SEG* 16.702 (Caria, ii/iii AD)'

**καταιβάτης 3**, for pres. def. read '*downward-plunging*'

**καταιβᾰ́τις**, add 'see also °καταβάτις'

**καταιβᾰτός**, add 'see also ‡καταβατός'

*__καταιϝεί__, *for ever*, αὐτὸν καὶ τὸ γένος κ. *Schwyzer* 362.4 (Locris, v BC).

*__καταῐερόω__, = καθιερόω, *JÖAI* 26 *Beibl.* 13 (Ephesus, ii AD), *SEG* 37.812 (Rome, sp. καταειερόω).

**καταινέω 1**, add 'abs., A.*Ch.* 706'

**καταΐξ**, for 'Eumel. 9' read 'A.R. 3.1376'

**καταίρω I**, for this section read '*take down* (in Aeolic form, in tm.), κὰδ δ' ἄερρε κυλίχναις μεγάλαις Alc. 346 L.-P.' **II 1**, before 'ἐς Δελφούς' insert 'cf. ὡς ἔθνος τι ἄπειρον κοράκων κατῆρε τότε' and transfer this quot. to follow 'Plu.*Rom.* 9'

*__καταίσχυντος__, *shameful*, Hsch. s.v. κατηφόνες.

*__καταιτιᾱτικός__, ή, όν, *noxious*, rest. in Vett.Val. 208.22, cf. αἰτιατικός I 2.

**κατακαίνω**, line 2, after '(X.)*An.* 3.2.12' insert '*BCH* 33.452 (Argos)'

**κατακᾰλέω I**, add '**2** *invite to participate* in games, *SEG* 30.1117, 1121, 1122 (all Entella, iii BC).'

*__κατακάρδιον__, τό, *down-turned twig* of the mulberry-tree, Cyran. 29 (1.12.29 K.).

**κατακαρφής**, after 'Nic.*fr.* 70.9' add '(cj.)'

**κατάκειμαι**, line 2, after 'Pl.*Smp.* 213b' insert 'Cypr. part. *ka-ta-ki-me-na* κατακιμένα *Kafizin* 270 (sense 3, 225/18 BC)' **1**, add '**b** *lie in a grave*, *IG* 10(2).1.352 (Thessalonica, iv AD), *SEG* 29.310 (Corinth, AD 529), ἐνθάδε κατάκιτε .. *TAM* 4(1).353.' add '**10** *to be given in pledge*, *Inscr.Cret.* 4.47.1, 10, al. (Gortyn, v BC); cf. κατατίθημι I 4 b.'

*__κατακένωσις__, εως, ἡ, *the process of emptying*, *CPR* 7.20.13 (iv AD).

**κατακέφᾰλα**, add 'παραφέρειν κ. sweep away *head over heels*, *POxy.* 1853.5 (vi/vii AD); perh. also of blows *on the head*, *PVindob.Salomons* 15.6 (v/vi AD)'

*__κατακήδευσις__, εως, ἡ, *burial*, *TAM* 2.620 (Tlos).

*__κατακήλησις__, εως, ἡ, *enchantment*, Cels.ap.Orig.*Cels.* 1.6 (pl.).

**κατακηλῑδόω**, after 'strengthd. for κηλιδόω' insert 'Phryn. 393 F.'

*__κατακληρουχία__, ἡ, *apportionment*, rest. in *BGU* 2444.93, 2445.24 (i BC).

*__κατακλῑτικός__, ή, όν, ἡ κ. ὥρα, ἡμέρα, the hour, day *of taking to one's bed*, Vett.Val. 205.3, 339.20.

**κατακλύζω I 1**, add 'humorously, with wine, ὅς μοι δοὺς τὸ πῶμα κατέκλυσεν E.*Cyc.* 677 (cj.)'

*__κατάκλυστος__, ον, *inundated*, πρὸς τῇ οὔσῃ κατακλύστῳ κλήρου ἀρούρας τρίς *PColl.Youtie* 27.10 (AD 165); perh. also *PMil.Vogl.* 105.20 (ii AD). **II** κατάκλυστον, τό, *floor which can be washed down*, *Inscr.Délos* 2420.

*__κατακνάπτω__, *tear to pieces*, in quot. fig., μελέα μήτηρ, ἣ τὰς μεγάλας ἐλπίδας ἐν σοὶ κατέκναψε βίου E.*Tr.* 1252 (cj.).

**κατακνάω**, add '*scratch all over*, κατὰ μὲν χρόα πάντ' ὀνύχεσσι δακνόμενος κνάσαιο Theoc. 7.110'

*__κατακόλλησις__, εως, ἡ, *glueing together*, τραπέζης *Delph.* 3(5).68 i 3 (iv BC).

**κατᾰκολουθέω**, add '*act in conformity with, live up to*, κατακολουθοῦσα τῇ ἑαυτῆς καλοκἀγαθίᾳ *SEG* 33.1036.5 (Aeolian Cyme, ii BC)'

**κατάκομος**, after '*with falling hair* or *beard*' insert '(?)Pi.*fr.* 356 S.-M.'; add 'transf., of trees, Ps.-Callisth. 3.6 cod. B.'

**κατάκοος**, delete the entry.

**κατακορακόω**, add '*SEG* 17.632 (Perge)'

**κατάκορος II**, adv. -ως, add '*abundantly, freely*, Androm.Jun.ap. Gal. 13.71.6'

**κατακράζω**, add 'κατέκραξαν κατ' αὐτῶν *SEG* 26.1813.23 (Nubia, iv/v AD)'

**κατακρᾰτέω**, line 1, delete 'pers.' and insert 'γαστρὸς οὐ κατακρα[τεῖς Hippon. 118.2 W.'

**κατακρέμᾰμαι**, delete the entry (v. sq.).

**κατακρεμάννῡμι**, line 5, pass., add 'Hdt. 4.72.4, Cratin. 175 K.-A.; w. gen., κώδωνες .. κατακρέμανται τῆς ἐσθῆτος Plu. 2.672a'

*__κατακρεμάς__, άδος, fem. adj., *overhanging* (precise sense uncertain in broken context), *Trag.adesp.* 653.7 K.-S.

**κατακρημνίζω**, line 1, for '*Carm.Pop.* 46.33' read 'Hermocl. 33'

*__κατακρημνῶν__, gloss on κατακρημνίζων, Hsch.

**κατάκρῐμα 1**, delete '*judgement*' and transfer '*Ep.Rom.* 5.16, 8.1' to this section. **2**, for this section read '*money paid under penalty*, *PAmh.* 2.114.8, *PCol.*v 3.170 (both ii AD)'

**κατακρίνω I**, add '**3** *place under obligation, bind*, αὐτὴν τὴν βασιλείαν κατακρίνομεν .. ὥστε .. προνοεῖν Just.*Nov.* 59.7.'

**κατάκρῐτος**, after 'ον' insert '(also η, ον, Hsch.)'; add 'κεφαλῆς κατάκριτον, = Lat. *capitis damnatum*, *SEG* 8.13 (Nazareth, rescript of Augustus or Tiberius)'

**κατακρούω 4**, for 'Perh. = διακρούω' read '*knock* or *hammer downwards*'

*__κατακρῠβῆ__, = κατακρύβδην, *PMich.*VIII 520.9 (iv AD).

**κατακτείνω**, line 3, aor. 1, add '3 sg. aor. subj. κατασκένηι *Inscr.Cret.* 4.41 I 14 (Gortyn, v BC)'; line 4, after '(Il. 6.)164' insert 'Aeol.part. κακκτάνοντες Alc. 129.19 L.-P.'

**κατακτενίζω**, add 'ψαρὸν .. ἵππον *Suppl.Hell.* 996.9 (i BC)'

**κατακύπτω**, line 2, after 'Il. 16.661' insert 'Men.*Dysc.* 538'

**κατάκυψις**, transfer the article after κατακυρόω.

**καταλαμβάνω I 1**, line 7, after '*arrive* at a place' insert 'Ἀθήνας Synes.*Ep.* 54' add '**b** *lay claim to*, Σῖμος κατέλαβε Ἀσκαληπιακόν (on the boundary stone of a mine), *SEG* 32.233 (Attica, *c.*350 BC).' add '**VI** = συλλαμβάνω IV, *conceive*, Aq.*Mi.* 6.14.'

**καταλαμπρύνω**, after '*splendid*' insert 'or *bright*'; add 'Sch.Pi.*O.* 3.35'

**καταλάμπω I**, add '**2** *illuminate mentally* or *intellectually*, καταλάμπεται .. πάντα ἀθρόως ὑπὸ τῶν θεῶν Procl.*Inst.* 143 D.'

*__κατάλαμψις__, v. °κατάληψις.

*__καταλᾰπαξῐκοίλιον__, τό, *evacuation of the stomach*, ὄνασις (ε)ἶ τοῦ κ. *Glotta* 34.45/7 and 297 n. 1 (graffiti on vases, Emporion and Apulia, iv BC).

**καταλέγω** (B), line 6, after '*Vit.Hom.* 21' insert 'cf. καταλέγεσθαι· ὀδύρεσθαι τὸν τεθνεῶτα Hsch.; cf. κατάλεγμα.'

**καταλείπω I 2**, add '**c** τὰ καταλελειμμένα *instructions*, Just.*Nov.* 1.1.1, al.' **III 1**, c. inf., add 'w. article, Arist.*Cat.* 7ᵃ37, *fr.* 58' **2 c**, at the beginning insert 'κ. τι ἐν τοῖς ἀκούουσι *leave* to the readers' intelligence, Aristid.*Rh.* 2 p. 523 S.' and after 'c. inf.' insert 'ib. p. 524 S.'

**καταλέκτρια**, delete 'Βύνης .. 217.5'; add 'v.s.v. καταδέκτρια'

*__κατάλευσμα__, ατος, τό, *stoning*, Sch.Lyc. 1181.

**καταλέχομαι**, add 'act., *put to sleep*, Hsch. s.vv. καταλέξας and κατέλεξας'

**καταλήγω**, line 4, for 'Arr.*Epict.* 6.20.21' read 'Arr.*Epict.* 1.6.20, 21' **2**, add 'in phonology, of words, εἰς τραχὺ γράμμα D.H.*Dem.* 40'

**καταληκτικός**, at end delete 'Arr.*Epict.* 2.23.46' (v. °ἀκατα-)

**καταληπτικός 2**, after 'Phld.*Rh.* 2.120 S.' insert 'Alex.Aphr. *de An.* 71.11'

**κατάληψις**, after lemma insert 'Dor. **κατάλαμψις**, *Lindos* 160.5 (ii BC)' **I 4**, add 'Alex.Aphr. *de An.* 71.12'

**καταλιμπάνω**, add 'Sapph. 94.2 L.-P., *IGBulg* 2236.45 (Thrace, iv AD)'

**καταλῑπᾰρέω**, after '*entreat earnestly*' insert 'Men.*Sam.* 721'

**κατάλλαγμα**, add '**II** *something given in exchange*, *Acta Joannis fr.* in *MH* 31.102.15.'

**καταλλάσσω**, line 1, after '*change* money' insert '*SEG* 26.13 (Attica, *c.*440/20 BC)'

**κατάλληλος II**, add '**2** in music, of tetrachords, *conjunct*, Aristid.Quint. 1.8; cf. °παράλληλος.'

**καταλογεῖον**, before '*POxy.* 73.34' insert '*PTeb.* 770.13 (iii BC)'

**καταλογή II**, line 2, delete 'codd. (-δοχή Reiske)'

*__καταλογισμός__, ὁ, *reckoning, account*, *PRyl.* 627.90 (iv AD).

*__καταλογιστής__, οῦ, ὁ, local official, perh. registrar or sim., *PGrenf.* 79.2.1 (iii AD).

**κατάλογος 2 a**, add 'pl., *enlisted men, troops*, Just.*Nov.* 102.2'

**κατάλοιπος**, add 'κατὰ τὸν κ]ατάλοιπον χρόνον τοῦ ἐνιαυτοῦ *SEG* 32.118.11 (Athens, 244/3 BC)'

**καταλοκίζω**, add 'κατηλόκιζε *Suppl.Hell.* 977.18'

**καταλούομαι**, for '*spend in bathing*' read '*wash away*, i.e. *squander in bathing*' add '**2** *bathe*, prob. of ceremonial washing, *JÖAI* 23 *Beibl.* 24 (Maeonia, ii AD; κατελούσετο).'

**καταλουστικοί**, for pres. ref. read '*TAM* 5(1).490.2, 8 (Lydia, ii AD)'

⁺__καταλοχία__, ἡ, *register*, οἱ Λευῖται .. ἀπὸ εἰκοσαετοῦς καὶ ἐπάνω ἐν διατάξει ἐν καταλοχίαις .. Lxx 2*Ch.* 31.18.

**καταλοχίζω 2**, add '**b** *enrol* into a group, class, etc., *PMich.*v 2.338.9 (i AD).' add '**3** *register* as owner of, διὰ τωι καταλελοχίσθαι αὐτὸν ἐπὶ τῶν αὐτῶν ἀρουρῶν *PMich.*XI 621.11 (AD 37).'

**καταλοχισμός 2**, add 'in official title, Εὐδαίμονι τῶι πρὸς καταλοχισμοῖς *POxy.* 3482.6 (73 BC)'

**καταλῡμαίνομαι**, add 'of cattle destroying crop-land, *PColl.Youtie* 77.4 (AD 324)'

**κατάλῡσις II**, add '**4** *accommodation* for animals, in quot., sheep, Lxx *Je.* 30.14(49.20).'

**καταλῠτήριον**, add 'Sch.Pi.*O.* 10.57'

**καταλύτης I**, add 'καταλύτου μονοημέρου Lxx *Wi.* 5.14'

**καταλύω II 2**, add 'Macho 350 G.'

**κατάμακτος**, add '*PVindob.Salomons* 2.24 (ii/iii AD)'

**καταμαντεύομαι 2**, add 'D. 60.34'

⁺__κατᾰμάω__ (A), *mow down*, κατ' αὖ νιν φοινία θεῶν τῶν νερτέρων ἀμᾷ κοπίς S.*Ant.* 601 (lyr.); *lay low, kill*, Euph. 84.3 (med.).

*__κατᾰμάω__ (B), *draw* or *scrape down* on to something (in quots., med.), τήν ῥα (sc. τὴν κόπρον) κυλινδόμενος καταμήσατο χερσὶν ἑῇσι Il. 24.165, τὸν χοῦν καταμήσονται (cj.) Pherecr. 126 K.-A., J.*BJ* 2.15.4, 21.3.

*__καταμείνας__, ὁ, perh. *resident, sitting tenant*, *POxy.* 2244.65, 3640.2 (vi AD).

*__κατᾰμελητέος__, α, ον, *not demanding attention*, *An.Boiss.* 5.381.

**καταμέμφομαι**, add 'Anacr. 13.7 P.'

*__καταμέριμνος__, ον, κ.· [*sollicitus*], *gloss.* in *PVindob.* L150 (*Tyche* 3.141ff., v AD); cf. ἐμμέριμνος.

*__κατάμερος__, τό, *partial payment*, ἐκ τοῦ καταμέρους (prob. to be understood as κατὰ μέρους) *PMich.*XV 748.8 (vii AD).

**καταμετρέω 2**, line 5, after '(Arist.)*Cat.* 4ᵇ33' insert 'ἑξακοσιάκις καὶ πεντηκοντάκις -εῖται ὁ κύκλος οὗτος ὑπὸ τῆς διαμέτρου τῆς σελήνης Papp. 6.556.15'

**καταμήνιος II 1**, delete the section.

**καταμιεῖ**, add '(**καταμνιεῖ** .. μνιεῖν La.)'

**καταμιμνήσκομαι**, add 'ἐμνήσαντο γάμου κάτα (= γ. κατεμνήσαντο) prob. in Call.*fr.* 75.18 Pf.'

**καταμίσγω**, add 'Emp. 93 D.-K.'

**καταμνημονεύω**, add '*SEG* 33.1183.19 (Lycia, 260/59 BC)'

**καταμοσχεύω**, add 'Anon.Alch. 364.20'

⁺__καταμπῠκόω__, *bind* as with a headband, στεφάνοισι κρᾶτα καταμπυκοῖς S.*fr.* 402 R.

*__καταμφωτοί__· αὐλοί τινες οὕτω καλοῦνται Hsch.

**καταναλίσκω 1**, line 8, after 'Ath. 8.345d' insert 'ταῦτα .. περὶ ἴδια τέκνα καὶ συγγενεῖς καταναλίσκειν *Cod.Just.* 1.3.41.3'

**καταναυμᾰχέω**, pass., add 'Isoc. 9.56'

**κατανομοθετέω**, after 'Pl.*Lg.* 861c' add '(v.l. κᾆτα νομ-)'

**κατάντημα**, add '**2** *destination* of a property, etc. *PMich.*inv. 4962.10 (*Aegyptus* 71.20, iii AD).'

**καταντης I**, line 2, after 'Ar.*Ra.* 127' insert 'ἄντρον *AP* 6.220.5 (Diosc.)'

**καταντλέω 1**, metaph., add '*Com.adesp.* 28 D.'

**κατανύσσω**, last line, for '*keep silence*' read '*be silenced*'

**καταξαίνω 2**, pass., add 'A.*fr.* 132c R.'

*__κατάξεσμα__, τό, = κατάξυσμα, Hsch., Suid. s.v. μύγματα (for ἀμύγματα).

**καταξέσματα**, delete the entry.

*__καταξιοπιστεύομαι__, *claim belief for*, ἑτέραν τέχνην Ptol.*Tetr.* 6; (cf. καταξιοπιστέομαι).

**καταξιος**, line 1, fem. -αξία, add '*SEG* 32.453.17 (Boeotia, ii BC)'

**καταξιόω II**, delete the section, transferring quots. to section I.

**καταξύω I 2**, add '**b** leg., *scratch out, cancel*, Sch.Ar.*Nu.* 774b K.'

**καταπᾰλαίω**, line 2, for 'τὰ ῥηθέντα' read 'ἐμέ'

**καταπάλλομαι**, line 2, after 'Il. 19.351' insert 'Stesich. 32.i.4 P.'

⁺__κατάπαξ__, v. ‡καθάπαξ.

*__καταπᾰρίζω__, perh. *"live in the house of Paris"*, Sch.Od. 8.517 (s.v.l.).

**καταπάσσω I**, line 5, pass., add 'καππεπάδμ[ Alc. 143.9 L.-P.'

**καταπάτησις I**, add 'λεκάνη τῆς κ., app. of a basin for washing the feet, Syr.*Ps.* 59(60).10' **2**, add '*PErlangen* 121 (iii AD), *SB* 11213.6 (AD 310)'

***καταπελτιστής**, οῦ, ὁ, *catapult-man*, Lyd.*Mag.* 48.19.

***καταπέντε**, wd. of unkn. meaning, perh. trade designation of Egyptian origin, Χαρίδημ(ος) καταπέντε *PMich.*IV 224.4059, 5533 (ii AD), *OMich.* 324.

+**κατάπερ**, v. καθάπερ s.v. ‡καθά.

**καταπέτασμα**, after 'Hld. 10.28' insert '(v.l. for παρα-)' add '**3** as personal possession, perh. item of clothing, *POxy.* 3150.37 (vi AD).'

**καταπίνω I**, add 'hyperb., καὶ μὴν ὁ Παφλαγὼν οὑτοσὶ προσέρχεται .. ὡς δὴ καταπιόμενός με Ar.*Eq.* 693, *V.* 1502, cf. ὁ ἀντίδικος ὑμῶν διάβολος ὡς λέων ὠρυόμενος περιπατεῖ ζητῶν τινα καταπιεῖν 1*Ep.Pet.* 5.8'

**καταπιπράσκω**, add '*SEG* 35.1439.9 (Lycia, ii AD)'

**καταπίπτω**, line 3, after '(Epid.)' insert 'Aeol. part. καππέτων Alc. 130.14 L.-P.'; line 4, after 'pf. -πέπτωκα' insert 'inf. -πεπτώκειν *SEG* 38.1476.95 (Xanthos)'; line 10, after 'οἰκίαι καταπεπτωκυῖαι' insert '*collapsed*' **2 a**, line 4, before '*base*' insert '*disheartened*, D.Chr. 18.15'

**καταπλάσσω I 3**, add 'τὸ καταπεπλάσθαι τὸν βίον (καταπεπλῆχθαι codd.) D. 37.43'

**καταπλαστός I**, after 'Ar.*Pl.* 717' insert '*Hippiatr.* 130.185.'

**καταπλέκω I 1**, add '**d** *entwine oneself round* a person, prob. in Nic.*Th.* 475.'

**καταπληκτικός**, add '**2** in pass. sense, gloss on ἔμπληκτος, Hsch.'

**καταπλήξ 2**, add 'Iamb.*Protr.* 21 λγ' (p. 124.13 P.)'

**κατάπληξις 1**, add '**b** *object of admiration, wonder*, Lucr. 4.1163.' **2**, after 'Arist.' insert '*EE* 1221ᵃ1, 1233ᵇ27'

**καταπλίσσομαι**, add 'act., καταπλίξας dub. rest. in Hippon. 104.16 W.'

***καταπλόϊν**, τό, perh. some sort of cloth (cf. καθαπλόω), *POxy.* 2729.37 (iv AD).

**καταπλοκή I**, add 'fig., εἰς κ. ἰέναι *arrive at a deadlock*, *PRainer Cent.* 161.17 (?v AD)'

**καταπνέω I 1**, add 'ῥοώδης, καταπνεόμενος ἀπὸ τῶν παρακειμένων ὀρῶν, ἐστὶν ὁ κατ' αὐτὴν διάπλους *Peripl.M.Rubr.* 25'

***καταποδίδωμι**, perh. *trade away*, ἐὰν δέ τις .. καταποδῷ τὰ δημόσια *JHS* 33.338.28 (Maced., ii AD).

**καταπονέω I 1**, line 5, delete 'πάντα .. Men. 744' add '**b** πρᾶγμα καταπονεῖν *get down to, put one's back into* a task or business, Men.*Dysc.* 392, *fr.* 526 K.-Th.'

***καταπόντισμα**, ατος, τό, app. = καταποντισμός, var. for καταπάτημα Lxx *La.* 2.8.

+**καταποντισμός**, ὁ, *submersion under the sea*, καταποντισμοὺς (*drownings*) καὶ τυφλώσεις Isoc. 12.122, ὁ κ. τῶν χρημάτων App.*Mac.* 16, καταποντισμοὶ πόλεων καὶ χωρῶν *Orac.Tiburt.* 137; transf., *destruction*, Lxx *Ps.* 51.6.

+**καταπρᾱΰνσις**· *mitigatio*, *Gloss.*

**καταπρηνίζω**, add ''Ηφαίστου πυρόεσσα κατεπρήνιζεν ἀϋτμή epigr. in *IUrb.Rom.* 1342.3'

***καταπρίσσομαι**, *tear off*, A.*fr.* 451h R.

**καταπρολείπω**, for '*forsake utterly*' read '*leave behind* in a place'

**καταπτύω**, add 'Iamb.*Protr.* 21 λβ' (p. 108.7 P.), al.'

***καταπῡ́γαινα**, ἡ, fem. form of καταπύγων, *Hesperia* 22.215 (Athens, vi/v BC).

***καταπῡγόω**, καταπυγῶν· κατασελγαίνων Phot., Suid.

**καταπῡ́γων I**, for '*given .. lewd*' read '*male passive homosexual*, sts. loosely as a term of abuse'; add '*AJA* 38.11 (Attic cup, Hymettus, ?vii BC), Lang *Ath.Agora* XXI C5 (vi BC), C18 (v BC), al.'

***κατᾰ́ρᾱσις**, εως, ἡ, *tamping*, *CID* II 139.16 (iii BC).

**κατᾰ́ρᾱτος**, add '*PHamb.* 192.9 (iii AD)'

**καταργέω I 2**, *to be rendered* or *lie idle*, add '*PMerton* 79 (ii AD), *PFlor.* 218 (AD 257)'

***κάταργος**, ον, *quite unwrought*, ξύλον, Call.*Dieg.* iv.28 (*fr.* 100 Pf.).

**κατάρδω 2**, for '*besprinkle*' read '*soak, dowse*'

+**κατάρης**, v. ‡κατώρης.

**καταρῑγηλός**, add 'perh. also Euph. in *Suppl.Hell.* 442.10'

***κατᾰρίθμητος**, ον, *numbered* in a class, category, etc., ἐν τοῖς ζῶσι Ps.-Callisth. 132.12.

***κατᾰρίθμιος**, *numbered* in a class, category, etc., ἐν φθιμένοις *GVI* 1984.3 (Ancyra, ?iv/v AD).

**καταρνέομαι**, add '*AB* 1.85.31'

**κάταρξις**, add '*PGrenf.* 2.87.21 (AD 602)'

+**καταρρᾰκόω**, *tear to shreds*, ἄναρθρος καὶ κατερρακωμένος sc. Heracles, S.*Tr.* 1103.

**καταρράκτης 3**, delete the section transferring quots. to section 5 (*sluice*) add '**7** some means of punitive restraint (whether dungeon, stocks, or other means), Lxx *Je.* 20.2, 36(29).26.'

**καταρρεπής**, for '= ἑτερορρεπής' read '*weighing* or *pressing down*' and add 'A.R. 2.593, Plu. 2.952e'

**καταρρέω I 1**, add 'fig. in part., of style, *flowing*, D.H.*Comp.* 20'

**καταρροφέω**, add 'Dor. -ρυφέω, Sophr. in *PSI* 1214*d*2'

**καταρρυθμίζω**, line 2, for 'passages *over-rhythmical*' read '*parts given rhythmical form*'

***καταρρύθμισις**, εως, ἡ, the process of *bringing into rhythm*, Ps.-Archyt. p. 32.3 T.

**κατάρρυθμος I**, for '*very rhythmical*' read '*having rhythmical form*'

**καταρτίζω II**, med., add 'φωνὴ κυρίου καταρτιζομένου ἐλάφους Lxx *Ps.* 28(29).9'

+**κατάρτιος**, ἡ, app. *ship's mast with yard*·(or the *yard* alone), ἔοικε γὰρ τῷ ἱστίῳ καὶ τῇ καταρτίῳ τῆς νεὼς ὅλης διὰ τὰς βύρσας καὶ τὰ κέρατα (sc. ταῦρος) Artem. 2.12, 53, 3.36, *EM* 478.23.

**καταρτισμός III**, add '*SEG* 17.545 (Pisidia, Rom.imp.), 32.1269 (Phrygia). **2** *completion, perfection* (of dentition), ἑτέροις δὲ μησὶ δυοκαίδεκα τὸν καταρτισμὸν φύει *Hippiatr.* 95.'

**κατάρτῡσις**, add 'Hippod.ap.Stob. 4.1.94 (*Pyth.Hell.* p. 100.22)'

***κάταρχος**, ὁ, app. title of an official, οἱ κάταρχοι καὶ ταβελλάριοι *BCH* 47.382.18 (Notium).

**κατάρχω I 1**, w. acc., add 'Alcm. 98 P., *Carm.Pop.* 5(b).5 P.' **2**, delete 'with reference to the religious sense infr. II 2' **II 2**, line 4, after 'Od. 3.445' add 'τὸ πρόθυμα .. κ. *Hesperia* 7.4 (Athens, iv BC)' **III**, add 'Lxx *Jl.* 2.17, *Na.* 1.12, etc.' **IV**, delete the section.

***κατασεβάζω**, *consecrate*, Sch.Pi.*O.* 3.35.

+**κατᾰσελγαίνω**, *to treat libidinously*, Phot., Suid.

**κατασημαίνομαι II**, delete the section transferring exx. to section I.

**κατασήπω 2**, add 'Plu. 2.231a'

**κατασκᾰφή**, add '*CPR* 6.1.14 (AD 125)'

**κατασκελετεύω**, line 2, after 'Sch.Ar.*Ra.* 153' insert 'transf., *cause* resources *to waste away* (in quot., abs.), Onas. 1.5'; line 3, delete 'Onos. 1.5 (Act.)'

+**κατασκελής**, ές, of style, *over-loaded*, D.H.*Isoc.* 2. **2** *elaborate, complicated*, τὸ τῶν ἐπιτεχνημάτων κ. Ptol.*Alm.* 13.2; μέθοδος id.*Harm.* 2.13 (comp.); [τοῦτο] κ. ἔχει [ὁ] τρόπος ib. 2 (comp.).

+**κατασκένω**, v. °κατακτείνω.

**κατασκευάζω**, line 4, after '(Tanagra, iii BC)' insert 'Cypr. *ka-te-se-ke-u-wa-se* κατεσκεύϜασε *ICS* 2.3'; line 5, after 'D. 42.30' insert '*SEG* 37.528 (Epirus, i BC)' **I 3**, line 4, after 'D. 18.71' insert 'τοῦτο τὸ ἡρῷον κατεσκεύασε *IEphes.* 3327 (ii/iii AD); ἑαυτῷ τὸ μνημεῖον κατεσκεύασεν Mitchell *N.Galatia* 201 (AD 218)'; line 11, for 'Id. 1.93, 2.17' read 'τἆλλα κ. id. 1.93.8; abs., id. 2.17.3' **11**, delete 'ὡς πολεμήσοντες Th. 2.7'

***κατασκεύασις**, εως, ἡ, = κατασκευή (in quot., III), *Cat.Cod.Astr.* 11(2).131.14.

**κατασκεύασμα I**, add 'of a piece of pottery, rest. in *Kafizin* 309 (225/18 BC)' add '**b** *construction* of a literary work, τὸ τραγικὸν κ. Sch.E.*Tr.* 1129.'

**κατασκευή I 1**, line 3, after 'Pl.*Grg.* 455b' insert 'τ]οῦ θεάτρου *IIlion* 1.10 (iv BC), τειχέων *SIG* 569.15 (Cos, Halasarna, *c.*201 BC)' **IV**, add 'Din. 1.53'

**κατασκευόω**, add 'εἰ δέ τι κατασκεώσαιτο *SEG* 25.606.11 (Doris, ii BC)'

**κατασκηνόω**, add 'w. acc., *occupy*, κατασκήνου τὴν γῆν Lxx *Ps.* 36(37).3, *Pr.* 2.21; transf., ἐγὼ ἡ σοφία κατεσκήνωσα βουλήν ib. 8.12'

**κατασκήνωμα I**, for 'A.*Ch.* 985' read 'A.*Ch.* 999'

**κατασκιάζω**, line 3, after 'Archil. 29' insert 'Anacr. 2 *fr.* 1.1 P. (tm.); προσώπου ἄνθος κατεσκιασμένη Men.*Dysc.* 951'

**κατασκοπέω**, line 5, after 'X.*Mem.* 2.1.22' insert 'ὑπτιάζων καὶ κατασκοπούμενος ἑαυτόν Aeschin. 1.132'

**κατασμικρῡ́νω II**, after 'Hierocl. p. 59 A.' insert 'Demetr.*Eloc.* 123'

**κατασπασμός 2**, add '*PSoterichos* 4.27 (AD 87)'

**κατασπάω IV**, *pull down*, add '*IG* 9(2).1229.27 (Thessaly, ii BC)' **V**, add 'τὴν φράσιν D.H.*Comp.* 20 (pass.)' add '**VIII** gloss on ξύει, *plane* or *shave wood*, Hsch., cj. in Thphr.*HP* 5.1.7.'

**κατασπείρω III**, line 3, for 'πλούτῳ Ἑλλάδα κ.' read 'κ. πλούτῳ Ἑλλάδα γῆν'

**κατάσπεισις I**, add 'Plu. 2.437b (sg.)'

**κατασπένδω I**, line 4, after 'Hdt. 2.151' insert '*AP* 7.260 (Carph.)' deleting this ref. from section II 2.

**κατασπεύδω 2**, delete the section.

***κατασπορεία**, ἡ, office of κατασπορεύς, *SB* 9050 vi 12 (i/ii AD).

**κατασπορεύς**, after '*sower*' insert 'Ath.*Sem.* 3 (*PG* 28.148a). **2** *inspector of crops*'

***Κατασπόρια**, τά, festival at Caunus, *JHS* 74.87.22, al.

***καταστᾰλαγμα**, ατος, τό, *drop of liquid*, Anon.Alch. 381.4.

**καταστᾰσιάζω 1**, pass., after 'D. 44.3' insert '52.7, 58.22, etc.'

**κατάστᾰσις II 2**, add '**b** *personal status*, Modest.*Dig.* 27.1.6.18, *Cod.Just.* 6.4.4.23.'

**καταστάτης 2**, add 'of a tax official, *POsl.* 88.16, 35 (iv AD)'

**καταστεγάζω**, after '*cover over*' insert 'rest. in Panyas. 15 B.'

**καταστέλλω I**, add 'fig., σὲ .. οἶκτον περιβαλὼν καταστελῶ E.*IA* 934' **II 2**, delete 'οἶκτον E.*IA* 934'; line 4, after 'Plu. 2.207e, cf. 547b, etc.' insert 'καταστίλατε τὴν ὀργὴν καὶ τὸν θυμὸν τοῦ (δεῖνος) *PPrag.* I 4.4 (v AD)'

***κατάστεμμα**, v. ‡κατάστημα.

**καταστενάζω**, after 'al.' insert 'w. acc. of person, Sch.E.*Tr.* 318'

***κατάστερος**, ον, perh. *sprinkled as with stars*, κ. δὲ πόντος .. ἐγάργαιρε σώμασιν Tim.*Pers.* 791.94 P. (s.v.l.).

**κατάστημα**, line 1, after 'Lxx 3*Ma.* 5.45' insert 'κατάστεμμα *POxy.* 3817.11 (iii/iv AD)' **1**, add '*POxy.* l.c.' **6**, add 'καὶ τοῖς μεταξὺ καταστήμασιν τῆς σελήνης *Peripl.M.Rubr.* 45'

***καταστοχαζόντως**, gloss on καταχρηστικῶς, Hsch.

***καταστρᾰτεία**, ἡ, *offensive expedition*, *BMCParthia* p. 40.

**καταστρᾰτοπεδεύω II**, for pres. def. read '*go* to a place *and camp there*' and add 'Lxx 2*Ma.* 4.22; cf. κατεστρατοπέδευσε· κατεπολέμησεν Hsch.' **III**, delete the section.

***καταστρωτέος**, gloss on στορνυτέος, Hsch.

**κατασφᾰγή**, add 'Heph.Astr. 1.21.15'

**κατασφρᾱγίζω**, penultimate line, after '(ii BC)' insert 'τὰ ὦτα Cels. ap.Orig.*Cels.* 5.64' add '**2** *shut up, confine*, Βασσαρίδων .. φάλαγγα εὐρώεντι κατεσφρήγισσε μελάθρῳ Nonn.*D.* 45.267.'

**κατάσχεσις II**, add '**2** *taking possession*, ἑτέρων Memn. 36 J.'

***κατασχετικός**, ή, όν, *retentive* (?), οἰκείωσις Hsch. s.v. σχετική.

**κατασχίζω**, line 4, after 'pass.' insert 'κὰδ δὲ λῶπος ἐσχίσθη Anacr. 96(*b*) P.'

**κατασχολέομαι**, add '**II** act. *release from the concerns* of, (ὕπνος) ψυχὰς ἀπὸ τῶν σωμάτων κατασχολῶν Afric.*Cest.* 1.17 p. 38 V.'

⁺**καταταράσσω**, gloss on καταπλήσσω, Hsch.

**κατατάσσω I 3**, for this section read '*allocate* funds, εἰς τὸ βασιλικόν *PSI* 510.13 (iii BC); med., εἰς ἀπόδοσιν τῷ θεῷ *IG* 11(2).224*A*7 (Delos, iii BC); pass., *SIG* 459.6 (Beroea, iii BC)'

**κατατείνω I 1**, add '**b** pass., of stringed instruments, Aristid.Quint. 2.16.' **4**, add 'ταῦτα (sc. δόγματα) .. ἐν ἔπεσι κατατεῖναι Arist.*fr.* 7'

***κατατελίσκω**, app. *dedicate*, ἱερεῖα κατατελισκόμενα *IEphes.* 10.8 (iii AD).

⁺**κατάτεχνος**, ον, *full of art*, ὦ κατατεχνοτάτου (v.l. κακοτ-) κινήματος *AP* 5.132 (Phld.); *artificial*, τὸ κ. Plu. 2.79b.

**κατατίθημι**, line 6, after 'Od. 19.17' insert 'pres. inf. act. καττιθέν *SEG* 9.4.38 (Cyrene, i BC), imper. κάθες Lang *Ath.Agora* XXI B1 (vi BC), Cypr. aor. act. 3 pl. *ka-te-ti-sa-ne* κατέθισαν *ICS* 94, *ka-te-ti-ja-ne* κατέθιjαν *ICS* 217.27' **I 3 b**, for this section read '*dedicate*, Cypr. *ka-te-ti-ja-ne i-ta-ti-o-ne* κατέθιjαν ἰ(ν) τὰ(ν) θιόν *ICS* 217.27; *ka-te-te-ke* κατέθεκε *ICS* 205, al.' **4 b**, after '*Leg.Gort.* 6.19' insert '(ὁ καταθένς who gives a slave as surety, ὁ καταθέμενος who receives one, cf. *Inscr.Cret.* 4.47.8, 4 (v BC))' **5**, add '*INikaia* 766, *TAM* 3(1).479, *SEG* 31.1425 (Palestine, vi AD), etc.' **II 4 b** add 'so perh. λύπην κ. αἰφνιδίῳ θανάτῳ *pay a tribute of* grief to .., *Inscr.Cret.* 2.iii 44.8 (Aptera, iii or iv AD)' **7**, add '*enter in one's accounts*, μισθούς *IG* 11.110.17 (Delos, iii BC)'

**κατατομή**, add '**V** *fraction* or *section*, *POxy.* 3465.14 (i AD).'

**κατατρέχω II 4**, *pursue*, add '*UPZ* 68.6 (152 BC)' add '**III** as term of accountancy, prob. *run on, be carried forward*, *PAnt.* 32.7, 8, al. (iv AD), cf. *PHib.* 255.5 (iii BC).'

**κατατρῑδομέω**, add '(reading uncertain, perh. κατ‹οικο›δομήσας, v. *BE* 1989.101)'

**κατατροχάζω I**, for '*cause to run* .. *promote*' read 'perh. *run to the attack* in a form of sham fight (v. *SEG* 32.678)'

***κατατρῡχόω**, = κατατρύχω, pass. aor. part. -ωθείς Memn. 40.4 J.

**κατατυμβοχοέω**, delete the entry ( v. °τυμβοχοέω).

**καταυγάζω**, line 2, after 'Hld. 1.1' insert 'fig., Ὀποῦντα κ. ὕμνοις Sch.Pi.*O.* 9.33' **II**, for 'Hld. 5.31' read 'Hld. 5.32'

**καταυλέω**, passim, for '*flute*' read '*aulos*'

**καταύλησις**, for '*flute*' read '*aulos*'

***καταῦτμενος**, ον, epith. of fine garments, perh. *floating with the breeze*, Sapph. 44.9 L.-P. (s.v.l.), cf. ib. 101.2.

**καταφέρω**, line 1, fut. -οίσομαι, read 'Il. 22.425 (med.), Arat. 871 (pass.)' **I 1**, add '**g** *hand down* property, *Cod.Just.* 1.5.18.5, 7.' **2 c**, add 'of wind, *come down*, Arat. 871' **d**, add 'of destruction by an earthquake, *SEG* 30.1254.B2 (Aphrodisias, AD 102/16)' **V**, add '**2** ὁπεί κε ὁ καιρὸς κατενέκει when the occasion *requires*, *BCH* 59.55 (Larissa, ii BC).'

**καταφθείρω 1**, at end for '*PMagd.* 11.9' read 'κατεφθαρμένην τὴν ὁδὸν ὑπὸ χρόνου ἀποκατέστησεν *TAM* 4(1).11' add '**b** pass., *remain idle, waste one's time* in a place, *PEnteux.* 27.7, 9.'

***καταφλεγμαίνω**, *to be inflamed*, Gal. 11.320.15.

**κατάφορτος**, add '*heavily laden*, of ships, Memn. 36 J.'

**καταφράζω**, line 3, after 'Hes.*Op.* 248' insert 'Hippon. 79.13 W.'

***καταφρακτάριος**, ον, Lat. *cataphractarius*, *mail-clad*, ἱππεῖς *BGU* 316.6 (iv AD).

**καταφρόνητος**, add 'Sch.E.*Or.* 1156'

**καταφρῠάττομαι**, delete 'τινι'

**καταφῠγή I**, add '**3** personified, Θεῷ Ὑψίστῳ καὶ Ἁγείᾳ Καταφυγῇ *SEG* 19.852 (Pisidia).'

**καταφύγιον**, add 'of a person, Χ(ριστ)ὲ ἡμῶν ἡ ἐλπὶς καὶ καταφύγιον *SEG* 35.733 (Beroea, iv AD)'

***καταφῦρω**, *foul, defile*, aor. 1 κατέφυρσε, Hsch. s.v. κατέδευσε.

**καταφῠτεύω I**, add '*PCair.Zen.* 157.3 (256 BC)'

**κατάχαλκος**, for 'a serpent *lapt in mail*, i.e. scales' read 'of a snake *covered with bronze* (-coloured scales)'

**καταχᾰρίζομαι**, lines 1/2, for '*corruptly make* .. thing *corruptly*' read '*give as a favour, make a present of* material or abstract things'; line 5, after 'D. 26.20' insert 'πάντα ταῦτα κ. 41.12' (deleting from section 3); after 'Arist.*Pol.* 1271ᵃ3' insert 'D.H. 6.30, 7.63'

**καταχέω I 2 c**, add '*pour out* song, ἠχέτα τέττιξ .. λιγυρὴν καταχεύετ' ἀοιδήν Hes.*Op.* 583, κακχέει λιγύραν ἀοίδαν Alc. 347(*b*).2 L.-P.'

**καταχθονίζω**, add '**2** fig., ἐλπίδας .. Μοῖρα κατεχθόνισεν *GVI* 1989.14 (Panticapaeum, ii/i BC).'

**καταχθόνιος**, add 'of Hecate, *SEG* 30.326 (i AD); of Hermes, *SEG* 26.1717 (tab.defix., Egypt, iii/iv AD)'

***καταχνόω**, *oppress*, Nic.*fr.* in *Suppl.Hell.* 562.8.

**καταχορεύω**, after 'Ael.*NA* 1.30' insert 'gloss on κατακωμάζω, Sch.E.*Ph.* 352'

**καταχράομαι II 1**, add 'Aeschin. 2.70' **2**, add 'μοχλοὶ .. κατεχρήσθησαν εἰς σφῆνας *IG* 2².1672.304 (Eleusis, 329/8 BC)'

**κατάχρεος**, add '**III** καταχρέως· ἐπαρκῶν εἰς μαρτυρίαν Hsch.'

**κατάχριστος**, after def. insert 'Heras ap.Gal. 13.779.4'; add 'also subst., ἡ κ. *Cat.Cod.Astr.* 8(3).148.11'

**κατάχρῡσος 4**, for 'Phld.*Po.* 5.15' read 'Phld.*Po.* 15.16'

***καταχρωμένως**, adv., (καταχράομαι) = καταχρηστικῶς, opp. κυρίως, Gal. 17(2).790.

***καταχύσιος**, ον, app. adj. fr. κατάχυσις in unkn. sense, *IMylasa* 308.4.

**κατάχυσμα 2**, for 'a bride .. Theopomp.Com. 14' read 'a bridegroom and bride, τὰ κ. κατάχει τοῦ νυμφίου καὶ τῆς κόρης Theopomp.Com. 15 K.-A.'

⁺**καταχωρέω**, *come in*, of revenue, *SEG* 2.481 (Scythia, iii AD).

**καταχωρίζω**, line 2, after 'Apollon.Cit. 2' insert 'spellings w. η for ι, e.g. κατεχώρησε Plu. 2.312b, κατεχώρηκεν *APF* 3.134, by itacism; cf. -ρεῖν, prob. for -ρίζειν *BGU* 981, etc.'

**καταψάλλω 2**, for this section read '*play music over*, in quot. pass., Procop.*Pers.* 2.23'

**καταψάω 2**, add 'καταψᾶν καὶ τιθασεύειν τὴν ὀργὴν τοῦ βασιλέως Demad.*fr.* 20 B.'

**καταψηφίζομαι I 1**, penultimate line, delete 'pf.'; last line, after '(D.H.) 5.8' add 'κατεψήφ[ισα]ν Call.*Dieg.* i.44 (dub., *fr.* 84 Pf.), καταψηφίζων Hsch. s.v. καταστίζων'

**καταψήχω II**, for '*stroke, caress*' read '*smooth down*'

**καταψύχω I 1**, after 'Epicur.*Fr.* 60' insert 'in curses, κραταιὲ Βεπτυτ, παραδίδωμί σοι Εὐτυχιανόν, .. ἵνα καταψύξῃς αὐτόν tab.defix. in *SEG* 35.213.3 (Athens, iii AD)'

***κᾰτέ**, = κατά, κ. ἐπιταγήν *TAM* 2(3).729, 730 (Lycia).

**κατέδω**, line 2, after 'Il. 24.415' insert 'applied to cannibalism, Emp.*fr.* 137.6 D.-K.'

**κατείβω II**, delete 'trans.' and for 'Ἔρος .. 36' read 'Ἔρως .. κατείβων καρδίαν ἰαίνει Alcm. 59(*a*) P.'

**κατεικονίζω**, add '**2** *register with an official description*, ἐγράφη κατεικονισθ(ὲν) διὰ γραφ(είου) [Τεβ]τύνεως διά τε Κρονίωνος γραμματέως *PMil.Vogl.* 145.28 (AD 174).'

**κάτειμι I**, add '**2** *to be descended*, οἱ κατιόντες *descendants*, *Cod.Just.* 6.4.4.14c.'

**κατείργω**, line 1, for 'Cypr. .. H.' read 'Cypr. *ka-te-wo-ro-ko-ne* κατέϝοργον (perh. -ē-) *ICS* 217.1'; line 3, after '*shut in*' insert 'τὰς μὲν ἐν ἡσυχίῃ κατέερξεν *h.Merc.* 356 (v.l. κατέρεξεν)'; line 7, for 'πτόλιν *Inscr.Cypr.* l.c.' read '*po-to-li-ne* πτόλιν *ICS* l.c.'

**κατεισαγωγή**, delete the article.

**κατελέγχω I**, line 1, for 'νόον' read 'νόος' **II**, delete the section, transferring quots. to follow 'Pi.*O.* 8.19' in section I. **III**, for '*betray*' read '*convict*'

***κατελευθερόω**, *liberate*, τῆς τυραννίδος Sch.Pi.*O.* 12.1 (pass.).

***κατέλευσις**, gloss on κατήλυσις, Hsch.

***κατέμπᾰλιν**, adv. *backwards*, *h.Merc.* 78 (tm.).

***κατεμπᾰτέω**, *trample*, κατεμπατοῦνται *POxy.* 3021 i 16 (i AD, s.v.l.).

***κατεναντίος**, α, ον, *face to face with*, w. gen., ἀνθρώπων κατεναντίη Arat. 102 (v.l. -ίον).

***κατενέργεια**, ἡ, *activity, study*, ὡς ἀποδείξω ἐκ πασῶν τῶν γραφῶν ἐν τῇ ἐμῇ κ. περὶ τοῦ σταθμοῦ Zos.Alch. 178.3.

***κατενωπός**, όν, *right opposite*, Theognost.*Can.* 69.

***κατεξανιστάω**, = κατεξανίσταμαι, gloss on καταπλήσσω, Hsch. s.v. καταπλήσσει.

**κατεπᾴδω I 1**, for '*soothe*' read '*blandish, cajole*' **II**, for '*to be always repeating*' read '*to recite in detail* or *at length*'

**κατεπείγω I 2**, add '*urge on* an action or performance, κατεπείγειν τὴν ἐξάνυσιν τῶν κεχρεωστημένων τίτλων *Cod.Just.* 10.19.9 pr.'

*__κατέπερθεν__, Aeol. adv., = *καθύπερθεν*, Alc. 357.3 L.-P., cf. °*ἔπερθα*.

**κατεπίθῡμος**, for 'inf.' read 'gen.'

*__κατέρᾱσις__, *εως, ἡ*, *pouring off*, Agath.Alch. 270.24.

*__κατέργω__, v. *κατείργω*.

**κατερείπω**, after 'Hdt. 7.140' insert 'Nic.*Th.* 724' and before 'Max.Tyr. 1.3' insert '*κατήριπεν δὲ ὁ χειμὼν τὰ θαυμαστὰ ἐκεῖνα πάντα*'

**κατερυθραίνομαι**, add 'act., *dye red*, Hsch. s.v. *καταβάπτει*'

**κατέρχομαι**, line 8, after 'etc.' insert '*Ἀϊδονῆος* Q.S. 3.15'

**κατεσθίω 2**, add '*τὸν κλῆρον* Hippon. 26.4 W.; (cf., w. play on literal sense of *θαλλός*), *ὅτι τὸν .. κατέφαγεν ἐραστήν ποτε Θαλλόν* Macho 425 G.'

**κατευφραίνω**, add '*κατ[ευ]φραίνει μάλιστα τὴν [ψυ]χὴν* Diog.Oen. *new fr.* 12.7 S.'

**κατευχή**, after '*vow*' insert 'Simon. 32 tit. P. (pl.)'

**κατέχω A I 1 a**, add '*embrace*, *Anacreont.* 41.7, 50.20 W.' add '**g** pass., *to be under a legal obligation*, *οἶδας γὰρ ἀκριβῶς ὅτι καὶ ἡ ταβέρνα καὶ οἱ δοῦλοί μου οὐδενὶ κατέχονται ἢ σοί* Scaev.*Dig.* 20.1.34.1, *Cod.Just.* 6.34.4.'

**κατηγορέω I 3**, add 'w. cogn. acc., *ταῖς κατηγορίαις ἃς .. κατηγοροῦσι* D. 8.8' **b**, add 'Gorg.*Pal.* 28, 32'

**κατήλῠσις I**, after '*AP* 10.3' insert '*way down into*, *κύρτοιο* Opp.*H.* 4.116' and for 'Simon. 179.1' read '*AP* 6.217.1 (Simon.)'

**κατήορος**, line 3, for '*AP* 5.259' read '*AP* 5.260'

**κατηρεφής 1**, line 5, delete '*χθονός*'

**κατῆτος**, before '= *κατὰ ἔτος*' insert 'adv., prob.'

*__καθῦτός__, v. °*καταθυτός*.

*__κάτια__, *τά*, unexpld. wd. found in household inventory, *BGU* 34.iii 4, al., iv 24 (?error for *ἀκάτια*).

+__κατῐᾰραίω__, Elean form of *καθιερεύω*, *utter an imprecation against, accuse*, *Schwyzer* 424.5 (iv BC); aor. opt. -*ιαραύσειε* (*τινος*) ib. 409.2 (v BC).

**κατιερόω**, *κατιέρωσις*, delete the entry.

**κατῑθύς**, for '*opposite*' read '*straight ahead* or *down from*'

*__κατιλλάριος__, *ὁ*, Lat. *catillarius*, *dish-maker*, *SEG* 35.1024.A3 (Arretium, i BC/i AD).

**κατίλλω**, for 'dub. sens.' read 'app. describing a distorted or constricted condition of the voice'

+__κατιλλώπτω__, perh. *look sideways at* or *through the slits of one's eyes*, *εὖ κατιλλώψας ἄθρει* A.*fr.* 226 R.; in erotic contexts, *τινι* Philem. 115 K.-A., *θῆλυ κ. AP* 5.119; cf. *κατιλλώπτειν, τὸ καταβλέπειν ἐπὶ χλευασμῷ* Poll. 2.52.

*__κατῑρόω__, v. *καθιερόω*.

**κάτισχνος**, add 'fig. of style, *jejune*, Sch.Flor. ad Call.*fr.* 1 Pf., lines 8/9 (rest.)'

**κατίσχω I**, add '*κάτισχε λῆμα καὶ σθένος θεοστυγές* Neophr. 2.4'

*__κατοικάδιος__, *ον*, = *κατοικίδιος*, *domestic*, *ἥρως IGBulg.* 1874 (Thrace).

**κατοικέω**, after lemma insert 'Aeol. pres. part. *κατοίκηντας IKyme* 13.76 (ii BC)' **I 2**, add 'fig., *ὁ κατοικὸν ἐν βοη(θείᾳ τοῦ ὑψίστου) SEG* 31.1598, 32.1573' **III**, for '*lie, be situated*' read '*exist as a settlement*' and add '*τὰς πόλεις τὰς ἐν Πελοποννήσῳ κατοικούσας* Isoc. 12.166'

**κατοικία 2**, = *colonia*, add '*IEphes.* 3327, 3239A, etc.'

**κατοικίδιος**, after '*a, ον*, only in *Gp.* 1.3.8' insert 'Just.*Nov.* 69.1.1'; line 2, for 'Theopomp.Hist. 258(*a*)' read 'Antig.*Mir.* 137' add '**2** *domiciled*, *BGU* 1816.8 (i BC).'

**κατοικίζω I**, line 7, for 'A.*Pr.* 252' read 'A.*Pr.* 250'

*__κατοκλάζω__, *squat down*, tm., *κατά τ' ὀκλάζουσιν ὁμοῖοι* Opp.*C.* 3.473.

*__κατόμοσις__, *εως, ἡ*, *affirmation on oath*, Hsch. s.v. *μά*.

**κατομφάλιος**, after '*navel*' insert '(or analogous part)'

*__κατόνησις__, Dor. -**όνᾱσις**, *εως, ἡ*, *enjoyment, right of profit from*, *καρποῦ SEG* 23.474 (Dodona, iv/iii BC).

**κατόνομαι**, add 'imper. *κατόνοσσο* Arat. 1142'

**κατόπιν** (s.v. *κατόπιθεν*) **II**, add '*κ. γίγνεσθαι to fall behind, be remiss*, Just.*Nov.* 59.3'

**κατόπισθεν II**, add '*h.Merc.* 407'

*__κατοπτάζομαι__, *discern, see*, Aesop. 266 P.

*__κατοπτευτήρ__, *ῆρος, ὁ*, *overseer*, Colluth. 54 (s.v.l.).

**κατοπτεύω I**, pass., add '*ὑπὸ λουτροῦ ἀληθινῶς κατωπτεύθησαν* X.*Oec.* 10.8' add '**III** w. dat., *adopt an unfavourable attitude towards*, *ἡμῖν POxy.* 2342.29 (ii AD).'

**κατορύσσω**, line 7, after 'X.*Mem.* 1.2.55' insert '*καταδῶ, κατορύττω, ἀφανίζω ἐξ ἀνθρώπων SPAW* 1934.1023 (tab.defix., Attica, iv BC)'

*__κατορύχω__, = *κατορύσσω*, *SPAW* 1934.1041 (tab.defix.).

**κατουλέω** and **κατούλη**, delete the entry (v. *JÖAI* 32.72).

*__κατοχεία__, *ἡ*, *fertilizing*, *τοῦ .. φοινικῶνος τὰς διακαθάρσις καὶ κατωχείας καὶ κατασπασμούς PSoterichos* 4.27 (AD 87).

**κατοχή II 1**, add '**b** pl., concr., *possessions*, *SEG* 30.568 (Maced., ii AD).'

*__κατόχημα__, *ατος, τό*, *residue*, Anon.Alch. 348.15.

+__κατοχμάζω__, *fasten down*, Opp.*H.* 5.226.

**κάτοχος**, line 2, after '*IG* 3.1425*a*' insert '*SEG* 8.13.12 (Nazareth, rescript of Augustus or Tiberius)'

*__καττάπερ__, v. °*καθά*.

*__κάττῡσις__, *εως, ἡ*, *stitching*, *ὑποδημάτων IG* 2².1672.190, 230 (Eleusis, 327 BC), v. *κασσύω*.

**κάτω II c**, add '*ἁ κάτω πόλις the lower quarter* of the city, *SEG* 23.563 (Crete, iii BC); cf. *ἄνω* (B) A II 1 d'

**κατῶβλεψ**, add 'Theognost.*Can.* 97'

**κατωκᾰρα**, add '[*κα*]*τωκάραι* Alc. 58.22 L.-P.'

**κατωμάδιος I**, add '*lying with shoulders down*, of the Great and Little Bears, *κατωμάδιαι φορέονται, ἔμπαλιν εἰς ὤμους τετραμμέναι* Arat. 29'

**κατώμοτος**, add '**2** *bound by an oath* (made against oneself), *κ. κατ' αὐτοῦ μὴ ἔστω Thasos* 18.4 (v/iv BC)'

*__κατωμόχᾱνος__, *ον*, (= *χαίνων κατ' ὤμου* Sch.) *Μιμνῆ κατωμόχανε* Hippon. 28 W.

*__κατωνῠμία__, *ἡ*, *designation*, Socr.Dion.*Lith.* 46.2 G.

**κατώρης**, add '*rushing downwards*, *ἄνεμος* Alc. 412 L.-P. (v.l. *κατάρης*), Sapph. 183 L.-P.'

**κατώτερος 1**, after '*Ep.Eph.* 4.9' insert '*κώμης Μαγαράτων κατωτέρας SEG* 32.1061 (AD 414)'

*__κατωχεία__, *ἡ*, v. °*κατοχεία*.

**κατωχεύει**, for '*πηδᾷ*' read '*πηδᾷ*'

**καυάζοντα**, add '(acc. to La. corrupt for *ὀκλάζοντα*)'

**καῦδος**, delete the entry.

+__καύης__, *ὁ*, Lydian wd. for *priest* or *priestess*: masc. Hippon. 4 W., *Sardis* 6(2).23.6 (iv BC), al.; fem. **καῦις** *καυεῖν* (for *καῦιν*, acc.) *Sardis* 7(1).51.3 (ii AD), al.

*__καυκεών__, *ῶνος, ὁ*, perh. deriv. of *καῦκος*; cf. *κυκεών*, Theognost. *Can.* 28.

**καυκίον**, add 'Lxx Sch.*Ge.* 44.2'

*__καυκουλάτωρ__, *ορος, ὁ*, Lat. *calculator*, *teacher of arithmetic*, *Edict.Diocl.* 7.67.

**καυληδόν II**, add 'Gal. 18(2).759.4, 788.17, 888.8'

*__καυλοκόπος__, *ὁ*, *stalk-cutter*, *PMil.Vogl.* 69.*B*23 (ii AD, *κολο-* pap.).

**καῦμα I 2**, add 'Pl.*Ti.* 86a (pl.)'

*__καυματινός__, *ή, όν*, *burning hot*, *κ. ὥρης ὑπαρχούσης Vit.Aesop.*(G) 28.

**καυνᾰκης**, for '*thick cloak*' read '*covering* (*blanket, rug*, or sim.)'; at end for '(Assyr. .. mantle)' read '(cf. Pahlavi *gonaka*, rug, bed-cover, of Iranian origin, Avest. *gaona*, hair, colour, *APAW* 1936(3).5)'

*__καύνη__, *ἡ*, cf. Lat. *canabae*, *settlement of camp-followers*, *Dura*[6] 434 (iii AD).

*__καυνιάζω__, *τὸ κλῆρον μακρόθεν ἡγοῦμαι* Hdn.*fr.* p. 27 H.; cf. *διακαυνιάζω*.

*__καυνιάρι(ο)ν__, *τό*, *gaming-table*, Hdn.*fr.* p. 27 H.

**Καύνιος**, add 'in a cult-title, *βασιλεῖ Καυνίωι SEG* 27.942.7 (Xanthus, Lycia, 337 BC)'

*__καυνός__ (B)· *κακός, σκληρός, κλῆρος* Hsch., gloss contaminated with *καυνός* (A).

**καυσία**, delete 'forming part of the regalia of their kings' and before 'Plu.*Ant.* 54' insert '*κ. διαδηματοφόρῳ*'

**καύσιμος**, line 2, *κ. ξύλα*, add '*IG* 1³.425.9'; at end add 'in uncertain sense, A.*fr.* 73b.5 R.'

**καῦσος** (A) **I**, add 'Hp.*Acut.* 5.66, *Aph.* 4.58, *Morb.* 1.3, 29, etc.'

**καύστειρα**, at end for 'in the form .. Nic. l.c.' read 'taken to be fr. **καυστειρός**, hence *καυστειροῖο* Opp.*H.* 2.509 (v.l. *καυστηρ-* both here and in Nic. l.c.), and perh. so Call. in *POxy.* 2375 ii 2'

+__καυστηρός__, v. ‡*καύστειρα*.

**καῦστις**, add '*παρὰ δὲ τοῖς τραγικοῖς καῦστις εἴρηται μεταφορικῶς ἡ μάχη. παρά τισι δὲ ἡ ὀσφῦς καὶ τὰ ἰσχία, παρὰ ἐνίοις δὲ ὁ ξηρὸς χόρτος. ἔνιοι δὲ τὸ αἰδοῖον* Phot. s.v. *ἀμφίκαυστις*'

+__καύστρα__, *ἡ*, *place of cremation*, Str. 5.3.8, *Rev.Phil.* 13.212 (Faustinopolis), *GVI* 1751.1 (Ion. -*η*, Termessus, ii/iii AD), *IEphes.* 2123, al. **b** *funerary urn*, *ITrall.* 203.

**καυσώδης**, add 'w. ellipsis of *πυρετοί*, Hp.*Coac.* 128, 134'

**καυτήριον**, after '*τό*' insert 'also **καυστ-**' **I**, add '*ἀκοῆς καυστήρια*, of persons, Cels.ap.Orig.*Cels.* 5.64' **III**, add 'Plin.*HN* 1.35'

**καύχημα 2**, add 'of Christ, *SEG* 32.1588 (vi/vii AD)'

*__καυχητικός__, *ή, όν*, *boastful*, *ᾠδή* Sch.Pi.*N.* 9.16.

**καυχός**, delete '**καυχοῦς**' and '*χαλκοῦς*'

*__καῦχος__, *εος, τό*, *boast, subject of boasting*, *Princeton Exp.Inscr.* III A no. 160 (v AD).

**καχεξία 2**, add '*Amyzon* 20 (*κακ-*)'

**κάχρυς**, line 1, after '*υδος* ib. 20' insert 'pl. acc. *κάχρῡς* Ar.*Nu.* 1358'

*__καψάριον__, *τό*, *cupboard for clothes*, *PHarris* 79.10 (iii AD).

**καψάριος**, after '*ὁ*' insert '*slave in charge of clothes*, esp. at baths'; after '*capsarius*' insert '*Edict.Diocl.* 7.75 (v.l. *καμψάριος*), *SB* 10258 i 11 (iv AD), *ITyr* 151 (*καμψ-*)'

**καψοί**, add '(*κάψαι· τεύχη* cj. La.)'

**κε**, line 1, for '*Inscr.Cypr.* 135.10 H.' read '*ICS* 217.10'

κεβλήπῠρις, delete 'nickname .. Hermipp. 72'
κεγχρεών, for pres. def. read 'some part of a foundry'
κεγχρίδιον, for 'κιχρηδῶν' read 'κιγχρηδῶν'
*κέγχρον, τό, prob. for κέγχρος, granulation on gold work, CPR 5.22.8 (?v AD).
κέγχρος II, add '4 grain of sand, Aq.Sm.Theod.Is. 48.19.'
κεδνός I 1, add 'pl. subst. ὦ μοῖρα κεδνῶν καὶ κακῶν κυνηγέτι Trag.adesp. 504' II, add 'E.Tr. 683, ἕν τι κεδνὸν αἱροῦ Thal. ap.D.L. 1.35'
κεδρία, line 1, after 'κεδρελάτη' insert 'or a preparation made from it' and add 'PSorb. I 34'
*Κεδρῑ́τᾱς, ὁ, title of Hermes, SEG 26.1046 (Crete, iii AD).
κέδρον, add 'III = στρούθειον (s.v. -ειος III), Ps.-Dsc. 2.163.'
κέδρος 2, delete 'for a beehive'
κεῖ, for '= κεῖθι, ἐκεῖθι' read '= ἐκεῖ' and after 'Herod. 1.26' add 'Call.Del. 195 (v.l., in POxy. 2225)'
+κεῖθεν, κεῖθι, v. ‡ἐκεῖ-.
*κειλαιδίκηνος, ὁ, title of Asclepius, SEG 30.717; also κειλαιδέκηνος, ib. 736, κειλαίσκηνος, ib. 727 (all Serdica, Thrace, ii/iii AD).
κεῖμαι, line 2, after 'IG 1².94.25' insert 'Cypr. ke-i-to-i κεῖτοι, ICS 11'; line 5, for 'Il. 24.567' read 'Il. 24.527'; line 6, after 'Aret.SD 2.4' insert 'Cret. κίαται Inscr.Cret. 4.174A22 (Gortyn, ii BC)'; line 14, after 'Od. 6.19' insert 'κέοντο Q.S. 3.728, (v.l.); κατεκείαθεν· κατεκοιμήθη Hsch.' I 6, for 'have a fall' read 'lie flat out after a fall (wrestling), fig.' and after 'Ar.Nu. 126' add 'Pl.R. 451a; Call.fr. 194.80 Pf.'
κειμηλιάρχης, add 'MAMA 3.349 (Corycus)'
κειμήλιον I, add 'κε̄μέλιον EAC 7.128 (Acanthus, vi BC)'
κειμηλιφῠλᾰ́κιον, add 'Just.Nov. 74.4.2'
κειρία II, add 'ribbon, Inscr.Délos 1439Abα70 (ii BC)'
κείρω, before 'fut.' insert 'Aeol. κέρρω Choerob.in Theod. 1.126'; line 9, after 'Luc.Lex. 5' insert 'part. κεκραμένος Schwyzer 686 (Pamphylia, iv BC)' II 2, add 'Thgn. 892 W.' 4, for this section read 'Cypr. e-ke-re-se ἐπίβασιν .. ἔκερσε made by cutting, hewed out, ICS 3'
κεκαδδίχθαι, delete the entry.
κεκᾰφηώς, lines 3/4, for 'fordone .. ib. 26.108' read 'exhausted, of persons, Nic.Al. 444; δέμας κεκαφηότα λιμῷ Nonn.D. 26.108'; line 6, after 'Opp.H. 3.572' insert 'κεκαφηότα γυῖα id.C. 4.206, Nonn.D. 2.539'
κεκῆνας, add 'cf. Κηκήν as a pr. n. in Inscr.Cret. 1.xxii 52 (ii/i BC)'
*κεκραγῖναι (κεκραδῖναι La.)· ἄγριαι θρίδακες Hsch.
*Κεκροπηΐς, ΐδος, = Κεκροπίς, SEG 21.748 (Athens, ii/iii AD).
Κεκροπία, add 'Ion. -ίη Suppl.Hell. 1044'
*κελαδαία, unexpld. wd. in damaged inscr., SEG 19.115.17 (Athens, ii/iii AD).
κελαδέω, line 4, after 'E.Hel. 371 (lyr.)' insert 'inf. κελαδέσαι prob. in Pi.I. 5.48 S.-M.' I 3, line 2, for 'grasshopper' read 'cicada'
κελαινός, add 'Myc. ke-ra-no, name of an ox'
κελέβειον, delete 'Ion. -ήϊον' and after 'Antim. 17' add '18, 19 Wy.'
κέλευθος IV, after 'of life' insert 'Simon. 36.13 P.'
κελευστής, add 'II house-steward, Mitchell N.Galatia 88.'
κελεύω I 9, add 'b w. ὥστε and inf., ἡ διάταξις κελεύει ὥστε πάντα δικαστὴν ἐν τῇ ἀποφάσει αὐτοῦ κελεύειν .. Cod.Just. 7.51.5 pr., 7.62.35; sim. w. ἵνα, ἡ διάταξις κελεύει ἵνα .. μὴ λαμβάνειν .. ib. 12.37.19 pr.'
*κελεφία, ἡ, a form of leprosy or sim., Cyran. 15; cf. ‡κελεφός.
κελεφός, add 'Epiph.Const. in PG 42.43'
κέλης I, add 'ἐπὶ (τοῦ) κέλητος in celebration of an ovatio, D.C. 54.8.3, 55.2.4. b obsc., w. ref. to a coital posture (cf. °κελητίζω), ἐπὶ τῶν κελήτων διαβεβήκασ' ὄρθριαι Ar.Lys. 60; cf., of a facetiously invented deity, ἥρῳ Κέλητι Pl.Com. 188.18 K.-A.; interpreted as female pudenda, Eust. 1539.34.' II, for 'fast-sailing .. oars' read 'a light fast-sailing ship' III, delete the section.
κελητίζω I, delete 'of one who leaps from horse to horse'; add 'pres. part., pl., of statues, figures riding on horseback, Plin.HN 34.75, 78' II, for this section read 'of a woman, to adopt a coital posture astride a man, Ar.V. 501, Th. 153, w. acc., Macho 171 G.'
*κελητισμός, ὁ, in obscene text, app. a coital position, cf. °κελητίζω II, AE 1957.48 (Attica, iii BC) (pl.).
*Κελκαία, ἡ, title of Artemis (identified w. Empress Sabina), SEG 37.522-5 (Epirus, ii AD).
*κελλαρεύω, to be a ‡κελλάριος, inscr. in ZPE 33.187 (Troad, v/vi AD).
*κελλαρικάριος, ὁ, cellarman, PKlein.Form. 1000 (v AD), CPap.Jud. 513.20 (AD 586).
*κελλαρικός, ή, όν, of a cellar or store-room, κελλαρικῶν εἰδῶν, provisions, PBeatty Panop. 1.219.
κελλάριος, after 'cellarman' insert 'Lat. cellarius, PRyl. 228.24 (i AD)'; at end add 'in pl., gloss on ταμίαι, Sch.Gen.Il. 19.44; fem. κελλαρία, ἡ, Hsch. s.v. ταμίη'
*κελλία, ἡ, = κέλλα, κελλίον, CPR 4.44.3, 7, 8 (v/vi AD).
κελλίβας, before 'PRyl. 136.10' insert 'PTeb. 793 vi 4 (ii BC)'
κελλικάριος, delete the entry.
κέλλω, line 2, fut., delete 'E.Hec. 1057' and after 'ἔκελσα' insert 'ἐπέκειλα Act.Ap. 27.41'
*κελλώνιον, unexpld. wd. cited as derived fr. κέλλω, Sch.E.Or. 800.
*κέλοξ, οκος, Lat. celox, small boat, πλοίῳ κ., gloss on κέλητι, Sch.Th. 8.38.
κέλῡφος 2, for 'sheath' read 'περὶ τοῦτον δ' (sc. καυλὸν) οἷον κέλυφός ἐστι τὸ καλούμενον αἰδοῖον'; line 6, for 'crustaceous fish' read 'crustacea'
κεμᾰ́δειον, delete '(prob.)'
κεμᾰδοσσόος, after 'chasing deer' insert 'Call.fr. 186.31 Pf.'
κεμάς, delete 'so Ar.Byz. ap.'
*κέμβερος, another name for λάλαξ, Hsch. s.v. λάλαγες (dub., v. ‡Κέρβερος).
*κεμήλιος, ὁ, prob. cult-title of Dionysus, Alc. 129.8 L.-P.
*κέμιον, τό, prob. a kind of vegetable, PRyl. 629.266, al. (iv AD); also καίμιον POxy. 1656.14 (iv/v AD); cf. °κεμοράφανος.
*κεμιοπώλης, ὁ, seller of κέμιον, SB 9902 B iii 6, T 7 (iii AD).
*κεμορᾰ́φανος, ὁ, a kind of vegetable, PRyl. 629.37, al. (iv AD), v. °κέμιον.
*Κεμπηνός, ὁ, title of Asclepius, IGBulg. 1².354 (Rom.imp.).
*Κενδρείσεια or -είσια, τά, name of a festival in Thrace, IGBulg. 889, al. (Philippopolis); written Κεντρ- IG 2².3169.20 (Athens, iii AD).
*κενεᾰ́ριον, v. ‡κενήριον.
κενεμβᾰτέω I 1, after 'Plu.Flam. 10' insert 'of the sun passing over an uninhabited region, ὥσπερ κ. Xenoph. in Placit. 2.24.9'
*κενεμεσία, ἡ, retching, Gal.ap.Aët. 9.10 (pl.).
*κένευϝον, ?τό, Cypr. e-pi-ke-ne-u-wo-ne perh. ἐπὶ κενεύϝο̄ν, cenotaph, ICS 94.
κενεών I 1, add 'of boats, Opp.H. 3.555'
κενήριον, add 'Dor. κενεάριον SEG 35.295 (Kynouria, late v BC; see also ib. 39.369)'
κενοδοξέω 2, add 'b glory in empty distinctions, D.Chr. 38.29.'
+κενολόγος· vanilocuus, Gloss.
κενοπᾰθέω, add 'Plu. 2.1106a'
κενός, line 9, for 'κενευϝός Schwyzer 683.4' read '°κένευϝον' I 2, line 16, delete 'ἐν κενοῖς S.Aj. 971' II 2, line 7, after 'Lxx Ge. 31.42' insert 'bereaved, ἐν κενοῖς S.Aj. 971' b, add 'of style, hollow, pretentious, D.H.Dem. 44; of an author, id.Is. 20; comp., ib. 19'
κενόσπουδος, line 3, for 'mere curiosity' read 'useless anxiety'
κενοτᾰ́φιον I, delete 'CIG 4340d, e' and add '2 place for corpse or sarcophagus, tomb chamber, SEG 2.702, 708, 6.667, Robert Hell. 10.172, SEG 17.601, 602, 630 (Pamphylia, Rom.imp.).'
*κενοφόβος, ον, gloss on ψοφοδεής, Hsch.
κενόω I 1, at end add 'make barren or desolate, ἐκενώθη ἡ τίκτουσα ἑπτά Lxx Je. 15.9'
*κενσίτωρ, ωρος, ὁ, Lat. censitor, registrar or taxation officer, PHerm. 32.11 (vi AD).
*κένταρχος, ὁ, centurion, IG 12(5).712.98 (Syros).
κεντέω, add 'II adorn with mosaics (cf. κέντησις II), Βυζάντιον 4.715 (Eresus, iv/v AD), REG 79.229 (Aetolia), ib. 82.462.'
κεντηνάριος, add 'SEG 24.911 (-άρις Thrace, iii/iv AD), BGU 2141.5 (AD 446)'
κέντησις II, add 'BCH suppl. 8 no. 226 (Philippi, iv AD)'
κεντητικός, add '2 engraved (κεντιτικός pap.), BGU 2359.2 (iii AD).'
*κέντινος, unexpld. adj. describing a horse, POxy. 922.11 (vi/vii AD), cf. ib. 1289.9 (v AD).
*κέντουκλον, τό, Lat. centunculus, a piece of cloth, Edict.Diocl. 7.52.
*κεντουρία, ἡ, Lat. centuria, CIG 5046, written -τυρία PLond. 142.4 (i AD), Aegyptus 62.171, Just.Nov. 128.1.
*κεντριστής, οῦ, ὁ, goader, driver, Hsch. s.v. κέντορες.
κεντρῑ́της I, for 'v. κεντρίνης III' read 'a venomous serpent' add 'IV perh. occupation term, maker of goads, MAMA 3.278.'
κέντρον 1, goad, as symbol of sovereignty, add 'Sol. 36.20 W.' 5 d, for '= πόσθη' read 'penis' add 'e in pl., antennae of the crayfish, Opp.H. 2.324.'
*κεντρορρᾰγής, v. κεντρομανής.
κέντρων, add 'III perh. goad, PMich.xv 717.4 (iii AD).'
κεντρωνάριον, for 'case for κέντρωνες' read 'perh. case for κέντρωνες II (pen-wipers)'
κεντρωτός 1, add 'φιάλαι Inscr.Délos 104-12.8 (iv BC)'
*κενωτέος, α, ον, needing to be purged, Gal. 11.211.8.
κέπφος 2, add 'Call.fr. 191.6 Pf. (cf. Sch.ad loc.)'
κεπφόω, for 'ensnare like a κέπφος' read 'make like a κ.' and after 'feather-brained' insert '(or changeable)'
κεραία II 3, for 'apex of a letter' read 'mark placed over letter to indicate length' and add 'stroke of a letter, SEG 32.1256 (Nicomedia)'
*Κεραιάτης, ὁ, v. ‡Κερεάτας.
κεραιός, add 'Myc. ke-ra-ja-pi (fem. instr. pl.)'

**κεραιοῦχος**, for '*upholding the right*, Hsch.' read 'κεραιοῦχον· δικαιοδότην ἀπὸ τοῦ ἐν τοῖς πλοίοις κεραιούχου Hsch.'

***κεράμάρχης**, ου, ὁ, prob. some annual magistrate, *BCH* suppl. 5 pp. 274-5 (three inscr., Thasos, iv/iii BC).

**κεράμβηλον**, add '*Et.Gen.* in Miller *Mélanges* 183'

**κεραμεύς**, add 'Myc. *ke-ra-me-u*'

**κεράμεύω 2**, after 'c. acc.' insert 'ἐκεράμευσεν ἐμέ *ABV* p. 349'

**κεραμεών**, after 'Ar.*Lys.* 200' add '(cj. κεραμών)'

***κεράμηγός**, όν, *carrying pottery*, of a boat (κύδαρος), *BGU* 2353.5 (AD 115).

***κεράμιδᾶς**, ᾶ, ὁ, *potter*, *PSI* 899.35 (iii AD, -ειδας pap.).

**κεράμικός**, after '*of* or *for pottery*' insert '*used in making pottery*' and add 'λίθου κεραμικοῦ *PMich.*v 238.143, 181'

***κεράμοδέτης**, ου, ὁ, kind of craftsman, perh. *tiler* or *pot-mender*, *Kerameikos* 3 p. 98.9 (iv BC).

**κεράμοπώλης**, add '*IG* $2^2$.1673.21 (iv BC)'

**κέράμος II 1 b**, insert at beginning 'χαλκέῳ δ' ἐν κεράμῳ Il. 5.387 (said to be used as a prison by the Cyprians: Theon.*Prog.* 13), cf. epitome Monac. of Thphr.*Char.* 6.6; pl., Nonn.*D.* 16.162' **2**, add 'also κέραμος, ἡ, *BCH* 56.293 (Stobi, ii AD)' **III**, delete the section.

***κέράμος**, τό, *pot*, κεράμε̄ πάντα *BE* 1989.305.

**⁺κεράοξόος**, ον, *carving* or *working in horn*, κ. τέκτων Il. 4.110, *AP* 6.113 (Simm.); masc. subst., *worker in horn*, Opp.*C.* 2.509.

**κεράός I**, before 'τράγος' insert 'Call.*fr.* 25.1 Pf.'; after 'Theoc. 1.4' insert 'Διώνυσος Nic.*Al.* 31'; add 'Bernand *IMEG* 107.1'

**κέρᾶς**, line 6, after 'Q.S. 6.225' insert 'dat. κεράασι [⏑–⏑⏑] A.R. 4.978' **III 1**, delete 'τόξον .. cf.' **2**, for '*flute*' read '*aulos*' **3**, for '*OGI* 214.43 (Didyma, iii BC)' read 'Didyma 424.43 (iii BC)' **V 5**, add 'perh. in wider sense, cf. κεραία II, *Peripl.M.Rubr.* 36' **7 b**, for 'πόσθη' read '*penis*' add '**IX** = κεράτιον II, as a coin, Epic. in *BKT* 5(1).120.61 (vi AD).' at end add 'Myc. *ke-ra-a* (pl.), *ke-ra-e* (dual)'

**κερασβόλος**, add '**III** κερασβόλα· οἱ περὶ τῶν κεράτων βοῶν δεσμοί, καὶ οἱ ἐν ταῖς ἀρχαίαις λύραις κόλλαβοι Hsch.'

**κεράστης I**, add 'κοχλίας κεράστας Achae. 42. **b** λύκος κ. *lynx* (from its tufted ears), *Edict.Diocl.* 8.35 (v.l.). **c** = °κερασφόρος I b, Nonn.*D.* 45.43.'

**κεραστίς I**, add 'of Cyprus (fr. shape of coastline), Hdn. 1.104.15'

**κεραστός**, add '*alloyed*, κ. νόμισμα Cels.ap.Orig.*Cels.* 6.22'

**κερασφόρος I**, add 'κ. κριόν Ph.Epic. in *Suppl.Hell.* 682' add '**b** ὁ κ. αὐλός the Phrygian pipe *having a horn-shaped addition* at the end, Aristid.Quint. 3.21; cf. κέρας III 2, °κεράστης, κεραύλης, ἐγκεραύλης.'

**⁺κερᾶτίζω**, *butt with horns, gore*, ἐὰν κερατίσῃ ταῦρος ἄνδρα Lxx *Ex.* 32.2, al.; fig., ἐν σοὶ τοὺς ἐχθροὺς ἡμῶν κερατιοῦμεν *Ps.* 43(44).5; abs., Ph. 1.57, Sch.Theoc. 3.5; w. ref. to a crocodile, perh. in mistranslation fr. Hebr., σὺ ὡς δράκων ὁ ἐν τῇ θαλάσσῃ καὶ ἐκεράτιζες τοῖς ποταμοῖς σου Lxx *Ez.* 32.2.

**κεράτινος**, add 'ον, τό, *vessel made of horn*, Gal. 13.139.5'

**κεράτιον II**, add 'abbrev. κρ *PVindob.Worp* 11.3, al. (vi AD)'

***κερᾶτόμορφος**, ον, *horned*, or *horn-shaped*, epith. of Egyptian god, *APAW* 1943(14).8 (Chalcis, iii AD).

**κερᾶτουργός**, for '= κερατοξόος' read '*worker in horn*' and add 'prob. *CPR* 7.50.16 (AD 636)'

**κερᾶτῶπις**, add '*PMag.* 4.2548'

***Κεραυνιασταί**, οἱ, association of worshippers of Zeus Keraunios, *SEG* 35.1483.B27-8 (Antioch, i AD).

**κεραύνιον II**, add '**2** some kind of design or pattern, πρόσωπον καὶ κύκλωι κεραύνια *Inscr.Délos* 1443*A*ii35, 1450*A*187.'

**κεραύνιος I 1**, at end for 'Call.*Aet.* 3.1.64' read 'Call.*fr.* 75.64 Pf.' and after '*VP* 17' insert 'without λίθος, Sm.*Ex.* 28.17' **II**, after '*Milet.* 1(7).278' insert '*SEG* 20.99 (Cilicia), 30.1617 (Cyprus, 44/31 BC), *POxy.* 885.44 (ii/iii AD), Paus.Ant. 10.2 J.; cf. Θεῷ μεγίστῳ κεραυνίῳ Βη‹το›χιχι *SEG* 32.1445 (Syria, iii AD)'

***κεραυνίτης** λίθος, perh. = κεραυνία λίθος, Cyran. 26.

***κεραυνοβίᾶς**, ᾱ, ὁ, *mighty by thunder*, prob. in B.*fr.* 20E.7 S.-M., *Coll.Alex.* p. 84, vi 9 (cj.).

**κεραυνοβολέω II**, add 'pass., Sch.E.*Med.* 144'

**κεραυνοβολία**, add '*hurling of a thunderbolt, stroke of lightning*, *SEG* 7.980 (Arabia, iii AD)'

**κεραυνός II**, for 'as a name .. *Arist.* 6' read 'nickname of Ptolemy, (?) elder son of Ptolemy Soter and Eurydice, Plb. 2.41.2, Plu.*Arist.* 6; given διὰ τὴν σκαιότητα καὶ ἀπόνοιαν, Memn. 5.6 J.'

**κεραυνοφόρος**, after 'D.C. 55.23' insert '*SEG* 31.1300 (AD 145/6)'

**Κερβεροκίνδῡνος**, delete the entry.

**Κέρβερος**, add '**III** kind of toad or frog, Sch.Nic.*Al.* 578 Ge., Hsch. s.v. λάλαγες (κεμβ- cod). **IV** = ὠχρός, Hsch.'

***κερβήσιος**, ὁ, *beer*, fr. Lat. *cervesia*, *Edict.Diocl.* 2.11.

***κερβικάριον**, τό, Lat. *cervicarium*, *pillow*, *POxy.* 1269.37 (ii AD), 921.8 (κερπ-; iii AD), *Stud.Pal.* 20.67.29 (ii/iii AD, κεβρ-), *BGU* 814.11 (iii AD); κ. θρόνου *PWisc.* 30 ii 14; as receptacle for dates, *PSI* 1331.12-14 (iii AD).

**κερβολέω**, add 'cf. σκερβόλλω'

**κερδαίνω I 1**, add '**b** *gain, win over* a person, *Ev.Matt.* 18.15, 1*Ep.Cor.* 9.19, 1*Ep.Pet.* 3.1.'

**κερδᾰλέος 1 b**, after 'Archil. 89.5' insert 'cf. ἄγρην κερδαλέην Opp.*H.* 2.119'; add 'of other creatures, κερδαλέαι .. σηπίαι Opp.*H.* 4.160'

***Κερδοῖον**, τό, *sanctuary of Apollo Κερδοῖος*, *SEG* 27.202.25 (Larissa, iii BC).

***Κερδοῖος**, ὁ, v. ‡κερδῷος.

**κερδοσύνη**, add 'sg. in epigr., *IGBulg.* 656 (Moesia, iv AD)'

***κέρδων**, ωνος, ὁ, attested by Lat. *cerdo*, *artisan*, Pers. 4.51, etc.

**κερδῷος I**, before '*IG* 9(2)' insert 'Thess. Κερδοῖος'; after '(Phalanna)' insert 'et al.'

***κερεᾰλιος**, α, ον, Lat. *cerealis*, οἱ κ. ἀγορανόμοι D.C. 43 (arg.), of an aedile, *SEG* 6.555 (Pisidia, ii AD).

**Κερεάτᾱς**, add 'also Κεραιάτης *SEG* 20.138 (Cyprus, iii BC)'

**κερητίζει**, delete the entry.

***κερητίζω**, prob. *play a game with a stick curved at the end and a ball*, Plu. 2.839c (cj. κελητ-, but v. *AD* 6 (1920/1) pp. 56-59). **2** κερητίζει· βασανίζει Hsch.

**κέρθιος**, for '*tree creeper, Certhia familiaris*' read '*short-toed tree-creeper, Certhia brachydactyla*'

**κερκίς II 1**, after 'Poll. 1.252' insert '*strut*, *IG* $2^2$.1668.52' and delete '*hair-pin* or' **7**, delete the section. **IV 1**, add 'Call.*fr.* 284 Pf. (cf. *Suppl.Hell.* 287.7)'

**κερκορῶνος**, delete 'perh. f.l. for κερκίων'

**κερκούριον**, delete 'only'; after 'Dim. of κέρκουρος' insert '*cargo vessel*, *BGU* 1933.2 (ii BC)'

**κέρκουρος**, line 2, delete 'esp. of the Cyprians'; add 'invented by the Cyprians acc. to Plin.*HN* 7.208'

**Κέρκῡρα**, add 'also *SEG* 23.474 (Dodona, iv/iii BC); Κέρκῡρ, athematic form, Alcm.*fr.* 114 P.; adj. Κερκῡραϊκός, ή, όν, Th. 1.118.1'

**κέρκωψ 2**, for '*knave*' read '*teller of false tales*'

**κέρμα**, line 1, for 'dub. l.' read 'prob.'

**κερμᾰτίζω I**, after 'Pl.*Men.* 79a' add 'οὐκ ἀναλίσκουσα τὸ ἐν οὐδὲ κερματίζουσα Plot. 5.5.4' **III**, add 'ἀργύριον κεκερματισμένον *small change*, Ar.*fr.* 215 K.-A.'

**κερμᾰτιον**, *cash*, add '*POxy.Hels.* 48.13, 19 (ii/iii AD)'

**κερμᾰτιστής**, add '*PUniv.Giss.* 30.11 (iii/iv AD)'

**κέρνας**, read 'κερνᾶς'

**κερνί[ον]**, read '**κερνίον**' and add 'Theognost.*Can.* 123'

**κερόεις**, for 'Simon. 30' read 'Pi.*fr.* 107a.4'

***κέρρω**, v. ‡κείρω.

***Κέρσουλλος**, ὁ, title of Zeus, *IHadr.* 3.3, also Κέρσουσσος ib. 4.7 (ii AD).

***κερτόκορος**, ὁ, perh. f.l. for **κερκόκορος**, *brush* (cf. κόρος (C)), made from an animal's tail (κέρκος), *SB* 9834b.28 (iii AD).

**κερτομέω**, lines 4/8, delete 'σὲ δὲ .. *Ph.* 1235' and 'c. dupl. acc. .. 1.62' add '**2** *mock* by false statement, *make game of*, σὲ δὲ κερτομέουσαν ὀΐω ταῦτ' ἀγορευέμεναι Od. 13.326, S.*Ph.* 1235, E.*Hel.* 619, *IA* 849; κοῦτι τυ κερτομέω Theoc. 1.62.'

***κέρχμων**, ονος, unexpld. wd. in Theognost.*Can.* 35.

**κέρχνος** (A), add 'also **χέρχνος** *IG* $1^3$.422.153 (Athens, v BC)'

**κέρχνωμα**, add 'also cj. in E.*Ph.* 1386'

***κεσσωνάριοι**, οἱ, app. Lat. *quaestionarii*, perh. for pap. κεσσωπαρ-, *SB* 2253.5 (*Berichtigungsl.* VII p. 180).

**κεστρεύς**, add 'κεστρεῖος (gen.) τῶ μέδονος *IGC* p. 99 B17'

**κέστρος II**, add '*SEG* 35.581 (Thessaly, ii BC)' add '**III** κέστρος· ὄχημα δίχα τροχῶν *Gloss.* II 200.5.'

***κευθμωνοδίτης**, ου, ὁ, *traveller in the underworld*, of Cerberus, *Suppl.Mag.* 42.3, 64 (iii/iv AD).

**κεύθω**, line 3, after '*Th.* 505' insert 'med., redupl. aor. κεκύθεσθε Call.*fr.* 238.6 Pf.'

**κεφᾰλαιος II 1**, add '**b** transf., *highest point*, τὸ κεφάλαιον τοῦ ἀντιπροσώπου θεάτρου X.*Eq.Mag.* 3.7.'

**κεφᾰλή I 1 b**, line 5, for 'in Archit., *upright*' read '*along the top*'; add 'also ἐπὶ κεφαλήν Hyp.*Lyc.* 17' **d**, lines 5/6, delete 'οὐ βουλόμενος .. *Lyc.* 17' **2**, lines 7 ff., delete 'periphr. .. sense' and 'ἡ κ. .. (iv AD)' inserting 'periphr. .. Hdt. 9.99' after 'Vett.Val. 74.7' add '**b** esp. as the unit on which personal taxation and compulsory service are imposed, ὑπὲρ συντερίας (i.e. συντελείας) τῆς καιφαλῆς *POxy.* 1331 (v AD); τὰ δημόσια τῆς αὐτοῦ κ. *PLond.* 1793 (v AD); τὰ ναύβια τῆς κ. αὐτοῦ καὶ τῶν αὐτῶν *PRein.* 57.8 (= Wilcken *Chr.* 390; iv AD).' **3**, add 'κ. κινδυνεύσει *PCair.Isidor.* 1.19 (AD 297)' add '**5** in leg. sense, = Lat. *caput*, *IGLS* 718.61 (i BC), see also °κατάκριτος.' **II b**, last line, after '*origin*' insert 'Hp.*Coac.* 498' **c**, add '*crest* of wave, *Peripl.M.Rubr.* 46' **e**, for '*PPetr.* 3 p. 72' read '*PPetr.* II p. 121' add '**f** *summit*, of mountains, Orph.*H.* 36.16, Q.S. 7.558.' **V 3**, add 'Philostr.*VA*

4.32' **4**, for '*band* of men' read '*column* of troops' add '**6** *capital city*, Μετοῦλον, ἡ τῶν Ἰαπόδων ἐστὶ κεφαλή App.*Ill.* 54.'

+**κεφᾰληγόνος**, ον, *producing heads*, Nic.*fr.* 74.25 G.-S.

***Κεφαλήν**, ῆνος, ὁ, epith. of Dionysus in Lesbos, Paus. 10.19.3.

**κεφᾰλίζω**, add '*POxy.* 2339.6 (i AD)'

**κεφᾰλικός IV**, delete the section.

***κεφᾰλιόω**, *hit on the head*, *Ev.Marc.* 12.4 (v.l., v. κεφαλαιόω II).

***κεφᾰλιτιόνη**, ἡ, = °κεφαλιτίων, *Cod.Just.* 10.16.1.

***κεφᾰλιτίων**, ωνος, ἡ, (cf. Lat. *capitatio*, also *capitum*, καππητόν) *food* or *fodder allowance* (sts. in cash), *Cod.Just.* 12.37.19.3.

**Κεφαλληνία**, add 'Dor. Κεφαλλᾱνία, *SEG* 23.189 (Argos, iv BC)'

**κεφᾰλοδέσμιον**, after 'τό' insert '*Edict.Diocl.* 28.7, *SB* 9746.31 (iv AD)'

***κεφᾰλόω**, pass. pf. part. κεκεφαλωμένος, *headed, having a head*, Simp. *in Cat.* 187.36.

***κεφᾰλώτιον**, τό, dim. of κεφαλωτόν, *head* of leek or other vegetable, *PRyl.* 627.81, al. (iv AD).

**κεχρημένος**, for 'χράω C VI' read 'χράω (B) C I'

***κεχρημένως**, adv., (χράομαι) w. dat., *in a manner requiring*, ἐπιτεύγμασι Phld.*Po.* 5.27.

**κεωρεῖν**, add 'κ⟨ν⟩εωρεῖν La.; cf. κνέωρον II'

**κῆβος**, add 'cf. *cephos*, Plin.*HN* 8.70'

***κῆδαρ**· πένθος Hsch.

**κηδεμονεύω**, after '*guardian*' insert '*EAM* 19.5-6 (Maced., ii/iii AD)' and before 'παίδων' insert 'spec., *be a tutor*'

**κηδεμονία**, after 'ἡ' insert 'Aeol. **καδ-** *SEG* 32.1243' add '**b** as legal t.t., the position of a *tutor* or *curator*, Modest.*Dig.* 19.2.49 pr., *Cod.Just.* 1.4.30 pr., Just.*Nov.* 72.2; of a *curator* alone, ib. 72.3.'

**κηδεμών**, line 1, after '(κήδω)' insert 'Aeol. **καδ-** *SEG* 32.1243' **I 2**, line 2, after 'X.*Mem.* 2.7.12' insert 'Men.*Dysc.* 737, al.'; lines 5/6, for 'of a legal *guardian*, *POxy.* 888.2 (iii/iv AD)' read 'legal t.t. for a guardian, encompassing *tutor* and *curator*, Modest.*Dig.* 26.6.2 pr., 4, *POxy.* 888.2 (iii/iv AD); *tutor* alone, Modest.*Dig.* 26.6.2.1, Just.*Nov.* 72.2'

**κηδεστής**, add '**4** κᾱδεστάς in Crete, *relative on the mother's side*, *Leg.Gort.* 2.18, 2.29 (v BC).'

**κηδέστρια 2**, for this section read '*mother* (or *daughter*)-*in-law*, *INikaia* 557.7, *Gloss.*'

***κηδευτικόν**, τό, *funeral fund*, *SEG* 30.1535 (Lycia, after AD 152).

**κῆδος I 2 a**, after '(v. infr. II)' insert 'Pi.*O.* 1.107, *N.* 1.54 S.-M.'; add 'Archil. 128.1 W., Pi.*I.* 8.7 S.-M., B. 19.36 S.-M., Thgn. 656 W.' **b**, delete 'cf. (Pi.)*N.* 1.54'

**κηδοσύνη**, add 'sg., *anxious care, solicitude*, Sch.E.*Or.* 1017'

**κήδω**, line 5, pf. κέκηδα, for '(in pres. sense)' read '(in sense of pres. med.)' **II 2**, add '*SEG* 32.1149 (AD 209). **b** *care for* as a *tutor*, Just.*Nov.* 94.1.'

+**κηθάριον**, τό, *cup* or *small basket* from which balls, pebbles, or sim. were poured into a voting-urn, Ar.*V.* 674, cf. Sch.ad loc.

**κηθίς**, add 'Myc. *ka-ti*, a type of jug'

**κήλας**, read 'κηλᾶς'

***κήλεα**, τά, = κᾶλα (v. κᾶλον), κήλεα νηῶν, *ship's timbers*, Hes.*fr.* 314 M.-W. (cj. κήελα).

**κηλέω**, at end after 'in good sense' for Pl. quot. read '*Trag.adesp.* 566 K.-S.'

**Κηληδόνες**, delete 'but harmless'; for 'Pi.*fr.* 53' read 'Pi.*Pae.* 8.71'

***κηλησμός**, ὁ, = κηληθμός, Hdn.*fr.* p. 24 H.

***κηλητής**, ὁ, *beguiler*, Hippon. 79.15 W. (κ[η]λητ[ῆ]).

**κηλικτᾶς**, after lemma insert 'or κηλίκτας'; add 'unless δεικηλίκτας is read'

**κῆλον**, for '*shaft .. arrow*' read 'means by which a god's miraculous power is manifested or deployed'; line 4, after 'Hes.*Th.* 708' insert 'cf. id.*fr.* 204.138 M.-W.'; delete 'metaph.' and line 6 fr. 'also' to the end; add 'perh. of Bacchic madness, Euph. in *Suppl.Hell.* 430 ii 18'

***κηλοτομέω**, *operate on for hernia*, Gal. 1.197.13 (pass.).

**κήλων**, after '(κῆλον)' insert 'Dor. **κάλων**, *AE* 1948/9.136 (Epid., iv BC)' **I**, delete '*PLond.* 1.131ʳ.303 (i AD)'

**κηλώνειον**, line 2, after 'Aen.Tact. 39.7' insert 'Men.*Dysc.* 536 (pl.)'

***κηλωνοστάσιον**, τό, dim. of °κηλωνόστασις, *PBerl.Leihg.* 13.14, *PLond.* 131ʳ.303 (i AD).

***κηλωνόστᾰσις**, εως, ἡ, *support* or *base for a swing-beam* (κήλων I), *SB* 12524 (17 BC).

**κημός II**, add '**3** *funnel-shaped device* on a fire-thrower, Plb. 21.7.1, 4.'

***κηνεῖ**, Dor. adv. *there*, *APAW* 1928(6).6 (Cos, iv BC).

***κηνσιτορεύω**, *serve as censitor*, *SB* 8246 (AD 340), *PColl.Youtie* 78.8 (AD 342).

**κῆνσος**, for '= Lat. *census*' read '*assessment* (for tax purposes)'; after '*Ev.Matt.*' insert '17.25' **II**, delete the section.

***κηνσουάλιος**, ὁ, Lat. *censualis*, *MAMA* 3.29, 206 (Cilicia), Just.*Nov.* 17.8 pr.

**κηνῶ**, (s.v. **κῆνος**), for 'ἐκεῖθεν' read 'ἐκεῖ'

**κήξ**, delete 'and καύηξ .. q.v.)'; add 'transf., καύαξ· πανοῦργος Suid.; cf. λάρος'

**κηπαῖος II 1**, after '*back-door*' insert '*IG* 1³.425.42 (Athens, v BC)'

***κηπεῖον**, τό, *garden*, *SEG* 33.168 B *fr.* a.1, 6 (Athens, iv BC), al.

***κηπεργός**, ὁ, *gardener*, *MAMA* 3.348, 687 (Corycus).

***κηπικός**, ὁ, *gardener*, *BGU* 1151.42, 51 (i BC).

***κηπίων**, ωνος, ὁ, name of a musical nome, Plu. 2.1132d.

+**κηποκόμος**· κηπουρός Hsch.

**κῆπος I**, line 4, for 'also of heaven' read 'prob. the garden of the Hesperides'; line 5, transpose 'cf. Pl.*Smp.* 203b' to follow '*S.fr.* 320 (lyr.)' and for 'eastern' read 'northern' **III**, add 'ὁ ἀφροδίσιος κ., Archipp. 2 D.'

**κηποτάφιον**, for '*tomb in a garden*' read '*garden with a tomb*'

**κηπότᾰφος**, after '(Ilias)' insert '*IUrbRom* 836'; add '*SB* 9801.2 (ii/iii AD)'

***κηπυριστής**, wd. without context in *SEG* 9.824 (Carthage). (Prob. for κηπουρ-; cf. κηπουρός).

**Κήρ**, line 1, after 'acc. Κῆρα' insert 'Dor. Κάρ, epigr. in *BCH* 116.599 (Ambracia, vi/v BC), acc. κᾶρα, Alcm. 88 P.' **II 2**, add 'οὐκ ὀλίγας κῆρας ἐν τῷ βίῳ διώσεαι, φθόνον καὶ ζῆλον καὶ δυσμενίην Democr. 191, 285 D.-K.'

**κῆρ**, line 2, before 'Trag.' insert 'in Pi., B., and'

+**κηρᾰφίς**, ίδος, ἡ, some kind of sea-creature, prob. crustacean, Nic.*Al.* 394; κ.· κάραβος Hsch.

**κηριαπτάριον**, (s.v. **κηριάπτης**), add '*container for wax*, *PVindob.*G 25737 (*ZPE* 64.75; vi/vii AD)'

***κηρίνθη**, ἡ, Lat. *cerintha*, *honeywort*, Verg.*G.* 4.63, Plin.*HN* 21.70 (-*e*).

**κήρινος II 1**, after '*as wax*' insert 'Hippon. 79.5 W.'

+**κηρίολος**, ὁ, Lat. *cereolus*, *wax taper*, *IEphes.* 2227, 3216.5 (ii AD); gloss on κηρίνη φρυαλλίς Hdn.*Philet.* 215 D.

**κηρίον I 2**, after '*AP* 9.190' insert 'Babr.*Prooem.* 18' **II**, add 'Hp.*Aff.* 35'

***κηριτρόφος**, ον, (κήρ) *death-breeding, deadly*, ὄφις Nic.*Th.* 192 (dub.; v.l. κηρο-).

***κηρογρᾰφεῖον**, τό, *implement for writing on wax*, *stylus*, Babylonian Talmud, Kelim, ch. 16 p. 48 (in Hebr. letters).

***κηροδόχος**, ὁ, *honeycomb*, Hsch. s.v. σμῆναι.

**κηρόκλυστος**, add 'perh. Cypr. *ke-ro-ku-lu-su-to-se* *ICS* 208 (addenda)'

**κηροπλάστης**, add '*PCair.Zen.* 782(*a*).64 (iii BC), Plot. 3.8.2'

**κηροπλαστικός**, add 'κηροπλαστικοῖς .. τύποις Procl. *in Prm.* 841.28'

**κηροποιός**, for 'Sch.Ar.*V.* 1075' read 'Sch.Ar.*V.* 1080'

**κηρός**, line 4, after '(*IG*) 14.1320' insert '*Anacreont.* 16.34, 17.25 W.'; after 'writing-tablets' insert 'Hdt. 7.239, *AP* 4.1.10 (Mel.), 7.36 (Eryc.)'

**κηροτρόφος** (A), after 'Nic.*Th.* 192' add '(v.l.)'

***κηρόω** (B), (?κήρ) pass. pf. part. κεκηρωμένη· κεκακωμένη Hsch.

**κήρυγμα**, line 1, after '(κηρύσσω)' insert 'Aeol. κάρυγμα *SEG* 32.1243'

**κηρῡκικός**, add 'ἑκατοστὴ κηρυκικῶν, = κηρύκειον II, *OBodl.* i 41 (ii BC): -κόν, τό, perh. = κηρύκειον II, *Inscr.Délos* 1408*A*ii50 (ii BC)'

***κηρῡκίσκος**, ὁ, perh. *crier*, ephebic official, *IG* 2².1723.7 (Athens, i AD, w. new fr., *SEG* 26.166.18).

**κῆρυξ** line 1, after 'Pi.*N.* 8.1' insert 'also Dor. *IG* 4².1.102 (Epid., iv BC), etc., Cypr. *ka-ru-xe*, alphabetic Κᾶρυξ pers. n., *ICS* 260' **I 4**, add 'τοὺς ἐρινάζοντας τοὺς ἐρινοὺς κήρυκας λέγουσι Hsch. s.v. κήρυκες' at end add 'Myc. *ka-ru-ke* (dat.)'

**κηρύσσω II 1**, lines 2/3, delete 'κ. τινά .. Ar.*Ach.* 748'

**κήρωμα 2**, after '*mud* or *clay*' insert '*mixed with oil*'

**κηρωματιστής**, before 'Sch.Ar.' insert 'suggested as equiv. of παιδοτρίβης'

***κηρωματίτης**, ου, ὁ, prob. the same as κηρωματιστής, *Edict.Diocl.* 7.64 (-είτης), *MAMA* 8.605 (κηρο- lapis).

**κηρών**, for '*bee-hive*' read 'unexpld. deriv. of κηρός' and add '*POxy.* 3412.6 (*c.*AD 360)'

**κήρωσις**, add '**II** *waxing*, a process applied to statues (cf. γάνωσις 1), εἰς τὴν κ. τοῦ ἀνδριάντος *Inscr.Délos* 290.130 (iii BC).'

***κηρωψός**, ὁ, *wax-maker*, *IGLBulg.* 106 (vi AD, cf. °μυροψός).

**κήτειος II**, add 'Ἀλκαῖος δέ φησι τὸν Κήτειον ἀντὶ τοῦ Μυσόν Sch.Od. 11.521 (= Alc. 413 L.-P.)'

**κητώεις**, for 'perh. *full of ravines*' read '*full of sea-creatures*'

**κηφήν**, line 2, for '*vagabond*' read '*parasite*'; line 3, after 'Ar.*V.* 1114' insert 'Timo in *Suppl.Hell.* 840.8' and after 'Pl.*R.* 552c' insert 'κηφήνων βοτάνη ib. 564e'; line 4, delete 'Plu. 2.42a'

***Κηφηνίδης**, name for a rich idler, Phld.*Rh.* 1.236 S.

***κῆφος**, v. °κῆβος.

***κιβαριάτωρ**, ορος, ὁ, fr. Lat. **cibariator*, army official issuing food and wine to the troops, *SB* 9457.2 (ii AD), *OWilck.* 1265 (ii AD; κιβαράτ-), 1142 (iii AD), *SB* 9230.3 (iii AD).

***κιβάριον**, τό, Lat. *cibarium*, *provisions*, *PLond.* 1159.8 (ii AD); pl. *IG* 4²(1).92.10 (Epid., iii/iv AD).

***κιβάριος**, ον, κ. ἄρτος, *household bread*, *IEphes.* 910, 3010, *PPetaus* 45.1 (ii AD); sim. ψωμίων κιβαρίων *PRyl.* 627.71.

κιβδηλιάω, for 'look like adulterated gold' read 'be pale or covered with °κίβδηλις'

*κίβδηλις, εως, ἡ, dross of metals, Hsch. s.v. κιβδηλιῶντας (-ίς cod.), EM 512.53.

κίβδηλος II, add 'κ. φίλος Trag.adesp. 638.17 K.-S.'

κίβισις, add 'Alc. 255.3 L.-P.' and for 'Call.fr. 177' read 'Call.fr. 177.31, 531 Pf.'

*κίβον· ἐνεόν. Πάφιοι Hsch.

κιβώριον, add 'III tomb, MAMA 6.339 (Acmonia; κιβώρεν); prob. to be read in IGLS 684 for κ(αὶ) Ἰβο[υ]ίου.'

κιβωτός, at end after 'opp. κίστη q.v.' insert 'perh. sarcophagus, Explor.arch.de Délos 30.148 (i AD)'

κίγκλος, for 'dabchick, Podiceps ruficollis' read 'wagtail, Motacilla'

κιθάρα I, add '2 the constellation Lyra, Nonn.D. 8.388, 13.359.'

κιθαρίζω, line 6, after 'Nu. 1357' insert 'distd. fr. ψάλλω as using a plectrum, opp. the fingers, SIG 578.18 (Teos, ii BC)'

κιθάρισμα, add '2 = κιθάρισις, SPAW 1934.1040 (tab.defix., Boeot.).'

κιθαρισμός, add 'distd. fr. ψαλμός, SIG 959.10 (Chios, ii/i BC)'

κιθαριστής I, after lemma insert 'non-Att.-Ion. -τάς SEG 35.989 (Knossos, ii BC)'; add 'distd. fr. ψάλτης, SIG 578.15 (Teos, ii BC)'

κίθαρος II, add 'IGC p. 99 B14 (Acraephia, iii/ii BC)'

*κιθαρῳδίστρια, ἡ, woman who plays and sings to the cithara, Heuzey-Daumet Mission Arch. de Macédoine no. 10.

κιθαρῳδός I, after 'as fem.' insert 'Plu. 2.397a, 972f (Glauce)'; after 'Alciphr. 3.33' add 'AP 5.98'

*κιθωνάριον, τό, dim. of κιθών, small tunic, IEphes. 4106.3 (iv AD).

*κίκερροι· ὠχροί. Μακεδόνες Hsch.

*κικεών, ῶνος, ὁ, castor-bean, Ricinus communis, Aq.Thd.Jn. 4.6.

*Κικήλλια, τά, festival at Alexandria (equiv. of the Saturnalia, acc. to Epiph.Const. p. 482 Dindorf), OGI 56.64 (iii BC).

κίκι, after 'κίκιος Hdn.Gr. 2.767' insert 'SB 9667.3 (iii BC), al.'; add '(cf. Hebr. qîqāyôn)'

*κικίννα· τριχόπλαστος Hsch. (κικιννᾶς· τριχοπλάστης La.).

κικιοφόρος, add 'PCair.Zen. 629.3, 5 (iii BC)'

*κικίς, ίδος, ἡ, castor-oil berry, κ. φρυγείσας ἐμβάλλοντες τῷ οἴνῳ Gp. 7.12.9 (v.l. κηκῖδας).

*κικκάμη, ἡ, screech-owl, Gloss.; cf. κικυμωίς.

*κικκάς, perh. = κίκκαβος, Hsch. s.v. οὐ μάλα κικκάς (cf. Stratt. 10).

*κικουργικός, ή, όν, used in making castor-oil, ὄργανον CPap.Jud. 452b.4 (ii AD).

κικυμίς, delete the entry.

*κικυμωίς, ίδος, ἡ, screech-owl, Call.fr. 608 Pf.; also -μηίς (-μωνίς La.) Hsch.; cf. κίκυμος Lat. cicuma.

*Κιλαδηνός, ὁ, cult-title of Asclepius in Thrace, SEG 30.720, 725, 742, etc.

*Κιλικάρχης, ου, ὁ, president of the provincial council of Cilicia, SEG 26.1457.10 (Tarsus, ii/iii AD).

Κιλικαρχία, thus, not Κιλικιαρχία.

Κιλίκιος, add 'neut. pl. Cilician cloths, PMich.inv. 4001 (ZPE 24.84, i/ii AD)'

κιλλακτήρ, add 'Hsch.; cf. pr. n. Κιλλάκτωρ (-κτήρ edd.) AP 5.28, 44'

*κιμαῖος, ὁ, or -ον, τό, mulberry juice, τῶι κιμαίωι Hippon. 78.14 W.; cf. κιμαί, κιμαός.

*Κιμιστηνός, ὁ, title of Zeus, SEG 25.825 (Dacia, ii/iii AD), al.

*κιναίδιος, name of a plant, a fish, a bird, a stone, Cyran. 24.

κιναιδολόγος, add 'Varro ap.Non. p. 79 L.'

κίναιδος I 2, for 'CIG 4926 (Philae)' read 'IPhilae 154'; add 'Plb. 5.37.10'

*κιναῖος, ὁ, (or adj. ος, α, ον?), κ. κάλαμος kind of reed, PRyl. 583.15, 61 (ii BC).

*κιναρᾶς, ὁ, artichoke-seller, ZPE 65.91 (SB 12497.39).

*κιναφεύειν· πανουργεύεσθαι Hsch.

*κινδαύει (κινδάνει cj.)· κινεῖται, κεραΐζει Hsch.; cf. κίνδαξ.

κινδυνεύω 2, w. preps., add 'w. εἰς, Cod.Just. 10.27.2.4, 12.60.7.7; w. περί and acc., ib. 1.40.13; w. ἐπί and dat., Just.Nov. 2.2.1' 4, add 'w. fut. inf., ἡγούμην .. κινδυνεύειν .. πάντων ἐνδεὴς γενήσεσθαι Isoc. 17.6' add '6 to be on trial, D. 30.2, 47.5, etc., Hyp.Lyc. 10, Is. 1.6, etc.'

κίνδυνος 1, line 15, for 'A.Th. 1033' read 'A.Th. 1048' 2, add 'metaph., κ. as a throw of the dice, ἀναρρῖψαι κ.· παρὰ τὸ ἀναρρῖψαι κύβον .. Phryn.PS 29.1' add 'II naut., ἡ ἐν πρῴρᾳ σελίς Hsch.'

κινέω I 1, add '(ellipt.) move (troops, household, etc.), Plb. 2.54.2, 9.18.6; ἐκίνησεν ἐκεῖθεν Ἀβραάμ Lxx Ge. 20.1' add '5 rack off, decant wine, POxy. 1631.17 (iii AD), al., SB 9778.9 (vi AD).' II 5, last line, for 'Alc. 82 (s.v.l.)' read 'Alc. 351 L.-P. (πύκινον codd.), cf. κί]νεις πάντα λί[θον id. 306(14) ii 31, v. λίθος v, πέτρος I'

κίνηθρον, delete the entry.

κινησίγαιος, after 'ον' insert 'earth-shaking, PMag. 4.1356'

κινητήρ, for '= κινητής' read 'shaker, of Poseidon'

*κινητήριον, τό, colloq. wd. for brothel, Eup. 99.27 K.-A.

*κινητιάω, = βινητιάω, Men.Dysc. 462, Vit.Aesop.(G) 32 (but βιν- ibid. W).

κινητικός I 1, add 'b suited to movement, of iambics and trochaic tetrameters, Arist.Po. 1460$^a$1.'

κιννάβαρι, for 'τεγγάβαρι' read 'τιγγάβαρι'

κινναμωμοφόρος, add 'Hld. 9.16, 19'

*κινόφθαλμος, ον, rolling the eyes suggestively, cited in support of reading κινάμυια (for κυνάμυια), Sch.Gen.Il. 21.394.

κινύρομαι 1, after 'lament' insert 'A.fr. 47a.ii 6 R.'

*κιονοκέφαλον, τό, capital of a column, CIJud. 781.5 (Side, iv AD).

*κίρκινος, ὁ, Lat. circinus, pair of compasses, Gal. 1.47.4.

*κιρκίτωρ, ορος, ὁ, Lat. circitor, inspector of frontier posts, SEG 9.356.35 (Ptolemais in Cyrenaica), 32.1554 (Arabia, both vi AD).

κιρροειδής, after 'Apollod.Hist. 214 J.' insert '(v.l. κηρο-)'

*κίρρος· ὀρός (cod. ὄρος), καὶ αἷμα, καὶ πόμα γάλακτος· Λάκωνες Hsch.

κιρρός, add 'b subst. κιρρόν, τό, app. as the colour of gold, Aq.Pr. 8.19, Is. 13.12 (Lxx τὸ χρυσίον τὸ ἄπυρον).'

*κιρρότης, ητος, ἡ, orange colour, Physici 2.295.22.

+κιρσουλκός, ὁ, sharp-pointed hook used in operation for varicocele, ἄγκιστρα τῶν σφόδρα μικροκαμπῶν, καλουμένων δὲ κιρσουλκῶν γαμμοειδῆ κατὰ τὴν καμπήν Orib. 45.18.5, Gal. 14.790.15.

*κίρυλος· ἰχθύς ποιος. καὶ ὀρνέου εἶδος Hsch.; cf. κηρύλος.

*κίρσιον, τό, type of thistle with soft spikes used for treating varicose veins, Dsc. 4.118, Plin.HN 27.61.

*κίρων· ἀδύνατος πρὸς συνουσίαν. καὶ αἰδοίου βλάβη. καὶ ἀπεσκολυμμένος. καὶ κυρίως μὲν ὁ σάτυρος, καὶ ἐντεταμένος, ὁ γυναικίας, καὶ μὴ δυνάμενος χρῆσθαι Hsch.

*κίσευρις, ἡ, some kind of herb, PColl.Youtie 87.8 (vi AD).

κίσηρις, after 'κίσηλις' insert 'AE 1948/9.137 (Epid., iv BC), PSI 1180.34 (ii AD)'; line 3, after 'Choerob.in Theod. 1.319 H.' insert '-ιος, SEG l.c.'

+κισηροειδής, ές, resembling pumice-stone, Thphr.HP 3.7.5; of heavenly bodies, as in some sense porous, Diog.Apoll. in Placit. 2.13.5, 2.20.10, 2.25.10; adv. -δῶς (s.v.l.), Epicur. in Placit. 2.20.14.

κίσθος, line 2, after 'HP 6.1.4, 6.2.1, 2' insert 'Theoc. 5.131'

κίσιρνις, add 'cf. κίσσιρις· εἶδος ὀρνέου, Suid.'

κίσσινος, after 'of ivy' insert 'στέφανοι Pi.Dith. 3.7'

*κισσῖτις, ιδος, ἡ, precious stone with markings resembling ivy-leaves, Plin.HN 37.188.

κισσοφόρος, add '3 of a coin, carrying a device of ivy, Inscr.Délos 1449Aabii23, 1450.102 (both ii BC).'

κισσόφυλλον I 1, after 'ivy-leaf' insert 'τροχίσκ[οι δύο ἔχοντε]ς κιττόφυλλ[α of decoration, SEG 34.95.46 (Athens, ii BC)'

κισσοχαίτης, add 'SEG 32.552.2 (Delphi, iv BC)'

*κισσύφιον, τό, = κισσύβιον, IG $2^2$.1424a.265 (Athens, iv BC).

*κισσώδης (B), ες, decorated with ivy-leaves, Nonn.D. 1.17.

*κίσταρχος, ὁ, official in charge of the κίστη, emendation fr. κτισαρχ-, BCH 14.538 (pl.).

κιστᾱφόρος, add 'as fem., AJA 37.246 (Latium, ii AD)'

*κιστέρνα· λάκκος φρέατος Hsch.; sp. κινστ- Just.Nov. 159 pr. (Lat. cisterna).

*κιστιόκοσμοι, οἱ, app. functionaries who arranged baskets for religious ceremonies, SEG 39.381 (Messene); also to be read in SEG 23.209.2, 210.2 (both Messene, iii BC).

*κιστιπλινθουργός, ὁ, app. maker of some kind of brick, Stud.Pal. 8.909.2 (ZPE 77.186).

*κιστοπλόκιον, τό, basket-maker's shop, PAmst.inv. 62 (Mnemosyne 30.146).

κιστοφόρος I, after 'processions' insert 'Sardis 7(1).195 (i BC)' II, add 'κ. τέτραχμον Inscr.Délos 1443Ai149 (ii BC), SEG 31.983 (ii/i BC)'

*κιτάτωρ, ὁ, Lat. citator, summoner, PHamb. 39.59 (p. 173) (ii AD).

*κιτρειαβολή, ἡ, (= κιτρια-), waving of the ethrog (citron), a ritual act in the Jewish Feast of Tabernacles, SB 9843.9 (ii AD).

*κίτρις, εως, ἡ, citrus-fruit, Al.Le. 23.40.

*κίττανος· ἡ κονιακὴ τίτανος Hsch.

κίχλη II, after 'Epich. 60' insert '(Dor. κίχλᾱ)'; add 'cf. ἴχλα'

κιχλιδιάω, add 'v. χλιδιάω'

*κιχυβεῖν· δυσωπεῖν Hsch.; cf. κίκυμος, κίκκυβος.

κίων, line 3, before 'al.' insert 'Cypr. ta-se-ki-jo-na-u-se, app. τὰς κιjοναυς (acc. pl.) ICS 10a (addenda)' I, add '3 of persons, Νάξου κίονας [Archil.] 325 W.; Τροίας κίονα, of Hector, Pi.O. 2.90.' at end add 'Myc. ki-wo'

κλᾰδᾰρός, for 'δοράτια' read 'δόρατα'

κλᾰδευτήριον II, add 'cut branches, Gloss.'

κλάδιον, add 'as sticks for burning, Edict.Diocl. 14.12'

κλάζω 2, for 'bark' read 'howl' and add 'Nic.Th. 674'

*κλᾳκοφορέω, hold office of κλᾳκοφόρος (of a woman), *SEG* 36.558 (Illyria, iii/ii BC).

κλᾳκτός, read κλαϊκτός; after κλειστός' insert '*closed, locked*'; add 'cf. κλῄζω (B) and forms fr. κλᾴζω s.v. κλείω'

κλᾶμμα, for pres. ref. read 'Alc. 119.11 L.-P.'

κλανίον, add 'also κλάνον or κλανόν, *PHamb.* 10.46 (ii AD), *POsl.* 46.9 (iii AD); cf. χλάνος, °χλανίαι'

*κλαουικουλάριοι, οἱ, Lat. *clavicularii*, officials of some kind, *POxy.* 2050.3 (vi AD), *SB* 2254.3.

*κλαρία· κλήματα ἀμπελόφυλλα Hsch.; cf. κλάριοι.

Κλάριος, before '*Rev.Phil.* 22.268 (iii AD)' insert '*SEG* 33.973 (Notion, iii/ii BC), ib. 26.1288.9 (Klaros, ii AD), al.'; after 'hence' insert 'Κλάρια, τά, name of a festival, *SEG* 4.479 (Colophon, iii BC)'

*κλᾱρογρᾰφέω, v. °κληρο-.

*κλᾱροπᾰληδόν, v. °κληρο-.

*κλάσσα, ἡ, Lat. *classis, fleet*, *BGU* 455.8 (i AD), 2492.7 (ii AD), *PColl. Youtie* 53.7 (ii AD), *IGRom.* 1.623 (Tomi, iii AD), al.

*κλασσικός, ή, όν, Lat. *classicus, naval*, *SEG* 34.1243.24, al. (Abydos, v AD).

*κλαστήρ, ῆρος, ὁ, = κλάστης, *vine-dresser*, *CPR* 10.56.3 (v AD).

κλαστήριον, add '**II** ξύλινα· κλίνης πόδες δύο καὶ κλαστήριον *Inscr.Délos* 1452*A*30 (ii BC), where κλασ- may be for κρασ- v.s.v. II.'

*κλαυδιανός, ὁ, *alloy of copper and lead*, Anon.Alch. 14.6, 24.3.

*Κλαύδιος, α, ον, *Claudian*, λεγ(ιῶνος) ια' Κλαυδίας *SEG* 33.1194 (i/ii AD).

*κλαύθομαι, *cry, weep*, epigr. in *PTeb.* 3.7.

κλαυμῠρίζομαι, for 'κλαυμαριόμενον' read 'κλαυμυριόμενον'

κλαυστικός, after '*mourning*' insert 'τὸ κ. opp. τὸ γελαστικόν, David *in Porph.* 203.19'

κλάω (A) **3**, for '*enfeebled* eyes' read '*drooping eyelids*'

κλειδᾶς, add '*MAMA* 3.689 (κλιδ-, Corycus)'

κλειδοποιός, after lemma insert '*PPetr.* II 39d 15 (iii BC)'; add '*SEG* 31.1517 (sp. κλιδ-; Egypt, Chr.)'

κλειδουχέω **I**, for '*to be her priestess*' read '*to be the guardian of her temple*' **II**, delete the section.

*κλειδουχικός, ή, όν, *of* or *for the* κλειδοῦχος, κλείς *Inscr.Délos* 1442*B*56, 1443*B*i163, 1444*Aa*47 (ii BC).

*κλειδοφορία, ἡ, *office of key-bearer*, τῆς Ἑκάτης *BCH* 51.97 (Panamara).

κλείδωσις, add '*AS* 9.113 (Pisidia)'

κλεῖθρον **II 4**, for 'Κλᾴθροις' read 'Κλάιθροις' and for '*Mnemos.* 42.332' read '*SEG* 33.336'

*κλεινοστατέω, perh. *close the lock-gates*, *PRein.* 117.8 (iii AD); cf. κλεινία (perh. = κλειδ-).

κλείς, line 2, after 'contr. κλεῖς, v. infr. III' insert 'also I 3 (Suppl.)'; line 8, for 'E.*Med.* 212 (anap.)' read 'E.*Med.* 212 (lyr.)' **I 3**, add 'acc. pl. κλεῖς *Inscr.Délos* 1450.199 (ii BC), *POxy.* 729.23 (ii AD), al.' **IV**, for '*rowing bench* in a ship' read '*hooked thole-pin*' at end add '(*κλᾱϝίς; Myc. compd. *ka-ra-wi-po-ro*)'

κλεισιάδες, at end for 'Usu. .. but' read 'written κλισ- *IG* 1³.425.42 (Athens, v BC) and often in codd.'

κλεισούρα, after 'ἡ' insert '(after Latin *clausura*)'

κλειτός, add 'Cypr. *ke-le-wi-to* κλεϝῑτō, *ICS* 402'

κλείω (A) **III 2**, delete the section.

*Κλεοπατρεῖον, τό, *shrine of Cleopatra*, *Bull.Soc.Alex.* 10.27 (i BC), Fraser *Ptol.Alex.* II 379 no. 319.

κλέος, line 2, for 'only nom. and acc. sg. and pl.' read 'usu. nom. or acc. (sg. and pl.); gen. sg. κλέους Antiph. 163.3, Corn.*ND* 14'; add 'cf. Myc. compd. n., as *e-te-wo-ke-re-we-i-jo* (possess. adj.)'

κλέπος, add '*Iamb.adesp.* 56 W.'

κλέπτω, line 6, for 'Ar.*V.* 57' read 'κέκλαμμαι Ar.*V.* 57 (sch.), Ath. 9.409c (cod. A), Choerob. *in Theod.* 2.188 H.'

*κλέψημα, gloss on κοία, Hsch.

κλεψίαμβος, before '*musical instrument*' insert '*stringed*'

*κλεψιγᾰμέω, gloss on κλοτοπεύειν, Hsch.

*κλεψιγᾰμία, ἡ, *illicit love*, Sch.Luc.*DMeretr.* 7.4 p. 280.16 R., Eust. 152.3.

κλεψίγᾰμος, add 'epigr. in Robert *Ét.Anat.* p. 97 (Troas)'

κλεψικοίτης, delete 'Ismenias ap.'

κλεψιμαῖος, adv. -αίως, add '*PMich.*x 581.7 (*ASP* vol. 6, ii AD)'

κλεψιποτέω, for '*drink unfairly*' read '*drink secretly*' and add 'epigr. in *IEphes.* 1062.7 (i AD)'

*κλεψίρρῠτος, ον, *secretly flowing*, κλεψίρρυτον ὕδωρ (?Call. *fr.* 771 Pf.)· τὸ τῆς κλεψύδρας Hsch. (v. κλεψύδρα).

*κλεψοπασχίτης, ὁ, *one who celebrates Easter in secret*, Leont.Byz.*HP* 2.2.10.

κλεψύδρα **III**, after 'Ar.*Av.* 1695 (lyr.)' insert '*Lys.* 913'

κλέω (A), line 8, before 'E.*fr.* 369.7' insert 'prob. in'

+κληδονισμός, ὁ, *soothsaying*, Lxx *De.* 18.14 (v.l.), *Is.* 2.6 (both pl.).

*κλῆδρος, ὁ, = κλήθρα, *alder*, *Gloss.*

κλῄζω (A), line 6, before 'ἔκλεισα' insert 'ἐκλήισσα *Suppl.Hell.* 953.16, Maiist. 38' and after '(Etruria)' insert 'κλῇξα Orph.*A.* 1004'; line 8, after 'Man. 6.571' insert 'aor. 3 pl. ἐκλήϊχθεν Orac.ap.Porph.*Plot.* 22'

κλῄζω (B), delete 'Pass., *AP* 9.62 (Even.)'

*κληΐς, Ion. for κλείς.

κλήθρα, add 'applied to a writing-tablet made of alder, Philet. 10.2'

*κλημάτιον, τό, dim. of κλῆμα I, *PPrag.* 109.4 (iii AD).

*κλημοφόρος, ὁ, = Lat. *vitifer*, i.e. *centurion*, *Gerasa* 219 (ii AD); cf. κλῆμα I 2.

κληρικός, after '*cleric*' insert 'freq. of lower cleric as opposed to bishop'

*κληρογρᾰφέω, Dor. κλᾱρ-, *write* a name *on a lot*, οἱ δὲ ἄρχοντες τὰ ὀνόματα κλαρογραφήσαντες χωρὶς ἑκατέρων ἐμβαλόντες ἐς ὑδρίας *SEG* 30.1119 (Nakone, iii BC).

κληροδοτέω, line 2, after '*Ps.* 77(78).55' insert 'cf. κληροδοτήσει υἱοὺς υἱῶν Lxx *Pr.* 13.22 (v.l.)'

κληρονομέω **III**, add '**b** w. acc., *give an inheritance to*, Ἰσραήλ Lxx *Si.* 46.1.(2).'

κληρονόμος, after 'ὁ' insert '(also ἡ, *SEG* 30.615, ib. 33.939 (of Artemis, Ephesus, ?iii AD), cf. D. 31.11)'; for '*heir*, freq. *the heir in possession*' read 'of an heir, (*designated*) *holder* or *possessor of an estate*'; line 7, after 'Mosch. 3.96' insert 'w. ἐξ, Scaev.*Dig.* 34.4.30.1, *Cod.Just.* 1.2.25 pr.'; add 'ἀπὸ κληρονόμων ποιεῖσθαι *disinherit*, *Cod.Just.* 6.4.4.24; so ἀπὸ κ. ποιεῖν, γράφειν, λέγειν Just.*Nov.* 115.3 pr., 115.3.14, 115.3.15'

*κληροπᾰληδόν, Dor. κλᾱρο-, *by the shaking of lots*, Stesich.*fr.* in *PMGF* 222b.223.

κλῆρος (A) **I 1**, add 'transf., of the dispensation of fate, πρωτότοκος Λούκις, δισσῷ κλήρῳ Θεόδοτος, παρθένος ἡ Δόμνα κλῆρον τρίτον ἐξετέλεσσεν *EG* 4.363 (c.AD 300)' **II 3 a**, add 'spec. *legacy*, opp. inheritance or *fideicommissum*, *Cod.Just.* 1.2.25.1, 1.3.45.1a'

κληρόω, add 'imper. κληρούσθωσαν *SEG* 31.122.25 (Attica, ii AD)'

κλήρωσις, add 'Dor. κλᾱρ-, *SEG* 31.825 (Halaesae, Sicily, ii BC)'

κληρωτήριον **III**, for '*list of citizens* .. lot' read '*device* in the form of a kind of hopper *for drawing lots*, (see *Hesperia* suppl. 1(1937) pp. 198 ff., *IG* 2².972, and so in Arist.*Ath.* ll.cc.)'

κληρωτής, add '*SEG* 26.120 (Athens, i BC)'

*κλήσιος, α, ον, perh. either *fame-bringing* or one *who locks*, as epith. of Artemis, Orph.*H.* 36.7.

κλῆσις **I**, add '**7** *designation as an heir*, *Cod.Just.* 6.4.4.12, 19b.' **IV**, for this section read 'cited in an etym. discussion of Lat. *classis*, D.H. 4.18'

κλῇσις, for 'cf. 7.70' read 'pl., *fastenings*, ἐπειρῶντο λύειν τὰς κλήσεις 7.70'

κλητήρ **II**, for this section read 'generally, *one who calls* or *summons*, esp. as a function of a herald, A.*Supp.* 622, Ἐρινύος κ. id.*Th.* 574, Ion Trag. 49, *Trag.adesp.* 664.33 K.-S.'

κλίμα **II 2**, add '**b** *geographical position*, Hero *Dioptr.* pp. 302, 304 S.' add '**6** *precinct, zone* of a city, Just.*Nov.* 43.1.1.' **IV**, for this section read '= κλιμακτήρ II, *SEG* 35.1060 (=*IG* 14.2431, Gaul, i AD)'

κλῑμᾰκίας, add 'but cf. Κλιμακίας Sicilian pers. n., Cic.*Verr.* 2.2.118'

κλῑμᾰκίς, add 'Amips. 12'

κλῑμακτηρικός, after 'Vett.Val. 148.20' insert 'κ. νόσος id. 289.27'

κλῖμαξ **I**, add '**3** in pl., *terraces*, E.*IT* 1462: sg. as pr. n., of a district, D.S. 19.21.' **IV**, after '*climax*' insert 'figure of speech in which the principal wd. of each clause is caught up and added to the next'

+κλῑνάρχης, ου, ὁ, *ruler of a feast*, Ph. 2.537, *OBodl.* III 372.

*κλῑνέα, ἡ, *small couch*, *PSoterichos* 3.28 (s.v.l., AD 89/90).

*κλίνεον, v. °κλινίον.

κλίνη **I 3**, add '*IEphes.* 3456' **II**, add 'κ. ἀμφικεφάλη *SEG* 29.146 (c.325 BC)'

κλῑνίον, add 'also κλίνεον, pl. κλίνεα *PFlor.* 369.2, [κλίν]ε̣ι̣α̣ *PSoterichos* 1.27, κλει̣νεα 2.22 (i AD)'

κλῑνοπετής, add '*PHels.* 2.22 (ii BC)'

*κλῖνος, τό, archit. term occurring in description of base of a temple, *Inscr.Délos* 500*A*8 (iii BC).

κλιντήρ, for '*couch*' read 'kind of couch, sts. dist. fr. κλίνη' and add 'κλῖναι πέντε: κλιντῆρες πεντήκοντα *SEG* 24.361 (Boeotia, 386/380 BC)'

*κλιντηρία, ἡ, *dining-couch*, Ps.-Callisth. 21.10.

κλιντηρίδιον, for 'foreg.' read 'sq.'

κλίνω, before 'fut.' insert 'Aeol. κλίννω (Choerob. in *An.Ox.* 2.227.19)' **IV 1**, add 'κλίνουσιν .. εὐθὺς ἀπὸ τοῦ στόματος τοῦ κόλπου *Peripl.M.Rubr.* 44'

κλισία, for '*place for lying down* or *reclining*' read '*lean-to* or *temporary shelter*' **I**, combine quots. fr. sections 1 and 2 under this def. **II 3**, delete '*nuptial*' and add '*AP* 5.127.2 (Marc.Arg.), 7.207.7 (Mel.) (pl.)'

κλισιάδες, for 'κλεισιάδες' read '‡κλεισιάδες'

***κλῐσιάρχης**, ου, ὁ, = κλινάρχης, *PMich.*v 246.14, 19 (i AD).

**κλῐ́σιον**, for '*outbuildings round a* κλισία or *herdsman's cot*' read 'prob. *lean-to shed* or *shelter*'

**κλίσις I**, add 'perh. *slope* of a hill, *IRhod.Peraia* 401 (ii BC)'

**κλισμία**, delete the entry.

***κλισμίον**, τό, *couch*, Call.*fr.* 75.16 Pf. (pl.), *IG* 11(2).287*B*20 (Delos, iii BC).

**κλοιός**, add '**4** κ.· μέρος τι τῆς νεώς Hsch.'

***κλοκελέα**, v. °γλυκελαία.

**κλόκιον**, after 'ἀμίς' insert 'Alex.Trall. 11.2 (v.l.)'

**κλοπῐμαῖος**, add '**II** astron. κ. ἡμέραι *epagomenal* days, cod. Vat.Gr. 1058.275ᵛ22, al.'

**κλουβίον**, add 'also **χλου-**, *PFay.* 72.4, *PTeb.* 413.14 (ii/iii AD); **χλι-**, *SB* 7365.16, al. (AD 104)'

**κλῠ́μενος**, add 'Myc. *ku-ru-me-no*, pers. n.'

**κλυντήρ**, for '*IGRom.* 1.730' read '*IGBulg.* 903' and after 'Philippopolis' insert 'ii AD'

***κλῠσιδρομάς**, άδος, fem. adj. *drenching as it speeds along*, αὔρα Tim.*Pers.* 92 (81 P.).

***κλυστηρίζω**, *apply a clyster*, in Lat., Cael.Aur.*Acut.* 3.4, Veg.*Vet.* 2.15.5 (both v AD).

***κλυστικός**, ή, όν, *used for clyster pipes*, Paul.Aeg. 7.3 (219.19 H.).

**κλῠτοεργός**, add 'also -γής, γέος (gen.), epigr. in *SEG* 37.1537 (Arabia, c.AD 400)'

***κλῠτοηχής**, ές, *of resounding fame*, Ph.Epic. in *Suppl.Hell.* 681.2.

**κλῠτός 2**, line 3, after '(Od.) 15.472' insert 'ὄρθρος Ibyc. 22(*b*) P.'; penultimate line, after 'Pi.*O.* 8.52' insert 'v. δαιτοκλυτός'

**κλῠτότοξος**, add 'hymn in *SEG* 39.355 (Epidaurus, Rom.imp.)'

**κλῠτόφημος**, after '*fame*' insert 'epigr. in *IHistriae* 1.171 (iv BC; -φαμ-)'

***κλυτωνος**, unkn. wd., perh. an error for *κλυτόνηος, *SB* 10769.99 (iii/iv AD).

**κλωγμός II**, add 'in uncertain sense, Cratin. 171.15 K.-A.'

**κλώθω II**, for this section read 'intr., in uncertain sense, ἀμφοῖιν κλώθοντος ἐν ἀρπέζῃσιν ἐρίνου Nic.*Th.* 647, cf. *Al.* 93, 528'

⁺**κλῶνος**, ὁ, *bundle, bunch*, or sim., in quot., of beans, *Edict.Diocl.* 6.33 (in Latin, *fascis*); cf. *ramus, Gloss.*

**κλῶσμα 1** and **2**, combine these sections under def. '*thread*'

**κλωστήρ I**, for this section read '*distaff*, Theoc. 24.70' **II 1**, add 'A.R. 4.1062'

**κλωστήριον**, add 'Suid. s.v. νῆτρον'

**κλωστός**, after '*spun*' insert 'E.*Tr.* 537' **2**, add 'τὸ κ. *the thread of fate*, *BCH* 112.451 no. 4.8 (Maced.)'

***Κνᾱκᾰλησία**, ἡ, epith. of Artemis at Caphyae in Arcadia, Paus. 8.23.3; cf. κνῆκος.

***Κνᾱκεᾶτις**, ιδος, ἡ, epith. of Artemis at Tegea, Paus. 8.53.11; cf. κνῆκος.

**κναπ-, καφ-, κναψ-**, see also γναπ-, etc.

**κνάπτω 1**, add '*dress* leather, οἷον ὅτε .. γναπτόμενοι μυδόωσιν ὑπ' ἀρβήλοισι λάθαργοι Nic.*Th.* 423'

*[κ]ναφαλλοϋφάντης, v. °[γ]ναφ-.

**κνᾰφεύς**, add 'Myc. *ka-na-pe-u*'

**κνᾰφικός**, line 2, after 's.v. κνάφος' insert 'κναφικός, ὁ, *fuller*, *PColl. Youtie* 83.8 (AD 353)'; line 3, after 'sc. ἐργασία' insert 'or τέχνη' and after '(i AD)' add 'cf. *GDI* 1904.6 (Delphi, ii BC)'

**κνᾰ́φος**, delete '**II** *carding-comb*' and append following part of article to section 1.

**κνάψις**, form γνάψις, add '*SB* 9834b.3 (iv AD)'

**κνέφαλλον**, add 'κνάφαλλον also in Hsch. s.v. γνάφαλλον'

**κνέφας**, after 'τό' insert 'ep. gen. κνέφαος Od. 18.370'; line 4, delete '(only in nom. and acc.)' **2**, add 'ὑπὸ κνέφας A.R. 2.1032'

**κνήδιον**, for 'κνίδια .. *nettle-seeds*' read 'Κνίδια, perh. *wine-jars*, v. Κνίδιος III'

**κνηκίς**, for 'Call.*fr.anon.* 36' read '*Suppl.Hell.* 1084, Call.*fr.* 238.17 Pf.'

**κνῆκος**, add 'Myc. *ka-na-ko*'

***κνηκουργός**, ὁ, *maker of oil from the plant* κνῆκος, *PMed.*inv. 68.38 R. ii 11 (*Aegyptus* 69.24, 13 BC/AD 32).

**κνήμη II**, after 'Eust. 598.4' insert 'cf. ὀκτάκνημος' add '**III** καὶ ὁδοὶ ἀνώμαλοι καὶ ἀναντώδεις Hsch. s.v. κνῆμαι.'

**κνημίδιον**, add 'sg., *IGLS* 1292 (Laodicea ad mare)'

**κνημίον**, delete the entry.

**κνημίς I**, add 'X.*An.* 1.2.16, al., Arist.*HA* 548ᵇ2'

**κνησμονή**, add '**2** transf., *annoyance*, Sch.E.*Hipp.* 14.'

**κνησμός**, add 'Hp.*Aff.* 35'

**κνηστήρ I**, for '*scraping-knife*' read '*grater*'

**κνήστριον**, delete 'ἰχθύων .. (Geronth.)'

**κνῆστρον**, for '(expl. .. 4.172' read '**b** = θυμελαία, prob. *Daphne Cnidium*, Dsc. 4.172. **2** *grater*, *Edict.Diocl.* 13.9, 10, Erot.'

***κνηστώδης**, ες, *grated*, ζειαὶ κνηστώδεις, ὁ κατειργασμένος σῖτος Hsch. s.v. πύρνοι.

***κνήσων**, dub. sens., ἐν τῷ κιβωτίῳ κνησῶνας τρεῖς *Inscr.Délos* 1444*Aa*37 (ii BC).

***κνίδειος**, α, ον, *of the nettle*, Theognost.*Can.* 54.

**Κνίδιος III**, after 'of wine' insert '*Pland.* 8.6 (ii AD)'; add 'hence perh. *wine-jars*, *Stud.Pal.* 22.75.7, 16 (iii AD), v. °κνήδιον; jar of perfumed oil, *POxy.* 3748.15 (AD 319)' **IV**, delete the section. add 'Myc. *ki-ni-di-ja* (fem.)'

**κνῑδόσπερμα**, add 'Paul.Aeg. 7.17.14 (350.24 H., 351.2 H.)'

**κνίζω I 2**, for this section read 'dub. reading in passage where context requires *chop up, grate* or sim., Thphr.*HP* 9.20.4 (perh. κνησθεῖσα)' **II**, for '*tickle*' read '*scrape* or *scratch* with the fingernails (without necessarily breaking the surface)' **2**, for '*chafe, tease*' read '*bother, irritate*' **b**, after '*provoke*' insert 'an emotion'

**κνῑπολόγος**, after 'ὁ' insert 'ἡ'; for pres. def. read '*common treecreeper*'; add 'κ. πιπώ Ant.Lib. 14.3'

**κνῑσάω**, delete '(never τὰς ἀγυιάς)' and add 'Orac.ap.D. 43.66, Luc.*Prom.* 19'; delete 'Orac.ap.' before 'D. 21.51'

***κνῑσευτήρ**, ῆρος, ὁ, priest who carried out burnt sacrifices, *ABSA* 42.206 (Cyprus).

**κνίσμα**, for 'in pl. *scratches*' read '*scratch*' and add '*AP* 5.157 (Mel.)'; for 'of lovers' *quarrels*' read 'of scratching, tickling, etc., used in love-play' and add '*AP* 12.209 (Strat.)' add '**b** *a small fragment broken off, chip, splinter* or sim., κ. πυρὸς θραύσας *AP* 12.82 (Mel.).'

***κνισμώδης**, ες, *marked with scratches*, Procl.CP *Hom.* 26.11.

**κνίψ**, line 2, delete 'and devour the fig-insect (ψήν)'

***κνοή**, ἡ, v. °κνόος.

⁺**κνόος**, ὁ, κνοῦς· ὁ ἐκ τοῦ ἄξονος ἦχος. λέγεται δὲ καὶ κνοή. καὶ ὁ τῶν ποδῶν ψόφος, ὡς Αἰσχύλος Σφιγγί (*fr.* 237 R.) Hsch.; perh. also (sp. χνόος) ἔτι χνόον .. ἄξονος .. ἵππος ἔναυλος ἔχει Call.*fr.* 384.5 Pf.

***κνούφιον**, τό, substance named after the Egyptian god Κνοῦφις, Anon.Alch. 9.14.

**κνύζα** (B), delete '(pl.)' and '(sg.)'

**κνύζα** (C), after 'Anacr.' insert '(432 P. κνυζή)'; delete 'cf. κνυζός'

**κνυζός II**, delete the section.

**κνωδάκιον**, add '*PUG* inv. 1164 (*ZPE* 58.92, iii AD)'

**κνώσσω**, for 'Simon. 37.6' read 'Simon. 38.9 P. (κνωσσ-, v.l.)'

***κοάζω**, of frogs, *croak*, Aesop. 307 H.

***κόαμος**· ὁ βασιλεύς Theognost.*Can.* 56 A.

***κοβάθια**, v. κωβάθια.

***κόβαθρον**, τό, = κύβεθρον, *PCol.* 188.9 (AD 320).

***κοβᾰ́λευμα**, ατος, τό, = κοβαλίκευμα, *Et.Gen.* in Miller *Mélanges* 191.

***κοβᾱλικεύομαι**, *cheat by tricks*, prob. in Ar.*Eq.* 270 (codd. ἐκκοβ-).

***κοβᾱλικός**, ή, όν, *knavish, scoundrelly*, ἀργυρίοισι κοβαλικοῖσι πεισθείς Timocr. 727.6 P.

**κόβᾱλος I**, add 'cf. κόβαλοι· δαίμονες .. περὶ τὸν Διόνυσον, Sch.Ar.*Pl.* 279, interpol. in Harp.'

***κογκῠλίδιον**, v. °γογγ-.

***κογνατικός**, ή, ον, *of* or *involving blood-relations* (*cognati*), Just.*Nov.* 84 pr.

***κογνᾶτος**, ὁ, Lat. *cognatus, blood-relation*, Just.*Nov.* 115.3.14.

**κόγχη I**, add 'applied to the pearl-oyster, Arr.*Ind.* 8.11' **II**, add '**3** *pudendum muliebre*, Sophr. 25, 26, cf. κογχυλαγόνες, and Plaut.*Rud.* 704.'

***κόγχισμα**, ατος, τό, kind of vessel or container, *POxy.* 2729.29, 34 (iv AD).

**κόγχος**, after 'ἡ' insert 'Epich. 42.8, 43'; line 2, after 'Crates Theb. 7' insert 'Call.*Epigr.* 5.1 Pf., Hedyle ap.Ath. 297b' **II**, add '**6** dub. sens., building inscr., *IAskl.Epid.* 52 B60 (iv BC, gen. pl. or fr. κόγχη).'

***κογχῠλεύς**, έως, ὁ, *purple-worker* (or *purple-fisher*), *MAMA* 3.309, al. (Corycus), κογχυλέως λιμένο(ς) Ἀστρονόης *ITyr* 8, al.

**κογχῠλευτής**, add '*ITyr* 7, al.'

***κογχῠλεύω**, app. *extract purple dye*, Hsch. (κογκ- cod.).

⁺**κογχῠ́λη**, ἡ, = κόγχη; spec. *murex*, v.l. in Ph. 1.536, *AP* 9.214 (Leo Phil.); cf. κογχύλαι· κηκῖδες Hsch.

**κογχῠ́λιον 1**, after 'Epich. 42.1' insert '(ῡ, cf. Lat. *conchȳlia*)'

***κογχῠλοκόπος**, ὁ, *producer of purple dye*, *ITyr* 72, 95 (abbreviated).

***κογχῠλοπλῠτής**, οῦ, ὁ, *purple-dyer*, *ITyr* 28, 198.

**κογχωτός**, for '*having a boss*' read '*having a boss* or *ornamentation in the form of a shell*' and add '*Inscr.Délos* 1444*Aa*6, 11 (ii BC)'

**κοδομεύς**, delete 'perh. to be read in *OStrassb.* etc.'

**Κόδρος**, add 'cf. Myc. *ko-do-ro*, pers. n.'

**κοδῠ́μᾱλον**, for 'Alcm. 90' read 'Alcm. 100 P.' and for 'καρύαι Περσικαί' read 'κάρυα Περσικά' add '**II** οἱ δὲ ἄνθους εἶδος, οἱ δὲ κόσμος περιτραχήλιος Hsch.'

⁺**κόθουρος**, ον, dub. sens., epith. of drones (κηφῆνες), Hes.*Op.* 304.

**κοία I**, read 'expld. by Hsch., etc., as *balls* or *stones*, κοίας ἐκ χειρῶν σκόπελον μέτα ῥιπτάζουσιν Antim. 89 Wy.'

***κοιαίστωρ**, ορος, ὁ, v. °κουαίστωρ.

***κοίας·** στρογγύλος Theognost.*Can.* 21.

***κοϊκᾶς**, ὁ, *maker of baskets from palm-leaves, PLaur.* 24 (*ZPE* 35.111-2, iii AD); cf. κοΐξ.

***κοΐκιον**, τό, *basket, PWash.Univ.* 30.6, *POsl.* 159.13 (both iii AD); cf. κοΐξ.

**κοιλαίνω I**, after 'Opp.*H.* 4.19' insert 'ἕλκος Numen. in *Suppl.Hell.* 590' add '**b** *open the recesses of*, μή ποτε κοιλήνῃς Παφίῃ νόον *AP* 9.443 (Paul.Sil.).'

**κοίλασμα**, after '*hollow*' insert 'of a pit hollowed out as trap'

**κοιλία II 4**, add 'meton., *offspring, Orac.Tiburt.* 148' **III**, add 'of a gulf, *Peripl.M.Rubr.* 40'

***κοιλίας**, gloss on κοστίας, Hsch.

**κοιλιολῦσία**, for '*looseness* .. medicine' read '*emptying of the bowels*, περὶ κ. γίνεσθαι'

**κοιλιολῦτέω**, for '*suffer from looseness of the bowels*' read '*empty one's bowels*'

***κοιλίον**, τό, perh. = κοῖλον (v. κοῖλος IV 1), point in a boundary, κατὰ τὸ κ. *Inscr.Cret.* 1.v 19*B*23 (Arcades, i BC).

***κοιλιόστροφος**, ον, *colicky*, Sch.Nic.*Al.* 597a Ge.

**κοῖλος 1**, line 16, after 'Hero *Bel.* 75.15)' insert '*curved*, perh. *hollow*, κλῇθρα S.*OT* 1262; σταθμὰ θυράων Theoc. 24.15'; line 18, before 'Ael.' insert '*Inscr.Délos* 1417*A*i102 (ii BC)' **III 2**, delete the section.

**κοιλόσταθμον**, add '*PMich.Zen.* 38.9, 20 (iii BC)'

**κοιλόσταθμος**, for '*with coffered ceilings, panelled*' read '*with curved or hollow supports*, precise signf. uncertain, but app. of wood'; after '*Hg.* 1.4' insert '*with wooden frames*' and after 'p. 143 (iii BC)' insert '*PCair.Zen.* 764.3 (iii BC)'; line 3, for '*coffered ceiling*' read '*curved* or *hollow door-jamb*'

***κοιλουργός**, ὁ, *maker of hollow ware*, perh. of gold and silver, *PSAAthen.* 1.1 (iii BC); < κοϝιλοϝοργός, Myc. *ko-wi-ro-wo-ko.*

**κοίλωμα I 1**, add 'of the black cavity or cup in the infundibulum of the teeth of horses, *Gp.* 16.1.16'

**κοιμάω**, line 2, after 'Med.' insert 'imper. κοιμοῦ *CIJud.* 1.281, cf. 150'; line 6, for 'Aeschrio 8.2' read '*AP* 7.345' **II 3**, add 'κοιμοῦ *CIJud.* 1.281 (κομοῦ ib. 150)'

**κοίμησις II**, add '**2** *laying to rest*, or *resting-place* i.e. tomb, κύμεσις Εὐφημίας δούλης Mitchell *N.Galatia* 468; κύμησις ib. 469.'

***κοιμητηρία**, ἡ, = κοιμητήριον, *EM* 550.56.

**+κοιμητήριον**, τό, *dormitory* for performing incubation in a temple, *SEG* 31.416 (Oropus, iv BC), Dosiad.ap.Ath. 4.143c. **II** *burial-place, SEG* 26.434, etc., 29.250, 31.286 (all Chr.); sp. κυμ- *SEG* 31.263, ib. 34.238 (-ιν), *INikaia* 284.

***κοίμητρον**, τό, *bed*, Sm.*Jd.* 4.18.

***κοινάζω**, *participate* in, w. gen. *SEG* 37.340.4 (Mantinea, iv BC).

**κοινᾱνέω**, add '*SEG* 12.371.24 (Thelphoussan inscr. at Cos, iii BC)'

**κοινεῖον II**, after '*common fund*' insert '*BCH* 78.322.17 (Ceos, iii BC)'

**κοινεών**, for '= κοινωνός' read 'form of κοινών'

***κοινοβίωσις**, εως, ἡ, *cohabitation, PDura* 32.10 (AD 254).

**κοινόβουλος II**, for '*IGRom.* 3.7' read '*TAM* 4(1).42' and add '*SEG* 30.1534 (Lycia, after AD 152)'

***κοινογρᾰφέω**, *write* a word *in the ordinary way*, Eust. 1553.28 (pass.).

**κοινοδῑκιον 2**, for '*PMagd.* 21.12, 23.9' read '*PEnteux.* 65.19, al.' and delete 'abbrev.'

***κοινόθᾱκος**, ον, perh. epith. of an ancestral tomb, *offering a common burial-place*, S.*fr.* 212.6.

***κοινοπᾰ́τωρ**, ορος, ὁ, ἡ, *having the same father*, Philicus in *Suppl.Hell.* 680.27.

**κοινοπρᾱγία**, after lemma insert '*SEG* 23.547.6 (Crete, iii BC)'

**κοινός I**, line 21, after 'Pl.*Mx.* 241c, etc.' insert 'ἐν Περγάμῳ κοινὸν Ἀσίας (sc. ἀγῶνα) *SEG* 34.1316.16 (Xanthos, i AD)'; line 23, before 'Iamb.' insert 'D.H.*Th.* 3' **IV 3**, *neutral*, add 'Isoc. 14.28'

**κοινοτᾰ́φης**, for '*Ath.Mitt.* 10.405' read '*CEG* 563'

**κοινών**, add '*accomplice*, sp. κονῶνα (acc.) *PVindob.Salomons* 15.12 (v/vi AD)'

**κοινωνέω I 2 a**, add 'rarely w. dat., ἐκοινώνησαν τῇ στρατείᾳ Sch.A Il. 2.339' **4**, add 'w. ἐν, ἐν τῇ ἁγιωτάτῃ ἐκκλησίᾳ κοινωνεῖν Just.*Nov.* 115.3.14'

***κοινωνησία**, ἡ, = κοινώνησις 2, *EA* 8.29 (Ephesus, Rom.imp.).

**κοινωνία I 1**, add 'ἀπὸ τῆς Ζήν[ω]νος κοινωνί[ας *Kafizin* 119' **2**, add 'ἐπὶ προεδρίᾳ καὶ κοινωνίᾳ θυσιῶν *SEG* 30.82.14 (Athens, c.AD 230)'

**κοινωνιμαῖος**, add 'κοινωνιμέων κτημάτων *POxy.* 2954.15 (iii AD)'

**κοινωνός 2**, add 'κοινωνοὶ οἱ περὶ Με[να]νδρον *SEG* 24.976 (Thrace, ii/iii AD)'

**κόϊξ 2**, add 'μικρὸν .. κόϊκα ἄρτων *PMich.*III 212 (ii/iii AD), al.'

**κοιόλης**, add 'cf. **κοίολις**· ἱερεύς, Theognost.*Can.* 21'

**κοιρᾰνία**, after '*sovereignty*' insert 'ἐπὶ τὰν κ[λειτὰ]ν κ. ὕπατον *dignity of the consulship*, (cf. ὕπατος III 1 at end), epigr. in *IG* 9(2).1135.8 (Demetrias, i AD)'

***κοιρανίδες**, αἱ, v. °κυρανίδες.

***κοιρᾰνόμοιρος**, ὁ, *Lord of Fate, PMag.* 4.1360.

**κοίρᾰνος 2**, add 'of Hades, νυκτὸς ἀΐδνᾶς ἀεργηλοῖό θ' ὕπνου κοίρανος *Lyr.adesp.* 78 P.; κώμου καὶ .. παννυχίδος *AP* 7.31 (Diosc.); ὕμνων (of Homer) ib. 213 (Arch.)'; after 'Orph.*fr.* 38' add '*IG* 9(1).270'

***κοισυροῦται**· κοσμεῖται Theognost.*Can.* 21; κεκοισυρωμένη· .. περιεσταλμένη Hsch.; cf. ἐγκοισυρόομαι.

**κοιτάριον**, after 'dim. of κοίτη' insert '*small couch, PUniv.Giss.* 20.35 (ii AD)'

**κοιτασμός**, after '*folding*' insert 'προβάτων *POsl.* 33.10, *PMich.*II 121ʳ iii 14 (both i AD)'

**κοίτη**, line 1, for '= κοῖτος 1' read '*bed*'

**κοῖτος I** and **II**, combine these sections under def. '*sleep, going to rest*' add (new) '**II** *resting-place*, of a sarcophagus, Λοχιγοῦ κοῖτος *SEG* 32.1515.'

**κοιτών**, line 4, after '*IG* 14.2143, al.' insert 'Θεοῦ Τ[ί]του ἐπὶ κοιτῶνος *IEphes.* 852 (c.AD 100)' **2**, add '*MAMA* 7.323 (Lycaonia), etc.'

***κοιτωνάριον**, τό, *resting-place, PPrincet.*inv. AM 8963.1 (*Tyche* 3.29).

**κόκκᾰλος**, add '*PLund* 11.1.19 (ii AD)'

***κοκκῐνόω**, *dye scarlet*, Hsch. s.v. ἠρυθροδάνωται.

**κοκκίζω**, for 'A.*fr.* 363, Ar.*fr.* 610' read 'A.*fr.* 363 R. (= Ar.*fr.* 623 K.-A.)'

**κόκκος**, after 'ὁ' insert '(ἡ, Lxx *Si.* 45.10)' **I 1**, add 'of mustard, *Ev.Matt.* 13.31' **II 1**, for '*berry (gall) of kermes oak*' read '*kermes* (thought to be a berry produced by the kermes oak)'; add '*scarlet thread*, κεκλωσμένῃ κόκκῳ, ἔργῳ τεχνίτου Lxx *Si.* 45.10'

***κοκκοῦσα**· συκῆ Hsch.

***κοκκοφάδιον**, τό, perh. *hoopoe, PMag.* 7.411.

***κόκκῡγος**, ὁ, = κόκκυξ, Alc. 416 L.-P.

**κόκκυξ I**, line 5, after 'Hsch.' insert '*AB* 1.27.24' **II**, add '*SEG* 32.450 (Boeotia, iii/ii BC)' **III**, for this section read '*early fruit*, κόκκυγας ἐρινάδος Nic.*Th.* 854' **V**, for this section read 'part of the συνωμία of an ass, κατάγραφος κ. (s.v.l.) *Hippiatr.* 14.3; of a horse, ib. 26.9, 115.3'

***κοκκώ**, v. °κωκώ.

***κόκκωρα**, τά, perh. *pomegranate*, Semus 3.

**κολάζω**, line 2, after 'Pl.*Lg.* 714d, etc.' insert 'κολῶ Hsch.'

***Κολαινιασταί**, οἱ, members of a cult-association of Artemis, *MDAI(A)* 67.165 (Attica, ii/iii AD), v. Κολαινίς.

***κολᾰκευμάτιον**, τό, dim. of κολάκευμα, Hsch. s.v. κοσκυλματίοις.

***κολανδιοφωντα**, τά, some kind of Indian ships, *Peripl.M.Rubr.* 60.

**κόλαξ I 1**, add 'ψόφῳ κ. ποιμένων S.*Ichn.* 154 (= 160 R.)'

**κολάπτω 2**, add 'med., *have engraved*, τὸ δὲ ἀλίασμα τόδε κολαψάμενοι οἱ ἄρχοντες ἐς χάλκωμα *SEG* 30.1119 (Entella, iii BC)'

***κολᾰ́σιμος**, η, ον, *deserving of punishment, Suppl.Mag.* 62.5 (v/vi AD), *PMich.*inv. 490 (*ZPE* 84.41, vi AD).

**κόλασις 2**, add '**b** *that which brings about punishment*, Lxx *Ez.* 14.4, al.'

**κολασμός**, after '= κόλασις' insert 'Call.*fr.* 114.12 Pf.'

**+κολεάζω**, *sheathe* a sword; transf., of sexual intercourse, κολεάζοντες· ὠθοῦντες ‹εἰς› κολεὸν[τες] περαίνοντες Hsch.

***κολεασμός**· τὸ περαίνεσθαι Hsch., v. °κολεάζω.

***κολέντερον**, τό, = Lat. *longao* (*longavo*), kind of sausage, *Gloss.* (perh. for *κωλέντερον).

**κολεός**, before 'ὁ' insert '(**κουλεός** Sch.E.*Ph.* 276, al.)' **I 2**, for this section read '*vagina*, Hsch. s.v. κολεάζοντες, v. °κολεάζω (also in mod. Gk.)'

***κολεός** (B), v. °κολιός.

**κολετράω**, add 'Hsch., s.v. κολετρῶσι'

**κολίανδρον**, for 'Sch.Ar.*Eq.* 679' read 'Sch.Ar.*Eq.* 682b'; add 'Al.*Nu.* 11.7, *Ex.* 16.31'

***κολιάσαι**· ὀρχήσασθαι Hsch., perh. also impf. ἐκολίαζε (written ϵϝολιαδη) *IG* 12 suppl. 244 (Syros, vi BC; unless obsc., cf. °κολεάζω).

***κόλιξ**, ικος, ἡ, v. °κύλιξ.

**κολιός**, add 'κολεοί *Edict.Diocl.* 4.41A, mistransl. Lat. *coturnices* (ὄρτυγες ib. 4.41), perh. for κολοιοί'

***κολίσκιον**, τό, perh. dim. of καυλίσκος, some kind of vegetable, *SEG* 7.434 (Dura).

**κόλλα 1**, after 'Hdt. 2.86' insert 'E.*fr.* 472.7 (anap.)' and add '*PKöln* 52.12,59 (AD 263)' add '**b** fig., ἁρμονίης κόλλησιν Emp. 96 D.-K.; δεσμοῦ τινος ἢ κόλλης τάξιν D.H.*Dem.* 40; Δημάδης κόλλαν [ὠνόμαζε] τὰ θεωρικὰ τῆς δημοκρατίας Plu. 2.1011b.'

**κολλάριον**, add '*PSI* 1116.8 (ii AD)'

**κολλάω I 1**, line 2, before 'ἐπιστύλια' insert '*attach firmly, join by mortising*, χσύλα ἐπιστύλια .. ἐγ δυοῖν κεκολλεμένον *IG* 1³.386 ii 107' **II**, lines 8/9, after '*Act.Ap.* 5.13' insert '*Vit.Aesop.*(G) 30' **III**, after 'Pi.*O.* 5.13' insert 'ἀντίθετα Plu. 2.350d'

***κολλεκτάριος**, ὁ, Lat. *collectarius, banker, PStrassb.* 35.11 (?vi AD).

**κόλλημα I**, line 3, after 'Antiph. 162' insert '*fastening*, ἀνάκλιντρα ἱμαντοδέτοις κολλήμασιν ἐπτυγμένα Ps.-Callisth. 120.2 K.'; add 'also *column* of writing, prob. in pap. in *APF* 4.97.3, al. (i AD), *PIand.* 7 ii 2, al. (ii/iii AD), see Youtie *Scriptiunculae* II 718'

**κόλλησις**, after lemma insert 'Dor. [κ]όλλᾱσις, *SEG* 24.277B.51 (Epid., iv BC)' add '**III** name for *holy vervain, Verbina supina*, περιστερεὼν ὕπτιος Ps.-Dsc. 4.60.'

⁺**κολλητίων**, ωνος, ὁ, perh. *filing clerk* employed by military police, *PFlor.* 91.27 (rest., ii AD), *POxy.* 1100.19 (AD 206), *BGU* 23.5, 6 (AD 207), *OBodl.* ii 1934.7 (iii AD).

**κολλόροβον I**, after '*crook*' insert 'gloss on καλαῦροψ, Sch.A.R. 4.974 (v.l.)' **I**, add '**2** *harpoon* or *gaff* for catching fish, *POxy.* 2234.15 (i AD).'

**κολλούρα**, omit '(?)' and add 'Sm. 1*Ki.* 10.3'; after 'cf. κολλύρα' add 'mod. Gk. κουλούρα, κουλούρι'

*****κολλουρίδιον**, τό, dim. of κολλούρα, *PPalau Rib.*inv. 66 (*APF* 23.272, i AD).

**κόλλοψ**, for '**II 2** metaph.' read '**III** (prob. a different word)'

*****κολλῠβίζω**, *cut into small pieces*, Suid. s.v. κολλάβους.

**κολλῠβιστής**, delete '*small*' and '*PPetr.* 3 p. 173 (prob. l.)' and substitute '*PTeb.* 1079.49 (iii/ii BC), *BGU* 1303.18 (i BC)'

*****κολλῡριακός**, ή, όν, *used in eye-salves*, Aët. 7.106 (369.6 O.).

*****Κολλυριών**, ὁ, month name, *SEG* 36.982c (Iasos, v BC).

**κολλώδης**, after 'Pl.*Cra.* 427b' insert 'Clearch.Com. 2.1 K.-A. (neut. pl. subst.), Hp.*Carn.* 3, 4, al.'

*****κολοβᾰφής**, v. ‡χολοβαφής.

*****κολοβᾰ́φινος**, v. ‡χολοβάφινος.

**κολοβιομαφόριον**, add '*PKöln Ketouba* line 17'

*****κολοβίων**, ωνος, ὁ, = κολόβιον 1, Sch.Aeschin. 1.131 S.

**κολοβόρῑνος**, delete the entry (read κολοβάφινος).

**κολοβός 2**, before 'ὄνος κ.' insert 'of animals, perh. spec. *with teeth worn away* (as an indication of age) (cf. *CPR* 6.20-1, 25), or more generally *docked* or *stunted*'

**κολοβοῦρος**, add 'as a pers. n., Κολοβούρῳ (dat.) *BGU* 2348.2 (iii AD)'

*****κολοβοφυής**, ές, *low-growing*, of grass for hay, *BGU* 2198.11 (vi AD).

*****κολοδιδός**, ή, όν, *yellow*, Anon.Alch. 330.13.

**κολοιάρχης**, read κολοίαρχος.

*****κολοιδορόω**, 3 sg. -οῖ, = ταράσσει, Theognost.*Can.* 56 A. (-δωροῖ codd.).

*****κολοίσιππος**, ὁ, prob. non-Hellenic wd. in a cult inscr., *Inscr.Cret.* 1.v 23.8 (Arcades, ii AD).

**κολοιτία I**, add 'cf. Lat. *colutea* (n. pl.), its fruit, Plaut.*Per.* 87 (cj.)'

**κολοίφρυξ**, after 'ἀλεκτρυών' insert 'καὶ ὄρος Βοιωτίας'

*****κολοκυνθᾰρῠ́ταινα**, ή, *scoop* or *dipper made of a gourd*, *Suppl.Hell.* 960.7.

**κόλον II**, add 'cf. κωλικός'

*****κολοός**, perh. = κολοιός, Hdn.*fr.* p. 17 H.

**κολοσσιαῖος**, after '*colossal*' insert 'εἰκόνα κ. *SEG* 33.1035 (Cyme, ii BC)'

**κολοσσός**, add '(v. *REA* 62.5 ff.)'

*****κολουᾶν**· θορυβεῖν Hsch.; cf. κολῳάω.

*****Κολουάς**, άδος, ἁ, an unexpl. topographical feature, ἐκ τοῦ Πετράχου ἐπὶ τὰν κολουάδα τὰν εὐδείελον· ἐκ τᾶς κολουάδος ἐπὶ τὰν σκοπι[άν] *BCH* 116.200.8, 9 (Phocis, iii BC).

*****Κολούρα**, ή, name of a hill, *SEG* 11.377.17-18 (Hermione, ii BC), app. referred to in Paus. 2.36.3 (v. Βολεοί, s.v. °βολεός), cf. κολουραῖος (Call.*fr.* 235 Pf.).

**κόλουρος**, add 'Ῥόλουρος pers. n., *SEG* 17.287 (Magnesia, vii BC)'

**κολοφών I**, add 'for a different expl. cf. Sch.Pl.*Tht.* 153c G.'

*****Κολοφωνιακός**, ή, όν, = Κολοφώνιος, Μιμνέρμου τοῦ Κ. *Suppl.Hell.* 1060.

*****κολπῑτεύω**, *smuggle*, *PVindob.Barbara* 8.4 (*ZPE* 40.139, iii BC), *PPhilad.* 35.22 (ii AD); cf. °διακολπιτεύω.

*****κολπῑτικός**, ή, όν, *smuggled, contraband*, *PTeb.* 38.12, 125, 1094.3 (-εικ-, all 114/13 BC).

**κολπόω**, line 1, after '*belly*' insert 'ἱστίον B. 13.130 S.-M.'

**κολυμβάς I**, last line, for 'Call.*Iamb.* 1.273' read 'Call.*fr.* 194.77 Pf.'

**κολυμβήθρα IV**, add 'Procop.*Arc.* 17.9'

**κόλυμβος II 1**, for '= κολύμβησις' read '*swimming*'; add 'humorously, of boiling food, Theodorid.ap.Ath. 6.229a' add '**III** *vat*, Pelag.Alch. 255.'

**κολχικόν**, add 'Plin.*HN* 28.129'

**κολῳάω**, for '*brawl, scold*' read '*cry out, shout*, cf. κολοιός, °κολουᾶν'

**κόλων**, add '*SEG* 34.630 (Maced., iii AD), al., *POxy.* 2476.32, 48'

**κολώνη**, line 1, for '*Lyr.adesp.* 74' read '*Lyr.adesp.* 65 P.' and add 'Ἀκράγαντος Pi.*P.* 12.3'; line 2, after '*peak*' insert 'A.R. 1.601'

**κολῳός**, for '*brawling, wrangling*' read '*tumult, uproar*' and add 'A.R. 2.1064; cf. κολοιός, κολοιή'

*****κομακτορία**, ή, *auction tax*, *PKöln* 83.12-13 (κωμακτορεία, AD 167), *POxy.* 1523.4 (iii AD).

**κομάκτωρ**, for 'dub. sens.' read 'prob. = Lat. *coactor* (cf. *comactores*: *argentarii Gloss.*)' and add '*PStrassb.* 79.3 (i BC, pl.)'

*****κόμανος**, ὁ, unexpld. wd., Hdn.*fr.* p. 28 H.

**κομάω I 2**, for 'of her lover' read 'of interpreters (of Erinna)'; for 'Opp.*C.* 3. 192' read 'Opp.*H.* 2.534'

*****Κόμβα**, ή, cult-name of Artemis, *TAM* 2(1).4 (Lycia).

**κόμβαλα**, for 'παίγματα' read 'πήγματα' and add 'perh. also Euph.in *Suppl.Hell.* 450 i 2'

*****κομβάλιον**, τό, part of the framework of a window, perh. *window-catch*, *PCair.Zen.* 847.18 (iii BC).

*****Κομβική**, ή, title of Artemis in Lycia, *Xanthos* 2, 3, *TAM* 2(2).407.

*****κομβίον** (B), τό, dim. of °κόμβος (B), *IIasos* 394 (cf. Robert *Ét.Anat.* 470); cf. °κάμβειν.

**κόμβος** (A), for '*roll, band, girth*' read '*knot, fastening*'

*****κόμβος** (B), ὁ, prob. *grandchild*, *IKeramos* 26.12, al., *Gnomon* 18.667 (*Didyma* 349).

**κόμβωμα**, add '(in pl.) *knots* or *buds* on a branch'

*****κομεᾶτος**, ὁ, Lat. *commeatus, supplies*, *PGiss.* 41.4, *POxy.* 1666.14 (iii AD); also κομι- *POxy.* 1477.7 (iii/iv AD), Hsch., Suid.

*****κομενταρήσιος**, v. °κομμεντ-.

*****κομεντάριον**, v. °κομμεντ-.

**κομέω** (A), at end after '(Karanis, iii BC)' insert 'A.R. 1.780, of the dead, *AP* 7.707 (Diosc.), of beehives, ib. 7.717'

**κομήεις**, add 'Myc. *ko-ma-we*, *-we-to* (gen.), pers. n. ("*long-haired*")'

**κόμης**, add 'πρὸς τὸν κόμιτα *POxy.* 3150.16 (vi AD), al.'

*****κομιᾶτος**, v. °κομεᾶτος.

**κομίζω**, line 1, before 'κομίσω' insert 'κομίσσω A.R. 1.419, al., Nonn.*D.* 1.446, al., *AP* 5.278.5 (Agath.)'; line 2, for 'only late, as' read '*IG* 11(4).1027.6 (Delos, iii BC)'; line 7, after '8.284' insert 'Lesb. [κο]μίσσασθαι (inf.) *IG* 12(2).29.9. Boeot. κομιττάμενοι (part.) *IG* 7.2406.8' **II 4**, delete 'ἔξω .. E.*Tr.* 167 (lyr.)'

**κόμιστρον I 1**, add 'A.*fr.* 154a.11 R.' **3**, for pres. def. read 'perh. *payment for porterage*' **II**, add 'cf. Poll. 6.186'

*****κομιτᾶτος**, ὁ, Lat. *comitatus, staff*, *SB* 7181.48 (AD 220), *PLips.* 34.6 (iv AD).

*****κομμέντα**, τά, Lat. *commenta, records*, *PSI* 951.2 (?iv AD), *POxy.* 1877.5 (v AD).

*****κομμενταρήσιος**, ὁ, Lat. *commentariensis, secretary* or *accountant*, w. var. spellings, e.g. κομεντ-, *PBerol.*inv. 7347 (*JJP* 19.93, iii AD), κομμεντ- *BGU* 2162.2 (AD 491); κομμετ-, *SEG* 32.1554A.18 (Arabia, vi AD).

*****κομμεντάριον**, τό, Lat. *commentarium, system of shorthand*, *IEphes.* 3054 (s.v.l.), sp. κομεντ-, *POxy.* 724.8 (ii AD).

*****κομμερκιάριος**, ὁ, Lat. *commerciarius, merchant*, *SEG* 32.1554A.5 (before vi AD), Just.*Nov.* 154.

*****κομμέρκιον**, τό, Lat. *commercium, trade*, ἀπὸ κομερκίων *BGU* 972.1 (vi/vii AD).

**κόμμι**, add 'acc. pl. κόμμιδες (for κόμμιδας) *BGU* 2357 ii 5 (iii AD)'

*****Κομμόδεια**, τά, *festival in honour of Commodus*, *Delph.* 3(6).143, καὶ ἐν Σμύρνῃ Κομόδεια Ὀλύμπια *TAM* 4(1).34; at Athens, *IG* $2^2$.2113.53, al.

*****Κόμμοδος**, ὁ, name given by Commodus to the eighth month, D.C. 72.15.

*****κομμονιτώριον**, τό, Lat. *commonitorium, letter of instructions*, *PMerton* 45.1 (v/vi AD), *PLond.* 1680.22, *SEG* 35.1360.5 (κομονητουρ-, Hadrianopolis, vi AD), Just.*Nov.* 128.17, Suid. (-μονητορ-); also κομμων- *Cod.Just.* 1.4.26.5, al.

*****κομμωτίζω**· ἐπιμελοῦμαι Suid.

*****κομόδιον**, τό, *gratuity* paid to officials, cf. Lat. *commodum*, *POxy.* 3358.4, 3424.3 (both iv AD).

*****κόμορος**, gloss on κοστίας, Hsch.

*****κομοτροφία**, ή, *letting the hair grow long*, Porph. in *Mél.Bidez* 149, prob. in Critodemus in *Cat.Cod.Astr.* 8(1).260 (codd. κωμο-).

*****Κομπεταλιασταί**, οἱ, guild which celebrated the Compitalia, *Inscr.Délos* 1761.18, al.

*****κομπλεύσιμος**, η, ον, *relating to the filling up of documents*, Lyd.*Mag.* 3.25.

*****κομπλεύω**, *fill up, complete* documents (as the function of a special clerk), *PUniv.Giss.* 33.2 (vi AD).

⁺**κομπολᾰ́κῡθος**, ὁ, *boaster*, an imaginary bird, Ar.*Ach.* 589, 1182; also **κομπολήκῡθος**, nickname for tragic poets, acc. to Choerob. *in Heph.* p. 230.21 C.

*****κομπολῠ́ρας**, α, ὁ, perh. *with noisy lyre*, rest. in A.*fr.* 451c.28 R. (lyr.).

**κόμπος** (A) II 2, add 'Pi.*fr.* 94b.13 S.-M.'

**κομπός** (B), after 'E.*Ph.* 600 (troch.)' insert 'Epicur.*Sent.Vat.* 45 A. (κόμπους cod., *WS* 49.33), Call.*fr.* 96 Pf.'

*****κομπρομισσάριος**, α, ον, *of* or *connected with a compromissum*, Just.*Nov.* 113.1.1.

*****κομπρόμισσον**, τό, Lat. *compromissum, an arbitrated compromise*, *SB* 10733.7 (iii (or v) AD), 9775.11 (vi AD); τὸν -ον (erron.) *CPR* 6.8.4 (AD 509).

**κονᾰβίζω**, line 3, for 'cf.' read 'trans., γαῖαν κ. ποσσίν'

*****κοναύθιον**, τό, type of river boat, *PHels.* 7.3 (ii BC).

*****κόνβεντος**, ὁ, Lat. *conventus, assembly*, cf. κονβενταρχέω, *IGRom.* 4.1169.

*****κονδέα**, ή, Sicil. word for "*fox*", *AB* 272.

*κονδικτίκιος, Lat. *condicticius*, ὁ *ex lege* κονδικτίκιος = *ex lege condictio*, *Cod.Just.* 1.3.45.6, Just.*Nov.* 162.1.2.

*κονδιτάριος, ὁ, *maker of spiced wine*, *PMed.* I 71.1, *PMich.*xv 740.14 (vi AD); also -ία, ἡ, Βικτωρίας κονδειταρίας τόπος *Not.Scav.* 1893.309 (Syracuse, v AD).

*κονδῖτον (or κονδεῖτον), τό, Lat. *conditum* (sc. *vinum*), *spiced wine*, *AP* 9.502 (Pall.), Alex.Trall. 8.2 (ii p. 341.5 P.), 11.1 (ii p. 469.12 P.), *PRyl.* 629.367 (iv AD, -διτ- pap.).

κονδοκέρατος, add 'cf. κοντός (B)'

*κονδόρῖς, ῖνος, *short-nosed*, κονδόρεινα (acc.) *POxy.* 3054.16 (AD 265); cf. °κοντόρρινος.

*κονδουκτορία, ἡ, cf. Lat. *conductor*, *office of contractors*, *POxy.* 900.6, 2110.4 (both iv AD).

*κονδουκτόριον, τό, *board of contractors*, *PCornell* 52.10 (iii AD), *POxy.* 2115.3 (iv AD).

*κονδούκτωρ, ορος, ὁ, Lat. *conductor*, *contractor*, *PBeatty Panop.* 1.60 (AD 298), *POxy.* 2115.6 (pl., iv AD), *PMich.*xi 624.24 (vi AD).

κόνδυ, line 3, delete 'as a measure'

κονδῠλωτός, after '*knobby*' insert 'perh. *embossed*, ποτήριον *Inscr.Délos* 104.16 (364 BC)'; neut. subst., add '*Inscr.Délos* 104.23'

*κόνητρον, τό, unexpld. wd. in Chr. inscr., Roueché *Aphrodisias* 80.

*κονθηλαί· ἀνοιδήσεις Hsch.; cf. κανθύλη.

*κονθινάρχειμι, *to be in command of the* *κονθινοι (dub. sens. cf. perh. κοντός (A) 2), κονθιναρχέντ[ου]ν *AE* 1932 suppl. 17 (Crannon, iii BC).

κονία I 1, add '*earth* (of the grave), τὸν ὀθνείῃ κείμενον ἐν κονίῃ *IHadr.* 61.4 (ii AD)'; at end after 'κονίῃσι' insert 'cf. κονίαισι Alc. 283.15 L.-P.'

*κονιᾱκόπος, ὁ, *plaster-grinder*, *POxy.* 2272.29 (ii AD).

*κονιᾱκός, ή, όν, *powdered*, κίττανος· ἡ κονιακὴ τίτανος Hsch.

κονίᾱσις, after '*Gp.* 2.27.5' insert '*POxy.* 3793.10 (AD 340)'

κονιᾱ́της, for '= foreg.' read '*plasterer* or *whitewasher*' and add '*ITyr* 186.2 (κονε-, Chr.), *PMich.*xi 620.137 (AD 239/40)'

*κονιδισμός, ὁ, disorder of the eyelids, Cyran. 35 (1.16.11 K.).

κονίζω, for 'v. κονίω' read 'pass., = κυλίεσθαι, prob. *roll in the dust*, Hsch.; fut. κονιεῖσθαι Ph. 2.173 (v.l.)'

*κόνικλος, v. °κουνίκολος.

κόνῑμα, for 'v. κόνισμα' read '= κονίστρα 2, *arena*, *SEG* 27.119.15 (Delphi, iii BC). **2** = κονίᾱμα, *plaster*, *Inscr.Délos* 365.48 (iii BC).'

κονιορτόω, add 'pass., Sch.Gen.Il. 23.764'

κόνιος II, add 'also of Demeter, *SEG* 31.368 (perh. unconnected with κόνις, *dust*)'

κόνισμα, for 'also κόνῑμα .. Delph., iii BC)' read 'v. °κόνῑμα)'

κονίστρα 2, add '**b** in pl., Call.*fr.* 328 Pf. (app. referring to παλαίστρα Κερκυόνος Paus. 1.39.3).'

κονίω, line 2, after 'fut.' insert 'κονίσομαι *APl.* 25 (Phil.)' and delete 'κονιοῦμαι .. κονίζεσθαι'; lines 5/6, for 'in Mss. .. 128' read 'mss. sts. incorrectly give forms fr. κονίζω' **I 1**, add 'οὖδας *A.Pers.* 163' **II**, last line, delete 'cf. *Pers.* 163 (troch.)'

κόνναρος, after 'κόνναρον, τό, *its fruit*' insert '*PHaun.* 20.10 (sp. κόναρ-; iv/v AD)'

κόννος 1, add '*Inscr.Délos* 1421*Ab*19 (ii BC)' **2**, for this section read '*fringe of hair, beard*, Luc.*Lex.* 5; cf. ἱέρωμα· τὸν κόννον Λάκωνες, ὃν τινες μαλλὸν ⟨ἢ⟩ σκόλλυν Hsch. κ.· ὁ πώγων, ἢ ὑπήνη. ἢ χάρις id.' **3**, delete the section.

*κονσιστώριον and κων-, τό, Lat. *consistorium*, *imperial assembly*, *POxy.* 140.5, *PMasp.* 32.15 (both vi AD).

*κονσουλάριος, α, ον, *consular*, Just.*Nov.* 8 not.inscr.

κοντάκιον, add 'Alex.Aphr.*in Metaph.* 548.18'

*κοντηλίτιον, τό, perh. dim. of κοντός (A), *PVindob.* G39847.916, 931 (*CPR* 5.110, iv AD).

*κοντῖλος, ὁ, *pole*, perh. used in vulgar sense for *penis*, cf. κ.· εἶδος ὀρνέου, ἢ ὄρτυξ. ἔστι δὲ καὶ ὄφις Hsch., Eup. 364 K.-A.

*κοντοβερνάλιος, ὁ, Lat. *contubernalis*, *comrade*, *aide*, *PGen.* 79.2, *PLips.* 40 ii 22 (both iv AD); also written κοντοβ- *Dura*[5] 39.

κοντοκῠνηγέσιον, delete the entry.

*κοντόρρῑνος, ον, *short-nosed*, Rhetor. in *Cat.Cod.Astr.* 7.202.7; cf. °κονδόρις.

κοντός (A) 1, delete '*punting-pole*' and add 'Plb. 21.7.2' **2**, before 'Luc.' insert 'Arr.*Tact.* 43.2'

*κοντροκῠνηγέσιον, τό, *wild-beast hunt with pikes*, *IGRom.* 4.1632.7 (Philadelphia, v. *SEG* 6.608).

*κοντώδης, ες, app. *armed with a pike*, Ἄρης, ἄφωνον πῆμα, κοντῶδες τέρας Gr.Naz.*Carm.* 2.1.11.

κόνυζα, add 'see also κνύζα, σκόνυζα'

*κοξάλια, τά, late Lat. *coxalia*, *loin-cloths*, *Edict.Diocl.* 27.2, 5.

*κόον, acc. (gender unkn.) κόον γάρ φασι κατὰ γλῶσσαν τὸ πρόβατον λέγεσθαι (sc. in Carian expl. of etym. of ἡ Κῶς) Eust. 318.40.

*κοορταλῖνος, ὁ, Lat. *cohortalinus*, *member of the lowest level of the staff of provincial governors*, *Cod.Just.* 1.5.12.6, 15.

*κοόρτη, ἡ, = κοόρτις, *IEphes.* 737.5 (iii AD).

κοπάζω, add '**2** trans., *curb, moderate*, Lxx *Si.* 39.28, 43.23, 46.7, 48.10.'

κόπᾰνον I, after '*pestle*' insert '*Inscr.Cret.* 1.xvii 2*b*2 (ii BC)'

κοπή 3, for this section read '*beating of the web*, i.e. *fulling*, as part of the weaving process; in quots., only in the title of officials to whom tax on fullers and weavers was paid or due, *PFay.* 58.7 (ii AD), *PAmh.* 2.119.4 (AD 200), *BGU* 2547.2 (iii AD)' **7**, add '*SEG* 32.794.10 (Olbia, *c.*325 BC)'

κοπιάτης, for 'also κοπιᾶς .. Philippi)' read '*SEG* 34.1330 (Lycaonia), perh. also Τίμωνος κωπιά[τ]ας χρηστέ, χαῖρε ib. 30.1622 (Cyprus, ii/iii AD)'

κοπιάω, line 2, for '*Apoc.* 2.3' read 'Onos. 22.1'

*κοπιδᾶς, ᾶ, ὁ, (κοπίς (B)) *maker of cleavers*, *MAMA* 3.573 (Corycus).

κοπίδερμος, add 'Aesop.*Prov.* 15 tit. P.'

κόπις (A), for '*prater, liar, wrangler*' read '*glib talker*'

κοπίς (B), line 3, for '*broad curved knife*' read 'applied to any chopping or cutting weapon'; line 4, after '(X.*Cyr.*) 6.2.10' insert 'by Lucanians, *AP* 6.129 (Leon.Tarent.)' **II**, add 'Molpis ap.Ath. 4.140b (= Molpis 1 J.), Hsch.'

κόπος II 3, add '*fruits of one's labour*, *Orac.Tiburt.* 116'

κοπόω, for '*weary*' read '*exhaust* with physical effort'; add '*SEG* 31.1474 (Arabia, AD 575/6)'

κοπρηγία, add '*PSoterichos* 1.24 (AD 69), *PFlor.* 143.5 (iii AD)'

κοπρηγός, after '*dung-cart*' insert '*PLond.* 131.30 (pl., AD 78/9)'

*κοπριαναίρετος, ον, *taken from the dunghill*, *PAmst.* 41.88, 114 (10/8 BC).

*κοπρίδιον, τό, ἀφόρδια· κοπρίδια Sch.Nic.*Al.* 140d Ge.

κοπρίζω, add 'πρασιαῖς κεκοπρισμέναις Dsc. 1.81, *BGU* 2354.12 (ii AD)'

*κοπριών, ῶνος, ὁ, Cret. for κοπρεών, κοπρών *Inscr.Cret.* 4.73*A*9-10 (Gortyn, v BC).

κόπρος I 1, add 'applied also to compost, X.*Oec.* 16.12, 20.11'

κοπτή II, for 'κοπτός II 2' read 'κοπτός II 1'

+κοπτικός, ή, όν, *of* or *for striking, chopping*, or sim., μέρη (sc. ξίφους) Sch.E.*Hec.* 543; adv. -κῶς Hdn.*Epim.* 134.

*κοπτοπώλης, ου, ὁ, *seller of pastries*, *AS* 20.43 no. 13.

κοπτός II 2, delete this section transferring exx. to section II 1.

κόπτω I 6, add '**b** *cut* letters (on wood), γράμματα Call.*fr.* 73.1 Pf.' **9**, add 'with the oars, in rowing, κ. ὕδωρ Call.*fr.* 18.11 Pf., A.R. 1.914'

*Κορᾱγωγός, ὁ, religious official, *IG* $2^2$.1247.20 (iii BC).

κορᾰκῖνος II, add '*IGC* p. 98 A8 (Acraephia, iii/ii BC)'

*κορᾰκοβρωσία, ἡ, *food for ravens*, *PMasp.* 353.A19 (vi AD, -οσια pap.).

*κορᾰκόπους, ποδος, ὁ, gloss on κορωνόπους, Hsch.

κορᾰκόω, add '*SEG* 17.630, 635 (Perge)'

*κορᾰκώδης, v. κορακοειδής.

κοράλλιον, add '*PSI* 1128.27 (iii AD)' and delete 'Alciphr. 1.39' (line 2), 'Luc.*Apol.* 1' (line 4) and at end 'sts. .. κωράλιον'

*κοράλλιον (B), τό, *figurine*, Alciphr. 1.39, Luc.*Apol.* 1 (κουρ-); cf. κωράλιον.

κοραλλιοπλάστης, for pres. def. read '*maker of figurines*'

*κοραλλίς, ίδος, ἡ, a precious stone (?*red jasper*), Plin.*HN* 37.153.

*κοραλλοαχᾰ́της, ου, ὁ, a kind of agate resembling coral, Plin.*HN* 37.139, 153.

*κόραλλος, *coral*, *PMag.* 4.2304, Theognost.*Can.* 56 A.

κόραξ, line 1, for '(not in Hom.)' read 'place-name in Hom., Κόρακος πέτρῃ Od. 13.408' **I 4**, add '*IUrbRom* 106, 107'

*κοράξαι· ἄγαν προσλιπαρῆσαι Hsch.; cf. κοράσσει.

κοραξός, add '*BGU* 1666.12 (i AD)'

κορᾱσίδιον, add '*SEG* 36.616 (Edessa, iii AD)'

*Κορᾱσιοδρόμος, ὁ, *courier serving the town of Corasium*, *MAMA* 3.415 (Corycus).

κοράσιον, line 2, after 'Philippid. 36' insert '(acc. to Phot. introduced as foreign word'; line 3, before '*IG* 7.3325' insert 'esp. of slave girls in manumission inscrs.' and before '*PStrassb.*' insert '*PCair.Zen.* 28.10 (iii BC), *SEG* 24.498, 530, 34.658 (Maced., ii/iii AD, sts. -ιν)'; add '(Maced. wd. acc. to Sch.bT Il. 20.404)'

*κορβάσει· τὸ καταπνεῖ, τὸ βλέπει Theognost.*Can.* 46 A.

*Κορδᾰκᾶ, ας, ἁ, title of Artemis in Elis, Paus. 6.22.1.

*κόρδᾰμον, = κάρδαμον, in pl. *Dura*[4] 129.

κόρδαξ, add '**2** name given to the trochaic metre, Cic.*Orat.* 193; cf. κορδακικός.'

*κορδούνια, τά, unexpld. wd., prob. a measure of (or receptacle for) grain, *OBodl.* III 295 (i AD).

*κορδυλίς [?ῠ], ίδος, ἡ, name of a fish, Ath. 7.306c; cf. κορδύλη III.

κορδύλος, add 'also some kind of creeping marine animal, mentioned with the octopus, Opp.*H.* 1.306'

κορεία (B), after 'D.Chr. 7.142' insert 'Nonn.*D.* 1.350 K., al.'

κόρειος II 2, for '*Ath.Mitt.* .. iii BC)' read '*SEG* 24.151.21-2, ib. 153.8 (Attica, iv BC)'

**κόρη**, line 5, after '*h.Cer.* 439)' insert 'voc. *κοῦρα* Call.*Dian.* 72, Naumach.ap.Stob. 4.23.7' and after '**κώρα**' insert '(also v.s.v.)'; line 6, after 'Theoc. 6.36' insert '(voc. *κῶρα* id. 27.52)' **I 1**, add 'of Athene, *γλαυϙὅπιδι ϙὅρει CEG* 182, al. (Athens, vi BC); *τῆ[ν ἡμ]ετέραν Κόρην* (perh. identified w. Aphrodite) *SEG* 18.578.2 (Cyprus, AD 14)' add '**5** the constellation *Virgo*, Doroth. 78, Nonn.*D.* 2.655 K.' at end add 'Myc. *ko-wa*' **B Κόρη**, after '**Κώρα** *GDI* 5047' insert '*Κούρα*, *Schwyzer* 262 (Cnidus, iii BC), *Κόρρα*, *SEG* 35.826 (Thrace, iv/iii BC)'

***Κορθιᾱτᾱς** (also **Κροθιᾱτᾱς**), ὁ, title of Pan, *Schwyzer* 67.3, 5 (Messenia, archaic).

+**κορθίλη**, ἡ, *κορθίλας καὶ κόρθιν· τοὺς σωρούς. καὶ τὴν συστροφήν* Hsch.; cf. -*ας ποιεῖν* a farming operation, *IG* 2$^2$.2493.16 (iv BC).

**κόρθιλος**, for '*βασιλίσκος*' read '*βασιλίσκος* III'

**κόρθυς**, delete 'lengthd. form of *κόρυς*'

***Κορία**, ἡ, title of Artemis in Arcadia, Call.*Dian.* 234 (-*ίη*). **2** of Athena, Paus. 8.21.4, Cic.*ND* 3.59.

***κοριανδρόκοκκος**, ὁ, *coriander-seed*, Lxx Sch.*Ex.* 16.31.

**κορίαννον**, after '*κορίαμβλον* Hsch.' insert 'also *κολίανδρον* (v.s.v.)' **I**, add '**b** given as alternative name for *κώνειον*, Sch. Nic.*Al.* 186a Ge.' at end add 'Myc. *ko-ri-ja-do-no* (**κορί(h)αδνον*), *ko-ri-a₂-da-na* (pl.)'

**κορίαξος**, after 'a kind of *fish*' insert '*Stud.Pal.* 20.224'

**κορίδιον I**, add '*Schwyzer* 462 (Tanagra, iii BC)'

**κορίζομαι**, for '*fondle, caress*' read '*speak fondly to*, w. acc.'

***κορῑκορώνη**, ἡ, *ἐκκόρει κορικορώνην* perh. in Horap. 1.8 (*ἐκκορὶ κορὶ κορώνη(ν)* codd.), Sch.Pi.*P.* 3.32 (*ἐκκόρει κόρει κορώνας*), cf. *Carm.Pop.* 35(*b*) P., a marriage cry; cf. *χελιχελώνη*.

**Κορίνθιος**, add 'Myc. *ko-ri-si-jo* (**Κορίνσιος*)'

**Κόρινθος I**, add 'cf. Myc. *ko-ri-to*, place name' **III**, *Κορινθόθεν*, for '*Michel* 1087' read '*SEG* 24.310'

**κόριον** (A), after '*little girl*' insert 'Eup. 30 K.-A.'

**κόρις II**, add '*SEG* 32.450 B.13 (Acraephia, iii/ii BC)'

***κόρκομα**, ἡ, Lat. *curcuma*, *basket*, Anon.Alch. 330.13.

+**κόρκορα**· *ὄρνις. Περγαῖοι* Hsch. (*κορκόρας* cj.)

***κορκορῠγέω**, *rumble*, of the bowels, Sch.Ar.*Nu.* 386.

**κορκορυγμός**, read '**κορκορῠγισμός** (v.l. -*υγμός*)'

***κορμηταί**· *κοσμηταί* Hsch.; cf. *κόρμος* (B).

**κορμίον II 2**, add 'cf. mod. Gk. *κορμί body*'

+**κορμολογία**, ἡ, perh. *gathering of logs* or *removal of stocks*, *SB* 5126.25 (AD 261), *PCol.* 179.18 (AD 300).

+**κορμός** (A), ὁ, *the trunk* or *stock* of a tree, Od. 23.196; *κ. ἐλάϊνοι PCair.Zen.* 431.4 (iii BC), *PLond.* 1972.2; in the measurement of a vineyard, *ἀπὸ κορμοῦ εἰς κορμόν PFlor.* 50 i 2, al. (iii AD). **2** *sawn-off trunk, log*, *κορμοὶ ξύλων* Hdt. 7.36, E.*Hec.* 575, *HF* 242, *κ. ἐλάας* Ar.*Lys.* 255, *PCair.Zen.* 154.2 (iii BC), poet. *κ. ναυτικοί*, i.e. oars, E.*Hel.* 1601.

**κορνικουλάριος**, add '*SEG* 31.1583 (iii AD); *κορνικολάριος POxy.* 2004, *κορνοκλάριος IGRom.* 3.59, *TAM* 4(1).112, *κολλικλάριος BGU* 435.8'

**κόροιβος**, after '*fool*' insert 'Suet.*Blasph.* p. 59 T.'; after '*Κόροιβος*' insert '*IG* 1$^3$.1147.44 ([*Κ*]*όροιβος*, v BC), Call.*fr.* 587 Pf.'

**κοροκόσμιον I**, for this section read '*small votive image of a nymph*, Clem.Al.*Protr.* 4.58 and Sch.ad loc. (false etym. in Sch.Theoc. 2.110)' **II**, add '(calque on Coptic expression)'

***κοροράτωρ**, *ορος*, ὁ, Lat. *colorator*, perh. *dyer* or *polisher*, *Edict.Diocl.* 7.54, cf. *Gloss.*

**κόρος** (B), add 'Myc. *ko-wo* (*κόρϝος*)'

**κόρος** (C), before 'Hsch.' insert 'perh. Bion. 2.17'; add 'cf. *κορέω* (A)'

**κόρος** (D), add '*PSI* 554.14 (259/8 BC)'

***κορόσπερμον**, *τό*, unexpld. wd., *PRyl.* 630*.8 (IV AD): perh. read *κορ‹ι›όσπερμον*, *coriander seed.*

***κορριγία**, ἡ, Lat. *corrigia*, *thong*, part of a harness, *Edict.Diocl.* 10.19 (sp. *χορηγία* in version in *SEG* 37.335).

**κόρση I 4**, add 'of the head of a plant, Nic.*Al.* 253'

***κορσίτης**, *ου*, ὁ, precious stone, prob. = *κορσοειδὴς λίθος*, *Lapid.Gr.* 171.12, 189.23.

***κορτήγι(ο)ν**, *τό*, wd. of unkn. meaning, perh. in a medical context, *PVindob.*G 39847.927 (*CPR* 5.110, iv AD).

***κορτιανός**, ὁ, fr. Lat., *member of a cohort*, *POxy.* 1253.4 (iv AD).

***κορτίνα**, ἡ, also *κορτίνη*, *PMasp.* 6 ii 48 (vi AD), Lat. *cortina*: **I** (archit.) *arch, vault*, *IGLS* 13.1.9135-6 (Bostra, vi AD). **II** as late Lat., *curtain*, *PMasp.* l.c., *PNess.* 180.7 (vi/vii AD).

***κόρτον**, *τό*, wd. occurring in inventory of utensils, perh. *sieve*, *SEG* 24.361.15 (Thespiae, 386/380 BC); cf. *κύρτη*, *κύρτος*.

**κορῠδός**, line 6, for '**κορυδαλλή**' read '**κορῡδαλλά** or **κορῠδαλλᾱ̆**' and add '*ASAA* 21/2 NS 275-8 (Sicily, iv/iii BC)' at end add 'cf. Myc. *ko-ru-da-ro-jo* (gen.), pers. n.'

***Κορύδων**, *ονος*, ἁ, name of a feast, *SEG* 32.1243.36 (Aeolian Cyme, 2 BC/AD 2).

**Κορυθαλλίστριαι**, add '(-*θαλίστ*- La.)'

***κορῠθήκη**, ἡ, *helmet-case*, *Inscr.Délos* 1417*A*i121 (ii BC).

**κόρῠθος II**, add 'Paus. 4.34.7, also *Κόρυνθος* (q.v. II)'

***κορύθων**· *ἀλεκτρυών* Hsch.; cf. *κορυνθεύς* II.

**κορυμβίας**, add '**II** kind of giant fennel, Plin.*HN* 19.175.'

**κορύμβιον**, add '**III** curled wig, Petron. 110.1, 5; cf. *κόρυμβος* II.'

***κορυμβίς**, *ίδος*, ἡ, = *κόρυμβος* II, Antim. 175 Wy.

**κορυμβίτης**, add '**II** kind of spurge, Plin.*HN* 26.70.'

**κόρυμβος I 1**, add 'of a hunting-net, *ἐπ' ἀκροτάτοισι κορύμβοις at the extreme ends*, Opp.*C.* 4.125'

**κορῠνήτης**, add 'Parth. in *Suppl.Hell.* 634'

**κόρυς**, add 'Myc. *ko-ru*, *ko-ru-to* (gen.), *ko-ru-pi* (instr. pl.)'

**κορύσσω I 1**, line 3, after 'Pi.*I.* 8(7).58' insert '*ἐμφύλιον αἷμα* Hes.*fr.* 190.2 M.-W., Semon. 7.105, Ibyc. 30(*b*) P.'

**κορυστής**, add 'Alcm. 1.5 P. (-*τᾶς*)'

**κορῠφαῖον III**, for '*ridge-beam*' read '*main rafter*'

**κορῠφαῖος I**, add '**2** = *κορύφαινα*, Cyran. 110.' **II 2**, sup., add '*Suppl.Hell.* 1176, Favorin.*fr.* 134 B.'

**κορῠφή I 1**, add 'in fig. phr., *ἀπὸ κορυφῆς ὡς ὀνύχων ἔπεσεν τὸ Βένετον SEG* 31.1492 (Egypt, AD 608/10)' **II 4**, add '*the Chief*, i.e. the emperor, *CPR* 5.17.4 (v AD)'

**κορῠφιστήρ 2**, add 'pl., gloss on *ἀμπυκτῆρες*, equated with *προμετωπίδια*, Sch.A.*Th.* 461'

+**κορῠφιστής**, *οῦ*, ὁ, *κ.*· *κόσμου γυναικείου τὸ περὶ τὴν κεφαλὴν χρυσίον. καὶ κεκρυφάλου τὸ μέσον ῥάμμα* Hsch., prob. also *κορυφισ[τής] SEG* 21.556 (Athens, iv BC).

**κόρῠφος III**, add '*POxy.* 3298.2 (iii AD)' add '**IV** a hair-style, Hsch.'

**κορώνη I 2**, after '*crow*' insert '*Corvus corone*'; line 2, for '*C. corone*' read '*C. frugilegus*' **II 6**, add '*κορώνας ἀναδούμενοι* Sophr. 163, cf. *κορωνίς* II 1, *χορωνός*' add '**8** *τὸ ἄκρον τοῦ αἰδοίου*, Suid., cf. perh. [Archil.] 331 W.' add '**III** a kind of fish, Hsch.'

**κορωνιάω II**, for 'leaves' read 'sheaves (of corn, fr. the ripeness of the ears)'; add 'also v.s.v. *κορυνιόεις* (v.l.)'

**κορώνιος I**, for this section read '*μηνοειδῆ ἔχων κέρατα βοῦς* Hsch.'

**κορωνίς II 2 a**, for 'Heph.*Poem.*' read 'Heph.*Sign.*'; at end for 'etc.' read 'D.H.*Comp.* 4 (p. 21)'

**κορωνισταί**, add '**II** sobriquet of gangs of young men in Cumae, *οὓς κ., ὡς ἔοικεν, ἀπὸ τῆς κόμης ὠνόμαζον* Plu. 2.261e.'

***κορωνοβόλον**, *τό*, app. *sling for shooting crows*, *AP* 7.546.

**κορωνοβόλος**, delete the entry.

**κορωνός**, line 1, after '*crooked*' insert 'Il. 2.746, al., as pers. n.'

**κοσκῐνευτής**, add 'included among employees at the circus, *OAshm.Shelton* 190'

***κοσκῐνοειδής**, *ές*, *sieve-like*, adv. -*ῶς*, Zos.Alch. 139.3.

**κόσκῐνον II**, for this section read '*κ. Ἐρατοσθένους*, method of finding prime numbers by elimination, Nicom.*Ar.* 1.13'

**κοσμαρίδιον**, add '*SB* 11075.15 (v AD)'

**κοσμάριον**, add '*BGU* 2217.12 (pl., written -*ιοι*, ii AD)'

**κοσμέω II 1**, line 5, after 'Pl.*Phd.* 97c' insert '*κοσμήσας τὴν διοίκησιν PThead.* 14 (iv AD)' add '**b** pass., *conform to, be guided by*, w. dat., D.H.*Amm.* 1.2; *κατά τι* ib. 1.1.' **2**, after '*κόσμος* III' insert '*Inscr.Cret.* 4.14 (vii/vi BC)'; after 'Plb. 22.15.1' insert 'w. acc., *perform* an act *as κ.*, Meiggs-Lewis 2.3.3 (Dreros, 650/600 BC)' **III 2**, add '*πάσῃ ἀγαθῇ ἀρε[τῇ] κεκοσμημένη* Mitchell *N.Galatia* 79, *MAMA* 8.449; also w. gen., *πάσης ἀρετῆς κεκοσμημένος MAMA* 1.228 (Laodicea Combusta); *embellish* a building, *SEG* 35.1471.(2)18 (Cyprus, vii AD)'

**κόσμησις**, line 3, after 'Arist.*Oec.* 1344$^a$19' insert '*SEG* 30.1786, 1787*A* (Cyrenaica, vi AD)'

**κοσμητεία**, add '*IEphes.* 4337.8 (-*ήα*, i AD)'

**κοσμητήρ II**, for this section read '*κοσμητῆρες*, *οἱ*, magistrates at Itanos, *Inscr.Cret.* 3.iv 3.22, 4.14'

**κοσμητής II**, add '**3** = *ἐνταφιαστής* (*Κουριεῖς*), Hsch.'

+**κοσμίζω**, *adorn, embellish*, *Cod.Just.* 8.11.3; cf. *σαρῶ· κοσμήσω* (cod. *κοσμίζω*) Hsch.

**κοσμικός I**, add '**2** *world-wide*, *ἀφορία* Longin. 44.1; *σεισμός IGRom.* 3.739 xiii 48 (Rhodiapolis, ii AD).' **II 1**, add 'neut. pl. as subst., Mitchell *N.Galatia* 465' add '**III** *fashionable*, Mart. 7.41.1,2.'

**κόσμιον**, add '*adornment*, Just.*Nov.* 14 pr. 1. **2** *votive image*, *AP* 9.326 (Leon.); cf. °*κοροκόσμιον*.'

**κοσμογένεια**, add '*creation*, applied to *Ge.* 1-2.7, Cels.ap.Orig.*Cels.* 6.29'

***κοσμογενής**, *ές*, *native of the universe*, *Gnomol.Vat.* in *WS* 10.237.

***κοσμογόνος**, *ον*, *producing the physical world*, *κ. στοιχεῖον τὸ ὕδωρ* Heraclit.*All.* 22.

**κοσμοκράτωρ**, delete 'epith. .. *H.* 4.3'

**κοσμοποίησις**, after '*ornamentation*' insert '*Inscr.Délos* 1443*B*ii 104 (ii BC)'

**κόσμος**, line 1, after 'ὁ' insert '(heterog. pl. *κόσμα POxy.* 494.10 (in sense II, ii AD); for form with rhotacism v.s.v. *κόρμος*)' **II**, add '*τὸν ναὸν καὶ τὸν ἐν αὐτῷ κόσμον IEphes.* 3757; of the equipping of a religious festival, τῶν μυστηρίων *SEG* 32.1243.14 (Aeolian Cyme, 2 BC/AD 2)' **IV 2**, add 'Arist.*Ph.* 252[b] 26'

***κοσμοτόκος**, ον, *giving birth to the world*, Heraclit.*All.* 64.7, 85.18.

***Κοσμοτορύνη**, ἡ, *World-stirrer* (of war), title of a satire by Varro, Nonius pp. 8, 231 L.

**κοσμοτρόφος**, after 'Man. 1.2' insert '*SB* 4313.2 (Alexandria, i/ii AD)'

***κοσούλλιον**, τό, unexpld. wd. in *Mim.adesp.* 15.32.

**κόσσῠφος**, line 1, after 'Att.' insert 'Boeot., Thess.' **II**, add 'κοττούφω (gen.) *SEG* 32.450. B9 (Acraephia, iii/ii BC), cf. pers. n. Κόττυφος D. 18.151, Aeschin. 3.124, al.'

***κόσταια**· ἄρτος κρίθινος Theognost.*Can.* 46 A.; cf. κοσταί, °γοσταί.

**κοστάριον**, for 'prob. = κόστος' read '*spice derived from* κόστος' and add '*PHaun.* 20.11 (iv/v AD)'

***κοστοῖνος**, η, ον, perh. *having the colour of* κόστος, *pale yellow*, *SB* 9307.3,6,9 (ii/iii AD).

**κόστον**, (s.v. κόστος), after 'Thphr.*Od.* 32' insert 'pl. κόστα *Dura*[4] 129' and delete '(but κόστα .. 15.19)'

***κόστον** (B), τό, in pl., wooden parts of a cart, *Edict.Diocl.* 15.19, cf. Lat. *costae*.

**κόστος**, add '*SB* 9834 b 22 (iv AD), cf. Skt. *kúṣṭha-*'

**+κοσύμβη**, ἡ, app. some kind of over-garment, D.Chr. 72.1, Poll. 2.30 (v.l. κορσύμβην, κοσσάμην), Hsch. (κοσσύμβη, κόσσυμβος), *EM* 311.5, 349.15.

**+κοτεινός**, ή, όν, dub. wd. in *PHib.* 225 iii 2 (perh. = κοτήεις); (also cj. for σκοτεινός in Pi.*N.* 7.61).

***κότθυβος**, an article of a soldier's equipment, *RA* 6.31 (Amphipolis, ii BC); perh. = °κοσύμβη.

**κοτίκας**, read '**κοτικᾶς**'

***κοτίλιον**, v. °κοτύλιον.

**κότῐνος**, line 1, after 'Theoc. 5.32' insert 'al.' add '**b** *olive-garland*, *SEG* 31.903.33 (Caria, iii AD).'

***κοτόνιον**, τό, app. kind of fig, *PKöln* 318.10 (vi/vii AD); cf. κόττανον.

***κότος**, τό(?), prob. for κύτος, *jar*, in inventory of utensils, *SEG* 24.361 (Thespiae, 386/380 BC).

**κότταβος 3**, add 'κότταβον βαλεῖν Pi.*fr.* 128'

**κοττάναθρον**, for 'κοττόβαθρον' read 'κοττανάβαθρον'

**κόττᾰνον**, add 'fig., καὶ ἡ παρθένος παρὰ Κρησί Hsch.'

***κοττιδιανός**, ή, όν, Lat. *cotidianus*, *daily*, *POxy.* 2408.10 (iv AD), Lyd.*Mag.* 107.18, 160.1.

**+κοττιστής**, οῦ, ὁ, *dice-player*, *Dura*[9] I p. 217 (iii AD), *Gloss.*

**κόττος III**, add '**2** κόττῳ *in a lump sum*, ἐὰν κόττῳ πραθῇ οἶνος *Basilica* 53.7.10 Sch.'

**κοτῠ́λη**, after lemma insert 'non-Att.-Ion. -ᾱ, *SEG* 25.343 (ϙοτύλλᾳ Corinth, viii/vi BC)' **3 b**, delete 'prob. also a smaller measure .. ὀξύβαφον' and transfer 'Hp.*Mul.* 1.6' to section 3 a.

**κοτυληδών 3**, add 'Hp.*Int.* 18, *Oss.* 16'

***κοτύλιον**, τό, dim. of κοτύλη, (κοτιλ- *Inscr.Délos* 1429Bii 25 (ii BC)) *small vessel* or *receptacle*, *Inscr.Délos* l.c., *SB* 1.22 (iii AD), *PLond.* 1657 (-ιν, iv/v AD).

**κοτυλίς**, delete the entry.

**κότῠλος**, add '*Schwyzer* 440.4 (Boeotia, vi BC)'

***κουαδράριος**, ὁ, Lat. *quadra(tar)ius*, *relating to stonemasonry*, *BGU* 21.1.5, *PGoodsp.Cair.* 12.i.6 (both iv AD), al.

***κουαιστορεία**, ἡ, *quaestorship*, *IGLS* 9112 (κυαι-; Bostra, iv AD)

***κουαίστωρ**, ορος, ὁ, Lat. *quaestor*, *IGRom.* 3.238.4; also **κυαίστωρ** ib. 4.1307.15; **κοιαίστωρ** Procop.*Arc.* 14.3; **κοιαίστωρ** *Cod.Just.* 1.12.8 pr.; **κυέστωρ** *Syria* 29.317 (Arabia, iii AD).

***κουαιστώριος**, ὁ, Lat. *quaestorius*, σκρεῖβα κ. λιβράριος *ILS* 8833, Ramsay *The Social Basis* 60.

***κουαττόρουιρ**, ου, ὁ, Lat. *quattuorvir*, *IG* 12(2).235.4 (Mytilene, ii AD).

***κουβαρίζω** (v.l. -ιάζω), gloss on μηρύω (v. μηρύομαι), Sch.Theoc. 1.29, as mod. Gk. *roll into a ball*.

**κουβηζός**, after 'στηβεύς' insert '(perh. read στιβεύς)'

***κουβικουλαρία**, ἡ, *chamberlain* (female), *SEG* 34.1262 (Bithynia, v AD), 8.175 (Jerusalem, vi AD).

***κουβικουλάριος**, ὁ, *chamberlain* (male), *IMylasa* 620.6.(sp. κουβουκλ-, v AD).

***κουβουκλεῖον**, τό, (Lat. *cubiculum*), *bedchamber*, Just.*Nov.*Ed.Not. 1, al. **2** *tomb*, κουβούκλιν *IG* 14,1451 (Rome, ii AD).

***κουδισάμιος**, ὁ, perh. *tool-grinder*, (cf. Lat. *cudis* and *samiarius*), *MAMA* 3.724 (Corycus).

***Κουέριος**, title of Poseidon, *Schwyzer* 559 (Thessaly, iii/ii BC).

***κοῦκεον**, τό, *fruit of the doum-palm*, *Ostr.Wilbour* 76 (prob. ii AD); also **κούκιον** *PHeid.* 333.29 (v AD, sp. κούκιν); cf. κόϊξ.

***κουκκούλλος**, ὁ, Lat. *cucullus*, *hood*, κουκκ[.]λον *POxy.* 3060.5 (ii AD).

***κουκούβη**, ἡ, species of *owl*, (cf. Lat. *cucubare*, *to hoot*), Eust. 1523.59.

***κουκουλάρι(ο)ς**, ὁ, maker of *cuculli*, *SEG* 39.649 (Augusta Traiana, ii/iii AD).

***κουκούλλιον**, τό, dim. formed on Lat. *cucullus* (-*lla*), *hood*, *PMich.*VIII 482.4 (ii AD, written κοκκούλιον), *POxy.* 1300.9 (v AD, written κούκλιν).

***κούμουλον**, τό, a measure, one thirtieth of an artaba (cf. Lat. *cumulus*), inscr. in *ZPE* 15.176 (v/vi AD), *PLond.* 1718.8, 9, al.; as tax or levy, *PFlor.* 75.21, *PVindob.* G13933[v].10 (*ZPE* 32.255, κούμολ-), *POxy.* 3395.12 (κούμηλ-), 3481.10 (κούμελ-, all iv AD).

**+κουνίκλος**, v. °κουνίκολος.

***κουνίκολος**, ὁ, Lat. *cuniculus*, *rabbit*, *Edict.Diocl.* 4.33A, also κουνίκλος Ath. 9.400f, κονίκλος Ael.*NA* 13.15, κυνίκλος Plb. 12.3.10 and prob. Gal. 6.666.

***κούνιον**, τό, *cradle*, Sch.Call.*Jov.* 48, cf. Lat. *cunae*, mod. Gk. κούνια (fem).

***κουνόπρειστις**, v. κυνόπρηστις.

***κοῦπα**, ἡ, Lat. *cupa*, *grave*, *niche*, *IUrbRom* 300, *Not.Scav.* 1931.369 (Catania, not before iii AD).

**κουρά II 1**, add 'ἀπονυχίσμασι καὶ κουραῖς Pythag.ap.D.L. 8.17'

**+κουράλιον**, v. ‡κοράλλιον (A) and (B).

**κουρατορεύω**, add 'trans., *act as guardian of* (a minor), in pass. οἱ ἐπιτροπευόμενοι ἢ κουρατορευόμενοι Modest.*Dig.* 27.1.15.3; also κουρατωρ-, *Cod.Just.* 3.10.1.1'

**κουρατορία**, add '*position of guardian*, Modest.*Dig.* 27.1.2; also κουρατωρεία, *Cod.Just.* 3.10.1.2'

**κουράτωρ**, after 'ορος' insert '(ωρος *Cod.Just.* 3.10.1.1)' and add '*JJP* 18.190 l. 3 (ii/iii AD)'

**κουρεῖον II**, delete the section.

***κούρειον**, τό, *victim offered for boys and feasted on by the* φράτερες *at the feast* κουρεῶτις, S.*fr.* 126, Is. 6.22 (κούριον codd.), *IG* 2[2].1237.28. **b** kid or lamb offered in spring to Hermes fr. each herd or flock, *Schwyzer* 721.13 (Thebes on Mycale, iv BC).

**Κούρεος**, delete 'from foreg. II'

***κούρευμα**, *hair cut off*, Hsch. s.v. κάρμα.

**κουρεύομαι**, add 'ἔγκαρτα· τοὺς κεκουρευμένους πυρούς Hsch.'

**κουρεύς I 1**, add '**b** Cypr. *ko-ro-u-se* perh. κōρούς or κο(ρ)ρούς, app. as title of official, *Kafizin* 117b, 118b, al. (in alphabetic script written κουρεύς).' **2**, add '*Edict.Diocl.* 7.22, 23'

**κουρευτής**, after '*barber*' insert '*UPZ* 96.10 (ii BC)'

**κούρητες II 1**, line 5, after 'worshipped in Crete' insert 'and elsewhere'; lines 7/9, for '(sg. only late)' read 'sg., *IG* 12(3).350, al. (ϙōρēς, Thera, perh. vii BC), *SEG* 9.107, 108, 110 (κωρ-, Cyrene, iv/iii BC)'; at end delete ')' after 'Dam.*Pr.* 267' **3**, add 'sg. κούρης *IEphes.* 47.30, al.'

***κουρητεύω**, *serve as* κουρῆτες II 3, *IEphes.* 47.7, 1060.9, 1061.8.

***κουρία**, ἡ, Lat. *curia*, D.C.fr. 5.8.

***κουριάτιος**, α, ον, Lat. *curiatius*, applied to an assembly, D.H. 9.41.2, *BMus.Inscr.* 3.544.

**κουρίδιος I 2**, after 'Archil. 18' insert 'κωριδίας τ' εὐνᾶς Alcm. in *POxy.* 2443.17'

**κουρικός I**, after '*hair*' insert 'σίδηρος *PMich.Zen.* 54.2 (iii BC)' add '**b** κουρική (sc. τέχνη), D.Chr. 7.117.'

***κουρῖτις**, ιδος, ἡ, a plant, = περιστερεὼν ὕπτιος, Ps.-Dsc. 4.60, Ps.-Apul.*Herb.* 4, 72.

***κουριῶσος**, ὁ, late Lat. *curiosus*, *inquiry agent*, *informer*, *PColl.Youtie* 74.4 (iii AD), *SEG* 35.1523 (-ιόσοι pl., Seleucia Pieria, vi AD), *BCH* suppl. 8 no. 150 (κουρίου[-, Thessalonica, v/vi AD).

***κουρκούτη**, ἡ, *gruel*, Sch.Ar.*Pl.* 673; cf. mod. Gk. κουρκούτι neut.

***κουροπερσονάριοι**, οἱ, fr. Lat. *cura* and *personalis*, officials of some kind, *POxy.* 2050.5. (vi AD), cf. *SB* 2254.4.

**κοῦρος** (B), for '*loppings* .. *tree*' read '= κορμός (A) 1' and add '*Inscr.Délos* 442A157 (ii BC)'

***κουροσόος**, ον, *child-saving*, cj. in *AP* 6.274.1 (Pers.).

**κουρότερος**, line 2, for 'Hes.*Op.*[447]' read 'Hes.*Op.* 447'

***Κουροτρόφιον**, τό, *shrine of* Γῆ Κουροτρόφος, *IG* 2[2].4756 (i/ii AD).

**κουροτρόφος**, line 4, after 'Od. 9.27' insert 'Εἰρήνη .. κ. Hes.*Op.* 228'

**κουρούλλιος** or **-ούλιος**, add 'also **κουρούλης** *IGRom.* 3.238.7 (Galatia), **κορούλης** *JRS* 49.96.11 (Cyrene, ii AD)'

***κουρσόριος**, α, ον, τροχάδια κ. for [*gal*]*licae cursuriae*, *Edict.Diocl.* 9.14, (but 14 A: τροχάδων κουρσόρων).

**+κούρσωρ**, ορος, ὁ, Lat. *cursor*, as a rank, *BCH* suppl. 8 no. 152 (-ουρος gen., Thessalonica, v/vi AD).

**κουσούλιον**, before '*cloak*' insert 'a garment, perh.' and add '*PHeid.* 333.7'

**κουστούμηνα**, add 'sg. (-μίνου), Hsch. s.v. ὄχνη'

**κουστωδία**, add 'al., *PRyl.* 189.2 (ii AD); also **κοστωδία**, prob. in *POxy.* 294.20 (AD 22)'

***κουφάριον**, τό, app. *cask* or sim., *PAmst.* 79.3 (iv/v AD); cf. κοῦφος 6.

***κουφήρης**, ες, unexpld. wd., *Lyr.adesp.* 5.3 P.

**κουφίζω II 2 b**, line 4, delete 'τῆς .. 16 J.' **3 b**, for this section read '*cancel* an entry in a register of tax-payers, κουφισθείσης αὐτῆς *PBremen* 24.7 (ii AD); κουφίσαι τὸ ὄνομα .. τοῦ πατρός *POxy.* 126.8 (vi AD); an item of property, τὰς γᾶς κουφισθῆναι ἀπὸ τοῦ ὀνόματος *PWürzb.* 18.10 (iv AD); med., *make an abatement* of claim, *PMasp.* 95.10 (vi AD); *reduce* a price, *BGU* 2332.13, 24 (AD 374)'

*κουφοκερᾰμεῖον, τό, *workshop* of a κουφοκεραμεύς, *POxy.* 1917.102 (vi AD).
*κουφοκερᾰμεύς, έως, ὁ, kind of potter, *POxy.* 1917.22 (vi AD), *PVindob.Tandem* 17.2 (vi/vii AD); cf. κοῦφος 6, neut. as subst., prob. referring to kind of lightweight ware.
*κουφοκερᾰμούργιον, τό, *pottery*, rest. in *CPR* 14.2.20 (vi/vii AD).
*κουφοκερᾰμουργός, ὁ, = κουφοκεραμεύς, *Stud.Pal.* 612.3 (vi AD), *BGU* 368.13, 29 (AD 615).
κοῦφος I 1, line 1, delete 'pl.' (v. section II 2) **6**, add '**b** transf. w. gen., συνέσεως κούφη Sch.S.*El.* 403.'
*κοφαλο-, incomplete wd., name of trade or profession in *PIand.*inv. 488 (*Aegyptus* 27.50, iii AD).
κόφῑνος II, after 'Boeotian' insert 'and Thess.' and add '*SEG* 34.558.28 (Larissa, ii BC)'
*κοφορέω, shortened form of κοπροφορέω, *convey manure*, *PHarris* 95.
*κοφορία, ἡ, *conveyance of manure*, *POxy.* 1220.8 (iii AD), v. °κοφορέω.
*κοχλαζοκύμων, ον, *with splashing wave*, *PMag.* 4.184.
κοχλιάζων, delete the entry.
*κοχλιάξων, ονος, ὁ, app. *shaft with screw-thread*, Orib. 49.20.6.
κοχλίας II, add '**6** *the pinna of the external ear* (opp. σκάφος), Poll. 2.85.'
κοχλιοειδής, delete '*spiral* .. πολύδονος'
*κοχλίον, τό, dim. of κόχλος, = τελλίνη, a type of mollusc, *Com.adesp.* 292.20 A.; in pl., Hsch. s.v. ξιφύδρια.
*κοχλιώδης, ες, *conchoid*, Ath. 3.86b.
κόχλος 1, line 3, after 'fem.' insert 'Theoc. l.c.' add '**b** κ. ναυτικός, type of mosaic design, *PCair.Zen.* 665 (iii BC).' **3**, for 'Eust. 728.47' read 'Eust. 728.48'
κοχῠδέω, add 'also **κοχυδεύω** dub. in Sophr. in *PSI* 1214*d*6'
+κόψα· ὑδρία Hsch.; cf. κοψία.
κραβᾰτιον, add 'also **κραββ-** Hsch. s.v. λέκτρα, also v.s.v. κράββατος'
*κραβᾰτοπόδιον, τό, *leg of a bed*, Sch.Od. 8.278 (gloss on ἑρμῖνες).
+κραβάτριος, ὁ, (κραβατάριος), masc. as subst., perh. *chamberlain*, *IPE* 2.297; cf. κραβακτήριος s.v. κράββατος, °κρεβαττάριος.
κράββᾰτος, line 6, after 'Virg.*Mor.* 5' insert 'γράβακτον *PMasp.* l.c.' and add 'also v.s.v. ‡κραβάτιον, °κραβάτριος, °κρεβαττάριος'
κρᾰδάω I, for '= κραδαίνω, only in part.' read '*brandish*' and after 'Il. 20.423' insert 'κραδάω τοῦδ' ὕπερ αἰγανέην epigr. in *IStraton.* 41(a)' add '**2** intr., *wave, quiver*, ἐπεὶ κελάδοντος ἀήτεω ταινίαι .. ἐφύπερθε διηέριαι κραδάουσι Opp.*C.* 4.410.' delete etym. note at end of article.
κρᾰδη I 1, delete '*quivering spray at the*' **III**, for this section read 'device for suspending actors above the stage, Ps.-Plu.*Prov.* 2.16, Poll. 4.128'
κράζω, p. 989, line 1, after 'Men.*Sam.* 204' insert 'κεκραγήσομαι Hsch. s.v. κεκραγήσει'; line 4, after 'ἔκρᾰγον (ἀν-)' insert 'Od. 14.467'; line 6, for 'late κέκρᾱγα' read 'l. κέκρᾱγ' in'; line 7, after 'κεκράγετε' insert '(κεκράγατε codd. RV)'; line 8, delete 'post-Hom.' **1**, add 'transf., perh. *babble*, κραζόμενα φάσκεις καὶ ἐγὼ φάσκω (pass.) *POxy.* 2353.2 (i AD)'
κραίνω I 1, line 3 fr. end, delete 'λάχῃ .. A.*Eu.* 347 (lyr.)' **III 1**, line 2, after 'Od. 8.391' insert 'Ephebic oath in *REG* 84.370 (κριν- in Poll. 8.106, Stob. 4.1.48)' **2**, add 'pass., *AP* 6.114'
κραιπᾰλόβοσκος, for '*which draws on drunkenness*' read '*provoked by a hangover*'
κραιπνός, add 'ἔβαινε κραιπνὸν βῆμα βαστάζων ποδός Ezek.*Exag.* 269 S.'
κράκτης, add 'v.l. in Ar.*Eq.* 304'
κράμβη, add '**4** prov., of stale repetition, Juv. 7.154, δὶς κ. θάνατος Sch.ad loc., Suid.'
κραμβήεις, for '*like a cabbage*' read '*of a cabbage*'
*κραμβιτάριος, ὁ, *cabbage-seller, greengrocer*, *ITyr* 31.
*κραμβιτᾶς, ᾶ, ὁ, perh. *vegetarian*, *AE* 1929.152 (κρανβ-, Thessalian Thebes), *Corinth* 8(3).563, *EHBS* 33.48 (pap., κραμπ-, all Byz.).
*κραμβοκέφᾰλος, ον, *cabbage-headed*, *PSI* 1259.7, *SB* 7997.7 (both ii/iii AD).
*κράμμη, ἡ, = κράμβη, *PCair.Zen.* 702.26 (iii BC).
κρᾶνα II, delete the section.
*Κραναΐδαι, οἱ, *sons of Cranaos*, i.e. people of Attica, E.*Supp.* 713 (cod. δαν-).
*Κραναῖος, α, ον, *Attic*, St.Byz. s.v. Κραναή.
*Κρᾱναῖος, v. ‡κρηναῖος.
κρᾰνάός 2, for '*hard*' read 'applied to things having a rough appearance' delete '**3** *stinging*' and add 'πίτυς *AP* 6.110'
κράνεια, line 3, after 'Od. 10.242' insert '(eaten by Diogenes, D.Chr. 6.62)'; line 4, for '*cherry-wood*' read '*cornel-wood*'; line 6, for '= *spear*' read '*spear of cornel-wood*' and before '*AP* 6.123 (Anyte)' insert '*AP* 6.122 (Nicias)'
κρᾰνειον, delete 'Amphis .. (prob.)'
*κρᾰνειος (A), α, ον, *of cornel-wood*, ἀστίλιον κράνειον *Edict.Diocl.* 14.4.
*Κράνειος (B), ὁ, name of a month at Buthrotum, P.Cabanes *L'Épire* no. 43 (iii/ii BC); perh. = Κάρνειος.
κράντωρ, at end for '*AP* 6.116 (Samos)' read '*AP* 6.166 (Samius)'
κράς I, add '*top, upper rim* of a *crater*, κρατῆρες .. ὧν κρᾶτ' ἔρεψον S.*OC* 473'
κράσπεδον 1, for this section read '*edge, border, fringe*, esp. of a garment, κράσπεδα στεμμάτων Ar.*V.* 475, Diph. 43.30, Theoc. 2.53, χρυσᾶ κ. Chamael.ap.Ath. 9.374a, Chrysipp.*Stoic.* 3.36.37; of a sail, E.*Med.* 524; in Jewish context, Lxx *Nu.* 15.38, 39, Sm.*Ez.* 5.3, al., *Ev.Matt.* 9.20; transf., τοῦ κρασπέδου τῆς κορυφῆς μου (app. = forelock), Aq.*Ez.* 8.3'
*κρασπέδωσις, εως, ἡ, *seaming of edges*, *PZen.Col.* 15.3, 5 (iii BC).
κραστήριον II, add 'perh. also *Inscr.Délos* 1452*A*30 (written κλαστήριον v.s.v.)'
*κραστιφόρος, ον, *producing fodder*, Pallad.ap.Ps.-Callisth. 3.13.
*κραστός, ά, όν, prob. past pass. part. of °κράω, cf. γράω, κράστις, etc., *fed at grass* (horses), *SEG* 25.556 (Haliartus, iii BC).
*κραταιγίς, ἡ, a name of the plant σατύριον, Plin.*HN* 26.99.
κρᾰταιόω I 2, add 'πολεμεῖν αὐτὸν ἐκραταιώθη Lxx 2*Ch.*35.22'
*Κρατεᾱνός, ὁ, cult-title of Apollo in Mysia, Robert *Hell.* 10.137ff.; -ή, ἡ, of Artemis, Ἀρτέμιδι Κρατιαν[ῇ] *SEG* 33.1101.3 (Paphlagonia).
*κρᾰτεραυγής, ές, (in dub. context, app.) *having powerful rays*, *Lyr.adesp.* 7(*d*).8 P.
κρᾰτερόφρων, for 'Διὸς .. *IG* 1².503' read 'Διὸς κρατερόφρ[ονι παιδί *CEG* 243 (cf. .. ]φρονι παιδί ib. 206)'
κρᾰτεύω, add 'in sense *hold in the hand*, *SEG* 23.220 (Messene, i AD)'
κρᾰτέω II 2, lines 1/2, delete '*prevail* .. 104' **4**, after '*master*' insert 'Pherecyd. 22(*a*) J.'; add '*to be restrained, held back*, οἱ δὲ ὀφθαλμοὶ αὐτῶν ἐκρατοῦντο τοῦ μὴ ἐπιγνῶναι αὐτόν *Ev.Luc.* 24.16' **IV 3**, add 'μὴ κρατεῖσθαι τὸν εἰς τόπον αὐτοῦ χειροτονηθέντα Modest.*Dig.* 27.1.13.5'
κρᾰτημα 3, add '*hilt* of a sword, prob. in Sch.E.*Hec.* 543'
κρᾱτήρ, add 'Myc. *ka-ra-te-ra*'
+κρᾱτηρίαρχος, a religious official in celebration of the Mysteries, *IGBulg.* 1.401.6 (-α[ρχ]ος, Thrace).
κρᾱτηρίζω II, add 'rest. in *IEryth.* 206.7-8 (iv BC), v.s.v. °κρατηρισμός'
κρᾱτηρίσκος, after 'ὁ' insert '*Inscr.Délos* 104.27 (364 BC)'
*κρᾱτηρισμός, ὁ, Ion. **κρητηρ-**, *serving of drink from a* κρατήρ *in a religious ceremony*, *IEryth.* 206.11 (iv BC).
κρᾱτηροφόρος, add 'of a coin, as subst., *Inscr.Délos* 1432*Bb*ii52 (ii BC)'
κρᾰτητής, add '**2** *pommel* of a sword, μύκης· τοῦ ξίφους ‹ὁ› κατὰ τὴν λαβὴν ὁ κ. καλούμενος Hsch.'
κράτιστος 2 b, (= *clarissimus*), add 'of a woman, *INikaia* 1062 (iii AD)'; add 'of a φυλή, *TAM* 4(1).238, 258; as cult-title of Zeus, Κράτιστος Μέγιστος Φροντιστής (= *Iupp.Opt.Max.Tutor*) *INikaia* 1141'
κράτος II 3, add 'as honorific appellation of the emperor, πρὸς τὸ ἡμέτερον κράτος Just.*Nov.* 113.1 pr.'
κραύγαζος, after 'Ptol.*Tetr.* 164' add '(v.l.)'
κραύγᾰσος, after '*shouter*' insert 'Ptol.*Tetr.* 164 (v.l.)'; add 'Hsch. s.v. βαβάκτης'
κραυγαστής, after '*AB* 223' insert 'Ptol.*Tetr.* 164'
*κρᾱφάγος, v. °κρεοφάγος.
*κράω, v. °γράω.
κρεάγρα, add 'written γρεάγρα *PLond.* 191.10; γρέγρα *PMich.*inv. 3163.44 (*TAPhA* 92.258, iii AD)'
κρέας, line 3, after 'etc.' insert 'κρεῖα *Schwyzer* 721.24 (Thebes-on-Mycale, iv BC), contr. κρῆ *ASAA* 33/4(1955/6).165, no. 14 (Ialysus)' and after 'κρεῶν .. 191' insert 'Cret., inscr. in *Kadmos* 9.126'; line 7, after 'κρέᾱ' insert 'Timocr. 1.11'
*κρεβαττάριος, α, ον, = κραβακτήριος (s.v. κράββατος), ἐνδρομίς *Edict.Diocl.* 19.5; cf. mod. Gk. τὸ κρεββάτι *bed*.
κρείων, line 4, after '(Il.) 11.751' insert 'w. gen. θεῶν κρείοντι Rhian. 1.21'; line 9, delete '3.10' and after '(lyr.)' insert 'οὐρανοῦ κ. Pi.*N.* 3.10'
κρεμάννῡμι, line 3 (form κρεμνάω), add 'also κριμν- *SEG* 33.1039 (Aeolian Cyme, ii BC)' **II 4**, delete the section.
κρεμασμός, line 3, for 'generally' read 'as employed in the reduction of dislocations'
κρέμβᾰλα, add 'Ath. 14.636c'
κρεμβᾰλιαστύς, add in final bracket 'also °βαμβαλιαστύς v.s.v.'
κρέξ II, after '*hair*' insert 'Call.*fr.* 288 Pf.'
+κρεοβόρος, ον, *feeding on meat*, cj. in A.*Supp.* 287 (cod. -βροτ-; cf. °κρεόβοτος).
*κρεόβοτος, ον, *fed on meat*, A.*Supp.* 287, rest. in *fr.* 451*l* R.
*κρεοδελός, ὁ, *spit for meat*, κρεοδ[ελός Ϝ]έξ inscr. in *PP* 42.42 (Tarentum, vi BC).
*κρεονομία, ἡ, *distribution of meat*, *Syria* 18.372 (Palmyra).

**κρεοπώλιον**, after '*butcher's shop*' insert '*meat market*' and add '*SEG* 23.207.34 (Messenia, ii AD)'

**κρεουργέω**, after '*mangle*' insert 'J.*AJ* 13.12.6, al.'

**κρεοφάγος**, add 'Dor. **κρᾱφάγος**, *Σώσι Νύμφων κραφάγε χαῖρε IG* 14.351 (Kephaloidion)'

***κρεοφῠλάκιον**, τό, perh. for *χρεωφυλάκιον* (rather than *meatstore*), *AE* 1936.32 (Cavalla, ii BC).

***κρεῦλλιον**, τό, dim. of *κρέας*, Theognost.*Can.* 126.

**κρήγυος 1**, for this section read '*good, honest, οὔ πώ ποτέ μοι τὸ κ. εἶπας* Il. 1.106, *ποτὶ οὐδὲν κράγυον σχολάζοντες* Lysis *Ep.* 3; of persons, *παρ' οἴνῳ κ. AP* 7.355 (Damag.), Herod. 4.46, 6.39; adv. *κρηγύως ἐπαιδεύθην* Call.*fr.* 193.30 Pf., *νομίμως καὶ κ.* Perict. ap.Stob. 3.28.21. **b** without moral connotation, *serviceable, desirable, ἄλλο μὲν οὐδὲν AP* 7.284 (Asclep.), *οὐδὲ γουνάτων πόνος κρήγυον a good symptom*, Hp.*Coac.* 31; of persons, *proficient, οὐκ ἐπίστανται, οὐδὲ κ. διδάσκαλοί εἰσι* Pl.*Alc.* 1.111e, *εἰ δ' εἰσὶ κ. τε καὶ παρὰ χρηστῶν* Theoc.*Ep.* 19.' **3**, delete the section.

**κρήδεμνον I**, add '**b** poet., of the tomb, *πέτρινα κ.* E.*Tr.* 508.' **II**, for this section read 'fig., of the walls or other defensive works of a city, pl., *Τροίης ἱερὰ κ.* Il. 16.100, Od. 13.388, *h.Cer.* 151, *h.Hom.* 6.2, B.*fr.* 20B.11 S.-M., Euph.*fr.* 54; sg., *Θήβης κρήδεμνον* Hes.*Sc.* 105. **b** of the stopper of a wine-jar, Od. 3.392.'

+**κρήδεσμον**, τό, *headband, κράδεσμα ἀργύρεα SEG* 19.618 (Metapontum, vi BC), Attic form in Hsch.

***Κρήζιμος**, ὁ, title of Zeus, *IEphes.* 3415 (ii/iii AD).

**κρήϊνον**, for '*larder*' read '*store-room for meat*'

***κρηματίς**, ίδος, ἡ, name of an article (perh. a cup) in a temple-inventory, *κ. ἱερά* in *IG* 7.3498.15, 20 (Oropus); cf. *κρημοφόρος*.

**κρήμνημι**, after lemma insert '(**κρίμν-**)'; line 2, for '*κρημνάντων*' read '*κριμνάντων*'; line 6, for '*κρημναμενᾶν*' read '*κριμναμενᾶν*'

**κρημνισμός**, add 'Heph.Astr. 2.24.8'

***κρημνοβᾰ́μων**, ον, gen. ονος, *cliff-walking, PMag.* 4.1365.

**κρημνοβάτης 2**, add 'Gr.Naz.*Carm.* 2.1.17.8 (*PG* 37.1267a)'

**κρημνός** (A) **1**, add 'prov. *ἐκ κρημνῶν γεννᾶσθαι* Heraclit.*Ep.* 4.2'

**κρηναῖος**, add '*Κρᾱναῖος*, title of Poseidon, *SEG* 35.590 (Larissa), fem., of Athena, *IG* 9(1).109 (Phocis)'

**κρήνη**, line 2, after '(Mytil.)' insert 'Alc. 150.5 L.-P.'; line 6, after '(Dreros, iii BC)' insert '*κράνα· κεφαλή source*, Hsch.'; add 'in title of Athena, *ἐν κράναις IG* 9(1).97.20 (Phocis, iii BC)'

***Κρηνίς**, ἡ, Dor. **Κρᾱν-**, ίδος, ἡ, *water-nymph*, Mosch. 3.29 (pl.).'

**κρηνῖτις**, add 'as epith. of nymphs, [*Νύμφαις ὑδρο*]*χόοις κρεινείτισιν* inscr. in *Gnomon* 59.612 (Lycaonia)'

***κρηπῑδάριος** (written *κριπ-*), ὁ, Lat. *crepidarius, maker of κρηπῖδες, AE* 1929.157 (Thess. Thebes, Chr.).

**κρηπῑδιαῖος**, for '*Rev.Phil.* 50.67 (Didyma, ii BC)' read '*Didyma* 41.27 (ii BC)'

+**κρηπΐδιον**, τό, archit., *floor-slab, SEG* 25.394 (Epid., iv BC), *Didyma* 39.33, 54, al. (all pl., ii BC).

***κρηπῑδόσφῠρος**, ὁ, ἡ, *one who wears boots covering the ankles*, of Athena, *PKöln* 245.10 (iii AD, verse).

**κρηπίς I 1 a**, for '*man's .. half-boot*' read '*shoe* with a platform sole attached by straps to the feet, worn by men and women'; after '*Parod.* 4' insert '(also interpr. as II 1 and as II 2)'; after 'Hist. 8' insert 'but *εἶδος ὑποδήματος, AB* 273, cf. Poll. 7.85; a man's shoe, *AB* l.c., cf. Plu. 2.760b; but there were women's *κρηπῖδες*, Luc.*Rh.Pr.* 15, cf. ‡*ὀπισθοκρηπίς*' **b**, for '*κρηπῖδες* .. themselves' read 'worn by Macedonians, Plu.*Ant.* 54, cf. Plu. 2 l.c.; by soldiers' **II**, line 4, after 'E.*Hel.* 547' insert '*step* of an altar, Lxx *Jl.* 2.17, 2*Ma.* 10.26'; line 7, before 'Onos. 4.4' insert 'Pl.*Lg.* 736e, *Plt.* 301e' **2**, add 'river-*bank*, Lxx *Jo.* 3.15, 4.18, 1*Ch.* 12.15'

**Κρής**, fem. *Κρῆσσα*, add '*SEG* 33.713 (Chalcis, iv BC)'

***Κρησίς**, ίδος, fem. adj. *Cretan, σίδη Κ.* Nic.*Al.* 490.

+**Κρῆσσα**, ἡ, v.s.v. *Κρής*. **2** as subst., = *κρήτη, chalk, Hippiatr.* 1.130.57, Hor.*Carm.* 1.36.10.

**κρηστήριον**, add '*IG* $2^2$.1424*a*277 (add.)'

**κρησφύγετον**, add 'Poll. 1.10'

***Κρητᾱγενέτας**, = °*Κρηταγενής, Amyzon* 14 (202/1 BC).

***Κρητᾱγενής**, ές, *born in Crete*, epith. of Zeus, *Inscr.Cret.* 2.xvii 1.18 (Lisos, iii BC), al.

**Κρητάρχης**, for '*CIG* 2744' read '*MAMA* 8.426' and add '*Inscr.Cret.* 4.250 (i BC)'

**Κρήτη**, add '(personified) *SEG* 31.923 (Caria, i/ii AD)'

***Κρητηνεύς**, ὁ, title of a sacred ox, *Schwyzer* 768 (written *Κρετενέος* gen., ?v/iv BC).

***κρητηρισμός**, v. °*κρατηρ-*.

**Κρητικός II 2**, add 'neut. as subst., *Κρητικόν· .. καὶ γένος ὀρχήσεως* Hsch.' add '**3** *Κρητική* (sc. *γῆ*) kind of earth used for fulling, *PHerm.* 12.8 (iv AD), cf. Lat. *creta.*'

**Κρητογενής**, delete the entry.

***κρήφιον**, τό, wd. of unkn. meaning (perh. a tool, cf. *κράφα*), included among articles given as security, *PMich.*III 173.11 (iii BC).

**κρῑβανάριος**, add 'perh. related to Persian *grībān "coat of mail"* rather than *κρίβανος*, cf. *κρίβανον breastplate* (Lampe)'

**κρῑβάνη**, for 'Alcm. 20 .. Ath.)' read 'Sosib. 6 (Ath. 3.115a, 14.646a)'

**κρῑβανος I 2**, add 'part of a hot-bath system, *SEG* 32.1502 (*κλιβ-*, Palestine, v AD)'

**κρῑβανωτός**, for 'Alcm. 20 (codd. Ath.)' read 'Alcm. 94 P.'

**κρῐγή I**, after 'also **κριγμός**' insert 'Ael.*NA* 5.51 (pl.)' **II**, delete the section transferring 'Hippon. 54' to section III and adding 'in this sense perh. parox.'

***κρίγκιον**, v. ‡*κρίκιον*.

**κρίζω**, for '*κεκριγότες*' read '*κεκρῑγότες*' and add '*κρίζει· ὀξὺ αὐλεῖ* Hsch.'

**κριθή**, add 'also *χριθή IG* $1^3$.232.16, 42, 250.22 (Attica, v BC); Myc. *ki-ri-ta*'

**κρῑθινος**, after '*beer*' insert 'X.*An.* 4.5.26'

***κρῑθόβωλον**, τό, perh. *barley cake for fodder, PCair.Zen.* 658.6 (iii BC); cf. *βωλόπυρος*.

***κρῑθολογέω**, *check* (*consignments of*) *grain for purity, κρι*[*θ*]*ο*[*λ*]*ογηθῆναι τὸν πυρόν PPetaus* 53.11 (ii AD), v. sqq.

***κρῑθολογία**, ἡ, *tax paid in compensation for adulteration of barley, POxy.* 2021.3 (vi/vii AD); also **κρῑθηλογία**, *Theb.Ostr.* 113 (ii/iii AD), *PIand.* 150 (iii AD).

**κρῑθολόγος**, delete 'hence .. 26.1'

***κρῑθόν**, τό, v. °*κριθός*.

***κρῑθοποιός**, όν, *used in preparing barley, κόσκινον* Poll. 10.114.

**κρῑθόπῡρον**, add '*EA* 13.40 (?Lydia, iii AD)'

**κρῑθοπώλης**, add '*SEG* 25.180 ii 55 (Athens, iv BC), *ITyr* 39C, 178 (Rom.imp.)'

***κρῑθός**, ὁ (or *-όν, τό*), error or variant for *κριθή, ἐν κριθῷ CPR* 7.45.7 (v AD), *PMich.*XI 608.6 (vi AD).

***κρῑθοσπορέω**, *sow with barley, τὴν κριθοσπορουμένην γῆν PThmouis* I 86.4 (ii AD).

**κρῑθοφόρος**, add '*PCair.Zen.* 728.4 (iii BC, fem. as subst. sc. *γῆ*)'

**κρίθων**, add '(*ἐπώνυμον ἀνδρὸς μοιχαλίου* La.)'

+**κρῑκέλλιον**, τό, *hoop, ring*, Sch.A.*Pr.* 74 (*-έλιον*), Alex.Trall. 8.2.

**κρίκιον**, after lemma insert '(*κρίγκιον* Sch.Od. 7.90, of a handle)'; add '(articles of jewellery, cf. Pontic *κρικί ear-ring*)'

***κρῑκολάγιον**, τό, wd. of uncertain meaning, perh. vessel with ring-shaped handle, *PVindob.* G16694 (*-ιν*, *ZPE* 35.130, vi AD).

**κρίκος 1**, for 'on a horse's breast-band' read 'on the middle of a yoke' **8**, add 'Str. 5.3.8' add '**10** *κρίκος· κίρκος ἔνθα ἡ κώπη εἰσέρχεται* Hsch.'

**κρίμα I 2**, add '*κρίματι βουλῆς TAM* 4(1).32' at end of article for 'ῐ .. poetry' read 'ῐ in inscr. in *JWI* 2.369 (i AD)'

***κρίμνημι**, = °*κρήμνημι*.

**κρίμνον**, after '*τό*' insert '(in codd. also *κρίμνον*)' **2**, delete the section. **3**, after '*crumbs*' insert '*AP* 6.302 (Leon.); *grains*'; after 'Herod. 6.6' insert 'Babr. 108.9, 32'

**κριμνός**, (in parenth.) for '*κριμνον*' read '*κριμμον*'

***κριμνοσπορέω**, *sow* (?)*barley, PStrassb.* 864.4 (ii AD).

**κρίνον I**, add '**3** a perfumed unguent, Pompon.*Dig.* 34.2.21.1.' **IV**, add '*MAMA* 9.61'

***κριντήρ**, ῆρος, ὁ, *judge*, epigr. in *Inscr.Cret.* 4.325 (Gortyn, v AD, pl.); cf. *κριτήρ, -ής*.

**κρῑνω**, line 9, after 'Aeol. **κρίννω**' insert 'Alc. 130.32 L.-P.' **II 1**, line 8, after 'Hdt. 3.31' insert '*οἱ κεκριμένοι classical authors*, Poll. 9.15, 153'; line 9, after 'Pi.*N.* 7.7' insert 'w. acc. resp., *Λεσβίαδες κριννόμεναι φύαν* Alc. l.c.'; line 11, after '(Leon.)' insert '**b** *admit* to a class, *number* in it'; line 12, after 'E.*Supp.* 969 (lyr.)' insert '*GVAK* 3.6'; line 13, after 'Luc.*Am.* 2' add 'esp. of admitting as a competitor in games, *κριθέντα Πύθεια JRS* 3.295 (Pisidian Antioch), *κ. ἐν Δελφοῖς IG* 12(2).388 (Mytilene)' **2 a**, add 'so *κρινθήμεναι* A.R. 2.148, *τὸ κριθέν* = (*senatus*) *consultum*, D.S. 14.113.7' **3 c**, add 'fig., *to be in a critical condition, τῆς πόλεως κρινομένης SEG* 24.1217 (i BC)' **7**, line 2, delete 'cf. *Supp.* 396' **8**, line 2, after '(ii BC)' insert 'Lxx *Is.* 41.6, al., Nic.Dam.*fr.* 47.8 J.'

**κριός IV**, add '**2** archit., perh. *buttress, PEnteux.* 8.11 (iii BC, pl.).'

**κρῑοτάφος**, add '*PTeb.* 61b.401 (118/7 BC), ostr. in *CE* 55.311'

+**κρῑοφάγος**, ον, *that eats ram's flesh, Θρήϊκες ἀμορβοὶ κριοφάγοι* Nic.*Th.* 50; cf. *κ.· θεός τις, ᾧ κριοὶ θύονται* Hsch.

**κρίσις II 1 b**, after this section insert '**c** = (*senatus*) *consultum*, D.S. 14.113.6; = *decretum*, D.Chr. 37.9; = *iurisdictio*, Str. 14.5.6; *ἐπὶ τῆς τῶν διαφορῶν κρίσεων* = *stlitibus iudicandis, IEphes.* 701 (i AD).'; for pres. '**c**' read '**d**' and add 'cf. *τὴν ὥραν τῆς κρίσεως SEG* 31.1419 (iii/iv AD); *the judgement* of God, *TAM* 4(1).375 (Jewish)' **III 2**, add '**b** *critical stage in life, climacteric*, Sen.*Ep.* 83.4.' add '**V** *class* or *category* of competitors in games, *ἀγωνισάμενον τὰς τρεῖς κ. παῖδα ἀγένειον ἄνδρα CIG* 2810*b*9 (Aphrodisias), *IGLS* 1265 (Laodicea, iii AD); *παῖς κρίσεως τῆς Ἀγησιλάου IG* 5(1).19.10, al. (Sparta), ib. 14.754 (Naples).'

**κρισσός I**, add 'X.*Eq.* 1.5'

*κρῑτεύω, serve as κριτής (iudex), SEG 35.714 (Maced., ii/iii AD).

κριτήριον 2 b, add 'of Fate, ISmyrna 541 (i AD)'

κρῑωπός, delete '= κριός VII, POxy. 1801.26'

κροαίνω, delete 'only pres. part.' (-ειν in Philostr.Im. 1.30 and VS 25)

*Κροθιᾱτᾱς, v. °Κορθιάτᾱς.

*Κροκᾱγόριος, ὁ, name of a month, Hesperia 27.75 (unkn. provenance, c.200 BC).

*κροκαλλίς, ίδος, ἡ, a precious stone, Plin.HN 37.154.

κροκᾶτον, delete 'Asin.' and add 'cf. Lat. crocatus'

*κροκάω, to be yellow, κροκόωντες κόρυμβοι Nic.fr. 74.22 G.-S.

*κροκεανόν, τό, alternative name for κώνειον, Sch.Nic.Al. 186a Ge.

κρόκη, line 2, for 'only in Hsch.' read 'Hsch., Theognost.Can. 40' for 'II' read 'κρόκη (B), ἡ,' and add 'cf. κρόκκαι'

*κρόκη (C)· πέμματος εἶδος Hsch.

+κροκίας, ου, ὁ, saffron-coloured, of a cock, Plu. 2.375e. 2 name of a precious stone, Plin.HN 37.191.

κρόκκαι, add '(κρόκαι La.; cf. °κρόκη (B))'

κροκοβαφής, for 'metaph., .. dying men' read 'of blood, as the colour associated w. fear'

*κροκόδεσμος, ον, bound with saffron, Theognost.Can. 21.9.

*κροκοδίανον, τό, a species of teasel, An.Boiss. 2.396.

κροκοδῑλέα, for 'dung' read 'a sweet-smelling substance from the intestines'

κροκόδῑλος, line 5, for 'cf. κροκύδιλος Hippon. 119 .. Indogerm.Forsch. 15.7)' read 'κερκύδιλος Hippon. 155, 155a W. (var. κρεκυ- and κροκύδειλος)' and add 'cocodrillus, Sen.QN 4a.2.13'; add 'sp. κορκόδειλος Peripl.M.Rubr. 15'

κροκόεις, add 'Tyrt. 18.2 W.'

*κροκοπώλης, ου, ὁ, app. saffron-seller, SEG 37.214 (iv BC).

κρόκος, line 1, insert in bracket 'also τό, v. section 4'

κροκόττας, for 'an Indian wild beast .. hyena' read 'a wild beast found in Ethiopia and India, prob. some kind of hyena'

κροκόω I, for 'crown with yellow ivy' read 'make yellow'

κροκύδιον, place before 'κροκυδισμός', deleting 'hence'

*κροκύδιστος, gloss on οὖλος, Sch.Gen.Il. 16.224, (cod. -δωτος).

κροκύς 1, add 'b pl., woollen cloth, AP 9.567 (Antip.).' add '3 a plant, Hsch.'

κροκύφαντος, after 'woven' insert 'BGU 1300.23 (iii/ii BC)' and after 'Subst.' insert 'Aq.Is. 3.19'

*κροκυφάντωτον, τό, network on a capital, Aq.Je. 52.22, 23.

*κροκών, ῶνος, ὁ, saffron-bed, Hdn.Gr. 1.29.

κροκώτινος, add 'IG 2².1529.17 (Attica, iv BC)'

κροκώτιον, add 'IG 2².1529.18 (Attica, iv BC)'

*κροκωτοβᾰφής, ές, saffron-dyed, Sch.E.Hec. 471.

κροκωτός 2, for 'worn by gay women' read 'worn by women on special occasions'; add 'also fem. in Lat., Naev.Trag. 43, Plaut.Aul. 832 (corc-)'

κρομμύδιον, add 'Rémondon, Le monastère de Phoibammon no. 21 (?iv AD)'

κρόμμυον I 1, after 'Bias ap.D.L. 1.83' add 'cf. Plu. 2.153e' II, line 5, for '(perh. metri gr.)' read 'Philem. 122'; add '[κρομμύων [ῡ] Nic.Al. 413]'

κρομμυόφακον, delete the entry.

Κρονίδης I, add 'of Chiron, Poet.de herb. 115, Orph.L. 11'

*Κρονίσκος, ὁ, dim. of Κρόνος; Κρονίσκοι ἑπτὰ ἐν ἑνί, title of a work by Galen, Gal.Libr.Propr. 12.

Κρονίων II, add 'BCH 116.279.1 (Colophon, ii BC)' add 'III Κρονίωνας· παλαιοὺς ἀνθρώπους Hsch.'

Κρόνος I 2, ἡ Κρόνου ἡμέρα, add 'T&MByz 7.323f. no. 15 (Thessalonica), SEG 31.830 (Sicily, both iv/v AD)'

κροσσοί, add 'sg., Hsch. s.v. θυσανόεσσα; Lxx Ex. 28.22'

κροτᾰλια, after 'each other' insert 'BGU 1300.25 (iii/ii BC)'

κρόταλον I, after 'in dances' insert 'Sapph. 44.25 L.-P.'; add 'Ath. Asklepieion v 75 (iii BC); see also °κρούπεζα 2'

*κροτεῦσαι· τὸ μὴ πλῆρες δοῦναι Theognost.Can. 21.

κροτέω II 2 a, after 'Thphr.Char. 11.3' insert 'cf. κροτήσατε Suid., = plaudite' 4, line 2, after 'weld together' insert 'AP 6.117 (Pancrat.)'

κρουματικός, after 'Plu. 2.1138b' insert 'Phot. s.v. νιγλαρεύων'

*κρουματογρᾰφία, ἡ, music., instrumental notation, Anon.Bellerm. 11.

κρουνός 1, add 'ὁ ἐν Κρουνοῖς, of Asclepius, IG 9²(1).631 (Naupactus, ii BC), al.' 4, after 'nozzle' insert 'App.Anth. 3.67 (Hedyl.), IG 11(2).287A.79'

*κρουνοφόρον· οὕτω καλεῖταί τι τῶν ἐν ταῖς ναυσίν Hsch.

*κρούπᾰλα, τά, perh. = °κρούπανα, ἀμφίλινα κρούπαλα S.fr. 44.

*κρούπανα· ξύλινα ὑποδήματα. καὶ κλεῖς Hsch.

*κρούπεζα, ἡ, usu. pl., clogs or wooden shoes worn by Boeotians and used in crushing olives, Paus.Gr. κ48 E., Phot. 2 clapper of wood or metal pressed by an aulos-player with his foot to mark the rhythm, Poll. 7.87 (sg.); οἱ δὲ κρόταλον, ὃ ἐπιψοφοῦσιν οἱ αὐληταί· τὸ βάταλον Phot.

+κρουπέζιον, τό, dim. of κρούπεζα, τὰ ξύλινα σανδάλια κρουπέζια λέγεται, καὶ ὑποδήματα ξύλινα, μεθ' ὧν τὰς ἐλαίας πατοῦσι Hsch. s.v. κρουπεζούμενος. 2 clapper used by αὐληταί, Poll. 7.87.

*κρούπετα· ὑψηλὰ ἢ ξύλινα ὑποδήματα, ἢ γυναικεῖα Hsch.

κρούστης, add 'for formation cf. Προκρούστης X.Mem. 2.1.14, etc.'

κρουστικός II 2, for this section read 'of a speaker, writer, or of style, forcible, emphatic, Ar.Eq. 1379, Luc.Dem.Enc. 32, Hermog.Id. 1.12'

κρούω 1, add 'of a scorpion, κρουστὶς (i.e. κρουσθεὶς) ὑπὸ σκορπίου Lefebvre RIGC no. 120' 5, line 2, for 'Simon. 183' read 'AP 7.24.6 ([Simon.])' 8, add 'perh. at SEG 35.915 (Naxos, vi BC)'

κρῠερός, line 4, after 'E.fr. 916.6 (anap.)' insert 'Phryn.Trag. 6 S.'; line 5, after 'icy-cold' insert 'Alc. 286(a).3 L.-P.'

κρῡμᾰλέος, after 'chilly' insert 'Eratosth. 16.10'

κρυπτάδιος, line 3, after 'Il. 1.542' insert '(neut. pl. as adv.)' and for 'Regul.Adv. .. 6.182' read 'also advs. -ίως Man. 2.195, 6.182, -ίῃ in hiding, Max. 339'

κρυπτή I, after 'Callix. 1' insert 'PSI 547.18 (iii BC), Str. 17.1.37, Ev.Luc. 11.33, Labeo Dig. 43.17.3.7' add 'b covered passage, arcade, Sen.Ep. 57.1, Juv. 5.106, CIL 1.1505.3.'

κρυπτήρ, add 'as subst., Inscr.Délos 1403Abii79 (ii AD)'

κρυπτός, add 'archit., τὸν κ. περίπατον Ath. 5.206a'

κρύπτω, line 3, after 'κρύψα 11.244' insert 'aor. 2 ἔκρυφε AP 7.423 (Antip.Sid.), 700 (Diod.), Q.S. 1.393, Nonn.D. 7.45, al.'

κρυσταίνομαι, delete 'with cold, freeze'

κρυστάλλινος I, add 'νίπτρα AP 9.330 (Nicarch.)' deleting this ref. in section II.

κρυσταλλοειδής I, at end delete 'Adv. .. 2.11.2' II, add 'Paul.Aeg. 3.22.30 (184.17, 20 H.); adv. -δῶς Placit. 2.11.2'

κρύσταλλος, after 'ὁ' insert 'also ἡ, v. sense II with Suppl.' II, after '(Claudian)' insert 'Q.S. 10.415'

*κρυσταλλοφόρος, ον, producing rock-crystal, Ps.-Callisth. 118.30.

*κρυφιμαῖος, α, ον, = κρύφιμος, IEphes. 4106.6 (iv AD).

κρύφω, delete the entry.

κρυψίδομος, delete the entry.

*κρυψίδρομος, ον, running secretly, Orph.H. 51.3.

κρωσσός 1, add 'also for unguents, Plu.Arist. 21' 2, after 'Mosch. 4.34' insert 'Lyc. 369 (pl.)'

+κρωτάνεροι (dub.)· βάναυσοι πολῖται, καὶ ἐξελευθεριωταί Hsch. (βάναυσοι. πολῖται. καὶ ἐξελεύθεροι. ἰδιῶται La.).

*κτάμιον, τό, special type of cultivated land, PMich.II 123ʳ iv 33 (AD 45), PMil.Vogl. 83.25, 105.19, 170.6, al. (all ii AD).

*κτάρα· ἰχθὺς βραχύτερος πάντων Hsch.

*Κτᾶρος, ὁ, epith. of Hermes, Lyc. 679.

κτέᾰνον, lines 8/10, for 'Hom. .. "wealth")' read 'dat.pl. κτεάνεσσι epigr. in IG 2².11120.8 (c.iii AD) (unless old dat. pl. of κτέαρ q.v.)'

+κτέαρ, ατος, τό, = κτέανον (which is prob. after old pl. of κτέαρ, *κτέανα), Hom. only in dat. pl. κτεάτεσσι, Il. 23.829, Od. 14.115, cf. Pi.O. 5.24, E.fr. 791.3: nom. and acc. sg. in later poetry, Maiist. 33, AP 9.52 (Carph.), 9.752 (Asclep. or Antip.Thess.), 11.27 (Maced.), Q.S. 4.543; dat. pl. κτέάτοις Hdn.Gr. 2.936.

*κτεᾰτισμα, ατος, τό, possession, hymn in BE 1991.419 (Berezan, i AD).

κτείνω 2, add 'τοῦ κτείνειν .. ἐξουσίαν = ius gladii, J.BJ 2.117'

κτείς, line 1, delete 'Edict.Diocl. 13.3' and transfer to end of section 1 6, after 'Art. 51' insert 'Call.fr. 343 Pf.' and delete 'Call.fr. 308' before 'AP 5.131'

*κτενᾶς, ᾶ, ὁ, comb-maker or wool-carder, MAMA 3.327, 739 (Corycus); cf. κτενιστής II.

κτενίζω, add 'II card, pass. pf. part., dub. in PIand.inv. 314 in Aegyptus 27.49 (ii/iii AD, ἐκτενισμ[.. pap.).'

κτένιον 1, add 'of κτείς, hair-comb, Edict.Diocl. 13.7'

+κτενιστής, οῦ, ὁ, hairdresser, Gal. 13.1038, Gloss. II wool-carder, PTeb. 322.23 (ii AD), BGU 1021.5 (iii AD), v. Aegyptus 26.41.

*κτενιστρίδιον, τό, hairdresser's shop, PAmst.inv. 62 (Mnemosyne 30.146).

κτῆμα 2, at end, estate, farm, etc., add 'Men.Dysc. 328, 737 S.'; vineyard, add 'SB 11240 (vi/vii AD); pl., SB 11009 (iii/iv AD)'

*κτηνάρχης, ου, ὁ, one in charge of providing transport animals, SB 11223.9 (AD 332).

*κτηναρχία, ἡ, provision of transport animals, SB 10202 (iii/iv AD), 11223.5, 9, al. (AD 332).

κτηναφαίρεσις, add 'PLond. 1677.35 (vi AD)'

+κτηνίτης, ου, ὁ, one having charge of (transport) animals, cattle-driver, Θησεὺς κτηνείτης ὁ λαλούμενος MAMA 8.569; as title of Hermes, Schwyzer 721.9 (Thebes-on-Mycale, iv BC).

κτῆνος, τό, line 1, before 'flocks and herds' insert 'possessions, esp.'; line 2, after 'h.Hom. 30.10' insert 'Hes.fr. 200.9 M.-W.'

*κτῆνος (B), ὁ, property, wealth, Hes.fr. 193.5, 198.6. M.-W.

κτηνοτροφεῖον, for 'cattle-stall' read 'place for cattle-breeding' and add 'Heph.Astr. 3.5.71'

κτηνοτροφέω, for 'keep cattle' read 'rear cattle' and add 'Heph.Astr. 3.5.35'

κτηνοτροφία, for 'cattle-keeping' read 'rearing of cattle'

**κτηνοτρόφος**, for '*keeping cattle, pastoral*' read '*raising cattle*' and for '*cattle-keeper*' read '*cattle-rearer*'

**κτήσιος I**, for '*belonging to property*' read '*that belongs to one, one's own*' and add 'transf., ἐπεὶ κτησίων φρενῶν ἐξέδυς S.*fr.* 210.36' **II**, add 'cf. Πάσιος'

**κτῆσις II 1**, for '(from pf.)' read '*thing possessed, possession*' **2**, add '*PPrincet.* 166.9 (ii/iii AD), κωμητικὴ κ. ib. 134.i.1 (iv AD)' add '**3** *title of possession*, καθὼς περιέχ(ε)ι ἡ κ. *Hierapolis* 88.1, cf. 216.8, 262.2.'

***κτήτης**, ου, ὁ, *proprietor*, Hsch. s.v. κτήτορες οἰκιῶν.

**κτίδεος**, after 'ἰκτίδεος' for '(which is not in use)' read '(Suid.)' and at end add 'prob. originally fr. misdivision of ἐπ' ἰκτιδέην in pre-Homeric version of 10.335'

**κτίζω**, add 'cf. Myc. athematic 3 pl. *ki-ti-je-si* (κτίενσι), part. *ki-ti-me-na*, cf. ἐϋκτίμενος'

**κτίλος I**, lines 3/4, delete 'ἱερέα .. Pi.*P.* 2.17' and for 'perh. their *cherished* eggs' read 'dub. sens.' **II**, for '*ram*' read '*the leading animal* (*ram*) *of a flock*' and add '*AP* 9.72 (Antip.)'

**κτίσμα 1**, *building*, add '*SEG* 31.1472, 34.327 (Chr.)'

**κτίστης I 1**, of Apollo, add '*SEG* 31.1287 (Side), 31.1575 (Cyrene)'; add 'of Heracles, *SEG* 35.842 (Moesia, ii/iii AD); of Hadrian, identified with Zeus Olympios, *SEG* 33.943, al.'; add 'granted as a title to outstanding citizens, *SEG* 31.910 (Caria, iii AD), etc.' add '**IV** name given to certain Thracian ascetics, οἳ χωρὶς γυναικὸς ζῶσιν, Posidon.ap.Str. 7.3.3.'

***κτιστικός**, ή, όν, of a κτιστής, *foundry*, *IHadr.* 132 (ii AD).

**κτιστύς**, for 'Ion. for κτίσις' read '= κτίσις' and add '*AAWW* 1948.305/6 (Egypt, Ptolemaic)'

**κτίστωρ**, add 'of Constantine, as "restorer", *Salamine* 202'

**κτίτης**, add 'Myc. *ki-ti-ta*'

**κτοίνα**, add 'Myc. *ko-to-na*, *ko-to-i-na*, *estate* (exact meaning uncertain)'

**κτοινᾱ́της**, read 'κτοινᾱ́τᾱς' and s.v. κτοινέτης, add 'Myc. *ko-to-ne-ta*'

***κτουπων** (?parox.), Cret. wd. of uncertain meaning and inflection, *SEG* 23.566.19 (Axos, iv BC).

**κτώ**, delete the entry.

**κῠάθειον**, before 'Nic.*Th.* 591' insert '*IG* 1³.405.10 (Athens, v BC)'

**κῠαθίζω II**, add 'repeated at Plu.*Marc.* 17.1'

**κῠαθίς**, add '*Inscr.Délos* 104.24 (pl., 364 BC)'

**κύᾰθος I**, delete 'Anacr. 63.5' add '**2** *vessel for cupping*, *Inscr.Perg.* 8(3).72.9 (sp. κύεθος).' **II**, add 'Anacr. 11(*a*).5 P., Nic.*Th.* 582, *Al.* 58'

***κυαίστωρ**, v. °κουαίστωρ.

***κυαιστώριος**, v. °κουαιστώριος.

**κῠᾰμιαῖος**, add '*Iiasos* 20.9 (iv BC)'

***κῠᾰμικός**, ή, όν, unexpl. deriv. of κύαμος, *IEphes.* 4123.19 (Rom.imp.).

**κῠᾰ́μινος**, add 'ἄχυρα *Gp.* 9.10.1'

***Κῠᾰμίτης**, ου, ὁ, god or hero *of the bean*, prob. Iacchus, Paus. 1.37.4, Hsch.

***κῠᾰμοπώλισσα**, ἡ, *seller of beans*, *PPanop.* 15 (iv AD).

**κύᾰμος**, add '**V** name of a small monetary unit, *Rh.Mus.* 60.331 (Tauromenium, i BC).'

**κῠᾰμωνίτης**, for '*bean-grower*' read '*one who works in bean-fields*'

***κῠᾰ́νασπις**, ιδος, ὁ, ἡ, *having a dark shield*, Anacr. 4.2 P.

**κῠᾰναυγής**, add 'of Circe, *Lyr.adesp.* 7(*c*).5 P.; of Persephone, *SEG* 35.1683 (Egypt, Hellen.)'

***κῠᾰναυγίς**, ίδος, ἡ, app. = κυαναυγής (in fem.), *Suppl.Hell.* 991.12 (poet. word-list, iii BC).

**κῠᾰναῦλαξ**, delete 'Orac.ap.'

**κῠᾰ́νεος II 1**, add 'late dat. pl. as fr. *κυανής, τίτλον περὶ τύμβῳ ἔγειρεν γράμμασι κυάνεσσι Mitchell *N.Galatia* 338' **2**, add 'applied to night, κυανέας [πο]λυόμματον [ποί]κιλμα νυκτ[ός lyr. in *POxy.* 2879 i 1'

***κῠᾰνοέθειρα**, fem. adj., *dark-haired*, *Suppl.Hell.* 991 (poet. word-list, iii BC).

***κῠᾰνόζῠγος**, ον, *having a dark yoke*, *Suppl.Hell.* 991 (poet. word-list, iii BC).

***κῠᾰνόκολπος**, ον, *having a dark recess*, *dark-bosomed*, *Suppl.Hell.* 991 (poet. word-list, iii BC).

**κῠᾰνόπεπλος**, after 'Hes.*Th.* 406' insert 'ὀμίχλη, of evening twilight, Musae. 113, 232'

**κύᾰνος I 4**, after '*cornflower*' insert '*AP* 4.1.54 (Mel.)' at end add 'Myc. *ku-wa-no*; cf. compd. *ku-wa-no-wo-ko-i* (dat. pl.) *cyanus-worker*'

***κῠᾰνόσελμος**, ον, *having dark benches*, δόρυ poet. in *POxy.* 2625 *fr.* 1.4.

***κῠᾰνοχίτων**, ωνος, ὁ, ἡ, *dark-robed*, Pi.*Dith.* 3.5.

**Κῠᾰνοψιών**, after 'month' insert 'in Chios, *SEG* 17.379.6 (v BC)'; after 'Κυανεψιών' insert '*SEG* 30.977 (Olbia, v BC)'

***κυβαλία** ἡ, app. some form of sexual perversion, *PMasp.* 97ᵛ(D)45 (vi AD); cf. κυβάλης.

**κύβδα**, after 'Ar.*Eq.* 365' insert 'εἰς γόνατα κύβδ' ἑστάναι id.*Pax* 897'

***Κύβδᾰσος**, ὁ, one of several invented names for gods of coition, Pl.Com. 174.17; cf. κύβδα.

**κύβεθρον**, for '= κυψέλη II' read 'a kind of container' and add 'see also °κόβαθρον'

**κύβελα**, delete the entry (gloss refers to Κύβελα, v.s.v. Κυβέλη).

***Κῠβελείη**, ἡ, title of Mother Goddess, Μητρὶ Κυβελείη(ι) *SEG* 22.511 (Chios, iv BC).

**Κυβέλη**, add 'archaic form Ϙυβάλα *SEG* 35.1820 (Locr.Epiz., vii/vi BC)'

**κῠβερνάω**, after lemma insert 'Cypr. κυμερέναι, s.v. κυμερνήτης, κυμερῆναι' **I 3**, after '*govern*' insert 'Heraclit. 41, Parm. 12.3'; add 'w. gen. κυβερνᾶν θεῶν τε καὶ ἀνθρώπων Pl.*Smp.* 197b'

**κῠβερνήτης**, line 1, add 'Dor. κυβερνάτας Alcm. 1.94 P., *SEG* 33.640 (Rhodes, ii/i BC)' **2**, add 'κ. Νείλου, title of a priest, *SB* 4100 (Philae), *OGI* 676 (Silsilis, ii AD)'

**κῠβερνητικός 1**, line 4, after '*Grg.* 511d' insert 'Arist.*EE* 1220ᵇ24, 1247ᵃ6'

**κῠβερνος**, add 'Hdn.*fr.* p. 25 H.'

**κῠβεύω I 2**, add '*Hell.Oxy.* 1.2 B.'

**κῡδᾰ́λιμος**, after 'also η, ον' insert 'Alc. 129.6 L.-P.'; add 'of a goddess, Ὄμπνια κυδαλίμη *SEG* 30.1272 (Caria, late Hellen.)'

***κυδάω**, unexpld. wd. in *POxy.* 2741 *fr.* 1b col.2.

**κύδιμος**, after '= κυδάλιμος' insert 'Doroth.*fr.* 38.11 S.'; add 'w. dat., Βιτιανὸν .. κύδιμον εὐνομίαις *SEG* 29.1139 (Miletus, iv/v AD)'

**κῡ́διστος 1**, add 'comp. κυδίων, ἕτερον δ' ἑτέρου κυδίον' ἔθηκεν Il.Pers. 5.2' **2**, add 'v. κυδρός at end'

***κύδνος**· κύκνος Hsch.

⁺**κῡδνός**, ή, όν, v.l. for κυδρός (in same sense), Hes.*Th.* 328, A.R. 4.1333, perh. also *GVI* 743.7.

**κῡδοιμός**, lines 4/5, delete '5.593; after 'Ar.*Pax* 255' insert 'as the weapon wielded by Eris, Il. 5.593'

**κῡδρός**, add 'X.*Eq.* 10.15'

⁺**Κῠδωνία**, Cret. town, Th. 2.85, Myc. *ku-do-ni-ja*, (mod. Khania). **2** *quince-tree*, cf. Κυδωνέα, *Gp.* 4.10.24.

***κυεσσωνάρ(ιοι)**, οἱ, app. Lat. *quaestionarii*, *POxy.* 2050.2 (vi AD).

***κυέστωρ**, ορος, ὁ, v. °κουαίστωρ.

**Κυζικηνός**, add 'also as ethnic of persons, Hdt. 4.76.3, etc.'

***κῡητικός**, ή, όν, *relating to conception*, Clem.Al.*Paed.* 2.10.

***κυήτωρ**, ορος, ὁ, ἡ, *parent*, of a bird, Cyran. 96 (pl.), cf. Eust. 1546.21.

***κυηφόρος**, ον, σωτήριος κ. δίφρος, app. kind of chair used for childbirth, Ps.-Callisth. 12.2.

**Κῠθέρεια**, form Κυθήρη, add '*SEG* 31.963 (Ephesus)'

**κύθρα**, etc., for '**κυθρόκαυλος**' read '**κυθρόγαυλος**'

***κυθροβρόχος**, ὁ, perh. *person who prepares clay for pots*, (cf. χύτρα), *PPrag.* 25.10 (vi/vii AD).

**κυΐσκομαι**, line 1, for 'pass.' read 'med.' **II**, after 'Gal. 4.513' insert 'pass., *to be conceived*, Ptol.*Tetr.* 121'

**κῠκάω II**, penultimate line, after 'Archil. 66' insert 'καρδίας κυκωμένης *Trag.adesp.* 664.23 K.-S.'

**κῠκεών**, line 2, after 'acc. κυκεῶνα' insert 'Hippon. 39 W.'

**κυκλᾰ́νεμον**, after 'τό' insert '*fan*' and delete '(dub. sens.)'

**κυκλάς I**, add '**3** κυκλάδες αὖραι *whirling breezes*, Nonn.*D.* 1.133.'

**κύκλευμα**, add 'applied to the κόσμος, τί ἐστι κόσμος; ἀκατάληπτος περιοχή .. ἀπλανὲς κύκλευμα Secund.*Sent.* 1'

⁺**κυκλευτήριον**, τό, app. *equipment* or *plant operated by a water-wheel*, (ἀρ.)ζ' ἐν αἷς τροχὸς καὶ κυκλευτήριον *PColl.Youtie* 65.49, 68 (*c.*AD 241), *PGiss.* 56.8 (vi AD).

**κυκλεύω I 2**, add '*SEG* 31.1116'

**κυκλέω I 3**, add '*give currency to*, λέξιν D.H.*Dem.* 56'

**κυκλικός I**, add '**5** of style, *rounded*, εὐρυθμία τῶν περιόδων D.H.*Pomp.* 6.' **II–IV**, for these sections read '**II** *of* or *belonging to the Epic Cycle*, θέλγει· ἡ -κή (sc. ἔκδοσις), θέλγεις Sch.Od. 16.195, 17.25; ἡ κ. Θηβαΐς Ath. 11.465e; κυκλικοί, οἱ, *poets of the Epic Cycle*, Sch.Il. 3.242, al.; adv. -κῶς, *in the manner of the Cyclic poets*, Sch.Il. 6.325, οὐ κ. τὰ ἐπίθετα προσέρριπται Sch.Od. 7.115; comp. -κώτερον Sch.Il. 9.222. **2** transf., *commonplace*, *conventional*, ἐχθαίρω τὸ ποίημα τὸ κ. Call.*Epigr.* 28.1 Pf.'

***κύκλιον**, τό, perh. *small reel of thread* or *ball of wool*, *PKöln* 124.3, al. (iv AD); *SB* 11289.6 (iv/v AD).

**κύκλιος I**, add '**2** metaph., τῆς ἀγωγῆς τῶν περιόδων τὸ κ. D.H.*Isoc.* 12.' **II 1**, line 8, before 'invented' insert 'κυκλίοις *SEG* 25.177.3 (Athens, 331 BC)'

**κύκλος II 1**, delete 'on the *janker*' **7**, add 'E.*Ph.* 1382' add '**12** an article of attire, *PZilliac.* 11.19, 22 (iii AD); cf. κυκλάς II.' **III**, add '**c** *roundabout phrasing*, *circumlocution*, Plu. 2.408f.'

**κύκλωμα**, line 4, after '**4**' insert '*kerb* running round base of altar, Lxx *Ez.* 43.17. **5**' at end delete 'κόσμος ἀπλανὲς κ. ib. 1' (v. °κύκλευμα)

***Κύκνεια**, fem. adj., *of Cycnus*, μάχα Pi.*O.* 10.15.

**κύκνειος II**, delete the section.

⁺**κυληβίς**· ἄκαρπος κράμβη Theognost.*Can.* 121; cf. κ.· κολοβή Hsch.

***κυλίβη** (v.l. κυλίνη)· ἡ ἄκαρπος κράμβη Suid., v. °κυληβίς.

**κύλινδρος**, add '**6** *cylindrical seal*, *Ath.Asklepieion* IV 124.99 (Athens, iii BC); app. also of a "sliced" cylinder, *κ. τετράγωνος πανταχεῖ ὑά[λινος]* ib. 101; cf. *κύλινδρος· σφραγῖδος εἶδος* Hsch.'

**κυλίνδω II 1**, line 3, for 'Alc. 18' read 'Alc. 326.2 L.-P.'

**κύλιξ**, after '*ἡ*' insert '*κόλιξ AE* 1953-4.205' and after '*wine-cup*' insert '*Ἐπαμείνονος ha* ϙ*ύλιξς SEG* 31.838 (Sicily, vii/vi BC), [ϙ]*ύλυιξ Corinth* 15(3) p. 360, no. 17'

***κυλίφακτος**, ?ά, prob. kind of vase, *SEG* 34.852 (Thera, vi BC).

**κυλίχνη I**, for '*small cup*' read '*cup* or *bowl*' and add '*ABSA* 59.42' **II**, for this section read '*κ.· φιάλη καὶ ἡ ἰατρικὴ πυξίς* Hsch.'

**κυλίω**, line 6, delete 'Call.'

**Κυλλήνιος**, insert 'Dor. **Κυλλάνιος** *Inscr.Cret.* 1.16.7 (Lato, ii/i BC)'; after 'of Hermes' insert 'Od. 24.1'; delete '*BCH* 27.295 (Crete)'

**κυλλός I 2**, for this section read 'of plants, *πὸτ τὰς ῥάπα[ς] κυλλάς SEG* 39.996.5 (Camarina, ii BC); in dub. sens. of some irrigation equipment, *κυλλῆς κυκλάδος μιᾶς PLond.* 3.776.10 (vi AD)' **II**, add '**2** fig., of a month of 29 days, Gal. 9.907.18.'

**κυλλόω**, pass., add 'Gal. 13.562.6, 576.3, 6'

***κυλοιάζω**, *κυλοιάζειν· τὸ τοὺς ὀφθαλμοὺς ἐπικλίνειν χλευάζοντα* Theognost.*Can.* 21.

***κυλτίς**, *ίδος, ἡ*, app. kind of filter for a water-wheel, (cf. *κυρτίς*), *POxy.* 3354.16 (AD 257).

**κῦμα I 2 a**, for '(A.*Th.*) 1083' read '1077' **b**, line 2, delete '*κακῶν*' and '*Th.* 758 (lyr.)' **II**, add 'A.R. 4.1492'

**κῡμαίνω I 2**, add '*ἰδών σε .. ἐκύμηνε τὰ σπλάγχνα* Herod. 1.56'

***κῡμᾰτιαῖος**, *α, ον*, *having a wave pattern, voluted*, *MDAI(I)* 19-20.238.25, 245 (Didyma).

**κῡμᾰ́τιον 1**, for 'of the *volute*' read 'a form of moulding, esp. of the *echinus* of an Ionic capital'

**κῡμᾰτωγή**, add 'Ps.-Hdt. *Vit.Hom.* 268, 488'

***κυμβᾰλία**, *ἡ*, prob. = *κυμβάλιον*, *PColl.Youtie* 87.12 (vi AD).

**κυμβᾰλίζω**, add 'transf., *κυμβαλίζει γὰρ ἡ κοίλη* (*ὁπλὴ ἵππου*) *μᾶλλον ἢ ἡ πλήρης καὶ σαρκώδης* [Simon.Ath.]*Eq.* 5'

**κύμβᾰλον**, add '**2** *stoup* for lustral water placed at the door of a house in which a corpse lay, Sch.E.*Alc.* 98.'

***κύμβᾰλος**, *ὁ*, = *κύμβαλον* 1, prob. rest. in Call.*fr.* 194.106 Pf.

**κύμβᾰχος**, line 2, after 'Il. 5.586' insert 'Call.*fr.* 195.29 Pf.'

***Κυμβελλείτης**, *ου, ὁ*, name of a kind of marble, *ISmyrna* 697.28 (ii AD).

**κύμβη** (A) **I**, add '**2** *shell* of a crab, Opp.*H.* 1.335.' add '**IV** *head*, *EM* 545.27.'

**+κύμβη** (B), *ἡ*, generic term for a bird (or class of birds), *πτεροβάμονες κύμβαι* Emp. 20.7.

***κυμβίδιον**, *τό*, dim. of *κύμβη* (A), in quot., *cup*, *IG* $2^2$.1534*A*119 (Athens, iii BC).

**κυμβίον**, add 'Astyd. 3.2 S., [D.]47.58'

**κύμβος**, for '= *κύμβη* (A), *cup*' read '*bowl* used for mixing' and add 'Sophr. 165'

***Κύμη**, *ἡ*, kind of wild cabbage, Nic.*fr.* 85.5 G.-S., Plin.*HN* 20.90 (cj.), (prob. identified w. place-name Cyme).

***κῡμήνασθαι**· *κείρεσθαι* Theognost.*Can.* 21; cf. ‡*κωμαίνω*.

***κῡμητήριον**, v. °*κοιμητήριον*.

***κῡμῑνᾶς**, *ᾶ, ὁ*, *seller of cummin*, *SEG* 8.143 (Jaffa, iii/iv AD), *ZPE* 11.15 (Cilicia, Chr.).

**κύμινδις**, last line, after 'cf.' insert 'Hippon. 61 W.'

**κύμῑνον**, add 'Myc. *ku-mi-no*'

**κῡμῑνοπρίστης**, add 'also *quibbler* or *logic-chopper*, D.C. 70.3.3'

**κῡμοπλήξ**, add 'v.l. for *κυματο-* in *AP* 10.7.1 (Arch.)'

**κῡμορρόον**, add '(or **κῡμόρροον**, cf. Theognost.*Can.* 121 (*κύμορον*))'

**+Κῡνᾱγίδᾱς**, title of Heracles in Macedonia, *EAM* 6, 20, al. (i BC/iii AD).

**κῠναγχικός**, add '**II** *κυναγχική, ἡ*, another name for the plant *ἀπόκυνον*, Ps.-Dsc. 4.80.'

***κῠναγχῖτις**, *ιδος, ἡ*, a plant used as a remedy for *κυνάγχη*, Ps.-Dsc. 3.24.

***κῠνάδακνος**, *ὁ*, *dog-bite*, *SEG* 6.802.36 (Salamis, Cyprus, ii/iii AD; pl., tab.defix.).

***κῠνᾰναιδής**, *ές*, *shameless*, rest. for *κυνάπαιδες* in Sophr.ap.Sch.Gen.Il. 21.394, also rest. in Euph. in *Suppl.Hell.* 415 i 12.

***κῠνανθρωπία**, *ἡ*, disease in which a man imagines himself to be a dog, Aët. 6.11 (151.21 O.).

**κῠνάπαιδες**, add 'v. °*κυναναιδής*'

**κῠνάριον**, add 'in later Gk. without dim. sense, Rémondon *Le monastère de Phoibammon* p. 34 no. 2 (?iv AD)'

**κύνειος**, after 'Ar.*V.* 898' insert 'cf. *κύνειον θάνατον· ἄγαν φοβερόν* Hsch.'

**κύνειρα**, for '*dog-leash*' read 'perh. = *πόρνη*'

**κῠνηγέσιον II 2**, add 'Plb. 30.26.1'

***κῠνηγέσιος**, *ὁ*, title of Hadrian identified w. Zeus, *BCH* 102.437.

**κῠνηγέτης**, add 'Myc. *ku-na-ke-ta-i* (dat. pl.)'

**κῠνηγέτις**, of Artemis, add '*SEG* 33.1174 (Lycia)'

***Κυνθήιος**, *ον*, app. = *Κύνθιος*, *δόμον Κυνθήιον SEG* 30.1237 (Africa, ii/iii AD).

***Κύνθιον**, *τό*, name of a sanctuary, *Inscr.Délos* 1417*A*ii47 (ii BC); cf. *Κύνθιος*.

**Κύνθιος**, add 'also epith. of Zeus at Delos, *SEG* 32.218.45, 85 (Athens, 103/1 BC), *Κυνθίη* of Athena, *Schwyzer* 769 (Paros, vi BC), cf. Lat. *Cynthia*, of Artemis'

***κυνιατοα**, prob. non-Hellenic name of a cult-object, *Inscr.Cret.* 1.xvii 2*b*2 (ii BC).

**+κύνικλος**, v. °*κουνίκολος*.

**κῠνοβᾰ́της**, add '[Simon Ath.]*Eq.* 5'

***κῠνοκεφᾰ́λειος**, *α, ον*, = *κυνοκέφαλος*, *PMag.* 4.2651.

**κῠνοκέφᾰλος**, for '*dog-faced baboon, Simia hamadryas*' read 'name for baboons and, prob., other kinds of monkey' and add '*Peripl.M.Rubr.* 50'

***κῠνοκοίτης**, *ου, ὁ*, *having sexual intercourse with dogs*, *Vit.Aesop.*(G) 49.

***κῠνοπότᾰμος**, *ὁ*, *beaver*, Cyran. 64.

**κῠνόπρηστις**, add '**II** kind of fish, *IGC* p. 98 A4 (*κουνόπρειστις*, Acraephia, iii/ii BC).'

**κῠνόρροδον**, add '**III** kind of lily, Plin.*HN* 21.24.'

***κῠνόσορχις**, *ἡ*, kind of orchid, Plin.*HN* 27.65.

**κῠνοσουρίς I**, add '**b** *κυνοσουρίδες· οἱ ἀπὸ ἀλωπέκων καὶ κυνῶν τικτόμενοι παῖδες AB* 452, Sch.Call.*Dian.* 94.'

***κῠνοτᾰ́φος**, *ὁ*, *dog-burier*, priest in an Egyptian temple, *PHib.* 213.9 (iii BC).

**κῠνουλκός**, add '*PSAAthen.* 2.2 (iii BC)'

**κῠνούχιον**, delete the entry.

**+κῠνοῦχος**, *ον*, *dog-restraining*, *τραχηλοδεσπότας κλοιοὺς κυνούχους AP* 6.107 (Phil.). **II** masc. subst., *bag, sack*, X.*Cyn.* 2.9, Ael.Dion.*fr.* 206, Poll. 10.64, Phot., Hsch.; for carrying money, *PCair.Zen.* 22.22 (iii BC), *Inscr.Délos* 442*A*7, 461*Aa*7 (ii BC), *AP* 6.298 (Leon.Tarent.).

**κύος**, delete '*IG* 12(5).646 (Ceos)'

***κῠοφόρημα**, *ατος, τό*, *that which is carried in the womb*, Sch.Gen.Il. 3.17.

**κῠοφόρος**, add '**2** subst. *womb* (or perh. applied to the penis as "producer of pregnancy"), *PLond.* 1821.161.'

***κῠπαιρίσκος**, *ὁ*, dim. of *κύπαιρος*, Alcm. 58 P.

**+κύπαιρος**, *ὁ*, *cyperus, galingale*, Myc. *ku-pa-ro, ku-pa-ro₂*, Alcm. 60 P.; cf. *κύπειρος, κύπερος*.

***κῠπᾰρίσσειος**, *α, ον*, Myc. *ku-pa-ri-se-ja* neut. pl., *made of cypress wood.*

***Κῠπᾰρισσία**, *ἡ*, title of Athena at Messene, *SEG* 23.209 (iii BC), *SEG* 39.381; cf. *Κυφαρισσία*.

**κυπαρισσόκομος**, add '*Lyr.adesp.* in *POxy.* 2736 *fr.* 2(b).12'

**κῠπᾰ́ρισσος I**, line 3, delete '*ἐλαφρά*' and for 'Pi.*fr.* 154' read 'Pi.*Pae.* 4.50' add '**III** *ποίη κυπάρισσος*, prob. = *χαμαικυπάρισσος*, Nic.*Th.* 910.' at end add 'cf. Myc. [*ku*-]*pa-ri-so*, place name, *ku-pa-ri-si-jo*, ethnic'

**κῠ́πασσις**, line 1, for 'Alc. 15.6' read 'Alc. 357.7 L.-P.'; line 2, for pres. def. read 'kind of chiton, of varying length and worn by both sexes'; line 3, after 'Lys.*fr.* 58 S.' add 'Herod. 8.31'; at end (*κυπασσίσκος*), for 'Hippon. 18' read 'Hippon. 32 W.'

***κῠπειρόεις**, *εσσα, εν*, form *κυπαιρόϝενς* Myc. *ku-pa-ro-we*, *scented with cyperus.*

**κύπειρος**, add 'Myc. *ku-pa-ro* (masc. or neut.), variant *ku-pa-ro₂*'

***κῠπελλοδόκος**, *ον*, *receiving cups* (cj. for *κυπελλοτόκ-*), *τράπεζα* Nonn.*D.* 47.62.

**κῠπελλοτόκος**, after 'Nonn.*D.* 47.62' add '(cod.; cj. *-δόκος*)'

***κῠ́περις**, *ιδος, ἡ*, = *κύπερος*, *PColl.Youtie* 87.14 (vi AD).

**Κυπρία**, (v. *Κύπριος* 2) add '*SEG* 30.1571, 32.1318 (Cyprus, iv BC)'

***Κυπριάρχης**, *ου, ὁ*, *governor of Cyprus*, Lxx 2*Ma.* 12.2.

**Κύπριος 1**, add '*Κυπρίας τε πόλεις* A.*Pers.* 891' at end add 'cf. Myc. *ku-pi-ri-jo*'

**Κύπρος**, add 'personified, *SEG* 31.924 (Caria, i/ii AD)'

**κυπτόν**, delete the entry.

***κυπτός**, *ή, όν*, *distorted*, *κυπτὸς ὀρθοῦται λόγος* A.*Ch.* 773 (v.l. *κρυπτὸς*).

**κύπτω 1**, last line, after 'Id.*Pax* 33' insert '‹*εἰς ἑαυτὸν*› *κύψαντα εὐωχεῖσθαι* Ath. 1.6a'

**κῦρα**, delete the entry.

***κῡρά**, v. °*κύριος*.'

***κυρανίδες** or **κοιρανίδες**, (sc. *βίβλοι*), *αἱ*, title of treatise, Cyran. 3.4.

**Κύρβας**, gen. pl., add '*Κυρβάνθων* inscr. in *PP* 4.73 (Rhodes, ii/i BC)'

**κυρβᾰσία**, add 'Ar.*fr.* 559 K.-A.'

**κύρβος**, delete the entry.

**Κυρηναϊκός**, add 'as the title of a Roman legion, *TAM* 2.1201 (Lycia, AD 145/6)'

**Κυρήνη**, after 'Ar.*Th.* 98' insert 'Call.*Dian.* 206, *Epigr.* 21 Pf.'

***Κυρηνιακός**, *ή, όν*, = ‡*Κυρηναϊκός*, *SB* 8802 (AD 82/3).

***Κυρήτειος** (?ῡ), ὁ, epith. of Poseidon, *Tit.Cam.* 31 (Camirus, iii BC), al.

**κῡριακός I**, κ. φίσκος, add '*SEG* 30.1349 (Miletus, *c.*AD 180/200)'; at end add 'ἰατροῦ τῆς κυριακῆς οἰκετείας *IEphes.* 3233.17 (iii AD)' **II**, κ. ἡμέρα, add '*POxy.* 3407.16 (iv AD)'

***κῡρίευσις**, εως, ἡ, *gaining possession of*, ἀπὸ τῆς Πτολεμαίου Αἰγύπτου κυριεύσεως *Marm.Par.* 109.

**κῡριεύω I 1 b**, delete 'Pass. .. Ptol.*Tetr.* 112'

**κύριος A II 3**, add 'also of place, S.*OT* 1453' **5**, add 'τὸ κύριον, *ordinary language*, ἐργῶδες ἐν τῷ κυρίῳ τραγικῶς ἅμα καὶ συμπαθῶς γράψαι' **B 1 a**, line 4, after '*PTeb.* 5.147 (ii BC)' insert '*owner* or *secure possessor*, εἰ τριακονταετὴς παρέλθοι χρόνος καὶ ἡ κατοχὴ κυρίους τοὺς λαβόντας καταστήσειε Just.*Nov.* 22.24'; add '(in later Gr. freq. written κύρις or κύρις w. late vowel shortening, e.g. *Vit.Aesop.*(G) 30), *SEG* 31.830 (iv/v AD)' **2**, line 4, for '**κύρα**' read '**κυρά**, *Vit.Aesop.*(G) 32' **3**, add 'of a *comes*, *AS* 35.96' add '**5** *trustee* (of a mortgage), *IG* 12(7).515.34 (ii BC).'

**κῡριότης**, line 1, after '*Ep.Eph.* 1.21' insert 'w. gen., Memn. 4.6 J.'

**κῡριόω**, after '= κυρόω' insert 'ἐκυριώθη *IGRom.* 4.661.31 (Acmonia, i AD)'

***κῦρις** (or **κύρις**), v. ‡κύριος.

***κῡριώνῠμος**, ον, *properly so-called*, αὕτη ἡ ἡμέρα ἡ κυριώνυμος Leont.Byz.*HP* 1.2.3.

**κῡρίως I**, for '*SIG* 1004' read '*SEG* 31.416' **IV**, last line, after '*EN* 1098ᵃ6' insert '*in more straightforward language*, D.H.*Th.* 29'

**κῡρόω 1**, line 13, after '*PRev.Laws* 48.17 (iii BC)' insert 'cf. Hsch. s.v. προσθεῖναι, where κυρῶσαι (κῦρσαι cod.) is explained as τὸ παραδοῦναι τῷ ἐωνημένῳ ὑπὸ κήρυκι'

***Κυρτᾶς**, ᾶ, ὁ, nickname of a fishmonger, *SEG* 11.169 (Corinth, vi AD); cf. κυρτοβόλος.

**κυρτίς**, add '*cage*, κ.· ὀρνιθοτροφεῖον Hsch.; cf. κύρτος 2'

***κυρτοπλοκεῖον**, τό, *basket-weaving shop*, *POxy.* 2719.11 (-ῖον, iii AD).

**κυρτός 1**, add '*full*, *brimming*, ὑπὸ κυρτοῖσι κυπέλλοις *Anacreont.* 50.22 W., (or ?*curved*); cf. κύρτωμα 2, κύρτωσις 2'

**κυρτωτός**, add 'rest. in *Didyma* 50.1*A*60'

**κῡρωτής**, add '*Hesperia* 5.401.2 (Athens, iv BC)'

***κῡρωτικός**, ή, όν, *ratifying*, *affirming*, κύριε· κυρωτικὲ καὶ τελεστικέ Sch.Pi.*P.* 2.106.

**κύσθος II**, add 'see also χύστος'

***κῡσοκνησιάω**, *suffer from anal pruritus* (or subst. -ία, ἡ in analogous sense), *POxy.* 2811.5a.13.

**κῡσοχήνη**, add 'rest. [in undefined sense], Hippon. 82.2 W.'

**κύστεροι**, add 'cf. κυρσερίδες'

**κυτῖσος**, for '(ἡ, Theoc. 5.128, 10.30)' read '(ἡ, Gal. 14.23, prob. in Theoc. 10.30, indeterminate id. 5.128)'; add 'form κύτεσος: Myc. *ku-te-so*, kind of wood; adj. *ku-te-se-jo*'

**κύτος 1**, add 'Alcm. 17.1 P.'

**κύττᾰρος 1**, add 'cf. κυρσερίδες, κύστεροι'

⁺**Κῠφᾰρισσίτας**, α, ὁ, epith. of Pan (or perh. Hermes), *Inscr.Cret.* 1.xvi 7 (Lato, ii/i BC).

**κῡφός**, line 4, for 'shrimps' read 'prawns'; line 5, before 'Eub.' insert 'Philox. 2.17 (cj.), Alexis 115.13 K.-A.'; line 6, delete '*shrimps .. squilla*'

**κῦφων I**, add 'perh. transf., of a heavy load, Men.*Dysc.* 102' **III**, for 'part of a woman's dress' read 'women's clothes, or kind of tunic' and after 'Posidipp. 44' add '(pl.)'

**κυψέλη I**, add 'S.*fr.* 441a.5 R.'

**κύψελος**, add 'Myc. *ku-pe-se-ro*, pers. n.'

**κύω II**, for 'in aor. act. .. A.*fr.* 44.4' read 'act., of the male, *impregnate*, transf., ὄμβρος ἔκυσε γαῖαν A.*fr.* 44.4 R.; *procreate*, οἱ δὲ (Ἐρωτιδεῖς) τραφέντες εὐθὺς πάλιν κύουσιν ἄλλους *Anacreont.* 25.16 W.'; line 9, after 'Lxx *Is.* 59.13' insert 'ὕε κύε, a cry at the Eleusinia, Hippol.*Haer.* 5.7, Procl. *in Ti.* 3.176 D., cf. *IG* 2².4876 (Athens, ?i AD)' at end delete 'The causal sense .. aor. ἔκυσα.'

**κύων II 1**, line 7, for 'also of offensive persons .. dogs' read 'as a derogatory term for non-Jews'; line 8, after '*Ep.Phil.* 3.2' insert 'Apoc. 22.15; of male sacred prostitutes, Lxx *De.* 23.18(19)' **IV**, line 3, after 'Ael.*NA* 1.55' insert 'κ. ποτάμιος, prob. *otter*, id. 14.21' **V**, add '**2** κύων πρότερος = the star Προκύων, Nonn.*D.* 16.202.' **IX**, add 'Nicostr.ap.Simp. *in Cat.* 26.24' add '**XIII** colloq. term for large kind of fly, = στρατιῶτις 3, Luc.*Musc.Enc.* 12. **XIV** νυκτερινοὶ κύνες acc. to Hsch. (s.v. νυκτ-) kind of women's shoes, *Suppl.Hell.* 1090.'

**κῶας**, add 'form *κῶϝος: Myc. *ko-wo*, *sheepskin*'

**κωβάθια**, add '*SB* 1049ᵛ.26-7 (sp. κοβ-, ii AD)'

***κωδικίλλος**, ὁ, also **κωδικέλλος** Arr.*Epict.* 3.7.30, *Cod.Just.* 6.48.8, usu. pl., Lat. *codicillus*, *official letter from the emperor*, Arr. l.c., *OGI* 543, *IGRom.* 3.175. **II** pl., *codicil* to a will, *TAM* 2.77, *Inscr.Cret.* 4.300, *Cod.Just.* l.c.

***κωδικιλλόω**, app. *add as a codicil*, *POxy.* 2283.11 (κοδ-, AD 586).

**κῴδιον I**, add '**2** pl., *strips of fleece* on the upper end of the forearm of the "sharp-thonged" type of boxing-glove, Philostr.*Her.* 6.'

***κώδιστρον**· ὀπὸς τῆς μήκωνος Theognost.*Can.* 56 A. (perh. ὁ ‹καρ›πός, cf. *EM* s.v. κώδη).

**κώδων**, line 1 (fem.), add 'κόδōν[α] νέαν inscr. in *PP* 42.42 (Tarentum, vi BC)' **2**, for '*crier's bell*' read '*bell* attached to warhorse or (perh.) other animal'; delete '"is his own trumpeter"'

**κώθων I**, add '(cf. Italian borrowing *qutun*, *Testimonia Linguae Etruscae* 28, 63, vii BC)' **II**, line 3, for 'Plu.*Ant.* 4, etc.' read 'Hegesand.ap.Ath. 11.477e; *feast*, Lxx *Es.* 8.17'

***κωθωνικός**, ή, όν, *drunken*, *PVindob.Tandem* 2.9 (iii AD).

**κωθωνιστής**, add '(v.l. φιλοκωθ-)'

***κωκῡμός**, ὁ, = κώκυμα, Call.*fr.* 177.14 Pf. (s.v.l.).

***κωκώ**, οῦς, ἡ, colloq. name for the penis at puberty, *AP* 12.3 (Strat.; cj. κοκκώ).

**κωλακρέτης**, add 'also **κωλοκράτης** *SEG* 39.148 (Attica, iv BC)'

***κωλάνεμος**, ὁ, *wind from the bowels*, on magical gem in *SO* 19.76.

***κώλαργος**· λευκόπους Theognost.*Can.* 56 A.

**κωλεός**, add '*Sokolowski* 1.71.6 (Casossus), ib. 63.6 (-ειός, Mylasa)'

**κωλῆ**, uncontracted form κωλέα, add '*SEG* 29.1088 (Caria, iii BC)'; κωλία, add '*SEG* 32.456 (Boeotia, *c.*235/0 BC)'

**κωλίζω**, after 'Olymp.Hist. p. 463 D.' insert 'Procl. *in R.* 2.218 K.'

***κωλιοθήρας**, ου, ὁ, perh. *mackerel-fisher* as pers. n., (for κολιο-), *IEphes.* 20.B27.

⁺**κωλοειδής**, ές, *formed* or *arranged in members*, Sopat.in Rh. 8.56.14 W., al.; adv. -δῶς ib. 8.9.24 W.

**κῶλον**, line 1, for 'A.*Pr.* 325' read 'A.*Pr.* 323' **2**, add '**b** *bone*, Juba 82 J., Poll. 4.75.'

***κωλοπέδῑλα**, τά, codd. in Theoc. 25.103 (v. ‡καλ-).

***κῶλος**, ὁ, *Lat. culus*, *buttocks*, *backside*, *Vit.Aesop.*(W) 77a.

**κώλῡσις**, add '**2** *prohibition*, *Cod.Just.* 1.4.25, 4.59.1.3.'

***κωλυσμός**, ὁ, = κώλῡσις, Heph.Astr. 2.30.16.

**κωλῡτήριος**, after '*preventive*' insert 'A.*fr.* 47a.15 R.'

***κωλῦτωρ**, ορος, ὁ, = κωλυτής, A.*fr.* 78a.20 R.

**κωλύω**, add '**II** *prohibit*, *forbid*, *Cod.Just.* 1.12.3.1a, 4.20.16 pr.'

**κῶμα**, line 1, after '*deep sleep*' insert '*trance*'

**κωμαίνω**, after 'κωμική' insert 'κωμήνασθαι Theognost.*Can.* 56 A.'

**κωμαῖος**, add '**2 Κωμαῖα**, τά, a festival at Thasos, *BCH* 82.195 (iv BC).'

***Κωμαιών**, ῶνος, ὁ, name of a month at Colophon, *AJP* 56.361 (iv BC), *REG* 47.29 (iii BC).

***κώμαρις**, ἡ, app. var. κόμαρος, Anon.Alch. 9.19, 278.16.

**κωμαρχέω**, add '**II** *to be leader of a* κῶμος or κώμη, *IG* 2².3104 (Attica, iv BC).'

***κωμάρχιος**, ον, name of a musical nome, Plu. 2.1132d.

**κώμαρχος I**, for 'Πολέμων 1.45' read '*IG* 2².3103.3' and add 'cf. *ARV* 26 no. 1'

**κωμᾰσία**, add '**II** *celebration of a* κῶμος in honour of a victor at the games, Sch.Pi.*N.* 4.17.'

**κωμαστήριον I**, after '(Taposiris)' add '*PBremen* 23.47 (ii AD)'

**κωμᾶται**, add 'κ.· λοιδορεῖται Theognost.*Can.* 56 A.'

***κωμᾰτικός**, v. °κωμη-.

**κωματώδης**, add 'adv. -δῶς, Paul.Aeg. 3.6.1 (144.32 H.)'

**κώμη**, add 'Dor. κώμᾱ, *BCH* 111.168 (Mantinea, iv BC)' **II**, add 'κώμας ἐκάλουν τοὺς στενωπούς Aphth.*Prog.* 8'

**κωμητικός**, after '*of a* κώμη' insert '*BGU* 802.8.9 (i AD)'; after '*PTeb.* 340 i 10 (iii AD)' insert 'κ. κτήσεως *PPrincet.* 134.1 (iv AD); Κωμᾱτικός, epith. of Zeus, Robert *Hell.* 10.38 (Thrace)'

***κωμογραμματικός**, ή, όν, *of* or *for a* κωμογραμματεύς; κ. κλῆρος, a κλῆρος whose profits supported a κωμογραμματεύς, *BGU* 2437.41 (i BC).

**κωμομισθωτής**, add '*PSI* 554.13 (iii BC)'

***κωμοπράκτωρ**, ορος, ὁ, *village tax-collector*, *PKöln* 137.37 (AD 88), *PAmst.* 29.2 (i/ii AD).

**κωμύδριον I**, add 'Suid. s.v. Καλλίμαχος'

**κῶνος II 2**, for '*cone* or *peak* of a helmet' read '*conical helmet*'; add '*RA* 6.31.3 (Amphipolis, ii BC)'

***κωνοψώμιον**, τό, kind of bread, prob. in the shape of a cone, or made fr. pine-kernels, κωνοψωμίῳ[ν] ὀψάρει(ον) Περσικόν *SEG* 26.382 (Athens, Rom.imp.).

**κώνωψ**, after '(Arist.*HA*) 552ᵇ5' insert 'Plu. 2.663d, *AP* 12.108 (Dionys.), *Gp.* 6.12, al.'

**Κῷος**, after 'Κώϊος' read 'Call.*fr.* 532 Pf., *TAM* 4(1).1.2 (iii BC)'

***κωπαστής**, οῦ, ὁ, *rower* or *pilot*, title of play by Aeschylus, A. *T* 78.2d R. (cf. *REG* 100.33).

**κωπεύς**, add '**II** = κωπηλάτης, *AB* 273.32.'

⁺**κωπεών**, ῶνος, ὁ, *handle*, *haft*, Thphr.*HP* 4.1.4, 5.1.7, *PMerton* 73.18, κωπαιῶνες *PReinach* inv. 2065.33, 38 (*JJP* 11/12.59; all ii AD).

**κωπήεις**, add '*hafted*, αἰγανέη Opp.*H.* 2.497'

***κωπίς**, ίδος, ἡ, *handle*, Theognost.*Can.* 56 A.

***κωπιών**, = °*κωπεών*, *Pap.Lugd.Bat.* XXVII 1.6 (ii AD).

***κωποδέτης**, ου, Dor. **-τᾱς**, ὁ, *one who binds an oar to the thole*, *Clara Rhodos* 8.228 (i BC).

***κωρᾰκίδιον**, τό, a fish found in the Nile (perh. = *κορακινίδιον*), *PAmst.* 92.4 (ii/iii AD).

**κωράλιον**, for 'cf. *κοράλλιον*' read 'v. °*κοράλλιον*'

***Κωρής**, Dor. for *Κουρής*, v. *Κουρῆτες* II 1.

***κώρτη**, v. °*χώρτη*.

**κώρῠκος I 2**, line 2, before 'Sor. 1.49' insert 'Dionys.Eleg. 3.3'; line 5, delete 'metaph.'

***κωταρχέω**, *hold the office of κωτάρχης*, *Didyma* 305.4, 451.1.

***κωτίαι**, *ταί*, perh. name of a priesthood or a festival, de Franciscis *Locr.Epiz.* p. 22 no. 8, p. 49 no. 35.

**κωτίλλω I**, after 'Thgn. 852' insert 'Sol. 34.3 W.'

***κωφαίνω**, 1 aor. *ἐκώφηνα*, *deafen*, *TAPhA* 68.54 (Beisan, tab.defix., iv AD).

***κωφεύς**, *έως*, ὁ, *deaf man*, Call.*fr.* 195.34 Pf., *Lexicon* in *An.Boiss.* 4.386.

**κωφίας**, for '*τύφλωψ*' read '*τυφλώψ*'

**κωφός II 1**, add '**b** of speech, *lacking sonority*, *flat*, *σύνθεσις* Demetr. *Eloc.* 68.' **2**, lines 3/5, delete '*οὐ* .. Cratin. 6' **b**, w. gen., add '*φύσει γάρ ἐστ' ἔρως τοῦ νουθετοῦντος κωφόν* Men.*fr.* 53 K.-Th.'

# Λ

+**λᾴα**, v. ‡λεία (B).

**λᾱάρχης**, add '*BGU* 1763.11'

**λᾶας**, line 5, for 'also masc. .. 93 H.' read 'also Cypr. masc. λᾶος *o-la-o o-te* ὁ λᾶος ὅδε *ICS* 84.1'; add 'cf. Myc. adj. *ra-e-ja*'

+**λαβδᾰκισμός**, ὁ, *excessive use of the letter lambda in pronunciation* or *composition, labdacism*, Quint.*Inst.* 1.5.32, Diom. p. 453 K., Donat. p. 393 K., Mart.Cap. 5.514.

*__λαβέλλιον__, τό, prob. dim. of Lat. *labellum, small basin, bowl*, *CPR* 8.65.18 (vi AD).

**λάβιον**, read '**λᾰβεῖον** (v.l. λαβίον)'

**λᾰβίς II 3**, add '*POxy.* 3473.21 (ii AD)'

*__λᾱβόλιον__, τό, = λιθοβολία, Alc. in *SLG* 262.3 (*PKöln* 59.3); cf. °λήβολος.

*__λᾶβολος__, v. °λήβολος.

**λαβράκτης**, delete the entry (v. °ἀοιδολαβράκτης).

*__λάβριχος__, ὁ, a fresh-water fish, *IGC* p. 99 B24 (Acraephia, iii/ii BC).

**λάβρος III**, adv., after '*furiously*' insert 'Alc. 72.3 L.-P.'

**λαβροσύνη**, line 1, delete '*greed*'

**λᾰβύρινθος I 1**, lines 4/5, for 'name of a building at Rome' read 'transf., of the underworld' **2**, line 5, after '*Icar.* 29' insert 'λαβυρίνθους σοφίας ἀνελίττων Aristid. 2.79 J.' add 'Myc. *da-pu₂-ri-to-jo* (gen.)'

**λᾰβῠρινθώδης**, add 'τὸ λ. τῆς φράσεως Eust.*Proem.* 9 in Sch.Pi. iii p. 289 D.'

+**λᾰγᾰνίζω**, perh. *be thin, blow weakly*, of the South wind, Hp.*Morb.Sacr.* 13 (γαληνίζω cj.).

**λάγᾰνον**, line 2, after '*Fr.* 116' insert '*PCair.Zen.* 569.89, 707.6 (both pl., iii BC)'

**λᾰγᾰρύζομαι**, add 'also act. form cited without expl. as example of -ύζω termination, Theognost.*Can.* 142'

*__λάγγουρος__, ὁ, name of stone, Socr.Dion.*Lith.* 41.1 G.

**λᾱγέτας**, add '(form λαϝαγέτας) Myc. *ra-wa-ke-ta*, title of high official; adj. *ra-wa-ke-si-jo*'

*__λαγκίον__, τό, cf. Lat. *lanx*, Charis. p. 42 K.

**λαγνεία II**, pl., add 'X.*Oec.* 1.22'

**λάγνης**, add 'non-Att.-Ion. gen. λάγνα *SEG* 34.370 (Boeotia, *c.*500 BC)'

*__λᾰγῡνάριος__, ὁ, *maker of flagons*, *MAMA* 3.236 (Corycus).

**λᾰγύνιον**, add '*PVindob.Worp* 11.7 (vi AD)'

*__λᾰγῡνίσκος__, ὁ, dim. of λάγῡνος, *Vit.Aesop.*(G) 87.

**λαγχάνω**, line 3, after 'al.' insert 'Aeol. λόχον Bernand *Inscr.Colosse Memnon* 29.17 (Balbilla)'; line 11, add 'med. aor. ἐλάχοντο Porph.*Plot.* 22'

**λᾰγωβολία**, for '*hare-shooting*' read '*hare-hunting* (using a throwing-stick)'

*__λᾰγωβόλος__, ον, *hunting* (with a throwing-stick), κούρη Nonn.*D.* 16.14.

**λᾰγών I 2**, after '*womb*' insert '*AP* 7.168 (Antip.Thess.), *SEG* 32.1615 (iv AD)'

*__λάη__, app. indecl. wine-measure, *SB* 1969 (vi AD), 1960 (vi/vii AD), *PStrassb.* 680.4 (early vii AD).

*__λάθησις__, εως, ἡ, given as expl. of Λητώ, Sch.Gen.Il. 1.36.

**λᾰθιπήμων**, delete the entry.

+**λᾰθίφρων**, ον, gen. ονος, *out of one's senses*, λύσσα Nonn.*D.* 47.741, Hsch.

**λαθρίδιος**, after '= λάθριος' insert '*AP* 7.457 (Aristo)' and after 'Luc.*Bis.Acc.* 33' insert 'epigr. in *SEG* 39.449.23 (Tanagra, v AD)'

**λάθριος II**, for 'Aphrodite' read 'Artemis' and after '(Leon.)' insert 'cf. Antim. 182 W., where expld. as = Προθυραία'

*__λαθροδάκτης__, gloss on σιγέρπης, Hsch.

**λαθροῦν**, for 'Cyr.' read 'Hsch.' and add '(βάπτειν Cyr.)'

**λάθῠρος**, add '**2** nickname of Ptolemy VIII, Plu.*Cor.* 11.'

*__λαΐα__, v. °λεία.

**λαίβα**, add 'cf. λαιός (B) end, °λαίδας'

**λαίγματα**, add 'cf. λαῖγμα· τὸ ἱερόν, θῦμα Theognost.*Can.* 27 A.'

+**λᾶϊγξ**, ιγγος, ἡ, *rounded stone* (of any size), *pebble*, etc., Od. 5.433, 6.95; A.R. 1.402, βαρείας .. λάιγγας id. 4.1678; πυρσοτόκους λάιγγας Nonn.*D.* 37.59.

*__λαίδας__· ἡ ἀσπὶς ἡ ἀπὸ βύρσης Theognost.*Can.* 27 A.; cf. ‡λαίβα.

+**λαίθαργος**, ον, (**λάθ-** Phryn.*PS* p. 87 B., **λήθ-** Hsch.) app. *making sudden surprise attacks*, of an apparently friendly dog, κοὐκ ὡς κύων λαίθαργος ὕστερον τρώγει Hippon. 66 W., S.*fr.* 885, Ar.*Eq.* 1068; λαιθάργῳ ποδί *Trag.adesp.* 227 K.-S.

*__λαιθυράζω__· τὸ διὰ τοῦ στόματος ψόφον τελεῖν ἐπὶ τῷ μαστῷ Theognost.*Can.* 27 A.; = χλευάζω Suid.

+**λαικάζω**, *practise fellatio on*, Ar.*Eq.* 167, *Th.* 57; Θειοδοσία λαικα̣δε̣[ι] εὖ Lang *Ath.Agora* XXI C33 (iv BC); καὶ πυγιζέσθω καὶ ληικαζέτω graffito in *Glotta* 62.167; in colloq. obscenities, med. λαικάσομ' ἄρα, i.e. I'll do anything rather, Cephisod. 3; οὐ λαικάσει φλυαρῶν; Men.*Dysc.* 892 S., Strato Com. 1.36; cf. *frigori laecasin dico* Petron. 42. **II** λαικάζω· ἀπατῶ Suid.

*__λαικάς__, -άδος, ἡ, = °λαικάστρια, Robert *Collection Froehner* p. 14 (Attic, iv BC), Aristaenet. 2.16.

**λαικαστής**, for '*wencher*' read '*fellator*'

**λαικάστρια**, for '*strumpet* .. 235' read '*fellatrix*, Pherecr. 152 K.-A.; loosely, *whore, tart*, Ar.*Ach.* 529, 537, Men.*Pk.* 485 S. **II** ἡ τίτθη παρὰ Λάκωσιν Orus ap.*Et.Gen.*' delete 'also .. (s.v.l.)'

**λᾱϊκός I 1**, add 'λαϊκὴ σύνταξις, *poll-tax*, *PMich.*v 241.35, 355.6, *PStrassb.* 522.6 (all i AD)' add '**3** adv. -κῶς *communally*, λαϊκῶς πανδημεὶ δειπνίζω *SEG* 35.747 (Maced., i AD).'

**λαῖλαψ**, at end after 'occurs in' insert '*PMag.* 4.182'

**λαιμάω**, after '= λαιμάσσω' insert 'λαιμᾷ δέ σοι τὸ χεῖλος ὡς ἐρω-διοῦ Hippon. 118.3 W.'

**λαιμώσσω**, delete 'Hippon. .. causa)'

**λᾱΐνεος**, add '*TAM* 4(1).48, Nonn.*D.* 37.68'

**λαΐνθη**, delete the entry.

*__λᾱϊνοουργός__, ὁ, *stone-mason*, *JRS* 57.43 no. 8.9 (Lycia, ?early i AD).

**λᾱϊνός 1**, after '*Trag.adesp.* 44' add '(= Ar.*Ach.* 449)'

*__λᾱϊνότευκτ(ος)__, ον, *built of stone*, perh. in epigr. in *OA* 6.43 (Cyprus, iii AD).

**λᾱϊον**, delete the entry.

*__λαῖον__, τό, *ploughshare*, A.R. 3.1335 (s.v.l.).

**λᾱΐον**, v. λήϊον (A).

**λαιός** (A), after 'Ant.Lib. 19.3' insert '(λάϊος)'

*__λαίσθα, λαίσθη__, Theognost.*Can.* 27 A. (prob. the same as λάσθη).

*__λαισκίδης__· ὁ βούπαις Theognost.*Can.* 27 A.; cf. λαόπαις.

**λαιφάσσω II**, add 'Hsch.'

**λαῖφος I**, for '*shabby, tattered garment*' read '*blanket* or sim., used as a cloak'

*__λαιφύη__· τὸ πρυτανεῖον Theognost.*Can.* 27 A.; cf. λαιμώρη II.

**λαιφύς**, after lemma insert '(‡λάφυξ, La.)'

+**λαίω**, λαίεται· καταλεύεται Hsch.; λαίειν· φθέγγεσθαι id., λαίω· τὸ βλέπω καὶ τὸ φονεύω Theognost.*Can.* 27 A.

**Λάκαινα**, line 2, for 'Helen' read 'Hermione'

**λᾰκάνη**, add '*POxy.* 1269.23 (ii AD)'

*__λᾰκάνιον__, τό, = λαγάνιον, *SB* 7572.3 (ii AD).

*__λᾰκᾰνιοργός__, ὁ, for *λεκανιουργός, *maker of* λεκάναι, *MAMA* 3.367 (Corycus).

**Λᾰκεδαιμόνιος**, add 'ἁ -ία, sc. γᾶ or πόλις, *AP* 9.320.4 (Leon.)'

**Λᾰκεδαίμων**, line 3, for 'Hdt. 1.67' read 'Hdt. 6.58.2, 7.234.2'

**λᾰκέρυζα**, line 2, after '*Op.* 747' insert 'Stesich. 32 i 9 P.'

*__λάκες__, pl., *bottles*, *CPR* 8.66.2 (vi AD).

*__Λακευτής__, ὁ, epith. of Apollo, perh. *utterer* or sim., cf. ληκητής, *SEG* 23.621 (Cyprus, iii BC).

**λάκημα**, for 'dub. sens.' read 'in accounts, in uncertain sense, perh. *lot*' and add '*PRyl.* 706ᵛ.1'

*__λάκησις__, εως, ἡ, *clucking* with tongue round palate, Hsch. s.v. κλωγμός.

*__λᾰκίνιον__, τό, *fragment*, cf. λακίς and Lat. *lacinia*, *Stud.Pal.* 20.244.18 (vi/vii AD).

**λᾰκίς**, line 2, for 'ἐμπίτνω .. 131' read 'λ. λινοσινεῖ A.*Supp.* 120'; line 3, after 'cf. 903' insert 'λακὶς χθονός *Trag.adesp.* 228 K.-S.'

*__Λακκίον__, dim. of λάκκος, as name of the Little Harbour at Syracuse, D.S. 14.7.

**λακκόπρωκτος**, for '*loose-breeched*' read 'compd. of °λάκκος (A) and πρωκτός as term of abuse' and add 'Lang *Ath.Agora* XXI C23 (v BC)'

+**λάκκος** (A), ὁ, (written λάκος, *PCair.Zen.* 176.276, iii BC) *pit, tank, cistern, vat* used for storing water, wine, or other things, (πίσσαν) ἐσχέουσι .. ἐς λάκκον ὀρωρυγμένον ἀγχοῦ τῆς λίμνης Hdt. 4.195, ἔτρεφον .. ὄρνιθας .. λιμναίους ἐν .. λάκκοισι ib. 7.119, Ar.*Ec.* 154,

D. 29.3; οἶνος πολὺς ἦν ὥστε ἐν λάκκοις κονιατοῖς εἶχον X.*An.* 4.2.22; Lxx *Ge.* 37.20, Thd.*Da.* 6.7(8), Alex. 174.9; contemptuously, of the Sea of Galilee, Porph.*Chr.* 55; obsc., of the female pudenda, Macho 282 G.; of the pit of death, Sheol, Lxx *Ps.* 27(28).1, al.; fig., ἀνήγαγέ με ἐκ λάκκου ταλαιπωρίας ib. 39(40).2. **b** Κούρτιος λ. = Lat. *lacus Curtius*, D.H. 2.42.

***λάκκος** (B), ὁ, λ. χρωματικός kind of dye, *lac*, *Peripl.M.Rubr.* 6, cf. Prakrit *lakkha.*

**λακκόω**, for '*hollow out*' read '*dye with lac*', v. °λάκκος (B).

**λάκτιμα**, after 'Hsch.' insert '(-ημα La.)' and after '*PGen.* 56.27' insert 'dub.'

***λακχάϊνος**, η, ον, *dyed with lac*, λακχά *Edict.Diocl.* 8.4.

**Λάκων II**, add 't.t. for method of forming line, Arr.*Tact.* 31.4, 32.1'

**Λᾰκωνίζω II**, add 'D. 59.36, Isoc. 4.110, etc.'

**Λᾰκωνικός II**, after 'as subst.' insert '**1** οἱ Λακωνικοί *Spartans*, Ar.*Pax* 212, *Nu.* 186.' and renumber pres. sections 1-4 as 2-5.

**Λᾰκωνισμός II**, add 'Isoc. 14.30, 15.318'

**λᾰλᾰγέω**, line 2, for 'grasshoppers' read 'cicadas'; line 3, for 'dub. l.' read 'cj.'

**λᾰλᾰγή**, for '*prattle*' read '*babble*'

**+λᾰλάγημα**, ατος, τό, *chattering*, in quot. meton., of tambourine, *AP* 6.220.15 (Diosc.).

**+λᾰλάζω**, *babble*, μηδ' ὥστε κῦμα πόντιον λάλαζε Anacr. 82 P.

***λαλαθάνατος**, wd. of uncertain meaning occurring in *defixiones*, *Kourion* 127.41, 131.29, etc.

**λαλαχεύομαι**, for '= λαχνόομαι' read 'perh. *live dissolutely* (cf. °λαλαχός)'

***λαλαχός**, gloss (with μοιχός) on τογέρα, Hsch.

**λάλησις**, add '*POxy.* 1083.16'

**λᾰλιά I 1**, add '**b** *a talk*, as a comparatively short and informal ἐπίδειξις of a sophist, Men.Rh. p. 434 S., al., Aristid.*Rh.* 2 p. 538 S.: pl., ib. p. 539 S.'

***λᾰλοβᾰρύοψ**, οπος, *loud-chattering*, Pratin. 3.13 S.

**λαλοβαρυπαραμελορυθμοβάτης**, delete the entry.

**λᾰλος**, line 2, after 'Theoc. 5.75' insert 'Call.*fr.* 192.14 Pf., *Epigr.* 16.3 Pf., Φάμα λ. *ISmyrna* 513.3 (ii BC)'; line 7, after '*VS* 2.30' insert 'D.H.*Dem.* 5'

***λᾰλοῦ**, colloq. wd. for the *penis* of boy before puberty, *AP* 12.3 (Strat., s.v.l.).

**λαμβάνω A I 1 b**, add 'w. captor indicated by εἰς, τοῦ πάππου .. ληφθέντος εἰς τοὺς πολεμίους Is. 7.8' **4**, line 5, for 'with Adj.' read 'w. predicative adj.' and add 'E.*HF* 223' **9 c**, line 6, after 'Plu.*Alc.* 18' insert 'w. εἰς, λαμβάνει οὐκ εἰς ἀδικίαν ὅσα πέπονθε Men.*Dysc.* 297, Aristid.*Or.* 26(14).76, Lib.*Or.* 11.161' **II 1 f**, after '*receive* an oath' insert 'Is. 2.39' **g**, line 2, after 'Hp.*Prorrh.* 2.24' insert 'in *double entendre* w. sense of *eat*, Macho 50, 52 G.' **i**, add 'λ. ἐξέτασίν τινος D. 18.246, 20.139, Call.*Epigr.* 59.3 Pf.'

***λᾰμιώδης**, ες, *like a Lamia*, Hsch. s.v. Λάμια.

**+λᾶμνα**, ἡ, Lat. *lamina, lamna*, (*metal*) *plate*, *Edict.Diocl.* 30.5, *PMag.* 4.2153, *PLond.* 124.26.

***λαμνίον**, τό, dim. of λᾶμνα, *PMag.* 4.3014, *PAnt.* 66.37, Iambl.Alch. 287.12.

***λαμπᾰδάριος**, ὁ, Lat. *lampadarius*, *torch-bearer*, Teuc.Bab. p. 42 B.

**λαμπᾰδηφόρος**, add 'of Hecate, *SEG* 26.819 (iii AD); as adj., λ. ἀνδριάντας *Didyma* 346.11, 16'

**λαμπᾰδίας**, add '**II** *torch-race*, *IG* 2².2119.230 (ii AD), *SEG* 29.147.9 (Athens, ii/iii AD).'

**λαμπάς** (A), add '**IV** Λαμπάδες, αἱ, nymphs attending Hecate, Alcm. 63 P.'

**λάμπη II**, delete the section.

***λάμπη** (B), v. °λάπη.

**λαμπηδών**, add '**3** app. *an inflamed swelling*, Hsch., s.v. φαύσιγγες.'

**λαμπρός II 1**, line 6, after '*IG* 14.911, 7.91, etc.' insert 'spec., the lowest of the three senatorial ranks, οὐδένα ἐμβάλλεσθαι ἐν φυλακῇ δίχα προστάξεως τῶν .. ἐνδόξων ἢ περιβλέπτων ἢ λαμπροτάτων ἀρχόντων *Cod.Just.* 1.4.22 pr.; applied to non-senatorial persons, *SEG* 31.1081'

***λαμπροτράπεζος**, ον, *keeping a fine table*, poet. in *SEG* 6.796.6 (Cappadocia, iii AD).

***λαμπροφοίτης**, ου, ὁ, *brightly-moving*, of the sun, *PMag.* 12.177.

***λαμπροφυής**, ές, *brilliant*, *PGron.*inv. 66.12 (*ZPE* 41.72).

***λαμπτηροῦχος**, ὁ, Boeot. **λαμπτηρῶχος**, *torch-holder*, λ. σιδάριοι τρῖς *SEG* 24.361.20 (Thespiae, iv BC).

**λαμπτηροφόρος**, add '*PCair.Zen.* 782(*a*).69 (iii BC)'

**λάμπω I 4**, add 'βέλτιστος πᾶσι δ' ἔλαμψα φίλος *SEG* 26.1808 (Egypt, Hellen.)' **II**, line 3, after '*Trag.adesp.* 33, etc.' insert 'fig., μή τις .. κῦδος ἔλαμψε νόθον *AP* 7.430 (Diosc.)'

**λᾰμῠρία**, add 'of both men and women, Str. 17.1.16'

***λᾰμῠρόω**, gloss on λαιθαρύζω, Hsch.; cf. λαμυρός.

***λαμψανώδης**, ες, *resembling the plant* λαμψάνη, Hsch. s.v. ῥαφίς.

***λανάριος**, ὁ, Lat. *lanarius*, *wool-worker*, *TAM* 5(1).85 (AD 145/6), *PStrassb.* 309ʳ.5 (iv AD), Βασσιανὸς λανάρις *IGBulg.* 1922.5, *Edict.Diocl.* 21.1, 1a.

**λανθᾰνόντως**, for '*secretly*' read '*surreptitiously*' and add 'Demetr.*Eloc.* 181'

**λανθάνω**, line 10, after 'Sol. 13.27' insert 'fem. part. λελαθυῖα Hes.*fr.* 343.13 M.-W.' **A 3**, add 'so perh. ὄμμα .. θέλγειν οὐ λάθε *AP* 5.282 (Agath.)' **4**, line 1, for 'relat. clause' read 'noun clause'; add 'without acc., οἱ πολλοὶ λανθάνουσιν ὅτι κολάζονται Plu. 2.554c' add '**6** w. acc. of respect, λ. τὴν ἀπόβασιν Th. 4.32.1; freq. w. neut. pron. or adj., id. 8.17, E.*IA* 516 (combined w. acc. pers., Th. 7.15.2).' **C I 1**, line 11, after '*Phdr.* 252a' insert 'plpf. w. acc. πάντ' ἐλέλασο Erinn. in *Suppl.Hell.* 401.28; w. inf., λάθοιο .. ἀπενθεῖν Theoc. 11.63'

**λάξ**, add 'cf. λ.· λάκτισμα Hsch.'

**λαξευτήριον**, add 'Sch.Th. 4.4; Hsch.'

***λάξιον**, τό, deriv. of λάξις, *allotment*, written λακσιον, *Kadmos* 9.145 (Crete, v BC).

**λάξις**, line 3, for 'so prob.' read 'so also'

**λᾱογράφος**, after '*Sammelb.*' insert '5661.2 (pl., i AD)'

***Λᾱοδῐκεών**, ῶνος, ὁ, name of month at Smyrna, *ISmyrna* 578.34, 709.13, al.

**λᾱοδόκος**, delete 'dub. in' and '(δαμοδόκων Bgk.)'

***λᾱοκρίσιον**, τό, *court-house of the* λαοκρίται, *PTeb.* 795.9 (ii BC).

**λᾱοξόος** (λαξός), add '*SEG* 33.1321 (Egypt, i/ii AD)'

**λᾱός**, add 'Myc. form λαϝο- in compds., e.g. *ra-wo-do-ko*, pers. n. = Λαόδοκος'

**λᾱοτύπος**, for '*cutting stones*' read '*of* or *for stone-working*' **II**, add '*SEG* 29.1187 (AD 165/6); cf. λατύπος'

**λᾱοφόρος I 1**, add 'transf., of a prostitute, λεωφ]όρε λεωφόρ' Ἡροτίμη Anacr. 1 *fr.*1.13 P.' **II**, delete the section

**λάπαθον**, add '**III** in pl., *faeces*, Sch.Gen.Il. 5.166.'

***Λάπατος**, name of month at Orchomenos, Arcadia, *Schwyzer* 667; Myc. month name *ra-pa-to.*

***Λαπηθιασταί**, οἱ, name of a guild, *IG* 12(1).867 (Lindos), *Clara Rhodos* 2.203.

***λαπιδόρχας**· ὁ μεγάλους ὄρχεις ἔχων Hsch.

***λᾱπίθης**, ου, ὁ, λ.· ὁ αὐχηματίας, παρὰ τὸ τοὺς λαοὺς εἰς ὄπιν ἄγειν καὶ ἐπιστροφήν, ὅς‹› ‹ἐ›κπείθει τινὰς περιαυτολογούμενος Suet.*Blasph.* 132 T., from the character of the Λαπίθαι, Il. 12.128, etc.

***λαπῷος**, α, ον, perh. = λαπώδης, Hdn.*fr.* p. 18 H.

***λαργιτιονάλια**, τά, perh. in *CPR* 7.26.19, 24, 33, 37, Lat. *largitionalia*, money tax on landed property.

***λαργιτίων**, ωνος (ονος), ἡ, Lat. *largitio*, *distribution of gifts*, *IEphes.* 38.11 (v AD); τῶν θείων λαργιτιόνων Just.*Const.* Δέδωκεν 9.

***λαργιτιωναλικός**, ή, όν, Lat. *largitionalis*, *concerned with the distribution of gifts*, πρόσοδοι *Stud.Pal.* 20.143.9 (v/vi AD), *PFlor.* 377.15 (vi AD).

**λᾱρδος**, for '*salted meat*' read '*bacon*, cf. Lat. *laridum, lardum*'; add '(cf. Λαρδᾶς as pers. n., *Amyzon* 53, Caria, ii BC)'

**Λᾱ́ρῖσα**, add 'see also °Λᾶσα'

**+λάρναξ**, ἄκος, ἡ (ὁ, v. infr. 2) *rectangular box, chest*, Il. 18.413, λάρνακι ἐν δαιδαλέαι Simon. 38.1 P., Hdt. 3.123.2, B. 5.141 S.-M., A.R. 1.622, D.S. 5.62, Plu. 2.968f, Luc.*Syr.D.* 12, Apollod. 1.7.2; used to hold the bones of the dead, (ὀστέα) χρυσείην ἐς λάρνακα θῆκαν Il. 24.795, λάρνακας κυπαρισσίνας ἄγουσιν ἅμαξαι .. · ἔνεστι δὲ τὰ ὀστᾶ κτλ. Th. 2.34.3; of the Ark of the Covenant, *AP* 1.62. **2** *trough*, ὁ λ. οὗτος *IG* 12(1).961 (Chalce).

**λᾰ́ρος**, add 'cf. λάρος· ὄρνις. καὶ ἰχθῦς ποιός Hsch.'

**λᾱρός 1**, lines 5/6. for 'Simon. 183.10' read '*AP* 7.24.10 ([Simon.])' **3**, add 'so λαροῖς ποσίν Hes.*fr.* 315 M.-W. (s.v.l.) acc. to Sch.A.R. 1.456 (glossed by ἁπαλός in *Et.Gen.*)'

**λάσα**, delete the entry.

***Λᾶσα**, = Λάρισα, Hsch.

**+Λᾱσαῖος**, = Λαρισαῖος (v. °Λᾶσα), *IG* 9(2).517.19 (Larissa, iii BC), also Λασσαῖος *BCH* 59.37 (Crannon).

**λᾰ́σᾰνα I**, for '*trivet* .. *pot*' read '*separate supports designed to hold any round-bottomed cooking-pot over a fire* (cf. *Hesperia* 54.393ff.)'

**λάσειος**, delete the entry.

**λασθαίνειν**, add 'ἐλασθαίνομεν· ἠκολασταίνομεν id.; μὴ δοκῇ με λασθαίνειν Hippon. 104.14 W.'

***λᾰσῐηκόμας**, masc. adj. *shaggy*, Κριός cj. in Mesom. 8.10 H. (λασιοκόμαν cod.).

**λάσιος II**, add 'of *laden* table, λ. τράπεζα· πληρεστάτη Hsch.'

**λάσταυρος**, after 'Phryn. 173' insert 'Men.*Sic.* 266 S.' and add 'Hsch. s.v.'

***λατερκουλίσιος**, ὁ, Lat. *laterculensis*, *employee of a laterculum*, Just.*Nov.* 23 epilogos.

***λατέρκουλον**, τό, Lat. *laterculum*, *registry of public offices*, Just.*Nov.* 25.6, al.

***λᾱτερπής**, ές, *delighting the people*, Pi.*fr.* 346b.3.

***λατίδιον**, τό, kind of fish (cf. °λάτις), *PAmst.* 92.5 (ii/iii AD).

*Λατῖνίς, ἴδος, ἡ, fem. adj. *Latin*, δέλτος Nonn.*D.* 41.160.

Λατῖνος, add 'adv. Λατίνως, *Orac.Tiburt.* 162'

*λάτις, ιδος, (gender uncertain), kind of fish, prob. *Nile-perch*, *Tilapia nilotica*, *PMich.*II 123ᵛ vii 19 (i AD), *Et.Gud.*; cf. λάτος.

*Λᾱτοῖος, ὁ, (sc. μήν) name of month at Byzantium, *Milet* 1(3).153 (ii BC); cf. °Λητώιος.

λᾱτομεῖον, line 1, before 'Str.' insert '*SEG* 26.134 (Attica, iv BC)' add '**II** *tomb hewn out of rock*, *BCH* 36.618-20 (Thrace; -ιον, -ιν), etc.'

λᾱτομικός, add 'λατομικῇ .. τέχνῃ *SEG* 30.1481'

λᾱτομίς, after '*stone-chisel*' insert '*PCair.Zen.* 759.1, 782(*a*).54 (both iii BC)'

*λατρευτής, οῦ, ὁ, *hired labourer*, *IEphes.* 1247b.8.

λάτρον, line 2, after '*EM* 557.35' insert 'cf. Varro *LL* 7.52' and before 'λάτρων' insert 'Call.*fr.* 276 Pf.'

λᾱτύπη, for '*Rev.Phil.* 50.67' read '*Didyma* 40.28, 41.54'

*Λᾱυδικηνόν, τό, prob. *Laodicean garment*, *Dura*⁴ 153 (cf. Λαδικηνός *Edict.Diocl.* 19.25, al., *Laudicea CIL* 3 p. 847).

*λαυκάνιον, τό, part of the throat, τὸ μεταξὺ τοῦ λ. καὶ τοῦ αὐχένος ἠχῶδες given as expl. of λήκυθος II, *Adam's apple*, Sch.Pl.*Hp.Mi.* 368c; cf. Hsch. s.v. λήκυθος, cf. λαυκανίη.

λαύκη, delete the entry.

*λαυνός, unexpld. wd. (noun in -αυνός), Hdn.*fr.* p. 27 H.

λαύρα **I**, add '*district* or *quarter* of a city, *SEG* 34.940.4 (Camarina, iv/iii BC)' **II**, for 'Hippon. .. 1089.10' read 'Hippon. 61, 92.10 W., Sotad. 2.1'

*λαύραρχος, ὁ, *chief of a district* or *quarter*, *BE* 1966 p. 445 no. 512.19, 25 (Tauromenium, i BC).

Λαφρία, after 'Ant.Lib. 40.2' insert 'τᾶι Ἀρτέμιτι τᾶι Λαφρίαι *SEG* 25.621.8 (Aetolia, ii AD), cf. τᾶι Βασιλείαι τᾶι ἐν Λάφροι ib. 25.640 (W. Locris, ii BC)'

Λαφριαῖος, add 'also in W.Locris *IG* 9²(3).624g.2, 638.3.3, 639.4.1; cf. °Λοφριαῖος'

+Λάφριος, ὁ, (after Λαφρία in *LSJ*), of Hermes, Lyc. 835, *SEG* 24.231 τὸν Λάφριν (Attica, ii AD). **II** month in Phocis, *GDI* 1719, al.; at Gytheion, *IG* 5(1).1145.28, etc.

Λάφριος, (after Λαφριάδαι in *LSJ*), delete the entry.

λαφύκτης, add 'Ath. 11.485a'

*λάφυξ· δάπανος, Drachmann *Cyrillglossar* (1936) p. 123; cf. λαιφύς.

*λᾰφῡρικός, ή, όν, *of booty*, de Franciscis *Locr.Epiz.* p. 41 no. 27.

+λᾰχᾰνάριον, τό, *vegetable pan*, *BGU* 2359.7, *PFam.Teb.* 49a ii 1, b ii 1 (iii AD), *Gloss.*

*λᾰχᾰνάρις, ὁ, *vegetable-grower*, *BIFAO* 70.42 no. 2.

λᾰχᾰνᾶς, add '*POxy.* 2421 (iv AD), *BGU* 2194.2 (vi AD)'

λᾰχᾰνευτής, after '= foreg.' insert '*PUniv.Giss.* 3.6 (ii BC)'

λᾰχᾰνεύω **I 2**, add 'Dsc. 1.91'

λᾰχᾰνιά, for '*garden-bed*' read '*vegetable-plot*' and add '*POxy.* 1913.17 (vi AD)'

+λᾰχᾰνικός, ή, όν, *of vegetables*: -κή, ἡ, *tax on vegetables*, *Inscr.Magn.* 116.42 (ii AD); so -όν, τό, *SB* 2085; perh. also *Ostr.* 787.1 (i AD).

λάχᾰνον **1**, add 'perh. *vegetable-seed*, *SB* 10402.4 (AD 125)'

λᾰχᾰνόπωλις, add '*CPR* 13.16.10 (iii BC), *PMich.*IV 224.2120 (ii AD)'

+λᾰχειδής, ές, epith. of kind of toad, perh. *green-hued*, Nic.*Al.* 568.

λάχη, delete 'τάφων .. A.*Th.* 914 (lyr.)' add '**2** collection of dues on *allotted rights of pasture*, *SEG* 3.357.2 (Acraephia, iii BC).'

*λᾰχή, ἡ, *digging*, A.*Th.* 914 (pl.).

λάχνη **I**, line 3, after '*O.* 1.68' insert 'of *hair* on the chest, Call.*fr.* 24.2 Pf.'; line 4, after 'Il. 2.219' insert 'cf. A.R. 4.1531'; at end before 'Opp.*H.* 2.369' insert 'so in sg.' **II**, delete 'Nic.*Al.* 410'

λάχος, add 'also Cypr. *la-ko-se* λάχος *ICS* 318 B vii'

*λαψάνιον, τό, = λαψάνη, *PAnt.* 92.26 (iv/v AD; λαμψανεια pap.).

λεαίνω **I 3**, add '*smooth so as to erase*, τὰς δέλτους *POxy.* 2741.1a i 19'

λέβης **I b**, for '*coin* .. Crete)' read 'as monetary unit, *Inscr.Cret.* 4.1, al. (vii/vi BC)' and add '*SEG* 37.752 (Lyttos, v BC)'

*λεβητίσκος, ὁ, dim. of λέβης, *IG* 2².1424*a*.147 (iv BC).

λεγεών, after 'λεγιών ib. 214.3, al.' insert '*TAM* 4(1).189; also written ληγιών Mitchell *N.Galatia* 289'; at end delete 'hence λεγιονάριος .. al.'

*λεγεωνάριος, ὁ, *legionary*, Modest.*Dig.* 27.1.8.6; also λεγιωνάριος *INikaia* 1551, *POxy.* 1419.7 (AD 265), *PLond.* 1254.5 (iv AD), λεγιονάριος *IGRom.* 3.214.3; ληγιωνάριος *BGU* 344 col. 2.4.

*λεγίτιμος, η, ον, Lat. *legitimus*, *based on law*, Just.*Nov.* 84.1 pr., al.

*λεγουμενᾶλε, Lat. neut. adj. *leguminale*, of a sieve, *Edict.Diocl.* 15.60.

λέγω (B) **I** after '**2**' insert 'act., *choose*, *pick*, Pl.*Lg.* 738a; pass., Il. 13.272, Pl.*Lg.* 737c'

λεία (B), line 1, after '(Pi.*O.* 10(11).44)' insert 'λαία *SEG* 23.324(a) (Delphi, 277 BC), sense 4, cf. Hsch., s.v. λαίαν' add 'form λᾱϝία in deriv. adj. Myc. *ra-wi-ja-ja* (fem. pl.); cf. ληΐάς'

λειαύστηρος, before 'Poll. 6.15' insert 'v.l. in'

*Λειβηθριάς, άδος, *of Libethrum*, τῶν Λειβηθριάδων νυμφῶν Str. 10.3.17, καὶ πηγαί–τὴν μὲν Λειβηθριάδα ὀνομάζουσιν Paus. 9.34.3; epith. of the Muses, κούρη Λειβηθριὰς ἔννεπε Μοῦσα Orph.*fr.* 342, *Suppl.Hell.* 993.7.

*Λειβηθρίς, ίδος, = °Λειβηθριάς, τῶν Λειβηθρίδων νυμφῶν Str. 9.2.25, *Suppl.Hell.* 980.1.

Λείβηθρον **II**, at end delete 'the Λειβηθρίδες .. 342'

*Λειβῆνος· ὁ Διόνυσος Hsch.

λειεντεριώδης, add 'Gal. 16.800.5'

λεῖμαξ **I 1**, line 2, after '(both lyr.)' insert '*IA* 1544 (interp.)'

*λείμψᾰνον, τό, = λείψανον, *ABSA* 59.19 (Aphrodisias).

λειμών **III**, line 2, delete '1.19'; last line, after '*Praef.* 6' insert 'λόγοι τῶν καλῶν λ. ἀφθόνους προτείνοντες Procl. *in R.* 1.161 K.'

λειμωνιάς, add 'Orph.*H.* 29.12'

λειμωνιάτης, delete the entry.

*λειμωνιᾶτις, ιδος, ἡ, a stone, = *smaragdos*, Plin.*HN* 37.172.

λειμώνιος, add 'as a divine epith., Κόρηι Λειμωνίαι *RA* 6.67 (Amphipolis, ii BC)'

*λειμωνῖτις, ἡ, a plant, = λειμωνία (s.v. λειμώνιος), Suid.

λεῖος, after 'α, ον' insert '(Ion. λέος, η, ον, *Didyma* 434.23, 25, 437.4 (both iii BC))' **I 3**, line 7, delete '3.14' **II**, line 2, before 'Dsc.' insert 'Arist.*HA* 534ᵇ23, *PA* 674ᵇ13'

*λειουργέω· καλλωπίζω Phot.

*λειπογᾰλαξία, ἡ, *absence of milk*, *agalactia*, νόσων γὰρ καὶ λειπογαλαξίας αἴτιος ἔσται Heph.Astr. 3.5.49.

λειπογνώμων, add 'also λειπε- *SEG* 26.136 (Athens, iv BC)'

*λειποτελής, ές, *in arrears with taxes*, *PTeb.* 711.4 (ii BC).

λείπω **I 3 a**, line 2, after 'ib. 903' insert 'ὡς ἡ μὲν λίπε μῦθον *thus she ceased talking*, Call.*fr.* 43.84 Pf.' **II 2 a**, add 'of prosecutor, *drop the case*, Arist.*Ath.* 16.8' **II 2**, line 8, before 'inf.' insert 'substantival' **b**, add 'med., *wane*, Orph.*H.* 9.4, Nonn.*D.* 5.164' **B II 3**, add 'τῶν κτεάνων .. τὸ λειπόμενον *deficiency* in possessions, *AP* 5.267.8 (Agath.)' add 'Myc. med. part. *re-qo-me-no*'

λειριόεις **1**, add 'ὀδμὴ .. λειριόεσσα Opp.*H.* 3.410'

λείριον **II**, before 'Dsc. 4.158' insert 'perh. *Narcissus poeticus*' add '**IV** flower of the plant ἔχις, Nic.*Th.* 543.'

*λειριόπρυμνος, ον, *lily-(?white-)prowed*, *Suppl.Hell.* 991.114 (poet. word-list, iii BC).

*λείριος, ον, *like a lily*, of white coral, λ. ἄνθεμον ποντίας ἐέρσας Pi.*N.* 7.79; ὄμματα B. 17.95 S.-M.; κηρία Opp.*C.* 1.128. **2** applied to melodious voice, ἵεσαν ἐκ στομάτων ὄπα λείριον (Σειρῆνες) A.R. 4.903, Orph.*A.* 253; cf. ‡λειριόεις.

*λειριόχροος, ον, *having lily-white skin*, Hdn.*fr.* p. 15 H.

λείστριον, delete '= λίστριον'; add '*IG* 2².1678*a*A5 (λιστρ- lapis; Athens, iv BC)'

*λείτορας, ὁ, = λείτωρ, (in quot., priest of Apollo), *SEG* 36.548 (Thessaly, iii BC).

λειτορεύω, for '= ἱερεύω' read 'serve as λείτωρ'; line 2, at beginning insert '*SEG* 8.714 (Thebes, Egypt, ii BC)'

λειτουργέω **I**, add 'of a house or family, οἴκων λητουργούντων D. 42.23'

λειτουργός **II 1**, add '**b** at Athens, *clerk* named at the end of list of magistrates and their assistants, *IG* 2².1728, 1729, 1731 (all i AD).'

λείτωρ, for '*priest*, ἀρωγὸς λ. *MDAI(A)* 12.283' read 'a kind of priest, Ἄρωγος λ. *IG* 2².4817.25, cf. λήτωρ, ἀλήτωρ (cf. Ἑλληνικά 8.229)'

λειχήν **3**, delete 'of animals'

λείχω, add 'in sens. obsc., *SEG* 34.1015 (Rome, ii/iii AD); cf. λείκτης'

*λειψᾰνοθήκη, ἡ, *repository for the remains of the dead*, *SEG* 31.630 (Rom.imp.).

λείψανον **2**, add 'also sg., *BCH* 102.413-4 fig. 3b (iii AD), etc.'

λέκκη, add 'also λέκτη, Theognost.*Can.* 27 A.'

λέκος, for '*dish*, *pot*, *pan*' read '*dish*, *bowl*' and insert '*SEG* 33.996 (Smyrna, vi BC), *IG* 1³.422.131 (Athens, v BC)'

*λεκτεῖκα, ἡ, Lat. *lectica*, *litter*, *SB* 7348.3 (i AD).

*λεκτικάριος, ὁ, Lat. *lecticarius*, *bearer* at funerals, Just.*Nov.* 43 pr., al., *PIand.* 8.154 (vi/vii AD), *ITyr* 29*B*, al.

λεκτίς, add '**II** *tomb*, masc. w. acc. λεκτεῖκα *SEG* 26.1314, 1320 (Sardis, iv/vi AD); cf. °λεκτεῖκα.'

λεκτός **I**, add 'βολὴ .. λεκτὴ πεντήϙοντ' ἀπὸ φυλῆς council *chosen* fifty from each tribe, *SEG* 16.485C.7 (Chios, vi BC)'

*λελεγίζω· τὸ κιθαρίζω Theognost.*Can.* 27 A.

*λεμβαρχέω, *command a* λέμβος, *IParion* 5.

*λεμησία, ἡ, wd. of unkn. meaning, *PYale* 902 + 906 (ii AD) in *YClS* 10.217, line 53; cf. λέμυσος, λεμεῖσα.

λέμμα **1**, add '*shell* of an egg, Ael.*VH* 10.3'

*λεμόνη, ἡ, *lemon*, Anon.Alch. 328.23.

*λεμψάνη, v. °λεψάνη.

*λεντιαρία, ἡ, female *linen-dealer*, *AAWW* 1956.230.10 (Lydia).

*λεντιάριον, τό, perh. *recess* or *cupboard for linen*, *ITomis* 389 (iii/iv AD)

***λεντιάριος**, ὁ, Lat. *lintearius*, perh. *cloakroom attendant* at gymnasium, *IG* $2^2$.2130.221, 14.2323. **2** *linen-dealer*, *Σευῆρος λεντιάρις IG-Bulg.* 1922.7.

**λέντιον**, delete 'hence *λεντιάριος* .. 14.2323'

***λέντιος**, *ον*, *made of linen*, *ἰλήματι καινῷ λεντίῳ POxy.* 3060.7 (ii AD).

***λενῶ·** *τὸ λυποῦμαι* Theognost.*Can.* 27 A.

***λεξιγράφος**, ὁ, = °*λεξογράφος*, *AB* 1094.

***λεξίδιον**, *τό*, *verbal expression*, Arr.*Epict.* 2.1.30, 2.23.43, etc., Gal. 13.575.8, etc.

**λεξιθηρέω**, delete 'Plu.ap.'

***λεξογράφος**, *one who records λέξεις*, *lexicographer*, Sch.Hes.*Op.* 633-40, Lyd.*Mag.* 11.16, 21.25 W; (see also *λεξικογράφος*).

***λεοδράκων**, *οντος*, ὁ, mythical creature, (*lion-serpent*), *Inscr.Cret.* 2.xix 7.19 (Phalasarna, iv BC).

**λεοντάγχης**, add 'of type of engraved agate, *Hippiatr.* 2.148.5'

**λεοντάριον I**, for 'Dim. of *λέων*' read '*statue* or *image of a lion*'

***Λεοντεῖον**, *τό*, app. *meeting-place of the λέοντες in the cult of Mithras*, *λεοντίῳ PBerol.* 21196.8 (*Tyche* suppl. 1992 p. 18, iv AD).

**λεόντειος**, add 'Myc. *re-wo-te-jo*'

**λεοντίς**, for pres. ref. read '*SEG* 33.946'

**λεοντοβότος II**, delete the section transferring 'Str. 16.1.24' to section I and add '*Νεμέης* .. *λεοντοβότου Inscr.Magn.* 181.9 (ii AD)'

**λεοντοδέρης**, for '*like* .. *tawny*' read '*lionskin*, name given to agate'

***λεοντόθυμος**, *ον*, *lion-hearted*, Hsch. s.v. *θυμολέοντα*.

**λεοντοπρόσωπος**, add 'Heph.Astr. 2.2.32'

***λεοντορήκτης** or **λεοντορήκτα**, ὁ, *lion-breaker*, Bonner *Studies in Magical Amulets* 169.

**λεοντόχασμα**, for '= *λεοντόκρουνον*' read '*spout in the form of a lion's mouth*' and add 'Aristo in *Gnomol.Vat.* in *WS* 10.23'

***λεοντοχασμάτιον**, *τό*, dim. of *λεοντόχασμα*, rest. in Sch.Pi.*Pae.* 6.7.

***λεοντοχασματύπανον**, *τό*, kind of wheel for raising water, *IGLS* 645.

**λέπαργος I**, for '*A.Fr.* 304.5' read '*S.fr.* 581.5' and for 'sheep or goat' read 'calf'; add '*βοὸς λεπάργου Trag.adesp.* 231' **II**, add '**2** *λέπαργος· ἡ χιών*, Theognost.*Can.* 27 A., Zonar.'

**λεπίδιον I**, add 'part used in the construction of a boat, *POxy.* 2195.141 (vi AD)'

**λεπιδίσκη**, delete the entry.

***λέπιδος**, *η*, *ον*, Lat. *lepidus*, *charming*, *agreeable*, *Λεοσθένης λέπιδος καὶ ἐράσμιος IG* 14.40.

***λεπιδῶτις**, *ιδος*, ἡ, gem, prob. the same as *λεπιδωτός* II 2, Plin.*HN* 37.171.

**λεπιδωτός I 2**, add 'Sm., Thd. *1Ki.* 17.5'

**λεπίς 3**, add 'Ptol.*Tetr.* 153'

**λεπιστής**, add '(or *λαπιστής*, see Hsch. s.h.v.)'

***λεπταμικτόριον**, *τό*, *a fine amictorium*, *PFouad* inv. 45.18 (*CE* 27.196, ii/iii AD).

***λεπτόδομος**, *ον*, perh. *slenderly fashioned*, *πείσματα* A.*Pers.* 112 (s.v.l., edd. °*λεπτότονος*, etc.).

***λεπτοκεραμικός**, *ή*, *όν*, *used for fine pottery*, *λίθος CPap.Jud.* 452*b*.5 (ii AD).

***λεπτόκλωνος**, *ον*, *having fine* or *thread-like branches*, *βεττονικὴ λ.* Paul.Aeg. 7.3 (200.19 H).

**λεπτοκοπέω**, add 'Heras ap.Gal. 13.558.12'

***λεπτοκυμία**, ἡ, gloss on *φρίξ*, Sch.Gen.Il. 23.692, Hsch.

***λεπτόπηνος**, *ον*, *made of fine fabric*, *λεπτοπήνοις ὑμέσιν* Eub. 67.5, 82.4 K.-A.

***λεπτοποιός**, ὁ, perh. *joiner* or *cabinet-maker*, Ramsay *Cities and Bishoprics* I p. 142 no. 31.

***λεπτοπρόσωπος**, *ον*, *thin-faced*, Heph.Astr. 1.1.58.

***λεπτοπυρέτιον**, *τό*, *slight fever*, Cyran. 59 (pl.).

**λεπτός III 2**, add 'in *Ev.Marc.* 12.42 equated with half a *quadrans*' add 'Myc. *re-po-to* (of linen, cf. I 3)'

***λεπτόσφυρος**, *ον*, *having thin ankles*, Hsch. s.v. *τανίσφυρος*, Rhetor. in *Cat.Cod.Astr.* 7.209.14.

**λεπτότης II**, add '**2** of literary or artistic style, *refinement*, *delicacy*, Hermog.*Id.* 2.12, D.H.*Isoc.* 3.'

***λεπτότονος**, *ον*, *finely-stretched*, *πείσματα*, cj. in A.*Pers.* 112 (but v. °*λεπτόδομος*).

***λεπτόχειλος**, *ον*, = *λεπτοχειλής*, Heph.Astr. 3.45.9.

**λέπτυνσις**, add 'Gal. 11.111.14'

**λέπυρον**, add 'of an eggshell, Ach.Tat.*Intr.Arat.* p. 33.19'

**λέπω II**, add '*τῷ ῥοπάλῳ τὰν κεφαλὰν λέπομες AP* 9.330 (Nicarch.)'

***λερνός**, *ή*, *όν*, unexpld. wd., Hdn.*fr.* p. 25 H.

***Λεσβιακός**, *ή*, *όν*, *Lesbian*, *Λ. λόγοι*, work by Dicaearchus, Cic.*Tusc.* 1.77; *Λεσβιακά*, *τά*, by Myrsilus (477 F 1-3 J.), also by Hellanicus (4 F 34-35), (or *Λεσβικά* (id. 33)).

**Λεσβιάς**, add '**2** *Λ.* (sc. *λίθος*), ἡ, a precious stone, Plin. *HN* 37.171.'

**λεσχαῖος**, add 'as title of Apollo, *IG* 9(2).1027 (Larissa, v BC)'

**λέσχη I 1**, line 2, after 'Camirus' insert 'vi BC, Dor. -ā' **3**, lines 5/6, for 'at Cnidus, *council-chamber*' read '*council-chamber* of the Cnidians at Delphi'

***λεσχήνευμα**, *ατος*, *τό*, *place for conversation*, *Inscr.Cret.* 2 v 51 (i AD).

***λεσχηνευτής**, *οῦ*, ὁ, = °*λεσχηνώτης*, *ὁ Ποντικὸς λ.* *"Talker"*, i.e. author of *Λέσχαι* Ath. 14.649c.

**Λεσχηνόριος**, line 4, after 'al.' insert 'written *Λεσχηνούριος*, *AE* 1927/8.123 (ii BC)'

***λεσχηνώτης**, *ου*, ὁ, *one who takes part in a discussion*, Thales ap.D.L. 1.43, Anaximen.ap.D.L. 2.4.

***λεσώνης**, *ου*, ὁ, = *λεσῶνις*, *SB* 6154.31 (i BC), *BGU* $37^v$ (i AD), *PTeb.* 313.6 (AD 210/1).

**λεσῶνις**, lines 2/3, delete 'later gen. .. *BGU* $37^v$ (i AD)'; line 3, after '(ii BC)' insert 'nom. pl. -*ῶνες BGU* 916.9, 25 (i AD)' (v. °*λεσώνης*)

***λεύδια**, v. °*γλεύδιον*.

**Λευκαθέα I**, add 'in Syria *SEG* 31.1392'

***λευκάνθεμος**, ἡ, = *λευκάνθεμον*, Sch.Nic.*Th.* 849 C.

**λεύκανσις**, add '**2** *whitening*, *whitewashing*, *ABSA* 61.306.122 (Epid., iii BC).'

**λευκαντής**, add '*SEG* 34.1124 (Ephesus, ii AD), *POxy.* 3743.7-8 (iv AD), *PWash.Univ.* 37.4 (v AD), *Corinth* 8(3).522 (v/vi AD)'

***λευκάριον**, *τό*, *λ. κωβαθίων* (*κο*- pap.), perh. *white powder*, *SB* $10492^v$.26 (ii AD).

**λευκάς II 2**, for this section read 'epith. of *ποίη*, Nic.*Th.* 849, *λ. π.* acc. to Sch. ad loc. being *ἡ λευκάνθεμος*'

**λευκασία**, add '**2** name of a skin disease, Cyran. 15.'

**λεύκασπις**, line 2, after 'X.*HG* 3.2.15' insert 'of a Tarentine corps, D.H. 20.1'

**λευκόγεως**, after '**λευκόγαιος**' insert 'cf. *leucogaeam*, Plin.*HN* 37.162'

***λευκογραφῖτις**, *ιδος*, another name for °*γαλακτῖτις*, Plin.*HN* 37.162.

***λευκόζωνος**, *ον*, dub. l., *white-girdled*, of Ino (Leucothea), *SEG* 26.683.5 (Thessaly, iii BC).

**Λευκοθέα I**, add 'pl., Alcm. S 5(b).12, *SEG* 32.1538 (Gerasa, ii/iii AD), 33.1262 (Syria, AD 268/9)'

**λευκόλινον**, for '*white flax*' read 'app. a kind of flax or hemp' and add '*PLond.* 1965.2 (iii BC)'

***λευκομέννιον**, *τό*, *white sprat*, *BGU* 2358.13 (iv AD).

**λευκομέτωπος II**, after 'bird' insert 'prob. *coot*'

***λευκοπίων**, *ον*, gen. *ονος*, *fat and white*, prob. in *POxy.* 1631.25 (iii AD); cf. Sch.Ar.*Ra.* 1124.

**λευκόπυρος**, add '*BGU* 1067.16 (ii AD)'

***λευκοπωρινός**, *ή*, *όν*, made of °*λευκόπωρος*, *BE* 1971.642 (Phrygia).

***λευκόπωρος**, ὁ, a kind of white marble, *BE* 1971.642 (Phrygia).

**λευκός I 1**, add '*Peripl.M.Rubr.* 38' **2**, line 3, after '(Phil.)' insert '*λ. ῥήσει* Babr. ii prooem. 13' **II 1 a**, add 'of person, *white-haired*, Call.*fr.* 194.52 Pf.' **2**, add '**b** of tortoise-shell, *pale*, *Peripl.M.Rubr.* 3, 30.' **3**, line 3, for 'Call.*Aet.* 1.1.2' read 'Call.*fr.* 178.2 Pf.'; line 4, for 'cf. Sch. .. 1094.39' read 'Call.*fr.* 191.37 Pf. (pl.)'; line 5, after '*Per.* 27' for '*ἡ λ.* .. Hsch.' read '**b** *white*, i.e. *favourable*, of a voting pebble, *ἡ λ. καὶ σῴζουσα ψῆφος* Luc.*Harm.* 3; *ψήφου διενεχθείσης ἐγένοντο πᾶσαι λευκαί SEG* 24.614 (Maced., ii AD), cf. *SEG* 9.354.25, *REG* 62.284.28, 286.21 (all Cyrenaica, i BC/i AD). **c** of place, *fortunate* or *glorious* (cf. 1), *ἡ τότε λ. Δῆλος AP* 9.421.5.' add 'Myc. *re-u-ko*'

**λευκότης**, add '**2** of style, *clearness*, *limpidity*, Eun.*VS* p. 458 B.'

**λευκουργός**, for '*BCH* 32.500 (Aphrodisias)' read '*La Carie* 162 (Apollonia of Salbake, *c*.AD 200)'

**λευκόφυλλος**, after 'Dsc. 4.103' insert '*PSoterichos* 4.17 (AD 87)'

***λευκόχαλκος**, ὁ, *τὸ δὲ λευκὸν τοῦ αὐτοῦ ᾠοῦ καλοῦσιν ὑδράργυρον, ὕδωρ ἀργυρικόν, λευκόχαλκον*, etc. Anon.Alch. 19.19.

***λευκοχίτων**, *ωνος*, ὁ, ἡ, = *λευκοχίτωνος*, *ζειά Lyr.adesp.* 11(*d*).5 P.

**λευκόχρωμος**, add '*ὄνος POxy.* 1708.10 (iv AD)'

**λευκόχρως**, for '*colourless*' read '*pale-skinned*'

**λευκώλενος**, of Hera, add '*λευϙ̄ολενōι ℎ̄ερᾱι JHS* 106.196 (vi BC)'

**λεύκωσις**, add '**III** *whitewashing*, *IG* $4^2$.102.305 (Epid., iv BC).'

**λευκωτής**, add '*SB* 10258 i 5 (iv AD)'

**λευρός I**, at end for 'Call.*Aet.Oxy.* 2080.67' read 'Call.*fr.* 43.65 Pf.'

**λεύσσω**, line 5, delete 'Poet.Verb .. *AB* 1096' **3**, for 'c. acc. cogn.' read 'w. cogn. or adverbial acc.'

***λευτο-**, Arcad. vb. *see*. part. *λεύτōν IG* 5(2).3, *λεύτοντες* ib. 5(2).16.

**λεύω**, line 1, after '*λεύσω*' insert '*A.fr.* 132c.1 R.'; line 3, after '*stone*' insert 'Hippon. 37 W.' and after 'Th. 5.60' insert '*τοὐμὸν σῶμα* A. l.c.'

**λεχεποίη**, delete '*h.Merc.* 88'

**λεχεποίης**, add '*h.Merc.* 88'

****λεχεστρωτήριον**, *τό*, Myc. *re-ke-to-ro-te-ri-jo*, name of a festival.

**λεχήρης**, add '*IEphes.* 2109'

**λέχομαι**, line 3, before 'Hsch.' insert 'Antim. 178 Wy.'

**λεχώ**, add 'on a funerary monument perh. indicating death in child-birth, *Inscr.Cret.* 2 x 12'

***λεχώζω**, *hatch*, Suid. s.v. *σελάχια*, cf. Phot. s.v. *σελάχιον*.

*__λεψάνη__, ἡ, = λαψάνη, *PLond.* 1771.10 (vi AD); also **λεμψάνη**, *PHamb.* 68.41 (vi AD).

*__Λέψυνος__, ὁ, epith. of Zeus, *Ilasos* 151.

*__λεώκερας__, τό, word in magical formula, *Inscr.Cret.* 2 xix 7.18 (Phalasarna, iv BC).

**λέων III**, after '*Th.* 643' insert 'Afric.*Cest.* p. 16 V.' **VI**, add '*Rev.Hist.Rel.* 109.63 (Rome)' add 'Myc. *re-wo-pi* (instr. pl.)'

*__Λεωνίδαια__, τά, festival at Larissa, *BCH* 59.515 (iii BC); also **Λεωνίδεια**, at Sparta, in honour of the hero of Thermopylae, *IG* 5(1).18.8, al.

*__Λεωνίδαιον__, τό, *shrine of Leonidas*, Paus. 5.15.2, 6.17.1.

*__λεῶρες__· τὸ ἄωρον Theognost.*Can.* 27 A.

+__λήβολος__, ον, Aeol. **λᾶβ-** Alc. 68.3 L.-P. (s.v.l.), *condemned to stoning*, λήβολε· λιθόβολε, ἄξιε λιθασθῆναι Hsch. (ληβόλε· λιθοβόλε cod., La.).

*__ληγατάριος__, ὁ, Lat. *legatarius*, *legatee*, *Cod.Just.* 6.4.4.18a; also **λεγ-** Modest.*Dig.* 26.6.2.3.

*__ληγατεύω__, *bequeath in the form of a legacy*, *Cod.Just.* 1.5.15.

*__ληγᾶτον__, τό, Lat. *legatum*, *legacy*, *BGU* 1.327.6, *IGRom* 3.828, Scaev.*Dig.* 33.8.23.2, *Cod.Just.* 1.2.25 pr., al.

*__ληγᾶτος__, ον, Lat. *legatus*, past pass. part. *bequeathed*, *SEG* 34.1213 (Lydia, ii AD).

*__ληγιών__, v. °λεγεών.

**λήγω II 1**, line 5, after 'Th. 7.6' insert 'abs., ληγούσης Πελοπηΐδος Call.*fr.* 384.11 Pf.'

**ληδεῖν** and **ληδήσας**, delete the entry.

+__λῆδος__, εος, τό, Dor. **λᾶδος**, a kind of *dress* (cf. ληδίον), λᾶδος Ϝημένα καλόν Alcm. 117 P., λᾶιδος· λῆδος, τριβώνιον Hsch.

**λήθαιος III**, add '= °ἀναγκίτης Orph.*L.* 197'

**ληθαργέω**, after '*forget*' insert '*SEG* 34.1065 (Aphrodisias, vi AD)'

**ληϊβοτήρ**, add 'Plu. 2.730b'

**ληΐδιος**, after '*captive*' insert 'Euph. in *Suppl.Hell.* 415 ii 18'

+__ληϊστής__, v. λῃστής.

**λήϊτον**, line 4, before 'λαιετόν' insert 'λαίετον' and before 'Suid.' insert 'λαιτρόν, Theognost.*Can.* 27 A.'

**ληκάω**, for '= λαικάζω' read '*have sexual intercourse with*'

*__ληκήτρια__, ἡ, λ. θεά Lyc. 1391, fem. of ληκητής.

**ληκυθίζω**, line 2, for 'Call.*fr.* 10.13 P.' read 'Call.*fr.* 215 Pf.'

*__ληκυθίς__, ίδος, ἡ, = λήκυθος, *Hesperia* 33.83.

**λήκυθος I 1**, after 'ἡ' insert 'Δηρίππō ἐμὶ λήϙυθος *SEG* 33.995 (Smyrna, vi BC)' **2**, add 'cf. Sch.Heph. p. 230.18 C.'

**λῆμα II 1**, at end after '*Ra.* 463' insert 'Call.*fr.* 43.59, 345 Pf.'

*__λημᾰτίζομαι__, *to be eager for*, λεληματίσθαι γὰρ τὸ τῇ διανοίᾳ πρὸς πᾶν ὁρμητικῶς ἔχειν Hsch. s.v. λελημένοι.

**λημάω**, line 3, after 'Ar.*Nu.* 327' insert 'χύτραις λημῶντες Luc.*Ind.* 23'

**λημματίζω**, add 'also **λημαт-** *PLond.* 995, 996, etc., λυμαт- *PHerm.* 24.3 (iv/v AD)'

**λημματικός**, add 'Zos.Alch. 213.2'

*__λημματισμός__, ὁ, *entry*, *crediting*, *SB* 9772.1 (pap. λιματ-; vi AD).

**λήμνιος**, add 'Myc. ethnic adj. *ra-mi-ni-ja*'

**Ληναϊκός**, for 'ἀγῶνες .. 7.414e' read 'Ληναϊκὴν .. Καλλιόπην Posidipp.ap.Ath. 10.414e (s.v.l.)'; add 'οἱ Ληναϊκοί *authors only qualified to compete at Lenaea*, Eratosth. in *POxy.* 2737; also perh. τὸ Ληναϊκ[όν], *Lenaean competition*, ib.'

*__Λήναιος__, ὁ, form of month Ληναιών given at *Hemerolog.Flor.* p. 70 (p. 4 K.).

**Ληναιών**, add '*SEG* 34.1175 (Miletus, ii AD), also Λη̣νεών *SEG* 30.977 (Olbia, v BC), 30.968 (Olbia, ii/iii AD)'

*__ληνίον__, τό, perh. *box*, Cyran. 26, 27.

**ληνίς II**, add 'in some similar sense, λ. ἀργυρᾶ *Inscr.Délos* 104.96'

*__ληνοβᾰτέω__, = ληνοπατέω, Cyran. 23; pass., ib. 22.

**ληνοβᾰτης**, add '*Anacreont.* 4.16 W.'

*__ληνοβᾰτικῶς__, adv., πατεῖν λ. i.e. in the wine-vat, Eust. 1574.8.

**ληνός 1**, line 2, after 'are pressed' insert '*IG* $1^3$.422.189, 425.34, 426.148 (cf. Poll. 10.130)' add '**b** *storage vessel* for wine, *POxy.* 1569, *PFlor.* 253 (iii AD).' add '**9** *bathing-tub*, λ. δημοσίας *MDAI(A)* 32.274 (Pergam., ii BC), *Inscr.Délos* 1423*Ba*ii4. **10** part of door, Maier *Griech.Mauerbauinschr.* 19.32 (Eleusis, iv BC).'

+__λῆνος__, εος, τό, *flock of wool*, A.*Eu.* 44, A.R. 4.173, 177, Call.*Suppl.Hell.* 257.6 (cf. *fr.* 722 Pf.), Nic.*Al.* 452, Epic.in *APF* 7.4, ?D.P.*fr.* 19ᵛ.20 L., Nonn.*D.* 6.146.

*__λῆνος__ (B), ὁ, prob. = βεβακχευμένος, *Schwyzer* 791 (Cumae, v BC); cf. λῆναι.

**λῆξις** (A) **I 1 c**, for 'pl., *fortunes*' read '*portion*, *lot*' and add 'Just.*Const.* Δέδωκεν 18, *Cod.Just.* 1.3.52.4,5, *PMasp.* 19.6 (vi AD)'

**λῆξις** (B) **I 2**, delete the section.

*__ληξοπῠρετος__, v. ληξιπ-.

**ληπτός I**, add '*Trag.adesp.* 168'

**λῆρος** (B), after '(Hedyl.)' insert '*Inscr.Délos* 1433.4 (ii BC)'

*__ληρότης__, ητος, ἡ, gloss on ὕθλος, Hsch.

**λῃστεία**, after '*piracy*' insert '*raiding*'

**λῃστεύω**, after '*practise .. piracy*' insert '*make raids*'

**λῃστήρ**, add 'of Hermes, *h.Merc.* 14'

*__λῃστογνώστης__, ου, ὁ, *associate of thieves*, Just.*Nov.* 13.4 pr., al.

+__λῃστοδιώκτης__, ου, ὁ, = Lat. *latrunculator*, *official* or *agent appointed to catch thieves*, Just.*Nov.* 8.13, al.

*__λῃστοδίωκτος__, ον, *pursued by pirates*, prob. cj. in X.Eph. 1.6.

*__λῃστολογέω__, app. *recruit* λῃσταί *as soldiers*, *IGBulg.* 1126 (iii/iv AD).

**λῃστρικός 2**, add 'comp. λῃστρικώτερον ἀφιγμένος i.e. *more concerned with plunder*, Plu.*Pyrrh.* 10'

**Λητοΐδης**, after 'Alc.*Supp.* 30.3' insert '*CEG* 785.1 (sp. Λετ-, v BC), *AP* 12.55'; after '(trisyll.)' add 'so Λατοίδα *CEG* 302.1 (vi BC); also Λητωΐδης *SEG* 23.126 (*c.*i BC)'

**Λητώ**, line 4, acc., add 'Λατών *SEG* 33.638, Λητοῦν *REG* 101.14 (Xanthos, iii BC)'

*__Λητωΐδης__, ὁ, = Λητοΐδης, *son of Leto*, i.e. *Apollo*, *SEG* 23.126 (*c.*i BC).

*__Λητωΐνη__, ἡ, *daughter of Leto*, i.e. *Artemis*, *Suppl.Hell.* 962.9.

*__Λητώϊος__, ὁ, *son of Leto*, i.e. *Apollo*, *TAM* 4(1).48.

**λήτωρ**, for '*priest*, prob. in' read 'a kind of priest (perh. as pers. n.)' and add 'cf. ἀλήτωρ'

**λιάζω** (B), for '[παρὰ .. 34.27' read 'λίην λιάζεις Archil. 113.8 W., Anacr. 85 P.'

**λιᾰρός**, line 2, after 'Od. 24.45, etc.' insert 'λιαροῖο (v.ll. λαρ-, λιπαρ-) .. γάλακτος Theoc. 25.105'

*__Λίβαιος__, ὁ, month in Cyprus beginning 2 Dec., *Cat.Cod.Astr.* 2.147.15, 148.13.

**λίβᾰνος I**, add 'fem. in Pi.*fr.* 122.3 S.-M., Nic.*Al.* 107' **II**, line 2, delete 'Pi.*fr.* 122.3'

*__λῐβᾰνοφλόγος__, ον, *incense-burning*, expl. of *turicremus* in Virgil gloss., *PNess.* 1.935 (vi AD).

**λῐβᾰνόχροος**, add '**2** λιβανόχρους (sc. λίθος), ἡ, a precious stone, Plin.*HN* 37.171.'

**λῐβᾰνωτίς** (B), add 'see also °λιβανωτρίς.'

*__λῐβᾰνωτοπώλιον__, τό, *incense-shop*, *IEphes.* 4102.2 (iii BC).

**λῐβᾰνωτός**, line 2, before 'Xenoph.' insert 'Sapph. 2.4 L.-P.'

**λῐβᾰνωτρίς**, for '*censer*' read '*box* or *casket for incense*'

*__λιβελλήσιος__, ὁ, Lat. *libellensis*, official in the imperial bureau dealing w. petitions, Just.*Nov.* 20.7.

**λιβέλλος**, after 'ὁ' insert '(neut. pl. λιβέλλα *Edict.Diocl.* 7.41)' and add '*Salamine* 29.4 (iii AD)'

*__Λιβερνάριος__, ὁ, = Λιβυρνάριος, *POxy.* 1902.4 (vi AD).

*__Λιβέρνιος__, α, ον, *Liburnian*, πλοῖον *POxy.* 2032.52, 54 (vi AD).

**λιβέρτος**, add 'fem. λιβέρτα *SEG* 35.1011 (Sicily, i BC)'

*__Λιβιανός__, ή, όν, *Livian*; κριθὴ Λ. barley *from Livia's estate*, *PKöln* 116.3 (iii AD).

*__λιβράριος__, ὁ, Lat. *librarius*, *scribe*, *BCH* 7.275 (ii AD), *SB* 6971, *Edict.Diocl.* 7.69, written λειβράρις *SEG* 26.1600 (Commagene).

*__Λιβύανδε__, adv., *to Libya*, *SEG* 9.3.19 (Cyrene, iv BC).

**Λιβυάρχης**, add '*SEG* 30.1785.1(e) (Cyrene, iv AD)'

**λιγάνταρ**, insert '(**λιγάντωρ** La.)'

*__λίγγω__, v. °λίγξε.

*__λίγλα__, ἡ, Lat. *ligula*, *spoon* (μυστίλη), Poll. 6.87; also **λίνγλα** (*lingula*, as measure), *BGU* 781 vi 3, 16 (i AD).

*__λιγμάτιον__, τό, dim. of λικμός (= λίκνον), *winnowing-fan*, *BGU* 2359.8 (iii AD).

*__λιγνύζω__ or **-νυΐζω**, *have a smoky colour*, of carbuncles, Plin.*HN* 37.94.

**λιγνύζω**, delete the entry.

**λιγνύς 1**, line 1, for 'Call.*fr.* 1.57 P.' read 'Call.*fr.* 228.57 Pf.'; add 'w. ref. to the colour of the Ethiopians, ἥλιος .. σκοτεινὸν ἄνθος ἐξέχρωσε λιγνύος εἰς σώματ' ἀνδρῶν Theodect. 17.2'

**λίγξε**, add '(cf. λίγγω· ἠχῶ Theognost.*Can.* 16)'

+__λιγουρά__, v. °λιγυρός.

+__λῐγουροκώτιλος__, v. °λιγυρο-.

**Λῐγυαστάδης**, before 'ου' insert '(or -ᾳστ-)'

**λιγύριον**, add 'Epiph.Const. in *Lapid.Gr.* 196.14, al.'

*__λῐγῠροκώτῐλος__, ον, app. *having a clear, seductive sound*, λιγουροκω[τί]λυ[ς (⏑⏑⏑–⏑–) ἐνοπῆς Corinn. 2(*b*).5 P. (Boeot.).

**λῐγῠρός**, line 1, after 'λιγουρά' for '(q.v.)' read '[⏑⏑–] Corinn. 11(*a*) P.' **I 1**, line 7, for 'poets' read 'poetry' add '**3** of style, *clear*, *lucid*, D.H.*Dem.* 5; adv. -ρῶς Plu. 2.874b; alternative expl. (= γλυκερῶς) offered by Sch.D.T. p. 173 H.' **II**, for '*pliant*, *flexible*' read '*fine*, *slender*'

*__Λιγυστίς__, ἡ, *Ligurian*, in quots., of Circe, E.*Tr.* 437, A.R. 4.553.

*__λῐγῠφεγγέτις__, ιδος, fem. adj., *shining clearly*, σεληναίη *App.Anth.* 6.140.6.

*__λῐθᾰγωγέω__, *transport stones*, *SEG* 34.122 (Attica, iv BC).

**λῐθάζω II**, after 'Pass.' insert 'Hsch. s.v.ληβόλε'

**λῐθᾰκός**, line 2, for 'Stesich.*Oxy.* 1087.48' read 'Stesich. 37 P.'

**λῐθάριον**, add '**3** *gravestone*, *SEG* 28.1582 (*c.*vi AD).'

***λιθάρτης**, ου, ὁ, (αἴρω) *stone-lifter*: as adj., καρκίνος λ. *IG* $2^2$.1424*a*.272 (Athens, iv BC).

**λῐθάς**, line 2, after '(Od.) 23.193' insert 'perh. as used in mosaic construction, *SEG* 19.408'

***Λιθήσιος**, ὁ, epith. of Apollo, St.Byz.; hence *Λιθέhια*, τά, festival in Laconia, *IG* 5(1).213.54, 60 (Sparta, v BC).

***λῐθία**, v. λιθεία.

**λιθίζω**, delete the entry.

**λίθιος**, add 'sp. λίτθ- *SEG* 31.572 (Crannon, *c*.200 BC)'

**λῐθογνώμων**, add 'title of work by Xenocr. (*Lap.* 89)'

**λῐθόδμητος**, after '*stone-built*' insert '*PHib.* 172.90 (iii BC)'

**λῐθοκόλλητος II**, delete the section.

**λῐθόκολλος**, for '*CIG* 2852.47' read '*Didyma* 424.47' and add '*Lindos* II 2 c 86, 87'

***λῐθοκονία**, ἡ, app. *pulverized stone*, Hsch. s.v. στία.

**λῐθοκόπος**, add '*IHadr.* 103.6 (Rom.imp.)'

**λῐθολογέω**, for '*build with unworked stones*' read '*build a stone foundation of*' **II**, for this section read '**2** perh. *reduce to the foundations*, Aq.*Mi.* 3.12.'

***λῐθολόγητος**, ον, *built with piled-up stones*, *Inscr.Délos* 1416*B*i11 (ii BC).

***λῐθόξεστος**, ον, *made of polished stone*, *IG* 12(1).842.9 (Lindos).

**λῐθοξόος**, line 1, after 'ὁ' insert '-ξοιος *IEryth.* 535' **1**, add '*SEG* 30.1397 (Lydia, ?iii/iv AD)'

**λῐθοποιέω**, add '*have inscribed on stone*, τὰ τοσαῦτα ὑμεῖν ἐλιθοποιήσαμεν γράμματα *SEG* 29.1476 (*c*.AD 200)'

**λῐθοπρίστης**, add '*EA* 12.118 no. 70 (Caria)'

**λίθος III**, for '*Epigr.* 8.1' read '*fr.* 64.7 Pf., *AP* 9.67.1, *SEG* 30.1269' **V**, for 'Alc. 82' read 'Alc. 351 L.-P.'; add 'cf. Aristid. 2.55 J.'

***λῐθοσσόος**, ον, *stone-moving*, of the sound of Amphion's lyre, Nonn.*D.* 25.428.

**λῐθόστρωτος 1**, add 'λ., ἡ, *paved road*, *Kourion* 111.7, 9'

**λῐθουλκός II**, for pres. def. read 'a kind of hook for extracting bladder-stone'

**λῐθουργός 1**, add '*gem-engraver, seal-cutter*, *App.Anth.* 3.79 (Posidipp.)'

***λῐθουρικός**, ή, όν, *suffering from* λιθουρία, Cyran. 116, al.

**λῐθοφόρος 1**, for '*IG* 3.296' read 'of a priest at Athens, *IG* $2^2$.3658, 5077 (w. ἱερεύς); λιθοφόρος τοῦ ἱεροῦ λίθου Clinton *Sacred Officials* pp. 50-1, line 15 (i BC)'

***λίθωμα**, ατος, τό, prob. *stone-work*, *AE* 1948/9.136 (Epid., iv BC).

**λικμάς**, add '*PStrassb.* 680.5 (early vii AD)'

**λικμάω**, line 4, delete '*make away with*' and '*crush, destroy*'

***λίκμησις**, εως, ἡ, *winnowing*, *PPetaus* 53.12 (ii AD), *PMich.*XI 609.22, *SB* 9409 iii 7.78 (both iii AD).

***λίκμητρα**, τά, *payment for winnowing*, *SB* 7373.15 (AD 29).

***λικναφόρος**, ον, = λικνοφόρος, *AJA* 37.250 (Latium, ii AD); in Bacchic θίασος, *IGBulg.* $1^2$.401.2 (Apollonia in Thrace).

***λῑμάσσω**, v. ‡λιμώσσω.

**λῐμεναρχέω**, add '*SEG* 34.1093 (Ephesus, ii/iii AD)'

***λῐμέναρχος**, ὁ, *harbour-master* (or, in quot., perh. = ἀγορανόμος, cf. λιμήν III), *SEG* 23.271 (Thespiae, iii BC).

**λῐμένιον**, after 'λιμήν' insert '*IG* $4^2$.76.27 (ii BC, λιμιν- lapis)'

**Λῐμένιος**, add 'also of Hera, Ναύμαχός με ἀνέθεκε τᾶι Ηέραι τᾶι *Λιμενίᾱι* *SEG* 11.226 (Perachora, vi BC)'

**λῐμενίτης**, add '**3** *dweller by the harbour*, *MAMA* 3.424, al. (Corycus).'

**λῐμήν**, add 'prob. Myc. *ri-me-ne* (dat.), (as part of place-name)'

**λῑμηρός**, add 'perh. in place-name Ἐπίδαυρος Λιμηρά Th. 4.56.2, 7.26.2, *barren*, expld. by Apollod.ap.Str. 8.6.1 as = εὐλίμενος'

**λῐμηρός**, delete the entry.

***λιμιταναῖος**, ὁ, = °λιμιτάνεος, *SEG* 32.1554 (vi AD).

***λιμιτάνεος**, ὁ, Lat. *limitaneus*, m. pl. *frontier troops*, Just.*Nov.* 103.3.1

***λιμιτόν**, τό, fr. Lat. *limes*, *frontier*, Just.*Nov.* 13.23, al., *SEG* 32.1554 (vi AD), 8.296.1 (Palestine), 782 (Syene, vi/vii AD).

***λιμιτοτρόφος**, ον, Lat. *limitotrophus*, *furnishing subsistence to troops stationed on the frontier*, *Cod.Theod.* 5.13.38, *Cod.Just.* 11.60.

**λιμνᾱγενής**, for '*BMus.Inscr.* 1009' read '*IKyzikos* 507'

**λιμνάζω**, lines 1/2, for '*form stagnant pools*' read '*form a lagoon* or *pool*'

**λιμναῖος I 1**, add 'of fish, *fresh-water*, *IGC* p. 99 B20 (λιμνήων: Acraephia, iii/ii BC)' **II**, delete the section.

***Λιμναῖος**, α, ον, of Limnae, on the borders of Laconia and Messenia; as epith. of Dionysius, Call.*fr.* 305 Pf.; of Artemis, Paus. 2.7.6; *Λιμναῖον*, τό, temple of Artemis at Limnae.

**λιμνήτης II**, add '[Ἀρ]τέμιτι Λιμνάτιδι *SEG* 36.558 (Illyria, iii/ii BC)'

**λιμνίον**, after 'Arist.*Mir.* 840$^b$33' insert '*PAAH* 1955.172 (Dodona)'

**λῑμός**, line 6, before 'Th. 2.54' insert 'Hdt. 7.171.2'

**λιμπάνω**, add '*GVAK* 19'

***λίμψᾰνον**, τό, = λείψανον (in quot., 2), *SEG* 31.1419 (iii/iv AD).

**λῑμώσσω**, add 'also **λιμάσσω** *Orac.Tiburt.* 117, Suid.'

***λῐναϊκός**, ή, όν, *made of linen*, *Inscr.Perg.* 8(3) p. 110 (Miletus, ii BC).

**Λίνδος**, after 'adv.' insert '**Λίνδοι** (loc.) *at Lindos*, *Clara Rhodos* 9.212 (Lindos, v/iv BC)'

***Λινδοῦχος**, ἡ, epith. of Athena, epigr. in *Lindos* II 177.4 (ii BC).

***λινέλαιον**, τό, *oil of flax*, Moses Alch. 311.18.

**λίνεος**, line 5, delete 'A.*fr.* 206'; line 6, after '(v.l. λιναία)' insert 'contr. λινῆ, τείναντες λινᾶς ἑξαχῶς *Didyma* 43.24'

***λῐνεργός**, όν, *spinning* or *working flax*, S.*fr.* 269a.43 R. (unless λινεργής q.v. is read); cf. λινουργός.

**λῐνεύς**, add '*SEG* 23.326 (Delphi, iii BC)'

**λῐνεψός**, add '*BGU* 2471.5 (ii AD)'

***λῐνοκατᾰγωγεύς**, έως, ὁ, *linen-transporter*, *POxy.* 3111.3 (AD 257).

**λῐνοκρῑθή**, delete the entry.

**λίνον II**, add '**6** λ. Καρπάσιον *asbestos*, Paus. 1.26.7.' at end add 'Myc. *ri-no*, cf. *ri-ne-ja* (fem.) *flax-workers*'

***λῐνοξός**, ὁ, perh. *instrument for beating flax, scutcher*, *MAMA* 3.40 (Meryemlik), 457, al. (Corycus).

**λῐνόπεπλος**, add '*SEG* 28.1585 (epitaph of Isis mystes)'

***λῐνόπηξος**, ον, *of combed linen*, *SB* 9570.8 (vi AD); sp. -πιξ-, *PMich.*XIV 684.8 (vi AD).

**λῐνοπλῦτής**, read '**λῐνοπλύτης**'; add '*PVindob.Tandem* 19.15 (v/vi AD); also **λινοπλύστης** (s.v.l.) *PRyl.* 640.8 (iv AD)'

**λῐνοπῦρος**, delete the entry.

**Λίνος I**, add '*SEG* 33.303 (Epid., iv BC)'

***λῐνοσῐνής**, ές, *damaging linen*, λακίς, prob. in A.*Supp.* 120, 131.

***λῐνόστημα**, ατος, τό, *cloth woven of flax and wool*, Isid.*Etym.* 19.22.17.

**λινούδιον**, add '*SEG* 37.1001 (Lydia, ii/iii AD)'

**λῐνοῦφος**, add 'subst., *linen-weaver*, *BGU* 2471.4, etc. (ii AD)'

**λῐνοφακός**, delete the entry.

***λῐνῠφαντάριος**, ὁ, *linen-weaver*, *MAMA* 3.450 (Corycus, written λεν-).

***λῐνῠφαρία**, ἡ, (*female*) *linen-weaver*, *Vita Epiph.* 1 (*PG* 41.24).

**λῐνῠφάριος**, for '= λίνυφος' read '*linen-weaver* or *owner of linen-weaving business*'

**λῐπαίνω I 2**, add 'pass., of man, *grow fat*, τοῦ κατὰ φύσιν πολὺ πλέον ἐλιπάνθη Memn. 4.7 J.'

***λῐπᾰραία**, ἡ, *liparaea*, a precious stone, Plin.*HN* 37.172, presum. fr. Lipara.

+**λῐπᾰράμπυξ**, ῠκος, ὁ, ἡ, *having a shining* or *gleaming headband*, *Μναμοσύνα* Pi.*N.* 7.15; humorously, of an oily sauce, Ar.*Ach.* 671.

**λῐπᾰρόθρονος**, add 'Theoc. 2.165 (*PAntin.*, -χροε codd.)'

**λῐπᾰρός I 2**, line 6, before 'adv.' insert 'also of flavours, Arist.*de An.* 422$^b$12'

***λῐπᾰρόσκηπτρος**, ον, *having a shining sceptre*, rest. in Simon. 14 *fr.* 60(*b*).4 P.

**λῐπᾰρόχροος**, line 2, after 'Theoc. 2.165' insert '(codd., -θρονε *PAntin.*), Παφίη λ. *Anacreont.* 20.7 W.'

***λῐπᾰρών**, ῶνος, ὁ, Alexandrian name for χνῆστρον, *Daphne oleoides*, Aët. 4.22 (368.28 O.), 6.68 (218.24 O.).

**λῐπερνέω**, line 3, after 'λιφερνοῦντες' insert '(cj. φιλερν-)'

**λῐπερνής**, for '*forlorn, outcast*' read '*deprived, destitute*'; for 'context doubtful in *BCH* 11.161' read '*GVAK* 11' and add 'perh. in A.*Supp.* 362'

***λῐποδᾶμία**, ἁ, *failure to serve the community*, *SEG* 25.447.9 (Arcadia, iii BC).

**λῐπόναυς**, delete '(or .. *fleet*)'

**λῐποναύτης**, add '*IG* 12(2).646*c*50 (Nesus)'

**λῐπόπνοος I**, for this section read '*with failing breath, dying*, *AP* 12.132 (Mel.), *APl.* 4.110.5 (Philostr.), 133.5 (Antip.)'

**λῐποτακτέω**, add '**2** *abscond*, *PHerm.* 21.17, *PLond.* 1247.14 (iv AD).'

***λῐποτρῐχία**, ἡ, *loss of hair*, γενείων Cyran. 52 (pl.).

***λῐπόχρως**, acc. masc. -οα, *sleek*, ταῦρος Nonn.*D.* 19.67.

**λῐπυρία**, add 'Gal. 11.586.7'

***λίς**, λινός, ἡ, app. *linen thread*, οὐ λίνας ἱστῶσιν, ἀλλὰ πίστει ζωγροῦσιν Leont.Byz.*HP* 1.7.9; cf. λῖτα.

**λίσπος**, add '(oxyt. acc. to A.D. in Suid. s.v. λίσπη); cf. λίσφος'

***λίστριον**, τό, *tool for smoothing stone*, *IG* $2^2$.1678 (Delos, iv BC); in Ar.*fr.* 847 K.-A. = κοχλιάριον, acc. to Phryn.*Ecl.* 292.

**λῖτα**, add 'Myc. adj. *ri-ta* (neut. pl.), *of linen*'

**λῐτᾰνευτικός**, add 'Sch.Pi.*P.* 4.385'

**λῐτή I**, at end after 'E.*Or.* 290' insert 'ὑπὲρ λειτᾶς perh. = *ex voto*, *IG* 4.584 (i AD)' add '**2** *religious procession* or *other ceremony*, Just.*Nov.* 123.32.'

***λῐτήσιος**, ον, *entreating*, Nonn.*D.* 43.137.

***Λιτοάμφοδον** [?ῐ], τό, name of block of houses, ἀπὸ τοῦ οἰκειδίου *Λιτοαμφόδου* τοῦ καλουμένου *Hesperia* 6.390 (Athens, tab.defix.).

**λῐτός I 1**, line 11, after 'Call.*Lav.Pall.* 25' insert 'cf. id.*fr.* 110.78 Pf.' **III**, line 3, after 'Call.*Ap.* 10' insert 'comp., id.*fr.* 384.32 Pf.'

**λῐτός** (A) and **λῐτός** (B), delete the entries.

+**λῐτός**, ή, όν, *suppliant, supplicatory*, θυσίαι Pi.*O.* 6.78, ἐπαοιδαί id.*P.* 4.217. **II** *prayed for*, Ἀώς id.*fr.* 21 S.-M. **III** dub. sens., perh.

*invoked in prayer* or *venerable*, γαῖα Alex.Aet. 1, Orph.*A.* 92; λιτὴ χθών· ἀπὸ τοῦ προσκυνεῖσθαι καὶ λιτανεύεσθαι Hsch.'

**λῑτότης I**, add 'of style, D.H.*Vett.Cens.* 5.2' **II**, delete '(cf. μείωσις)'

***λῑτούργιον**, v. λειτούργιον.

**λῐ́τρα I**, after 'Posidipp. 8' insert 'in early use, metal bar used as currency, *Archeologia Classica* 38-40.13 (Sicily, vi BC)' **II**, after 'J.*AJ* 14.7.1' insert 'inscribed on weights, *IEphes.* 3493, 4364, etc.' and after '*AP* 10.97 (Pall.)' add '*Cod.Just.* 10.72.5' **III**, add 'written on *amphora*, λί(τραι) *SEG* 31.813 (i BC/i AD)'

**λιτρισμός**, after '*delivery by weight*' insert '*Edict.Diocl.* 19.6'

**λίτρον I**, line 2, after 'Ar.*fr.* 320.1' insert '*IG* 1³.422.150 (Athens, v BC)'

***λῐφερνέω**, v. ‡λιπερνέω, also φιλερνέω.

***λιχνικάριος**, ὁ, perh. for *λικνικάριος, *winnower*, or *λυχνικάριος, *lamp-maker*, *MPER* xv 141.3 (vi AD).

**λίχνος I 1**, delete 'metaph. .. Pl.*R.* 579b' **2**, for this section read '*greedy* (for knowledge), *inquisitive*, Pl.*R.* 579b, Crates Theb. 4; λ. ἐσσί [γὰρ] καὶ τό μεν πυθέσθαι Call.*fr.* 196.45 Pf., of lover's eyes, id.*fr.* 571 Pf.'

**λίψ** (C), delete the entry.

**λοβός II 1**, add 'used as binding material with dried mud in building, *IG* 2².463.68'

**λογᾰριάζω**, line 1, after 'Ar.*Pl.* 381' insert 'pass. λογαριασθῆναι, *have one's accounts audited*, expl. of εὐθύνας δοῦναι, Anon. *in Rh.* 204.20'

***λογᾰριαστής**, οῦ, ὁ, *calculator*, Alex.Aphr. *in SE* 12.36.

***λογᾰρίτης**, ου, ὁ, *cashier*, *MAMA* 3.280 (Corycus).

**λογάς** (A), add '**3** λογάδες, αἱ, *the eyes* (perh. as "chosen companions"), Sophr. 49, Call.*fr.* 85.15 Pf., Nic.*Th.* 292, *AP* 5.269 (Paul.Sil.); sg. expld. as *white of the eye*, Poll. 2.70.'

**λογάς** (B), delete the entry.

**λογγάζω**, add 'possible reading in *PMich.*VIII 486.18 (ii AD)'

***Λογγᾶτις**, ιδος, ἡ, epith. of Athena, Lyc. 520, 1032.

**λογεῖον**, add 'τὸ λογεῖον δεικτηρίου *SEG* 23.207 (Messene, i BC/i AD)'

**λογευτήριον**, add '*PHels.* 24.1 (ii BC)'

***λογέω**, v. λογάω II.

***λογή**, ἡ, *attention, heed*, λογήν μου μὴ ἔχουσαν *PMich.*III 217.6 (iii AD), *PAmst.* 95.18 (iii AD); cf. mod. Gk. τί λογῆς.

***Λογῖνα**, ά, female counterpart to Λόγος in title of play by Epicharmus, Epich.*fr.* 87-9.

***λογίσκος**, ὁ, *a little conversation* or *debate*, cj. in Antiph. 207.

**λογισμός I**, add '**3** pl., = Lat. *rationes, property, assets*, Just.*Nov.* 117.10.'

***λογιστήρ**, ὁ, = λογιστής, de Franciscis *Locr.Epiz.* no. 32.

**λογιστήριον I 1**, add 'used as place of detention, *PBeatty Panop.* 1.228, 346, 350 (AD 298)'

***λογιστορικόν**, τό, any one of collection of dialogues by Varro, Gell. 4.19.2, 20.11.4.

***λογιστός**, ή, όν, (λογίζομαι) *to be counted* or *calculated*, Call.*fr.* 196.47 Pf.

**λογοθεσία I**, *audit*, add '*Cod.Just.* 10.30.4.4'

***λογοθέσιον**, τό, *audit of accounts*, *POxy.* 3627.2, *CPR* 7.21.11 (both iv AD), Just.*Nov.* 128.18. **2** pl., *account-books*, Palchos in *Cat.Cod.Astr.* 1.94.17. **II** *documents containing* or *dealing with contracts*, Just.*Nov.* 136.5 pr.

**+λογοθέσιος**, ὁ, *accountant*, Palchos in *Cat.Cod.Astr.* 1.95.26.

***λογομάχος**, gloss on ὑπήρατος, Hsch.; cf. ἐπήρεια, etc.

**λογοποιέω II**, add '**2** *remonstrate*, *PMich.*V 229.18, 230.16, *POxy.* 2234.17 (all i AD).'

***λογοπρᾱγία**, ἡ, function of a λογοπράκτης, *ODouch* 57.

**+λογοπράκτωρ**, ορος, ὁ, app. kind of *accountant*, *PBaden* 26.40 (iii AD), perh. also *PHarris* 96.26 (i/ii AD), *POxy.* 3564 (iii AD).

**λόγος I 1 a**, at end, metaph., add 'εἰ δέ τις ἐνχειρήσει, ἕξι τὸν λόγον πρὸς ‹?τὸν Θεόν› *SEG* 30.1546 (iv/v AD); also of other things than money, οἰνικὸς λ. *Stud.Pal.* 20.85 ii 1, λ. κριθῆς *PCair.Zen.* 464.1 (iii BC)' add '**c** ἐκ λόγου, in accounts, *brought forward*, freq. in papyri, ἐγ λ. λήμματος τοῦ δεκάτου ἔτους *PLond.* 131 (i AD); ἐγ λ. τοῦ μηνὸς ἐλοιπογραφήθησαν there were entered as balance from the month's *account*, *BGU* 362 vi 9 (iii AD); τὸ ἐγ λ. τοῦ Φαμενὼθ the *balance* from Ph., *PCair.Zen.* 333.1 (iii BC); ὃ ἔχεις ἐγ λ. the *balance* you have in hand, ib. 593.12 (iii BC): see also °ἔκλογος (C).' **2**, line 4, after 'Hdt. 8.100' insert 'ἴ τις δὲ τολμῇ ἀνῦξεν, δώσι Κυρίῳ λόγον *BCH* suppl. 8 no. 58 (Beroea, iii/iv AD)'; line 13, after 'al.' insert 'εἰς μισθοῦ λ. Plu. 2.240d'; line 14, after 'Arist.*HA* 517ᵇ27' insert 'Plb. 9.20.3' **4**, line 15, after 'v. infr. VI 2 e)' insert 'οὐδ' ἐν λόγῳ ἄνδρα τιθείην Tyrt. 12.1' **II 2**, add 'λόγον ἔχειν πρός τι *be in proportion to*, Plu. 2.147a' **VI 1 a**, at end after 'also in sg.' insert 'τὰ μὲν ἂν Μοίσαι .. ἐμβαίεν λόγ[ῳ] Ibyc. 1(*a*).24 P.' **3 a**, add 'παρεῖναι ἐν λ., i.e. where there is *speaking*, οἱ π. ἐν λ. who hear my words, E.*Rh.* 149 (v.l.), Ar.*Ach.* 513; in direct address to the audience, ὦνδρες οἱ παρόντες ἐν λ. id.*Av.* 30; ἀπὸ λόγου app. *orally*, *PMich.*VIII 492.5, 19 (ii AD)' **e**, add 'also *rhetoric*, as discipline, *GVI* 1081.3' **VII 2**, line 4, after 'Luc.*Alex.* 9, etc.' insert 'ἵνα τὸ τοῦ λόγου πάθω Men.*Dysc.* 633 S.' add '**6** *declaration of legal immunity*, τοὺς καλουμένους λόγους Just.*Nov.* 17.6; cf. οἷς ἂν ἐθέλοιεν λόγον ἀσυλίας παρέχοντας id.*Edict.* 2 pr. **7** ὁ διὰ λόγων, expression used to add a person's official name, *according to official documents called* .., *BGU* 2263.7 (ii AD).'

***λογχοβόλος**, ὁ, *spearman*, Ps.-Callisth. 53.22.

**λοιβή I**, add 'λυβά *SEG* 25.556 (Haliartus, iii BC, Boeot. decr.)'

***λοιγίζω**, λοιγισθῆναι· ἀπολέσθαι Theognost.*Can.* 22.

***λοιγωπός**, όν, (*one*) *whose eyes spread destruction*, of Athena, *PKöln* 245.8 (iii AD).

**λοιδορέω II**, line 3, delete 'τινος Ach.Tat. 1.6'; line 4, after 'πρός τινα' insert 'Macho 215 G.'

**λοιμώδης**, add 'adv. -δῶς, ὁπότε λ. ἐνόσησεν ἐν Συρίᾳ Gal. 12.285.6'

**+λοιπογρᾰφέω**, *enter as the amount of arrears*, *PGoodsp.Cair.* 7.7, *PHamb.* 3*A*3, *B*2 (i AD); in granting deferment of payment, δύο συνγραφὰς ἐλ. χωρὶς ἀργυρίου κομιδῆς *IG* 12(5).860.23 (Tenos, i BC). **b** of the debtor who acknowledges the debt, *PGiss.* 46.5 (ii AD). **2** *carry over as balance*, *BGU* 362 vi 9, xiv 17, al. (iii AD): metaph., χρόνους -ουμένους the *balance*, Nech.ap.Vett.Val. 279.12. **II** w. acc. pers., *enter as in arrears* or *in debt*, *PFay.* 109.7 (i BC/i AD); so prob. in pass., μηδὲν αὐτὸν -εῖσθαι *PLond.* 940 (iii AD). **b** *allow* person *to defer payment*, ἀφ' ὧν ἐλ. αὐτόν *BGU* 362iii21, *PPetr.* 3 p. 154 (iii BC).

**+λοιπογρᾰφή**, ἡ, *balance carried over*, *Stud.Pal.* 20.85ᵛ*B*5 (iv AD); λοιπογρα[φὰς] ἑαυτοῖς προσῆψαν (of magistrates leaving office) i.e. acknowledged *balance owing* from them, *IEphes.* 15.5 (ii AD).

**+λοιπός**, ή, όν, (-ός, όν *IG* 1³.365.32) *that which remains* (after other parts have been accounted for), *the rest of*, οἱ λοιποὶ Λυδοί Hdt. 1.13.1, ἡ λοιπὴ πᾶσα Ἀσίη id. 1.192.1; Th. 3.95.2, τὴν λοιπὴν (sc. ὁδὸν) πορευσόμεθα X.*An.* 3.4.46, J.*BJ* 1.4.6, δύο τὰ λοιπὰ (sc. τάγματα) id.*AJ* 17.10.9; w. partit. gen., ἡ λοιπὴ τῆς Λιβύης Hdt. 4.191.2, τὰς λοιπὰς τῶν νεῶν Th. 7.72.3. **b** οἱ λοιποί, *the rest, the others*, Hdt. 1.207.7, Th. 3.18.2, J.*AJ* 12.7.1. **c** τὰ λοιπά, *the rest*, τὰ λ. μου κλύουσα A.*Pr.* 476, τὰ δ' ἄλλα, οἶδας γὰρ ὁποῖα τὰ λ. Aristaenet. 1.16. **2** *that remains* (to make up the full total), τὸ λ. γένος Hp.*Aër.* 23, Apollod. 3.6.8, τὸν δὲ τρίτον (sc. πύργον) .. ὁ δὲ λοιπός .. J.*BJ* 4.9.11, τὰ γένη τὰ τρία τὰ λοιπά Plot. 6.2.19, Heph.Astr. 1.2.11. **b** *the other parts of, the rest of* (apart from the one specified), τοῦ δὲ λοιποῦ ἔργου *IG* 1³.474.40, μέλι .. οὐ πολλῷ τοῦ λοιποῦ χεῖρον J.*BJ* 4.8.3; subst. τὰ λοιπά, Ἰουδαίους .. πρὸς τὰ λ. καρτερῶς ἀντέχοντας ἐκάκωσαν οἱ πύργοι ib. 5.7.2; ἐν τοῖς λοιποῖς *among other things*, *SEG* 26.426.18 (*c.*AD 200). **c** λοιπόν, *for the rest*, i.e. to complete the account, argument, etc., Dsc. 2.83, λ., ἀδελφοί, χαίρετε 2*Ep.Cor.* 13.11, Arr.*Epict.* 1.24.1, *BGU* 969.19 (ii AD). **3** *the remaining* (unspecified), τῇ .. λοιπῇ τῇ κατὰ τὴν δίαιταν ἐπιμελείᾳ Plb. 1.59.12, παρασκευῇ id. 4.63.2; neut. pl. subst., εἰ δὲ ταῦτα, καὶ βῆχα καὶ πταρμὸν .. καὶ τὰ λοιπά Plu. 2.1084c, Heph.Astr. 1.23.3. **4** *left over*, ὅλωλα κοὐδὲν λοιπὸν .. κακῶν E.*Hec.* 784, τί λοιπὸν ἔσται τοῖς ἀντιλέγουσιν ..; Isoc. 5.57, cf. Pl.*R.* 466b. **b** w. inf., λοιπὸν οὖν ἐστιν οὐδὲν ἄλλο πλὴν .. ἐπανελθεῖν nothing *remains* but to .., Isoc. 12.88, οὐκοῦν λοιπὸν ἂν εἴη .. ἀποδεικνύναι X.*Smp.* 4.1. **c** λοιπόν, *in respect of the time remaining, by that time, by then*, ὅτε λ. ἐνόσει ἐπὶ θανάτῳ Ael.*VH* 8.14, ἦσαν δὲ λ. μέσαι νύκτες Ach.Tat. 2.26.1, ἑσπέρα δὲ ἦν λ. Jul.*Or.* 1.24c. **d** expr. the consequence, *as a result*, Plb. 1.15.11, 1.30.8, al. **5** *that is yet to come, future*, λ. βίοτος Pi.*O.* 1.97, γένος ib. 2.15, εὐχαί ib. 4.15, μηκέτι τῆς λοιπῆς φιλίας κοινωνεῖν D. 21.118; λοιποί *men of the future*, Pi.*I.* 4.39. **b** of time, ὁ λ. χρόνος Pi.*N.* 7.67; w. partit. gen., πρὸς τὸν λοιπὸν τοῦ χρόνου D. 15.16; in advl. phrs., τὸν λ. χρόνον S.*Ph.* 84; τοῦ λ. χρόνου id.*El.* 817; ἐν τῷ λοιπῷ χρόνῳ *IG* 1³.101.36; εἰς τὸν λ. χρόνον Pl.*Ep.* 358b; ἐκ τοῦ λ. χρόνου D. 59.46; neut. subst. τὸ λοιπὸν τῆς ἡμέρας X.*An.* 3.4.16. **c** τὸ λοιπόν, *henceforward, for the future*, Pi.*P.* 5.118, *N.* 7.45, A.*Eu.* 1031, S.*OT* 795, *IG* 1³.14.14, al.; τὸ λ. εἰς ἅπαντα χρόνον A.*Eu.* 763, τὸ λ. ἤδη Plb. 5.4.5, καθεύδετε τὸ λ. *Ev.Matt.* 26.45; also τὰ λοιπά A.*Th.* 66, E.*Hel.* 698, Th. 8.21, X.*HG* 1.1.27; τοῦ λοιποῦ Hdt. 1.189, Ar.*Pax* 1084, D. 4.15. **d** w. preps., in advl. phrs., ἐκ τοῦ λοιποῦ X.*Smp.* 4.56; ἐκ τῶν λοιπῶν Pl.*Lg.* 709e; ἐς τὸ λοιπόν A.*Pers.* 526, *Eu.* 708, Th. 3.44.3; εἰς τὰ λοιπά J.*BJ* 3.6.1; πρὸς τὸ λοιπόν J.*AJ* 8.12.3.

***λοκόπινος**, ὁ (?for *λευκο-), λ. ἐστιν ὁ βάπτων εἰς βάθος καὶ μὴ ἀποπτύων Anon.Alch. 10.19.

***λομας**, app. adj. in agreement with ἀρούρας, *BGU* 2245.11 (i AD).

**+λοξόβᾱμος**, ον, *walking slantwise*, Gr.Naz.*Carm.* 1.2.1.714, Hsch.

**λοξοκέλευθος**, after 'Nonn.*D.* 5.233' insert '(cj.)'

**λοξότης**, add '**3** *collateral relationship*, Theophil.Antec. 3.6 pr.'

**λοξόφθαλμος**, after '*oblique-eyed*' insert 'Ptol.*Tetr.* 144'

***λοξώδης**, ες, *oblique*, Gal. 2.297.3.

***λοπάδη**, ἡ, = λοπάς, *dish* in list of kitchen equipment, Lang *Ath.Agora* XXI B14 (iv/iii BC).

**λοπάδιον**, add 'in list of kitchen equipment, Lang *Ath.Agora* XXI B12'

**λοπάς I** and **II**, for these sections read 'kind of cooking-pot, *casserole* or sim., Ar.*Eq.* 1034, *V.* 511, Eub. 108 K.-A., Pl.Com. 173.12, Men.*Sam.* 365 S., Dsc. 2.142. **b** *food served in a casserole, AP* 12.44, Gal. 6.653.13. **2** (see quot.) λοπάς· παρὰ Συρακοσίοις τὸ τήγανον· παρὰ δὲ Θεοπόμπῳ (Com. 2 K.-A.) ἡ σορός, καὶ παρὰ τοῖς κωμικοῖς Suid.'

**λοπάω I**, add 'of the peeling of the skin, A.*fr.* 73b.6 R.; cf. λοπῶντα· λεπιζόμενον ἢ λοπιζόμενον Hsch.'

**λοπίδιον**, add '*Inscr.Délos* 1441*A*ii62 (ii BC)'

**λοπίζω**, after 'Hsch.' insert 'hence pf. part. pass. *having the gilding flaked off,* θυμιατήριον .. περικεχρυσωμένον, τινὰ δὲ λελοπισμένον *Inscr.Délos* 1429*A*ii12, 13 (ii BC)'

***λόπιμον**, τό, *sweet chestnut,* Nic.*fr.* 76 G.-S., Ath. 2.53b, Dsc. 1.106, Hsch.

**+λόπιμος**, ὁ, = λόπιμον, Gal. 6.621.12, 12.420.7.

**+λοπίς**, ίδος, *scale* of fish or reptile, Ar.*V.* 790, Nic.*Al.* 467, *Th.* 154. **2** (*metal*) *plate,* Aen.Tact. 20.3.3. **3** *fragment* of ἀκρόβασις, *Inscr.Délos* 1432*Ab*ii14. **4** *dish, Schwyzer* 89.20 (Argos, iii BC).

**λορδόω**, line 2, after 'Hp.*Art.* 46' insert 'Men.*Dysc.* 533 S.'

**λόρδων**, for '*the demon of impure* λόρδωσις' read 'humorously invented erotic deity'

***λουδάριοι**, οἱ, perh. the staff of a *ludus* other than the gladiators, φαμιλία μονομάχων καὶ λουδαρίων *IGRom.* 4.1453 (Smyrna), see Robert *Les Gladiateurs* pp. 209, 285 n. 2.

***λοῦδος**, ὁ, Lat. *ludus, gladiatorial school, IGRom.* 4.1072, *PLips.* 57.11, *SEG* 30.1308 (Trajan), *Inscr.Perg.* 8(3).99.

***λουέτιον**, τό, perh. = λουτήριον, λοέτιον χαλκõν τετρε̄μένο[ν] *IG* 4.1588.17 (Aegina), unless λοετρόν (λουτρόν) is to be read; cf. χαλκίον ἐγλοτέριον *IG* 4.39.18.

***λουκάνικον**, τό, Lat. *lucanicum, sausage, PLond.* 1259.30, *PRyl.* 627.208, al. (iv AD), Charis. 94.12 K.

***λούπα**, ἡ· λέγεται δὲ οὕτως παρὰ Ἰταλιώταις ἡ λύκαινα, Lat. *lupa,* Suet.*Blasph.* 32 T.

**λοῦσις**, after '*Gloss.*' insert 'see also λῶτις'; line 2, for '*cleaning*' to end, read '*free bathing* (granted as an amenity to a city), *BCH* 76.655.17 (Delphi, iv AD), *IGRom.* 3.584 (Lycia); for meaning see *BE* 1954.146'

***λουσώριον**, τό, *place for games,* inscr. in *RAL* 1993 p.267.12 (Iasos, iii AD). **2** *pleasure-ship,* cf. Lat. *lusoria navis, IGRom.* 3.481 (Termessus, iii AD).

**λουτήρ**, delete '*Supp.Epigr.* .. i AD)' and '*IGRom.* 4.454 .. i AD)'; add 'as container for oil, *IGRom.* 4.454.10, *SEG* 4.263.10 (both i AD), *OGI* 479.10 (Dorylaeum)'

***λούτρα**, ἡ, *sarcophagus, coffin, MAMA* 3.210, al. (Corycus); cf. μάκρα, πυρία.

**+λουτρίς**, ίδος, ἡ, *temple servant employed for washing,* Hsch., Phot. **II** ᾤα λ., app. *loin-cloth* or sim. worn during bathing, Theopomp.Com. 38 K.-A.

**λουτρόν I 2**, add '*BCH* suppl. 8 no. 5' **II**, line 2, delete 'E.*Ph.* 1667' add 'form λεϝοτρ- in Myc. adj. *re-wo-te-re-jo*'

**λουτροφορέω**, add '*hold office of* λουτροφόρος, λουτροφορήσαντα δίς *IIasos* 115.8'

**λουτροφόρος 1**, add '**b** temple assistant who carried water for ritual purposes, *Didyma* 330.4, *IIasos* 628.3.'

**λουτροχόος**, add 'Myc. *re-wo-to-ro-ko-wo* (= λεϝοτροχόϝος)'

**λουτρών**, for 'baptismal font' read 'baptistery'

***λουτρωνίδιον**, τό, (*small*) *bathing establishment, PHels.* 12 (163 BC).

**λουτρωνικός**, add '*Cod.Just.* 10.30.4 pr.'

**λούω I**, add '**c** *provide free baths, IGRom.* 4.555, Demitsas Μακεδ. 51, τὸ βαλανεῖον λούειν μελέτω τοῖς ἐπιμελη[ταῖς *SEG* 30.1382 C (AD 301); v. °λοῦσις.'

**λόφα**, add '(λοφαδίσκος La.)'

***λοφαδίσκος**, v. ‡λόφα.

**λοφίδιον**, after 'λόφος II' insert 'Men.*Dysc.* 100, *Asp.* 59 S.'

**λοφορρῶγα**, add 'cf. Hippon. 104.39 W.'

**λόφος**, line 1, for 'of a horse, *withers*' read 'in a horse, including the mane'; after 'Il. 23.508' insert 'cf. Ael.*NA* 16.20'

**λόφουρος**, add 'λ.· ἐπίσημος Hsch.'

***Λοφριαῖος**, = Λαφρ., *IG* $9^2$(1).100, 105, $9^2$(3).634.12, (Aetolia, ii BC); cf. ἐν Λοφρίῳ *SIG* 366.4.

**λοχᾱγέτας**, after 'A.*Th.* 42' insert '*fr.* 451k.4 R. (pl.)'

**λοχᾱγός**, after 'D.H. 2.7' insert '**3** an ephebic office at Athens, *IG* $2^2$.2976 (iv BC), al. **4** leader of an ἄγειμα (ἄγημα), *SEG* 23.271 (Thespiae, iii BC).'

**λοχαῖος I**, line 1, for '= λόχιος' read '*set in ambush*' **II**, for this section read '*teeming,* σχῖνος Arat. 1057; σῖτος Phot. (expld. as βαθύς); so prob. in Thphr.*CP* 3.21.5, 23.5; as epith. of Δαμία, *IG* 12(3).361'

**λοχεῖος 1**, line 3, delete 'θυέτωσαν .. 204*b*9'; line 5, delete 'cf. λοχαῖος'

***λοχευτικός**, ή, όν, *connected with childbirth,* ἡ λ., *midwife,* in quot. fig., λ. τῶν γενεσιουργῶν λόγων Procl.*in R.* 1.18.28.

**λοχεύτρια II**, add 'Λοχεύτριαι, in the cult of Hera at Argos, Hagias-Derkylos 4 J.'

**λοχεύω**, add '**IV** λοχεύοντες· ἐνεδρεύοντες Hsch.'

**+λοχή**, ἡ, *thicket,* = λόχμη, *IMylasa* 254.7.

***λοχιάς**, άδος, ἡ, *midwife,* dub. in *POxy.* 3642.16 (ii AD); epith. of Hecate, *PMag.* 4.2285.

**λοχίδιον**, for 'dub. sense' read 'perh. *couch used in childbirth*'

**λοχίζω**, add '**IV** λοχισθέν· γεννηθὲν ἢ σφαγέν (σφαλέν La., as "caught in ambush").'

***λόχιον**, τό, perh. *birth-house* (as shrine of Isis), *PColl.Youtie* 51 (ii/iii AD).

**λόχιος II**, add 'of Isis, *SEG* 34.622, al. (Maced.)' **III 1**, add 'offered in sacrifice, Antim. 182 Wy.; αἱ τὰ λόχια ἐκπορευόμεναι καὶ ζωννύμεναι *Milet* 1(7) 204*b*9219'

***λόχις**· λῆξις Theognost.*Can.* 58 A. (prob. Aeol. for *λαχίς).

**λοχισμός**, add '**II** in pl., *formations into* λόχοι, cj. in A.*Ag.* 404 (lyr.; λογχίμους codd.); cf. λοχίζω II.'

***λόχον**, v. °λαγχάνω.

**Λυαῖος**, line 2, after '(cf. Lat. *Lyaeus*)' insert '*AP* 6.154 (Leon. or Gaet.)'

**λυγγούριον**, for 'a kind of *amber*' read 'perh. *yellow* or *brown tourmaline*'

***λύγγουρος**, ὁ, = λυγγούριον, Cyran. 28.3.

**λυγγώδης**, add 'Gal. in *CMG* 5.9.(1).329.10, 12 al.'

**λύγδινος 1**, line 2, after '*marble*' insert 'στάλα *SEG* 9.3.17 (Cyrene, iv BC)'

**λύγκειος**, for '(Λυγκεύς) *of Lynceus*' read '(λύγξ) *of a lynx*'; add 'δέρμα λύνγιον *Edict.Diocl.* 8.35'

***λυγκίδιον**, τό, dim. of λύγξ (A), Aesop. 37 H. (cj., λυκ- codd.).

**λύγξ** (A), after 'gen. λυγκός' insert 'also λυγγός Ael.*NA* 7.47, al; acc. λύγγα, E.*fr.* 863'; delete '(λύγγα .. λύγγιος)' add '**III** perh. species of ape, Gal. 2.430.9, 535.11.'

***Λῡδηίς**, ίδος, fem. adj., *Lydian,* Hermesian. 7.41.

***Λῡδιεργής**, ές, *of Lydian workmanship,* Call.*fr.* 196.29 Pf.

**λύζω I**, add 'Archig.ap.Gal. 11.836.15, 13.176.8'

***λῡήεις**, εσσα, εν, *discordant,* τὸ δὲ λυῆς λυῆντος ἀπὸ τοῦ λυήεις Hdn.Gr. 1.59.

***λύημβρος**, ὁ or ἡ, kind of fish, = βεμβράς (v. μεμβράς), Cyran. 46.15.

***λῡῆς**, v. °λυήεις.

***λυθίραμβος** (v.l. **λυθίραμμος**), v. διθύραμβος at end.

**λύθρον**, lines 3/4, for 'Ph.ap.' read 'Ph.Tars.ap.'; add '*Trag.adesp.* 235 K.-S.'

***λυκαιχμίας**, ὁ, unexpld. wd., perh. *wolf-battle,* i.e. wolf-like or guerrilla fighting, οἷος ἐοίκησα λυκαιχμίαις Alc. 130.25 L.-P, commentary on Alc. in *POxy.* 3711 ii 32.

**Λύκειον I**, add 'also temple of Apollo at Argos, *SEG* 30.355. **2** app. an offering to Apollo in the form of a monument or sim., *IG* 12(3).389, 12 suppl. p. 86.'

***Λῠκιάδες** (cj. **Λυκηιάδες**)· κόραι τὸν ἀριθμὸν λ', αἱ τὸ ὕδωρ κομίζουσαι εἰς τὸ Λύκειον Ἀθηναίων Hsch.

**λῠκῐδεύς**, add 'Plu. 2.462e'

**λύκιον I 2**, line 2, before 'Dsc.' insert '*Peripl.M.Rubr.* 49' **II**, add 'also λύκιος, ὁ, *SEG* 32.1618 (iii/ii BC)'

**Λύκιος II**, add 'Pi.*P.* 1.39'

***λῠκοπρόσωπος**, ον, *wolf-faced,* Teuc.Bab. p. 47.4 B.

**λύκος I**, add '**b** λ. κεράστης *lynx, Edict.Diocl.* 8.35.'

**+λῠκοσπάς**, άδος, ὁ, ἡ, app. breed of horse found in southern Italy or round the Adriatic coast, Call.*fr.* 488 Pf., Ael.*NA* 16.24; in conjectural explanations of its etym., Plu. 2.641f, Choerob.*in Theod.* 1.287, Hsch.; in unexpld. context, Nic.*Th.* 742.

**+λῠκόσπαστος**, ον, *torn by wolves,* Hsch. s.v. λελυκωμένα.

***Λυκούλλιος**, α, ον, name of kind of marble, *Edict.Diocl.* 33.4.

***Λῠκωρεῖος**, ὁ, = sq., A.R. 4.1490.

***Λῠκωρεύς**, έως (έος), ὁ, cult-title of Apollo at Delphi, Call.*Ap.* 19, Euph. 80.3.

**λῦμα** (A) **III**, after 'A.*fr.* 692' insert 'Orph.*H.* 14.14'

***λῡμᾰγωνεία**, ἡ, app. *offence against the rules of a contest, BGU* 1823.24 (i BC).

***λῡμᾰγωνέω**, app. *offend against the rules of a contest, SEG* 27.261.69 (Beroea, ii BC).

**λῡμαίνομαι** (B), line 3, after 'A.*Ch.* 290' insert 'fut. λυμανθήσομαι A.*fr.* 47a.12 R.'

**λῡμάντωρ**, add '*SEG* 9.1.70 (Cyrene, iv BC)'

***λῡμᾰτίζω**, v. °λημματίζω.

**λυμνός**, add '*SEG* 29.308 (v AD)'

***λῡπηροτόκος**, ον, perh. = λυποτόκος, *ZPE* 48.279 (Cilicia).

**λύρα**, for 'a stringed instrument .. shell of a tortoise' read 'in earlier period applied equally to a bowl lyre (with tortoise-shell soundbox) and to a box lyre, but later spec. to the former; cf. κιθάρα, φόρμιγξ'

**λῠρᾰοιδός**, delete 'Plu.*Sull.* 33'
**λῠριστής**, add '*IG* 14.2030 (Rome), *SEG* 17.438 (Malta, iii AD)'
***λῠροκτῠ́πος**, ον, *striking the lyre*, *GVI* 1522a, Bernand *IMEG* 167.2, 170.2.
**+λῠρόκτῠπος**, ον, *sounding like a lyre*, of a bowstring, Lyc. 918.
**Λῡσάνδρια**, add '*AA* 1965.440 (Samos, written -εια)'
***λῠ́σειος**, v. λύσιος.
**λῡσίζωνος II**, add '*IG* 12(5) ii p. 332, no. 582'
**λῡσιμέριμνος**, add 'of eternity, αἰῶνα .. τὸν λ. *SEG* 30.1256'
***λῡσίνοσος**, ον, *curing disease*, φάρμακα *REG* 69.127.
**λῡσιπόλεμος**, after 'ὁ' insert '*ender of wars*, of a person, *SEG* 26.1835.3 (Cyrene, iv BC)'
**λῡσίπονος**, add 'ὕπνος *AP* 12.127 (Mel.), *SEG* 33.563 (iii AD), of baths, Robert *Hell.* 4.76, al.'
**λῡσιῳδός**, line 2, after 'Plu.*Sull.*' insert '33 (codd. λυρῳδ-)'
**λύσσα II 1**, add '*cases of frenzy* in human beings, Hp.*VM* 19'
**λῠτήρ**, add '**III** *destroyer*, *Byzantion* 5.10 (Stobi, iv AD).'
**λῠτήριος I**, line 6, delete 'τὸ .. 758' **II**, after '= λύτρον' insert 'Stesich. 222b.226 (p. 214 D.)'; line 3, after 'Pi.*P.* 5.106' insert 'πημονῆς, of drunkenness, S.*fr.* 758 (where τὸ μεθύειν are words of Ath.)'
**λύτρον I 1 a**, add 'also sg. *SEG* 23.460'
**λυχναπτέομαι**, delete the entry.
***λυχναπτέω**, *light lamps* (in quot. pass.), *Sokolowski* 1.28.13.
***λυχνάπτης**, ου, ὁ, *lamplighter* (in temple), written λυχνάτ- *MAMA* 3.437; ?erron. pl., λυχνάπτοι *POxy.* 1453.4, 8 (i BC); cf. Hsch. s.v. δᾳδοῦχος.
**λυχνάπτρια**, add '*SEG* 34.655 (Maced.)'
**+λυχναψία**, ἡ, *lamplighting*, app. the same as λυχνοκαΐα, *TAM* 4(1).16 (AD 122/3), *PAmh.* 2.70.11 (ii AD), *IGRom.* 4.1176 (Aegae), Ath. 15.701b.
**λυχνεύς**, delete 'cf. Ath. 15.699d'
***λυχνιάζω**, *burn* a lamp, ἐλαίῳ λ. (sc. λύχνον) *PWarren* 21.1 (iii AD).
***λυχνικόν**, τό, perh. *lampholder*, *MAMA* 6.361.
**λύχνιον**, add '**3** kind of eyesalve, Asclep.Jun.ap.Gal. 12.744.6.'
**λυχνίς I**, add '**3** app. for λυχνῖτις *candle wick*, *Edict.Diocl.* 18.5.'
**λυχνί̄της II**, for this section read 'λ. λίθος, kind of Parian marble, prob. *"of a luminous quality* or *translucent"* but supposed to be so called because quarried by lamplight, Varro ap.Plin.*HN* 36.14'
**λυχνῖτις**, add '**II** *made from* λυχνίτης II, λ. ζώνη *Suppl.Hell.* 978.6.'
***λυχνοδότης**, ου, ὁ, *lantern-giver*, priest in Egyptian temple, *PHib.* 213.12 (iii BC).
**λυχνοκαΐα**, add 'written λυχνοκαιία, *SEG* 9.13.16 (Cyrene, iv BC)'
**+λυχνοκαυτία**, ἡ, *lamplighting*, app. the same as λυχνοκαΐα and °λυχναψία, Cephisod. 11 (Ath. 15.701b).
**λύχνον**, add '*CEG* 463 (vi BC)'
***λύχνος**, ους, τό, = λύχνος, ὁ, Lxx *Da.* 5.1.
**λύχνος**, ὁ, **I 1**, add 'pl., used as title of book, *sunt etiam qui λύχνους inscripserint*, Gell.*Praef.* 7'
***λυχνουρέοντες**, οἱ, unknown objects (made of bronze, ?parts of a lamp), *Inscr.Délos* 1417*B*i37 (ii BC), al.
**λυχνοῦχος**, for '*lampstand*' read '(portable) *lampholder*'
**λύω**, line 8, for 'opt. plpf.' read 'opt. pf.' **I 2 c**, at end delete '*buy from a pimp*'; after 'Ar.*V.* 1353' insert '(under influence of Rabbinical phr.) ὃ ἐὰν λύσῃς ἐπὶ τῆς γῆς, ἔσται λελυμένον ἐν τοῖς οὐρανοῖς *Ev.Matt.* 16.19, 18.18' **II 1**, line 3, after 'Od. 2.69, etc.' insert 'λ. τάξιν, *break* formation, Polyaen. 7.28.2' **IV**, add 'med., *pay in quittance from a vow*, Πύθερμός με ὁ Νέλωνος ἐλύσατο τῆς Ἑσιος ἄγαλμα *Schwyzer* 749 (*c.*500 BC)'
**λῶ**, line 7, subj., add 'λείει *SEG* 36.855 (Sicily, vi/v BC)'; med., line 3, after 'Hsch.' insert 'pf. λέληνται *POxy.* 2256 *fr.* 8.7'
***λώβηξ**, ηκος, ὁ, bird identified with γύψ, Cyran. 28 (1.11.1,7 K.).
**+λώβησις**, εως, ἡ, *maiming*, *impairment*, Ptol.*Tetr.* 151, Sch.E.*Hec.* 1098.
***λωγεῖ**· μαίνεται Theognost.*Can.* 58 A.
**λώγη**, read **λωγή**.
***λωγήρυχος**· ὁ ἀναλαμβάνων τὰ πίπτοντα τοῦ σίτου ἐν τῷ ἀμητῷ Theognost.*Can.* 58 A.
***λωδικάριος**, ὁ, *maker of coverlets* or *blankets*, Teuc.Bab. p. 45 B.
**λωΐων I**, add 'ἐπὶ λωιτέρῳ *SEG* 34.1628 (Egypt, ii/iii AD)'
***λώλια**· σῦκα κεκομμένα Theognost.*Can.* 58 A.
***λώλωμα**· παιδικὸν βρῶμα Theognost.*Can.* 58 A.
**λῶμα**, add 'Sch.Call.*Dian.* 12; Myc. *wo-ro-ma-ta* (pl., = Ϝλώματα) (?)*wrappings*'
**Λῷος**, add 'in Asia Minor, *Hemerolog.Flor.* p. 75 (14 K., Ephesus), p. 77 (18 K., Tyre), *SEG* 31.1389 (Syria); in Egypt, *SEG* 34.1598 (AD 323)'
***λωπάς**, άδος, ἡ, kind of bottle, Anon.Alch. 33.1.
**λωποδῠσία**, for '*highway-robbery*' read '*clothes-stealing*' and add '*PMilan.* 30.1 (ii BC)'
***λωποδῠτία**, ἡ, = λωποδυσία, Poll. 7.42.
**λῶπος** (s.v. λώπη) before 'Herod. 8.36' insert '*SEG* 11.1112 (λõπος Arcad. decr., vi/v BC)'
***λωραμέντα**, τά, Lat. *loramenta*, *harness*, *Edict.Diocl.* 8.8, 10.1.
***λωρῖκα**, ἡ, Lat. *lorica*, *breastplate*, *POxy.* 812 (i BC), *PBeatty Panop.* 1.343 (AD 298).
**λωρίκιον**, add 'Just.*Nov.* 85.4'
**λῶρος I**, add 'neut. pl. λῶρα, Hsch. s.vv. ἡνίαι, ἡνία σιγαλόεντα'
***λωροτόμος**, ὁ, *strap-cutter*, *MPER* xv 111.30 (vi/vii AD).
**λωτέω**, for '*play the flute*' read '*play the aulos*' and add 'Theognost.*Can.* 58 A.'
***λωτίζω**, ?*wash* (cf. °λῶτις), εἴ τις .. τὰ πρόβατα ποτάγοι πρὸ τᾶ[ς λ]ώτιος λωτίξας ἀπαγέτω *Delph.* 3(4).352 (190 BC).
**λώτῐνος I**, add 'λ. ποίαις *Anacreont.* 32.2 W.' **II 1**, add 'αὐλίσκων ὑπὸ λωτίνων Pi.*fr.* 94b.14' add '**4** perh. *lotus-coloured*, τοῦ ἐριδίου τοῦ λωδίνου *POxy.* 3060.11 (ii AD).'
**λῶτις**, for 'dub. sens.' read 'perh. (*ritual*) *bath*, app. NWGk. form for λοῦσις (< *λόϜετις)' and add 'gen. λώτιος *Delph.* 3(4).352 (190 BC); cf. λωτίζω'
**λωτός III 1 a**, for 'flutes' read 'auloi' **b**, line 2, delete '(lyr.)' and for '*flute*' read '*aulos*'; add 'E.*HF* 11'
***λωτοσπορεύς**, έως, ὁ, *sower of fodder plants*, *PTeb.* 893 (ii BC).

# M

**μά** (A) **I**, at end for '*μὰ ναί Inscr.Cypr.* 109 H.' read 'Cypr. *ma-na-i μὰ ναί*, *ICS* 8.6'
***μᾰγᾰδίζω**, *produce an* (*octave*) *concord*, of singers, *μαγαδίζουσι ταύτην* (sc. *τὴν διὰ πασῶν συμφωνίαν*), *ἄλλην δὲ οὐδεμίαν* Arist.*Pr.* 918.40; *μ. ἐν τῇ διὰ πασῶν συμφωνίᾳ* ib. 921ᵃ12; metaph., Theophil. 7.2.
**μάγᾰδις**, for '*magadis*' to end read '*an octave concord*, *ψάλλω δ' εἴκοσι χορδαῖσι μάγαδιν †ἔχων* Anacr. 29 P.; *πηκτίδων ἀντιζύγοις ὁλκοῖς κρεκούσας μάγαδιν* Diog.Ath. 1.10 S.; *κέρασι .. καὶ σάλπιγξιν .. οἷον μάγαδιν* (v.l. *μαγάδι*) *σαλπίζοντες* X.*An.* 7.3.32; of an effect on the cithara, Philoch. 23 J., Hsch.; in related senses, perh. Alcm. 101 P., Telest. 4.2 P., Canthar. 12 K.-A. **II** of musical instrument, *Λυδός τε μ. αὐλός* Ion Trag. 23 S. (dub. sens.); Aristox.*fr.* 97-99 W. and later antiquarians (v. Ath. 14.634c-7a, Poll. 4.61, Hsch., Phot.) interpreted earlier refs. as referring to some instrument (harp or aulos); in S.*fr.* 238, *πηκταὶ δὲ λύραι καὶ μαγάδιδες*, the last two wds. do not scan normally and are prob. a gloss.'
***μᾰγᾰρεύς**, *έως*, *ὁ*, initiate of a group who gathered in a megaron, *SEG* 39.649 (Thrace, ii/iii AD); cf. °*ἀρχιμαγαρεύς*.
***μᾰγᾰρον**, *τό*, *underground pit* into which young pigs were thrown in worship of Demeter, Men.*fr.* 870 K.-Th., Phot.; also sp. *μέγαρα* (always pl.) Paus. 9.8.1, Porph.*Antr.* 6, Sch.Luc.*D.Meretr.* 1, cf. Hebr. *mᵉʿārāh*, *cave*, mod. Gk. *μαγαρίζω make foul*, *dirty*, see also °*ἀρχιμαγαρεύς*.
**μαγγᾰνάριος II**, add 'in context of building, *IGRom.* 3.1165 (AD 485)'
***μαγγᾰνικός**, *ή*, *όν*, *of* or *for a pulley-block*, *μ. ξύλον PMich.*xiii 660.10 (vi AD).
**μάγγανον II**, add '*φεσκάσιον· μάγγανον πλοϊκόν* Phot., Suid.'
***μαγδάλλει**· *τίλλει*, *ἐσθίει* Hsch.
***μᾰγειρῑα**, *ἡ*, prob. *tax on* or *licence for butchers* (cf. *μαγειρικός* 4), *IG* 12 suppl. 125.18 (Eresus).
**μᾰγειρικός 1**, for '*fit for a cook* or *cookery*' read '*of a butcher* or *cook*'; after 'Pl.*Grg.* 500b' insert '*SEG* 31.983.8-9 *μαγε[ιρικοὺς] ἐργάτας* (Priene, ii/i BC)' **4**, for this section read '*tax on butchers*, *SB* 7645.13 (iii BC), *PUniv.Giss.* 2.5 (ii BC), *Inscr.Magn.* 116.42 (ii AD)' add '**5** name of kind of plaster, *μ. ἔμπλαστρος PSI* 1180.44 (ii AD).'
***μᾰγείριος** or -*ίριος*, epith. of Apollo in Cyprus, *to-a-po-lo-ni to-ma-ki-ri-o ICS* 304 (iii BC).
**μᾰγευτής**, add 'cf. *μαγευτὰν αὐλόν· τὸν μαγεύοντα τοὺς ἀκροωμένους* Hsch.'
**μᾰγεύω III 2**, for '*call forth by magic arts*' read '*apply magic arts to*'; before 'Luc.*Asin.* 11' insert '*ἔρωτα*'
**μᾰγιανός**, for '*inscribed with charms*' read '*magic*'
***μάγιστερ**, *ὁ*, Lat. *magister*, *PSI* 481.10 (v/vi AD), Just.*Nov.* 30.2.
***μαγιστράτη**, *ἡ*, *magistracy*, *IGRom.* 1.599 (Istros, AD 201).
***μαγίστρατος**, *ὁ*, *magistrate*, *BE* 1970.398 (Tropaeum Traiani, iii AD).
***μαγιστριανός**, *ὁ*, Lat. *magistrianus*, official on the staff of the *magister officiorum*, *POxy.* 904.2 (v AD), *Cod.Just.* 12.60.7.2.
***μαγιστρόκηνσος**, *ὁ*, Lat. *magister census*, *registrar* of the senate and city of Constantinople, *Cod.Just.* 1.2.17.2, 2a.
***μάγιστρος**, *ὁ*, Lat. *magister*, *BGU* 927.5 (iii AD), *MAMA* 1.216 (iv AD), *Cod.Just.* 10.11.8.12.
***μαγιστρότης**, *ητος*, *ἡ*, *office of the magister*, *PAmh.* 138.11 (iv AD).
***μαγίστωρ**, *ορος*, *ὁ*, cf. Lat. *magister*, *SEG* 34.1095 (Ephesus, iii AD), *PLond.* 1790.10 (v/vi AD, -*σσ*- pap.); written *μαΐστωρ* Suid.
***μαγκίπισσα**, *ἡ*, *female baker*, Lxx Sch. 1*Ki.* 8.13.
***μάγκιψ**, *ιπος*, Lat. *manceps*, *contractor*, *MAMA* 3.409, al. (Corycus).
**μάγμα**, for '*thick unguent*' read '*mouldable sediment deposited in unguents*, etc.' and before 'Plin.*HN* 13.19' insert '*faecem unguenti magma appellant*'
**Μαγνησίη**, add 'also *Μαγνησία* Th. 1.138.5, 8.50.2, *SEG* 23.189 (Argos, iv BC)'
**Μάγνησσα**, add '*Μάγνησσαν κόραν Lyr.adesp.* 107 P., A.R. 1.584, etc.'
**Μάγος I 2**, add '**b** perh. a priest in Mithraic worship, Mitchell *N.Galatia* 404.' **II**, after '*magical*' insert '*ἐπῳδαί* Sosiph. 1'
***μάγουλον**, *τό*, *cheek*, as mod. Gk., Melamp. p. 503 F.
***μᾰγουσαῖος**, *ὁ*, = *μάγος* I 2, Bardes. 3.16 J., Suid. s.v. *γοητεία*.
***μάγωζ**(?α), *τά*, *treasuries*, *ἐν μαγώζοις* Aq.Sm.*Ez.* 27.24 (v.l. *μαγούζοις*).
**μᾰδᾰγένειος**, for 'Dor. for *μαδηγένειος*' read '*smooth-chinned*, (non-Att.-Ion., cf. *μαδιγένειος*)'
**μᾰδᾰρός 2**, add 'applied as a nickname, Cic.*Att.* 14.2.2, cf. perh. *Μάδρος IG* 5(2).387 (Lusi, v BC)'
**μᾰδᾰρόω**, after '*bald*' insert 'rest. in *Inscr.Cret.* 1.xvi 6.i-iii.24 (Lato, ii BC)'
**μᾰδάω 1**, for 'of a disease in fig-trees' read 'of the wood of diseased trees' **2**, add '**b** *become bare* by chafing, *πᾶς ὦμος μαδῶν* Lxx *Ez.* 29.18.'
**μαδηγένειος**, delete the entry.
**μάδησις**, add 'Gal. in *CMG* 5.10.(2).2 62.15'
**μᾰδῐγένειος**, line 2, delete 'prob. *μαδηγένειοι*'
**μαδωνάϊς**, add '(*μαδωνία* cj.)'
**μᾶζα**, line 1, for '(*μάσσω* .. 258 P.)' read 'or **μάζα** (on the accentuation see Hdn.Gr. 2.937, Moeris p. 258 P.)'; add 'see also *μᾶδδα*'
**μαζονομεῖον**, add '*SEG* 29.146b II 5 (Attica, iv BC)'; form -*νόμιον*, add 'Poll. 6.87'
**μαζονόμον**, after '(Didyma, iii BC)' insert 'Varro *RR* 3.4.3, Hor.*Sat.* 2.8.86'
***μαζόω**, *agglomerate*, Anon.Alch. 333.17.
**μᾰθητής**, add 'perh. of a trainee athlete, *Hesperia* 54.217 no. 3 (iii AD); *μ. ἱππέων*, transl. Lat. *discens equitum*, *SEG* 31.1116; see also *μαθετάς*'
***μαθκων** or **μαθκωνον**, pl. *μαθκωνα*, name of a garment, *SEG* 7.417, 419 (Semitic wd.).
**μαῖα I 3**, add 'Robert *Les stèles funéraires de Byzance* 176'
***Μαιαδεύς**, *έως*, *ὁ*, a name of Hermes, Hippon. 32.1 W., see *Μαῖα*, *Μαιάς*.
**Μαίανδρος I**, add 'as a divinity, *Schwyzer* 721.11 (Thebes at Mycale, v/iv BC)' **II**, add 'expld. as *κόσμος τις ὀροφικὸς παρὰ τοῖς ἀρχιτέκτοσι*, Sch.*AP* 6.286; as *εἶδος ἱππασίας παρὰ τοῖς ἱπποδαμασταῖς*, ib.'
**Μαιμακτήρ**, delete 'prop. = *Μαιμάκτης*' and add 'at Ephesus, *IEphes.* 690, al.; at Cyme, *SEG* 33.1040. **II** pl. *Μαιμακτῆρες*, divinities at Mytilene, *IG* 12(2).70.'
***Μαιμακτήρια**, *τά*, autumn festival in Thasos, *BCH* 82.195 (iv BC).
**Μαιμακτηριών**, add 'also in Samothrace, *SEG* 31.803'
**Μαιμάκτης**, add 'at Naxos, *Διὸς Μ. IG* 12(5).47; *Μ.· μειλίχιος*, *καθάρσιος* Hsch.'
**μαινάς II**, for 'esp. of love' read 'applied to the *ἴυγξ*'; after '*P.* 4.216' add '*μαινάδα βότρυν AP* 4.1.25 (Mel.)'
**μαινόλης I**, line 1, after lemma insert 'Dor.Aeol. -*λᾱς*' and after 'Sapph. 1.18' insert 'L.-P.; *θίασος* Phot., Suid. s.v. *θίασος*'; line 3, after 'gen.' insert 'Archil. 196a.30 W.' and delete '*ἀσέβεια* .. *Or.* 823 (lyr.)'; add 'pl. *μαινόλιδες* (*μεν*- lapis) *Bacchants*, *SEG* 17.772 (iii AD)' **II**, delete '(From *μαίνομαι* .. *φαίνομαι*)'
**μαινόλιος**, add 'epith. of Zeus, *IG* 12(2).484.16 (Mytilene)'
**μαίνομαι**, line 4, after 'also' insert '*μεμάνηκα* Arg.Men.*Oxy.* 1235.66 (*μεμενηκέναι* pap.), and '; before 'Theoc.' insert 'Men.*Epit.* 879'; line 5, after 'aor. med.' insert '(*ἐπ*)*εμήνατο* Il. 6.160'
***μαῖοι**, *οἱ*, *adoptive parents*, *IG* 12(5).199 (Paros); cf. *μαῖα* 2.
***Μαιουμάρχης**, *ὁ*, *one who presides over the Maioumas*, (v. °*Μαιουμᾶς*) Roueché *Aphrodisias* 40 (v AD).
***Μαιουμᾶς**, *ᾶ*, *ὁ*, festival in Syria and elsewh., Jul.*Mis.* 362D, *INikaia* 63, *Gerasa* 279 (vi AD).
***μαιουμίζω**, *celebrate the Maioumas*, (v. °*Μαιουμᾶς*) *ITyr* 151.
***μαιριάω**, *Ταραντῖνοι δὲ μαιριῆν τὸ κακῶς ἔχειν* Hsch. s.v. *Μαῖρα*.
***μάκαμον**, *τό*, *beer*, *κερβησίας ἤτοι μακάμου Edict.Diocl.* 2.11.
**μᾰκαρ**, line 7, after 'Sol. 14' insert 'Hippon. 43, 117 W.' **III**, add 'in epitaphs, *GVI* 795 (iii/iv AD)'
**μᾰκᾰρι**, add 'cf. mod. Gk.'
**μᾰκᾰριστός**, adv. -*ῶς*, add '*GVI* 788 (ii/iii AD)'
**μακαρῖτις**, add 'acc. -*ῖτιν MAMA* 9.75 (ii/iii AD)'
**μᾰκεδνός**, line 1, after 'Od. 7.106' insert 'prob. rest. in A.*fr.* 451*l*.13 R.'
***Μᾰκεδονιαρχέω**, *exercise the office of Μακεδονιάρχης*, *SEG* 24.497 (Maced., ii AD).
***Μᾰκεδονιάρχης**, *ου*, *ὁ*, app. some religious officer in Maced., *AA* 1942.176, al., *SEG* 24.479 (Maced., iii AD).
***Μᾰκεδονιαρχικός**, *ή*, *όν*, *of the office of Μακεδονιάρχης*, *ἐν προβολαῖς Μ. AA* 1942.176.
***Μᾰκεδονιάρχισσα**, *ἡ*, fem. of °*Μακεδονιάρχης*, *AA* 1942.176.

**Μᾰκεδών**, add 'ἐξελιγμὸς *M.*, a form of military manœuvre, Arr.*Tact.* 23.1, 24.1; w. ellipsis of ἐξελιγμός, ib. 31.4'

***μάκειρ**, v. ‡μάκιρ.

**μᾰκέλας**, read 'μᾰκελᾶς' and add 'see also °βακέλας'

**μᾰκελλάριος**, (s.v. μάκελλον), add '*BASP* 12.153 (?iii AD; sp. μακελάρειως), *SEG* 29.327 (Corinth, v/vi AD)'

**μᾰκελλον II**, line 4, after 'Aesop. 134' insert '*SEG* 29.327 (Corinth)'

**μᾰκελλωτός**, add 'cf. *macellotae* fem. pl., for *ostia*, Varro *LL* 5.146'

***Μᾰκηδονίς**, ίδος, ἡ, *Macedonian*, Hom.*fr.* 24 D., *GVI* 1015.1 (Alexandria, i/ii AD), Nonn.*D.* 2.400.

**μάκιρ**, after '*malabarica*' insert 'or sim. tree'

**μακραίων 1**, add 'Emp. 115.5 D.-K.'

***μάκριον**, τό, dim. of μάκρα (*sarcophagus*), *ITyr* 81, 82 (v/vi AD).

***μακροβιοτεία**, ἡ, *longevity*, Phld.*Sign.* 17.

**μακροημέρευσις**, add '*SEG* 34.1515 (Arabia, vi AD)'

**μακροκέντης**, add '*JJP* 19.110 (uncertain sense in broken context)'

***μακρόκνημος**, ον, *long-shanked*, Heph.Astr. 3.45.9.

***μακρόουρος**, ον, *long-tailed*, Cyran. 65 (2.22 K.).

***μακροπαράληκτος**, ον, *having the penultimate syllable long*, Sch.Il. 6.268, Eust. 407.36.

**μακρόπορος**, before '*ravelling*' insert '*having a long course* or *orbit* (opp. βραχύπ-), Procl.*in R.* 2.20 K.'

**μακροπώγων**, add '*Cat.Cod.Astr.* 11(2).138.10'

**μακρός I 1**, add 'app. w. ellipsis of δρόμος *CEG* 374.2 (Laconia, vi BC)' **II**, add '**4** μακρόν, τό, part of the parabasis of a comedy = πνῖγος, Sch.Ar.*Ach.* 659, *Nu.* 518, Poll. 4.112.' **III 2**, add 'ἐς τὸ μακρόν *in height*, Call.*fr.* 196.31 Pf.'

**μακρότης**, add 'τοῦ ῥυθμοῦ, i.e. predominance of long syllables, Demetr.*Eloc.* 40'

***μακρόχειρον**, τό, = Lat. *tunica manicata*, *long-sleeved tunic*, *Dura*[4] 98.

***μακροχρονία**, ἡ, *long duration*, βίου Moses Alch. 315.17.

**†μακροψῡχία**, ἡ, *fact* or *power of taking a long view*, Cic.*Att.* 9.11.4.

**μακτήριον I**, delete '= μάκτρα Plu. 2.159d' and for 'Call.*fr.* 7.32 P.' read 'Call.*fr.* 23.11 Pf.'

***μακτήριος**, α, ον, *of a kneader*, Plu. 2.159d.

**μάκτρον**, add '*IEphes.* 456 (iv AD; written μακρον)'

**μᾰλα II**, line 2, delete 'only in' and after 'Tyrt. 12.6' insert 'Call.*fr.* 67.13 Pf.' **III 1**, line 3, after 'id.*Grg.* 510b' insert 'ὡς ἔνι μάλιστα Men.*Dysc.* 699 S.'

**μᾱλάβαθρον**, after 'Plin.*HN* 12.129' insert '*SB* 9834b.22 (iv AD, written -βατρα pl.); also **μηλόβαθρον** Androm.ap.Gal. 14.41, βαλάβαθρον *SB* 9804.5 (ii AD), *BGU* 953.2 (iii/iv AD)'

**μᾰλαγμα II**, add 'cf. μάλαγμα *moecharum* (applied by Augustus to Maecenas), Macr.*Sat.* 2.4.12'

***μάλαθρον**, τό, gloss on ἄνηθον, Sch.Theoc. 7.63; cf. μάραθρον.

**μᾰλᾰκια**, for 'i.e. .. *shells*' read 'ὅσα ἄναιμα ὄντα ἐκτὸς ἔχει τὸ σαρκῶδες, ἐντὸς δ' εἴ τι ἔχει στερεόν'

**μᾰλᾰκίων**, for 'term of endearment, *darling*' read 'term of contempt, *softy*'

***μᾰλᾰκόμμᾰτος**, ον, *soothing the eyes*, ὕπνος *Lyr.adesp.* 11(*g*).1 P.

**μᾰλᾰκός I 1**, add 'w. implication of rottenness, δρῦν *AP*6.254 (Myrin.); of ἀμυσγέλαι almonds, *fresh* (opp. σκληραί), *SEG* 9.41.17, al. (Cyrene, ii BC)' **III 2 d**, for 'παθητικός' read '*pathic*' add '**3** of style, *gentle*, D.H.*Dem.* 20; adv. -κῶς id.*Pomp.* 6.'

**μᾰλᾰκόσωμος**, add 'Paul.Aeg. 7.3 (237.10 H.)'

**μᾰλᾰκόφρων**, for '(Orph.*H.*) 69.13' read '69.17'

**μᾰλᾰκόφωνος**, add 'Sch.Pi.*O.* 9.34c'

**μᾰλακτήρ**, delete 'χρυσοῦ μ. καί'

**μᾰλᾰχη 1**, for 'μολόχη .. (cod. F)' read 'see also μολάχη, ‡μολόχη'

**†μαλάχιον**, τό, dim. of μαλάχη, *mallow*, *PIndiana Univ.* 4.1 (*CPh* 43.112, iii AD). **II** sp. μαλάκιον, a woman's ornament worn round the neck, Ar.*fr.* 332.10 K.-A. (ap. Poll. 7.95; μαλάχιον Phot. s.v.), Poll. 5.87, Hsch.; **μολόχιον** Clem.Al.*Paed.* 2.124.2.'

***Μᾰλεᾱ́τας**, ὁ, cult-name of Apollo, *IG* 4[2].128 (*c.*280 BC), *SEG* 33.306, Paus. 2.27.7.

***Μᾰλεᾱ́τεια**, τά, *festival of Apollo of Malea*, *IG* 5(1).213.57 (Sparta, v BC).

**μᾰλερός II**, for this section read 'μαλερὰς φρένας *Suppl.Hell.* 1087 (μαλερὰς φρένας· ἀσθενεῖς Hsch.)'

**μᾰλευρον**, delete 'Alc. 70, Achae. 51' and after 'Theoc. 15.116' insert 'Call.*fr.* 177.18 Pf.'; add 'cf. Myc. *me-re-u-ro* (form *μέλευρον)'

***μαλεων**, gen. pl., app. some implement or object used in construction work, ὑπὲρ τι(μῆς) κάμ‹π›τρας μαλεων *PWash.Univ.* 28.7 (vi/vii AD).

**μᾰλη 1**, add 'perh. Myc. *ma-ra-pi* (loc. pl.)' **2**, for '*underhand, secretly*' read 'ὑπὸ μάλης (done) *in an underhand manner, secretly*' and add 'αἱ ὑπὸ μάλης πράξεις Plu. 2.64e'

**μάληκος**, after 'pr. n. in inscrr.' insert 'e.g. Μαλε͂ϙō (gen.) *Corinth* 15(3).1 (*c.*700 BC), Μάλε͂κος *IG* 5(2).425 (Phigaleia, v BC)'; add 'cf. μαληκῷ παιδίῳ· χοιριδίῳ δεσμῷ Hsch. (μαλήκῳ πέδᾳ· μοιριδίῳ δεσμῷ La.)'

***μάλημπτος**, Lat. *male emptus*, *bought as a bad bargain*, *SEG* 39.1062 (Rhegium, i BC/i AD).

***μαλθᾰκιάζω**, *make soft* or *effeminate*, Cyran. 25 (1.10 K.).

**μαλθᾰκός**, after lemma insert 'Lacon. μαλσακός Alcm. 4 *fr.* 1.5 P.'

***μᾱλία**, Aeol. for μηλέα, Sapph. 2.3 L.-P.

***μᾱλίς**, v. μηλίς (A).

**μαλιώτερα**, after 'Hsch.' insert 'fr. a comp. form of μάλα'

***μαλκιόεις**, εσσα, εν, = μάλκιος, *Suppl.Hell.* 1167.

**μάλκιος**, last line, delete 'the latter .. Nic.*Th.* 382'

**μαλλός 1**, add '(cf. Myc. *wool* ideogram app. *ma+ru*)' **2**, for this section read 'of men's hair, πλοκάμων μαλλοί E.*Ba.* 113, cf. Hsch.; of a bird's neck-feathers, Ezek.*Exag.* 260 S.'

***μαλλουργέω**, *work the flock of wool*, i.e. prob. *card*, *SB* 10209 (ii/i BC).

***μαλλοφρονέω**, *to be wiser*, τῆς γὰρ ἐπιστήμης μαλλοφρονεῖν ἔμαθες *GVI* 1934 (unless error for μᾶλλον φρονεῖν).

**μαλλωτός**, add 'of shoes, *Edict.Diocl.* 9.25'

***Μᾱλόεις**, εντος, ὁ, (cf. μῆλον (B), -oϝεντ- suffix) epith. of Apollo in Lesbos, Th. 3.3.3, etc., as place-name, *IG* 12(2).74.5 (Mytilene, iii BC). **II** poet. for *Lesbian*, Μαλόες (Dor. = Μαλόεις) ἦλθε χορός Call.*fr.* 485 Pf.

**μᾱλοκόμος**, **μᾶλον**, for 'Dor.' read 'hyperdor.'

**μᾱλοπᾱ́ραυος**, for 'Aeol. .. Hsch.' read '*white-cheeked* (μᾱλός (A); cf. Hsch. μαλλοπάραυος· λευκοπάρειος) or perh. *apple-cheeked* (μῆλον (B)), Alc. 261(*b*)i 5 L.-P. (rest.)'

**μᾱλός** (A), after 'Hsch.' add 's.v. μαλλός'

**†μᾱ́λουρις**, fem. of μάλουρος, Hsch.; as subst., of an animal, in quot. prob. a cat or sim., Call.*Cer.* 110.

**†μᾱ́λουρος**· λεύκουρος Hsch.

***μαλφιον**, τό, unexpld. item in accounts of a business establishment, *PMich.*inv. 1933 (*BASP* 16.82, ii AD).

**μάματα**, after 'ποιήματα' insert '(πέμματα cj. Meineke)'

**μαμμᾰ́κυθος**, after lemma insert '*one who hides in his mother's skirts* (κεύθω)'

**μάμμη I**, add 'voc. μάμμᾰ Ar.Byz.' **III**, add 'written μάμη, *AAWW* 1961.124 (Lydia, iii AD)'

**μαμμία**, add '*IG* 2[2].10743 (iv BC)'

**μαμμοπᾰ́τωρ**, for '*Inscr.Cypr.* 159 H.' read 'Cypr. *ma-mo-pa-to-re* μα(μ)μοπάτōρ *ICS* 277'

**μανδάκης**, after 'ὁ' insert '(or **μανδάκη**, ἡ)'

**μανδάκιον**, add '*PHamb.* 21.5 (iv AD, μαντακ- pap.)'

**μάνδᾰλος**, add 'Hsch. s.v. καβλή‹ς›'

***μάνδαξ**, ακος, ὁ, = μανδάκης, *PRein.* 110.8, 10 (iii AD).

***μανδᾶτον**, τό, Lat. *mandatum*, form of *consensual contract*, Just.*Edict.* 9.3, al.

***μανδάτωρ**, ωρος, ὁ, Lat. *mandator*, *guarantor*, Just.*Nov.* 4.1, al.

***μανδατωρεύω**, = Lat. *mandare*, *mandate*, Just.*Nov.* 4.1.

**μανδήλη**, after '(v AD)' insert 'also **μαντ-** Poll. 7.74'

***μάνδιξ**, ικος, ὁ, = Lat. *mantica*, *wallet*, *Vit.Aesop.*(G) 4, al.

**μάνδρα 1**, after 'Plu. 2.648a' insert 'for sheep, Nonn.*D.* 34.252' add '**b** *monastery*, Epiph.Const. 42.340a M., etc.' **2**, for this section read 'a place of human habitation, *Peripl.M.Rubr.* 2, 20, *POxy.* 984 (i AD)'

***μανδρᾰγόριον**, τό, dim. of μανδραγόρας, Cyran. 48.

***μανδράρχης**, ὁ, person in charge of a μάνδρα, *PHib.* 211.6 (iii BC).

***Μάνδρος**, ὁ, a divinity in Asia Minor, with the title Καίων, *IKyme* 37.5-6, also in theophoric pers. n. Ἀναξίμανδρος etc.

***μανέανον**, τό, an unidentified tool or instrument, *BGU* 544.25 (ii AD).

**μᾱ́νης I**, line 3, read 'μάνᾱς' **II**, for '*small bronze figure*' read 'part of stand' **III**, at beginning insert 'Μᾱ́νης (perh. diff. wd.), also acc. pl. Μᾶνας Ar.*Av.* 522'

**μᾰνιάκης**, add 'cf. Iran. *mani-*, *necklace*'

***μανίζω**, prob. *damage*, fut. μανίσει Ramsay *Cities and Bishoprics* 1.157, unless fr. μηνίω.

**μάννα**, line 2, delete 'but .. λίβανος'

**μαννάριον**, delete 'perh. .. μαμμάριον' and add 'cf. mod. Gk. μάννα *mother*'

**μανός I**, add '**2** metaph., *mentally weak*, Suid. s.v. μανόν.' **II 2**, after '-νῶς' insert 'Hermog.*Id.* 2.12'

**μανόσπορος**, add 'A.*fr.* 113a.1 R.'

***μανούβριον**, τό, Lat. *manubrium*, *handle*, *BGU* 544.22 (ii AD, pl.).

**μανόφυλλος**, add 'read by Zenod. in Od. 13.346 (w. Att. scansion ⏑⏑–⏑)'

**μαντεία**, after lemma insert 'Arg. μαντήα *Schwyzer* 89 (iii BC)'

**μαντευτικός**, add 'Diog.Oen.*fr.* 122 i 5 S.'

***μαντηλαρία**, ἡ, = °μαντηλάριος (ἡ), *IEphes.* 1078.14 (iii AD).

***μαντηλάριος**, ὁ and ἡ, *slave who brought towels* or *napkins* at a banquet (cf. Verg.*G.* 4.377), *SEG* 34.1126 (Ephesus), *IEphes.* 1060.14; cf. ‡μανδήλη.

***μαντήλη**, v. °μανδήλη.

*μαντιαρχέω, serve as μαντιάρχης, aor. part. Cypr. alphabetical μανζιαρχήσαντος, *Kafizin* 258(b) (iii BC).

μαντιάρχης, add 'Cypr. *ma-ti-a-*[, *perh.* μα(ν)τια[ρχō, *Kourion* 9'

+μαντίαρχος, ὁ, = μαντιάρχης, *SEG* 20.162 (vii/vi BC), 23.621 (iii BC, both Cyprus).

μαντικός I 1, line 1, for '*prophetic*' read '*of prophetic utterances*'; add 'μαντικώτερα εἰρῆσθαι Plu.*Cat.Mi.* 52, *Pomp.* 60' **II**, line 3, after 'Luc.*Hes.* 7' insert 'μαντικώτατος of Romulus, *devoted to divinations*, Plu.*Cam.* 32.5'

μαντίον, add 'Lyd.*Mag.* 69.1'

μάντις I 1, add 'as a civic office, *SEG* 26.694 (Ambracia, *c.*150 BC)' **II**, delete 'a kind of *grasshopper*'

*μάντος, ὁ, Lat. *mantus*, *short cloak*, *Edict.Diocl.* 19.71.

μαντοσύνη, add '**2** in pl., *oracular response*, *APl.* 296 (Antip.).'

μαντῷος, add 'Olymp. *in Alc.* p. 201'

*μᾱνῠτειρα, ἡ, Dor. fem. of μηνυτήρ, στάλα *SEG* 8.482 (Egypt, i BC/i AD).

μάνωσις, add 'ἡ τῶν ἄστρων ἀνταύγεια καὶ μ. the stars' *power of rarefying* the light they reflect, Hp.*Hebd.* 1.2'

*Μαξιμιάνειος, α, ον, *named in honour of Maximianus*, ἀγών *JRS* 3.289, al. (Antioch in Pisidia).

*μάππα, ἡ, Lat. *mappa*, *napkin*, *Vit.Aesop.*(G) 44.

μαππάριος, add 'written μαμπ- *PGrenf.* 2.111.12 (v/vi AD)'

+μαππίον, τό, dim. of °μάππα, *Gloss.*; sp. μαπιν *POxy.* 1051.17 (iii AD); neut. pl. μαπα (dub.) ibid. 19, μαμπία ib. 1741.17, μαπία *PRyl.* 627.20 (iv AD).

μάραγδος, after 'σμάραγδος' insert 'Men.*fr.* 315 K.-Th.'

*μαραθᾶς, ᾶ, ὁ, *seller of fennel*, dub. in *IG* 12(9).522 (Euboea) (cf. *Rev.Phil.* 18.52).

μάρᾰθον, add '(form μάραθϝον) Myc. *ma-ra-tu-wo*'

Μᾰρᾰθῶνάδε, add 'Euc.ap.Arist.*Po.* 1458ᵇ9'

μᾰραίνω, line 5, delete '(leg. -αμμ-)' and after 'Plu.*Pomp.* 31' insert 'cf. μεμαραμένη *GVI* 1801.2 (Bithynia, late Rom.imp.)'

μαράσσαι, add 'cf. ἀμαράσαι, μαρίν'

*μαργᾰρεος, ὁ, = μαργαρίτης, Gr.Naz.*Carm.* 2.1.38.34.

μαργᾰρίτης, add '**III** an Egyptian plant, Arist.*Plant.* 1.4.1 (819ᵃ11 ed. Apelt).'

μαργάω, after 'only in part.' insert '(except μαργᾷ· μαργαίνει Hsch.)'

μάργος 1, after 'of wine' insert '*maddening*'; add '(s.v.l.)' **3**, add 'Arist.*Phgn.* 808ᵇ6'

μάρδος, for '*flute*' read '*reed-pipe*'

μάρη, delete the entry (v. °μάρος).

Μᾰρῐανδῡνοί, (s.v. Μαριανδυνία), add 'as name of a helot class at Heracleia, Str. 12.3.4'

μᾰριεύς, for 'Hsch. (μαριζεύς cod.)' read 'cf. °μαριζεύς'

*Μαριεύς, έως, ὁ, *of the town Marion* in Cyprus, S.*fr.* 69, D.S. 19.62, 79.2.

*μαριζεύς· λίθος τις, ὃς ἐπισταζομένου ὕδατος καίεται Hsch.; cf. μαριεύς.

+μᾰρῑκᾶς, μαρικᾶν· κίναιδον. οἱ δὲ ὑποκόρισμα παιδίου ἄρρενος βαρβαρικόν Hsch.; Μαρικᾶς represented Hyperbolus in a play of this title by Eup., cf. Ar.*Nu.* 553.

μαρίν, add 'cf. μαράσσαι, ἀμαράσαι'

*μάριον, τό, dim. of μάρις, *POxy.* 1297.3 (iv AD).

μάρις, add 'Hallock *Persepolis Fortification Texts* p. 2 (*c.*500 BC). **2** μ. .. καλεῖται δὲ ὁμωνύμως καὶ τὸ μακρὸν πέπερι Hsch.'

μαρίω, delete the entry.

*μαρκαζήτα, ἡ, *marcassite*, *white iron pyrites*, Anon.Alch. 333.28.

μαρμαράριος, after 'ὁ' insert 'cf. Lat. *marmorarius*'; add '*Edict.Diocl.* 7.5, *MAMA* 3.21 (Seleucia), *Inscr.Olymp.* 657 (v/vi AD), *ITyr* 152 '

μαρμάρεος II, add 'see also °μαρμάριος (A)'

μαρμᾰρίζω, line 2, for '-ιζούσας Pi.*fr.* 123.2' read '-ιζοίσας Pi.*fr.* 123.3 S.-M. (v.l. -υζοίσας)'

μαρμᾰρικός, add 'Zos.Alch. 186.2, cf. (for sense) Μαρμαρικοῦ .. πολέμοιο *SEG* 26.1835 (Cyrene)'

μαρμᾰρινος, line 3, after 'λίθος' insert 'kind of stone wrongly identified with onyx, *Lapid.Gr.* 198.2'; add 'neut. pl. subst., (?)*marble tablets*, *SEG* 33.1040 (Cyme, ii BC)'

*μαρμάριος (A), α, ον, Aeol. for μαρμάρεος II, *IKyme* 19. **II** Μαρμάριος, ὁ, epith. of Apollo at Delos, *Inscr.Délos* 2473.

*μαρμάριος (B), prob. = μαρμαράριος, *MAMA* 3.683 (Corycus), *MAMA* 3.25 (-άρις, Seleucia).

μαρμᾰρῖτις, add '**III** the plant *fumitory*, Ps.-Dsc. 4.109.'

μαρμᾰρόεις, for '= μαρμάρεος' read '*gleaming*' and add '**II** *of marble*, μ. στήλη *IG* 9(2).650, cf. 14.1603.'

*μαρμᾰρόπαιστος, ον, *struck out of marble*, εἰκών epigr. in *JHS* 73.139 (*c.*ii AD).

*μαρμᾰρύζω, v. μαρμαρίζω.

μαρμᾰρωσις, add 'Keil-Premerstein *Dritter Bericht* 64 (iv AD), *ICilicie* 34.4 (v/vi AD). **2** *marble paving*, *JHS* 28.195 (Side).'

*μᾶρος, ους, τό, *hand*, Pi.*fr.* 310 (Sch.Il. 15.137); cf. εὐμαρής, εὐμάρεια.

*Μαρσήλλιος, ὁ, name of a month, *Amyzon* 2 (321/0 BC).

μάρσιππος, add 'a kind of sackcloth, *PHels.* 7.7 (ii BC)'

+μαρτῠρητικός, ή, όν, *providing evidence*, *testimonial*, ψηφίσματα μαρτυρητικὰ καὶ τε[ι]μητικά *La Carie* 78.18.

μαρτῠρία I, lines 4/5, delete 'μαρτυριῶν .. 1316'; line 8, after '*commendation*' insert 'D.H.*Th.* 35'

μαρτῠριον III, add '*AS* 35.96 (iv AD), *SEG* 34.1212 (-ρειν for -ριν, Lydia)'

*μαρτῠρολόγος, ὁ, *reader at the commemoration of a martyr*, *PLand.* 154.8 (v/vi AD).

μαρτῠρομαι, add '**5** *give testimony*, Modest.*Dig.* 27.1.13.8.'

μαρτῠροποιΐα, after 'Ptol.*Tetr.* 183 (pl.)' insert '(v.l.)'

μάρτυς I, add '**b** as adj., μάρτυρι σιγῇ Nonn.*D.* 3.123; μ. πομπῇ ib. 4.207.'

Μάρων, line 2, after 'Od. 9.197' insert '(great-grandson of Dionysus, Hes.*fr.* 238 M.-W., a companion of D., pap. in *Aegyptus* 6.192)'

μᾰσάομαι I, line 5, after 'Cass.Fel. 32' insert 'as a gesture of contempt, Philostr.*VA* 7.21' and delete 'or Att. Prose' **II**, delete the section.

μάσημα, add '**2** part of the head-harness of a horse, = Lat. *salivarium*, *Edict.Diocl.* in *SEG* 37.335 iii 10.'

*μᾰσητρίς, ίδος, ἡ, fem. of μασητήρ, Hsch. s.v. νάρθη.

*μασθέλιον, τό, in pl., some part of a pack-camel's equipment, perh. *straps* or *harness*, *PNess.* 74.7 (vii AD).

μάσθλης, line 3, for 'Sapph. 19' read 'Sapph. 39.2 L.-P., perh. in Alc. 143.12 L.-P.'

*μασθοδοσία, v. °μαστο-.

*μασθός (B), Dor. for μαδός, Heraclid.ap.Eust. 1562.4.

μασκαύλης, add '?cf. βασκαύλης'

*μάσλης, v. ‡μάσθλης.

*μασονάφι(ο)ν, τό, perh. = μασουάφιον, *PVindob.* G39847.928 (*CPR* 5.110, iv AD).

*μασσανδάνια, τά, unexpld. wd., ostr. in *BASP* 23.25.

*μάσσινος, ὁ, *rope*, *ICilicie* 108.5 (v/vi AD).

μάσσω, line 6, after '[ᾰ]' insert '(μαεν *Schwyzer* 230 (Arcesilas vase, vi BC) has been interpreted as = μαγέν, sc. τὸ σίλφιον)' **II**, add 'see also *SEG* 30.1364' **III**, insert 'fig.' before '*take the impression of*'

μάσσων, add 'see also μασσότερον'

μάσταξ II, add 'unless = sense III *locust* (or its grub), also perh. in Theoc. l.c.' **III**, add 'Artem. 2.21'

μαστῑγοφόρος I, add 'λύθρον μ. *Trag.adesp.* 235 K.-S.'

μαστίζω, line 2, after 'Il. 5.768' insert 'ἐμάστιξα Lxx 3*Ma.* 2.21'; line 3, after '(Leon.Alex.)' insert 'also μαστισθείς *SEG* 8.246.17 (Palestine, ii AD)'

*μαστικτήρ, ῆρος, ὁ, *that stabs* as with a goad, ἤκουσα μαστικτῆρα (cj.) καρδίας λόγον A.*Supp.* 466.

μάστιξ II, add '**b** of persons, transl. Hebr. wd. from root meaning "smite", but Hebr. perh. corrupt, Lxx *Ps.* 34(35).15 (πλῆκται in Aq., Sm. ad loc.).'

μαστῖχη, add 'also μαστύχη, *Edict.Diocl.* 36.63'

*μαστοδοσία, ἡ, (μασθο-), *suckling*, ἐν ταῖς μασθοδοσίαις τῶν βρεφῶν Heph.Astr. 3.5.49.

*μαστοδοτέω, *suckle*, Cyran. 74.

*μαστρεῖον, τό, *assembly of the* μαστροί, *Tit.Cam.* 110.44, rest. in *Lindos* 419.25 (i AD).

*μαστρεύω, *serve as* μαστρός, *Lindos* 420*a*6, al. (i AD).

μαστρικός, add 'masc. subst., perh. = μαστρός, *Tit.Cam.* 89.7'

+μαστροπεύω, of a pimp, *procure*, X.*Smp.* 4.57, Luc.*Tim.* 16, Ach.Tat. 6.3; fig., οὐκοῦν σύ με .. μαστροπεύσεις πρὸς τὴν πόλιν ..; (i.e. public life), X.*Smp.* 8.42; μαστροπεύουσι δὲ αὐτῇ (sc. ἡδονῇ) .. τὸν ἔρωτα αἰσθήσεις μ. ἡδονῇ Ph. 1.40, 156.

μαστροπός I, after '*pimp* or *procuress*' insert 'Sophr. 69 (dub. gender)'; line 2, delete 'metaph.'

μαστρός, add 'at Olympia, *SEG* 31.358 (v BC)'

+μαστύς, ύος, ἡ, *search* (cf. μάστευσις), Call.*fr.* 10 Pf.

*μαστύχη, v. °μαστίχη.

μασύντης, add 'cf. Μασυντίας Ar.*V.* 433'

*μασχᾰλῆν (or -ᾶν)· τὸ τοῖς λευκίνοις σχοινίοις τὰς ἀγκύρας σχάσαντες περὶ τὸν ἀγκυρίτην λίθον περιθεῖναι Hsch.

μασχᾰλίζω, add 'perh. Boeot. form in Hsch.: μασχαλίττει· ὑπὸ κόλπον καὶ μάλην φέρει'

μασχᾰλίσματα 2, add '*SEG* 36.206.16, 17 (Attica, *c.*300 BC)'

*μάσχιον, τό, = μασχάλη II 2, *OBodl.* II 1756 (ii AD, pl.).

μᾰταιος I, add '**3** μάταια, τά, *empty beings*, *phantoms*, Lxx *Le.* 17.7, 2*Ch.* 11.15.'

+μᾰταϊσμός, ὁ, *miscarriage*, Seleuc.ap.Ath. 2.76f, Plato Com. 61 (ibid.).

*μᾱτερία, ἡ, Lat. *materia*, *dough*, Chrysipp.Tyan.ap.Ath. 3.113b,c.

*μάτημι (A), line 2, before ':– Pass.' insert 'elsewhere ματέω, ματεῖ·

ζητεῖ Hsch., aor. part. ματίσας (for -ήσας) *PUniv.Giss.* 32.16 (iii/iv AD), cf. inf. ματίσαι Hsch.'; at end delete the entry in brackets.
**μάτημι (B), Aeol. for πατέω, *tread*, μάτει Alc. 74.3 L.-P., pres. part. fem. pl. μάτεισαι *Incert.auct.* 16.3 L.-P., fut. inf. ματήσην Alc. 200 L.-P; ματεῖ· πατεῖ Hsch.
*μᾰτίδιον, τό, a measure (app. dim. of μάτιον), *PCol.* 188.18 (iv AD).
μᾰτίζω, delete the entry.
*ματίς· μέγας. τινὲς ἐπὶ τοῦ βασιλέως Hsch.
*μάτλα, ἡ, Lat. *matula, chamber-pot*, *SB* 1160.6 (ostr.).
*ματρικάριος, ὁ, public servant employed app. in maintaining order, Just.*Nov.* 13.5.
*μάτριξ, ικος, ἡ, Lat. *matrix, roll, list*, *PBeatty Panop.* 1.17, al. (AD 298), edict of Anastasius I in *SEG* 9.356.6, 13 (Cyrenaica, vi AD), *PMonac.* 2.8 (vi AD), *LW* 1906*d*, *e* (Bostra, prob. vi AD), Lyd.*Mag.* 3.2.
*ματρώνα, ἡ, Lat. *matrona, married woman*, *IGRom.* 3.244, *PFlor.* 16.2 (iii AD).
*ματρωνίκιον, τό, *women's part of baths*, *PFlor.* 384.7, 14 (v AD); pl., *women's quarters*, attached to monastery hospice, *PNess.* 79.29, al. (early vii AD, ματρον- pap.).
*μαυλάκι(ο)ν, τό, prob. dim. of μαῦλις (B), *PFouad* 84 (ii AD).
μαῦλις (B), for 'Call.*Aet.* 3.1.9' read 'Call.*fr.* 75.9 Pf.'
μαυρός, add 'cf. mod. Gk. μαῦρος'
μαυρόω, add 'v.l. for ἀμαυρόω (q.v.), Hes.*Op.* 693'
Μαύσσωλλος, for 'Μαυσωλεῖον' read 'Μαυσώλειον'
*μᾰφάρι(ο)ν, τό, = μαφόριον, *Dura*[4] 93, 129.
μᾰφόριον, add 'Lyd.*Mens.* 1.20; see also °βαφωρι-'
μᾰφόρτης, for '*veil* .. priests (cf. *Gloss.*)' read '*short cloak with a hood*'; add 'cf. Hebr. *ma'ᵃpōreṯ*'
μᾰφόρτιον, add '*Edict.Diocl.* 29.29'
μᾰχαιρᾶς, add '*MAMA* 3.628 (Corycus)'
μᾰχαιρίδιον, delete 'Luc.*Pisc.* 45'
*μᾰχαιρον, τό, = μάχαιρα, *POxy.* 1289.4,7 (v AD, μαχερ- pap.).
*μαχάτης, ὁ, or -άτη, ἡ, or -άτι‹ο›ν, τό, a measure of cubic capacity, *SB* 9303.5 (iii AD).
μάχη I 1, add '**b** *brawl, affray*, *SEG* 31.122 (c.AD 121/2); μ. παροίνους *Anacreont.* 42.13 W.'
μᾰχητής, add 'cf. Myc. *ma-ka-ta*, pers. n.'
*μᾰχικός, ή, όν, = μάχιμος, *An.Ox.* 4.266.4.
*μᾰχιμικός, ή, όν, *belonging to a* μάχιμος, [κλῆρος] *PVarsov.* 3.35 (ii AD); so also *PRyl.* 202.5 (i AD); γῆ μ. perh. to be read in *BGU* 958*b* (ii/iii AD); cf. *PLond.* 193.34 (i AD): see *APF* 12.95.
μάχιμος, after '*PTeb.* 61(*a*).109 (ii BC), etc.' insert 'sg. μ. ἑπτάρουρος *PColl.Youtie* 16.3 (109 BC)'
*μαχλίς· ἑταίρα, πόρνη Hsch.
μάχλος 1, line 3, for 'Aeschrio 8.6' read 'Aeschrio in *Suppl.Hell.* 4.6'
*μαχλῶντες· πορνεύοντες Hsch.
*μέ, v. °μετά.
*μεγαβρόντης, ου, m. adj., *loudly-thundering*, codd. in Ar.*V.* 323.
μεγαίνητος, add '*IG* 2².3632.10'
*Μέγαιρα, ἡ, name of one of the Erinyes, Corn.*ND* 10.
+μεγᾰκήτης, ες, *having the form* or *appearance of a monster* (usu. marine), δελφίς Il. 21.22, νηῦς 8.222, 11.5, 600; ὄρκυνοι μεγακήτεες Opp.*H.* 3.132, 546; of the Trojan Horse, Q.S. 12.151. **2** of the sea, *full of monsters*, μεγακήτεα πόντον Od. 3.158, A.R. 4.318.
μεγακλεής I, add 'gen. -κλέος Euph. in *Suppl.Hell.* 416.1'
μεγᾰλάμπρως, delete the entry.
μεγᾰλάμφοδος, add 'Sch.Gen.Il. 16.635'
Μεγαλάρτια, add 'at Delphi, *CID* 1.9*D*10 (v BC)'
*μεγᾰλᾶτος, ον, *involved in great ruin*, A.*Pers.* 1016, *Eu.* 791, 821.
μεγαλαυχής, for '= μεγάλαυχος' read '*lofty, proud*' and before 'Vett.Val. 272.8' insert 'in pejorative sense, *haughty, conceited*'
μεγᾰλαυχία, add '**3** in good sense, *pride*, *SEG* 18.293.14.'
*μεγᾰλευκτος, ον, *greatly prayed for*, sup., πίστιν .. τὰν μεγαλευκτοτάταν cj. for μεταλευκοτάταν in paean ap.Plu.*Flam.* 16.
*μεγᾰλία, ἡ, as honorific title, *highness*, [τ]ὴν [σὴν] μεγαλίαν *PCol.* 173.7 (iv AD).
*μεγᾰλοευπώγων, ωνος, ὁ, *having a large fine beard*, *Cat.Cod.Astr.* 7.217 (perh. μεγαλοπ- or εὐπ-).
+μεγᾰλόηχος, ον, *stirring up tumult, turbulent*, Sch.Pi.*P.* 12.38, *I.* 8.45, Hsch. s.v. ἐριβρεμέτης, ἐρίβρομον.
*μεγᾰλόθρονος, ον, *mightily enthroned* (unless to be derived from θρόνον), Ἥρη hymn in *SEG* 8.548.21 (Egypt, i BC).
μεγᾰλόθῡμος, add 'Plu. 2.614b'
*μεγᾰλόκλονος, ον, *loud-sounding*, *Trag.adesp.* 109d K.-S.
μεγᾰλομέρεια III, add '*SEG* 23.447 (ii AD)'
*μεγᾰλοναύτης, gloss on βουβάρας, Hsch.
μεγᾰλοπᾰρηος, thus, not -πάρηος.
*μεγᾰλόπλευρος, ον, *with big flanks*, gloss on ἐρίπλευρος, Sch.Pi.*P.* 4.419.
μεγᾰλοπολίτης, add 'also *citizen of Megalopolis*, *SEG* 23.226, 227'
*μεγᾰλοπόρως, adv. *bountifully*, *SB* 8267.30.
μεγᾰλοπρεπής I 2, sup. as honorific title, add '*SEG* 31.1401 (Palestine, v AD)' **3**, add 'of a writer, D.H.*Isoc.* 3'
μεγᾰλοσώματος, after '*large-bodied*' insert 'Plu.*fr.* 149 (p. 177 B.)'
μεγᾰλότης, add 'Plu. 2.441b (pl.)'
μεγᾰλοτρᾰχηλος, add 'Sch.D.Il. 10.305'
μεγᾰλόφθαλμος, after 'Ptol.*Tetr.* 143' insert '(v.l.)'
*μεγᾰλοφροσύνως, adv. *generously*, *IGRom.* 3.739 xvi 49, xviii 13 (Rhodiapolis, ii AD).
μεγᾰλύνω I, add '**2** *make long*, μεγαλύνουσι τὰ κράσπεδα i.e. *wear long tassels*, *Ev.Matt.* 23.5.'
μεγᾰλώνῠμος I, delete '*giving glory*' and insert '(?)Alc. 304.3 L.-P.'
μεγᾰλωστί II 1, before 'v.l.' insert '*greatly*, Phld.*Oec.* p. 6 J.'
μεγᾰνωρ, add '*GVAK* 11.3'
*μεγᾰρίζω (B), perform the rite of the μέγαρα, (v. °μάγαρον), Clem.Al.*Protr.* 2.17.1.
μέγᾰρον, read 'μέγαρον (A)' **IV**, delete the section.
*μέγᾰρον (B), v. °μάγαρον.
μέγας, line 3, after 'μεγάλα, etc.' insert 'Pamph. fem. acc. πόλι μhε[ι]άλα *IPamph.* 3.5 (Sillyon, iv BC)'; line 4, for 'and only once .. (anap.)' read 'voc. masc. μεγάλε A.*Th.* 822, *AP* 14.100, Them.*Or.* 13.163c' **C 1**, line 6, after 'Plu.*Lyc.* 19' insert 'μέδδων *IGC* p. 98 A24, 27, al. (Acraephia)'; line 7, μειζότερος, after 'elder' insert '*SEG* 33.1299 (Tiberias, iv AD)' **2**, add 'as title of gods, Διὶ τῶι Μεγίστωι *SEG* 33.675 (ii BC), etc.; cf. Demetrius Poliorcetes, Moretti *ISE* 7.2 (303/2 BC); of Emperors, Αὐτοκράτορα μέγιστον Νέρωνα Καίσαρα *SEG* 32.251, etc.; transl. Lat. *pontifex maximus*, ἀρχιερέα μέγιστον *SEG* 30.1635, etc.' add 'Myc. form of compar. *μέζως, *me-zo*, *me-zo-e* (pl.); sup. *me-ki-ta* (neut. pl.)'
μεγασθενής, line 2, for 'also' read 'of non-personal agents' and add 'οἶστρος Ἀφροδίτας Simon. 36.10 P.'
μεγαυχής, for '= μεγάλαυχος' read '*worthy of pride, glorious*'
μεγαύχητος, add 'epigr. in *Inscr.Cret.* 1.viii 33 (Cnossus, ii BC), Ph.Epic. in *Suppl.Hell.* 681.3'
μέγεθος II 1, add '*strength, force*, ἀνέμου Thphr.*Sign.* 29' **III**, add '**3** *body having magnitude, mass*, Arist.*GC* 321ᵇ16, al.'
μεγεθύνω I 1, line 2, after 'Iamb.*Protr.* 21 ιζ'' insert 'κόμην *let* .. *grow*, Aq.*Nu.* 6.5'
*μεγιστοῦχος, *holder of the highest office* (app. *high-priest*), Ph.Epic. in *Suppl.Hell.* 683.2.
*μεδιανόν, τό, Lat. *medianum, central hall*, *ISmyrna* 192.
μέδιμνος, before 'ὁ' insert 'Cret. ϝέδιμνος *Inscr.Cret.* 4.184.16 (Gortyn, ii BC)'; line 3, after 'corn-measure' insert '*SEG* 30.380 (Tiryns, vii BC)'
*Μεδίμῳ· ἥρωι Hsch.
μεθαιρέω, line 1, delete 'only' add '**II** *change over to*, ἥν περ μεθεῖλες τὴν τέχνην A.*fr.* 78c.56 R. **III** *remove*, μεθελόντω τὰ ἀναθήματα ἐς ἄλ[λον τ]όπον *ASAA* 30/32(1952/4).249, no. 1, line 21 (Rhodes). **IV** med., *change*, τὰ οἰκία *SIG* 344.72 (Teos, iv BC); [τὰ ἄρμενα] Teles p. 10 H.'
μεθάλλομαι II, add 'fig., ἐπ' ἄλλα ἀσύνδετα Longin. 20.2'
*μεθαύριον, v. °μεταύριον.
μεθελίτης, for 'dub. sens.' read 'perh. *mutton-butcher* (cf. μέθλην)'; line 2, after 'ib. 674' insert '*SB* 11003.7 (iv/v AD)'
μεθέπω, line 1, for 'Sapph.*Supp.* 23.8' read 'Sapph. 94.8 L.-P.' **I**, add '**4** *look after*, Il. 10.516 (tm.), Sapph. l.c.' **II**, for this section read '*pursue, follow* a course, occupation, γεηπονίην Ps.-Phoc. 161, αἶσαν Pi.*N.* 6, μοῦσαν *App.Anth.* 3.157.3; *go for, undertake*, ἕκοντι .. νώτῳ μεθέπων δίδυμον ἄχθος ἄγγελος ἔβαν Pi.*N.* 6.57. **2** *possess, have*, Nonn.*D.* 48.355, 362, al.'
*μεθερμηνεία, ἡ, *interpretation*, Zos.Alch. 118.14.
μεθημοσύνη, add '*TAM* 4(1).382'
μεθιδρύω, line 2, delete 'pass.'
μεθίημι, line 8, for 'Colluth. 127' read 'Coluth. 128' **II 2 b**, delete the section.
μεθιστάνω, form -άω, add '*Cod.Just.* 1.3.55.2'
μεθίστημι A II 2, place 'so in med. .. 18.9.5' in a parenthesis and add 'ἑαυτὸν ἐκ τοῦ ζῆν D.S. 3.5, cf. 4.55; τοῦ ζῆν μ. [τινα] *BGU* 36.13 (ii AD)' **B I 2**, line 5, for 'σκότος' read 'σκότον' and after 'Pl.*R.* 518a' insert 'ἐκ τοῦ ζῆν *PLond.* 354.10 (i BC)'
μεθοδεία, add '**III** *trade, employment*, Just.*Nov.* 122 pr.'
μεθοδευτής, add '**3** *investigator*, τῆς λεκιθώδους ὕλης Zos.Alch. 144.16.'
μεθοδεύω 3, after '*get round*' insert '*POxy.* 2342.27 (ii AD)' **5**, add '*SEG* 32.1554 (Arabia, vi AD)'
μεθόδιον II, for 'cf.' read '**III** *ingenious device*'
μέθοδος II, add '**6** *occupation, trade*, Just.*Nov.* 122.1, τὴν μέθοδον κραυβιτᾶς *AE* 1929.151 (Thessaly, v/vi AD).'
μεθόριος, line 10, after 'Plu.*Crass.* 22' insert 'ἐν μεθορίᾳ γῆς καὶ οὐρανοῦ Max.Tyr. 14(8).11; ἡ μεθορία *banishment*, Philostorgius in *PG* 65.480A'
Μεθυμναῖος, add 'perh. jocular version of °Μηθυμναῖος'

*μεθυποτίθημι, *pawn, mortgage*, *PPanop.* 21.20 (iv AD), *POxy.* 3355.13 (vi AD).

μεθύσκω, line 1, at end insert 'first at Hdt. 1.106 (κατ)εμέθυσα'

μεθύστερος II, line 2, for '*in a moment*' read '*never thereafter*'

μεθυτρόφος, for 'ἡμερίς Simon. 183.1' read '*AP* 7.24.1 ([Simon.])'

μείγνυμι, line 19, after '*S.fr.* 271 (anap.)' insert 'Critias Trag. 5.11 S.' B 4, add 'perh. also act. ellipt. in same sense, Ἐγέστρατος μοὶ μίσγη (?for μίσγει or ἐμίγη) Lang *Ath.Agora* XXI C8'

Μειλινόη, add 'cf. *Jahrb.Ergänzungsheft* vi(1905).13.26 (Pergamum, iii AD) (Μηλ-)'

μειλίσσω II, delete '*to be subdued* .. A.R. 3.531' III 2, line 2, after '*subdue*' insert 'πυρὸς μειλίσσετ' ἀυτμήν A.R. 3.531'

μειλίχιος I, add 'μειλίχιόν τε καὶ αἰνετὸν ἔργον *SEG* 31.1288 (iii AD)'

μείλιχος, line 1, for 'cj. in Sapph. 100' read 'Sapph. 2.11, 112.4 (cj.) L.-P.'

*μειξόκρουστος, ον, adj. of uncertain meaning describing clothing, *PVindob.* G16846 (*Tyche* 2.6; v. also ib. 7.63; vii AD).

μειονεκτέω, line 4, before 'c. gen. rei' insert 'Call.*fr.* 196.44 Pf., *to be at a disadvantage*, Arr.*An.* 3.8.7'

μειότης I, for '*minimizing*' read '*reduction to a minimum* (in context indicated by γέ in τουτό γέ μοι χάρισαι)'

μειόω II, line 2, after 'Pl.*Cra.* 409c' insert '(cited in supposed etym. of μείς)'

μειρᾰκιώδης I, delete 'τὸ μ., of style .. Longin. 3.4' II, after '*characteristic of youth*' insert '(as lacking in restraint, taste, etc.), *juvenile*' and add 'D.H.*Isoc.* 12, *Pomp.* 2, Longin. 3.4; adv. D.H.*Dem.* 29'

μείρομαι (A), line 5, after 'ἐμμόραντι' insert '(ἐμμόρατι La.)' II 2, for this section read '2 *fall to one's lot*, σε .. ἔμμορε κῦδος A.R. 4.1749. 3 w. predicative adj., *become by fate* such and such, πᾶν δὲ νόημα ἔμπληκτον μεμόρηκε Nic.*Al.* 213.' III, line 10, after '*destiny*' insert 'Antipho 1.21'; at end after 'μεμόρηται' insert 'A.R. 1.646' and after 'Man. 6.13' insert 'μεμόρητο A.R. 1.973'; delete 'but μεμορημένον .. μορέω (q.v.)' IV, add 'pf. part. μεμορημένος Nic.*Al.* 229'

μείς 3, add 'cf. Myc. adj. *me-no-e-ja*' at end add 'Myc. *me-no* (gen.)'

μεῖχμα, for 'Alc.*Supp.* 13.7' read 'Alc. 34(*b*).7 L.-P.'

μείων, line 4, after '(Tegea)' insert 'Boeot. μίων *BCH* 60.28 (Acraephia, ii BC)'; line 6, after '*less*' insert 'Il. 2.528, al., *smaller*, μείων κεφαλῇ Ἀγαμέμνονος Il. 3.193'; line 7, after 'A.*Supp.* 596 (lyr.)' insert 'Epich. 62'; line 8, delete '(not in other works of Hp.)'; line 9, delete 'or Com.'; line 10, before '*younger*' insert 'pl., *fewer*, Xenoph. l.c.; χρόνῳ μ. γεγώς'; at end add 'form μεϜjως(?), Myc. *me-wi-jo*, *me-u-jo*'

μείωσις, add 'b = °μειότης I, A.D.*Synt.* 267.25.'

*μελαγκᾰλᾶμον, τό, *ink and pen*, *PFouad* 74.9 (cj., cf. *Glotta* 35.299; v AD).

+μελαγκρήπις, ῖδος, fem. adj., perh. *having black shoes*, *Suppl.Hell.* 991.3 (poet. word-list, iii BC), Eust. 174.9, 1437.53.

μελάγχιμος, line 3, after 'A.*Pers.* 301' insert 'μελάγχιμον ἰόν A.R. 4.1508'

*μελαγχολαίνω, = μελαγχολάω, Sch.Gen.Il. 6.202.

*μελαγχρινός, ή, όν, = μελάγχροος, *Cat.Cod.Astr.* 12.149.1; cf. mod. Gk. μελαχρινός.

*μελαιναῖος, α, ον, *dark* (= μελανός), *Orac.Sib.* 5.349 (s.v.l.).

μελαινάς, delete the entry.

μελαίνω I 1, line 4, after 'Nic.*Al.* 472' insert '*darken*, Plu. 2.373d'; line 6, for 'D.H.*Pomp.* 2' read 'D.H.*Dem.* 5'; add 'of the moon, *to be darkened*, Plu.*Aem.* 17'

μελαμπέτᾰλος, add 'rest. in *Suppl.Hell.* 991.1 (poet. word-list, iii BC).'

Μελαμποδεῖον, add '*Schwyzer* 664.5 (Orchomenos, Arcadia, iv BC)'

μελάμπῡγος, after 'Archil. 110' insert 'Philostr.*VA* 2.36'

μελαμφᾱρής, add '*Trag.adesp.* 660.6 K.-S., *Suppl.Hell.* 991.4 (poet. word-list, iii BC)'

*μελάμφᾱρος, ον, = μελαμφαρής, *Hymn.Is.* 43, *ISmyrna* 728 (ii/iii AD).

μελάμφυλλος II, after 'Subst.' insert 'Μελάμφυλλος, ή, old name of Samos, Str. 10.2.17, 14.1.15, Iamb.*VP* 2.3'

μέλαν I 2, for this section read 'μ. Ἰνδικόν *indigo* or *Indian ink*, *Peripl.M.Rubr.* 39, cf. Plin.*HN* 35.43, 46' add '3 *lamp-black*, Ael.*NA* 17.25.'

μελᾰνάθήρ, for '(-αίθηρ Hsch.)' read 'also μελαναίθηρ *PCair.Zen.* 731.11 (iii BC), Hsch.'

μελανδίνης, after '*dark-eddying*' insert 'μελανδίναι .. ῥόες (-δεινη .. ροσσ lapis) *GVI* 1684.9 (Chersonesus, i/ii AD)'

μελάνζοφος, before '*EM*' insert 'Simon. 125 P.'

μελᾰνία I, line 2, before 'Str. 12.8.18' insert 'Thphr.*HP* 5.3.1' add '2 *darkening* (of the sky), X.*An.* 1.8.8; (morbid) *darkening* of the skin or flesh, Lxx Sch.*Le.* 13.39; pl., (in quot. fig.) Plb. 1.81.7.' II, delete the section.

μελάνιον, after '*ink*' insert '*Edict.Diocl.* 18.11, 11a'

*μελᾰνόβᾰφον, τό, perh. *ink-bottle*, *AJA* 63.275 (Sicily, iii BC).

*μελᾰνοπτεροφαιολοσώμᾰτος, ον, *having dark wings with a wholly grey body*, χελιδών *GLP* 1.95.9.

*μελᾰνοχαίτης, ου, masc. adj. *dark-haired*, Theognost.*Can.* 85.

*μελαντικός, ή, όν, *blackening*, ὕδωρ μ. τριχῶν Paul.Aeg. 3.2.3 (132.25 H.).

*μελάνωσις, εως, ή, = μέλανσις, Moses Alch. 309.10 (lemma).

μέλας I, line 7, after 'Od. 4.359' insert 'πόντος μ. E.*IT* 107'

μέλασμα I, add 'Gal. 12.266.13'

μελασμός I 1, add 'Gal. 17(2).803.2, 5 (pl.), 18(2).556.18'

μέλε (B), lines 5/6, delete '(who says .. women only)' and for '*Eq.* 668' read '*Eq.* 671'

*Μελεάγρεια, τά, festival in honour of Meleagros, *AS* 39.50 (Balbura), *SEG* 29.1439, 1441.

+μελεδαίνω, *be concerned about, worry* or *care about*, w. gen., πενίης Thgn. 1129, Theocr. 9.12; w. acc., Archil. 14 W., οὐ μελεδαίνει τὸν τὸ πιεῖν ἐγχεῦντα Theocr. 10.52. II *devote care to, take care of*, w. acc., *SIG* 2 (Sigeum, vi BC); τοὺς νοσέοντας Hdt. 8.115.3, τὰς ὑστέρας Hp.*Mul.* 1.17; id.*Morb.Sacr.* 8 (pass.), Aret.*CA* 6.10; see also μελεταίνω.

*μελεδών (B) (or -ῶν)· φροντιστής, μεριμνητής, ἐπίτροπος, οἰκονόμος, προεστώς, φύλαξ Hsch.

*μελεοκοπέω, = μελοκοπέω, Heph.Astr. 2.18.66, 2.25.11.

μελεταίνω, add 'cf. °μελεδαίνω'

*μελετητής, οῦ, ὁ, *trainer, coach*, Aristid.*Or.* 50(26).28.

μελετητικός, add 'III μελετητικὴ ποιότης ῥημάτων *desiderative* (e.g. *lecturio*), Dosith. p. 406 K.'

μέλι I, add 'Myc. *me-ri*, *me-ri-to* (gen.); adj. *me-ri-ti-jo*' II, for pres. def. read 'perh. *honeydew*'

μελία I, add 'μελίας καρπός· τὸ τῶν ἀνθρώπων γένος Hsch.'

μελίαμβοι, after 'Cercidas' insert '(Κερκιδᾶ κυνὸς μ. title in *POxy.* 1082 *fr.* 4)'

*μελῐανθής, ές, *honey-scented*, μελιανθέος οἴνης Nic.*Al.* 58.

μελῐβόας, for '*sweet-singing*' read '*with honeyed tones*, ὕμνος Lasus 1 P.'

μελίεφθον, for '*honey-jar*' read 'app. *pan for boiling honey*'

*μελίέψιον, τό, *boiled honey, something boiled with honey*, *BGU* 2355.5 (ii/iii AD).

*μελιεψός, ὁ, *honey-boiler*, *SB* 11003.8.

μελίζω (B), line 3, after 'Med.' insert 'κάλλα μελισδομέναι Alcm. 35 P.'

μελίθροος, add '*SEG* 33.563 (Thrace, iii AD)'

*μελῐκηρίδιον, τό, dim. of °μελικήριον, *POxy.* 3406.11 (iv AD).

μελῐκήριον, for '*honey-comb*' read '*honey-cake*'

μελικτής, for '*singer, player*, esp. *flute-player*' read '*musician*'

μελίνη I, after '*S.fr.* 608' insert '-ην ἀντὶ πυρῶν ἀλλάττεσθαι Aristid.*Or.* 34(50).6, *Edict.Diocl.* 1.6' II, for '*Edict.Diocl.* .. *Aeg.*)' read '*Edict.Diocl.* 8.29'

*μελίουργός, ὁ, *honey-maker*, *Gp.* 15.3.7.

μελίσκιον, delete 'Alcm. 65 .. A.D.)'

*μελίσκον, τό, dim. of μέλος, *a little song*, Alcm. 36 P.

μέλισσα III, line 2, after 'S.*OC* 481' insert 'Nic.*Al.* 374'

μελίσσειος II, add 'cf. mod. Gk. μελίσσι'

μελισσοβότᾰνον, for '*balm, Melissa officinalis*' read 'expl. of μελίτεια'

*μελισσός, ὁ, name of a bird, Cyran. 92 (3.27.1 K.).

+μελισσόφυλλον, τό, name given to one or more fragrant herbs, Thphr.*HP* 6.1.4, Dsc. 3.103, 104.

μελισσόφῠτον, τό, read '-φῦτος, ή'

*μελιτᾶ(s), ὁ, *honey-merchant*, Παύλου τοῦ μελιτα[. *SB* 13036 (*Tyche* 6.232).

+μελίτεια, ή, a fragrant herb, perh. the same as °μελισσόφυλλον, Theoc. 4.25, 5.130.

μελῐτερπής, for 'Simon. 184.9' read '*AP* 7.25.9 ([Simon.])'

*μελίτευχής, ές, *honey-producing*, παγά *B.fr.* 28.14 S.-M.

μελίτῖνος, for pres. def. read '*made* or *flavoured with honey*'; after 'Diog.ap.D.L. 6.51' insert 'οἴνου μελιτ(ίνου) Lang *Ath.Agora* XXI He30'; before 'στεφάνια' insert '2 *honey-coloured*' and add '*POxy.* 3201.3 (iii AD)'

*μελίτρῐχος, ον, *having honey-coloured hair*, *Cat.Cod.Astr.* 10.187, 190, 216.

μελίφρων I, add 'of persons, *AP* 13.12 (Hegesipp.)'

*μελίφωνος, ον, *honey-voiced*, Sapph. 185 L.-P., *AP* 9.66 (Antip.Sid.).

μελίχλωρος, add '2 μ. (sc. λίθος), ή, a precious stone, Plin.*HN* 37.191.'

μελίχροος I 2, before 'in gen.' insert 'Lat. *melichrus*, Lucr. 4.1160; τὸν ὠχρὸν ὑποκοριζόμενος μελίχρουν Plu. 2.45a' add 'III μελίχρους (sc. λίθος), ή, a precious stone, Plin.*HN* 37.191.'

μέλλαξ, add '*SEG* 26.1717 (tab.defix., Egypt, iii/iv AD)'

μελλάρχων, add 'inscr. in *Syria* 29.326 (Arabia, iii AD)'

μελ(λ)είρην, after 'at Sparta' substitute '*boy about to become an* εἴρην, in sixth year of public education, i.e. in thirteenth of his age, Plu.*Lyc.* 17, Ἡροδότου Λέξεις in Stein Hdt. ii p. 465 (Berlin 1871)'

*μελ(λ)έπαρχος, ὁ, *eparch-designate*, *Ann.Épigr.* 1984.839b (?v AD).

μελλέφηβος, before 'Censorin.' insert '*IG* $2^2$.2986 (ii BC), 2991 (i BC)'

μελλησμός I, add '*PVindob.Tandem* 2.22 (iii AD)'

μελλητικός, add 'II τὸ μ. app. = τὸ μέλλον, κατὰ τοῦ μ. μηδὶς ἀνοίξῃ *CIJud.* 1.652 (Syracuse; -τεικοῦ).'

*μελλῐχόμειδος, ον, voc. -ε (or -ες fr. μελλιχομείδης), *gently smiling*, Alc. 384 L.-P.

+μελλόγαμβρος· μελλονύμφιος Hsch.

*μελλογραμμᾰτεύς, έως, ὁ, *γραμματεύς-designate*, *CIJud.* 1.121, 279 (Rome).

μελλογυμνᾰσίαρχος, add '*POxy.Hels.* 15.6 (i AD)'

*μελλολέων, λέοντος, ὁ, *one about to be a λέων* VI, the final grade in Mithraic initiation, *MDAI(R)* 49.206 (Dura, pl.).

*μελλονύμφη, ἡ, = μελλόνυμφος, ἡ, *CIJud.* 1.106 (Rome), cf. Poll. 3.45.

*μελλονύμφιος, = μελλόνυμφος, of a man, Phryn.Com. 78, *CIJud.* 1.148 (Rome), Hsch. s.v. μελλόγαμβρος.

μελλόνυμφος, lines 3/4, delete 'Phryn. .. -νύμφιος)'

μελλοπρύτανις, after '*πρύτανις-designate*' insert '*IEphes.* 1051.4 (i/ii AD)'

μέλλω IV, add 'with day of the week, ἐν τῇ μελλούσῃ παρασκευῇ *Hesperia* 54.214 no. 1 (iii AD)'

μελοποιέω II 1, add '*SEG* 11.52c (Isthmus, ii AD)'

μέλος A, add '4 *member* of a group, (Lat. *membrum*), Just.*Nov.* 109 pr.'

μέλπω II, line 5, after 'Paus. 1.2.5' insert '*IG* $2^2$.5056, 5060'

*μελύγιον, *intoxicating drink made from honey*, gloss. in *POxy.* 1802.36 (ii/iii AD); μελύγειον *EM* 578.8, μελίγυον Zonar.

μέλω A III 2, at end for 'aor. .. 200' read 'also καὶ μέλονται πρός τινος ἢ Διὸς ἢ .. Ἀθάνας *Trag.adesp.* 167c.4 K.-S., cf. μεληθὲν βάρβιτον *AP* 5.200 (s.v.l.)' B II, line 4, after 'c. dat.' insert 'τῇ παιδὶ .. μεμέλησο *AP* 5.220.7 (Agath.)'

μελῳδία II, add 'μ. ἡ τραγῳδία τὸ παλαιὸν ἐλέγετο Call.*fr.* 462 Pf.'

+μελῳδικός, ή, όν, *of* or *involving singing*, μ. κίνησις Cleonid.*Harm.* 2, Ptol.*Harm.* 3.5; πειθώ Aristid.Quint. 2.10; opp. λογικός, Aristox.*Harm.* 10.

μέμνεο, etc., for 'μιμνῄσκω' read 'μιμνήσκω'

Μεμνόνειον I, add 'pl., *Suppl.Hell.* 984.11'

*μεμοριάλιος, ὁ, Lat. *memorialis*, class of clerk in the civil service, *Cod.Just.* 4.59.1.2.

+μεμόριον, τό, *grave-monument*, (fr. cross-influence between μνημεῖον and Lat. *memoria*), *IGRom.* 4.1650 (Philadelphia), Ramsay *Cities and Bishoprics* 2.736 (iii/iv AD), *T&MByz.* 7.323 no. 15 (iv/v AD); also μημόριον *SEG* 2.393, 404 (Maced.), μιμόριον *IG* 10(2).353 (Thessalonica, iv AD); μημώριον *SEG* 31.855; μημούρηων *BCH* suppl. 8 no. 294 (v AD); applied to a *martyrium*, *BCH* suppl. 8 no. 1 (v/vi AD); see also ‡μνημόριον.

μεμπτός, after '*blameworthy*' insert 'Alc. 1.8 L.-P.'

*Μεμφίτης, ου, ὁ, v. °τεφρίας.

μέμφομαι 3, add 'b w. dat. of thing censured only, *AP* 5.299.6 (Agath.), 6.71.10 (Paul.Sil.).' 6, for '*GDI* 4998 (Gortyn)' read '*Inscr.Cret.* 4.41 vii 13 (Gortyn, v BC), al., Just.*Nov.* 100.1.1, al.'

*μεμψῐμοίρημα, ατος, τό, perh. *document of public censure*, μ]εμψιμοιρηματ[ .. *SEG* 33.888 (Ephesus).

μέμψις, add '3 legal *complaint*, *charge*, *Cod.Just.* 1.4.29.8, 1.4.34.7; κινῆσαι τὴν κατὰ τῆς διαθήκης μέμψιν ib. 6.4.4.16.'

*Μενδήσιον, τό, *temple of Mendes* (prob. identified w. *Pan*), *POxy.* 3332.5 (i AD).

μενεδήϊος, after 'Il. 12.247' insert 'τὸ πάρος μενεδήϊος ἦσθα'

μενέδουπος, add 'Hsch. s.v. βρυαλίκται'

Μενέλᾱος, line 2, after 'Dor.' insert 'nom. Μενέλας Jeffery *LSAG* pl. 69 no. 47 (*c.*600 BC)'

μενετός, after '*patient*' insert 'κριταί Cratin. 171.6 K.-A.'

μενέχαρμος, add '*GDRK* 17'.9'

μενοεικής, add 'A.R. 3.984, Opp.*H.* 5.374'

μένος, add 'as element in pers. n., already in Myc. *e-u-me-ne* Εὐμένης'

μένω, line 2, after '(Tegea, iv BC)' insert '*BCH* 111.168.6 (Mantinea, iv BC)' I 2 b, add 'in pregnant sense, *CR* 46.250 (Asia Minor)' II 1, line 5, after 'E.*Ph.* 740' insert '*wait for the end of*, χειμῶνα Hes.*Op.* 652; χεῖμα *AP* 6.221 (Leon.Tarent.), Q.S. 7.137; λαίλαπα id. 8.379'

*μεραρχέω, perh. *to be governor of a district*, Robert *Hell.* 10.24 (?Byzantium).

μέρδει, add 'act. aor. μέρσε, *IParion* 52.10; cf. ἀμέρδω'

μέρεια, after lemma insert '(or μερεία)'

μερίζω I 2, add '*distribute* by testamentary disposition, *PUps.Frid* 1.6, 9,14 (AD 48)'

μεριμνάω, 4 lines fr. end, before 'pass.' insert 'med., μεμεριμνημένους περὶ τὸν πορισμόν Onos. 1.20'

μεριμνητής, add 'gloss on °μελεδών, Hsch.'

μερίς I 1, add 'βελτίων μερίς Men.*Dysc.* 283' II, for this section read '*category*, *division*, E.*Supp.* 238, D. 18.64; *faction*, ἡ Σύλλα μερίς Plu. 2.203b'; transfer 'Pl.*Lg.* 692b' to section I 1 and 'Jul.*ad Them.* 253c' to section I 3 d.

*μέρισις, εως, ἡ, = μερισμός, *PLond.* 394.13, 15 (vi/vii AD).

μέρισμα, add 'II prob. *inlaid work*, *IGLS* 3.733.'

μεριστής, add 'II pl., financial officials at Istria, *IHistriae* 6, al. (iii BC).'

μερῑτεία I, add '*PMich.*II $121^v$ i 9 (i AD), al.; written μεριτία in *APF* 10.214 (ii AD)'

μέρμερος I, line 1, delete '(only in Il.)'; line 3, delete 'in Hom. always' II, add 'cf. pers. n. Μέρμερος Il. 14.513, -ίδης Od. 1.259'

μερμηρίζω II, line 4, after '(Od.) 16.256' insert 'Call.*Epigr.* 8.5 Pf.'

μερμηρικοί, for 'πειρᾶται' read 'πειραταί'

μερμίλλων, after 'μορμίλλων' insert '*SEG* 32.1145 (Erythrae)'

μέρμῑς, for 'dat. pl. .. Zonar.' read 'also μέρμῑθος, ὁ, -α, ἡ, -ον, τό, μερμίθαις Agatharch. 47, μέρμιθα· μέρμιθον, σπαρτίον, λεπτὸν σχοινίον, ἢ ἀργυροῦν δεσμόν Hsch., μέρμιθος· ἡ σχοῖνος Zonar.'

*μερμνάδαι· οἱ τρίορχοι (Lydian), Andron ap.*POxy.* 1802.46; as name of Lydian dynasty, Hdt. 1.7.1.

μέρμνος, delete 'Call.*Aet.Oxy.* 2080.68'; add 'gen. μέρμνου (nom. incert.), Call.*fr.* 43.66 Pf.; cf. pers. n. Μέρμνων Theocr. 3.35'

*μεροΐς, ίδος, ἡ, plant with lettuce-like leaves found at Meroë, also called αἰθιοπίς, Plin.*HN* 24.163.

*μέροξος, ὁ, = λευκογραφίς, Paul.Aeg. 7.3 (237.7 H.).

μέρος II 2, add 'Ἀρχὸν ἐξ Ὑπνίας κὰτ τὸ μέρος ἐλέσσθ[ων] *SEG* 23.305 (Delphi, 190 BC)' IV 1, add '*act* of a play, M.Ant. 12.36, Platon.*Diff.Com.* p. 4' add '6 *the part facing in a particular direction, side*, Hdt. 4.101.1, Th. 7.80.2; ἐξ ἀμφοτέρων μερῶν τοῦ δρόμου *OGI* 56.52 (Canopus, iii BC), cf. *PPetr.* 3 p. $43(2)^v$ iv 11 (247/6 BC), Lxx *Ex.* 32.15.'

μέροψ I, add 'of devotees in relation to a god, σῶν μερόπων Luc.*Trag.* 193, *IG* $2^2$.4533.5 (iii AD)' add '2 spec., of the supposed original inhabitants of Cos descended from Merops (Il. 2.831, al.), Κόως .. πόλις Μερόπων ἀνθρώπων *h.Ap.* 42; subst., Pi.*N.* 4.26, *I.* 6.31, *Suppl.Hell.* 903A.1, 13. 3 μέροπες· οἱ ἄφρονες ὑπὸ Εὐβοέων, in *POxy.* 1802.47.'

*μές (B), Thess. *until*, w. gen. μὲς μὲν τᾶς τετράδος *SEG* 31.577, μὲς τᾶς πέμπτας *BCH* 59.55 (both Larissa, ii BC); cf. μέστε, μέσφα, etc.

μέσᾰβον, line 3, for '(Call.)*Fr.* 513' read '*fr.* 651 Pf.' and after 'γλυφαί)' insert '177.5 Pf.'

μεσᾰβόω, for '*yoke, put to*' read '*fasten to the yoke*'

μεσάγκῠλον, add 'II *the thong* of such a javelin, Philostr.*Gym.* 31.'

μεσάζω, line 1, after 'D.S. 1.32' insert 'of a person, Aq. 1*Ki.* 17.4' add 'III *be in control*, *PMerton* 46.7, 12 (vi AD).'

*μεσαιπόλος, ον, perh. *going in the middle*, Ἀδρία βαθύπλου .. μεσαιπόλε πόντου Mesom. 6.2 H.

μέσακλον, for '*weaver's beam*' read '*heddle-rod*' and after '1*Ki.* 17.7' insert '(vv.ll. μέσακνον, μεσάντιον)'

*μεσάλουργής, ές, *middling purple*, χιτωνίσκος *IG* $2^2$.1524.189 (Brauron, iv BC).

*μεσᾰρίστερος, ον, of a horse, prob. the one in a team of four next to the left-hand side of the pole, *SEG* 34.1437 (Syrian, Apamea, v/vi AD).

*μεσάρκειος, v. °μεσερκ-.

*μεσαυλικός, ή, όν, of °μεσαύλιον (B), μεσαυλικὰ κρούματα Aristid. Quint. 1.11.

+μεσαύλιον (A), τό, *inner courtyard*, *Vit.Aesop.* in *POxy.* 2083.27.

*μεσαύλιον (B), τό, *piece of aulos music played in the intervals of a choral ode*, Eust. 862.19.

μέσαυλος I, add 'Ar.*fr.* 387 K.-A. b μέσαυλον καὶ νῦν κατοικία ἀγροτική, τουτέστιν ἔπαυλις Eust. 1664.26.' II, for 'Att. .. in full' read 'adj., of the door *between the* αὐλή *and the inner part of the house*' add 'III μέσαυλον, τό, *colonnaded court* of a church, synagogue, etc., *Rev.Phil.* 32.36 (Side, v/vi AD).'

μεσεγγύη, after '*party*' insert '*PAnt.* 35 ii 14 (iv AD)'

μεσέγγυος II, add '*in trust*, μ. τὴν μείρακα καταθέσθαι Ar.*fr.* 746 K.-A.'

*μεσεγγύωσις, ἡ, *depositing of security*, prob. in Charis. 33 K.

*μεσεμβρίη, v. ‡μεσημβρία.

μεσέρκειος, add 'written μεσσάρκειος *Tit.Cam.* 126 (vi BC), μεσάρ- ib. 127'

μέση I, add '2 perh. the name of a Delphic Muse, Νήτας. Μέσσας. Ὑπάτας (from the strings of the lyre) *SEG* 30.382 (Argos, *c.*300 BC), cf. Plu. 2.744c.' add 'IV (sc. ἡμέρα) *midday*, *SEG* 32.1149 (Magnesia on the Maeander, AD 209), the *south*, Call.*Del.* 280.'

μεσηγύ, line 2, delete 'only in' and insert 'A.R. 4.602' I 2, add 'μεσσηγὺς τοῦ τε ὤμου καὶ τοῦ τραχήλου J.*AJ* 19.1.14' II, add 'A.R. 3.723, 930'

*μεσηλικία, ἡ, *middle age*, *SB* 6133.9, *MAMA* 7.263.

μεσημβρία, line 2, after 'Arr.*Ind.* 3.8, al.' insert 'also μεσεμβρίη *SEG* 37.576 (Maced., iv BC)'

**μεσημβρίζω**, add '**2** of stars, *shine at midday*, Nonn.*D.* 7.297.'
**μεσημέριος**, add 'cf. mod. Gk. μεσημέρι'
**μεσήρης**, after '*midmost*' insert 'μεσέρε̄ς perh. on vase in *AION* (*A*) 6.281ff.'
**μεσῑτεία**, after '*mortgaging*' insert '(used in connection with catoecic land)' and add '*BGU* 2473.11 (*c*.AD 100)'
**μεσῑτεύω I 3**, for this section read '*pledge*, *mortgage* in connexion with catoecic land, *CPR* 1.1.19 (ii AD)'
**μεσίτης I 1**, add '**b** official entrusted with collection and disbursement of taxes, *CPR* 6.9.1, 2 (v/vi AD), *REG* 70.120 (Palestine, vi/vii AD).'
**μέσκος**, add '(in Hsch.), unless mistake for πέσκος'
***μεσμίρω**, *become runny*, *flow*, Anon.Alch. 323.24.
**μεσόγαιος I**, add 'μεσόγειος, ον, *Peripl.M.Rubr.* 2' **II 1**, add 'μεσόγειος, ἡ, spec., *the interior region of Attica*, Arist.*Ath.* 21.4'
***μεσοκώμιον**, τό, *centre of a village*, Mitchell *N.Galatia* 181 (AD 145).
**μεσονύκτιον**, at end, μεσανύκτιον, add '*SEG* 30.622 (Maced., i AD); cf. mod. Gk. μεσάνυχτα, neut. pl., μεσόνυχτι, τό (poet.)'
***μεσοπλᾰτείτης**, ου, ὁ, *resident in "the middle street"*, cj. in *IMylasa* 403; cf. °ξυστοπλατείτης.
**μεσοπόρος**, read '**μεσόπορος**' and for '*going .. middle*' read '*of the mid-passage*: μ. πελάγεσσιν *in the deep-sea ways*'
***Μεσοποτᾰμηνός**, όν, *of Mesopotamia*, *POxy.* 3053.16 (AD 252).
***μεσόπυργος**, ἡ, *a construction between towers*, *AArch.Syr.* 15.75 (Syria, vi AD), rest. at *SEG* 25.733 (Moesia, i BC).
***Μεσορή, Μεσορί**, name of a month, *AP* 9.383.12, *PSI* 635.15 (iii BC), *SEG* 24.1237 (Egypt), 33.1445 (Cyrenaica), al.
**μέσος I 3 b**, add 'applied to a go-between, ὁ διδοὺς καὶ ὁ λαμβάνων καὶ ὁ μέσος γενόμενος Just.*Nov.* 123.2.1, al.' **III 1 a**, line 8, after 'id.*Hec.* 1150' insert 'ἐν μhέσōι Κεφαλε̂ς τε καὶ ἄστεος *CEG* 304.1 (Attica, vi BC)' **c**, line 2, after '(D.) 18.294' insert 'ἀπελθ' ἐκ τοῦ μ. Men.*Dysc.* 81 S.' **e**, add 'also ἀνὰ μ. = μεταξύ, *SEG* 9.8.64 (Cyrene, i AD)' **3**, add 'τὸ μ. *moderation*, E.*Hyps.fr.* 1 iii 33 B.' **IV**, add 'ἡ μέση τῶν ποταμῶν (sc. χώρα) *Mesopotamia*, Hdn.Gr. 1.331, Philostr.*VA* 1.20'
**μεσοστροφωνίαι**, add '(perh. read μεσσοστροφώνιαι, see *REA* 62.303/4)'
**μεσόστῡλον**, before 'Sch.Od.' insert '*MDAI(A)* 31.431 (ii BC)'; add 'also app. a structure erected in such a space, *Cod.Just.* 1.4.26.8'
**μεσόσφαιρος**, add 'Plin.*HN* 12.44'
**μεσότακτος**, delete the entry.
***μεσοτέλεστος**, ον, *half-finished*, Aetolian acc. to gloss. in *POxy.* 1802.51 (ii/iii AD).
***μεσοτοίχιον**, τό, *party-wall*, *PDura* 19.13 (i AD).
**μεσουρᾰνέω II**, add 'Ptol.*Tetr.* 33'
**μεσουράνησις**, delete 'Plot. 3.1.5 (pl.)'
**μεσόφθαλμος**, after '*eyes*' insert 'Ptol.*Tetr.* 143'
***μεσόφρυς**, υος, ἡ, = μεσόφρυον, *PSI* 1140.12 (ii AD); in pl., ib. 907.21 (i AD), *PSoterichos* 25.9 (AD 109), *POxford* 11.7 (ii AD).
***μεσοχορέω**, *serve as* μεσόχορος I, *IHistriae* 167, 207 (ii AD).
**μεσόχορος I**, add '*IHistriae* 100 (iii AD), v. °μουσόχορος'
**μεσόω 1**, of time, add 'μεσο(ῦντος) Νο(εμβρίου) *SEG* 30.1648 (ii/iii AD), *Salamine* 27 (Cyprus, ii/iii AD)'
**μέσπιλον**, for 'ῐ Archil. .. Eub. 74.4' read 'ῑ *APl.* 255, ῐ Eub. 74.4 K.-A.'
**⁺μέσσᾱβον**, v. ‡μέσαβον.
**μέσσᾰτος**, line 3, after 'D.P. 204' insert 'ἐν μεσάτοισι κλύδωνος ἀνωίστου τε κυδοιμοῦ orac.ap.Porph.*Plot.* 22'; add 'Myc. *me-sa-ta* (?nom. pl. fem.), *of middle size* or *quality*'
***μεσσίκιος**, v. °μισσίκιος.
***μεσσοδόμα**, v. μεσόδμη II.
**μέσσα**, line 2, after '(Cyrene)' insert 'v.l. in Call.*Cer.* 92, 111'
**μέσφα 2**, line 2, for '(Call.)*Hec.* 1.1.4' read '*fr.* 260.4 Pf.' add 'see also °μές, μεσπόδι, μέστα, μέστε, μέττα'
**μετά**, line 2, after 'πεδά (q.v.)' insert 'which is a different word; μέ *IG* 7.2712.95 (Acraephia, i AD) (cf. μεταυτα for μετὰ ταῦτα)'; line 3, after 'acc.' insert 'Myc. *me-ta* (w. dat.)' **C II 3**, lines 6/7, for 'A.*Th.* 1080' read 'A.*Th.* 1074' **IV**, add 'ἔχων μετὰ χεῖρα τὴν Ἀνθίαν holding A. *by* the hand, X.Eph. 1.12.1'
**μεταβαίνω II**, after 'μεταβῆσαι' insert 'and perh. in fut. μεταβήσειν' and after 'Pi.*O.* 1.42' insert 'μεταβάσοντας ἐλθεῖν Ποίαντος υἱόν id.*P.* 1.52 (cj.)'
**μεταβάλλω A III 1**, at end delete 'c. gen. rei' and after 'καιναὶ καινῶν' insert '(or καίν' ἐκ καινῶν)'
***μεταβαστάζω**, expl. of Lat. *convecto* in Virgil gloss. (cf. Verg.*A.* 7.749), *PNess.* 1.865 (vi AD).
**μεταβλέπω II**, for '*look after*' read '*look towards*'
**μεταβλητός**, add 'Procl.*Inst.* 76 D., al.'
**μεταβολή II**, add '**8** *translation*, Modest.*Dig.* 27.1.1.1.'
**⁺μεταβουλία**, ἡ, *change of heart*, Simon. 38.23 P.
**μεταγγίζω**, line 2, after 'Gal. 11.215' insert '*SEG* 33.1221a (Bactria, ii BC)'

**Μεταγειτνιών**, add '**Μεταγειτονιῶ[νος]** *Inscr.Délos* 338*Aa*42 (iii BC)'
**μεταγενής 2**, after 'D.H.*Th.* 9' insert 'Modest.*Dig.* 1.4.4'
**⁺μεταγίγνομαι**, *fall as a share* to, ᾧ δ' αὖτε γάμου μετὰ μοῖρα γένηται Hes.*Th.* 607. **2** *migrate*, Lxx *2Ma.* 2.1.
**μετᾰγω I 1**, add 'pass., *to be diverted*, of funds, *IEphes.* 17.52 (i AD)'
**μεταδετέον**, for '*one must untie*' read '*one must change the tethering* (from one place to another)'
**μεταδιατᾰγή**, after '*POxy.* 899.40' insert 'al.'
**μεταδιατίθεμαι**, add '*PMich.*inv. 4719 (*BASP* 22.327, i AD)'
**μεταδίδωμι 2**, add 'πάντα τῇ ψυχῇ καλά *GVI* 1113a.5 (Apamea, ii AD), 1978.17'
**μεταδιεράω**, add '**2** as t.t. in wrestling (precise sense unclear), *POxy.* 466.11 (ii AD).'
***μετάδοτος**, η, ον, *shared*, prob. in *Stud.Pal.* 22.184.32 (ii AD).
**μετάδουπος**, for '*falling at haphazard*, *indifferent*' read '*thundering* (?)*changeably*, i.e. *of uncertain portent*'
**Μετάδως**, for 'αἰδώς' read 'δώς'
**μέταζε**, for '= μεταξύ' read 'τὰ μ. *afterwards*' and delete 'but .. Δωριεῖς'
**μεταθόω**, for '*appease by sacrifice*' read '*repeat an offering* (only med. attested)'
**μεταιβολία**, delete the entry.
**μεταίρω II**, for '*depart*' read '*move* (*elsewhere*)'
**μεταίτης**, for 'Ph. 2.516' read 'Ph. 2.526'
**μεταίχμιος**, line 8, after 'Arist.*PA* 676ᵃ2' insert '*Iamb.adesp.* 2 W.'
**μετακατασκευάζω**, add '*SEG* 33.1040.4 (Aeolian Cyme, ii BC), *TAM* 5(1).242 (AD 209/210)'
***μετακηδεύω**, *move to another tomb*, *TAM* 2(3).1166.11 (Lycia) (pass.).
**μετακιᾰθω I**, add '**2** *follow up*, *continue the example of*, πατρὸς λώβην Nic.*Th.* 132.'
**μετακῑνέω 1**, after 'Hdt. 9.74' insert '*IG* 2².13200 (Attica, AD 160)' and transfer '*IG* 5(1).1390' to section 2. **2**, add '*PVindob.* G25945.12 (*Tyche* 2.48, iii AD)'
**μετακίνησις 1**, add '*change of formation* of troops, τὰς μεταβολάς τε τῶν τάξεων καὶ τὰς μ. Arr.*Tact.* 9.4'
**μετακινητέος**, add '**2** *to be changed*, ἔθος Gal. 6.410.12.'
**⁺μετακῑνητός**, ή, όν, *able to be changed*, ὁμολογία Th. 5.21.2; νόμοι Solon ap.Plu. 2.152a.
***μετάκλωσμα**, ατος, τό, *that which is interwoven*, fig., μοιρῶν ἀνάγκης τε μετάκλωσμα Cyran. 5 (ἐπίκλωσμα K.).
**⁺μετακομῐδή**, ἡ, *moving from one place to another*, *transportation* of grain *SEG* 39.1180.74 (Ephesus, i AD); *moving* from one bed to another, pl., Gal. 18(2).503.14.
**μετακομίζω**, add '**2** *transpose* into a different dialect, D.H.*Dem.* 41.'
**μετακύνιον**, add 'Simon.Ath.*Eq.* 5'
**μεταλαμβάνω V**, add '**3** *write down from dictation*, Porph.*Plot.* 8.'
***μετάλημψις**, εως, ἡ, = μετάληψις, *POxy.* 1200.36 (iii AD).
***μετάληξις**, subst. corresponding to μεταλήγω, only as pers. n., *SEG* 23.87 (Attica, iv BC).
***μεταληπτός**, gloss on πεδάγρετος, Hsch.
**μετάληψις II 4**, line 2, after 'Trypho *Trop.* 5, etc.' insert 'D.H.*Th.* 31'
**μεταλλεύω I 4**, add '*IKyzikos* 560' add '**6** fig., *exploit as if a mine*, prob. in Phld.*Oec.* p. 26 J.; cf. mod. Gk. ἐκμεταλλεύομαι *exploit*.'
**μεταλλίζω**, add '*Basilica* 35.1.9 Sch.'
**μέταλλον II**, add '**b** Lat. *metallum*, *marble paving-slab*, *JS* 1988.30 (Apamea, Chr.).'
***μεταλλωρῠχος**, ὁ, *sapper*, *FGrH* no. 533 2.20 J. (pl., ii AD).
***μεταμειπτός**, όν, *exchangeable*, rest. in Hes.*fr.* 43(a).43 M.-W.
***μεταμελλοδῠνᾱ**, ἁ, *remorse*, Cerc. 2(b).13 D.³.
**μετάμελος II**, add 'δύνασθαι τὸν μετάμελον .. ἀνακαλεῖσθαι (sc. τὴν δωρεάν) Just.*Nov.* 87 pr.'
***μεταμπελεύω**, ?*transplant vines*, Heph.Astr. 3.5.69.
***μεταναγρᾰφή**, ἡ, *re-registration*, *transfer in the books*, prob. in *IEphes.* 14.34 (i AD).
**μεταναστεύω 2**, for 'ib. 61(62).6' read 'ib. 61(62).7'
**μετανάστης**, for '(μεταναστῆναι, cf. ὑπερανάστης)' read '(sts. taken as μετανά-στης or for *μεταναστάτης, but prob. to be analysed as μετα-νάστης; cf. μεταναίω, °νάστης)'
**⁺μετανέομαι**, *visit*, *approach*, εὐνήν Musae. 205, Nonn.*D.* 14.89, ἄλλον ἐνηείῃ μετανεύμενος, ἄλλον ἀπειλῇ ib. 29.7, 36.161.
**μετανίσομαι**, after lemma insert 'or **μετανίσσομαι**'; line 1, for '*pass over*' read '*change position*, *cross over*'; line 2, after 'Od. 9.58' insert 'of the polar axis, οὐδ' ὀλίγον μετανίσεται Arat. 21'
**μεταξάβλαττα**, read '**μεταξαβλάττη**'
**μεταξάριος**, add '*SEG* 32.1439 (Syria, AD 516), *ITyr* 22, 98'
***μεταξένια**, τά, app. some form of offerings, *CID* 7 A 26 (v BC).
***μέταξος**, ἡ, = μέταξον, Just.*Nov.* app. 5.
**μεταξύ I 2 b**, add 'Plu. 2.240a,b; μ. ἐβίω Ruf.*Ren.Ves.* 2.4' **II 1**, after '*POxy.* 914.8 (v AD)' insert '*Cod.Just.* 1.3.45.13, 1.4.33.2'
***μεταπαραβολή**, ἡ, astron., *conjunction*, Simp. *in Cael.* 471.9.

*μεταπερισπάω, prob. *divert*, τοῦ Δημητρίου μεταπερισπασθέντος εἰς δημοσίαν χρείαν *PFam.Teb.* 24.54 (ii AD).

μεταπιπράσκω, add '*PVatic.Aphrod.* 10.13 (vi AD)'

μεταπίπτω I 1 a, line 4, after 'A.D.*Adv.* 188.25' insert 'ὁ λόγος θαμινὰ μ., of *changes* of construction, D.H.*Dem.* 39'

*μεταπλᾰνάομαι, *disperse* or *wander off into*, w. acc., ζῷα ἄλογα μεταπλανώμεναι λοιπὸν διατελέσετε, of metempsychosis, Herm. ap.Stob. 1.49.44.

μεταποιέω I, line 4, after 'Sol. 20.3' insert 'cf. Sch.A Il. 20.273, al.'

*μεταποικίλλομαι, *embroider*, in quot. fig., Agath. pr. 17.

*μεταπολέω, *go along* with, τῶν ἑτέρων τοῖς ἑτέροις ἐπακολουθούντων καὶ μεταπολουμένων Chrysipp.*Stoic.* 2.293 (unless this is fr. °μεταπόλλυμι *perish in succession*).

*μεταπόλλυμι, v. °μεταπολέω.

*μεταπολογίζομαι, *transfer to another account*, *MAMA* 8.413(*b*).4.

μεταπορεύομαι I 2, add '**b** *claim at law*, *SEG* 9.8.121 (Cyrene, i BC, senatus consultum).'

μετάπρᾱσις, add 'ἔρια εἰς μετάπρασιν ὠνεῖσθαι Heph.Astr. 3.5.39, 43'

μεταπρέπω, add 'pass. form in same sense, μεταπρεφθεὶς ἑτάροισιν *GVI* 1519.5 (Moesia, i BC); cf. ἐμπρέπω'

μεταρίθμιος, add '**2** *of account among*, ἰχθύσι δ' οὔτε δίκη μ. οὔτε τις αἰδώς Opp.*H.* 2.43.'

μεταρρυθμίζω I 2, add 'τοὺς ἀδικοῦντας μεταρυθμίζειν ἐπὶ βελτίονα βιωτήν, *Βυζάντιον* 6.366 (Sardis, vi AD)'

μέταρσις, add '**2** *arrogance, conceit*, Aq. 1*Ki.* 2.3.'

*μεταρυθμίζω, v. °μεταρρυθμίζω.

*μετασᾰλεύω, *remove, alter*, οὐδ[ενὶ ἐξέσται] μετασαλεῦσαί τι (exhortation against disturbing a grave) *SEG* 34.1144 (Ephesus).

*μετασκούτλωσις, εως, ἡ, prob. *replacement panelling* or *paving* in a theatre, *JRA* suppl.2 pp. 20, 28 (Aphrodisias, ii/iii AD).

μετάστᾰσις II 1 a, add '*change of position*, τανυπτερύγου μυίας μ. Simon. 16.4 P.' **b**, delete 'τοῦ βίου μεταστάσεις id.*fr.* 554' and 'Simon. 32' **2**, after 'γνώμης' insert 'βίου' and after '*Andr.* 1003' insert '*fr.* 554'

+μεταστείχω, *go in search of, go after*, E.*Hec.* 509, *Supp.* 90, A.R. 3.451, Ἰνδὸν Ἄρηα μετέστιχε θυιὰς Ἐνυώ Nonn.*D.* 29.279.

μετατάσσω, line 2, for '*adjourn*' read '*rearrange, change* (the date of)'

μετατίθημι II 1, add '**b** *transfer* to another purpose, τὸ δὲ ἀρχαῖον τὸ ἐπιδιδόμενον .. εἰς ταῦτα μὴ ἐξέστω μεταθεῖναι εἰς ἄλλο μηθέν *IG* 12(7).515 (ii BC). **c** *transfer* to another *the right to* or *possession of*, *Cod.Just.* 1.3.41.11, Just.*Nov.* 22.20.2.'

μετάτροπος 2, for this section read '*having a change of mind* or *attitude*, δαίμων γὰρ ὅδ' αὖ μετάτροπος ἐπ' ἐμοί A.*Pers.* 943, A.R. 3.818' add '**3** μετάτροπα ἔργα *reversal, restitution*, Hes.*Th.* 89.'

*μετατροπόω, *convert*, τούτους (sc. τοὺς ἐχθροὺς) εἰς φιλίαν *Gnomol.Vat.* in *WS* 11.225.

μεταυγάζω, for '*look keenly after* .. τινα' read '*discern from a distance, spot*'

μεταύριον, add 'διὰ τῆς μεθαύριον *POxy.* 1844.4, 5 (vi/vii AD); cf. mod. Gk. μεθαύριο'

μεταυτίκα, add 'Theoc. 25.222 (v.l. παρ-)'

μεταφέρω, add '**5** *transport*, *PKöln* 274.4, *PPetr.* 3 p. 46 i 16, *PCair.Zen.* 520.10, 620.11 (iii BC).'

*μεταφορεῖος, ον, *of* or *concerning transport*, *Kafizin* 227.

*μεταφορεύς, έως, ὁ, *courier, messenger*, Ἁρποκρατίωνι μεταφορ(ε)ῖ *PPetaus* 34.11 (AD 184).

+μεταφορέω, *convey* from one place to another, *shift*, Hdt. 1.64.2, 2.125.4.

μεταφῠτεύω, add 'Pythag.ap.Iamb.*Protr.* 21 λη' p. 125.12 P.'

μεταχάσκω, for 'Apostol. 7.20 (*Journ.Philol.* 4.320)' read '*Com.adesp.* 41 D.'

μεταχειρίζω 5 a, line 2, delete 'τὸν .. 1.20'

μεταχέω, add 'Myc. pf. part. pass. *me-ta-ke-ku-me-na* (fem.), app. *taken to pieces*'

μεταχθόνιος, delete the entry (read μεταχρόνιος).

μεταχρόνιος II, lines 3/4, delete 'μεταχθόνιος .. μεταχρόνιος'

*μετεγγῠητής, οῦ, ὁ, *joint-security*, *SB* 4884.

*μετεικάς, άδος, ἡ, (sc. ἡμέρη) *twenty-first day of the month*, Hes.*Op.* 820 (s.v.l.).

μέτειμι (εἰμί *sum*) II 1, lines 5/6, delete 'οὐδὲν μᾶλλον .. cf.'

μέτειμι (εἶμι *ibo*), for 'Att. fut. of μετέρχομαι' read 'used as fut. of μετέρχομαι'

*μετεκβάλλω, *cause to change* from a practice, μετεκβάλωσι τοῦ νυνὶ τρόπου ?Cratin. in *PCGF* 76 *fr.* 1 col. i.3.

*μετέκθεσις, εως, ἡ, *supplementary list*, *PMich.*inv. 4607 (*TAPhA* 83.78.1, iv AD, -εχ- pap.), *PMasp.* 138 ii[r].47 (-εχ- pap.).

*μετεκποιέω, *finish making*, μεταεξεποίησεν τρίχωμα *Pap.Lugd.Bat.* xxv 16.5.

μετεξέτεροι, for '= ἔνιοι, *some among many, certain*' read '*some among others*' and add 'Nic.*fr.* 76, *Th.* 414 (interp.)'

μετέπειτα, add 'Heph.Astr. 1.1.9'

μετεπιγράφω I, add '*SEG* 17.729 (Lycia, Rom.imp.)'

μετέρχομαι, line 1, after 'Theoc. 29.25' insert 'πεδελθέτω Alc. 129.13 L.-P.' **IV 1**, add 'esp. *go to fetch* a bride, *AP* 7.367 (Antip.Thess.), διὰ κηρύκων Plu. 2.297c' **3**, line 5, delete '*narrate* them'

μετεωρισμός I, add 'μετεωρισμὸν ὀφθαλμῶν (i.e. a haughty look) μὴ δῷς μοι Lxx *Si.* 23.4, 26.9'

μετεωρολέσχης, add 'perh. w. ref. to sophists, Ar.*fr.* 401 K.-A.'

μετέωρος, line 16, for '*more rapid*' read '*shallower*' **II 3**, add 'μέλη .. μετέωρα ἐντόνοις ὅμοια Zeno *Stoic.* 1.58' **III 3**, add 'ἐν μετεώρῳ *in suspense*, Just.*Nov.* 30.8 pr.' add 'cf. Dor. πεδάορος, πεδήορος'

μετῆλαι, for 'Poll. 1.243' read 'Poll. 1.143'

μέτηλυς I, delete '*PFlor.* .. iii AD)'

μετοικεσία, for 'μετοικία I' read '*removal to a foreign country*' and for 'also .. leal"' read '**2** *place of residence abroad*, πλεόνων μ. *the abode of the majority*, i.e. the dead'

μετοικέω II, add 'transf., of the status of citizens under an oligarchy, Isoc. 4.105'

μετοίκιον I, after 'X.*Vect.* 2.1' insert '*Hesperia* 5.401.126 (Athens, iv BC)'; after 'Luc.*Deor.Conc.* 3' insert 'πρὸς τὸ μ. τινα ἀπάγειν in connection with, i.e. for not paying, *this tax*, Plu. 2.842b, cf. id.*Flam.* 12'

μετοικοδομέω, after '*build elsewhere*' insert 'με]τοικοδομήσειν Men. *Dysc.* 446 S.'

μέτοικος 1, after 'esp. at Athens' insert '*SEG* 34.47 (verse, Attica, 506 BC; form μετάοικος)' **2**, delete the section.

*μέτοπις, ιδος, ἡ, *vengeance*, Διός Hom.*Epigr.* 8.4 (nisi leg. μέτ' ὄπις).

*μέτοπον, τό, *metope* (archit.), *IG* 1³.474 i 30; cf. μετόπη, μεθόπιον.

μετόρχιον, add 'prob. rest. in *PRyl.* 583.20, 71 (ii BC)'

μετουσία I, add 'w. πρός and acc., Just.*Const.* Δέδωκεν 20a, *Cod.Just.* 1.3.43 pr.' **II**, add '*PHamb.* 128.59 (iii BC)'

μετούσιος, add '**II** *participating* in, Alcin.*Intr.* p. 164.9 H.'

μετοχετεύω, line 1, for '*convey in a channel*' read '*channel*' and after '*divert*' insert 'D.Chr. 18(35).20'; line 4, after 'p. 165 A.' insert 'fig., D.H.*Vett.Cens.* 1'

μετοχή III, delete the section.

*μετόχλησις, εως, ἡ, *removal by means of a lever*, θύρας μετοχλήσει Heph.Astr. 3.46.

μετρέω III 4, add '*SEG* 30.1121 (iii BC)' add '**5** *adjust, accommodate to*, ὁ νόμος πρὸς .. τὸ παρασυμβαῖνον μετρηθείς Just.*Nov.* 7.2 pr.

μετρηδόν, after 'adv.' insert '*by measure*, Nic.*Al.* 203'; after 'Nonn.*D.* 7.115' insert '22.271, al.'

*μετρηματιαῖος, ὁ, *hired labourer*, *SB* 9406.16, *PFlor.* 322.20 (both iii AD).

μετρητής II, add 'abbrev. με. *SEG* 31.983 (ii/i BC)'

μετριάζω I 1, add 'of (the use of) figures of speech, D.H.*Dem.* 4'

μέτριος A II, add 'μετρίων ἡμερῶν Thphr.*Sign.* 24' **B I 1**, line 6, after 'Pl.*Euthd.* 305d' insert 'w. adj., μετρίως .. ἐπίπονον Pl.*R.* 329d, D. 6.19, Theoc. 30.3'

μετριότης II, add 'freq. in a self-depreciatory sense, *PSI* 449.9, *PBeatty Panop.* 1.69 (AD 298)'

μετρονόμοι, add '*SEG* 24.157 (Attica, iii BC)'

*μετροποιός, ὁ, *maker of measures*, *PTeb.* 277.2 (iii AD, pl.).

μέττα, add 'μετ(τ)' as prep. or w. ἐς = *up to* (a place), *BCH* 109.163B.8 (Crete)'

μετωνῠμία, line 2, before 'Cic.' insert 'D.H.*Dem.* 5 (pl.)'

μετωπηδόν, line 2, after 'Hdt. 7.100' insert 'Sosyl. 1 iii 13 J.'

μέτωπον II 1, lines 6/7, delete 'dub. sens. .. 30' (v. °μέτοπον); penultimate line, after '(X.*Cyr.*) 2.4.3' insert 'ἐπὶ μετώπου ἐλαύνειν id.*Eq.Mag.* 3.6'

μέχρι III 1, line 4, delete 'Call.*Sos.* 5.4 and 5.5' **2**, line 3, for 'μέχρις .. Men. 633' read 'μέχρι .. Men.*fr.* 525 K.-Th.'; line 4, after '*Ench.* 11' insert 'μέχρις κε μένῃ Call.*fr.* 388.9 Pf.'

μή A 8, add 'μὴ προφάσεις *AP* 5.193(192) (Diosc.), cf. 53(52) (id.; πρόφασις cod.); also w. nom., v. βαιών' **C II 1**, lines 1/2, for 'with .. *apprehension*' read 'where fear is implied'; line 3, for 'περισκοπῶ .. *El.* 898' read 'εἰσόμεσθα μή τι .. καλύπτει S.*Ant.* 1253' **D 2**, after 'μή is sts. repeated' insert 'cf. οὐ C'

μηδᾰμά, line 2, delete 'and of Manner, *not at all*' and insert 'μηδάμα μηδ' ἕνα *never anyone*, Alc. 129.16 L.-P., and so'

μηδέ, line 9, for 'οὐδέ' read 'οὐ' and for 'A II 3' read 'A II 8'

*Μήδεια, ἡ, epith. of Artemis (prob. ethnic), *SEG* 32.1612 (iii BC).

μηδείς, line 2, after '(Mytil.)' insert 'also fem. μεδενία *SEG* 26.461 (Sparta, v BC); acc. μαδέμινα (for μηδένα) *SEG* 36.548 (Metropolis, Thessaly, iii BC)'

μηδεπώποτε, add 'Plu.*Ages.* 19.6, D.L. 6.54'

μηδέτερος, line 3, after 'id. 7.5.9' insert '[Isoc.] 1.42'

Μηδικός I, add '**2** as an imperial title, *ISelge* 13 (after AD 175).'

*Μηδίσκιον, τό, *silken garment*, *PDura* 30.20 (iii AD); cf. Μηδικός I.

*Μήδισσα (sc. γυνή), ἡ, = Μηδίς, *IG* 2².9354 (iii/ii BC).

**μήδομαι**, at end after 'only in lyr. exc. A.*Pr.*l.c.' insert '*Ch.* 991'
**μῆδος** (A), add 'in Myc. compd. n., as *e-ke-me-de* = Ἐχεμήδης, *pe-ri-me-de* = Περιμήδης'
**Μῆδος**, add 'Cypr. *ma-to-i* Μᾶδοι *ICS* 217.1'
**μηθείς**, line 4, delete 'but rarely .. *NT*' and add '*Dura*$^5$ (1)12.8'
**μηθέτερος**, add 'Lxx *Pr.* 24.21 (B)'
***Μηθυμναῖος**· ὁ Διόνυσος Hsch., app. *from Methymna*, but see ‡Μεθυμναῖος.
***μηιονιστί**, adv., *in the Maeonian language*, Hippon. 3a W.
***μὴ καί**, like μὴ ὅπως I 1, *not just not*, folld. by ἀλλά, οὐδέ τις ἔτλη, μὴ καὶ λευκανίηνδε φορεύμενος, ἀλλ' ἀποτηλοῦ ἑστηώς A.R. 2.192; after a neg. sentence, *much less*, id. 3.589.
**μηκόθεν**, add 'διαγνῶναι ἀπὸ μ. Sch.E.*Ph.* 1118'
**μήκων IV**, add '**2** *socket of the eye*, Hsch. s.v. κρατηρίσκοι.'
***μηκωνίας**, Dor. **μᾱκ-**, α, ὁ, = μηκώνειος, μακωνιᾶν ἄρτων rest. in Alcm. 19.2 P.
**μηκωνίς II**, delete the section.
**μηλᾰφάω**, for 'Sophr. in *Cod.* .. 82' read 'Sophr. 146b O.'
**μηλέα**, line 5, after 'Thphr.*HP* 4.13.2' insert 'μ. ὀξεῖα *crab-apple, Pyrus acerba*, ib.'
**μήλινος II**, for 'μύρον μ.' read 'μήλινον, τό, *quince-perfume*' **2**, add 'Ezek.*Exag.* 262 S.'
**Μηλίς**, (s.v. Μηλιεύς), after '(Hdt.) 8.31' insert 'cf. Μαλίς· Ἀθηνᾶ Hsch., Hippon. 40 W.'
***μηλῖτις**, ιδος, ἡ, (μῆλον B) a precious stone (named from its colour), Plin.*HN* 37.191.
***μηλόκερως**, ων, *having sheep's horns*, Ps.-Callisth. 27.20, 33.12.
**μηλολόνθη**, add 'see also μηλάνθη I'
**μηλονόμος**, after '(lyr.)' insert '*PMasp.* 2 iii 4, al. (vi AD)'
**μηλοπάρειος**, delete the entry.
***μηλοπεπόνιον**, τό, dim. of μηλοπέπων, *melon*, *OAshm.Shelton* 217 (written μελοπεπόνιν).
**μηλοσκόπος**, add '**II** *watcher over sheep*, of Pan, *GDRK* 17ʳ.11.'
**μηλοσόη**, read '**μηλοσόα**'
***μηλόται**, v. μηλάτης.
**μηλοφόρος**, line 4, after '*IG* 14.268 (v BC)' insert 'ib. 271; also θεᾷ Μαλοφόρῳ *IGBulg.* $1^2$.370 bis'
**μήλοψ**, read '**μῆλοψ**'
**μηλόω II**, for this section read '*dye* wool, Hsch. (s.v. μηλῶσαι), Poll. 7.169; med., Eust. 1394.32'
**μήλωθρον II**, add 'μήλωθρα· βάμματα. οἱ δὲ τὸ τῶν δερμάτων βάμμα. ἄλλοι τὸ παρύφασμα τῆς πορφύρας. οἱ δὲ καλλωπίσματα Hsch.'
**μηλώσιος**, add 'or perh. *dressed in a sheepskin* (μηλωτή)'
**⁺μήμη**, prob. *great-grandmother*, *Didyma* 345.12 (i BC/i AD), *SEG* 30.1286 (Didyma, i AD).
***μημόριον**, v. °μεμόριον.
**μήν**, read '**μήν** (A)' **II 2**, line 6, after 'S.*Ant.* 626 (anap.)' delete 'etc.'; line 10, for 'καὶ μὴν καί' read 'καὶ μὴν .. καί'
**μήν**, ὁ, read '**μήν** (B), ὁ' **II**, delete the section.
***Μήν** (C), an Anatolian divinity, *IG* $2^2$.1365, 1366, etc.; nom. sg. **Μείς**, *SEG* 4.647.2, 648.3 (Lydia).
**μηνᾰγύρτης**, for '*Rhea*' read 'perh. of °Μήν C'
**μηνιαῖος I 1**, add 'τὰ μ., also *monthly payment, salary*, *Edict.Diocl.* 7.64, al.'
***μηνιακός**, ή, όν, *recurring monthly*, ἡμέραι *SB* 5959.10 (iii AD).
**μηνιάρχης**, after '*prefect*' insert '*OBodl.* II 1986 (ii/iii AD)'
**μηνιεῖος**, for 'λοιπογραφομένου' read 'λοιπογραφουμένου'; add 'cf. Myc. *me-ni-jo* (*μήνιον), *monthly ration*'
**μῆνις**, line 1, for 'gen. μήνιος Pl.*R.* 390e' read 'Ep. gen. μήνιος Od. 3.135 (used by Pl.*R.* 390e in ref. to Iliad)'
***μήνῖσις**, εως, ἡ, *anger*, *Psalm.Salom.* 2.25(23).
***μηνίσκιον**, τό, dim. of μηνίσκος, as an ornament, *PMich.*II 121ʳ II ii 2.8 (i AD), *PHamb.* 10.45 (ii AD).
***μήνισμα**, ατος, τό, = μήνιμα, Πολέμων 1.213 (Iolcus, iii BC).
**μηνῑτής**, after lemma insert '(or μηνίτης)'
***μηνσώριον**, τό, Lat. *mensorium*, *basket*, *Stud.Pal.* 20.151.3, 14 (vi AD, μηνσωρρ-).
***μήνυον**· εἶδος ἄνθους Theognost.*Can.* 130.
***μήνυος**, ὁ, *informer*, *SEG* 29.980 (Italy, late Rom.imp.).
**μηνῡτής II**, after 'Cratin. 428' add '*PKöln* 266.20 (iii BC)'
**μηνύω I 4**, add 'Arist.*de An.* 403$^a$19' **II**, line 1, after 'Athens' insert 'and elsewhere'; line 5, after 'D. 24.11' insert 'w. εἰς, *lay information* before, *Cod.Just.* 1.4.26.4'
***μηνωπός**, όν, perh. *moonlit*, cj. in *POxy.* 3724 *fr.* 1 vii 9 (list of epigrams, i AD).
**μήποτε I 2**, add 'Cypr. *ICS* 264'
**Μηριόνης II**, delete '*pudenda muliebria*'; after '*AP*' insert '12.97 (Antip.)'
**μηρός**, after lemma insert 'also neut. pl. μῆρα q.v.' add '**4** transf., *flank*, ἐν μηροῖς ὄρους Lxx *Jd.* 19.1. **5** archit., *the segment between the grooves of a triglyph*, Vitr. 4.3.5.'
**μηρυκάζω**, add 'med., τῶν μαρυκαζομένων ζῴων Hsch. s.v. ἤνυστρον'
**μήρῡμα I**, line 1, after '*strand*' insert 'of rope, *IG* $2^2$.1627.70, 150, 1128.335, al.'
**μήρυξ**, read '**μῆρυξ**'
**μηρύομαι I 2 a**, add '*Carm.Pop.* 30(*c*).2 P.' **II**, add 'also μηρύω δὲ τὸ κουβαρίζω Sch.Theoc. 1.29; πλατύνειν· μηρύειν Hsch.'
***μητᾶτον**, τό, Lat. *metatum*, pl., *quarters, billet*, edict of Anastasius I in *SEG* 9.356.43, 44 (Cyrenaica, vi AD), ib. 40 (μιτᾶτα), Just.*Nov.* 130.9.
***μητατορικός**, ή, όν, (for -ωρικός) *concerning measuring*, fr. Lat. *metatorius*, ἐνδοματικὰ μ. Lyd.*Mag.* 3.70.
**μήτε 1**, add '(μήτε .. ἤ in codd. of Ph. 2.137, Porph.*Abst.* 4.8)'
***μητεύω**, *commander* for military quarters, Just.*Nov.* app. 4 rubric, 4.1.
**μήτηρ I 1**, add °Ἰουλίαν Δόμναν .. μητέρα κάστρων *SEG* 24.953, *Amyzon* 71, etc., μήτηρ συναγωγῆς *CIJud.* 496 (ii/iii AD)' **2**, Μήτηρ θεῶν, add '*SEG* 32.268 (ii AD), *TAM* 4(1).90, etc.; Μήτηρ ἀπὸ σπηλέου *SEG* 34.1293' add 'form μάτηρ, Myc. *ma-te*, *ma-te-re* (dat.)'
**μητίετα**, after '(Tegea)' insert 'gen. μητιέταο Max. 445'
***μητρίδιον**, τό, app. dim. of μήτηρ on the model of πατρίδιον, Ar.*Lys.* 549.
**μητρίδιος**, delete the entry.
**μητροκᾰσιγνήτη**, add '**2** *mother's sister*, Nonn.*D.* 3.425, 21.182.'
***μητροκᾰσίγνητος**, ὁ, *uterine brother*, *CEG* 166 (Sicinus, v BC).
**μητροκωμία**, add '*PBeatty Panop.* 2.228 (AD 298)'
**μητροπάτωρ**, add 'title of Apollo at Clarus, *AC* 35.417 n.1'
**μητρόπολις**, line 3, after 'ἕως' insert '(Μητροπόλιος, *REG* 101.14-16, 89, Xanthos, iii BC, place-name)' **I 2**, for 'Ph.ap.Plu. 2.718e' read 'Philol.ap.Plu. 2.718e'; add 'τὴν φιλαργυρίαν εἶπε μητρόπολιν πάντων τῶν κακῶν Diog.ap.D.L. 6.50'
**μητροπολίτης II**, add '*SEG* 30.1713 (Arabia, AD 624)'
**μητροπολῑτικός I**, add '*POxy.* 1521.3 (ii AD)'
**μητρυιά**, line 2, after '(Lesbos)' insert '**μητρυά** Pl.*Lg.* 672b, 930b, *Com.adesp.* 12.4 D.'
***μητρωϊκός**, ή, όν, perh. = μητρικός, τύπος μ. *Inscr.Délos* 1409*Ba*ii100 (ii BC).
**μητρῷος I 1**, at end after 'τὰ μ.' insert '*Leg.Gort.* 4.44, *Inscr.Cret.* 4.20 (vii/vi BC)' add '**3** fem. subst., *maternal aunt*, ἁ ματρόα Mitchell *N.Galatia* 28.' **II 2 b**, after 'Duris 16 J.' insert 'Plu. 2.763a'
**μήτρως**, line 2, after 'acc. ωα and ων' insert 'ως *SEG* 34.1226 (Lydia, AD 158/9)' **2**, add '*Leg.Gort.* 8.52 πὰρ τοῖς [μ]άτρōσι τράπε(θ)θαι (= τρέφεσθαι); ib. 9.4 το]νς ματρόανς'
**μηχᾰνάριος**, after '*engineer*' insert '*mechanic*'
**μηχᾰνεύομαι**, after '= μηχανάομαι' insert '*Trag.adesp.* 573'
**μηχᾰνεύς**, add '**2** *engineer*, *PPetaus* 103.38 (ii AD, written μιχ-).'
**μηχᾰνή I 1**, add 'for grinding corn, μ. σιταλητική *PMich.*inv. 257.3 (*BASP* 13.3, iii AD), *BGU* 405.7 (iv AD)' **II 1**, at end after 'Pl.*Phd.* 72d' insert '*Alc.* 1.130b' **2**, add 'ἐκ πάσης μηχανῆς *Cod.Just.* 1.3.45.3a'
***μηχᾰνία**, ἡ, *trickery*, Hsch. s.v. μαγγανεία.
**μηχᾰνικός II**, add 'w. ref. to architecture, σοφίᾳ τῇ καλουμένῃ μηχανικῇ Procop.*Aed.* 1.1.2 K.'
***μηχᾰνιον**, τό, dim. of μηχανή, *apparatus, equipment*, *PHarris* 112.10 (v AD).
***μηχᾰνοδέτης**, ου, ὁ, *workman who assembles machines*, *MAMA* 3.752 (Corycus).
**⁺μηχᾰνοποιΐα**, ἡ, *construction, engineering*, of engines of war, Ath.Mech. 10.9; of a clock, *Inscr.Perg.* 8(3).103.
**μηχανοποιός 1**, add '**b** *architect, builder*, Procop.*Aed.* 1.1.24.'
**⁺μηχᾰνουργός**, ὁ, *artificer, mechanic* or sim., *APl.* 5.382, *POxy.* 1970.14, 34 (vi AD); transf., as gloss on ῥᾳδιουργός, Hsch.
**μῐαίνω 1**, delete the section transferring exx. to section 2. **3**, at end after '(Iulis)' insert 'v BC' and add '*PMich.*v 244.17 (i AD)'
***μῐαιόω**, *defile*, ἀνθ' ὧν αὐταὶ ἐμιαίωσαν αὐτὰς ἐν φυρμῷ ἀναμείξεως *Psalm.Salom.* 2.15(13).
**μῐαιφονία**, line 2, after '*murder*' insert '*AP* 5.215 (Mel.), 9.157'
**μῐαιφόνος**, line 2, after '(Il.) 844, al.' insert 'of human beings, A.*Pr.* 868, Arist.*EN* 1177$^b$10'; line 3, after 'B.*Scol.Oxy.fr.* 5.1' insert '(= *fr.* 20A.16 S.-M.), μ. γάμων S.*El.* 492'; add 'see also μιηφόνος'
***μιακαιεικάς**, άδος, ἡ, *the twenty-first of the month*, *BGU* 2042.2, 3 (AD 105).
***μῐᾰρολόγος**, ον, *foul-mouthed*, Sch.Luc. 205.7.
**μῐᾰρός 4**, penultimate line, after 'Pl.*R.* 562d' insert 'D. 18.296, al.; Aeschin. 1.42, al.' add 'see also μιερός'
**μίγα**, add 'Orph.*A.* 791'
**μίγδην**, add 'μίγδαν Pi.*fr.* 52m.7 S.-M.'
**μῐγής**, after 'Nic.*fr.* 68.4' insert 'cf. μιγός (perh. read μιγή)'
**μίγμα I**, add 'transf. of style, D.H.*Dem.* 5' **2**, line 2, for 'μ. σμύρνης' read 'sg., Lxx *Si.* 38.8; μίγμα σμύρνης' add 'cf. ‡μεῖχμα'
***μῐγός**, ή, όν, *not sorted out*, ἐρέα *Edict.Diocl.* 25.11, cf. ‡μιγής.

**μιεῖν**, add '(dub., v. μνίειν and °καταμιεῖ)'
***μῐεστήρ**, prob. = *μιαστήρ (= μιάστωρ), gloss in *POxy.* 1802.61 (ii/iii AD); (cf. χιέζω = χιάζω, πιάζω = πιέζω).
**μῐκῐχιζόμενος**, for '*under age*' read '*in third year of public education*, i.e. nine years old'; lines 3/4, for 'is expld. .. *year*' read '= foreg.'
**μικκός**, line 1, after 'μικρός' insert 'A.*fr.* 47a i 23, ii 15 R.'
**μῖκός**, add 'cf. stem of Myc. pers. n. *mi-ka-ri-jo*'
***μῑκροκέρᾰμον**, τό, *small pot*, *PBremen* 22.7 (ii AD).
**μῑκρολογία II 2**, add 'Ptol.*Tetr.* 192'
***μῑκρολῡπία**, ἡ, *annoyance at trifles*, pap. in *Aegyptus* 63.154-5.
***μῑκρόπρος**, adv., *about, more or less*, ζήσας .. τὸν [πάντα βίον ἔτη π]εντήκοντα μικρόπρος *SEG* 32.1064 (late Rom.imp.); also **μικροῦ πρός** *SEG* 31.1431 (AD 582), **μικρῷ πρός**, *ACO* 2(1).186.31.
**μῑκρός I 1**, add 'in place-names, ἀπὸ Διοπολείτου μικροῦ *SEG* 30.1720, μηκρᾶς Ἀ[σ]ίας ib. 26.790 (Byzantium, vi AD)' **II 1**, line 2, after 'Pl.*R.* 498d' insert 'πρὸς μικρόν *GVI* 1842.3 (Egypt, i/ii AD)' **III 5 a**, for 'Antipho .. 4.129' read 'Hdt. 4.129.5; *in detail*, Antipho 6.18 (s.v.l.)' at end delete 'ῐ only .. *fr.* 36.17 J.'
**μῑκρόσφαιρον**, read '**-σφαιρος**, ον' and add 'Plin.*HN* 12.44'
**μῑκρόφθαλμος**, after 'Hp.*Epid.* 6.7.1' insert 'Ptol.*Tetr.* 143'
**μῑκρόφωνος I**, add 'comp., Plu. 2.963a'
**μῑκροψῡχία**, line 3, delete 'Cic.*Att.* 9.11.4'
**μῑκῠ́θειος**, for 'α, ον' read 'ον'; add 'ἀργυρίς, κύλιξ, ib. 442*B*142, 172 (ii BC)'
**μῖλαξ II**, delete the section.
***μῖλαξ** (B), = μέλλαξ, Hermipp. 33, Hsch.
**Μῑλήσιος**, add 'form Μιλάτιος, Myc. *mi-ra-ti-ja* (fem. pl.)'
**Μῑ́λητος**, line 1, after 'Theoc. 28.21' insert 'Μίλατος *SEG* 23.189 (Argos, *c*.330 BC); also a town in Crete, Μίλητος Il. 2.647, ethnic Μιλάτιοι, *Inscr.Cret.* 1.8.6.36'
**μῑλιάριον II**, add '**b** *mile*, τέσσαρες (sic) μειλιάρια ἡμεῖν ἐπίκεινται *JRS* 46.46 line 6 (Phrygia, iii AD).'
**μῑ́λιον**, add 'ἀπὸ Ἁλικαρνασσοῦ μί(λια) β' *SEG* 31.932 (iii/iv AD)'
**μίλλος**, add 'also in pers. n., e.g. Μίλων, Afric.Euseb. I 201 (vi BC)'
***μιλτόεις**, εσσα, εν, form μιλτόϝευς, Myc. *mi-to-we-sa* (fem. pl.), *painted red.*
**μιλτοκάρηνος**, for '*red-headed*' read '*red-topped*, λόφων ἀπὸ μιλτοκαρήνων'
**μιλτοπάρηος**, after 'ον' insert 'Dor. **-πάρᾱος** *Suppl.Hell.* 991.36 (poet. word-list, iii BC)'; line 3, for 'Macho ap.Ath. 3.135b' read 'Matro ap.Ath. 4.135b'
**μιλτόπρεπτος**, for 'A.*Fr.* 116' read 'A.*fr.* 47a.24, 116 R.'
**μιλτόπρῳρος**, add '*Suppl.Hell.* 991.33 (poet. word-list, iii BC)'
**μίλτος I 2**, delete the section transferring exx. to section 1.
**μιλτόω**, add 'ψιάθους .. μεμιλτομένας (for -ωμένας) *POxy.* 3505.5 (ii AD)'
**μῐμαίκῠλον**, after '*fruit of* κόμαρος' insert 'Ar.*fr.* 698 K.-A.'; add 'cf. pers. n. Μυμαικύλη *SEG* 30.238 (Attica)'
**⁺μῐ́μαρκυς**, ἡ, dish composed of offal and blood, acc. to Hsch. usu. of hare, Ar.*Ach.* 1112, Pherecr. 255 K.-A., Diph. 1 K.-A.
**μῑ́μαυλος**, for 'flute' read 'aulos'
**μῑμέομαι II**, line 5, delete 'of μῖμοι .. X.*Smp.* 2.21'
***μῑμερά** (or **-ηρά**)· ἡ μιμητικὴ τέχνη, καὶ ἡ μίμησις Hsch.
**μῑμηλός II**, delete this section transferring exx. to section I and adding 'Plu. 2.215a, Nonn.*D.* 42.217, al.'
**μῑ́μημα 1**, for '*anything imitated, counterfeit, copy*' read '*copy, imitation*, whether intended to represent, counterfeit, or for any other purpose' **2**, delete the section transferring exx. to section 1 and adding 'Ph. 2.146, al., καλάθου μίμημα τρόπαιον *SEG* 36.1260 (late ii AD), Plot. 1.2.2, al. Nonn.*D.* 1.373, al.'
**μιμνήσκω B I 3**, line 4, for 'etc.' read 'μέμνημαι .. σου λέγοντος ib. 8; μ. Κριτίᾳ συνόντα σε Pl.*Chrm.* 156a' and for 'relat.' read 'clause' **III**, line 4, at end insert 'κ(ύρι)ε, μνήσθητι τοῦ δούλου σου *SEG* 31.1474 (Arabia, vi AD)' add 'Μνᾶσι- Μνησι- in pers. n., Myc. *ma-na-si-we-ko*'
**μιν**, add 'Myc. enclitic *-mi*'
**μίνθα**, for 'also μίνθος, ἡ, .. 732b' read 'μίνθα· τὸ ἡδύοσμον. καὶ ἀνθρωπεία κόπρος Hsch.' add 'Myc. *mi-ta*' (see also °μίνθος)
**μινθόβαψ**, delete the entry.
**⁺μίνθος**, ὁ, ἡ, *mint*, (masc.), Mnesim. 4.63, Plu. 2.732b; (fem.), Thphr.*CP* 2.16.2; used in comedy for κόπρος acc. to Eust. 1524.12, cf. μίνθα, μινθόω.
***μίνθων**, ωνος, ὁ, app. a kind of sexual pervert, Phld.*Vit.* p. 37 J., Luc.*Lex.* 12, Hsch. s.v. κικκίδαι.
**μίνθωνος**, delete the entry.
***μινίκιον**, τό, *bangle, necklet, armlet*, *SEG* 2.776 (Dura, iii AD).
***μινοδολόεσσα**· ἀριθμῶν σύνταξις παρὰ Χαλδαίοις gloss. in *POxy.* 1802.67 (ii/iii AD); cf. Hsch. s.v. μινδαλοεσσα(ς).
**μινύζηον**, read 'μινύζωον'
***μῐνυθάνω**, form of μινύθω, *PMich.*I 11.7.

**μῐνῠ́θω**, after lemma insert '[ῠ, but ῡ in μινύθει B. 3.90 S.-M., cf. 5.151 (cj.)]' **II**, line 6, after '*Mochl.* 19' insert 'πόθῳ μ. *h.Cer.* 201, 304'
**μῐνυθώδης**, add '**2** app. *weak-willed*, Suet.*Blasph.* 111 T.'
**μίνυνθα**, line 4, after 'B. 5.151' insert '(μίνῡθεν cj.)'
**μῐνῠ́ρομαι**, for 'of the nightingale, *warble*' read 'in quot., of the nightingale'
**μῐνῠώριος**, after '*AP* 9.362.26' insert 'ἀστέρα λέκτρων Musae. 305'
**μῐνῠ́ωρος**, delete 'cf. Musae. 305'
***μῐνῷδες**, v. °Μίνως.
**Μῑνώϊος**, add 'also Μῑνόϊος, *SEG* 36.731.22, 33 (Delos, iii BC)'
**Μῑ́νως**, delete 'but also ῐ Pl.Com. 15 D.' (prob. pr. n. Μίνων); line 3, after 'Hdt. 1.173' insert 'Pl.*Lg.* 624a, *AP* 7.727 (Theaet.)'; line 6, after 'Hsch.' insert 'cf. **μινῷδες**· ἄμπελοί τινες οὕτω λέγονται παρὰ Ῥοδ[ίοις, gloss. in *POxy.* 1802.71 (ii/iii AD)'
**μιξοβόας**, add 'Simon. 14 i 5 P.'
***Μιρίϙυθος**, graffito, both pers. n. and n. of an insect, *REA* 49.36 (Delphi, vii/vi BC).
**μίρμα**, add '(μίργμα La.)'
**μῑσάνθρωπος**, before 'Pl.*Phd.* 89d' insert 'οὔτε μισόδημος ὢν οὔτε μισάνθρωπος Isoc. 15.131'
**μῑ́σηθρον**, add '*POxy.* 433.27 (sp. μείσ-)'
**μῑσητός II**, (μίσητος), for this section read '*lecherous, promiscuous*, μίσετος *ho* πα[ῖς Lang *Ath.Agora* XXI C1 (vii BC), γυνή (?)Archil. 206 W., Cratin. 354 K.-A., Suet.*Blasph.* 24 T., Ammon. 322 N.'
**μισθαποδότης**, add '*IGLBulg.* 207 (iv AD)'
***μισθογέωργος**, ὁ, perh. *hired farm-manager*, *PLond.* 1076 (vii AD).
**μισθοδοτέω**, line 4, pass., for '*receive pay*' read '*be paid*' and add '*Hell.Oxy.* 14.2'
**μισθοφορία II**, add '*income*, Luc.*Nav.* 13; *rent*, *BGU* 2139.12 (AD 432)'
***μισθωσίδιον**, τό, dim. of μίσθωσις, *SB* 7530.4, 18 (i BC).
**μισθώσιμος**, add '*PMerton* 24.13 (ii/iii AD)'
**μῑσοβάρβᾰρος**, before 'Luc.*Dem.Enc.* 6' insert '**2** *hating barbarism* (in language)'
**μῑσόδημος**, after 'And. 4.16' insert 'Pl.*R.* 566c'
***Μῑσοκύων**, κύνος, ὁ, title of a book on misfortunes by Hermagoras of Amphipolis, *Stoic.* 1.102.
***μῑσομήτωρ**, τορος, *hating one's mother*, *Orac.Tiburt.* 174.
**μῑσοπονηρία 1**, line 3, after 'etc.' insert '**b** *severity* in dealing with wrongdoing, τυχεῖν τῆς προσηκούσης μ. *UPZ* 8.30 (ii BC).'
**μῑσοπόνηρος**, after 'adv. -ρως' insert '*with severity towards wrongdoing*'; delete 'simply, *with hostile sentiments*' and add '*ICilicie* 70 (iii BC)'
***μῑσόχρῡσος**, ον, *hating gold*, i.e. not mercenary, of a physician, *Not.Scav.* 1941.193 (Rome, ii AD).
***μισσιβίλια**, τά, Lat. *missibilia*, *throwing-spears*, Just.*Nov.* 85.4.
***μισσίκιος**, ὁ, Lat. *missicius*, *a discharged soldier*, *PGnom.* 53, 54 (ii AD), sp. μεσσίκιος, *TAPhA* 90.139.
***μίσσος**, ὁ, Lat. *missus*, μίσσος ἡνιόχων *chariot-race* (as an event in a programme), *POxy.* 2707.3,6, al. (vi AD).
***μισσώριον**, τό, Lat. *missorium*, *dish, bowl*, *CPR* 8.66.14 (μυσσ- pap., vi AD).
***μίσχη**· πιλήματα, ταινίαι, μαλλοὶ οἱ τῶν ἐρίων Hsch.
**μῐτόομαι**, line 3, for '*let one's .. a string*' read '(describing the stridulation of a grasshopper or sim.)'
**μίτρα I 2**, after '*girdle*' insert 'Hes.*fr.* 1.4 M.-W.' and add '*AP* 5.199, 6.272' **3**, for '*wrestlers*' read '*charioteers*'
***μιτρᾰ́να**, ἁ, *headband*, Sapph. 98(*a*).10, (*b*).3 L.-P.
**μιτροφόρος**, delete the entry.
**μῐ́τῠλος**, after '**μύτῐλος**' insert 'or **μύτᾰλος**' **II**, before 'μίτυλον' insert 'αἷμα πιεῖν μύταλον Call.*fr.* 691 Pf.'
**μιχθᾰλόεις**, add 'μιχθαλόεσσα *Suppl.Hell.* 991.65 (poet. word-list, iii BC)'
**μνᾶ I**, add '*IEphes.* 3437a'
***μνᾶ** (B), Aeol. for μνεία, *IEryth.* 122.28.
**μνᾱαῖος**, line 4, after '(iv AD)' insert 'κιθάρω μέδδονος μναΐῳ *IGC* p. 99 B15 (Acraephia, iii BC)'; line 5, after '*POxy.* 265.18 (i AD)' insert '905.6 (ii AD, μναγαῖον)'
**μνανόοι**, for 'extra ordinem, fort. μνακόοι' read 'dub., cj. μνακόοι or μναμονόοι'
**μνάομαι I**, line 3, after 'Call.*Ap.* 95' insert 'w. acc., μνώεο .. οὔνομα Μηδείης A.R. 3.1069; Προμηθέα .. μνώμεναι, ὥς κείνοιο θεοπροπίῃσι Κρονίων δῶκε Θέτιν Πηλῆι Q.S. 5.338'
**μνάσιον**, add 'fr. Egyptian *mnw*'
***μνᾱσιχολέω**, v. °μνησιχολέω.
**μνεία I**, for 'ἐμὴν μ. dub. in Ael.*VH* 6.1' read 'μ. τὴν ἐμήν Ael.*NA* 12.32'; add 'μ‹ν›είας χάριν *IG* 9(2).1311, etc.; μνίας χ. *SEG* 30.1044; μνείας ἕνεκεν *SEG* 34.1028 (ii/iii AD)' add '**III** αἱ Μνεῖαι local name for the Muses, Plu. 2.743d.'
**μνῆμα I 2**, after 'D. 18.208' insert 'pl. as a place-name, *SEG* 23.236 (Arcadia, iii BC)'
**μνημεῖον 2**, add 'of a stele, ζῶν φρονῶν ἑαυτῷ τὸ μνημῖον κατεσκεύασεν Mitchell *N.Galatia* 204 (iii AD)'

**μνήμη**, after 'Dor. **μνάμα**' insert '(late sp. **μνήσμη** *SEG* 6.390 (Lycaonia, iv/v AD))' **I 1**, of the dead, add '*εὐσεβοῦς μνήμης* *Cod.Just.* 1.1.3.3'

***μνῆμις**, ἡ, *memorial*, *μνῆμις Λόκρου κελευστοῦ* Mitchell *N.Galatia* 88 (Byz., s.v.l.).

***μνημόδουλος**, ὁ, app. *slave looking after a monument*, *TAM* 2.794 (Arycanda).

**μνημοδόχος**, delete the entry.

**μνημονευκτικός II**, after 'Ptol.*Tetr.* 155' insert '(v.l., v. °*μνημονικός*)'

**μνημονεύω I 1**, add 'w. part., Pl.*Ep.* 319a' **III**, add '*μναμονεύϝεν* (inf.) *SEG* 27.631 (Lyttos, *c.*500 BC)'

**μνημονικός I 2**, for this section read '*of or connected with the μνημονεῖον*, *περὶ τῶν γραμμάτων τῶν μνημονικῶν* *SEG* 33.679 (Paros, ii BC), *μ. συγγραφῆς* *CPapJud.* 142 (14 BC)' **II**, add 'Ptol.*Tetr.* 155 (v.l. *μνημονευτικός*)'

**μνημόριον**, add '*IG* 3.3513, *SEG* 25.806 (Moesia, Rom.imp.); cf. °*μεμόριον*'

**μνημοσύνη**, after 'Pi.*O.* 8.74' insert 'E.*Hyps.fr.* 1 ii 27 B.' and delete 'in Att. only as pr. n.'

**μνημόσῠνον 1**, add '**b** *funerary monument*, *TAM* 4(1).179.'

***μνημόσῠνος**, η, ον, *of record* or *remembrance*, *γράμματα records*, Lxx *Es.* 6.1; *ἡμέραι* ib. 9.27 cod. A; *ἀσπάσματα πικρᾶς μνημόσυνα τύχης* *SEG* 34.1259 (i AD). **2** of monuments, *memorial*, *βωμόν μνημόσυνον* Mitchell *N.Galatia* 50.

**μνήμων II 2**, for this section read 'see quot.: *οἱ γὰρ ἐν Σικελίᾳ Δωριεῖς ὡς ἔοικε τὸν ἐπίσταθμον μνάμονα προσηγόρευον* Plu. 2.612c' **3**, after '*Leg.Gort.* 11.16' insert '*SEG* 33.679 (Paros, ii BC)'

**μνησίκᾰκος**, add 'adv. -*ως*, *μ. ἔχοι* Onos. 42.22'

***μνῆσις**, εως, ἡ, *memory*, orac. in *SEG* 33.1056B.10 (Cyzicus, ii AD).

***μνησιχολέω**, μνᾱσ-, *harbour a grudge*, *SEG* 25.447.4-5 (Alipheira, iii BC).

***μνηστεῖα**· *sponsalia*, *Gloss.*; cf. *μνή‹σ›τεια· γάμου δῶρα* Hsch.

**μνήστειρα**, for '*bride* .. (Agath.)' read '*betrothed*, *AP* 5.276.1 (Agath.)'

**μνηστεύω**, line 9, after 'censured by' insert 'Hdn.*Philet.* 161' **II**, delete '*promise in marriage* .. E.*El.* 313'

**μνηστήρ**, add '**III** *mindful*, Hsch.; cf. *μνήστειρα* II and *μνήστωρ*.'

⁺**μνηστηροφονία**, ἡ, *slaughter of suitors*, esp. w. ref. to book 22 of the Odyssey, Str. 1.2.11, Plu. 2.194c, Ath. 5.192d, Longin. 9.14.

**μνηστός I**, after 'abs.' insert '*h.Ap.* 208; *betrothed*'; add 'Procop.*Goth.* 3.1.44, *Arc.* 4.37, Just.*Nov.* 123.40' **II**, before '*memorable*' insert '(fem. -*ός*)'

***μνῆστρα**, τά, *betrothal*, = Lat. *sponsalia*, Charis. p. 34.7 K.

**μνῆστρον**, delete the entry.

**μνῐᾰρός**, for '*mossy*' read '*covered in seaweed*' **2**, for '*soft as moss*' read '*soft as seaweed*'

**μνίον**, last line, after '[ῐ]', insert 'Nic.*Th.* 787'

**μνιός**, for 'Hsch. s.v. *μνοῖον*' read '°*μνόϊος*'

***μνόϊος** or **μνοῖος**, α, ον, (*μνόος*) *soft*, *downy*, Hsch.; *ὦ μνοίων μαστῶν* *AP* 5.132(131) (Phld.) (cj., *μοιν* cod.); cf. *μνιός*.

**μνόος II**, delete '(codd. Ath., s.v.l.)' and add '*IMylasa* 302.12'

***μνωιονόμοι**· *τῶν Εἰλωτῶν ἄρχοντες* Hsch. (La.; *μονονομοιτῶν* cod.); cf. *μνοΐα*.

***μογγιλάλος**, ον, *talking hoarsely*, Ptol.*Tetr.* 150 (v.l.), v. *μογι-*; cf. *μογγός*.

**μογγός**, add 'cf. mod. Gk. *μουγγός dumb*'

**μογερός I**, for 'Ar.*Ach.* 1207' read 'Ar.*Ach.* 1209' and add '*AP* 7.457 (Aristo)'

**μογέω I 2**, line 3, after 'E.*Alc.* 849' insert 'w. acc., *τὰς κόρας μ. suffer* from eyestrain, *HE* 3173 G.-P. (Posidipp.)' **II**, delete the section.

**μογιλάλος**, line 2, after '*Tetr.* 150' insert '(v.l.)'

**μόγῐς**, after '**μύγις**' insert 'Sapph. 62.7 L.-P.'; last line, delete '[ῑ metri gr., Il. 22.412]'

***μογόεις**, εσσα, εν, *painful*, *κακόν* Q.S. 4.402.

**μόγος 2**, after '(lyr.)' insert 'Nic.*Th.* 428'

***μοδεράτωρ**, τορος, ὁ, *governor of a province*, Just.*Nov.* 20 pr., al.

***μόδινος**, ὁ, = *μόδιος*, *EA* 13.44 no. 3 (W.Phrygia, ii AD).

**μόδιος 1**, add 'Plb. 21.43.19, Lang *Ath.Agora* XXI Ha 44 (v/vi AD)'

***μοικίω**, v. °*μοιχάω*.

***μοικλός**, v. °*μυκλός* I.

**μοῖρα A I 3**, after 'army' insert 'J.*BJ* 4.9.1.487'; add '*class*, *grade* in a religious society (the Essenes), J.*BJ* 2.8.10.150' **5**, after 'etc.' insert '*μ. τοπική*, *μ. χρονική*, 1/360 of the ecliptic, or of the time of the daily revolution, Hypsicl. p. 5 M.'; before 'Procl.*Hyp.* 3.52' insert '*SEG* 30.1795 (AD 327)' **III 1**, at end for 'Alc.*Supp.* 14.10' read 'Alc. 39.10 L.-P.; *ζώω μοῖραν ἔχων ἀγροϊωτίκαν* a rustic's *lot*, id. 130.17 L.-P.' **B**, line 7, delete 'of the Furies, Id.*Eu.* 172'; line 8, after '(Halic., iv/iii BC)' insert '*SEG* 24.1128 (early ii BC)'

**μοιρᾱγέτης**, after '*IG* 1².80.12' insert '*Schwyzer* 696 (Chios, ?iv BC)'

**μοιραῖος**, add 'adv. -*ως*, *τὸν ἄνδρα μ. ἀντιτιμηθῆναι* *VDI* 1960(3).154 (Chersonese)'

***μοιράφιον**, τό, dim. of *μοῖρα*, Theognost.*Can.* 127.

**μοιράω I**, add '*τέτραχα μοιρηθέντα* .. *ἕδρανα κόσμου* Nonn.*D.* 48.385' **II**, for '*divided* .. hair' read '*gave a share of* their locks, i.e. cut off their locks and laid them on the corpse'

***μοιρηφόρητος**, = *μοιρο-*, Sch.Gen.Il. 8.527.

***μοιρίζω**, *share*, (cf. *μοιράω*), *ὅταν μοι[ρί]ζωμεν* *SEG* 17.415.1 (Thasos, iv BC).

**μοιχάω**, after lemma insert 'properly Dor., also ***μοιχέω**: Cret. *μοικίῖν*, pres. part. *Leg. Gort.* ii 21'

***μολάχη**, v. °*μολόχη*.

**μόλῐβος**, line 1, delete 'Ep.'; add 'cf. *μόλυβος*'

**μολῐβουργός**, add '*POxy.* 915.1 (vi AD); written *μολυβ-* *OWilck.* 1188'

**μόλις**, line 8, after 'Philem. 88.8' insert 'Plu.*Alc.* 2.5'

**Μολίων**, add 'cf. perh. Myc. pers. n. *mo-ri-wo*'

⁺**μολοβρίτης**, εω, ὁ, *σῦς μ. wild boar*, Hippon. 114b W.

**μολοβρός**, line 2, after 'Lyc. 775' insert 'as Spartan pers. n., Th. 4.8.9, cf. Myc. pers. n. *mo-ro-qo-ro*'

***μολοκός**· *ἀνδρώς* Theognost.*Can.* 60 A.

⁺**μολουρίς**, ίδος, ἡ, *locust*, unless related to ‡*μόλουρος*, Nic.*Th.* 416; pl., *βατραχίδες καὶ τῶν σταχύων τὰ γόνατα* Hsch.; cf. *μελουρίς*, *μολυρίς*.

***μολοῦρις**· *αἰδοῖον· κολοβὴ λόγχη· ἢ μόλις οὐρῶν* Hsch.

**μόλουρος**, after 'a kind of *serpent*' insert 'or some small reptile'; add 'cf. pers. n. *Μόλουρος* *SEG* 33.460 (Larissa, ii BC)'

**μολόχη**, (s.v. *μαλάχη* 1), add 'cf. Cret. place-name *ἐμ Μολοχᾶντι* *SIG* 940; also *μολάχη* *Epigr.Gr.* 1135'

**μολόχινος**, for '*made of mallow-fibre*' read '*of mallow*, trade term applied to garments made from a type of fine cloth (prob. cotton) which were imported from India'

***μολόχιον** (B), τό, dim. of *μολόχη*, *mallow*, *PIndiana Univ.* 4.1 (iii AD).

**μολπάζω**, add '*ὕμνον ἀμφί τινα* *A.fr.* 204b.9 R. (lyr.)'

**μολπαρχέω**, for '*lead the song and dance*' read 'to be leader of the *μολποί*'

**μολπαστής**, add 'of Apollo, *μολπαστής· συμπαίκτης* Hsch.'

**μολποδώρα**, delete the entry.

**μολποί**, add 'at Olbia, *MH* 31.211 (v BC); at Hierapolis, *ZPE* 1.185.23 (ii AD)'

**μολύβδιον**, add '**III** *lead tablet*, *SEG* 38.13.B4 (Rhamnous, *c.* 500/480 BC).'

**μολυβδόδετος**, after '*lead*' insert '[*μ*]*ύκε̄ χὂ μ.* *IG* 1³.425.38 (Athens, v BC)'

**μόλυβδος II 1**, delete the section transferring exx. to section I. add 'Myc. *mo-ri-wo-do*; see also *βόλυβδος*'

**μολυβδοχοέω 2**, add '*TAM* 2.437 (Patara; *μολυβο-*)'

**μολυβδόω 2**, add '*ἐπαέτιον ξύλινον μεμολυβδωμένον* *Inscr.Délos* 442*B*168 (ii BC)'

***μολυμός** [?ῡ], ὁ, perh. = *μολυσμός*, *MAMA* 4.280 (Dionysopolis).

**μόλυχνον**, add '(cj. *δεισαλέον*)'

***μολυχνάζω**, *thicken* (intr.), Anon.Alch. 334.28.

**μόμφος**, after '(Mantinea, v BC)' insert '*ἰν μόνφον* interpr. by some as adj. *ἰνμονφον*, i.e. *ἔμμομφον*, *liable to blame*, but cf. *ἐμμεμφής* (*ἰνμενφές* line 23)'

***μονάδιον**, τό, *little monastery*, [.. *τῷ εὐαγεῖ μο*]*ναδίῳ* rest. at *BCH* 98.780.1 (Argos, v/vi AD).

**μονάζω I 1**, add '**b** *to be a monk*, *PKöln* 151.7 (AD 423).'

**μονάξ**, delete the entry.

***μονάρταβος**, ον, *taxed at one ἀρτάβη per ἄρουρα*, *POxy.Hels.* 9.12 (AD 26), *PSI* 1328.47 (ii/iii AD), [*ἐκ*] *μοναρτάβ*[*ο*]*υ* *POxy.* 2143ʳ (iii AD).

**μοναρχία**, add 'fig., opp. *ἰσονομία*, *τὴν δ' ἐν αὐτοῖς* (sc. *δυνάμεσιν*) *μοναρχίαν νόσου ποιητικήν* Alcmaeon 4 D.-K.'

**μονάς II 3**, of weight, add '*ἀργυρίου μονάδα̣ μία‹ν›* *POxy.* 3402.4 (iv AD)'

**μοναστήριος II 1**, for '*hermit's cell*' read '*room set aside for solitary religious exercises*' **2**, after '*monastery*' insert '(for male or female communities)' and add '*Cod.Just.* 1.3.46.6'

**μονάστρια**, add 'also *μονήστρια* *MAMA* 3.45'

**μοναυλέω**, for '*play a solo on the flute*' read '*playing the single aulos*'

**μοναυλία** (A), for '*solo on the flute*' read '*playing the single aulos*'

**μοναύλιον**, for '*solo instrument*' read '*single aulos*'

***μοναύλιος**, α, ον, *living alone*, *celibate*, *EA* 12.151 no. 5.16 (Lydia or Mysia, iii AD), Suid.

**μόναυλος** (passim), for '(*single*) *flute*' read '*single aulos*'

**μονᾰχός 1**, add '**b** of a garment, *single*, *made with a single cloth*, or perh. *unlined*, *PHamb.* 10.26 (ii AD), *POxy.* 1273.13 (iii AD); *μ.*, ἡ, *Peripl.M.Rubr.* 6.' **II**, add '*SEG* 37.1058 (Bithynia)'

***μονείμων**, ον, gen. ονος, *wearing one garment*, Sch.A.R. 3.646; see also *μονοείμων*.

**μονή II 2**, add '*SB* 9683.12 (iv AD), *BCH* suppl. 8 no. 255 (v/vi AD)'

**μονήρης I 1**, add 'of a (Christian) ascetic, *Cod.Just.* 1.3.52.15. **b** *single*' and transfer 'Nic.*Al.* 400' here **II**, for '*with one man to each oar*' read '*having a single bank of oars*' and transfer 'Plb. 21.43.13' fr. section I 1.

*__μονήτης__ (gen.), *mint*, ἱερᾶς μ. *POxy.* 3618.15 (iv AD), cf. Lat. *moneta.*
**μονία** (A) **1**, for '*changelessness*' read '*abiding, rest*' and add '(also interpr. as *μονία* (B))'; for 'Emp. 27.4' read 'Emp. 28.2 D.-K.'
**μονία** (B), add 'v. °*μονία* (A)'
**μονόβολον**, add 'also name of a game of chance, *Cod.Just.* 3.43.1.4'
**μονόγᾰμος**, add '*μουνό-*, *AS* 5.31.5 (N.Phrygia, iv AD)'
+**μονόγραμμος**, ον, *existing only in outline*, in mocking ref. to Epicurus' gods, Cic.*ND* 2.59; of very thin men, Lucil. 59, 725 M. (Non.Marc. 37.9 M.). **II** *marked by a single streak*, of a variety of *iaspis*, Plin.*HN* 37.118.
*__μονογρᾰφεῖον__, τό, *office of a notary*, *APF* 33.24,27 (?iii BC).
**μονοδεσμία**, for 'a tax of uncertain nature' read 'a kind of tax on land originally paid in kind' and add 'μ. χόρτου *BGU* 2285.4 (AD 194/5)'
**μονοδραχμία**, delete the entry.
**μονόδραχμος**, delete the entry.
*__μονόειδος__, ον, = *μονοειδής*, Zos.Alch. 113.6.
**μονόζυξ II**, add '**2** of a limb, *containing one bone*, Paul.Aeg. 6.107 (v.l. *ὁμοζύγων*).'
**μονοθρηνέω**, for '*mourn in solitude*' read '*sing a solo dirge*'
*__μονοικίδιον__, τό, *detached house*, *PKlein.Form.* 239.3, al. (vi/vii AD).
*__μονοκᾰδιον__, τό, a liquid measure, *PPrincet.* in *Tyche* 3.29ff.
*__μονόκερος__, ὁ, *unicorn*, *PMag.* 3.504.
**μονόκερως I**, for 'poet. .. 181' read '*μουνο-* Archil. 276 W. (Hsch.)' **II**, for '*wild ox*' read 'used mistakenly to translate word meaning *wild ox*'
*__μονόκοπος__, ὁ, *a single cutting*, χόρτου μ. *PMichael.* 43.8 (vi AD).
*__μονοκόρωνον__, τό, *a single crow*, *Vit.Aesop.*(G) 77.
**μονόκροτος**, for pres. def. read '*manned by a single bank of oars*'
*__μονόλεκτρος__, ον, *sleeping alone*, λέχος εἰ μονόλεκτρον ἴαυες *SEG* 30.1142.
**μονόμαλλος**, add '*Dura*[4] 93, 153'
**μονομᾰχης**, add '*ITrall.* 100'
**μονομάχος II**, add 'sg. J.*AJ* 19.1.15'
*__μονόμεσος__, ον, *having only one intermediate*, Olymp.*in Cat.* 137.32, Elias *in Cat.* 243.31.
*__μονόμυξος__, ον, *having one wick*, *Inscr.Délos* 1417*A*i59, 72 (ii BC).
*__μονόνυμφος__, ἡ, *having one husband*, metrical epitaph, *IGLS* 1366 (Apamea).
**μονόξῠλος**, for 'πλοῖα *canoes*' read 'πλοῖον *dug-out canoe*' and add 'Aeschin. 2.124'; line 3, delete 'cf. Pl.*Lg.* 956a'
**μονοπᾰλη**, after '**-πάλη**' insert 'Ion. **μουνο-**'
**μονόπελμος**, for '*Edict.Diocl.* 9.16' read '*Edict.Diocl.* 9.13,16' and add 'Callistr.ap.Harp. s.v. ἁπλᾶς'
*__μονόπληγος__, *involving a single stroke*, τῷ δ' ἑτέρῳ (σκαφητῷ) θερινῷ μονοπλήγῳ *PSoterichos* 1.22 (AD 69), 2.18 (AD 71).
**μονοπρόσωπος I 1**, add 'as epith. of Hecate, Ἑκάτη τρίμορφε Ἑκάτη μονοπρόσωπε *SEG* 30.326 (i AD)' **2**, add '*PCair.Zen.* 764.3 (iii BC)'
*__μονοπωλάριος__, ὁ, app. = *μονοπώλης*, *PHamb.* 228.4 (vi AD).
*__μονοπώλης__, ου, ὁ, app. *trader, retailer*, Mitchell *N.Galatia* 418.
**μονοπωλία**, add '*PMich.*I 60.6 (iii BC)'
**μονοπώλιον**, line 2, delete '*PSI* 619.10 (iii BC)'
+**μονόπωλος**, ον, *driving a single horse*, E.*Or.* 1004 (dub.).
**μονορῠχης**, after lemma insert 'Ion. **μουν-**'
**μόνος**, line 4, delete 'by E. only in *μούναρχος*' **I**, add '**3** of a magistrate (normally having colleagues) *sole*, *IEphes.* 3493.' add '**V** *ace, throw of one* at dice, *BCH* 8.501-3 (*μοῦνος*).'
*__μονοσάμβᾰλος__, ον, = *μονοσάνδαλος*, Sch.Pi.*P.* 4.133.
**μονόστεγος**, for '*of one story*' read '*having a single continuous roof*' and add '*PMich.*XII 627.6 (AD 298)'
*__μονοσύνθρονος__, ον, *only sharer of the throne*, of Christ, μ. παῖς πατρὸς ἀθανάτου *PKöln* 172.12 (iv/v AD).
*__μονόσωμος__, ον, *for one body*, κοιμητήριον (lapis κυμ-) *BCH* suppl. 8 no. 153 (v AD), *SEG* 19.443 (Philippi).
*__μονοτᾰφιον__, τό, *single tomb*, Rott *Kleinas.Denkmäler* p. 369 no. 74; perh. also *SEG* 31.1419 (Palestine, iii/iv AD).
*__μονόφᾰκος__, ὁ, *lentil*, *CPR* 10.52.9 (iv/v AD).
*__μονοχῖτων__, ωνος, ὁ, kind of tunic, perh. unlined, -ων μελίτιν(ος) *POxy.* 3201.3 (iii AD).
*__μονοχῖτωνος__, ον, adj. of uncertain sense, cf. °*μονοχίτων*, σ]τολὴν πορφυρῆν μονοκίτονον (sic) *PFam.Teb.* 21.20 (ii AD); cf. *διχίτωνος*, *λευκοχίτωνος*.
**μονόχορδος**, add '(*Arabian*) *one-stringed lute*' and transfer 'Poll. 4.60' to follow.
**μονόχωρον**, add '**2** *single room*, *POxy.* 3057 (i/ii AD), 1957 (v AD), 1964 (vi AD).'
**μονόω II 2 b**, for 'c. gen. rei' read 'without sense of desertion, *deprived* of' and add 'εἰ μετὰ μὲν μαρτύρων .. μονούμενος δὲ μαρτύρων Antipho Soph. 44 A col. 1.20 D.-K.'

*__μόνωρος__, ον, *of a single age*, τῶν δύο ἀδελφῶν αἱ θυγατέρες, μόνωροι καὶ ἴσωροι *IEryth.* 525.5.
**μόργιον**, add 'unless f.l. for *μόρτιον*; cf. *μορτή*'
**μόργος**, add '**III** μ.· (corr. for *μόριος*) ἄπληστος Hsch.; cf. *μοργίας*.'
*__μοργός__, ὁ, = *ἀμοργός*, (cf. *ἀμαυρός*, *μαυρός*) Suid.
**μορέω**, delete the entry.
**μόριον III**, add '**3** (gramm.) *particle*, Aristid.*Rh.* 2.532, 533 S.'
**μόριος**, for '*of burial*' read '*allotted by fate*'
*__μορίτης__, ου, ὁ, perh. a wine made from mulberries (*μόρα*), Zos.Alch. 184.16.
**μορμολῠκεῖον 1**, line 1, after '*Phd.* 77e' insert '(pl.)'
*__μορμολῠκιον__, τό, = *μορμολυκεῖον*, as term of opprobrium, *Vit. Aesop.*(W) 77b, (unless late sp. of *μορμολυκεῖον*).
**μορμολύττομαι**, delete 'Act. *μορμολύττω* is f.l. in'
*__μορμόρυξις__, εως, ἡ, *frightening, scaring*, rest. in Pi.*Pae.* 20.6 S.-M.
**μόρμυλος**, read **μορμῠλος**
**μορμῠρω**, line 3, after 'A.R. 1.543' insert '*APl.* 182 (Leon.Tarent.)'
**μορμωτός**, add 'also as pers. n. Μόρμωττος, L.Robert *Monnaies antiques en Troade* pp. 120-121'
+**μορόεις**, εσσα, εν, app. *mulberry-like*, perh. *having a shiny, bubbled pattern*, like a mulberry or blackberry, (*μόρον*, but referred by ancient lexicographers to *μόρος* *"fate"*), ἕρματα ..τρίγληνα μορόεντα Il. 14.183, Od. 18.298; in unexpld. sense, perh. *glistening*, τεύχη Q.S. 1.152; ποτόν Nic.*Al.* 130, 136; ἐλαίῃ ib. 455; φρυνός ib. 569; expld. by Hsch. as μετὰ πολλοῦ καμάτου πεπονημένος, cf. Eust. 976.40; by Apollon.*Lex.* as ἀθάνατα, μόρου μὴ μετέχοντα.
*__μόρρα__, perh. hyperaeolic form for *μοῖρα*, Sappho commentary, *SLG* 261A *fr.* 2 i 8.
**μορτή**, add 'cf. perh. ‡*μόργιον* (= ?*μόρτιον*)'
**μορτός**, add 'Hsch. (*μόρτος* La., also glossed *μέλας*, *φαιός*); cf. °*ἄμβροτος* and non-Att.-Ion. pers. n. Ἀγέμορτος, Κλεόμορτος, Χαρίμορτος, etc.'
**Μόρυχος I**, add 'also name of a glutton in Att. comedy, Ar.*Ach.* 887, *Pax* 1008, etc.'
**μορφάζω**, add '**II** *make specious* or *adorn*, τὰ ψευδῆ Eust. 1691.8.'
*__μορφίζομαι__, *simulate, make a show of*, μ. τὴν εὐσέβειαν Gel.Cyz. *HE* 3.16.6.
*__μορφόλῠκος__, ον, *having the form of a wolf*, *PMag.* 4.2812.
**μόρφωμα**, add '**2** pl., *idols*, Aq. 1*Ki.* 15.23.'
*__μόσθιον__, τό, dim. of *μοῦστος*, a measure of wine, *POxy.* 1589.17 (iv AD); cf. *μουστάριον*.
*__μοσμένιον__, τό, *little horse*, pap. in *Aegyptus* 6.187.
*__μοσμονᾰριος__, ὁ, (?)*keeper* of *μοσμένια*, pap. in *Aegyptus* 6.187.
**μόσσυν**, at end for 'A.R. 2.1017, Call.*Aet.Oxy.* 2080.70' read 'A.R. 2.381b, Call.*fr.* 43.68 Pf.'
*__μοσχάλιον__, τό, = *μασχάλιον*, *OStrassb.* 677 (ii AD; -λει-).
**μοσχανοσῖτος**, add 'read perh. two words *μοσχανὸς σῖτος* (‡*μόσχος* I)'
**μοσχέλαιον**, add '*μουσχελ*[.. *PLouvre* inv. 6745 app. 177 (*WS* 96 (NF 17).69)'
*__μοσχευτικός__, ή, όν, *used for* (*cutting*) *suckers*, δρέπανα *PCair.Zen.* 851*a*24 (iii BC).
*__μόσχημα__, = *μόσχευμα*, *PCair.Zen.* 839.2 (sp. *βοσχ-*), 4 (iii BC).
**μόσχινος**, add '-ον, τό, prob. *calfskin*, *CPR* 10.52.8 (iv/v AD); perh. also *calf* or *calfmeat*, *PNess.* 85.6 (vii AD)'
**μοσχίον**, add '**II** ἁπαλὰ φυτά .. ἢ κρομμύου τὸ σπέρμα Hsch.'
**μόσχιος**, after lemma insert '= *μόσχειος*' add '**II** name of a month, *SEG* 17.829.5 (*c.*200 BC; unkn. provenance).'
**μοσχοθύτης**, add '*PMich.*IV 225.1814 (ii AD), *SB* 9902 L6, M6 (iii AD)'
*__μοσχολόγος__, ὁ, a kind of *actor* or *mime*, *Inscr.Cret.* 4.223 (Gortyn).
**μόσχος** (A) and (B), read as sections I and II under same lemma **II 3**, delete '*any young* .. even'
**μοσχοτρόφος**, line 2, for '*τιθηνός*' read '*τιθήνη*'
*__μοσχών__, ῶνος, ὁ, *byre for calves*, *PCair.Zen.* 642.3 (iii BC).
**μοτός I**, at end for 'Call.*Fr.* 7.40 P.' read 'Sch.Call.*fr.* 23.21 Pf.' and after 'Hsch.' insert 's.v., *Et.Gen.* s.v. *ἄμοτον*'
**μοτόω**, add '*BGU* 1903.3 (iii BC)'
**μουγκρίζω**, for '*slobber*, or perh. *snarl*' read '*growl, groan*'; add 'cf. mod. Gk. *μουγγρίζω*'
*__μουζίκιον__, τό, *box inlaid with mosaic*, *PColorado* inv. 2 (*ZPE* 93.213, v AD).
*__Μουκίεια__, τά, *games in honour of Q.Mucius Scaevola*, *IGRom.* 4.188.4 (Poemanenum, i BC).
*__μουλᾰγόρας__, ου, ὁ, perh. *mule-seller*, *MAMA* 3.86 (Diocaesarea).
**μούλη**, read **μοῦλα**
*__μουλιατρός__, ὁ, = Lat. *mulomedicus*, *mule-doctor*, prob. in *Edict.Diocl.* 7.20A.
*__μουλικός__, ή, όν, *of* or *for mules*, χαλεινοῦ μουλικοῦ *Edict.Diocl.* in *SEG* 37.335 iii 10.6, al.
**μουλίων**, after '*muleteer*' insert '*TAM* 4(1).39 (iii AD)'

*μοῦλος, ὁ, Lat. *mulus, mule, PMich.*xi 620 v[v] 284, *SB* 9409 *fr.* 7.110, *PCornell* 39.3.

**μουνᾰδόν**, for '= *μόνον*' read '*individually*' and after 'Opp.' insert '*H.* 1.444'

**μουνάξ**, add 'Arat. 119, Euph. 98'

***μουνικίπιον**, *τό*, Lat. *municipium, a self-governing community, IEphes.* 3048.13.

***μουνίφεξ**, *ικος, ὁ*, Lat. *munifex, private soldier without exemption from military duties, PBeatty Panop.* 2.28 (AD 300).

**Μουνῠχία**, read '**Μουνῐχία**' (and so in all derivatives; sts. sp. *Μουνυχ-*, e.g. in Sch.E.*Hipp.* 759, St.Byz.)

***μοῦργος**, *ὁ*, prob. the *brown* one, of a horse or mule, (unless *ὁμουργός* is read), *POxy.* 922.19 (vi/vii AD); cf. mod. Gk. = *watchdog.*

**Μοῦσα II 1**, add '**b** *ἀπὸ μούσης* = *ἀπόμουσον, ἄμουσον, οὐκ ἔστιν ἀπὸ μούσης* it is not *out of place*, Ael.*NA* 12.34, al.'

***μουσανᾰγωγός**, *ἡ*, *leader of the Muses*, title of Isis at Canopus, *POxy.* 1380.62 (ii AD).

**Μούσαρχος**, delete 'Dor. **Μώσαρχος**' and for 'Terp. .. Diehl)' read '*Lyr.adesp.* 23 P. (*Μωσ-* Bgk.); of a man, *IHistriae* 167 (ii AD), 100 (iii AD)'

**Μουσεῖον I 1**, add 'E.*Melanipp.Sap.*prol. 19' **3**, add 'at Ephesus, *IEphes.* 3239' **II**, before 'Paus. 1.25.8' insert '*SEG* 28.60 (Athens, 270/69 BC)' **IV**, add '*SEG* 23.271 (Thespiae, iii BC)'

**μουσῐκεύομαι 1**, add 'Sch.Pi.*P.* 4.526'

**μουσικός I**, line 3, after '*Lg.* 828c' insert '*εὐφωνία* D.H.*Isoc.* 3' **II**, lines 3/4, delete '*lyric poet* .. 243a (but .. p. 96 K.)'

⁺**μούσμων**, *ωνος, ὁ*, Lat. *musmo*, wild sheep found in Sardinia, perh. *mouflon*, Str. 5.2.7.

***μουσόγρᾰφος**, *ον*, app. *written in verse*, *μουσογράφους φοιτῶν ἀρτιμαθεῖς σελίδας SEG* 28.541.

***μουσοεπής**, *ές*, *speaking in verse*, *φάμα καρύσσω μουσοεπεῖ στόματι GVI* 1179.2 (Smyrna, ii BC).

***μουσόθετος**, *ον*, *set up by music*, *Θήβης τείχεα μ. SEG* 8.528 (Egypt, ii/iii AD).

**μουσοποιέω II**, add 'abs., *Trag.adesp.* 496.1 K.-S.'

**μουσοπόλος I**, add '*ὡς δ' ὅτε μουσοπόλων ἔργων ἄπο παῖδες ἴωσιν*, i.e. from school tasks, Opp.*H.* 1.680'

***Μουσότροφος**, *nurtured by the Muses*, in quot., name of a horse, *SEG* 7.213.22 (Beirut).

**μουσουργία**, for '*singing, making poetry*' read '*the work of the Muses*, i.e. *music, poetry*, etc.' and add 'Hld. 2.24'

**μουσόχορος**, for '*-χαρής*' read '*μεσόχορος* (q.v.) rather than for *μουσοχαρής*'

***μουστάριος**, *α, ον*, *of must*, perh. in *CPR* 8.63.2 (vi AD).

***μουσχάτιον**, *τό*, *muscatel*, *PMed.Rez.* 17 (vii AD); cf.*μόσχος* (C).

***μουσχοροσᾶτον**, *τό*, *?wine flavoured with rose-water*, *PMed.Rez.* 17 (vii AD).

***μούσωσις**, *εως, ἡ*, *mosaic*, *SEG* 37.367 (Patrae, ?vi AD).

***μουσωτής**, *οῦ, ὁ*, *worker in mosaic*, *Syria* 1.302 (vi AD); cf. °*παξαμᾶς* II.

**μόχθος**, line 4, delete 'of the *labours* of Heracles'; add '*ἐκ τῶν ἰδείων μόχθων*, by one's own *efforts*, i.e. at one's own expense, *BCH* suppl. 8 no. 62'

**μοχλεία**, line 1, for '= sq. 1' read '*leverage*', for '*Supp.Epigr.* 2.569.19 (Didyma, ii BC)' read '*Didyma* 40.25 (ii BC)' and add 'Plot. 5.9.6'

**μῦ**, add 'cf. Hebr. *mēm*, see also *μῶ*' **2**, delete the section.

***μῦ** (B), used to represent *a muttering sound* made with the lips, *μῦ λαλεῖν to mutter*, Hippon.ap.S.E.*M.* 1.275 (read as *μοιμύλλειν fr.* 124 W.); to imitate the sound of an aulos lament, *μῦ μῦ μῦ μῦ* Ar.*Eq.* 10; cf. *μύζω* (A).

**μῠάγρα**, after '*mouse-trap*' insert 'Ar.*fr.* 576 K.-A.'

***μῠάκανθα**, *ἡ*, = *μυάκανθος*, *Gp.* 10.21.6.

**μυάκιον**, after 'dim. of *μύαξ*' insert '**II** *spoon*' and add '*BGU* 2360.6 (iii/iv AD)'

***μυγερός**, *ὁ*, = *νυκτικόραξ*, Cyran. 29.

**μύγματα**, delete the entry (v. *ἀμύγματα*).

**μυδαλέος**, read '**μῡδᾰλέος**' and delete note on quantity.

**μυδάω**, after lemma insert 'aor. *μυδῆσαι* Hsch., pf. *μεμύδηκα* Dsc. (v. infra)'

***μυδροστᾰσία**, *ἡ*, *place of an anvil, forge*, Roueché *Aphrodisias* 208 (Chr.).

**μυελός 1**, add 'perh. as the vital fluid, A.*Ag.* 76' deleting this ref. fr. section 4.

**μυέω I**, add 'in this sense Myc. *mu-jo-me-no*, but for form see °*μύω*' **II**, add 'w. gen., *οὔτε γὰρ εὐεπίης Μου[σ]ῶν φιλίων ἐμυήθης* Mitchell *N.Galatia* 146'

**μύζω** (B), add 'Archil. 42.2 W. (cj.), Hsch.'

***μῦθαρ**· *μῦθος* Hsch.

**μυθίζω**, med., after 'Perict.ap.Stob. 4.28.19' insert '*AP* 12.181 (Strato)'

**μυθολογεύω**, delete 'prob. rest. in Sapph.*Supp.* 7.4'

**μυθολόγος II 1**, for 'Call.*Aet.* 3.1.55' read 'Call.*fr.* 75.55 Pf.'

**μῦθος II 2**, add '*λέγοντος δέ μου ταῦτα, ἀπεκρίνατό μοι ὅτι μύθους λέγοιμι* D. 50.40' **III**, add 'Sch.Od. 21.71'

**μυίαγρος**, line 2, for 'prob.' read 'v.l. Myiacores'

**μῡκάομαι 2**, line 6, after 'Theoc. 22.75' insert 'of the sound made by a water-clock, Mesom. 8.28 H. (*μηκ-* cod.)'

**μύκημα**, line 2, after 'A.R. 1.1269, etc.' insert 'Longus 1.21'; add 'of the noise made by a water-clock to indicate the time, Luc.*Hipp.* 8'

**μύκης**, line 2, before 'Dor.' insert 'Att.nom.sg. [*μ*]*ύκη IG* 1[3].425.38 (v BC)' **II 1**, after 'Hdt. 3.64' insert 'Nic.*Al.* 103' **6**, delete the pres. section, transferring quot. to section 1 and substitute '*πῖλος καὶ δερμάτινον ὑπηρέσιον* Hsch.'

⁺**μύκλα**, *ἡ*, in pl., black *lines* on a donkey's back or legs, Hsch.; cf. °*μύκλος* II.

⁺**μύκλος**, *ὁ*, *lustful* person, Archil. 270 W., Lyc. 771; as epith. of a donkey, ib. 816; perh. as designation of a donkey, *PTeb.* 409.7 (*μοικλ-*, i AD); cf. *μυχλός*. **II** (perh. different wd.) as °*μύκλα*, *fold* or *line* on a donkey's coat, Hsch., *EM* 594.21; cf. *ἐννεάμυκλος ὄνος* Call.*fr.* 650 Pf.

***Μῠκονιάς**, *άδος*, fem. adj., *of Myconos*, *SIG* 1024.14 (Myconos).

**μῠλαῖος I**, for '*working in a mill*' read '*occupied at the (hand)mill*'

**μῠλακρίς II**, add '**2** *knee-cap*, Hippon. 162 W. (Poll. 2.188).'

***Μυλάντειοι** *θεοί*· *ἐπιμύλιοι* (*ἐπιμύλιον* cod.) Hsch.; connected with Mylas, one of the *Τελχῖνες* at Camirus, St.Byz. s.v. *Μυλαντία* (a promontory at Camirus).

***Μυλάντιος**, epith. of Apollo at Camirus, *Tit.Cam.* 15 B 10, al.

**μῠλάσασθαι**, add 'cf. mod. Chiot *μουλιάζω drench*'

**μῠληβόρος**, for '*millstone-eating*' read '*feeding at a mill*'

***μῠλινάριος**, *ὁ*, *miller*, *IG* 4.411 (Corinth, v/vi AD).

**μῠλίτης II**, for '*molar tooth*' read '*wisdom tooth*' and after 'Gal. 14.722' insert '*An.Ox.* 3.82.26'

**μυλλός** (A), add '**II** *καὶ παροιμία ἐπὶ τῶν ἀκουόντων καὶ ‹κωφότητα› προσποιουμένων, ἔστι δὲ καὶ κωμῳδιῶν ποιητὴς οὕτω καλούμενος* Hsch.'

**μυλόεις**, add 'cf. *Μυλόεις· ποταμὸς Ἀρκαδίας* Hsch.'

**μῠλοκόπος**, for '*millstone-worker*' read '*millstone-cutter*' and add '*PPetaus* 103.43 (ii AD), *POxy.* 3641.6 (vi AD)'

***μῠλοκρῐβᾰνιον**, *τό*, *milling-bakery*, *POxy.* 1890.6, 19 (vi AD).

**μύλος I 2**, add '*BGU* 2477.9 (i AD)' and delete 'generally, *stone*' **3**, add 'Hsch.'

**μῠλωθρικός II**, for '*IG* 2.860' read '*IG* 2[2].1707 (181/180 BC)'

**μῠλωθρός**, after 'Poll. 7.180' insert 'also *mill-worker*, *Hesperia* 28.232, Ath. 14.619b'

***μῠλώναρχος**, *ὁ*, = *μυλωνάρχης*, *POxy.* 1890.3 (vi AD, *μυλον-* pap.).

**μῠλωνίον**, add 'Aët. 2.183 (220.8 O.)'

**μῦμα**, add '*θριδάκων τρῖμμα, καὶ ὑπόχυμά τι* Hsch.'

**μῡνάομαι**, for lemma read '*μύναμαι*' and for 'Alc. 89' read 'Alc. 392 L.-P.'

**μυναρός**, add 'perh. for *μυνδαρός*, cf. *μυνδός*'

**μυνδός**, add 'Hsch.; cf. mod. Gk. *μουντός dull*'

**μυξωτῆρες**, add '**II** sg., *vessel for pouring* oil into a lamp, Lxx *Za.* 4.12.'

***μυόγᾰλος**, *ὁ*, = *μύγαλος*, Cyran. 42.

**μυόσωτίς II**, for 'Dsc.-Dsc.' read 'Ps.-Dsc.'

***μυότροχον**, *τό*, = *μυοσωτίς* II, Ps.-Dsc. 4.86 (*μυόρτοκον* codd.).

**μύουρος** (A) **1**, after '*mouse-tailed*)' insert '*μύουρα καὶ βραχέα* A.*fr.* 78a.29 R.' **2**, line 3, before 'Ath. 14.632e' insert 'Plu. 2.611b' at end after '*μῦ-*' insert 'A. l.c.'

***μύραινος**· *ἡ μύραινα ἀρσενικῶς* Hsch. (*sea-eel*, cf. *μῦρος*).

**μῠράφιον**, add '*Dura*[4] 128, *POxy.* 2596 (iii AD)'

***μῠρεψᾶς**, *ᾶ, ὁ*, = *μυρεψός*, *MAMA* 3.712 (Corycus).

**μῠρεψικός**, after 'ib.*Ca.* 8.2' insert '*ἀγγεῖον μ.* Aët. 12.55' and add 'adv. *-κῶς in the manner of an unguent*, Asclep.Jun.ap.Gal. 13.1031.7'

**μῠρεψός**, add 'Lxx *Si.* 38.8(7), 49.1, also written °*μυροψός*'

**μῠρηρός**, add '*κύαθος IG* 2[2].1424a321'

**μῡριᾰγωγός**, add '**II** *leader of ten thousand*, epith. of God, *JÖAI* 32.80 (amulet).'

**μῡρῐάκις**, for '*numberless times*' read 'usu. indicating a very large number' and add '*POxy.* 3063.3 (ii AD), Gal. 4.355.11'

***μῡρῐακός**, *ή, όν*, *of* or *belonging to the ten thousand* (in quot., full citizens), *ἀρχαί SEG* 9.1.46 (Cyrene, iv BC).

***μῡρῐάριθμος**, *ον*, *of countless number*, *ὄχλος* Ps.-Callisth. 1.19 cod.C.

**μῡριάς II**, add '*μου[ρι]άδεσσι λάϋς* Corinn. 1(*a*) i 34 P. (s.v.l.)'

***μυρικόω**, *make mute, strike dumb*, *Suppl.Mag.* 55 D-G 1, 8 (iii AD), perh. also ib. 95.4 (v AD).

***μῡρῐοανάγωγος**, *ον*, *that leads up ten thousand*, i.e. *a countless number*, Rott *Kleinas.Denkmäler* p. 375.

***μῡρῐόκλαυστος**, *ον*, *ten thousand times bewailed*, *GVI* 1941.1 (Thisbe, ii/iii AD).

***μῡρῐονταπλάσιος**, *ον*, *ten thousand times as great*, w. gen., Simp. *in Ph.* 479.2.

**μῡρίος I 2**, line 6, delete 'in Ion. prose' and insert '*κραυγὴ μ.* Hanno

*Peripl.* 14'  **4**, add 'also sg., ὑπέρτεροι μυρίον ἄλλων *ICilicie* 49 (iii/v AD)'

**μῡρῐοτευχής**, add '**2** *having ten thousand arms*, μ. ἕδος (i.e. a *tropaeum*), *SEG* 23.451 (i AD).'

***μῡρῐοψήφιστος**, ον, that gives ten thousand ψῆφοι (cf. *Apoc.* 2.17) Rott *Kleinas.Denkmäler* p. 375.

**μῡρῐώνῠμος**, add 'of Hecate, *SEG* 26.819 (iii AD)'

**μύρκος**, add 'cf. Lat. *murcus*'

**μύρμη**, after lemma insert 'in Dor. form μύρμᾱ'

**μυρμηκίζω**, add '**III** med., *have itching palms*, (?) interpol. in Gal. *Med.Phil.* 2.'

***μυρμηκιόεις**, εσσα, εν, *warty*, Marc.Sid. 97 (*GDRK* 2 p. 22, -κώεντα codd.).

**⁺μυρμηκολέων**, οντος, ὁ, an animal not precisely identified (cf. Str. 16.4.15), but in quot. app. used simply as synonym for "lion", Lxx *Jb.* 4.11.

**μύρμηξ** **IV**, add 'Sch.A.R. 2.52'

**μύρμος** **I**, add 'Call.*fr.* 753 Pf.'

***μῠροναρδοπώλης**, ου, ὁ, seller of μύρον and νάρδος, *ZPE* 61.78.

**μῠρόπνοος**, add '4.1.9 (Mel.)'

***μῠροποιέω**, *make perfume*, *SB* 10296.7 (i BC).

**μῦρος**, after 'ap.Ath. 7.312f' insert 'Ael.*NA* 14.15, μούρω *IGC* p. 98 l. 12 (Acraephia, iii/ii BC)'

***μῠρουργός**, ὁ, *perfume-maker*, Heph.Astr. 2.19.16, Cypr. *mu-ro-wo-ro-ko* μυροϝοργό(ς) *Rantidi* 2.

***μῠροψός**, ὁ, *unguent-maker*, *MAMA* 3.289a, 448, 699, see also μυρεψός.

***μυρραῖος**, α, ον, *of the myrrh-tree*, *AP* 4.1.29 (Mel., cj.).

***μυρσῐνεών**, ῶνος, ὁ, *myrtle-grove*, Aq., Sm.*Za.* 1.8.

**μυρσῐνίτης** **II 2**, add 'also τιθύμαλλος μ. Afric.*Cest.* p. 15 V.'

**⁺μύρσος**· κόφινος ὦτα ἔχων, ὃς καὶ ἄρριχος Hsch., cf. Call.*fr.* 756 Pf.

***Μυρτάτης**, ου, ὁ, epith. of Apollo, *SEG* 23.655 (Paphos, iii BC).

**μύρτον** **II**, add '*AP* 7.406 (Theodorid.)'

**μύρω** **II 1**, line 5, for 'opt.' read 'subj.'

**μῦς** **I**, add 'μ. ἐλιοί *dormice*, *Edict.Diocl.* 4.38, v. ἐλειός'  **V**, for this section read '*gag, muzzle* (sts. taken as separate word), Herod. 3.85, 5.68' (deleting this from section I 1)

**μύσαγμα**, add '*PMag.* 4.2576, 2645'

**μυσάλμαι**, delete the entry.

***μυσάλμης**, ου, ὁ, *one who lives very cheaply*, Eust. 1828.15, cf. 1507.2, μυσάλμαι· πολὺ πεινῶντες καὶ ‹τὰ εὐτελέστατα› (‹ὁτιοῦν› La.) ἐσθίοντες Hsch.

**μυσάρχης**, delete the entry.

***Μῡσάρχης**, ου, ὁ, *leader of the Mysians*, Lxx *2Ma.* 5.24.

***Μυσαχέων**, gen. pl., name of a kinship group at Naupactus, *IG* 9²*.*718.22, 28 (Locris, v BC).

**μῠσαχνός**, after '*defiled*' insert 'Hippon. 105.10 W.' and for 'Archil. 184' read 'Archil. 209 W.'

**μύσαχος**, delete the entry.

***μυσαχρόν**· μυσαρόν, μυσαχθές Hsch.

***Μῡσία**, ἡ, *Mysia*, Hdt. 160.4, X.*An.* 7.8.8, etc.  **II** Lat. *Moesia*, *SEG* 31.1116, J.*BJ* 4.10.6, Plu.*Oth.* 4, etc.

***μυσίδιον**, τό, (written μυσίδην) Iambl.Alch. 286.18, 288.3, dim. of μίσυ I.

**Μύσιος**, add 'στιχάριον *M. PWash.* 58.5 (v AD)'

***μύσκελος**· στραβόπους Cyr., cf. pers. n. Μύσκελος *GDI* 345.75, Μύσκων Th. 8.85.3.

**μυσπολέω**, delete 'with a play on μυστιπολέω'

**μυστᾰγωγία**, add '**IV** fig., of initiation into the business of tax-farming, *PTeb.* 812.5 (ii BC).'

**μύσταξ**, delete 'Dor. and Lacon. .. fem.' and add 'cf. βύσταξ'

**μυστάρχης**, add '*SEG* 24.1050 (Moesia, ii AD)'

***μυσταρχικός** (sc. βωμός), *of* or *for a* μυστάρχης, Robert *Ét.Anat.* 291 (Amastris).

***μυστηγορία**, ἡ, *mystical discourse*, Procl. *in Prm.* p. 779.15.

**μυστηριακός**, after 'Ptol.*Tetr.* 163' insert '167 (both of persons)'

**μυστηριάρχης**, add '*TAM* 4(1).262'

**μυστήριον** **I 1**, add 'applied also to Chr. rites, Just.*Nov.* 123.31, al.'  **2**, add '**c** *hall used by* μύσται, *Sardis* 7(1).17.6.  **d** *tomb*, *SEG* 31.1388 (Syria, Jewish).'  **3**, add '**b** *secret sign*, *PVindob.* G30052 + 13607.11 (*Pap.Flor.* VII 337, c.AD 300).'

**μύστης** **1**, add 'μύστα λέων *SEG* 30.1562 (epigr. on image of lion, w. ref. to grade in Mithraism)'

**⁺μυστίλη**, ἡ, *spoon*, Aret.*CA* 1.4, 10, *CD* 3, Ath. 3.126a.  **b** a crust of bread scooped out to the form of a spoon, Ar.*Eq.* 1168, Pherecr. 113.5 K.-A., Poll. 6.87.

***μυστιονίκης**, ου, ὁ, victor in some unidentified games or event, (cf. perh. °μυστικὸς ἀγών, ἱερονίκης) *POxy.Hels.* 25.31 (AD 264, sp. -νείκ-).

**μυστιπόλος**, add 'masc. subst. Orph.*H.* 18.18, 25.10, al.'

**μύστις**, add 'μύστισι σὺν βάκχαις *POxy.* 3723.13 (ii AD)'

**μυστοδόκος**, add '*PMag.* 20 ii 8'

***μυστρικός**, written μουστρικός, ὁ, *spoon-maker*, *MAMA* 4.100 (Synnada, vi AD).

**μυστρίον** **II**, delete the section transferring quot. to section I; add '*PMich.*XIV 684.14 (vi AD, sp. μιστ-); cf. mod. Gk. μυστρί'

**μύστρον** **2**, add '*bricklayer's trowel*, *Vit.Aesop.*(G) 116'

**μῡτᾰκισμός**, delete 'Diom. p. 453 K.' and after '*Gloss.*, etc.' insert 'a fault of pronunciation, Diom. p. 453 K. (pl.)'

**⁺μύτης** (μύτις La.)· ἰχθὺς θήλεια ἥτις ἄνευ ἄρρενος οὐ νέμεται· καὶ ὁ ἐνεός· καὶ ὁ μὴ λαλῶν καὶ ὁ πρὸς τὰ ἀφροδίσια ἐκλελυμένος Hsch.

**μύτις** **II**, add 'cf. mod. Gk. μύτη'  **III**, add 'see also °μύτης'

**μύττακες**, after 'Ἴωνες' insert '(Λάκωνες vel Κρῆτες cj. La.)'

**μυττωτός**, add 'title of work by Parthenius'

**μύχατος**, add 'ἐνὶ μυχάτοισι δόμοιο Q.S. 13.385 codd.'

**μυχή**, delete the entry.

**μυχθίζω** **1**, for this section read 'app. *moan noisily*, A.*fr.* 461 R. (perh. referring to ἀναμυχθίζομαι A.*fr.* 473, cf. ἐκ δὲ τοῦ μύζειν καὶ ὁ μυκτὴρ λέγεται καὶ ὁ μυγμὸς καὶ τὸ μυχθίζειν παρά τε Αἰσχύλῳ καὶ ἄλλοις Eust. 440.25; see also ib. 1965.47), Call.*Dian.* 61 (cj., codd. μοχθ-)'

**μῠχός** **1**, add 'φρένων .. ἐν μύχῳ Theoc. 29.3'

**μύω** **I 2**, after 'S.*fr.* 774' insert 'πρὶν μύσαι id.*Inach.* (*fr.* 269c.24 R.)'  add 'cf. Myc. *mu-jo-me-no* (part., prob. dat. sg.), but in sense as μυέω'

**μῠωξία**, add 'Gr.Naz.*Ep.* 4'

**μῠωπάζω**, add 'Heph.Astr. 3.45.2'

**μῠωπίζω**, for pres. def. read '*spur* or *goad*'

**μύωψ** **I**, add 'transf., of a flower which closes when the sun is obscured, κόρκορον Nic.*Th.* 626'

***μωιδων**, unexpld. wd., Pi. in Hdn.*fr.* 7 H.; cf. Hsch. μωδεῖ· λαλεῖ, ᾄδει.

**μώϊον**, after 'measure of capacity' insert 'equivalent to 2 γόμοι (cf. T.Reekmans, *Sixth Century Account of Hay* (= *SB* 9920), p. 31 no. 2)'

**μῶκος**, delete 'cj. in Epich. 148'

***μωληθμός**· μάχη Theognost.*Can.* 60 A. (-λιθ- codd.).

***μωλία**, ἡ, *battle*, Hsch.; cf. μῶλος.

***μῶλον**, τό, kind of garlic, Plin.*HN* 26.33; cf. μῶλυ II.

***μῶλος** (B), ὁ, = Lat. *moles*, *mole*, *breakwater*, *Cod.Just.* 10.30.4 pr.

**μωλῡτική**, delete the entry.

***μωλῡτικός**, ή, όν, *coming to a head*, of a tumour, prob. cj. in Praxag.ap.Orib. 44.18.2.  **2** -ή· φοβερά Hsch.

**μωνιή**, μωνιόν, add 'app. artificial formations after μεταμώνιος'

**μώριος** **3**, for this section read 'neut. μώριον· πόα τις, ᾗ πρὸς φίλτρα χρῶνται Hsch.'

***μωροκυστα**, epith. of a harlot, cf. κύσθος, *Dura*⁹ 1.212 (iii AD).

***μῶρον**, = μόρον 1, Hsch.; = μόρον 2, Theognost.*Can.* 131; cf. Lat. *morum.*

**μωρός** **3**, for 'things' read 'acts, etc.'

***μωρός** (B), ά, όν, μωρόν· ὀξύ, μάταιον, ἀμβλύ etc. Hsch.

***μῶρυ**· ὄξος δριμύ Theognost.*Can.* 60 A., Zonar.

**μώψ**, add 'cf. μύωψ, νώψ'

# N

**νάβλα**, for pres. def. read 'a Phoenician *harp*'; line 2, delete 'cj. in S.*Fr.* 849'; line 3, after 'cf. ναῦλον I ' insert 'ναῦλα'

*__ναβλᾶς__, ᾶ, ὁ, player of the instrument νάβλα, *GDI* 5258 (Acrae; for reading see *La Carie* p. 283 no. 6).

*__ναβλίστρια__, ἡ, fem. of ναβλιστής, Heuzey-Daumet *Mission Arch.de Macédoine* no. 10.

**νάερρα**, add 'app. Aeol. ending -ερρα for -ειρα, (ναιέτ>ερρα cj.)'

**ναεύω**, for '*Leg.Gort.* 1.39' read '*Leg.Gort.* 1.40, 43' and add '*Inscr.Cret.* 4.41 iv 8, 47.31 (all Gortyn, v BC); cf. ναύω II'

**ναί I 1**, add 'in a dependent inf. clause, αἴ κ' αὐτὸν αἰτίηται ναὶ ἀποδό(θ)θαι ἢ ἀποκρύψαι *Inscr.Cret.* 4.47.27 (v BC)' **2**, line 3, after '*HG* 4.4.10' insert 'with petitions'; add 'E.*Ph.* 1665, Ar.*Pax* 1113, *Nu.* 784, al., *GVI* 1920 ([ν]αὶ λίτομαι), Herodes Att. ap.Philostr. *VS* 2.5.3' **II 1**, line 2, after '(lyr.)' insert 'Hdt. 1.159.4'

**ναΐδιον**, add '*IEphes.* 3327 (ii/iii AD)'

**ναιετάω II**, for '*to be situated, lie*' read '*to be inhabited, provide habitation*'; line 2, delete 'hence *exist*'

**νᾱ́ϊος**, read 'νᾱ́ϊος (A)'

*__νᾱ́ϊος__ (B), α, ον, non-Att.-Ion., *of a temple*, Myc. *na-wi-jo* (m. acc. sg.), cj. in Pi.*P.* 6.4.

**Ναΐς** (s.v. Ναϊάς), at end after 'Ναΐδες' insert 'Alcm. 63 P.'

**ναΐσκος**, after '*shrine*' insert '*SEG* 30.1220 (ii/i BC)'

*__ναιτάω__, = ναιετάω, poet. in *MAMA* 1.412 (E. Phrygia).

**ναίχι**, before 'S.*OT* 684' insert '*SEG* 24.73 (Attica, *c.*500 BC)'; add 'coupled w. εὖγε, *ARV*² 28 no. 11, 1620'

**ναίω**, line 1, after 'poet. verb' insert 'also in late prose, e.g. Plu. 2.606f' **II 1**, line 3, after '*h.Ap.* 298' insert '(dub., cj. ἔλασσαν)' **III**, after 'Il. 14.119' insert 'Call.*fr.* 680 Pf.' at end add '(cf. °νάω)'

**Νακόρειον**, read '**νᾱκορεῖον**'

*__νᾰκοτίλης__, ου, ὁ, = νακοτίλτης, *SEG* 17.529.

**νᾰκοτίλτης**, add '*CEG* 626 (iv/iii BC)'

**νακτός I**, for 'τὰ νακτά *felt*, Hsch.' read 'νακτά· τοὺς πίλους. καὶ τὰ ἐμπίλια Hsch.' and add '*frontlet bands*, Aq.*Ex.* 13.16, *De.* 6.8' **II**, for this section read '*choked* (of a river), *SEG* 7.12.10 (Susa, i BC)'

**νᾰκύριον**, add '(νᾰκύδριον La.)'

*__νάμα__, *homage, reverence*, Iranian wd. used in Mithraic inscrr., νάμα θεῷ Μίθρᾳ, νάμα πατράσι *Dura*⁷ 87 no. 848, al.

*__ναμαραν__, (m. acc. sg.) perh. *candelabrum*, *Inscr.Délos* 2240, 2241, app. Semitic wd.

**ναμαρᾶς**, delete the entry.

*__νᾱμόφορος__, ον, *carried on the stream*, *CE* 47.288.

*__ναννούδιον__, τό, dim. of νᾶνος, νάννος, *lap-dog*, Sch.Luc.*Conv.* 19.

**νᾶνος I**, add 'as adj., of ponies, Cinna *Poet.* 9(1)' **II**, add '**b** kind of shallow water-vessel, Varro *LL* 5.119, Paul.*Fest.* p. 176 M.'

*__νᾱοθέσιον__, τό, (?) *temple area*, *PReinach* 2066.36 (ii AD) in *JJP* 11/12.75.

**νᾱολέκτης**, delete the entry.

*__ναοπηγός__, v. °ναυπηγός.

**νᾱός I**, antepenultimate line, after 'Aeol. ναῦος' insert 'perh. in Sapph. 2.1 L.-P. (ναυγον ostr., i.e. ?ναυϝον)' and for 'Alc. 9' read 'Alc. 325 L.-P.' **IV**, line 3, after '(Phaestus, ii BC)' insert '*Inscr.Cret.* 1.xvii 21, al.' add '**V** (*Christian*) *church*, Eus.*HE* 10.2.1, Mitchell *N.Galatia* 211, *SEG* 30.1711 (AD 596).' add 'cf. Myc. adj. *na-wi-jo, of shrines*'

*__νᾱοφῠλᾰκέω__, *to be guardian of a temple*, *IEphes.* 3263 (ii/iii AD).

*__νᾱοφῠλᾰκία__, ἡ, *office of temple guardian*, *IEphes.* 4330.5 (*c.*iii AD).

**νᾱόω I**, for 'τὰν ἀγέλαν .. (Crete)' read '**1** for a ceremony in which the ἀγέλα took the oath to the constitution, *Inscr.Cret.* 1.xix 1.24 (iii BC). **2** in order to give asylum, ib. 4.83.5 (v BC).'

**νάπος**, add '**II** γυναικὸς αἰδοῖον Hsch.'

**νάρδος**, at end for '(Semitic .. *lardu*)' read 'fr. Skt. *náladam*, perh. through Semitic, cf. Hebr. *nērd*, Aram. *nārd(ēn)*, Akk. *lardu*'

*__ναρδοσμῖλαξ__, ακος, ἡ, uncertain whether an otherwise unattested plant, or a combination of νάρδος and σμῖλαξ, *PMed.Rez.* 8.11.

*__Ναρηνός__, ὁ, title of Zeus in Dacia, *SEG* 25.828, al. (Rom.imp.).

*__Ναρθάκιον__, τό, place-name in Thessalian Phthiotis, Xen.*HG* 4.3.8, Str. 9.5.10, etc.

*__ναρθᾱκιῶντες__· νάρθηξι πλήσσοντες Hsch.

**ναρθηκιάω**, delete the entry.

**ναρθήκιον**, add '**III** *medicine chest*, Cic.*Fin.* 2.22, Mart. 14.78.1.'

**ναρθηκοφόρος 2**, add '*TAM* 5(1).822 (AD 198/9)'

**νάρθηξ**, line 1, after lemma insert '(originally -ᾱκ- suffix, v. °Ναρθάκιον, °ναρθᾱκιῶντες, νάθραξ)'; lines 4/6, for 'as a schoolmaster's *cane* .. Onos. 10.4' read 'used as a stick for striking, as a dummy weapon, etc., X.*Cyr.* 2.3.20, Arist.*Pr.* 948ᵃ10, Onos. 10.4; by a schoolmaster, *AP* 6.294 (Phan.); used as a splint, Hp.*Off.* 12, Gal. 10.437.18'

**ναρκίον**, after lemma insert '(A)'; add 'and also perh. νάρναξ'

*__ναρκίον__ (B), τό, dim. of νάρκη II, *electric ray*, Philox.Leuc. (*b*).11 P.

**ναρκισσίτης**, before 'Plin.' insert 'also fem. ἡ ναρκισσῖτις'

**νάρκισσος**, line 2, after 'Theoc. 1.133' insert '*AP* 5.147 (Mel.), *GVI* 1409'

*__Ναρνάκιος__, ὁ, title of Poseidon, from Larnaca, Cyprus, *APF* 13.14 n. 2; cf. νάρναξ.

*__νασαμωνῖτις__, ιδος, ἡ, a precious stone, Plin.*HN* 37.175 (fr. Libyan tribal or place-name).

**νασμός**, add 'of a deluge of rain, Lyc. 80'

*__νᾶσος__, v. ‡νῆσος.

**ναστήρ**, add '*MAMA* 7.584 (pl.)'

⁺**νάστης**· οἰκιστὴς καὶ κύριον ὄνομα Hsch.; cf. Νάστης pers. n., Il. 2.867, °μετανάστης.

**ναστός I 3**, add 'neut. pl., ναστά· ψαιστά. Ῥόδιοι. καὶ Ἀττικοὶ ἄρτους καὶ ἱερὰ πέμματα Hsch.'

*__ναστοφᾰ́γος__, ον, *that eats* ναστοί (*cakes*), orac. in Paus. 8.42.6 (v.l. ἀναστο-).

*__νατήρ__ [?ᾱ cf. νᾰ́τωρ], ῆρος, ὁ, *tile*, *AE* 1948/9.136 A 12, 17 (Epid., iv BC), νατῆρες· ὑπηρέται (s.v.l.). ἡ κεραμίδες Hsch.

**νατῆρες**, delete the entry.

**ναυαρχέω II**, add 'perh. also *TAM* 4(1).215.7'

**Ναυαρχίς II**, add '**2** cult-title of Aphrodite, *IPE* 2.25 (i BC).'

*__ναυδόμος__, ὁ, Myc. *na-u-do-mo* (pl.), *ship-builders.*

*__ναυκλᾱ́ριος__, α, ον, *of merchant shipping*, ναυκλᾱρίου Ποσειδῶνος *Inscr.Délos* 2483 (i BC); cf. ναύκληρος, ναυκλήριον.

*__ναυκλήρισσα__, ἡ, *female boat-owner*, *BE* 1961.457 (Cos).

*?__ναυλεπλοῖον__, τό, in formula χωρὶς ναυλεπλοίου, *free of freight charges*, *PMich.*vi 400, 401, etc. (iv AD), unless misreading for χωρὶς ναύλ(ων) πλοί(ων), cf. *PMich.*vi 399.

**ναῦλον II**, add '*SEG* 26.382 (Athens)'

**ναυλόχιον**, add 'Plu.*Them.* 9.2'

**ναύλοχος II**, add '**b** as a place-name, *SEG* 23.189 (Argos, iv BC), *OGI* 1.2. **2** name of a hero, *Inscr.Prien.* 196, *SEG* 33.640, al. (Rhodes, ii/i BC).'

*__ναύλωσις__, εως, ἡ, *hiring* or *chartering of ships*, *SB* 8754.8 (i AD), 9212.10 (iii AD).

**ναυλωτικός**, fem. subst., add '*Ann.Épig.* 1984.227a'

**ναυμᾰχία**, add '**II** *mock naval battle* presented as a spectacle, Vell. 2.56.1, Suet.*Jul.* 39.1. **b** an artificial *lake* for this purpose, Suet. *Nero* 27.2. **III** prob. *game of chance*, Lucil. 14.460 K., Poll. 7.206, cf. *BCH* 79.547.'

*__ναυμᾰ́χιον__, τό, = °ναυμαχία II b, *Acta Petr. et Paul.* 79.

**ναυπηγέω**, line 2, after 'Pl.*Alc.* 1.107c' insert 'Arist.*EE* 1247ᵃ25'

**ναυπήγιον**, add '*IG* 1³.182.10 (*SEG* 26.21)'

**ναυπηγός**, add 'ναοπηγός *SB* 3506, ναυπᾱγός *SEG* 33.640 (Rhodes, ii/i BC)'

**ναύπλιος**, add 'Plin.*HN* 9.94, also adj., τῶν ν. (written ναυπλοίων) κόχλων Ps.-Democr. 357.16'

**ναῦς**, line 11, after 'Phryn. 147' insert 'νέας Polyaen. 4.7.6, v.l. in J.*Vit.* 33'; line 13, after 'νεός' insert '(Hdn. 2.675)' and after 'Od. 9.283' insert 'dat., νεΐ prob. in *AP* 7.637 (Antip.)'; line 17, after 'Dem.Bith. 4.6' insert 'dat. pl. νήεσιν Q.S. 3.744, 8.362' and after 'νεῦς' insert 'cf. *AP* 13.27 (Phal.)'; line 21, before ':– Dor.' insert 'cf. **νηῦς**, νηῦν, Hdn.Gr. 2.645, prob. in prov. in Suid. s.v. ἐγένετο (= Zen. 3.44)'; line 25, for 'f.l. .. 22.17' read '*Hymn.Curet.* 58 (prob. monosyll.)' and after 'sg.' insert 'acc. νᾶα prob. in Alc. 117(*b*).21 L.-P.' add '**II** app. representing Hebr. wd. for *anus*, Lxx 1*Ki.* 5.6 (ita B, ἕδρας A).'

**ναυστολόγος**, add '**2** *levying seamen*, Str. 8.6.15 (cf. *ZPE* 9.204).'

**ναύστολος**, delete the entry.

**ναύτης I**, add 'ὥστε μή μ' ἄγειν ναύτην *take along on a voyage*, S.*Ph.*

901, cf. Pl.Ep. 347a' add 'III owner or manager of a boat, PRoss.-Georg. III 5$^r$.5, 10 (iii AD), PSI 948.6 (iv AD), POxy. 1947.5, 1948.7 (vi AD).'

ναυτικός I 1, add 'ναυτικὸς ὄχλος the class of poorer citizens at Athens who rowed in the fleet, Arist.Pol. 1304$^a$22, 1322$^b$7'

ναυτιώδης 1, delete 'Plu. .. 128d' 2, after 'disposed to nausea' insert 'of persons, Plu. 2.128d; ὀρέξεις ib. 127a'

*ναυτοκολυμβητής, οῦ, ὁ, sailor-diver, PMich. III 174.4 (ii AD).

ναυτολόγος, delete the entry (v. °ναυστ-).

*ναυτοτίρων, ωνος, ὁ, naval recruit, PSI 781.9 (iv AD), cf. Lat. tiro.

*ναυφράγιον, τό, shipwreck, v. ποιήσαντες Maecian.Dig. 14.2.9 (calque of Lat. naufragium facere).

ναυφῠλᾰκέω, add 'w. acc., θαλαμηγόν PTeb. 802.5 (ii BC)'

*ναυφῠλάκια, τά, wages of ναυφύλακες I, BCH 80.64 (Rhamnus, iii BC).

ναυφύλαξ I, add 'Ulp.Dig. 4.9.1.3, Suid. s.v. ναυτοδίκαι'

νάφθα, for 'Lxx Da. 3.64' read 'Thd.Da. 3.46'; add 'var. forms νεφθαρ, νεφθαι Lxx 2Ma. 1.36, see also ἄφθα'

*νάω (B), = ναίω, prob. read by Zenod. in Il. 6.34, 13.172; Lyr. ap.Clem.Al.Strom. 4.26.167.

*νεάδιον, τό, unexpld. wd., Stud.Pal. 20.233.2 (vi/vii AD).

νεάζω, line 2, after '(Lucill.)' insert 'part. AP 9.261 (Epig.)' III, add 'Gp. 2.19.1'

νεᾱνίας I, add '3 as an Attic cult-hero, IG 2$^2$.1358B.21, SEG 33.147.27.'

+νεᾱνικότης, ητος, ἡ, youthful vigour, prowess, Sext.Ps. 9.1, 109(110).3.

*νεᾱνιότης, ητος, ἡ, = °νεανικότης, Aq.Ps. 9.1, 45(46).1.

νεᾱνισκάρχης, for 'official in charge of ἔφηβοι' read 'official in charge of organization of νεανίσκοι' and add 'οἱ νεανίσκοι οἱ γυμναστικοὶ ἐτείμησαν Διόφαντον .. τὸν νεανισκάρχην SEG 29.1201 (Lydia)'

*νεᾱνισκεία, ἡ, vigour, SEG 13.261.3 (iii AD).

*νεᾱνισκολόγος, ὁ, app. convener of νεανίσκοι, SEG 17.662 (Aspendus), cf. Sch.Juv. 8.191.

νεᾱνίσκος 1, after 'young man' insert 'freq. treated as a particular class' and add 'INikaia 1086, SEG 29.1201'

+νεάοιδος, ὁ, young singer, prob. with unbroken voice, treble, AP 7.13 (Leon.Tarent. or Mel.); cf. νεαρῳδός.

Νεᾱπολίτης, add 'fem. Νεαπολῖτις AR 35 p. 112'

νεᾱροπρεπής, delete 'possessing .. Aristid.Rh. 2 p. 551 S.'; add 'transf., suited to the modern style, Aristid.Rh. 2 p. 551 S.'

*νέαρχος, ου, ὁ, leader of the νέοι, IEphes. 1143, 1145 (i/ii AD).

νέᾱσις, add 'Gaius Dig. 50.16.30.3'

νεάτη, add '2 perh. personified as a Delphic Muse, Νήτας. Μέσσας. Ὑπάτας SEG 30.382 (Argos, c.300 BC), cf. Plu. 2.744c.'

νέᾰτος (A), line 1, after 'η, ον' insert '(also ος, ον Arat. 60)'; line 10, after 'to be situated)' insert 'neut. pl. νείατα as adv., deep down, Nic.Al. 120'

νέᾰτος (B), after 'ον' insert 'νῆτ(ος) SEG 34.940 (Camarina, iv/iii BC)'

*νεβελ, Hebr. wd. = wineskin, νεβελ οἴνου Lxx 1Ki. 1.24, 2Ki. 16.1, Ho. 3.2.

*νεβεύω, perform some function in the cult of Artemis, (?for *νεβ(ρ)εύω, cf. °νεβρίζω) Πολέμων 1.249 (Larissa), IG 9(2).1123 (Demetrias, ii BC), SEG 34.489; cf. °ἐπινεβεύω.

*νέβρειον, τό, name of a plant, = ἐλαφόβοσκον, Ps.-Dsc. 3.69.

νέβρειος, for 'αὐλοί .. 244' read 'Call.Dian. 244; v. αὐλοί pipes made from fawn(-bone)'

+νεβρίζω, dress (initiates) in a fawnskin (in Sabazian revels), D. 18.259, cf. Harpocr.

*νέβριον, τό, dim. of νεβρός, ἴσα νεβρίοισιν prob. in Sapph. 58.16 L.-P.

νεβρῑ́της, before 'Orph.' insert 'rest. for νευρ- in' and after 'Orph.L. 748' insert 'Lapid.Gr. 187.20'

νεβρός, add 'Theoc. 11.40, al.'

νεβροτόκος, after 'bringing forth fawns' insert 'as subst. = deer'

+νεβροφόνος, ον, fawn-killing, πούς A.fr. 47a ii 18 R.; a kind of eagle, = πύγαργος, Arist.HA 218$^b$20; epith. of Dionysus, Nonn.D. 44.198.

+νεήμελκτος, η, ον, newly-milked, νεημέλκτῃ ἐνὶ πέλλῃ, i.e. filled with new milk, Nic.Al. 311.

*νεητόκος, ον, = νεοτόκος, Nonn.D. 25.553, al.

νεήτομος, for 'cut .. young' read 'newly castrated'

νειάτιος, add 'rest. in Call.fr. 384.49 Pf.'

*νεικεογενής, ές, engendered in strife, Simp. in Ph. 161.12.

νεικέσσιος, add 'perh. read νείκεσσι· πολέμοις'

νεῖκλον, for 'cf. νίκλον' read 'cf. °νίκλον, °νικλεῖν'

Νειλεῖον, delete the entry.

*Νείλεως, v. °Νηλεύς.

*νεῖλιος, ὁ, a dull green precious stone, Plin.HN 37.114.

νειλοκᾰλάμη, add '(unless by metathesis for λινοκαλάμη)'

Νειλομέτριον, for 'rod' read 'scale'

Νειλόρῠτος, add 'GVI 766 (Tithorea)'

νειοκόρος, for '(Pancrat.)' read '(Pancrat., fem.)'

νειός 2, at end delete 'IG 2$^2$.334.17'

νεῖος (A), for 'A.R. 1.125, Hsch.' read 'neut. as adv. newly, lately, Call.fr. 384.5 Pf., A.R. 1.125'

νεκροποιός, for 'killing' read 'making lifeless' and add 'Alex.Aphr. in Top. 376.27'

*νεκροστολιστής, οῦ, ὁ, prob. = νεκροστόλος, CE 26.157 (i AD).

*νεκροτάφιον, τό, tomb, BGU 34 iv 17 (pl.).

+νεκροφόρος, ὁ, one who carries out a corpse for burial, Plu.Cat.Ma. 9.2, id. 2.199e, Gloss.

νεκρώδης, after 'corpse-like' insert 'Plu.Phoc. 28.5'

*νεκταίρουσιν· κολάζουσιν Hsch. (νεκταροῦσιν La.; cf. νεκτάρας).

νεκτᾰρεος, add 'also as subst. = νέκταρ, Antip.Sid., Philol. 101.104.7'

νεκτάρθη, add '(ἐζημιώθη La.)'

*νεκύα, ἡ, v. νέκυια IV.

+νεκῠδαίμων, ονος, ὁ, spirit of a dead person (esp. one who has died before his time), SB 4947.1 (iii AD), PMag. 4.368, al., Hesperia 54.232 no. 12; cf. νεκυοδαίμων.

νεκύδᾰλος, for 'nympha' read 'pupa'

*νεκύειον, τό, corpse, MAMA 7.402.

νέκυια I, add 'applied to Caesar's alleged conjuring-up of outcasts of society as his entourage, Cic.Att. 9.10.7, 9.11.2, 9.18.2' III, delete the section.

νεκῠομαντεία, line 1, after 'ἡ' insert 'necromancy, PMag. 7.285'

νεκῠομαντεῖον, delete 'in pl., PMag.Lond. 121.285'

νεκύσια, add 'cj. in Plu.Crass. 19'

νεκυσσόος, for 'rousing the dead to life' read 'epith. of Persephone, speeding the dead on their way'

Νεμέα, line 3, after 'ib. 7.82, etc.' insert 'in title of Nemean Zeus, τοῦ Διὸς τοῦ Νεμέαι SEG 30.360, 34.282'

Νέμεα, add 'Νεμέαια, BCH 81.684'

Νεμεᾰκός, add 'Plu. 2.677b'

Νεμεάς, after 'Pi.N. 3.2' insert 'subst., ἡ N. the Nemean games, ASAA 30/32(1952/4).290 no. 66, lines 16, 17 (Rhodes)'

νεμέθω, line 1, after 'νεμέθων' insert 'devouring'

*νεμεσήμων, ον, gen. ονος, indignant, resentful, Call.fr. 96.1 Pf., Nonn.D. 25.125.

νέμεσις, lines 8/9, delete 'πενθεῖν .. anap.)' B 1, line 6, after 'S. l.c.' insert 'as a statue, AS 37.56 no. 3'; add 'Βωμὸς Νεμέσεων SEG 30.860 (Dacia, iii AD)'

νεμήϊος, for '(expld. .. νέμω)' read '= Νέμειος'

*νέμημα, ατος, τό, bounty, SB 9132.8 (iii/iv AD).

+νεμητής, οῦ, ὁ, distributor, dispenser, IEphes. 1604.4, Poll. 8.136; cf. ἀπονεμητής.

νεμήτρια, add '(Rome, iv AD)'

νέμος, add 'of a sacred grove (perh. influenced by Lat. nemus), Philostr.VA 3.1, 4.36, 7.8' add 'II = τὸ γυναικεῖον αἰδοῖον Hsch. III = τὸ τοῦ ὀφθαλμοῦ κοῖλον (read κύλον) id.'

νέμω A II 1, add 'have legal possession of, (= Lat. possidere), Cod.Just. 10.11.8.5a, 5b, Just.Nov. 119.7' B I, line 1, delete 'drive to pasture'

νέννος, lines 3/4, delete 'q.v.'; add 'Inscr.Cret. 2.xiii 5.2'

*νεόβακχος, ὁ, prob. newly initiated Bacchanal, Sokolowski 3.90.7 (Callatis, ii BC); worshippers of Zeus Dionysus, AJA 66.286 (Phrygia, as adj., μύσται .. νεόβακχοι).

νεόβλαστος, after 'sprouting afresh' insert 'Simon. in POxy. 3965 fr. 27.16'

*νεόβλεπτος (cj.), ον, newly seen, Hsch. s.v. νεώπας.

νεογῡ́νης, delete the entry.

νεόδμητος (A) and (B), after 'ον' insert '(also η, ον, Hsch.)'

νεοζῠγής, after 'metaph.' insert 'νεοζυγὲς ἅρμα Choeril. 1.5'

νεόθηκτος, after 'newly whetted' insert 'Plu.Cic. 19.2'

*νεόθηρος, ον, perh. newly caught, of Chr. converts, MAMA 6.227 (Apamea).

*νεόθνητος, ον, app. who was to die young, epigr. in SEG 36.602 (Maced.).

νεοίη, add 'pl. = ἀφροσύναι Hsch.'

Νεοκαισαρεών, add 'IEphes. 614B.7'

*νεοκέλᾱδος, ον, newly or youthfully resounding, χορός B.fr. 61.2 S.-M.

*νεοκένωτος, ον, newly emptied, κεράμιον Afric.Cest. p. 179 V.

νεόκλωστος, for 'fresh-spun' read 'newly woven'

νεοκμής I, for this section read 'newly made, Nic.Th. 707; newly got, fresh, ποίας νεοκμῆτας ib. 498 (cj.)'

νεόκμητος I, delete the section.

νεόκουφον, delete the entry (read ‡καινόκουφον).

νεόκτῑτος, add 'cj. in A.fr. 78c.51 R.'

*νεόλεκτρος, ον, newly married, prob. in A.fr. 168.20 R.

*Νεομήνιος, v. νουμήνιος.

*νεόπιστος, ον, newly believing, Swoboda Denkmäler 61 (Vasada).

*νεοποιός, v. °νεωποιός.

*νέοπος, ον, perh. uttering new things, Trag.adesp. 654.18 K.-S.

Νεοπτόλεμος, before 'S.Ph. 4, 241' insert 'Pi.N. 7.35'

νέορτος, at end delete 'νεοργόν or -ουργόν codd. Plu.'

νέος I 1 a, add 'w. pr. n., to distinguish generations, εὐτυχῶς Ἡσυχίῳ νέῳ *SEG* 30.1785 (iv AD)' **II 1**, add 'w. name of a god, as title of imperial family, *Μάγνητες θεὸν θεοῦ υἱὸν Τίτον Καίσαρα νέον Ἀπόλλωνα εὐεργέτην SEG* 23.450; *Δομετίαν νέαν Ἥραν τὴν γυναῖκα τοῦ Σεβαστοῦ IStraton.* 1008; w. other celebrated names in honorific inscriptions, *Ἰούλιον Νικάνορα νέον Ὅμηρον καὶ νέον Θεμιστοκλέα IG* 2².3788 (Augustus), etc. **b** *Νέος Σεβαστός*, a month in Egypt, = Hathyr, named in honour of Tiberius, *PTeb.* 561 (AD 14), *BGU* 1.4 (iii AD).' **III**, add 'ἐ[ς] νέω app. for ἐκ νέου *anew*, *SEG* 9.72.127 (Cyrene, iv BC), v.l. in Theoc. 15.143' penultimate line, after 'νεϝόστατος q.v.' insert 'Νεϝόπολις *IPamph.* p. 201 no. 17' at end add 'Myc. *ne-wo*'

**νεοσφᾰγής**, add 'κεφαλή Plu.*Cam.* 31.4'

***νεοτᾱτεύω**, *to be a member of a* νεότας (v. νεότης III), *Inscr.Cret.* 4.164 (iii BC).

**νεότης III**, add 'also, *body of* νέοι at Tanagra, poet. in *IG* 7.581 (*Hermes* 72.233; i AD, ἐν νεότᾳ)'

**νεότικτος**, delete the entry.

**νεοτρῐβής**, for '*freshly ground*' read '*newly threshed*'

**νεοφῠτεῖον**, after '*Gloss.*' insert 'ἀμπελικὸν ν. *PHamb.* 68.23 (vi AD, -ιον pap.)'

***νεοφώτιστος**, ον, *newly enlightened*, i.e. *newly baptized*, *SEG* 4.20 (Syracuse), 8.45.5 (Scythopolis, iv/v AD), *BCH* suppl. 8 no. 123 (Thessalonica, iv AD).

**νεοχμός I**, line 5, after 'Cratin. 145' insert 'A.*fr.* 78c.50 R. (satyr-play)'

***νεόχωτος**, ον, (χώννυμι) *newly heaped up*, ἠρίον *IG* 12(2).489.9 (Lesbos).

**νέπους**, line 4, for 'Call.*fr.* 77' read 'Call.*fr.* 222 Pf., pl., id.*fr.* 66, 186'; line 8, for 'Call.*fr.* 260' read 'Call.*fr.* 533, where sense is ambiguous'

***Νερουαίδεια**, τά, festival in honour of Nerva, *IG* 5(1).667 (Sparta, *c.*AD 97).

***Νερωναῖος**, ὁ, a month in Cyprus beginning 2 March, *Cat.Cod.Astr.* 2.145.5, 146.10.

***Νερώνειος**, ὁ, an Egyptian month in Caligula's calendar, *POxy.* 355 (AD 40/41), *BGU* 713.26 (AD 41/42); **Νερώνειος Σεβαστός**, ὁ, an Egyptian month in the time of Nero, = Choiak, *BGU* 1599.6 (AD 54; -ιος), *PFay.* 153ᵛ.8 in *APF* 4.98 (i AD; Νερωνι); also without Σεβαστός, *PFay.* 153ᵛ.10, 33 (*APF* 4.98f.; abbreviated).

**Νερωνιανός**, add '(sc. λίθος) the *Neronian stone*, name given to the green (πρασώδης) σμάραγδος, Socr.Dion.*Lith.* 26.9 H.-S.'

**νεῦμα I 1**, add 'λαιῆς ὑπὸ νεύματι χειρός i.e. *on the left*, D.P. 517; *nodding* in time to music, Luc.*Ner.* 6' **II 1**, delete the section **2**, add 'fig. ν. ποδῶν Simm.*Ov.* 11'

**νευρά 2**, add 'so ψαλάξεις νευρᾶς κτύπον Lyc. 139, perh. w. play on νεῦρον v' **4** and **5**, delete these sections.

**νευρί̄της**, for 'Orph.*L.* 748' read '*Lapid.Gr.* 187.20'

***νευρόδετος**, ον, *stringed*, ὄργανα Aristid.Quint. 2.19.

**νεῦρον V**, add 'Call.*fr.* 199 Pf.'

**νευροσπαστέω II**, delete the section.

**νευρόσπαστος**, add 'also fem. subst., a kind of caper berry, Plin.*HN* 24.121'

**νευρότονον**, delete the entry.

***νευρότονος**, ον, *gut-strung*, καταπάλτης *IG* 2².1487.88-90.

***νευρότροπος**, ὁ, *sufferer from an injury to the sinews*, Cyran. 105.18.

***νευρόχονδρος**, ον, *neuro-cartilaginous*, Gal. 18(2).612.10.

**νεύω I**, add '**5** *diverge*, *deviate*, νεύσας .. ἄπωθεν ὁδοῦ *AP* 6.220.6 (Diosc.).'

***νεφάριος**, α, ον, Lat. *nefarius*, *immoral*, ἐξ ἰγκέστων ἢ νεφαρίων γάμων *Cod.Just.* 1.3.44.3.

**νεφέλη III**, line 2, for 'Call.*Aet.* 3.1.37' read 'Call.*fr.* 75.37 Pf.'

**νεφεληγερέτα**, add 'nom. -έτης, Nonn.*D.* 38.203'

***νεφελίς**, ίδος, ἡ, = νεφέλιον II 2, *Cat.Cod.Astr.* 8(3).148.11.

**νεφελοειδής**, add 'epith. of (Jewish) God, *PMag.* 4.3068'

***νέφθαρ**, v. °νάφθα.

**νεφόομαι**, add '**2** *to be formed into a cloud*, of dust, Aristodem. 1.8.'

**νέφος I 2**, add 'ἔθανον λοιμοῦ ν[έ]φει ἐνκαταληφθείς *MAMA* 9.79.4 (Aezani, ii AD)' add '**III** *fine hunting-net*, Hsch. s.v. νέφεα; cf. νεφέλη III.'

**νεφρός**, add 'perh. at *SEG* 30.1283.4 (sg. rest.) (Didyma, vi BC). **2** *nephros Adadu*, *the kidneys of the Syrian god Hadad*, name of a gem, Plin.*HN* 37.186.'

**νέφωσις**, for 'Al.*Jb.* 3.5' read '*Aq.Jb.* 3.5'

**νέω** (A), line 3, delete 'poet. νέον Alc. 143'

**νέω** (B), line 5, before 'S.*fr.* 439' insert '(app. implying the double process of spinning and weaving)'; line 6, after 'Pl.*Plt.* 282e' insert 'hemp, καννάβεως ἐνεσμένης εἰς ‹σ›χοιν[ίο]ν *Edict.Diocl.* 36.9; gold (thread), χρυσοῦ ἐνησμένου ib. 30.2 (nisi leg. ἐνηγμένου)'

**νέω** (D), delete the entry.

**νεωκορέω I 1**, line 1, after '*tend*' insert 'νενεωκόρηκεν *BCH* 83.364.45 (Thasos, i BC)'

**νεωκόριον**, add '*Lindos* II 419.24 (i AD); νᾱκορήιον *SEG* 24.277.12 (Epid., iv BC)'

**νεωκόρος**, after 'ὁ' insert '(also ἡ, *IG* 11(2).287*A*78 (Delos, iii BC), Paus. 2.10.4)'; line 4, after 'ii AD)' insert 'Paus. 10.12.5'; line 5, after 'poet.' insert '**νειοκόρος** *AP* 6.356 (Pancrat.)' and after '*AP* 9.22 (Phil.)' insert '**νεακόρος** *Xanthos* 15; **νεοκόρος** *TAM* 4(1).34, *SEG* 31.1548 (Egypt, AD 126)' **II**, add 'νεωκόρος βουλή *SEG* 33.1123 (Phrygia)'

**νεωλκέω**, for 'metaph. .. *Mort.* 28' read '**2** transf., *pull along like a ship*, *haul*, νεωλκῶν τὴν ὁδόν (sc. πρόβατον) Men.*Dysc.* 399 S., τὸ [ν]ενεω[λκημένο]ν (sc. corpse) ἐν τῇ κλίνῃ Phld.*Mort.* 28.1.'

**νεώλκιον**, add 'sg., Sch.A Il. 14.35'

**νέωμα**, add '*CIG* 6850 (unkn. provenance, pl.)'

**νεωποιεῖον**, add '-**ποεῖον**, *BCH* 59.478 (Samos)'

**νεωποίιον**, for '= νεωποιία' read '= νεωποιεῖον'; add 'written ναοποιον in *BCH* 59.9 (Delph., iii BC)'

**νεωποιός**, line 1, after '*IG* 2².1678*bA*14' insert 'νεοποιός *IEphes.* 957, (ii AD), al.' **I**, add '**νᾱποός** *IG* 12(5).173 ii (Paros), 1016 (Naxos)'

**νεώρης**, add 'E.*fr.* 964.6'

***νεωρί̄διον**, τό, dim. of νεώριον, *Inscr.Délos* 1417*B*ii118, 119 (ii BC).

**νεώριον**, at beginning insert 'Dor. **νᾱώριον** *IG* 9(1).692.5, 11 (Corc., ii BC)' add '**2** name of a building on Delos, *SEG* 36.731 (*c.*272 BC).'

**νέωρος**, add '*IG* 2².1.30'

**νέωτα**, after lemma insert '[disyll. in Theoc. 15.143 (s.v.l.)]'; add 'for Lat. *designatus*, οἱ ἐς ν. ἄρχοντες D.C. 56.34.2'

**νεωτεροποιία**, add '**2** *fondness for experiment* in literary style, D.H.*Dem.* 2.'

**νεώτερος I 1**, after 'Th. 3.26' insert 'w. gen., νεωτέρους ἐτῶν τριάκοντα *IG* 12(7).515 (ii BC)'; add 'of the New Comedy, Poll. 6.34, al. **b** *the younger*, *junior*, following a name, [Κάλλι]ππος νεώ(τερος) *IG* 2².2323a, Πομπήϊον τὸν νεώτερον Polyaen. 8.23.16, *SEG* 30.1286 (i AD), 33.589 (iii AD), etc.'

***νεώψ**, νεῶπας· ἀντὶ τοῦ νεοβλέπτους, ἢ νέας Hsch.

**νη-**, add 'for Myc. v. °ἀνωφελής'

**νή**, after lemma insert 'Boeot., Arc. νεί q.v.' add '**III** without constr., in answer to a greeting, χαῖρε .. νὴ καὶ σύ Men.*Sam.* 129, Luc.*Tim.* 46, *Fug.* 29, al. **IV** *yes* (= ναί), Men.*Carch.* 33 S., *Dysc.* 510, *Epitr.* 1120, *Sam.* 385, 389, Satyr.*Vit.Eur.fr.* 39 xiii 23.'

***νηδεής**, ές, *fearless*, cj. in Alcm. 26.4 P.

***νήδυιος**, unexpld. wd., Call. in *Suppl.Hell.* 306.

**νηδύς 4**, add 'meton., *gestation*, νηδύος ἐκ τριτάτης Opp.*C.* 3.60'

***νηῐδία**, Ion. -ίη, ἡ, *ignorance*, *SEG* 36.790 (Thasos, v BC).

**νήϊος**, line 4, for 'νήϊα alone' read 'ν. πτερά'

**νῆϊς** (A) **I**, lines 2 & 5, for '(Call.)*Aet.* 1.1.33' read '*fr.* 178.33 Pf.'; line 4, for '*Aet.* 3.1.49' read '*fr.* 75.49 Pf.'; line 5, for '*Aet.Oxy.* 2079.2' read '*fr.* 1.2 Pf.'

**νήκεστος**, add '*h.Cer.* 258 (cj., cod. μήκιστον)'

***νήλας**, hyper-Aeol. = νηλής, Balbill. in *SEG* 8.716.12.

***Νηλεῖον**, τό, *temple of* Νηλεύς (Νείλεως), founder of Miletus, *IG* 1³.84.27 (written Νελ-, 418/7 BC).

***νηλείτης**, ου, ὁ, masc. adj., *guiltless*, Antim. 177 Wy., νηλείταις· ἀναμαρτήτοις, *Iamb.adesp.* 44 W.

**νηλεῖτις**, line 3, after 'vv. ll.' insert 'also νηλ[ει]τιε[ς] Hom. as cited in *PMil.Vogl.* 17 ii 9'

**Νηλεύς II**, for this section read '= Νείλεως (cf. Hdn. 2.450.26), founder of Miletus, *IG* 1³.84.4, al. (written Νελ-, 418/417 BC), Call.*Dian.* 226; cf. °Νηλεῖον'

***Νηληΐς**, ίδος, ἡ, fem. adj., epith. of Artemis at Miletus, Call.*fr.* 80.18 Pf., Plu. 2.254a, Polyaen. 8.35.

**νηλής I**, after 'E.*Cyc.* 369 (lyr.)' insert 'of smoke, Hes.*fr.* 270 M.-W., *Suppl.Hell.* 1164'

**νηλίπους**, after 'gen. ποδος' insert 'acc. νηλίπουν A.*fr.* 451p.21 R.'; after 'Max.Tyr. 30.6' insert 'νηλίπουν κέλευθον A. l.c.'

**νῆμα**, add '**b** loosely for ὕφασμα, *woven work*, *AP* 6.286.5 (Leon. Tarent.).'

**νηματικός**, for '*woven*' read '*spun*'

**νημερτής**, line 1, for 'the only .. A.*Pers.* 246' read 'A.*fr.* 168.16 R. and cj. in *Pers.* 246'; line 3, after 'Hes.*Th.* 235' insert 'νύμφαι ναμερτεῖς A.*fr.* 168.16 R.'; line 7, before 'Sup.' insert 'ζόη Herod. 4.68 (prob.)'

**νηνεμία**, add 'Arist.*de An.* 404ᵃ20'

**νηνίατον**, for 'Hippon. 129' read 'Hippon. 163 W. (= Poll. 4.79)'; add 'cf. νηνίατος (cj. for νινήατος)· νόμος παιδιαρώδης καὶ Φρύγιον μέλος Hsch.'

***νηοσσόος** (B), ον, *driving ships*, αὔρη Nonn.*D.* 39.177, 40.344.

**νηπᾰθής**, add '*SEG* 32.1608 (Cyrene, AD 251/2)'

**νηπιάζω**, add '**2** *to be a child*, Memn. 14.1 J.'

***νηπιόεις**, εσσα, εν, = νήπιος, *AB* 1089.

**νήπιος**, line 1, after 'also ος, ον Lyc. 638' insert '*SEG* 30.1485 (Phrygia, AD 305/6)'

***Νηπιοτροφικός**, ὁ, (sc. λόγος), *on the rearing of children*, title of work by Mnesith.Ath., Sch.Orib.*inc.* 19 Dar. (= 37 Raeder).

**νηπῡτία**, delete the entry.

**νηπύτιος I**, line 3, after '(Il.) 20.200' insert 'ἐξέτι νηπυτίης = ἐκ νέας, *from childhood*, A.R. 4.791' add 'cf. Myc. *na-pu-ti-jo*, pers. n.'

**νηρείτης**, add 'see also °ἀναρίτας, ἀνηρίτης'

**νήριθμος**, add 'epigr. in *SEG* 37.712 (Chios, ii AD)'

**νῆρις III**, delete the section.

***νηρίς**, ίδος, ἡ, *hollow rock, cavern*, Hsch. (pl.).

**νήρῑτος**, line 3, after 'Od. 9.22' insert '(either place-name or adj. here and at 13.351) cf. pers. n. Νήριτος Od. 17.207'

**νηρῑτοτρόφος**, add '(or **νηρῑτοτρόφος**, *breeding a multitude* (of creatures))'

**νησαῖος**, after '*insular*' insert '*of an island* or *islands*'; add 'γέρων A.*fr.* 46a.15 R.'

**νησιάς**, after 'in pl.' insert '*PBaden* 86.20 (i AD)'

**⁺νησίγδα**, name of a prepared food, ἐν Νυκτί (Philem. 55 K.-A.) ἀποδιδόασι μάσημά τι ποιόν Hsch.

**νησίς**, after '*islet*' insert 'Hippon. 103.3 W.'

**νηστης**, (νασῖτις), delete 'γῆ *PEleph.* 20.48 (iii BC)'

**νησιώτης I 1**, add 'fem. (-ῶτις) Ach.Tat. 1.18, Charito 5.1' **2**, delete the section **II 1**, line 3, after '(lyr.)' insert 'ἡσυχία Plu. 2.602e'

**νησιωτικός**, for '*of* or *from an island*' read '*of* or *connected with islanders*'; line 4, for '*insular situation*' read '*matters*, etc., *concerning the islanders*'; add 'adv. -κῶς, ἀρχιερασάμενον -κῶς, having been ἀρχιερεὺς νήσου *SEG* 23.638 (Cyprus, AD 17 or 18)'

**νῆσος**, line 1, after 'νᾶσος' insert '(νᾶσσος *IG* 12(1).70, Rhodes)' add '**3** *peninsula*, Hdn.Gr. 1.91.13, *EM* 75.1 (of Ἀλωπεκόννησος); cf. χερσονησίζω, Πελοπόννησος.'

**νῆστις I 1**, at end delete 'metaph., .. (lyr.)' **II 3**, delete the section. add 'see also ἄνηστις'

***Νῆστις**, ιδος, ἡ, name of a Sicilian water-goddess, Emp. 6.3, 96.2, Alex. 323 K.-A. (= Emp. 6.3).

***νῆτος**, v. νέατος (B).

**⁺Νηφᾰλιεύς**, ὁ, *sober*, epith. of Apollo (opp. Dionysus), *AP* 9.525 (acc. -ῆα, v.l. νηφαλέον τε *APl.*).

**νηφάλιος I**, penultimate line, after 'Crates Hist. 5' insert 'Hsch.'

**νήφω**, line 7, before 'S.*OC* 100' insert '(i.e. with wineless libations)'

***νίβα**· χιόνα. καὶ κρήνην Hsch.

**νίζω II**, add 'αἷμα νίψαι D.*fr.* 20 S. (*AB* 1.360)'

***νῑκάεις**, v. νικήεις.

**νῑκαῖος**, after '*belonging to victory*' insert 'ἐφύμνιον Call.*fr.* 384.39 Pf., νικαίων ἔργων *PLit.Lond.* 62 (i BC)'

**νικάριον**, add 'Aët. 7.117 (394.13 O.)'

***νῑκάς**, άδος, ἡ, *figure of Victory*, *SEG* 7.1076 (Syria).

**νίκαστρον**, add '(νίκατρον La.)'

**νῑκάω**, line 5, before 'pf.' insert 'aor. part. νικέρας *CEG* 321a (Eretria, *c.*500 BC)' **I 1**, five lines fr. end, c. dupl. acc., add 'Ἴσθμια .. ἐνίκα ἅλμα, ποδωκείην, δίσκον, ἄκοντα, πάλην *APl.* 3 (Simon.)', cf., w. triple acc., ἄνδρας .. πυγμὰν .. Ὀλύμπια *AP* 6.256 (Antip.)' **4**, add '*Apoc.* 5.5' **II 1 a**, line 8, after 'etc.' insert 'τοὺς νικῶντας ἐκ τοῦ θηρίου those *victorious over* the beast, *Apoc.* 15.2 (Semiticism)'

***Νικέρως**, ὁ, a god (cf. Νίκη, Ἔρως), *Inscr.Perg.* 8(3).142.

**νίκη II 1**, add '**b** represented by a statue, *IG* 1³.52.B3, 323.52, etc., Νίκας δύο χαλκᾶς *SEG* 37.693 (*Inscr.Délos* 1403, ii BC). **c** as an attribute of the Roman emperors, *SEG* 30.1245, 31.916, etc.'

**νίκημα**, line 2, before '*Delph.*' insert 'Satyr. *Vit.Eur.fr.* 39 xv 7'

**νῑκητής**, after 'Eust. 157.1' insert 'of the Emperor Constantine, *SEG* 31.1324 (Cappadocia)'

**νικητικός I**, add '**2** *of* or *marking victory*, τὴν νικητικὴν ψῆφον Just.*Nov.* 126.2.'

***Νῑκηφόριον**, τό, a commemorative grove at Pergamum planted by Eumenes I, Liv. 32.33.5.

**νῑκηφόρος II**, line 5, after '*PTeb.* 43.28 (ii BC)' insert 'of the Roman emperors, *T&MByz.* 9.271 no. 3'; add 'as name of a legion (= Lat. *Victrix*), λεγ[εῶ]νος Ϛ' Νεικηφόρου *SEG* 23.317 (Delphi, AD 85)'

***νικλεῖν**· λικμᾶν Hsch.

***νίκλον**· τὸ λίκνον Hsch.; cf. νεῖκλον.

**⁺νῖκος**, εος, τό, later form for νίκη (in Lxx translating root represented by Hebr. *niṣṣēaḥ* "conquer", *neṣaḥ* "eternity", etc.) *victory*, Lxx 1*Es.* 3.9, 2*Ma.* 10.38, *BGU* 1002.14 (i BC), *IG* 12(5).764.2 (Andros, prob. i AD; written νεῖκος), *Ev.Mat.* 12.20, Vett.Val. 358.5, Orph.*A.* 587, *APl.* 5.381, read by Aristarch. in Il. 12.276. **2** *pre-eminence, glory*, Lxx *La.* 3.18 (v.l. νεῖκος). **II** *eternity*, εἰς νῖκος, *for ever*, Lxx 2*Ki.* 2.26, *Jb.* 36.7, *La.* 5.20, etc.

***νικύλεον**, τό, a kind of fig, Cretan, Hermonax ap.Ath. 3.76e, cf. perh. Myc. ideogram NI for *figs*.

***νίκωρ**, unexpld. wd. in Sophr. 133 (Hdn.Gr. 2.938.4).

**νιν 2**, add '*Pae.Delph.* 11'

***Νινεύδιος**, ὁ, cult-title of Zeus at Aphrodisias, *BCH* 9.80 no. 10, *MAMA* 8.410, *ABSA* 59.16ff. no. 19.

***νίνισσα**, ἡ, perh. *midwife*, *MAMA* 7.554 (?or to be read as termination of a preceding pr. n.).

**νιννίον**, read 'νίννιον'; add 'cf. *ninnium*, Pl.*Poen.* 371 (dub. sens.)'

***νιπτέον**, *one must wash*, τοὺς πόδας Aët. 16.64.

***νίπτης**, ου, ὁ, *washer, cleaner*, *POxy.* 1917.39 (vi AD).

***νίτρῐνος**, η, ον, *of* or *derived from* νίτρον, χοῖσκος, *Inscr.Délos* 1426Ai15.

***νιτρίς**, ίδος, ἡ, some form or derivative of νίτρον, *Inscr.Délos* 1417Ai65.

**νίτρον**, penultimate line, for 'mixed with oil as a soap' read 'used in cleaning, ῥύμματι καὶ ν. Χαλαστραίῳ'

**νιτροπηγικός**, add 'Paul.Aeg. 7.13.17 (326.14 H.)'

***νιτροπώλης**, ου, ὁ, *seller of* νίτρον, *SB* 3913 (Antinoopolis, Chr.), *PVindob.*G 14296 (*Tyche* 6.118, v/vi AD).

**νιτρώδης I 1**, after 'impregnated with ν.' insert '*alkaline*' **2**, delete the section transferring quot. to section 1. **II**, add '*CIL* 10.6786, 6789 (tit. Lat.)'

**νῐφετός 1**, add '*AP* 7.8 (Antip.Sid.)'

**νῐφόεις II**, add 'Nic.*Th.* 291'

**νῐφοστῐβής**, for '*piled with snow*' read '*walking over the snow*'

***Νοέμβριος**, ον, Lat. *Novembris*, *IGRom.* 1.176, πρὸ γ' ἰδῶν Νοεμβρ[ίων] ib. 4.347 (AD 117), *SB* 10305.1 (AD 124), καλανδῶν Νοεμβρίων *SEG* 31.830 (Sicily, iv/v AD), etc.

**νοερός**, lines 1/2, delete 'ψυχαὶ .. (v.l., Comp.)' add '**b** *intelligent, quick*, ἐάνπερ γε ᾖ ὁ πυλωρὸς νοερός Aen.Tact. 28.2, Onos. 1.7.'

**νοέω**, line 8 and **I 3**, line 10, for 'Anacr. 10' read 'Anacr. 24 P.'

**νόημα**, line 2, after 'νόημα 105.3)' insert 'Aeol. **νόημμα** Sapph. 60.3 L.-P., etc.' **I 4**, for this section read '*ingenious saying, conceit*, Eust. 1634.14 (referring to Epich. 87)'

**νοθεύω III**, after 's.v. Ἴλιον' insert 'Ath. 10.455c'

***νοθογένης**, ου, ὁ, app. *cross-bred offspring*, ψήληκες· τῶν ἀλεκτρυόνων οἱ νοθογένναι Hsch., Suid.

***νοθολογέω**, perh. *speak deceptively* or *disingenuously*, ‹ἐξ ἐθνῶν μὲν› ὥσπερ κιλικίζειν τὸ νοθολογεῖν Suet.*Blasph.* 251 T.

**νόθος II**, line 7, for '*meretricious*' read '*not genuine* (opp. ἁπλοῦς)'

***νομάδιον**, τό, *guinea-fowl chick*, *SB* 10270.33.5, 34.3 (iii AD).

**⁺νομαῖος**, α, ον, *reared* or *growing in pastures*, χίμαρος *AP* 6.157 (Theodorid.); ἕρπυλλον Nic.*Th.* 67.

**νόμαιος 1**, add 'ἀλάλαγμα ν. Call.*fr.* 719 Pf.'

***νομάριον** (B), τό, perh. dim. of νομός or νομή, *SB* 7530.19 (i BC).

**νομάς II**, line 1, delete 'fem.'; line 2, delete 'calf *of the pastures*, i.e. fatted' **4**, delete the section.

**νομευτικός II**, for this section read 'of persons, *occupied* or *employed in herding*, νεανίσκος Plu. 2.149c; ἄνδρες Ael.*NA* 14.16'

**νομεύω 2**, delete the section.

**νομή IV**, add 'Lxx 2*Ma.* 5.14 (cod. Ven.), prob. in 3*Ma.* 1.5'

**νομίζω I 1**, transfer 'ν. θειότατον νόμον Gorg.*fr.* 6 D.' to section II 1.

**⁺νομικάριος**, ὁ, app. some official in a νομός, *PBeatty Panop.* 1.252 (AD 298), *POxy.* 3190.4 (iii/iv AD), *PMich.*inv. 439 (*BASP* 16.146, iv AD), etc.

**νομικός**, line 1, after 'ή, όν' insert '(also ός, όν *SEG* 26.821 (Thrace, *c.*100 BC)' **I 1**, add '**b** *having the character of law*, νομικώτεροι οἱ νόμοι Men.Rh. p. 375 S.' **2**, at end after 'Plu.*Cic.* 26' insert 'νομική (sc. τέχνη) *jurisprudence*, *GVI* 2021.3 (Amasia, i/ii AD)'

**νόμιμος I 1**, add 'ν. γάμος *lawful* wedlock, Mitteis *Chr.* II.372, VI.7 (ii AD), *AP* 5.267.7 (Agath.); ν. ἐπίτροπος = Lat. *tutor legitimus*, Modest.*Dig.* 27.1.10.7; ν. κληρονομία = Lat. *legitima hereditas*, legacy *in accordance with the civil law* (on intestacy), ib. 26.6.2.1; ἐμπόριον ν., *officially regulated* port, *Peripl.M.Rubr.* 4, 21, 35' **II 1**, at end, sg., add 'ἡ παροῦσα διάταξις .. κελεύει .. τὸ αὐτὸ νόμιμον κρατεῖν *Cod.Just.* 4.35.24'

***νόμιμος** (B), ον, *pasture-*, *perh.* in *IMylasa* 273.2, 274.8, 275.6 (papp., νομίμου γῆς)).

**νόμος** (A) **2**, for this section read 'ν. τέλος *pasture-dues*, *IG* 7.2870.16 (Coronea, ii AD); so νόμιον, τό, *PStrassb.* 21.14 (ii AD)'

**νόμισμα II**, add 'spec. = χρυσοῦς I 3 (Lat. *aureus*), D.C. 55.12.4, Scaev.*Dig.* 40.4.60'

**νομιστί**, add 'combining sense of *by law*, M.Ant. 7.31'

***νομμοκλάριος**, ὁ, perh. = Lat. *nummularius*, *money-changer*, *MAMA* 3.302 (Corycus).

***νομογρᾰφεῖον**, τό, office of the νομογράφοι, *POxy.* 2726.27 (ii AD).

***νομοδεικτέω**, *act as* νομοδείκτης, *POxy.Hels.* 25.21 (AD 264).

**νομοθετέω II**, add 'foll. by ὥστε, *Cod.Just.* 1.11.10.5, 8.10.12.7'

**νομοθέτημα I**, add 'representing Lat. *rogatio*, D.C. 38.6.1'

**νομοθέτης II**, add '**2** at Rome, used for *decemviri*, D.S. 12.24.1, D.H. 10.57.1.'

***νομοθετητόν**, gloss on θεμιστευτόν, Hsch.

**νομομᾰθής**, add '*CIJud.* 113, 193, 333 (Rome, ii/iii AD)'

**νομός I 3**, add 'cf. °νόμος I 1 e' **II 1**, delete the section transferring quots. to section I 1

**νόμος I 1 e**, line 6, after 'Hdt. 9.48' insert '(in this and similar phrases νομός, *distribution*, shd. perh. be read); cf. νομή IV' add '**f**

adverbial acc., w. gen. *after the practice* of, τετράποδος νόμον Pl.*Phdr.* 250e.'

**⁺νομώνης**, ου, Boeot. **-ώνας**, ὁ, official who collects dues for the use of public pasture, *IG* 7.3171.43 (Orchomenus).

***νόνναι** v. °νῶναι.

**⁺νόννος**, v. νέννος.

***νοουίκιος**, ον, =Lat. *novicius, of recent standing*, νοουίκιον δοῦλον ἢ δούλην *SEG* 39.1180 117 (Ephesus, i AD).

**νόος**, line 3, after '(iamb.)' insert 'A.*Pr.* 164 (lyr.)'; line 9, after 'ibid.' insert '(gen. pl. νῶν Plot. 4.3.14)'

**νορύη**, add 'rest. in Lang *Ath.Agora* XXI B19'

**νοσᾰκερός**, for 'Vulgar' read 'Com.'

***νοσεύομαι**, in pf. 'τὰ ἐν τῷ ὀγδόῳ μηνὶ νενοσευμένα the *illnesses suffered* in the eighth month, Hp.*Septim.* 2'

**νοσέω I 1**, line 4, after 'A.*Pr.* 386' insert 'ὁ νοσέων the *patient*, Hp.*Epid.* 1.23, al.'

**νοσηλεύω**, before 'τινα' insert '*CEG* 37 (Athens, vi BC)'

**νοσηλός**, after '(q.v.)' insert 'νοσηλότερον τὸ σωμάτιον ἔχει she is *in poor health, poorly*, *POxy.* 939.26 (iv AD)'

**νοσημάτιον**, add '*SEG* 39.883.6 (Chios, Rom.imp.)'

**νοσοκομεῖον**, add '*CIG* 9256'

**νοσοκομέω**, before 'Iamb.' insert 'w. acc.'

**νόσος**, line 1, after 'Ion.' insert 'also A.*Supp.* 684 (lyr.)' **I**, add '(εἶναι) ἐν νόσῳ *SEG* 34.657 (Maced., iii AD)'

***νοσοτροφέω**, *nurse an illness*, Jul.*Or.* 6.181d.

**νοσοτῡφέω**, delete the entry.

***νοσσάριον**, τό, for *νεοσσάριον, dim. of νεοσσός, classed as non-Att. by Phryn. 182 (177 F.).

**νοσσάς**, add '*PHib.* 181.13 (iii BC)'

**νόσφι**, add 'in prose, *CID* I 13.7 (iv BC)'

***νόσφισμα**, ατος, τό, *stealing, peculation*, *PSI* 1120.4 (i AD).

***νοτάριος**, ὁ, Lat. *notarius, secretary*, Jul.*Ep.* 23.378 B, *IGRom.* 4.235.13, *BCH* 7.244 (Isauria), *Edict.Diocl.* 7.68, etc.; *PGoth.* 18.5.12, *PGrenf.* 63.16f, etc., τριβοῦνος νοταρίων *BCH* suppl. 8 no. 247 (v AD), τριβ(ούνου) νοταρίου *SEG* 28.1284 (Cilicia, vi AD).

**νοτία**, add '**IV** a plant, perh. white bryony, Plin.*HN* 24.175, Ps.-Dsc. 4.182.'

**νότιος I 2**, delete the section **II**, at end after 'Comp. -ώτερος' insert 'Arat. 238, 490'

**νοτίς**, for 'A.*fr.* 481' read '*Trag.adesp.* 261 K.-S.'

**νοτόθεν**, after '*from the south*' insert '*on the south side*, *IG* 1$^3$.426.70, *SEG* 32.161 (Athens, 402/1 BC)'

**νότος II**, after '*PTeb.* 164.17 (ii BC), etc.' insert 'without gen., τὰ οἰκήματα τά τε ἀπὸ νότου .. καὶ τὸ ἀπὸ βορρᾶ *SEG* 23.678 (Cyprus, ii BC)'

**νουθετέω 1**, before 'Pass.' insert 'w. inf. of act advised, D.Chr. 63.6'

**⁺νοῦθος**, adj. *soft, quiet* (of sound), Hes.*fr.* 158 M.-W.; cf. νυθός; but expld. by Hdn.Gr. 2.947 as a subst. meaning ψόφος ἐν οὔδει.

***νουμενάρια**, τά, *window-glass* (= Lat. *luminaria*), *PGot.* 7.5 (iv AD).

***νουμεράριος**, ὁ, Lat. *numerarius, keeper of accounts*, *SEG* 29.642 (Thessalonica), 32.1554 (Arabia, both early vi AD), *PFlor.* 295.8 (vi AD), *Cod.Just.* 1.42.2, 12.49.13.1.

***νούμερος**, ὁ, Lat. *numerus*, in sense of *military unit*, *IGRom.* 3.2, *BGU* 316.8 (iv AD), *BCH* 33.34 (v/vi AD), *MDAI(A)* 13.251.

**νουμηνία**, line 2, after 'Hdt. 6.57 (pl.)' insert '*SEG* 30.980 (Olbia, v BC)'; line 4, after '*PCair.Zen.* 167.5 (iii BC)' insert '**νομηνία** *SEG* 30.957 (Maced., AD 132); **νεμηνία** *SEG* 30.1121 (Entella, iii BC)'

**νουμήνιος I**, delete 'Att. contr. for νεομήνιος' and add 'as title of Apollo, *SEG* 32.337 (*c*.300 BC), uncontracted form Νεομήνιος, Philoch. 88b J.'

***Νουμίδαι**, οἱ, *Numidians*; Νουμίδαι Ἰουστινιανοί, body of soldiers stationed in Egypt, *BGU* 2197.7 (vi AD).

***νούμμιον**, τό, = νοῦμμος 3, *PKlein.Form.* 972.3 (iv AD), *POxy.* 1165.6 (vi AD); written **νούμιον**, *PKlein.Form.* 87.3, *PMasp.* 9$^v$.24 (both vi AD).

**νοῦμμος 2**, for 'λίτρα .. pound' read 'twenty-fourth part of old Sicilian talent'

**⁺νουνεχόντως**, v. °ἐχόντως.

**νυγμή I**, for '= sq.' read '*prick, puncture*'

**νυκτᾰλωψ**, add '**III** another name for the plant νυκτήγρετον, Plin.*HN* 21.62.'

***νύκταρχος**, ὁ, *officer of the night-watch*, *MAMA* 3.428 (Corycus).

***νυκταστράπτης**, ου, ὁ, *emitter of lightning-flashes by night*, *PMag.* 4.182.

**⁺νυκτερεύω**, *spend the night in the open, be out at night*, X.*Cyr.* 4.2.22, *An.* 4.4.11, 6.4.27, ν. ἀθλίως Timocl. 16.1; med., of night-revellers, Timachidas ap.Ath. 699e. **b** of things, *be left out at night*, Aen. Tact. 30.2.

**νυκτηγρεσία**, add 'as name of the tenth book of the Iliad, Sch.Hippon. 118 B 6 W. (cf. νυκτεγερσία)'

**νυκτῐβόας**, add 'expl. of *bubo* in Virgil gloss., *PNess.* 1.955 (vi AD, -βόα pap.)'

**νυκτῐλᾰλος**, for '*nightly-sounding*' read '*sounding by night*'

**νυκτῐπᾰταιπλᾰγιος**, for '*nightly-roaming-to-and-fro*' read '*roaming by night*'

**νυκτίπλαγκτος**, for '*causing to wander .. bed*' read '*marked by nocturnal wandering*'

***νυκτιτρόμος**, ον, *trembling by night*, *Suppl.Mag.* 49.48, 57 (iii/iv AD).

**νυκτῐφᾰνής**, for '= foreg.' read '*appearing at night*'

***νυκτῐχροος**, ον, *night-* (*i.e. dark-*)*skinned*, Ps.-Callisth. 83.6.

***νυκτογρᾰφος**, ὁ, *one who writes by night*, *PMich.* II 123$^v$ ii 14, 23, al.

**νυκτοπλοέω**, add 'μὴ ἐξέστω αὐτῷ νυγτοπλοεῖν (sic) *POxy.* 3250.22 (AD 63)'

***νυκτοπῡρετος**, ὁ, *night-fever*, *PTeb.* 275.22 (iii AD).

***νυκτοφᾰνής**, ές, *appearing by night*, epith. of Hecate, *SEG* 26.819 (after AD 212).

**νυκτοφῠλαξ**, add 'as a Christian office, *SEG* 29.643 (AD 532)'

**νυκτοφῠλάξια**, for '*guard-house*' read 'name of a festival'

**νυμφᾱγέτης**, add 'of Apollo, *SEG* 34.440 (Phocis, ii BC)'

***νυμφᾱγέτιος**, ον, = νυμφαγέτης, (?)Πᾶν]α Νυφαγέτιο[ν (sic) *SEG* 17.82 (Athens, iv BC).

**νυμφᾰγωγός I 2**, delete the section transferring exx. to section 1.

**νυμφαῖος II**, add '**2** Νυμφαῖα, τά, *festival of the Nymphs* at Apollonia, *Inscr.Délos* 1957, *Hesperia* 4.84 (Athens) (both ii BC).'

**νυμφεῖος**, add '**II** *of the* Νύμφαι (νύμφη II 2), *Didyma* 159 i 9 (iii AD).'

**νύμφη**, line 3, after 'νύμφᾱ' insert 'sp. νύφη *IG* 1$^3$.974, 2$^2$.4650, *Kafizin* 21, al.' **I 3**, add '*SEG* 31.1020 (Lydia, AD 82/3), 31.1037 (Lydia, AD 210/1), cf. mod. Gk. νύφη; perh. also *sister-in-law*, *SEG* 34.1221 (Lydia, AD 91/2)' **II 1**, add 'sg., goddess at Kafizin, Cyprus, *Kafizin* 5, al.; of Isis, *SEG* 24.561 (ii AD); nymphs represented in statuary, *SEG* 24.496 (ii/iii AD)' **2**, line 3, after '*water*' insert 'Nic.*Th.* 623, al.'

**νυμφιάω**, for 'mares' read 'horses'

**νυμφικός I**, after 'adv. -κῶς' insert 'Plu.*fr.* 157.6 S.'

**νυμφίος I 2**, after '*Jd.* 15.6' insert '(v.l. γαμβρός)' **II**, after 'Pi.*P.* 3.16' insert '(cj.)'; after 'λέκτρα' insert 'Call.*fr.* 63.11 Pf'; for '*Epigr.Gr.* 373' read '*GVI* 1668'; add 'αἷμα Nonn.*D.* 32.34'

**νυμφοκόμος**, line 2, after 'Hsch.' insert 'transf., A.*fr.* 168.23 R.'

**νυμφόληπτος**, add '**2** *intoxicated* or *possessed by water*, ν. καὶ βάκχοι τοῦ νήφειν Philostr.*VA* 2.37.'

***νύμφος**, ὁ, grade in Mithraic initiation, *MDAI(R)* 49.206 (Dura), Jerome *Ep.* 107.

**νῦν I 1**, line 9, after 'ἀπὸ ν. *AP* 5.40 (Rufin.)' insert '*CRAI* 1982.62' **5**, add 'νῦν ὅτε, (*it is*) *now that*, dub. in A.*Supp.* 630, *Th.* 705, cj. in Alex.Aet. 3.21' add '**6** *in the present passage*, Sch.E.*Med.* 68, al., Sch.Ar.*Av.* 851, al.'

**νῦν δή I 1**, for '*Grg.* 462b' read '*Phdr.* 250c, *Ly.* 217e' and delete '*Com.adesp.* 597, etc.' **2**, add 'Ar.*Pax* 5, al.' **3**, add '*in these circumstances*, Th. 6.24.2'

**νύξ I 1**, line 9, before 'Hdt. 7.12' insert 'Od. 15.34'; line 18, after 'Pl.*R.* 621b' insert 'νύκτα μέσην Hdt. 8.9.1' **2**, line 7, after 'Pl.*Criti.* 117e' insert 'ὁ διὰ νυκτὸς στρατηγός *commander of the night-watch*, *Laodicée* p. 261 no. 3'; line 8, after 'ἐκ νυκτῶν' insert 'Od. 12.286'

**Νῦσα**, add '**III** pl., prob. the designation of some group of nymphs, *ABV* 39 no. 15.'

**⁺νύσσᾰ**, ἡ, *marker* erected at either end of a race-course: **1** acting as the *turning-point*, Il. 23.332, 344, al., Theoc. 18.15, Nonn.*D.* 37.112, Gal.*UP* 16.4. **b** transf., of other circular or continuous courses, Nonn.*D.* 11.165, 39.336; of celestial orbits, ib. 1.169, al.; of recurrent temporal processes, etc., ib. 3.35, 37.6, al. **2** as the *starting-point* of a race, τοῖσι δ' ἀπὸ νύσσης τέτατο δρόμος Il. 23.758, Od. 8.121, Opp.*H.* 5.642, Lyc. 15. **3** as the *finishing-post*, fig., ν. ἀοιδῆς ἰθύνειν Opp.*H.* 3.11, Nonn.*D.* 12.87.

**νύσταγμα**, for '*nap, short sleep*' read '(*period of*) *sleep* or *drowsiness*'

***νυσταλωπιᾶν**· νυστάζειν Hsch. (but v. νυκταλωπάω).

**νῠχιος**, line 1, delete 'Tim. .. by'; line 2, delete '*nightly*, i.e.' add '**4** Νυχίη, ἡ, a form or title of Dione, *SEG* 34.1436 (Syria, *c*.iii AD).'

**νύχος**, add 'inscribed on gaming-board, with uncertain significance, *SEG* 23.620 (Cyprus, iii BC)'

***νώβυστρον**, τό, a term of abuse, perh. *blockhead* (νοῦς, βύω), Herod. 6.16.

**νωγᾰλέος**, add '-έον· πυρρόν Theognost.*Can.* 62 A.'

**νωθής I**, add '**3** *indistinct*, Arat. 228.'

***νωθραίνω**, *to be unwell*, *POxy.* 2609 (iv AD).

**νῶκαρ**, after lemma delete 'ἄρος' **I**, before 'Hsch.' insert 'ν.· νύσταξις, νώθεια, κακόσχολος ἔννοια' **II**, for this section read 'νῶκαρ· ὁ δυσκίνητος Suid.'

**νωλεμές**, after 'A.R. 2.605' insert 'cf. νωλεμέα· ἰσχυράν, νωλεμές· ἰσχυρόν Theognost.*Can.* 62 A.'

**νωμάω II 2**, add 'also of the voice, στονόεσσαν ἀϋτὴν ν. A.R. 4.1006; med., νωμᾶται .. ἔθειραν B. 5.26 S.-M.'

***νωμενκλάτωρ**, ορος, ὁ, Lat. *nomenclator*, *POxy.* 1244ᵛ, without context (ii AD, pl.).

***Νῶναι**, αἱ, Lat. *Nonae*, *the Nones*, *N. Μαρτίων IGRom.* 4.661.31 (Acmonia, i AD), *BCH* suppl. 8 no. 130 (Thessalonica, AD 469); also *νόνναι* Plu. 2.269d.

***νωνυμνί**, adv., *without being named*, Call.*fr.* 43.55 Pf.

**νώνυμος I 2**, add 'Arat. 370' **II**, delete 'Call.*Aet.* .. *being named*)'

***νῶος**· *μωρός* Theognost.*Can.* 62 A.

**νωπέομαι**, for '*to be downcast*, Ion Hist. 1' read '*to be abashed*, Ion Hist. 6 J.' and add 'cf. *προνωπής*'

***νωπήεις**, εσσα, εν, perh. = *νώψ*, Theognost.*Can.* 62 A.

***νώρικον** or **ος**, Phryg. for *ἀσκός*, acc. to Ps.-Plu.*Fluv.* 10.2.

***νωρυμνόν**· *οὐχ ὑψηλόν, οὐκ ἐρυμνόν* Theognost.*Can.* 62 A.

**νωτηγός**, for '*ἵπποι*' read '*ἡμίονοι*'

**νωτιαῖος**, before '*spinal*' insert 'of the back, *ἐρέας λαγείας νωτιαίας Edict.Diocl.* 1.10 (*ZPE* 42.283)'

**νῶτον II 3**, for this section read '*the convex side of a shield*, *AP* 6.125, Lxx *Jb.* 15.26; also a part (?*rim*) of a wheel (translating the same Hebr. wd.), 3*Ki.* 7.33, *Ez.* 1.18, al.'

***νωφελής**, ές, v. *ἀνωφελής*.

**νωχελής II**, for '*abortion*' read '*that which is dilatory in moving*'

***νωχλεύω**, = *νωχελεύομαι*, *Vit.Aesop.*(W) 76.

# Ξ

**ξαίνω I 1**, line 6, after 'etc.' insert 'οὐ ξένουσιν (read ξαίν-) οὐδὲ νήθουσιν v.l. in *Ev.Matt.* 6.28 (cod.Sinaiticus, v. Metzger *Textual Commentary on the Greek N.T.* p. 18)'

***ξανάα**, τά, *crippling of the fingers* caused by cold and weariness, perh. orig. from carding wool, Sch.Nic.*Th.* 383.

***ξανθηρότης**, ητος, ἡ, *golden colour*, Sch.Hes.*Th.* 350.

**ξανθίζω I**, add '*Trag.adesp.* 441'

**ξανθοδερκής**, for '*with fiery eyes*, of a dragon' read '*yellow-eyed*, δράκων'

**ξανθός I 2**, line 4, for 'B.*fr.* 3.4' read 'B.*fr.* 4.65 S.-M.; ξ. πεύκαις Pi.*Dith.* 2.11 S.-M.' and after 'A.*Pers.* 617' insert 'ἔλαιον E.*IT* 633, ξανθοῦ μέλιτος Lang *Ath.Agora* XXI He36 (iv AD)'; penultimate line, after 'comp. -ότερος' insert 'ξανθοτέραις ἔχη[..] ταὶς κόμαις δάϊδος Sapph. 98(*a*).6 L.-P.' **II 3**, add 'cf. Myc. *ka-sa-to*, pers. n.'

***ξανθότρῐχος**, ον, *tawny-haired*, Hsch. s.v. πυρσοκόρσου λέοντος.

***ξανθόχλωρος**, ον, *yellow-green*, ὕδωρ Zos.Alch. 142.8.

**ξείρης**, for 'v. ξυρίς' read 'v. ‡ξυρίς'

***ξείτης, ξεῖτος, ξεῖθος**, = ἑξίτης, *the throw of six* at dice, *PASA* 2.88, 89.

**ξενᾱπάτης**, line 2, after 'ξειν-' insert 'Aeol. **ξ[εν]ναπάτας** Alc. 283.5 L.-P.' **2**, for 'Ibyc.*Oxy.* 1790 i 10' read 'Alc. l.c., Ibyc. 1.10 P.'

**ξένη 1**, add 'ὅτις ξέν[αν] γεγάμηκε *IG* 5(2).343 (Orchomenus, Arcadia, iv BC)' **2**, add 'designating a place other than one's legal residence, *PMich.*x 580.7, *POxy.* 251.11, 252.10, al.'

***ξενηδόκος**, Ion. ξεινη-, ον, = ξενοδόκος, Nonn.*D.* 13.104, 18.307.

**ξενηδόχος**, delete the entry.

**ξενηλᾰτέω**, after '*banish foreigners*' insert 'Plu. 2.727e'

**ξενία I**, add '**4** *sojourn in an alien state*, *Schwyzer* 366.A4, 6 (Locris, iii BC).' **II**, before '*PSI*' insert '*PBremen* 15.4 (ii AD)' and after '(iv/v AD)' insert 'so perh. καλεῖ σε εἰς τὴν ξ. ἑαυτοῦ *POxy.* 747.1 (ii/iii AD)'

**⁺ξενιᾱγός**, ὁ, bringer of ξένια, *PZen.Pestm.* 54.32 (iii BC).

**ξενίζω**, line 5, after 'E.*Alc.* 1013, etc.' insert 'ξένος πεφυκὼς τοὺς ξενίζοντας σέβου Men.*Mon.* 556'

***ξενικοκέρᾰμος**, ὁ, *foreign jar* (of wine), *SB* 10918.5 (iii AD).

**ξενικός I 1**, after 'D. 57.34' insert 'at Ephesus, *IEphes.* 884 i 1 (i AD)' **3**, after 'Pl.*Lg.* 702c' insert 'Διονύσια τὰ ξ. transf., of games in honour of Dionysus, *SEG* 24.1023 (Callatis, iii/ii BC)'

**ξένιος II 2**, neut. subst., add 'of offerings to a deity, Sophr. in *GLP* 73.18' add 'form ξένϝιος, in Myc. *ke-se-ni-wi-jo, ke-se-nu-wi-ja*'

***ξένισμα**, τό, gloss on θαῦμα, Hsch.

***ξενοδάϊκτος**, ον, *that murders guests* or *strangers*, *Suppl.Hell.* 991.96 (poet. word-list, iii BC).

***ξενοδαιτῠμών**, όνος, ὁ, *one that feasts on guests* or *strangers*, E.*Cyc.* 610 (cj.).

**ξενοδοκέω**, add 'Pl.*R.* 419a'

**ξενοδόκος I**, line 4, after 'Od. 8.210' insert 'A.*fr.* 451h.3 R., Call.*fr.* 59.19 Pf.' **II**, for 'Simon. 84.7' read 'Simon.*eleg.* 87 W.²'; add '*AD* 11.61 (Larissa)'

**ξενοκρίται**, for '= ξενοδίκαι' read '*foreign judges* in μετάπεμπτα δικαστήρια'; for '(Patara)' read '(Pinara)'; for 'title of official at Sparta' read 'description of Spartan sent as judge to Alabanda' add '**2** the title of certain Roman judges in Egypt, *POxy.* 3016 (AD 148).'

***ξενοκυσθᾰπάτη**, ἡ, *nonce-wd. of uncertain sexual meaning* (cf. ξεναπάτης), *AP* 11.7 (Nicandr. or Nicarch., -κυστ- codd.).

**ξενοκυστᾰπάτη**, delete the entry.

**ξενοπᾰθέω**, for '*have .. feeling*' read '*feel shy* or *ill-at-ease*'

***ξενοπάροχος**, ὁ, *official entertainer of foreigners*, Arcad.Charis.*Dig.* 50.4.18.10.

**ξένος**, line 5, after '(sed v. fin.)' insert 'ξῆνος, in Dor. pers. n., *Schwyzer* 277A (Rhodes, vi/v BC), *IG* 4.618 i 6 (Argos), *GDI* 4834 b 10, 15 (Cyrene), see also °ξηνεῖος' **A III A**, add 'στρατηγὸς ἐπὶ τῶν ξένων = *praetor peregrinus*, *IG* 9².242 (Acarnania, i BC)' **2**, delete the section transferring quot. to section 1. **B I**, add '**2** perh. as epith. of Zeus, = ξένιος, *SEG* 32.1026 (written ξείνο gen., Paestum, *c.*550 BC).' **III 2**, line 1, for '*fresh*' read '*different*'; add '(irreg. sup.)'

***ξενοτρόφιον**, τό, prob. *payment for mercenaries*, *IMylasa* 651.6 (iii/ii BC, Cret. dialect).

**ξενόω II 2**, line 4, before 'ξενωθεὶς ὑπὸ' insert '*to give* someone *the rights of a* ξένος'

**ξενών**, add 'used to house the sick, *Cod.Just.* 1.3.45.1, 6.4.4.2'

**ξένωσις**, for '*entertainment of a guest*' read '*aberration*'

***ξερεύω**, *become dry* (w. ξερ- for ξηρ-, cf. mod. Gk. ξερός), only found in pf. part. ἐξερευκός, -ότα, as epith. of κεράμιον (-α), referring to sun-dried produce, *SB* 9132.3, 7, 12 (iii/iv AD).

***ξεστικῶς**, adv. app. *so as to shave the surface*, ὅρα τὸ ἐπιλίγδην ἀντὶ τοῦ ξεστικῶς καὶ ἐπιπολῆς Eust. 1119.54.

***ξεστισμός**, ὁ, *quota of sextarii* (measures of wine due in payment), *POxy.* 2114.13 (iv AD).

**ξέω II 1**, add 'fig., of style, Poll. 6.140, 141'

***ξηνεῖος**, α, ον, *relating to aliens*, κσενεῖαι δίκα[ι δι]κάδδε(θ)θαι *Inscr.Cret.* 4.80.8 (Gortyn, v BC).

**ξηραίνω 1**, pass., add 'of corn, *be ripened*, *Apoc.* 14.15'

**ξήρᾰσις**, for '*siccitas*' read '*desiccation*' and add 'Gal. 16.415.11'

***ξηροκήπιον**, τό, *dry garden* (cf. ξηροὶ καρποί, for sun-drying produce, or possibly with little water supply), *PNess.* 31.20 (vi AD).

***ξηροκόπιον**, τό, καισεκπρώπιον· δρέπανον, ξηροκόπιον Hsch.

**ξηρός I 1**, line 1, for 'χειμάρρους' read 'ἔκρους'; line 9, after '(iii BC)' insert 'abs., without χόρτος, *PZen.Col.* iv 95.6 (iii BC)' **2**, for this section read 'of various bodily conditions, λιμῷ γένηται ξηρός Hippon. 10 W.; ξ. κοιλίη, i.e. *costive*, Hp.*Aph.* 2.20; of limbs withered by paralysis, *Ev.Matt.* 12.10, *Marc.* 3.3, *Luc.* 6.6, al.; as a result of fear, Theocr. 24.61; externally, from lack of unguents, E.*El.* 239; adv. ξηρῶς βήττειν have a *dry* cough, Gal. 9.626.8'

**ξῐφήρης**, after 'Hdn. 7.5.3' insert '*POxy.* 3561 (AD 165)'

**ξῐφηφορέω**, add 'D.C. 53.13.7 (*ius gladii habere*)'

**ξίφος I 2**, for this section read 'as a symbol of judgement, Philostr.*VS* 1.25.2; of the praetorian guard, τὸ μὲν βασιλεῖον ξ. .. ἦν ἐπ' Αἰλιανῷ τότε ib. 4.42' **II**, for this section read '*pen* of the squid (τευθίς), Arist.*HA* 524$^{b}$24, *PA* 654$^{a}$21; *sword* of the swordfish, id.*fr.* 325, Opp.*H.* 3.558' add 'Myc. *qi-si-pe-e* (dual); see also σκίφος'

***ξοᾰνός**, ή, όν, app. adj. in Hsch. ξοανῶν προθύρων· ἐξεσμένων; cf. ξόανον.

**ξοΐς**, add '*PMich.*xv 721.57 (iii/iv AD)'

***ξοΐτης**, ου, ὁ, prob. *one who works with an engraving-tool*, χαλκεὺς ξ. Swoboda *Denkmäler* no. 117 (Isauria).

**ξουθός**, add '**III** masc. as subst., a dark yellow semi-precious stone, Plin.*HN* 37.128.' at end add 'Myc. *ko-so-u-to*, name of an ox; also pers. n. (so later Ξοῦθος)'

***ξύθος**· σμάρις (a fish), Cyran. 116 (4.46.1, 2 K.).

***ξῠϊδόγλῠφος**, ον, *carved with a chisel*, *GVAK* 15.6 (Phrygia); cf. ξοΐς.

**ξυλαλόη**, read 'ξῠλᾰλόη' and delete 'scanned .. *An.Ox.* 3.277'

**ξῠλᾰμή**, add '*POxy.* 1124.15 (i AD)'

**ξῠλᾰμητής**, add '*PTeb.* 886.62, 64 (ii BC)'

***ξυλάμητρον**, τό, *wages for sowing*, *PWash.Univ.* 77.25.

***ξῠλᾰμιστής**, οῦ, ὁ, *sower* of green fodder plants, *PCair.Zen.* 727.12 (iii BC).

***ξῠλέμπορος**, ὁ, *wood-merchant*, *Orientalia* 35.135 fig. 73.

***ξύλη**, ἡ, *timber*, *SEG* 36.1087 (Sardis, 213 BC).

**ξῠληγός**, add 'also ή, όν, *naves* -άς Ulp.*Dig.* 32.55.5'

***ξῠλικάριος**, ὁ, *carpenter* or *joiner*, *MAMA* 3.84, 95 (Diocaesarea), 3.731 (Corycus).

**ξῠλικός**, penultimate line, after '*PTeb.* 8.26 (iii/ii BC)' read 'ξυλικόν, τό, a wooden construction in a garden, perh. fencing or supports for plants, κῆπον σὺν τῷ πεπηγμένῳ ξ. *SEG* 17.545.11 (Pisidia, Rom.imp.); cf. *lignarium*, *pulpitum*, *Gloss.*'

***ξῠλῑνᾶς**, ᾶ, ὁ, *woodcutter*, *IEphes.* 4312a (Chr.).

***ξῠλῑνοβαστάκιον**, τό, perh. that part of a waggon which carries the load, *flooring*, *PMasp.* 303.15 (vi AD).

**ξύλῐνος**, after lemma insert '(sp. σύλιν- *IG* 2².1623.331, iv BC)' **I 1**, line 5, after 'Ath. 3.78d' insert 'cf. *lina xylina*, cloth *made of cotton*, Plin.*HN* 19.14' **II**, delete the section.

**ξύλιον**, delete the entry.

**ξυλλείομαι**, add '(also expl. as form of σκύλλω or συλλέγω)'

**ξῠλόγλῠκον**, add '*ICilicie* 108.18 (v/vi AD)'

***ξῠλογλύφος**, ὁ, *wood-carver*, *BCH* 102.413 (iii AD), Hsch.

***ξῠλοκᾰβαλ(λάριος)**, ὁ, perh. *rider armed with wooden lance* (in quot., applied to a bandit), *SEG* 35.1360.7 (Hadrianopolis, Paphlagonia, vi AD).

***ξῠλοκάρος**, ὁ, *woodcutter*, *IPrusa ad Olympum* 149 (ii AD).

**ξῠλοκοπέω I**, add 'Hsch. s.v. *καλοκοπῆσαι*' **II**, after 'Arr.*Epict.* 3.7.33' insert '*POxy.* 2811 *fr.* 5a.4 (ii AD)'

***ξῠλοκοπικός**, *ή, όν*, *for cutting wood*, *PTeb.* 794.13 (iii BC).

***ξῠλομαστῖχη**, *ἡ*, *mastic wood*, *POxy.* 3733.29, 3766.11 (both iv AD).

**ξύλον I 2**, delete the section transferring quot. to section 1. **II 3 b**, for '*stocks*' read '*wooden frame*' and add '*ξύλον ἔχοντα ἐν τοῖς ποσίν, ὥστε μὴ δυνηθῆναι ἐκ τοῦ πλοίου λαθεῖν καὶ διαφυγεῖν PKöln* 281.12 (vi AD)' **5**, for 'theatre' read 'court or assembly' **III**, line 3, for 'Call.*Cer.* 41' read 'Call.*Cer.* 40'

**ξῠλοπάκτων**, add '*PBeatty Panop.* 1.12 (AD 298)'

***ξῠλοπέδη**, *ἡ*, *wooden frame* or *fetter for restraining the feet* (cf. ‡*ξύλον* II 3 b), Aq.*Jb.* 13.27, 33.11, Lyd.*Mag.* 48.2.

***ξῠλοπύριος**, *ον*, perh. *sharpened by fire*, *σανίς Poliorc.* 271.11.

***ξῠλοπωλία**, Ion. *-ίη*, *ἡ*, *sale of wood*, *SEG* 2.579.8, 12 (Teos, iv BC).

***ξῠλοσάγγᾰθον**, *τό*, (or *-ος*, *ὁ*), an unidentified plant (recorded as commodity used in a mint), *POxy.* 3618.12 (iv AD); cf. ‡*σάγγαθον*.

***ξῠλοσέλῖνον**, *τό*, variety of *celery*, or sim. plant, *PMil.Vogl.* 302.185 (ii AD).

**ξῠλοσπόγγιον**, add 'in Lat. inscrs., *PMich.*VIII 471.29, *Ann.Épigr.* 41.5'

***ξῠλοτομέω**, *cut wood*, *PRoss.-Georg.* II 19.31 (AD 141).

**ξῠλοτομία**, after '*POxy.*' insert '729.29 (ii AD)'

***ξῠλοτόμιον**, *τό*, *axe for cutting wood*, *SB* 9587 (for reading *ξυλοτόμιν* v. *Mnemosyne* 30.142, vi/vii AD).

**ξῠλοφθόρον**, after '*τό*' insert '(also *-ος*, *ὁ*, Hsch.)'

**ξῠλοχάρτια**, delete the entry.

***ξῠλοχάρτιος**, *ον*, neut. pl. subst., *τὰ ξυλοχάρτια paper made from papyrus*, Eust. 1913.41 (*BASP* 9.27, 28); *document written on this material*, *τὸ ξυλοχάρτιον κοντάκιον* Steph.*in Rh.* 277.29.

**ξῠλόω II**, after '*make of wood*' insert 'or *cover with wood*' and for '*γαῦλον*' read '*γαυλόν*'

**ξύλωμα**, after '*piece of woodwork*' insert 'or *wooden panelling*'

***ξῡνέτης**, *ου*, *ὁ*, *ξυνέται· συμπολῖται* Hsch.

**ξῡνήων I**, after 'Hes.*Th.* 601' insert '(*ὁ δεῖνα*) *τῆ(ν) στέγην ἐποίησεν κοὶ ξυνεῶνες* Robert *Hell.* 9.78 (Hellespont, vi BC)' **II**, after 'as adj.' insert '*common to all*, *ξυνήονι πότμῳ* Nonn.*D.* 12.266'

***ξύνιστρον**· *νόμισμα* Hsch.

**ξῡνόω**, after lemma insert '*make common*, Sch.Pi.*O.* 7.36'

***Ξύρεος**, *ὁ*, name of a god, *Θεῷ Ξυρέῳ IHadr.* 19; identified with Apollo, *MAMA* 9.60 (ii/iii AD); also **Ξυρᾶς**, *Θεὸς Ξ. IHadr.* 20.

**ξύρησις**, for '*baldness*' read '*shaving of the head* as sign of mourning'

***ξῠρησίταυρος**, *ὁ*, one who *shaves off* his pubic hair (v. *ταῦρος* III); pl., name of a *τάγμα* (set) at Sardis, Ap.Ty.*Ep.* 39.

***ξῠρητικός**, *ή, όν*, *of shaving*: *-κή* (sc. *τέχνη*), *ἡ*, *An.Ox.* 4.248.10.

**ξῠρίς**, line 3, after '*ξειρίς*' insert '*SEG* 13.550.6 (Caesarea, Rom.imp.)'

**ξυστάδες**, delete the entry (v. °*ξυστάς*).

**ξυστάλλιον**, for '*ξῦστρον*' read '*ξύστρα*'

**ξυστάρχης**, last line, for 'Smyrna' read 'Thyatira'

***ξυστάς**, *άδος*, *ἡ*, *closely-planted vineyard*, Poll. 7.147 (v.l. *ζυγάς*), Hsch. (pl.); cf. *συσταδόν*.

**ξυστήρ**, line 2, delete '*graving-tool*'

***ξύστης**, *ου*, *ὁ*, = *ξυστήρ*, *CPHerm.* 127 xviii 9 (iii AD).

**ξυστίς**, after '*ἴδος*' insert '(**ξύστις**, *ιδος*, acc. to Sch.Ar.*Nu.* 70)'

***ξυστοπλᾰτείτης**, *ου*, *ὁ*, *resident in the* **ξυστοπλατεῖα* (prob. *street of the ξυστός*), *συμβίωσις -ειτῶν ISmyrna* 714 (ii AD).

**ξυστός**, line 2, after 'Aristias 5' insert 'Philostr.*VA* 4.3' **I 1**, for 'and statuary, Vitr. 5.11.5' read 'Vitr. 5.11.4' add '**III** a carpenter's tool, Gal. 1.47.4 (s.v.l.).'

**ξύστρα I**, add '**2** *ξ. ἁλιευτική*, app. *instrument for scaling fish*, *PWürzb.* 5.9, 12 (i BC).'

***ξυστροληκῦθον**· *κάδη καὶ βησσία ἐλαίου λουτρικά* Hsch.

**ξυστρολήκυθος**, delete the entry.

**ξυστρωτός**, after 'of pillars' insert '*SAWW* 179(6).63 (Cilicia, i/ii AD)'

# O

**ὁ, ἡ, τό**, line 10, for '*Inscr.Cypr.* 135.20 H.' read '*ICS* 217.30, al.'; line 22 (p. 1194 col. 1, line 10), after 'Sapph. 16' insert 'Thess. gen. sg. *τοῖ SEG* 31.572 (*c.*200 BC), al.' **A VII 2**, line 2, for '*καί μοι κάλει*' read '*ἀφικνοῦμαι ὡς*'; line 3, for 'Pl.*Lg.* 784d' read 'Pl.*Lg.* 784c' **VIII 5 b**, add 'v. *πρό* A II 1' at end add 'Myc. *to-jo* (gen. sg.), *to-i* (dat. pl.)' **B II 5**, line 4, before 'freq. with advs.' insert '**6**'; line 9, after '*Or.* 1412 (lyr.)' insert 'also *τὸ εἰκῇ* Pl.*Grg.* 506d, al.; *τὸ μόλις* D.H.*Comp.* 20' add '**7** w. numerals, indicating number of tenures of office, *ὕπατος τὸ ζ' TAM* 4(1).11 (AD 116); indicating a date, *τῷ ζμσ'* (sc. *ἔτει*) *SEG* 32.1537 (AD 184).' **C**, line 4, for '*ὃ ἐξορύξῃ* .. (Cyprus)' read 'Cypr. *o-e-xe o-ru-xe*, *ὃ ἐξορύξε̄ he who* expels him, *ICS* 217.12, 25'; line 10, delete 'Com. or'

**ὄα** (A), add 'cf. *αἶα* (C)'

**ὀάρισμα**, for '*familiar converse*' read '*lore*'

**Ὀασιτικός**, add '*PCair.Zen.* 299 (iii BC), *POxy.* 2567 (iii AD), 3425 (iv AD), etc.'

***ὄβαν**, v. °*ὄουαν*.

⁺**ὄβδη**, *ἡ*, = *ὄψις*, *Μούσῃ γὰρ ἦλθον εἰς ὄβδην* Call.*fr.* 218 Pf., unless one wd., as certainly in *ποιεῖσθαι τὴν ἀπογραφὴν εἰσόβδην* = *palam, in propatulo*, *ILampsakos* 9.42-4 (ii BC); cf. **ὄβδην** and **ἐσόβδην** cited as advs. by A.D.*Adv.* 198.7.

**ὀβελεία**, add 'Lang *Ath.Agora* XXI B12 (iv/iii BC, sp. *ὀβελίαι*)'

***ὀβελισκοποιός**, *ὁ*, *maker of ὀβελίσκοι*, *IG* $1^{3}$.426.13 (Athens, v BC).

**ὀβελίσκος I 3**, add 'so in Dor. form *ὀδελίσκος ABSA* 61.264.13 (Epid., *c.*370 BC)' **5**, add 'also, *bar* protecting outlet of drain' transferring here quots. fr. section IV **IV**, delete the section.

**ὀβελός I 3**, for '*IG* $1^{2}$.6.95, al.' read '*IG* $1^{3}$.4.A20 (Athens, v BC), 7.1739.8 (Thespiae, iii BC)'

***ὀβιφέρι** (gen.), *wild sheep*, fr. Lat. *ovis fera*, *Edict.Diocl.* 8.25 (sp. *ὀβιβέρι* at *SEG* 37.335 ii 20).

**ὀβολίσκος I**, add '**b** perh. *water-tank*, *POxy.* 2406 (ground-plan of a house) (ii AD).'

***ὀβολοκερε** (?for *ὀβολοκέρεα* = *-κέρατα* or *-κέρεια*), perh. *pin* or *skewer made of horn*, *SEG* 29.972 (label for surgeon's implements, Italy, iv BC).

**ὀβολός I**, line 2, for '*IG* $1^{2}$.140.5, al.' read '*IG* $1^{3}$.6.C12, 237'

**ὀβρίκἄλα**, after lemma insert 'or *-οι, οἱ*'; line 2, at end insert 'Phot., Ar.Byz.*fr.* 203B S.; forms *ὀβρίκια*, *ὄβριας* Poll. 5.15, see also *ἰβρίκαλοι*, °*ὄβριχα*'

***ὀβριμάδες**, *αἱ*, wd. of unkn. meaning, perh. pr. n., epigr. in *BCH* 75.195 (Crete).

***ὀβρῐμότοξος**, *ον*, *equipped with a strong bow*, Antim. 174 Wy.

***ὄβριχα**, *τά*, (or *-οι, οἱ*), = *ὀβρίκαλα*, *ὑστρίχων τ' ὀβρίχοισ[ι* A.*fr.* 47a.809 R.

**ὀβρυζιακός**, add '*POxy.* 126.15, 27 (vi AD)'

**ὄβρυζος**, for '(cf. Lat. *obrussa*)' read '(prob. fr. Hitt. *ḫubrušḫi*, *clay container*, presumably used in gold refining; Lat. *obrussa* fr. Gk.), see also °*βρύζα*'

***ὄγγας**· *ὁ ἀπὸ πολλῶν ὑγρός* Theognost.*Can.* 46 A.

**ὀγδόδιον**, add '(*ὀγδοαῖον* La.)'

**ὀγδοήκοντα**, add 'written *hογδοήκοντα Tab.Heracl.* I 43, II 70'

**ὀγδοηκοντούτης**, line 3, after 'Simon. 146' insert 'fem. **-αέτις** *AP* 7.733 (Diotim.)'

⁺**ὄγδοος**, *η, ον*, (*[ὀγ]δόϝα* fem., Aetol. *IG* $9^{2}$(1).152) *eighth*, Il. 7.223, etc., *ὄγδον Δαμοίτας Νικομείδ[εος] SEG* 23.273 (ii BC); as designation of a legion, *ἐκλεχθεὶς ἰς ὀγδ[όαν Αὐ]γούσταν SEG* 31.1116; *ὀγδόα, ἁ*, a monetary unit (cf. *ἕκτη*), *SEG* 26.1084 (Megara Hyblaea, vi BC); *ὀγδόη* (sc. *ἡμέρα*), *ὀγδόῃ τῆς πρυτανείας IG* $1^{3}$.475.284, *Πανάμμοι ὀδδόα ἐφ' ἰκάδι SEG* 31.577 (Thessaly, ii BC), Plu.*Thes.* 36; *ὀγδόη* (sc. *μοῖρα*), *eighth part*, *SEG* 33.1034 (Aeolis, iii BC), cf. *ὀγδόα· ἡμιχοινικόν* Hsch.; neut. (sc. *ἔτος*) *εἴκοστον χὤγδοον GVI* 1091 (Dyme, ii/iii AD).

**ὀγκάομαι**, delete 'Theopomp.Com. 4'; for 'Call.*Aet.Oxy.* 2079.31' read 'Call.*fr.* 1.31 Pf.'

***ὀγκαρίζω**, = *ὀγκάομαι*, Aq.*Ge.* 49.14 (v.l.).

***ὀγκάς**, *άδος, ὁ*, *brayer*, Theopomp.Com. 5 K.-A.

***ὀγκιαρήσιον**, *τό*, perh. a coin (fr. *ὀγκία*, *uncia*, cf. *μιλιαρήσιον*), *PIand.* 103.14 (vi AD).

**ὄγκος** (B) **I 4**, for this section read '*the animal body with respect to its workings, system*, *τῆς χολῆς ἀναχεομένης εἰς τὸν ὄγκον* Ruf.*Anat.* 30, Ph. 1.391, Sor. 1.26, *ταράττειν τὸν ὄγκον* Plu. 2.652e, 653f, Gal. 1.272.17' **II 3**, add 'Longin. 3.4'

**ὀγκώδης** (A) **I 2**, add 'of persons, D.Chr. 30.19'

**ὄγμος I**, add '**4** perh. *wheel-rut*, Nic.*Th.* 371.' **II**, after '*h.Hom.* 32.11' insert '*ἠέρος ὄγμοι* Call.*fr.* 335 Pf.'

**ὀδᾱγός**, add '*SEG* 23.271 (Thespiae, iii BC); as pers. n., Cypr. *o-ta-ko-se Kadmos* 29.143 (iv BC)'

**ὀδαῖος II**, for this section read '*ὀδαῖα, τά*, *freight, merchandise*, Od. 8.163, 15.445'

***ὀδᾰνόν**· *εὐῶδες μύρον* Theognost.*Can.* 51 A.; cf. *ἑδανός*.

**ὀδαξησμός**, add 'also **ἀδαξησμός** Erot. 107.21'

**ὀδάξω II**, add 'abs., *τῆς γὰρ ὀδαξαμένης* when it has *bitten*, Nic.*Th.* 306'

**ὀδάχα**, read '**ὀδαχᾶς**'

**ὅδε**, line 5, for '*τῶνδεων* Alc. 126' read '*τωνδέων* Alc. 130.21 L.-P.' **I**, after '**6**' insert '*such and such*, *διὰ τήνδε τὴν αἰτίαν* Pl.*Phdr.* 271d, cf. 272a; *πορευσόμεθα εἰς τήνδε τὴν πόλιν Ep.Jac.* 4.13. **b** *ὅδε καὶ ὅδε*, *this man and that, A and B*, D.Chr. 40.13, 33.48 (pl.).'; before 'in Arist.' insert '**c**' and at end delete '*πορευσόμεθα* .. 4.13' **III 2**, line 6, delete 'v. .. 1.2'; add '*ὅδε* and *οὗτος*, of the same person or thing, S.*Ant.* 189, 297, Th. 1.143, etc.' add '**4** *τόδ' ἐκεῖνο* E.*Med.* 98, like *τοῦτ' ἐκεῖνο* (v. *οὗτος* B III 5).' **IV 2**, add 'also neut. pl., *SEG* 31.1525 (Egypt, iii/ii BC)'

**ὀδελονόμος**, after 'financial official ' insert 'at Argos, *BCH* suppl. 22 p. 235 (v BC)'

***ὀδευτός**, *ή, όν*, *furnished with roads*, *γῆν ὀ. ἐποίησεν* D.Chr. 3.127.

**ὀδηγός**, add '*σκίπων AP* 7.457 (Aristo)'; see also ‡*ὀδαγός*.

**ὀδῑ́της**, add '*ὀδῖτα* (voc.) epigr. in *REG* 80.282 (Chios)'

**ὁδοιπορέω**, line 4, after 'S.*OT* 801' insert 'Crates Com. 16.3 K.-A.'

**ὁδοιπορικός**, line 2, after 'Poll. 1.181' insert '*ὁ. πήδησις*, t.t. for a leap in armour on to a cantering horse, Arr.*Tact.* 43.4'

**ὁδοιπόρος**, add '*AP* 7.502 (Nicaenet.), *SEG* 31.379 (*c.*100 BC)'

***ὀδοντίδας**· *πολυφάγος* Hsch.; cf. *ὀδοντίας*.

**ὀδοντισμός**, add '*εἶδος αὐλήσεως ὅτε ἡ γλῶττα προσβάλλεται πρὸς τὸν ὀδόντα* Hsch.'

***ὀδοντῖτις**, *ἡ*, a plant said to cure toothache, Plin.*HN* 27.108.

**ὀδοντοτῠ́ραννος**, for 'large animal, prob. *crocodile*' read 'fabulous animal, perh. based on accounts of the crocodile'

**ὁδός III 3**, add '*ἐκ πάσης ὁδοῦ by every means*, *Cod.Just.* 1.3.45.3a; sim. *διὰ πάσης ὁδοῦ* ib. 1.4.34.6'

**ὁδουρός**, add '**III** = *ὁδίτης*, *traveller*, Nic.*Th.* 180.'

**ὀδούς**, line 1, after '*EN* $1161^{b}23$' insert '*Mech.* $854^{a}28$' **I 1**, add '*ὀδόντες ἐλεφάντων tusks*, *Didyma* 394.16 (i BC), cf. Opp.*C.* 2.493' **II**, for '*ploughshare*' read '*tine*'

***ὀδυρμοχᾰρής**, *ές*, *delighting in lamentation*, *IHadr.* 168 (ii/iii AD).

***ὀδῡρομένως**, adv. fr. part. pres. of *ὀδύρομαι*, *ζῆν ὀ. in lamentation*, Favorin.*Exil.* 10.45.

***ὀδῡ́ρω**, act. form of *ὀδύρομαι*, *GVI* 969.7 (Daldis, i AD).

*°**Ὀδῠ́σειος**, v. °*Ὀδυσσεύς*.

**Ὀδυσσεύς**, at end after 'Od. 18.353' add '°**Ὀδύσειος** Stesich. 32 i 2 P.'

**ὄζαινα II**, for this section read 'another name for *ὀσμύλη* (*ὀσμύλιον*, etc.), Call.*fr.* 406 Pf. (Ath. 329a)'

**ὀζαινῑ́της**, delete the entry.

⁺**ὀζαινῖτις**, *ίτιδος, ἡ*, a kind of nard, supposed from its name to be evil-smelling, but prob. fr. the Indian town of Ozene (Ujjain), Plin.*HN* 12.42.

**ὀζᾰλέος**, for '*branching*' read '*knobbed*'

***ὀζηλίς**· *ἡ βοτάνη* Theognost.*Can.* 45 A.

**ὄζος II**, add '**2** rhet. term of unkn. significance, *οἷον Λικύμνιος ποιεῖ ἐν τῇ τέχνῃ ἐπούρωσιν ὀνομάζων καὶ ἀποπλάνησιν καὶ ὄζους* Arist.*Rh.* $1414^{b}18$.'

**ὄζος**, Cret., after 'Gortyn' insert 'vii/vi BC'

***ὀζόχρωτος**, *ον*, app. *having knotty skin*, Heph.Astr. 3.45.2; cf. *hircosus*, *Gloss.*

**ὄζω**, line 1, after 'impf. *ὦζε*' insert 'Hippon. 92.10 W.'

***ὀθεύς**· *εὐνοῦχος* Theognost.*Can.* 53 A. (*ὄθης* Zonar.).

**ὄθι**, line 3, after '*Phd.* 108b' insert 'Ant.Lib. 33.3, 4'

***ὀθία**, = *ὄθιζα*, Zonar.

**ὄθιζα**, after 'cf.' insert '°*ὀθία*, °*ὀθυσία*'

**ὄθμα**, for 'Call.*Aet.* .. 37' read 'Call.*fr.* 186.29 Pf.'

**ὀθνεῖος I**, add 'ὀθνέην ὁδόν Archil. 244 W.'

***ὀθονεμπλουμάριος**, ὁ, *linen-embroiderer*, *PAmst.*inv. 39 (*CE* 48.128, iv/v AD), cf. Lat. *plumarius.*

**ὀθονιακός I**, add 'written ὀθων- *BCH* suppl. 8 no. 33 (v/vi AD)'

***ὀθονιάπωλις**, ιδος, ἡ, fem. of ὀθονιοπώλης, *SB* 10162.538.2 (iii/iv AD).

**ὀθόνιον 1**, add '**b** ὀ. Σηρικόν *silk*, *Peripl.M.Rubr.* 64.'

***ὀθονιοπράτης**, ου, ὁ, *linen-seller*, *SEG* 27.874 (Ancyra, Chr.), *IGLBulg.* 249 (Odessos, vi AD).

**ὀθονιοπώλης**, add '*MAMA* 3.225, 4.349'

***ὀθονιοπώλιον**, τό, *linen-shop*, *PAmst.*inv. 62 (*Mnemosyne* 30.146, ii AD).

**ὀθούνεκα**, after lemma insert 'Ion. ὁτεύνεκα Herod. 5.20, al.' **I**, add 'E.*Hel.* 104, etc.' **II**, add 'E.*Alc.* 796'

**ὀθούνεκεν**, after lemma insert 'Ion. ὁτεύνεκεν, *Iamb.adesp.* 38.12 W., Herod. 7.103'; after '= foreg.' read '*because*' and after 'Timo 34' insert 'Theoc. 25.76. **II** *that*, A.R. 3.933.'

***ὀθύλλομαι**, glossed by διανοέομαι, Hsch. s.v. ὠθύλλετο; cf. ὀθέω, etc.

***ὀθυσία**, = ὄθιζα, Theognost.*Can.* 53 A.; cf. °ὀθία.

***ὀθύω**, impf. ὤθυνον, = ἄγω, Theognost.*Can.* 53 A.; cf. ὀθεύει, ὀθρεῖν.

***ὀθωνοπώλης**, ου, ὁ, = ὀθονιοπώλης, *TAPhA* 90.140.18.

**οἴγω**, penultimate line, for 'Alc. 225 Lobel' read '*Lesb.fr.adesp.* 20 L.-P.' and continue 'ὀΐγοντ' [ί] ἔαρος πύλ[αι Alc. 296(*b*).3 L.-P.'

**οἰδημάτιον**, after 'Hp.*Fract.* 5' insert 'Gal. 18(2).389.4, 390.12'; delete 'name of an eye-salve'

**οἶδμα II**, delete the section.

***οἴεον**, τό, *sheepfold*, κλεῖθρα κατασκευάσαντι τοῖς οἴκοις τοῖς ἐν τῶι οἰέωι *Inscr.Délos* 290.78 (iii BC).

**οἰέτεας**, add 'Mosch. 2.29 G.'

**ϝοιζηάζω**, delete the entry.

**ὀϊζυρός**, line 6, at end insert 'Ion Trag. 38.2 S.'; line 7, delete 'by Trag., nor'

**οἴζω**, add 'med. οἴζομαι dub. in S.*fr.* 269c.47 R.'

**οἶις**, delete 'but .. is prob.'

**οἴκαδε I**, add 'Telecl. 1.6 K.-A.; w. gen. *to the home of*, οἴ. τοῦ ξένου Eup. 99.84 K.-A.' **II**, delete the section.

**οἰκεῖος IV 2 b**, for this section read '*familiar* with, *at home* with, w. gen., βασιλεῖς .. καίπερ οἰκεῖοι σοφίας γεγονότες Str. 17.1.5, τοὺς οἰκείους τῆς πίστεως *Ep.Gal.* 6.10, Iamb.*VP* 30.176' **B II**, add '**5** w. gen., *in conformity with*, *ICilicie* 70 (ii BC)'.

**οἰκειότης III**, delete the section.

**οἰκειόω II 1**, line 3, delete 'abs. .. Aen.Tact. 24.5'

***οἴκελος**, v. °οἴκυλα.

**οἰκετεία 1**, after lemma insert 'ϝοικετεία *SEG* 23.566 (Crete, iv BC)'; add '*Inscr.Cret.* 1.xvi 17.16 (ii BC), *Ev.Matt.* 24.45, ἰατροῦ τῆς κυριακῆς οἰκετείας *IEphes.* 3233 (iii AD)'

**οἰκέτης I 2**, line 3, delete 'hence opp. δοῦλοι' and for '(Pl.*Lg.*) 853e' read '(Pl.*Lg.*) 853d' **II**, at beginning insert 'perh. *residing divinity*, ὅδε σηκὸς οἰκέταν εὐδοξίαν Ἑλλάδος εἵλετο Simon. 26.6 P.'; after '(Sparta)' insert 'Paus. 3.13.4'

***οἰκετιεύς**, v. οἰκιτιεύς.

**οἰκέτις**, add 'οἰκέτιδα (acc.), epigr. in *SEG* 37.450 (Thessaly, ii/iii AD)'

***οἰκέτισσα**, ἡ, = οἰκέτις I, *female household slave*, *TAM* 3(1).282 (Termessus; sp. ὑκαίτισσα).

***οἰκεύω**, = οἰκέω, (in quot.) *colonize*, *SEG* 23.474 (Dodona, iv/iii BC).

**οἰκέω**, line 1, (ϝοικέω), add '*SEG* 11.244 (Sicyon, v BC), also ϝοικίω, *SEG* 23.589 (Gortyn, iii/ii BC)'; line 2, after 'Aeol. pres.' insert 'οἴκημμ‹ι› Alc. 130.31 L.-P.' and for 'Alc. 69' read 'id. 328 L.-P.'; line 4, after 'Hdt. 1.1' insert 'Aeol. ἐοίκησα Alc. 130.25 L.-P.' **A 1**, line 4, after 'E. l.c.' insert 'πᾶσι τοῖς οἰκοῦσι μοναστήρια *Cod.Just.* 1.3.43 pr.'

**οἴκημα II 1**, for 'Isoc.' read 'Is.'

**οἰκία**, line 1, (ϝοικία) add '*SEG* 32.496, 34.355; also ϝυκία (all Boeotia, iv/iii BC); see also βοικία' **I 3**, delete the section.

**οἰκίδιον 1**, add 'applied to a (Christian) tomb (or perh. chapel), *SEG* 30.1068 (Tenos)'

**οἰκιήτης**, before 'ϝοικιάτας' insert 'also at Epid.'; line 3, after '(*IG*) 262.16' insert '*SEG* 26.449.6'

**οἰκίον**, add 'in form οἰκίν, of a (Christian) *tomb*, *ITyr* 90'

***οἴκισμα**, τό, = οἴκημα, *dwelling-place*, *SEG* 18.615.7 (Syria, iv AD).

**οἰκισμός**, add '*SEG* 25.486 (Boeotia, iii BC)'

***οἰκιστεία**, ἡ, app. *founding*, rest. in *SEG* 12.380.9 (decree of Gela at Cos, iii BC).

***οἰκοδεσπᾶ**, ἡ, = οἰκοδέσποινα, inscr. in Robert *Collection Froehner* i p. 111 (Cibyratis).

**οἰκοδεσποσύνη**, delete '*CIG* 2987 (Ephesus)'; for 'Keil-Premerstein .. 170.13' read '*TAM* 5(1).688 (i AD)' add '**2** *family*, *IEphes.* 622.17.'

**οἰκοδεσπότης I 1**, add '*master of an estate*, *PPhilad.* 1.48 (ii AD)'

**οἰκοδεσποτικός I**, for this section read '*of* or *proper to the head of a household*, Cic.*Att.* 12.44.2, τῇ συμβίῳ Δημητριάδι ζησάσῃ τὸν βίον οἰκοδεσποτικὸν ἔτη λ' *TAM* 4(1).128'

**οἰκοδομεύς**, delete the entry (v. °οἰκοδόμος).

**οἰκοδομέω 1 a**, add 'οἰκία ᾠκοδομημένη, i.e. not made of mud, *PAmh.* 2.51.11, 23 (i BC), *PLond.* 880.27 (ii BC)' **I 3**, line 3, delete 'cf. ἀνοικοδομέω' add '**4** = ἀνοικοδομέω, *rebuild*, *repair*, *IG* 11(2).161*A*120 (Delos).'

**οἰκοδομή I**, line 4, after 'Plu.*Cam.* 32' insert 'γεφυρῶν οἰκοδομῆς Just.*Nov.* 131.5; fig., *building up of faith*, *edification*, *POxy.* 2785 (iv AD)'

**οἰκοδομητός**, add 'also ᾠκο- *SEG* 33.955 (Ephesus)'

***οἰκοδόμητρα**, τά, *wages for building*, πάθνης *PLips.* 106.8 (i AD).

**οἰκοδόμος**, add 'dat. pl. οἰκοδόμεις, w. dissimilation of οι-οι to οι-ει (as in λοιπεῖς *IG* 2².1028.12, and οἴκει), *OStrassb.* 583 (iii BC)'

***οἰκοδομουργός**, v. °ὁμουργός.

**οἴκοθεν**, after lemma insert 'ϝοίϙοθεν *SEG* 30.380 (Tiryns, vii BC)'; line 1, after 'οἴκοθε' insert 'Call.*fr.* 275 Pf.' **3**, add '*Cod.Just.* 4.21.22.4, etc.'

***οἰκονομήτρια**, ἡ, *that gives effect to a dispensation*, ἡ ἡμέρα (i.e. Easter) ἡ .. τῶν πενήτων οἰκονομήτρια Ps.-Chrys.*HP* 2.7.

**οἰκονομία I 4**, add 'at Priene, *SIG* 1003.29 (ii BC)'

***οἰκονομίδιον**, τό, *document of a transaction*, *POxy.* 2679 (ii AD).

**οἰκονομικός**, line 6, for '*the duties of domestic life*' read '*estate management*'; at end for 'also in literary sense .. Sch.Th. 1.63' read '**2** *concerning arrangement* of literary material, D.H.*Dem.* 51, *Th.* 9, Quint.*Inst.* 7.10.11; adv., *in an ordered manner*, Sch.Th. 1.63.'

**⁺οἰκονόμισσα**, ἡ, *female estate manager*, *JHS* 24.283 (v AD), *MAMA* 8.399, *INikaia* 1466.

**οἰκονόμος**, after 'ὁ, ἡ' insert 'written οἰκονόνοι (pl.), *Hesperia* 58.118 (Crete, ii BC)' **I 1**, *steward of an estate*, add 'Mitchell *N.Galatia* 34, *INikaia* 753; transf., οὕτως ἡμᾶς λογιζέσθω ἄνθρωπος ὡς ὑπηρέτας Χριστοῦ καὶ οἰκονόμους μυστηρίων Θεοῦ *1Ep.Cor.* 4.1, *Ep.Tit.* 1.7' **2 b**, at end for 'θεοῦ .. *1Ep.Cor.* 4.1' read 'as the title of a Christian official, *SEG* 32.1492 (v AD), etc.'

**οἰκόπεδον 1**, last line, after 'πόλεως' insert 'Demad. 26'

**οἶκος I 1**, line 3, after 'Lxx *Ge.* 31.33' insert 'or the country, town, etc., where one lives or belongs' and add 'οἱ ἐν οἴκῳ Ἀθηναῖοι X.*HG* 1.5.16, *Cyr.* 7.2.1, *An.* 2.4.8, al.' **2**, last line, after '*within*' insert 'A.*Ag.* 427' **3**, lines 2/3, delete 'Δεκελειῶν .. 33'; line 4, for '*IG* 4.1580 (Aegina)' read 'ℎοῖϙος *SEG* 32.356 (Aegina, *c.*550 BC)'; at end after 'funerary monument' insert 'Ἀρκι[.]άλης μηποίεσεν (= με ἐποίησεν) οἶϙον Δαμε[.] *SEG* 30.1058 (Naxos, vii BC), *IEphes.* 1630' add '**IV** = φρατρία (s.v. φράτρα) II 1, prob. in *IG* 2².1237.33 (Attica, iv BC), 12(5).528.15, 1061.16 (both Ceos, iii BC). **2** *guild*, τῶν ναυκλήρων *BCH* 25.36 (Amastris).' at end after 'ϝοῖκος' insert '*Kafizin* 266b, 267b (iii BC), Myc. *wo-i-ko*'

***οἰκοσιτέω**, *take one's meals at home*, Luc.*Sacr.* 9 (s.v.l.).

**οἰκόσιτος II** and **III**, delete the sections.

**οἰκοτρᾰφής**, after 'οἰκότριψ' insert '*Vit.Aesop.*(G) 45'

**οἰκότριψ**, delete 'Attic for οἰκογενής'; add '(in conjectural context)'

***οἰκοτροφής**, ές, *house-bred*, κοράσιον *Delph.* 3(6).37.6.

**οἰκότροφος**, delete '*house-bred* .. (Priene, iv BC)'

**⁺οἰκότως**, v. εἰκότως.

**οἰκουμένη II**, add 'personified, *RA* 1987.98 (Phrygia, iii AD)'

**οἰκουμενικός**, after '*IG* 3.129 (iii AD)' insert '*SEG* 31.1288 (Pamphylia, iii AD)' and for '*Rev.Arch.* 1874.113' read '*SEG* 36.1051 (Miletus, ii AD)'

**οἰκουρός I**, add 'used loosely of other domestic creatures, νῆσσαι οἰκουροί Arat. 970'

**οἰκτίζω 2**, line 2, after 'Din. 1.110' insert '*set forth pathetically*, Memn. 35.3 J.'

**οἰκτιρμός**, add '*SEG* 31.1562 (iv/v AD)'

**οἰκτροπᾰθής**, add 'transf., of feelings, πένθος epigr. in *Inscr.Cret.* 2.v 50 (i AD)'

***οἰκτροτόκεια**, fem. adj. *pitiable in child-bearing*, *GVI* 467 (Amorgos, ii/iii AD).

***οἰκτρόφονος**, ον, *of pitiful killing*, *ISmyrna* 522(b).10 (ii/i BC).

**οἴκυλα**, for '*grain*' read '*pulse*', cf. Lat. *vicia*; also **οἴκυλος**· ὄσπριον Theognost.*Can.* 21; **οἴκελος** ὁ πίσος ib. 20'

***οἰκών**, ῶνος, ὁ, = οἶκος, cj. in *CIJud.* 672 (Acmonia in Phrygia).

**οἶμα**, add 'of a cuttle-fish, Opp.*H.* 1.312'

**οἰμάω**, line 1, for 'οἴμη' read 'cf. οἶμα'

**οἴμη**, for '= οἶμος' read '*song*, *poem*, etc.'; line 3, for 'οἴ. .. τέττιγι' read 'λιγυρὴν δ' ἔδωκεν (sc. Φοῖβος) οἴμην to the cicada'; line 4, for '*Anacreont.* 32.14' read '*Anacreont.* 34.14 W.'

**οἴμοι**, lines 2/3, delete 'first in Thgn. and Trag. (v. infr.)' and 'and Com.' and insert '*SEG* 3.56 (Attica, *c.*540 BC), *SIG* 11 (*c.*525/500 BC), *CEG* 49 (*c.*525/500 BC), *Not.Scav.* 1899.411 (?vi BC, see Jeffery *LSAG* p. 269), Emp. 139.1 D.-K.'

***οἰμωκτιᾶν**· τὸ οἰμῶξαι Hsch., Phot.

**οἰνάνθη**, **II**, delete the section transferring quots. to section I. **I**, add 'as fem. pers. n., *SEG* 25.59 (Athens, vi BC)' **III 1**, line 3, for 'Plin.*HN* 21.65' read 'Plin.*HN* 21.167' **2**, add 'cf. Plin.*HN* 10.87' **3**, add '**b** an unguent, *IStraton.* 247.20, al. (ii AD).'

**οἰνανθίς**, for '= οἰνάνθη II' read '= οἰνάνθη I'

**οἰνάρεος**, for 'σποδίη' read 'σποδιή'

***οἰναρχεῖον**· συμπόσιον Theognost.*Can.* 22.

**οἰνάς I 3**, add 'Myc. *wo-na-si* (dat. pl.), perh. *vineyards*' **II**, for '*a wild pigeon .. Columba livia*' read 'kind of pigeon, prob. corruption of Hebr. *yônāh*' at end add 'cf. γοινάκες, γοινέες'

**οἰνέμπορος**, after '*wine-merchant*' insert 'Ptol.*Tetr.* 179'; for '*Supp.Epigr.* 3.537' read '*IGBulg.* 1590.10'

***οἰνεών**, ῶνος, ὁ, = οἰνών, *Gloss.*

**⁺οἰνηγός**, όν, *wine-carrying*, *PSI* 568.2 (iii BC); masc. subst. *wine-shipper*, *MAMA* 3.682, 709 (Corycus), *OGI* 521.22 (v/vi AD).

**οἰνηρός II**, at end after '*IG* 2².1707' for '(iii BC)' read '(181/0 BC)'

**οἰνικός**, add 'neut. subst. *contribution of wine*, *SEG* 31.122 (i AD)'

**οἰνοβρώς**, for '*eaten with wine*' read 'perh. *consisting of juicy flesh*, οἰνοβρῶτα βορήν, of the pomegranate'

***οἰνογεύστης**, ου, ὁ, *winetaster*, *POxy.* 3517 (iii AD).

**οἰνοδοτέω**, add '*distribute wine* (in a cult-organization), *SEG* 34.1107 (Ephesus)'

**οἰνομετρέω**, add '*SEG* 25.790 (Moesia, ii BC)'

**οἰνοποιέω**, add 'trans., *make into wine*, οἰνοποιηθέντων τῶν καρπῶν *PRyl.* 583.7, 49 (ii BC)'

***οἰνοποίημα**, τό, *wine-making*, *BGU* 2357 ii 9 (iii AD).

***οἰνοποσιάρχης**, ου, ὁ, *organizer of a (village) drinking-party*, *INikaia* 1071 (i/ii AD), 726 (iii AD).

**οἰνοποσίαρχος**, delete the entry.

**⁺οἰνοπόσιον**, τό, *drinking-party*, *TAM* 4(1).16 (AD 122/3); sp. -ποσιν (unless to be taken as acc. of *οἰνόποσις), *TAM* 4(1).17 (AD 184/5), 4(1).68, *IHistriae* 57.32 (iii AD).

**οἰνοποτέω**, for 'Call.*Aet.* 1.1.12' read 'Call.*fr.* 178.12 Pf. (pap.; see also °ζωροποτέω)'

**οἰνοπότης**, add 'also -πώτης Phot. α 595 Th.'

**οἰνοπώλιον**, add 'Plaut.*As.* 200'

***οἰνοπώτης**, v. °οἰνοπότης.

**οἶνος**, line 7, after 'παρ' οἶνον' insert 'Hedyl.ap.Ath. 11.473a'; at end for '*Inscr.Cypr.* 148 H.' read 'Cypr. *to-wo-i-no* τῶ Ϝοίνō, *ICS* 285' and add 'Myc. *wo-no*'

**οἰνόσπονδος**, add 'Hsch. s.v. νηφάλια ξύλα'

***οἰνουργός**, ὁ, *wine-maker*, Μυρῖνος Θεοφίλῳ οἰνουργῷ *PAmst.* 53.1 (AD 433).

**οἰνοχίτων**, for 'Call.*Fr.anon.* 211' read '*Suppl.Hell.* 1093' and for 'ib. 158' read '*Suppl.Hell.* 1076'

**οἰνοχοέω**, lines 4/5, for 'Aeol. -όεισα .. codd. Ath.)' read 'Aeol. aor. imper. -όαισον Sapph. 2.16 L.-P.'

**οἰνοχόη**, line 4, for 'οἱ. θεῶν σωτήρων' read 'οἰνοχόα θεῶν σωτήρων μία'

***οἰνοχόϊον**, τό, *vessel for pouring wine*, Ϝοινοχόϊα χαλκία *SEG* 24.361 (Thespiae, 386/0 BC).

**οἰνοχόος**, add '**2** -ος, ον, *used for wine-pouring*, δέπας *AP* 5.266.6 (Paul.Sil.).'

***οἰνοχοποιός**, ὁ, *maker of* οἰνοχόαι, *Delph.* 3(4).285.3 (ii BC).

***οἰνοχῡτεῖον**, τό, *wine-cellar*, *Dura*⁷·⁸ 171 (ii AD).

**⁺οἶνοψ**, οπος, adj. used in Homer as epith. of the sea (conventionally translated as *wine-dark*), Il. 23.316, Od. 5.132, 2.421, etc.; also as epith. of oxen, βόε οἴνοπε Il. 13.703, Od. 13.32; cf. Myc. *wo-no-qo-so* (descr. of an ox). **2** used to describe complexion of the skin, cf. °οἰνωπος, οἶ. Βάκχος *AP* 6.44 (Leon.Tarent.), Θεραπναίη .. νύμφη οἴνοπα πῆχυν ἀνεῖλκε Tryph. 521.

***ϝοινώα**, ἁ, perh. *vineyard* (if not a pr. n.), πὰρ τὰς Ϝοινώας *Mél.Navarre* 354 (Thespiae).

***οἴνωθρον**, v. οἴνωτρον.

**οἰνωπός**, line 1, for 'Semon. 180' read '*AP* 7.20 ([Simon.])'; line 4, for 'but, *dark-complexioned*' read 'indicating a complexion midway between ὑπέρλευκος and μέλας'

**οἴνωτρον**, add 'also **οἴνωθρον**, *GVI* 1625.4 (Rhodes, i BC, cf. Robert *Hell.* 10.282 n.2)'

**οἰνώψ**, add '**II Οἰνῶπες**, οἱ, one of the Ionic tribes, *SIG* 57.1 (Miletus, v BC), etc.; sg., of a member of the tribe, ib. 798.2 (Cyzicus, i AD).'

**οἰόζωνος**, after '*wayfarer*' insert 'perh. euphem. for a robber'

**οἰόκερως**, add 'rest. in Call. in *Suppl.Hell.* 288.1'

**οἴομαι**, line 12, after 'ὀΐω' insert '(also A.*Pr.* 187 (anap.))' **VI 3**, after 'Lys. 12.26' insert '(s.v.l.)' and delete 'cf. Pl. .. *Ep.* 324b' add '**4** ὡς ᾤου (after an adv.) *as you thought* (sc. erroneously), Pl.*Ep.* 319b, cf. Pers.*Stoic.* 100 (ap.Ath. 607c).'

**οἱονεί**, add 'introducing a hypothetical etymological form, κάμηλος οἱονεὶ κάμμηρος Artem. 1.4'

**οἰονόμος I**, delete 'ἐπ' οἰονόμοιο .. (Leon.)' **II**, add 'perh. also neut., ἐπ' οἰονόμοιο *in the sheep-pasture*, *APl.* 230 (Leon.Tarent.)'

**οἰοπέδη**, delete the entry.

**οἰοπόλος I**, after 'Pi.*P.* 4.28' insert 'θεαί A.R. 4.1322, 1413' deleting these refs. fr. section II.

**οἶος**, line 1, for 'οἶϝος *Inscr.Cypr.* 135.14 H.' read '*o-i-wo-i* οἰϜōι *ICS* 217.14' **I 1**, add 'μαζὸν δ' ἀμφοτέροισι παρίσχεται, οἷον ἑκάστῳ, i.e. one to each for itself, Opp.*H.* 1.660'

**οἷος III 1 a**, line 2, after 'a thing' insert 'or the quality leading to, or shown in, an action'; line 5, after '*R.* 415e' insert 'Thphr.*Char.* 1.2, al.' **b**, line 3, after 'Is. 8.21' insert 'Sosip. 1.20'; line 4, for 'Antig.Car.ap.Ath. 7.345d' read 'Antig.Car.ap.Ath. 8.345d'; add 'cf. *PEnteux.* 26.3, al. (iii BC)' **3**, line 3, for 'ἐστίν' read '[ἐστίν]' **V 2 b**, add 'οἷον ὡς Arist. 1013ᵃ4, Thphr.*Od.* 9' **3**, after 'a part.,' insert 'οἷα Ἕλλησι ὁμιλήσαντα Hdt. 4.95' **VI**, line 3, after 'Arist.*EN* 1114ᵇ17' insert 'οἱουδήποτε γένους *SEG* 33.1177 (Lycia, AD 43), *PColl.Youtie* 92.35 (vi AD)'; line 5, delete 'οἱοσδήπως .. AD)' (read οἱῳδήποτε); before 'οἱοσδητισοῦν' insert 'οἱοσδήτις Plu. 2.1043c'; line 6, before 'οἱοσποτοῦν' insert '**οἷός περ**, see section II 1; **οἱόσποτε** *SEG* 29.250 (?iv AD)'

***οἰριάζων**· τραχυνόμενος Theognost.*Can.* 23.

***οἴριος**· ἀποστερητής Theognost.*Can.* 23.

**οἰρών**, at end delete 'cf. ἱρών' add '**II** Cypr. *i-to-i-ro-ni*, perh. ἰ(ν) τ(ōι) οἰρōνι, *region*, *ICS* 217.8, 31.'

**ὄϊς**, line 3, after 'Call.*Ap.* 53' insert 'ὄϊς Opp.*C.* 2.377'

**οἶσος**, line 3, after 'Hsch.' insert 'cj. in Antim. 121 Wy.' and delete 'perh.'

**ὀϊστεύω II**, after '*shoot with an arrow*' insert 'A.R. 1.759'

**οἰστικός**, after 'Orib.*fr.* 72' insert 'Procl.*Inst.* 63, al.'

**οἰστός**, line 2, after 'Arist.*Ph.* 239ᵇ30' insert 'Iamb.*VP* 28.140'

**ὀϊστοῦχος**, add '*SEG* 37.1175 (ii AD)'

**οἰστρήεις II**, for 'Nonn.*D.* 21.188' read 'Nonn.*D.* 21.190'

**οἴστρημα**, for '*ravings* of madness' read '*spur* to madness'

**οἰστροβολέω**, for '*strike with the sting*, τινα esp.' read '*sting*, τινα'

**οἶστρος II 2**, line 2, after '*passion*' insert 'Simon. 36.10 P.'

**οἰσῠοπλόκος**, add 'also οἰσιο- *Gloss.*'

**οἰσύπη**, after '**οἴσυπος**' insert '(neut. *oesypum* in Lat., Ov.*Ars* 3.213, Cels. 6.18.7.A, Plin.*HN* 12.74, etc.)'

***οἰσυπλοκή**, ἡ, *wickerwork*, πε‹ρ›ὶ οἰσυπλοκῶν *Edict.Diocl.* 12.19, (perh. οἰσυ(ΐνων) πλοκῶν).

**οἰφόλης**, after '*lewd*' insert 'τοΐφωλη (= τοῦ οἰφόλη) *SEG* 32.724 (vi BC)'

***οἰφόλιος**, ὁ, prob. a title of Dionysus, in Archil. 251.5 W.

**οἴφω**, line 3, delete 'Mimn. 15 Diehl.'

**οἴχομαι**, line 3, for 'ᾤχωκε' read 'οἴχωκε' and after 'A.*Pers.* 13' insert 'παρ-οίχωκεν Il. 10.252'

***οἰωνευτής**, οῦ, ὁ, = οἰωνιστής, *SB* 9309ᵛ.3 (iv AD).

**ὄκα**, line 1, after 'ὅτε' insert 'Stesich.*S.* 15 ii 15 (p. 160 D.)'

**ὀκέλλω I 2**, for this section read 'to *sail* a course, in quots. transf., πλόον Nic.*Th.* 295, στίβον ib. 321'

***ὀκίστια**, τά, (or ?ὀκίστια) perh. *harrows*, *IG* 1³.422.135 (v BC), (cf. Lat. *occare*, Welsh *oged*, etc.).

**ὄκκᾱ**, penultimate line, after '*AP* 6.353.4' insert '(Noss.)'

**ὄκκαβος**, add '*occabus* in Lat. inscr., *CIL* 13.1751'

***Ὀκκονηνός**, ὁ, cult-title of Zeus, *IGBulg.* 599, 718 (Ὀκον-), *INikaia* 1118, 1119; also perh. **Οὐκονηνός** *SEG* 32.679 (Thrace).

**ὀκλάζω I 2**, line 3, for 'Hld. 5.23' read 'Hld. 5.24'

**ὀκνέω**, line 4, after '(Il.) 20.155' insert 'w. part., D.Chr. 7.129' **I 3**, last line, for 'ὀ. μή ..' read 'ὀ. μή w. subj.' and after 'D. 1.18' insert 'w. opt., X.*An.* 2.4.22; w. ind., Call.*Epigr.* 27.2 Pf.'

***ὀκνηλός**, = ὀκνηρός, Theognost.*Can.* 62.

***ὀκνία**, ἡ, = ὄκνος I 2, Sch.E.*Or.* 708.

***ὀκνόλακκος**, ὁ, = °ὄκνος λάκκου, *POxy.* 2197.130, al. (vi AD).

**ὄκνος IV**, add '**2** perh. kind of derrick or crane, *PLond.* 1164*h*8 (iii AD); ὄκνος λάκκου, perh. a *shadoof*, *PMerton* 41.2, *PMich.*XIV 682.1 (both V AD).'

**ὀκρίβας**, line 1, after 'Odeum' insert '(or perh. the theatre)'

***Ὀκτάβαῖος**, ὁ, a month in Cyprus beginning 2 January, *Cat.Cod.Astr.* 2.148.14.

***ὀκταβάριος**, ὁ, collector of the *octavae* (tax), *IGChr.* 10 (Hellespont, iv/v AD).

**ὀκτάβλωμος**, add 'cf. βλωμός'

***ὀκταδράχμιος**, α, ον, *of eight drachmas*, ὀκταδραχμίας σπονδῆς Διονύσου *PMich.*inv. 1337 (*BASP* 16.194, AD 156).

**ὀκτάδραχμος**, add '**3** ὀκτάδραχμος, ἡ, *eight-drachma tax*, *POxy.* 1185.19 (*c.*AD 200).'

**ὀκταέτης**, add 'fem. Μαρκαίνα ὀκταέτης *SEG* 31.564 (Delphi, ii AD)'

**ὀκτάκις**, after '*eight times*' insert 'Plu. 2.1003f'; after 'ὀκτάκι' for '*Epigr.Gr.* 356.4 (Hadriani)' read '*IHadr.* 94.8 (i/ii AD)'

**ὀκτακότῠλος**, after '*cotylae*' insert 'σταμνία *PSI* 535.49 (iii BC)'

**ὀκτάμηνος**, at end after 'Arist.*HA* 583ᵇ33' add '(dub.)'

***ὀκταξεστιαῖος**, ον, *of eight sextarii*, *PMich.*XV 734.16 (AD 572).

**ὀκταούγκιον**, add '*Cod.Just.* 6.4.4.16c'

**ὀκτάρουρος**, add 'also **ὀκτώ-** *PHamb.* 65.15 (ii AD)'

**ὀκτάς I**, add 'Procl. *in Ti.* 2.213.31, 215.22' **II**, add '**2** *set of eight* or a *one-eighth measure* (in quot., written ὑκτάς, in an inventory of utensils), *SEG* 24.361.23 (Thespiae, iv BC).'

***ὀκτασσαριαῖος**, ον, τόκος ὀ. interest of *eight asses* a month on 100 denarii, i.e. 6% per annum, *REG* 19.247 (Aphrodisias).

**ὀκτάχορδος**, add '*octochordos* at Vitr. 10.8.2'

***ὄκτις**, ἡ, an unidentified bird, *PAmst.* 13.12 (v AD).

**ὀκτώ**, line 2, after '(v/iv BC)' insert 'Thess. ὄττου *SEG* 26.672.13, etc., (Larissa)'

**ὀκτώβολοι**, delete the entry.

***ὀκτώβολος**, ον, *at eight obols* a mina, εἰσφορά *IG* 5(1).1432.3 (Messene, i AD).

***Ὀκτώβριος**, α, ον, Lat. *October*, τῇ πρὸ ἐννέα καλανδῶν Ὀκτωβρίων *SEG* 15.815.51 (Apamea, *c.*9 BC); *SEG* 32.871 (Crete, ii AD); also Ὀκτόβριος Mitchell *N.Galatia* 181 (AD 145); Ὠκτόβριος *SEG* 28.1574 (v/vi AD).

**ὀκτωκαιδεκαέτης**, before 'Luc.*DMort.* 27.7' insert '*SEG* 32.611 (Pharsalus, i BC)'

**ὀκτωκαιδεκέτης**, after '(Halic., iv BC)' insert '*GVI* 1976.6 (Rome, ii AD), ὀκτοωκαιδεχέτης (sic) *SEG* 24.1239 (Egypt, iii BC)'; after 'Theoc. 15.129' insert 'fem., *GVI* l.c.'

***ὀκτώρουρος**, v. ‡ὀκτάρουρος.

***ὀκτώχορδος**, v. ‡ὀκτάχορδος.

**ὀκώχιμος**, delete the entry.

***ὀλαίγειος**, ον, *of pure goat's hair*, ὀλαίγεον καρακάλλιν *POxy.* 3871.2 (vi/vii AD).

**ὀλβιοδώτης**, after 'Orph.*H.* 34.2' insert 'Hymn ap.Stob. 1.1.31'

***ὀλβιοτελής**, ές, compd. of ὄλβιος and -τελής in indeterminable sense, Simon. 14 *fr.* 157.4 P.

**ὀλβοθύλακος**, for 'Cerc. 10' read 'Cerc. 4.2'

**ὄλβος**, line 6, after '(lyr.)' insert '*wealth, money*, [ἐξ] ἰδίων ὄλβων *TAM* 4(1).223 (Rom.imp.)'

**ὀλβοφόρος**, for '*bringing* .. θεοί' read '*wealthy, fortunate*' and add '*SEG* 36.694c (Berezan, late vi BC)'

**ὄλεθρος**, after lemma insert 'Cret. ὄλετρος *Inscr.Cret.* 4.51.10 (Gortyn, v BC)'

***ὀλεπίγραφος**, ον, *fully taxed*, *PThmouis* col. 74.10, 81.3, 156.13.

**+ὀλερός**, ά, όν, alleged to be Att. for θολερός, perh. ghost-word, Hp.ap.Gal. 19.126, Hsch.; of a wind that brings dirty clouds, cj. in Str. 1.2.21, (cf. perh. ὀλός, ὁ).

***ὀλιαρχία**, ἡ, v. ‡ὀλιγαρχία.

***ὀλιαρχικός**, v. ‡ὀλιγαρχικός.

**ὀλῐγαναφορία**, for '*quickness in rising*' read '*low elevation of rising*'

**ὀλῐγανάφορος**, for '*quick in rising*' read '*rising a little way*'

**ὀλῐγανδρία**, for '*scantiness of men*' read '*scarceness of men*' and add '*BGU* 1835.10 (51/50 BC), ὀλιανδρ- pap.)'

***ὀλῐγανθής**, ές, *flowering briefly*, ὥρῃ *Sodalitas* I 440 (Phrygia).

**ὀλῐγαρχία**, line 1, after 'etc.' insert 'also **ὀλιαρχία** *IG* 2².448.61 (iv BC)'; line 4, after 'Pl.*Ap.* 32c' insert '*SEG* 28.46.5'

**ὀλῐγαρχικός**, line 1, before '*oligarchical*' insert 'also ὀλιαρχικός pap. in Men.*Sic.* 156' **2**, add 'sup., Plu.*Sol.* 13'

**ὀλῐγήριος**, delete 'or perh. .. ἠρίον'

**ὀλῐγογράμμᾰτος**, add '**2** *not fully literate*, Just.*Nov.* 73.8 pr.'

**ὀλῐγοδρᾰνέω**, line 2, before 'also in late Prose' insert 'Ion Trag. 53 S.'; line 4, after 'pres. ind.' insert 'Anon.iamb.ap.Ath. 3.126f'

***ὀλῐγοήμερος**, ον, = ὀλιγήμερος, Eust. 18.8.

**ὀλίγος I 1**, line 4, after 'Theoc. 1.47' insert 'Cypr. ὀλίζων (v. infra VI 1), *the younger*, *Karnak* 13' and delete 'οὐκ ὀλίγης .. 2080.85' **2**, add 'in adverbial sense, ὀλίγη ὡμίλει *she seldom consorted* with them, Arat. 115' **3**, add 'cf. Call.*Epig.* 1.15 Pf.' **IV 9**, line 2, before '*to within*' insert 'παρ' ὀλίγον ἢ διέφευγον ἢ ἀπώλλυντο there was a *narrow margin* between escape and destruction, Th. 7.71.3' add '**11** πρὸς ὀλίγον *for short while*, *SEG* 33.1000. **12** ὀλίγου γ' οὕνεκα *for a little time*, Ar.*Lys.* 74. **13** ὀλίγα πράσσειν as contradictory to πολλὰ π. (πράσσω III 4), ὀ. πρῆσσε, φησίν, εἰ μέλλεις εὐθυμήσειν M.Ant. 4.24 (cf. Democr. 3).' **V**, add 'prob. rest. in Call.*fr.* 43.83 Pf., cj. ib. 80+82.21 Pf. (Add. II; -ους pap.)' **VI 1**, line 3, for 'the older form .. Hom.' read 'early form prob. ὀλίζων < *ὀλιγ-γων; ὀλείζων perh. in some ancient texts of Homer'; line 8, insert 'Cypr. *o-li-zo-ne*, ὀλίζων *Karnak* 13' add '**b** app. in sense of ὀλίγος *AP* 9.521, cj. in Choeril. in *Suppl.Hell.* 329.1.' **2**, delete 'always of Number or Quantity'

**ὀλῐγοστός I**, line 1, at end insert 'Men.*fr.* 208 K.-Th.'

**ὀλῐγοσύλλᾰβος**, add 'comp., Procl. *in Cra.* p. 34 P.'

**ὀλῐγοτρόφος II**, delete the section.

***ὀλῐγότροφος**, ον, *taking little nourishment*, Arist.*PA* 682ᵃ21, *Pr.* 898ᵇ21.

**ὀλῐγοϋπνία**, for '*little* or *short*' read '*moderation in*'

**ὀλῐγοχρόνιος I**, line 2, for 'Thgn. 1020, Mimn. 5.5' read 'Mimn. 5.4'

**ὀλῐγωρέω**, line 1, after '(Imbros, ii BC)' insert '*IG* 12 Suppl. 644.34, 43 (Chalcis, iii BC)' **2**, add 'also πρός τι Modest.*Dig.* 27.1.13.1' **3**, for '*PAvrom.* 1.25' read '*PAvrom.* 1A25' add '**4** *to be worried* or *concerned*, περὶ σοῦ *PSI* 1404.14 (i AD), *PHerm.* 14.6 (iv AD); *PMerton* 46.8 (vi AD).'

***ὄλιος** (ὀλίς La.)· σκίουρος, ἔλειος Hsch.; cf. ὄλειρ.

**ὀλίος I**, line 2, for '300 BC' read '*c.*300 BC'; add 'cf. °ὀλιαρχία, ὠλιώρησα s.v. ὀλιγωρέω'

***ὀλισβοδόκος**, ον, *receiving the* ὄλισβος (perh. in sense "plectrum"), rest. in Sapph. 99 i 5 L.-P.

**ὀλισθᾰνος**, after lemma insert '(or oxyt.)'

**ὀλισθάνω**, line 8, after 'infr.)' insert '2 sg. ὤλισθας, *GVI* 1861.9 (i BC/i AD)' **I 1**, add 'of a building in a state of collapse, Just.*Const. Δέδωκεν* 7a' **2**, line 2, after '*Cra.* 427b' insert 'λέξις ὀ. διὰ τῆς ἀκοῆς D.H.*Comp.* 22' **II 2**, for this section read 'fig., *cause to slip*, ἀναστήσονται οἱ Πέρσαι πρὸς κραταιὸν πόλεμον καὶ ὀλισθήσονται ὑπὸ Ῥωμαίων *Orac.Tibur.* 112; w. abst. obj., τὰς διανοίας Lxx *Si.* 3.24'

**ὀλισθοποιέω**, add 'cf. *tavefactus* (transl. as if *labefactus*) ὀλισθοποιηθὶς *PNess.* 1.847 (Virgil gloss., vi AD)'

**ὄλισθος I 2**, after 'cf.' insert '?Call.*fr.* 754 Pf.'

***ὀλίσθρημα**, ατος, τό, *intrigue*, κατισχύσει βασιλείας ἐν ὀλισθρήμασιν Thd.*Da.* 11.21.

**+ὁλκαῖον**, τό, *stem* of a ship, A.R. 1.1314. **II** *bucket* or *bowl*, Antioch.ap.Poll. 6.100.

**ὁλκάς 1**, add '*POxy.* 3342.31 (AD 204/6); transf., of the ether as carrier of the cosmos, Philol. 12'

**ὁλκεῖον II**, add 'καὶ ὁλκία δὲ τὰ πηδάλια ἐν Ναυπλίῳ ὠνόμασε (sc. S.*fr.* 438) Poll. 10.134'

**ὁλκή III 2**, add 'Lang *Ath.Agora* XXI Hb2 (iii BC)'

***ὁλκίδιον**, τό, dim. of ὁλκεῖον, *PIand.* 150 ii 4 (iii AD).

**ὁλκός**, ή, όν, **I**, after '*attractive*' insert '*absorbent*' **III**, for this section read 'ὁλκά· δυνατά Hsch.; θoὐλκότατον· βαρύτατον id.'

**ὁλκός**, ὁ, **I 2**, for '*strap, rein*' read '*leather strip, thong*'

**+ὁλκότης**· τὰ αὐτά (i.e. the glosses on ὁλκός in Hsch.), prob. *weight*, Hsch.

**ὄλλῡμι B III**, line 3, for 'of the *dead*' read 'of the *slain*'

**+ὅλμος**, ὁ, *mortar*, χεῖρας ἀπὸ ξίφεϊ τμήξας ἀπό τ' αὐχένα κόψας, ὅλμον δ' ὣς ἔσσευε κυλίνδεσθαι δι' ὁμίλου Il. 11.147, Hes.*Op.* 423, Hdt. 1.200, Ar.*V.* 201, 238, *IG* 1³.422.22, 25, 423.10 (written ὁόλμος, V BC), καθίσας τὸν ἄνθρωπον ὀκλὰξ ἐπὶ ὅλμων δύο Hp.*Haem.* 4, Men.*Dysc.* 631, *CID* I 10.24, *IG* 12(5).872.82 (iii BC), *PLille* 9.9 (iii BC), etc.; prov. ὅ. ὑπὲρ κεφαλῆς Lib.*Ep.* 473.4. **II** transf., of things with a deep circular depression: **1** the part of the tripod on which the Pythia sat, Poll. 10.81; prov., ἐν ὅλμῳ κοιμᾶσθαι Plu.*Prov.* 2.14; ἐν ὅ. εὐνάσω Zen. 3.63. **2** drinking-vessel, Menesth. 1. **3** *bulb* between the main tube and mouthpiece of an aulos, Eup. 289 K.-A., cf. Poll. 4.70, and v. ὑφόλμιον II. **4** form of sundial, ὅλμου τοῦ λιθίνου ὃς ἐκαλεῖτο Ἑλληνιστὶ [γν]ώμων *PHib.* 27.26 (iii BC). **5** τὸ ὑπὸ ταῖς ὑπογλουτίσιν ἑκατέρωθεν κοῖλον Hsch.

***ὀλοεῖται**· ὑγιαίνει Hsch.; cf. °ὀλοός (B), οὔλω, ὀλός I 2.

**ὄλοισος**, add '(ὄλυσος La.)'

**ὁλοκᾰλᾰμος**, add '**2** *full-grown reed*, *PCol.* 230.5 (?iii AD).'

**ὁλοκαυτέω**, for '*offer whole*' read '*burn an offering entire*'

**ὁλόκαυτος 1**, after '*burnt whole*' insert 'οἶς Sokolowski 2.19.84 (iv BC)'; for 'Call.*Fr.* 1.49 P.' read 'Call.*fr.* 228.49 Pf.'; delete 'τὸ ὁ.' and transfer 'Lxx .. (16)' after 'θυσία'

***ὁλοκίτρινος**, ον, *entirely citron-yellow*, epith. of the λίθος ἀχάτης, Socr.Dion.*Lith.* 17 G.

**ὁλοκληρία**, line 1, after '*soundness in all parts*' insert '*good health*'; line 3, for '(Phrygia, i/ii AD)' read '(Lydia, ii/iii AD); *Sardis* 7(1).94'

**ὁλόκληρος**, line 11, before 'Adv.' insert 'subst. τὸ -ον Modest.*Dig.* 27.1.1.2; ἐξ ὁλοκλήρου *in its entirety*, Just.*Nov.* 22.44.9'

**ὁλόκνημος**, for 'σκελὶς' read 'σχελὶς'

***ὁλοκότιον**, τό, = ὁλοκόττινος, *BGU* 1082.5 (iv AD).

***ὁλοκό(τ)τινος**, ὁ, Lat. *solidus*, a gold coin, *Edict.Diocl.* 30.1a, *POxy.* 1223.32 (iv AD), 1026.5 (v AD); also -ον, τό, *PMasp.* 70.1 (vi AD).

**+ὁλολαμπής**, ές, *shining all over*, coined as etym. of Ὄλυμπος, Arist. *Mu.* 400ᵃ8.

***ὁλόλῐνος**, ον, *made of pure linen*, *PMag.* 36.268 (iv AD).

**ὁλόλῐτος**, delete the entry.

**ὄλολοι**, add 'cf. ὄλολυς'

**ὀλολῡγή**, line 3, after '*h.Ven.* 19 (pl.)' insert 'Alc. 130.35 L.-P.'

**ὀλόλυγμα**, add '**2** *cause of wailing*, *Syria* 14.385 (Mesopotamia).'

**ὀλολῡγών II**, for this section read 'meton., *frog*, (sts. app. spec. a *tree-frog*), Eub. 102.6 K.-A., Thphr.*Sign.* 42, Theoc. 7.139, Arat. 948, *AP* 5.291.5 (Agath.); cf. *qua vocem emittunt* (*rani*) *mares, cum vocantur ololygones*, Plin.*HN* 11.173'

**ὀλολύζω**, add 'see also °ἐλελύζω'

**ὄλολυς**, add 'cf. ὄλολοι'

**ὀλοός I**, penultimate line, delete 'θάρσος .. Nonn.*D.* 13.416' and insert '**ὀλοῖος**, Procl.*H.* 5.15'

***ὀλοός** (B), ἡ, όν, = ὅλος, καὶ ὁ ἀγαθὸς ὀλοός, ὁ φρόνιμος καὶ ὑγιής Sch.Nic.*Al.* 75b, Suid.

***ὀλοπίναρος**, α, ον, *consisting entirely of pearls*, *PMasp.* 340ᵛ.31.

***ὀλοπόλιος**, v. °ἀλοπόλιος.

**ὀλοπράσινος**, add 'Zos.Alch. 142.26'

**ὀλόπτω**, after '*tear out*' insert 'τρίχα ὤλοψε Euph. in *Suppl.Hell.* 415c ii 16'; after 'Call.*Dian.* 77' insert '*fr.* 573 Pf.'; after '(Antip.Sid.)' insert 'Nonn.*D.* 21.70'

**ὀλόπῡρος**, after '*of unground wheat*' insert 'ὀλοπύρων (sc. ἄρτων) *PIand.* 146 iii 8 (ii BC)' and for 'esp. *of wheat boiled whole*' read 'ὀλόπυρος, ὁ, *a dish made from this*'

***ὀλορούσιος**, ον, *completely red*, *POxy.* 1978.7 (vi AD).

**ὅλος I 2**, add '*IG* $4^2$.126 (Epid.)' **3**, add 'w. gen., *entirely concerned* with or *intent* on, οὕτω τῶν .. πραγμάτων καὶ τῆς ἀληθείας ὅλοι Just.*Nov.* 78.4 pr.' **4**, line 5, after 'Pl.*Plt.* 302b' insert 'abbrev. ὅ. before numbers, *in total*, *SEG* 30.1535 (ii AD), etc.; also fem., ὅλαν *entirely*, *Inscr.Cret.* 4.77*B*4 (Gortyn, v BC)' add 'ἐν ὅλαις *altogether, in all*, *CPR* 7.8.16, *PGoodsp.Cair.* 30 xxxi 12 (ii/iii AD)'

**ὀλοσηρικός**, after 'Cyran. 120' insert '*PVindob.* G16846 (*Tyche* 2.6-7)'

**ὀλοστήμων**, add 'στιχαρομαφόριον *POxy.* 1978.6, al. (vi AD, -στυμ-pap.)'

**ὀλόσφῡρος**, add 'Alcid.*Od.* 26'

**ὀλοσχερής I 3**, penultimate line, after 'Plot. 1.6.9' insert 'D.H. *Din.* 4'

**ὀλοσώματος**, add 'ἀνδριάς *IG* 12(7).240.29 (Amorgos, iii AD)'

**ὀλοφλυκτίς**, before 'ἴδος' insert '(-φυκτίς Hsch., Phot.)'

**ὀλόφυρσις**, add 'Aret.*SD* 1.5'

**⁺ὀλοφυς**· οἶκτος, ἔλεος, θρῆνος Hsch.; Theognost.*Can.* 57 A.; Sapph. 21.3 L.-P.

**ὀλόχροος**, add 'Hsch. s.v. ἀμυσχρόν'

***ὀλοχωρία**, ἡ, *whole area* or *site*, ἱεροῦ *PSI* 1145.14 (ii AD).

**ὄλπη**, line 1, after 'ἡ' insert '**ὄλπα** *SEG* 26.399 (Corinth, *c.*580 BC)'

****Ὀλυμπεῖος**, α, ον, late form of -ίειος, *Olympian*, μίαν ἐν τῷ Ἡρακλείῳ καὶ μίαν ἐν τῷ Ὀλυμπείῳ γυμνασίοις *SEG* 30.1383A (Hypaera, AD 301).

**Ὀλύμπια**, for '*the Olympic games .. Zeus*' read 'a religious festival with agonistic games held in honour of Olympian Zeus, at Pisa'; add 'at other places, *IG* $2^2$.3162.10, 18, ibid. 16 (sp. -εια), *TAM* 4(1).34 (Smyrna), *SEG* 31.1103 (Phrygia), etc.'

**Ὀλυμπιάς II 3**, add '= Lat. *quinquennium*, *lustrum*, *PKöln* 10.4 (i BC)'

****Ὀλυμπιασταί**, οἱ, name of a guild of worshippers named after a woman called Ὀλυμπιάς, *MDAI(A)* 25.109 (Rhodes).

**Ὀλυμπίεια**, after '*his festival*' insert '(including agonistic games)'; delete 'later Ὀλύμπεια .. al.'

**Ὀλυμπιεῖον I**, after 'Th. .. 70, al.' insert '*IG* 7.1, al. (Megara, iv BC)'

**Ὀλυμπικός 2**, add 'Ὀλυμπικὰν στοὰν *SEG* 23.207 (i BC/i AD)'

**Ὀλυμπιονίκη**, delete 'Id. 4.17' and '(both pl.)'

****Ὀλυμπιονῑκία**, ἡ, *victory at Olympia*, δύο τ' Ὀλυμπιονικίας ἀείδειν (-κας pap.) B. 4.17 S.-M.

**Ὀλυμπιονίκος**, for 'ib. 5.21' read 'Pi.*O.* 5.23' and add 'Lang *Ath.Agora* XXI C5 (vi BC)'

**Ὀλύμπιος**, line 2, after 'Men.*Sam.* 187' insert '*SEG* 34.1093 (ii/iii AD)'; line 6, after '(Elis, vi BC)' insert 'τôι Δὶ τôι Ὀλυπίōι *SEG* 31.344 (?Laconia, *c.*500 BC)' add '**2** *proper to* or *characteristic of the Olympian gods*, Plu. 2.458c.'

****Ὀλυμπομέδων**, οντος, ὁ, *lord of Olympus*, *PHib.* 172.74.

**Ὄλυμπος**, line 4, after 'cf. 113' insert 'Parm. 11.2'

**ὄλῡρα**, lines 1/2, for '= ζειαί (q.v.)' read 'prob. *emmer*'

***ὀλῡρίδιον**, τό, dim. of ὄλυρα, *PHib.* 207.6 (iii BC).

***ὀλῡροκοπία**, ἡ, *the milling of* ὄλυραι, *POxy.* 3807.26.

***ὀλῡροπράτης**, ου, ὁ, *dealer in* ὄλυραι, rest. in *BGU* 1288.2 (ii BC).

***ὀλυρός**· τραχύς Theognost.*Can.* 57 A.

**ὅμαδος III**, for 'Pi.*I.* 8(7).27' read 'Pi.*I.* 8.25a S.-M.' and insert 'Orph.*L.* 560'

***ὁμαίχμια**, τά, = ὁμαιχμία, app. referring to taking Cretans into citizenship, *Milet* 2.12 (verse, *c.*200 BC).

**ὁμᾰλίζω I 1**, for 'cf. Damox. 2.50' read '*BGU* 2354.6 (ii AD)' **2**, add '*make even* (in tempo), Damox. 2.50'

***ὁμᾱλίκιος**, v. °ὁμηλίκιος.

***ὁμᾰλιστικός**, ή, όν, *used for levelling* the ground, μηχανή *PWarren* 15.4 (ii AD).

**ὁμᾰλός I 4**, line 3, after 'Epicur.*Ep.* 2 p. 53 U.;' insert 'of style, D.H.*Dem.* 20'

**ὁμάς**, after '*the whole*' insert 'ἐκ τῆς ἡμῶν ὁμάδος *PNess.* 24.4 (vi AD)' and after '*Gp.* 10.2.3' insert 'καθ' ὁμάδα, of succession to an estate *as a whole*, *Cod.Just.* 6.48.1.3'

**ὁμαῦλαξ**, after '*lands*' insert '(of persons) Call.in *Suppl.Hell.* 238.9'; after '(Antip.)' insert '(of places) ὁ. ἀρούρας A.R. 2.787'

**ὅμαυλος II**, for 'γήρας' read 'γῆρυς'

**ὀμβρία**, add '**II** kind of meteorite, = νοτία III, Plin.*HN* 37.176.'

**ὄμβριμος I**, add 'Διὸς Ὀμβρίμου (on an altar), *IHistriae* 334'

**ὄμβριος**, add 'fem., personified as a goddess, Θεὰ ἡ Ὀμβρίος *Salamine* 60'

***ὀμβριστήρ**, ῆρος, ὁ, = °ἐξομβριστήρ, *PRyl.* 583.16, 63 (ii BC).

***ὄ(μ)βρυσις**, ἡ, prob. some extra charge or tax, μετὰ τῆς ὀμβρύσεως καὶ τοῦ ἀναλώματος *SB* 10568.7 (AD 393/4); app. an assaying charge, *POxy.* 3147.19 (iv/v AD).

**ὁμευνέτις**, add '*SEG* 23.220 (Messene, i AD)'

**ὁμήθης 1**, for 'Call.*Aet.* 1.1.5' read 'Call.*fr.* 178.5 Pf.' **2**, for '*accustomed*' read '*congenial*'

***ὁμηλίκιος**, α, ον, Dor. **ὁμᾱλίκιος**, *of the same age*, *GVI* 1155.5 (Arcesine, ii/i BC).

**ὁμῆλιξ**, for 'ὑμᾶλιξ' read 'ὑμαλιξ' and add 'Sapph. 30.7, 103.11 L.-P.'

***ὅμηλυς**, υδος, ὁ, *companion*, Nonn.*D.* 14.25 (pl.).

**Ὁμήρειον**, add '**II** at Smyrna also name of a copper coin, Str. 14.1.37.'

**ὁμήρης**, for '= ὅμηρος' read '*mixed*'

**Ὁμηρικός**, add '**III** ὁμηρικόν, τό, some article of clothing, *PRyl.* 627.21 (iv AD).'

**Ὁμηρομάστιξ**, before 'Gal. 10.19' insert 'Vitr. 7.1.8'

**Ὅμηρος**, lines 1/2, after '(dub.)' insert 'Callin. 6' and before 'Hdt.' insert 'Simon. 59 P.'

**ὅμηρος**, add 'also neut. sg., παῖς ὧν ὅμηρον ἐδόθη βασιλεῖ, ὅ ἐστιν ἐνέχυρον *Vit.Hom.* 6.44'

***ὁμῑλητήρ**, ῆρος, ὁ, pl. as gloss on θέραπες, Hsch.

**ὅμῑλος**, line 4, delete 'rare in Att. prose'

***ὁμιχλοφάνής**, ές, *misty, cloudy*, as a description of the sun as constituting an omen, *Orac.Tiburt.* 27.

**ὄμμα I**, add '**3** the *eye* of gods, etc., considered as watching over human affairs, ὄ. Δίκης S.*fr.* 12 R., Orph.*H.* 62.1, *SEG* 11.325 (iv/v AD); ὄ. Διός Orph.*H.* 59.13, ὄ. δαιμόνων *Trag.adesp.* 499.' add '**VI** ὄ. βοός = βούφθαλμον, *AP* 4.1.52 (Mel.).'

***ὀμμᾰτωρυξία**, ἡ, *the gouging-out of eyes*, *PMasp.* 353.19 (vi AD).

**ὄμνῡμι**, line 15, after '[D.] 19.318' insert 'Cypr. 1 pers. *o-mo-mo-ko-ne*, ὀμόμοκον, *ICS* 8.6' **III**, line 5, for 'rarely .. σιδαρέοισι' read 'w. dat., τῷ γὰρ ὄμνυτε; *what do you swear by?*'

**ὁμοβώμιος**, add '*MAMA* 9.16 (i AD), Plu.*fr.* 157.3 S.'

***ὁμογᾰρικός**, v. °ὠμογαρικός.

***ὁμογενέτωρ**, ορος, ὁ, *brother*, E.*Ph.* 165 (lyr.).

**ὁμόγρᾰφος II**, add '*SEG* 35.665B.37 (Ambracia, ii BC)'

**ὁμόδελφυς**, for 'Call.*Fr.* 168 .. *Fr.* 1.73 P.' read 'Call.*fr.* 228.73, 524 Pf.'

**ὁμόδουλος 3**, add 'Just.*Nov.* 166 pr.'

***ὁμοδῠνᾰμος**, ον, *of the same power*, Paul.Aeg. 3.46.7 (254.15 H.).

**ὁμοζῠγία**, add '**2** of married life, epigr. in *IGBulg.* 814 (written -ζυγέης), *SEG* 36.843 (Sicily, v AD).'

**ὁμόζῠγος I 1**, add '**b** ὁμόζυγος· γαμετή Hsch.' **II**, for '*corresponding*' read '*joined in a pair*'

**ὁμόζυξ**, add '**II** κώλων, as synon. with διζύγων, v.l. in Paul.Aeg. 6.107.'

**ὁμόθηλος**, before 'Hsch.' insert '*Delph.* 3(3).277.3 (i BC/i AD)'

**ὁμόθρονος**, add '**2** *holding the same rank*, Just.*Nov.* 31 epilogos.'

**ὁμοίιος** (A), line 4, after 'cf. ξυνός' insert 'or perh. *levelling*'; line 5, after 'νεῖκος Il. 4.444' insert 'Theoc. 22.172'

**ὁμοίιος** (B), before 'for ὁμοῖος' insert 'perh. the same as ὁμοίιος (A), used by misunderstanding'

***ὁμοιόζηλος**, ον, *showing similar zeal*, *BCH* suppl. 8 no. 179 (Thessalonica, iv/v AD).

**ὁμοιομερής**, add 'adv. -ῶς, *homogeneously*, Gal. 7.99.6'

**ὅμοιος**, line 3, Arc., add 'ὑμοῖος *BCH* 111.167' **B 5**, penultimate line, after 'E.*Or.* 697' insert 'folld. by ἤπερ, Aristid.*Rh.* 2 p. 531 S.'

**ὁμοιοσχήμων**, lines 4ff., form ὁμοιόσχημος, add 'ὑποδήματα ὁμοιόσχημα Leont.Byz.*HP* 2.3'

**ὁμοιοτῡπής**, after 'Λητοῦς' insert 'διδύμοις' and after 'Sidyma' insert 'ii AD'

**ὁμοιόω I**, add '**3** *make equal* (before the law), τὴν μητέρα .. ὡμοιώσαμεν τῷ πατρί Just.*Nov.* 2.3 pr.' **II**, after '*to be like*' insert 'Aristid.Quint. 3.10'

**ὁμοκλάω**, add 'w. fut. inf., A.R. 4.1006'

***ὁμοκτηματικός**, ή, όν, *belonging to the same estate* or *farm*, γεωργοί *POxy.* 1983.11 (vi AD).

***ὁμολέγω**, *agree, concur*, *PCol.* 175.59 (AD 339).

**⁺ὁμολεχής**, ές, *sharing the same bed*, *Lyr.adesp.* 119.29 P.

**ὁμολογία 3 c**, add 'meton., *amount specified in agreement*, Just.*Nov.* 123.2.1'

**Ὁμολώϊος**, line 3, after '(Naupactus), etc.' insert '-ια, τά, festival at Orchomenos, *IG* 7.48, 3196, 3197' and after 'fem.' insert 'Ὁμολωΐς, ίδος, cult-epith. of Athena, Lyc. 520'

***ὁμομαχία**, gloss on ὁμοαιχμία, Hsch.

**ὁμομήτωρ**, after 'Orph.*fr.* 15' insert 'Plu. 2.482a'

**ὁμονοητικός**, line 2, after 'Arist.*Pol.* 1330ᵃ18' insert 'of persons, Iamb.*VP* 221'

**'Ομονῶος**, add 'also *'Ομόνοιος SEG* 36.750 (Mytilene, iv BC)'

***ὁμοπαντεπόπτης**, ου, ὁ, *he who sees everything at the same time*, *PMasp.* 188ᵛ.2 (vi AD).

**ὀμόργνῡμι**, add 'med. aor. μόρξατο, Q.S. 4.270, 374 (app. fr. false division of ἀπομόρξατο), see also ὄμαρξον'

***ὁμορρεύστης**, ες, *flowing together*, Anon.Alch. 449.23.

**ὁμόρροθος**, after 'Theoc.*Ep.* 3.5' insert 'fig., ἀπὸ φρενὸς ὁμορρόθου Simon. 14 *fr.*35(*b*).10 P.'

***ὁμόρροπος**, ον, *of the same value as, on a level with*, τοῖς ἐμοῖς παισίν *GVI* 1875.29 (Alexandria, i BC).

**ὁμός**, line 5, after 'Hes.*Sc.* 50' insert '(οὐκέθ' ὁμὰ codd.); οὐ καθ' ὁμὰ ζώοντες not living *together*, Ps.-Babr. *Μυθικά* 10 p. 217 C.' last two lines, for 'c. gen. .. 26' read 'ἑτέρων ἴχνια μὴ καθ' ὁμὰ [δίφρον ἐλ]ᾶν Call.*fr.* 1.26 Pf.; w. dat. prob. cj. in Nic.*Th.* 817'

***ὁμοσόδιον**, τό, a space in a building (?assembly room, cf. ὁμόσε - ὁδός), θύραι τοῦ αὐτοῦ ὁμοσοδίου *CPR* 7.44.9 (v/vi AD).

**ὁμόσπονδος**, add 'Ion Trag. 53f S.'

***ὁμόστῐβοι** (-βεῖς cj.)· συμπράττοντες Hsch.

**ὁμόστοιχος**, line 2, after 'Dam.*Pr.* 312' insert 'of girls dancing, Alcm. 33 P.'

**ὁμότᾰφος**, add '**2** masc. subst., *member of a burial club*, Sol.*Lg.fr.* 76a R.'

***ὁμότᾰχος**, ον, *having the same speed*, τὸν δρόμον οὕτως ὁμόταχον ῥυθμίζων Hld. 10.29.

***ὁμοτεμενής**, ές, *sharing the same* τέμενος, *Inscr.Cret.* 2.xvii 1.16 (Lisos, iii BC).

***ὁμοτέχνης**, ου, ὁ, *craft-fellow, member of the same guild*, *SB* 6266.3 (vi AD).

***ὁμοτεχνία**, ἡ, *guild of workmen*, *MAMA* 9.49 (ii AD).

***ὁμοτεχνίτης**, ου, ὁ, = °ὁμοτέχνης, *ZPE* 61.74 (AD 386).

**ὁμότεχνος II 2**, for this section read 'ὁμότεχνον, τό, *guild*, ὁ. τῶν λαναρίων *TAM* 5(1).85, ὁ. τῶν γναφέων ib. 86, ὁ. τῶν ὑφαντῶν *SEG* 33.1017 (all Saittae, ii AD)'

**ὀμότης**, after '*swears*' insert 'prob. of magistrates who swear to observe a law, *Meiggs-Lewis* 2 (Dreros, vii BC), cf.'

**ὁμοτρεχής**, read '**ὁμοτρεκής**'

**ὁμότροπος 1**, line 2, after 'Pl.*Phd.* 83d' insert 'ὁ. αὐτῷ νυμφίον Men.*Dysc.* 337'

**ὁμουργός**, for '*mate* .. (vi AD)' read 'perh. in *SEG* 33.932 (Ephesus; or ?*[οἰκοδ]ομουργοί)'

**ὁμοφῡλία**, add '*SEG* 30.1723 (Egypt, i/ii AD; sp. ὁμοφιλία)'

**ὁμόφωνος II 2**, after 'Ptol.*Harm.* 1.7' insert '*on the same note*, of successive syllables, D.H.*Comp.* 11.63'; adv., after 'S.E.*P.* 3.239' add '*SEG* 34.1065 (Aphrodisias, vi AD)'

**ὁμόχροος**, add 'λαχάνοις τοὺς ἀνθρώπους ὁμόχροας *Vit.Aesop.*(G) 124'

**ὁμόψῡχος I**, after 'Lxx 4*Ma.* 14.20' insert 'Gorg.*Hel.* 2'

***ὄμπια**, v. °ὄμπνιος.

**ὀμπνηρόν**, add 'also ὀμπνιηρόν, ὀπνιηρόν, v. *Suppl.Hell.* 1094'

**ὄμπνιος I 1**, after '*nourishing*' insert 'ὄμπνιον ὕδωρ Call.*fr.* 357 Pf.'; add 'ὄμπια (sic)· παντόδαπα τρωγάλια Hsch.' **2**, for 'cf. *BCH* 11.161 (Lagina)' read 'perh. also of Hecate, *SEG* 30.1272 (Lagina, ?ii/i BC); cf. ὄμπνια Μήνη Nonn.*D.* 5.488, 38.124'

**ὀμφᾰκηρός**, delete '(ὀμφακηρὰ α' .. numeral)' and add 'ὀμφακηρά, ἡ, *rounded vessel, flagon*, *PLond.* 239.13 (iv AD), *POxy.* 1870.13 (v AD)'

**ὀμφάκινος 1**, for '*unripe grapes*' read '*unripe fruit*'; add '*Edict.Diocl.* 31a; κηκῖδος ὀμφακίνης Gal. 14.198.17'

***ὀμφᾰλάριον**, τό, some kind of vessel, *PHerm.* 23.7 (iv AD); also **ὀμφαράριον** *PVindob.Worp.* 11.6 (vi AD); cf. °ἀμφοράριον.

**ὀμφᾰλητομία**, line 1, delete '*midwifery*'

**ὀμφᾰλός III**, add '**6** part of the νόμος κιθαρῳδικός, Poll. 4.66.'

***ὀμφᾰράριον**, v. °ὀμφαλάριον.

**ὀμφή**, line 6, delete 'signified by the flight of birds'

**ὀμφήεις**, add '*Didyma* 497.5'

***ὁμωμότας**, α, ὁ, *one who supports a person's oath by swearing with him*, .]μομότας *Inscr.Cret.* 1.xviii 5.13, 4.4.3.

**ὁμωνυμία I**, after lemma insert '(Ion. -ίη *SEG* 34.1116)'; before '*AP* 6.100' insert 'ὁμωνυμίῃ παῖς πατρὸς Ἀντιφάνης'

**ὁμῶς**, line 2, delete '*in equal parts*, Hes.*Th.* 74'

***ὀναλόω**, Thessalian for ἀναλόω, *SEG* 31.572.A7-8 (Crannon, *c.*200 BC).

**ὄνᾰρ II**, line 8, κατ' ὄναρ, add '*TAM* 4(1).67, *SEG* 31.1259 (Pisidia, ii AD)'

**ὀνάριον**, add 'in undetermined sense, Lang *Ath.Agora* XXI B10 (iv BC)'

**ὀνᾶς II**, delete the section.

***ὀνάς**, άδος, ἡ, *she-ass*, Aq., Sm.*Za.* 9.9, Al.*Ge.* 45.23, *POxy.* 3416.18 (iv AD); *Gloss.*

***ὀνγράφω**, v. °ἀναγράφω.

**ὄνε**, add 'also Cypr. *o-ne* ὄνε *ICS* 306.5; *to-ne* τō(ι)νε (dat. sg.), 306.2, 7'

**ὄνειαρ I 2**, delete the section transferring exx. to section 1. **II**, line 2, for 'Call.*Epigr.* 49' read 'Call.*Epigr.* 48 Pf.'

**ὀνειδίζω I**, line 9, after 'S.*Ph.* 523' insert 'also w. acc. of person, τοιαῦτ' ὀνειδίζεις με id.*OC* 1002'; at end after 'Hdt. 8.143' insert 'w. pred. adj. ἐπειδή .. τυφλόν μ' ὠνείδισας S.*OT* 412' **II 2**, delete 'c. acc. .. *OT* 412'

**ὄνειος** (B), lines 5/6, for 'ὀνήϊστον .. A.R. 2.335' read 'w. acc. and inf., τἄλλα μεθέντας ὀνήϊστον πονέεσθαι θαρσαλέως A.R. 2.335'

**ὀνειραιτησία**, add 'sp. ὀνειρετησία *POxy.* 3298.41 (iii AD)'

***ὀνειριάζω**, *dream*, Cyran. 1.5.13 K.

***ὀνειροκρῖτία**, ἡ, = -κρισία, *PMag.* 1.330.

**ὀνειροπολέω**, line 4, after 'Luc.*Merc.Cond.* 20' insert 'Ach.Tat. 5.26; med. S.E.*M.* 8.57'

***ὀνειροπρόσωπος**, ὁ, name of a wild poppy, Ps.-Apul. 53.13 (*oniroprosopos*).

**ὄνειρος 1**, add 'κατ' ὄνειρον *SEG* 36.484 (Thespiae, i/ii AD), 36.533 (Acarnania, ii AD)'

***ὀνειρόφοιτος**, ον, *frequenting dreams*, i.e. *appearing frequently in the dreams* of his worshippers, epith. of Egyptian god, *APAW* 1943(14).8 (Chalcis, iii AD).

***ὀνειρωκτικός**, ή, όν, *of* or *occurring in dreams*, θεάματα Procl. *in R.* 1.121.9 (codd. -ρακτ-); φαντασίαι Sch.Theoc. 9.16.

***ὄνη**, ἡ, *she-ass*, *BGU* 228.3 (ii/iii AD), *PMich.*XI 620.218 (iii AD).

**ὀνηλάτης**, add '*Salamine* 22 (Cyprus, i AD)'

**ὀνηλᾰτικός**, add 'ἐργασία *POsl.* 135.6 (iii AD)'

**ὄνησις**, line 9, after 'βίου ὄ.' insert 'E.*Med.* 254'

**ὀνητός I**, add 'cf. Myc. neut. subst. *o-na-to*, *beneficial use of land*'

**ὀνήτωρ**, add 'form ὀνᾱτήρ, Myc. *o-na-te-re* (pl.)'

***ὀνθομετάφορος**, ὁ, *dung-transporter*, *PPrincet.* 154.3 (vi AD).

**ὀνθοφόρος**, add '*CPR* 10.116.5 (AD 446)'

**ὀνικός**, add 'σάγμα ὀ. *PSI* 527.2 (iii BC)'

***ὀνίλαμον**, τό, name of an *eye-salve*, Aët. 7.106 (370.4 O.).

***οννα**, unexpld. wd. in list of comestibles, ψωμίων τῆς οννα *BGU* 2358.10 (iv AD.).

***ὀνοθήλεια**, ἡ, *female donkey*, *PNess.* 89.31, 34 (vi/vii AD, ὠνοθελ- pap.).

***ὀνοκαρδία**, ἡ, precious stone of scarlet colour, Plin.*HN* 37.176.

**ὀνοκένταυρα**, read **ὀνοκενταύρα**.

**ὀνοκίνδιος**, add 'said by Pollux to be Doric, Poll. 7.185'

**ὄνομα I**, lines 4ff., form οὔνομα, add 'μὴ παρακούσῃς τὸ οὔνομα τοῦ Θεοῦ *SEG* 31.1594'; line 10, delete 'in Hom. always of a person' (cf. section II, line 1); line 17, add 'also ἐξ ὀνόματος *IHistriae* 57.28 (ii AD)' add '**4** *name* considered as having magical properties, *Gp.* 20.18.' **IV 1**, add 'ἐν ἑνὶ ὀνόματι θανάτου Lxx *Wi.* 18.12' **2**, add 'ὑπεύθυνον εἶναι Ὑπαιπηνῶν βουλῇ προστείμου ὀνόματι βφ' *IEphes.* 3829; εἰς ὄνομα *in the name of*, εἰς ὄ. Θατρῆτος *POxy.* 3903; sim. ἐπ' ὀνόματος ib. 3908. 3909 (s.v.ll., all AD 99)' **V**, add 'D. 23.36'

***ὀνομάγγων**, ωνος, ὁ, *donkey-seller*, *POxy.* 3192.10, 3728.4 (iv AD), cf. Lat. *mango*.

**ὀνομάζω**, line 2, after 'etc.' insert 'Aeol. ὠνύμασσαν Alc. 129.8 L.-P.; unaugmented aorist ὀνόμαξαν *CEG* 894.14 (Delphi, iv BC)' **IV**, add '**2** *put into words, express*, τὰ πραχθέντα D.H.*Th.* 26; pass., ib.'

**ὄνομαι**, add 'A.*Supp.* 337'

**ὀνομᾰσία I 1**, for '*name*' read '*nomenclature, naming*' add '**3** *listing of names*, Just.*Nov.* 1.1.1.'

***ὀνόμᾰσις**, εως, ἡ, *naming*, Pl.*Smp.* 199b (v.l.).

***ὀνομασμός**, ὁ, = ὀνομασία, Alex.Aphr. *in SE* 12.9.

**ὀνομαστής II**, add '*SEG* 32.1554 (Arabia, vi AD)'

**ὀνομαστί**, line 3, for 'Call.*Aet.Oxy.* 2080.81' read 'Call.*fr.* 43.79 Pf., Theoc. 24.78'

**ὀνομαστός I**, after '*named, to be named*' insert 'Arat. 381, 385'

**ὀνομᾰτικός**, line 3, after 'Hermog.*Id.* 1.6' insert 'ἀπαγγελία Aristid.*Rh.* 1 p. 499 S.'

**ὀνομᾰτοθέτης**, add 'Alcin.*Intr.* p. 160 H.'

**ὀνόπορδον**, before 'Hsch.' insert 'τὴν ἑλξίνην· ἔστι δὲ λάχανον ἄγριον. καὶ εἶδος κογχυλίου'

**ὄνος I 1**, line 5, for 'when caught .. ὀστρακίνδα' read 'when failing in a game' and add 'Pl.*Tht.* 146a' **6**, add 'ὄνος (ολος pap.) ἄγειν δοκῶ μοι τὴν ἑορτήν Men.*Dysc.* 550' **IV**, delete '= τρωξαλλίς' **VII 2**, line 1, after 'round' insert 'ὄ. ἀλέτας *Inscr.Cret.* 4.75B7 (v BC)'; line 2, after 'Alex. 13, 204' insert '*IG* 1³.422.24 (Athens, v BC)' add 'Myc. *o-no*'

**ὀνοτάζω**, med., add 'Ion Trag. 17 S.'

**ὀνοφορβός**, add 'D.Chr. 7.134'

⁺**ὀνόφυλλον**, τό, gloss on ὄνος (in sense = ὀνῖτις), Sch.Nic.*Th.* 628.

**ὄντα II**, add 'Just.*Const.* Δέδωκεν 7d'

***ὀντίθημι**, v. °ἀνατίθημι.

**ὄντως**, line 6, after 'also with nouns' insert 'or adjs.' and add '*SEG* 31.286, 962'; lines 8/10, for 'not used by Th. .. earlier' read 'Arist.*EE* 1238ᵃ19; Ion. ἐόντως cj. in Hdt. 7.143.1'

**ὄνυ**, line 1, after 'ὅδε' insert '(also sts. in Crete, *Inscr.Cret.* 2.xii 11.3, ib. 22*B*14 (Eleutherna, vi/v BC), ib. v 20*A*5 (Oaxos, iii BC)), pron. referring back to something or somebody previously mentioned; see also °τῶνυ'; line 2, after 'nom. sg. masc.' read '*o-nu* ὄνυ, *ICS* 216(b), acc. *to-nu* τόνυ, *ICS* 215(b)'

**ὀνύδιν**, for 'ὀνάριον' read 'ὀνίδιον, *little ass*'

**ὄνυξ I**, line 6, for 'of horses and oxen' read 'of ungulates'; line 8, delete 'metaph. .. στόνυχα)' and insert 'poet., of the point of a spear, *AP* 6.123 (Anyt.)' **1**, add 'ἀπὸ κορυφῆς ὡς ὀνύχων *SEG* 31.1492 (Alexandria, AD 608/10)' **3**, add 'σέ τε ἀκούων ἄνδρα, οἷον ἐξ ὄνυχος ἤδη ὁρῶ Philostr.*VA* 1.32' **II**, for '*anything like a claw*' read 'transf., of other pointed or claw-like objects, τρητὸς ὄνυξ πετραῖος (used for anchoring) Nonn.*D*. 3.48, οὐ πόδα .. ἀπέδιλον ὄνυξ ἐχάραξε κολώνης ib. 14.385' **III**, for '*anything like a nail*' read 'transf., of things displaying the appearance of a nail' add 'Myc. *o-nu-ka*, *o-nu-ke* (pl.), some kind of ornamentation on textiles'

***ὀνῠχανθές**, οῦς, τό, kind of plant, Ps.-Apul. 10.15.

**ὀνῠχίζω I**, add 'in animal husbandry, *trim the hooves*, *PMil.Vogl.* 308.162'

**ὀνῠχισμός**, add '*trimming of hooves*, *Edict.Diocl.* 7.20'

**ὄνωνις**, for 'Call.*fr.anon.* 366' read '*Suppl.Hell.* 1138'

***ὀξειοβᾰρής**, ές, *pungent and heavy*, Ael.*NA* 7.5 (s.v.l., cj. ὀξοβ-).

**ὀξίζω**, add '**2** trans., *treat with vinegar*, πόδας χοίρου ὀξίσας (-ύσας cod.) *Vit.Aesop.*(G) 42.'

**ὀξίς 1**, after 'Ar.*V.* 1509' insert 'Iamb.*Protr.* 21θ''

**ὀξῠβελής II**, masc. subst., add 'J.*BJ* 2.19.9.553, 3.5.2.80, al.'

**ὀξῠβρέχω**, delete the entry.

***ὀξυγγοσᾰπουνον**, τό, *lard-soap*, Anon.Alch. 380.18 (lemma), cf. Lat. *axungia*, *sapo*, σαπώνιον.

***ὀξυγραφία**, ἡ, *tachygraphy*, Simeon Metaphrastes *Vita Luciani* 1.4.

**ὀξυγράφος**, add 'masc. subst. ὁ. τῆς ἐξακτορίας *PLond.* 1105, *PRoss.-Georg.* v 61B.13 (iv AD)'

***°Ὀξῠδέρκᾱ**, epith. of a goddess (cf. Ὀξυδερκώ), *IG* $4^2$.491 (Epid.).

**ὀξῠδερκικός**, delete the entry.

**ὀξῠδορκικός**, for '= .. (q.v.)' read '*making the sight sharp*'; add 'Antyll.ap.Orib. 10.23.29, v.l. in Dsc. 2.163'

**ὀξυδρόμος**, add 'sup. Hld. 10.4'

***ὀξυζώμιον**, τό, *acid liquid*, Anon.Alch. 271.2.

**⁺ὀξῠκόμινα**, τά, prob. *food pickled in vinegar and cumin*, Petron. 66.7.

**ὀξῠόεις**, add 'of a crane's beak, perh. by mistaken derivation fr. ὀξύς, ὀξυόεντι γενείῳ Nonn.*D*. 14.335'

***ὀξῠόρμητος**, ον, *quick to start*, Heph.Astr. 3.45.3.

**ὀξῠπεινος**, after 'Cic.*Att.* 2.12.2' insert 'adv. -ως ἔχει Men.*Dysc.* 777'

**ὀξῠπετής**, for 'Sch.Od. 3.372' read '*Suppl.Hell.* 1165'

***ὀξῠπίδας**, ὁ, perh. non-Hellenic name of cult-object, *Inscr.Cret.* 1.v 23.16 (Arcades, ii AD).

***ὀξῠπόδης**, ου, ὁ, = ὀξύπους, *EA* 13.3 no. 496 (Mylasa, Rom.imp.), Hsch. s.v. καλπάζει.

**ὀξῠπόρος I**, for '*with pointed mouth*' read '*piercing sharply*' **II**, transfer to ὀξύπορος.

**ὀξύπτερος**, line 3, before '*De.* 14.13' insert 'Lxx' and after it 'Cyran. 95'

**ὀξῠπώγων**, after '*beard*' insert '*BGU* 1080$^v$ (i AD)'

**ὀξύρρῖνος**, after 'ον' insert '*Cat.Cod.Astr.* 12.194.18'

**ὀξύρροπος**, for 'τὸ ὀ. τῆς πεύσεως .. Longin. 18.1' read 'τὸ ὀξύρροπον *sudden change*, τὸ ὀ. τῆς πεύσεως Longin. 18.1, τὸ ὀ. τῆς τύχης Hld. 10.2'

**ὀξυρρυγχῖτικόν**, for '(sc. μέτρον)' read '(sc. κεράμιον)'

**ὀξύρρυγχος 2**, after 'Egyptian fish' insert 'one or other species of *Mormyrus*' add '**b** app. *sturgeon*, Ael.*NA* 17.32.'

***ὀξύρ(ρ)υτος**, ον, unexpld. adj. in description of siege-engine, *Poliorc.* 225.17.

**ὀξύς**, εῖα, ύ, line 2, delete 'and so Babr. 73.1 metri gr.' **IV**, lines 8/9, for 'ὀ. καιρός .. 6.1, al.' read 'ὀ. καιρός *fleeting* opportunity, Hp.*Aph.* 1, *PHib.* 15.42 (iii BC); *urgent* crisis, Onos. 6.1, al., Longin. 27.1'

***ὀξῠτοκία**, v. ὠκυτοκία.

**⁺ὀξῠτόρος**, ον, *sharply piercing*, ὀ. χαλινῷ v.l. in S.*Ant.* 108, πίτυς ὀ. (i.e. sharp-leaved) *AP* 4.1.16 (Mel.).

**ὀξυτυρία**, delete the entry.

***ὀξῠτύριος**, α, ον, "*bright Tyrian*", name of a grade of purple, *Edict.Diocl.* 24.4,20, 29.19,25,31; also **-τέριος** ib. 24.20.

***°Ὀξυχία**, ἁ, epith. of Artemis, *SEG* 25.1018 (Crete, ii/iii AD).

***ὄουαν** (acc. sg.), represents Lat. *ovationem* (cf. εὔας), Plu.*Crass.* 11; written **ὄβαν** id.*Marc.* 22.

**ὀπᾱ́ων I 1**, add 'as the title of a hero divinity, ⟨Ὀ⟩πάονι Μελανθίῳ *SEG* 23.643 (Cyprus, i BC)'

**ὄπεᾰς**, line 2, after 'Hdt. 4.70' insert '[.]πέατι Hippon. 78.6 W.'

***ὀπεί, ὀπειδεί**, v. °ἐπεί.

**ὀπέρ**, add 'so *hoπήρ* *BCH* 70.262 (Boeotia, ?iii BC); see also ὀπεραμερία s.v. ὑπερημερία'

***ὀπεράριος**, ου, ὁ, Lat. *operarius*, *workman*, *ICilicie* 46 (i/ii AD).

**ὀπή I**, after lemma insert '(ὄψομαι, ὄπωπα)' **II**, add 'fig., *window* on the mind, Favorin.*Exil.* 16.5, 9' **III**, delete '(ὄψομαι, ὄπωπα)'

**ὄπη II**, line 4, after 'etc.' insert '*hόπε̄* νόμος ἀποστάτο̄ *IG* 5(1).1155 (Laconia, v BC)'

**ὀπηδέω**, line 10, for 'A.*Fr.* 475' read '*Trag.adesp.* 493 K.-S.'

**ὀπηδός**, after 'ὁ' insert 'ἡ'; add 'Procl.*Inst.* 185'

***ὀπί** (A), Myc. *o-pi*, prep. w. dat. (app. = ἐπί); also in compds.

***ὀπί** (B), (?) app. conditional particle, Cypr. *o-pi-si-si-ke* perh. ὀπί σίς κε (= ἐάν τις), *ICS* 217.29.

**ὀπιθόμβροτος**, delete 'poet. for ὀπισθόμβροτος'

***ὀπινάτωρ**, ορος, ὁ, Lat. *opinator*, soldier detailed to collect money for the issue of pay and donatives, *PBeatty Panop.* 2.41, 54, al. (AD 300), ὀπιν[ν?]άτωρ *POxy.* 2114.10 (AD 316).

***ὀπινίω**, ωνος, ἡ, Lat. *opinio*, *legal opinion*, *POxy.* 2130.1 (ὀπεινίω pap.), 25 (iii AD), *PSI* 1076.14 (iii AD).

**ὀπιπᾶ**, at end for 'πυρροπίπης' read 'πυροπίπης'

***ὀπῖπάζει**· εὐλαβεῖται Theognost.*Can.* 65 A.

**ὀπῑπεύω**, at end after 'ὀπ-ωπα' add 'freq. written ὀπιπτεύω in codd.'

**ὄπισθεν I 1**, add 'αἱ ὄπισθε θεαί, an unidentified group of goddesses, *IEryth.* 207.21, 25; also sg., ἡ ὄπισθε θεός *Michel* 832.27'

**ὀπίσθιος**, line 3, after 'Arist.*HA* 500$^b$30' insert 'without σκέλος, *IG* $2^2$.1424a.19, 56 (iv BC)'; line 5, after '(Arist.)*IA* 706$^b$1' insert 'τὰ ὀ., *back*, *buttocks*, *PLond.* 191.15 (ii AD)'

**ὀπισθόδομος I**, add '**ὑπισθόδομος** *IG* 4.1588.9'

**ὀπισθοκρηπίς**, add '*IG* $2^2$.1424a.337 (woman's shoe, Poll. 7.94)'

***ὀπισθόποινος**, ον, (?)*retributive*, *Suppl.Hell.* 991.26 (poet. word-list, iii BC).

**ὀπισθοπόρος**, add '**2** *travelling backwards*, app. of a hand writing from right to left, ib. 4.268.'

***ὀπισθότατον**· τελευταῖον, ἔσχατον Hsch.; cf. ὀπίστατος.

**ὀπισθῠπέρα**, for '*brace of a sail*' read '*brace* that maintains tension away from the helmsman in opposition to the ὑπέρα'; add 'also **ὀπισθοπ-** *PZen.Col.* 100.8 (iii BC)'

***ὀπίσσωτρον**, v. ‡ἐπίσωτρον.

**ὀπίσω**, line 2, for 'Sapph.*Supp.* 8.9' read 'Sapph. 19.10 L.-P., **ὐπίσσω** *Lyr.adesp.* 1A.14 P.'

***ὀπίσωθεν**, adv. *from behind*, ὀ. ἀκολουθήσας *Tab.Defix.Aud.* 187.61 (ὀπίσοθεν tab.), cf. Arc. 129.10.

***°Ὀπιταΐς**, ίδος, ἡ, epith. of Artemis in Zacynthus, *IG* 9(1).600, *SEG* 14.481 (Thrace, iii BC).

**ὁπλῑτοδρομέω**, for 'Paus. 1.23.11' read 'Paus. 1.23.9'

**ὁπλοθήκη**, add '**3** perh. *compartment* (on a ship) *for storing tackle*, *PMich.*inv. 4001 (*ZPE* 24.83, i/ii AD).'

***ὁπλοκτῠπία**, ἡ, app. *fighting with weapons*, Ps.-Callisth. 14.8.

**ὁπλομᾰχέω II**, for '*drill-sergeant*' read '*weapon-instructor*'

**ὁπλομᾰχης**, add '*IG* $2^2$.766.10 (iii BC)'

**⁺ὁπλομᾰχος**, ον, *fighting with heavy arms*, ὁπλομάχοι ἄνδρες Alciphr. 1.11, Lxx *Is.* 13.5; masc. subst., Plb. 2.65.11. **II** masc. subst., *instructor in fighting with weapons*, X.*Lac.* 11.8, Thphr.*Char.* 5.10, Teles p. 50 H., *PCair.Zen.* 298 (iii BC), *SIG* 697*E*11 (Delph., ii BC), *SEG* 26.176 (Athens, ii AD).

**ὅπλον III** 6, line 2, after 'Hdt. 7.218, etc.' insert 'ταλαντάρχην δι' ὅπλων *SEG* 32.660 (Thrace, ii/iii AD)'; third line from end, after '*Cyr.* 7.2.8' insert 'κατὰ τὰ ὅ. εἶναι Aen.Tact. 27.5'

**ὁπλοποιία**, add '**2** *place where arms are made*, *arms factory*, Just.*Nov.* 85.1.'

**ὁπλότερος**, add 'cf. Nonn.*D*. 33.343, *AP* 5.218.3 (Agath.)'

***ὁπλοφᾰνία**, ἡ, *display of arms*, *AE* 1932 suppl. 20 (Phthiotid Thebes, iii BC, pl.).

**ὁπλοφορέω I**, delete '*BCH* .. B.C.)' and add 'in a religious rite, Διὶ Κυνθίῳ *Inscr.Délos* 1897.3 (ii BC)'

**ὁπλοφόρος II**, of Pallas, add '*PKöln* 245.7 (iii AD)'

***ὀπνιηρόν**, v. °ὀμπνηρόν.

**ὁπόθι 1**, add 'also in prose, *IG* 5(2).343.A20 (Orchom., iv BC)'

**ὅποι**, after 'Ion. κοι' insert 'Aeol. **ὄπποι** (or **ὄππoι**) *IKyme* 113.14, etc.'

**ὁποῖος III**, delete '1076'; add '*AP* 7.295.7 (Leon.Tarent.), Lyc. 74, 182; also sg., προσώποις τισίν .. ὁποῖον δή τε παισὶ καὶ ἐγγόνοις Just.*Nov.* 1 pr. 2, 29.1'

***ὀπόκισσος**, ὁ, *gum derived from the fruit of ivy*, Alex.Trall. 2.258.

***ὀποπευκέδᾰνον**, τό, *gum derived from the roots of Peucedanum* (*sulphurwort*), Alex.Trall. 1.72, 2.147.

**ὀπός II**, at end after 'alone' insert 'Nic.*Th.* 907'

**ὁπόσος**, line 3, after 'Ion. ὁκόσος' insert 'cf. *ZPE* 68.119 (Emporion, vi BC)'

**ὁπότε I**, line 3, for 'only ὅτε is so used' read 'ὅτε is normally used (but ὁπότε ἦσαν *Hell.Oxy.* 14.2)' add '**3** with some causal force, *in circumstances in which*, *when*, Thgn. 749, Hdt. 2.125.7, Lys. 6.23, D. 23.86, Is. 2.39, Pl.*Lg.* 895c; ὁπότε γε S.*OC* 1699, X.*Cyr.* 8.3.7.' **B**, line 2, after 'Pl.*Lg.* 895c' insert 'A.R. 1.83'

**ὁπότερος**, line 1, after 'Hom.' insert '(also Aeol. *SEG* 34.1238, *c.*200 BC)'

**ὅπου I 1**, after 'Relat.' insert 'X.*An.* 7.1.27'; for 'πόλεως .. cf.' read 'πόλιος ὅκου ἦν ἐπιτηδειότατον' **2**, line 2, after 'S.*OT* 924' insert 'Pl.*R.* 415d' **B**, before 'Plu. 2.427c' insert 'J.*BJ procem.* 1'

***οπουπα**, unexpld. designation after a name, *BGU* 2280a ii 14; also ουπουπα *BGU* 1087 iii 5 (iii AD).

**ὀπτάνιον II**, delete the section.

**ὀπτάω 4**, line 3, after 'fire of love' insert 'ὤπτηται μέγα δή τι Call.*Epigr.* 43.5 Pf.'

**⁺ὀπτευτήρ**, ῆρος, ὁ, *one who has the oversight* of, σιδήρου, of Hephaestus, cj. in Colluth. 54 (see also °κατοπτευτήρ).

**ὀπτήρια 2**, after '*presents*' insert 'or *sacrifice*'; add 'sg., gloss on γενέθλιον δόσιν Sch.A.*Eu.* 7, also Nonn.*D.* 5.139; as adj., ὀπτήριον ὕδωρ ib. 6.129'

***ὀπύ**, v. ὑπό.

**ὄπυι**, before '*SIG* 56.39' insert '*SEG* 30.380 (Tiryns, vii BC), *SEG* 26.461.5 (Sparta, v BC)'

**ὀπυίω**, line 1, after 'ὀπύω' insert 'Cypr. *o-pu-we-ne* ὀπύ(*F*)ε̄ν, *ICS* 213a'; line 2, delete '(Hsch. .. γεγαμηκότες)' **I 1**, for '*marry, take to wife*' read '*be married to, be the husband of*' **2**, for '*to be married*' read '*be the wife of*'

***ὀπυόλαι** (ὀπυι- La.)· γεγαμηκότες Hsch.

**ὀπωπή II 2**, before 'Opp.*C.* 3.75' insert 'transf., of a leopard's spots'

**ὀπώρα I**, add 'personified, *SEG* 26.473 (Elis, iii BC)'; add 'also ὑπώρα *OMich.* 90.4 (iii/ii BC), *POxy.* 298.38 (i AD)'

**ὀπωρικός 1**, add 'of crops, *grown for fruit*, *IEphes.* 3217(b).36 (ii AD)'

**ὅπως A I 2 b**, add 'ὅπως κε οὖν .. βολλεύσαιτο ἀ βολλά *Milet* 3.152A.8 (ii BC)' **6**, delete the section.

**ὅπως ποτέ**, add 'ὁπωσποτοῦν *in any way whatever*, Alcin.*Intr.* 32 p. 186 H.'

**ὁρᾱματιστής**, after 'Sm.' insert '(more prob. Aq.)'

***ὁρᾱπεία**, ἡ, office of °ὁρᾶπις, *SB* 9346.8, 9658.12 (both ii AD).

***ὁρᾶπις**, ιδος, ὁ, perh. Egyptian *high priest*, *PRyl.* 676.7 (i AD).

**ὁράριον**, add '*Vit.Aesop.*(G) 21, *Stud.Pal.* 20.245.24 (vi AD); also ὠράριον, *Edict.Diocl.* 27.8, 23, *PBodm.* 29.332 (iv AD), Hsch. s.v. σιμικίνθια, Syr.*Ge.* 38.18'

**ὅρᾱσις**, add '**IV** as name of bird, the *Seeing-bird*, of the eagle, pap. in *SHAW* 1923(2).17 (but perh. an unrelated Egyptian word).'

**ὁρᾱτικός I**, add 'of mental vision, Plot. 5.3.10' transferring here '-κὴ διάνοια id. (Ph.) 2.19' from line 3.

***ὁρατίων**, ωνος, ἡ, Lat. *oratio, legislative proposal of the Emperor*, usu. read to the senate by his quaestor, Modest.*Dig.* 27.1.1.4.

**ὁρᾱτός**, delete 'Plu. 2.1029e'

**ὁράω**, lines 14/16, for 'whereas .. Gr.' read 'and always to be restored in early Att. writers; later ἑώρακα, Men.*fr.* 208.2 K.-Th. (proved by metre)'; lines 17/18, delete '(ἑώρακειν .. 5 D.)' **II**, line 1, for '(v. ὄψ)' read '(v. ὄψ (B))' add '**VI** *pertain, refer to*, w. εἰς, τὸ .. τοῦ Διὸς ἄγαλμα ἐς Δία πάντα ὁρῇ καὶ κεφαλὴν καὶ εἵματα καὶ ἕδρην Luc.*Syr.D.* 32; πάντα τὰ εἰς ἐκκλησιαστικὴν ὁρῶντα κατάστασιν *Cod.Just.* 1.1.7 pr.; w. πρός, 1.3.29.1; also trans., τοῦτο σὲ ὁρᾷ τὸν ληγατάριον Theophil.Antec. 2.20.20.'

***ὀρβᾶς**, ᾶ, ὁ, *lentil merchant*, *SB* 9463.9 (*ZPE* 72.267).

**ὀρβικλᾶτον**, delete the entry.

***ὀρβικουλᾶτος**, ον, μῆλον -ον, Lat. *malum orbiculatum*, a variety of apple, Androm.ap.Gal. 13.289.14; also ὀρβικλ- Diph.Siph.ap.Ath. 3.80f, Dsc. 1.115.4.

***ὄρβιον**, v. °ὀρόβιον.

**ὀργᾰνάριος**, add '**2** *waterwork engineer*, *CPR* 14.41.5 (vi/vii AD).'

**ὀργᾰνικός**, line 10, after '(Tanagra, ii BC)' insert 'ὁ. μοῦσα, opp. ᾠδική D.H.*Comp.* 11.62'; adv. -κῶς, add '**2** as affecting the organ (as a whole), Gal. 7.99.6.'

***ὀργᾰνισμός**, ὁ, *apparatus*, Zos.Alch. 252.15.

***ὀργᾰνιστός**, ή, όν, *coming from an apparatus*, ὕδατα Anon.Alch. 281.11.

**ὄργᾰνον I 2 b**, at end before 'of plants' insert 'of the vocal organs, τοῖς ἡμετέροις ὀ. Aristid.Quint. 3.20, τὸ φωνητικὸν ὄ. id. 2.13'; for 'Id.*de An.*' read 'Arist.*de An.*' **3**, for 'Simon. 31' read 'Pi.*fr.* 107b S.-M.' **II**, add '**2** *piece of land irrigated by one installation* (cf. μηχανή I 4), *PLond.* 1690.9, *PMasp.* 87.6, 307.4 (vi AD).' **III**, add 'applied to techniques of literary style, τέσσαρα ὥσπερ ὄ. τῆς Θουκυδίδου λέξεως D.H.*Amm.* 2.2'

**ὀργᾰνος**, line 1, for 'ὀργάνη χείρ' read 'ὀργάνᾱ χείρ'; line 2, for '*BCH* 52.52' read '*IG* 12 suppl. 380' and for '*IG* 2.1329' read '*Inscr.Délos* 63 (v/iv BC), *IG* 2².2939'

**ὀργάς 2**, at end delete 'similarly .. (s.v.l.)'

***ὀργεύς**, έως, ὁ, = ὀργεών, gen. pl. -έων Lys.*fr.* 112 S., to be read also in A.*fr.* 144 R. (πρῶτος ὀργεών codd.), Arist.*EE* 1241ᵇ25 (ὀργίων codd.), *Hesperia* 10.56 (Athens, *c.*300 BC; cf. *HThR* 37.82).

**ὀργεών**, lines 3/4, delete 'poet., .. *Fr.* 144'; lines 6/7, delete 'a gen. pl. .. ὀργεώνων:—'

**ὀργή II 1**, add '**b** applied to Dionysiac frenzy, Pi.*fr.* 70b.20 S.-M.'

***ὀργή** (B), Ionian for πίσσα acc. to Sch.Ar.*Av.* 839.

***ὀργή** (C), perh. fem. of adj. *ὀργός, opp. βέβηλος, *initiated* (cf. ὄργια) sc. γυνή Herod. 4.46.

**ὄργια I**, add '**2** *secret cult-objects*, Theoc. 26.13, *GVI* 1344; sg., Clem.Al.*Protr.* 2.22.'

**ὀργιάζω II 2**, add 'pass., Euphron. 2'

**ὀργιαστίς**, delete the entry.

**ὀργίζω II**, lines 10/11, for 'ἐπί τινος D. 21.183' read '(but ἐπὶ πάντων in all cases, D. 21.183; cf. ἐπί A III 3)' add '**2** *feel passion* against, *SEG* 35.26.25, 218.34, 220.19 (curse-tablets, Athens, iii AD).'

**⁺ὀργιοφάντης**, ου, ὁ, *one who displays cult-objects* (°ὄργια I 2) and *initiates into mysteries*; cf. ἱεροφάντης, *AP* 9.688, Orph.*H.* 6.11, 31.5.

**ὄργυια 3**, line 2, delete 'poet.'

**ὀργυιαῖος**, add 'τᾶν ὀργυιαιᾶν perh. of the Graces on the throne of Phidias' Zeus, Call.*fr.* 196.43 Pf.(-υι- scanned as short syll.)'

***ὀργώδης**, ες, *passionate*, cj. for ὀφεώδης in Pl.*R.* 590a (see Jaeger *Scripta Minora* II 309ff.).

***ὀρδινάριος**, α, ον, Lat. *ordinarius*; sp. ὡρδινάριος, *OGI* 568 (Tlos, iii AD); ὡρδενάριος, *MAMA* 1.168 (Laodicea Combusta, iv AD).

***ὀρδινᾶτος**, ὁ, (also sp. ὠρδ-), Lat. *ordinatus*, ἑκατόνταρχος ὀ. = *centurio ordinatus*, *PBeatty Panop.* 2.60, 190 (AD 200); so ὀπτίων [ὠρ]δινᾶτος = *optio ordinatus*, *SEG* 31.1116 (Phrygia, Chr.).

**ὀρέγω II 1**, lines 2/3, delete 'ἀνδρὸς .. *Epigr.Gr.* 448.4 (Syria)' **3**, after 'acc.' insert 'ἀνδρὸς .. ποτὶ στόμα χεῖρ' ὀρέγεσθαι Il. 24.506'; add '*GVI* 270.4 (Syria)'

***ὀρεθής**· ἄδικος Theognost.*Can.* 67 A.

**ὀρειδρόμος**, after '*running on the hills*' insert 'Simon. 14 *fr.*35(*b*).7 P.'

**ὀρεινός III**, add 'also fem. subst., *desert canal*, *SB* 10541.5, 10543.6'

**ὄρειος**, line 1, after '(Luc.)*DDeor.* 20.3' insert 'Aristid.*Or.* 26(14).101'; after '*IG* 12(7).75 (Amorgos)' insert 'epith. of Aphrodite, *The Swedish Cyprus Expedition* 1927-31 vol. iii p. 626 no. 12; of Dionysus, *IEphes.* 1267 (both ii AD)'

**ὀρείχαλκος**, add 'see also °ὠρόχαλκος'

***ὀρεκτύς**, ύος, ἡ, ὀρεκτύων· ὀρέξεων Hsch.

***ὀρεονόμος**, η, ον, = ὀρεινόμος, in quot. w. ref. to the particular hill at Kafizin, Νύμφηι ὀρεονόμηι *Kafizin* 8, 12, 13.

***ὀρεσιδίαιτος**, ον, *dwelling in the mountains*, *APAW* 1943(14).8 (Chalcis, iii AD).

**ὀρεσκῷος**, after 'Od. 9.155' insert 'Alcm. 89.4 P.'

**ὀρεσσιπόλος**, add '*PVindob.Rainer* 29801.17 (Gow *Buc.Gr.* p. 169)'

**Ὀρέστης**, add 'cf. Myc. *o-re-ta*, pers. n.'

**ὀρεύς I**, add 'ὀρέας *Dialex.* 2.11'

**ὀρθᾰγορίσκος 1**, add 'βορθαγορίσκεα'

**ϝορθασία**, before 'v. sq.' insert 'also Ϝροθασία *SEG* 2.67 (Laconia, vi BC)'

**Ὀρθεία**, line 4, before 'Βωρθεία' insert '**Ϝωρθέα** *IG* 5(1).289 (Laconia, ii AD)' and before ''Ορθεία' insert '**Βορθίη** *IG* 5(1).1376'; line 5, after '(name of a ship)' insert '**Ϝροθαία, Ϝορφαία** *IG* 5(1).252a, b (Laconia, vi BC)'

**ὀρθιάζω II 1**, for '*set upright*' read '*cause to stand*, μηρῶν ῥόπαλον' add '**b** abs., *have a sexual erection* (cf. °ὀρθιάω), Paul. Aeg. 6.70 (112.23 H.); cf. ἐξανδρόομαι III.' **2**, delete the section.

**⁺ὀρθιάω**, *have a sexual erection*, Sch.Pi.*P.* 10.56, Cyran. 16 (1.5.13 K.), 26 (1.10.64 K.).'

***ὀρθιλάτης**, ου, ὁ, unexpld. military office, κοιμητήριον Αὐρ(ηλίου) Γεροντίου ὀρθιλάτου *BCH* suppl. 8 no. 131 (AD 507).

**ὄρθιος I 2**, at end for 'of animals .. 10.36' read 'w. ref. to sexual erection, ὕβριν ὀρθίαν κνωδάλων Pi.*P.* 10.36' **II 2 a**, penultimate line, delete 'μελῳδία .. 1140f' **b**, for this section read 'ὄρθιος, ὁ, metrical foot having an arsis of four *morae* and a thesis of eight *morae*, Aristid.Quint. 1.16, 2.15, Plu. 2.1140f (but differently defined at Bacch.*Harm.* 101); of a melody, *written in such a rhythm*, τῆς ὀρθίου μελῳδίας ibid.' **VI**, add 'perh. different wd.; cf. *'Ορθεία*'

***ὀρθόβλεψις**, εως, ἡ, *orthodoxy*, *IGLS* 1801 (iii AD).

**ὀρθογρᾰφέω**, add '**2** *to be an* ὀρθογράφος, *GVI* 1836 (Athens, ii AD).'

***ὀρθογρᾰφικός**, ή, όν, *orthographic*, τὸ ὀ. = ὀρθογραφία, Sch.D.T. 302.8.

**ὀρθογρᾰφος**, add '**2** perh. scribe employed to make fair copies of documents, *GVI* 592, *POxy.* 3138.2 (iii AD).'

***ὀρθοεπής**, ές, *speaking correctly*, Posidipp. in *Suppl.Hell.* 705.24.

***ὀρθοπλάγιος**, ον, perh. *having a design of straight and oblique motifs*, τυλοτάπητα ὀρθοπλάκιν *SB* 13597 (V AD).

**ὀρθόπλουμος**, for '*embroidered with feathers*' read 'app. *embroidered with a vertical design*' and add '*Edict.Diocl.* 29.12, 13'

**ὀρθόπνοια**, add 'Androm.ap.Gal. 12.120.8, 13.114.2; in animals, Afric.*Cest.* p. 31 V.'

**ὀρθοπνοϊκός**, add 'masc. pl., sufferers from ὀρθόπνοια, Androm.ap.Gal. 13.106.4, 113.10'

**ὀρθοποδέω**, for '*walk .. uprightly*' read '*advance, make progress*'

***ὀρθοποδία**, ἡ, *straight forward movement*, transf., (*successful*) *progress*, *PMil.Vogl.* 24.8 (ii AD).

**ὀρθός II 1**, add '**b** ἡ ὀρθὴ τῆς ἐπιπέδου βάσεως *rectilinear*, i.e. enclosed by straight lines, Pl.*Ti.* 53c.' add '**3** transf., *direct*; ἐξ ὀρθοῦ *directly*, ὡς ἐξ ὀρθοῦ περὶ τὴν ἰδίαν οὐσίαν μεγάλα βλαπτόμενος *Cod.Just.* 4.21.22.2.' **III 6**, add 'of style, *tense*, D.H.*Comp.* 4.27' **V**, add 'but opp. ἐγκλινόμενα, perh. *indicative* verbs as opp. those in other moods, D.H.*Comp.* 5.37. **2** αἱ ὀρθαὶ περίοδοι (opp. αἱ ἀντεστραμμέναι), those in which the dependent clause precedes the principal clause, Sch.D.T. p. 27 H.' **VI**, at end after 'βορθαγορίσκοι = ὀ.' insert 'pers. n. Ϝορθαγόρας *SEG* 11.336 (Argos, vii BC)'

***Ὄρθος**, ὁ, better attested reading for Ὄρθρος q.v., perh. with dissimilation of ρ.

**ὀρθόσημος**, for '*Edict.Diocl.* 29.24, cf. 44' read '*Edict.Diocl.* 29.17, 29'

**ὀρθοστάτης I 2**, delete the section transferring exx. to section I 1.

***ὀρθόστρωτος**, ον, of upright surfaces, *faced with marble*, τοῖχοι, Hierocl. p. 54.16 A.; subst., πῶς ἐν ὀρθοστρώτοις οἰκῇς Arr.*Epict.* 4.7.37.

***ὀρθόσφυρος**, ον, *having straight ankles*, Hsch. s.v. τανίσφυρος.

**ὀρθότης III**, for '*the* .. narrative' read '*use of nominatives and finite verbs*, cf. °ὄρθωσις 2'

**ὀρθοτομέω**, for 'metaph. .. *teach* it *aright*' read 'fig., ἐργάτην ἀνεπαίσχυντον, ὀρθοτομοῦντα τὸν λόγον τῆς ἀληθείας, i.e. not distorting it'

**ὀρθοϋφος**, for '*weaver* .. *weaving*' read '*weaver at a vertical loom*' and add '*PLaur.* 24 (v. *ZPE* 35.112), *BGU* 2471.4 (ii AD)'

**ὀρθόω III**, for 'intr. .. πλαγιάζω)' read '*express by means of nominatives and finite verbs*, τὰ ἐννοήματα Aristid.*Rh.* 1.465 S. (pass.): abs., opp. πλαγιάζω ib. 2.533 S.'

**ὀρθρεύω**, add '**2** *rise early, make an early start*, Lxx *To.* 9.6.'

***ὀρθρίζω**, *rise early, make an early start*, Lxx *Ge.* 19.2, 27, *Jo.* 3.1, 1*Ki.* 1.19, etc., *Ev.Luc.* 21.38; προήγεν ὀρθρίζων καὶ ὀψίζων, i.e. early in the morning and late in the evening, Thd. 1*Ki.* 17.16. **2** *look diligently* for (calque of Hebr. *šiḥēr*), Lxx *Jb.* 7.21, πρὸς σὲ ὀρθρίζω *Ps.* 62(63).1, etc.

**ὄρθρος I**, for '*the time* .. *cock-crow*' read '*the period preceding daybreak while it is still dark* (see *TAPhA* 119.201ff.)' (and so throughout the section); add 'fig., ὄρθρου ἀποστέλλων, i.e. insistently (calque on Hebr.), Lxx *Je.* 25.4, 33(26).5. **2** *daybreak, first light*, J.*AJ* 1.28, Plu.*Pomp.* 36.4, Hsch. (s.v. ἔωθεν).'

**ὄρθωσις 2**, for '*use of the nominative case*' read '*use of nominatives and finite verbs*'

**ὀρία**, add '*IG* 9²(1).177.13 (Delphi, ?iii BC)'

***ὀρῑγᾰνόεις**, εσσα, εν, *of* ὀρίγανον, ὀριγανόεσσα .. χαίτη Nic.*Th.* 65.

**ὀρῑγᾰνον**, line 1, before 'τό' insert '[usu. 'ῑ, but ῐ Tim.*fr.* 23 P.]'

***ὀριεντάλιος**, ον, Lat. *orientalis, eastern*, λεγεώνων .. ὀριενταλίων *PBeatty Panop.* 2.187, 192 (AD 300).

**ὁρίζω**, line 2, after 'Hdt. 3.142' insert 'Boeot. ὀριττ[ά]ντων *IG* 7.2792, ὥριττα *SEG* 23.297' **II 2**, add '**b** abs., *establish boundary-markers*, *IG*, *SEG* ll.cc.; of line, *act as boundary*, *Tab.Heracl.* 1.13.'

***ὀρῐκοίτης**, Dor. -τᾱς, ᾱ, ὁ, *lying down to sleep on the hills*, Κένταυρος *Lyr.adesp.* 6.10 P. (= B.*fr.* 66 S.-M.).

**ὀρῐκός**, line 3, after 'ὀρεικός' insert '(cf. βοεικός)' and delete '(interpol.)'

**ὁρῐκός 2**, after '-κῶς' insert 'perh. *according to the* ὅρια (v. ὅριον I 2)'; add '(s.v.l.)'

***ὀρινοβάτης**, ου, ὁ, *ranging the mountains*, ὀ. γαστραφέτης type of cross- or stomach-bow used in mountain-warfare, Bito 64.4.

***ὁριοδεικτία**, ἡ, (in paps. usu. sp. -δικτία; ὁρωδ- *PMerton* 31.4, AD 307), administrative district in Egypt, *PCol.* 136.36, 51 (AD 296/8), *PCair.Isidor.* 5.5, 7.8, etc. (iii/iv AD), *PColl.Youtie* 78.7 (AD 342).

**ὅριον**, add 'ὅριν χω(ρίου) ἰδιοκτήτου Ἑρμοῦ *ICilicie* 33 (iii/iv AD); form Ϝόρϝιον, Myc. *wo-wi-ja* (pl.) ?'

**ὅριος I**, for 'ον' read 'α, ον' and add 'Διὸς Ὁρίου καὶ Ἀθηνᾶς Ὁρίας *SEG* 30.93 (Eleusis, 20/19 BC)'

***ὀρῖτις**, ιδος, ἡ, a precious stone, Plin.*HN* 37.176; cf. ὀρείτης.

**ὀριχᾶται**, add 'cf. ὀριγνάομαι'

****Ορκαμανῖτης**, ου, cult-title of Zeus, *SEG* 33.1118-20 (Phrygia, iii AD), *MAMA* 6.242-3.

**ὀρκάνη**, add 'Lycurg.*fr.* 76'

***ὀρκίολος**, ὁ (or -ον, τό), Lat. *urceolus, little water-jar*, *TAM* 4(1).6, *IG* 12 suppl. 413 (Thasos, ii AD; -ίωλ-), *Gloss.*

**ὅρκιον II 1**, line 12, after '(Il.) 4.157' insert 'cf. Alc. 129.23 L.-P.' and for 'ib. 269' read 'Il. 4.269'

**ὅρκιος 1**, comp., for 'ὁρκιωτέραν δ' ἤμην' read 'ὀρκιōτέραν δ' ἔμēν' and add '*Inscr.Cret.* 4.42*B*5 (both v BC)'

**ὁρκισμός**, after 'Plb. 6.33.1' insert '*SEG* 31.1594 (on an amulet)'

**ὅρκος**, line 8, after 'Od. 2.377' insert 'X.*An.* 2.5.7'

**ὁρκωμόσια II**, (sg. exx.), add '*SEG* 33.147.12, 52 (Attica, iv BC)'

***ὅρκωσις**, εως, ἡ, *the swearing of an oath*, *SEG* 23.271.64 (Thespiae, 220/208 BC).

***ὁρκωτήριον**, τό, *place of oath-taking*, *PHal.* 215 (pl., iii BC).

****Ορλύγιος**, epith. of Zeus, *ASAA* 30/32(1952-54).262, no. 6 (Rhodes).

**ὁρμᾰθός I**, lines 5/6, delete 'perh. .. Polystr. p.9 W., cf.'

**ὁρμαίνω I 1**, add 'γάμον ὁ. A.*fr.* 47a ii 24 R. (anap.)'

***ὁρμαστρίς**, ίδος, ἡ, *fiancée*, *SEG* 26.1657 (Palestine, s.v.l.).

**ὁρμάω A 1**, lines 7/8, delete 'ὁρμηθεὶς .. 8.499' **B 2 b**, after 'Th. 1.64, 2.69, al.' insert 'indicating person's original place of residence, *SEG* 26.791 (Byzantium, vi AD)'

**ὅρμενος**, line 2, after 'Ath. 2.62f' insert '*Edict.Diocl.* 6.11'

**ὁρμή I 2**, add 'ὁρμὴ ὕδατος *current, gush*, Lxx *Pr.* 21.1' **II 1**, add '**b** personified, Ὁρμῇ ἐπιταγὴν Φιλημάτιν *IG* 2².4734 (i AD), Paus. 1.17.1.'

**ὅρμημα I 1**, line 3, after 'pl.' insert 'τοῦ ποταμοῦ τὰ ὁ. *gushing streams*, Lxx *Ps.* 45(46).5' transferring 'θαλάσσης .. *Ptol.* 4' fr. section 2 to follow it. **2**, line 3, after 'Lxx *Ho.* 5.10' insert '*sexual impulse*, Sm.*Ez.* 23.20'

***ὅρμινθον**, τό, app. the same as ὅρμινον, Sch.Nic.*Al.* 602a; also ὁρμίνθιον, ib. 601c.

**ὅρμος I 3**, for 'Luc.*Salt.* 11' read 'Luc.*Salt.* 12' **II 1**, add '*PWash. Univ.* 1.34 (i AD)' **2**, line 2, after '(lyr.)' insert 'Lib.*Ep.* 1088'

**ὁρμοφύλαξ**, add '*PTeb.* 370.5 (pl., ii/iii AD)'

**ὀρνεάζομαι**, delete '*carry the head* .. birds'; add 'ὠρνεάζετο· μετέωρον ἐπῆρε τὴν κεφαλήν Hsch.' add '**2** act., *twitter like a bird, chatter*, Aq.*Is.* 8.19 (L.-R.), prob. in Aq.*Is.* 38.14 (for ὀρνίζω).'

**ὀρνεόφοιτος**, for '*frequented by birds*' read 'perh. *going after birds*'

**ὀρνίζω**, add '(s.v.l.; v. °ὀρνεάζομαι)'

**ὀρνῑθειος**, add 'form ὀρνίθιος, Myc. *o-ni-ti-ja-pi* (fem. instr. pl.) *decorated with birds*'

**ὀρνῑθιον**, after 'Stratt. 58' add 'ostr. in *ZPE* 98.133 no. 22 (sp. ὠρν-, Egypt)'

***ὀρνῑθοπούλλιον**, τό, *young fowl*, *PKlein.Form.* 1329 (vi/vii AD).

**ὀρνῑθοτροφεῖον**, add '*PLund* 4.11 i 15 (ii AD), Hsch. s.v. κυρτίς'

**ὀρνῑθοτρόφος**, add '*SB* 10270.1.1 (iii AD)'

**ὄρνις**, line 2, after 'Hom.' insert '(in Cret. written ὄνν[ι]θα, *Inscr.Cret.* 4.41 iii 8 (Gortyn))'; line 3, delete 'in acc.'; line 4, after 'etc.)' insert 'later also nom. pl. ὄρνις Luc.*Ep.Sat.* 35'; line 8, after 'iv BC)' insert 'ὀρνίκων *PTeb.* 875.19 (ii BC)' **II 2**, at end after '(Ar.)*Av.* 719 sqq.' insert 'ὄρνιθος οὔνεκα A.*fr.* 78c.54 R.'

**ὄρνῡμι 4**, line 2, after '(A.R.) 3.457' insert '*AP* 11.158 (Antip.Thess.)'

**ὀρόβιον**, add 'also **ὄρβιον** *PMich.*XI 619.1 (c.AD 182)'

**ὄροβος**, line 2, for '*of its seeds*' read '*of the pulse*'

***ὀροθέτης**, ου, ὁ, *official appointed to fix boundaries*, *Inscr.Cret.* 3.iii 25, al. (i AD), *IGBulg.* 1401.9 (ii AD).

**ὄρομαι**, add 'Myc. part. *o-ro-me-no*'

**Ὀρομπᾱτας**, add 'cf. ὀρεμπόται'

**ὄρον**, delete 'ὄρος .. 130' (v. °ὄρος (B)).

**ὄρος 3**, for 'in Egypt, *desert*' read 'in Egypt, spec. of the infertile hilly terrain bordering the Nile valley'

***ὄρος** (B), εος, τό, wooden *implement for pressing olives*, *SEG* 11.244 (Sicyon, v BC), Poll. 7.150, 10.130; cf. ὄρον.

**ὀρός 2**, add 'Nic.*Th.* 708' penultimate line, after '**οὐρός**' insert 'or **οὐρόν**'

**ὅρος**, line 1, after lemma insert '**ϝόρος** *SEG* 25.517 (Thebes, ?v BC)'; line 4, for 'Megarian .. 885' read 'Megar. ὄρρος *Schwyzer* 172 (Heraclea Pontica); ὄρρους, acc. pl., *SEG* 37.576 (Maced., iv BC)' **I 1**, add 'of a race-course, *SEG* 35.218.13, 26 (Athens, iii AD)' **II b**, line 7, delete 'Thphr.*Char.* 10.9' **c**, add 'τὴν ἐκ τῶν ὅρων .. ἀσφάλειαν, i.e. sanctuary provided in sacred land, Just.*Nov.* 17.7 pr.' **III 1**, lines 1/2, delete 'ἦν .. E.*IT* 1219' add 'form ϜόρϜος, Myc. *wo-wo*'

**ὀροτῠπος**, for '*dashing down a mountain*' read '*smiting the mountain*' add '**II** of the giants, *striking with mountains* (as missiles), *Trag.adesp.* 594b K.-S., Hsch.'

**ὀροφικός**, after '*of* or *for a roof*' insert '*Inscr.Délos* 1417*A*ii17 (ii BC)'

**ὄροφος II 1**, add 'synecd., *house*, *SEG* 9.72.16 (Cyrene, iv BC)'

***ὀροφῠλᾰκέω**, *to be a mountain-guard*, *La Carie* 162.9 (Apollonia Salbace, ii/iii AD).

**ὀροφῠλᾰκέω**, delete the entry.

***ὀροφῠλᾰκία**, ἡ, *mountain guard* or *defence*, *SEG* 29.1516.8 (Lycia, ii BC).

***ὀροφῠλᾰκος**, ὁ, = ὀροφύλαξ, *Amyzon* 2.

***ὄροχθος**, ὁ, ὄρογκοι· τῶν ὀρῶν τὰ ὀγκώδη, ἃ καὶ ὀρόχθους καλοῦσιν Hsch.

****Οροχωρείτης**, ου, ὁ, cult-title of Zeus, *SEG* 32.1271 (ii AD), 33.1158 (undated, both Phrygia).

**ὄρπηξ I 2**, for this section read '*rod* or *stick cut from a tree* or *shrub*: used for driving animals, Hes.*Op.* 468; Θεσσαλὸν ὄρπακα i.e. *lance*, E.*Hipp.* 221'

**ὀρρωδέω**, line 1, after 'al.' insert 'S.*fr.* 951 R.'

**ὀρσοδάκνη**, for '*which eats the buds of plants*' read 'born from a larva in cabbages'; at end for '(The word .. found' read '(cf. ὄρρος perh., but etym. uncertain)'

**ὀρσολόπος**, for 'perh. *eager for the fray, tempestuous*' read 'app. *who* *thrashes* (a fleeing enemy, cf. ὄρρος, λέπω II)' and for 'Anacr. 70' read 'Anacr. 48 P.'

**ὀρτῠγοκόπος**, add 'Pl.*Alc.* 1.120a'

**ὀρτῠγομήτρα**, add '(Hsch. explains ὀ. as ὄρτυξ ὑπερμεγέθης, and this may be the meaning in Lxx ll.cc., al.)'

**ὄρτυξ**, for 'ὕγος .. 245' read 'ὕγος (also ὗκος, Philem. 192 K.-A.), ὁ (also ἡ, Lyc. 401), (ῡ Att. as in δοίδυκα, κήρυκα acc. to Demetr.Ixion ap.Ath. 9.393b, but ῠ in all determinable instances)'

**ὀρῠγή 1**, add '**b** ἡ ὀρυγὴ ἐξέδρας the *dug-out* (i.e. underground) exedra, *Syria* 17.260 (Palmyra, iii AD).'

***ὀρυζιοπωλική** (sc. τέχνη), ἡ, *rice-selling, PTeb.* 612 (i/ii AD).

**ὀρυζοτροφέω**, delete the entry; cf. ῥιζοτροφέω.

**+ὀρυκτήρ**, ῆρος, ὁ, *digger*, Thphr.*fr.* 30.2.

**ὀρύκτης I**, after 'Aesop. 99' add '*mole*, the animal who digs, (calque on Hebr.), Aq.*Is.* 2.20'

**ὀρυκτός II**, add 'ἁλὸς ὀρυκτοῦ *PSorb.* 35 (AD 225)'

**ὄρυς**, for 'Hdt. 4.192' read 'Hdt. 4.192.1'

**ὀρύσσω I**, for '*dig*' read '*form by digging, excavate*' **III**, for '*dig through* .. διορύσσειν' read '*dig up, excavate*'; add '*destroy by digging*, ὅπως μηδεὶς ὀρύσσῃ τὰς ὁδοὺς *Dig.* 43.10.1.2'

**ὀρφᾰνιος**, for '= foreg., *desolate*' read '*childless*'

**ὀρφᾰνιστής**, add 'also at Istros, *IHistriae* 184 (iii BC)'

**ὀρφᾰνοδῐκασταί**, after '*orphans*' insert 'or *guardians of orphans*'; add '*Inscr.Cret.* 4.72.12 7'

**ὀρφᾰνόομαι**, add '*to be bereaved of*, Sch.Pi.*I.* 7.14'

**+ὀρφᾰνοφύλαξ**, ακος, ὁ, ἡ, *publicly appointed guardian of orphans*, X.*Vect.* 2.7, *Delph.* 3(2).168.27 (ii BC); fem., *SEG* 23.353 (Naupactus, ii BC).

**ὀρφνήεις**, for 'poet. for ὀρφνός' read '= ὄρφνινος'

**ὄρφνῐνος**, add 'Orph.*A.* 965'

**ὄρφνιος**, delete 'but .. corrupt'

**ὀρφνῑτης**, for 'dub. epith. of τάλαρος' read 'perh. *working at night*, εἰροκόμος'

**ὀρφοβότης**, after 'ὁ' insert 'also **ὀρφοβώτᾱς** *SEG* 39.1008.6 (Sicily, iii BC)'

**ὀρφώς**, add '**2** an unidentified fish (sp. ὀρφός) said to be kept for omens by priests at Lycian temple of Apollo, Ael.*NA* 12.1.'

**ὄρχᾰμος**, for 'Ep. word' to end read 'ὀ. στρατοῦ A.*Pers.* 129, ὄρχαμε γαίης Opp.*H.* 1.70; without gen., A.*fr.* 451q R., *AP* 11.284 (Pall.)'

**ὀρχέομαι**, line 2 (impf.), after '(v. infr.)' insert 'ϙὠρκε̃το (prob. = καὶ ὠρχεῖτο)' **I 2**, add 'Ath. 10.454f.' **II**, add '**b** prob. sens. obsc., *IG* 12(3).536 (Thera, viii BC).'

**ὀρχηστής**, line 2, after '*IG* 1².785' insert '(v BC)' and after '(*IG*) 919' insert 'Dipylon vase, *c.*725 BC, perh. here in erotic sense, cf. °ὀρχέομαι II b'; add 'as adj., πόδα *AP* 7.37 (Diosc.)'

**ὀρχηστοπᾰλάριος**, add 'ὀρχιστοπαλαρίων πρασίνων *IEphes.* 2949'

**ὄρχις I**, after '*testicle*' insert 'τὸν ὄρχιν Hippon. 92.3 W.'

**Ὀρχομενός**, add 'Myc. *e-ko-me-no* (place-name)'

**ὅς, ἥ, ὅ B IV 6 a**, add 'perh. at *IG* 1³.533 (v. *SEG* 10.410)' **Ab IV 2**, delete 'in Att.' and after 'Ar.*Ec.* 338' insert 'Men.*Dysc.* 485, Call.*Jov.* 1.67, *Epigr.* 11.1 Pf.' **3**, add 'also pl. ἅ Isoc. 12.181'

**ὅς, ἥ, ὅν I**, line 1, after '*his, her*' insert '*their*'; line 5, before 'sts. also in lyr.' insert 'Hes.*Th.* 71, A.R. 1.384'; last line, after 'never in Attic prose' add 'exc. τὰ ἃ δάκρυα Pl.*R.* 394a (archaizing passage)'

**ὁσάκις**, add 'Cret. **ὀθάκις, ὀθθάκιν, ὀττάκιν**, *Inscr.Cret.* 1.x 2.10 (Eltynia, v BC), vii 5 *bis* (Cnossus, iii BC), 4.73*A*6 (Gortyn, v BC)'

**ὅσδε**, add '*IG* 7.1686 (Plataea, iv AD), *GVI* 1181, etc.'

**ὁσημέραι**, line 4, before 'Hyp.*Ath.* 19' insert 'Pl.*Chrm.* 176b'; line 6, after 'Ar.*Th.* 624' insert 'D.H. 1.24, al.'

**ὁσία I**, add 'ἐξ ὁσίης *SEG* 33.736 (epigr., Crete, ii AD)' **II 2**, add 'Just.*Nov.* 43 pr.' **III**, add 'ὁσίας χάριν Modest.*Dig.* 26.6.21'

**ὅσιος I**, add '**3** ὅσια· ἄλφιτα δεδευμένα ἐλαίῳ καὶ οἴνῳ Hsch., cf. Suid. s.v. ἀφοσιοῦσθαι.' **II 1**, add 'sup. as honorific title of church dignitary, Mitchell *N.Galatia* 226 (*c.*AD 580), *SEG* 31.1446 (AD 639)' **3**, add 'Διὶ ὁσίῳ ἐπηκόῳ *INikaia* 1057 (iii AD). **b** masc. or neut., personified as a deity, Ὁσίῳ Δικαίῳ *IHadr.* 136 (ii AD), *SEG* 31.1130, 33.1003 (both iii AD). **c** sup. as title of Roman emperor, τοῦ ὁσιωτάτου Αὐτοκράτορος Καίσαρος .. *IEphes.* 3217 (AD 113/120).' **III**, adv., add 'ᾧ τάφον οὐχ ὁσίως .. ἀνέγειρα (i.e. perh. "prematurely") *ITomi* 384 (iii/iv AD)'

**°Ὀσῑριασταί**, οἱ, *guild of worshippers of Osiris*, σύνοδος Ὀσειριαστᾶν *Inscr.Cos* 54.1 (ii BC).

**ὀσμή II**, lines 3/4, after 'it occurs also in' insert 'Hippon. 92.11 W.'

**ὀσμηρός 2**, delete the section.

***ὀσμός**, ὁ, name of a leguminous plant, Dsc. 2.147, cf. *Eranos* 53.31.

**°Ὀσορᾱπεῖον**, τό, = Σαραπεῖον, temple of Sarapis, *PSI* 1128.22 (iii AD).

**°Ὀσορᾶπις**, ιδος, ὁ, = Σάραπις, *UPZ* 19.3, al. (ii BC) (written Ὀσεράπις *SB* 5103).

**ὅσος IV 1 a**, after 'Arist.*Rh.*1376ᵃ34' insert 'cf. *AP* 5.216.3, 4 (Agath.), 9.581.3' **V**, add '**3** without comp. or sup., ὅσῳ περὶ τοῦτο ἡμεῖς πονούμεθα, τοσούτῳ πᾶσαν ἐξεῦρον οἱ βουλευταὶ τέχνην .. Just.*Nov.* 38 pr. 1.' **VI 2**, before 'Ar.' insert 'Hdt. 1.174.3' add '**3** ἐξ ὅσου *since*, Hdt. 2.98.1, 3.63.2 (v.l.).'

**ὅσπερ II 1**, after '(s.v.l.)' insert '*SIG* 888.10 (AD 238), etc.' **4**, add 'κατὰ ταῦτά σφιν ἔστō hᾶιπερ Κνōσίοις *Schwyzer* 83.B28 (Argos, *c.*450 BC)'

***ὅσπις**, ὁ, dat. ὅσπι, Lat. *hospes, lodger, POxy.* 3860.10, 15, 42 (iv AD).

***ὁσπίτιον**, τό, Lat. *hospitium, house, PLips.* 40 iii 18 (iv/v AD); **ὀσπήτιον**, Sch.Gen.Il. 1.396, Suid. **2** *establishment for the sick* or *destitute, hospital, PVindob.Worp.* 15, *PBasel* 19 (both vi/vii AD).

***ὀσπρεάχῠρον**, τό, *pulse-chaff, CRAI* (1945) p. 379 (Berytus, v AD).

**ὀσπρεύω**, add '*IG* 1³.252.13 (v BC)'

**ὀσπρηγοί**, for '*OGI* .. v/vi AD)' read '*SEG* 34.1243 (sp. ὀσπριγοί: Abydos, *c.*AD 492)'

***ὀσπριγίτης**, ου, ὁ, *pulse-merchant, PKlein.Form.* 1091 (vi AD), *POxy.* 2000.14 (vi/vii AD, ωσπρ- pap.).

**ὀσπριοπώλης**, add 'also ὀσπρεο- *REG* 70.120.13 (Caesarea, vi/vii AD)'

***ὅσπρον**, τό, perh. *decorated material, Tyche* 1.167 (Alexandria, vi/vii AD); cf. Hsch. ὄσπρα· ποικίλα.

**ὄσσα 4**, add 'Πυθίαν .. ὄσσαν Neophr. 1.2'

**ὄσσομαι II 2**, add 'ὀσσόμενοι φρ[εσὶ] γῆρ[ας Hes.*fr.* 1.10 M.-W.'

***ὄσσος**, ὁ, *pupil of the eye*, Sch.rec.E.*Ph.* 370 (interpr. of δι' ὄσσων).

**ὀστᾰκός**, after 'Ὄστακος' insert '*IG* 11(2).107.8 (iii BC)'

**ὅστε**, line 7, after '*Eu.* 25, 1024' insert 'v.l. in E.*Rh.* 972'; line 9, for 'antec.' read 'demonstr.'

***ὀστεοθήκη**, ἡ, = ὀστοθήκη, *TAM* 2(3).780.1 (Lycia).

***ὀστιάριος**, ὁ, Lat. *ostiarius, door-keeper, porter, SEG* 9.346.32 (Cyrenaica, vi AD); written ἀστ- *PFlor.* 71.518 (iv AD), *BGU* 672 (vi AD).

**ὅστις**, line 5, for 'Alc. 45' read 'Alc. 66 L.-P., Arc. ὅζις *SEG* 11.112 (vi/v BC), dat. ὀнέοι *IG* 5(2).262 (v BC)'; line 6, after 'Od. 1.124' insert 'Aeol. ὀττέω *SEG* 34.1238 (*c.*200 BC)'; line 14, after '*IG* 2².1126.25' insert 'cf. Theoc. 16.68'; line 24, after 'Hes.*Op.* 31' insert 'οὔτινος Theoc. 25.35, Dor. ὥτινος id. 14.19' **II 1**, add 'ὅστις is less freq. in later Greek, but where used may = ὅς, τῇ ἐπαύριον ἥτις ἐστί κτλ. *Ev.Matt.* 27.62, cf. *POxy.* 110.3, *PFay.* 108.7 (both ii AD)' add 'Myc. neut. *jo-qi* = ὅ, τι'

***ὀστογενής**, v.l. for ὀστεογενής.

**ὀστοθήκη**, delete '*sarcophagus*' and add 'see also °ὀστεοθήκη'

**ὀστολογέω**, add 'Men.*Asp.* 77'

***ὀστοφάγος**, ὁ, *ossuary*, graffito in *PalEQ* 1937.130 (Jerusalem, i BC/i AD).

***ὀστρᾰκη**, ἡ, = ὄστρακον, *jar*, Lang *Ath.Agora* XXI Hb12 (iv AD).

**ὄστρεον**, line 3, for 'ὀστρία' read 'ὄστρια' **III**, add 'ὀστρείου *SEG* 24.277.B60 (Epid., iv BC)'

***ὀστρῖτις**, ιδος, ἡ, = ὀστρίτης, Plin.*HN* 37.177.

***ὀστροφά**, v. °ἀναστροφή.

***ὀσχίον**, τό, dim. of (?) ὄσχος, *SEG* 7.1065 (Arabia).

**ὄσχος**, for 'ὦσχος' read 'ὤσχος'

**ὅταν I 2**, line 6, after '(*Ev.*)*Marc.* 3.11' insert '*GVI* 1113a.8 (Apamea)'; line 8, after '(s.v.l.)' insert 'cf. *PHamb.* 70.19 (ii AD)'

**ὅτε**, line 1, before 'Cypr.' insert 'Myc. *o-te*' and for '*Inscr.Cypr.* 135.1 H.' read '*o-te ICS* 217.1' **A I**, add '**4** ellipt., ὅκα τὸ τέταρτον *for the fourth time, Inscr.Cret.* 4.184.2 (ii BC), cf. ib. 250.3 (i BC).' **III 2**, add 'also ὁτεδήποτε Heph.Astr. 1.24.4'

**ὀτεῖος**, for 'τεῖος' read 'τεῖον'

***ὀτεύνεκα**, v. °ὁθούνεκα.

***ὀτεύνεκεν**, v. °ὁθούνεκεν.

**ὅτι A II**, add '**3** ὅτι may be resumed by ὡς, Hdt. 3.71.5, 9.6, etc., or vice versa; cf. ὡς B I 1.' add '**V** introducing a consec. cl., οὕτως ἡμῖν τῶν βουλευτηρίων μέλει .. ὅτι δίδομεν .. Just.*Nov.* 89.2.3.'

**ὀτιή**, line 1, after '*because*' insert 'A.*fr.* 281a.9 R.' **2**, delete '*Eq.* 360'

**ὀτλεύω**, add 'Procl.*H.* 1.31'

**ὄτλημα**, for 'Theognost.*Can.* 13' read 'Theognost.*Can.* 44 A.'

**ὀτλήμων**, delete '(ὁ τλήμων .. Schmidt)'

**ὄτοβος**, add 'ὄτοβος ἄλιμος *Trag.adesp.* 247 K.-S.'

***ὄρτος**, v. °οὗτος.

**ὄτρεα**, delete the entry.

**οὐ G**, line 13, insert 'Cypr. *o-u-ki ICS* 306.5 may be either οὐκί or οὐχί' at end add 'Myc. *o-u-* (*prefixed to vbs.*)'

**οὗ, οἷ, ἕ**, line 2, after 'ἑοῦ' insert 'read by Zenod. in Il. 19.384, also Hes.*Th.* 401 (v.l.), A.R. 4.803'; lines 11ff. (form ϝοι), add 'also written γοι *SEG* 8.715.7 (Egypt, ii AD), γοί· αὐτῷ Hsch.'

***οὐά** (B), ἡ, v. ᾠβά.

***οὖας**, v. οὖς.

**+οὐάτιον**, τό, *pupil of the eye, PMag.* 5.92, 12.229.

**οὐατόεις**, add '**3** applied to a tree with hanging branches, Hsch. s.v. οὐατόεν.'

**οὐγγία**, add 'κ' ο(ὐ)γ(κίαι) (i.e. 20 oz.) Lang *Ath.Agora* XXI Hb3 (iii BC). **2** *the twelfth part of an inheritance*, Just.*Nov.* 18.1, 89.12.3.'

**οὐγκιασμός** (s.v. οὐγγία), add 'Zos.Alch. 164.2. **2** *assignation of shares in an inheritance*, Just.*Nov.* 107.1.'

**οὐδᾰμόθεν**, add 'ἐκείνοις οὐδαμόθεν προσήκει D. 15.26, 21.196, al.'

**οὐδέ A II 2**, line 10, after 'D. 22.4' insert 'w. ellipsis of main neg., γῆ δ' οὐδ' ἀὴρ οὐδ' οὐρανὸς ἦν Ar.*Av.* 694, E.*Tr.* 477, χεῖρας δὲ οὐδὲ πόδας προσθίους ἔχει Arist.*HA* 503$^b$34; υἱὸς ἄρσην οὐδὲ θυγάτηρ Lxx *To.* 6.12 S.'

**οὐδός** (A), line 6, after '(Epid., iii BC)' insert 'app. aspirated form *hυπὸ τôι hοδôι τᾶς θύρας* Lang *Ath.Agora* XXI B1 (vi BC)'

**οὐδών**, add 'cf. Lat. *udo*'

**οὐδώνιον**, for '*Edict.Diocl.* .. (Asine)' read '*Edict.Diocl.* 7.47'

***οὐεῖλλος**, neut. pl. οὐεῖλλα, perh. = Lat. *vilia*, *Dura*$^4$ 133.

***οὐεριδάριος**, ὁ, Lat. *veredarius*, *imperial courier*, οὐ.· βεριδάριος Hsch.

***οὐέρνας**, ὁ, Lat. *verna*, *BCH* 28.196, *MDAI(A)* 13.242.

***οὐέρτραγος**, ὁ, Lat. *vertragus*, *greyhound*, Celtic wd., Arr.*Cyn.* 3.6.

**οὐετερανός**, line 2, after '**οὐετρανός** ib. 99, 142, etc.' insert '*PBerol.*inv. 11624.16 (*JJP* 18.35, iv AD); ὀε(τρανός) *SEG* 32.1447 (Syria, AD 150)' and after 'Zonar.' insert '*IGRom.* 4.730, etc., and **βετερανός** *IG* 14.1470'

***οὐετρανικός**, ὁ, app. *a man of veteran status*, *Princeton Exp.Inscr.* 765$^{13}$, *LW* 3.2227, 2546.

***οὐετράριος**, ὁ, Lat. *vitrarius*, *glass-worker*, *ITyr* 117.

***οὐηλάριον**, τό, Lat. *velarium*, *curtain*, *SB* 7033.39 (v AD).

***οὐθένεια**, v. οὐδενία.

***οὐιάτωρ**, ορος, ὁ, Lat. *viator*, *agent* for a Roman magistrate, *SB* 976 (inscr., Roman period).

***οὐίγουλ**, or **οὐίγουλος**, ὁ, = Lat. *vigil*, *watchman*, *IEphes.* 615.13 (ii AD), ἔπαρχος οὐιγούλων *SB* 9898.2, *JJP* 18.323 (*POxy.* 2231, both iii AD).

***οὐικάριος**, ὁ, Lat. *vicarius*, *deputy*, *vicar*, *SEG* 34.1163 (Ephesus, Chr.); cf. °βικάριος.

***οὐικεννάλια**, τά, Lat. *vicennalia*, festival celebrated every twenty years, *PStrassb.* 138.12 (AD 325); also sg., *POxy.* 2187.21.

***οὐικήσιμα**, τά, Lat. *vicesima*, *a twentieth part*, *BGU* 388.1.7 (ii/iii AD).

***οὐι(ν)δίκτα**, ἡ, Lat. *vindicta*, form of manumission, *PGnom.* 21.64 (ii AD).

***οὐινδικτάριος**, ὁ, Lat. **vindictarius*, slave emancipated by *vindicta*, *IGRom.* 3.801.20, 802.25 (Syllium).

***οὐιξιλλατίων**, ωνος, ἡ, Lat. *vexillatio*, *troop*, *squadron*, *PCair.Preis.* 39 (AD 347); οὐξελλ[ατίων] *BGU* 600.13, etc.; see also °βιξ-.

***οὐιξίλλον**, τό, Lat. *vexillum*, *ensign*, *SEG* 34.1306 (AD 275/6).

***οὐιόκουρος**, ὁ, Lat. *viocurus*, *curator of roads*, *Ann.Épigr.* 66.376 (*IGBulg.* 884).

**οὐλαί**, after '**ὀλαί**' insert '(also in Epid., *BCH* 73.366 (iv BC))'

**οὐλᾰμός II**, after 'Plb. 6.28.3' insert '(transl. Lat. *turma*)'; add 'Sch.Lyc. 32 (cf. γόλαμος; Homeric metre indicates initial ϝ)'

**οὐλάς II**, lines 2/3, for 'Call.*Fr.* 360 .. κεναί)' read 'Call.*fr.* 724 Pf. (οὐλαὶ ἀεὶ κεναί codd. Suid.), ib. 24.10 (prob. rest.)'; line 4, after 'Sch.Theoc. 1.53' insert 'Sch.Lyc. 183'

***οὐλένιον**, v. °ὠλένιον.

**οὐλή**, add '**2** *a corneal opacity*, Paul.Aeg. 3.22.24 (181.1-2 H.).'

**οὖλιγξ**, read '**οὔλιγξ**'

***οὖλιξ**· οὐρανίσκος Zonar. 1478; cf. οὖλον.

**οὐλόδετον**, for 'ib. 30' read 'Phot. α 1110 Th., Eust. 1162.30'

**οὐλοκάρηνος II**, delete '(cf. οὐλοκίκιννα)'

**οὐλοκίκιννα**, delete the entry.

***οὐλοκίκιννος**, ον, *having close ringlets*, Telesill. 8 P.

**οὐλόκομος**, add '**II** *having thick, bushy foliage*, κίτρις Al.*Le.* 23.40.'

**οὐλόμενος I**, add 'of a fatal drink, οὐλόμενον δέπας *SEG* 33.1108 (Paphlagonia)'

**οὖλος** (B), line 6, after 'Hdt. 7.70' insert 'as subst., οὔλη λευκή Hsch.' **3**, line 7, after 'so perh.' insert 'οὖλον ἀείδειν *AP* 7.27 (Antip.Sid.)'; add 'cf. ἴουλος'

**οὖλος** (C), line 6, delete 'οὖλον ἀείδειν ib. 27 (Antip.Sid.)'

**οὐλοφυής**, for '*rough, raw, undifferentiated* .. (τύποι χθονός)' read '"*whole-natured*" precise significance unclear)'

**οὔλω**, after '*h.Ap.* 466' insert 'οὖλε expld. by χαῖρε, ὑγίαινε, *PRyl.* 16(*a*) *fr.* 2$^v$ (iii BC)'

**οὖν II 1**, line 4, delete 'Hdt. and' **2**, lines 2/3, for 'but only, it seems' read 'chiefly'; at end before '*AP* 12.226' insert 'Call.*Cer.* 75, *fr.* 64.5, 384.5 Pf.'

***οὐνέδων**, ωνος, ὁ, Lat. *unedo*, Gal. in *CMG* 5.4.(2) 304.23.

**οὕνεκα II**, line 5, after 'ἕνεκα)' insert '*CEG* 92, οὕνεκεν χρόνου *in respect of* years, poet. in *PMich.*I 77.9 (iii BC), *IG* 2$^2$.2943.18 (iii AD), Q.S. 1.724, 4.497, al.'; delete 'It has been' to end of article.

***οὐνή**, ἡ, v. °ὠνή.

***Οὐννικός**, ή, όν, *of the Huns*, στράτευμα Procop.*Pers.* 2.4.4, *Vand.* 3.18.13, etc.

***Οὖννοι**, οἱ, *the Huns*, Procop.*Pers.* 1.3.4, 2.1.14, etc.

***οὐξελλατίων**, v. °οὐιξιλλ-.

***Οὐπησία**, ἡ, cult-title of Artemis, *SEG* 23.208 (Messene, AD 42).

**Οὖπις I**, add 'in Thrace, Sch.Lyc. 936' **III**, before 'maiden' insert 'Hyperborean' and after 'Delos' insert 'Call.*Del.* 292'

**οὐρά I 1**, line 5, after 'Arist.*PA* 689$^b$30, al.' insert 'Arat. 625'; for 'not used .. *HA* 504$^a$31' read 'of birds, Arat. 600, 628, but cf. οὐρὰν μὲν οὐκ ἔχουσιν (ὄρνιθες), ὀρροπύγιον δέ Arist.*HA* 504$^a$31'

***οὐρᾶγιον**· ἔσχατον Hsch.; cf. οὐραγός.

***Οὐράνια**, τά, games celebrated at Sparta in honour of Zeus Οὐράνιος, *IG* 5(1).658.11 (i AD), *Inscr.Magn.* 180.12 (ii AD); τῶν μεγάλων Οὐ. *IG* 5(1).32*B*9 (ii AD); τῶν μεγίστων Οὐ. ib. 667.1 (i AD).

**Οὐρᾰνία II**, add 'of Hecate, *SEG* 30.326 (i AD); of Μήν, *INikaia* 1515 (iii AD), *TAM* 5(1).349, Θεὰ Οὐρανία goddess with cult in Lydia, *SEG* 31.999 (AD 202/3)'

**Οὐρᾰνιάς**, for '*Urania*' read '*Zeus Οὐράνιος*'

**οὐρᾰνιος I 2**, line 4, after 'Pi.*O.* 11(10).2' insert 'Hp.*Aër.* 12'

**Οὐρᾰνίωνες**, add 'in Chr. context, *BCH* suppl. 8.265'

**οὐρᾰνοειδής**, add 'epith. of (Jewish) god, *PMag.* 4.3068'

**οὐρᾰνόεις II**, for this section read '*of the roof of the mouth*, οὐρανόεσσαν ὑπήνην, perh. the inside of the upper lip, Nic.*Al.* 16'

***οὐρᾰνολέσχης**, ου, ὁ, *one whose boasts tower heaven-high*, Eust. 1687.48.

**οὐρᾰνός I**, add '**7** as the abode of the souls of the dead, *IAssos* 74a.' **III**, add '*SEG* 34.1463'

**οὐρᾰνοστεγής**, delete 'cf. ὑποστενάζω II'

**οὐρᾰχός IV**, for '*stems* or *stalks*' read '*rachilla*'

***οὐρβανικιανός**, ή, όν, Lat. *urbanicianus*, χειλίαρχος *IApam.* 8.8 (iii AD).

**οὐρβανός**, add '**2** κολλήγιον οὐρβανῶν, Lat. *collegium urbanorum*, *SEG* 37.559 (6) (Cassandreia, Maced.).'

**⁺οὐρεύς**, ῆος, ὁ, Ion. for ὀρεύς (q.v.), *mule*, Il. 1.50, 10.84 (also understood as οὖρος *guard*, cf. Arist.*Po.* 1461$^a$10), A.R. 3.841.

***οὐρητρίδιον**, τό, dim. of οὐρητρίς, *chamber-pot*, *PMichael.* 18.11.10 (iii AD, οὐρι- pap.).

**οὐριοστάτης**, after '(ἵστημι)' insert 'as adj.'; add '*Trag.adesp.* 659.16 K.-S.'

**οὖρος** (B), add 'Cret. ὦρος, in pl., title of officials, *Inscr.Cret.* 4.184a.13 (Gortyn, ii BC); prob. in Hsch. (cod. ὥρου· ὥρια. φύλακος; [ὧρια] φύλακος cj. S.), cf. ὠρεῖον, οὐρεύω'

**οὖς**, line 5, for 'Simon. 37.14' read 'Simon. 38.20 P.' and add '*AP* 7.409.3'; line 10, after 'Dor.' insert 'ὦας Sophr. in *PSI* 1214*a*4 (= *GLP* 1.73.4)' and for 'Alcm. 41' read 'Alcm. 80 P., cf. ὦατα Balbilla in *SEG* 8.716.9'; line 24, after 'id.*Smp.* 216a' insert 'οὖς ἀνέχειν *prick up one's ears, pay heed*, Thgn. 887, A.*fr.* 126 R.' **II 1**, add 'cf. Myc. compds. *ti-ri-jo-we*, *three-handled*, *qe-to-ro-we*, *four-handled*' **4**, delete '(οὔατα Hp.)' and for 'Hp.*Cord.* 8' read 'Hp.*Morb.Sacr.* 17, *Cord.* 8 (οὔατα)' add 'see also ἆτα, ὦας'

**οὐσία I**, lines 5/7, delete 'καλῶς .. iv BC)'

**οὐσιακός**, after '*pertaining to an estate*' insert 'οὐσιακοῦ γεωργοῦ *PSorbonne* inv. 2364.5 (*BASP* XII 2 p. 87, AD 26)'; add 'οὐσιακά, τά, *revenues from (imperial) estates*, *PMich.*X 599.1 (AD 177)'

***οὐσιαστικός**, ή, όν, *substantial*, *solid*, χαλκοῦ, σιδήρου, μολύβδου καὶ τῶν οὐσιαστικῶν μετάλλων Anon.Alch. 270.1; cf. οὐσία IV.

**οὐσιότης**, after '*quality of existence*' insert 'Alcin.*Intr.* p. 164.30 H.'

**οὖσον**, add 'cf. °σοῦσον'

***οὐσούφρουκτος**, ὁ, Lat. *usufructus*, *usufruct*, Just.*Nov.* 7 pr., al.

**οὔτε**, add 'Myc. *o-u-qe*'

**οὔτις**, line 4, for 'only twice in E., *Fr.* 45, 325' read 'E.*fr.* 45, 325, *Alc.* 194, 293, al.' and add 'Democr. 116 D.-K.'

**οὗτος A**, line 12, after 'v BC), al.' insert 'in Crete sts. written ὄϝτος, *Inscr.Cret.* 4.3.6 (Gortyn, vii/vi BC), cf. ib. 2.xii 3.5 (Eleutherna); ἐτοῦτο (for τοῦτο, as mod. Gk.) *IKyzikos* 266' **C I**, add '**6** *such-and-such*, Pl.*Phdr.* 272a, *Prm.* 160e, Arist.*Cat.* 5$^b$36, *Ev.Matt.* 8.9, etc.' **VII 4**, for 'at end of a formula' read 'to clinch a statement' **VIII 3**, line 3, after 'Hdt. 1.161, al.' insert 'and Antipho'; add 'τοῦτο δέ alone, *or again*, X.*Ath.* 3.11'

**οὕτως A I**, add '**8** καὶ οὔ. introducing a consequential action, *and so*, Acusil. 22 J. (prob.), X.*An.* 3.4.8, Arr.*Epict.* 4.8.13, al.' **IV**, delete 'in Hom. .. Hdt. 1.5'; line 6, for 'cf. 1.20' read 'ὁρῶν ὥσπερ ἂν ἄλλον τινὰ οὑτωσί D. 39.27'

**ὀφειλέτης**, add 'cf. Myc. *O-pe-re-ta*, pers. n.'

**ὀφείλω I 1**, lines 14/15, delete 'metaph., .. *Fr.* 126' **2**, line 3, after 'Ael.*VH* 10.5' insert 'w. gen., *to be indebted* for something, ἦ κάρτ' ὀφείλω τῶνδέ σοι A.*fr.* 78a.3 R., Ar.*Nu.* 22'; add 'ὕπνος ὀφειλόμενος of death, *AP* 7.78 (Dionys.), 219 (Pomp.), 419 (Mel.)' **II 3 c**, w. acc. and inf., add 'Demad. 26' add 'Myc. 3 pl. *o-pe-ro-si*, 3 pl. aor. *o-po-ro* (= ὄφλον)'

**ὀφέλλω** (B), line 11, after 'Pi.*P.* 4.260' insert 'μητέρα μοι ζώουσαν ὀφέλλετε (imper.) Call.*fr.* 602.3 Pf.'

**ὄφελος**, add 'Myc. *o-pe-ro*, *deficit*'

**ὀφεώδης**, add 'see also °ὀργώδης'

**ὀφθαλμίζομαι**, add '**III** perh. also act. -ίζω, *cast the evil eye on*, ὀφθαλμίσαι· φθονῆσαι Phot. (s.v.l., cj. -ιάσαι).'

**ὀφθαλμός VI**, add 'Gal. 18(1).837.17, 18(2).732.3, 9' add '**VIII**

name of a plant, ὀφθαλμὸς Τυφῶνος (*oftalmos Tifonos*) Ps.-Apul.*Herb.* 42.17; cf. ὀφθαλμὸς Πύθωνος [Diosc.] 3.26.'

***ὀφθαουηρ**, app. Gk. transcription of an Egyptian priestly title, perh. = στολιστής, *BGU* 2469 i 6 (ὀθφαουηρ) and 9 (ὀφθαουηρ) (ii AD).

***ὄφιδνα·** δράκαινα Theognost.*Can.* 80 A.; cf. ὄφις, ἔχιδνα.

***ὀφικιάλιος** (also **ὀφφ-**,) τό, Lat. *officialis*, *BGU* 657 ii 9 (ii AD), *POxy.* 1646.3 (iii AD), *CRAI* 1952.593 (Caria, iii AD), *SEG* 32.1554 (Arabia, vi AD).

***ὀφίκιον** (also **ὀφφ-**,) τό, Lat. *officium*, *official appointment*, ἵνα ὀπίκια (sic) λάβῃ *POxy.* 3312 (ii AD), *IGRom.* 3.130, *PSI* 281.51 (ii AD).

***ὀφῐόκοιλος**, ὁ, precious stone, *Lapid.Gr.* 191.16.

**ὀφῐοπλόκᾰμος**, after 'Orph.*H.* 69.12' insert '70.10'

**ὀφιοφόρος**, add '(lapis, -φοριος)'

**ὄφις**, after 'ὁ' insert '(also ἡ, Plu. 2.988a, of the serpent Python)' **I**, add 'ἐν κόλπῳ ἔχειν ὄφιν Thgn. 602' **III**, add 'but in Nonn.*D.* 2.290 Ὄφις Ἀμάξης is the constellation *Draco*'

**ὀφλισκάνω**, line 7, after 'And. 1.73' insert 'aor. pass. part. ὀφληθέν Just.*Nov.* 59.3' **I 2**, add 'pass. τὴν δίκην δικαίως ὠφλημένην D. 29.55'

**ὄφρα A I**, lines 8/9, for 'but Hom. thrice uses it' read 'in Hom.'; after 'Il.' insert '8.110' and after '16.242' insert '19.70'

**ὀφρύη**, add '**II** for ὀφρῦς I 1, Hp.*Dieb.Judic.* 2.'

**ὀφρύκνηστον**, add 'Archil. 58.10 W.'

**ὀφρῠόεις**, after 'εν' insert '(neut. -όειν where long syll. required, Call.*fr.* 186.20 Pf.)'

**ὀφρῦς I 1**, 7 lines fr. end, after '*IA* 648' insert 'cf. τὰς ὀ. ἄνες Men.*Dysc.* 423' **II**, add '*ornamental stone* projecting above a lintel, Lib.*Or.* 5.51'

***ὀφρύωμα**, ατος, τό, *"eyebrow"*, name given to part of liver, Heph.Astr. 3.6.15.

***ὀφφικ-**, v. °ὀφικ-.

**ὀχεία I 2**, add 'ὠχίας *PSI* 33.22 (iii AD)'

**ὀχετεία**, add 'Max.Tyr. 21.6'

***ὀχετογνώμονες**, v. ‡ἐχετογνώμονες.

**ὀχετόκρᾱνον**, for '*Mnemos.* 42.332' read '*SEG* 33.336'

**ὀχευτικός**, after 'Thphr.*fr.* 183' insert 'comp. and sup., Ath. 9.391e, d'

**ὀχεύω I**, add 'fig., ἄμφω ὅπως ποταμὸς λαγόνων ῥείθροισιν ὀχεύσι *TAM* 3.907-8 (ii/iii AD)'; at end after 'Ph. 2.307' insert '(of bestiality)'

**Ὀχεών**, delete the entry (v. °Ἀντιοχεών).

**ὀχή I**, add 'Hp.*Mochl.* 20'

**ὄχημα I**, after 'E.*Tr.* 884' insert 'cf. οὗτός (sc. ὁ ἠήρ) τε γῆς ὄχημα Hp.*Flat.* 3; app. some form of support used in hydraulic works, τὰ φράγματα καὶ ὀχήματα *SEG* 32.4663 (Boeotia, i AD)'

**ὀχθέω**, line 1, for 'present only .. q.v.' read 'present not found'

***ὄχινος**, ὁ, unexpld. wd., μυλαῖος *PTeb.* 793 i 26 (ii BC).

**⁺ὀχλάζω**, *to be turbulent* or *obstreperous*, Aq.*Ps.* 58.7, 15, *Pr.* 7.11, *Je.* 4.19.

**ὀχληρία**, add '*PHamb.* 182.2 (249 BC)'

**ὀχλίζω**, line 2, delete '*by a lever*' **II**, add 'cf. Nic.*Al.* 505'

**ὀχλικός**, add 'adv. -ῶς dub. in *PFouad* 31.2 (ii AD)'

***ὀχλοκρᾰτησία**, ἡ, = ὀχλοκρατία, ὑπὸ ὀχλοκρατησίας καὶ φόνους Heph.Astr. 1.21.20.

**ὄχλος I 1**, add 'pl., *crowd*, D.S. 13.94; *the masses*, *people in general*, Heraclit.*Ep.* 7.4' **2**, add '**b** perh. referring to the non-citizen population, *SEG* 26.1817 (Cyrene, ii/i BC).'

**ὄχμα**, add 'cf. ὄχανον'

**ὄχος**, add 'cf. Myc. *wo-ka* (app. fem.) *vehicle*'

**ὀχῡρός 2**, add 'comp., Plu.*Arat.* 50'

**ὀχυρόω II**, add 'μεγίστοις ἐπιτιμίοις ὀχυροῦντες τὰ παρ' ἡμῶν ὁρισθέντα *Cod.Just.* 1.3.38.5'

**ὀχύρωσις**, add 'cf. °ἐχύρωσις'

**ὄψ** (B), for 'gen. ὀπός' read 'nom. only'; add 'cf. Myc. compds. *ka-ro-qo*, *po-ki-ro-qo*, pers. n., *o-po-qo* (dual) = *ὀπώπω (cf. μέτωπον), *blinkers*'

***ὀψᾰρέλαιον**, τό, *fish-oil*, Afric.*Cest.* p. 80 V.

**ὀψᾰ́ριον**, after 'dim. of ὄψον' insert '*foodstuff*, esp. *fish*' and add 'κωνοψωμίω[ν] ὀψάρει(ον) Περσικόν, ναύλου ὀψάρει(ον) κοινόν *SEG* 26.382 (Athens)'

**ὀψᾰριοπωλεῖον**, delete the entry.

***ὀψᾰριόπωλις**, ιδος, ἡ, *fish-shop*, τὰς ἐν τῇ ὀψαριοπώλεισι μαρμαρίνας τραπέζας *ITrall.* 77.19 (ii AD).

**ὀψέ**, line 1, after 'ὄψι (q.v.)' insert 'also app. Cret. ὀψῶι *SEG* 23.566, Pamph. *ὄψα (v. °ὀψιγενής)'

**ὀψῐγενής**, add 'also Ὀψαγένης *IPamph.* 49 (pers. n., ii BC)'

**ὀψῐ́γονος 2**, line 2, after '*h.Cer.* 165' insert 'Stesich 45 i 2 P.' for '4' read '**II** (parox.)'

**ὀψίζω**, add '**II** οὐ ἐὰν ὀψίσῃ, i.e. finds himself at nightfall, Lxx *Si.* 36.27; προήγεν ὀρθρίζων καὶ ὀψίζων, i.e. early in the morning and late at night, Thd. 1*Ki.* 17.16.'

**ὀψῐμᾰθής I**, add 'adv. ὀψιμαθῶς Gal. 8.601.5'

**ὀψίμοθος**, add 'cj. ἀψίμοθος'

**ὄψιος**, line 1, after 'α, ον' insert '(also ος, ον, Arat. 1027)' and before 'ὅταν' insert 'δείλης ὀ. Plb. 18.8.1'

**ὄψις I 1**, line 7, after 'id.(Th.) 7.44' insert 'δεῖ τὰ ἐκκλησιαστικὰ ἐμφυτεύειν διὰ τὴν ἀποκατάστασιν τῆς ὄψεως i.e. visible condition, *Cod.Just.* 1.24.5' **II 1 a**, for 'Emp. 4.10' read 'Emp. 3.10' add '**III** astrol., *aspect* of a planet in relation to one in a zodiacal sign on its left, Heph.Astr. 1.16; cf. ἀκτίς I 3.'

***ὀψῐ́τευκτος**, ον, *late-made*, Eust. 1235.17.

**ὄψον II**, for 'Ar.*frr.* 247, 545, cf.' read 'Ar.*fr.* 258 K.-A., cf. ib. 557'

**⁺ὀψοπόνος**, ὁ, *cook*, *AP* 6.306.

**ὄψος**, add '*PCornell* 35.15, 16 (iii AD)'

**ὀψοφάγος**, add 'Ael.*VH* 1.28'

**ὀψοφόρος**, add '*SEG* 30.1894'

**ὀψωνιαστής**, add 'prob. in graffito in W.Ruppel *Der Tempel von Dakke* 3 p. 60 no. 78'

***ὀψωνιάτωρ**, ορος, ὁ, = ὀψωνάτωρ, *caterer*, Phot. α 239 Th.

# Π

**πᾱγᾱνός 3**, add '*TAM* 5(2).109.2'

**πᾱγαρχία**, after 'district under a π.' insert '*POxy.* 3307.1 (iv AD)'

***παγγεννήτειρα**, ἡ, *mother of all*, *PMag.* 4.2556; cf. παγγενέτειρα.

**πάγγεος**, add 'πάνγεος .. δῆμος *IHadr.* 80 (ii AD)'

***παγγέραστος**, ον, *honoured by all*, Anon.Alch. 4.5.

***παγγόνος**, ὁ, epith. of Helios, *procreator of all*, cf. παγγενέτωρ, *IG* 4².529 (Epid., ?ii BC).

***πάγγωνος**, ὁ, (γωνία) precious stone, Plin.*HN* 37.178.

**πᾰγερός I**, add 'transf., of death, *SEG* 23.137b.4 (iv BC)'

**πάγη 2**, add 'Iamb.*VP* 17.76'

**πάγιος II**, add 'ἐπιστῆμαι, opp. στοχαστικαί, Phld.*Rh.* 1.26, 59 S.'

**πᾰγίς**, line 1, for 'Call.*Fr.* 458' read 'Call.*fr.* 177.17 Pf.'

***Παγκάμης**, ὁ, cult-title of Heracles, *SEG* 26.429 (Argos, i AD).

***πάγκαρπον**, τό, form of contest in the arena between men and beasts, Just.*Nov.* 105.1.

***παγκλυστής**, οῦ, ὁ, temple-official, *SB* 7336.18 (iii AD, παν- pap.).

**παγκοίτης**, add 'Simon. in *SLG* 348.8'

***παγκρᾰτεύς**, έως, ὁ, = παγκρατιαστής, Pi.*N.* 2 tit.

**παγκρᾰτής 2**, for 'B.*fr.* 10' read 'B.*fr.* 14.4 S.-M.' and add 'Simon. 36.5 P.'

**⁺παγκράτωρ**, ορος, *all-powerful*, Σούχου π. *SEG* 8.551.23 (i BC), θεός π. *SEG* 7.13, γῆ Robert *Hell.* 2.121 (all verse).

***παγκυκλικός**, όν, adj. of uncertain application referring to celestial orbits, Anon.Astr. in *PMich.*III 149 x 12 (ii AD).

**πάγξενος**, add 'B. 11.28, 13.95 S.-M.'

***πᾰγόδετος**, ον, *frostbound*, ὕδωρ Mesom. 10.3 H.

**πᾰγος**, after 'ὁ' insert '(also **πάγος**, εος, τό, v. II 1, 5)' **II 1**, after '*frost*' insert 'κρ]ύερος πάγος Alc. 286(*a*).3 L.-P.' **4**, after '*coagulation*' insert 'στερεῷ γῆς πάγῳ Pl.*Ti.* 43c' **5**, for 'confused *mass*' read '*undivided firmament*' and after 'Hp.*Hebd.* 6' insert 'ap.Gal. 19.73'

**πᾰγουρος**, add '**II** *tongs*, Hsch. s.v. πυράγρη; cf. καρκίνος.'

**πάγρος**, for 'perh. = φάγρος' read 'an unknown bird' and add 'Ael.*NA* 5.48'

**⁺πάδος**, ἡ, a kind of tree, perh. the same as πηδός, Thphr. 4.1.3.

**πᾰθεινός**, for '*suffering, mournful*' read '*mourning, grieving*'; add '*PMich.*v 234.18 (AD 43)'

**πᾰθημα I**, add '**2** *damage*, *Inscr.Cret.* 4.144.13, al. (v/iv BC).'

**πᾰθητικός I 2**, line 3, after 'Cic.*Orat.* 37' insert 'of an author, Plu.*Nic.* 1 (sup.)'; add '*in* or *by feeling*, τὰ δίκαια μὴ π. μόνον ἀλλ' ἐπιλογιστικῶς κατανοεῖν Phld.*Rh.* 2.254 S.' **II 1**, add 'Procl.*Inst.* 124'

**πᾰθητός II 1**, add '**b** τὸ π. *capability of emotion*, Phld.*D.* 1.11.'

**⁺πᾰθικευόμαι**, *act as a catamite*, *AP* 11.73 (Nicarch.).

**⁺πᾰθικός**, ή, όν, in sexual sense, *pathic*; in Lat. form *pathicus*, Cat. 16.2, 57.2, Juv. 2.99.

**πάθνη**, after 'φάτνη' insert '*PLips.* 106.8 (i AD)'

**πᾰθος I 2 b**, add 'Th. 1.106.2' **IV 2 b**, add '*AP* 9.330 (Nicarch.)'

**παι**, for '*Inscr.Cypr.* .. al.' read '*ka-sa-pa-i* κάς παι *ICS* 217.4, *i-te-pa-i* ἰδὲ παι 217.12, *ta-sa-pa-i* τᾶς παι 261'

**Παιάν I 2**, title of Apollo, add 'Ἀπόλλων Παῶνος *SEG* 39.427 (Boeotia, iii/ii BC)' at end add '[The first syll. is sts. short in Trag.lyr., A.*Ag.* 146, etc.]' and 'Myc. *pa-ja-wo-ne* (dat.), divine name'

**⁺παιᾱνίς**, ιδος, fem. adj., *having the form of a paean*, ἀοιδαί Pi.*fr.* 128c S.-M.

**Παιᾱνισταί**, after 'at Rome' insert 'pap. in Men.*Dysc.* 230 (cj. °Πανιστ-)' and add '*SEG* 32.232, *POxy.* 3018'

**παιγνία II**, for '= ἑορτή' read '*festivity, party*' and add 'Herod. 3.55'

**παίγνιον**, before 'τό' insert '(παίχνιον in Theoc. 15.50 (*PAntin.*), Call.*fr.* 202.28, 33 Pf.; cf. mod. Gk. παιχνίδι)' **I 1**, after 'Ephipp. 24' insert 'Lang *Ath.Agora* XXI Hd14 (iii AD)' **III 2**, for '*comic performance*' read '*diversion, amusement*' and delete 'Suet.*Aug.* 99'

**παίγνιος**, for '*AP* 7.12.212' read '*AP* 12.212.6'

**παιδᾰρίδιον**, add '*SEG* 36.618 (Edessa, iii AD)'

**παιδᾰρικός**, add 'πεδαρικόν *ITyr* 47'

**παιδᾰριον II**, after '*young slave*' insert '(perh. sts. without ref. to age)'; add '*POxy.* 3960.28 (AD 621)'

**παιδᾰρίσκος**, add 'Sch.Ar.*Th.* 291'

**παιδᾰριώδης**, after '(Sup.)' insert 'of literary work, D.H.*Dem.* 44; of an author, id.*Is.* 19'

***παιδᾰρίων**, ωνος, ὁ, gloss on προύνικος, Hsch.; cf. °πατερίων.

**παιδέρως I**, add '**2** pl. = παιδεραστία, *IKyzikos* 520 (iii/ii BC).' **II 1 a**, delete the section. **b**, add 'Paus. 2.10.5-6, cf. Plin.*HN* 22.76; cf. pl. παιδὸς ἔρωτες Nic.*fr.* 75.55 G.-S.' **2**, add '**b** a kind of *amethyst*, Plin.*HN* 37.123.'

**παίδευμα I**, for 'πόντου παιδεύματα, of fish' read 'χθονίων τ' ἀερίων τε παιδεύματα i.e. animals and birds' **II 2**, add 'πρὸς ἀρετήν D.H.*Isoc.* 4'

**παίδευσις I**, add '**4** *chastisement*, Just.*Nov.* 122 pr.'

**⁺παιδευτής**, οῦ, ὁ, *person in charge of education, educator, instructor*, Pl.*R.* 493c, al., *Lg.* 811d, al.; as municipal appointment, *IG* 2².1011.35, *TAM* 5(1).700 (i AD). **2** *one who imposes discipline, corrector*, *Ep.Hebr.* 12.9.

**παιδεύω II**, line 15, after 'Aeschin. 3.148' insert 'τράγον ἄεθλα *AP* 6.312 (Anyte)'

***παιδιακόν**, v. °πεδιακόν.

**παιδιακός**, delete the entry.

**παιδικός I**, line 5, after 'Lys. 21.4' insert 'ὕμνοι π. B.*fr.* 4.80 S.-M.' **II**, delete 'ὕμνοι .. 3.12' **III 1**, after '(i BC)' insert '**b** *child's garment*, *Edict.Diocl.* 7.58, 59, *Dura*⁴ 97, 100 (πεδ-).'

**παιδικῡνηγεσία**, delete the entry.

**παιδιόθεν**, add '(sp. πεδ-) ἐκ π. *AJA* 36.460 (S.Galatia)'

**παιδίον III**, after '*convulsions*' insert 'Ruf.ap.Orib.*inc.* 38(20).27'

**παιδισκάριον**, line 2, before 'Hld. 1.11' insert '*PSI* 1359.4 (ii/iii AD)' add '**2** *stone used in spinning*, Hsch.'

**παιδισκεῖος II**, add '(with uncertain significance) τὸν θᾶκον σὺν τοῖς κατ' αὐτοῦ ἐπικειμένοις παιδισκηίοις *IEphes.* 455 (ii AD)'

**παιδίσκος**, add 'also *young slave*, Ammon.*Diff.* 378 N.'

**παιδνός**, line 2, delete 'for παιδὸς χ.'

***παιδογόνιον**, τό, *birth of a child*, παιδογονίου ἄρρενος, θηλείας *PMich.*v 243.5 (i AD).

***παιδογρᾰφία**, ἡ, *register of birth*, ἡ .. ἡλικία δείκνυται ἢ ἐξ παιδογραφιῶν ἢ ἐξ ἑτέρων ἀποδείξεων νομίμων Modest.*Dig.* 27.1.2.1.

**παιδόθεν**, delete 'Ibyc. 1.10'

***παιδοκλέπτης**, ου, ὁ, *boy-stealer*, Call.*Dieg.* vii.6 (*fr.* 194 Pf.).

**παιδομᾰθής**, delete '*precociously quick*' and add 'Quint.*Inst.* 1.12.9'

**παιδονομέω**, after '*hold office of* παιδονόμος' insert '*SEG* 29.527 (Thessaly, i BC), *TAM* 4(1).42'

**⁺παιδοπίπης**, ου, ὁ, *one who eyes boys amorously*, Ath. 13.563e; cf. παρθενοπίπης, ὀπιπεύω.

**παιδοποιός 1**, add 'E.*Rh.* 980'

**παιδοτρόφος 1**, for 'Simon. 12.4' read 'Simon. 3.6 P., A.*fr.* 47a.2.8 R. (lyr.)'

**παιδουργέω**, add 'Plu. *in Hes.* 74'

**παιδουργία I**, add 'Plu. *in Hes.* 74'

**παιδοφιλέω**, after 'Sol. 25' insert 'Pl.Com. 279 K.-A.' and delete 'Pass. .. 247'

**παιδοφίλης**, add '*AP* 12.44 (Glauc.)'

**παιδοφόντης**, after 'Ph. 2.581' insert '(*Trag.adesp.* 327b K.-S.)'

***παιζόγελως**, ων, *playfully jesting*, *Cat.Cod.Astr.* 12.190.9.

**παίζω**, line 2, for 'παιδδωᾶν' read 'παιδδωᾶν'

**παίκτης**, for '*dancer* or *player*' read '*dice-player, gambler*' and after '(Leon.)' insert 'Man. 4.448'

**πάϊλλος**, add 'Peek *AV* 120 (*c.*300 BC), Hsch.; fem. πάϊλλα, prob. in Epich. in *CGFP* 85.347'

***παίνουλα**, v. φαινόλη.

**Παιονικός**, add 'as title of Dionysus, *SEG* 37.561 (Maced., ii AD)'

**παιπάλημα**, for '*piece of subtlety*' read 'slang term, perh. conveying the idea of slander or innuendo w. obscene allusion (cf. Maxwell-Stuart *AJP* 96.11' and for 'Aeschrio 8.8' read '*AP* 7.345'

**παιπᾰλιμος**, for 'Theognost.*Can.* 10' read 'Theognost.*Can.* 31 A.'

***παιπᾰλώσσω**· τὸ παίζω καὶ τὸ παροινῶ Theognost.*Can.* 31 A.

**παῖς**, line 1, after 'ὁ, ἡ' insert 'acc. sg. παῖδαν *SEG* 32.611 (Thessaly, i BC)'; line 2, dat. pl. παίδεσσι, add '*SEG* 23.416 (Thessaly, v BC)'; line 9, before 'ι' insert 'see also πᾶς (B)' **I**, line 2, delete '(with special reference to the father, opp. τέκνον, q.v.)'; line 6, for '*Inscr.Cypr.* 135.11 H.' read 'Cypr. *pa-i-ta-se* παῖδας *ICS* 217.11' **3**, after 'periphr.' insert 'παισὶν .. Αἰτναίων Pi.*N.* 9.30' **II**, add 'at Sparta, *boy in fifth year of public education*, i.e. eleven years old, Λέξεις Ἡροδότου in Stein Hdt. ii p. 465 (Berlin 1871)' **III**, after '(of all ages)' insert 'Hippon. 13 W.' add '**IV** pl. voc., as a form of familiar address to equals, Ar.*Eq.* 419, Theoc. 10.52, 13.52. **b** as an exclamation, approximating to sense of παπαῖ, Men.*Dysc.* 500, *Mis.* 216, *Sam.* 678, 690, etc., Macho 215 G.'

***παῖσκος**, ὁ, *child*, *Kafizin* 117 (221/0 BC); also **πηῖσκος** *Inscr.Cret.* 1.x 2.5, 7.

**παιφάσσω 1**, line 2, for 'A.R. 4.1440' read 'A.R. 4.1442'

+**παίχνιον**, v. °παίγνιον.

**παίω I 1**, add '**c** of a scorpion, *sting*, Ael.*NA* 5.14, 6.23, 10.23.' **4**, for '*Pax* 874' read '*Pax* 899'

**παιωνίζω**, last line, after 'παιαν- in' insert 'B. 17.129 S.-M.'

***πακτάριος**, ὁ, fr. Lat. *pactum*, *contractor*, *POxy.* 2024.11, 2032.55 (vi AD), 138.9, 40 (vii AD).

***πακτείκια**, τά, fr. Lat. *pacticius*, perh. *agreed payments* in manumissions, *Inscr.Perg.* 8(3).44.

**πάκτον**, add 'Just.*Nov.* 120.1.1; perh. *agreed sum*, *POxy.* 3958.22, 30 (AD 614)'

***πακτονάριον**, τό, dim. of πάκτων, *small boat*, *PVindob.*G 39847.463 (*CPR* 5.98) (iv AD), *PLond.* 1904.6 (v/vi AD) (written φακ-), *SB* 4323.9 (written πακτων-).

**πακτόω 1**, line 1, after 'Archil. 187' insert 'θύρην ἐπάκτωσα Hippon. 104.19 W.'

**πακτωτής**, add '*Bodl.Ms.Gr.Class.* c. 88 (P.) (iii BC). **2** Christian church-official, ἀναγνώστης καὶ π. *Inscr.Cret.* 4.481 (Gortyn, v/vi AD).'

***πακτωτόν**, τό, = πάκτων, *BGU* 1933 (ii AD).

***πάλᾱ**, v. πάλη (A).

***πᾶλα**, ἡ, Lat. *pala*, *spade*, *Edict.Diocl.* 15.45.

**πᾰλάθη**, add '*Carm.Pop.* 2.6 P.'

**πάλαι**, line 2, after '*time*' insert 'Sapph. 49 L.-P.'; line 8, delete 'cf. Eup. 11' and substitute 'Ar.*Pax* 414, 475'

**πᾰλαιγενής**, line 3, for 'Μοῖραι' read 'μοῖραι'; add 'epic. in *Coll.Alex.* p. 82 ii 5'

**πᾰλαιμοσύνη**, s.v. παλαισμοσύνη, add '*CEG* 805 (iv BC)'

**Παλαίμων**, after 'Hsch.' insert 'pl. Παλαίμονες, sea-gods, Call.*fr.* 197.19, 23 Pf.'

***πᾰλαιοκέρᾰμος**, ὁ, *old wine-jar*, *SB* 9569.2 (pl., AD 91); cf. °καινοκέραμος.

***πᾰλαιοπόρνη**, ἡ, *aged harlot*, *Dura*[4] 1.213 (iii AD).

**πᾰλαιός**, after 'ά, όν' insert '(also ός, όν, Hp.*Epid.* 7.82)' **I 2**, add '**b** name of kind of jasper, Epiph. in *Lapid.Gr.* 196.11.' **II**, add '**4** applied to the original or principal sum of money involved in a transaction, Lys.*fr.* 6.' add 'Myc. *pa-ra-jo*'

***πᾰλαιοσεβής**, ές, *of ancient reverence*, *Suppl.Hell.* 974.6 (written παληο-, iii BC (s.v.l.)).

**πᾰλαιουργός**, add '*SEG* 39.235 (Athens, iv BC)'

***πᾰλαιόφῠτος**, ον, *planted long ago*, *ASAE* 39.292 (Panopolis).

**πᾰλαίπλουτος**, for '*Quarterly* .. iii AD)' read '*SEG* 8.269.9 (Gaza, iii/ii BC)'

**πᾰλαιστᾰγής**, for '*that has become oily from age*' read '*pressed long ago*'

**πᾰλαιστή**, delete 'Aeol.' to end of article.

***Πᾰλαιστίνη**, ἡ, *Palestine*, Hdt. 1.105.1, al.; also Π. χώρα Str. 16.4.18.

**πᾰλαιστρᾰτιώτης**, add 'Modest.*Dig.* 27.1.8 pr., al., *SEG* 33.1188 (Iconium, iii AD)'

**πᾰλαιστρίδιον**, add 'Call.*Dieg.* viii.35'

**πᾰλαιστροφύλαξ**, for '*superintendent of a wrestling-school*' read '*attendant in a wrestling-school*'

**πᾰλαιφάμενος**, for '= sq., .. *anon.* 102' read 'of a tree, *long spoken of, legendary*, (?)Call.*fr.* 756 Pf.'

**πᾰλαίωμα**, after '*Jb.* 36.28, al.' insert '(the corresponding Hebrew wd. means "clouds, the heavens")'

**πᾰλαίωσις**, last line, after 'Lxx *Na.* 1.15(2.1)' insert 'Sm.*Ps.* 71(72).7, 91(92).11'

**πᾰλάμη I 1**, add '**b** applied to a bear's paws, Opp.*C.* 4.417.' **II**, line 2, after 'sense' insert 'παλάμαν ἔχει Alc. 249.7 L.-P.'; line 3, after 'of the gods' insert 'Κυπρογενήας παλάμαισιν Alc. 380 L.-P.'

**πᾰλαμναῖος I 2**, add 'applied to the mountain appointed for the sacrifice of Isaac, amulet in *SEG* 31.1594' add '**III** name of month at Locri Epizephyrii, de Franciscis *Locr.Epiz.* 22, 24, 31.'

***παλάριος**, α, ον, app. Lat. *palaris*, *with a stake*, ὅπλον παλάριν *BGU* 40.5 (ii/iii AD).

**πᾰλάσιον**, delete 'παλάθιον Suid.' and add 'παλάσια ἃ καὶ Κρατῖνος (*fr.* 390 K.-A.) ἰσχάδα κοπτὴν καλεῖ Poll. 6.81'

**πᾰλαστή**, line 4, after '*PLit.Lond.* 183' insert 'Aeol. **παλάστα** Alc. 350.6 L.-P.'

***πᾰλαστῶσαι**· χειροτονῆσαι Hsch.

+**Παλατῖνος**, η, ον, *of the Palatine*, D.H. 2.70. **II** *palace official*, *TAM* 4(1).255, Μημόριν Βαρδίωνος παλατίνου *BCH* suppl. 8.151 (v/vi AD), *Cod.Just.* 1.5.18.11, al.

+**Παλάτιον**, τό, Lat. *Palatium*, *the Palatine hill* in Rome, D.H. 1.31, etc., D.C. 53.16.5. **II** *the palace* or *court of the Roman emperor*, D.C. l.c., *TAM* 4(1).255, 285, *PBeatty Panop.* 1.260, Just.*Const.Δέδωκεν* pr.

***πᾰλεός**, v. παλαιός.

**πᾰλευτής**, for '*decoy-bird*' read '*setter of decoy-traps*'

**πᾰλεύω I**, after '(Ar.*Av.*) 1087' insert 'w. acc., *decoy*, Ael.*NA* 4.16' **II**, after '*entrap*' insert 'Lyc. 405'

**πᾰλέω**, line 2, before 'elsewh.' insert '*to be wrecked*, of a ship, πεπαληκός *SB* 9367.10.10'

***παλεωράφιον**, τό, *cobbler's shop*, *PAmst.*inv. 62 (*Mnemosyne* 30.146), *Gloss.*

**πάλη** (A) **I**, add 'νικάσας Νέμεα ἀγενείους πάλαν *Lindos* 699a, b'

***πᾰλησεβής**, v. παλαιοσεβής.

**πᾰλιγγενεσία I 1**, after '*AJ* 11.3.9' insert 'cf. Memn. 40.2 J.'

**πᾰλιγκάπηλεύω**, add 'prob. in *Berytus* 12.124.48 (Cyrene, iv BC)'

**πᾰλίγκτιστος**, add 'expl. of Lat. *recidivus* in Virgil gloss., *PNess.* 1.762 (vi AD)'

**πᾰλίμβολος**, at end for '*turned* or *patched*' read 'perh. *second-hand*'

**πᾰλιμβουλία**, for 'f.l. for -βολία' read 'perh. *the giving of contrary advice*'

**πᾰλίμβουλος**, for 'f.l. for -βολος' read '*giving contrary or untrustworthy advice*' and add 'Heph.Astr. 3.16.5'

**πᾰλίμπισσα**, after 'Dsc. 1.72' insert '**-πιττα** *Inscr.Délos* 1441*A*ii 19, al. (ii BC); **παλίνπιττα**, ἑφθὴ πίττα Hsch., παλινπίττης *IG* $2^2$.1673.22 (iv BC): **παλίνπισσα** *SIG* 1171.14 (Lebena)'; delete 'cf. παλίνπιττα'

***πᾰλιμπλᾰνήτης**, ου, ὁ, = παλιμπλανής, Lyc. 1239.

**πᾰλιμπλεκής**, for '*twined* or *plaited back*' read '*plaited back*, i.e. narrowing at the top'

+**πᾰλίμπλῠτος**, *rewashed*, *AP* 7.708 (Diosc.).

**πᾰλίμπνοος**, for '*breathing*' read '*breathed*'; after 'Nonn.*D.* 37.295' insert 'al.'

+**πᾰλίμποτον**, τό, kind of drinking-vessel, perh. the same as ῥυτόν, *Didyma* 424.37, 40, *PLond.* 1960.16.

**πᾰλίμπρᾱτος 1**, add 'cf. Call.*fr.* 203.55 Pf. (-πρη-)'

***πᾰλιμφροσύνη**, ἡ, *repentance*, *remorse*, orac. in *SEG* 33.1056B.4 (Cyzicus, ii AD; παλινφ- lapis).

***πᾰλίμψηστρον**, τό, = παλίμψηκτρον, *SEG* 33.1177 (Lycia, AD 43).

**πάλιν III**, after 'Ar.*Ach.* 342' insert 'Men.*Dysc.* 113, Macho 206 G.'

***πᾰλίνδουλος**, ὁ, = ὁ πολλάκις δουλεύσας Hsch. s.v. παλιγκάπηλος.

**πᾰλίνζῳος**, delete the entry.

***πᾰλίνζωος**, ον, *coming back to life*, Opp.*H.* 1.319.

***πᾰλίνπιττα**, v. °παλίμπισσα.

+**πᾰλίνσοος**, ον, *safe again*, *AP* 1.49.

***πᾰλιντροπή**, ἡ, *changing back*, Zos.Alch. 196.1 (unless to be taken as two words).

**πᾰλινῳδία**, add '**3** *repetition*, Clem.Al.*Paed.* 3.11.60, *Theol.Ar.* 57 A.'

**πᾰλιουροφόρος**, after 'παλίουρος I' insert '(s.v.l.)'

**πᾰλίωξις**, delete '[ῑ metri gr.]'

**πάλλα**, add 'cf. παλίζεσθαι'

**Παλλάδιον II**, add 'also used in connection with the cults of Zeus and Athena, *SEG* 30.85 (Athens, i BC)'

***Παλλάδιος**, α, ον, *of Pallas*, ἔλαιον Marc.Sid. 75.

**παλλᾰκίς**, line 2, after 'Od. 14.203' insert 'X.*Cyr.* 4.3.1'; line 4, for '(of ritual prostitution)' read 'applied to a temple prostitute as being the concubine of a god'

***παλλάντιον**, τό, a plant, = πολύγονον or ὀστεόκολλος, *Hippiatr.* 66.

**Παλλάς II**, for '*maiden-priestess*' read '*temple-prostitute*' and after 'Str. 17.1.46' insert '(perh. ghost-word)'

**Παλλειών**, add 'also Παλλεών *Amyzon* 36 (ii BC)'

***παλλιόλιον**, τό, dim. of Lat. *palliolum*, *small cloak*, *PMich.*III 201.9 (i AD, παλλιώλιν), *PTeb.* 405.3 (iii AD, παλλιόλιν).

***παλλίολον**, τό, Lat. *palliolum*, *POxy.* 3724 v 29, *BGU* 781.6.6 (i AD).

***πάλλιον**, τό, Lat. *pallium*, *cloak*, Aesop.*Prov.* 120 tit. P.; in forms πάλλιν and πάλιν, *Dura*[4] 97, 93, *BGU* 22.17 (ii AD).

**πάλλω**, line 8, after 'ἐφάλλομαι' insert 'though there was prob. early confusion between the vbs. through misdivision of ἐπ-ᾶλτο as ἔ-παλτο' **II**, line 6, after 'Ar.*Ra.* 345' insert '*throb*, οἱ κρόταφοι πάλλονται Hp.*Acut.* 30' **III**, add '**2** *twitch*, μηρὸς εὐώνυμος πάλλων *PFlor.* 391.8 (iii AD).'

***πάλμα**, ατος, τό, *leaping*, given as etym. of name Παλλάς, *POxy.* 2260 ii 5 (ii AD).

**παλμός 1**, add 'περὶ παλμῶν μαντική, work by Melamp.'

***πάλμυρον**, τό, unexpld. wd., Theognost.*Can.* 131.

**παλμώδης**, add 'adv. -δῶς, Gal. 7.65.18 (s.v.l.)'

**πᾰλος 2**, after '*lot*' insert 'Alcm. 65 P.'

**παλτός I**, for '(lyr.)' read '(anap.)' **II**, line 2, after '*Fr.* 16' insert 'παλτῷ, i.e. in spear-throwing contest, *MDAI(A)* 62.4 (ii BC)'

**παμβᾰσῐλεύς**, after 'έως' insert 'poet. also ῆος Opp.*H.* 1.78'; add 'of Marcus Aurelius, Opp. l.c.; of Zeus, Orph.*H.* 73.3'

**παμβῶτις**, add 'ἐλπίς *Trag.adesp.* 252 K.-S. (Hsch.)'

***παμμᾰκάριος**, v. °παμμαχάριος.

**παμμᾰκάριστος**, after '= foreg. (πάμμακαρ)' insert 'Antip.Sid. in *Inscr.Délos* 2549.11'

***παμμᾰχάριος**, ὁ, = παγκρατιαστής, Ambros. *in Ps.* 36.55 (*PL* 14.993); prob. in Firm.*Math.* 8.8.1 (codd. *macharios*); also sp. παμμακ-, ἀθλητὰς παμμακαρίους, λωποδύτας Teuc.Bab. p. 43.27 B.

***παμμεδέων**, οντος, ὁ, *ruler of all*, Ζεύς Nonn.*D.* 40.97.

***πάμμνηστος**, ον, *ever remembered*, *CIJud.* 1.661 (Tortosa, vi AD), cf. πάμνηστος.

**πάμμουσος**, add 'as a sobriquet, Mitchell *N.Galatia* 370 (i AD)'

***πάμπαιδες**, οἱ, app. the lowest age-group in athletic contests, *IG* 12(9).952.5 (Chalcis, ii BC), 7.1764.13 (Thespiae, ii/i BC), 2871.21 (ii/i BC).

***παμπάσιον**, τό, *entire possession*, Ἠπειρωτικὰ Χρονικά 10.253 (written πανπασιον), cf. ‡παμπησία.

**παμπήδην**, for '(A.)*Fr.* 56' read '*fr.* 154a.16 R.'

**παμπησία**, add 'non-Att.-Ion. **πανπᾶσία**, Ἠπειρωτικὰ Χρονικά 10.254 (Dodona, iv BC); cf. °παμπάσιον'

**πάμπολυς II**, after 'etc.' insert 'w. comp., πάμπολυ .. κυριώτεροι Pl.*Ep.* 7.345b, cf. Is. 8.33'

**παμπρᾶσία**, add 'also sp. παππρασια, *Kafizin* 266(a) (225/4 BC), 267(a) (223/2 BC)'

***παμπρᾶσιον**, τό, app. = παμπρασία, *unreserved sale of property*, *POxy.* 3015.21, 27 (ii AD).

***παμφανός**, prob. *shining*, Hdn.*fr.* p. 28 H.

***παμφίλητος**, ον, *beloved of all*, *Not.Scav.* 1937.473 (Sicily, Chr.).

**πάμφιλος**, for 'prob.' read 'cj.'

***πάμφοιτος**, ον, *wandering everywhere*, πάνφο[ιτ]ον ἄνασσαν *TAM* 4(1).92.

***πάμφρητρος**, ον, *consisting of all the phratries*, παμφρήτροις .. ἀγέλαις *Didyma* 537.6.

***Παμφῡλαία**, ἁ, *of all the* φῦλα, cult-title of Artemis, *IG* 4².503 (Epid., ii BC).

***Παμφῡλίς**, ίδος, fem. adj. *Pamphylian*, D.P. 46, al., Nonn.*D.* 2.38, Π. γαίη *GVI* 815.6 (Attalea, ii AD).

**πάμφῡλος I**, add '**2** *of all the* φῦλα, cult-title of Zeus, *SEG* 37.370 (Megara, v BC).' **II**, line 3, before 'gen. pl.' insert 'nom. sg. Πανφύλας *SEG* 13.239 (Argos, v BC)'

**πάμψογος**, add 'Heph.Astr. 2.15.11'

**πᾰνᾰγής I**, add 'βίος *SEG* 37.1175.10 (verse, Pisidia, ii AD)' **II**, add '*accursed*, Phld.*Sto.* 339.8'

***πᾰναγρυπνία**, ἡ, *complete wakefulness*, *PMag.* 4.3274.

**πᾰνᾱγῡριάρχας**, etc., delete '-αγύριος'

***Πᾰνᾱγύριος**, ὁ (sc. μήν), month at Amphissa, *Delph.* 3(3).32 (ii BC).

**Πᾰνᾰθηναϊκός**, add 'τὸ π. scent (prob. sold in miniature Panathenaic amphorae), Apollon.ap.Ath. 15.688f, Plin.*HN* 13.6'

**πᾰνάθλιος**, add 'Hld. 5.2'

**πᾰνάκεια II**, add 'Πανάκιαν Σῴζουσαν *Inscr.Perg.* 8(3).128'

**πᾰνάκη**, add '**II** = πανάκεια II, Herod. 4.6.'

**πᾰνᾰκήρᾰτος**, add 'πανακήρατον ἔλλαχον εὖχος *SEG* 24.1243'

***πᾰναλγής**, ές, *full of sorrow*, n. acc. pl. as adv., -έα κωκύσασα *IKyzikos* 518.21 (verse, i AD).

**Πᾰνᾰμάρεια**, add 'sp. Παναμάρια, *SEG* 30.1274 (Caria, c.AD 200)'

***πᾰνᾰμῠ́μων**, ον, gen. ονος, *utterly blameless*, *GVI* 199 (Pontus, ii/iii AD).

**πάναξ**, add 'Eudem. in *Suppl.Hell.* 412A.5'

**πᾰνάπηρής**, for '*all-unmutilated*' read '*quite unharmed*, πόδες' and for 'Call.*Cer.* 126' read 'Call.*Cer.* 125'

***πᾰναργῠ́ρεος**, α, ον, *all silver*, ἄμφω ταῦτα -εα Antip.Sid. in *Inscr.Délos* 2549.6.

***πᾰνάρεστος**, ον, *pleasing in every way*, *GVI* 874.1 (Smyrna, ?ii AD).

**⁺πᾰνάριον**, τό, *chest* or *box for keeping bread*, *POxy.* 300.4 (i AD), 1272.8 (ii AD), S.E.*M.* 1.234, *SB* 9834b.23 (iv AD).'

***πανταυτᾰ́δελφος**, ον, *entirely fraternal*, Dioscorus in *Byz.-neugr.Jahrb.* 10.342.

**Πᾰνᾰχαιά**, after 'Demeter' insert 'Δάματρι Παναχαιᾶι *SEG* 25.643 (Thessaly, Hellen.)'

***Πᾰνᾰχαϊκός**, ή, όν, *of all the Achaeans*, τῶι Παναχαϊκῶι συνεδρίωι *SEG* 35.304 (Epid., after 68/7 BC).

**πᾰνᾰώριος**, add 'adv., παναώρια *GVI* 318.1 (Thessalonica, ?iii AD)'

***πανδᾶμικοί**· παιδικοὶ χιτῶνες ἐν ταῖς πομπαῖς Hsch.

**πανδέκτης I 1**, add 'cf. Plin.*HN praef.* 24' add '**3** *medicine-chest*, Sch.Ar.*Pl.* 711.'

***πάνδεκτος**, ον, *receiving all*, πάνδεκτον Φερσεφόνης θάλαμον *CEG* 489.4 (Attica, iv BC).

***Πανδήμεια**, τά, *festival of Zeus Pandemos*, *IHadr.* 128 (iii AD).

**πάνδημος I**, of Zeus, add '*IHadr.* 125 (ii/iii AD), 126, 127; also of Dionysus, *SEG* 32.1243 (2 BC/AD 2)' add '**2** -ον, τό, *confederation of demes*, κωμῶν δύο Swoboda *Denkmäler* 282.' **II**, line 4, after 'π. ἐρασταί' insert 'ἐραστής' and after 'Pl.*Smp.* 181e' insert '183e' add '**b** *from all the town*, π. ἐραστής *AP* 5.302.9 (Agath.).'

***πάνδοξος**, ον, *all-glorious*, Pi.*fr.* 94b.8/9 S.-M.

**πάνδουρος**, add '**II** = πανδουριστής, Roueché *Aphrodisias* 113 (v/vi AD), Hsch. s.v. πανδοῦρα.'

**πανδῠ́νᾰμος**, add 'Plot. 5.9.9'

**πάνδυρτος**, for 'poet. for' read 'edd. metr. gr. for'

**πανδῠσία**, for '*total .. star*' read '*the period during which the Pleiades and Orion are setting* (at sunrise), οἱ ναυτικοί ap.Procl.in Hes.*Op.* 618-26'

**πανδώτειρα**, add '*PMag.* 4.2280'

**Πᾰνεῖος II**, add 'τὰ ὅρια τοῦ Πανίου *SEG* 32.1499 (Diocletian)'

***πᾰνελευθερία**, ἡ, *entire freedom*, *IG* 7.1780.7.

***Πᾰνελλάς**, άδος, ἡ, *the whole of Greece*, Pi.*Pae.* 6.62 S.-M., Philod.Scarph. iii.32, Call.*fr.* 106 Pf.

**Πᾰνελλήνιος I**, add '**2** title of Hadrian, *SEG* 32.185 (Athens).' **II 2**, add 'ὁ ἄρχων τοῦ Πανελληνίου *SEG* 28.1566 (Cyrene, AD 154)'

***πᾰνέντῑμος**, ον, *held in all honour*, ὁ π. οἶκος οὗτος *BCH* suppl. 8.103 (Thessalonica, v AD).

***πᾰνεορτεύω**, *keep a solemn festival*, *IPhilae* 159.3 (i AD).

**⁺πᾰνεπάρκιος**, ον, *all-sufficient*, *Suppl.Hell.* 937.27, 1181.1.

***Πανεπις**, ὁ, Egyptian deity, "bull of Apis", *JEA* 12.34 (v BC).

***πᾰνέραστος** (sc. λίθος), ἡ, = πανέρως, Plin.*HN* 37.178.

**πανεύφημος**, add 'Just.*Nov.* 8 iusiurandum 43'

***πᾰνηγῠριαρχία**, ἡ, office of πανηγυριάρχης, *Didyma* 157 I(c).

***πᾰνηγῠριαρχικός**, ή, όν, *of a* πανηγυριάρχης, τιμή *PASA* 2.396 (Caria).

***πᾰνηγῠ́ρίη**, ἡ, = πανήγυρις, *SEG* 8.549.24 (hymn, i BC).

**πᾰνηγῠρικός I**, add 'προφήτης *Didyma* 264.1, 238 II 2, al.; ταμίας ib. 408.3, 410.1'

**πᾰνήγῠρις**, before 'Dor.' insert 'Aeol.' **I 1**, add '**b** *market-day*, Just.*Const.Δέδωκεν* 8c.'

**πᾰνημᾰδόν**, add '*SEG* 13.277 (Patrae, iv/v AD)'

**πᾰνῆμαρ**, add '*Trag.adesp.* in *PKöln* 241 A i 1'

***πανθάπᾶσι**, = παντάπασι, *PCol.* 175.9,53 (AD 339).

**πάνθειος I**, before 'ον' insert 'α'; add 'epith. of Zeus and Athena, *SEG* 20.719.12, 13 (Cyrene, ii BC)'

**πανθέλκτειρα**, for 'Simon. 183.1' read '*AP* 7.24.1 ([Simon.])'

**Πανθεών**, add 'at Olynthus, *SEG* 39.617 (iv BC)'

**πανθοινία**, add 'Cels.ap.Orig.*Cels.* 8.24'

***πανθυπᾰκουστής**, οῦ, ὁ, *one who hears everything*, *PMag.* 4.1369.

**πᾰνίμερος II**, for 'prob.' read 'cj.'

**Πάνιος**, add '**II** name of month, *SEG* 17.829 (unkn. provenance, c.200 BC).'

***πᾰνίρευς**, εος, ὁ, title of priest at Mytilene, *IG* 12(2).61.3 (written -ειρ-), 102, cf. ἱρεύς.

**Πᾰνίσκος**, after 'Πάν' insert '*Inscr.Délos* 1416*A*i51 (ii BC)'; add '(Cic.) *Div.* 1.14.23'

***Πᾰνιστής**, οῦ, ὁ, *worshipper of Pan*, Men.*Dysc.* 230 (παιανιστ- pap.).

**πᾰνίχνιον**, for '*the whole track*' read 'pl., *all kinds of tracks*'

**Πᾰνίωνες**, delete 'Πανιώνιον' to end.

***Πᾰνιώνιος**, ον, *of* or *associated with the* Πανίωνες; as title of Apollo, *IEphes.* 814; of Hadrian, ib. 1501; ὁ κρατὴρ ὁ Π., *sacred vessel* at Delos, *Inscr.Délos* 104.129, Hyp.*fr.* 69. **b** *Πανιώνιον, τό, temple and meeting-place of the* Πανίωνες at Mycale, Hdt. 1.141.4, al., *CIG* 2909 (Mycale). **c** *Πανιώνια, τά, festival of the* Πανίωνες, Hdt. 1.148.1.

***Πανλίμνιος**, ὁ, title of Apollo, *SEG* 29.515 (Thessaly, ii BC).

**παννῠ́χιος**, before 'ον' insert 'α'

**πᾰνομφαῖος**, for '*sender of ominous voices*' read '*universally prophetic*'

***πᾰνόπαια**, ἡ, epith. of Hecate, *PMag.* 4.2612, 2965, v. ἀνοπαῖα 2.

***πᾰνόρφᾰνος**, ον, *very much an orphan*, *SEG* 14.563.15 (epigr., Chios, i BC).

***πᾰνόσιος**, ον, pl. οἱ πανόσιοι, *the number* or *company of the holy ones*, Phld.*Sto.* 339.17.

**πᾰνοσπρία**, add '**b** gloss on πάγκαρπα θύματα, Sch.S.*El.* 635, cf. Hsch.'

**πᾰνουργέω I**, add '**b** διὰ σχημάτων π. *play tricks* with figures (of diction), Longin. 17.1, cf. 2.'

**πᾰνουργία I 1**, add '**b** transl. Hebr. *'ormāh*, elsewhere *craftiness* but here app. in good sense, *shrewdness*, Sm.*Pr.* 8.12.'

**πᾰνοῦργος II**, line 4, after 'Plu. 2.28a' insert 'Lxx *Pr.* 27.12, *Si.* 21.12'

***πανπᾶσία**, v. °παμπησία.

**πάνριζος**, add 'also πάρριζος, π. μολεῖν Ἀίδου μέγαν κευθμῶνα poet. in Robert *Collection Froehner* I no. 77 (Alexandria, i BC)'

**πανσᾰγία**, add 'Ion. **πασσαγίη**, Call.*fr.* 359 Pf.'

***πανσευδί**, adv., written πανσεϜδί, = πανσυδί, prob. in *Inscr.Cret.* 1.xxviii 7 (vi BC).

***πανσοφία**, ἡ, poet. πασσοφίη, *complete wisdom*, *Epigraphica* 10.76 (Leptis Magna).

**πάνσοφος**, for '*most clever*' read '*clever in every way*'; line 3, for '*Trag.Adesp.* 470.3' read 'A.*fr.* 181a.3 R.' and add '*SEG* 30.1179 (Ostia, iii AD)'; line 4, after '(Tenos)' insert '*PHerm.* 4.14 (iv AD)'

*πανσπερμεί, adv., all seeds (or kinds) together, φύετο στάχυς ἄμμιγα κριθαῖς πασπερμεί Lyr.adesp. 11(d).4 P.
πανσπερμία, add 'cf. πασπερμεῖον'
*πανσπέρμιον, τό, = πανσπερμία, Anon.Alch. 18.14.
πανσῠδί, add 'cf. πασσυδόν, πασσυδιάζω, see also °πανσευδί'
πανσῠδίᾳ II, delete the section transferring quots. to section I. add 'II utterly, AP 7.299 (Nicomachus).'
*πανταβροκτον, τό, app. for *παντά-βροχον, vessel for soaking dried foods, Kafizin 230(a) (225/18 BC).
πανταπᾶσι, line 1, before 'before a vowel' insert 'usually' and add 'before a consonant, e.g. παντάπασιν καὶ .., SEG 37.1003 (Sardis, c.200 BC)'
παντᾰπώλης, add 'PTeb. 841 (ii BC)'
πανταχόσε, after 'Plu.Agis 14' add 'Just.Nov. 4 epilogos'
παντεβιπᾶσιν, delete the entry.
παντελής, line 1, for 'σάγην' read 'σαγὴν'
*Παντελίη, ἡ, name for Demeter, IG $4^2$.551.1 (Epid., metr.inscr., Roman); cf. παντέλεια I, παντέλειος.
*παντευλογ(έω), uncertain reading, perh. pray constantly, SEG 36.970.A5 (Aphrodisias, iii AD).
+πάντεχνος, ον, belonging to or dealing with all the skills, παντέχ[νοις] Ἁφαίστου παλάμαις Pi.fr. 52i.65 S.-M.; παντέχνου πυρὸς σέλας A.Pr. 7.
παντογενής, add 'Αὖραι Orph.H. 81.1 (cj.)'
παντοδύνᾰμος, delete 'Plot. 5.9.9' (v. °πανδύναμος)
παντοδῠνάστης, add 'PMag. 12.267'
παντοθᾰλής 2, for 'BMus.Inscr. 1067.15' read 'BMus.Inscr. 1075.14'
παντοῖος II, adv., add '2 in every way, i.e. absolutely, Just.Nov. 105.2.2, 109.1.'
παντοκρᾰτειρα, line 2, delete 'pecul.'; add 'SEG 8.548.2'
παντοκρᾰτωρ, line 2, for 'almighty' read 'ruler over all'; add 'as cult-title of Zeus, INikaia 1512 (ii/iii AD), 1121 (iii AD); of the Emperor Julian, BCH suppl. 8 no. 86'
πάντολμος, after 'all-daring' insert 'τὸ πάντολμον σθένος Ἡρακλέος Pi.fr. 29.4 S.-M.' and for 'shameless' read 'w. pejorative force'; add 'AP 5.218.4 (Agath.), 248 (Paul.Sil.)'
*παντοπωλικός, ή, όν, selling all varieties of goods, PSI 692.2, 12, 13 (AD 52/3).
+παντόπωλις, ιδος, ἡ, of a market, etc., selling all kinds of goods, τὰν παντόπωλιν στοάν SEG 23.207 (Messene, Augustus); as subst., general dealer, PRyl. 227.3 (iii AD).
πάντοτε, add '2 in every instance, Plu. 2.550b, Peripl.M.Rubr. 29.'
*παντόφωνος, ον, producing the whole range of sounds, ὄργανα Dain Inscr.du Louvre 60.20 (Heraclea ad Latmum).
πάντρητος, for 'the part .. holes are' read 'perh. perforated collar enabling additional holes to be opened'
πάντροπος, add 'III versatile, Μουσέων π. ἦν θεράπων MDAI(A) 20.228 (Rhodes, i BC).'
πάντως I, line 5, for 'A.Pr. 335' read 'A.Pr. 333'
πᾰνῠπέρτατος 2, after 'supreme' insert 'Alcmaeonis fr. 3 p. 33 B.' and add 'Ζηνὶ πανυπερτάτῳ INikaia 1071 (i/ii AD)'
*πᾰνυπεύκυκλος, ον, well-rounded all over, π. ἀνθεμίς Poet.de herb. 134 (cj., codd. παρ-).
πᾰνῳδός, before 'ἀχώ' insert '(or Πᾱνῳδός, of the music of Pan)'
*πᾰνώλεος, ον, = πανώλης II 1, γένοισαν ἐξώλεοι καὶ πανώλεοι IMylasa 476.8 (Rom.imp.).
+πᾰνώνιος, ον, Cypr. pa-no-ni-o-se, prob. having full rights of sale or enjoyment, ICS 217 A10, B22 (also Addenda p. 415).
πάξ, after 'Diph. 96' insert 'AP 5.181 (Asclep.)'
παξαμᾶς, add 'II in μουσωτοῦ παξαμᾶ Syria 1.302 (Sidon, vi AD), π. may denote a special kind of mosaic (or the maker of it).'
*πάομαι, last line, after 'ii BC)' insert 'IG 4.752.13 (Troezen, ii BC)'
*πᾱόνιος, α, ον, of a peacock, Edict.Diocl. 18.9; cf. πάων, Lat. pavo.
*παπειν (acc. sg. masc.) perh. local title, metr.inscr. in Robert Hell. 7.198.10 (Tarsus, ii/iii AD).
+πᾱπίας (παππ-), ου, ὁ, dad, childish or familiar term for father, Ar.V. 297, Pax 128, Men.Dysc. 856, Ephipp. 21 (all voc.); applied familiarly to an old man not one's father, Men.Dysc. 930.
*πάπος, ὁ, = πάππος I 1, MDAI(A) 27.307 (Maced., pl.), AAWW 1961.124 (Lydia, AD 233/4), SEG 30.1485 (Phrygia, AD 305/6). II something used as incense, εἰς ἀποκαυσμὸν τῶν π. Ramsay Cities and Bishoprics I 119 (see also SEG 6.272: perh. = papaver), Rev.Phil. 36.73 (Iconium), cf. perh. πάππος II, which must be a different wd. fr. sense I.
παππάζω II, add 'w. internal acc., παρακάτθετο Βάκχος Ἀθήνῃ Εὔια παππάζοντα Nonn.D. 48.954'
πάππας, after 'nom. πάπας' insert 'A.fr. 47a ii 14 R. (lyr.) (prob.), Men.Dysc. 194, 204' and after 'acc. πάπαν' insert 'Men.Dysc. 648, cf. 494' add 'II (Christian) priest, SEG 32.1474 (Syria), PLond. 1914.25 (iv AD), al.'
παππίας, v. °παπίας.

παππικός, add 'PGrenf. 55.23 (ii AD); also ός, όν, ITyr 33A.4'
*παππωνῠμικός, ή, όν, derived from one's grandfather's name, [ὄνομα] Sch.E.Rh. 36; adv. -ῶς Sch.Gen.Il. 9.191, Suid. s.v. Ἀλκείδης; cf. πατρω-, μητρω-, μαμμω-νυμικός, -ῶς.
παππωνῠμικῶς, delete the entry.
παππῷος, add 'CPR 7.3.7 (AD 150); perh. also cult-title of Zeus, INikaia 1513'
πᾱπῠλιών, after 'Edict.Diocl. 19.4' insert 'PMich.III 214.26 (iii AD)'
πάπῡρος, at end after '∪∪∪' add 'cf. Moer. p. 311 P.'
πᾰρά, line 3, after 'Att.' insert 'once in Ion.' and after '(Paros)' insert 'SEG 30.1456 (Sinope, c.470/50 BC), ib. 366 (Argos, c.460/50 BC)' B II 2, line 10, for 'Pl.Phlb. 29f' read 'Pl.Phlb. 29e; παρ' ἐμαυτῷ in my own mind, id.Phd. 107b'; add 'πὰρ Ἥραι (i.e. in or near her temple), SEG 34.282 (Nemea, iv BC)' C I 2 b, add 'ἀποδώσω παρὰ τὸν εὔθυνον τὸ καθῆκον IG $1^3$.244.B7' III 8, for 'of a .. possibility' read 'with expressions of possibility and permission'; transfer the reference to Arrian to follow 'Av. 846' inserting 'also' before 'πεῖσαι'; add 'π. τοῦτο ἔσται καὶ ὁ κύων ἄνθρωπος S.E.P. 2.23' F, add 'also for πάρειμι, Cratin. 113 K.-A., Hermipp. 52 K.-A.' G, after 'IN COMPOS.' insert '(sts. w. apocope)' at end add 'Myc. pa-ro, prep. w. dat. = παρό'
*παραβάδην, v. °παρβάδαν.
παραβαίνω, line 3, after '*παραβάω' insert 'also w. apocope of preverb, παρβαίνοντι IG $9^2$.609.15 (Locris, vi/v BC), part. παρβεῶντας SEG 9.3.42, 47 (Cyrene, iv BC)'
*παραβᾰλᾰνεύς, έως, ὁ, sick-nurse, ACO 2(1).179, PIand. 154 (vi/vii AD); (cf. Lat. parabalani, parabolani).
παραβάλλω, after lemma insert '(w. apocope of preverb, e.g. παρβάλλοιτο, Schwyzer 323.C26 (Delphi, iv BC))' B, add 'VI (in med.) transgress, εἰ δέ κα παρβάλληται Sokolowski 2.33A.9 (Dyme, iii BC), Leg.Sacr. ii.74C7, D18/9.'
παράβᾰσις II, line 3, after 'Plu. Comp.Ages.Pomp. 1' insert 'as t.t. in law, συνθηκῶν παραβάσεως (sc. δίκη) Poll. 8.31'
παραβάτης II, add 'ὁ π. the Transgressor, i.e. the Emperor Julian, Suid. s.v. Ἰουλιανός, Eust. 83.41' add 'III passer-by, κεῖνος ἂν εὐδαίμων εἴη μᾶλλον παραβάτας IG 9(1).256.11 (Halae).'
παραβῐάζομαι I, for this section read 'act in defiance of some constraint, Lxx De. 1.43, Plb. 24.8.3'
*παραβίᾰσις, εως, ἡ, the use of violence, Epicur.fr. 29.39.2 A.
παραβῐβάζω 1, for 'put aside, remove' read 'transfer'
*παραβιβρώσκω, nibble at, παραβέβρωται Vit.Aesop.(G) 45; Hsch. s.v. παρεσθίε[ται].
παραβλέπω I, add '3 see by the side, in quot. pass., Archim.Aren. 13.'
παράβλημα I, after 'fodder' insert 'Hsch. s.v. κάπητον' II, add 'PRyl. 558.3 (iii BC)'
παραβολᾶνοι, delete the entry (v. °παραβαλανεύς).
παραβολεύομαι, after '(v.l. παραβουλ-)' insert 'μὴ παραβολεύεσθαι PSI 1241.27 (ii AD)'
παραβολή VI, after 'multiplication' insert 'Nicom.Ar. 2.27' and delete 'hence .. Ar. 2.27'
*παραβολινθέω, unexpld. wd., PAberd. 190.3 (i AD, pass.).
παράβολος II 2, line 7, for 'τὰ π. .. Longin. 32.4' read 'neut. subst. audaciousness of language, Longin. 22.4; pl., ib. 32.4'
*παραβρᾰδύνω, tarry, Luc.Alex. 44 (v.l.).
παράβυστος II 1, add 'prob. in IG $2^2$.1646.12' 2, add 'Procop.Arc. 1.17'
παραβύω I, add 'in chariot-racing, perh. push aside, SEG 34.1437 (Syria, v/vi AD)'
παραβώμιος 3, add 'παραβ[ώ]μια ῥέξαι epigr. in SEG 39.855 (Patmos, iii/iv AD)'
παραγαύδιον, after 'Edict.Diocl. 19.29' insert 'Dura[4] 93'
παραγγελία II 1, add 'Din.fr. IVa (p. 78.10 C.)' 2, add 'b notice of legal proceedings, Just.Nov. 88.1.'
παραγγέλλω III 3, add 'of the complainant, pap. in Illinois Cl.Studies 3.100' IV 2, for 'App.BC 1.21' read 'App.BC 1.121' and add 'w. dat., εἰ .. τις .. τῶν αἱρετικῶν .. οἱῳδήποτε δημοσίῳ φροντίσματι παραγγείλειεν Cod.Just. 1.5.18.10'
*παραγειτνιάω, to be neighbour, τισι Sch.E.Rh. 5.
παραγίγνομαι, line 2, after 'Plb. 3.99.2, etc.' insert 'w. apocope of preverb, παργίνομαι, SEG 31.575 (Larissa, 171 BC), aor. part. pass. παργεναθέντες SEG 30.1119 (Entella, iii BC)' I 4, for this section read '(have a right) to be present at a feast, IG 12(7).515 (Amorgos, ii BC); παραγενόμ[εν]ος .. ἀπὸ Πλατίννας (i.e. through his descent from P.), Inscr.Cos 405' at end add 'form παρο-, prob. Myc. 3 sg. aor. med. pa-ro-ke-ne-[to]'
παράγραμμα, add 'III play on words, pun, Cic.Fam. 7.32.2.'
παραγραμματίζω I, for '= foreg.' read 'τινα make a pun on the name of'
παράγρᾰφος, add '2 masc., pencil for drawing lines, CGL 3.639.3.'
+παραγράψιμος, ον, open to objection, S.E.M. 7.170; disqualified, Modest.Dig. 27.1.13.6.

**παρᾰγωγεύς**, after '*introducer*' insert 'or perh. official who collected a παραγώγιον from initiates'

**παράγωγή I 6**, after '*furnishing*' insert '*Didyma* 41.34'

***παρᾰγώγιμος**, ον, *that is in transit*, π. φορτίον *SEG* 14.639.B13 (Caunus, i AD).

**παραδειγματίζω**, delete '*Ev.Matt.* 1.19' (v. δειγματίζω).

**παραδείκνῡμι**, add '**7** of a creditor, π. εἰς ἐνεχυρασίαν *indicate* a property *as having become liable to distraint*, *PRyl.* 176.5 (iii AD, rest. as med.), *PLand.* 145.3 (iii AD; act.), etc.'

**παράδεισος I 3 b**, add 'pl., παραδίζοισι κατοικῶ *AS* 5.32.24 (N. Phrygia, iv AD)'

***παραδεισοφύλαξ**, ᾰκος, ὁ, *custodian of a* παράδεισος, *PCair.Zen.* 690.22 (pl., iii BC).

***παραδεισών**, ῶνος, ὁ, *orchard*, *PHamb.* 99.9 (i AD).

***παραδεξιόω**, perh. *make convenient*, *BGU* 1844.19 (i BC).

**παραδέχομαι**, line 1, after 'Pl.*Tht.* 155c' insert 'w. apocope of preverb, παρδέξαι *SEG* 35.1011 (Sicily, i BC)'

***παραδηθύνω**, *linger upon*, Orph.*L.* 634 (cj.).

**παραδηλόω**, after 'Plu.*Crass.* 18, etc.' insert 'w. inf., Hld. 7.9'

***παραδήλωσις**, εως, ἡ, *intimation*, Poll. 4.33 (pl.).

**παραδίδωμι**, line 2, after 'AD' insert 'w. apocope of preverb, παρδῶντι *Tab.Heracl.* 1.106' **I 4 a**, add 'κατὰ τὸ παραδεδομένον *according to tradition*, *SEG* 30.622 (Thessalonica, i AD)'

**παραδιώκω I**, for this section read '*drive out, eject*, from office, *SEG* 7.1.13 (Susa, i AD; pass.); *reject* a reading, A.D.*Synt.* 145.20'

**παραδοξονίκης**, of athletes, add '*SEG* 34.1317 (Lycia, c.AD 90)'

**παράδοξος II**, add 'in list of kouretes, *SEG* 33.937 (Ephesus, ii AD)'

**παράδοσις**, line 2, after 'ἡ' insert '**πάρδοσις** *Brit.Mus.Quarterly* 11.13 (on gem, ii/iii AD)'

**παραδρομάδην**, for '*in running* or *passing by*' read '*in passing, briefly*'

**παραδρομή**, add '**III** perh. = παραδρομίς, *CPR* 7.44.2 (v/vi AD, s.v.l.). **IV** *passage* of time, *Cod.Just.* 1.3.43.13, 10.19.9.1.'

**παραζηλόω I 2**, for this section read '*to be overzealous*, ἔν τινι Lxx *Ps.* 36(37).1, 7; abs. ib. 8'

+**παράθερμος**, ον, *excessively hot-blooded* or *violent*, D.S. 24.3, Plu. *Comp.Pel.Marc.* 3; transf., of actions, π. καινουργία Hierocl. p. 52 A.

**παράθεσις II**, add '*IG* 12(7).515.77' **III**, delete '*IG* 12(7).515.77' **IV**, add '**b** *entry on a file*, *PColl.Youtie* 73.14 (AD 289).'

**παραθέω III**, add 'fig., χρυσὸν δ' εὐδικίη παραθεῖ Call.*fr.* 384.14 Pf.'

**παραθήκη**, add '**b** *place of deposit*, *SEG* 31.1072 (Pontus, ii/iii AD). **2** of a tablet entrusted to supernatural powers for the execution of the curse it bears, *Tab.Defix.Aud.* 22.39, 32.27 (both Cyprus).'

**παραθρώσκω**, for 'Oikonomos .. (ii BC)' read '*SEG* 32.644 (Pydna, iii BC)'

**παράθυμα**, delete the entry.

**παραιβαδόν**, for 'prob. in Opp.*C.* 1.484' read 'cj. in Opp.*C.* 1.484 (cod. παραὶ βατόν)'

***παραιθου** (gen.), unidentified ingredient in a medicament, *POxy.* 1088.15 (i AD).

**παραιθύσσω II 1**, delete 'λαίφεα'

**παραινετήρ**, add 'w. adjectival force, παραινετῆρας ἐξαντλῶ λ[όγους] *Trag.adesp.* in *PKöln* 242.2'

**παραιτέομαι II 2 a**, line 8, delete 'Iamb. *VP* 2.7'; add '*reject* a candidate, Onos. 1.19' **b**, add 'abs., Modest.*Dig.* 26.5.21.2'

**παραιτητέος 1**, add 'id. *VP* 2.7'

***παραιτία**, ἡ, *responsibility, blame*, *PMed.*inv. 68.38ʳ ii 11 (*Aegyptus* 69.19, i BC/i AD).

**παραίτιος 1**, line 3, transfer 'τῶν δ' .. A.*fr.* 44.7 R.' fr. section 2 to follow 'A.l.c.'; line 4, after 'αἴτιος' insert 'Plb. 4.57.10'

+**παραιφᾱσίη**, v. °παραφασία.

+**παραίφᾰσις**, v. ‡παράφασις.

**παρακᾰλέω**, line 1, after 'Lxx *Jb.* 7.13, al.' insert 'w. apocope of preverb, παρκαλῖ *SEG* 32.456 (Haliartos, iii BC)'

**παρακάλυμμα 1**, add 'so prob. in *Inscr.Délos* 442A229 (ii BC)'

***παρακᾰπηλεύω**, *carry on unauthorised trade*, *ZPE* 27.211 (Samos, iii BC).

***παρακατάγνυμι**, *break off in part*, ῥυτὸν δίκρουνον παρακατεαγὸς τοῦ χείλ[ους] *Inscr.Délos* 1441Aii86 (ii BC).

**παρακαταθήκη**, line 1, after 'ἡ' insert '(παρκα(τ)θέκα *Schwyzer* 54.B1 (Tegea, but not Arc., v BC), Boeot. παρκαταθείκα *IG* 7.2420.34)'

**παρακατάσχεσις**, add '*PMasp.* 295 ii 9'

**παρακατατίθημι**, after lemma insert 'w. apocope of preverbs, παρκαττίθεται *SEG* 30.1163 (Heraclea, Italy, iv/iii BC)'

**παράκειμαι I**, line 4, after 'Telecl. 1.7, etc.' insert 'of parallel anchors, *Peripl.M.Rubr.* 4' **2**, delete 'cf. Plb. 5.34.7' **II 2**, add 'Ath. 9.409b' add '**III** trans., *to have put in* or *deposited* a document (cf. ‡παρατίθημι B 2 a), ἐπὶ ῥαδιουργίᾳ παρακεῖσθαι αὐτὸν τὴν συγχώρησιν *UPZ* 162 vi 4, cf. 21, vii 3, 21, viii 2, 33 (ii BC); παρέκειτο τὴν δηλουμένην διαγραφὴν *SB* 4512.67 (ii BC); εἴ τινα ἀπόδειξιν παράκειται *UPZ* 161.35 (ii BC).'

**παρακελευστής**, add 'app. title of an office, *one who calls upon* (a deity), Πολιάδος Ἀθάνας π. *IG* 12(2).484.17'

**παρακίναιδος**, delete 'f.l. in'

**παρακῑνέω**, line 2, after 'II 2)' insert 'Men.*Dysc.* 961; *incite* against the government, Plu.*Pel.* 6'

**παρακίρναμαι**, add 'act. παρεκίρνα· παρέμισγε Hsch.'

+**παρακλαίω**, *weep beside*, *AP* 5.103 (Rufin.); cf. παρακλαυσίθυρον; Sch.Ar.*V.* 977.

**παρακλῑνω I 3**, line 4, after '*HA* 540ᵃ1' insert 'Ant.Lib. 17.6' **4**, delete the section.

**παρακοιμάομαι 2**, add '**b** of sexual intercourse, Sch.Pi.*P.* 4.449.'

***παρακοιτάζω**, *lie beside*, Hsch. s.v. παρευνάζων.

**παρακοιτέω**, abs., add '*SEG* 24.154.13 (Attica, iii BC)'

**παρακολλητικός**, add 'Heras ap.Gal. 13.781.13'

**παράκολλος I**, for 'χαμεῦνα, .. 10.36)' read 'χάμευνα, low couch *with ornamental wood-work glued on*, *IG* 1³.421.204 (Athens, v BC), cf. Poll. 10.36'

**παρᾰκολουθητέον**, add 'Gal.*Anim.Pass.* 5.8 (*CMG* 5.4(1).1, 18.10)'

***παρᾰκολουθητής**, οῦ, ὁ, *assistant*, *PFam.Teb.* 15.103 (ii AD).

**παρᾰκολουθητικός**, after '*for following* or *understanding*' insert 'τὴν δὲ τριβὴν καὶ τὴν ἐξ αὐτῆς ἕξιν εἶναι πολλοῖς παρακολουθητικὴν Phld.*Rh.* 1.52 S.' **2**, delete the section.

***παρᾰκολουθήτρια**, ἡ, *supervisor*, *POxy.* 3921.6, 49 (AD 219).

**παρακολυμβάω**, add 'part. Παρακολυμβῶσα, title of comedy by Nicostratus, Phot. α 1197 Th.'

**παρακομίζω 2**, after '*transport*' insert 'παρακομίσεν *ZPE* 72.100.5 (Emporion, vi BC)'

+**παρᾰκοντίζω**, *throw a javelin beyond* (others), Luc.*Par.* 61.

**παρακοπτικός**, add 'adv. -κῶς Gal. 17(2).454.12'

**παρακόπτω II 1**, add 'w. gen. χρησμῶν παρεκόπης i.e. you were diverted from the proper understanding of them, A.*Ag.* 1252 (cj.)'

**παρᾰκούω IV 1**, add 'w. acc., μὴ παρακούσῃς τὸ οὔνομα τοῦ Θεοῦ *SEG* 31.1594'

**παρακρέμαμαι**, delete the entry.

**παρακρεμάννῡμι**, add 'pass., Luc.*Asin.* 23; metaph., *to be dependent*, τὰ παρακρεμάμενα μέρη *the dependencies* of an empire, Plb. 5.35.10'

***παρακύϊσμα**, ατος, τό, name of the sign Ͳ (later ⅂), Sch.D.T. p. 496 H. (s.v.l.); see Ϻ (p. 1562 at end of π entries).

**παρακῡρόω**, delete the entry.

+**παράλαμψις** (A), εως, ἡ, *shining spot on the cornea*, Hp.*Prorrh.* 2.20, Gal. 19.127.

***παράλαμψις** (B), Dor. for ‡παράληψις.

**παραλέγω III 1**, delete 'Med., .. 1.101 S.'

**παραλειπτέον**, line 2, after 'Isoc.' insert '15.149'

***παραλημπτής**, v. ‡παραληπτής.

**παραληπτής**, add '*steward, estate-manager*, *CPR* 6.31.2 (cf. pp. 61 & 79) (iii/iv AD)'

**παραληπτικός**, add '*POxy.Hels.* 41.39 (iii AD, sp. παραλημφθ-)'

**παράληψις**, line 1, after '-ληψις' insert 'Dor. -**λαμψις**, *Clara Rhodos* 2.175.9 (ii BC)' **2**, add '*SEG* 30.1274 (Caria, c.AD 200)'

**παράλιος I**, add '**2** as title of Artemis, di Cesnola *Salaminia* p. 96.' **III**, after '= οἱ Πάραλοι' insert '(v. πάραλος II) Arist.*Ath.* 13.4'

**παραλλᾰγή I 2**, add 'ἐκ παραλλαγῆς γίνεσθαι τὰ σωλάρια *first one side* (of the road) *and then the other*, *Cod.Just.* 8.10.12.5b' **II**, add 'παρὰ τὴν προτέραν D.H.*Comp.* 15'

**παραλληλισμός I**, add '*POxy.* 1916.10 (vi AD)'

**παράλληλος**, add '**4** in music, of tetrachords, *disjunct* (opp. °κατάλληλος), Aristid.Quint. 1.8.'

**παραλογεύομαι**, add 'act., *SEG* 8.466.23, 41 (Egypt, i BC)'

***παραλόγια**, τά, app. *false arguments*, *PMacquarie* inv. 358 (*Atti Napoli* III 827).

**παραλογισμός I**, line 3, before 'Arist.*Po.* 1455ᵃ13' for 'θεάτρου' read 'θατέρου' **II**, add 'ἐπὶ παραλογισμῷ *with fraudulent intent*, *PColl.Youtie* 12.7 (177 BC)'

**παράλογος I 1**, at end before 'sup.' insert 'comp. -ώτερον Plu.*Tim.* 1' **2**, before 'adv.' insert 'comp., Plu. 2.1123a' **II**, add 'ἐκ παραλόγου *abnormally*, Pompon.*Dig.* 1.3.3'

**πάρᾰλος III 2**, after 'cf. παραλίτης' insert '‡παράλιος III' **IV**, delete 'ἡ π.'

+**παραλοῦμαι**, *wash beside*, πάντας χρὴ παραλοῦσθαι καὶ τοὺς σπόγγους ἐᾶν Ar.*fr.* 59 K.-A., cf. 537; act., παραλούειν Phot., Suid.

**παραλῡπέω**, add '*SEG* 32.1149 (Ionia, AD 209)'

**παράλῠτος**, for '= foreg.' read '*paralysed*, D.H. 9.21'

**παραλύω I 1 b**, delete the section. **II**, line 10, after 'Plu.*Cleom.* 37' insert '*disband*, ἅρματα Lxx 2*Ki.* 8.4'

**παραμελέω**, line 4, after '*neglect*' delete 'a duty' and insert 'τῶν ἀγρῶν Arist.*Ath.* 16.5'

***παραμελορυθμοβάτας**, ὁ, nonce-wd., *one who ruins melody and rhythm as he goes*, Pratin. 3.13 S.

**παραμεμπτέον**, delete the entry.

**παραμένω** **II 2**, add 'med., παραμενῶμαι ἐπεὶ (for ἐπὶ) τῆς Ἀλεξ-ανδρείας *POxy.* 3396.19 (iv AD)'

***παραμίσθωμα**, ατος, τό, *supplementary hired hand, SEG* 38.1462.23, 44 (Oenoanda, ii AD).

+**παραμονάριος**, ὁ, *guardian of a rest-house,* Aesop. 252 P.; also *of a church, monastery,* etc., *Cod.Just.* 1.3.45.3, *SEG* 30.1688 (sp. -μων-, Palestine, vi AD). **II** *one acting as an assistant under the terms of a* παραμονή (q.v., sense 1), *POxy.* 3960 (AD 621), *SB* 4490 (vii AD).

**παραμονή** **1**, for '*obligation* .. deferred' read '*obligation to remain with a person,* esp. of a manumitted slave with his ex-master, for a stated period until the completion of a contract, or sim.'

**παράμονος**, after 'rarer form of foreg.' insert 'freq. as pers. n.' and delete '(q.v.)'

**παραμῡθία**, add '**6** *special allowance,* οἷς ἡ τοιαύτη ἀφώρισται π. .. ἀποπληροῦσθαι τὴν αὐτῶν π. *SEG* 9.356.21, 24 (Cyrene, vi AD), *BGU* 1024 vii 12, *PPrincet.* 96.6-7, etc., *Cod.Just.* 3.2.4.8. **7** *interest* on a mortgage, *BGU* 2150.12 (AD 472).'

**παραμῡθιακός**, delete the entry (read °Φαρμουθιακός).

**παραμύθιον** **1**, add 'ὕπνου *AP* 7.195 (Mel.)'

***παραναίομαι**, *dwell beside,* ἡμῖν δὲ κακὸς παρενάσσατο γείτων Call.*fr.* 294.2 Pf. **2** trans., *cause to dwell* in, καί μιν .. σφετέρῃ παρενάσσατο χώρῃ D.P. 776.

**παραναίω**, delete the entry.

***παρανακᾰλέω**, *exhort, POxy.* 1841.2 (vi AD).

***παράναυλον**, τό, kind of transport charge, *PRyl.* 213.47 (ii AD).

**παρανθέω**, add '**III** fig., *lose the bloom of beauty,* cj. in X.*Smp.* 8.17 (based on reading of *PGiss.* 1 ii 4 παρανοήσῃ).'

**παρανθῐνολογέω**, for 'dub. sens. in' read '*over-harvest the flowers of*'

**παρανίσσομαι**, after lemma insert 'or better **παρανῑ́σομαι**'; add 'abs., *come to aid,* Arat. 426'

***παρανύμφη**, *woman who conducts a bride,* Isid. 9.7.8; cf. mod. Gk. παρανύμφη (*sponsor*).

**παράνυμφος** **I**, after '*best man,*' insert 'one of the *dramatis personae* in Ar.*Ach.*', and delete this reference from section II.

***παράνω**, *just above,* prep. w. gen., *PMasp.* 169bis 49 (569 AD); cf. παρακάτω.

***παράνωθεν**, adv. *over the top,* Anon.Alch. 324.11.

**παραξῐφίς**, add 'pl., as a title of book of miscellanea, Gell.*Praef.* 7'

**παράπαιγμα**, add 'perh. inscription on a gaming counter, *SEG* 34.1534 (παρα..γμα, Alexandria, i AD)'

***παραπαλάριος**, ὁ, mentioned among entertainers of various kinds, perh. to be connected w. Lat. *palaria, the exercise of tilting against a stake,* Teuc.Bab. p. 44 B.

**παράπαν**, for 'in correct writers .. Art.' read 'usu. joined w. art.' and after 'Th. 6.80, etc.' insert 'without art., Th. 6.18.7'

**παρᾰπᾰτάω**, after 'A.*Eu.* 728' insert '(codd., cj. παρηπάφησας (παραπαφίσκω))'

**παρᾰπᾰφίσκω**, line 1, after 'παρήπαφον' insert '(but v. °παραπατάω)'

**παραπείθω**, line 2, for 'Il. 24.208' read 'Il. 14.208'

**παραπεμπτέος** **II 1**, add 'Gal. 14.305.15'

**παραπέμπω** **I 3**, after '*IG* 12(7).53.19 (Amorgos)' insert '*escort* a prisoner, *PKöln* 281.16 (vi AD)' **III 2**, after '*give up, omit*' insert 'τὸν κατὰ μέρος λόγον Hipparch. 1.10.24'

**παραπιπράσκω** **II**, delete the section transferring quot. to section I, changing ref. to '*ISmyrna* 723'.

**παραπλᾰγιάζω**, for 'Hsch.' read 'trans., *divert,* Hsch. s.v. παροχετεύει'

**παραπλέκω** **II**, line 2, for 'π. ἑαυτόν *becurl* himself' read 'w. pers. obj.'

**παραπλεύριος**, add 'π. ἄκανθαι, of dolphins, Sch.Pi.*P.* 4.29'

**παραπλήξ** **II**, after '*mad*' insert 'B. 11.45 S.-M.'

**παραπληξία** **I**, delete '*IG* 12(9).1179' **II**, after 'Lxx *De.* 28.28' insert '(quoted in *IG* 12(9).1179)'

**παραπλομένοισι**, add '(cf. περιπέλομαι)'

***παραπλωΐζω** (-πλωζ- cod.), *to be situated* or *move alongside the road,* Hsch.; cf. πλόος 4 b.

***παραποδίδωμι**, med., *sell below market price,* παρααποδόσθαι (sic) *IHistriae* 20 (ii BC); cf. παράπρασις.

**παραποθνήσκω**, add 'Men.*Dysc.* 379 (s.v.l.)'

**παραποίησις**, after '*forgery*' insert '*AS* 10.71 no.124 (pl.) (Pisidia, ii AD)'

***παραπόκειμαι**, *to be laid up in store, PBeatty Panop.* 1.208 (AD 298).

**παραπομπή**, add '**III** *delegation* of jurisdiction, εἴτε αὐτόθεν κατὰ τὴν φύσιν τῆς οἰκείας δικάσειεν ἀρχῆς εἴτε καὶ ἐκ παραπομπῆς ἡμετέρας Just.*Nov.* 20.7.'

**παραπομπικά**, add '*Cod.Just.* 10.30.4.4'

**παραπομπός** **I 1**, add 'as subst., *escort* (= Lat. *prosecutor*), *POxy.* 3635.3 (v AD)' add '**III** app. functionary in religious processions, *BCH* 11.12 (Caria).'

**παραπόντιος**, add 'also α, ον, ἐπὶ τῆς ἀγχιθαλάσσου δὲ παραποντίας *EA* 14 p.22 l.34 (Ephesus, i AD)'

**παραπόρφυρος**, after '*edged with purple*' insert 'Plu. 2.330a'

***παραπότᾰμος**, ον, of land, *riverside, POxy.* 2847 i 9 (iii AD).

**παράπτομαι** **II 1**, add 'μηδὲν ὅλως παραψάμενος τῶν ἁγίων (sc. χρημάτων) *BCH* 56.293 (Stobi, ii/iii AD)'

**παράπτωμα** **I 3**, add '*SEG* 31.1562 (iv/v AD)'

***παραράβδωσις**, εως, ἡ, prob. *fence* or *railing, AS* 12.198 (Cilicia, i/ii AD).

***παράρραπτος**, ον, *sewn as a fringe, IG* 7.2421.7 (Thebes, παρραπτ-).

**παραρρέω** **II 2**, for 'also .. etc.' read 'abs., *drift from course, err*'

**παράρρυθμος** **I**, add '(*dancing*) *in irregular measure,* of the Curetes, Orph.*H.* 31.3 [παράρυθμοι]' **II**, delete the section.

**παράρρῡμα**, (sp. παράρ-), add 'παραρύματα λευ[κά] (?canvas), *SEG* 24.159(b).328; π. τρί[χινα] ib. 330 (326/5 BC)'

**παράρτημα** **II**, for 'dub. sens. in' read '*appendix, supplement*'; add 'cf. mod. Gk. παράρτημα'

+**παραρτίζομαι**, *prepare,* ναῦς παραρτισάμενος Plu.*Luc.* 7.6; παραρτίζεσθαι· παρασκευάζεσθαι Hsch.

**παραρτύω** **II**, delete the section.

***παρασεβέω**, *to be impious, Sokolowski* 2.33.A11 (Dyme, iii BC).

**παράσειρος** **I**, add '**2** παράσειρον, τό, app. kind of large sack, τὸ .. παράσιρον τὸ στυπέϊνον ἐν ὧι τὰς λʹ ἀρτάβας τῶν ἀλφίτων κατήγαγον *Pap.Lugd.Bat.* xx 54.10 (iii BC).'

**παρασεύω**, for '*rush past*' read '*speed past* or *alongside*' and add 'Nonn.*D.* 37.387'

**παρασημαίνομαι** **I**, add 'also act., παρασημαίνει· παραχαράττει, παραδηλοῖ Hsch.'

**παράσημον** **I**, after 'or *note*' insert 'or *diacritical sign*' **II 1 a**, add '*distinguishing characteristic,* τῆς Δημοσθένους συνθέσεως D.H.*Dem.* 50'

+**παράσῑρον**, τό, v. °παράσειρος.

**παράσῑτος** **II 1**, add '*OGI* 195.2 (Egypt, i BC)'

***παρασκᾰφίτης**, ου, ὁ, *boatman,* Teuc.Bab. p. 47 B. (-σκαρ- cod.), v. Robert *Hell.* 1.143.

**παρασκευάζω** **A 1**, add '**b** intr., *get ready,* ἕκαστος ἐν τῷ καθ' ἑαυτὸν παρασκευάσει δικαστηρίῳ Just.*Const.Δέδωκεν* 24.' **2**, line 4, after 'D. 28.17' insert '*produce, cause,* τοὺς ὄγκους καὶ τὰ καύματα Diocl.*fr.* 43' **3**, line 5, delete '*accustom*'; line 6, delete '*accustom* it not to ..' and after '*Eq.* 2.3' insert 'w. acc. & inf., τὸν πόλεμον μέχρις ἀπειλῶν προκόψαι Memn. 15 J.; φρονεῖν ὑμᾶς D.Chr. 33.23' **5**, delete the section (transferred to section 2). **B I 2**, line 7, for 'Is. 8.3' read 'τοῦτον π. πράγμαθ' ἡμῖν παρέχειν Is. 8.3'

**παρασκευαστικός** **3**, add 'τὰ π., title of treatise by Heraclid.Cum., Ath. 4.145a'

**παρασκευή** **II**, add 'in Chr. use, *Friday, BCH* suppl. 8 no. 270 (v/vi AD), *Cod.Just.* 1.4.22.1'

**παρασκηνόω** **I**, delete the section.

***παρασπαίρω**, *gasp beside,* w. dat., θυηλαῖς Nic.*fr.* 62.2.

**παρασπιστής**, after '*companion in arms*' insert 'A.*fr.* 303 R.'

**παρασπορά** **1**, after '*sowing*' insert '*PStrassb.* 267.10 (AD 126/8)'

***παρασταθμία**, ἡ, *deficiency in weight, PAmst.*inv. 39.21 (*CE* 1973.128, iv/v AD), *POxy.* 132 (*CE* l.c., vi/vii AD).

**παραστάς** **1**, line 1, after 'ἡ' insert 'acc. sg. -στάδαν *IHadr.* 1 (ii AD)'; line 5, for 'also in sg.' read 'sg., part of a catapult'

**παράστᾰσις** **I 3**, add '*delivery* to a person, εἰς παράστασιν στρατηγοῦ (?for -ῷ) *POxy.* 2139.3, *SB* 10270.1, 5, 9, etc. (see *BASP* 11.46)' **5**, add '**b** perh. *presentation* of a candidate (for entry to a tribe, deme, etc.), *POxy.* 3463.19 (AD 58).' **II 2**, delete the section.

**παραστᾰ́τις**, after lemma insert '(παρστάτις, epigr. in *Hesperia* 23.63 (Athens))'

**παραστεγάζω**, delete the entry.

**παράστημα**, after 'Dor.' insert 'Boeot.' and after '(Epid., iii BC)' insert '*BCH* 20.324 (Lebadea)'

***παραστόμιον**, τό, *muzzle,* Hsch. s.v. φίμα (read φιμά or φιμός).

***παραστόμιος**, ον, *of* or *belonging to the side of the mouth,* in quot. app. of an article of harness, *IG* $1^3$.422.239.

**παραστρᾰτεύομαι**, add '*POxy.* 2902 ii 9 (AD 272)'

***παρασυγγρᾰφή**, ἡ, *breach of contract, PSI* 903.22 (i AD).

***παρασυμβαίνω**, *occur additionally,* Just.*Nov.* 7.2 pr.

***παρασυνᾰ́γω**, *hold heretical assemblies,* Just.*Nov.* 132.

**παρασύναξις**, for '*clandestine religious assembly*' read '*the holding of a heretical assembly*' and for '*Cod.Just.* 1.5.8.3, 5' read '*Cod.Just.* 1.5.14, 1.5.20.2; in Lat. transliteration, ib. 1.5.8.3, 5'

**παρασύνθημα**, for pres. def. read '*countersign*'

**παρασύρω** **2**, before 'Plb. 16.4.14' insert 'Tim.*Pers.* 6'

***παρασφρᾱγιστής**, οῦ, ὁ, *maker of counterfeit seals,* Teuc.Bab. p. 42 B.

**παρασχιστής**, after 'D.S. 1.91' insert 'Ptol.*Tetr.* 179'

**παρασωρεύω**, add 'τροφὴν π. Aesop. 6 P.'

**παρατᾰτικός**, adv. -ῶς, add '*in an extended sense,* Julian *Dig.* 38.7.1, Ulp.*Dig.* 42.4.2.4'

**παρατείνω** **I 2**, add 'Men.*Sam.* 544'

***παρατέλειος**, α, ον, prob. nearly *full-sized, PHaw.* 208.9, al. (*ZPE* 93.206, i AD).

***παρατενίζω**, *turn one's gaze aside* (*immodestly*), π. ὀφθαλμοῖς (?)Aq.*Is.* 3.16 (L.-R.); cf. ἀτενίζω.

**παρατίθημι A 3**, add 'τὴν ἀσπίδα ἐπίθημα τῷ φρέατι π. Ar.*fr.* 306 K.-A.' **B 2 a**, lines 4/5, delete 'Plb. 3.17.10' and after '*deposit*' insert 'or *put into official hands*'; before '*POxy.*' insert '*UPZ* 162 ix 7 (ii BC), Wilcken *Chr.* 26.35 (ii AD); pass. *to be appended*' **b**, after '*store up*' insert 'χρήματα Plb. 3.17.10' **5**, last line, for 'v.l. in Id.*Comp.*' read 'cf. id.*Is.* 13'

**+παράτιτλον**, τό, *marginal scholium* or *note*, *Cod.Just.* 1.17.2.21, Just. *Const.*Δέδωκεν 21.

***παράτομος**, ὁ, *section*, of a field, *SB* 9134.4, 5 (ii AD), also perh. *PPrincet.* 172.10 (ii AD, *ZPE* 70.141).

***παρατουρᾶς**, ᾶ, ὁ, *maker* or *seller of furnishing materials*, *ITyr* 133.

**παρᾱτούριον**, delete '(Lat. *antepannus*)'

**παρατρᾰγῳδέω**, before 'Poll.' insert 'Stratt. 50 K.-A.; παρατραγῳδήσαί τι μοι ἐκ[ Com. in *Lex.Mess.* fol. 282ᵛ4'

***παρατρᾰ́πιος**, η, ον, (ἀτραπός) *situated by the wayside*, *AP* 9.706.5 (Antip.).

***παρατρεπτικός**, ή, όν, *averting*, Sch.E.*Andr.* 527.

**παρατρέπω 7**, add 'Afric.*Cest.* p. 59 V.'

**παρατρέχω 5**, delete 'abs., of time, Hdn. 2.12.4' add '**6** *run* or *extend alongside*, ἀλλ' αὔτως λείη παραδέδρομεν *Suppl.Hell.* 944.8. **7** of a period of time, *elapse*, Hdn. 2.12.4, *Cod.Just.* 1.4.32.2, Just.*Nov.* 1.4 pr.'

**παράτρητος**, for '*pierced at the side* .. airs' read 'of a tube, etc., *having an orifice set to one side*: αὐλὸς π. kind of pipe making a sound suitable for mournful music'

**παρατρῖβή 2**, for 'Ath. 14.626e' read 'Plb. 4.21.5' and add '30.27.2'

**παράτροπος II**, delete 'where Sch. expl. παρατροπικός'

**παρατροχάζω 2**, after '*APl.* 4.169' insert '*SEG* 34.342 (Achaea, ii/iii AD)'

***παράτῠλος**, ὁ, archit., *collateral* metal *thole* linking two blocks, *Didyma* 41.47 (ii BC).

**παραύα I**, for 'prob. in Theoc. 30.5' read 'Theoc. 30.4' add 'cf. Myc. *pa-ra-wa-jo* (dual), *cheek-pieces* of helmet'

**+παραυλέω**, cited by Pollux as compd. of αὐλέω without indication of sense, Poll. 4.67.

**παραφαίνω I 1**, line 3, after 'Ar.*Ec.* 94' insert 'γυμνὸς .. παρεφαίνετο μαζός Call.*Dian.* 214'

***παραφᾰσία**, ή, poet. παραιφασίη, *consolation*, *comfort*, Musae.*fr.* 22 D.-K., *Epigr.Gr.* 421.2, Nonn.*D.* 11.207, 48.133; (w. gen.) *consolation* for, Nonn.*D.* 11.365. **2** *advice*, *persuasion*, A.R. 2.324, 3.554, Euph. in *Suppl.Hell.* 415 i 10, poet. in *Suppl.Hell.* 956.3 (all pl.).

**παράφᾰσις** (A) **1**, after 'Il. 11.793' insert 'Aret.*SD* 1.2, Them.*Or.* 8.106d, Nonn.*D.* 40.115' and after '*APl.* 5.373.3' add 'πόνου *AP* 5.284; εὗρε σοφὸς λιμοῦ με παραίφασιν poet.ap.Orion s.v. πεσσοί, *SEG* 31.291 (Corinth, *c.*v AD)'

***παραφερνικαῖος**, α, ον, = °παραφερνιμαῖος, προικιμαῖα καὶ παραφερνικαῖα πράγματα *PNess.* 33.14 (vi AD).

***παραφερνιμαῖος**, α, ον, *that is in addition to a dowry*, *extradotal*, *PNess.* 18.25 (vi AD).

**παραφέρω III 1**, line 4, after 'Hp.*Art.* 12' insert 'π. τὰς κώπας Arr.*An.* 2.21.9' **IV**, line 3, after 'Plu. 2.432b' insert 'metaph., π. κατακέφαλα *POxy.* 1853.5 (vi/vii AD)'

***παραφησῠχάζω**, *settle down* in one's relations with, *PCair.Isidor.* 75.20 (iv AD; sp. παραπ-).

***παραφοβέω**, *drive aside in fright*, Ion Trag. 43c S.

***παραφόρετρον**, τό, *charge for transport*, *POxy.* 3169.178 (ii/iii AD).

**παράφορος I 3**, add '-φόρως *in a frenzied manner*, Gal. 8.484.16, 9.188.11'

**παραφρῡγᾰνισμός**, for 'ib. p. 100' read '*PPetr.* 2 p. 17 (iii BC)'

***παραφῠλᾰκεία**, ή, *office of a* παραφύλαξ, Robert *Hell.* 10.250 (Acmonia, iii AD); also -ία, *TAM* 2(3).838d7 (Lycia, ii AD), *IGRom.* 3.649.7.

***παραφῠλᾰκεῖον**, τό, *police-* or *garrison-building*, *TAM* 3(1).14A14 (Termessus, ii AD).

**παραφῠλᾰκή II 1 b**, after '*garrison-duty*' read 'form -ακά, *SEG* 26.1817 (Arsinoe Cyrenaica, ii/i BC), *Notiz.Arch.* 4.20.15 (Cyrene, Augustus)' add '**III** *precautionary stipulation*, εἴ τις δὲ παρὰ ταύτην τὴν παραφυλακὴν γυναῖκα ἐν τῷ ἰδίῳ οἴκῳ σχῇ Just.*Nov.* 123.29.'

***παραφῠλᾰκία**, v. °παραφυλακεία.

**παραφῠλᾰκίτης**, for '*IGRom.* 4.896 (Phrygia), *CIG* 4366*x* (Pisidia)' read 'Ramsay *The Social Basis* 106 (Cappadocia)'

**παραφύλαξ**, for '*watcher, guard*' read 'name of an official, perh. *chief of police*, *OGI* 527 (Hierapolis)'; for '(Aphrodisias)' read '(Apollonia Salbace), *MDAI(A)* 68.23 (Samos, ii AD), *IEphes.* 612a, 1579, al., *JHS* 29.166 (ii AD)'

**παραφυλάσσω III**, after 'παραφύλαξ' insert '(q.v. with Suppl.)'; add '*OGI* 485.7 (Magnesia ad Maeandrum), *SEG* 34.1107 (Ephesus)'

**παραχειμάζω**, add '**II** pass., app. *to be blown off course by a storm*, *CPR* 7.60.14 (vi/vii AD).'

**παραχειμαστικός**, add '**2** neut. pl., π. λεγιώνων *winter-quarters* or *tax for maintenance in winter-quarters*, *MEFR* 55.57 (Thyatira, ii AD).'

***παράχορδος**, ον, *discordant*, Phot. s.v. παρακεχόρδικεν.

**παραχρῆμα 1**, add 'εὐθὺς καὶ παραχρῆμα *Cod.Just.* 1.3.52.6'

**+παραψῐδάζω**, perh. *spatter*, Hippon. 92 W.; cf. perh. ψίδες *droplets*.

***παρβάδᾱν**, adv. *by transgression*, A.*Eu.* 553 (sch., codd. περβάδαν, περαιβάδαν; see παραβάτης II).

**παρβαίνω**, before '-βασία' insert '-βάλλω'; for 'poet. for παραβ-' read 'see παραβ-'

***παργίγνομαι**, v. ‡παραγίγνομαι.

**πάρδᾰλις I**, add 'applied to prostitute, τὴν πόρδαλιν καλοῦσι τὴν κασαλβάδα Ar.*fr.* 494 K.-A.'

***παρδίδωμι, πάρδοσις**, v. παραδίδωμι, ‡παράδοσις.

***παρεγγρᾰφή**, ή, perh. *interpolation*, *SEG* 33.1177.9, 29, 40 (Lycia, i AD).

**παρέγγρᾰφος**, add 'Philoch. 119 J.'

**παρεδρεία I**, add 'οἱ ἀπὸ τῆς π., perh. = οἱ πάρεδροι *PSI* 1357.9 (ii AD)'

**παρεδριάω**, add 'παρεδριώ‹ο›ντι *IG* 10(2).1.447.10 (Thessalonica, ii/iii AD)'

**πάρεδρος II 1**, penultimate line, after '*Hell.Oxy.* 10.1' insert '(s.v.l.)'

**παρείκω I 2**, delete the section.

**πάρειμι** (εἰμί) **II**, add 'Ar.*Eq.* 330'

**παρείρω**, line 2, after 'Plb. 18.18.13' insert 'λόγον εἰς τοὺς Φιλιππικοὺς Did.*in D.* 13.17'

**παρεισβαίνω**, delete the entry (v. °παρεκβαίνω).

**παρεισδύνω**, line 2, after 'Demad. 3' insert 'Call.*Epigr.* 44.5 Pf.'; after 'A.D.*Synt.* 319.24' insert 'Hld. 1.12, 7.27'

**παρείσοδος**, add 'of a stage entrance, Sch.S.*Aj.* 66'

**παρεισπορεύομαι**, for '*enter*' read '*infiltrate*'

**παρέκ A II 3**, after '*contrary to*' insert 'Call.*fr.* 186.7 Pf.' **4**, after '*beside*' insert 'τέρψιές εἰσι θεῆς πολλαὶ .. παρὲξ τὸ θεῖον χρῆμα Archil. 196a.13 W.' **B 4**, at end after 'Plb. 3.23.3' insert 'Lxx *Ez.* 15.4'

***παρεκάτεροι**, οἱ, *those on each side*, *Vit.Aesop.*(G) 25 (παρακ- cod.).

**παρεκβαίνω**, before '*step*' insert 'Cret. **παρεσβ-** poet. in *Inscr.Cret.* 1.xxiii 3 (Phaestus, ii BC)'

**παρεκδέχομαι**, after '*misconstrue*' insert 'Plb. 15.25.35'

***παρέκκειμαι**, *to be put aside*, Porph.*in Harm.* p. 88 D.

**παρεκνέομαι**, after 'A.R. 2' insert '651' and after '941' add '1243'

***παρεκπέτομαι**, *fly out and past*, παρεξέπτη Plu. 2.806e.

**παρεκπίπτω**, add '**II** *fall to pieces*, of papyri, prob. in *PFam.Teb.* 15.71 (i/ii AD).'

**παρεκτείνω I**, add '**b** *stretch out beyond*, w. gen., εἰ .. μὴ τοῦ ἀναγκαίου πουλὺ παρεξετάθης *AP* 9.643 (Agath.). **2** *make coextensive with*, τῇ ναυμαχίᾳ τὴν βύβλον π. D.H.*Th.* 12. **3** pass., *to be strained*, τὸ .. -τεταμένον *intensity*, Aristid.Quint. 2.10.'

**παρεκτός I**, add '*SEG* 26.434'

***παρελαιν**, ὁ, prob. non-Hellenic name of a cult-object, *Inscr.Cret.* 1.v 23.5 (Arcades, ii AD).

**παρελαύνω II 1 b**, add 'fig., Parm. 8.61'

**παρέλκω II**, abs., add '*EA* 12.150 no. 3, l. 4 (Lydia, ii/iii AD)'; after 'Luc.*Am.* 54' insert 'παρελκύσαντος δὲ αὐτοῦ χρόνον *SEG* 35.1164.8 (Lydia, ii AD)'

**παρεμβαίνω**, for 'τεθρίππῳ .. etc.' read '**2** παρεμβεβηκὼς *riding as a passenger in*, τεθρίππῳ D.H. 2.34; ἐφ' ἁρματείου δίφρου id. 5.47.'

**παρεμβολή III**, for this section read '*ramming at an oblique angle*, Plb. 21.7.4 (cj. παραβ-)'

**+παρεμβολικός**, ή, όν, *of* or *connected with a* (*military*) *camp*, δεῖπνα Plu. 2.643d; of the possessions of a dead soldier, *PWisc.* 14 (AD 131).

***παρέμβροχος**, ον, *slightly tipsy*, *Vit.Aesop.*(G) 68.

**παρεμπίπτω I 3**, add 'of a word *inserted* for euphony, D.H.*Dem.* 40'

**παρέμπτωσις 2**, for 'D.H.*Amm.* 2.2' read 'D.H.*Th.* 24 (pl.)'

**παρεμφερής**, add 'Isid.Trag. 1'

**παρεμφέρω I**, add '**2** med., *to be in association with*, *PBonn.*inv. 2.16 (*JJP* 18.43).' **II 2**, for '*float in as well*' read '*be suspended*'

**παρεμφύομαι**, add 'Alcin.*Intr.* p. 178.27 H.'

**παρενδείκνυμαι 1**, add '**b** w. nom. and inf., *assume arrogantly*, Call.*Dieg.* vii.4 (*fr.* 194 Pf.).'

**παρενδημέω**, add 'τοῖς παρενδα[με]όντοις decr. in *ZPE* 101.128 (Dyme, ii BC)'

**παρένθετος II**, add '*SEG* 32.1554 (Arabia, vi AD)'

**παρενθήκη**, add '**III** *surety*, *guarantor* (cf. Lat. *intercessor*), Just.*Nov.* 4.1.'

***παρενσκάζω**, app. *hobble along*, Aq.*Is.* 3.16 L.-R.

**παρεντίθημι I**, add '**3** *add*, μὴ ἐγγράφου γενομένου τοῦ δανείσματος μηδὲ ἐπερωτήσεως παρεντεθείσης Just.*Nov.* 136.4.'

**παρεξᾰμείβω**, add '**II** (tm.) παρὲκ γόνυ γουνὸς ἀμείβων perh. *getting* his knee *past* the other's knee, A.R. 2.94.'

**παρεξετάζω**, line 2, after '*τί τινι*' insert 'D.H.*Dem.* 36'

***παρεξοχή**, *ἡ*, wd. of uncertain meaning, *Poliorc.* 220.20, etc.

***παρεπικόπτω**, *satirize by the way*, w. acc., Call.*Dieg.* vi.30 (*fr.* 192 Pf., *παρεκοπτων* pap.), 37.

***Παρεπιλυκάρχης**, *ου*, *ὁ*, leader of the *Παρεπίλυκοι*, I.Nicolaou *viii*[e] *Congrès international d'épigraphie: Communications* p. 111.

***Παρεπίλυκοι**, *οἱ*, members of an otherwise unknown society, *ἔδοξεν τοῖς ἐπὶ Λυκίης καὶ Παρεπιλύκ[οις]* I.Nicolaou, op. cit. s.v. °*Παρεπιλυκάρχης*.

⁺**παρεπιφέρω**, *carry towards one's destination*, *Peripl.M.Rubr.* 57 (cod.).

***παρέργιον**, *τό*, perh. *waste piece*, *offcut* or sim., rest. in *PKöln* 52.34, 83 (AD 263).

**πάρεργος I**, add '**2** of persons, *unimportant*, *Ἑλλήνων οὐχ ὁ παρεργότατος GVI* 1876.4 (Termessus, ?ii AD).' **II**, neut. subst., add '*μᾶλλον τὸ πάρεργον ἐπεκράτησ' ἢ τοὔνομα* (the subst. *μᾶνία* prevailed over the name *Μᾶνία*) Macho 210 G.'

**παρέρχομαι III 1**, add 'abs., X.*Smp.* 1.7'

***παρερῶ**, (fut.) = *παράφημι* 2, Sch.Pi.*O.* 7.111, 117.

**παρέστιος**, add 'w. dat., *at home* in, Opp.*H.* 1.249'

***παρεσχᾰρίτης**, *ου*, *ὁ*, *one who sits by the hearth*, Eust. 1564.28.

**παρετέον I**, add 'Arist.*EN* 1172[a]26'

***παρετικός**, *ή*, *όν*, *palsied*, Asclep.Jun.ap.Gal. 13.1022.2.

**παρετοιμᾰσία**, add '*apparatus* or *equipment*, Sch.B Il. 21.490'

***παρετῠμολογία**, *ἡ*, *allusion to etymology*, *An.Ox.* 3.383.21.

**παρευτακτέω**, for '*BCH* 55.439' read '*Inscr.Délos* 2598'

⁺**παρεύτακτος**, *ὁ*, *a former ephebe* (cf. *εὔτακτος*), *Inscr.Délos* 2593.52, al., 2598.6 (ii BC), Lucil. 321, 752 M., *IG* 2².2998, 2999 (i BC), 2094 (ii AD); fem. *pareutactae* prob. in Varro *gram.* 89.

⁺**παρεφηβεία**, *ἡ*, *status of a* °*παρέφηβος*, *GVI* 1154 (Samos, ii/i BC).

***παρέφηβος**, *ὁ*, *a young man of the age succeeding that of ἔφηβος*, *IG* 12(3).339.23, 340.19 (Thera, i AD).

**παρέχω**, line 4, after 'Hes.*Th.* 639' insert 'opt. *παρασχέθοι* A.*fr.* 78a.13 R.' and after 'Ar.*Eq.* 321' insert '(troch.)' **A II 3**, at end for '*δέμασὰ κέντητον*' read '*δέμας ἀκέντητον*' **III 2**, line 4, after '*El.* 1080' insert 'without dat., prob. in Favorin.*Exil.* 23.11' **B**, line 2, after 'Lys. 9.8' insert '1 aor. inf. *παρέξασθαι IGBulg.* 43.19 (Odessus, i BC)'

***παρηγόριος**, *ὁ*, perh. *consoler*, *PMich.*xv 740.21 (vi AD), *PMasp.* 58.

**παρήγορος**, line 3, for '*Epigr.Gr.* 344' read '*IHadr.* 80 (ii AD)'

***παρηΐδιος**, *α*, *ον*, *of the cheeks*, *μᾶλα AP* 9.556 (Zon.).

**παρήκω I**, add '*lie beside* in the grave, *TAM* 4(1).267' **III 3**, add '**b** *ἐκ τοῦ παρήκοντος as it happens*, *fortuitously*, Just.*Nov.* 1.1.4, 90.2.'

⁺**παρῆλιξ**, *ικος*, *ὁ*, *ἡ*, *not of a suitable age*: *over age*, *too old*, Plu.*Alex.* 32; comp. -*έστερος* Sor. 1.15. **2** *under age*, *PVindob.Salomons* 5.12, 25, 29 (ii AD), *POxy.* 1257.2 (iii AD); transf., of actions, *AP* 12.228 (Strat.).

**πάρημαι 1**, line 2, after 'only part.' insert 'in Homer' **2**, add 'impf. *παρείατο* used as sg., *κούρη δὲ π. δακρυχέουσα* Call.*fr.* 497 Pf.'

***παρημερινός**, *ή*, *όν*, = *παρήμερος* II, *PTeb.* 275.22 (iii AD).

**παρήχημα**, for pres. def. read '*instance of παρήχησις*'

**παρήχησις**, for '= foreg.' read '*the use of words alike in sound but different in meaning*'

**παρηχητικός**, for '*alliterative*' read '*of* or *belonging to παρήχησις*'; for 'Eust. 1638.17' read '*with παρήχησις*, Eust. 1638.15'

**παρθενεία**, last line, of a man, add 'Just.*Nov.* 6.1.3'

**παρθένειος**, line 2, after 'Pi.*N.* 8.2' insert '*παρθενήϊα φρονεῖν* id.*fr.* 94b.34 S.-M.'

**παρθένευμα 2**, for this section read '= *παρθενεία*, E.*Ion* 1473'

**παρθενεύω 2**, add '*Cod.Just.* 1.3.52.14'

**παρθένια**, add '**II** = *παρθένεια* I, *τέ[κτονι πα]ρθενίων σοφῶν Ἀλκμᾶ[νι* poet. in *POxy.* 2389 *fr.* 9.'

**παρθενική**, add '**2** a plant, app. = *παρθένιον* 1, *feverfew*, Cat. 61.187.'

**παρθενικός II**, neut. subst., add '**2** = *π. χιτών*, *Dura*[4] 100 (pl.).'

**παρθένιος I 2**, add 'without *ἀνήρ*, *bridegroom*, *AP* 7.384.7 (Marc.Arg.)'

**παρθένος I**, add '**6** metaph., of the number seven, Hierocl.*in CA* p. 465 M.' add 'see also *φαρθένος*'

**παρθενών II**, lines 2/3, for 'also, of the cella' read '**b** the apartment occupied by virgin priestesses' and add 'also in other temples'

**Παρθικός**, add 'as title of Roman emperors, *SEG* 32.461, 33.1130, etc.'

**πάρθυμα**, delete the entry.

***παρθῡμαται**, nom. pl. (masc. or fem.), perh. *additional sacrificial victims*, *Inscr.Cret.* 4.65.9 (Gortyn, vi BC).

***παριαμβίζω**, v. *ἰαμβαυλεῖν*.

***παριαμβίς**, *ίδος*, *ἡ*, prob. kind of music or rhythm played on the lyre, later interpreted as an instrument, Epich. 109, Apollod.ap.Hsch.

**παρίαμβος III**, for '*harp*' read '*κιθάρα*'

**παρίημι**, line 3, after '*HP* 5.3.6' insert 'med. aor. 2 *παρείμην* S.*OC* 1666'; line 4, delete 'aor. 2 .. 1666' **II 3**, add '*εὖτ' ἂν τὸ νέον παρῇ let go by*, S.*OC* 1229 (lyr.), cf. Pl.*R.* 460e'

**Πάρινα**, delete the entry.

***πάρινος**, *η*, *ον*, *of marble*, Lxx *Es.* 1.6, *ABSA* 56.5 (Paphos, ii BC), *Syria* 17.260.5 (iii AD), 18.372 (both Palmyra).

**Πάριος** (s.v. *Πάρος*), after 'D.S. 2.52' add 'cf. °*πάρινος*. **b** as cult-title of Demeter, *SEG* 33.684 (Paros).'

**παρίστημι B**, after 'aor. 2' insert '(2 sg. imper. *παράστα* Men.*fr.* 110 K.-Th., *Th.* 28, perh. w. transference to thematic inflexion, cf. *ἀπόστα*)'; after 'plpf. act.' insert '(also fut. pf. *παρεστήξεις* Men.*Dysc.* 364)' add '**VIII** *γῆ παρεσταμένη rented* or *mortgaged* farmland, Hsch.; cf. *ἵστημι* B II 2 at end.'

**παριστορέω I**, for '*inquire by the way*' read '*learn by the way*' **II**, add 'Did.ap.Porph. *in Harm.* p. 28.25 D., Sch.Theoc. 1.117'

***παριωνικός**, *ή*, *όν*, *quasi-Ionic*, *μέτρον*, of the Anacreontic verse, *POxy.* 220[r] vii 7.

***παρμενίσκος**, *ὁ*, ornament of a door, *Inscr.Délos* 1428ii67, 1429*B*ii13 (ii BC); also a common pers.n.

***Παρνᾱσιάς**, *άδος*, fem. adj., *of Parnassus*, E.*Ion* 86 (cod. *Παρνησ-*).

***Παρνᾱσιος** or **Παρνάσσιος**, *α*, *ον*, (also *ος*, *ον*, E.*IT* 1244 (lyr.)), *Parnassian*, Pi.*P.* 10.8, Limen. 22, etc: also **Παρνήσσιος**, *IG* 2².1258.24 (iv BC); as cult-title of Zeus, *[Δι]ὸς Παρ[ν]ησσίο SEG* 34.39 (Athens, 500/480 BC), *[Διὸς Πα]ρνεσίο SEG* 33.244 (Attica).

***Παρνᾱσίς** (*Παρνασσ-*), *ίδος*, fem. adj., *of Parnassus*, *Pae.Delph.* 4; also *Παρνησσίς* A.*Ch.* 563.

⁺**Παρνᾱσός** or **Παρνασσός**, Ion. **Παρνησός** or **Παρνησσός**, *ὁ*, *Parnassus*, Od. 19.432, Hes.*Th.* 499, Th. 3.95.1, etc.

***πάρο**, Aeol., = *πάρεστι*, Alc. 130.12 L.-P.; cf. *ἐνό*, *ἔνο*, *ἐξό*.

***παρό** (B), Myc. *pa-ro*, v. ‡*παρά*.

**παροδεύω**, add '**4** *enter the arena*, inscr. in *ZPE* 1.105-6 (Side, iii AD).'

**παροδοιπόρος**, add '*GVI* 428.1 (Ephesus, ii BC)'

**πάροδος** (B) **II b**, for 'on the stage' read 'into the orchestra, *IG* 12(9).207.55 (prob.) (Eretria, *c.*290 BC)'

**παροικίζω**, after '*τινά τινι*' insert '*AP* 7.287 (Antip.), 448 (Leon. Tarent.)'

***παροίνησις**, *εως*, *ἡ*, = *παροινία*, Anon. *in Rh.* 327.13 (pl.).

**παροίνια**, add 'transf., *rowdiness*, *PMich.*inv. 6979 (*ZPE* 76.251, 215 BC)'

**παροίνιος II**, after 'Ph. 1.353' insert '*αὐλοί* Poll. 4.80' and after 'Sch.Ar.*V.* 1217, 1231' insert '*τὸ π. βοήσω Anacreont.* 2.8 W.'

**παροίτερος I 1**, line 2, after '*in front of*' insert 'Arat. 306'

**παροίχομαι I 2**, add '*ὑπὲρ τοῦ παρῳχηθέντος ὀγδόου ἔτους PMich.*xi 617.17 (ii AD)'

**παρολκή III**, delete the section.

***πάρολκον**, *τό*, ?*towrope*, *OBodl.* 72 (ii AD), *PLond.* 1164(h).10 (iii AD), *POxy.* 997 (iv AD), Sch.Th. 4.25.

**πάρολκος I**, delete the section.

***παρομφάλιος**, *ον*, *along* or *near the middle*, v.l. for *κατομφ-*, Nic.*Th.* 290.

**παρονομᾰσία I 1**, line 2, after 'Cic.*de Orat.* 2.63.256' insert 'D.H.*Th.* 48' **II**, for '*derivative*' read '*pronoun*'; delete '*by-name* .. (pl.)'

**παρονομᾰτοποιέω**, delete the entry (read *ὀνοματοποιέω*).

**παροξυντικός I 2**, after 'Hp.*Prorrh.* 1.50' insert 'Gal. 11.393.11, 14'

**πάροξυς**, add '**III** *somewhat sharp* in taste, in quot. gloss on *ὀμφακίας* Hsch.'

***παρόρεγμα**, *ατος*, *τό*, *allowance*, *honorarium*, *δαμιεργοῖς SEG* 9.11.19, al. (Cyrene, iv BC).

**παρόρειος**, for 'the form *παρώρειος* .. Subst.' read 'see also °*παρώρειος*'

**παρορίζω I**, delete the section.

⁺**παρόριος** (A), v. *παρόρειος*.

⁺**παρόριος** (B), *ον*, *situated along a boundary*, Plu. 2.366b; w. dat., *τῇ Αἰθιοπίᾳ OGI* 168.57 (Syene, ii BC); *τὰ παρόρια space along boundaries*, *POxy.* 1475.22 (iii AD).

**παρορισμός**, for '*removal of landmarks*' read '*infringement of boundaries*, *encroachment*' and add '*PGen.* 99 (ii AD)'

**παρορκέω**, add '*SEG* 26.1386 (Phrygia)'

***παρορκία**, *ἡ*, *perjury*, *MDAI(A)* 29.331 (*GRBS* 17.265, Phrygia).

***παρορμητήριον**, *τό*, gloss on *ῥωστήριον*, Phot.

***παρορμήτης**, *ου*, *ὁ*, *encourager*, Hsch. s.v. *τάρροθοι*.

**παρορμίζω**, for '*Μουνυχίασιν*' read '*[Μουνυχίασιν]*'; add 'pap. in *SHAW* (1923)2.23'

***παρορῠγή**, *ἡ*, *burying*, *digging in alongside*, *σκολόπων* Rh. 1.436.18 (pl.); cf. *ὀρύσσω* IV.

**πάρος**, line 1, after 'poet. Particle' insert '(also in prose, *SEG* 37.340.14 (Mantinea, iv BC))'

**παρουλίς**, line 1, for '*οὐλή*' read '*οὖλον*'

**παρουσία I 3**, delete the section adding 'S.*El.* 1251' to section I 1.

**παροχέομαι**, for '*sit beside in a chariot*' read '*ride beside* another *in a vehicle*' and add 'spec. of the groomsman at a wedding, Men.*Sic.* 404 S.; cf. ‡*πάροχος* (A)'

**παροχετευτέον**, add 'Gal. 10.861.9'

***παροχία**, ἡ, = παροχή, *provision*, *SB* 9907.23 (AD 388).

**πάροχος** (A), line 1, for '*one who sits beside* another *in a chariot*' read '*one who rides beside* another *in a vehicle*'; line 4, for 'συμπαρέστη' read 'συμπάρεστι'

**παρρησία 3**, add '*freedom and fearlessness* of aspect, Sch.Pi.*N.* 10.73'

***πάρριζος**, v. ‡πάνριζος.

***παρστᾰτις**, v. ‡παραστάτις.

***παρτέλλεται**· παραινεῖται (read παρανεῖται) Hsch.

**παρυπάρχω**, before '*attend*' insert '*partly begin*, pf. part. pass. παρυπηργμένον prob. in *IG* 2².1522.20. **2**' at end add 'cf. Plu. *Lib.* 5'

***παρυπερέχω**, *project partly beyond*, Hero *Bel.* 88.

***παρυπεύκυκλος**, ον, *somewhat round*, Poet.*de herb.* 134 (codd.).

***παρυποκρούω**, perh. *offend by meddling*, Call.*Dieg.* vii.3 (*fr.* 194 Pf.).

***παρύπτιος**, ον, *"concave"*, used of a geometrical plane figure *with a re-entrant angle*, Papp. 652.20; cf. °ὕπτιος VII.

**παρφ-**, for compds. of παρά v. παραφ-.

**πάρφαινε**, delete the entry.

***παρφυροῦς**, v. °πορφύρεος.

***παρῴδησις**, εως, ἡ, defined as ὅταν ὁ ῥήτωρ κῶλον ἀρχαῖον τίθησι καὶ χωρίον ἑαυτοῦ i.e. when the rhetor quotes a passage of classic literature and adds his own continuation, Sch.Aristid. p. 462 D.

**παρῳδός II 2**, add '*IG* 11(2).120.48 (Delos, iii BC)'

**παρωθέω I 1**, line 2, after 'Hp.*Art.* 18' insert 'so prob. in *h.Merc.* 305 (tm.)'

**παρωνύμιος II 1**, add 'in a pun, παραμύθιον ἦσθα παρωνύμιόν τε γονεῦσι *CEG* 564 (Athens, iv BC)' **2**, for '= Lat. .. *agnomen*' read '*by-name*, Arist.*Ath.* 17.3'

***παρώρειος**, ον, = παρόρειος, *PTeb.* 787.4 (ii BC), Str. 12.8.13.

**παρωροφίς**, after 'Poll. 1.81' add '(defined as τὸ μεταξὺ τοῦ ὀρόφου καὶ τοῦ στέγους, i.e. *cornice* or *gable*)'

**πᾶς**, lines 1/2, for 'Sapph. .. Alc.*Supp.* 12.6, 25.8' read 'Sapph. 31.14, 44.14, Alc. 34.6, al. L.-P., *SEG* 32.1243 (Cyme, 2 BC/AD 2)'; line 6, after 'πᾶσι' insert 'πάνσι *BCH* 109.189-194 (Crete, ii/i BC)'; line 10, after '*Je.* 13.11' insert 'also πᾶν τὸν χρόνον *IG* 9²(1).583.56, cf. *IG* 9(1).39.3' **B II**, line 6, after 'v. infr. δ.' insert '**III**' **D II 4**, add '*all the time*, ἡ γῆ νιφετῷ τὰ π. χρᾶται Hdt. 4.50.2, cf. Luc.*Asin.* 22, Ach.Tat. 5.13, 7.16'

⁺**πᾶς** (B), Cypr. *pa-se*, *pa-sa*, = παῖς, *ICS* 80.2, 92.2, 157.2.

**πασίγνωστος**, add 'Anon.Alch. 344.13'

**πᾱσιθέα I**, add '= ἀρτεμισία I 2, Poet.*de herb.* 27; = παιωνία ἄρρην, ib. 144, prob. in Ps.-Dsc. 3.140 (-θέη)'

**Πασικράτεια**, after '(Selinus' insert 'v BC'

⁺**Πᾱσικράτη**, ἡ, Dor. -α, *universal queen*, θεᾶς Πασικράτας *SEG* 32.636 (Maced., AD 286); identified w. Artemis, *AE* 1910.307 (Ambracia).

***πᾱσιμέλητος**, ον, *cared for by all*, *SEG* 19.794 (Pisidia).

⁺**πασίολος**, v. ‡φασίολος.

**Πάσιος**, add '**II** name of a month, *Hesperia* 27.75 (unkn. provenance, c.200 BC).'

**πᾱσίφίλητος**, add '*IG* 5(1).1494 (Messene, iii/iv AD)'

**πᾱσίφιλος**, for '= foreg.' read '*loving* or *friendly to all*'

***Πᾱσιχάρηα**, ἁ, *"gratifying-all"*, name coined by Alcm. 107 P. to suit a promiscuous woman.

***πασπερμεί**, v. °πανσπερμεί.

⁺**πασσᾰγία**, v. ‡πανσαγία.

***πάσσακον**· πάσσαλον Hsch. (perh. πασσάκων· πασσάλων).

**πασσᾰλιον**, add 'Poll. 7.114'

**πασσᾰλιστής**, for 'κυνδαλοπαίστης' read 'κυνδάλη'

**πάσσᾰλος**, line 1, after '(v. infr.' insert 'cf. πασσαλόφιν· τοῦ πασσάλου. ὁ δὲ σχηματισμὸς Βοιώτιος Hsch.'

**πάσσον**, delete the entry.

***πάσσος**, ον, Lat. *passus*, πάσσος οἶνος *raisin wine* (*vinum passum*), Eust. 1178.17; also neut. (?masc.) subst., Plb. 6.11a.4, Lang *Ath.Agora* XXI Hd9 (ii AD), 12 (ii/iii AD).

***πασσοφία** (-ίη), v. °πανσοφία.

***πάσσοφος**, v. °πάνσοφος.

**πασταί**, add 'Ar.*fr.* 702 K.-A.'

**παστάς I 2**, add 'of a gymnasium, *SEG* 23.233 (Arcadia, ii BC)' **3**, delete '*AP* 6.172' **II**, after '*bridal chamber*' insert 'but perh. to be understood as *porch* (I 1) v. J. Roux in *REG* 74.43ff.'

**πάστας**, add '*BCH* 107.401 (Knossos, i AD)'

**παστή**, before '*case, container*' insert 'perh.' and add 'παστὰς χαλκᾶς *PFreib.* 52.4'

***παστίλη**, v. σπατίλη II.

**παστιλλᾶς**, after '= foreg.' insert '*POxy.* 3390.3 (AD 358)'

⁺**παστός**, ὁ, *bridal canopy* or *curtain* (freq. used loosely as a symbol of marriage), Lxx *Ps.* 18(19).5, *SEG* 1.567.5 (Karanis, iii BC), *AP* 5.51, 7.182, *GVI* 719, 804, etc., Luc.*DMort.* 23.3, Nonn.*D.* 5.214, Poll. 3.37. **2** *bed-canopy* (in non-marriage context), D.Chr. 62.6; also in ritual use, Herod. 4.56, *ISmyrna* 753.

**παστοφόριον**, add '*PBonn.*inv. 208.3 (*JJP* 18.52; sp. παστοφοροιον, ii AD)'

**παστοφόρισσα**, add '*OBodl.* 1821'

**παστοφόρος**, for 'priests appointed for this purpose' read 'a class of priests of unknown function'

***παστῷος**, α, ον, perh. *of the* παστός, Hdn.*fr.* p. 18 H.

***πάστωρ**, ορος, ὁ, Lat. *pastor*, *herdsman*, *SB* 801 (ii/iii AD).

**πάσχω**, line 3, after 'Il. 9.492, etc.' insert 'Lac. πάσον Alcm. 1.35 P.' **III 1 a**, line 9, after 'with subst.' insert '*POxy.* 1121.7 (iii AD), *PGen.* 58.16 (iv AD), *Cod.Just.* 6.4.4.23' **2 a**, add 'but also πάσχειν τι *to be affected, disturbed*, Men.*Kith.* 49, D.H. 9.3.5, Plu. 2.682b' **III 4**, lines 3 ff. (τί παθών), add 'Ar.*Nu.* 340'

⁺**πάσωλος**, v. ‡φασίολος.

***πᾰτάγγης**, ου, ὁ, = σπατάγγης, a kind of *sea-urchin*, Poll. 6.47.

**πᾰτᾰγέω I**, add 'Pl.*Euthd.* 293d' **II**, last line, for '*Lyr.adesp.* 121' read '(?)Call.*fr.* 761 Pf.'

***πᾰταγμός**, ὁ, *striking, smack*, Rh. 3.520.30.

**Παταίκεια**, delete 'sg. Παταίκειον' to end.

***Παταίκειος**, *belonging to the fund of the* Παταίκεια, φιάλη *Inscr.Délos* 438.2, 442*B*54 (ii BC).

***πᾰτάκτρια**, ἡ, *striker*, τῶν ζῴων, of a καλαῦροψ, Rh. 3.607.8.

**πᾰτάσσω II**, line 7, after '*sting*' insert 'of a scorpion, Arist.*HA* 607ᵃ17'

***πᾰταχρον**, τό, *idol*, Lxx *Is.* 8.21 (pl.); also masc. sg. τὸν π. ib. 37.38 (prob.). (Cf. Aram. *patakrā*).

**πατελλίδιον**, delete the entry.

***πᾰτελλίκιον**, τό, *dish*, *CPR* 8.66.10 (v AD), *POxy.* 1901.34, 68, 2419.9 (vi AD), *Gloss.*

**πᾰτερεύω**, add 'of women, app. as indication of rank, *CPR* 10.127.6 (vi AD)'

**πᾰτερία**, add '*POxy.* 2780.8 (vi AD)'

⁺**πᾰτέριον**, τό, dim. of πατήρ, in quots. only as voc., used in addressing an old man, Luc.*Nec.* 21; also **πατερίων**, *Vit.Aesop.*(G) 56 P. (*POxy.* 2083ʳ.7, iv/v AD), al.

**πᾰτημα I**, add '**2** perh. *trodden grapes*, used as fodder, *POxy.* 1142.3, 1156.9 (both iii AD) or *pounded spice*, *POxy.* 2570(b).5, 3733.19, 3766.102.'

**πᾰτήρ**, line 2, at end insert 'dat. πατῆρι *SEG* 30.1502 (Phrygia)' **II**, add 'alone, of Zeus, *BCH* 109.189 (Cnossos, ii/i BC)' **V**, after '*IG* 14.1272' insert '*MDAI(R)* 49.203 (Dura)' **VI**, after 'similarly' insert 'πατέρα δήμου Ῥώμης, of Vespasian, *Salamine* 138'; for 'π. τῆς πόλεως .. Methone)' substitute '**2** π. τῆς πόλεως = *curator (pater) ciuitatis*, *IG* 5(1).1417.11 (Methone), *SEG* 29.1070, *PMich.*inv. 3999 (*ZPE* 75.268), *Cod.Just.* 1.5.12.7, etc. (all vi AD).' add 'Myc. *pa-te*'

**πᾰτητής**, before 'Hsch.' insert '*SB* 4640 (v/vi AD)'

***πᾰτίλη**, v. σπατίλη.

**πᾰτος** (A) **I 1**, add '**b** *action of going, course*, Nic.*Th.* 479.' **2**, add '*ISalamis* 45 (v AD), *Cod.Just.* 8.10.12.3a' **3**, add 'Plu. 2.670b'

⁺**πᾰτος** (B), εος, τό, *robe woven for Hera*, Call.*fr.* 66.3 Pf.

**πάτρα III**, add '*SEG* 33.1016 (Lydia, AD 103/4), epigr. in 26.456.11 (Laconia, ii/iii AD)'; form πατρεία, add '*EA* 15.80 no. 31.9 (Lydia, i AD)'

**πατρᾰδελφεία**, for '*cousin by the father's side*' read 'collect. noun for *paternal cousins*' and transfer entry before **πατραδελφεός**.

**πατρᾰδελφος**, before 'Is. 4.23' insert 'ἀνεψιὸς ὢν αὐτοῖς ἐκ πατραδέλφων'

**πατριά I**, add 'πατριᾶφι (instr. pl.) *with their lineages*, *SEG* 37.340.17 (Mantinea, iv BC); cf. °πατροφιστί, ἐπιπατρόφιον'

**πατριάρχης II**, add '*SEG* 33.1298 (Palestine, iv AD)'

***πατριᾶφι**, v. °πατριά.

***πατρικιᾶτος**, ον, Lat. *patriciatus*, *patrician*, κάλτιοι π. rest. in *Edict. Diocl.* 9.7.

**πατρικός**, after 'ή, όν' insert 'Aeol. **πάτριχος** acc. to Sch.D.T. p. 532.30 H.' **I**, add '**2** as a cult-epith. (cf. °πάτριος), Ἀρτέμι πατρικ[ῇ] *SEG* 29.1159 (Lydia).'

***πατριμώνιον**, τό, Lat. *patrimonium*, *IEphes.* 3056.4 (ii AD), *PFlor.* 320.4 (written πατριμούνιον, iv AD).

**πάτριος II**, add '**2** as a cult-epith., of Μήν, *SEG* 31.1132, 1210, 1232, etc.; fem., of Hestia, *SEG* 31.728 (Delos, ii BC).'

**πατρίς**, line 1, after 'ἴδος' insert 'Aeol. acc. πάτριν *IG* 12(2).242 (Mytilene), *SEG* 33.1037 (Cyme, ii BC)' **II**, line 4, after 'Ar.*Pl.* 1151' insert 'for πατὴρ πατρίδος v. πατήρ VI; personified, *IStraton.* 1026 (Flavian)'; line 5, after '*UPZ* 9.5 (ii BC)' insert 'D.S. 15.11.2, etc.'

***πατρόβουλος**, ὁ, *son of a member of a* βουλή, *designated by his father to succeed him*, *IEphes.* 972, 1044, *IG* 12(5).141.7 (Paros), Jul.*Ep.* 54, *PLond.* 971.7 (iv AD).

***πατρογενίδης**, ου, *descended on the father's side*, τῶν ἀπὸ Ἄρδυος Ἡρακλειδῶν π. Robert *Hell.* 10.276 (Claros, ii AD).

⁺**πατρογέρων**, οντος, ὁ, *son of a member of a* γερουσία, *designated to succeed him*, *IEphes.* 26, 972, 1573.

***πατροθεῖος**, ον, *hereditary*, πατροθίου καθαρουργ(οῦ) *PAlex.* (1964)32.4 (v AD).

***πατροκτασία**, ἡ, = πατροκτονία, *PMasp.* 353.A.11 (vi AD).

**πατροκτόνος I**, add '**2** subst., *parricide*, Plu. 2.1065, *Rom.* 22.4.'

**πατρομήτωρ 1**, after 'Luc.*Alex.* 58' add '(v.l., see °προμήτωρ)'

***πατρομύστης**, ου, ὁ, *son of a* μύστης, *designated by his father to succeed him*, *ISmyrna* 731.17-8, 732.

⁺**πατροποίητος**, ὁ, *adoptive father*, Mitchell *N.Galatia* 358 (sp. -φοιητ-), 387 (sp. -ποητ-), *AJA* 36.460 (border of Lycaonia and Galatia), Heuzey-Daumet *Mission Arch.de Macédoine* no. 135 (Ressova).

**πατροτυψία**, add 'Sopat.Rh. 8.199 W.'

***πατροφιστί**, adv. *with the father's name*, *SEG* 23.178.6 (Nemea, 229 BC); cf. πατριστί, πατριαστί, πατριᾶφι (s.v. °πατριά).

**πατρωϊῶχος**, add 'Ἠπειρωτικὰ Χρονικά 1.255 (Dodona, v/iv BC)'

**πάτρων I**, add 'π. τῆς πόλεως *CIJud.* 619d (iii/iv AD); sim. π. τῆς μητροπόλεως *ITomis* 2.101 (iii AD)'

**πατρωνεύω**, line 1, after '(Delph., i BC)' insert '*IGBulg.* 314 (Mesembria)'; line 2, after 'D.S. 40.5' insert '*INikaia* 1201'

**πατρωνικός**, add 'also -ονικός Theophil.Antec. 3.7.2'

**πατρώνισσα**, add 'also -όνισσα Theophil.Antec. 3.7.3'

**πατρώνῠμος**, add '*POxy.* 3273 (i AD)'

**πατρῷος I**, add 'also as epith. of Hermes, *SEG* 32.751 (Berezan, v BC), 30.93 (Eleusis, i BC); of Athene, *SEG* 37.295 (Epid.)'

**πάτρως**, line 2, for 'Stesich. 17' read 'Stesich. 51 P. (in signf. ὁ κατὰ πατέρα πρόγονος, Eust. l.c. infr.)'; line 4, after '*BCH* 11.471 (Lydia)' insert 'πάτρως *SEG* 33.1016 (Lydia, AD 103/4)'

**πάτωρ**, delete the entry.

***παύγλα**, ἡ, app. = Lat. *pavicula*, *rammer*, παῦγλα ἤτοι γλεύδια *Edict.Diocl.* 15.43.

***Παύλεια**, τά, games at Alexandria Troas, Σμίνθεια Π. *Buckler Anat. Studies* 245-8.

**παυνί**, add 'also app. παῦνι (in broken context), Hippon. 79.16 W.'

***παῦνι**, also **παῦν**, **παοῖνι**, **παῦνει**, month name in N.Africa, *AP* 9.383, *SEG* 33.1401, 1459, 1486 (all Cyrenaica), *POxy.* 267.39, *PHib.* 46.21, *SB* 1167, 3776, etc.

**παυράκις**, add 'also παυράκι, ἃ παυράκι γίνεται ἀνδρί Thgn. 859'

**παυροεπής**, for '*words*' read '*verses*'

**παῦρος 1**, line 2, after '*Op.* 538' insert 'ἰχθύες A.R. 1.573'; line 4, after 'Q.S. 7.613' insert 'sup., παύριστον τό κεν .. τις ἴδοιτο a thing of which one can see *extremely little*, Call.*fr.* 384.55 Pf.'

**παυσανίας**, delete '(ubi .. A.)'

***παυσικραίπᾰλος**, ὁ or ἡ, *"stop-the-hangover"*, inscr. on a drinking-cup, dub. in *Hesperia* 16.240 (Corinth, ii BC).

**παῦσις**, add 'π. πυρετῶν Hp.*Epid.* 7.49'

***παυσιτοκεῖα**, τά, *an offering marking the end of childbirth*, *BE* 1973.247.

**Πάφιος** (s.v. Πάφος), after 'abs.' insert 'Cypr. *ta-se-pa-pi-a-se* (τᾶς Παφίας), *ICS* 262 (*c.*500 BC)'

***Παφλᾰγόνισσα**, ἡ, *Paphlagonian*, Εὐπορία Μανοῦ Π. *IG* 2².10052 (Piraeus, i BC).

**παφλάζω**, for 'Alc.*Supp.* 25.4 (p. 28 Lobel)' read 'Alc. 72.5 L.-P.'

**πάχνη 1**, add 'transf., πάντα πάχνης ἦν πλέα καὶ πυρός of a sick man, Aristid.*Or.* 48(24).46'

***πᾰχόω**, *thicken*, ἕψε ἕως παχῶσαι prescription in *Hermes* 33.343 (nisi leg. παχνῶσαι).

**πᾰχῠμερής I**, add 'adv. -μερῶς, *in large portions* or *pieces*, Asclep. Jun.ap.Gal. 13.1022.9'

**πᾰχύπους**, add 'Hsch.'

**πᾰχύς I 6**, add 'Λύδη καὶ παχὺ γράμμα καὶ οὐ τορόν Call.*fr.* 398 Pf.'

**πᾰχύτης II**, add '**2** of style, τὴν π. τῶν ποιημάτων Sch.D.P. 3 (*GGM* II p. 427ᵇ4 adn.).'

***Παχών**, month name in N.Africa, *AP* 9.383, *SEG* 24.1178 (Alexandria, iii BC), 33.1395 (Cyrenaica), etc.

**πε**, for 'of πετ(ά) = μετά' read 'of πετ = πεδά'

⁺**πεδά**, non-Att.-Ion. prep. (corresponding in use to μετά) **A** w. gen., *with*, *among*, Sapph. 55.4 L.-P., Alc. 70.4, 73.10 L.-P., al., Ibyc. 40.3 P., Theoc. 28.21; following a noun, id. 29.38. **B** w. acc., *after*, Sapph. 99 i 1 L.-P., Alc. 387 L.-P., Alcm. 1.58, 17.5 P., *Leg.Gort.* 3.27, *Schwyzer* 619.20. **2** *to*, Alcm. 3 *fr.* 1.8 P., *Schwyzer* 177.5. **3** *according to*, π. θῦμον Sapph. 60.5 L.-P. **C** w. dat., *among*, τοῖς π. Ibyc. 1.46 P., unless πέδα here = μέτεστι. Myc. *pe-da*.

**πεδάγρετος**, add 'cj. in Alc. 358.3 L.-P.'

***πεδάλιον**, τό, app. = Lat. *podium*, *JRA* suppl.2 p.28 (Aphrodisias, ii/iii AD).

***πεδάμοιρος**, ον, *having a share*, *IRhod.Peraia* 351 (vi AD).

***Πεδανασσεύς**, epith. of Apollo, *Didyma* 70 (*SEG* 30.1293).

**πεδᾰνός I**, for this section read '*low-growing*, ῥυτῆς βλάσται Nic.*Al.* 306; *flat*, *squat*, ἀλκαίη, οὐρή, σαῦροι id.*Th.* 226, 289, 817'

**πεδᾰορος**, for 'Alc. 100' read 'Alc. 315 L.-P.' and add 'A.*Ch.* 590 (lyr., cj.)'

***πέδε**, v. °πέντε.

***πέδειμι**, Dor. = μέτειμι (εἰμί *sum*), [ἀ]ρχᾶν πεδεί̣μ[εν] ..], *ASAA* 27/29(1952).112 (Acrae, v BC).

****πέδρεις**, εσσα, εν, Myc. *pe-de-we-sa*, of an ἐσχάρα, *equipped with feet*.

***πεδεπιθύω**, Cret., prob. *sacrifice together with others*, *Inscr.Cret.* 4.146.3 (Gortyn, v/iv BC).

⁺**πεδέρχομαι**, Aeol. and Dor. in senses of μετέρχομαι, *pursue*, πεδελθέτω Alc. 123.13 L.-P. **2** *follow*, *ensue*, Pi.*N.* 7.74. **3** *beseech*, Theoc. 29.25.

**πεδέχω**, add '*SEG* 23.474 (Dodona, iv/iii BC)'

**πέδη I**, add '**4** a kind of brake, π. καὶ ἄξων *IG* 1³.422.122 (Athens, v BC); cf. τροχοπέδη. **5** *leather-covered ring* for securing the rudder or mast of a ship, Hsch.; cf. ἱστοπέδη.'

***πεδῐακόν**, τό, *land record-book*, π. ἐπικρίσεως pap. in *Aegyptus* 15.210 (iii AD), *POxy.* 1287.2 (ii AD), *PSI* 450.69 (παιδ-; ii/iii AD).

**πεδῐακός I**, add 'πεδιακὴ ὁδός, *fieldpath*, *BGU* 2055.12 (ii AD)'

***πεδῐαρχέω**, *to be a "controller of the plain"*, (app. office connected w. the Pythian games), *BCH* 80.592 (Locris, vi/v BC).

**πεδιάς I**, add 'fem. subst., *flat land*, *BGU* 2159.8 (AD 485)'

***πεδῐάσιμος**, ον, *of the plain*, *POxy.* 1537.12 (ii/iii AD); cf. πεδιασιμαῖος.

**πεδῐεῖς**, add 'Myc. *pe-di-je-we* name of a class of men; cf. deriv. *pe-di-je-wi-ja*, perh. *infantry spears*'

***πεδικόν**, v. °παιδικός.

**πέδῑλον**, add 'Myc. *pe-di-ra* (pl.)'

***πεδιόθεν**, v. °παιδιόθεν.

⁺**πέδιjος**, α, ον, Cypr. *pe-ti-ja-i*, *situated in the plain*, *ICS* 217 B18.

**πεδιοφύλαξ**, add '*PVindob.Tandem* 16.23 (v/vi AD)'

⁺**πέδοι**, adv. *to the ground*, A.*Pr.* 272, Luc.*Lex.* 1.

**πέδον 4**, penultimate line, for 'as also for πέδον' read '**b** πέδον *to the ground*'; add 'Call.*Del.* 227'

⁺**πεδοσκᾰφής**, *digging out the earth*, πεδοσκαφέεσσι μακέλλαις Nonn.*D.* 4.255, 12.331. **II** *hollowed out of the earth*, ib. 26.112, 30.145, al.

***πεδοτρεφής**, *grown* or *nourished in the earth*, πεδοτρεφέων .. δρακόντων Nonn.*D.* 2.47, λέκτρα πεδοτρεφέων ὑμεναίων ib. 29.337, al.

**πεδότριψ**, add 'Ph. 2.446'

**πέζα II**, add '**b** *stylobate* of a colonnade, *Suppl.Hell.* 978.7.'

***πεζάρχης**, ου, ὁ, *leader of infantry*, *GVI* 1928.7.

**πέζαρχος**, add '*IG* 2².175.8 (iv BC)'

**πεζίδιον**, delete the entry.

**πεζίς**, add 'Leont.Byz.*HP* 2.2.10'

***πεζίτιον**, τό, *ribbon*, Suid. s.v. ταινίαι, and so Phot. (-ζήτ-), *EM* 749.37 (-ζέτ-), *Gloss.* (-ζίδ-).

**πεζός II**, line 1, for 'πεζὸς' read 'πεζὸν'; line 2, for 'Call.*Aet.* 4.1.9' read 'Call.*fr.* 112.9 Pf.'

**πεῖ**, adv., after 'Sophr. 5' insert 'Theoc. 15.33 (*PAntin.*)'

***πειθηνίς**, ίδος, fem. adj., = πειθήνιος II, πατρὸς π. βουλῇ *Orac.Chald.* 81.2 P.

**πείθω II**, at end delete 'Pi. uses .. *P.* 3.28' and for '*I.* 4(3).72' read 'Pi.*I.* 4.90 S.-M.'

**Πειθώ I**, add '*SEG* 33.643 (Rhodes, 100 BC). **2** as epith. of Aphrodite, *IG* 9(2).236 (Pharsalus, v BC), *ABSA* 47.190 (Cnidus, iv/iii BC).'

***πεῖλα**, ἡ, Lat. *pila*, *pier*, *mole*, *IEphes.* 23.17 (ii AD) (pl.).

***πειλῑπής**, v. πιλιπής.

**πειράζω II 1**, add 'pass., πειράζεται τὰ νήπια ποίας τινὰς ἔχει τὰς τῆς ψυχῆς διαθέσεις D.S. 2.58'

***Πειραῖα**, τά, *the Dionysia in Piraeus*, *IG* 2².1028.16 (100 BC), etc.

**πεῖραρ I 2**, add 'π. κουροσύνας *AP* 6.281 (Leon.Tarent.)'

***πειρᾱτ(ε)ῖαι**, αἱ, *treacherous attacks*, Hsch. s.v. πεῖραι.

**πειρᾱτεύω II**, add 'πειρατευ[όν]των Θραικῶν οὐκ [ὀλίγων τὴν [.. χ]ώραν *IHistriae* 15.9 (iii/ii BC)'

**πειράω A IV 2**, for '*make an attempt on* a woman's honour' read '*attempt to seduce*' and add 'παῖδας ἐπείρων Ar.*Pax* 763, *V.* 1025'

***πείρημα**, ατος, τό, *limit*, codd. in *App.Anth.* 3.186, Gr.Naz.*Carm.* 2.1.38.9.

**πειρητίζω**, line 1, delete 'Ep. form of πειράω' and insert 'πειρατίζω Hsch.'

**πείρινς**, line 4, after 'Hsch.' insert '(cf. dat. πυρίνθω in *PMasp.* 303.14 (vi AD))'

***πειστικόν**, τό, *"room of the faithful"*, (or perh. = Lat. *posticum*), ἡ ψηφεὶς (mosaic work) τοῦ π., R.Stillwell *Antioch-on-the-Orontes* (1933-36) 33, 42 (v AD).

***Πειστίχη**, ἡ, (πείθω) *goddess of persuasion*, epith. of Aphrodite, *Inscr.Délos* 2396, 2397; without Ἀφροδίτη, ib. 2398 (Πιστίχῃ).

⁺**πειώλης**, ου, ὁ, = κίναιδος, Suid., *EM* 668.36, Eust. 1684.29; cf. πεοίδης, πεώδης.

***πεκουλιάριον**, τό, *personal property*, *EAM* 22 (ii/iii AD).

**πεκούλιον**, add '*EA* 6.63 no. 5, Just.*Nov.* 162.2.1'

**πεκτήρ**, add 'cf. Myc. fem. *pe-ki-ti-ra₂*, πέκτριαι'

***πεκτοραλίων**, (gen. pl.), Lat. *pectorale*, *breastplate*, *PMich.*xv 742.5 (vi AD).

**πελᾰγόστροφος**, for '*roving through the sea*' read '*that haunts the deep sea*'
**πελάζω A II**, add 'cf., of snakes, poet. in *PKöln* 244.17 (iii AD)' **C I 3**, add 'ἐν πανηγύρει δαιμιόνων πελαζόμενος Aesop.*Prov.* 39 P.'
**πελᾰνός**, line 4, for 'π. αἱματοσταγής .. slaughter' read 'π. αἱματοσφαγής'
**πελαργός I**, add '**b** π.· ἄγγος τι κεράμεον Hsch. cf. *PBSR* N.S. 59.177ff.'
**πέλας II**, add 'τοὶς πέλας ἀμμέων Alc. 353.1 L.-P.'
*__πελᾰτεύω__, *to be a* πελάτης, i.e. to depend on like a client, [κ]ηδεστῶν τρόπον οἶσιν [ἔ]ντροφος (-τροπος pap.) πελατεύσεις *A.fr.* 47a ii 22 R. (lyr.).
*__πελεθραία__, ά, subdivision of a πέλεθρον, *SEG* 13.395 (Larissa, iii BC); also **πελεθριαία**, ib. 394; cf. πλεθριαῖος.
*__πελεθριαῖον__, τό, = °πελεθραία, *SEG* 26.676.6 (Larissa, iii BC).
**πελειάς**, line 3, after 'Opp.*C.* 1.351' insert 'πεληϊάσιν *GVI* 270.3 (Trachonitis, ii/iii AD)'
**πελείους 2**, for this section read '*livid*, Lxx *Prov.* 23.29'
*__πελεκᾶς__ (B), ὁ, *axe-maker*, prob. in *OWilck.* 2.720 (i BC).
**πελεκῖνος III**, add 'a kind of fastening for a sarcophagus-lid, ἐγχωνεύσει τοὺς π. *SEG* 17.633.9 (Perge); τὸ πῶμα πελεκείνοις διεί[λ]ηται *TAM* 3.574 (Termessus). **IV** a kind of *sundial*, Vitr. 9.8.1.'
**πέλεκυς I 2**, add 'meton., for "lictor", id. 3.87.7' **6**, for 'prob. in *Inscr.Cypr.* 135.26 H.' read 'prob. interpr. of Cypr. *pe* standing for a sum of money, *ICS* 217 A15, B26' add '**7** an ancient weight of six or twelve minae, Hsch.'
*__πελεκυφόρᾱς__, α, ὁ, masc. adj., *bearing* (the brand of) *an axe*, π. ἵππον Pi.*fr.* 339a S.-M.
*__πελέμαιγις__, ιδος, *shaking the aegis*, epith. of Athena, perh. to be read rather than πολέμαιγις in B. 17.7 S.-M.
⁺__πελιγᾶνες__ (-όνες Str.7 *fr.* 2), *elders* in Macedonian communities or colonies, *IGLS* 4.1261.22 (ii BC), cj. in Plb. 5.54.10, Hsch.
**πελιδνόομαι**, add 'πελιδνώθεισα Alc. 298.11 L.-P. (s.v.l.), Call.*fr.* 374 Pf.'
**πέλιξ**, add 'Myc. *pe-ri-ke* (pl.)'
**πελῐόομαι**, add 'act., *mark with a livid bruise*, Eust. 1681.53'
*__πελῐωμάτιον__, τό, *slight contusion*, *POxy.* 3195.48 (AD 331).
*__πελῐωπός__, όν, *of livid aspect*, Theognost.*Can.* 69.
**πέλλα**, line 1, after 'Il. 16.642' insert 'Hippon. 14.1 W.' **2**, delete the section.
**πελλητήρ** (s.v. πελλαντήρ), before 'Clitarch.' insert 'perh. *milking-pail*' and after 'ibid.' insert '(Boeot.)'
*__πελλοδόχος__, ὁ, dub. sens., *PIand.* 17.4 (vi/vii AD).
**πέλμα II**, for '*stalk*' read '*base* (*eye*, i.e. remains of calyx)' add '**III** *ground area*, *ICilicie* 61 (Samos, Byz.).'
*__πελματοπώλης__, εω, ὁ, *seller of shoe-soles*, *IEphes.* 2.25, 27 (340/320 BC).
**Πελοποννησιακός**, add '*SEG* 26.121 (Athens, i BC)'
*__πέλτα__, τά, *tomb* or some part of a tomb (perh. *platform*, cf. Hitt. *palzaḫḫa*), *SEG* 6.307, 428, 434 (Lycaonia), *MAMA* 1.31, 60 (Phrygia); cf. πλάτας, πλάτος (B).
*__πελτᾱφόρας__, v. πελτοφόρος.
**πέλτη II 1**, for '*small light shield* .. orig. Thracian' read '*small wooden or wicker shield with covering of skin*'; after '*IG* 1².282.120' insert 'X.*Mem.* 3.9.2'; add 'used loosely for any shield, π. Δωρίς *AP* 7.430 (Dioscor.)'
**πέλτης**, delete '*salted*'
⁺__πελτίδιον__, τό, v.l. for πελτάριον (in same sense), Luc.*DMort.* 12.2.
**πέλτον**, delete the entry (v. °πέλτα).
**πέλω**, add 'Myc. part. *qe-ro-me-no*'
**πελωριάς**, delete 'cf. *AP* 6.224 (Theodorid.)'
⁺__πεμπάκι__, delete the entry (v. °πεντάκις).
**πεμπᾱμερος**, for '*Inscr.Cypr.* 134 H.' read '*to-pe-pa-me-ro-ne*, τô πε(μ)παμερōν *ICS* 220.2'
**πέμπε**, add '*SEG* 26.672 (Thessaly, 200/190 BC)'
*__πεμπείκοντα__, = πεντήκοντα, *SEG* 26.672 (Thessaly, 200/190 BC).
*__πεμπεικονταέν__, = *πεντηκονταέν, *fifty-one*, *SEG* 26.672 (Thessaly, 200/190 BC).
**πεμπταΐζω**, after '*fifth day*' insert '(or incorrectly, *in the fifth generation*)'
**πέμπτος I**, add 'in a legionary title, λε[γ](ιῶνος) πέμπτης Μακεδ(ονικῆς) *ICilicie* 31 (ii AD)'
*__πεμπτοστάτης__, ου, ὁ, *priest in the fifth grade*, πεμπτοστάτου Διός *SEG* 32.1483 (Syria, i/ii AD).
*__πέμφελα__· δύσκολα, τραχέα, βαθέα Hsch.; cf. δυσπέμφελος.
**πέμφιξ 3**, add 'φλύκταιναι πέμφιξιν ἐειδόμεναι ὑετοῖο Nic.*Th.* 273' deleting this quot. from section 4. **4**, line 6, for 'Call.*Fr.* 483 .. 43' read 'Call.*fr.* 43.41 Pf.'
**πενθαλέος 1**, add '-οῖσιν ὀδυρμοῖς *Bithynische St.* III 1.1'
**πενθάς**, for 'cf. Nonn.*D.* 14.271' read 'π. φωνῇ Nonn.*D.* 11.314'
**πένθεια**, for 'poet. form of πένθος' read 'perh. *female mourner*' and after 'lyr.' insert 's.v.l.'
**πενθερά**, after '*mother-in-law*' insert '(at first only *wife's mother*, acc. to Ar.Byz.ap.Eust. 648.54)'
*__πενθεράς__, άδος, ἡ, = πενθερά, *mother-in-law*, *MAMA* 7.430.
**πενθερίδης**, add '*SEG* 34.1224 (AD 96/7)'
**πενθέριος**, for 'πενθερός' read 'πενθερά' **II**, after 'cf.' insert '*Thasos* 141.21 (iv BC)'
**πενθερός**, after '*father-in-law*' insert '(at first only *wife's father*, acc. to Ar.Byz.ap.Eust. 648.54)' **II**, add '*MAMA* 8.271 (Lycaonia)'
⁺__πενθέτηρος__, ον, *of five years' standing*, πενθετήροις [π]ροπό[λοις] Philod.Scarph. in *SEG* 32.552.131; cf. πεντετηρικός, etc.
*__πενθέτης__, = πεντέτης, cj. in Alex. 125.10 (for πεμφθείς; read πένθετες).
**πενθημερία**, delete the entry (read πενθ(ήμερος)).
**πενθημιαρτᾰβη**, for this lemma read '**πενθημιαρτᾰβιον**, τό'
*__πενθημιδακτῠλιος__, α, ον, *of five half-fingers' breadth*, *BCH* 20.324.66 (Lebadea, ii BC).
**πενθήρης**, add '*Trag.adesp.* 705.1 K.-S. (iamb.trim.)'
*__πενθίδιος__, ον, *mournful*, στεναχαί, *CEG* 587 (Athens, iv BC).
**πενθῐκός**, line 2, after '*mournful*' insert 'πενθικὸν μηδὲν ποιείτω μηδείς *Thasos* 141.3 (iv BC)'
**πένθῐμος**, add 'πενθίμοις σχήμασι J.*AJ* 2.6.8, etc.; sup. διαθεὶς αὐτὸν -ώτατον ib. 19.1.18'
**πένομαι**, line 1, add 'pf.part. πεπεμμένοις *IG* 4.752.13 (Troezen, ii BC)'
*__πένουλα__, v. φαινόλη.
*__πεντᾰβασμος__, ον, *having five steps* or *rungs*, *Inscr.Délos* 1417*A*i76 (ii BC); cf. πεντέβαθμος.
*__πεντᾰβαφος__, ον, *quintuple-dyed*, πενταβάφου πορφύρας *PColl.Youtie* 85.3,4, *POxy.* 1978.9 (both vi AD).
*__πεντᾰγωνοειδής__, ές, *pentagon-shaped*, *Poliorc.* 206.15.
**πεντᾰδάκτῠλος II**, for 'as Subst. = πεντέφυλλον' read 'πεντα-δάκτυλον, τό, = πεντάφυλλον' and add 'sp. πεντεδ- *PMag.* 2.34'
**πεντᾰετηρικός**, add 'masc. subst. (sc. ἀγών) *SEG* 34.1316 (Lycia, AD 90); also neut. pl., τῶν μεγάλων πενταετηρικῶν *MAMA* 9.19 (Rom.imp.)'
**πεντᾰέτηρος I**, line 3, delete 'cf. .. (vi AD)' **II**, add 'ἀρχὸν πενταέτηρον *BCH* 78.74.4 (Achaea, iv/v AD); also πεντεϝέτειρος, Ἀρχ.Δελτ. 14 Pl. i 27 (Thespiae, iii BC)'
**πενταθλέω**, add 'also **πενταϝεθλέω**, πενταϝεθλέōν νίκα *Hesperia* 28.322 (*SEG* 26.407; inscr. on ἁλτήρ, Isthmia, early vi BC)'
⁺__πεντᾰκέλευθος__, ἡ, *meeting-place of five roads*, orac. in Paus. 8.9.4.
**πεντάκις**, for 'later **πεντάκι**' read 'also **πεντάκι**' and add '*CEG* 346 (Delphi, 475/50 BC); also **πενπάκι** ib. 374 (Sparta, *c.*530/500 BC); erron. for πεντάκι or due to poet. influence'
*__πεντᾰκορίνθιος__, ὁ, app. coin of the value of five Corinthian staters, χρυσίω πεντακορινθίω (gen.) de Franciscis *Locr.Epiz.* 35 (iv/iii BC).
*__πεντᾰκότῠλος__, ον, *holding five* κοτύλαι, *Inscr.Délos* 1432*Ab*ii32 (ii BC).
*__πεντᾰκωμία__, ἡ, *union of five villages*, *ABSA* 51.154 (Caralitis, AD 133), cf. ib. 156.
⁺__πενταλκία__, ἡ, conjectural rest. in sense of a measure (? *πενταολκία cf. ὁλκή), *Inscr.Cret.* 4.79.6 (v BC).
**πεντᾰμετρος**, for 'Hermesian. 7.36' to end read 'Sch.D.T. 173.13; also πεντάμετρον, τό, Hermesian. 7.36, Call.*fr.* 203.31, 45 Pf.; π. ἐλεγειακόν D.H.*Comp.* 25, [τροχαικὸν] π. Heph. 6.2'
**πεντᾰμηνιαῖος**, for '*Epigr.Gr.* 344.17 (Bithynia)' read '*IHadr.* 80 (ii AD)'
**πεντᾰμηνος 2**, for 'ὁ π. (sc. χρόνος)' read 'περὶ πεντάμηνον (prob. for (τὴν) πεντέμηνον περίοδον)'
**πεντᾰμναῖος**, add '-μνεως, *SEG* 16.497.3 (Chios, iii/ii BC)'
*__πεντᾰναυβία__, ἡ, *duty of performing five* ναύβια, *PColl.Youtie* 21.14 (AD 80/1).
*__πεντᾰνευρον__, τό, species of *plantain*, *An.Boiss.* 2.395, Anon.Alch. 326.4.
**πενταξεστιαῖον**, delete the entry.
*__πενταξεστιαῖος__, ον, *containing five sextarii*, *PColl.Youtie* 93.8, *PSI* 881.5, *CPR* 8.63.2 (all vi AD).
*__πεντᾰπάλαστος__, ον, = πενταπάλαιστος, *measuring five handbreadths*, *Inscr.Délos* 1432*Bb*ii16 (ii BC); cf. πεντεπάλαστος.
*__πεντάπλησον__, aor. imper. *multiply by five*, perh. erron. for πεντάπλωσον (i.e. °πενταπλόω) *PCair.* 10758 (vi AD), or -πλασον (-πλάζω, cf. διπλάζω).
**πεντάπλοκος**, add '*PSoterichos* 4.18 (AD 87), *PVindob.Boswinkel* 8.13 (AD 332)'
*__πενταπλόω__, *multiply by five*, v. °πεντάπλησον.
*__Πεντᾰπολῖται__, οἱ, *citizens of a* πεντάπολις, *BCH* 62.37 (Maced., Rom.imp.).
*__πεντάπρωτοι__, οἱ, (*board of*) *five leading men*, *SEG* 32.1467 (Syria, Chr.).
**πεντᾰρουρος**, add 'also **πεντεάρουρος**, *PHamb.* 65.18 (ii AD)'
*__πένταρχος__, ὁ, *member of a* πενταρχία, *SEG* 31.745 (Naxos, Hellen.).
**πεντάς**, add 'also **πεντεάς** *SEG* 33.848 (Mauretania, i AD)'

*πεντασσός, ἡ, όν, fivefold, PHeid. 323 c 12 (written with the symbol ϵ–, cf. τετρασσός, etc., AD 310).

*πεντάστῡλος, ον, having five posts or pillars, κλίνεια πεντάστυλα PSoterichos 1.27 (AD 69), 2.23 (AD 71), PFlor. 369.2 (ii AD).

πέντε, add 'Pamph. πέδε, IPamph. 3.5 (iv BC)'

*πεντεδάκτῠλον, v. °πενταδάκτυλος.

*πεντεδεκᾰέτης, ές, = πεντεκαιδεκαετής, SEG 6.137.30 (Phrygia, iv AD).

πεντεδραχμία, add 'five-drachma tax, Ath.Agora XIX P26.475, 479 (342 BC)'

*πεντεϝέτειρος, v. °πενταέτηρος.

*πεντεκαιδεκάδρομος, ὁ, youth who has reached fifteen years, πεντεκαιδεκαδρομō (gen.) Inscr.Cret. 4.72 xi 54.

*πεντεκαιδεκᾰμηνος, ον, of fifteen months, neut. sg. as subst., π. ἔχων .. ἤρθην GVI 1244 (Athens, ii/iii AD).

*πεντεκαιδεκᾰμοιρία, ἡ, space of fifteen degrees, Heph.Astr. 3.5.62, 63, al.

*πεντεκαιδεκᾰπους, ποδος, fifteen foot long, IG 2².1672.156 (pl.).

*πεντεκαιδεκάστεγος, ον, of fifteen storeys, Poliorc. 239.2.

πεντεκαιδέκᾰτος, add '-η, ἡ, fifteenth day, IMylasa 103 (ii/i BC), TAM 5(1).230 (AD 253/4)'

*πεντεκαιδεκάτροπος, ον, app. consisting of fifteen divisions, Procl. in Ti. 2.170.11 D.

πεντεκαιεικοσιέτης, add 'also -εικοσέτης CEG 176 (Panticapaeum, v BC), GVI 1233 (Egypt, ii/i BC)'

*πέντεκτος, η, ον, one-fifth, SEG 36.1116.B1 (Cyzicus, iv BC).

*πεντέλῑτρον, τό, weight of five λῖτραι, Dacia 3/4.611 (Perinthus).

πεντέμηνον, delete 'τό' (cf. ‡πεντάμηνος)

πεντέπους, line 3, for 'Arr.Peripl.M.Eux. 3' read 'Arr.Peripl.M.Eux. 2'

πεντετηρικός, after 'every five years' insert '(in alternative reckoning, every four years)'

πεντηκοντακάρηνος, delete the entry.

⁺πεντηκοντᾰκέφαλος, ον, (in quots. scanned -κεφᾰλος) fifty-headed, Hes.Th. 312, Pi.fr. 93 S.-M. (πεντηκοντο-).

πεντηκοντᾰπαις II, for 'Δαναός' read 'ἀδελφός'

*πεντηκοντᾰπους, ποδος, fifty foot long, στῦλος PGiss. 69.13 (ii AD).

πεντηκόσιοι, add 'IG 12(3) suppl. 330.22 (Arcesine, ii BC)'

πεντηκοστολόγος, add 'at Byzantium, Arist.EE 1247ᵃ19'

πεντηκοστύς, add 'at Argos, Schwyzer 90.13 (iii BC)'

*πεντημίεκτος, η, ον, two-fifths, SEG 36.1116.A9 (Cyzicus, iv BC).

*πεντῆντα, = πεντήκοντα, CIJud. 596 (Venusia); cf. mod. Gk. πενῆντα.

*πεντόγκιον, τό, = πενταούγκιον, Epich. 9.

πεντόροβος 2, before 'IG 11(2).161B19' insert 'IG 1³.383.176'

*πέντος, α, ον, = πέμπτος, GDI 4991 ii 39.

*πεντωβόλειος, α, ον, = πεντώβολος, τόκου πεντωβολείου PSI 1328.34 (AD 201).

*πεντώβολον, τό, five obols, δραχμᾶν δύο πεντωβόλου IG 4².109 ii 123 (Epid.).

πεντώβολος, line 4, delete 'δραχμᾶν .. (Epid.)'

πεντώγκιον, delete the entry.

πεντώρῠγος, add 'IG 2².1627.356 (iv BC)'

πεξόν, delete the entry.

*πεξός, ἡ, όν, Lat. pexus, of materials, brushed, Edict.Diocl. 20.12, al.; cf. πεξὸν ἱμάτιον, prosa pexa tunica, Gloss.

πέος, after 'Ar.Ach. 158' insert 'AP 11.224 (Antip.Thess.)'

πεπαίνω, line 5, delete 'but' and substitute 'mature meat by hanging'; line 6, for 'by being boiled with it' read 'i.e. by hanging the bird in a fig-tree'

πέπανσις, after 'fruits' insert 'etc., Hp.Hebd. 4'

πέπερι 2, add 'Peripl.M.Rubr. 49' add '3 λευκὸν π. white pepper, SEG 37.1019 (Pergamon, ii AD).' at end, in parenth., add 'πιπέρεος SEG 37 l.c., acc. sg. πίπεριν SEG 30.326 (Athens, i AD)'

*πεπεροπαστάριον, τό, container for pepper, PVindob. G29709 (ZPE 64.77, v/vi AD).

πεπλᾰνημένως II, add 'Gal. 16.815.2'

πεπλογρᾰφία, for 'title .. Worthies' read 'Cicero's description of work by Varro, prob. the Imagines'

πεπλοθήκη, for 'wardrobe' read 'chest for storing the (Panathenaic) peplos'

*πεπόνιον, τό, dim. of πέπων I 2, melon, PRyl. 630*. 21, al. (IV AD); cf. mod. Gk. πεπόνι.

*πεπόνιος, α, ον, app. melon-coloured, δερματικὸν π. PMichael. 18 ii 2 (iii AD).

πεπρωΐων, delete the entry.

*Πεπρώϊοι or Πεπρῷοι, app. name of a χιλιαστύς, IEryth. 17.15-16 (iv BC).

*πέπτης, ου, ὁ, perh. baker, POxy. 3492.27 (AD 161/9).

πέρᾱ (A), add 'Myc. compd. pe-ra₃-ko-ra-i-ja, (Περαιγολαΐα) name of the Further Province'

πέρα (B), line 2, after '(lyr.)' insert 'αἴ τίς κα πέραι συναλ[λάκ]σει ἐ̄ς πέρ[α]ν ἐπιθέντι μὲ ἀποδιδõι Inscr.Cret. 4.72 ix 43 (Gortyn)'; add 'πέρᾱν app. acc. and πέρᾱ (A) instr. fr. this appellat.'

περαίνω IV, add 'cf. °διαπειραίνω'

περαιόω II, lines 1/2, for 'etc., Leg.Gort. .. vii 15' read '(app. cancel the sale of a slave and return him) Inscr.Cret. 4.41 vii 15, 4.72 vii 11'

περαίτερος I, add 'sup. περαίτατον Hsch.'

περαίωσις, add 'II end, expiry of a period of time, PKöln 104.20 (vi AD); completion of a process, Cod.Just. 9.4.6.3.'

⁺πέρᾱμα, ατος, τό, act of crossing a river, Palladius ap.Ps.-Callisth. 3.10. 2 place across the water, Just.Nov. 14, 59.5 (bis).

πέρας II 2, add 'πέρατι παραδοῦναι Cod.Just. 1.3.41.29' 4, add 'rhet., = ὁρισμός II, Cratin.Jun. 7.4' IV, at end after '(Men. Epit.) 470' insert 'Dysc. 117'

περᾱτικός, add 'SEG 24.633 (Thrace, Chr.); of kind of gum, Bdellium peraticum, Plin.HN 12.35'

*περάτρια· ἡ παραγγέλλουσα τὴν ὥραν ταῖς κεκτημέναις Hsch. (post Πέρδικος).

*Περγαῖος, α, ον, of Perge in Pamphylia, SEG 34.1305; title of Artemis, ib. 25.693, IPamph. pp. 160-1 (sp. Πρειας).

Περγᾰμηνός, after 'ή, όν' insert 'of Pergamum, SEG 23.362, etc.; title of Asclepius, SEG 24.978, 27.373'; line 3, before 'Suid.' insert 'Edict.Diocl. 7.38'

πέργουλος, add 'cf. σπέργουλος, σπόργιλος'

*περδικίτης, ου, ὁ, sc. λίθος, Alex.Trall. 12, Paul.Aeg. 7.17.75 (365.12-13 H.).

πέρδιξ, after 'partridge' insert '(in quots. either rock or chukar partridge)'

πέρδομαι, after '(Ar.)Pax 335' insert 'Eup. 99.10 K.-A.'

πέρθω, line 6, after 'poet. verb' insert '(used by Arist. in pun on Πέρσαι, Rh. 1412ᵇ2)'

περί, line 2, after 'A.v' insert 'Cypr. ta-ne-pe-re-ta-li-o-ne, τὰν πὲρ Ἐδάλιον ICS 217.27' F, add 'cf. Myc. pe-ri-me-de, pe-ri-qo-ta, etc.' G, for 'not in Trag. .. 634)' read 'in Trag. περέβαλον A.Ag. 1147, περεσκήνωσεν id.Eu. 634 (s.v.ll.)'

περιαγκωνίζω, after 'Lxx 4Ma. 6.3' insert 'aor. part. pass. περιαγκωνισθείς Aesop. 200 P.)'

περιαγνίζω, add 'med., περιαγνισαμένη Sokolowski 1.18.14 (Maeonia, ii BC)'

περιάγω 2 b, for 'cf. Luc. .. 187e' read 'lead in circuitous argument, περιαγόμενος τῷ λόγῳ Pl.La. 187e, Luc.Nigr. 8'

περιᾰγωγεύς, before 'windlass' insert 'capstan or'

*περιάκτρια, ἡ, prob. machine for changing scenery on stage (cf. μηχαναὶ περίακτοι), SEG 9.13.13 (Cyrene, iv BC).

περίαλλος I, line 2, delete '2.217'; line 3, after '(lyr.)' insert 'w. gen., π. θεῶν A.R. 2.217'

*περιαργύρωσις, εως, ἡ, plating with silver, Anon.Alch. 378.15.

περίαυλον, add 'also περίαυλος, ὁ, EM 361.39'

περιβάλλω, line 1, for '(v. infr.)' read '(περέβαλον is prob. cj. for περεβάλοντο in A.Ag. 1147)' II 1, add 'pass., ξύλον σιδήρῳ περιβεβλημένον bound round, App.BC 5.118' IV 1, lines 4/6, for 'pf. Pass.' read 'plpf.' and before 'δυναστείας' insert 'pf. part.', deleting 'cf. 2.25'

περίβλεπτος, penultimate line, after 'title of honour' insert '= Lat. spectabilis, ranking between illustris and clarissimus, POxy. 3481.3 (AD 442), SEG 32.1554 (early vi AD), Cod.Just. 1.4.22 pr.'

*Περιβλήμαια, τά, festival at Lyttus, ἐν τοῖς Περιβλημα[ίοις] Inscr.Cret. 1.xix 1.21 (Malla, c.221 BC).

περιβολᾴδιον, after 'wrapper' insert 'BGU 1848.13 (i BC)'

*περιβόλαιος, ον, encircling, Hsch. s.v. κόρυθα περίδρομον.

περίβολος II 1, add 'b περίβολον, τό, surrounding wall, Bernard Akoris 2, id. Les portes 33 (sp. -βωλον) (both i AD).'

*περιβρᾰχίων, ονος, ὁ, armlet, Inscr.Délos 1421Bbii10 (ii BC).

περιβρέμω, after 'round about' insert 'περὶ δὲ βρέμει ἄχω Alc. 130.33 L.-P.'

*περιβροχή, ἡ, moistening round about, Gal. 18(1).571.4 (unless ἐπιβρ- is read).

περίβωτος, after 'περιβόητος' insert 'APl. 49 (Apollonid.)'

περιγηθής, after 'very joyful' insert 'Emp. 27.4'

περιγίγνομαι II 2, add 'τὰ περιγενόμενα surplus, see PMich.VI 385. 42 n.'

*περίγναμπτος, η, ον, curved, prob. in Q.S. 1.149.

περιγρᾰφή II 3, for 'compass of expression' read 'sentence or clause embracing a thought' and add 'structure, framework of a sentence, D.H.Th. 26'

περιγράφω I 2, for 'being self-contained' read 'i.e. expressed in separate sentences'

περιδαίω, add 'also act., inflame with love, A.R. 4.869 (in tm.)'

περιδέξιος I 1, for 'AP 12.247 (Strat.)' read 'metaph., Call.fr. 360 Pf., AP 12.247 (Strat.)' 2, after '(lyr.)' insert 'w. inf., APl. 378'

περιδέρκομαι, before 'Nonn.' insert 'intr. in' and for 'AP .. (Agath.)' read 'trans. in AP 5.289.5, 16.169.1 (both Agath.)'

***περίδερμα**, gloss on ἀνθήλιον (q.v.), Hsch.

**περιδινέω**, add '**b** *twist out, dislocate,* Plu. 2.327a.'

***περιδῑνοπλᾰνήτης**, ου, ὁ, *one who wanders round, PMag.* 3.557.

**περίδῑνος**, delete 'ἡ' and for '*rover, pirate*' read '*brigand*'

***περιδίνω**, *tread round in threshing,* δινομένην πέρι βουσὶν ἐμὴν ἐφύλασσον ἅλωα Call.*fr.* 255 Pf.

**περίδριος**, ον, (δρίος) συκῆσι *surrounded by a cluster* of haemorrhoids, Marc.Sid. 62 (codd.).

**περιδρομή II**, for 'J.*AJ* 20.12.1' read 'J.*AJ* 20.11.2' and delete 'ἐκ π. Ptol.*Tetr.* 55' add '**IV** *enclosing framework,* Sm.*Ez.* 43.14.'

***περιδωμάω**, *build round,* poet. in *POxy.* 2812 *fr.*1(a) ii 25.

**περίειμι** (εἰμί) **III 1**, add 'of surviving members of a family, Τοκης ὁ πατὴρ καὶ Οὐαδέα ἡ μήτηρ περιόντες *SEG* 30.612 (ii AD)'

**περιέλᾰσις I**, add '**2** *driving round* in procession, dub. rest. in *IG* 1³.241.11.'

***περιέξ**, prep. w. gen., *around,* πάντων τῶν π. αὐτῆς οἰκημάτων *SB* 6000.9 (vi AD).

***περιέξοθεν**, v. °περιέξωθεν.

***περιέξωθεν** or **περιέξοθεν**, adv., *round the outside, all round,* αἱ π. ἄρουραι *PMich.*XIII 666.11, 23, 32; *PKöln* 104.6, *PHamb.* 68.16 (all vi AD).

**περιεργία 1**, after '*needless questioning*' insert 'Isoc. 10.2'

**περίεργος II 1**, after 'adv. -γως' insert 'D.H.*Isoc.* 3' add '**b** *taking particular trouble*; comp. adv. -ότερον, *Cod.Just.* 4.21.22.2.'

**περιέρπω II**, add 'Call.*Dieg.* iv.31'

**περιέρχομαι II 1**, line 9, after 'Hdt. 8.106' insert 'Paus. 4.17.4, 8.53.3'

***περιεστίαρχος**, ὁ, = περιστίαρχος, Poll. 8.104, Phot.

***Περιεστώ**, ἡ, a goddess of healing, *BE* 1991.221 (Thrace, *c.*400 BC).

**περιέσχατα**, add 'D.C. 36.49 (τῶν περὶ ἔσχατα D.H. 1.79 (s.v.l.))'

**περιέχω I 4**, transfer '*Supp.Epigr.* 3.421.33' to precede 'impers.'; add 'impers. pass., καθὰ τῇ θείᾳ ἡμῶν ταύτῃ περιέχεται νομοθεσίᾳ *Cod.Just.* 1.3.41.18'

***περιζᾰμενής**, ές, *violent,* π]νείοντος Βορέαο περιζαμενὲς Διὸς αἴσῃ Hes.*fr.* 204.126 M.-W.

***περίζῠγος**, ον, = περίζυξ, δᾳδίον τὸ π. prob. in *Inscr.Délos* 1442*B*70 (ii BC).

**περίζυξ I**, line 5, for 'Teos .. sens.' read 'Teos, iv BC): these exx. could be referred to °περίζυγος but nom. περίζυξ occurs'; line 6, after '*IG* 2².1469.75' add '(iv BC)'

**περίζωμα**, line 1, for '*girdle* .. *loins*' read '*loin-cloth*'; line 4, after 'Arr.*Epict.* 4.8.16' insert 'by the cult-statue of a goddess, *GDI* 5702.23 (Samos, iv BC)'

**περιζώννυμι**, before '*gird*' insert '(-ζωννύω Lxx *Ps.* 17(18).33)' add '**2** metaph., τινά τι Lxx *Ps.* l.c., ib. 40.'

**περιήγησις**, after lemma insert 'Dor. **περιάγησις** *SEG* 23.178 (*c.*229 BC)'

*__περιήκω__, *to lie around, surround*: part. *surrounding,* πέτραν [τὸν ὄχθον] περιήκουσαν Philostr.*VA* 3.13, κύκλῳ περὶ τὸ σπήλαιον π. ἄμπελος D.Chr. 2.41. **II** *to have come round to in the course of events,* w. acc., τοῦτον τὸν ἄνδρα φαμὲν περιήκειν τὰ πρῶτα Hdt. 6.86.α', τὰ σὲ περιήκοντα 7.16.α'.1, ἔμελλε .. δίκη περιήξειν καὶ Φιλοποίμενα Paus. 8.51.5. **b** w. εἰς, ἐπεὶ δ' εἰς τὸν φονέα ἡ ἀρχὴ περιήκει X.*Cyr.* 4.6.6, Arr.*An.* 4.13.4. **2** abs. of time, *to have come round,* καιρῷ περιήκοντι Plu.*Ages.* 35, ἔτει δεκάτῳ περιήκοντι Aristid.*Or.* 50(26).1, *Parth.* 30.2. **III** *to have turned* into, w. εἰς, [κεφαλαὶ] εἰς κρανία π. Philostr.*Im.* 2.19.

***περιηχής**, ές, = περιηχητικός, Rh. 1.450.9.

**περιήχησις**, add '**2** *rumour, hearsay, PBerol.*inv. 7347 (*JJP* 19.93).'

**περιηχητικός**, after '*resonant*' insert 'Thphr.*fr.* 89.10 (comp.)'

**περιθειόω**, add 'med. περιθειούμενος, Plu. 2.168d'

**περίθετος**, for 'a mask *with a wig attached*' read 'app. some sort of female headdress'

***περιθεώρησις**, εως, ἡ, *careful consideration,* Plu. 2.820a.

***περίθλασμα**, ατος, τό, app. *adjacent bruising, Hippiatr.* 104.7 (v.l. ὑπόθ-).

**περιθραύω**, add '**3** *break at the edges,* pf. part. περιτεθραυσμένον *Inscr.Délos* 1450*A*35.'

***περιθριγκίζω**, *fence round,* σὺν τῷ περιτετριγχισμένῳ τόπῳ *TAM* 4(1).239; cf. περιθριγκόω, θριγκός (τριγχός).

***περιθύρα**, ἡ, = περίθυρον, *CPR* 7.44.23 (v/vi AD).

**περίθῠρον**, for '*Ephes.* 4(1) no. 28' read '*IEphes.* 4128 (iv AD), 495 (vi AD), *ISmyrna* 849 (v/vi AD; sp. -θοιρ-)'

***περιθύτης**, ου, ὁ, office-holder in the temple of Asclepius at Pergamum, π. καὶ θεραπευτής *Inscr.Perg.* 8(3).79, 140, 152.6 (ii AD).

***περιθῠτικός**, ή, όν, *of* or *connected with the* °περιθύτης, *Inscr.Perg.* 8(3).140 (ii AD).

***περιθύω**, *perform the office of* περιθύτης, *BE* 1971.146 (Astypalaea).

***περιθωρᾱκίζω**, *gird about with a breastplate* (in quot. fig.), *IGLS* 524 (v AD).

**περιιάπτω**, after 'Theoc. 2.82' add '(dub., πυρὶ θυμὸς ἰάφθη *PAntin.*)'

**περιιστάω**, delete 'Chamael.ap.'

**περιίστημι B I 3**, delete '*come round* .. Th. 1.76' and add 'cf. *BCH* 59.37 (Crannon, πεστάντας = περιστάντας)' **II 3**, add 'ἡμῖν .. ἀδοξία τὸ πλέον ἢ ἔπαινος περιέστη Th. 1.76.4'

**περικᾰής**, after 'adv. -καῶς' insert '*with a very high fever,* π. πυρέττειν Gal. 7.722.17, 9.291.10'

**περικάθαρμα II**, add 'sg., *POxy.* 2331 ii 10 (iii AD)'

**περικαίω I**, add 'Ζώπυρος -όμενος, a comedy by Strattis, Stratt. 9, 10 K.-A.; Ἡρακλῆς π., a tragedy by Spintharus, Suid.'

***περικαλδής**, ές, = περικαλλής, dub. readings in *CEG* 327, 335 (both Boeotian, vi BC).

***περικᾰλυψις**, εως, ἡ, *covering round,* Procl.*in Ti.* 2.285.4 D.

***περικατάμαγμα**, ατος, τό, *offscouring,* Hsch. s.v. περίψημα.

**περίκειμαι I 1**, add 'of areas, *lie round,* τὸν περικείμενον τόπον *TAM* 4(1).276'

***περικεκομμένως**, *with excessive concision,* βαρβάρως καὶ π. εἰρῆσθαι Sch.Luc. p. 194.23.

***περικεφᾰλᾴδιον** (written -αιδιον), τό, dim. of περικεφαλαία, *Inscr.Délos* 1439*Aa*i16 (ii BC).

**περικεφᾰλαιος II 2**, for '*disorder of the oak*' read '*disorder affecting the head,* (of pigs)'

**περικήδομαι**, add '*PKöln* 63.16 (?Hellen. epic)'

**περικλαίω**, add 'med., Call.*fr.* 228.68 Pf.'

**περικλάω II 1**, add '**b** in chariot-racing, *wheel round the turning-post, SEG* 34.1437 (v/vi AD).'

**περικλεής**, after 'περικλειτός' insert 'Ibyc. 1(*a*).2 P.; cf. pers. n. Περικλέης, Archil. 13.1 W., etc.'

**Περίκλειος**, add 'also Περικλήϊος, Π. αἶμα λελογχώς *Corinth* 8(1).88'

**περικλειτός**, after '*far-famed*' insert 'B.10.19 S.-M.'

**περικλήϊστος**, after '*far-famed*' insert '*GVI* 1632.5 (Istropolis, ii/iii AD)'

***περίκλινος**, ον, unexpld. adj., στάβλον *LW* 3.2161 (Syria, ?vi AD), perh. = περικλινής.

**περικλίνω III**, for 'dub. sens. in' read '*shirk,* [ἐν τοῖς πράγμ]ασιν οὐ περιέκλινεν διὰ τὸ γῆρας *MDAI(A)* 31.431 (ii BC)'

**περικλῠμενον**, after 'Dsc. 4.14' insert 'Nic.*Th.* 510; also **-ος**, ὁ, Hsch.'

***Περικλύμενος** (-κλυμος cod.)· ὁ Πλούτων Hsch.; cf. Κλύμενος.

**περικολούω**, after 'Nic.*Al.* 267' add '528'

**περίκομος**, add '**II** *covered with hair, hairy,* Poll. 4.37.'

**περικρᾱνιον** (s.v. περικράνιος II), add 'Gal. 8.205.14; χαλεινοῦ μουλικοῦ μετὰ τοῦ περικρανίου (Lat. *frenum mulare cum capistello*) *Edict.Diocl.* in *SEG* 37.335 iii 6'

**περικρᾰτέω**, line 3, for '*Carm.Pop.* 46.24' read 'Hermocl. 24'

**περικρούω 1**, add 'ὃς ἂν τοῦτο τὸ μνημεῖον περικρούσῃ *IKyzikos* 560' **5**, for 'ib. 499a' read 'Men.*Dysc.* 414, Plu. 2.499a'

***περικυκλόκοσμος**, ὁ, prob. *carved surround in the form of a garland, EA* 10.101ff.

**περικῠλινδέω**, line 5, for '*roll about*' read '*revolve*'

***περικῡμάτιος**, ον, *having a wavy border,* ἱμάτιον *IG* 2².1514.18; cf. παρακυμάτιος.

**περίλευκος**, add '**3** περίλευκος, ἡ, name of a kind of agate, Epiph. in *Lapid.Gr.* 197.5, Plin.*HN* 37.180.'

**περίλοιπος**, add 'Myc. *pe-ri-ro-qo*'

**περιλῡω I**, after '*loosen round about*' insert 'Plu. 2.586a'

**περίμετρον**, add '**II** *round loaf,* Aq. 1*Ki.* 10.3.'

***περίμηρα**, τά, = περιμήρια, Ps.-Callisth. 108.7.

***περιμύω**, of a wound, *close,* μῦσεν δὲ πέρι βροτόεσσ' ὠτειλή Hom.*fr.* 8 D.

***περίνᾱος**, ον, *round the temple,* Ἄμμωνι καὶ τοῖς περινάοις (sc. θεοῖς) *SEG* 20.719.20 (Cyrene, ii BC); cf. περιναΐος.

**περινέμομαι**, after 'Plu.*Dio* 46' add '*Cam.* 34.4'

**περίνησος**, after 'cf.' insert '*Inscr.Délos* 1442*B*57 (ii BC)'

**περιοδεία I 1**, after '*circuit*' insert '*PRein.* 109.14 (ii BC, -δηα pap.)'

**περιοδονίκης**, after '*all the great games*' insert '(orig. the four panhellenic festivals, afterwards applied to different grades of multiple victor)'

**περίοδος**, ὁ, after lemma insert '(A)' add '**2** = ‡περιοδονίκης, *IG* 14.1107 (Rom.imp.), *IGRom.* 4.1251 (Thyatira, iii AD; to be read for περὶ ὁδῶν); τρὶς π. κῆρυξ *Inscr.Olymp.* 243 (iii AD).'

**περίοδος**, ἡ, after lemma insert '(B)' **I 1**, add '**b** *detour,* Modest.*Dig.* 27.1.10.3.' **2**, for '*slow walk*' read '*perambulation*' **II**, add '**2** *circuitous method* of investigation, Pl.*Phdr.* 274a, *R.* 504b.'

**περίοικος III**, for '*on the same* .. *of us*' read '*between the same parallels of latitude but 180° to the E. or W.*'

***περιοίχομαι**, v. °περοίχομαι.

**περιολισθάνω**, line 4, delete 'later **-ολισθαίνω**'

***περίοργος**, ον, = περιοργής, A.*Ag.* 216 (cj.), codd. περιόργως, v. περιοργής.

**περιορίζω I 1**, add 'w. acc., περιορίσας τὴν πόλιν *SEG* 34.1309 (Lycia, AD 161/9)'

***περιόριον**, τό, *precinct surrounding a tomb, MAMA* 6.83 (pl., Attouda).

*περιουλόομαι, pass., *to be cicatrized round*, Aët. 7.36 (287.10 O.).
περιουσία, add '**IV** *property, estate*, *Cod.Just.* 1.3.52.1, 1.3.55.4; of the private property of the emperor, ib. 1.33.4, 1.34.1. **2** *possession* (opp. ownership), Theophil.Antec. 3.2.2.'
περιοχή **I 3 c**, add 'of *arguments* of plays, π. τῶν Μενάνδρου δραμάτων Suid. s.v. Ὅμηρος, Σέλλιος κτλ.' **II**, for '*section* .. book' read '*passage* in a book or other writing, D.H.*Th.* 25' **III 2**, add '*wall of circumvallation*, Lxx *Ez.* 4.2'
περιπάλαξις, delete the entry.
*περιπᾰλάσσομαι, περιπαλαχθῆναι· περιπαλακῆναι Hsch.
περιπείρω, line 2, after '1*Ep.Ti.* 6.10' insert 'ἑαυτὴν π. κακοῖς Sopat.Rh. 8.30.6 W.'
*περιπέτασμα, τό, = Lat. *velamen* (in transl. of Verg.*A.* 1.649), *PRyl.* 478.144.
περιπίπτω **II 3**, add 'med., ἀώροις περιπέσοιτο συνφοραῖς *EA* 13.19 no. 4'
περιπλέκω **1**, med., add 'fig. Ἥλιον ὠκύμορον Κεία γαμέτην με ποθοῦσα καὶ μήτηρ τύμβῳ Ἰούλλα περιπλέκεται *SEG* 34.1280 (Paphlagonia, iii AD)'
περιπλήθω, add '**b** of groups, *be full in number, teem*, βουκολίοισι περιπλήθουσι Theoc. 25.13.' deleting this ref. in line 3.
περιπλοκή **I 1**, for '*interlacing*' read '*embracing*'; delete 'cf. Luc. .. etc.'; add '*embrace*, Luc.*Alex.* 39, Stob. 3.39.32'
περίπλοος, ὁ, add '**III** perh. naval manœuvre in which a ship circled round to ram an opponent amidships, Th. 7.36.3, X.*HG* 1.6.31.' deleting this from section I.
περίπλῠσις, add 'π. ἐρυθρά Gal. 16.623.17'
περιπνοή, for '-πνοία' read 'περίπνοια'
*περίπνῡα, ἡ, perh. = περίπνοια, app. some kind of illness (?περιπνευμονία), εὔξετο .. ὑπὲρ τῶν τέκνων διὰ τὴν περίπνυαν *TAM* 5(1).247 (AD 257/8).
περιποιέω **II 1**, at end delete '*make gain*' and transfer 'X.*Mem.* 4.2.38' to follow 'X.*Mem.* 2.7.3' add '**III** *make, construct round*, *SEG* 32.356 (Aegina, *c.*550 BC).'
*περιπολαρχέω, *command* περίπολοι, Robert *Hell.* 10.284 (iii BC), *SEG* 32.626 (Illyria, iii BC)'
περιπολέω **II 1**, add '**b** w. acc. pers., *attend on*, Sch.S.*OT* 1322 explaining ἐπίπολος.'
*περιπολία, Ion. -ίη, ἡ, *revolution* of heavenly bodies, Hp.*Hebd.* 2.
περιπολλόν, add 'also περιπολλά (neut. pl.) Arat. 914'
περίπολος **2**, after 'Eup. 341' insert 'Anon.Hist. (*FGrH* 105) *fr.* 2 J.'
*περιπορπίς, ίδος, ἡ, *clasp*, cj. in A.R. 1.767.
*περιπορφῠροῦς, ᾶ, οῦν, = περιπόρφυρος 1, χιτὼν *Inscr.Délos* 1417*A*i30 (ii BC).
*περιπρῖσμα, ατος, τό, = πρίσμα I 1, ἐλεφαντίνων π. *IG* $2^2$.1408.13, 1409.6, etc.
περιπτύσσω **I 1**, at end delete 'Pass.' and transfer 'Aristaenet. 1.1' to the end of section I 3; after it add 'fig., τὴν τῶν Ἀκεράλων ἄνοιαν περιπτυσσάμενοι Just.*Nov.* 115.3.14'
περίπτωμα **1**, add '*sudden illness*, *TAM* 5(1).331, cf. Robert *Hell.* 10.102 n. 10'
περίρραμμα, add '*Thasos* 155.8 (iv BC)'
περιρρέω **II 3**, line 4, after 'Luc. *VH* 2.11' insert 'τὸ πῦρ αὐτῷ περιέρρει, Call.*Dieg.* viii.12 (*fr.* 197 Pf.)' **4**, line 4, after 'Plu.*Per.* 16' insert '[λέξις] περιρρέουσα τοῖς νοήμασιν *overflowing* with ideas, D.H.*Dem.* 18'
περιρρογχάζω, add '*PCol.* 242.4 (v AD)'
*περίσαος, ον, app. *remaining*, ϝέτεα *BCH* 60.182.22, 24 (Thespiae, iii BC).
*περισκᾰπετεύω, *dig a ditch round*, χοῦρον περρεσκαπετευμένον πέλεθρα IIII *IGC* p. 11 l. 18 (Larissa, iii BC); cf. σκάπετος.
περισκέλια, for '*drawers*' read '*trousers*' and after it insert 'Hsch.'
*περισκελίδιον, τό, dim. of περισκελίς, *IG* $2^2$.1534.78 (Athens, iii BC), *Inscr.Délos* 1409*Ba*i98 (ii BC), *CPR* 5.22.4, 7 (?v AD).
περίσκεπτος **2**, delete '*admired*, Χαρίτεσσι'
περισκέπω, add '*SEG* 31.1288 (Side, AD 249/52)'
*περισκηνάω or -έω, *surround with* σκηναί, Poll. 8.20 (cod.), cf. *JHS* 75.117.
*περισκηνόω, aor. περεσκήνωσα, *drape round* like a tent, φᾶρος A.*Eu.* 634.
περισκληρύνω, add 'Gal. 18(1).391.1'
περισκοπέω **II 1**, after 'Arat. 199' insert '464, 852 (tm.)' add '**b** w. gen., *look out for*, Εὔροιο περισκοπέειν ἀνέμοιο Arat. 435, 925, 987.'
*περισμῡχηρός, όν, *smouldering, covered in smoke*, Amyntas in *Suppl.Hell.* 44.5 (pap. -ζμυ-).
περισμύχω, after '*fire*' insert 'transf., of rust'
*περισπαίρω, *twitch convulsively upon* a point, barb, or blade, of the dying, γλωχῖσι Opp.*H.* 5.547 (prob. cj.); δουρί Q.S. 1.624; cf. λώβῃ, i.e. wound inflicted by scorpion, Nic.*Th.* 773: abs., dub. in Lyc. 68.
περισπασμός **I**, for '*wheeling round*' read 'in military manœuvres, *about turn*' **II**, line 5, delete 'θυμοῦ .. *Ec.* 2.23' add '**b** *preoccupation*, πᾶσαι αἱ ἡμέραι αὐτοῦ ἀλγημάτων καὶ θυμοῦ περισπασμὸς αὐτοῦ Lxx *Ec.* 2.23.'
περισπάω **II**, lines 1/2, delete 'intr. .. 116.5' **III 1 a**, add 'π. [τὰ χρήματα] εἰς τὴν ἄδικον ἐπιθυμίαν προϊσταμένων *IEphes.* 18 b 8 (i AD)' **3**, after '*distract*' insert 'Plb. 3.116.5'
περισπογγίζω, add 'sp. περισφ- Paul.Aeg. 6.34.3 (72.20 H.)'
περισπορία, for '*suburbs*' read '*surrounding country*'
περισπουδάζω, add 'rest. in *SEG* 39.1056 (Neapolis, i BC)'
περισσοδάκτῠλος, for '*with* .. *toes*' read '*having toes of unequal length*, of a hen'
περισσός **II 1**, line 11, after '(Lucill.)' insert 'Theoc. 26.24'; add 'followed by ὑπέρ, τὸ περισσὸν ὑπὲρ τὸ τετραούγκιον *Cod.Just.* 6.4.4.18a' **2**, line 3, for 'A.*Pr.* 385' read 'A.*Pr.* 383'
*περισσότευκτος, ον, *elaborately worked*, βωμὸν περισσότευκτον ἀγλαόν θ' ἕδος *IHadr.* 132 (ii AD).
*περισσοφροσύνη, ἡ, *excessive cleverness*, Them.*Or.* 21.259b.
περιστᾰδόν, for 'Call.*Hec.* 1.1.4' read 'Call.*fr.* 260.14 Pf.'
περίστᾰσις **I 2 a**, add '*walled area*, *PHels.* 12 (ii BC)' **II 1 b**, add 'τραγῳδία ἐστὶν ἡρωικῆς τύχης π. Thphr.ap.Diom. p. 487.12 K. (unless π. here = περιπέτεια III 1)'
περιστᾰχῠώδης, for '*with an ear* .. *on it*' read '*set round spike-fashion*'
*περιστεγνοποιΐα, ἡ, *building of roofed hutments*, *RA* 3.40 (Amphipolis, iii/ii BC).
περιστέλλω **II**, add '**2** abs., of the lips in pronouncing ω, D.H.*Comp.* 14.' **III 2**, after '*defend*' insert 'A.*fr.* 154a.18 R.'
περιστέριον, add '**III** = περιστερίς II, Hsch.'
*περιστερόπουλλος, ὁ, *small dove*, *CPR* 7.42 ii 1 (v AD).
περίστια, line 2, after 'Ar.*Ec.* 128' insert 'sg., π., τό, *purificatory offering* after return from a funeral, Hsch.'
*περιστῐγής, ές, *spotted all over, variegated*, ἔρφος Nic.*Th.* 376 (v.l.); μυρμήκειον ib. 749.
περιστοιχέω, add '**2** fig., *hem in, confine*, in quot. pass., Procl.*in R.* 1.124 K. (nisi leg. -ισμένων).'
περιστοιχίζω, for '*surround as with toils* or *nets*' read '*surround with a fence*'
περιστολή **I 3**, for '*adornments*' read '*covering, cloak*, or sim.'
περιστροφίς, add 'Alc. 143.8 L.-P. (indeterminate sense)'
περίστρωμα, add '*SEG* 28.53 (Athens, iv BC)'
*περίστρωμον, τό, or -ος, ὁ, = περίστρωμα, *Dura*[4] p. 100 no. 227.
περίστῡλος **II**, add 'τὸ π. τοῦ γυμνασίου *SEG* 30.1535 (Lycia, after AD 152)'
περίστῳον, add 'sp. περίστωον *IEphes.* 3239 (ii/iii AD), περίστοον ib. 3233 (iii AD)'
*περισυνός, prob. for περυσινός, ἐπὶ τοῖς π. ὁρίοις *PFlor.* 383.77, 104 (iii AD), *PMasp.* 128.15 (vi AD).
περισύρω **II 1**, after 'Lxx *Ge.* 30.37' add 'fig., Ph. 1.178' deleting this ref. fr. section 2.
περισφάλεια, delete the entry.
περισφάλλω, pass., add 'Gal. 18(1).327.9'
*περισφογγίζω, v. °περισπ-.
περισφρῑγάω, before 'gloss' insert '*swell greatly*, A.R. 3.1258 (tm.)'
περισχοινισμός, for '*BCH* 23.566 (Delphi)' read '*SEG* 27.119.13 (Delphi, iii BC)'
περισῴζω, add 'in Chr. sense, *save* from damnation, *Cod.Just.* 1.3.41.3, 1.3.42 pr.'
*περιτειχόω, = περιτειχίζω, *EA* 12.109 no. 43 (Caria, Rom.imp.).
*περίτῑμος, ον, *highly honoured*, Call.*fr.* 75.52 Pf.
περιτῑνάσσω, add 'med., *hop about* in pain, Aesop. 235 P.'
Περίτιος, add '*SEG* 31.1003 (Lydia, AD 84/5), 32.1555 (Arabia, AD 178), 37.590 (sp. Περειτ-, Maced., AD 189)'
περιτόναιον, after 'Hp.*Epid.* 7.20' insert '(pl.)'
*περιτρέφω, pf. -τέτροφα A.R. 2.738, Nic.*Th.* 299, 542:– (*cause to*) *form* or *grow round*, ἀυτμὴ πηγυλὶς .. ἀργινόεσσαν ἀεὶ περιτέτροφε πάχνην A.R. 2.738; pass., περιτρέφεται κυκόωντι, i.e. it (the curds) forms as you stir, Il. 5.90, σακέεσσι περιτρέφετο κρύσταλλος Od. 14.477, τὸ περιτεθραμμένον σαρκίδιον M.Ant. 12.1, Gal. 2.504.3. **2** act., *grow round*, τῆς (ῥίζης) ἀκανθοβόλος μὲν ἀεὶ περιτέτροφε χαίτη, λείρια δ' ὡς ἴα τοῖα περιτρέφει Nic.*Th.* 542, 543; w. abst. subj., κραδίην .. κακὸν περιτέτροφεν ἄλγος ib. 299.
περιτρέχω **II 1**, add '**c** *make a rapid survey of* a subject, D.H.*Din.* 11.'
*περιτρινχίζω, v. °περιθριγκίζω.
περίτριμμα **I**, add 'as term of abuse, ὁ μολοβρός· αἰσχρός, ἀναιδής. περίτριμμα Hsch.'
περιτροπή, add 'κατὰ περιτροπήν Sopat.Rh. 8.132.7 W.'
περίτροπος, for 'prob. l. in Plu.*Lys.* 12' read 'cj.in Plu.*Lys.* 12 (v. παράτροπος)'
*περιτῠλόομαι, *become callous all round*, Crito ap.Gal. 13.798, Cass.*Pr.* 13.
περιτῠλόω, delete the entry.

*__περιφαιδρύνω__, *cleanse round*, κάρη A.R. 4.663 (v.l. ἐπι-).

*__περιφαίνομαι__, *establish*, aberrant pf., περιπεφανούμενα ἐκφόρια *BGU* 2390.30 (160/59 BC).

__περίφαντος II__, for '*famous*' read '*conspicuous from every side*' and add 'Orph.*H.* 20.1'

__περιφέγγω__, after '*illuminate round about*' insert 'Plu.*fr.* 14 S. (περιφευγ- codd.)'

__περιφέρεια II__, for '*wandering, error*' read '*madness*'

__περιφερής I 1__, delete 'Hermipp. 4' __2 a__, add 'Hermipp. 73 K.-A.'

__περιφθείρομαι II__, for this section read '*wander about wretchedly*, Isoc.*Ep.* 9.10, Lycurg. 40, Men.*Dysc.* 101'

*__περιφῐᾰλισμός__, ὁ, *digging a basin round a plant*, *PCol.* 179.18 (AD 300) in *TAPhA* 92.469, cf. ib. 93.164.

*__περιφῑμίζω__, *bind fast* by a spell, *SPAW* 1934.1041 (tab.defix., Boeotia; -φιμμ-); cf. °φιμόω, *muzzle*, περιφιμόω.

__περιφλεγής__, line 1, after '*burning*' insert 'καῦμα (*fever*) X.*HG* 5.3.19 (v.l. πυρι-)'

__περιφλίω__, read '__περιφλῖω__'

*__περιφλίωμα__, ατος, τό, *door-frame*, *MAMA* 8.498 (Aphrodisias, ii AD).

__περιφορά II 5__, for '*error*' read '*madness*' __IV__, after '*turntable*(?)' insert '(unless = *margin, period of grace*)' add '__V__ pl., *rotating objects*, τὰς ἐπ' ἄκρου σφαιροειδεῖς π., of the angler-fish's lures, Ael.*NA* 9.24.'

__περιφόρῖνος__, delete 'cf. περίφουρνος'

__περίφουρνος__, delete the entry (v. °φοῦρνος).

__περίφραγμα I__, add '__2__ *the toils of a hunting-net*, Sch.Pi.*N.* 3.89 (pl.).'

__περιφρᾰδής__, adv., add 'ὅπῃ[ως τοῦ]το περιφραδέως σὺ τελέσσῃς *SEG* 31.1288 (Side, AD 249/52)'

__περιφροσύνη 1__, for '*cunning*' read '*cleverness, skill*' and after 'Them.*Or.* 21.259b' insert '(dub., v. °περισσοφ-)' add '__2__ *contempt*, Plu. *Comp.Alc.Cor.* 3.'

__περίφρων I__, add 'Mitchell *N.Galatia* 14 (Rom.imp.)'

__περίχαλκος__, add '*PMich.*inv. 1718.18 (*APF* 33.57, iv AD)'

__περιχαλκόω__, add 'θυμιατήριον ξύλινον περικεχαλκωμένον *Inscr.Délos* 1442*B*45 (ii BC)'

__περιχειρίδιον__ (s.v. περίχειρον), before 'Hsch.' insert '*Inscr.Délos* 1417*B*ii46'

__περίχειρον__, add '*Inscr.Délos* 1442*B*24'

*__περιχρήσιμος__, ον, *very useful*, Ps.-Callisth. 131.17.

__περιχύτης__, after 'Ptol.*Tetr.* 179' insert '(v.l.)'; add '*Stud.Pal.* 22.75.39 (iii AD, περι[χ]οιτ- pap.)'

__περιχωματίζω__, after '*surround with a dyke*' insert '*PTeb.* 775.9 (ii BC)'

__περιχώριος__, add 'Sch.S.*OC* 1059; π. [ἀγῶνες] Sch.Pi.*I.* 1.11'

__περίχωρος__, last line, after '*Ev.Matt.* 14.35' insert '*SEG* 36.1095 (Sardis, iii AD), *Res Gestae Saporis* 34 (pl.); τὸ π. *IG* 5(2).3.10 (Tegea, iv BC)'

__περιψάω__, after '*wipe clean*' insert 'Hippon. 104.18 W.'

__περίψημα__, add 'perh. also *something of no value*, π. σοι ποίει, *Vit. Aesop.*(G) 35'

__περίψηφος__, add '__II__ subst. περίψηφον, Dor. -ψᾶφον, τό, prob. *balance, surplus*, *Lindos* 419.12 (i AD).'

*__περιωπής__, ές, *seeing in all directions*, διφυῆ π. .. Ἔρωτα Orph.*A.* 14; *seen from all directions* or *having views all round*, π. νηόν epigr. in *IGBulg.* 2086.

__περίωπος__, delete 'in Orph.*A.* 14' to end.

__πέρνημι__, line 7, after 'aor. ἔπρησα' inset '(dub., v. *Meiggs-Lewis* 16)'; after '__πιπράσκομαι__' for 'first .. 224a' read 'Lys. 18.20, Pl.*Sph.* 224a, *Phd.* 69b (s.v.l.)'; after '__πιπράσκω__ first found in' insert 'Thphr.*fr.* 98 (if the wd. is fr. Thphr.), then'

*__περοίχομαι__, *run* or *extend round*, Hes.*Th.* 733 (s.v.l.).

__περόνη I 1__, after '(*IG*) 2².1388.20' insert 'δίβολος περόνᾱ *AP* 6.282 (Theod.)'

*__Περϙοθάριοι__, οἱ, class of refugees at Locris, *IG* 9²(1).718.27 (v BC).

*__περροδων__ (gen. pl.), unexpld. wd. in list mainly of foodstuffs, *PWash. Univ.* 52.3 (iv AD).

__περσέα__, for '*Mimusops Schimperi*' read '*Cordia myxa*, *sebesten* (a plum-like tree)'

__περσεῖος__ (s.v. πέρσειον), add '*PMich.*inv. 4001 (*ZPE* 24.83, i/ii AD, sp. περσοίνου)'

__Περσεφόνη__, line 2, for 'Φερσεφόνη' read 'Φερσεφόνᾱ'; line 3, after 'etc.' insert 'cf. Φερσοπόνη *Inscr.Cret.* 2.xvi 10 (ii AD)'; after '*CIG* 4588' insert '(Φερσεφόνεια Hsch.)'; add 'also v.s.v. Πηριφόνα, °Πηρεφόνεια, Φερσέφασσα (where some refs. are repeated)'

*__περσῆ__ ὀξύ(μαλα), τά, app. *peaches*, Lang *Ath.Agora* XXI B20.

__Πέρσης I a__, line 3, before 'The Greeks ..' insert 'fr. Old Iran. *Pārsa*' add '__2__ as epith. of Zeus, *TAM* 5(1).267.'

*__περσίδιον__, v. πέρσειον.

*__περσικοποιός__, ὁ, *maker of slippers* (Περσικός 2), *IG* 2².11689 (iv BC).

__Περσικός 5__, before 'Cratin. 259' for 'ὁ Π. alone' read 'Π. ἀλέκτωρ' add '__9__ as epith. of Artemis, *BCH* 11.447-8 no. 5, *SEG* 31.998, etc.'

*__Περσῖνος__, η, ον, *Persian*, σουβρικάλλιον Περσεῖνον *Stud.Pal.* 20.41ᵛ.3 (s.v.l., v. *Tyche* 2.10, ii AD).

__πέρσις__, for 'εως' read 'ιδος' and after 'ἡ' insert 'acc. -ιν Arist.*Po.* 1456ᵃ16'

*__περσονάλιος__, α, ον, *personal*, ταῖς περσοναλίαις (sc. ἀγωγαῖς = *actionibus in personam*) Just.*Nov.* 136.5 pr.

__πέρσυ__, after '(Cyzicus)' insert '*POxy.* 1299.8 (iv AD)'; cf. ‡πέρυσι, mod. Gk. πέρσι'

*__περτέδοκε__, v. °προσδίδωμι.

__πέρῠσι__, add '*PFlor.* 189.4 (iii AD), *PSI* 81.14 (v/vi AD)'; cf. ‡πέρσυ'

*__Περφερέτᾱς__, α, ὁ, epith. of Zeus in Thessaly, *Liv.Ann.* 3.155 (*RPh.* 35.128ff., Mopsium), *SEG* 23.444 (Larissa, both i BC); also Φερφερέτας *IG* 9(2).1057.1 (Mopsium, i BC).

*__πεσσά__, ἡ, part of a building, perh. the same as °πεσσός III 2, *PMichael.* 58A2 (vi AD).

*__πεσσᾰράκοντα__, v. ‡τεσσαράκοντα.

__πεσσεύω__, lines 3/4, for 'fortune .. affairs' read 'i.e. *shifts* them up and down *like pieces on a board*'

*__πεσσοβολία__, ἡ, *casting of* πεσσοί, used as dice, *PNess.* 21.20, 22.10 (both sp. πεισσ-, vi AD).

*__πεσσοποιέομαι__, app. *make oneself a pessary of*, Poet.*de herb.* 103.

__πεσσός II__, line 2, after '*pessary*' insert 'Hp.*Jusj.*' __3__, for '*JHS* 8.118 (Iasos)' read '*IIasos* 20' __III__, for this section read 'archit., *pier* (supporting an arch), Str. 16.1.5, Procop.*Aed.* 1.1.37. __2__ perh. *terrace*, *POxy.* 1272.6 (ii AD).'

*__πέσωμα__, ατος, τό, *fall*, Kretschmer *GV* p. 122.

__πετᾰλία I__, for '*crate*(?)' read '*basket*'; after '*PCair.Zen.* 99.3' insert '*SB* 9091, ostr. in *SB* 7402.2, al.' and insert 'all ' before 'iii BC' __II__, delete the section.

__πέτᾰλον I__, line 4, after '(lyr.), etc.' insert '*cornstalk*, κορωνιόωντα πέτηλα βριθόμενα σταχύων Hes.*Sc.* 289' __II 1__, add '__b__ κόλλης π. *sheet* of glue, *IG* 11(2).203*B*97 (Delos, iii BC).'

__πετᾰλουργός__, add 'subst., Anon.Alch. 379.7'

__πέτᾰσος III__, for '*OGI* 510.4' read '*IEphes.* 2039-41'

*__πεταστικός__, ή, όν, wd. of uncertain meaning, π. διάκρισις *Physici* 2.228.5.

__πετασών__, add 'Varro *RR* 2.4.10, Mart. 3.77.6, etc., *Edict.Diocl.* 4.8'

__πετεινός__, 3 lines fr. end, after 'Lycurg. 132' insert 'πετεινός, ὁ, *cock*, opp. ὄρνις (hen), Diogenian. 3.50'

__πετευριστής__, add '*POxy.* 2860.16 (ii AD)'

__πέτευρον II 2__, for '*platform, stage*' read 'applied to a narrow platform at the top of a σαμβύκη II' __III__, for '*springe, trap*' read 'dub. sens. in passage where Hebr. means *depths*' __IV__, add 'Call.*fr.* 186.4 Pf., Lyc. 884'

__πετηνίς__, for 'κόρις' read 'ἀκρίς (La.)'

*__πετίτωρ__, ορος, ὁ, *applicant*, app. a Mithraic title, *Dura⁷* p. 87 no. 848, cf. Lat. *petitor*.

__πέτομαι__, line 19, (pf. πέπτηκα), after '(v. ποτάομαι)' insert 'pf. intrans. (κατ)έπτηκα Men.*Kol.* 40' __II 1__, line 3, delete 'of fickle natures'; line 6, before 'of fame' insert 'τῶν μαινομένων πέτεται θυμός τε νόος τε *soar unchecked*, Thgn. 1053'

__πετρᾰκισχείλιη__, add 'δραχμὰ[ς] πετρακισχιλίας *BCH* 60.178.24 (Thespiae, iii BC)'

*__πετρᾰκοντᾰεττά__, = τεσσαρακονταεπτά, *forty-seven*, *SEG* 26.672.31 (Larissa, ii BC).

*__πετρᾰκοντᾰπέμπε__, = τεσσαρακονταπέντε, *forty-five*, *SEG* 26.672.42 (Larissa, ii BC).

__πετράς__, add 'also Thess., *SEG* 31.577 (136/5 BC)'

*__πέτρες__, = τέσσαρες, *four*, *SEG* 26.672.43 (Larissa, ii BC).

*__Πετρησιάρχης__, εω, or -ος, ὁ, prob. ruler of a district of Ceos, *IG* 12(5).610.2 (Ceos, iii BC).

__πέτρῐνος III__, for this section read 'π. ἀκοντισμός, term (acc. to Arrian, Celtic) for manœuvre in which javelin is thrown from horseback while on the turn, Arr.*Tact.* 37.4'

*__πετροκόλαπτος__, ον, *engraved on stone*, π. ἔπος *SEG* 32.896 (Crete, ii/i BC).

__πετρορριφής__, for '*hurled from a rock*' read '*pelted with stones*'

__πέτρος I 1__, add '__b__ *tombstone*, *AP* 7.465 (Heraclit.; = *EG* 1524 P.).' __II__, add '(app. fr. misunderstanding of Skt. *pattra* "leaf")'

__πετροφυής I__, add 'Τιθορεί[α] πετροφ[υ]εῖ *GVI* 766'

__πετρόω I 1__, after '(Theodorid.)' insert 'Nonn.*D.* 47.591' __2__, delete the section.

__πετρών__, add '*Princeton Exp.Inscr.* 1019'

__πεττᾰράκοντα__, add '*BCH* 60.179.37 (Thespiae, iii BC)'

__πέτταρες__, add 'also Thess., *SEG* 31.575 (171 BC), ib. 13.394 (iii AD), etc.'

*__πεύθω__, aor. part. πεύσανς *Inscr.Cret.* 4.83 (Gortyn, v BC), πούσας ib. 1.xix 1.13 (Malla, iii BC), pass. πευσθένς ib. 4.83, *lay information against*, *Leg.Gort.* 8.55, *Inscr.Cret.* 4.162.7.

__πεύκη II__, add '__3__ *oar*, Tim.*Pers.* 13, 76 P.'

*__πευκώδης__, ες, *covered with pine-trees*, λόφος *Inscr.Olymp.* 46.36 (ii BC).

**πεφεισμένως**, after '*cautiously*' insert 'Phld.*Rh.* 2.140 S.'

**πεφλάζει**, add 'cf. παφλάζω'

***πεφοριῶσθαι**· πεπαχύνθαι τὸ δέρμα τοῦ ὀφθαλμοῦ Phot., Harp.

**πῇ II 3**, add 'ὅπηι μὲν .., πῇ δὲ .. *SEG* 32.1502 (Palestine, v AD)'

**πήγᾰνον**, π. ἄγριον, add '*PColl.Youtie* 4.7 (iii AD)'

***πηγάσιος**, α, ον, *belonging to the spring*, Νάρκισ<σ>ος π. *Syria* 31 Pl.C (facing p. 198); cf. Πήγασος.

**πηγή I 1**, after 'Dor. πᾱγά' insert '(also Boeot., e.g. *SEG* 23.297, Lebadea, iv/iii BC)'; line 2, after 'cf.' insert 'Hes.*Th.* 282, Stesich. 7.2 P.'; lines 3/4, delete 'κρουνῷ .. 22.147' **II 1**, after '*source*' insert 'Il. 21.312, 22.147'; add '**b** where π. is dist. fr. κρήνη, π. is the *spring*, κρήνη the artificially constructed *fountain*, Th. 2.15, Paus. 2.3.3, 4.31.6; cf. οὐδ' ἀπὸ κρήνης πίνω Call.*Epigr.* 28 Pf.'

**πῆγμα I 4**, add 'κατὰ π. καὶ κατὰ τὴν ἀρχαίαν συνήθιαν perh. a *fixed rule* or *tariff* (cf. πήγνυμι IV), pap. in *ASNP* ser. II.6.1 (v AD)' add '**IV** *block* (of land), ἰδιωτικῆς καὶ βασιλεικῆς πάσης οὔσης ἐν ἑνὶ πήγματι *PNew York* 20.11 (AD 302).'

**πήγνῡμι III**, add 'J.*BJ* 6.3.4'

**πηγός II 2**, add 'Antim. 145 Wy.'

**πηδᾰλιοῦχος**, add 'Dor. **πᾱδᾰλιοῦχος**, in lit. sense, *Clara Rhodos* 8.228 (Rhodes), *SEG* 33.640 (Rhodes, ii/i BC)'

**πηδός**, line 2, for 'πάδος (q.v.)' read '‡παδός'

**πηῑσκος**, delete 'Dim. of παῖς'; for '*Supp.Epigr.* 2.509.5 (Crete, v BC)' read '*Inscr.Cret.* 1.x 2.5, 7 (Eltynia, vi/v BC)'

**πηκτίς I 1**, after '*stringed instrument*' insert 'a form of *harp*' and add 'Anacr. 28, 41 P., Diog.Ath. 1.9 S.'; after '= λύρα' insert '*AP* 9.270 (Marc.Arg.), Philostr.*Im.* 1.10.3, *Anacreont.* 43.10 W.' **2**, add '*IG* 4.53 (Aegina, Rom.imp.)'

**πηκτός III**, line 4, for 'salt *obtained from brine*' read '*rock salt*'

**πηλᾰμύς**, add 'also **πηλᾰμίς** Hsch. La. s.v. θύννον'

***πηλεύς**, ὁ, wd. of unkn. meaning in damaged pap., *CPR* 7.44.12 (v/vi AD).

**πήληξ 1**, after '(Il.) 16.797' insert 'Od. 1.256'; add 'cf. Πήληξ, citizen of the Attic deme Πήληκες, Aeschin. 2.83' add '**3** ὄργανόν τι ψαλτήριον Poll. 4.61 (prob. a crested harp).'

***πηλοάρτης**, ου, ὁ, (αἴρω) *clay-* or *mortar-lifter*, *PRein.* 2065.47, 48 (ii AD) in *JJP* 11/12.66, cf. *PRyl.* 642.11 (iv AD).

**πηλόγονος**, for '= γηγενής, used of the giants' read 'used of the human race'

***πηλοκάρβων**, ωνος, ὁ, kind of lute (clay), Anon.Alch. 38.1.

**πηλοπᾰτέω**, add '**II** *tread clay*, as term in pottery-making, *PMich.*v 241.33 (i AD).'

**πηλοποιός**, add 'Gal. 10.395.11'

**πηλός**, line 2, after 'Phryn. 38' insert 'pl., Plu. 2.993e' **I 2**, after '*mire*' insert 'Heraclit. 5'

**πηλόω**, line 3, after 'Plu. 2.980e' insert 'πηλοῦσθαι τῷ θεῷ Aristid.*Or.* 48(24).74'

**πῆλυξ**, read '**πήλυξ**' and add 'cf. σπήλυγξ'

+**πήλωμα**, ατος, τό, *mud-pit* (in a gymnasium), *lutinae* πήλωμα Char. p. 33 K.; perh. also *CIG* 2758 (*ZPE* 79.289).

**πηνίκα**, line 4, (πηνίκα ἄττα), after 'Ar.*Av.* 1514' insert '*fr.* 617 K.-A.'

**πηνίον I**, add '**3** *thread*, Sch.E.*Hec.* 444, 471.'

**πήνισμα**, for '*woof on the spool*' read '*thread* (for the woof)'

**πῆξις I 2**, for '*fixing*' read '*determination, computation*'

***Πηρεφόνεια**, = Περσεφόνη (Lacon.), Hsch.; cf. Πηριφόνα.

**πηρίν**, delete 'ἐλάφου πηρίς Hsch.'

**πηρός**, before 'Dor.' insert 'accented πῆρος in Att. acc. to Hdn.Gr. 1.190'; line 3, delete '(cf. .. 57)'; line 4, after 'Hp.*Mul.* 2.131' insert '*blind*, Aesop. 37 P., *AP* 9.46 (Antip.Thess.)'

**πῆρος**, for '*dotage*' read '*injury*' and for 'Alc. 98' read 'Alc. 10.4 L.-P.'

***πηροφόρος**, ὁ, *one who carries a wallet*, Hsch. s.v. θυλακοφόροι (πυρο- cod.).

**πήρωσις**, add 'fig., πήρωσις ἄπαις βίος *AP* 9.359.7 (Posidipp. or Pl.Com.; = *EG* 1694 P.)'

**πηχυαῖος**, add 'also **πηχιαῖος**, *IG* 12(2).11.14 (Mytilene, iii BC)'

**πηχῦνω**, for '*take in one's arms, embrace*' read '*take in the crook of one's arm*'; delete 'χείρεσσι .. (Rhian.)'

**πῆχυς**, line 1, for '**πᾶχυς** Alc. 33' read 'and Dor. **πᾶχυς** Alc. 350.7 L.-P., Call.*fr.* 196.38 Pf.'; line 3, after 'πήχεως' insert '*IG* 2².1013.34, al. (ii BC)' **III 1**, line 1, after '(the bridge)' insert '*h.Merc.* 50'

**πιαίνω I**, add 'Arist.*Oec.* 1345ᵃ3' deleting this ref. in section II 3.

***πιάκλον**, τό, Lat. *piaculum, expiatory offering*, *SEG* 7.351 (Dura, iii AD).

**πιάτρα**, after '*TAM* 2 .. (Tlos)' insert '870.6; also πιέτρα ib. 847, 848'

**πιβρᾶτος**, after '*privatus*' insert 'βαλανεῖ πιβράτου *private bath attendant*'

**πιγκέρνης**, for '*cupbearer*' read '*bar-keeper*' and add '*CPR* 8.56.20 (v/vi AD)'

**πῑδῠλίς**, for '= πιδακόεσσα' read 'πέτρα ἐξ ἧς ὕδωρ ῥέει' and add 'Call.*fr.* 67.12 Pf. (cj.)'

**πῑδύω**, after '*gush forth*' insert 'Hp.*Epid.* 5.16'

**πιέζω I**, add '**2** in chariot-racing, perh. *bore*, μὴ πιάσωσιν, μὴ παραβύσωσιν *SEG* 34.1437 (Syria, v/vi AD).' **II**, add '**6** *imprison*, *SB* 9786.7 (iv AD).'

***πιειρῶς**, adv. fr. πίειρα, *richly*, πιειρῶς καὶ λιπαρῶς Sch.Pi.*N.* 1.16.

**Πῑερία**, add 'cf. Myc. *pi-we-ri-ja-ta*, pers. n.; *pi-we-ri-di* (dat.), fem. n.'

**Πῑερίδες**, after '*P.* 1.14, etc.' insert 'sg. Πιερίς prob. in Pratin. 3.4 S.; epigr. in *SEG* 37.1175.10 (Pisidia, ii AD)'

**Πῑερικός**, after 'Hdt. 4.195' insert '*AP* 7.34 (Antip.Sid.; = *EG* 3444 P.)'

**πιεστήρ**, line 2, for '(pl.)' read '(πιεστῆ[ρας], but perh. πιεστή[ρια] shd. be rest.'

**πιεστήριος II**, after '*press*' insert '*IG* 1³.425.12 (Athens, v BC; pl.)'

**πῑθάκνιον**, add 'also φιδάκνιον *IG* 1³.425.24 (Athens, v BC), 2².1627.313, 316 (Athens, iv BC)'

**πῑθεών**, for 'later form of πιθών' read '= πιθών' and add '*TAPhA* 65.128 (Olynthus, iv BC)'

+**πιθήκη**, ἡ, *monkey-spider*, also called ὀρειβάτης, ὑλοδρόμος, ψύλλα, Ael.*NA* 6.26.

**πιθηκίζω**, after 'of flatterers' insert 'ὑπό τι μικρὸν ἐπιθήκισα Ar.*V.* 1290 (lyr.)'

**πῐθήκιον II**, for pres. def. read 'device attached to the centre of a platform between two ships supporting a siege-engine to steady it in rough weather'

**πίθηκος**, after 'Dor. **πίθᾱκος**' insert '*Naukratis* ii p. 68, Ar.*Ach.* 907; (as pers. n. *SEG* 29.938, Selinous, vi BC)'

**πῐθοιγίς**, for 'Call.*Aet.* 1.1.1' read 'Call.*fr.* 178.1 Pf.'

**πῐθος I 1**, at end for 'Hdn. 8.4.5' read 'Hdn. 8.4.4'

**πικρία**, add '**4** of style, *severity*, D.H.*Vett.Cens.* 2.5.'

**πικρίδιον**, after '*Endivia*' insert 'prob. in com. in *PTeb.* 693.20'

+**πικρόλωτος**, ὁ, a kind of lotus, Gal. 14.159.13.

**πικρός**, line 1, after 'Od. 4.406' insert 'Maced. βικρός acc. to Plu. 2.292e'

**πικρότης II**, add '**2** of style, *harshness*, D.H.*Pomp.* 6.9.'

***πικροφᾰγία**, ἡ, *bitter diet*, *An.Boiss.* 3.415.

***πικροχολία**, ἡ, *bitter bile, biliousness*, Gal. 7.727.1.

**πῖλίον 1**, add 'as a freedman's cap, cf. Lat. *pileus*, Plb. 30.18.3'

***πῖλιος**, α, ον, *made of felt*, *Inscr.Délos* 1441*A*i13 (ii BC).

***πιλνόν**· φαιόν, Κύπριοι Hsch.

**πῖλοποιός**, add '*SEG* 29.1195 (Lydia, AD 194/5)'

**πῑμελοσαρκοφᾰγος**, for '*sepulchre of fat*' read '*eater of fat flesh*'

**πῑμεντάριος**, after '*apothecary*' insert '*MAMA* 8.574 (Aphrodisias, ii/iii AD)'

**Πιμπληΐδες**, add 'sg., the nymph *Pimpleis*, mother of the Muses, Epich. 41'

**πίμπλημι I**, add '**4** *complete* a period of time, τρισσὸν ἐπ' εἰκοστῶι πλήσας ἔτος *GVI* 842 (ii/i BC), *SEG* 33.1458. **5** *fulfil* destiny, etc., ζωὰν πλήσατ' ἐμεῦ τέκεος *SEG* 37.990 (Miletus, ii BC), *IEphes.* 2101A.'

**πίμπρημι**, line 6, after 'E.*Andr.* 390, etc.' insert 'Πρῆσαι *CEG* 2.7' **I**, third line from end, delete 'of wounds, .. Id.*Al.* 438)' **II**, after '*distend*' insert '*inflame*'; after 'Nic.*Al.* 477' insert 'al.' and after 'Dsc. 4.32' insert 'Nic.*Al.* 438, 571; med., ib. 345'

**πῐνᾰκοθήκη**, after '*picture-gallery*' insert 'Varro *RR* 1.2.10, al.'

***πῐνᾰκοπλήστης**, ου, ὁ, ?*one who fills plates*, *PAmst.*inv. 21 (*ZPE* 9.49).

**πίναξ 2**, add 'Lang *Ath.Agora* XXI B12 (iv/iii BC)' **3**, for 'Simon. 178' read '*AP* 5.159.4 ([Simon.]; = *EG* 317 P.)'

**πῑνᾰρός**, after 'Eup. 251' insert 'τὰ πάλαι πιναρᾷ κεκαλυμμένα λάθᾳ ξόανα epigr. in *Inscr.Délos* 2548 (i BC)'

***πῑνεγχύτης**, ου, ὁ, *cup-bearer*, Ps.-Callisth. 83.13,15.

***πιννωνᾶς**, ᾶ, ὁ, *setter of pearls*, *JHS* 58.255 (Jewish medallion; vi AD).

**πῖνον**, delete 'cj. .. BC)'

**πῖνος 2**, add 'π. *litterarum*, Cic.*Att.* 14.7.2'

**πίνω**, lines 9/10, imper. πίει, add '*SEG* 32.31, 33.64(b) (Att., vi BC); also πῖ *TAM* 4(1).324 (Rom.imp.); πίον *SEG* 30.1129 (Alena, iii BC)'; line 20, after 'aor. ἐπόθην' insert 'Nic.*Th.* 622, *Al.* 432'; line 22, after '*EM* 698.52' insert '(Alc. 401 L.-P.) πῶ also *GDI* 1376, 1377 (Dodona), *CR* 57.102 (Attic vase, vi BC); Cypr. *po-ti* πῶθι *ICS* 264.1' **III**, add 'ἔρωτα πίνων Anacr. 105 P.'

***πίνωσις**, εως, ἡ, ?*tarnishing*, Al.*Pr.* 25.12.

***πιπερῖτις**, ιδος, ἡ, perh. *pepperwort*, *Lepidium latifolium*, (in second ref. perh. also *Polygonum hydropiper*), Plin.*HN* 19.187, 20.174.

***Πίπλειαι**· αἱ Μοῦσαι ἐν τῷ Μακεδονικῷ Ὀλύμπῳ Hsch.; cf. Πίμπλεια.

**πίπτω**, line 12, for 'Simon. 183.7' read '*AP* 7.24.7 ([Simon.]; = *EG* 348 P.)' **A 1**, line 7, for 'Simon. l.c.' read '*AP*([Simon.]) l.c.' **B I**, add '**3** *lie down, take one's place at table*, πρὸς δαῖτα E.*Ion* 652; cf. ἀναπίπτω 5.' **V 3**, add 'πέπτωκε in receipts is freq. folld. by the payer's name in nom. and the amount in acc. (but usu. a symbol only), πέπτωκεν Θέωνι .. Τεώς .. (δραχμὰς) ἑβδομήκοντα *SB* 1178, *OWilck.* 1491, 316, al. (iii BC)' **VII**, last line, before 'ὅσα' insert '*fall within the range of*'; add 'D.S. 3.44'

***πίπυλος**, ὁ, gloss on κορυδαλλός, Sch.Theoc. 10.50.

**Πῖσα**, at end after 'Pi.' insert 'and B.'
**Πισαῖος**, add 'of the Olympic games, *Πισαῖον ἀγῶνα* *SEG* 23.113 (Attica, iii AD)'
**πισγίς**, for 'dub. sens. in' read '= *πυξίς*'
***Πισιδικός**, *ή, όν*, *Pisidian*, *θεῶν Πισιδικῶν* *SEG* 32.1289 (Phrygia, Rom.imp.).
***πισκάριον**, *τό*, Lat. *piscarium (forum)*, *fish-market*, *SEG* 19.115.23 (Athens, ii/iii AD).
***πισκεῖνα**, *ή*, Lat. *piscina*, *basin*, *IHadr.* 47 (i/ii AD); sp. *φισκῖνα* *CIL* 3.14894 (Salona).
***πίσσαι**, *αί*, *peas* (cf. *πίσος*), *SEG* 9.35 (Cyrene, ii BC).
***πισσάριον** (B), *τό*, gloss on *ἔτνος* *soup*, Sch.Pl.*Hp.Ma.* 290d; cf. *πίσος*, *πίσινος*.
***πισσία** or -**εία**, *ή*, (**πιττ-**), *treatment with pitch*, Gal. 18(2).900.5.
***πισσοκωνάω**, *cover with pitch*, Hsch. s.v. *κωνῆσαι*.
**πισσόω I**, add '*κούφ(ων) πεπισσωμένων* *PVindob.* G23243 (*ZPE* 64.80, vi/vii AD)'
**πιστάκιον**, add '*PVindob.Worp* 11.14 (vi AD)'
***πιστίκιον**, *τό*, a cereal, prob. *hulled emmer* (Egyptian wheat), *Edict. Diocl.* 1.7, *PCair.Isidor.* 11 iii 39 (iv AD), al., *EPap* 5.102-103 (nos. 24.2.4, 25.2.5, both iv AD).
⁺**πιστικός** (A), *ή, όν*, adj. describing nard, perh. = *πιστικός* (B), in sense *genuine*, *Ev.Marc.* 14.3, *Ev.Jo.* 12.3.
**πιστικός** (B), add '**3** *ὁ*, *trustee*, *custodian*, *CPR* 8.67.19 (vi/vii AD), 85.2 (vii/viii AD; pap. has *πι*[).'
**πίστιον**, delete the entry.
***πίστιος**, *α, ον*, *reliable*, *trustworthy*, *TAM* 2.338 (Xanthus).
**πίστις I 1**, line 6, after '*OT* 1445, etc.' insert '*εἰς πίστιν ἐλθεῖν Χρόνῳ* Men.*Dysc.* 282' **2 c**, after '*PGnom.* 180 (ii AD)' insert 'Just.*Nov.* 119.7; sim. *κακὴ πίστις* ib.' **4**, add '**b** *creed*, *belief*, *Cod.Just.* 1.1.3.2, 3.' **VI**, after '*Fides*' insert '*ἐν τῷ ναῷ τῷ τῆς Π.* *Thasos* 174E.7 (80 BC)'
⁺**πιστός** (A), *ή, όν*, of medicines, *to be drunk*, A.*Pr.* 480.
**πιστός** (B) **A I 1**, add 'as the title of a legion (transl. Lat. *fidelis*), *SEG* 33.1194 (Cappadocia, i/ii AD), 32.1390 (Commagene, ii AD), etc.' **B 3**, add '*οἱ πιστοί* *the company of believers*, *ITyr* 15'
**πιστόω III 3**, at end delete '*τίς ἂν* .. Opp.*C.* 3.355' add '**4** *feel sure* of, *be convinced* by, Onas. 13.3; *τίς ἂν τάδε πιστώσαιτο*, .. *ὅτι* Opp.*C.* 3.355, 417.'
***πιστρίνη**, *ή*, Lat. *pistrina*, *bakery*, *ODouch* 39, 57.
**πίτνημι**, lines 6/7, delete '*θαλάμων*'
**πιττακιάρχης**, add '*PFlor.* 18.1 (ii AD), *Stud.Pal.* 20.236.1 (v/vi AD)'
***πῐτῠοφόρος**, *ον*, *pine-bearing*, expl. of *pinifer* in Virgil gloss., *PNess.* 1.605 (vi AD).
**πίτυς**, add 'A.*fr.* 78c.39 R.'
**πιτύστεπτος**, delete 'poet. for *πιτυόστ-'
**πῐτῠώδης**, after '*abounding in pines*' insert '*π*[*ι*]*τυώδεϊ δείρᾱι* B. 12(11).39 S.-M.'
***πιτυών**, *ῶνος*, *ὁ*, *pine-grove*, *platanonas et aerios pityonas*, Mart. 12.50.1.
**πίων I**, add '**3** of the eyes, *fatty in appearance*, *glistening*: of a snake, Nic.*Th.* 443; of a person in fever, *τὰ λευκὰ τῶν ὀφθαλμῶν λαμπρώτατα καὶ πίονα* Aret.*SA* 2.1, 3.10.' **III**, sup., add 'Hp.*Genit.* 1'
**πλᾰγιάζω III 1**, add '**b** *use a construction other than nominative and finite verb*, opp. *ὀρθόω* III, Aristid.*Rh.* 2 p. 533 S.; pass., ib. 1 p. 465 S.'
***πλαγιάριος**, *ὁ*, Lat. *plagiarius*, *kidnapper*, ?Teuc.Bab. p. 50 B.
⁺**πλᾰγιαυλίζω**, *play the πλαγίαυλος*, Eust. 1157.40.
⁺**πλᾰγίαυλος**, either *aulos with reed mouthpiece inserted at the side* or *flute*, Theoc. 20.29, Bion *fr.* 10.7 G., *AP* 11.34.5 (Phld.); = *φῶτιγξ*, Juba 16 J.
**πλάγιος I 1**, add '**b** subst., *ἡ πλαγία* (sc. *θύρα*), *side* or *back door*, *POxy.* 3642.28-9 (ii AD), *CPR* 5.17.8 (v AD). **c** *πλάγιος αὐλός*, = °*πλαγίαυλος*, Luc.*VH* 2.5, Longus 1.4.3, 4.26.2, Ael.*NA* 6.19.' **4**, *ἐκ πλαγίου*, add 'transf., indicating collateral relationship, *Cod.Just.* 6.4.4.14e, f' **II**, last line, for 'Ph. 2.173' read 'Ph. 2.172'
**πλαγκτύς**, for 'Call.*Aet.* 1.2.7' read 'Call.*fr.* 26.7 Pf.'
⁺**πλᾰδάω**, *to have an excess of moisture*, *be moist* or *wet*, *φλύκταιναι* Nic.*Th.* 241, *σκύλα* 422, *ῥινοί* 429; of unripe corn, Ph. 1.179; of soil, A.R. 2.662; of unhealthy flesh, Hp.*Aër.* 10. **2** of liquids, *to be thin* or *watery*, *οὐρόν* Nic.*Th.* 708, *πλαδόωντι ποτῷ* id.*Al.* 119; cf. *πῆξις πλαδῶσα* Arist.*HA* 516ᵃ3; transf., w. ref. to looseness of the stomach, *π. τὸν στόμαχον* Dsc.*Eup.* 2.9, Gal. 13.145.10. **3** fig., of the mind, understanding, etc., *to be green* or *unformed*, Ph. 1.441, 459, 2.411. **4** in causal sense, *ἐπλάδα· κατέδευεν* Hsch.
***πλάδιμος**, *η, ον*, perh. for *πλάθιμος, *moulded*, *decorated with moulding*, *ἰσώστας πλαδίμους* *MAMA* 8.552.10.
**πλᾰθά**, after '*figure*' insert '*AP* 13.21 (Theodorid.; = *EG* 3148 P.)'
**πλᾰθᾰνίτης**, for '*baked in a mould*' read '*kneaded on a board*'
**πλᾰθᾰνον**, for '*dish* or *mould* in which bread, cakes, etc., were baked' read '*kneading-board* or *tray*'
***πλᾰθᾰνος**, *ὁ*, *π. ἄγγος τι* *POxy.* 3000 *sch.* 13; cf. °*πλάθανον*.
**πλάθω**, line 1, delete 'in lyr.'
**πλᾰκίτης**, add 'Anon.Alch. 286.26'
***πλᾰκοπρίστης**, *ου, ὁ*, *sawyer-mason*, *PMerton* 97 (vi AD).
***πλᾰκός**, *οῦ, ὁ*, = *πλάξ*, *slab* of stone, *BE* 1966.512 (Sicily).
***πλακοτόν**, *τό*, (?for *πλακωτόν*), *pavement*, *SEG* 26.1627 (Apamea, AD 533).
**πλᾰκουντάριος**, add '*Vit.Aesop.*(G) 63'
***πλᾰκουντοφᾰγέω**, *eat cakes*, Hsch. s.v. *να*[*υ*]*στοφαγεῖν*.
**πλακοῦς II**, delete the section.
**πλᾰκόω**, add 'Anon.Alch. 325.1'
**πλᾰνάω II 4**, line 4, after 'Hp.*Prog.* 24' insert '*πεπλ. μέτρα* *irregular* rhythms (in prose), D.H.*Comp.* 25, 26'
**πλᾰνής I 2**, after '*planets*' insert '(incl. sun and moon, Nonn.*D.* 5. 67-84)'
***πλᾰνησίμοιρος**, *ον*, *causing fate to go astray*, *PMag.* 4.1368.
**πλᾰνητικός**, add '**II** *misleading*, *λόγοι* Sch.E.*Hipp.* 486.'
***πλανιτικόν**, *τό*, wd. occurring in list of garments, *PMich.*XIV 684.9 (vi AD); cf. *πλανίς*.
**πλάσις 1**, add 'D.S. 1.16.1'
**πλασμᾰτώδης**, add '**2** *artificial*, *contrived*, *π. ἐστὶν ἡ ὑπόθεσις καὶ ἡρμοσμένη* Hipparch. 1.4.6.'
**πλάσσω**, line 18, after 'Gal. 6.313' insert 'Poll. 6.74, 10.112, Hsch. s.v. *πλάθανον*' **I 2**, delete the section.
**πλάστης I**, at end for 'perh. = *τριχοπλάστης*' read '*hairdresser* (cf. *κεροπλάστης*)'
**πλάστιγξ**, add '**V** *μέρος τι τοῦ αὐλοῦ, καὶ σύριγγος τὸ ζύγωμα* Hsch. **VI** the constellation *Libra*, Man. 4.242.'
**πλαστός I 1**, add '*μήτε πλαστὰν μήτε γραπτὰν* .. [*εἰκόνα*] Plu. 2.215a (*Ἀποφθέγματα Λακωνικά*)'
**πλᾰτᾰγή**, add 'Plu. 2.714e'
***πλάταμος**, *ὁ*, object acting as boundary-marker, perh. = *πλαταμών*, *IG* 14.352 ii 12,17.
**πλᾰτᾰμών 5**, delete the section transferring exx. to section 1.
***πλᾰτᾰνώδης**, *ες*, *like a plane-tree*, *σπίλαξ· μῶλος ὁ πλατανώδης* Hsch.
**πλᾰτας**, after '(Aphrodisias)' insert 'also *tomb*, *MAMA* 8.538; cf. °*πέλτα*'
***πλᾰτειάρχης**, *ου, ὁ*, *leader of a πλατεῖα*, *SEG* 30.1449c (sp. *πλατεάρχ-*, Pontus, iii AD).
**πλάτη I 1**, for this section read '*blade of an oar*, A.*Ag.* 695, S.*Aj.* 358, E.*Hec.* 39, Arist.*PA* 684ᵃ3, 13 (in describing the feet or other extremities of var. creatures). **b** *use of oars*, *sea-voyage*, S.*Ph.* 220, 335, E.*IT* 242. **c** *fleet*, E.*IA* 236, Hel. 192.' **4**, before '*AP*' insert 'cj. in'
**πλᾰτικός II 2**, line 2, delete 'or *involving breadth*' and after 'id.*in Cael.* 579.16' insert '**b** *involving extension*'; line 7, adv. -*κῶς*, add '*POxy.* 3420.12 (iv AD)'
***πλατιϝοίναρχος** [?ᾱ], *ὁ*, president of college of °*πλατιϝοίνοι*, *SEG* 30.380 (Tiryns, late vii BC).
***πλατιϝοίνοι** [?ᾱ], *οἱ*, members of a religious college, perh. in charge of libations of wine, *SEG* 30.380 (Tiryns, late vii BC).
**πλάτος** (A) **I 7**, delete the section. **VI**, for '= *δραχμαί*' read 'prob. = *τετράδραχμα*'; add 'cf. *RN* 1935.1 (Delphi, i BC); cf. °*πλότος*'
**πλᾰτος** (B), add '*Hierapolis* 322; cf. °*πλάτας*, °*πέλτα*'
***πλᾰτῠγόνᾰτος**, *ον*, *having broad knees*, Rhetor. in *Cat.Cod.Astr.* 7.224.13.
***πλᾰτῠλίσγιον**, *τό*, *rake*, Ph.*Bel.* 100.10, Apollod.*Poliorc.* 220.18.
**πλᾰτύς I 5**, add '*πλατὺς ψυχῇ* *arrogant* (calque on Hebr.), Aq.*Pr.* 28.25' **II a**, add '*Τρόφιμον* .. *ἡ πλατεῖα τῶν λειτουργῶν ἐτείμησαν* *SEG* 31.1026 (ii AD)'
***πλᾰτύτοξος**, *ον*, *of the broad bow*, epith. of Apollo, *CEG* 331 (Boeotia, v BC).
**Πλατώνειος**, after '*α, ον*' insert '(also -*ος*, -*ον*, *GVI* 1451 (Rhodes, iii BC))'
**Πλατωνικός**, after '*Π. φιλόσοφος*' insert '*IEphes.* 3901 (i AD)'
**πλέγμα I 1**, for 'Simon. 183.2' read '*AP* 7.24.2 ([Simon.]; = *EG* 343 P.)'
⁺**πλεθρίζω**, app. *extend to the length of a πλέθρον*, *ταῦτα πλεθρίζων*, i.e. *exaggerating*, Thphr.*Char.* 23.2.
⁺**πλέθρισμα**· *δρόμημα* Hsch., Phot.
**πλέθρον**, add 'see also *πέλεθρον*'
**πλειστηριάζω**, add '*TAM* 4(1).3.2 (sp. *πληστ-*)'
**πλειστονίκης**, add '*POxy.Hels.* 25.21, al. (AD 264)'
**πλεῖστος IV**, add '**7** *ἐκ πλείστου* *from the greatest distance*, Aen.Tact. 6.5.'
**πλείων A I 1**, line 9, after 'id.*R.* 435d' insert '*ἐκ πλείονος* *from a fair distance*, Aen.Tact. 26.1; so *ἐκ π. χωρίου* id. 26.9' **2**, add '**b** *οἱ πλε(ί)ονες* *the full initiates*, of the Essenes, J.*BJ* 2.8.9, 14.6; of the Christians, 2*Ep.Cor.* 2.6.' **II 2 e**, add '*πλεόνως* Hdt. 3.34.2, 5.18.5' **B**, after 'FORMS' for 'Ep.' read 'poets'; line 2, for 'Call.*Aet.Oxy.* 2080.85' read 'Call.*fr.* 43.83 Pf.'; line 5, after 'iv BC))'

insert 'neut. sg. also πλέος, ἧμ π. ἢ εἷς κατείπωσι *Thasos* 18.2, 10 (see also πλός)'; line 8, form πλήων, add '*SEG* 32.1243 (Cyme, 2 BC/AD 2)'

**πλειών**, after 'Hes.*Op.* 617' insert '(also interpr. as *seed*; cf. πλειόνει)'

**πλεκτή I 3**, for '*fishing-basket* or *weel*' read '*net* or *trap* for game'

**πλέκω I 1**, after '*plait*' insert 'or *make by plaiting*' **II 2**, after 'Pl.*Hp.Mi.* 369b' insert 'cf. πλέξομεν ὕμνοις [τ]ὰν .. Τρ[οῖ]αν *Scol.* 917(*b*).4 P.'

***πλέννα**, πλένναι· μύξαι Hsch., βλένα· μύξα. οἱ δὲ διὰ τοῦ π πλένα καὶ πλέννα τὰ ἀσθενῆ καὶ δυσκίνητα id.; cf. βλέννα.

**πλένναι**, delete the entry.

**πλεονάζω II 1**, line 4, after 'id. 3.3.7' insert 'πλεονάζει δ' Ἀριστόξενος .. "ἐπηλλαγμένα" λέγων τὰ "συνημμένα" Sch.Il. 13.358, πλεονάζει δ' ἐπὶ τῆς λοιδόρου Suet.*Blasph.* 25, 94 T.' **2**, after 'Epicur.*Sent.* 4' insert 'ἔν τινι Plu. 2.613c'

**πλεονάκις I**, add 'πληονάκι *SEG* 34.1198 (Lydia, ii BC)'

**πλεονασμός**, add '**5** *additional tax*, *BGU* 2055.18 (ii AD).'

**πλεύμων**, line 3, for 'ὁ π.' read 'π.' **II**, line 2, after 'term of abuse' insert '(in sense "*windbag*")'

**πλευρά III C**, for '*side* of a square or cube' read '*side* of square or *edge* of solid figure'

***πλευρίς**, ίδος, ἡ, pl., *ribs of beef*, Hsch. s.v. σχελίδες.

**+πλευρωνία**, ἡ, quoted as deriv. of πλευρά, Them. *in PN* 11.24, Mich. *in PN* 25.20.

***πλεύστης**, ου, ὁ, *seafarer*, Rhetor. in *Cat.Cod.Astr.* 8(4).212.

**πλέω I**, add 'impers. pass., *Peripl.M.Rubr.* 14, 28. **2** εἰς τὸν βορέαν ἤδη πλέοντος (ἀπονεύοντος cj.) τοῦ πλοός *with the course heading* (northwards), etc., ib. 62.' **II 2**, add '**b** ὀφθαλμοὶ πλέοντες *swimming* eyes, as a morbid symptom, Hp.*Epid.* 7.17.'

**πλέως**, line 3, for 'πλῆ .. 912' read 'πλῆ Diog.Apoll. 10 D.-K. (Hdn.Gr. 2.912)' **II 2**, delete 'Comp. πλειότερος .. *Et.Gen.*' add '**III** comp. πλειότερος *fuller*, Od. 11.359; *longer*, Arat. 1080; *stronger*, id. 644; *thicker*, Nic.*Th.* 119; π. φάρυγι Call.*fr.* 757 Pf., π. στόματι *AP* 6.350 (Crin.; = *EG* 5047 P.) = *pleniore ore*; but πλειότεροι Arat. 1005 = πλείονες.'

***πληγόω**, = πλήσσω, πληγῶσαι αὐτὸν πληγαῖς βιαίαις Sch.Lyc. 780.

**πληθυντικός**, adv. -κῶς, add 'D.H.*Comp.* 6'

**πληθύς**, line 3, delete '= δῆμος, *Leg.Gort.* 6.52' add '**II** *sum* of money, *Leg.Gort.* 6.52. **III** the *full* of the moon, Arat. 774, 799.'

**πληθύω II**, line 2, after 'is trans.' insert '(*fill*)'

**πλημμέλημα**, add '(*legal*) *wrongdoing*), Just.*Nov.* 8.10 pr.'

**πλήμῡρα 1**, line 3, after 'of the Nile' insert 'Ph. 2.526 (pl.)'

***πληνάριος**, α, ον, *comprehensive*, *full*, ἀμεριμνίας μερικάς τε καὶ πληναρίας Just.*Nov.* 128.3.

***πληξίᾰλος**, Dor. **πλᾱξ-**, ον, *striking the sea*, Simon. 14 *fr.*55(*a*).6 P.

***πληρατός**, ή, όν, *complete*, *PMilan.* 48.10 (v/vi AD); cf. πλήρης (w. Lat. suffix).

***πληρέω**, = πληρόω, prob. in *JA* 246.2/3 (Kandahar, iii BC).

**πλήρης III 3**, line 2, after '(Arist.*Ath.*) 69.1' insert '*IG* $2^2$.1641.32 (iv BC)' **6**, add 'εἰς πλῆρες *fully*, *Cod.Just.* 1.3.35.3'

***πληροφορητικός**, ή, όν, *giving full assurance*, ὅρκος Steph. *in Rh.* 289.18.

**πληρόω III 3**, add 'ἐν εἰνδ(ικτιῶνι) ε' πληρ‹ο›υμ(ένῃ) *SEG* 34.1262 (Bithynia, v AD)' **6**, add 'ἐπλήροσεν τὴν εὐχ{ι}ήν *ICilicie* 118'

***πλήρω**, = πληρόω, pap. in *ZPE* 78.146 (AD 475).

**πληρωτής I**, after '*one who completes*' insert 'εὐδαιμονίας D.H. 1.38' **II**, for this section read 'a subordinate official concerned with the preparation or completion of documents, *PFay.* 23 intr., γραμματεύς πληρωτῶν *PHamb.* 59 (both ii AD); under a πριμισκρίνιος, Lyd. 3.11, 68; under a διαιτητής, *Cod.Just.* 2.12.27.3'

***πληρώτρια**, ἡ, fem. of πληρωτής I, *joint-lender*, *Hesperia* suppl. 9.17 (Athens, mortgage-stone, ?iv BC).

**πλησιάζω II 3**, add 'abs., Plu. 2.718a, Phryn.*PS* 12.5, Sor. in *CMG* 4 p. 46.10'

**πλησιαστής**, add '**2** *adherent*, *follower*, Simp. *in Ph.* 25.20.'

**πλησίμοχθος**, delete the entry.

**πλησίος I 3**, add 'fem. subst. ἡ πλησία (sc. χώρα) *the neighbourhood*, ἀπὸ πλησίας *Kafizin* 66(a) (iii BC); sp. πλεσ- ib. 76(b)'

**πλησιόχωρος**, add 'sp. πλησιόχορος *IG* 9(2).521.34 (Larissa, iii BC)'

**πλῆσμα**, add '**II** *stuffing* (of cushions), *TAPhA* 90.140.20 (pl.) (written πλησζμ-).'

**πλήσμιος**, add 'adv. πλησμίως Gal. 7.751.2'

**πλήσσω I 1 b**, before '*Sammelb.*' insert 'Arist.*HA* $607^a$20, Ach.Tat. 2.7' **2**, for 'Call.*Aet.* 3.1.37' read 'Call.*fr.* 75.37 Pf.'

**πλίγμα I**, after 'Hsch.' insert 'τὸ π. γνῶναι in wrestling, cj. in Gorg. 8 D.-K.'

**πλινθεῖον III**, add '**3** perh. *statue-base*, τὴν Νείκην σὺν τῷ πλ‹ι›νθείῳ *IEphes.* 504 (i AD).'

**πλινθευτής**, after 'Poll. 7.163' insert '*PGoodsp.* 30.2.9 (ii AD)'

***πλινθευτική**, ἡ, *brick-making*, χειρωνάξιον πλινθευτικῆς *SB* 7588.3 (AD 118).

***πλινθευτικός**, ή, όν, *pertaining to brick-making*, π. τόπος *brickyard*, *PKöln* 104.9-10 (vi AD).

***πλινθηγός**, όν, *used for brick-carrying*, *BGU* 2353.6 (AD 115).

**πλινθικός**, add 'adv. πλινθικῶς *in the* (*geometrical*) *form of a brick*, Procl.*in R.* 2.39.28'

**πλινθίς 6**, add '*SEG* 25.392 (Epid., iv BC)'

**πλινθοειδής**, after '*brick-like*' insert '*PSI* 1178.8 (ii AD)'

***πλινθορκία**, ἡ, = πλινθουλκία, *Stud.Pal.* 22.35.20 (i AD).

**πλινθουργεῖον**, add '*BGU* 1992a i 2 (ii BC)'

**πλινθούργιον**, after '*brickworks*' insert '*PLond.* 1166.12 (i AD)'

**πλινθοφόρος 2**, add '*Inscr.Délos* 1415.3 (ii BC)'

**πλοιαφέσια**, add 'Apul.*Met.* 11.17'

**πλοκᾰμίς**, line 1, after '*braid of hair*' insert 'Men.*fr.* 901 K.-Th.'

**πλόκᾰμος I 1**, line 5, for 'Call.in *PSI* 1092.47' read 'Call.*fr.* 110.47 Pf.' add '**3** *leaf*, *Anacreont.* 43.6 W., *AP* 7.22 (Simm.; = *EG* 930 P.). **4** *smoke ring*, Poll. 2.27.'

**πλοκή III 1**, add '**e** στίχων πλοκαί a *succession* of verses, Sch.E.*Or.* 165.'

**πλόκιον II**, add '*PVindob.* G41866.2 (*Tyche* 1.89; vi AD, or *headband*)'

**πλόκιος**, delete the entry.

***πλοκοκόπιον**, τό, ?*garland-maker's shop*, *PAmst.*inv. 62 (*Mnemosyne* 30.146).

**πλόος 1**, penultimate line, before 'metaph.' insert 'τριηρ[ῶν τῶ]ν ἐν ‹τοῖς› νεωρίοις καὶ τῶν ἐμ πλῶι οὐσῶ[ν *IG* $2^2$.1631 (iv BC); ἀποδημήσα[ς] [κα]τὰ πλοῦν *SEG* 24.1095 (Moesia, iii/ii BC), πεζοὶ καὶ κατὰ πλοῦν (?)*travellers by land and sea*, *TAM* 4(1).295'

***πλότος**, εος, τό, app. Cypr. for πλάτος (A) (dat. *po-lo-te-i*), *tablet*, *ostrakon*, *ICS* 318 B vii 2.

**πλουμᾱρικός**, add 'also φλουμαρικός *PSI* 1082.14 (iv AD)'

**πλουμᾱ́ριος**, add 'also φλουμάριος (written -άρης) *POxy.* 2421.32 (iv AD)'

***πλουμᾱρίσιμος**, η, ον, *embroidered*, *PAnt.* 44.9 (iv/v AD), cf. Lat. *plumarius*, *brocaded.*

***πλουμᾱ́ρισσα**, ἡ, *embroideress*, *PAberd.* 59 i 7 (iv/v AD).

***πλοῦμος**, ὁ, or **πλοῦμον**, τό, *down*, *Edict.Diocl.* 18.1, al., cf. Lat. *pluma*, *feather*, *down.*

**Πλουτεύς**, line 2, after 'Πλουτῆος' insert '*SB* 4313.2 (Alexandria, i/ii AD)' add 'cf. Myc. *po-ro-u-te-u*, pers. n.'

**πλουτέω I 2**, for 'πλουτῖον .. *IG* 12(8).442.8' read 'πλουτῖον τέκνων λίπετο δῶμα πό[σει] *BCH* 91.621 no. 81'

***πλουτηφόρος**, ον, *wealth-bringing*, epith. of Ammon, Ps.-Callisth. 6.4.

***πλουτίνδα**, adv. *according to wealth*, [αἱρε]τοὺς π. καὶ ἀριστίνδα *IG* 7.188.9 (Pagae, prob. iii BC).

***πλουτίς**, ίδος, ἡ, (sc. ἑταιρεία) the *wealthy faction* at Miletus, opp. ἡ χειρομάχα, Plu. 2.298c, Eust. 1425.64.

**πλουτοδότειρα**, add 'of Isis, epigr. in *Inscr.Cret.* 4.244 (ii BC)'

**πλουτοδότης**, add 'of Ammon, Bernand *Akôris* 18 (?ii AD)'

***πλουτοδότις**, ἡ, *Giver of wealth*, title of Hermuthis, *SEG* 8.548.1 (Egypt, i BC).

***πλουτοποιέω**, *enrich*, Sch.Pi.*O.* 7.60.

**πλοῦτος II**, line 3, after 'Antiph. 259' insert 'also pl.; as title of comedy by Cratinus, Ath. 3.94e, etc., cf. Πλοῦτοι δ' ἐκαλούμεθ' ὅτ' [ἦρχε Κρόνος] Cratin.*fr.* 171 K.-A.'

**πλῠ́νω**, line 8, transfer 'Hp.*Acut.* (*Sp.*) 65' to follow 'part. πεπλυμένος' **II**, line 2, after '*abuse*' insert 'A.*fr.* 78a.71 R.'

***πλῠσιμάριος**, ὁ, *laundryman*, *POxy.* 3598.7 (iv AD), 3599.7 (v AD).

***πλυτάριος**, α, ον, π. ἐρισκός, name given by soldiers to a clay drinking-vessel, Suid. s.v. κώθωνες.

**πλωΐζω**, after 'Arr.*Peripl.M.Eux.* 23' insert 'pass., τὰ πλοϊζόμενα *parts sailed over*, *Peripl.M.Rubr.* 45' and add 'cf. Myc. *po-ro-wi-to*, perh. πλώϝιστος, name of month'

***πλωϊσμόν**, τό, *shipment*, τῷ αὐτῷ ὑπὲρ πλοεισμοῦ *PVindob.Tandem* 19.2 (v/vi AD), εἰς τὸ πλοεισμ‹..› *PMasp.* 57 i 3 (vi AD).

**+πλώς**, πλωτός, ὁ, *swimmer*, i.e. fish, πλῶτες ἁλός Opp.*H.* 3.63; app. used spec. for the grey mullet (κεστρεύς), Epich. 44, Xenocr. ap.Orib. 2.58.29.

**πλωτήρ I 1**, line 2, before 'Ar.*Ec.* 1087' insert 'E.*IT* 449, *Hel.* 1070'

***πλώτωρ**, ορος, ὁ, = πλωτήρ, *AP* 7.295 (Leon.Tarent.; = *EG* 2066 P.).

**πνεῦμα III**, add '**2** *inspiration*, *genius*, Longin. 9.13, D.H.*Th.* 23, Luc.*Dem.Enc.* 14.' **V**, π. πονηρόν, add '*SEG* 30.1794 (Jewish, iii AD)'

**πνευμᾰτέμφορος**, for '= πνευματόφορος' read 'expld. as ὑπὸ πνεύματος πεπληρωμένος'

***πνευμᾰτηλάτης**, ου, ὁ, *spirit-driver*, of Cerberus, *Suppl.Mag.* I 42 (iii/iv AD).

**πνευμᾰτοφόρος**, delete 'προφῆται ib.*Ze.* 3.4'

***πνευμᾰτόφορος**, ον, *borne by the wind*, *light*, *frivolous*, προφῆται Lxx *Ze.* 3.4.

**πνευμᾰτώδης 2**, for '*windy*, *exposed to the wind*' read '*characterized by*

*wind, windy*' and add 'αἱ ἅλωνες περὶ τὴν σελήνην πνευματώδεις μᾶλλον ἢ περὶ ἥλιον Thphr.*Sign.* 31'
**πνευστιάω**, after 'Hp.*Int.* 44' insert '*Com.adesp.* 362'
**πνέω I**, three lines fr. end, after 'Poll. 4.72' insert 'w. acc., ἔπνεε Δαρδανίδας *piped* the D. (i.e. songs celebrating them), *APl.* 7 (Alc.Mess.)' **IV**, add 'τὴν .. πνεύσασαν .. ὕστατα *AP* 7.166 (Diosc.; = *EG* 2968 P.)'
**πνῑγίζω**, for '= πνίγω' read 'humorous conflation of πνίγω and πυγίζω'
***πνῑγμοσύνη**, ἡ, = πνῖγμα, Anon. *in Rh.* 204.20.
**πνίγω I 3**, add 'S.*Ichn.* 393'
***πνιχμός**, ὁ, = πνιγμός (in quot., sense 1), Nic.*Al.* 365 (v.l.).
**πνοή II 2**, after '*breath*' insert 'Γοργόνες .. ἃς .. οὐδεὶς εἰσιδὼν ἕξει πνοάς A.*Pr.* 800'
**πόα**, line 1, before 'E.*Cyc.* 333' insert 'A.*fr.* 28, 29 R.'; lines 2/3, delete 'Boeot. **πύας** .. iii BC)' **I 2 a**, add 'ποίη κυπάρισσος = χαμαικυπάρισσος, Nic.*Th.* 910' **4**, line 3, delete '*meadow, Schwyzer* l.c. (pl.)' (now read γύας, v. γύης)
**ποδαγρικός 1**, before 'Plb.' insert '*SB* 7638.4 (iii BC)'
**ποδᾱπός 2**, add '**b** indef., *of any kind, Vit.Aesop.*(G) 32, al. (ποτ-).'
**πόδαργος**, add 'Myc. *po-da-ko*, description of an ox'
***ποδάριοι**, οἱ, members of an association of performers, perh. *scabillarii, TAM* 5(1).92 (ii AD), *Gloss.*
**ποδάριον**, add '*PHaun.* 25.10 (iv/v AD)'
**ποδηγετέω**, after lemma insert 'Dor. ποδᾱγ- *GVI* 1859.5 (Teos, ii/i BC)'
**ποδιαῖος I 2**, for '[γραμμή]' read '[δύναμις]'
**ποδιστήρ II**, after '*tripod*' insert 'Lxx 2*Ch.* 4.16'
**ποδοκοίλιον**, add 'in lists of rations, *OAshm.Shelton* 78, 80'
***ποδοκοπέω**, *strike with the feet*, Hsch. s.v. κωλαβρισθείησαν.
**ποδόψηστρον**, add 'Herod. 5.30'
**ποδοψόφος**, add 'cf. °ποδάριοι'
**πόδωμα 1**, before '*OGI* 510.5' insert '*Gerasa* 51 (AD 81/3)'
**⁺ποέχομαι**, Cypr. for προσέχομαι, part. *po-e-ko-me-no-ne adjoining, ICS* 217.19, 21.
**ποηφάγος**, add 'Call.*fr.* 365 Pf.'
***ποθαιρέομαι**, etc., v. °προσαιρέομαι.
***ποθᾱλόω**, v. °προσηλόω.
***ποθεδρεία**, ἡ, = προσεδρεία (in quot., sense 2), *IG* 12(3).247.8.
**ποθεινός I 2**, add 'sup. as form of address, τῷ εὐλογο[υ]μένῳ καὶ ἀληθῶς ποθεινοτάτῳ υἱ[ῷ] *PMich.*inv. 3999 (*ZPE* 75.268, vi AD)' **III**, for 'Subst. .. paint' read 'perh. colour epith. (cf. πόθος III)'
***ποθεινότης**, ητος, ἡ, *quality of being dear, dearness*, in a complimentary address, τῇ σῇ ποθεινότητι *PKöln* 281, *PStrassb.* 279, *PHerm.Rees* 50 (all vi AD).
**ποθητός**, add '*SEG* 33.1475 (Cyrenaica, i/ii AD), *IG* 5(2).491 (Megalopolis, ii/iii AD)'
**ποθῑ́κω**, add 'part. οἱ ποθίκοντες, *relatives*, orac.ap.D. 43.66'
**πόθος II 1**, after 'E.*Andr.* 824' insert '*Tr.* 116, *Hel.* 763' add '**b** of the beloved person, Ἡράκλειτος, ἐμὸς πόθος *AP* 12.152.'
**⁺ποῖ A** *to what place?, whither?*: ποῖ πατεῖς πύλας; A.*Ch.* 732; ποῖ με χρὴ μολεῖν; S.*El.* 812; ποῖ τις φύγῃ; Ar.*Pl.* 438. **b** (w. gen.), ποῖ φύγωμεν Ἀπίας χθονός; A.*Supp.* 777, S.*Tr.* 984. **II** *to what point of time?, till when?, how long?*: ποῖ χρὴν ἀναμεῖναι; Ar.*Lys.* 526; ποῖ κῆχος; – ἐγγὺς ἡμερῶν τεττάρων Pherecr.*fr.* 175 K.-A. **III** *to what end* or *result?, in what (final, eventual) circumstances?*: πῶς καὶ ποῖ τελευτᾶν; A.*Pers.* 735; ποῖ κρανεῖ, ποῖ καταλήξει .. μένος ἄτης; A.*Ch.* 1075; ἃ δ' ὑπέσχεο ποῖ καταθήσεις; S.*OC* 227; τὸ δ' ἔνθεν ποῖ τελεύτησαί με χρή; ib. 476; (in indirect qn.), ἔνισπε ποῖ κεκύρωται τέλος A.*Supp.* 603. **b** w. gen., ποῖ τις φροντίδος ἔλθῃ; S.*OC* 170; ποῖ φρενῶν ἔλθω ib. 310; (indirect) οὐκ ἔχω ποῖ γνώμης πέσω ib.*Tr.* 705. **IV** in repeating indignantly another speaker's words (as ποῖος), *indeed*: .. λευκὸν ἵππον .. – ποῖ λευκὸν ἵππον; Ar. *Lys.* 193, 383.
***ποιαλίς**, v. °πυελίς.
***ποίβολος**, ὁ, *peripheral zone*, de Franciscis *Locr.Epiz.* 16, NWGk. equiv. of *πρόσβολος; cf. περίβολος.
**ποιδέομαι**, for 'προσδέομαι' read '°προσδέω (B)'
**ποιέω A III**, line 11, for 'ποιεῖσθαι .. friend' read 'κασιγνήτῳ ἶσον π. ἑταῖρον *treat* a friend as a brother'
**ποίημα I 1**, after '*work*' insert '*artefact*, τō Παρίō ποίημα Κριτωνίδεω εὔχομ[αι εἶναι] *CEG* 413 (*c.*525/500 BC)' **3**, for '*fiction*' read '*literary production in prose*' and add 'Isoc.*Ep.* 1.2'
***ποιητίκευμα**, τό, *poetical expression*, Steph.*in Rh.* 312.8.
**ποιητικεύομαι II**, after '*poetically*' insert 'Steph.*in Rh.* 312.5'
**ποιητικός I**, add '**3** gramm., of a verb, *active*, D.H.*Amm.* 2.7, 8 (i pp. 427f.).' **II 1**, add 'comp., D.H.*Th.* 46'
**⁺ποικιλίας**, ου, ὁ, an unidentified fish of the river Aroanius, Philosteph.Hist. 20, Paus. 8.21.1.
**ποικίλλω I 2**, line 8, after 'Pl.*Ti.* 87a' insert '*produce a varied* utterance, ποικίλλουσα .. κρωγμὸν πολύφωνα κορώνη Arat. 1001'
***ποικῐλογνώμων**, ονος, *having a versatile mind*, Heph.Astr. 3.45.5.
**⁺ποικῐλόθρονος**, ον, *on a richly-worked throne* (or *adorned with variegated flowers*), Ἀφροδίτα Sapph. 1.1 L.-P. (v.l. ποικιλόφρον).
**ποικῐλόνωτος**, add 'ποικιλόνωτον .. ἴτυν ἄστρων Nonn.*D.* 2.575; prob. in A.*fr.* 47a.26 R.'
***ποικῐλόπρυμνος**, ον, *having a variegated stern*, *Suppl.Hell.* 991.112 (poet. wd.-list, iii BC).
**ποικῖλος II 1**, add '**b** of mosaic work, *SEG* 26.1628 (Apamea, vi AD)' **2**, transfer 'Od. 8.448' to section III 3. **III 1**, add 'of deities (?Μοῖραι), θεαί .. ποικίλαι *SEG* 23.206 (Messenia, ii/iii AD)' **3 c**, add 'as a complimentary term in an epitaph, *SEG* 25.1088(b) (Cyprus, ii/iii AD)' add 'cf. Myc. compds. *po-ki-ro-nu-ka*, epith. of cloth; *po-ki-ro-qo*, pers. n.'
***ποικῐλοτειρής**, ές, *varied with stars*, πόλον π. rest. in *IG* 2².4494.7 (i AD).
**ποικιλόφρων**, for 'Alc.*Supp.* 22.7' read 'Alc. 69.7 L.-P.'
**⁺ποιμανδρία**, ἡ, kind of vessel, identified w. τανάγρα, Lyc. 326 (Ποιμανδρία is said to be an old name for Τάναγρα, St.Byz.).
**ποιμήν II 2**, delete '*teacher*' and after 'etc.' insert 'of a sophist, Lib.*Or.* 1.25' add 'Myc. *po-me, po-me-no* (gen.)'
**ποίμνη**, line 4, after 'etc.' insert 'αἶγές τε καὶ ποῖμναι καὶ βόες Philostr.*VA* 2.13'
**ποίμνιον II**, after '*Ev.Luc.* 12.32, al.' insert '*body* or *congregation of Christians*' and after '1*Ep.Pet.* 5.2' add '*IHadr.* 120 (iv AD)'
**ποιναῖος**, add '**II** perh. *expressing thanks, CEG* 356 (Isthmia, v BC).'
***ποινῑκάζω**, v. °φοινικάζω.
***ποινῑκαστᾱ́ς**, v. °φοινικιστάς.
**ποιολογέω**, for '*put up corn in sheaves*' read '*gather grass* or *hay*'
***ποιόφῠτος**, ον, *planted with grass, growing grass*, σηκοί A.*fr.* 273a.1 R.
***ποιπνῦτροισι**, unkn. sens. and accent, Antim. 186 Wy.; cf. ποιπνύτροισι· σπουδαίοις Hsch. (s.v.l.).
***Ποιτρόπια**, τά, a Delphic festival, *CID* I 9.D5 (v BC); cf. Ποιτρόπιος (form dial. equiv. of προστρόπιος).
**ποίφυγμα**, add '**2** σχῆμα ὀρχηστικόν Hsch.'
**ποιφύσσω**, add '**III** trans., *frighten*, Hsch.'
***ποίωμα**, ατος, τό, *qualification, added quality*, Simp. *in Cat.* 254.12.
**Πόκιος**, add '*SEG* 25.606 (Doris, ii BC)'
**ποκκί**, for '= πρός τί, but' read 'of dub. origin'
**πόκος I**, add 'fem. acc. pl. πόκας *SEG* 23.305 (Delphi, *c.*190 BC)' add 'Myc. *po-ka* (pl.), *fleeces*'
***πολάζω**, *to be common, abound*, Θρηικίῃσιν .. νήσοισι πολάζει Nic.*Th.* 482 (codd. πελ-; cf. ἐπιπολάζω).
**πολεμιστής II**, add '**2** of other things, *martial*, πολεμιστὰ (acc. masc.) σίδηρον Orph.*L.* 312.'
**πόλεμος**, add 'gen. alone, *in time of war*, καὶ πολέμō καὶ εἰρήνης *SEG* 31.969 (Erythrae, 351/44 BC), 30.990 (Delos, iv/iii BC). **2** applied to rioting, *PLond.* 1912 (i AD), *POxy.* 2339 (i AD), 3065 (iii AD).' **II 2**, delete the section. add 'cf. Myc. *po-to-re-ma-ta*, man's name (cf. πολεμητής)'
**πολεύω II**, for '*turn up* the soil with the plough' read '*go over* (i.e. plough) land'
**πολέω I**, for 'intr. .. *haunt*' read '*range over, haunt*, w. acc.'; after '*Pers.* 307' insert 'intr. *go about*' **II**, for '*turn up* the soil with the plough' read '*go over* (i.e. plough) land'
**πολιά**, add 'transf., of trees, οὐδ' αὐτὰ (sc. δένδρα) γέροντος ἤδη χρόνου πολιὰ καθαύαινεν Luc.*Am.* 12'
***πολιϝάναξ**, ακτος, ὁ, (cj.) *lord of the city*, Ποτιδᾶ‹ι› Πολιϝάνα‹κ›τι (sic) *ZPE* 60.90 (*IG* 4.222; Corinth, vi BC).
**πολιαρχέω**, add 'Thess. τολλιαρχέω *SEG* 23.437 (Crannon, iii BC) fr. °πτολιαρχέω'
**πολιαρχία**, add 'Just.*Nov.* 13 pr.'
**πολίαρχος**, add 'cf. πτολίαρχος, fr. which the Thess. form is assimilated'
***πολιάω**, *go grey, age*, οὐ πολιᾷ· οὐ γηράσκει Hsch.
***πολιδῠνάστης**, ου, ὁ, *city-despot*, Plb. 5.4.3 (cj.).
**Πολιεύς**, line 2, after 'etc.' insert 'of Sarapis, *JHS* 21.275 (Xois, Egypt)'
**πολιήτης**, after 'E.*El.* 119' insert 'Ion Trag. 41 S.'
**πολιῆτις**, after 'A.R. 1.867' insert 'Posidipp. in *Suppl.Hell.* 705.1'
**πολιορκέω**, line 4, before '(πόλις' insert 'written **πολιουρκέω** *Marm. Par.* 113, v.l. in Str. 17.3.15, Lyd.*Mens.* p. 184 W. cod., v.l. in Procop.*Goth.* 2.24'
**πολιορκία**, after 'ἡ' insert 'written **πολιουρκία** *IG* 12(7).387.6 (Amorgos, iii BC), *Marm.Par.* 113'
**πολιός I 1**, line 5, before 'γάλα' insert 'εὔιον γέροντα of wine (w. play on 2), Men.*Dysc.* 946' **2**, line 3, for 'Alc.*Supp.* 20.2' read 'Alc. 50.2 L.-P; σάρκες E.*Supp.* 50 (lyr.); χείρ *AP* 9.568 (Diosc.; = *EG* 2943 P.)' add '**III** πολιά, ἡ, (sc. λίθος) a precious stone, Plin.*HN* 37.191. Myc. *po-ri-wa* (neut. pl.)'
**πολιοῦχος** (A), sp. πολίοχος, add '*Inscr.Cret.* 4.171.14'

**πόλις**, line 13, after '*An.Ox.* 1.361' insert 'Thess. πόλλιος *BCH* 59.37 (disyll., Crannon)' **II**, line 1, after '*country*' insert 'orig.'; add 'Αἴγυπτον καὶ Λιβύην τῶ πόλεε decr.ap.Crater.in Sch.T Il. 14.230'

**πόλισμα**, line 5, after 'Th. 1.10, 4.54' insert 'Plu.*Pomp.* 28.1, D.C. 40.36.4, al.'

***πόλιστος**, = πλεῖστος, *IG* 14.645.130 (Heraclea, iv BC).

**πολῑταρχέω**, add '*SEG* 24.580 (sp. πολειττ-, Maced., ii BC), 33.520 (Maced., ii AD)'

**πολῑτάρχης**, add '*SEG* 30.568.16 (Maced., ii AD)'

***πολῑταρχικός**, ὁ, *one who has served as* πολιτάρχης, *IG* 10(2).162.15, 197.13 (Thessalonica, iii AD).

**πολῑτεία I 3**, for pres. ref. read 'Arist.*Ath.* 4.3, *IG* 9(2).517.17 (Larissa, iii BC)'

**πολῑτευμα I**, add 'ἀρετῆς ἕνεκεν .. κατὰ τὸ πολίτευμα καὶ ἐν τοῖς ἄλλοις πᾶσιν *Amyzon* 24'

**πολῑτευτής**, add '**2** member of the πολίτευμα (as a governing body), *SEG* 9.1.31, 67 (Cyrene, iv BC).'

**πολῑτεύω B I**, add '**b** *to live doing one's civic duty, Act.Ap.* 23.1, *Ep.Phil.* 1.27.'

**πολῑ́της I**, add '**3** *city-dweller*, Just.*Nov.* 52.1, 89.2.2.'

**πολῑτικός I 1 a**, add 'πολιτική, ἡ, perh. *city tax*, *EA* 7.74 (Sardis, 213 BC)' **b**, after '*in a town*' insert 'τῇ π. ἐργασίᾳ *Vit.Aesop.*(G) 2'; add '*appointed* or *authorized by the city*, ἀρτοπώλης *Sardis* 7(1) no. 166 (-ειτ-)' **2**, adv., add 'sup. πολιτικώτατα Arist.*Ath.* 40.3' **3**, add 'ἡ πολιτική, prob. *the body of citizens*, *SEG* 36.1087 (Sardis, 213 BC)' **IV**, for '*concubine, mistress*' read '*prostitute, whore*'

**πολῑτογρᾰφία**, add '*SEG* 26.96 (Athens, *c.*220 BC)'

**Πολιχνῖται**, add '*IG* 1³.260 viii 17 (Athens, v BC)'

**πολλάκις**, line 2, delete 'never in prose' **I**, add 'πολλάκι δὲ γράφων *Amyzon* 15 (201 BC), Phld.*Ir.* 9.28'

***Πολλᾰλέγων**, οντος, ὁ, *"Saying-much"* or *"Heeding-much"* (cf. Οὐκαλέγων Il.3.148), name coined by Alcm. 107 P.

**πολλοστός I 1**, adv, add 'sp. πολλαστῶ[ς, *PVindob.*G 29.386.11 (*Tyche* 7.56, vi/vii AD)' **3**, transfer 'X.*Mem.* 4.6.7' to exx. w. οὐδέ in the following line.

***πολοειδής**, ές, *cylindrical*, ὄργανα Anon.Alch. 275.16, 277.7.

**πολῠάϊκος**, after 'Sch.E.*Med.* 10' add 's.v.l.'

**πολῠανδρος I 2**, after 'Onos. 21.5' insert 'ἔθνη -ρότατα D.Chr. 35.14'

**πολῠανθής**, add 'πολυανθέων Ἐρώτων *Anacreont.* 55.7 W.'

***πολῠ́αρνος**, ον, *rich in lambs*, Hsch. s.v. πολύρρην.

***πολῠαύχητος**, ον, *much-vaunted*, epigr. in *Lindos* 177.6 (ii AD).

***πολῠβιβλογενής**, ές, perh. *producing much papyrus*, *PGron.*inv. 66 in *ZPE* 41.82 (ii AD).

***πολῠ́βλεπτος**, ον, *much-observed*, *PMasp.* 141 rᵛ.31 (vi AD).

***πολῠ́βοια**, fem. adj., *rich in cattle*, εἰρήνη π. Euph. in *Suppl.Hell.* 415 ii 4, cf. *fr.* 177.2 (Powell).

**πολῠβούτης**, at end for 'Carm. .. K.)' read '*Carm.Naup.* 2 B.'

**πολῠ́γιος**, for 'Paus. 2.31.13' read 'Paus. 2.31.10 (perh. corrupted fr. ‡πολυγώνιος)'

**πολύγονον**, add 'also **πολύγονος**, ἡ, Plin.*HN* 27.113, Cyran. 34.19'

**πολῠ́γραμμος**, add 'of kind of jasper, Plin.*HN* 37.118'

***πολῠ́γραπτος**, ον, *fully-painted*, *SEG* 28.541 (32.633; Maced., late Hellen.).

**πολῠγώνιος**, add 'voc. sg., Call.*fr.* 114.2 Pf., prob. addressed to cult-stone representing Apollo, cf. Paus. 2.31.10 where πολυγώνιος shd. perh. be read for πολύγιος'

**πολῠδάκρῡτος I**, after '*Tr.* 1105 (lyr.)' insert 'adv. -ως *with many tears*, Sch.S.*OC* 1646' and add 'sup. *SEG* 24.1075 (Moesia, iii/iv AD)'

**πολῠ́δενδρος**, add 'Simon. in *POxy.* 3965 *fr.* 27.8, Theoc. 17.9'

**πολῠδῐκέω**, add '*SEG* 9.1.47 (Cyrene, iv BC)'

**πολῠ́δῐκος**, after '*litigious*' insert 'Heraclid.*Pol.* 4.5'

***πολῠ́δῖνος**, ον, *whirling round and round*, Nonn.*D.* 2.457.

**πολύδριον**, after 'πόλις' insert 'J.*AJ* 18.249 (s.v.l.)'

**πολῠδῠ́νᾰμος 2**, add '*JRS* 40.78.24 (Cyrene, letter of Hadrian)'

**πολῠ́δωρος**, after '**II**' insert '*bountiful*, γῆ epigr. in *MAMA* 8.130 (Dinek Saray)'

**⁺πολῠείδεια**, ἡ, = πολυειδία, Call.*Dieg.* ix.34 (*fr.* 203 Pf.).

**πολυειδής**, line 5, after '(Sup.)' insert 'νεὼς π. *having a rich variety* of ornament, Aristid.*Or.* 50(26).28'

***πολῠέλιξ**, ικος, ὁ, ἡ, gloss on τετραέλιξ, Hsch.

**πολῠ́εργος I**, delete 'perh. f.l. for ἀμπελοεργοί' **II**, add '*SEG* 31.1284 (Antioch in Pisidia)'

***πολῠέτηρος**, ον, Ep. **πουλυ-**, = πολυετής II, Nonn.*D.* 14.103 (s.v.l.).

**πολῠηγερέες**, before 'read' insert '*gathered from many quarters*'

***πολῠθᾰλής**, ές, *of many blooms*, metaph., π. λοχεύματα gloss on λόχια τριθάλεια, Sch.Antim. 182 Wy.; also π. δῶρα ibid.

**πολῠθαύμαστος**, after '*much-admired*' insert 'Sch.E.*Hipp.* 168'

***πολῠθενία**, ἡ, *abundance, prosperity*, *SEG* 14.787 (Dorylaeum).

**πολυθλῐβής**, add '*PSI* 253.134 (v AD)'

***πολῠ́θριγκος**, ον, *having many* θριγκοί (?*friezes*), π. τέραμνα (houses) Dain *Inscr. du Louvre* 60.13 (Heraclea ad Latmum; hymn).

**πολῠ́θριδαξ**, read '-θρῖδαξ'

**πολῠ́θριξ II**, add '**b** a precious stone, Plin.*HN* 37.190.'

**πολυθρόνιος**, delete 'πολύθρονος' to end of article.

***πολῠ́θρονος**, ον, = πολυθρόνιος, Call.*fr.* 364 Pf., v.l. in Nic.*Th.* 875.

**πολῠ́θροος**, add '*of manifold utterance*, Μοῦσα Opp.*C.* 3.461'

***πολῠ́καλλος**, ον, *endowed with great virtue*, *MAMA* 7.78.

***πολῠκάνδηλος**, ὁ, (or **-ον**, τό) *chandelier*, *Corinth* 8(3).618 (rest. in *T&MByz* 9.366 no. 74).

**πολῠκέφᾰλος**, add 'sup., Max.Tyr. 38.7'

**πολῠ́κλαυστος I**, after 'η, ον' insert '*AP* 7.712 (Erinn.)' and after '*lamented*' insert 'Archil. 94.3 W.' **II**, after '*causing much lamentation*' insert 'ὦ πολύκλαυθ' Ἅιδη *CEG* 591.5 (Attica, *c.*350 BC)'

**πολῠ́κοινος I**, add 'in kinship, i.e. *sister to many*, π. Ἀμφιτρίταν S.*fr.* 673'

**⁺πολῠ́κοπος**, ον, *accompanied by much striking* or *beating*, ὄρχησις Ath. 1.20e (cj. πολυπρόσωπος, cf. Plu. 2.711f). **2** *much-buffeted* (by experience), *Cat.Cod.Astr.* 11(2).189.9.

**πολῠ́κοσμος**, after '*much-adorned*' insert 'τῆς π. χρόας Ael.*NA* 10.13'

**πολῠ́κρᾱνος**, after '*many-headed*' insert '(or *huge-headed*)'

**πολῠ́κροτος I**, for '*ringing loud* or *clearly*' read '*rowdy, noisy*' **II**, add 'Call.*fr.* 67.3 Pf.; cf. κροτέω II 4, κρότημα'

**πολυκτόνος**, add 'of Hades, *SEG* 34.325 (*c.*100 BC)'

***πολῠκωπίτης**, ου, ὁ, one of the crew of a πολύκωπον (πλοῖον) *PLond.* 1712.6, 37 (AD 569); perh. also *PMasp.* 136.16, 287.18.

***πολῠ́λᾱϊς**, ϊδος, *giver of much booty*, Ἀθάνα π. Alc. in *SLG* 262.9.

**πολῠ́λάλητος**, add '**III** *much spoken-of*, ἥρως epigr. in *IGBulg.* 796.3 (ii/iii AD; -λαλατος).'

***πολῠ́μαστος**, ἡ, *many-breasted*, (*Dianam Ephesiam*) *multimammiam, quam Graeci π. vocant*, Jerome *in Ep.Eph.* prolog. (*PL* 26.441).

**πολῠμεμφής**, after '*much-blaming*' insert 'Arat. 109 (v.l. περι-). **II** *blameworthy*, epigr. in *IHadr.* 36 (i BC/i AD).'

**πολῠ́μετρος II**, after '*metres*' insert 'στροφαί D.H.*Comp.* 26'

**⁺πολῠ́μῐτος**, ον, *having tapestry-woven decoration in many colours*, πέπλοι π. A.*Supp.* 432, Cratin. 481 K.-A., Plin.*HN* 8.196, *Peripl.M.Rubr.* 39, al., προσκεφάλαια *SB* 7033.37 (v AD).

**πολυμνήστη**, delete 'πολυμνάστοιο .. (Pers.)'

**πολύμνηστος I**, add 'πολυμνάστοιο .. Τισίδος *AP* 6.274 (Pers.)' **II**, for this section read '*much-remembered*, πολυμνήστοιο Δαμαίου Nic.*fr.* 110 G.-S., Orph.*H.* 50.2; perh. also A.*Ag.* 1459 (lyr.)'

**Πολύμνια**, add 'as appellat., πολύμνια παντερπὴς κόρα *Lyr.adesp.* 24 P.)'

**⁺πολῠ́μνῑος**, α, ον, *full of seaweed* or *waterweed*, v.l. (ap.Sch.) in Nic.*Th.* 950; cf. πολυμνία· ἡ θάλασσα, ἡ πολὺ φυκίον ἔχουσα Hsch.

**πολῠ́μορφος I**, after '*manifold*' insert '*varied*'; after 'Arist.*PA* 646ᵇ32' insert 'of mosaic work, *SEG* 26.1629 (Apamea, vi AD)'; for 'Him.*Or.* 34.4' read 'Him.*Or.* (34)35 (p. 147.33 C.), D.H.*Comp.* 16'

**πολῠ́μοχθος I**, add 'Orph.*H.* 29.15, 37.4, al.'

**πολῠ́μῡθος I**, for 'Call.*Iamb.* 1.170' read 'Call.*fr.* 192.14 Pf.'; add '*AP* 7.713 (Antip.); *talkative*, Call.l.c., *Epigr.* 16.1 Pf.' **III**, delete 'cf. Call.*Epigr.* 18'

**πολῠνεικής**, after '(A.)*Th.* 830 (anap.)' insert '*Lyr.adesp.* 96 P.'

**πόλυντρα**, delete '(i.e. Lat. *polenta*)' and add '(Aeol. for *πάλυντρα)'

**πολῠ́ξῠλος**, add '**2** *containing many sticks*, or *many* (i.e. *varying numbers of*) ξύλα (v. ξύλον v) *in length*, δέσμαι *Theb.Ostr.* 144 (i AD).'

**πολῠόμματος**, add 'transf., of the night sky, κυανέας [πο]λυόμματον [ποί]κιλμα νυκτ[ός] *POxy.* 2879 i 1 (= *SLG* 458)'

**⁺πολῠόμφᾰλος**, ον, *having many bosses* or *knobs*, πολυόμφαλα .. πόπανα, i.e. sacrificial cakes, *PDerveni* ii 7 (*ZPE* 47, post 300 pp. 1-12, iv BC); πεδίον π., poet. expression for the formation of shields in a Roman *testudo*, Opp.*C.* 1.218.

**πολῠόφθαλμος 1**, add '**b** also perh. *large-eyed*, *POxy.* 1380.129.'

***πολῠόχλητος**, ον, *much-disturbed*, Anon.*in Rh.* 34.12.

**πολῠπάθεια I**, add '*SEG* 35.304 (Epid., after AD 67/8)'

**πολῠπαίπᾰλος II**, for this section read 'πολυπαί(πα)λος αἰθήρ· ποικιλμένος. οὐχ ὁμαλός Hsch. (*Suppl.Hell.* 1100)'

***πολῠπᾰ́λακτος**, ον, *sprinkled with much blood*, cj. in A.*Ch.* 425.

**πολῠ́παλτος**, for 'Call.*Sos.* 4.1' read 'Call.*fr.* 388.1 Pf.'

**πολύπαταξ**, read '**πολυπᾰ́ταξ**'

**πολῠ́πειρος**, add '**2** = πολυπείρων 1, Orph.*H.* 12.13.'

**πολῠπείρων 1**, add 'οἴμους θηρῶν τ' οἰωνῶν τε Orph.*A.* 33' **2**, delete the section.

**πολῠπήμων II**, after '*much-suffering*' insert 'Alcm. 5 *fr.*2 i 9 P.'

**πολῠ́πηνος**, for '*thick-woven, close-woven*' read '*of elaborate pattern*'

**πολυπλάνητος II**, before 'A.*Ch.* 425' insert 'cj. in'

**πολυπλήθεια**, after 'Aen.Tact. 3.1' insert 'ὄχλου Men.*Dysc.* 166'

**πολῠ́πλοκος 2 a**, lines 4/5, delete 'neut. as .. *Sign.* 40'

**πολῠπόθητος**, add 'of the dead, *T&MByz* 7.319 no. 12 (AD 535)'

**πολῠποίκιλος 1**, add 'of the sun, as having oracular significance,

*Orac.Tiburt.* 22, 23' add '**3** of a craftsman, *versatile*, *SEG* 31.1284 (Antioch in Pisidia).'

**πολύπους** (A), after 'S.*El.* 488 (lyr.)' insert '(or *having swift feet*)'

**πολύπους** (B), line 9, for 'in Poets .. from' read 'poet. also' and after '**πούλυπος**' insert '*AP* 9.10 (Antip.Thess.)'; line 12, after 'Hp.*Aff.* 5 (v.l.)' insert 'acc. πώλυπον Simon. 9 P.' add '**V** in form πῶλυψ, name of a throw in dicing, *BIFAO* 30.6 (Alexandria).' add 'Myc. *po-ru-po-de* (dat.)'

**πολυπραγμονέω 3**, for '*to be curious after*' read '*busy oneself with*' and after 'etc.' insert 'σημία θεάμενος ἐπολυπράγμοσα (as if pres. -μόνω) *HThR* 27.61 (Nubia).'

**πολυπραγμόνησις**, delete 'dub. l. in'

***πολύπωος**, υ, *grazed by many flocks*, πολ]υπώεος ἄγχι Πελίννη[ς Euph. in *Suppl.Hell.* 429.19.

**πολύρρηνος**, after 'A.*Eleg.* 3' insert '*EG* 1620 P. (Posidipp.)'

**πολύρρητος**, add 'as pers. n., *SEG* 26.577 (Orchomenos, *c.*250 BC)'

***πολύρρῠπος**, ον, *full of dirt*, gloss on πουλυπινές in E.*Rh.* 716 cod. A.

**πολύς**, lines 4ff., acc. sg., add 'πολέα (masc.) *Suppl.Hell.* 1013'; line 8, after '(Il.) 11.708' insert 'cf. A.R. 2.898' **I 2 b**, add '*possessing full physical strength*, ὠμογέρων ἔτι πουλὺς ἀνήρ Call.*fr.* 24.5 Pf., cf. *Epigr.* 61.1 Pf.; βούπαις οὔπω πολλός A.R. 1.760' add 'Myc. *po-ru-* (in compds.)'

***πολῠσήσᾰμος**, ον, *containing plenty of sesame*, πλακοῦς *Vit.Aesop.*(W) 58.

***πολῠσιγμος**, ον, *containing many sigmas*, Mart.Cap. 5.514.

**πολύσκαλμος**, for '*many-oared*' read '*with many rowlocks* (contrasted w. a small boat)' and after '*AP* 7.295' add '(Leon.Tarent.)'

**πολυσκᾰριστος**, add 'Sch.Il. 2.814 (= *POxy.* 1086.105)'

***πολυσκεδής**, ές, *widely scattered*, A.*fr.* 132c.16 R.

***πολυσκελής**, ές, *stout-limbed*, *stout-legged*, Clem.Al.*Strom.* 5.8 (*GCS* 52.362).

***πολύσπορος**, ον, of men, *abounding in seed*, Ptol.*Tetr.* 72, *Cat.Cod.Astr.* 7.212; of deities controlling procreation, Πρωτόγονος Orph.*H.* 6.10, Φύσις ib. 10.19; of astrological influences, Ptol.*Tetr.* 34, Vett.Val. 6.6; adv. -ρως, *with a multiplicity of seed*, S.E.*M.* 5.58. **2** transf., of countries, *fertile* or *teeming with inhabitants*, Ἀσιάδος πολυσπόρου E.*Tr.* 748, Πάρθων τε πολύσπορος .. αἶα Opp.*C.* 3.23.

**πολυστέφᾰνος II**, for this section read '*Πολυστέφανος*, ἡ, a Sicilian goddess, *SEG* 34.959 (iii BC), *IG* 14.262, 2406.67'

**πολυστεφής I**, line 3, for '*wreathed with*' read '*richly crowned with*'

***πολύστρεβλος**, ον, *given to extortion*, Al.*Pr.* 28.16.

**πολύστροφος 2**, for '*versatile*' read '*changeable*' add '**b** *variable*, τοῦ πάχετος μῆκός τε πολύστροφον Nic.*Th.* 465.'

***πολῠσύντῠχος**, ον, perh. *gregarious*, *Cat.Cod.Astr.* 11(2).189.5.

**πολῠτέλεια**, add '**3** lit. crit., *abundance of matter*, Phld.*Po.* 5.5.'

**πολῠτελής I**, add '**2** lit. crit., *in rich abundance*, διανοήματα Phld. *Po.* 5.9. Adv. πολυτελῶς *with a full treatment*, opp. εὐτελῶς, ib. 5.4.' **II**, add 'adv. also -έως, *SEG* 32.1243'

***πολῠτερπος**, ον, = πολυτερπής, *CEG* 452 (Corinth, *c.*580 BC), unless pers. n.

***πολῠτευκτος**, ον, *much-wrought*, *GVI* 477.3 (Smyrna, i/ii AD).

***πολυτῑμιος**, ον, = πολύτῑμος I, *SEG* 6.159.14 (Phrygia, iii AD).

**πολῠτῑμος I**, add 'γονέων πολυτείμων *SEG* 30.1507, μνήμην .. πολύτειμον ib. 31.1284 (both Pisidia)'

**πολῠτρῐχος I**, add 'Heras ap.Gal. 12.430.13'

**πολῠτροπος III**, after '*various, manifold*' insert 'Diog.Apoll. 5 D.-K.'

**πολῠτροφος I**, delete 'Ptol.*Tetr.* 163'

***πολῠτροχος**, ον, *much-rolling*, Orph.*L.* 649.

**πολῠυμνος**, after '*famous*' insert 'δῆρις Ibyc. 1(*a*).6 P.'

***πολῠφήμητος**, ον, = πολύφημος III, *famous*, *BCH* 15.455.

**πολῠφήτωρ**, after 'Sch.' insert 'B' and add 'cf. Porph.ap.Sch.B Il. 14.200'

**πολύφθογγος**, add '**II** *having a full voice*, Arr.*Cyn.* 5.4.'

**πολυφροσύνη**, add '*ICilicie* 102 (iii AD)'

**πολῠφυλλος**, add 'π., τό, name of a plant, Ps.-Dsc. 2.147'

**πολῠφωνία**, add '*diversity of utterance*, Max.Tyr. 1.1 (pl.)'

***πολῠχᾰρις**, ὁ, ἡ, *very grateful*, εὐχήν epigr. in *SEG* 16.683 (Caria, Rom.imp.).

**πολῠχειρ I**, after 'S.*El.* 488 (lyr.)' insert '(or *having strong hands*)'

**πολῠχορδος**, for 'Simon. 46' read '*Lyr.adesp.* 29(*b*).2 P.'

***πολυχρήσιμος**, ον, *useful in many ways*, Zos.Alch. 215.2.

***πολυχρονέω**, *take a long time* (to rise), Ptol.*Tetr.* 132.

**πολυχρονία**, add '**b** *long life*, *POxy.* 465.174 (ii AD).'

**πολυχρονίζω**, delete 'abs. .. *Tetr.* 132'

***πολῠχωρον**, τό, measure of capacity used in Egypt, *CPR* 7.20.14, 18 (iv AD).

**πολῠχωρος I**, sup., add 'Alcin.*Intr.* p. 168.1 H.'

**πολῠώδῠνος II**, add 'πάτερ *SEG* 6.140.19 (Phrygia, iv AD)'

**πόλχος**, for 'coin inscription of doubtful meaning' read 'prob. pers. n.'

***πομπᾰγωγός**, ὁ, *organizer of a procession*, *SB* 9161, 9162, *BGU* 2118.4, *POxy.* 2768.5 (all iii AD).

**πομπεῖον II**, add '*IG* 2².1673.20 (iv BC), Plin.*HN* 35.140, Plu. 2.839c; also in Thrace, *SEG* 37.607 (iv BC)'

***πόμπευμα**, τό, *procession*, Ps.-Callisth. 1.10.

**πομπευτής 2**, for this section read '*one who takes part in a procession*, τοῖς πομπευταῖς (v.l. πομπεύουσιν) Luc.*Nec.* 16'

**πομπεύω I 2**, for this section read '*carry* or *escort in a ritual procession*, πομπευέτωσαν .. τὸν βοῦν ἐκ τοῦ πρυτανείου *IG* 12(7).515 (Amorgos, ii BC), αὐτὴν (sc. Vestal Virgin) .. πομπεύσαντες δι' ἀγορᾶς D.H. 8.89.5' **II 2**, after 'Procop.*Vand.* 2.9' insert 'transf., of the procession to the underworld, πομπεύων τὴν ἀδίαυλον ὁδόν epigr. in *IG* 9(2).648.11 (Larissa, Rom.imp.)' and for 'metaph.' read 'fig.'

***Πομπηϊασταί**, οἱ, guild of *worshippers of Pompeius*, *Inscr.Délos* 1641, 1797 (i BC).

**πομπικός 1**, add 'ὁδός Lang *Ath.Ag.* XIX L9.57 (343/2 BC)' **2**, after 'Longin. 8.3' insert 'comp., Eun.*VS* p. 500 B.'

**πόμπιμος I**, add 'Plu. 2.86e'

***πομποστόλος**, ον, *of a procession*, πομποστόλον ἆμαρ ἄγει poet. in *Inscr.Délos* 2548 (i BC); **πομποστόλοι**, οἱ, *members of a procession*, *Inscr.Délos* 2607.4, 2608.4.

**πομφόλυξ I**, add '**2** *blister*, = πομφός, Nic.*Th.* 240.' **IV**, before 'Paul.Aeg.' insert 'Plin.*HN* 34.128'

**πονέω A**, line 7, after 'A.R. 2.263' insert 'Aeol. pres. part. πονήμενοι perh. in Alc. 5.9, 119.17 L.-P.; also perh. πονάω, v.infra' **II**, add 'so in pass., id. 1.752' **B**, line 9, after 'Dor.' insert '(?Aeol.)' and after 'Pi.*O.* 6.11' insert 'pf. part. πεπονᾱμένον id.*P.* 9.93' **I**, add '**4** act., impers., πονεῖ μοι ὅτι .. *IHadr.* 157.'

**πονηρία I**, after '*condition*' insert 'Hippon. 39.4 W.'

**πόνος I 5**, delete the section. **III**, line 4, transfer 'πόνον .. anap.)' to section I 2, line 2, after 'Hes.*Op.* 470'; add 'of poems, Call.*Epigr.* 6.1 Pf., *AP* 7.11.1 (Asclep.)'

**ποντιάς**, add '**2** = Ποντικός, *AP* 7.497 (Damag.).'

**ποντίζω**, after 'A.*Ag.* 1013 (lyr.)' insert '*fr.* 47a.16 R.'

***ποντικοφάρμᾰκον**, τό, *litharge*, Anon.Alch. 335.1.

**πόντιος I a**, add 'epith. of Aphrodite, *IHistriae* 173.2 (ii BC); of Athena, Ἀθηναίης Ποντίης *SEG* 28.707 (Paros, iv BC)'

***ποντόγνητος**, η, ον, = ποντογενής, *Suppl.Hell.* 991.61 (poet. word-list, iii BC).

***ποντόγονος**, ον, = ποντογενής, *Suppl.Hell.* 991.60 (poet. word-list, iii BC) (παντ- pap.).

**πόντος II 2**, add 'as a Roman province, *TAM* 4(1).25'

**ποντόφαρυξ**, read '**ποντοφάρυξ**'

***πονωπόνηρος**, *very wicked*, comic formation in Ar.*V.* 466, *Lys.* 350 (πόνῳ πόν- cod. Rav.).

**πόπᾰνον**, line 3, for 'Men. 129.4' read 'Men.*Dysc.* 450'; add 'πόπανον ῥαβδωτὸν ἐννεόμφαλον *Inscr.Perg.* 8(3).161.3'

**ποππύζω II**, before 'pass.' insert 'also in showing disapproval, *tut-tut*' **IV**, for this section read '*tootle* (on a crude musical pipe), Theoc. 5.7'

***πορβιοπώλης**, v. °φορβιο-.

***πορδηκίδαι**, term of abuse, mock-patronymic formed fr. πορδή, *fr.iamb.adesp.* 33 in *Anth.Lyr.* i(3) D.³ (Hsch. s.v. πατρόθεν II).

**πορεία II 3**, add '**b** philos., *way, path*, in life, Socr.*Ep.* 29.5.' **4**, for this section read '*means of transport*, *IG* 1³.127.34, *PRev.Laws* 50.11 (iii BC), *PGrenf.* 43.8 (ii BC)'

**πορεῖον I**, add '**2** pl., *transport animals*, *PCair.Zen.* 720.7 (iii BC), *PTeb.* 704.20 (iii BC), 750.6, al. (ii BC).'

***πορευτής**, οῦ, ὁ, *ferryman*, *OWilck.* 1507 (ii BC).

**πορεύω I**, add '**4** *convey, channel* information, Eur.*Melanipp.Capt.fr.* 6.17 (*GLP* 13.13).'

***πορθμάριος**, ὁ, = πορθμεύς, *ferryman*, *POxy.* 2421.8 (iv AD), *PMil.Vogl.* 188 ii 29, 33, *PSI* 808.2 (?iii AD), (all sp. προθμ-).

**πορθμεῖον III**, add '**2** *ferryboat tax*, *PKöln* 95.2, 15 (written προθ-, ii/iii AD), perh. also *PColl.Youtie* 31.4 (AD 199), *PRyl.* 185.6.'

**πορθμεύω II**, delete 'Act. intr.' and before 'τίς ἀστήρ' insert 'abs.'; add '*IG* 1³.41 (446/445 BC)'

**πορθμός II**, delete 'χωρεῖ .. 341c'

**πορθμοφῠλᾰκία**, delete the entry (only in abbrev. form, perh. read ‡πορθμεῖον).

**πόριμος II 2**, delete the section transferring exx. to section I.

***Πόρισος**, epith. of Zeus, Διὸς Πορίσου Κτησίου Robert *Hell.* 10.63 (Rom.imp.), unless to be read as Πορισ‹τ›οῦ.

**ποριστής 1**, add '**c** *purveyor, provision-merchant*, Ph. 2.525 (pl.).'

**πόρκος I**, add 'perh. also π. Ἰστριεὺς τετρασκελής Lyc. 74 (kind of animal acc. to Sch. ad loc.)'

**πόρνη**, for 'Archil. 142' read 'Archil. 302 W.' and add 'Alc. 117(*b*).26 L.-P., al., Hippon. 104.34 W.; πόρνας (gen. sg.) *SEG* 37.661 (Chersonesus, iv BC)'

**πορνοβοσκέω**, after 'Ar.*Pax* 849' insert 'D. 59.68'

***πορνολύτᾱς**, α, ὁ, perh. *one who resorts to prostitutes*, graffito in *Glotta* 40.50 (Tarentum, iv/iii BC).

**Πορνόπιος**, add '*SEG* 34.1238 (Aeolis, *c*.200 BC)'

**πόρνος 1**, add '*IG* 12(3).536 (vii/vi BC)'

***πορνότεκνον**, τό, *child of a prostitute, PAlex.* 76ʳ.

**πόρος I 1**, add 'Th. 7.78.3, 80.6' **IV**, after 'personified' insert 'as a cosmological principle, Alcm. 1.14 Sch.A, 5 *fr.* 2 ii 19 P.'

**πόρπαξ I**, add 'Critias 37 D.-K.'

**πορπάω**, after 'A.*Pr.* 61' insert 'med. aor. ἐπορπήσατο Hsch. s.v. περονήσατο; plpf. ἐπεπόρπηντο, id. s.v. δωριάζειν'

**πόρπη**, line 3, after '(E.)*Hec.* 1170' insert 'πόρπη χρυσῆ *Inscr.Délos* 439*a*77 (181 BC)'; line 6, for '*IGRom.* .. (Egypt)' read '*IPhilae* 159.1 (acc. πόρπαν)'

**πορπίον**, for pres. ref. read '*Inscr.Délos* 1417*A*3, 1442*A*53 (both ii BC)'

**πορσύνω**, line 3, before 'πορσαίνεσκον' insert 'πορσαίνεσκεν Hes.*fr.* 43a.69 M.-W.' **II 3**, after 'pass.' insert 'στόλος πορσύνεται S.*Ph.* 781' at end of article add 'a form πορσύεται is found in *GVI* 1923.12 (Cyzicus, i AD); perh. πόρσυε shd. be read for πόρθυε ib. 2039.9 (Mytilene, ?i/ii AD)'

**⁺πόρταξ**, ἄκος, ὁ, *calf*, Il. 17.4 (= ἄρρην βοῦς Hsch.); cf. as pers. n., *SEG* 31.827, 32.927 (Sicily, Hellen.).

***πορταρῆσις**, ὁ, Lat. *portarensis, *gate-watchman, ODouch* 31.1, 41.1, 6.

**πορτᾶς**, after '*dealer in calves*' insert '(or *gate-keeper*, fr. Lat. *porta*)'

***πορτευθών**, v. °προσέρχομαι.

***πορτί**, v. πρός.

***πορτιπōνέν**, v. ‡προσφωνέω.

**πόρτις**, add 'Myc. *po-ti-pi* (instr. pl.)'

**πορφύρα III**, add 'granted as an honour to an agonothete, *Gerasa* 192.9, 15 (ii AD)' transferring '*IGRom.* 3.1422' fr. section IV.

***πορφῠρᾶς**, ᾶ, ὁ, *dealer in purple, MAMA* 8.562 (Aphrodisias, ii AD), *ITyr* 118b, 119, 120.

***πορφῠρᾱφορία**, v. ‡πορφυροφορία.

**⁺πορφύρεος**, α, ον, Att. **-ροῦς**, ᾶ, οῦν, Aeol. **-ύριος** Sapph. 54 L.-P., Alc. 45 L.-P.; dat. πορφύρωι Sapph. 98(*a*).4, neut. sg. πόρφυρον ?Sapph. 105(*c*).2, neut. pl. πορφύρā Sapph. 44.9; -ύριος also in *IG* 5(1).1390.179 (Andania, i BC); παρφυροῦς *Dura*⁴ 93,97. **I** *purple-dyed, purple*, of stuffs, clothes, etc., π. φᾶρος Il. 8.221; χλαῖνα Od. 4.115; πέπλοι Il. 24.796; δίπλαξ 3.126, Od. 19.242; ῥήγεα Il. 24.645; τάπητες 9.200, Od. 20.151; σφαῖρα 8.273; χλάμυς Sapph. 54 L.-P.; σπάργανα, πτερά, Pi.*P.* 4.114, 183; χλανίς, χιτών Simon. 38.16 P., B. 18.52 S.-M., cf. A.*Pers.* 317, Hdt. 1.50.1, E.*Or.* 1457 codd. (lyr.), etc.; adv. -ῶς, *with purple dye*, στύφειν *PHolm.* 24.37. **2** *purple-clad, in purple*, Luc.*Tim.* 20. **II** *purple-coloured*: **1** of the sea, ἐς .. ἅλα πορφυρέην μεγάλα στενάχουσι ῥέουσαι Il. 16.391; ἀμφὶ δὲ κῦμα στείρῃ πορφύρεον μεγάλ' ἴαχε νηὸς ἰούσης 1.482, Od. 2.428; π. κῦμα .. ποταμοῖο ἵστατ' ἀειρόμενον Il. 21.326, cf. Od. 11.243; θάλασσα Alc. l.c. **2** of human complexion, *bright-red, rosy*, π. Ἀφροδίτη Anacr. 12.3 P.; στόμα Simon. 80.1 P.; παρῇδες Phryn.Trag. 13 S.; χείλη *GVI* 746 (iii/iv AD); also of birds' plumage, τὸ .. νῶτον αὐτῷ πορφυροῖς ἠγλάϊσται Ael.*NA* 17.33. **3** of blood, αἵματι δὲ χθὼν δεύετο π. Il. 17.361; hence of death in battle, ib. 5.83, al. **4** *dark*, of hair, *Anacreont.* 16.11 W. **b** ὁ π. alone, of Death (perh. the *Dark One*), *AP* 11.13.2 (Ammian.). **5** of the rainbow, Il. 17.547; to which a supernatural π. νεφέλη is compared, ib. 551, cf. Xenoph. 32.2. **6** πορφυροῦν (sc. ἄνθος), τό, *Woodfordia floribunda* (an Indian shrub), Ctes. 45(38)J. Form *πορφύρειος, Myc. *po-pu-re-jo*.

***πορφῠροβᾰφικός** or **-βαπτικός**, ή, όν, *connected with purple-dyeing*, ἡ π. (sc. τέχνη), Phld.*Rh.* 1.16.12.

**πορφῠροβάφος**, after '*dyer of purple*' insert 'Ion Hist. 6 J., *SEG* 25.180 (*c*.330/22 BC)'; delete 'Ath. 13.604b'

**πορφῠροπώλης**, add '*IMiletoupolis* 35 (i/ii AD), *PHerm.* 52 (AD 399), etc.'

***πορφῠρόσημος**, ον, *marked with purple*, δερματίκιον σειπποένον πορφυρόσημον *PMich.*inv. 1373 (*ZPE* 21.26).

***πορφῠρόστολος**, ον, *having a purple robe*, Zos.Alch. 246.22.

**πορφυροφορία**, add 'also **πορφῠρᾱφορία** *SEG* 37.855 (Caria, i AD)'

***πορφῠρόω**, *empurple*, fig., *glorify*, καὶ ἐν δόξῃ αὐτῶν πορφυρωθήσεσθε Aq.*Is.* 61.6.

**πορφύρω 1**, line 7, after 'id. 4.668' insert 'of storm clouds, *AP* 5.64 (Asclep.)' **2**, line 4, before 'Q.S. 2.85' insert 'A.R. 1.461, 3.397'

***πόρω II 1**, add 'τὸ πεπρωμένον μοίρης ἀπέδωκα *SEG* 32.605 (ii AD)'

**Ποσειδῶν**, form Ποσειδάων, add 'Myc. *po-se-da-o, po-se-da-ono* (gen.)'; line 7, after 'B. 16.79' insert 'A.*fr.* 78c.47 R. (lyr.)'; line 14, after '(Megarian)' insert 'but ᾰ *Tit.Calymn.* xii 30 (Cos, iii BC)'; add 'Ποσειδᾶν, acc. (app. conflation of Attic Ποσειδῶ and Doric Ποτ(ε)ιδᾶν, *Suppl.Hell.* 990.6)'

**Ποσειδώνιος**, add 'also as month-name (cf. Ποσιδάϊος, etc.), μηνὸς Ποσειδανίου *SEG* 32.871 (Crete, ii AD)'

**πόσθων I**, add 'as pers. n., *SEG* 35.30 (Sounion, *c*.500 BC)' **II**, add 'Men.*fr.* 415 K.-Th.'

***ποσιαστής**, οῦ, ὁ, prob. *member of* a religious association called a συμπόσιον, *BCH* 60.337 (Philippi, ii/iii AD).

**Ποσιδήϊος**, add 'cf. Myc. *po-si-da-e-ja*, name of a goddess'

**Ποσιδηϊών**, add 'sp. ποσειδι(ών) *SEG* 30.977 (Olbia, v BC)'

**πόσις**, ὁ, line 5, for '*Inscr.Cypr.* 93 H.' read 'Cypr. *po-si-se* πόσις, *ICS* 84.2'

**πόσος II 1**, ἐπὶ ποσόν, after 'Plb. 2.34.15, etc.' insert '*to a certain extent* or *degree, Peripl.M.Rubr.* 20' for '**III**' read '**II 3**' and after 'ποσῶς' insert '*to some degree* or *extent*'

**ποσσίκροτος I**, add '*CEG* 785.2 (Histiaea, v BC)'

**πόταγε**, delete the entry.

***ποτάγω**, v. προσάγω.

***ποτᾰμοδίαιτος**, ον, *dwelling in rivers, APAW* 1943(14).8 (Chalcis, iii AD).

**ποτᾰμός I 1**, add 'in a rallying cry, τοὺς ἐχθρούς σου τῷ ποταμῷ *SEG* 34.1056 (Aphrodisias, vi AD)' **II**, add 'Ἱερὸς Π. *SEG* 31.933 (Caria, ii AD), Mitchell *N.Galatia* 1, 2, 3, al. (Rom.imp.)' add '**IV** ἐπὶ τοῦ ἥπατος σημεῖον Hsch.'

**ποτᾰμοφόρητος**, after '*river*' insert '*BGU* 1216.98 (ii BC)'

**ποταμοφῠλᾰκίδες**, delete the entry.

***ποτᾰμοφῠλᾰκίς**, ίδος, ἡ, *guard- or patrol-ship on a river*, ὑπὲρ μερισμοῦ ποταμοφυλακίδος *SB* 4354.4 (AD 112), 4356 (AD 117), al.; pl., *OWilck.* 293 (i AD), *PFlor.* 91.4 (ii AD).

***ποτᾰμοφύλαξ**, ἄκος, ὁ, *river-guard*, rest. in *PAmh.* II 32.13 (ii BC), *PBremen* 11.32 (ii AD), *PLond.* 2561 (Milne *GSM* No. 715 (ποταφυλαξ)).

***ποτᾰμόω**, pass., *to be formed into a river, flow together* (in quots., fig., of nations), Aq.*Je.* 28(51).44 (v.l. ποταμισθήσονται), *Is.* 2.2 (L.-R.).

**ποτάομαι**, line 3, for 'ποτῆται' read 'ποτήται'

**πότε II**, line 3, for 'in μήποτε .. 144 H.' read '*po-te, ICS* 261, cf. μήποτε'; line 4, Aeol. ποτα, add '*SEG* 31.572 (*c*.200 BC)' **II 3**, at end for 'Part.' read 'particle'; after '(dub.)' add 'ποτὲ μέν .. ἄλλοτε δέ *AP* 12.156' **III 1**, add 'as first word in story, Aesop. 232 P.'

**πότερος III**, line 4, for '*SIG* 421' read '*IG* 9²(1).3*A*31'

**ποτή** (A), after '*h.Merc.* 544' insert 'ποτὴν ὄρνιθι ἐοικώς Arat. 278 M.'

**ποτήρ**, add '*PCol.* 240 (iv/v AD)'

***ποτηρία**, ἡ, *drinking-cup*, ha ποτερία *IG* 9(1).303 (s.v.l., Locri, v BC).

**ποτηρίδιον**, add 'sp. βοτηρίδιν *SEG* 28.1586 (Rom.imp.)'

**ποτήριον**, for 'Alc. 52, Sapph.*Supp.* 20a.10' read '*CEG* 454.1 (Ischia, viii BC), *SEG* 32.859 (Eretria, vii BC), *Lyr.adesp.* 34 P., Sapph. 44.10 L.-P., Alc. 376 P.'

**ποτής**, add 'S.*fr.* 314.274 R.'

**πότης**, for 'usu. in fem. .. v. infr.' read 'Call.*fr.* 191.43 Pf.; fem. πότις'

**ποτί**, line 1, for 'Dor. for πρός' read 'dial. equiv. of πρός'; line 16, for 'also πο-' read 'also πο(τ)- w. simplified spelling' add 'Myc. *po-si* (also in compds.), prob. *ποσί (cf. πός B) rather than *πορσί (cf. πρός, πορτί)'

***ποτι-, ποθ-**, for compd. wds. w. this first element see also s.v. προσ-.

**ποτίζω 1**, line 2, after '*Aph.* 7.46' insert 'νέκταρ ἐπότισεν Pl.*Phdr.* 247e' **2**, for 'τοὺς ἵππους .. 247e' read 'πεπότικε μὲν γὰρ ὥσπερ ἰατρός μ', ἔφη, ἃ δεῖ Macho 4 G.' **3**, line 3, before 'also *water*' insert 'π. τοῖς ποσὶν αὐτῶν Lxx *De.* 11.10; cf. πούς I 6 k'

***ποτικαταρτίζω**, Dor. for *προσ-, *add by way of equipment*, rest. in *IRhod.Peraia* 201.9 (i BC).

**ποτικός 1**, after 'etc.' insert 'comp., id. 2.352f'

**ποτίκρᾱνον**, for 'Dor. form of προσκρ- (which is not found)' read 'Dor. for *πρόσκρ- (hypothetical formation in Hsch. s.v. ποτίκρανον)'

***ποτιποιέω**, *make in addition, SEG* 32.356 (Aegina, *c*.550 BC); cf. προσποιέω.

**ποτισμός**, for 'Call.*Fr.anon.* 121' read '*Suppl.Hell.* 1032'

**ποτιστρίς**, add '**2** adj., ἐν τῇ μέσῃ ποτιστρίδι διώρυγι *PCair.Zen.* 825.19 (iii BC).'

**ποτιψαύω**, after 'Dor.' insert 'and poet.' and after 'Pi.*fr.* 121.3' add 'S.*Tr.* 1214'

**πότμος I 1**, add 'Plu. 2.591c (poet. language)' last line, after '*fr.* 871.1' add 'E.*Hec.* 971, *Ion* 1605'

**πότνα**, after '(nom.)' insert 'π. γυναικῶν *AP* 6.287 (Antip.Thess.)'

**πότνια**, penultimate line, after '*Ion* 873, al.' insert 'Ar.*Ra.* 337, *Pax* 445, 975 (anap.), al.' add 'Myc. *po-ti-ni-ja*, title of goddess'

**πότος**, ὁ, add '**2** *something to drink, draught*, Nic.*Al.* 59.'

***ποτουδίζω**, v. °προσουδίζω.

***πουιών**, ῶνος, ὁ, perh. = πουλβῖνον, *PWarren* 18.12 (iii AD).

***πουκρίς**, ίδος, ἡ, kind of freshwater fish, *IGC* p. 99 B27 (Acraephia, iii/ii BC).

**πουλβῖνον**, add 'also φουλβῖνον (q.v.)'

***πουλβῖνος**, ὁ, *bed-tick, Edict.Diocl.* 28.56 (sp. -βει-).

***πουλικάριος**, α, ον, adj. describing kind of blanket, *Edict.Diocl.* 8.43.

*__πουλλίον__, τό, dim. of °ποῦλλος, in context perh. *cockerel*, *SB* 5301, 5302 (Byz.), *PColl.Youtie* 95.9 (vii AD); cf. mod. Gk. πουλί *bird*.

*__ποῦλλος__, ὁ, *chicken*, *POxy.* 1913.26 (vi AD).

*__πουλῠβοώτης__, ὁ, ἡ, v. πολυβούτης.

*__ποῦνδα__, v. °φοῦνδα.

*__πουρα[μ]ω__ (gen.), kind of freshwater fish, *IGC* p. 99 B30 (Acraephia, iii/ii BC).

*__πούραυμα__ (for *πῦρ-), ατος, τό, perh. *brazier*, *BCH* 62.149 (Boeotia).

*__πουρείνιον__, τό, dim. of πουρεινίς, = πυρήνιον, *IG* 7.2421.8 (Tanagra, iii BC).

**πούς I 1**, last line, after 'Od. 4.149' insert '*AP* 5.55 (Diosc.)' **4 b**, line 6, after 'Prov.ap.Suid.' insert 'cf. Mesom. 3.9 H., Ps.-Babr. Μυθικά 17 p. 219 C.' **c**, after '*close at hand*' insert 'τῶν δ' (ἰβίων) ἐν ποσὶ .. εἱλευμένων τοῖσι ἀνθρώποις Hdt. 2.76.1' **6 k**, lines 3/4, for 'perh. .. wheel' read '*by the foot*, i.e. measure, (during the inundation)' and before 'τόπον' insert 'ἀπὸ π. ποτισμός *SIFC* 13.366 (cf. °ποτίζω 3)' **II 1**, add 'ἐν ποδὶ λῃγούσης Πελοπηΐδος at the *extremity* of the Peloponnese, referring to the Isthmus of Corinth, Call.*fr.* 384.11 Pf.; πὰρ ποδὶ .. Νείλου νειατίῳ by the outermost (i.e. most easterly) *mouth* of the Nile, ib. 48; app. w. ref. to a form of interlinear glossing, τῇ κατὰ πόδα καλουμένῃ χρήσασθαι τῶν νόμων ἑρμηνείᾳ Just.*Const.* Δέδωκεν 21' **III**, for '6 fingers' read '16 fingers' at end add 'Myc. *po-de* (dat.), *po-pi* (*πόπφι, instr. pl.), *foot* of cauldron, table'

**ποῦ‹τ›ριν**, add '(= Lat. *putris*)'

**πρᾶγμα II 8**, after '*question*' insert 'S.*fr.* 314.332 R.' **III 3**, line 5, after '= κτήματα, Hp.(*Lex* 5?)ap.Erot.' insert 'τὰ πράγματα τοῦ αὐτοῦ μοναστηρίου κινητὰ καὶ ἀκίνητα καὶ αὐτοκίνητα *Cod.Just.* 1.3.43.4; τῆς τῶν πραγμάτων διακρίσεως (transl. Lat. *separatio bonorum*) Just.*Const.* Δέδωκεν 7d'

**πραγμᾰτεία II 1**, add '*appurtenances of one's business*, i.e. *merchandise*, *wares*, Just.*Nov.*appendix 5'

**πραγμᾰτεύομαι I 2**, add 'ἐπί τι *IEphes.* 1503.10 (ii AD)'

**πραγμᾰτευτής**, add 'of slave (or freedman) estate-managers, *SEG* 31.1143, *INikaia* 1203 (Rom.imp.)'

**πραγμᾰτευτικός I**, after '*business*' insert 'Ptol.*Tetr.* 178'

**πραγμᾰτικός I 1**, line 4, delete 'men *of affairs*'

+__πραγμᾰτολογέω__, *state one's case*, Arist.*Rh.Al.* 1438ᵇ20, Ph. 1.554, 655, D.L. 9.52.

**παιδεύω**, after 'δηώσαντες' insert 'Sch.E.*Ph.* 202-15'

*__πραικόκ(κ)ιον__, τό, *apricot*, Orib. 1.48 (*CMG* 6.1(1).23), al., Gal. 6.811.12; also **πρεκόκκιον** Gal. 6.585.9, 594.6; cf. βερικόκκιον, Lat. *praecox*.

**πραίκων**, after '*praeco*' insert '*SEG* 36.595 (Maced., ii/iii AD)'

**πραιπόσιτος**, add 'in non-military context, πρεποσείτου θησαυρῶν *SEG* 32.1061 (Rome, AD 414)'

*__πραῖς__, ὁ, *Lat. praes*, *surety*, *SEG* 39.1180.102 (Ephesus, i AD).

*__πραισεντάλιος__, α, ον, Lat. *praesentalis*, *serving in the imperial palace*, Just.*Edict.* 13.2.

*__πραίσεντον__, τό, *troops serving in the imperial palace*, Just.*Nov.* 22 epilogos.

*__πραιτέριτος__, ὁ, Lat. *praeteritus*, *former comrade*, *CPR* 6.76.6.

*__πραιτούρα__, ἡ, Lat. *praetura*, Just.*Nov.* 13.4 pr.

*__πραίτωρ__, ορος, ὁ, Lat. *praetor*, *IGRom.* 3.188 (Ancyra), al., *BCH* 7.20, Porph.*Plot.* 7.35, Lyd.*Mag.* 1.27, al.

*__πραιτωριανός__, ή, όν, *praetorian*, Just.*Nov.* 24.1.

**πραιτώριον I**, after '*Ev.Matt.* 27.27' insert '*PPetaus* 47.44, 48.2 (sp. πλετ-) (both AD 185)' **II**, add 'ἔπαρχος τῶν ἱερῶν τῆς ἔω πραιτορίων *IEphes.* 1345'

*__πραιτώριος__, α, ον, Lat. *praetorius*, κοόρτης δεκάτης πραιτωρίας Φιλιππιανῆς *IEphes.* 737.6.

*__πραίφεκτος__, ὁ, Lat. *praefectus*, *IG* 14.680 (ii AD), *IGRom.* 1.10, Lyd.*Mag.* 2.6; cf. Plb. 6.26.5.

**πρακτικός I 1**, add '**b** *concerned with real life*, opp. μυθικός, Longin. 9.14.'

**πράκτιμος**, before '*SIG*' insert 'w. gen.' and add '*Delph.* 3(6).69.13 (ii/i BC)'

**πρακτορεύω**, add '*JRCil.* 1.19 (Side, iii AD)'

**πρακτορικός**, add 'πρακτορικόν, τό, an extra charge *made by* or *for the* πράκτορες, *PTeb.* 298.63 (ii AD), *BGU* 471.13, 17'

**πράκτωρ II 2**, add '**b** court official, = Lat. *exsecutor*, *Cod.Just.* 3.2.4.8.'

*__πράμνιον__, τό, *pick*, *BGU* 2359.4 (iii AD).

*__πραξᾰγᾰθος__, ον, *beneficent*, θεῶν π. (-αγαθαν lap.) καὶ σωτήρων *BCH* 79.340 (Arcadian Gortys, ii BC).

**πράξιμος I**, add '**b** of persons, *liable to distraint*, *Inscr.Délos* 1522.18 (i/ii AD).'

**πρᾶξις**, add '**IX** *certificate*, διὰ τάχους ἀποστεῖλαι τὴν πρᾶξιν μετὰ τοῦ γραμματηφόρου *PWash.Univ.* 8.6, π. ὑπομνημάτων *PFlor.* 293 (both vi AD).'

**πρᾳόνως**, after 'Ar.*Ra.* 856' insert 'Lys. 24.15'; for '(Formed .. -νους' read '(presupposes a comp. *πρᾳων; cf. ἐλασσόνως)'

**πρᾶος**, line 4, after 'Lyr.(' insert 'first in Alc. 68.3 L.-P. (πρᾶυ)'; line 15, after 'cf. Phot.' insert 'ἔχει δὲ τὸ ἰῶτα' **I 3**, add 'τὸ πρᾶον *modesty*, *humility*, τὸ πρᾶον θαύμαζε τῶν κτισμάτων *SEG* 31.1472 (Arabia, AD 603)'

*__πρᾰσᾶς__, ᾶ, ὁ, *grower* or *seller of leeks*, *IG* 12(5).1104 (Syros, ii AD).

**πρᾰσινος 2**, add 'Epiph.Const. in *Lapid.Gr.* 194.23 (given as equiv. of σμάραγδος)' **3**, add 'τῶν νέων Πρασίνων, i.e. organized youngsters within the green faction, *SEG* 31.1493 (Alexandria, *c.*AD 608)'

**πρᾰσιον I 1**, line 3, for 'Nic.*Th.* 550' read 'Nic.*Al.* 47'

*__πρᾰσιος__, ἡ, = πράσιον, Nic.*Th.* 550.

**πρᾰσοκουρίς**, for '*milliped*' read 'kind of caterpillar'

**πράσσω**, line 16, after 'A.*Pr.* 75' insert 'pf. part. pass. πεπρᾱμένος *SEG* 26.121 (late i BC)' **III 3**, delete the section. **VII**, delete the section.

**πρατήνιον**, delete the entry.

*__πρατήνιος__, ον, [?ᾱ] epith. of a ram, perh. *yearling*, κριὸς π. *Sokolowski* 2.94.6, 11 (Camirus, iii BC, cf. also 104); cf. Phot. s.v. προτήνιον, Hsch. s.v. πρατήνιον, see also πρητήν.

**πρᾱτήρ II**, add 'so π. alone, ἔστησεν ἐπὶ τοῦ πρατῆρος *Vit.Aesop.*(G) 21'

*__Πρατίνειος__, ον, of Pratinas, the reputed inventor of satyric drama, λῆμμα Πρατίνειον epigr. in *Chiron* 19.505 (*c.*200 BC).

**πρᾱτοπάμπαις**, for 'chief of the πάμπαιδες (v. Addenda)' read 'member of one of the age-groups in Spartan education'

**πρᾱτός**, add 'οἶν πρατόν *SEG* 26.136 (Athens, iv BC), ἐν πρατῷ *for sale*, *SEG* 34.558 (Larissa, ii BC)'

**πρᾶτος**, line 2, delete '436'; add 'τῷ ἔτει τῷ π. *next following*, *IG* 12(3).436.7 (Thera, iv BC); as the name of a month, Πράτου μενός *AA* 4.681-7 (Phocis, v BC)'

**πρᾱϋμενής**, after '*of gentle spirit*' insert 'Sch.E.*Or.* 119'

**πρᾱΰνοος**, after '*of gentle mind*' insert 'πειθώ Simm. 24.10'

**πρεῖγυς**, line 4, after 'al.' insert 'title of a magistrate, *Inscr.Cret.* 4.184.13 (Gortyn, ii BC)'; line 7, for 'ib. 2562' read '*Inscr.Cret.* 4.3.7.23'; add 'see also ‡πρέσβυς'

*__Πρειέτιος__, v. °Πριέτιος.

*__Πρείετος__, v. °Πρίετος.

*__πρειμ-__, for transliterated compds. of Lat. *primus* v. °πριμ-.

*__πρεκνόν__· ποικιλόχροον ἔλαφον Hsch.; cf. περκνός, πρακνόν.

*__πρέποντος__, ον, (back-formation fr. πρεπόντως) *fitting*, ἔδοξε .. πρέποντον ἔμμεν *BCH* 59.37 (Crannon, ii BC).

**πρεπόντως 1**, add 'δι' ὅλης τῆς ἀρχῆς ἀνεστράφη π. *SEG* 33.696 (Amorgos, iii BC)'

**πρεπτός**, add 'S.*fr.* 314.330 R.'

**πρέπω I 2**, for this section read '*to be clearly audible*, A.*Ag.* 321, S.*fr.* 314.231 R.' **3**, delete the section. **III 3**, add 'w. inf., γείτονες οὐ τρισσαὶ μοῦνον Τύχαι ἔπρεπον εἶναι *APl.* 40 (Crin.)'

**πρεσβεῖον I 3**, add '**b** = Lat. *legatum*, *legacy*, *Cod.Just.* 1.2.5.1, 1.3.45.13, 14.'

**πρέσβειρα**, after 'πρέσβυς' insert 'S.*fr.* 314.339 R.'

+__πρεσβεύτειρα__, ἡ, fem. of πρεσβευτής, in quot. fig., of scent, as an emissary coming to hunting-dogs, Opp.*C.* 1.464 (πρεσβύτ- codd.).

**πρεσβευτής II 2**, add 'πρεσβευτὴς Σεβαστῶν ἀντιστράτηγος *SEG* 31.908 (Aphrodisias, iii AD)'

**πρεσβευτικός**, add '**2** -κά, τά, *expenses of an embassy*, or perh. *court-fees*, *PMerton* 35 (iv AD).'

**πρεσβεύω**, after lemma insert 'πρεσγεύω *GDI* 5148' **I 1 c**, delete 'also .. 352d' **2**, line 7, for 'time' read 'value' **II 3 b**, delete the section.

**πρέσβις** (A), after '*ambassador*' insert 'Prisc. pp. 286, 320 D.'

**πρέσβις** (B) **II 1**, for 'Aesop. 107ᵇ V Chambry)' read 'Aesop. 57(II) H. (v.l. -υς)' and add 'cj. for πρέσβυν in Lyc. 331'

**πρέσβυς**, line 1, for 'ὁ' read 'or υος (v. infra III 2 b), ὁ (also ἡ Lyc. 331 codd.)'; line 18, after '*PCair.Zen.* 447.9 (iii BC)' insert 'πρεσβυτέρα, ἡ, *old lady*, *PHaun.* 15.11 (ii BC)' and after 'η, ον' insert '(πρεσβυτερώτατος *PSI* 1159.5 (ii AD), πρεσχύτατος epigr. in *ZPE* 12.175 (Egypt, v BC), πρίγιστος *Glotta* 41.65 (Crete))' **II**, add 'of a Roman senator, Plb. 21.18.7, 10; πρισγουτέρυς *SEG* 23.271 (Thespiae, iii BC)' **III 2**, line 7, after 'Ptolemaïs Hermiu, i AD)' insert 'τὸν πρεσβύτερον τῆς κώμης *JJP* 18.35 (iv AD)'; line 8, after '*Ev.Matt.* 16.21, etc.' insert 'fem. πρεσβυτέρα *CIJud.* 731c (Crete, iv/v AD)' add '**b** *guardian*, πρέσβυος τῶν ὁσίων *BCH* 87.203 (Delphi, ?i AD).' 4/5 lines fr. end of article for 'Cret.' read 'Dor.' and before 'πρεῖγυς' insert 'πρέσγυς'

*__πρεσβῠτεράρχης__, ου, ὁ, official at local games, π. τῶν Ὀλυμπίων καὶ ἱεροφάντης *SEG* 24.479 (Maced., iii AD).

*__πρεσβῠτερία__, ἡ, *seniority*, εἰς πρεσβυτερίας λόγον *PMich.*v 326.11 (i AD).

*__πρεσβῠτέρισσα__, ἡ, *elder*, (Jewish), *SEG* 27.1201 (Tripolitania, iv/v AD).

**Πρέσβων**, delete the entry.

***Πρεσβωνοι**, οἱ, (dub. accent), *the Elders*, name of family or χιλιαστύς, *ABSA* 58.56 (Chios, v/iv BC), *SEG* 15.537.

***πρεσγεύω**, v. °πρεσβεύω.

***πρέσγυς**, v. °πρέσβυς.

**πρηγιστεύω**, add '*SEG* 32.869 (Crete, ii AD)'

**πρήθω**, line 2, for 'A.R. seems .. 1537' read 'pres. part. πρήσ(σ)οντα, -οντος A.R. 4.819, 1537 (cj. πρήθ-)'

***πρήμ(ν)η**, ἡ, = πρημνάς, Hsch., Phot.

***πρηρόαρχος**, ὁ, ἡ, epith. of victim sacrificed at the πρηρόσια, Δαίρᾳ ἀμνὴ πρηρόαρχος *IG* 1³.250*A*16.

+**πρηρόσια**, v. °προηρόσιος.

**πρηστήρ II**, delete the section transferring exx. to section I and inserting 'transf., of the hot blast produced by bellows' before 'A.R. 4.777'

**πρίᾰμαι**, add 'Myc. aor. 3 sg. *qi-ri-ja-to*'

***Πρῐᾱπίδιον**, τό, *small image of Priapus*, *Inscr.Délos* 1442*A*4 (ii BC).

**πρῐᾱπίζω**, for '*to be lewd*' read '*behave toward like Priapus*'; delete '*to be ithyphallic*' to end of article.

**Πρίᾱπος**, delete '(also written Πρίεπος ..)' v. °Πρίετος

***πριβάτιος**, α, ον, Lat. *privatus*, *PKlein.Form.* 1033 (vi AD).

***πριβᾶτον**, τό, *private bath*, (fr. Lat.), *IGLS* 3(2).545 (v AD). **II** pl., *the private property* of the Emperor (Lat. *res privata*), *Cod.Just.* 1.5.18.9, Procop.*Arc.* 22.12.

***πρίγκεψ(-ιψ)**, ιπος, ὁ, Lat. *princeps*, (in quots., as legionary rank), Plb. 6.21.7, al., *IGRom.* 3.264, 1157, 1230, *POxy.* 1424, *BCH* 23.419.

***πριγκιπάλιος**, ὁ, Lat. *principalis*, *PFlor.* 278 iii 14, iv 12 (ii AD).

***πριγκιπᾶρις**, ὁ, Lat. *principalis*, π. γέγονα ἐφ' ἔτους *SB* 8088.5 (ii AD).

**πρίγκιπες**, delete the entry.

***πριγκίπια**, τά, Lat. *principia*, *headquarters*, *SB* 10530.4, 18 (AD 143).

**Πριέπιος**, delete the entry (v. °Πριέτιος).

**Πρίεπος**, delete the entry (v. °Πρίετος).

***Πριέτεια**, τά, *festival of the god Prietos*, *SEG* 36.1155 (sp. -ηα, Nicomedia, ii AD).

***Πριέτιος**, (sc. μήν), ὁ, name of a Bithynian month, *TAM* 4(1).19, 35, 59, al., (sp. Πρειέτειος, Πριέτηος. Alleged forms Πριεπ-, Περιεπ- do not exist, v. *AE* 1979.231-6).

***Πρίετος**, ὁ, a Bithynian god, *TAM* 4(1).74, al. (Πρειετ-; Πρίεττος at *SEG* 36.1155); app. confused w. Πρίαπος in Luc.*Salt.* 21, Arr.*fr.* 23 J., see note at end of foreg.

***πριμάριος**, ὁ, Lat. *primarius*, *BGU* 958d (iv/v AD, pl.).

***πριμικήρ**, ῆρος, ὁ, = °πριμικήριος, *PBodm.* 29.49, 126 (iv AD).

***πριμικήριος**, ὁ, Lat. *primicerius*, *BCH* 33.34 (iv AD, written πρημηκιρις), *JHS* 11.162, *PColl.Youtie* 89.3 (AD 485), Just.*Edict.* 4.1.

***πριμιπιλάριος**, ὁ, Lat. *primipilaris*, *IGRom.* 3.55 (πρειμι-), 810, etc., *INikaia* 1551 (iii AD); transf., πιθήκων π. *Vit.Aesop.*(G) 87 (-ηπη-). Also **πρειμοπειλάριος**, *BCH* 4.377, etc.; πριμοπιλάρ(ιν) *SEG* 34.1591 (Egypt).

***πριμιπῖλον**, τό, *office of primipilus*, Modest.*Dig.* 27.1.8.12, 27.1.10.5, *POxy.* 1905.10, 2001.3, *PThead.* 48, *PCol.* 141.52.

***πριμισκρίνιος**, ὁ, Lat. *primiscrinius*, *chief secretary*, *SEG* 9.356.17, 71 (Cyrenaica, vi AD), 32.1554 (Arabia, vi AD).

**πρίν**, line 4, add 'see also φρίν' **A I**, add '**b** folld. by πρίν B, Il. 1.97, Od. 19.585, al. (v. infra); by ἔστ' ἄν, A.R. 2.251.' **II**, add '**5** *sooner*, folld. by πρίν B, Il. 7.481, Od. 19.475, al. (v. infra).'

***πρῑνεύς**, έως, ὁ, *ilex-grove* (possibly a place-name), *IEryth.* 151.20 (iv BC).

***πρῑνεών**, ῶνος, ὁ, *ilex-grove*, Aq.*Ge.* 14.3,8.

***Πρινοφόρος**, ὁ, *bearer of the holm-oak* (cult-title of Dionysus), *IG* 10.2(1).260.B2 (iii AD).

**πρῑνών**, delete '*IG* 1².328.1 (dub.)'

***πρῑονοποιός** or **πρῑονοπώλης**, ου, ὁ, *maker* (or *seller*) *of saws*, rest. in *SEG* 12.84 (Athens, v BC).

***πριόρες**, οἱ, Lat. *priores*, (*military*) *officers*, Just.*Nov.* 117.11.

***πρισγούτερος**, v. °πρέσβυς.

**πρῖσμα**, before 'Thphr.*HP* 5.6.3' insert 'Aen.Tact. 35'

***πρισμή**, ἡ, *sawing*, ἐγλαβόντι τὴν π. τῶν ξύλων *IG* 11(2).199*A*89 (Delos, iii BC).

+**πρισμός**, ὁ, *sawing*, *Theb.Ostr.* 144.2 (πρυσμ-, i AD). **2** *gripping* as with the teeth, πρισμοῖς· ταῖς βιαίοις κατοχαῖς Hsch.

***πρισόριον**, τό, app. Lat. *pressorium*, *?clothes-press*, *PMich.*XIV 684 (*Tyche* 6.233, vi AD).

**πρίων** (A) **1**, add 'τὸν φθόνον ἔφη πρίονα εἶναι ψυχῆς *Gnomol.Vat.* in *WS* 11.63' add '**4** πρίονας χερῶν· τοὺς δεσμούς Hsch.'

+**πρίων** (B), ὁ, nonce-wd., app. one who calls out πρίω (buy), Ar.*Ach.* 36; cf. πρίων· ἀγοράζων Hsch.; the force of a pun on πρίων (A) is not clear.

**πρό A I 3**, lines 5/6, delete 'E.*Alc.* 18, 645'; line 10, for 'cf.' read 'θανὼν π. κείνου E.*Alc.* 18, cf. 645' **II 1**, (p. 1465 b, line 4), after 'Pl.*Smp.* 173a' insert '*Trag.adesp.* 664 i 12 K.-S.'; (line 5) delete 'προ τοῦ ἤ .. (Thisbe)' add '**b** προ τοῦ as conj. = πρίν, πρὸ τοῦ ἤ Γαίος Λοκρέτιος τὸ στρατόπεδον .. προήγαγεν *IG* 7.2225.22 (Thisbe, ii BC), π. τοῦ εἰσέλθοις *BGU* 814.14 (iii AD), π. τοῦ τις ἐνέγκῃ *PFay.* 136.6 (iv AD).' **2 b**, add '*SEG* 31.830 (Sicily, iv/v AD)' **D**, add 'Myc. *po-ro-ko-wo* (πρόχοος), *po-ro-te-ke* (προύθηκε), *po-ro-ko-re-te* (*po-ro-* in sense of "*in place of, vice-*"), etc.'

**προάγγελος II**, after '*harbinger*' insert '*Trag.adesp.* 664 ii 11 K.-S.'

***προαγγελτήρ**, ῆρος, ὁ, = προάγγελος II, prob. in *SEG* 9.72.137 (iv BC).

+**προᾰγοραστής**, οῦ, ὁ, app. *servant who buys stores for the household*, *MAMA* 3.668a.

**προᾰγωγή**, add '**IV** *rhetorical delivery*, Corn.*Rh.* p. 397 H. **V** *production* (of documents, etc.) *in court*, Just.*Edict.* 7.1.'

***προᾰγων**, οντος, ὁ, title of an official in Ormele, *PASA* ii nos. 41*A*, 43, prob. in no. 89.

**προᾰγών 1**, after 'etc.' insert '(or a *rehearsal*)'

**προαιρέτης**, for '*steward, keeper*' read 'title of official (of uncertain function)' and add '*ODouch* 54'

**προαιρέω II 1 b**, add '*SEG* 23.447 (Thessaly, iii AD)'

**προαισθάνομαι**, add 'D. 18.63, al.'

***προακμαστικῶς**, adv., *before the climax*, Aët. 5.53 (32.16 O.).

**προακτικός**, add '**II** *advancing, promoting*, Ascl. *in Metaph.* 146.6, Phlp. *in de An.* 207.15.'

**προᾱλίζω**, add 'Aen.Tact. 17.4 (cj., cod. προσ-)'

**προαλιώτας**, delete the entry.

***προαναγγέλλω**, aor. 1 part. προαναγγείλαντος cj. for προσαν- in Sch.Pi.*O.* 7.83.

**προανᾰγω**, add '**II** *add beforehand to stock*, ὅταν τὸ ἴσον πλῆθος προαναχθῇ, Ἑλληνικά 7.179 (Chalcis, iii BC).'

**προανακόπτω**, add '**2** *cut off in advance, preclude*, Just.*Nov.* 159.3.'

**προανακρούομαι II**, add '**b** *begin a speech by saying*, προανακρουσάμενος ὅτι ?Duris in *POxy.* 2399.46-8; cf. ἀνακρούω II 2.'

***προανακτάομαι**, *repair beforehand*, κάματον διὰ τῆς τροφῆς Porph. ap.Sch.B Il. 19.222 (προσ- cod.).

***προανανεύω**, *deny in advance*, *Pap.Bub.* 4 lxii 5 (iii AD).

**προαναπαύω I**, for pres. def. read '*prescribe rest before*' **II**, add '*IApam.* 133, *BE* 1980.303 (Epirus, both Chr.), *SEG* 26.790 (Byzantium, vi AD)'

**προαναπλέω**, add '**2** *sail up* a river *first*, *PMich.Zen.* 57.12 (iii BC).'

**προανασκευάζομαι**, for 'plpf.' to end of article read '*remove beforehand*, [κειμήλια] ib. 1.13.9; [ἀνδράποδα] prob. in D.H. 6.3'

***προανάσυρμα**, ατος, τό, app. *indecent exposure*, Εὔβουλος δὲ ὁ κωμικὸς τὸ λαθρίδιον γέννημα προανάσυρμα παρθένου καταγελάστως ὠνόμασεν (*fr.* 138 K.-A.) Poll. 3.21.

**προανατείνω**, add 'med., *make apparent beforehand*, Onas. 6.11'

**προανατίθημι**, add '*Inscr.Perg.* 8(3).72'

**προαναφώνησις I 2**, add '*foreshadowing* of what is to come, Sch.T Il. 1.45, Sch.A Il. 11.604'

***πρόαντα** (acc.), τόν, perh. *row of columns in front*, *IStraton.* 200.8.

**προαπαγγέλλω**, add '*SEG* 31.983 (Ionia, ii/i BC)'

**προαπειλέω**, after '*PCair.Zen.* 230.3' insert '(med.)'

**προαποβάλλω**, add 'εἴτε .. προαποβάλοι τὸν ἄνδρα i.e. *lose by his prior decease*, Just.*Nov.* 74.5 pr.'

**προαποδίδωμι I**, add '**3** *act as* °προαποδότης, *GDI* 1990.9 (Delphi, 195 BC).'

**προαποδότης**, for '*one who .. surety*' read '*substitute for the seller, warrantor*'

**προαποθνήσκω I**, add '*TAM* 4(1).217'

***προαποκλάω**, *break off before*, ὁ κριὸς τῆς ἄλλης ἐμβολῆς προαπεκλάσθη Memn. 34.1 J.

**προαπόλλῡμι I**, after '*destroy first*' insert 'προαπολεῖ με Men.*Dysc.* 391 (προσ- pap.)'

***προαποτίλλω**, *pluck out before*, Asclep.Jun.ap.Gal. 12.742.8.

***προαρρᾰβωνίζω**, *betroth beforehand*, π. αὐτὸν ἐμαυτῇ *Vit.Aesop.*(G) 30.

***πρόαρχος**, ὁ, *president*, ὁ ἱερεὺς τοῦ Διὸς τοῦ Τροφωνίου καὶ πρόαρχος τοῦ βακχείου *SEG* 32.475 (Boeotia, iii AD).

**προασθενέω**, add 'Paul.Aeg. 3.78 (299.16 H.)'

***προαστιανός**, όν, *of* or *belonging to the* προάστιον, θεοί *Inscr.Magn.* 309.

**προάστιον**, for '*suburb*' read '*land outside a town* (so also in derivatives)' add '**3** of a temple outside a town, cf. °προαστιανός, *SEG* 8.536, 537 (Egypt, i BC; προαστιν).'

**προαστίτης**, add '*POxy.* 3941.19 (AD 605)'

***πρόαστυ**, εος, τό, = προάστιον, *IGBulg.* 2086.3 (epigr.).

***προάτριον**, τό, *forecourt*, τὸ π. τοῦ μεγάλου γυμνασίου *TAM* 5(2).926.6.

**προαυλέω**, -ημα, -ία, for '*flute*' read '*aulos*'

**προαφίημι**, add 'Aen.Tact. 32.6'

***πρόβα**, ἡ, Lat. *proba*, *test sample*, *SEG* 34.1243 (Abydos, c.AD 492).

**προβάλλω A II 4**, delete the section. **B I 4**, add 'And. 1.132' **III 1**, line 15, after 'D. 21.139' insert 'of a boxer, *to be on guard*'; line 16, after 'id. 4.40' insert 'προβεβλημένος *in the attitude of defence*, Arist.*fr.* 569'

***προβᾰσῐλεύς**, έως, ὁ, title of a magistrate at Argos, *SEG* 29.361 (*c.*400 BC).

**προβᾰσῐλεύω**, add '*Cod.Just.* 1.11.9.3'

**πρόβᾰσις**, add '**III** prob. *marching in front, leading* (a procession), τιμηθέντα προβάσει *Delph.* 3(1).555.26 (iii AD).'

**προβασκᾰνία**, add 'προβασκανίαν is perh. to be read for πρὸς βασκανίαν in *Vit.Aesop.*(W) 16'

**προβασκᾰ́νιον**, add 'prob. for προσβάσκανον in *Vit.Aesop.*(G) 16'

***προβᾰτάγριος**, ον, *of a wild sheep*, δέρμα *Edict.Diocl.* in *SEG* 37.335 ii 20 (where other versions have προβάτειον).

**προβᾰτεύς**, add '*IG* 9².748.41, 43 (Locris, *c.*190 BC)'

***προβᾰτικόν**, τό, *tax on sheep*, *Hesperia* 27.75.13 (*c.*200 BC).

**προβᾰ́τιον**, delete '*little*' before '*sheep*' and add '*PHerm.* 27.5 (V AD)'

**προβᾰτοβοσκός**, after '*shepherd*' insert '*IGBulg.* 851 (-χός)'

**προβᾰτοδόρας**, for 'Procl. .. 502' read 'Sch.Hes.*Op.* 504'

**πρόβᾰτον**, line 2, after 'Hsch.' insert '*Vit.Aesop.*(G) 97 (βρώμασι cod.)' **I**, add 'of a pack-animal, *SEG* 33.1120 (Phrygia, iii AD)'

***προβᾰτονόμος**, ὁ, perh. *sheep-rearer*, Ἰακω προβατον(όμος) *SEG* 36.970.B13 (Aphrodisias, iii AD).

**προβᾰτώδης**, for pres. def. read '*sheep-like*' and for 's.v. βαίκυλος' read 's.vv. βαίκυλος, βλήχημα, βληχήματα'

***προβατωρία**, ἡ, Lat. *probatoria* (sc. *epistola*), *imperial letter of commendation*, *SEG* 9.356.78 (Cyrenaica, vi AD), Lyd.*Mag.* 3.2; sp. προβατορ- *Cod.Just.* 11.8.16.1.

***προβέβαιος**, ον, *very firm*, *PMichael.* 45.31 (vi AD).

***πρόβειος**, α, ον, = προβάτειος, *An.Ox.* 2.56, *An.Boiss.* 3.408, *PLond.* 113.10.13 (vii AD), cf. *CQ* 33.31.

**προβιβάζω 3**, for '*teach*' read '*inculcate in, impress on*'

**προβλώσκω**, add 'from one's country, Ἀπαμείας πατρίδος ἐκ προμολῶν *SEG* 24.637 (Thrace, i BC)'

***προβοκάτωρ**, ορος, ὁ, Lat. *provocator*, kind of gladiator, Robert *Les gladiateurs* no. 30 (Plotinopolis), 194 (Miletus, written πρω-), 291 (Cyzicus), *ITomis* 288 (iii AD), 30.1800 (iii AD).

**πρόβολος I**, add '**4** *face* of a seal-stone, *App.Anth.* 3.79 (Posidipp.; = *HE* 20.6 G.-P.).'

**προβουλή II**, for 'dub. in *BCH* 26.168' read '*IGLS* 1185'

***προβουλία**, ἡ, gloss on προμηθία, Sch.E.*Med.* 741; προβουλίης in fragmentary context, *IHadr.* 159 (Rom.imp.).

***προβουλικός**, ή, όν, *of probouleutic rank*, ἄνδρα ἐκ πατέρων π. *AS* 12.199.5 (Cilicia Trachea), *SEG* 35.1416 (Pamphylia, Rom.imp.).

**προγᾰμιαῖος**, add '*Cod.Just.* 5.17.12'

**προγᾰ́μιος I**, add 'ἥρως π. prob. *honoured by those about to wed*, Swoboda *Denkmäler* p. 15 (Misthia (Fassiler) in Pisidia)'

**⁺πρόγᾰμος**, ον, *approaching the time of marriage, about to marry*, Tryph. 341, Mitchell *N.Galatia* 234; subst. *Progamus*, title of play by Caecilius.

**⁺προγαργᾰλίζω**, *tickle beforehand*, ὥσπερ προγαργαλίσαντες (sc. themselves) οὐ γαργαλίζονται Arist.*EN* 1150ᵇ22.

***προγαστρότης**, ητος, ἡ, *proluvies* προγαστρότης, Charis. p. 46.1 B.

**προγεωργός**,add '*POxy.* 899ᵛii (p. 226) (AD 200)'

**προγνώμων**, after 'c. gen.' insert 'or acc.'

**⁺προγνωσία**, ἡ, *foreknowledge*, Sch.E.*Hec.* 1137. **2** *preliminary knowledge* of a subject, *Corp.Herm.* 2.17b.

**προγόνη**, add 'rest. in *TAM* 3(1).338 (Pisidia); *step-daughter*, Sch.Lyc. 183'

***προγονία**, ἡ, *line of descent, prosapia* ἡ π. Charis. p. 33.9 B.

**προγονικός**, add 'τοὺς προγονικοὺς θεούς *TAM* 4(1).45; adv. -ῶς, *in the ancestral manner*, Mitchell *N.Galatia* 195 (s.v.l.)'

***προγόνιον**, τό, wd. of uncertain meaning in calendar of Eleusis (?*sacrificial new-born lamb*), *IG* 2².1357.30, 1363.9 (iv/iii BC).

**προγόνιος**, delete the entry (v. °προγόνιον).

**πρόγονος I 1**, delete '*SIG* 1038.9 (Eleusis, iv/iii BC)' **2**, add 'ἀθάνατον μνήμην παισί τε καὶ προγόνοις *IEryth.* 210a.4 (= *CEG* 858, iv/iii BC)'

**⁺προγρᾰφή**, ἡ, *public notice, announcement*, X.*Eq.Mag.* 4.9, Plb. 25.3.2, *SIG* 976.37 (Samos, ii BC), D.C. 47.13, 56.25. **2** *notice of sale*, Thphr.*fr.* 97.2; (cf. sense II) Plu. 2.205c. **II** (= Lat. *proscriptio*) *proscription*, Str. 5.4.11, σφαγαὶ καὶ π. Plu.*Brut.* 27, *Cic.* 47, ἐπὶ θανάτῳ προγραφαί App.*BC* 1.2. **b** *warrant for arrest*, *BGU* 372.8 (ii AD). **III** *advance notice*, *IMylasa* 605 (AD 209/11); *published forecast* of an astronomical cycle, D.S. 12.36. **IV** *introduction* or *preamble* (specifying contents, programme, etc.), Plb. 11.1a.1, *BGU* 780.2 (ii AD), Men.Prot. p. 16 D., Gal. 13.777.3.

**προγρᾰ́φω I 1**, add '*INikaia* 766' **III**, add 'προγραφέντος τῆς βουλῆς *La Carie* 67.5 (Heraclea Salbace)'

***προδᾰμάζω**, *tame* or *subdue previously*, Heph.Astr. 3.19.1.

**⁺προδᾰνείζω**, *advance*, esp. to public funds, *on behalf of someone* for the time being unable to pay, τὸ δὲ ἀργύριον τὸ εἰς τὴν θυσίαν προδανεῖσαι τὸν ταμίαν τοῦ δήμου *IG* 7.4254.38 (Oropus, iv BC), Arist.*Ath.* 16.2, *PCair.Zen.* 377 (iii BC), Plu. 2.852b; med. χρήματα εἰς τὸ θεωρικόν, χρήματα εἰς τὴν διοίκησιν π. Hyp.*Dem.fr.* 4. **II** *lend to the public funds*, ὅσοι ἂν προδανείσωσιν ἄτοκα *OGI* 46.5 (Halic., iii BC), ἀξιωθεὶς προδανεῖσαι χρήματα ἔδω[κεν] *IG* 12(8).156 (Samothrace, iii BC), D.C. 51.17. **2** fig., εἰς τὴν γένεσιν τῷ πόνῳ προδανεισθεὶς χρόνος Plu.*Per.* 13, cf. Luc.*Sacr.* 3.

**⁺προδᾰνεισμός**, ὁ, *advance of funds on behalf of another*, *IG* 2².835.5-6, *Milet* 3 no. 138.31 (iii BC), *IMylasa* 601.11 (i AD).

**⁺προδᾰνειστής**, οῦ, ὁ, *one who advances money on behalf of another*, *OGI* 46.9 (pl., Halic., iii BC), *IG* 11(2).287*A*122 (Delos, iii BC), *IMylasa* 802.5.

**προδᾰπᾰνάω 2**, add '*SEG* 32.453 (Boeotia, ii BC)'

**προδείκνῡμι**, line 2, after '(v. infr.)' insert 'pf. med. (or pass.) Aeol. προδεδείχμενον Alc. 75.4 L.-P.'

**προδιάζω**, delete the entry.

***προδιαίρεσις**, εως, ἡ, *preliminary division*, *PFouad* 35.9 (i AD).

**προδιαιρέω 2**, for this section read 'med., *make a preliminary division*, *PMil.Vogl.* 23.22 (ii AD)'

**προδιαλαμβάνω I**, add 'cj. in Th. 7.73.1'

***προδιᾰμαρτάνω**, *lose before*, Memn. 29.1 J. (pass.).

***προδιαπορίαι**, αἱ, *preliminary problems*, subscr. Thphr.*Metaph.* p. 38 R.-F. (v.l. προδιαπορήσεις).

**προδιασείω**, after '*stir beforehand*' insert 'Men.*Arg.* p. 148.65 K.-Th.'

***προδιασκευάζω**, *plan in advance*, τῶν .. γενησομένων προδιασκευάζων ἰνδάλματα Procop.*Aed.* 1.1.24.

***προδιαψηλᾰ́φημα**, τό, *preliminary fingering, testing*, τὰ π. τῶν κιθαρῳδῶν Phlp.*in APo.* 242.14.

**προδικία I**, add '*SEG* 25.591 (Phocis, ii BC)'

**προδοματικός**, add '*PMich.*II 121ʳ II vii.1 (i AD)'

***προδομόνδε**, adv., *to the* πρόδομος, rest. in Euph. in *Suppl.Hell.* 413.8.

**προδουπέω**, for '*before*' read '*forward*'

**πρόδρομος I 2**, add '**b** masc. pl., name given to winds preceding the Etesian winds, Arist.*Mete.* 361ᵇ24, *Pr.* 941ᵇ7, Thphr.*Vent.* 11. **c** name given to early figs, τάχα .. οἱ πρόδρομοι διὰ τὴν μαλακότητα τοῦ ἀέρος προτεροῦσι Thphr.*CP* 5.1.5, 7, al.; cf. πρόδρομα· τὰ προακμάζοντα σῦκα Hsch.' **4**, for this section read 'ὅτι Μιτυληναῖοι τὸν παρ' αὐτοῖς γλυκὺν οἶνον πρόδρομον καλοῦσι, ἄλλοι δὲ πρότροπον Ath. 1.30b' add '**5** πρόδρομα· τὰ ἐν τῷ ἄξονι ξύλα Hsch.' **II**, delete the section.

**⁺προεγγόνη**, v. °προεκγόνη.

**⁺προέγγονος**, v. προέκγονος.

***προεγγρᾰφεύς**, έως, ὁ, some kind of petty official or clerk, *Kerameikos* 3.11 (i BC).

**προέγκειμαι**, add 'τοῖς προενκημένοις μου τέκ[νοις *TAM* 4(1).187'

***προεγκηδεύω**, *bury in before*, *SEG* 2.602.3 (Sivrihissar).

**προέδρα I**, add '**3** Call.*fr.* 43.30 Pf. (in unkn. sense).'

**προεδρεύω I**, add '*SEG* 36.788 (Samothrace, iii BC)'

**προεδρία 2**, add '**b** body of πρόεδροι, *Hierapolis* 342.'

**πρόεδρος**, add '**III** as adj., -ος, ον, τιμαί epigr. in *TAM* 3(1).18 (Pisidia).'

**προεῖδον II**, add '**b** w. acc., χρὴ προΐδην πλόον Alc. 249.6 L.-P.'

**πρόειμι** (εἰμί *sum*) **I**, add '**2** t.t. in philosophy, *to be prior to existence*, Procl.*Inst.* 116, 122 D.'

**προεισβάλλω II 2**, add 'Gal. 9.704.10'

***προεκγόνη**, ἡ, *great-granddaughter*, *IEphes.* 1066.3, 3072.14, 3274.5; *TAM* 2.278 (Xanthus); also προεγγόνη (cf. next), rest. in *IEphes.* 980.15, *Cod.Just.* 6.48.1.12.

***προέκγονος**, ὁ, *great-grandson*, *IGRom.* 4.990 (Samos); also προέγγονος (the forms are not separable), *IEphes.* 3017.2, 3070.4, *CIG* 4380*b*¹.7 (Cibyra), Just.*Nov.* 18.4 pr.

**προεκδίδωμι**, add '**III** *give in marriage before*, Sch.E.*Andr.* 32 (pass.).'

**προεκλείπω**, after 'Hp.*Ep.* 10' insert '*fail, be wanting*, ὅτι ἐνταῦθα προεκλείπει ἡ δύναμις Sopat.Rh. 8.55.4 W.' and for '*evacuated*' read '*abandoned*'

**προεκπίπτω II**, for 'π. τὸ ἀδύνατον' read 'εἰς πᾶν προεκπίπτον ἀδύνατον'

**προεκπλέω**, add '*IMylasa* 101.2'

**προεκφέρω I 2**, add 'D.H.*Dem.* 39'

**προελευθερόομαι**, add '*Cod.Just.* 6.4.4.10'

**προέλευσις**, add '**4** *appearance as plaintiff*, ἕκαστος τῶν ἠδικημένων τὴν π. πεποίηνται *PMich.*V 231.8 (i AD).'

**προέλκω**, after '*drag forth*' insert 'Men.*Dysc.* 898 (προσ- pap.)'

**προενδίδωμι**, after 'Plu. 2.444c' add '(cj., codd. προσεν-)'

***προενθάπτω**, *bury in before*, τῷ προεντεθαμμένῳ αὐτῆς ἀνδρί *TAM* 3(1).309.2 (Pisidia).

***προενθήκη**, ἡ, *sum previously laid by*, *SEG* 30.1535 (Lycia, ?ii AD).

***προέννοια**, ἡ, *previous notion*, Porph.*in Prm.* 2.20 (cj., codd. προσ-).

***προεντῠπόω**, *engrave on in advance*: fig. ἀθανάτοις ἑαυτὸν προεντυπωσάμενος τοῦ βίου ὑπομνήσεσιν *MAMA* 8.477 (Aphrodisias).

**προεξαιρέω I**, after '*BC* 2.64' insert 'med., προεξελόμενος ἐκ τῶν λαφύρων ὅσα .. D.H. 11.48'

**προεξᾰριθμέομαι**, add 'pass. -ηριθμημένα *enumerated above*, *BGU* 1816.25 (i BC)'

**προεξοδιάζω**, add '*Salamine* 22 (i AD)'

**προεξορμάω II 1**, add 'w. inf., *hasten prematurely to* .., J.*AJ* 19.1.16'

**προεπισκέπτομαι**, add 'Ptol.*Tetr.* 74'

**προερευνάω**, add 'pass., Aen.Tact. 27.15'

**προευπορέω I**, add '*SEG* 24.154 (Attica, iii BC)'

⁺**πρόεχμα**, ατος, τό, perh. *advantage* or *protection*, J.*AJ* 17.10.7 (s.v.l.).

***πρόζῡμα**, τό, = ζύμη, *PMil.Vogl.* 152 ii 36,53 (sp. προσζ-), 153 i 5, 15 (all ii AD).

**προηγέομαι 5**, add 'Just.*Nov.* 134.1'

**προηγέτης 1**, add 'applied to gods, -ῶν θεῶν Ἀρτέμιδος καὶ Ἀπόλλωνος *TAM* 2.188.7'

**προηγορέω I 1**, line 1, after 'Plu. 2.386b' insert '*SEG* 19.835.9 (Pisidia)'

**προήγορος I**, add 'cf. οἱ προήγοροι ὑπὲρ τῆς θεοῦ κατε[δι]κάσαντο, etc. *IEphes.* 2.1 (iv BC)'

***προηγός**, ὁ, gloss on ἄρχων, Sch.S.*Aj.* 934.

**προηγουμένως II 2**, after 'Hermog.*Id.* 1.1, 7' insert 'Longin. 44.12'

***προηροσιάς**, άδος, fem. adj., *of* or *connected with the* Προηρόσια, προε̄ροσιάδο̄ν χριθο̄ν *IG* 1³.250*A*21.

**προηρόσιος**, line 1, after 'ον' insert 'also **πρηρ-**'; line 5, after 'τά' insert '(not always distinguishable fr. -οσία)' and add 'προε̄ρόσια *IG* 1³.250*B*8 (*c.*400 BC), πρηρ- *SEG* 26.136 (Athens, 400/350 BC), Hsch.'; line 6, sg., add '*IG* 1³.250*B*18' **II**, add 'Max.Tyr. 30(24).4'

**πρόθεμα I**, add 'Just.*Nov.* 137'

**πρόθεσις I 5**, line 3, after '(*UPZ*) 31 (ii BC)' insert 'τὴν π. ἐκπληρῶσαι *PWürzb.* 4.12 (ii BC)'

***προθμάριος**, ὁ, v. °πορθμάριος.

***προθμεῖον**, v. ‡πορθμεῖον.

**πρόθῡμα**, add '**2** *sacrifice on behalf of*, w. gen., E.*Hyps.fr.* 60.62 B.'

***προθῡ́μημα**, ατος, τό, *courage, spirit*, Sch.Pi.*P.* 8.61.

**προθύραιος I**, of Artemis, after 'Orph.*H.* 2.4, 12' insert 'cf. Sch.Antim. 182 Wy., *Inscr.Perg.* 8(3).161 (ii AD)'; line 3, before 'Procl.' insert 'rest.in'

***προθύριον**, τό, dim. of πρόθυρον, ἀπὸ τῆς γωνίας τοῦ π. *Inscr.Délos* 1417*C*45 (ii BC).

**πρόθῠρον**, line 1, after 'τό' insert 'πρόθιουρον *Schwyzer* 504 (Boeotia, ii BC)'

***προθῠσία**, ἡ, *right of priority in sacrificing*, *SEG* 37.866 (Caria, Hellen.), Robert *Ét.épigr.* 18 (Delphi, Rom.imp.).

**πρόθῠσις**, add '**II** *preliminary sacrifice*, *BCH* 73.366 (Epid., iv BC).'

**προθύτης**, for '*BCH* 24.386 (Bithynia, iii AD)' read '*INikaia* 726 (AD 288/9)'

***προΐερα**, τά, *preliminary rites*, *SEG* 25.445.29 (Stymphalus, ii BC).

**προΐημι B I 3**, line 2, after 'etc.' insert 'abs. (sc. κόπρον), Macho 212 G.'

**προικῐμαῖος 2**, before 'πράγματα' insert '*PColl.Youtie* 67.25 (iii AD)'

**προίκιος**, for 'Call.*Fr.* 542 = *Oxy.* 2079.34' read 'Call.*fr.* 1.34 Pf.'

***προικοφάγα**, (?voc.), app. *"dowry-eater"* (applied to the coffin of a child whose dowry was spent on it), *Corinth* 8(3).630 (v/vi AD).

**προικοφόρος**, add '**II** πρ., ὁ, gloss on ἐεδνωτής, *Cod.Vat.Gr.* 1456.'

**προικῷος**, add '*PFlor.* 93.17, *PMasp.* 3.18 (both vi AD); -ῷον, τό, *dowry*, Just.*Nov.* 18.11, pl., ib. 138.4'

**προίξ**, line 1, after 'ἡ' insert 'also **προοίξ** *PMich.*inv. 3249 (*ZPE* 31.173.6,11, ii AD)' **II**, add 'προῖκα βουλευτής *councillor who did not have to pay an entrance-fee*, Mitchell *N.Galatia* 181.49 (AD 145)'

**προΐστημι B**, line 1, after 'προὔστην' insert '(Aeol. aor. inf. πρόσταν, = προστῆναι, *IEryth.* 122 (ii BC))' **II 3**, add 'προστάντα τῆς πατρίδος ἐν καιροῖς ἀναγκαίοις *SEG* 37.957 (Claros, ii BC)'

***προϊσχνόω**, *thin beforehand*, Gal. 17(2).846.17, 848.8.

**πρόκα**, for 'in Call. in *PSI* 9.1092.52' read 'Call.*fr.* 110.52 Pf.'

***προκαθᾱγός**, ὁ, *leader* (as epith. of gods), ἀθανάτων προκαθαγὲ μάκαρ .. Παιάν epigr. in *SEG* 24.1244 (Nubia, ii/iii AD).

**προκαθαίρω**, after 'Dsc.*Eup.* 1.19' insert 'Gal. 17(2).330.4' add '**2** transf., *purge first* of defects, Just.*Nov.* 74.1.'

**προκαθάρσιον**, add 'Alcin.*Intr.* p. 182 H.'

**προκαθηγεμών**, add 'also ὁ, epith. of Apollo, *GDI* 3589c; of Dionysus, *SEG* 34.1289; of Heracles, *SEG* 31.1102 (both Phrygia, ii AD)'

**προκαθηγέτης**, add 'of Zeus, *SEG* 30.1524 (Lycia, iii AD)'

**προκαθηγέτις**, after '(Phaselis)' insert 'of Hecate, *TAM* 2.189*a*7'

**προκαθίστημι I 2**, add '**b** act., fig., *use as a screen*, τὸν νόμον π. Antipho 6.21.'

⁺**προκαίω**, *burn before* or *first*, *Kerameikos* 3.50; aor. pass., ἵνα μὴ προκαῇ (v.l. προκαυθῇ) τὸ φάρμακον Aët. 15.14 (p. 61 Z.).

**προκαλίζομαι**, add 'εἰς Ἀφροδίτην Nonn.*D.* 35.138'

**προκαταβαίνω**, add 'of boats, *descend* the river *first* or *as a preliminary* (to a sea voyage), *Peripl.M.Rubr.* 55'

**προκαταβάλλω I**, add '**2** *pay in advance, pay on account*, *IG* 12(7).515 (ii BC).'

**προκαταβολή I**, add 'glossed by ἐνθήκη, Hsch.'

***προκαταγρᾰφή**, *previous contract of sale*, *PPanop.* 22.12 (iv AD).

**προκατάκειμαι**, add '**2** *lie in the tomb before*, i.e. predecease, *TAM* 4(1).249.'

**προκατάληψις I 1**, add '**b** prob. *previous occupation* (of a property), *PEdfou* 5.15 (iii BC) in *CE* 14.376, (written προκαλήψ- in *JEA* 45.75.6).'

**προκατάρχω II 2**, add '*SB* 9786.1 (iv AD) Just.*Nov.* 112.3.2'

**προκατασκευάζω II**, add 'med., π. τινα πράγματα *makes* certain points *for himself in the preliminary survey*, D.H.*Is.* 15'

**προκατασκευή 3**, before 'Hermog.' insert 'D.H.*Lys.* 15, *Is.* 3,15'

***προκατάσκοπος**, ον, *foreseeing*, gloss on ὕποπτος, Sch.E.*Hec.* 1135.

**προκαταστοχάζομαι**, delete the entry.

**προκατατίθημι II**, add '**3** *bury before*, *TAM* 2.1144.3 (Lycia).'

**προκαταχέω**, add 'fig., τοὺς δὲ λόγων δεομένους ἢ παιδείας διὰ τὸ προκατακεχυμένον κλέος οὐκ ἐλάνθανεν Eun.*VS* p. 465 B.'

***προκατοίχομαι**, *predecease*, *TAM* 2.1029, al. (Lycia).

***προκενοσπουδέω**, *bustle about impatiently*, orac.in *DAW* 85.37 (Cilicia).

**προκέφᾰλος I**, add '*Vit.Aesop.*(G) 1, Ar.*fr.* 112, 568 K.-A.'

**προκήρυγμα**, add '**2** *public auction*, *PEnteux.* 37.3 (iii BC).'

***προκῐθᾰριστής**, οῦ, ὁ, *leading player on the cithara*, *Didyma* 182.17, 264.7.

**πρόκληροι**, delete the entry.

***πρόκληρος**, ον, app. *preceding the drawing of lots*, προκλήρου οὐδεν[ὸς .. ἐξου]σίαν προπατῆσαι *SEG* 30.1382 (Lydia, AD 301), *MAMA* 8.497.

⁺**προκλησία**, ἡ, perh. *formal offer* or *guarantee* (?of quality), ἔνδος τᾶς προκλησίας .. ἔξος τᾶς προκλησίας *SEG* 9.11 ff. (Cyrenaica, iv BC).

***προκλυστέον**, *one must purge beforehand with a clyster*, Paul.Aeg. 2.41 (113.19 H.).

***προκοιτᾱτήριον**, τό, *room* or *space at the entrance to a bedroom*, *IAskl.Epid.* 52A.42 (iv BC).

⁺**προκομῐδή**, ἡ, *bringing forth*, *production* of a document, *Cod.Just.* 4.21.22 pr., 1, 2; cf. π.· *prolatio Gloss.*

**προκομίζω**, add '**III** προκομιόμενος, ὁ, *Spartan boy in second year of public education*, i.e. eight years old, 'Ηροδότου Λέξεις in H.B. Rosén, *Eine Laut- und Formenlehre der herodotischen Sprachform*, (Heidelberg 1962), pp. 222 ff.'

**προκόμιον I**, add '*IG* 11(2).203*B*41 (iii BC)' deleting this ref. in section II.

**προκοπή 2 a**, lines 2/3, for 'opinion-forming' read 'self-conceit'

⁺**πρόκοπος**, ον, (προκόπτω) *advanced*, Sor. 1.34 (comp.), Aret.*SD* 2.4.

**προκόπτω**, add '**III** *pound* in a mortar *beforehand*, Gal. 14.86.5.'

***προκουράτωρ**, ορος, ὁ, Lat. *procurator*, rest. in *BGU* 815.5 (ii AD), *PHerm.* 71.2 (v AD), *Stud.Pal.* 20.143.1 (v/vi AD).

***προκράζω**, *call out before* or *first*, *BGU* 1141.48 (i BC).

**προκρίνω II**, add '**2** of law, ruling, etc., *prejudge* another legal situation, ἀνήβοις δὲ ἢ καὶ ἐλάττοσι τὴν ἡλικίαν οὐδὲν ὁ παρ' ἡμῶν προκρίνει νόμος Just.*Nov.* 1.4.1.'

**προκτητικός**, after '*ownership*' insert '*BGU* 1148.34 (i BC)'

**προκύκλιος I**, for this section read '*having the nature of a procuress*, Herod. 6.90' **III**, add 'also in Aeolis, *SEG* 34.1238 (*c.*200 BC)'

**προκῠλίομαι II**, add 'προεκυλίοντό τε τοῦ τεμένους X.Eph. 5.13'

**Προκύων II**, for this section read 'pl., transf., of the hangers-on of a critic or sim. figure, Phld.*Rh.* 1.242 S., Hippias Erythr. 1 J., πικροὶ καὶ ξηροὶ Καλλιμάχου πρόκυνες *AP* 11.322 (Antiphan.)'

**πρόκωπος 1**, after '(lyr.)' insert 'Luc.*Dom.* 30' **3**, delete the section.

**προλάκκιον**, for '*ante-chamber*' read '*tank attached to a main cistern*'

**προλαμβάνω II 1**, of the dead, add 'abs., *ICilicie* 36 (vi AD)'

***προλαμπάς**, άδος, ἡ, wd. occurring in context w. λαμπάς in unpubl. inscr. fr. Cos relating to cult of Hermes Enagonios, v. *Sokolowski* 1.129.

***πρόλαμψις**, εως, ἡ, *shining forth*, Procl.*in Ti.* 1.361.3 D.

**προλεαίνω**, add 'Alcin.*Intr.* p. 163 H.'

**πρόληψις I 1**, add 'Alex.Aphr.*Fat.* 165.15, 25' add '**3** *presumption of law*, Just.*Const.* Δέδωκεν 5.'

***προλιμπάνω**, poet. = προλείπω, *GVI* 1752 (Demetrias, iii/ii BC).

**προλογία**, add '*PVindob.* G29779.43 (*WJA* N.F. 1.71)'

**προλοχίζω II**, before 'Plu.*Sert.*' insert 'D.H. 1.79'

***προμᾰ́θημα**, ατος, τό, *preparatory education*, Hsch. s.v. προπαιδεύματα.

***πρόμαια**, ἡ, *great-grandmother*, *JHS* 73.34 (Caunus, i BC).

**πρόμᾰλος**, after 'ἡ' insert '(but προμαλόιο .. αἰζήεντος Theopomp.Coloph. in *Coll.Alex.* p. 28)'

**προμαντεύομαι**, add '**2** prob. *consult the oracle first*, προθύοντα καὶ -όμενον *CID* I 9.D40 (Delphi, v/iv BC).'

***προμαρτῠ́ρια**, ἡ, *evidence given beforehand*, Rh. 6.124.14.

***προμαρτῠροποιέω**, *testify beforehand*, *SB* 10288.1a.8 (AD 125).

**πρόμᾰχος I 1 a**, add 'X.*Hier.* 11.12'

⁺**προμέτρης**, ου, ὁ, *official who measures out corn allocation*, *IEphes.* 2299, 3216, Lyd.*Mag.* 1.46.

**προμετωπίδιος II 2**, delete 'but *chest-piece*'

***προμετώπιον**, τό, perh. *façade* of a temple, *Amyzon* 3, 7.

⁺**προμετωπίς**, ίδος, ἡ, *ornament worn on an animal's forehead*, Callix. 2

J. (Ath. 5.200e, 202a). II part of a tomb, perh. a piece of ornamentation set above the coffin, ἡ σορὸς καὶ ἡ προμετωπὶς καὶ ἡ στήλη Inscr.Magn. 281 (i AD), 282.

προμηθέομαι, line 2, after '2 sg.' insert 'imper. aor.' and for 'Archil. (?) in PLit.Lond. 54' read 'Archil. 106 W.'

προμηνύω, for 'denounce beforehand' read 'reveal beforehand'

*προμητάτωρ, ὁ, Lat. *prometator, surveyor sent on ahead of a unit, Just.Nov. 130.6.

προμήτωρ II, add 'Luc.Alex. 58 (v.l. πατρομήτορος)' III, add '2 of Aphrodite, as mother of the imperial family, SEG 30.1254 (Aphrodisias, AD 102/116).'

προμικκ‹ιχ›ιδδόμενος, delete the entry (v. °προκομίζω).

προμισθωτής, for 'Ἀρχ.Ἐφ. 1910.371' read 'SEG 33.466 (Larissa, i BC)' and add 'SEG 30.593 (Serrae, ii/iii AD)'

*πρόμνημα, ατος, τό, memorial, BCH 7.503.

προμολή, line 3, for 'mouth of a river' read 'approaches of a town' and before 'Opp.C. 2.134' insert 'fountain-head of a river'

*πρόμορος, ον, = πρόμοιρος (in quot., sense 2), GVI 1931.4 (Laconia, ii AD).

πρόμος, line 8, after '(Claudiopolis)' insert 'ξυστοῦ πρόμος SEG 23.395 (Corcyra, ii AD)'

πρόνᾱος II, line 2, for 'BMus.Inscr. .. ii AD)' read 'IEphes. 27.272 (ii AD)' and add 'ἐν τῶι Προνεωι (of the Parthenon), IG $1^{3}$.292-316 (v BC)'

*προνᾱόω, perh. build the façade of a temple, in quot., fig., ὅταν δέηι τὸν ἔπαινον πολλοῖς θεοῖς προναῶσαι SEG 26.821 (Maroneia, c.100 BC).

προνήσιον, for 'veranda' read 'bench built on to the wall of a house'

*προνῑκότης, ητος, ἡ, = προυνικία, Vit.Aesop.(G) 15.

*πρόνιννος, ἡ, app. grandmother, SEG 37.590 (AD 189).

προνοέω A II 1, add 'w. inf., π. κατασκευασθῆναι .. τὸ ὑδρεκδοχ(ε)ῖον provided for the ὑ. to be built, IEphes. 695 (AD 80/1)' 3, add 'aor. pass. προνοιηθῆναι SEG 23.447 (Thessaly, ii BC)' B, line 11, after 'ib. 37' insert 'imper. προνοηθήτωσαν SEG 33.1039 (Aeolis, ii BC)' and for 'Id. 26.15' read 'Lys. 26.15'

*προνόημα, ατος, τό, forethought, Sch.E.Hipp. 1102 (pl.).

προνοητής, add 'POxy. 2479.19 (vi AD)'

προνομή 4, after '3Ki. 10.23' insert '(the Hebrew refers to forced labour)'

προνομοθετέω, pass., add 'SEG 30.1980.80 (Athens, i BC)'

*πρόνομος, ὁ (or -νομον, τό), = δικαίωμα, θεσμός, anon.ap.Suid. (pl.).

προξενέω II 1, at end delete 'π. τινὶ .. X.Ap. 7'

προξενητής, after 'agent' insert 'Sen.Ep. 119.1, Mart. 10.3.4'

προξενητικός, add 'fig., of the Sphinx, φόνου π. Sch.E.Ph. 1024'

*προξενικός, ή, όν, relating to πρόξενοι, νόμος Milet 3 no. 140.34 (iii BC).

*προξένιον, τό, Cypr. po-ro-xe-ni-o, gift offered to a πρόξενος, Kafizin 117b.

πρόξενος I 3, after 'witnesses' insert 'to a treaty, πρόξενοι ὁ Ζεὺς κ' Ὀπόλōν κ' ὦλλοι θεοὶ πόλις Ποσειδανία Meiggs-Lewis 10 (Sybarite, vi BC)' II, fem., add 'IEphes. 3124'

*προοδηγέω, lead the way, escort, Hsch. s.v. προηγεῖται.

*προοικοδόμημα, ατος, τό, frontal building, τὸ π. τῆς συνοικίας Inscr.Délos 1417 C52 (ii BC).

προοίμιον I 2, add 'ἐν προοιμίῳ τῆς ἐπιούσης πρώτης ἰνδικτιῶνος SEG 32.1554 (Arabia, vi AD)'

*προοίξ, v. ‡προίξ.

*προολοφῡ́ρομαι, lament before, Sch.Gen.Il. 1.414.

πρόοπτος, delete 'manifest' and add 'D. 3.13'

προοράω II, delete 'with pf. and plpf. pass.' and section 1 2, add 'w. part., προορωμένη τοῦ ζῆν καταστροφήν τινα αὐτῇ παροῦσαν Men.Pk. 132' 3, add 'ἄγγαρος ὄντως κοὐδενὸς προορώμενος Men.fr. 349 K.-Th.'

προορύσσω, add 'τοὺς .. γυροὺς προορύττειν Thphr.HP 2.5.1'

πρόπαις, for 'boy .. year' read 'in fourth year of public education, i.e. ten years old'

*πρόπακος, ον, unexpl. adj. referring to bread, ἀρτίδια πρόπακα PVindob. G39847.696 (CPR 5.104, iv AD).

πρόπαππος 2, delete the section transferring quot. to section 1; add 'pl., ancestors, Call.fr. 229.5 Pf.'

πρόπαρ I 1, add 'A.Ag. 1020'

*προπαρατυγχάνω, happen upon previously, acquire a prior knowledge of, Sch.Pi.O. 7.98.

προπαροξῡ́νω II, for 'have .. fever' read 'of a fever, to be provoked prematurely'

πρόπᾱς, add 'Nic.Th. 338'

προπᾰτέω, add 'grapes, SEG 30.1382 (Lydia, AD 301)'

*προπερίσπᾰσις, εως, ἡ, circumflexion of the penultimate, Eust. 341.14.

προπέτεια I, add 'Call.Epigr. 42.4 Pf.'

προπετεύομαι, add 'Just.Nov. 22.18'

προπῖνα, add 'Just.Nov. 117.15 pr.'

*προπιναρία, ἡ, fem. of °προπινάριος, Μαρία πραπιναρέα (sic) SEG 31.1082 (Galatia, v AD).

*προπινάριος, ὁ, Lat. popinarius (but influenced by προπίνω), keeper of low eating-house, MAMA 3.168 (written πρω-, Corasium), CRAI 1945.379.8 (Berytus, Byz.).

προπίνω I 2, for 'take a snack before dinner' read 'take a drink before dinner' II 1, after 'προπινομένη ποίησις Dionys.Eleg. 1' add 'cf. qui mortalibus versus propinas Enn.Sat. 7'

*πρόπιον· μάντευμα Suid.; cf. θεοπρόπιον.

προπιπράσκω, add 'pass., pf. προπέπραται AA 21.20 (Milet., i AD)'

προπιστεύω, add 'II entrust beforehand, PFreib. 69.7.'

*πρόπλασμα, τό, sculptor's clay model, Plin.HN 35.155; transf., rough draft, Cic.Att. 12.41.4.

*προποδέω, lead the way in a dance, Call.fr. 228.2 Pf.

*προποθέω, have a previous desire for, μὴ προποθέσας ὑγιείας Gal.Thras. 29.

προπολεύω, add 'SEG 33.1056 (Cyzicus, ii AD)'

προπολέω I, add 'Critias 6.7 (cod. A Ath.)' II, delete the section.

προπολιόομαι, delete the entry.

*προπολιόω, become grey first or previously, τοὺς πώγωνας προπολιοῦντας Heph.Astr. 2.2.36, Sch.Pi.O. 4.39; med., Diod.Cron.fr. 129 D.

προπολῑτεύομαι II, after 'Them.Or. 16.205c' insert 'pres. part. equiv. to Lat. principalis' and add 'POxy. 2343.17 (iii AD)'

πρόπολος, line 1, for 'ον .. before' read 'ὁ, ἡ'

πρόπομα I, add 'POxy. 2047.2 (v AD)' II, delete the section transferring 'Plu. 2.624c' to section I.

πρόποσις 2, for 'BMus.Inscr. 1036 (Caria)' read 'Amyzon 65.3 (Caria, ii BC)' add '4 drinking-party, συμβολικὴ π. AP 5.134 (Posidipp.).'

προποτίζω 2, add 'Sch.Il. 11.515'

*προπράκτωρ, ορος, ὁ, champion, A.fr. 47a.i 5 R.

*προπρεσβεύω, perh. act as leader of an embassy (or in place of ambassador), IEphes. 2026 (AD 200/5), Xanthos 56.

προπτόρθιον, delete the entry.

*προπτόρθιος, ον, adj. applied to a sacrificial animal, prob. an indication of its age, ἔριφος προπτόρθι[ος] Sokolowski 3.18.46.

προπῠ́λαιος I, add 'IGBulg. 1768, 1770'

*προπῠ́λιος, α (Ion. η), ον, = προπύλαιος, IGBulg. 2123.

*προπωλή, ἡ, brokerage, Vett.Val. 4.23.

προπώλης, delete 'Vett.Val. 4.23'

προπωλητής, after 'foreg.' insert 'PStrassb. 87.16 (ii BC)'

πρόρρησις II 2, add 'of a private announcement, TAM 3(1).714 (iii AD)'

πρός, line 5, form πορτί, add 'IMylasa 660.9 in EA 19.12 (ii BC)'; lines 7/8, for 'Inscr.Cypr. 135.19 H.' read 'ICS 217.19' C II, for 'v. infr. III 5' read 'v. infr. III 4 and 5' III 4, add 'πρὸς ἔτος, = κατ' ἔτος, Sokolowski 2.86.5 (Lindos, c.AD 200)' D, line 5, after 'Hdt. 5.67' insert 'beginning sentence, without δέ or other particle, Lxx Ca. 1.16'

προσάγιος, delete the entry.

προσᾰγόρευσις, add '2 concr., letter, PWarren 20.9 (iii AD).'

προσᾰγορεύω, line 6, before 'address' insert 'Dor. ποταγορεύσαντος PP 42.114 (Cos, iii/ii BC)'

*προσαγορία, v. ‡προσηγ-.

προσάγω, line 2, before 'once ποσάγω' insert 'ποτάγω SEG 23.305, 570 (Delphi), SIG 1010 (Chalcedon), etc.' I 8 a, add 'introduce to the Mysteries, SEG 30.1980.61 (Athens, iv BC)'

προσαγωγεύς II, delete 'hence fem.' to end.

προσᾰγωγή II 3, for this section read 'approach to a place or thing, D.S. 13.46. b facility for approach, access, Plu.Aem. 13; access for ships to put in, Plb. 10.1.6, Peripl.M.Rubr. 46.'

*προσᾰγωγικός, ή, όν, = προσαγωγός, Sch.Luc. 165.8.

*προσᾰγωγίς, ίδος, ἡ, (ὁ), Dor. ποταγωγίς Arist.Pol. $1313^{b}13$, transport boat, BGU 2400.12-13, PLille 21.8, PPetr. 3 p. 254, 257, etc. (all iii BC). II talebearer, informer, οἷον περὶ Συρακούσας αἱ ποταγωγίδες καλούμεναι Arist. l.c.; masc., τοὺς καλουμένους προσαγωγίδας Plu.Dio 28, 2.523a.

προσαιρέομαι, after lemma insert 'Dor. ποθαιρέομαι (καὶ αἴ τινάς κα ἄλλως τοὶ πολιανόμοι ποθέλωνται Schwyzer 62.118 (Heraclea, iv BC), aor. imper. ποθελέσθων SEG 23.305 (Delphi, c.190 BC)); also ποτ- SEG 26.1817 (Cyrenaica, ii/i BC)'

προσαιτέω II, line 4, after 'c. gen.' insert '(s.v.l.)'

προσαίτησις, add '2 additional demand, POxy. 3424.1 (iv AD).'

*προσᾰλεύω, shake beforehand, PIand. 139.29 (ii AD, pass.).

προσᾰλίζομαι, delete the entry.

*προσᾰλίζω, assemble or collect in addition, Aen.Tact. 17.4 (cod., v. °προαλίζω).

*προσᾰμαρτάνω, commit an offence against, w. dat., SEG 32.1222 (i AD), ἴ τίς τι ταύτῃ προσαμάρτῃ τῇ στήλλῃ 33.1029 (ii AD), 34.1233 (iii AD); form ποσ- 31.1003 (i AD), 1013 (ii AD, all Lydia).

προσαμπέχω, for 'veil besides' read 'embrace'

***προσαναγγέλλω**, *report, make known, CodJust.* 1.3.41.28.

**προσαναγράφω**, add 'also ποταναγράφω, *SEG* 34.282 (Nemea, late iv BC)'

**προσαναδέχομαι**, add '**II** *undertake further, Inscr.Délos* 1838 (ii BC).'

**προσανακλίνω**, after '*lean on*' insert ''Ἑρμῆν .. προσανακεκλιμένον πρὸς δενδρυφίωι *Inscr.Délos* 1417*B*i97 (ii BC)'

***προσανακομίζω**, *bring up in addition, PTeb.* 703.190 (iii BC, pass.).

***προσαναμάσσω**, in med., *sully* or *tarnish in addition*, τῆς πόλεως χαλεπῶς φερούσης ἐπὶ τῷ τὴν ἐνίων ἀγνωμοσύνην προσαναμάττεσθαι τοὔνομ' αὐτῆς Ph. 2.537 (τῆς .. ἀγνωμοσύνης .. αὐτῇ cj. Mangey), Just.*Nov.*74.1.

**προσαναμείγνυμι**, add 'προσαναμέμικται γὰρ αὐτοῖς Just.*Const. Δέδωκεν* 8a'

**προσαναπίπτω**, add '**II** of the arm of a torsion engine, *strike against in the recoil*, w. dat., Hero *Bel.* 91.10.'

**προσαναπλέκω**, add 'Just.*Const. Δέδωκεν* 7'

**προσαναφέρω**, after lemma insert 'aor. imper. προσανενενκάτωσαν *SEG* 31.952.8 (Ephesus, ii AD)'

***προσαναφορά**, ἡ, (*supplementary*) *report, IG* 12(5).721.12 (Andros, i BC); Thess. ποτομφορά *SEG* 13.390.

***προσαναψύχω**, *chill in addition*, Paul.Aeg. 2.46 (117.5 H.).

+**προσανοικοδομέω**, *build on as an annex* or *support*, fig. ἐλεημοσύνη .. πατρὸς .. ἀντὶ ἁμαρτιῶν προσανοικοδομηθήσεταί σοι Lxx *Si.* 3.14.

***προσανομολογέομαι**, *agree in addition*, προσανωμολογήσατο δὲ καὶ Ὑβρίλαος ἔχειν .. *PColl.Youtie* 8.7 (224 BC).

**προσαντλητέον**, after 'Paul.Aeg. 3.28' add 'Aët. 16.74 (p. 119 Z.)'

**προσάπαξ**, add '*in a single payment, CPR* 5.18.12 (vi AD)'

***προσαποβιάζομαι**, fut. -βιῶμαι, *make an effort to produce more, PCair. Zen.* 611.19 (iii BC).

**προσαποκρίνομαι**, add '**2** *give a further answer*, Aristid. 2.94 J.'

***προσαπολείπω**, *leave out in addition*, λιθείας ἧς προσαπολείπεις *PCair. Zen.* 771.27 (iii BC).

***προσαπολογίζομαι**, *state in addition, REG* 101.14 (Xanthos, 206/5 BC); w. acc. and inf., *UPZ* 162 vi 1 (ii BC).

**προσαποπέμπω**, add '*SEG* 34.122.70 (Eleusis, iv BC)'

***προσαποτιννύω**, *pay in addition as a penalty*, Scaev.*Dig.* 50.9.6.

***προσαποτυπανίζω**, *attack with cudgels, PMich.*inv. 6979 (*ZPE* 76.291, 215 BC); cf. °ἀποτυμπανίζω.

***προσαποχράομαι**, *embezzle, BGU* 432 ii(2).2-3, 2467.21 (AD 190).

**προσάσσω**, delete '(unless from προεισάγω)'

***προσατιμάζω**, *dishonour in addition*, Sch.E.*Ph.* 877 (pass.).

**προσαυλέω**, for '*perform on the flute*' read '*play in accompaniment on the pipe*'; line 3, after 'Plu. 2.632c' insert 'τί μοι προσαυλεῖς; Men.*Dysc.* 880'

**προσαύλησις**, for '*flute*' read '*pipe*'

***προσβάθρα**, ἡ, perh. *step, IG* $2^2$.1672.144 (pl.) (Eleusis, 327 BC).

**προσβαίνω 2**, add 'abs., E.*Phaëth.* 97 D.; of the Nile in flood, *PSI* 1333.18 (iii AD)'

**προσβάλλω I 1**, add '**c** *extend a structure across* to, w. πρός *AJPh* 56.362.22 (Colophon, iv BC).'

**πρόσβασις 1**, add 'part of the dromos of an Egyptian temple, *SEG* 24.1173 (Alexandria, 29 BC)'

***Προσβατήριος**, ὁ, epith. of Poseidon, *SEG* 30.1980 (Eleusis, i BC).

***προσβεία, προσβευτάς, προσβεύω**, = πρεσβ-, *SEG* 25.445 (Arcadia, *c.*189 BC).

**προσβολή**, lines 1/2, delete 'e.g. .. pl.)' **II 3**, line 1, after '*impact*' insert 'of bronze, A.*Ag.* 391'

***προσγαληνιάω**, *display calm conditions*, of the sea, Hsch. s.v. ὁ Κρὴς τὴν θάλατταν.

**προσγλίχομαι**, add 'οὐ δεῖ θαυμάζειν ὅπως .. οὐδὲ προσγλίχεσθαι (i.e. desire to know as well) ὅπως .. Procl. *in Ti.* 1.80 D.'

**πρόσγραφος II**, add '*SEG* 31.122 (Attica, ii AD)'

**προσγυμναστής**, for '*fellow-wrestler*' read '*wrestling-partner*'

**προσδεκτός**, add '(attested as pers. n., *SEG* 32.1214 (Lydia, ii AD), etc.; fem. -ή, *EA* 16.96 (Prusa ad Olympum)'

**προσδέχομαι**, line 3, after 'D.S. 15.70' insert 'ποδεξαστα (= προσδέξασθαι) *SEG* 36.548 (Thessaly, iii BC)'

**προσδέω** (A), line 1, before '*bind on*' insert '(Dor. aor. inf. ποιδῆσαι *IG* $4^2$.122.41 (Epid., iv BC))'

**προσδέω** (B) **II 1**, line 2, after 'Theoc. 5.63' insert 'also ποιδεῖσθαι *IG* $4^2$.121.13 (Epid., iv BC)'

***προσδιασήπω**, *corrupt in addition*, Gal. 17(1).735.8.

**προσδιαστέλλω II 1**, add 'pass. impers. w. acc. and inf., *UPZ* 118.12 (ii BC)'

***προσδιατυπόω**, *lay down additionally* in a decree, Just.*Nov.* 162 epilogos.

**προσδίδωμι**, add 'Pamph. aor. περτέδōκε *IPamph.* 17 (iii BC), written -έδωκε ib. 18 (ii BC)'

**προσδοκία 1**, line 3, after 'in good sense' insert 'π. βιοτᾶς E.*Hyps. fr.* 64.108 B.' **2**, add '**b** personified as deity, *Pap.Lugd.Bat.* xxv 8 iii 14 (after AD 231).'

***προσδοτέον**, *one must give in addition*, Gal. 10.576.6.

***προσεγκόπτω**, *engrave in addition*, τὸ ψήφισμα ἐς τὴν στήλην *GDI* 5496.21 (Miletus, iv BC).

***προσεγχυματιστέον**, *one must inject besides*, Aspasia ap.Aët. 16.94 (p. 141 Z.).

**προσεδρεύω 1**, after '*watch* the rise of the Nile' insert 'as a local function or office' and add 'Bernand *Akôris* 29, 30, al.'; add '*reflect upon, concentrate upon*, Democr. 191 D.-K.'

***προσειλημμενῖται**, οἱ, (cf. προσλαμβάνω I 2) *inhabitants of the added land*, Ptol.*Geog.* 5.4.10(8).

**πρόσειμι** (*sum*) **1**, add 'τῷ προσιόντι προσεῖναι *associate with* him who seeks your company, Hes.*Op.* 353'

**πρόσειμι** (*ibo*) **2**, delete 'καὶ φιλέοντα .. εἶναι)' add '**6** *enter on an inheritance*, Just.*Nov.* 1.1.1.'

**προσεισευπορέω**, add '*IHistriae* 18.24 (ii BC)'

***προσεκδέχομαι**, perh. *to be additional surety* for, *PColl.Youtie* 16.27 (109 BC).

***προσεκκρέμαμαι**, *to be suspended in addition*, Gal. 18(1).334.13.

***προσεκουτωρία**, ἡ, Lat. *prosecutoria, covering note, letter of authorization, CPR* 7.26.17, 31 (vi AD).

**προσεκπίπτω**, delete 'metaph. .. Longin. 15.8'

***προσεκσκύλλω**, app. *ransack, PColl.Youtie* 16.29a (109 BC).

**προσεκτικός II**, add 'Longin. 26.3 (comp.)'

**προσέλευσις**, add '**II** *appearance in court* as a prosecutor, *POxy.* 283.19 (i AD); cf. προσέρχομαι I 5. **III** *entrance on an inheritance*, Just.*Nov.* 1.1.1.'

**προσεμπίπρημι**, before 'Lxx *Ex.* 22.6' insert 'Aristodem. 1.2.3 J.'

**προσεμφερής**, before 'X.*Smp.*' insert 'Ar.*fr.* 476 K.-A.' and after '(Sup.)' insert 'τὼ προσεμφερῆ Plat.Com. 54 K.-A.'

**προσεμφέρω**, add '**II** *pay* or *contribute in addition*, ἕτερα νομίσματα δεκατέσσερα .. προσενενεχθῆναι *PMich.*XIII 659.70 (vi AD).'

**προσέναγχος**, add '(dub., cj. πρὸς ‹ἔμ'› ἔναγχος)'

**προσενίημι**, add 'Gal. 11.129.1'

**προσεννέπω 1**, after 'll.cc.' insert 'A.*Ag.* 323' **2**, delete the section.

**προσεξαπλόω**, before 'S.E.*M.* 1.56' delete 'dub. in'

**προσεπαυξάνω**, after '*further*' insert '*Inscr.Prien.* 107.21 (ii BC)'; add 'Robert *Hell.* 9.8 (Sardis); pf. part. προσεπευξηκώς (sic) *IGRom.* 4.293a ii 49 (Pergamum, ii BC)'

***προσεπεμβαίνω**, προσεπεμβαίνει· ἐπιβαίνει, ἐπιτωθάζει, ἐπιγελᾷ Hsch.

**προσεπιβάλλω II**, add '*SEG* 36.1087 (Sardis, 213 BC)'

**προσεπιγράφω**, add '**II** *assign responsibility for*, Sopat.Rh. 8.159.6 W.'

+**προσεπιδέχομαι**, *receive besides, PTheb.Bank* 12.12 (ii BC); *take upon oneself besides*, Ph.*fr.* 63 H. (v.ll.προσενδ-, προσδ-).

**προσεπιδέω**, add 'Gal. 18(1).819.11, 823.16'

***προσεπιδιδάσκω**, *teach in addition*, Them. *in APo.* 50.9.

**προσεπιδίδωμι**, after 'Pl.*Sph.* 222e' insert 'ἔτι προσεπέδωκε *IG* $2^2$.553.9'

**προσεπιπλάσσω II**, for '*work into* a plaster' read '*plaster on*'

***προσεπισκευόω**, = προσεπισκευάζω, *Inscr.Cret.* 3.ii 1.6 (ii BC).

**προσεπισκήπτω**, add '**2** *enjoin in addition*, Just.*Nov.* 78.2 pr.'

**προσεπιτεχνάομαι**, add 'Just.*Nov.* 97.2'

**προσεπιχέω**, add 'Heras ap.Gal. 13.1045.18'

**προσεπιψηφίζομαι**, add '*Thasos* 185.6 (i AD)'

**προσέρδω**, after '*sacrifice*' insert '*in addition*'

***προσερισμός**, ὁ, *rebellion*, prob. in Aq. 1*Ki.* 15.23.

**προσέρχομαι**, line 3, after 'aor. .. -ῆλθον' insert 'part. πορτευθών = προσελθών, *Inscr.Cret.* 1.xvii 11 (Lebena); pass. -ελεύσθην, part. -ελευσθείς (in sense I 5), Just.*Nov.* 82.7.1, *CodJust.* 2.3.18 ' **I**, add '**8** *enter upon an inheritance* (= Lat. *adire*), Just.*Nov.* 1.1.1.'

***προσεσταλμένως**, *in a well girt up manner*, gloss on εὐσταλέως, Gal. 18(2).692.2.

**πρόσευξις**, for '= προσευχή' read '*prayer, petition*'; add '*BMus.Inscr.* 421.2'

**προσευχή I**, add 'ἀναθέντα ἐκ τῶν ἰδίων ἐπὶ προσευχῇ τοῦ θεοῦ *SEG* 32.810 (Delos, iii/ii BC, Samaritan)'

**προσεχής I 2**, add 'διὰ τὸ προσεχῆ τὸν τόπον εἶναι τῷ βορέᾳ *Peripl.M.Rubr.* 12'

**προσέχω**, after lemma for 'Cypr. ποέχω (q.v.)' read 'Cypr. med. °ποέχομαι' **I 3**, add '**b** *bring* to a person's attention, σοὶ γὰρ προσέχω ὅτι .. *OFlorida* 14.8.'

**προσηγορία**, add '**b** concr., *letter, PRoss.-Georg.* III 9.7 (iv AD), *PKöln* 111.3 (v/vi AD); προσεκτήσαντο τὴν προσαγορίαν *SEG* 28.1566 (Cyrene, AD 154).'

**προσήκω III 2**, add 'ὥσπερ ἐστὶ προσῆκον, βάρβαρον Ἕλλησι D. 3.24, cf. Just.*Const. Δέδωκεν* 18, etc.' **3**, οἱ προσήκοντες, add '*subordinates, PBeatty Panop.* 2.98'

**προσηλόω**, after lemma insert 'dial. ποθᾱλόω, *IRhod.Peraea* 201.18 (i BC)'

**προσημαίνω I**, of medical symptoms, add 'Gal. 17(2).396.1'

**προσήνεια**, add 'w. ref. to characterization (in quot., by E.), D.Chr. 18.7'

**προσήπω**,for 'προσαπέντα' read 'προσαπέντων'

**πρόσθεμα II**, for 'πόσθη' read '*penis*'

**πρόσθεν**, line 1, delete 'Ion.' and after 'Hdt. 1.11, al.' insert 'Isoc. 18.61, D. 20.94, *Hell.Oxy.* 16.5, *IG* 12 suppl. p. 119 n. 714.18 (Andros, iv BC)'

**πρόσθεσις I**, add '**3** (architectural) *extension*, ἐψηφώθη ἡ πρόσθεσις [τοῦ] ναοῦ *IGLS* 1321 (vi AD).'

**προσθήκη I 1 b**, add 'π. κυρώσεως *POxy.* 3345.48 (AD 209)'

***προσθῠρᾶς**, ὁ, *doorkeeper*, *PPetaus* 34.10 (*c.*AD 184).

***προσικτός**, ή, όν, *attainable*, ὁδός *TAM* 3(1).34*D*59 (Termessus); cf. ἀπρόσικτος.

**προσίστημι I 2**, for this section read '*weigh in addition, include in the weighing*, μάγειρε, μὴ προσίστα τοῦτό μοι τοὐστοῦν Macho 20 G.' **4**, for 'Arist. l.c.' read 'Arist.*Pr.* 870$^a$32' **II 1**, add 'ὅπως προσιστῆται τὸ πλῆθος πρὸς τὴν ἐπικύρωσιν τῆς χειροτονίας Arist.*Ath.* 41.3'

**προσκαθέζομαι**, line 3, for 'πολιορκία' read 'πολιορκίᾳ'

**προσκαθίζω 1**, add '**b** transf., τὸ προσκεκαθικὸς τῆς ψυχῆς τοῖς τέκνοις its *being fixed upon*, Sch.S.*OC* 1119.' **3**, delete the section.

***προσκαθιστάω**, = προσκαθίστημι, Just.*Nov.* 134.2.

**προσκαθίστημι**, for '*supply* labour *besides*' read '*supply besides*' and after '(iii BC)' insert 'κύνας προσκατέστησε *SEG* 24.154 (Attica, iii BC)'

**πρόσκαιρος II**, delete '*Ev.Matt.* 13.21' add '**2** of persons, *concerned only with the moment*, i.e. *lacking staying power*, *Ev.Matt.* 13.21, *Ev.Marc.* 4.17.'

***προσκᾰλίζω**, *hoe previously*, prob. in *PTeb.* 953.11 (ii BC).

**προσκαρτερέω 4**, add 'of things, ἵνα πλοιάριον προσκαρτερῇ αὐτῷ *Ev.Marc.* 3.9'

**προσκαρτέρησις**, add '**2** *devotion to one's profession*, *IG* 12 suppl. 249.8 (Andros, ii BC).'

**προσκαταβάλλω**, add 'ἐνὶ στήθεσσιν ἐμοῖς ποτικάμβαλες αὐδ[ὴν] θέσπιν *PBodm.* 29 (iv AD)'

***προσκαταπλέω**, *sail to a place against*, w. dat., Duris 24 J.

**προσκαταχωρίζω I**, add 'transf., *record additional* grievances, *SEG* 29.1130 (ποτι-, Clazomenae, ii BC)'

***προσκατεγγυάω**, *seize additionally as security*, *PTurku* 1.46 in *Tyche* 6.101 (Theadelphia, ii BC).

**πρόσκειμαι III 1**, line 3, after 'Hdt. 1.196' insert 'προσκεῖσθαι δὲ αὐτῷ καὶ τὴν στρυπτηρίαν, *Schwyzer* 722.14 (Thebes-on-Mycale, iii BC)'

**προσκεφᾰλάδιον**, add '*SB* 9834b.16 (iv AD)'

***προσκεφᾰλᾱτικόν**, τό, = προσκεφάλαιον, *cushion*, *PKlein.Form.* 1089.2 (*CE* 58.232, vii AD).

+**προσκηδής**, ές, *full of sorrow, distressed*, ξεινοσύνη Od. 21.35, A.R. 4.717. **II** *tied by marriage or kinship*, Hdt. 8.136; masc. pl. subst., *AP* 7.444 (Theaet.). **2** *friendly*, A.R. 3.588.

**προσκηρύσσω I**, add '*IG* $1^3$.125.24 (405/4 BC)'

**προσκῑνέομαι**, for 'sens. obsc., of women' read 'describing a form of responsive action during sexual intercourse'

**προσκληρόω**, after lemma insert 'dial. ποτικλᾱρόω' add '**2** *choose by lot in addition*, ἐκ τῶν λοιπῶν πολιτᾶν ποτικλαρώντω .. *SEG* 30.1119 (Entella, iii BC).'

**πρόσκλησις**, for '*summons* to quoit-throwing' read '*summons* of the discus (i.e. gong)'

**προσκνυζάομαι**, after 'Philostr.*Her.Prooem.*' insert 'of a lion, id.*VA* 5.42'

***προσκολλητέον**, *one must stick on*, Archig.ap.Gal. 12.676.16.

**προσκολλητός**, add '**2** -όν, τό, *annex*, *CPR* 14.13.19 (form -ᾱτόν, vi/vii AD).'

**πρόσκολλος**, add 'adv., w. gen., *adjoining*, πρόσκολλα τοῦ οἴκου *Stud.Pal.* 10.125.3 (v/vi AD)'

***Προσκόπα**, η, (πρόσκοπος) title of Artemis, Ἀρτέμιτι Προσκόπαι *SEG* 39.550 (Apollonia, Illyria, iii BC).

**προσκοσμέω**, add '**2** *attach to the ranks* of: med., *side with*, προσεκεκόσμηντο δὲ τούτοις Arist.*Ath.* 13.5.'

**πρόσκρῐσις I**, add 'τὴν σάρκα .. εἶναι ἐν συνεχεῖ ἀποκρίσει τε καὶ προσκρίσει Alex.Aphr.*Mixt.* 235.22'

***προσκρῐτικός**, ή, όν, *of* or *concerning assimilation*, ἡ θρεπτικὴ δύναμις, ἡ μεταβλητικὴ δὴ καὶ προσκριτικὴ τῆς τροφῆς Alex.Aphr.*Mixt.* 234.14.

**πρόσκρουσμα II**, add '**2** *charge, imputation*, Charito 4.6.2, Ach.Tat. 8.10.'

**προσκύλλω**, for '*molest before*' read '*violate the chastity of before*' and delete 'women *with a past*'

**προσκῠνέω I 2**, add 'w. gen., Τύχης τῆς Δούρας *SEG* 7.571 (Dura)'

**προσκῠνητήρ**, add 'Ramsay *Cities and Bishoprics* 1.338 (Phrygia)'

**προσκῠνητήριον**, add 'προσκυνητ[ήρι]α *BCH* 3.482 (Phrygia)'

**προσκῠνητός**, add 'as epith. of a place of worship, προσκυνητῇ .. προσευχῇ Mitchell *N.Galatia* 209b (?iii AD)'

**προσκῠρέω 3**, line 4, delete '(*SB*) 4208.7 (ii BC)'

+**προσκῡρόω**, *confirm the ownership* or *possession*, τὴν προσκυρωθεῖσάν σοι παρ' ἐμοῦ δεσποτείαν (gift of part of a house), *PLond.* 1044.15 (ii AD), *Cod.Just.* 1.5.15, 1.11.9.2; cf. προσκῡροῖ· βεβαιοῖ Hsch., *Gloss.*

***προσλᾰλημα**, τό, *subject of talk*, *An.Boiss.* 4.447.

**προσλέγω I**, after 'med. 1 aor. ἐλεξάμην' insert 'κακὰ προσελέξατο θυμῷ Hes.*Op.* 499'; at end delete 'metaph. .. 499'

***προσληπτήριον**, τό, unexpld. item in inventory, *Inscr.Délos* 104(28)b.B12.

***προσμαρτύρησις**, εως, ἡ, *witness*, *POxy.* 3807.33 (i AD).

**προσμαρτῠ́ρομαι**, add '*PAnt.* 40.7 (iv BC)'

**προσμείγνῡμι I 3**, add 'Gal. 10.910.12'

**προσμένω I 2**, add '*SEG* 26.729 (Maced., AD 195)' add '**3** τὸ προσμένον *the matter awaiting confirmation*, Epicur. [2, 38] 6, [5] xxiv 2, 5 A., D.L. 10.34.'

**πρόσμορος**, add 'πρόσμορον or πρὸς μόρον, dub. sens. (perh. for πρόμορον = πρόμοιρον), *Inscr.Cret.* 1.xviii 177 (Lyttus)'

**πρόσνευσις II**, after 'of a planet' insert 'Ptol.*Tetr.* 4'

***προσοδαρχέω**, *to be treasurer of a* πρόσοδος (sense I 3), *MDAI(A)* 6.42 (Cyzicus).

**προσοδάρχων**, delete the entry.

**προσοδιάζω**, add '**2** *to be supplied with provisions*, *ABSA* 51.154.5 (unless προσωδιάσθη is to be understood for -σθην).'

**προσόδιος**, add '**II** προσόδιον, τό, *income, revenue*, *Inscr.Cret.* 1 xvii 2b.8.'

**πρόσοδος II 1**, add '**b** fig., *profit, advantage*, π. ἔσεσθαί τισι epist.ap.D. 18.78.'

**προσοδῠ́ρομαι**, add '*complain of before* a person, ὃς οὐ πρότερον αὐτῷ προσωδύρατο πάθη Just.*Nov.* 30.9 pr.'

***προσομιλητής**, οῦ, ὁ, *disciple*, Aët. 3.80 (292.13 O.).

***προσονίνημι**, *benefit moreover*, Numen.*fr.* 14 P.

**προσονομάζω**, add '**II** *name* (i.e. *appoint*) *in addition*, Just.*Nov.* 30.4.'

**προσοργίζομαι**, before 'J.*BJ* 2.14.6 (v.l.)' insert 'Arist.*Ath.* 19.5'

***προσορισμός**, ὁ, *inclusion within boundaries, addition* to a territory, etc., *MDAI(A)* 72.243.22 (Samos, ii BC).

***προσόρνῡμι**, in pf. part. προσορωρ[ότες] *rushing* at him, dub. in *BGU* 1252.21 (ii BC).

**προσουδίζω**, after '(οὖδας)' insert 'dial. ποτουδίζω, aor. ἐποτούδιξε (-ιζε cod. Hsch.) Sophr. 141'

**προσουσία**, add '(as pers. n., Lang *Ath.Agora* XXI C31, *c.*400/390 BC, etc.)'

**προσοχθίζω**, after '*to be wroth with*' insert 'τῷ γένει Satyr.*Vit.Eur.fr.* 39 xii 21; τῷ ἐπιχωρίῳ φθόνῳ *fr.* 39 xv 22'

**πρόσοψις I**, add '**b** *facing* of a building, *POxy.* 2197.4, al. (vi AD).'

**προσπαίζω II 2**, for this section read '*play teasingly with*, Luc.*Dom.* 24, Ael.*NA* 4.45; *make fun of, tease*, Pl.*Euthd.* 285a, τοὺς ῥήτορας id.*Mx.* 235c, τὸν Ὀδυσσέα οἱ μνηστῆρες D.Chr. 9.9'

**προσπάσχω II**, line 5, for 'abs., Macho 2.2' read 'w. dat. understood, Macho 468 G.'

***προσπελαστός**, ή, όν, *approachable*, Phot. s.v. πλατά.

**προσπέμπω**, add 'w. ref. to lovers' messages, *Hesperia* 54.225-6 no. 8'

***προσπεριέχομαι**, *cling to, desire, in addition*, dub. in *APF* 2.519 (ii BC).

***προσπεριτειχισμός**, ὁ, *additional fortification of surrounding wall*, εἰς τὸν προσπεριτειχισμὸν τῆς πόλεως *Amyzon* 35.

**προσπέτομαι**, line 2, after '(v. infr.)' insert 'also aor. part. προσπετάσας (sic) Aesop. 296 P.'

**προσπίπτω II 5 b**, for this section read 'τὰ ποτιπίπτοντα ποτὶ τὰν αἴσθησιν that *strike* on the senses, Archyt. 1, cf. Thphr.*Sens.* 5.41; σοι .. προσπιπτέτω *let it* (the thought) *present itself to* you, M.Ant. 7.19, cf. 13, 9.24, 11.7, Longin. 14.1; π. μεγαλορρημονέστερα *have a more impressive effect*, id. 23.2, cf. 29.1; π. δι' ἑαυτοῦ or αὐτόθεν *to be self-evident*, S.E.*P.* 2.168, *M.* 1.300'

***πρόσπλᾰσις**, εως, ἡ, *moulding on, adhesion*, Procl.*in Ti.* 2.60.15 D.

**προσπλάσσω**, line 4, delete '*to be smeared upon*'

**προσπλέκω**, line 4, after 'Arg. 1 Ar.*Ra.*' insert 'J.*Ap.* 1.222'

**προσπλοκή 1**, delete 'cf. Aq.*Ex.* 28.32'

+**πρόσπλοκος**, η, ον, *plaited on*, συμβολὴν προσπλόκην Aq.*Ex.* 28.32. **2** fig., *involved in a relation* with, θεῷ προσπλόκους Rhetor. in *Cat.Cod.Astr.* 8(4).148.

***προσπνίγω**, *choke, throttle*, *POxy.* 2331 iii 20 (verse, iii AD).

**προσποιέω I 1**, delete 'cf. Plot. 6.1.21' **2**, after '*MAMA* 4.27' add '(perh. calque on Phrygian αδδακετ κακουν)' **II 4**, add '**b** w. acc. and inf. *pretend* or *claim* that .., Ἑρμῆν δεδωκέναι [τοὺς νόμους] D.S. 1.94.'

**προσποίησις**, add '**4** *pretence*, D.C. 42.8.'

**προσποιητικός**, add '*fictitious*, πένθος Anon.Astr. in *PMich.* III 148 ii 7 (i AD)'

**προσπορεύομαι**, line 1, **ποτιπορ-**, add '*SEG* 26.701 (Dodona, *c*.205 BC)'

**προσπορίζω 1**, line 4, after '*POxy.* 133.6 (v AD)' insert '*CodJust.* 12.33.8.5'

**προσρέω I**, line 3, after 'Plu. 2.760a' insert 'abs., προσερρύη Men.*Dysc.* 225'

**προσσημαίνω**, delete '*besides*'

**⁺προσσημ(ε)ιόω**, *brand in addition*, δεκυείροις (= *a decemviris*) ἐπὶ ποδὸς προσσημιωθήσεται *IEphes.* 215.13 (ii AD); med. προσσημειοῦμαι· *adnoto*, *Gloss.*

***προσσκῦλάω**, *plunder in addition*, dub. rest. in *UPZ* 6.19 (ii BC); cf. ‡προσσυλάω.

**προσσπεύδω**, add '**II** *demand urgently in addition*, πλέονα μισθόν *PBremen* 63.16 (ii AD, written προσπ-).'

**προσστερνίζομαι**, add '*SEG* 34.1259 (Bithynia, i AD)'

**προσσῡλάω**, before '*UPZ* 6.19' insert 'dub. in'; add 'cf. °προσσκῦλάω'

**προσσωρεύω II**, delete 'Luc.*Anach.* 25' (v. °προσω-)

**προστάσιμον**, delete the entry.

**πρόστᾰσις IV**, for this section read 'perh. *balance brought forward*, or an error for πρόθεσις, *public notice*, *BGU* 2467.24b (AD 190)'

**προστᾰτήριος III**, add '*IG* 7.2405-2406 (Thebes, 229 BC)'

**προστάτης II 3**, add 'οἱ πέντε π[ρο]στάται κώμης *POxy.* 1275.7 (iii AD)' add '**4** perh. *foreman*, ἱστῶνος πρόστατα καλλιπέπλου *INikaia* 103 (epigr., ?i AD).' **III**, add '**4** *guarantor* of a loan, *AA* 1987.681 (v BC).' **IV**, add '**2** official in a temple, of Aphrodite, *SEG* 23.209 (Messene, iii BC), of Demeter, *SEG* 34.981 (i BC).'

**⁺προστείχω**, *step forward*, *advance*, vv.ll. in S.*OC* 30, 320.

***πρόστεν**, = πρόσθεν, *CEG* 119 (Thessaly, *c*.450 BC).

***προστερνίδιος**, ον, *fitted to the front of the chest*, *PAnt.* 67 ii 1.

***προστετῠπωμένως**, *so as to shape by pressure*, Paul.Aeg. 3.35.1 (221.8 H.).

**προστηθίδιος**, delete 'of horses' and add '*SEG* 37.491 (Thessaly, v/iv BC)'

**προστίθημι**, line 7, after 'Dor.' insert 'aor. ποτθεθῆι *Schwyzer* 323.C39' **A I 2**, add '*deliver* to a purchaser at an auction, Hsch. s.v. προσθεῖναι' **III**, add '**6** *bury additionally* in a grave, *EA* 19.37.8 (Pessinos, Rom.imp.).'

***προστικτέον**, *one must punctuate before*, Sch.Il. 7.390.

**προστῑμάω**, add '**2** pass., of an offender, w. acc. of penalty, *to be fined*, *CodJust.* 10.56.1.4, 11.54.2.1.'

**πρόστῑμον**, add '**3** prob. *surety*, *deposit*, *CPR* 5.5.3 (iii AD).'

**προστρᾰγῳδέω I**, add 'Simp.*in Ph.* 1015.8'

**προστρέχω II 1**, add 'ἀνέσεως τόπον εὑρὼν τοῖς ἀποστόλοις προσδραμών Mitchell *N.Galatia* 466'

**προστρόπιος**, add 'cf. Ποιτρόπιος, °Ποιτρόπια'

**προστροπος**, add '**III** = προσάντης, Hsch.'

***πρόστρωσις**, εως, ἡ, app. *paving*, π]ρόστρωσιν *SEG* 33.1277 (Jerusalem, 18/7 BC).'

**προστῷον**, after 'written' insert 'προστοῖον in *Inscr.Délos* 1417*Ai* 162 (ii BC)'; before '*IGRom.*' insert '*JHS* 54.142 (Delos, ii BC)'

***προσυγχωρέω**, *grant previously*, τινι *PFam.Teb.* 21.22 (ii AD).

**προσυποτίθημι I**, add 'Satyr.*Vit.Eur.fr.* 39 xvii 7' **II**, after 'Med.' insert '*prescribe besides* (in teaching), D.H.*Comp.* 20. **b**'

***προσφᾰγιάζω**, *offer sacrifice* at a tomb, cj. in Robert *Ét.Anat.* 308.

**⁺πρόσφαγμα**, ατος, τό, *blood-offering made to dead before burial* or *before* ἐκφορά, A.*Ag.* 1278, E.*Alc.* 845, *Hec.* 41, Plu.*Comp.Thes.Rom.* 1(2); pl., of a single victim, E.*Hec.* 265, *Tr.* 628. **2** *sacrificial victim* in general, E.*IT* 243.

**προσφέρω A I 4**, for '*address* proposals, offer, etc.' read '*put forward*, *propose*, τῶν διορθωμάτων τῶν ὕστερον ποτιφερομένων *SEG* 23.305 (Delphi, *c*.190 BC); w. noun clause, ὡς διαλέγωντι .. ποτήνεγκαν *BCH* 88.570 (Argos, ii/i BC); esp. w. λόγον, λόγους'

**πρόσφημι**, after lemma insert 'dial. ποτίφᾱμι, ποτέφα Stesich. *S.* 11.3'

**προσφῐλής I**, add 'in epitaphs, Μάντα Ἀριστοφῶντος προσφιλὴς χαῖρε *SEG* 31.785 (Thasos, Rom.imp.), etc.'

***προσφοραῖος**, ον, perh. *concerned with* προσφορά, Hdn.*fr.* 26 H. (= Ion Trag. 49a S.).

**πρόσφορος I 2**, add 'ἡδονὴν ἐμποιῆσαι προσφορώτατοι Men.Rh. 393.16 R.-W.' add '**4** of judges, *having jurisdiction*, *competent*, *CodJust.* 7.51.5.1.'

**προσφύή**, after '*supernumerary teeth*' insert '*wolf-teeth* (*dentes lupini*)'

**προσφωνέω I**, add '**5** *call to appear in court*, *bring charge against*, πορτιπõνε̄ν δ' ἅιπερ τõν ἄλ(λ)õν *Inscr.Cret.* 2.v 9.8 (Axos, early v BC).' **II**, add '**3** app. *promise* a thing to someone, *PKöln* 109.15 (iv/v AD).'

**προσφωνητικός**, before 'adv.' delete 'only in' and insert 'Men.Rh. 382.2, 414.31 R.-W.'

***προσχαριστήρια**, v. προχαριστήρια.

**προσχεθεῖν**, for '*ward off from*' read '*hold in front of*'

**πρόσχημα II 1**, at end, of person, add '*Chiron* 17.238 (Pamphylia)'

**πρόσχολος**, after '*assistant schoolmaster*' insert '*IG* $2^2$.10949'

***προσχρηματίζω**, *to be called beside*, *have an additional name* (cf. χρηματίζω III 1), *SEG* 32.1243 (2 BC/AD 2), *TAM* 3(1).213 (Pisidia, i/ii AD).

**προσχωρέω II 1**, line 3, abs., add 'ταῖς προσχωρούσαις πόλεσι Onas. 38.1'

***προσῴζω**, *save before*, Sch.E.*Med.* 526.

**προσωνῠμία I**, for '*surname*' read '*name* (w. particular ref. to its deriv. fr. an eponym or other source)'

***προσωπικός**, ή, όν, *personal*, προσωπικὴν ἀσφάλειαν *CodJust.* 12.60.7.2; adv. -κῶς, *individually*, ib. 6.4.4.19b. **2** adv., *in respect of grammatical person*, Choerob.*in Theod.* 2.29 H.

**προσωπικῶς**, delete the entry.

**προσώπιον I**, add '*Inscr.Délos* 1409*Ba* 10 (ii BC)'

***προσωπίτης**, ου, ὁ, measure, so called fr. the Prosopite Nome, *POxy.* 919.5 (ii AD) (s.v.l.).

?***προσωπίτιον**, τό, app. = °προσωπίτης, προσωπῖδιν *Stud.Pal.* 56.23 (ii/iii AD).

**προσωπῖτις**, add 'Paul.Aeg. 7.3 (196.3 H.)'

**πρόσωπον**, line 7, after '(Leon.)' insert 'Alciphr. 3.40'; line 20, after '*Ev.Matt.* 22.16' insert 'ἐν προσώπῳ σου *before your face*, Sopat.Rh. 8.339.17 W.' **III**, line 5, after '*portrait*' insert '*SEG* 33.946 (Ephesus, i AD)' **IV 2**, for '*legal personality*' read '*standing*, *social position*' add '**6** εἰς πρόσωπόν τινος *on behalf of*, *to the account of*, *CodJust.* 1.2.15 pr., 1.2.24.3.'

**προσωρεύω**, add 'Luc.*Anach.* 25'

**πρότανις**, add 'also πρώτανις, *Chiron* 22 p.377 (Mytilene, i BC)'

***προτᾰρῑχεία**, ἡ, *previous maceration*, Anon.Alch. 270.2.

**πρότᾰσις I 2**, delete the section transferring the quot. to section 1.

**προτάσσω I 1**, at end, after '*POxy.* 1112.18 (ii AD)' insert '*IEphes.* 3239 (ii/iii AD)'

**προτᾰτικός**, add '**II** *of the* πρότασις (I.4): προτατικὸν πρόσωπον character introduced at the beginning to explain the action of play, Donat.*praef.* Ter.*An.* I. 8, Euanthius in *CGF* p. 65 K.'

**προτείνω I 1**, add '**b** *stretch out* for flogging, *Act.Ap.* 22.25.'

**προτέλειος**, add '**πρωτέλειος** is Att. acc. to Phryn.*PS* p. 105 B. (πρωτο- cod.); cf. προτέλειαι in Hsch. after πρῶτα (cf. πρωπέρυσιν s.v. προπέρυσι)'

**προτέλεσμα**, add 'Heph.Astr. 1.20.9'

**προτελευτάω**, add '*ICilicie* 35 (vi AD)'

**προτέμνω II**, for '*prune* vines' read '*prepare* vines *before pruning*, cf. Świderek *La propriété foncière* 67'

**προτεραῖος III**, delete the section.

**προτεράσιος**, add '*SEG* 37.340.13 (Mantinea, iv BC)'

***προτερᾰτεύομαι**, *first describe a portent*, Call.*Dieg.* xi.21 (II p. 46 Pf.).

**προτέρημα**, line 3, after 'M.Ant. 1.16' insert 'τὰ ἀπὸ τύχης π. inscr. in *APF* 6.10 (Delos, ii BC)'

**προτερικόν**, delete the entry.

**πρότερος** and **πρῶτος**, line 2, add '(προτεραίτερος humorous comp. of πρότερος Ar.*Eq.* 1165)' **A IV**, add '**2** προτέρως is used in Arist.*Phys.* 195ᵃ30 of being a cause *in a prior way*, cf. °ὕστερος A IV.' **B I 2**, add 'in dates, ἔτ(ους) σλθ' μηνὸς πρώτου *SEG* 34.1301 (Phrygia, ii AD)' **3**, add '**e** in the title of a legion, *SEG* 31.1116 (Phrygia, Rom.imp.).' **4**, add 'πρῶτος τῆς συγκλήτου (= Lat. *princeps senatus*), Plb. 32.6.5; π. βασιλεύς as title of Sun-god, *AR* 1985-6.47 (ii/i BC)' **III 2**, after 'Babr. 45.14' insert '*CodJust.* 1.4.29 pr.' **IV 2**, add '*SEG* 23.638 (Cyprus, i AD)'

**προτέταρτον**, add '*Inscr.Cret.* 4.75.A6, 81.9 (Gortyn, v BC)'

***προτήκτωρ**, ορος, ὁ, Lat. *protector*, *PPrincet.* 119.1 (iv AD), *SEG* 32.1553 (Arabia, undated), *CIG* 9448 (AD 518, sp. προτικτ-), *TAM* 4(1).383, al. (sp. πρω-).

**προτίθημι II 3**, add 'imper., introducing text of edict, πρόθες *IEphes.* 3217 (i AD)'

***προτῑμή**, ἡ, *special honour*, *Michel* 459.21 (Caria, ii BC).

***προτομάδιον**, τό, dim. of προτομή, *PAlex.* (1964) 23.8 (i/ii AD).

**προτομή 1**, transfer '*OGI* 214.41' to section 2 **3**, add 'of a god, *INikaia* 1085 (iii AD)'

**⁺προτονίζω**, *let* the sail *belly out against the forestay*, *AP* 10.2 (Antip. Sid.).

**⁺προτόνιον**, τό, *apron* worn by sacrificing priestess, Poll. 10.191, Hsch., Phot.; cf. °προγόνιον.

**πρότονοι II**, delete the section transferring quots. to section I.

***προτοῦ** or **πρὸ τοῦ**, v. ‡πρό A II 1, ὁ, ἡ, τό A VIII 5 b.

***προτρέφω**, *suckle*, *SB* 10235 (i AD).

**προτρέχω**, line 1, after 'X.*An.* 1.5.2' insert 'προέδραμεν *Trag.adesp.* 664 i 15 K.-S.'

**προτριακάς**, add '*Inscr.Cos* 43, *SEG* 32.1149 (Ionia, AD 209)'

**πρότρῖτα**, add 'πρότριτα παρέμμεναι *SEG* 34.1238 (Aeolis, *c*.200 BC); sg. πρότριτον *on the third day before*, *Inscr.Cret.* 4.81.5 (Gortyn, v BC); cf. προτέταρτον'

**προτροπάδην**, add '*Suppl.Hell.* 946.5'

**πρότροχος**, add '**2** a form of wheeled siege-engine, *Poliorc.* 199.13.'

***προτῡπής**, ές, *insistent*, φαντασία Plot. 1.2.5.20 (s.v.l.).
**προτύπτω II** and **III**, for these sections read '**II** *strike beforehand*, A.*Ag.* 132 (lyr.); *strike first*, Procop.*Vand.* 1.18.'
***προύγᾰμος**, ον, προύγαμον βίον ζήσει, app. = πρόγαμος II, *MAMA* 7.485.
**προϋιωνός**, add '*SEG* 29.1173 (ii AD)'
**προϋπεξορμάω**, delete the entry.
**προϋπόκειμαι**, add '**III** *to be buried first*, *TAM* 2.1163.3 (Lycia).'
**προϋπόστᾰσις**, for '= προῦπαρξις' read '*previous existence*'
***προϋποσυλλέγω**, perh. *compile* or *collect in advance*, *SEG* 28.1566 (Cyrene, letter of Hadrian).
**προϋποχρίω**, add 'Gal. 18(2).524.2'
***προυρίς**, v. °φρουρίς.
***προυρρά**, v. ‡φρουρά.
***Προυσιακός**, ή, όν, *of Prusias*, τετράχμον *Inscr.Délos* 1443*A*i140 (ii BC).
***Προυσιάς**, άδος, ή, upright drinking-vessel, named after Prusias, king of Bithynia, *Didyma* 463.22 (*c.*179 BC), cf. Ath. 11.496d.
**προυφῆτις**, delete '(metri gratia)'; add '(ii AD)'
**προϋφίσταμαι**, line 2, before 'but usu.' insert '(pres. -ίσταται ταύτης D.H.*Comp.* 2)'
**προφᾰνής I**, add 'πρόφανες Alc. 132.6 L.-P.'
***προφαντάζω**, *cause* one *to have a presentiment*, τὸν ἀκροατήν Sch.B Il. 11.45.
**προφᾰσίζομαι**, line 3, after 'D.C. 59.26' insert 'act. aor. part. προφασίσας, Hsch. s.v. σκήψας'
**πρόφᾰσις I 2 c**, add '*AP* 5.53 (Diosc.), 193'
**προφᾰσιστικός**, for '*reproachful*' read '*consisting of false allegations*'
**προφέρω**, line 1, after 'προφέρεσκον' insert 'Theoc. 25.138' **I 3 a**, add '*express*, ταὐτὸν ὑποθετικῶς Demetr.*Eloc.* 296' **b**, delete 'Med.' to end of section. **4**, line 7, after '(Daphne, ii BC)' insert '*urge in objection*, w. acc. and inf., *CRAI* 1932.242.10' **5**, add 'ὁπόσσω κα προφέρηται *for whatever sum is ordained*, *SEG* 9.72.123'
**προφητεύω III**, add '*IHadr.* 6 (ii AD), al.'
**προφθάνω 2**, add '**b** *to be before*, τὸ προφθάσαν γένος the family *in previous days*, Sch.Pi.*N.* 6.97.'
***προφθέγγομαι**, *address*, *SB* 7635.6 (v/vi AD; unless προσφθ- is intended).
**προφθίμενος**, add 'perh. also *SEG* 34.274 (Corinth, iii AD)'
***προφῐλανθρωπέω**, *grant an indulgence before*, pass., ἐν τοῖς προπεφιλανθρωπημένοις *PTeb.* 124.36 (ii BC).
**πρόφρων I 2**, add 'εἰ δὴ μὴ π. γε Ποσειδάων .. ἐθέλῃσιν ὀλέσσαι *on purpose*, Hes.*Op.* 667, cf. Thgn. 404, *CEG* 5.5'
**προφωνέω I**, add '*bear witness, declare formally*, *Inscr.Cret.* 4.81.9 (written προπōνέτō, v BC; cf. ἀποφωνέω)'
***προχειριστικός**, ή, όν, *productive*, Phlp.*in de An.* 349.31.
**προχειροτονία**, delete 'περὶ .. id.*fr.* 436'
**προχειροφόρος**, add '*POxy.* 3197.7 (AD 111), *PPetaus* 34.24 (AD 184)'
**⁺πρόχνῠ**, adv. *on one's knees*, π. καθεζομένη, i.e. kneeling or crouching, Il. 9.570; ὥς κε .. ἀπόλωνται π. κακῶς Il. 21.460, ὀλέσθαι π. Od. 14.69, perh. perish *after being brought to one's knees*, but expld. by Sch. as = παντελῶς. **2** *thoroughly*, π. γεράνδρυον A.R. 1.1118; so app. in Antim. 5 Wy. **3** *in truth*, εἰ δὴ π. γέρας τόδε πάρθετο δαίμων A.R. 2.249. (The aspirate is difficult but cf. γνύπετος, Skt. adj. *prajñu-* (dub. sens.); senses 2 and 3 presumably fr. misunderstanding of Homer.)
**προχοή** (A), lines 1/2, for '*outpouring*, i.e. *mouth* of a river' read '*flowing waters, streams* of a river'
**προχοΐς II**, for this section read '*beaker, wine-jug*, *Didyma* 426.4 (276/5 BC), *AB* 294'
**πρόχοος II**, add '*SEG* 33.1036 (Aeolis, ii BC)' add 'Myc. *po-ro-ko-wo* (pl.)'
**προχορεύω**, add 'also med., abs., ΠυρϜίας προχορευόμενος *CEG* 452 (Corinth, *c.*580 BC)'
**πρόχρονος**, add '**2** *untimely*, *Thasos* 334.26; adv. πρόχρονα, ib. 332.7.'
**προχωρέω I 3 a**, delete the section **b**, after '*sell*' insert '*Peripl.M.Rubr.* 6, al.'
**προχώρησις**, add '**III** *proceeds*, Just.*Nov.* 98.1.'
***προωθισμός**, ὁ, *pushing forward*, Simp.*in Cael.* 543.23.
**προωνέομαι**, add '*TAM* 4(1).366'
***προωνητικός**, ή, όν, *bought previously*, προωνητικῷ δικαίῳ *on the basis of a former purchase*, *PColl.Youtie* 71.20 (AD 281).
**πρόωρος**, add 'adv. προώρως, Paul.Aeg. 3.76.1 (295.3 H.)'
**πρύλις**, for 'Cret.' read 'Cypr.'; after 'πυρρίχη' insert 'ι'
**πρύμνᾰ I 2**, add 'prov., πρῷρα καὶ πρύμνα, i.e. all that is most important, τῆς Ἑλλάδος D.Chr. 37.36'
**πρύμνηθεν**, for 'Il. 15.716 .. *IT* 1349' read 'A.*Th.* 209, Luc.*Lex.* 15; *by the stern*, π. λάβε Il. 15.716; *stern-foremost*, Arat. 348; dub. sens., E.*IT* 1349'
**πρυμνόθεν II**, after '*from the bottom*' insert 'Opp.*H.* 1.455'
**πρῠτᾰνεία** (A) **I**, add '**b** *the body of* πρυτάνεις, *IG* 2².415.15 (iv BC), cf. ib. 330.8, 35 (all pl.).'
**πρῠτᾰνεῖον II 2**, add 'of other funds, τοῖς μνήμοσιν δοῦναι τοὺς ἄρχοντας .. ἀπὸ τῶν πρυτανείων δραχμὰς ΔΔΔ *SEG* 33.679 (Paros, ii BC)'
**πρῠτᾰνειος**, add '**2** as title of Hermes, *SEG* 39.870 (Ceos, v BC).'
**πρῠτᾰνευμα**, for '*principate*, i.e. *prince*' read '*presidency*, i.e. *president*'; for 'Epigr. in *Rev.Phil.* 19.178' read '*Suppl.Hell.* 982.14'
**πρῠτᾰνεύω III 1**, delete 'παρά τινος' and 'by one'
***πρωβοκάτωρ**, ὁ, v. °προβοκάτωρ.
**πρώην**, line 1, after 'πρῴαν' read 'Theoc. 8.23, 14.5, Mosch. 3.69; πρόαν Theoc. 4.60, 5.4, 15.15' **I**, add '**3** generally *in the past, earlier*, *Cod.Just.* 1.3.41.11, 8.10.12.4.' at end delete '(The first syll.' to end of article.
***πρῳηρότης** or **πρωϊ-** (scanned ⏑⏑), εω, ὁ, (ἀρόω) *early plougher*, prob. in Hes.*Op.* 490 (cj., vv.ll. πρωτηρότης, προη-).
**πρωθήβης**, line 4, after 'App.*Hisp.* 65' insert 'π. φοίνιξ *SEG* 7.195 (Syria, iv AD)'
***πρωθῐερεύς**, έως, ὁ, *chief priest*, *Inscr.Cret.* 1.xxii 12 (Olus, i AD); v. °πρωτοϊερεύς.
**πρωθύπνιον**, delete the entry.
**πρωΐ**, line 2, add 'πρωΐ Men.*Inc.* 58'
**⁺πρωϊζός**, όν, πρῳζός Call.*fr.* 559 Pf. (in corrupt *fr.*); π.· προχθεσινός, ὑπόγυος *EM* 691.54. **II** neut. as adv., *the day before*, pl., χθιζά τε καὶ π. Il. 2.303. **2** *very early*, pl., οὕτω δὴ π. κατέδραθες Theoc. 18.9; sg., π. ὁδεύων *Epic.Alex.adesp.* 4.6; in indeterminate sense, τὸ π. Lys.*fr.* 68.
**πρωΐθεν**, add 'ἀπὸ πρωΐθεν *previously*, *SEG* 31.983 (Ionia, ii/i BC)'
**πρώϊμος**, delete 'cj. in Call.*fr.* 482 (*Hermes* 24.453)'; adv., comp., add 'περὶ τὸν αὐτὸν καιρὸν .., προιμώτερον δέ *Peripl.M.Rubr.* 28'
**πρώϊος I 2**, line 3, πρωΐας as adv., add 'Archig.ap.Gal. 12.444.5' **II**, line 2, after 'Hdt. 8.130' insert 'φῖτυ π. S.*fr.* 889 R.' add '**III** *early in one's life*, *AP* 7.439 (Theodorid.), 716 (Dionys.).'
**⁺πρώκῐος**, η, ον, *dewy*, cj. in Call.*fr.* 1.34 Pf.
**πρωκτός**, after '*anus*' insert 'Hippon. 104.32 W.'
***πρωρά**, v. °φρουρά.
**πρῷρα I 2**, add 'of the face, = πρόσωπον, Hsch.; cf. πρωραχθής, ἀνδρόπρῳρος, καλλίπρῳρος'
**πρῳρᾰτης**, add 'Ion. -ήτης, *CID* I 7.A11 (v BC)'
**πρωτᾰγωνιστέω**, add ' of leadership in war, *JHS* 68.47.30 (Lycia, ?ii BC), *SEG* 34.1198 (Lydia, ii BC)'
***πρωταναγνώστης**, ου, ὁ, *chief lector* (in a church), (?τόπος) πρωταναγνώστου *Sardis* 7(1).188 (?iv AD); also **πρωτοαν-** *CPR* 10.122.9 (vi AD).
***πρωταπογρᾰφέω**, *register for the first time*; med. or pass., cj. in *PFay.* 31.18 (ii AD).
**πρωταπογρᾰφομαι**, delete the entry.
***πρωταπόγρᾰφος**, ὁ or -ον, τό, *list of persons registered for the first time*, ἀ[πογράφεσθαι] ἐν πρωταπογράφῳ pap. in *Aegyptus* 15.209 (iii AD).
**πρωταύλης**, for '*flute-player*' read '*piper*' and add '*POxy.* 2721.5 (AD 234)'
**πρωτεῖος**, after '*of the first quality*' insert '*Edict.Diocl.* 8.11'
***πρωτέλειος**, v. °προτέλειος.
**πρωτεύω I**, lines 3ff., *hold position of* πρῶτος, add 'πρωτεύσαντα τῶν ἱερῶ[ν *SEG* 34.1107 (Ephesus); of chief official in Egyptian town or village, *CPR* 6.79.2 (v AD)'
***πρωτεπιστήμων**, ονος, app. *having newly acquired the skill* or *knowledge*, ἱππηλάται π. Anon.*in Rh.* 15.18.
***πρωτέφηβος**, ὁ, *leader of* ἔφηβοι, *Inscr.Délos* 1956 (i BC).
***πρωτήκτωρ**, v. °προτήκτωρ.
***πρώτηλα**, τά, *pair of oxen*, cf. Lat. *protelum*, dub. in *JRS* 46.46.4 (Phrygia, iii AD).
***πρωτηρότης**, v. °πρῳηρότης.
***πρωτοαναγνώστης**, v. °πρωταναγνώστης.
**πρωτοβόλος I 1**, delete '(Rufin.)'
***πρωτογενέτωρ**, ορος, ὁ, *first-begetter*, of God, *PMasp.* 188ᵛ.1.
**πρωτόγνᾰφος**, for '*fresh from the fullers*' read '*carded once only* i.e. *almost new*' and add '*PMichael.* 18 ii 3, al. (iii AD), *Peripl.M.Rubr.* 6'
***πρωτογονᾶτος**, ον, *firstborn*, *MDAI(A)* 33.149 no.11 (Constantinople).
**πρωτόγονος I 3**, for this section read 'a name of the Orphic divinity Φάνης, Orph.*fr.* 54, 86, *H.* 6.1. **b** fem. -η, a name of Persephone, Paus. 1.31.4.'
***πρωτοδρᾰκωνάριος**, ὁ, *chief* °δρακωνάριος, τῷ αἰδε(σι)μ(ωτάτῳ) Δομιτιανῷ (π)ρωτοδρακοναρίῳ *ITyr* 33C.
***πρωτόθετος**, ον, gramm. of a word, *primitive*, opp. *derivative*, = πρωτότυπος, Ar.Byz.*fr.* 241G S.
***πρωτοϊερεύς**, έως, ὁ, *chief priest* or *member of a sub-class of* ἱερεῖς, *BGU* 2469 ii 8 (ii AD), Chapouthier *Les Dioscures* 26 (Dorylaeum); v. °πρωθιερεύς.
***πρωτοκλῑναρχος**, ὁ, *chief president of an Isiac confraternity*, *IPhilae* 199.5 (AD 456/7).
**πρωτοκλῑσία**, after 'etc.' insert 'ἐν ταῖς ἄλλαις συνόδοις πάσαις πρωτοκλισία *Inscr.Délos* 1520.33 (ii BC)'

**πρωτοκοσμέω**, add '*SEG* 32.869 (Crete, ii AD)'

***πρωτοκούρης**, ητος, ὁ, *president of a college of* κουρῆτες (sense II 3), *IEphes.* 974, 1042a, 1061, etc. (ii/iii AD).

**πρωτόκτιστος**, add '**2** *first built*, of a gate, Sch.E.*Ph.* 1113.'

**πρωτολοχία**, add '*SEG* 13.403 (Maced., ii BC)'

***πρωτόμηνος**, ὁ, one of the νεωποῖαι *in office in the first month of the year*, *IEphes.* 3513a (i BC/i AD); cf. σύμμηνος.

***πρωτονεωποιός**, ὁ, *first* νεωποιός, *CIG* 2800, *REG* 19.145 (both Aphrodisias in Caria; -νεοπ-).

**πρωτόπᾱλος**, add '*SEG* 32.605 (Larissa, ii AD)'

**πρωτόπολις**, add '**2** v. °πρωτόπτολις.'

**πρωτοπολίτης**, after '*Gloss.*' insert '*Vit.Aesop.*(G) 93; sg., *eminent citizen*, *IG* 10.2(1).204 (Thessalonica; -είτης)'

**πρωτοπορεία**, add '*BGU* 2424.7 (86 BC)'

**πρωτοπρεσβῦτερος**, add '*SEG* 19.443 (Philippi); πρωτοπρεσβοιτέρου *BCH* suppl. 8.238, προτο- *ICilicie* 119, etc.'

***πρωτοπροφήτης**, ου, ὁ, *chief* or *first prophet*, Μωυσῆς π. *PJen.*inv. 536 (*APF* 27.61, v/vi AD).

***πρωτόπτολις**, εως, ἡ, *first*, i.e. *oldest*, *among cities*, Τάρσος ἀειδομένη π. Nonn.*D.* 41.357.

**πρωτοστάτης II**, add '**2** *chief magistrate* of a village, *PCair.Isidor.* 64.10 (iii AD), *SB* 9502.'

⁺**πρωτοστολιστής**, οῦ, ὁ, *keeper of sacred vestments* (*of the first class*), *PGrenf.* 44 ii 2 (ii BC), *IPhilae* 196, 197 (AD 452).

***πρωτοσφήν**, ῆνος, ὁ, *first wedge*, οἱ π. Hero *Stereom.* 2.31, al.

***πρωτοτόκεος**, ον, = πρωτοτόκος, *having borne offspring for the first time*, Boeot. πρᾶτο- *SEG* 25.556 (*c.*210/200 BC).

**πρωτότῠπος II 1**, add 'Just.*Nov.* 4.1'

***πρωτουργικός**, ή, όν, *providing the initial impetus*, αἰτία Procl. *in R.* 1.180 K.

***πρωτοφεγγής**, ές, *shining with first light*, τῆς π. ἡμέρας *Trag.adesp.* 664 ii 11 K.-S..

***πρωτόχθων**, gen. ονος, ὁ, ἡ, *aboriginal*, (of Sardis), *SEG* 36.1095, ἡ π. καὶ μητρόπολις τῆς Ἀσίας καὶ Λυδίας ἁπάσης ib. 1096 (iii AD), *IUrb.Rom.* 85.

**πταῖμα**, add '*TAM* 4(1).1.40 (Bithynia, ii BC)'

**πταῖσμα I 1**, add '**b** *blow* or *bruise* on the toes, Poll. 2.199; cf. °ἐπίπταισμα, πρόσπταισμα.'

**πταίω II 2**, line 7, transfer 'also .. S.*Ph.* 215 (lyr.)' to section 1.

***πτᾶσα**, v. πέτομαι.

**πτελέα**, add 'also πελέα *IG* $4^2$(1).102.44 (Epid.); form πτελέϝα, Myc. *pte-re-wa*, *elm-wood*'

***πτερᾰφορία**, ἡ, *office of* πτεροφόρος, *PTeb.* 298.21 (ii AD, -εία pap.).

**πτερίς I**, after 'Dsc. 4.185' insert 'πτερίδα D.Chr. 7.75'

***πτεριστής**, οῦ, ὁ, perh. *embroiderer*, *IG* 3.3441 (πταιρ-).

**πτέρνη I 2**, add '*AP* 9.225.4 (Honest.), and so prob. in Call.*fr.* 2.4 Pf.' **III**, delete 'f.l.' to end of article and add 'Myc. *pte-no* (dual), some part of a chariot'

**πτερνίζω I 1**, after '*strike with the heel*' insert 'of a rider urging on his horse' **2**, for this section read '*trip up from behind*, *PVindob. Salomons* 15.10 (v/vi AD); fig., as metaphor fr. wrestling, *circumvent*, *outwit*, Lxx *Ge.* 27.36, *Ho.* 12.4, *Ma.* 3.8, Ph. 1.125'

**πτερνισμός**, for '*supplanting*' read '*overturning* (as if by lifting the heel), in quot., fig.'

***πτέρνομαι**, = πτάρνυμαι, 3 sg. πτέρνεται, gloss on χρέμπτεται, Cyr.

**πτερόεις I**, add 'prob. of Eros, τὸν πτερόεντα θεόν *IHadr.* 29 (i BC/i AD)' **II**, for '*winged* words' read '*flighted* words'

**πτερόν III 2**, add 'πέμπειν χρύσεον Μουσᾶν Ἀλεξάνδρῳ π. B.*fr.* 20B.4 S.-M.' **3**, delete the section. **4**, for this section read '= σκιάδειον, *Com.adesp.* 1129' **8 b**, for '*battlements*' read 'protective structure built on to city wall, πτερὰ τὴν οἰκοδομίαν καλοῦσι ταύτην ἐπεὶ ὥσπερ ἀποκρέμασθαι τοῦ τείχους δοκεῖ' **c**, for '*portcullis* .. gateways' read 'metal plating let down to cover city gate in the manner of portcullis' add '**10** *column* in tables, *Cat.Cod.Astr.* 8(2).13. F. 47-87.'

**πτεροφόρος III**, for this section read 'kind of priest, = πτεροφόρας I, *PGrenf.* 44 ii 3 (ii BC), *SEG* 31.1556 (Thebes, Egypt, ii/i BC)'

**πτεροφυής**, add '*PMag.* 12.46'

**πτερύγιον II**, add '**11** *cloudy spot* in the beryl, Plin.*HN* 37.79.'

**πτερῠγοειδής**, delete 'only' before 'adv.' and insert 'ἐκφύσεις Gal. 2.439.7, ὀστᾶ 441.10, 443.4'

**πτέρυξ II 1**, line 3, for 'tortoise' read 'turtle' **7**, read 'unspecified part of a building' add '**12** pl., the *extremities* of the world or a land, ἐπὶ πτερύγων τῆς γῆς Lxx *Jb.* 37.3, 38.13, *Is.* 24.16; imagined as four corners, *Is.* 11.12, *Ez.* 7.2.'

**πτηνοπέδῑλος**, add '*PMag.* 5.404'

**πτίλον**, line 1, for '(q.v.)' read '(cf. Ψίλαξ B)'; line 3, after 'Suid.)' insert 'ἁπαλὸν ψ. cj. in Alcm. 3 *fr.*3 ii 68 P.'

**πτῐλωτός**, add '**3** *decorated with feather pattern*, φιάλαι *IG* $2^2$.1443.135.'

***πτισᾶνᾶς**, ᾶ, ὁ, seller of *barley-gruel* (πτισάνη II), *AP* 11.351 (Pall., cj. πτιστής).

**πτισάνης**, delete the entry.

**πτοέω**, line 2, after 'Call.*Dian.* 191' insert 'Dor. ἐπτοάθην E.*IA* 586 (lyr.)' **II**, line 5, after '(= Thgn. 1018)' insert 'φρένας ἐπτοέαται Anacr. 1 *fr.*1.12 P.'; at end after 'E.*IA* 586 (lyr.)' insert 'Hsch. s.v. πτοιώμενον'

**Πτολεμαϊκός**, add '**3** designation of an age group in athletics, *SEG* 27.1114.19 (Egypt, iii BC).'

***πτολιαρχέω**, in Thess. form *τταλιαρχέω, v.s.v. °πολιαρχέω.

**πτόλις**, line 4, for '*Inscr.Cypr.* 135.1 H.' read '*po-to-li-se*, *ICS* 217.2;' line 8, for 'πτόλιϝι *Inscr.Cypr.* 135 6 H.' read '*po-to-li-wi* πτόλιϝι *ICS* 217.6'

**πτόρθιος**, add '(unless, reading as *Sokolowski* 3.11.A16 Ποσειδῶνι πτόρθι[ος], some kind of sacrificial offering, cf. °προπτόρθιος)'

***πτῠάζω** or **πτῠίζω**, *winnow*, λελικμημένη· κοσκινευθεῖσα, πτυασθεῖσα (πτυισ- La.) ἐπ' ἀνέμῳ Hsch.

**πτύον**, add 'and is restored in *IG* $1^3$.422.134 [π]τέō (dual) (v BC)'

**πτῠρομαι**, add 'act. **πτύρω** as expl. of *terreo* in Virgil gloss., *PNess.* 1.778 (vi AD), *Gloss.*'

***πτῠχίδιον**, τό, *tablet*, *PMil.Vogl.* 152 ii 52.

**πτύχιον I**, add '**2** prob. *leaf* of a folding door, *PMerton* 39.5 (iv/v AD).'

⁺**πτύχιος**, α, ον, quoted as adj. fr. πτύξ, *EM* 64.28; spec., *folded* or *broken*, of reeds, *BGU* 2210.19 (AD 617).

**πτῶμα II 2**, line 6, after 'Lys.*fr.* 203 S.' insert '*PFay.* 102.20 (ii AD), *BGU* 2483.4 (iii AD)'

**πτωμᾰτισμός**, add '*SEG* 30.1794 (iii AD)'

**πτῶσις III**, add '**2** of the categories, *mode*, Arist.*EE* $1217^b$30, *Metaph.* $1089^a$27.'

**πτωτικός**, add '**3** *liable to fall* (or *cause falling*), ὀλισθηρόν· πτωτικόν Hsch.'

**πτωχικός**, add '**2** *of a poorhouse*, πτωχικοῦ πράγματος Just.*Nov.* 7.3 pr.'

**πτωχός**, line 1, delete 'S.*OC* 444'; lines 7/8, delete '(so πτωχός (fem.), S.*OC* 444)' **II**, after '*Ep.Gal.* 4.9' insert 'νοήματα (in a comparison) D.H.*Comp.* 4'

**πτωχοφᾰνής**, for '*like a beggar*' read '*having the appearance of a beggar*'

***πῠάνη**, ἡ, dub. sens., Sch.A Il. 12.459 (perh. = λάρναξ).

**πῠάνος**, after 'Hsch.' insert 'πύανοι, μῖγμα παντοδαπῶν ὀσπρίων, Theognost.*Can.* 23 (cod. πτυ-)'

**πύας**, delete the entry.

***πῡγιαῖα**, τά, *padding to accentuate the buttocks*, Hsch.

**πῡγίζω**, add '*SEG* 31.824 (Sicily, v BC), 8.574 (Egypt, iii AD), etc.'

***πῡγίον**, τό, dim. of πυγή, *SDAW* 1934.1040 (tab.defix.).

***πῡγιστής**, οῦ, ὁ, *sodomite*, *SB* 6872 (graffito).

**πυγμᾰχος**, add '(on accent) Ath. 4.154f.'

**πῡέλιον**, after 'πύελος' insert '*Inscr.Cret.* 1.xvii 12*A*6 (Lebena, ii/i BC)'

**πῡελίς II**, add 'also ποιαλίς *TAM* 2.347, 348, 706, *IMylasa* 468.8'

**πῠελος**, after 'πύαλος' insert '**ποίελος, πύαιλος, ποίαλος**' **4**, add '*TAM* 4(1).258, 361, 363, etc.'

**Πῡθᾰγόρειος**, after '*Pythagorean*' insert 'Pl.*R.* 600b, etc.'; before 'Pl.*R.* 530d' insert '-ειοι, οἱ'; add 'Iamb.*VP* 18.80, etc.'

**Πῡθᾰγορικός**, before 'τὰ Π.' insert 'οἱ Π., Plu. 2.488, *Num.* 11.1'; after 'D.L. 7.4' insert 'a work by Aristotle, Arist.*fr.* 204, 205 (τὸ Π. *fr.* 199)'

**Πῡθαεύς**, add 'also **Πῡθαιεύς** *SEG* 11.890 (Cynuria, vi BC)'

***πῡθάζω**, v. °πυθαΐζω.

**πῡθαΐζω**, add 'also **πυθάζω**, πυθασταὶ τοὶ πυθάξαν[τες] *SEG* 25.852, 853 (Telos, iii/ii BC)'

**πῡθαϊστής**, after 'member of such a mission' insert '*SEG* 21.541 ii 50, al. (Erchiae, iv BC)'; add 'also πῡθασταί (pl.) *SEG* 28.852, 853 (Telos, iii/ii BC), cf. ‡πυθιασταί'

***πῡθάρχᾱς**, α, ὁ, leader of πυθαϊσταί, *SEG* 25.852 (Telos, iii BC).

***πῡθαρχέω**, *to hold the office of* °πυθάρχας, *Didyma* 87.4.

***πῡθασταί**, v. °πῡθαϊστής.

**Πῡθία II**, add '*SEG* 30.1286 (Didyma)'

**Πύθια**, add 'also **Πύτια** *SEG* 23.566 (Crete, iv BC)'

**Πῡθιασταί**, add '*Tit.Cam.* 78.10 (i BC), cf. °πυθαϊστής'

**Πῡθικός I**, line 4, before 'νικήσαντα' insert 'Π. αὐλός, kind of aulos, app. αὐλὸς χορικός (cf. Πυθαύλης, χοραύλης), Poll. 4.81, Aristid.Quint. 2.16; cf. τὸ .. τῶν ψιλῶν κιθαριστῶν ὄργανον, ὃ καὶ Πυθικὸν ὀνομάζεται Poll. 4.66; as an athletic category (of boys aged 12-14 years)'; line 5, for 'cf. 1064.7' read '*SIG* 1065.7' add '**2** Πυθικοί, οἱ, association of musicians at Saittai, *SEG* 29.1200.'

**Πύθιον**, add 'at Icarion, *IG* $2^2$.4976 (iv BC), etc.'

**Πῡθιονίκης I**, line 2, after 'Hld. 5.19' insert ' also nom. **Πυθιονίκα** *IG* 7.1888b9'

**Πύθιος**, add 'also **Πύτιος** *Schwyzer* 686 (Pamphylia, iv BC), 198 (Crete, ii BC); **Πύττιος** *SEG* 33.638 (Crete, ii BC)'

**πυθμήν III**, for '*lowest number*' read '*lowest term*'

**Πῡθόνῑκος**, add '*GDI* 1504*B*b4 (Opus)'

**Πῡθόχρηστος II 1**, add 'εἶναι Βαγαδάτην νεωκόρον τῆς Ἀρτέμιδος πυθόχρηστον αὐτῶι γενόμενον *Amyzon* 2.10 (iv BC)' **2**, for 'epith. of' read 'applied to the names of gods for whom cults were approved by the Pythian oracle'

**Πῡθώδε**, add '*Πυθόδ' ἀνέθεκ[ε] CEG* 369 (Delphi, *c.*600/550 BC)'

**Πῡθῶθεν**, add '*IG* 1³.256.4 (v BC)'

***πυκακίνη**, ἡ, type of garment, prob. made fr. thick fabric, *PVindob.* G39847.881 (*CPR* 5.109) (iv AD).

**πῠκῐνοκίνητος**, add 'Gal. 18(1).415.8, 10'

***πυκλιή**, gloss on *βαθάρα* (Maced.), Hsch. (entered as if *βατ-*; cf. °*πυρλός*).

**πυκνός A III**, add '**3** *τὸ π. density* of style, D.H.*Th.* 24; cf. *πυκνόω* II b.' **V 1**, at end delete '*τὸ π.* .. 24'

**πυκτᾰλεύω**, after 'Sophr. 111' add '(*PSI* 1214*a*16)'

**⁺πυκτᾰλίζω**, = *πυκτεύω*, Anacr. 1 *fr.*4.1 P., 51 P., perh. also *πυ]κταλίζουσι* Hippon. 102.8 W.

**πυκτεύω**, line 5, of gladiators, add '*SEG* 32.605 (Larissa, ii AD)'

**πυκτικός 2**, after '*of* or *for boxers*' insert '*ἱμάντας .. πυκτικούς* Eup. 350 K.-A.'

**⁺πυκτίς** (B), *ίδος*, ἡ, supposed to be some kind of animal, Ar.*Ach.* 879, but perh. example of *πυκτίς* (A) inserted for word-play w. following *ἰκτῖδας*.

**Πῠλαία I 1**, add '*IG* 1³.96' **2**, for this section read '*Amphictyonic rights*, D. 6.22, 8.65, cf. 5.23 (which may belong to 1)' **II**, add 'prov., app. of a trivial fiction, *ἐκ πίνακος καὶ πυλαίας* Plu. 2.386b'

**πῠλαῖος 1**, add 'title of Poseidon, *Ποτειδῶνι Κραναίωι Πυλαίωι SEG* 15.377 (Larissa, iv BC)'

**πῠλαωρός**, at end after 'Il. 24.681' insert '*GVI* 1179.7 (Smyrna, ii BC)'

**πῠλεών II**, for this section read '*wreath*, Alcm. 3 *fr.*3 ii 65 P., 60.2 P., Pamphil.ap.Ath. 15.678a; *circlet*, Call.*fr.* 80.5 Pf., Aristaenet. 1.15 (*πόλεων* cod.), cf. Poll. 5.96'

**πῠ́λη I 2**, add 'of a temple, *SEG* 32.1260 (Paphlagonia, AD 192/3)' **4**, add '*ὁ πρὸς τῇ πύλῃ*, i.e. *customs officer*, *PRein.* 95.1' **II 1 c**, after 'metaph.' insert '*ἔαρος π.* Alc. 296(*b*).3 L.-P.'

**πῠλοκλειστής**, for pres. ref. read '*SEG* 26.1835 (Cyrene, ii AD)'

***?πῠλονόμος**, ὁ, *customs officer*, *Κάστορος πυλωνόμο[υ] Ἑρμοπολείτου κώμης Anagennesis* 3.82 (*SEG* 33.1363, Egypt, Chr.).

**Πύλος**, add 'Myc. *pu-ro*'

***πῠλουχίς**, *ίδος*, ἡ, *guardian of the gate*, *Ἡρωΐνησι Πυλοχίσι SEG* 26.136 (Athens, iv BC).

**πῠλοῦχος**, add '**2** of a deity, *guardian of the gate*, rest. *πυ[λόχωι SEG* 26.136 (Athens, iv BC); cf. *πυλάοχος*.'

**πῠλών**, add 'on a race-track, *τοὺς πυλῶνας τῶν ἱππαφίων Tab. Defix.Aud.* 234 (ii/iii AD)'

**πυλώριον**, add 'perh. also *πυλωρ[ίου] SEG* 25.318 (Attica, i AD)'

***πύννος**· *ὁ πρωκτός* Hsch., cf. *Didyma* p. 100*a*.51 (graffito); v. *πουνιάζειν*.

**πυξίδιον II**, after '*πυξίς*' insert '*Inscr.Délos* 1417*B* i139 (ii BC)'

**πῠοποιέω**, add 'Heras ap.Gal. 13.766.5'

**πῡός**, line 3, for 'supr.' read '*πύον* II'

**πῦρ I 4**, add '*Πῦρ ἄφθαρτον IEphes.* 1058, 1060, al.'

**πῡρά**, *τά*, line 8, delete 'metaph.'

**πῡρά**, *ᾶς*, **1 b**, add '*SEG* 32.655 (AD 102/3)' **3**, add 'a *pile of wood* for burning, *bonfire*, *Act.Ap.* 28.2.'

**πῠ́ραγρα 1**, add 'Nic.*Al.* 50, Luc.*DDeor.* 5.4, 7.2'

***πῡραίθης** (or **πύραιθος**), *ου*, ὁ, *fire-kindler* (title of a priest), *POxy.* 2722.3, 6 (AD 154), 3567.3 (AD 252).

***πῠράκτωσις**, ἡ, *heating of a cautery-iron*, Aët. 1.233 (98.6 O.), 7.32 (280.23, 281.24 O.).

**πῡρᾰμίς II**, add '**2** perh. *candle*, Arist.*Ph.* 245ᵇ.11.'

***πῠράπτης**, *ου*, ὁ, *fire-lighter* (perh. a religious office, cf. *λυχνάπτης*), *SEG* 19.661 (Alabanda, Rom.imp.).

**πῠραυγής**, add '(first syll. long in Orph.*H.* 19.1 s.v.l.)'

**πῠ́ραυνος I**, line 1, after '*coals*' insert 'Pl.Com. 142 K.-A.'

**πῠραύστρα**, add 'Myc. *pu-ra-u-to-ro* (dual), *fire-tongs*'

***πύργᾰλος**, ὁ, kind of bird (cf. *πυργίτης*), *PAmst.* 13.8 (sp. *πρυγ-*; v AD).

**πυργηρέομαι**, add 'act., *πυργηροῦμεν· φυλάττομεν τὰ τείχη* Hsch.'

***Πυργία**, ἡ, *goddess of the tower*, title of Athena in Locris, *SDAW* 1935.695; cf. *ἐπιπυργῖτις*.

**πυργίον**, add '**2** part of a funerary monument, *LW* 1639. **3** *dice-box*, Sch.Aeschin. 1.59. **4** part of a trireme, Hsch.'

**πυργίσκος 1**, read 'perh. *pillar* supporting a sarcophagus, *TAM* 2.51, 63, 64a, b, 65, 66'

**πυργίτης**, after '*of a tower*' insert '(cf. *πύργος* I 3)'

**πυργοποιΐα**, add 'de Franciscis *Locr.Epiz.* 3, 6, 10, etc. (sp. *-ποία*, iv/iii BC)'

**πύργος I 1**, line 3, delete '*city walls*' **3**, for '*the part of a house .. and worked*' read 'any separate structure built for protection, watch-keeping, etc., esp. in the open country (estate, vineyard, etc.)' and delete remaining definitions of section. add '**b** a structure forming part of a tomb, *TAM* 2.245.'

***πυργοσηκών**, *ῶνος*, ὁ, app. *fortified enclosure*, *IGLS* 316.

**πύρδᾰλον**, for '*Lyr.Alex.Adesp.* 31' read 'Call.*fr.* 197.42 Pf.'

**πῠ́ρεθρον**, delete 'cf. *πυρῖτις* II'

**πυρετέω**, delete the entry.

**πῠρετός II**, add 'personified as a deity, *Θεῷ Πυρετῷ Inschr.Hierap.* 7'

**πῠρετώδης 1**, add 'adv. *-δῶς* Gal. 18(1).551.9'

**πῡρήν VI**, for 'Str. 4.6.10' read 'Plb. 34.10.9'

**πῡρία I 4**, for '= *εἰσώστη*' read '*sarcophagus*' and delete '*tomb-chamber*'

**πῡρίᾱσις**, add 'Erasistr.ap.Gal. 11.200.14'

**πῡριάω 3**, add 'Erasistr.ap.Gal. 11.206.13'

***πῠρῐδάής**, *ές*, *flashing with fire*, *ὄμμα* B.*fr.* 64.21 S.-M.

***πῠριλόχευτος**, *ον*, *fire-born*, of Dionysus, Ps.-Callisth. 55.5.

**⁺πῡρίνη**, ἡ, stone of a fruit (= *πυρήν* I), v.l. in Hp.*Mul.* 2.138 (8.298.18 L.), *Gp.* 6.11, 9.18 (v.l.), Hsch.

**πυριρρόθιος**, delete the entry.

**πῡρῖτις I 1**, for this section read 'perh. *convolvulus*, Nic.*Th.* 683; as adj., *ῥιζάδα .. πυρίτιδα* id.*Al.* 531'

**πῠρίφευκτος**, add 'Anon.Alch. 19.19'

**πῠριφλεγέθων I**, add '**2** *blazing with fire*, [*κεραυνός*] *SPAW* 1934.1046 (tab.defix.), *SEG* 34.1308 (Side, i BC/i AD).'

**πῠριφλεγής 1**, add 'sup., Plu.*Daed.* 5'

***πῠρίχροος**, *ον*, contr. *-χρους*, *ουν*, = *πυρίχρως*, Xenocr.*Lap.* 90.

**πυρκαεύς**, add 'Poll. 9.156; *Προμηθεὺς π.* title of play by A., id. 10.64'

**πυρκαϊά I 2**, add 'Heraclit. 43 D.-K.'

***πυρκόρος**, ὁ, prob. *tender of the sacred fire* (cf. *νεωκόρος*), *AE* 1934/5.140 (Atrax in Thessaly, v BC).

***πυρλός**, gloss on *βαθάρα* (entered as if *βατ-*) (*Ἀθαμᾶνες*), Hsch.; cf. °*πυκλιή*.

***πῡροβόλησις**, *εως*, ἡ, *sowing of wheat*, *BGU* 1850.25 (?i BC; *προβ-* pap.).

**πῠρόεις**, after '*εν*' insert '(poet. also *ειν*, Nic.*Th.* 748)'

***πῠροελκής**, *ές*, *characterized by fiery ulcers*, *λοιμοῦ π. GVI* 993.1 (Rome, ii/iii AD).

***πῡρόκοπρος**, (?)ἡ, *fire of (dried) dung*, Moses Alch. 301.21, 311.16.

***πῡροσπορεία**, ἡ, *sowing of wheat*, *PMil.Vogl.* 131.5, 140.34.

**πῡροσπορέω**, add '*POxy.* 1629.9 (44 BC), *PVindob.Worp* 2.13 (21 BC)'

***πῠροσώματος**, *ον*, *having a fiery body*, in invocation of *Ἄρκτος*, *PMag.* 7.701.

**πυρπολέω II 2**, for 'Med. .. *fire*' read 'pass.'

***πύρρινος**, *η*, *ον*, *fiery red*, *BGU* 2217 ii 17 (ii AD; unless to be taken as fem. subst. *fire-pot*, or sim.); of a garment, *PVindob.* G25.950 (*Die Sprache* 34(1).192, v/vi AD).

**πυρρίχη 1**, add '*χοραγήσαντα πυρρίχαι SEG* 39.759.19 (Rhodes, i BC); *καλεῖται δ' ἡ πυρρίχη καὶ χειρονομία* Ath. 14.631c'

**πυρρῐχίζω**, add 'Ath. 14.631a'

**πυρρίχιος II**, after '*πυρρίχη*' insert 'D.H.*Comp.* 18'; add '*ῥυθμός* D.H.*Comp.* 17'

**πυρρῐχισμός**, add '**2** the *use of a pyrrhic foot* at the end of a hexameter, Eust. 1577.52 (referring to Il. 12.208 (v. *ὄφις*)).'

**πυρρῐχιστής**, add 'glossed by *λουδιώνης* (Lat. *ludiones*), *POxy.* 3452.14 (ii AD)'

***πυρροκέφᾰλος**, *ον*, *red-headed*, Hsch. s.v. *πυρσοκόρσου λέοντος*.

***πυρροκόκκῐνος**, *ον*, *scarlet*, *Cat.Cod.Astr.* 11(2).157.7.

**πυρρός I 2**, for '*with red hair*' read '*having a ruddy complexion* (or sts. *having red hair*)' add 'cf. Myc. *pu-wo* (masc.), *pu-wa* (fem.), pers. n. and see also °*φυρρός*'

**πυρρότης**, after 'of hair' insert '(or complexion)'; add 'Hp.*Aër.* 20'

***πυρρόχαλκος**, ὁ, *yellow copper*, Moses Alch. 310.18.

***πυρρόω**, *dye red*, Hsch. s.v. *ἠρυθροδάνωται*.

**πυρσαυγής**, before 'Orph.' insert 'dub. cj. in'

***πυρσόπνευστος**, *ον*, *fire-breathing*, *Suppl.Mag.* I 42 (iii/iv AD).

***πυρφλέγων**, *οντος*, ὁ, = *πυριφ.*, *SPAW* 1934.1043 (tab.defix.).

**πυρφορέω II**, after 'Charito 2.4' add '(*ἐπυρπό[λει POxy.* 2948)'

**πυρφόρος I b**, line 4, for '*engine .. fire dart*' read '*fire-basket* (in an incendiary device)' and before 'Jul.*Or.* 2.62d' insert 'prob. *fire-dart*' **II**, line 6, delete 'satyric' **2**, add 'also in the Eleusinian mysteries, *SEG* 30.93 (Eleusis, 20/19 BC)'

**πῠρώδης I**, line 4, before 'Sup.' insert 'comp., *ἀὴρ πυρωδέστερος ὢν* Aen.Tact. 23.1'

**πῠρωπός II**, before 'Plin.' insert 'Prop. 4.10.21'

***πύσμᾰδε**, adv., *to interrogation*, *προσαγαγεῖν PCol.* 175.37 (iv AD).

**πυτίζω**, line 1, delete '*frequently*' and after 'mouth' insert '*Placit.* 3.5.9'

**πῡτίνη**, add 'Ar.*fr.* 880 K.-A.'

**⁺πῶ** (verb), v. ‡*πίνω*.

**πώγων 1**, after '*beard*' insert 'Alc. 143.6 L.-P.' **4**, add 'poet. in *POxy.* 2817.3; also the feathered end of an arrow, Nonn.*D.* 16.9'

**⁺πῶθι**, v. ‡*πίνω*.

***πωλάδιον**, τό, = πωλάριον, *PCair.Isidor.* 136.6 (iii/iv AD, πολαδ‹ιο›ν pap.).

**πωλάριον**, add '*PMich.*XI 620.218 (AD 239/40)'

***πωλάς**, άδος, ἡ, *female foal*, τὴν πωλάδαν (*sic*) ὄνον *PCair.Isidor.* 86.11 (iv AD).

**πωλέομαι**, line 4, after 'Il. 5.350' insert 'Aeol. 3 pl. πώλενται Alc. 130.33 L.-P.'

**πωλέω**, lines 4/5, delete 'prob. in *IG* 1².60.10'

**πωλητήρ**, add '*SEG* 12.380.30 (Cos, fr. Gela-Phintias, iii BC)'

**πωλητικός**, add 'κατὰ τὸν πωλητικὸν νόμον *IMylasa* 208.13 (i BC), al.'

**πωλικός 1**, add 'νικάσαντα κέλητι πωλικῶι Kontorini *AER* 2.168 no. 74 (Rhodes, i BC)'

**πωλίον**, add '**III** gloss on ἀκρίς, Sch.Theoc. 5.34.'

**πῶλος I 2**, delete 'of the dog .. (Strat.)' **3**, add 'οἱ κύνεοι π. *AP* 12.238 (Strat.)' add 'Myc. *po-ro* (dual)'

**⁺Πωλώ**, οῦς, ἡ, epith. of Artemis on Thasos, *IG* 12 suppl. 382, 383; on Paros, suppl. 202.

**πῶμα** (B) **II**, after '*drinking-cup*' insert 'E.*Ion* 1212'

***πωμαρικός**, ή, όν, *of* or *concerning fruit-growing*, *PHamb.* 222.18 (vi/vii AD).

**πωμάριον**, after '*orchard*' insert '*POxy.* 707.19 (ii AD)'; add 'π. φοινίκων *PMasp.* 170 (AD 564)'

**πώποκα**, add 'see also πήποκα'

**πώποτε I**, add 'followed by neg., ὅτι πώποτε οὐκ ἐρρέθη λόγος τοιοῦτος περὶ Σουσαννης Thd.*Su.* 27'

***πώπως**, *in any way whatever*, τὰ ἀφιερωμένα πόπως (*sic*) *SEG* 32.1423.12 (Syria, AD 192/3).

***πώρη**, ὃ δηλοῖ τὸ πένθος Sch.E.*Or.* 392 (expl. of ταλαίπωρος).

**πῶρος 4**, add '**b** stone-like tumour in other parts of the body, Orib. 45.6.1, 7.'

**πῶς III 5**, after '*Ach.* 24' insert 'E.*Hec.* 1160' **V**, delete 'π. .. *Matt.* 21.20'

***πώσποτε**, indef. adv., *in any way whatever*, *Sardis* 7(1).20.16 (vi AD).

***πωσφόρος**, v. °φωσφόρος.

**πῶυ**, line 5, after 'Nonn.*D.* 3.302' insert 'νέων ἵνα πῶϋ *GDRK* 30.89'

# Ρ

**ῥαβδίον 4**, for this section read 'of items in temple inventories, *ῥαβδία ἀκοντίων Inscr.Délos* 104-28*bB*17, ?λί]θος φηγοειδὴς ῥαβδίωι ἠρτημένος ἀργυρῶι *IG* 2².1534.103 (iii BC)'

**ῥαβδισμός**, add '*PTeb.* 229 (i BC)'

**ῥαβδιστής**, after 'ὁ' insert '*beater* (prob. in some process of cloth-making), *PMich.*II 123ʳ vi 19, xiv 17 (i AD); *fuller*, *BGU* 2547.3 (iii AD)'

**ῥαβδομαντεία**, for '*a wand*' read '*rods* or *sticks*'; add 'Jerome *in Ezech. PL* 25.206'

**ῥάβδος I 1**, at end for '*divining-rod*' read '*rod* or *stick* used in divining' **III**, line 4, after 'D.S. 5.37' insert 'cf. Hsch.' **IV 1**, after '*verse*' insert '(in expl. of *ῥαψῳδός*) Menaechm. 9 J.'

**ῥαβδουχέω**, after 'badge of office' insert '*ῥαβδōχε̄ν τὸς hιεροποιός IG* 1³.250A9 (Attica, v BC)'

**ῥαβδοῦχος**, add '**3** *cattle-drover*, *POxy.* 1626.9 (iv AD); perh. also *SEG* 29.307 (Corinth, v/vi AD).'

**ῥαβδωτός II**, add 'of a kind of sacrificial cake, *πόπανον ῥ. Inscr.Perg.* 8(3).161.3 (ii AD)'

***ῥᾰγᾰδώδης**, ες, *cracked, fissured*, of soil, *SB* 6797.26 (iii BC).

**ῥᾰγάς**, line 1, after 'Ephor. 65(e) J.' insert '*SB* 6797.9 (iii BC)'

⁺**ῥᾰδᾰλός**, ή, όν, perh. *quivering*, read by Zenod. for *ῥοδανός* (q.v.) in Il. 18.576, Nicaenet. 1.4.

***ῥάδᾰμος**, ὁ, v. *ὀρόδαμνος*.

**ῥᾰδᾰνίζω**, for '*ῥοδάνη*' read '*ῥοδανίζω*'

**ῥᾰδινός**, line 1, for '*βράδινος*' read '(‡*βράδινος*)'

**ῥᾴδιος**, line 2, after '*α, ον*' insert 'also *ος, ον* (E.*Med.* 1375, Pl.*Plt.* 278d, D.*Ep.* 3.23)' **B**, line 1, after 'Aeol. *βραΐδίως*' insert 'Alc. 129.22 L.-P.' **2**, line 2, after '*recklessly*' insert '*βραΐδίως πόσιν ἔμβαις ἐπ' ὀρκίοισι* Alc. l.c.'

**ῥᾳδιουργία**, add '*δίχα .. οἱασδήποτε ῥαδηουργίας PColl.Youtie* 92.35 (AD 569)'

**ῥᾳδιουργός**, line 3, for '*knave, rogue*' read '*bandit*'

**ῥᾱθῡμέω**, line 3, after 'etc.' insert 'w. gen., *μαθημάτων* Clem.Al.*Strom.* 4.5, *τοῦ νόμου Cod.Just.* 3.2.4.7, *PMasp.* 151.194 (vi AD); w. inf., *τοῦτο πρᾶξαι Cod.Just.* 1.3.45.6' **3**, add '*οὐδὲ γὰρ χρὴ μόνας τὰς ἐκπομπὰς κατεπείγεσθαι, ῥαθυμεῖσθαι δὲ τὰ στρατιωτικὰ δαπανήματα Cod.Just.* 12.37.18'

**ῥᾴθῡμος I 3**, for '*slipshod*' read '*lacking in drive, perfunctory*'

***ῥαίανος**, unexpld. adj., cf. *ῥαίαν*, Hdn.*fr.* p. 28 H.

***ῥαιβοκερεῖς**· *στρεβλοκέρατοι* Hsch. (*ῥαικακερεῖς* cod.).

**ῥαῖδα**, for '*rhaeda*' read '*raeda*'

***ῥαιδαστίζει**· *τὸ σκώπτει* Theognost.*Can.* 32 A.

**ῥαικακερεῖς**, delete the entry.

***ῥαικάμη**· *ἡ ῥᾳστώνη* (*ease*), Theognost.*Can.* 32 A.; cf. *ῥαθάμη*.

**ῥαίω II**, for 'Pass., .. S.*Tr.* 268' read 'pass., A.*Pr.* 189, S.*Tr.* 268, *AP* 7.529 (Theodorid.)'

**ῥακά**, before 'Hebr.' insert 'Aramaic or'; add 'cf. °*ῥαχᾶς*'

***ῥᾰκάδιον**, τό, app. *rag* used as wrapping, ostr. in *ZPE* 98.138 no. 29.4 (Egypt); cf. °*ῥακίδιον*.

**ῥάκανα**, add 'cf. Lat. *rachana, Edict.Diocl.* 19.5, also °*ῥάχνη*'

***ῥᾰκίδιον**, τό, dim. of *ῥάκος*, *little rag*, Paul.Aeg. 2.46 (117.27 H.).

⁺**ῥάκιον**, τό, (*ῥάκ- GVI* 1920.9 (Athens, i AD)), *rag*, *χαλκὸν ἀδόκιμον ἐν ῥ. Inscr.Délos* 1450*A*103; app. of a flag, Them.*Or.* 16.210b; fig., *ῥάκιόν τι τοῦ παλαιοῦ δράματος* Ar.*Ach.* 415; in pl., id.*Ach.* 412, *V.* 128, al.; perh. for use as bandages, *IG* 1³.421.163 (Athens, v BC).

**ῥάκος I 2**, for 'even .. flesh' read 'of flesh torn to *rags*'

**ῥᾰκώδης 1**, after '*ragged*' insert '*προσκεφάλαια IG* 11(2).147*B*13, *χιτώνιον IG* 2².1518.66'

**ῥάκωσις**, add 'in unexpld. context, *CPR* 7.8.58 (ii/iii AD)'

**ῥάμμα** (B) **3**, add '*APF* 2.2.15'

***ῥαμμάτιον**, τό, perh. *small piece of thread*, Anon.Alch. 323.3.

**ῥαμματώδης**, add '*ἕλιξ τὸ τῆς ἀμπέλου ῥαμματῶδες* gloss in Cod.Vat.Gr. 23'

**Ῥαμνούσιος**, add '*Ῥαμνόσιοι SEG* 35.24 (Attica, v BC)'

**ῥάμφος**, before 'Plu.' insert 'Call.*fr.* 647 Pf.'

**ῥᾰνίζω**, add '*Suppl.Hell.* 975.4 (iii BC)'

***ῥάνσις**, εως, ἡ, (*ῥαίνω*) *sprinkling* of temple with wine, *SB* 9199.15, 16, 19 (ii AD); written *ρεανσις Stud.Pal.* 22.183.109 (ii AD); cf. °*ῥάντης*.

**ῥαντήρ II**, after '*sprinkler*' insert '(a vessel)' and for '(Adanda)' read '(Cilicia, i/ii AD)'

**ῥάντης**, delete square brackets in lemma; after '*sprinkler*' insert 'of priestly official or servant, *Gnomol.Vat.* in *WS* 11.230 no. 527, cf.'; after '(ii/iii AD)' insert '*BGU* 185.10 (ii A.D; *ρεαντης*, cf. °*ῥάνσις*)'; add 'as surname or title, Paus. 5.21.12'

***ῥαντοπόλιος**, ον, *having a sprinkling of grey hairs*, gloss on *μεσαιπόλιος*, Sch.Gen.Il. 13.361.

**ῥαντός**, add '*ῥαντά, τά*, *beads sprinkled* on the hair, Sext.*Ca.* 1.11'

**ῥάξ 1**, after '*grape*' insert '*καλὰ ῥάξ SEG* 32.806 (Tyras, *c.*575/50 BC)'

⁺**ῥάπα**, v. *ῥάψ*.

**ῥᾰπίζω I**, line 5, for '*ῥεραπισμένα* .. 166' read '*ῥεραπισμένῳ νώτῳ* Anacr. 112 P.'

**ῥάπτης**, add '*TAM* 4(1).132 (Rom.imp.), *Hesperia* 41.41 no. 33 (Corinth, v/vi AD), etc.; cf. form **ῥαπτήρ*, Myc. *ra-pte, ra-pte-re* (pl.)'

**ῥαπτός II**, after '*worked with the needle*' insert 'perh. *embroidered*, *ῥ. κερβικάριον SB* 9834 b 6 (iv AD; sp. *ῥεβτόν*, for pronunciation cf. mod. Gk. *ῥαφτός*)'

**ῥάπτρια**, add 'Myc. *ra-pi-ti-ra₂*'

**ῥάπτω**, add 'Myc. pf. part. pass. *e-ra-pe-me-na*'

*°**Ῥᾱρία** (s.v. *Ῥᾶρος*), add '*IG* 2².1672.119, 120, 253 (iv BC)'

*°**Ῥάριος**, adj. included in alphabetical list, *SB* 10769.139 (iii/iv AD), perh. pr. n., cf. *Ῥᾶρος*.

**ῥάσμα**, add '*ὅσσας εἴχ' Ἀχιλεὺς νῆας τόσα ῥάσματ' ὀφείλεις PCair. Zen.* 535.2 (iii BC)'

**ῥάσσω 2**, add '**b** *dash down*, in pass., Euph. 9.6 vGr.'

**ῥᾳστωνεύω**, delete '= *ῥαθυμέω*'; for 'dub. l. in Ael.*fr.* 281' read 'Ael.*NA* 16.23'

**ῥᾰφᾰνίδιον**, add 'also **ῥεφᾰν-** *Dura* 125 no. 861'

**ῥᾰφάνινος**, add 'also **ῥεφάνινος**, Moses Alch. 300.17'

**ῥάφᾰνος II**, add '*AP* 9.520 (Alc.Mess.)'

***ῥᾰφᾰνόσπερμον**, *radish seed*, *SB* 10532.14-15, 24 (AD 87/8).

**ῥᾰφιδᾶς**, add '**2** *cobbler*, *AP* 11.288 (Pall.).'

**ῥᾰφιδεύς**, delete the entry (v. °*ῥαφιδᾶς*).

**ῥᾰφιδοποιός**, add '*BGU* 2351.6 (ii AD)'

***ῥᾰφικός**, ή, όν, = *ῥαπτικός*, Sch.D.T. 445.22.

***ῥᾰφίον** (or ?**ῥᾰφεῖον**), τό, *ῥαφίῳ· τῷ κεντηρίῳ ᾧ διακεντοῦντες οἱ τεχνῖται τῶν τοιούτων ἐπιτηδείους ὀπὰς τῇ τοῦ λίνου διέρσει παρασκευάζουσι* Gal. 19.134.

**ῥᾰφίς II**, add '*IGC* p. 98 A23 (Acraephia, iii/ii BC)'

***ῥαχᾶς**, ᾶ, ὁ, dub. sens., as nickname, *SB* 7638.7 (iii BC), cf. *Ev.Matt.* 5.22.

**ῥᾰχίζω I**, add '*τὰ δερόμενά τε καὶ ῥαχιζόμενα τῶν ἱερείων* Philostr.*VA* 5.42' **II**, for '*play the braggart, boast*' read '*tell outrageous untruths*'

**ῥᾰχις I 2**, add 'for *ἱερὴ ῥ.* see ‡*ἱερός* IV 10'

**ῥᾰχιστής II**, for '*boaster, braggart*' read '*teller of tall stories, liar*' and after '*ῥαχιστήρ* .. Hsch.' add '*SB* 9806.2 (iii AD)'

***ῥάχνη**, ἡ, perh. *cloak*, *POsl.* 161.5 (late iii AD), *PGen.* 80.7 (iv AD), *CPR* 8.65.6, 7, etc. (vi AD); cf. *ῥάκανα*.

***ῥαχνίον**, τό, dim. of °*ῥάχνη*, *POxy.* 2058.22 (vi AD).

**ῥάχνος**, delete the entry.

**ῥᾱχός**, line 3, for '*thorn-hedge*' read '*growth of bushes, thicket, brushwood*' and add '*PKöln* 144.24 (ii BC), *POxy.* 3558 (after AD 150)'; line 4, delete 'in Hdt. l.c. .. *wattled fence*'

***ῥάψ**, *ῥαπός*, *reed*, *ποτ τὰς ῥάπα[ς] κυλλάς SEG* 27.650.4 (Camarina, ii BC), *ῥάπα· τὴν καλάμην* Hsch.

*°**Ῥαψώ**, οῦς, ἡ, name of goddess or nymph, *IG* 2².4547 (Phalerum, iv BC).

***ῥαψῴδημα**· *ψεῦσμα, φλυαρία* Hsch.

***ῥαψῳδοτοιοῦτος**, ὁ, *sort of rhapsode*, Strato Com. 1.48 K.-A.

**Ῥέᾱ**, lines 2/3, delete "*Ῥεῖα δ'* .. *δμηθεῖσα*)'

⁺**ῥέανσις**, v. °*ῥάνσις*.

⁺**ῥεάντης**, v. °*ῥάντης*.

***ῥεγεωνάριος**, ὁ, Lat. *regionarius, police-officer* at Antioch in Pisidia, *JRS* 2.81.

**ῥέζω** (A), line 9, after 'Cleonae' insert 'prob. 575/550 BC' at end add 'form perh. **ϝόρζω* (<**wr̥gyō*) Myc. 3 sg. *wo-ze*, inf. *wo-ze-e*, part. *wo-zo*, pass. part. *wo-zo-me-no*'

**ῥεθομᾱλίδας**, for 'Alc. 150' read 'Aeol. acc. to Sch.Il. 22.68'

⁺**ῥέθος**, εος, τό, *face, countenance*, S.*Ant.* 529 (anap.), E.*HF* 1204 (lyr.),

Call.*fr.* 67.13 Pf., A.R. 2.68, Lyc. 173: Aeol. in this sense acc. to Sch.Il. 22.68, cf. Sapph. 22.3 L.-P. (dub. sens.), Theoc. 29.16. **2** in pl., perh. *nose and mouth*, ψυχὴ δ' ἐκ ῥεθέων πταμένη Il. 16.856. **II** in pl., fr. misunderstanding of sense I 2, *limbs, body*, ῥεθέων ἐκ θυμὸν ἕληται Il. 22.68, cf. Theoc. 23.39.

***ῥέκος·** ζώνη Hsch., Phot., Suid. (prob. a dialect form of ῥάκος).

**ῥέκτης**, add '**2** Dor. ῥέκτας, *priest*, prob. in *IG* 14.431.'

***ῥελατωρία**, ἡ, perh. *receipt brought back after delivery*, *POxy.* 3125.6 (AD 325), cf. Lat. *relatoria*.

**ῥεμβάς**, add 'Heph.Astr. 2.21.28'

**ῥέμβος**, add 'one who qualifies for corn dole, perh. in rotation, after completion of public service, *POxy.* 2908 iii 37; 2927.7, 21; 2928 i 1'

**ῥέμω**, for 'Theognost.*Can.* 11' read 'Theognost.*Can.* 32 A.'

***ῥεπαρατίων**, ωνος, ἡ, Lat. *reparatio*, *Stud.Pal.* 20.123.33 (V AD).

***ῥεποστώριον**, τό, Lat. *repos(i)torium*, *stand for serving courses at meal*, *Pap.Lugd.Bat.* XIII 6.9.

***ῥεπούδιον**, τό, Lat. *repudium*, *Cod.Just.* 1.3.52.15, *POxy.* 129.1 (VI AD).

**ῥέπω II**, line 1, after 'trans.' for 'only' read 'ῥ. τὸν νοῦν καὶ πείθειν ἑαυτόν Epict.*fr.* 8 (τρέπειν Gesner); otherwise'

***ῥέσκριπτος**, ὁ, *rescript*, *SB* 9763.33 (V AD), fr. Lat. *rescriptus, -um*.

***ῥεφᾰνίδιον**, v. ‡ῥαφαν-.

***ῥεφᾰνικός**, ή, όν, = ῥαφάνινος, Zos.Alch. 184.8.

***ῥεφέκλα**, ἡ, plant, perh. kind of cyclamen, Anon.Alch. 13.6.

***ῥεφερενδάριος**, ὁ, Lat. *referendarius*, imperial official, *Cod.Just.* 1.15.2.1, 4.59.1.1.

**ῥέω I 1**, line 24, after 'also w. gen.' insert 'Pl.*Phdr.* 230b' **2**, add 'ῥέει φάτις prob. in Nic.*Th.* 484. **b** of plague, *spread*, Hp.*Ep.* 27. **c** εὖ ῥεῖν of enterprises, *prosper*, Thgn. 639, cj. in Sol. 13.34 W. **d** of time, *pass*, πολλοῦ ῥυέντος χρόνου Memn. 14.1 J., ῥέοντι .. χρόνῳ Just.*Nov.* 1.1.4.'

***ῥέωνος·** εὔωνος †ἀνδρός Hsch., cf. Theognost.*Can.* 32 A.

**ῥηγεύς**, add 'also **ῥᾱγεύς**, *EM* 703.28'

***ῥῆγλα**, ἡ, *part of wagon* (perh. Lat. *regula*, bar), *Edict.Diocl.* 15.13; ῥῆγλαι· σιδηρᾶ ὡς ῥάβδοι Hsch.; cf. °ῥηγλίον.

***ῥηγλίον**, τό, *bar* of gold, *Edict.Diocl.* 30.1a, cf. Lat. *regula, regularis*.

***ῥηγλοχύτης**, ου, ὁ, *ingot mould*, Anon.Alch. 322.24, 325.10, (ρυ-, ρι-); cf. °ῥηγλίον.

**ῥηγμίν** or **-μίς**, line 2, for 'neither form is found' read 'these forms only in Hsch.'

**ῥήγνῡμι**, line 3, after 'cf. 4.22' insert '*Gnomol.Vat.* in *WS* 9.185'; line 7, after 'ῥῆξα Il. 6.6' insert 'Aeol. ἐρρηξε Alc. 179.2 L.-P.' **A 4**, add 'D. 9.61' **5**, line 4, after 'Lxx *Is.* 49.13' insert 'θυμὸν ἔρρηξας ib.*Jb.* 15.13'

**ῥηκτός**, add 'A.R. 3.848'

***ῥημᾰτίζω**, *speechify*, A.*fr.* 78a.30 R.

**ῥημᾰτιον**, after '*phrase*' insert 'or *word*'

**ῥήν**, for 'ἡ' read 'ὁ' and delete '*sheep*' add 'cf. Myc. adj. *we-re-ne-ja* (fem.)'

***'Ῥηνοπότης**, ου, ὁ, *one who drinks the water of the Rhine*, verse oracle in *SEG* 31.851 (Ardea, AD 78/81).

***ῥῆνος**, εος, τό, = ῥήν, dub. in Hsch. s.vv. πολύρρην and ῥήνεα.

***ῥήξ**, ῥηγός, ὁ, Lat. *rex*, *king* (in the west), Procop. 5.1.26, 6.14.38. **II** pl., name of infantry unit at Rome, id. 5.23.3.

**ῥηξίχθων**, for '*bursting forth from the earth*' read '*breaking* or *splitting the earth*' and add '(?)of a pig, Strato Com. 1.19 K.-A. (v.l. ἐρυσίχθ- in Ath. 8.382e)' add 'also ῥηξίχθιον *Suppl.Mag.* I 12'

**ῥῆον**, after '*rhubarb*' insert 'Androm.ap.Gal. 14.40'

***ϝρητᾱ́**, ἁ, Cypr. for ῥήτρα, *treaty, agreement*, acc. pl. *we-re-ta-se* ϝρέτας *ICS* 217.28.

***ϝρητάομαι**, *make an agreement*, Cypr. aor. *e-(u-)we-re-ta-sa-tu* ἐϝρετάσατυ, *ICS* 217.4, 14.

***ῥητορεῖον**, τό, perh. *prize for rhetoric*, Anon.*in Rh.* 98.11, 12.

**ῥητορικός**, add '**4** ῥ. λεξικόν, *Lex.Rhet.* ap.Eust. 200.1, al.: pl., id. 1921.57.'

**ῥητός I 1**, line 7, after 'Plb. 32.6.7' insert 'ἐκ τῶμ μὴ ῥητῆι (sc. ἡμέρα), perh. *from those which do not fall on a stated* day of sacrifice, *IG* $2^2$.1357a.25 (403/2 BC), cf. Hsch. s.v. ῥητήν' and after 'ῥητόν, τό' insert '*compact, treaty*, *Inscr.Cret.* 4.197.17 (τῶι .. ῥη]τῶι ii BC)'; at end for 'so perh. ἀπὸ ῥητῶν .. p. ix' read 'ἀπὸ ῥε̄το̄ν perh. *in the aforesaid manner*, *Hesperia* 33.385 (Eretria, V BC)'

**ῥήτρα**, after 'Elean ϝράτρα' insert 'Cypr. ‡ϝρήτα' **I**, add 'ἐπὶ ῥήτρῃσι λαβεῖν receive *on conditions*, Call.*fr.* 85.6 Pf.' **II 4**, after '*Cyr.* 1.6.33' insert '*Meiggs-Lewis* 8.2 (Chios, VI BC)'

**ῥηχμός**, add '(= *SEG* 36.336, iv BC) perh. to be interpr. as place-name'

**ῥῑγέω**, line 3, delete 'Dor. 3 pl. ἐρρίγαντι Theoc. 16.77'

**ῥῑγοπῡρετίον** (s.v. ῥιγοπύρετος), add '*PCair.* 10263.16 (iv/v AD), *Suppl.Mag.* I 23'

***'Ῥίεια**, τά, *festival* of Poseidon *at Rhium* in Locris, *IG* 4.428.10 (Sicyon).

**ῥίζα I**, line 3, after '*root*' insert '(sts. extended to include *stock*)' and add 'τὰς ἀκάνθας δὲ αὐτοῦ (sc. ῥόδου) τὰς παρὰ τὴν ῥίζαν Luc.*Hist.Conscr.* 28' add 'form *ϝρίζα, Myc. *wi-ri-za*, of wool'

***ῥιζάριον**, τό, *small root*, Moses Alch. 306.5.

**ῥίζις**, delete 'of the elephant kind'

***ῥιζοκᾰλᾰμος**, ὁ, *reed*, αὐξηρῶν δονάκων μεγάλων ῥιζοκαλάμων Sch. Nic.*Al.* 588b Ge.

**ῥιζοκέφᾰλος**, for '*of which .. root*' read '*having a bulbous root*'

***ῥιζοκρίκι(ο)ν**, τό, app. *ring attached to the base*, μοχλὸν .. σιδηροῦν ῥιζοκρίκιν ἔχοντα *Poliorc.* 254.1.

***ῥιζοποιός**, όν, *engendering roots* (or, for ῥοιζο-, *hissing*, or, for ῥυζο-, *snarling*), magical formula in *Suppl.Mag.* II 96 A 27, E ↓3 (both sp. ῥιζοπυέ), ib. F *fr.* A5 (sp. ῥυσοπηέ).

**ῥιζοφυής II**, add 'ῥιζοφυὴς Μουσέων πτόρθος *SEG* 36.975 (Halic., late Hellen. epigr.)'

***ῥιζωτήρ**, ῆρος, ὁ, *causing to strike roots*, epith. of the sun, but prob. f.l. for ῥοιζήτωρ, Orph.*H.* 8.6.

**ῥικνός**, after 'ή, όν' insert '(cf. pers. n. ϝρικνίδας, *SEG* 36.341, Argos, VI BC)'

**ῥικνώδης**, add '**II** *dancing in a twisted, contorted manner* (cf. ῥικνόομαι II), of Dionysus, *AP* 9.524.18.'

**ῥίκνωσις**, add 'Gal. in *CMG* 5.10(2).2.172.22, 173.8'

**ῥῖμμα**, add '**2** *outcast*, Sch.E.*Hec.* 1076.'

**ῥῑνάω** (B), add 'cf. καταρρινάω'

***ῥῑνεστήρ**, ῆρος, ὁ, prob. *halter*, *PTeb.* 886.68 (ii BC).

**ῥίνη I**, add 'perh. also ῥίνε̄ *SEG* 30.1148 (Capua, 460/50 BC)' **II**, add 'ῥίνα *IGC* p. 98 A22 (Acraephia, iii/ii BC)'

**ῥῑνηλάτης**, for 'Poll. 2.74' read '*Trag.adesp.* 426 K.-S. (Poll. 2.74)'

**ῥῑνόβᾰτος**, add '*IGC* p. 98 A20 (Acraephia, iii/ii BC)'

**ῥῑνόκερως 2**, delete the section transferring quots. to section 1.

**ῥῑνός I**, line 1, before 'Od. 5.426' insert 'pl.'; line 2, after 'etc.' insert 'Nic.*Th.* 429' add 'form *ϝρινός, Myc. *wi-ri-no*, adj. *wi-ri-ni-jo*'

**ῥῑνοῦχος**, delete '(ῥίς II)'

***ῥῑνωτηρία**, ἡ, some part of a ship, Poll. 1.86.

**ῥίον 2**, place-name, add 'Myc. *ri-jo*'

***ῥιπαρία**, ἡ, *office* or *function of riparius*, *POxy.* 2032.50, *PMasp.* 287 iv 30, *CPR* 10.48.3 (all VI AD).

***ῥῑπήεις**, εσσα, εν, *stormy*, prob. in *PMich.*inv. 4926a (*ZPE* 93.157).

***ῥῑπίδιον**, τό, *small bellows* or *fan*, *PMich.*XIV 680.7 (iii/iv AD), *CPR* 10.7.45, Hdn.*Epim.* 118. **2** μέρος τῆς νεώς Hsch.

**ῥῑπίς III**, add 'Ael.*NA* 13.10 S.'

**ῥῖπος**, for 'ἀχύρων ῥ. .. 1.86, al.' read 'as measure of straw, ἀχύρων ῥ. *SEG* 9.11, 12, 15, 28, cf. ib. 35.1834'

**ῥιπτάζω**, line 6, for 'ὕφη γυναικῶν .. ἐρριπτάζετο S.*fr.* 210 iii 12' read 'ὕφη γυναικῶν ἀνδ[ρὸ]ς ἐρριπτ[ά]ζετο S.*fr.* 210.68 R.'

**ῥίπτω**, line 12, for 'ῥερίφθαι' read 'ῥερῖφθαι'

**ῥίς II**, for 'prob. *brow .. spur of land*' read 'perh. some kind of canal, cf. *SEG* 37.758'

**ῥισηγέτης** (s.v. ῥισῆς), add 'written ῥισηιγήτ- *SB* 5246.3 (iii/ii BC)'

**ῥίσκος**, add 'see also °ἐρίσκος'

**ῥισκοφῠλάκιον**, add '*PSI* 858.30 (iii BC)'

**ῥίψασπις**, for '*craven*' read '(as a sign of cowardice, freq. in fig. contexts)' and add 'Lys. 11.5'

**ῥιψόφθαλμος**, after '*casting the eyes about*' insert 'in a covetous or lustful manner'

**ῥόα**, line 1, before 'ῥοιά' delete 'later' and after it insert 'Ar.*Pax* 1001' **II 2**, for '*knob .. pomegranate*' read '*ornament in the form of a pomegranate*' and delete '*tassel* .. ῥοΐσκος'

***ῥόγα**, ἡ, (*money*) *allowance*, τὴν ῥόγαν τῶν λιμιταναίω[ν καὶ τῶν στρ]ατιωτῶν *SEG* 32.1554 (Arabia, VI AD), *CPR* 8.74.3 (VII AD); *rations*, *PMasp.* 76.4, 145.4 (VI AD); cf. °ῥογεύω and *Eranos* 89.121-2.

***ῥογεύω**, *pay in kind*, cf. Lat. *erogare*, οἶνον *PMasp.* 76.8, 145.1, etc. (VI AD), Just.*Nov.* 130.1.

**ῥόδεος I**, after '*of roses*' insert 'κάλυκες *h.Cer.* 427' **II**, after '*rosy*' insert 'χείρ *AP* 9.745 (Anyt.)'

***'Ῥοδιασταί**, οἱ, *devotees of the goddess* °'Ῥόδος, *IG* 12(1).157 (Rhodes, i AD).

**ῥοδίζω II 2**, for this section read '*decorate* the grave of a person *with roses*, at the Rosalia, *INikaia* 1422; pass., ib. 95'

**ῥοδῐνοπορφῠροῦς**, ᾶ, οῦν, read '**ῥοδῐνοπόρφῠρος**, ον (v. *Tyche* 6.234)'

**ῥόδινος I**, for 'Anacr. 83' read 'Anacr. 89.2 P., Stesich. 10.3 P. (pl.)' **II**, add '**b** subst., ῥ. ἡ, kind of hyacinth stone, Epiph.Const. in *Lapid.Gr.* 196.25.'

***?ρο]δῐνόχρωα**, perh. *rose-coloured*, *PNag.Ham.* 3.8 (iii/iv AD).

**ῥοδισμός**, for '*ceremony*' read '= Lat. *Rosalia*, *a festival*'

**ῥοδοδάκτῠλος**, add 'epith. of Helios, *SEG* 34.1294 (Phrygia)'

**ῥοδόεις**, add 'form *ϝορδόϝενς, Myc. *wo-do-we* (neut.)'

**ῥόδον I 1**, add '**b** flower of the ῥοδοδάφνη, Luc.*Asin.* 17. **c** of gold, etc., in a necklace, *IG* $1^3$.360.4 (V BC), $2^2$.1376.6 (v/iv BC).' **II**, add '*BCH* 24.306, 60.337 (Philippi)'

**'Ῥόδος**, add 'as a divinity, *SEG* 23.547 (Crete, 201/0 BC)'

**ʽΡοδοσκάρφα**, delete the entry.

***ῥοδοφορία**, ἡ, *ceremony involving carrying of roses*, *POxy.* 3694.6 (AD 218/25); cf. ῥοδοφόρια.

**ῥοΐδιον**, after 'ῥούδιον' insert 'unless this is dim. of ῥοῦς, *sumach*'

**ῥοιζέω**, lines 5/6, after 'Arist.*HA* 535ᵇ27' insert 'of beetles, Hippon. 92.10 W.' add '**2** used Aq.*Ge.* 31.51 for *set up* (by mistake due to the ambiguity of the Hebr. wd.).'

**ῥοιζήτωρ**, for '(Orph.*H.*) 8.6' read 'cj. for °ῥιζωτήρ ib. 8.6'

***ῥοῖον**, τό, app. *stream*, (cf. ῥόος, ῥοία), *SEG* 23.236.3 (Phizalea, iii BC) (unless to be read as the first letters of a pr. n.).

***ῥοισπις**, wd. occurring in list of bird names, *PAmst.* 13.11 (v AD).

**ῥόμβος A I**, for this section read '*bull-roarer*, instrument whirled on a string to make a whirring noise, used in the worship of Rhea and Dionysus, E.*Hel.* 1362, Ar.*fr.* 315 K.-A., Archyt. 1, Diog.Ath. 1.3 S., Orph.*fr.* 34; described, Sch.Clem.Al.*Protr.* 2.17.2, cf. Hsch.; used in love-magic, Theoc. 2.30 (but expld. by sch. as = ἴυγξ 1), cf. Luc.*DMeretr.* 4.5, Propertius 2.28.35, Ov.*Am.* 1.8.7. **2** perh. *whipping-top*, *AP* 6.309 (Leon.Tarent.), M.Ant. 5.36, Sch.A.R. 1.1134, cf. 4.144.' **II**, line 6, after 'Orph.*H.* 8.7' insert 'meton., θύννων ῥ. *AP*6.33.3 (Maec.)' **B**, add '**5** = ψωλή, *PLond.* 1821.164 (vi AD). **6** a cavalry formation, Ael.*Tact.* 19.5, Arr.*Tact.* 17.'

**ῥομβωτός**, for 'J.*AJ* 12.2.10' read 'J.*AJ* 12.2.9'

**ῥόος**, line 1, for '*Inscr.Cypr.* 135.19 H.' read 'acc. *ro-wo*, *ICS* 217.19'; line 3, after '*Peripl.M.Rubr.* 46' insert 'nom. pl. ῥόες (ροσσ lapis) *GVI* 1684.9 (Chersonesus, i/ii AD), perh. acc. pl.: εἰς ῥόις ὕδατ(ος) *SB* 10549.8 (AD 204)'

**ῥοπή I 2 a**, add 'κα‹ὶ› νόσō ῥοπᾶι *SEG* 39.1019 (Selinous, v BC)'

**ῥόπτον**, for '*operating table*' read 'something to which a patient is tied for an operation'

⁺**ῥόπτρον**, τό, (ῥέπω) part of a trap, consisting of heavy piece which falls on the victim when dislodged (cf. Eng. deadfall), Archil. 186 W., Poll. 7.115; fig., δίκης ἔπαισεν αὐτὸν ῥ. E.*Hipp.* 1172. **II** *knocker* on door, E.*Ion* 1612, Ar.*fr.* 40 K.-A., Lys. 6.1, X.*HG* 6.4.36. **2** colloq., *penis*, Hsch. **III** in pl., an instrument consisting of two small cymbal-heads struck together by shaking, used esp. by Corybantes, *rattle*, *clapper*, or sim., Corn.*ND* 30, Luc.*Trag.* 36, Orph.*frr.* 105b, 152, *AP* 6.74 (Agath.), Nonn.*D.* 9.116, al. **2** as part of a Parthian percussion device used in battle, ῥ. βυρσοπαγῆ καὶ κοῖλα περιτείναντες ἠχείοις χαλκοῖς Plu.*Crass.* 23.

***ῥοσικόν**, τό, commodity, perh. cognate of ῥούσιος, *red pigment*, *rouge*, *BGU* 2357 ii 16 (iii AD; unless for ῥωστικόν, i.e. *strengthening agent*).

***ῥόσσα**· ἡ κίχλη Theognost.*Can.* 102.

**ῥοταρία**, add 'cf. late Lat. *rotarius*, "*of a wheel*"'

**ῥούδιον**, add '**II** v. ‡ῥοΐδιον.'

**ῥοῦς I**, add '**3** shrub related to the sumach, *Coriaria myrtifolia*, Plin.*HN* 24.91.' add '**III** = ῥόον (q.v.), *dried mulberry fruit*.'

**ῥούσιος I**, add 'στρῶμα ῥ. *PVindob.* G25737 (*ZPE* 64.77, vi/vii AD)'

***ῥοφεῖον**, τό, item in list of kitchen vessels, Lang *Ath.Agora* XXI B12 (pl., iv/iii BC).

**ῥοφέω**, line 8, for 'Hippon. 132' read 'Hippon. 165 W. and is freq. in the best codd. of Hp.; also Dor., Sophr. in *PSI* 1214*d*2 (κατα-)'

***ῥύγή**, ἡ, *growling*, *snarling*, *Trag.adesp.* 653.9 K.-S.

**ῥύγχος**, after 'τό' insert '(acc. ῥύ]γχον *IEryth.* 203.4 (iv BC))'

**ῥῦδόν**, after 'Od. 15.426' insert 'ῥ. ἀφνύνονται Call.*fr.* 366 Pf.'

***ῥύζα**, ἡ, (ἐρύω A), *drawing* of a bow, Hsch.

**ῥυθμίζω II**, after '(Arist.)*Spir.* 485ᵇ2' insert '*CodJust.* 6.48.1.26 (AD 528/9)'

***ῥυθμοποιός**, ὁ, = ὁ μέλη καὶ ῥυθμοὺς ποιῶν Hsch.

**ῥυθμός VI**, add '*Peripl.M.Rubr.* 6'

**ῥῠκάνη**, after '*plane*' insert '(tool)'; add 'Varro *LL* 6.96'

***ῥῠκάνισμα**, ατος, τό, *plane-shaving*, *Poliorc.* 223.18.

**ῥῦμα** (B), after '*protection*' insert 'τούτους ηὐξήσατε ῥύματα δόντες i.e. bodyguards Sol. 11.3 W.'

***ῥυμβάδας**· λάϊγγας τὰς διεσχισμένας Hsch.

***ῥῡμεῖον**, v. °ῥυμίον.

***ῥύμιγξ**· χείμαρρος Hsch.

***ῥῡμίον**, τό, dim. of ῥύμη II, *lane*, *alley*, *PMeyer* 20ᵛ.5 (iii AD); also ῥυμεῖον, ἐν τυφλῷ ῥυμείῳ *SB* 9902 A i 25, ii 1 (iii AD).

**ῥύμμα II**, for 'Sch.Nic.*Al.* 95' read 'Nic.*Al.* 96'

**ῥῡμός I 2**, line 2, for '*log* .. fuel' read 'perh. *spit* or other instrument used in roasting sacrificial victims' **II**, for '*trace*' read '*rein*' **IV**, for 'perh. *shelf* or *row*' read '*steelyard*, *IG* 1³.386.21, al, 387.40; meton., *amount weighed at a time*, *beam-load*'

**ῥῠπᾰρός 2**, add 'λόγου μόριον D.H.*Comp.* 12' **3**, for 'of coins .. alloy' read 'of payments including the extra charge' and add '*BGU* 2554.6' **4**, for 'prob. = ἀδειγμάτιστος' read 'of grain, *unpolished*' and delete '*unwinnowed*'

**ῥῠπάω**, add 'transf., of moral turpitude, Just.*Nov.* 80.8'

***ῥῠποπώλης**, ου, ὁ, *seller of rubbish*, Sch.Ar.*Pl.* 17; cf. γρυτοπώλης.

**ῥύπος I 2**, add 'Ar.*fr.* 931 K.-A.'

**ῥῡσαλέος**, add 'γραῖα *GVI* 1185.1 (Palestine, ii/iii AD)'

**ῥῡσίπτολις**, after 'ῥυσίπολις' insert 'A.*fr.* 451q.7 R. (lyr.)'

**ῥύσις I**, add '**b** fig., τῆς λέξεως D.H.*Dem.* 40, cf. *Comp.* 23.' **III**, after 'Math.' insert 'ῥύσει σημείου συνίσταται γραμμή Ph. 1.23'

**ῥυστάζω**, line 3, after 'Il. 24.755' insert 'Call.*fr.* 588 Pf.'

**ῥυστήρ II 2**, for this section read '= ἀρυστήρ, *ladle* of irrigating-machine (shadoof), prob. in *Aegyptus* 6.191 (pap. ρηστηρ)'

***ῥύτειρα** (A), ἡ, fem. of ῥυτήρ (A), Ἄρταμι ῥ. τόξων (?)Alcm. 170 P.

⁺**ῥύτειρα** (B), ἡ, fem. of ῥυτήρ (B), Suid.

**ῥῡτήρ** (B), before 'ῥυτῆρες' insert 'δήμου ῥ. *AA* 21.38 (Miletus, ii BC)'

**ῥῡτός II**, line 4, after 'Plu.*Alex.* 67' insert 'prob. in Phld.*Rh.* 2.54 S., where the ν of τόν may be the initial of the lost wd.'

***ῥῡτοφῐάλιον**, τό, *small* φιάλη *designed to facilitate pouring*, *Ath. Asklepieion* v 71 (iii BC).

**ῥύτωρ** (A), add 'ῥ. τόξου the constellation *Sagittarius*, Arat. 301'

**ῥωβίδας**, for '*of less* .. *old*' read '*in the first year of public education*, i.e. seven years old'

**ῥωγάς**, for 'ὁ, ἡ' read 'fem. adj.' add '**II** as subst., ἡ, *cloven rock*, Nonn.*D.* 3.56, 10.175 (cod.).'

***ῥωθῶς**· σφόδρα Theognost.*Can.* 68 A.

***ʽΡωμαΐα**, v.s.v. ‡ʽΡωμαῖος.

***ʽΡωμαϊκόν**, τό, some article of clothing, *PRyl.* 627.18 (iv AD).

**ʽΡωμαϊκός**, line 1, after 'al.' insert 'ἀρυσάς .. -οῖς γράμμασιν ἐπιγεγραμμένος *Inscr.Délos* 442*B*139 (ii BC)' add '**2** *Roman* (i.e. civil opp. ecclesiastical), ʽΡ. ἐλευθερία Just.*Nov.* 144.2.4.'

***ʽΡωμαῖον**, τό, *temple of Roma*, *Milet* 7 p. 17 (i BC).

**ʽΡωμαῖος**, after 'Plb. 10.36.3, etc.' insert 'applied to Roman citizens in other parts of the Empire, *SEG* 29.690 (Histria), etc.'; τὰ ʽΡ., add '*SEG* 33.1039 (Cyme, ii BC), 33.644 (Rhodes, i BC), etc.)'

**ʽΡωμαϊστής**, add '*SEG* 31.1535 (Philae, ?i AD)'

**ῥωμᾰλέος 2**, add '**b** *strengthening*, of food, Diocl.*fr.* 133 (comp.).'

***ῥωμᾰλεότης**, ητος, ἡ, *physical strength*, Rh. 3.599.15.

***ʽΡωμανήσιος**, ον, = Lat. *Romanensis*, archit., of kind of construction, *CodJust.* 8.10.12.5 (sp. ʽΡωμανίσιος).

**ʽΡώμη**, add '**2** ἡ νέα ʽΡ. i.e. Constantinople, Just.*Nov.* 70.1; Βυζαντιὰς ʽΡ. *APl.* 56.1; ἑκατέρα ʽΡ. Just.*Nov.* 81.1.'

**ῥώννῡμι II 3**, lines 4/5, after 'D. 18.152, 19.248' insert 'τῇ θυσίᾳ Men.*Dysc.* 264, 520'

⁺**ῥώπᾱες**, wd. glossed by ἀλσώδες, Arc. 143 (perh. for ῥωπᾶεν, v. ῥωπήεις).

**ῥωπεύω I**, for '*AP* 6.226' read 'ῥωπεύειν· ξυλεύεσθαι Suid.'

**ῥωπογράφος**, for '(ῥῶπος) .. masters' read '(ῥώψ A) *painter of forest scenery*'

**ῥωποπώλης**, line 3, after 'ῥοπο-' insert 'cf. LXX 3*Ki.* 10.15 (v.l. for ἐμπόρων in A.)'

***ῥως**, perh. = ῥῶσις, *strength*, poet. in *Pap.Lugd.Bat.* XXV 1.6.

***ῥωσιτάριον**, τό, wd. in list of dyestuffs, perh. = ῥωστήριον, *POxy.* 1922.4 (v AD).

⁺**ῥωσκομένως**, adv. fr. part., perh. of Ion. *ῥώσκομαι (related to ῥώομαι or ῥώννυμι), *with violent motion*, Hp.*Cord.* 1 (nisi leg. θρωσκομένως).

***ῥωστέον**, *one must strengthen*, Archig.ap.Gal. 13.167.16.

⁺**ῥωστήριον**, τό, glossed by παρορμητικόν, Hsch.; cf. Phot.

**ῥωχμή**, for '*fissures*' read '*wrinkles*'

# Σ

**σʹ II**, add ʻτάμὰ καὶ σʹ id.*El.* 273ʼ

**Σαβαζιασταί**, add ʻ*SEG* 33.639 (Rhodes, *c.*100 BC)ʼ

**Σάβάζιος**, lines 4f., before ʻ(Ar.)*Lys.* 388ʼ insert ʻ*χὠ τυμπανισμὸς χοἰ πυκνοὶ Σαβάζιοι cries of "Sabazios!"*ʼ; for ʻθεῷ .. *CIG* 3791ʼ read ʻ*θεῷ Σαβαζίῳ Παγισαρανῷ TAM* 4(1).79ʼ; add ʻ*Διὶ Σαουαζίῳ INikaia* (AD 122/3)ʼ

***Σάβάθικός**, app. = *Σαβάζιος*, *GVAK* 8 (Bithynia, i BC/i AD).

***σάβαθον**, v. °*σάμβαθον*.

**+σάβάκός**, *ή*, *όν*, *disabled, debilitated*, Hp.*Morb.* 1.31, *σαβακῶν σαλμακίδων AP* 7.222 (Phld.), Hsch.

**σάβάκτης**, read ʻ**Σάβάκτης**ʼ and for ʻ*shatterer* .. pots' read ʻ*Shatterer*, one of a number of demons supposed to be active in a potteryʼ

**σάβάνον**, after ʻ*towel*ʼ insert ʻ*Edict.Diocl.* 28.57, al.ʼ

**σαβαύτια**, add ʻ*PMich.*inv. 419.6 (*ZPE* 31.176, iii/iv AD)ʼ

**Σάβος**, add ʻ**2** place dedicated to the service of Sabazios, Sch.Ar.*Av.* 874, Harp. s.v. *Σάβοι*.ʼ

***σάβουρᾶτος**, *ον*, Lat. *saburratus, filled with ballast*, *σκάφος PMerton* 46.10 (vi AD).

**σάβουρος**, for ʻ*without ballast*ʼ read ʻperh. *in ballast, empty*ʼ; add ʻcf. Lat. *saburra, ballast*ʼ

**σάβυττος I**, after ʻ*hair*ʼ insert ʻ*ἐξυρημένος σαβύττους* Eup. 313 K.-A.ʼ

**+σαγάλινος**, *η*, *ον*, *of teak*, *ξύλων σ.* cod. *Peripl.M.Rubr.* 36.

**σάγανα**, add ʻ*PPrag.* I 90.10 (vi/vii AD)ʼ

**+σαγγαικόν** (or ?-αϊκόν), *τό*, app. some ritual garment, *σ. βεβαμμένον κόκκινον ἐν κιβωταρίῳ Inscr.Délos* 1416*A*58, 1417*B*i60, 1452*A*40, (perh. shoe, cf. *σαγγάριος*, *τζάγγη*).

**σάγεσφ[όρος]**, for ʻdub.ʼ read ʻprob. *mule*ʼ; add ʻcf. °*σαγηφόρος*ʼ

***σάγήνιον**, *τό*, dim. of *σαγήνη*, *net*, *ICilicie* 108 (v/vi AD).

***σάγηφόρος**, *ό*, beast of burden, prob. *mule*, *AAWW* 1948.322/3 (epigr., Panopolis, Rom.imp.); cf. ‡*σαγεσφ[όρος]*.

**σάγίον**, add ʻ*saddle cloth* (for camel), *PMich.*XV 717.1 (iii AD)ʼ

***σαγιττάριος**, *ό*, Lat. *sagittarius*, *SEG* 34.1598 (Egypt, AD 323), *SB* 4223.8 (pl., iv AD), *BCH* suppl. 8.63 (Maced., v/vi AD).

**σάγμα II**, *pack-saddle*, add ʻ*PRyl.* 562.30 (250 BC)ʼ

***σαγματικός**, *ή*, *όν*, *of or for a pack-saddle*, *βελόνη Edict.Diocl.* 16.10.

**σαθαρυγά**, add ʻcf. °*σαιθάρυγξ*ʼ

**σάθων**, add ʻtitle of work by Antisthenes against Plato, whom he so nicknamed, Ath. 5.220d, D.L. 3.35ʼ

***σαιθάρυγξ**· *ἡ ταραχή* Theognost.*Can.* 33 A.; cf. *σαθαρυγά*.

***σαίνα**· *τὸ αἰδοῖον* Theognost.*Can.* 33 A.

***σαίνος**· *ὁ ἀριστερεών* Theognost.*Can.* 33 A.

**σαιστός**, add ʻ*ἐλαίας κλάδος* Theognost.*Can.* 33 A. (*σαῖστος* codd.)ʼ

**σάκεσφόρος I**, after ʻAjaxʼ insert ʻB. 13.104 S.-M.ʼ

**σάκηφόρος**, for ʻ*Supp.Epigr.* 4.522ʼ read ʻ*IEphes.* 293, 1250ʼ

***σάκκαρος**, *ό*, perh. item of military equipment, *SB* 7181*B*36.

**σακκηγία**, add ʻ*PUps.Frid* 1.12 (iii AD)ʼ

***σακκοπάθνιον**, gloss on *χλιδός*, Hsch., prob. *nose-bag*, cf. *φάτνη*, *φατνίον*.

**σακκοπλόκος**, add ʻ*SEG* 19.657 (Caria, Rom.imp.)ʼ

***σακκοποιός**, *ό*, *sack-maker*, *POxy.* 3642.28 (ii AD), *PKlein.Form.* 124 (vi AD).

***σακκορ(ρ)άφος**, *η*, *ον*, *used for sewing sacks*, *βελόνη Edict.Diocl.* 16.10 (*σαρκο-*), *SB* 7181*B*12.

**σάκκος II 1**, for ʻ*Ostr.* .. al.ʼ read ʻof grain, *OWilck.* 1091, 1096, 1101 (all ii AD); of wine, *OMich.* 249 (iv AD)ʼ

***σάκκουν**, *τό*, (or **-ους**, *ό*), perh. article of women's clothing made of hair, *Pap.Lugd.Bat.* XXV 49.9, *PHamb.* 223.2 (ii AD).

**σακκοφορικός**, add ʻsubst., *σ.*, *τό*, tax paid by *σακκοφόροι*, *PGoodsp. Cair.* 14.7 (iv AD), *POxy.* 3395.13 (AD 371)ʼ

**σάκρα**, delete the entry.

***σάκρος**, *α*, *ον*, Lat. *sacer, sacred* used w. ref. to the imperial household, *ἐν σάκρῳ αὐδιτορίῳ* Just.*Nov.* 50 pr.; fem. pl. subst., *imperial archives*, *PSI* 481.13 (v/vi AD).

***σάκωμα**, v. ‡*σήκωμα*.

**+σάλάγέω**, *agitate vigorously*, colloq., of man in sexual intercourse, Luc.*Alex.* 50 (verse); in some manifestation of mourning, *σαλαγεῖ* (cod. *σασαλ-*)· *θρηνεῖ* Hsch.; cf. mod. Gk. *σαλαγῶ drive a flock by shouting*, *σάλαγος* of the noise so made.

**σάλάγη**, delete ʻ(cf. *σελαγή*)ʼ

*(?)**σαλακᾶς**, *ᾶτος*, *ό*, perh. = *σαλάκων*, *POxy.* 3617.11 (iii AD).

***σαλακονδεῖτον**, *τό*, Lat. *sal conditum, spiced salt*, *Edict.Diocl.* 3.9.

***σαλακωνηδα**, wd. occurring in list of bird-names, *PAmst.* 13.7 (v AD).

***σαλαμακάπηλος**, *ό*, = °*σαλγαμάριος*, *SB* 11077.13 (iv/v AD).

**Σάλάμίνιος I**, add ʻ**2** in Cyprus, *IG* $1^3$.113.1, etc., Cypr. *Σελαμίνιος* (*se-la-mi-ni-o-se*) *ICS* 166.2, 338.ʼ

**Σάλάμίς**, delete ʻin Gramm.ʼ and after ʻ**Σάλάμίν**ʼ insert ʻEun.*VS* p. 494 B.ʼ

**σαλάριον**, add ʻModest.*Dig.* 27.1.6, 11ʼ

**+σάλάσσω**, *shake, make unstable*, Nic.*Al.* 457, *σεσαλαγμένος οἴνῳ APl.* 306.1 (Leon.Tarent.); *AP* 6.56 (Maced.Thess. II), 11.57 (Agath.).

***σαλάχιον**, *τό*, prob. = *σελάχιον*, *PMich.*II 127 ii 32, *Gloss.*, cf. mod. Gk. *σαλάχι*.

***σαλγαμαρικός**, *ή*, *όν*, *of a pickle-seller*, *ἐργαστήριον σ. CPap.Jud.* 511.11 (vi AD), *PRoss.-Georg.* III 38.11 (*σαλκ-*, vi AD).

***σαλγαμάριος**, *ό*, Lat. *salgamarius, seller of pickled foods*, *Corinth* 8(3).540, 551 (v/vi AD).

***σάλγαμον**, *τό*, *pickling material*, *PBeatty Panop.* 2.246, 286 (AD 300).

**σάλευτός**, add ʻcj. in Procl. *in R.* 1.103 K.ʼ

**σάλεύω**, line 11, after ʻ*Si.* 28.14ʼ insert ʻ*disturb* a tomb, *ABSA* 51.148 (Caralitis, ii AD), etc.ʼ **II 3**, for ʻwith the hip-joints far apartʼ read ʻwith a displaced hip-jointʼ

***Σάλιος**, *ό*, *member of the priesthood of Salii*, D.H. 2.70.1, 3.32.4, *IGRom.* 4.960 (i AD), Luc.*Salt.* 20.

***σαλκαμαρικός**, v. °*σαλγαμαρικός*.

***σαλοῦσα**· *φροντίζουσα* Hsch.

**σαλπιγγωτός**, add ʻ*SB* 9319 (AD 116), 8745-7 (*c.*AD 170), etc.ʼ

***σαλπιγκτήρ**, *ῆρος*, *ό*, = *σαλπιγκτής*, Hsch. s.v. *ὀτρυντήρ*.

**σάλπιγξ III**, for ʻ*στρόμβος* 2ʼ read ʻ*στρόμβος* 3ʼ

***σαλπίζηνος**, *ό*, name of a kind of opal, Socr.Dion.*Lith.* 38 H.-S.

**σαλπίζω**, line 7, after ʻ*An.Ox.* 4.325ʼ insert ʻCret. *-ίνδω*, inf. *-ίνδε[ν]* *Inscr.Cret.* 4.146.9 (Gortyn, iv BC)ʼ

**σαλτάριος**, add ʻalso **σαλτουάριος** *TAM* 5(1).616 (iii AD)ʼ

**+σαλώτιον**, *τό*, unidentified comestible, pl. *σαλώτια δώδεκα PRyl.* 172.15; sg., perh. *OBodl.* i P295.9. **2** item in list of vessels and implements, *POxy.* 3060.8 (ii AD), *SB* 1.25 (iii AD).

**+σάμαθον**, v. °*σάμβαθον*.

***σάμβαθον**, *τό*, kind of earthenware jar and corresponding liquid measure, *σάμβαθον βωριδίων POxy.* 2728.33, 2729.9 (iii/iv AD); also **σάμφατον** *PSI* 1423.23 (iv AD); **σάμαθον** *POxy.* 1290.1 (v AD); *σάβαθον PHaun.* 21.4 (iii/iv AD).

**σαμβύκη I 1**, for this section read ʻ*small arched harp*, Aristox.*fr.* 97 W., Neanth. 5 J., Plb. 8.4.11, (?)Juba 15 J., Str. 10.3.17, Plu. 2.827a, Ath. 14.633f, Aristid.Quint. 2.16; var. form *ζαμβύκη*, see also °*ἰαμβύκη*ʼ

**σαμβῡκίστρια**, add ʻ*PHib.* 270.1 (iii BC)ʼ

***σαμκάμυκος**, *ον*, app. designation of kind of cloth, *τῶν ἑκατὸν λίνων Σινυραιτικῶν σαμκαμύκων CPap.Jud.* 414 (AD 21).

***Σαμναῖος**, *ό*, epith. of Apollo, *SEG* 14.688, 690.62 (Caria, ii/i BC); as an ethnic, Kontorini *AER* 2 p. 19 no. 17 (Rhodes, ii AD).

**Σάμόθρᾳξ**, add ʻ*SEG* 33.644 (i BC)ʼ

***σάμφατον**, v. °*σάμβαθον*.

**σάμψουχον**, line 3, before ʻAret.ʼ insert ʻNic. l.c., id.*fr.* 74.53, *AP* 4.1.11 (Mel.)ʼ

***σάμψυχος**, *ό*, = *σάμψουχον*, *PColl.Youtie* 4.4 (iii AD).

***σάμψῡχος**, *ή*, = *σάμψουχον*, Hsch. s.v. *ὕσωπίς*.

***σανάπαι**, Thracian for *μέθυσοι*, Hecat. 34 J.

**σανδάλιον III**, add ʻ(so perh. **σαντάλιν** *SB* 7635.14, v/vi AD)ʼ

**σανδάλίσκος**, for ʻHippon. 18ʼ read ʻHippon. 32.5 W.ʼ; add ʻHerod. 7.125ʼ

**σανδάλοθήκη**, add ʻ*Inscr.Délos* 1450.139, 1451*A*38 (ii BC)ʼ

**σάνδάλον I**, for ʻSapph. 98ʼ read ʻSapph. 110(*a*).2 L.-P.ʼ; add ʻCall.*fr.* 631 Pf.ʼ

***σανδάσηρος**, *ό* or *ή*, *Lapid.Gr.* 208, 1179; cf. *adfert aliquando errorem similitudo nominis sandaresi. Nicander sandaserion vocat*, Plin.*HN* 37.102.

**σανδύκιον**, add ʻ*Stud.Pal.* 20.96.10ʼ

**σάνδυξ II**, after ʻ*casket*, Id.ʼ insert ʻcf. *σενδούκη*, *-ουκι*, Sch.Ar.*Pl.* 711, 809ʼ

**σᾰνῐδώδης**, add 'ξύλον σ. κάταργον, of the ξόανον of Hera at Samos, Call.*Dieg.* iv.27 (*fr.* 100 Pf.)'
**σᾰνῐδωτός**, for 'al.' read '*Inscr.Délos* 1403*Bb*ii33, 1417*A*ii55 (ii BC), Hsch. s.v. φατνωτῶν, *Gloss.*'
**σᾰνίς 3**, for '*ship's deck*' read 'in the hull of a ship'
**σᾰνίσκη**, for 'Herod. 4.36' read 'Herod. 4.62'
**σαννάδας**, delete the entry.
***σαννάς**, άδος, ἡ, *wild goat*, Hsch., Cret. acc. to Polemon ap. Sch.Hippon. 118 W.
+**σάννᾱς**, ου, ὁ, *clown, buffoon*, Cratin. 489 K.-A.
***σαντᾰλι(ο)ν**, v. °σανδάλιον.
+**σᾰόπτολις**, v. °σώπολις.
**σάος**, at end delete 'cf. σάως'
***σάπημα**, ατος, τό, *decay*, οὔλων *Lapid.Gr.* 182.19 (pl.).
***σᾱπουνᾶς**, ὁ, *soap-merchant*, *IGLBulg.* 105 (vi AD).
**σαπρία**, add '**2** *filth, squalor*, *Vit.Aesop.*(G) 29.'
***σαπρόδης** (for -ώδης), ες, of wine, *lacking a bouquet*, inscr. in *RAL* 1993 p.267.17.
***σαπρόμορφος**, ον, *of squalid appearance*, *Vit.Aesop.*(G) 121.
**σαπρός II 3**, add 'fig., εἰρήνη σ. Ar.*Pax* 554' **4**, delete the section.
**σαπρόστομος**, add 'perh. in *POxy.* 3725 *fr.* 1 ii 9 (i/ii AD), subject-heading to *AP* 11.241 (Nicarch. II)'
***σᾱπωνίζω**, *wash with soap*, Anon.Alch. 324.6.
**σᾰρᾱπιακός**, add 'καδίσκος σ. *Inscr.Délos* 1417*A*ii134 (ii BC); of a type of garland, *PAlex.*(1964) 22.4 (ii AD)'
***Σᾰρᾱπίδειον**, τό, *temple of Sarapis*, Call.*Dieg.* vi.4 (*fr.* 191 Pf.).
**Σᾰρᾱπιεῖα** (s.v. Σάραπις), add 'at Naxos (written -ηα), *IG* 12(5).38.4, 11, 18'
**Σᾰρᾱπις**, line 1, after 'ιδος' insert '(also ιος, Robert *Hell.* 11.85, *Inscr.Délos* 1412*a*61, al.)'
**σαργάνη 2**, after '*basket*' insert '*IG* 1³.422.150 (Athens, v BC)'
***σαρδᾰχᾰτης**, ου, ὁ, kind of agate, Socr.Dion.*Lith.* 43 H.-S.
**σάρδιος**, add 'λίθος σάρδιος .. σαρδίῳ τῷ ἰχθύι τεταριχευμένῳ ἐοικώς Epiph.Const. in *Lapid.Gr.* 194.6'
***σάρδις**, Lydian for *year*, Lyd.*Mens.* 3.20.
**σαρδισμός**, add 'prob. in Sch.D.T. 447.25 (σαρκασμός codd.)'
***σαρδονῠχιον**, τό, = σαρδόνυξ, *EA* 19.25 l. 7 (Pessinus, i/ii AD), prob. in Al.*Jb.* 28.16.
**σαρήσιον**, delete the entry.
***σαρκῑναρίων**, ωνος, ὁ, app. *butcher*, Teuc.Bab. p. 43.3 B.
**σαρκόω**, add '**IV** Chr., *to endow with human nature, incarnate*, *Cod.Just.* 1.1.5.1, 1.1.6.7.'
**σάρκωσις**, add '**II** Chr., *incarnation*, *Cod.Just.* 1.1.5.3.'
**σαρμός**, add 'Hippon. 165a W.'
**σάρξ**, line 13, after '*Ba.* 746' insert 'so in pl., αἱ σάρκες αἱ κεναὶ φρενῶν id.*El.* 387' add '**c** ὁ ἀνὰ σάρκα *anasarca*, Aret.*SD* 2.1.7 H.'
**σάρον II**, for 'of sea weed' read 'in an abusive reference to Delos, Ἀστερίη, πόντοιο κακὸν σάρον' **III**, delete 'dub.' and transfer quot. to section I.
**σάροννύω**, add 'σαρωνύουσι *OBodl.* ii 1722 (ii AD)'
***Σαρπηδόνεια**, τά, *games in honour of Sarpedon*, *SEG* 28.1248 (Xanthos).
***Σαρτιωβιάριος**, ὁ, month name in Crete, *Inscr.Cret.* 1.xvi 4A.22.
**σαρωνίς**, for 'Poet.ap.Parth. 11.4' read 'Parth. 11.4 (= *Suppl.Hell.* 646.4)'
***σάρωνύω**, v. °σαροννύω.
+**σάσᾰμον**, **σᾱσᾰμόπαστος**, etc., v. ‡σησαμ-.
**σαστήρ**, after '*Supp.Epigr.* 3.602' insert '*BE* 1950.151'
***σαταβαρα**, ὁ, office included in list of priests fr. Cilicia, *ICilicie* 11c (ii AD).
**σατρᾰπεύω**, add 'also ἐξαιθραπεύω, ἐξαιτραπεύω (qq. v.)'
**σατράπης 1**, add 'also ξαδράπης *SEG* 27.942 (Lycia, 337 BC)'
**σᾰτῠρικός 2**, add 'σατυρικαὶ κωμῳδίαι of certain Latin comedies, Nic.Dam.ap.Ath. 6.261c, Lyd.*Mag.* 1.41'
**σᾰτῠριον II**, for '*fritillary .. graeca*' read 'perh. *heart-flowered orchis, Serapias cordigera*'
**Σᾰτῠρίσκος I**, before 'Theoc.' insert '*Inscr.Délos* 104.18 (iv BC)'
**Σᾰτῠρος**, for '**Τίτυρος**' read '**Τῐτῠρος**' **II**, add 'also sg. Demetr. *Eloc.* 169'
***σαύη**· ὁ κόσμος. Βαβυλώνιοι Hsch. (late Babylonian *šawê*, *heavens*; cod. σάνη).
**σαυκρόπους**, add 'cf. ψαυκρόπους'
**σαυκρός**, add 'cf. ψαυκρός'
**σαυλοπρωκτιάω**, for '*walk in a swaggering way*' read '*walk in an affected way*'
**σαυνιαστής**, lines 2/3, for 'Dor. -τάς' read 'dial. -τάς' and for 'or perh. .. 31.25' read 'rest. in Call.*fr.* 197.48 Pf.'
**Σαυρομάτης**, line 4, (Σαρματία), add 'also Σαρμαθία *SEG* 31.1116 (Phrygia, late Rom.imp.)'; line 6, (Σαρματικός), add 'as an imperial title, of Commodus, *ICilicie* 77 (AD 178)'

**σᾰφής II 4**, after '-εστέρως' insert 'Antipho 3.2.5'
**σᾰφήτωρ**, for 'a variant' read 'coined as an etymon'
***σαφρικόν**, τό, *casia*, *Gloss.*
**σᾱφώνιον**, add '*PVindob.Worp* 11.8 (vi AD), *PAnt.* 202(a).10 (vi/vii AD)'
**σάω**, delete 'Med.' and for 'σαόω' read 'σάωμι (v. σῴζω)'
**σβεστήρ**, add '**2** as adj., ῥόος σ. Nonn.*D.* 23.291.'
**σεβάζομαι 2**, add 'also act. (cf. σέβω II), poet. in Favorin.*Exil.* 11.5 B.'
**σέβας I**, add '**2** in Chr. prose, *reverence*, *Cod.Just.* 1.4.34.11.'
**σέβασμα I**, add 'Hld. 9.22'
**σεβάσμιος I**, add 'comp., σεβασμιωτέρας ἢ κατὰ ἄνθρωπον ὁμιλίας Charito 2.4; sup., Θεαῖς Νεμέσεσιν Ζμυρναίαις σεβασμιωτάταις *SEG* 32.1082 (Smyrna, iii AD)' **II**, add 'τοῦ οἴκου τοῦ σ. *SEG* 31.372 (ii AD)' add '**3** σεβάσμιος, ὁ, type of coin, *PKöln* 166.10 (vi/vii AD).'
**Σεβαστεῖον I**, add '*SEG* 23.207 (Messene, time of Augustus)'
**σεβαστικός**, delete 'Iamb.*Protr.* 21 κε´'
***Σεβαστολόγος**, ὁ, official who pronounced panegyrics of the Emperor, *Milet* 7.65.10 (Robert *Hell.* 7.206ff.).
**Σεβαστον(ε)ίκης**, for '*in Imperial games*' read 'in the Σεβαστά, v. σεβαστός II 4'; after '(Ancyra)' insert '*GDI* 4107 (Rhodes), *PLond.* 1178.67'
**σεβαστονεικηφόρια**, for '*Imperial games*' read 'festival of Augustus and Athene Nicephoros'
+**Σεβαστόνεως**, ω, ὁ, official in the cult of Caligula, *Milet* 7.65.10 (Robert *Hell.* 7.206ff.).
**σεβαστός I**, for this section read '*venerable, reverend, august*: of gods, Ἑστίας Σεβαστῆς *ICilicie* 44 (i/ii AD), Διὶ Σεβαστῷ *INikaia* 1129 (AD 131); of places, ἐν Σεβαστῇι Πάφωι *SEG* 23.638 (Paphos, AD 18/9). **2** θεοὶ σεβαστοί of deified emperors, *SEG* 30.1245 (Caria, i BC/i AD), 29.677 (Thrace, AD 78, etc.); without θεοί, *SEG* 30.1534 (Lycia, ii AD), *IEphes.* 691, 693 (AD 209/11).' **II 1**, fem., add '*SEG* 33.1132 (Phrygia, ii AD), etc.' **2**, add '*SEG* 34.398 (Delphi, i AD), 24.612 (Maced., ii AD)'
**σεβαστοφάντης**, after '*flamen Augusti*' insert '*SEG* 31.901 (Caria, mid i AD)'
**Σεβαστοφόροι**, after '*Mens.* 4.138' insert '*BCH* 24.340.30 (Oenoanda, iii AD), Suid. s.v. Αὐγουστεῖον'
**σεβένινος**, add 'also **σιβένινος** *PLond.* 1414.13'
**σεβένιον**, for '*palm-fibre*' read '*fibrous spathe of male date-palm*'
**σέβερος**, for 'Theognost.*Can.* 11' read 'Theognost.*Can.* 33 A. (cf. Lat. *severus*)'
***σέβετος**· ὁ κοχλίας Theognost.*Can.* 33 A.; cf. σελάτης.
***Σεβήρεια**, τά, festival of Severus at Athens, *SEG* 26.184 (iii AD); also Σευήρεια *IG* 2².3169 (iii AD), *JHS* 99.161-2 no. 4 (Lycia, AD 231/5).
**σέβισμα**, add '*BGU* 1764.12'
**σέβομαι**, line 3, after '*Plot.* 12' insert 'med. aor. inf. σέψασθαι Hsch.'
**σεγέστρον**, add 'cf. Lat. *segestre*, ‡στέγαστρον'
**σείνιοι**, delete the entry (ghost word).
**σειρά IV**, add 'κατὰ σειράν = Lat. *in stirpes, ex stirpibus*, *Cod.Just.* 6.4.4.19b' **V**, add 'Procl.*Inst.* 97 D., etc.'
**σειραίνω**, after '*parch*' insert 'Euph.in *Suppl.Hell.* 443.6'
**σειραῖος 2**, add 'σειραῖα δεσμά S.*fr.* 25'
**Σειρήν I**, add 'masc., ἀνέθεσαν .. σε̄ρῆνα ἀργύρεον *SEG* 12.391 (Samos, vi BC)' **III**, add 'but in Ael.*VH* 4.2 app. *drone*, cf. Plin.*HN* 11.48' **IV**, for this section read 'in Lxx used to translate words rendered as *ostrich* (or *desert-owl*) and *jackal*, *Jb.* 30.29, *Mi.* 1.8, *Is.* 13.21, 34.13, 43.20, *Je.* 27(50).39'
**σείριος**, line 4, after '*Op.* 417' insert 'Σήριον ἄστρον Alcm. 1.62 P.'; line 6, for 'of *stars* .. 23.62' read 'subst. neut., of all *stars*, σείρια παμφανόωντα Ibyc. 33 P.' and delete 'cf. E.*fr.* 779.8 cod. Longin.'
***σείρωμα**, ατος, τό, *sediment*, defined as κάθισμα ὑδατῶδες ὀποβαλσάμου, Aët. 1.132 (67.14 O., cf. 68.1-2 O.).
***σειρώτης**, ου, ὁ, liquid measure, οἴνου σιρ(ωταί) *PPrag.* I 92.1 (vi/vii AD), σ. οἴνου ἢ ἄλλου τινὸς ὑγροῦ *simussator* (i.e. *cim-*), *Gloss.*
**σεισμός 2**, add 'σ. πυρφόρου *whirring* of a fire-dart, Lxx *Jb.* 41.20'
***σειστημάρχης**, v. °συστημάρχης.
**σεκουνδαρούδης**, for '*secunda rude insignis*' read 'fr. Lat. *secunda rudis*'; add '*IGRom.* 4.831 (Hierapolis), *SEG* 36.595 (Maced., ii/iii AD)'
***σεκούτωρ**, ορος, ὁ, Lat. *secutor*, type of gladiator, *SEG* 32.605 (Thessaly, ii AD), πρωτόπαλος σεκουτόρων D.C. 72.22.
***σέκρετον**, v. °σηκ-.
***Σεκυών**, v. ‡Σικυών.
**σελᾰγέω II**, for 'Opp.*C.* 1.210, 3.136' read 'χαλκὸν σελαγεῦντα Opp.*C.* 1.210, τοῖσι σελαγεῦσιν ὀδόντες ib. 3.352'
**σελᾰγίζω**, after '= σελαγέω II' insert 'Call.*fr.* 238.26 Pf.'
***σελάγινος**, v. °σελγ-.
***Σελᾰμίνιος**, v. °Σαλαμίνιος.
**σελάσκω**, for 'Theognost.*Can.* 11' read 'Theognost.*Can.* 33 A.'
**σέλᾰχος**, after 'τό' insert '*AP* 6.222 (Theodorid.)'

*σελγινος, η, ον, dub. sens., ἱμάτιον σελγινον περιπόρφυρ[ον], *SEG* 38.1210 (Milet., ii BC).
**σεληνάριον**, add 'also perh. *crescent* of land, ἐν τῷ σεληναρί(ῳ) *PMich.*xv 721.47 (iii/iv AD)'
**σεληνῖτις**, add '*PMag.* 4.2360'
**σεληνόβλητος**, delete '*epileptic*'
*σεληνόγονος, ον, *born of the moon*, *PMag.* 3.331.
*σεληνοπετής, ές, *fallen from the moon*, of Musaeus, rest. in Ion ap.Phld.*Piet.* p. 13 (v. *ZPE* 57.54).
*σελία, ἡ, *seat* (= σέλλα), Swoboda *Denkmäler* 110.
**σέλῖνον II**, for 'Sch. .. 10' read '*Carm.Pop.* 6 P.' at end add 'Myc. *se-ri-no*'
**σελῖνοφόρος**, for '*Jahresh.* 18 *Beibl.* 287 (Ephesus, i BC)' read '*IEphes.* 14.20 (i BC)' add '**2** adj., ἅρμα σελινοφόρον *crowned with celery*, Call.*fr.* 384.4 Pf. (οἱ γὰρ νικῶντες τὰ Ἴσθμια σελίνῳ στέφονται Sch.ad loc.).'
**σελίς II**, line 3, for '(Jul.)' read '(Phil.)'
*σελλάριος, ὁ, Lat. *sellarius*, gloss on κέλης, Sch.Gen.Il. 15.679, Suid. s.v. κελητίζειν.
*σελλίς, ίδος, ἡ, *chair* or *bench* (cf. σέλλα), *EM* 398.17.
*σελλοξύλινον, τό, perh. *wooden saddle*, *CPR* 14.32.19 (vii AD).
*σελλοποιός, ὁ, ?*saddle-maker*, *CPR* 14.32.8, 34 (vii AD).
*σελλοφόρος, ὁ, prob. the same as διφροφόρος, *litter-bearer*, Roueché *Aphrodisias* 80 (v/vi AD).
**σέλμα II 1**, add 'Ath.Mech. 18.12'
*σέμεστα, τά, term used w. ref. to linen, perh. either of a measure or of a manufactured item, λινᾶ σ. *POxy.* 3979.15 (iii AD).
**σεμίδᾱλις**, line 4, add 'σιμίδαλιν *SEG* 31.122 (Attica, *c.*AD 121/2)'
+σεμνεῖον, τό, room or building for private or communal worship (in quots., w. ref. to a contemplative sect), Ph. 2.475, 476, Suid., *Gloss.*
**σεμνολόγημα**, add '**III** σχόλια· σεμνολογήματα Hsch.'
*σεμνοπολεύω, *perform sacred rites*, Dioscorus 24.16 (*GDRK* i 150).
**σεμνοπρέπεια**, add 'Ptol.*Tetr.* 206'
**σεμνοπρεπής**, after '*dignified*' insert 'epigr. in *TAM* 2.203.10'; after 'D.L. 8.11' insert 'Mitchell *N.Galatia* 436'
**σεμνοτροπία**, after 'Ptol.*Tetr.* 206 B.' add '(v.l.)'
*σενάτωρ, v. °σινάτωρ.
*Σεουηριανός, ή, όν, *of Severus*, *TAM* 4(1).25, *ICilicie* 30 (AD 222/35).
*σέρκος· ἀλεκτρυών. καὶ ἀλεκτορίδες σέλκες Hsch.
+Σευήρεια, v. °Σεβήρεια.
**σεύω**, line 16, after '(Dor. σῶμαι Epil. 3' insert 'σῶται Hsch.' **II**, line 6, after 'so in trag.' insert '(lyr. exc. E.*IT* 1294)'
**σηκίς**, add 'Sch.Ar.*Pax* 185'
**σηκός III**, add 'Lys. 7.2, 5, 10, al.'
*σήκρητον, τό, Lat. *secretum*, ἐν τῷ σηκρήτῳ in *court*, *POxy.* 1204.12 (AD 299); cf. σέκρετον· συνέδριον Hsch.
**σήκωμα**, after 'Dor. **σᾱ́κωμα**' insert 'also non-Att.-Ion., Lang *Ath.Agora* XXI Hb4 (i BC)' **1 b**, after 'standard *measure*' insert '(variously 5, 6 or 8 *sextarii*)'; add 'Cypr. *sa-ko-ma SEG* 23.608 (v/iv BC)'
**σηλαγγεύς**, for '*gold-refiner*' read '*gold-washer*'
**σῆμα**, for 'Dor.' read 'dial.' **3**, add '**b** *memorial*, ξόανον .. θῆκεν σᾶμ' ἱεραπολίας epigr. in *SEG* 13.422 (Delos, iii BC).' **6**, delete 'mostly in pl.' and add 'Arat. 72, 233, al.'
**σημαίνω A I 1**, at end after 'Pl.*Lg.* 682a' insert 'σ. τι w. gen. of reference, ἀστέρας οἵ κε μάλιστα τετυγμένα σημαίνοιεν .. ὡράων Arat. 12, 757' **3**, line 4, after 'Th. 2.8' insert 'cf. ἐφ' ὕδατι σ. Arat. 873' **B II**, line 4, after '*Ath.* 8' insert 'συνθήκας *REA* 33.8 (Theangela, iv/iii BC)'
**σημάντρια 2**, for this section read 'σαμάντριαν .. πυρᾶς .. ἰωάν *sign*, Call.*fr.* 228.40 Pf.'
**σήμαντρον**, line 3, before 'metaph.' insert '**2** *brand mark*, ἀνδράποδα .. σεσημασμένα τῷ δημοσίῳ σημάντρῳ X.*Vect.* 4.21.'
**σημάντωρ**, line 1, after 'ὁ' insert 'Dor. **σᾱμ-** Simon. 14.62(*a*).3 P., Pi.*Pae.* 13(*a*).24 S.-M.'
**σημᾰσία IV**, for '*Bull.Soc.* .. vi AD)' read 'when the water is at its highest, also the occasion of a festival Σημασία, Bernand *Akôris* 41 (iv AD)'
**σημεία I 2**, add 'κατὰ σημαίαν *by maniples*, Plb. 18.32.11'
*σημειολῠ́της, ου, ὁ, *interpreter of portents*, *Vit.Aesop.*(G) 86, Ps.-Callisth. 1.4.10 (pl.).
**σημεῖον I**, add '**10** *signpost*, Demetr.*Eloc.* 202. **b** of the mark of the Nile at its highest point, Bernand *Akôris* 40, 41 (sp. σημῖον, iv AD); cf. ‡σημασία.' **II 1**, add 'of the image of a Syrian goddess (app. misunderstanding of wd. based on the divine name Semea or Simea), καλέεται δὲ σημήιον καὶ ὑπ' αὐτῶν Ἀσσυρίων, οὐδέ τι οὔνομα ἴδιον αὐτῷ ἔθεντο Luc.*Syr.D.* 33. **b** sent as proof of the genuineness of a communication, etc., *PCair.Zen.* 192 (iii BC), *PPetaus* 28.8, 17 (ii AD), *POxy.* 1683 (iv AD), etc.' add '**IV** = Lat. *signum*, *second name*, *IG* 14.935; cf. °σίγνον III.'
**σημειόω I 1**, add 'σεσημ‹ει›ωμένος *patterned*, *Edict.Diocl.* 19.8' **II 1**, line 3, after 'ii 25 (i AD)' insert '*SEG* 31.1560 (Egypt, Rom.imp.)'
*σημειώσιμος, ον, *entered under the seal* of, εἰς ἐφημερίδα Ἰουλίων Θέωνος καὶ Θέωνος σημιώσιμον Ματρέου *POxy.* 3588.3 (ii AD).
**σημείωσις I**, add '*SEG* 33.1177 (Lycia, AD 43). **2** as a term for *pronoun*, A.D.*Pron.* 4.2.'
**σημειωτός**, add '**II** *patterned*, φακιάλια *Edict.Diocl.* 29.38.'
+σημήϊον, v. ‡σημεῖον.
*σημήτωρ, ορος, ὁ, *indicator*, γραφὴν σημήτορα τύμβου *GVI* 233 (Cius).
+σημοθέτος, ον, poet. **σᾱμ-**, *making a mark*, *AP* 6.295 (Phan.).
*σημοφόρος, ον, *standard-bearing*, κάμαξ epigr. in *SAWW* 224(1).39 (Egypt, ii/i BC).
**σηνοῦροι**, read '**σήνουροι**' and add 'cf. σαίνουρος'
**σηπία**, line 1, after 'ἡ' insert '**σηπίη** Hippon. 166 W.'; line 2, delete 'at Athens'
**σηπιάς**, add 'perh. also σηπιά[δων ..] *SEG* 23.326 (Delphi, iii BC)'
*σηπόγαστρος, ὁ, kind of earthenware vessel, Anon.Alch. 323.18.
**σήπω II 1**, line 6, after 'σέσημμαι' insert 'Ps.-Luc.*Philopatr.* 20'
**σήρ**, delete the article.
*σηρίον· θηρίον Hsch., Lacon.; cf. σηροκτόνος.
**σησᾰμικός**, after '*pertaining to sesame*' insert 'τῶι σησαμ[ι]κῶι σπόρωι [ι *PVat.Gr.* 65 (*Tyche* 5.102)'
**σησᾰ́μινος**, line 3, for 'δοκοί' read 'φαλάγγων σασαμίνων' add '**2** of *sissoo-wood* (*Dalbergia Sissoo*), ξύλα Dsc. 1.129.'
**σήσᾰμον I 2**, add 'Men.*fr.* 709 K.-Th.' add 'form σασάμα or σάσαμον, Myc. *sa-sa-ma*'
**σησᾰμόπαστος**, for 'Dor. **σασ-**' read 'Dor. **σᾱσ-**'
*σησᾰμοσπορεύω, *sow with sesame*, pass. aor. subj. -ευθῆι prob. in *PCair.Zen.* 816.6 (iii BC).
*σησκουπλικάριος, ὁ, Lat. *sesquiplicarius*, *PHamb.* 39.21 (p. 169) (ii AD); also **-κιάριος** *BGU* 614.2.11/12 (iii AD).
**σῆτες**, add 'form prob. *τσάϝετες, Myc. *za-we-te*'
**σητόβρωτος**, add '*PFam.Teb.* 15.36 (ii AD)'
**σῆψις**, line 2, for 'Emp. 121' read '*Orac.Chald.* 134 P.'
**σθενᾰρός**, add 'sp. στεναρός, *SEG* 32.605 (Larissa, ii AD)'
**σθενής**, for 'κρατερός' read 'καρτερός'
*σθενόγαυρος, ον, *exulting in strength*, prob. in *GVI* 263.3 (Phrygia, ii AD).
**σθένος I 1**, line 11, delete 'the only phrase .. (cf. infr. III)'; add 'ἀλλ' εἴτε δόλῳ ἔχουσι αὐτὴν κτησάμενοι, δόλῳ ἀπαιρεθῆναι ὑπὸ ὑμέων, εἴτε καὶ σθένεϊ τεῳ κατεργασάμενοι, σθένεϊ κατὰ τὸ καρτερὸν ἀνασώσασθαι Hdt. 3.65.6'
*σθλιβόω, [?ῑ], *rub*, Anon.Alch. 323.4; cf. θλίβω.
*σιακυκα, ἁ, prob. non-Hellenic name of a cult-object, *Inscr.Cret.* 1.v 23.15 (Arcades, ii AD).
**σίᾰλον I**, add 'pl., Nic.*Th.* 86'
**σίᾰλος**, add 'form σίhαλος, Myc. *si-a₂-ro*'
**Σίβυλλα**, add '**II** *prophetess* generally, Βαλουβουργ Σήνονι (?for Σέμνονι) σιβύλλα̣ *SB* 6221.8 (ostr., ii AD).'
**σῐβύνη**, form συβίνη, add '*SEG* 31.1574 (Cyrene, ii BC)'
**σῑγᾰλόω**, add 'Sch.Pi.*O.* 3.8'
**σῑγάλωμα**, for 'σιγαλόεντα' read 'σιγαλόεν'
**σῑγάω I 2**, after 'E.*Alc.* 78' insert 'τὸν σιγώμενον τόπον *the place where no sound is heard*, Aen.Tact. 22.13'
**σιγγλάριος I**, line 3, for 'etc.' read '*ITyr* 161, *SEG* 29.319 (Corinth, v/vi AD); in late inscrs. and papyri the wd. refers generally to a *courier*, v. *REA* 62.358-9' **II**, add 'cf. *SEG* 28.1624'
*σιγελλᾶτος, η, ον, Lat. *sigillatus*, *figured*, (*embroidered*) *with figures*, ἀγκονάριον ὁλοσιρικὸν σιγελλᾶτον *Tyche* 2.7 (vii AD).
**σῑγητής**, for '*AJA* 37.262' read '*AJA* 37.269'
**σίγλα**, add '**II** *abbreviation*, Just.*Const.* Δέδωκεν 22.'
**σίγλος I 1**, add 'Cypr. *si-ko-lo-ne*, *ICS* 309.13 (coin; at *ICS* 224, 368 abbrev. *si* for weight)' **2**, add 'also σίγλων χρυσείων χιλιάς Alex.Aet. 4.3' **II**, before 'Phot.' insert '*IG* 2².1544.22 (Eleusis, iv BC)' and delete 'cf. sq.'
**σίγμα II 1**, for '*Princeton* .. 560' read '*IGLS* 9122 (v AD), *CIJud.* 781.4 (sp. σῖμμα; Side, Byz.); add 'of a topographical feature of Alexandria, *POxy.* 3756.2 (AD 325)'
**σίγνον I**, add '**2** of the sign of the Cross adopted by Constantine, *Salamine* 238E.' **II**, after '*store*, *prison*, etc.' insert '*GVI* 849.3 (Phrygia, i AD), *POxy.* 3616.5 (iii AD), ὀστιάρ‹ιο›ν σίγνοισι βαλών poet. in *PBodm.* 29.131 (iv AD)' add '**III** *second name*, *GVI* 1096.3 (Propontis, ?i AD), 446.4 (Athens, iii/iv AD); cf. °σημεῖον.'
**σίδη I**, add 'Alcm. in *PMGF* i p. 68 D.'
**σίδηρεος**, line 2, before '*SIG* 144.14' insert 'S.*fr.* 20 R., E.*Ph.* 26, Th. 2.76.4'; line 4, after '**σιδάρεος** [ᾰ]' insert '*CEG* 1 (early v BC)'; line 5, after 'Aeol. σιδάριος' insert '*SEG* 24.361 (early iv BC)' **I 1**, add 'as the name of Roman legion (transl. *Ferrata*), λεγιῶνος ἕκτης Σιδηρᾶς *SEG* 33.1089 (i AD), *IGRom.* 4.266 (iv AD)'
+σῐδηρίσκος, ὁ, Dor. σιδᾱρ-, some unidentified iron implement, *Inscr.Cret.* 4.145 (*SEG* 28.734, v/iv BC).
**σῐδηρίτης I 1**, for 'Eup. 263' read 'A.*fr.* 78a.67 R., Eup. 283 K.-A.'

*σῐδηροδαΐκτης, ου, ὁ, cleaving or destroying with iron, rest. in Trag.adesp. 720k K.-S. (σιδηρο..ίκτης Suppl.Hell. 991.99).

σῐδηρόδετος, add 'of the smith's craft, SEG 31.1284 (Pisidia)'

σῐδηροκόντρα, for 'Ausonia 6.9*' read 'Inscr.Cret. 4.305' and after 'Gortyn' insert 'iii AD'

*σῐδηροπέρσης, ου, ὁ, destroying with iron, Suppl.Hell. 991.93 (poet. word-list, iii BC).

+σῐδηρόπληκτος, Dor. σιδᾱρο-, ον, struck by iron, σιδαρόπληκτοι μὲν ὧδ' ἔχουσιν (i.e. by iron weapons), σιδαρόπληκτοι δὲ τοὺς μένουσιν .. τάφων πατρῴων λαχαί (i.e. by iron tools), A.Th. 911-912.

*σῐδηρόροφος, ον, iron-roofed, Nonn.D. 8.137 (cj.).

*σῐδηροσάνδᾰλος, ον, wearing iron sandals, τ[ὴν σιδη]ροσάνδαλον Suppl.Mag. I 49.59 (ii/iii AD).

σῐδηροφᾰ́γος, add 'Anon.Alch. 344.28'

σῐδηρόψῡχος, add 'PMag. 7.356'

*σίδλι(ο)ν, v. °σιτλίον.

+σῑειδής, ές, godlike (v. σιός), Alcm. 1.71 P.

*σικάριον, τό, fr. Lat. sica, dagger, POxy. 1294.8 (ii/iii AD).

Σῐκελία, add 'personified, SEG 31.925 (Caria, i/ii AD)'

Σῐκελός, delete 'rare in prose' and add 'Σύμμαχος Τιττάλου Σικελός SEG 33.455; IG 2².10291, 10292, al.'

*σικλάριον, τό, prob. dim. of Lat. sicula, small dagger, CPR 8.65.10 (vi AD).

σῐκῠήρᾱτον (s.v. σικυήλατον), add 'also σικύρατον PHamb. 99.7 (i AD), PPrinect. 39.4 (iii AD)'

*σῐκυΐα, ἡ, = σικύα, Them.in APo. 60.1, Suid.; prob. to be rest. in ἐπέθηκε τὰν σικ[υΐαν ἐ]πὶ τὰν γαστέρα Inscr.Cret. 1.xvii 9 (Lebena; if an iambic line).

*σῐκῠοπώλης, ου, ὁ, gourd-seller, PKöln 195.21 (ii/iii AD).

*σῐκύριον, τό, cucumber, PPrinect. 39.7 (iii AD; cf. σικύδιον).

σῐκῠών, line 7, for 'Σικυώνοθε' read 'Σικυωνόθε' and add '[Σ]εκυδναθεν IG 9².209 (Melitea, ?v BC, v. REG 54.61-62'; line 8, for 'the people .. ii BC)' read 'also Σεκυών, Σεκυδ[νι] SEG 11.257 (= 14.310, Sicyon, v BC), cf. ἡ Σικυὼν Σεκυὼν παρὰ Σικυωνίοις acc. to A.D.Adv. 144.20; in inscrs. at Delphi: ΣεϙυϝόνιοςBCH 61.57-60 (vii/vi BC), Σεκυώνιοι GDI 2581.273 (ii BC), but Σικυδνιοι SIG 31.8 (Dor., v BC), Σικυδνιος IG 5.1.1565 p. xxi (iv BC)'

Σῐκῠώνια, add 'also sg., Macho 158 G.'

σικχάζομαι, delete the entry.

*σικχαζόμενος· σκωπτόμενος Hsch.

*σιλβος, η, ον, unexpld. description of kind of tunic, στιχαρομαφόρην (-φόριον) σιλβον PWash.Univ. 58.4 (v AD, ?emend to στιλβόν).

σιλεντιάριος, add 'sp. σελ-, SEG 26.436 (Argos, v/vi AD)'

Σῑληνός, for 'E.Cyc. 13, 82, 269' read 'E.Cyc. 539' 2, add 'b of fountain, orig. in the form of a statue of Silenus, silanos (fr. Dor. Σῑλᾱνός) ad aquarum, Lucr. 6.1265, CIL 8.692, etc.'

+σιληπορδέω, Dor. σιλᾱ-, colloq. wd. popularly associated w. πέρδομαι, behave in a vulgar manner, Sophr. 164, Posidon. 253.46 E.-K.; cf. mod. Gk. τσιληπουρδῶ.

+σιληπορδία, ἡ, vulgar arrogance, Luc.Lex. 21, v. °σιληπορδέω.

σιλίγνιον, for '= Lat. siligo, winter wheat, ibid. (pl.)' read 'prob. = Lat. siligineum, small wheat-loaf, CPR 7.42 i 1, ii 3, 13 (v AD); PKlein.Form. 957.4 (v/vi AD), cf. PMerton 85.9 n.'

+σίλλῡβον, τό, fringe, tassel, τοὺς .. θυσάνους καὶ σίλλυβα οἱ παλαιοὶ καλοῦσιν Poll. 7.64; cf. σίλλυβα· κροσσοί. οἱ δὲ τὰ ἀνθέμια καὶ κοροκόσμια Hsch. 2 kind of thistle, Dsc. 4.155, Ruf.ap.Orib. 7.26.38.

*σῑμᾰ́λος, η, ον, = σιμός, Sch.Gen.Il. 15.705; as pers. n., Anacr. 41 P., al.

*σιμιαις, αιτος, an unidentified food crop, PTeb. 419 (iii AD).

*σιμίσιον, τό, = Lat. semissis, half a gold solidus, Inscr.Cret. 1.xxii 65 (Olus, iv AD).

Σῖμος I, add 'Myc. si-mo, pers. n. (masc.)'

*σιμπλάριος, α, ον, Lat. simplarius, of money, the simple amount paid, πεντήκοντα μυριάδας σινπλαρίας ὃς ἔδωκ[εν BCH 76.655 (Delphi, iv BC).

σίμωρ, for 'field mouse' read 'small mouse-like animal'

σινᾰ́πιον, after 'σίναπι' insert 'Edict.Diocl. 1.34, 35'

*σινάτωρ, ὁ, Lat. senator, TAM 4(1).367.2.

*σινγιλίων, ωνος, ὁ, Lat. singilio, kind of shirt or tunic, Edict.Diocl. 19.47, al.

*σινγουλάριος, -άρις, v. ‡σιγγλάριος.

*σινδόνη, ἡ, cotton garment, Peripl.M.Rubr. 6, 48, 51, al.

*σινδονίσκη, ἡ, dim. of σινδών (garment), Michel 832.24 (Samos, iv BC), Plu. 2.340d: v. MDAI(A) 68.47.24.

σινδονίσκος, delete the entry.

σινδών, line 2, after 'εἰκών' insert 'sp. σιμδώμ ZPE 34.131 (SEG 28.53 + 29.146)'

σίνις I, delete 'ἔθρεψεν .. Ag. 718' and 'as Adj. destroying' II, after 'Corinth' insert 'B. 18.20'

σίνομαι, line 6, after 'σίνω' insert 'Plu. 2.913e'

*σινόργανον, τό, prob. an instrument, or part of machine, for raising water, PMerton 39.2 (iv/v AD), POxy. 1985.11 (vi AD).

σινπλαρία, delete the entry (v. °σιμπλάριος).

+σίντης, εω, ὁ, predator, of the lion, Il. 11.481, 20.165; of the wolf, 16.353; of a snake, Nic.Th. 625; w. fem. subst., σίνταο φάλαγγος ib. 715; acc. to Hsch. s.v. μακεσίκρανος also applied to the hoopoe. 2 robber, despoiler, Opp.H. 4.602, Cat.Cod.Astr. 7.115; humorously, of mice, Call.fr. 177.29 Pf.

*σιόδμᾱτος, v. ‡θεόδμητος.

σῑοειδής, for 'like σίον' read '= θεοειδής' and add 'cf. °σιειδής'

*σιόεις, εσσα, εν, overgrown with σίον, An.Ox. 3.401.34.

*σιοκόλος, ὁ, Lacon. for θεοκόλος, Eup. 480 K.-A. (cj.).

σιοκόμος, delete the entry.

σιός, add 'σιόφιν = θεόφιν, Alcm. 12.4 P.'

σιππινόμεστος, add '(pap. σιπποιν-, cf. °σίππινος)'

*σίππινος, η, ον, made of tow, σάκκος PRyl. 606.22 (iii AD); also σιππόινος (pap. σειππόεινος) SB 11575.11 (iii AD).

*σιπποϊνοπώλης, ου, ὁ, = στυππειοπώλης (cf. σίππιον), PPetaus 92.20 (ii AD).

*σιπποποιός, ὁ, tow-maker, POxy. 2799 (vi AD).

σιπῠΐς, for 'jar' read 'jar similar to pyxis' and add 'RAL 1965.454ff. no. 10 (Gela, iv BC)'

+σίρωμα, v. °σείρωμα.

+σιρώτης, v. °σειρώτης.

σισακικία, delete the entry (v. Tyche 5.180).

σισύμβριον I, for 'bergamot-mint' read 'calamint' II, before 'Poll. 5.101' insert 'Pherecr. 2.3 K.-A.'

*σισύριον, τό, dim. of σισύρα, σεισυριν PDura 33.13 (iii AD).

σίσυς, add 'Semon. 31b W.'

Σῑσῠφία χθών (s.v. Σίσυφος), add 'SEG 31.291 (Corinth, v AD)'

*Σῑσῠφίδαι, οἱ, descendants of Sisyphus, χὠ τᾶς ἀσώτου Σισυφιδᾶν γενεᾶς (i.e. Odysseus) S.Aj. 189; poet. for Corinthians, Call.fr. 384.10 Pf.

σῑτᾰλετικός, add 'μηχανὴ σιταλητικὴ PMich.inv. 257.3 (BASP 13.3, iii AD)'

σῑταποδοχεῖον, for 'Partsch' read 'Patsch'

σῐ́ταρχος (s.v. σιτάρχης), add 'SEG 23.305 (Delphi, c.190 BC)'

*σῑτεκλήμπτωρ, ορος, ὁ, collector of corn, rest. in PAnt. 33.24 (iv AD); cf. ἐκλή(μ)πτωρ.

σῑτεύσιμος, add 'Stud.Pal. 20.233.1 (vi/vii AD)'

σῑτευτάριος, add 'Corinth 8(3).559 (v/vi AD)'

σῑτευωνέω, delete the entry.

σῑτηρέσιον, add 'payment in kind, POxy. 2892, al. (iii AD), PLips. 84 iii 20 (iv AD), PVindob.Tandem 19.15 (v/vi AD)'

σῑτηρός, add 'IV σιτηρά, ἡ (sc. (?)ἀποθήκη), corn-magazine, SB 8754.15, BGU 1742.16, 1743.13 (all i BC).'

*σῑτηρουσία, ἡ, unexpld. compd. of σῖτος (unless for -ουχία), Hsch. s.v. στάχυς.

σῑτικός, line 1, after 'corn' insert 'σ. ἐμπόριον Arist.Ath. 51.4' add 'b σιτική, ἡ, corn-market, SEG 8.43 (Palestine, i AD), ICilicie 124 (i/ii AD), SEG 27.947 (Tarsus, iii AD).'

σῑτισμός, after 'feeding' insert 'IGRom. 4.144.8 (Cyzicus, i AD)'

*σῑτιστάριος, ὁ, fattener of poultry or cattle, Corinth 8(3).559 (v/vi AD).

*σῑτιστός, ή, όν, fattened (= σιτευτός), PMil.Vogl. 145.10 (AD 174).

σίτλα, add 'CPR 8.65.19 (vi AD)'

σιτλίον, add 'written σίδλιν, pap. in JEA 20.27 (v/vi AD)'

σῑτοβολεῖον (s.v. -βολών), add ''Ελληνικά 7.179 (Chalcis, iii BC), IG 9(2).243 (Thessaly)'

*σῑτοθέτης, ου, ὁ, official concerned with supply of corn, SEG 36.788 (Samothrace, iii BC).

σῑτοκᾰ́πηλος, after 'corn-factor' insert 'SB 10447ᵛ.5 (?iii BC), PLond. 44.33 (ii BC)'

σῑτόκρῑθον, for 'mixture of wheat and barley' read 'wheat and barley together' and add 'POxy. 2766 (AD 305), CPR 5.16.11 (AD 486)'

*σῑτομ(ε)ίλης, ου, ὁ, miller, PLond. 387.18 (vi/vii AD).

σῑτομετρέω 2, line 4, after 'IGRom. 3.679 (Tlos)' insert '(ἄνδρες) σιτομετρούμενοι members of privileged class in some Lycian cities, who received special allocation of grain, SEG 27.938, 30.1535.8 (both ii AD), TAM 2.578'

σῑτομέτρης, add ''Ολυμπίου σιτομέτρου ITyr 188, 189 (Rom.imp.)'

*σῑτομετρικός, ή, όν, of or concerned with measuring corn, σειτομετρ[ι]κῶν [χρησ]τηρίων PVindob.Salomons 5.13 (AD 192).

σῑτοπώλης, add 'σιτοπῶλη (nom. pl.) SEG 23.271 (Thespiae, late iii BC)'

σῖτος, line 2, delete 'only' and after 'Delph. 3(5).3 ii 19 (iv BC)' insert 'de Franciscis Locr.Epiz. no. 28' I 1, add 'b meton., corn-market, SEG 26.72.18 (Athens, iv BC).' add 'Myc. si-to'

*σῑτοσπορία, ἡ, sowing of grain, POxy. 2973.25 (AD 103; sp. σειτ-).

*σῑτοτᾰμῐεύω, serve as *σιτοταμίας (corn-treasurer), AE 1933 suppl. 2, IG 9(2).1029, 1093 (all Thessaly).

*σῑτοφάκη, = °σιτόφακον, PRainer Cent. 137 (vi AD).

***σῑτόφᾰκον**, τό, *wheat and lentils*, *POxy.* 3406.4 (iv AD).

***σῑτοφθόρος**, ον, *grain-destroying*, τὰ κοπροφόρα καὶ σιτοφθόρα ζῷα Sch.Nic.*Al.* 115a Ge.

**σῑτοφύλᾰκες I**, add '*SEG* 26.72 (Athens, 375/4 BC)'

****σῑτοχόϝος**, ὁ, *one who dispenses grain*, Myc. *si-to-ko-wo*.

***σῑτόχρωμος**, ον, *wheat-coloured*, ἵππος μο[υ θ]ήλεια σειτόχρωμο[ς *PMich.*IX 527.8 (ii AD).

***Σιττηνή**, ἡ, local name for a mother-goddess, *IHadr.* 33 (AD 160/1).

**σῑτών**, add '**2** *granary*, *SEG* 9.354 (Cyrenaica, ?i AD), Gr.Naz.*Carm.* 2.1.11.1267.'

**σῑτωνέω**, for '*buy corn*' read '*serve* or *hold office as* σιτώνης' and add '*TAM* 4(1).262.3'

⁺**σῑτωνικόν**, v. °σιτωνικός.

***σῑτωνικός**, ή, όν, *concerned with the purchase of corn*, [ἐπι]δόσεις -κάς *Didyma* 296.4, χρήματα *PASA* 3.612 (Ilias); n. sg. subst., *wheat-fund*, *Inscr.Délos* 399 A 73 (ii BC), σ. καταναλισκομένου *IG* 4.2.8 (Aegina, i BC); n. pl., *IG* 2$^2$.1272.3 (iii BC), 1708 (ii BC), *IGRom.* 4.580 (Aezani).

**σιφλός I**, delete 'of fish, *mad on food*, *greedy*' and transfer 'Opp.*H.* 3.183' to section II, prefixing 'perh.'

***σίφνον**· σιπύα Hsch. cf. id. s.v. σιπύη.

**σῑωπή I 1**, add '**b** *pause* between sounds, D.H.*Comp.* 22.'

**σιωπηρός**, add '**2** *tacit*, *implied*, σ. ἐλευθερίαν Just.*Nov.* 22.11; adv. -ρῶς ib. 118.5.'

***σῑωπητικόν**, τό, *novice's fee* in mystery cult, *PMich.*VIII 511.3 (iii AD).

**σκαιωρία**, after '*mischief*' insert 'Procl.CP *Hom.* 27.2.4, Just.*Nov.* 63.1'

**σκᾰλεύω**, add 'fig., Aq.*Ps.* 76(77).7'

***σκᾰλῐδευτής**, οῦ, ὁ, *hoer*, *PCair.Zen.* 816.9 (iii BC), *SB* 797.8, 25 (iii BC).

**σκᾰλίς**, delete 'or *shovel*' and add '*IG* 1$^3$.422.140 (v BC)'

***σκᾰλιστρον**, τό, prob. = σκαλιστήριον, Aq.Sm.*Je.* 50.10.

***σκαλλόν**, σκαλλίον .. οἱ δὲ σκαλλόν Hsch.

**σκάλλω**, add '*hoe in*, *Gp.* 2.24.1'

***σκᾰλοβᾰτικός**, ή, όν, *of climbing a ladder*, ἡ σ. (sc. τέχνη) Rh. 5.22.25.

***σκαλώνια**· τὰ ἀσκαλώνια (ἀσκωρώνια cod.) Hsch.

***σκαμβίς**· θερμοποτίς Hsch.

***σκαμνοκάγκελος**, ὁ, app. *railing separating benches*, *ISmyrna* 844 (iv/v AD), cf. Lat. *scamnum*, *cancellus*.

**σκάμνος**, add '**σκάμνον**, τό, *PDura* 33.12 (iii AD)'

**σκανδῑκοπώλης**, for 'as Ar. called Euripides' read 'sobriquet applied in comedy to Euripides from his mother's alleged occupation'

**σκᾰπᾰνεύς**, add 'Cret. καπανεύς *Inscr.Cret.* 1 xxv 2 (Pyloros, ii BC); cf. σκάπετος, κάπετος'

**σκᾰπᾰνη II**, add 'Men.*Dysc.* 542'

***σκάπαρδος**· ὁ ταραχώδης καὶ ἀνάγωγος Hsch. Also **σκάπερδος**, σ.· ὁ δυσχερής Suet.*Blasph.* 122 T.

**σκαπέρδα**, add 'acc. to Hsch., πᾶν τὸ δυσχερὲς σκαπέρδα λέγεται καὶ ὁ πάσχων σκαπέρδης'

***σκαπέρδης**, v. °σκαπέρδα.

***σκαπλάριον**, τό, prob. = Lat. *scapulare*, *PRyl.* 713$^v$.2 (iv AD).

***σκάρηνα**, ἡ, name of fish, *IGC* p. 98 B23 (Acraephia, iii/ii BC).

**σκᾰρισμός**, add 'ὄνον σκαρ(ισμῷ) ἴχνους *PColl.Youtie* 47.3 (AD 145)'

**σκᾰρῖφος**, after 'Hsch.' insert 'τῶν δέκα ῥητόρων σ., their *score*, i.e. a *list* of them giving the number of speeches each made, Sch.Aeschin. 2.18'

***σκαστός**, v. °σχαστός.

**σκᾰτοφᾰγέω**, add 'Men.*Sam.* 427'

**σκαῦρος**, for '*with deviating hoof*' read 'of the feet, *bent* or *twisted outwards*'

***σκαφεία** (?), ἁ, perh. a kind of σκαφεῖον, *spade*, σκαφ[είας] (gen.) rest. in list of temple implements, *PP* 42.42 (Tarentum, vi BC).

**σκάφη I 4**, for '*grave*' read '*sarcophagus*'

**σκᾰφηφορέω**, add 'Harp., Phot.'

**σκᾰφηφόρος**, for 'Phot.' read 'σκαφηφόροι .. ἀντὶ τοῦ μέτοικοι· οὗτοι γὰρ ἐσκαφηφόρουν Ἀθήνησι Harp.'

**σκᾰφιον** (A) **II 2 c**, add 'Gal. 18(1).777.5'

**σκᾰφιστήριον**, add 'cf. Lat. *caphisterium*'

**σκᾰφοειδής**, after '*Arat.* 19' insert 'of the *scaphoid* bone of the ankle' transferring 'Gal.*UP* 3.6' to follow this and adding 'id. 2.776, cf. *PLit.Lond.* 167.27'

**σκᾰφόπλωρος**, delete the entry.

***σκαφόπρωρος**, ον, prob. *round-prowed*, *POxy.* 3031 (AD 302), *PCair.Preis.* 34.16 (iv AD); also rest. in *BGU* 812 ii 2 (ii/iii AD).

**σκεδάννῡμι**, line 1, after 'Nic.*Al.* 583' insert '**σκεδάζω**, Hsch.; poet. also **κεδάννυμι**, **κεδαίω**, qq.v.'

**σκεδασμός**, add 'Procl.*Inst.* 13 D.'

***σκειρᾰφέω**, v. °σκιραφέω.

***Σκειρόμαντις**· ὁ ἐπὶ Σκ[ε]ίρῳ μαντευόμενος Hsch.; cf. Σκίρος.

**σκέλος**, add 'prob. Myc. *ke-re-a$_2$*, *legs* of tripod-cauldron'

***σκέλος** (B), εος, τό, app. some form of tax or other payment, *PAvrom.* 2.A9, B10 (i BC); perh. = σίγλος, σίκλος.

***σκεπᾰνισμός**, ὁ, *covering*, prob. of woven material, *PTeb.* 1077.6 (iii BC).

***σκεπαρνᾶς**, ᾶ, ὁ, *maker of adzes*, *SEG* 29.628 (Maced.).

**σκεπαρνηδόν**, add 'Gal. 18(2).728.12'

**σκέπαρνον I**, line 2, after 'Homeric passages' insert '*A.fr.* 78c.51 R.'; add 'app. set up as (temporary) memorial for the dead, τῷ ἀνδρὶ αὐτῆς ἔθηκε τὸ σκέπαρνον *IGBulg.* 2254 (ii/iii AD)' at end delete '[Hom. .. Σκάμανδρος.]'

**σκέπη II**, add '**3** *temporary dispensation from public duties* (cf. Lat. *vacatio*), *SEG* 38.1462.102 (Oenoanda, AD 124/6).' add '**III** transl. Lat. *castellum*, *garrison*, in bilingual inscr., *SEG* 31.952 (Ephesus, Trajan).'

**σκέπτομαι II**, line 6, after '*Cra.* 401a' insert 'w. gen., τῶν ἄμυδις πάντων ἐσκεμμένος Arat. 1153'

***σκεπτώριον**, τό, *mirror*, *PMasp.* 340$^v$.40 (-ωριν).

**σκέπω**, after 'freq. in later prose' insert '*Peripl.M.Rubr.* 8'; add 'imper. in invocations, θ(εοτό)κε, σκέπε *SEG* 30.1262 (Halic.), 1266 (Hyllarima, both Byzantine)'

***σκεπώνιον**, τό, *storehouse*, *PAberd.* 191.8 (pl., iii AD).

**σκευᾰγωγέω**, add 'Philostr.*VA* 2.14'

**σκευάζω I 2**, line 2, after 'ib. 313' insert '*construct*, *put up* monument, *TAM* 4(1).115 (Rom.imp.).'

***σκευαρίδιον**, τό, *small vessel*, ἐν ἑτέροις σκευαριδίοις *SB* 11075.6, 16 (v AD).

***σκευᾶς**, ᾶ, ὁ, Lat. *scaeva*, *gladiator fighting with his left hand*, Robert *Les Gladiateurs* no. 34 (Philippopolis), no. 178 (Iasos).

***σκευαστικός**, ή, όν, *artificial*, *prepared*, τὸ ἐφήμερον σκευαστικόν ἐστι φάρμακον Sch.Nic.*Al.* 249b Ge.

**σκευοθήκη**, add 'written **σχεοθ-** *SB* 7182.46 (i BC)'

***σκεῦον**, τό, = σκεῦος I, *Inscr.Cret.* 1.xvii 2a8 (Lebena, ii BC).

**σκεῦος IV**, for this section read '*sarcophagus*, *IEphes.* 2227 (ii AD), *SEG* 24.568(b) (Maced., ii/iii AD), *MAMA* 8.580 (Aphrodisias, iii AD)'

**σκέψις 3**, *the Sceptic philosophy*, add 'personified, *SEG* 34.1667 (v AD)'

***σκηνᾰγωγός**, ὁ, *boat with an awning*, *BGU* 1933.4 (ii BC).

**σκηνίτης I 1**, line 4, after '*a stall*' insert 'Isoc. 17.33' **2**, delete the section.

***σκηνοπάροχος**, ὁ, *one who furnishes stage-scenery*, *SEG* 38.1462.44 (Oenoanda, AD 124/6).

**σκηνορράφος**, add '(sp. σκηνοράφος) *IGBulg.* 2198'

***σκηπτίτης**, ου, ὁ, precious stone, Socr.Dion.*Lith.* 32.1 G.

**σκηπτός**, line 3, for 'metaph. also of a dust-*storm*' read 'applied to a violent eddy of dust'; line 4, delete '*hurricane*' and transfer quots. to exx. of '*thunderbolt*'

**σκηπτοῦχος 1**, add 'as title of the emperor Theodosius III (died AD 450), *BCH* suppl. 8 no. 88; pl. of cosmic powers, Orph.*H.* 10.25'

⁺**σκηπτοφόρος**, v. °σκηπτρο-.

**σκῆπτρον I**, line 3, for 'used by the lame or aged' read 'used as an aid in walking' **II 1**, last line, delete 'S.*OT* 811' **2**, add 'Just.*Const.* Δέδωκεν 23' add '**3** as a symbol of divine power, invoked in imprecations, *SEG* 32.1222 (Lydia, i AD), 33.1029 (ii AD), etc.'

**σκηπτροφόρος**, for '*Delph.* 3(1).510.3 (iv BC)' read '*BCH* 116.589, 593 (Athenian epigr. at Delphi, iv BC)' and add 'also Dor. σκᾶπτρο- *AP* 7.428 (Mel., v.l. σκαπτο-). **b** subst., *staff-bearer*, of annual priests at Seleuceia Pieriae, *OGI* 245.22, 45 (ii BC).'

**σκήπτω I 2**, add 'σκήπτομαι κατὰ χειμῶνα, of a trierarch, *enter a plea* (*that the ship was destroyed*) *by storm*, *IG* 2$^2$.1631.344; also pass., of a ship about which such a plea was entered, ib. 1629.746.1.' **II 1**, for 'med. .. A.*Eu.* 801 (s.v.l.)' read 'μήτε τῇδε γῇ βαρὺν κότον σκήψητε A.*Eu.* 801 (cj.)' and delete 'Pass. .. *IG* l.c.'

**σκῆψις**, line 7, delete '(sc. τὰ τέκνα)'

**σκῐά 2**, add '*mirror-image*, Diogenian. 2.4'

**σκῐᾰγρᾰφέω 1**, add 'Bas.Sel.*HP* 3.29 (sp. σκιογ-)'

***σκῐᾰγρᾰφή**, ἡ, = σκιαγραφία, Poll. 7.128 (v.l. σκιαγραμμή).

**σκῐᾰεις**, add 'χθονὸς ὀμφαλὸν σκιάεντα prob. in Pi.*Pae.* 6.17 S.-M.'

**σκῐάζω**, line 3, after 'pf. ἐσκίασμαι' insert 'Sapph. 2.7 L.-P.'

**σκίαινα**, add 'Gal. 6.724, Ath. 7.322f, Opp.*H.* 1.132, al.'

**Σκῐᾰποδες**, add 'Alcm. 148 P.'

***Σκιέρεια**, τά, festival of Dionysus at Alea, Arcadia, Paus. 8.23.1.

***σκιλλίτης**, ου, ὁ, (*wine*) *seasoned with squill*, Afric.*Cest.* 2.6.12 V.

⁺**σκίμπους**, ποδος, ὁ, simple kind of bed or pallet, *IG* 1$^3$.423.8, 425.11, Ar.*Nu.* 254, 709, Pl.*Prt.* 310c, X.*An.* 6.1.4; suspended as a litter, Gal. 6.150.

**σκίμπτομαι**, for '*press forward*' read '*press*, or *throw*, *down*' add '**IV** act. intr., Hsch. s.vv. σκίμψαι and σκίμπτει.'

***σκινδακίζω**, denominative vb. fr. *σκίνδαξ (cf. κίνδαξ, σκίναξ), σκινδακίσαι· τὸ νύκτωρ ἐπαναστῆναί τινι ἀσελγῶς Phot., Hsch. (s.v. σκίνδαρον).

***σκινδάρ(ε)ιος**· ὄρχησις οὕτω καλουμένη Hsch.

***σκίνιψ**, ὁ, = σκνίψ, contemptuous term for an old miser, Suet.*Blasph.* 217 T. (cod. κύνιψ), cf. *sciniphes* Petron. 98.1.

***σκῐογρᾰφέω**, v. °σκιαγ-.
**σκίπων**, add 'as an emblem of rank, Plb. 32.1.3'
**σκῑρᾰφεῖον**, add 'Luc.*Lex.* 10'
***σκῑρᾰφέω**, *behave deceitfully*, σκειραφεῖν· κακοπραγμονεῖν Hsch.
**σκῑρᾰφος**, add 'Suet.*Lud.* 1 T.'
**Σκίρος**, add 'see also °Σκειρόμαντις'
***σκιρρωδῶς**, v. °σκιρώδης.
**Σκίρτος**, add 'also as a name for gladiators, *SEG* 30.1257 (Aphrodisias)'
**σκῑρώδης**, add 'adv., σκιρρωδῶς *so as to form a callus*, Gal. 8.475.10, 9.163.9, 12.59.6'
**Σκίρων I**, add 'τοῦ Θρασκίου μὲν ἐν τῷ Πόντῳ, Σ. δὲ ἐν τῇ Ἑλλάδι καλουμένου *Peripl.M.Eux.* 4.2'
⁺**σκίφη**, ἡ, dub. sens., cf. perh. σκνιπός (A), καί τινος ποιητοῦ σκίφης μεστοὺς εἶναι τοὺς στίχους Crantor ap.D.L. 4.27.
⁺**σκῖφος**· ὁ παρ' ἡμῖν λεγόμενος σκνιπός, ἢ τὸ ξίφος (v. σκῖφός) Suid.
**σκληρός I 2**, add 'Arr.*An.* 1.17.6'
***σκληρουργός**, ὁ, *quarryman*, *SEG* 31.1557 (Egypt), inscr. in *ZPE* 98.122 no. 11 (Egypt, i AD).
***σκληρόχειρ**, gloss on λαϊνόχειρ, Hsch.
**σκνῑπός** (A), add 'Sch.Ar.*Pl.* 84'
**σκνίψ**, for 'acc. σκνίπας [ῐ] Ezek.*Exag.* 135' read 'acc. σκνῖπας Ezek. *Exag.* 135a S.' and add 'cf. °σκίνιψ'
***σκοδίσκος**, ὁ, wd. occurring in inventory of household furniture, *PLond.* 191.4 (ii AD).
**σκοῖδος**, add '*EAM* 74 (iii/ii BC)'
**σκόλεφραι**, after 'κατακεκαυμέναι' insert '(κατακεχυμέναι Theognost.*Can.* 71 A.)'; add 'cf. σκολοφρή'
⁺**σκολιοδρόμος**, ον, *running on an indirect course*, of the nymphs of underground streams, Orph.*H.* 51.4; of the moon, Man. 4.478.
**σκόλιον**, for '*song which went round crookedly at banquets*' read 'kind of drinking-song'
***σκολλύφιον**, τό, app. kind of hair-style, Hsch. s.v. κόρυφος.
**σκολόπενδρα 2**, before 'Ael.*NA* 7.26' insert '*AP* 6.222 (Theodorid.), 223 (Antip.)'
**σκολοπισμός**, add '**II** *protection by palisades*, prob. in *SB* 7188.13 (ii BC); cf. σκολοπίζω.'
**σκολοφρή**, add 'cf. ‡σκόλεφραι'
***σκόλυπνον**· κεκακωμένον Theognost.*Can.* 71 A.
**σκολύφρα**, add 'σ.· πόρνη Theognost.*Can.* 71 A.'
***σκοπελάριος**, ὁ, *watchtower guard*, *OFlorida* 6.8 (?ii AD), *SB* 9549(4).8 (iii AD).
***Σκοπελία**, ἡ, cult-title of Artemis, *IG* 4².505 (Epid.).
***Σκοπελῖτις**, ιδος, ἡ, cult-title of Artemis, *SEG* 35.989.10 (Knossos, ii/i BC).
**σκοπή I**, add 'of observation point for divination through birds, *Inscr.Perg.* 8(3).115'
**σκοπιάζω I 2**, for 'Isis-worshippers' read 'fishermen' and for '(Callipolis)' read '(Parium), cf. Robert *Hell.* 9.81'
**σκοραδᾶν**, for '*Docum.* .. (Cyrene)' read '*SEG* 9.35 (iii BC), 41 (ii BC, both Cyrene)'
**σκορδᾶτον**, add 'perh. also *POxy.* 1923.15 (v/vi AD)'
**σκορδευτής**, add '*BGU* 1530.7'
**σκόρδιον 1**, add 'ostr. in *ZPE* 98.138 no. 29.4 (Egypt)'
***σκορδίσκος**, ὁ, *saddle*, σκορδίσκον στρατιωτικόν *Edict.Diocl.* 10.2 (*SEG* 37.335 iii 2).
***σκορδόω**, = σκοροδόω, Poll. 5.93.
**σκόροδον I**, add 'Ar.*Th.* 494, etc., perh. w. play on obscene sense "penis" (cf. *Philol.* 127.139ff.)'
***σκοροδύλη**· θαλάσσιος ἰχθύς. ἔνιοι κορδύλη Hsch.; cf. σκορδύλη.
**σκορπέρως**, τος, for '*BCH* 2.323' read '*Inscr.Délos* 1414*a*i17 (ii BC)'
**σκορπίζω 1**, add '*spread* manure, *PSoterichos* 1.26 (AD 69), 2.21 (AD 71), *BGU* 2354.8 (ii AD)'
**σκορπιόδηκτος**, add 'Heras ap.Gal. 13.786.13'
**σκορπίος II**, add '*IGC* p. 98 A24 (Acraephia, iii/ii BC)'
**σκορπισμός**, add 'ἄμμου *PMil.Vogl.* 52.106, 117 (ii AD)'
**σκοτερός**, after '= σκότιος' insert 'θάλαμος epigr. in *IG* 9².340.8 (Thyrrheum, ii/i BC)'
***σκόρτια**, ἡ, Lat. *scortea*, *coat made of hide*, *Edict.Diocl.* 10.16, 16a (*SEG* 37.335 iii 16, 16a).
**σκοτία III**, for this section read 'Σκοτία, epith. of Aphrodite in Phaestus, Crete, *EM* 543.49; cf. perh. σκότιος I 2; also in Egypt, Hsch.'
**σκότιος I 1**, line 8, for 'rare in Prose .. Charax 6' read 'poetic term for "illegitimate", Plu.*Thes.* 2, νόθος καὶ σκότιος id. 2.751f; παῖς σ. Charax 6'
***σκοτοείμων**, ον, gen. ονος, *dark-clad*, χθών *Hymn.Is.* 27.
**σκοτοιβόρος**, add 'also **σκοτοιβόρᾱς** Suet.*Blasph.* 99 T.'
**σκοτομήνιος**, add 'νύκτ[ες .. σκοτο]μήνιοι Hes.*fr.* 66.5 M.-W.'
***σκοτόταφρος**, ὁ, ?*hidden trench*, cod. B in Ps.-Callisth. 3.23.
***σκοτουλᾶτος**, v. ‡σκουτουλᾶτος.
**σκοτόω**, line 1, after '*Aj.* 85' insert '*fr.* 269a.30 R.'
**σκουτάριος**, add '*SEG* 37.1081 (Nikomedeia, iv AD)'
**σκουτλάριος**, delete 'or .. *flooring*'
**σκουτλόω**, for '*mosaics*' read '*a covering of thin plates of marble arranged in patterns* (*opus sectile*)'; add 'τὰς εἰσόδους καὶ ἐξόδους *AC* 2.74 (Aphrodisias; lapis κουκλόσαντα after wd. ending in -ς)'
**σκούτλωσις**, after '*chequered work*' insert '*decoration with opus sectile*, v. °σκουτλόω'
⁺**σκουτουλᾶτος**, ον, Lat. *scutulatus*, *with a checked pattern*, of material, *Peripl.M.Rubr.* 24 (written σκοτ-), *Edict.Diocl.* 20.11 (σκουτλ-), Lyd. *Mag.* 1.10.
***σκρείβας**, α, ὁ, Lat. *scriba*, *BCH* 7.275 (ii AD), *POxy.* 59.9 (iii AD), *PColl.Youtie* 79.12 (iv AD).
***σκριβηνδάριος**, ὁ, app. *secretary*, *SEG* 36.1335 (Beersheba, vi AD).
***σκρίβων**, ωνος, ὁ, officer of the imperial guard, Agath. 3.14.5, *scribon(o)s* *SEG* 34.927 (Crete, vi AD).
**σκρῑνιάριος**, add '*MAMA* 5.309 (Nacolea, v/vi AD; sp. ἰσκρην-)'
**σκύζομαι**, before '*to be angry with*' insert '*to growl at*'; line 5, after '(Il.) 9.198' insert 'Theoc. 16.8, 25.245; also act. 'σκύζουσιν· ἡσυχῇ ὑποφθέγγονται, ὥσπερ κύνες Hsch.; cf. σκύζειν (cod. σκυζᾶν) Poll. 5.86'
**σκυθάριον**, for 'θάψος' read '*smoke-tree*, *Rhus cotinus*'
**Σκύθης I 1**, for 'Hes.*fr.* 55' read 'Hes.*fr.* 150.16 M.-W.'; add 'prov., ἡ ἀπὸ Σκυθῶν ῥῆσις of brutal plainness of speech, Demetr.*Eloc.* 216, D.L. 1.101' **II**, for 'τοξότης III' read 'τοξότης II'
**Σκυθία**, after '**Σκυθίηνδε**, ib. 256' insert '**Σκυθίηθεν**, epigr. in *SEG* 39.855 (Patmos, iii/iv AD)'
**Σκῠθικός I**, add 'as the title of a Roman legion, *SEG* 33.1194 (Cappadocia, i/ii AD), λεγεῶνος τετάρτης Σκυθικῆς *ICilicie* 87 (ii AD)' **II**, add 'also Σκυδικαί, Hsch.'
**σκῠλάκαινα**, add 'applied to Hecate, εἰνοδία σ. θεά *AAWW* 1961.125 (Maeonia, ii AD)'
⁺**σκῠλάκευμα**, ατος, τό, *whelp*, *cub*, *AP* 7.433 (Tymn.); pl., Διὸς σ. (σκυλεύματα cod.), of Amphion and Zethus, *AP* 3.7 (Inscr.Cyzic.), ib.16.91 (ii BC).
**σκῠλακῖτις**, for '*protectress of dogs*' read '*mistress of dogs*'
**σκῠλακοκτόνος**, add '= *Lyr.adesp.* 1029.2 P.'
**σκῠλακώδης**, after '*dog*' insert 'φωνή *PMag.* 4.2810'
**σκῡλάω**, delete 'dub. .. Cyzic.' and add '**2** *plunder*, τὸν ναόν *UPZ* 6.22, cf. 15 (ii BC). **3** = σκύλλω I 2, *AP* 3.6, *GVI* 1946.14 (Nicaea, Bithynia, ii/iii AD).'
**σκῡλεύω 1**, line 7, for '*BCH* .. Cypr.' read '*SEG* 6.802 (Salamis, Cyprus, ii/iii AD)'; add 'obsc., κατευδούσης τῆς μητρὸς ἐσκύλευε τὸν βρύσσον Hippon. 70.8 W.'
**σκυλήτρια**, add 'Eust. 1072.64'
***σκυλίζω**, = σκυλεύω, ἐσκούλιξε *Boeot.adesp.* 39 *fr.* 5.3 P.
**σκύλλω I 1**, line 4, before 'Pass.' insert '*tear* or *rend apart*'; add '*SEG* 39.340 (Corinth, Rom.imp.)' **2**, for '*AP* 3.6 (Inscr.Cyzic.)' read 'cj. in *AP* 3.6 (Inscr.Cyzic.) v. ‡σκυλάω'
**σκυλτικός**, add 'Heph.Astr. 2.33.15, 2.36.15,16'
***Σκῡριανός**, ή, όν, of Scyros; name of a kind of marble, *Edict.Diocl.* 33.14.
***σκύρον** (B), ὦ σ., wd. of uncertain meaning, Alc. 167.3 L.-P. (cf. 58.13, 174.2), app. voc.sg. of *σκύρων.
**σκῦρος**, for 'cf. Poll. 9.104; cf. σκῖρος' read 'the centre line in the game ἐπίσκυρος, as marked out w. stone chippings, Poll. 9.104; hence perh. ἐπὶ σκύρῳ (or σκύρων; ἐπισκυρῶν cod.) πολέμοιο Call.*fr.* 567 Pf.(v. *CR* 73.101ff.)'
**σκῠτάλη**, line 11, after 'ἀχνυμένη σκυτάλη' for '(dub. sens.)' read '(v. *CQ* N.S. 38.42ff.)' add '**VI** σκυτάλαι· αἱ ἱππικαὶ ἶλαι .. ἢ θύλακες δερμάτινοι Hsch.'
**σκῠτάλιον I 2**, delete '*flute*' and 'perh. so in Thphr.*HP* 4.4.12' **5**, for '*BCH* 29.546 (Delos, ii BC)' read '*Inscr.Délos* 1432*Ba*i12, 1409*Aa*i111 (ii BC)'
**σκῠτάλος**, add '*BGU* 2361a i 3 (iv AD)'
***σκῠτᾰλοφορέω**, *carry a* σκυτάλη, of heralds, Sch.Pi.*O.* 6.154a (prob. for σκυτοφορεῖν).
**σκυτίς**, for '*amulet*' read '*amulet-case*'
**σκῠτοτομεῖον**, for 'Macho ap.Ath. 13.581d' read 'Macho 359 G.' and for 'v.l.' read 'cod.'
**σκῠφίον**, after 'σκύφος' insert '*Inscr.Délos* 320*B*53 (iii BC), 1409*Aa*i105 (pl.)'
***σκῠφισμός**, ὁ, form of *operation on the scalp*, *An.Boiss.* 1.230.
**σκύφος**, penultimate line, before 'Anaximand.' insert 'Anacr. 88 P.'; add 'sp. σκόφος *SEG* 24.361 (Thespiae, iv BC)'
***σκώη**· παιδίσκη Theognost.*Can.* 71 A.; cf. σκῶ.
***σκωληκοβρωσία**, ἡ, *eating by worms*, *PMasp.* 325 II$^{v}$ 16 (vi AD).
***σκωληκοέρημος**, ον, perh. *laid waste by worms*, *PTeb.* 1043.40 (ii BC).
**σκώληξ**, after 'ὁ' insert '(also ἡ acc. to Eust. 1504.39)'

**σκῶλον II**, for '*stumbling-block* .. σκάνδαλον' read '*thorn in the flesh, affliction*'

***σκωπελαδᾷ**· τὸ σχηματίζεται Theognost.*Can.* 71 A.; cf. σκώψ 2.

**σκωπτικός**, after '*jesting*' insert 'Ph. 1.215.19'

**σκωπτόλης**, add 'Philostr.*VA* 1.7'

**σκωρσελεινα**, add 'written **σκωρσελήνης** in *PMich.*III 212.8 (ii/iii AD); perh. *celeriac* (σκῶρ, σέλινον)'

**σλιφομαχος**, for 'Cyrenaic' read 'Arcesilas'

**σμᾰράγδιον**, add 'written **ζμαράγδιον** in *Inscr.Délos* 1409*Ba*ii02 (ii BC)'

**σμᾰραγδος I**, ζμάραγδος, add 'also in pers. n., *SEG* 24.1076 (Moesia, ii/iii AD)'

**⁺Σμᾰρᾰγος**, ὁ, mischievous demon supposed to cause pots to break during firing, Hom.*Epigr.* 14.9.

***σμενία**, app. Dor. for σμινύη, *PP* 42.42.9 (ii BC).

***σμερδᾰλεότης**, ητος, ἡ, *awesomeness*, Eust. 1702.46.

**σμηματοθήκη**, add '*IG* 2².1469.97'

***σμῆνιγξ**, ιγγος, ἡ, = μῆνιγξ, prob. in Nic.*Th.* 557.

***σμηνών**, ῶνος, ὁ, = σμηνιών, *BCH* 22.402 (ζμη-; Olymus, i BC).

***Σμῑκρίνης**, ου, ὁ, a typical skinflint, pers. n. in com. Men.*Epit.*, *Asp.*, Jul.*Caes.* 311a, Them.*Or.* 34 p. 462 D.

***σμῑλεύω**, *carve*, ἐσμιλευμένος κατακεκομμένος Hsch. (cod. ἐσμηλ-).

**Σμίνθεια**, add '*Ilion* 125.8, 14 (ii/iii AD)'

***Σμινθεῖον**, τό, *sanctuary of the Smithian Apollo*, *IGRom.* 4.246.3 (Troas).

**Σμινθεύς**, add 'cf. Myc. *si-mi-te-u*, pers. n.'

***σμῐνύδιον**, τό, dim. of σμινύη, Ar.*fr.* 889 K.-A.

**σμιρεύς**, add '[σμ]ιρεύς *SEG* 18.743 (Cyrene, iii BC); app. abbrev. *ΣΜ*, *SEG* 9.44 (Cyrene)'

**Σμῑσιών**, after 'name of month' insert 'deriv. of Σμίνθος'

**σμόρδωνες**, add 'cf. pers. n. Σμόρδōν *SEG* 28.37 (Camarina, vi BC)'

**⁺σμῡρίζω**, = μυρίζω, ἐσμυριχμένας Archil. 48.5 W.; cf. Hsch. ἐσμυριχμέναι.

**σμύρις**, line 3, after 'Orib. 15.1.20 codd.' insert '**σμεῖρις**, εως, ἡ, *IEphes.* 23.18 (ii AD)'

**σμύρνα**, after '**ζμύρνα** as in' insert 'Hyp.*Ath.* 6'

***σμυρνίτης**, ου, ὁ, λίθος σ., precious stone, Socr.Dion.*Lith.* 46.1 H.-S.

**σμῶδιξ**, line 3, after 'cf.' insert 'Lyc. 783'

**σοβᾰρεύομαι**, add 'Hsch. s.vv. σοβαρεύεσθαι and σοβαρεύεται'

**σοβᾰρός II**, add '**3** adv. -ρῶς, colloq., *tremendously*, *POxy.* 3356.14 (i AD).'

**σόγχος**, delete '(where ἐξογκοῖτ' is a pun on ἐκσογκοῖτ')'

***σόκκος** (B), ὁ, Lat. *soccus*, *slipper*, *Edict.Diocl.* 20A, 21, al.

***σόλδιον**, τό, name of coin, Anon.Alch. 324.15, cf. Lat. *solidus*.

***σολέμνιος**, α, ον, Lat. *sollemnis*, *customary*, Just.*Edict.* 13.13; neut. pl. subst., *customary services* or *expenditures*, ib. 13.14, 21.

**σόλιον**, after '*PSI* 206.9 (iii AD)' insert '(sg. used to denote a pair)'

***σολίτης**, ου, ὁ, *sandal-maker* or *-seller*, σο‹λ›ίτι καὶ καμισογοραστῇ *Corinth* 8(3).522.

**σολοικιστής**, add 'cf. Hsch. s.v. Βρίγες'

***σολοιτῡπ[ίη**, *product of forging at Soli*, i.e. bronze, dub. rest. in Call.*fr.* 85.11 Pf. (αμφισολοιτυπ[ pap.; could be divided ἀμφὶς ὀλοιτυπ[).

**σολοιτύπος II**, before '*forged*' insert '(proparox.)'; add '(prob. alternative expls. of wd. w. single meaning)'

***σονωπτώριον**, τό, wd. in inventory of receptacles and vessels, *BGU* 2360.9 (iii/iv AD), perh. for συν-, cf. συνοπτάω.

***σορέλλην**, νος, ὁ, app. = σορέλλη, Suet.*Blasph.* 213 T.

**⁺σορίδιον**, τό, *little coffin* or *urn*, Hierocl.*Facet.* 97; τὸ σορίδιον ἄγγος *TAM* 2(3).1164.2 (Lycia).

***σορικόν**, τό, name of an eyesalve, Aët. 7.107 (374.9 O.) (s.v.l.).

**σόριον**, add 'σόριν ὑποκίμενον *ITyr* 31'

**σοροπηγός**, add 'Lib.*Or.* 1.225'

**σορόπληκτος**, add '= Suet.*Blasph.* 211 T.'

**σορός**, line 1, after 'ἡ' insert '(app. ὁ, *ITyr* 10)' **I**, transfer 'Ar.*V.* 1365' fr. section II, and add 'on an ossuary, *SEG* 31.1405 (Jericho, i AD); of a mummy, *PHaun.* 17.14 (ii AD)' **II**, for this section read 'derogatory term for old man, Macho 301 G., Luc.*D.Meretr.* 11'

**σορώϊον**, for '*cerecloth*' read '*mummy-dressing*'

***σουβαδιούβας**, α, ὁ, Lat. *subadiuva*, *under-assistant*, *POxy.* 1042.13 (vi AD), *BCH* suppl. 8 no. 148 (Thessalonica, v/vi AD).

***σουβαλάρι(ο)ν**, τό, Lat. *subalare*, *SEG* 37.335 iii 10 (*Edict.Diocl.* 10.10).

**σοῦβος**, for 'an unknown animal' read '*wild sheep* or *goat*'

**σουβρίκιον**, after '*subricula*' insert '(dim. of σουβρικός, cf. *rica*)' and add '*PMich.*III 201.8 (i AD)'

**⁺σουβρικός**, ὁ, article of clothing, *PCornell* inv. I 11 (*ZPE* 22.53, AD 59), σουβρικός *superaria*, *Gloss.*

***σουβσκριβενδάριος**, ὁ, app. *under-secretary*, *SEG* 9.356.66 (Cyrene), 32.1554A (Arabia, both vi AD); cf. °σκριβενδάριος.

***σουγγεστίων**, ονος, ἡ, Lat. *suggestio*, *the supplying of an answer to one's own question*, *Cod.Just.* 4.59.1.1.

***σουγλάριον**· ἐργαλ(ει)οθήκη Hsch.

***σουμάριον**, τό, Lat. *summarium*, *summary*, Iambl.Alch. 289.9.

***σουμμάριος**, ὁ, Lat. *summarius*, title of official on the staff of a *comes*, Just.*Nov.* 30.1.1, 30.7.1.

***σουμμαρούδης**, ὁ, fr. Lat. *summa rudis*, chief instructor at a gladiatorial school, *AS* 20.39 no. 4 (*BE* 1971.670), *SEG* 36.595 (Maced., ii/iii AD).

***σοῦμμος**, ὁ, Lat. *summus*, *highest in rank*, σ. κουράτωρ *PBeatty Panop.* 1.393, 395, 2.28; σ. εἴλης fr. Lat. *summus alae*, *CPR* 6.76.8 (ii/iii AD). **2** a position on the board in the game of τάβλη, *AP* 9.482.9 (Agath.).

**Σουνιεύς**, add 'ἐξουννιέων (i.e. ἐκ Σ.) *SEG* 24.226 (i BC/i AD)'

***σουπερνουμεράριος**, ὁ, Lat. *supernumerarius*, *supernumerary*, (ἑκατοντάρχῳ) σουπερνουμεραρίῳ *PBeatty Panop.* 2.183, 264, 269, 289 (AD 300).

***σοῦφον**, τό, app. kind of vessel or measure, cf. ὀκτάσουφος, τρίσ-, *PMich.*inv. 3725 (*ZPE* 61.80, iv AD).

***σουφρουμεντάριος**, ὁ, Lat. **suffrumentarius*, *corn supply assistant*, *POxy.* 1903.7 (vi AD).

**σοῦχος**, after 'ὁ' insert '(Egypt. *sehu*)'

**σοφία**, line 1, delete 'prop.' **2**, add 'Lxx *Pr.* 1.7' **4**, for this section read 'personified in Jewish "wisdom" literature, Lxx *Pr.* 8, *Si.* 24, etc.'

**σοφιστικός 1**, after 'id.*Sph.* 224c' insert 'σ. σχήματα *characteristic of sophists*, Hermog.*Meth.* 13'

**σοφίστρια**, add 'Cels.ap.Orig.*Cels.* 5.64'

***σοφοδῐδάσκᾰλος**, ὁ, *teacher of wisdom*, prob. of a rabbi, inscr. in *Sardis from Prehistoric to Roman Times. Results of the archaeological exploration of Sardis 1958-1975*, ed. G.M.A. Hanfmann, (Cambridge Mass. 1983), pp. 183, 189 (v AD).

***σπάδη**, ἡ, = σπάθη, *SEG* 7.376.17 (Palmyra, ii AD).

****σπᾱδίκινος** (?), v. °σπανδίκινος.

***σπᾱδίκιον**, τό, dim. of σπάδιξ, *IG* 14.956*B*25 (Rome, iv AD).

**σπᾰδων**, add '**2** *gelding*, *PCair.Zen.* 802.22, 28, 33 (iii BC).'

**σπᾰθᾰρικόν**, for '*thin upper-garment*' read 'prob. *closely woven veil*'

***σπᾰθᾰρικός**, ή, όν, *of* or *used by a* σπαθάριος, σπαθαρικὴ μάχαιρα *BGU* 2328.10 (v AD).

***σπᾰθᾶς**, ᾶ, perh. *cutter* or *swordsmith*, *PBerl.Bork.* (*Tyche* 6.235).

**σπᾰθάω II 1**, add 'σπαθήσῃ (v.l. -εις) ἐπὶ τούτῳ (sc. ἔρωτι) *you will waste your strength* on this, Luc.*Luct.* 17'

**σπᾰθη 5**, add 'synecd. *sword*, *SB* 1.21 (iii AD), Just.*Nov.* 85.4' add '**10** perh. a vase-shape, *AJA* 45.598 (graffito on amphora).'

**σπᾰθίζω**, add 'Aët. 15.13 Z.'

***σπᾰθινος**, η, ον, *woven* or perh. *close-woven*: τὰ σ. articles of dress, Aq.*Is.* 3.19 (L.-R.); cf. σπαθαρικόν.

**σπαίρω**, for 'of dying fish' read 'esp. when near to death' and add 'Apollod. 3.13.6'

**⁺σπάλαθρον**, = σπάλαυθρον, σκάλευθρον, etc., *fire rake* or *poker*, Poll. 10.113; fig., of an officious person, Suet.*Blasph.* 164 T.; prob. Myc. *qa-ra-to-ro*, app. a utensil.

***σπανδίκινος**, η, ον, app. colour term describing a στρόφος, (perh. for *σπαδίκινος, cf. σπάδιξ 2, *bay*, *red*), *SEG* 38.1210.19 (Miletus, ii BC).

**σπάνιος I**, add 'of precious stones, λίθοις ποικίλιος τοῖς ἀρίστοις καὶ σπανιωτάτοις πολυτελείᾳ *SEG* 39.1055.10 (Neapolis, AD 194); λίθος ὁ σ. the *rare* stone (owned only by the king of Persia), Socr.Dion.*Lith.* 28.1 H.-S.'

**σπᾰνός**, line 1, after 'Hsch.' insert '*beardless* (as mod. Gk.), Anatolius in *Cat.Cod.Astr.* 8(3).188'; after 'Ptol.*Tetr.* 144' insert '(v.l.)'

**Σπᾱνός 1**, add '(λιθάργυρος) Σπάνη Dsc. 5.87; masc. pl. subst., ἔπαρχο]ν σπείρης β' Σπανῶν *INikaia* 56 (Hadrian). **b** ἐλαιὸν Σπανόν, a kind of oil, *PSorb.* 62.1, *POxy.* 2052 (vi AD); also Σπανόν, τό, *Gp.* 9.26, *POxy.* 1862.' **2**, before '*grey*' insert '*Spanish*, referring to a certain textile colour'

***σπᾰνοτεκνία**, ἡ, *paucity of offspring*, rest. in *Cat.Cod.Astr.* 2.163.9.

**⁺σπαπιπρώτας**, α, ὁ, app. a priest with some function at sacrifices, *IPamph.* 3.17, 24 (Sillyon, iv BC).

***σπᾰρακτός**, ή, όν, *torn*, rest. in A.*fr.* 451s.10.2 R.

**σπαρνός**, for 'poet. for σπανός, σπάνιος' read '*sparse*, *scarce*' and add 'Hes.*fr.* 66.6 M.-W.'

**σπαρτίνη**, add 'Poll. 7.114'

***σπαστήρ**, ῆρος, ὁ, perh. = ἐπισπαστήρ, *SEG* 21.559.7 (Athens, iv BC).

**σπάω III 1**, lines 3/4, after 'Alex. 5, cf. 285' insert 'w. gen., ἀκράτου Ath. 613a'

***σπεγκρᾶνίς**, v. °ἐπεγκρανίς.

***σπειλες**, pl., perh. *gut strings*, *BGU* 2361b i 11 (iv AD); cf. σπίλα Hsch.

**σπεῖρα I 8**, add '*PHib.* 217.20, al. (ii AD)'

**σπείρᾱμα 1**, delete 'metaph. .. *App.Anth.* 3.186'

**σπειράομαι**, line 2, delete 'πέριξ ..'

**σπειράρχης**, after 'σπεῖρα II 2' insert '*RA* 6.31 (Amphipolis, ii BC), *IGBulg.* 1517.4 (Philippopolis, iii AD)' *__σπειρόω__ (B) (or ?__σπορόω__), *sow*, εἰ δὲ σποιρώσωμε φασούρια ἐπ' ἔτη *PMich.*xiii 666.33 (vi AD).

**σπείρω I 3**, line 5, after 'S.*El.* 642' insert 'cf. A.*fr.* 78a.65 R.'

*__σπείρωμα__, ατος, τό, dub. sens., Aq.*Je.* 50.10 (v.l.).

**σπεκλάριον**, add 'Cyran. 25.1, Zos.Alch. 139.2'

**σπέκλον 1**, add '**b** prob. *window-pane*, *PWisc.* 66.1, 5 (AD 584), *POxy.* 1921.12, 13 (AD 621).'

**σπεκουλάτωρ**, line 1, before 'ορος' insert '(σπεκλάτωρ *BE* 1959.260 (Tomi))'

*__σπεκταβίλιος__, α, ον, Lat. *spectabilis*, title of the middle rank of Roman senators, cf. ‡περίβλεπτος, Just.*Nov.* 24.4, al.

**σπένδω**, line 6, after 'Plu.*Rom.* 19' insert 'subj. σπε̄σθέωσι *SIG* 57.8 (Milet., v BC)' **I 1**, at end before 'οὗτος θεοῖσι' insert 'ὅταν οἱ κρητῆρες σπε̄σθέωσι *SIG* l.c., βωμὸς Διὸς .. μέλιτι σπένδεται *IG* 12(5).1027 (Paros, *c.*500 BC)'

**σπέος**, for '*Inscr.Cypr.* 98 H.' read '*se-pe-o-se*, *ICS* 2.2; 3.3'

**σπέρμα I 1**, add '*crops* generally, τὰ σ. Lxx 1*Ki.* 8.15, *SEG* 33.1041 (late ii BC)' **II 1**, for 'φέρειν' read 'φέρων' and for 'to be pregnant *of*' read 'bearing *the seed* of' add 'Myc. *pe-ma*, var. sp. *pe-mo*'

**σπερμαίνω 2**, after 'Hes.*Op.* 736' insert '*fr.* 1.16 M.-W. (cf. *CPh.* 81.221-222)' and add 'of the female, Gal. 4.536.9, 593.10; w. internal acc., γόνιμον σπερμαίνειν id.*UP* 14.7 (II 302.13 H.)'

*__σπευδίας__, α, ὁ, kind of wheat having a light yield, Plin.*HN* 18.64.

**σπεύδω**, line 1, after 'σπεύσω' insert 'A.*Ag.* 601'

*__σπευσίδωρος__, ον, *eagerly bringing gifts*, of Prometheus, A.*fr.* 204b.12 R.

**σπήλαιον 1**, add 'in cult-title, Μητρὶ ἀπὸ σπηλαίου *SEG* 34.1293 (Phrygia, Rom.imp.)' **2**, delete the section.

**σπῐλάς** (A) **I**, at end for 'Simon.(?) 179' read '*AP* 6.217.2 ([Simon.])'

**σπινθήρ**, after 'Plb. 18.39.2' insert 'σπινθῆρα τῆς ψυχῆς (i.e. spark of life) εὗρεν ἐν αὐτῇ Philostr.*VA* 4.45'

**σπινθηρίζω I**, add '**2** transf., *sparkle*, Epiph.Const. in *Lapid.Gr.* 195.10.'

**σπῑνός**, for '= ἰσχνός' read '*gaunt*, *lean*' and add 'Ptol.*Tetr.* 144'

*__σπλαγχνοεντεριφόρον__, τό, tray for carrying σπλάγχνα and ἔντερα, σπλα̣ν̣χνοεντεριφό̣ρ̣ον *Kafizin* 285 (iii/ii BC).

**σπλάγχνον**, line 1, at end insert 'also fem. pl., σπλάνχνας *SEG* 31.895 (Africa)'

**σπογγίτης**, after '*like a sponge*' insert 'ἄρτος σ. Hsch. s.v. κύστη' and delete 'only' before 'fem.'

*__σπογγοκέφᾰλος__, ὁ, *spongehead*, pers. description in *CPap.Jud.* 512.1 (vi/vii AD), *SB* 4668.6, 7 (vii AD).

+__σποδησιλαύρα__, term for a prostitute, σ.· ἡ πόρνη, λεγομένη οὕτω παρὰ τὸ διατρίβειν τὰ πολλὰ ἐν ὁδοῖς ἢ καὶ δημοσίᾳ συμπλέκεσθαι Suet.*Blasph.* 33 T., κατὰ τὴν κωμῳδουμένην σποδησιλαύραν Eust. 1088.37, Hsch.; cf. σποδέω.

*__σπολάδιον__, τό, dim. of σπολάς, rest. in *IG* $2^2$.1648.20 (Delos, v. *BCH* 62.249f.).

**σπονδαυλέω, σπονδαύλης**, for '*flute*' read '*pipe(s)* or *aulos*'

*__σπονδειοδάκτῠλος__, ὁ, *metrical foot consisting of spondee and dactyl*, Rh. 6.103.20.

**σπονδεῖον I**, add '**4** τὰ σπονδεῖα a festival of Heracles, *SEG* 39.148 (Attica, iv BC).'

*__σπονδέριον__, τό, perh. = σπονδάριον, *PAmst.* 68.25 (ii/iii AD).

**σπονδή II 1**, line 10, for 'less freq., .. 5.76' read 'σ. ποιεῖν *arrange a truce*, Th. 5.76.2, ἐκείνων (sc. τῶν θεῶν) .. σ. ποιούντων Ar.*Pax* 211'

*__σπονδιστήριον__, τό, perh. *place for drink-offering*, *SEG* 38.1321.2 (Pisidia, ii/iii AD).

**σπονδοποιός**, add '*Sokolowski* 1.57 (Caria)'

*__σπονδοφόρον__, τό, *libation-tray*, *CISem.* 2.3923 (Palmyra).

*__σπονδῠλοκόπος__, ὁ, app. some kind of unqualified practitioner, *quack*, οἱ σπονδυλοκόποι μιμοῦνται τοὺς γραμματικοὺς καὶ εὐδοκιμοῦσιν ἐν αὐτοῖς Sch.Hermog.*Id.* 2.5 in Rh. 5.536; cf. σφόνδυλος, etc.

**σπορά I 1 b**, add 'designating the father (opp. mother), ἡ γαστὴρ τῆς σπορᾶς προκρινέσθω Just.*Nov.* 162.3'

*__σπορᾰ́διος__, α, ον, *scattered*, *sporadic*, ἀμπ(ελοι) σπ[ο]ράδιοι καὶ ἐλάινα καὶ ἕτερα φυτά *PPetaus* 17.4 (*c.*AD 184).

**σποραῖος**, after '= σπόριμος' insert '*CPR* 1.45.7, perh. also *PMich.*inv. 3761 (*Tyche* 1.181)'

*__Σποργίλος__, ὁ, pers. n., w. play on name of bird, prob. *sparrow*, Ar.*Av.* 300; cf. (σ)πέργουλος, mod. Gk. σπουργίτης.

**σπορητός 3**, add 'Gal. 17(1).18.2'

*__σπορητός__ (B), ή, όν, = σπορευτός, ἐν ἀμπέλοις, ἐλαιῶσιν, σπορητοῖς τόπ[οις] *BCTH* NS 19b.109.

**σπόριμος 1**, fem. -η, add 'σποριμην αὔλακα Call.*fr.* 22 Pf.'; line 5, for '*BCH* 51.149 (Salamis Cypr.)' read '*SEG* 6.802 (Salamis, Cyprus, ii/iii AD)'

**σπόρος I**, add '**3** *sown land*, *PLond.* 1980.4 (iii BC), *PEnteux.* 60.4.9.' **II 4**, after '*semen genitale*' insert 'Nic.*Al.* 582'

*__σπορόω__, v. °σπειρόω (B).

**σπουδαιότης**, add '*CPR* 8.20.2 (iii AD)'

**σπουδάρχης**, for 'σπουδαρχίας' read 'σπουδαρχίαις'

**σπουδαστής**, add 'also prob. *student* (as in mod. Gr.), *CPR* 8.10.10 (ii/iii AD)'

**σπουδή II 1 a**, add 'σπουδῇ w. gen., *by the efforts of*, *SEG* 30.1687 (Palestine), 1690 (Arabia, both vii AD)' **III**, add 'acc. as adv. (unless error for dat.) *zealously*, Mitchell *N.Galatia* 120 (AD 124)'

**σπύλιον**, after '*IG* $2^2$.1358' insert '*B*10'

**σπύλων**, delete the entry.

+__σπῡρᾰ́μῐνος__, η, ον, Dor. form of πυράμινος; neut. pl. as subst. *wheat-flour*, *SEG* 9.13 (Cyrene, iv BC, prose); cf. °σπυρός.

**σπῠράς**, add 'Eup. 15 K.-A.'

**σπῠρίς**, form σφυρίς, add 'Men.*Sam.* 297, *PSI* 543.54 (iii BC)'

+__σπῡρός__, ὁ, Doric form of πυρός, *IG* $4^2$.40.8, 46.38 (Epid., v BC), *SIG* 1026.9, 1027.11 (Cos, iv BC), *SEG* 9.11, 12, al. (iv BC), 18.743 (iii BC), 9.42, 43 (ii BC, all Cyrene), *An.Ox.* 1.362, *EM* 724.33.

**σταβλάριον**, delete the entry (v. ‡ταβλάριος).

**σταβλίτης**, for '*official in the posting service*' read '*stableman*' and add '*SB* 9920 ii 7.1, 9.12, 10.2 (σταυλ- pap.; vi AD)'

**στάβλον**, add 'for race-horses, *SEG* 34.1437 (Syria, v/vi AD)'

**σταγματοπώλης**, add '*POxy.* 3748.6 (AD 319)'

*__στᾰδιάρχης__, ου, ὁ, *one in charge of the race-course* or *arena*: transf., of Christ (w. prothetic vowel), εἰσταδιάρχη νικηφόρε Χ(ριστ)έ *SEG* 32.1588 (Egypt, vi/vii AD); cf. as pr. n. of bull, Robert *Les Gladiateurs* 191C (Cos).

**στᾰ́διον II 3**, add 'κυκλοῦντες τὸ σ. going round *the walk*, Lxx *Su.* 37'

*__στᾰδόν__, adv., (ἵστημι) *in standing position*, Theognost.*Can.* 58 A.

**στάζω II 1**, add 'fig., of divine anger, Lxx *Je.* 49(42).18, 51(44).6'

**σταθμάω II 2**, add 'τἀρετῇ σταθμώμενος τὰ πάντα *Trag.adesp.* 327 K.-S.'

*__σταθμηδόν__, gloss on στήδην, Sch.Nic.*Al.* 327a Ge.

**Σταθμία**, add 'of Ennodia, *IG* 9(2).577 (Larissa)'

**σταθμός I 1**, line 10, for 'A.*Pr.* 398' read 'A.*Pr.* 396' add 'Myc. *ta-to-mo*, *sheepfold*, *pillar*, perh. also weight'

**σταθμοῦχος I**, add '*BASP* 16(3).196.6 (iii AD)' add '**III** prob. *subdivision of an* ἄμφοδον, *SB* 9869 a3, b3 (AD 160).'

**σταῖς I**, line 1, after 'not στᾶς' insert 'but στάς "ἄνευ τοῦ ι" in Attic acc. to Phot., dat. στᾱτί (sic) Sch.Hippon. 118D6 W.'

*__στᾰ́λαχμος__ or -υχμος, ὁ, cj. for σταλαγμός in Sapph. 37 L.-P.

**στᾰ́λιξ**, add 'transf., of the spines of the sargue, Opp.*H.* 4.606'

*__στᾱλογρᾰ́φος__, v. °στηλο-.

**στάλσις**, add '**2** gloss on στόλος, Sch.Pi.*P.* 8.140, Sch.Pi.*N.* 3.27.'

**στᾰμίν**, add 'of structures in house, epigr. in *SEG* 30.1272.4 (Caria, Hellen./Rom.imp.)'

**σταμνίον 1**, for 'Men. 129' read 'Men.*Dysc.* 448'

*__σταμνίσκιον__, τό, *small jar*, Phot. α 1198 Th.

*__στάμνον__, τό, = στάμνος, Φιλοξένης τὸ στάμνον *SEG* 33.1238 (Bactria, ii BC, s.v.l.).

**στάμνος**, line 4, after 'D. 35.32' insert '*vase*, *IG* $1^3$.425.48ff.'; line 8, as a measure, add 'Lang *Ath.Agora* xxi Ha54'

*__στάς__, αδός, fem. adj., *standing*, στάδα λίμνην *Suppl.Hell.* 1055.

**στᾰ́σιμος II 1 b**, line 5, for '*BCH* .. Cypr.)' read '*SEG* 6.802 (Salamis, Cyprus, ii/iii AD)'

**στάσις B I 2 a**, add '*military station*, *garrison*, Lxx *Jd.* 9.61' **III 2**, after '*discord*' insert 'Alc. 130.26 L.-P.'

*__στᾱτίας__, ὁ, kind of bread or cake, gloss on σποπία, Hsch.; cf. σταιτίας, ‡σταῖς.

*__στᾰ́τιον__, τό, dim. of στατός I 2, *Inscr.Délos* 1441*A*ii34 (ii BC).

+__στατίων__ or __στατιών__, ωνος, ἡ, (ὁ, *OGI* 755.4 (Miletus)), *military guard-post*, *TAM* 2.1165 (acc. στατίωναν), *SEG* 2.666 (Bithynia, iii AD). **2** *association of foreigners* in town or their meeting-place, *OGI* 595.5, al., 755.4, Robert *Hell.* 7.198 (Puteoli, ii AD).

**στατιωνάριος**, for '= *stationarius*, *IG* 14.830.32' read 'member of a °στατίων (sense 2), Robert *Hell.* 7.21'

*__στατοῦτος__, η, ον, Lat. *statutus*, *fixed*, *determined*, στατοῦτον ἀριθμόν Just.*Nov.* 16 rubric; neut. subst. *fixed amount*, *complement*, etc., ib. 3.2.1.

**σταυροειδής**, adv., before 'Hsch.' insert 'Anon.Alch. 321.11'

*__σταυροποιία__, ἡ, *crucifixion*, *POxy.* 2339.25 (i AD).

*__σταυροφόρος__, ὁ, *bearer of the cross*, Ἰησοῦ Χ(ριστ)ῷ] κυρ(ίῳ) σταυροφόρῳ *SEG* 30.1542 (Lycaonia, iv AD).

**στᾰφιδευταῖος**, add '*PColl.Youtie* 87.11 (vi AD)'

*__στᾰφίδιον__, τό, *dried grape*, *raisin*, *PFreib.* 4.67 (ii/iii AD).

**στᾰφίς I**, for '(q.v.)' read '(q.v. with Suppl.); *SEG* 9.11, 12, al. (Cyrene, iv BC), Hp.*Acut.* 64, Theoc. 27.10, *AP* 5.304'

**στᾰφῠλή I**, add '**3** τοῦ ζυγοῦ τὸ μέσον Hsch. **4** kind of sea-weed, Ael.*NA* 13.3 S.'

**στᾰφῠλητόμος**, after 'Nonn.*D.* 7.165' add '(cj. for -κόμ-)'

*__στᾰφῠλικός__, ή, όν, *of* or *concerning grapes*, τῆς σταφυλικῆς προσόδου *SEG* 33.1041.23 (Cyme, Aeolia, ii BC).

*__στᾰφῠλῑνάριον__, τό, dim. of σταφυλίνος I, *PRyl.* 629.214 (iv AD).

***σταφυλοβόλος**, ον, perh. *of* or *for grape-pressing*, πλίνθοι *IG* 1³.425.39 (Athens, v BC).

***σταφυλοπατητής**, οῦ, ὁ, *grape-treader*, *PVindob.Salomons* 8.25 (AD 325).

***σταφυλοτόμος**, ον, = σταφυλητόμος, *excising the uvula*, *Suppl.Mag.* I 1 (iii AD).

**στάχι**, add '(Egyptian wd., Theognost.*Can.* 78)'

**σταχυηκόμος**, add 'epigr. in *SEG* 13.277 (Patrae, iv/v AD)'

**σταχυητρόφος**, add '*GVI* 720'

***σταχύινος**, η, ον, *of ears of wheat*, στέφανος *Inscr.Olymp.* 56.15.

**στάχυς** VII, delete the section.

**στέαρ**, line 1, for '**στέαρ** .. sub. fin.]' read '**στέᾱρ**, 'ατος, τό'; at end for '[Gen. .. στεάτιον]' read '[gen. στέατος disyll. by synizesis, Od. l.c.]'

***στεατῖτις**, ιδος, ἡ, a precious stone, Plin.*HN* 37.186.

***στεατότριπτος**, ον, *rubbed with fat*, rest. (as σταιατο-) in *PSoterichos* 4.17 (*Tyche* 3.277-8, AD 87).

**στεγανόπους I**, delete the section, adding 'Alcm. 148 P.' to section II.

**στεγανός I**, add '**3** *costive*, νηδύς Nic.*Al.* 367.' **II 1**, add 'neut. as subst., οἱ δὲ Ῥωμαῖοι στεγανὰ ποιήσαντες παρεχείμαζον D.S.*fr.* 33 (ap. Suid. s.v.)'

***στέγαξις**, v. στέγασις.

**⁺στεγάσιμος**, ον, *used for awning* or *roofing*, πάπυροι σ. *PLond.* 1940.58 (iii BC).

**στέγασις**, line 3, at end for 'iv BC' read 'iii BC'

***στεγάστριον**, v. °στέγαστρον.

**στέγαστρον 1**, add 'also **στέγεστρον**, *PRyl.* 627.38 (iv AD), *Edict.Diocl.* 8.42A; cf. ‡σέγεστρον; also **στεγέστριον**, ib. 8.43A; cf. **στεγάστριον**, Hsch. s.v. λαρίεθος'

**στέγη II 1**, after '*room*' insert 'A.*fr.* 362.3 R.'

***στεγνοκοίλιος**, α, ον, *suffering from constricted bowels, constipated*, Aët. 3.92 (295.9 O.).

***στεγνοποιΐα**, ἡ, *building of shelters*, rest. at *SEG* 14.656.14-15 (Caunus, ii BC); cf. περιστεγνοποιΐα.

**στεγνοποιέω**, after 'Med.' insert '*PHal.* 1.172 (iii BC)'

**στεγονόμια**, add '**2** *buildings, premises*, Just.*Nov.* 40 pr. 1.'

***στεγόω**, *roof over*, Sch.Pi.*P.* 4.426.

***στεία**, v. °στία.

**στεῖρα** (B) **I**, after 'Od. 10.522' insert 'Theoc. 9.3'

***στελλάριον**, τό, *star-shaped object*, or = στειλειάριον, *haft* (v.s.v. στελεός), *CPR* 8.66.12, 17 (vi AD).

**⁺στέλμα**, ατος, τό, some personal item, perh. *girdle*, listed in a magic spell, *PMag.* 7.785; cf. στέλμα· στέφος, στέμμα Hsch.

**στέμμα I 1**, add 'fig., ἀρετῆς .. πάσης στέμμασιν κοσμούμενος *SEG* 30.1562 (?ii AD)'

**στέμφυλον**, add '**III** used to translate wd. meaning "dross", Aq.*Is.* 1.22 (L.-R.), 25.'

***στεμφυλουργικός**, ή, όν, *of* or *for wine-pressing*, στεμφυλουργικὸν ὄργανον *POsl.* 145.3 (ii/iii AD), *POxy.* 2723.9 (iii AD).

**στενακτικός**, after '= sq. 2' insert 'Sch.E.*Hipp.* 415'

**στεναχή**, add '*SEG* 23.233 (Tegea, ii BC, verse)'

**στενολεσχέω**, add '**2** *use compression in discourse*, Eust. 1552.52.'

**στενός II 3**, line 7, after '(Hdt.) 7.175' insert 'Call.*fr.* 1.28 Pf.'

**στενότης**, add '**III** *financial straits*, *BCH* 59.440 (Acraephia, i AD).'

**στενοχωρέω**, line 1, for '*confined*' read '*short of room*' and for 'Macho ap.Ath. 13.582b' read 'Macho 396 G., σ. σταθμοῖς *PPetr.* 2 p. 28 (iii BC)'

**στένω**, add prose exx.: **1**, D. 18.217, 323, id.*Ep.* 3.44; Plu. 2.117a, b, 193f, Luc.*DDeor.* 6.2, *DMort.* 2.1, 27.2. **2**, w. ἐπί, D. 18.244. **3**, Luc.*Asin.* 21.

**⁺στεργάνος** (dub.)· κοπρών (κόπρων cod.) Hsch., cf. Lat. *stercus*, *sterculinum*.

**στέργηθρον I**, add 'Plin.*HN* 25.160'

**στέργω III 2**, add 'Lys. 33.4' **3**, add 'Isoc. 8.23, al.'

**στερεός I 1 b**, after 'σ. τάλαντα' insert '(in context app. = Ἀττικὰ τάλαντα)'; for '*SIG* 826*D*20' read '*Delph.* 3(4).279' and after this quot. insert 'τῶν στερεῶν ὀνομάτων, perh. *substantial* accounts, *POxy.* 2861 (ii AD)' add '**6** *sure, reliable*, adv. -ρεῶς, *with certainty*, φωνῆσαι Sch.Nic.*Th.* 1 C.'

**στέρεσις**, add '*SEG* 35.1439 (Lycia, ii AD)'

***στέρνα**, ἡ, = στέρνον, *POxy.* 108.11, al. (ii/iii AD).

**στέρνον II 1**, add 'Pi.*Pae.* 4.14 S.-M.' **2**, after 'Nic.*Th.* 924' insert 'ἐν στέρνῳ .. θυείης ib. 91'

***στερνοτύπος**, ον, = στερνοτυπής, γόος epigr. in *JEA* 40.119.19 (Egypt, ii BC); ἀνῖαι *GVI* 1006.5 (Rhenea, i BC).

**Στερόπης**, add 'see also °ἀστεροπός'

**στερρότης I**, after 'Ph. 1.276' add '*POxy.* 3581 (iv/v AD)'

**στέρφος I**, after 'cf. τέρφος, ἔρφος' add 'στρέφος'

**στέρψανον**, add 'cf. στρέφανον'

***στεφανᾶς**, ᾶ, ὁ, *wreath-maker*, *ISmyrna* 504.

**στεφάνη I 2 a**, add 'perh. forming part of the decoration of a prow, *SEG* 37.692 (Delos, ii BC)'

**στεφανηφορία**, add '**III** *office of* στεφανηφόρος, *SEG* 30.1390 (Lydia, c.AD 150).'

**στεφανηφόρος I**, add 'poet., of spring, *Anacreont.* 55.1 W.' **III**, for this section read 'of Attic drachmas of the New Style bearing wreath on the reverse, ἀργυρίου Ἀττικοῦ -ου δραχμαί *Inscr.Délos* 1415.12; δραχμαὶ (τοῦ) στεφανηφόρου (sc. ἀργυρίου) *IG* 2².1013.33, 1028.30, al.; also δραχμὴ στεφανηφόρος, τέτραχμον -ον *Inscr.Délos* 1443*A*ii62, 1442*A*70, al. (all ii BC)'

***στεφανοπωλία**, ἡ, *selling of crowns* or *chaplets*, *Anatolia* 9.38.58.

**στεφανόπωλις**, after 'ιδος' insert 'Arist.*Ath.* 14.4'

**στέφανος II 3**, add 'Swoboda *Denkmäler* 168, 245 (Palaia Isaura)'

**στεφάνωμα**, line 2, after 'Thgn. 1001' insert '*Inscr.Délos* 1421*Bb*ii3 (ii BC)'

**στεφάνωσις**, add 'tab.defix. in *SEG* 34.1437 (Syria, v/vi AD)'

**στεφανωτικόν** (s.v. στεφανωτικός), add '*SEG* 33.1123 (Phrygia, iii AD)'

***στεφάριον**, τό, an unidentified archit. term, *AE* 1925/6 39.6 (Oropus, ii BC).

**στέφος 2**, for 'of libations' read 'of offerings placed on a grave' add '**3** στέφεα· στεφῶνες Hsch.'

**στέφω II 1**, lines 9/10, delete 'τινος Nonn.*D.* 5.282'; line 14, after '(ii AD)' insert 'fig., στεφθήσονται γνῶσιν Thd.*Pr.* 14.18'

**⁺στεφών**, ῶνος, ὁ, pl., gloss on στέφεα Hsch.; of the edge of hill or cliff (cf. στεφάνη II), ὡς ὁ σ. περιφέρει κύκλῳ *IEphes.* 3.8 (c.290 BC); cf. στεφών· ‹τόπος› ὑψηλός, ἀπόκρημνος Hsch.

***στηβεύς**, gloss on κουβηζός, Hsch. (prob. for στιβεύς, cf. Hebr. *kōbēs*, "fuller").

**στῆθος IV**, add 'X.*HG* 5.4.50'

***στηλάριον**, τό, *commemorative pillar*, ἐστήσαμεν τὸ στιλλάριν *IHadr.* 87 (iii AD), στηλλάριον Ramsay *Cities and Bishoprics* 1.150, *TAM* 5(1).239.

**στήλη**, line 1, after 'ἡ' insert 'εἰς στήλην written as one word (εἰστήλην), *IG* 12(7).515 (Aigiale, Amorgos, ii BC), *SEG* 30.546 (Maced., ii/i BC)' **II**, add '**6** *inscribed charm*, *PMag.* 4.1115, al., 5.96, al., 7.215, etc.'

**στηλίδιον**, add 'pl., *IG* 2².1498.11'

**στηλίον**, add '*IGBulg.* 679 (Nicopolis ad Istrum, iii AD)'

**στηλίς**, add 'στηλλεῖδα *SEG* 30.855 (Moesia, ii AD), στιλίδα *BCH* suppl. 8 no. 58 (Maced., iii/iv AD)'

**στηλίτευμα**, for '*invective*' read '*inscription on a pillar*'

***στηλλάριον**, v. °στηλάριον.

**στηλογραφέω**, add 'στηλλογραφῶ *SEG* 34.656 (Maced., AD 191), ἐστηλλογράφησα *SEG* 34.1217 (Lydia, c.AD 198)'

**στηλογραφία**, for 'Arab.' read 'Akkadian' add '**II** *inscribing on a tablet*, *IG* 9(2).13.4, 14*a*3.'

***στηλογράφος**, ὁ, *inscriber*, σταλογράφοι *SEG* 37.340.18 (Mantinea, iv BC).

**στηλοκοπέω**, before 'as a form of punishment' insert 'ἐσταλοκόπεισαν τὰ δεδο[γμένα] *SEG* 38.377 (Acraephia, c.200 BC)'

**στηλόω**, line 2, for 'τάφον .. (Amyntas)' read 'τίς δὲ τάφον στάλωσε; (i.e. set up with an inscription), Amyntas in *Suppl.Hell.* 43'

**στηµάτιον I**, for 'al.' read 'Bito 47.7 M.'

**στήμων II**, lines 5/7, delete 'σ. .. 728' add '**III** *pole* of a wagon, *Edict.Diocl.* 15.11.'

**στήριγμα 5**, delete the section transferring quot. to section 1 and adding '2*Ki.* 20.21'

**στηρίζω I 1**, add '**b** *fix* one's eye, gaze, etc., on (in anger, etc.), στηριῶ τοὺς ὀφθαλμούς μου ἐπ' αὐτοὺς εἰς κακὰ καὶ οὐκ εἰς ἀγαθά Lxx *Am.* 9.4, οὐ στηριῶ τὸ πρόσωπόν μου ἐφ' ὑμᾶς *Je.* 3.12, *Ez.* 6.2, etc.'

**⁺στήριον**· ἱεράκιον (ἱέρακι cod.; perh. read στήριον ‹ἢ στόριον›). Σέλευκος Hsch.; cf. mod. Gk. στόρι.

**στησίχορος**, line 2, after 'χοροί' insert 'στεσίχορον hύμνον ἄγοισαι, verse fr. on Attic vase, *Lyr.adesp.* 20(c) P.'

**στία**, add 'στεῖαι γὰρ αἱ ψῆφοι τῆς θαλάσσης Sch.Nic.*Al.* 466c Ge.'

**στιβάς 2**, add '*Inscr.Perg.* 8(3).161 (ii AD)' **3**, add 'of funeral bier, *Alcmaeonis fr.* 2.2 p. 33 B.'

**στιβήεις**, for 'ἀγχοῦρος' read 'ἄγχαυρος' and for 'Call.*Hec.* .. 10' read 'Call.*fr.* 260.64 Pf.'

**στίβική**, for '*PCair.Zen.* 136.247' read '*PCair.Zen.* 176.247'

***στιγμαῖος**, α, ον, = στιγμιαῖος, Plu. 2.117e.

**στιγμή I 1** and **2**, for these sections read '*tattooed mark*, D.S. 34/5.2.1; also a natural *mark* or *speck* on a bird's plumage, Alex. Mynd.ap.Ath. 9.398d. **2** *minimal mark*, point, οἷον ὅτι ταὐτὸν .. στιγμὴ ἐν γραμμῇ καὶ μονὰς ἐν ἀριθμῷ· ἑκάτερον γὰρ ἀρχή Arist.*Top.* 108ᵇ26, *EN* 1174ᵇ12, *de An.* 427ᵃ10, Apollod.*Stoic.* 3.259. **b** the smallest division of a degree of the zodiac, *IG* 12(1).913 (Rhodes, ii/i BC).'

**στιγμιαῖος**, delete '117e' and 'στιγμαῖος is f.l. in Plu. 2.117e'

***στιλλάριον**, v. °στηλάριον.

**στιλπνός**, add 'of clothes, *SEG* 31.1288 (Side, AD 249/52)'
**στῖμι**, add '*Peripl.M.Rubr.* 49, 56'
**στίξ 1**, add 'ἀνιηραὶ θέρεος στίχες, i.e. swarms of flies, Opp.*H.* 2.448'
***στιπένδιον**, τό, Lat. *stipendium, year's service*, ἐτῶν κε' ἰστοπενδίων ξ' *JÖAI* 30 *Beibl.* 28 (Ancyra).
**στιπποκογχιστής**, add '*POxy.* 1980.6 (vi AD)'
**στιππουργός**, add '*CPR* 14.5.10 (vi AD)'
**στιφρός**, read 'στῑφρός'
**στιφρότης**, read '**στῑφρότης**'
**στῐχάριον**, for '*variegated tunic*' read 'kind of tunic'; delete 'also **στιχαρο**(sic)**μαφόριον**' to end.
***στῐχἄρομᾰφόριον**, τό, kind of cloak, *SB* 6024, 7033 (v AD), *Stud.Pal.* 20.275, *POxy.* 1978.
***στῐχἄροφελώνιον**, τό, kind of cloak, *PMichael.* 38.2 (vi AD).
**στίχη**, delete 'prob. in' and add '*Edict.Diocl.* 22.9'
**στῐχολόγος**, add '**2** *reciter of psalms*, *ASAA* 30/32(1952/4).302.88 (Rhodes; v. *BE* 1956.197); *MEFR* 64.107 no. 23 (Caesarea Mauretaniae; v. *BE* 1953.261).'
**στιχοπλανήτης**, delete the entry.
**στῖχος IV**, delete 'II' after 'συστοιχία' add '**V** a *tax* in general, *CPR* 8.79.2 (vii AD).'
**στλεγγίς**, add 'also στλιγγίς, *Inscr.Délos* 104.88, 113, 115 (iv BC, Attic text)'
**στοιβάς**, for 'v. στιβάς' read '= στιβάς 5, *Ilasos* 393'
**στοιχάς I 1**, add 'σ. νεφέλας Nonn.*D.* 18.282'
**στοιχέω**, line 4, after 'Poll. 8.105' insert '(ὅπου ἂν στειχήσω Robert *Ét.épigr.* 302 (iv BC))' **II**, add 'med. *Inscr. Cret.* 3 iv 9.18. **2** med., *to be sufficiently available* to, Modest.*Dig.* 34.1.4 pr.'
**στοιχομῡθέω**, before 'Phot.' insert 'ἐφεξῆς λέγειν' and add 'glossed by μακρηγορέω, Hsch. s.v. στοχίζῃ'
***στολάριον**, τό, app. some article of clothing, *Vit.Aesop.*(G) 21 (s.v.l.).
**στολάρχης**, add '**II** prob. *controller of clothing*, *PAnt.* 33.9 (iv AD), and so perh. in *PCair.Zen.* l.c.'
***στολᾶτα**, Lat. *stolata*, ματρῶνα σ. *POxy.* 907.4 (iii AD), *PFlor.* 16.1 (iii AD), *TAM* 5(1).758 (iii AD).
**στόλιον**, for 'Dim. of στολή II, *scanty garment*' read '*garment* (in dim. or pejorative sense)'
**†στόλοκρος**, στόλοκρον· τὸ περικεκομμένον τὰς κόμας, καὶ γεγονὸς ψιλόν, εἴτε δένδρον, εἴτε ἄνθρωπος. δηλοῖ δὲ καὶ ἀνειδὲς καὶ σκληρόν Hsch.; of a shorn boy, Anacr. 2 *fr.* 1.3 P.; applied to goats not having fully developed horns, Hsch. s.v. κόλον.
**στόλος 3**, *fleet*, add 'στόλου Π(οντικοῦ) *SEG* 33.1095' **4**, λόγου σ., for '*set narrative*' read 'course of argument'
**στόμα I 3 b**, add 'ἀπὸ στόματος προσαγορεύειν greet with a kiss, Porph.*Plot.* 2.17' **III 2**, after 'X.*Ages.* 11.15' insert '(s.v.l.)'
**στόμαργος**, add 'Myc. *to-ma-ko*, description of an ox'
**στομαυλέω**, for '*flute*' read '*pipe* or *aulos*'
**στομᾰχικός 1**, before 'πάθος' insert 'πόνος *Inscr.Cret.* 1.xvii 11 (Lebena, ii BC)'
***στομᾰχώδης**, ες, *irascible*, *Vit.Aesop.*(G) 28.
**στομίς I**, add 'Hsch. s.v. φορβειά'
***στονύει**· τὸ ὀξέως λέγει Theognost.*Can.* 73 A.
**στόνυξ**, line 5, for '*fangs*' read '*claws*'; line 6, for 'nail-removing *prongs*, i.e. nail-scissors' read 'perh. instrument for manicuring nails, *clippers*'
**στοργή 2**, add '*defixio* in *Hesperia* 54.227 no. 9 (iii AD)'
**στοργικός**, after 'όν' insert '*affectionate*, *PMil.Vogl.* 73.7 (ii AD)'
**στόρνυμι**, line 4, after 'A.*Ag.* 909' insert '(codd.)' and delete '*Com.adesp.* 1211' **II**, at end for 'dub. sens.' read '*floored* and decked'
***στουπίον**, v. °στυππεῖον.
***στοῦπρον**, τό, Lat. *stuprum*, *illicit sexual intercourse*, *Cod.Just.* 5.4.29.8.
**στοχάζομαι II 1**, add 'τί στοχασώμεθά σου; *what are we to infer about you?*, *AP* 7.422 (Leon.Tarent.)' **2**, add 'Just.*Const.* Δέδωκεν 13'
**στοχασμός I 1**, after '*use of circumstantial evidence*' insert 'for solving a question of fact'
**στοχαστής 2**, add 'πᾶς ποιητὴς ψυχαγωγίας .. σ. Agatharch. in *GGM* i p. 117'
**στοχαστικός 1 a**, add 'adv., πρὸς τὰ ἔνδοξα -κῶς ἔχειν id. *Rh.* 1355ᵃ17; comp., -κωτέρως Gal. 9.249.8' **2**, for '*guesswork*' read '‡στοχασμός'; lines 4/5, after 'Syrian.*in Hermog.* 2.34 R.' insert 'στάσις ib. 157' and delete 'πρὸς .. Arist.*Rh.* 1355ᵃ17'
***στρᾰβόπους**, ὁ, ἡ, gen. ποδος, = στραβοπόδης, gloss on μύσκιλος, Cyr.
***στρᾰγάλος**, ὁ, = ἀστράγαλος, *Vit.Aesop.*(G) 69.
***στραγγουριτία**, ἡ, = στραγγουρία, *POxy.* 1384.30 (v AD).
***στραγγουρίωσις**, εως, ἡ, = στραγγουρία, *JS* 1881.87.
***στρᾶτα**, ἡ, Lat. *strata*, *street*, *SEG* 37.496 (Thessaly, iv/v AD).
**στρᾰταρχικός**, add 'Heph.Astr. 3.4.12'
**στρᾰτεία**, add '**6** service in the imperial administration (whether civil or military), *Cod.Just.* 4.59.1.2; spec. of military service, ἔνοπλον στρατείαν ib. 1.3.52.5.'
**στρᾰ́τειος**, fem. -εία, add '*Ilasos* 222, 223'
**στρᾰτεύω**, add 'Boeot. στροτεύω, *SEG* 30.1980 (Orchomenos, iii BC)'
**στρᾰτηγέτης**, line 2, before 'Cret.' insert 'Dor. στραταγέτας B.17.121, 18.7 S.-M.'
**στρᾰτηγέω I 1 a**, add 'so στρατηγεῖν κατὰ πόλιν, ἐπὶ τῶν ξένων *to be praetor urbanus* or *peregrinus*, *IG* 9²(1).242.3-5 (Thyrrheum, 94 BC)' **d**, add 'στρατηγήσας ἐπ' Ἴμβρον *SEG* 24.194(b) (Attica, i BC)'
**στρᾰτηγίς**, add 'as epith. of Aphrodite, *IG* 9²(1).256.3 (Thyrrheum, ii/i BC)'
**στρᾰτηγός**, add '**III** ἥρως Στρατηγός at Athens, *Hesperia* 15.221 (*c*.200 BC), *IG* 2².1035.53 (ii AD).'
***στρᾰτηλᾰτιανός**, ὁ, officer of the staff of the στρατηλάτης, *IG* 10(2).1.791 (Thessalonica, iv AD or later), *PSI* 176.16, 183.3 (v AD), *PWash.Univ.* 17.5 (vi AD).
***στρατηλάτισσα**, ἡ, fem. of στρατηλάτης, *CPR* 10.127.4 (vi AD).
**στρᾰτιά I**, add '**3** used as poet. equivalent of *legio*, στρατιῆς τε τεταγμένος ἐσθλῆς πρώτων Ἀρμενίων inscr. in *Phoenix* 26.183-6 (Cilicia, iv AD).'
**στρᾰτιώτης I**, add '**3** officer in the imperial civil service, Lib.*Ep.* 841.1.'
**στρᾰτιωτικός I**, add 'δῶρα στρατιωτικά (= Lat. *dona militaria*), *SEG* 31.1300.15 (Lycia, in an addition to *TAM* 2.1201A, AD 145/6)'
**στρᾰτιῶτις 3**, for '*soldier-fly*' read 'colloq. term for large kind of fly'
**στρᾰτολογία**, add '*SEG* 31.675 (Thrace, *c*.AD 90/100)'
***Στρᾰτόνῑκος**, ὁ, month in an Asiatic calendar, *Hemerolog.Flor.* p. 73 (p. 10 K.).
**στρᾰτοπεδάρχης**, for '*military commander*' read '*commander of a force in the field*' and add '*SEG* 31.1590 (ii BC), Heph.Astr. 1.1.151'
**στρᾰτοπεδαρχικός**, add '*IGLBulg.* 240 (v/vi AD)'
**στρᾰτόπεδον I**, add '**3** *headquarters*, of the Emperor Julian at Constantinople, Jul.*Ep.* 46.'
**στράτωρ**, add '*SEG* 7.951 (Arabia, iii AD)'
**στρέβλωσις**, add '**2** *vexation, harassment*, Just.*Edict.* 7.7, *CPR* 10.121.5 (vi AD).'
**στρεβλωτήριος**, after '4*Ma.* 8.13' insert 'Sopat.Rh. 8.34.17 W.'
***στρειφωτήρ**, ῆρος, ὁ, wd. in list of nautical building materials, cf. στροφωτήρ, *PMich.*inv. 4001 (*ZPE* 24.84, i/ii AD).
***στρέπτειρα**, ἡ, *spinner*, βίου σ. Μοῖρα *GVI* 1154.9 (Samos, ii BC).
**στρεπτοφόρος**, add 'masc. subst., category of legionary soldier, Lyd. *Mag.* p. 47.18 W.'
**στρέφανον**, add 'cf. στέρψανον'
**στρεψίμαλλος**, before 'in reference' insert 'perh.'; add 'an obsc. ref. may be intended, v. *Glotta* 69.139'
**στρίβος**, for '*a weak fine voice*' read '*a thin shrill cry*'
***στρίγλα**, ἡ, = Λάμια, Sch.Aristid. p. 42 D.
***στρικτωρία**, ἡ, Lat. *strictoria*, *shirt with long sleeves*, *Edict.Diocl.* 22.7.
**στροβῑλᾶς**, add '*CPR* 13.29.75'
**στρόβῑλος 6**, add 'Ps.-Hdt.*Vit.Hom.* 280; used as flavouring, *Vit. Aesop.*(G) 63' **9**, for '*winch*, or perh. *rotating shaft*' read 'perh. *bell-shaped lower millstone*' and add '*POxy.* 3639.11 (AD 412)'
***στροβῑλοφόρος** (στροβηλ- cod.), ον, *bearing cones*, Hsch. s.v. κωνοφόρον.
***στρογγῠλαῖος**, α, ον, *circular*, of gymnasium, *PKöln* 52.10, 58 (AD 263).
***στρογγῠ́λιας**, v. στραβαλός.
**†στρογγύλλω**, *make round in form* or *section*, *AP* 7.726 (Leon.Tarent.); pass., of morbid growths, Aret.*SA* 1.8 H., Archig.ap.Gal. 8.90.
**στρογγῠ́λος I**, add '**6** of sputum, *nummular*, Hp.*Prog.* 14.'
***στρογγῠλώδης**, ες, *having a round form*, Alex.Aphr. *in Top.* 382.13.
**στρογγῠ́λωμα**, delete 'or *mosquito-net*'
**στρογγῠ́λωσις II**, for '*trench*' read '*circular encampment*'
**στρομβεῖον**, for 'Dim. of στρόμβος 5' read '*round pellet*'
***στροτεύω**, v. ‡στρατεύω.
***στρούκτωρ**, ωρος, ὁ, Lat. *structor*, *one who serves at table*, Ath. 4.170e, Zos.Alch. 138.7.
**στροφᾰλίζω**, after 'στρέφω' insert '*move round rapidly, twirl*'
**στροφέω**, add '(prob. f.l. for στρέφει)'
**στρόφιγξ 4**, for this section read 'applied to the *conical hill* at Kafizin in Cyprus, *ta-i-e-pi-to-i-so-to-ro-pi-ki* [νύμφαι] τᾶι ἐπὶ τῶι στρόφι(γ)γι *Kafizin* 218b, al.; (sp. στόρφ-, ib. 50, 286, al.; στόφ-, ib. 14, 305, al.)'
**στρόφις**, for 'ἡ' read 'ὁ'
**στροφίς**, add 'acc. -ιν *PP* 42.42'
**στροφωτήρ**, add 'cf. perh. °στρειφωτήρ'
**†στρυπτηρία**, v. °στυπτ-.
**στρυφνός III**, delete 'Hp.*VM* 14, 15'
***στρωτή**, ἡ, perh. *pavement*, *ABSA* 58.59 (Chios, i BC).

**στρώτης**, add '*POxy.* 1951.2, 7 (v AD)'

**στρωφάω I**, line 10, delete 'i.e. claiming a husband's rights' and after 'A.*Ag.* 1224' insert 'ἐν δεμνίῳ .. [φρον]τίσιν στρωφωμένη *Trag.adesp.* 664.25 K.-S.'

***στύβον**, τό, gloss on ἱππόφεως (*spurge*), Gal. 19.106.14.

***στυγνοπρόσωπος**, ον, *having a gloomy* or *glowering expression*, Heph.Astr. 3.45.2.

***στῡλεῖον**, τό, *pillar*, (unless adj. στύλειος, *of pillars*, is understood), *SEG* 31.841 (Syracuse, vi BC; see also Dubois *IGDS* 86).

**στῡλίς I**, at end for 'pecul. acc. .. Smyrna)' read 'acc. στυλλίδαν *SEG* 33.1084; στυλλεῖδαν *TAM* 4(1).134 (both Nicomedia, Rom.imp.)'

**στῡλοβάτης**, for '*base of a column*' read '*continuous base supporting row of columns*'

***στῡλοπαραστάς**, άδος, ἡ, *pilaster*, *SEG* 30.1258, *Milet* 1(2).102 (i BC).

**στῡλοπῑνάκιον**, for '*pillar* .. *on it*' read '*tablet forming part of a pillar*'

***στῡλοποιός**, ὁ, *maker of pillars*, *SB* 4771.9.

**στῦλος**, line 2, after 'ib. 109 iii 92 (iii BC)' insert 'w. prothetic vowel, τοὺς ἰστύλους *SEG* 32.1269 (Phrygia, Rom.imp.)'

**στῡλόω**, line 2, after '(ii BC)' insert 'ἰπνὼν ἐστυλωμένος *IG* 11(2).287*A*166 (Delos, iii BC)'

**στύμεον**, for 'dub. sens.' read '= στόμιον (in quot. prob. *cave*)'

***στύμνιον**, τό, τυπαστήριον· τὸ τῶν ἁλιέων στύμνιον Hsch.

**Στυμφᾱλίς**, before 'A.R. 2.1053' insert 'Pi.*O.* 6.84'

**στυππεῖον**, add 'also στουπίον *Edict.Diocl.* 26.2'

**⁺στυππειοπλόκος**, ὁ, *tow-spinner*, *IG* 2$^2$.1673.15, 41 (Eleusis, iv BC).

**στυπτηρία**, after 'Ion. -ίη' insert 'also **στρυπτ-**' **II**, add '**2** *tax on the sale of alum*, *Inscr.Prien.* 364.15 (iii/ii BC, form στρυπτ-).' add 'Myc. *tu-ru-pte-ri-ja*'

**στύραξ** (B), before 'X.*HG* 6.2.19' insert '*IG* 1$^3$.422.266'; line 2, delete '*shaft*'

***στῡρόν**, τό, = στύραξ (A) I, Call.*fr.* 43.88 Pf. (cf. στυρόν· τὸ μύρον Zonar., Theognost.*Can.* 130).

**Στωϊκός**, before '**Στοϊκός**' insert 'Scanned –◡◡ by Cerc. 3 A.5 D.$^3$'

**στωμύλλω II**, lines 3/4, delete 'also .. *Pax* 995'

**σύ**, line 3, after 'Boeot.' insert '**τΰ** *CEG* 326.2 (*c.*700/675 BC), 110 (*c.*500 BC)'; line 5, after 'ib. 50.27, 55.6' insert 'τύν tab.defix. in *SDAW* 1934.1040 (Boeotia)'; line 14, for 'Alcm. 17' read 'Alcm. 48 P., *AP* 7.464.5 (Antip.Sid.)' p. 1659$^a$, lines 7/8, for 'also τεΐ Alcm. 53' read 'also τεΐ (transmitted as τεὶ) Alcm. 70(*b*) P.' transferring this to the end of section I 1 **III**, for 'ὑμεῖς' read 'ὑμεῖς'

**σῠάγρειος**, before 'ον' insert '(-εος, *PCair.Zen.* 12.52)'

**σύαρτον**, add 'rest. in *SEG* 23.326 (Delphi, iii BC)'

***σύβακχοι**, οἱ, name for the φαρμακοί in Athens, Hellad.ap.Phot.*Bibl.* p. 534a H. (v.l. σύμβ-, q.v.).

**⁺σῠβήνη**, ἡ, *case* for arrows, *IG* 1$^3$.350.82 (427/6 BC), Ar.*Th.* 1197, 1215, Sch.Ar.*Th.* 1197; for αὐλοί, Poll. 7.153, 10.153; cf. σ.· αὐλοθήκη ἢ τοξοθήκη. ἢ ὁ ναυτικὸς χιτών Hsch.

**σῠβόσιον II**, delete the section.

**συβριασμός**, for 'ἡ ἐν' read 'ὁ ἐν'

**σῠβώτης**, add 'Myc. *su-qo-ta*'

***σῠγάτηρ**, v. °θυγάτηρ.

**συγγᾰμέτης**, add '*INikaia* 1101 (perh. fem., iii/iv AD)'

**συγγένεια I 1**, add 'defined: ἡ συγγένεια ὄνομά ἐστι γενικόν, διαιρεῖται δὲ εἰς τρία, εἰς ἀνιόντας εἰς κατιόντας καὶ τοὺς ἐκ πλαγίου Theophil.Antec. 1.10.1; limited to cognates, *Cod.Just.* 6.4.4.20'

**συγγένειος**, add '**II** app. *belonging to the family*, Mitchell *N.Galatia* 399.'

**συγγενεύς**, add '*TAM* 4(1).284'

**συγγενής II 1 b**, add 'including children, Just.*Nov.* 115.3.12, *Cod.Just.* 6.4.4.23'

**συγγενικός II 1**, add 'of a family tomb, *TAM* 4(1).231, 257, al.; τὸ συγγενικόν, *kindred*, *kinsmen*, *INikaia* 1035 (ii AD), 1034 (iii AD), *MAMA* 6.24. **b** cult-title of Zeus, *INikaia* 1130 (Rom.imp.).'

**⁺συγγέωργος**, ὁ, *fellow-cultivator*, Ar.*Pl.* 223, *PSI* 1043.20 (ii AD). **b** member of association of γεωργοί, *SB* 7457.3 (ii BC), 8267.16, 20, al. (i BC).

**συγγίγνομαι**, line 2, after '-εγενόμην' insert 'Cypr. *su-ne-ke-no-to* (3 sg.) *ICS* 309 A 1'

***συγγνωστεύω**, *witness jointly* regarding, συγγνωστεύω τὸν Θῶνιν ὡς πρόκειται *PMich.*XIV 676.32, 34 (AD 272).

**συγγονή**, add '*CPR* 6.77.33 (ii/iii AD)'

***συγγόνιον**, τό, unexpld. wd., some kind of division within nome, νομοφύλ(αξ) β′ συγγονίου Θεμίστου, *PFreib.* 4.62 (ii AD).

**συγγρᾰφεύς I**, line 4, after 'Ar.*Ach.* 1150' insert '(s.v.l.)'

**συγγρᾰφοδιαθήκη**, add '*testamentary covenant*, *POxy.* 1102.14 (ii AD)'

**συγγράφω II 2**, line 2, delete '*get speeches composed*'

**συγγώνιον**, add 'adj. -ιος, ‡ὑπότονοι *Inscr.Délos* 442*A*229 (ii BC)'

***συγκαθάπτω**, *join to by grasping*, σ. χεῖρά τινι Men.*Dysc.* 953.

**συγκάθεδρος**, for '*colleague*' read '*adviser*' and after 'συνθάκων' insert 'νομικὸς σ. ἀνθυπάτου *IGRom.* 1.933 (Sicca, ii AD)'

**συγκαθίζω I 1**, delete 'τὰ συνέδρια *Hell.Oxy.* 11.4' **II 1**, after '*sit together*' insert 'ἐν τῷ συνεδρίῳ *SEG* 12.87.14-15 (Athens, 336 BC); τὰ συνέδρια .. ἐν τῇ Καδμείᾳ συνεκαθίζεν *Hell.Oxy.* 16(11).4 fin. B.'

**συγκαθίστημι I 2**, add 'pass. μετὰ τῶν συνκαθεσταμένων ἐνδίκων *IMylasa* 134.5 (ii BC)'

**σύγκαιρος**, for 'Anon.ap.Suid.' read 'Ael.*fr.* 81'

**συγκᾰλέω 1**, for '*call to council*' read '*call together*' and after 'Ar.*Av.* 201' insert 'Th. 7.60.5'

**συγκαταβαίνω 4, 5 & 6**, for these sections read '**4** *commit oneself* to a battle or sim., εἰς τὸν ὑπὲρ τῶν ὅλων κίνδυνον Plb. 3.89.8, εἰς ὁλοσχερῆ κρίσιν id. 30.90.5, D.S. 12.30, 17.98, al.; w. ref. to negotiations, εἰς πᾶν Plb. 3.10.1. **5** *agree* or *submit* to, συγκαταβάντες εἰς φόρους καὶ συνθήκας Plb. 4.45.4, τοῖς ἀξιουμένοις Onas. 4.3. **6** *descend* to unworthy measures, dealings, etc., Plb. 26.1.3, εἰς λοιδορίαν Phld.*Rh.* 1.383 S.'

**συγκαταβῐβάζω I**, add '*SEG* 32.605 (Larissa, ii AD)'

**συγκαταγιγνώσκω**, add '**II** *join in thinking ill of* a person, *UPZ* 146.17 (ii BC).'

**συγκατάθεσις**, add '**4** perh. *joint dedication*, *IEphes.* 3239 (ii/iii AD).'

**συγκατακλείω**, after 'Luc.*DMort.* 14.4' insert 'βύκτας δ' ἐν ἀσκῷ συγκατακλείσας βοός Lyc. 738'

***συγκαταμένω**, *reside together*, *SEG* 26.645 (Thessaly, *c.*AD 400).

***συγκαταξιόω**, *choose*, *elect*, ἐκ τῶν συγκατηξιωμένων φιλτάτων *IEphes.* 3029.7 (ii AD).

**συγκατασκευάζω**, add '**2** *join in building*, *IEphes.* 3712 (ii/iii AD).'

**συγκατασκηνόω**, for '*establish* .. *quarters*' read '*help to settle* men *in their tents*'

**συγκατασχίζω**, delete the entry.

**συγκατατίθημι 1**, add '*MAMA* 6.264 (Phrygia, i AD)'

**συγκαταφέρω**, add '**2** *help in conveying to the grave* (perh. by contributing to expenses), *IGRom.* 4.1453.'

**συγκαταχωρίζω II**, after '*BGU* 578.19 (ii AD)' insert 'τῷ συνκαταχωρισθέντι μαρτυροποιήματι *JJP* 18.180 (ii AD)'

***συγκατηγόρημα**, ατος, τό, that which in a sentence is neither subject nor predicate, Priscian.*Inst.* 2.15.

**συγκατορύσσω**, after 'τί τινι' insert 'Men.*Dysc.* 814'

**σύγκειμαι**, add '**IV** *to have been committed*, *delivered* for transmission (cf. συντίθημι III), of instructions, *UPZ* 110.50 (ii BC).'

**⁺συγκέλλω**, *bring ashore* or *into harbour together*, transf., ἐν δ' ἄρα τῇσι (sc. κυρτίσι) στρόμβους συγκέλσαντες ὁμοῦ χήμῃσι τίθενται (sc. fishermen) Opp.*H.* 5.602.

**συγκεραστός**, add '[*com*]*mixtum* συνκεραστὸν ἢ κρᾶσις *PVindob.Lat.* 27 (*Tyche* 5.37, iv AD)'

***συγκηδεμών**, όνος, ὁ, *fellow* ‡κηδεμών, Just.*Nov.* 72.2.

**συγκῑνέω I**, line 4, for '*sympathetic emotion*' read '*excitement*'

**συγκλάω**, line 4, after 'Phld.*Mus.* p. 23 K.' insert '*PVindob.Tandem* 6.12 (v AD)'

***συγκλειδοφορέω**, (of a temple official) *to be a fellow key-bearer*, w. dat., *IStraton.* 663.5, al.

**σύγκλεισμα**, for '3*Ki.* 7.29' read '3*Ki.* 7.16(29)' and add '4*Ki.* 16.17'

**συγκλεισμός**, add '**2** *fastness*, *refuge*, Lxx 2*Ki.* 22.46, *Mi.* 7.17.' **II**, add '*fulfilment* of a task, *PMichael.* 46.13, 54.4 (vi AD, -κλισμ- papp.)'

**συγκληρονομέω**, add 'Just.*Nov.* 53.6.1; perh. also μή τι[νες συνεκλη]ρ[ο]νόμησαν τῇ γυναικί; rest. in *POxy.* 3758.113 (AD 325)'

**συγκληρονόμος**, add 'Scaev.*Dig.* 31.88'

**σύγκληρος I**, add 'w. dat., Νύμφαις σ. *Suppl.Hell.* 978.14'

**⁺σύγκλῑνος**, ὁ, *table-companion*, Men.*fr.* 916 K.-Th.; pl., *IG* 2$^2$.2350 (iv/iii BC).

**συγκλίτης**, add '*SEG* 31.638 (Maced.)'

**συγκλύζω I 1**, add 'συνεκλύσθη πόρος Ἐρυθρᾶς Θαλάσσης Ezek.*Exag.* 241'

**⁺συγκολλάω**, *glue*, *cement*, *solder*, etc., *together*, *IG* 2$^2$.1668.82 (iv BC), Luc.*Alex.* 14, *PVindob.Salomons* 2.7 (ii/iii AD); fig., Ar.*V.* 1041, Pl.*Mx.* 236$^b$. **2** transf., *join together*, *unite*, Pl.*Ti.* 43a; pass., of a wound, Sor. 1.36; of a building, *to be joined on* to, *PNess.* 31.1 (vi AD).

***συγκολλήγας**, ὁ, *colleague*, *POxy.* 3917.4 (rest., ii AD), *PCol.* 188.26 (AD 320).

**συγκόλλησις**, after 'Clearch. 44' insert '*PFam.Teb.* 15.3, al. (ii AD)'

***συγκολλητός**, όν, *glued* or *fixed together*, *Ath.Asklepieion* III 29 (iv BC).

**συγκομίζω I 2**, add 'of other foodstuffs, τὸς ταρίχōς ἐς οἶκον συνκόμισον καὶ σφήκ' ἴσα (lapis σφηκισα) *SEG* 37.665 (Carcinitis, *c.*400 BC)'

**συγκοπιάω**, add 'w. acc., *share the work on*, σ. τὴν ἐντομίδα ἐκ τῶν κοινῶν κόπων *IG* 10(2).478 (Thessalonica, iii AD)'

***συγκρᾱσία**, ἡ, perh. = σύγκρασις I b, Vett.Val. 248.26.

**σύγκρᾱσις II**, add '**2** *aggregate* of different classes, types, etc., in quot., in register of wheat lands, *PMich.*inv. 335$^v$ (*ZPE* 32.238, iii/iv AD).'

**συγκρᾱτύνω**, add 'Gal. 17(1).821.7'

**συγκρίνω II**, add '**2** gramm., in pass., *have degrees of comparison*, τῶν κυρίων οὐ συγκρινομένων A.D.*Pron.* 64.12.'

**σύγκρῐσις II**, add 'in the process of selection, συγκρίσεις ἀρχιτεκτόνων *SEG* 33.1040 (Cyme, ii BC)'

**συγκροτέω II 2 c**, add 'transf., *knock together, contrive*, δικαστήρια παρὰ τῇ σῇ ἐπιεικίᾳ πρός μαι συγκροτῆσαςε *POxy.* 3126 i 11 (AD 328)'

**συγκρότησις II**, add '*CRAI* 1945.379.8 (Berytus, Byz.), Just.*Nov.* 109.1'

**συγκρουσμός**, add '**2** perh. *hammering out* of a matter under dispute, συγκρουσμὸν .. ἡμῶν ἐργάζεσθαι *CPR* 8.30.6 (iv AD).'

⁺**σύγκτησις**, εως, ἡ, *joint possession*, *SEG* 30.1383 (Hypaepa, AD 301). **II** *agglomeration of properties*, Modest.*Dig.* 31.34.1, Scaev.*Dig.* 34.30.1.

**συγκῠλίομαι 1**, add '**b** *roll (down) with*, v. συγκατακυλίνδομαι.'

***συγκῠνηγέτις**, ιδος, ἡ, *fellow-huntress*, τῇ Ἀρτέμιδι Sch.E.*Hipp.* 1130.

**συγκωμαστής** (after σύγκωμος), before 'Tz.*H.*' insert 'D.C.*fr.* 39.10'

***συγκωμήτης**, ου, ὁ, *fellow-villager*, *PDura* 26.2, 9 (iii AD), Just.*Nov.* 52.1.

***συγξενόδοκος**, ὁ, *fellow-ξενοδόκος*, *SEG* 29.500, 502 (Thessaly).

**συγξέω**, for 'by *scraping* .. *Comp.* 22' read 'stones *so that they fit together*, τῶν λογάδην συντιθεμένων λίθων αἱ μὴ συνεξεσμέναι βάσεις D.H.*Comp.* 22; metaph., of literary work, in pass., *to be polished, smooth*, Alcid.*Soph.* 20 R.'

**συγχειμάζω**, line 1, for 'App.*BC* 5.77' read 'App.*BC* 5.75'

**συγχέω I 1**, add '**b** *melt together*, πολλὰ τῶν χρυσῶν ἀναθημάτων Plu. 2.401f.'

**συγχίς**, for '*shoe* or *sock*' read '*sandal*'

**σύγχρησις**, for '*common* .. *use*' read '*commercial dealings*'

**συγχρισμός**, before 'Paul.' insert '*SB* 9199.13 (ii AD), *Stud.Pal.* 22.183.105 (ii AD)'

**συγχρονέω I 1**, add '**b** *spend time with*, τινι *PMich.*VIII 497.15 (ii AD).'

**σύγχροος I**, add '**2** perh. *of blended colours*, *PHarris* 73.44 (*ZPE* 37.234).'

***συγχρυλεος**, α, ον, unexpld. adj. (accent unkn.), κίονες πλείονες χαμαὶ συνχρυλεαι *IGC* 1 p. 11, lines 22, 24 (Larissa, ?iii BC).

**συγχυσμός**, delete the entry (v. °συγχρισμός).

**συγχωρέω I**, add '**2** *move together, close up*, Ar.*V.* 1516.' **II**, lines 1ff., delete '*get out of the way* .. (anap.)'; for '*give way, yield, defer to*' read '*fall in with, agree with*' and delete 'Pl. l.c.' add '**b** of events, *conform with one's wishes* or *intentions*, Pl.*Tht.* 191c.' **2**, add '*Cod.Just.* 10.11.8.3' **3**, add 'τὸν δὲ τόπον συνεχώρησαν .. εἰς τὰς ὀρτασίμους ἡμέρας *TAM* 4(1).100'

**συγχώρησις 1**, for this section read '*agreement, assent* to an argument or proposition, τὴν .. σιγήν σου συγχώρησιν θήσω Pl.*Cra.* 435b, *Lg.* 770c, τὴν τῷ λόγῳ συγχώρησιν ib. 837e, Aristid.Quint. 2.10 (pl.); coupled w. συνδρομή Hermog.*Id.* 2.1. **b** *agreement, consent* to a course of action, *IEphes.* 3260.9, etc.; by the emperor, ib. 25.9, 38.8; w. κατά, κατὰ συνχώρησι[ν τῆς] Σελευκέων προβ[ουλῆς] *SEG* 36.1297 (Syria, i/ii AD), *IMylasa* 470.' **3**, add 'Just.*Nov.* 139 rubric'

**συζεύγνυμι 1**, add 'in building, ταύτας (sc. μεσόμνας) τρήσαντι καὶ συζεύξαντι *IG* $2^2$.1673.36 (Eleusis, iv BC)'

***συζῠγικός**, ή, όν, *of conjugates, conjugational*, Iamb. *in Nic.* 15.7 P.

**σύζῠγος**, add 'Aeol. σύνδυγος, Sapph. 213 L.-P.' **2**, after 'masc.' insert '*spouse*, *MAMA* 7.366'

**σύζυξ II**, add '**2** neut. pl. subst., *consonants* (cf. ἄζυγα, *vowels*), Nonn.*D.* 4.262.'

***σῡηνίς**, ἡ, app. = sq., συηνὶς στικτή *Livre d'écolier* 147 (iii BC).

***σῡηνίτης**, ου, ὁ, *red granite quarried at Syene*, Plin.*HN* 36.63.

**σῡΐδιον**, delete '*porker*'

**σῡκάζω II**, add 'ἀποσυκάζω' add '**III** = ἐπηρεάζω, Artem. 1.73 P.'

**σῡκαλλός** (s.v. συκαλίς), add '*Edict.Diocl.* 4.36'

**σῡκᾰμῑνέα**, after 'Gal. 6.589' insert '*PFlor.* 50.32, 66 (iii AD); συκαμειναί *CPHerm.* 7 ii 18'

**σῡκᾰμῑνεών**, delete '*PFlor.* .. AD)'

**σῡκάμῑνον I**, transfer 'Lxx *Am.* 7.14' to section II.

**σῡκάμῑνος II**, add 'Lxx 3*Ki.* 10.27, *Is.* 9.10(9)' and after '*Ev.Luc.* 17.6' insert '(perh. in sense I)'

***σῡκᾰμῑνών**, ῶνος, ὁ, *plantation of* συκάμινοι, Ulp.*Dig.* 47.11.10.

***σῡκαμπελών**, ῶνος, ὁ, *vineyard with fig-trees*, *PNess.* 32.9 (vi AD).

**σῡκάριον**, add '*PFlor.* 176.9 (iii AD)'

**σῡκέα II**, delete the section, transferring quot. to section I. at end add 'form prob. *σύτσα < **sūkyā*, Myc. *su-za*'

⁺**σῡκίδιον**, τό, *(young) fig-tree*, τὰ νέα σ. Ar.*Pax* 598.

**σύκινος I 1**, line 4, after 'Ar.*V.* 897' insert '(perh. to be understood as sense II)' **2**, after 'metaph.' insert '*of no account*, Hippon. 41 W.'

**σῡκομορέα**, add '*Hippiatr.* ii p. 165.16 O.-H., *Gp.* 10.3.7'

**σῡκόμορος**, for '*sycamore-fig*' read '*sycomore*'

***σῡκοτρᾰ́πεζος**, ον, *living on a diet of figs*, i.e. *cheaply, poorly*, *Iamb.adesp.* 46 W.

**σῡκοφαντέω**, add '**III** *guide, act as courier for*, *PNess.* 89.22 (vi/vii AD).'

**σῡλέω II**, add '*SEG* 25.606 (Doris, ii BC)'

**σῡ́λη**, line 7, delete '[to fear]' **II**, line 2, after '*booty*' insert 'Hedyl.ap.Ath. 11.486b'

**σῡ́λησις**, add 'Ptol.*Tetr.* 197 B., *PBerol.*inv. 11624.14 (*JJP* 18.35, iv AD)'

***σῠ́λινος**, v. °ξύλινος.

**συλλᾰβή II 4**, add 'sg., ἄλφα σ. Herod. 3.22'

**συλλαγχάνω**, add 'pl., *to be chosen by lot together*, *SEG* 30.1119 (Entella, iii BC)'

**συλλαμβάνω VI 1**, add '**b** w. acc., *take as an associate*, *PBremen* 9.8, *PGiss.* 11.12 (both ii AD).'

***συλλαμπᾰδεύω**, *carry a torch with*, rest. in Sch.min.Il. 6.21 (cf. Alcm. 63 P.).

***συλλαυρίτης**, ου, ὁ, *resident in the same street*, *POxy.* 3979.6 (sp. συνλαυρείτ-), *PRyl.* 606.37 (both iii AD).

**συλλέγω I 1**, add '**b** *contract* an illness, Aristid.*Or.* 50(26).1 K. (pass.).' **2**, for this section read 'med., *regain control of, collect* oneself, one's faculties, etc., σύλλεξαι σθένος E.*Ph.* 850, συνειλεγμένον τὰς ἀφάς Pl.*Ax.* 365a, ἐκ τῆς ἀσθενείας σ. ἐμαυτόν ib. 370e; abs., αὐτὴν (sc. ψυχὴν) εἰς αὑτὴν ξυλλέγεσθαι καὶ ἀθροίζεσθαι Pl.*Phd.* 83a'

***συλλείωσις**, ἡ, *agglomeration*, Anon.Alch. 7.5; cf. λείωσις.

***συλλέκτης**, ου, ὁ, *collector*, συνλέκ(ται) ἀχ(ύρου) *PKöln* 122.2, π]ερὶ συνλέκτου οἴνου *POxy.* 1415.9 (both iii AD).

***συλλεκτικός**, ή, όν, *acquisitive*, δωρεῶν Vett.Val. 46.14; abs., id. 48.19.

***συλλήμπτωρ**, ορος, ὁ, = συλλήπτωρ, *DAW* 85.38 (Cilicia).

**συλλῐθηγία**, add '*OMich.* 1.311, 322 (iii AD)'

**συλλογεύς 1**, delete ' at Athens' to end add '**2** *summoner, convener*, *IG* $2^2$.1257 passim, 1496.83, 114, etc., τõ δήμō συλλογῆς *SEG* 26.72 (Athens, iv BC).'

**συλλογισμός I 1**, add 'Lxx *Ex.* 30.12, *Wi.* 4.20'

**σύλλῠσις**, add '*BGU* 1926.8, 13 (ii BC)'

**σῡλόνυξ**, for '*paring the nails*' read '(instrument for) *cleaning the nails*'

**συμβαίνω III 1 b**, delete 'mostly impers.' and add 'τοιαύτη .. γὰρ ἡ ἀπορία οὖσα συνέβαινεν D. 47.44'

**σύμβακχος**, add 'subst., οἱ σ., *members of a Dionysiac cult association*, *SEG* 31.983 (Ionia, ii/i BC; cf. °συβακχοί)'

**συμβάλλω II 4**, add 'πρὶν ἢ συμβάλῃ τῇ χώρᾳ *Peripl.M.Rubr.* 38'

***συμβαλτός**, ή, όν, = συμβλητός (in quot., IV), θύρα Anon. *in Rh.* 184.26.

**συμβᾰμᾰτικός**, after 'Ptol.*Tetr.* 203' insert '(v.l. συμβατικός)'

**συμβᾰσῐλιστής**, for '*fellow* .. (q.v.)' read 'pl., *guild* or *worshippers of a deified Ptolemy* (in quot., Ptol. III; cf. βασιλιστής)'

***συμβετέρανος**, ὁ, = Lat. *conveteranus*, *fellow-veteran*, Modest.*Dig.* 27.1.8.6.

**συμβῐ́βᾰσις I**, after '*reconciliation*' insert 'Ammon.*Diff.* 133 N.'

**σύμβῐος**, after '*husband*' for '*Epigr.Gr.* 399 (Ancyra)' read '*GVI* 242 (Ancyra, i/ii AD)' and add '*SEG* 30.1187, 1209 (both Italy)'

**συμβῐόω 1**, add 'of a wife, *SEG* 29.1197 (Lydia, AD 209/10), *TAM* 4(1).306'

**συμβίωσις I 2**, delete the section. **II**, add '*Inscr.Perg.* 8(3).85, *SEG* 31.1010 (Lydia, ii AD), etc.'

**συμβιωτής**, add '**III** *member of a* συμβίωσις II, Ramsay *Cities and Bishoprics* 2.470, *IG* $9^2$(1).248.6 (Thyrrheum, ii BC), *IGRom.* 4.796.7 (Apamea), *SEG* 33.1165 (Side, iii AD), etc.'

**συμβόλαιον II 2**, line 2, after 'E.*Ion* 411' insert 'Men.*Dysc.* 469, 470'

***συμβολᾱφόρος**, ὁ, *bearer of sacred symbols*, *DAW* 80.39 (Maeonia), *TAM* 4(1).76.

**συμβολικός 2**, add 'ψῆφος *AP* 6.248 (Marc.Arg.; = *Garl.* 1422 G.-P.); n. pl. as subst., ib. 5.135' **4**, add 'sg., *PGrenf.* 2.41.11 (i AD)'

***συμβολογρᾰ́φος**, ὁ, *notary*, *SB* 5326.5 (Byz.).

**σύμβολον III 1**, line 4, delete '*clue*, S.*OT* 221' and transfer quot. to section I 1 a (fig.); last line, transfer 'εἰράνας .. *AP* 6.151 (Tymn.)' to follow '*prearranged signal*' in section 4.

**συμβούλιον II**, add 'sp. -ειον, *POxy.* 3019.8'

**συμβροχέω**, for '= συμβρέχω' read 'pass., of land, *to be watered thoroughly*' and add '*PFlor.* 383.88 (iii AD)'

***συμβροχίζω**, *inundate, irrigate*, *BGU* 2063.23 (ii AD), 938.8 (iv AD). **2** *ret*, reduplicated pf. σεσυνβρ[ο]χι[σμένης *PColl.Youtie* 80.22 (AD 315).

***συμβροχικός**, ή, όν, *subject to inundation*, *PHerm.* 26.7 (v AD).

***συμβροχισμός**, ὁ, *retting*, *PLeit.* 2.3. (ii AD), *PColl.Youtie* 68.19 (iii AD), *POxy.* 3256.16 (AD 317/18).

***συμμᾰλακτέον**, *one must soften together*, Paul.Aeg. 7.3 (217.1 H.).

**συμμᾰ́χομαι**, at end delete '–Prose word .. Poets'

**σύμμᾰχος 1**, line 2, after '*ally*' insert 'Archil. 108.1 W.'

**συμμειρακιώδης**, delete the entry.

***συμμερισμός**, ὁ, *distribution of shares*, *SEG* 25.744 (Callatis, ii BC).

***συμμεταμορφόω**, *transform with*, τὴν φαντασίαν τοῖς ὑποκειμένοις πράγμασιν Procl. *in R.* 164 K.

**συμμέτοχος**, subst., add '*PKöln* 144.13, 28, 33 (152 BC), also perh. *spouse*, *EA* 12.111 no. 47 (Caria)'

**σύμμετρος II 1**, add 'w. gen., Aristid. 109 J. (= 1.50 L.-B.)' **4**, add '*κώμη σ.* Peripl.M.Rubr. 4'
**σύμμιγμα**, add '*σπέρμα ἀνθρώπου ἅρπαγμα καὶ σ. τοῦ τῶν προγόνων γένους* Zeno *Stoic.* 1.36 (ap.Gal. 19.370)'
**σύμμιξις II**, add 'Arist.*Ath.* 3.5'
***συμμοιχεύω**, *to be an adulterer with*, w. dat., Heraclit.*Ep.* 7.3.
**συμμορία 4**, for '*a company* in general' read '*a group of associates*' and after '*δειπνεῖν κατὰ σ.* J.*AJ* 5.7.3' insert '*οἷον κατὰ σ.* Longin. 20.1'
**συμμορφίζω**, add '(v. °*συμφορτίζω*)'
***συμπαιγνία**, ἡ, app. calque of Lat. *collusio, collusion*, *Cod.Just.* 6.4.4.6, Just.*Nov.* 54.2 pr., *Gloss.*
**συμπαραδίδωμι**, add '**2** *hand over together*, Just.*Nov.* 6 epilogos 1.'
**συμπαρακαθέζομαι**, line 1, for 'aor.' read 'impf.'
**συμπαρατάσσομαι**, add 'also act. **-παρατάσσω**, *set alongside*, *συμπαρα[τά]ξας μοι τὸν ἑαυτοῦ γραμματέα* *PTurku* 1.12 in *Tyche* 6.100 (Theadelpheia, ii BC)'
**συμπαρατυγχάνω**, for '*Cat.Cod.Astr.* 6.70' read 'Heph.Astr. 2.18.40, 43'
**συμπάρειμι** (*εἰμί sum*) **2**, add '*SEG* 37.979 (Claros, ii AD)'
***συμπαρεμπλέκω**, *insert, include simultaneously*, Anon. *in Rh.* 243.28, 31.
***συμπαρεμπλοκή**, ἡ, *simultaneous insertion, inclusion*, Anon. *in Rh.* 243.30.
***συμπαρθενεύω**, *live together in celibacy*, *PMed.*inv. 4969.11 (*ZPE* 93.155, v/vi AD).
**σύμπας**, add 'form *ξύμπας*, Myc. *ku-su-pa*'
***σύμπαχος**, ον, *thick*, *Poliorc.* 224.6, 244.8.
***σύμπεισις**, εως, ἡ, *persuasion*, Men.*Epit.* 716.
***συμπένθερος**, ὁ, *joint father-in-law*, said of a bride's father in relation to the bridegroom's father, Sch.Od. 4.22.
**συμπεραίνω II 1**, add '*τὸ πρᾶγμα περὶ οὗ μοι ἐπεστείλατε συνεπέρανα* *POxy.* 2862.3 (iii AD)'
**συμπεραντικός**, after '*tending to a conclusion*' insert 'Alex.Aphr. *in Top.* 563.6' and delete 'only in'
***συμπεριελαύνω**, *round up together*, *τάς τε βόας καὶ τὰ πρόβατα* *PTeb.* 729.7 (ii BC).
**συμπεριποιέω**, add '*Amyzon* 37'
**συμπερίπολος**, for '*Philol.* 71.92' read '*BCH* suppl. 9 p. 345 no. 9' and add '*SEG* 32.626 (Illyria, iii BC)'
**συμπεριφέρω II 3**, add '**b** *ἀγνοίᾳ σ. go about, live one's life in* ignorance, J.*AJ* 19.147'
**συμπεριφορά 2**, line 5, before '*σ. ποιεῖσθαι χρημάτων*' insert '**b** *indulgence, remission*' and add '*PMich.*IX 568.8 (I AD), *POxy.* 1590 (iv AD)'
**†σύμπλεγμα**, ατος, τό, *complex* of sculptured figures, *IEphes.* 509, 518, 857, 858 (i/ii AD); cf. *Pana et Olympum luctantes .. quod est alterum in terris symplegma nobile*, Plin.*HN* 36.35.
**συμπλήγδην**, delete the entry (v. °*ἐκπλήγδην*).
***συμπλήξ**, ῆγος, ὁ, ἡ, = *συμπληγάς*, Antim. in *Suppl.Hell.* 64.3 (s.v.l.).
**συμπληρωτικός 1**, add 'Iamb.*Protr.* 21 *ιγ'*, Procl.*Inst.* 75 D.'
**συμπλοκή 1**, line 4, after 'Pl.*Plt.* 281a, cf. 306a, al.' insert 'of scale armour, Hld. 9.15' and before '*ἡ ἁπάντων* ..' insert 'fig.'; after '*Stoic.* 2.284' add 'of intermarriage, *REG* 101.14' **2**, add 'with bandits, *IHadr.* 84.6 (i/ii AD). **b** *quarrel*, *POxy.* 3981.4 (AD 312).'
**συμποδισμός**, after 'ὁ' insert '*entanglement*, Alex.Aphr. *in SE* 135.13'
***σύμποκος**, ον, *complete with fleece*, i.e. *unshorn*, *πρόβατα* *PThead.* 22.9, 23.11 (iv AD).
***συμπολῑτευτής**, οῦ, ὁ, *fellow-citizen*, Diog.Oen.*fr.* 39 S.
**συμπολῑτεύω**, add '**3** *have the same legal force*, Just.*Const. Δέδωκεν* 23.'
**συμπομπή**, add '*σουννομπάν* *SEG* 32.456 (Boeotia, *c.*235/0 BC)'
**συμπονέω**, line 5, after 'S.*Ant.* 41' insert 'D. 2.9'
**σύμπονος**, add '*POxy.* 1942.4 (vi AD), Just.*Nov.* 119.5'
**σύμπορος**, add 'masc. subst. *ZPE* 7.225 no. 19 (Miletus, verse)'
**συμποσίαρχος**, after '(Palmyra, iii AD)' insert 'also ostr. in *BASP* 20.49.11'
***συμποσιαστής**, οῦ, ὁ, member of a cult-association, *IGBulg.* 1626 (Traiana Aug., *συν-*).
**συμπόσιος**, add 'epigr. in *SEG* 34.1266 (Bithynia)'
**σύμπους**, add 'neut. pl. *τὰ ζῷα .. ἔχοντα .. οὐ διεστηκότας τοὺς πόδας , ἀλλ' ἑστῶτα σύμποδα* Sch.Pl.*Men.* 97d G.'
***συμπραγματευτής**, οῦ, ὁ, *collaborator*, *PMasp.* 158.11 (vi AD).
***σύμπρᾱσις**, εως, ἡ, *joint purchase* or (perh.) *requisition*, (*ἐν συμπράσει*, *by way of requisition*) *PRyl.* 215.7, *PColl.Youtie* 32.7 (both ii AD).
**συμπράσσω I**, line 7, after 'Plb. 28.7.2' insert '*τινὶ ἔς τι* App.*BC* 5.7.31, D.C. 37.21.4'
**συμπρεσβύτερος**, for '*fellow-presbyter*' read '*fellow-elder*' and add '*PColl.Youtie* 21.9 (i AD), Mitchell *N.Galatia* 329 (iii/iv AD)'
**συμπροβαίνω**, before '3 sg.' insert '*οἱ λόγοι τῷ χρόνῳ σ. advance with the advance of time*, Aristid.*Or.* 2.103 J.'
**συμπρονοέω**, add '*SEG* 19.790.5 (Pisidia)'
**συμπροσγίγνομαι 1**, after 'Dor. **συμποτιγίν-**' insert 'Thess. **συμπογγῖν-** *BCH* 59.56 (Larissa, w. -γγ- for -gg-, not -ng-)'
**συμπρόσειμι**, for '*to be present together*' read '*to be present with as a support*' and add '*POxy.* 1061.10 (i BC)'
***συμπροσίημι**, aor. med. -*ήκαντο*, *let approach together*, *πρέσβεις* Did. *in D.* viii.10.
***συμπροστρέπω**, *support a supplication*, *συμπροστρέψω τὴν οἰκοδομὴν ποιῆσαι* *PMil.Vogl.* 255.2 (ii/iii AD).
**συμπροτρέπω**, add 'med., *IG* $2^2$.1039.29 (i BC)'
**συμπρύτᾰνις**, add '*SEG* 26.694 (Epirus, *c.*150 BC)'
***συμπρωτοκωμήτης**, ου, ὁ, *associate πρωτοκωμήτης*, *PFlor.* 296.41 (vi AD).
***σύμπρωτος**, η, ον, *the very first*, adv. -*ον* Pi.*fr.* 128c.8 (s.v.l.).
***συμπτώσιμος**, ον, *collapsing*, *οἰκία* *PGoodsp.Cair.* 13.4 (iv AD).
**σύμπτωσις I**, for '*CIG* 3293 (Smyrna)' read '*TAM* 4(1).134 (Nicomedia)' and add '*ἐν συμπτώσει in a state of ruin* or *collapse*, of a house, *SB* 9902 A, IV 2, etc. (iii AD), of a site, *PFlor.* 50.61'
**συμφᾰνής**, line 1, before '*manifest*' insert '*clearly visible*, *Amyzon* 38' and after '*evident*' insert '*συμφανῶν* (*ξυμφώνων* codd.) *πράξεων* Pl.*Lg.* 864b'
**σύμφανσις**, delete the entry (v. °*σύμφαυσις*).
***σύμφαυσις**, εως, ἡ, *shining together*, Eust. 1060.53.
***συμφεροντής**, ου, ὁ, perh. *fellow-benefactor*, *καρπίων ἀνέθηκε .. εὐχὴν μετὰ συνφαιρονταῖς* (*sic*) *IG* $2^2$.4794.
**συμφέρω A I 4**, add 'w. gen., *κακῶν τῶν σῶν ξυνοίσω* E.*fr.* 909.12'
**σύμφθαρσις 2**, for this section read '*breaking down into a homogeneous substance*, of the digestion of food, Syrian. *in Hermog.* 1.66 R.; transf., of abstract things, Hermog.*Id.* 1.22, Iamb. *in Nic.* p. 80 P.'
**συμφθείρω II**, for this section read '*break down into a unified mass*, *φαρμάκων συντριβέντων καὶ συμφθαρέντων ἀλλήλοις* Plu. 2.436b; transf., sounds, D.H.*Dem.* 48; *συνεφθαρμένα ἀλλήλοις* of *π* and *σ* forming *ψ*, id.*Comp.* 14; abstract qualities, Iamb. *in Nic.* p. 81 P.'
**συμφιλοκᾰλέω**, add '*support in the quest of distinction*, J.*AJ* 11.312'
***σύμφιμος**, ον, *tightly closed*, Iambl.Alch. 287.5.
***σύμφοιτος**, ον, gloss on *ὁμόφοιτος*, Sch.Pi.*N.* 8.54.
**συμφορά II 2**, after '*misfortune*' insert 'Alc. 69.2 L.-P.'
***συμφορτίζω**, *burden together with others*, v.l. in *Ep.Phil.* 3.10 (v. *συμμορφίζω*).
**σύμφραξις**, add '**2** *fencing round*, *Tit.Calymn.* 52.12 (iii BC).'
**σύμφρουρος II**, add '*SEG* 23.444 (Thessaly, i BC)'
**συμφῠγάς**, add 'Isoc. 16.14, 26, etc.'
**συμφυής II**, add '**4** adv. *συμφυῶς*, *in fusion*, Simp.*in de An.* 59.25.' **III**, add 'Nonn.*D.* 14.212'
**συμφύλαξ**, add 'cf. *ὁ γὰρ φόβος δεινὸς δοκεῖ σ. εἶναι* X.*Eq.Mag.* 7.7'
**σύμφωνος II 3**, line 2, before '*ἐκ συμφώνου*' insert 'neut. subst., *agreement, pact*, *Cod.Just.* 1.3.55.1; also *clause in an agreement*, ib. 4.65.34'; line 3, after '*Cod.Just.* 8.10.12' insert '*κατὰ σύμφωνον* *AR* 1985/6.63 (W. Maced., iv BC)'
***συμψειρικός**, v. ‡*συψ-*.
***σύμψημα**, ατος, τό, pl. *scrapings*, Hsch. s.v. *συρματὶς στρατιά*.
***συμψηφισμός**, ὁ, expl. as *σύνθεσις ψήφων*, Alex.Aphr. *in Top.* 9.18.
**σύμψηφος 1**, add '**b** *conforming to one's views, agreeable*, *POxy.* 2711.7 (iii AD).'
***συμψῑλίζω**, perh. *join in stripping*, *PVindob.* G29946 i 22 (Gallo *Frammenti biografici* II p. 266).
**σύν**, lines 2 ff., w. gen., add '*MAMA* 1.193, 208, 212, 217, etc.'; line 16, for 'Sapph. 75' read 'Sapph. 121 L.-P. (codd.); *ξυνιείς* Pi.*N.* 4.31 (codd.)'; line 17, after '(Locr., v BC) etc.' insert 'Cypr. *ICS* 217.28' **A 5**, add 'of attendant burden, *σ. γήρᾳ βαρεῖς* S.*OT* 17; *σ. νόσοις ἀλγεινὸς ἐξεπέμπετο* id.*OC* 1663' add '(form *ξύν*) Myc. *ku-su*'
**συνᾰγείρω**, line 2, after 'Theoc. 22.76' insert 'Aeol. 3 sg. pf. *συναγάγρεται* Alc. 119.10 L.-P.'
**συναγέσκεο**, delete the entry.
***συνᾰγορᾱνόμος**, ὁ, *colleague as ἀγορανόμος*, *MUB* 26.62 (Tyre, i AD); w. dat., *SEG* 11.499 (Sparta, ii AD).
***συνᾱγοριστικός**, v. *συνηγ-*.
**συναγρίς**, after '*sea-fish*' insert 'perh. *sea-bream, Dentex vulgaris*, cf. mod. Gr. *συναγρίδα*'
**συναγχικός**, line 1, after '*συνάγχη*' insert 'Ar.Byz.*Epit.* 2.178'; line 2, delete '*of* .. Gal. 15.790'
**σύναγχος**, add 'Gal. 15.790.8'
**συνάγω II 3**, add '**b** in logic, *reduce* to, *συνάγει* (*τὰ τέτταρα*) *εἰς τὰ δύο* Arist.*GC* 330b20.' add '**III** perh. *compel, oblige* (calque of Lat. *cogo*), *Cod.Just.* 1.2.24.2.'
***συνᾰγωνοθέτης**, ου, ὁ, *colleague as ἀγωνοθέτης*, rest. in *Inscr.Prien.* 111.174, 118.4, 11 (i BC), *Hesperia* 28.324 (Isthmia, Rom.imp.).
**συνάδελφος I**, add 'Mitchell *N.Galatia* 252 (after AD 212)'
**συνᾴδω I 1**, line 3, after 'Ar.*Av.* 858 (lyr.)' insert '(cj. *συναυλείτω*)' **II**, for 'trans.' read 'w. acc. pers.'
***συνᾱθλητής**, οῦ, ὁ, *fellow-athlete*, *MAMA* 8.417.32 (dub.).

**συνάθροισμα**, add 'Sch.E.*Hec.* 100-24'

**⁺συναΐδιος**, ον, *coeternal, Cod.Just.* 1.1.5.1; συναΐδιος· συνυπάρχων Hsch.

**συναίρεμα I**, add 'sp. συνέρεμα *POxy.* 3170.23 (iii AD)'

**συναιρέω II 1**, line 4, after 'Sch. ad loc.)' insert 'S.*Tr.* 884' add '**III** *choose together with*, αἱρεθεὶς θεωρὸς .. μετὰ τῶν συναιρεθέντων *JHS* 68.48.73, 77 (Lycia, ?ii BC).'

**συναισθητικός**, before 'adv.' delete 'only' and insert '*conscious* (to oneself), εἰς αὑτήν Plot. 2.2.1.10'

***συναίσθομαι**, = συναισθάνομαι (in quot., III), *PLit.Lond.* 138 vii 7 (i AD).

**συναιχμᾰλωτις**, add 'Sch.S.*Tr.* 318 (ξυν-)'

**συνακμάζω**, for '*blossom* or *flourish at the same time*' read '*reach the peak* of one's growth, development, fortune, etc., *at the same time*'

**συνακοντίζω I**, for 'Antipho 3.4.5' read 'Antipho 3.4.6 G.'

**συνακροάομαι**, add '**2** *to be a fellow judge*, ὥστε τὸν κοιαίστωρα συνακροᾶσθαι αὐτῷ *Cod.Just.* 7.62.35.'

***συνακροατής**, οῦ, ὁ, *fellow judge*, Just.*Nov.* 86 rubric.

**συνακτήριον**, add '*Cod.Just.* 1.5.14'

**συνᾰλίσγομαι**, read **συνᾰλισγέομαι** (v.l. **συνᾰλίσγομαι**).

***συναλλάζω**, v. °συναλλάσσω.

***συναλλακτήρ**, ῆρος, ὁ, = συναλλακτής (in quot., II), *SEG* 34.940 (Camarina, *c.*300 BC).

**συναλλακτής**, add '**III** *party in a contract*, Just.*Edict.* 7.3.'

**συνάλλαξις 2**, add 'ἡ τῶν καρπῶν σ. the *contract* concerning, *BGU* 1120.52 (i BC)' **3**, delete the section.

**συναλλάσσω**, line 1, after 'Att. -ττω' insert 'Dor. -ζω, *SEG* 11.244 (Sicyon, *c.*500 BC)' **II 2**, add '**b** *enter into a contract of* marriage, τῶν δευτέρων γάμων, οὓς μετὰ τόνδε ἡμῶν συναλλάξαιεν τὸν νόμον Just.*Nov.* 22.48 pr.; also abs., ib. 157.1.'

**συναλοάω**, add '**3** *beat up, thrash*, Longus 4.29.'

**συνᾰλύω**, add 'Philostr.*VA* 8.11'

***συναμφιβολεύς**, έως, ὁ, *fellow-(net) fisherman, PCornell* 46.7 (ii AD).

**συναναζεύγνῡμι**, add '*BGU* 1257.20 (iii BC)'

**συνανάκειμαι**, add '**2** euphem., of sexual intercourse, Sopat.Rh. 8.258.22 W.'

***συνανάκλῐσις**, εως, ἡ, *lying down together, coitus*, tab.defix. in *SEG* 35.224.13 (Attica, iii AD).

**συναναπέμπω**, add '**2** *admit to an inheritance equally with*, θυγατράσι δὲ συνανεπέμπετο (ἡ μήτηρ) Just.*Nov.* 22.47.2.'

**συναναπίπτω**, before '*concubo*' insert '*lie down together*, tab.defix. in *SEG* 35.219.7, 17, 221.4 (Attica, iii AD)'

**συναναρτάομαι**, add 'w. dat., Socr.*Ep.* 6.10'

**συνανασκευάζω**, delete 'Gal.*Opt.Doctr.* 6' and transfer 'S.E.*M.* 7.214' to follow 'Phld.*Sign.* 12, al.'

**συναναστρέφω II 2**, delete the section.

***συνανάτᾰσις**, εως, ἡ, (τείνω) *straining, effort*, Phld.*Rh.Suppl.* 45.14 S.

***συναναφύρομαι**, *to frequent together*, get *mixed up with*, μὴ ἐν τῷ κο[ι]νῷ γυμνασίῳ συναναφύρωνται τοῖς .. *SEG* 28.1566 (Cyrene, AD 143); cf. ἀναφύρω.

***συναντагωνιστής**, οῦ, ὁ, *fellow-competitor*, Sch.Pi.*N.* 11 p. 185.4 D.

**συναντάω II**, add 'of a topographical feature, *meet* the traveller, i.e. *come next*, *Peripl.M.Rubr.* 33 C.' **III**, add 'τοῦν συναντακόντουν (pf. part.) φιλανθρούπουν παρ' αὐτοῖο πὸτ τὰν πόλιν *SEG* 31.572 (Thessaly, *c.*200 BC)'

**συνάντησις**, after 'of heavenly bodies' insert 'Ptol.*Tetr.* 150 B.'

***συναπαιτητής**, οῦ, ὁ, *fellow tax-collector, SB* 9840.10 (s.v.l., iv AD).

***συνάπαξ**, *all at one time*, Gal. 2.381.17.

***συναπελευθέρα**, ἡ, *fellow freedwoman, ISestos* 2 (?i BC).

**συναπελεύθερος**, add '*IGLS* 9032'

***συναπηχέω**, *sound at the same time*, Polyaen. 8.23.2; cf. συνεπηχέω.

***συναπογέννησις**, εως, ἡ, *joint procreation*, Procl. *in R.* 1.134, 2.366 K.

**συναπογράφομαι**, add '**III** act., dub. sens., *Inscr.Cret.* 4.160*B*5 (Gortyn, iv/iii BC).'

***συναποκηρύττω**, *banish, disown together with* another, Men.*Sam.* 509; cf. ἀποκηρύττω II.

**συναποκλῑνω I**, add '**2** *cause to veer away with* another, w. dat., Memn. 38.5 J.'

**συναποστέλλω**, after lemma insert '*send out together*, ὅποι .. ἂν .. μέρος τι τῆς πόλεως συναποσταλῇ D. 4.45'

***συναποτάσσω**, *assign* troops *together to a detachment*, *SEG* 34.558 (Larissa, *c.*150/130 BC).

***συναποχή**, ἡ, *joint receipt, POxy.* 1891.18 (v AD).

**συναποχωρέω**, add 'of physical conditions, w. dat., ταυτὶ .. τὰ νοσήματα .. ξυναποχωρεῖ ποτε τῇ φύσει Philostr.*Gym.* 28'

**συνάπτω A I 2**, line 11, delete 'but .. Theopomp.Com. 22' **II 2 b**, line 2, after 'id.*Ph.* 1241' insert 'σ. τὸν λόγον Theopomp.Com. 23 K.-A.' **III 3**, for 'what *conclusion follows*' read '*what hypothetical proposition is made*' and for 'Call.*Fr.* 70.3' read 'Call.*fr.* 393.3 Pf.'

**συνᾰρέσκω**, line 7, after 'c. dat.' insert 'Arist.*Ath.* 33.2'

***συνᾰρήγω**, compd. of ἀρήγω in *Suppl.Hell.* 937.8 (fragmentary hex.).

**⁺συναρθμέω**, *cause to agree with*, σ. ἐπέεσσι A.R. 4.418.

**συνᾰριθμέω I**, after 'Is. 5.18' insert 'Call. *fr.* 587 Pf.'

***συνᾱρίστιον**, τό, *lunch-club, IG* 12(3).93, 94 (Nisyros, iii BC).

**συναρμόζω I 1 a**, at end, *to be joined in wedlock*, add 'also in act., Memn. 4.4 J.' add '**c** *fit* on, στεφάνους .. κροτάφοισι ῥοδίνους συναρμόσαντες *Anacreont.* 43.2 W.'

**συναρπᾰγή**, after '= *obreptio*' insert '*Cod.Just.* 1.4.26.4' **2**, for '*Cat.Cod.Astr.* 1.104' read '*Cat.Cod.Astr.* 1.106' and add '*PCarlsberg* 49ʳ i 22 (v AD; *APF* 32.17)'

**συναρτύω II**, for '*to be joint*-ἄρτυνος' read '*to be joint*-ἀρτύνας'

**συναρχία II**, in sg., add '*SEG* 23.447 (Thessaly, ii BC)'

**συναρχῐεράομαι**, add '*SEG* 26.784 (Thrace, AD 162/3)'

**συνάρχω II 2**, add 'Gal. 9.563.11'

**συνασεβέω**, add '*SEG* 32.1423d (Syria, AD 192/3)'

**συνασπίζω**, line 1, before 'Hsch.' insert 'Lxx 3*Ma.* 3.10'

**⁺συναυλέω**, *play the aulos in accompaniment* to, Ar.*Av.* 857 (cj.), συναυλεῖν τοῖς χοροῖς Ath. 14.617b. **2** of pipes, pipers, *play together*, Luc. *Dem.* 16, Longus 2.35.

**συναυλία** (A), for '*symphony* .. Hsch.' read '*playing together by two or more auletes*, Sch.Ar.*Eq.* 9 J. (cf. Hsch., Poll. 4.83)'

***συναυξητικός**, ή, όν, *capable of increase*, φύσις Gal. 19.473.

**συνᾰφή I**, line 6, after 'Epicur.*Nat.* .. 9' insert 'Procl.*Inst.* 32 D., al.'; line 7, at end insert 'ἡμῖν δὲ πρὸς ἐκείνους (sc. τοὺς θεούς) γίνεται σ. Sallust. 15.3 R.'

**συνᾰφής**, lines 1/2, delete 'κόλποι .. 21'; line 3, after 'Hp.*Morb.* 4.49' insert 'τὸ ἐκείνῳ (sc. τῷ πρώτῳ) σ. πλῆθος Procl.*Inst.* 149 D.'; line 4, after 'Aret.*SD* 1.7' insert 'topogr., κόλποι σ. ἀλλήλοις Arist.*Mu.* 393ᵃ21, *Peripl.M.Rubr.* 2 (w. gen.), 20, al.'

***συναφιερόω**, *consecrate*, *SEG* 32.1425, 1426 (Syria, ii AD).

**συναφίημι 1**, add '**b** *manumit together*, *SEG* 28.455 (Boeotia, iii BC).'

***συνδᾱμέτας**, α, ὁ, = συνδημότης, *IRhod.Peraea* 201.15 (i BC).

**συνδᾰπᾰνάω**, add '*IGLS* 2707 (i AD)'

**συνδαυχνᾱφόρος**, after 'Thess.' insert '(v BC)'

***συνδέξιος**, ὁ, member of a society of Mithraic μύσται, *Dura*[7,8] p. 87 no. 848, cf. Firm.*De err.prof.relig.* 5.2.

**σύνδεσμος I 1**, add 'σ. αὐτοῦ (sc. crocodile) ὥσπερ σμιρίτης λίθος Lxx *Jb.* 41.6(7)' **V**, delete the section transferring quot. to section IV. add '**VII** perh. *puzzle, enigma*, Thd.*Da.* 5.12.'

**συνδηλόω**, line 3, for 'τῷ' read 'τοῖς'

**συνδημιουργέω**, after '*create*' insert 'or *fashion*' and add '*ISelge* 16'

**συνδιαλέγομαι**, after '*converse with* or *together*' insert '*ZPE* 77.56.7 (Cilicia, iii BC), D.S. 12.75.3'

**συνδιαπνέω 2**, for this section read '*exude together* with, ἱδρῶτος γενομένῳ συνδιέπνευσε τούτῳ τὸ ζέσαν τῆς μελαίνης Gal. 18(2).279.9'

**συνδιατελέω**, for '*continue with to the end*' read 'w. dat., *continue with* one *to the end*'

**συνδιατίθημι**, line 1, after '*help in arranging*' insert 'χσυνδιαθέσεν τὸν ἀ[γôνα] *IG* 1³.3.8 (Marathon, v BC)'

***συνδιεξάγω**, *administer together*, part. συνδιεξηχώς *SEG* 25.112.14 (Athens, early ii BC).

**συνδικαστής**, add '*fellow-judge*, Just.*Nov.* 53.3 pr.'

**σύνδῐκος I 3**, add '= Lat. *defensor civitatis, PCol.* 175 (iv AD)'

**συνδιοικέω**, line 3, after 'D. 24.160' insert 'Sallust. 21.1 R., Iamb.*De An.* ap.Stob. 1.49.67'

**συνδοκῐμάζω**, for 'J.*AJ* 20.2.2' read 'J.*AJ* 20.2.3'

***σύνδορπνος**, ον, perh. *companion at table*, *Dura*[6] p. 40.

***συνδουλίων**, ωνος, ὁ, *fellow-slave, Vit.Aesop.*(G) 16 (pl., -ίονες cod.).

**σύνδουλος 1**, after 'Babr. 3.6' add '*IKios* 49 (Rom.imp.)'

**συνδρομάς**, for 'pecul. fem. of σύνδρομος' read '*running together, meeting*' and after 'Theoc. 13.22' insert 'of a type of door consisting of two leaves, *IG* 1³.422.15, Poll. 10.24'

**συνδρομή 2 a**, add 'of rhetorical characteristics, D.H.*Dem.* 50'

**συνδυάζω III**, after 'Just.*Nov.* 130.7' insert '(sp. συνδοι-)'

***συνδύασμα**, ατος, τό, *combination of two elements*, Alcin.*Intr.* 10 (p. 166.3 H.).

**σύνδῠο**, last line, for 'Plb. 8.4.2' read 'Plb. 8.6.2'

***συνεγγηράσκω**, *grow old along with*, *SEG* 32.1243.21 (Aeolian Cyme, 2 BC/AD 2).

**συνεγγισμός**, line 3, delete 'πρὸς τὴν ἀρετήν'

***συνεγγυητής**, οῦ, ὁ, *joint surety, MDAI(A)* 59.42 (Attica, iv BC).

***συνεγκᾰλέω**, *charge jointly*, in pass., οἱ συνεγκαλούμενοι the *joint defendants*, *UPZ* 161.38, 56 (ii BC).

**συνεδρεύω III 1**, line 3, after 'Aët. 15.10' insert 'Συνεδρεύοντα, title of a book of the physician Praxagoras, Gal. 18(1).7.16'

**συνέδριον 1**, line 13, after 'Gal. 6.332' insert '= Lat. *consistorium principis*, Lib.*Or.* 18.154' **2**, after 'X.*HG* 2.4.23' insert 'Men.*Dysc.* 177' add '**II** *base for a number of statues*, *Michel* 537 (Cyzicus, i BC).'

**σύνεδρος I 2**, for '*sitting together, friendly*' read '*perching together*' add

'**3** *keeping company with*, ἔνθα σύνεδρος Φωσφόρῳ ἠδὲ καλῷ Ἑσπέρῳ ὄφρα πέλω of a deceased infant, *SEG* 31.846 (Italy, iii AD).' **II** **2**, add 'of the Roman senate, *BCH* 109.597-607 (Augustus)'

°**συνειδός**, ότος, τό, v. σύνοιδα (sense I, p. 1721ᵃ line 14 and sense v 2).

**συνειλέω**, add 'εἰς αὐτὸν συνειλοῦ *withdraw into yourself*, M.Ant. 7.28'

**συνείμαρται**, after 'Plu. 2.569f' insert 'M.Ant. 12.3'

**σύνειμι** (εἰμί) **5**, after '*take part in, attend*' insert '*SEG* 29.1088 (Caria, iii BC)'

**σύνειμι** (εἶμι) **II** **3**, add 'ἐκτείνεσθαι καὶ συνίεναι Arist.*Mete.* 387ᵃ14; id.*PA* 689ᵃ30'

**συνείσακτος 1**, add 'Just.*Nov.* 137.1'

°**συνείσδοσις**, εως, ἡ, app. *communal donation*, *BCH* 9.76 (Aphrodisias).

**συνεισφορά**, add '**2** transl. Lat. *collatio bonorum, joint contribution to estate by those emancipated by decedent in his lifetime*, Just.*Nov.* 18.6.'

°**συνεκδᾰνείζω**, *join in lending out*, rest. in *SEG* 31.122 (Attica, c.AD 121).

°**συνεκκαθαίρω**, *purge together*, Gal. 14.137.14.

**συνεκμαρτῠρέω**, add '**2** med., *acknowledge jointly as one's child*, συνεκμαρτυρεῖσθαι .. τὸν γεγονότα αὐτῷ ἐκ τῆς Τνεφερσόιτος *POxy.Hels.* 35.36 (AD 151).'

**συνεκπέμπω 1**, add '**b** *escort away*, in quot., the dead, Call.*fr.* 194.50 Pf. (tm.).'

**συνεκπίπτω**, add '**VII** *fall into* or *be included* in a schedule, ὃ δ' ἂν φανῇ ὑπολειπόμενον καὶ τούτων συνεκπεσεῖτε (i.e. πεσεῖται) τῇδε τῇ καταγραφῇ *PColl.Youtie* 65.75 (AD 241).'

**συνεκπῠρόω**, add 'Procl.*Inst.* 129 D.'

**συνεκσῴζω**, after 'S.*OC* 566' insert 'Men.*Dysc.* 753'

**συνεκτικός I 2**, for '*firmly gripping*' read '*holding oneself back, cautious*'

**συνεκφέρω 1**, add '*SEG* 33.1039 (Cyme, ii BC)'

**συνελαύνω I 2**, add '*Cod.Just.* 1.3.38.2' add '**3** in chariot-racing, *drive together* with, τοὺς σὺν αὐτῷ συνελαύνοντας *SEG* 34.1437 (v/vi AD).'

**συνελεουρέω**, read **συνελεορέω** (cf. °ἐλεορέω)

**συνελευθερόω**, add '**II** *manumit* several slaves *together*, *Cod.Just.* 6.4.4.10, 11.'

**συνέμφᾰσις**, add 'Alcin.*Intr.* 35 (p. 189.19 H.)'

**συνενεργέω**, delete 'Plot. 3.4.6' (read συνεργέω) and after 'Ascl. *in Metaph.* 282.5' add '(cj.)'

**συνεξελαύνω**, add 'Just.*Nov.* 42.3 pr.'

**συνεξέρχομαι 1**, add '**b** of two athletes, *step out of the ring together* after a drawn fight, *Inscr.Magn.* 180.16 (ii AD).'

°**συνεπαγγέλλομαι**, *join in making an* ἐπαγγελία, *SEG* 30.1073.14 (Chios, c.189/8 BC).

**συνεπάγω 2**, lines 5/6, delete '*draw* .. cf.'

**συνεπέρχομαι**, add '**2** *approach together with*, in quot., of an epiphany, *SEG* 34.1216 (Lydia, AD 295/6).'

**συνεπιβαίνω II**, add 'abs., Men.*Dysc.* 954'

**συνεπιβάλλω**, add '**III** *add to an existing amount*, καὶ συνεπιβαλῖν τῷ λοιπῷ ἄνω *PFreib.* 53.23 (i BC). **IV** *affix* a seal *jointly*, συνεπιβαλλέτω τὸν δακτύλιον ὁ ἐγ [Μυ]ανίας καὶ ἐξ Ὑπνίας βούλαρχος *SEG* 23.305 (Delphi, c.190 BC).'

**συνεπιδείκνῡμι**, line 2, after 'Iamb.*Myst.* 2.7' insert 'of a ὁριοδείκτης, σ. ἀρούρας *PRyl.* 656.22 (AD 300)'

**συνεπιδίδωμι I 1**, add '**b** abs., *devote oneself wholeheartedly*, *SEG* 18.570 (Lycia, ii BC).'

**συνεπικιρνάω**, after '*mix with besides*' insert 'Ptol.*Tetr.* 146, Heph.Astr. 2.12.16'

**συνεπινοέω II**, add 'also act., Alcin.*Intr.* 10 (p. 164.14 H.)'

**συνεπιπλέω**, for '*join in a naval expedition*' read '*sail together on an expedition*' and add '*SEG* 34.558 (Larissa, ii BC)'

°**συνεπιτηρέω**, *serve as joint-superintendent* with, τὰς ἡμέρας ἃς μόνας αὐτῷ Διδύμῳ συνεπετήρησα *PMich.*xi 616 (AD 182).

**συνεπίτροπος**, add '*PHamb.* 70.2 (ii AD), *IEphes.* 3131'

°**συνεποικιανός**, ὁ, *fellow-member of a settlement*, *TAM* 5(1).712 (Gordus, ii AD; -εποκ-).

**συνερᾰνιστής**, add '*SEG* 31.122 (Attica, ii AD)'

**συνεργᾰσία**, add 'ἡ σ. τῶν λινουργῶν *SEG* 32.1234 (Lydia, AD 192/3)'

°**συνεργεπιστᾰ́της**, ου, ὁ, *joint superintendent of works*, *IEphes.* 674 (ii AD).

⁺**συνέργιον**, *guild of workmen*, *PMich.Zen.* 57.2 (iii BC), *ICilicie* 46.4 (i/ii AD). **2** τὸ Μέγα Συνέργιον, a quarter in the city of Side (see also *Rev.Phil.* 32.19ff.), *IGRom.* 3.810.9.

**συνερείδω II 2**, line 3, delete '*press on* .. Arr.*Tact.* 12.3'

°**συνερέτης**, ου, ὁ, *fellow oarsman*, Hsch. s.v. ξυνερέται.

**συνέρῑθος**, before 'less freq.' insert 'fem. sup. συνεριθοτάταν Βρομίῳ *most faithful handmaid* to B., prob. in Telest. 1(c).1 P.'

**συνέρχομαι II 3**, add 'of accomplices, *TAM* 4(1).269' **b**, line 5, after '*PGnom.* 71, al. (ii AD), etc.' insert 'σύνηλθε (for σύνελθε, on the bezel of a ring) *RIB* II(3).2422.35' add '**IV** w. dat., *help* (cf. Lat. *subvenio*), Just.*Edict.* 7.8.1.'

°**συνέστᾱς**, α, ὁ, member of a society or college, perh. of sim. standing to a παράσιτος, *IG* 9²(1).434.9 (pl.) (Acarnania, ii BC).

**συνέστιος 1**, lines 2/3, delete 'ξυνέστιοι .. A.*Th.* 773 (lyr.)' **2**, for this section read 'Ζεὺς ξυνέστιος Zeus *patron of those who share the same hearth*, A.*Ag.* 704. **b** θεοὶ ξυνέστιοι gods *who share an altar*, id.*Th.* 773 (s.v.l.); perh. also συνεσ]τίοις θεοῖς *PGiss.* 99.26 (ii AD).'

**συνευᾰρεστέω**, add '*SEG* 25.708, 36.590 (both Maced., Rom.imp.)'

°**συνευᾰρέστησις**, εως, ἡ, *consent*, *Delph.* 3(6).48.16 (ii BC).

°**συνευφημία**, ἡ, *panegyric to match* another, *parallel laudation*, cj. in Jul.*Or.* 3.106b.

**συνεχής I 1**, line 2, for 'of quantity' read 'of types of measurable quantity'; add '*consecutive in space*, ἄλλοι συνεχεῖς ὅρμοι' **II 1**, line 9, delete 'τὸ σ. ἔργου (prob. for ἔργον) Anaxandr. 63'

°**συνεχῖτις**, ιδος, ἡ, name for γαλαξίας II, Plin.*HN* 37.162.

**συνέχω I 1**, line 10, after 'Ar.*V.* 95' insert 'συνέχει τὰς ῥῖνας *holds* his nose, Sch.Ar.*Pax* 10'; line 13, for '*Is.* 52.16' read '*Is.* 52.15' **3**, add '**b** *compose, make up*, πέντε δὲ ἄλλαι (πόλεις) τὸν Πολεμωνιακὸν συνέχουσι Πόντον Just.*Nov.* 82.1 pr.'

**συνηβάω**, for 'παῖς ἐθέλει' read '‹παῖς ἐ›θέλει' and for 'Anacr. 24' read 'Anacr. 33 P.'

**συνηβολίη**, for '*occurrence*' read '*meeting*'

°**συνηγεμών**, όνος, ὁ, *fellow commander*, *SEG* 31.1348 (Cyprus, iii BC).

**συνηγορία 1**, add '**b** as an official service, *Cod.Just.* 1.5.18.10.'

**συνήθεια I**, add '**3** *club, guild*, τῶν πορφυροβάφων *IG* 10.2(1).291.1; τῶν ὄνων *ABSA* 18.155 (Beroea).' **III**, pl., add '*SEG* 34.1243 (Abydos, c.AD 492). **2** perh. a type of dike-tax, *PKöln* 104.15 (vi AD), *PHamb.* 56 vi 15 (vi/vii AD).'

**συνήθης I**, add 'Ἑρμεῖ καὶ συνήθεσι, in a dedication, *BCH* 90.450 (Delos, ii/i BC)' **III 2**, add '*Peripl.M.Rubr.* 14, 36, 38'

**συνήκω II**, for 'of walls, *meet* in a point' read 'of structures, formations, etc., *converge*'

°**συνήλῠσις**, εως, ἡ, *meeting, assembly*, (transl. Lat. *conciliabulum*), *IEphes.* 4101.16 (Trajan).

**συνημοσύνη II**, delete 'sg. .. φιλημοσύνη'

**συνήορος**, add '**3** *brother, sister*, Hsch. s.v. ξυνάοροι.'

°**συνθεᾱ́γος**, ὁ, *fellow*-θεαγός, τῶν ἐξαγορείων *SB* 7634.13 (AD 249).

°**συνθερᾰπευτής**, οῦ, ὁ, *fellow-devotee* of Asclepius, *Inscr.Perg.* 8(3).28.

**συνθεσία 1**, at end delete 'περὶ .. codd.)'

**σύνθεσις I 2 g**, add 'of spices and incense, Lxx *Ex.* 30.32, 37; ἡ σ. θυμιάματος, τὸ θυμίαμα τῆς σ. ib. 35.28, 31.11' add '**h** *mosaic work*, τόπον τὸν ἐνθάδ' ἐκόσμησε Παῦλος τῆι πολυμόρφωι συνθέσει *SEG* 26.1629 (Apameia, vi AD).' add '**3** *joint tomb*, Robert *Ét. Anat.* pp. 224-5.'

**σύνθετος I 1**, add 'πλίνθος *PMich.*v 285-6.4 (i AD)'

**συνθήκη**, after lemma insert 'non-Att.-Ion. -θήκα' and add '*SEG* 36.548 (Thessaly, iii BC)'

**συνθηκοφύλαξ**, after '*covenant*' insert '*Vit.Aesop.*(G) 71'

⁺**συνθηρᾱτής**, οῦ, ὁ, *one who joins in hunting*, in quot., of hunters' horses, Philostr.*Gym.* 26; transf., *one who joins in the quest of*, τῶν φίλων X.*Mem.* 3.11.15.

**συνθραύω**, after 'Plu.*Arist.* 18' insert '*SEG* 35.209 (c.AD 150)'

**σύνθρονος**, add 'of a soul in the underworld, *ISmyrna* 529 (verse, i AD)'

°**συνθυίω**, *rush together with*, τινι Sch.min.Il. 6.21.

**συνθύξω**, add 'perh. fut. of συντυγχάνω'

**συνθῠσία I**, add 'personified, *SEG* 35.1736-7 (cf. *RA* 1987.98, Phrygia, iii AD)'

**σύνθωκος I**, before 'Jul.*Or.* 5.166b' insert 'of the Mother of the gods' and add 'Μίνω σ. εἰμι poet. in inscr. in *APF* 5.164 (iii/ii BC)'

**συνῑαίνω**, for '*cheer together*' read '*simultaneously gladden*'

°**συνῑερογλῠ́φος**, ὁ, *fellow hieroglyph-carver*, *POxy.* 1029.6 (pl., ii AD).

**συνιππεύω**, before 'θυέλλαις' insert 'ἀέλλαις Opp.*H.* 5.344'

°**συνισθμιάζω**, *join in the celebration of the Isthmian games*, A.*fr.* 78c.58 R.

**συνῑσόομαι**, add 'act., Hsch. s.v. συγκρίνει'

**συνίστημι A VI 2**, add 'Modest.*Dig.* 27.1.13.7' **B II**, add '**4** *stand by* a principle, attitude, etc., *insist on*, συστῆναι ταῖς κατηγορίαις *Cod.Just.* 1.4.34.18, συνίστασθαι τοῖς ἑαυτοῦ δικαίοις ib. 10.11.8.5.'

**συνίστωρ 2**, line 3, after 'σώματα' insert 'αὐτοῖς'

**συνισχναίνω 2**, after 'ξυνισχνᾰνεῖ' insert '(or ξυνισχᾰνεῖ; codd. συνανίσχει)'

**συνναύτης II**, for 'worshippers of Isis' read 'fishermen' and for '(Callipolis)' read '(Parium), cf. Robert *Hell.* 9.81'

°**συννεκροτᾰ́φος**, ὁ, *fellow burier of the dead*, *PRyl.* 574.2 (pl., i BC).

**συννέμω 1**, add '**b** *manage together*, αὕτη δὲ συνένεμε τὸ ἐργαστήριον *PLond.* 1976.12 (iii BC).'

**συννομή III**, add 'and at Lindos, *Lindos* 454.9'

°**συννομιτεύομαι**, *share quarters*, οὔτε ἐν τῇ κώμῃ συννομιτεύεται *PMich.*inv. 160 (*ZPE* 23.133, AD 162).

**σύννομος** (A) **I 2**, lines 5/6, for 'which *lie between* two seas' read '*which consort with* the sea'

**σύννοος 3**, add 'Aen.Tact. 20.1'
**σύννυμφος**, add '*JRCil.* 1.24 (late Rom.imp.)'
**συνοδία III**, delete the section.
***συνοδιακός**, ή, όν, ἰνσπέσιμον σ. *of assembled troops*, *SEG* 9.356.25 (Ptolemais in Cyrenaica, vi AD).
**σύνοδος** (B), line 1, after 'deliberation' insert 'Alc. 130.30 L.-P.' **2,** add 'personified, *SEG* 35.1377 (cf. *RA* 1987.103, Phrygia, iii AD)' **3,** add 'ἡ σ. τῶν τεκτόνων *SEG* 29.1186 (Lydia, AD 165/6); of religious associations, *SEG* 32.453 (Boeotia, ii BC)'
**συνόδους**, at end for 'σινόδους, συνώδοντα' read 'σινόδων'
**συνοικειόω 1**, at end before 'Plu.*Lyc.* 4' insert '*SEG* 38.1476.31 (Xanthos, 206/5 BC)'
**συνοικέω I 2**, after '*PEnteux.* 91.2 (iii BC), etc.' insert 'w. acc., *SEG* 38.1476.29 (Xanthos, 206/5 BC)'
**συνοίκησις I**, add 'fig., ἡ ψυχὴ .. διὰ τὴν συνοίκησίν τε καὶ πρὸς τὸ σῶμα ὁμιλίαν Max.Tyr. 1.7'
**συνοικιάζω**, delete the entry (v. °ἐνοικιάζω).
**συνοικίζω II**, add '*SEG* 38.1476.79 (Xanthos, 206/5 BC)'
***συνοίκιον**, τό, *joint lodging*, *PMil.Vogl.* 287.5 (ii AD).
**συνοικῐσία 1**, for 'Pontus' read 'Maeander'
**συνοικισμός II**, after '= foreg.' insert '*SEG* 30.1120 (Entella, ?iii BC), *SEG* 25.445 (Stymphalus, Arcadia, *c.*189 BC)'
**συνοικιστήρ**, for 'Pi.*fr.* 186' read 'Epic.ap.A.D.*Synt.* 138.13'
**συνοικιστής**, after '*of a colony*' insert '*SEG* 12.379.9 (Cos, fr. Camarina, iii BC)'
**σύνοικος 2**, add '**c** αἱρεῖσθαι [Δίκαν] σ. B. 15.56 S.-M.'
**συνοκωχή**, add 'συνοκωχά· νόσος, λοιδορία, μάχη Hsch.'
**συνόμαιμος**, add '*SEG* 28.541 (Maced., Hellen., in quot., *sister*)'
***συνομβρέω**, *flood, cover with a deluge*, pass., *PMichael.* 4.11 (ii AD).
**συνόμευνος**, for '*bedfellow*' read '*consort*' and add 'Κρόνου συνόμευνε Orph.*H.* 27.12, *INikaia* 1248'
**συνόμῑλος**, before 'Hsch.' insert '*GVAK* 17 (Phrygia)'
***συνομόφῡλος**, ὁ, ἡ, *member of the same profession*, *POxy.* 3500.12 (iii AD).
***συνονομάζω**, *name together* with, *POxy.* 3498.25, 43 (AD 274).
**συνοπᾱδός**, add 'Iamb.*Protr.* 14.5 P.'
**συνόριον**, add '*SEG* 35.665A.24, 25 (pl., Ambracia, ii BC)'
***συνορχηστής**, οῦ, ὁ, *fellow dancer*, παιδὶ συνορχηστὴν θύρσον *POxy.* 3723.16 (elegy, ?ii AD).
**συνουσίασμα**, for '*Berl.Sitzb.* 1934.1041' read '*SEG* 37.389.12'
**συνουσιαστής**, add '*fellow member of a social club*, Lys. 8 tit.'
***συνοφρῡάζω**, *contract the brows, frown*, Sch.S.*Ant.* 528.
**συνοχή II 6**, delete the section.
**συνόχωκα**, for 'of *συνοχόω' read 'an artificial form, perh. of συνέχω, cf. *ὄκωχα'
**συντακτικός**, add '**IV** perh. *placed in the same category*, συντακτικοῖς καὶ ὑπερθέτοις *PRyl.* 585.29 (ii BC).' transposing entry to follow **συντακτήριος**
**συντᾰμίας**, before '*colleague in the quaestorship*' insert '*fellow-treasurer*, *Didyma* 393.3, 400.8'
***συντᾰφιαστής**, οῦ, ὁ, *member of a burial-society*, rest. in *PRyl.* 590.13 (i BC).
***συντέκτων**, ονος, ὁ, *fellow craftsman*, *SEG* 28.1368 (Palestine, iii AD).
**συντέλεια IV**, delete the section.
**συντελέω I 1**, line 3, delete 'σ. εἰς τὰ ἑκατὸν .. X.*Cyr.* 6.1.50' **2,** add '**b** act., *happen to be*, *Cod.Just.* 1.3.35.3.' **4,** for '*destroy*' read '*exterminate* (calque of Hebr. *killāh*)' add '**5** *pucker up in scorn*, στόμα Aq.*Is.* 52.16.' **II 1,** add 'ἐπειρᾶτο συντελεῖν αὐτῷ εἰς τὰ ἑκατὸν ἅρματα X.*Cyr.* 6.1.50' **III 2,** line 4, for '*tributaries*' read '*regions united* to it'
⁺**συντέμνω**, Ion. -τάμνω Hdt. 5.41.2, 7.123.1, fut. -τεμῶ, aor. -έτεμον, *make* or *form by cutting*, ξ. τὰς πρῴρας ἐς ἔλασσον Th. 7.36.2, σ. χιτῶνας (i.e. uppers of shoes) X.*Cyr.* 8.2.5, σ. τὰς πλεκτάνας Alex. 187, cf. 84, Arr.*An.* 7.19.3; transf., συντέμνει δ' ὅρος ὑγρᾶς θαλάσσης the sea *cuts short* (my realm), A.*Supp.* 258; abs., *shorten one's course, take a short route*, σ. ἀπ' Ἀμπέλου ἄκρης ἐπὶ Καναστραῖον ἄκρην Hdt. 7.123.1. **2** *cut* a path, καινὴν .. καὶ ἐρήμην ἀνοδίαν Porph.*Chr.* 1. **II** *curtail* in quantity, degree, extent, etc., τιμὰς σὺ μὴ σύντεμνε τὰς ἐμὰς λόγῳ A.*Eu.* 227, εἰς ἓν .. πάντα τὰ μέλη ξυντεμῶ Ar.*Ra.* 1262, τὸν ἐνιαυτὸν σ. .. εἰς μῆν' ἕνα Philippid. 25.1 K.-A. **2** *cut* expenses, σ. τὴν μισθοφορὰν Th. 8.45.2; σ. τὰς δαπάνας εἰς τὰ καθ' ἡμέραν *cut down* one's expenses to one's daily wants, X.*Hier.* 4.9; humorously, by expressing items in the form of diminutives, Mnesim. 3.4 K.-A. **3** *curtail* narrative, expression, etc., ἐν βραχεῖ πολλοὺς λόγους Ar.*Th.* 178, cf. Aeschin. 2.31, Pl.*Prt.* 334d, Heph.Astr. 2.15.2; w. ellipsis of obj., ὡς δὲ συντέμω E.*Tr.* 441, *Hec.* 1180, οἶνον εἰπὲ συντεμών Antiph. 55.12 K.-A., cf. D. 39.4, Anaxil. 22.30 K.-A. **4** *cut short* a process, πόνους E.*Rh.* 450; med., πάντα τοι συντέμνεται Κύπρις .. βουλεύματα S.*fr.* 941.16 R.; w. ellipsis of obj., τοῦ χρόνου συντάμνοντος as time *cut* the matter *short*, Hdt. 5.41; *stop* a person *in his course*, συντέμνουσι γὰρ θεῶν ποδώκεις τοὺς κακόφρονας Βλάβαι S.*Ant.* 1104. **III** *join with a cut*, ἵνα συντμηθῇ πάντα καὶ γένηται μία ἕλκωσις Heliod. ap.Orib. 44.23.69. **IV** *join in cutting, assist in making a distinction*, Pl.*Sph.* 227d, *Plt.* 261a.
**συντεχνίτης**, add '*PHamb.* 56 v 1 (p. 207) (vi/vii AD)'
***συντηκτικῶς**, of feverish patients, *wastingly*, Paul.Aeg. 7.19.3 (375.24 H.).
**συντίμησις**, before '*valuation*' insert '*total*'
***σύντμησις**, εως, ἡ, *cutting short*, e.g. ἱερομηνία for ἱερονουμηνία, Sch.Pi.*N.* 3.4.
**συντομία I**, add '**2** *cutting of delay, dispatch*, διὰ πάσης συντομίας *SB* 9752.3 (vii AD).'
**σύντομος I 2**, add '**b** of speakers, writers, Aeschin. 2.51, Call.*Epigr.* 11 Pf., Poll. 4.20, 6.149.' **4,** delete the section.
**συντονάριος**, after '*pedicularius*' insert 'perh. referring to musician who accompanies his playing with foot-operated clapper (v. °κρούπεζα 2)'
**συντρέχω I 2**, before 'Hdt. 8.71' insert 'Archil. 102 W.'
**Σύντριψ**, for 'lubber-fiend .. kitchen' read 'demon supposed to break pots during manufacture'
**σύντροφος I 1**, at end before 'cf. συντρόφη' insert 'also fem., *foster-sister*, *SEG* 34.1205 (Lydia, AD 170/1), 31.991 (Lydia, AD 234/5), al.' **3,** delete 'c. gen. .. S.*Ph.* 203, cf. σύντροπος'
**συνυμνέω**, after '*sing hymns together*' insert '*SEG* 37.961 (Claros, ii AD)'
**συνυπάγω**, after 'Sch.E.*Or.* 854' insert '*subject jointly* to, τὴν τοῦ γήμαντος οὐσίαν συνυπάγει ταῖς συνθήκαις Just.*Nov.* 22.40' and after 'pass., *to be brought under the power of*' insert '*Cod.Just.* 1.2.17 pr.'
**συνυποδέχομαι**, add '**2** *receive, obtain jointly*, Just.*Nov.* 11.24.'
***συνυπομένω**, *endure together* with, Sopat.Rh. 8.173.23 W.
**συνυπουργέω**, add '*BCH* 7.502 (Phrygia, AD 433)'
**συνῠφή 1**, add 'applied to the girdle of the ephod, Lxx *Ex.* 36.28 (39.20)'
**συνωθέω**, add '**III** *force, compel*, *Cod.Just.* 1.3.38.3, 1.4.26.3, ὅπερ ἔλαβε .. ἀποδοῦναι συνωθείσθω Just.*Nov.* 123.28.'
**συνωμόσιος**, add 'as a title of Zeus, *OGI* 65 (Egypt, iii BC)'
***συνωρία**, ἡ, *carriage-service*, οἱ μουλίωνες οἱ ἐπεστῶντες (= ἐφεστῶτες) συνωρίᾳ *TAM* 4(1).39.
**συνώριος**, delete 'doubtful .. (Bithynia)'
***συοσκύαμος**, ὁ, = ὑοσκύαμος, prob. in Nic.*Al.* 415.
⁺**συππινᾶς**, ᾶδος, ὁ, *worker* or *dealer in tow*, τῇ συμβιώσει τῶν συππινάδων *ISmyrna* 218.13; cf. στυππεῖον, στιππύον, σίππιον.
**συρβάβυττα**, delete the entry.
***σῡρήνεμος**, ον, (σύρω, ἄνεμος) *drawing breeze*, ῥιπίδας, cj. for πυρ- in *AP* 6.101.2 (Phil.); cf. ‡ἀνεμόσυρις.
**σῡρία**, for '*garment*' read '*stuff* or *material*'
***Συριακός**, v. °Σύρος.
**σῡρίγγιον 3**, add 'Gal. 13.402.15, 403.6'
**σῡριγγώδης**, add '**2** *sounding like a pan-pipe*, Heph.Astr. 1.1.119, 139, al.'
**σῦριγξ I 1**, after 'Hes.*Sc.* 278' insert 'E.*Ion* 498, *IA* 1038; sg., Ion Trag. 45 S.' add '**b** σ. μονοκάλαμος *flute*, Euph.ap.Ath. 4.184a, *AB* 265.21, *EM* 480.1.' **3,** for '*mouthpiece of the* αὐλός' read 'an attachment to the αὐλός allowing modification of the sound, Aristox.*Harm.* 21, Arist.*Aud.* 804ᵃ14' **II 2,** after '(A.)*Supp.* 181' insert 'but *the nave* itself in' **11,** for 'perh. *loop*' read '*sheath*'
**σῡρίζω I**, add '**2** *play the aulos in its top register*, Aristox.*Harm.* 21; cf. °σῦριγξ I 3.' **II,** after '*hiss* like a serpent' insert 'Hippon. 79.11 W.'
⁺**Σύριος**, v. ‡Σύρος.
⁺**συρίσκος, σύρισσος, σύριχος**, ὁ, v. ὑριχός.
**σύρισμα**, after 'the former in' insert 'Longus 2.30'
**σῡριστής I**, add '*hissing*, of snakes, Opp.*C.* 1.521'
**Σύρος**, line 3, after 'v. infr.)' insert 'of Assyrians, Aristid.*Or.* 26(14).91'; line 16, after '(v. πύλη II 2)' insert 'Συρίᾳ Θεῷ *SEG* 34.885 (Chalcis); *Assyrian*, Σ. γράμματα, i.e., in this case, cuneiform, D.S. 2.13'
⁺**σύρρα**, phonetic sp. of σύν ῥα, v.l. in Il. 8.61; understood as simple equiv. of σύν, Orph.*fr.* 167.5, Hsch.
**σύρροος**, line 2, delete '101e' (v. °σύσσοος)
**σύρροπον**, delete the entry.
***σύρροπος**, ον, prob. = ἰσόρροπος, of a weight which is equal to a control weight, *IGLS* 1272b (ii AD); also cited in Sch.D.T. p. 465.5 H.
***συρρυσμόω** (Ion. for συρρυθμόω), *bring into combination*, συνρυσμοῦσθαι (συνριθμοῦσθαι cod.)· συγκρίνεσθαι Hsch.
***συρτάριον**, τό, *instrument for making metal thread*, Anon.Alch. 323.6.
**σύρτης I**, add '**2** app. *thong*, παράμματα μετὰ τῶν συρτῶν *Edict.Diocl.* in *SEG* 37.335 iii 3 (μετὰ φλαγέλλου in another version).'
**συρτός**, ή, όν, **II**, after 'Cyran. 58' add 'τοῦ θηρίου συρτοῦ *Orac.Tiburt.* 151'

**σύρω 2**, line 5, after 'Plu. 2.5f' insert 'abs., ὕδωρ ἐν φάραγγι σῦρον Lxx *Is.* 30.28'

**συσκέπτομαι**, add 'Sopat.Rh. 8.44.27, 48.19 W.'

***συσκεύασμα**, ατος, τό, *contrivance*, gloss on κάττυμα Hsch.

**συσκύλλομαι**, add '*POxy.* 2275.19 (iv AD)'

**συσπάω I**, line 5, for 'fire' read 'drought'

**συσσᾰρᾱπιαστής**, for '*fellow-worshipper*' read 'pl., *guild of worshippers*' and after 'Thasos' insert 'ii BC'

**συσσίτιον I 2**, add '*soldier's mess*, Aen.Tact. 27.13'

***συσσῑτολογέω**, pf. συνσεσιτολόγηκα, *to be* σιτολόγος *jointly*, μετά τινος *PTeb.* 774.8 (ii BC).

**σύσσῑτος**, add 'D. 54.4, Aeschin. 2.22, al.; pl., of members of a religious association, *SEG* 32.505 (Thespiae, *c.*300 BC)'

***σύσσοος**, ον, *coherent, solid*, οὐδὲ γὰρ ἔτι εἴη κα σύνσοον καὶ ἓν τὸ ζῷον Ti.Locr. 101d M.

**συσταθμία**, after 'Dsc. 1.54' insert '*PMerton* 12.17 (i AD)'

**+συσταλτικός**, ή, όν, medic., *systolic*, Gal. 9.298.3. **2** of music, *tending to produce lowness of spirits, depressive*, Cleonid.*Harm.* 13, Aristid.Quint. 1.12.

**συστάς 1**, add '*Ath.Agora* XIX Ph9 (370/69 BC)'

**σύστᾰσις B I 4**, after '*conspiracy*' insert '*Inscr.Perg.* 160.6 (συσστ-; ii BC)'

**συστᾰ́της II**, for this section read 'official, perh. only at Oxyrhynchus, who replaced the φύλαρχος at the end of the 3rd century AD, responsible for: appointments to liturgies, *POxy.* 1627, *PFlor.* 39; registration of births and deaths, *PSI* 164, *POxy.* 1551; poll-tax collection, *PSI* 163, *PFouad I Univ.* 19, etc.'

**συστᾰτός 2**, add 'Pl.*Ti.* 33a'

**συστέλλω I 2 a**, add 'συσταλμένος of time, *limited*, 1*Ep.Cor.* 7.29' **b**, add 'Gal. 11.240.8'

**συστέφομαι**, add 'συνστεφθεὶς παίδων πάλην *SEG* 30.1524 (Lycia, iii AD)'

**σύστημα 2 - 5**, for these sections read '**2** *organized body* or *association*, political, ethnic, etc., Pl.*Lg.* 686b, Arist.*EN* 1168$^{b}$32, Plb. 2.38.6, προσέθηκε τὴν πόλιν πρὸς τὸ τῶν Ἀχαιῶν σύστημα id. 2.41.5, cf. 6.10.14, 9.28.2, Diog.Bab.*Stoic.* 3.241, τὸ Ἀμφικτιονικὸν σύστημα *Delph.* 3(1).48.16 (i BC), ὅπου ποτὲ σύστημα τοῦ γενοῦς ἐστιν ἡμῶν J.*Ap.* 1.7. **b** of a professional, administrative, etc., body, θήκη διαφέρουσα τῷ συστήματι τῶν λημενητῶν λινοπωλῶν *MAMA* 3.770, cf. *SEG* 30.1382c (Lydia, AD 301), *IMylasa* 144.5, al.; of priests, Plb. 21.13.11, Str. 17.1.29; τὸ δὲ σύστημα σενᾶτον προσηγόρευσεν Plu.*Rom.* 13, cf. Lib.*Or.* 11.146, σ. τῆς γερουσίας *ITrall.* 77.1. **c** of a body of troops, τὸ σ. τῶν μισθοφόρων Plb. 1.81.11, cf. 5.53.3, 30.25.8, etc.; of a gang, J.*AJ* 20.9.4; of a ship's crew, Alciphr. 1.8. **d** of a herd, etc., of animals, Plb. 10.27.2, 12.4.10.'

***συστρᾰτιωτικός**, ή, όν, *of an association of* συστρατιῶται, *PRyl.* 585.11 (ii BC).

**συστρέφω IV**, add '**2** act., perh. *collect, accumulate*, ἐλαϊκὴν δὲ συστρέφειν ἕκαστ[ον] τῶν ἐλα[ι]οπωλῶν *PHamb.* 182.10 (iii BC).'

**συστροφή I 2**, add '**b** *dazzling* of the eyes, Simp. *in de An.* 46.1; *dizziness*, Hsch.' **II 1**, add 'cf. Myc. *ku-su-to-ro-qa*, *total*' add '**6** pl., *wrinkles*, Sch.Gen.Il. 9.503.'

***σύστρωσις**, εως, ἡ, perh. = σύστρωμα, *IGRom.* 3.365.7.

***συστῡφόομαι**, = ‡συστύφω, Hsch. s.v. συνεστυφωμένοι.

**συστῡ́φω**, for 'Pass.' to end read 'glossed by (συ)σκυθρωπάζω, *look gloomy*, Hsch. s.vv. συνέστυβας, -βεν, συνστύψαι'

***σύστωρ**, prob. error for συνίστωρ, *JÖAI* 8.143 (tab.defix.).

***συσφᾰγιάζομαι**, pass., *to be slaughtered along with*, τῇ θυγατρί Sch.E.*Hec.* 399.

**συσφαιριστής**, delete 'dat. pl. .. *IG* $2^2$.4794' (v. °συμφεροντής)

**συσφίγγω**, line 1, after 'Herod. 5.25' insert 'so as to check the flow of blood, Ath. 2.41b'; line 2, before 'τὸ λόγιον' insert '*fasten close*'; line 3, after 'ib. 3*Ki.* 18.46' insert '*clench*, ib.*De.* 15.7'

**συψειρικόν**, delete the entry.

***συψειρικός**, όν, also συμψ-, συνψ-, Lat. *subsericus*, *partly silk*, στίχη *Edict.Diocl.* 19.10, 20.1; σειρακίῳ ἐργαζομένῳ εἰς συψειρικὸν τρεφομένῳ ib. 20.9, al.

**σῠώδης**, add 'comp. -έστερος Eun.ap.Phot.*Bibl.* 77'

**σφᾰγίς**, add '*butcher's knife*, *AP* 6.306 (Aristo)'

**σφᾰγῖτις**, add 'Hp.*Acut.* 9'

***σφαγνίον**, τό, commodity (?plant) occurring in price lists, *POxy.* 37.33.24, 3766.106 (iv AD).

**σφάζω 6**, for 'metaph. *torment*' read 'hyperb. *"kill"*' and add 'Men.*fr.* 746 K.-Th.'

**σφαῖρα 4**, for 'a weapon of boxers .. σφαιρομαχίαι' read 'prob. *padded glove* used in boxing practice' **6**, for 'sea-*balls*' read 'kind of zoophytes, = ἁλοσάχναι' **8**, add 'Nic.*Th.* 584' add '**10** *ball* used in voting, *SEG* 9.8 i 25 (Cyrene, 7/6 BC).'

**σφαιρίον I**, line 2, after 'Pl.*Ep.* 312d' insert 'ὑελοῦν *glass ball*, *PFam.Teb.* 49a ii 3 (iii AD)'

***σφαιρολήκῡθος**, ὁ, app. *globular oil-flask*, *POxy.* 3080.8 (ii AD).

**σφαιρομᾰχέω 1**, add 'fig., Men.*Dysc.* 605'

**σφαιρομᾰχία**, add '**2** *ball-contest* (description of °ἐπίσκυρος), Poll. 9.107.'

**+σφαιρωτήρ**, ῆρος, ὁ, *ornamental knob*, on a seven-branched candlestick, Lxx *Ex.* 25.31, 33, al.; pl., as heraldic device, *Tab.Heracl.* 1.184. **2** transl. Hebr. wd. meaning 'thong' (v.l. σφυρ-), Lxx *Ge.* 14.23. **b** in an inventory in unexpld. sense, *PLond.* 402$^{v}$.22 (ii BC).

**σφᾰκος I**, for '*sage-apple*, *Salvia calycina*' read 'kind of sage, *Salvia* species which forms an edible gall-apple, cf. mod. Gk. φασκόμηλο' and add 'Men.*Dysc.* 517 S.' add 'cf. Myc. adj. *pa-ko-we*, σφακόϝεν'

***Σφαλεώτας**, α, ὁ, epith. of Dionysus, *SEG* 19.399.*a*3, al. (Delphi, ii BC).

**σφάλλον**, add 'prob. Aeol. = σφῆλον fr. σφάλλω'

**σφεδᾰνός I**, delete 'κάρηαρ Nic.*Th.* 642' and add '**2** perh. *having a rough surface*, κάρηαρ Nic.*Th.* 642.'

**σφειδρόν**, for 'Theognost.*Can.* 12' read 'Theognost.*Can.* 37 A.'

**σφεῖς A I 3**, add 'Arc. σφέσιν *SEG* 37.340.15, (Mantinea, iv BC)' **II**, line 7, for '*Riv.Ist.Arch.* 2.19' read '*Inscr.Cret.* 4.83.2 (v BC)' **B I 3**, line 6, after 'al.' insert 'And. 3.11; πλεῖν ἐπὶ σφᾶς αὐτούς *against themselves* or *their own country*, Th. 8.86.4'; add 'as 2 pers. pl., σφᾶς αὐτοὺς ἐπεφόβησθε And. 2.8' add 'Myc. *pe-i* (dat. pl. σφεhι)'

**σφεκλαράριος**, delete the entry.

***σφεκλαρᾶς**, ᾶ, ὁ, = Lat. *specularius*, *glazier*, *SEG* 7.197 (Berytus, v/vi AD).

**σφέκλον**, add 'Olymp. *in Grg.* p. 252.7 W.'

**σφέλας III**, for this section read '*block* for pounding or chopping, ἢ σφέλᾳ ἢ ὅλμῳ κεάσας Nic.*Th.* 644'

**σφενδάμνινος**, for 'metaph. .. *hearts of oak*' read 'fig., in uncertain significance'

**σφενδονάω I 1**, add 'generally, *pelt*, σ. βώλοις λίθοις Men.*Dysc.* 120' **II 2**, for '*move like a swing*' read '*move like a sling*'

**σφενδονήτης**, for 'Ἀρχ.Δελτ. 14 Pl. iv 26' read '*SEG* 23.271'

**σφηκιά**, before 'Lxx *Ex.* 23.28' insert '*swarm of wasps*'

***σφήκιον**, τό, perh. *rafter*, *SEG* 37.665.3 (N. coast of Black Sea, *c.*400 BC; see also *BE* 1989.478); cf. σφηκίσκος, ἡμισφήκιον.

**+σφηκισμός**· εἶδος αὐλήσεως εἰρημένον ἀπὸ τῆς ἐμφερείας τῶν βομβῶν Hsch.

**σφήνωσις 1**, add 'Gal. 18(2).594.2'

**σφίγγω II 1**, add 'ἡ δὲ ἀμέρεια σφίγγουσα καὶ συσπειρῶσα (τὴν ἑκάστου δύναμιν) Procl.*Inst.* 86 D.'

**Σφίγξ**, line 2, for 'where .. Sch.' read 'v.l.' at end, form Σφίξ, add '*CEG* 120 (?*c.*450 BC)'

**σφόδρα I 4**, line 5, after 'Pl.*Phd.* 100a' insert 'οὐδέπω γεγονὼς σ. εἴκοσιν ἔτη not *quite* twenty, Pl.*Alc.* 1.123d'

**σφοδρός II**, line 5, after '-ότερον' insert 'Thphr.*Sign.* 32'

**σφόνδῠλος II 1**, add 'perh. also Aen.Tact. 36.2' **4**, delete the section.

**σφρᾱγίς I 1**, add 'fig., of the final moment, ἐν δ' ὥραις ὀλίγαις Μοιρῶν γὰρ σφραγεῖδες ἐπῆλθον *GVI* 1166 (Rome, iii AD)' add '**VI** name of a section of the νόμος κιθαρῳδικός, Poll. 4.66.'

***σφρᾱ́γιστρα**, τά, app. *fee for attaching a seal* or *warrant* to a sacrificial victim, *PMoen* inv. 5 (*CE* 54.275).

***Σφρᾱγιτίδες** [?ᾱ], αἱ, nymphs associated w. prophecy on Mt. Cithaeron, Plu.*Arist.* 19.6, id. 2.628f, cf. the cave Σφραγίδιον, Paus. 9.3.9; cf. Σφραγιτίδων.

***σφρᾱγῖτις**, ιδος, ἡ, kind of medicament, cf. σφραγίς V, τῇ Πολυείδου σφραγίτιδι Aët. 9.38.18.

***σφῡρίζω**, *pound, crush*, Anon.Alch. 329.23, 27.

**+σφῠρίς**, v. σπυρίς.

**σφῠρόν I**, add 'prov., ἀνώτερον τοῦ σ. λέγειν *talk of matters outside one's knowledge*, Ath. 8.351a, cf. *ne supra crepidam sutor*'

**σφῠρωτήρ**, before 'Lxx' insert 'v.l. in'; for 'cod. .. cett.)' read '(cf. °σφαιρωτήρ)'

**σφωΐτερος II**, delete '= σφέτερος' and section 1. **4**, after '1.1286' insert '4.454'

**σχᾰ́διον**, after '= ἰσχάδιον' insert '*PRyl.* 629.32 (iv AD), al.'

**+σχᾰδοκᾰ́ρυα**, v. °ἰσχαδοκάρυον.

***σχαστός**, ή, όν, perh. *out of line, askew*, *SEG* 39.442.36 (Oropus, iv BC; sp. σκαστ-; cf. ἄσχαστος).

**σχεδιάζω**, add '**3** *approach*, Hsch.; cf. σχέδιος I 1.'

***σχεδιαστής**, οῦ, ὁ, *improviser*, Teuc.Bab. p. 44 B.

**σχεδικός**, for '*riddling*' read '*of* or *belonging to* σχέδη (°σχέδος 2)' and for '*riddle-composers*' read '*makers of* σχέδη'

***σχεδιοναύτης**, ου, ὁ, *raft-navigator*, *SEG* 28.1040 (Nicomedia).

**σχεδογρᾰφία**, for '*art of parsing*' read '*writing of* σχέδη (°σχέδος 2)'

**σχεδόθεν**, add 'σχεδόθεν δὲ κακῷ κακόν .. ἀκειομένη, *shortsightedly* trying to cure one wrong with another, A.R. 4.1081'

**σχέδος**, for '*riddle*' read 'in later Gk., *account of a word* w. ref. to origin, sp., etc., *An.Boiss.* 2.349; hence **2** *riddle* based on alternative sps. and division of wds.'

**σχεδουργός**, for '*riddle-maker*' read '*maker of* σχέδη (°σχέδος 2)'

***σχέθω I 2**, line 2, after '(Od.) 14.490' insert 'εὔνοον θῦμον σκέθοντες Alc. 129.10 L.-P.'

**σχελίς**, add 'cf. σχέλος = σκέλος (q.v.)'

**σχέμα II**, delete the section.

**σχερός II**, for 'Theognost.*Can.* 12' read 'Theognost.*Can.* 38 A.'

**σχετλιασμός**, add '**2** gramm., *interjection* (of indignation), Charis. p. 470.19 B. (given as equiv. of Lat. *interiectio*).'

**σχετλιαστικός**, line 2, delete 'A.D. .. al.'; at end for 'ἐπίρρημα' read '°ἐπίρρημα D.T. 642.2, A.D.*Pron.* 34.30, *Adv.* 127.19'

**σχῆμα 5**, add '**b** *calling*, τὸ μοναχικὸν σχῆμα *Cod.Just.* 1.3.52.9, τοῦδε τοῦ σχήματος (sc. office of καγκελλάριος) Lyd.*Mag.* 3.38.' **8 d**, add 'also of dice used in prophecy, Paus. 7.25.10'

***σχημᾰτίζω**, *shape with protuberances and hollows*, i.e. opp. smooth, Alex.Aphr. *in Sens.* 58.12.

***σχημᾰτιστικός**, ή, όν, *fitted for giving shape*, ἐνέργεια Procl. *in Ti.* 2.216.22 D.

**σχίζω I 1**, line 6, after 'Pi. l.c.' insert '*SB* 9123.7 (ii BC)'

**σχῖνος I**, for 'trodden on by goats' read 'browsed upon by goats, Eup. 13.4 K.-A.' **II**, delete 'Thphr.*CP* 5.6.10, *Sign.* 55'

**σχίσμα I**, add 'of the *vulva*, Ruf.*Onom.* 110' **III**, delete the section.

**σχισμή**, add '*split*, Heraclid.Pont.ap.Sch.Pi.*O.* 6.119'

***σχοινάριον**, τό, perh. *ball of twine*, *PMich.*inv. 4001 (*ZPE* 24.84, i/ii AD), *PRyl.* 627.170 (iv AD).

***σχοινεύομαι**, app. *measure by* σχοῖνοι (σχοῖνος III), Hsch. s.v. καίνυσθαι.

**σχοινιά II**, for '*CIG* (add.) 2056*g*' read '*IGBulg.* 57.7 (Tiberius)'

**σχοινίον I 2 c**, add '*PGen.* 99 (ii AD)'

***σχοίνιος**, α, ον, prob. = σχοίνινος, ῥῦμα *PZen.Col.* 43.3 (iii BC).

**σχοινίς** (A) **I 2**, for this section read '*raised band of decoration*, *Didyma* 39.17; on silver cup, ib. 424.55. **b** perh. *enclosure wall*, *TAM* 2.850.'

**σχοινίων II**, delete '*effeminate*' and for '*flute*' read '*aulos*'

**σχοινοειδής**, for 'J.*AJ* 12.2.9' read 'J.*AJ* 12.2.8'

***σχοινοκοπέω**, *cut rushes*, Hsch. s.v. καλοκοπῆσαι.

**σχοῖνος**, line 6, after 'σ. εὐώδης' insert '*AP* 4.1.26 [Mel.]' and delete 'Hp.*Mul.* .. *Nat.Mul.* 33'; transfer 'Aret.*CA* 2.8' to follow 'Dsc. 1.17' **I 3**, add 'Lxx *Ps.* 138(139).3' **III**, add '**b** as a measure of area, *Tab.Heracl.* 1.19, al.' add 'Myc. *ko-no*, var. *ko-i-no*'

***σχοινουλκία**, ή, *survey*, *PMerton* 5.33 (ii BC).

***σχοινωτός**, ή, όν, perh. *rope- or rush-patterned*, ψέλια *PMichael.* 18Ai5 (iii AD).

**σχολάζω II**, add '**2** *to be annulled*, θεσπίζομεν ὥστε πᾶσαν ἐκποίησιν πραγμάτων .. τοῖς σεβασμίοις οἴκοις διαφερόντων .. σχολάζειν *Cod.Just.* 1.2.17.1, Just.*Nov.* 120.11; *to be idle*, *be in abeyance*, *Cod.Just.* 10.16.13.1. **3** of period of time, *expire*, Just.*Nov.* 111.1.'

**σχολάριος**, add '*SEG* 37.1076 (Bithynia)'

**σχολεῖον II**, for this section read '*place for sitting* or *resting*, *exedra*, *BCH* 10.414 (Thyatira), *IEphes.* 2407'

**σχολή I**, add '**4** *absence* of, σχολὴν .. τῆς τῶν πραγμάτων νομῆς Just.*Nov.* 167.1.' **III**, add 'κόμ(ης) σχολῆ(ς) γεντιλίων ἰωνιόρων *Chiron* 6.305 no. 12 (Phrygia, vi AD)'

**σχολικός I 1**, at end after 'D.H.*Comp.* 22' insert '*academic*, *artificial*, πάθη Longin. 3.5, cf. 10.7' **2**, delete the section.

***σωβῆρις**· ναῦς, πορθμίς. ἔνιοι τὴν παλαιάν Hsch.

***σώειλον**, τό, unexpld. wd. in *CPR* 7.44.22 *bis* (v/vi AD).

**σῴζω**, line 17, after 'ἐσώσθην only in Hsch.' insert 'σωσθείς (sp. σοσθίς) *SEG* 32.1084 (Spain, v AD)' forms, **2**, line 3, before 'fut.' insert '2 sg. impf. ἐσάους *Inscr.Délos* 1658' **3**, for 'Call. l.c.' read 'Call.*Lav.Pall.* 142, *Cer.* 134, *fr.* 112.8 Pf.' **I 3**, line 7, after 'Procl.*Hyp.* 5.10' insert 'cf. Hipparch. 2.3.23; σ. τὴν ὑπόθεσιν Arist.*Cael.* 306$^a$30' add '**b** part. σῳζόμενος, *being currently in force*, τοῦ σῳζομένου κανόνος *Cod.Just.* 1.2.24.5.' **II 2**, add '*Peripl.M.Rubr.* 56 (cod.)' **7 b**, add '*SEG* 31.1310 (Lycia); fem. Μοίραις σῳζούσαις *SEG* 24.902 (Thrace)'

**σωκέω 2**, add 'cf. σωκῶ· ἀντὶ τοῦ ἰσχύω. οἱ δὲ νεώτεροι ἀντὶ τοῦ σῴζω Sch.S.*El.* 119'

***σωλάριον**, τό, Lat. *solarium*, *sun-terrace*, archit., as a feature of tombs in Asia Minor, *IEphes.* 1645, 2200b, al., *ISmyrna* 191.7, 8, 212.3, al.; attached to a private dwelling, *Cod.Just.* 8.10.12.5.

**σωλήν 4**, delete the section transferring exx. to section 2 **6**, add 'Sophr. 24'

***σωληνοποιός**, ὁ, *pipe-maker*, *IEphes.* 4315.

**σῶμα I 2**, lines 3/4, for 'σῴζειν or -εσθαι' read 'σῴζεσθαι' and delete 'D. 22.55'; add 'fig., of an institution, εἰς τὸ τῆς πόλεως σῶμ' ἀποβλέψαντες Din. 1.110, Hyp.*Dem.* col. 25' **3**, line 2, before 'Pl.*Grg.* 493a' insert '*CEG* 10 (v BC)'; line 3, after 'Pl.*R.* 328d' insert '**b** *person*, opp. property, [τὸ σ.] σῶσαι *keep* it *untouched*, D. 22.55'; add 'opp. ὄνομα, Hdt. 1.139, E.*Or.* 390'

**σωμάλοιφος**, add '(cj. **σωμάλοιφος**· κατηλιμμένος. **σωμάτια**· τὰ σκύτινα αἰδοῖα)'

**σωμάτειον**, add '**2** *a body*, i.e. component individual, ὡς ἐλλειπόντων δῆθεν τοῖς ἀριθμοῖς σωματείων *Cod.Just.* 1.2.20.'

***σωμᾰτεμπόριον**, τό, *stock of slaves for sale*, *Vit.Aesop.*(G) 15, al.

**σωμᾰτίζω II 2**, add '**b** *register for taxation*, *BGU* 2488.3 (ii AD), *PWarren* 3.13 (vi AD).'

***σωμᾰτομιξία**, ή, *sexual intercourse*, Ps.-Callisth. 3.12 (pl.).

**σωμᾰτοφύλαξ**, after '*bodyguard*' insert '*SEG* 31.80 (Athens, 307/1 BC)'

***σωμόβουβλον**, τό, *beef*, *Stud.Pal.* 20.250.3 (vi/vii AD).

***σωμφιακός**, ή, όν, adj. describing some aspect of embalming, τὴν σωμφιακὴν τέχνην *PHeid.* 327.8 (AD 99).

***Σώπολις**, εως, ὁ, = σωσίπολις, name of a deity, *IEphes.* 1060, 1233. **2** as an honorific title (artificial epic form σαόπτ-), Δῆμος ὁ Μιλήτοιο σαόπτολιν ὧδε γεραίρει Βιτιανὸν στήλῃ *SEG* 29.1139 (Miletus, iv/v AD).

***σωράκιον**, τό, dim. of σώρακος, *PMil.Vogl.* 61.26 (ii AD); v. σωρακίς II.

**σωροβόλιον**, for '*LW* .. (Mylasa)' read '*IMylasa* 814.10, 253.5, 256.2, 7'

**σῶς** (A), last line, after 'ΣαϝοκλέϜης' insert '*ICS* 383 (Abytos)'

***σωσικόλωνος**, ή, *saviour of the coloni*, epith. of Artemis, *Inscr.Délos* 2377.

***σωσικόσμιος**, ὁ, member of an Alexandrian phyle founded by Nero, fr. an epith. of the Emperor, *SB* 10780.4, 10894.6, 15, 11165.1 (all ii AD); v. °σωσίκοσμος.

***σωσίκοσμος**, ὁ, *saviour of the world*, *Suppl.Mag.* 49.61 (ii/iii AD).

***σωσίνεως**, ω, ὁ, *saviour of ships*, epith. of Poseidon, *CIRB* 30 (Panticapaeum, i BC).

**σωσίπολις**, add 'of a tutelary hero, Paus. 6.20.2.4, etc.; of a human benefactor, *REG* 72.213 (Aenus, Rom.imp.)'

***σωστεύματα**· τὰ τοῦ τροχοῦ ξύλα Hsch. (σωστρ- Musurus; cf. s.v. σωτεύματα).

**σωτήρ I 2 b**, add 'of Heracles, *SEG* 33.555 (Epirus, ii BC)' **3**, line 4, after 'al.' insert 'pl. of Ptolemy I and Berenice, Call.*Del.* 166, cf. *APF* 5.156 (Egypt, iii BC; θεοὺς σ.)' **II**, for 'γονῆς .. *Th.* 225' read 'A.*Ag.* 664, S.*OT* 80-1, *Ph.* 1471, E.*Med.* 360 (anap.)' add '**IV** *grain of salt*, Hsch.'

**σωτηρία I 1**, add 'in opening formula, Ἀγαθᾶι τύχαι καὶ ἐπὶ σωτηρίαι *SEG* 32.623 (Illyria, ii/i BC)'

**σωτήριος II 2**, add 'οἱ ἀγωνοθέται τῶν μεγάλων Σωτηρίων καὶ Ῥωμαίων *SEG* 33.1039 (Cyme, ii BC)'

***σωφρόνη**, ή, = σωφροσύνη, dub. cj. at E.*Ba.* 1002 (as pr. n., Men.*Epit.*, *GVI* 683, etc.).

***σωφρονητικός**, ή, όν, = σωφρονικός 2, Rh. 1.231.6.

**σωφρονισμός**, add '**2** euphem. *punishment*, *chastisement*, *Cod.Just.* 1.1.5.4, 4.20.15 pr.'

**σωφροσύνη**, add '**4** -ης ἄρχων, poet. for σωφρονιστής II, *IG* $2^2$.3768.13 (iii AD).'

# T

ταβελλάριος, add '*BGU* 2355.3 (ii/iii AD)'

*ταβέρνα, ἡ, Lat. *taberna, shop, stall,* Scaev.*Dig.* 20.1.34.1, *SEG* 33.1123 (iii AD).

*ταβερνάριος, ὁ, Lat. *tabernarius, shopkeeper, MAMA* 3.311.

*ταβέρνιον, τό, *small shop* or *stall, PRyl.* 627.293, al. (iv AD).

*τᾰβης, v. °τάπης.

*ταβλάριον, v. °ταβουλάριον.

ταβλάριος, add 'also sp. ταβουλάριος *MAMA* 7.524 (pl.), *PHamb.* 31.17 (pl., ii AD), *POxy.* 2268.14 (v AD), 3867.8 (vi AD), Mitchell *N.Galatia* 474, Just.*Edict.* 9.4; cf. °ταβουλάριον'

*ταβλοειδής, ές, adv. -ῶς, app. *in the form of a tablet,* Anon.Alch. 325.7.

*ταβουλάριον, τό, Lat. *tabularium, archives, POxy.* 2116.10 (iii AD); perh. also ταβλάριον, ἐν [τῷ τ]αβλαρίῳ *POxy.* 676.38 (iii AD; v. *ZPE* 91.81).

+τᾱγά, ἁ, *office* of ταγός, hence *time when there is a* ταγός (i.e. wartime), κἐν ταγᾶ κἐν ἀταγίαι *SIG* 55 (Thessaly, v BC); (also expld. as special sense of τᾰγή, *mobilisation*); perh. in dub. reading *officers in charge,* Ἑλλάδος ἥβας ξύμφρονα ταγάν A.*Ag.* 110.

τᾱγεύω I 3, add 'of a female ταγός, *SEG* 34.481 (Thessaly, *c.*150 BC)'

τᾰγή 1, for 'κἂν ἐκ τᾶς ταγᾶς' read 'καἴ κ' ἐκ τᾶς ταγᾶς' **3**, add '*INikaia* 1071, Ps.-Callisth. *Hist.Alex.Magn.* pp. 35.19, 45.7, 57.13 K.' after '**6**' insert '*tribute* paid to the Great King by the satrapies, Arist.*Oec.* $1345^{b}25$, cf. Hsch. τ. βασιλικὴ δωρεά'

τάγμα III, add '**d** *staff* of an official, Just.*Nov.* 13.4 pr. **e** *club* (at Sardis), Ap.Ty.*Ep.* 39, 40, 41.'

τᾱγός, line 2, delete 'ξύμφρονε .. A.*Ag.* 110 (lyr.)' **II 2**, at end for '*Inscr.Cypr.* 116, 170 H.' read 'alleged Cypr. exs. are dub., v. *ICS* 258'

ταθρίσιον, delete the entry (v. °θρίσσιον).

ταινιόω, line 2, after 'X.*HG* 5.1.3' insert '*SEG* 24.156(a) (Eleusis, *c.*238/7 BC)'

τακτικός I 1, delete 'adv. comp. .. Sch.E.*Ph.* 1141' (v. °τατικός) add '**III** -ός, ὁ, Ephebic official at Thebes, *IG* 7.2440 (?i BC).'

τακτόμισθος, for '*PLond.ined.* 2243' read '*PLond.* 1986'

τακτός, adv. τακτῶς, for 'v.l. in Plot. 3.1.2' read 'cj. in Plot. 3.1.3'

*τακτώριος, ὁ, name of a variety of σμάραγδος, treatise περὶ λίθων in *WS* 20.319.

τᾰλᾰεργός, add 'of a spinning-woman, A.R. 4.1062'

*ταλαμών, v. °τελαμών.

*τᾰλαντάρχης, ου, ὁ, title given to one who has power over the life and death of gladiators (w. ref. to Il. 22.209 ff.), τὸν ἱερέα καὶ ταλαντάρχην δι' ὅπλων *SEG* 32.660 (ii/iii AD).

τᾰλαντιαῖος I 1, add 'τοῦ ἐράνου τοῦ ταλαντιαίō *SEG* 23.96 (iv BC)'

τᾰλαντόομαι, add 'act. fut. ταλαντώσω, Hsch.'

τᾰλᾰπείριος 1, line 3, after '(Od.) 14.511' insert 'Πέργαμον Ibyc. 1(*a*).8 P.'; add '*Trag.adesp.* 599 K.-S.'

τᾰλᾰρος 1, add 'fig., Μουσέων τ. of the Museum, Timo 12' **2**, delete the section.

τᾰλας, before 'τάλαινα' insert '(hyper-Ion. **τάλης** Herod. 3.35, 7.88 (but τάλας 5.55))'; line 2, after 'also' insert 'gen. τάλαντος, Hsch.'

+τᾰλᾰσήϊος, ον, *of* or *related to wool-working,* τ. ἔργα A.R. 3.292, Orph.*fr.* 178, τ. ἱδρώς Nonn.*D.* 6.142.

τᾰλᾰσία, for '*wool-spinning*' read '*wool-working*' add 'Myc. *ta-ra-si-ja, portion of raw material for manufacture*'

τᾰλᾰσιουργέω, for '*spin wool*' read '*work with wool*'

τᾰλᾰσιουργικός, for '*of .. wool-spinning*' read '*of .. wool-working*'

τᾰλᾰσιουργός, for '*wool-spinner*' read '*wool-worker*' and add '*IG* $2^{2}$.1554.2, *SEG* 25.180.8, 28, al. (Athens, iv BC)'

+τᾶλις, ἡ, gen. τάλιδος S.*Ant.* 629, acc. τᾶλιν Call.*fr.* 75.3 Pf., dat. τάλῑ (τάλῃι codd.) Sch.Il. 14.296, *betrothed woman*; cf. τᾶλις· ἡ μελλόγαμος παρθένος καὶ κατωνομασμένη τινί, οἱ δὲ γυναῖκα γαμετήν, οἱ δὲ νύμφην Hsch. (Aeol. acc. to Sch.S. l.c.).

τᾰμεία, add 'also sp. **ταμία** Wolters *Kabirenheiligtum* 79, *TAM* 2(3).838 *f* 7 (Lycia)'

τᾰμία, after 'Il. 24.302' insert 'Ar.*fr.* 305.2 K.-A.'

τᾰμῐακός, line 2, after '*fiscalis*' insert 'τ. λόγος *POxy.* 1414.8 (iii AD)'

τᾰμίας II 2, add 'Plb. 1.52.7, al., *IG* 14.951 (AD 78)'

τᾰμῐεῖον, add 'w. ἱερώτατον, of the imperial treasury, *IEphes.* 3712 (ii/iii AD), *INikaia* 766 (iii AD)'

*τᾰμῐεύς, έως, ὁ, *store-keeper,* St.Byz. s.v. ταμιεῖον, cf. *SB* 5223.8.

τᾰμῐευτικός I, add '**2** *of a steward,* βυβλία *PCornell* 1.16 (iii BC).' add '**III** *belonging to the Elatean* ταμίαι, χρήματα *IG* 9(1).144.8 (Elatea, ii AD). **IV** -ός, ὁ, = ταμίας, *TAM* 2(3).845.7 (Lycia).'

τᾶν, delete 'only Att.' and add 'Pi.*fr.* 215b.4, Epich. 87'; line 3, for 'not in Ar.' read 'Ar.*Pl.* 66, al.'

Ταναγραῖος, add 'fem. Ταναγραία *SEG* 31.473 (Boeotia)'

*Ταναγρεύς, έως, ὁ, = Ταναγραῖος, *IG* $2^{2}$.10405 (iii BC).

*Ταναγρίδαι· οἱ Ταναγρεῖς Hsch.

τᾰνᾰήκης, line 1, after 'edge' insert '*tapering to a point*'; lines 2/3, delete '**II** *tall*' transferring exx. to section I.

τᾰνᾰός, after '*h.Cer.* 454' insert 'διέβα ταναοῖς πο[σί] Alcm. 3.70 P.' add 'Myc. *ta-na-wa,* of wheels, prob. *thin*'

τᾰνῠήκης I, add 'ἰοί B.*fr.* 20D.7 S.-M.'

τᾰνυκνήμῑς, add '**2** of mountains, *having extensive spurs,* Nonn.*D.* 13.67; cf. °βαθυκνήμις.'

*τᾰνυπρήων, ωνος, *having a towering reach,* τανυπρήωνος .. [Ἑ]λικ[ῶνος *Suppl.Hell.* 938.5 (hex.).

τᾰνυπτέρυξ, line 3, gen. pl., add 'νώτων *AP* 9.59 (Antip. Thess.)'

τᾰνύσφῠρος, add '(v. τανίσφυρος)'

τᾰνῠφυλλος I, delete 'prob. .. 426.7' at end add '(v. τανίφυλλος)'

τᾰνῠω I, add 'w. ref. to crucifixion, τὸ ξύλον .. ἐν ᾧ Χριστὸς μέλλει τανύεσθαι *Orac.Tiburt.* 72' **II**, add 'τὰ σκέλεα τανύσας τῆς γυναικός Hp.*Steril.* 244'

ταξείδιον, add 'also **ταξίδιον**, *journey, PMich.*VIII 501.24 (pl., ii AD); cf. mod. Gk. ταξίδι'

ταξίλοχος, for 'Arist.*Pepl.* 9' read 'Arist.*Pepl.* 34'

ταξιόομαι, delete the entry.

*ταξιόω, *post, station* as for battle: med., μή ποτε σφετέρας ἄτερθε ταξιοῦσθαι δαμασιμβρότου αἰχμᾶς Pi.*O.* 9.78. **2** transf., *place* in a rank, ἵνα .. ταξιώσις με μετὰ τῶν ἐγκλε[κτ]ῶν σου Mitchell *N.Galatia* 87 (Byz.).

*ταξιπᾰτέω, perh. *trample on* (w. ἐπί), Procl.CP *Hom.* 29.33.

τάξις I 4 c, for this section read 'the body of subordinates of a high military or civil official (= Lat. *officium*), Lib.*Or.* 27.7, *Cod.Just.* 1.5.12.15, 1.5.18.10, 6.48.1.10, *BCH* suppl. 8 no. 148 (Thessalonica, v/vi AD)' **IV 1**, add '**b** *category, class* of relatives, in order of entitlement to inheritance, *Cod.Just.* 6.48.1.5.'

τᾰπεινός 4, add '*T&MByz* 7.312 no. 6 (Thessalonica, *c.*AD 491/7)'

τᾰπης, add 'τάβης *Edict.Diocl.* 7.62'

*τᾰπητᾶς, ᾶ, ὁ, *rug-merchant, POxy.* 3044.5, 3045.3 (iv AD).

Ταραντῑναρχος, for 'Ἀρχ. Δελτ. 14 Pl. iv 19' read '*SEG* 23.271.19'

τᾰραξίας, add 'Choerob. *in Theod.* 1.141.32'

Τάρας, pr. n. of the river-hero, add '*SEG* 34.1020, 1021 (ii AD), *Inscr.Perg.* 8(3).132'

τᾰρᾰχή 4, add 'D.C. 37.31.1, 41.3.3'

*τᾰρᾰχίζεσθαι, gloss on θολερεῖν, Hsch.

τᾰρᾰχος, add 'of digestive upsets, Hp.*VM* 14, *Flat.* 14'

ταρβέω, line 1, after 'Hdn.Gr. 2.930' insert 'Aeol. **τάρβημι** Alc. 302.12 L.-P.'

*ταρθωτής, οῦ, ὁ, app. for ταρσωτής, *revetter* of a dike with brushwood, *POxy.* 1053.25 (vi/vii AD).

*τᾰρῑχηρά, ἡ, *tax on pickling business, OMRL* 67.26 (i AD; sp. -χιρ-).

τᾰρῑχιον, add 'Pherecr. 26 K.-A., Axionic. 4.16 K.-A.'

τᾰρῑχοπώλης, add '*SEG* 25.180 (Athens, iv BC)'

*τᾰρῑχόπωλις, ιδος, ἡ (sc. ἀγορά; cf. ἰχθυόπωλις), = ταριχοπωλεῖον *Gnomol.Vat.* 340 (*WS* 11.44).

τᾰρῑχον (s.v. τάρῑχος), delete 'Philippid. 9' and 'Axionic. 3.15'

τᾰρῑχος II, line 2, after '*fish*' insert 'Epich. 162' and after '*Ach.* 967' insert '*SEG* 37.665 (N. shore of Black Sea, *c.*400 BC)'

ταρσικάριος, before '*PLips.* 26.9' insert '*SB* 8268 (ii/iii AD)'

*ταρσίκιον, τό, perh. *crate for drying figs, POxy.* 2273.8 (iii AD).

ταρσός II 3, line 2, before 'Babr.' insert 'Mosch. 2.61'; line 4, delete 'of a peacock's *tail,* Mosch. 2.60' add '**7** λίθος ὁ κάτω τιθέμενος ἐν τῷ ἰπνῷ Hsch.'

*ταρτᾰροειδής, ές, = ταρταρώδης, of the sun viewed as an omen, ὁ τρίτος ἥλιος αἱματοειδής, παμμεγέθης, πῦρ φλέγον *Orac.Tiburt.* 24, 25.

**Τάρταρος I**, add 'transf., of a river-bottom, τάρταρον ἰλυόεσσαν Nic. l.c. (*Th.* 203)'

***ταρτημοριαῖος**, α, ον, shortened form of τεταρτημοριαῖος, τ. τινα καλοῦσιν οἷον διχάλκου ἄξιον Phot. s.v. ταρτημόριον (cf. *EM*747.18).

***Τάρφη**· πόλις Λοκρίδος, οἱ δὲ σποδός, τέφρα. ἢ βλαστός Hsch.

***ταρφήεντα** ἐντάφια· τεφρώδη Hsch. (ταρφίεντα cod.; cf. °Τάρφη).

***τάρχεα**· τὰ νενομισμένα τοῖς νεκροῖς Sch.A Il. 7.85, cf. Sch.Gen.ibid.; Sch.B has **ταρχύματα**, Sch.T **ταρχῶα**.

**τάσσω**, line 1, after 'Pl.*Prt.* 262e, etc.' insert 'Boeot. τάδδεσθη (pass. inf.) *SEG* 32.496 (Thespiae, *c.*250 BC)'; line 4, after 'pass. sense)' insert 'E.*Supp.* 521 (ἐπι-)' **I 2**, line 9, add 'in fig. phr., τῆς ὑστέρας τεταγμένος Pl.*Criti.* 108c; also act., Isoc. 12.180' add '**3** *organize* a state, ὁ δὲ (sc. Νουμᾶς) αὐτὴν (sc. τὴν πόλιν) νόμοις τάξας τε καὶ κατακοσμήσας Just.*Nov.* 47 pr.'

***ταταῖ**, an exclamation of pain, Herod. 3.79; cf. ἀτταταῖ; *tatae*, Plaut.*St.* 771.

**τατί**, add 'perh. also θαθί Lang *Ath.Agora* XXI F11'

**τατικός 2**, add 'adv. comp., *with greater force*, Sch.E.*Ph.* 1141'

**Ταΰγετον**, add 'also τὰ Ταΰγετα ὄρη Iamb.*VP* 19.92'

***ταυράς**, άδος, ἡ, *cow*, XVIII *Int.Cong.Pap.* II 83 (*Tyche* 4.237).

**Ταυρεασταί**, add 'at Istria, *IHistriae* 60, 61 (iii/ii BC); also **Ταυριασταί** ib. 57 (ii AD)'

**ταυρεία**, add '**3** *helmet of ox-hide*, Hsch.'

**Ταυρεών**, after 'Herod. 7.86, etc.' insert 'name of first month at Olbia, *SEG* 30.977, 980 (V BC)'

***Ταύρια**· ἑορτή τις ἀγομένη Ποσειδῶνος Hsch.; cf. ταύρεος II.

**ταυρινάδαι**, delete the entry.

***ταυρινᾶς**, ᾶδος, ὁ, *shoemaker*, *MAMA* 6.234 (Apamea); συνεργασία πλήθους -άδων *IEphes.* 2080, 2081 (ταυρειν- lapides).

**ταυροβολικός**, ή, όν, *connected with the* ταυροβόλιον, *ara taurobolica*, *CIL* 9.1538 (AD 228).

**ταυροβόλιον**, add '**2** *bullfight*, as an entertainment, *IIlion* 12.14 (i BC), *TAM* 2.508 (Lycia, i BC).'

**ταυροθύσια**, for '*Supp.Epigr.* 4.180.6' read '*IKeramos* 7.6, 9.10'

**ταυροκαθάπτης**, add '*IG* 2².3156 (Athens)'

**ταυροκαθάψια**, add '*SEG* 32.660 (Thrace, ii/iii AD)'

**+ταυρόκερως**, ω (also dat. -κέρωτι Euph. 14.1 vGr.), ὁ, ἡ, *bull-horned*, of Dionysus, E.*Ba.* 100 (lyr.), Euph. l.c., Orph.*H.* 52.2; of Io, Agatharch.ap.Phot.*Bibl.* 443a.25; of Μήνη, Orph.*H.* 9.2; of Attalus of Pergamum, orac.ap.D.S. 34/35.13, Paus. 10.15.3.

**ταυρομαχία**, delete '*IGRom.* 3.631.14 (Xanthus)'

***ταυρομάχια**, τά, *fighting with bulls*, *TAM* 2.287.14.

**Ταυροπόλια**, for 'Ἀρχ.Ἐφ. .. iv BC)' read '*SEG* 34.103 (Attica, iv BC)' and add '*SEG* 31.615 (Maced.)'

**ταυροπόλος**, add '*SEG* 31.614 (Maced., 179/1 BC); Ταυροπόλαι· ἡ Ἄρτεμις καὶ ἡ Ἀθηνᾶ Hsch.'

**ταῦρος I 2**, add 'cf. ταῦροι· οἱ παρὰ Ἐφεσίοις οἰνοχόοι Hsch.'

**ταυροσφαγέω**, for '*cut a bull's throat*' read '*slaughter a bull* or *bulls*'

***ταυροτάφος**, ὁ, *one who prepares (sacred) bulls for burial*, *PMich.*inv. 855 (*ZPE* 27.147, i AD).

***ταυροτρόφος**, ὁ, *bull-breeder*, Roueché *Performers and partisans* no.44 (Aphrodisias, Chr.).

***Ταυροφόνια**, τά, festival at Mylasa, *IMylasa* 201.

**ταυροχόλια**, for 'Κυζικῷ' read 'Κυζίκῳ'

***ταυρόω**, v. ταυρόομαι 2.

**ταύτᾳ**, after lemma insert '(or **ταυτᾷ**)' and add 'cj. in Theoc. 15.18 (perh. in origin ταυτᾶ instr.)'

**ταυτότης III**, delete '*maintenance of identity*, Plot. 1.2.7' (v. αὐλότης)

**ταφή 2**, for this section read '*burial place*, *tomb*, pl., Hdt. 4.71.3, 5.63.4, S.*Aj.* 1090, 1109; sg., *SB* 6028, al. (i BC), *INikaia* 767 (iv AD); μιᾷ καὶ μόνῃ ταφῇ, i.e. urn or tomb which would require no renewal, *GVI* 1975.24. **b** *mummy*, *POxy.* 736.13 (i AD), Wilcken *Chr.* 499 (ii/iii AD); of the covering of a mummy, whether linen wrappings or mummy-case, δευτέρα τ. *PGiss.* 68.7 (ii AD), *APF* 4.133 (ii AD).'

***ταφία**, ἡ, *tombstone*, *SEG* 3.674.A4 (Rhodes, ii BC); also ταφίη *MAMA* 9.89.1 (Phrygia, Rom.imp.).

**τάφιος II**, delete 'but also .. (Rhodes, ii BC)'

**τάφρη**, add 'Dor. **τράφα**, *IRhod.Peraea* 353A.8 (*c.*200 BC)'

**τάχα II**, line 7, after 'with aor. ind.' insert 'S.*Ph.* 305'

***ταχύγουνος**, ον, *having swift legs*, Nonn.*D.* 1.91, 9.155, al.

***ταχυδιάνοιος**, gloss on λειόμερος (q.v.), Hsch.

***ταχύλογος**, ον, *speaking rapidly*, *Physiogn.* 1.332.11, 17.

**ταχυμάχης**, for 'ὠκυβόας' read 'ὠκυβόαι'

**ταχύπλοος**, for 'ὠκύπλους' read 'ὠκύαλος'

**ταχύπους**, add 'ταχύπουν κέλευθον *Trag.adesp.* 127.6 K.-S. (codd.)'

**ταχύς B** adv. **I**, line 2, after 'etc.' insert '*soon*, Sapph. 1.21, 23 L.-P.' add '**b** *early*, Plu. 2.178e.' **C I 3**, line 4, for 'Men. 402.16' read 'Men.*fr.* 333.16 K.-Th., *AP* 11.23 (Antip.Thess.)' **II 3**, as adv., add 'ἵνα .. τὰν ταχίσταν συντελεσθέοισιν *IKyme* 13.15 (ii BC)'

***ταχύω**, *make haste*, *hurry*, *Suppl.Mag.* 34 (vi AD).

***ταωνίτης**, ου, ὁ, precious stone, = ταώς II, *Lapid.Gr.* 168.25.

**τε A II**, lines 16/17, delete 'διάνδιχα .. Il. 8.168' add 'Myc. *-qe*'

***τεάφη**, ἡ, *sulphur*, Anon.Alch. 323.9 (written τι- ib. 327.11).

***τέγεα**, v. °τένεα.

**Τεγεάτης**, after 'Ion. -ήτης' insert 'Arc. **-ᾱτᾱς** *SEG* 33.319 (iii BC)'

***τεγκοσχ(..)**, prob. type of reed, *SB* 9699.491 (i AD).

***τεγοποιέω**, *cover with a roof*, w. acc., *Inscr.Délos* 444*B*95 (ii BC).

**τέθηπα 1**, line 5, for '*amazed*, *astonied*' read '*dazed*'

**+τεινεσμώδης**, ες, *affected by* τεινεσμός, Hp.*Epid.* 1.26.γ', προθυμίαι -ώδεες Aret.*SA* 2.5, cf. Sor. 2.20; *suffering from* τεινεσμός, Gal. 12.325.12. Adv. -δῶς Ruf.ap.Orib. 8.24.24.

***τειρωνολογέω**, *recruit for the army*, *BE* 1960.230 (*IGBulg.* 517).

**τειχεσιπλήτης**, add 'Orph.*H.* 65.2'

**τειχήρης**, add 'Aen.Tact. 1.3, 23.4'

***τειχητός**, ή, όν, *walled* or *fortified*, εἰς τὸν τειχητὸν [.. *Ath.Agora* XIX P26.534 (iv BC).

**τειχίζω II**, add 'of non-physical protection, τὰ κοινὰ πράγματα τῇ τοῦ φιλανθρώπου θεοῦ χάριτι τειχίζεσθαι πεπιστεύκαμεν *Cod.Just.* 1.3.42 pr.'

**τειχισμός**, add '*SEG* 25.486 (Oropus, iii BC), *REG* 101.14 (Xanthos, 206/5 BC)'

**τειχοδομέω**, add '**2** *fortify with a wall*, Θήβη ἐτειχοδομήθη Sch.E.*Ph.* 287.'

**τειχομαχέω**, line 5, for 'App.*Hann.* 92' read 'App.*Hisp.* 92'

***τειχοποιής**, v. °τειχοποιός.

**τειχοποιία**, add '*SEG* 36.1277 (Edessa, iii AD)'

**τειχοποιός**, add '-ποιής *SEG* 32.795 (Olbia, *c.*325/300 BC)'

***τειχοσεισμοποιός**, όν, *causing earthquakes destructive of walls*, *PMag.* 4.183.

**τεκμαίρομαι A I**, for '*assign*, *ordain*' read '*mark out*, *indicate*, *designate*'; line 10, for 'with a notion of foretelling' read 'of a prophet' **III**, for this section read '*indicate* (to an observer), show, ὁλκόν, οὖρον (= ὅρον) D.P. 101, 135, 178; πόμα Nic.*Al.* 105, τοῦ μὲν ὑπὲρ κυνόδοντε δύω χροῒ τεκμαίρονται ἰὸν ἐρευγόμενοι id.*Th.* 231.'

**τέκμαρ**, line 1, delete 'never elsewhere' and insert 'A.R. 3.493, etc., Opp.*H.* 4.26, Q.S. 3.503, etc., Synes.*Hymn.* 1.491; sp. τέκμορ *SEG* 31.1203 (Rom.imp.)' **I 2**, add 'a principle in Alcman's cosmology, τέκμωρ Alcm. 5 *fr.* 2 ii 14 sqq. P., v. *CQ* NS 13.155-6'

***τεκνοθεσία**, ἡ, *placing in adoption*, *PZen.Col.* 58.9 (iii BC), παρὰ Ἰσιδώρας τῆς Ἀπολλωνίο(υ) .. κατὰ δὲ τεκνοθεσίαν Διονυσίο(υ) *POxy.* 3271.4 (i AD).

**τεκνοποιΐα I**, add '*PPanop.* 28.5 (AD 329)'

***τεκνοτρόφος**, ον, *bringing up children*, ἀνὴρ ἀξιόλογος καὶ τ. *IG* 12(7).394.5 (Amorgos); prob. subst. in *GVI* 977.8 (Mauretania, ii/iii AD).

**τεκνοφάγος**, add '*SEG* 31.1285 (Pisidia, Rom.imp.), Thphl.Ant.*Autol.* 1.9.3, 3.3.16'

**τέκνωμα**, add 'Dosiad.*Ara* 4'

**τέκτων**, add '**5** kind of spider, Hsch.' add 'Myc. *te-ko-to-ne* (pl.)'

**τελαμών I 2**, after 'E.*Ph.* 1669' insert 'κατεδήσατο τελαμῶνι τοὺς ὀφθαλμοὺς αὐτοῦ Lxx 3*Ki.* 21(20).38' **3**, add 'Aq.*Is.* 3.18' **II 2**, add 'sp. ταλαμών Robert *Hell.* 7.32ff. (Bithynia)'

**τέλειος I 2 a**, add 'τέλειοι αὐλοί *full-sized*, the second largest of five sizes of aulos, Aristox.*fr.* 101 W., Arist.*Aud.* 804ᵃ11, Ath. 4.176f, Poll. 4.81' **3 b**, line 9, after '(ii AD)' insert 'τ. ἀριθμητικόν *complete* land-tax, *SB* 4415.4 (ii AD); εἰς τέλειον *absolutely*, *Cod.Just.* 11.1.1 pr.' **VII 3**, add '*IHadr.* 77 (i/ii AD)'

**τελειόω II 4**, add '*TAM* 4(1).356'

***τελέσεργος**, ὁ, dub. l. for τελεσιουργός 3, Διὸς τ. *IG* 12 suppl. 380.2 (ΤΕΛΣΕΕΡ- lapis; Thasos, v BC).

**τελεσιουργός 3**, add 'of Athena, *IG* 2².4338a'

***Τέλεσσαι**, αἱ, name of goddesses at Cyrene, *PP* 15.294 (ii BC).

**τελεστήριον II**, for '*thank-offering for success*' read '*offerings to a sanctuary*' add '**2** = Att. τέλη (v. τέλος I 6), Wolters *Kabirenheiligtum* 27 no. 4 (iii/ii BC) (τελεστειρ- lapis).'

**τελεστής**, add 'Myc. *te-re-ta*, title of an official'

**τέλεστρα**, for '*admission to priesthood*' read '*initiation*'

**τελεσφορία 1**, for '*initiation in the mysteries*' read '*mystery rites*' and delete '*Cer.* 130' add '**III** *ripening* of fruit, etc., περὶ καρπῶν τελεσφορίας *ABSA* 49.15 (Dorylaeum; τηλ-); χαλεπὴν .. τελεσφορίην rest. in Call.*fr.* 85.13 Pf.'

**Τελεσφόρος III**, add '*Inscr.Perg.* 8(3).125, 126'

**τελεταρχέω**, delete the entry.

***τελετουργός**, όν, *working by means of a rite*, θεοί Procl. *in R.* 2.153.23 K.

**τελευταῖος I 1**, add 'sup. *Peripl.M.Rubr.* 16, 18, 21' **2**, add 'τεῖ τελευτ[αίαι ἐμέραι] *IG* 1³.364.22 (433/2 BC)'

**τελευτάω II 1**, delete 'ἐλπίδες E.*Ba.* 908 (lyr.)' **2 b**, line 3, after 'A.*Supp.* 211' insert 'ἐλπίδες τ. ἐν ὄλβῳ E.*Ba.* 908 (lyr.) (s.v.l.)'

**τελέω I 7**, line 1, transfer 'ὅτε δὲ .. Od. 5.390' to section 5. **8**, after 'S.*El.* 147 (lyr.)' insert 'epigr. in *Phoenix* 26.183 (iv AD)'; after '*to be*' insert '*ἐπὶ τῇ ἐξουσίᾳ τελοῦντα* Cod.Just. 1.2.24.1' **III 3,** add 'cf. *τελεῖν τὰν Ἀφροδίταν Anacreont.* 36.16 W.'

*__τελίαμβος__, *ὁ*, dactylic hexameter having an iambus in place of the final spondee, *novam potius hanc speciem quam miuron existimant versum et teliambon appellant* Mar.Vict. (Aphth.) in *Gramm.Lat.* 6.68 K.

**τέλμα I,** add '*Ath.Agora* XIX P26.161, L6.140, 142, L10.40 (iv BC)'

*__τελμάτιον__, *τό*, dim. of *τέλμα* I, Simp. *in Cael.* 66.9.

**τέλος I 2,** line 4, after 'Semon. 1.1' insert 'cf. Archil. 298 W., Alc. 200.10 L.-P.' **III 2,** add 'epigr. in *SEG* 23.278 (Thebes, iii BC)'

**τέλσον,** add 'transf., of the edge of a threshing-floor, Nic.*Th.* 546'

**Τελχίνιος I,** after 'Paus. l.c.' insert '*Ἥραι Θελχινίαι Sokolowski* 3.18.7 (Erchiae, iv BC)'

**τέλωρ,** for '*τελώριον*' read '*πελώριον*'

**τεμᾰχοπώλης,** add 'perh. at *SB* 10258 i 14 (iv AD)'

**τέμᾰχος,** line 6, after 'Paul.Aeg. 7.11' insert '*τ. γάλακτος* i.e. of cheese, Al. 1*Ki.* 17.18'

**τεμενίζω,** add '**b** *οἱ τεμενίζοντες* members of a religious association at Miletus, *SEG* 30.1339 (Miletus, ii/i BC).'

**τεμένιος I,** add 'subst., *τεμένια, τά, REA* 44.35.45 (Olus, ii BC)' **II,** add 'also of Artemis, *SEG* 25.938 (Naxos, iv BC)'

**τεμενίτης,** add '**2** pl., members of a religious association at Miletus, *Τεμενεῖται οἵδε SEG* 30.1340 (Miletus, ii/i BC).'

**τέμενος,** after lemma insert 'Cypr. nom. *te-me-no-se ICS* 265.2 (in quot., sense II)' **III,** after '*temple*' insert 'Pl.*Ax.* 367c' at end add 'Myc. *te-me-no* (sense I)'

**τέμνω** (A), line 10, after 'Il. 19.197' insert 'Aeol. part. *τόμοντες* Alc. 129.15 L.-P.' **I 3,** pass., add '*TAM* 4(1).367' **III 2,** after 'so in Med., 9.580' insert 'A.R. 1.868' **IV 3,** line 4, after 'Th. 2.19, 55' insert '*POxy.* 3575.11 (iv AD)'

**Τέμπεα II,** add 'sg. *τέμπος*, Sch.E.*Ph.* 600, *EM* 527.46'

*__τέμπλον__, *τό*, Lat. *templum*, (in quot., unexpld. archit. term), *τὸ τένπλον τοῦ τίχους τοῦτο ICilicie* 24 (v/vi AD).

**τενᾰγῖτις,** after '*ιδος*' insert 'acc. *τεναγῖτιν*'

**τένεα,** add 'cf. *τέγε(α)· κόρυζα, Κῷοι* id.'

*__τένται__, v. *τέλομαι*.

**τένων I,** line 7, for 'for the foot' read 'in ref. to the sole of the foot'; last line, delete '*τένοντα* .. 62.3' add '**b** *neck*, Lyc. 1112, Luc.*Cat.* 19, Babr. 62.3, Ael.*NA* 2.39, al.' **II,** after 'mountain-*ridge*' insert '*δύσβατον ἀμφὶ τ.* Nonn.*D.* 11.193'

**τέξις,** add '*birth, nativity*, Ptol.*Tetr.* 105'

**τεός,** line 3, after 'E.*Heracl.* 911' insert '(cj.)'

*__τερᾰτοειδῶς__, adv., *in monstrous form, as a prodigy, κατελθεῖν* Sch.E.*Ph.* 806.

**Τερβινθεύς,** add 'also *Τερμ-* *SEG* 36.1047 (iii BC), 1048 (ii BC, both Miletus)'

**τερεβινθίζω,** add '*terebinthizusa*, a variety of the stone *iaspis*, Plin.*HN* 37.116'

**τερετίζω I,** for '*hum*' read '*warble, trill*, or sim.' and add '**4** of *αὐλοί*, Philostr.*VA* 6.36.'

*__τερετίστρια__, *ἡ*, *chirruper*, of the cicada, *Vit.Aesop.*(W) 99.

**τέρην,** line 1, after '*εν*' insert '(*ειν* Hsch.)'

**τέρθρον,** add '*τίς .. ἦλθεν ἐπὶ τέρθρον θυράων;* Apollod.Lyr. 1 P.'

*__τερμαστής__, *οῦ, ὁ*, *boundary-commissioner*, *SEG* 35.665.B35, 43 (Epirus, ii BC).

**τερμᾰτίζω,** after '*limit, bound*' insert 'Hippon. 103.3 W.'

**Τερμέρειον 2,** delete the section.

*__Τερμινθεύς__, v. °*Τερβινθεύς*.

**τέρμινθος I 1,** add 'reported to grow parasitically on the olive, Thphr.*CP* 2.17.14. **b** used w. ref. to the pistachio-tree, *Pistacia vera*, *φασὶ δ' εἶναι καὶ τέρμινθον, οἱ δ' ὅμοιον τερμίνθῳ*, .. id.*HP* 4.4.7; also its fruit, *θυμίαμα καὶ στακτὴν καὶ τερέμινθον καὶ κάρυα* LXX *Ge.* 43.11.' **II & III,** for these sections read '**II** *τέρμινθος· φυτὸν ἐμφερὲς τῷ λίνῳ ἐξ οὗ πλέκουσιν παρ' Ἀθηναίοις [παρ]ορμιάς* Hsch., Phot., *EM* 753.10.'

**τερμιόεις,** line 1, for '*fringed*' read '*having a decorated border*'; add 'form *τερμιδϝενς*, Myc. *te-mi-dwe, te-mi-dwe-ta* (neut. pl.), of wheels'

**τέρος,** for 'dub. .. 65 H.' read 'dub. in Cypr. *i-te-re-i* perh. *ἰ(ν) τέρει ICS* 244'

**τερπνός II,** for 'Call.*Fr.* 256 .. 1218*c*6' read 'Call.*fr.* 369, 536 Pf.; hyper-characterized adv. *-ίστατα* ib. 93.3'

**τέρτα,** delete the entry.

*__τέρτος__, *ᾱ, ον*, Aeol. for *τρίτος*, *τέρτον τόνδε* Alc. 129.7 L.-P., cf. Choerob.in *An.Ox.* 2.275, Hsch. s.v. *τέρτα*; perh. also Boeot. **τορτ-** (in pers. n. *Τορτέας SEG* 23.271, iii BC).

**Τερφεῖος,** add '*IKyme* 13 i, ii, *SEG* 33.1039 (Aeolian Cyme, all ii BC)'

⁺__τέρφος__, *εος, τό*, = *στέρφος*, *outer covering, integument, skin*, of snake, Nic.*Th.* 323, of chestnut, id.*Al.* 268.

**τέρχνος,** for '*twig, young shoot*' read '*shoot, young plant* or *sapling*, Call.*VB* in *Suppl.Hell.* 257.25'; line 3, for '*plants* .. 9 H.' read '(*te-re-ki-ni-ja*) *plants*, *ICS* 217.9, al.'

**τερψίχορος,** add '*σοφία CEG* 797 (Larissa, iv BC)'

**τεσσᾰρᾰκαιδεκέτης,** before '**-δεκετής**' insert '**-δεχετής** *GVI* 1709 (Thessalonica, ii/i BC), cf. °*ἔτος*; also *τεττ-* *SEG* 34.1271 (*τετρασκαιδεκέτης* lapis)'; delete 'fem. .. Arist.*Ath.* 56.7.'

*__τεσσᾰρᾰκαιδεκέτις__, *ιδος*, fem. of *τεσσαρακαιδεκέτης*, Arist.*Ath.* 56.7, *GVI* 1461.4.

**τεσσᾰρᾰκαιεικοσίπους,** delete the entry.

**τεσσᾰράκοντα,** after '*τεσσεράκοντα* (q.v.)' insert '*τεΤαράϙοντα IEphes.* 1 A1, B8 (vi BC)'; line 3, form *τετρώ-*, add '*SEG* 34.940 (Sicily, iv/iii BC)'; line 6, after '**πετταράκοντα** (q.v.)' insert 'Aeol. *πεσ(σ)αράκο[ντα] EA* 11 p. 4 (Assos, late vi BC)' and after 'indecl.' insert 'exc. Aeol. gen. *τεσσ[ερ]ακόντων Schwyzer* 688*C*14 (Chios, v BC)'

**τεσσᾰρᾰκονταχοίνικος,** add '*PMich.*III 145 iii 7 (ii AD)'

**τεσσᾰρᾰκόσιοι,** add 'also **τετταρακ-** *Inscr.Délos* 1401*C*8 (ii BC)'

**τεσσᾰρᾰκοστόγδοος,** add '*τεσσαρακοστόγδοον, τό*, *forty-eighth part*, *SB* 10497.23-4 (*τεσσαρακοσθωγδον* pap., AD 213).'

**τεσσᾰρᾰκοστός I,** add '*τεττ-* *Inscr.Magn.* 16 (207/203 BC)' **II,** add '*μισθωτὴν τεσσερακοστῆς ἐρεῶν POxy.* 3104 (AD 228)'

**τεσσᾰράριος,** add '*Ἐπίγονος τεσσεράρις SEG* 26.1853 (Cyrenaica, i AD)'

**τέσσᾰρες,** line 19, after 'Theoc. 14.16' insert '**τέζαρα** *SEG* 19.618 (Metapontum, v BC)'; add '*τέσσαρες ἄνδρες* = Lat. *quattuorviri*, *Xanthos* 50.2 (AD 96/9)'

**τεσσᾰρεσκαίδεκα,** add '**τεττ-** *IG* 2².1673 (Eleusis, iv BC)'

**τεσσᾰρεσκαιδεκᾰσύλλᾰβος,** add 'Sch.Theoc. 29 *prooem.*'

**τεσσᾰρεσκαιδέκᾰτος,** add 'neut. as adv., *for the fourteenth time*, *AS* 36.139 no. 1 (5/4 BC)'

⁺__τεσσερακαιεβδο‹μη›κοντούτης__, *ες*, *seventy-four years old*, *Ἀ(σ)σων τε(σ)σερακαιεβδοκοντότης ἐὼν τὰς οἰκίας ἐχσεποίησεν IG* 12(5).219 (Paros, vi BC).

**τεσσερᾰ́κοντα,** add '*τεσεράκαντα SEG* 31.883 (Tridentum, v AD)'; delete 'but also' to end of article.

*__τεσσεράριος__, v. ‡*τεσσαρ-*.

*__τεστάτωρ__, *ορος, ὁ*, Lat. *testator*, Just.*Nov.* 19.9, 159 pr.

**τετᾰνός I,** line 2, for '*smooth*' read '*taut, stretched*' and for '*πῆχυς*' read '*πρίων*'; line 4, after 'Crito ap.Gal. 12.825' insert '*μελίχρως, τετανός, στρογγυλοπρόσωπος SB* 7169.17 (ii BC)'

**τέτᾰνος I,** add 'humorously, in obsc. sense, *κᾆτ' ἐντέξῃ τέτανον τερπνὸν τοῖς ἀνδράσι καὶ ῥοπαλισμούς* Ar.*Lys.* 553' **II,** delete the section.

*__τετᾰνοτρῐ́χῐνος__, *ον*, = *τετανόθριξ*, *PMich.*V 298 introd. 6 (i AD).

**τεταρταῖος 2,** after 'Id.*Ti.* 86a' insert '*πυρετοὶ τ. πολυχρόνιοι* Hp.*Aër.* 7'; add 'personified as a god in Samos, *ZPE* 3.149ff.'

*__τεταρτολογία__, *ἡ*, *payment of duty of one-fourth*, *PVindob.* G40822 (*BASP* 23.74).

**τέταρτος I,** add 'in the title of a legion, *λεγεῶνος τετάρτης Σκυθικῆς ICilicie* 87 (ii AD)' **II,** add '**3** coin, *Πτολεμαϊκὰ τ. Inscr.Délos* 444*B*32, al. (ii BC); *quarter of a mina*, *SEG* 31.1626; *of a stater*, *BE* 1989.324 (Didyma, ii BC), cf. Hsch. *τέταρτον ἥμισυ· τὸ τέταρτον ἡμιστάτηρον*.'

*__τεταρτώνης__, *ου, ὁ*, *collector of the quarter-tax*, *Syria* 22.263, 264 (Palmyra, ii AD).

**τέτμον 1,** penultimate line, after 'opt.' insert '*τέτμοι* Call.*Del.* 159'

⁺__τετρᾰβόλος__, *ον*, *shedding the teeth a fourth time*, *ὄνοι θήλειαι τετραβόλοι PSI* 79.10 (iii AD).

*__τετράγκαθος__, *ὁ*, *gum tragacanth*, Anon.Alch. 331.9.

**τετράγραμμος,** add '**2** = *τετραγραμμιαῖος*, Hsch. s.v. *στατήρ*.'

**τετρᾰγωνικός,** before 'Iamb. *in Nic.*' insert 'Hero *Dioptr.* 28 (p. 280 line 2)'

*__τετρᾰγώνιον__, *τό*, *square object*, *CPR* 8.66.1 (vi AD); perh. *a square container* (or *?square coin*), Just.*Nov.* 105.2.1, 3.

*__τετρᾰγώνιος__, *ον*, = *τετράγωνος* I 1, *CPR* 8.66.8 (vi AD) and I 4, Ptol.*Tetr.* 115.

*__τετρᾰγωνίτης__, *ου*, epith. of Hermes, cf. °*τετράγωνος*, *PASA* 3.342*D*66 (Pisidia).

**τετράγωνος I 2,** add '**c** cubic measure of wood, prob. a cubic *ξύλον* (v. *ξύλον* V) *PBremen* 15.12 (ii AD), *POxy.* 669.21 (iii AD); so prob. *τὴν ὄργυαν τὴν τετράγωνον Inscr.Délos* 290.167 (iii BC).' add '**V** epith. of Hermes, Babr. 48.1, *PMag.* 5.401, 7.669, *TAM* 3(1).34*D*71 (Pisidia).'

*__τετραδία__, *ἡ*, dub. sens., *κοιμητήριον Σεργίου μικροῦ τετραδίας Ἰάννου νέου IG* 3.3486.

**τετρᾰδισταί I,** for this section read 'members of a *θίασος* who met for celebration on the fourth day of the month, Alex. 260.1 K.-A., Ath. 14.659d (Men.*Kol.fr.* 1 S.)'

**τετράδραχμον,** line 1, delete '*silver*'

**τετρᾰ́δωρος,** add 'Call.*fr.* 196.27 Pf.'

**τετρᾰετηρικός,** add '*TAM* 2(1).307.6'

**τετρᾰετηρίς,** for '*CIG* 2741.22, 2812' read '*MAMA* 8.506, 519' and add '*SEG* 35.1415 (Pamphylia, ii/iii AD)'

**τετρᾰετής I,** add 'Men.*Sic.* 355 S., Call.*Cer.* 58, *τ. δαμάλην Suppl.Hell.*

396.2 (Dorieus), *AP* 6.155 (Theodorid.), 6.356 (Pancrat.)' **II**, add '[τ]ε[τ]ραετῆ .. ἀλικί̣α̣[ν *CEG* 691.2 (Rhodes, iv BC)'

**τετρᾰκαιεικοστός**, before '*PFay.* 82.12' insert '-όν, τό, *twenty-fourth part*' and add '*SB* 10359.4 (ii AD)'

**τετρᾰκαιεξηκοστόν**, after '*part*' insert '*BGU* 234.12, 17 (ii AD)'

***τετρᾰκεράτιον**, τό, name of a tax, cf. °δικεράτιον, *REG* 70.120 (Palestine, vi/vii AD).

**τετρᾰκι**, before '*MAMA* 4.157' insert 'w. ref. to the repetition of a name through four generations' and add '*SEG* 34.1302 (Pamphylia), al.'

***τετρᾰκοντόγδοος**, ον, *forty-eighth*, *SB* 9760.4 (vii AD).

**τετρᾰκόσιοι**, form -κάτιοι, add 'τζετρακάτιαι *IG* 5(2).159.10, (Tegea, v BC, engraved by Arcadian)'

**τετρακτύς II**, for '6:8:9:10' read '6:8:9:12'

**τετρακωμία**, add '*INikaia* 726 (AD 288/9)'

***τετρᾰλῑτρος**, ον, of a ξέστης, *containing four* λῖτραι, *SB* 9751.2 (vii AD).

**τετρᾰμαίνω**, after '= τρέμω' insert 'Archil. 23.9 W.'

**τετραμηνιαῖος**, add '*SEG* 32.1554 (Arabia, vi AD); τ. βρέβια lists of supplies *for four months*, *Cod.Just.* 1.42.2'

***τετραμηνιακός**, ή, όν, neut. pl. subst., *supplies for four months*, *SEG* 9.356.82 (Ptolemais in Cyrenaica, vi AD).

**τετρᾰμηνος**, line 4, ἡ πρώτη τ., add '*OStrassb.* 178.2, *OHeid.* 254 (both ii BC)'

**τετρᾰμορος**, for '*four parts*' read '*a quarter*' and after 'Nic.*Th.* 106' insert 'ταμίσοιο ib. 712'

**τετρᾰούγκιον**, for '= *triens* (i.e. *coin of four unciae*)' read '*four-twelfths*, i.e. *one-third*, *of an estate*, = Lat. *triens*' and add 'Just.*Nov.* 134.10.2'

**τετρᾰπᾰλαστος 1**, add '(sp. -παλαιστ-) *PSoterichos* 1.21 (AD 69), 2.17 (AD 71), *IG* 12(2).11.15' **2**, add 'Hsch. s.v. τετράφυον'

**τετρᾰπεδος I**, transfer '*IG* 4$^2$(1).119.14, al. (Epid.)' to section II after '*four feet*' and for 'Plb. 8.4.4' read 'Plb. 8.6.4'

**τετραπλάσιος**, after 'cf. 756e' insert 'τούτῳ (ἀποδώσεις) τὸ̣ τ̣ε̣τ̣ρ̣ᾶ-α-πλάσειον ἢ ὅσου πέπραται τὰ ὑπάρχοντα *PWisc.* 81.7 (ii AD)'

**τετραπλεθρία**, for '(Corcyra)' read '(Crete, iii BC)'

***τετραπλεῖ**, adv., *Inscr.Cret.* 4.41.4.2 (Gortyn, v BC), cf. τετραπλῆ.

***τετρᾰποδί**, adv., *on all fours*, ἅτε βρέφος ἑρπύζουσι Nic.*Al.* 543.

**τετρᾰπολος**, add '*PCornell* 39.6 (iii/iv AD)'

**τετρᾰπος**, delete 'Cret. nom. .. (Gortyn)'

**τετρᾰπους I 1**, line 2, after 'Pl.*Ti.* 92a' insert 'τετράπουν μῖμον ἔχων θηρός E.*Rh.* 255 (lyr.)' add 'Cret. τετράπος, *Schwyzer* 181 iii 7 (Gortyn), Myc. *qe-to-ro-po-pi* (instr. pl.) (both in sense I 2)'

**τετραπρόσωπος**, add 'Μήτηρ *MAMA* 5.101, θεά *ABSA* 49.13 (both Dorylaeum), *PMag.* 4.2818'

**τετρᾰπυργία**, after 'Str. 17.3.22' insert 'also in Lydia, *TAM* 5(1).230 (iii AD)'

**τετρᾰπωλον**, after 'τέθριππον' insert '*PLond.* 1912.45 (i AD)'

**τετράς I**, after '**2**' read '*the fourth day* of the first, middle, or last decad of the month' and add 'μέχρι τετρὰς ἐπιλάμψει (?-ψῃ) δεκάδι (i.e. the fourteenth day) Ezek.*Exag.* 178 S.' add '**5** in general, *fourth*, Guarducci *EG* 4.363 (c.AD 300). **6** *group of four*, τετράδας ἐς πίσυρας κρηνῶν προχέεις σέο κάλλος *SEG* 32.1502 (v AD).'

**τετράσπαστος**, delete the entry.

***τετραστᾰσιος**, ον, *of four times the value*, *weight*, etc., *CID* II 62 iiA 5.

**τετράστοον**, add '*Ann.Épigr.* 1990.957 (Aphrodisias, iv AD; sp. -στω-)'

***τετράστροφος**, ον, *consisting of four strophes*, Serv. in *Gramm.Lat.* 4.468.21 K.

**τετράτομος 2**, for this section read 'of a papyrus roll, *consisting of four* τόμοι, χάρτας τετρατόμους *PLond.ined.* 2134 (*JHS* 55.95, ii AD); -ον, τό, such a *roll*, *PFreib.* 53.25'

**τέτρᾰτος**, add 'Thess. **πετριτ-**, παρ πέτριτεν ἔτες, i.e. *every fourth year*, *SEG* 37.494.10 (Metropolis, late iii BC)'

***τετρᾰϋφαντος**, ον, *having a quadruple web*, ἱστοῦ τ. *PMasp.* 6$^v$.49.

***τετρᾰφυλλος**, ον, *of four leaves*, στεφάνιον χρυσοῦν τετράφυλλον ἄστατον *Inscr.Délos* 1416*A*i57 (ii BC).

**τέτρᾰχᾰ**, add 'Ἰνδικήτας μεμερισμένους τέτραχα Str. 3.4.1; Nonn.*D.* 2.248, etc.; *in four ways*, Opp.*H.* 3.72. **b** *four times*, *APl.* 336 (vi AD).'

***τετρᾰχάλκιον**, τό, = °τετράχαλκον, *IEphes.* 13 ii 27.

***τετρᾰχαλκον**, τό, *quadruple chalcus*, a coin = half of an obol, *BMC Ionia* 340; also -ος, ὁ, Hsch. s.v. ἵπποπορ.

**τετρᾰχοίνικος**, after '*holding four* χοίνικες' insert '*PTeb.* 796.11 (ii BC)'

**τετρᾰχους**, after '*holding four* χόες' insert 'τετρ]άχουν Lang *Ath.Agora* XXI Ha13 (iii BC)'

***τετρωβολεῖος**, ον, = τετρώβολος, *PStrassb.* 52.13 (ii AD).

**τετρώβολος II**, after 'τετρώβολον' insert '(often written τετροβ- in papyri and ostraca)'

***τετρῷος**, ὁ, *throw of four* at dice, *TAM* 3(1).34*D*67 (Termessus); pl., *BCH* 8.502, 503; also sg. τετρῴ ib. 502 (Phrygia).

**τεῦγμα**, for '*work*' read '*structure* or *artefact*' and add 'χρυσέοις τεύγμασιν *Didyma* 118.9 (ii BC)'

**τευμάομαι**, for 'Antim. 3' read 'Antim. 3.2 W.' and add '*Suppl.Hell.* 1044'

**τεῦχος IV**, add 'τ. δημόσιον *BCH* 60.131 (Delphi, i AD), *Delph.* 3(6).35.19, al.' at end add 'Myc. *te-u-ke-pi* (instr. pl.) *equipment*'

**τεύχω I 1**, add 'ἐλεγεῖον, -α τ. *CEG* 819.13, *SEG* 28.1245.B19' **2**, τετυγμένος, add '*fixed*, *definite*, Arat. 12, 757' at end add 'Myc. pf. part. *te-tu-ko-wo-a₂* = τετυχϝoha'

**τέφρα**, at end delete 'Gr. θέπτανος'

**τεφράς**, for 'τέττιξ' read 'cicada'

***τεφρίας**, ου, ὁ, kind of serpentine (ὀφίτης), also called Μεμφίτης, Plin.*HN* 36.56.

***τεφρῖτις**, ιδος, ἡ, precious stone, Plin.*HN* 37.184.

**τεχνάζω II 3**, line 3, after '*Philopatr.* 26' insert 'in aor. part. *AP* 6.4 (Leon.Tarent.)'

**τεχνάρχης**, add 'w. ref. to an association of sculptors, *Salamine* 43 (ii/iii AD)'

**τέχνασμα II**, add 'Aen.Tact. 37.8'

**τεχνήεις II**, after 'Q.S. 8.296' insert 'τ. καὶ δεινὸν καὶ πόριμον Gorg. 11a.25 D.-K., τεχνήεντι νόῳ *Suppl.Hell.* 938.11, δόλῳ Nonn.*D.* 37.202'

**τεχνικός II**, before 'Thphr.*Lap.* 55' insert 'Pl.*Lg.* 889a'

**τεχνίτης III**, add 'γόης καὶ τ. ἄνθρωπος, opp. ἰδιώταις ἀνθρώποις, Luc.*Peregr.* 13'

**τῆ**, after lemma insert 'Cypr. τᾶ (*ta*) *ICS* 346, 347'

**τηθία**, after '*old woman*' insert 'Men.*Mis.* 13, Ar.Byz.*fr.* 243C S.'

**Τηθύς I**, as type of very old woman, for 'Call. .. 174' read 'Call.*fr.* 194.52 Pf.' and add 'Suet.*Blasph.* 216 T., *Com.adesp.* 57 D.'

***τηλέγνωτος**, ον, *recognized from afar*, A.*fr.* 204c R. (dub.).

***τήλεμος**, ον, perh. *distant*, Theognost.*Can.* 64.

**τηλέπορος 1**, add 'Nonn.*D.* 17.339, 37.692'

***Τηλέφεια**, τά, name of a tetralogy of plays relating to the Telephus legend, Σοφοκλῆς ἐδίδασκε Τηλέφειαν *IG* 2$^2$.3091.8 (early iv BC).

**τηλεφόρος**, for 'Nonn.*D.* 19.149' read 'Nonn.*D.* 18.262 cod., 19.149 cod.'

***τῆλις**, delete the entry.

**τηλόθεν 1**, add 'σήμηνε .. Il. 23.359' (fr. section 2) **2**, for this section read 'w. gen., *far from*, Πελειάδων μὴ τηλόθεν Pi.*N.* 2.12, τοῦ Τελαμῶνος τηλόθεν οἴκου S.*Aj.* 204, E.*HF* 1112'

**τηλοῦ 1 a**, add '*Trag.adesp.* 77 K.-S.' **2**, add 'E.*fr.* 884'

**τηνεσμός**, for 'f.l. for τεινεσμός' read '= τεινεσμός'

***τηνεσμώδης**, ες, = τεινεσμώδης, Sch.Nic.*Al.* 382 Ge.

**τηρέω II 1**, after '*observe*' insert 'ἀνάλωσιν Thgn. 903' **III 1**, add '*keep* a regulation, rule, etc., *IEphes.* 3217 (AD 113/20)'

**τητινός**, add 'ἐ[φ]ήβων τητινῶν *SEG* 29.806 (Euboea, 120/100 BC)'

***Τιβέριος**, ὁ, name of an Asiatic month beginning Oct. 24, *Hemerolog.Flor.* 79 (22 K.).

***Τιβηνός**, ὁ, wine, app. named after the village of Τίβας in Lydia, Gal. 6.806.7, 14.16.9, al.

***τιβιάζομαι**, app. *play the tibia*, *Mim.adesp.* 15.6, 42.

**τιγρήϊος**, delete the entry.

***τῑθασμός**, ὁ, *nursing at the breast*, Procl.CP *Hom.* 26.11.

**τίθημι**, lines 25/26, after 'ἔθηκαν' insert '(E.*HF* 590)' and after 'Attic' insert 'inscrr.' **A III 2**, after 'E.*Ph.* 576' insert 'βόστρυχον Call.*fr.* 110.8 Pf.' **B II 1**, at beginning delete 'when Med. is more freq. than Act.' at end add 'Myc. 3 aor. *te-ke* (in sense B I 1)'

**τῑθηνήτειρα**, add 'ὦ Βάχχοιο τιθηνήτειρα *SEG* 26.683 (Thessaly, iii BC)'

**τῑθῠμαλλίς 3**, delete the section.

**τῑθῠμαλλος**, for 'used for poisoning water in warfare' read 'used as poison' and add 'Ael.*NH* 1.58'

**τίκτω**, line 6, aor. 1 ἔτεξα, add 'subj. τέξῃ Hes.*fr.* 343.8 M.-W., *Epigr.Gr.* 706.2'; lines 13f., aor. pass. ἐτέχθην, add '*IHadr.* 80 (ii AD)'

**τίλλω I 2**, line 6, delete 'as a description of an idle fellow'

**τίλτρον**, delete '*PRyl.* .. (iv AD)'

***τῑμαδά**, adv., app. *in proportion to one's rank*, *SEG* 23.566 (Crete, iv BC).

**τῑμαῖος**, add 'as cult-epith. of Zeus, Διὶ Τειμαίῳ *TAM* 5(1).267'

**τῑμάξιος**, after '*worthy of honour*' insert '*PAmh.* 153$^v$.1 (vi/vii AD)'

***τῑμᾰχεῖον**, τό, place where the τιμᾶχος (τιμοῦχος) exercises his office, *SEG* 9.5 (Cyrene, 109/8 BC); perh. also *SEG* 9.18 (iv BC), 9.33 (iii BC).

**τῑμάω I**, line 20, τιμᾶν τινα τάφῳ, γόοις, etc., add '*SEG* 31.1003 (Lydia, i AD), Mitchell *N.Galatia* 28 (Rom.imp.), etc.'; add '*honour* with a bequest, ληγάτῳ .. τιμηθέντες *Cod.Just.* 1.5.15, 1.5.18.4, al.' **III**, line 7, for 'sentence of death' read 'condemnation'

***τῑμευτητικός**, ή, όν, *of* or *concerned with valuation*, τειμευτητικῶι νόμωι *SEG* 39.1180.98 (Ephesus, i AD).

**τῑμή**, line 1, add 'dial. τιμά *GVAK* 13' **I 4**, add 'of a monument,

*IEphes.* 3233 (iii AD)' **II 2**, before 'valuation' insert '*the process of evaluating*, πάντως οὐ σὴ αὕτη ἡ τιμή Pl.*Grg.* 497b; τὰς τιμὰς τὰς τῶν πολλῶν ἀνθρώπων ib. 526d' **III**, line 5, delete 'οὐ σὴ .. 497b'

**τιμήεις**, line 1, delete 'acc. τιμήϝεντα .. (Sicily)' **1**, add 'ἥβη τιμήεσσα Mimn. 5.5 W.'

**τίμημα 1**, add 'pl., rest. in *SEG* 19.835.3 (Pisidia)' **4**, add 'τὸ τείμημά σου τὸ πολιτικόν app. your *fine* due to the city, *POxy.* 3105 (iii AD)'

**τιμητεία**, add '*SEG* 30.1442 (iii AD)'

**τιμητεύω**, after 'D.C. 41.14' insert 'in Bithynia, *MDAI(A)* 12.178 (Prusias, iii AD), cf. °βουλογραφέω'; add '*ISalamis* 11.5 (c.AD 60)'

**τιμητός**, add '**IV** as honorific epith. of emperors, *Xanthos* 49 (ii AD).'

**τιμίζω**, *declare the value of*, οὗ δὲ ἂν ἀναγράψηται καὶ τιμίζηται εἰσαγωγήν *SEG* 39.1180.50 (Ephesus, i AD).

**τίμιος I**, sup., add '*SEG* 31.1281 (ii AD)' **II 3**, add 'adv. τιμίως *honourably*, *IHadr.* 71'

**τιμιουλκέω**, after 'Hsch.' insert 'where also **τιμουλκέω**'

**τιμογράφέω**, add 'w. gen., *assess, estimate*, *PCol.* 98.4 (iii BC), *PCornell* inv. 1.34 (*BASP* 22.87, i AD)'

***Τιμοθεαστής**, οῦ, ὁ, *follower of Timotheus*, perh. the citharode of Miletus, rest. in *Didyma* 181.5 (iii AD).

***τιμουλκέω**, v. °τιμιουλκέω.

**τιμουχέω**, add '*SEG* 31.985D (also fr. Teos, written τιμοχ-, 480/450 BC)'

**τιμοῦχος I**, add 'epith. of Aphrodite, *IG* 12(5).222 (Paros, ii BC)' **II**, line 3, after 'Teos' insert '*SEG* 31.985D (480/450 BC, written τιμōχ-)'

**τιμωρέω I 1**, line 6, transfer 'Democr. 261' to section II 1.

**τίναγμα**, add '*SEG* 15.853.11 (Alexandria, ii BC)'

**τινάσσω**, penultimate line, for 'poet. Verb' read 'rare in early prose but'

**τινθάλέος**, after '= sq.' insert 'λοετρά Call. in *Suppl.Hell.* 287(b).5' and for 'Epic. .. 7.7' read 'Dionys.Bassar.*fr.* 81.4 L.'

**τίνω**, lines 4/5, for '*Inscr.Cypr.* 135.12 H.' read '*ICS* 217.12'; line 6, after 'etc.' insert 'Cypr. subj. *pe-i-se* πείσē, *ICS* 306'

**τίπτε**, line 1, after 'τί ποτε;' insert '*why ever?*'

**τίρων**, add '*SEG* 24.1218 (Egypt, iv/v AD); also sp. τήρ- *SEG* 31.1116 (Phrygia, Chr.)'

**τίς**, line 4, for 'Cypr. .. 10 H.' read 'Cypr. *si-se* σις *ICS* 217.10, al.; perh. acc. pl. *si-na-se* σινας *ICS* 10a.4' **A II 11**, add '**d** after neg. τί ποτε *anything at all*, οὐ δύνομαι (*sic*) τί ποτε πρᾶξαι *SB* 9616ʳ 6 (vi AD).' **B**, line 7, after 'Pi.*N.* 7.57' insert '(but prob. in *h.Cer.* 404)' **I 8 c**, line 2, after 'etc.' insert 'w. inf., *AP* 5.178.2 (Mel.)' **II 1 a**, add '*SEG* 31.1003 (Lydia, AD 84/5)'

***τισάνη**, ἡ, = πτισάνη, *POxy.* 736.51 (i AD).

**τιταίνω I 3**, add 'of a charioteer, Nonn.*D.* 37.290'

**Τιτάν I**, add '**2** as adj., Τιτῆνι σιδήρῳ, of the knife with which the Titans killed Dionysus, Nonn.*D.* 6.174.'

**Τιτᾱνίς**, add 'pl., Acus. 7 J.'

**τίτλος I 1**, add 'also **τίτλον**, τό, *CIG* 8621.10 (v AD), *MAMA* 7.484; **τίτουλος**, ὁ, *REA* 64.59 (Vienne (Isère)); **τίτυλος**, ὁ, Theognost.*Can.* 61' add '**III** *tax*, *CPR* 8.54.2 (v AD), *Cod.Just.* 10.19.9 pr.'

***τίτουλος**, v. °τίτλος.

**τιτρώσκω**, line 4, for '*Historia* .. (Gortyn)' read '*Inscr.Cret.* 1.x 2.1, 9 (Eltynia, vi/v BC)'

***τίτυλος**, v. °τίτλος.

**τίω I**, at end after 'id.*Ag.* 706 (lyr.)' insert 'τίεσκε μύθους *Trag.adesp.* 268 K.-S.'

***Τλᾱπολέμεια**, τά, *games held in honour of Tlepolemos* at Rhodes, *SIG* 1067.8 (ii AD).

**τλήμων III 2**, after '*miserably*' insert 'prob. in Anacr. 2 *fr.*1.7 P.'

***τληπενθής**, Dor. τλᾱ-, ές, *sorrowful*, Νιόβα B.*fr.* 20D.4 S.-M.

**τμήγω**, line 2, after 'aor. 1 ἔτμηξα' insert 'Il.Pers. 4.4 B.'; line 3, after '(prob.)' insert 'also Aeol., τμᾶξα Balbill. in *SEG* 8.716.9'

**τμῆμα**, add '**5** geom., *division* (*degree*), Ptol.*Alm.* 1 p. 31 H., al.'

**τμητικός 3**, add '**b** *solemnly sworn*, ὅρκος Steph.*in Rh.* 289.18.'

***τόγα**, ἡ, Lat. *toga*, *IHadr.* 1 (ii AD).

***τόγε** (i.e. τό γε), *at least*, δοκοῦντος τοῦ ἀφισταμένου τῷ μετὰ τῶν ἄλλων διαίτης ἀναχωρεῖν τόγε ἐπὶ τῷ συνοικεσίῳ *Cod.Just.* 1.3.52.15, 1.3.55.4.

**τοῖος I 1**, add '**b** *such as this* (that follows), *the following*, ἐφθέγξατο τοῖα Call.*Del.* 108, *Cer.* 97; τοίην ἀρχήν Batr. 8; τ. μῦθον ib. 77.' add '**4** introducing a reason for something said, πάντα δ' ἐνίκα ῥηϊδίως· τοίη οἱ ἐπίρροθος ἦεν Ἀθήνη Il. 4.390, cf. S.*Aj.* 562, *Ant.* 124.' **V**, add 'also neut. pl. τοῖα Nic.*Th.* 429'

**τοιοῦτος**, line 4, delete '*Ag.* 315' **6**, for this section read 'introducing a reason for something said, S.*Tr.* 46; βασιλεὺς οὐδεὶς ἄλλος .. ἔσται· τοιαῦτα ἔχω φάρμακα Hdt. 3.85.2' and renumber the pres. section 6 as 7; after 'S.*OT* 1327' insert '*App.Anth.* 5.17 (Hedyl.)'

**τοιχίον**, add 'pl., prob. in *Inscr.Cret.* 4.85 (Gortyn, v BC)'

***τοιχοποιός**, ὁ, *official responsible for wall-construction*, de Franciscis *Locr.Epiz.* p. 17 no. 3.

***τοίχισμα**, ατος, τό, *wall, side* (of a ship), Poll. 1.120 (?interp.).

***τοιχογράφος**, ὁ, *wall-painter*, *Edict.Diocl.* 7.8.

****τοιχοδόμος**, ὁ, (cf. τοιχοδομέω), Myc. *to-ko-do-mo*, *builder, mason.*

**τοῖχος 3**, add 'of a bed, Artem. 1.74'

**τοιχωρύχος**, after 'ὁ' insert 'also ἡ, Men.*Dysc.* 588'

***τοκάριον**, τό, *interest*, *PHaun.* 41.6 (iv AD).

**τοκεών**, for 'elsewh. .. 1.137' read 'Call.*fr.* 191.72 Pf.'

**τόκιον**, add '*SEG* 37.422 (Phocis, v BC), *SB* 5344.9'

**τόκος II 4**, for this section read 'homoeophonic substitute for Hebr. *tōk* (oppression), Lxx *Ps.* 71(72).14, *Je.* 9.6'

**τόλμα**, line 9, after '(*O.*) 13.11' insert 'and prob. Aeol., cf. Sapph. 24(*b*).6 L.-P.'

***τολμηρία**, ἡ, *audacity*, *UPZ* 196.66 (ii BC).

**τομή II**, add '**8** transf., *cutting out, excision*, τελείᾳ τομῇ πάσης τῆς κατ' αὐτοῦ ζητήσεως *PMich.*XIII 659.212, 238 (vi AD).' **III 4**, add 'δεῖν ῥήθημεν γενικῷ νόμῳ τῇ .. παρούσῃ ζητήσει δοῦναι τομήν Just.*Nov.* 2.3.pr.'

**τονθορύζω**, after '(Opp.*C.*) 3.169' insert '*squeal*, of pigs, *Vit.Aesop.*(G) 48'

***τονομυρικόω**, *make dumb the voice of*, τονομυρίκοσον αὐτόν *Suppl.Mag.* 55.17 (iii AD).

**τονωτικός**, after 'Gal. 6.577' insert 'adv. -κῶς, τ. θεραπεύειν treat *bracingly*, Aët. 12.46 O.'

**τοξαλκέτης**, after '= sq.' insert 'epith. of Apollo' and add 'applied to Artemis by Antisthenes of Paphos, *Philol.* 101.105.15'

**τοξαρχέω**, add '*SEG* 23.481 (Illyricum, ii/i BC)'

**τοξάρχης**, (s.v. τόξαρχος), add '*SEG* 24.1095 (Moesia, iii/ii BC)'

**τοξία**, for '= τοξῖτις' read '*associated with the bow*, epith. of Artemis' and add '(sp. τοκσίαν)'

**τοξικός 1**, add '*BGU* 2085.13 (AD 119)'

**τοξοδάμας**, add '*Μίνως* B. 26.12 S.-M.'

***τοξοϝοργός**, v. °τοξουργός.

**τοξοποιός**, add '*SB* 10558.3 (vi/vii AD), *PLond.* 1028 (p. 276).20 (vii AD)'

**τοξότης**, add 'Myc. *to-ko-so-ta*, subst. or pers. n.'

***τοξουργός**, ὁ, Cypr. *to-ko-zo-wo-ro-ko* τοξοϝοργό(ς), *bow-maker*, *ICS* 352d (Addenda p. 421); Myc. *to-ko-so-wo-ko.*

***τοπειώδης**, ες, of a *landscape*; -ες, τό, *a landscape scene*, Vitr. 5.6.9.

***τοπιάρι(ο)ς**, ὁ, Lat. *topiarius*, *ornamental gardener*, *TAM* 5(1).53, 524 (ii AD).

**τοπικός I 2**, after '*PFlor.* 58.8 (iii AD)' insert '*Peripl.M.Rubr.* 12, δικαστήρια *JÖAI* 4 *Beibl.* 37 (Phrygia)'

**τόπιον I**, add 'τόπεν *ICilicie* 92 (v/vi AD)'

***τοπογραμμάτικός**, *of* or *for a* τοπογραμματεύς; τ. κλῆρος, a κλῆρος whose profits supported a τοπογραμματεύς, *BGU* 2437.2, 52 (i BC).

**τοπογράφος**, for '*topographer*' read '*painter of landscapes*' and add '*Inscr.Délos* 2618.17 (?i BC)'

**τόπος I 1**, add 'applied to localities other than towns, *Cod.Just.* 1.2.25, ἐν οἱῳδήποτε τόπῳ ἢ πόλει ib. 4.59.1 pr.; *place* reserved for particular purpose, τόπος Κυριακοῦ βρακαρίου *IGChr.* 262' **5**, add '*ITyr* 8; also of a religious sanctuary, *SEG* 32.453 (Boeotia, ii BC), *IEphes.* 3418a' **9**, add '*SEG* 34.1437 (Syria, v/vi AD)' add '**IV** *rank, position*, *TAM* 4(1).32, 40, 42, *Cod.Just.* 12.33.8.3.'

**τοποτηρητής**, add '**2** *delegate, representative*, Just.*Nov.* 8.4, 128.19.'

***τοποφύλαξ**, ακος, *guardian of a place* (in quot., a cemetery), *CIG* 9546 (Italy, Chr.)

***τόρανος**, ὁ, *instrument used for drilling wells*, *AE* 1948/9.133ff.

**τορευτός**, add 'τορευτὰ ἀργυρώματα *Peripl.M.Rubr.* 24'

**τορεύω II 1**, add 'ἀργυρώματα τετορευμένα *Peripl.M.Rubr.* 28'

***τόρμα** (B), Lat. *turma*, *troop, squadron*, *Syria* 22.219 (Arabia, ii AD).'

**τορνευτός I**, for 'ποτήρια Men. 977' read 'ποτήριον Men.*fr.* 921 K.-Th. (v.l.)'

***τορνοσύνθετος**, ον, *built in a circle*, Anon.Alch. 39.15.

**τόρος**, after 'etc.' insert '*IG* 1³.422.141, 426.22 (Athens, v BC)'

***τορύνιον**, τό, gloss on ‡ροταρία, Hsch.

**τόσος**, add 'Myc. *to-so*'

**τοσόσδε**, add 'Myc. *to-so-de*'

**τότε I 1**, line 8, before 'Pl.*R.* 557b' insert 'E.*El.* 42, Ar.*Ra.* 169'

***τοτη, τοτοτε**, words written on black-figure epinetron, perh. representing sound of trumpet, *BCH* 108.99ff.

***τοῦμα**· στόμα Hsch.

***τοῦρτα**, ἡ, Lat. *torta*, *twisted loaf, twist*, Erot. s.v. ἄρτον ἐγκρυφίαν.

***τουρτίον**, τό, dim. of °τούρτα, *PRyl.* 629.26 (iv AD).

**τουτάκις I 2**, delete the section.

***τουταυτοῦν** (= τοῦτ(ο) αὐτὸ οὖν), *exactly the same thing*, *PMich.*XI 624.29 (vi AD).

***τοφιών**, ῶνος, ὁ, *burial-ground* (= ταφεών, cf. ἐντοφήϊα, etc.), *Tab. Heracl.* 1.137.

**τραγαλέον**, add 'cf. τρηγαλέον, ὑρειγαλέον, ῥωγαλέος, τρ- and ὑρ- being prob. written for Ϝρ; cf. Ϝρῆξις = ῥῆξις'

***τραγεῖον**· πόας εἶδος Hsch.; cf. τράγιον.

***Τράγιος** (B), title of Apollo at Tragia in Naxos, St.Byz. s.v. Τραγία.

**τρᾰγοπρόσωπος**, add '*PMag.* 13.31'

***τρᾰκάς**, = τριακάς II 1, μεινὸς [Ἀγαγυ]λίοι τρακάδι *Schwyzer* 614.6 (Thessaly, ii BC).

***τρᾰκισχίλιοι**, αι, α, *three thousand*, πέλεθρα [τρ]ακισχίλια *SEG* 26.672 (Larissa, 200/190 BC).

***τρᾰ́κοντα**, (= τριάκοντα), *thirty*, πέλεθρα ἑκατὸν τράκοντα δύα *SEG* 26.672.10 (Larissa, 200/190 BC).

**τρακταΐζω II**, add '**2** *treat, discuss*, Just.*Nov.* 111.1, 118.4.'

***τρακτατίων**, ωνος, ἡ, Lat. *tractatio*, *tax-list*, *PMasp.* 329 ii 5, al. (vi AD).

***τρακτᾶτον**, τό, *administration*, τοῦ τρακτάτου τῆς ἐπαρχίας *Cod.Just.* 12.49.13.1.

***τράκτυλος**, ὁ, given as alternative name for μαλάβαθρον, Gal. 19.735.

**τρᾰ́πεζα I**, add '**3** (*Christian*) *altar*, *Cod.Just.* 1.4.35.4.' **II 1**, line 2, after 'Plu. 2.70e' insert 'μεταξὺ τῶν τραπεζῶν *SEG* 26.72.5, 46 (Athens, 375/4 BC)' **III 3**, add '*TAM* 4(1).87 (ii AD)' at end add 'Myc. *to-pe-za* (form **torpedza*)'

**τρᾰπέζιον I**, after '*table*' insert 'rest. in *IG* $1^3$.426.28 (Athens, v BC)'

**τρᾰπεζιτεία**, add 'λαβεῖν τὴν τραπεζιτίαν *PHarris* 54.4 (*ZPE* 18.256, vi AD)'

**τρᾰπεζίτης I 1**, add '*PMich.*xiv 681.2 (v AD)' add '**3** *assayer*, Clem.Al.*Strom.* 2.15.4, 6.81.2, al., Arr.*Epict.* 3.3.3.'

**τρᾰπεζοποιός**, after '*table*' insert '*IG* $1^3$.422.73 (Athens, v BC)'

**τρᾰπητός**, add 'cf. Lat. *trapetus*'

***τράππαγον**, τό, type of Indian galley, μακρῶν πλοίων ἃ λέγεται τράππαγα καὶ κότυμβα *Peripl.M.Rubr.* 44.

***τραύλισμα**, ατος, τό, *imperfect speech* as of children, νηπιάχοις τραυλίσμασι *GVI* 977.1 (Mauretania, ii/iii AD).

**τραύξανα**, after 'Suid.)' insert '= °τρώξανα, *Edict.Diocl.* 14.12' and delete 'Cf. τρώξανον'

**τρᾰφερός II**, add 'coupled w. διερή Dionys.Bassar.*fr.* 34 (b/c).3 L.'

**τρᾰ́φω**, after 'Hes.*Th.* 480' insert '(Byz. cj., τρεφ- codd. plerique)'; add 'aor. ἔθραψα epigr. in *Inscr.Cret.* 1.xxii 58 (Olus, ii/iii AD)'

**τρᾰχηλίζω II 2**, add 'fig., *get a neck-lock* (on the wind), i.e. twist to the right quarter, *Peripl.M.Rubr.* 57'

**τρᾰχήλιον**, add '**2** *collar*, *PMich.*xv 752.42 (ii AD).'

**τρᾰχηλοειδής**, add 'Gal. 18(2).350.3'

**τρᾰ́χηλος I 1**, line 3, after '*throat*' insert 'Hippon. 103.1 W.'

**τρᾰχηλώδης**, add 'Gal. 18(2).349.13, 351.2'

**τρᾱχύς**, line 2, after 'Theoc. 25.74' insert 'τρηχύν fem. acc. sg., id. 25.256' **I**, add '**5** of coins, *in mint condition*, τὴν .. τιμὴν ἀπόστειλόν μοι ἐν μαρσιππίῳ ἐσφραγισμένον ἐν 'τραχαίοις (perh. for τραχέοις) *POxy.* 2728.28 (iii/iv AD)'

**τρᾰχών**, as pr. n., add 'Str. 16.2.16, 20, *IEphes.* 3157 (ii AD)'

**τρεῖος**, add 'cf. *BCH* 8.501 ff.'

**τρεῖς**, line 4, add 'neut. pl. τρά *SEG* 26.675 (Larissa, ii BC)'; line 5, after 'τρῖς' insert '*IG* 4.1588.23 (Aegina, v BC)'; line 9, after 'Pi.*N.* 7.48' insert 'τρεῖς ἄνδρες (= Lat. *tres viri*) *triumvirate*, *SEG* 31.952 (Ephesus, ii AD); indicating the day of the month, τῇ τρισὶ τοῦ Δίου μηνός *SEG* 32.638 (Maced., iii AD)'; line 14, after '(cf. τριάζω)' insert 'so τὰ τρί' ἡ δάφνη κεῖται Call.*fr.* 194.80 Pf.' at end add 'Myc. *ti-ri-si* (dat.)'

**τρεισκαιδέκᾰτος**, add 'fem. subst. *thirteenth day*, Od. 19.202, Hes. l.c.; ἐπὰν ἐπιτελῶσιν τὰς θυσίας .. τῇ τρισκαιδεκάτηι *SEG* 33.1039.38 (Aeolis, ii BC), *Amyzon* 36 (ii BC)'

***τρεισκαιδεκᾰ́πολις**, v. °τρισ-.

***τρεκινάριος**, ὁ, Lat. *trecenarius*, centurion in command of the 300 *speculatores* in the praetorian guard, *IGRom.* 3.1432.

***τρελλός**, ή, όν, *crazy*, as pers. n., *IG* $2^2$.12552 (Τρέλλος, iv BC), cf. mod. Gk. adj. for meaning.

**τρέπεδδα**, line 3, after 'BC)' insert 'also **τράπεδδα**, *IG* 7.3172.170, 173 (Orchomenus, iii BC)' add '**2** *table*, *SEG* 24.361 (Boeotia, iv BC).' and delete '(Not from .. for τράπεζα)'

**τρέπω**, line 11, delete 'once' and after 'Pl.*Cra.* 395d' insert '(προ-) id.*Prt.* 348c'

**τρέφω**, line 5, after 'Plb. 12.25$^h$.5' insert 'also τετράφηκα (ἀνα-) *TAM* 2(3).1104.16 (Lycia)' **II 1**, add 'aor. part. as subst., *foster-parent*, οἱ θρέψαντες *SEG* 33.1060, Ἀνδρομέδαν τὴν ἑαυτοῦ θρέψασαν 34.1223 (Lydia, AD 218/9); pass., *foster-child*, Μουσονίῳ τῷ υἱῷ μου [καὶ ..] Σακέρδωτι νέῳ τραφέντι μου *TAM* 4(1).262' **III 1**, add 'perh. οἱ θρέψαντες class of people in a religious association, *SEG* 30.622 (Thessalonica, i AD)'

**τρέχω**, line 7, after '(v. infr.)' insert 'Aeol. subj. δρό[μωμεν] Alc. 6.8 L.-P.' **I 2**, add '**b** transf., of time, *Cod.Just.* 1.4.32.2.'

***τρήρων**, ωνος, ὁ, ἡ, epith. of, or name for, dove (cf. τρέω), τρήρωσι πελειάσιν Il. 5.778, 22.140, 23.853, Od. 12.63, *h.Ap.* 114, Ar.*Av.* 575, A.R. 3.541; τ. alone, Moero 1.3; in fig. contexts (oracular) referring to women, λεύσσω θέοντα γρυνὸν ἐπτερωμένον τρήρωνος εἰς ἅρπαγμα Lyc. 87, 423. **b** applied to other birds, κέπφοι τρήρωνες Ar.*Pax* 1067.

***τρῐᾱκᾰδίζω**, ἐτριακάδιξεν· εἰς τριακάδας ἐνέγραψε, Σικελοί Hsch. (cj., ἐτριέκοψεν cod.).

**τρῐᾱκάς III**, for this section read '*group of thirty persons*, a division of the population in some cities: at Sparta, Hdt. 1.65.5; at Athens, *IG* $2^2$.1214.18; at Phlius or Corinth, *SEG* 30.990 (*c.*325/275 BC)' at end add 'see also °τρακάς'

**τρῐᾱκάσιοι**, add 'also at Mantinea, *SEG* 37.340.24 (iv BC)'

***τρῐᾱκᾰτιαρχέω**, *to be a* τριακατιάρχας, athematic part. -αρχέντες, *SB* 9937.1 (Cyrene, iii BC).

**τρῐᾱ́κις**, after '*IG* 5(1).222' insert '(*c.*530/500 BC)'

***τρῐᾱκονθετηρίς**, ίδος, ἡ, = τριακονταετηρίς, *SEG* 18.633.3 (217 BC).

**τρῐᾱκονθήμερος 2**, for 'τριακονθήμερον, τό' read 'τριακονθήμερος, ἡ'

**τρῐᾱ́κοντα**, delete '[In late Epigr. .. etc.]' and add 'see also °τράκοντα'

**τρῐᾱκοντᾰ́δραχμοι**, add '**2** τρ., οἱ, a census-class, *Schwyzer* 366*A*22 (iii BC).'

***τρῐᾱκοντᾰ́μεροι**, οἱ, prob. a *board of officials* performing duties *for thirty days*, *IG* 14.256.27 (Phintias Geloorum); cf. πεντάμεροι.

**τρῐᾱκοντάμερος**, delete the entry.

***τρῐᾱκονταμναῖος**, add '*worth thirty minae*, ἔρανος *GDI* 1772.17 (Delphi, ii BC)'

**τρῐᾱκοντόριον**, add '*PCol.* 115j'

***τρῐᾱκόσθεκτος**, η, ον, *thirty-sixth*, *PMich.*iii 186.39, 187.42, 43 (both i AD); sp. τριακοστ- *PMich.*iii 186.8.

**τρῐᾱκοσιαστός**, for '*JHS* 33.338' read '*SEG* 30.568'

***τρῐᾱκοσιόδραχμα**, τά, *loans of 300 drachmas*, *IG* $1^3$.248.28, 35 (Rhamnus, v BC), cf. °διακοσιόδραχμα.

**τρῐᾱκόσιοι**, line 2, after 'Il. 11.697' insert '(τρῑη-)' **1**, add 'sg., τριηκοσίης δρόμον Ἠοῦς passage of *three hundred* days, Nonn.*D.* 25.308 (-κοστῆς cod.), cf. διακόσιοι' **II 2**, after 'Id. 19.295' insert 'at Thasos, *Thasos* 7.8 (v BC)'

***τρῐᾱκόστεκτος**, v. °τριακόσθεκτος.

**τρῐᾱκοστός II**, add '**2** *the thirtieth day*, κατὰ τριακοστήν Mitchell *N.Galatia* 257 (AD 140).'

**τρῐάντα**, add 'ἔ[θ]ανε πέντε κὲ τρειάντα ἐτῶν *TAM* 4(1).132 (Rom. imp.)'

***τρῐανταήμερος**, ἡ, *period of thirty days*, *Vit.Aesop.*(G) 120.

***τρῐαντόφυλλος**, ον, *having thirty leaves*, Anon.Alch. 331.7.

**τρῐᾰ́ριοι**, add 'Plb. 2.33.4, 14.8.5, al.; sg. ὀπτίων τριάρες *SEG* 31.1116 (Phrygia, late Rom.imp.)'

**τρῐάς**, add '**5** in wrestling, *triple throw*, *SEG* 30.1616 (Cyprus, iii AD).'

***τρῐαστής**, οῦ, ὁ, *victor in the triple throw* (type of wrestling), *POsl.* 85.6 (iii AD), cf. τριάζω, τριακτήρ.

***τρῐβαῖον**, τό, prob. = τριβαία, *Dacia* 1988.146ff. (*c.*AD 200).

***τρῐβᾰ́κηλος**, ὁ, *the Thrice-Effeminate*, title of comedy by Naevius, Donat. in Ter.*Adelph.* 521 (*tribaselo* codd.).

**τρῐβᾰκός I 2**, delete the section transferring quot. to section 1.

**Τρῐβαλλοί**, add 'sg. as pers. n., Lang *Ath.Agora* xxi F62 (v BC)'

**τρῐβάς I**, for pres. def. read '"*masculine*" *lesbian*' add '**III** fem. adj., *worn*, τύλη *PFam.Teb.* 49aii4 (iii AD).'

***τρῐ́βιβλος**, ον, *consisting of three books*, Gal. 1.408.5.

***τρῐ́βλιον**, v. °τρύβλιον.

**τρῐβολεκτρᾰ́πελος**, for 'deal in *coarse rude jests*' read 'rattle on about *thorny, abstruse matters*'

**τρῐ́βολος II**, for this section read '*threshing-board* (perh. confused w. Lat. *tribulum*), Ph.*Bel.* 85.37, τριβόλους ἀχυρότριβας *AP* 6.104 (Phil.), Longus 3.30, τ. ξύλινος *Edict.Diocl.* 14.41. **2** transl. Hebr. wd. denoting some cutting instrument, Lxx 2*Ki.* 12.31.' **VI**, add 'cf. τρίβολον ἄκοντα· τρίαιναν Hsch.'

**τρῖβος II 1**, add 'fig. τρίβῳ κατέξαινον ἄνθος Ἀργείων A.*Ag.* 197' **2**, add '**b** *hinge*, *BGU* 2359.1 (iii AD).' **3**, delete the section.

***τριβοῦνος**, ὁ, Lat. *tribunus*, *tribune*, *IGRom.* 3.279, *PFlor.* 89.6, *SEG* 34.1515 (Arabia, vi AD); τριβ(ούνου) νοταρίου *ICilicie* 91 (vi AD).

**τρῐ́βων** (A), for '*worn garment, threadbare cloak*' read '*cloak* (sts. w. implication of being worn or threadbare, cf. τρίβω II), *IG* $1^3$.422.120 (Athens, v BC)'

**τρῐ́βων** (B) **2**, delete the section.

**τρῐβωνάριον**, add '*POxy.* 3617.12 (iii AD)'

**τρῐγέρων**, after 'A.*Ch.* 314 (anap.)' insert 'of wine, *AP* 9.409 (Antiphan.); of persons, *AP* 7.295 (Leon.Tarent.), 421.6 (Mel.)'

**τρίγληνος I**, for this section read '*having three eyeballs*: in quots. as epith. of ear-rings consisting of a cluster of three round stones, ἕρματα τρίγληνα Il. 14.183, Od. 18.298; cf. ‡τρίκοκκος'

**τριγλῖτις**, add '**2** precious stone, *triglitis mulli .. colore cognominatur*, Plin.*HN* 37.187.'

**τρίγλῠφος II**, at end before 'pl.' insert 'also neut., ἡ δὲ τῆς κρηπῖδος καὶ τοῦ τριγλύφου (ποίησις) ἀτελής Arist.*EN* 1174$^a$26'

**τρίγωνος I 1**, add 'of type of harp (cf. II 2), *τ. πηκτίδες* Diog.Ath. 1.9 S., *τ. ψαλτήρια* Arist.*Pr.* 919$^{b}$12' **II 2**, for this section read '*triangular harp*, masc., S.*frr.* 239, 412 R., Eup. 88.2, 148.4 K.-A., Ar.*fr.* 255 K.-A., Pherecr. 47 K.-A., Pl.*R.* 399c; neut., Pl.Com. 71.13 K.-A. (s.v.l.), Arist.*Pol.* 1341$^{a}$41 (s.v.l.), Aristox.*fr.* 97 W.' add '**6** masc., name for the plant *μηδική* (v. *Μηδικός* II 1), Ps.-Dsc. 2.147, Hsch.'

**+τρίδουλος**, ον, *triply a slave*, i.e. *a slave through and through*, A.*fr.* 78c.5 R., *οὐδ' ἐὰν τρίτης ἐγὼ μητρὸς φανῶ τρίδουλος* S.*OT* 1063, Ach.Tat. 8.1.2; literally, of one descended through three generations of slaves, Theopomp.Hist. 244. **II** *consisting of three slaves*, *ζεῦγος τ.* Ar.*fr.* 580 K.-A.

**τριέλικτος**, line 2, after 'Orac.ap.Hdt. 6.77' insert '*τ. ἁλωή triple* halo, Arat. 816'

**τριετήρης**, delete the entry.

***τριετηρία**, ἡ, = *τριετηρίς* 2, *Inscr.Cret.* 4.146.7 (iv BC; sp. *τριϝετηριαν*).

**τριέτης II**, add 'Aristonous 1.37'

***τριετίρης**, ενος, ὁ, prob. a *third-year* (ε)ἰρήν, i.e. fifteen years old, *IG* 5(1).1120 (Geronthrae, v BC; v. *AC* 27.105f.). (*τριτ-* shd. perh. be read, cf. *τριτίρενες*, *πρωτείρης*.)

**τρίζω**, line 3, after 'Il. 2.314' insert 'fut. *τρίσω* Sm.*Is.* 38.14, *τριζήσω* Aq.*Am.* 2.13' **2**, line 8, for 'Call.*Hec.* 1.4.14' read 'Call.*fr.* 260.68 Pf., Aq. l.c.'

***τριήδαρχος**, ὁ, perh. for *τριη‹κά›δαρχ-*, *POxy.* 43$^{v}$ ii 27 (iii AD); cf. *τριακάδαρχος*.

***τριημιπηχιαῖος**, α, ον, = *τριημίπηχυς*, *a cubit and a half long*, *IG* 12(2).11.14.

***τριημιστατήρ**, ῆρος, ὁ, *one and a half staters*, *SEG* 34.122 (Eleusis, 333/2 BC).

**τριημιστατῆρα**, delete the entry.

**τριηραύλης**, for '*flute-player*' read '*piper*'

**τριηριτικός**, line 2, after '*IG* 2$^{2}$.1629.70, 100, 134' insert '*κρατήρ* ib. 1424a.153, 1425.361, 1649.3'

**+τριηροποιός**, ὁ, *builder of triremes*, *IG* 1$^{3}$.153, 182 (both v BC), Arist.*Ath.* 46.1.

**+τριθάλεια**, ἡ, epith. of Artemis, Antim. 182 Wy. (v.l.), cf. *τριθαλλίαι* (read *τριθαλείαι*)· *μεγάλως τοῦ θάλλειν αἴτιαι* Hsch.

***τρικάμαρος**, ον, *having three vaults*, *PNess.* 22.19 (vi AD).

***τρικαρανοστρεφής**, οῦς, of Cerberus, *turning three heads*, *Suppl.Mag.* 42 (iii/iv AD).

***τρικέλευθος**, ον, *having three ways*, *SEG* 25.449 (Arcadia, iii/ii BC).

***τρικέλλαρον**, τό, name of some implement, *POxy.* 1290.5 (v AD).

***τρικενναλικός**, ή, όν, *of a tricennial festival*, *SB* 10988.2 (vi AD), cf. late Lat. *tricennalis*, °*οὐικεννάλια*.

***τρικίναιδος**, ὁ, app. *thoroughgoing catamite*, perh. in *POxy.* 3724 *fr.* 1 ii 29 (list of epigrams, i AD).

**+τρίκογχος**, ον, archit., *having three niches*, *τὸ τρίκονχον σίγμα* (i.e. Σ-shaped) *IGLS* 9122 (AD 488).

**τρίκοκκος**, after '*with three grains* or *berries*' insert '(in quot., as gloss on °*τρίγληνος*)'

**τρικόλωνος**, add '*οἱ Τρικόλωνοι*, app. as name of an estate, Lang *Ath.Agora* XXI I4 (iv AD)'

**τρικόνητος**, for 'cf. *ἐπικονέω*, *κονή*' read 'cf. °*δια-*, *ἐπι-*'

**+τρίκορυς**, υθος, *having triple helmets* (the exact significance is unclear), *Κορύβαντες* E.*Ba.* 123.

**τρικότυλος I**, add '*TAPhA* 79.184 (Attic vase, v BC)'

**τρίκροτος**, for '*rowed with triple stroke*' read '*rowed by three banks of oars*'

***τρίκτοινοι**, οἱ, name of association in Rhodes, *ASAA* 17/18 (1939-40).149.18.

***τρικτύαρχος**, v. °*τριττύαρχος*.

**+τρικύλιστος**, ον, perh. *carried on three wheels* (i.e. a three-wheeled chair), Epicur.*fr.* 125 (*CPh* 35.183).

***τρίλλη**, ἡ, part of the body (in quot., w. ref. to horses), *Hippiatr.* 2.239, cf. perh. *δρῖλος*, Simon Ath.ap.Suid.

**+τρίλλιστος**, ον, (for *τρισ-λιστος*), *thrice*, i.e. *earnestly*, *addressed in prayer* or *entreated*, *νύξ* Il. 8.488; as epith. of Demeter, Call.*Cer.* 138; adv. *-τως* *AP* 5.271 (Maced.Thess. II).

**τριμερής**, after 'adv. *τριμερῶς*' insert '*in three instalments*, *Cod.Just.* 10.16.13.5, 7' add '**II** *τριμερές*, *τό*, *a third*, *PLond.* 1674.56, *PMasp.* 45.2 (both vi AD).'

**τρίμηνος**, line 3, delete '*τὸ τ.*'

**τριμιτάριος**, before '*PLond.*' insert '*PAnt.* 33.10 (iv AD)'; at end add 'also *-ία*, ἡ, *Ζωσίμη τριμιταρία Not.Scav.* 1895.482 no.159 (Syracuse).

**τριόδιον**, after '= foreg.' insert '*BGU* 958e (iii/iv AD)'

**τριοδίτης II 1 a**, after 'Chariclid. 1' insert '*Hesperia* 6.391.18 (tab. defix., Athens)'

**τρίοδος I 2**, add '**b** as adj., epith. of Hecate, *SEG* 26.819 (Thrace, after AD 212).'

**τριόδους II 1**, line 4, for 'cf. *AP* 11.126' read 'Opp.*H.* 4.639'

**τριούγκιον**, after '= *quadrans*' insert 'as a proportion of an inheritance, *Cod.Just.* 6.4.4.16'

***τρίοψ**· *ὁ ὑπὸ τῶν Πυθαγορικῶν ἐν Δελφοῖς τρίπους ‹οὕτως καλούμενος›* Hsch., cf. *Τριόπιος*.

**τρίπεδος**, add '*Inscr.Cret.* 4.30 (?vi BC; indeterminable context)'

**τριπετής**, delete the entry.

**τρίπλευρος II**, add 'sg., *ASAA* NS 33/4 (1955-6).165 no. 14 (Ialysus)' add '**III** *τρίπλευρον*, *τό*, *spherical triangle*, Menelaus ap.Papp. 6.476.16.'

***τρίπλησον**, aor. imper. *multiply by three*, perh. error for *τρίπλωσον* (*τριπλόω*), *PCair.* 10758 (vi AD), cf. °*πεντάπλησον*.

**τριπλόος**, after '*PRev.Laws* 19.14 (iii BC)' insert '*ἀποτεινέτω προσ[τ]είμου τὸ τριπλοῦν SEG* 31.122 (Attica, ii AD)'

**τριποδίσκος**, add 'Myc. *ti-ri-po-di-ko* (pers. name)'

**τρίπους**, add '(form *τρίπος*) Myc. *ti-ri-po*, *ti-ri-po-de* (dual) (in sense IV 1)'

***τρίππος**, ὁ, app. *team of three horses*, *trigae τρίππος* Charis. p. 35 B., cf. *τρίππον*.

**τρισέληνος 1**, before '*AP* 9.441' insert '*POxy.* 2331 ii 4a (*CR* 71.189, iii AD)'

***τρίσελλος**, ον, *having three seats*, *PFay.* 117.17 (ii AD).

***τρισευμοιρος**, ον, *thrice fortunate*, Anon.Alch. 28.14.

***τρισήρως**, ὁ, Myc. *ti-ri-se-ro-e* (dat.), divine name.

***τρισκαιδεκάπολις**, ιδος, ἡ, *confederacy of thirteen* Ionian *cities*, *Didyma* 356.7 (ii AD).

**τρισκακοδαίμων**, for 'Men. 404.1' read 'Men.*Pk.* 400, *Epit.* 19, al.: adv., *τρισκακοδαιμόνως ἔχω* dub. l. in id.*Dysc.* 523'

**τρισπερίοδος**, delete the entry.

***τρισσάδιος**, α, ον, = *τρισσός*, *πεντάδα τρισσαδίην ἐτέων*, *IG* 10.2(1).447.5 (Thessalonica, ii/iii AD).

**τρισσός**, add 'cf. *Ps.* 79(80).6. **VI** = *τριστάτης*, Aq.*Ex.* 14.7, al.'

**+τριστάτης**, ου, ὁ, app. calque of Hebr. *šālîš*, military *officer* of high rank, LXX *Ex.* 14.7, 15.4, *4Ki.* 10.25; esp. officer attending on the king, *ὁ τ. αὐτοῦ 4Ki.* 15.25, cf. Hsch. (Expld. in Sch.Od. 3.324 as, in pl., the *three who stood* on an Egyptian chariot).

**τρίστιχος**, add '*IGRom.* 1.1162 (i AD, *-ικ-*)'

**τρίστοος**, add 'fem. subst., *atrium* of church, *τὴν πᾶσαν ἐκαλέργησεν* (for *ἐκαλλιέργησεν*) *τρίστωον DOP* 6.87 (Nicopolis, vi AD)'

**τρισχίλιοι II**, add 'X.*HG* 2.3.51, al., Lys. 25.22'

**τριταῖος**, add '**IV** app. in non-temporal sense (v. *SEG* 36.1538), *SEG* 36.903 (Italy).'

**τρίτατος**, add '*τριτάτην ἤματος* (app. on the third day of her illness) *ὀλλυμένην GVI* 662'

***τριτεῖος**, α, ον, *of third-class quality*, *ἔρεα Edict.Diocl.* 21.4; cf. *τριτεῖα*.

**τριτημόριος II 2**, add '**b** as a weight, *τριτε(μόριον) SEG* 31.154(a) (Athens, v BC); *Ath.Agora* X LW17, al.'

**τριτημόρον**, add '*Inscr.Délos* 104.73 (iv BC); perh. used as adj., *ληκύθια τριτάμορα ZPE* 12.267 (Sicily, v BC)'

**τριτίρενες**, add '(Cf. °*τριετίρης*)'

***τριτόδιος**, ὁ, epith. of Zeus, *SEG* 33.453, 454 (Atrax, Thessaly, v, iii BC).

**τρίτομος**, add '*τρίτομον*, *τό*, papyrus roll consisting of three sections, *PFreib.* 53.25'

**τρίτος II 2**, *τρίτη* (a weight), add '*SEG* 31.154(g) (Athens)' **IV**, add '*τὸν ἀπὸ τρίτου ἑκατοστῆς ἀποδιδότω τόκον* (i.e. $\frac{1}{3}$ percent) Just.*Nov.* 22.44.4; sim. *ἐκ τρίτου* ib. 7'

***τριτοστολιστής**, οῦ, ὁ, app. *στολιστής of the third rank*, *PSelect.* 21.5.

**τρίτρα**, after '*times*' insert 'or *a third of*' and for '*GDI* .. (Gort.)' read '*Inscr.Cret.* 4.43*Ab*9 (Gortyn, v BC)'

**τριττύς III**, for '*a third of the φυλή*' read 'app. *a tripartite civil division*, understood as a third of a *φυλή*'

***τριχᾶς**, ᾶ, ὁ, *hairdresser*, *PAmst.*inv. 62.54 (*Mnemos.* ser. 4 30.146, ii AD).

**τριχιάω**, add '**III** *τριχιῶν*, ὁ, calque of Hebr. *śā'îr* "hairy one" (in context, a goat-formed demon), Aq.*Is.* 13.21, Aq., Sm., Thd.*Is.* 34.14 (cf. *τριχίας* I).'

**τρίχιον**, add 'item in inventory of travelling equipment, *PRyl.* 627.171 (iv AD; ?*wig*, ed.)'

**τριχοίνικος**, neut. as subst., add '*IEphes.* 3437'

***τριχόπλαστος**, *having one's hair set in curls*, Hsch. s.v. *κικίννα*.

**+τρίχορδος**, ον, *having three strings*, *λύρα* D.S. 1.16.1, *κιθάρα* St.Byz. 130.20; *based on three notes*, of the music of Olympus and Terpander, Plu. 2.1137b. **II** subst., *τ.*, ὁ, a three-stringed instrument, prob. *lute*, Anaxil. 15 K.-A.; later neut., *τρίχορδον*, *τό*, Poll. 4.60.

***τριχόρροια**, ἡ, *shedding of the hair*, Cyran. 63.16, 74.4 K.

***τρίχους**, ουν, *holding three χόες*, cj. in *PErasm.* 19.4 (ii BC).

**τρίχωμα**, add 'of the sacred *hair* of Isis, *παρὰ τοῖς τριχώμασι ἐν Κοπτῷ PMich.*VIII 502.5 (ii AD); in title, *Ἴσιδι τριχώματος θεᾷ μεγίστηι SEG* 18.704 (32.1583, Egypt, AD 105); of a coral reef, Agatharch. 108'

**τρίχωρος I**, add '*κλεῖθρον τρίχωρον PMag.* 4.2337'

**τρίχωσις I 1**, add '**b** *plumage*, Sch.Pi.*P.* 4.380, 381.'

**τρῐωβολεῖος**, add 'applied to a person as an indication of worthlessness, *Act.Alexandr.* iv 13.18'

*__τρῐωβόλιον__, τό, = τριώβολον, dub. in Steph. *in Rh.* 286.22 (pl.).

*__τρῐώβολος__, ὁ, = τριώβολον, *Inscr.Délos* 1429*B*ii25 (ii BC).

**τρῐῳδέομαι**, add 'Procl.*in R.* 2.21.16, 2.22.2 K., al.'

**τρίωτον**, delete the entry (v. °τρίωτος).

*__τρίωτος__, ον, Cret. δρίωτος, *Inscr.Cret.* 4.145.6 (Gortyn, v/iv BC), *three-handled*, καναστ(ραῖ)ον *Inscr.Cret.* l.c.; -ον, τό, *three-handled jar*, *BGU* 544.17 (ii AD).

**τροπᾰϊκόν**, add '*SEG* 32.599 (Thessaly, i BC/i AD); also -κός, ὁ, *SB* 10288.1a.7 (τροπαιεικος pap., Palestine, AD 125)'

**τροπαῖον**, add 'of a monument for a successful athlete, *SEG* 34.1316 (Lycia, *c.*AD 90). **2** *memorial monument*, *SEG* 36.1260 (Paphos, end ii AD).'

**τροπαιοῦχος**, Ζεὺς τ., add '*ICilicie* 16; also Ἑρμῆς τ. ib. 17 (both early iii AD)'; at end add 'transf., of deeds, τροπαιούχοισιν ἐπ' ἔργοις Orph.*H.* 33.4'

**τροπαιοφόρος I 2**, before 'a coin' insert 'neut. subst.'

**τρόπις**, add 'form *τόρπις Myc. *to-qi-de* (dat.), prob. *spiral*; deriv. adj. *to-qi-de-we-sa* (fem.), *$*torq^widwessa$*, cf. Lat. *torqueo*'

**τρόπος II**, line 6, after 'etc.' insert 'ὁ γενεαλογικός, ὁ πραγματικός τ. [τῆς ἱστορίας] *kind*, Plb. 9 *fr.* 1.1.4, 2.4' **4 b**, line 2, after 'Id.*Lg.* 638c' insert 'κατὰ τ. ἔχειν, εἶναι, *to be all right, be in order*, Men.*Dysc.* 134, 215' add '**c** w. gen., *by way of*, κατ' ἰσχύος τρόπον A.*fr.* 281a.20 R.'

**τροπόω** (A), add 'pass., ἐτροπώθη ὁ πόλεμος *reached a turning-point*, Lxx 3*Ki.* 22.35'

**τροῦλλα**, for '*BMus.Inscr.* 980' read '*Salamine* 30' and add 'also τρυλλα *BGU* 2360.3'

**τροφεία**, before 'ἡ' insert '(also **τροφέα** *GDI* 2254.6 (Delphi, i BC))'

**τροφεύς 1**, add 'transf., πάντα νικᾷ ὁ τροφεὺς τῆς ὅλης οἰκουμένης *Suppl.Mag.* 7' **4**, add '*BMC Phrygia* p. 399 (Synnada, i AD), cf. D.Chr. 48.10'

**τροφεύω**, add 'w. acc., τοῦτον, γύναι, τρόφευε Ezek.*Exag.* 29'

**τρόφιμος II 1**, add 'cf. *IG* $2^2$.6731'

*__Τροφωνιάς__, άδος, fem. adj., *of Trophonius*, Τροφ]ωνιάδος γᾶς *SEG* 23.297 (Lebadea, iv/iii BC).

**Τροφώνιος**, Ζεὺς τ., add '*SEG* 32.475 (Boeotia, after AD 213)'

**τροχᾰ́διa**, for '*walking-shoes*' read '*running-shoes*' and add '*PMon.* 142.17 (vi AD)'

**τροχιά II**, for '*the round of a wheel*' read '*wheel*' and transfer 'Nic.*Th.* 816' to section I after '*rut*'

*__τροχινός__, ή, όν, *round, liable to roll*, εὐτροχάλοιο· τοῦ τροχινοῦ Sch. Nic.*Al.* 134d Ge. (s.v.l.).

**τροχίσκος 1**, add '**b** item of temple equipment, μέτρα χαλ(κᾶ) ἱερατικὰ β' σὺν τροχίσκῳ σιδηρῷ α' *POxy.* 3473.25 (ii AD).' **2**, for '*troche* or *trochisk*' read '*ellipsoid*' **3**, for '*ear-ring*' read '*pendant*'

**τροχός B I 1**, after 'E.*Med.* 46' insert '(or *hoop*, cf. section A II)'

⁺**τροχωτός**, όν, *round*, *PHarris* 88.20 (v AD).

**τρύβλιον I**, add 'Lang *Ath.Agora* XXI B12 (iv/iii BC), *Kafizin* 49; sp. τρίβλ- *Inscr.Délos* 104.16, 23 (364 BC)'

**τρῠγάω I 1**, lines 3/4, for 'metaph. .. Ar.*Pax* 1338 (lyr.)' read 'w. sexual innuendo, τρυγήσομεν αὐτήν (sc. Ὀπώραν) Ar.*Pax* 1338'

**τρύγη I 1**, add 'cf. τρύγη· ὁ πυρός, καὶ ἡ κριθή, καὶ πᾶς ἄλλος καρπός, καὶ ποιὰ βοτάνη Hsch.'

*__τρῠγών__, line 1, after 'ἡ,' insert 'also ὁ, Lxx *Ca.* 2.12'

*__τρῠγώνι(ο)ν__, τό, a bird, dim. of τρυγών, *PAmst.* 13.4 (v AD).

*__τρύεινος__, η, ον, perh. = θρύινος, *of reed rope*, *BGU* 2361a ii 6 (iv AD).

**τρύξ I**, after '*PTeb.* 555 (ii AD)' insert 'fig. ἔοικας ὦ πρεσβῦτα νεοπλούτῳ τρυγί Ar.*V.* 1309; cf., in pun w. sense II 1, συνεκποτέ' ἐστί σοι καὶ τὴν τρύγα.— ἀλλ' ἔστι κομιδῇ τρὺξ παλαιὰ καὶ σαπρά id.*Pl.* 1086' **II 4**, delete 'metaph. also .. 1086'

**τρῠ́πᾰνον IV 1**, delete the section. **2**, append this section to section I, adding '**3** term of opprobrium in list of words app. indicating noisy chatterers, Suet.*Blasph.* 21, 167 T.'

**τρῡσίππιον**, add 'wheel-shaped, acc. to Hsch. s.v. ἵππου τροχός'

**τρῠφεροδίαιτος**, after 'foreg.' insert 'Ptol.*Tetr.* 166'

**τρύφος**, add 'Call.*fr.* 261.1 Pf. (= *Suppl.Hell.* 289.1), A.R. 1.1168'

**Τρῳᾰδεύς**, add '*Inscr.Perg.* 8(3).74'

**τρωγλοδύνων**, before 'Batr.' insert 'interpol. in'

**τρώγω**, line 4, before 'ἐν-' insert 'ἀπο-, δια-' and after 'παρα-' insert 'ὑπεκ-' **III**, add 'ἀθήραν τρώγειν *eat porridge* or *gruel*, perh. prov., *be spoon-fed* or *pampered*, *SB* 10567.36 (iii AD)'

**τρωκτός I**, transfer '*eatable*, Hdt. 2.92' to section II.

**τρωξαλλίς**, line 1, after 'Alex. 15.12' insert 'Ael.*NA* 6.19'

*__τρώξᾰνα__, τά, *dry twigs*, Thphr.*CP* 3.2.2, cf. ‡τραύξανα.

**τρώξανον**, delete the entry.

**τυγχάνω A I 3 a**, line 13, after 'ἄν' insert 'or ἦν' and after '*it may be*' insert 'E.*Ph.* 765, *Or.* 780' **B II 2 d**, add 'X.*Cyn.* 1.8'

⁺**τυί** (or **τυῖ**)· ὧδε, Κρῆτες Hsch., i.e. *hither* (cf. υἱ).

⁺**τυῖδε**, (written as τυΐδε, rather than τυῖδε, in papyri of Sapph. and Alc., but always scanned disyll.), Aeol. adv., *to this place, hither*, Sapph. 1.5 L.-P., al., perh. at Alc. 142.3 L.-P., cj. in Hes.*Op.* 635, Theoc. 28.5, *Epigr.Gr.* 988.3 (Balbilla), Sch.T *Il.* 14.289.

**τῠ́κισμα**, after 'E.*Tr.* 814' insert '(codd. τεκ-, τυκτ-)'; after '*fr.* 125.3, cf. *HF* 1096' insert '(codd. τειχ-)'

**τυλάριον 1**, after 'τύλη' insert '*cushion*'; add 'also τύλαρον, *PSI* 825.17 (iv/v AD, pl.)'

*__τῠλοεργός__, ὁ, *cushion-* or *mattress-maker*, *PIand.* 150ii3 (iii AD).

**τῠ́λος 3**, add '*Tab.Defix.* 74.17' add '**5** = τύλη 2 and 3, *pad* or *cushion* for horses, dual [τ]υλō prob. to be read at *IG* $1^3$.421.187, v. *SEG* 33.20 (414/13 BC).'

*__τῠλοτάπης__, ητος, ὁ, perh. kind of cushion, *PRyl.* 627.36 (iv AD), *SB* 13597 (v AD).

**τύλωσις II**, add 'but see *BCH* 80.516-18'

**τυμβαύλης**, for '*flute*' read '*pipe*'

**τύμβιος**, after '(Macedonia)' insert 'λώβην .. τύμβιον *TAM* 3(1) p. 361, *SEG* 33.111 (Paphlagonia)'

**τύμβος 2**, add 'Pl.*Lg.* 872b, Plu.*Alex.* 72.5, Luc.*Charid.* 22' add '**III** *altar*, Lyc. 313 (of Apollo), 613 (of Hera).'

**τυμβοχοέω**, add '*Suppl.Hell.* 1002'

*__τυμβωρῠ́χιον__, τό, *grave-robbing*, τυμβωρυχίου ἐνκλήματι ὑπεύθυνος ἔσται *IKalch.* 73.4.

**τυμβωρῠ́χος**, for '*CIG* 2826, al.' read '*MAMA* 8.544, 547, 550, al.' and add '*SEG* 32.1423D (Syria, ii AD)'

*__τῡμολῑτική__, ἡ, kind of jar or sim. vessel, τὴν ἑτέραν τυμολειτικήν *POxy.Hels.* 46.3 (i/ii AD), *POxy.* 1759.8 (ii AD), 1760.13-14 (ii AD).

**τυμπᾰνικός**, after 'ὕδρωψ' insert 'Plin.*HN* 25.60'

**τύμπᾰνον I**, for '*kettle-drum*' read '*frame drum, tambour*' **II 1**, add 'meton., ὦ τύμπανα· ὦ ἐπιτήδειοι τυμπανισθῆναι Hsch.' **3**, delete the section transferring quot. to section 1

*__τύν__, v. °σύ.

**Τυνδᾰρίδης**, add 'Τινδαρίδαι, perh. dat. dual without final ν, to be read at *IG* 5(1).937, v. *SEG* 36.354 (Kythera, iv BC)'

**τυννός**, for '*so small, so little*' read '*small, little*' and for 'Call.*Fr.* 420' read 'Call.*fr.* 471 Pf.'

**τῠπικός**, after '**2**' insert '*carved in relief*, [σύμπαντι τῷ τ]υπικῷ [κόσμῳ] *TAM* 3.21 (early iii AD)'

⁺**τῠ́πιον**, τό, dim. of τύπος, in quot., *small moulded figure*, *IG* $2^2$.1534.205, al., 11(2).161.B119 (Delos, iii BC).

**τῠπίς**, for 'Call. in *PSI* 9.1092.50' read 'Call.*fr.* 110.50 Pf.'

**τύπος IV**, add '**2** *drawing, painting*, γραπτοὶ τ. E.*fr.* 764, *AP* 7.730 (Pers.); τ. alone, *APl.* 136, 143.' **V**, delete 'γραπτοὶ τ. .. *AP* 7.730 (Pers.)'

**τῠπόω II 1**, add '**b** *paint, portray*, *APl.* 138.' add '**3** *assign to a type, classify*, Aristox.*Harm.* 4.'

**τύπτω I 1**, add 'inscribed on an astragalus as an injunction, τύπτ[ε] *SEG* 30.949 (Olbia)'

**τύπωμα 1**, add 'ἀνέθηκε δὲ καὶ τύπωμα χρύσεον *IHadr.* 1 (ii AD)'

**τῠπωτός**, before 'Lyc.' insert 'τόρμα' and add 'φιάλη *Didyma* 426.8, 435.5, 436.7'

*__τῡρᾶς__, ᾶ, ὁ, *cheesemonger*, *SEG* 26.1673 (Palestine, iv AD).

*__Τυρβηνός__, ὁ, cult-name of Apollo, Hsch.

**Τύριος**, add 'as epith. of Heracles, *RIB* 1129'

*__τύριος__, ὁ, = *tetradrachm*, *SB* 10305.5; perh. also ib. 10304.10 (both ii AD).

**τῡροκνηστις**, add 'τυροκνάσστιδες τρῖς *SEG* 24.361 (Thespiae, iv BC)'

**τῡροποιός**, add '*ITyr* 43'

**τῡροπώλης**, add '*SEG* 25.180 (Athens, iv BC)'

*__τῡρόπωλις__, ιδος, ἡ, *cheesemonger*, *SB* $10447^v$ i 12 (iii BC).

**τῡρός**, add 'Myc. $tu\text{-}ro_2$, perh. τυρροί *cheeses*'

**τύρσις**, delete 'also .. *fortified house*'

**τυφλάγκιστρον**, before '*blunt hook*' insert 'a surgical instrument'

**τυφλός I 2**, for 'τοξεύματα' read 'βέλη' and for '*HF* 199' read 'B. 5.132 S.-M.' **4**, after 'metaph.' insert 'ἐλπίδες A.*Pr.* 250' **II 1**, lines 1/2, for 'ἐλπίδες A.*Pr.* 252' read '*unseen*' and after 'Id.*Fr.* 593.6 (lyr.)' insert 'of weapons, E.*HF* 199'

*__τῡφομένως__, *smoulderingly*, Gal. *de Crisibus* 122.8 A.

*__τῡφός__, ὁ, term of abuse for an old man, cf. τυφογέρων, τῦφος, etc., Suet.*Blasph.* 209 T.

**Τῡφῶν I**, lines 2-6, for 'represented .. Sch.Pl.*Phdr.* 230a' read 'another form of Typhoëus, Typhos, Hes.l.c., *h.Ap.* ll.cc., A.*Pr.* 354, *Th.* 493, etc.'; line 8, identified w. Set, add '*Hesperia* 54.214 no. 1 (iii AD)'

*__Τῡφωνιακός__, ή, όν, = Τυφωνικός, *PMag.* 7.468.

**Τῡφώς II**, as appellat., add 'E.*Ph.* 1154'

**τῠχαῖος II**, add '**2** neut. pl. subst., *Genialia* τύχαια, Charis. p. 37 B.; cf. τύχεια. **b** small statuettes of Τύχη, ἔμπορος τυχαίων *IG* 14.419 (Messene, iii AD).' **III**, delete the section.

**τῠ́χη**, line 2, after 'iii BC)' insert 'Cypr. also dat. *to-ka-i* *Kafizin* 133a, 177' **III 1**, add 'Ἀπόλλωνι .. ὑπὲρ Κλέονος τοῦ υἱοῦ ἀνέθεκεν ἐν *τύχηι SEG* 23.621 (Cyprus, iii BC), *Kafizin* 113a (iii BC), 177, al.' **4**, add 'τυχἀγαθᾶι *Delph.* 3(2).137' **IV 1**, add 'νικᾷ ἡ τύχη τοῦ Δόρου (a charioteer) *SEG* 31.1486, 1492 (both Alexandria, AD 608/10)'; personified, add '*SEG* 31.537 (Delphi, *c.*280 BC), etc.'

***τώμεντον**, τό, Lat. *tomentum, wool, flock, Edict.Diocl.* 18.7.

***τώνᾱ**, ἁ, Cret. for ζώνη, Hsch.

***τῶνυ**, adv., *thence*, τῶνυ ἀι ἁ ὁδὸς ἐπὶ τὸ .. *CRAI* 1985.255 (Crete, *c.*500 BC) cf. ὄνυ.

***τώρα**, adv., *now*, *Syria* 23.179.37 (iii AD), as mod. Gk., < τῇ ὥρᾳ (ταύτῃ).

**τώς I**, add 'Alcm. 1.46 P.' **II**, line 2, after 'A.*Th.* 637' insert '(cj. in *Ag.* 242)'

# Y

***ὑαινίτης**, ου, ὁ, kind of precious stone, cf. ὑαίνιος, Socr.Dion.*Lith.* 53 H.-S.

**ὑᾰκίνθῐνος**, line 1, after 'Od. 6.231' insert 'ἄρουραι Anacr. 1. *fr.* 1.7 P.' and at end add 'ἐν ποτηρίοις σμαραγδίνοις καὶ ὑακινθίνοις Ps.-Callisth. 63.21, cf. 63.33'

***ὑακίνθιος**, ον, perh. sp. for *-θειος, *consisting of* or *like the stone* ὑάκινθος, λιθάριον ὑ. *SEG* 37.1001.3-4 (Lydia, ii/iii AD).

**Ὑᾰκίνθιος**, add '*SEG* 25.1110(*f*) (Cyprus, Hellen.)'

**ὑάκινθος I 1**, for '*wild hyacinth* .. *Scilla bifolia*' read 'plant, perh. *Hyacinthus orientalis*' **II**, for '*aquamarine*' read '*sapphire*'

**ὑᾰλᾶς I**, add 'also **ὑελ-** *POxy.* 3428.14 (written οἰελᾶ, iv AD)'

**ὑάλεος**, add 'cf. Myc. adj. *we-a₂-re-jo*, prob. *decorated with rock crystal*'

**ὑᾰλοειδής 1**, for '*crystalline* lens of the eye' read '*retina*' **2**, for '*topaz*' read '*peridot*'

**ὕᾰλος**, line 6, after '*Apoc.* 21.18' insert 'penultimate syll. long in Mesom. 13.1, 5 H. (ὑελο- cod.; ὑελλ- is v.l. in Hdt. 3.24.1, Luc. *VH* 2.11)'

**ὑᾰλουργός**, form ὑελ-, add '*POxy.* 3265.5, 3742.3 (both early iv AD)'

**ὑᾰλοψός**, add '*PBaden* 97.35 (vii AD)'

**ὑβρίζω II 4**, add 'οὐδὲν τῶν ὑβρισμένων no *ostentatious* gift, Ael. *VH* 1.31 D.'

**ὑβριστής I 1**, add 'E.*Andr.* 977, *Supp.* 575, 728'

**⁺ὑβριστοδίκαι**, οἱ, nonce-wd., *"outrageous jurymen"*, title of comedy by Eupolis, Eup. p. 466 K.-A.

**ὑγῐαίνω I 4**, line 4, after '*BMus.Inscr.* 1123a (inc.loc.)' insert 'cf. καθ' ἣν ὑγιαίνομεν ὥρην *at the time of day when we say farewells*, *AP* 12.177 (Strat.)' **II**, after 'pass.' insert 'Hp.*Morb.* 1.20, 21'

**ὑγίεια A**, line 4, after '(Herod.) 4.20' insert '(perh. ῡ here and in Call.*fr.* 203.21 Pf.)' **II**, add '**b** generally any gift received by the sacrificer, πᾶν τὸ ἐκ θεοῦ φερόμενον εἴτε μύρον εἴτε θαλλός Hsch., cf. θαλλός III.' **III**, for this section read '*cure, medicine*, ὕπνος δὲ πάσης ἐστὶν ὑγιεία νόσου Men.*Mon.* 783. **2** name of a medicine, Alex.Trall. 5.4 (II p.159.3 P.); also, of plaster, Androm.ap.Gal. 13.932.3, Heras ap.Gal. 13.766.6.' **B**, after 'Call.Com. 6 (hex.)' insert '*SEG* 30.1330 (Rom.imp.); identified with Athena, *IG* I$^3$.506 (v BC)'

**ὑγιής II**, for '*sound in mind*' read '*sound* (as applied to the mind, character, etc.)' and delete '*virtuous*' **III 2**, after '*POxy.* 1031.18 (iii AD), etc.' insert '*Corinth* 8(3).486 (iii AD)'

***ὕγῐος**, v. ὕγειος.

**ὑγῐόω**, add '*PMasp.* 283 I 15, ὑγιοῦν· τὸ σα[ρρ]οῦν. τὸ θεραπεύειν Hsch.'

**ὑγρᾰσία**, add 'euphem. *urine*, Lxx *Ez.* 7.17, 21.12'

**ὑγροβᾰφής**, add 'see also °ὑδροβαφής'

***ὑγρομαντεία**, ἡ, *water-divination*, *Cat.Cod.Astr.* 8(2).143.

**ὑγρόπορος**, for '= ὑγροκέλευθος' read '*going through the water*'

**ὑγρός I 1**, add '**b** as quality of the air, αἰθήρ Pi.*N.* 8.41, E.*Ion* 796; ἀήρ Emp. B 38.3 D.-K., Arist.*GC* 330$^b$4, *Mete.* 348$^b$28.'

**ὑδάτῐνος II**, delete the section transferring quots. to section III.

**ὑδᾰτόεις I**, add 'νέφη ὑδατόεντα Theoc. 25.89' **II**, for '*transparent* .. *fine*' read 'of garments, *flowing*' and for 'cf. ὑδάτινος II' read 'cf. °ὑδάτινος'

***ὑδᾰτομαντεία**, ἡ, *water-divination*, Tz.*Alleg.Il.* 18.195.

**ὑδᾰτοτρεφής**, add '(-τροφής Hsch. and codd. at Ath. 2.41a in a citation of Od. l.c.)'

**ὑδᾰτώδης I**, add 'adv. -δῶς Gal. 16.761.15'

**ὑδᾰτώλενος**, for 'dub. sens.' read '*having watery arms*' and add '(ii/i BC)'

**ὑδερώδης**, add '**b** *suffering from dropsy*, Gal. 12.177.7, 13.224.2.'

***ὑδρᾰγώγημα**, ατος, τό, *irrigation-channel*, Sch.Gen.Il. 21.257.

**⁺ὑδραγωγία**, ἡ, *system of irrigation*, Arist.*PA* 668$^a$14, Duris 89 J.; transf. of veins, etc., Pl.*Ti.* 77e, cf. ὑδρεία I 2.

**ὑδρᾰγωγός I**, add 'τόπος *where water gathers*, Horap. 1.49 S.' **II 2 a**, add 'gloss on ὀχετηγός, Sch.bT Il. 21.257'

***ὑδρᾰλετάριος**, ὁ, app. *operator of a water-mill*, Teuc.Bab. p. 46.7 B.

***ὑδρᾰλετᾶς**, ᾶ, ὁ, *water-mill engineer*, *Sardis* 7(1).169 (iv/v AD); delete ὑεραλέτης II.

**ὑδράλμη**, add 'Anon.Alch. 348.9'

**ὑδραντικός**, delete the entry.

***ὑδραντλητικός**, ή, όν, *for water-pumping*, ὑδραντλητικὴ παροχία *SB* 9907.23 (AD 388); prob. in *PFlor.* 58.10-11.

**ὑδραύλης**, add '*IEphes.* 1601a.8'

***ὑδραυλικός**, ή, όν, *hydrostatic*, *machinas hydraulicas*, Vitr. 1.1.9, 9.8.4; *hydraulicis organis*, Plin.*HN* 7.125, Suet.*Nero* 41.2; also neut. subst. τὸ -όν, *hydrostatic organ*, Aristocles ap.Ath. 4.174c, Hero *Spir.* 1.42.

**ὕδραυλις**, for '*hydraulic*' read '*hydrostatic*' and delete 'so τὸ -αυλικόν .. 1.42'

**ὑδρεῖον II**, add '**2** some part of public baths, *SEG* 26.784 (Thrace, AD 162/3), *IEphes.* 435.'

**⁺ὑδρεκδοχεῖον**, τό, *water-tank*, *IEphes.* 695.9 (i AD), ib. 424 (ii AD), *MAMA* 8.449.4 (the last two sp. -εγδ-).

**⁺Ὕδρεος**, ὁ, Syrian deity, *Inscr.Délos* 2155, 2160; also **Ὕδρειος**, ib. 2087 (all after mid-ii BC)

**ὕδρευμα**, after '*tank*' insert '*Inscr.Cret.* 3.iv 18 (iii BC)'

**ὑδρία II 2**, delete 'esp. in law courts, etc.'

**ὑδρίσκη**, add 'written **ἑδρύσκη**, *PMich.Teb.* 121$^r$ II ii 8 (i AD), etc.'

**⁺ὑδροβαφής**, ές, ὑδροβαφὲς (?sc. ἱμάτιον) ὃ νῦν ψυχροβαφὲς καλοῦσιν *a garment dyed with* only (cold) *water* added to the dyestuff, Poll. 7.56 (v.l. ὑγρο-).

**⁺ὑδροβάφος**, ὁ, perh. *one who carries out ceremonial immersions*, cf. καταλουστικοί, *IEphes.* 3414, 3415 (ii/iii AD, cf. *BE* 1982.293).

**ὑδροβόλος**, for '*Epigr.Gr.* 1036' read '*TAM* 5(2).92 (revised text)'

***ὑδρογέρων**, οντος, ὁ, another name for ἠριγέρων, Apul.*Herb.* 76.22 (cj.).

***ὑδροδότης**, ου, ὁ, *provider of water*, *SB* 9653 i 16 (ii AD).

**ὑδροκόμος**, for 'prob. *well-bucket*' read 'prob. *drive-cable* of water-wheel'

***ὑδρολογία**, ἡ, *work on the water-supply*, *CPR* 8.22.49 (AD 314).

**ὑδρομαντεία**, add 'Plin.*HN* 37.192'

**ὑδρόμελι**, add '*SEG* 32.1601 (Nubia, iv/v AD)'

***ὑδρομίκτης**, ου, ὁ, *seller of wine mixed with water*, *SEG* 26.817 (sp. -μήκτ-; Thrace).

**⁺ὑδροπαροχία** (-εία) ἡ, *supply of water for irrigation*, *IEphes.* 4337.10 (i AD), *POxy.* 137.22, *PVindob.Salomons* 9.8 (both vi AD).

***ὑδροπαροχικός**, όν, *of the supply of water for irrigation*, *POxy.* 3582.6 (v AD).

**ὑδροπάροχος**, add '*PVindob.Salomons* 9.9 (vi AD)'

***ὑδροπίσσιον**, τό, (?)*liquid pitch*, *CRAI* 1945.378 (Berytus, Byz.).

**ὑδροπότης**, delete 'used .. fellow' and add 'Ath. 2.44b, *SEG* 25.774 (Moesia, Rom.imp.), 31.238 (*GVI* 1841, Athens, iii AD); also -πώτης Macho 46 G., Phot. α 595 Th.'

**ὕδρος I**, add 'ὕδρον ἐν Λέρνῃ Hippon. 102.10 W. (= Ὕδρα)' add 'Myc. *u-do-ro*, *water-pot* (cf. ὑδρία)'

**ὑδροσκόπιον 2**, add '*Cat.Cod.Astr.* 8(2).113.17'

**ὑδροφόβος II**, add 'Heras ap.Gal. 13.431.16'

***ὑδροφορείη**, ἡ, poet. = ὑδροφορία, κεκασμένη ὑδροφορείῃ *Didyma* 344.3.

**ὑδροφορία II**, add 'ostr. in *CE* 61.275 (i/ii AD)'

**ὑδροφόρια**, lines 1/2, for 'a festival .. Sch.Pi.*N.* 5.81' read 'race in honour of Apollo at Aegina run by carriers of amphorae, Call.*Dieg.* viii.32 (*fr.* 198 Pf.), v. °ἀμφορίτης'; lines 3/4, delete 'name of .. Διηγήσεις viii.32'

**ὑδροφόρος II**, of priestess, add '*SEG* 30.1286 (Didyma, i AD), 36.1060 (Miletus)' add '**2** ὑδροφόρον, τό, *vessel for carrying water*, *Kafizin* 267 (223/222 BC).'

**ὕδρω**, delete 'apparently' and add '*IG* 14.1890.11'

**ὕδρωψ**, line 1, after 'ὁ' insert '(also ἡ Nic.*Th.* 467)'

**ὕδωρ**, line 2, for 'Call.*fr.* 475' read 'Call.*fr.* 268 Pf.; acc. pl. ὑδάτη *Nautarum Cantiuncula* 4' **I 1**, add '**b** *water-supply*, *IEphes.* 3217 (ii AD), *SEG* 35.189 (v/vi AD).' **5**, add 'perh. also Lang *Ath.Agora* XXI Hd 16 (iii AD)' add '**6** pl., ὕδατα, τά, *urine*, Sm.*Ez.* 7.17, 21.12.'

**ὕειος**, add 'form perh. *ὑήϝιος, cf. Myc. *we-e-wi-ja*'

***ὑελᾶς**, v. °ὑαλᾶς.

**ὑέτιος I 1**, add 'Θεὸς Ὑέτιὸς *SEG* 39.958 (Eleutherna)'

**ὑεύχομαι**, delete the entry (v. *ICS* 181).

**⁺ὑϝαις**, dub. in Cypr. *u-wa-i-se za-ne*, app. *in perpetuity*, *for ever*, *ICS* 217.10, 23, 28.

***ὑϊδεύς**, έως, ὁ, = ὑϊδοῦς, *TAM* 5(1).786, Hsch.; also υἱιδεύς Isoc.*Ep.* 8.1.

**ὑΐδιον** (B), add 'τῷ φιλ]τάτω υἱιδίῳ *SEG* 30.606 (Maced., ii/iii AD)'

***ὑϊδός**, ὁ, = ὑϊδοῦς, Hsch.

***υἱή**, ἡ, *daughter*, *SB* 101 (i AD): also Aeol. **ὐά** *Schwyzer* 625 (Mytilene, ?i AD).

**υἱήν**, add 'cf. Myc. *we-je-we* υἱῆϝες app. *vines*'

***υἱιδεύς**, v. °ὑϊδεύς.

**ὑϊκός**, after 'ἱερεῖον ὑϊκόν .. *Milet.* 7.18' insert 'neut. subst. ὑϊκόν, τό, *SEG* 31.122 (Attica, c.AD 121/2)'

**υἱοθεσία**, sp. ὑο-, add '*SEG* 30.1007, *AR* 1985/6.99 (both Rhodes)'

**υἱοποιία**, add 'rest. in *SEG* 23.317 (Delphi, i AD), Just.*Nov.* 89.7'

**υἱός**, line 6, for 'ὑύς .. 686' read 'hυύς *IG* 1³.783, 791, 865, hῦς *SEG* 23.38 (Attica, vi BC)' **3**, add 'υἱοὶ τῶν συμμίξεων *children of mixed race*, Lxx 4*Ki.* 14.14 (mistranslation of Hebr. phr. meaning "hostages")', deleting this quot. fr. section 4 add '**10** *heir*, *SB* 9902A ii 13 (iii AD).'

**υἱωνός**, add 'also ὑωνός *SEG* 33.1016 (Lydia, AD 103/4), *PFlor.* 71.235 (iv AD)'

***ὑκερός**, v. °ἐκυρός.

***ὑκτάς**, v. °ὀκτάς.

**ὑλαῖος I**, add 'τὴν ὄρνειθαν ὑλήαν (unidentified bird), *OFlorida* 15.4 (ii AD)'

**ὑλακτέω I**, after 'Eup. 207' insert 'Herod. 6.14' **II**, transfer 'hence Vespasian .. D.C. 66.13' to section I 1.

***Ὑλᾶτης**, ὁ, Cypr. *u-la-ta-i*, *ICS* 2.4, 85.1, al.; epith. of Apollo, Bernand *Les Portes* no. 47 (iii BC), Lyc. 448, Nonn.*D.* 13.444.

***ὑλιᾶσθαι·** κινεῖσθαι Theognost.*Can.* 21 A.

***ὑλιελινᾶτες**, unexpld. wd. in list of tradesmen, *PAmst.*inv. 21 (*ZPE* 9.49).

***ὑλινόμος**, v. ‡ὑλονόμος.

***ὕλιος**, α, ον, *muddy*, app. in place-name, Πλακὸς Ὑλίας (gen.) *IG* 9²(1).609 (Locr., v BC).

**ὑλιστήριον**, add 'also ὑλιστάριον *SB* 9483.13 (ii AD)'

**ὑλίτης**, before 'v. ὑλήτις' insert '*BGU* 2430.23 (ὑλείτης pap., i BC)'

***Ὑλλεῖς**, οἱ, one of the three Dorian tribes, Tyrt. 19.8 W., Hdt. 5.68.2, *Ath.Agora* XVII 4.3 (458 BC); fem. **Ὑλλίδες**, αἱ, *Tit.Calymn.* 88.18, al. (ii BC).

**ὑλομᾰνέω 2**, add 'Philostr.*VS* 2.32.2'

**ὑλονόμος**, for 'Simon.(?) 179.7' read '*AP* 6.217.7 ([Simon.])' and add 'also **ὑλινόμος**' *IAskl.Epid.* 167

**ὑλοξιδής**, after '*woodcutter*' insert 'or *glass-maker* (for ὑελο-), but the second element is unexpld., v. *ICilicie* p. 221 n. 2'

**ὑλοτομικός**, add 'Alex.Aphr.*in Top.* 237.25'

***ὑλώνης**, ου, ὁ, *buyer of wood*, *Ath.Agora* XIX L8.103, 141 (Oropus, c.330 BC).

**ὑλωρέω**, add '*SEG* 34.564 (Thessaly, c.200/190 BC)'

**ὑμέναιος I**, add 'also app. ὑμέναια, τά, Mitchell *N.Galatia* 118' **II**, line 1, for "Ὑμήν' read '‡Ὡμήν'

**ὑμενώδης I**, add '**2** app. *thin as a membrane, filmy*, χιών *SEG* 29.1477.'

**ὑμέτερος I**, line 7, for 'sts.' read 'normally'; add 'in addresses to a single person with whom others are associated, Sol. 19.2 W., Call.*Del.* 204' deleting these refs. fr. section II.

**ὑμήν**, line 2, after 'Arist. .. 519ᵇ4, al.' insert '*POxy.* 3195.42 (AD 331)'

***ὑμνᾰγωγός**, ὁ, *leader of hymns* in Eleusinian worship, *SEG* 30.90 (Eleusis, 20/19 BC).

**ὑμνέω I 1**, line 9, after 'c. dupl. acc.' insert '*praise* in song, τὰ νομισθέντα γὰρ αἰεὶ Διόνυσον ὑμνήσω E.*Ba.* 72'; at end delete 'impers. .. 1203.5'

**ὕμνησις**, after '*praising*' insert 'Pi.*Pae.* 12.5 S.-M. (rest.)'

***ὑμνηστός**, ή, όν, = ὑμνητός (cf. ὑμνήστρια), *celebrated, praised*, Εὐλάλις ἀνὴ[ρ] ὑμν(ι)στος (sic ed.) Mitchell *N.Galatia* 323 (iii/iv AD).

***ὑμνίδιος**, ον, app. *produced by (insects') wings* (fr. syncopated dim. of ὑμήν), ὑμνιδίῳ .. πατάγῳ *AP* 7.198.6 (Leon.Tarent., s.v.l.).

***ὑμνοδιδασκᾰλέω**, *act as* ὑμνοδιδάσκαλος, *La Carie* II p. 216.

**ὑμνολογέω**, add 'epigr. in *SEG* 30.1367 (Smyrna, late Hellen.)'

**ὑμνοποιός**, after 'E.*Rh.* 651' insert 'μάθησις *IG* 12(7).449.7 (Amorgos, ii BC)'

**ὑμνοπόλος II**, for 'Simon. 184' read '*AP* 7.25.2 ([Simon.])'

**ὑμνῳδέω I**, add 'οἱ ὑμνῳδήσαντες κοῦροι *SEG* 37.962 (Ionia, ii AD)'

**ὑμνῳδός**, add 'also sg. *CEG* 578'

***ὕμως**, Aeol. for ὅμως, Sapph. 58.21 L.-P.

***ὑναφορέω**, Cypr. for ἀναφορέω, *Kafizin* 266b (= *ICS* 231).

***Ὕγγιος**, v. °Ἰύγγιος.

**ὑνεύχομαι**, delete the entry (v. *ICS* 181, *Kourion* 25).

***ὑνιερόω**, v. °ἀνιερόω.

**ὕννος**, add 'ὗνοι pl. perh. in *AAWW* 1948.322-3 (Panopolis, Rom.imp., see also *BE* 1958.139)'

***ὑντίθημι**, Cypr. for ἀνατίθημι, aor. *u-ne-te-ke* ὐνέθε̄κε *ICS* 181; also Arc., 3rd pl. imper. aor. ὐνθεάντω *SEG* 25.447 (Aliphera, iii BC).

**ὑοβοσκός**, after 'Arist.*HA* 603ᵇ5' insert '*POsl.* 160.3 (iii AD)'

**ὑπαγκᾰλίζω**, for 'Pass.' read 'med.'

**ὑπαγκάλισμα**, after 'S.*Tr.* 540' insert 'Διὸς ὑ. σεμνόν (i.e. Hera) E.*Hel.* 242'

***ὑπᾰγορᾱνόμος**, ὁ, *deputy agoranomos*, *AR* 1989/90.33 (Messene, late Rom.).

***ὑπᾰγωνοθετέω**, *act as sub-*ἀγωνοθέτης, rest. in *IGRom.* 4.850 (Laodicea ad Lycum), v. *REA* 62.296.

***ὑπάετος** or **-αίετος**, ὁ, kind of eagle, = ὀρειπέλαργος, Arist.*HA* 618ᵇ34, Ant.Lib.*fab.* 20.6 (cj.), cod. oxyt., cf. °γυπαιετούς.

***ὑπαίθρειος**, ον, = ὑπαίθριος, cj. in *S.Ant.* 357.

**ὑπᾰκούω II 5**, delete fr. 'ὑπάκουουσι' to end of section **IV**, delete the section.

***ὑπακωνίδιον**, τό, dim. of °ὑπακώνιον, *PSI* 1355.4 (ii BC).

***ὑπακώνιον**, τό, perh. article of clothing, *PSI* 1355.6 (ii BC).

***ὑπᾰλαζών**, όνος, ὁ, *something of a charlatan*, Men.*Asp.* 375 S.

**ὑπᾰλεύομαι**, after 'ib. 760' insert '*AP* 7.472b (Leon.Tarent.), *SEG* 31.1288 (Side, AD 249/252)'

**ὑπαλλακτέον**, add 'Gal. 17(1).98.18'

**ὑπαλλακτικός**, before 'adv.' for 'only in' read 'gramm., *involving an interchange of relation*, ὑπαλλακτικὴν (στάσιν) Quint.*Inst.* 3.6.47'

**ὑπᾰμάω**, add 'prob. also A.*fr.* 273a.3 R. (in tm.)'

***ὑπαμπετίν**, written ὑπανπετίν, adv., app. *going round under*, *SEG* 35.991.B8,10 (Lyttos, v BC), cf. περιαμπετίξ.

***ὑπανατέλλω**, *rise somewhat, begin to rise*, of a star, Ael.*NA* 14.24, of a fountain, ib. 15.4'

**ὑπαναφύομαι**, add 'also act., τραχύτητας ὑπαναφύει Ael.*NA* 10.13'

**ὕπανδρος I**, add 'θυγατέρας ὑπάνδρους *SEG* 24.911 (iv AD)'

***ὑπανελεύθερος**, ον, *somewhat deficient in liberality, niggardly*, Gallo *Framm.Biogr.* II 274.

**ὑπανίημι II**, line 2, delete 'so .. al.'

**ὑπανίσχω**, delete '*slowly*'

**ὑπαντάω I 1**, add 'also in pass., ὑπηντήθη τῷ στρατηγῷ *Vit.Aesop.*(G) 65'

**ὕπαρ**, for '*Schwyzer* 686.2' read 'in sense A II 4, Ϝίλσιος ὕπαρ *for the sake of preventing*, *IPamph.* 3.2 (iv BC)'

***ὑπαρχιτεκτονικόν**, τό, *budgetary money of the* ὑπαρχιτέκτων, *CID* II.1 ii 46 (iv BC).

**ὕπαρχος I 2 b**, add 'ὁ τῶν ἀννόνων ὑ. = Lat. *praefectus annonae*, Just.*Nov.* 82.2 pr.'

**ὑπάρχω B III 2**, for '*to be devoted to*' read '*give support to*'

**ὑπασπιστής 2**, add '*SEG* 31.1574 (Cyrene, late ii BC); sg., member of this unit, *SEG* 13.403 (= *EAM* 87, ii BC)'

**ὑπασχολέομαι**, add '*BGU* 1159.23 (i BC/i AD)'

**ὑπάτη**, add '**2** name of a Delphic Muse, *SEG* 30.382 (Argos, c.300 BC), cf. Plu. 2.744c, see also °μέση I 2.'

***ὑπᾰτικιανός**, ή, όν, *associated with an officer of consular status*, ταξεωτῶν *Mir.Demetr.* p. 157.19 L.

***ὑπάτισσα**, ἡ, *wife* or *widow of a consul*, *POxy.* 2243a.86 (vi AD), *CIG* 9008.

**ὕπᾰτος II**, add 'νόος ὕπατος λόγω καὶ διανοίας Archyt.ap.Iamb.*Protr.* 4' **III 1**, after '*Mon.Anc.Gr.* 5.1' insert 'Jul.*Caes.* 332b'

**ὑπαυλέω**, for '*flute*' read '*aulos*'

***ὕπαυλις**, εως, ἡ, part of house, perh. *covered yard*, οἰκίδιον .. ἐν ᾧ ὑ. καταπεπ[τωκυῖα *PMich.*XII 627.7 (AD 298).'

**ὑπαυλισμός**, for '*flute*' read '*aulos*'

***ὕπαυτα**, v. ὑπό C III 2, line 20.

**ὑπειδόμην**, line 1, after 'ὑπιδόμενος' insert '(ὑφ- *BCH* 10.301.20 (Alabanda, ii BC))'

**ὑπειλέομαι**, of bandage, add 'Gal. 18(1).789.5'

**ὑπεισέρχομαι I 4**, add '*succeed to in place of another*, ἵνα τοῦ πρώτου παραιτουμένου ὁ μετὰ ταῦτα βαθμὸς ὑπεισέρχηται *Cod.Just.* 6.4.4.20a; εἰς τὰ τῶν ἰδίων γονέων δίκαια Just.*Nov.* 118.3'

***ὑπεκδέχομαι**, *have under oneself*, μαστῷ πόρτιν ὑ., v.l. in *AP* 9.722 (Antip.Sid.).

**ὑπέκθεσις**, add 'cf. ὑπέκθεσις· ὑπόθεσις Hsch.'

**ὑπεκκᾰλύπτω**, for '*uncover from below* or *a little*' read '*expose* by removing the top covering'

**ὑπεκπροθέω**, add '**2** *run out before* another's advance, Emp. B 35.12 D.-K.'

**ὑπεκπροφεύγω**, add '*INikaia* 1045 (iii AD)'

**ὑπεκτρώγω**, after '*gnaw secretly away*' insert 'in quot., fig., i.e. *filch*'

**ὑπεκφέρω II 2**, add 'Lesb.Rh. 2.7' **IV**, delete the section.

**ὑπελάσσων**, add 'Just.*Nov.* 115.5 pr.'

***Ὑπελλαῖος**, -αία, epith. of Zeus and Athena, *SEG* 20.719.A16 (Cyrene, ii BC).

***ὑπέμφᾰσις**, εως, ἡ, perh. *indication*, κατ' ἀντίθεσιν καὶ ἀπόθεσιν καὶ ὑ. Zos.Alch. 134.13.

**ὑπεναντίος II**, add 'also neut. sg., w. gen., ὑπεναντίον τῶν νόμων Just.*Nov.* 134.4'

**ὑπεξαίρεσις**, line 6, delete ': hence' and insert '*exception*, *Cod.Just.* 4.35.24'

***ὑπεξᾰκούω**, *listen fully to* (w. gen.), of arbitrators, prob. in *Inscr.Perg.* 245.6 (rest., ὑπεξ[ lapis, ii BC).

**ὑπεξέρχομαι II**, add '*Cod.Just.* 1.5.18.11'

**ὑπεξουσιότης**, add 'Just.*Nov.* 81 pr., al.'

**ὑπεπιστάτης**, add '*SB* 4638, *PBatav.* 4 ii 14'

**ὑπέρ**, line 2, after 'Arc. ὀπέρ (q.v.)' insert 'Pamph. ‡ὑπάρ; ὑπερί *SEG* 33.1152 (ii AD), *TAM* 4(1).370 (v. *SEG* 30.1438, Nicomedeia, Chr.)' **A I**, add '**4** *above, in excess of*, *MAMA* 8.252B (iii AD).' **B III**, add 'ὑπὲρ ἥμισυ Κᾶρες ἐφάνησαν Th. 1.8.1' **IV**, add '**2** *later than*, *Cod.Just.* 9.47.26.3, 10.11.8.7a.' **V**, add '*SEG* 25.447 (Arcadia, iii BC), 23.207 (Messene, Augustus)' **C**, add '*Cod.Just.* 10.11.8.4b (s.v.l.)'

**ὑπέρα II**, delete the section.

***ὑπεράγιος**, α, ον, *supremely holy*, *MAMA* 7.190 (Hadrianoupolis).

***ὑπεραιρέω**, *take in addition*, τὸ ἐπιτιμηθέν *IG* 11(2).199*A*74, cf. 84, 85 (Delos, iii BC).

**ὑπεραισχῦνομαι**, add 'w. aposiopesis, ὑπεραισχύνομαι γυναιξὶν ἐν ταὐτῷ - Men.*Dysc.* 871'

**ὑπεραιώρησις**, add 'Gal. 18(2).488.11'

**ὑπεράλλομαι I**, add '**2** abs., *jump further* (than others), Luc.*Anach.* 8.'

**ὑπερανατείνομαι**, add 'act. intr., Hsch. s.v. ὑπερτενή'

***ὑπερανατέλλω**, = ὑπερτέλλω, Hsch.

**ὑπεράνω 4**, add '*BCH* 60.119 (Delphi, i BC), *SEG* 31.825 (Sicily, ii BC)'

***ὑπεράξιος**, ον, *well worthy*, Ael.*NA* 4.29.

**ὑπεραπαιτέω**, add '*Cod.Just.* 3.10.1.2'

***ὑπεραρθρισμός**, ὁ, *hyperbatic use of the article*, Sch.D.T. 460.13.

**ὑπεράριθμος**, after '*supernumerary*' insert '*PTeb.* 703.155 (iii BC)'

**ὑπέραρσις**, for '*exaltation*' read '*high-water mark*'

**ὑπεράστειος**, add '**2** *exceedingly refined, over-elegant*, ὄψιν ὑπεράστειος Men.*Mis.* A93 p. 353 S.'

**ὑπεραυγέω**, add '**2** *irradiate from above*, τὴν γῆν Eudox. 20.9.'

**ὑπερβαίνω III**, after '*protect*' insert 'Aq., Sm., Thd.*Is.* 31.5, perh. also *ITyr* 75'

**ὑπέρβᾰσις I**, add 'Aq.*Ex.* 12.11'

***ὑπερβάτης**, ου, ὁ, *housebreaker*, *PMich.*inv. 3736 (*Anagennesis* 4.141, iv/v AD).

**Ὑπερβερεταῖος II**, add '*Schwyzer* 590.9 (Larissa, 214 BC), *ICilicie* 109 (AD 99), *SEG* 32.1537 (Arabia, AD 184), etc.; sp. -βερταῖος *SEG* 34.1208 (Lydia, AD 111/2); μη(νὸς) Ὑπερβερτέου *SEG* 31.991 (Lydia, AD 234/5)'

**ὑπερβῐβασμός**, add '*An.Par.* 4.31.28'

**ὑπέρβῐος II**, line 3, ὑ. ἦτορ ἔχειν, add 'Hes.*Th.* 139, 898'

***Ὑπερβόϊος**, v. °Ὑπερβώϊος.

**ὑπερβολή I 4**, add 'qualifying adv. εὖ Macho 168 G.'

**ὑπερβολία**, add '**II** dat. (-βολίῃ) = ὑπερβολῇ, *exceedingly*, *MAMA* 8.208.'

**ὑπερβώϊα**, add 'also -βόϊα'

***Ὑπερβώϊος** (or **Ὑπερβῷος**), ὁ, name of month in Crete, τὸ Ὑπερβōῖō μηνός *SEG* 23.530 (vii BC).

**ὑπεργεμίζω**, add '*PHib.* 182 xiii 183 (iii BC)'

***ὑπέργω**, ὑπηργμένη in unkn. sense in fragmentary inscr., *SEG* 24.139 (Athens, ii BC).

***ὑπερδᾰπᾰνάω**, *overspend*, *BGU* 1838 (ii BC), *PLond.* 1171.21 (i BC).

**ὑπερδάπανον**, delete the entry.

**ὑπερδέξιος**, line 1, after 'ον' insert 'sts. fem. -α, Ion. -η, of Athena' **II**, add '**4** *possessing superiority*, epith. of Apollo, Plu.*Arat.* 7.2; of Zeus, *IGC* p. 11, line 12 (Larissa, ii BC); of Athena, *IG* 12(1).22 (Rhodes, Hellen.); of Zeus and Athena, *Thasos* 124 (ii/i BC), *SEG* 15.517 A II 5 (Paros, iii BC), cf. Robert *Hell.* 10.63 ff., 295 and v. °καθυπερδέξιος.'

**ὑπερδικέω**, add '*SEG* 34.1238.48 (Aeolis, *c.*200 BC)'

**ὑπερείδω I 2**, delete the section transferring quot. to section II.

**ὑπερέπαρσις**, for '*excessive exaltation*' read '*raising up* (to safety)'

**ὑπερεπιθῡμέω**, for 'Porph.*Plot.* 19' read 'Longin.ap.Porph.*Plot.* 19.25'

***ὑπερεπιτηδείως**, *very suitably*, *Com.adesp.* 22.38 D.

***ὑπερεχής**, ές, *that exceeds the proper, normal, etc., amount, excess*, neut. as subst., τὸ ὑ. τοῦ τόκου καὶ τοῦ ἡμιολίου *IG* 12(7).515.35 (Amorgos, ii BC).

**ὑπερήκω**, add '**2** *jut out beyond*, w. gen., τούτου .. ὑπερήκει τοῦ κόλπου ἀκρωτήριον *Peripl.M.Rubr.* 40.'

**ὑπερημερία**, line 2, after 'Lebad.' insert 'iv BC'

***ὑπερηνόρεος**, ον, app. *arrogant*, Aeol. ὑπερᾱν-, dub. in Theoc. 29.19.

**ὕπερθεν**, (ὕπερθε), line 1, at end insert 'E.*Ion* 1153 (trimeters)'

**ὑπέρθετος**, add 'title of official in Egypt (Lat. *superpositus*), σ]υντακτικοῖς καὶ ὑπερθέτοις *PRyl.* 585.29 (ii BC)'

**ὑπέρθῡρον**, add '*Carm.Pop.* 2.14 P.'

***ὑπερί**, v. °ὑπέρ.

**ὑπεριδρύω**, before 'in pass.' insert '*set* or *establish above*, Procl. *in R.* 1.174 K.'

**ὑπερίστᾰμαι 1**, after 'and pf. act.' insert 'cf. also ὑπερεστήξει· ὑπερσταθήσεται Hsch.'

**Ὑπερίων**, add '*MAMA* 1.390'

***ὑπερκᾰκέω**, ὑπερκακεῖν· ὃ νῦν ἐκκακεῖν Hsch.

**ὑπερκεράω**, line 2, for '*stretch beyond*' read '*curve beyond*'

***ὑπερλαμβάνω**, unexpld. wd. in broken text, *POxy.* 2344.15 (iv AD).

**ὑπέρλαμπρος I 1**, add 'of an appearance of the sun considered as omen, *Orac.Tiburt.* 23'

**ὑπερμαζάω**, add 'Poll. 7.24'

**ὑπερμεγέθης**, line 5, after '*Cyr.* 1.6.8' insert 'of youths, perh. *oversized*, ephebic list in *JEA* 37.89.50 (Memphis, iii AD)'

**ὑπερμενής**, add 'epith. of Θεοὶ Σωτῆρες, *RIB* 461'

***ὑπερμεριμνάω**, *to be exceedingly concerned about*, ὑγίαν *PBerl.Zill.* 14.3 (vi AD), cf. *Gnomon* 22.143ff.

**ὑπερμετρέω**, add 'ὑπερμετρῆσαι rest. in *PAnt.* 55 *fr.*(*b*)$^v$ 10'

***ὑπερμηρίδια**, τά, *parts of a sacrificial victim above the thigh*, *BCH* 113.449 (Crete, iv BC); perh. also in *SEG* 15.564 (cf. ib. 39.954; Dreros, *c.*600 BC).

***ὑπερνήχομαι**, *swim past* or *over*, ὑπερνήχεται· ὑπερέχει, ὑπερβαίνει Hsch.

***ὑπέρνομος**, ον, *supralegal*, προαίρεσις *An.Boiss.* 2.45.

**ὑπεροικοδομέω**, add '*Berytus* 33.52'

***Ὑπεροῖος**, v. ὑπερῷος 2.

***ὕπερον**, τό, (perh. also ὕπερος, ὁ, Hes.*Op.* 423 v.l.), *pestle*, λεήναντες ὑπέροισι Hdt. 1.200, Plb. 1.22.7, Luc.*Philops.* 35, Poll. 1.245, ὕπερα σιδηρᾶ id. 7.107 (cf. .. έροις σιδηροῖς, the mutilated title of a comedy in *IG* 14.1097), 10.114, *EM* 779.48, Lang *Ath.Agora* XXI B19, *IG* $1^3$.422.265, 425.105 (Athens, v BC), *PRyl.* 167.14; prov., of never-ending and ineffectual labour, ὑπέρου μοι περιτροπὴ γενήσεται Pl.Com. 1 K.-A., Pl.*Tht.* 209d (cf. Philem. 30 K.-A.), Plu. 2.1072b; used as lever for stretching dislocated joints, Hp.*Fract.* 13, *Art.* 78, al.; as a club, Plu.*Alex.* 63.9; as a staff, Luc.*Demon.* 48. **II** like πηνίον, *pupa* of geometrid moth, Arist.*HA* 551$^b$6.

**ὑπέροπλος I**, add 'comp. -ότεροι A.*fr.* 168.4 R. (s.v.l.)'

***ὑπεροπτεία**, ἡ, *haughtiness*, cj. in S.*Ant.* 130.

***ὑπερόπτις**, ιδος, ἡ, fem. of ὑπερόπτης, acc. -ιν Rh. 1.559.6.

**ὑπερόριος I 1**, add 'adv. -ίως, ἐξορίζομαι *Cod.Just.* 11.41.7'

***ὕπερος**, ὁ, v. °ὕπερον, τό.

**ὑπέροχος**, after 'Ion. ὑπείρ-' insert 'Ὑπάροχος pers. n. *BCH* 114.460 (Doris, *c.*500 BC)'

**ὑπερπᾰθής**, for '*grievous*' read '*affected by great emotion*' and for 'Phleg.*fr.* 36.1 J.' read 'Phleg.*fr.* 36.1.5 J.' and insert 'Alcin.*Intr.* p. 184.22 H.'; after 'adv. -θῶς' insert '*excessively*, Ptol.*Tetr.* 188 B., cf.'

**ὑπερπαίω**, last line, before '*Supp.*' insert '*surplus*'; add 'so ἐκ τῶν ὑπερπαιόντων *IGBulg.* 1565'

***ὑπερπαρέχω**, *provide on behalf of*, *SEG* 30.380 (Tiryns, vii BC).

***ὑπέρπεδον**· ὄρος, βουνός, ἔπαρμα γῆς Phot.

**ὑπέρπικρος**, add 'Men.*Dysc.* 129'

**ὑπερπράξιον**, add '*ZPE* 56.89 (wax tablet, Egypt, v/vi AD)'

**ὑπερπράσσω**, add 'Just.*Nov.* 17.4'

**ὑπέρπῡρος 2**, add 'σίτω οὐπερπούρω *SEG* 25.556 (Boeotia, *c.*210/200 BC); n. subst., τὰ οὐπέρπουρα *SEG* 32.456 (Boeotia, iii BC)'

**ὑπερσαρκέω 1**, add 'Androm.min.ap.Gal. 13.729.10'

**ὑπερτέλειος 1**, for '*beyond completeness* or *perfection*' read '*larger than* °τέλειος (I 2 a), designation of a type of aulos'

**ὑπερτερέω 1**, add 'Certamen 149'

**ὑπέρτερος I 1**, add '**b** w. gen., *on the upper part*, τᾶς τήνω φλιᾶς καθ' ὑπέρτερον Theoc. 2.60; *in the parts above*, καθ' ὑπέρτερα γαίης Arat. 498.' **II**, add '*older*, Mitchell *N.Galatia* 392'

**ὑπερτίθημι I 3 a**, line 3, after 'D.S. 13.3' insert 'οὐδὸν ὑπερθεμένη *APl.* 58'

**ὑπερφῐλοσοφέω**, add 'Philostr.*VA* 7.37'

***ὑπέρφορβος**, ὁ, *exceedingly bountiful*, τὸ νῦν ἅζομαι θεῶν πατ[έρα] βροτῶν πάσας γενεᾶς ὑπ[έρ]φορβον *SEG* 36.350 (Epid., Rom.imp., new text of *IG* $4^2$.134, which has [πολύ]φορβον).

***Ὑπερφορεύς**, έως, ὁ, epith. of Zeus, *SEG* 20.719A (Cyrene, ii BC).

***ὑπερφρονητής**, οῦ, ὁ, *despiser*, *An.Boiss.* 5.340.

**ὑπέρφρων 1**, add 'of persons, τοὺς ἄγαν ὑπέρφρονας *Trag.adesp.* 521 K.-S.'

**ὑπερχᾰρής**, add '*SEG* 23.206 (Messene, AD 2/3)'

**ὑπερχειλής**, for '*over the brim, running over*' read '*full to the brim*'

***ὑπερχράομαι**, *use to excess*, Sch.B Il. 1.193.

**ὑπέρχρεως**, add '**2** of estates, *encumbered*, v.l. for ὑπόχ- (q.v.) in Is. 10.16, 17.'

***ὑπερχύνω**, *overflow*, Socr.Dion.*Lith.* 37 G.

***ὑπεστιοῦχος**, ὁ, functionary in the cult of Hestia, *IEphes.* 1078.16, cf. °ἑστιοῦχος.

**ὑπεύθῡνος II**, add '**4** *defendant*, *BGU* 2173.3 (AD 498), *Cod.Just.* 2.2.4 pr.'

**ὑπευλᾰβέομαι**, for '*to be somewhat afraid*' read '*to be cautious* or *wary of*' and add 'συμβολὴν μάχης Memn. 29.1 J.'

**ὑπήνη 2**, add 'οὐρανόεσσαν ὑπήνην perh. the inside of the upper lip, Nic.*Al.* 16'

***ὑπηνῆτις**, ιδος, *of the upper lip*, θρίξ *An.Boiss.* 4.431.

**ὑπηρεσία I**, for '*body of rowers, ship's crew*' read 'collective term for the assistants to the trierarch over and above the rowers'; line 7, delete '*crews*' **II 2**, add 'εἰς ἀπρεπεῖς αὐτῷ (sc. ὕδατι) ὑπηρε[σίας καταχρωμένους] *IEphes.* 3217 (ii AD) and then in naval contexts' and transfer fr. section I quots. Plb. 5.109.1, 1.25.3, *Gp.* 18.9.3.

**ὑπηρετέω I**, for '*as a rower*' read '*serve as a member of a* °ὑπηρεσία' **II 3 d**, add 'in other cults, Mitchell *N.Galatia* 204 (AD 227)'

**ὑπηρέτης II 1**, add '*temple servant*, *SEG* 23.209 (Messene, iii BC)'

***ὑπήχησις**, εως, ἡ, *subterranean noise*, Paus. 7.24.8 (cj., v. ὑφήγησις II).

***ὑπισθόδομος**, v. °ὀπισθόδομος.

***ὑπιωγή**, ὑπιωγαί· ὑπαγωγαί, ὑποδρομαὶ τῆς πέτρας διὰ σκέπην, σκεπηνὰ μέρη Hsch.

***ὑπνέω**, = ὑπνόω, Anon.*Fig.* p. 172.11 S.

**ὑπνοδῶτις**, delete the entry.

**ὕπνος I 3**, after '(Plu.) *Alex.* 50' insert 'καθ' ὕπνου *Sardis* 7(1).94'

**ὑπνόω II**, add '*AP* 5.23 (Call.), 5.184 (Mel.)'

***ὑπνωτέον**, *one must sleep*, *An.Boiss.* 3.327.

**ὑπό**, at the end of first paragraph add 'Myc. *u-po*' **C II**, add '**2** *subject to* conditions, etc., ὑπὸ ἐκκλησιαστικὸν ἐπιτίμιον *Cod.Just.* 1.4.29.10; ὑπὸ τὸν ἔσχατον κίνδυνον ib. 9.47.26.2.' **III**, add '*in the time of*, hυπὸ δὲ Ἐχεμένε̄ ἔφορο[ν] *Schwyzer* 12.66 (Sparta, v BC)' add '**V** ὑπό τι *up to a point, somewhat*, ὑπό τι ἄτοπα Pl.*Grg.* 493c; ὑ. τι ἀσεβῆ id.*Phdr.* 242d; ὑ. τι μικρὸν ἐπιθήκισα Ar.*V.* 1290 (lyr.), ὑ. τι ‹δὴ› σκυθρωπάσας Macho 247 G.'

**ὑποβάλλω I 3**, add '*Cod.Just.* 1.1.5.4, 1.3.29.1' add '**4** ὑ. ψήφους *cast* voting-pebbles *surreptitiously*, Arist.*Ath.* 68.3, cf. Call.*fr.* 85.8 Pf.' **III**, add '**2** *propose* (as an official measure), οἱ κωμάρχαι τῆς Θεαδελφίας ὑπέβαλον, ὥς σου ἀπενεγκόντος .. *PPrag.* I 108.3 (Theadelphia, iii AD).'

**ὑπόβᾰσις**, add '**IV** ὑπόβασις· ὁ ἐνδότατος χιτών, ἢ περίζωμα Hsch.'

**ὑποβιβλιοθηκοφύλαξ**, delete the entry.

***ὑποβιβλιοφύλαξ**, ἄκος, ὁ, *sub-librarian*, *BGU* 660.9, 14 (ii AD).

**ὑπόβλητος**, line 3, after '*OC* 794' insert '*PMich.*III 174.9, 11 (ii AD)'

**ὑπογάστριον II**, add '*IGC* p. 99 B5 (Acraephia, iii/ii BC)'

**ὑπογραμμᾰτεύς**, add 'of an ephebic officer, *SEG* 26.184, 188, 194, 198 (iii AD)'

**ὑπογραμμᾰτεύω**, add 'τοῦ Λυκίων ἔθνους *SEG* 17.711.8-9 (Balbura, ii AD)'

**ὑπογρᾰφεύς 2**, for '*person .. another*' read '*writer acting on behalf of an illiterate*'

**ὑπογρᾰφή I 1**, add '**d** *signature*, *Cod.Just.* 1.2.24.9.'

**ὑπογράφω**, add '**VI** *register, enter* as, (cf. ἐπιγράφω III 4) ἐὰν ἰδιωτικὴν μὲν ὑπογραφόμενοι τύχην, δύνανται βασανισθῆναι *Cod.Just.* 4.20.15.1.'

**ὑπόγυιος II**, neut. as adv., add 'Gal. 7.949.8, 8.858.2, 9.520.9'

**ὑποδακρύω 2**, add 'Gal. 11.318.11'

**ὑπόδειγμα I 2**, add 'συγκρίσεις ἀρχιτεκτόνων γέγοναν μεθ' ὑποδειγμάτων *SEG* 33.1040 (Cyme)'

***ὑποδειλικός**, όν, unexpld. adj., in quot. of a shirt, καμίσιν ὑποδειλικόν *PMich.*XI 607.31 (AD 569), perh. cf. ὑποδειρίς.

***ὑποδείριον**, gloss on ὑποδέραιον, Hsch.

**ὑποδεσμεύω**, add 'med., Ister 36 J.'

**ὑποδεσμός I**, add '*Edict.Diocl.* 8.7 (pl.)'

**ὑποδέχομαι**, add 'also act. ὑποδέχω *POxy.* 3400.5, 18, 23 (iv AD)'

***ὑποδηλωτέον**, *one must indicate*, Aristox.*Harm.* p. 4 M.

**ὑπόδημα**, add 'sg. used w. force of pl., *PMich.*VIII 477.27 (ii AD)' add '**b** applied to °κρούπεζα 2, Poll. 7.87, 10.153.'

**ὑποδημᾰτοποιός**, add '*IG* $2^2$.1559.48'

***ὑποδημᾰτοπώλης**, εω, ὁ, *sandal-seller*, *IEphes.* 2.29 (see also *SEG* 36.1011, iv BC).

+**ὑποδημᾰτουργός**, ὁ, *sandal-maker*, *JHS* 22.124 (v. Robert *Castabala* 34, Iconium).

***ὑποδημιουργός**, ὁ, *official* or *magistrate ranking below* δημιουργός, *DAW* 44(6).27 no. 59 (v. Robert *Castabala* 34, Cilicia).

***ὑποδημόσιον**, τό, *the sub-office of the public archives*, *Hierapolis* 341.

**ὑποδιᾱκονέω**, for '*serve under another* .. (loc.inc.)' read '*serve under a* διάκονος, *SEG* 37.527 (Epirus, Rom.imp.)'

**ὑποδιάκονος**, before '*MAMA* 3.462' insert '*subdeacon* in the Chr. Church' and add '*ITyr* 36, *SEG* 30.1701 (v AD), *Cod.Just.* 1.4.34.5, etc.'

**ὑποδιάκων**, for '= ὑποδιάκονος' read '*subdeacon* (cf. °ὑποδιάκονος)' and add '*SEG* 24.899, etc.'

**ὑπόδικος**, line 6, after 'iii BC)' insert 'w. gen. of the penalty, κεφαλῆς *SEG* 9.8.66 (Cyrene, i AD)'; line 10, before 'ὑ. ἀσεβείας' insert '*liable to an action* before'; line 11, after 'Pl.*Lg.* 868d' insert '*Ath.Agora* XIX L4A.96 (363 BC)'

**ὑποδίπλωσις**, add 'applied to the scaly formation of a crocodile's skin, *double layer*, Sm.*Jb.* 41.5'

+**ὑπόδουπος**, understood as adj. "reverberating" by ed. in Hdn.Gr. 2.947, quoting Hes.*fr.* 158 M.-W. (ὕπο δοῦπος cod.).

**ὑποδοχεῖον II**, after '*socket* of door-hinge' insert 'or perh. *groove* for metal rollers'

**ὑποδοχή IV 2**, add 'transf., ἀρθρῖτις καὶ ποδάγρα πολλῶν ἄλλων κακῶν ὑποδοχαί εἰσιν Ruf.ap.Orib. 45.30.62' **3**, for this section read 'philos., the *receptacle* or *space* in which things are created, πάσης .. γενέσεως ὑποδοχήν Pl.*Ti.* 49a, 51a, Plot. 2.4.1, al., ὑποδοχαὶ τῶν μαθηματικῶν εἰδῶν Iamb.*Comm.Math.* 3 (p. 14.9 F.), cf. ὕλην τε καὶ ὑ. ib. 4 (p. 16.20 F.; cod. ἀπο-)'

**ὑποδράξ**, for 'Call.*Fr.anon.* 63' read 'Call.*frr.* 194.101, 374.1 Pf.'

+**ὑποδρομέω**, Aeol. ὑπα-, *run under*, w. dat., λέπτον .. χρῶι πῦρ ὑπαδεδρόμηκεν Sapph. 31.10 L.-P.

**ὑπόδρομος** (A) **2**, delete the section.

**ὑπόδροσος**, for '*somewhat dewy*' read '*wet with dew*'

**ὑποζεύγνῡμι I b**, add '*to be inferior to*, ὑπέζευκται .. Ὁμήρῳ *AP* 7.409.9 (Antip.Sid.)'

***ὑπόζω**, *begin to smell*, *PRyl.Zen.* 11.24 (v. *Aegyptus* 14.119; cj. -ζ(έ)οντα).

**ὑπόθεμα**, after '**II**' insert '= ὑποθήκη II, *PMich.*III 173.11, al. (iii BC), *PTeb.* 891.5 (ii BC)'

**ὑποθετικός III**, for '*by way of suggestion*' read '*by way of precept*'

**ὑποθήκη I**, line 6, delete '*instructions*, Cic.*Att.* 2.17.3' and at end, after '(Gal.) 6.405' add 'cf. *ad me ab eo quasi* ὑποθήκας *adferes*, Cic.*Att.* 2.17.3' **II**, add 'of the object given as security, *Cod.Just.* 1.3.45.12'

**ὑποθηκῐμαῖος**, add 'pl. -αῖα, τά, *mortgaged property*, *POxy.* 2411.50 (ii AD)'

***ὑποϊεράρχης**, ου, ὁ, *under-hierarch*, dub. in Wolters *Kabirenheiligtum* p. 30 no. 5a (cf. p. 79).

***ὑποϊερεύς**, v. °ὑφιερεύς.

***ὑποικίδιος**, ον, *belonging, functioning*, etc., *within the house*, ὑ. κιθάραι paraphrase of φόρμιγγες ὑπωρόφιαι Sch.Pi.*P.* 1.188.

**ὑποικοδομέω**, after '*IG* $2^2$.463.114' insert '(iv BC), 11(2).287*A*60, 61 (Delos, iii BC)'

**ὑποκᾰθαρσις**, add 'Gal. 11.85.3'

**ὑποκάθημαι I**, add '**3** *to be situated below*, τὰ ὑποκαθήμενα πεδία *POxy.* 3167.5 (AD 195/198).'

**ὑποκαθίημι I**, add '**2** *secretly cause to act, suborn to act*, *PTeb.* 820.30 (iii BC).'

***ὑποκᾰλᾰθηφόρος**, ἡ, *assistant woman basket-bearer*, *IEphes.* 1072.9, cf. °καλαθηφόρος.

**ὑποκατάστᾰσις**, add '*appointing of a substitute heir* or *legatee* in the event of the original ones not accepting, *Cod.Just.* 1.3.52.13, Just.*Nov.* 1.1.3'

**ὑποκαταστάτης**, for '*substitute*' read '*assistant* °καταστάτης'

**ὑποκατάστᾰτος I**, add '**2** *substitute heir* (cf. °ὑποκατάστασις), Just.*Nov.* 22.44.9.'

**ὑπόκειμαι I 2**, add '*to be before* the audience in the theatre, Sch.Ar.*Nu.* 889c H.' **II 7**, after '*to be pledged* or *mortgaged*' insert '(whether the creditor or debtor is in possession)'

**ὑποκεντέω**, for 'τινὰ δόρασιν' read 'γεφύρας δόρασιν'

***ὑποκῆρυξ**, ῦκος, ὁ, *assistant* κῆρυξ, rest. in *SEG* 18.83.6, v. *BE* 1961.269 (Athens, ii AD), but dub., v. S. Follet *Athènes au II^e et au III^e siècle*, Paris 1976, pp. 280-281.

***ὑποκῐθᾰριστής**, οῦ, ὁ, *supporting lyre-player*, *PMich.*inv. 4682.15 (*Illinois Class.Stud.* 3.135, ii/iii AD).

***ὑποκλείδιον**, τό, perh. *clasp* of a belt, *SEG* 38.1210.21 (Miletus, ii BC).

**ὑποκλέπτω I 1**, pass., add 'w. retained acc., τοὺς εὐνὰς ὑποκλεπτομένους S.*El.* 114' **2**, delete the section. **II 1**, after '*keep secret*' insert 'ζῆλον Nonn.*D.* 1.71, al.' **2**, for this section read '*evade*, ζῆλον *AP* 5.269.5 (Agath.), ὄμμα ib. 290 (Paul.Sil.); *cheat, beguile*, μόχθον Nonn.*D.* 18.58, μερίμνας ib. 42.215'

**ὑποκλύω**, after 'A.R. 3.477' add '(v.l. ὑπ- for ἐπέκλυες)'

***ὑποκόκκῐνος**, η, ον, *scarlet-tinged*, *PGrenf.* II 28.5 (ii BC, ὑποκκιν- pap.).

**ὑποκόλπιος I 2**, add 'transf., ὑποκόλπιον τοῦ χοροῦ· στάσεως χῶραι αἱ ἄτιμοι Hsch.'

***ὑποκολπόω**, *spread round stealthily*, αὐτίκα οἵ γε ἠρέμα τὰ κέρα ὑποκολπώσαντες περιβάλλουσιν ἅπαντας Agath. 3.22.6.

**ὑπόκοπρος**, for '*slightly faecal*' read '*containing faecal matter*'

***ὑποκορῠφαῖος**, ὁ, *assistant* κορυφαῖος, rest. in *BGU* 347 I 13, II 11 (ii AD).

**ὑπόκρημνος**, delete the entry.

**ὑποκρῐ́νομαι II 4**, add 'ὑπεκρίνατο μανίαν Ael.*VH* 13.12'

**ὑπόκρῐσις II 1**, add 'transf., *imitation*, ἐρεθίζομαι πρὸς αὐτὰ[ν] ἁλίου δελφῖνος ὑπόκρισιν Pi.*fr.* 140b.15 S.-M.' **4**, delete the section.

***ὑποκρύσταλλος**, ον, *crystalline*, *PWash.Univ.* inv. 181, 221 (*ZPE* 74.85, ii/iii AD).

**˟ὑποκῠᾰνίζω**, *to have a darkish blue colour*, λίθος ἕτερος λάγγουρος· οὗτος ὑποκυανίζων Socr.Dion.*Lith.* 41.1 G.
**ὑπολανθάνω**, add '**II** perh. *go in ignorance of*, πάνθ' ὑπολανθάνετε τὰ βίου συνεχῶς μυστήρια σεμνά *IUrb.Rom.* 1169 (iii/iv AD).'
**ὑπολείβω**, after 'A.*Ag.* 69 (anap.)' insert '(codd., edd. ἀπο-)' and for 'pass.' read 'med.'
**˟ὑπόλειος**, ον, *rather soft* or *smooth*, μειράκιον .. ὑπόλειον Men.*Sic.* 201.
**ὑπόληψις II 3 b**, delete the section.
**ὑπολογή II**, add '*Hesperia* 9.68.105 (= revision of *IG* 2².463, 307/6 BC)'
**˟Ὑπολυμπιδία**, fem. adj. (*worshipped*) *at the foot of Olympus*, Ἀφροδείτηι Ὑπολυμπιδίαι *SEG* 34.630 (Maced., ii/iii AD).
**+ὑπολύριος**, ον, *placed under the lyre*, δόναξ Ar.*Ra.* 232, δόνακα δέ τινα ὑπολύριον οἱ κωμικοὶ ὠνόμαζον, ὡς πάλαι ἀντὶ κεράτων ὑποτιθέμενον ταῖς λύραις Poll. 4.62 (cf. *h.Merc.* 47ff.).
**ὑπομᾰλάκος**, add 'Ptol.*Tetr.* 162'
**ὑπομαρτῠρέω**, delete the entry (v. *Glotta* 50.95).
**ὕπομβρος**, after 'Ph.*Bel.* 82.28, 97.27' insert '*rain-affected, damp*, τὸν σῖτον *PMich.*inv. 3207 (*ZPE* 100.76, ii BC)'
**ὑπομένω II 2**, add '**b** *await in hope*, ὃ γὰρ βλέπει, τίς ὑπομένει; v.l. in *Ep.Rom.* 8.24; abs., Lxx *La.* 3.21.' add '**III** *undertake, shoulder* a task or office, *SEG* 18.27.3 (Attica, ii BC), *SEG* 31.122 (Attica, c.AD 121/2).'
**ὑπομήκης**, for '= ὑπόμακρος' read '*elongated*'
**+ὑπομηλίς**, ίδος, ἡ, perh, *service-berry, Sorbum torminale*, Pallad.*Agric.* 13.4; of gold objects in imitation of the fruit, used to adorn Artemis, *Didyma* 432.17 (iii BC), al.
**ὑπομιμνήσκω I**, add '**5** *summon to court*, *Cod.Just.* 3.2.4 pr., 10.11.8.5b.'
**ὑπόμνημα**, line 1, insert 'Dor., Aeol. ὑπόμνᾱμα *SEG* 30.1122 (Entella, iii BC), 32.1243 (Cyme), etc.' **I 2**, for this section read '*funerary monument*, *SEG* 33.1059, 1060 (Cyzicus, early Rom.imp.), etc., 24.1075 (Tomi, iii/iv AD)' **II 4**, add '**b** *registry of public documents*, *Cod.Just.* 1.3.45.14, 4.21.22.7.' **IV**, add 'addressed to a king, *SEG* 13.403 (Maced., iv BC)'
**ὑπομνημᾰτίζομαι**, add 'perh. also act., *SEG* 30.82 (Athens, c.AD 230)'
**ὑπομνημᾰτικός**, add '**II** subst., ὑπομνηματικός, ὁ, *commentator*, St.Byz. s.v. Ἄβιοι.'
**ὑπομνημᾰτισμός**, lines 1/2, delete 'of a shopping list' and for '*PFreib.* .. *UPZ* 62.12' read '*PFreib.* 53'
**ὑπομνημᾰτογρᾰφέω II**, add 'so act., *enter in minutes*, *PMerton* 26.16 (iii AD)'
**ὑπόμνησις**, add '**5** *notification of a summons*, *Cod.Just.* 2.2.4 pr., 10.11.8.4.'
**˟ὑπομόλυβδος**, ον, *containing a mixture of lead*, of adulterated coinage, *SEG* 26.72 (Athens, iv BC).
**ὑπομονή II 1**, add 'Lxx 4*Ma.* 1.11, al.; *enduring to do*, αἰσχρῶν ἔργων Thphr.*Char.* 6.1' **III**, for this section read '*hope*, Lxx *Ps.* 9.19, 61.5, etc. **2** that in which one's hope is placed, Lxx *Jb.* 14.19, ὑπομονὴ Ἰσραὴλ κύριε *Je.* 14.8, 17.13.'
**ὑπόμυξος**, for '*somewhat charged with mucus*' read '*characterized by mucus*'
**+ὑπομυξώδης**, ες, *having a mucous quality*, Gal. 18(1).363 14.
**ὑποναίω**, add '(unless to be taken as two wds.)'
**˟ὑπονᾱκόρεω**, *serve as* °ὑπονακόρος, *Lindos* 301 (i BC).
**˟ὑπονᾱκόρος**, ὁ, *sub-warden of a temple*, *Lindos* 295 (i BC).
**ὑπόνομος II 3**, add 'cf. *OGI* 483.163 (Pergamum, ii AD)'
**ὑπονόστησις**, of the Nile, add '*PBeatty Panop.* 2.8, 46 (AD 300)'
**ὑπόξῠλος**, transfer 'A.*Fr.* 286' to follow '*counterfeit*' in section 2
**ὑποοπλομᾰχος**, for '*Hesperia* 2.507' read 'in an ephebic catalogue, *SEG* 33.158.50'
**˟ὑποπαραδείκνῡμι**, *set down in a report* or (?)*sell by the procedures of* παράδειξις, *PTeb.* 1101.11 (AD 114).
**+ὑποπετρίδιος**, *dwelling under rocks*, ὄνειροι Alcm. 1.49 P. (wrongly expld. by Hdn. 2.237 as = ὑπόπτερος).
**ὑποπῐθηκίζω**, delete the entry (v. °πιθηκίζω).
**ὑποπῑμελος**, for '*somewhat fat*' read '*containing fat, fatty*'
**ὑποπίπτω I 2**, line 4, after 'Isoc. 7.12' insert '*Peripl.M.Rubr.* 16'
**ὑποπόδιον**, add 'ὑ. διπλοῦν, a device used for beating time with the foot, cf. °βάταλον, Sch.Aeschin. 1.126'
**ὑποπορφῠρίζω**, add 'Epiph.Const. in *Lapid.Gr.* 196.23'
**˟ὑποπρακτικός**, ή, όν, *subordinate*, Ptol.*Tetr.* 182 (s.v.l.; cf. ‡ὑποτακτικός in parallel passage in Heph.Astr. 2.19.21).
**ὑποπρό II**, for '*before*' read '*just previously*'
**ὑποπτάζομαι**, add 'act., *suspect*, *POxy.* 2274.8 (iii AD) as corrected in *TAPhA* 87.68'
**ὑποπτεύω**, add '**IV** in mystery rites, *hold the rank of* °ὑπόπτης, *SEG* 29.799 (Samothrace, late Hellen.).'
**ὑπόπτης**, add '**II** a rank of initiate (app. below μύστης), *SEG* 29.799 (Samothrace, late Hellen.); cf. ἐπόπτης II.'
**ὕποπτος**, add 'also **ὕποπτος** *BE* 1967.582 (Phrygia)'
**ὑπόπυος I**, after 'Hp.*VC* 15' insert '*Nat.Hom.* 12'
**˟ὑποπύργιον**, τό, rest., name of a tax, ἀπὸ ἐπικεφ(αλαίου) κ(αὶ) ὑποπυρ(γίου) *REG* 70.120.9 (Caesarea, vi/vii AD).
**ὑπόπῡρος 1**, for '*with .. secret fire*' read '*fiery*' **2**, after 'metaph.' insert '*fevered*'
**ὑπορθόω**, add 'vines, *PMich.*XIII 666.17 (vi AD)'
**ὑπορρᾰφή**, add 'written ὑποραφή *Edict.Diocl.* 7.48, 50, 51 (see also *SEG* 37.335)'
**˟ὑπόρραψις**, εως, ἡ, = ὑπορραφή, *Edict.Diocl.* 7.49.
**ὑπόρρῡσις I 2**, add 'Heras ap.Gal. 13.775.2'
**ὑπορύσσω**, line 2, after '(Hdt.) 6.18' insert 'Aen.Tact. 32.8, 37.7, al.'
**˟ὑπορώξ** or **ὑπορρώξ**, ῶγος, ἡ, perh. *underground passage*, prob. in Aq.*Is.* 2.19 (L.-R.).
**ὑποσείω I**, for this section read '*set in violent motion, twist back and forth*, οἱ δέ τ' ἔνερθεν ὑποσσείουσιν ἱμάντι Od. 9.385. **2** *cause to have a fit of trembling*, Hp.*Coac.* 159; *PMerton* 59.6 (ii BC). **3** *agitate, shake*, v.l. in Gal. 6.481.15 (v. ὑποσήθω); ἄρτους ὑποσείων (under the nose of dogs) Ael.*NA* 7.13 (codd.).' **II**, delete the section
**ὑποσήπω**, after 'ib. (Ael.*NA*) 1.51' add 'intr., ib. 15.18'
**ὑποσιώπησις**, after '*silence*' insert 'Ptol.*Tetr.* 192'
**ὑπόσκληρος**, add 'Gal. 13.421.17'
**ὑπόσομφος 1**, before 'Them.*Or.* 18.222d' insert 'fig. τὴν πόλιν ἀντὶ λαγαρᾶς καὶ ὑποσόμφου μεστὴν ἐποίησεν ἀγλαΐας'
**ὑποσόριον**, add '*SEG* 30.1395 (Philadelphia)'
**ὑποσπασμός**, for '*drawing secretly away*' read '*withdrawing* (of claims)'
**˟ὑποσπειρίτης**, ου, ὁ, *plinth, base*, *IGChr.* 10 (Panderma, iv/v AD).
**˟ὑπόσσομαι**, *contemplate* (*mentally*), ὑποσσόμενοι πραπίδεσσιν hex. in *POxy.* 3535 i 16 (ii AD).
**˟ὑπόσταθμον**, τό, *base, stand*, καρδόπου *IG* 1³.422.35 (Athens, v BC).
**˟ὑπόσταξις**, εως, ἡ, *discharge*, παρακολουθεῖ δὲ ἀεὶ τοῖς τὸ ἀκόνιτον πεπωκόσιν .. ὑγρὰ ὑπόσταξις Sch.Nic.*Al.* 24d Ge. (cf. ἀπόσταξις).
**ὑπόστᾰσις A 2**, for this section read '*upward pressure*, τοῦ κύματος (v.l. πνεύματος) Arist.*Mete.* 368ᵇ12, Hp.*Off.* 3' add '**4** κοιλίης ὑ. *constipation*, Hp.*Coac.* 108 (v.l. ἐπι-), 295.' **B II 4**, add 'Φοινίκων τοὺς γείτονας προσέλαβεν εἰς τὴν αὐτὴν ὁρμήν τε καὶ ὑ. Ael.*fr.* 59' add '**VII** *sum* or *amount on deposit*, *BGU* 432 ii(2).6 (AD 190; see *BGU* 2467).'
**ὑποστᾰ́της II**, delete '*Theol.Plat.* 3.7'
**+ὑποστάτις**, ιδος, ἡ, *that creates*, αἰτία Procl.*Theol.Plat.* 3.7.
**ὑποστέλλω I 2**, add '**b** *reduce* one's diet, Erasistr.ap.Gal. 11.201.7, *PPrincet.* 114.43 (*BASP* 12.77), cf. usage in section II 1.'
**+ὑπόστεμα**, v. ‡ὑπόστημα.
**ὑποστενᾰχίζω**, delete 'Δι'
**ὑπόστη**, after 'part of a tomb' insert 'perh. = *loculus*' and for '*BCH* 12.280, 281' read '*SEG* 16.696'
**ὑπόστημα**, add '**VI** (written -στεμα), *property in land* (cf. ὑπόστασις B VI), *PWürzb.* 18.12 (iv AD), *PMichael.* 33.7 (v AD).'
**ὑπόστολοι**, for 'officials .. Thessaly' read 'an organized group of worshippers, esp. of the Egyptian gods' and add '*SEG* 36.583 (Maced., 67/66 BC)'
**ὑπόστροφος**, delete 'cf. ὑπόφορος'
**˟ὑποστῡ́λωσις**, εως, ἡ, *under- or supporting colonnade*, *Poliorc.* 224.5.
**˟ὑποσφρᾱγίς**, ῖδος, ἡ, app. *seal at foot of document*, περίστροφος· ὁ τῆς ὑποσφραγῖδος τόπος Hsch.
**ὑποτάκτης**, add 'an ephebic official, *IG* 2².2051.101 (ὑβο- lapis)'
**ὑποτακτικός 4**, insert '*subordinate* (in quot., opp. αὐθεντικός)' Heph.*Astr.* 2.19.21 (cf. °ὑποπρακτικός)'; before '-τακτικόν' prefix '**b**'
**ὑποτάσσω** line 1, fut. ὑποταγήσομαι, for 'Cyran. 15' read '1*Ep.Cor.* 15.28, Cyran. 1.4.49 K.' **I**, add '*IG* 12(7).515 (Amorgos, ii BC)'
**ὑποτελής I**, add '**2** subst., *subject* (of a ruler), *Cod.Just.* 1.4.26.11.'
**ὑποτίθημι I 1**, add 'pass., *to be presented* to sight of audience, Sch.Ar.*Nu.* 1 H., cf. °ὑπόκειμαι I 2' **VII**, add '**3** *enter in one's accounts*, *IG* 2².1228.5 (ii BC).'
**ὑποτίμησις**, add '**3** *underestimating, toning-down*, ἡ γὰρ ὑ., φασίν, ἰᾶται τὰ τολμηρά Longin. 32.3.'
**ὑποτίμητος**, delete the entry.
**˟ὑπότονος**, ὁ, perh. = ὑποτόναιον, *threshold*, *Inscr.Délos* 442*A*229 (ii BC).
**ὑποτρίζω**, line 1, for 'cats' read 'γαλέαι' **2**, after 'of things' insert '*emit a sharp sound*'
**ὑπότροφος**, add '**II** subst., ἡ, *under-nurse*, in list of temple officials, *Inscr.Magn.* 117.10 (ii AD).'
**ὑπότρῡγος**, add 'Gal. 19.149.17'
**ὑποτρύζω**, for '[ὑποτρύ]ζουσιν ἀοιδῇ .. 1219.1' read 'θεσπεσίῃ λάλον ὕμνον ὑποτρύζοντος ἀοιδῇ Nonn.*D.* 39.359, cf. 17.374'
**ὑπουργέω 1**, add '**b** w. gen., *serve, be employed* in, Ἀκακίου ὑπουργοῦντος σιτικῆς *ITyr* 16.'
**˟ὑπούργησις**, εως, ἡ, *assistance*, *ICilicie* 113 (AD 590).
**ὑπουργία 1**, for '(Theangela)' read '*JÖAI* 11.71 (both Theangela,

iii/ii BC)' **2**, before 'pl.' insert '*work performed as a task*, Lib.*Or.* 11.89' add '**3** *job*, *office*, *Cod.Just.* 1.2.24.15.'

**ὑποφέρω**, line 2, after 'Il. 5.885' insert 'aor. subj. ὑποίσω *AP* 7.26.7 (Antip.Sid.)' **I 1**, add '*be borne* or *go underneath*, τῷ ἡλίῳ περὶ αὐτὴν (sc. γῆν) ὑποφερομένῳ Plu. 2.1006e' **V 2**, line 1, for '*bring* .. *BC* 5.6' read '*cause to fall*, *bring down*, App.*BC* 5.6 (in numbers); εἰς θρύψιν Lib.*Or.* 59.149'; line 3, after '(Hp.) 17.ιγ'' insert 'Arist.*Ath.* 25.1, 36.1'

*__ὑποφεύξιμος__, ον, *providing a way of escape*, Sch.A.R. 1.246.

**ὑποφήτης**, add '*BCH* 116.280.31 (Colophon, ii BC)'

**ὑποφθέγγομαι 2**, for '*reply*' read '*speak as if from the abdomen*' and transfer here fr. section 1 'ἐντὸς ὑ. .. Pl.*Sph.* 252c'

**ὑποφοινίσσομαι**, for 'pass.' read 'med.' and add 'also act., Hsch. s.v. ψαιθόν'

**ὑποφόρος I**, transfer 'τισι' to precede 'Plu. 2.774c'

*__ὑποφυάς__, άδος, ἡ, ?*undergrowth*, Hsch. s.v. μόλσον.

**ὑποφῠλᾰκία**, add '*TAM* 2(1).189, 284'

*__ὑπόφυλλα__, τά, app. part of an olive crown, *IG* 2².1476.11, *SEG* 38.143.18, *Ath.Asklepieion* v 29 (iii BC, s.v.ll.).

*__ὑποφυλλόω__, *strip off leaves at the base* of a vine, *SB* 10768.22 (iii BC).

*__ὑποχειριστής__, οῦ, ὁ, *administrative assistant*, *PVindob.Tandem* 22.6 (ὑποχιρ-, AD 64).

**ὑποχεύς**, add 'app. some device for catching fish, cf. ὑποχή, *POxy.* 3268.10, 3269.2 (iii AD)'

*__ὑποχλωρίζω__, perh. *to be yellowish*, Epiph.Const. in *Lapid.Gr.* 194.11.

*__ὑπόχνοος__, ον, *downy*, of a peach, Rh. 1.523.19.

*__ὑποχορήγημα__, ατος, τό, app. *something furnished* or *supplied*, *SEG* 30.1073.16 (Chios, 189/8 BC), unless to be divided as two wds., ὑπὸ χορηγημάτων.

+__ὑποχραίνω__, *make dirty underneath*, μὴ πόδες ἱμερόεντες ὑποχραίνοιντο κονίῃς Colluth. 232.

*__ὑποχρηστεύω__, *serve as* ὑποχρήστης (*assistant oracle-giver*), *Didyma* 353.18, 381.14.

*__ὑπόχρῑσις__, εως, ἡ, *smearing underneath*, Anon.Alch. 379.13 (ὑπόχρησιν codd.).

**ὑπόχρῡσος III**, delete '*gleaming* .. 1.31' add '**IV** *gleaming with gold*, μῆλα Philostr.*Im.* 1.31.'

*__ὑποχρύσωμα__, τό, perh. either *thin adhesive layer used as base for applying gold-leaf* or *gold paint*, *PKöln* 52.12, 60 (AD 263).

*__ὑπόχρως__, ῥυπόεις· ὑπόχρως Sch.Nic.*Al.* 470c Ge.

**ὑποχωρέω I 1**, line 6, after 'νέμεσθαι ὑποχωροῦντας' insert 'i.e. *walking backwards*' add '**4** of a coastline, *recede*, *Peripl.M.Rubr.* 12, 15, 29.'

**ὑποχώρησις I 2**, before '*CIG* 3705' insert 'perh. *latrine*'

*__ὑποψάλτης__, ου, ὁ, in Chr. worship, *subchanter*, *succentor*, *ITyr* 222B.

*__ὑποψῠχρόομαι__, *begin to grow cold*, Sch.Pi.*N.* 10.137.

**ὕπτιος II**, add 'ὑπτίου ποδός *of the upturned sole of the foot*, S.*fr.* 501.2 R.' add '**VII** ὕπτιον, τό, math., a *quadrilateral with no parallel sides*, Papp. 652.20; cf. °παρύπτιος.'

*__ὑπύ__, v. ὑπό.

*__ὑπώρα__, v. ‡ὀπώρα.

**ὑπωρόφιος 2**, line 3, (ὑπωρυφία), after '(Epid., iv BC)' insert 'also Aeol., *SEG* 30.1040 (Cyme, ii BC)'

**ὑρῐχός**, line 3, after '**συρίσκος**' insert 'Poll. 7.174'

+__ὕρχη__, ἡ, *earthenware jar*, Ar.*Vesp.* 676, ὕρχας οἴνου Poll. 10.74 (Ar.*fr.* 435 K.-A.), ὕ. ταρίχου *PSI* 428.8 (iii BC), ὑπογαστρίων ὕ. ib. 84; ὕρχη· ἐφ' ἧς τὰ φορτία φέρουσιν οἱ ναῦται Hsch.; perh. also τὸν (sc. λέβητα) ἐπ' *hυρ‹ϲ›κᾶι SEG* 30.500(b) (Delphi, vi BC); Aeolic acc. to Poll. 6.14, cf. αὐτίκα τὸ ὕρχας Αἰολικὸν ὂν ψιλοῦται.

**ὗς** (A), add '**IV** *pudenda muliebria*, Macho 332 G.'

**ὑσγῖνον**, line 5, after 'ἰσγένης ib.(*Edict.Diocl.*) 24.9-12' insert 'also γισγίνης ib. 19.41A'

**ὑσγῑνόσημος**, after '*Edict.Diocl.* 29.36, al.' insert 'γισγινοσήμων ib. 29.10'

**Ὕσπορος**, add '(app. a Hellenized form of a foreign name, also Ὑπόβαρος, Plin.*HN* 37.39 (= Ctes. 450 p.500 J.))'

**ὑσσωπίτης**, add 'perh. also *SEG* 30.956 (abbrev., Olbia, iii BC)'

+__ὕσταριν__, adv., accent uncertain, Elean equiv. of ὕστερον, *afterwards*, *Schwyzer* 424 (iv BC).

**ὑστέρημα**, add '*SB* 9257ʳ.6 (232 BC)'

*__ὑστερόμητις__, -ιος or -ιδος, masc. adj., *late in counsel*, Nonn.*D.* 13.540.

**ὑστερόποτμος**, add 'also applied to a second marriage, app. after the death of a first spouse, Hsch.'

**ὕστερος A II 1**, line 5, δεκάτῃ ὑ., add 'δεκάτει ὑστέραι *SEG* 32.110 (Athens, 273/2 BC)' **IV 1**, for this section read 'adv. ὕστερον, of place, *behind*, ὀπαδεῖν .. ὕ. *Trag.adesp.* 493 K.-S.; w. gen., ὕ. τῶν ἱππέων γίγνεσθαι X.*Cyr.* 5.3.42' **2 a**, add 'τῶι ὕστερον *SEG* 37.340.12-13 (Mantinea, iv BC)' **3**, ἐξ ὑστέρου, add 'Hp.*Coac.* 418, *PHels.* 10.15 (ii BC)' add '**4** of logical relationship, ὑστέρως *in a secondary* or *posterior way*, Arist.*Ph.* 195ᵃ30, cf. °πρότερος A IV 2.'

**ὕφαιμος**, line 5, for 'Men.*Epit.* 479' read 'Men.*Epit.* 900 S.'

**ὑφαίνω II**, line 8, after '*Hymn.Is.* 14' add 'πολλοὶ γὰρ φθόνῳ δίκας οὐκ ἀδικήματός τινος .. ὑφαίνοντες *Cod.Just.* 8.10.12.7'

**ὕφαλμος**, after '*somewhat salt*' insert '*brackish*' and add 'Paul.Aeg. 7.3 (231.8 H.)'

**ὕφᾰλος I 1**, line 1, after '*under the sea*' insert 'ὕ. τείρετο, of Danae, A.*fr.* 47a.2.31 R. (anap.)' **II**, after '*somewhat salt*' insert '*brackish*'

**ὑφάπτω I 2**, add 'E.*Ba.* 778'

*__ὑφέννῡμι__, app. *wear as an undergarment*, pass. plpf. στάδιον ὑφέεστο χιτῶνα Call.*fr.* 293 Pf., cf. ὑποέστης.

**ὕφεσις**, add '**IV** act of *passing up* to, ἡ ἐκ τῆς ἀριστερᾶς χειρὸς ἐς τὴν δεξιὰν ὕφεσις τῶν ἀκοντίων ὀξεῖα Arr.*Tact.* 38.3.' deleting this quot. fr. section I 1.

**ὑφέσπερος**, for '*AP* 5.304 (better divisim)' read '*AP* 5.305'

*__ὑφηγηλάζω__, *go before*, *guide*, Arat. 893 (tm.).

**ὑφήγησις II**, add '(v. °ὑπήχησις)'

**ὑφηγητικός**, after '*fitted for guiding*' insert 'Alcin.*Intr.* 6 p. 158 H.'

*__ὑφῆλιξ__, ικος, ὁ, ἡ, *below in age*, *BE* 1974.368 (Callatis).

*__ὑφῐερεύς__, έως, ὁ, *assistant priest*, *SEG* 16.452 (Delos, 109/8 BC), *IG* 5(2).49 (Tegea, AD 78); also ὑποϊερεύς, *IMylasa* 544.5.

**ὑφίημι II**, line 2, after 'c. gen.' insert 'δρόμω Alc. 117(*b*).6 L.-P.'

*__ὑφιππάρχης__, ου, ὁ, *deputy to a* ἱππάρχης, *SEG* 16.864 (Abu Simbel).

**ὑφιστάνω**, add 'Procl.*Inst.* 25 D.'

**ὑφίστημι A I 4**, line 2, delete '*treat as* .. 5.1.4' **B I**, add '**3** w. dat., *stand in the way* of, i.e. *block from sight*, νύκτα δὲ γαῖα τίθησιν ὑφισταμένη φάεεσσι Emp. B 48 D.-K.' **V**, add 'cf. Hp.*Coac.* 281'

**ὑφόλμιον II**, for 'part .. II 5' read 'cup-shaped mouthpiece of an aulos, in which the reed was inserted'

+__ὐχηρος__, ά, Cypr. prob. = ἐπίχειρον II 1, *wage*, gen. sg. *u-ke-ro-ne* ὐχέρōν *ICS* 217.5, 15 (Idalion, v BC).

**ὑψαύχην 2**, add 'ἢ διέπεις ὄχθους ὑψαύχενας ἀκρωρείους Orph.*H.* 32.4' **3**, add 'also in prose, Him.*Or.* 18.5, 47.1, 63.6 C., Sopat.Rh. 8.188.13 W.'

*__ὑψηλοποιέω__, *raise*, *pile up*, Sch.E.*Or.* 402.

*__ὑψηλόπορος__, ον, *moving on high*, Hsch. s.v. ὑψιφοίτης.

**ὑψηλός 1**, add '**b** *on the high sea*, *Peripl.M.Rubr.* 57, cf. °ὕψος I 2. **c** ὑψηλόν, τό, perh. *long robe*, *PHarris* 109.5 (iii/iv AD), *POxy.* 2054.4 (vii AD).'

*__ὑψηλοτᾰπεινότης__, ητος, ἡ, *difference between the top and the bottom*, Anon.Alch. 435.17.

*__ὑψηλόφρονος__, ον, *lofty-minded*, *PMag.* 5.482.

**ὑψῐβίας**, add 'rest. in *IG* 4²(1).129.5'

**ὑψίβρομος**, delete the entry (v. °ὑψίδρομος).

**ὑψίγονος**, add 'as pers. n., e.g. *SEG* 25.771 (Moesia, Rom.imp.)'

*__ὑψίδρομος__, ον, *travelling on a lofty course*, Orph.*H.* 19.1, Nonn.*D.* 38.310. **b** of water, *running at a high* or *flood level*, ib. 13.523, 23.253.

*__ὑψιέπης__, ες, *high-flown*, υψιέπης rest. in *PMich.*inv. 6 (*ZPE* 93.166, iii AD).

*__ὑψῐκελεύθης__, ου, masc. adj., *treading a lofty path*, *PMag.* 2.89.

*__ὑψῐκέρᾱς__, ᾱτος, *having lofty horns*, ὑψικέρατα πέτραν a *high-peaked* rock, Pi.*fr.* 325 S.-M.: acc. fem., ὑψικέραν βοῦν B. 16.22 S.-M.; also -κέρης, ητος, Choerob.*in Theod.* 1.166 H.

*__ὑψῐκέραυνος__, ον, *making lightning on high*, Hsch. (gloss defective).

+__ὑψῐκέρης__, v. °ὑψικέρας.

**ὑψίκερως**, delete 'metaplast. acc.' to end; v. °ὑψικέρας.

**ὑψίκρημνος I**, add '*Trag.adesp.* 445a K.-S.'

**ὑψῐπᾰγής**, for '*high-built*, *towering*' read 'perh. *ice-capped*'

+__ὑψῐπόδης__, ου, masc. adj., *standing to a great height*, Nonn.*D.* 20.81, 37.686.

**ὑψίπολις**, for 'citizen .. ἄπολις' read '*having a lofty city*'

**ὑψίπους**, for '*high-footed* .. *lofty*' read '*standing in the heights*, i.e. of heavenly nature'

**ὑψίπῠλος**, after 'Il. 16.698' insert 'Ibyc. 1(*a*).14 P.'

*__ὑψίτῠπος__ or **-τῠπος**, ον, perh. *striking at a great height*, *Lyr.adesp.* 7(*d*).7 P.

**ὑψιφᾰής**, add '*BKT* 5.2 p. 143.4'

*__ὑψῐφρονέω__, *to have proud thoughts*, Sch.Pi.*P.* 2.91.

+__ὑψῐχαίτᾱς__, ᾱ, ὁ, perh. *having proud* or *splendid locks*, Pi.*P.* 4.172 S.-M.

**ὕψος I**, add '**2** *high* (*open*) *sea*, *Peripl.M.Rubr.* 33. **3** astrol. = ὕψωμα I 2, opp. βάθος, Vett.Val. 241.25.'

**ὑψόω**, before '*lift high*' insert '(ὑψέω in Hp.*Praec.* 7, v. infra)'

**ὕω I 2**, lines 6/7, for 'prayer .. earth' read 'cry at the Eleusinia'

+__ὑωνός__, v. ‡υἱωνός.

# Φ

φάαντερος, after '*more brilliant*' insert 'Call.*fr.* 238.16 Pf.'

φάβα, Lat. *faba*, add '*BGU* 2359.10 (iii AD)'

*φᾱβᾶτον, τό, *bean flour* or *cake*, *PRyl.* 630*.406 (IV AD), [φ]οβάθου (sic) *PPrag.* I 90.9 (vi/vii AD).

*φαβρικήσιος, ὁ, *armourer*, φαβρικησίου καὶ δουκηναρίου *SEG* 26.1314, 1320 (both Sardis, iv/vi AD).

*φάβριξ, ικος, ἡ, *workshop*, *PBeatty Panop.* 1.214 (AD 298), *SEG* 24.911.6 (Thrace, iv AD), cf. Lat. *fabrica*.

*φᾰγεδαινίζω, *afflict with ulcerous sores*, Aq. 1*Ki.* 5.6, 7.10.

*φᾰγίον, τό, *food*, *Mim.adesp.* 15.34 (ed. proparox., but cf. mod. Gk. το φαγί), also prob. at *ODouch* 34.

*φᾱγός, v. φηγός.

φᾱεινός, line 2, after 'φαεννός' insert '(pers. n. Φαβεννός *SIG* 422.7, Delphi, w. -β- for -ϝ-)'

φᾱεσίμβροτος, after '(Eleusis, ii/iii AD)' insert 'of Christ, *PBodm.* 29.168 (iv AD)'

φαιδῐμόεις, add '*GVAK* 11.2'

φαίνω, line 11, after 'Sophr. 83' insert 'Aeol. πέφαννε Alc. 206.5 L.-P.'; line 16, (fut. φανήσομαι), add 'Pl.*Hp.Ma.* 300d' **B II 1**, four lines fr. end delete 'ὡς' before 'ἀγαθοί'

φαιοχῑ́των, for '(where .. causa)' read 'app. φαϊο-'

*φαιώδης, ες, *dark* in complexion, *Vit.Sapph.* in *POxy.* 1800 *fr.* 1.22.

φακῆ, for 'pearls before swine' read 'of an incongruous juxtaposition of the precious and the common'

φάκιον, add '**II** (?)*small flask*, *Pap.Lugd.Bat.* XXV 13.12 (Byz.).'

*φακτιωνάριος, ὁ, Lat. *factionarius*, *leader of a faction*; φ. Ἀλεξανδρίας καλλιείνων *leader of the* Blue *faction* at Alexandria, *PCair.Isidor.* 58.13 (iv AD); Ἀμμω(νίου) το(ῦ) καλοῦ φακ(τιωναρίου) *SEG* 34.1562 (Egypt).

*φάκτον, τό, μέτρον παρὰ Ἀρκάσι, κοτύλαι ἀττικαὶ τρεῖς Cyr.; cf. Myc. *pa-ko-to* (dual), name of a vessel.

φακτονάριον, delete the entry (v. °πακτ-).

*φᾰλαγγικός, ὁ, *soldier in a phalanx*, πεζοὶ μὲν ἐν μέσοισι καὶ φαλαγγικοί Ezek.*Exag.* 198 S.

*φᾰλαίνιος, ὁ, *resembling a whale* (as nickname), Διόγνητος ὁ φ. ἐπικαλούμενος *Hist.adesp.* in *POxy.* 2399.35 (i BC).

φᾰλακρός **I 1**, line 4, after 'E.*Cyc.* 227' insert 'cf. A.*fr.* 47a.24 R.; τὸ -όν, S.*fr.* 171.3, 314.368 R.'

*Φαλερνός, ὁ, *Falernian wine*, Lang *Ath.Agora* XXI He27 (iii AD).

*φᾰλητάριον, τό, dim. of φάλης, *Mim.adesp.* 15.29.

φαλίπτει, add 'cf. φαλός II'

φάλλαινα **II**, after 'Sch.)' insert '**III** ἡ ἐν τῇ κεφαλῇ θρίξ Hsch.'

*φαλλίων, ονος, = φαλλοφόρος, Suid. s.v. Φαλῆς.

*φαλλῳδός, όν, *singing phallic songs*, Atil.Fort. p. 293.23.

φᾱμιστός, for '*Bull.* .. i AD)' read '*GVI* 1861 (lapis -σθα; Leontopolis, i AD)'

φᾰνερός **I 5 b**, line 6, for 'rarely .. *Ages.* 5.7' read 'more rarely ἐν φ., Th. 4.73.2, X.*Ages.* 5.7, *AP* 12.66'

*φᾰνίζω, = φανερόω, *Stud.Pal.* 20.75 (iv AD).

φᾰνός, ἡ, όν **I 1**, add 'neut. pl. *well-lit parts*, X.*Oec.* 9.3'

*φαντήρ, ῆρος, ὁ, epith. of Zeus, *that displays* or *brings to light*, *SEG* 17.406 (Chios, iv BC).

φάος **I 3**, pl. *eyes*, add 'Call.*Dian.* 53, 71, 211, Nic.*Al.* 24, al.'

*φᾱοσφόρος, v. φωσφόρος.

φᾰραγγίτης, add 'epith. of (prob.) Heracles, [Ἡρακ]λῇ Φαραγγείτῃ *SEG* 24.1037 (Moesia, ii/iii AD)'

φαρκίς, after '*wrinkle*' insert 'Simon. in *POxy.* 3965 *fr.* 27.15'

φάρμᾰκον **I 1**, add 'φ. δηλητήρια *SIG* 37*A*1 (Teos, v BC), 985.18 (Philadelphia), 1180.2 (Cnidus)' **4**, delete 'φ. δηλητήρια .. v BC)' at end add 'perh. Myc. *pa-ma-ko*'

φαρμᾰκοποσία **1**, after 'Hp.' insert '*Nat.Hom.* 7'

*Φαρμουθιακός, ή, όν, *of the Egyptian month* Φαρμοῦθι (March-April), Φ. ἐργασία *POxy.* 1631.13, 3354.12 (both iii AD).

φάρξις, add '= φράξις II'

φᾶρος, at end add '(form φάρϝος) Myc. *pa-we-a* (pl.)'

φάρος, ὁ (or ἡ), add '**II** medic., *lozenge*, Asclep.Jun.ap.Gal. 13.97.4.'

φάρος, τό, for 'Alcm. 23.61' read 'Alcm. 1.61 P.' and for 'Antim.*Eleg.* p. 293 B.' read 'Antim. 119 Wy.'

*φαρσάγγιον, τό, = παρασάγγης, *parasang*, *Cat.Cod.Astr.* 7.102.30.

+φάρω, v. ‡φέρω.

*φᾱσᾱνάριος, v. °φασιανάριος.

φάσγᾰνον, after 'Pi.*N.* 1.52[b]' insert 'A.*Ag.* 1262'; at end add 'Myc. *pa-ka-na* (pl.), *swords* or *daggers*'

φασήλιον **1**, after 'dim. of φάσηλος' insert '(*bean*)' add '**II** *small boat*, Βερενίκης φ. ἀγωγῆς διακοσίων *PRyl.* 576.7 (ii BC).'

φάσηλος, line 1, for parenthesis read '(fem. in Colum. 10.377)' **II**, delete 'hence Lat. *phaselus*' and add 'App.*BC* 5.95'

*φᾱσιᾱνάριος, ὁ, *pheasant-farmer*, *Dig.* 32.1.66; in form φασαν- *IG* 10(2).1.857 (iii AD), *Corinth* 8(3).561 (v/vi AD).

φᾱσιᾱνός, add 'also φασιανὴ θήλεια, the female bird, *Edict.Diocl.* 4.19'

φᾱσίολος, add 'πάσωλος *Gloss.*'

φάσις (B) **II 4**, after '*sentence*' insert 'Thd.*Su.* 55'

φασκία, after '*Dura*[4] 93 (iii AD)' insert 'pl., *PRyl.* 627 ii 41, as some kind of garment, ζεῦγος φασκιῶν *PKöln Ketouba* 17'

*φασκιάρια, τά, fr. Lat. *fascis*, *bundle*, *SEG* 37.1186.43 (Takina, AD 212/213).

*φασκίδιον, τό, perh. dim. of φασκία, *bandage*, *PWarren* 18.16 (iii AD).

*φασκίς, gloss on διάφυσον, Hsch. (διάφυσος La.), also pl. φασκίδες, gloss on βασκευταί, id.

*φᾰσούλιον, = φασήλιον (in quot., sense 1); sp. φασούρ-, *PMich.*XIII 666.33 (vi AD), cf. mod. Gk. φασόλι, φασούλι.

φάσσα, at end for 'Luc.*Sol.* 7 coined a masc. form φάττος' read 'masc. φάττος suggested in a *reductio ad absurdum*, Luc.*Sol.* 7'

*φᾱταρχ-, v. °φρᾱτριαρχ-.

φᾰτίζω **III**, before 'Pass.' insert '*give a name to*, Rhian. 13'

φᾰτις **II 2**, add '*AP* 7.352 (?Mel.)'

φατνωματικός, for 'in form .. (cf.' read 'τὸ φ. (in form παθνω-, cf.'

*φατριασμός, v. φρατριασμός.

*φατρῖται, οἱ, members of a φ(ρ)άτρα, *IG* 5(2). 446.8 (Megalopolis, i BC).

φάττος, for 'φάσσα' read '‡φάσσα'

φαῦλος, line 3, add 'Hdt. 2.173.2' **II 5**, after 'Hp.*Aph.* 2.32' insert 'Macho 71 G.'

φαυροφόρος, for 'Call.*Fr.anon.* 132 .. cod. B)' read '*Suppl.Hell.* 1042'

φαυστήρ, for pres. def. read '*window*' and add 'cf. φωστήρ II'

φαύω, add 'Cypr. *Kafizin* 47'

*Φεβρουάριος, Lat. *Februarius*, *February*, also Φεβράριος, etc., Plu.*Rom.* 21.3, *Num.* 18.2, al., Lyd.*Mens.* 1.17, *SEG* 30.1212 (Rome), Mitchell *N.Galatia* 466, *IG* 14.142.

*φέγγασπις, ιδος, ἡ, *having a shield of light*, of Athena, poet. in *PKöln* 245.9 (iii AD).

φέγγος **I 1 d**, for 'Sosiph. 3.1' read 'Sosiph. 3.3 S.'

Φειδιακός, for '*made by Phidias*' read '*made in the style of Phidias*' and add 'neut. subst. *JRCil.* 1.271'

φείδομαι **IV**, line 9, after 'from doing' insert 'Call.*Epigr.* 1.13 Pf.'

φειδωλία **II**, for 'τόξου' read 'τόξων'

φελλεύς **II**, delete the section transferring quots. to section I.

*φελλοχᾰλαστέω, *release the cork floats* from fishing nets, *IParion* 5.10.

*φεμινάλια, τά, Lat. *feminalia*, *trousers* or *leggings*, Hsch. (s.v. ἀναξυρίδας; sp. φημ-); also φιμινάλια, Phot. α 1578 Th. (s.v. ἀναξυρίδας), *PVindob.*G 41673.2 (*Tyche* 1.88, vi/vii AD).

*φενέστρα, ἡ, Lat. *fenestra*, *window*, *PLond.* 481[v].28 (iv AD).

*φενίκουλα, ἡ, Lat. **faenicula*, perh. some kind of hay-implement or equipment, *Edict.Diocl.* 15.21.

φεννίς, add 'Eust. 1554.35'

φερέζῠγος, add '**2** *benched*, νᾶα φ[ερ]έσδυγον Alc. 249.3 L.-P. (cf. ζυγόν III 1).'

*φερεντάριοι, Lat. *ferentarii*, τάγμα στρατιωτικόν Hsch.

φερέοικος **I**, add 'of Byzas, Cadmus, Nonn.*D.* 3.365, 4.33'

φερεπτόλεμος, for '*Jahresh.* 18 *Beibl.* 35' read '*GVAK* 47.2'

*φερέπῡρος, ον, *wheat-bearing*, *Didyma* 496*B*5 (ii AD).

φερέσβῐος, add 'A.*fr.* 204b.12 R., Ion Trag. 7 S.'

φερνά (= φερνή II), for '*portion* of victim' read '*portion* of offerings'

*φερνίκουλον, τό, *dowry*, *PMich.*inv. 1373 (*ZPE* 21.26, iii AD).

*φερνιμαία, ἡ, app. some legal process involving a dowry, *SEG* 33.1177 (Lycia, AD 43).

*φερνῷος, ον, *of a dowry*, *BE* 1970.512 (Lydia).

*Φερρόφαττα, v. °Περσεφόνη.

*Φερσέφασσα, v. Περσεφόνη.

*Φερσεφόνα, -όνεια, -όνειος, v. Περσεφόνη.

*Φερσοπόνη, v. °Περσεφόνη.

*Φερσοφάσα, v. °Περσεφόνη.

φέρτατος I 2, (form φέριστος), delete 'mostly voc.' and add 'SEG 31.291 (Corinth, late Rom.imp.)'

*Φερφερέτᾱς, v. °Περφερέτας.

φέρω, line 1, φάρω, add 'EM 114.20' I, line 7, after 'E.Hec. 762' insert 'med. [τὴν] ὠδεῖνα μίην γα[στρὸς] ἐνεγκαμένη Mitchell N.Galatia 149'

Φετιάλιοι, line 2, after 'sg.' insert 'Φητιᾶλις Mon.Anc.Gr. 4.7'

*Φετταλός, v. Θεσσαλός.

φηγῐνέος, read 'φηγῑνεος' and after 'Maec.' insert 'or Maccius'

*φηγοειδής, ές, acorn-shaped, Ath.Asklepieion iv 126.103 (iii BC).

*φηλάρρην, ενος, ὁ, sham-male, φ. μοιχός Sen.Contr. 1.2.23.

φήληξ, add 'Ar.fr. 541 K.-A.'

φήμη I 1, line 10, delete 'φήμη .. Hel. 820' add 'b vehicle of a prophetic voice, oracle, E.Hel. 820, Pl.Lg. 738c.'

φημί, line 21, after 'Hdt. 3.153' insert 'Antipho 5.51, Isoc. 5.119'; line 32, after 'Pi.N. 9.43' insert 'Arc. subj. 3 sg. φᾶτοι SEG 37.340.21 (Mantinea, iv BC)'; line 33, for 'A.R. 2.500' read 'A.R. 1.988, 4.555 II, add 'w. acc., φησὶ τούσδε τοὺς στίχους Certamen 95' III, line 4, after 'οὔ φημι' insert '(so οὐκέτι, οὔπω, etc. φ.)'; line 10, before 'id.(Pl.)Phdr.' insert 'Ar.Nu. 1325' IV, add 'w. acc. of person, Ἑρμῆς γάρ νιν ἔφησε θεαῖς Ταθνηι προπολεύειν CEG 860 (Cnidos, vi BC)' at end add '(form φαμί) Myc. 3 sg. pa-si'

φημίζω I 3, for 'Call.Aet. 3.1.14, 58' read 'Call.fr. 75.14, 58 Pf.' 4, delete 'ὃ ἐφήμισεν .. xi 3'

φήρ, line 2, after 'sg.' insert 'Alc. 286(b).3 L.-P.'

φήρεα, delete the entry.

*φήρε(ι)ος, α, ον, belonging to satyrs, satyr-like; neut. pl. subst. swelling of glands near or beneath the ears (such as are attributed to satyrs), Hp.Epid. 6.3.6; perh. also in Gal. 19.151.

φθείρ I 1, after 'louse' insert 'or tick' 2, after 'lice' insert 'or other parasites' III, add 'Sch.Lyc. 1383'

φθείρω II 1, after '1' insert '(cf. ἀνα-, εἰσ-, προσ-, συμπερι-)'

*φθῑνάριον, = φθίνα II, kind of olive, SB 10727.2 (ii/iii AD).

φθῐνοπωρίς I, add 'φ. ὧραι rest. in Call.fr. 43.40 Pf. (addenda)'

φθίω II, add 'τό τε φέρον καὶ τὸ ἀλλοιοῦν καὶ τὸ αὖξον ἢ φθίνον Arist.Ph. $243^{e}39$'

Φθῑώτης (s.v. Φθία), line 2, delete 'cf. E.Tr. 575' and after 'as adj.' insert 'Φθιώτας .. ναούς E.Tr. 575'

φθογγή, line 1, after 'poet. form of φθόγγος' insert '(also in late prose, e.g. Plu. 2.613e, Cat.Ma. 13.4, Crass. 23.8)'

*φθοϊκός, ή, όν, consumptive, Asclep.Jun.ap.Gal. 13.101.13.

φθόϊς, before 'ὁ' insert '(also φθοῖς Eust. 1753.2)'; line 3, before 'acc.' insert 'nom. and' and after 'φθοῖς' insert 'Clem.Al.Protr. 2.19'

φθόνος I 1 b, add 'AP 7.117 (Zenodotus)'

φθορία, delete the entry.

-φῐ, -φῐν, delete the article.

φῐάλη, after lemma insert 'non-Att.-Ion. φιάλα, Cypr. pi-a-la, ICS 177 (vi BC)' I 2, line 2, after 'libations' insert 'Sapph. 44.29 L.-P.' at end for 'The form φιέλη .. p. 389 P.' read 'forms: φιέλη IMylasa 301.16, ILabraunda 92.1-2, cf. Moer. p. 389 P.; φιηάλα, φιέλα Myc. pi-a$_2$-ra, pi-je-ra$_3$ (pl.)'

φῐαληφόρος, after 'Locrian priestess' insert 'an office originally held by a boy, ὁ φιαληφόρος' and add 'fem., pl., at Athens in the cult of the Great Mother, IG $2^2$.1328.10 (ii BC)'

φῐάλιον, add 'also φιέλιον IMylasa 897 (in EA 13.9)'

φῐάλλω, add 'cf. ἐφίαλεν· ἐπεχείρησεν and ἠφίαλεν· ἐπεχείρησεν Hsch.'

φίβλα, delete 'Suppl.Epigr. 2.776 (Dura)'

*φιβλατώριον, τό, cloak fastened by a fibula, Edict.Diocl. 19.65, al., φιβουλατώριον ib. 19.24, al.; φιβλατώριον περιβόλαιον Περσικόν Suid., cf. °ἱμφειβλατώριον.

*φίβλον, τό, equiv. of Lat. fibula, SEG 7.371 (Dura, ii AD), 2.776 (iii AD).

*φιδάκνιον, v. ‡πιθάκνιον.

*φιδεικομ(μ)ισσάριος, α, ον, Lat. fideicommissarius, ἐπιστολή PMasp. 151.54, 312.25 (both vi AD).

*φιδεικόμμισσον, τό, Lat. fideicommissum, Just.Const. Δέδωκεν 6; sp. φιδικ- Cod.Just. 6.48.1.1.

*φίδνα· ῥίζα ἡ Ἀχίλλειος καλουμένη Hsch.

*φίκατι, v. °εἴκοσι.

φικιδίζω, delete the entry (v. Aristopho 3 K.-A.).

*φίκις, ιδος, ἡ, app. buttocks, POxy. 3070.5, perh. PHeid. 190 fr. 1.75, v. ZPE 30.36 (for accent: Hdn.Gr. 1.88.35 codd. [Κίκις L.]).

+φικιῶ, desiderat. fr. same stem as φίκις, Suid. (v. ZPE 52.56).

φῑκοπήδᾰλος, for 'dub. sens.' read 'having a rudder in the shape of a fig-leaf' and add 'PCair.inv. 10580/10488 (ZPE 20.158)'

*φῐλαβάρσακος, ὁ, friend of (the town) Abarsacus, IApam. 103.1 (Pylai).

*φῐλάγγελοι, οἱ, members of a religious (app. Chr.) society, Φιλαγγέλων συνβίωσις SEG 31.1130 (Phrygia, iii AD).

*φῐλαγρίππας, ου, ὁ, member of a cult of Agrippa, Robert Hell. 11/12.226.

φῐλᾰδέλφεια, add 'neut. sg. also of a building in commemoration of Φ., Inscr.Délos 400.38 (ii BC)'.

φῐλᾰδελφία, add 'ICilicie 16 (AD 209/11)'

φῐλάδελφος, add 'epith. of the Nymph at Kafizin, Kafizin 300 (225/218 BC); fem. -α IPamph. 154'

*φῐλᾰδελφοσύνη, ἡ, love of brother or sister, An.Boiss. 4.408.

φῐλᾰθήναιος, add 'Isoc.Ep. 5.2'

+φῐλάκανθις (cod. -θίς), ιδος, fem. adj. bony, of fish, AP 6.304 (Phan.).

*φιλάκουον, τό, Egyptian name for κληματῖτις, Ps.-Dsc. 4.180.

φῐλάκρᾱτος, line 2, for 'Simon. 183.5' read 'AP 7.24.5 ([Simon.])'

φῐλαλληλία, after 'mutual love' insert 'Diog.Oen.fr. 21.8 S.'

φῐλαναγνώστης, after 'of reading' insert 'D.S. 1.77.1'

φῐλανδρία I, add 'TAM 4(1).124' II, for this section read 'excessive desire (of women) for men, E.Andr. 229, cf. Hermog.Id. 2.5'

φῐλανθρωπεύομαι I 1, add 'abs., Men.Dysc. 573'

φῐλάνθρωπος I 1, add 'as an honorific description, SEG 31.901 (Caria, i AD)' 2, add 'of Asclepius, SEG 37.1019 (Pergamum, ii AD)'

φῐλάοιδος, line 1, delete 'or singers'; line 2, after 'musical' insert 'φιλάοιδον λιγύραν χελύνναν Sapph. 58.12 L.-P.' and after '(Antip. Sid.)' insert 'Nonn.D. 1.415'

*φῐλᾰπᾰμεύς, έως, ὁ, friend of Apamea, τὸ συνέδριον τῶν φιλαπαμέων IApam. T 8 (Perinthos).

φῐλαπεχθημοσύνη, after 'D. 54.37' insert 'Isoc. 15.315'

φῐλαπεχθήμων, after 'D. 24.6' insert 'of words' and transfer 'Isoc. 8.65' to follow, adding 'id. 12.249, al.'

φίλαυλος, for 'flute' read 'aulos'

φῐλᾰχαιός, add 'cf. pers. n. Φιλάχαιος IG 5(2).159 (Tegea, Lacon. dial., v BC)'

φῐλεκᾱγᾰθία, delete the entry.

*φῐλέννομος, ον, loving those who keep the law, φιλόθεος φ. Χριστοῦ MAMA 1.237 (Laodicea Combusta).

*φῐλεξᾰπάτης, ου, ὁ, ἡ, fond of deceit, AP 5.164 (Asclep.).

φῐλέρημος, line 3, for 'AP 5.8' read 'AP 5.9'

φίλερως, after 'amorous' insert 'AP 5.206 (Leon.Tarent.), Nic.fr. 16 G.-S.'

+φῐλευνος, ον, libidinous, Anacreont. 1.7 W. 2 devoted to one's marriage(-bed), SB 10162(546).2 (iii/iv AD).

φῐλεύτακτος, for 'devoted to discipline' read 'well disciplined'

*φῐλεφέσιος, ὁ, loving the Ephesians, IEphes. 1381a.11, 1545.6.

*φῐληγορία, ἡ, poet. -ίη, friendly speech, GVI 1864 (Athens, ii/iii AD).

φῐληδέω, at end after 'c. part.' insert 'φ. διέλκων Ar.l.c.'

Φῐλήσιος I, add 'Arr.Peripl.M.Eux. 2.2'

φῐλήτης, line 8, for 'Call.Hec. 1.4.11' read 'Call.fr. 260.65 Pf.'; line 11, after 'the papyri of' insert 'Hippon. 79.10, 102.12 W.'

φῐλητός I, add 'γυνὴ φ. IG 12(3).910; sup. -τότατος GVI 1899.2 (Pisidia, ii/iii AD)'

φίλητρον, delete 'f.l. .. (Crates)'

φῐλήτωρ I 1, for '(Cretan)' read '(Cretan acc. to Str. l.c.), Call.fr. 23.4 Pf.' 2, delete '(τῷδε .. darling)'

φῐλιακός 1, add 'PRyl. 28.99 (iv AD)'

φῐλικός, add '2 φ. μέλος a love-song, Theoc. 10.22.'

φίλιος I 2, add 'of the Muses, Mitchell N.Galatia 146'

Φῐλίππειος I, add 'epith. of Zeus, IG 12(2).526 (Eresus, end iv BC)'

φίλιππος, add '?Alcm. 168 P., B. 3.69 S.-M.'

*φῐλοβάναυσος, ον, fond of vulgarity, μνησικάκους, φιλοβαναύσους, ἀνευφράντους Heph.Astr. 2.15.12.

*φῐλοβάσᾰνος, ον, fond of torment, Ptol.Tetr. 161.

φῐλοβάσκᾰνος, delete the entry (v. °φιλοβάσανος).

*φῐλόβροτος, ον, fond of mortals, MAMA 7.582; cf. φιλόμβροτος.

+φῐλογέρων, οντος, ὁ, loyal to the Elders (γερουσία), Hesperia suppl. 6.163 no. 52.5 (Apamea, ii AD = IGRom 4.783).

*φιλόγῠνος, ον, = φιλογύνης, Lys.fr. 122 S.

*φῐλοδέμνιος, for 'loving the bed' read 'libidinous'

*φῐλοδεσποτεύομαι, love acting as a despot, Anaxil. 42 K.-A.

*Φῐλοδιόνῡσοι, οἱ, friends of Dionysus, name of an association, Didyma 502.1 (ii AD).

φῐλόδοξος, line 2, delete 'Pl.R. 480a' add '2 fond of (mere) belief, (opp. true knowledge), Pl.R. 480a.'

φιλοζέφῠρος, add 'as epith. of Arsinoe, Hedylus ap.Ath. 11.497d'

φιλόζωος I 2 b, delete the section transferring quots. to section 2 a.

*φῐλοθάλᾰμος, ον, loving the bridal-chamber, epith. of Aphrodite, Ps.-Callisth. 12.16.

*φῐλοθάλασσος, loving the sea, OA 6.46 (Cyprus, iii/iv AD); also -θάλαττος, Cat.Cod.Astr. 7.201.1.

φῐλόθεος, add 'as honorific epith., SEG 32.501 (Thespiae, i BC/i AD), TAM 5(1).457'

φῐλοθύτης, add 'Philostr. VA 4.19, 5.21'

*φῐλοΐδιος, α, ον, *loving one's own*, in quot., of a good wife, *DAW* 1896(6) no. 178.

*φίλοικος, ον, *loving one's home*, τρόπον φίλανδρον [καὶ φίλ]οικον *SEG* 29.1199 (Lydia, AD 212).

**φῐλοκάθᾰρος**, delete 'Ptol.*Tetr.* 63'

**φῐλοκᾰλέω 5**, pass., add '*SEG* 31.1476 (Arabia, vi AD)'

**φῐλοκέρτομος**, add '*Trag.adesp.* 365a K.-S.'

**φῐλοκτίστης**, add '*SEG* 34.1053 (Caria, vi AD), ib. 36.1341 (Caesarea Maritima, vi AD)'

**φῐλοκύνηγος**, add 'as member of a guild of huntsmen' and transfer '*Supp.Epigr.* 3.499' to follow, adding '*SEG* 32.1218 (Lydia, iii AD)'

**φῐλοκωθωνιστής**, delete 'f.l. for κωθωνιστής' and add '(cf. °κωθωνιστής)'

**φιλόκωμος**, for 'Simon. 183.5' read '*AP* 7.24.5 ([Simon.])'

**φῐλόλᾱος**, add '**2** *loving his people* (in epitaph of a Jew ), *CIJud.* 1.203.'

*φίλολβος, *loving prosperity*, Εἰρήνα *Hymn.Curet.* 40.

*φιλόλεκτρος, ον, *devoted to one's marriage (bed)*, *IUrb.Rom.* 1284 (ii/iii AD).

**φῐλόλογος II 2**, add 'as honorific description in an epitaph, *TAM* 4(1).232 (Rom.imp.)'

**φῐλολοίδορος**, add 'φιλολοιδόροιο γλώττης *Anacreont.* 42.11 W.'

**φῐλολουτρέω**, add 'Gal. 11.34.7'

**φῐλόλουτρος**, add 'Gal. 11.137.8'

*φῐλολύκιος, ον, *friend of the Lycians*, *BCH* 83.498.24 (i AD).

**φῐλομᾰλᾰκος**, after 'Ptol.*Tetr.* 162' add '(v.l. °ὑπομάλακος)'

**φῐλόμβροτος**, add 'also Φιλόμροτος pers. n., *SEG* 24.405 (Thessaly, v BC)'

**φιλομέτριος**, for '*loving moderation*' read '*friend of the poor*'

**φῐλόμολπος**, after '*song*' insert 'Stesich. 16.10 P.'; add 'Call.*Del.* 197'

*φῐλομόνᾰχος, v. °φιλομονόμαχος.

*φῐλομονόμᾰχος, ον, *fond of individual combats*, Ptol.*Tetr.* 180, *Cat. Cod.Astr.* 8(2).86 (cod. φιλομόναχος).

**φῐλόμωμος**, after 'Ptol.*Tetr.* 162' insert '(v.l. °ἐπίμωμος)'

**φῐλονῑκέω 1**, add '**b** pass., of words, *to be uttered contentiously*, Pl.*Lg.* 907c.'

**φῐλονῑκία 1**, line 2, after 'in bad sense' insert 'Simon. 36.11 P. (pl.)'

**φῐλοξενία**, after '*hospitality*' insert 'Thgn. 1358, B. 3.16 S.-M.'

**φιλόπαις I**, for 'Simon. 183.6' read '*AP* 7.24.6 ([Simon.])'

**φιλόπαππος**, delete '-παπποι θεοί .. 176' (v. *ASAE* 19.49)

**φῐλοπάτωρ**, add 'of Cleopatra, *SEG* 24.1217 (Egypt, 39 BC)'; at end add 'cf. Myc. *pi-ro-pa-ta-ra*, fem. pers. n. (*Φιλοπάτρα)'

*φῐλοπένης, ητος, ὁ, ἡ, *loving the poor*, *CIJud.* 1.203 (Rome).

**φῐλοπευστέω**, add '*PRyl.* 624.10'

*φῐλόπῐλος, v. °φιλόφιλος.

*φῐλόπιστος, ον, app. *lover of the faithful*, Mitchell *N.Galatia* 271.

*φῐλοπλία, ἡ, perh. *association of young men supporting gladiators*, *IEphes.* 2226.3.

**φίλοπλος**, delete '*Ephes.* .. 70' add '**b** masc. subst., member of a °φιλοπλία, *IEphes.* 3055, 3070.'

*φῐλοποίμνιος, ον, *loving the flock*, κύων Theoc. 5.106.

**φῐλόπολις II**, add 'as a complimentary term in an epitaph, *SEG* 33.1087 (Bithynia, AD 215/217)'

**φῐλοπολίτης**, add 'as an honorific term in an inscr., *SEG* 31.901, 913 (Aphrodisias, i AD), *IEphes.* 1390.3'

*φῐλοπραγμᾰτία, ἡ, *meddlesomeness*, *POxy.* 2267.6 (iv AD).

*φῐλορήτωρ, ορος, ὁ, ἡ, *fond of orators and oratory*, Cic.*Att.* 1.13.5, Phld.*Rh.* 2.218.15 S.

*φιλόρκειος, ον, *ready to make vows*, *Kafizin* 102.

**φῐλορώμαιος**, after '*friend to the Romans*' insert 'Mitchell *N.Galatia* 188 (43/40 BC)'

**φῖλος**, delete the entry.

**φίλος**, line 1, delete 'also ος, ον, Pi.*O.* 2.93' (but cf. *ZPE* 35.264-5) **I**, line 8, after 'Ar.*Nu.* 1168 (lyr.)' insert 'also Theoc., Bion; in prose, Longin. 6'; lines 19/20, for '(in bad sense, *Lac.* 2.13)' read 'φίλος Ἡρᾶς *SEG* 32.847.B55 (graffito, Thasos, iv BC)' add '**e** as a member of an association, *comrade, fellow*, *SEG* 29.1188, 1195 (Lydia, ii AD), *TAM* 5(1).93 (iii AD).' **IV 1**, add 'sup. as masc. or fem. pers. n., cf. Myc. *pi-ri-ta*' **4**, for 'Call.*Fr.* 146' read 'as pers. n. Φιλωτέρα Call.*fr.* 228.43 Pf.' and add 'Φιλοτέρα *SEG* 31.526 (Boeotia, iv BC)'

**φῐλοσάρᾱπις**, add 'also **φιλοσέρᾱπις** (dat. -πι) *IG* 12(5).712.25 (Syros)'

**φῐλοσοφέω II 3**, add 'Macho 374 G.'

**φῐλοσοφία 3**, add 'Hp.*VM* 20'

**φῐλόσοφος I 1**, add 'perh. as official title, *IG* 2².791.30 (Attica, iii BC), Λ. Φλ. Ἀρριανὸ[ν] ὑπατικὸν φιλό[σο]φο[ν] *SEG* 30.159 (Attica, ii AD)'

**φῐλοσυγγενής**, after p.56 A insert '*TAM* 5(1).12.12 (AD 80/81).

**φῐλοτεκνία**, add '*ISelge* 15.9-10 (Rom.imp.)'

**φῐλότεκνος**, add '*SEG* 28.1493 (Egypt, i/ii AD), *ISelge* 15.21 (Rom.imp.)'

**φῐλότεχνος**, line 2, after 'Ath. 15.700c, etc.' insert 'of a smith, *SEG* 31.1284 (Antioch in Pisidia)'

**φιλότης 2**, after 'Il. 3.73, cf. 94, 323' insert 'ἐπὶ φιλότατι *Olympia Bericht* 7.207 (Sybaris at Olympia, vi BC)'

**φῐλοτήσιος**, line 1, for 'Dor.' read 'dial.' **II**, add 'also (?)neut. φιλοτάσιον *CEG* 445 (Boeotia, vi BC); φιλ]οτέσιον Lang *Ath.Agora* XXI C6 (*c.*500 BC)'

**φῐλοτῑμέομαι III**, add 'Θεῷ Πρειέτῳ Δημόφιλος .. τὸν βωμὸν ἐφιλοτειμησάμην *TAM* 4(1).77'

**φῐλοτῑμητέον**, add '**b** *one must contend*, Gal. 8.553.16.'

**φῐλοτῑμία I 4**, add '**b** *fund of staple commodities* or *money* out of which disbursements were made to professionals and craftsmen as honoraria, *PLond.* 1305 (*Tyche* 5.63ff.; vi AD). **c** *donation, bounty*, *Cod.Just.* 1.3.44.3, Just.*Nov.* 22.23.'

*φῐλοτίμιος, ον, = φιλότιμος, only as adv. -ίως *Inscr.Cret.* 4.168.10 (iii BC, unless fr. φιλότιμος, w. analogical adv. suffix).

**φῐλότῑμος I 2**, add 'φ. τῆς δοχῆς Macho 106 G.' **II**, comp., -ότερον, add '*SEG* 32.794.11 (Olbia, 325 BC)'

**φῐλότρῠφος**, delete the entry.

*φῐλοφαρές, τό, name for the plant πράσιον, Dsc. 3.105.1.

**φῐλόφῐλος**, add 'written φιλόπιλε (voc.) *SEG* 30.1769 (inscr., Egypt, ii/iv AD)'

**φῐλόψῐλος**, for 'Alcm. 152' read 'Alcm. 32 P.' and after 'ψιλεύς' add '(so Phot., Suid., but perh. error for φιλόφῐλος = *φιλόπτιλος, *loving down*)'

**φῐλοψῡχέω**, line 3, for 'φ. ὑπὲρ τῆς ἀρετῆς' read 'ὑπὲρ δὲ τῆς ἀρετῆς οὐ φιλοψυχήσαντες'

**φίλτᾰτος**, add '*SEG* 30.1470 (Phrygia, iii AD), *TAM* 4(1).352 (Chr.)'

**φιλτροκατάδεσμος**, for '*PMag.Par.* 1.296' read '*PMag.* 4.296, *Suppl.Mag.* 38.8 (ii AD)'

*φιλτροπόσιμος, ον, *having the qualities of a love-potion*, Cyran. 3.37.23 K., al.; neut. as subst., *love potion*, ib. 1.22.29, al.

**φιλυπόστροφος**, add 'in non-medical context, *Corp.Herm.fr.* 23.67 N.-F.'

**φῐλῳδός**, add 'cf. φιλάοιδος'

*φιμά, ά, = φιμός, Hsch.

*φιμινάλια, τά, v. °φεμινάλια.

**φῑμός III**, add '*qui .. mitteret in phimum talos* Hor.*Sat.* 2.7.17'

**φῑμόω**, line 4, after 'Ev.*Matt.* 22.34' insert 'by a spell, *Tab.Defix.Aud.* 22.42 (Cyprus), al.; τὰ στόματα πάντων ib. 15.24 (Syria)'

**φίμωσις II**, for '*stopping up an orifice*' read '*contraction of an orifice* (so that it cannot be opened)'

**φιμωτικός**, after '*silencing*' insert 'παραθήκην φ. τινος *Tab.Defix.Aud.* 22.39, 32.27 (both Cyprus)'

**-φιν**, delete the entry.

*φίντων, ωνος, ὁ, *beloved*, (cf. φίντατος, pers. n. Φιντεία, Φιντίας), A.*fr.* 47a.802 R.

**φίσκος II**, add 'Just.*Nov.* 117.8.2; perh. of other treasuries, *SEG* 29.980 (Italy, late Rom.imp.)'

**φιτρός I**, for 'Call.*Fr.* 246 (= *PSI* 11.1218*a*2)' read 'Call.*fr.* 177.2, 785 Pf.'

**φῖτυ**, before 'Ar.' insert 'S.*fr.* 889 R.'

*φλάγελλα, ἡ, Lat. *flagellum, whip*, φλαγέλλας μαστιγωθῆναι *POxy.* 2339.10 (i AD), see also φραγέλλη.

**φλαγέλλιον**, add 'see also ‡φραγέλλιον'

*φλάγελλον, τό, Lat. *flagellum, whip, lash*, *Edict.Diocl.* 10.3, 18.

**φλᾱμέντας**, lines 1/2, for '*IG* .. φλάμινα' read 'gen. φλαμένος *IGRom.* 3.1332 (Bostra); acc. φλαμίνα'; after '(Pisidia)' insert 'φλαμ. (abbrev.) *IG* 2².5206'; add 'φλαμένιος *AE* (1934/5) παρ. 15 (Thebes)'

**φλαῦρος**, line 1, after 'first in Sol. 13.15' insert '(dub. in Alc. 59(*a*) L.-P.)'

**φλάω**, line 2, for '(Ahrens, φλασῶ codd.)' read '(v.l. φλασῶ)'; line 4, for '(Ahrens, φλάσαιμι codd.)' read '(v.l. φλάσαιμι)'

**φλεβοτομέω**, pass., add '*Inscr.Perg.* 8(3).139 (Rom.imp.)'

**φλεγμαίνω II 3**, add 'of literary style, παχὺ καὶ φλεγμαῖνον Eust. 285.27'

**φλεγμᾰτόεις**, add '(= *Suppl.Hell.* 1116)'

**Φλεύς**, after '(Hdn.Gr.) 2.911' insert 'dat. Φλεῖ *IEryth.* 207.61 (ii BC)'

**φλέψ 3**, add '**b** *vein* in a stone, Epiph.Const. in *Lapid.Gr.* 196.2.' add '**4** of the caverns of the underworld, βυθίων φλέβα πᾶσαν ἐναύλων Nonn.*D.* 36.103.'

**φληνᾰφία**, add 'perh. φληναφε̣ί̣[α *POxy.* 2802.3'

**φλήνᾰφος I**, transfer 'Amelius ap.Porph.*Plot.* 17' to section II.

**φληνᾰφώδης**, add 'Sch.Hes.*Op.* 160'

**φλιά**, line 1, delete '(later .. Oropus, i BC)' (τὰ στεφάρια is now read, v. °στεφάριον) **1**, line 3, (in sg.), after 'Theoc. 23.18' insert 'Call.*Epigr.* 42.6 Pf.'; line 4, (παρὰ φλιῇ), for 'Call.*Iamb.* 1.220' read 'Call.*fr.* 194.24 Pf.' and add 'ἐπὶ φλιῆς ib. 91' **2**, transfer pres. quots. to section 1 and for this section read 'used to translate Hebr.

wd. usu. understood as "lintel", Lxx *Ex.* 12.7, 22, 23' at end add 'Myc. *pi-ri-ja-o* (gen. pl.)'

**Φλῐάσιος**, for 'cf. *Φλυήσιος*' read 'see also °*Φλυήσιος*'

**φλόγῐνος**, add '**III** *φλόγινος* (sc. *λίθος*), ἡ, a precious stone, Plin.*HN* 37.179.'

**φλογίον**, add 'ostr. in *BASP* 23.28'

***φλογοῦχος**, ὁ, *flame-holder*, *SEG* 16.741 (Pergamum, Rom.imp.).

***φλογοφόρος**, ον, *flashing*, of the moonstone, *Physici* 2.204.16.

**φλόγωσις 1**, add 'pl., Hld. 8.11'

***Φλοιά**, ᾶ, Lacon. name for Persephone, Hsch.

***Φλοιάσιος**, v. *Φλιάσιος*.

**φλοιός**, line 2, for 'Call.*Fr.* 101' read 'Call.*fr.* 73 Pf. (cj.)'

**φλόξ I 3**, for 'of the *heat* of the sun' read 'of the *fire* of the sun' and after 'S.*Tr.* 696' insert 'Simon. 76.3 P., Orph.*H.* 69.10'; for 'the *blade* of a sword' read 'of a flashing sword' **II**, add '*AP* 4.1.51 (Mel.)'

**φλόος**, line 4, for 'cf.' read '*bast*'; line 5, delete 'the *slough* of' and for '**φλους**' read '**φλοῦς**'

***φλουμάρης**, v. °*πλουμάριος*.

***φλουμαρικός**, v. °*πλουμαρικός*.

**φλῠαρία**, add 'applied to a libellous statement, *Cod.Just.* 1.5.12.17'

**φλυζάκιον**, delete 'cf. *φυσάκια*'

***Φλῠήσιος**, ὁ, title of Hermes, Hsch., cf. *τὸν Φλυησίων Ἑρμῆν* Hippon. 47 W. and ‡*Φλιάσιος*.

**φλύω**, line 8, for '*φλύζειν*' read '*φλύζων*'

***φοβερόμματος**, ον, *having terrible eyes*, voc., *PMag.* 5.437, Bonner *Magical Amulets* 168.

***φοβερόφθαλμος**, ον, *having terrible eyes*, gloss on *γοργῶπιν* (acc.), Hsch.

***φοβεσᾱ́νωρ**, νορος, ὁ, ἡ, *man- or warrior-scaring*, *θυμός* *GVI* 1918 (Crete, ii/i BC).

**φοβέω A I**, add 'Th. 7.30.1'

**φόβος II 1**, line 9, after '*Act.Ap.* 9.31' insert 'of a woman for her husband, *SEG* 35.1427.5 (pl., Side, iii AD)'

**φοιβάω I 1**, after '*purify*' insert 'E.*Phaëth.* 57 D.'

**Φοίβη**, of Artemis, add '*SEG* 32.1068 (Italy, *c.*AD 150)'

***Φοιβίη**, ἡ, (Ion.) title of three-headed female deity, perh. Dione as Hecate, *SEG* 34.1436 (Syria, *c.*iii AD).

**φοῖβος I**, add 'comp. *φοιβότερος*, orac. in *SEG* 33.1056.C6 (Cyzicus, ii AD)'

***φοιδερατικός**, ή, όν, *connected with a treaty* or *alliance*, Just.*Nov.* 148.2, al.

***φοιδερᾶτος**, ὁ, Lat. *foederatus*, *bound* (to Rome) *by a treaty*, *Cod.Just.* 1.5.12.17, 12.37.19.2, Just.*Nov.* 117.11.

***φοῖδες**, v. *φωῖς*.

***φοινῑκάζω**, *write*, *act as scribe*, *ποινικάζεν* (inf.) *SEG* 27.631.A5 (Lyttos, Crete, *c.*500 BC), cf. *ἐκφοινίσσω*, °*φοινικαστᾱ́ς*, °*φοινικογραφέω*.

**Φοινῑκαῖος**, add '*SEG* 26.704.5, 37.510 (both Dodona, ii BC), *IG* 2².951 add. (Ambracia, ii BC), etc., cf. °*Φοινίκη*.'

***φοινῑκαστᾱ́ς**, ᾶ, ὁ, *scribe*, *ποινικαστάν* (acc.) *SEG* 27.631.A11, B1, al. (Lyttos, Crete, *c.*500 BC), cf. °*φοινικιστής*.

**φοινῑ́κεος**, line 4, for 'metaph. .. Diehl²' read 'perh. w. ref. to blushing, ..]*νικεος αἰδώς* Erinn. in *Suppl.Hell.* 401.34'

**Φοινῑ́κη**, add **IV** 'title of Athena at Corinth, Lyc. 658 and Sch.'

***φοινικηγός**, όν, wd. of uncertain meaning in list of building supplies, *BGU* 2361a ii 4 (iv AD) (*φυνικηγός* pap.).

**φοινῑκήϊος II**, delete '*γράμματα*' and '*Φ.* alone'

**Φοινῑκίζω**, for 'of unnatural vice' read 'of cunnilingus'

**Φοινῑκικός**, after 'ή, όν' insert '(freq. var. **Φοινῑκός**)'

**φοινῑ́κινος I a**, line 3, after 'Id. 8.2' insert 'of honey, *Edict.Diocl.* 3.12' add '**III** = *φοινίκεος*, *red*, Hsch. s.v. *φοίνικι φαεινόν*.'

**φοινῑ́κιον III**, for this section read 'item in a list of medical supplies, *Inscr.Cret.* 4.145 (Gortyn, ?v/iv BC)' add 'Myc. *po-ni-ki-jo*, name of a spice'

**φοινῑ́κιος I**, delete '*φ. οἶνος*' to end of section add 'Myc. *po-ni-ki-ja* (fem.), of chariots, *crimson* or *of palm-wood*'

**φοινῑκιστής II**, for '*wearer of purple .. rank*' read 'perh. *secretary*, *scribe*, cf. °*φοινικαστᾱ́ς*'

***Φοινῑκῖτις**, ιδος, ἡ, a precious stone, Plin.*HN* 37.180, 188.

***φοινῑκογρᾰφέω**, *act as secretary* or *scribe*, *SEG* 31.985D (Teos, v BC), cf. °*φοινικάζω*, *φοινικογράφος*.

***φοινῑκοέᾱνος**, ον, *purple-robed*, *φοινικοεάνων* .. *Ὡρᾶν* Pi.*fr.* 75.14 S.-M. (rest.).

**φοινῑκοπᾰ́ρηος**, add 'Dor. *φοινικοπάραος* *Suppl.Hell.* 991.34 (poet. word-list, iii BC)'

***φοινῑκοπάστιλλος**, ὁ, (?)*red dye from palm-tree*, Anon.Alch. 346.10.

***φοινῑκόπρῳρος**, ον, *having a red prow*, *Suppl.Hell.* 991.35 (poet. word-list, iii BC).

**φοινῑκόπτερυξ**, read **φοινῑκοπτέρυξ** and for 'Lyr. in *Mitteil.* .. 139' read '*Lyr.adesp.* 11(*f*).2 P.'

***Φοινῑκός**, v. °*Φοινικικός*.

***φοινῑκόχλοος**· *ξανθόχλοος* Hsch.

**Φοῖνιξ A I 2**, after 'Od. 15.417' insert 'of Europa, as daughter of Phoenix, B. 17.54 S.-M.'; last line, for '*ἄμπεχος*' read '*ἄμπελος*' and add 'cf. Hsch.' **B I 2**, line 2, after 'Pi.' insert 'B.'; line 4, after '*P.* 1.24' insert 'B. 18.56 S.-M.' **IV**, for 'like a *guitar*' read 'type of lyre' and add 'Alc.ap.Cyr. in cod. Matrit. (*GRBS* 9.272)' **X**, for '*εὐρύνοτος*' read '*εὐρόνοτος* a south-easterly wind' **XII**, add 'Asclep.Jun.ap.Gal. 12.776.4, 10' at end add 'Myc. *po-ni-ke* (dat.), *po-ni-ki-pi* (instr. pl.), prob. *palm-tree*'

**φοίνιος**, at end for 'Rare in Com.' read 'com. only paratrag.'

**φοινίσσω I 1**, lines 4/5, delete '*empurple*, *μόρον* S.*Fr.* 395' and transfer ref. to section II.

**φοινός 1**, add 'app. masc. subst., *red poppy*, Lang *Ath.Agora* XXI B19'

**φοῖς**, read '**φοΐς**' and for '*φῴς*' read '*φωΐς*'

**φοιτᾰλέος**, after 'E.*Or.* 327 (lyr.)' insert '*φοιτᾱλ-* A.*Pr.* 598, E. l.c.'; after '*roaming wildly about*' insert 'Euph.*fr.* 97 vGr.'

**φοιτάω**, line 1, after '(Hdt.) 7.126' insert 'Call.*fr.* 194.32, 202.67 Pf. (v. Add. in vol. II)' **II**, add '**2** of decrees, etc., *to be issued*, *Cod.Just.* 1.3.52.11, 1.3.55.2.'

***φοιτητικός**, ή, όν, *wandering*, *moving*, Sch.E.*Ph.* 1024.

**φοῖτος**, add 'Sch.A.R. 4.55'

**φόλετρον**, add '*PMich.*xv 741.5, 11 (vi AD)'

***φολιᾶτον**, τό, Lat. *foliatum*, a perfumed oil made from aromatic leaves, *Edict.Diocl.* 36.88; see also *φουλιᾶτα*.

***φολιᾶτος**, ον, Lat. *foliatus*, *bearing foliage*, *ἀρσενίκιον* Anon.Alch. 318.7.

**φολίς**, line 3, after 'Epic.ap.Sch.Nic.*Th.* 257' insert '(= *Suppl.Hell.* 1166)'

***φολλατώριον**, τό, Lat. *fullatorium*, *fuller's shop*, *PLond.* 191.5 (ii AD).

**φόλλις II**, add '**2** sum of money equal to 12,500 denarii, *PBeatty Panop.* 2.302 (AD 300).'

**φονεύς**, add 'see also *φονής*'

**φονεύω 1**, line 4, after 'cf. *El.* 34' insert '*οὐ φονεύσεις* Lxx *Ex.* 20.15' **2**, after 'of an animal' insert 'considered legally as a murderer' add '**II** *slaughter* animals, *Peripl.M.Rubr.* 4.'

**φόνιος II 3**, add 'adv. *φονίως*, Sch.E.*Tr.* 539'

**φόνος**, line 15, after 'D.S. 19.8' insert '*ἐν φόνῳ* .. Lxx *Nu.* 21.24' fr. section II.

**φορά B 3**, line 6, after 'D.S. 16.54' insert 'Men.*Pk.* 533 S.'

***φοράριος**, ὁ, perh. *shopkeeper*, fr. Lat. **forarius*, *IGRom.* 3.93 (written -*ις*, Sinope), cf. °*φόρος* (B).

**φορβειά I**, for '*halter* .. *manger*' read '*halter* for horses, camels, etc.' and add '*PCair.Zen.* 781.12, *PHib.* 211.17 (both iii BC), *PMich.*xv 717 (iii AD)' **II**, for this section read 'kind of halter used by players of wind instruments to support the mouthpiece against the lips, Ar.*V.* 582, Plu. 2.456b; in fig. phr., app. w. ref. to lack of restraint, *ἀγρίαις φύσαισι φορβειᾶς ἄτερ* S.*fr.* 768 R.' at end add 'form **φορβηϝια*, Myc. *po-qe-wi-ja*'

**φορβή**, add 'Myc. *po-qa*'

***φορβιοπώλης**, ου, ὁ, *seller of φόρβιον*, or perh. *of fodder*, *POxy.* 1037.4 (v AD; *πορβιο-*).

**φόρετρον**, add '**2** *transport*, *carriage*, *BGU* 2269.9 (AD 138/9). See also ‡*φόλετρον*.'

**φορεύς**, add '**IV** *shield-strap*, Hsch.'

**φορέω I 1**, add '**b** prob. of road or door, *lead to* (as *φέρω* A VII 1), Call.*fr.* 504 Pf.'

**φόριμος II**, add 'also *τὸ φ.*, Plin.*HN* 35.184, Gal. 12.917.7'

***φορίνιον**, τό, see quot.; *φορίνιον γὰρ λέγεται τὸ παχυνθὲν δέρμα τοῦ ὀφθαλμοῦ* Phot. s.v. *πεφοριῶσθαι*.

**φορμαλεία**, line 2, for 'perh.' read 'prob.' and after '*φρουμαρία*' insert '*list of supplies to be delivered*' add '**2** *official receipt for supplies*, *PLond.* 1663.25 (vi AD), cf. *PMasp.* l.c.'

***φόρμη** (**φώρμη**, **φούρμη**), ἡ, Lat. *forma*, *quality* or *class*, *ταπήτια διπρόσωπα δύο τῆς πρώτης φούρμας* *PMich.*XIV 680.11 (iii/iv AD), *πρώτης φόρμης* *Edict.Diocl.* 8.2, al. **II** *cobbler's last*, *περὶ φορμῶν καλικαρικῶν* ib. 9.1.

**φόρμιγξ 1**, add '*Φ. ἀστερόεσσα* the constellation *Lyra*, Nonn.*D.* 1.257; *ἡδυμελῆ* .. *οὐρανίῃ Φόρμιγγι τεὴν σύριγγα συνάψω* ib. 467'

***φορμίδιον**, gloss on *φορμίον*, Hsch.

**φορμός 1**, transfer 'prov., .. Arist.*Rh.* 1385ᵃ28' to end of section 2. **3**, delete the section adding quots. to section 2.

**φορμοφόρος**, add 'rest. in *Schwyzer* 230 (ed. pr. *ἱρμο-*, v. *ZPE* 33.88-9)'

**φορολόγος**, add '*POxy.* 3273.3 (i AD), *SEG* 32.676 (Thrace, iii AD)'

**φόρον**, for 'cf.' read 'as a court of law' adding '*PMasp.* 312.7 (vi AD), *Cod.Just.* 4.20.15.3, 8.10.12.8'

**φόρος 1**, add '**b** *rent paid in kind*, *PMich.*xv 727.3 (iv/v AD).'

***φόρος** (B), ὁ, *forum*, *market-place*, *φ. Θεοδοσιανός* *IEphes.* 1534 (Chr.), *φόρος· ὁ τόπος, τὸ πωλητήριον* Suid., cf. ‡*φόρον*.

***φορτηγέσιον**, τό, app. *the business of carrying merchandise* or the *equipment* for it, *SEG* 26.845.3 (Berezan, vi/v BC).

**⁺φορτηγός**, *όν*, *carrying loads* or *cargoes*, of ships, ἄκατοι Critias 2.11 W.; νῆες Plb. 1.52.6, 5.68.4, etc.; πλοῖα D.S. 14.55, 20.85; of men, *engaged in transporting cargoes*, ναυβάτην A.*fr.* 263 R., Metag. 4.4 K.-A. (hex.); subst., *porter*, Thgn. 679, Cratin. 171.73 K.-A., cf. Poll. 7.131.

**φορτίον I**, line 2, for 'Sapph.*Supp.* 9.13' read 'Sapph. 20.13 L.-P.' and delete '*Pl.* 352' add '**b** pl., *contents of a building, fixtures*, *POxy.* 242.16, 243.27, *PMich.*x 584.25 (all i AD).' **2 a**, add 'so perh. sg. in Ar.*Pl.* 352 is *piece of goods* offered, *bargain* offered' **3**, delete 'ἔρωτος .. Anacr. 170'

**φόρτος I 1**, line 4, after 'φ. ἔρωτος' insert 'dub. sens., Anacr. 115 P.'

**φορῶ**, delete 'prob. abbreviation of'; add (cf. demotic and Coptic πορο).

***Φορωνιάς**, άδος, ἡ, epith. of Hera, epigr. in *Lindos* 698 (*c.*200 BC).

**φόσσᾶτον**, for '*CIG* .. Anastasii)' read '*SEG* 9.356.36 (Ptolemais in Cyrenaica, vi AD)'

**φουλβῖνον**, add 'cf. πουλβῖνον'

**φουλιᾶτα**, add 'see also °φολιᾶτος, -ον'

***φούλλων**, ωνος, ὁ, Lat. *fullo, fuller, launderer, Edict.Diocl.* 22.1.

**⁺φοῦνδα**, ἡ, Lat. *funda, belt for carrying money, Ann.Épigr.* 1907.22 (Aphrodisias), *PHamb.* 10.34, 38; φ.· *ventralis Gloss.* (cf. mod. Gk. = *tassel*); also **ποῦνδα** *PMich.*inv. 3163.42 (*TAPhA* 92.258, iii AD).

***φοῦρκα**, ἡ, Lat. *furca*, in quot., *forked frame for a cart, Edict.Diocl.* 15.9.

***φούρμη**, v. °φόρμη.

***φουρνάκιον**, τό, *small oven*, Anon.Alch. 367.15, 17, 19.

***φουρνέλλον**, τό, *oven, furnace*, Anon.Alch. 321.9, al.

**φοῦρνος**, add '**II** περὶ φούρνων οἰκεί(ων) app. kind of slipper, *Edict.Diocl.* 9.20 (περιφορίνων 20A., q.v.).'

***φουσκάριος**, ὁ, *seller of* φοῦσκα, *PLond.* 1028.5 (vii AD).

***φράγδην**, adv., *as a defence, defensively*, Batr. 266.

**φραγέλλη**, add 'see also °φλάγελλα'

**φραγέλλιον I**, add '-ιν μουλιωνικόν *Edict.Diocl.* in *SEG* 37.335 iii 18, cf. φλαγέλλιον' **II**, delete the section transferring quot. to section I (cf. *ZPE* 94.285)

***φραγηλίτης**, ὁ, app. for φραγελλίτης, kind of policeman employed to guard church property, *ITyr* 10.

**φρᾱδᾱτήρ**, add '*SEG* 34.940 (Camarina, iv/iii BC)'

**φρᾱδή**, after lemma insert 'dial. φραδά *IG* 5(2).261.15 (v. infra under sense II)'

***φρᾰδητός**, ή, όν, *known*, Sch.Pi.*N.* 3.45 (explaining φράδασε in Pi. *N.*3.26 S.-M.).

**φράδμων**, add 'also φράσμων, φ.· προσέχων Hsch.'

**φράζω**, after lemma insert 'Boeot. φράττω Corinn. 34 P.'

**⁺φρασμοσύνη**, ἡ, *injunction*, ἀνέθεκε .. μάντειόν (i.e. μάντεων) φρασμοσύνᾶι *CEG* 243 (Athens, v BC); cf. φραδμοσύνη.

***φράσμων**, v. °φράδμων.

**φράσσω**, line 6, after 'Il. 15.566' insert 'subj. φαρξώμεθα Alc. 6.7 L.-P.'

***φρᾱτερικός**, ή, όν, *of a phratry*, φ. γραμματεῖον D. 44.41.

**φρατορικός**, delete the entry.

**φρᾱτριαρχέω**, add 'also **φᾱταρχέω** de Franciscis *Locr.Epiz.* 20; see also φρηταρχέω'

***φρᾱτριάρχιον**, τό, *temple of a phratry*; in form φᾱτάρχιον, de Franciscis *Locr.Epiz.* 14, 16.

**φρᾱτρίαρχος**, add 'also **φᾱ́ταρχος**, de Franciscis *Locr.Epiz.* 8, 22, 23, 34; see also φρήταρχος'

**φρᾱτρικός**, after '= φρατριακός' insert 'app. *belonging to a phratry*, *SEG* 26.676 (Larissa, 200/190 BC)'

**φρᾱ́τριος III**, add 'at Scepsis, *JÖAI* 3.55, where see other refs.'

**φράττω**, add 'also Boeot. for °φράζω'

**φρέᾱρ**, line 1, before 'Ep.' insert '**φρῆρ** *Tit.Cam.* 64a.1, *PLond.* 1948.7 (iii BC); **φρῆν** *SEG* 39.1002.4 (Camarina, ii/i BC)' **1**, add 'Lang *Ath.Agora* XXI K1 (vi BC)' **2**, delete '**b** .. 810' transferring the ref. to line 2 of section 2, after 'Th. 2.48, 49' at end add '(cf. ‡στέᾱρ)'

**φρεᾱτία, φρεᾱ́τιον**, add 'see also φρητία, °φρήτιον'

***φρένησις**, εως, ἡ, = φρενῖτις, Cels. 3.18.1.

**φρενοβλᾰβής**, add '*Trag.adesp.* 625.45 K.-S.'

**φρενοβλᾰβία**, add 'Heph.Astr. 2.31.16 (pl.)'

**φρενοδαλής**, for '-δᾱλ-' read '-**δαλ**- [prob. -δᾱλ-]'

**φρενώλης**, after '*frenzied*' insert 'Hippon. 77.5 W.'

***φρεωρῠχικός**, ή, όν, *for digging wells*, ἐργαλεῖον φ. Hsch. s.v. τόρος.

***φρῆν**, v. °φρέαρ.

***φρῆρ**, v. °φρέαρ.

***φρήτιον**, τό, = φρεάτιον, *IG* 14.217 (Sicily, pl.).

***φριγιδάριον**, τό, Lat. *frigidarium, cooling-room* in a bath, *SEG* 26.784 (φριγδ-; Thrace, AD 162/3).

***φρῑμαγμός**, ὁ, sound uttered by animals in a state of excitement, *snorting*: by horses, Lyc. 244; by goats, Poll. 5.888, D.H.*Comp.* 16.

**φρῑμάσσομαι**, for '*snort and leap: wanton*' read '*snort in excitement*' and after 'of goats' insert 'Pi.*fr.* 332 S.-M.'

**φρίξ II 2**, after 'Hp.*Morb.* 2.68' insert 'Nic.*Th.* 778'

***φριξοχαίτης**, ου, ὁ, *having bristling hair*, S.*fr.* 10d.5 R.

**φριξωποβρόνταξ**, delete the entry.

***φριξωποβρονταξαστράπτης**, ου, ὁ, *hurler of frightful thunder and lightning*, *PMag.* 5.19.

**φρονέω IV**, line 13, ζῶν καὶ φρονῶν, add 'fem. ζῶσα προνοῦσα (sic) Mitchell *N.Galatia* 242 (Rom.imp.)'

***φροντάριον**, τό, (cf. Lat. *frontalia*), *ornament for* (?*horse's*) *forehead*, in pl., pap. in *JÖByz* 33.13.5 (vi AD).

**φροντίζω II 2**, line 16, for '*to be concerned* or *anxious* about' read '*give consideration* or *attention* to'

**φροντίς III 2**, add '*SEG* 32.1554 (Arabia, vi AD)'

***φροντιστεία**, ἡ, prob. *office of* φροντιστής II 1, *SEG* 19.882 (Syria, ii AD).

**φροντιστής II 1**, add 'as title of Zeus, *INikaia* 1141 (ii AD)'; at end, as transl. of Lat. *procurator*, add 'Modest.*Dig.* 26.6.2.5'

**φροῦδος 2**, add '*POxy.* 3069.19 (iii/iv AD)'

***φρουμαρία**, v. ‡φορμαλεία.

**⁺φρουμεντάριος**, α, ον, Lat. *frumentarius*, of military personnel, *concerned with victualling*, *SIG* 830.5 (Delphi, ii AD), *IG* 10(2).207.6 (Thessalonica, iii AD), *SEG* 31.905 (Caria, iii AD).

**φρουρά II**, add 'sp. πρωρά *SEG* 25.447 (Arcadia, iii BC), προύρρα *SEG* 37.494 (Matropolis, Thessaly, iii BC)'

**⁺φρουρίς**, ίδος, fem. adj., *watch-, guard-*: as subst. sc. ναῦς, *guard-ship*, *IG* 1³.21.85, Th. 4.13.2, X.*HG* 1.3.17; also φρουρίς, αἱ πρ. καλούμεναι πύλαι (at Abdera), Call.*Dieg.* ii.34 (*fr.* 90 Pf.) (perh. pr. n.).

**φρουρός**, add 'see also προυρός'

**φρῠ́αγμα II**, after '*insolence*' insert 'Men.*fr.* 333.13 K.-Th.'

**φρῠ́γᾰνον I**, add 'applied to driftwood, Ael.*NA* 5.23'

***Φρῠγιᾰκός**, ή, όν, *Phrygian*, Macho 191 G., Str. 10.3.15, *Edict.Diocl.* 19.53, 62.

***Φρῠγικός**, ή, όν, *Phrygian*, D.H. 1.29, St.Byz. s.v. Φρυγία.

**Φρῠ́γιος**, line 1, after 'ος, ον' insert 'Arist.*Pol.* 1276ᵇ9' and after 'Luc.*Harm.* 1' insert 'etc.' **I 1**, add 'Μητρὶ Φρυγε[ίηι] *the Phrygian goddess, Ilasos* 229.2'

**φρυκτός 2**, add 'cf. ἐπὶ φρυκτῶ παρίηι *CID* I 13.15-16 (precise interpr. uncertain, Delphi, iv BC); as sacrifice, perh. rest. at ib. 7.7-8 (Andrian law, v BC)'

***φρῡνεός**, ὁ, = φρύνη, Pratin. 3.10 S. (φρυναιου cod. A of Ath. 14.617e), *EM* 801.29.

**φρύνη III**, for 'nickname .. complexion' read 'as fem. pers. n.' and add 'Φρύνᾱν *SEG* 31.824 (Gela, v BC)'

***φρῠ́νινον**, τό, = φρύνιον 1, kind of plant, Paul.Aeg. 7.3 (254.7 H.).

***φρῡνίτης**, ου, ὁ, kind of precious stone, Socr.Dion.*Lith.* 52 H.-S.

***φρῡνοποπεῖον**, τό, perh. kind of skillet, *SEG* 24.361 (Boeotia, iv BC).

***φρώριον**, v. φρούριον.

***φυγαδείω**, v. ‡φυγαδεύω.

***φῠγᾰδευτής**, οῦ, ὁ, *that which drives away* (snakes), of the stone σιδηρίτης, Orph.*Lith.Kerygm.* 15.25 G.

**φῠγᾰδεύω**, after 'Elean φυγαδείω .. (iv BC)' insert 'also aor.subj. φυγαδεύαντι ib. line 6' **II**, transfer 'Plb. 10.22.1' to precede 'fut.'

**φύγεθρον**, add 'Hp.*Aff.* 35'

***φῠγελίτης**, ου, ὁ, name of a Lydian wine, from Phygela or Pygela, Dsc. 5.10.

**φῠγή II**, line 10, after 'pl.' insert 'Alc. 129.12 L.-P.'

**φῠγοπτόλεμος**, for 'poet. for *φυγοπόλεμος' read 'also φυγοπόλεμον (acc.) Hsch. s.v. φύξηλιν'

**φύη**, delete the entry.

**⁺φῡκάριον**, τό, *rouge obtained from seaweed*, Hsch. s.v. ἄφυκα, Zonar.; sp. φουκάριον *PMich.*VIII 508.6 (ii/iii AD), cf. φῦκος II.

**φῡκίον I 1**, for '= φῦκος I' read '*seaweed*' and add 'Hippon. 75.2, 115.10 W.'

**φῦκος II**, add 'Lxx *Wi.* 13.14'

**φῠ́λαγμα I 2**, add 'of the tomb, φύλαγμα σωμάτων epigr. in *TAM* 4(1).303 (Rom.imp.)'

**φῠλᾰκή II 1**, line 9, after 'Id. 8.39' insert 'Θησεὺς .. διὰ πάσης ἦν φυλακῆς τῷ πατρὶ Αἰγεῖ Call.*Dieg.* x.21 (*fr.* 230 Pf.)'

**φῠλᾰκίς**, add 'φ. τριημολίαι *Hesperia* 11.292 no. 57 (Athens, iii AD, v. Robert *Hell.* 2.124)'

**φῠλᾰκῑτικός**, line 2, after '*pertaining to police*' insert 'φ. κλῆρος *PTeb.* 808.3 (?ii BC)'

**φῠλᾰκός I**, last line, for 'Call.*Hec.* 1.2.12' read 'Call.*fr.* 260.28 Pf.' **II**, after '(Il. 2.695, etc.)' insert 'Φυλάκα, title of Demeter, *IG* 9(2).573, *SEG* 17.288 (Larissa, i BC or later)'

***φῠλακρισία**, ἡ, perh. *registration of members of a tribe*, *PHarris* 64.7, al. (iii/iv AD).

**φῠλακτέος II 1**, add 'Gal. 10.838.2'

**φῠλακτήριον 1**, for '*guarded post, fort, castle*' read '*fortified guard post*' and add '*SEG* 24.154 (Attica, iii BC); fig., Pl.*R.* 424d' **2**, for '*amulet*' (line 7) to end read '*magical inscription worn as an amulet*, *PMag.* 4.1626, 7.298, 580'

**φῠλακτικός II**, after 'Adv. -κῶς' insert 'Men.*Dysc.* 95'

**φῠλάκτωρ**, for '*Bull.* .. 244' read '*GVI* 1861'

***φυλαουργέω**, v. °φυλλα-.

**φῠλαρχέω**, line 3, c. gen., add 'φυλαρχήσας φυλῆς Ποσειδωνιάδος *TAM* 4(1).223, 299 (Rom.imp.)'

**φῠλαρχία**, add '**II** = πομπή τις Hsch.'

**φύλαρχος I a**, for '*CIG* 3773' read '*TAM* 4(1).42' **II**, after 'Hdt. 5.69' add 'Ar.*Av.* 799, Pl.*Lg.* 755c, al., Lys. 15.5, Arist.*Ath.* 30.2, al., etc.'

**φῠλάσσω**, line 12, imper., add 'φεφύλαχσο *Schwyzer* 538 (Acraephia, vi BC)'

***φυλατός**· ἡ λέξις παρὰ Βλαίσῳ (Blaes.*fr.* 5). σημαίνει δὲ ᾠδήν Hsch. (app. Italic wd.).

**φῠλετικός I 2**, delete 'ἡ φ. .. *BC* 3.30'; v. °φυλέτις.

***φῠλέτις**, ιδος, fem. adj., φ. ἐκκλησία, = Lat. *comitia tributa*, App.*BC* 3.30.

**φυλλάζω**, add '*frondentesq(ue)*· καὶ φυλλαζούσας Virgil gloss. in *PNess.* 1.851'

***φυλλαουργέω**, *strip the foliage* (from vines), *PMich.*XIII 666.17 (written φυλα-, vi AD).

***φυλλάω**, = φυλάσσω, (cf. mod. Gk. φυλάγω), φύλλατε ἀὴ τō σō δούλō *SEG* 36.1269 (Armenia, late Rom.imp.).

***φυλλίδιον**, τό, dim. of φυλλίς, *salad*, σάκκος φυλιδίων *BGU* 2359.5 (iii AD).

**Φυλλικός** (s.v. φυλλικός II), add '*SEG* 23.412 (189/8 BC), 32.599 (Augustus)'

**φυλλίνης**, add '**2** εἶδος τι κυκεῶν‹ος› Hsch.'

**φύλλον I 2**, for 'of flowers, *petal*' read '*flower*'; add '*AP* 6.154 (Leon.Tarent. or Gaet.)' **II**, after '*PTeb.* 38.3, 78.4 (ii BC)' insert 'κατὰ φύλλον *according to crops*, w. ref. to taxes, *BGU* 1120.20 (ii BC; v. *ZPE* 19.284)' add '**III** *something shaped like a leaf*, applied to segment of the covering of a ball, *AP* 14.62.'

**φύξηλις**, for '*cowardly*' read '*apt to run away*, *fugitive*' and add 'poet., of thunderbolt, Nonn.*D.* 1.320'

**φύξῐμος I**, line 4, after 'Id. 9.29.4' insert 'τὸν να[ὸν] φ. *Chiron* 19.134.48 (Sardes, i BC)'

**φύξιος 2**, add '**b** *repellent*, φ. ὀδμήν Nic.*Th.* 54 (cj.).'

**φύος**, add '*PSI* 892.82 (?iv AD)'

***φῠρᾱματικά**, τά, perh. some form of interior decoration, cf. κονιατικά, *MAMA* 8.498.26 (Aphrodisias).

**φύρᾱσις**, line 2, for '*mixture*' read '*kneading*'

**φύρκος**, delete 'Dor. φοῦρκος'

***φυρός**, v. °φυρρός.

***φυρόχρωμος**, ον, perh. *tawny-coloured*, of cow, *PBaden* 19.5 (ii AD), v. °φυρρός.

***φυρρός**, ά, όν, app. = πυρρός, *tawny*, of a camel, *PVindob.Worp* 9.5 (AD 158); also **φυρός**, *PLond.* 1132b.5 (AD 142), of an ox, *PGen.* 48.8 (AD 346).

**φῡσάω I**, line 11, after 'Antiph. 117 (troch.)' insert 'w. ὡς, *boast* that, φυσήσας ὡς κλαύσοιτο ὁ Φρυνίων εἰ .. D. 59.38'

***φύσγων**, v. °φύσκων.

***φῦσελος**, ὁ, or -ον, τό, *wind* in the stomach, Sch.Nic.*Al.* 287 Ge.; cf. φύσαλος.

**φύσησις**, add '**2** *swelling*, of waves, Sch.A.R. 1.1167.'

**φῦσιγξ I**, add '(unless erron. for φαῦσιγξ)'

***φῠσιδρόμος**, ον, (sp. φυσιτρ-), *nature-roaming* (cf. φύσις VII), epith. of a demon, *Suppl.Mag.* 49.57 (iii/iv AD).

**φύσις III**, line 2, before 'κατὰ φύσιν' insert 'ἐκ τῆς φύσεως *in the course of nature*, ὡς ἐκ τῆς φύσεως τὸν θάνατον ἴσον ἔσχεν *SEG* 26.821 (Thrace, *c.*100 BC)' add '**b** ἐν φύσει *in living form*, opp. the state of those not yet born, μὴ μόνον οἱ ἐν φύσει .. ἀλλὰ καὶ οἱ κυοφορούμενοι *Cod.Just.* 6.4.4.21, 6.48.1.2.' **VII 2**, for 'testes' read 'vagina and anus'

***φῠσίσοφος**, ον, *wise by nature*, μέλισσα Rh. 3.530.

***φῠσιτρόμος**, v. °φυσιδρ-.

**φύσκων**, for 'Alc. 37B' read 'Alc. 429 L.-P.; written φύσγων id. 129.21 L.-P.'

**φυστή**, line 1, for 'kind of *light pastry* or *puff*' read 'cake made of coarse meal and wine'; line 2, for '(Leon.)' read '(Leon.Tarent.), Teles p. 4.12 H.'

**φῠτᾰλιά I**, line 3, after '(Il.) 20.185' insert '*Inscr.Cret.* 4.43*Ba* 2 (v BC)' and add '*AP* 6.44 (Leon.Tarent.)' **II**, delete 'also of the *vine* .. (?))' and for 'ib.' read '*AP* 6.44' at end add 'Myc. *pu-ta-ri-ja*'

**φύτευσις**, for '= φυτεία' read '*planting*' and add 'φιτευσιος δαφνέων *SEG* 24.277.A29 (Epid., iv BC)'

**φῠτεύω I 4**, for this section read '*implant*, ταύτην (sc. ψυχὴν) μὴ φυτεῦσαι εἰς μηδεμίαν θήρειον φύσιν Pl.*Phdr.* 248d'

**φῠτηκόμος**, add 'also as adj., *causing plants to grow*, μαρμαρυγὴν πέμπουσα φυτηκόμον Nonn.*D.* 7.303'

***φῠτήκομος**, ον, *covered with vegetation*, φ.· σύνδενδρος τόπος Hsch.

**φῦτλον**, for pres. ref. read 'orac. in *TAM* 4(1).92'

***φῠτοεργείη**, ἡ, *cultivation of plants*, Gr.Naz.*Carm.* 1.2.1.257 (*PG* 37.542a), cf. ‡φυτουργία.

**φῠτοεργός**, add 'Nonn.*D.* 47.58, al.'

**φῠτόν I 1**, add '**b** *stem of wood*, μονόδροπον φυτόν Pi.*P.* 5.42.' at end add 'Myc. *pu-ta* (pl.)'

**φῠτός I**, for this section read '*naturally-formed*, πυάλους δύω, μίαν μὲν φοιτήν (sic) *TAM* 4(1).276.8 (iii/iv AD)'

**φῠτοσπορία**, add '**2** *generation of offspring*, *IHadr.* 166 (Rom.imp.).'

**φῠτοσπόρος**, after 'S.*Tr.* 359' insert '*SEG* 23.220 (Messene, i AD)'

**φῠτουργία 1**, add '*PKöln* 144.29 (152 BC)' at end add 'see also °φυτοεργείη'

**φύω B II 2**, lines 3/4, delete 'πολλῷ γ' ἀμείνων .. A.*Pr.* 337'

**φωΐς**, add 'Cratin. 226 K.-A.'

**Φωκαΐς**, as a coin, add '*Inscr.Perg.* 8(3).161.32 (ii AD)'

***φωκαρία**, ἡ, Lat. *focaria*, *housekeeper*, *concubine*, *BGU* 614.13 (iii AD).

***φωκάριον**, τό, *concubine*, *BGU* 600.21 (ii/iii AD); φωκάριν *PPrincet.* 57 (ii AD).

***φώλαρχος**, ὁ, app. some kind of cult official, *PP* 18.385-6 (Velia, Italy; see also *SEG* 30.1225, cf. perh. Φωλευτήριος).

**φωλεός I**, add 'Hippon. 86.4 W.' **II**, add 'Call.*fr.* 68.2 Pf.'

***Φωλευτήριος**, ὁ, epith. of Apollo, *IHistriae* 105 (iii BC, see also *SEG* 30.798; cf. perh. °φώλαρχος).

**φωνέω I 3**, for '(written πωνίω)' read '3rd sg. pres. part. πōνίοντες, etc., cf. Cret. forms of ἀποφωνέω, °προσφωνέω' **III**, add 'pass., *to be proclaimed*, *AP* 7.430 (Diosc.)'

**φωνή II 2**, after '*language*' insert 'or *dialect*'; at end after 'cf. 409e' insert '(or perh. w. ref. to orthography, v. *REG* 80.234 ff.)'

**φωνήεις 1**, add 'poet., of a lyre, Sapph. 118 L.-P.; of a song, Pi.*O.* 9.2; transf., of speech, B.*fr.* 26.2 S.-M.' **2, 3 & 4**, delete these sections.

**φωράω I**, add '*search* a person, Plu. 2.248f'

**φώριος I**, add '**b** *of a robber*, ἐπήλυσις Call.*fr.* 331 Pf.'

**φωσφόριον II**, add '*IGBulg.* 1731.29 (Thrace, iv/iii BC)' **III**, add '*PVindob.Tandem* 26.14 (AD 143)'

**φωσφόρος**, line 2, after 'Call.*Dian.* 204, etc.' insert 'w. dissimilation of aspirates, πωσφ- *Hesperia* 4.138 (sense II, pl., Athens, ii/iii AD), *SEG* 26.413 (lamp signature, Isthmia, ii AD), 31.1285 (Pisidia, Rom.imp.)'

***φωταθύρίς**, v. ‡φωτοθυρίς.

**φωτεινός I**, add 'sup., *Orac.Tiburt.* 22'

**φῶτιγξ**, for '*flute*' read '*transverse pipe*' and add 'app. distd. fr. πλαγίαυλος by Nicom.*Harm.* 4'

***φωτιστήριον**, διαφανῆ φ. λυχνικά gloss on Lat. *luminaria*, *Gloss.* **2** *baptistery*, *SEG* 8.318 (Mt. Nebo, vi AD), 30.1697, 33.1270 (Palestine, vi AD), 31.1476 (Arabia, vi AD).

**φωτοθῦρίς**, add 'also φωταθ-, *PMil.Vogl.* 99.12, *PLond.* 1179.62 (both ii AD)'

**φωτοφόρος**, add '**2** fem. subst., app. *lampstand*, *SEG* 16.741 (written φωιτοφόρος, Pergamum, Rom.imp.).'

# X

X, line 3, before 'stands' insert 'more often'

**χαβότια**, for 'dub. sens., perh. *honey-pots*' read 'perh. *small pots*, cf. °καβίδιον'

**χαβῶνες**, for 'ἀπό' read 'ἀπό'; add 'see also χαυών, °χαμῶνας'

***χαβώνιον**, v. °καβόνιον.

**χάζω B 2**, line 5, for 'nor in truth .. hit him' read 'of a stone, i.e. it nearly hit the man' and after '(Il.) 16.736' insert '(s.v.l.)'

***χαιμαφάριον**, τό, app. some kind of oil or lubricant in medical use, perh. *camphor*, *PRyl.* 529.13 (iii AD).

**χαιρετίζω**, add '*SEG* 26.730 (Maced., ii/i BC)'

**χαίρω III 1 a**, lines 6/7, transfer 'S.*Ph.* 462' to section 2 a; add 'cf. w. χαίρω as response, κῆρυξ Ἀχαιῶν χαῖρε .. – χαίρω A.*Ag.* 538; also opt., χάροις (sic) παροδεῖτα *INikaia* 767' **b**, for this section read 'inf. after vb. of speaking, χαίρειν δὲ τὸν κήρυκα προὐννέπω S.*Tr.* 227; ὅτι προσειπών τινα χαίρειν οὐκ ἀντιπροσερρήθη X.*Mem.* 3.13.1; inf. alone, πόλλα μοι τὰν Πωλυανάκτιδα παῖδα χαίρην Sapph. 155 L.-P., Pl.*Ion* 530a; Κῦρος Κυαξάρῃ χαίρειν X.*Cyr.* 4.5.27, Theoc. 14.1' **c**, delete the section. **2 a**, add 'inf. after vbs. of speaking, *MDAI(A)*56.131 (= *GVI* 1344.1) (Miletus, Hellen.), Luc.*Dem.Enc.* 50' deleting these refs. from section 2 c, together w. 'Sapph. 86, Ar.*Pl.* 322, Eup. 308, X.*HG* 4.1.31'

**χαίτη 1**, add 'χαίτην (-ας) σείειν *shake one's locks*, Anacr. 77 P., E.*Med.* 1191; poet., of trees, Call.*Del.* 81, *Anacreont.* 18.12 W.' **3 b**, for 'hedgehog' read 'porcupine' **5**, for this section read '*tuft* of the papyrus plant, βύβλος .. ἐπ' ἄκρῳ χαίτην ἔχουσα Str. 17.1.15; *thistledown*, Theoc. 6.16'

***χάκαξ** (?), gen. χάκακος, name of a freshwater fish, *IGC* p. 99 B 30 (Acraephia, iii/ii BC) (cf. χάραξ IV).

**χαλάδριον**, after '**χαλάτριον**' insert '*POxy.* 3354.16 (iii AD)'; add 'also **χελάδριον**, *POxy.* 1142.13 (iii AD); **χαράδριον** *PTeb.* 815 *fr.* 2 iii 74 (iii AD); see also χαλατριόομαι'

**χᾰλαζα II 1**, add '**b** *eruption of pimples*, Nic.*Th.* 252, 778.'

**χᾰλαζήεις II**, for '*whose sting causes an icy chill*' read '*causing* (by its sting) *skin eruptions*'

***χᾰλάζησις**, ἡ, *pimple* or *tubercle* in flesh of swine, Alex.Aphr.*Pr.* 3.139 *bis*.

***χᾰλαζίτης**, ου, ὁ, stone resembling hailstone (= χαλαζίας, χαλάζιος), Orph.*Lith.Kerygm.* 25 H.-S.

**χᾰλάζωσις**, add '*CIL* 13.10021 (181)'

***χαλαίβασις**· ἀπὸ τοῦ χαλαρῶς βαδίζειν Suet.*Blasph.* 66 T.

**χᾰλᾰσις 3**, for '*University* .. 3(2).58' read '*SEG* 8.647.3 (Egypt, iv AD)'

**χᾰλασμα 2**, add '*gap* between part of the surface of pavement blocks and the bed on which they rest, *IG* 7.3073.114 (Lebadea, ii BC; delete from section 3).' add '**8** *over-measure* (leaving an allowance for error), of land, *PGiss.* 36.17 (ii BC).'

***χᾰλαστάριον**, τό, prob. *necklace*, dim. of χαλαστόν, *PKöln* 166.4 (-ταριν pap.) (vi/vii AD).

**⁺χαλβᾰνίς**, ίδος, *made from the plant all-heal*, Nic.*Th.* 938, subst. Androm.ap.Gal. 14.41 (= *GDRK* 2.62.164).

***χαλβᾰνόριον μέλι**, τό, kind of honey, made from the resinous juice of all-heal (χαλβάνη), Alex.Aphr.*Pr.* 3.2.

**χᾰλεπός B II 1**, lines 6/7, for 'χ. λαμβάνειν περί τινος Th. 6.61' read 'also χαλεπῶς λαμβάνειν, w. ellipse of obj., Th. 6.61.1'

**χᾰλέπτω I 1**, add 'Κύπριδα χ. *AP* 5.263.5 (Agath.); τὴν παῖδα ib. 300.3 (Paul.Sil.)' **II**, at beginning, delete '*provoke* .. (Agath.)' and add 'Call.*Cer.* 48' **III**, for this section read 'act. intr., *to be angry*, Nonn.*D.* 16.34; w. dat., Bion *fr.* 14.2 G.'

***χᾰλικός**, ή, όν, *of cement*, χαλικὴ ἡμμιτία on a tile, app. indicating a measure, *SEG* 16.848 (Caesarea).

**χᾰλῑνός I 2**, add 'of a string of words full of difficult sounds, used for practice in articulation, Quint.*Inst.* 1.1.37' **III**, after 'part of the tackle of a ship' insert 'perh. *parrel*' **IV 1**, add 'of a snake's mouth, Nic.*Th.* 234' **2**, delete the section.

**χᾰλις I**, for '*Docum.* .. 101' read '*SEG* 26.1835 (dub. l.)' and add 'Nonn.*D.* 15.25'

**⁺χαλκάνθη**, ἡ, = χάλκανθον, Heras ap.Gal. 13.558.8, v.l. in Dsc. 3.80.

**χάλκειος**, add 'Myc. *ka-ke-ja-pi* (fem. instr. pl.)'

**χαλκέλᾰτος**, for 'poet. for' read 'var. of'

**⁺χαλκεόγομφος**, ον, *fastened with bronze nails*, ἐν ἀτερπέϊ δούρατι χαλκεογόμφῳ Simon. 38.10 P.

***χαλκεόζωνος**, ον, *girt with bronze*, of Heracles, *Suppl.Hell.* 1033, cf. χαλκόζωνος.

**χάλκεος II**, add 'form χάλκιος, Myc. *ka-ki-jo*'

***χαλκεότευκτος**, ον, *fashioned of bronze*, εἰκόνι .. χαλκεοτεύκτῳ *SEG* 18.137.B4 (Isthmus, iii AD), see also χαλκότευκτος.

**χαλκεόφωνος**, add 'χαλκεόφωνον ἐπισπέρχουσαν ἀοιδὴν Μελπομένην *AP* 9.505.15'

**χαλκεύς**, add 'Myc. *ka-ke-u*'

**χαλκεών 1**, add 'serving as repository for bronze implements, *SEG* 11.244 (sp. χαλκιόν, Sicyon, vi/v BC)'

**χαλκηδόνιον**, add '**II** prob. *chalcedony*, *PRyl.* 627.162 (iv AD), χαλκεδ-).'

***χαλκηδόνιος** (sc. λίθος), ὁ, *chalcedony*, Sm.*Is.* 54.12.

**Χαλκῐδικός IV**, for this section read 'neut. subst., app. room or recess built into the end of a basilica, Vitr. 5.1.4'

**χαλκίον I 1–3** for these sections read '**1** *bronze* (*object*), *IG* 1³.510, ἐν τῷ χαλκίῳ (sc. of a shield) ἐνορῶ .. Ar.*Ach.* 1128. **2** *bronze cauldron*, Ar.*fr.* 345 K.-A., Eup. 99.41, 272 K.-A., X.*Oec.* 8.19, *IEphes.* 3757; χ. θερμαντήριον *IG* 1³.421.96, Gal. 13.663.15; χ. ἐγλουτήριον *IG* 4.39.18 (Aegina); of the cauldron at the oracle of Zeus at Dodona, used prov. for a chatterbox, Men.*fr.* 60.3 K.-Th. **b** *bronze basin* used in the game of κότταβος, Poll. 6.110.'

***χαλκῑτάριον**, τό, *chalcite*, Anon.Alch. 5.8.

**χαλκόδετος**, add 'Myc. *ka-ko-de-ta* (neut. pl.)'

**⁺χαλκοκέραυνος**, ον, epith. of the sea, app. *bronze-thundering*, A.*fr.* 192.3 R. (s.v.l.).

***χαλκοκορώνη**, ἡ, dub. sens., Rh. 6.90.30.

***χαλκοπῡρίτης**, ου, ὁ, *copper pyrites*, Anon.Alch. 16.6.

**χαλκοπώλης**, add '*SEG* 32.239 (Athens, *c.*400 BC)'

**χαλκός**, line 1, for '*GDI* 5011.4 (iii BC)' read '*Inscr.Cret.* 4.162.3 (Gortyn, iii BC)'; line 11, before 'alloyed' insert 'χ. Μαριεύς fr. Marion in Cyprus, *IG* 2².1675.17' **II 4**, add 'humorously, of a moneyed man, *AP* 9.241 (Antip.Thess.)'

***χαλκοστεγίς** (or -στεγής -ές), *bronze-roofed*, *Gramm.Lat.* 4.197.22 K. (*Appendix Probi*).

**χαλκότευκτος**, add 'see also °χαλκεότευκτος'

**χαλκοτῠπική**, add 'w. τέχνη added, *PSI* 871.12 (i AD)'

**χαλκοῦς II**, add 'sobriquet of a moneyed man, Ἀριστομήδης ὁ χαλκοῦς λεγόμενος Did.*in D.* 9.52; cf. °χαλκός II 4'

**χαλκόχρους**, add 'ὄνον ἄρρενα χαλκόχρωον *POxy.* 3143.10 (AD 305)'

**χαλκωμάτιον**, add '*SB* 9834a4, 9 (iii AD)'

**χαλκωρῠχος**, after '*miner*' insert '*SB* 7200.19 (ii AD, -ορ- pap.)'

***χαλκωτός**, ή, όν, app. *covered with bronze*, *Inscr.Délos* 104-28.bB.15.

***χαλτουλάριος**, v. ‡χαρτουλάριος.

***χάλχη**, v. κάλχη.

**χᾰμᾶθεν I**, add '**2** legal t.t. = Lat. *de plano*, *informally*, Modest.*Dig.* 27.1.13.10.'

**χᾰμαί I 1**, line 4, after 'Hdt. 4.67' insert '*IG* 1³.474.103'; line 5, after '*IG* 2².1672.305' insert 'χ. ἐγένοντο Call.*Epigr.* 43.4 Pf.'; add 'τὸ χαμαί *the ground*, τοῦτον τὸν τόπον ἐξέκλεισεν τὸ χαμὲ ὀρύξας *SEG* 36.935 (Rome)'

**χᾰμαιδικαστής**, add '*PLips.* 64, *PLond.* 980 (both iv AD), *Cod.Just.* 7.15.5.4; also **χαμο-** Hsch. s.v. σήλεκτος'

**χᾰμαιευνάς**, (s.v. -εύνης), add 'θύμβρη Nic.*Th.* 532; see also χαμευνάς'

***χᾰμαιλίχων**, οντος, ὁ, kind of fishing-net, Sch.Th. 7.25.

**χᾰμαιρῑφής I**, for this section read '*thrown* or *knocked to the ground*, Eust. 1279.45; of a building, epigr. in *SEG* 9.189 (Cyrene, ii AD); of a person, *PCair.Isidor.* 63.25 (AD 296; sp. χαμερ-). **2** of infants, *exposed*, *abandoned*, Hsch. s.v. ὑποβολιμαῖον, *EM* 781.36. **b** = *collecticius*, *Gloss.*'

***χαμέτρυος**, v. χαμαίδρυς.

***χᾰμευνάδιος**, α, ον, *sleeping on the ground*, *Eleg.adesp.* in *Suppl.Hell.* 958.17 (s.v.l.).

**χᾰμευνάς II**, for '*lair*' read '*bed on the ground*'

**χᾰμεύνιον**, after 'χαμεύνη' insert 'Hippon. 62 W.'

***χᾰμεύρετος**, ον, *found exposed*, *foundling*, of babies, Just.*Nov.* 153.

***χᾰμοκέντησις**, εως, ἡ, *floor-mosaic*, *BE* 1966 p. 386 no. 229 (two inscrs.; Eurytania, Aetolia; v/vi AD).

+**χᾰμοσόριον**, τό, *tomb hollowed out of the ground* or *rock*, *BCH* suppl. 8.231, 232 (Maced., iii/iv AD), *MAMA* 3.27, 30, al.

**χάμψα**, for 'ὁ' read 'ἡ (or -ης, ὁ)' and delete 'cj. in A.*Supp.* 878 (lyr.)'

***χαμῶνας**· στέαρ ἢ τὰ ἐκ στέατος τικτόμενα Hsch., cf. χαβῶνες, χαυών. (Prob. Semitic, cf. Akk. *kamānu*, Hebr. *kawwān* "sacrificial cake").

***χανάκτιον**· τὸ μωρόν, Δωριεῖς Hsch.

**χανδάνω II**, line 6, after '*h.Ven.* 252' insert 'Q.S. 12.328'

**χανδόν**, for 'Call.*Aet.* 1.1.11' read 'Call.*fr.* 178.11 Pf.'

**χᾰόω**, after 'Simp.*in Epict.* p. 47 D.' add 'tab.defix. in *SPAW* 1934.1043'

***χαράβδη**, ἡ, a disease of corn, Hsch.

***χᾰράγιον**, τό, = χάραγμα 2, *Cat.Cod.Astr.* 8(2).165.14.

**χάραγμα**, add '**5** *loaf* (cf. χαραγμή), *PWash.Univ.* 56.16 (v/vi AD).'

***χαράδριον** (B), v. ‡χαλάδριον.

**χᾰραδρος**, add 'cf. Myc. *ka-ra-do-ro*, place-name'

**χᾰρᾰκίας III**, add '*IGC* p. 98 A33 (Acraephia, iii/ii BC)'

**χᾰρᾰκισμός**, for '*JHS* 33.338 (Maced., iii AD)' read '*SEG* 30.568 (Maced., ii AD)'

**χᾰρᾰκίτης 1**, for this section read 'perh. a bird, *the Egyptian great reed warbler*, typically noisy and aggressive, βυβλιακοί (v.l. βιβλ-) .. χ. Timo in *Suppl.Hell.* 786.2'

**χᾰρᾰκοβολία**, for '*forming a palisade*' read '*erection of a palisade*'

***χᾰρᾰκοκόπος**, ον, *used for cutting stakes*, δρέπανα *PCair.Zen.* 851a26 (iii BC).

**χᾰρακτήρ I 1**, line 2, for '*IPE* $1^2$.16*A* 14' read '*IPE* $1^2$.32*A*18' **II 1**, line 4, after '(Arist.)*Ath.* 10.2' insert 'ἔχον τὸν αὐτὸγ χαρακτῆρα τῶι Ἀττικῶι *SEG* 26.72.9' **2**, line 6, after '*brand*' insert 'on a slave, *PHib.* 198.87 (iii BC)'

**χᾰρακτηρίζω 2**, after 'Iamb.*Comm.Math.* 4' add 'Procl.*Inst.* 102, 121, 158 D., al.'

**χᾰρᾰκών**, for 'perh. *vineyard containing staked vines*' read 'perh. *paling, palisade*' and add '*CPR* 7.38.10n. (iv AD)'

**χᾰράσσω II 1**, line 3, after '(Apollonid.)' insert '*PMil.Vogl.* 69.B38, 83, 84 (ii AD), v. °ἐκτάσσω'

**χᾰρίεις**, line 1, for '*Mon.Piot* 2.138' read '*CEG* 326'; line 3, after 'dat. -εντι' insert 'fem. pl. χαρίεσσιν Orph.*H.* 46.5'

**χᾰρίζω II 3**, add 'of the gift of a slave to a deity, *SEG* 34.656 (Maced., ii AD)'

**χᾰρις V 2**, add 'θῦμα ἐκ τριῶν ποπάνων συγκείμενον, τινὲς δὲ πλακούντων εἴδη, καὶ ἀρτοχάριτας καλεῖσθαι Hsch.' **VI 1**, line 4, after 'A.*Ch.* 266' insert 'ἔμαν χάριν Alc. 304 i 7 L.-P.' **2 a**, after 'κατὰ χάριν Pl.*Lg.* 740c' insert '*Cod.Just.* 1.1.7.5'

**χᾰρισμός**, delete '*gratifying*' and add 'Phld.*Mort.* 21'

***χᾰριστεία**, ἡ, *thank-offering*, ἀρὰν καὶ χαριστήιαν *SEG* 23.593 (Gortyn, i BC), cf. χαριστεῖον, -ήιον.

**χᾰριστέον I**, add 'Isoc. 19.22'

**χᾰριστήριος II**, neut. subst., add 'χαριστέριο(ν) τόδε *Kafizin* 6; pl. χαριτήρια (sic), ib. 278'

**χᾰριστίων**, add 'in a list of kitchen equipment, *PAlex.* (1964)31.6 (iii/iv AD)'

**χᾰρῑτήσιον III**, for '(Orchom. .. lapis)' read '(-είσια lapis), *SEG* 34.356 (both Orchom., in Boeotia)' **IV**, add '*SEG* 28.953.57.62 (Kyzikos, i AD)'

**χαρίτινος**, after 'dub. sens.' insert 'perh. the same as °χάρτινος'

**χᾰρῑτώπης**, delete the entry.

***χᾰρῑτῶπις**, ιδος, fem. adj., *of charming aspect*, *IG* $2^2$.12828.7.

***χαρουχάριος** or ***χαρουχᾶς**, v. ‡καρουχάριος.

***Χάροψ**, οπος, Boeotian deity, *SEG* 23.102.c.i, ii, 28.457 (vi BC, see also 36.428); identified w. Heracles, *AD* 1916.218ff. (iii/ii BC), *SEG* 28.455 (iii BC), Paus. 9.34.5.

***χαρταλάμι(ο)ν**, τό, perh. *belt*, *SB* 9754.3 (AD 647).

***χαρταρίδιον**, τό, dim. of χαρτάριον, *PMich.*VIII 510.23 (ii/iii AD).

**χαρτάριον**, after '*small piece of papyrus*' insert '*PMich.*II $123^{v}$ix 30 (i AD)'

***χαρτάριος**, ὁ, app. = χαρτουλάριος, *BGU* 466.12 (ii/iii AD), *GVI* 477.2 (χαρτάρις, Smyrna, i/ii AD).

***χαρτᾱτικόν**, τό, *payment for an official document*, *clerk's fee*, *SEG* 9.356.18, 79 (edict of Anastasius, Cyrenaica, vi AD; pl.); also **χαρτιατικόν**, *CIG* 5187c21 (Ptolemais), Ulp.*Dig.* 48.20.6 (Lat. *chartiaticum*).

**χάρτης 1**, add '**b** *official document*, Just.*Nov.* 8.1, *Cod.Just.* 4.21.16 pr., 4.21.22.11.'

**χαρτιατικά**, read χαρτιατικόν, v. °χαρτατικόν.

***χάρτῐνος**, η, ον, *of* or *for papyrus*, ἐκ τεύχους χαρτίνου *SEG* 32.1149 (Magnesia on the Maeander, AD 209).

**χαρτίον**, add '**2** perh. *tax on papyrus*, *BGU* 2370.66 (i BC).'

**χάρτισμα**, delete the entry (v. ‡χόρτασμα).

**χαρτός 2**, after 'of persons' insert 'μὴ χαρταὶ γενώμεθ' ἐχθροῖς Call.*fr.* 194.98 Pf.'

***χαρτουλάριον**, τό, perh. *secretariat*, ἐν τῷ χαρτουλαρίῳ *POxy.* 3960.21, 26 (AD 621).

**χαρτουλάριος**, add 'sp. χαλτουλάριος Teuc.Bab. p. 47.28 B.'

***χᾰρυβδεύω**, *to fish in a* °χάρυβδις 2 b, *POxy.* 3269.4, (iii AD), 3270.10 (iv AD).

**χάρυβδις 2**, add '**b** *pool* in a river, *POxy.* 3267.5.'

***χαρχᾰρόπεπλος**, v. °καρχαρό-.

**χᾰρων I**, after 'Lyc. 455' insert 'Call.*fr.* 339 Pf.'

**χάσιος**, add 'cf. χάϊος'

+**χάσκαξ**, ᾱκος, ὁ, = *pathicus*, Eust. 1909.54 (cf. °χαυνόπρωκτος).

**χάσκω I 2**, add 'w. περί, *develop an appetite* for, κεχηνέναι περὶ τὰς ἐπιθυμίας Clem.Al.*Paed.* 2.10.102'

**χάσμα I**, add (fr. section II) 'χάρυβδις .. ἅρμα περιβαλοῦσα χάσματι E.*Supp.* 501' **II**, for this section read '*gaping mouth* of an animal, Plu. 2.670c, Σκύλλης χάσμασιν *AP* 11.379 (Agath.); w. defining gen., χ. φάρυγος *AP* 6.218 (Alc.), χ. ὀδόντων *Anacreont.* 24.4 W.; synecd. *gaping-mouthed head*, E.*HF* 363 (lyr.), *Rh.* 209, Plu. 2.366a'

***χασμωδιώδης**, ες, *with hiatus*, Rh. 3.544.11.

***χαυλιαστής**, οῦ, ὁ, dub., perh. an occupational designation, ἀπὸ δομεστίκων χαυλιαστίς *MAMA* 5.5 (Dorylaeum, iv/v AD).

+**χαυνόπρωκτος**, ον, nonce-wd., humorous term of abuse, *loose-arsed*, Ar.*Ach.* 104, 106.

**χαυνότης**, line 2, after 'X.*Oec.* 19.11' insert 'Plu.*Sert.* 17.3'

***χαυνοτρίβωνες**, οἱ, app. members of some guild (?clay-moulders), *SEG* 32.931 (Sicily, iv/iii BC).

***χαυνών**, v. ‡χαυών.

**χαύνωσις II 1**, for '*making confused, mystification*' read '*making a case out of nothing*'

**χαυών**, for '*kavvân*' read '*kawwān*'; add 'cf. χαβῶνες'

**χεῖ**, after '*IG* $2^2$.1491.33' insert '(τὸ χεῖ perh. *crosswise*)'

***χειλογρᾰφία**, v. °χειρο-.

**χεῖλος I 2**, add 'Hippon. 118.3 W., Call.*fr.* 194.82 Pf.' **II**, line 4, after 'Ar.*Ach.* 459' insert 'of a ship, Eup. 353 K.-A., *AP* 7.215 (Anyt.)'; penultimate line, for 'τείχους' read 'τεύχους'

***χείλωμα** (B), ατος, τό, = ‡χήλωμα.

***χειλωμάτιον**, v. °χηλωμάτιον.

***χειλῶνες**· τῶν ἀλεκτρυόνων τινές Hsch. (perh. *χίλωνες, i.e. *fatted cockerels*).

**χειμάρροος II 1**, add '*AP* 7.411 (Diosc.)' **2**, delete the section transferring quot. to section 4.

**χειμάω**, for 'ῥιγέω' read 'ῥιγόω'

***χειμώδης**, ες, *stormy*, Sch.E.*Rh.* 247.

**χειμωνικός I**, add 'πωμάριον *PKlein.Form.* 951 (v/vi AD)'

**χειμωνόθεν**, for '*in a storm*' read '*from stormy weather*'

**χείρ**, line 15, for 'Aeol. .. Theoc. 28.9' read 'Aeol. acc. χέρρ', Alc. 58.21 L.-P.; pl., χέρρας, Theoc. 28.9' **I 3**, add 'of a horse, *SEG* 34.1437 (Apamea, v/vi AD)' **II 4**, add 'in making an agreement, ἔδοσαν χεῖρας *SEG* 30.568 (Maced., ii AD)' **6 g**, add '*SEG* 26.701 (Dodona, *c.*205 BC)' **i**, add 'ἔχων μετὰ χεῖρα τὴν Ἀνθίαν holding A. *by the hand*, X.Eph. 1.12.1' **IV**, add '**2** *dominion, rule*, Lxx 2*Ki.* 8.3, 1*Ch.* 18.3. **3** in Roman law = *manus*, as the power of a paterfamilias, Modest.*Dig.* 27.1.8.8, 11.' **V**, line 4, delete 'δεδωμάτωμαι .. A.*Supp.* 958' **VII 4**, add '(transl. Hebr. *yad*) *signpost*, Lxx *Ez.* 21.20 (25)'

***χείρα**, ἡ, = χειράς I, Hsch.

+**χειράγρα**, ἡ, *pain in the hand* (incl. *gout*), Gal. 13.1026.13, Ptol.*Tetr.* 153 (pl.); cf. Lat. *cheragra* (*cheir-*, *chir-*), Cels. 1.9.1, Plin.*HN* 24.188, etc.

**χειραγρικός**, add 'cf. *podagrici pedibus suis male dicunt, chiragrici manibus*, Petr. 132.14'

**χειραπτέω**, add '*misuse*, *SB* 9066 i 14 (ii AD)'

***χείραργος**, ον, *having a useless hand*, gloss on κολόχειρ, Hsch.

***χειρέμβολον**, τό, perh. *official receipt of goods for transport*, Ulp.*Dig.* 4.9.1.3.

***χειρετέροπλος**, ον, (χείρ, ἕτερος, ὅπλον) *having one hand armed*, of a gladiator, epigr. in *ITomis* 288 (ii/iii AD).

**χειρίδιον**, add '**2** kind of loose *sleeve* (cf. χειρίς 2), *PMich.*XV 752.42 (χιρίδ- pap., ii AD).'

**χειρίζω II 3**, line 2, after '(iii AD)' insert 'also act., χειρίσαι πρεσβευτήν *Thasos* 170.27 (ii/i BC)'

+**χειρικός**, ή, όν, (in quots., **χερ-**), *manual*, ἔργα *POxy.* 1692.5 (ii AD), *PGiss.* 56.11 (vi AD), ἐργασία *PHamb.* 23.22 (vi AD).

**χειρισμογράφος**, after '*Stud.Pal.* 20.81.4 (iv AD)' insert '(cf. *ZPE* 22.103, χιρισ- pap.)'

**χειριστής**, after '*manager, administrator*' insert 'minor official who acted as agent for the πράκτωρ in the collection of dues' and add '*PMich.*XII 640.1 (i AD), *IEphes.* 3239 (ii/iii AD)'

***χειρίτεχνος**, ον, *hand-made*, ἔρια κερίθεκνα *Inscr.Cret.* 4.75*B*4 (Gortyn, v BC), cf. χειροτεχνία, °χειρότεχνος.

**χειροβοσκός**, add 'S.*fr.* 164a R.'

***χειρογρᾰφή**, ἡ, *contract of loan*, *PMich.*II $123^{v}$iii 12, al. (i AD).

**χειρογρᾰφία 2**, add 'sp. χειλο- by dissim., *PVindob.Worp* 17.1 (AD 58)'

***χειροδάκτῠλος**, ὁ, *fingerstall*, χειροδάκτυλοι ἀργυροῖ Anon.Alch. 366.2.

***χειροκμής**, ῆτος, ὁ, *manual labourer*, Steph. *in Rh.* 270.16 (pl.), cf. χειρόκμητος.

***χειρονίπτριον**, τό, dim. of χειρόνιπτρον, *hand-basin*, *POxy.* 3860.35 (iv AD; sp. -νίπτιν).

**χειρόνιπτρον I**, after 'Eup. 118.1' insert '*IG* 1[3].405.5 (*c.*412 BC)' and add 'sp. χερο- Eust. 1353.53'

***χειρονιψάτης**, perh. *basin for washing hands*, *BGU* 2360.1 (iii/iv AD).

**χειρονομέω I**, add 'of a pantomimic actor, *SEG* 31.1072 (Pontus, ii/iii AD)'

**χειρονόμος**, for '*one who .. posture-master*' read '· ὀρχηστής' and after 'Hsch.' add 'but *shadow-boxer*, *Didyma* 179.3'

***χειροπόνιον**, τό, *expense of manufacture*, σὺν χειροπονίοις καὶ πάσαις δαπάναις *SEG* 33.1179 (Lycia, i/ii AD), cf. χειροπόνια.

***χειρότεχνος**, ὁ, = χειροτέχνης, *POxy.* 38.17 (i AD).

**χειροτονέω II 1 b**, add 'spec., *ordain by laying on hands*, *CPR* 5.11.4 (iv AD)'

**+χειροτονητής**, οῦ, ὁ, *one who appoints* or *elects to a position*, *POxy.* 2894 ii 37, 2936 ii 9, 12, al. (iii AD); = *creator*, *Gloss.*

**χειροτονία II**, add '**4** *power of appointing*, *disposition*, *Cod.Just.* 1.3.38.6.'

**χειρουργικός I 2**, add 'χειρουργικὸν μέρος τῆς τέχνης Gal. 18(2).667.7'

***χειροχρήστης**, ου, ὁ, *scribe*, pap. in *ZPE* 99.118 (Arabia, ii AD).

***χειροψέλ(λ)ιον**, τό, *bracelet*, *POxy.* 3491.5 (ii AD), *PKöln* 166.20, 22 (vi/vii AD).

***χελάδριον**, v. ‡χαλάδριον.

**χέλειον I**, delete '*crab's shell*' and transfer 'Nic.*Al.* 561 .. χέλιον cod.)' to follow '*testudinum*' **II**, for '*Philol.* 90.137' read '*Suppl.Hell.* 415.1.24'

***χελῑδονιακός**, ή, όν, *shaped like a swallow's tail*, *chelidoniacus gladius*, Isid.*Etym.* 18.6.7.

**χελῑδόνιος**, after 'also ος, ον' insert 'Macho 427 G., Dsc. 5.32' **II 1**, at end delete 'χελιδόνια (sc. σῦκα) .. Epigen. 1.2)'

**χελῑδονισμός**, add 'Eust. 1914.16'

***χελῑδονοειδής**, ές, *coloured like the swallow*, *PMasp.* 6[v].83 (vi AD).

**χελῑδών III 5**, delete '(with play on Ar.*Lys.* 770 (hex.))' and 'cf. Juv. 6.365(6)' add '**IV** kind of (russet-coloured) fig, Ar.*fr.* 581.4 K.-A.'

**χελιχελώνη**, add 'cf. °κορικορώνη'

**χελῡ́νη II**, add 'Dor. **χελύνα̅** Call.*fr.* 196.22 Pf.'

**χελῡ́νιον**, for '*Mitteil.* .. 160' read '*PRain.* (*NS*) 1.28 (p. 160)'

**χελώνη I**, χελώνη χερσαία, add '*Peripl.M.Rubr.* 3, 30' **III 6**, for '*JHS* 10.82' read '*TAM* 2.448' add '**10** *ship's keel*, Hsch.'

**χέρᾰδος**, line 5, after 'Pi. l.c.' insert '(cf. Sch. ad loc.)'

***χερικός**, v. °χειρικός.

**Χέρνᾱσος**, for 'prob.' read 'Ep. Χέρνησος'; after 'Χερσόνησος' insert 'A.R. 1.925 (v.l.), 4.1175'; for '*Docum.* .. 94' read '*SEG* 9.76 (Cyrene, iv BC)'

**χερνῐβόξεστον**, add '*PWash.Univ.* 59.14 (v AD)'

**χέρνιψ**, add 'Myc. *ke-ni-qa* (acc.), also deriv. *ke-ni-qe-te-we* (pl.)'

**χερόνησος**, delete 'A.R. 1.925' (v. °Χέρνασος)

**+χερόνιπτρον**, v. ‡χειρόνιπτρον.

**χερσαῖος I**, add '**2** *consisting of dry land*, *PPetaus* 25.22 (ii AD).'

***χερσιμῑμάς**, άδος, ἡ, *hand-mime actress*, *SB* 10769.204.

***χερσοκᾰλᾰμία**, ἡ, *land overgrown with reeds*, *PMich.*V 310.7, al. (i AD).

**χερσονομή**, add '*PPetaus* 43.23 (ii AD)'

***χερσοπᾰρᾰ́δεισος**, ὁ, *garden land*, *POxy.* 3205.11, 52, 58 (iii/iv AD).

**χέρσος** line 8, after '(Pi.)*N.* 1.62' insert '9.43' **II**, line 3, delete 'ἐν κονίᾳ .. ib. 9.43'; cf. κόνιος I.

***ἔρχνος**, ὁ, v. °κέρχνος A.

**χέω I 3 b**, add '*APl.* 119 (Posidipp.)'

***χηβάδις**, ἡ, *ewer* or sim. *vessel*, Anon.Alch. 322.16.

**χηλή II 1**, line 3, after 'sg.' insert '*App.Anth.* 3.80 (Posidipp.)'

**χήλωμα**, add '**II** *box*, *chest*, *POxy.* 1294.5 (χειλ-, ii/iii AD), cf. χηλός.'

***χηλωμάτιον**, τό, dim. of χήλωμα, *small box*, *chest*, *POxy.* 1294.3 (χειλ-, ii/iii AD).

***χηλωτός**, ή, όν, adj. app. fr. χηλή or χηλός (*chest*), *PRyl.* 627.63 (iv AD).

**χηνάγριον 1**, delete '*young*' and add '*PMil.Vogl.* 305.22 (ii AD)'

***χηνᾶς**, ᾶ, ὁ, *goose-keeper*, *SB* 5377 (*ZPE* 20.231).

**+χηνιάζω**, *make a noise like a goose*, of an incompetent piper, Diph. 78 K.-A.'

***χηνίς**, ίδος, ἡ, perh. *gosling*, *IG* 11(2).224A11 (Delos, iii BC).

***χηνοβοσκία**, gloss on χηνοβοσία, Hsch.

***χηνόπους**, ποδος, ὁ, ἡ, app. *flat-footed*, of a woman, *IG* 12(3).388.

**χηρᾰμός**, line 6, after 'Hom.' insert 'and Lyc.'

***χήρειος**, α, ον, *bereaved* of a relative: of a husband, λέκτρα *AP* 9.192 (Antiphil.); Ion. χηρήϊος, of children, οἶκος Antim. 81 Wy.

**χηρεύω II**, after 'E.*Cyc.* 440' insert '(dub. l.)' and for 'χηρεύσει' read 'χηρεύει'

**χῆτος**, add 'Hes.*Th.* 605, Philostr.*VA* 2.39'

**χθεσινός**, add 'of bread, Aët. 3.177 (349.28 O.)'

**χθιζός**, last line, after 'Il. 19.195' insert 'A.R. 4.1397, *AP* 9.305 (Antip.Thess.)'

***χθονικός**, ή, όν, = χθόνιος, Ἑρμῆν χθονικόν *Tab.Defix.* 107.3.

**χθόνιος I**, add '**2** *characteristic of* or *suitable to the underworld*, i.e. *gloomy*, *severe*, Anacr. 60 P., ῥυσμοί id. 71.2 P., cf. Suet.*Blasph.* 98 T.'

**χῐ́ασμα 1**, add '*PFlor.* 233 (*ZPE* 78.98)'

***χῑδροβρόχον**, τό, app. *vessel for soaking* χῖδρα, *Kafizin* 219 (223/222 BC).

**χῖδρον**, delete '*unripe*'

***χιθών**, v. °χιτών.

***χιλᾶς**, ᾶ, ὁ, perh. a trade designation (?*dealer in fodder*), *SEG* 36.970.B29 (Aphrodisias, iii AD).

**χῐλεύω I**, add 'χειλεύει στρατόν Hsch.'

***χῑλιᾰγωγός**, ὁ, *leader of a thousand*, epith. of God, *JÖAI* 32.80 (amulet).

**χῑλιαρχία II 3**, for '*AJA* .. BC)' read '*Sardis* 7 no. 1i6 (iii/ii BC)'

**χῑλιαστήρ**, add '*BCH* 59.478 (Samos)'

**χῑ́λιοι 3**, add 'also masc. (sc. στατῆρες), *SEG* 32.794 (Olbia, *c.*325 BC)'

**χῑλιοπλᾰσίων**, for '= foreg.' read '*a thousand times as much* (*as many*, *as great*)'

**χῑλός 1**, line 1, before '*green*' insert '(also χιλόν, τό, Hsch.)' **2**, add 'pl., Nic.*Th.* 569'

***χιλωκτός**, ή, όν, or **χιλωκτόν**, τό, [?ῐ] perh. *fodder-bag*, *PMich.*VI 421.24 (i AD).

**χῐ́λωμα I**, add '*PLond.* 190.45 (?iii AD)'

**χῐ́μᾰρος**, after 'Ar.*Eq.* 661' insert '*SEG* 33.167.20 (Attica, 440/30 BC)'

***χῐονοβροχοπᾰγής**, ές, *snow- and rain-congealing*, *PMag.* 4.1358.

***χῐονοδροσοφερής**, ές, *bringing snow and dew*, *PMag.* 4.1362.

***χῐονοειδής**, ές, *snowy in appearance*, of the sun appearing as an omen, *Orac.Tiburt.* 27 (cf. χιονώδης).

**+χῐονόομαι**, *to be snowed on*, Lxx *Ps.* 67(68).15 (see also χιονίζω).

**Χῖος I 1 b**, add '(see also χῖον, ἡμίχιον)' **II**, line 3, after '*ace-dot*' insert '*Epigr.Gr.* 1038 (χεῖ-)'; line 5, for '(Poll.) 205' read '(Poll.) 9.100'

***χῑρίδιον**, v. °χειρ-.

***χῑρισμογρᾰ́φος**, v. ‡χειρ-.

**χῐτών I 1**, add 'sp. χιθών, *BGU* 816.18' **2**, add 'as ceremonial garment for goddess, *IEphes.* 2 (*c.*340/320 BC)' at end add 'Myc. *ki-to*, *ki-to-ne* (pl.)'

**Χῐτώνη**, add '**Κιθωνέα**, Hsch.'

**χῐτωνίσκιον**, add '*IG* 2[2].1515.20; also χιθωνίσκιον, ib. 1516.7'

**χλαῖνα**, line 10, delete 'of husband and wife'

***χλᾰμῠδαρχικός**, ὁ, app. *one in charge of military cloaks*, *PPanop.* 17.2, 18.2 (both AD 329).

***χλᾰμῠδηφορέω**, *wear a chlamys* (as an ἔφηβος), *SEG* 28.1458 (Antinoopolis, ii AD), *JEA* 37.87.2 (Memphis, iii AD); also **χλαμυδοφ-** *PMich.*VI 426.18 (ii/iii AD); glossed by Θετταλίζειν, Poll. 7.46; also written χλαμυρο-, *POxy.* 2895.6 (iii AD).

**χλᾰμῠδηφόρος**, add 'as epith. of Hermes, *PMag.* 5.403'

**+χλᾰμῠδοφορέω**, v. °χλαμυδηφορέω.

***χλανίαι**· περιβολαί Hsch. (cf. χλανίτιδες, κλανίον, etc.).

**χλᾰνίδιον** (form χλάνδιον), add '*SEG* 38.1210.22 (Miletus, ii BC)'

***χλᾰνῑδοφόρος**, ον, *wearing a* χλανίς, Archipp. 50 K.-A.

***χλαρ(ον)**, perh. a kind of gem, *PRyl.* 627.159 (iv AD).

**χλεύη**, for 'Aeschrio 8' read '*AP* 7.345 (Aeschrio)'

**+χλῆδος**, ὁ, app. *rubble*, *debris*, A.*fr.* 16 R., D. 55.22, 27; transf., ἀργυρίου χλῆδον λαβών Crates Com. 31 K.-A.

**χλιαίνω**, line 10, delete 'al.' and after '(Mel.)' insert '*AP* 12.136'

***χλιᾰροπᾰγής**, ές, *easily fusible*, Anon.Alch. 31.3.

**χλιᾰρός 1**, add '**b** neut. pl. subst., *warm baths*, *SEG* 32.1502, 1503 (Palestine, v AD).'

**χλιάω**, delete '(sed leg. χλιαρόν)' and for 'ἀτὰρ .. *Hesperia* 5.95' read 'μὴ κούρας ἅτ' ἀρηγὸς (= ἀρωγὸς) ἀφάσσων στέρνα πόθῳ χλιάοι *Hesperia* 5.95'

**+χλιβίον**, v. ‡κλουβίον.

***χλῐδωίδιον**, τό, app. = sq., *SEG* 39.163 (Attica, iv BC).

**χλῐ́δων**, for 'Plu. 2.145a (prob. l.)' read 'Plu. 2.317f'

**χλῐδώνιον**, add '*IG* 2[2].1457.8'

**χλοΐα**, before '*IG* 2[2].949.7' insert '*IG* 1[3].250.A26, B31 (v BC)'

**χλόος**, add '**II** pl., *green foodstuffs*, *PMich.*VIII 496.17 (ii AD).'

***χλούβιον**, v. ‡κλουβίον.

**χλωρικός**, add '-κόν, τό, *green fodder*, τῷ θ' (ἔτει) χλωρικῷ ξυλ(αμῆσαι) *POxy.* 3911.25 (AD 199)'

***χλωρόπαστος**, ὁ, *shot with green*, name of a stone, Socr.Dion.*Lith.* 39.1 G.

**χλωρός I 1**, lines 8/9, for 'ἡ .. scenery' read 'ἡ or τά, something required for depicting a river (perh. personified) in a mime, perh. *green stain* or *green draperies*' and add '**b** χλωρά, τά, *green crops*, opp.

*πυρός*, *POxy.* 501.16 (ii AD).' **III**, lines 6/7, delete 'of fish .. 7.309b'

**χλωρότης I**, for '*greenness*' read '*green* or *yellowish colour*'; line 2, after 'Lxx *Ps.* 67(68).14' insert 'Plu. 2.952c; of the pallor of gold mixed w. silver, ib. 395d' **II**, delete the section.

*__χλωροφᾰγία__, ἡ, *green fodder*, *PLond.* 1165.3 (ii AD), *PMasp.* 87.13, *BGU* 2139.14 (AD 432).

*__χλωροφόρος__, ον, *bearing (green) fodder*, χ. (sc. γῆ) *PMich.*II 123ʳiii.6 (i AD), *PTeb.* 553 (i/ii AD).

**χνοάω**, line 1, for 'cheeks' read 'breasts'

**χνόος**, line 4, after 'Od. 6.226' insert 'Hippon. 115.9 W.' **II 1**, add 'applied to the first coat of a foal, *AP* 6.156 (Theodorid.)'

*__χνόος__ (B), v. °κνόος.

**χοᾰνεύω II**, add '**2** *melt down* metal objects, Just.*Nov.* 120.10.'

*__χοᾰνιον__, τό, dim. of χοάνη, rest. in *IG* 1³.427.57 (Athens, v BC).

*__χοαχυτίς__, ίδος, ἡ, fem. of χοαχύτης, *keeper of mummies*, *UPZ* 189.4 (ii BC).

**χοδέαντες**, delete the entry (v. °χοδέω).

*__χοδέω__, *defecate*, = χοδιτεύω (v. χοδιτεύειν), Sophr. in *PSI* 1214*d*5.

+__χοΐδιον__, τό, *small pouring vessel*, *SEG* 21.557.9 (Athens, iv BC).

**χοιρίσκος**, after 'dim. of χοῖρος' insert '*IG* 5(1).1390.68 (Andania, i BC)'

*__χοιρόγυνος__, ὁ, a Nile fish, *PYale* 56 (100 BC), cf. χοῖρος II.

*__χοιροθῠσία__, ἡ, *sacrifice of young pig*, *POxy.* 3866.3 (χυρ-, vi AD).

*__χοιροκατᾰγωγεύς__, έως, ὁ, *pig-drover*, cj. in *BGU* 92 (ii AD; v. ‡καταγωγεύς).

**χοῖρος**, line 1, after '*Ach.* 764' insert '*SEG* 33.147 (Athens, v or iv BC), Herod. 8.2'

**χοιροσφᾰγεῖον**, add '*PCair.*Cat. 10703 (*Aegyptus* 68.38; vi/vii AD)'

*__χοιρότριψ__, ῖβος, ὁ, obsc. compd. of χοῖρος I 2 and -τριψ (τρίβω), Hdn.Gr. 1.246.26.

*__χοιροτρόφος__, ὁ, *swineherd*, Hsch. s.v. συβώτης.

*__χοΐσκιον__, τό, dim. of χοΐσκος, *IG* 2².1533.102.

+__χοΐσκος__, ὁ, *pouring vessel*, (dim. of χοῦς A), *IG* 2².1533.115 (Athens, iv BC), *Inscr.Délos* 1426*A*i15 (ii BC).

**χολέδρα 2**, add 'written χολέτρα, *POxy.* 3285.32, 35, 37 (ii AD)'

**χολή I 2**, sg., add 'Nic.*Th.* 561' deleting this ref. fr. section II. **3**, line 1, for 'Poets' read 'Com.'

*__χολιάζω__, *make angry*, *SEG* 38.1233 (ii AD).

**χολοβάφης**, add 'Alex.Aphr. *in SE* 48.22; also **κολοβάφης**, Hsch. s.v. κολοβάφινα'

**χολοβάφῐνος**, add 'also **κολοβ-**, ἀγαλμάτιον κολοβάφινον ἐν ναϊδίῳ *Inscr.Délos* 1416*A*i12 (ii BC), βοιδάριον ib. 17, 1423*Ba*ii22, δακτυλίδιον 1439*Bb*ii94, cf. Hsch.'

*__χολοποιέω__, *produce bile*, *Vit.Aesop.*(G) 3.

**χόλος I**, add '**2** snake's *venom*, *AP* 7.172.6 (Antip.Sid.).'

*__χονδήν__, adv., *in capacity*, φιδάκνας ἀμφορέων χ. *SEG* 21.644.19 (Attica, iv BC) (acc. of *χονδή, cf. χανδάνω).'

*__χονδρίᾱσις__, ἡ, *the condition of swelling with clots of milk*, of women's breasts, Aët. 16.36 (p. 52 Z.).

*__χονδρόγᾰλα__, τό, *mash of milk and crushed grain*, *SEG* 32.1243 (Cyme, Aeolia, 2 BC/AD 2).

*__χονδροκόπος__, ὁ, *grinder of groats*, *CE* 42.356 (iii BC).

**χονδροσύνδεσμος**, delete the entry (read χόνδρῳ σύνδεσμος).

**χοοφορία**, add '*PSoterichos* 1.24 (AD 69), 2.20 (AD 71)'

**χοραυλέω, -αύλης**, for '*flute*' read '*aulos*'

**χορεῖος I**, after '*of* .. *dance*' insert 'ῥυθμός (cf. II) Men.*Dysc.* 951'; delete 'cf. Ael.*NA* 2.11'; epith. of Dionysus, add '*SEG* 30.86 (ii AD)'

**χορεύω**, line 3, delete 'E.*Ion* 1084 (lyr.)' **I 3**, read 'fig., take part (in a particular group) Pl. *Tht.*173c; w. dat., *to be a votary of*, παιδείᾳ Phld.*Rh.* 1.141, φιλοσοφίᾳ ib. 2.271.' **2**, add 'in erotic contexts, Nonn.*D.* 8.228, 16.67, σὲ γὰρ τέκε χάλκεος Ἄρης Κύπριδος ἐν λεχέεσσιν Ἐρωτοτόκοιο χορεύων ib. 34.117' **III**, line 2, after '(lyr.)' insert 'so prob. in A.*fr.* 204b. 1 R. (lyr.), unless in sense II 2'

*__χορηγεσία__, ἡ, Dor. χορᾱγ-, = χορηγία I 1, epigr. in *Lindos* 197f6 (ii BC).

*__χορηγητῶς__, adv., Dor. χορᾱγ-, *on a grand scale*, *AS* 17.81.9 (Bithynia, ii AD).

**χορηγία I 1**, add 'ποιησάμ[ε]νος τὰν χοραγίαν *SEG* 32.1243.45 (Cyme, 2BC/AD 2); personified, ἄνασσα Χοραγία *SEG* 30.133 (Athens, after AD 130)' **II 2 b**, add '*furniture* of the Temple, Lxx 2*Es.* 5.3; pl., *supplies*, Diog.Oen. 64 ii 1 S.'

**χορῑτεία**, after '= χορεία' insert '(unless a mistake for that word)'

*__χοροδῐδασκᾰλέω__, *train a chorus*: fig., ἐντέχνως χ. ἐν φιλοσοφίᾳ Phld. *Lib.* col. 3 line 9.

**χοροιτῠπία**, sg., add 'Panyas. 16.15 B.'

**χοροστᾰτέω**, before 'Hsch.' insert '*IGRom.* 1.562 (Nicopolis ad Istrum)'

**χορτάριον**, add '**2** *hay*, *BGU* 625.33 (ii/iii AD), *POxy.* 1862.37 (vii AD).'

**χόρτασμα 1**, after '*fodder, forage* for cattle' insert '*PHamb.* 27.17 (iii BC)'

**χορτᾰχῠρον**, for '*chopped hay*' read '*grass straw*' and add '*PMich.*XII 650.27 (iii AD)'

*__χόρτη__, v. °χώρτη.

**χορτηγός**, add 'ὑποζύγια *PCair.Zen.* 292.480 (iii BC)'

*__χορτόβρωμα__, ατος, τό, *grazing*, *PSI* 1327ʳ7 (ii AD).

**χορτοκοπή**, add '*PSI* 1327ʳ6 (ii AD)'

**χορτοκόπιον**, add '*IGBulg.* 1401.7 (ii AD), *IMylasa* 257.9'

*__χορτοπᾰτημα__, ατος, τό, *threshed straw*, *POxy.* 2985.2, 6, 2986.7, 8 (both ii/iii AD).

**χόρτος II 1**, add 'χ[όρτ]ου ἀρακίνου ἀρουρῶν δέκα τριῶν *PVindob.Worp* 3.19 (AD 321)'

*__χορτωνέω__, *purchase food*, *PCair.* 10311.9 (*APF* 33.5; iii AD).

*__χούζιον__, τό, perh. a kind of gourd, *ICilicie* 108.6 (v/vi AD).

**χοῦς** (A), line 1, delete 'Nic.*Th.* 103'; line 2, before 'measure of capacity' insert 'vessel or'

**χραισμέω 2**, add '**b** w. dat. of thing, *have an antidote* for, χραισμήσεις ὀφίεσσι Nic.*Th.* 551.'

**χραίσμημα**, delete the entry.

**χραίσμησις**, delete 'Nic.*Th.* 926'

*__χραύω II__, for this section read 'med. w. gen., Cypr. *to-ka-ra-u-o-me-no-ne* τὸ(ν) χραυόμενον Ὀ(γ)καντος ἄλϜō *be adjacent to, adjoin*, *ICS* 217.9; app. variant *to-ka-ra-u-zo-me-no-ne* *ICS* 217.18'

**χράω** (B), line 5, after 'Hermesian. 7.89' insert 'A.R. 1.302' **C III 4 a**, ἔς τι, add 'E.*Med.* 821, D. 19.30'; πρός τι, add 'Hdt. 4.87.2, Lys. 24.24'; ἐπί τι, add 'Pl.*Grg.* 508b' **VII**, at end delete 'Hsch.' and 'has' and after 'χρησιμεύσει' insert 'Hsch.; also perf., Phryn. 206'

**χρεία**, line 2, for 'Call. in *PSI* 11.1216.43' read 'Call.*fr.* 195.33 Pf., Cretan χρήια *BCH* 109.189ff.' **V**, line 3, for 'Theon *Prog.* 5, etc.' read 'Men.Rh. 392.31 R.-W.'; line 4, delete 'Aristipp. etc.'

+__χρειᾰκός__, ὁ, app. *employee, agent*, or sim., *Peripl.M.Rubr.* 16, *BGU* 14 ii 9 (iii AD); in the service of a temple, pap. in *Mélanges Desrousseaux* p. 199 (ii AD).

+__χρεονόμος__, ὁ, title of an official, *SEG* 25.447 (Arcadia, iii BC), *ABSA* 26.166 (Sparta, ii AD).

+__χρεοφῠλᾰκιον, -φῠλᾰκέω__, etc., v. ‡χρεω-.

*__χρεῦμα__· ῥεῦμα, ὕδωρ Hsch. (prob. conflated fr. χεῦμα and ῥεῦμα).

**χρεών II**, add 'μετέστη εἰς τὸ χρεών i.e. died, Mitchell *N.Galatia* 223 (AD 165)'

*__χρεωστικός__, ἡ, όν, of a χρεώστης, ἀσφάλεια *BGU* 472.2.11 (ii AD).

**χρεωφῠλᾰκικός**, add 'and *YClS* 3.26-47'

**χρεωφῠλᾰκιον**, for '*office* .. *is kept*' read '*office of the* °χρεωφύλαξ' and add 'τῶν ἐν τῶι χρεοφυλακίωι βυβλίων *Salamine* 90 (ii BC)'

**χρεωφῠλαξ**, for '*keeper of the register of public debtors*' read '*keeper of documents relating to debts*' and add '*Salamine* 90 (ii BC)'

**χρή I 1**, add '**b** εἰ χρή *if it is proper, if one should*, ὦ μῶρος, εἰ χρὴ δεσπότας εἰπεῖν τόδε E.*Med.* 61, *IT* 1288, resumed by χρὴ δέ id.*El.* 300, *HF* 141.'

**χρῄζω**, line 5, after '*SIG* 56.23 (Argos, v BC)' insert '*SEG* 34.282 (Nemea, iv BC)'

**χρῆμα II 1**, line 6, for 'τεκμαίρει .. *O.* 6.74' read 'χ. ἕκαστον *everything*, Pi.*O.* 6.74, 9.104' **III**, for '*oracle*' read '*oracular pronouncement* or *decree*' and add 'Swoboda *Denkmäler* 107'

**χρημᾰτῐσις**, after '-ῐσις' insert '(-ιξις *Inscr.Cret.* 4.232.3 (Gortyn, ii BC))'

**χρημᾰτισμός I 5**, add '*INikaia* 1071 (i/ii AD)'

**χρηματιστής**, add '**III** *giver of oracles*, Θεοὶ χρηματισταί *Pap.Lugd.Bat.* XXV 8 i 1 (after AD 231).'

*__χρημᾰτοθήκη__, ἡ, *treasury*, τὰς ἱερὰς χρηματοθήκας *JEA* 56.179 (63 BC).

+__χρημᾰτοφύλαξ__, ακος, ὁ, *treasurer*, *PErasm.* 10 (ii BC), *PRyl.* 586.9, al., (i BC); used to translate Lat. *praefectus aerarii*, Vett.Val. 38.34 (38.6 P.).

**χρήσῐμος I 1**, add 'w. inf., ἀποπολεμεῖν χ. Pl.*Phdr.* 260b'

**χρησιμότης**, add '*Epigraphica* 10.76.23 (Leptis Magna, ii/iii AD)'

**χρῆσις II**, add '*oracular saying*, *Inscr.Perg.* 8(3).34.16'

**χρησμοδοτέω**, line 1, after 'Poll. 1.17' insert '*prophesy*, ἀληθείας Ramsay *Cities and Bishoprics* 2.566 (iv AD)'

**χρησμολόγος II**, add '*BCH* 116.279.4 (Colophon, ii BC)'

**χρηστεύομαι**, add 'Lxx *Ps.Sal.* 9.6'

**χρήστης II 2**, line 2, after 'D. 32.12' insert '*AP* 7.732 (Theodorid.)'

**χρηστομᾰθής**, for '*an adept in polite*' read '*desirous of*'

*__χρηστομουσία__, ἡ, *an excellent abode of learning*, Γάδαρα χ. *RA* 35 (1899/2).49 (Palestine).

**χρηστός II 6**, delete the section. **III**, line 1, after 'Hp.*Art.* 32' insert 'Arist.*EE* 1214ᵃ21' add '**IV** in treaty between Sparta and Tegea χρηστὸν ποιεῖν was interpr. by Arist. (*fr.* 592) as = ἀποκτιννύναι, and χ. there may be *good* as euphemism for *dead*.'

*__χρηστοσύνη__, ἡ, *goodness*, *IG* 9².662 (Locris, ?iii BC).

*__χριθή__, ἡ, v. ‡κριθή.

**χρῖσμα III**, add '*La Carie* p. 363'

**χρίω**, line 9, delete 'only in late poets, as' **I 1**, line 4, after 'Il. 23.186' insert 'w. gen., ἐλαίου στέρνα χρίουσιν Achae. 4 S.'

**χροιά II**, line 7, for '*μεμεγμένας*' read '*μεμιγμένας*'

***χροῖα**, τά, app. used as pl. to χρώς II, Emp. 71.3 D.-K.

**χροΐζω I**, line 3, after 'of a woman' insert 'Call.*fr.* 21.4 Pf.'

***χρονέω**, = χρονίζω (in quot., sense I 4), χρονέεσκε *AP* 5.77 (Rufin.).

**χρόνιος I 3**, add 'ὕλας τὰς χρονίας *Salamine* 204 (v AD)' add '**6** *pertaining to the lapse of time*, χ. παραγραφή *Cod.Just.* 1.3.45.12.'

***χρόνῐσις**, εως, ἡ, *expenditure of time*, ἐπί τινι πράγματι χ. Anon. *in Rh.* 176.29.

**χρονογρᾰφία I**, delete 'αἱ χ. καὶ ἡ Ἀτθίς'; add 'cf. *Hesperia* 26.164.23'

**χρονοκρᾰτορία**, add 'Heph.Astr. 2.30 tit., 2.31 tit., al.'

**χρονοκρᾰτωρ**, for 'Ptol.*Tetr.* 209' read 'Ptol.*Tetr.* 290' and add 'Heph.Astr. 2.26.18, 19, 2.29.1, 11'

**χρόνος I 3 a**, add 'τίνα χρόνον; at what time? (if the following words are sound), Call.*Del.* 1' **b**, add 'χρόνου *for a while*, Ael.*NA* 4.45, ἤδη χρόνου ib. 5.33' **IV**, add 'χρόνον ἐμποεῖν τῷ πράγματι Men.*Dysc.* 186'

**χρῡσαλλίς II**, delete 'old' before 'name'

***Χρῡσαμπελῖται**, οἱ, name of a guild at Attouda, *MAMA* 6.84.

**χρῡσάμπυξ**, lines 2/3, delete 'epith. .. Od.'; line 4, after 'B. 5.13' insert '**2** *with golden headband*, of the gods' horses, Il. 5.358, 363, al.'

**χρῡσάνθεμον 4**, delete the section.

**χρῡσανθής I**, add 'κιθών *PMich.*II 121ʳ IV i 3 (i AD)'

**χρῡσάνθινα**, add 'perh. also *SEG* 31.1044 (Sardis)'

***χρῡσάνθιον**, τό, *sulphate*, Maria Alch.ap.Zos.Alch. 146.13, Anon.Alch. 15.13.

**Χρῡσᾱορεῖς**, (s.v. χρυσάορος), add '*Amyzon* 16 (iii/ii BC)'

***Χρῡσᾱορικός**, ή, όν, *of* or *belonging to the Χρυσαορεῖς*, *Amyzon* 28 (ii BC).

***χρῡσαστρᾰγάλος**, ον, *having gold bosses*, φίαλαι Sapph. 192 L.-P.

**χρῡσᾰ́φιον**, add '*PMich.*inv. 1363 (*BASP* 16(3).196; iii AD), χρυσάφιν *PSI* 836.13 (vi AD), cf. mod. Gk. χρυσάφι'

***χρῡσειδής**, ές, = χρυσοειδής, *Hymn.Is.* 109.

**χρῡσεῖον**, read '**χρῡ́σειον**' and add 'Pl.*Lg.* 742d'

***χρῡσελᾰ́της**, ου, ὁ, *goldbeater*, *Edict.Diocl.* 30.5; also **-ηλᾰ́της**, Anon. Alch. 379.8.

***χρῡσέλᾰτος**, ον, = χρυσήλατος, epigr. in Mansel *Ausgrabungen in Side* (1951).54.

**χρῡσέμπαικτος**, delete the entry (v. °χρυσέμπαιστος).

***χρῡσέμπαιστος**, ον, *embossed with gold*, *BGU* 781 iv 1 (i AD).

***χρῡσεόκαρπος**, v. ‡χρυσόκαρπος.

**χρῡσεόκυκλος**, add 'epith. of Horus, *PMag.* 4.460'

**χρῡσεομίτρης** and **-μίτρα**, add 'also **-μιτρος**, ον, *AS* 9.104 (Pisidia, ii AD)'

**χρύσεος I 3**, add '= Lat. *aureus* (cf. °χρύσινος), Just.*Nov.* 121.1' **III 1 a**, add 'epith. of Zeus, Robert *Hell.* 10.105; χ. Παρθένος, partner of Hosion Dikaion, ib. 107; of Artemis, *INikaia* 1501 (Rom.imp.)' **b**, before 'Luc.*Laps.* 1' insert 'Men.*Dysc.* 675'

***χρῡσεόστροφος**, ον, *wearing a golden girdle*, Ibyc. 1(*a*).40 P.

***χρῡσετήσιος** (sc. λίθος), a stone also known as αἱματίτης, Anon.Alch. 8.1.

***χρῡσηλᾰ́της**, v. °χρυσελάτης.

**χρῡσήλᾰτος**, add 'cf. °χρυσέλατος'

**χρῡσήνιος**, add 'of Apollo, *TAM* 4(1).48 (Rom.imp.), *PMag.* 2.91'

**χρῡσίζω**, **I** add 'τῷ χρώματι χλωροὶ καὶ χρυσίζοντες (ὄφεις) *Peripl.M.Rubr.* 40'

**χρῡ́σῐνος I**, add '= Lat. *aureus* (cf. °νόμισμα II), *Cod.Just.* 6.4.4.10'

**χρῡσίτης I**, add 'Plin.*HN* 33.106 (*chrysitis, -im*)' **II 1**, add 'cf. Plin.*HN* 37.179'

***χρῡσογραμμία**, ἡ, *writing in letters of gold*, Anon.Alch. 327.1.

***χρῡσόδεσμος**, ον, *having gold fastenings*, Hsch. s.v. χρυσάμπυκες.

***χρῡσοδότης**, ου, ὁ, *distributor of gold*, epigr. in *TAM* 3(1).127.5 (Termessus); of Ammon, *SEG* 26.1721 (Egypt).

**χρῡσοέθειρ**, line 3, fem. -έθειρα, add 'Ibyc. 1(*a*).9 P.'

**χρῡσόζωνος**, for 'Hes.*fr.* 278.4' read '*Suppl.Hell.* 1168.4'

**χρῡσόκαρπος**, add 'also χρῡσεό-, κλάδα χρυσεόκαρπον *Suppl.Hell.* 1056'

***χρῡσοκελεύθης**, ου, ὁ, *travelling a golden path*, χρυσοκέλευθα, voc., of Apollo, *PMag.* 2.91.

**χρῡσοκέλευθος**, delete the entry.

**χρῡσοκόλλα I**, for '*basic copper carbonate*' read 'or other green copper mineral' add '**2** see quot.: τὸ .. δι' οὔρου παιδὸς σκευαζόμενον φάρμακον ὃ καλοῦσιν ἔνιοι χρυσοκόλλαν, ἐπειδὴ πρὸς τὴν τοῦ χρυσοῦ κόλλησιν αὐτῷ χρῶνται Gal. 12.286.15.'

**χρῡσόκομος**, after '*golden-haired*' insert 'χρυσόκομ' Ἄπολλον *CEG* 308' and after '(Mnasalc.)' insert '(s.v.l.)'

***χρῡσοκοράλλιον**, τό, dim. of χρυσοκόραλλος, Moses Alch. 307.5.

***χρῡσοκόσμητος**, ον, *adorned with gold*, Sch.E.*Rh.* 382.

***χρῡσολάμπετος**, ον, *sparkling with gold*, ῥάβδῳ Hippon. 79.7 W.

**χρῡσολαμπίς II**, add 'Socr.Dion.*Lith.* 45 G.'

***χρῡσολευκόλῐθος**, ον, (made) *of gold and white marble*, Sch.D.T. 378.11; also **χρυσεο-** Hdn. 2.849.1.

**χρῡσόλῐθος**, for '*topaz*' read 'yellowish precious stone, perh. *peridot*' and add '*Peripl.M.Rubr.* 39, 49, 56'

**χρῡσολύρης**, delete 'Pi.*Pae.* 5.41'

**χρῡσόμαλλος**, add 'τὸ χρυσόμαλλον Αἰήτου δέρος *Trag.adesp.* 37a K.-S.'

**χρῡσομᾰνής**, add 'μελέτη *AP* 10.76.4 (Paul.Sil.)'

**χρῡσομίτρης**, add 'also χρυσόμιτρος, Hsch. s.v. χρυσάμπυκας'

***χρῡσόμιτρος**, v. ‡χρυσομίτρης.

***χρῡσονεστριεύς**, έως, ὁ, *gold-spinner*, *Edict.Diocl.* 30.6.

***χρῡσονομέω**, *serve as* ‡χρυσονόμος II or *treasurer*, *SEG* 30.1340 (Miletus, ii/i BC), al.

***χρῡσονομία**, ἡ, office of ‡χρυσονόμος II, *Didyma* 486 (188/7 BC).

**χρῡσονόμος II**, add 'title of a treasurer at Miletus, *SEG* 30.1343 (49/8 BC)'

**χρῡσόπαστος**, add '**2** subst., χρ., ὁ, precious stone, Epiph.Const. in *Lapid.Gr.* 197.19.

***χρῡσόπεζα**, ἡ, *gold-footed* or *-sandalled*, *POxy.* 2444.3.9 (perh. Pi.).

***χρῡσοπέτᾰλον**, τό, *gold-leaf*, Anon.Alch. 377.7 (lemma).

**χρῡσοποιός**, add '*SB* 10769.206 (iii/iv AD)'

**χρῡσόπτερος I**, add 'χρυσόπτερε παρθένε (the Muse), Stesich. 16.11 P.'

**χρῡσοπτέρῡγος**, add '*IKourion* 104.16 (ii AD)'

**χρῡσορόης**, add 'also χρυσοροᾶς *NC* 144(1984).52ff. no. 43 (Hierapolis, coin of Annia Faustina)'

**χρῡσόροφος**, add '*SEG* 36.1099 (Sardis, v/vi AD)'

**χρῡσός 2**, add '**b** a coin, = Lat. *aureus* (cf. °χρύσινος), *Cod.Just.* 3.2.2 pr. 1.' **3**, after 'Pi.*O.* 7.50' insert 'applied to a lover, *BCH* 106.3 ff.' at end for '(Borrowed .. yellow)' read 'Myc. *ku-ru-so*, also app. as adj. (Semitic borrowing, cf. Akk. *ḫurāṣu*, Hebr. *hārûṣ*, etc.)'

***χρῡσοσημέω**, *embroider with gold*, *CPR* 8.65.6, 8, 14, 15 (vi AD).

***χρῡσόσκαλμος**, ον, *with golden oar-pins*, of a ship, *BIFAO* 70.13.

***χρῡσοτέλεια**, ἡ, = Lat. *aurum coronarium*, *REG* 70.120 (Caesarea, vi/vii AD).

**χρῡσότῡπος**, before 'E.*El.* 470' for 'κρᾶνος' read 'χρυσοτύπῳ κράνει'

**χρῡσουργός**, add 'form χρυσοϝοργός, Myc. *ku-ru-so-wo-ko*'

**χρῡσοφᾰ́ής**, add 'Nonn.*D.* 42.495'

***χρυσοφόρμιγξ**, ιγγος, (prosody uncertain) *possessing* or *associated with a golden lyre*, Ἀπόλλων Simon. 6.*fr.* 1(*a*).5 P.

**χρῡσοφόρος I 2**, add '*IEphes.* 3263 (ii/iii AD)'

***χρῡσόφυλλον**, τό, kind of chrysolite, Epiph.Const. in *Lapid.Gr.* 197.16.

***χρῡσοχαλῖνωτος**, ον, gloss on χρυσάμπυξ, Sch.Gen.Il. 5.358.

***χρῡσόχαλκος**, ὁ, app. = *aurichalcum*, a copper alloy, *SEG* 39.1180.67 (Ephesus, i AD).

***χρῡσοχεύς**, έως, ὁ, *goldsmith*, *PCol.* 214.6 (AD 85/86).

***χρῡσοχοοποίησις**, εως, ἡ, *fusion of gold*, Comarius Alch. 291.11.

**χρῡσοχόος 2**, add '*PPetaus* 69.34'

**χρῡσόχροος**, add 'χρυσόχ‹ροε› Παιάν rest. in epigr. in *SEG* 24.1244.2 (Nubia, ii/iii AD)'

**χρῡσυποδέκτης**, add '*ITyr* 90 (χρυσουπο-, Chr.)'

**χρῡσῶπις**, add '**III** χ. (sc. λίθος), ἡ, precious stone, Plin.*HN* 37.156.'

***χρῡσώρῠφος**, v. ‡χρυσωρύχος.

**χρῡσωρύχος**, for '*Supp.* .. iv AD' read '*GVI* 1170 (Phrygia, iv AD, lapis χρυσώρυφα' and at end delete 'cf. χρυσώρυφος'

**χρῡ́σωσις**, after '*gilding*' insert '*Inscr.Délos* 290.231, 234 (iii BC)'

**χρῴζω 1**, line 1, after 'E.*Ph.* 1625' insert 'pass., ὡς μάτην κεχρῴσμεθα κακοῦ πρὸς ἀνδρός id.*Med.* 497' deleting this passage in section 3.

**χρῶμα II 2**, add '**b** τὰ χ. the *paints*, i.e. *painting*, Chor. p. 280 F.-R.'

**χρωμᾰ́τῐνος**, after '*coloured*' insert 'or *for colouring*' and add '*SEG* 36.267 (61/0 BC)'

***χρωμᾰτογρᾰ́φος**, ὁ, *painter*, Anon.*in Rh.* 26.17.

***χρωμᾰτωτός**, όν, *coloured*, στιχάριν ἔμπλουμον χρωματωτόν *Stud.Pal.* 20.275.4 (vi AD).

**χρώς I 2**, lines 3/4, after 'Pherecr. 30' insert 'εἰς χρόα κειράμενοι *AP* 7.446 (Hegesipp.)'

**χρωτίζω**, add '**2** med., = χροΐζομαι, *Mim.adesp.* 1.36 C. (without dat.); fut. pass. ib. 26.'

**χῠδαῖος II**, add '**3** geom., *square* (as opp. to ἀγελαῖος *cubic*), *POxy.* 3455.8, al. (iii/iv AD).'

**χύδην**, line 1, for 'Call.*fr.* 1.11 P.' read 'Call.*fr.* 228.11 Pf.' **I**, after 'Pl.*Phdr.* 264b' insert '*IG* $2^2$.1491.7 (Athens, iv BC)'

**χύμα 3**, add '*quantity* (of powdered, granular, or sim. substance), κασίας χύμα πλεῖστον *Peripl.M.Rubr.* 10'

***χῡμᾰτίζω**, gloss on κλύζω, Sch.Nic.*Al.* 140a Ge.

**χῡμός I 2**, line 1, after 'Hp.*VM* 18' insert 'Gorg.*Hel.* 14'

***χῠτάργῡρος**, ὁ, *liquid silver*, Anon.Alch. 16.14.

**χύτλον** **1**, for '*Berl.Sitzb.* 1927.161' read '*SEG* 9.72.49'
**χύτρα**, line 4, add 'ϙύτρα Lang *Ath.Agora* xxi K2 (vi BC)' **I 1**, at end delete 'children .. χυτρίζω'
**χυτρόγαυλος**, add 'Men.*Dysc.* 505, 506'
**χύτρος** **I 1**, add '*SEG* 35.113 (Attica, *c.*300 BC)' **II 2**, add 'τοὺς Κύθρους *IG* 2².2130.69 (ii AD)'
**χωλός** **II 2**, after 'Demetr.*Eloc.* 301' insert 'Call.*fr.* 203.14, 66 Pf.'
**χωλόω**, for 'Did. ad D. 11.22' read 'Did. *in D.* 13.6 P.-S.'
**χώλωμα**, delete '(Hp.*Art.*) 64' and add 'applied also to impairment or deformity of the arms, Hp.*Art.* 64'
**χώλωσις**, after '*lameness*' delete 'Hp.*Art.* 66' and add 'applied also to impairment or deformity of the arms, Hp.*Art.* 66'
**χῶμα** **I 4**, for '*mole* .. *jetty*' read '*mole* or *causeway* projecting into the sea' **5**, delete the section. **II**, after 'Hdt. 1.93, 9.85' insert 'A.*Supp.* 870 (acc. to sch. = ἄκρα)' **III**, for '*mass of soil* in which roots are found' read '*deposit of soil*' add '**b** applied to a dunghill, ἐκ χώματος κοπρηγείας *PHaun.* 24.5 (i/ii AD).'
ˣ**χωμᾰτεία**, ἡ, *work on the dikes*, *PSI* 901 (i AD; -ηα).
**χωμᾰτεκβολεύς**, add 'Πιᾶς χωματοεγβολ(εύς) *PPetaus* 88.8 (*c.*AD 185)'
ˣ**χωμᾰτεπιμελητεία**, ἡ, *superintendence of dikes*, *POxy.* 3508.23, 25 (AD 70).
**χωμᾰτεπιμελητής**, before '*BGU*' insert '*PColl.Youtie* 21.10 (AD 80/81)'
ˣ**χωμᾰτοεγβολεύς**, -έως, ὁ, v. ‡χωματεκβ-.
**χωμᾰτοφύλαξ**, add '*PPetaus* 44.28 (AD 184)'
**χωνεία**, add '*PMich.*xv 706.8 (ii/iii AD). **2** perh. *cementing* (unless to be taken as misspelling of κονία), χάλικα μεταφέροντες εἰς χωνίαν ληνῶν *PMich.*xi 620.132, 136 (iii AD).'
**χωνευτήρ**, add 'Moses Alch. 311.17'
**χωνευτός**, for 'al.' read 'subst., χωνευτόν, τό, ib.*Jd.* 18.20, *Is.* 42.17 (pl.)'
**χώρα** **I 2**, line 5, after 'Paus. 5.17.6' insert '*enclosed space* between two main beams of a building, *room*, *IG* 2².1668.77 (iv BC), *ITrall.* 147' add '**6** χ. λαμβάνειν, *have place*, *be possible*, *Cod.Just.* 1.3.45.4; sim. w. εἶναι, οὐκ εἶναι χώραν ἐκκλήτῳ ib. 1.4.29.3, 6.4.4.11a.' **II 1**, add 'transl. Lat. *territorium*, *IEphes.* 4101.17 (Trajan)' **2 a**, add 'so perh. ἀγεώργητοι μενοῦσιν αἱ χῶραι *IGLS* 1998.30 (Hama, i AD)'
**χωράζω**, add '*SEG* 23.201 (Messenia, ii BC)'
**χωρᾰ́φιον**, add '*Inscr.Cret.* 4.338.6 (i/ii AD), cf. mod. Gk. χωράφι'
ˣ**χωρεῖον**, τό, = χωρίον, in quot. transl. Lat. *forum*, *SEG* 31.952 (Ephesus, ii AD).
**χωρεπίσκοπος**, for '*coadjutor* or *suffragan-bishop*' read '*superintendent of country districts* at a distance from the bishop's seat' and add '*SEG* 30.1675 (sp. χωροεπ-, Syria, vi AD), *Cod.Just.* 1.3.38.2'
**χωρέω** **II 1**, add '**c** χωρεῖν ἐπί τινα *take legal action* against, *Cod.Just.* 1.3.55.4.' **5**, add '*to be transferred* or *paid out*, χωροῦντος το[ῦ ἡμι]σέου μέρους εἰς τὸ δημόσιον *SEG* 24.614 (Maced., ii AD).' **III 1**, line 10, before '*to be capable of*' insert '*to be big enough to grasp*, *take in* (mentally), τὴν τοῦ θεοῦ δύναμιν Longin. 9.9'
**χωρητικός** **1**, add 'neut. sg. subst., *capacity*, ἃ καὶ εὔστερνα ὡς πλατέα διὰ τὸ χ. καλεῖ Simp.*in de An.* 68.10'
**χωρίδιον**, after 'Lys. 19.28' insert 'Men.*Dysc.* 23' and after '[ῐ in' insert 'Men. l.c.'
**χωρίον** **2**, after '*town*' insert 'or *village*' and add 'Mitchell *N.Galatia* 84; fortified, *Amyzon* 19' **3**, after '*IG* 1².325.10' insert 'Mitchell *N.Galatia* 34; pl., *rural areas*, Just.*Nov.* 73.9, 85.3 pr.'
⁺**χωρισμός**, ὁ, *separation*, λύσις καὶ χ. ψυχῆς ἀπὸ σώματος Pl.*Phd.* 67d, Thphr.*CP* 6.7.3; χ. τῆς ἀφέδρου, ἀκαθαρσίας, *menstrual discharge*, Lxx *Le.* 12.2, 18.19; of abst. things, Arist.*EN* 1175ª20, Plot. 4.7.8; *separation* of a person from an association, ὁ ἀπὸ θεοῦ χ. Hierocl. *in CA* 24 p. 103.24 K. **II** *going away*, *departure*, Plb. 5.16.6, D.S. 2.60, 17.10.
**χωριστός** **I**, delete the section transferring quots. to section II.
**χωρίτης** **1**, after 'Muson.*Fr.* 11 p. 60 H.' insert 'Alciphr. 3.70.1'
**χῶρος** **II**, add '**5** subdivision of τριττύς, *BCH* 78.317 (Ceos, iv BC).'
ˣ**χωροφῠλᾰκέω**, *act as a* χωροφύλαξ, *SEG* 23.305 (Delphi, *c.*190 BC).
ˣ**χώρτη**, ἡ, = Lat. *cohors*, χ. ἑνδεκάτης ὀρβανῆς *JÖAI* 4.207 (near Selymbria, i/ii AD), cf. *IGRom.* 3.359 (Sagalassus, Pisidia), *SEG* 30.818 (Moesia, ii/iv AD), etc.; στρατιώτης χόρ(της) η' πρ(αιτωρίας) *IG* 14.1661 (Rome); also **κώρτη** *IUrb.Rom.* 134 (iii AD).
⁺**χῶς**, v. χοῦς (A).
ˣ**χώστρα**, ἡ, *melting-pot*, Anon.Alch. 271.22, 287.25.
**χωφόριον**, add '*POxy.* 3511.24 (iv AD)'

# ψ

**ψάγδᾱν**, for 'or **σάγδας**' read 'also **ψάγδας** (Hsch.), **σάγδας**'; line 6, for 'nom. .. Hsch.' read '*σάγδης*, app. fem.gen. Ath. 15.690e, *σάγδας* 16.691c.'

**ψαιστός**, add '*AP* 6.300, 334 (Leon.Tarent.)'

***ψάκαστρον**, v. *βουτόρος*.

***ψᾰλαγμα**, *ατος, τό, light touch, ψαλάγματα· ψηλαφήματα* Hsch.

**ψᾰλάσσω**, add 'Ion Trag. 13a K.-S.'

***ψάλιος**, *ὁ*, see quot.: *σημαίνει γὰρ ἡ μὲν* (*λέξις*, sc. *ψάλιος*) *τὸ τιθασευόμενος ἵππος* Sch.E.*Ph.* 793.

+**ψᾰλίς**, *ἴδος, ἡ, U-shaped cutting tool* or *shears*, Ar.*fr.* 332.1 K.-A., *AP* 6.307 (Phan.), 11.368 (Jul.Antec.), Poll. 2.32, 10.140, perh. *PTeb.* 331.13 (ii AD). **II** *U-shaped bracelet*, S.*fr.* 407a R. **2** *U-shaped band* for affixing hangings to columns or the like, Lxx *Ex.* 27.10, 11, 30.4, 37.6. **III** *vaulted chamber* or *passage*, *στενὴν δ' ἔδυμεν ψαλίδα* S.*fr.* 367 R., *ψαλίδα προμήκη λίθων ποτίμων* Pl.*Lg.* 947d, *SEG* 27.119.30, 34 (Delphi, iii BC), Ph.*Bel.* 80.46, D.S. 2.9, Str. 17.1.42, *MAMA* 8.435 (Aphrodisias, sp. *ψελίς*), *IGLS* 438.4, *POxy.* 2804.221 (vi AD). **IV** glossed by *ταχεῖα κίνησις* (alternative explanation), Sch.Pl.*Lg.* 947d G.

**ψᾰλίττεται**, add '(perh. *run a U-shaped course*, i.e. round a turning-point and back)'

**ψάλλω II 2**, add 'Chr., *sing psalms*, *Cod.Just.* 1.3.41.24'

***ψαλμοποιός**, prob. = *ψαλμῳδός*, *SB* 10769.211 (iii/iv AD).

***ψαλταναγνώστης**, *ου, ὁ, intoner*, *MAMA* 6.237 (Apamea); also *ψαρτ-* *SEG* 30.1323 (Ephesus).

***ψαλτήρ**, *ῆρος, ὁ,* = *ψάλτης*, Hsch.

**ψαλτήριον**, for '*stringed instrument, psaltery, harp*' read 'stringed musical instrument, prob. usu. some form of *harp*, but perh. also extended to include a *psaltery*'; for 'Hippias' read 'Alcid.'

**ψάλτης**, add '**2** *psalm-singer, cantor*, *Cod.Just.* 1.3.44 pr., *POxy.* 3958.11 (AD 614).'

**ψάμμη**, add 'cf. *ψαμμήν· ἄλφιτα* Hsch.'

**ψάμμος**, line 1, before '*sand*' insert 'Aeol. °**ψόμμος**'

***ψαμμόχωστος**, *ον*, = *ἀμμόχωστος*, *piled up with sand*, *POxy.* 1911.89 (vi AD).

**ψάρος** or **ψᾶρος**, add '**2** a sea fish, Cyran. 4.75.1 K., cf. *ψόρος*.'

***ψαρταναγνώστης**, v. °*ψαλτ-*.

**ψαυκροπόδης**, add '(v. *Suppl.Hell.* 1122)'

**ψαυκρός**, add '(v. *Suppl.Hell.* 1123)'

**ψαῦσις**, after 'Democr. 11' insert 'Hp.*Vict.* 1.23'

**ψαύω I 5**, add '**b** *ψ. οὐρανοῦ grasp heaven*, i.e. reach the supreme heights, Sapph. 52 L.-P., Plu.*Demetr.* 22, Ael.*VH* 12.41; cf. *ἡμιθέων ψ.* Synes.*Ep.* 142.55.' add '**7** *put one's hand to, attempt*, Herod. 4.75, Plb. 3.32.5, 18.53.1.'

***ψάφεα**· *ψωμία* Hsch., cf. *ψάθεα*.

***ψᾱφοτρῖβέων**· *περὶ τοὺς λόγους* (cj. *λογισμούς*) *τριβομένων* Hsch.

**ψέλιον I 1**, after '*armlet* or *anklet*' insert '(U-shaped, i.e. in the form of an interrupted circle)' **2**, for pres. def. read 'a kind of shears' penultimate line, within parentheses, insert 'see also °*ψελιοῦχος*' at end add 'see also *σπέλλιον*'

***ψελιοῦχος**, *ον*, *bridle-chain holding*, *ἅρμα ψ.* *Suppl.Hell.* 996.10 (technopaignion, i BC).

**ψελιοφόρος**, add 'in pl., gloss on Lat. wds. *βραχιᾶτοι/ἀρμιλλίγεροι* Lyd.*Mag.* 47.19 W.'

**ψελλός**, add 'cf. Myc. *pe-se-ro*, pers. n.'

***ψενδύλοι** (cod. *ψελύνοι*)· *σπόνδυλοι* Hsch.

**ψευδής I 1**, line 5, delete '*ψ. λόγοι* Hes.*Th.* 229'

**ψευδογρᾰφία**, for '= foreg.' read '*fallacy* in geometry or arithmetic'

***ψευδογρᾰφικός**, *ή, όν, of* or *belonging to fallacious proof*, *ἡ ψ.* (sc. *τέχνη*) Alex.Aphr. *in SE* 195.18.

***ψευδοδιάτοιχος**, *ὁ*, archit., *false parpen*, *MDAI(I)* 19-20.238.25.

***ψευδοδοξάζω**, *suppose erroneously*, Plb. 10.2.3 (v.l.).

**ψευδοδοξέω**, after 'Plb. 10.2.3' insert '(v.l., v. °*ψευδοδοξάζω*)'

***ψευδοκᾰμῑνάριος**, *ὁ*, *false potter*, *Σωτήριχε, κίναιδε ψευδοκαμινάρι* nonce-wd. in *SEG* 39.1062 (Rhegium, i BC/i AD).

***ψευδοπαρηχητικός**, *ή, όν*, *connected with ψευδοπαρήχησις*, Eust. 1586.21.

***ψευδορήτωρ**, *ορος, ὁ*, *false orator* or *rhetorician*, Rh. 6.577.6.

**ψεῦδος I 1**, add 'pl., personified, Hes.*Th.* 229' **II 2**, add '*App.Anth.* 3.79 (Posidipp.)'

**ψευδοσέλῑνον**, add '*Cat.Cod.Astr.* 7.234.4'

**ψευδοσοφιστής**, add 'Cyran. 1.12.29 K. (pl.)'

**ψεύδω B I 3**, add 'w. cogn. acc., *ψεῦδος λυσιτελέστερον .. ἐψεύσατο* Pl.*Lg.* 663d'

**ψεῦσμα**, after '*τό*' insert 'also *ψεῦμα* Numen. l.c.' and after 'Plu.*Art.* 13' add 'Numen.*fr.* 27.70, 71 P.'

**ψήκτρα**, add 'implement used by a barber, made of reed, perh. *comb*, *AP* 6.307 (Phan.).'

***ψηφηδᾰκέω**, *bite* (i.e. *injure*) *with one's vote*, Ar.*Ach.* 376 (cf. *POxy.* 856 i 23).

**ψηφίζω**, line 2, after 'Th. 2.24' insert 'med., *ἐψαφίξατο* *SEG* 31.572 (Thessaly, *c.*200 BC)' **III**, line 2, after 'also found in' insert '*Inscr.Cret.* 4.78.1 (Gortyn, v BC), al.' add '**IV** app. (as *ψηφόω*) *adorn with mosaic*, *SEG* 32.1468 (Syria, Chr.).'

**ψηφίον**, add '**2** *mosaic*, *CIJud.* 803 (Syria, iv AD), *SEG* 32.1440 (Syria, vi AD); pl., *SEG* 30.1715 (Arabia, vi AD).'

**ψηφίς I 1**, add '**b** as collect. sg., *shingle*, Hippon. 128.3 W.' **2**, add '**b** *pebble for voting*, *πά]ντες ὑπὸ ψηφῖδα κακὴν βάλον* Call.*fr.* 85.8 Pf., cf. *ψῆφος* II 5 and °*ὑποβάλλω*.' **3**, after '*tessellated work*' insert '*mosaic*' and add '*SEG* 24.1197(e) (Egypt, iv AD), 31.1396 (Syria, v AD)'

**ψήφισμα**, form *ψάφισμα*, add 'also Aeol., *IKyme* 13, etc.' add '**III** *mosaic work*, *SEG* 32.1517 (Palestine, vi AD).'

***ψηφιωτής**, *οῦ, ὁ, maker of mosaics*, *IGChr.* 226(5) (sp. *ψιφιοτῶν*).

***ψηφοθεσία**, *ἡ*, *laying of a mosaic pavement*, *ISmyrna* 733.5 (ii/iii AD), *SEG* 20.462.5 (Palestine).

**ψηφοθεσμία**, add 'unless error for °*ψηφοθεσία*'

**ψηφοθέτης**, after '*pavements*' insert '*Edict.Diocl.* 7.7'

**ψηφολογέω**, add '**2** *calculate by counters*, Anon. *in SE* 2.39.'

**ψηφολογικός**, for '*juggling*' read '*legerdemain*'

+**ψηφοπεριβομβήτρια**, *ἡ*, app. cup constructed with cavity containing clay pellets, causing it to make rattling sound, Eub. 56 K.-A. (cf. *JHS* 90.200).

**ψῆφος I 2**, add 'of a pearl, Ael.*NA* 15.8' add '**3** applied to the pupil of the eye (or the eyeball), w. play on sense II 1, Artem. 1.26 (p. 32 P.).' **II 5**, line 11, after 'Antipho 5.47' insert '*περὶ τούτου ψήφου διενεχθείσης* a *vote having been taken*, *BCH* 86.58.25 (Maced., ii AD)' add '**8** *judgement* as a faculty, *ψ. ὀρθήν* Lib.*Ep.* 19.10.'

***ψηφοφορικός**, *ή, όν*, *accustomed to manipulation of counters*, Anon. *in SE* 2.38.

**ψηφόω II**, add '*SEG* 23.653 (Cyprus, v/vi AD), 31.1473 (Arabia, vi AD)'

**ψήφωσις**, add '**II** *adorning with mosaics*, *IGLS* 1320 (Apamea, AD 391), 770 (Antioch, ?vi AD), *SEG* 8.21 (near Ptolemais, vi AD).'

**ψηχρός**, after '*fine*' insert 'Nic.*Th.* 559 (v.l. *ψῆγμα*)'

**ψήχω I 2**, for '*δέρην μέτωπά τ'*' read '*δέρην* (sc. *ταύρου*)'

**ψῐά**, add 'perh. also Archil. 48.20 W.'

**ψῐᾰθιον**, delete 'perh.' and add '*BGU* 812 i 5, 8 (iii/ii BC)'

**ψῐᾰθοπλόκος**, add '*CPR* 13.11.39 (iii BC), *SB* 9375.21 (*ψιαθω-*, ii AD)'

**ψῐᾰθος III**, for 'perh. *sack*' read '*rush-basket*' and add '*BGU* 2334.5 (*ψειέθων* pap., iv AD)'

***ψιθωμία‹ν›**· *Λάκωνες τὸν ἀσθενῆ* Hsch.

**ψῑλῆται**, after 'Eust. 1222.53' insert '(*ψιλῖται* ib. 907.38)'

**ψῐλιον**, after '*armlet*' insert '*SEG* 37.994 (Priene, vii BC)'

**ψῑλότης II 2**, for '(pl.)' read '(pl.; opp. *δασύτητες*); Phld.*Po.* 2.18 (opp. *πρόσπνευσις*)'

***ψιμεῖον**, v. °*ψιμμίον*.

***ψιμμίον**, *τό*, = *ψιμύθιον*, *white lead*, Zos.Alch. 248.11, perh. also *ψιμεῖον* *Stud.Pal.* 20.96.9 (iv AD).

**ψιμύθιον**, add '*ψημίθι(ο)ν* *PVindob.* G39847.936 (*CPR* 5.110, iv AD)'

**ψιμυθοειδής**, add 'Zos.Alch. 111.9'

***ψιττᾰκινος**, (*η*,) *ον*, *green-coloured*, of cloth, *SB* 9122.10 (i AD); *collyrium psittacinum a colore ita dictum*, Scrib.Larg. 27.

***ψιχόμαλλον**, *τό*, perh. f.l. for ***ψιλο-**, *smooth* (?)*woollen garment*, *Stud.Pal.* 20.245.15 (vi AD), cf. *ZPE* 76.114.

***ψοαλγικός**, *ή, όν*, *suffering from pain in the loins*, Aët. 12.70.

***ψοθέω**, = *ψοφέω*, Call.*fr.* 194.106 Pf.

+**ψόμμος**, *ὁ*, Aeol. for *ψάμμος*, *sand* or *dust*, Alc. 306 *fr.* 14 ii 2, 6 L.-P.; cf. *ψόμμος· ἀκαθαρσία, καπνός* Hsch.

**ψόρος**, add '*SEG* 23.326 (Delphi, iii BC)'

**ψοφοειδής**, for 'φωνήεντα' read 'τὰ ψ. = those consonants which are not mutes, *continuants*'

***ψυγμογνᾰφεύς**, έως, ὁ, *dry-cleaner*, *PFlor.* 388.80 (i/ii AD).

**ψυγμός II**, add 'ἔψυξαν ἑαυτοῖς ψυγμούς Lxx *Nu.* 11.32' **III**, delete the section.

**ψυδρεύς**, add 'also in Epirus, *SEG* 32.623 (Buthrotus, ii/i BC)'

**ψυδρός**, before 'Lyc.' insert 'Simon. in *POxy.* 3965 *fr.* 26.16'

**ψύλλα II 1**, add 'cf. Ael.*NA* 6.26' **3**, delete the section.

**ψύλλιον**, add 'also **ψύλλιος**, ὁ or ἡ, Cyran. 1.23.1, 2.45.4 K.'

**ψῡχᾰγωγέω II 1**, add '**b** *divert*, *amuse*, Alciphr. 3.18, Jul.*Or.* 1.40a. **c** *console*, αὐτούς ib. 8.244b, cf. 248c.'

**ψυχάριον**, add '*SEG* 33.947 (Ephesus, i BC)'

**ψῡχή I 2**, line 4, after 'endearing name' insert 'Theoc. 24.8, Macho 223 G.' **IV 3**, line 5, after 'Arist.*EN* 1168$^b$7' insert 'perh. also E.*Or.* 1046'

**ψῡχογονικός**, after '*of* or *for* ψυχογονία' insert 'ψ. διαιρέσεις Procl. *in R.* 2.192.26'

**ψῡχολέτης**, add 'of the devil, *PYale* inv. 1336 (*BASP* 22.333ff., iv/v AD)'

**ψῡχολῖπής**, after '*lifeless*' insert '*GVI* 1154 (ii BC)'

***ψῡχόλυτρος**, ὁ, *one whose soul is ransomed*, *PBerl.* 17612.8 (*APF* 21.78, vi AD).

**ψῡχομαντεῖον**, add 'pl., *rites of necromancy*, Cic.*Div.* 1.132'

**ψῡχορρᾰγέω**, for '*break loose*' read '*break up, collapse*'

**ψῡχοστᾰσία**, add 'as alternative name for νέκυια as part of Odyssey (bk. 11 or 24), Philostr.*VA* 8.7.7, *Her.* 51.7'

**ψῡχότροφον**, delete the entry (v. °ψυχρότροφον).

***ψύχρανσις**, ἡ, *chilling*, Alex.Aphr.*Febr.* 12.8 (opp. θέρμανσις).

**ψῡχροβᾰφής II**, for this section read 'of dyes, *used in cold immersion*, ὥσπερ τῶν ἀνθῶν τὰ μὲν ψυχροβαφῆ τὰ δὲ θερμοβαφῆ Thphr.*Od.* 22'

***ψῡχ‹ρ›οθερμοφῠσησος**, epith. of Typhos, *breathing cold and hot*, *PMag.* 4.183.

**ψῡχροποτέω**, add 'Gal. 17(2).199.12'

**ψῡχρός I**, line 9, transfer 'of a snake, Theoc. 15.58' to precede 'esp. of dead things' and add 'Thgn. 602'

***ψῡχρότροφον**, name for the plant κέστρον 1, cf. Plin.*HN* 25.84.

**ψῡχροφόρον**, after '*Gloss.*' add 'τῶν δύο ψ. *POxy.* 896.11 (iv AD)'

**ψύχωσις**, after 'M.Ant. 12.24' insert 'pl., Procl.*Inst.* 63 D.'

***ψωλοκοπέομαι**, *to be affected with priapism*, Lucilius 304 M.; act. in causative sense, ψωλοκοπῶ τὸν ἀναγιγνώσκοντα in margin of *PLond.* 604 *B* col. 7 (i AD).

***ψωμή**, ἡ, = ψωμός, Anon.Alch. 16.7 (pl.).

**⁺ψωμίον**, τό, dim. of ψωμός, *piece of bread*, *PTeb.* 33.14 (ii BC), *Ev.Jo.* 13.26, M.Ant. 7.3, D.L. 6.37, *BGU* 2357 iii 12 (iii AD).

**ψωμός**, after 'Od. 9.374' insert 'Hippon. 75.4 W.'

**ψώρα I**, for '*scurvy*' read '*scabies*' and add 'Hp.*Aff.* 35'

**ψωρανθεμίς**, for '= λιβανωτίς' read 'kind of λιβανωτίς (A)'

**ψωράω**, add 'Friedländer *Epigrammata* p. 164'

**ψωρός II**, add 'perh. also *SEG* 32.771 (Berezan, vi BC, unless for ψωλός)'

**ψώχω**, for '*rub small*' read '*rub so as to break up, separate*, etc.' and before '(pass.)' insert 'Diog.Oen.*fr.* 9 ii 13 S.'

# Ω

**ὦ** and **ὤ** i, add '**2** w. acc., *ὦ τὸν Ἄδωνιν* Sapph. 168 L.-P., *GVI* 1386, *ὤ ἐμὲ δειλάν* Call.*Lav.Pall.* 89.'

**ὦ** add **III**, 'perh. also in Myc. *o-*, *how* (usu. prefixed to verbs)'

**ᾠα** (A) **I**, for this section read '*covering for the body made from sheepskin, a loincloth* or sim., *περιζωσάμενος ᾤαν λουτρίδα κατάδεσμον ἥβης* Theopomp.Com. 38 K.-A., Hermipp. 56, 76 K.-A., *στέγασμα, εἴ τι βδ́λεστε, ἀποπέμψαι ἢ ὤας ἢ διφθέρας ὡς εὐτελεστά(τα)ς καὶ μὴ σισυρωτάς* *SIG* 1259 (Athens, iv BC); cf. *τὸ δέρμα ᾧ ὑποζώννυνται αἱ λουόμεναι γυναῖκες ἢ οἱ λούοντες αὐτάς, ᾤαν λουτρίδα ἔξεστι καλεῖν .. οὕτω δὲ τὴν μηλωτὴν ἐκαλοῦν ἴσως ἀπὸ τῆς ὄιος* Poll. 10.181, Hsch.' **II**, at the beginning insert 'perh. orig. different word'

**Ὠγύγιος 1**, *primeval*, add '*νόμου ὠγυγίου* Orph.*H.* 59.10, 64.10' **2**, add '*πελειάων ὠγύγιον τέμενος* epigr. in *SEG* 39.1673.10 (Arabia, ii AD)'

**ὧδε II 1**, penultimate line, *ὧδε καὶ ὧδε*, *this way* and *that*, add 'Call.*Epigr.* 28.2 Pf.' **2**, for '*τηνεῖ δρύες* .. Theoc. 1.106' read 'Theoc. 5.45'; add 'Call.*Epigr.* 47.4 Pf., '*Υγινὴ ὧδε κῖτε* *SEG* 26.376 (Athens), 33.1315 (Egypt, i BC/i AD)'

***ᾤδησις**, *εως, ἡ*, *singing*, *POxy.* 3555.13 (i/ii AD).

+**ὠδῑνολύτης**, *ου, ὁ*, name given to a fish (*ἐχενηΐς* II) from its supposed power of facilitating childbirth, Plin.*HN* 32.6.

**ὠδίνω I 2**, after 'Lxx *Ca.* 8.5' insert 'cf. *τέκνα μου, οὓς πάλιν ὠδίνω* *Ep.Gal.* 4.19'; add 'transf., of a fountain, *ὠδείνουσι τεὸν μένος ὄβριμον ἠνεκ[ὲς αἰέν* *SEG* 32.1502 (Palestine, *c.*AD 455)' add '**3** causal, *cause to go into labour*, [*φωνὴ Κυρίου*] *ὠδίνοντος ἐλάφους* Aq.*Ps.* 28(29).9'

**ὠδίς I 2**, line 6, delete '*τοῦ ᾠοῦ* .. 560$^b$22'

***ᾠδοδῐδάσκᾰλος**, *ὁ*, *singing-master*, *OGI* 56.70 (iii BC).

**ὠθέω**, line 10, for '(plpf.) *ἐῴκει*' read '*ἐώκει*' **II 1**, add 'fig., *πενίην* *AP* 6.117 (Pancrat.); *ἀμαθίαν* Plu. 2.47f'

**ὠθίζω**, add '**III** *refuse*, *deny* an applicant, *ἀλόγως παραιτησάμενος ὠθισθήσεται* *Cod.Just.* 3.1.12.1.'

***Ὠκεάνη** (v.l. -**μη**), *ἡ*, alleged to be the oldest name of *the Nile*, D.S. 1.19.4 (cf. 1.12.6 and °*Ὠκεανός* IV).

**Ὠκεάνης**, delete the entry.

**Ὠκεᾰνός IV**, add '*οἱ Αἰγύπτιοι Ὠκεανὸν νομίζουσι τὸν Νεῖλον* D.S. 1.12.6, *BMus.Inscr.* 1077 (Sudan)'

***ᾠκοδομητός**, v. ‡*οἰκο-*.

***Ὠκτόβριος**, v. °*Ὀκτώβριος*.

**ὠκῠ́πλοος**, for '(Hsch. s.v. *ὁ*) *ὠκύκλοος*' read '*ὠκύπλοος*'

**ὠκῠ́ς I**, add '**3** of (the passage of) time, *βίου ὠκυτάτου* *TAM* 5(1).201; comp. adv. *ὠκυτέρως* Gal. 9.454.17.'

**ὠκῠτόκιος II**, add '**b** title of a collection of synonyms by Telephus of Pergamum, designed for speedy selection, Suid. s.v. *Τήλεφος Περγαμηνός*.'

***ϝωλᾱ́**, v. °*βουλή*.

***ὠλεία**, *ἡ*, *destruction*, *JRCil.* 2.234.

***Ὠλέναδε**, *to Olenos*, *Ὠ.· ὡς ἄγραδε* Hsch. (v. *Suppl.Hell.* 1126).

**ὠλένη 1**, line 8, delete 'is dub. l.'

***ὠλένιον**, *τό*, dim. of *ὠλήν*, *mat*, used in brick-making, *BGU* 2361a i 11, ii 9 (iv AD).

***ὠλῐτόφρονας**, v. °*ἀλιτόφρων*.

**ὡμᾰλία**, line 1, after '*average*' insert 'only in phrase *ἐφ' ὡμαλίαν* *IG* $2^2$.1673.8 (iv BC)'

**ὠμηστής 1**, line 6, after '= *ὠμάδιος* I' insert 'Alc. 129.9 L.-P.'

+**ὠμία**, *ἡ*, *shoulder*, Lxx 1*Ki.* 9.2. **2** transf., *the "shoulder" of a building* formed by the convergence of the roof and upright wall, Lxx 3*Ki.* 6.13(8), 2*Ch.* 23.10, al. **b** *shoulder-piece* or *flange* to support a sacred vessel, Lxx 3*Ki.* 7.17. **II** *bend* in a river, *PTeb.* 828.9 (ii BC).

***ὠμίς**, *ίδος, ἡ*, kind of sea fish, Cyran. 1.24.1, al. K.

**ὠμοβόειος**, line 6, after 'etc.' insert '*IG* $2^2$.1471.57'

**ὠμοβόρος**, before 'A.R. 1.636' insert 'S.*fr.* 10g.13a/b.3 R.'

***ὠμογᾰρικός**, *ή, όν*, neut. pl. subst., perh. vessels *containing* °*ὠμόγαρον*, *PGot.* 17$^v$.2 (sp. *ὀμο-*).

***ὠμόγᾰρον**, *τό*, *uncooked garum*, *PVindob.Worp* 11.7 (vi AD).

**ὠμογέρων I**, after 'Il. 23.791' insert 'Call.*fr.* 24.5 Pf.'

***ὠμόδαιτος**, *ον*, *feasting on raw meat*, prob. cj. in Ps.-Callisth. 58.11 K.

**ὠμόλῐνον**, add '**III** *linen sack*, *Vit.Aesop.*(G) 34 P.'

***ὠμόπλινθος**, *ὁ*, *unbaked brick*, *PLond.* 1708.91, *PKlein.Form.* 1092 (both vi AD).

**ὦμος I 2**, add '**b** of meat, *SEG* 31.416 (Boeotia, iv BC).' add '**4** object used in wine or oil production, perh. part of a *press* or *carrying-pole*, *PFlor.* 233.2, *PRyl.* 236.23 (both iii AD), cf. *τοῖς ἀπ' ὤμων ἐμβαλλομένοις ἐργάταις* *PHels.* 4D ii 10 (ii AD, unless *ὦμος* here is to be taken literally).'

**ὠμός I 4**, add 'comp., Alc. 119.16 L.-P.'

**ὠμοτᾱ́ρῑχος**, for 'prob. *pickled flesh of the tunny's shoulder*' read '*raw pickled fish*'

***ὠμοτόκετος**, *ὁ*, *premature child-birth*, *PFouad* 75.5 (i AD); *-τοκητ-*).

***ὠνανθεσία**, *ἡ*, *manumission through sale*, *SEG* 36.518.15, 23 (Delphi, *c.*AD 100); cf. ‡*ἱερανθεσία*.

***ὠνάρχης**, *ου, ὁ*, title of a Milesian officer, perh. = *ἀρχώνης*, *Didyma* 315.7.

**ὠνέομαι**, line 10, after 'D. 37.5)' insert 'Ion. pf. inf. *ὠνῆσθαι* *ZPE* 68.121.4 (lead letter, Emporion, v BC)' **II**, line 2, for 'dub. in pres. since' read 'pres. *Cod.Just.* 1.3.52.11'; line 3, after 'part.' insert '*ὀνονημένος* *SEG* 12.391 (see also 34.868) (Samos, vi BC)'

**ὠνή**, line 1, after 'ii BC' insert '*οὐνή* *TAPhA* 65.125, 128, 130 (Olynthus, iv BC)' **II 2**, add 'also *TAPhA* 65 l.c., *TAM* 4(1).276 (Rom.imp.)' **III**, add 'Cypr. *o-na ὠνά* *ICS* 299.7'

***ὠνηνικός**, *ή, όν*, prob. f.l. for °*ὠνητικός*, *πράσεις* *PMichael.* 45.7 (vi AD).

+**ὠνητικός**, *ή, όν*, *of* or *concerning sale*, *PPanop.* 21.22 (AD 315), *PHerm.* 18.16 (AD 323); adv. *-κῶς*, *ὠ. ἔχειν*, *to be disposed to buy*, Ph. 2.465, 468.

***ὠοῖ** (or **ὠοί**), cry of distress, *POxy.* 3722 *fr.*17 ii 7 (lemma in Anacr. commentary, ii AD).

+**ὠοιοί**, var. of *ὠαιαί*, A.D.*Adv.* 127.28, 31.

**ᾠόν 4**, line 2, after 'Dinon 14' insert 'cf. *Inscr.Délos* 1417*A*ii140'

***ᾠοπώλης**, *ου, ὁ*, *egg-seller*, *POxy.* 83.4 (iv AD; written *ὀω-*).

**ᾠοσκοπία**, delete '*divination from them*'

**ᾠοσκοπικά**, for '*a treatise thereon*' read '*a treatise*, app. *on divination from eggs*'

***Ωπ**, *ὁ*, a Syrian divinity, *IGLS* 1.230, 6.2916.

**Ὦπις**, for 'cf. Hdt. 4.35' read '**2** name of a Hyperborean maiden at Delos, Hdt. 4.35, Apollod. 1.4.5.'

***ὠποθηκάριος**, v. °*ἀποθηκάριος*.

**ὥρα** (C) **A I 3**, line 7, after 'Theoc. 15.74' insert '*ἐρεῖτε τάδε Εἰς ὥρας· καὶ σὺ ὑγιαίνων καὶ ὁ οἰκός σου* Lxx 1*Ki.* 25.6' **II 2 b**, add '*πρὸ μιῆς ὥρης* perh. = *πρὸ πρώτης ὥρας* Call.*fr.* 550 Pf.' **B I 1**, at end delete 'freq. .. etc.' **4**, line 6, (*αὐτῆς ὥρας*), add 'Plu. 2.239b'; line 14, after 'Plu. 2.784b' insert '*καθ' ὥραν* also, *at this very moment*, *καθ' ὥραν γράφω ἐπιστολήν* *POxy.* 3150.17 (vi AD)' **C**, add '*SEG* 33.115 (Athens, iii BC)'

**ὡραΐζω II 2**, delete '(leg. *ὡρᾴζεθ'*)' and for 'Men. 855' read 'Men.*fr.* 788 K.-Th.'

**ὡραῖος I 2**, add '**b** *ὡραῖα· νεκύσια, οἱ δὲ δαιμόνια* Hsch.' **V**, add 'Gal. 13.162.4'

***ὡράϊσμα**, *ατος, τό*, *youth*, Sch.Pi.*N.* 8.1.

**ὡρᾱκιάω**, after '*swoon away*' insert 'S.*fr.* 120 R.'

***ὠράριον**, v. °*ὀράριον*.

***ὠρδινάριος** (**ὠρδεν-**), *α, ον*, v. °*ὀρδινάριος*.

***Ὠρειόνια**, v. °*Ὠριόνια*.

***Ὠρείτης**, *ου, ὁ*, title of Apollo, perh. *of Oreus* in Euboea, *Anecd.Stud.* 267 (v. *ZPE* 54.132).

***Ὠριόνια**, *τά*, *festival in honour of Orion*, [*ἀγωνοθ*]*έτης Ὠρειονίων* *IG* 12 suppl. 646.16 (Chalcis, perh. fr. Tanagra, iii AD).

**ὥριος** (A) **I**, line 1, after '*ος, ον*' insert '*GDI* 1775.22 (Delphi, ii BC)'; line 3, delete 'Theoc. 7.62' **II 1**, line 2, after 'Hes.*Op.* 392, 422' insert '*κρύος* ib. 543' at end add '*ταῖς -οις* (sc. *ἡμέραις*) *GDI* l.c.'

**ὡρίτης**, delete '*Ἀπόλλωνος* .. *Anecd.Stud.* 267'

**ὡρολόγιον**, line 6, for '*CIG* .. (loc. incert.)' read '*SEG* 37.527 (Nicopolis, Epirus, Rom.imp.)'

**ὦρος** (A), for 'Call.*Fr.* 150 .. 28)' read 'Call.*fr.* 177.28 Pf.'

**ὦρος** (B), add 'also Cret. for °*οὖρος* (B)'

**ὦρος** (C), delete '(C)' and transpose to follow (new) *ὦρος* (C)

**ὦρος** (D), read '*ὦρος* (C)' and delete '(better *ὦρος*)'

**ὡροσκοπεῖον I**, after '**-σκόπιον**' insert '*SEG* 18.739 (Cyrene, ii BC), *IEphes.* 3223A'

*__ὡρόχαλκος__, ὁ, = ὀρείχαλκος, *brass*, *Peripl.M.Rubr.* 6, *PGiss.* 47.6 (ii AD).

**ὤρυγμα**, add '*roaring* of a lion, Sm., Thd.*Is.* 5.29'

**ὠρύομαι**, for '[ῡ]' read '[ῡ exc. Pl.Com. 138.2 K.-A., D.P. 83]'

**ὡς Ab 1**, add 'θεὸς ὥς X.*Cyn.* 1.6 (perh. in paraphrase of poetry)' **B III 3**, after 'omitted' insert 'in Hdt.'

**ὡσάν I 3**, add 'Gal. 6.360.15, cf. mod. Gk. σάν'

*__ὡσκοφόροι__, v. °ὠσχοφόροι.

*__ὡσομοίως__, or better **ὡς ὁμοίως**, perh. = ὡσαύτως, *Delph.* 3(3).421.6 (i AD).

**ὥστε A II**, add 'τὸν ὄγδοον, ὥστε Κόροιβον, οὐ συναριθμέομεν Call.*fr.* 587 Pf.'

**ὠσχός**, read ὦσχος.

**ὠσχοφόροι**, add '*Ath.Agora* XIX L4a.21, 49 (363/2 BC)'

**ὦτε**, after 'A.D.*Pron.* 48.28' insert 'also Arc., *SEG* 37.340.12 (ἄφωτε, Mantinea, iv BC)'

**ὠτειλή II**, line 2, at end insert 'E.*Supp.* 945 (pl.)'; penultimate line, after 'ii.488)' insert '**ὠτέλλα** (-η cod.) Theognost.*Can.* 111'

**ὠφέλεια**, add '**III** Ὠφελία, personified as a divinity, *Pap.Lugd.Bat.* xxv 8 iii 15 (iii AD).'

**ὠφέλημα I 1**, add 'τὸν μηδὲν ὠφέλημα applied iron. to a useless person, Macho 385 G.'

**ὠφέλησις**, add 'Diog.Apoll. B 2 D.-K., Phld.*Po.* 13.23 J.'

**ὠφέλιμος**, after 'Pl.*R.* 607d' insert '*Men.* 98c'

*__Ὠφέλιος__, ὁ, *helper*, cult-title of Zeus, *IHadr.* 10 (ii/iii AD).